A HANDBOOK OF MATERIA MEDICA

AND

HOMOEOPATHIC THERAPEUTICS

A HANDBOOK OF MATERIA MEDICA

AND

HOMOEOPATHIC THERAPEUTICS

By

TIMOTHY FIELD ALLEN, A.M., M.D., LL.D.

GYAN

Published by

Gyan Publishing House
5, Ansari Road
Daryaganj, New Delhi-110002
Phone: 011-47034999, 9811692060
E-mail: books@gyanbooks.com

Distribution Network
gyanbooks.com
India, USA, Canada, UK, Australia, France

ISBN : 978-81-212-9864-3 (PB)
First Published, 1889

2nd Impression 2023

Printed at: Gyan Press, Delhi.

A HANDBOOK OF MATERIA MEDICA AND HOMOEOPATHIC THERAPEUTICS
Author: TIMOTHY FIELD ALLEN

A

HANDBOOK

OF

MATERIA MEDICA

AND

HOMŒOPATHIC THERAPEUTICS

BY

TIMOTHY FIELD ALLEN, A.M., M.D., LL.D.

PROFESSOR OF MATERIA MEDICA AND THERAPEUTICS IN THE NEW YORK HOMŒOPATHIC MEDICAL COLLEGE AND HOSPITAL;
FELLOW OF THE NEW YORK ACADEMY OF SCIENCES; HONORARY MEMBER OF THE HOMŒOPATHIC
MEDICAL SOCIETY OF FRANCE; CORRESPONDING MEMBER OF THE BRITISH
HOMŒOPATHIC MEDICAL SOCIETY, ETC.

1889

PREFACE.

THE preparation of this Handbook was commenced immediately after the completion of the Encyclopedia, and in accordance with a desire, strongly and unanimously expressed by a number of prominent physicians at a dinner given by the publishers to the Author of that work, to possess a condensed volume for ready reference. The first labor undertaken was to correct the errors and supply the omissions which to some extent marred the Encyclopedia; this work proved to be gigantic, involving, as it did, a review of nearly every symptom in comparison with the originals; the whole Encyclopedia could, almost as well, have been re-cast.

To this revised material have been added most of the provings and many cases of poisoning which have accumulated during the past ten years, omitting only such as seemed to rest upon a doubtful basis or which would not be of any practical value. A number of drugs included in the Encyclopedia have been omitted in the Handbook by reason of their inutility or unreliability (for example, the provings of Mure and Houatt), since scarcely any of them have been found valuable; all of Houatt's contributions have been thrown aside on account of their inherent improbability: the "Lacs" have been left to Dr. Swan's announced Materia Medica of the Nosodes, to which also Hydrophobinum, Syphilinum, *et cetera,* have been referred. This procedure has been forced upon the Author by the necessity to provide the profession with a working handbook; but should the work find so much favor that a new edition be called for, the wishes of the profession generally would be considered in adding some of the drugs that have been omitted, especially if these shall have proved themselves reliable. The material thus selected has been condensed in accordance with a system uniformly adhered to, omitting nothing important and avoiding repetition.

The following example will serve to illustrate the method employed.

Under Agaricus, as condensed:

Vertex.—Stitches; itching. Tearing; lancinating, to l. ear. *Aching;* morning; morning, > after rising; at night; > open air; pulsating, with despair bordering on rage.

Same not condensed:

Stitches in vertex. Itching stitches in vertex. Tearing in vertex. Lancinating tearing in vertex, extending to left ear. *Aching in vertex.* Aching in vertex in morning. Aching in vertex in morning, relieved after rising. Aching in vertex at night. Aching in vertex, relieved in open air. Pulsating pain in vertex, with despair bordering on rage.

In the above paragraph all symptoms belong to the *Vertex.* In the first *period* only *Stitches.* In the second *period, Tearings.* In the third *period* all are *Achings; but each semicolon closes a symptom;* thus Aching in the vertex at night is not said to be > *in the open air;* but the *Aching in the vertex > open air* is a separate semicolon and a separate symptom. In the last semicolon the "pulsating" still refers to the *aching,* which dominates the whole period; the last period might read as follows:

Vertex, Aching.
" " in morning.
" " " > after rising.
" " at night.
" " > open air.
" " —pulsating, with despair, etc.

This plan of making a *dominating sensation* cover a whole period, and dividing that period into semicolons for each symptom, affords a good method of condensation. It is confidently believed that no confusion will arise from following this plan.

In some places very long paragraphs have been divided even when the whole refer to one locality.

The sensations have been arranged in accordance with the general idea of the Encyclopedia of giving *first* in a paragraph the objective symptoms, namely, those to be apprehended by the observer alone, including the appearance, the motions or lack of motion, *et cetera;* second, the sensations arranged *in the order of acuteness:* sharp pains first, followed by dull pains or sensations.

Very few signs or abbreviations have been used:

<, means getting worse from, aggravated by, or sometimes simply worse.

"< r. side" means "worse on the right side."

>, means getting better, *et cetera.*

r. means right.

l. means left.

The initial letter of a dominating word is sometimes repeated to avoid the possibility of confusion.

Comparisons of each drug have been made with a few of its allies, but it has been deemed advisable to limit these to a *very few.* Comparison is often confounded with *contrast,* and to attempt both would greatly swell the size of the book, without any increase of its usefulness; the limited number of comparisons admitted will be found reliable and a real help to those not quite satisfied with the remedy under inspection and looking for one generally similar to it and to the case in hand.

The *clinical* sections have given the author a great amount of tribulation. To sift the enormous mass of reported cures is no light task; much has been rejected, some modified and admitted after comparison with the observations of the most careful prescribers. There is no doubt that much fault can be found, with admissions as well as with rejections; doubtless some reliable clinical indications have escaped notice, but it is believed that what is here gathered fairly represents the therapeutic range of our drugs as at present known.

Much might be said concerning the *reliability* of our symptomatology; the errors that have been perpetuated from year to year in old material, and in new material obtained by faulty methods, are well known. There is no doubt that some of even Hahnemann's symptoms were observed in the sick, both as apparent results of drug action and as probable cures; it is also true that most provers have allowed themselves to record, as effects of drugs taken for experiment, symptoms which would have arisen spontaneously or which were "suggestions" of a mind watching for such effects. There is no doubt that many if not most symptoms have been observed in only one or two persons as the effect of a drug, and that many of these would fail of confirmation by repeated experiment, *but* after all these allowances have been made there remains a good and true pathogenesis sufficient for a working materia medica and capable of justifying itself by unfailing results when put to the test of homœopathic therapeutics. Numerous provings, each consisting of but a single observation, even the result of but a single dose, appeal to our knowledge of the effects of analogous drugs as genuine; they must be utilized, their symptoms guide us unerringly to the saving of life, and they cannot be discarded. We acknowledge the lack of accuracy in observation, the failure of confirmation required for scientific accuracy; we are cognizant of the absolute necessity of rebuilding the whole symptomatology from the very foundation, but during the years, or rather, generations which will elapse till this be done, we must cure the sick as best we may, and use sometimes doubtful material to accomplish our results. During this interim we must endeavor to keep separate the *probably* pure pathogenesis and the merely clinical history of each drug, for by doing this our pathogenesis will undergo a slow regeneration, good observations will replace the bad and our therapeutics will rest upon an ever-increasingly strong foundation.

The arrangement of a symptomatology for daily work in therapeutics is a matter of the utmost importance. Attempts have been made to construct working materia medicas for homœopathists on the plan of grouping the symptoms of each prover by themselves, but they fail of ready usefulness and we find ourselves obliged to work on the lines of our great master, Hahnemann. The actual need is a grouping of symptoms under the regions of the body, and under rubrics so that the symptoms of our patients may readily be compared with those of a drug thought to be applicable. We are compelled to prescribe for symptoms, and drug-symptoms must constantly be compared with those of the patient. It is rarely possible to find identity of expression between patient and prover; even the designation of similar pains varies; frequently the peculiar pain of the sick person has never been experienced by any prover in exactly the same locality, but drug-analogies may be followed and a remedy successfully selected. The necessity of looking through the symptoms referred to any locality constantly forces itself upon us. The "Schema" of Hahnemann must then be followed for all ordinary work. For extraordinary symptoms repertories of various sorts are needed; usually Bœnninghausen's method can be followed, namely, get the drugs affecting the part, get the drugs causing the particular sensation noted, get the conditions; then turn to the "Schema" and see which of the selected drugs applies best to the patient. Sometimes also we feel the need of some sort of a concordance to hunt up remarkable symptoms.

Systematic study of a drug requires a very different sort of an arrangement; for this the student needs to consult impartially all provings which have been made in good faith, to note the evolution of drug-effects, to compare the day books of the different provers, and to determine, if possible, the true characters of the drug-disease. A full collection of all provings would be most valuable.

In the study of provings or of the "Schema" it should be kept constantly in mind that just as groups of symptoms vary in individuals sick with any definite "disease," pathologically considered, so the groupings of symptoms in the provings vary, and it is extremely rare, if indeed it has ever happened, to find the total symptoms of any

any patient out of *all* the provers, it is constantly necessary to make up the nearest possible to the total from *several* provers, and it really matters not where the individual symptoms come from, so they be reliable; even parts of symptoms may be pieced together, a pain here, a locality there, a *condition* from another or from several (the "condition" should dominate the whole), to complete the picture *and the cure.* Hence it follows that in condensing our symptomatology great liberties may be taken, if only the exact meaning be preserved. Liberties have not been taken, after this fashion, in the preparation of this book, but smaller books could readily and safely be made from this by condensing after the above method.

The Selection of the Remedy.

The first duty of the therapeutist is to note carefully and completely the various complaints of his patient and add thereto his own observations concerning his condition, that is to say, he must get all of the subjective and objective symptoms. This duty is frequently quite apart from that performed in making a diagnosis and requires quite a different line of investigation; this duty may, indeed, be performed without making a diagnosis, though it is not wise to attempt it. Having "taken the case," one sets about finding the remedy which corresponds most closely to the symptoms. Three things must be done before this *Handbook* is consulted: (1) get a list of the drugs which affect the localities complained of by the patient; (2) get a list of the drugs which correspond to the sensations, and (3) get the drugs which have the same aggravations and ameliorations. *The importance* of these groups is *inverse* to the order above mentioned; the last is most important. These lists are to be obtained from the "*Pocket-book of Therapeutics,*" based on Bœnninghausen's work.

Select from these lists those drugs which occur most frequently, compare their symptoms in the Handbook with those of the patient, and select the drug which best covers the case. These directions are simple, easily followed by any one, whether educated or not, and will frequently lead to success. It must, however, be remembered that there are great and important differences in the symptoms of the sick, not only as regards their influence over a diagnosis, but also as regards their importance in influencing the choice of a remedy. It must also be recognized that a thorough knowledge of the peculiarities of a drug may lead to its selection, even if it may have but few of the symptoms of the patient. The above sort of knowledge distinguishes the "professional" from the un-professional therapeutist, the leader from the imitator.

In the case of the patient, it may be said that there are comparatively few simple diseases to prescribe for. Most symptom-lists are extremely complicated; in chronic complaints the observation that one organ after another has become involved furnishes series of symptoms from new foci, as it were, the lately developed symptoms often overpower and obscure previous affections; in acute diseases the immediate symptoms are complicated by a series of old chronic troubles which, likely as not, have so affected the vitality of the individual that the acute disease has become possible. In the latter case (frequently in scarlatina and the other so-called zymotic diseases), we find our patient unresponsive to the remedy selected for the most numerous and apparently important symptoms, and are compelled to fall back upon a careful analysis of a few chronic troubles.

It seems to be true that an individual, free from inherited and acquired disease, will not be affected by any zymosis whatever, and that a person sick with a zymotic disease will, if freed from the incubus of his chronic complaint, speedily recover. In such a case, then, we may safely say that the *totality* of the symptoms is not to be regarded.

Still we must prescribe very frequently for a few severe and distressing symptoms, and postpone for a time the investigation of the past history and present complications of the malady. This symptom-palliation is usually followed by most practitioners to the exclusion of thorough work in therapeutics, but he who practices it exclusively or even habitually is liable to administer as many different medicines as there are urgent symptoms, and finally to resort to physiological palliation and become almost wholly empirical in his practice.

In these acute diseases a knowledge of the nature of the morbid process enables the expert to separate the symptoms due to the recent malady from those which are contingent and individual and which must be considered most seriously. In the vast majority of cases the most brilliant cures are made and life actually saved by the selection of a remedy which corresponds to the fewer individual rather than to the more numerous generic symptoms. Herein lies the secret of getting at what is characteristic in the patient.

In chronic diseases the conditions are somewhat different, and as a rule the symptoms are less complicated, but it frequently becomes necessary to exercise great partiality toward a few symptoms to the exclusion of the many. In most of the chronic maladies which show no tendency to recover, but rather to involve one organ after another, the original symptoms become obscured. For example, in cancer, the tumor, with its destructive metamorphoses, has developed from the underlying cachexia which has determined its manifestations. This secondary development gives rise to new and obtrusive symptoms which may entirely mask the real disease. Consumption develops from the scrofulous habit. The Lithæmic diathesis gives rise to a host of degenerative changes in various organs and tissues which develop new sets of symptoms. In all of these and other similar diseases it becomes our duty to investigate thoroughly the nature of the morbid processes, to study the evolution of the malady and separate the symptoms into groups. While it may be true that the absolute totality of all the symptoms would include the original, determining and essential symptoms of the case, yet he who fails to grasp the full significance of all the symptoms will fail to appreciate the overpowering value of the few. It is then necessary to get at what is characteristic in the patient in all forms of sickness.

Drugs must be studied in much the same way; provings are to be followed step by step as they develop in the day books of the provers. Unfortunately the earlier provers have given us no day books, and too many of the later disciples have followed their example; but when possible study the originals and note the peculiarities of each drug, observe the predominating sensations, study the conditions under which these sensations appear or are modified, note the organs affected; this study is to be pursued during quiet hours, and need not be associated with the selection of a remedy for a patient.

In the selection of the remedy it must always be remembered that there is no specific for a "disease," that the symptoms only of the sick are to be treated, and that these symptoms vary in each individual. It may also be recognized that these groups of symptoms, varying so constantly in individuals, are to be met by varying groups of drug symptoms, and that these groups must be made up from different provers. The recognition of this fact determines the arrangement of our symptomatology for practical work in therapeutics; it seems clear that in no other way can homœopathy be practiced successfully.

Nothing need be said concerning the size of the dose further than it bears upon the relative value of symptoms. It is contended by some that the order of evolution of upon the size of dose of the drug to be administered to the sick who suffer from symptoms which appear in a similar way.

It may be said in reply that the practical experience of the best prescribers negatives such a hypothesis, and it may further be asserted that there is no fixed order of evolution either in prover or patient. Provers vary greatly in their susceptibility to drugs, and any given amount of a drug may be large relatively to the sensitiveness of one prover and small as regards the sensitiveness of another, so that the order of evolution of effects is constantly changing. The same is true of the sick; a dose large for one individual is small for another, and the only guide to the size of dose for any patient is his individual susceptibility to drugs in general or to any particular drug at any particular time. It has been fully established by experience that it matters not (for therapeutics) by what sort of dose an effect has been produced; only let a symptom be reliable, it will be cured by different doses for different people. The amount of drug necessary to produce it varies with the susceptibility of the prover, the amount needed for its removal varies with the susceptibility of the patient.

It is confidently hoped that this Handbook will contribute to the more certain application of homœopathic therapeutics to the symptoms of the sick, by the critical examination of which the best results are to be attained.

NEW YORK, April, 1889.

REMEDIES.

MATERIA MEDICA

AND

THERAPEUTICS.

Abies Canadensis.

Common name, hemlock or hemlock spruce. Natural order: Coniferæ. The fresh bark and young buds are bruised and mixed with double their weight of alcohol.

General Effects.—Weakness, faintness; lies with legs drawn up. Mood irritable. Head light; vertex feels congested. Mouth dry. Hunger, with rumbling in the bowels after eating; craving for meat, pickles and coarse food, with gnawing in the epigastrium. Thirst. Belching of wind. Distention of stomach, with burning in it. Weakness in epigastrium. The region of the liver feels hard, with a pain behind the r. scapula. Sick feeling in bowels, with an irritable feeling in the region of the spleen. Constipation. Burning in the rectum. Frequent micturition. Uterus has a soft, weak feeling, with soreness of the fundus, relieved by pressure. Respiration labored. Action of heart increased and labored. In sacral region a weak feeling. Night restless, with tossing about. During the day yawning and drowsiness. Cold shiverings as if the blood were ice-water. Chills run down the back. Feeling of cold water between the shoulders. Hands cold, shrunken. Skin clammy.

Compare with *Abies nigra.*

Abies Nigra.

A tree growing in northern United States and Canada, belonging to the Coniferæ. A tincture is prepared by dissolving the gum in alcohol.

General Action.—As far as we are now able to judge from the provings, and from our clinical experience with this drug, its most marked effect is upon the digestion; and in disorders of the stomach its only laurels have been won. Most, if not all, of the symptoms hitherto observed are intimately associated with gastric disturbances.

Generalities.—Weariness. Bone pains (Eupat. perf.).

Mind.—Melancholy; nervous; unable to think; dull during the day, but wakeful at night.

Head.—Vertigo. Dull headache. Head and face hot (Bry.). Pain in l. ear.

Choking sensation in throat.

Hunger at noon and night; *loss of appetite in morning* (Nux v.); *sensation of a hard-boiled egg in stomach;* pain after eating (Bry., Nux v.); P. extending to l. side. Constipation.

Menstruation suppressed (Bry.).

Dyspnœa; worse on lying down; sense of suffocation as if one could not expand the lungs; sharp cutting pain in the heart; heart's action heavy and slow.

Pain in the small of the back.

Night restless, with bad dreams.

Coldness, alternating with heat.

Clinical.—The most characteristic indication for Abies in indigestion is the distress as if something were knotted up in the stomach. It has often proved curative in the dyspepsia resulting from the use of tea and tobacco.

Abrotanum.

The Southernwood (Artemisia Abrotanum, L.) is still cultivated in old gardens; a low shrub about three feet in height, with finely divided leaves of an intensely bitter taste. A tincture is prepared from the chopped and bruised leaves.

General Action.—The indications of a central disturbance (hyperæmia) of the nervous system, producing anæsthesia and paralysis, are very marked; this is accompanied by neuralgic pains, which cause restlessness and are relieved by motion.

Group for Study—Absinth., Rhus tox., Con., Gels., Caust., Argent. n., Phos., Cimicif., Zinc.

Generalities.—Trembling all over. (Argent. n., Cimicif., Gels.) Often unconsciously dropped the reins while driving. (Compare Con.) Pains in afternoon, with necessity to lie down, great sleepiness, but inability to sleep. P. in back, hips and knees, in afternoon. P. all day in side and back of neck and shoulders, limbs, back and hips, with numbness of arms and hands.

Darting pain in various parts of body and limbs; in various parts, in forenoon, most severe above and near r. elbow. Itching, then darting pains in different parts, most in lower lobes of lungs and below knees. Lameness, morning on waking, especially in back, muscular soreness on motion, with pain in back of neck, shoulders, r. side of chest and limbs, with lameness of r. hip, so as to cause limping.

Weakness, in forenoon, with lameness; weak, sickly feeling, with internal trembling when excited. Disposed to lie prone.

Mind.—Nervous, excited, loquacious, felt like shouting, good humored, happy. Taciturn, irritable, violent. Peevish, feels as if she would like to do something cruel. Desponding. Thinks her brain is softening. No capacity for thinking. Feebleness and dulness.

Head.—Aching; and fulness. Creeping chills along convolutions of brain, with prickling. L. brain seems especially weak, easily fatigued by conversation or mental effort. Head weak, could not hold it up. Squeezed feeling in temporal region. Pain in l. temple, morning on waking, continuing all forenoon. Scalp sore, < l. side. Itching of scalp.

Eyes.—Smarting in evening, with pain in l., and inability to open it.

Ears.—Wind rushes out of right. Humming like a bee, but when in bed a sound like distant talking, > listening intently, but returning as he turned his mind from it.

Nose.—Watery discharge.

Mouth.—Tongue sore. Mouth hot and dry, morning on waking. Mouth dry and sore; sore, < night, with salivation; soreness mostly confined to gums near l., upper molars.

Throat.—Scraping.

Stomach.—Appetite poor. Gnawing hunger. Eructations of air tasting of the plant; of air tasting of salt mackerel in evening. Nausea; with sour eructations; in evening, with burning and soreness of stomach; felt sick all forenoon, > open air. Stomach sour. Burning like acidity. Heat; in epigastrium at night, with pain.

Abdomen.—Bloated and painful at 10 P.M.; bloated at midnight, so that it was difficult to walk or bend, and feeling as if bowels could be kept from passing out at anus only by keeping legs close together. Pain; all night, with several stools. P. and heat. Weak, sinking feeling (Gels., Phos.). P. in l. hypochondriac region, with empty eructations. P. in region of liver and kidneys, sick, sore, faint, almost amounting to faintness, with inability to walk in the street.

Anus and Stool.—Piles, becoming worse as the rheumatic pains abated, with frequent inclination to stool, hardly anything but blood being passed. Urgent desire for stool; with loose stools at 6 and 7 A.M. Frequent loose stools. Stool, with straining, and feeling as if large and indurated, though quite the reverse. Constipation.

Urinary Organs.—Bladder full, urging to urinate.

Sexual Organs.—Pain in testicles and back. Twitching in ovarian regions, extending to back. Darting pain in region of l. ovary.

Respiratory Organs.—Sudden hoarseness (Gels., Seneg.). Voice weak (Caust., Gels.). Raw feeling caused by cold air. Sensation as if breathing hot air. Breathing difficult.

Chest.—Pricking pain in r. Pain just below heart, then crawling and eructations. P. in l. lung; P. in base of both lungs through the day, with darting pains in limbs and ankles. Sore P. in lungs; in lower part of l. lung, morning on waking. Burning through r. chest.

Pulse.—Quick.

Neck and Back.—Pulling in muscles of neck beneath r. angle of jaw. Back lame, and painful. Heavy pain in lumbar region at 5 P.M.; extending to testicles. Weakness of back, with ovarian pains.

Extremities.—Pain all day in shoulders, arms and hips; in arms, legs and feet on waking, > after motion, with lameness (Rhus t.). Sore feeling in all, morning on waking, mostly in joints. Joints sore and lame (Rhus t.). Joints stiff, with prickling (Rhus t.). Prickling and burning in joints. Weakness of extremities; of arms and limbs, with numb feeling (Rhus t.); of legs, in evening, and painfulness and lameness of hands.

Upper Extremities.—Pain in axillæ as if a sore were forming. Shoulders pain. P. from joint to elbows; *sharp pain* in l. on waking; fugitive P. all night, preventing sleep; lameness and soreness, morning on waking.

Arms.—Pain above elbows; above r. elbow in afternoon; above l. elbow at 1 A.M. when rising. Sore pain above l. elbow at 11 P.M. Arms feel as if tied to body. Lameness and aching on outer and under side, above l. elbow, when riding; then lameness of arm all day. Lameness and weakness of r. arm. Weakness.

Pain in l elbow and r. hand; in r. elbow all forenoon. Hands sore and painful all day, with difficulty in handling everything. Lameness of r. hand; l. hand at 10 A.M., so that he could not sit still. Aching in first r. finger, then in other fingers of r. and l. hand. Numb sensation in fingers (Con., Phos., Sec. corn.).

Lower Extremities.—Aching pain all day across hips. P. in hips, severe in r. hip and thigh. Lameness of hips and legs. Thighs lame and painful, with sore feeling, but they are not sore to touch.

Knees.—Pain; l.; sore P. in evening, r. then l. Lameness and painfulness of r. knee in morning. Lame, aching p. on inside of r. knee, then on outside of l. Lameness of knees at 11 A.M. Weakness of r. knee and ankle.

Legs.—Sudden pain. P. in middle of l.; then r. tibia. Legs and feet lame and painful. Sore lameness in head of l. fibula in evening. Ankles and legs so painful that he could not sit still at 11.30 A.M. (Rhus t.). Pain in ankles and knees, with lame and painful feet. Aching P. in ankles and feet, especially outside of l. ankle.

Skin.—A large sore forms from a small scratch. The old eruption feels sore, with violent pricking itching extending to head and arms. Itching of limbs; of a corn on second left toe.

Sleep.—Yawning and eructations all day. Sleepiness all day. Sleep unrefreshing. Sleep restless; with springing up and constant jumping and thrashing of arms. Night restless, with heat and pain at epigastrium. Dreams frightful, and waking frightened and trembling.

Fever.—Chilliness.

Absinthium.

Artemisia absinthium. Common wormwood. A shrub of the natural order Compositæ, wild in Europe, naturalized in the United States. A tincture is prepared by bruising the young leaves and blossoms and adding two parts of alcohol.

General Action.—The most marked general effect of Absinthium is epilepsy. The convulsions attack suddenly one who has been in the habit of drinking absinth for a long time, especially if at any time he indulges in excess. A large number of these convulsions are apt to occur in rapid succession for a few hours, coming on with screaming. The convulsions begin in the face and extend to the body and limbs, which are at first rigid, and then affected by clonic spasms; with cyanotic face, irregular and stertorous respiration. The convulsions are followed by stupidity, lack of sensibility and loss of memory. The general or associated symptoms are as follows:

Generalities.—Faintness. Symptoms of general paralysis. General anæsthesia or general hyperæsthesia. Trembling, especially of the lips, tongue and limbs, worse in the morning. Frequent hysterical spasms, not amounting to epilepsy, the convulsions consisting of rigidity of the limbs and some irregular motions. Tendency to lie with head low.

Mind.—Crying and wishing to die. Delirium. Dread of assassination. Various hallucinations. Idiocy. Irritable mood. Kleptomania. Loquacity. Complete loss of memory. Sudden attacks of stupor and unconsciousness. Frightful visions. Expression foolish.

Head.—General confusion, with headache. Constriction of the temples. Pain above the eyes. Vertigo on rising, or with tendency to fall backward.

Eyes brilliant. Conjunctiva injected. Sclerotic yellow. Pupils dilated unequally. Lids heavy.

Loss of appetite and loathing of food. Thirst. Eructations. Nausea; retching; vomiting of bitter mucus. Coldness and oppression in stomach. Food lies heavy. Flatulent distention of the abdomen, which is hard. Wind colic. Liver becomes enlarged. Constipation.

Micturition frequent. Urine deep orange, of a strong odor; red; in some cases albuminous.

Darting pain in r. ovary.

Voice feeble, speech hesitating; voice trembling and hoarse. Cough, with expectoration. Crepitant râles. Heart's action irregular, tumultuous; trembling of the heart felt through to the back. Oppression of chest.

Unsteady, tottering gait. Sciatica.

Clinical.—This drug has been used as a remedy for prolonged spasms of children, and in a few cases of epileptiform convulsions of older persons. Its clinical history is, however, very imperfect.

Acalypha Indica.

A weed found in India, belonging to the Euphorbiaceæ. A tincture is prepared from the fresh plant.

Severe fit of dry cough, followed by spitting of blood.

NOTE.—This symptom, doubtless a clinical observation, enabled Dr. Holcomb, of New Orleans, to cure a most obstinate case of hæmoptysis, after other means had failed.

Acetic Acid.

For use, prepare dilutions with distilled water.

General Action.—This acid produces directly gastro-enteritis, and also (in one case, at least) membranous laryngo-tracheitis. Its remote effects are a profound anæmia, with diarrhœa, night-sweats, feeble pulse, emaciation and cough.

Generalities.—Emaciation. Attacks of faintness. General oppression and heaviness. Weakness. General trembling. (Convulsions, with insensibility.)

Mind.—Irritability. Nervousness. Anxiety. Alarm. Excitement. Delirium. Confusion. Inertia. Unconsciousness.

Head.—Vertigo. Heaviness. Dull pain in forehead and vertex. Dull aching in r. frontal eminence, then in l. In the temples distention of bloodvessels. Shooting P. through temples.

Eyes.—Sunken, surrounded by dark circles. Pupils dilated. Lachrymation.

Face.—Red, hot and perspiring, with flushed cheeks. Pale, waxy. Expression wild.

Mouth and Stomach.—Salivation. Tongue pale and flabby; dry and cold. Thirst. Eructations, hot. Loss of appetite; aversion to cold food; to salt food. Nausea; vomiting; vomiting after eating. In the stomach, pain, burning, gnawing, ulcerative. Heat. Soreness. Fermentation, with distress. Cold drinks cause distress. Soreness in one spot as from an ulcer, with gnawing; with agony and vomiting of thick, yellow matter, like yeast. Epigastrium painful to pressure.

Abdomen.—Burning pain. Distention. Griping. Rumbling. Feeling as if it would sink in, which caused dyspnœa. Relief by lying on abdomen.

Stools.—Watery, with colic. Bloody.

Urine increased and light-colored.

Mother's Milk impoverished, bluish, deficient in caseine and butter; the child drooped, had diarrhœa, and died of marasmus; the mother was pale, emaciated, and had chronic hemorrhages.

Respiratory Organs.—Voice lost. Croup, with hissing respiration, rattling, formation of false membrane in windpipe. Cough dry, then moist, with fever; dyspnœa, emaciation, œdema and diarrhœa. Respiration difficult, feeble, hurried.

Chest.—Burning pain. (Chronic inflammation.)

Pulse.—Rapid, small, weak.

Extremities.—Weak. Wrist and hand feel paralyzed. Hands cold, prickling, dry. Œdema of lower extremities. Diminished sensibility of feet.

Skin.—Pale and waxy. Red and burning. Desquamation.

Fever.—Temperature diminished, with cold feet. Flushes of heat, with perspiration. Hectic, emaciation, diarrhœa, night-sweats, dyspnœa, and swelling of lower extremities. Low fever, with delirium, diarrhœa, tympanitis, constipation; also with stupor. Sweats profuse, cold, nocturnal.

Clinical.—General anæmia, with a waxy skin, anasarca, emaciation and sweats. Delirium in low fever, with profuse sweats and diarrhœa. Membranous croup, with bright-red face and perspiration. It should be given in anæmia of nursing women. (See above.)

Aconitum.

Aconitum napellus, or A. stœrkianum. Natural order: Ranunculaceæ. The monkshood, though cultivated in America, is a native of Europe. A tincture is made from the whole plant, gathered at the time of flowering

General Action.—Aconite in small doses accelerates the heart's action, and causes a rise of temperature; then follow alternate chill and fever, tumultuous action of the heart, sweat and great weakness. From larger doses, paralysis of the heart, feeble pulse, cold sweat, paralysis of sensory and motor nerves, vomiting and purging, convulsions and death. *Mental distress is exceedingly characteristic;* it is produced by all doses, in all cases of poisoning, in all provings, and even in experiments on animals; this peculiar anxiety distinguishes Aconite from all other drugs. The tingling and numbness, which are experienced even from small doses, and the neuralgias, affecting particularly the upper portion of the body, are, likewise, characteristic. Aconite causes only functional disturbance; there is scarcely any evidence of power to produce tissue change; its action is brief, and shows no marked periodicity.

Groups for Study and Comparison.—Other species of Aconite, Veratrum (and liliaceous plants, such as Convallaria, Adonis, Colchicum), Digitalis, Camphor (Opium), Arsenicum, Iodine.

Antidotes.—Belladonna, Nux vom., Digitalis, Camphor (each in part only).

Generalities.—Lies on l. side (Spong.); on back, with l. hand flat under head during morning sleep. Cannot lie on r. side or back (Nux v.).

Jaundice. Swelling of whole body. Cracking of joints.

Convulsions; alternating with relaxation; tetanic (Sec. corn.); convulsions, with distortion of eyes, clenched jaws, body rigid and bent backward, limbs distorted (Jasmin). Convulsions, with eyes drawn upward, fists clenched across the throat, grating of the teeth, ropy saliva and involuntary discharges. Convulsions of face and upper extremities, relieved by vomiting. Convulsions at intervals of 20 minutes, ushered in with a shuddering noise; arms became rigid and raised above head, which was thrown back, and lower limbs extended rigidly, features distorted to one side or other, eyes closed, no general convulsions, face pale, consciousness unimpaired, could not speak owing to spasms of respiratory muscles, during intervals spoke well. Falls down insensible, icy cold, imperceptible pulse, hands and arms fixed in front of chest, face pale, lips blue, eyes sunken, twitching of eyeballs (Sec. c.). Limbs strongly flexed, with cold, clammy sweat, eyes turned upward, followed by general relaxation, aphonia and vomiting. Tetanus, with clenched fists, arms drawn backward and flexed, with opisthotonos. Convulsions of lower extremities, with clenched, cold, numb hands and slow pulse. Limbs drawn inward, thumbs clenched into palms (Hyosc.). Legs in constant motion, with cold sweat on face; cracking of joints.

Prickling and electric shocks through whole body. Hysterical condition (Ign., Plat.). Twitching; of tendons (Bell., Hyos., Op., Stram.); of muscles of face, fingers and toes; attempting by jerks to change her position in bed. Threw himself about violently, and attempted to bite attendants.

Trembling (Lach.); anxious. Trembling like a boiling and seething, with coldness. Nervousness; on falling asleep, and fear; and agitation (Arg. nit., Tarent., Thea.).

Stitches here and there (Bry.); electric, in forehead, back, sides of chest, back of hands and in other parts; flying, here and there in evening, in ribs, abdominal parietes and joints (Puls.). *Stinging or stinging-burning pain in many parts, as if in skin* (Nux v.), *sometimes with heaviness, numbness or swelling; tearing stitches in nearly all joints alternately.* Lancinating P., especially in joints (Kali carb.).

Drawing, wandering, tearing, mostly alternating with heart symptoms. Pain, *in joints;* P. around waist. Drawing P., here and there; throbbing, here and there; wandering, sometimes in nape, loins, intestines, or right groin, or one or another joint (Puls.). Drawing, here and there in joints. Rheumatic P. *Bruised sensations:* Constriction. General oppression. Malaise.

Swollen feeling over almost whole body, especially l. side, changing to a numb feeling, with bruised feeling in muscles and pressing or bruised feeling in bones, also with the swollen feeling changing to numbness there is a bruised feeling in ribs, upper part of chest and arms, and a crampy feeling about heart. *Swollen feeling in many parts* (Rhus, Spig.), *generally with shuddering-cold or rigor.*

Soreness and stiffness of all muscles (Rhus). General sore, tired feeling (Arn., Baptis., Rhus).

Sensitive to fresh air (Dulc., Kali c.). *Sensitiveness of whole body to touch* (Bell., Chin., Nux v., Spig.).

Restlessness and tossing about (Ars.).

Weakness (Gelsem.) morning on waking, > on rising; *from walking and talking;* walking, < ascending stairs; with sleepiness; in joints, with unsteadiness; of muscles and ligaments, so that he could not sit nor stand unsupported; intermittent, with insensibility. Depression, with faintness, livid face and feeble pulse (Dig.). Nervous prostration. Laziness. Collapse (Sec. c.). Faintness, *on attempting to sit up* (Carbo v., Gelsem.), evening when urinating, with rush of blood to head; after urinating, with whirling around of everything and with cold sweat on hands, with shivering.

Numbness; *with tingling* (Plat., Rhus, Sec. c.).

Crawling, like a mixture of formication, prickling and tickling, first on tip of tongue, then over upper surface of tongue and lips, extending to posterior part of mouth, then beginning in tips of fingers, then in face, above all in suprahyoid region and on chin, then in cheeks and tip of toes, on perineum, chest, abdomen, and lastly on back, more violent in former regions, < change of temperature.

Heaviness (Nux v., Rhus). Leaden of body, from shoulders downward, with pressure from all sides and from above, seeming to make the body, except head and neck, smaller. Feeling as if the bedclothes were a dreadful weight.

Paralytic condition; in l., then r. side. Loss of equilibrium.

Clinical.—The *convulsions* arrested or prevented by Aconite are not dependent upon a chronic constitutional taint, but result from a sudden nervous shock, such as fright, or are of recent origin, as in the puerperal state; the face is red, hot and sweaty, with other symptoms as above. In hysterical spasms, neuralgias, congestions, hæmorrhages, and effects of shock from injury or fright, the terrible mental distress characteristic of the drug must be the guide to its successful use; also after exposure to sun or great heat, with a plethoric appearance, some anæsthesia or great sensitiveness to touch, Acon. may be used always with mental anxiety and acute sensitiveness to pain. The pains are usually acute, sticking, and often associated with or followed by numbness. Restlessness and agonized tossing about are essential in a case requiring Aconite.

General Conditions.—*Aggravation,* in evening; in close room (Iod.); on rising from lying down (Bry., Op., Dig.).

Amelioration, in open air (Bry., Plat.); in cool air (Bry., Op., Puls.); after eating (Puls.); after watery stool; after sweat (Rhus); after vomiting (Dig., Sec. c.); after drinking (Cedron); after wine or coffee (transient).

Mind.—Raving, with jumping out of bed (Bell.); intermittent. Delirium; *chattered childish nonsense* (Hyosc.); *said he was dying, with restless jerking and jumping about* (Ars.). Mixture of dulness and excitement.

Activity of mind. Clearness. (Clairvoyance.) Buried in thought. Occupied with one subject Disinclined to think; to read. Distraction. Inability to think; stupid, also in evening, or with fretfulness, from tobacco smoke. Unsteadiness of thought. Confusion. Coma, eyes half closed, pupils insensible (Op.). Memory active (during excitement); impaired (reaction). Hallucinations, that his head was three times its natural size, that his mental operations transpired in the pit of his stomach. **Anxiety;** *with the shivering; inconsolable;* as of an impending misfortune. Agony. **Fear. Apprehension.** Dread, of misfortune; *of approaching death* (Ars., Op., Plat.); of staggering and falling. *Solicitude.* Despair (Arsen.); plaintive cries. *Sadness.* (Ign.); from music, which is unendurable and goes through every limb (Tarent.); weeping. **Whining.** *Piteous howlings* (Verat.). **Vexation** about trifles (Nux v.). Complaints and reproaches, often about trifles. Misanthropic. Quarrelsome (Nux v.). Fretful. *Restless, variable mood* (Ign., Plat.). Impatience. Hurry in all actions, in speech (Arg. n., Lil. tig.). Gayety; happiness, inclined to sing and dance. Apathy; disinclined to talk; indifferent; desire to be alone (Plat.). Anthropophobia (Aur.). Obstinacy.

Clinical.—In delirium, with ravings about death, hot face and head; effects of fright; fear of crowds or of death, with anguish, etc.

Head.—Sticking pain (Caps. < rest); jerking sticking, especially in forehead; sticking on coughing (Arn., Carbo v.). *Shooting pulsating.* Aching; on stooping < mental effort; < speaking. A., as from a band (Gels., Merc. sol.); as from a hot iron band; as if eyes would fall out; as if brain were pressing out; as if brain were raised here and there; bruised, < motion, drinking and speaking. *A., burning, as if brain were agitated by boiling water.* A., constrictive and pressing, especially in upper part of forehead, < light and noise, > sleep, with obscured vision; as if skull were compressed from all sides (Anac.), especially in l. orbit; constrictive pain over whole skull, especially l. side and over l. eye, > cool hand. A. in head and face, extending over body. Neuralgic pain, then in lower extremities.

Compression, as if aponeurosis were too tight; as from a vise; in evening, at times worse in l. orbit; recurring at same hour. **Fulness** (Glo.), with erratic pain in r. supraorbital, temporal and frontal regions. Congestion; sudden and frequent, with anxiety, then rigor over back. Apoplectic. Heaviness; in morning, with vertigo; with ringing in ears, < yawning, dizzy, especially in frontal region, with nausea and sinking in pit of stomach, also on stooping. Drawing, especially in temporal muscles and behind ears; feeling as if something were drawn out of head, causing lids to be drawn up. Confusion; morning on waking; after every effort; while eating; in evening with pressure in forehead; forenoon, with flushes of heat and vertigo; < motion; as after intoxicating drinks. Emptiness; morning, as after intoxication. Lightness. Head feels smaller to hand, with warmth of head. Pulsation (Bell., Fer., Glo.); fine, here and there. Waving and shaking of brain. Roaring in head and ears, < reading. Tingling, benumbed. Feeling as if head were forcibly turned around.

Vertigo; morning on waking (Lach.); forenoon, with confusion of head; forenoon, when walking, changing in house to stupefaction; driving or walking; *on rising up* (Bry., Phos.); on rising, with heavy headache in temporal muscles above ears, nausea and gush of cold sweat; on rising, with flickering before eyes, roaring in ears, pain in head and face, nausea and weakness; when standing; on *stooping* (Sulph.); stooping, with vision of sparks and fog; after walking, with reeling; vertigo aggravated, open air, after dinner, *shaking head, when there is blackness before eyes,* stooping **with nausea,** *rising from a seat* (Bry.); > *walking and sitting,* by *deep breathing.* Vertigo, with distraction of mind; with headache; obscuration of vision; feeling as if about to fall; staggering, especially to r.; vertigo, with feeling that his legs were going away from him. Everything goes around in a circle. Vertigo, to falling.

Forehead.—Stitches in r.; after eating, extending to temple; alternating with same in occiput; nauseating over orbits, *extending to upper jaw;* stitches at times pulsating or pressive-aching, on walking, > sitting. Drawing; *drawing pressive feeling in nerve trigeminus; tense drawing in trigeminus, then shooting, wandering, intermittent, then constant pain, sometimes pressure.* Crepitation (as of gold tinsel bent back and forth), and in temples and nose. Aching; morning, on waking; night; < evening; over eye; r. half; especially over r. superciliary ridge, with dread of jar by riding; in spot above l. superciliary ridge, morning after waking, > after a nap; l. eminence; in sinciput; forehead and occiput, < towards evening. Contractive. In r. protuberance, extending towards orbit, with flushes of heat, especially in face and ears; involving r. eyebrow. Outpressing. Stupefying, < towards 6 P.M. Wedge-like pressing asunder, near l. brow, < in room.

Feeling as of a board before forehead. Corrugated between brows. Squeezing; in bones, with sick feeling as if madness would ensue; over nose, with feeling as if she would lose her reason, < walking in open air. Nailed-up feeling in a warm room. Swelling; swollen feeling, < l. Tension; squeezing, tensive pain behind orbits. **Fulness** (Glon.); **in sinuses, with heaviness and feeling as if something would come out,** the latter also on stooping. Heaviness; in sinciput, with numbness. Pulsation towards both eyes; *l. side, with attacks of blows in r. side.* Confusion; r.; dizzy, in r., when walking in open air.

Temples.—*Stitches in r. muscles;* stitches in l. temple, < entering house, with drawing pain; stitches from temple into head; twitching stitches in l. Tearing in l. Drawing from muscles into external meatus, causing tense feeling there. Aching; l.; r. (Sang.); behind r. mastoid process; bursting (Glon.); as if compressed with screws; as from pressure of a thumb behind r. ear; pressing-out, evenings, with fulness in forehead, pricking and biting in lips, as in beginning of coryza, with flushes of heat; stupefying, drawing, pressing-inward in l.; shooting pulsating; neuralgic in r. Tingling; with sense of enlargement of forehead and disturbance of vision. Pulsation of arteries during chill. Contraction of muscles. Swelling. Swollen feeling, < l.

Vertex.—Stitches (Bry.); aching; forenoon, evenings; *nightly;* > washing with cold water; light, < stooping and moving head; < motion; then extending to forehead, where it caused heaviness and fulness; aching on both sides; aching, with tension, aching, as from a *cap,* also > *motion in open air;* A., extending towards temporal region, < stooping; A., as from a weight. Heaviness, compression extending to whole head.

Parietals.—Jerking, shooting, drawing, tearing pain in r. side of head superiorly. Aching; in l. side of head; evening and night; > cold water; in l. side, as if compressed. Heaviness in bones; heaviness in r. side of head, with pressing out. Semi-lateral drawing in head.

Occiput.—Stitches; in bone; alternating with same in root of nose. Twitching, tearing. Aching; < stooping, and in forehead; acute about base of brain and in back of neck, with spasms in arms; distending; by fits and starts; twitching. Injected feeling in brain. Drawing numbness in l. Weight.

Scalp.—Bristling of hair on vertex; *scalp feels as if the hair stood on end, also in spots. Stitches under scalp. Sensation as if swollen and numb. Sensitiveness to touch;* in spots, *and to cold air, < strong wind.* Sensation as if some one drew him up by the hair. *Formication; > heat. Creeping in l. side as from a brush.* Tickling on touching hair, especially on vertex. Itching.

Clinical.—The headache associated with fever is a hot, full, pulsating, bursting pain, with flushed face, etc., reminding one of Bell.; the neuralgia of scalp and skull varies, usually sharp, shooting along nerves (Spig.), drawing, tense, numb (Verbasc.), or pulsating (Glon.). The anterior portion of head is usually involved. The peculiar mental distress accompanies all the headaches (clinically).

Eyes.—*Bloodshot.* Yellowish. Protruding. *Dull, with blue rings.* Expressionless. Wandering look. Glaring. Staring. Glassy. Sparkling. *Distorted.* Turned upward. Twitching—pain; < looking down or around, with heat in them; pain as if crushed; *P. anteriorly as if it would be pushed out when lids are opened* (Sang.), extending to supraorbital region and interior of brain. Sharp P. through r., leaving an ache. Feeling as if they would drop from their sockets. **Painful inflammation.** Swollen feeling. Constriction. Tightness across eyes and nose. *Burning;* burning alternately in each; burning and pressure in l., and over brow. Warmth and undulation, with half-closing of lids and feeling as if it were too dark to read in a well-lighted room. (Cold feeling in open air.) **Sensitiveness to air.** Itching.

Lachrymation; when coughing; < evening and night.

Balls.—Fine sticking in r. *Enlarged feeling, as if coming out of orbits and stretching lids* (Nat. m., Par.). Pressure; in l. ball and r. orbital region; as if pressed into orbit; upper part feels as if pressed out of orbit on moving it, > stooping, changing to dull pain on bending head backward; pressure in front, not quite superficial, part, sometimes stinging or burning.

Pupil.—*Contraction;* then dilatation; alternating with dilatation. Mobility, then dilatation, with dim vision, and blinking on looking at bright objects. Dilatation; r. nearly oval; l. irregularly polygonal. Insensible to light.

Lids.—Swollen. Twitching. Blinking on looking at strongly lighted objects. Closed convulsively. Will not keep closed, so that there is sleeplessness. *Burning.* Itching. Heaviness. Hard red swelling of r. upper, with tension, < morning. Pressure alternately in each upper. L. upper feels as if long, heavy and hanging down paralyzed. *Dryness of upper.* Pain deep-seated in r. inner canthus. *Sensation of sand in l. inner canthus. Margins sore, red and inflamed* (Apis). Irritation of margins. Itching on margins, with smarting.

Conjunctiva, injected; especially towards inner canthus; *of lids and balls red.*

Orbits.—Sudden compressive pain in upper margin of r. *Shooting in supraorbital ridge, branching across forehead to scalp, to r. temple, cheek, and into some teeth,* < pressure and towards evening, when there was constant cough, followed by swelling of ridge. Tearing in l. margin; tearing in l., with constriction as if ball would be pressed outward. Pain. Tension.

Vision.—Acute. Confused. Dazzled. *Dim;* with vertigo. *Lost.* Weak. Amblyopia. Diplopia. *Photophobia.* Flickering; in evening on going from half-dark room into street, worse at short than long distances. Black floating spots. Sparks. White bright spot, changing to straw color, then the whole field of vision became lilac-hued, followed by a bright azure spot. All sorts of hallucinations.

Clinical.—In the first stage of acute inflammations of various tissues of the eye and its appendages, with heat, dryness and sharp pain, before any exudation has taken place. Acute inflammation from foreign bodies, etc. In acute aggravations of chronic disease (catarrh, trachoma, etc.). In recent paralysis from cold. In ciliary and orbital neuralgia. Acute symptoms from overstrain of muscles.

Ears.—Stitches in l. in forenoon, with twinges and stoppage; acute stoppage in r. meatus externus; drawing stitches in l. Tearing in l. Pain; *in r.;* l.; below r.; burning P. shooting into l.; drawing P. Burning, itching and darting when yawning, < in evening and in open air, > after eating. Feeling as if a drop of hot water were in l. Stoppage; of r.; stopped feeling in l. Tickling in r. as from a worm in it. Swollen sensation in bone around external ear. Prickling burning in palate, throat, and Eustachian tube, < swallowing. Stiffening sensation in r. Eustachian tube, compelling swallowing.

Hearing impaired. **Sensitiveness to every noise** (Bell., Mur. ac., etc.). Buzzing before ears, then faintness. Humming. Humming hissing. *Ringing;* with yawning. *Roaring;* l.; < reading. Seething. Singing. Loud noises.

Clinical.—Inflammation of external parts, even involving the tympanum, with fever, excruciating pain, caused by a draught of cold air. Neuralgia, involving ear and parts about it.

Nose.—Stitches at root alternating with same in occiput. *Pain at base between orbits* (Ign., Kali bi.). Stupefying compression at root. Constriction. Obstruction in r. nostril. Tightness across nose and eyes. Raw feeling in posterior nares. *Dry feeling in posterior nares.* Sneezing frequently; with pain in abdomen; with shootings in chest; sneezing interrupted by pain in l. chest. Desired to sneeze, but could not. *Clear fluid flows from nose;* hot fluid drops out; frothy mucus from nose and mouth; profuse discharge with stuffing in head; discharge of thick yellow mucus. Coryza; *fluent,* beginning with violent chill about midnight, then copious sweat; *severe coryza,* with lachrymation; **Epistaxis** (Cact. mil.); *blows out bright blood mornings* (Bry.). **Great sensibility of olfactory nerves** (Bell.); *bad smells have a powerful effect.*

Clinical.—Incipient coryza, nares hot and dry, or with hot fluid discharge, with chills and fever. Hæmorrhage of bright, hot blood, with anxiety (Ham., Secale, Phos., Croc., blood dark).

Face.—Dusky. *Pale;* and anxious. *Red;* with tension; flushed over cheek bones, otherwise pallid. *Livid.* Livid purple, with white blotches. Sunken. Expressionless. **Expression of agony**; of astonishment; **of anxiety; of fright**, and imbecility; heavy, depressed; *hippocratic; restless;* pinched. Swelling. Distortion; < change of temperature. *Twitching. Pain; creeping,* *on cheeks; P. in zygomatic process as* from an internal ulcer; pressive and digging pain in chin. Lower and anterior part feels compressed from both sides. Contracted feeling in muscles and numb, heavy, paralytic feeling in whole face. Drawing in cheeks, upper jaw and forehead. Distorted feeling; as if a muscle bulged out, then as if whole jaw were thrust to one side, or as if the lower jaw were pushed up or raised into the cavity of the mouth. **Swollen feeling**; < l. side; *of cheeks. Tingling;* benumbed. Rigidity. Numbness; of cheeks and tongue, extending over shoulder and back and down the arms, then hyperæsthesia.

Lips.—*Black.* Blue. Pale. *Swollen.* **Pain.** Feeling as if swollen. Inflammation. Burning; extending to stomach. Heat. Feeling as if drawn up. Dryness; then in mouth, with heat rising from chest to head. Tickling. Tingling. Numbness; extending to stomach. Swollen feeling.

Jaws dropping. *Involuntary closure with salivation. Trismus; in paroxysms.* Shooting jerks in lower. *Rigidity.* Aching of lower; in joint on chewing; burning aching in upper; piercing as if they would fall off; pressing on lower. Drawing in lower with stinging. Creeping, and in tongue, with burning, so that the teeth seemed to wabble. Tingling in angles and down side of neck. Leaden heaviness of upper. Numbness. Dead feeling in lower. Paralysis of lower.

Clinical.—The expression in fever is flushed and anxious, in neuralgia pinched and suffering, in tetanus drawn and rigid. The neuralgia commonly cured results from cold, is of recent origin, and usually associated with tingling and numbness (Verbascum). Several cases of tetanus have been cured.

Mouth.—Teeth. Stitches; in r. molars, also with drawing. Aching; r.; l. upper; drawing burning pain on r. lower margin of a socket. Feeling as if they would fall out. Sore feeling. Peculiar feeling in roots. Cold feeling in incisors. *Sensitiveness to open air.* Numbness extending over cheek bone to inner canthus, then over almost whole body, with feeling in head as if brain were larger and pressed forcibly against the skull, with chilliness over back and paleness and coldness of face. *Gums hot.*

Tongue.—Hanging out of mouth. Moved constantly, at times thrust beyond lips and moved from side to side. **Swollen.** *Burning vesicles on tip.* (Nat. Sul.) Coated; in morning; white; yellow. Stitches in r. under surface; at back; through it fine, in tip; flying. Cramp at root. Feeling as if getting longer. Biting, < towards tip. *Burning;* after eating; of sides; *tip;* under tongue. Cold (Camph. Verat. a.); feeling as of cold air passing over it; biting cooling, with salivation, then crawling. Drawn-up feeling; feeling in root as if drawn spasmodically to both sides. *Dry and rough feeling in middle.* Leathery feeling. Crawling, and on lips, then on face, spreading over body, with itching in skin and drawing up of face, dry skin, afterwards crawling increased and caused such restlessness that he walked the room almost all night as if crazy; crawling, as from peppermint, extending to lips and lower part of palate. Prickling; spreading over lips and to fauces, then to tips of fingers and toes, to face and then over whole body, with formication and tickling. Tingling; of tip; extending to lips. Numbness. Paralysis. **Articulation** difficult. Thick speech. Unintelligible sounds.

Mouth in general.—Twitching. Drawn to one side. Redness. Burning biting. Burning; with congestion, and in lips, with roughness in throat, especially in posterior nares, which compels hawking, and feeling as if tough mucus were drawn through choanæ, with dryness, < tobacco smoke. Inflammation and pain. Soreness of salivary ducts. **Dryness**; at night; dry feeling in front part; with coolness. Feeling as if the breath were fetid, in morning on waking. Fuzziness in spots. Tingling; benumbed. *Numbness.* Discharge of frothy mucus and from nose. *Salivation;* frothy; saliva streaked with red; hawked up thin, sour saliva; watery. *Breath hot;* breath fetid.

Taste.—Astringent. **Bitter.** Diminished. Fishy. Flat, nauseous, sweet, compelling hawking of tough mucus, then swallowing it. Lost for things that formerly tasted strong and well. Nauseous at root of tongue, > while eating. Pasty in morning. Peppery; especially on tip of tongue; at root of tongue, extending forward over whole tongue, with increased saliva; in pharynx. Of rotten eggs. Sour. Sweet. Offensive.

Clinical.—Neuralgic toothache. Teething with hot inflamed gums, great distress, etc. The tongue often feels swollen with the fever: *acute glossitis,* with dry hot mouth (Mercur. with salivation).

Throat.—Frequent pulling at. Bruised feeling from l. side of throat to shoulder-joint and a portion of dorsal muscles, < lying, > moving and open air, with stiffness, alternating with a similar feeling in upper and lower limbs. Drawing from side of to ears; *D. in muscles. Redness.* Mucus. Cramp. *Stitches; at back part; causing frequent swallowing. Pain; < deglutition;* l. side, with profuse swallowing of saliva; in fauces and soft palate, with tension. Soreness. Raw feeling with mucus in larynx. Roughness. *Raw scraping feeling in back part, with desire to hawk.* Scraping; > clearing throat; *in throat and soft palate, with burning as from peppermint.* Constriction in pharynx.

Peppery feeling. *Burning* (Canth.); *at back part,* also causing hawking; cooling, then on tongue. *Heat;* alternately with heat in face. Coldness, as after peppermint. *Dryness* (Bell. Dubois); at night; < tobacco smoke; *with irritation to cough; as if something stuck in it. Throat seemed to swell.* Constriction; at back part. Sensation of mucus; feeling as if mucus hung at palate, with nausea. Creeping. Tickling. Burning-tingling. Numbness; with prickling. Paralytic attack. Sticking choking in a spot, < swallowing and speaking, l. then r. Strangling sensation.

Redness of soft palate; arch of palate; tonsils; uvula; r. tonsil. *Burning in soft palate.* Coldness as from peppermint in soft palate in evening, soon extending to pharynx. *Dryness of soft palate; palate and posterior nares.* Scraping in soft palate, extending to hard palate and tip of tongue, with burning in same, and with redness of soft palate. *Constriction in soft palate and uvula, with scratching, causing hawking, spitting and nausea.*

Swelling of tonsils; feeling as if uvula rested on tongue (Alumina); swelling and elongation of uvula, *with arborescently injected dark red fauces and pharynx,* feeling as if an angular many-pointed body were sticking in throat, with sticking burning in palate, throat and along Eustachian tube, < swallowing, with dull pain behind sternum, headache and salivation, the throat symptoms < walking in open air, > after eating.

Œsophagus.—Pressive and burning pain extending

into stomach. Constriction. Burning. Coldness as from peppermint. Crawling during passage of food. Dryness and scraping.

Clinical.—Acute inflammation of various portions of the throat, with swelling, dryness, sticking pain (rarely, if ever, indicated after infiltration, exudation or ulceration has taken place).

Stomach.—Hunger. Appetite diminished; *lost. Loathing of food;* of bread. **Thirst;** *at night;* after vomiting; *for beer during heat;* for beer, which lies heavy on the stomach; **for cold water.** (Hiccough after eating and drinking); spasmodic action of stomach and diaphragm like hiccough and retching at the same time.

Eructations; empty, also after eating; empty, > after breakfast, with nausea; ineffectual attempts at; frequent, loud; with mineral taste; offensive; sour; of sweetish water, with roaring in ears; sweetish water with nausea; risings from pit of stomach, amounting to nausea when fasting. Waterbrash.

Nausea; from flesh broth; from food; at sight of food; when walking in open air; > eating; in pit, then under sternum and lastly in throat; on rising, with vertigo, heavy headache above ears and gush of cold sweat; with sinking in pit, < sitting, > walking; with sinking in pit and scraping from pit to throat; with sinking in pit and heaviness in head; with weight in stomach; with sweet taste; as after disagreeably sweet or fat substances. Retching; violent, with confusion of head.

Vomiting; after each drink; with purging; with stools, cardialgia and colic; *bilious,* also fetid and black (with relief); blood-streaked; *dark grumous liquid;* all food; food, then frothy mucus; gravy-like, with stringy mucus; *greenish-gray, watery; green* (Verat.); *green masses, with diarrhœa of same appearance; mucus;* olive-yellow fluid; violent.

Sticking in epigastrium after a full meal, with tension. Sharp pain, and in bowels, then discharge of flatus. *Aching;* while eating; after dinner; in epigastric region; in pit; in pit while sitting, walking and standing; in pit, changing to constriction of chest; burning, also with tenderness on pressure; burning in epigastrium; *burning, extending to mouth, with dryness;* as from something indigestible at noon, then sensitiveness and warmth till evening; *as from a stone in pit,* extending through to back, with squeezing like a stiffness; spasmodic; in pit as if swollen internally. Feeling of a ball rising from pit and spreading cool air over vertex and occiput. Epigastric region tender to touch. Burning; after dinner; heartburn morning on waking, almost taking away the breath, > rising; warmth in epigastric region; heat in pit (Ars.); warmth in pit while eating, with tenderness.

Anxiety in pit, < warm room, with vertigo. Distress after eating. Discomfort in pit and upper abdomen after eating, with pressure. Contractive feeling as from an astringent. Spasmodic constriction. Swelling. Fulness. Feeling of a lump. Repletion at pit. Tension in pit, >offensive eructations. Empty feeling; at noon, with eructations. Collapse alternating with distention. *Sensitiveness to touch;* at pit. Uneasiness in epigastrium. *Anxious pulsation in pit, with shooting.* Numbness.

Clinical.—Acon. is indicated in distress at the stomach, retching and vomiting (especially of green substances), associated with fever (at the outset of an eruptive disease), or without fever following a severe shock, such as fright, or with sudden suppression of menstruation or perspiration, with anxiety and restlessness; occasionally also in infants during dentition when the general state corresponds. Hæmatemesis.

Abdomen.—Flatus; emission of; hot. Gurgling, > emission of flatus; G., with itching in rectum and call to stool. Splashing. Rumbling; after eating; >discharge of flatus; all night, with grumbling; with shooting and contractive pain here and there; with tension; as after a purge, during soft stools. Fermentation. **Swelling.**

Stitches (Sulph.). *Griping; with swelling,* > emission of flatus. *Pain;* from sneezing; during stool; >emission of flatus, with distention; burning P., also with tenderness or pressure; drawing P. here and there; flatulent P., also in different parts. **Cutting;** morning in bed; during stool; extending towards r. shoulder, during stool. Feeling as if diarrhœa would occur. **Burning** (Ars.). *Chilliness* (Camph.). Colicky stretching. **Sensitiveness** (Bell.). Raw feeling. Seemed full of water. Weakness as from abuse of purgatives. Paralyzed feeling; especially in transverse colon. Amelioration of many symptoms after warm soup.

Hypochondria.—Stitches in l. (Dig.); in spleen when walking; in liver; *in hepatic region, hindering deep breathing* (Bry. Iod.); in hepatic region, with soreness; inward in region of spleen, < pressure and deep inspiration. Griping in upper abdomen, with distention of abdomen. Pain in upper abdomen, with ineffectual straining at stool; *in hepatic region, obstructing breathing. Constriction, < r., preventing deep breathing;* in region of gall-bladder on sitting, preventing breathing. Anxiety. *Fulness. Weight.* Coldness in upper abdomen. Feeling as if something cold pressed outward, above and to l. of umbilicus.

Umbilicus.—Retraction, < morning before eating. Griping about. Clawing in region, with scraping. Pinching in region, also before diarrhœa; above umbilicus. Drawing pain in both sides of umbilicus; on bending abdomen together. Jerk-like pressure. Compression. Feeling as if a ball rose from region and spread cool air over vertex and occiput. **Burning;** spreading towards pit of stomach.

Hypogastrium.—Gurgling. Stitches in l. Pinching, especially in r. flank, affecting inspiration. *Pain as from a flatulent purgative.* Drawing from l. towards back, with pain in sides of abdomen on pressure. *Sensitiveness to touch* (Op.). Faintness.

Flatulent pain in parietes and r. side of abdomen. Pressing pain in parietes, r. then l., recurring for days. Flying stitches here and there in parietes, ribs and joints, in evening.

Muscles.—Drawing pain in recti abdominia, which were stretched as hard as a board. Tension; in r. groin. Contraction (Sulph.). Twitchings in hepatic region, taking away breath. Spasmodic action of muscles of abdomen, chest and limbs (Verat.).

Clinical.—In various inflammatory processes, peritonitis, enteritis, in the early stage with severe, agonizing pain, tossing about, high fever, etc.; violent colic from cold; early inflammatory symptoms in the hepatic region; severe inflammation or engorgement of the pelvic viscera when the other conditions correspond, Aconite has been promptly efficacious.

Rectum.—*Pain. Tenesmus* (Caps.). *Urging to stool;* with colic, also during stool. Itching, with gurgling in abdomen and call to stool.

Anus.—*Shootings.* Sore feeling. Cramplike constriction. *Painful contractions* (Sil.). *Pressure.* Burning at night, with scraping. Sensation of a warm fluid escaping. *Bleeding hæmorrhoids* (Ham., Nit. ac.); *burning and heat in hæmorrhoidal vessels* (Æsc. hip., Sulph.), itching and pressure in hæmorrhoidal vessels. Paralysis.

Stool.—Diarrhœa; with grumbling in abdomen; with pain in abdomen; with faint feeling; urgent, offensive. Pasty. *Watery;* and copious, urgent, also with colic. Gushing of yellow water mixed with white foam, preceded by gurgling. Constipation. Hard, with effort; hard and earlier than usual. *Green* (Dulc.). Black and fetid. Clay-colored. *White; with red urine.* Whitish-yellow. Copious; after urging, followed by painful pinching. Scanty; and soft and frequent, with straining. Frequent. Involuntary; during a faint; with a feeling as if passing only flatus.

Clinical.—Violent pain in rectum, with chill and fever, inflammation, tenesmus and bloody discharges (dysentery), in early stage. Bleeding piles, with heat and sharp stitches, blood bright. Diarrhœa, stools green, watery, after a chill or fright. Choleraic discharges with collapse, deathly anxiety and restlessness.

Urinary Organs. — Bladder. Pain on walking. Splashing feeling on urinating. *Tenesmus at neck. Burning in neck when not urinating* (Canth.). Paralysis of neck. Micturition at night. Desire to urinate on touching abdomen; desire, with scanty discharge, also with difficult discharge; **anxious desire.** *Anxiety always on beginning to urinate. Difficult. Frequent.* Involuntary.

Urethra.—Stitches; on walking. *Burning when urinating.* Stitches in meatus; morning on urinating. Stitches in fossa navicularis always on urinating. *Burning in fossa navicularis* (Petrosel.).

Urine. Copious; and watery. *Scanty; and saturated;* scanty and loaded with albumen and casts; afterwards copious. Suppressed. Pale. *Red;* with white fæces. Brown; with dirty brown sediment; with brick-dust sediment. **Dark and hot;** *dark and scanty. Hot* (Borax). Clouded. *Deposits blood.* Salts diminished. Acid, precipitating phosphates.

Clinical.—Acute inflammation of various parts, with fever, hot urine, great agony at the thought of micturition, etc. Retention of urine (especially in infants). In fever the urine is dark, hot and scanty, but with no evidence of nephritis. Rare cases of congestion of the kidney, with bloody urine, pain in kidneys, fever, etc. Acute prostratitis, from cold especially, supervening on chronic disease.

Sexual Organs.—Crawling, stinging in glans. Stitches in glans and prepuce; l. side of prepuce; in glans when urinating; in glans, as from a galvanic current. Pinching in glans on urinating. Frequent erections. Retraction of scrotum (Petrol.) *Swollen and hard feeling in testicles* (Rhod., Spong.). Drawing pain in testicles; r. *Bruised pain in testicles* (Rhod.); *r.;* l. (Nit. ac., Thuj.). Desire diminished; increased, also in evening; (alternating with relaxation). Emissions; only in morning; frequent, also at night.

Menses which had ceased the day before reappeared. Metrorrhagia. Milk increased.

Clinical.—Suppressed or painful menstruation from violent emotions (fright), sudden chill, with anguish, fever, etc. Metrorrhagia, bright and hot, with general Aconite symptoms. Acute orchitis, with general fever.

Respiratory Organs. — Larynx. *Pain on coughing* (Osm.). **Sensitiveness to inspired air** (Osm.). Irritation, < going from warm room into open air, with dry cough. *Tickling, provoking cough* (Sang.); tickling from smoking. Drink and food get into larynx, causing cough. Compression on both sides. Burning pain, with choking. Burning in glottis. *Aphonia* from debility. *Weak voice.* **Hoarseness** (Bell. Iod.).

Trachea.—Rattling and vibration. Pressive and burning pain, extending to pit of stomach, caused by cough. Raw feeling, causing short cough. Wide feeling in air-passages during respiration. Dry feeling. Numbness and asleep sensation under sternum.

Cough in morning, with *blood-streaked expectoration* (Sulph.); towards evening; after drinking; (during heat of body); when exercising; from irritation in larynx; from tobacco smoke, also with hemming; < towards evening, with pain and oppression in chest; with shooting in chest (Bry. Kali carb.). *Disturbing night's rest.* Distressing. Violent; *with shootings in different parts of chest,* compelling him to lie on the back. Dull-toned, straining chest. Hacking, from tickling at epiglottis (Wyeth.). *Short;* every half-hour after midnight, from tickling in larynx, < attempts to repress it. **Dry;** *from irritation in larynx* (Puls.); from change of temperature, with raw pain in chest; < warm room; < deep breathing and change of temperature, with smarting and soreness behind sternum; with raw pain in chest and smarting in larynx; and harsh; **and hoarse ringing** (Bro. Iod. Spo.); *and short, from scratching in throat.* Constant, irritation to. *Frequent,* **with expectoration of bright blood** (Cact. Ip. Led. Phos.).

Expectoration.—**Of blood;** *of blood and mucus, with raw feeling behind sternum. Rusty* (Phos.). *Thin, frothy, white mucus, with streaks of bright blood* (Sulph.). Gelatinous mucus. Tenacious, slimy. Cough brings up a sweetish salt fluid into mouth, tasted only at root of tongue.

Respiration.—Asthmatic. *Fear of suffocation* (Phos.). Choking; easy; easy while swallowing; in paroxysms. *Difficult;* > cough; *impeded by anxiety, with sweat on forehead; with necessity to breathe deeply;* with pressure under sternum and transient heat; and rapid; and slow. *Inspiration through nose impeded, < in sleep. Short;* in sleep after midnight; in shocks and weak; scarcely perceptible. Gasping. Groaning at each respiration. *Sighing;* on account of slow circulation and congested feeling in lungs; *deep. Loud, with open mouth.* Mucous râles; posteriorly. Irregular. (Inspiration with a double jerk, like the bleating of a goat, in sleep.) Superficial. *Slow;* in sleep. Frequent, deep. *Stertorous.* No respiration or circulation, yet kept moving some part of body.

Clinical.—The Aconite cough is dry, either short hacking or hard ringing and croupy, it hurts the larynx (in laryngitis) or the chest (in pleurisy or pneumonia). In the first stage of membranous croup, with high fever, great anxiety and restlessness, it will often abate the attack. (Iodine is also applicable at this stage of high fever, but the patient is quiet and the exudation has already become plastic; after the fever abates neither Acon. nor Iodine is indicated.) The cough is aggravated by warmth (on expiration) usually. In congestion of the lungs, with great oppression, distress and anxiety, expectoration of bright, hot blood. In the hyperæmic stage of inflammations of the thoracic viscera (with the general indications), prior to exudation, Acon. will be found invaluable. After Acon. either Iodine or Bryonia follows well; both these have high fever without anguish, both seem to be associated with an exudative process. Acute symptoms occurring during the progress of chronic diseases occasionally require Acon.

Chest.—Spasmodic action of muscles of chest, abdomen and limbs. **Stitches;** on **inspiration** (Borax, Ran. bulb.); when sneezing; in r. side of sternum; in centre of sternum towards evening; beneath sternum and between scapulæ; near l. axilla; in l. pectoralis major and intercostals; towards false ribs; *side* (Squill.); under l. ribs on inspiration (Sulph.); under r. ribs on laughing aloud (Borax); *sides and between scapulæ, on deep breathing;* in l. lower, > lying; in various parts, also < bending sideways; **with cough** (Borax); in r., with suspension of breathing (Borax); with anxiety and peevishness, a sticking, then throbbing in the side, then headache; burning stitches in l. half; *fine burning; constrictive, in r. side;* drawing, also in l.; in region of eighth, ninth, tenth and eleventh ribs, l., then r., often extending to loins; in side, extending towards back; stitches about last r. rib, through to small of back; *from lowest r. rib to apex of shoulder-blade; at every inspiration;* extending inward in l.; as from flatus; in l. upper; flying along sternum and between ribs; interrupting respiration; now here, now there; periodical stitches, with dry cough; now superficial, now deep, and in cardiac region.

Pain at night; > bending backward; r.; r., then l.; l. on sneezing; in sternum; from sternum to spine; beneath sternum, compelling frequent deep breathing; in region of second l. rib, near sternum, < deep inspiration; l. side superiorly, with sensitiveness to touch; < towards evening, with oppression, in the evening associated with drawing stiffness in nape and pain in scapulæ, wine relieved the chest symptoms, but aggravated the head symptoms; on chest, especially on posterior r. side and lower part, with tightness; creeping; drawing, in various parts; externally in spots, < r. side.

Squeezing pain; under sternum. Constriction; to r. of sternum; as if ribs of both sides were drawn towards each other. Compression from all sides; compression in middle of sternum and anterior part of chest, affecting inspiration; in central anterior part, or constriction, especially in r. ribs, hindering deep breathing. Tightness; *in side;* with strong, loud respiration. *Anxiety* (Spig.). *Oppression* (Phos., Ferr., Chin. Sul.); *in r. side,* then in whole chest; at night, with frequent deep breathing; of lungs after drinking; between shoulders on deep breathing, with anxiety and stitches; > deep inspiration; *compelling frequent inspiration. Heaviness; under sternum, preventing deep inspiration. Fulness;* forenoons on walking, *with heaviness, internal uneasiness, anxiety and palpitation,* > motion in open air.

Painful shocks in l. side superiorly, < breathing. Raw pain under sternum on inspiration. Soreness on posterior surface of sternum, as if bruised, evenings. Bruised feeling in ribs and upper part of chest; in last rib, < touch; in middle of sternum, < touch. Pinching digging in r. side between third and fourth ribs. Gnawing pain in r. clavicle. Shooting, boring, burrowing in l. side between fourth and sixth ribs. Crawling as from beetles.

Heat (Bry.); with weakness; *burning under sternum, with pressure* (Phos.); in lungs, also with a feeling as if hot fluid would come into the mouth. Feeling as if hot water were poured into chest, then icy coldness, almost with faintness, with frequent shivering and headache in r. temple. Chilliness evenings. Weakness. Aggravation of symptoms in evening. It is characteristic that wine relieves the chest symptoms, namely, the venous congestion, while it aggravates the active trouble in the fibrous structures of the skull and meninges.

Heart.—Stitches; forenoons, < walking; *in præcordial region;* in region as if in pleura costalis, morning on rising, preventing upright posture and deep breathing, with inclination to cough, > rubbing, then soreness on touch. Cramp about. Aching; in region. **Anxiety about** (Amyl, Camph.); *with quicker, stronger beat;* when sitting after much motion, with contracted pulse and constricted chest. *Compression in præcordial region. Oppression of præcordial region* (Chin.). Pressure inward in region. Weight about. Heat, and disagreeable feeling. Congealed feeling in bloodvessels. Feeling as if circulation were impeded in all vessels. Slow twitchings in region, towards surface of chest.

Palpitation; after eating; on walking; > quiet (Chin.); **and anxiety,** *with increased heat, especially in face; and anxiety, with restlessness and pressive pain in region of heart; with anxiety, difficult breathing, weariness in limbs, sensation of something rushing into head, confusion and flying heat in face.* Tumultuous beating, systole and diastole inseparable to ear. Trembling. Fluttering feebly. Impulse weak. Beating but once to every three beats of pulse. Intermittent beating. Irregular beating. Beating quickly while pulse is slow, apparently intermittent. Movement of r. auricle rapid, irregular, not related to beats of ventricle.

Symptoms alternate with wandering, drawing tearing pains.

Clinical.—Exceedingly valuable in acute inflammations, with fever, stitches at heart, violent beating and anguish. The febrile pulse of Acon. is full, hard and rapid. In cardiac inflammations requiring Acon., the patient must lie on the back with the head raised.

Pulse.—Contracted, full, strong, febrile, rapid. Rapid at one time, at another slow. *Slow;* and full, strong. *Small and soft.* Tendency to dicrotism. *Weak.* Imperceptible. *Intermittent.* Thready. Tremulous. Twitching. *Beat of temporal and carotid arteries felt when sitting.*

Neck.—Twitching of muscles. Stitches externally. Neuralgic pain in l. side and shoulder. Pain in r. cervical muscles and shoulder-joint, so that he could bend the arm backward only with great pain. Drawing pain; in muscles of r. side of throat and neck; from r. side of neck into ear and shoulder; to l. of nape and in scapula, on moving neck. Pain extending down neck towards r. shoulder. *Drawing in muscles* (Baptis.); drawing in side. Constriction. Pressure inward as with a finger-tip. Tension in muscles, especially in sterno-cleido-mastoid, and in its attachment to mastoid process, on turning head. Stiffness of r. side, with tenderness on pressure.

Nape.—Stitches; in l. side, with drawing, also < entering house, > open air. Pain in l. side of cervical vertebræ; in nape and about base of brain, with spasms in arms; *rheumatic, on moving neck* (Cimicif.). Sensation as if the flesh were separated, with a feeling as if the neck would not support the head, and with shootings on moving head. Bruised pain in single muscles, < evenings and nights on lying down. Stiffness (Agar. Rhus t. *Sil.*); in evening; with jerking pain.

Back.—Stitches. Cutting, extending over l. hip round to abdomen, in a circle. Shooting digging in whole l. side, < inspiration. Pain; < stooping (Æsc. h.); in lower part; rheumatic, in muscles of back and shoulders, in places where the chilly or numb sensations had been most marked. Stiffness (Berb.). Feeling of heartburn all down. Numb feeling.

Spine, crawling pain, as from beetles. Pain extending down spine.

Scapulæ.—Stitches between; on deep breathing. Digging boring from r. to front of chest, < deep inspiration. *Bruised pain between scapulæ.* Drawings in r. Drawing pain in lower angle of l. Drawing tearing. Burning gnawing near r. side of dorsal vertebræ.

Lumbar region.—Stitches, with creeping; with drawing. Tearing, < pressure. Boring in l. side. Pain; (Æsc. h., Berb.); r.; l. regions of kidneys; region of l. kidney. Drawing P., < motion of trunk, standing up, stretching, stooping or sitting down, with pain on pressure; while walking, > bending in small of back; drawing pain in sacro-lumbalis and longissimus dorsi, < pressure and motion. Labor-like pain when walking. *Tensive pain* (Berb.); < *stepping, and in sacral region;* tensive pain in vertebræ, or bruised feeling, and with gripes as from flatulence. Paralytic pain, > movement and bending inward. *Bruised pain extending to nape;* bruised pain at union of last lumbar vertebræ with sacrum, with feeling as if small of back were beaten to pieces (Arn.). Tension (Berb.); > bending backward; with drawing, compelling bending backward, sensitiveness; in renal region. Uneasiness in region of r. kidney. Numb feeling, extending into legs.

Sacral region.—Pain; burning P.; sticking crawling in sacroiliac region, which gradually changed to a paralytic pressive pain, lasting nearly all day. Sensitiveness. Stiffness in sacral and hip-joints. Sticking burning in region of coccyx, with a feeling of heat.

Extremities.—Twitching of fingers and toes. *Trembling* when walking; with tingling and shooting; convulsive distortions; distorted sensation. Stretched involuntarily. Moved incessantly; motions as if muscular sense failed. Paralysis of l. arm and leg, also l., then r. arm and leg; paralyzed feeling in arm and thigh, alternately r. and l., also in arms and feet, with trembling in whole body, especially limbs.

Stitches in feet and arms; backs of hands and feet; drawing gnawing, especially in forearms. Tearing in r. upper arm and upper third of thigh; in r. upper arm towards elbow and in thigh towards knee; alternately in both thighs, r. knee and r. forearm; *drawing.* Sharp pain in l. knee, then in l. ulnar nerve. Pain in elbows, knees and hip-joint after walking, > pressure; like bone-pain in metacarpal and long bones; drawing, also in joints; stretching. Shattered feeling. Bruised pain; in shoulder and hip-joints after sleep.

Drawing alternately in elbow, knee and calf. Tingling, prickling; in tips of fingers and toes at night. Asleep sensation. Feeling as if circulation stopped. Heaviness; when walking and in open air, with sensitiveness. Motion difficult. Stiffness. Numbness; > walking; in tips of fingers and toes. Weakness; even in bed; after walking; arms and legs; r. knee and l. elbow; especially feet, with sleepiness and ill humor; of joints, especially knee and joints of foot, with twitching in tendons.

Clinical.—Neuralgia, especially of the upper extremities, with numbness of the limb as if the blood did not circulate freely, resulting from a sudden check of perspiration, finds a prompt remedy in Acon. (Aconitum uncinatum, from Virginia, has made some brilliant cures of this sort.) Neuralgic pains in the lower limbs point to its use in sciatica. Acute muscular rheumatism of the back and limbs occasionally demands Acon., but it is rarely useful in true arthritic inflammations. It will be noticed that the pains are usually drawing, tense and numb and relieved by open air.

Upper Extremities.—*Shoulder.* Stitches in l.; joint and elbow. Tearing in l. joint; to fingers, almost only on motion, with blueness of hand; drawing, in joint. Pain; joints; l. joint; with feeling as if it would sink down; drawing pain, also in l. shoulder and arm, on which he lies, with soreness. Drawing in r., then drawing and tearing in same, with lameness in head of left humerus. Numbness. Weakness of r. joint.

Arm.—Tossed about; backward, above head. Trembling. Stitches. Tearing in r., with prickling-like formication. Pinching in spots near bend of l. elbow. Pain; drawing; drawing and paralytic; drawing and tearing extending along r. forearm, in wrist and fingers. Bruised pain; with sinking down. Boring in l. Contracted sensation from shoulders to finger-tips, with numb, heavy and paralytic feeling. Prickling. Tingling. *Numbness*; l.; and of hands, with tingling as from a galvanic current. Weariness.

Upper Arm.—Stitches anteriorly in middle of r. at rest; sudden and drawing posteriorly in r. Pressure in r. Drawing pain in r. Drawing on outside, with paralytic stiffness. Drawing numbness on posterior anterior side of l. Weariness of l.

Elbow.—Stitches; extending to wrists, on outside of arms, on flexing fingers to wrists. Tearing in bend; drawing. tearing. Pain; after walking; drawing; rheumatic, l., r. Bruised pain in r.

Forearm.—Twitching of muscles. Sticking in inner surface of lower and of l.; drawing, in bones on motion. Tearing drawing, also on outside of r.; undulating, on upper end of l.; in l. forearm, hand and fingers. Pain, cramplike, in l.; in r., as if in bone, with aching in wrist; jerking drawing pain along lower and internal surface of l. to palm; drawing and tearing pain along r. forearm, in wrist and fingers; pain in r. extending along flexor tendon of little finger, < motion. Bruised pain. Weight. Paralytic feeling in r. forearm and hand when writing, > violent motion.

Wrist.—Trembling on moving hand. Stitches. Tearing. Drawing, paralytic pain in r. Drawing. Numbness; painful.

Hand.—Trembling. Wild movements. Pulseless. Stitches in l.; l. metacarpal bones; in dorsum of l.; pulsating stitches in r. palm. Pain in metacarpal bones like bone-pains; constrictive pain in l. palm; cramplike P. in r., also > motion, with shooting; flying growing P. in metacarpi, also in forenoon, and in the finger-joints; lame pain in metacarpi. Sprained feeling in r. metacarpus; in joints of r. Drawn-up feeling. *Numbness* (Phos.); of palms; and tingling, as from a galvanic current. Paralytic tinglings in l., later in ulnar region of r. Weight.

Fingers.—Clenched. *Blueness of nails* (Nux v., Op.). Twitching. Cutting in inner side of r. index. Pain in r. thumb-joint; *creeping;* as from dislocation, in r. thumb-joint on motion. Drawing P. in r., also l. thumb; in r. index; in l. middle finger after getting into bed; drawing lame P. in r. index. Flying growing P. in joints; intermittent lame growing P. in distant joint of l. index. Paralytic P. in thumbs. Twitching P. in r. thumb. Drawn-up feeling; with tingling. Feeling as if asleep on grasping anything. Prickling and tingling; hot prickling in tips, nights.

Numbness; of tips (Sec. c., Phos.). Stiffness of r. index. Weight.

Lower Extremities.—Tottering. Reeling as if drunk, as after a blow on the head. Giving out. Moved perpetually. Paralysis. Drawing pain here and there in l. Drawing along, with discomfort in knees, < l. knee, as after long squatting; drawing in tendinous expansions. Leaden heaviness, < ascending stairs. Numbness, with heaviness and inability to raise them from the ground (Con.); numbness even when walking, so that he has frequently to stop to move the feet back and forth to get rid of the sensation (Ars.). Loses the sensation of standing firmly, as if the feet would rise up.

Thigh.—Paralysis of l. Stitches in muscles. Drawing tearing. Pain in hips; r. hip; hips after walking; hip-joint when walking; r. hip, > walking in open air; as from a bandage, while walking, with fatigue; bruised pain, also in middle of thigh; almost crushing pain in head of femur after lying, with weakness. Drawing pain in r. when walking; in head of l. femur when standing and sitting, < walking; *in l. hip-joint on motion*; in border of l. hip-bone, extending towards hip-joint; alternately in each, while moving, then in both. Short feeling in tendons of ham. Soreness on touch. Numbness (Ars.). Weakness; after sitting; in head of femur, with pain.

Knee.—Cracking. *Unsteadiness;* especially of one. Contraction of cords under knee, with bruised pain in l. patella. *Stitches in l.;* l. patella; deep, slow, over r.; drawing in l.; *flying, in evening*, with icy coldness; tearing, in r. Tearing in r. knee and leg; drawing tearing; jerking, in inside; sudden, in l. Pressing gnawing in patella. Pain (Benz. ac.); after walking (Bry.); r.; in patella, also on walking; bruised, also in patella; drawing, to heel and back again; rheumatic (Benz. ac.); tense, in r. patella; intermittent, in l. patella on walking in open air. Tension of cap; in l., then r. patella, < descending stairs. Weakness; in evening, extending over r. thigh and leg; in tendons, with twitching.

Leg.—Failure; on attempting to ascend stairs. Cramp; *in calves*; r. calf. Pricking. Pain; in r.; in r. calf, with tension. Drawing pain in r.; on inside of l. Paralytic and bruised pain. Drawing at inside of both legs, < walking, with sensitiveness of leg to touch and pain as if sore; drawing in tibiæ, with stretching; paralytic drawing in r. leg and tendo-achillis to heel. Feeling as if going away from him, with vertigo. Heaviness; of r.; with swollen feeling; in calves, < r., with tension; feeling of a weight of the size of a palm on the outside of each. Asleep sensation in lower part. Tingling (Calc. ph.). Numbness; of lower part; of calves. Weakness; after sitting; on beginning to walk.

Ankle.—Tearing going upward in l. outer. Pain; > compression; drawing pain in l.; rheumatic pain in anterior part of l. Sensation as if tied in morning.

Foot.—Cramp in sole. Stitches on dorsum of l.; on r.; from heel to popliteal space. Pain in r. instep; in r. heel, < treading; drawing, in r. heel after getting into bed; burning, in r. foot; in tendo-achillis; drawing, in r. tendo-achillis; intermittent, in r. tendo-achillis on walking in open air, and in dorsum of l. foot. Shortened feeling in tendo-achillis; with bent feeling. Contracted feeling in both tendons achillis, so that, especially in evening after sitting or in morning on rising, it was difficult to stand erect without bending the knees. Paralytic drawing. Heaviness; leaden, also while sitting and standing. Tingling. Prickling. Asleep sensation; r. while sitting. Numbness; spreading upward, with tingling; sudden. Weakness; < ascending steps; < during rest; in tendons of joints, with twitching.

Toes.—Twitching. Stitches in r. fourth; in third and fourth r., when sitting; flying, in third and fourth r., after getting into bed; hot stitches at night. Lancinating pain in r. great, < on inside of ball, after getting into bed, and in third and fourth r. toes and in l. metatarsal bones. *Asleep when walking*, r. Numbness gradually spreading over whole body. Numbness of tips.

Skin.—**Gooseflesh.** Duskiness. Horripilation. Blackness of all parts. Pallor; of fingers. Yellow. *Redness of cheeks; of face*, with heat; red spots. Discolorations on limbs. Elasticity and smoothness. Shrivelling. *Dryness;* with rustling and coldness; like parchment. Tightness, with dry heat. Desquamation; of face. Vesicles; on temples; humid on l. side of scrotum; itching; painful on lower limbs, also on l. lower limb. Heat-rash on forehead. Nettle-rash on backs of hands. *Spots like flea-bites on hands, face, etc.* Pimples on forehead; like flea-bites on backs of hands; itching and biting, here and there, and filled with yellow lymph; itching on upper lip; red, on flexor side of thumb, index and middle fingers, and painful to pressure. Painful furuncle at tip of nose. Tremor in muscles of shoulder, with bruised pain on touch.

Burning and scratching stitches. Dartings here and there, with a raw feeling, ending with pain as if wounded. Sensation as if epidermis were separated from cutis by an intervening layer, < r. leg. Sensation as when in a vapor bath. Prickling on face. Tickling on face; tickling, causing uneasiness, < change of temperature. Feeling as from electric sparks; especially on wings of nose.

Formication; extending through whole body, < arms and legs; with burning; in temporal region; face; face, with burning in skin; r. cheek; back, arms and thighs; limbs; arms; r. forearm; hands; *fingers;* finger-tips; *fingers while writing;* fingers, on getting into a warm bath, with tingling; in l. middle and index fingers, with warmth; especially of hairy parts, except head, with biting; here and there with shuddering, < upper arm and lower leg. Fuzziness where the formication had been. Insensibility.

Irritation of cheeks. Itching; in muscular parts, < forearms; face; back; legs; < about nose; scrotum; prepuce, > rubbing, but returning; voluptuous, on glans penis; tickling, on inside of l. upper arm; on inside of leg; burning, < inside lower limbs and about knees.

Clinical.—While Acon. is not applicable to the cure of diseases of the skin dependent on a constitutional dyscrasia, yet its power to produce vesicles associated with the neuralgic pains naturally leads to its use in the prodromal stage of Herpes zoster (Ran. b.). The nervous sensations, especially formication and the asleep-sensation, point to its use in certain neuroses.

Sleep.—*Yawning;* morning on rising, with shivering; interrupted; spasmodic; *without sleepiness*; desire to yawn and stretch. Sleepiness; towards noon; afternoon; after eating; falls asleep standing. Feels as if sleeping in the air with no firm bed under him. Feels herself sleeping while still awake. Stupid sleep. Waking difficult. Sleeplessness; till 4 A.M. **Restless night**; leaves the bed frequently. *Starting up, moving and talking in sleep;* starts up in sleep and says some one is holding her. Twitchings on falling asleep; in limbs. Waking frequently.

Dreams. **Anxious** (Rhus t.); before midnight; **and waking with a start.** *Fearful. Nightmare.* That she was falling from a height. *Vivid; about the events of the day.* Half the night, of a subject which occupies his attention long after waking. Towards morning, containing an explanation of what was a riddle to him while awake. Confused; and long. Of subjects that have been foreign to his thoughts. Extravagant, in a half-sleep. Strange, found himself laughing on waking. Delightful. Of thieves. Vexatious, quarrelsome. In which he talked. Lascivious (Phos. ac.). Waking dreaminess, imagining that he is far from home.

Chilliness; morning on rising, with yawning; afternoon; evenings; evenings with headache; **towards evening,** *with thirst,* **hot head and face, red cheeks and out-pressing headache** (Bry.); towards evening, with white cold hands; at night, with heat, thirst and restlessness; at night, then copious sweat; at night on lying down, then sweat in latter part of night; after siesta general feeling of rigor and coldness in r. upper arm, then in evening warm feeling, like a catarrhal fever; *on slightest motion;* after eating; after eating, with weakness and sleepiness, at night heat and tossing about and sleep interrupted by dreams; in open air; when walking, > by wine, with distended abdomen, salivation and general sick feeling; with anxiety, also during most of the symptoms; with anxiety as if blood would overflow vessels, especially coldness in face, > by open air and motion; with pain in r. temple; *cold body, with hot forehead, hot lobules of ears and inward dry heat;* especially in soles and knees, with confused head, heat of face, then full, hard, rapid pulse, flushes of pleasant warmth over body, anxiety and warmth about heart, inclined to sweat on forehead and temples, sweat over whole body, especially on head, nape, chest and abdomen, while soles always seem blown upon by a cool wind; with paleness and sunken features; with stiffness of whole body; **one cheek being red and hot, the other pale and cold**; with blueness of face and hands; *with desire to be covered with many clothes;* with yawning and stretching; with faintness; with sweat.

Shuddering at night on lying down. Shaking chill at night, then hot dry skin, then sweat. *Sensitiveness to cold draught.* Feeling as if he would take cold. Symptoms of having caught cold, violent coryza, shivering over back, < towards evening, difficult breathing, pressure beneath sternum, at times flushes of heat, pulse full, accelerated. Chilliness alternating with heat; *at night,* also with spots of gooseflesh, which disappear on breaking out of sweat; after coldness; with tingling and nervousness, then dry heat, soreness on touch and anxiety. Sudden chilliness, > by eating. External, with pallor and internal heat; with dryness, and with rustling of skin; with sweat. Long-lasting, then transient heat and copious sweat, with waving and swaying of head.

Scalp sensitive to cold air; cold sensation in scalp; forehead cold; rigor from vertex down to coccyx, then agreeable warmth in skin; feeling as if a cool air were spreading over vertex and occiput from a ball which seemed to rise from umbilical region. In face, internally, with external heat. *Shivers upward towards chest.*

Chills over back; shivering over back; chilliness in back and limbs; and arms; and upper arms; down back, < evening; in afternoon and towards evening, and in feet, with heaviness in forehead and vertex; along spine, also with gooseflesh creeping along galea aponeurotica; with a feeling of numbness in small of back, extending into lower limbs, and while sitting or standing it seems as if the lower limbs went to sleep, > walking; when in open air after breakfast, and in chest, then heat (with frontal headache), which motion renewed; creeping over back and thighs; extending over legs, with cold sweat and cold feeling in face, then heat and rapid pulse and symptoms of coryza; from middle of spine to lumbar muscles of both sides, with flushes of heat in head; between shoulders and down back, with formication, < motion, with cold tips of fingers and toes; internal, extending from back over lower limbs, while upper limbs are warm, with cold sweat and face icy-cold to touch.

From præcordia to limbs after midnight, then dry heat, with febrile pulse, which he could hear in his head, then sweat in morning. *In limbs;* creeping; in lower, then upper, as often as he moved, *extending to whole body,* between skin and muscle, with gooseflesh, > violent exercise in open air, returning when standing or lying; especially in limbs, with blueness of nails of fingers and toes; in limbs, with blueness of hands, fingers, chin and jaw.

Coldness of arms; < l.; shuddering, < upper arms and thighs; and legs, with shivering, even in face. Hands; of one, with insensibility; *and feet, while face is hot;* and feet, evenings, also with flushing of face, < evening; and feet, with shuddering over back, while head and body are warm; at noon, and in feet, with heat of head, cheeks and hands in afternoon, and with frequent alternations of temperature; towards evening, and in feet, then nausea about middle of sternum, nausea > eating, then heat of face. Fingers with blue nails; *tips of fingers and toes.*

Spreads over all lower limbs, fingers are deathly pale; down inside of lower limb from middle of thigh, < on knee and sole. Down fore part of thighs, as from trickling of water. Legs, < warm room and walking; creeping, on inside of leg. Knee, in evening, with flying shootings. **Feet** (China), *< toes; feet,* with sweat of toes and soles; soles. Under skin; shivering as if between skin and flesh, < back and abdomen, even during sweat.

Heat; in afternoon; afternoon, with weakness, < limbs; evening, with rapid pulse and symptoms of coryza; towards evening, continuing next day and for a week, with difficult breathing, distress in region of heart and intermittent pulse, five beats were full, hard and rapid and the sixth intermittent, with pallor, emaciation and sickly look (at night, with dyspnœa, restlessness and pain); *waking at night, with dryness of mouth and throat* and confusion of head and vertex. Aggravation in evening, with swollen veins; after getting into bed; on going to bed, < lower limbs; indoors. Amelioration in morning. With thrist. Drinks but little during the heat, yet has dry lips. Feeling all day of impending fever, with nausea, want of appetite, and aching pains in whole body, especially in limbs. *With throwing off of clothes.* (China. Op. Verat.)

Hot sensation over whole body, with red cheeks, childish mirth, *and headache on turning eyes upward and sideways, or with red cheeks and heat of head, shuddering over whole body, or with red cheeks, rigor, weeping and headache.* Internal heat; at night; with thirst; *with moderate thrist for beer;* with chilliness and nausea, fever, > going into open air and walking; with prostration. Flushing heat; in evening; < entering house. *Dry heat;* with tightness of skin, also with numbness and tingling spreading from feet. Heat extending over whole body, especially stomach and abdomen, with sweat.

Hot feeling in upper part of body, especially face, as if sweat would break out. **In head;** *with forehead hot to touch, and with rigor over rest of body on motion;* externally on vertex; suddenly in head and face. *Face; < evening;* cheeks; *cheeks, with redness and* **feeling as if face were growing larger;** heat in cheeks and palms in evening; l. cheek seemed swollen and hot, but was cool to touch; heat alternately in face and throat; **dry, in face towards evening, with anxiety;** flushing, especially of face and ears, with pressing pain in region of l. frontal eminence, extending towards upper orbital margin. In region of coccyx, with sticking burning. *Pleasant, from back over whole body, especially in back, with sweat;* creeping, over back; flushing in back. Hot sensation in hands, then over whole body, even in chest, without external heat; heat in palms evenings; burning along dorsum of index. *Heat of skin;* then coldness. *Burning through all mucous membranes.*

Sweat; at night; after midnight, *relieving all symptoms;* < after stool. Profuse; in morning (after nightly delirium); after convulsions. Exhausting. *Sour. Steaming. Cold;* on head; forehead; on brow, with almost imperceptible pulse and sparkling eyes; back; hands; palms; feet. Cold and clammy; on face; forehead; hands and feet. Gushing cold sweat, with nausea, vertigo and headache. On forehead and præcordia. Under nose; on face; abdomen after stool; around waist and lower limbs; chest; hands; *on whichever cheek he lies on;* l. wrist; inside of thighs and on scrotum, in bed, with itching, > cold water.

Clinical.—The Aconite fever is sthenic in type and for the most part not remittent, though the aggravation towards evening is decided. It is not useful in fever as a symptom of any form of malarial or septic poisoning, *nor of a localized inflammatory process,* but is adapted to a general febrile state without a pathological lesion (in this respect differing from Iodine, Bryonia, Gelsemium, etc.). The never-failing characteristic is the *mental anguish,* without which Aconite is useless; if the patient be quiet and apathetic Acon. is not the remedy, no matter how high the temperature; thirst and restlessness are present. Frequently there are alternations of chill and fever, but the sweat is usually critical and terminates the attack. It is valuable in the chilly as well as the febrile stage preceding the development of many eruptions and lesions, but when the preliminary storm has passed and the lesion has become established, the picture changes from Aconite to some other remedy.

Aconitum Ferox.

A plant allied to A. Napellus, L., but more deadly in its effects. In India it is called Bisch or Bikh. It contains both Aconitine and pseudoaconitine, but more of the latter (differing thus from A. Napellus, which contains more of the former) and a third alkaloid.

General Action.—Its action is quite similar in a general way to that of A. Napellus, more violent; it seems not to cause neuralgia of the trigeminus.

Weakness; on waking; muscular. Sensibility diminished. Touch blunted, feeling as if he had on gloves, and as if he walked on woolen carpets, no pain on pinching cheek. Amelioration in afternoon; A. after coffee. Mental activity increased; then diminished so that he could do no mental work. Anxiety. Constant talking. Confusion of mind; of head. Dulness of head on waking. Vertigo; on attempting to sit by the stove, with flickering, trembling of limbs, oppression and nausea. Pupils dilated, sluggish. Lachrymation (from local application), > by cold applications, with burning, swelling and burning of upper lid, photophobia, next day lids and ball red. Cheeks felt fuzzy. Burning of lips; < by hot drinks. Boring in nose. Sneezing.

Tongue coated yellowish-white; formication on tongue involving whole mouth; T. insensible, like leather. Salivation. Taste flat, pasty; T. sharp, burning. Burning in mouth; and throat; < by food, > by cold water; in pharynx; in tongue. Constriction of throat. Little appetite. Eructations. Nausea; after breakfast. Vomiting. Pain in stomach; after eating; on pressure; drawing in region of S. and sacrum, spreading over abdomen, < by pressure. Heat in stomach. Rumbling in abdomen. Gurgling. Stools dark, semi-liquid. Diarrhœa, with pain. Micturition frequent and copious. Urine light, then dark.

Inclination to cough. *Dyspnœa; must sit up with head leaning on hands. Respiration rapid. Anxiety, with suffocation from feeling of paralysis in respiratory muscles.* Pulse slow; P. small and weak. Limbs weak and trembling. Walking uncertain, difficult and fatiguing. Formication < over face; over whole body, changing from one nerve to another, causing painful uneasiness, constant change of position, weakness on attempting to rise, vertigo, blackness before eyes, trembling and nausea, all > by lying. Sleepiness. Sleeplessness. Desire for warmth. Icy coldness of body, especially of limbs. Skin cold; and dry, rustling; must be covered. Temperature increased. Sensation as if glowing hot wires were stuck into him, > by sweat. Sweat, with calor mordax.

Clinical.—It has proved palliative in cardiac dyspnœa (Curare, Phos.) (with "Cheyne-Stokes'" respiration).

Aconitinum.

An alkaloid obtained from Aconitum Napellus, L.; composition $C_{33}H_{43}NO_{12}$. (Commercial aconitine is mixed with pseudoaconitine, both obtained from the above species.)

General Action.—Paralysis, first peripheral then central. Loss of sensation, then also of motion. Depression of heart's action, of blood pressure, of respiration and temperature. Intense hyperæmia of nerve centers, brain and spine; heat from head extending over body; neuralgia, especially of trigeminus.

Antidotes.—Strychnine, Atropia. In poisoning, stimulants, ammonia, heat, digitalis, etc., according to indications.

Generalities.—Throws himself about the bed continually. Sudden change, limbs turned colder, heart's sounds and pulse disappeared, skin turned of a marble color, face turgescent, pupils dilated, conjunctiva injected, cold, clammy sweat over whole body, breathing more laborious and superficial, tracheal rattling, peculiar, clear, short moaning, tonic spasms beginning in fingers, then in face, trismus, after a while general clonic convulsions, unconsciousness, this paroxysm lasted about five or six minutes, on return of consciousness he thought he had had bad dreams, in fifteen minutes return of convulsions, during which respiration almost stopped. Convulsive movements excited by touching him. Glowing tingling over whole body. Oppression. Malaise. Restlessness. Weakness; from least effort. Sensibility diminished, < on hands and cheeks. Numbness, < in face and throat, with tingling.

Mind.—Irritable and quick in his replies. Distraction. Power of attention impaired. Ideas sluggish. Memory weak.

Head.—Aching; < by mental or physical exertion, with faceache; with heat and tightness. Fulness. Heaviness; and dulness. Vertigo. Temples, constriction; aching, and along infraorbital nerve; fulness; throbbing; painful tension and prickling, involving face. In forehead, cheeks, upper jaws (over whole tract of trigeminal) drawing pressing stretching, alternating with pain, becoming steady and severe, < by motion and mental effort. Pain in supraorbital nerve.

Eyes and Ears.—Strained feeling in eyes. Lachrymation (from local application), with swelling of lids and redness. Pupils very mobile, finally dilated; dilated, sluggish; contracted, sluggish. Lids numb. Vision dim. The lamplight was disagreeable. Blind and deaf. Ringing in ears; and pressure. Roaring.

Face.—Distorted, < about mouth (facies hippocratica). Darting pain, sometimes with vomiting. Tense and swollen feeling. Fulness in cheeks. Sensitive and swollen. Tingling, and in mouth. Lips burning; with numbness, extending over tongue, mouth and throat.

Mouth and Throat.—Burning on tip of tongue; inside mouth after supper; in mouth, spreading to throat and stomach, with acridity, then burning and numbness of lips, tongue and pharynx, with salivation. Salivation. Taste disgustingly bitter. Throat dry. Every attempt to swallow was followed by spasmodic contractions, as in hydrophobia. Swallowing difficult, with pains in nape and behind jaws in parotid region, so that in eating he had to press the nape with his hands. Burning in throat; and over larynx; in gullet.

Stomach, Etc.—Appetite lost. Eructations. Nausea; when erect; on rising from a recumbent position, with inability to see. Vomiting; violent, from sudden jerking of abdominal muscles, accompanied by a loud shout. Gastric and cardiac anguish, with sensation as if all parts except head were filled with lead. Heat in stomach. Rumbling in abdomen. Micturition difficult. Dysuria and occasionally retention, with hypogastric pains. Urine increased; and dark; micturition delayed. Nocturnal emissions.

Respiratory Organs, Etc.—Cough, with easy expectoration. Respiration difficult; and short, irregular, superficial, sometimes 40 per minute, a few minutes later much slower; oppressed and sighing; slow and deep, with slow pulse. Moaning. Chest oppressed; anxious pressure. Heart's action feeble; and irregular, quick, sounds heard only at apex and scarcely distinguishable. Pulse rises; at first more frequent, during the heat, then slow, small, weak, and at times dicrotic; small, irregular, dicrotous, sometimes scarcely to be felt.

Extremities.—Bruised feeling, with difficulty in grasping objects. Relaxation. Numbness; of forearms and hands, with heaviness. Tingling in fingers. Gait heavy. Legs tremble.

Skin.—Red spots as from punctures. Pallor, coldness and sweat; pallor and coldness, < limbs, which were bedewed with cold, clammy sweat. Prickling, < on face and limbs; face and forearms; P. following a nerve; in forearms and hands, with numbness and heaviness of them; tingling, in legs, running to spine and head. Formication, < by quiet; F. on forearms; on face, with feeling as if epidermis were scaling off.

Sleep.—Yawning. Sleepiness. Sleep disturbed; and dreamy. Frequent waking.

Fever.—Coldness. Heat; with pricking and smarting; numbing glow; of skin (from external application), with lancinations and pricklings, then heaviness and numbness of the part affected, skin seemed raised up and contracted by muscles beneath, anæsthesia; sudden, in head and face, extending over body, < in region of stomach, with sweat. Sweat.

Actæa Spicata.

Actæa spicata, L. A tincture is prepared from the fresh root.

Relations.—Cimicifuga, Clematis, Aconite.

The pains are generally *tearing,* drawing. Fermentation in blood. Pulsations. Weakness after eating; from talking; walking in open air; sudden. *Delirium,* during fever; *furious.* Unconsciousness. Headache persisting after the fever; headache in skull and periosteum. Boring in head. Vertigo, with nausea. Head symptoms < at night and by walking; mostly periodical. Pressure in forehead from the broad daylight. Twitching pains in temples. Pain in vertex; hammering, in occiput. Sensation of horripilation on scalp. Pimples on scalp. Ophthalmia like catarrhal inflammation. Suggillations in conjunctiva. Burning lachrymation. Vision blue; vision of spots when looking steadily.

Twitching pain in ears, when sneezing or blowing nose. Ear sore to touch. Murmuring in ears after sleep, < by anxiety. Nostril red. Bruised pain in nose. Nasal mucus tinged with blood. Nosebleed during oppression of chest. Yellow around mouth. *Rheumatic pain in face* (Acon.). Lips chapped. Salivation. Fetid breath. Pain in submaxillary glands when chewing. Tearing in throat, < by cold morning or evening air. Throat sore when speaking.

Appetite sharp in morning. Hunger, with aversion to food. Nausea. *Vomiting; sour* (Calc. c.). Sticking in epigastrium on deep inspiration. Pain at stomach pit; in stomach, with difficult breathing. Cramp in stomach; drawing in epigastric region. Uneasiness in stomach after eating. Emission of flatus. Spasmodic contractions of bowels. Compression in abdomen. Pain in r. hypochondrium on pressure; P. as before diarrhœa; as before or during menses. Painful shock in abdomen at each inspiration. Uneasiness in A. Pulsations in r. hypochondrium. Left hypochondrium almost insensible. Stool pappy; omitted. Frequent urging to urinate; with painful micturition. White sediment in urine.

Respiration difficult, with pain in stomach; with pain in hip; inspiration; on account of weakness, especially expiration. Bruised pain in sacral region when lying on side. Pulsation in kidney region. **Swelling of joints after slight fatigue.** *Pain in hands as from paralytic weakness.* Lower limbs swollen; boring, > by stretching; weakness after changes of temperature. Thighs tremble when lifted. Knees weary. Horripilation after drinking; H., then heat with vomiting. Cold, numb and discolored fingers. Sweat on head (Calc .c.); cheek on which he lies; viscid; cold, with malaise (Calc. c.).

Clinical.—Almost the only use of this drug has been for subacute rheumatic gout of the small joints, associated with sour stomach.

Æsculus Hippocastanum.

Æsculus hippocastanum, L. (Horse-chestnut.) Natural order Sapindaceæ.

A tincture is prepared from the fresh, ripe, hulled nuts.

General Action.—Most marked on lower bowel (engorged hæmorrhoidal veins). Excessive pains in back and hips. Irritation of mucous membrane of throat.

Allies.—Aloe, Bap., Bell., Berb., Diosc., Nit. ac., Phyto., Pod., Sulph.

Generalities.—Tearing in back, r. side and shoulders. Pain on walking; walking erect. Soreness; on motion; on waking; of arm, back, lower limbs, < small of back; morning on waking, < calves, thighs, back, shoulders, neck, upper limbs and chest. Fulness; of dependent parts. Heart, lungs, stomach and brain feel as if too full of blood. Malaise; with dull stupefying feeling in head. Disinclined to rise after waking. *Weakness;* from walking; in joints; as from walking far. *Faintness.* Joints stiff. Amelioration from eructation.

Mind.—*Inability to fix attention.* Cheerfulness. Clearness, with light feeling in anterior lobes, but heaviness and dulness in occiput. Confusion. Feeling as if death were impending during the darting pain in trachea, followed by exalted condition of brain and nervous system. Disinclination to work. Gloomy forebodings. *Irritability.* Memory lost. *Sadness.* Stupidity. Thoughts rapid. Unconsciousness on waking.

Clinical.—The patients, as a rule, are despondent and irritable.

Head.—Aching; dull here and there, especially in r. temple and occiput, then dull stitches in forehead and temple. Feeling of a board upon it. *Confusion; with vertigo.* Heaviness; dull, especially in region of r. ear. Intoxicated feeling. Vertigo; afternoon; with balancing in head. **Forehead.** Aching; with fluent coryza; *with constrictive feeling in skin of forehead;* as during cold in head; flying, and in temples; neuralgic. *Pressure; with nausea.* Throbbing in eminence. *Aching over l. eye;* over r. eye. Region of causality, neuralgic pain, r. darting towards l., with constriction in skin of forehead; uneasiness l. Sinus, fulness. **Temples.** Aching l., acute, r.; with soreness; flying. Dulness. Stitches, l., with nausea. **Vertex.** Fulness; and pressure. Parietal, aching above r. temple. **Occiput.** Aching, with flushes of heat in integument of occiput, nape and shoulders; extending to ears. Bruised feeling, with lameness in nape. Heaviness. Pressure on cerebellum. **Scalp.** Hyperæsthesia. Soreness of r. side from lying on it.

Eyes.—Heat. Pain, light and giddy in r. when near light; shooting pain in l. Smarting. Twitching r. *Weight.* Deep-seated burning and stinging in l. orbit, as if pain surrounded ball, with coldness in eye. Twitching of lids. Tries to keep from winking. Burning in inner canthi. *Lachrymation.* Eyeballs sore. Pupils dilated, contracting slowly. Vision. Flickering. Illusions.

Ears.—Burning. Fulness. Pressure about r.

Nose.—Coryza; with cool feeling on inspiration; with fulness in nose and forehead; with pressure in forehead, especially at root of nose; fluent, with frontal headache; fluent, with twisting in front part of nose. Drawing in right nostril as in coryza. Mucus more watery; l. nostril full of thick mucus. Pain, shooting. Sensitiveness to inspired air. *Sneezing.* Feeling as after snuff. Soreness and fulness. Pain in r. bone; pressure in l. bone. Mucous membrane, sensitiveness, causing a cold feeling; swollen sensation. Pressure at root. Posterior nares *dry;* also palate; *stinging and burning, and in soft palate.*

Face.—Flushed after rubbing. *Pale, miserable appearance.* Twitching of muscles under l. eye. Lips feel hot.

Mouth.—Teeth. Oily feeling. Pain in sound. Tongue. Coat thick yellow; dirty white. Pain sharp, biting. *Scalded feeling;* with constriction of fauces. Swollen feeling. Uncontrollable, causing inability to speak long words distinctly. Tip, biting and stinging; soreness. Mouth. Burning; and in œsophagus. Dryness; and in pharynx, with soreness. Scraping, irritation or burning, extending to stomach. *Salivation;* with oily taste; with coppery taste. Taste *bitter;* flat; like licorice; *metallic;* slimy; sweet. Submaxillary glands, increased secretion. Parotid glands sore when exposed to wind.

Throat.—Acrid feeling. Biting. Congestion. Inspired air feels cooler. *Constriction* (Bap.); with dull pain on each side of tonsils. *Burning;* when swallowing. *Dryness* (Bell.); after eating; increase of dry feeling, then secretion of mucus; *with contraction. Excoriation* (Phyto.). Formication. Feeling as if something had lodged in it. Mucus, causing cough. Pain > eating a grape; sharp, biting pain; pain as if burnt. *Pricking* and pressing, with fulness in epigastrium and eructations. *Raw feeling.* Shooting. Soreness in forenoon, > in afternoon. Stinging. *Swallowing difficult; inclined to swallow, with dryness* and stiffness in throat (Bell.), with pain in tonsils, with neuralgic pain in fauces. Tickling causing cough. Upper part, fulness. Pharynx, dryness; irritated feeling, and in mouth. Tonsils and soft palate congested; with aching. Œsophagus, burning; constricted, scraped feeling; and in throat, causing disposition to hawk; dryness.

Clinical.—Is a valuable remedy for follicular inflammation of the posterior wall of the pharynx, with the symptoms above emphasized; it is to be compared especially with Phytolacca.

Stomach.—Appetite little. Increased; with sick feeling in stomach. *Eructations; of air;* of air with waterbrash; of mucus; periodical, of viscid mucus. *Nausea;* with burning and salivation; with eructations; with ineffectual urging to stool. *Retching. Violent vomiting.* Stomach aching and rumbling; aching extending downward. Burning; as if it contained water. Cutting. *Distress;* with pain in bowels; *in epigastrium; distress, with nausea; burning, in epigastric region,* and in umbilical region, with aching in lumbar region, < walking; burning, in cardiac portion. Dyspepsia. Faintness in pit. Fulness; after eating; *in* *epigastrium.* Fluttering in pit. Fulness; at epigastrium. Gnawing and emptiness in morning. Griping in epigastrium. Flatulent griping from stomach to umbilical region. Heat; in epigastrium. *Pain;* after eating; in epigastrium; about and below pyloric extremity; acute; burning; in pyloric portion; dull, in cardiac portion; *extending to r. lobe of liver;* below pit, causing faint feeling; neuralgic in region. *Pressure as from a stone at pit.* Soreness; of epigastrium. Periodical tightness at pit, with labored breathing. Twisting at pit.

Abdomen.—Distention; > by general sweat. Rumbling. *Emission of flatus; fetid;* with griping. Cramp-like contraction before stool. Cramp. Constriction. Griping at each inspiration. Pinching before stool. Pain alternating with pain in chest; P. extending to small of back; flying. *Soreness on touch.* Distress. Feeling as after severe diarrhœa. Burning.

Stitches in r. hypochondrium; in l.; deep-seated above r. hip. Pinching in r. hypochondrium. Aching in hypochondria; through to back, < by inspiration; in r., < by walking; *in r. lower lobe of liver;* r. lobe of liver; in region of gall-bladder (Diosc.); shifting, in l. hypochondrium. *Soreness in r. hypochondrium* (Bry.). *Fulness in r. hypochondrium* (Pod.). *Distress in liver.* Umbilical region, fine stitches; cutting; pinching below umbilicus; *pain;* pain after stool; pain after difficult stool, and in hypogastric region; soreness; distress; distress, and in hypogastric region, with urging to stool and rumbling; burning distress. Rumbling in hypogastrium. Cutting in l. groin. Pain in hypogastric region. Neuralgic pain in r. groin.

Clinical.—The action of this drug on the liver associated with engorged portal circulation, especially in large hæmorrhoids, is extremely marked; see symptoms above and compare with Pod.

Rectum.—**Burning after stool** (Alœ, Nit. ac., Sulph.). *Constriction;* after stool. **Dryness; with heat** (Aloe); followed by moisture. *Fulness. Itching and dryness* (Sul.), with stiffness of skin and adjacent cellular tissue. *Feeling as if mucous membrane were thick and obstructed stool, and as if rectum would protrude if the effort were continued.* Pressure; with inclination to stool and eructations. *Soreness;* with sensation as if something would pass off all the time. **Feeling as if full of small sticks** (Nit. ac.). **Anus.** Extreme flow of blood to, from rubbing. **Burning** (Sul. Nit. ac., Alœ). Sphincter unable to contract. *Cutting after stool* (Alœ). **Fulness** (Aloe); *after walking, with itching.* Heat (Sul.). **Itching** (Sul.). Pain. **Pressure** (Sul.). *Prolapsus; prolapsed feeling after stool; prolapsed feeling, with backache. Raw feeling.* **Soreness** (Berb.). **Urging to stool** with every eructation; with stool; after stool; with distress in umbilical and hypogastric regions, and rumbling; with desire to remain long at stool; with shivering; constant; constant, with pain in r. hypochondrium and stomach. *Ineffectual.*

Clinical.—For protruding, purple piles with the symptoms noted this drug has been found extremely valuable, and for these troubles it has won its greatest laurels; especially associated with them and almost characteristic of the drug are the severe pains in the sacrum and small of back and the fulness in the region of the liver.

Stool.—Black and soft; first part black and hard, last part almost as white as milk, then tearing in anus. Copious and soft, followed by burning and feeling of swelling and constriction in rectum. First half dark, rest light. Diarrhœa; of ingesta. Difficult; then soreness, aching and fulness in rectum; difficult and dry; and scanty; and *large, hard, then pain and feeling as if anus protruded.* Frequent. Hard, with soreness of anus. Knotty. Light-colored. Liquid; preceded by griping. Mixed in character. Mushy, with pain in lumbar region. Omitted. Rope-like. Scanty. Small. Thin.

Micturiction.—*Frequent.* Urging to. Urine dark, *scanty, scalding. Hot.* Increased in amount. Retained.

Genital Organs.—Pain. Penis, dull and heavy shooting pain through or near belt. Testicles; drawing l.; soreness. *Leucorrhœa.*

Respiratory Organs.—Glottis and pharyngo-laryngeal mucous membrane dry and stiff. Larynx dry (Bell.); and tickling; tickling, scraping, and in pharynx; tickling, causing cough, with mucous expectoration. Trachea, throbbing, darting pain, causing tickling. Cough; dry; dry hacking, from constriction of fauces, with irritation of epiglottis. Expectoration frequent; thick, then watery mucus; ropy mucus; sweetish mucus. Respiration labored.

Chest.—Constriction; in lower part. Burning distress. Heat in; with coldness rising up. *Pain in r. lung on motion upward and downward when breathing;* pain, alternating with pain in abdomen; pain as if stone lay on pit of stomach. *Raw feeling.* Shooting pain in sternum. Soreness in and over lungs, with rush of blood, on full inspiration. Stitches l.; then r.; in l. side; in lower lobe of l. lung, > passing urine. Pain in sternum as if a piece were torn out. *Tightness.* Twitching, to l. shoulder. Warmth.

Heart.—Burning in region. Pain in apex; acute pain in apex; burning in apex; darting in region, with fulness and palpitation; neuralgic, in apex; neuralgic, in region, arresting breath. Palpitation; periodical; periodical, with anxiety. Stitches in region. *Twitching over region.* Pulse accelerated; soft and weak.

Neck and Back.—**Neck.**—Glands enlarged and sore to touch. Lameness and weariness in nape. *Pain; in nape;* dull, heavy in nape. Soreness, with pricking. **Back.**—*Aching; < moving;* between shoulders; in **small of back** (Berb., Phyto.), < motion (Phyto.); **in sacram and hips** (Berb.), < **walking and stooping;** *making it difficult to get up after sitting.* Distress in dorsal region. Lameness and weariness in small of back; lameness and strained feeling in r. lumbar region, extending to gluteal muscle. Pain; between shoulders; *lumbar region;* small of back and hips when getting up, > motion; *sacrum; in lumbosacral region, and on stooping;* sacral and lower lumbar region, after difficult stool. Stiffness. Stitches. *Tearing in small of back and hips when walking* (Berb.). Weariness.

Clinical.—These pronounced symptoms of the back are usually associated with hæmorrhoids, but the drug has also been used for lumbago not associated with any hepatic or hæmorrhoidal disease; even dysmenorrhœa with the peculiar sacro-iliac pains has been relieved.

Limbs.—Heaviness. Spasms. Nails blue. *Stretching.* Shoulders, pain. Arms, aching; neuralgic pain; paralysis of r.; tearing and jerking of r. Forearms, numbness with prickling; darting pain in l. Cannot control muscles to write well. Hands, pricking after washing; stinging. Tottering. Limbs ache when weight of body rests on them. *Knees ache.* Legs ache; weak. Calves sore. *Tendo-achillis sore.* Feet swell; after walking. Corns sore.

Skin.—Formication in front of temple; on nose. Fulness, as from too much blood in body. Gooseskin. Itching all over, especially around waist; itching of testicles. Redness and flying heat of l. side of face, red spot on forehead from pressure of hat; large red spots on face on rubbing after washing.

Sleep.—*Yawning; constant.* Sleepiness; stupefying. Frequent waking. Dreams distressing; dreams that he is fighting in a battle; that he saw a man in his room.

Fever.—Chilliness; from riding in cool air; of skin, when cold air strikes it, with chattering of teeth. Rigors. Heat; general; of head; integuments of occiput, extending to ears; burning of l. cheek; hands hot and dry; burning of palms and soles; skin hot and dry; in flashes over body; flying, before eructations. General sweat, with decline of abdominal distension.

Æthusa.

Æthusa cynapium, L. *Natural order* of plants, Umbelliferæ. A tincture is prepared from the whole plant when in flower.

General Action.—This plant, formerly supposed to be poisonous, is now proved to be harmless; large quantities can be taken with impunity; it seems, however, to possess a disagreeable essential oil which provokes nausea and vomiting and causes other symptoms. It is particularly useful in gastro-intestinal disorders of children (vomiting, diarrhœa, and even convulsions).

Allied Drugs.—Sulph., *Sul. ac.*, Tart. emet., Kali b., Ox. ac., Ip., *Grat.*, *Gam.*

Generalities.—Hands, head and face seem swollen after walking in open air, > in the house. Clothes seem loose. Secretions diminished. Stabbing pain. Seething in blood in morning on waking. Uneasiness. Weakness, with sleepiness in afternoon. Amelioration in open air; after entering house; after broth.

Clinical.—A case of infantile paralysis, with the characteristic indications for Æthusa, is reported cured.

Mind.—Anxiety. Dulness like intoxication. Earnestness. Excited, lively in forenoon, apprehensive, sad in afternoon. Fixed idea of a garment which she had made the previous day, and of which she dreamed. Fretfulness; in afternoon; in open air, > in house; > towards noon. Does not talk willingly.

Head.—Aching; seeming to come from teeth; pulsating on entering house. Brain seems bound up. Constriction. Drawing upward in. Dulness. Pulsation, especially r. side and backward, with heaviness; pulsation and sticking in afternoon. Raging here and there on entering house. Painful screwing together from both sides. Shattered feeling in afternoon. Vertigo; in open air; during and after rising from a seat; > open air; sudden while sitting, > rising.

Forehead.—Aching; crampy, with disposition to contract eyebrows; intermittent, in lines vertically over each eye; pulsating l. In forepart of head, pain as if compressed posteriorly and superiorly. Constriction from points vertically over each eye, > pressure; constriction and yet pressure outward; constriction of brows. Heaviness which seems to press head downward, when sitting; heaviness which presses down eyelids, during dinner. Pressure in sinuses. Pulsation. Shooting up over eyes. Sticking, in afternoon on turning head to r. Jerking tearing in l. sinus while sitting. Tension as from a band fastened at each zygoma. Sensation as if something were turning around in it.

Temple.—Aching as if a bloodvessel had been torn out of l. Pulsation, l. Sticking shooting in l. Sticking, l.; and pulsation, > pressure. Sudden tearing in r., in afternoon. Aching in l. mastoid process.

Vertex.—Aching. Painful sticking and beating, in afternoon, > rubbing.

Parietals.—Sticking in l. half of head; inward in upper part of l. bone; sticking and pulsating in upper part of r. bone. Tearing and pulsation in r.; sticking tearing in l. Twitching in r., in afternoon.

Occiput.—Aching in r.; occasional. Heaviness. Sticking and pulsation in upper part of r.; tearing stitches extending forward from, in afternoon. Tearing in r. side, shooting through whole head and extending to r. side, in afternoon.

Eye.—Burning as from smoke, in house. Watery.

Ear.—Sticking shooting in l. Sticking in l.; into r.; in r.; > boring, > rubbing; in r.; preceded by stitches in r. hypochondrium, in afternoon; in l., with sensation of heat coming out of it, alternating with stitches in l. costal region. Stopped sensation, with hardness of hearing, which lasted longer in l. ear. Stuffiness in r. Tearing, > rubbing; sticking, in afternoon, in r.; about l., extending to top of head. Twitching.

Clinical.—It is reported to have cured a discharge from the r. ear associated with spasms, stupor and vomiting of milk.

Nose.—Much thick mucus. Ulcerative pain, as if there were an open spot in left fossa. Pressure in upper passages. Sneezing; inclination to, in l. nostril. Stitches externally, l. side. Stoppage; sudden, morning, after waking.

Face.—Sensation of fulness and heat. Hollow-cheeked. Stitch like the tapping of a finger in middle of l. cheek, with tearing. Malar bones; crampy aching, < l.; sticking and tearing, in r.; tearing in l. in cold air. Lips dry. Tearing in lower lip extending into neighboring teeth, in afternoon. Tearing in r. lower jaw.

Mouth.—Teeth; grumbling in a r. lower back tooth; a r. lower **decayed** molar, sensitive, < touch; tickling in l. upper teeth. Gums, stitches here and there; sticking and tearing, now r., now l. Tongue dry. Mouth, burning; dryness; salivation. Taste insipid; metallic; slimy, with dryness; sweetish; sweetish morning after waking; tastelessness to food.

Throat.—Burning. Dryness. Hawking, frequent; inclination for hawking and for spitting. Stitches when not swallowing. Desire to swallow, as if to keep something down; sensation as if she could not swallow, with spasmodic contraction in r. side of throat and ear, in afternoon while sitting. Œsophagus, burning; warmth and uneasiness.

Stomach.—Indisposed to eat, with fair appetite. Thirst. Eructations, tasting of broth; eructations burning œsophagus and throat; empty in afternoon; of food; rancid; hot, sour waterbrash. *Nausea; at sight of food;* in mouth and pharynx; extending down œsophagus to stomach, with rumbling and gurgling in stomach and upper abdomen and fluttering in stomach. Hiccough in afternoon. *Retching and throwing up phlegm.* Burning. Feeling as before diarrhœa, and in bowels. Griping. Heaviness. Feeling of indigestion; and in upper abdomen. Feeling as after a spree. Sticking in side near stomach, extending deeply inward on sitting bent, > becoming erect. Feeling as if something turned about, then heat rising into chest. Uneasiness, as before gastric catarrh; uneasiness and warmth.

Clinical.—For vomiting of milk (in young children), especially of curdled milk, this remedy is unrivalled: associated with this condition or consequent upon the gastric derangment there may be diarrhœa of a thin yellow or greenish character (Gratiola, Gamboge). Some very obstinate cases of gastrointestinal catarrh have been cured by Æthusa, and it has even arrested convulsions and paralytic symptoms, which doubtless had their origin in indigestion. The vomiting or evacuation by the bowels of curds of milk is quite a characteristic indication.

Abdomen.—Coldness; in region of transverse colon; in upper. Cramps in small intestines quickly shifting from place to place. Cutting above umbilicus; cutting in lower, with urging to stool. Griping in umbilicus, then two soft stools. Gurgling and rumbling in upper, and in stomach, with nausea and fluttering in stomach. Sensation of a load in upper. Sensation in upper, as after a dose of medicine. Movements, then a stool, which is first hard, then soft; painful movements below navel, with desire for stool, after morning broth. Pain as before diarrhœa; pain in upper, and in stomach, as from something indigestible. Pressure in l. hypochondrium and burning, with stitches. Rush as of boiling water in umbilical region. Stitch in r. hypochondrium, then in r. ear, in afternoon; in l. hypochondrium; in l. hypochondrium, with burning, > rubbing; burning stitches at one time in r. hypochondrium, at another in l. loin; sticking in hypochondriac region, extending backward, in afternoon. Warmth in upper.

Anus.—Clawing, with straining, during hard stool. Tenesmus after soft stool. Urging to stool, with cutting in abdomen; urging after morning broth, with painful movements below navel. Stool hard; first part hard, then soft; loose, yellow and sour; two soft.

Urine.—Diminished. Increased; pale, of sweet odor.

Sexual desire diminished; strong, on waking.

Cough.—Dry, in paroxysms, after dinner. Frequent short, hacking.

Chest.—Burning, as from a glowing iron, in a spot below l. breast. Crampy constriction r. Digging and tension in front of r. axilla. Stitch in region of r. ribs, in afternoon; beneath l. mamma in afternoon, < inspiration; in middle of chest, 6.30 P.M., during inspiration on rising after sitting bent, < deep breathing; acute in middle of sternum, then burning in same spot, > pressure, but returning; in l. costal region, alternating with sticking in and sensation of heat coming out of l. ear; deep internally beneath l. female breast, in afternoon. Tension in front of r. axilla, evening when knitting.

Heart.—Crampy constriction, with a feeling as if he could not take a long breath. Pulse rapid; slow and soft.

Neck and Back.—Neck.—Drawing pain as if a tendon or bloodvessel would be torn out, in r. side, > rubbing. Stitch inward in l. muscles. Tearing in a spot on r. side; in tendons of r. side; pulsating in spot on tendons of l. side. Sticking twitching in nape. **Back.**—Aching in small of; heavy aching across kidneys, morning on waking. Drawing in r. lumbar region while walking, > sitting. Pain between scapulæ, morning on waking. Screwed-together feeling in small of. Stitch between scapulæ; in r. lumbar region, then pressure; burning at one time in l. loin, then in r. hypochondriac region.

Superior Extremities.—Shoulder, paralyzed feeling in l., then in r. forearm; painful tension in l., then r. forearm, paralytic pain in l. while sitting; sticking in tendons of r. while using hand; sticking tearing in middle of l., along upper surface, to wrist; tearing in spot on inner surface of l.; tension in tendons of l. while knitting, > moving fingers; sudden weakness while knitting; weakness near r. wrist extending to little finger. Stitch in l. external styloid process. Hand; tearing on back of r., in tendons of thumb; tearing in metacarpal bone of index, l. and r. Thumb, sticking in ball of l., on flexing, > extending thumb; stiff feeling l.; twitching tearing as in marrow, between first and second joints of l.; twitching of l. Fingers, fine sticking on l. side of tip of r. index, > pressure; tearing on lower surface of third joint of r. little; tearing between little and ring, < stretching them.

Inferior Extremities.—Weakness. Hip, pinching externally, in r.; sticking and drawing into l. thigh; tension in r. in afternoon. Thigh, paralytic pain in middle of r. while sitting, > motion; sticking in upper part of l. Sticking in r. knee in evening when standing. Tearing deep in r. instep in afternoon. Tearing sticking in r. heel, extending into sole as far as ball of foot. Sticking in r. sole below heel.

Skin.—Dry, white, leathery, pinched look. Face red. Skin of hands dry and shrunken, especially palmar surface. Painful boil on sacral region.

Sleepiness; in afternoon; > open air.

Fever.—Chilliness, internal and external; internal and external, with sleepiness, in forenoon; coldness in, around and behind r. ear, seeming to be in bone; of feet and limbs, nearly to knees. Shivering on entering house. Heat general; glowing feeling over whole body; morning on waking; heat of head; and burning in face; rushing to head; in forehead, with pressure; in face; with full sensation; burning on r. side of nose, then as with a glowing needle externally in pit of stomach; heat extending up back in afternoon; burning externally in small of back, > rubbing; general peripheral warmth. Sweat; on forehead.

Agaricus.

This poisonous mushroom, Agaricus muscarius, is not uncommon in dry forests. It is usually distinguished by its scarlet, mottled top. A tincture is made from the younger fresh plants.

General Action.—Agaricus acts energetically upon the circulation, respiration, peristalsis and secretion. It irritates and excites the cardiac filaments of the pneumogastric, causes tonic contractions of arterioles and smooth muscle fibre (intestines, bladder, iris), increases secretions from the salivary glands, liver, pancreas, mucous membrane of intestinal canal, etc., and causes contraction of the pupil and spasm of accommodation. Paralysis results as a reaction from prolonged spasm or as the primary effect of large doses. Numerous effects (motor and sensory) may be referred to an anæmia of nerve centres (brain and spine), caused by persistent spasm of bloodvessels.

Allies.—Secale corn, Physostigma, *Pilocarpine*, Nicotine.

Antagonist.—Belladonna.

Generalities.—Emaciation. Cracking in joints on motion. *Convulsions;* > vomiting, with anxiety and pain at epigastric region; alternating with stupor; frequent convulsions in posterior part of chest, passing obliquely through, then in epigastrium, then in hypogastrium, especially r. side in evening, when standing, with a feeling as if the whole body were shaken. Spasm more like a trembling than a convulsion, with delirium. Convulsive motions of head and upper part of trunk, with startings in limbs. *Frequent twitching of different muscles* (Zinc.); twitching and jumping of single fingers. Twitching when lying, sometimes in one group of muscles, sometimes in another; sometimes with electric stitches here and there in the skin. Restlessness; of every voluntary muscle at 3 A.M., then quivering of whole body, especially of lower jaw, then action of muscles as in St. Vitus' dance. *Trembling;* internal. Sudden shaking of body and pulling of r. arm from under his head down to the trunk when lying, then fine stitches in condyles of elbows. Commotion of nervous system. Tumbling about in a grotesque way. Awkwardness in evening.

Stitches in various parts of the body, especially between skin and flesh, no part of the body seems free from them, sometimes with electric shivering and restless sleep. Tearing now and then in tendinous expansions, especially on l. outer thigh. Pain simultaneously in several parts, especially on both sides above small of back; pain of various kinds simultaneously in all parts when sitting; intermitting, in bones in morning, <noon,> afternoon and evening, especially located in l. tibia, sometimes appearing in condyle of l. elbow, resembling syphilitic bone-pains, except that they are > warmth of bed. Cramplike pain in various muscles and parts of body, even within l. ear, or of all muscles when sitting. Bruised feeling, < sitting; bruised feeling in joints. Boring in head, thighs, tibæ and bones of tarsus, when sitting, with somnolence and general relaxation. General malaise, *discomfort* in whole body; all forenoon; in evening; with tired feeling in legs, preventing sleep, though very sleepy. Sensitiveness of all parts to pressure. Pulsations in all parts, especially in epigastrium. It seems as if the whole body were diminishing. Constant inclination to bend backward and forward and to stretch. Impulse to fall backward. Rising in morning difficult.

Weakness; morning on waking, with confusion; weakness after afternoon nap, with painfulness and lameness of limbs; in bed; after an embrace; on least motion, with palpitation; on waking; when walking; after walking; after short but quick walking; < sitting; >walking in open air; with delirium, much like that in a dynamic fever; with cold and viscid sweat; with vertigo; alternating with itching on face, nose, ears and scalp. Fainting; faint feeling on ascending a hill, with sweat. Supernatural strength. Light feeling, as if she could run as never before. Blunting of senses; heaviness of whole body; morning on waking, with heat; at night; especially of calves. The whole body seems paralyzed. Much affected from walking; much affected by being in the air, which is not hot. Aggravation in morning, fasting and after eating; aggravation of symptoms of muscles when sitting, seldom when walking. Amelioration from vomiting and stool. He feels best when walking very slowly.

Clinical.—Chorea and chorea-like twitchings, neuralgia and various troubles due to weak irritable nerves, with an irritable, anæmic spine, frequently find their remedy in Agaricus. General aggravation from walking in the open air and relief from being warm in bed predominate. There is no evidence of any chronic constitutional dyscrasia, such as underlies epilepsy. Tremor and tremulous tongue in low fever, with delirium and attempts to get out of bed.

Mind.—Delirium; imagines himself a military officer; imagines himself at the gate of hell and that the mushroom tells him to fall on his knees and confess his sins, which he does. Phantasy that he saw his dead sister in heaven. Calling for his hatchet, alternately with religious excitement. Fury; desires to rip up his bowels, which he imagines the mushroom has ordered. Fearless, menacing, mischievous frenzy, also frenzy, so that he injures himself, with great strength. Talking incoherently, passing rapidly from one subject to another. Merry, incoherent loquacity, with convulsions of facial and cervical muscles, < r., drawing head towards r. shoulder, and with movement of flexion and extension alternately in lower limbs while walking, followed by quiet, then nausea and malaise. Telling secrets. Singing; and talking, but does not answer questions. Alternately sings and is vexed, embraces his companions and kisses their hands. Timid craziness. Delirium, with increase of strength. Running and walking involuntarily in dangerous places. Intoxicated, they carry heavy loads, take long steps and jump over small objects as if over trunks of trees. A small hole seems like a frightful chasm and a spoonful of water an immense lake. (Cannab. ind.). Leaping. Dancing. Romping with children. Wild cries. Ecstasy, prophecies and making verses. Courage. Bold, revengeful projects.

Gayety; with increase of strength, then sleep, then prostration on waking. Now gay, now melancholy. Laughter, owing to a mixed sensation of happiness and misery; involuntary laughter after each yawning; laughter about their not standing and walking straight. *Disinclination to speak;* or work, also with uneasiness and weakness. *Ill humor;* morning on waking; *ill humor, with disinclination to answer questions.* Loathing of life. Quarrelsome. Vexed with herself and pities herself. Anxiety; with tremors and lassitude; with sweat; about his present and future condition; as if something unpleasant were going to happen to her. Depression of spirits; from slight causes; so that he shut himself up in his room, lest he should be obliged to talk. Weeping; with anguish. Uneasiness of mind and body. *Indifference.* Indolence. *Aversion to mental work;* with thoughtless staring.

Imbecility. Coma. Unconsciousness; with closed eyes; with red, puffy face. Attack as if he would lose consciousness in evening after lying down. Understands with difficulty what he reads, and even if it is easy to understand he *reads with difficulty because the type seems to move, with itching and burning in eyes.* Attention not fixed by reading. Stupefaction; morning on waking; > open air, with drowsiness; with spasmodic agitation; alternating with convulsions. Confusion in morning on waking. Cannot find the words he wishes to use. Memory weak; lost, also thought he had made a journey. Nervous activity indescribably deranged.

Head.—*Falling backward, as if a weight were attached to occiput.* Swaying back and forth. Convulsions of muscles of head and neck. Involuntary motions. Shooting. Tearing in different places in skull; in tendinous expansions of skull; as if brain would be torn to pieces; jerking tearing, especially behind r. ear. Aching; morning in bed; on waking at 3 A.M.; after dinner, especially in occiput; deep-seated, *dull, especially in forehead, obliging constant motion of head and closure of eyes;* > copious stool, with flushes of heat; dull, stunning, with thirst and heat, especially in face; extending over skull, < touch, with constricted feeling in brain and inability to keep his mind on any subject. Externally in forenoon, especially in posterior half. Drawing aching; > sleep at night; morning on waking, with pressure in eyeballs. Intermittent aching before sleep. Sudden aching extending into l. ear, as if something would stop it, when lying down on account of vertigo. Grinding. Stupefying aching. Leaden pressure of brain on skull, extending to nose. Sensation as if pain would appear; > thinking about it.

Burrowing in brain. Drawing in all directions, with sensation as if he would lose his senses. Intoxicated feeling; pleasant intoxication. Stupefaction; forenoon; dizzy sensation on putting head out of window, with roaring in l. ear. *Confusion* towards noon, with cool creeping in scalp of vertex, and tension in scalp. *Dulness,* < walking in open air; with fulness in head and drawing towards temples; dizzy, also in afternoon, < reading or looking into the light. Enlarged feeling. Fulness. *Heaviness;* as after intoxication; as if pressed in, especially in forehead. Congestion; rush of blood on mental effort, with throbbing in arteries, heat in face and disturbance of thought.

Vertigo; morning; morning, with stupefaction; *morning, from strong sunlight;* forenoon, with stupefying headache; from afternoon, till late in evening, with impulse to fall backward; *from heat of sun;* while walking; from walking in open air and meditating; in room on turning around; on entering dark room from open air, with nausea; < open air; > open air; > room; > turning quickly or moving head; > thinking of something else, with indistinct vision; with stupefaction; with burning in vertex; with drawing pain in forehead; intermittent vertigo; sudden as if turning around.

Forehead.—Twitching of l. muscles; in r. superciliary ridge, with dragging. *Stitches* in r. and l.; over eyes; stitches in r. eminence from a noise at breakfast; in a spot in l. eminence; over l. brow, > scratching; in l. superciliary ridge, towards outside, morning on waking; in l. superciliary ridge, with twisting; alternately in each eminence; in front, always after rising, gradually extending to occiput; jerking deep in cerebrum; piercing cerebrum like lightning when walking in open air, with feeling as if he would lose consciousness. *Tearing* in bones; above nose; intermittent drawing. Drawing cutting when standing, becoming pressive stunning when sitting. *Aching;* in morning, with contraction of muscles of forehead and lids; on waking; when sitting, with vertigo; < open air; > towards evening; in cavities; in l. side; l. eminence; over l. eye; above eyes, with stitches; in middle, > pressure upon temples; in superciliary ridges, also l., then r.; in r. superciliary ridge, in morning; in r. superciliary ridge, > washing body with cold water, then worse again; in r. supraorbital region on walking in open air; above r. side, with burning; in r., with morning dulness of head; alternately in each eminence; in frontal and sagittal sutures. Deep-seated aching at margin of hair of forehead; deep-seated in r. eminence in morning on waking. Aching extending inward; extending to eyes, with twitching; pressing upon upper half of eyeballs. Sensation during the day as if headache were coming on, which appeared towards evening in spots upon F. and temples. Aching in sinciput as if sides of head were pressed together. Piercing r. superciliary ridge; itching piercing over l. brow, > scratching. Grinding in l. eminence. *Burning* pain above r. eye, with lachrymation; burning pain in l. eyebrow and occiput, with sensitiveness to touch and pressure. *Drawing* pain; *between superciliary ridges;* in middle; in l.; r. side in morning on waking; from l. towards r. side while sitting; in l. eminence, oppressing eye; in forehead, eye and occiput, with pressure; intermittent, extending to eyes, also during the day. **Drawing in bone from both sides, as far as root of nose.** *Boring;* > pressure; in l. superciliary ridge. Burrowing in l. eminence and over l. eye; in l. forehead and occiput; in l. eminence, along sagittal suture, through whole hemisphere to occiput, when walking in open air in forenoon; in l. eminence as if everything in brain were stirred up; as if the brain were an ant-hill, with fulness of head. Sore feeling above l. brow. Enlarged feeling and sensation as if the brain were promiscuously mixed up, with aching in temples. Fulness. Confusion. Heaviness; painful.

Temples.—*Twitching* in l.; about temples and ears; in temples and cheeks; in l. temple and zygoma; in r. temple and along zygoma, with shooting; rhythmical in l. temporal and frontal regions. *Stitches;* l.; over r. eye; r. after talking, then l., then pressure in l.; < l. region; l. mastoid process. Tearing in r. *Aching* in temples; l.; r.; r. bone; l., then r., then in l. lower jaw, like a decayed tooth beginning to ache; aching at noon; in spot in l. region after breakfast; above l. concha, reaching deep into the brain, < touching hair, with depressed spirits; cramplike, in l.; drawing; in r., more stupefying than throbbing; boring throbbing in squamous portion of bones. Burrowing in l. at midnight, > pressure; dull burrowing in l. after dinner. Dragging downward, extending as far as half of the ears, < during the day and by touch.

Vertex.—Stitches; itching. Tearing; lancinating, to l. ear. *Aching;* morning; morning, > after rising; at night; > open air; pulsating, with despair bordering on rage. Deep-seated boring.

Sides.—Twitching in r. Flashlike stroke externally in l. *Shooting;* r.; l.; from l. parietal bone into r. temple; in l. half from 10 A.M. till 2 P.M., then periodical stitches. *Tearing* in r. upper; in r. parietal bone, over ear, < touch, with sensation as of a festering spot; in l. circumference of brain, with pressing, especially in orbit and zygoma, and with confusion of head; fine, behind and over l. ear. *Aching* in r.; l.; l. on waking, > after rising; l., with urging to urinate; in l. side of skull, with tearing; in l. half, becoming a burrowing; *in r. as from a nail;* boring in l. skull and in ascending ramus of lower jaw.

Occiput.—*Stitches* across; flying stitches in forenoon;

periodical; tearing from one side to the other in morning. *Tearing* in r.; r. half of bone; behind head and over l. ear; intermittent tearing in l. *Aching;* in l. half of bone *when seated;* < lying and becoming burning and extending between superciliary ridges when lying on back; throbbing. Drawing pain; in afternoon; morning in bed, < stretching and holding breath. Drawing. *Boring. Burrowing* between occipital region and nape in forenoon, with weariness in lower limbs and sleepiness; in r. half of occiput in morning in bed, with stitches in middle of r. cheek. Bruised feeling in occiput and nape; in r. side of occiput. Creaking towards l., < pressure, with pain on touch. Tension; especially in spots; extending towards occiput, there developing into aching, with heaviness. Heaviness; towards neck-joint, with tension. Dull fulness after waking. *Atlas-joint.* Stitches. Jarring, extending into head.

Scalp.—Elevations on occiput and along sagittal sutures, with biting burning after scratching. Scurf in spots. *Pimples;* painful on vertex at roots of hair, bleeding easily and leaving red pimples. Vesicles on forehead. Twitching over l. ear; *above r. eye. Stitches* on top of l. side, changing to pressive pain in vertex; biting, in l. side of scalp, in parietal bone and splinter stitches in r. temporal region near ear. Tearing and drawing pain in scalp and skull at night, < pressure, especially a spot on vertex, which pains as from an internal festering. Tearing tensive sensation in occiput. Tension. Sensitiveness of l. to touch; sensitiveness in spots; of eyebrows; as if ulcerated. Formication on scalp. Itching; < getting up; here and there, with sensitiveness to touch; like the healing of wounds; on vertex, with pimples; on occiput towards nape; on occiput, with pimples; burrowing, on occiput; biting, on forehead and on various parts; biting corroding, on l. side.

Clinical.—Vertigo from the sun. Severe neuralgic headaches mostly in small spots, sharp piercing pain as from a nail (Ign.). Dull headache from prolonged desk-work.

Eyes.—Yellow. Red. Fierce expression. Rolling; upward. Staring wildly. Sticking, with tension; scraping sticking under r. upper lid. *Pain;* on moving them or exerting by candle light; after dinner with inclination to close them without sleepiness; towards inside; above upper lids, < when closed, with fatigue of eyes after great exertion in too strong a light; P. as from a grain of sand in l., also under r. upper lid at noon, with lachrymation; drawing P.; twitching pain in l.; P. as from something inward in eyes and upon forehead; burning pain. *Burning;* always after closing lids; burning after opening and closing; burning after yawning; burning with itching; burning, with weariness. Hot to touch. Dryness. Contracted feeling in evening; contracted feeling in r., with clearer vision, then biting pain in eyeball and lachrymation, then twitchings in l. eye (which had existed in r.), > wine. Painful stretching in morning on waking. Sensation as if they had to be wiped constantly. *Itching* in morning; in r., > rubbing, with pressure; in r., with pricking; in l., with tickling. Sensitiveness. Weak feeling. Insensibility to light. Lachrymation; r.; while reading.

Ball.—Pulled upward towards angles of orbits and fixed. *Twitched here and there;* also with lachrymation of l.; *twitched in l. while reading, with pressing;* painful twitching in r. Sudden tearing in r. *Pain;* when moved; on touch; in l.; in l. in morning; *in l., with spasms;* in upper and outer part of r.; drawing P.; pain as from pressure of a hand; piercing in r.; intermittent pain towards top and outward in r. *Drawing* in ball after dinner, < l., extending into forehead, with pressing. Painful worrying under l. lid, as if on ball, or itching. Burning, < moving them, with pressing. Motion of ball difficult. Enlarged feeling; in l. after vomiting.

Pupils.—Contracted, then dilated. *Dilated,* then contracted.

Lids.—Half-opened; without swelling and often with twitching and winking of lids. Agglutination as by slimy threads. Mucus. Twitching; in a small spot and extending towards one canthus. *Winking.* Pressure, < r., with sleepiness. Biting and contracted feeling. *Contraction.* Burning; after being closed. Difficult opening. *Upper lid, trembling;* r.; l., morning and noon; twitching l.; stitches in l. *Lower lid,* twitching of l.; winking of r., with throbbing in an artery on l. side, at back of nose, and twitches in skin of l. side of nose; winking of l., with itching. *Margins of lids,* redness, and of the conjunctiva palpebrarum, with sticking and tension in eyes. Stitches; biting stitches in r. upper; itching stitches in l. upper at roots of ciliæ; biting in morning on waking; itching.

Canthi.—*Agglutination, with yellow humor,* < morning and evening; of inner. Mucus; in inner. Swelling towards l. inner. Left caruncula enlarged. Scraping *stitches* in l.; in inner, also in morning on waking, with mucus; smarting stitches in l. inner. Pressure in l. as from a foreign body. Jerking worrying in l. *Burning* in l. outer; in inner, < touch; in inner when lids are closed firmly. Contraction of l. inner. *Itching of l., with twitching.*

Brow.—Falling out of hairs. Soreness on touch. Cramplike pain under r., making it difficult to open eyes.

Orbits.—Coarse stitches at exit of l. infraorbital nerve. Burning and pressure.

Vision.—Lost; while reading. Decreasing gradually when walking in open air. Weak. *Dim; if she looks long at any object; while reading; also with flickering;* with burning in l. outer canthus and pressure as from sand under l. upper lid; as from cobwebs; *as from a mist. Short-sighted.* Photophobia. Sensitiveness to candle light. Double; in evening. Dizzy in evening. *Motion of type while reading, with itching and burning. Flickering; while writing* (Seneg.). Black spot hovering before l. eye. Yellow spots when looking at light objects. Brown spot before l. eye towards inner canthus in gloomy weather; brown oblong spot hovering obliquely towards l. inner canthus on closing r. eye.

Clinical.—An exceedingly valuable remedy in asthenopia from prolonged strain, spasm of accommodation (Physostig.), twitching of eyes and lids; weakness of the muscles, with "swimming" of the type; myopia, with chronic chorioiditis.

Ears.—Redness, burning and itching, as if they had been frozen. Twitching of muscles close to l. ear; in cartilage; of tensor tympani, also with sound as if a leather-covered metal valve were set in motion; in r. tympanic cavity, with rattling or fluttering; rolling inside r. tympanum.

Stitches in l. auditory canal; twitching stitches inside l. ear. Tearing in r.; in l., with itching and desire to bore deep, the tearing < lying on same side; in r. meatus, extending to upper jaw, caused and < by cold air. Cramplike pain inside l. *Itching in ear, with burning; itching behind;* in l. external auditory tube, with cold stitches in middle ear; tickling itching in r. Eustachian tube alternating with ringing in l. ear. Feeling as if wax flowed out. Wax increased.

Hearing.—Acute. Dull. *Deaf* in l., as if something were before it; deafness, with headache. Stoppage of l. ear. *Ringing* in l.; r. when walking in open air. Rushing and ringing; or noise like a distant tea-kettle beginning to boil, with heat in head; rushing in r., like the sound of a locomotive, when lying, > rising. Roaring; l.; r., then l.; bubbling, roaring in l.; constant roaring in l., with creaking in both on empty swallowing. Sound in l. ear, as of a clock striking at a great distance. Whirring. Humming at night like a spinning-wheel. Sound as if a nail were being driven into a board at a distance. Creaking, as of a wooden screw, when swallowing. Intermittent clicking in r.

Clinical.—The subjective symptoms are extremely interesting, but there are very few clinical verifications; the frost-bitten sensation is, however, characteristic here as elsewhere. Spasm of the muscles of the pinna of the ear, especially of the attollens, persistent spasms, so that they attracted attention.

Nose.—Blueness; of tip, with paleness. Inflammation and soreness of inner wall. Creaking in bones. Stinging in l. side of root. *Pressure* in bones; at root, with a feeling as if nose were stopped, without stoppage; throbbing in bone, with feeling as if a swollen body in upper passage would force itself down; sudden, on superior part of dorsum. Burning pain. Cutting boring from l. nostril into frontal bone, as from an electric shock. Cutting soreness in upper part of l. nostril on inspiration. Sensitiveness high up in l. nostril in afternoon when breathing; S. of inner walls. *Dryness,* with sensation of a cold in the head; with bleeding when cleaned. *Stopped* feeling at night; feeling, < stooping. Fulness in upper passage, with a feeling as if a ball were forcing itself down the nasal canal. Biting in mucous membrane of l. nostril; in mucous membrane, with sneezing and with jumping of muscles of l. loin. Prickling in r. nostril and eye, as before sneezing. Itching in nose, and pungent smell, as if about to sneeze; tickling itching in l. nostril. *Sneezing;* morning on waking; from sunlight; from nausea; always twice in succession; *frequent* in morning; frequent during sleep; *frequent,* without coryza. Violent sneezing in morning in bed; violent after every attack of cough.

Coryza; every morning, with sneezing; with confusion of head; with discharge causing eruption on nose and upper lip. *Fluent coryza;* towards evening; attacking l. half of nose and l. eye, then r. half and r. eye, which discharged acrid, burning moisture, then nose swelled, was bluish-red, sore to touch, then desquamated. Discharge of copious mucus; with burning of upper lip; of scanty white, dry mucus, with sensation as if there were much mucus; much viscid mucus after snuff. *Clear water drops, without a cold in head;* clear water drops on stooping. Watery discharge, with a feeling of stopped coryza (*Nux v.*). Bleeding; *in morning after blowing;* (passive bleeding in old people). *Smell sensitive;* in r. nostril, but lost in l.

Clinical.—The symptoms of irritation in the nose, and the spasmodic sneezing as well as the discharge of pure water from nostrils without inflammatory symptoms, all point to its use in nervous complaints, with these peculiarities (whooping cough, chorea, etc.).

Face.—Pale; and sunken; *with bluish appearance around eyes, nose and mouth.* Red; after eating, with heat; *with itching and burning, as after freezing.* Red cheeks, < l. Yellow, especially about nostrils and corners of mouth. Puffiness; with a ghastly, leaden appearance; pale, with blue circles around eyes, and blueness of nose and lips; red. **Twitching;** of upper half of l. side; near r. malar-bone; pulsating twitching in r. cheek. *Stitches* in l. cheek; middle of r. cheek, in l. cheek, near exit of infraorbital nerve; in r. cheek, where infraorbital nerve forms plexus; in r. malar-bone; in chin; biting, on point of chin; sudden, in l. cheek near eye; electric, in l. malar-bone, with frequent twitches, especially in l. cheek; in r. cheek, close to lower edge of orbit, changing to a coarse pain, as if in bone; fine, in r. side. *Pain* in l. zygoma; on r. side of chin; in facial bones, especially socket of eye, in morning; *lancinating and drawing, in r. cheek. Pulsation* in l. cheek, with shooting stitches from l. eye into upper jaw.

Lips.—Blue, and pale. *Upper chapped, with burning smarting.* Middle of lower cracked, burning and painful. Peeling of epithelium of upper when smoking; of inner surface of upper. *Herpetic eruption on upper.* Painful pimples on upper; burning, changing to blisters. *Vesicles* on upper; around r. corner of mouth; burning, on lower; burning, on red part; changing into ulcers, with swelling. *Twitching of upper.* Trembling. *Stitches* in r. upper; in middle of upper, near nose. Tearing. Burning. *Dryness; with burning pimples, changing to vesicles filled with yellow serum.*

Jaws.—Convulsions of lower. Twitching of r. muscle of mastication. Trembling of muscles of lower, and in chin. Clenched. Rigid. Spasmodic drawing in lower; tensive drawing in r., extending towards ear. *Stitches* in joint; in l. lower jaw, extending into cheek; fine, on margin of lower; in r. lower, *as if splinters were forced between skin and flesh. Tearing in r. lower;* l. lower; sticking, in horizontal ramus of lower. Pain in l. joint on waking, < opening mouth; in joint, with soreness on touch; tearing drawing, in r. upper jaw and r. cheek.

Clinical.—The neuralgic prosopalgia of Agaricus is electric-like, as of splinters between skin and flesh, mostly in the infra-orbital nerve, and along the jaws. The symptoms of the lips are very marked, and have been nearly all verified. These eruptions about the mouth have been repeatedly cured in growing children given to jerkings, licking the lips, and with more or less chorea-like symptoms.

Mouth.—Teeth. Gnashing in sleep. Twitching in a loose tooth after drinking water. Lancinations in lower incisors, with drawing, the lancinations continued towards l. angle of lower jaw. *Tearing* in l.; in lower, < cold; in all upper, waking at 1 A.M. *Gnawing* in upper molars in afternoon, then itching in l. ear, then toothache. *Pulsation* in l. upper molars in afternoon, with tearing. Grumbling in l. upper. Drawing in lower incisors. Elongated feeling in incisors, < evening. Toothache in l. molars; in roots of l. upper teeth, involving upper incisors; in upper incisors *after looking out of window in cool air,* with drawing; drawing aching in lower incisors; drawing cutting in hollow molar, while abdominal symptoms disappear, and *vice versa;* drawing and tearing pains in teeth and side of head, disturbing sleep, with stupefying vertigo and palpitation, > rising from bed, but returning violently, with frequent chilliness.

Gums.—Bleeding. *Swelling.* Pain, with acrid taste to saliva. Sensitiveness.

Tongue.—Pale. Painful ulcer at side of frænum. *Coat* in morning; *white;* white, with dirty yellow apthæ at tip, with feeling as if the skin would peel off after a meal; yellow; yellow at back; dirty yellow; slimy; tough, in morning; tough mucus, < morning; thick, tough mucus, especially in morning, with fuzziness and prominence of papillæ, especially towards the back, and with a dry, astringent feeling. *Stitches* at tip. Biting in back part of l. edge, with an acrid sensation behind tongue on same side. *Soreness;* at tip, < touch and lasting all the evening; at tip, where there seemed to be a blister. *Burning* at tip; at r. lower side, with sore spots, which seemed furred; burning as from sharp tobacco. *Dryness;* with contraction. Itching, prickling in l. half.

Foam at mouth; at corners. Black blood-blister. Splinter-like stitches in l. sublingual salivary glands, then salivation. *Soreness,* especially of roof; of roof as if skin were off; of hard palate, with blisters. *Dryness;* and in fauces, with sensitiveness to air in those parts; of palate, especially uncomfortable when swallowing, with stitches towards r. ear and r. salivary gland. Saliva acrid. *Salivation;* in forenoon, with nausea; after stitches in l. sublingual salivary gland; with pain in abdomen; *with dryness of throat;* sudden, on moving mouth; flowing from mouth. *Constant spitting.* Breath bad; in morning, with foul taste; nauseous and sour; smell as from horse-radish.

Taste.—Foul in morning; on smoking; < after breakfast. *Bad* at root of tongue, with nausea. Clayey. Insipid; when stomach is empty. Pappy. Astringent. Metallic. Rancid. Biting in l. half of tongue. Slimy, glutinous. Bitter; morning; before dinner; sharp bitter at root of tongue; sweetish bitter when smoking, especially at root of tongue. *Sweet;* < afternoon; sweetish acrid; sweet, gummy, offensive, after breakfast, with distention of abdomen. Salt; to a cigar, especially at root of tongue.

Clinical.—Neuralgic toothache < in open air. Neuralgic, splinter-like pains in tongue, with salivation.

Throat.—Tension externally in region of thyroid gland, < evening. *Distention, with feeling as if the cravat were too tight* (Lach.). Hawking of masses of mucus from fauces and posterior nares. Stitches internally on external touch; towards parotid and submaxillary glands; *extending along Eustachian tube towards r. ear* (Gels.°). Tearing; as if something were torn on swallowing saliva. Aching in r. side; as from a foreign body, also < while vomiting. Sensation as if a particle of food stuck there. Scratching; behind root of tongue. Roughness; mornings. Burning; extending into l. side of chest, with scratching; scratching burning, and in posterior fauces; cool burning, and in stomach. Coldness as from a pungent cress, from pharynx to stomach. *Dryness;* palate to pharynx in morning on waking; of pharynx, with stitches towards parotid and submaxillary glands; contractive dry feeling in fauces and palate mornings on waking, extending to pharynx, causing *contraction there as after an astringent drink. Contraction.* Paralysis of muscles of pharynx and gullet. Swallowing impaired. Œsophagus. Choking after eating. Burning along after breakfast; cool burning.

Stomach.—Appetite. Excessive; morning; towards evening, with sweat and with weakness and trembling of limbs; soon after eating. *Much hunger but no relish;* in morning. Sudden hunger; towards evening. Hurried eating. Lost; for breakfast; for dinner; lost, with thirst. Quick repletion at dinner, even before hunger is satisfied. Little appetite; for dinner; mostly for bread and butter. He does not eat bread with pleasure. Aversion when eating; to taste of food and drink; to roast meat; to food, with pressive pain in stomach and nausea; to tobacco.

Thirst in forenoon; while walking in forenoon; for beer in forenoon; in afternoon. Unquenchable. No thirst.

Eructations after dinner, with nausea; with nausea. Frequent; in afternoon. Violent. Imperfect; dying away in lower part of œsophagus; rising to region of larynx. *Empty;* alternating with hiccough, also while smoking. Watery, with nausea. Salt fluid. *Tasting of rotten eggs. Tasting like apples;* in forenoon. Rancid. Sour; in forenoon. Tasting of food; in morning. *Hiccough;* afternoon; frequent.

Nausea; at 1 A.M., with difficult vomiting of undigested food; in forenoon; towards noon; after breakfast; after dinner; after eating, also > eructations; after drinking cold water; when coughing; > open air; < morning, with emptiness in stomach; with pain in stomach; with crawling in pit of stomach; with vertigo, as if about to lose consciousness; with anxiety rising from abdomen; with cutting in abdomen; with faintness and anxiety; as far as mouth; sudden from smoking a cigar, with vomiting of food.

Ineffectual retching. *Vomiting.* Frequent, with frequent stools. Violent. Food. Breakfast, with the odor of alcohol. Watery, with shock to the whole body. Mucus. Spongy matter, with stools, which relieve. Bitter; fluid; bitter, with shuddering creeping over body.

Gurgling in stomach. Rumbling in epigastrium. Painful retraction during diarrhœa, and of abdomen. Trembling, then of whole body. Stitches in pit. Tearing in pit. *Pinching;* in epigastrium towards evening, with cutting; in pit, as with tongs. Pain; in region mornings on waking; after breakfast; after eating a little, not < by continued eating; with inclination to sigh; in epigastric region; in pit; in pit and along sternum. *Pain* causing patient to roll on the ground and utter sharp cries; at midnight, as if flatus were pressing it out, > emission of offensive flatus; tensive pains from pit to left clavicle, towards evening during deep breathing. Painful tension in epigastrium. Cramplike constrictive pain in pit, extending far into abdomen. Cramplike compression in pit, with shooting. *Cramp* at noon. *Boring.* Boring in epigastrium in afternoon, > evening by emission of flatus. *Gnawing* in pit.

Sensation as if a stone lay in it. Sensation as if it were sinking like a heavy weight towards abdomen. *Oppression* after eating; with sharp pains; with inclination for stool; at pyloric orifice; in pit, extending to sternum; in pit after breakfast; in pit after dinner, with drawing and pressure in eyeballs and indolence; in upper and lower border when standing and walking. Heaviness; in pit; in pit, with tightness. *Fulness,* with a flat feeling and feeling as if fastened to pharynx; fulness, with inclination to vomit rising into throat; feeling of fulness and flatus after dinner; after dinner, with pressure and flatulence. Feeling as if he would eructate, resembling distending pressure in orifice of stomach. *Drawing* and pressing, < pressure of hand; drawing downward after breakfast, > passage of flatus, with pressive pain; spasmodic drawing in region of pit towards evening, extending as far as chest. *Burning*; after meat; after breakfast, with twisting sensation; with aversion; in pit; cool burning. Coolness. Shuddering, extending over whole body. *Crawling* at pit, with nausea. Discomfort; after breakfast. Digestion bad. *Empty* feeling; in pit; with repletion. *Faintness;* with an empty feeling that sometimes alternated with pressure as of a heavy body. Feeling of flabbiness; in forenoon.

Abdomen.—Painful retraction during diarrhœa, and of stomach. Twitching; of walls. *Meteorismus.* **Distention;** after breakfast; after food; after light food; after supper, with fulness and with oppression of chest; after scanty stool; making sitting and breathing difficult. Feels distended, but is not. Fermentation; feeling of fermentation. Rattling; as if peas rolled about. **Rumbling;** morning; after stool; with pain deep in umbilical region, < pressure; like distant thunder in evening, with inclination for stool. Gurgling; after breakfast, with rattling; after a pappy stool, with rattling.

Flatus troubled him at night. Urging of flatus towards anus. Sensation of flatus after breakfast, with searching. **Emission of flatus;** before hard stool; during stool, with pinching in abdomen, with warmth in abdomen; with feeling as in diarrhœa; **much inodorous;** fetid; smelling of garlic; cadaverous during stool; painful, or preceded by colic.

Stitches; outward in walls, also forenoon, when walking. **Cutting**; late in evening; during stool; before stool; before soft, crumbling stool; griping in forenoon and afternoon, with accumulation of flatus; as from a purgative, > liquid stools. Pinching; during liquid stools; before and during stools, with cutting. **Griping**; morning, on waking, then two liquid stools; forenoon and afternoon; at noon, with emission of flatus; after breakfast; after walking in open air, with burning pain in lower abdomen; with dragging and with cutting in anus and dry stools; here and there, more against walls than in intestines; with diarrhœa; with clawing in upper abdomen, stitches and then cutting; cutting griping; that urged to stool, > by stool, accompanied by cutting in abdomen; beginning with a stitch. *Writhing. Pain;* morning, after stool; after light food. Searching. Burrowing at 9 A.M., with griping and ineffectual urging of flatus towards anus. Feeling as before diarrhœa. Dragging in intestines, in inguinal canal and in pelvis. Oppression from flatus. Heaviness; after dinner, with griping and ineffectual urging of flatus towards anus. Urging. Soreness. Tension. Nausea; with pressure. Burning; after breakfast. Sensation of a cold. Discomfort. Restlessness; sinking into abdomen. Faintness. Empty feeling. Flabby feeling. Crawling and coursing, extending through all nerves. Symptoms disappear during drawing cutting pain in a hollow back tooth, and *vice versa.*

Upper abdomen.—Twitching; undulating. Cutting, colicky spasms just below diaphragm, when sitting, extending towards spine. Clawing stitches, then cutting. Discomfort, with nausea.

Umbilical region.—Distention. Flatus accumulates. Pressure of flatus under umbilicus. **Stitches;** morning, on waking; biting. Tearing above umbilicus, in a fine line. Cutting. Pinching; *below umbilicus,* with bloated abdomen; clucking pinching; crawling pinching. Griping; after breakfast; till dinner-time; between umbilicus and right hypochondrium. *Pain;* in morning, when half awake; sometimes rising into right chest; deep-seated. Fulness. Heaviness; after a scanty stool; under umbilicus, also after breakfast; below umbilicus, with feeling of a ball of the size of a small fist. Urging under umbilicus. Discomfort.

Sides.—Twitching in l.; writhing jumping of recti muscles in evening in bed. Griping in left; in l., with rumbling in abdomen. Pain in l., causing nauseated ill feeling in same spot; spasmodic in l., urging to stool and arousing him at midnight; sprained pain in muscles on stooping. Nausea in l. with pain.

Hypochondria.—*Stitches in liver;* when breathing; in r. lobe of liver, radiating from surface towards centre; in liver and pit of stomach, with nausea; sudden stitches in liver towards noon; occasional stitches in r. hypochondrium, < pressure; deep-seated stitches in r., mornings; extending from r. and from umbilicus to behind sternum; *under l. short ribs* on inspiration; < sitting with a stooped chest; in region of spleen in afternoon. **Pain** in liver mornings; in r. hypochondrium, more towards the back, also with occasional stitches, < bending to the l.; in r. extending upward; at l. last true rib, with pain as from a gunshot wound in corresponding place on r. side; in region of spleen, also > walking; in region of spleen in evening, when lying on l. side, > turning to r. side; deep contractive pain in region of spleen; cramplike pain in region of spleen; pulsative pain below l. hypochondrium, rising as far as third and fourth ribs. **Soreness** in hypochondria and in region of pit of stomach as if contents of thorax were compressed, < after eating. Pressive tension below ribs after an emission. Heaviness in r. hypochondrium, with drawing as if liver had increased and would be torn from its ligaments.

Hypogastrium.—Distention after a copious pappy stool, with sensitiveness; with cutting and movements of flatus. Rumbling. Gurgling; in l., with rattling. Twitching in l. flank; of pyramidal muscles. **Stitches** in r. flank; extending from pelvis to r. side, along r. flank to r. ribs, growing weaker in their course; in region of cœcum from sneezing; sudden stitches in l. Drawing tearing from l. inguinal region to middle of fore side of thigh. Cutting; in evening, as before diarrhœa. **Griping** after a pappy stool, and in forenoon while walking in open air; with burning pressive pain; in l., with rattling in intestines; in l. ilium, between umbilicus and symphysis pubis, extending to r. ilium, > pressure; cutting griping in forenoon and afternoon, with accumulation of flatus. Pinching above l. hip, > passage of flatus. **Pain** in groin; sprained pain in l. groin when walking; tensive pain in r. inguinal region. **Drawing** pain in hypogastrium, extending towards lumbar muscles; pain in pelvis towards umbilicus and r. flank; rheumatic drawing externally in r.

ilium under gluteals, in l. in afternoon, < sitting, > walking. Spasmodic drawing in l. groin when urinating. Dragging in l. groin. Heaviness; after breakfast, also after a copious pappy stool; in pelvis, with dragging. Urging in hypogastrium. **Tension**; in pelvis; in r. inguinal region, < drawing up and stretching out thigh, afterwards > walking, but recurred while sitting or lying. Burning.

Clinical.—The gastro-enteric symptoms are due to an acute catarrhal inflammation with severe sharp pains, often with purging or only with great flatulence. The profuse inodorous flatus is often found in the nervous affections requiring Agaricus. The pains in the region of the liver may indicate the drug in hepatic disease, but probably not in an acute inflammation.

Rectum.—Discharge of light-red blood after stool, with great straining; of much mucus, with wind. Stitches; as of flatus forcing to anus, but which there caused a recurrent motion into pelvis. Tenesmus after stools. **Urging** to stool; mornings; with painful straining towards the front of rectum; with a kind of tenesmus and with burning sticking deep in spine; ineffectual, also with emission of much wind; sudden. Feeling as if diarrhœa would set in. Acrid pain during and after stool; when passing wind. Distending pain, then emission of flatus. Prickling; as from worms. Cutting itching just above anus in evening, as after acrid diarrhœa, > pressing out anus.

Anus.—**Hæmorrhoids,** burning, also painful; inflamed; swollen. Stitches. Pressure at noon. Disagreeable sensation, like heaviness and fulness, at noon, > while sitting. **Burning**; heat at noon, with itching; and itching mornings, as with tenesmus during stool; after stool; after hard stool; after soft stool. Dry feeling, with inclination to retract it. Moist feeling. Smarting after easy stool, with inclination to retract anus. Itching; after a copious pappy stool, then burning; with tickling. Prickling. Closed feeling, with urging to stool. Paralytic weakness of sphincter.

Stool.—At noon and evening, which is unusual. *Dysenteric flux.* Liquid; with burning in anus; semi-liquid, also scanty. **Watery** early in morning, with colic and tenesmus; at night, with pain in region of spleen. Dark-green, liquid, afternoons. **Diarrhœa** early in morning, *with violent pinching;* frequent, with griping and *emission of much flatus;* frequent, with swelling of hæmorrhoids and bearing down of intestines into inguinal canal and pelvic cavity. Pasty; with much wind; then heaviness. Slimy, with much wind; with tenesmus and pain. Soft and crumbling. Crumbling preceded by a moist feeling in anus.

Hard; every other day; after dinner, with scraping; then pappy stools, then diarhœa. Knotty at night; easy in morning, preceded by colic, then liquid, with colic, fermentation and nausea, after a quarter of an hour watery. Delayed, hard and scanty. Dark. Leek-green. Yellow. Offensive. Tough, sticky, copious, after sudden urging. Causing burning. Copious. Scanty. Difficult. Frequent; at night. Omitted; every other day. Stoppage of excretions.

Urinary Organs.—Twitching pain in bladder. Tensive pain in region of bladder in forenoon while driving. Paralytic weakness of sphincter vesicæ. Retention of urine. Frequent **urging** to urinate; and violent, and copious urine, with stitches in meatus urinarius; violent urging at night and much urine; with scanty urine. Micturition frequent; and profuse; *rare;* rare and scanty; intermittent; after several attempts; followed by dripping, also with cold, shrunken penis.

Urethra.—*Effusion of viscid mucus. Stitches;* when urinating. **Burning** while urinating; at orifice at night. Feeling as if a drop of cold urine passed. Sensation as if he had not done urinating. Disagreeable sensation at end, along glans, inducing pressure. Crawling itching in glans, seemingly in urethra. Prickling and itching at orifice. Tickling as from a small foreign body in fossa navicularis.

Urine.—*Copious;* at night; with stool; with relaxed penis; and pale. *Scanty;* and dark; and reddish. *Clear, lemon-colored.* Hot and dark. Watery. Milky after standing.

Clinical.—The nervous invalid who requires Agaricus usually passes little urine (unlike Ignatia), though the bladder may be irritable.

Sexual Organs.—Irritation. No pleasurable sensation in an embrace in spite of strong excitement. Erections in morning; *frequent,* also at night; continual at night; no erection in evening when he desired an embrace, in the ensuing night several emissions. *Testicles* retracted. Drawing in testicles in evening, with uneasiness, awkwardness and sleepiness; spasmodic, in l. testicle and spermatic cord. Desire excessive; in morning; after a nap after dinner; *with relaxed penis.* Aversion to sexual intercourse. Desire diminished. Emission; copious during an embrace; at night; at night without lascivious dreams; tardy emission during embrace; insufficient. Menses increased; and earlier, *with violent tearing pressive pain in back and abdomen and itching of external genitals.*

Clinical.—Violent spasmodic dysmenorrhœa, with terrible bearing-down pains. Itching of genitals, neuralgic pains in pudenda.

Respiratory Organs.—**Larynx,** *constriction;* with oppression; aching in r. side, with irritation to cough; tickling, causing cough. Saliva runs into trachea, < raising head, and causes hawking. Scratching irritation in windpipe, causing dry cough. Voice husky, with piercing pains in chest; rough, with sticking in larynx on deep breathing.

Cough; in morning; in morning, then sneezing; in forenoon, with sneezing; in afternoon, with vomiting; at night; at night, with sweat; on waking, with expectoration; after dinner, with sneezing; < towards evening; with sneezing; with gagging; with lachrymation and nausea. Frequent; after eating. Fatiguing, frequent at night on waking, with thick expectoration. Labored, frequent, mostly dry, during the day. Labored, on waking, mostly dry, with expectoration of thick, white mucus. *Convulsive cough;* during the day; in morning, with expectoration of mucus; in forenoon; waking from sleep, with tickling in upper part of larynx and extending down throat. Deep, almost wheezing inspiration, then short, clear-sounding shocks of cough, often with doubling up of body, nausea and lachrymation. *Paroxysmal,* with a kind of confusion of whole body and thick mucous expectoration, the cough so sudden and violent that he was obliged to double up, contract his legs and move his arms, but the later attacks were not so violent, brought no expectoration, and associated with soreness of chest. Shaking the whole body, at night, from tickling in trachea, seldom with expectoration. At night obliging him to sit up in bed. *Sudden, violent* *attacks* during the day. *Violent and isolated attacks*, ending with repeated sneezing. Violent during the day; in morning, also on waking; at noon, with repeated sneezing; violent cough in afternoon; at night; night and morning, with expectoration of mucus. Inclination to violent cough during the day, <when smoking tobacco. *Constant irritation to cough, which can be mostly suppressed, but if not there are painful shocks, mostly of dry cough. Dry;* forenoon; after eating; after dinner, disturbing his nap while sitting; with wheezing under sternum, causing burning; mostly dry, sometimes with rattling of mucus in afternoon and evening, with blowing of much mucus from nose, and in morning coughing up of mucus. *Hacking* in forenoon; after dinner; convulsive, with oppressive sweat. **Loose**, labored, from irritation in windpipe. Coughing up mucus in morning; in morning on waking; forenoon; lumpy mucus during the day; large brown flakes of mucus, < morning.

Expectoration.—Mucous; *of ball of mucus, almost without cough;* small gelatinous, transparent, moulded lumps of mucus, with great relief to lungs, by forcible expiration, without cough. Like coagulated starch-paste.

Respiration.—Suffocative attack. Short; when walking slowly, and asthmatic. *Difficult;* towards 11 A.M.; *noisy;* is obliged to stand still several times when walking to take breath; *as if chest were too full*, he is obliged to breathe deeper, which causes sticking in pit of stomach. *Deep; frequent sighing;* with rapid pulse. Superficial. *Noisy* at night, with wheezing in chest. Accelerated; on rising from a seat; and catarrhal, with oppressed chest, not >by deep breathing and involuntary bursts of cough. As if chest were filled with blood.

Clinical.—Spasmodic, convulsive, nervous cough, which may provoke a secondary hæmorrhage.

Chest.—Twitching of pectoral muscles; r. pectoral; l. intercostals. Catarrh. Rattling of mucus; in morning, then cough; when lying on back.

Stitches; towards noon, with tension; in l. axilla; in muscles of anterior wall of r. axilla; in l. side from dry cough; in region of lungs; in one or other lung, < bending forward or backward; in r. lung; in r. lung on walking; in middle of r. lung, < every respiration; in r. lung while sitting, arresting breathing, > pressure of hand; in l. lung; in l. lung, between fifth and sixth ribs, < breathing; in l. muscles; in r. muscles; in muscles near l. nipple; in intercostals below r. nipple; in r. muscles, then r. ribs; below nipples; between l. nipple and sternum, < every respiration; in ribs; l. ribs; near lower ribs; where l. ribs end, during inspiration; where l. ribs end, when sitting with chest bent forward; behind sternum, also < at end of expiration; behind sternum, impeding respiration; in centre of chest, also with pressure and fulness; through upper part of l.; in upper chest, with pressure, like a burning pain; in chest and back, especially under scapulæ and corresponding parts in front, inducing deep breathing. Sudden stitches in l. lung; sudden in l. chest; sudden in region of borders of dorsal vertebræ, evenings when sitting. Jerking stitches in r. lung. Heavy stitches in chest; stitches extending from behind forward; extending outward in lower half in forenoon when walking; outward from l. nipple, seemingly more in muscles. Feeling of motion in muscles of chest and neck on deep breathing, almost a sticking.

Tearing; in region of l. clavicle; in anterior wall of l. lower rib region; in l. lower wall; in l. side, extending over surface of nearly whole body; piercing tearing in small spots. **Pinching** from l. mamma to umbilicus. **Sprained** feeling internally in evening, < deep inspiration; burning piercing under r. nipple, arresting breathing, caused by a leap. **Bruised** pain in l. side; in front wall, with difficult breathing. **Aching**; at night; after breakfast, also with tension; after convulsive cough; after rising; here and there in afternoon; aching in some parts of chest and abdomen, on deep breathing, with feeling as if something dislocated itself; in r. chest, also after rising; aching near r. nipple in evening; near r. nipple when walking, with sensation as if deep breathing would remove the cause; intercostals of upper part of l. breast; l. intercostals, with drawing; in centre, with burning; along sternum; behind sternum, also < at end of expiration; under sternum when coughing; on upper half of sternum; in middle of sternum, < inspiration; to l. of lower third of sternum; in l. lower rib region. **Drawing** pain; behind r. margin of sternum; burning drawing pain from without inward in r., with oppression. **Tensive** pain. **Burning** pain in l. half; below sternum after breakfast. **Burning**; after dinner; under sternum; in sternal region, with roughness; fine burning in different places, especially upon sternum, with prickling.

Horrible **shuddering** within chest and throat, waking him, with crying out; this shuddering seemed to begin in diaphragm and extended along œsophagus or trachea, in posterior mediasternum, and pushed forcibly against larynx, which produced a shrill cry.

Anxiety; < rising from a seat; causing unsteadiness of hand when writing; with rapid and audible breathing; suffocative, under sternum at night, with stopped sensation in nose. Anxious restlessness, as when expecting something unusual.

Constriction *obliging frequent and deep inspiration, < walking.* Contracted feeling of sternum. **Tension** across; after breakfast; anterior walls, also with short breath; both sides, from behind forward, after dinner, with backache; *lower part taking away breath, when moving and sitting.* Pain in lower part, especially in region of pit of stomach, as if contents of thorax were compressed, < after dinner. **Oppression**; forenoon sitting, with stitches; after supper, with distention of abdomen; with throbbing of arteries; with burning inside; behind sternum at rest, with palpitation; in upper part, with deep inspirations on walking and sitting, with pressure behind sternum and at sides of it, coming and going, with sensation of a load on chest; *in region of diaphragm, with drawing pain; especially behind borders of sternum, with visible beating of heart;* compelling deep breathing; preventing slow and deep inspiration; *in cardiac region, as if chest were narrowed.* Anxious feeling of oppression, which in reality did not exist. **Heaviness**; on chest. **Rawness**, with indications of cough in morning. Sore pain on anterior surface, < r., near sternum, seemingly under ribs, > stool; below sternum, also after breakfast; pulsative; in places, < r. half.

Clinical.—Most of the sensations are of a neuralgic character, but many seem to be dependent on the abnormal circulation in the lungs, caused by Agaricus. (Dyspnœa caused by contracted bloodvessels and unoxygenized blood.) The pains are mostly aggravated by exercise and after eating. Spasmodic cough at night after falling asleep. (Night-sweats in phthisis. Laryngeal catarrh, with expectoration of small hard lumps (Stan.) and soreness in larynx.)

Heart.—Stitches in region; with intermittent pulse, the stitches obstructing breathing; in region, with rapid pulse; burning, from region of heart to l. scapula, on deep inspiration, < coughing, sneezing and hiccough. *Aching* near; 4 P.M. till evening. Burning aching, with palpitation; intermittent burning, in region at noon. *Anxiety*. Compressed feeling. *Oppression* and violent beating on stooping; anxious, with irregular violent action, also < sitting. *Blows* at night on lying down and morning on waking, at slightest noise, with trembling in pit of stomach and anxiety. Painful shocks at night, with anxiety; twitching shocks. **Palpitation**; morning on waking; 3 to 5 P.M.; evening; in evening, with anxiousness, that ended in restless drowsiness; on least motion; when standing; when vexed. Increased pulsation, with red face. Violent pulsation, perceptible even in coccyx. Irregular strong beats, on sitting down, with oppression. Visible strong beats. Trembling of heart on waking; trembling, with anxiety.

Clinical.—A valuable remedy for irregular tumultuous palpitation, especially for the irritable heart of tea and coffee drinkers and of tobacco-smokers (compare Arsenic and Spigelia).

Pulse.—Double. Full and rapid. Rapid and hard; rapid, also with sighing. *Intermittent;* > morning; > drinking coffee. *Irregular*. Imperceptible. *Small;* and hard; and quick, in morning. Tremulous. *Slow;* > drinking coffee; and *weak*.

Neck.—Twitching of muscles from l. side to l. side of throat. Chirping in occipital region, as if a cricket were in cervical canal, mornings in bed. Stitches in cervical vertebræ; when stooping. Sudden aching between neck and shoulders. Tensive aching in occipital region and on both sides of atlas. **Bruised** feeling in l. neck and shoulder region; feeling in region of posterior cervical muscles in morning in bed and afterwards when sitting, with a feeling on bending forward as if too short. **Sprained** feeling in muscles; on turning backwards towards the l. **Tension** of nape. Tensive drawing in sterno-cleido mastoid muscles, causing stiffness in nape. *Stiffness of nape* (Ignatia). With heat and pain, < moving head to side, especially to r. side.

Back.—Coarse stitches between skin and flesh. Tearing when walking, extending now to r., now to l. side of lumbar vertebræ. *Aching;* in evening; at night, and across chest, loins and r. thigh; after dinner; after garden work, and in small of back; < motion; *after dinner, especially in a spot in middle, with sensitiveness on touch and motion. Spasmodic and drawing pain, extending to middle of chest and into œsophagus*, in afternoon. *Pain as after continual stooping.* Twitching pain in l. side. **Bruised** *feeling in muscles; with a feeling as if too short on bending forward;* with sprained pain, and disposition to stretch the back. Drawing towards evening, and in loins. Stiffness; on rising from a seat and righting body, > sitting, with violent pain in l. loin. Weakness; of muscles; convulsive shock, extending to entire r. side of body.

Spine.—**Stitches; deep-seated burning. Aching along spine and limbs**; along spine in bed; *in several places on increased motion;* **along spinal cord when stooping**; < turning body; *on turning, especially in region of last dorsal and first and second lumbar vertebræ, which become pulsative on increased motion; drawing tensive along, with occasional flying pain in cord. Pain when stooping as if too weak to support the body.* Dragging, crackling and creaking along spine during increased motion of body, especially at or near atlas-joint on more rapid motion of body. **Soreness, on touch**; in spots; *mornings, so that leaning against a chair is painful; when washing with a sponge.* Sensitiveness, then pain all along spine, especially dorsal vertebræ, and it seems as if the cough had its origin in the spine. Pulsation in spinal canal. Prickling along spine and occiput.

Scapulæ.—Twitching between; rhythmical in l. and in l. deltoid. **Stitches** between; coarse on surface below r.; sudden below l.; gnawing stitches under. Tearing between. Drawing between. Sore pain at lower angle of l. as if chapped. *Weakness between, extending into neck, with stiffness.*

Dorsal region.—Stitches in vertebræ; at night on waking; in dorsal and lumbar vertebræ; between dorsal and lumbar vertebræ, then the well-known feeling as if the spinal marrow were touched with an icy object, then sticking in cervical vertebræ. **Aching** in muscles on sitting; between eighth and ninth vertebræ on turning trunk; in twelfth dorsal and first and second lumbar vertebræ, with coldness in gluteal muscles and formication of feet. **Drawing** pain between eighth and ninth dorsal vertebræ, extending periodically to hyoid bone. **Boring** in middle of back. **Soreness** between eighth and ninth dorsal vertebræ on touch, and pulsation pushing downward, synchronous with pulse, > pressure.

Lumbar region.—Crackling in vertebræ on stooping, and in neck. Electric shock in an upper vertebra, extending to lower part of body. Shivering shock in vertebra, extending to whole body. **Twitching**; l.; r. in evening; in muscles and tendons extending from an upper vertebra, with convulsive shuddering in lower part of body. **Stitches** in region of r. kidney; in small of back on raising thigh when sitting; in r. loin, also during day; in superior anterior process of iliac bones; darting from spinal marrow of sacro-lumbar region towards r. gluteal muscle; *sudden in small of back at noon while walking in open air, with* dizzy nausea, the knees gave way and he leaned against a wall to prevent falling. Tearing in lumbar muscles on walking or sitting. *Lumbago extending along spine to nape.* **Aching** in loins; with weakness of feet when walking out of doors; on rising from a seat, preventing righting body and moving thighs; when sitting or lying, > motion. **Aching** in l., < standing, walking and touch; in region of r. kidney, disturbing sleep; after exertion at stool, soon extending to lower limbs; as from hæmorrhoids; tensive drawing aching; tensive in sacro-lumbar vertebræ, mornings when lying on l. side, moving into region of l. hip, and > lying on r. side. Painful tension in tendons and ligaments of r. sacro-lumbar region, extending to great trochanter, > lying on l. side. *Cramplike* pain from ilium down towards muscles of anterior surface of r. thigh. *Pain* in pelvic bones as if separated from sacrum, < morning in bed. *Bruised* feeling in loins; < standing; < lying and sitting. Sprained feeling in l. loin. Drawing in loins; internal from pelvic muscles into legs, becoming an external trembling. Dragging. Fulness in loins, with heaviness. **Tension** in vertebræ, < stooping; across always on stooping, extending into sides of abdomen, where it resembled a sprained pain in abdominal muscles. Urging in l. loin. **Weakness** in loins on descending stairs and walking in open air, extending to feet; in loins, with pressive tensive pain. Heaviness. Paralytic pain in back part of loins, < walking and standing. Paralyzed feeling near vertebræ, above border of r. ilium.

Sacrum.—Twitching, and in lower limbs. Stitches. *Crick in l.* Tearing like growing pain in sacrum and hip, increasing and decreasing. Aching; when leaning against seat while at stool; in both sides; < evenings and walking; with weakness when walking; aching as if it would burst; bruised feeling when sitting.

Clinical.—Symptoms of spinal irritation, with pains, often dull but usually sharp, sticking, with excessive sensitiveness of the spine to touch, most severe in upper dorsal region, have been repeatedly verified. Lumbago, with a host of severe muscular pains, *all worse on walking in the open air.*

Extremities.—Stretching. *Trembling.* Shocks; sometimes in l. hip, sometimes in r. hand, originating in corresponding joints; electric, and in different fingers. *Twitching of muscles;* with jerking up of one thumb, then another, and of separate fingers; electric. Restlessness and quivering trembling of l. upper arm and thigh muscles, with shocks in those limbs and jumping of muscles in different positions of body. **Pain,** in every part, here, there and everywhere; mostly sharp stitches, tearing, also aching, drawing, piercing, bruised; < walking or after motion; > after continued motion; with crawling, as after freezing. Soreness of muscles; weakness, with sensitiveness, trembling, restlessness. Extremities fall asleep.

Clinical.—Neuralgic pains, sharp, shooting, as if under the skin, often shifting from place to place, worse on motion. Sensations as if a part (especially of feet) had been frozen and was burning on being restored. Neuralgia in locomotor ataxia.

Upper Extremities.—*Convulsive shocks* in various muscles from shoulder to fingers. Twitchings everywhere. Tearings. Pain; bruised, drawing, tensive, sprained, *as from splinters, as if burnt on surface.* Tremblings. Weakness. Lameness. Numbness and sensitiveness to cold, especially in fingers. Asleep feeling. General aggravation to touch.

Lower Limbs.—The symptoms fall into the following groups, not characterized by locality, and they affect every part, from hip to toes. *Twitchings* and convulsive shocks. *Tearings. Stitches.* Tremblings, with unsteady muscles and weakness, heaviness and giving way. *Pains,* cramplike, burning, bruised, boring and piercing. Tension and stiffness. Pains usually < when walking and ascending, > sitting. In the heel soreness and feeling of splinters. Joints feel dislocated. Corns become sore. *Feet feel frost-bitten.*

Skin.—Smooth and oily, especially on face. Pallor. **Redness** *of face, with itching* and burning, as after freezing; redness of face without heat; of l. side of scrotum, with swelling, itching and twingling; *of fingers, with burning itching as if frozen.* **Icterus,** especially of neck, face and chest, after the convulsions. *Twitching above r. eye. Itching* eruption, spreading to abdomen and thighs. *Desquamation.* **Pimples;** on forehead; painful on vertex; itching and sore to touch, in and between brows; inflamed pimples on r. cheek; itching, on side of mouth; whitish, itching and burning, on lower abdomen, about umbilicus, pubis and inner thighs, the itching and burning < scratching; inflamed, on back, discharging bloody matter; on arms, with burning itching; *inflamed,* on dorsum of l. hand; biting, above l. knee, with burning after scratching. Pustule in beard; itching and burning in breast, with red areola; between l. index and thumb and on r. side of neck, with itching. **Boil** on r. natis; painful, on front side of l. thigh and on the natis, the one on natis discharging blood without matter. Suppurating, painful abscess in middle of r. deltoid. Vesicles on forehead; in r. wing of nose; on chin; white vesicles on chin.

Stitches here and there; near umbilicus; r. side of neck; r. calf; electric stitches on anterior surface of r. thigh; itching stitches in various parts. *Soreness* of r. hand from wrist to thumb and forefinger, with burning. Formication on various parts of body and extremities; with burning; with itching; with pricking. Biting inducing scratching, on legs during the day when walking; corrosive biting and burning on various parts during the day. **Itching** of every part of the body, of large and small areas, mostly shifting from place to place; voluptuous; corrosive; *burning,* especially after scratching; often coming on in evening, growing worse in the night and relieved towards morning, with sweat; *with burning redness and swelling as after a frost-bite* (fingers, toes, ears).

Clinical.—The sensations in the skin are due apparently to a pure neurosis and not to any tissue change in the skin itself. The burning itching and redness as after a frost-bite are the chief characteristic indications.

Sleep.—*Sleepiness* at any and all times. *Yawning.* Violent, convulsive, < walking in open air. Sleeplessness from 1.30 to 2.30 A.M. Sleep light, with many dreams. Restless drowsiness in evening. Restlessness at intervals during a bad dream. Restless sleep; at night; at night, with constant tossing about, owing to shuddering in whole body, in head as well as chest, abdomen and feet; restlessness at night from itching on abdomen, thighs, arms and scalp. Electric shocks on falling asleep, with twitchings through legs, < l. and complete waking. Sleep unrefreshing. *Sleep bad, with headache and depression* bordering on melancholy.

Dreams, anxious; frightful, with outcries as if some one were murdering him; bad; disconnected; unremembered; vivid; vivid, partly agreeable, partly disagreeable.

Fever.—*Chilliness;* forenoon, with disagreeable sensation over back, especially spine; forenoon, with flushes of heat; evening, also with flushes of heat; evening alternating with heat; night on raising cover; going into open air; *on slight motion,* and in cooler air and if a cool finger touched a warm part; < morning. Sensitiveness to cool air; especially in hands and feet, with pale, wan face. Chill, with hot head, confusion and loss of ideas; with dull headache, stupefying vertigo and palpitation; chill, with thirst or subsequent heat, also every evening; with warm face, hands and feet; with yawning, also with frequent desire to urinate, weakness and disinclination to move, < internal. Shaking; in evening, also on undressing; on lifting bed-covers; over whole body, also afternoon and evening; over whole body, with gooseflesh, then heat of head, with painful beating in forehead and sweat on forehead; with doubling up on sofa, teeth chattered, pain in face, hands blue, no thirst, headache, groaned much in sleep, then towards morning general sweat, which relieved. Chilliness over whole body, especially in feet, then heat over whole body, especially lower limbs, which he must uncover, the blood seemed to stream glowing hot through veins, circulation excited, febrile, pulse hard and tense, and thirst at night. *In region of coronal suture after scratching, spreading to forehead; internal chilliness in scalp on r. frontal bone, with external warmth;* in head, especially occiput; creeping chill in scalp of vertex, with sensation as if scalp were drawn tightly over skull.

Chill through back and limbs, now and then; in spots on ribs, before l. scapula; close to coccyx; feeling in lumbar region as if spinal marrow or its membranes were touched by ice; feeling as if cold air were spreading over body from spine; when leaning against a chair, as if water were running down back; in spine and upper limbs, then shaking chill, with blue face and hands, which are icy cold, small, hard pulse and heavy head. *Shivering* in back; along spine and uper limbs. Coldness in r. axilla and inner condyle of foot, mornings in warmth of bed (familiar), in limbs, with blueness; of tip of r. elbow; over metacarpal joint of r. middle finger; hands; hands, with blue nails; lower limbs; l. natis; r. natis at every beat of pulse; in spots on nates and coldness extending to ankles, especially great toe (familiar); l. natis and region of trochanter (familiar); r. natis and below r. scapula, also between skin and muscles. Quicksilver sensation in r. gluteal, also in a lengthwise spot; in l. gluteal (familiar) after dinner; quicksilver sensation in r. popliteal space (familiar). **Coldness** in track of a nerve on posterior surface of thigh; on posterior side of l. thigh; in whole l. leg, rousing from sleep; thrill of C. down l. leg to foot; C. of ankles and toes; feet; of skin, with swollen veins. Gooseskin from slightest contact of cool air.

Heat; morning on waking, with heaviness; all afternoon in attacks, with sweat and dull headache without thirst, heat and sweat, < evening on putting on hat, with rapid breathing and weakness; in evening, with thirst and cold hands; H. at night, but chill if she turns or raises covers; at night, then sweat; at night, with glowing face, sweat towards morning. Radiating warmth from whole body. General orgasms of blood. **Burning** in different places. Heat of head; to touch; especially on vertex, partly also in eyes; burning in vertex; burning in l. superciliary ridge, near temple, < pressure and pain on pressure. *Heat* **in ears**; *with itching;* in face in morning on waking, with bloated feeling, especially in cheeks, and with heat of head; in face at 4 P.M., and redness, with tension of cheeks; in face in evening, especially near malar-bone; in face on waking from deep sleep, especially in cheeks; in face after eating, with redness; in face, with anxiety, > sweat; burning of cheeks; in cheeks in flushes; in face in flushes, with sweat on forehead; in attacks in face and upper part of body. Burning of lips. Heat creeping through back on slow walking in open air, with twitching in l. side of face. Warmth in dorsal region, with a rough feeling. Biting burning in dorsal portion of spinal column. **Burning** above l. elbow; in r. thumb in afternoon; in gluteals; in r. tibia; legs in morning, > rising; in l. leg; r. leg; r. leg in morning; r. leg in evening; r. leg after dinner; in skin of r. leg; in r. calf; skin about r. malleolus, as in incipient erysipelas; in feet as if blood were glowing in veins, in warm bed; warmth as from a hand at top of tibia and fibula; burning in a corn on r. little toe. Warm skin, with distended veins.

Sweat; after a quiet night; in forenoon; towards evening; evening in bed, especially on legs, with sensation as if they were fanned by a cool breeze; at night; at night after an embrace, with weakness; at night, especially about legs; on waking; on walking; on ascending a hill, with faintness; from anxiety. Cold and viscid sweat, with weakness; cold sweat on face, neck and chest. Sweat on hairy scalp; on chest at night; on upper part of chest and shoulder after an embrace, then on abdomen and at anus; on palms; about lower limbs at night; inner surfaces of legs evenings in bed; about legs, also in morning, with lassitude; on r. leg; on legs in morning; on legs at night.

Agnus Castus.

The chaste tree, Vitex Agnus-Castus, L., is a shrub four or five feet in height, indigenous in Southern Europe. A tincture is prepared from the bruised berries.

General Action.—The most prominent effect seems to be the loss of sexual power (followed in provers by an increased desire). Our meagre provings show a corresponding loss of nervous energy. (See Mind especially.)

Group for Study.—Gelsem., Phosph., Picric. ac.

Generalities.—Bruised feeling all over. Weakness; when standing, as from anguish, with sensation as before diarrhœa.

Mind.—*Absence of mind, with loss of memory* (Anac.). *Inability to fix his attention when reading* (Gels., Phos., Cimicif.). *Sadness, saying that she shall die soon* (Aurum). Melancholy, feeling as if nothing existed around him, dissatisfied with himself, incapable of attending to business, *indifference to things about him.* Feeling as if he were nobody, and would rather be dead than have that feeling, *with no courage,* when free from it he feels exalted, would like to read like an orator, etc. (Compare Plat.)

Clinical.—The symptom of sadness, with the impression of speedy death, has led to the successful use of this drug in puerperal mania, in which the patient even hinted that she intended to commit suicide.

Head.—Contractive aching when reading. Confusion; like a drawing. Heaviness, with pressure in nape, and sensation as if head would fall forward. Intoxication. Vertigo, as if everything turned in a circle. Tensive tearing in forehead; tearing in l. frontal eminence, with pressure.

Temples.—Tearing in l.; r., < motion; with pressure. Tearing, especially above r. eye, < motion, and in other parts of the brain, with sticking; *tearing in temples and forehead, in brain,* < motion, *with pressure.* Contractive pain above temples.

Pressure in region of l. parietal bones. Pain in upper part of r. side, more a smarting and sticking, as if in bone, ending in a corner of the forehead, < in evening, felt even in sleep. Fine stitches in scalp, then sticking itching, > scratching. Biting itching spots on scalp.

Eyes.—Pain towards temple, as from a blow, < touch. Burning in evening when reading. Lachrymation in the house. Smarting stitches in r. ball, >

rubbing. Pupils dilated. Corrosive itching in upper lids.

Ears.—*Ringing, or rather roaring.* Hardness of hearing.

Nose.—Aching as from pressure of a stone, on dorsum, on r. nasal bone and between r. brow and root of nose, > pressure. Much sneezing, with dry nose. Illusion of smell, of herring, and sometimes of musk.

Face.—Paralytic tearing in r. malar-bone. *Tearing deep in r. ramus of lower jaw, below the sockets;* tearing in r. ramus of lower jaw, with pressure.

Mouth and Throat.—Teeth pain when touched by warm food or drink. Acute drawing in region of l. parotid gland. Taste coppery, as if mouth had been galvanized. Mouth dry, with saliva so tough that it can be drawn out in threads, velum perdulum palati and uvula red, scratching in throat, obliging him to cough, and while coughing the mucus feels viscid, like a piece of cloth hanging in the throat. Corrosive itching in pit of throat. Sensation of tenacious mucus in throat.

Stomach.—Great appetite. Thirst; *want of thirst;* aversion to drink. Frequent hiccough. Eructations; both the eructations and the flatus emitted by rectum smell like old urine in clothes. Nausea in pit; when standing, afterwards in abdomen, as if the bowels sank down. Pinching in pit when sitting bent. Food made him feel uneasy and replete.

Abdomen.—Rumbling; *in sleep.* Feeling as before diarrhœa. Pressure in upper, after dinner; shifting pressure in upper, with cutting. Stitches in r. inguinal region; in superior and anterior spinous process of l. os ilium. Cutting above l. os ilium.

Anus and Stool.—Pain as from subcutaneous suppuration in flesh near anus when walking. Twitching in sphincters. Loose stools; with pain in abdomen. *Constipation.* Stool inclined to re-enter rectum.

Urinary Organs.—*Discharge of prostatic fluid when straining at stool* (Phos. ac.) Urine copious, passes in a strong stream. Frequent micturition, with copious, dark urine. Disagreeable feeling in back part of urethra after micturition. Yellow discharge from urethra.

Sexual Organs.—Itching; corrosive in membranes of penis. Drawing along spermatic cords. **Penis relaxed, not excited by voluptuous fancies.** Erections *feeble, without desire; frequent erections;* painful in morning; violent, in morning after rising. *Crawling in testes.* **Testicles cold.** Desire increased; *diminished. Emission at night after an embrace* (Phos.); *semen discharged in a stream, without ejaculation* (Gelsem.), *scanty and has but little smell.*

Clinical.—Agnus castus is an extremely valuable remedy for loss of sexual power in men, amounting even to complete impotency. The indication for the use of this drug is coldness of the genital organs, with complete loss of sexual instinct; it has also been used for loss of sexual power following gonorrhœa, or associated with a chronic gleety discharge. It may be used for great relaxation of the genital organs of women, with leucorrhœa, or with these symptoms, scanty and diminishing secretion of milk, perfect abhorrence of sexual intercourse.

Respiratory Organs and Chest.—Voice sounds as if passing through wool. Cough, evening in bed. Pressure in chest; above r. nipple, < expiration and touch; in region of last true and the first rib of r. side, < touch; in xiphoid cartilage, directly above pit of stomach; externally in region of sternum, < during deep inspiration.

Pulse, slow and weak.

Back.—Cracking in dorsal vertebræ like rubbing a thumb along a board. Stitches above crest of r. ilium, near spine; deep, sharp S. in coccyx; intermittent, deep S. on l. side, near os sacrum and coccyx.

Upper Extremities.—*Pressure in r. axilla, < touch.* Tearing stitches on top of l. shoulder. Tearing in r. shoulder-joint, < motion and inspiration, with pressure. *Pressure in upper arm, superiorly, externally, < touch.* Prickings on external surface, just above l. elbow. Pressure on r. elbow, < motion. Twitching in region of r. elbow, > moving arm. Dull stitch in outer side of r. ulna, a few inches above wrist. Paralytic pain in l. wrist, on turning hand. Drawing pain in metacarpal bones. Paralytic twitching drawing in metacarpal bone of l. index, < touch. Swelling of a finger-joint, with arthritic tearing. Sticking in r. fingers in evening; in eminence of lower joint of index; in upper joint of r. thumb. Pressure in muscles of l. thumb. Buzzing and humming of r. index.

Lower Extremities.—Tearing. Pricking high up in r. side of r. thigh. Lancinating pain in r. hip-joint, sometimes extending above and below joint, < motion, > rest, when it is more a tearing with pressure, accompanied by weakness. Crampy pain externally, near l. hip when walking. Shooting in bend of r. knee when standing. Sticking drawing pain in bends of knees, extending into thighs and legs, < motion, in rest changing to drawing, with pressure. Stitching in external side of l. fibula, a little above foot, > pressure. Tearing in inner side of l. leg, from knee to foot. Aching in r. tibia when standing. Paralytic twitching drawing in muscles of l. leg, from knee to foot, when walking and on touch. Sharp intermittent stitches in region where the fibula and tibia join the tarsus anteriorly. Ankles turn easily when walking on pavement; in morning. *Heaviness of foot as from a load attached to r. tarsal bones.* Sticking in one part of outer side of foot when standing still. Dull intermittent sticking in sole near heel. Fine lancinations in soles. Stitches in l. big toe; causing whole limb to jerk. *Tearing in anterior joints of l. toes, < walking.*

Skin.—Red itching spots on inner surface of l. forearm. Formication of r. cheek; under skin of hands. Sensation in upper part of l. calf as if pulled at with a string. Itching stinging in different parts; in inguinal region. Itching around an ulcer in evening. Stinging itching in places on face, beginning with a long stitch on each side. I. as from fleas, especially up back. *Corrosive I., > scratching, but returns.*

Sleep.—Drowsiness. Long sleep. Restless S. Starting in S. Dreams anxious; constant, unremembered; voluptuous.

Fever.—Chilliness; *without thirst,* or subsequent heat; C. in scalp, with tension, however it feels warm. **Testes cold** *at night, objectively, not subjectively. Internal coldness, with external warmth, except of hands; internal, with trembling and external warmth.* Shuddering, alternating with heat, without thirst. Heat in l. external ear; face, with dry mouth, then thirst when the H. is over. Pleasant warmth of l. hand and forearm. Creeping H. in whole body, evening in bed, with cold knees. Sweat of l. hand, especially interior sides of fingers, in open air, previous to heat.

Ailanthus.

The Chinese Sumach (Ailanthus glandulosa, Desf.) is a medium-sized tree which is commonly cultivated in the United States. A tincture is prepared from the fresh young shoots, leaves and flowers.

General Action.—It causes nausea and vomiting, diarrhœa and even dysentery; a low type of fever, with muttering delirium and restlessness; a rash resembling scarlatina; general malaise and great weakness.

Allied Drugs.—*Rhus tox.* (Quasia, Cedron), Anacardium, Baptisia.

Generalities.—Malaise. Restlessness (Rhus tox). Dulness over whole body. Electric thrill extending to finger-tips. *Tingling and prickling in whole body* (Rhus tox). Heavy feeling. Faint feeling, with nausea. Incapable of standing long. *Weakness;* on exertion. Aggravation from sight of food.

Mind.—*Unconsciousness.* Muttering delirium (Hyosc.). Confusion of intellect. Mental alienation. Inability to concentrate mind. Memory lost (Anacard.). Recklessness. Stoical indifference. Anxiety. Fright (Stram.). Low spirits.

Clinical.—With the low fever general stupor or indifference, with sighing.

Head.—Aching; with burning in eyes; A., with nausea and vertigo; with chills, then flushes of heat. Confusion. Dull compressed feeling, with confusion and pain in forehead. Fulness; after wine; with sleepiness; F., with intoxicated feeling; F., with burning on brain; apoplectic F. Heaviness, > pressure, with pain over eyes. Thick, heavy feeling. Electric thrill extending from brain to limbs. Vertigo; < stooping; with nausea; with vomiting; staggering, when rising or moving.

Aching in forehead; in centre of F., more to l.; heavy A. between 1 and 2 P.M., with drowsiness; peculiar heavy, dull A., incapacitating for mental labor. Aching in temples; on waking; in r., with nausea; darting A. in temples and occiput, with confusion of ideas; lancinating in both, and fine prickling pain in l.; acute prickling. Tightness in temples. Tender bruised feeling over parieto-*frontal* sutures. Sensation of an electric current through l. side of head. Pain behind ears; P. in occiput, with dizziness and ringing pain in forehead and swelling below l. eye and upon cheek; darting aching in occiput. Beating in occipital arteries.

Clinical.—Constant frontal headache of a neuralgic character. Headache paroxysmal, with drowsiness during the day, confused mind, mental depression.

Eyes.—Smarting and aching as from astringents. Rough and irritated feeling, as from sand and dust. Burning; with headache. Lachrymation in open air or by bright light. Lids agglutinated in morning, with purulent discharge. Conjunctivitis, with redness and inflammation extending around outer canthus. Brows fall out. *Photophobia.* Dim vision. Blurring of figures and letters.

Ears.—Feeling in r. as from a blow. Ringing in r.; ringing in ears like music.

Nose.—Swelling. *Soreness* on l. side, with pain. Dryness. Catarrhal obstruction. Difficult breathing through nose. Sneezing, with sensation of cold about the eyes and gnawing in chest. Chronic catarrh. Bleeding; of bright blood. Smell lost.

Face.—Pale. Sallow and inactive complexion. *Dusky,* bilious complexion. Dark circles around eyes. Capillary congestion in irregular spots. Neuralgic pain, forcing him to walk. Hot, red. Feeling about articulations of jaws like mumps.

Mouth.—Teeth feel as after an acid. Gums swollen and bleeding. Tongue coated; with a pasty taste in morning; thick white coat, *brown in centre.* Oozing of blood from denuded surface of mouth. Dryness of M., with bleeding from roof and sides. Pain in M. Soreness of M., with rawness and burning. Discharge of blood and stringy saliva. Flat taste to everything. Brackish and flat taste to water.

Throat.—Parotid and thyroid glands enlarged and sore. Redness. Spreading ulcers, feeling as after application of nitrate of silver. *Inflammation of fauces and tonsils, with spots of incipient ulceration. Thick œdematous, and dry, choky feeling. Irritability. Dry, rough and scrapy,* < morning. Feeling as after an astringent. Constriction; with sensation of a foreign body. Full feeling; just above sternum, with desire to hawk up something. *Hawking up mucus;* hawks up greenish purulent matter. *Soreness on swallowing* or on admission of air; S. on swallowing, extending to ears.

Clinical.—Diphtheritic scarlatina, with ichorous discharge from the nose, throat dusky red, with grayish exudation, great swelling both internal and external.

Stomach.—Appetite capricious. Appetite lost; for breakfast; for dinner; no hunger, but eats his usual quantity. Disgust at food. No thirst except when eating. Nausea; every morning; in morning, with diarrhœa, sometimes with vomiting; with anguish, and also with tightness in temples; with sharp pain in r. temple; with vertigo, and also with headache; with sour eructations; with faint feeling; as from fat meat; intermittent; in women, similar to that of pregnancy. Retching. Vomiting; in sleep without waking; all food soon; sour; with diarrhœa. Pain; sharp prickling, and in temples; as from pins. Burning; with darting pain through it. Emptiness; in pit. Faintness after dinner. Inactive condition, as if its contractive power were impaired.

Abdomen.—Rumbling. Tympanitis. Griping. Pain; before soft stool; with soft stool. Feeling as before diarrhœa; feeling as of "insecurity," as if he would be attacked by diarrhœa any minute. Looseness, more in large intestine. Nausea. Burning. Stricture below short ribs, with the nausea. Tenderness over hepatic region. Oppression below hypochondria, with pain and with the nausea. Pain in hypogastrium and hips.

Stool.—Dysentery, frequent, painful stool, little fæcal matter, much bloody mucus, with little fever. Watery, expelled with great force. Frequent diarrhœa, with pain in abomen. Easy, frequent. Constipation.

Urine difficult to pass.

Respiratory Organs.—*Cough in violent fits before retiring and on rising; painful C.; deep;* and exhausting, with asthmatic expansion of lungs. Oppressed, with muco-purulent expectoration, free in morning, sticky and scanty during the day. Expectoration difficult, in small flakes. *Hawking up mucus.* Whitish expectoration. Yellow mucus from throat. Asthmatic oppression of larger bronchi. Asthmatic wheezing. Croupy choking. Crepitant ronchus. Oppressed breathing. Sighing. Rapid breathing.

Chest.—Stitches, with aching; S. in lungs; l. lung. Cutting to l. of lower part of sternum. Gnawing. Soreness internally; S. of lungs. Aching under clavicle, extending sometimes to sternum; A. through lungs; in lungs, < a long breath; l. lung; in anterior part of l. lung, extending to posterior part; especially through centre of l. lung, sternal edge, with a contracted feeling; A. in chest, with constriction. Burning pain under l. shoulder. Burning, as from breathing hot steam or air; B. in r. lung. Heaviness in sternal region. Oppression as if strapped; O. of bronchi. Sensation as if air-cells stuck together, can hear air-cells open (?) as lungs expand. Tired feeling in lungs.

Pulse.—Rapid; then slow. Slow; then rapid; and full. Small, rapid.

Neck.—Pain; in nape and upper part of back. Soreness of glands, with pain under l. scapula. Swollen feeling in muscles.

Back.—Aching, pressed feeling in dorsal vertebræ. Pain; between shoulders; deep-seated in r. scapula, also preventing motion; P. close on either side of dorsal vertebræ; P. in small of back; pain in back, head, neck, with numbness under l. scapula, extending as a band down to l. hip.

Extremities.—Aching restlessness. Heaviness. Asleep. Shooting pain in shoulders. Numbness of l. arm, with sensation in fingers as if asleep. Tingling of l. arm and hand; morning on waking. Bruised feeling on r. forearm. Numbness of l. hand. Tingling and pricking in fingers.

Tottering gait. Lancinating pain in lower limbs. Lower limbs tired. Pain in r. hip-joint; hips and hypogastrium; shooting P. in hips. Trembling of legs. Numbness of l. leg, with tingling, pricking pain in foot and toes. Pain in r. foot, preventing walking; P. in l. foot when walking, a kind of tension.

Skin.—Jaundice. Erysipelatous swelling of face. Sore on prepuce like incipient chancre. *Eruption; livid;* E. like measles, but without the concomitants of that exanthem. *Miliary rash, almost livid, more profuse on forehead and face, especially on forehead, with dingy patches between the spots of eruption, with muttering delirium, small, rapid pulse, cold dry surface, the livid color of the skin when pressed out returned very slowly, the whole a complete picture of torpor.* Elevations filled with turbid liquid looking like pus, with inflamed areola. Vesicular inflammation, resembling the eruption caused by Rhus, on uncovered parts. Dryness. Itching and an uneasy feeling around nose.

Sleep.—Sleepiness; all day; morning or forenoon; after wine, with fulness of head; S., with restlessness. Sleep in afternoon. S. heavy at night; S. disturbed and unrefreshing.

Fever.—Chilliness; with sweat; preceded by miliary eruption, most profuse on forehead and face, during the chill hunger, with a distressing sense of general emptiness, speedy vomiting of food, pain in back of neck, upper part of back and in r. hip-joint, during the hot stage thirst, delirium and desire for brandy. C. over whole body, as from water.

Heat, then coldness; H. during the day, with nausea; head burning hot; burning on brain. Heat in face, with redness. Heat in skin, < morning, lasting till noon, with dryness. Cold sweat; with the nausea and vertigo.

Clinical.—Scarlet fever, with symptoms of depression, eruption slow in appearing, of a livid hue, or with petechiæ; patient stupid, with diphtheritic infiltration and much swelling of the throat; scarlet fever, deep coma, tip of nose and extremities cold, rash pale violet, involuntary discharges.

Aletris Farinosa.

Aletris farinosa, Linn. (natural order Hæmodoraceæ), colic root. A tincture is prepared from the root.

General Action.—It seems to be an irritant to mucous membranes (see nose, mouth and gastro-intestinal canal), and to produce an engorgement of the lower abdomen, with symptoms in women of a heavy uterus.

Allies.—Colch., Arum tri., Aloes, Lil. tig., Kali c., Iris, Crocus, Dioscorea.

Generalities and Mind.—Uneasiness. Faint feeling in evening, with nausea. *Tired; all the afternoon, with dull, heavy, confused feeling in head and inability to concentrate the mind or study.* Mind confused and wandering. Mind tends to run on pleasant thoughts, but it does not continue on one object long. Rapidity of thought not lessened, but the *power and energy of mind weakened.*

Head.—Aching; in morning on waking; every morning, with nauseous, faint, all-gone feeling in stomach, > eating; in different parts. Strange feeling, gradually settling down, with aching in occiput. Feeling as if in a vise. Pressure over eyes, with a queer sensation behind ears. Pain over r. eye, running down into eyeball, > closing lids, at same time nausea and pain in lower abdomen. Forepart felt as if in a vise; feeling in forehead as if in a vise, with dull pain running from r. temple over eye down into eyeball. Aching in r. temple. Temples feel as if in a vise; T. feel as if pressed together, with an occasional twinge in r. temple. Pain in vertex, < bending it forward and by straining at stool; P. in vertex, with weight in occiput. Heaviness in vertex and over eyes.

Occiput. Pain; and in neck; then weight; on l. side, just behind ear; and heaviness, with sharp pain running down r. trapezius, which was < bending head forward, > bending it backward. Queer feeling. Weight, with aching over eyes and through head from temple to temple. Heaviness, as if a weight would draw it backward, and the neck had not the strength to prevent it, > during breakfast, with a feeling as if the scalp were contracting across the back, drawing the sides of the occiput together.

Eyes, Ears, Nose and Face.—Lancinating pain in r. eyeball. Eyelids feel as if pressed down. Pain back of ear, running down sterno-mastoid muscle, leaving soreness to touch; P. back of r. ear, extending down anterior surface of sterno-mastoid muscle. Ears feel as if open through from one to another. Deaf in l. E., stuffed feeling. Nose sore inside of tip; inside, on l. of tip; inside, < r. side (a crack just inside r. nostril). Watery discharge from nose. Lips dry and cracked (Arum tr.).

Throat.—Pain; in r. side all the afternoon, and at 5 P.M. in l. side close up under jaw, with thirst and hyperæmia of mucous membrane of pharynx and larynx; in r. side (in r. anterior pillar), intermittent, like shocks of an electro-magnetic machine run slowly but strong, < any movement of head that stretched the muscles. Soreness in morning on waking.

Stomach.—Appetite lost. Thirst; during fever. Eructations of air after eating; of food in evening, with burning in throat. Nausea, with giddiness, then vomiting and purging; N. < by coffee; with pressure in forehead, the nausea > dinner, but returning with gagging at the sight or thought of grease. All-gone feeling in morning on rising, causing faintness, > eating.

Abdomen.—Cramps. Griping (Diosc.). Pain all through, settling into lower part, > passing flatus and scanty diarrhœic stool (Colch.); P. all through, < bending forward, > bending backward, then the pain increased and it seemed as if all the insides had sunken to lower abdomen and were cut with knives (Verat.); > scanty diarrhœic stool (Colch.); intermittent, mostly in lower part, > **scanty** diarrhœic stool, tenesmus during and after stool, with feeling as if lower part of rectum were closed. Aching in hypogastrium; and across back of hips.

Stool.—Frequent ineffectual urgings. Loose, painful, offensive, frequent. Thin, with hard lumps in it. Hard; and delayed, small, scanty, difficult; and delayed, scanty, difficult, than constant desire to urinate for half an hour; frequent, the first small; urgent, dark, offensive, excoriating. Bad odor to S. and flatus.

Urinary Organs.—Micturition rare. Incontinence, < walking fast or sneezing. Amount and specific gravity of urine diminished at first. Phosphates slightly increased.

Sexual Organs.—Pain in uterine region; in morning on waking, menses almost black, scanty and sour, with malaise. Menses too soon, light-colored, with colic and bearing-down pains (Aloes), lasted 52 hours (always six days), then leucorrhœa, white, stringy; *too soon and profuse, with labor-like pains.*

Clinical.—It has been found useful for prolapsus uteri associated with general anæmia and scanty menstruation; the pains are griping clutching in the right inguinal region extending down the thigh; it has also been used for leucorrhœa and endometritis. It cured hæmorrhoids in one of the provers.

Cough.—Tickling, short, dry, hard, on waking, becoming spasmodic, < by talking, discharge of urine during C., later C. incessant, and like whooping C., lose my breath and become cyanotic C., > suddenly on occurrence of menstruation (eight days too soon).

Chest.—Pain in l. breast as if a knife ran into it; sharp P. in l. breast, then extending through into back, to left of lower part of r. scapula.

Pulse.—Irregular and intermittent.

Neck and Back.—Pain in centre of nape, running off into l. shoulder, then the pain in nape moved up to occiput, where it lasted all the evening. Sharp pain from lower point of l. scapula through to l. breast. Pain in dorsal region. Sensation as if the back would break just above waist, afterwards the same pain higher up. Backache, with dragging in sacral region and stringy, colorless leucorrhœa, beginning when walking.

Extremities.—Sharp pain in r. shoulder-joint, streaked down arm, then into l. chest, where it located just above nipple. Pain running down tops of thighs, all night. Knees painless in forenoon during motion, painful in afternoon while sitting. R. leg feels paralyzed below knee and numb, could not bear weight on it.

Skin.—Itching, papillary eruption across chest and upper part of back, with hyperæmia and hyperæsthesia of surrounding integument, the itching < scratching with the nails, but > rubbing with the palms.

Sleep.—Restlessness at night, < fore part, preventing sleep; R. every night, late falling asleep, then immediately terrible dreams, which wakened, till late in morning, then resting well; with many dreams. Unrefreshing. Sleeplessness till 12 or 1 o'clock, then restless sleep till late in morning, then undisturbed sleep; S. < fore part of night, with physical and mental restlessness, the mind continually wandering on occurrences of his past life, no tendency to brood over sorrow, thoughts very pleasant.

Fever.—Chills, face flushed. Limbs cold, head and face hot and flushed. Feverish.

Allium Cepa.

Natural order, Liliaceæ. A tincture is prepared from the common red onion.

General Action.—The first and most marked effects are catarrhal, nose, eyes and larynx; less marked on intestinal tract. Neuralgic pains in various parts like a fine thread. General aggravation from warm air.

Allies.—Iod., Brom., Arsenicum, Squilla., Arum., Puls.

Generalities.—Shock, with eructations of wind. Indescribable revolution in whole body. Feeling as after taking cold, feverish, < evenings, with heat in face, tongue and mouth feel burnt and dry, without thirst, drinks only a small quantity, restlessness in limbs (Ars.), next day tongue coated. Troubles as after taking cold, pains in all bones, with aching in throat, prostration, etc. Restlessness, with pain in abdomen. Deathly faintness after profuse micturition. Weakness (Ars.). Amelioration afternoon and evenings; after dinner; after supper; by diarrhœa.

Mind.—Confusion and absent-mindedness from much business in afternoon, after wine and coffee. *Indefinable anxiety* and apprehension with the abdominal pain (Ars.).

Head.—Electric shocks through. *Aching;* morning, also especially in temples; **evenings in room, with coryza** (Iod.); *< evening, with coryza; > open air, also with nasal discharge;* deep within, extending forward and outward to ears; moving from deep within to ears like threads, remaining in spots; oppressive. *Confusion.* Dulness; with coryza and lachrymation. Fulness; with heaviness as if bound up and with flickering before eyes; F., with pressure in stomach. Heaviness. Sensation as if wrapped up in warm water during the headache.

Forehead.—Stitches externally over l., in evening, drawing into ear, upper jaw and teeth of same side. Aching in region of organ of "concentration;" over r. eye; over r. eye, extending to root of nose; neuralgic, over r. eye, extending into root of nose; deep-seated aching over l. brow; oppressive, over eyes, frequently going through head like an electric shock. Confusion. Dulness as after chloroform, and in whole head. Heaviness; over both eyes.

Aching in temples, < r., < winking, afterwards extending over forehead, < l. side. Tingling pain behind l. mastoid process. Aching in vertex; l. side of vertex. Swollen and heavy feeling on crown. Aching from both sides of head, downward and inward towards middle.

Occiput.—Aching; both sides, > in evening after

beer, with dull confusion from crown backward and downward. A. on both sides of occiput, then in two round places in upper posterior part of head, then a general and humming sensation of the part being asleep. Pressure in upper part of O. in evening, becoming about 11 o'clock a sensation as if asleep in bone. Confusion on both sides of and towards upper part, pressing down sideways, then behind ears around whole occiput.

Clinical.—The headache of Allium cepa is mostly in the forehead, extending to temples and downward to eyes and into the face, associated with coryza.

Eyes.—Redness, < l. Stitches in l. in morning. *Biting* sensation as if there were smoke under upper lids, < night. *Pain; as if they hung loose posteriorly on a string*, could be bored into with the fingers and torn out. **Lachrymation of l., with redness of ball**; *L. < l.*; L. in morning; *L. < in evening, in warm room*; **L., with coryza.** Burning of lids; in outside of r. upper lid. Irritation of l. upper lid; after drinking coffee, < warm room, > open air. Dim vision by candle light. Dazzling vision in the distance and dim near by. Flickering and blindness. *Sensitiveness to light, < l.*

Clinical.—Eyes. The inflammation of the eyes and nose is characterized by the symptoms as emphasized. The lachrymation is generally very profuse, with burning and smarting, but, as a rule, does not excoriate the lids, while the discharge from the nose is watery and extremely acrid. With these symptoms there are generally associated the violent laryngeal symptoms noted further on. For acute fluent coryza of this character the drug stands unrivalled.

Ears—Affection. Stitches through r., in morning. Pecking behind r. Humming on lying down. Ringing; distant, < r. Roaring in l. in afternoon.

Nose.—Pain like a thread in a nerve, extending outward and downward from nose in morning. Soreness; in morning. Dryness of nostrils. Irritation in r. nostril in morning. Crawling in right nostril as before sneezing. *Sneezing*; morning; **frequent,** *also in evening on entering warm room.* Catarrhal troubles > in cool room; (violent C. after rain and northeast wind); C. **evenings in room, with headache**; *C., with headache, also < evenings*; **C., with larchrymation**; *C., with heat, lachrymation, headache, and acrid burning discharge making lip red and sensitive. Discharge, > open air, with headache*; **copious watery** D.; *dropping, in evening, in the street, without sensation of coryza; watery*; blowing thin mucus from nose.

Face.—Swelling of cheeks, with toothache. Drawing pains in l. cheek, extending into l. eye; < cold air. Pain like a thread in a nerve in r. upper jaw, downward from the medium line to the side, deep within the bone, in evening.

Mouth.—Teeth. Smutty-yellow. Pressure in r. back on entering warm room. Aching in back, at breakfast, from bread; from warm cocoa, > cold water; in back, in sleep, with feeling as if too long, > rising; in r. back, after traveling against northwest wind, with desire to bore into and suck them, which relieves, also < warm soup, > cold water; aching in l. eye-tooth, in root, disturbing sleep, with swollen feeling and heat in cheeks; A. root of l. eye-tooth, with inflammation of gum, the pain ceasing suddenly and beginning in a r. back tooth, in the eye-tooth it is pressive growling, the toothache > cold water and cold generally; A., with swelling of cheeks; A. raging, in a broken tooth. Drawing in first upper, from root to crown, r. then l. Pecking in two last back.

Coated tongue; morning; back part, < morning; slimy. Dryness on r. side of root of T. Pain under T., with a half-circle of sore elevations at lower insertion of frænum. Burnt and dry feeling in mouth and tongue, without thirst. Dryness of mouth, without thirst. Scalded feeling in mouth and tongue. Offensive breath. Burning taste, more on gums and upper part. Nauseous taste; on waking. Sweet taste; sickly-sweet.

Throat.—Redness of back part of r. side of palate. *Constrictive pain in region of os hyoides, then low down posteriorly on r. side.* Drawing pain in l. side, > cold air. Pain; *extending to ear.* Pain as from a sore lump, morning on swallowing and elevating tongue. Pain below larynx as after swallowing too large a mouthful, or as if swollen, in afternoon, extending every little while into r. ear. Feeling in pharynx as if food stuck behind the breast-bone.

Raw feeling in morning, with tickling in region of epiglottis, r., then l. side, with sensation of weakness in stomach, hiccough, uprising of frothy salivary mucous fluid, eructations of wind and passage of offensive flatus, constant inclination to hacking to relieve the tickling in larynx. Dryness; of soft palate after breakfast; D. in morning, with tickling and hacking cough. Heat low down, extending into stomach. In throat and orifice of Eustachian tube, chilling or burning twitching and gnawing, not painful; chilling or burning twitching in region of r. Eustachian tube, then above it a kind of gnawing, neither painful. Numbness in back part. Mucus; behind choanæ towards evening; in posterior fauces, choanæ, and on posterior surface of soft palate, bland mucus constantly in evening, which must be swallowed or hawked up.

Stomach.—Appetite, which disappears as soon as he begins to eat, food is disgusting. *Thirst;* in evening, after beer and herring; *evenings, with heat;* evening after flushes of heat; T. after chilliness. Eructations; in morning; of air in morning and in evening. Hiccough; morning. Nausea; > eructations; deathly, after eating, > eructations; in posterior part of throat, forced up as with a thrust. Vomiting; frothy slimy fluid. Rumbling in epigastrium after breakfast. Pain; with fulness in head, < after coffee; in region of pylorus; on l. side; deep within epigastrium, as if at orifice, and posteriorly, at 10 P.M. Heat extending into S. Empty feeling and drawing back and forth, with pain. Weak feeling; in morning.

Abdomen.—Rumbling in morning; after breakfast. Flatulency. Emission of flatus in morning; E. during ineffectual urging to stool; difficult, also in evening; frequent, also at night; loud; *offensive*, also in morning; *offensive and moist, also in morning* (Sulph.). Gurgling and rumbling; < l. side. Distention; before dinner; with pain, > emission of flatus. Swollen feeling before and after diarrhœa, with sharp pain and oppression of breathing. Pain; morning; < after eating; < sitting, > emission of flatus, while moving about; > emission of flatus; more pressing than burning, especially in l. inguinal region, < afternoon after coffee, with heat in A. Heat, with nausea; H. afternoon after coffee, with pain. Nausea, extending into throat, then confusion of head. Feeling of diarrhœa, and soft stool without diarrhœa.

Rumbling in transverse colon in evening, with urging to stool. Pain about umbilicus; after dinner. Aching in hepatic region, extending through abdomen. Pain in liver in evening; in r. hypochondrium at 9 P.M., with cold shudders down back; contractive in l. hypochondrium, with sensation of wind moving about; drawing P. from region of liver through whole abdomen.

Burning glow or chilling sensation as if scattered, in r. side, with confused feeling, then emission of offensive flatus; warm or chilling sensation in r. side, as if a glow within beat against it and over external and upper part of thighs, in evening. Stitches in l. side evening and morning; l. side < lying; l. side, with ineffectual urging to stool. Pain in l. side; l. side, especially in middle and lower part, and in region of bladder, with troubles in urinating, no stool, *violent thirst, expression on face of anxiety and doubt*, skin hot, especially in painful and sensitive places, pulse rapid, full, hardish, indefinable anxiety, apprehension and restlessness (Ars.). Pain in l. side as if punched. Pain in l. flank.

Rumbling in l. side of lower abdomen. Stitches in inguinal ring posteriorly and in spermatic cord, with pressive pain. *Sudden burning or chilling cutting, as thin as a thread, from sides of hypogastrium inward towards middle and upward.* Cutting, with a twisting motion, the pain moving in a small space, deep-seated above l. groin, midway on a line between symphysis pubis and anterior superior spinous process of ilium. Pain deep in pelvis (in prostate?); extending from inguinal region along spermatic cord; painful spot deep in r. pelvis in evening. Pressure on a spot on inside of pelvic cavity, above and inside r. groin, in evening. Periodic pain in pubic region, < sitting. Heaviness in lower abdomen as if pressed upon before and after standing, > after bathing.

Clinical.—The abdominal symptoms seem to be of a catarrhal character, and are in many respects similar to those of Sulphur, with which it should be compared.

Rectum and Anus.—Stitches down into lower part of rectum afternoons. Urging to stool; ineffectual, also with emission of flatus; ineffectual, with stitch in l. side of abdomen; strong urging to a soft stool; sudden urging, also with rumbling. Biting in anus. Feeling of cracks inside anus during stool. Creeping as of a cool worm in anus and in some protruding hæmorrhoids, < l. side.

Stool.—Diarrhœa; night or towards morning; after midnight and towards morning. Bloody. Difficult, but not hard. Long and thick. Absent; with severe pain in abdomen.

Urinary Organs.—Aching in bladder; and in prostate, deep in pelvis, morning and forenoon after coitus. Burning pressure in region of bladder at 10 P.M. Full feeling in bladder. Irritability of B. and pain over kidney region. Sensitiveness of B. Urging to micturition; frequent; frequent, excessive, with burning dribbling. Difficult micturition. *Frequent micturition, with burning in urethra; and red urine;* < evenings; with shuddering and chilliness. Burning in urethra. *Urine copious in afternoon.* Frothy U. Iridescent film. Red U., with reddish-yellow, sandy sediment.

Sexual Organs.—Drawings in r. spermatic cord. Sticking and pressive pain in spermatic cord and posteriorly in inguinal ring. Burning pain in forepart of glans. Erections morning on waking, with painful tension, without sexual desire. Virility increased. Violent pain in uterine region and in region of bladder.

Respiratory Organs.—Tickling in epiglottis; T., with *constant inclination to hack*, also in morning; T. in larynx, with mucus in fauces. *Throbbing and contracted sensation in larynx* (Brom.). **Hoarseness** (Brom.). **Hacking cough on inspiring cold air** (Brom.). Hacking cough in morning. *Constant inclination to hack to relieve the tickling in larynx* (Brom.). Free expectoration of mucus in evening; hawks up sweetish nauseous mucus; thick, white, frothy mucus expectorated from fauces, without cough. Asthmatic breathing, as often before, at 11 P.M., after smoking tobacco. Oppressed breathing, with ascites. *Obstruction* to breathing *in middle of upper chest*, evenings.

Clinical.—The cough of this drug is sometimes associated with extreme hoarseness, and in addition to the symptoms given there has been clinically noted a feeling as if the larynx would split, or as if the mucous membrane would be torn out on coughing, with excessive watering of the eyes.

Chest.—Stitches in l., on deep inspiration; in l., with burning pain in various parts, especially in region of cartilages of fifth and sixth ribs. Pain below sternum, especially to the r. side, at 10 P.M., on moving in bed; below sternum, morning, on stooping; as if food lodged behind sternum.

Heart.—Circulation aroused. Pulse accelerated, full, hardish; excited after 2 A.M. Harder pulse in evening.

Back.—Stitches in r. scapula, running to elbow, with burning pain. Pain below r. shoulder, more towards spine, after long sitting. Stitches in lumbar region. Burning pressure in small of back; at 10 P.M. Pain in kidney region; in l.; l., then less severe in r.; r., with fulness in bladder and frequent urging to urinate. Pain in loins, as from retention of stool.

Extremities.—Restlessness. Rheumatic pain in joints. *Soreness, especially on arms, as if it were all scratched off, with tired feeling therein.* Weak feeling, with flatulent troubles. Stitches in arms. Weak feeling in arms. Pain in r. elbow as from a blow, at noon. Numb sensation in l. elbow; forenoons, < motion. Painful affection of l. forearm, especially of radius, evening, when resting on arm in writing. Pain in middle of l. radius, > taking hold of it and rubbing it. Pain on back and extensor side of r. wrist in evening. Dryness and redness of hands, as if he had been in the cold. Lameness of joints of l. hand. Trembling of r. hand; in evening. Pain in l. middle finger; pain in r. fourth and fifth finger.

Clinical.—This drug has been used for neuralgias following amputations or injuries of nerves, characterized by fine, threadlike pains, shooting, but not burning like those of Arsenic.

Lower Extremities.—Thigh. Bruised feeling on side of l. near knee. Pain on outer side near knee; l., also r.; almost burning pressure in upper part of l. thigh, towards outer side. Weakness of hips nights; in region of hips late in evening on rising from a seat and on walking, < ascending steps; of hips; preventing him from finishing coition.

Stitches outward in front of r. knee, as if coming from the bone. Paralytic pain in knee. Shooting in

l. leg and r. foot. Burning pressure on a spot externally in middle of l. leg in evening, then low down on r. Pain in r. ankle mornings; P. l.; burning P. around l. outer ankle, then lower down, and a burning pressure externally, then internally. Pain in r. foot evenings; ticking pain in metatarsal bone of l. great toe evenings. Painful twitching in inner side of l. heel. *Pain in external soft parts of r. great toe, and in l. middle finger.*

Skin.—A wart between l. shoulder and side of neck begins to pain, is red and is scratched off. Hard swelling under l. ear, with pain extending into ear, < pressure. Stitches, especially on head, forehead, brows, in throat and on r. arm. Itching in supraorbital region, < *l.;* burning, in brows, supraorbital region and upper lids, in evening; corrosive, voluptuous, especially on palmar side of l. thumb, from first to second phalanx, not on ball, in evening; corrosive, with redness, and points which cannot be well described or seen, and desire to be rubbed or washed, evenings, < after going out.

Sleep.—Yawning; with headache and pressure in stomach; frequent internal Y., in evening. Sleepiness; mornings; mornings after rising, with disinclination to work; S., evening. Sleeplessness after 2 A.M. Dreams of battles, fight, precipices, storms at sea, difficulty in reaching the coast, and efforts to get out of wells. Dreams of being near the water two nights in succession.

Fever.—Chilliness; alternating with heat, evenings during coryza. Internal C., then heat and thirst. Shivering in back; cold shiverings down back, evenings, with liver-pains, also at 9 P.M., with pain in r. hypochondrium; shivering down back, < nights in bed, with feverishness in all veins and sweat, especially in axilla and palms; cold shivering creeping along back; cold creeping along back.

Heat at 2 A.M., without thirst, > morning, < after *breakfast;* H., with thirst; after coldness. Heat from much walking, without thirst. Heat of head. In *l.* eyebrow. Of face; warm spots on r. cheek. Glowing sensation on outer side and upper part of thighs. Warmth of skin; hot skin, especially on the painful and sensitive parts of abdomen and region of bladder. Flashes, in evening, with thirst. *Flitting H., now and then;* evenings, with thirst. Internal H., with rumbling in abdomen. Sweat; towards morning; while working; in axilla; on palms.

Alnus.

Clinical.—This drug has been used for strumous disorders, enlarged submaxillary glands, leucorrhœas, with erosions of cervix, which bleed easily, amenorrhœa, burning pain from back to pubis.

Aloe.

This Liliaceous plant inhabits Africa; the leaves afford a juice which, when inspissated, forms the Aloes of commerce, from this a tincture is prepared.

General Action.—The most pronounced action of Aloes is the engorgement of the pelvic viscera (Uterus, Rectum), increasing hæmorrhoidal congestion and uterine hæmorrhage. The diarrhœa is very characteristic, and with the portal congestion are associated the frontal pains, flatulence and various secondary phenomena. The arthritic pains are significant, but have been neglected clinically.

Allies.—*Æsculus hipp.*, (Bell.), (Bry.), *Lycopod.*, Podophyllum, *Sulphur*, Berberis, Iris, (Phos.), (Puls.).

Generalities.—Anxious starting-up. Sticking in joints. Bruised or sprained pain in various places. Drawing in various places, as if it involved the bones; paralytic D. in various muscles. Ebullition of blood. Sensitiveness of whole body. Restlessness; anxious. *Disinclination to move. Disinclination to go into the open air, though there is relief from it.* Indolence; at noon. Weakness; evening; on motion; after vomiting; *alternating with activity. Aggravation* in afternoon, especially of symptoms of mucous membranes (Lyc.).; symptoms appear in evening particularly. *Amelioration* in open air (Lyc.); from exercise in open air; emission of offensive flatus in evening; emission of hot flatus upward and downward; smelling camphor.

Mind.—Disinclination to mental labor (Phos.). *Speedy fatigue from mental labor.* Incapacity for labor, with peevish restlessness. Anguish. Anxiety; from vertigo. Apprehension and oppression. Sadness. Peevish about himself (Sulph.); so that he insults and blasphemes, < afternoons. Anthrophobia. Quarrelsome. Wilful. Hard to please and crying at least provocation (Puls.). Disgust at everything during pain. Phlegmatic. Indifferent in evening. Excitement. Contentment. Happy mood in evening.

Head.—Tearing here and there. Shaking in, as if brain were loose, when walking at 11 A.M., < fresh, cold air and on laying head down, then and awhile after rising up pulsating pain, especially in occiput, > after eating. *Aching;* in morning, until after breakfast, with languor; in morning, after incomplete stool. > by a second stool; *after griping in bowels and after stool;* (from heat of sun); on touch; < in dark, > in light; < motion, especially stooping; < in warm, > cool air; > eating; with nausea; *alternating with lumbago;* alternating with pain in loins, also periodically; pulsating A.; sluggish drawing A., more externally.

Congestion. Attack, with nausea, as from indigestion. Heaviness. Tension. Confusion; painful, every morning. Murky feeling, compelling him to make the eyes small. Widened feeling, as if pressed out on all sides. Shock from arm into head, thereupon sensation of a wind extending from head into abdomen. *Vertigo;* while standing and walking, making him anxious; > by nasal catarrh, l., then r., with copious mucus, which soon became thick; paroxysmal; as if everything whirled about with her, < ascending stairs and turning quickly; as if he sat on a high chair, while sitting after eating.

Forehead.—Stitches over brows, and also in frontal prominences; in l. brow outward to eye, afternoon and evening; in r. side between forehead and vertex, from the top inward. **Aching;** *afternoon;* r. side; *in sinciput;* **in supraorbital region;** *in middle of F., downward and inward towards nose;* with abdominal symptoms; **above forehead, with heaviness in eyes and nausea;** extending to half of face (Bry.); involving orbits; pressing A., down into forehead; A. pressing outward towards temples; *A. in forehead and on vertex, as from a weight.* Drawings to bottom of r. side from above r. brow, every evening; D. over r. side, with sticking; darting, over l. eye and outward through eye. Confusion in sinciput, especially with chilliness.

Temples.—Stitches in l., < every step; in l. towards ear; through l. into brain; drawing, over r. (Aching in r.); intermittent, < l. Pressing outward to T., with periodic heat in face and flickering vision. Pressive boring in l., in afternoon.

Vertex.—Aching; as from subcutaneous ulceration, on r. side, < touching hair; as from subcutaneous ulceration behind vertex, with standing up of hair on that spot. *Weight on.*

Parietals.—Sudden shootings upward in r. side of head, evening and morning. Aching on l. side of head; on l. side of top of bone; in middle of r. half of brain; leaping pain in r. bone, towards vertex. Pulsation in l. wall of head, at first painless.

Occiput.—Stitches after stooping. *Aching in r. angle,* in evening. Dull drawing in l. Pulsation at night when lying down. External soreness.

Scalp.—Dryness of hair. Aching on occiput like a pressure. Sensitive spot on l. upper occiput in morning when combing hair, and towards evening on r. side of vertex. Beaten feeling near l. vertex, so that pressure is painful, yet feels good. Numbness moving over scalp, with warmth.

Clinical.—Frontal headache is most characteristic of this drug; it is generally associated with abdominal symptoms; it is rarely useful for neuralgic headaches.

Eyes.—Compelled to make small, during the pain in forehead. Heaviness, with aching above forehead and nausea. Tearing at bottom of r. Pain as from a hot current in r., along axis of vision; outward drawing pain in and over l. Pressure in r. ball, evenings from light. Pustules surrounded by red vessels at external angle of r. *Pain deep in orbits, as if in muscles,* < *r.* Outward drawing pain in brow, extending to l. eye. Vision dim at night; when writing. Flickering; with scotoma; with the pressing outward to temples and periodic heat of face. *Yellow rings move before the eyes.* Shining bodies shoot across eyes.

Ears.—Drawing sticking in middle ear, l. then r. Drawing from, into a lower back tooth. Twinging in r.; in evening. Aching during menses; in, and externally behind and below l., during menses; in l. external meatus, < pressing teeth together; towards midday drawing pain from before backward, below r. external meatus, behind the lobules, in mastoid process and in ear passage itself. Heat in middle and outer. On pressing teeth together a numbness behind ear, drawing down through a lower back tooth. Sudden explosion in l., after getting into bed, as from the breaking of glass, the clink of the glass was heard at bottom of head and extended towards r. ear. Rustlings in r., on moving jaw.

Nose.—Redness in cold open air. Scurfiness on inner surface of r. wing, with sensitiveness. Pain on motion, < morning. Burning in l. nostril. Dryness, morning in bed. Sneezing; till evening, with watery mucus; ineffectual attempts at, also in morning. Coryza; < afternoon; with burning in nose; with pain in nose; with soreness in r. nostril; dry; fluent; sensation of C., with husky voice and chilliness. Discharge of copious mucus, which soon becomes thick, from l., then r. nostril, after the anxious vertigo; thin mucus. Bleeding in morning; from r. nostril, morning in bed; flowing of blood in afternoon; feeling as if it would bleed.

Face.—Redness, with heat, wide-awake and excited; red round spot on l. border of lower jaw, between lower border, angle of jaw and chin. In l. half, confusion and pain coming from an inflamed spot in mouth and from forehead. Fine crackings in r. maxillary joint at 9 P.M., when reading aloud.

Lips.—Red; in evening. Swelling, pain, dryness, and scurf; swelling of lower, with a vesicle covered with a yellowish hard skin. Moist spongy scurf. Cracking; inner side of upper, when laughing; painful C. of lower, near angle. Dryness; after dinner, > evening, with whiteness; D., with white scaly epidermis, licked continually with the tongue.

Mouth.—Teeth. Yellow. Stitches in a third hollow back tooth. *Concave edges seem sharp and hurt the tongue.* Sensitiveness in a hollow back tooth, < eating, afterwards pain when not touched, and then a pustule appears in front of its gum. Gnawing in a l. lower hollow tooth in evening and periodically through night, < eating. Drawing in lower incisors. Tongue coated yellowish-white. Trembling and shock in larynx and tongue. Dry tongue; evenings; D. and stiff; and red. Pain in back part of r. side of tongue, < touching teeth. Coldness of l. side of tongue.

Inflamed spots in mouth; inflammation and sore pain in l. cavity. Dry mucus; thick mucus on waking at 3 o'clock and in fauces. Dryness; evenings; after dinner, > evening. Dry heat. Burnt and inflamed feeling in hard palate and about last teeth, > swallowing food. Sore feeling in inner side of l. cheek, afternoons. Salivation; after breakfast, with hunger. Sickening smell to the breath. *Taste metallic, with dry irritative hacking;* of ink or iron, with irritation to cough; bitter; *bitter, nauseous;* like senna, between root of tongue and soft palate; sour; clayey.

Throat.—Pain; with sense of rawness and swelling, < swallowing, with hawking of thick mucus on waking at 3 A.M.; with expectoration of thick lumpy mucus from fauces and choanæ; in arches of velum palati when chewing hard food; in back part on swallowing; in arches of palate on empty swallowing and on yawning, afterwards when not swallowing, > swallowing food; in soft palate when yawning; in soft palate as if sore or burnt, on chewing, < evening. Soreness of l. arch of palate on opening mouth wide.

Swollen feeling in morning, < afternoon; at 8 or 9 A.M., or pressure; in palate at 3 A.M.; in soft palate and uvula in evening, < morning, > noon. Fulness, sometimes with eructations. Constriction. Rawness, especially in upper part, in soft palate and uvula, > after breakfast, returning in open and cold air in afternoon, with raw voice. Scraping, provoking cough; in morning. Tickling irritation to cough, evening and morning, with taste in mouth of ink or iron. Dryness; with inflammation, cough and expectoration. Affection after skating, and again in evening in middle of soft palate posteriorly. Hawking up thick mucus; thick, tough, lumpy mucus, easily loosened, in morning after rising.

Stomach—Appetite increased; at 6 A.M.; 7 A.M. on waking; afternoon; evenings; evenings, with yawning; after breakfast, so that water accumulates in mouth; for bread; for fruit; for juicy food; for stimulating food, with fulness of stomach; canine hunger in forenoon; canine, after morning stool. Frequent appetite, but not great. Diminished appetite; in morning; at noon. Appetite good at noon, but went away on working. Appetite lost, with dyspepsia and constipation; lost, with febrile sensation; no appetite for meat.

Thirst; evenings; at night; after dinner and supper; for water in afternoon; especially for beer. Aversion to drinks, especially cold drinks. Eructations; of air; *bitter;* bitter, after drinking water; sour; tasting of food; acrid, after dinner; bilious. **Nausea;** (after sour things, with lassitude); must sit still in order not to vomit; with inability to vomit; with headache; **with aching above forehead and heaviness in eyes;** with empty feeling in stomach; with diarrhœa and pain in umbilical region, < pressure; with weakness. Hæmatemesis.

Distention; after drinking water, with bilious eructations; *in epigastrium,* also with appetite for stimulants; in region of stomach (Lyc.). Flatus rising towards throat, with nausea. Pain; in r. side; in pit after breakfast, > eructations; *in pit when making a false step on stone pavement;* in r. epigastrium, with tension; from epigastric region into both sides of chest; from epigastric region into pharynx; extending into pharynx; from pit through to back, like a weight, with sore pain, sometimes this pain rises into chest and then sinks down again with eructations. Pain drawing up into sides of chest, < motion, with nausea. Snatching under pit (in a mesmerized person). Oppression; < eructations; with eructations. Twitchings in epigastrium; cutting, tearing, sticking, in epigastric region. Crawlings. Torpidity, so that he did not know when his appetite was satisfied. Warmth, with hunger. Weakness in pit like a weight and burning.

Abdomen.—Distention (Lyc.); **with motion of flatus** (Puls.); D., with periodic movement, < after eating; after a meal, also during menses, also mornings, especially in hypochondrium. Rumbling. *Gurgling,* before a thin stool; with constipation; *moving about, also after supper.* Rattling, mostly in hypogastrium, as from movement of uterus. Motions, especially in lower part; M., with urging to stool; M., with writhing.

Emission of flatus after every meal; in noon repose; *on attempting to go to stool;* **burning and offensive** (Sulph.); **offensive** *in evening; O., with stool;* O. after eating; *hot; loud, with stool; frequent and loud,* also morning and evening; *easy, with inclination as for soft stool;* vigorous, evenings; copious in evening, also at night, *also with stool,* also **with little fæces;** copious, long, lazy, offensive, after stool; copious, offensive, after noon nap and towards evening; *the more copious the harder and more delayed the stool, and offensive,* < in morning.

Stitches before stool. Cutting; morning after rising; when eating; after vinegar; with diarrhœa; drawing across through abdomen, with ill humor, anthropophobia, *not disposed to go into open air, though it is better thereby.* Griping; *before stool, also during and after stool;* after midnight, with diarrhœa; with small stools; as from taking cold, also from 10 to 12 A.M., after a thin stool. *Pain;* at night before and after diarrhœa; *in muscles when rising from lying, with pressing to stool, as from taking cold,* also *morning and evening;* compelling one to bend body. Anxious feeling. Inflammation; on intestinal mucous membrane, with ulceration. Sensation of a stone in abdomen if she lies on it, but the stone seems to be in the side if she lies on the side; with sweat, next day dry coryza and diarrhœa. *Dragging down.* Drawing, crawling; pleasant, with diarrhœa. Soreness on pressure. Chilliness. Feeling as if he had taken cold, after morning stool. *Heat.* Determination of blood; ebullition of blood in organs. Pulsation; at night when lying down; (during rest, < lying at night). Indolent feeling with the stool. **Weak feeling, as if diarrhœa would occur.**

Upper abdomen.—Distention (Lyc.). Aching in upper and middle part of abdomen, going downward. Griping in upper, after dinner and supper, with twisting; G. in upper and around umbilicus, > sitting bent and emission of offensive burning flatus, with twisting and ineffctual urging to stool. Cutting; in afternoon, < motion, especially stretching body outward, > sitting bent; in small intestines, also with gurgling.

Sides.—Stitches now in l., now in r. Aching in r. *Soreness, especially in sides and down sides of umbilicus, on touch, with pain.*

Hypochondria.—*Distention,* > passage of flatus, with pain in l. hypochondrium. Stitches in hepatic region; from liver into chest, interrupting respiration; periodic, in hepatic region, sometimes moving into chest, interrupting respiration; in spleen; drawing, from splenic region into loins, waking at night; extending from splenic region through l. breast; in l. hypochondrium, as if in l. ligaments of womb and in ovaries; now in r., now in l. hypochondrium; from hypochondria, around umbilicus, and then into rectum. Cutting; in afternoon, < by motion, especially stretching body outward, > by sitting bent. Cramplike pain in region of spleen. *Pain; < by standing, so that he stoops;* in hepatic region (Lyc., Sul., Pod.); > by emission of flatus; *towards morning, with distention, pain in forehead and diarrhœa,* with painful weakness of leg, diarrhœa and chilliness; in r., with tension; jerking in l., extending downward and inward in morning when walking; hard, alternating with the same under upper part of sternum. Inner pressure. Pinching in both. Bile increased and irritation of liver. *Uneasiness in region of liver, with heat, pressure and tension* (Pod.). Strained feeling in liver by the last ribs.

Umbilicus.—Motions in region, at 6 A. M., with urging to stool and hunger. Retraction. Stitches; on sneezing; throbbing boring S. in region. Pinching around. Cutting about, after stool. Raking in a circle about, as from a blow, morning on rising, < pressure, with yellowish diarrhœa and nausea. *Pain in region;* < pressure, with diarrhœa and nausea; P. especially in region, < touch, especially in deeper tissues, < morning; P. in a spot in middle abdomen, in morning, > lying bent and pressing upon it, passing into cutting after rising, then two pappy stools. Griping in umbilical region, with shivering through whole body. Digging around. Boring in region. Twisting about.

Lower Abdomen.—Distention; flatulent, along colon, < motion, > passage of hot flatus, with a pressing outward pain; moving along colon in evening, then copious discharge of flatus. Rumbling, with pinching. *Gurgling at night, with sudden urging to stool.* Shocks over hips, with distention. Stitches over arch of pubis. Pain as if another stool would follow after a stool; *P. as before menses* (in a nursing woman); in groins. **Sensation of a plug between symphysis pubis and os coccygis** (compare Bell.), **with urging to stool.** Pressure and drawing, with drawing in spermatic cord, then griping in transverse colon, > by passing flatus. **Heaviness.** *Determination of blood to large intestines;* to pelvic region. Cramps, and in r. groin, passing beyond r. knee. Soreness, with tension. Inflammation of lower part of intestinal canal. Irritation at end of intestine. Periodic drawing in r. inguinal region. Affection of lower end of intestinal canal and of pelvic organs.

Clinical.—The abdominal symptoms are apt to be associated with pressure and fulness in the region of the liver. There is always great accumulation of flatus, which presses downward and causes distress in the lower bowel.

Rectum.—Stinging. Cutting during solid stool. **Heat** (Æsc. h.), *with diarrhœa;* when fæces pass. *Soreness.* Annoying sensation, caused by pain in loins. *Loose sensation.* **Heaviness.** *Dragging down, during menses, with full sensation in pelvis;* D. near anus. Feeling as if the stool were solid during a natural, also during a pappy one. **Fear least stool should escape with flatus; feeling as if thin stool would escape on passing urine; with the stool always a feeling as if more were at hand.** *Tenesmus as if more stool would follow, which must be held back on account of soreness of anus, yet on account of this pain he does not dare to draw the anus together.* **Urging to stool, with passage of urine** (Merc. c.). *Urging to stool;* in morning; *morning on waking;* at 3 A. M.; in evening; *at night, also during micturition;* **after eating;** *when rising from lying; or standing;* during stool, when he thought he had finished more came; *after stool; after thin stool; continual;* also at night; *frequent,* with heaviness in pelvis; *sudden in morning on rising; sudden, with liquid stool; ineffectual, also with emission of flatus,* also with a feeling of softness, also with debility; as for a solid stool, which was soft; near anus, more towards perineum. Tenesmus, with diarrhœa.

Anus.—Drawing stitches on walking after morning stool, more on l. side and forward to region of prostate gland and vesiculæ seminales. Stitches, extending into loins; S. during stool, as if it would be torn forward, then after stool pain which compels him to draw it together frequently, whereby it becomes tense and aches. *Sticking, cutting after stool.* Pain, > drinking beer. *Burning* (Berb., Sulph.); *after stool; after emission of hot flatus. Fulness and pressing out;* fulness and pressure after a small thin stool. Pulsation while sitting after dinner. *Sore feeling* (Berb.. Æsc. h., Iris); during stool, with chapped feeling. Crawling after stool. *Itching;* in afternoon. Ulcers on edge. **Hæmorrhoids sore** on wiping after stool. **H. swollen and sore** (Æsc. h., Sulph.), <through day; sore during stool; sticking in H. in evening on rising from a seat and later when sitting; smarting when sitting and lying; painful during diarrhœa; protrude during stool; protrude, with a full feeling; itching in afternoon; itching, with sticking; itching of soft H. evening and morning. Discharge of blood from anus; during stool, also with pain in loins; after stool; of membranous looking mucus. *Weakness of sphincter, so that cleanliness was difficult.* Soreness of perineum after walking; soft, painless varicose tumors on perineum.

Stool.—*Liquid;* with sudden urging. Watery, with tenesmus. Thin mornings. *Diarrhœa; morning on rising,* with raking about umbilicus as from a blow, and with nausea; in evening, with tenesmus; yellowish green after midnight, with griping in abdomen; with pain in hypochondria and chilliness; yellow; *yellow, towards morning, also with distention and dull pain under ribs;* pappy, after constipation; pappy, towards the end, at 2 A.M.; *yellow pappy,* with pain in umbilical region, which is < pressure. *Pasty.*

Constipation; after diarrhœa; C., with growling in abdomen. Omitted; with unendurable condition of mind. Hard; first part, latter part thin, pappy, also at 2 A.M.; H. and indolent; small and tough. Crumbling; and scanty, with feeling as if more ought to come (Sulph.). Lumpy. Dark, pappy and scanty. *Yellow;* grayish-yellow. Green (in an infant). Bloody; with pain in loins. Undigested; with traces of blood. *Brownish, small, slimy, half-fluid.* Evacuation of mucus in large conglomerate pieces; yellow mucus. *Small, yellowish, shining stool at 9 A.M., with sputtering flatus, with dread lest fæces and urine escape together, while he would force out, yet he held back.* Bilious; partly of bilious-streaked mucus mixed with fæces, partly of thin yellow fæces, after grumblings and motions in abdomen, then crawling in anus.

Copious; late in evening; and difficult; *and thin, after waking at 3 o'clock;* and forcible, with noisy flatus, then drawing in bowels and limbs. Small; and soft, after much straining; and thin. Sputtering. **Involuntary, with passage of flatus** (Sulph.). **Falling out without exertion;** *almost unnoticed.* Indolent. Difficult; distending rectum at first. Frequent; with flatulence and tenesmus. Stool at an unusual time; S. **during micturition** (Mur. ac.), *also at 5 A.M., with micturition; morning after rising; after breakfast.*

Clinical.—Engorgement of the hæmorrhoidal veins is one of the most constant effects of Aloes, and it is one of the best remedies for hæmorrhoids as above characterized. The diarrhœa is particularly treacherous; that is, the patient does not have a proper sense of the accumulation of fæcal matter in the rectum, and there is loss of power in the sphincter, so that the stool escapes easily, and when the desire for stool comes the patient is scarcely able to attend to it. Aloes has been prescribed with success in constipation with heavy pressure in the lower part of the abdomen, particularly with a feeling of a plug in the pelvis, as above mentioned; in chronic dysentery, with the abdominal symptoms of flatulence and the burning in anus and rectum, the discharge sometimes of jelly-like lumps, intense pain and soreness in rectum after the stool.

Urinary Organs.—Urging to urinate; frequently at night. Difficult micturition. Interrupted micturition. Frequent M. in afternoon, with copious and light-colored urine. *Burning on urinating.* Blood from urethra. Urine scanty; and hot; copious; C. and pale, after stool; dark; D. and scanty, with slimy sediment; bloody; fine granular cloudiness, with whitish sediment and putrid ammoniacal smell; yellow sediment, like bran.

Sexual Organs.—Tickling of prepuce, with crawling and spotty redness. Pollution in midday nap. Increase of leucorrhœa. Pain in female genitals as if torn. Cramps in uterus, with loss of white mucus. *Determination of blood to uterus* (Bell.). Heaviness in uterus, with pain in back; with pain in loins, and groins. Menses appeared in a woman nursing a child two months old. Menses too early; and too copious (Bell.); increased, with colic; long-lashing. Menstrual blood dark and clotted (Bell.).

Clinical.—Valuable for uterine hæmorrhage, with feeling of great heaviness of uterus and the sensation of a plug above noted. The uterus always feels too heavy and engorged, as if hæmorrhage would take place at any time.

Respiratory Organs.—Stitching in r. side of larynx with each paroxysm of cough. Scraping in larynx, with tickling in fold of neck. Raw pain in larynx when spitting. Trembling and shocks in larynx and tongue.

Hoarseness; in back of fauces; deep in fauces, after a dream that he was in danger, but could not scream on account of hoarseness, > after breakfast. Raw voice in morning. Cough; from scraping in throat, also in morning; dry, < towards evening; dry, sometimes from determination of blood to chest: hoarse, crepitant, deep-sounding cough, as if trachea were raw, dry and full of mucus.

Expectoration constantly, from scraping and tickling in larynx; lumpy; yellow tenacious, after cough; thick, also in morning, also at 3 A.M.; jelly-like in morning after rising. Hæmoptysis. Asthma and wheezing. Dyspnœa. Inspiration wheezing, panting, evenings after smoking. Whistling in throat. Whistling and labored respiration.

Chest.—Cutting, tearing, sticking jerks, which suddenly stop the breath, < recovering himself from a stooping or twisted posture. Stitches; through l., also when crouching on account of pain in abdomen; in lower, with dyspnœa; in l. breast, < bending body; under r. mamma; anteriorly in region of l. sixth rib, at 9 P.M., < deep respiration; moving about; obstructing respiration; pinching at back of l. side and under l. nipple, on bending to the left, sometimes impeding respiration; twitching, also when lying, impeding respiration, with palpitation.

Pain in ribs under r. axilla, extending in region of shoulder towards back; behind sternum; *under sternum;* in anterior part on deep inspiration; at costal attachments of muscles that go to arms, on motion of arms; as if she would choke; hard, under upper part of sternum, alternating with some pain in region of r. lower ribs. Sprained pain behind middle of sternum on rising, only on moving arms, on stooping and crouching together, > stretching chest and throwing it forward. Bruised feeling between bones and flesh in anterior part and sides up into axillæ. Sticking drawing in region of l. sixth and seventh ribs in morning on stretching, superficial but preventing respiration. Constriction, with periodic pressure and squeezing, < l. Determination of blood. Weakness; on bodily exertion.

Heart and Pulse.—Stitches in præcordium on deep inspiration. Pain in præcordial region, extending to l. scapula, also extending under l. scapula. Palpitation, with stitches in chest. Heart's action strong. Action quicker, in bed, < after 2 A.M., with frequently a strong beat. Pulse rapid; slow; intermittent; irregular in force and frequency; sunken; sunken after vomiting; weak and changeable; weak and suppressed.

Neck.—Cracking of cervical vertebræ at 8 A.M., on motion. Drawing pain in r. side, only on moving neck after rising from midday rest, afterwards the same pain on motion, but tensive, almost burning. Drawing; tensive, burning in r. side, as if in muscles, forenoon when sitting, > motion, and on sitting in afternoon the same tensive drawing, and on stooping in morning and afternoon, burning. Tension in nape behind ears, with compression. Soreness on r. side, on motion, as if a muscle were stretched.

Back.—Pain at nights; P., with heaviness in uterus. Bruised pain in whole back, on and between scapulæ, as after long stooping. Stitches under the scapula, with outward-pressing pain; S. between scapulæ, < r. side, with squeezing. Pain in region of last dorsal vertebræ, as if in spinal cord, at night after eating much, < lying on back, > rising.

Sacral Region.—Stitches in r., shooting towards anus, hips and lower abdomen. *Lumbago alternating with headache.* Pain; morning on rising, also < evening; at appearance of menses; involving pelvis; drawing about in sacrum during the day, < sitting, with heaviness; drawing, in sacrum, spreading over pelvis, < evenings, with ill humor; acute drawing through flank into middle of thigh. Drawing, with burning; D. in r. kidney region, with pressure. *Heaviness, < sitting, > motion, with pressure;* H. involving pelvis and rectum. Weight on rising from a seat, and in pelvis. Stiff feeling after sitting. Biting, burning and sticking as from a mustard plaster, between skin and flesh, in afternoon.

Coccyx.—Bruised feeling. Periodic clucking in region.

Extremities.—Jerking, drawing, dull sticking in the finger, knee and elbow-joints. Asleep on lying down after eating. Cracking in l. shoulder-joint, morning on moving it. Sticking in shoulder, extending into ulna. Outward pressing pain in S.; in l. S. Shock extending from arm into head. Pressive or paralytic drawing in r. arm near shoulder. Heaviness of r. arm. Arms weak. Pain in elbow.

Forearm.—Pain ending in wrist; beginning in middle of r., ending in wrist, where it seemed as if it would press the bones asunder, at night in bed. Paralytic drawing in anterior parts; jerking drawing in l., as if in flesh, extending into palm, 3 to 4 P.M., when sitting still and writing.

Stitches in metacarpal joint. Pressing-asunder pain in bones of wrist. Weakness of wrists. Swelling of hand, 8 to 10 P.M., especially balls of thumb, with heat and tickling-itching, feeling as as if frozen. On stretching out l. hand it feels as if the nerves were too short and were dragged like an electric shock. Drawing in metacarpal bones and joints of r. middle finger at 3 P.M. Drawing into palm. L. hand asleep, forenoon, sitting in a wagon. In l. hand and forearm sensation as if internally asleep, and now and then an internal jerking. Symptom of chilblains on hands.

Fingers.—Stitches; in joints; tearing S. in second joint of l. fourth; twitching drawing S. in joints. Sprained feeling or as after taking cold, in last joint of l. fourth. Pain in lower condyles of first phalanges of r. hand, evenings; under nail of l. index; in r. fourth, with stiffness; drawing, in l. middle, especially in metacarpal joint, with stiffness; drawing, in metacarpal joint of fourth, with sticking; jerking drawing, in metacarpal joint of l. fourth. Drawing in joint of l. thumb, also in forenoon and in midday rest.

Lower Extremities.—Weariness and heaviness.

Thigh.—Cracking in r. hip-joint morning on rising and on walking. Shocks from hips towards inguinal regions, preceded by chilliness. Stitches in middle of buttock when stooping. Tearing in r. thigh; above r. knee. Pain in inside of l.; outward-pressing P. Drawing in l. buttock. Heaviness in thigh; in r. upper, with pain from prostration.

Stitches in r. knee; while walking. Pain in knee. Drawing in knee; r. on sitting still; in r. tibia. Heaviness of legs. Painful weakness of legs, with pain in hypochondrium. Whole l. leg asleep. Sprained feeling in outer bone of l. ankle when walking; sprained feeling in ankle, evening in bed and in morning, or in l. great toe, or in a finger or thumb that had been sprained a few months before. Weak ankles.

Cramp in r. foot. Pain in foot; in sole during rest; in soles as after a long journey, when walking on pavement; P. on inner margin of metatarsal bone of l. great toe, beginning as a pressure, then becoming a drawing. Painful pullings in r. foot. Sprained and bruised feeling in tendo-achillis, < l. in evening. Sprained pain in great toe, sometimes r., sometimes l., in joint, at night on every motion, with chilliness. Pain in r. little toe as from chilblains; pain in r. third toe as if frozen, afternoon on walking.

Skin.—*Golden-colored.* Redness, especially of face. Eruption around mouth. Swelling in various places, with pain. Blotches on abdomen. Painful nodules; under chin behind r. jaw. Pimples on various places; under lower jaw; small elevated, raw, itching P, with circumscribed redness, on abdomen. Cracks and discharge of thick matter. Inflammation of a comedone on l. side of upper lip, becoming a yellow pustule. Furuncle on upper arm. Suppuration where hard skin had been torn from foot. Red, inflamed ulcerous spot on r. third finger, with tearing. Ill-looking vesicles on genitals.

Pain after being scratched sore. Feeling of a hair on back of hand and backs of fingers. Feeling as if the hairs on last phalanges of l. fingers rose slowly. Crawling, itching, biting on various places; on knee-caps, calves and inner surface of thigh. Itching at umbilicus; around anus; of arms; of hands, with heat and swelling, as if frozen; of inner side of l. thigh; inner side of l. thigh above knee; on popliteal space, also l., then < r.; behind knee and on scalp; in various parts; biting, at umbilicus in evening.

Sleep.—Yawning in evening, with hunger; much at 8 P.M.; frequently and violently after midday sleep, also in evening in open air without sleepiness; violently in forenoon, with stretching. Sleepiness at midday; evenings, also with indifference; after eating; half senseless after eating; dozy sleep long in morning, also only at noon, also after dinner; dozy lying after waking. Midday sleep with chasing visions. Sleeplessness; before midnight; from midnight to 5 A.M.; in evening. Sleep restless. Waking early. Sleep interrupted by hæmorrhoidal irritation and sexual excitement; during sleep emission without dream. Dreams confused; D. that he was in danger but could not cry on account of hoarseness; towards morning, that he had defecated in his breeches; heavy; indistinct.

Fever.—Chilliness; at night; at appearance of menses; during stool; during soft stool; on moving; with diarrhœa and pain in hypochondria; with confusion of sinciput. Cold feeling in occiput, with throbbing of arteries; tip of nose externally, in evening; legs and feet; hands, to touch; feet, afterwards heat of them. Shivering; through whole body, with griping in umbilical region. Heat. Internal fever, with rapid pulse and loss of appetite. Warm sensation on scalp. Heat in inner and outer ear. Burning in nose, with coryza. Warmth and redness of face; periodic heat of face, with pressure in temples and flickering vision; in r. foot. Sweat at night; at night after drinking; at night after drinking cold water; in axilla; under axilla; offensive, < night.

Alstonia Scholaris.

A tincture is prepared from the bark of this tree (natural order Apocynaceæ).

Violent purging and cramp in the bowels, vertigo and general weakness; sharp purging, with pain, uneasiness in bowels and heat and irritation in the lower bowel.

Clinical.—Camp diarrhœa of undigested food; bloody; especially of malarial origin, from drinking bad water, or even dysenteric symptoms, with great prostration. Has been used in India for the malarial fevers of that country, and it has also been found valuable as a tonic in the debility following exhausting fevers.

Alum.

Alumen, the common potash alum, a double sulphate of Aluminium and Potassium, $K_2\ Al_2\ (SO_4)_4$, 24 H_2O, is triturated with sugar of milk for use.

General Action.—It has a strong chemical affinity for albumen, so that it causes contraction, paleness and dryness of tissues; it contracts capillaries. In large doses it is an emetic, and produces a general gastro-enteritis.

Relationship.—Alumina, Tannin.

Generalities.—Convulsive movements (Gallic acid). Trembling of muscles. Nervous tremor and excitability, as from unpleasant news. Wandering cramps. Bruised pain in whole body. Rheumatic pain in whole body. Ebullition of blood going upward. Pulsation through whole body when standing long on one spot, with palpitation. Restlessness; with fever. Faintness; with dim vision; F., as from hunger. Weakness; morning after rising; W. from short walk, then pain in lumbar region. Amelioration when walking.

Mind.—Excitement; morning after rising. Agitation. Anguish. Anxiety. Sadness from 9 A.M. till noon.

Head.—Rush of blood to. Aching; at night on waking, > cold water, with nausea; heavy, especially in occiput; intermittent wandering aching in forenoon; < morning on waking, at one time shooting from one temple to the other, at another heavy on vertex, as from a weight, with intermittent nausea, with chilliness and feeling as if cold water were poured down back, at another time great heat through body, in fact feeling exactly as when attacked by smallpox.

Vertigo; in evening, > lying, with headache; as if he would fall forwards, when looking down; sensation as if vertigo were coming on in evening when lying on back, > opening eyes and turning on r. side, with weakness in pit of stomach. Aching in r. side of forehead; over eyes in morning; over l. eye; over eyes on waking, till 10 A.M., > cold water, reappeared next morning and at 9.30 P.M., > after lying down, with vertigo; jerking in l. side of forehead at 8 A.M. Stinging in vertex, when stooping, afternoon till evening. Aching on vertex. Aching in occiput.

Eyes.—Burning, itching on r. lower lid. Itching, burning on border of lower lid, r. then l. Bruised feeling on inferior edge of l. orbit on pressure and on moving lids. *Watery* discharge, afterwards glutinous and watery. Burning in r. external canthus, with itching.

Ears.—Heat in both and in l. side of face at midnight, > going to bed. Hears everything in sleep. Ringing in r.

Nose.—Dryness; D. in choanæ, from throat. *Sneezing;* when out of doors.

Face.—Expression animated, with fever. Pain in

l. articulation of jaw close to ear. Twitching of lower lip.

Mouth. — Tongue, stitches, < tip; rough and as if scraped, in morning; burning also on r. side; dry feeling in morning, < fore part, with sufficient saliva; burning on tongue. Roof coated with phlegm. Pain in mouth, burning pain. Burning. Contraction. Dryness. *Salivation*, with a dry feeling on tongue. Taste metallic; T. sourish; sourish on r. side of tongue; disgusting, sweetish.

Throat.—Thick mucus, and on palate. *Scraping with the cough.* Pain. Soreness; in both sides, when talking, and when swallowing, with dryness. Prickling in both sides, with dryness, which extended to posterior nares and rose into throat, with constant desire to drink. Dryness. Heat; and in larynx. *Burning pain down the œsophagus.* Tickling, causing cough. Swallowing impossible. Acute pain in gullet.

Stomach. — Appetite increased; lost; none for breakfast; loathing of food. Thirst, with fever. Eructations; tasteless. Nausea; at night on waking and in morning; in morning, with faintness; in morning, with weakness; with headache; with chilliness; with cold sweat; in morning, with pain and convulsive bearing in stomach like the deathly sickness of pregnancy; sudden. Retching. Easy vomiting; without previous nausea. Vomiting of blood only.

Distention after breakfast; D., with good appetite; of epigastrium; of epigastrium and stomach after eating; of pit, also after eating; of pit, urging him to take a deep breath, which he cannot do. Gas. Inflammation, and of bowels. Griping. Pain in epigastrium; in pit in evening when lying on back, then pulsation; pain to left of pit, at 8 P.M., when walking in open air, > standing still and pressing, disappearing by bending double, when continuing to walk the pain returned a little lower, < by every step. Burning pain. Sudden pain at noon, with pallor, blue lips, knees drawn up against breast, then vertigo, nausea, coldness, weakness and headache, which last all the afternoon. Sudden jerking pain up into swallow at 3 P.M. when sitting, > walking, with twitching of lower lip and weak feeling in pit of stomach. Sharp pain at 4 P.M., while sitting in church, with deathlike faintness, sickness, weakness, cold sweat, rush of blood to head, then sensation as if blood left the head and extremities, cold limbs, dim vision, feeling as if pain in stomach would draw her double, then heat, rush of blood to head, so that she could hardly hold it up or keep her eyes open, then weakness, especially in back, in evening when taking a long breath it seemed to come from a spot on each side of spine, on a line with inferior angles of scapulæ. Cramplike drawing in epigastric region.

Burning. Heat in morning, > cold water; H. in pit, with full feeling. Warm creeps from pit down over abdomen. Dry and burning sensation. Contracted feeling. Heaviness; with throbbing as in an ulcer, also after eating. Throbbing at 11 A.M., after eating; after eating; at pit, in evening when lying on back; in epigastrium, extending to heart, with palpitation. Sinking, > eating; 11 A.M., > eating. Weakness in pit; in pit when sitting, has to rise; in pit, as during pregnancy. Uneasiness in pit, with rapid short breathing.

Abdomen.—Distention. Flatulence; shifting. Stitching down median line, into penis, as if it followed a thread. *Griping.* Pain; burning P. in small intestines. Burning in lower part, and in small of back, can scarcely get up, with feeling as if back would break. Inflammation of intestinal canal. Contractions of muscles from sides towards linea alba; in evening; jerking C. of muscles. Weakness.

Rectum and Anus.—Urging to stool, with much borborygmus. Smarting and burning in rectum after a solid stool. Hæmorrhoids after a hard stool; H., with aching within anus; hæmorrhoidal irritation. Beating in anus; after a stool. Itching in anus all the evening.

Stool.—Diarrhœa; *yellow, like an infant's;* afterwards constipation. Constipation. Hard, bloody. Copious, solid. Frequent. Rare, scanty. Difficult. *Blood with stool.*

Urinary Organs.—*Urging to urinate. Frequent micturition.* Metallic sensation about orifice of urethra, with feeling in clitoris as if urethra lay there, and as if urine could not be retained on account of pressure on clitoris. Itching in orifice of urethra; in evening, and on scrotum. Urine, brown, muddy; bluish, iridescent film; looks as if cheesy milk had been stirred into it; increased; acid; *free and watery*, afterwards scanty and dark.

Sexual Organs.—Cutting in l. side of penis. Erections during dinner. Emission of thick semen at night. Menses watery.

Respiratory Organs.—Larynx, *tickling from talking, causing cough;* heat. Voice hoarse, < talking; hoarse and shrill, cannot talk loud, varying, sometimes high, sometimes low; *lost*, with sore throat; partially lost; feeling as if she had lost her *voice.* Windpipe contracted. Cough when exercising; from tickling in throat; slight irritative, *dry, in evening after lying down* (Nux v.); tickling, morning after rising; irritation to C. in morning after rising. Expectoration; of coagulated blood in morning, after rising. Respiration rapid.

Chest.—Stitching down middle, later in r. side. Pain; in clavicle, when inhaling; under r. clavicle and r. shoulder, when inhaling; on sides; l., in morning; l., when sitting, < bending forward; in l., near middle of sternum, when washing and dressing, lasting till 9 A.M.; in breast, < r., or a binding sensation, > lying; as if distended, in afternoon, < after supper; rheumatic, in r. side; sore, under r. nipple in morning, < bending double. Rawness. Scraping, scratching to middle of sternum. Anxiety, heaviness like a stone, with inclination to take a long breath. Fulness. Tightness; across upper part, with heat. Warmth inside, opposite l. shoulder. Weakness in lower part, and in abdomen.

Heart.—Pain shooting to lower part of r. lung. Palpitation; when standing long on one spot, with pulsation through whole body; rapid and violent, < lying on r. side, and lying long in one position. Throbbing; like the heavy blows of a hammer, with long intervals. Intermittent beating. Pulse rapid; intermittent; small and rapid, afterwards intermittent and thready.

Neck.—Pain on side; r. side. Cramplike drawing, and stiffness.

Back.—Stinging between scapulæ. Tearing at lower angles of scapulæ from 2 P.M. till evening, when sitting still, > moving. Pain at edge of r. scapula, near spine; on a line with inferior angles of scapulæ all the evening, on every deep inspiration; rheumatic, under l. scalpula; on both sides, near middle, on deep inspiration. Breaking sensation. Cramp in back, just below hips, in morning, extending up l. side, with warm ebullitions. Weakness; in region of scapulæ, > stooping.

Extremities.—Twitching in morning, after rising, especially in arms, with excitement; T. in forenoon. Bruised pain in joints of arms, hands and feet.

Upper Extremities.—Shoulder, pain in l.; l., > motion; rheumatic pain in l., < motion; drawing tearing, especially in l. shoulder. Pain in arms; as if distended in afternoon, < after supper; rheumatic pain in bones of arms, < r.; pain as from a cord around r. arm; pain as from a cord around r., just below shoulder, causing fulness of bloodvessels and weakness, the pain sudden, intermittent and extending in lines in different directions. Unpleasant sensation in arms in morning, then heat, more in l. hand. Weakness; a kind of numbness in l. arm, and particularly in l. shoulder.

Elbow.—Pain; extending into arm; rheumatic, in bend, morning on waking, when extending arm, > rising and walking. Sprained pain in r. wrist at 12 M., thence it goes into first phalangeal joint of r. forefinger, where it is a tearing, with weakness of hands during menses. Trembling of hands. Rheumatic pain in l. hand, and in all finger joints.

Lower Extremities.—Bruised pain when standing, as after a severe cold. Weakness; l.; on ascending stairs. Pain in knee when walking, < r. Uneasiness in knees, with pains just above them. Sensation as if a cord were tied under r. knee, the pain extending upward and downward in lower leg. Numb feeling in r. leg from knee into foot, when lying on it. Pain in l. ankle in morning when walking, < ascending steps. Pain in l. foot and ball of foot. Pain in sole, between ball of little toe and heel. *Cramplike drawing in plantar surface of r. foot.* Sensitiveness of feet to pressure and when walking, especially soles. Stitches in r. great toe; in under part, in evening when walking in street and when pressing on it.

Skin.—Bleeding of chin from a slight scratch in morning when shaving. Itching on scrotum in evening; I. on r. shoulder; burning I. on l. hip.

Sleep.—Drowsiness. Sleep delayed by warm ebullitions. Restless S., when he does sleep it is so light that he hears his birds move in their cage. Sleeplessness, with fever. In the night, half waking, half dreaming, she hears what happens around her, but dreams on, of dead bodies, that her father had died, together with fear, but feeling that the dream would pass over if she could turn on her side, which she could not do on account of heaviness in her bones.

Fever.—Chilliness; at noon; C. with nausea; then heat; alternating with heat. Sensitiveness to cold. Cold head and hands; skin; limbs. Cold hands; < motion; afternoon and evening, with cold legs. Cold legs; cold feet. *Chill*, with metallic taste, nausea, palpitation, pain striking from heart across to lower extremity of r. lung, sensation of cold water poured down back, numbing coldnesss of feet, afterwards a general chill, with deathlike faintness.

Heat; with thirst, nausea and vomiting; inward, all forenoon. Warm ebullitions in morning. Ebullitions like spasms spreading over trunk, especially in back. Flushes to head. Warm creeps run over abdomen. Burning on r. side of neck. Heat in arm; in hands; in l. hand. Heat and tingling after creeping and coldness. Fever, with thirst, nausea, vomiting, sleeplessness, agitation, animated expression of face, pain and distention of epigastric region, frequent pulse and burning pain in mouth, pharynx and stomach. Cold sweat during cramp in stomach.

Alumina.

Pure clay, a tri-hydrate of Aluminum, is triturated with sugar of milk for use.

General Action.—On mucous membranes, causing a form of dry catarrh, on the spinal system of nerves and on tissues.

Relations.—The alkaline earths, especially Kali c., Mag. c., Bar. c., Nat. m., Caust.; also *Graph.*, *Silicea*, Rhus t., Niccol. and Zinc.

Generalities.—Twitching; > rising. His arm and head are jerked backward several times, with apprehension. When he attempts to sleep while sitting after dinner, a jerk through head and limbs, like an electric shock, with stupefaction. Tremor after supper; during leucorrhœa, with lassitude. Involuntary motions. Tremulous excitement of nervous system. Lightning-like shooting to and fro in r. shoulder, small of back and abdomen, then bruised feeling. Pain all over at night; (aching in bones, especially of legs, chest and back). *Takes cold easily* (Kali c.). Orgasm of blood, with increased pulse, and trembling of hands when writing, also after a meal, with heat of whole body and sweat of face. Shaking pulsations through whole body. Restlessness at night, with pain all over body; R. when sitting or lying; anxious R.

Unconquerable disposition to lie down. Faintness and weariness; feverish faintness, with internal heat. *Weakness* (Kali c.); morning on rising; morning on waking; after a short conversation or walk; during menses; of mind and body after menses; < *talking;* < after walking in open air, and by lying down, with yawning, stretching, drowsiness and *inclination to lie down*, the weakness < lying; > sleep in forenoon; with chilliness and headache; *tremulous.* Paralyzed feeling in all muscles. Most symptoms appear in morning; most S. come on when sitting. Aggravation towards evening; after an emission; after dinner. Amelioration every other day; at night; evening in open air; after eating; from walking.

Clinical.—Bœnninghausen cured four cases of locomotor ataxia.

Mind.—Excitement of intellectual and physical powers. Absence of mind; alternating with animation. Inattention when reading. Dulness. *Stupor; with dread of falling forward.* Various objects occupy his mind, but not one is distinctly impressed upon his recollection. Memory weak; want of memory. Inability for connected thought. Indisposition for mental labor, with inability for it. Weakness of mind and body after menses. Chooses different expressions from what he intended. Reflective.

Horrible thoughts on seeing blood or knives, she feels, for instance, as if she would commit suicide, though she has the greatest aversion to it. Sad, disagreeable images. Despair. *Anxiety;* at night on waking, with dyspnœa and sweat; in morning, as if threatened with epilepsy; with external heat and *uneasiness* as *if she had done something bad;* with palpitation and pulsations in some parts of breast and abdomen. Anguish, with restlessness; A. on waking towards morning, caused by pains imagined in sleep.

Apprehension; of losing his thoughts and understanding. Dread when talking on entering house after a walk, with nausea. Fright; when he wishes to urinate; and starting on hearing least thing fall. *Uneasiness in evening as if evil impended.*

Peevishness. Whining. Weeping against his will; W. and howling. Depression of spirits on account of his disease; believes that he cannot recover; *depressed, as with grief, morning on waking,* without perfect consciousness. Dissatisfaction with everything. *Ennui.* Desire to be alone in forenoon. *Obstinacy.* Opposition to the wishes of others. Quarrelsome in afternoon. Indifference. Irresolution. Laziness; *in forenoon, with ennui.* Exacting. *Seriousness. Changing mood; assurance alternating with timidity.* Did not answer, then anxious groaning, then laughter alternating with weeping. Contemptuous laughter at everything; convulsive L., also evening in bed. Cheerfulness; after walking in open air, with staring.

Head.—Stitches through, at every step; *in brain, with nausea;* going around brain; outward in afternoon. Tearing; in forenoon; evening, with pressure from both sides of head and with chills. Thrusts shooting through H. as from knives now and then. Pinching and griping externally in evening, < stooping, with a sensation of ague towards occiput.

Aching at night in bed; > *morning on rising,* with pain in nape; on waking, before menses; and in forehead, during menses, < blowing nose, with a cold; A. < walking; < walking in open air; > appearance of menses; > laying head down quietly in bed, with chilliness and lassitude; as if bruised, with red cheeks; as if brain were dashed to pieces, as in putrid fever; in afternoon, obliging one to lie down, with dry heat and cough during sleep; pulsative, on ascending stairs after dinner; as if screwed together at 2 P.M. when standing, with stitches in forehead and such heaviness in vertex that the head threatens to fall on stooping; as if a worm were crawling under skull, the pain is also cutting and corrosive.

Intoxication from smoking; from weakest spirituous drinks; intoxicated feeling alternating with pain in kidneys. Confusion; morning, > rising; afternoon; 4 P.M.; with dread of losing consciousness; with heat of face, as if consciousness were outside of his body, when he says anything it seems as if some one else said it, or when he sees anything as if some else had seen it, or as if he could only see through some one else's eyes. Paroxysmal stupefaction in morning; dizzy paroxysmal S. when at bodily labor. Heaviness; morning, with heat; heaviness in forenoon; afternoon; 4 P.M., with confusion of forehead and sensitiveness of vertex to touch; H., with pale face and lassitude; H. as if it would fall forward at 1 P.M. when sitting erect, < stooping. Weakness; from dreams.

Blood rushes to, with blackness before eyes, vertigo, ringing in ears and drowsiness. Rhythmical pulsation in afternoon when walking and morning in bed. Surging synchronous with pulse after dinner, on stooping, > becoming erect. Feeling as if brain would fall forward, after dinner on stooping, > raising head, with heat. *Vertigo in morning;* evening before urging to stool; *as soon as she opens her eyes;* when sitting; on walking; < stooping; > wiping eyes; with nausea; *everything turns around him,* also at 4 P.M.; *as if she would turn around, in morning, with fainting nausea,* the nausea > wheat bread, then sour taste.

Forehead.—Stitches in afternoon; in evening; S. on going to sleep; S. after eating, < towards evening, and in occiput. Tearing in forenoon; afternoon; evening, > open air; T. pressing back over vertex at 10.30 P.M. Aching; above eyes; in a spot on upper part when touched, in morning; *burning and pressive, when standing or sitting after dinner,* with warmth, the pain > by open air; pressing in; pressing out after dinner; *as from a tight hat,* and on occiput. Constriction. Beating and stitches in forehead and r. side of head in afternoon.

Temples.—Stitches in r. as with a large blunt instrument, leaving soreness; stitches in r. when singing. Tearing, shooting in r. and on vertex, with the cough. Tearing externally in r., then internal boring and beating; in r., then burning after rubbing; upward in l., then stitches in r. Compressive aching, extending above eyes; in evening. Pressing-in pain in r. after dinner. Boring in r. in evening; in l. in evening, with drawing pain; in forenoon, with tearing. Pulsation in r. in afternoon, with weight on vertex. Stupefying tension in a spot in r. in forenoon, > pressure. Crawling between skin and flesh, going to forehead and pressing outward there.

Vertex.—*Pulsative aching* over r. temple, early on waking. Aching in l. as if raised by a lock of hair. *Pulsation and raging* in forenoon.

Sides.—Stitches in r. in morning; S. as with an awl, on outside close to vertex, on l. side; S. in r. when stooping during labor. Tearing in r. in forenoon, with stitches, and in the evening in l. frontal eminence. Sensation as if r. were screwed towards the other at 8.30 A.M., and as if vertex were oppressed by a heavy load. Painful drawing in r. Pulsation in r. in afternoon, with stitches; P. in upper part of r. at 1 P.M., with tearing.

Occiput.—Aching; during cough. Bruised feeling, > lying. Drawing and pulsative tension in r. side in forenoon.

Scalp.—Sore pain on touching hair. Hair dry; H. fell out. Pimples in a cluster behind r. ear, with painful tension. Itching here and there, with formication.

Eyes.—*Squinting.* Staring after walking in open air, with cheerfulness. Twitching. Trembling of l. as if it would leap out, < towards evening and on looking down, > closing eye, or looking up or holding eye with hand, with sensitiveness to light. Dimness morning on waking, > washing, with biting. Mucus in r.; dry M. morning on waking; much M. at night. *Pressure;* in r. in evening when reading or writing; below l. upper lid as from a foreign body. Tension around l. Biting in morning, with burning pain; in l. as from soap, in evening; tearing. *Burning* (Nicc.); morning on waking; < by looking up; at night and in morning, with itching and increased secretion of mucus; burning and pressure in eyes and nose as if she would be attacked by a cold. Dryness in evening, with dulness. Excoriated feeling in interior in evening, after which they are continually closed. Itching. *Lachrymation;* morning after waking; in open air. Pressure on l. ball.

Lids.—*Agglutination in morning on waking, with burn-*

ing when opened and with dread of light. Falling out of lashes. Tearing in r. upper on looking down, and on looking up feeling as if upper lid were longer and hanging down, in morning, then stitches in r. side of head. Feeling as if l. upper were hanging down. Upper lid feels paralyzed, hangs down and covers only half of eye. Weakness in afternoon as if they would close. Pressure so that she could not open them; alternating pressure.

Canthi.—Stitches. *Itching*, and in lids. Burning. Biting, with stinging and burning, as from an acrid humor.

Inflammation of r. conjunctiva in evening. Tearing in upper border of orbit. Trembling sensation in brows.

Vision.—*Photophobia in morning;* l. sensitive to light. *Dim;* evening; in open air; *obliging her to wipe her eyes constantly, with sensation as if lids would adhere in the corners*, as if a feather or hair were before r. eye. Weak after long looking. Black, with rush of blood to head, vertigo, ringing in ears and drowsiness. Flickering and spots, with a kind of vertigo. Bright on closing eyes. White sparkling stars after blowing nose. Yellow.

Clinical.—Squinting in children during teething. Subacute and catarrhal inflammation of conjunctiva, particularly with dryness and smarting, great loss of power of the eyelids so that it is difficult to open the lids. The most important indications for this drug are the burning and dryness without much discharge and without destruction of tissue. It is useful in asthenopia from irritated conjunctivæ, also in granular lids and chronic blepharitis.

Ears.—*Redness and heat evenings.* Sticking; l.; into hollow; deep in r. at night; into ear; outward through. Tearing in, behind and below; T. evenings, > pressure, with stitches. Boring in morning and in hollow of ear in afternoon, and on pressure. Tension. Pulsation. Feeling as if something were lying before r. externally. Itching; in meatus, with tingling. Obstruction on blowing nose, opening again on swallowing. Crackling on swallowing; C. in tympanum, < chewing. It seems in r. ear as if he had a different voice. Ringing, with rush of blood to head, blackness before eyes, vertigo and drowsiness. Roaring in morning and at same time stools are more solid than usual; R. in evening; before ears, as of large bells, morning after rising. Whistling. Whizzing.

Nose.—*Swelling of l. wing, with hardness and pain* on touch; *S. of septum* (Caust.), *with redness and pain on touch*, the pain < in evening. *Ulcerated nostrils. Soreness in r. nostril, with scabs and thick yellowish discharge* (Graph.). Tearing in and near r. fossa, > pressure. Intermittent burning pain in r. wing in evening. Sneezing; morning on waking. Cold comes on during menses, with pain in nose, head and forehead, < blowing nose, then diarrhœa and colic; sensation in nose evenings as if a cold would come on; unwell as from a cold which cannot develop. Coryza, with sneezing and obstruction of nose; dry C., also < night, with dryness of mouth; fluent C., also afternoon and morning; fluent, with frequent sneezing and lachrymation; sudden fluent in l. nostril, with obstruction of r.; fluent then dry. Discharge of water from r. nostril without catarrh. Thick mucus runs from posterior nares into mouth, also thick viscid mucus. *Obstruction;* of l. nostril. Rattling and piping in afternoon, with rough voice. Bleeding. Blood only is blown out. Smell acute; weak; sour smell in nose in morning.

Clinical.—Chronic nasal catarrh, with scurfy nostrils or discharge of indurated masses of mucus, nose is sore internally, and sometimes ulcerated; the tip of the nose is somewhat swollen and red, associated with internal soreness. In post-nasal catarrh, with loss of smell and pain in root of nose (Nat. m.).

Face.—Redness of cheeks; coppery. Pallor; alternating quickly with redness. Expression sullen, low-spirited. Tearing in sides, < r., in zygoma, > rubbing, sometimes with tearing in r. teeth. Painful red spots on r. cheek. Drawing and tearing in l. cheek and gums in afternoon. Tension and heat in l. side in evening. Swollen feeling; after dinner, with feeling as if eyes were smaller, so that vision is impaired. Chin feels as if covered with a cobweb (Graph.).

Jaws.—Firmly set. Lower J. shortened. Swelling, so that he cannot open mouth without pain, with stitches into malar-bone and temple. Tension and drawing in jaw and cheeks, with salivation; painful tension in articulation when chewing or opening mouth.

Lips.—*Chapped.* Desquamation. Blueness of vermilion border during and after the fever. Swelling of lower; swelling and vesicles; swollen feeling. Bright vesicle on internal surface. Crusty eruption on lower. Dryness.

Mouth.—Teeth. Thick, badly smelling mucus on. Catching of two rotten molars (one above, the other below) into each other on opening mouth. Ulceration of all roots. Tearing in r.; in molars, sometimes as high as temples. Cutting in open air and in evening on lying down in bed. Gnawing in a lower front molar, < 9 P.M. > sitting up in bed, with tearing behind ear, as if the ear would be torn out, after midnight there is only the gnawing in the tooth. Drawing and tearing in lower incisors, extending to zygoma and temples. Aching on chewing; A. > rising; in incisor; in upper molar on touch; in hollow, when food gets into them; extending to ear; extending to larynx, with irritation of nerves as after catching cold or using too much chamomile; drawing, in r. in evening, > lying down; as if loose on setting them together; in a stump as if pushed into socket, on biting on it; jerking, in one of the first l. upper molars; jerking and tearing wake him after midnight, > after rising; ulcerative, in roots on chewing. Boring in hollow. Tearing, grinding, boring in evening. Bruised feeling in a r. upper molar, > pressure, which makes it feel loose. *Elongated feeling.* Pulsations in roots at night in bed. Cold feeling, with sensitiveness. Tickling after dinner, and in their roots.

Gums.—*Swelling.* Ulcer on l. lower, discharging saltish blood. Drawing pain as if sore.

Tongue.—Coated white; yellowish-white, with bitter taste. Sticking to palate on waking, with dryness of mouth. Crawling (stinging). Rough feeling. Itching of tip.

Mouth in general.—*Ulcers.* Much mucus; in morning; while throat is dry. Painfulness of inner mouth, palate, tongue and gums, with soreness so that he can scarcely eat. Scraping after stool and during digestion, and in stomach. Burnt feeling after dinner. Heat. Crawling on inner surfaces of cheeks. Dryness; on waking; *although saliva is not wanting*, causing frequent painful swallowing. Musty smell. Salivation; with sense of contraction in mouth or crawling upon surface of cheeks; evening in bed; < afternoon, > night; sweetish or sourish S. Spitting much saliva and mucus in morning.

Taste.—Astringent, acrid. Bitter; evening after apples; B. and slimy in morning on rising; B. and nauseous to beer, causing retchings. Bloody. Sour after wheat bread. Sourish, saltish. Flat, to everything; flat, metallic in morning. Meat, especially, has no taste. Food seems tasteless and unsalted, < evenings.

Throat.—*Inflammatory redness in back part* (Arg. m.). Inflammation terminated by a livid border around buccal cavity. Mucus choking him till he swallows it; deep-seated mucus; saltish mucus after dinner; *thick, viscid M.*, < *evening and morning on waking*, increasing the soreness of throat, expectorated in little lumps with difficulty (Arg. m.). Stitches on empty swallowing; *shooting here and there, in evening, and sometimes on swallowing something pointed seems to stick in the throat* (Nit. ac.). Pressure in, with internal heat of hands; P. *as from a lump, with soreness, rough voice and dry throat.* Constrictive pain in evening, with much mucus in mouth. Spasmodically drawing pain in one side and in ear, nights, < deglutition. Pressive and tensive pain in r. inner side, as far as ear. Drawing and tensive pain in r. side, < moving tongue. *Soreness after difficult clearing; S. on swallowing;* aching, during empty swallowing in evening (caused by a swelling); burning, in evening when swallowing and afterwards.

Scraping high up; griping; as if he had swallowed pepper. *Rawness and roughness* in evening, causing cough. Roughness in morning on waking, with oppression of chest and sneezing; R., with scraping, obliging cough; *causing hawking, evening and night, with accumulation of mucus.* Burning in evening; like heartburn, with roughness. Dryness; *at night;* **in evening, inducing frequent clearing** (Bar. c., Zinc.), *with scraping;* D., with much mucus in mouth. *Tickling causing cough.* Taste sour after milk-soup in evening, then bitter eructations; sudden sourish in forenoon; sweet in morning, with vertigo, then expectoration of mucus mixed with blood. Amelioration of symptoms from warm food and drink.

Tonsils.—Swelling. Stitches in r. in morning. Aching in l. when swallowing and afterwards. Swallowing impeded at night, as from spasmodic constriction.

Œsophagus.—*Pain as if a part were contracted or compressed,* in middle of chest, < during deglutition (Zinc.), with oppression of chest alternating with palpitation, < after eating. *Constricted feeling every time he swallows food.* Contraction in morning on waking, with want of action.

Clinical.—The characteristic sore throat, especially in speakers, with great dryness of the mucous membrane, which is inflamed, not pale; with the sore throat the uvula may be relaxed and cause a persistent tickling cough, with constant inclination to clear the throat, but almost always with dryness, sometimes with a sharp splintery feeling in the throat; dryness, irritability and relaxation seem to be the characteristic indications for this drug.

Stomach.—Appetite. He is almost always hungry. Rabid. Strong for vegetables, fruit and soft food. Hungry, but eats nothing with relish. Diminished A.; with fulness in abdomen. *No appetite and no taste to food. Aversion to meat*; even to vomiting. Aversion to smoking. Smoking does not agree with him. Thirst; all day; at dinner.

Eructations; after supper; E. while eating, with pressive pain in chest. Acrid, corroding. Bitter in evening after potatoes, with loathing, which makes him shiver; in evening after milk-soup. Tasting of milk-soup from supper till he lay down. Rancid after breakfast soup; R. < after dinner; leaving a burning. Sweetish, and sweetish mucous expectoration mornings. *Sour;* forenoon; evening in bed; of liquid; of mucus, < after soup for breakfast, then burning in throat like heartburn: acidity rises into mouth in forenoon, with heat in mouth. Waterbrash. Hiccough; after eating, at noon and in evening; H. after dinner.

Nausea; morning; morning on waking, with stickings over eyes, pain in kidneys during motion, and lassitude; in morning on waking, with physical depression as if sleep had not recruited her, and with quick feverish pulse and internal heat; at 4 P.M.; at 4 P.M. with vertigo; from evening till next forenoon, with vertigo, palpitation and anxiety; when standing; after supper, with tremor; after supper, with weariness; when talking or entering room after a walk in open air, with dread; with good appetite; with stitches in brain; with chilliness; after eructation of air, with chilliness which rises from feet into abdomen; arresting the breath at night; *faint-like in morning,* > wheat bread, *together with vertigo;* fainting in morning, > after breakfast.

Retching; in throat in morning. **Vomiting, with the dry hacking cough;** V. of phlegm and water.

Stitches in pit and chest, extending upward; S. in stomach and chest coming out at shoulder, after dinner till evening, with short breath and anguish. Tearing from pit down into abdomen, a sore pain as if everything would be torn out. Cutting in region in afternoon, with pain on touch. Griping in pit in evening in bed. Pinching in afternoon, Pain; in evening, with sensitiveness to pressure; after dinner, with bloated feeling, pain on external touch, empty eructations and fermentations or loud rumbling and rollings in abdomen; after potatoes, with nausea, then colic; drawing; drawing, extending into pharynx, with difficult breathing. Pressure in pit, < walking; in pit, with crawling as from a worm; at pit and from thence oppression of chest, preventing walking; in stomach and upper abdomen in afternoon, with soreness transversely across them; as from a stone, in evening, after milk-soup, > eructations.

Oppression towards noon or evening; upon eating; after potatoes in morning, extending to throat, > eructations. Soreness in pit during cough; ulcerative S. in pit morning on turning in bed. Twisting and constriction extending into chest and throat, with difficult breathing. Gnawing in region after dinner. Empty feeling without much appetite. Fulness; in evening, > emission of flatus. Drawing after dinner, causing tension in whole body and weakness. Contractions; > eructations. *Burning;* after supper; after drinking water; heat in forenoon, rising into head. Coldness as after cold water in evening, and in forenoon, > afternoon.

Abdomen.—Distention; after dinner, > stool; during menses; after supper; after eating, with orgasm towards chest; with rumbling, empty eructations and soft stools; painful, at night, with retention of stool. Rumbling; after dinner, with rolling. Grumbling; after eating. Moving to and fro, with painless clutching. Loud emission of flatus; copious emission upon walking; bad smelling in night and after dinner; frequent desire to emit F.

Stitches.—Tearing mornings after rising. Cutting; as if she would have diarrhœa during stool before menses, with pinching, writhing and pressing, like labor-pains; transversely across when sitting bent; rising to abdomen like a twisting, with rumbling, then aching in chest from 4 to 11 P. M., arresting breath. Pinching; after every meal, at noon and in evening; evening in bed; ending in salivation; towards evening, with tearing and with chilliness in body, > warm cloths; at midnight, > towards morning, with rumbling; on waking, with tenesmus and faintness; after every cold that she takes or as soon as she goes into cold air; during menses, with weakness; with writhing; with heat in stomach; sudden, here and there in afternoon, passing to small of back, where it causes gnawing.

Pain; before menses; during menses; before or with diarrhœa; before a scanty, sometimes solid, sometimes soft stool; drawing; *flatulent;* as after a copious stool, which leaves behind a desire for stool. Bruised feeling; after diarrhœa, especially at the place where she had had an internal ulcer, > rubbing and laying the hand on it while the body was bent. Heaviness. Seems to hang down heavily in afternoon when walking. Tension of muscles from reaching high. Pulsation. Burning; with chills; sudden B. in afternoon. Cold feeling internally in afternoon. Seems inactive for want of peristaltic motion. Hernia protrudes; towards evening, becoming constricted in lumbar region, > sitting quietly, with pain obliging her to bend double and preventing walking.

Upper Abdomen.—Pain as before diarrhœa, then soft stools. After stool, ineffectual desire, and in sides, without tenesmus.

Hypochondria.—Stitches; in r. when standing, > by sitting; in l. in evening, extending to pit of stomach; alternately under l. lower ribs and in r. side of abdomen; as if in liver, on rising from stooping, with arrest of breath. Tearing in liver; from r. into hip in forenoon. Pain in liver when stooping, with sensitiveness; drawing in r. when sitting or walking. Feel pressed or screwed towards each other in forenoon; seemed pressed towards each other, with pain on touch. Burning in r. in afternoon, with stitches, as if cut into by a band.

Umbilicus.—Pinching around in evening; below, during breakfast, with distention of abdomen. Pressure inward in region in afternoon when standing, with stitches. Worrying around, as after a cold, in afternoon.

Sides.—Stitches in l.; *in region of ring, with tension as far as side of abdomen,* and at same time a tumor like a strangulated hernia may be felt; *from l. to middle of chest* with every inspiration, when stooping and afterwards when standing erect. Tearing on exertion, extending to thighs. Pinching in l., afternoon and night, extending to hypochondriac region and sternum, with tearing stitches. Aching in l. after eating. Pulsative pain near l. ring when sitting. Ulcerative pain in l., with nausea. Aching in l. after eating.

Hypogastrium.—Stitches in r. iliac region. Pinching in groins and lumbar region on ascending stairs, with stitches. Pressure in groins, towards sexual organs in evening; in r. ilium as if both sides were pressed together in a vise. Drawing pain in muscles over l. groin when dancing or walking fast. Cutting from forenoon till evening, with burning. An inguinal hernia protrudes violently.

Rectum.—Seems paralyzed. *Dried and constricted feeling during stool.* **Pressure and sense of excoriation after a small hard stool.** *Tenesmus during diarrhœa;* T. of both rectum and bladder after urinating; of rectum and bladder, better after an evacuation; ineffectual, also after dinner, also on waking. Much urging before stool. Bearing down during knotty and scanty stool. Itching, burning and stinging. Crawling as from worms.

Anus.—Varix decreases during night's rest; enlarges in evening and becomes moist and burning; moist and stinging; protruding, < walking, > night's rest. Stitches after a difficult stool. *Excoriated feeling after a stool attended with contraction of rectum and constriction of anus* (Sil.). Pressure; *during stool, with pain.* Burning during soft stools; after liquid stools; with sticking, and with stiffness in back. Itching, < scratching; *burning;* as if it would pulsate. Weak feeling of sphincter, with emission of flatus. Discharge of dark blood when walking.

Perineum.—Stitches. Bruised pain on touch. Pressure; during coition; at beginning of coition and during erections; on blowing nose. Inflamed feeling between scrotum and anus.

Stool.—Diarrhœa in evening; D. during menses; with colic; with tenesmus; frequent, after constipation. Liquid; with colic; first part liquid and expelled with a jerk, the last part appearing burned. Soft, at night. **Hard,** in balls (Mag. c.). *In shape of laurel berries, difficult, with cutting in anus as if too narrow, then a stream of blood, followed by soreness in anus and along rectum.* Bloody; *dropping of blood during stool.* Bloody mucus during and between stools. Bright-colored. **Scanty.** *Difficult.* Early. Frequent. Retained.

Clinical.—Constipation is the rule in cases requiring Alumina; the rectum is inactive, the stools are hard, often associated with soreness of the rectum and anus, which bleed readily, so that the hard stool is frequently followed by blood. It is particularly useful in the constipation of children, with dry and inflamed rectum and bleeding. Has to strain at stool in order to pass urine.

Urinary Organs.—Bladder. Spasmodic pain extending to chest, > breakfast. Pressure and drawing in region of, especially at neck. Tenesmus; after urinating, with tenesmus of rectum. *Weak feeling in B. and in genitals* in evening, so that he fears he shall wet the bed. Urging to urinate, with increased urine; U. in morning on waking, with difficult and tardy emission in a thin stream from the female urethra. Frequent micturition; at night; in evening, in small quantities; during menses, corroding genitals. Involuntary U. when pressing at stool. Seldom but copious U. (U. in a twisted stream). No urine.

Urethra.—Tearings and shootings, ascending through hypogastrium, when walking in open air. Drawing in morning on waking, with biting. Heat, > lying still. Burning before micturition; during micturition, < evening; B. after micturition. (No inconvenience in urinating after sitting a long time, but as soon as he moves about he feels a burning.) Itching, burning. Voluptuous itching, and between testicles. (Dry feeling in anterior portion, as if skin were insensible, < morning.)

Urine.—Decreased in morning, with cutting in anterior part of urethra, none in forenoon, but in afternoon frequent emissions of copious reddish urine, which becomes turbid during the night and deposits a sediment; little urine, with a sediment of red sand. Increased; I., pale, hot; pale, with a turbid sediment. White and turbid, as if chalk had been stirred into it. Deep yellow, soon depositing a large, loose cloud. Turbid at night.

Sexual Organs.—Pressure. *Tickling*, and on thighs. Smegma behind glans. Drawing pinching in penis as far as glans, when moving hand along penis. Drawing from glans through urethra. Compressed feeling in glans. Itching of glans. Formication of glans. Soreness of inner surface of prepuce. Violent erections; numerous E. in evening, during night in bed, and in afternoon when sitting; (priapisms during night). Contractive pain in r. spermatic cord, at the same time the r. testicle is drawn up, sore and painful. Itching of scrotum. Hardness of l. testicle, with pain on touch. Desire increased at first, then decreased; want of D.; indifference; lessened at first, with increased erections, then D. increased although erection is wanting. Emissions; at night; at night, with voluptuous dreams; during afternoon nap; jelly-like E. during coition.

Twitching stitches in l. side of pudendum, extending into chest. Itching in pudendum during leucorrhœa. Pain in l. side of vagina, like the ticking of a watch, with ulcerative throbbing. Leucorrhœa; after menses; *acrid* (Graph.); *acrid after menses* (Mag. c.), *with burning in genitals and more in rectum, these parts seemed inflamed and corroded, so that walking was difficult, > washing with cold water, L. flowed almost over her feet,* at same time discharge of blood resembling meat washings (N. ac.); like meat washings in afternoon and night; *profuse transparent L. only in daytime; like water or transparent mucus, stiffening the linen; yellow;* copious before menses, with tremor, lassitude and sensation as if everything would fall out of abdomen. Menses too profuse, with bloated abdomen; M. scanty; scanty and short; scanty and pale; too early, preceded by headache, which returned on the second day, and continued during the period, menses less copious than usual; too early, preceded by pain in abdomen, and accompanied by diarrhœa.

Clinical.—Involuntary emissions, particularly when straining at stool, have been found to be a valuable indication for the use of this drug in sexual weakness, especially in elderly people.

Gonorrhœal bubo, with a yellowish gonorrhœal discharge, with burning and itching along urethra, particularly at meatus.

Respiratory Organs.—*Irritation in larynx inducing cough.* Hoarseness; in morning; in afternoon, with rancidity of throat; > walking in open air. Voice lost suddenly, > afternoon and evening.

Cough; < *in morning,* with much expectoration; in afternoon sleep; in evening, from rawness and roughness in throat; from scraping and roughness in throat; from tickling in throat; irritation to C., with frequent spitting. *Dry at night;* **continual dry hacking, with vomiting and arrest of breathing** and sticking extending from l. side of abdomen to hypochondrium and pit of stomach; before midnight, with chilliness, then with dry heat; violent during the day; violent morning after rising, later expectoration; short; frequent short, forenoon and evening; suddenly coming and passing off quickly in morning. In short fits, with tearing shooting in r. temple and at vertex. Sudden violent, but short, in afternoon, by making an effort he expectorates a piece of phlegm mixed with blood. Fatiguing *C., with much expectoration,* < morning (Calc. c.).

Respiration difficult in forenoon. Dyspnœa at night on waking, with anxiety and sweat. Short R. in afternoon, with pressure on chest; S. at night when lying on back, > lying on side, with pressure on chest. Groaning; anxious; unconscious groaning and sighing. Sighing. Whistling and smothering in chest.

Chest.—Rattling, caused by mucus. Stitches in l. mamma at 9 A.M.; under sternum, < talking, with compression of chest; in upper part; high up in sides during exercise, > sitting or walking, with pressure and arrest of breath; here and there, sometimes, < by breathing, sometimes burning. Pinching in upper part in evening, when sitting. Cramp and oppression at night, having walked much the day before. Cutting and pressure internally when walking fast, > sitting.

Pain in forenoon, sometimes extending to back, < walking, then empty eructations; while eating; during and after cough, with paralytic pain extending through arms; here and there; high up on sides when sitting or walking; high up on sides during exercise, > sitting and lying; on sternum, < evening when walking; externally at lower part, > friction; intermittent, with shortness of breath and irritation to cough; spasmodic, in middle on swallowing food and drink; as if cut or sore, after dinner, till 10 P.M., > lying down, returning next morning during cough, with a weak feeling on chest, empty eructations and short breath. Oppression; when stooping, while writing; *oppressive pain, also at night,* < bending head forward; oppressive pain in middle, alternating with constriction and violent palpitation of heart, < after a meal. Contracted feeling, with apprehension. Constriction in afternoon when stooping, while sitting, > becoming erect; when stooping at work, > walking in open air; in a spot below r. side.

Soreness; in forenoon, caused by cough; in chest and pit of stomach, with fatiguing cough, lachrymation and tenacious expectoration; S. internally when moving or turning body. Excoriated feeling in lower part of sternum, extending to stomach, then hoarseness. Boring, sometimes in middle, sometimes in sides, < breathing, sometimes in evening, > becoming erect and walking. Heat in middle; in fore part when breathing. Burning in r. side in afternoon, with twinges and sticking in a r. false rib. Chilliness in interior of sternum. Dryness in both sides; oppressive, under sternum. Pulsations; in breast.

Heart and Pulse.—Anxiety about heart, > after rising; A. as if sweat would break out at 4 or 5 A.M., > rising. Constriction and violent palpitation alternating with oppressive pain in middle of chest, < after a meal. *Palpitation;* on waking; on waking before menses; with irregular beats, large and small ones being intermixed; anxious, with sudden heat and sweat. Pulse feverish morning on waking. Pulse increased.

Neck.—*Swelling of glands of l. side.* Stitches in glands of r. side, with drawing pressure in those of l. Stitches in nape; > friction; in r. side, > friction; externally on l. side, > pressure, with tearing in head and stitches in ears. Tearing, shooting and pinching, in nape as far as r. shoulder, with cough and sneezing. Pain in nape and head at night in bed, > morning on rising;

in nape on moving head. Drawing and pressure in glands of l. side. Painful drawing in muscles in forenoon. Tension in nape in afternoon. Stiffness, > motion; in neck and upper part of back, in morning, > motion, with drawing pain; so that she cannot turn the head to the left; in nape extending towards head. Feeling of swelling in sides, with stinging.

Back.—Stitches extending to ribs. Pressure before protrusion of a varix from rectum. *Bruised feeling;* and in limbs, as in fever and ague. Grumbling in back and sacrum after itching, crawling (stinging). Stiffness.

Scapulæ.—Stitches between and on, also arresting breathing; with cutting and with chilliness; gnawing. Tearing in l., also in arms, hands and legs, < evening. Painful tension between, in forenoon. Painful stiffness between, extending afterwards towards ribs and kidneys.

Intermittent stitches in middle.

Loins.—Tearing stitches in evening in bed; tearing stitches in r. extending to l. side of chest, through pit of stomach, when inspiring. Tearing over hips and on upper brim of pelvis. Tearing twitchings, < during motion. Gnawing, rising to between shoulders. Pain in evening, with vertigo, then urging to stool, during which pure blood was passed, with a paralyzed feeling in small of back; during motion, and in legs; when walking and in legs; P. after walking; < walking and stooping; in kidneys in morning, > afternoon; in kidneys, alternating with intoxicated feeling in head; *in lower vertebræ as if a hot iron were thrust through. Bruised feeling;* when walking, and in hips and muscles of calf; and in morning in coccyx on touch; over hips when walking; in kidney region, < stooping and turning, as if a hook were plunged into her. Pulsation after a stool.

Coccyx.—Painful twitches at point, in afternoon. Gnawing in evening, > stretching. Tearing in os innominatum.

Extremities.—Twitching; before falling asleep; in lower, especially in legs and feet, then disposition to turn arms and stretch them upward. Tearing in arms, hands, legs and l. scapula, < evening. *Pain as if squeezed narrower, with pressure in joints.* Sense of contraction in r. index and foot, as if tendons were too short, when he touches something with his finger he feels as if electrified. *Drawings.* Burning tension in dorsa of feet and hands, as from a swelling. Rigidity of hands and feet as if asleep on waking. The fourth and fifth fingers, the r. knee, and at last the heel, go to sleep after sitting. Cramplike sensation, like numbness, ascending the whole l. leg, during bodily labor, also in l. arm, with dizzy stupefaction of head, in interrupted paroxysms. Uneasiness at night. Paralytic weakness in morning, in paroxysms, with stupefaction of head.

Upper Extremities.—Axillæ, tearing; intermittent tearing in afternoon. Shoulder, sudden twitching or concussion in r.; stitches, and in axillæ and arms, also at night; tearing in; *sprained pain in joint,* < raising arm.

Arm.—Tearing. Paralytic pain, as from a bruise, sometimes across small of back, coming to r. upper and l. lower and *vice versa.* Tight feeling, as from a cold. Weariness; of one. Heaviness.

Upper arm.—Stitches in muscles of l. Tearing extending from back part of upper to scapula, when sneezing and coughing; extending to fingers, and from fingers and wrists to shoulders; (sticking) as if in bone, in forenoon, and in *elbow.* Pain in l. as if dislocated; drawing, in l. humerus. Burning (and tension), as from a glowing iron, and in fingers and l. elbow.

Elbow.—Sticking as if sprained, and in wrist. Tearing. Pain above point, < leaning on it, as from a pressure on upper arm. Boring in point.

Forearm.—Twitching of r. forearm and in lower joint of l. thumb. Tearing; apparently upon bone; T. as far as fingers. Drawing and tearing pain morning on waking. Painful drawing when at rest. Heaviness in forearm and hands, and her arms seem shorter. Asleep and pricking sensation in l.

Trembling of hands when writing. Veins of hands distended in afternoon and evening. R. hand is asleep on waking. Fingers. Swelling. Brittleness of nails. Tearing in and between fingers. Pain in middle, on motion; insufferable P. in bones, after itching around lowest joints; drawing P. in thumb and index; as if dislocated in r. index. *Gnawing beneath nails,* with crawling along arm as far as clavicle. Falling asleep of l. thumb in afternoon, then crawling.

Lower Extremities.—Heaviness and staggering *in evening. Slow tottering.* Staggering; > walking.

Thigh.—Stitches from l. hip to loins, repeated when breathing; when breathing. *Tearing in thighs and legs* when sitting and lying, < night; T. and sticking in hip-joint and just *above* knee, in paroxysms. Cutting transversely across r. natis in forenoon. Pain in r. hip-joint. Bruised feeling in l. hip in morning, < pressure. *Tension almost like a cramp in thighs and legs,* (Nat. m.), *intermittent, extending downward. Nates fall asleep when sitting.*

Knee.—*Trembling.* Cracking in r. when walking. Stitches in l. only when walking, > walking in open air; in r. in evening, with tearing. *Tearing* (Rhus t.); *coming out at toes,* in afternoon, > walking, with sensation of swelling; in r.; *in patella;* on inside of l. in evening; sticking, in evening before sleep. Pain in patella on pressure or on bending knee; in bend of l., < stepping; in bend of l. when walking after rising from a seat; in bend at night, extending to heel; drawing in bend on ascending stairs; twitching inward at patella. Boring in r. Appeared to be longer during the pain. Falling asleep of r. after sitting.

Leg.—Stitches in r. tibia in evening in bed; cramplike, in r. in afternoon nap when sitting, and after waking, with numbness. Tearing; in calves. Pain during motion, and in loins; after a walk, and in loins; tensive, at inside of calves when walking. Bruised feeling in r. tibia, < during motion. Gnawing. Cramp in calves on crossing feet or on stepping on toes; *frequent in calves;* in calves as if tendons were too short, after rising from a seat, > walking. Gastrocnemii muscles appear too short and tense when walking (Sil.). Tension and burning on external surface of r. calf in evening. Drawing; painless down calves. Pulsation in l. calf in morning. Uneasiness several evenings at 7 P.M. *Weariness;* **when sitting;** especially in middle of tibiæ, with bruised feeling when standing and feeling as if she would sink down, < evening. *Heaviness.*

Malleolus.—Tearing, and in feet. Tearing drawings from externus up leg.

Foot.—Stitches in soles, with tickling; burning S. in

r. sole, evening and morning, > rubbing; *smarting*, in *corns*. Tearing in each tendo-achillis in evening. Pains in corns; drawing, in tendo-achillis when at rest; *in sole as if soft and swollen when stepping on it* (Zinc.). Sensitiveness of r. sole. Compression in l. heel from both sides. Tension on sole in forenoon. Weakness in afternoon. *Heaviness, with lassitude of legs;* heaviness, with tearing. *Numbness of heel on stepping.* Falling asleep of r., with crawling in it.

Toe.—Cutting in r. great, in morning when walking.

Skin.—Swelling (soft, red) of arm and violent stitches in it. Fine eruption on inside of r. thigh, with itching. Itching rash without redness, on arms and legs, exuding watery blood when scratched. Roughness of face, especially of forehead. Herpes between toes. Boil on nose; one after another on l. cheek; suppurating on r. hip. Small red elevations, with a pointed vesicle in middle, across shoulders, burning only in the evening. Vesicles on r. ear; on r. half of chest and on throat, with burning pain, and with heat in face and chills in rest of body; V. on r. side of neck.

Pimples on forehead; l. cheek; chin; neck; back; itching, on forehead, r. side of nose and l. angle of mouth, running together on pressure; hard, itching, under skin of neck and chest; red, rough on r. cheek; painful to touch on r. cheek; on l. lower eyelid, with stinging; on r. side of nose, with burning and stinging.

Stinging here and there, < evenings; in almost cured ulcer in sole when stepping upon it in the room after walking in open air. Soreness and inflammation of small injuries. Aching pain in hard skin of feet, with sensitiveness. *Tension of face, even around eyes, as if the white of an egg had dried on it* (Graph.), after dinner when walking in open air. Tickling of soles; of sexual organs and thighs.

Formication in r. side of face, with stinging in hollow of ear and tearing in r. knee; on glans; l. thumb; calves after supper; in big toe as if frozen; on r. fingers in evening, with burning stinging; itching, on r. side of lower jaw; on l. clavicle (and over r. half of chest, with biting itching), the spot burns on scratching, and burning vesicles appear.

Itching in various parts, < evenings, on being heated, generally > scratching. Itching, with gnawing; with burning after scratching. Burning itching. Crawling (and stinging) itching in whole back and in sacrum. Stinging itching in back and side of abdomen.

Clinical.—General dryness of the skin is marked in patients requiring this drug. Intolerable itching, forcing scratching until the skin bleeds, on getting warm in bed, has been found associated with the characteristic constipation.

Sleep.—Yawning; morning on rising; before dinner, without drowsiness. **Sleepiness**; in morning; in evening, even when standing; > open air; irresistible S. in forenoon. Falls asleep early. Too sound. Deep towards morning, with dreams which fatigue the head.

Sleeplessness before midnight, also on account of heaviness of arms. Falls asleep late on account of images crowding on his fancy; falls asleep late and sleeps longer next morning. Restless sleep before midnight, with weeping and grief; restless sleep before menses, with many dreams, and on waking she has orgasm, heat in face, headache and palpitation; with anxiety and heat and with twitchings in limbs and startings before sleep. Starting in sleep before midnight. Snoring in afternoon nap. Rising from bed without being aware of it and going anxiously from one room to another, rubbing his firmly-closed eyes. Speaking loud, laughing and weeping in sleep. Sobbing and groaning in sleep. *Frequent waking.* Anxious waking; from dreams.

Dreams.—*Anxious;* towards morning; after midnight. *Confused. Nightmare.*

Fever.—Chilliness; in forenoon, with lassitude, and in afternoon shaking chilliness in back; from 4 A.M. till evening, with contraction of stomach, > empty eructations, then four liquid stools, with constant chilliness; from 7 to 8 P.M.; evening during stool; every other day towards evening, with want of appetite, sleeplessness and tossing about the bed; in evening, with headache; in evening, < motion, with flushes of heat in face; at 5 P.M., especially in back and feet, then sweat; C. before midnight, with dry cough, then dry heat with the cough; all night, with uneasy sleep; in open air; during stool; with headache and weariness; with eructations, bitter taste, salivation, weakness and headache as if it would burst, especially in vertex, and vertigo.

Cold shiverings and sweat on every motion after walking in open air, with chilliness of head, afterwards when going to sleep heat of head, hands and feet. Chilliness followed by heat of body and sweat of face. Frequent C. during the day, with feeling in limbs as if he had caught cold, then heat of face in evening. C. alternating with warmth, in evening, face hot, with chills and shivering in rest of body. Creeping C., 4 to 6 P.M., with pulsating pain in forehead and occiput, > pressure.

Internal C., with external heat, especially of cheeks; internal C., with hot hands and hot lobules of ears; internal C., with hot cheeks and cold hands; *internal*, with stretching and bending of limbs, < *after warm drinks.* Chilliness in hands; with hot cheeks; in feet rising into abdomen, with nausea; in feet, with heat in head, and chilliness in whole body. Sensitive to cold air, especially in feet.

Heat; towards evening, especially in feet, then shivering, all without thirst; H. before midnight; *H.* at night, *with anxiety* and sweat; H. in bed; at night in bed, then sweat; H. of whole body after eating, with sweat on face. Sensation when sitting as after violent heat.

Dry heat in afternoon sleep. External heat. Flushing H.; with weakness, obtuseness and anxiety; of face. Internal; morning on waking; in forehead, with dulness of mind; I. in hands. Running over whole body during bodily effort, then chills, with burning in abdomen. Sudden, with sweat and anxious palpitation. Itching burning of anterior border of r. ear.

Heat in head in morning; beginning in head, in evening; in head after dinner. Pleasant warmth in r. side of face in afternoon. Burning in superior angle of l. scapula, > friction. Heat of r. arm, internally and externally.

Sweat after 6 A.M. in bed; at night on waking, with anxiety and dyspnœa; on every motion, then cold shivers.

Ambra.

Ambergris seems to be a morbid product of whales; it floats on the sea and is tossed occasionally upon the shore. A trituration is prepared for use. (It dissolves in alcohol.)

General Action.—Nervous phenomena predominate, convulsive cough, eructations, etc. It has been used for hysterical complaints for a long time.

Relations.—Mosch., Phos., Zinc., Camph., Agar., Chin. s.

Generalities.—Pulsation like the ticking of a watch. Uneasiness; by day; in blood when walking in open air, with rapid circulation and weakness. Inclination to stretch. *Weakness;* morning in bed, also especially in upper part of body, with confusion in head, sensation as if eyes had been tightly closed, nausea in pit of stomach and disinclination to rise; at midnight on waking, with nausea, pressure in pit of stomach and in abdomen, violent erections without voluptuous sensation, dryness in mouth and insensibility of surface of body; on waking, with dryness of mouth and pressure in upper abdomen, which is > lying on abdomen, then tearing in small of back, which is > by lying on back; > walking; sudden in morning in a hot room, with cold sweat on hands and forehead; with giving way of knees; with pain in all limbs; with heaviness. Amelioration while walking in open air, but symptoms return while sitting.

Clinical.—Useful for persons who are debilitated either by age or overwork, who are anæmic, sleepless, have twitching of the muscles.

Mind.—Memory bad, with weakness of thought, so that he has to read everything three or four times and then does not seize the meaning. Stupid feeling. Distorted images, grimaces, diabolical faces crowd upon his fancy and he cannot get rid of them. Lewd fancies, even when dreaming, the mind and sexual organs, however, are but little excited by them. Excitement; and loquacity, with fatigue from talking, inability to sleep at night, headache as from a load, oppression, necessity to sit up in bed, anguish and general sweat. Hurry in mental occupations. Uneasiness; with oppression of chest. *Despair. Anguish in evening;* A., with tremor. Anxiety; after eating. Sadness; with sinking about heart. Easily aroused to indignation. Impatience. Irritation from talking, with general trembling, especially in lower limbs, and necessity to be alone to rest. Whining, then peevish and quarrelsome. Indifference to joy or grief, but more depressed than composed. Dreamy condition. Constant alternation of depression of spirits with vehemence of temper.

Head.—Lancinations on exertion and at every step, > lying, with cutting. Tearing through. Aching; at night on waking, > rising; when blowing nose; > walking in open air; especially over and on top of head, with tearing; with stitches; as if a cold would come on; external, and in neck and nape, as from a strain in lifting, with pain on touch. Aching confusion after eating, < during motion; compressing confusion. Drawings and tearings to and fro. Empty feeling every morning, as if she had revelled all night. Stupefying tension. (Twitching in.) Congestion of blood; rush of blood caused by music. *Vertigo; afternoon;* forenoon and afternoon on walking in open air; in afternoon, *with feeling of weakness in stomach. Weakness, with vertigo;* W., with chilliness of head.

Forehead.—Tearing, as far as upper part of face. Aching; in l. eminence; over eyes, always after midnight till 7 or 8 o'clock, with nausea; A., with apprehension of becoming insane; paroxysmal, over nose, becoming a tearing and leaving behind confusion of occiput. Pressure downward, and in vertex, every other day, beginning in morning, < afternoon, with heat in head, burning in eyes and paleness of face. Feeling as when a cold is about to break out, and in eyes.

Temples.—Stitch over l. Tearing in l. as high as vertex, and in r. frontal eminence and *behind l. ear.* Compressing headache starting from T. Roaring around T.

Vertex.—*Tearing and apparently in whole upper part of brain,* with paleness of face and coldness of l. hand. Aching. Painless pressure on, in evening, with heaviness of head.

Occiput.—Stitches ascending towards, in evening. Tearing, ascending to vertex and forehead; to forehead in evening in bed, after having fallen asleep; in l. towards nape and behind ear. Aching, and in nape; in a spot. *Confusion.* Uneasiness after midnight.

Scalp.—*Hair falls out.* Sore pain on r. side on touching hair.

Eyes.—Distended veins in white. Tearing around l. after eating, then around r.; T. in short jerks in and around r. *Pain as if they had been too firmly closed, < morning.* Pressure in, with difficult opening; P. upon as if they were deep in orbits, with tearing headache, extending downward from forehead or from ear through occiput. Burning pain in r. Biting; with pressure as from dust; B., with lachrymation. Burning in lids. *Itching of lids* as if a stye would form. Pressure on l. brow. Vision dim.

Ears.—Tearing in r.; T. in lobule and *behind* it. Itching and tickling in. Crawling in. Crepitation and creaking in l. as when winding a watch. *Roaring and whistling* in afternoon. *Deafness in one. Hearing decreases every day.*

Nose.—Spasm of r. wing, towards malar bone. Tingling as if one would sneeze. Dryness; with irritation as if one would sneeze. Obstruction, with internal sore feeling. Sneezing; with dry nose. Coryza, with cough and expectoration of white mucus; dry C. **Bleeding,** < *in morning; dried blood in nose.*

Face.—Pale. Red spot on cheek. *Jaundice-colored.* Trembling of muscles. Twitchings in evening in bed. Painful swelling of cheek on upper jaw, with throbbing in gums. Tearing in upper part, especially near r. wing of nose. Tension in cheek as from swelling. Stitches in jaws. Pain as if jaws were screwed together or asunder. Spasm of lower lip, with sensation as if pressed against gums and torn away. Pain in corners of lips as if cracked.

Mouth.—Teeth. Aching in hollow T. in evening; more lancinating than tearing, in a hollow T. after dinner; in a hollow T. as if a nerve were touched, < in open air; *drawing, sometimes in r., sometimes in l.;* drawing, in one or another, < warmth, > cold and after eating, with swelling of inner side of gums; burrowing, under l. lower molars, in evening in bed. Drawing in an incisor as if air rushed in, causing a stitch; pinching, in r. upper molars. Gums bleed; r. lower; G. painful and swollen.

Tongue.—Coated gray-yellow. Lumps under T., which feel excoriated. Rheumatic pain posteriorly when not swallowing, and in pharynx. Numb and dry feeling in morning on waking, and in mouth and lips.

Vesicles in mouth, paining as if burnt. Tearing in palate as far as into l. ear. Scraping on palate. Smarting in mouth, with excoriated feeling and pain which prevented swallowing anything solid. Dry mouth in morning on waking, without thirst. Contracted feeling in salivary glands when eating, especially the first mouthfuls. Salivation. *Fetor;* early after waking. Sourish taste after milk. (Bitter taste early when waking.)

Throat.—Pain in a submaxillary gland, which seemed swollen. *Secretion of mucus, with roughness and scraping; grayish M. which is difficult to hawk up, with scraping;* hawking up mucus in morning. Tearing; upper back part; in back part during dinner, and on l. side of palate. (Soreness *after a draft, stitches shooting from neck into r. ear,* pain < moving tongue); (S. not when swallowing food but during empty swallowing and on external pressure, with tension of cervical glands as if swollen); in a **spot** when coughing; as if something impeded swallowing. Sensation as if something lodged; as if food lodged in pit, after eating. *Raw sensation in region of velum pendulum palati.* Scraping; after cough; S. as in a cold. Biting in back part; between acts of swallowing. *Tickling* causing cough. *Itching* when coughing, and in thyroid gland. Dryness in morning.

Stomach.—Eructation at night; **frequent E., with violent convulsive cough;** *empty; sour;* bitter; insipid, in afternoon; violent, after dinner. Hiccough from smoking tobacco. Nausea; always after midnight till 7 or 8 o'clock, with pain over eyes; (after breakfast); (clawing). Retching and vomiting can hardly be avoided when hawking up phlegm. Spasm. *Spoiled sensation every evening and eructations of acrid substances as high as larynx, like heartburn.* Stitches in region, with pressure. Pressure in epigastrium; > walking in open air, returning when sitting; in epigastrium, with cold hands and feet; in region of stomach, with tension. Burning; when walking in open air, with suppressed eructations; in region and higher up. (Weakness about pit after every evacuation.)

Abdomen.—Distention; after midnight; after eating or drinking, with tension. Fermentation at night; F., with rumbling. Flatus emitted at night. Spasms. Twitchings of muscles evening. Cutting mornings, with soft stools; C. in evening; in bed after midnight, with sweat; with soft stool. Pinching, then cutting in epigastrium, > eructations. Pain; then emission of flatus; changing to pinching; from incarcerated flatus, < l. side. Compressed feeling; morning. Excitement as if menses would come on. **Cold internally** (Camph., Phos.). (Burning.) Tenesmus after stool.

Aching in side below pit of stomach when coughing. Pressure below pit of stomach, > eructation, with burning; P. below pit of stomach and in hypogastrium, from time to time and at night. Stitches around umbilicus when moving abdomen, < retracting abdomen. Pressure in umbilical region when coughing; P. in umbilical region, > eructations, with heartburn. *Coldness of one side. Aching in region of liver; > touch.*

Hypogastrium.—Flatulent distention after midnight, with pressure downward. Stitches when retracting abdomen and on pressure; S. over hips. Pinching in r.; P. morning in bed, > rising, renewed by lying down, especially lying on back, with fermentation and gurgling, especially in epigastrium; P., < r. side, after ineffectual urging. Pressure; *deep in after stool;* over r. hip; sharp, over r. hip, or a dull stitch.

Rectum.—Tenesmus. *Frequent ineffectual urging to stool, with anxiety and* **intolerance of the presence of people.** Tickling. (Drawing.) Itching and biting, > rubbing. Stitches in anus. *Itching in anus.*

Stool.—Soft, copious, light-brown. Much blood, with a soft stool. *Constipation.* Frequent. Scanty.

Urinary Organs.—Pain in bladder and rectum at the same time. Urging to urinate early after rising, so that often he cannot retain the urine. Feeling in urethra as if a few drops passed out. Burning in orifice of U. and in anus. (Twitchings in U.)

Urine copious; *at night;* < morning, then dull pain in kidney region. Scanty; with reddish sediment. Brown; *dark B. and turbid during emission. Turbid even during emission,* yellow-brown, forming a **brown sediment,** while the clear urine above it was yellow. Bloody. Reddish cloud. Wheyey. Of penetrating odor after standing.

Sexual Organs.—Tearing in glans. Pain in glans as from ulceration. Violent erections early on waking, without desire, the parts being externally numb, after the erection subsides tingling-tearing in fore part of urethra. Twitching in testicles. Burning internally in region of vesiculæ seminales. Voluptuously delightful feeling internally without external irritation.

Female.—Burning, < after a walk and after a hard stool, with discharge of a little blood. **Itching of pudendum;** *with soreness and swelling.* Burning, biting, tickling and itching on vulva when urinating, and in urethra. (Profuse leucorrhœa at night); (of thick mucus, increasing from day to day, with a stitch in vagina before each discharge). (Mucus in bluish-white clots from vagina.) Hæmorrhage from uterus. *Menses too early.*

Respiratory Organs.—Burning and itching titillation from larynx down to abdomen. Hoarse, rough voice, with tenacious mucus in throat; rough, deep voice alternating with thick mucus in larynx, which he easily throws up when clearing throat or by a slight cough. Cough; *every evening with pain under l. ribs as if something were torn loose; only at night,* from irritation in throat; from tickling in throat; **violent, convulsive, with frequent eructations** *and hoarseness; a kind of whooping; deep, dry,* with salivation, then scraping in throat. *Salt expectoration when coughing.*

Clinical.—Nervous spasmodic cough, with frequent eructations, distress about the heart, etc. These coughs are of a nervous kind, paroxysmal, cough especially on waking in the morning, ending with violent eructations; the chest becomes very sore to external touch; the cough is aggravated by the presence of people; it may be hollow and barking, but the eructations are particularly characteristic.

Chest.—*Wheezing.* Stitch extending to back; dull S. in r., interrupting respiration. *Tearing in l.* Pressure on upper part; below (in ?) l. half; deep in r. half during strong expiration; paroxysmal, in upper part. Bruised pain over pit of stomach, > eructations; B. pain in last true r. rib, more towards back. Rheumatic pain below r. arm. Burning pain near one r. rib, < pressure, then in l. chest. Burning; in external parts. *Raw feeling.* Oppression (Phos.); in chest and back, between scapulæ, > after eating; with uneasiness. Tension. Tightness so that she cannot breathe deeply nor yawn fully.

Heart.—Pressure in præcordial region. Anxiety,

even to arrest of breathing, with heat. Palpitation; when walking in open air, with pale face; *with pressure in chest as from a lump lodged there, or as if chest were obstructed* (Phos.).

Neck.—Drawing ache in nape. Pressive drawing ascending from nape and extending through head towards forehead, considerable pressure remaining, especially in occiput.

Back.—Pain as if intestines were compressed, with heaviness in back as if not able to right himself. Oppression extending to chest. Weight extending from spinal marrow to abdomen, with sprained sensation. Stitches in l. scapula. Rheumatic pain on r. scapula; in r. side of back. Stitches in loins when sitting; in loins, < motion. Pressure in lower part of loins. Painful tension in muscles of loins.

Extremities.—Twitching; at night, with coldness of body. Uneasiness like a formication, only by day, with anguish.

Upper Extremities.—Shoulder, dull stitch on r.; tearing; *tearing in l. joint*; drawing in evening, *with a sprained and paralyzed feeling.* Arms, twitching; tearing in r. in morning; sense of clucking. Falling asleep of arms when lying on them; l. at rest during the day; r. at night, with a numb feeling. (Paralysis of r. upper arm.) Tearing in r. elbow; on r.; r. elbow and forearm. Drawing aching in r. forearm as far as elbow.

Hands.—Cramp. Stinging as from fleas, and in fingers. Tearing in interior of middle of r. Asleep at night. Paralysis.

Fingers.—Drawn inward in evening. Paroxysmal trembling of thumb in evening. Stitches at times in r. index, at times in r. thumb. Tearing in r. index; in lowest joint of l. index; under nail of r. middle; in tip of r. little; in two last, in evening before sleep; in muscles of thumb. Lancinating pain in tip of l. thumb, and when touched lightly feeling as of a splinter under nail, > hard pressure. Rheumatic pain in lowest joint of thumb, through metacarpal bone to wrist. *Drawing in F.* and thumb. Weakness at night. (Stiffness in lowest joints in evening, < after not exercising them, with swelling of lowest joint of thumb and pain on bending it.)

Lower Extremities.—Stretching and relaxation. *Cramp, and almost every night cramp in calves. Tearing in l. in morning;* rheumatic in r. *Heaviness.* Sensation as if asleep, step not firm. Tearing in r. natis; l. hip, then r.; T. in front of thigh, just below l. hip; clucking T. under l. natis. Sprained pain above knee, < after sitting. Tension in thigh as if tendons were too short, < when walking.

Tearing on r. knee. Drawing in knees and ankles. Soreness of bend of knee, < evening. Stiffness in bend of knee in morning. Paralysis of knee. Swelling of legs, especially feet. Tearing in upper part of l. tibia; in lower part of l. leg; intermittent, on l. calf. Painful spots on shins. Sense of grumbling in calves and feet. Weakness of legs in morning. Swelling of l. inner malleolus, with pain only on walking, > continued walking. Tearing in ankles.

Foot.—Stitches in l.; in heel. Tearing in external border of l.; in l., with stitches. Pain in joint of l. when walking; in heel when walking; in corns, with a sore feeling; arthritic in joints. Weakness, with insensibility. Tingling, with numbness, after rising he felt faint, it became dark before his eyes, had to vomit bile and lie down again. Tension in l. at noon. Stiffness.

Toes.—Stitch in ball of big. Tearing in l. middle. Arthritic pain in ball of big.

Skin.—Blueness of leg from distended veins during menses, with aching. Wrinkling on finger-tips in morning. Tetter reproduced; itching T. between thumb and index. Itch eruption reproduced, with much itching. Pimples on face; in whiskers, with itching; red P. on forehead close to hair, with soreness on touch; painful P. on forehead; itching P. above male parts of generation.

Soreness of a wart on finger. Itching nearly all over, even on abdomen; of glans; in palms; finger-tips; knees; ankles; *inside of sole;* toes; I. above malleoli in evening when lying down, and after rubbing a sore and bruised feeling; gnawing and tingling, on face. Tickling in tip of great toe; itching T. around eyes. Formication in tip of finger as if asleep, > pressure. Insensibility as far as knee early on waking, the hands have an indistinct sensation, the skin seems asleep.

Sleep.—Sleepiness by day. Sleeplessness; before midnight; at night, without knowing the cause; S. nights with slumber early in morning full of fantasies.

Falls asleep late, afterwards uneasy sleep, owing to pressure in epigastrium, < r. side; falls asleep late, afterwards has anxious dreams as if he were abused and too weak to defend himself, on waking he is weak in upper part of body, with pinching pressure under pit of stomach and nausea, then symptoms reappear when lying down and falling asleep again and are then accompanied by pressure in l. side of abdomen, the symptoms > when wide awake, sitting up and moving about, ending with emission of flatus, fermentation in abdomen and eructation. Starts in fright when falling asleep in evening, imagines the room is too light and jumps out of bed with anguish. *Uneasy sleep at night;* on account of coldness of body and twitchings in limbs; *anxious dreams,* with talking and desire to drink. Sleeps at night on his back with bent knees, the occiput being supported by both hands, and has vivid dreams.

Waking early, then frequently interrupted but deep sleep. Waking frequently, and about 2 A. M. uneasiness in whole body, especially in occiput. Many dreams. *Vexing,* anxious *D.*, with talking. Vivid uneasy D. as soon as he falls asleep. D. full of work.

Fever.—Chilliness in forenoon, > dinner, with weariness and sleepiness; C. in evening; C. after diarrhœa, with weariness and headache; C. before dinner. Internal C. at night. (Coldness of skin over whole body, except face, neck and genital organs.) Cold hands; in evening. Cold feet. Coldness of r. leg, especially knee; of legs, more internally than externally. Heat; every quarter of an hour; two evenings from 7 to 8. Burning places in skin. Heat in head; *in face in flushes;* hot lips. Burning in l. scapula; B. of soles. Sweat all day; every morning, especially on affected side; S. at night; in bed after midnight, with cutting colic; copious at night; copious when walking, especially on abdomen and thighs; strong-smelling, after midnight many nights.

Ammoniacum.

Gum Ammoniac is obtained from Dorema Ammoniacum, Don, natural order Umbelliferæ. For use the gum (inspissated juice) is first triturated.

In general Ammoniac acts on all the mucous membranes, at first causing diminished then increased secretions (see eye, throat, bowels and bronchi). The pains developed by the provings are noteworthy, especially violent in the lower extremities; notice the pains referred to the cæcal region; the disturbance of vision, etc. It was formerly used largely as an expectorant in chronic bronchitis and asthma.

Allies.—Asap., Senega, Ammon mur., *Ferrum.*

Generalities.—Stitches in various parts in evening, on l. great toe, l. knee and in chest. Fermentation here and there. Pulsation in whole body, with restlessness, delaying sleep, though he had drunk less beer than usual. Sluggishness on rising, with drowsiness, depression of spirits, physical heaviness and weariness. Weariness on least motion; weariness, with bruised feeling in limbs.

Mind.—Melancholy; and discomfort. Ill humor; with uneasiness. Disinclination for anything. Incapacity for mental exertion.

Head.—Stitches through. Aching; at night, preventing sleep; in whole head at noon, especially in supraorbital region and occiput. Confusion in afternoon; in evening; with heaviness and aching, and with drowsiness; with sleepiness, weariness of limbs and pain in crural nerve. Heaviness. Vertigo while reading, passing into headache, which lasted into the night.

Forehead, aching; < all day till evening; r. half; and over eyes; and over eyes, stronger in temporal region, > after dinner; with confusion of head and drowsiness. Confusion in sinciput, with weakness of sight and heaviness in loins. Stitching in l. temple. Tearing in l. side of head. Fuzzy sensation at occiput. Pustules where hair ceased. Itching vesicles on l. occiput where the hair ceased and a vesicle in beard in r. side of face. Stitches as from a knife in middle of scalp. Itching; more in vertex and below; on l. side of occiput where hair ceased; on occiput where hair ceased, with pustules under the hair. Prickling when scratched.

Eyes.—Drawing stitching. Tension and dull stitching, < stooping. Dry feeling, with sensation of a foreign body between l. upper lid and ball. Weariness after reading. Aching in upper part of ball. Prickling in upper half of ball. Purulent matter in inner canthi, < r., morning on waking. Stitches in r. lower lid, < moving lids, touching them or stooping; throbbing pricking in l. upper, followed by pressure. Pains in lower had disappeared and only a hard pellicle could be felt in r. Feeling as if a gland were swollen under lid.

Vision.—Beams of light and sparks proceeding from eyes and a burning light surrounded by brilliant colored rings. *Dim, almost lost, in evening,* with stars and fiery points moving before eyes; dim in evening, < morning after rising, with warmth in eyes; as through a thick mist or cloud of dust in evening. Of a waving cloud of dust. Of floating dust before eyes (which were heavy from sleep), with pressure upon orbital region. Daylight hurts eyes. Cannot read without straining eyes.

Ears.—Stitches in r.; at noon. Deep-seated tearings in r. external auditory passage. Humming. Clinking in l. at 10 P.M. when scratching occiput.

Nose.—Mouth and throat dry on waking. Profuse mucous discharge from nose. Frequent sneezing.

Face.—Countenance changed and she became pale. Drawing in l. zygoma late in evening, extending to temples. Lips dry and burning.

Mouth.—Short rheumatic stitches in l. eye-tooth. Dull stitching jerking pains in two l. lower incisors at 7 o'clock. Yellowish coat on tongue; with bitter taste. Dry roughness in tip of tongue and in hard palate; in posterior part of hard palate, with pressure in pit of stomach. Dryness of mouth and oppression of chest, < morning. Taste clayey; flat, somewhat sweetish, in morning; bitter; no taste in fore part of tongue, but nauseating, bitter in pharynx, > after eating.

Throat.—Sticking from region of r. submaxillary glands into mouth. Feeling of something sticking deep in throat, necessitating swallowing. Scraping and burning in throat and œsophagus. Roughness; and dryness. Fulness extending up into throat at 10 A.M.; fulness in throat and gullet, almost inducing nausea. Peculiar sensation, causing cough, > after eating. Sensation after swallowing as from a dry cough. Scraping in œsophagus.

Stomach.—Eructations; of resinous odor; of resinous bitter taste; violent. Nausea. Pressure; after supper; in pit, with tension; in pit, alternating with pressure and heaviness in pubic region. Burning in pit; with pressure.

Abdomen.—Rumbling after 1 P.M.; rumbling, with confusion in sinciput; rumbling, then soft stool, with much flatus. Flatus copious at night; copious sour in morning; strong smelling. Cutting. Griping. Pain; in afternoon; with borborygmus.

Stitches under ribs and navel, < l. side; under l. short ribs and between superior and anterior spinous processes of ilium and l. side of navel; under r. short ribs, in cæcal region, and after rising, in r. ear; under r. short ribs at 9 o'clock, also at 8 A.M., noon and evening; fleeting, under short ribs in morning on waking, and in cæcum. Pain about navel, with tension as if pressed together. Stitches in cæcum at 7 o'clock; the stitches in cæcum alternated with similar pains in corresponding part of l. side; jerking, in cæcum, returning on change of posture, < reclining towards l., when lying. Pain in cæcum, then in corresponding point on l. side.

Hypogastrium.—Stitches between crest of l. ilium and navel, then in cæcal region; in r. pubic region, almost in spermatic cord, returning in the evening. Cutting below navel after dinner. Pain and tension below l. side of navel, from which there was developed a stitching (apparently superficial). Pain *in pubic region; with heaviness,* also the same alternating with pain in pit of stomach; drawing pains about lower abdomen; rheumatic pain in l. side of pelvis. Jerking, drawing in l. groin.

Rectum.—Pressure on while sitting.

Stools.—Fluid. Copious; and mucous. Pappy, in morning; in afternoon, with rumbling in abdomen; frequently after 1 P.M. Soft; and dark brown; and unsatisfactory. Insufficient in morning, then a pappy one at 1.30, after dinner; stools diminished while urine was increased, with increase of the pain in pubic region. Delayed till evening; delayed and firm. Hard, sluggish. Difficult, even when there was slight urging the rectum was so inactive that the stool was affected only by effort and with interruptions.

Urinary Organs.—Stitches through fossa navicularis. Burning at orifice of urethra, diminishing interiorly. Some drops of urine were discharged after urinating. Urine and sweat increased, with diminished stools. Urine had a peculiar smell; contained much mucus. Uric acid increased.

Sexual Organs.—Stitches at root of penis; in spermatic cord and in l. pubic region; r. spermatic cord in evening; r. spermatic cord while walking; drawing, in l. spermatic cord at 11 o'clock. Aching drawing in testicles. Drawing pain along spermatic cord; in evening. Drawing in r. spermatic cord; intermittent, in region of l. spermatic cord.

Respiratory Organs.—Tickling in trachea. Voice hoarse. Coughing up mornings thickish mucus from larnyx. *Mucous expectoration. Dyspnœa and oppression of chest.* Respiration accelerated. *Respiration short and more in upper part of lungs, with anxiety and discomfort.*

Clinical.—Ammoniacum has obtained some repute for the relief of humid asthma, and catarrhal affections of the air passages, as an expectorant. It has relieved severe bronchitis with free mucus, expectoration, stitches in chest, frontal headache, dim vision, etc. Violent bronchial cough at night, with very free expectoration of stringy mucus. Often used for chronic bronchorrhœa with very tenacious expectoration, sometimes with a feeling as if something would be torn loose, and the patient clutches at the sternum, generally worse at night.

Chest.—Jerking stitches about l. short ribs, more upward towards chest. *Oppression when inspiring, with stitches in l. half. Constriction, with pain. Pressure in.* Affection of lower half of l., then deep-seated pain there.

Heart and Pulse.—Palpitation in evening, with restless sleep; in chest and carotids in evening after lying down, making it difficult to get to sleep. Throbbing of heart and arteries at night when lying down; strong throbbing of heart extending below pit of stomach, at night on going to bed, < lying on back or l. side, preventing sleep. Pulse *tense;* and small. Rapid; and hard.

Back.—Stitches in l. lumbar region, < expiration. Heaviness and pressure at end of lumbar vertebræ.

Extremities.—Tearing in wrists and ankles; in r. shoulder-joint, knee and tarsus, and l. tarsal bone. Stitches in r. knee and l. elbow. Rheumatic pains in l. shoulder, knee and r. ankle. Weariness. Heaviness in evening.

Upper Extremities.—Shoulder. Stitches in r.; in l. joint; in l., with tearing; in l. joint, extending over deltoid, > pressure; in shoulder and axilla, extending to elbow; in glands of r. axilla in evening; drawing S. in r. deltoid at 9 A.M. Rheumatic pain in r. shoulder.

Arm.—Bruised pain, especially about elbow. Rheumatic pain in r. about 12 o'clock; in r., now at one point, now at another. Paralyzed feeling in l. Tensive itching aching on fleshy parts of extensors of r. forearm and elbow. Drawing and tearing in r. wrist. Bruised feeling in l. wrist, then r. Rheumatic pain in r. metacarpal bones, in elbow and shoulder. Rheumatic pain in l. index. Drawing in r. middle finger.

Lower Extremities.—Thigh. Stitches in r. trochanter major from 3.50 to 5.30 P.M., with weariness of leg; in r. hip-joint, at 10 A.M., when sitting; above r. hip-joint, < sitting bent up. Pain above r. knee, < walking; in crural nerve, extending towards inguinal ring and spermatic cord; jerking, in l. crural nerve in evening; drawing, in r. trochanter at 4 A.M.; drawing, in r. trochanter and l. knee in evening, extending to spermatic cord. Weariness of r.; in r. trochanter major; in hip-joints in evening.

Knee.—Stitches in l. side of r. towards morning. Indefinable pain in l. Tension in r. when walking. Swollen feeling in l. at 9 P.M. while sitting, with heat in knee and pricking in bend of knee.

Leg.—Stitches and pressure on l., at side of l. knee, at protuberance of tibia. Tearing in r. shin. Pain above r. ankle; below knee when walking. Ankles, tearing; cracking in l. ankle in evening when moving.

Foot.—Stitches in r. metatarsus; below r. metatarsus; on outer dorsum of l. foot; in l. metatarsus, with burning. Tearing and drawing in l. sole. Pain in middle of l. sole. Painful drawing in l. foot. Heaviness in r. sole, so that he trips when ascending stairs.

Toes.—Stitches in r. great toe, after a burning in it; S. in l. little toe, at left of joint, where skin was thickened. Gouty pain in l. great toe, < walking. Drawing in l. middle, at 10 A.M.

Skin.—Itching returns in evening; itching in r. groin.

Sleep.—Yawning frequently bringing tears into eyes; Y. because the stomach felt empty, after soft stool. *Sleepiness;* all day, with late falling asleep in evening, then frightful dreams always as soon as he fell asleep, which woke him, then difficult falling asleep again. Falls asleep late. Interrupted sleep from 12 to 3 o'clock, then sleeplessness. Restless sleep; interrupted and unrefreshing. Waking frequently. Dreams distressing; confused; continued; remembered; many, also after 4 A.M.

Fever.—Chills running from feet up over back at 10 o'clock; the same after dinner, at 1 o'clock. Burning in l. metatarsus; in r. great toe, then stitches. *Disposed to sweat.*

Ammonium Bromatum.

The Bromide of Ammonia ($NH_4Br.$) is triturated with sugar of milk for homœopathic use.

General Action.—Large doses of Bromide of Ammonia produce mental dulness and physical depression; locally applied, anæsthesia results, in short the general symptoms common to all the bromides. Special attention should be directed to the symptoms of the throat and the cough, so clearly developed by Dr. Cushing's proving.

Allied Drugs.—Bromine, Ammon., Caust., Kali c.

Generalities.—Circulation excited; with nervous excitement as after wine; vascular excitement, with exhilaration as after morphine, then drowsiness. Feeling as after a dose of opium, though less excited.

Head.—Indescribable pain. *Pain in side near l. eye;* back of eyes, < l.; near r. eye as if a nail were driven in. *Feeling of a band above ears,* pressing hardest just above ears. Tightness in temples.

Eyes.—Redness; with soreness; in morning, < l., with soreness and with white mucus in corners.

R. full of white stringy mucus. Pain around eyes, extending into head. Soreness; r.; sore feeling, with sensation as if sand were in them. Smarting in evening. R. feels as if bathed in hot water. At 3 P.M. bad feeling. Enlarged feeling in evening, with blurred vision; r. feels large and smarts, and he has to wear a shade in the evening to read and write. Balls feel large and sore in evening. Lids, swollen; mucus on lashes; agglutinated; agglutinated in morning; drooping of lids evenings, with pain on raising them. Pain around orbits. Redness between orbit and inner canthus, and appearance as if a membrane were growing over it.

Ears.—Sharp pain in lower part of l. at 8 P.M., extending to cheek and neck.

Nose.—Stoppage; then discharge of clear fluid. Watery discharge from l. nostril.

Face.—Flushing.

Mouth.—Tongue. Soreness; of top, sides and tip. *Smarting as if burnt in morning.* Burnt feeling, < talking or reading; B. feeling, especially near tip. Biting in l. side of tip. Dryness in morning, with soreness and stiffness. Stiffness. Mouth and throat full of white sticky mucus in morning; white frothy mucus in mouth; stringy tasteless mucus in mouth. Mouth feels burnt; in morning. Mouth dry in morning. Salivation. Taste of food eaten several hours before.

Throat.—Redness. Mucus; in posterior fauces; sticky M.; white, *sticky, blood-streaked;* white, thick. Stinging, > sneezing, with inclination to cough. Pain in tonsils. Smarting; when hawking up white sticky mucus. Scalded feeling in fauces and top of tongue for half its length. *Soreness;* < l. side; with mottled look, as if diphtheritic deposit were beginning; with white sticky mucus from nose and throat; at 8 P.M., preparing to swallow is painful, but the act of swallowing is not. *Irritation; with inclination to cough.* Tickling; in morning and at 11 A.M., with inclination to cough; in evening; with cough. Heat at midnight when walking, and in lungs. Feeling as if hot air passed up r. side, though the stomach feels cold. Distress in œsophagus and stomach on swallowing anything cold.

Stomach.—Eructations of sour gas. Indigestion. Rising of something from pit, impeding breathing and causing faint and disagreeable feeling, > eructations; feeling as if something, not wind, were rising from stomach, causing faint feeling. Cutting. Distress; > afternoon; in upper part of epigastrium, extending to back and hypochondria, with inability to sit still, empty eructations, impeded breathing and general sweat. Sore lame feeling. Faintness in epigastrium or suffocation, in afternoon and evening, rising on sides of sternum to throat, causing sighing, walking about and fear that he might die.

Abdomen.—Uneasiness towards evening, next day diarrhœa and feeling as if distended by flatus. Twisting pain above crest of r. ilium.

Rectum.—Old hæmorrhoid returned with hardness and soreness, but speedily disappeared. Sudden urging to stool and loose stool.

Sexual Organs.—**Clinical.**—It has cured neuralgia of the l. ovary.

Respiratory Organs.—Cough, with tickling in throat. Deep C.; deeper in afternoon and evening from tickling below tonsils and causing pain in tonsils; deep from tickling on both sides of throat. Sudden C.; *in evening from tickling in throat,* < sides; from tickling below *tonsils;* with white mucous expectoration; sudden deep; sudden hacking, in evening, with watery nasal discharge; short sudden, in morning on rising, from sensation of mucus in throat; spasmodic sudden from tickling in throat. Frequent C. Inclination to cough from deep in throat; sudden, from tickling in throat, also causing strangling; sudden, from tickling just below both tonsils; almost constant. *Expectoration of white sticky mucus;* and occasionally of blood; of gelatinous mucus. Suffocating sensation from lungs, causing him to move around. Inclination to draw a long breath.

Clinical.—Valuable in the chronic laryngeal catarrh of speakers, or with dry spasmodic cough, which becomes almost continuous, especially at night, with tickling, heat and burning.

Chest.—Pain under middle of l. clavicle; in lungs: r. lung; in lungs in forenoon, especially in *pleura;* worse in upper part of r. lung; constrictive, across chest. Tightness; with pain in lungs. Coldness inside lung.

Pulse.—Rapid.

Back.—Pressure over r. kidney, > *pressure,* but leaving a pulling. Sore spot over r. kidney.

Extremities.—Weight on r. shoulder at 9 P.M. Pain posteriorly in middle of thigh, l. then r. Pain as from a cord around middle of r. thigh in forenoon, causing limping, the same pain below l. knee in afternoon, in ankle in evening, then in l. foot. Legs ache; from coldness of feet. L. ankle and foot lame.

Skin.—Villous and papillated rash in flexures of neck. Prickling.

Sleep.—Nodding. Slept but two hours at night. Dreamed of trying to pass urine into a bottle, but could not do so on account of being in a crowd of men and women.

Fever.—Coldness; with flashes of heat; cold back; *cold feet,* also in evening. Heat in flashes, as if sweat would break out.

Ammonium Carbonicum.

Carbonate of Ammonium (volatile salts) is prepared for use by dissolving one part in nine parts of pure water.

General Action.—(Compare Ammon. caust.).

Allies.—Kali c., Ammon mur.

Generalities.—Emaciation. Marasmus. Spasms. Tetanus. A jerk in upper part of body and in arms at 3 A.M., with tearing, then faintness. Trembling of whole body when walking. Blackness before eyes, motion of letters and arrest of breathing, with previous lassitude, and upon rising quickly from a seat rigidity of whole body, arms and legs being stretched out, while the fingers were so clenched that he had to use force to stretch them, which made them again movable. Tearing in whole body, especially in thighs. *Bruised feeling* in whole body early after rising, with weakness and weeping mood. Pain on motion in bed. Pain in occiput, in chest and from scapulæ down along ribs. Rheumatic drawing pain through limbs, hands, feet, nape, head, etc. Indisposition in morning; sudden, towards evening, with faintness, > walking in open air, but still she felt stitches in r. side.

Restlessness everywhere and success in nothing; R., which becomes a convulsive trembling; in a child every day from 7 till 10 P.M., with waking, tossing about, screaming, bloated and burning feeling in head, then sound sleep till morning, when the face is covered with spots as if scarlatina would break out. *Weakness all day;* in morning; morning and forenoon, > walking in open air; morning and evening; in forenoon, with sleepiness; evening; *after stool;* W. on leaving her bed; when walking in open air, with trembling and discouragement; *during menses, especially in thighs, with yawning, toothache, pain in small of back, and chilliness;* during menses, with pain in thighs as if they would fall off, or as if tendons would tear off, alternating with pain in small of back; with lying down for several hours as if senseless and weary. Numbness of r. side when lying on it.

Clinical.—Generally useful in great prostration with falling temperature. Hæmorrhages, especially under the skin, with general anæmia. Sometimes useful after hæmorrhage from the bowels, with very low temperature.

It is of use in poisoning by charcoal fumes; (Arnica is sometimes used in these cases, also Bovista.)

Sensitiveness to open air; in evening. Lying on l. side easier than on r.

Aggravation on r. side of body; in open air. Cannot bear evening air, with heaviness of feet and soreness of whole body; affected by talking much and hearing people talk, her hands and feet becoming cold in consequence of it; talking difficult after dinner; affected by walking in open air; all symptoms relieved after a good meal.

Mind.—Does not seem to be in his senses. Dreams at night while awake. Thoughtless in his head. Arrangement of ideas difficult. Absence of mind, with anxiety, and when speaking he is at at loss to finish his speech. Loss of train of thought when telling a story, and hitting upon wrong thoughts and expressions. Incorrect speech, using one word for another. Uses wrong letters and figures in writing and ciphering. Memory lost; with headache when reflecting. Tormented by disagreeable memories.

Anguish as if she had committed a crime, every afternoon between 5 and 6 o'clock, > towards evening. Anxiety at 7 P.M.; in evening in bed; afternoons, > towards evening, with weakness; at night, as if she had to die, with cold sweat, audible palpitation, lachrymation, inability to move her eyes or speak, audible heavy breathing and trembling of hands; on account of her illness. Apprehension in forenoon, with chilliness. Easily frightened.

Anger; in evening, with scolding. Ill humor; in morning; in forenoon, sometimes with headache. Intolerance of contradiction; of noise. Irritability after the fever, > glass of "bishop;" during menses; with reluctance to answer. Obstinacy in a child. Dissatisfaction. Finding fault with everything.

Grief. Weeping mood, with thoughts of death. Sadness; the whole morning; towards evening; with the abdominal complaints that occurred every evening; at night, and sometimes excitement; during cloudy weather; during menses; with no inclination to go out; with restlessness. Excessive mirth. Laughing immoderately at trifles. Excitement. Exaltation. Earnestness. Fear of work. Mood better after supper. Stupor and insensibility.

Clinical.—Patients requiring this drug are generally listless and lethargic.

Head.—Stitches; here and there deep in brain, < r. side, > in open air. Aching; morning, with heaviness of forehead, < in afternoon; morning in bed, with nausea rising to throat; morning, with nausea, > as soon as he took his pipe into his mouth; in afternoon; evening; after dinner; *after walking in open air,* and lasting through evening; on waking, with cold in head; > after supper; with pale face, pain at stomach and ill humor; over whole head after getting heated; now here, now there in brain, with sticking over one brow. Clawing aching. Aching as before, especially a sensation as after drunkenness; A. like a knocking or hacking with a sharp instrument, < motion; A. as if water or something else were in his head; ulceration A., on moving head and on pressure, especially at a gland in occiput. Boring at night, with lancinations. Drawing and tearing.

Distended feeling in brain, < r. side. Stupefaction. Confusion; caused by stopped coryza; with emptiness. *Light feeling.* Heaviness; with confusion; with fulness. Rush of blood, < towards evening; at night, with heat in face on waking. Congestion in afternoon after coffee, with inability to stand upright well. Loose feeling of brain. Feeling as if brain fell towards the side where he stoops, sometimes with stinging, giving no rest, even nights. Vertigo; in morning; morning, with flickering before eyes, so that she must sit down; morning, > walking, with nausea; at night; on turning body; with nausea and want of appetite; with trembling of feet; with cold sweat, as usually in a fainting fit; after sitting still, as from intoxication; at night, as if everything turned with her, so that she had to sit up in bed; morning after rising, as if things turned with him in a circle, < towards evening, felt at night on moving head.

Forehead.—Stitches over r. eye; over l. eye after dinner, causing eyes to contract; boring, deep in brain behind r. eminence, during dinner. Aching; *throbbing, as if it would burst;* throbbing, in l.; burning, in sinciput; drawing, in periosteum, waking her mornings, > rising. *Fulness, and in vertex, as if head would burst; F. as from vapor of coal. Heaviness after dinner, with throbbing;* H. in sinciput, with confusion. Throbbing. Uproar behind r. eminence, as if everything would come out.

Temples.—Stitches in l., < chewing; in l., as with a blunt instrument. Tearing morning and evening; in r. during dinner; behind l. ear as far as vertex, with sensation as if head were cleft. Painful beating in temple, l. side of head and l. side of occiput, sometimes with yawning.

Vertex painful. Heaviness in l. side of head, < in bed; r. side seems heavier than l., with sensation as if it would fall to that side.

Scalp.—Aching on touching hair; causing shuddering. Sensation as if hair stood on end, on entering house, with crawling over head and cold feeling there. *Itching,* especially of occiput; I., with sensitiveness when scratched.

Clinical.—Vertigo or feeling of looseness in the brain as if it fell from side to side, whichever way the head was turned. Sometimes in the beginning of cerebro-spinal meningitis the patient falls into a stupid non-reactive state; he is cold, the surface is cyanotic; pulse weak; in such cases this drug will bring about a reaction; then you may select some more specific remedy which will cure the trouble.

Eyes.—Inflammation and dimness; r. Pressure; with cutting; with fine stitches. Sore sensation in afternoon if he does not sleep. Burning, < morning on waking, with photophobia, and in evening on lying down. Biting, with itching of borders of lids. Itching and biting in morning, > rubbing. Weakness, with continual winking. Lachrymation, < r.; L., when reading; while the white of the eye is full of red veins, also in r. Pupils alternately contracted and dilated. Twitching in r. outer canthus, with veiled vision. Agglutination in morning; with running in daytime. Stye on r. upper lid becomes inflamed, with tension. Inflammation of r. inner canthus, without pain. Pressure in lids on waking and when falling asleep, with inability to open them, although he is internally awake. Vision double on looking at a distance 'and on accommodating for near vision. Flickering. Indistinct V. Sparks at night on waking. White sparkling stars, when sneezing. A black spot hovers before eyes after sewing.

Clinical.—Muscular asthenopia from prolonged use of the eyes, with appearance of yellow spots on looking at white objects.

Ears.—Hard swelling of parotid glands. Twitches in middle, with pinching; twitches and tension around l., and in cheek-bone and temples, with swelling of cervical glands. Tearing below and behind (< moving head), sometimes as far as vertex, occiput, nape of neck and shoulder. Stitches in r.; l. Pinching in r. in evening, as before. Crawling and burrowing in l., afterwards extending to lower jaw. Pulsation in l. at night when lying on it. Tension behind r. Hearing diminished. Sensitiveness of a deaf ear to a loud sound, causing trembling. Ringing; in r. Roaring before l.; in l. at night. Rushing in r. every night after midnight, when lying on it. *Buzzing before*, as if hearing were dull and as if something were lying before ears. Sound like a distant shot.

Nose.—Vesicle on fore part of septum. Swelling and tenderness internally in wing; swelling in r. nostril, with soreness and itching, with crawling in nose, as from incipient catarrh, and with discharge. Twitching in l. side, seeming to draw up wing. Tearing in l. nostril and at same time in bone of l. elbow, extending towards hand. Pain when breathing strongly through it. *Sensation in tip when stooping as if blood accumulated there.* Dryness of nose and lips. *Obstruction; at night; without any cold;* at 1 A.M., with anxiety as if choking, and pain in chest on account of difficult breathing. *Sneezing; frequently morning in bed;* violent.

Coryza; *during menses;* C., with burning in region of stomach and deafness; with obstruction of l. nostril; with obstruction and rattling in nose and roughness of voice; *dry, < night, without slightest air passing nose;* dry in bed in evening and night, with obstruction of nose; *fluent*, also with cough, also with tearing in l. cheek. Catarrhal irritation, with scraping and scratching in throat, with pain as from excoriation and difficult hawking of phlegm. *Acrid fluid running from nose;* during menses. Blowing out bloody mucus. *Water runs from nose when stooping;* dropping of water without coryza. Pus drops from one nostril on blowing nose in morning. **Bleeding**; after dinner; from l. nostril on blowing nose. Smell like a profuse sour sweat.

Clinical.—In children, catarrh, stoppage and acrid burning discharge, inability to sleep on account of the stoppage, starts up; also nosebleed on washing the face or hands or after eating.

Face.—Redness of l. cheek. Pallor; before and during menses; with nausea and mental and physical weakness; with bloating. Wretched look. Tearing in r. side, with painful tension. Pain in zygoma; in r. side; in glands beneath chin, and when moving mouth tension; drawing, in cheek bones. Sensation of stretching, with necessity to rub eyes and face, as if sleepy.

Lips.—Pimple on lower, with burning pain. Burning vesicles on vermilion borders. Cracked and corners of mouth sore; crack in middle of lower, with bleeding and burning pain. Dry; and stuck together; D., cracked, burning and feeling as if covered with blisters. Pain in upper as if cracked. Itching. Pain in jaws caused by coughing.

Mouth.—Teeth. Falling out of sound ones. The decay progresses rapidly. Blood comes from a molar on sucking. Stitches; in teeth and lower jaw of one side when a warm liquid gets into mouth; *in molars on pressing them together;* in healthy molar in open air; in upper hollow tooth on touch of tongue. Tearing in upper; in teeth and jaws as far as ears, before midnight; during menses, with pain when biting on them, and with restlessness; in l. upper molars, with salivation and gnawing in l. shoulder; in roots of l. upper, as if an ulcer would form. Tearing twitching, extending into ears, also at night in a hollow molar, > smelling Hepar sulph. *Toothache in evening as soon as she gets into bed*, lasting all night; at night, with swelling of cheek next day, afterwards nose enlarged and red spots on face and neck; *on biting together;* when chewing, < air rushing into mouth; during menses, also < during and after eating, > warm cloths and pressure; in anterior inferior incisor on biting during menses; with heat of same side of face; throbbing; darting, in a decayed molar after dinner, > picking; drawing, during menses, also > eating; drawing, which seems to be in the jaws and extends to ear and cheek, only when eating and biting upon tooth; as if squeezed, in evening; in two molars, as when sweets get into a hollow tooth. Drawing; at night and on waking; in a molar after a journey in damp weather, with tearing. *Elongated feeling.* Soreness of hollow molar. Dulness; in molars, with a loose sensation when biting. Feeling as if there were no power to bite. Feeling of an abscess at roots which threatens to burst on access of air on biting.

Gums.—Abscess discharging pus. Inclination to bleed. Redness and sensitiveness. Swelling, and of cheek; swelling and sensitiveness, especially of lower teeth, with a yellow painful vesicle between lip and lower canine tooth; sensation of swelling, and swelling and inflammation. Stitches in r. inner and upper. Sensitiveness to touch of tongue. Itching, with bleeding when scratched.

Tongue.—Flabby, white, with creamy coating. Redness, and of whole inside of mouth, especially the excoriated spot on palate. *Vesicles*, especially at border; at tip, with burning pain. Ulcer on tip, with a sore feeling when tongue is moved. Pustules, especially on border and under tongue, with burning and stinging pain. Painful erosion on middle. Burning at tip, < touch. Coldness on taking medicine, then warmth. Pithy feeling in anterior half.

Mouth in general.—Redness, especially beneath tongue; < towards evening, with tenderness; and inflammation of mouth and throat, with pain as if excoriated. Burning vesicles on inner side of lower lip; painful white, on inner side of lower lip; inside of cheeks full of vesicles. Excoriated spot on palate caused by a hard crust. Swelling on jaw beneath gum, painful on chewing; hard swellings on inner side of lower lip. Swollen sensation. Much mucus in afternoon and evening, and in nose; mucus, with scraping; loose mucus.

Pain in palate as if ulcerated on touch of tongue, then exfoliation. Scraping soreness in mouth, especially in inside of upper gums, with softness of one spot. Roughness, with bloody taste, then cough and expectoration of light-colored blood, with burning and heaviness in chest, heat and redness in face and trembling of whole body. Narrow feeling, so that she fears to open her mouth or move her tongue lest she should hurt some part by touch of tongue. Dry feeling in morning; dryness in evening, not > by drinking; at night, with heat. Itching. Salivation; with scraping; salt; watery. *Much spitting.* Smell bad; in morning, and taste. Taste bitter in morning and on waking; bitter at root of tongue; pungent, cool, then burning; salt; nasty and sourish; *sourish and metallic to food;* sour after drinking milk; sweet, with bloody saliva; bloody.

Throat.—R. submaxillary gland tender to touch. Swelling of tonsils, < morning and evening, with difficult swallowing. Stinging and drawing or tearing, < speaking. Sensation of something sticking in it, morning and evening, with choking pressure; sensation as if something were sticking in r. side, making swallowing difficult. *Pain during deglutition as if r. tonsil were swollen.* Pressure in, with external swelling on sides. Aching and shooting in afternoon and towards evening in a thyroid gland, which had been swollen and numb for years. Full and obstructed feeling. Soreness; towards evening. Roughness, < speaking; *R., with scraping.* Scraping; causing cough. Burning, and in œsophagus; in pharynx; *down œsophagus,* as from alcohol. Dryness; and in mouth, morning on waking, and afternoons and evenings, with thirst. Hawking frequently on account of mucus in throat; hawking of salt mucus at night.

Stomach.—*Appetite violent;* great at dinner; increased at dinner, *but satiety after eating a little;* great hunger with but little appetite. Appetite lost; in morning; with continual thirst; for meat or boiled things during menses, with desire only for bread and cold things. Milk is distasteful. Little appetite and hunger, though he relishes his meal. Thirst; in afternoon; for beer. She cannot eat dinner without drinking. No thirst.

Empty eructations; evening and after dinner. Eructations tasting of food; during and after supper. *Frequent but suppressed E.* Sour E., after milk. Hiccough. *Nausea;* in morning, with coated tongue; after rising in morning, till afternoon (during menses), with chilliness and vomiting of sour water; in attacks at night; every day after dinner; *after eating;* during and after dinner (during menses), with weakness; with flatulent disturbance. Vomiting when walking.

Distention after eating. Rumbling. A stitch at pit at every attack of cough. Pinching; with rumbling and gurgling. Gnawing at r. side. Boring, extending to first lumbar vertebræ, with tearing. *Pain; at night; on pressure;* after dinner; > after supper; with loathing of supper; with disposition to watery risings; with nausea and sensitiveness at pit; at pit after eating, then nausea and vomiting of ingesta, then sour taste; extending in a vibratory motion towards l. nipple. *Clothes press upon.* Tenderness at epigastrium. *Overloaded feeling until three hours after eating. Oppression after eating;* after supper; with sense of contraction (also in chest), with loathing and nausea; in morning, passing into nausea. Full feeling during menses, with trembling. Discomfort after eating, with pressure in stomach and forehead. Heaviness in pit; in epigastrium. Emptiness. *Burning;* in pit; then in bowels; extending into intestines, as from strong wine. Coldness in region.

Abdomen.—Distention; with retention of stool; painful D. Accumulation of flatus, with griping; *much flatus in evening;* emitted in afternoon, evening and night; fetid. Rumbling in afternoon, with discharge of flatus; R., with movings; with pain; as from spasms, or when fasting, every time when she swallows something.

Stitches, < walking. *Tearing during menses,* which appeared too soon. Pinching in forenoon when walking in open air, > lying on abdomen and applying warm cloths, with contraction and rumbling, appearing again in evening and in the cold next morning, afterwards > in room; P., with obstruction. Griping with flatus. Cutting and biting as from worms, with contractive pain at stomach, chilliness, sweat and sleeplessness till morning, with return of pain on waking; *cutting before and after a loose stool.* Pain at 7 A.M.; waking at 3 A.M., two days before menses; afternoons from wet and cold; nights, > emission of strong flatus; after breakfast; before menses, and in small of back; during menses, with griping, pressure, and with tension between scapulæ; resulting in diarrhœa; as before diarrhœa; disposition to flatulent P. Sudden painful contraction, as far as stomach, > by compression and passing off after lying down. Heaviness. Symptoms recur regularly every evening.

Contractive and pinching pain in upper, then in lower part, in morning before menses, causing nausea, salivation, faintness and chilliness. Pressure over umbilicus as from a button. Sore pain in liver. Aching under r. ribs, in region of liver; in small intestines.

Sides.—Stitches in l. in evening when stooping; below l. ribs in evening. Pain in l. in morning; in l. during dinner, > emission of flatus. Compression on both, when sitting, > motion and stretching. Burning deep in l.

Elastic swelling in l. *groin* in evening after lying down, *with bruised pain,* pain < by lying on that side. Aching swelling of l. inguinal glands, > towards noon, replaced by headache and ill feeling, which lasted till evening and recurred next day. Transverse stitches deep in hypogastrium when standing. (Pinching in r. groin when stretching, with stitches); P. moving transversely across towards sacrum and rectum, during stool, > bending body, ceasing after stool. Contractive cramp deep in hypogastrium on stooping, also in small of back. Cutting in lower A., during which the abdomen is very small. Pressure in groin and bend of thigh; in hypogastrium, also during dinner. Sense of fulness and distention in l. groin. Hernia protrudes in l. groin.

Rectum.—Varices form, moist and painful, as from excoriation; protrude, > lying; protrude during stool and are *painful* afterwards, so that she cannot walk. Cutting, with good stools. Burning pain at night, with urging to stool. Tenesmus with the stools;

urging before usual hour. *Discharge of blood during and after stool.* Bleeding from intestines.

Anus.—*Itching.* Scratching after stool, then burning.

Stool.—*Diarrhœa;* twice a day; in morning, with colic; *preceded and followed by cutting in abdomen;* very early, then headache and much rigor; of fæces and mucus, with cutting in abdomen before and during stools. Liquid. *Hard, retarded* and difficult; H., surrounded by streaks of blood; and painful, with prickings in anus. *Retained, then loose.* Constipation. Mixed with mucus. Surrounded by watery mucus, at 7 A.M.

Urinary Organs.—Tenesmus of bladder, even at night, with diminished urine accompanied by burning; *frequent urging to urinate, also at night,* also < in afternoon, with increased urine; T., with cutting. Discharge of a milky prostatic fluid after a hard stool. *Involuntary micturition in a boy while asleep* towards morning. *Frequent micturition; at night,* sometimes copious; frequent and copious, < evening. Blood from urethra. Traction in fore part of urethra in evening after urinating. Urine copious; and turbid; in afternoon, with loose stool. Red. Urine reddish, like water mixed with blood, after dinner; pale at noon, for the first time since last evening; white, *sandy;* turbid U. of peculiar smell and with copious sediment; turbid, high-colored and fetid; alkaline (it had been acid).

Clinical.—Indicated in uræmia with the characteristic symptoms of the drug.

Sexual Organs.—Itching; of glans penis; of mons veneris. Erections; continual in morning. *Choking pain in scrotum* and spermatic cords, with pain of scrotum on touch, and involuntary erections. Drawing pain in scrotum. Drawings in scrotum, > by raising it. Weight of scrotum. Relaxation of scrotum. Itching of scrotum. Desire vehement, without remarkably voluptuous thoughts and almost without erection; voluptuous, with trembling of body almost without erection; dormant. Aversion to the other sex. Emissions almost every night.

Itching of pudendum; with swelling and burning. Soreness of pudendum and anus, < urinating. *Leucorrhœa;* watery, burning. *Menses too early;* too early after a cold drive and *very copious, < at night and when sitting and driving, previously griping colic,* with want of appetite; delayed, with one complete interruption; pale; copious; *copious, blackish, often in clots, passing off with spasmodic pain in abdomen, and hard stools; with tenesmus; acrid, causing soreness and burning pain in thighs.*

Clinical.—Catarrhal leucorrhœa, acrid, burning. Tendency to hæmorrhage; menses too frequent and too profuse.

Respiratory Organs.—*Accumulation of mucus in larynx,* then rough voice. Drawing and stinging itching in larynx. Constriction in larynx from both sides of neck. *Hoarseness;* with roughness in throat. Difficulty in talking after eating; D. as from weakness of organs of speech, or on account of pains resembling pains at stomach. Mucus in trachea increased. Rattling in trachea as from mucus.

Cough; all day and in morning, with mucous expectoration; morning in bed, with mucous expectoration, affecting chest and head; in evening in bed; evening in bed, with asthma; *at night;* from 12 to 1 o'clock at night, with stuffed cold and sleeplessness; with mucous expectoration and soreness in air-passages; C. < ascending a hill, *with expectoration of bloody mucus,* heaviness on chest and short breathing *with asthma;* from deep in chest. *Violent, every day at 3 to 4 A.M., in a child. Dry C., from scratching in throat; dry,* < *night,* as *from dust in throat; violent dry in middle of night.* Irritative cough. Short and suppressed hacking, from irritation in larynx, with sensation of spasmodic asthma. Expectoration; bloody, when clearing throat.

Asthma after every effort, with palpitation; < ascending steps, > in open air, with pallor and inability to do anything when in a warm room, except to sit still. *Oppressed breathing;* at night; making him hack. Sighing. Short breathing, < ascending steps; S., with stitches in chest. Wheezing.

Clinical.—Chronic cough of old people, with tickling in larynx or under the sternum, dyspnœa, great shortness of breath; the cough is apt to be worse in the early morning hours; sometimes with bloody expectoration. Chronic bronchitis of old people, with emphysema.

Chest.—Cracking of sternum when bending chest backward, with pressure in middle of chest. Stitches after supper; S. when stooping, > straightening up; *in r. breast when stooping;* in l. breast at night, < lying on l. side; at side of l. nipple when breathing, < when sitting; S. under r. breast, close by lowest ribs; at last true rib when breathing and singing; in sternum, caused by cough; in r. side when walking; upon sternum, in r. side of chest and under l. breast, with bruised pain in the parts on touch; in l. side, beginning in præcordial region and moving downward towards side and afterwards towards back.

Pain; at lower part of sternum, caused by cough; at r. breast on touch; as after sitting bent, < r. side; intermittent, < l. side. Bruised pain in middle, in morning. Oppression, < lying; O., with desire to cough in order to be relieved; with difficulty in speaking, coryza and mucous expectoration, < morning; compressive. Contraction from cough; contraction of middle, with bruised pain on pressure. Soreness under sternum, as from excoriation, caused by cough. Rough feeling, with hoarseness when calling aloud. Distress. Drawing downward sensation during expiration and preventing it. Lungs feel drawn down when standing. Heaviness when walking in open air, with tightness; H. at sternum at night, with oppression; as from accumulation of blood. Rush of blood after writing. Heat internally. Coldness internally. Weakness; with coryza.

Clinical.—This drug is indicated in pneumonia when there is great debility, with symptoms pointing to the formation of heart clot.

Heart.—Stitches. Oppression. Palpitation; after every effort, with asthma; (after coition, with excited circulation); with blood rising to neck and difficult breathing when hand is pressed on heart; with retraction of epigastrium and weakness in præcordial region. *Pulse quick;* strong.

Neck.—Drawing pain in nape, with stitches over temples and bloated face. Drawing down from neck. Stiffness when turning head. Tension in nape on stooping, with pain in forehead as if it would burst.

Back.—Twitching at night when asleep. Pain; during motion.

Loins.—Sudden stitches in r. Shooting. *Pain; during menses;* when walking; < motion and walking; when stooping, with feeling as if muscles were too weak to support the body, which threatens to fall forward; drawing, extending to legs; drawing and pressive pain at rest, > walking; gnawing, and in hips, extending to abdomen and moving again backward; throbbing, when at rest. Bruised pain. Sudden darting when walking out into open air, < rising after long sitting.

Stinging in coccyx, preceded by itching.

Extremities.—Stretching; morning. Prickings in tips of fingers and toes. Pain at night, with gnawing pain in small of back; P. in forenoon and night, with gnawing pain in small of back, > rest. Sticking drawing, sometimes in r. arm, sometimes in legs. Bruised feeling; in evening. Weakness, < evening, in knees and legs; with disinclination to work; in morning, as if he had not slept enough; as after a fever. Hands and feet go to sleep when sitting, > moving about. Heaviness.

Upper Extremities.—Tearing in joints. Pain in glands of axilla, with swelling. Paralytic drawing from l. axilla to wrist.

Shoulder.—Tearing; in l. towards chest. Shooting and tearing in r. joint. Pressure upon l. Drawing pain in r. joint. Bruised pain in l.; in l. shoulder and elbow in evening.

Arm.—*Spasm of r., drawing it backward,* then heat of body and turbid white urine. Pain at 3 or 4 A.M., with coldness and stiffness of arm, heaviness in elbow, and on motion of arm or when it is in bed tearing in shoulder, elbow and wrist. Drawing pain, and in hands. *R. appeared to weigh a hundred-weight and to be without strength.* Weakness of r., with coldness, numbness and lifelessness, then tingling. Paralyzed feeling in r.; in r., with heaviness, weakness and necessity to let it hang down, with swelling and coldness of hand.

Upper Arm.—Twitches in r. Insensibility, where he had been pricked.

Elbow.—Cracking during motion. Stitches. Tearing in bone, as far as little finger; in bone of l., extending towards hand, and at same time in l. nostril. Boring in fossa that receives olecranon process. Creaking pain on stretching arm out straight before him. Stiffness.

Pain in middle of l. forearm, evening in bed, with feeling as if bone would curve inward forcibly and break. Tearing in wrist, as far as fingers, > warmth of bed; tearing in l. W., as if in marrow, towards l. finger. Tension in wrist, < motion.

Hand.—Trembling. Distention of veins after washing in cold water, with blueness. Stitches when breathing, and in fingers. Pain on dorsum, waking her at night. R. goes to sleep at night when lying on it.

Fingers.—Swelling of middle joint of r. middle, with pain when touched or bent. Twitching in l. thumb. Cramp in posterior phalanx of a finger, morning till night, when in the cold, < stretching, with stitches. Tearing in fingers, and in articulations of thumb. Pinching on stretching them apart. Jerking griping in l. thumb, as if in bone. Drawing pain from tips as far as hand, as from mesmerizing. Bruised feeling in l. thumb in cold air.

Lower Extremities.—Staggering when rising. Cracking in joints when walking. Sudden weakness after dinner.

Thigh.—Tearing. Pain in hip-joint when walking; in hip-joint, as if beaten asunder, every morning in bed, < turning, > rising and walking; over bend of l. knee, as if tendons were too short, on pressure and when sitting upon them. Drawing pain descending from l. hip. Pain in r. thigh as if inmost marrow were shaken, < lying and sitting. Bruised feeling; when taking much exercise; in middle of both, during menses; over r. knee, > rubbing. Sprained feeling in l., with weakness and sudden bending of legs when walking. Jerklike scraping upon bones of thighs and legs in evening, obliging her to twitch up the leg and walk about. Sudden pulsation about r. hip in evening. Stiffness when walking. Weakness, and of legs.

Knee.—Cracking on motion. Twitches, and in legs; T. in patellæ in evening. Tearing. Sprained feeling on sitting down and turning leg. Boring in and upon patella; boring and drawing in knee, causing uneasiness in legs.

Leg.—Twitches towards evening. Stitches deep in calves. Tearing below knee and at l. tibia. Sprained feeling in l. when walking. Straining in calf (from a cold?). Sore and bruised feeling in muscles. Seem contracted. Shortened feeling in tendons of muscles. Cramp when lying, < rising; C., especially in muscles of tibiæ and feet; C. in calf when walking in open air. Heaviness in evening. *Restlessness.* Pain as from paralysis, as if they were going to sleep, > walking. Asleep when sitting and standing, and at night when lying on the limb.

Malleolus.—Tearing, and in joints of feet, extending to toes, > warmth of bed. Drawing pain in external.

Foot.—Swelling as far as calves; of ball of r. in morning on rising, and tenderness as from frost. Trembling. Tearing twitches in r. heel. Stitches in ball of r.; (over r. heel). Tearing in soles. Pain in ball of l. in evening; in heel on waking, as if the bone were perforated by ulceration. Sensitiveness to wet and cold. Burning in the swollen ball of l., with pain. Crawling in dorsum of l. as if asleep. Tingling in l. heel, with ulcerated feeling when touched; in sole when lying in evening, with itching and with burning after scratching. Weakness.

Toes.—*Redness of big toe, < evening in bed, with swelling and pain, and with swelling of whole foot;* tender red swelling of r. toes, like chilblains, in evening. Painful twitches in ball of big toe (which had been frozen when a child). Stitches in balls of big toes, with drawing as if frozen, < evening on going to sleep; tearing S. in big toe, with twitches. Piercing pain in ball of big toe, evening in bed. Pain in ball of big toe as from subcutaneous ulceration, when walking.

Skin.—*Redness, like scarlatina, of whole upper part of body;* R. of a dormant herpetic eruption, with itching and burning, then disappearance in a few days. Blue spot over knee, with burning. Hard swelling of cheek, as well as glands of ear and neck. Deep-seated induration over r. knee, with pain on pressure. Hardness, with chaps. Desquamation of palm. Scaling of chin, with itching. Eruption at mouth; miliary, around chin. Herpes-like, scaly eruption around mouth. White herpes-like spots on cheek, continually exfoliating. Rash on r. side of neck and on l. forearm; red rash on chest. Inflammation of warts.

Pimples on forehead and tip of nose; increased in number on face; on forehead, with vesicles; on l.

cheek near ear, with pain on pressure; on legs, with inflammation; burning, on nape and forearms; itching, on thighs and hands; itching, on podex; on podex, painful at night on lying down. Small tubercles on elbow and large ones on neck, with cutting, only a few ulcerating.

Boils on forehead; tip of nose; on cheek and around ear; on cheek, at corners of mouth, and on chin boils and indurations, discharging blood and water; above r. breast, with redness and pain on touch; on l. shoulder; on l. nates in evening, with pain; on r. thigh, discharging much pus and blood when cut open; deep-seated burning, on knee, preceded by itching; on l. instep, with pain on touch. Pustules over whole body; on forehead, temple, cheek and chin; side of nose; tip of nose; cheeks during menses; r. commissure of mouth, with boring, preceded by several pustules on l. cheek and on thighs. Vesicles on r. corner of mouth and on upper lip; V. on l. scapula, with stinging as from fleas. Soreness between a child's legs. Offensiveness of the fluid in an ulcer.

Sensitiveness to cold. Burning in accidental scratches on fingers, then subcutaneous pustules. Contraction on forehead and face. Tension of face (nose and lips), as if face were swollen, morning on waking. Itching here and there, usually > after scratching, or painfully burning; I. here and there, then after scratching burning vesicles, or pimples or hard nodes.

Sleep.—Yawning; with salivation, weakness, discomfort or chilliness; spasmodic, in evening. *Sleepiness* by day; in afternoon; in evening, but uneasy sleep at night; when not busy; unconquerable S. after supper, but he does not sleep well at night.

Sleeplessness from 11 till 1 o'clock; till 12.30, with straining and pressure on abdomen and discharge of flatus; for two hours after 1 or 2 o'clock; from midnight till 4 A.M., with pain in stomach; till 4 A.M., then oppressive sleep, during which he sweats till 7 o'clock; from itching and stinging of skin. Falls asleep late; on account of uneasiness, dry heat and sometimes burning at stomach. Sleeps better the sooner she goes to bed. Light sleep. *Restless S.; and unrefreshing;* < during menses, with frequent waking. *Startings in sleep at night*, then fear; *startings after midnight*, then sleeplessness for a long time. Waking frequently; with groaning and sobbing; with chilliness. Waking every half hour, then weariness in morning.

Dreams.—Terrifying. (Nightmare on falling asleep.) Anxious; with anxiety at the end, waking him at 3 A.M. Lewd, of coition, and on waking sensation as after an emission. Vivid. Confused; about things that happened many years ago.

Fever.—Chilliness; during the day; in morning, then hiccough; in evening; towards evening, > after going to bed; *in evening*, with bristling of hair, blue hands and nails, chattering of teeth and shaking, sometimes followed by nightly heat and sweat in morning; at night in sleep, > on waking; at night, especially in feet; in open air or on entering room; when undressing; C. on going out, fresh air causes sneezing and slight sore throat. Chilliness, with sweat, afterwards heat with thirst; alternating with heat, in bed from 9 to 12 P.M., together with uneasiness; alternating with heat during menses, with sensitiveness to cold, nausea, thirst, pressure at chest, stitches in l. side of chest, tearing in forehead, confusion of head, alternate redness and paleness of cheeks, pressure at stomach, disposition to eructations, violent coryza and sleeplessness.

Shivering; before sleep. Rigor when walking across the street. Rigor, with weakness, then heat in face. Rigor alternating with heat, especially heat in face. Chills and heat for several days, mostly shaking chills, then dry heat, with sweat only in morning. Head gets cold easily. Cold feeling in longitudinal sinus of head. Cold hands and feet. Cold feet; *in evening, < when going to bed;* cold feet, with heat in head.

Heat; at 9 A.M.; in forenoon, before menses, with anxiety; evenings, with headache; at night; from walking in open air. Hectic fever. Orgasms of blood at night. Heat in head when coughing; in sinciput, with pressure; in head and face, with red cheeks; especially in head and face, with burning in lobe of l. ear and around nostrils; *in face during and after dinner; in face during mental exertion;* especially in abdomen during forenoon. Burning in nape in morning. Burning in back, especially in small of back; on a small spot of upper and lower arm; in hands and feet about noon; in bend of r. knee and along leg, with redness and *increase of the pain on touch of cold hand. Heat of l. big toe, with pain as if burnt,* < damp weather and on pressure of boot, > resting foot firmly on floor and by walking.

Sweat; *in morning;* towards morning; night; early every night, and heat in morning; < night; profuse, fetid; as from weakness, *on forehead;* on joints in morning; on legs at night; on scrotum.

Clinical.—**It is a useful remedy in scarlatina, low type, with somnolence and other characteristic symptoms.**

Ammonium Causticum.

Hydrate of Ammonium, Aqua Ammonia, a transparent colorless liquid, holding in solution ten per cent. of Ammonia gas, specific grav. 0.959, may be taken as the first decimal dilution.

General Action.—A powerful cardiac stimulant; it lowers blood pressure. Applied to mucous membranes, inhaled or swallowed it is an irritant and causes œdema and ulceration. The symptoms here given are from cases of poisoning.

Relatives.—Alcohol, Kali caust.

Generalities.—Beating the bed-clothes. Trembling; at least effort, with inability to stand on getting out of bed. Cramps. Bleedings from mouth, nose, eyes and ears, causing faintness. Emaciation, with constant vomiting, weak, frequent pulse, hectic flush on cheeks, eyes sunken, tongue foul, headache, constipation and weakness.

Semi-conscious, pupils dilated, breathing noisy and hurried, pulse rapid, sweat, pain in abdomen, vomiting of blood, mucus and shreds of mucous membrane, afterwards hoarseness, heavy, drowsy condition, face dusky, skin dry, heat, later lips swollen, tongue dry, mucous membrane of mouth eroded, mucous membrane of fauces looking œdematous, softened and inflamed, pain and tenderness of abdomen on touch, tympanitis, burning pain in throat and pit of stomach, coma and incessant retching.

Face pale, anxious and covered with clammy sweat, extremities cold, pulse rapid and feeble, mouth and throat red and inflamed, burning pain in throat, difficult swallowing, feeling of impending suffocation, voice reduced to a whisper, breathing noisy, frequent and laborious, vomiting of mucus tinged with blood, tenacious mucus in throat inducing fits of cough and sickness.

White patches on tongue and inner side of cheeks, congestion of mucous membrane of tonsils and pharynx, swallowing difficult, frequent vomiting, respiration rapid and shallow, with râles, cyanosis, afterwards unconscious with half-open eyes, pupils moderately contracted, convulsions.

Muscular pains, especially in thighs. Weakness. Amelioration from drinking vinegar and water.

Mind.—Anguish; with suffocation and constriction of throat. Anxiety. Despondency. Despair. Excitement in evening, with small, quick pulse and increased oppression. Timidity. Fell back, insensible, as if choked. Coma.

Head.—Confusion, with pressure in temple; confusion, with rumbling in abdomen. Sensation in brain as if pressed asunder in the middle, towards the front and to both sides. Pressure in frontal region, with feeling as if the head would split. Forehead, where the vessels are full of blood, hot to touch. Pressure in occiput.

Eyes.—Red and shining. Spasmodically turned upward and lids closed. Haggard, injected, and lids swollen. Sunken and pupil dilated. Lachrymation. Pupils contracted; dilated and eyes inverted. Yellowish chemosis. Conjunctiva yellow.

Ears.—Deafness.

Nose.—Coryza. Watery fluid running from, and air is completely excluded. Much serous liquid. Flow of bloody fluid, and from mouth.

Face.—*Pale;* with suffering expression. Red; during exacerbations of fever; upper part violet red, lower part blanched. Distorted, with red spots. Expression of anxiety; of anguish. Lips swollen; lower swollen; cyanotic; livid; black coating on middle of lower; lips and tongue red and denuded; mucous membrane of lips and nose destroyed; inside of upper lip, tongue, roof of mouth and fauces white and other parts excoriated.

Mouth.—Tongue white; and palate and œsophagus as far as visible, with blisters; tongue coated white, painful and tender, with patches of its membrane pulled off. Black coat at tip. Tongue, mouth and fauces red and raw, and when asked where the pain was he pointed to ponum adami, under l. ear. Curled pieces of white skin detached from tongue and throat, and those parts are red. Dry tongue. Burning and scraping at root of tongue and at posterior wall of fauces. Teeth clenched. Mouth and throat dark red, swollen, tender, with epithelium detached in places. Burning, and in œsophagus and stomach. Burning pain from mouth to stomach. Foaming. Salivation; bloody. Much mucus; much limpid mucus from salivary glands and mucous membrane of pharynx. Albuminous, viscid, bloody secretion pouring from mouth and nares.

Throat.—Redness externally and swelling of soft parts; deep redness of velum, its pillars, tonsils and posterior wall of pharynx; deep redness of posterior wall of pharynx, of epiglottis and mouth, with pain in throat. Uvula contracted and covered with white mucus. Pain, and especially in epigastric region. Heat. Burning pain; with feeling of suffocation; burning pain down throat and in epigastrium and l. hypochondrium, with tenderness to pressure on these parts. Scraping; and lancination. Hawking of frothy mucus; constant hawking, causing pain, with expectoration. Swallowing difficult; painful; impossible. Dryness of œsophagus. Burning pain in œsophagus, with tenderness of stomach on pressure.

Stomach.—Thirst; with difficulty in swallowing; with inability to swallow. Eructations. Ineffectual retching. Vomiting; blood; matter like soap-suds; mucus, constantly; stringy mucus, light, then dark; throws up by mouth and nostrils a burning whitish fluid, smelling like sal volatile liniment. Pain; from a hearty meal; in epigastric region, also < pressure; pain in epigastrium and l. hypochondrium, with tenderness. Epigastrium tender and swollen; epigastric region sensitive at 4 P.M., with small pulse and shiverings. Heartburn. Heat, and in chest; feeling as if on fire from stomach to mouth. Burning pain, and in throat.

Abdomen.—Rumbling; with confusion of head. Soft. Pain; in lower A. and in back and sacral region; inexpressible, in upper part of intestinal tube.

Rectum and Stool.—Spasmodic contraction of rectum, an injection spouted forcibly from it as soon as thrown up. Much blood from anus; with tenesmus. Stools frequent, bloody. Profuse, liquid, fetid, of much disorganized blood. Solid, with cessation of confusion of head. Involuntary. Several, after vomiting, causing burning at anus. None.

Urine.—Incontinence of. Suppressed. Scanty, red. Alkaline and dark. High-colored, thick, with abundant heavy lateritious elimination. Smelling of ammonia. Albuminuria. Much sediment, consisting of urates.

Menses.—Too early and profuse.

Respiratory Organs.—Voice lost; weak and indistinct; hoarse; hoarse and weak; deep and weak; speech fatiguing, interrupted, also with low weak voice. Glottis, œdema; spasm, with asphyxia. Tickling in larynx, with pain in epigastrium. Coarse mucous râles in larynx and trachea. Trachea spasmodically rising and falling. *Bronchitis, with profuse expectoration.*

Cough and much expectoration, < after drinking; with much mucous expectoration; when he tries to drink, with expectoration, also with mucous expectoration; obstinate; sonorous, moist, like suffocative catarrh, with tracheal râles; spasmodic, with expectoration of much membrane. Bloody expectoration. Profuse mucous expectoration.

Suffocation; rousing from sleep. Choking sensation on swallowing. *Respiration difficult;* and stertorous, quick; stridulous; hoarse, croaking; heavy and rattling; rapid. Inclination to draw a long breath, which is prevented by pain in back of chest, in œsophageal region. Gasping for breath.

Clinical.—Loss of voice, with great debility or with burning rawness in throat. Spasm of the glottis (or paralysis), with suffocation, the patient gasps for breath.

Chest.—Mucous rattling. Cutting opposite fifth and sixth cervical vertebræ, at bottom of pharynx. Pain, with suffocative anguish; pain on speaking. Oppression; with increased rattling and threatened suffocation. Catarrh of lungs. Heat, and in stomach.

Heart.—Anguish in præcordia, with oppression of chest. Præcordial region distended and painful. Tumultuous action. Carotids beat violently. Pulse rapid; rapid and hard; rapid, small and weak; slow and irregular; pulse and heart's action slow and intermittent; pulse small; small and hard; small, depressed; weak; weak and irregular.

Extremities.—Nails violet. Twitches of r. arm.

Clinical.—Muscular rheumatism of the shoulders.

Skin.—Pale, cold and inelastic. Dry. Redness over nose and frontal sinuses. Rosaceous spots on inner and anterior surface of forearms, then on whole inner surface of arm, generally following the lymphatics. Red erythematous spots with yellow borders, especially along lymphatics. Erysipelas. Skin is taken off by a blister plaster, but no serum is secreted.

Sleep.—Restless night. Sleeplessness.

Fever.—Coldness; of limbs; of skin; of skin, especially of limbs. Hot skin; hot, dry skin. Sweat; cold.

Ammonium Muriaticum.

Sal Ammoniac, NH_4Cl, is dissolved in water for use.

General Action.—It causes profuse secretions from mucous membranes, especially of the air passages, and when decomposed in the blood acts as a heart-stimulant (see Caustic Ammonia).

Relations.—Ammon. caust., Kali, Alumina, Mur. ac.

Generalities.—Loss of fat. Stitches in l. side of abdomen, then in r. side of chest, then in r. scapula, then in small of back, with chilliness and sleepiness during the day. Pressive burning and stinging now here, now there, in forenoon. Painful twitching, or jerking tearing now here, now there, the pain most severely beats, as if it would suppurate, 6 to 10 P.M., on sitting, > lying in bed. Pain and bruised feeling in all bones, when slumbering or sitting still. Bruised pain in morning after rising, < during motion, especially in back, with tearing in shoulders and nape. Contracted feeling in whole body, in morning, so that walking was difficult, > long walking. Orgasm of blood; with anxiety. Sudden faintness after dinner, when taking exercise in open air, with weakness. Weakness mornings. Weakness, inactivity, general depression (in fever). Weakness, with constriction of throat and difficult respiration. Amelioration in open air. Coffee restricts the action of the drug.

Clinical.—The mucous secretions are generally increased; free in the air passages; cover the stool; profuse leucorrhœas; free discharge from nose, etc.

Mind.—Excitement when talking on an important subject. Anxiety, sometimes with weeping; anxiety, with melancholy. Irritable, peevish and easily frightened; irritable and peevish in forenoon, > after dinner; peevish in morning, and confused, as if she had not slept enough. Ill-humored in evening, absorbed in her thoughts and can scarcely be induced to speak. Antipathy to certain persons. Timidity. Seriousness.

Head.—Stitches, in the house, especially in l. side, with pressure. Aching. Confusion as after intoxication. Heaviness; after rising. Vertigo, with *fulness and heaviness;* V. in morning, > open air, with confusion; V. as if she would fall to one side, < motion, > open air (Kali c.).

Forehead.—Sudden fine stitches in l. in afternoon. Tearing when sitting. Boring. Aching; throbbing aching in evening, < touch, with weakness, so that he can scarcely walk, and chills on going to bed. Pressure in morning, after an uneasy night, with heat there; pressure downward towards root of nose, morning after rising, with sensation as if the brain were torn. Heaviness in front of; H., with internal heat and sweat.

Temples.—Stitches in l. in forenoon. Tearing in r., extending into side of face; fine tearing upward in r. bone during menses; sudden tearing upward in r. in forenoon. Burning pain in l., and sometimes stitches. Painful twitches upward in l.

Vertex.—Stitches on stooping from 3 to 6 P.M.; stitches in morning, with sensation as if head were bursting. Pain as if head were broken in two.

Side.—Fine stitches in l., in forenoon. Tearing in upper part of r., while sitting.

Occiput.—Compression as from a vise, then in sides of head, with ill humor. Pinching in a spot on l. side in forenoon.

Scalp.—Itching. Itching pimples on r. side of occiput in evening, > at night.

Eyes.—Pain. Sensation as if a body were rising in l., forenoons, preventing vision. Burning in morning after rising, if she looks at the light; in evening, and closing as from sleep, > by light; at night, with lachrymation; of r., continuing long in open air. Twitching of l., > long rubbing. Lachrymation morning after rising. Tearing in balls. Twitching in l. ball, > rubbing.

Lids.—Agglutination in morning on waking, with burning in canthi after washing. Twitching of lower, < l. Tearing in external canthus. Burning in canthi; morning, < looking at the light, > washing.

Vesicle in white. Redness of white, with itching of eyes. Tearing in upper border of r. in afternoon, while sitting, first <, then > by pressure. Hammering over margin of r. orbit in morning, or sensation as if a large body were pushing there. Vision misty in morning, > washing; she distinguishes nothing in the open air, even in the sunlight, sees better in the house. Yellow spots when sewing and when looking out the window into the garden. Eyes weak, glassy, watery.

Ears.—Fine stitches in l. in afternoon in open air; S. inward in r. when walking in open air, then burning extending outward from l.; outward from r., also as with an awl; fine, outward in l. when walking in open air. Boring and stitching outward from r. Boring twitching in r. Clawing and tearing in r. Twisting in l. and behind it, where there is a moist herpes. Burrowing and turmoil in r. on which he lay at night, as if something would come out. Tickling in r. Itching in both, with discharge of liquid wax. Grumbling and thundering noise in r. when sitting and at night, with pulsations.

Nose.—External swelling of l. side, then discharge of bloody crusts. Mucous membrane of nose and lips destroyed. Sore on the inside and around margins of nostrils. Ulcerative pain in l. nostril, < touch. Obstruction at night, with pain at r. nasal fossa; l. nostril stopped by mucus, > blowing. Itching in nose, with desire to blow it, sensation as if a large, rough body were sticking high up, and obstruction. Sensation in upper part as before a cold. *Sneezing frequently;* without a cold, rousing from sleep, with *crawling in throat,* causing cough and salivation.

Clear water running from nose and corroding lips.

Coryza, with eruptions in nostrils; C., with obstruction of nose and loss of smell; with obstructed feeling and difficult discharge of much mucus; dry, but clear water runs out of nose; at one nostril, out of which runs thick, yellow matter, with tearing in cheek-bone and teeth of l. side. Brown blood with the mucus on blowing. Bleeding, morning on washing face; B. from l. nostril, with relief of the itching. Bloody froth from nose and mouth.

Clinical.—Coryza, with acrid, watery discharge, ulcerative pain in nostril, nose very sore to touch. Discharge scalding hot, *also with cold feeling between shoulders.* Loss of smell.

Face.—Pallor. Distortion, expression of anxiety. Swelling of cheek, with enlargement of a gland below r. angle of jaw, with throbbing and lancinating pain. Tearing in bones of r. side, evening while sitting; in l. malar-bone; in r. malar-bone in forenoon, extending into temples; in cheeks in evening, alternating with tearing in sides of neck. Twitching pains in a spot in r. upper part, in forenoon, > during touch. Tearing stitches in r. side of chin. Tearing in l. lower jaw, then in upper incisors. Drawing in lower jaw. Lips chapped; dry, wrinkled and chapped, she had to moisten them constantly with the tongue; itching pimples around upper; blisters on upper, becoming inflamed and ulcerated; excoriated spot on r. side of upper, with burning soreness; contracted, with greasy feeling; burning; burning stinging of upper.

Mouth.—Teeth, tearing; in all at 8 P.M., > in bed; in upper, evening in bed, r., then l.; in a decayed root of l. upper, in afternoon when sitting, > pressure. Stinging in upper incisors. Swelling of gums of lower back teeth, with stitches extending to l. temple. Tongue white; coated more than usual on rising; coated white; white mucous coat in spots on tongue and mouth, like a false membrane; *vesicles at tip, with burning pain; burning vesicles at tip.* Could scarcely speak and complained of burning pain in throat and chest. Taste bitter, also in morning, > after eating, with frequent bitter eructations; bitter, during the anxiety, with nauseating bitter eructations; sourish, also morning on waking; pappy, morning after rising; disagreeable, with salivation.

Throat.—Swelling, external and internal, with pressive pain when swallowing, and drawing and stinging pain in the swollen submaxillary glands. Stinging; when yawning. Stinging raw sensation. Soreness, with rawness. Burning pain in throat and chest; with difficulty in speaking. Constriction, with difficult respiration. Roughness, > after dinner. Dryness. Itching, then expectoration of blood. *Throbbing in tonsils,* as if in an artery, with uneasiness and anxiety. Constant hawking from tickling in throat, without much expectoration. Hawking up mucus in morning. Hawking with expectoration of small pieces of mucus. Mucus difficult to hawk up. Mucus which he can neither swallow nor hawk up. Swallowing almost impossible.

Clinical.—Swelling of tonsils so that he can scarcely swallow, after taking cold.

Stomach.—Appetite capricious, sometimes lost, sometimes ravenous, with constipation or diarrhœa; want of; want of, in evening, with frequent yawning; none, yet he takes his usual food. Thirst; evening; before the chill, before 5 P.M.; satisfied only with lemonade; unquenchable, afternoons; absence of.

Eructations of air; of food; oppressive, tasting of ingesta; bitter; bitter in forenoon, with taste of food; of bitter, sour water in afternoon, the taste of which remained till she ate again. Hiccough; after dinner; frequent H. or bitter eructations, with the hiccough stitches in l. breast.

Nausea in attacks; N. in forenoon on walking in open air; after dinner, > eructations and in open air; after every dinner and supper, with waterbrash and horripilation; with oppression at stomach, yet inclination to eat.

Stinging at pit at 8 A.M., extending into r. axilla and muscles of r. upper arm, with burning. Heat in morning. Burning in afternoon, with pressure, becoming a stinging; burning towards pharynx, like heartburn. *Gnawing;* or grinding, as from worms. Grinding in morning, > after breakfast, with writhing. Pressure, with nausea. Sensation as if everything would turn around in forenoon on walking in open air, > by eructations, renewed while sitting, with necessity to go into the open air, where it disappeared, with disposition to waterbrash, nausea and vomiting. Emptiness or hunger; E. without desire for food; E., yet he can hardly persuade himself to eat. Sensation of fasting, yet it feels full, < after breakfast. Fulness in afternoon, with oppression. Drawing.

Abdomen.—Inflation in morning during and after a purge; in evening before menses, > emission of flatus; in evening, > by two stools, with tension of stomach. Rumbling; in afternoon; morning on waking, from fermentation in sides, extending to chest. Growling and noises, with emission of much flatus. Frequent emissions of flatus; loud emission; emission of offensive flatus, without sensation of flatus.

Cutting from 2 to 4 A.M.; at 7 P.M., extending to groins and small of back, > stool. Gripings, with motions; G. here and there in afternoon, without sensation of flatus. Pinching at every inspiration; P. before a loose stool; P. in abdomen and groins morning after rising, as before menses. *Colic.* Pain after diarrhœa; P. > stools. Soreness internally after morning diarrhœa, with pain as if beaten; sensation as if the intestines were turning around at 10.45 P.M. Painful pressure as with a hand in l. side. Weight, > sleep, with anxiety. Oppression. Fulness. Pressive tension in l. side near ring, as if something were pressing out. Drawing in side.

Burning pain in a spot in upper. Splenetic stitches even when sitting. Stitches in l. hypochondriac region when spinning. Stitches in region of r. ribs in afternoon when walking, with burning. Pinching in hypochondria.

Umbilicus.—Rumbling around; then soft stool, with urging. Cutting around, in evening, with shooting. Griping below, at 6 P.M. Grinding near, after dinner. Pinching to left of, while standing, < stooping; around, at 7 P.M., then two stools. Pain around, in afternoon, with five half-liquid stools; *pain below,* at 4 P.M., *then usual stool,* with stinging in anus. Discomfort below and to left of navel.

Pinching in lower, with griping and dyspnœa. Intermittent griping in lower, in forenoon. Pain in lower, with soft stool. Stitches over l. hip when sitting, and when stooping while standing.

Groin.—Sense of distention of l., becoming painful on sitting; D. of r., with a tensive sensation and grinding. Stitches in r. when sitting, coming out behind hip.

Tearing when walking, with tensive pain. Ulcerative pain in r. when walking. Cutting after 8 P.M., as far as small of back, with stitches and urging to urinate. Gripings in evening, afterwards extending to navel, > by a purge. Pain in r., often extending to hip and small of back. Sprained pain in l. obliging him to walk crooked. Burning in r. flank in afternoon when sitting.

Clinical.—Chronic congestion of the liver, with depression of spirits, stools coated with mucus.

Rectum and Anus.—*Itching soreness of rectum with pustules by the side of it. Burning in rectum during and after soft stools* (Mur. ac.). *Burning in anus during soft stool* (Mur. ac.). Itching in anus, > after nosebleed, with pressure. Hæmorrhoidal flux produced or increased. *Tearing in perineum* when walking. *Stinging tearing in perineum* in evening.

Stool.—*Contained glassy, tough mucus. Covered with mucus. Green slimy diarrhœa* mornings. Diarrhœa in morning; after every meal, with pain in abdomen, back, small of back and in limbs. *Soft;* at an unusual time; *and frequent,* also with much micturition; and profuse; yellow, with urging, then tenesmus and burning in rectum; next day none. Frequent, almost fluid, with mucus. **Hard, crumbling, scanty,** but after dinner the usual stool, then burning in anus (Mur. ac.). *Hard, covered with mucus.* Hard; first part, last part soft, also during menses, with straining, then burning in anus, then usual stool in afternoon. Of two small pieces, passed with pressure, then soft stool. No stool; for two days, with colic and sensation as if diarrhœa would come on.

Clinical.—Constipation, with hard, crumbly stool, or the fæces are covered with glairy mucus. Chronic diarrhœa during menstruation, green mucous stools; sometimes diarrhœa alternates with constipation.

Urinary Organs.—Pinching in bladder when lying, as far as urethra, with stitching. Tenesmus of bladder after 4 A.M. Urging to urinate at 10 A.M. Desire to urinate, with emission of only a few drops, then micturition with the stool. *Micturition frequent and copious at night;* frequent in morning; M. slow. Urine copious; at night, before menses; C., strongly ammoniacal; with a stale smell. Urine diminished in amount; and in frequency. Urine hot and copious. Urine bright yellow, saturated, with a loose cloudy sediment. Turbid, with urates on cooling. Clayey sediment.

Sexual Organs.—Erection at 8 A.M.; morning in bed; frequent, with little desire. Stitches in l. spermatic cord, with beating. In female genital organs sensation in morning as after an embrace. Leucorrhœa, with distention of abdomen; *L. like the white of an egg after pinching around navel;* brown, slimy L. after micturition. *Menses too soon; with pain in abdomen and small of back, flow more profuse at night.* Discharge of a quantity of blood with the stool during menses.

Clinical.—Many abdominal symptoms during menstruation and pregnancy, constipation as above, liver swollen and sensitive, with jaundice, flatulent distention of abdomen. Menstruation too early and free, flows more at night. During pregnancy pain in l. side of abdomen as if sprained.

Respiratory Organs.—Irritation in morning, causing hawking, with expectoration of a piece of mucus and a raw sensation, then soreness behind uvula. *Hoarseness* in afternoon, *with burning in region of larynx.* Aphonia.

Cough when breathing deeply, < lying on r. side. *Dry;* in morning, also with sticking in fore part of chest; from 6 to 9 P.M., from tickling in throat, > after lying down; *at night, preventing sleep;* dry mornings, loosens in afternoon, most frequently with sticking in l. hypochondrium; *dry hacking, also from tickling in throat,* which continues when not coughing, in forenoon. Violent cough at 10 P.M. in bed, during which water comes into her mouth. Cough, with expectoration; in morning; C. during the day, with hawking and expectoration of mucus; *C. at night when lying on back,* loose, with sticking in l. middle false ribs, extending to last false ribs and preventing "coughing out," < turning on to side. Expectoration of tough mucus in afternoon.

Desire to breathe deeply and to cough long, with slight expectoration. Short breath. Suffocation threatened. Breath lost when walking, obliged to breathe deeply but slowly.

Clinical.—Pulmonary catarrh, with hacking, scraping cough; cough < by lying on back or r. side. The dry cough, with stitches in chest, may become loose in the afternoon or at night. Profuse expectoration, with rattling of mucus in old people, with coldness between the shoulders.

Chest.—*Rattling.* Stitches in middle of l. rib region; behind r. ribs on motion; below r. breast during menses; below r. female breast in afternoon when sitting bent; below l. female breast while standing; in fore part in afternoon, > sitting; in fore part in afternoon and next morning, with pressure; sudden fine, come out of l. in forenoon; rhythmical, in l. in evening while sitting; upward, as with an awl, in l., afternoons with every inspiration; tearing, in a spot in l. clavicle, with bruised pain on touch. Tearing in a spot in l. clavicle, with bruised pain on pressure. Bruised pain beneath r. breast, frequently intermittent, also often with short breath. Pressure in fore part in evening; upon l. mamma when taking exercise in open air, and in l. side of chest on going from warm room into open air; *in middle,* in afternoon, *with stitches,* as if a morsel stuck there.

Heaviness when walking in open air; at night, waking him, with restlessness, which prevents sleep, this heaviness awoke him again at 3 A.M., he was kept in a half-sleep, in which he was partly conscious and dreamed that he had been hanged and the chest had been hard pressed. *Oppression* in morning after rising, > eructations, which came on in open air; when moving arms forcibly and when stooping; like a dry catarrh. Tightness on respiration. Painful tension under r. mamma, frequently intermittent, after dinner. Tension or compression as with a vise in front at lower part, when standing.

Rawness at 8 P.M. Sticking crawling in l. when sitting. Burning spot when walking in open air; burning spot on r. side. Beating after dinner, extending to pharynx, with heat in face and uneasy mood; B. like a pulse in a spot in l. cavity, morning when standing.

Clinical.—In catarrhal pneumonia of children, with ropy, tenacious expectoration.

Heart and Pulse.—Tearing in præcordial region, extending suddenly into l. forearm. Pulse intermittent; weak, irregular, rapid; small, soft, rapid.

Neck.—Swelling of cervical glands. Tearing stitches

in neck and l. clavicle on moving head. Tearing in cords of l. side; intermittent, in cords of r. side, during menses; in sides in evening, alternating with tearing in cheeks. *Throbbing in glands*, with flushes of heat *and want of air in throat. Stiffness*, with pain on turning it, from nape to between shoulders. Tension in nape at 10 P.M., > after lying down, with stiffness. Drawing in tendons of nape.

Back.—Aching at 10 A. M., during menses, then weakness of thighs. Pain when sitting, > motion, with compression as from a vise. Bruised pain, < lying upon it; bruised pain at night, < lying upon it. Sprained and bruised pain in r. side, extending to middle ribs and axilla, waking at night, on turning the body, stretching arms, sneezing, yawning and breathing. Tension, preceded by itching of l. scapula.

Stitches in l. scapula during rest; S. in l. scapula, < lowering shoulder and turning the trunk to the left. Pinching in flesh of r. scapula. Pain between scapulæ as from a wrench or bruise, or as if muscles were stretched asunder. Drawing and pressing inward in middle lumbar vertebræ, forcing him to stretch the abdomen forward.

Small of Back.—Pain when rising after stooping; waking at night; when walking, so that she could not walk straight; with incarceration of flatus; from 1 till 4 A. M., with paralytic pain in hips and in external surface above knee, and the parts were still painful to touch the next forenoon. *Pain as if shattered; as if beaten and shattered*, waking between 11 and 12 P.M., with necessity to turn constantly, the pain lasting till 1 P.M. next day. Bruised pain at night; at night, so that she can hardly lie; in afternoon while spinning, > after motion. *Painful stiffness, even when sitting, < raising the body erect.* Sensation as if something elastic like air were pressing out, in forenoon, after yawning.

Bruised pain in coccyx when sitting, < when slumbering.

Extremities.—*Shooting and tearing in tips of fingers and toes*, then in r. upper arm, now here, now there, 6 to 10 P.M., > after lying down, with anxiety. Tearing in l. arm and foot; in fingers and toes at 8 P.M. on spinning, > by lying; now here, now there, evening when sitting, > after lying down. Stinging in tips of fingers and toes in afternoon when walking in open air. Stinging, jerking and crawling in tips of fingers and toes from 1 to 2 P.M. Burning crawling when standing, now in tips of fingers, now in tips of toes, as if they would go to sleep. Weakness. R. more affected than l.

Clinical.—This drug has been used in the treatment of chronic sprains. It is one of the remedies when there is contraction of the hamstring tendons, which seem tight when walking, > by continued motion. Cures sciatica; the pains < by sitting, somewhat > by walking, entirely > by lying. It has been used for the neuralgic pains in stumps of amputated limbs. It is useful for tearing, stitching pains from ulceration in heels, < at night in bed, > by rubbing.

Upper Extremities.—Shoulder. Tearing on waking before midnight. Rheumatic pain in joint on motion, r., then l. Burning in r., with pressure. Throbbing in r., as with a finger, morning in bed, and during the day. Drawing in joint, as after a cold, in afternoon at rest.

Axilla.—*Swollen gland*, resembling a hard, red ulcer, which separated constantly into parts, like a large pimple. Rapid intermittent throbbing in l., while sitting.

Arm.—Tearing in l., as if in tendons, extending into fingers, > motion. *Heaviness and rigid feeling* in r. in evening when spinning.

Upper Arm.—Tearing in middle, in afternoon, with sensitiveness of arm to pressure; T., below shoulder-joint, as if in the marrow, as far as wrist, in afternoon. Compression in l. when leaning it against the table, > motion of arm. R. seems paralyzed and rigid in morning.

Forearm.—Pressure in l., in bed, > motion, renewed by leaning arm upon the table when writing. Drawing from r. elbow to little finger, in afternoon, becoming a tearing, > motion. Heaviness and feeling as if asleep in r., in afternoon.

Wrist.—Tearing in tendons of internal surface of l., in afternoon; in tendons of internal surface of l., with twitching.

Hand.—Stitches in l., < motion, with beating. Lancination through hollow of r., while walking in open air. Twitching, tearing behind l. thumb, with swelling. Sprained pain in dorsa, at lower ends of metacarpal bones, especially on last thumb-joint, when seizing something, afternoons, > extending hand, when pressing on the thumb-joint the pain passes off with a cracking sound. Beating in r. palm, as with a little hammer, > motion. Feeling of paralysis in r., and in first phalanx of r. middle finger, when sitting and knitting.

Fingers.—Twitching. Tearing and stitches in various places, here and there, > pressure and rubbing. Cramplike pain in middle phalanx of r. middle finger, as if in tendons, on bending fingers inward. Painful throbbing under l. thumb-nail from 1 to 5 P.M. Aching in first joint of l. index on stretching it out while knitting, > bending it. Crawling in tip of r. thumb and index, as if going to sleep, in evening when sitting.

Lower Extremities.—Boring. **Thigh.** Twitching in l. popliteal region, on walking the cords seem too short, > long walking. *Tearing in front of thigh when sitting; in external surface of r. in evening* **when sitting down**; *intermittent in l. hip, extending down thigh in afternoon when sitting, at first > by rising.* Sticking on external surface of *l. hip*, at night from 12.30 till 2, > pressure, with copious passage of flatus, and it seems as if the pain were caused by flatus. *Pain in l. hip as if tendons were too short, in forenoon, so that she limps*, when sitting there is gnawing pain in bone. *Hamstrings painful, as if too short when walking.* Contraction about popliteal region, as if dried up or too short, morning on rising, so that she could not descend stairs, > by long and violent exercise.

Knee.—Stitches at 9 P.M. *when sitting.* Stinging in l. when walking in forenoon, then tearing.

Leg.—Trembling of l., with sensitiveness to touch. Slow fine stitches in inner surface below l. knee while sitting; stitches in l. calf when sitting; stinging in l. calf during rest after walking. *Drawing tension when sitting or lying, obliging him to walk crooked, after which the symptoms pass off.* Tension in tendons, with traction so that walking was difficult, with lassitude in legs. Spasmodic contraction around lower part of l. in forenoon. Weakness, > night. Insensibility of l. in afternoon when sitting (dead feeling).

Malleolus.—Spasmodic contraction or tearing below and around r. inner, when sitting. Trobbing as from an ulcer in l. outer; on walking, and in r. foot.

Foot.—Tearing in external border when standing, > motion. *Heel, ulcerative pain in r.*, > vigorous rubbing; tearing in r. heel at 3 A.M., in bed, with ulcerative pain; sticking tearing in l. heel, and ulcerative pain; pain in bones of heels as if bruised and contracted when walking; spasmodic, painful contraction in r. heel evening in bed. Asleep sensation in r. foot at night, in l. next forenoon.

Toes.—Sticking in l. great, afternoons, slowly increasing and decreasing; fine S. in r. little on standing and walking. Tearing in l. great, while standing; in r. great, in afternoon while sitting; in external surface of r. great, while sitting.

Skin.—Red spots on l. side of chest, with burning itching, turning pale on pressure. Desquamation between thumbs and index fingers. Eruptions on face. Dry and tettery herpes on face. Rash over whole body. Miliary eruption (sudamina) after profuse sweat. Psoric eruption over greater part of back and lower limbs.

Deep-seated nodes around and below r. wrist, with itching, after scratching they burn, become inflamed and seem about to suppurate, but do not, with swelling, a reddish brown scurf on those which are much scratched. Pimples after itching and scratching, on fore part of forehead; on inner side of l. forearm. Itching pimple on external concha of r. ear; on r. forearm; on r. side of neck and on l. hand, in evening; on dorsa of hands in evening and at night, with desquamation of the itching places the next morning. Painful pimple on antihelix of r. ear. Sensitive and inflamed pimple on top of r. scapula.

Boil on r. side of abdomen; on l. shoulder, with tensive pain. Vesicle on l. side of face. Vesicles, with itching, then burning, on r. wrist; on front of chest and on l. leg. Tensive burning vesicles on r. shoulder, forming scurf. Vesicles on a hard base, on and about r. wrist, mostly on its upper surface, with itching, then burning, some becoming scurfy from scratching, inflamed for a long time, new ones appearing daily.

Crawling in tips of fingers and toes. Subcutaneous formication over whole body. Itching, now here, now there, over whole body, evenings before lying down; over whole body, > evening after lying down. Sensation as from flea-bites at spots on l. mamma in evening, > scratching.

Sleep.—Constant yawning in morning, without sleepiness. Sudden sleepiness at 6 P.M., > when light is brought into the room. Starting up in evening on falling asleep. Sleep restless; after midnight, with frequent waking and turning, amidst dreams. Sleepless after midnight; sleepless till towards morning; till 3 A.M., without cause; till 3 A.M., then sweat in morning on waking; sleepless night, with chilliness from 3 to 4 A.M., then heat, then sweat, all without thirst. Sleep full of dreams. Frightful dreams all night. Lewd dreams.

Fever.—*Chilliness evenings after lying down and* **as often as she wakes,** *without thirst;* evenings after lying down and all night. Cold feet evening in bed; coldness of feet prevents sleep till midnight. Coldness from 7 till 9 P.M., with thirst; chilliness at 6 P.M., > lying down, with thirst; < evening and night, with shivering; in evening, coldness running down back; creeping between skin and flesh. Shivering creeping over her at 5 P.M. *Coldness in back and between shoulders*, at the spot of a previous pain, only internal, the coldness ending in itching. Chilliness at 5.30 P.M., then sweat before midnight. C. and shivering at 6 P.M., and next morning at 7, then sweat in bed, all without thirst. C. alternating with heat, then sweat in evening. Intermittent fever, paroxysm of cold, heat and profuse sweat. Fever paroxysms begin with chill and heat and end with sweat.

More heat than coldness. Heat in face, > open air. Heat on r. side of head every evening; in head before midnight, preventing sleep; in head in morning after rising, with fulness; creeping over head; flushing; in head in afternoon; dry, in head on entering room, then thirst in evening. Heat in evening, without thirst; in forenoon, thirst in morning after rising; H. in afternoon, with sweat, then thirst. Attacks of fever, then chills and heat, with bloated red face, and thirst during the chills and heat. Heat in palms, soles and face in evening after lying down, with thirst, then sweat. H. over whole body when exercising in open air, with redness of face and sweat; over whole body in a warm room and after quick motion, with redness of face and stinging heat, especially externally over chest; in whole body as if sweat would break out; at night in bed, then sweat in morning. Frequent flashes of heat, then sweat. Hot sensation after rising, with sweat of hands and odorous sweat of feet. Hot hands.

Sweat after midnight; S. on every exertion; general, nights; profuse; profuse morning in bed, without previous heat or chill.

Clinical.—*Cold feeling between shoulders.*

Ammonium Phosphoricum.

Clinical.—It has been used successfully in some cases of nodosities of the joints of the fingers and backs of the hands, and also for chronic bronchitis in patients suffering from chronic rheumatic gout. It has also been used with success in facial paralysis.

Ammonium Picrate.

Clinical.—Periodical neuralgia in r. side of occiput, boring extending to the ear, orbit and jaw, vertigo on rising, especially in irregular menstruation.

Amyl Nitrosum.

A yellow ethereal liquid ($C_5H_{11}NO_2$). It is dissolved in alcohol for internal use.

General Action.—A direct and powerful dilator of arterioles and capillaries, causing flushing of upper part of body, with rapid tumultuous action of heart. Action rapid, evanescent.

Relatives.—Glon., Cactus, Mellilotus, etc.

Generalities.—Stiffness as after taking cold. Restlessness. Uncertain trembling sensation over whole body. Tingling in different parts. Numb feeling along the arteries after the weakness had passed off. *Weakness;* with tendency to perspire on slight exertion. Muscles generally seemed relaxed and heavy, causing sensation of unsteadiness while walking. All symptoms ameliorated by exercise in open air (Glon.).

Clinical.—Temporarily relieved epileptiform convulsions. Hysterical symptoms, with flushes, profuse menstruation, etc.

Mind.—*Anxiety as if something might happen* (Mosch.), *must have fresh air.* Oblivious of recent conversation.

Stupefaction, with flushing of face and scalp, sudden smarting of conjunctivæ, injection of ocular conjunctivæ, dim vision as through a film, smartings in præcordial region, then r. renal region, then r. axilla, then mid-sternum, then lumbar region, then lower lobe of r. lung, at apex of heart, and in lower lobe of l. lung, with tenderness on pressure, increasing dyspnœa, sneezings, nasal catarrh and sighing, pulse 68, small and feeble, smartings changing position rapidly, being most persistent in eyes, bases of lungs and spine, then gaspings.

Head.—Aching; morning on rising, with nausea; from violent exercise, afterwards heat of room caused the headache to extend from temple to occiput, < *l. side* and remained long in occiput. Heavy aching. Crushing pain upon head, that gathered into a feeling of confusion, threatening to make him unconscious, with throbbing in head, glowing of face, general sweat, < palms, and sensation as if scalp were jerked from occiput towards forehead, ceasing just before it reached that point, then dull headache.

Feeling of a band about (Acon., Gels.). Heaviness. Intoxicated feeling. *Surging of blood to head and face* (Bell., Glon., Mellilot.). *Fulness;* with flushing of face, increasing to agony (Acon.), with palpitation, which shook the whole body, then sinking to the floor, then unconsciousness, with livid red color of face and eyes, followed by anæsthesia of second phalanges of l. middle and ring fingers.

Confusion; full confused feeling, mostly frontal, then throbbing and bursting sensation. *Throbbing; and heat* (Bell.). Throbbing, with bursting-out feeling in ears and constriction of throat and heart. Throbbing and fulness, then a confused weak feeling and a weight in top of head as if it would be crushed in. Vertigo; morning on rising; with heaviness of head; with nausea, also < when eyes are closed.

Forehead.—Aching. Fronto-orbital pain. Aching over eyes; as if a weight were within. Bursting pain. Heavy pain across in morning. Heaviness over eyebrows. Heaviness in forehead, head would fall to one side, then the other. Heaviness and pressure outward in forehead and temples, with a stupid, drowsy sensation and burning in stomach extending up to throat. Oppression in fronto-parietal suture, then proceeding to frontal bone. Dull feeling. Humming.

Temples.—Aching; r. *Throbbing* (Glon., Chin.). Pressure outward while walking, < l., with heavy pain in occipital region, extending to nape.

Vertex.—*Sensation of something rushing upward and throbbing in.* Throbbing, and in carotids, with redness and heat in face, head and neck. Humming.

Parietals.—Aching in l. Constriction as if pressed in. Dull throbbing in sides and back of head.

Occiput.—Boring. Aching; r.; < r.; < heat of room and writing, > when forehead was painful; sub-occipital aching, < fatigue and evenings. Throbbing.

Clinical.—Valuable for violent neuralgic headaches, with great flushing of the face, gasping for breath, tremulousness, dyspnœa, or alternating paleness and coldness of the face, especially of one side. Sometimes useful in the results of sunstroke with the characteristic surging of the blood to the head and face, oppressed respiration, staring eyes, choking in throat.

Eyes.—Glassy and rolling vacantly. Arteries of optic disk small, while *veins were dilated, varicose and tortuous.* Pain in sunlight, with lachrymation, then sneezing, weakness. Sudden sharp pain under l. Smarting of balls in evening, with injection of conjunctivæ. Pupils dilated. Twitching under l. outer canthus. Conjunctivæ bloodshot. Pain back of eye on looking at near objects. Vision dim; blurred when reading; wavering; yellow; primrose halo, even with eyes closed and shaded.

Clinical.—Exophthalmic goitre, the result of grief, with the characteristic flushings of the drug, enlarged thyroid gland, irregular, tumultuous action of heart, dyspnœa.

Ears.—*Throbbing;* behind ear. Sensation of a piston working up and down in. Sensation as if membrana tympani would be forced out with each beat of heart.

Nose.—Pressure over root. *Numb feeling in bones.* Sneezing; after rising; constant desire for. Bleeding from l. nostril.

Face.—**Flushed**; *then turgidity of facial veins;* then pale. Grayish white. *Sensation as if blood would start through skin, with heat and redness,* and with lachrymation. Creeping in l. cheek; r. cheek below malar-bone, then twitching and creeping under l. eye. Vesication of lips, nostrils, etc.

Mouth.—Wide open.

Throat.—Swelling and inflammation of l. tonsil. *Collar seemed too tight. Constriction;* > motion; *on each side of trachea, along carotids; extended to chest and caused dyspnoea and asthmatic feeling in larynx and trachea,* with desire to eructate. Sensation as from fumes of a match, with desire to cough. Tickling. Dry sensation in throat and mouth at 5 A.M., on waking, with stiffness and dryness of lips.

Stomach.—Appetite lost. Eructations. Nausea. Crampy pain in epigastric region. Burning; with empty eructations. Fulness and pressure, with belching of gas. Discomfort.

Abdomen.—Rumbling. Stool, with rumbling, then empty feeling. Distention, with pain. Griping. Pain, < when lying down. Oppression near liver. Griping in umbilical region. Crampy pain in umbilical region. Contraction of muscles of lower A. as if drawn together over region of uterus, with hard feeling on pressure in region of uterus, fallopian tubes and ovaries.

Urine.—Acid, contained a cloud of an oxalate (probably lime), with traces of sugar, specific gravity increased.

Menstrual flow begins at once, but ceases when no longer under influence of drug.

Clinical.—Effects of suppression of the menses, or after the cessation of menses, flushing headache or general flushes over the face and upper part of the body. Said to be valuable in hour-glass contraction of the uterus and hæmorrhages from the uterus. Valuable for after-pains which are associated with flushing of the face.

Respiratory Organs.—Cough; inclination to, with indescribable feeling of fulness about chest; hacking. Respiration accelerated. Peculiar sensation of choking. Suffocated feeling from palpitation. Dyspnœa with inclination to cough. Respiration difficult and rapid, with feeling of weight on sternum. Respiration spasmodic and irregular, a few breaths very rapid, then slow and long-drawn, finally they became barely perceptible. Sighing; desire to sigh convulsively. Easier and deeper, apparently from dilatation of bronchi.

Clinical.—Cough, spasmodic, suffocative, with great oppression of chest. Dyspnœa of Bright's disease.

Chest.—Aching in r. Drawing pain in l., between seventh and ninth ribs. Peculiar sensation in r. lung or chest, not exactly a pain. Oppression on walking; especially at lower part of sternum; at end of sternum on descending stairs. Contraction at left of heart. Warmth in.

Heart.—**Præcordial anxiety** (Acon., Cact.). Stitching and constriction in cardiac region. Pain in region of heart, > eructations; pain in region of, extending round to back; *pain and constriction around* (Cact.). Constriction and pressure over præcordial region as if he wanted to rub it. *Cardiac oppression and tumultuous heart action.* **Marked beating of heart and carotids.** Palpitation; after exercise, *action accelerated.* Blood pressure diminished. Pulse rapid; and small, then full; and irregular; irregular and jerking, then so slow and feeble that it could not be detected at the wrist; slow and *strong*, then quicker and jerking; pulse distinctly felt in fingers (Glon.).

Clinical.—Heart. Cardiac oppression, tumultuous action of the heart, violent pulsation in carotids. A valuable palliative in hypertrophy of the heart, with insufficiency of the aortic valves.

Neck.—Stiffness and pain, neuralgic or rheumatic, in r. side, and in r. shoulder, extending to wrist. Aching in morning, moving to suboccipital region.

Back.—Twinges near dorsal vertebræ. Aching across loins; on waking and lying down at night; < fatigue and evening. Aching in r. renal region. Pain and weariness in lower lumbar region in morning.

Extremities.—Trembling, with feeling of weakness. Shifting pains caused by movement, on dorsal surface of r. hand, on l. patella and from l. thumb to axilla. Rheumatic pain in l. leg and knee, then soreness of r. arm and shoulder, then lameness of r. scapula. Soreness of extensor muscles. Uneasy feeling. *Tired.*

Discomfort in r. shoulder. Arms trembling; pain and stiffness of r. arm, especially near wrist, < motion; lameness of flexor muscles of r. arm. *Tremulousness of hands,* with stiffness and numbness of fingers. Hand tired when writing, with crampy feeling in wrist and thumb, and the thumb grasps the pen so tightly that it is difficult to guide it. Drawing tensive pain in l. wrist and fingers.

Lower extremities stiff. Sharp pain in l. calf.

Sleep.—Drowsiness; and confusion; overpowering. Sleep restless, full of anxious dreams, frequent waking, with aching in temples, stomach and abdomen.

Fever.—Chill creeping over back and sides. Cold and clammy skin, suffused with adhesive perspiration supersaturated with Amyl. Heat. *Heat about head; with throbbing;* and along œsophagus to stomach. Heat *of face; with redness.* Burning of r. cheek, extending into eye and around r. ear. Heat in l. ear. Warmth of neck. *Sweat;* profuse, with cold chills running down back; on forehead; on hands, with warm feeling of head and body, especially abdomen.

Anacardium.

The marking nut, Semecarpus Anacardium, a native of the East Indies, is a small tree belonging to the Anacardiaceæ. A tincture is prepared from the crushed seeds.

General Action.—Essentially similar to Rhus tox. The mental symptoms are very pronounced and characteristic: the characteristic sensation is that of a "*plug.*"

Allies.—Anacardium occidentale (the cashew nut), Rhus, Ailanthus, Comocladia, Nit. acid, Merc.

Generalities.—Emaciation. Startings when awake in evening in bed. Trembling from weakness at every motion. Motions more energetic and persevering, muscles contract more vigorously, but on motion the fibres seem stretched too much or as if there were not sufficient fluid in the joints. Indolence; after siesta, so that he can scarcely move his limbs, and loathes speaking.

Stitches externally at several places, pectoral muscles, forehead, wrist, etc. Aching internally in whole body; in all tendons, so that he cannot walk and sinks down; like a boil in affected parts, so that he dare not touch them; burning in affected parts. Bruised sensation in all bones, morning in bed, with stiffness of nape of neck and small of back, and headache in forehead and temples, all > rising (Rhus t.). Drawing and pressive pain in almost all parts. Drawing in abdomen and thighs, with subsequent burning, then pain in bones on touch, so that she cannot fall asleep.

Uneasiness every other night, so that he could scarcely sleep; feverish, in afternoon, as during a cold, with faintness and tremor of limbs. Weakness after eating; W. during a short walk; after a short walk; *so that he wants to sit or lie all the time. Faintness on ascending stairs;* when walking, > continued walking, with heaviness of feet. Dulness of senses, with confusion of head and prostration. Heaviness in morning, with disinclination to rise; H. and fulness of body from playing on piano. (Any part which he does not move immediately goes to sleep). *Paralysis of some parts.* Panting, languishing condition, like paralysis, in afternoon after a short walk. *Disappearance of most symptoms during dinner, but reappearance of them two hours afterwards.* Periodicity in appearance of symptoms, the attacks ceasing for one or two days and then continuing again for a couple of days. Open air is unpleasant to him and feels too rough.

Clinical.—Alcoholism, restlessness, sleeplessness, twitching of muscles, he hears voices saying that he is going to die. It has been found useful in injuries of tendons and in chronic rheumatic troubles.

Mind.—*Labor is difficult, like absentmindedness.* Stupidity; after waking. *Vanishing of thought. Deficiency of ideas and loss of his subject without knowing it. Weakness of understanding. Loss of comprehension in morning, with confusion and emptiness of head.* Confusion of the present with the future; C. as if a cold were coming on. Dreamy state day and night, without sleeping, with anxiety about his business. **Memory weak** (Merc., Nit. ac., Rhus t.); *in morning, especially as regards single names; < forenoon;* in afternoon, with diminution of imagination; confused; lost, with impaired speech; vivid. Animation and liking for acute analysis, but every effort of this kind causes tearing pressive headache in forehead, temples and occiput.

He constantly thinks of some new object to which the mind forcibly clings. Excitement of fancy from 9 to 10 P.M., with many projects, but without ability to control his attention, and the mind gradually becomes dull, so that he is without ideas. *Illusions of fancy, with apprehension; melancholy I.* that he or his friend is lying on a bier in the side room.

He is separated from the whole world and despairs of being able to do what is required of him. Dread of labor. Disinclination to read in the morning. Despondency.

Anxiety (Rhus t.); *in evening; about every trifle; with dulness of senses;* **as if pursued, with suspicion of everything around him** (Merc.), when standing and walking; A. driving him out of bed. *Anxious actions and imagination that he is surrounded by enemies,* then warmth and boiling of blood. *Apprehension;* in evening; A. when meditating upon his destiny, with thoughtfulness. Lack of confidence in his own strength. *Sadness;* after eating; S. in forenoon, with awkwardness and indolence.

Excessive anger at a slight offense, breaking out in personal violence. Irritability; with desire to go into the open air; *irritable and contradicting. Takes everything in bad part and becomes violent.* Great susceptibility to insults. Impatience and activity; I. with the play of his children, which usually pleased him. *Indifference.* Listlessness in morning. Irresolution, awkwardness and querulousness. Laughing when he should be serious. Great cheerfulness; and more disposed to work in afternoon, as soon as the sleepiness after dinner is past.

Clinical.—Loss of memory, with melancholia, great difficulty in collecting the thoughts; the weakness of memory and mental depression have been relieved in syphilitic patients, but without marked relief of the general syphilitic symptoms. Melancholia, with fixed ideas of demons. At times inclination to swear; or the idea that he is possessed of two persons or wills. Fears that he is pursued or suspected. In general it cures a great variety of troubles associated with profound melancholy and hypochondriasis, associated with complete loss of memory, or with tendency to use violent language. Extremely valuable for brain fag.

Head.—Swelling. Twitchings from behind forward, reaching across l. side of vertex and forehead. *Tearing during hard labor;* T., returning every third day, with chills in whole body, low spirits and restlessness. Aching; < motion; with stitches in l. temple; occasionally; grinding in evening; stupefying, especially in forehead, exciting vertigo, so that he threatened to fall to the left when sitting; throbbing. Pressure inward in small places. Bruised feeling on waking from vivid dreams; in brain from mental effort. Confusion; in morning after rising, with heaviness; painful, when he lies in an uncomfortable position. Heaviness. Vertigo; afternoon after a walk; with blackness before eyes; *as if turning in a circle, on stooping;* as if all objects were too distant, when walking; as after spirituous drinks.

Forehead.—Stitches when coughing, or in side of head; tearing S. over r. eye. Pinching in fore part of head, with tearings towards forehead. Grinding in r. half of fore part of head, especially along the border of the orbit, > strong pressure and when eating, with pain as if a heavy load were forced in, the pain being > in evening when lying with the painful spot on the arm. Compression and dull pressure below l. eminence. Aching in morning; A. in angle between frontal and nasal bones; in centre of forehead, gradually extending deeper and over whole front of head, in evening; drawing, and in occiput and l. vertex; *constrictive,* from 5 P.M. till morning, with peevishness and a grinding pain, which is > by strong pressure, afterwards extending to whole head, with painful feeling of a band reaching from nape to ears; constrictive A. in r. side, especially at external border of orbit. Pressure from without over l. brow; outward at r. side; coming out at r. eminence; as if brain were shaken, every morning on waking, < walking. Painful confusion, extending to root of nose. Soreness.

Temples.—Twitchings in head in front of l. ear. Stitches in l., with jerking tearings; S., drawing from temple into forehead, when breathing. *Tearing in l.;* in brain, just above r.; piercing and biting, extending into brain. Neuralgia in r. *Pressure in r.;* inward in l.; *inward,* > towards evening, with squeezing in temples and *constriction* in vertex; tearing, in l. Compression in both.

Vertex.—**Pressure as from a plug** *on l. side. Aching when coughing or inspiring deeply.*

Sides.—Stitches through l., extending deep into brain; incipient tremulous S. in upper part of l. Tearing in r. side of head, face and neck, then humming before l. ear. Pressure in r., changing to stitches; P. in r., interrupted by stitches. Drawing pain in l. Confusion in l., then r.

Occiput.—Twitching shoots and tearing, < bending head backward, and in temples. Tearing in successive attacks, reaching to temple; T. in lower part of r., extending to forehead. Aching in r.; during cough.

Scalp.—Boils, feeling sore when touched or scratched. Soreness at 4 P.M., or of dura mater. Itching.

Clinical.—The headaches are digging, throbbing in character, > by eating, but < by any attempt to use the mind or by overwork.

Eyes.—Rheumatic tearing in l. (more in lids), extending to temples. Pain. Pressure upon, < l., and in l. external canthus when looking long at one object. Tearing in balls and orbits, mornings when walking. Pressure in balls from before backward or from above downward. Sensation as of something between ball and upper lid, which caused rubbing, something seems to rub between ball and lower lid. Pupils dilated. *Pupil contracted;* r. contracted.

Lids.—Twitching. Swelling; l.; swollen feeling. Pressure below l. external canthus; as from a stye in r. inner canthus and neighboring tarsal cartilages. **Pressure as with a plug** *on upper border of r. orbit,* extending into brain, with stupefaction of whole side of head. Sensation *as if a plug pressed* in under upper border of orbits and touched the balls. *Vision dim* in evening, as if eyes were full of water, obliging winking. Flickering; of a flame, > looking steadily. *Halo around light in evening.* Sensitiveness to light. *Short-sighted.* Every object appeared a long way off on waking from a nap.

Ears.—Twitches in external. Stitches in l.; tearing S. in tip of l. antitragus. Tearing in l., extending down cheek; T. along upper border of r. cartilage; sticking T. in l. external; suppurative tearing and beating in cartilage and inner ear, < boring in with finger, *and there arises a stopped feeling in meatus.* Twinging in r. meatus. Painful twitchings in l. meatus as if a nerve were put on the stretch, or like electric shocks. *Painful drawing in l. meatus internus.* Cramplike pain in meatus externus. *Cramplike contraction in l. meatus,* **with pressure against tympanum**; cramplike contraction in l. concha.

Ulcerative pain when biting teeth together; when swallowing. *Obstructed feeling, as from cotton,* in l., with impaired hearing (verified clinically, < during storms). Itching in, with discharge of brownish matter. Tingling in r. Pressure upon external. Drawing pain behind l. Sensation behind ears as if the part would become sore, obliging rubbing. *Roaring before. Humming.* Hearing sometimes acute, sometimes feeble.

Clinical.—Deafness, with loss of memory.

Nose.—Red sore pustules in r. nostril, on septum. Pain as from too great cold, causing lachrymation, also in fore part. Bruised feeling in l. bone. Obstruction of posterior nares. Sneezing. Coryza; in evening; with inability to get warm, heat in head, coldness of hands and feet, afterwards dry heat, tension in tendons of legs, cramp of calves and uneasiness about heart; dry; fluent, with frequent sneezing and lachrymation. Bleeding after violent blowing. *Illusory smell, as from burning tinder, morning on rising; like pigeon or chicken dung,* < *smelling his clothes or his own body; almost lost.*

Face.—*Pale.* Swelling, beginning at the eyes. Look sickly, hollow-eyed, with blue rings around eyes. Squeezing in middle of cheeks. Pressure upon l. cheek-bone; P. extending upward upon l. side of chin, with external burning of chin. Drawing pain in r. cheek-bone. Twitching of mouth and fingers in sleep. Dryness of lips and their corners; burning dryness of external borders of lips. Drawing pain in lower jaw, < evening. Tearing in joints of jaws; T. in r. joint.

Mouth.—Teeth. Tearing in l.; intermittent T. Aching in a lower incisor as from stirring a tooth-pick in it, < contact of tongue and open air; jerking A., more pressive than drawing, on taking something warm into mouth; drawing, in roots and gums of l. lower molars; cramplike drawing, in r. lower, reaching to ear; tensive and drawing, in a hollow molar, extending to ear, several days at 10 P.M. Elongated feeling at night in bed, with aching. *Gums bleed on slight rubbing.* Gums swell.

Tongue.—White and rough; heavy and swollen feeling. Difficulty in speaking certain words, as if tongue were too heavy. Speech firmer and surer in afternoon than in forenoon. *Painful vesicles in mouth.* Liquid comes into mouth and throat, causing nausea in chest. Bitter dryness. Taste bitter to bread; B. after smoking. Tobacco does not relish, it only causes biting. Everything tastes like herring-brine. Insipid taste; to beer; *insipid, foul taste to food.*

Throat.—*Firm and tough mucus, at same time obstructing posterior nares.* Stitches here and there externally. Slow thrusts coming from both sides of the ears and in their cavities, as if two blunt plugs were penetrating to meet in centre. *Scraping.* Roughness; after eating, with a deep tone to the voice. Rawness and soreness. Pressure in pit; on both sides of larynx, sometimes interfering with deglutition; sudden, in l. side. Dryness in forenoon, > eating; bitter D. Itching.

Stomach.—Appetite great, pressure at stomach and nausea unto vomiting, after eating; lost; lost for dinner, yet he relishes it; violent at times, none at all at other times. Thirst; after eating; constant T. Eructations in morning; after drinks and liquid food; after stool; with spasmodic pain at stomach; burning the throat, after eating; of fluid, choking him. Hiccough.

Nausea in morning; in morning, with a fasting sensation; towards evening, with salivation, then vomiting followed by great acidity in mouth; from food of which he is generally very fond; with retching, returning after drinking cold water, then vomiting of this water, with a sensation as if the œsophagus were pressed asunder by a large ball. Qualmishness at pit between meals, with anxiety as from a sprain, but without real nausea, and with good taste and good appetite.

Rumbling and fermenting in pit. Compressive stitches in pit, on inspiration and expiration. Contractive pain, > stooping, < lifting arm and turning body. Drawing and pressive pain below pit, when walking. Pressure after eating; from mental effort; in pit when walking in open air, > *after eating,* with drawing; after eating, with weakness and thirst; in pit after every meal, with tension; intermittent, over and near pit, when eating; slowly coming and going in pit; in region towards abdomen after a slight breakfast, as if he had eaten too much. Fasting sensation in pit, then pressure in stomach and feeling as of obstructed emission of flatus both above and below, with want of appetite. Burning rising into throat. Heartburn after soup, like sour air in œsophagus, with a constricted sensation. Shaking in pit at every step after eating. Tickling beneath pit, obliging laughing when occupied with serious things, but when occupied with ludicrous things he can refrain from laughing.

Clinical.—Morning sickness of pregnancy, relieved while eating, but the symptoms soon return.

Abdomen.—Inflation after dinner. *Rumbling,* with pinching. Flatus moving about, as from a purgative, after eating. Wavelike shooting, like lightning. Cutting and pinching, as from flatulence or cold, with tenesmus. Pinching. Griping; in morning. Pain more cutting than pinching, when flatus is incarcerated; P. as if intestines were spasmodically shortened, in forenoon on bending backward; as if something would twist together, then pressure; P. twisting and turning transversely across, with the tenesmus.

Hypochondriac dejection after a meal, there is pressure upward in abdomen, with weakness of body and mind. Stitches in region of spleen, seeming to be partly in chest and partly in abdominal cavity; S. in l. hypochondrium; S. sometimes in r., sometimes in l. hypochondrium, when inspiring; pulsating burning S. externally below r. short ribs; short stitches in muscles below l. short ribs. Pressure in liver region after eating.

Cutting suddenly once in r. side. Intermittent pressure outward over ring.

Umbilical region.—Rumbling. Stitches in cavity; S. on r. side over umbilicus; S. l. side; intermittent S. at umbilicus. *Thrusts as from a blunt tool in r.* Pressure in a small spot above and below U., and in l. side of abdomen; below U. after eating, < pressure and breathing; in muscles below umbilicus during stool, and especially after it, < inspiration; as if something hard had formed, with a sensation when breathing, speaking, and especially when coughing, as if the abdomen would burst, and when touched pain like a pressure and tension; *around umbilicus* **as if a blunt plug were squeezed into intestines.** Pinching contraction in l. when breathing.

Hypogastrium.—Stitches; deeply penetrating, at spinous processes of l. iliac bones. Pinching during stool. Griping.

Rectum and Anus.—*Tenesmus, but he cannot expel anything, and the rectum seems plugged up; frequent T. during the day, without ability to expel anything. Urging to* *stool after eating, more in upper part of intestines;* frequent urging, with scanty, first soft, then hard stools. Straining at stool, even when soft. Itching at anus; after an embrace.

Stool.—Diarrhœa at night, then constipation; frequent D., watery, but difficult. Pale. Frequent but difficult S. Constipation.

Clinical.—Stools very sluggish, the rectum seems plugged up; the attempt to have a stool causes distress in abdomen.

Urinary Organs.—Discharge of prostatic fluid after micturition; D. during stool. Constant desire to urinate; frequent desire, but little passes. Irritability of bladder. Micturition at night. Itching in urethra. Frequent, clear, watery urine, before breakfast; frequent, clear, watery urine, in small quantities. Dark green urine. Urine turbid when emitted, depositing a dirty sediment.

Sexual Organs.—Tearing in mons veneris. Cutting along penis. Desire; morning after waking; D. from voluptuous itching on scrotum; lack of D. Emission at night without amorous dreams.

Respiratory Organs.—Cough in morning; evening in bed, causing blood to rush to head; nightly, with rawness of throat; after dinner, with vomiting of food; < night; with vain desire to sneeze; resembling whooping-cough, whenever he talks; shaking, at night, preventing sleep; in severe attacks, with shivering; beginning with tickling in larynx and suffocation; periodical, only by day, with arrest of breathing; hacking, after eating, affecting throat as if it were raw; short, with purulent expectoration; short, < afternoon, with tenacious, gray-yellow expectoration. Expectoration of blood when coughing. Asthma. Short respiration, < after eating and when sitting; *S.*, with oppression in region of sternum. Interrupted respiration when drinking.

Chest.—Twitching of pectoral muscle, when raising arm. Stitches; a hand's breadth below l. axilla; in upper part of l. mamma, preventing rising from her seat, afterwards a weight at that place; pulsating above heart; intermittent pulsating, close to l. side of throat; constrictive, externally at l. false ribs; corrosively itching, at last false rib. Tearing in l., reaching to heart, with pressure as if the whole were being crushed, < sitting bent.

Pressure upon part of r. border of sternum; P. on chest, < sitting, with fulness and desire to get rid of this symptom by vomiting; **dull P., as from a plug,** in r.; sudden P. close to r. axilla, and at the same time on opposite side of back; P. upon sternum, as from a blow, when falling asleep during the day; inward P. over r. nipple. Oppression; during expiration, with pressure upon sternum; with internal anxiety and heat; with weeping, which relieves it; extending towards axillæ, with difficulty of breathing. Oppressive anxiety in region of sternum, as if he must go into the open air and be busy. Drawing pain in muscles. Wavelike drawing in l. chest. Soreness in a spot behind sternum; S. in chest, < inspiration, with rawness.

Heart and Pulse.—*Stitches in præcordial region when breathing;* at night when breathing; in l. præcordial region, < breathing and walking; *in præcordial region, extending to small of back;* short, through and through heart, succeeding each other two by two. Cutting in præcordial region. Uneasiness apparently about heart; < forenoon. Weak feeling, as if working too slowly. Pulse weak and accelerated. Slow P.

Clinical.—Palpitation, especially in old people, when complicated with such slight difficulties as an ordinary coryza, rheumatic affections of the pericardium. Rheumatic pericarditis, with double stitches through the cardiac region, one stitch is quickly followed by another, then there is a long interval.

Neck.—Cracking in cervical vertebræ when stooping. Intermittent pressure at angle formed by neck and top of l. shoulder; *intermittent, as from a heavy burden,* on r. side of neck and on top of l. shoulder, apparently in bone. Rheumatic drawing downward along nape.

Stiffness of nape; painful, in r. side of neck, mornings on waking after lying on that side, < turning head toward painful side; with tensive pain, < turning head quickly after keeping it still, less during constant motion; in nape, occiput and between scapulæ on waking, with pressive tension; painful contractive, on l. side close to occiput, when at rest, not affected by motion.

Back.—Painful stiffness when raising oneself while sitting, > sitting bent.

Scapulæ.—Cracking on raising arm. Stitches in external side of l.; *in l., returning slowly* and causing a tearing to extend to all sides; tearing, near r., extending outward. Tearing between scapulæ. Intermittent thrusts externally in r. half of external surface of l. Pain in r., near spine, as from continually sitting bent. Neuralgic pain over r. Cramplike pressure inward, under and near scapulæ; lancinating P. close under l. Bruised pain in r. scapula and upper arm, < lifting arm. Formication, or sensation as if asleep.

Small of Back.—Stitches.

Clinical.—Diseases of the spinal cord, sensation of a band around the body, feeling of a plug in the spine so that any motion of the body causes a pain as if the plug were sticking still further into the body, paralyzed feeling in knees, the patient is scarcely able to walk, feeling as if the knees were bandaged.

Extremities.—Paroxysmal tearings simultaneously through upper and lower. Neuralgia in region of outer metatarsal bone of l. foot and in fingers and knees. Heaviness in l. arm and leg when walking.

Upper Extremities.—Itching pricking below shoulders, > rubbing.

Arm.—Tearing in l., with drawing. Pressure in bones and muscles of r., with lassitude in them. Bruised feeling if he lies on them at night. Lancinating tension from joints down flexor muscles, on stretching and extending them, and on bending arms back there is a cracking in the joints, especially in shoulders, with pain as if dislocated. Rheumatic sensation in r. Pulsation when sitting quietly after they had been loosely crossed, and even in whole body (after exercise). Going to sleep of l.

Upper Arm.—Painful twitching above bend of l. elbow. Intermittent pressure, like a grumbling in l., apparently in marrow. Aching (spasmodically) in muscles in evening when walking in open air and when sitting. Rheumatic drawing pain from r. shoulder to bend of elbow, with stiff feeling in arm. *Pulsation as with a heavy body in middle of l.*

Elbow.—Pressure in bend of l., which draws the arm down and makes its motion difficult, when walking in the open air.

Forearm.—Cramplike twitches a hand's breadth above l. wrist. Cramplike pain in l. at night in bed, and in back of hand. Cramplike pressure in l., <

pressure, becoming a tearing pressure on motion. *Pressure inward here and there.* Cramplike drawing in r., from wrist to elbow. Pressive drawing on upper surface of l. Aching in muscles when writing. Pressive scratchings on bone when at rest.

Wrist.—Twitches in flexor tendons.

Hand.—Stitches on back of l.; on external knuckle of r., with itching; burning S. in border of l. where little finger joins metacarpus; tearing S. in ball of r. Tearing on back. Cutting at metacarpal bone of r. index. Sprained feeling in metacarpal bone of r. little finger. Cramplike drawing in region of metacarpal bone of little finger. Cramplike contraction of l., so that she cannot straighten her finger.

Pain in palm on moving it; *cramplike, where r. metacarpal bones join phalanges;* cramplike, where l. index joins metacarpal bone; intermittent lancinating, cramplike, on l. border where little finger joins metacarpus; cramplike, twitching, in anterior extremities of metacarpal bones; pressive spasmodic, in muscles transversely across back of l.; grumbling, between metacarpal bones of l. index and middle fingers, just behind knuckles.

Fingers.—*Cramplike twitches* in lowest phalanges of l., synchronous with pulse. Tearings in little; in r. thumb, extending to elbow, as if a whitlow would form. Intermittent cramplike pain in lowest joints of r. thumb and index. Intermittent neuralgia in flexors of r. thumb, < pressure. Contractive lancinating pain in muscles of l. thumb, > motion and touch. Tickling itching in little, seemingly seated deeper than the flesh, evening after lying down. Numbness.

Lower Extremities.—Uneasiness when standing, as if they ought to be drawn up, with anxiety. Weariness, as from too much walking, with sleepiness.

Thigh.—Cracking in r. hip-joint on moving it while sitting. Twitchings and drawings, especially in and about knees, as after a long walk, with painful uneasiness when sitting, like a tremulous agitation. Boring stitch in muscles of lower part of r. in front; burning S. here and there in muscles, obliging scratching; itching, in l., > rubbing. Sprained and bruised pain over r. hip when rising from a seat and when moving trunk while sitting, < then by rising, and compelling him to walk stooping.

Pressure at inner side of r. thigh, with twitching sensation; *P. in thigh sometimes intermittent, rhythmical; as from a plug* in l. gluteal muscles; in middle of external side of r. thigh, synchronous with pulse and always accompanied by a lancination; cramplike, anteriorly and posteriorly in l. Dull pain just above l. knee; above knee on lifting foot high, with soreness, and with painful weakness about knees and cramplike pinching between bend of knee and calf. Drawing pain down outer side of r.; drawing pain above knees when sitting, felt as mere weakness when walking. Tearing contraction in spot on external side of l., then pain as from subcutaneous ulceration. Painless weakness above knees when walking, with pain when sitting as after great fatigue.

Knee.—Stitches in r. Pain on long stooping, and in muscles above and below them; at inner side when walking, also with drawing; drawing, in l. when bending it (while sitting), > stretching; drawing, at internal surface of r. when sitting; drawing, apparently behind r. patella. Burning sore pain at outer side of l., as if scraped. *Painful uneasiness when sitting, with stiff feeling as if bandaged or made tense.* Weakness when standing after eating, with sleepiness and indisposition to work. *Paralyzed feeling, with stiffness and lassitude.*

Leg.—Tottering when standing. Pulsation and twitches in muscles. Painful twitches, like electric shocks, in l. tibia, over malleolus; wavelike twitches here and there in legs when sitting. Cramp in calves at night; cramp in calves when walking. Stitches on surface of tibia, over r. ankle; dull S. or thrusts just below r. knee when treading. Neuralgic twinges in l. calf; about r. calf and ankle. Aching upon l. tibia when sitting, with uneasiness of whole limb, which decreases when leg is drawn up. *Cramplike pressure in calves,* more towards outer side, towards tibia; rheumatic tensive P. transversely across tibia, on extending leg when walking; tearing, in tibia, just below ankle, at anterior surface. Pressive lancinating pain in tibia and muscles of legs, sometimes with boring. Burning pain in middle of leg, on anterior and rather on outer part. Drawing in legs; here and there after a walk; with pressure and heaviness, the heaviness > by extending foot; *cramplike, intermittent, from heels into calves; painful, in tibia;* downward in legs when sitting. Tightness in l. calf; *in calf when walking* and at night in bed, as if muscles were too short. Uneasiness extending up and down, when sitting, > walking and returning on sitting, causing pressure inward at places; U. when sitting, as if everything were alive in them and descended in a turning motion into feet, which felt heavy and almost as if they would go to sleep. Heaviness.

Ankle.—*Sprained feeling in l. tarsal articulation when setting foot on ground.* Neuralgic twinges, now and then. Drawing pain in tarsal articulation when he seats himself. Drawing downward over outer malleoli, when standing, with pain in soles.

Foot.—Cramplike drawing of r. sole into a curve. Painful twitchings internally on back of foot. Stitches on back of l. Tearing and grinding pain in heel in morning in bed. Cramplike pressure in l. heel; intermittent P. at inner border of sole. Burning sore pain above heel. Painful weakness of feet when sitting.

Toes.—Intermittent twitching in r. great. Tearings in great; T. transversely across roots, > moving them. Spasmodic drawing and tearing, extending into back of foot.

Skin.—Mulatto-like appearence of hands, white, with black spots. Redness of arm (affected part), with pimples, then swelling and redness of face, then redness of abdomen and thighs on which the arm had rested, swelling and redness of l. hand, forearm and lower half of upper arm, vesicles and pustules on forearm, especially at back of forearm, the redness > pressure, raised spots on back of r. hand, front of wrist and on lower abdomen, surmounted by white pustules, redness and swelling of eyes (l. closed), upper lip, chin and back of r. cheek, with red raised spots, the color being sharply defined, yellow crusts like eczema on chin, a red patch, with transparent vesicles on inner side of each thigh, the eruption causing itching.

Desquamation, excessive. Roughness around mouth, with exfoliation, herpes and crawling itching. Destruction; leaving an inflamed surface covered with miliary, itching pustules, the itching < at night and in warmth, especially when gloves were worn, the pustules discharging a yellow liquid forming crusts, with swelling and heat of whole back of hand.

Swelling of head; of face, beginning at eyes; of l. side of face, with pocklike blisters; passing gradually from eyes down to thighs; of neck after the head; of affected parts, so that the patient looked like a hogshead; with itching, so that the places were scratched sore. Hypertrophied appearance of skin, with swollen and indurated papillæ and wheals and formation of thick folds, which impede motion.

Inflammation of affected parts (hands), with pain and itching, then pustules discharging thin pus, coalescing, appearing like blisters, the blistering being confined to hands and lips, which had been rubbed, while the swelling and pustules extended to other parts, the penis and scrotum were enormously distended, but the eruption was confined to the scrotum, and there were some fever and thirst with the first appearance of the swelling.

Warts covering the hands, even the palms. Itching eruption around knees, as far as calves. Scarlet eruptions of whole body, especially of thigh in contact with the nut, and of abdomen. White, scaly herpes on r. cheek, close by upper lip. Pimple on side of l. index, after nightly itching in hollow of hand and between fingers which was >, not removed by violent friction; P., with red areola at top of l. temple and at angle of r. wing of nose.

Pustules, with red areola on lower part of upper arm, with itching during motion of arm; P. on index, with red areola and stinging, voluptuous itching, which spreads over whole palm, red and white lymph and afterwards a scurf appear, beneath which is a plug of pus, with a drawing sore pain in the ulcer in the evening. Hard, red, sore pustules on forehead and in angle of l. wing of nose. Suppuration and pain under chin where there was a boil two years ago. Blisters on backs of hands; on chin, discharging liquid when broken; discharging a yellowish transparent liquid, which hardened to a crust in open air. Raised crusts on chest, neck, axillæ, upper arms, abdomen, scrotum, thighs, discharging a thick yellowish liquid, partly changing into wartlike excrescences, with thickened epidermis, the intermediate skin being of an erythematous redness and the itching fearful.

Itching; at night; < in evening and when he went to bed; burning, at affected parts, < scratching; burning, on thighs in evening; the burning changes to painful itching, with stitching, like stings of insects; stinging, here and there, especially on back and thighs, > for a short time by scratching; voluptuous, over whole body, < scratching; voluptuous, on scrotum, which excites sexual desire. Itching of the wound (on l. wrist), then vesicles, with heat, inflammation and redness, extending above elbow, covering anterior and under aspects of the limb, the itching < at night, followed by soreness, redness and inflammation of scrotum, then eyelids and upper part of r. cheek appeared as in erysipelas, with heat, stiffness and burning in skin, also red patches on bend of r. arm and on r. hand, afterwards swelling and tension of r. arm, with redness, which disappeared on pressure.

Irritation, with feverishness, loss of appetite and constipation. Desire to scratch in many places, without itching, > scratching. Tetters which had itched before now burn and sting. *Dry feeling in hands and fingers.* Insensibility to itching irritants.

Clinical.—Extremely valuable in eczema, especially with great irritability of mind, the eruptions itch excessively and burn. The symptoms of this drug are to be compared with Rhus, to which they are very similar.

Sleep.—Yawning after an attack of cough; Y. after stool. Sleepiness in afternoon when sitting or reading, with weariness; evening and morning in bed, with weakness; at 8 P.M., after dinner; after eating, with indisposition to work; as from weakness. *Sound sleep till* 9 A.M. Difficult waking in morning. Slumber day and night, with heat, thirst, heat of skin, and with grumbling and anxious sighing when asleep.

Sleeplessness; often for half hours at night; till 2 A.M., with uneasiness. Frequent waking, with general sweat. Anxious sleep, his head lay either too low or too high, which caused confusion. Anxious screams in sleep.

Dreams of *fire.* Anxious, full of danger; A. about fire. That he had to preach without having committed his sermon, causing anxious meditation, without ability to accomplish it. *Of dead bodies*, a near tomb or a steep precipice. Of loathsome diseases of others. That his face is covered with white, ugly pustules. Of the smell of tinder and sulphur, with continuance of the illusion after waking. Mixed with plans he had made. *Vivid;* about old events; with great mental exertion. Oppressive, that everything one did would end in vanity and vexation, and that nothing could extricate me from poverty.

Fever.—Chilliness; after midday nap; of limbs in morning, causing trembling; of hands and feet; of feet in morning; of feet when walking; of feet, < walking. Cold creepings. Shivering as if he had caught cold; S. in back, as from cold water thrown over him; over whole body, with heat in face, without thirst.

Heat; in head; face; face and brain in afternoon, with redness of cheeks; face after dinner, with accumulation of sweetish saliva and thirst; H. in face every day at 4 P.M., with nausea and heaviness in whole body, obliging lying down, > eating; in face after eating, with weakness; spreading quickly over face after supper, followed by thirst. Burning in chin; B. between chin and lower lip, as if scraped with a dull razor. Heat of palms; with coldness of backs of hands. Legs burn as from glowing sparks. Soles burn when sitting. Heat on upper part of body, with thirst, sweat and hot breath, complaints of chilliness, causing him to shake, and coldness of feet, which were formerly sweaty.

Dry heat, < night, with thirst; D. in face and over head, with confusion of head, pale look and heat of skin; of hands. External heat in evening in bed, with burning itching and irritation as from much scratching, the burning < by scratching; E., with thirst and dry burnt lips; after waking, with stupidity, red cheeks, cold forehead, heat in head, thirst, and sore, painful dryness in throat; over whole body, with complaints of chilliness. Itching burning here and there in skin, > scratching. Internal heat; in evening, with cold sweat over and over, especially in head, with short breath, thirst and weakness in abdomen and knees, even to falling; with heat in face and palms, without thirst.

Sweat in evening after walking; at night; general, by an open window, with thirst for milk; in abdomen, back and forehead in evening by an open window; in chest and abdomen at night; clammy, on palms, < l.

Anagallis.

The scarlet pimpernel (poor man's weather-glass) is a small weed belonging to the Primulaceæ. A tincture is prepared from the fresh plant.

Trembling, like shivering, in evening; trembling of heart, evening in bed, before and during a dull pain in a hollow tooth, with trembling and shivering in whole body and anxiety in chest. Liveliness. Pleasure in everything. Inability to collect his thoughts during a sermon on account of joy, without thinking of anything in particular. Thinking about everything, and vigor of mind. Aching in sinciput after a draft of cold air. Spasmodic stitches in temples, extending to eyes, with pressure in middle of eyes. Twinges in r. ear.

Dry feeling and scraping in throat, in evening. Itching in rectum, with pressure in loins, as in hæmorrhoidal troubles. Desire for stool. Burning pain on urinating, < morning, with agglutination of orifice, requiring violent pressure before urine passes, which it does in several streams; burning tensive pain, during the erection before coition, > coition. Tickling prickling, half painful, especially at orifice, inclining to coition. Desire for coition.

Sudden feeling internally in chest as if struck with a cushion full of pins. Anxiety in chest in evening. Tensive drawing from l. shoulder to nape, renewed on raising l. arm violently and extending it forcibly downward. Dull drawing pain in metacarpal bone of thumb, < r., sometimes like a tearing, returning at uncertain intervals. Cramp in ball of thumb on cutting with shears in evening, becoming a dull drawing, when it leaves this place it appears in l. thumb. Sleep bad, restless, falls asleep late, wakes early and has not slept enough in the morning. Heat rising to head, and sensation of sweat on forehead, then sticking in eyeballs and tickling prickling in urethra, which inclines to coition.

Angustura.

We omit the symptomatology of Angustura vera. Formerly Angustura spuria was confounded with it, and an almost hopeless mixture resulted. The spuria being obtained from a species of Strychnos gave rise probably to its vaunted power over tetanic and spasmodic affections. (Angustura vera has been found to be useful in caries, especially of the long bones?)

Anthemis Nobilis.

The Roman Chamomile is a small weed belonging to the Compositæ. A tincture is prepared from the fresh flowering plant.

Allies.—Chamomilla.

Generalities.—Malaise. Laziness. Dislike to going out of doors.

Mind.—Wandering of thoughts, little command over mind, distaste for hard study. Peevishness. Nervous and afraid of being run over in the evening on going out. Low spirits; feeling as if something were about to happen, with desire to be alone to unburden himself by crying, < 3 to 5 P.M.

Head.—Aching in forehead during the fever; boring oppressive, in forehead at 6 P.M., > before morning, with general languor; A. in forehead as from congestion at 8.30 A.M., < bending head down after eating. Aching on top as from pressure from within and feeling as if the top of the head were blown off.

Eyes.—Lachrymation, < exposure to cold; after rising, < indoors, with running of *clear water* from l. nostril, < indoors and entering colder room. Pain as if something pressed against posterior part of ball, < bending head downward.

Nose and Mouth.—Sneezing when indoors. Lips dry. Face pale. Tongue coated white, with islands on it. Taste intensified; T. bitter.

Throat.—Constriction about junction with œsophagus, when drinking causing difficulty in swallowing liquids, but not solids. Contracted feeling on swallowing tea, especially in posterior part. Raw feeling in back part, increasing from morning till evening, < swallowing saliva and in open cold air; rawness, with disposition to swallow saliva.

Stomach.—Appetite increased, especially for meat; lost. Thirst; lost. Nausea < indoors. Warmth; pleasant, *then desire for food.*

Abdomen.—Aching in liver region, < walking; in r. hypochondrium, as from distention, with fæces, then urging to stool, which resulted in the passage of only hard mucus, the pain continued all day; corresponding to transverse colon, beginning on r. side and going to l., then diarrhœa, which was first *white*, then *putty-like*, then vomiting, with griping and ineffectual urging to stool, griping, and coldness and chilliness inside abdomen, passing into legs as far as knees.

Anus and Stool.—Itching in anus as from ascarides, < in evening, when sitting. Stools freer, softer; omitted; hard, dark; yellow; pale yellow.

Urinary and Genital Organs.—Pain as from distention in and over bladder, extending along spermatic cords (as far as contained in inguinal canal), which felt as if varicose. Desire to urinate on waking at 2 A.M., and every time he woke afterwards; desire to urinate, with pain at neck of bladder, as from distention. Frequent micturition; at night, with a small quantity each time. Seminal emission about 4 A.M.

Cough, dry, paroxysmal, in afternoon, from tickling at back of larynx, which was relieved by the cough, with aggravation of the cough in warm room, but not at night in bed.

Pulse rapid, full and soft.

Neck and Back.—Carotid vessels in neck feel turgid, especially marked below, decreasing upward. Aching in loins; < l., as from exertion, at 9.30 A.M., < walking, > 3 P.M.

Skin and Sleep.—Itching of soles as from chilblains. Waking frequently and walking about the room.

Fever.—Cold feeling when dressing, beginning in legs, where it was most felt, then in neck, then in whole body, when it became general it was most felt in neck, at 10.45 A.M., with nausea at 11.30, nausea went off at 1 P.M. on going into open air, but coldness increased, with dull frontal headache, dull aching pains in limbs, especially in large joints and loins, great lassitude, especially in gluteal region, tenderness of eyeballs on pressure, skin dry, cutis anserina, veins of limbs reduced in size, cold creeping over whole body, especially in scalp where it began, < on leaving fire, no appetite, tongue with a moist white coating, especially in centre, no thirst, pulse rapid, small and weak. Coldness of limbs from wrists and ankles downward. Dislike to touch or drink anything cold from forenoon till evening. Heat after walking, with sweat, especially on head and face.

Antimonium Arsenitum.

Triturate with sugar of milk.

General sick feeling. Sense of weakness. Congestion of head. Pain in forehead; temples; orbits. Conjunctivitis. Œdema of face. Loss of appetite. Nausea. Diarrhœa slight, without pain in abdomen. Pulse 90. Wandering pains along sciatic nerves. **Excessive dyspnœa in cases of emphysema.**

Clinical.—Useful in emphysema with excessive dyspnœa and cough, < eating and lying down.

Antimonium Crudum.

The crude mineral, Stibnite, a crude ter-sulphuret of Antimony, is pulverized under water, and the black insoluble powder is triturated with sugar of milk for use.

General Action.—A general tissue remedy; its chief manifestations hitherto being on the mucous membranes and skin. Gastric catarrh, with very white tongue. The disposition generally determines its choice.

Allies.—Sulphur, Ars., Lyc., Nux v., Puls., Zinc., Ran. b.

Generalities.—*Getting fat* (Kali c.). Swelling of whole body. Emaciation and exhaustion. Lies on his back at night. *Convulsions, with vomiting.* Twitchings of mucles in many parts. Disposition to start at slight noises. Heavy, pressive pains, sometimes in chest, sometimes in back, sometimes in both these parts. Sensation of general vascular ebullition. Uneasiness. Weariness; in morning, with indisposition to rise; at 7 P.M., especially of feet, with peevishness. Indolence and disposition to lie down after dinner. Feels badly in heat of sun and in warm air, even on slight motion and work. Aggravation on l. side of body; *A. from wine* (Ars., Lyc., Nux v., Zinc.). Feels best in rest and cold air (Lyc., Puls.).

Clinical.—There is general aggravation from cold water, whether taken internally or applied externally. Is suited to the bad effects of Rhenish sour wines.

Mind.—Dementia, did not leave the bed, spoke nothing without being asked, desired neither to eat nor to drink, but ate with pleasure if anything was offered, and she felt hungry, constantly pulled her neckcloth, or folded and unfolded a handkerchief, or pulled feathers out of the bed and gathered them together, with such insensibility that she did not feel the sores formed by the evacuations on which she was lying.

Sulky (Sulph.), *does not wish to speak.* Does not speak. **Peevish,** *vexed without cause.* Disposition to shoot himself at night (Ars.), > leaving the bed. Anxiety from 3 to 5 A.M.; about himself during the day; in attacks. Discouragement, making the head feel warm in front. Dejection of spirits during the day. Sadness in evening. Grief in forenoon, the sound of bells and the sight of his surroundings move him to tears, with short and heavy breathing.

Clinical.—Extreme irritability and fretfulness is the keynote to its use in a great variety of gastric disorders, especially in children; the child cannot bear to be touched or looked at.

Head.—Apoplexy; with much watery foam from nose and mouth. Intoxication. Tearing, > walking in open air; here and there, from morning till night; at noon, with heat in it. **Aching; after bathing in the river,** with weakness of limbs and repugnance to food; then nosebleed; dull stupefying pain when smoking, with nausea in pharynx. Emptiness, as after continual working in a cold room. Vertigo; with nausea. Weakness.

Forehead.—*Aching,* < *ascending stairs,* and *in vertex;* A. as if it would burst, with intoxicated feeling, sitting alone and refusing to speak; within skull, at r. eyebrow, as if pressed asunder; stupefying, externally when walking in open air, with sweat from anxiety. Pressure inward in l. side, at times drawing. Boring outward, and in temples. *Heaviness.*

Drawing pain over l. temporal bone, > pressure, then returning more violent. Pulsation externally at l. temple, < when it is not especially noticed, with fine prickings extending towards eyebrows. Painful spot on l. parietal bone, when touched, as if the periosteum were swollen. Flat tubercles on scalp, painful to pressure, with crawling all around. Single sharp stitches on scalp.

Clinical.—The headaches are the result of disordered stomach, especially of eating candy. There is great disposition to take cold about the head, especially after getting wet or after a bath.

Eyes.—*Inflammation; and redness,* with itching and nightly agglutination (Nat. m.). Redness of l., with photophobia on rising in morning and mucus in inner canthus. Fine stitches in fore part of ball in forenoon, without pain. Redness of lid, with fine stitches in ball. Twitching of l. lids. *Gum in canthi* in forenoon; mucus in r. canthus in morning and dry gum in both lids. Moist place at outer canthus, painful on sweat coming in contact with it. Itching in outer canthus. Sharp stitches below l. brow. Blindness.

Clinical.—Valuable in chronic blepharitis, with soreness, the eyes red, agglutinated at night.

Ears.—Redness of l., with burning and swelling, as from a mosquito bite. Swelling of internal concha, with redness and periodical itching. Stitches; itching, at border of r. concha, above helix, > touch. Drawing pain through r. ear into Eustachian tube, almost to the mouth, after dinner. Sensation of burrowing or swarming (of animals), < lying still. Crawling in r. meatus auditorius. R. seems blocked up in evening. Deafness, as from a leaflet before tympanum. Ringing before. Roaring, < afternoon; < during stillness; [R. after violent vomiting, then loss of hearing]. D. in as if some one were beating against the door of the house. Swashing as of water, when moving jaws.

Nose.—*Nostrils chapped and covered with crusts* (Ran. b.); *l. nostril chapped and painful. Pain when breathing, as from cold air or acrid vapor. Sore nostrils,* with drawing pain; *soreness in anterior angle of r. nostril,* with pain as in a cold; sore feeling when inspiring, < r. nostril, which is obstructed. Obstruction in evening (Lyc.). Dryness when walking in open air, so that he can hardly speak (Lyc.). Coryza; *with sore, crusty nostrils; dry;* fluent, also in morning. Bleeding, *every evening;* flowing out of blood.

Clinical.—A kind of eczema about nostrils, which became sore, cracked and scurfy.

Face.—Twitches in l. side; at corners of mouth. Sensation on touch at and below the chin as if the hand moved over *sore places, with honey-colored granules here and there.* Burning, stinging, as from a spark, on chin and upper lip. *Cracks in corners of lips, with pain like sores* (Arum t., Zinc.). *Dry lips.* Formication upon upper lip. Red pustules on upper lip and at r. corner, with dull pain.

Mouth.—Teeth. Grinding, waking from siesta. *Stitches on inspiration. Aching in a hollow tooth, < at night,* a fine stinging, pulling and grinding, as if in the nerve, moving downward, then upward into head, *and on touching the tooth with the tongue, pain as if the nerve were scratched.* Aching renewed after eating, < applying cold water, > in open air. A. nightly, with heat coming from chest; twinging, evening in bed and after eating. *Bleeding. Gums stand off from teeth and bleed easily.*

Tongue.—**Coated white** (Puls.) in forenoon. Blisters. Fine stitches in front, on l. border, after dinner. Intermittent sore feeling on r. border, with redness.

Rawness of palate when clearing throat, with expectoration of much mucus. Fine pinching in palate all night, < swallowing, > morning by hawking up the phlegm collected on sides of palate, leaving rawness. *Dry mouth* at night. Salivation; *salt.* Smell as in ptyalism from mercury.

Clinical.—Valuable for toothache in hollow teeth extending into head, < cold water. On the face pustular eruption with yellow crusts, which are painful, small boils and pimples on the face, especially about the mouth and nose, associated with white tongue and disordered digestion. Tongue thickly coated white; this is a very marked symptom. Especially valuable in the indigestion of children from sweets, associated with very peevish disposition; with this tongue there are loathing of food, nausea and even vomiting, headache, after-taste of the food, great thirst, especially at night.

Throat.—Clearing, and hawking when walking in open air. Roughness in morning, with dryness. Soreness on l. side, as from a swelling or plug. A foreign body seems to hang in it, he tries in vain to swallow or expel it. Scraping on velum palati from phlegm, which often could not be expelled. Much viscid mucus. Thick yellowish mucus must be drawn from posterior nares into throat and expectorated. Swallowing impeded.

Clinical.—Diphtheria, the child was very cross, whining and crying because it was looked at; especially on waking, with the characteristic crusts around nostrils and in the corners of the mouth.

Stomach.—Appetite little; lost. Goat's milk refreshes him. *Thirst; in evening; at night; with dryness of lips.* **Eructation of a fluid tasting of the ingesta,** afternoons; E. of a raw taste; bitter, like bile; loud. Hiccough; when smoking tobacco. Nausea; *after a glass of wine* (Ars., Nux v., Zinc.); with vertigo, vomiting; *with convulsions* (Nux v., Zinc.); *with diarrhœa;* with diarrhœa and anguish.

Cramp. Burning in pit like heartburn, with good appetite. Burning spasmodic pain in pit, driving him to the resolution of drowning himself. Pinching in region; on r. side, over and by side of pit. Cutting in region. Pressure in morning, with thirst; P., which is more like a dull cutting, < drawing in abdomen. Pain on pressure. *Pain as from fulness,* without fulness and with appetite; *as after too much eating, with distended but not hard abdomen* (Lyc.). Fulness after eating, with inflation, often alternating with lightness, vigor and activity of mind and body. Sense of hunger in morning on waking, without appetite, not > by eating, with emptiness in pit of stomach and want of animal heat.

Clinical.—Catarrhal inflammation of the stomach, with thickly coated white tongue, nausea, vomiting, after-taste of the food, etc. After nursing the child vomits its milk in little white curds and refuses to nurse afterwards.

Abdomen.—*Distention* (Lyc.); < after eating; causing pain as from internal pressure. Loud rumbling; in forenoon, as from emptiness; rumbling as when bubbles arise in water. Flatus after eating, moving about audibly, < r. side, some being expelled; rumbling F. bursts forth immediately after eating, some smells badly, some before passing off moves downward and meets other flatus, especially in r. side; inconsiderable flatus passes off, with a pressing-asunder sensation as if a copious stool would occur. Sensation after a moderate dinner as if the body were filled with moving flatus.

Cutting; with nausea in abdomen and accumulation of water on tongue; with oppression coming from stomach, indisposition to work, dry humor and pain at stomach on eructations. Pain. Sudden compressive colic, with gulping up of water. Sudden pinching in evening, especially on r. side towards back, < motion. Sensation as after violent diarrhœa, causing weakness. Empty sensation, > after eating.

Tight feeling below stomach, with empty eructations. Tension in hypochondria. Pinching on l. side of navel; like the beat of a pulse low down in l. side in afternoon; as from a swelling, in the cartilage or periosteum of upper part of crest of ilium. Hard gland in l. groin over Poupart's ligament, running parallel with it and painful on pressure. Hardness in groins as from swollen glands, with pain as from swelling felt on pressure.

Rectum and Anus.—*Rectum,* protusion during stool; *sore pain during stool, as if an ulcer had been torn apart;* itching; *discharge of mucus,* with emission of flatus; continual discharge of blood and solid portions. Varices protrude more than usual. Crawling in hæmorrhoids, evening in bed till falling asleep, with burning. *Itching in anus* (Sulph.). Burning in anus at night, with itching and smarting. Drawing pain in anus.

Clinical.—Hæmorrhoids, with oozing of yellow mucus, constipated during hot weather.

Stool.—Urging after dinner and quick expulsion of ordinary fæces, with straining (Trombid.). *First natural, then several small, loose evacuations, then small hard evacuations, with violent straining in rectum and anus till all are passed. Liquid.* Thin; after vinegar, with pain in rectum. Diarrhœa at night and in morning; disposition to diarrhœa, which does not take place. Pappy, frequent. Hard in morning; in evening, with pressing in rectum and cutting in abdomen. *Difficult and hard;* with previous pressing in rectum. *Constipation.*

Clinical.—Alternating diarrhœa and constipation in old people.

Urinary Organs.—Painful contracted feeling at neck of bladder. Tenesmus at night, rousing from sleep; constant urging, with dysuria; frequent tenesmus though little urine is passed; *frequent and violent desire and much urine each time. Frequent micturition; with* *burning in urethra during emission;* at night, with copious urine; with scanty watery urine; with scanty urine expelled in great haste; with dark urine. Urine expelled more rapidly. Burning in urethra. Urine copious; scanty at night, in an intermitting stream, with painful erections. Brown-red. Gold-yellow, thin, with scarcely perceptible cloud. Small red corpuscles after standing.

Sexual Organs.—Burning at penis. Itching at penis; at extremity. Erections. Biting-itching at l. side of scrotum, as from salt. Drawing pain in spermatic cord, < standing, > stooping, while there was a boil at perineum. Sexual desire, with uneasiness in whole body; desire diminished. Irritation as if a pollution would come on, even when leaning the back against something. Pollution at night, with many dreams; without voluptuous dreams. Discharge of water from vagina, causing biting down thighs. *Pressure in womb as if something would come out.*

Clinical.—Suppression of menses with the gastric and mental symptoms of the drug. Prolapsus uteri when there is constant bearing down as if something were pushing out of the vagina, and tenderness over the ovarian region, particularly when the menses have been suppressed by cold bathing. The leucorrhœa is watery and contains little lumps.

Respiratory Organs.—*Spasm of larynx and pharynx as if the throat were filled with a plug, which became alternately thicker and thinner, with a sore feeling.* **Voice lost** as often as he became hot, > by resting himself; *weak;* rough. Cough in morning after rising, coming from abdomen, *in paroxysms, each becoming weaker, so that the last attack is only a hacking cough.* Dry cough frequently; dry, in a sudden short attack, with scratching in trachea. C. in morning, with discharge of viscid thin phlegm from deep in chest. Asthma. Suffocative catarrh. *Dyspnœa.* Difficult breathing during supper; after supper. Sighing as from fulness of chest afternoon and after eating.

Chest.—Stitches in middle, with constrictive pinching; S. when breathing deeply, on r. side under two first ribs, then under upper part of sternum; in l. when breathing, with cough and headache; sharp, in l. during expiration while standing. Pain half pressive, half sticking, under l. clavicle, apparently in air passages, when breathing. Pressive pain in interior of r. chest in evening when lying down. Pain in pectoralis major as from contusion or too great effort, in morning when extending and lifting arm or on pressure. Oppression; morning on waking. *Burning, with dry cough and dyspnœa; B. at every cough, with hot breath.*

Heart and Pulse.—Palpitation. Pulse, sometimes a few quick, then three or four slow beats.

Neck.—Swelling of cervical glands. Spasmodic drawing pain in muscles of nape, as far as scapulæ, in evening after lying down and in morning, caused and < by stooping, exerting arm and turning head to left. Spasmodic drawing downward in one of the r. cervical muscles in evening when sitting. Inward pressing drawing on l. lower part. Tightness when stooping, in nape and between scapulæ.

Back.—Spasmodic stitches in r. scapula when sitting. Tearing in back from morning till night. Pain in small of B., > night; in small of B. when rising from a seat, > walking.

Extremities.—*Discolored nails.* Enlarged feeling. Tremulous fatigue and heaviness after dinner, as if coming out of abdomen, with trembling of hands when writing, then much offensive flatus, the abdomen being distended.

Upper Extremities.—Twitches in r. deltoid. A stitch under both arms when walking in open air. Upper arm, drawing jerk transversely through r.; quivering drawing in muscles, > warmth, renewed in a draft; paralytic pain in muscles when bending arms; as if contracted too much or weakened by the contraction. Cracking in elbow on turning it to and fro. Drawing in forearm; down r. forearm; paralytic drawing in r.; drawing on inside of lower part, with sensation of pressure from without. Cracking in metacarpal joint of thumb on motion. *Finger-nails did not grow as fast as formerly, and the skin beneath the nails was sensitive. Drawing pains in fingers and their joints.* Gouty pains in joints of r. fourth finger.

Clinical.—Acute rheumatism in fingers with the gastric disturbances, also the nails of the fingers became horny and split, or horny growths formed beneath the nails. Soles became very sensitive when walking, corns became inflamed, and new corns formed on the soles or toes.

Lower Extremities.—Painless drawing beginning at r. knee or os ischium, going down thigh and tibia to foot, so that he has to lift it and change its position several times. Twitches in l. natis in evening when sitting. Drawing in one natis, around hip-joint into thigh. Clucking in lower part of r. natis when standing.

Thigh.—Drawing pain at anterior and internal sides; in posterior muscles of l.; in hip-joints, towards os sacrum; in l. hip; *in l. hip-joint* in evening and when walking, < when bending thigh backward. Pain in r. hip-joint. Tension high up in r. thigh, like a spasm. Sensation of a spasm at external border of thigh in afternoon, as if muscles became slowly contracted and extended.

Knee.—Sudden stitch on outside; stitch in l., causing jerking in leg. Drawing pain in r. Stiffness; painful, obliging limping.

Leg.—Deep stitches down tibia; sharp stitches outward in shaft of r. tibia when sitting. Drawing pain as high as knee; drawing pain at lower part of l. tibia; on inside of l. calf. Bruised feeling in a spot on outside of l. calf when touched. Pain just below knee as if tied tightly, in evening. Painless intermittent pinching low down on r. calf. Clucking posteriorly in r. leg, then stitches in ankle.

Malleolus.—Sprained pain in r. outer, when turning foot outward, with cracking of joint when bending or stretching it.

Foot.—Mortification after the violent vomiting had subsided, with burning, lancinating and tearing pain, but insensibility to touch or prick of pin, followed after amputation by suffocative catarrh. Chilblains in summer, with pain and redness. Heaviness so that she cannot lift it. R. feels benumbed when walking and goes to sleep. Heel, drawing pain in l.; cramplike drawing at outer side of l. *Soles, horny places close to where the toes begin, with pain as in corns; sensitiveness of soles when walking, < on a stone pavement; fine prickings in soles.*

Toes.—Cracking of great toe, at every motion requiring effort. Tearing and drawing through r. great. Rhythmical cutting under l. great. Burning pain in ball of r. great. A corn on l. little toe became painful as if pressed upon.

Clinical.—Useful in soreness of the heels.

Skin.—Bluish spots on thighs; on tibiæ. Liver-colored spots on shoulders; liver-colored spots and dots here and there, especially on arms. Red points on chest, with itching, not > by rubbing. Red points, with white dots in centre; on front of neck, with stinging on moving hand over beard; red points, with white tips, below l. corner of mouth. Rash; behind ears, as far as nape and over scapulæ; on middle of upper arms. Nettle-rash in face, especially on cheeks; on face and limbs, as far as the swollen fingers, with thirst and nausea.

Pimples coming on at night; on styloid process of l. radius; on r. natis; as from mosquito bites on face, also on r. cheek, also on r. knee; that itch on getting warm in bed and prevent sleep; itching at bend of elbow, also in ball of hand, on muscle of thumb. *Pimples and vesicles as from stings of insects*, beginning with itching, in many parts, *especially on face and joints* of limbs. P. painful to touch, on neck and under chin; red, hard, painful to touch, on l. temple, where cartilage of ear begins. Red, on top of r. shoulder, passing off for a short time on pressure. Red, hard elevation on each side of forehead, with itching, coming and going. Hard pea-shaped body under skin on l. side of nape, felt on stretching skin when bending head. Flat pimples, itching when touched, on cheeks, with yellowish scurf. Red, itchlike P., stinging on touch, on carpal joint of r. thumb, with brown scurf.

Eruption on l. cheek towards chin, with yellow crust, painful to touch, and which may be knocked off easily. Red, burning, suppurating eruption on face. *Pustules here and there, with brown scurf;* painful to pressure, on both sides of nose; hard, long-continuing, like pocks, below neck; hard, on l. natis, with itching and tensive pain. Boil on perineum, with burning and pain far around. White tubercle, painful on touch, above eyebrows. White, hard tubercles, with red areola, on leg, after itching. Vesicle on styloid process of r. ulna; on outer border of l. hand; itching, on l. hand. Like varioloid, with stinging on pressure, in several places; on face and nose; on knee. Red heat V., with yellow dots over r. shoulder, afterwards they look like gooseflesh and scale off.

Stitches here and there on neck; in r. sole, evening in bed after a walk, > rubbing. Tickling and itching stitches from within outward here and there, especially in upper arm and under r. natis. Sensitiveness of neck, sore feeling when rubbed hard on account of itching, also upon chest. Crawling along l. calf. *Itching, especially on neck and limbs; on back; on chest;* here and there, waking him, with blisters; waking him, with pimples at several places; on chest, then sore feeling after rubbing, skin sensitive as after blisters; of arm, and after rubbing reddish blisters like mosquito bites; on inside of r. knee, and after rubbing a painful blister; on chest, as if blisters were healing. Stinging itching of r. thigh not > by scratching, then a flat, yellowish pimple.

Sleep.—*Sleepiness during the day* and in morning after waking; in forenoon; in afternoon when sitting; *overwhelmed with sleep* every day at 7 P.M., and she continues to sleep during the night; at 6 P.M., and peevish, at 8 he cannot refrain from sleeping, sleeps soundly all night and in the morning is so tired that he can scarcely open his eyes. Sleepless till midnight; every evening, with shiverings, especially over whole l. side, upon which he does not lie, or with sexual desire when getting warm, and erections making him more awake. *Waking frequently at night, as from fright;* waking frequently at night, and on falling asleep dreams about solemnities.

Fanciful delusions in sleep; she hears a knocking outside or is called. Horrible dreams about the mutilation of men. Anxious D., as if he were to be hurt, he starts up from sleep and struggles with his hands and feet. Sleep interrupted by disagreeable dreams about quarrels with his relatives. Pleasant D. of seeing an old schoolmate. Voluptuous, at night, with pollutions.

Fever.—Chilliness; internal. Cold feet; till 1 A.M. Shiverings over whole back, without thirst; S. over whole body in morning, with heat in forehead, without thirst. Chills towards noon, with thirst for beer, then sleep, then heat and thirst. Hot feeling from slightest exercise, especially from heat of sun, with heat in throat. Warmth all over body on waking at 2 A.M., with burning itching and excoriated feeling in anus. *Heat at night in bed, with sweat.* Sweat during sleep; general in morning on waking; general, making finger-tips soft and wrinkled; returning at the same hour on three days in succession.

Antimonium Sulf. Auratum.

The golden sulphuret of Antimony, a reddish-brown powder, is triturated for use.

General Action.—A tissue remedy similar to Antimony and Sulphur. Its clinical application has hitherto been confined mainly to diseases of the respiratory apparatus, coughs, etc., one case of chronic pleuro-pneumonia, with extensive pleuretic effusion, is reported cured.

Generalities.—Thick crusts, could only be removed with pain. Burning sticking in whole l. side, especially in lumbar muscles. Rheumatic symptoms in all parts. Weakness in morning; in morning, > afternoon, with tendency to tremor, etc., with disposition to stretch and yawn.

Clinical.—**Of very great value in acute and chronic nasal and bronchial catarrh and in acne.**

Mind.—Apprehensiveness.

Head.—*Aching;* with fulness and pain in r. ear; heavy; onesided, especially in l. temporal region. Tightness, with restlessness. Confusion; on account of urging in abdomen; especially in cerebrum. Vertigo and stopped feeling as from fresh catarrh, mind sluggish, with singing in l. side of head, dull feeling in front of head. Forehead confused. Forehead heavy at 10 P.M., with singing, flushed face, ill humor and rather an independent, indifferent, reckless kind of feeling.

Vertex.—Lancinating pain in r. side in evening, extending to r. inner angle of eye. Aching in morning, with rush of blood to head on stooping, producing throbbing headache, with weakness; in r. side during rest, throbbing and severe during motion, extending to back of ear; during motion, < any jar while walking, when it seemed as if the skull would be raised to relieve the pressure on the brain; pulsative, and in frontal region, with feeling as if the skull would be raised with every pulsation of arteries.

Eyes, Nose and Lips.—Eyes weak, afterwards moist.

Increased secretion in nose and throat. Coryza in morning, with impeded respiration; C., with loss of smell; fluent, with confused head, impeded respiration and impaired appetite. **Nosebleed on washing.** Lips dry.

Mouth.—Boring tearing toothache. Tongue coated reddish-yellow; thick white coat, with dryness of mouth and much saliva. Salivation. *Taste pasty in morning;* P., with slimy-coated tongue; sweetish bitter and flat taste. Metallic styptic taste; extending into pharynx; extending to stomach; extending to lower part of pharynx, with nausea, fulness in head, heaviness about eyebrows and dull feeling in centre of forehead.

Throat.—Increased secretion of mucus in back part. Offensive-smelling mucus. Pressure as from a plug. Pressure and tensive feeling, < at larynx. Scraping pain, especially in larynx, with heat in fauces. Scraping slimy feeling. Scratching rough feeling in morning. Soreness, with hard cough; S. in morning after getting out of bed, with hacking cough and expectoration of much mucus.

Stomach.—Hunger. Appetite at dinner too much, then stupid feeling, with sleepiness, A. strong again at 6 P.M., with a good deal of thirst (fever?). Appetite lost; with almost loathing of food; with nausea. Nausea; > cup of tea; with tearing in the stomach, the latter > rest. Vomiting. Weakness, disordered digestion, with nausea. Pressure; in pit; in epigastric region. Fulness. Emptiness. Feeling as of an acid, with nausea; feeling as of an acid, which appeared to increase and boil up. Weight in lower part of epigastrium, with nausea, excitement and ill humor.

Abdomen.—Flatulency. Passage of much flatus, with sudden urging to stool, stool at first solid, then bright yellow, pasty, then colic and rumbling around navel. Tension and fulness; T. and sensitiveness, especially about navel. Colic as from a drastic purge. Twisting. Pressure in region of navel, with fulness. Sensitiveness of colon and especially at anus.

Rectum and Stool.—Constant urging to stool. Smarting and aching in rectum and anus. Pressing in R. after stool, with smarting; pressing in R. after stool, with burning smarting. Stools soft, reddish-brown; half solid, half soft; irregular, in hard balls, then pain and smarting in rectum, felt for several hours when walking; in hard balls; hard, difficult; hard and difficult, then smarting, pressing and throbbing in rectum; hard and delayed; hard and delayed, then heat and pressure in rectum. Stools increased, with nausea. No stool. Constipation, with tenesmus and burning pain in anus.

Urinary and Sexual Organs.—Heat in urethra during micturition, then smarting extending about an inch into urethra. Tickling in urethra, with twitching and increased urine. *Urine increased, dark-red;* increased, reddish-brown; increased, with tension and tickling in penis. Sensitiveness of genitals. Itching of genitals, anus and perineum. Itching of scrotum, < towards morning, then redness, next day dry pustulous eruption, with constipation, afterwards the itching and eruption extended more towards perineum. Desire excited.

Respiratory Organs.—Tickling in larynx as from mucus without ability to expectorate; in larynx and trachea as from mucus. *Increased mucus, with fulness in bronchi* and full, hard breathing; increased tough mucus during the restless night; tough mucus in bronchi and larynx. Pressure in bronchi, with constriction. Fulness in bronchi; with difficult respiration. Increased mucous expectoration mixed with blood, of a sweetish taste. *Respiration difficult;* difficult, full; hard, full of râles.

Heart and Pulse.—Heaviness in præcordium, with apprehension. Pulse soft; small, suppressed; slower in evening than in the morning.

Neck and Back.—Tensive pressing feeling in cervical vertebræ, nape of neck and thoracic ribs. Tensive drawing pain in loins.

Extremities.—Tensive feeling in muscles of shoulder and thigh. Tensive and tickling sensation. Weakness. Joints, drawing tearing; gouty, rheumatic, drawing tearing; rheumatic pains; stiff tensive pains, in morning; tension, with increased sensitiveness, especially in shoulders and knees. Tensive pain in l. shoulder-joint. Arm, boring tearing in joints and in wrist; rheumatic pains in joints; heavy in morning; painful immobility of l. Twitchings in ulnar nerves like electric shocks, especially in elbow. Pressure in forearm, with heaviness and pain. Fingers swollen; tensive swollen feeling in F. Lower limbs weary and heavy. Tensive rheumatic troubles in hip-joint and inguinal region. Swelling of ankles and especially knees.

Skin.—Reddish swelling behind r. ear, which leaves redness and scurfiness. Elevated, dry pustules on inner surface of thighs, which itch, feel tense, pain on walking and involve the whole leg in sympathy, after nearly three weeks they dry and desquamate. Itching, especially on scrotum and inner surface of thighs; in bend of r. arm in afternoon, with redness like scarlet rash; of one, then another finger.

Sleep.—Deep sleep, with sweat. Soporous S., not refreshing. Heavy S., from which he was several times partially aroused by headache, mostly in r. frontal eminence. Sleepy early, but after going to bed wakeful, restless, with aching in legs, from knees to feet, with paralyzed feeling, and tingling and itching over face, on thighs and hips. Restless night. Broken, soporous sleep. Disturbed and restless S. at night, with headache, > rising in morning. Sudden waking at midnight, with confused head and pressure above forehead towards vertex, fulness in stomach, pressure and tense feeling in throat, especially larynx, pasty taste, bronchi full, hard respiration, then slumber soporous, not refreshing; sudden W. after midnight, with excitement, restlessness, sexual desire, then light sleep; after three hours' sleep, with heavy, confused head, pressure in stomach, difficult breathing, fulness of bronchi, tossing about, warmth and sweat.

Dreamy sleep; and waking after midnight with dull headache; with sudden wakings after midnight, with gouty and rheumatic troubles in limbs; and frequent waking with confused head, tension and dulness in brain. Vivid dreams, with sudden waking after midnight, with restlessness, drawing, tensive, rheumatic pains over thorax and spine, difficult and rattling respiration, with profuse mucus.

Fever.—General chilliness, with shivering down over whole spine. Febrile symptoms, which started along spine, extended towards the whole abdomen and limbs, then heat, with sweat, pulse full and soft, lungs sensitive, < l. lung. Chill alternates with heat; towards evening. Heat. Sweat at night.

Antimon. et Potass. Tart.

Tartar emetic, a tartrate of Antimony and Potash, is dissolved in pure water for use.

General Action.—It increases the secretions generally, but produces nausea and vomiting and profound depressions of the heart, pulse and temperature. It promotes rapid waste of tissues.

Allies.—Ars., Phos., Kali bi., (Cad.), Camph., Verat., Sec. c.

Generalities.—Emaciation. Blood loses fibrin and becomes thinner. *Convulsions; with tetanic spasms;* with unconsciousness; epileptic, with vomiting; convulsive movements. Springing into the air as soon as he got warm in bed. Distortion from cramps and rigidity as if dead, with gangrene of one foot and violent pain. Contraction of all muscles, especially of abdomen and upper limbs. **Trembling**; *internal; of head, with paralytic trembling of hands on every motion. Unsteadiness alternating with syncope.*

Tearing in limbs, chest, abdomen, testicles and eyes; T. in abdomen and limbs, with drawing. Pain < violent and quick motions, especially when sitting down afterwards; rheumatic P. in whole l. side. Bruised feeling. Drawings here and there. *The child wishes to be carried constantly.* Malaise; after supper. General distress; alternating now with chills, now with heat. *Pulsation in all vessels,* perceptible externally. *Restlessness; or nausea;* morning on rising, with weariness; from pain in abdomen; < 5 P.M., especially in epigastric region. The touch of anything is disagreeable, with inclination to unbutton his collar. Indolence, with sleepiness. *Faintness; from vomiting.* Relaxed condition of whole body. *Weakness* (Ars., Verat. a.); *after vomiting* (Ars.); on waking; from waist to toes, with coldness; *as if death were close at hand* (Verat. a.). Sensation lost. Aggravation while sitting. Amelioration after frequent emission of pale urine.

Mind.—*Furious delirium* (Verat. a.). *Talking to himself.* Unconnected wandering. Unconsciousness. Stupor interrupted by spasms. Restlessness. Excitement. (Suicidal mood, with raving.) *Anxiety increasing with the nausea,* with pressure and warmth in the abdomen, which moves about as from flatus. Apprehension, with fulness about heart and heat; A., with restlessness; about his recovery. Dreaded to be left alone lest he "should be dreadfully nervous and not know what to do with himself." Despondency *towards evening,* with pain in chest, sleepiness and chilliness. Fright at every trifle. Quarrelsome. *Whining and crying if touched,* with drawing inward of toes and fingers. Ill humor; on waking, with rubbing of his eyes as if in a stupid sleep, and howling if one looked at him; with intolerance of noise. *Gayety,* then towards evening peevishness and anxiety about the future.

Head.—Stitches from 11 A.M. till evening; S. on motion. Aching; in brain; with pressure and throbbing in forehead and temples; with sensitiveness in epigastric region; stupefying; tensive, in afternoon, with drawings and burrowings as far as root of nose; *tensive,* especially in forehead, mornings on waking, > *cold water.* Inflammation of meninges of brain. Congestion. Compression. *Intoxicated condition, as from wine.* Stupefaction as if confined. Confusion; morning; *morning,* > rising; *with a feeling as if he ought to sleep;* with warm forehead, depression of vigor and indifference; with nausea; with heaviness and pressure in sinciput; like a pressure in temples. *Heaviness;* with confusion; in morning on waking, with confusion and discomfort; requiring a support behind. Vertigo; on closing eyes; *on lifting head from pillow* (Cact.); on walking; tottering from V. when walking; with flickering before eyes. Internal weakness; external, with inability to hold it erect.

Forehead.—Twitching and drawing, especially over l. eye, with tension. Sticking (or rather tearing) from 2 P.M. till 3 A.M. Boring below r. eminence. Bruised feeling. Aching; < motion; above nose; over nose and one eye; in sinciput and occiput; in r. side in evening and in l. half in night, both with sensation as if brain were balled into lumps; in l., with pressure on eyes, *as from a band;* wavelike, on r. eminence; drawing about, in F. and vertex, with tension and pressure; *more like a sticking, extending into l. eye,* with inclination to close eyes; which sometimes becomes a sticking, which extends to temple, < cough. *Throbbing in r. side.*

Temples.—Sticking. *Drawing pain in r.; extending to zygoma and upper jaw.* Pressure inward in l. Compression. Tension as if squeezed, with stupefaction. Pulsation in bloodvessels.

Aching on vertex; on waking. Tension on vertex. Tearing drawing from behind forward in l. half of head; intermittent T. in r. side of head. Tensive pressing-in aching in l. half of skull. Stupefaction in l. half of head, with tension. Feeling in occiput as if something fell forward on stooping. Heaviness in occiput, with an anxious oppressive sensation. Hair falls out.

Eyes.—Fixed and turned upward. Squinting. Surrounded by blue rings and lying deep in their sockets. Swollen. *Bloodshot.* Yellow sclerotic. Pressure on. Burning in evening. *Weak;* and dim. Swimming and dim. Sudden tensive pain in upper part of r. ball. Bruised feeling in ball, < touch. Pupil dilated. *Inclined to press lids together tightly.* Lids difficult to move. Electric stitches in inner canthi, with pressure in eyes. Burning in r. inner canthus, with biting and with redness of conjunctiva. Conjunctiva congested. *Flickering before eyes; < rising from a seat, with vision as through a veil* and vertigo. Sparks. Vanishing of vision; and of hearing.

Clinical.—It has been found useful in herpes of the conjunctiva, photophobia, ill humor and weakness.

Ears.—Roaring.

Nose.—Pointed. Ulceration in anterior corner of nostril, with pain (Ant. c.). *Stupefying tension across root, as from a band* (Cad.). *Sneezing; with fluent coryza, chilliness, loss of taste and smell* (Camph.). Coryza towards evening; fluent C.; fluent, with tickling cough, eructations, retching and vomiting of tough watery mucus. Bleeding at 3 P.M., then fluent coryza, with sneezing.

Face.—Pale and sunken (Verat. a., Ars.). Red. Smutty-colored. Swollen. *Livid.* Bluish. *Twitching.* Distorted, with tetanic spasm of jaws as if endeavoring to bite everything within reach. Expression anxious; of great suffering; lethargic. Pressure on l. malar-bone; preceded by drawing. Tensive feeling, and in neck. Drawing from chin along r. side of lower jaw. *Lips dry, scurvy;* livid; cracked at night.

Mouth.—Toothache; in morning; rheumatic, in r. lower back teeth. Gums bleed. Gums appear like pink velvet with raised pile. Tongue white; T. coated; *thick, white, pasty coat;* thick yellow C. in morning, thicker in afternoon; pasty C.; slimy; gray. Dryness and redness of T. (Verat. a., Rhus t.); in centre (Verat. v.). Tearing posteriorly on l. side of root of T. on swallowing. *Motion of T. painful;* motion difficult. Speech difficult.

Pustules in M. and on tongue. False membranes in M., < on tongue, in irregularly rounded patches, whitish or grayish, somewhat thick, consistent and firmly adherent, in the œsophagus they are small, delicate, pale and easily detached, beneath the pseudo-membrane, the lingual mucous structure is excoriated, ecchymosed, wrinkled, and forms an elevated margin around the plastic deposit, which is red, the œsophagus is ulcerated, the borders of this ulceration not elevated but enclosed by a gray circle, the base being soft and grayish, and, at some points ecchymosed. Dryness. Salivation (Verat. a.); with a qualmish filthy taste; tasteless water runs out, with retching and bringing up of a little clear mucus. Taste bitter; B. in morning; B. and pasty; clammy; C. in morning on rising; metallic; salt; too sweet, to drinks; > drinking cold water. No taste to food (Verat. a.). Tobacco is not relished.

Clinical.—Tongue red and dry in the middle or red in streaks, with great prostration, or sometimes brown and dry in pneumonia.

Throat.—Pustules, some leaving soft superficial ulcers. Redness of soft palate and pharynx, with vesicles, many of which are opened, swollen and covered with mucus. Swelling of tonsils and cervical glands. Mucus; with short breath. *Pain.* Choking sensation. Burning; and in œsophagus. Disagreeable feeling caused by nausea; disagreeable feeling on palate. Soreness and constriction. Rawness, with difficult and painful swallowing. *Swallowing difficult;* > drinking cold water. Burning pain in œsophagus (Ars.). Sensitiveness of œsophagus.

Stomach.—Appetite increased; *great, for apples, with thirst for cool water* (Verat. a.); canine (Verat. a.) on walking in open air; *diminished;* D., with much thirst; soon satisfied, almost nauseated; lost; lost in morning. Aversion to food. No desire for tobacco. Thirst increased; at night; increased, *next day lost;* with internal heat; *for acids* and for strong liquors; **no thirst.**

Eructations; then rising of fluid (as of food), which she swallows, then sour taste and scraping down throat; *empty;* hiccough-like; of milk and acrid fluid; bitter; bitter and acid. Gagging. Nauseous. Salt, nauseous fluid. Sharp, salt, watery fluid. Sour. Waterbrash. Hiccough.

Nausea; *at noon when his appetite is nearly satisfied; at night, with vomiting and frequent stools; after dinner;* after eating; after drinking; at sight of food; from swallowing saliva; *with pressure in pit of stomach, then aching in forehead;* with swelling and pain in epigastric region; with vomiting of mucus and acceleration of pulse; with disagreeable taste and salivation; with aversion to food; with aversion to food and pinchings in abdomen; with discomfort and depression; *followed by yawning, with lachrymation, then vomiting.* **Anxious nausea** (Ars.); rising suddenly from umbilicus and epigastric region in repeated attacks.

Retching; at noon after soup; after vomiting; with sweat on forehead, weakness of limbs and flow of water from mouth, then weakness; ineffectual.

Vomiting after eating (Ars., Verat.); after pressure on stomach; > lying on r. side; *with headache and trembling of hands; with frequent stools, also with weakness* (Ars.); *with anguish* (Ars.); *then constant involuntary watery stools* (Ars.). *Difficult V.;* of bitter, bad-smelling, pasty fluid with an acid reaction. V. of food; from cough; food and drink. Of curdled milk. Whitish liquid. Green; in masses, with great effort. Dark. Of mucus; tenacious, with bile; painful, of mucus and bile mixed with blood. Of bile. Of blood, with colic and rolling about in agony.

Flatulent, audible motions in epigastric region. Sticking in epigastric region; below pit, < retracting abdomen; in stomach, extending downward into l. side of abdomen and again upward, with aching when touched; burning. Cutting in pit, extending upward. *Cramp.* Pain; > eructations; *in pit; in epigastrium, also with tension;* in epigastrium on pressure; in epigastrium, with retching and thirst; with heat; anxious, in pit, with distention and sensitiveness to touch; in pit as from incarcerated flatus, in evening, with forcible expulsions of flatus, which relieve; burning, after eating.

Enteritis. Anxiety in pit. *Fulness; at night, with eructations like foul eggs and restless sleep;* after dinner, with nausea, griping in umbilical region and sticking in sinciput and occiput. *Heaviness;* and in whole abdomen, > open air and eructations, < in house, causing malaise. Emptiness. Digestion diminished. Weakness. Warmth; causing restlessness. Feeling of cold water in pit, with faintness, then heat in head. Tension in epigastric and liver regions. Whirling in pit evenings on going to sleep, with violent rapid beating of heart. Pulsation in epigastric region. Soreness on touch; in epigastric region. Creeping. Malaise, and in abdomen, on touch the pain increases in stomach but diminishes in abdomen.

Clinical.—Continual nausea, with vomiting or efforts to vomit, with perspiration on forehead, great prostration and trembling, usually without thirst; or vomiting of tough, slimy matter, with great thirst and disgust for food.

Abdomen.—Distention; with gurgling. *Meteorism.* Offensive flatus. Gurgling. Rumbling; after eating; before diarrhœa; during stool, with pressure; as from water, > eructations and emissions of flatus. Commotion. Stitches; extending through rectum. Tearing, with drawing. Griping; > emissions of flatus; after eating, with cutting; > passage of wind upward and downward, with cutting and nausea. Pinching, with tension.

Cutting; towards 9 P.M.; *with heaviness across lower abdomen, ineffectual retchings, then ineffectual tendency to diarrhœa, difficult vomiting,* vomiting of food with sour taste, *trembling in abdomen and bending together,* then scraping in throat, then chill, *then two diarrhœic stools, the last like water;* with twisting, and with tearing from hypogastrium through thighs to knees, like labor-pains, stitches at navel, nausea and waterbrash, then diarrhœa, preceded by rumbling.

Pain; in evening after eating, > bending backward and stooping; after eating; P. after vomiting; before diarrhœa; < movement; on rising and on going to bed, sometimes changing into flatus, the emissions of which relieve, also > standing, returning when sitting,

< bending; extending towards rectum, > emission of hot flatus; drawing, with fluid stools; (spasmodic, with closure of eyes and necessity to sleep); *as from stones*, < *sitting and stooping*, at times changing to griping about umbilicus. *Sensation as if full of stones after long sitting at work, though it does not feel hard. Inflammation.* Nausea, like approaching griping. Tension, especially over bladder; < towards 6 P.M. Pulsation. Crawling in afternoon, becoming griping and flatulence. Sensitiveness to touch. Uneasiness. Discomfort, starting from A., with groaning, moaning and restlessness. Relaxed.

Upper.—Distention, with pain. Spasmodic motion as the nausea paroxysmally increases and retching arises in throat. Stitches. Tearing in l. Pain; in a spot in l. on retracting abdomen. Painful tension below short ribs, < sitting, from incarcerated flatus, which is emitted at times. Struggle in upper and lower A. between nausea and tendency to diarrhœa, at times > empty eructations and emissions of flatus. Discomfort in upper and lower, with necessity to lie and stretch out.

Dulness over liver, especially at base. Liver sensitive to touch. Aching in mesogastric region, with horripilation and gooseflesh; A. in umbilicus in morning. Pinching below umbilicus. Stitches over pubis. Sticking tearing in a spot in l. lower. Pressure in hypogastrium, with aching and cold shivers, as before menses. Pain in lower part of l. side. Burning in lower. Rheumatic sensation in l. pelvic bones.

Clinical.—Violent colic, as if the bowels would be cut to pieces, tearing from above downward; accumulation of water in mouth, and perhaps diarrhœa. Shifting of flatus, with sharp cutting colic, with nausea.

Rectum.—Sticking. Burning irritation like a tickling, extending through urethra to glans, where the tickling is most severe. Irritability and soreness. Ineffectual desire for stool though bowels seemed full and pressing. (Hæmorrhoids.) Heat in anus during stool; burning in anus after a stool. Tension in perineum, < walking, with urging to urinate.

Stool.—Watery; at night; and greenish; like opaque rice-water, with vomiting, pulse feeble, features shrunken, skin cold and bluish, < on hands and feet, fingers and toes dark livid or purplish, fingers shrunken like a washerwoman's, cramps in extremities, pain in stomach and bowels (Verat.). Half fluid. Diarrhœa; *with vomiting; offensive;* bilious, mucous; involuntary; yellowish-brown; like yeast, with cadaverous smell. Pasty; after repeated desire, though it seemed almost fluid. Hard; sometimes hard, sometimes soft; hard at first, then pasty, with tenesmus. Constipation. Blood-streaked. Bilious. Containing dead round worms. Mucous. *Copious.* Difficult. Involuntary. *Frequent, with vomiting, and with weakness.* Stool after eating.

Clinical.—Stools grass-green, slimy, with vomiting, colic, etc.

Urinary Organs.—Sticking in lower part of bladder. Micturition frequent; difficult and painful; involuntary M.; urging at night; *urging increased, with burning in urethra and scanty urine, the last drops of which are bloody and accompanied by pain in bladder.* Sticking in posterior part of urethra in forenoon. Tearing in fore part of urethra. *Burning in urethra when urinating; B. after urinating.* Diuresis. Copious urine forenoon and evening; copious and watery; copious, dark and turbid. Urine retained, then fatal eclampsia. *U. brownish-red, turbid and of strong odor;* red inflammatory look and deposit of bloody red fibres. Turbid U. at first clear like water, deposits milky sediment. U. contained desquamated epithelium of uniferous tubes. U. albuminous (Arsen.).

Sexual Organs.—Swelling of external. Excited, then relaxed. Desire aroused.

Respiratory Organs.—Pain in larynx, with short cough on talking. Hoarseness in morning; H. < talking (K. bi.); H., with cough, hawking and expectoration. Voice small, changed, in evening. Weak, slow speech. Fulness and oppression in bronchi. Tickling in trachea, causing short cough. Tough mucus in bronchi and trachea (K. bi.).

Cough; in morning, with easy hawking of mucus; about 2 or 3 A.M., with expectoration; before midnight; when angry; after eating, with vomiting of food and mucus; with sneezing; painful; dry; dry and short; difficult, with expectoration. Irritation to C. from catarrh, though she has no power to cough; irritation to C., with tough mucus in throat, oppressed breathing and stitches in l. chest. Expectoration of sweet transparent mucus; white frothy sputa.

Asthma. *Suffocation at 3 A.M., with necessity to sit up* (K. iod.), > *cough and expectoration; S. in evening in bed, with necessity to sit up all night.* Breath arrested. *Dyspnœa; with necessity to be supported in a sitting position in bed* (Ars.). *Short breath.* Slow and labored B. Breathing hindered by swelling of pharynx and accumulation of tough mucus, with fever and delirium. *Heavy, anxious B.* Deep B. Sighing. Snoring expiration in sleep, with intermittent inspiration to two jerks. *Rapid B.* Snuffing for air before she got the strength to cough. Rough B. on auscultation.

Clinical.—Bronchitis in children, with rattling of mucus, which accumulates in the bronchial tubes and seems to fill up the air-passages so that there is great shortness of breath, cold sweat; the child coughs always on getting angry. Threatening suffocation, with wheezing and rattling and cyanosis, cannot clear the lungs, dyspnœa on falling asleep. In pneumonia of old people or those greatly debilitated, with rattling in the chest, cold perspiration, threatening paralysis of the lungs. The cough is usually short, without expectoration. Sometimes valuable in œdema of the lungs, with great dyspnœa and cyanosis, with dilated heart.

Chest.—**Rattling of mucus,** *with oppression* (Phos.). Pain behind and at base, < deep breathing; deep in C. and pharynx after violent sneezing. Pressure on, in sleep. *Oppression* (Phos.). *Constriction;* with cough. *Fulness; in lungs.* Anxiety, and around heart; *A., with oppression of chest* (Phos.) *and rising of warmth from heart.* Rawness. Almost sore twitching feeling towards evening, especially in l. side, with despair. Burning in (before each of his epileptic attacks), which rises into throat.

Heart.—Pressure or heaviness in præcordium. *Oppression* (Phos.). Anxiety in præcordium. Apprehension and warmth about heart, with sensation as if he felt the beat of the heart in the head. *Warmth about.* Heavy feeling in præcordium. *Palpitation;* with purging. Whirling every night, with beating, > sweat. Action rapid; and irregular; small and irregular; intermittent and feeble; weak, afterwards forcible.

Pulse.—**Rapid, weak and trembling** (Ars.); R. during nausea, rising till he vomits, then slow and weak; and almost audible, with general pulsation, which she believes must be audible. Excited. Full; irregular and rapid; *F. and slow.* Slow and weak. *Contracted.* Imperceptible. Intermittent.

Neck.—Cramp in muscles. Sudden aching over l. then over r. scapula on turning head and on touch. Weakness of muscles close to occiput, < r. side.

Back.—Stitching tearing, especially near r. hip. Pain as from weakness, < after eating *and while sitting.* Stitches in kidney region on moving arm. Pain in loins; as if he had carried a weight there, before and on rising from bed, > after rising; rheumatic P. above sacrum in morning.

Clinical.—Lumbago and sciatica, the vertebræ feel as if rubbed against each other.

Extremities.—Inclination to stretch. Tearing; and drawing; T. and D. in joints. Rheumatic drawings through r. hand, then drawings through legs from above downward, especially in region of knee and noticed on walking. Rheumatic and bruised feeling before and on rising. *Weariness.* Heaviness; of feet and arms. *Insensibility, with coldness* (Sec. c.).

Upper Extremities.—Cracking in shoulder-joint, with tearing to hands. Pain in r. shoulder-joint as if dislocated. Short rheumatic pain in and around shoulder-joint and l. breast. Twitching in r. arm; of tendons of arms and hands; tearing, in arm and l. side. Paroxysmal drawing along outer surface of l. upper arm, almost as if in bone. Rheumatic pain in l. elbow. Tearing in muscles of l. forearm. *Trembling of hands* (Agar.). Stitches on back of l. hand on touching hairs. Fingers contracted upon shoulders, with rigidity of every muscle. Deadness of tips of fingers, with dryness, hardness and insensibility.

Lower Extremities.—Cramp. Sticking upward in varices. Drawing, tensive pain. Tension and tearing. Heaviness and stiffness.

Thigh—Spasmodic twitching of muscles. Sticking in hip and knee in evening in bed. Rheumatic pain in and over l. hip; below l. hip. Rheumatic drawing in upper part of r., (spasmodic drawing in T., extending to abdomen). *Tension in hamstrings in evening on walking* (Rhus t.). Burning pricking in knees. Aching in knee as if the limb had no power and as if tendons were stretched, in morning in bed and on rising. Weakness of knees.

Leg.—Tetanic spasms, > straightening. Twitching in l. calf. Cramp in leg, > forcible extension; C. in calves; in calves afternoons, > walking; in calves, waking him. Slow rhythmical picking below l. knee. Upward sticking in varices. Rheumatic pain on l.; side of l. calf; rheumatic between l. calf and malleolus. Spasmodic drawing in calves. Weariness in legs. Numbness and coldness.

Swelling of r. malleolus, with stiffness. Sudden pricking as from a blow in l. instep; near inner malleolus. Tension on dorsum of foot during the day while walking. Weariness of feet. *Feet go to sleep on sitting down* (Sec. c.). Sudden painful rhythmical picking in l. great toe.

Skin.—Pallor of whole body; bluish. Yellow spots on fingers. Sallowness increasing to jaundice. Eruption; itching. Spots like flea bites on hands. Rash; on arms, breast and occiput; reddish; itching, suppurating. Pimples on genitals; itching, from waist to knees; like the itch, on arm near wrist and on upper arm, the itching > by scratching; small red, conical, hard, with inflamed base like *lichen simplex,* on breast, anterior surfaces of upper arms, wrists, hypogastrium and inner surfaces of thighs.

Pocklike eruption, often pustular; pimples like pocks on side of chin, with tickling. Pustules; *on genitals;* on *scrotum* and penis; *as in small-pox on inner surface of forearm, then on back, painful, then forming crusts;* on chest and neck, like cow-pox, with red areola, then a crust leaving a deep scar; *itching; painful. Vesicles over whole body.* Suppurating places become confluent and discharge blood and matter.

Itching; on scrotum; around an ulcer; crawling, in the sores in evening on lying down in bed; painful burning, in leg, where there are varices, as if a suppurating inflammatory swelling would ensue; biting; in r. sole evenings in bed, with biting.

Clinical.—Pustular eruptions with red areola. Said to be useful in adynamic types of small-pox.

Sleep.—*Yawning;* and stretching, also forenoons. **Sleepiness;** at 10 A.M., also with weak and gone-to-sleep limbs; 11 A.M., with sleep if he sits still and vivid dreams of a continuation *of his previous thoughts; early in evening;* in evening, then wide awake till late at night; after dinner; on horseback in strong air; when riding in open air, with vertigo; *with inactivity.* Sleep as soon as he sat down in the daytime; S. after dinner. Sleeps with head erect; on back, with l. hand under his head. Stupid sleep. Heavy sleep; and on waking knows nothing about it.

Sleeplessness; till midnight; till 1 A.M., then dream that he is wading in deep water and cannot get out. Late falling asleep, with frequent waking and tossing about. Difficult falling asleep. *Shocks and jerks coming* from abdomen *in first sleep,* throwing of one or other arm from the body, now of a foot, now throwing of the whole body into the air. Starting in sleep in forenoon. Screaming in sleep, with staring eyes and *trembling and drawing up of arms and feet.* Talking in sleep. Restless sleep; with confused heavy dreams. Short sleep. Light sleep, full of historic dreams. Waking often from anxious dreams.

Dreams anxious; vivid, heavy, anxious; heavy. Historic. Of fire, from which he must fly. That he preaches without having memorized and "gets stuck." Fatiguing. Nightmare.

Fever.—Chilliness; forenoons; at night and on rising in morning. Rigor at 5 A.M., then heat, with rapid and full and strong pulse, hot skin, red face, heat in head, palpitation, burning at stomach, fulness and nausea, impeded respiration, pressure and constriction of chest, cough, rough respiration and pain under l. nipple on deep inspiration. Chill at 3 P.M., with trembling. C. at 6 P.M., then after eating heat with drawing in occiput; at 8 P.M., with flushes of heat.

Cold limbs; hands; l. hand; *hands, with moisture; cold hands and finger-tips;* feet; *skin;* skin of r. arm, hand and both great toes; cold shivering through skin during stool. Chill, with gooseflesh and cold skin, which remained longest on hands; C., with drowsiness and weakness; with heat of certain parts, especially of face. Rigor, with burning in head and beating of heart. C. alternating with heat; till 8 P.M.; on motion; with heat in head.

Shivering. *Trembling chill on going into open air.* Chill, as if cold water were dashed over him, with gooseflesh on arms and yawning. Creeping chill, with heat, nausea and faintness. *Chill from within outward, with trembling* and general sick feeling; C. from within outward, spreading from spine over abdomen and limbs; extending from spine to limbs and especially to abdomen, with feverishness. C. running through all vessels.

Heat; afternoon, < motion, especially in head; H. in evening, especially in face; at 6 o'clock, with want of appetite, then increased pain in abdomen; in head, also < motion; on forehead in morning; of face; in middle of spine; of skin; with full hard pulse; with weak pulse; with restlessness, thirst and headache, followed at night by sweat. Heat and moisture of hands on coughing, with sweat of head. Heat and sweat of forehead on coughing, so that she became dizzy. Burning in joints, with tearing. Heat rising to head in flushes. Dry H., driving him out of bed. Fatiguing H. at night, interrupting sleep. H. of same kind at the same hour two days.

Sweat in morning on waking; at night; in sleep; when vomiting; S. on head and chest; forehead and neck; forehead, with coldness of head; especially of affected parts. *General. Cold; and clammg;* cold on forehead; *cold on face;* clammy on face; clammy on forehead during nausea. Anxious, when vomiting.

Antipyrine.

An alkaloid synthetically prepared, Dimethyl-oxy-chinicine. Solutions in distilled water or triturations.

Properties.—It reduces the temperature of the body, allays pain, promotes sleep and causes perspiration.

Swollen body, great pains in limbs. Numbness. Anxiety. "I don't know what is the matter with me, I remember nothing, I am becoming like an idiot, I am going mad." Loss of consciousness. Headache. Dizziness. Snapping in head so that she ran up and down the room screaming, partially losing control of herself and apprehending insanity. Singing in ears, with congestion. Sneezing violently, about twenty times without pause, face and eyes suffused, tears flowed, mucus flowed from nose, breathing labored, with feeling of suffocation, inability to lie down, violent cough, with expectoration of much mucus, with profuse sweat. Itching and burning in mouth and throat, < in roof of mouth, the feeling soon extended to eyes, nose and ears, violent sneezing at least fifty times, with copious watery fluid running from nose and eyes, such turgescence of mucous membrane that she could not breathe through nose, afterwards stupid, tormenting feeling, with swelling of nose and eyes till exhausted she fell asleep, sleep disturbed and tiresome. Coppery taste in violent bouts, with intermittent coppery smell.

No appetite. Vomiting. Epigastric pain causing her to bend forward and cry out. Gastro-enteritis. Expanding sensation rising from stomach, instead of the nausea which she had had. Pain in abdomen. Incontinence of urine. Urine diminished. Hoarseness. Dyspnœa, breathing hard, with feeling of suffocation. Pain in chest. Tightness of chest. Depressing effect upon heart from large doses, causing disturbed circulation and respiration, cyanosis and vomiting, the final result is paralysis, these are the secondary action. Pulse rapid and full. Pulse increases, temperature decreases.

Œdema of arms and hands. Skin covered with red spots. Eruptions appear and disappear suddenly. Erythematous eruption appearing first in arms, passing down, appearing last on legs. Erythematous patches on arms, eyes felt uncomfortable, she slept scarcely at all, feet cold, next morning face was red and swollen, eyes almost closed, the rash was general and of the color of pomegranate, the intervals between the patches scarcely noticeable at first sight, appetite poor, sensation as if inside of body were filled with ice, little itching, next day catarrhal conjunctivitis, irritation of nasal fossæ and hoarseness, pulse twice as fast as usual, 78 to the minute, buzzing in ears, for sometime afterwards prostration and intermittent sensations of cold. Itching on inside of thighs, with urticaria, which soon extended to abdomen. Urticaria, especially in women; general U., with intense itching, she tears herself with her nails. Sleepiness. Intermittent coldness. Heat. Cold sweat, then quick rise in temperature, with chill and full, rapid pulse.

Clinical.—High fever in morning on rising, wanting water, head aches, pain in frontal sinuses. Erythema.

Apis.

Live bees (Apis mellifica) are shaken in a bottle, and then digested in dilute alcohol for several days.

General Action.—Erysipelatous inflammation and destruction of tissue (of dermoid tissue), acute inflammation of kidneys and some other parenchymatous tissues.

Allies.—Canth., Rhus t., Gelsem, Ledum, Secale corn., *Lyc.*, Phos., *Mag. m.*, Merc., Sulph.

Generalities.—*Swelling of whole body;* with pallid, deathlike look of face; of whole side of body, first in joints; of face, neck, chest and limbs. Blood colorless and only red in the centre of the vessel. (No blood when venesection is attempted.) Failed to respond when spoken to. Falling to the ground. Twitching; burning, like a prickling contraction from without inward, in r. thumb and other places. Convulsions; from the offer of water, which was desired, with expression of fear in face as in hydrophobia, also C. when touched on r. index (the place of the sting); generally tonic, but in a measure clonic, with knees drawn up to breast and hands and arms moved convulsively, partially conscious and continually moaning. Electric shocks, thrilling ends of fingers and toes. Trembling.

Burning stitches here and there, especially on back, which itched. Neuralgic rheumatism. General bruised sensation. *Prickling over whole body* (Sec. corn.), externally and internally. General sensation of fulness and weakness of co-ordinating power, especially in hands. Malaise. Strange, indefinable feeling; with stinging feeling and white and red spots in palms, on arms and feet. Sensation in whole body as if everything were too large. Restlessness; in afternoon, with weakness; alternating with depression approaching syncope; nervous, the latter half of the night. Necessity to lie down; sudden, without weakness or faintness. Sensation as if dying. Faintness; with nausea; F., with weakness, anxiety and distress at stomach, oppression of chest, dyspnœa, short, rapid breathing and rapid pulse. **Weakness**; evening, with vertigo; *during diarrhœa; with trembling;* with desire to be let alone; *as if bruised in every limb, especially in back, < rising from a seat,* with necessity to stretch.

Sudden weakness; with coldness; with vomiting, profuse diarrhœa, cold limbs, pale face, griping in abdomen, pulse weak, after abatement of these symptoms redness of part stung. General sensation diminished. Numbness over whole body. Amelioration from sleep.

Clinical.—There is general aggravation of all symptoms about 5 P.M. The pains are always sudden, stinging. As a rule, the patients are not restless, but in some cases of hydrocephalus there is great restlessness, with rolling of the head from side to side. The effects generally travel from r. to l., pain, erysipelas, inflammations. In paralysis following diphtheria or typhoid fever it is sometimes indicated; sometimes, but rarely, in rheumatic affections. Cases are reported in which there was diminished sensibility with paralysis, could not tell when the foot touched the ground, with soreness of the spine and pains. General inclination to dropsical effusions and anasarca, with stinging pains. General intolerance of the heat of the bed.

Mind.—Excitement; approaching delirium. Violent affection of whole nervous system. Fear; of death, or sensation as if he could not breathe again. Anxiety; with excitement and restlessness. Sadness; in forenoon, with longing for death. Irritability; allowed no one but his mother to come near him. Dissatisfaction with everything. Restlessness, with dulness of head. Listless. Concentration impossible. Inability to fix attention on a book requiring thought (Gelsem.). Inability to think clearly and to express himself. Confusion; when reading. Unconsciousness.

Clinical.—Stupor or even unconsciousness, with or without symptoms of inflammation of the meninges of the brain. As a rule, it is characterized by sudden starts with screaming, as from some terrible pain in the head. In meningitis from suppressed eruptions with stupor, apparently the result of effusion, interrupted by short cries. In the stupor occurring during the progress of low types of fever or malarial disease, as in typhus, diphtheria, etc. Mania resulting from the suppression of the menses, with stupor alternating with attacks of errotic mania. Impairment of mind so that the patient seems preoccupied, lets things fall from her hands, and seems to be unconscious of things transpiring about her. As a rule, the mental state in erysipelas, diphtheria, low fevers, etc., requiring Apis, is one of apathy, indifference, or even unconsciousness.

Head.—Aching from 8 to 10 P. M., with chilliness and toothache, pain in forehead, alternately in l. and r. side, afterwards in r. side of vertex, where it is sensitive to touch, then in temples, then r. side of forehead, next morning in l. side of forehead; A. in evening during cough; during cough; when rising from reclining or from sitting; < reading; > *pressure;* > during diarrhœa; *mostly confined to forehead, with fever;* with fulness and heaviness in occiput; and in eyeballs; *dull, heavy, from rising till* 3 P.M.; oppressive, when in a warm room and reading; expansive, on exertion, with vertigo and palpitation; bursting, with vertigo and confusion of mind. *Confusion; with pain in sinciput; with pain in forehead.* Anxiety, with swelling of face. Fulness, with heaviness, pressure and sometimes sudden rush of blood. Throbbing, < moving and stooping, > *pressure. Whole brain seems weary,* asleep and crawling (Con.). Head feels swollen. Heaviness, with pressure; H. as if she could hardly hold it up, < during day and by motion, coughing, etc., with throbbing. **Vertigo;** evenings after sleeping on the sofa, **with headache;** with blindness; with nausea; *confused, worse when sitting than when walking, extreme when lying and closing eyes.*

Forehead.—Stitches, and in temples; *over r. eye, extending to eyeball;* burning, in l. superciliary ridge. *Aching, and in temples;* after sneezing, with vertigo; with dulness and confusion; inwardly above outer end of l. eyebrow, in afternoon, lasting all day, < when coughing; in upper part as if it would burst, extending to temples; in l. side in evening, with stitches under l. ear, chilliness, yawning, and pain in umbilical region; in sinciput, with vertigo; heavy tensive, over eyes, with pain through orbits; dull heavy, > pressure, and in sides of head. Dulness just over eyes. Confusion from supraorbital ridges to protuberances, > after breakfast.

Temples.—Stitch in l. in evening. *Aching in l.;* and in organs of causality, comparison, mirthfulness and ideality; in single jerks to middle of forehead, < 10 A.M., with sensitiveness of head to touch, burning of eyes and itching of nose; sharp, in r.; heavy, in morning on waking, r., then l.; throbbing. Boring; every morning on waking; intermittent. Bursting sensation (Bell.).

Heaviness in vertex, with fulness. Pressure deep inward in l. side of vertex when drawing on boots. Headache in l. side and vertex when coughing. Heavy pain in r. parietal protuberance. Aching in occiput; < shaking head. Blow in suboccipital region. Swelling of head; inflammatory S. and twitching, so that apoplexy was feared. Hair falls out. Itching; in afternoon; extending to face and neck, afterwards to thighs and hands.

Clinical.—The headache is usually a hot, heavy feeling, with congestion and with sudden stabbing pains, almost universally relieved by external pressure and aggravated by any motion. In meningitis, acute or chronic, or tubercular hydrocephalus, extremely valuable when the peculiar symptoms are present, the child bores the head into the pillow, is stupid and occasionally screams out.

Eyes.—Scleræ injected. Bloodshot; and protruding, pupil dilated and immovable, and was obliged to change from convex to concave glasses (from sting in cornea). *Piercing* in evening, *with necessity to remove the spectacles while reading and writing* (in a near-sighted woman). Boring forenoon, with piercing. *Burning stinging in r.,* beginning with heaviness and *causing lachrymation.* Sensation as if a mass of mucus were in l. Heaviness, with inclination to close them, and after being closed for sometime desire to rub and press them.

Twitching in l. < at night. *Stinging itching, and in lids and around eyes* (Sulph.), on l. side, and especially in inner canthus. Piercing itching around eyes, in brows, lids and eyes themselves, < l., and more at inner canthi, with desire to rub eyes while pressing them hard, *with soreness and smarting in margins of lids, in canthi and in eye itself* (Sulph.), quivering of l. ball and sensation of mucus in them, < l., full feeling in eyes and weak vision. *Weakness, with photophobia; W., with pain when used. Lachrymation;* l.; of l., in evening, with pain in l. side of forehead; *of l., with burning and sensation of a foreign body in it, weakness of both eyes, with pain and sensitiveness to light in evening when sewing;* of r.; of r. at night in bed, with flow of mucus; of r. from a biting piercing sensation; *with pain in eyes; with pain when looking at a bright light.*

Piercing in balls. *Aching in l. ball, mosty in lower part;* A. around l. ball, then around both. Pupils insensible to light. **Lids swollen, red, œdematous** (Rhus t.). *Upper lids so swollen that they hang like sacs over face. Agglutination;* with soreness of margins and canthi. Twitching of r. lid. Stinging in r. lower, in morning. *Burning in margins of lids* (Sulph.), *causing lachrymation.* Stinging in r. caruncula. Sensation of a foreign body in l. outer canthus after constant profuse lachrymation. Itching on margins; I. of r., with prickling; paroxysmal, of r.; *of l. inner canthus.* Conjunctiva injected. *Burning stinging around l. eye and in superciliary ridge. Aching over and about eyes, > pressure. Pain around orbits;* in l. orbit, mostly lower part. Photophobia. Vision obscured; difficult, with a whirling sensation in sight. Blindness; in afternoon when stooping.

Clinical.—An extremely valuable remedy in a great variety of diseases of the eyes; in inflammation of the lids, which are œdematous, often everted so that the lid actually rolls over on to the cheek, the conjunctiva is inflamed and œdematous, with hot lachrymation, photophobia, violent stinging pains; the lids even may become ulcerated. It is often found valuable in purulent ophthalmia, with infiltration of the balls and lids, great œdema and sharp pains are sufficiently characteristic. In inflammations of the cornea of various sorts, scrofulous, parenchymatous, with or without destruction of the tissues, especially in ophthalmia following eruptive diseases, with great œdema, burning stinging pains. There is, as a rule, temporary relief from the application of cold water. Sometimes indicated in staphyloma of the cornea or sclerotic. In serous inflammation within the eyeball, in serous iritis or aquacapsulitis, with punctiform deposit on the inner surface of the cornea. In muscular asthenopia, with sharp stinging pain on attempting to use the eyes, swelling of lids, etc. In short, it is an extremely valuable remedy in inflammatory affections of the eyes, always characterized by serous exudation, œdema, with sudden piercing pains.

Ears.—Swelling; of a lymphatic gland behind ear. Purple. Stitches under l. Pain in r. middle; behind l. Itching in r., then l.; in ears and glands near root of tongue, increasing in two years to sharp itching and burning in throat just back of palate, finally working into bronchial tubes, down around lungs, and resulting in asthma. Ringing in r. Rumbling. Hearing diminished.

Clinical.—Erysipelatous inflammation of the external ear. Deafness in fever.

Nose.—Swelling. Obstruction. Sneezing; on going into open air; violent; with watery discharge from nose and eyes. Coryza, < evening, with dull sensation in nose, and now and then some dropping; with dread of cold but < *from warmth;* with feeling as if it would swell. C. at 4 P.M., with dryness of nose, then burning of lips, with sensation as if they would chap. Blowing of blood; mornings.

Clinical.—In erysipelatous inflammation of the nose externally, red swelling, sharp stinging pains. Coldness of the tip of the nose when the throat begins to be sore is a pretty sure indication for Apis.

Face.—*Swollen; red and œdematous, especially nose,* eyelids and cheeks; and head. Inflammatory S., r. eye completely closed, l. almost, the cheeks hung down to the breast; and eyelids puffed up, lips turned upward, inside out; and cyanotic. Shrunken, wan and anxious. Pale. *Red;* then purple; *with heat, burning piercing pain and swelling.* Stinging in l. malar-bone; burning, in chin and malar-bones. Sensation as if l. side would swell, especially about eye.

Jaw.—Drawing back and forth of lower. Stiffness of lower extending to mouth and throat, making speech difficult and unintelligible, with constriction in throat exciting spasmodic hacking cough, with difficulty in breathing, < on inspiration, throat swollen, < uvula and arches of palate, < on l. side, deflecting uvula to the right.

Lips.—Swollen; upper; and sensation of swelling, then eruption about lips and dryness and desquamation of lower lip. Cyanotic. Livid and open. Lower chapped. Dark streak along epithelium, with cracks and desquamation. Dryness, with a black stripe in red portion. Roughness, < upper, with tension. Prickling, with bruised and swollen feeling; P., and on tongue, extending over face, temples and head, thence over entire body.

Clinical.—The appearance of the face varies with the character of the other affections; in disease of the kidneys in pregnancy the face is œdematous and pale; during fever it is generally hot and bright red; sometimes almost livid; in erysipelas it is swollen and inflamed, with severe stinging pains; the erysipelas is characterized by puffiness and œdematous infiltration, which, as a rule, does not pit on pressure; the swelling is out of proportion to the intensity of the pain.

Mouth.—Jerking grinding of teeth on biting them together, in swallowing, after yawning, etc. Toothache in evening in r. upper jaw, during which she feels the biting-together of the teeth in her head, with chilliness. Jumping pain in l. upper molars. Gums bleed. Gums painful.

Tongue.—*Swollen;* then S. of face and whole body, *with inability to swallow,* move tongue or speak. *A row of vesicles somewhat to l. of tip, with soreness and rawness;* V. on tip and l. side, with red spots. Covered with a dirty white fur, pale, soft and flabby. Pain, with burning rawness, stinging, and with vesicles along edge. *Rawness on margin, with scalding and pimples and stinging. Dryness, with redness and tenderness of mouth* (Rhus t.). Prickling heat. Burning extending into stomach, with eructations and gathering of tasteless water in mouth, the eructations < after drinking water, almost suffocating her.

Scalding in mouth and throat. Burning in mouth in forenoon, with thirst. Dryness; under tongue at 6 P.M., > moving tongue much; of palate, also with roughness. Salivation; soapy, mornings, and in fauces. Taste bitter at back of tongue and in fauces; B., afterwards more pungent, spreading to fauces, with affection of tongue as after chewing pyrethrum, at same time symptoms in all parts of mouth as after alcohol. Taste as of sweet almonds. Loss of taste.

Clinical.—During acute febrile states the tongue is red and hot, even dry and hot, and in low fevers it may even tremble, reminding one of Lachesis. Sometimes in scarlet fever it is cracked, sore and covered with blisters or ulcerated, but is rarely red and dry. In diphtheria it is swollen, not heavily coated.

Throat.—*Swollen; with hoarseness, difficulty in breathing, difficulty on swallowing* from irritability of epiglottis, and with *white spot to left of glottis;* and posterior part of hard palate, base of tongue and inside of cheeks, the parts bright red, dry and shining. Viscid mucus deep in T. in morning, compelling frequent hawking; thick M. in pharynx. Pressure as from a foreign body in upper back part. Rawness, with inclination to hawk; R., with viscid saliva adhering to hard palate, velum and tongue; extending to pit of stomach, with hoarse, hard, spasmodic, hollow cough, caused by a sensation of filling up in throat, as if he needed to raise something, eating drove the soreness downward and he continued to eat till soreness and cough disappeared. Full and choking sensation, as if filling up; F., constriction and suffocation, < horizontal position, with difficult, anxious breathing. *Constriction, with sensation of a foreign body in it and painful swallowing. Deep-seated stinging itching, at lower part of neck,* *with constriction.* *Dryness; with heat* (Bell., Æsc. h.). Swallowing difficult. Nausea apparently from T.

Clinical.—In severe inflammations of the throat, with general stupor and prostration, even in diphtheria, we will find in Apis an extremely valuable and frequently indicated remedy. It is almost a specific in true diphtheria, always indicated when the throat is very much swollen and œdematous, with severe stinging pains on attempting to swallow, with great inertia or even complete stupor. In suspected scarlet fever, in the early stage, when rash is seen upon the hard palate and the throat is œdematous and bright red, with great pain on swallowing and the eruption is mottled, without thirst.

Stomach.—Appetite lost; and he refused drink. Thirst. Eructations; after eating; tasting like the yolk of eggs; violent empty during headache. Hot vapor seems to rise from S., *with dry throat, without thirst*, with burning cheeks and cold feet. Aversion, with chilliness and cold limbs. Nausea; at night, with rumbling in abdomen as before diarrhœa; with vertigo; with vomiting and faintness; with pain in whole body. Gagging. Vomiting at night in sleep, with thirst; *V., with diarrhœa;* of food; of bile; then a thin bitter fluid with pain across lower abdomen; yellow and bitter. Prickling as from needles. Pressure in region of orifice; in pit. Crampy pain, and in abdomen, then vomiting and diarrhœa. Oppression at pit; at epigastrium. *Sore feeling, and in abdomen. Burning.*

Clinical.—The absence of thirst is the rule in Apis cases, though sometimes there may be great thirst; in these circumstances the condition of stupor and the afternoon aggravation at 5 o'clock will overbalance the presence of thirst. The vomiting of food and frequent effort to vomit must be associated with the Apis symptoms in meningitis or in the early stage of scarlet fever and in various other troubles. It has occasionally been found useful in the nausea of pregnancy.

Abdomen.—*Distention;* after a moderate meal, and dyspnœa when lying, strong desire for stool, passed flatus and urine freely. Rumbling, with urging to stool; R. as before diarrhœa. Loud offensive flatus. Sputtering flatus after stool. Cutting. Griping. Sickly feeling, inclining him to continue a quiet sitting posture. Pain; mornings, with hard scanty stools; in morning, with urging to stool, also with pain when straining, after dreaming at night that she had pain in abdomen and diarrhœa; P. < **pressure, touch and horizontal position, with sensitiveness**; with urging to pass flatus; with a feverish trembling feeling; contractive, at 11 P.M. when walking, compelling her to bend forward. **Soreness; morning; when sneezing or on pressure.** Compression. Nausea.

Faintness and nausea from short ribs across the whole abdomen. Pain under l. last ribs; in umbilical region, with chilliness; from hips towards umbilicus, forenoon; in hypogastrium, with bloating of abdomen; in hypogastrium, with bearing down in uterus, as if menses were coming on. Shooting deep in pelvis. Throbbing boring over crest of l. ilium, > eructations. Soreness deep within, below and beside r. hip, with burning and numbness.

Clinical.—Abdominal dropsy, sometimes with diarrhœa and vomiting, great oppression of breath with the other general symptoms indicating Apis. With all the abdominal affections there is present the characteristic bruised feeling in the abdominal walls, which are extremely tender (Lyc.), sometimes even when the abdomen is not swollen; we may even meet with this symptom in hydrocephalus. Stool sometimes involuntary on every motion; this symptom indicates Apis in diarrhœa and cholera infantum, especially in great stupor with disinclination to take food or drink. In dysentery with a low type of fever, apathy, bloody, almost painless stools, abdomen sore, anus raw, tongue raw, dry, sometimes with tenesmus. Cholera infantum with constant relapses, with threatening brain troubles, sunken abdomen; the child gets stupid and starts suddenly, especially during dentition. There may be constipation, with fever or with hydrocephalus.

Rectum and Anus.—Electric shock in R. then urging to stool. Frequent urging. Tenesmus. **Anus, raw sensation, with diarrhœa**; pain in A.; throbbing in A.; sensation of stuffing; heat.

Clinical.—Hæmorrhoids, with stinging pain, the anus becomes extremely sore (Æsc. h.). Piles after confinement, with sharp, stinging pain. Ascarides, with delirium, screaming, etc.

Stool.—*Watery, yellow; frequent yellow, W., with griping;* W. copious. *Soft, mixed with serum, orange-colored. Loose in morning; and urgent;* loose, lumpy. *Copious diarrhœa, with vomiting;* lumpy D., with vomiting, *then watery and fetid stools*, then pappy mixed with mucus and blood, then stools like dysentery, with tenesmus and crushed sensation in intestines. *Copious, blackish brown, green and whitish.* Frequent. Scanty, pappy, light yellow. Natural, preceded by emission of flatus, and almost colorless water, containing lumps, or fragments of jellylike mucus, streaked with blood. Omitted.

Clinical.—Diarrhœa, watery, yellow, sometimes painless. Chronic diarrhœa, cannot urinate without having a stool, or the stools become dark and fetid, worse after eating (compare with Aloes).

Urinary Organs.—*Burning and soreness when urinating.* Excitement. Disagreeable feeling in bladder, with bearing down in region of sphincter, frequent desire to urinate and during micturition burning smarting and uneasy feeling in spermatic cords. Urging, with scanty urine and dribbling. Frequent desire to urinate; with burning in urethra and with uneasiness in spermatic cord; frequent desire, and when passing burning and sensation as if the flow were obstructed by contraction near glans. Involuntary micturition. No micturition for thirty-six hours. Stitches in urethra. Burning in urethra before and after micturition. *Urine high-colored, and frequent emissions of small quantities.* Urine copious; < *outdoor exercise*, with flatulence and diarrhœa; pale, with red or mealy sediment, frequent urging and strangury. Scanty; with frequent micturition. Offensive.

Clinical.—In acute inflammation of the kidneys, frequently with great aching in the lumbar region, with soreness over the region of the kidneys (Merc. c., Phyto.), and excessively bruised sensation in the abdominal walls on deep pressure. Acute inflammation of the kidneys, particularly during or subsequent to eruptive diseases; the urine may be almost entirely suppressed, loaded with casts; the dropsy also is very great, comes on rapidly, is especially marked in the face and upper part of the body, with stupor, absence of thirst; with restlessness and dryness of skin. In inflammation of the bladder, which becomes very irritable; frequent or even involuntary micturition; at times when urine is passed there is stinging pain or there may be strangury (Canthar.). The urine is rarely bloody, very frequently high-colored. The urine is sometimes retained in the bladder, rarely suppressed (Stram.). As a rule, in diphtheria, erysipelas, scarlet fever, etc., when there is no inflammation of the urinary passages the urine is quite free and pale, even though the patient drinks but little. In subacute or chronic Bright's disease Apis has been found serviceable in temporary exacerbations with an increase of dropsy, sometimes about the head, when the patient is stupid, sometimes in the chest, when there is great difficulty in breathing and the patient is suffocated on lying down. Incontinence of urine in old people.

Sexual Organs.—Frequent and long-lasting erections. Scrotum tense and translucent, looking as in hydrocele. Testicle swollen, with tension and itching; l. T. sore;

fulness in r., with aching. Excitement. Desire when sitting at home and when driving.

Deep penetrating pain in clitoris, extending into vagina, with swelling, dryness and hardness of labia minora, which is covered with a crust, hindering the beginning of micturition, > in evening by applications of cold water. Hæmorrhage from uterus. *Metrorrhagia in second month, with profuse discharge of blood, heaviness of abdomen, faintness, restlessness and yawning. Miscarriage at second month; at third month.* Bearing down as in early stage of parturition; *B., with sensation as before menses;* in r. ovarian region. Cutting in l. ovarian region across to r. in evening when stretching in bed. Strained pain in l. ovarian region at 6 P.M., < walking, then in corresponding spot on r. side, with lame feeling in scapulæ. Drawing in r. ovarian region.

Clinical.—Erysipelatous inflammation of penis, with excessive œdema, great soreness and stinging pain. Hydrocele with the characteristic symptoms. Inflammation and swelling of r. testicle. Inflammation of prepuce, with warty excrescences. It particularly affects the r. ovary (Lyc.); curative in various forms of inflammation and neuralgia, always with extremely sensitive sharp stinging pains. Has cured cystic tumor of the ovary (ovarian dropsies), with bruised sore pain in abdominal walls (Lyc.). In inflammation of the cellular tissue of the pelvis (pelvic cellulitis), with excessive soreness over the lower abdominal region and sharp pain (Ars.). In enlarged and inflamed uterus following pregnancy, etc. While menstruation is sometimes profuse, as an accompaniment in various diseases, it has been found useful in the suppression of menses with the cerebral symptoms above noted, also with local inflammatory symptoms, bearing down, extreme tenderness, with flushing of face and head, especially in girls. Dysmenorrhœa, with severe ovarian pains, with a puffed, waxy appearance of face, etc. It has averted threatening abortion with soreness of the ovaries, hæmorrhage. Erysipelas of the mammary glands or swelling like tumors, with stinging boring pains.

Respiratory Organs.—Raw sensation in larynx, with sensitiveness. *Hoarseness.* Cannot speak above a whisper. Cough in shocks when roused from sleep before midnight, from a crawling in windpipe at pit of throat, > when something is loosened and swallowed, at every shock increased headache in l. side and upper part; *severe C.* before midnight, < *after lying and sleeping*, from tickling in posterior wall in windpipe, with desire to brush the spot, l. side of head aches while coughing, he must bend head back and hold it so that the shock cannot act with so much violence, cough < warmth and rest, > loosening mucus; deep, hard ringing, from constriction of throat, reaching down to upper part of lungs, which were very sore.

Expectoration of copious, transparent, frothy, bloody mucus. **Sensation as if he could not breathe again. Suffocation;** *with inability to bear anything about throat* (Lach.), dusky face and bluish lips. Asthma. *Dyspnœa;* and at each inspiration a crowing sound that could be heard across the street; with sleepiness and shortness of breath when walking (Curare). *Breathing hurried and difficult, with fever and headache;* H., superficial and sighing; H. nights, and short. Closed rooms, especially if overheated, are insupportable. Inspiration croupy; I. laborious, loud. Breathing slow, heavy, œdema of lungs developing. Sighing.

Clinical.—Œdema of the larynx, with great distress for breath. Hydrothorax, with suffocation on lying down, either the result of pleurisy or dependent on disease of the kidneys; in these cases there is especially present with the dyspnœa a feeling as if he could not draw another breath. The cough is usually suffocative, spasmodic, from irritation in upper part of chest or suprasternal fossa, short and dry. Fit of coughing brought on by pressure on the larynx (Lach.).

Chest.—Stitches; *at night, and through back;* just below heart; in side; *in l. side;* under l. arm, near fourth or fifth rib; in r. nipple extending into lung; in forenoon, where cartilages of ribs bend towards hypochondria, l. then r., with darkness before eyes, in which she felt boring sticking. Tearing, drawing, starting from l. lower side of sternum, drawing back and forth in chest, upward, and finally into lower jaw, and at same time pain in back.

Pain; at night; in upper part; under l. short ribs; near last ribs, in or below heart; *in l. side, near middle of sternum, with fulness in chest* and short breath; sudden, to l. on lower part of sternum; *sudden, just below heart, soon extending towards r. chest, with suffocation,* face and hands purple, falling down, feeling as of rapid swelling of lining membrane of air-passages, including nose, which was stopped. *Bruised pain. Sore feeling* (Phos.). Fulness, with tension and pressure; feeling of F., constriction or suffocation, < horizontal position, with difficult, anxious breathing. Oppression; at bottom of sternum; with frequent desire for a deep inspiration (Phos.). Trembling in forenoon, with pressure and oppressed breathing. Heat in morning, and in stomach. *Melting heat in region of diaphragm as from running violently.*

Heart and Pulse.—Stinging in region of H. Intermittent pain. Oppression in region of H., with slight suffocation reaching to throat. Palpitation. Rapid, feeble beats of H. Pulse rapid; full and strong; and weak; and small; P. decreased; feeble; scarcely perceptible. Slow, irregular, afterwards rapid. Pulseless at wrist.

Clinical.—Pericarditis, with scanty urine, swollen limbs, bluish lips, great soreness over the region of the heart.

Neck.—Swollen glands. Flushed. Rheumatic stitches in r. side of nape; in muscles of r. side, morning on rising, < moving head in that direction, > moving head in any other direction. Piercing burning pain in spot on l. side, also on occiput and l. arm. Tensive pain extending back of l. ear and over l. side of head. Drawing from nape, extending behind l. ear and over l. side of head. Tension in r. side, beneath and back of ear. Stiffness of l. tendons, painful if he moved the head to opposite side; S. of nape, and small of back. Weight at nape, with tension.

Back.—Inward trembling down, with shuddering without coldness, 3 to 5 P.M., more in upper half. Weakness in both sides of spine, as if she could not lie upon it. Pain under scapulæ, < r.; under scapulæ, with sore feeling on moving the parts; under scapulæ, < moving. Pressure on last ribs, posteriorly on l. side of spine, hindering breathing. Bruised sensation near last ribs, < l. Burning stitch in upper part of small of B. Stiffness of small of B.

Extremities.—*Œdematous swelling.* Blood settled under toe and finger nails. Twitching. Unpleasant sensation in inner side of arm from elbow to axilla, and in anterior and inner part of each thigh from near knee to inguinal region.

Clinical.—Synovitis, especially in the knee, which is swollen and shiny, with stinging pains, extreme sensitiveness (from a bruise). Limbs swollen from dropsy, associated with inflamed kidneys. Inflammation around a nail (panaritium), with burning stinging and great soreness. Sometimes indicated in dissecting wounds with great swelling.

Upper Extremities.—Weakness. Great increase and intensity of odor from axillary glands. Cramp in l.

shoulder. Pain in shoulder and upper arm; r. Tensive pain extending from l. shoulder into nape. Drawing in l. biceps. Cramp in r. arm. Swelling of arm and hand, with pain; S. of whole r. arm from sting on r. hand, with enlargement of axillary and cervical glands. Itching sticking in back of arm. Aching in r. ulnar nerve; down l. ulnar nerve, in bones of arms and fingers. Drawing in r. arm, with burning of anterior surface. Crawling in arm as if asleep, < l. Sudden darting pain in l. elbow.

Stinging and burning in hands, especially palms, > cold water. Sore and red spots on palms. Want of power, with incomplete anæsthesia of hands. Benumbed feeling in r. hand, then itching in palm. Swelling of second r. finger, except tip, especially middle joint, in morning, with redness and heat, burning stinging, with tingling, extending up arm to body and down r. side and leg to foot, pain < 5 P.M. to 8 A.M., preventing sleep, < cold applications, > hot applications and gentle rubbing or pinching of end of finger. Burning pricking in finger-tips. Tingling of l. fingers. *Numbness of fingers, especially tips,* about roots of nails, with sensation as if he could shake off the nails; N. of index; l. ulnar fingers. Inward burning about a hang-nail on outside of r. fourth finger.

Lower Extremities.—Staggering. Pain as if in bones. Sore feeling in flesh, > walking, returning while sitting. Pain in l. hip; in l. knee, outside, over and under knee, especially in front and laterally. Burning stinging in knee. Crawling as if asleep from l. knee to foot. Darting pain in l. outer malleolus. **Foot and toes feel swollen and stiff.** *Feet swollen in evening when taking off boots and socks; with fulness, heaviness and stiffness,* with itching, redness and bungling feeling of upper part, fulness and pain in soles and balls of toes, and sensation as if stepping on cushions. Pricking in little toes.

Skin.—Purple spots on extremities and purple skin of feet and purple nails of fingers and toes. Redness of hands as far as wrists and feet and ankles. Red stripes along fingers and arms. Red spots on extremities. Red and white spots on palms, arms and feet. Erythematous redness of trunk, arms and chest, and the body appeared bloated. Elevations, with sensitiveness, without change of color. Swelling on back of neck, so that the head pressed upon the chest. Throbbing in the swelling. Painful red swelling; inflammatory S., r. eye entirely closed, l. almost, cheek and nose level, cheek hung upon the breast, the breast swollen like a great loaf; S. about joints, with inflammation and itching. *Swellings after bites of insects, sore and sensitive to touch;* at outer corner of eyebrow.

Itching of face, arms and legs, with redness and with hard, white elevated patches and ridges, the application of cold water distressed him, occasionally the legs became cold and blue but in five or ten minutes they were again red and hot. Itching, red elevations over body, extremities and even ears. Wales covering body, without itching or burning, but with disappearance of other symptoms; *white wales covering body. Red and white blotches.* Red blotches, with sensitiveness of skin to touch. Blotches on body and on back of hand, with stinging. Inflammation over whole body, with pressure when rubbed, and white spots like mosquito bites; I., with pain and gangrene; *cellular I. ending in suppuration.*

Erysipelas of face, with fever, coated tongue and thirst; E. of forearm, with disorder of muscular nerves and with heat, redness, swelling and pain. *Erysipelatous swelling, hard and white in middle, with sharp pain. Nettle-rash; after fever; over whole body, also with lessening of previous symptoms;* over whole body except feet; paler than usual color of skin, with swelling of face and whole body. Sensitive pimples; in inner cartilage of l. ear. *Furuncles and* **large swellings** *of every description,* or local inflammation attended them *with stinging.* Sore pustules, with red areola in hair of pubes, with soreness and pain.

Stinging, with swelling and inflammation; *itching S. in different parts,* especially lower limbs. Stinging prickling, burning, smarting and itching all over skin. *Prickling; all over body;* especially on back and palms of hands, face, forehead and under eyes, chiefly in circumscribed spots. *Burning in various portions, with stinging;* especially on back, which itched. Burning like prickly heat on back, arms and hands and after scratching, itching and blotches like nettle-rash.

Sensitiveness to touch; every hair is painful when touched. Full and constricted feeling on forehead and face, then swelling, with red streaks on face, swelling extending to body and limbs, and urticaria over whole body. Crawling in l. fingers; as from insects on inner side of r. knee in morning; of feet, with itching; as after freezing.

Itching; > scratching; over r. eyebrow; on back of hands and upper part of feet; of r. hand, with chapping; *and after scratching blotches like nettle-rash;* on outer part of l. wing of nose, with soreness and redness; *biting, in eyebrow, sometimes r., sometimes l.;* I. or stinging of face, ears, throat, hands and wrists. Stinging itching on posterior surface of r. thigh, like flea bites, in afternoon, > scratching, then on r. arm. Burning itching, on l. thigh, especially posteriorly; in spots in palm, < l.; at 9 P.M., on backs of hands, knuckles, joints of fingers, < r., then chapping; *in evening, beginning in arms, spreading over whole body; over whole body,* with red pimples, thicker on chest and back than on face and arms.

Clinical.—**Valuable for urticaria, erysipelas and œdematous swellings, always with extreme sensitiveness to touch and with stinging burning pains.**

Sleep.—Yawning; mornings. **Sleepiness**; *in morning;* in morning, will not rise, feels as if beaten, must stretch herself, with vertigo. Sleeplessness; and the brain has no rest day or night, with restlessness and loose, urgent stools at night. Restless sleep, with inclination to frequent waking and incessant dreams. Terrified starting in evening sleep from a noise. Frequent waking, with vexatious dreams of business cares. *Dreams;* full of care and toil, of traveling, mostly by railroad.

Fever.—Chilliness; at noon, with red face and red spots on body; in evening, with cold fingers, < l.; in evening while sitting, caused by previous slight movement, with heat in face and headache; when eating; with cold limbs and nausea; with hot hands; with racking pain through head, weakness and shivering; then fever at night. Shuddering, with diarrhœa; S., then nettle-rash. *Chill every day at 3 P.M. running over back, with shuddering, < in warmth, with dead feeling in hands, then after an hour heat, with hoarse cough, heat of cheeks and hands,* **without thirst,** *then heaviness and weakness.* Cold extremities; hands. Coldness and pallor of fingers up to first phalanx, and of toes, nails cyanotic. Cold, clammy skin. Cold feet, with hot head. Heat; at night, with agitation; with general oppression; over whole body, with stinging. In flushes; mixed with chills. Internal, without external, with trembling, and rapid pulse, then vertigo while standing, as if about to faint, pallor, nausea and vomiting, then sleep, with *anxious starting* and cough, then quiet sleep after turning on to other side. Heat of head; in upper part of l. ear; in spots on hands; in finger-tips; in feet; in face, with full sensation. *Burning in head, < motion and stooping, > firm pressure, with throbbing and with occasional sweat.* Sudden heat over back, with pain at l. ilio-sacral junction. Burning of toes, with redness and heat in them while the feet are cold. B. of toes, with erysipelatous redness and heat in a patch on foot and coldness of the rest of the feet. *Sweat; after trembling and fainting, then nettle-rash;* alternating with dry skin; cold, on feet.

Clinical.—In intermittent fever the characteristic symptom for Apis is chill at 4 to 5 P.M., with thirst, < external heat or slightest motion, with oppression of breath as if he would smother; heat without thirst, with some sensitiveness; the sweating stage is usually very slight or wanting; there is generally sleepiness throughout the paroxysm. In typho-malarial fever; in which there are the unconsciousness, dry tongue, involuntary stools, stupor, intense thirst.

Apium Graveolens.

A tincture is prepared from the seeds of this plant (the common celery; Nat. order, Umbelliferæ).

Generalities.—Bruised sensation in flesh after scratching, with sometimes a raw sensation. Inability to sit still or lie still, from feeling of "fidgets," cannot keep from thinking. Weakness; in evening. Remission of symptoms in morning and forenoon.

Head.—Aching all day, > when eating and in open air; frontal; sharp, over r. eye and temple on going to bed and lasting all night, > during breakfast; in r. temple from noon till evening, with nausea (chronic headache always began in l. temple); in l. temple, spreading over l. side of face and to top of head; < deep in l. temple, as from a jar, almost throbbing, < by light, must keep eyes partly closed, reading tires head, the headache afterwards distinctly throbbing deep in and through temples and somewhat in forehead, most of the time can count the beats in the head, the pain < by stooping, moving head and eating, > by complete rest and quiet, but the throbbing continued when at rest, expiration through nose makes the throbbing painful, afterwards the pain > for some minutes by three mouthfuls of cold water, also > by hot compresses to forehead till he began to move, > on waking if he waked without moving, stopped short on eating Indian meal gruel. Sore feeling over whole top. Scalp sore to touch.

Eyes and Nose.—Eyes feel sunken. Tickling in nose in forenoon, with desire to sneeze. Nose stuffed; with pain in forehead. Sneezing in morning, with tickling and running from nose; S. in morning, with watery discharge from nose and tickling in r. nostril.

Lips, Mouth and Throat.—Itching of lips and desire to rub them with the teeth. Sore pain in l. teeth. Sore spot on tip of tongue, feeling like a canker sore. Soft palate red and sore; soft palate and fauces swollen and dark red. Back part of throat hurt by air rushing down posterior nares. Throat sore.

Stomach.—Appetite lost; ate nothing from Sunday morning till Wednesday night. Nausea. Spitting up food. Unpleasant sensation, with belching tasting of celery. Heartburn. Gone feeling in pit, partially > by eating.

Stool and Urine.—Two urgent, well-formed stools in the day, preceded by pain in abdomen going directly into rectum, with feeling as if she could not retain the stool a moment, next day three stools of the same kind. Urine retained.

Respiratory Organs and Heart.—Tickling in top of windpipe at night, causing dry cough. Cough. Wheezing at night. Heart's beats can be counted by hearing or feeling in chest.

Neck, Back and Extremities.—Muscles of nape pain on motion and seem sore from severity of headache. Sacral pain, with bellyache, the S. pain > after getting out of bed, < on lying down again; S. pain < after lying down, > by moving about, with pain in lower abdomen on first lying down, > after continued lying, the same S. pain afterwards on rising, but extending further up back and more on l. side. Growing pain in r. leg before going to bed and lasting most of the night.

Skin.—Itching blotches on l. sacral region. Red, itching eruption on upper inner part of thighs, < l., extending to groins, towards night. Itching on different parts, < after undressing and at night; and as soon as it was allayed in one place it appeared in another. Itching leaving burning after scratching, about face; on l. jaw, extending to whole l. side of face and nose. Itching of l. cheek and jaw in evening, after scratching red blotches, then burning; I. on l. lower jaw, then after scratching red blotches, then itching red blotches on l. instep and outside of l. ankle; I. on l. buttock at night, after scratching felt a blotch like an insect bite; I. like the bite of an insect in different parts, causing shuddering or trembling of the part, then little red elevated itching pimples, the I. somewhat > by scratching, then burning creeping sensation.

Sleep.—Broken. Sleepless all night; till 4.30 A.M.; from Sunday till Wednesday. Could not go to sleep without great exertion and then would wake unrefreshed in ten minutes.

Fever.—Chill from any change of temperature, < in back or where the lower temperature strikes the body. Hot feeling on vertex. Intermittent burning inside thighs, which look like a raw surface, extending to groins, < on l., with itching, which is < at night. Sweat on forehead on waking at 4 A.M.

Clinical.—Profuse discharge from granulating ulcers, intense constriction over sternum, with drawing feeling through to back on lying down.

Apocynum Androsæmifolium.

This "dog's bane" is a perennial herb belonging to the Apocynaceæ. A tincture is prepared from the fresh root.

Allies.—Apocynum cannab.

Trembling. Pain in different parts; P. on turning to l. side; *P. in all joints;* flying P. in different parts. Swollen sensation in body and face. Heaviness of body, with great sleepiness. Weakness. Fulness in head. Headache; in l. side; pulsating A. in occiput;

A. in back of head and neck, with stiffness. Great itching and irritation in l. nostril. Great sneezing. Everything smelled like honey. Twitching of facial muscles. Violent pain in l. zygomatic process. *Pain in all l. lower teeth.* Taste delightful. Nausea. Vomiting; with purging; effort at V. Flying pain in stomach.

Shooting pain in l. groin. Feeling as if something would pass the bowels, with fulness and pain in r. side. Diarrhœa, with pain and rumbling, only two stools, but copious and affording much relief; D. and constipation on alternate days. *Constipation.* Frequent bilious stools; painful bilious diarrhœa. Micturition frequent. Urine profuse. *Menses profuse,* lasting eight days, with violent pressing pain.

Dull heavy pain when breathing, seeming to go from above downward. Pain in nape extending to front of neck. Stiff neck. Pulsating pain in r. forearm. Pain above wrists. Hands and feet swell. Pain *in knee and in r. shoulder. Cramp in soles, < r., with burning and with pain in joint of l. big toe* and heat in r. leg and knee. *Tingling pain in toes,* sharp pain in middle toe. *Itching* of body and face; of face, with burning. Inability to sleep. S. unrefreshing. Violent dreams. Chilliness. Heat of head and neck; H. in r. leg and knee. Profuse *sweat* of whole body, with *violent heat* in soles.

Clinical.—Has been found useful in acute rheumatism with great stiffness. General rheumatic pains. It has been used for renal calculi and gravel.

Apocynum Cannabinum.

The Indian hemp is a perennial herb belonging to the Apocynaceæ. A tincture is prepared from the fresh root.

General Action.—Increases the amount of urine; causes free action of the bowels, with weakness of sphincters of rectum and bladder, and with hæmorrhoidal congestion. It has a powerfully depressing action on the heart, causing irregularity and great weakness of pulse.

Allies.—Alstonia, *Digitalis,* Asclēpias, Arsen., Phos., Aloe, Pod., Oleander, Colch., Verat.

Generalities.—Weight diminished. Rheumatic pain in joints. Restlessness at night; on going to bed. Weakness in morning; at night, especially in all muscles; after stool; < motion; with diarrhœa; muscular; muscular, all the evening. Aggravation from motion.

Mind.—*Bewildered.* Cannot concentrate thoughts. Dull and unable to think well. Fancy exalted with flow of good spirits. No ambition. Inability for labor.

Head.—Aching; morning on waking; on waking before 5 A.M.; extending to meatus auditorius externus; confused; confused after stool; confused, extending to orbits. Dulness. Heaviness in evening, with aching in small of back and limbs; dull, after stool. Vertigo in morning on rising from stooping; on rising from stooping; when rising, < yawning or stretching; after stool; < ascending; as if he would fall, *suddenly appearing and disappearing.*

Forehead.—Aching; darting; throbbing, and in vertex; heavy drawing, especially about superciliary ridges. Fulness. Heaviness; over eyes.

Temples.—Sticking in r. Aching; in r.; r. after stool; r., then stabbing pain, then confusion of head, then vertigo; with heaviness and pain in eyes as if he had used them too much; piercing, in r., also after stool, with vertigo and ringing in r. ear; piercing, in r., with nausea; A. darting from l. to r., and *vice versa.* Throbbing in temporal artery.

Eyes.—Irritation in l. as from sand in morning on waking, with heat and redness. Pain in l. as if wearied, with drooping of lids. Pain in orbital region and dull heavy feeling over eyes.

Ears.—Sticking in l.; r. Partial deafness in l. after singing.

Nose.—Sneezing long-continued and violent. Discharge increased. Nostrils and throat filled with thick well-concocted yellow mucus in morning on waking.

Face.—Pale; with cold sweat (Dig., Verat.). Red and hot look. Dull heavy pain in both sides of face and nose, < l., passing into forehead.

Mouth.—Tongue sticks to the roof in morning. Dryness in morning; on waking. Salivation, then dryness in fauces. Mucus and saliva in mouth and fauces increased. Spittle thick and tenacious. Tonsils and throat coated with dried mucus.

Stomach.—Hunger (Oleander, Verat.); all the time; ravenous. *Thirst* on waking. Hiccough night and morning. Nausea; in evening; at night when waking; after sleep; after stool; < about 7 or 7.30 P.M.; with inability to vomit; with piercing pain in r. temple; with flashes of heat in different parts, beginning in throat and extending downward. Vomiting; after sleep. Retching. Pinching shooting from r. to l. of epigastrium. **Oppression in epigastrium and chest** (Phos.), *impeding breathing, after lighter meals than usual;* distressing O. in epigastrium after meals; distressing, in epigastrium, > walking. Gnawing; 10 A.M., after a hearty breakfast; after dinner. Burning pain (Colch.). Burning while at breakfast. At pyloric region sensation as if a ball pressed against the inside of the wall. Dull, heavy, sick feeling all the morning, and in abdomen. Working in S. after meals; as from flatus, > empty eructations. Sinking; on waking; in pit. Weakness.

Abdomen.—Rumbling; during stool, with emission of flatus. Flatulence; emission of flatus in evening; emission before stool; emission during stool. *Distention;* about stomach, liver and spleen, < after a moderate dinner (Lyc.). Distended feeling, with pain as if flatus were moving in different parts, then sudden urging to stool. Feeling as if he had drunk too much water. Grumbling; and disagreeable feeling. Pain while at breakfast, > stool; after stool, compelling him to sit down again, when nothing but wind passed; darting in different parts, with feeling as if flatus expanded the intestines; of moving flatus before stool. Feeling as if diarrhœa would occur. Uneasiness. Empty feeling after stool (Pod., Sul. ac., Phos.). Weak feeling (Oleander, Phos.).

Short pinching across middle. Aching in umbilical region; after stool. Grumbling pain in umbilical region. Feeling of goneness in umbilical region after a stool. Feeling as if something were passing up colon, with a grumbling sensation. Feeling as if something were passing through liver. Pulsation in r. hypochondrium in evening. Distended feeling in lower after eating. Darting pain in lower, with rumbling. Weak feeling in lower.

Rectum.—*Tenesmus* (Colch.); after stool; after stool, with aching in hypogastric region. Urging to stool; after eating; after pain in abdomen; with emission of only flatus; sudden. Bearing down; after stool, even protrusion. Soreness; after a stool, with bearing down. Heaviness. Weak feeling.

Anus.—Protruding inflamed hæmorrhoids, with pain in anus as if a wedge were forced into it by a hammer; inclination to hæmorrhoids. *Bearing down pain* (Cact.). Pressure and weight, > walking. Burning. Itching. Open feeling after stool. Loss of power in sphincter (Aloe).

Stool.—**Watery,** small, with much flatus, then soreness in anus; watery and large, with bearing down pain in anus and soreness in rectum (Aloe). Thin, frequent, with the force and sound of a cork from a champagne bottle, lemon-colored, frothy, containing undigested food (Pod.); thin, at latter part; copious, thin at first, towards the end containing lumps of fæces; thin, light-yellow, mixed with mucus. Loose, bilious, but not very copious. Loose in morning; loose, small, frequent, with much flatus, sometimes difficult, sometimes expelled with force. Diarrhœa scanty, difficult, with much flatus. Furious painless diarrhœa at night. Early, mushy, expelled with a rush and much flatus. Frothy. Bloody. Involuntary when intending to emit flatus (Aloe). Mushy, copious, darkish-brown, very fetid. *Scanty;* and difficult. Bowels sluggish but fæces not hard or costive. So large after the diarrhœa ceased that the expulsion was painful. Symptoms *always* immediately after eating.

Urinary Organs.—Bladder seemed much distended, then turbid hot urine, with a thick mucous sediment, with burning in urethra after micturition. Aching at neck of bladder after urinating, with sensation as if the sphincter were trying to close but could not (Jug. r.). Little expulsive power in bladder. Weakness of sphincter of neck of B. Constant desire to urinate with copious discharge. The scanty urine flowed as easily as oil. Could hardly tell when urine was passing; hardly knew when he was through, the urine still seemed to want to dribble away. Smarting and burning in urethra when urinating. Aching in urethra after urinating. Discharge of thin watery fluid from urethra. *Urine copious;* and lighter-colored; with a sediment, which in many respects resembled albumen. *Scanty urine.* Hot U. (Aloe), leaving tingling in urethra.

Respiratory Organs.—*Cough short, dry.* Sudden, hard and frequent C. evening and nights. Expectoration of white mucus; of white gelatinous mucus. *Respiration short and unsatisfactory.* Disposition to sigh (Op.). Constant sighing from a peculiar sensation in chest. Suffocated feeling.

Heart.—Darting pain in region in afternoon and evening. Catching pain. Weak feeling near. Palpitation. Increased action; with fluttering and sensation as if it would force itself through the wall of the chest. Action fluttering and feeble, then slow and labored, now and then losing a beat, with a clicking sound. Impulse felt against wall of chest. Pulse rapid; slow; diminished; full, irregular, slow, intermittent, dicrotic, at times feeble.

Back.—Pain. Sticking in inferior angle of scapula. Pain at inferior angle of l. scapula; pain in r. S. and in muscles of forearm. Prickling tingling in region of l. S. at 2 P.M., with lameness of muscles. Aching in kidney region; in lower part of l. loin when walking. Soreness in kidney region when using muscles. Aching in sacrum and at times sharp and sticking pain, appearing occasionally in hip, knee and ankle-joints.

Extremities.—Bruised feeling in morning on waking, > after walking, and in all joints, and especially in small of back. Sore feeling in morning, and in muscles. Weakness of arms. Lower limbs feel stiff. Pain in knees, < l.; so that he feared inflammatory rheumatism.

Skin.—Boils on face and thighs. Erysipelas of face and head. Itching on back, sides and limbs at 6 P.M., and on going to bed found large papules, like hives, covering the body, red when scratched, which did not relieve, appearing in greatest number on lumbar region and around waist.

Sleep.—Sleepiness; on going to bed, without ability to sleep. Little sleep at night. Sleep unrefreshing. Waking early. Disturbed by dreams.

Fever.—Cold hands and feet. Burning in red part of upper lip. Heat of skin on going to bed (Sil.). Flashes of heat; in face; in different parts, with nausea. Sweat; cold on face (Dig., Colch., Verat.); copious, also at night.

Clinical.—It has been used chiefly for dropsical effusions dependent upon diseases of the liver; it has not been so useful in albuminuria. Cases of hydrocephalus have been cured; patients do not have the screaming out which characterizes Apis. Hydrothorax with scanty urine; ascites; general anasarca; in all these cases there is generally great thirst, but drinking causes distress or nausea and vomiting; the stomach is very irritable and there is great distention on taking anything into it. For neuralgia of the sciatic and lumbar nerves in r. groin and trochanter extending up into lumbar region, pain very severe. Excessive hæmorrhage from the uterus, vomiting. It has arrested post-partum hæmorrhage. Purpura, with suppression of urine, has been cured. The general indications in dropsies of various sorts seem to be the presence of great thirst and the extreme irritability of the stomach; in this respect it resembles Arsenicum. It is supposed that the aqueous infusion is more efficacious than the tincture.

Apomorphinum.

An alkaloid obtained from the decomposition of morphine by means of hydrochloric acid. Formula $C_{17}H_{17}NO_2$. For use, the alkaloid is triturated with sugar of milk.

General Action.—The chief interest attached to this substance lies in its remarkable power to produce emesis (which it does in doses of from five to seven millegrams in adults). This irritating action upon the nerve centre is similar to that of Sanguinaria, Veratrum, Ipecac., Copper and Zinc.

Generalities.—Pandiculations. Depression. Faintness. Weakness; with sweat on face, which was pale; so that eyes closed involuntarily.

Head.—Aching. Heaviness. Vertigo; with chilliness. Dulness, sometimes described as headache, sometimes as heaviness or vertigo, often with roaring in ears and feeling of heat, at times sudden anxiety in præcordial region and pressure in chest, with the reaction there is generally inclination to sleep, prostration and in a few cases nausea and retching without warning, the relaxation during the prodromal state was very great, with sweat, salivation and paleness, especially of face, the vomiting is easy, or after the stomach has been emptied difficult with eructations and retching, between the acts of vomiting the patient is quiet, weak, yawns and perspires, sleepy after the vomiting ceases.

Injection of conjunctivæ and lachrymation. Pupils dilated. Face red; pale. Salivation. **Violent in-**

clination to vomit. **Vomiting; without previous nausea; easy;** *of water as soon as it was drunk, also milk.* Retching; as soon as stomach had been emptied. Weight at stomach. Respiration irregular; rapid. Pulse rapid and irregular; rapid, small and soft. Extremities heavy; weak. Inclined to yawn. Sleepiness, with sweat. Sleep. Heat running suddenly all over body, then vomiting. Hot feeling all over body, especially in head. Sweat.

Clinical.—The applicability of this drug to the relief of various troubles requiring prompt emesis will be apparent to every one. (Its use in poisoning by Opium is dangerous.) The hypodermic injection of $\frac{1}{16}$ of a grain will cause full emesis within 5 to 15 minutes in an adult. It has been found useful in vomiting of various sorts, sometimes with violent spasms and empty retching and headache, sometimes with heartburn, pain between shoulder-blades; sometimes it has cured the vomiting of food, sometimes palliated the vomiting of pregnancy or uterine displacements or uterine tumors, sometimes relieved seasickness; in one case the 2d trit. cured vomiting which had lasted several days without any organic disease, apparently of nervous origin.

Aralia Racemosa.

The American spikenard is an herbaceous plant belonging to the Araliaceæ. A tincture is prepared from the fresh root.

General Action.—See respiratory organs.

Allies.—Iodine, Ars., Ip.

Severe cold, no cough. Weak, half sick and filled with vague nausea. Feeling on rising at 8.30 as after a "spree," with nausea in throat and stomach and sensation as if diarrhœa would set in, and at 3.15 P.M. stool, difficult, soft, yellow, about a teaspoonful, with protrusion of mucous membrane of rectum like a tumor (have had hæmorrhoids), after stool aching pain in rectum extending upward and on l. side. Headache.

Lips red, swollen, lips and mouth feel parched, wants to keep the tongue moving to keep it moist, although there is profuse salivation, saliva running from mouth, < by lying, roof of mouth covered with ulcers, irregular in size and shape, having a yellowish-white covering (not membrane), looking like pus, throat swollen and sore, swallowing difficult on account of a sensation of a "bunch" in throat, voice weak and husky. Nausea. Discomfort in stomach, with flatulency. Griping. Irritation in anus at night. Mucous discharge from rectum. Diarrhœa; preceded by belching.

Asthma on lying down at night, dry wheezing respiration when lying on back, with sense of impending suffocation, rapidly increasing dyspnœa, loud musical whistlings during inspiration and expiration, *but louder during inspiration,* inability to lie down, warm, salt, mucous expectoration, greater oppression of r. than of l. lung, afterwards when lying on r. side all oppression and discomfort were in r. lung, but on turning over the l. lung was affected and *the r. relieved entirely,* constant desire to clear chest of something, *all obstruction being during inspiration,* on forcible expiration raw, burning, sore feeling behind whole length of sternum and in lungs, most intense behind sternum, in morning easy expectoration of loose phlegm, afterwards fear that r. lung is diseased, and cough now and then, with raising of phlegm, which is swallowed involuntarily.

Sweat in sleep at night.

Clinical.—It has been found useful for asthma with spasmodic cough at night, in general < lying down. Spasmodic cough at night *after the first sleep,* cough caused by tickling in throat, associated with constriction of chest, has to sit up and cough violently; sometimes caused by a feeling of a foreign body in the throat. Asthma, with oppressed breathing all day, as from a weight on stomach, < night on lying down, when the patient is awakened by the violent cough, > raising a little tough mucus. Hay fever, frequent sneezing, with asthmatic attacks and whistling respiration, must sit up. It has cured leucorrhœa, acrid, offensive, with bearing down pains.

Aranea.

The papal-cross Spider (Aranea Diadema), *Linn.* A tincture is prepared by crushing the live spider and digesting with alcohol.

General Action.—The most characteristic feature of this drug is the tendency to a periodic recurrence of the symptoms at exactly the same hour. Continued coldness without reaction characterizes the attack.

Related Remedies.—(Tarantula), Camphora (not periodic), Argent. met., Arnica, Cedron, Secale corn.

Generalities.—Weakness; with confusion of head.

Head.—Aching; till evening, > *in open air;* > smoking in open air; > walking, with burning in eyes and heat in face; especially in forehead, > smoking; *with confusion, both > by smoking.* Drawing extending down lower jaw. **Confusion** in evening when studying, and pressive pain, as if on bones of r. temple and upper part of forehead, > resting head on hand; after eating; with weakness. *Heat in forehead and eyes, a flickering in them on reading or writing, which aggravated the headache.*

Ears and Nose.—Twinging pain in ear and parotid gland, r., then l. Coryza; with thirst.

Mouth.—*Sudden violent pain in all teeth at night after lying down.* Sensitive cold sensation in r. lower incisor, at the same hour two days, < drawing in air. Sticking in palate and larynx. Taste bitter, > smoking; nauseous bitter, with coated tongue; unpleasant T. of milk after drinking it.

Stomach, Abdomen and Stool.—Thirst. Heaviness and fulness in lower abdomen, as from a stone, **at the same time two days,** with nausea in pit of stomach, *griping in abdomen,* heaviness in thighs and confusion in head. *Stool fluid,* passed only a part at a time and with straining, *with pain in abdomen,* which is > by rubbing, fermenting in abdomen after the stool.

Sexual and Respiratory Organs.—*Menses too early, too strong and too copious. Hæmorrhage from the lungs.*

Extremities.—*Dull, burrowing bone-pain; in r. arm and tibia in morning in bed and at intervals through the day.* Twitching in muscles of l. upper arm in afternoon. *In ring and little fingers a feeling as if they had gone to sleep and of formication.* Dull, burrowing bone-pain in r. os calcis on motion, > continued motion.

Sleep restless, with frequent waking, and always with a sensation as if hands and forearms were swollen and heavy. (**Feverish attacks, consisting mostly of coldness,** *with pain in long bones, troubles in the abdomen, which are usually accompanied by a chill,* and mostly come on towards evening, and pimples here and there.) Heat in face; especially in eyes.

Clinical.—Tremulous, sensitive, nervous exhaustion, nightly sensation as if her hands and arms were enormously enlarged, often causing her to strike a light to see if it were really so. In headache, continuous for fifteen months, at base of brain, < in damp weather. Toothache, < in damp weather and as soon as the patient gets into bed. Lumbar abdominal neuralgia, intermittent, from being uncovered at night, < from 8 to 11 A.M., with yawning or vomiting. Enlarged spleen, always < in damp weather. Diarrhœa, great loss of appetite and sleep. Bronchitis, cough < on lying down at night, tickling in throat brought on cough. Asthma, unable to lie down day or night, white, frothy expectoration, nausea and disgust for food. Diseases of os calcis, with boring; digging in that bone; this may be due to simple periostitis or may be associated with caries; sometimes bones feel like ice. Sleeplessness in subjects suffering from asthma; nervous cough. Chronic intermittent fever, with swelling of spleen, living in a damp place, patient chilly day and night, always < during a rain. Quotidian fever. The attacks recur at the same hour and consist mostly of coldness, which lasts a long time and is not followed by heat or sweat. The patient is exceedingly weak, but while thirsty has none of the restlessness of Arsenic. These conditions have been found mostly in old people.

Argentum Metallicum.

Pure precipitated silver is prepared for use by trituration with sugar of milk.

General Action.—Silver exerts a marked and general action on the mucous membranes from the pharynx through stomach and bowels, genito-urinary tract and respiratory apparatus. Independently also it seems to cause spinal irritability, with numerous pains in body and extremities, with tendency to spasmodic action of muscles.

Allied Drugs.—Aluminium, Ferrum, *Zincum*, Lyc., Chin., Sulf., Gelsem., Hyperic., *Agaric.*

Generalities.—Electric shocks through upper part of body, in forenoon, exploding close to foramen magnum (compare Chin., Sulf.). Twitching and pulsation of several muscles, especially in r. thigh; of r. temporal, r. frontal muscles, muscles of neck near thyroid cartilage and towards nape, it repelled the hand, with quivering pain.

Burrowing, tensive, stiff, bruised and broken feeling in bones. Drawing pain, now in l. forehead, now in occiput, now in l. elbow, when at rest; alternately in different joints, upper arm, calf and forehead, when at rest. Soreness between nates, around anus and in groin, when walking. Painful tension alternating between tendon of r. psoas and triceps humeris, with bruised pain on pressure.

Weakness in morning on waking (Chin., Alumin.), with depression; after waking, especially of upper arm; at 11 A.M., especially of upper arms, with sleepiness; when sitting or walking, especially of thighs, with sleepiness; when walking in open air, with heat and anguish as if the clothes were too tight; paralytic W. on motion; in limbs in morning, > rising, with tensive bruised pain in nape. **The attacks recur every day at noon** (Gelsem.).

Clinical.—General tendency to emaciation, with sallow, pale complexion. General anæmia, with œdematous feet. Rheumatic pains in limbs and back, generally < lying down. General loss of power, threatening paralysis.

Mind.—*Cheerful and talkative* (reaction). Merry when pleased, but crying long about a trifle. Ill-humored.

Head.—(Stitches in morning, with redness of one eye.) Shooting and tearing. Stinging burning pain in head. Intoxicated condition; dizzy sleepy intoxication. Creeping and crawling, as if tipsy. Dizzy stupefaction. Confusion; at 10 A.M.; as from smoke in brain; as from vertigo. Hollow feeling, with aching in brain and chilliness. Soreness on pressure. *Vertigo, with difficulty in controlling his senses;* when sitting and reflecting; on coming in from a walk, with shivering; *suddenly, with mist before eyes* (Gelsem.).

Forehead.—Tearing in r.; deep in r. eminence, extending towards r. temple; in l. eminence; under l. eminence, with compression in globe of eye. **Aching,** *with drawing pressure in occiput and stupor;* over brows; deep in r. eminence extending obliquely to r. temporal region; drawing, in eminences. Intermittent boring anteriorly in l. side, < evening after lying down.

Temples.—Cutting stitches in skull or on surface of brain, in front of l. ear, forward. Tearing in l.; *region of r. and l. bone, < touch;* in l. bone and over l. mastoid process. **Aching** in l.; externally in bones; over r. ear, extending backward, with drawing; *drawing, in l. temple,* also at rest, also when sitting. **Pinching** in r., with intermittent stitches extending inward. Drawing downward from mastoid process for an inch, > on pressure when at rest.

Parietals.—Aching externally in bones; externally in l. bones; drawing throbbing, deep in r. half of brain during rest; drawing, in l. side of head, as if in brain substance, at 8 P.M. when crossing the room, becoming a tearing as if a nerve were torn out, ending suddenly. Drawings deep in r. half of brain in evening, increasing to tearings and extending towards forehead and occiput.

Occiput.—Drawing pain in l. when at rest, alternating with the same in ball of l. thumb; drawing pain externally from bone obliquely across r. temporal bone to middle of frontal bone; between l. protuberance and mastoid process when at rest.

Clinical.—Attacks of vertigo, with crawling and whirling in head as if intoxicated; on looking at running water; feeling of emptiness in head.

Eyes.—(*Redness and thickness of lids.*) Sticking vertically through l. upper lid in afternoon; in canthi; l. inner canthus at 3 P.M.; l. canthi, with itching. Itching in inner canthi; stinging, in canthi.

Clinical.—Sometimes useful in blepharitis, but rarely in purulent ophthalmia, the edges of the lids thickened.

Ears.—*Stitches* in fossa behind r. lobule, penetrating head; inward in fossa behind l. lobule; cutting, in l. middle, as far as brain. *Tearing* over l. *Drawing* pain within l.; in fossa behind r. lobule, extending downward in a crescent form, during rest; drawing pain from fossa under r. lobule to skin of cheek, extending to lower jaw, as if in periosteum; intermittent drawing, in fossa behind l. lobule; drawing, extending downward from mastoid process, > at rest on pressure. Stopped sensation in r.

Nose.—Throbbing in fore part of l. nostril, with tension in external skin of nose as if bones were compressed and tickling prickling in l. nostril, causing violent sneezing. Biting in l. nostril. Irritation as if a cold would come on. Obstruction in fore part. *Tingling and itching in, then bleeding. Fluent coryza; with frequent sneezing.* Bleeding on blowing nose.

Face.—Stitches in r. malar-bone. Tearing on l. zygoma; *drawing T. in r. zygoma.* Gnawing pressure in bones of r. side, especially malar-bone. Drawing pain in muscles, especially in region of cheek-bones. Throbbing over l. cheek, as if muscles would be raised, with swollen feeling in l. cheek, chilly burning in skin, and redness of both cheeks. *Swelling of lip under nose* (Hep., Merc. c.). Cutting stitches inward under r. lower jaw, apparently in gland.

Mouth.—Teeth. Lower row sticks to upper, as if covered with sticky cement (Zinc.). Aching in the hollow l. lower wisdom tooth; in an incisor on pressure forward. Gum painful, < touch. Tongue, *sore and burning vesicle* (Lyc.); dryness, and of hard palate; dry in middle; dry feeling, with moisture; burning on tip, in afternoon. *Mouth dry.* Salivation morning in bed; during afternoon nap, then dryness of mouth so the tongue stuck to the palate; with shaking chill; viscid, impeding speech.

Clinical.—Sticky, tough saliva on palate, causing scratching.

Throat.—*Swelling of region of submaxillary gland, making neck stiff, with tension on motion and difficult swallowing as from internal swelling of throat.* **Mucus, viscid, gray, jellylike, in morning, easily hawked up** (Alumina). Cutting towards parotid gland as after an acrid acid, when chewing, felt in Eustachian tube. Boring and digging. Drawing pain in r. submaxillary and parotid glands; drawing pain, in l. parotid gland. **Rawness and soreness**; during expiration and deglutition. **Roughness,** with scratching. Scraping constantly in velum pendulum palati, as if a rough body were glued to it, worse during empty swallowing than when swallowing a morsel, forcing him to swallow saliva, afterwards descending deeper into fauces. *Painful tension when yawning, as from a swelling.* Itching crawling in pharyngeal orifice of r. Eustachian tube, extending to tympanum, r. then l. (compare Gels.). Pulsation of carotids, < l. Nausea, then general heat, especially about head, with red face, without thirst.

Clinical.—Catarrhal sore throat. Chronic pharyngeal catarrh, with hawking of jellylike mucus which is viscid and gray, < morning. *Rawness and soreness when coughing, not on swallowing.*

Stomach.—Hunger in morning; at 6.30 on waking; in forenoon, with nausea as from emptiness of stomach and scraping irritation in bronchial tubes, causing dry cough; during afternoon nap, with nausea; with nausea, contraction of pharynx and inclination to swallow saliva; with drawing-in of pit of stomach. *Excessive appetite; even when stomach feels full* (Lyc.); in paroxysms. Appetite gone; in morning; gone, with loathing of food when thinking of it. (Great desire for wine). Hiccough when smoking. Nausea; caused by anxious dreams. Retching, by which a bitter, acrid, bad-tasting liquid is brought into mouth, leaving behind scratching, roughness and burning in fauces. Vomiting in afternoon during stool.

Pinching over S. and in l. hypochondrium. Pressure in pit. Burning; sudden in pit, when standing and reading, with dull compression of brain from all sides, approaching vertigo, nausea in region of sternum, sudden heat in whole body, but more in face, and sweat on chest and face.

Abdomen.—Painful distention at night, > emission of flatus (Lyc.). Rumbling; at night, with emission of flatus; with fermenting, as if water were poured from one intestine to another. **Cutting** transversely across internally. Contractive pain when sitting after morning stool. Pain as in diarrhœa. Tension in muscles when walking, so that he has to stoop, with contraction. Burning in morning as far as chest.

Flatulence in upper, with fulness and hungry feeling (Lyc.). Tympanic distention of r. side of A., with bruised pain on hard pressure, > emission of flatus. *Rumbling in l. like the croaking of frogs.* Stitching between r. hypochondrium and epigastrium, then hunger and rumbling in bowels; cutting, in rings; extending outward in muscles near two last ribs, ending in pinching, > rubbing. Bruised feeling on l. surface when walking, with sprained feeling.

Hypogastrium. — Stitches extending backward. Pressure after beginning to eat, extending towards pubic region, < during inspiration, > rising from the seat. Drawing pain through r. inguinal ring, down to testicles, at 4 P.M., during rest, with pasty stool; drawing tensive, in r. inguinal region, along psoas muscle when at rest. Straining during and after a soft stool; sensation in bend of l. groin as if tendon of psoas muscle were strained, with bruised pain on pressure. *Bruised pain in groin over l. hip and on l. side of pelvis.* Boring just over r. groin. Tension in l. iliac region, along psoas muscles; in l. groin and thigh, with drawing.

Pelvis.—Drawing stitches in r. towards back part, during rest. Drawing pain externally on l. posterior part, during rest. Drawing on r. side of posterior brim, and in small of back. Sprained pain around back of l., on motion; on external posterior rim on motion after rising; on l. posterior surface of outer rim (at insertion of gluteus maximus) in afternoon after walking, renewed at every step; at back, < l. side, caused by difficult stool and micturition. Bruised pain around back of l.; bruised and sprained P. on l. surface when walking.

Rectum.—*Frequent and successful desire for stool in lower part, with small soft stool.*

Anus.—Sensation as if a worm forced its way through sphincter (Ferrum). Sensation as if a living threadworm hung out, which on stooping caused itching (Sulph.), but no need to scratch. Itching at 8 P.M. while walking, and along fossa between nates. Feeling as if small bubbles of air escaped.

Stool.—Brownish-yellow, pasty, with ineffectual pressure at end. *Dry and like sand after dinner.* Hard, insufficient. Frequent, preceded by pinching and urging, the last almost diarrhœic. Difficult.

Urinary Organs.—*Micturition frequent; and copious* (Gels.). Burning when urinating. Stitch forward in urethra.

Clinical.—Polyuria, diabates insipidus and possibly glycosuria, urine very profuse and turbid, of sweet odor.

Sexual Organs.—Tearing along spermatic cord into testicles at 4 P.M., when resting after a walk. **Crushed pain in r. testicle** *when walking, < pressure of clothes* (Rhod., Zinc.); *in testicles* in evening in bed. *Bruised pain in l. testicle.* Digging deep in substance of r. testicle when at rest, with fear and anxiety. Desire diminished. Emissions at night; without lewd dreams; incomplete, in sleep.

Clinical.—Seminal emissions without sexual excitement or with loss of sexual power. Chronic gleet. Affections of l. ovary, it feels as if it were very large. Prolapsus of uterus with great bearing down and pain in l. ovary, pain extending up back and down l. thigh, with leucorrhœa, yellow, excoriating, ichorous, of an intolerable odor. In women suffering from uterine disease, pain in joints and limbs. Ulceration of uterus, cervix swollen, spongy, corroded, with foul discharge. Palliative in scirrhus of uterus. Sore feeling extending to the whole abdomen < riding in a carriage.

Respiratory Organs.—Crashing, shattering, with a reverberation (like that heard from ice breaking up in the spring). *Mucus on laughing, causing cough. Mucus in air-passages on stooping, expelled by a single cough.* Pain in cricoid cartilage, caused by a draft, with feeling of a stopper in throat and bruised pain on pressure. *Cutting in windpipe, becoming a stitch, causing shocks of cough*, watery expectoration with the cough.

Cough (in morning). Hacking, dry C. in morning after rising. *Attacks of short rattling C. by day, > at night and in open air, with thick, white,* **easy expectoration, looking like boiled starch** (Agar.). On inspiration two tones (as from a bassoon, low and high), at the same time low down in throat, in evening before sleep.

Clinical.—Loss of voice after singing or talking. Chronic hoarseness, cannot speak; larynx feels sore, and there is expectoration of gray gelatinous mucus, the rawness extends as far as the bifurcation of the trachea. When eating fruit it seems as if a little piece stuck; it feels in upper and front part as if something lay in a little spot, almost as if chilling and somewhat pressing, which constantly irritates him to cough, without being removed by doing so. *Rawness and soreness in upper part of larynx when coughing, not when swallowing* (Brom.). Feeling of a raw spot in windpipe, in region of suprasternal fossa, < speaking, talking or singing. Cough from laughing. Cough caused by irritation in larynx and trachea and from accumulation of mucus, the expectoration is characteristic, looking like grayish, boiled starch or like gray jelly. A valuable remedy for the chronic laryngitis of singers and speakers, the expectoration is characteristic.

Chest.—Twitching from r. anterior clavicular region towards shoulder-joint (in a fibre of pectoralis major) during rest. Stitches under l. third true rib; between r. sixth and seventh true ribs, < deep inspiration; under l. last ribs; near r. nipple; beneath r. nipple; on r. side near handle of sternum; under xiphoid cartilage; *outward in r. side, when sitting, arresting breathing;* boring stitches in r. axilla; cutting transversely across below l. last rib, when stooping sideways and leaning on arm; drawing, as in an ulcer, in lowest rib near spine; extending outward inside upper part of sternum; intermittent, under cartilages of l. last true ribs, over pit of stomach, evening in bed, as if in pleura, in præcordial region; pressing, on r. side of chest and sternum, < deep inspiration.

Tearing beneath r. axilla. Cutting on l. side, near pit of stomach, in cartilages of false ribs, morning in bed, changing to a pain in same place on r. side, which is more like an indistinct pressure; on left of pit of stomach, extending across cartilages of false ribs, morning after waking, with bruised pain on pressure; outward in both sides, in region of lowest ribs, < deep inspiration; horizontal, on l. side, in cartilage of false rib, when quiet after breakfast. **Pinching** in spot below r. axilla at noon while at rest, with bruised pain after pressure; sticking pinching in l. side of sternum, < sitting bent. Aching externally in sternum; internally on middle of sternum, < motion, especially stooping and then rising again; over heart, with oppression; spasmodic, in ribs, with tension; drawing below r. axilla during rest after dinner, with bruised pain on strong pressure; as if something pressed hard on r. ribs; pressing outward in spot under second or third r. rib, during deep inspiration; cramplike in l.; then soreness on touch. Oppression. Sprained feeling in posterior wall of r. axilla on exertion, > rest; cutting sprained feeling in cartilage of l. false rib, horizontally across rib, near pit of stomach. Gnawing scratching on l. side when at rest. Mucus, with cough and expectoration.

Heart.—*Spasmodic twitching of cardiac muscle, < lying on back*, with the thought that he would have apoplexy. (Oppressive burning in region.) Pulse quick in evening in bed, with thirst.

Neck.—Pressure on l. outer side when walking in open air. Drawing pain in r. side close to foramen magnum. Tensive bruised feeling along sterno-cleido muscles in morning when stretched, on sitting in open air. Stiff feeling in nape, with drawing and pressing on occiput. Painful tension on both sides of foramen magnum in morning after waking, < motion.

Back.—Cutting stitches at ends of r. ribs, near spine, < curving back. Bruised feeling in morning after waking, and in loins. Tickling itching stitches between scapulæ. Tearing in upper part of l. scapula when sitting, > rising from a seat; in glenoid cavity of scapula, extending to clavicle. Pressure inside scapulæ. Sprained feeling in uppermost muscles of r. scapula on exerting the outstretched arm.

Loins.—Stitches in second lumbar vertebræ; burning stitches in r. loin when sitting, but when rising and on pressure the pain is burning without stitches. Pressure in side of back opposite bowels, then oppressive stitches on least motion or when breathing, so that he had to walk bent, when lying still with griping as in a malignant ulcer and with oppression of chest. Drawing tensive pain in l. loin and below inguinal ring at 7 P.M., after walking, extending to thigh. Bruised feeling in small of back; morning on waking, < motion, and in loins and nape. Deep-seated sprained feeling in lumbo-sacral region, < adduction of l. thigh, compelling limping, then bruised pain on outer side of l. knee.

Extremities.—Tearing in ends of long bones; in metacarpal bone of thumb and in metatarsal bone and proximal phalanx of big toes, < touch, with aching. Drawing and tensive pain in bends of elbows and knees, > strong pressure. Cramplike drawing in back of r. hand and foot. Sprained feeling in top of r. shoulder on walking, and in l. inner malleolus. Discomfort and weakness. Weakness in morning; > after rising.

Upper Extremities.—Shoulder. Electric shocks, extending through l. arm, when sleeping, with hands under head. Twitches around r. joint, at one time in posterior margin of axilla, at another in front of clavicle extending to top of shoulder. Tearing in r. joint; on top of S. and in region of head of humerus; on articular eminence of r. at 5 P.M. while at rest; from articular eminence of r. to nape during rest; pressive T. below joint. Tearing drawing pain in r. joint at rest, with paralytic weakness; drawing pain in r. deltoid; drawing pain in l. deltoid at rest, with bruised pain on pressure; drawing digging pain under r. deltoid; boring scratching pain in r. shoulder-joint in morning when walking. Bruised pain on top of l. when walking. Sprained feeling in l. joint during rest. Weakness on waking at 6.30.

Arm.—Tensive drawing, like stitches, in different places. Inclination to fall asleep in morning when lying on it. Paralysis of r. arm and hand. Paralytic feeling during motion, especially in elbows.

Upper Arm.—Cramp in middle, < lifting arm. Burning stitch anteriorly in middle of l. Tearing in l.; drawing tearing near condyles of l. elbow at 3 P.M., at rest. Pinching in r. Aching in flesh, < touch; drawing, in muscles of r., near bend of elbow, during rest, with paralytic weakness; drawing, in anterior surface of r. *when at rest*, with paralytic weakness in the same place and inclination to stretch arm. Paralytic drawing on outside of l., *with bruised feeling on pressure*. Weakness; in morning after waking, > after rising, with stiffness of neck; about shoulders in morning on waking.

Elbow.—Twitching in l. at 3 P.M. during rest; in bend of r. during rest and bruised pain on top of r. shoulder. Stitches in tips; in tip of l. during rest. Burning pain in a spot at 6 P.M. during rest. Drawing pain through radial joint of r. at noon during rest; spasmodic, in bend of r., as if arm had been sprained, during motion, < extending arm. Tension externally at tip when bending arm.

Forearm.—Stitches at beginning of radius, behind wrist; intermittent, in r. radius, more in muscles. Tearing in posterior muscles between bones of l. elbow and radius, as far as wrist; drawing, above wrist at 2 P.M.; jerking, in middle of radius, r. then l., then in proximal joint of r. middle finger. Spasmodic pressure in inner side of l., with drawing pain. Drawing pain in radius, beginning above wrist, in morning in bed, then the same pain in r. shoulder. Paralytic drawing pain from middle of flexor side of l. radius to elbow during rest; from condyles of elbow, along ulnar side in evening in bed, r. then l. Paralytic drawing in r. radius, beginning above anterior condyle in evening.

Wrist.—Tearing in bones. Drawing pain in radial part of l. during rest, > moving hand, *with bruised pain on pressure.*

Fingers.—Twitchings of whole r. thumb while writing, so that it is abducted from fingers. Tearing in middle joint of r. little; in proximal joint and metacarpal bone of l. fourth, < seizing something, with spasmodic clenching of finger; drawing T. in middle joint of l. index, in bed, afterwards throbbing. Paralytic pain in r. joints. Drawing pain in middle joint of r. index at 1 P.M. during rest, with sudden paralytic weakness in it; drawing P. in ball of l. thumb, during rest, alternating with the same in l. occiput; in bone of proximal joint of ring finger at noon, during rest. Drawing in joints of l. three middle.

Lower Extremities.—Stiffness in evening. Weakness after waking; with giving way of knees when walking; after rising from bed, especially in region of trochanters, with painful *sprained* tension around trochanters and buttocks, < walking, with *bruised pain* on pressure.

Thigh.—Electric shocks starting from l. then r. hip-joint during after-dinner nap. Twitches above l. patella. Tearing stitches over l. patella; throbbing S. in l. trochanter, synchronous with pulse, along neck of femur to socket in morning in bed. Pressure in r. hip-joint when he steps on l. foot in running. Drawing pain in l. hip at noon during rest. Paralytic drawing in r. hip-bone. Bruised feeling in gluteal muscles on walking, stooping, adducting thigh and lying on parts; behind l. hip during motion; in anterior surface of l. thigh and knee. Sprained pain in r. hip-joint; l. hip, caused by sneezing; in hip-joint on every step. Burning soreness between nates after walking. Tingling humming in l. thigh, with drawing in anterior muscles. Stiffness of muscles about hip-joint on dressing. Weakness of thigh when walking in street; paralytic, in thigh and hip; paralytic, in r. hip-joint when walking, < moving leg forward, with stitches when setting foot down, causing limping.

Knee.—Electric shock in r., in forenoon, then two similar shocks through upper part of body, exploding close to foramen magnum, preventing sleep. Twitching in outer side of l. when sitting, with a clucking sensation. Tearing in l. when sitting. Aching when sitting, and extending outward in muscles of l. leg; cramplike incisive, over l., on both sides, when he does not move; drawing, in condyles of l. Drawing from r. popliteal space through knee to outer margin of patella at 10 P.M. in bed. Bruised feeling, < sitting; on inside of r.; l. patella; on l. side of r. patella, < walking, > sitting, with weakness of limbs; in r. *on motion* with pain as if dislocated; throbbing, on anterior and inner surface of r. knee when standing. Sprained pain in l. patella, on motion; in r. knee in morning on walking, with cramp in calf; inward in r. knee, > during rest. Knees give way on ascending stairs; on walking.

Leg.—Cramp in l. calf, < rest. Burning corrosive stitches in l. tibia, not far from knee in evening in bed, causing twitching of foot. Tearing in and below head of fibula, now l., now r.; throbbing, in middle of r. tibia. Cutting in l. fibula on standing. Pain consisting of digging, tension, rigidity and bruised feeling, in fibula, at 3 P.M. when walking, with weakness, repeated at 6 P.M.; pain in muscles of calf as if too short when descending stairs; drawing throbbing, in middle of l. tibia at rest; paralytic, in periosteum or bone of l. fibula during rest; drawing paralytic, through marrow of r. tibia at 6 P.M. when walking across the room. Paralytic drawing in middle of l. tibia, as if in periosteum, during rest; cramplike drawing in lowest part of r. calf at 10.30 A.M. Sprained pain in inner condyle of r. tibia on walking in open air.

Ankle.—Cutting-outward stitches in outer malleoli when sitting, > walking, < resting foot on a small support. Tearing in l. inner malleolus, extending upward, during rest. *Bruised pain on l. inner malleolus.* Sprained pain in l. outer malleolus when walking; in r. inner malleolus on motion after rising. Paralytic drawing pain near l. outer malleolus at rest. Feeling as if l. foot were detached, and cartilage of joints did not touch when walking.

Foot.—*Tearing, at times on soles, at times on dorsa, or on heels, toes (especially proximal joints), in tarsal or metatarsal bones, with sometimes a tearing extending beyond malleoli.* Pain in a corn; in heel when stepping, feeling as if pithy; drawing, in l. metatarsal bones and ankle, with burning in corn of l. toe; drawing, on dorsum of r., in metatarsal bones, while sitting, then throbbing P. Bruised feeling in joints, < sitting, with throbbing. Pulsation in joints of feet and lower part of legs, as from weakness, < rest, > motion, with tingling and stinging in skin of leg. Toes. Tearing on back of l. middle toes at 6 P.M. Burning pain in a corn on l. little toe in evening.

Skin.—Furuncle on l. last rib, sensitive to touch. Pimple on l. temple, with pain on touch; (P. on tibia, with burning pain.) Sticking as from fleas; here and there, as from electric sparks; in middle of extensor side of l. forearm at 11 A.M., then in skin of r. chest. Titillation in r. palm. Crawling in fold of external ear; on l. scapula as if asleep. Itching over whole body; external ear; l. ear; inner surface of l. lobule; between scapulæ; on elbows; *corrosive, in lobules in morning after rising;* corroding, in fossa of r. auricle; biting, on forehead; biting, on r. elbow; biting, on inside of l. knee; in folds of concha, afternoons, with burning sore pain after scratching; burning, here and there.

Sleep.—Inclined to, fore part of night, but could not on account of heat and stinging in skin, with vertigo when half awake, so that he thought the head would fall out of bed, then shaking of body as in epilepsy, with vertigo and sleeplessness. Sleepless after 3.30 A.M. *Restless at night.* At beginning of afternoon nap electric shocks of l. lower limb, starting from knee. Waking frequently. Dreams anxious; of care and fright; that he was followed by a large, powerful enemy, then early waking and weakness, especially in hip-joints; unremembered, of loathsome things; of the day's business; of the events of the day; vivid.

Fever.—Chilliness under skin morning in bed; in afternoon till he fell asleep, then sweat after midnight; over upper part of body at night on lifting covers; under skin of upper part of body morning in bed, with weakness of limbs, especially upper arms, hunger and nausea; on back and on feet, extending above ankle; on r. side of pelvis, near sacrum, when sitting, returning after dinner. Creeping chilliness in skin on uncovering upper part of body. Shivering; over r. side of scalp; creeping through outer side of l. lower limb when standing in a room.

Heat in forenoon, with feeling of heat over whole body, less about head, without thirst, with sweat on abdomen and chest. Hot sensation in face without redness. Burning on r. side of small of back when rising and on pressure; on tip of r. elbow; paroxysmal; in a corn; in r. heel and tendo-achillis as if asleep; itching, under skin of inner side of l. wrist, with stinging. Warmth in concha of l. ear, with itching.

Sweat, easy, < during and after eating.

Clinical.—Hectic fever every day from 11 till 12 or 1 o'clock.

Argentum Nitricum.

Nitrate of silver is prepared for use by dissolving the pure salt in distilled water.

General Action.—An irritant poison causing violent inflammation and ulceration of throat and stomach and mucous membranes generally. It attacks and destroys the red corpuscles of the blood causing general malnutrition, especially ecchymoses. It increases the flow of bile and causes degenerative conges in the liver and albuminuria. It depresses the temperature. It produces violent tetanic convulsions, followed by paralysis.

General Peculiarities.—Sharp splinter-like pains in mucous membranes (Nit. ac.), free muco-purulent discharge. Tremulous weakness, with coldness.

Allied Drugs.—Aurum, Cuprum, Mercur, Plumbi., Zinc., Nitric acid and compounds, *Picric ac.*, *Gelsem.*, Hydrastis.

Generalities.—Emaciation. Dropsy; œdema of legs and ascites. *Convulsions; and twitchings.* **Trembling and tremulous sensation** (*Gels.*, *Cupr.*, *Merc.*). Excitation of muscles and nerves, with consensual excitation of nerves of stomach. Pressure in groins at 10 P.M. while sitting, and in hollow of r. knee, in l. little finger and on back of l. foot. Pain in sides in morning after a restless night, with bruised feeling in limbs; in groins, below and in front of l. trochanter, when walking, causing knees to bend; drawing, in groins, thighs, calves, especially in tibia and l. thigh.

Clucking sensation in spots in upper arm or thigh, hand, one ear and on l. cheek; also the same, or in one leg, or else drawing in finger-joints, or in one knee, or in spot of r. upper arm, if the pain in forehead decreased for some time. *Expanding sensation, especially in face and head* (Glon., Gels.), *with a feeling as if bones of skull separated, and with heat.* Disagreeable sensation moving about, now in limbs, especially in r. upper, now in head, especially about r. temple. **Orgasms** in whole body, with heat (Sulph.). Restlessness at night, with headache and stupefaction (Sulph.). Presentiment of the approaching epileptic fit.

Weakness; morning on waking, with apathy; morning on rising, with oppression of body and mind; morning after rising, with trembling and irritated and apprehensive mood; after breakfast, with nervousness, trembling and fear to undertake anything; in afternoon; afternoon, with heat; after a short walk; *with rigidity of calves;* with despondency; **tremulous,** *with debility* and apathy. Insensibility of body. Aggravation during the day; of mental and head symptoms at night, but of general symptoms in morning; on l. side. Amelioration from emission of flatus.

Clinical.—General tremulous weakness, with nervous restlessness, emaciation and sighing respiration. Epileptiform convulsions or even true epilepsy, the patient is very restless or tremulous before or after the attacks. Especially useful in epilepsy caused by fright, or associated with menstruation. For chronic nervous results of alcoholic stimulants or the effects of excessive sexual indulgence, very restless, afraid to be alone, very melancholy, especially worse after eating, with flatulent distention, palpitation, etc. Paralysis from diseases of the spine, with great exhaustion and restlessness, sighing respiration. It has probably cured some cases of locomotor ataxia. Paralysis involving the diaphragm and lungs, sighing, gasping for breath. Post-diphtheritic paralysis. In all these cases there must be present more or less of the characteristic mental and abdominal symptoms of the drug.

Mind.—Unconsciousness. Stupefaction, with suffering look. Imbecile appearance, with childish manner, and on lying down, even in the day, to relieve his head visions and distorted faces hover before his imagination. Sluggishness. Difficulty in conceiving an idea, with heat and fulness in head. Absence of thought. Confusion of senses, with stupid demeanor. Wandering of thoughts. Memory weak, with inability to think correctly (Merc., Nit. ac.). Faltering speech from inability to find suitable words. Alternation of clear consciousness and indifference. *Mental and physical affection, he does not undertake anything lest he should not succeed.* Anxiety in morning after rising, with irritability, nervousness, weakness and trembling; making him walk rapidly. Apprehension that she will lose her senses, with chilliness. Fixed moody thoughts. Depression; after eating; without desire to do anything. Gloomy at 11 A.M., with drawing pain in forehead, yellowish complexion, sweetish-bitter mucous taste, dry, viscid lips, weakness, febrile sensation and weakness of legs. *Nightly nervousness; with heat and fulness in head* (Sulph.). *Nervous, faintish and tremulous sensation.* Taciturnity; hypochondriac, with dulness in head and beating in whole body. Laziness.

Clinical.—Melancholia, apprehension of serious disease; during the attacks of great anxiety or depression she becomes very weak or she has diarrhœa (the diarrhœa as the result of mental emotion is a marked indication for this drug). Melancholia, with impulse to throw herself from the window. Valuable in the mental depression or irritability which results from brain fag, with general debility and trembling of the whole body.

Head.—Aching; morning on waking from dreamy sleep, with confusion; beginning in morning on waking, < movement, with fulness, heaviness and stupidity; morning on waking, obliging him to gnash his teeth; deep in brain *on waking*, with chilliness all the forenoon; *from mental exertion;* < strong and agreeable odors; > **binding head tightly** (Pic. ac.); **aching, with** enlarged **feeling** (Bell.); with toothache; with eructations and chilliness; *generally with chilliness, sometimes with heat;* especially in forehead, with weakness and restlessness; especially in forehead, with dejection and restlessness; disturbing sleep; stupefying, at night, especially extending to temples and forehead, with heaviness of whole head, restless dreams and nausea; as if it would burst, from mental exertion (Pic. ac.).

Boring in different spots. Digging-up moving about in parenchyma of brain; pressing digging headache, with chilliness and bruised feeling in limbs. *Drawing in bands over surface of brain, apparently in membranes or sinuses. Congestion, with throbbing of carotids, heaviness and stupefying dulness in head, melancholy, weakness of mind and inability to express himself suitably and coherently.* Fulness; morning on waking, with confusion and with heavy aching, especially at l. frontal eminence, temples and occiput, with at times cessation of occipital pain but increase of temporal pains, with enlarged and weighty feeling in head, and with vertigo suddenly appearing and ceasing, the pain > tightly binding or pressing head aud by cold air; at night, with heat and excitement; > pressure, with pushing and heat; with dulness; *painful F. in afternoon, with heaviness, inability to recollect* and glowing heat in head and cheeks.

Stupid feeling when writing. Dulness in morning on waking from a sleep full of dreams. Confusion; over night, with stupid feeling, changing in morning on waking to fulness in forehead, with stinging digging in same, < after rising; after dinner, with beating in whole body and hypochondriac taciturnity; < after coffee; especially in occiput, l. side of head and forehead; with whizzing in ears and hard hearing. Heaviness; morning on rising; at night, with dulness and heat; and fulness, especially in frontal sinus. Sensation of sinking down from head. Tender, to cold.

Vertigo; morning; morning, with headache; before falling asleep; more before eyes; with blindness; with dulness of sense and as if he had lost sensation, with drowsiness; *with buzzing in ears,* **weakness of limbs and trembling**; with nausea and confusion of senses; with staggering (Gels.); *as if intoxicated, with weakness of lower limbs; as if turning in a circle, in morning, with headache;* faintlike.

Forehead.—*Stitches, intermittent,* in l. eminence, < afternoon, *with digging; in l. frontal and parietal regions, extending to malar-bone, and then digging pain.* Tearing in r. bone; l. side; l. eminence; here and there; in sinciput, with pressure and heaviness; extending into l. eye and side of face, with lachrymation of red and glistening eye. Aching; r. bone; r. upper; r. half in morning on waking, especially in eyebrows; after waking, > after dinner, with dulness; < evening; < after coffee, dull drawing, then sticking; over forehead and below l. eye, with drawing; extending to eyes, with sneezing; as if grasped, and in vertex; *as from a band, on l. bone, especially on eminence, at times more violent, < walking.* **Boring in l. frontal eminence** (Aurum); *above l. eye;* in l. frontal bone; l., then r. side; *l. side* when walking; above, on l. side, with tearing; in eminences, with heaviness of front part of head; in a spot in bone; in spots, with tearing, and in sides of head; moving about above forehead. Pushing in r. as from a load. Drawing; on l.; on l. eminence; in l. eminence, with sticking; *in l. eminence, with digging,* afterwards with drawing tearing, extending along l. arm; over, with pressing. *Pulsations in l.;* undulating pulsations. Cool feeling as from a current from r. eminence into r. eye. Heaviness all day in sinciput, < stooping, with pressure; in sinciput, < walking in open air, > towards evening, with pressure; over eyes, which open with difficulty, < stooping, > towards evening; in forehead, with pressure.

Temples.—Tearing at 6 A.M. in bed; in r., extending to face; drawing T., extending from r. to upper jaw and some teeth. Cutting in l. Aching in r. Boring; in r. at 10.30 P.M., increasing in shocks, the same in l. at 10 P.M. when sitting.

Vertex.—Tearing on r.; at 8 A.M., more violent diagonally. Drawing extending from top of skull to above and behind l. ear. Aching over coronal sutures, passing to eyes and root of nose.

Sides of Head.—Stinging and digging in l. half of brain, alternately anteriorly and posteriorly. Tearing on r. side of head at night on waking; now in r., now in l.; on l. side of skull; in spots on r. skull. **Aching in one side, with enlarged feeling in corresponding eye**; in r.; in r. in evening, consisting of heaviness, fulness and pressure; dragging beating A. in r., with general discomfort. Boring in r. at 8 A.M.; in r. upper at 8 A.M.; in spots in r. upper at 1 P.M. when walking, increasing in shocks. Digging in r. side of head; *in r. hemisphere in evening, with raging till he lost his senses,* if it abates in forehead, it increases in side of head and towards occiput, whence it extends to nape, pain < during motion, when there is vertigo so that he walks to the left. Drawing in side; on top of l. side, also as if crawling and pricking; in r. side, < motion, > rest, with pressure and heaviness; sudden drawing upward on r. parietal bone at 10.30 P.M., when sitting, then pressing on l. side of forehead, then pressing deep in r. wrist.

Occiput.—*Intermittent digging cutting motion, extending through l. hemisphere to frontal protuberance, increasing and decreasing rapidly.* Boring in r. Narrow traction, extending into middle of brain.

Scalp.—Tumorlike, itching elevations, and in nape. Wandering tearing in l. upper forehead. Tender. *Itching; with creeping crawling and sensation as if roots of hair were pulled upward;* at boundary of neck and scalp at night; with biting, and on nape; pricking, in a spot in hair at nape. Creeping towards morning.

Clinical.—Hemicrania, deep-seated, periodical headache, a boring pain, > tight bandaging, brought on by any depressing cause; sometimes the bones of the head feel as if they would separate and the head feels very large, the patient almost loses her senses, it ends in vomiting, or the pain may extend to the face (compare with the gastric symptoms).

Eyes.—Bloodshot; and unable to read at night. Wild rolling, with dilated and insensible pupil. Hollow. Bleared; and dry, with circumscribed congestion and ecchymoses in conjunctiva bulbi (Arn.,θ Plumb.), after itching in the preceding evening. Opaque spot on cornea. *Filled with mucus;* morning on waking, with confusion of head, especially in forehead and root of nose. *Ophthalmia, with pain.* Photophobia; with smarting and burning after long use. Deep-seated aching in morning. Smarting; on closing them; by gaslight. Pricking; in l. Pressure as if too full, with heat and pain in ball on motion and touch, with mucous flocks in daytime, infiltration of conjunctiva bulbi and palpebrarum, with stinging itching pain as from a grain of sand, *gray spots and* **bodies in shape of serpents moving before vision,** misty vision, narrowing of aperture between lids, frequent winking, general debility and heat of skin. Sore pain in upper and inner part of r. when reading. Burning, morning on waking, with dryness and trouble in opening them. Itching in l., with biting. Lachrymation. Sticking in l. ball; in inner angles of balls; in l. ball at 6 A.M. on rising, more in lower part; in r. ball at 10 P.M.; burning sticking on external surface of l. ball. Pupil contracted.

Scurf in lashes. Agglutination; of r. at night; with smarting on waking. Stitches in r., < evening, with burning. Canthi, **blood-red, with swelling of caruncula lachrymalis and with clusters of red vessels extending from inner canthus to cornea** (Zinc.), *puckering and interstitial distention of conjunctiva, increased secretion of tears and gum;* stitches in inner; *itching;* biting in r. outer. *Red swelling around cornea, towards inner canthus* (Zinc.). *Redness of conjunctiva of eyes and lids.*

Orbits.—Tearing in centre of r. lower ridge in attacks while sitting, with pressing. Pressure on l. lower border; in l. eyebrow. *Neuralgic pain in l. infraorbital region.* Boring on surface of l.; on lower margin of l.; on upper margin of r.; on lower margin of r.; deep in r. lower ridge; on both sides of glabella. Drawing on lower margin of r.; in centre of r. lower ridge.

Vision.—Blindness; *caused by mucus* (Euphras.) Obscuration, with anxiety, heat in face and lachrymation. Weakness, with moisture of eyes; sudden W. at twilight. Blurring of letters, with vanishing of vision when reading and writing (Nat. m.). Farsighted. Fiery bodies and flashes in morning in the dark.

Clinical.—With the headache and nervous symptoms there is frequently great photophobia, with general loss of muscular co-ordination, is unable to keep the eyes fixed steadily (Conium) and everything is blurred. The inflammatory symptoms are usually very violent; purulent ophthalmia, with great swelling of the conjunctiva, and especially of the caruncula, the discharge is very abundant and purulent; even when the cornea is involved and ulceration results it is sometimes found to check the progress of the disease. Especially in new-born infants, purulent ophthalmia, with much profuse discharge, threatening, or actual ulceration. Chronic ulceration of the margins of the lids, with profuse discharge, sometimes calls for Arg. nit., but more frequently for Arg. met., if the edges of the lid are thickened.

Ears.—Tearing behind r. Twinging pain; in r., with tearing. Stitches deep in l.; deep in r. and all around it; in r. when walking. Aching above l., morning after rising. Painful stoppage, with headache. Boring above r.; in front of l. Feeling of a board before l. Drawing in front of and above r., like a crawling and pricking. *Whizzing in l., with feeling of obstruction and hard hearing;* W. before, with dulness of head. Ringing; morning in bed; *with deafness* (China); before ears, passing into momentary deafness, with roaring.

Nose.—Ulcers in; covered with yellow crusts. Bleeding pimple on septum. Pain in r. wing, with swelling. Sore pain in, when compressing wings. Bruised pain in l. bones. *Itching in.* Smarting in. Rigidity in cavity, with clawing. Obstruction; at night, with itching; in room, but in open air flow of thin mucus; in upper part. *Sneezing.* Scurfs in; causing pain and bleeding when detached. *Discharge of white pus, with clots of blood;* white pus, mixed with lumps; pus like brain substance; purulent mucus, with spots of blood when sneezing. *Coryza; with chilliness, sickly look, lachrymation, sneezing and stupefying headache, obliging her to lie down in afternoon;* with sneezing, then tingling in nose and posterior nares; dry, then loose, changing to rattling cough, with yellow expectoration, sweat, bad look, hollow eyes and disturbed sleep, and as the cough improved blowing from nose purulent mucus mixed with blood. Bleeding from r. nostril at 8 A.M.; blows blood from r. nostril; blows blood and puriform mucus from nose. *Sense of smell dull.* Smell of pus before nose at night.

Clinical.—Loss of smell and hæmorrhages.

Face.—*Sunken, pale, bluish.* Pale. Leaden-colored, with nausea. *Sickly appearance.* Expression of old age, with tight drawing of skin over bones. Convulsions, the mouth being almost locked. Twitching under skin close to l. side of nose, with creeping. Stitches; in l. cheek; on zygoma; in l. cheek, with drawing; burning S. on l. zygoma at 4 P.M., then r.; deep in l. side of chin. Tearing on r. cheek; in l. zygoma, with boring. Pain wandering about in l. cheek like a crawling. Boring in r. cheek; deep in sides of chin. Drawing in cheek; under skin, above chin.

Lips.—Bluish, and soft parts of mouth. Purple-red spots on margins and about chin, with a whitish-gray crust covering interior of mouth. Hard pimples on vermilion border, paler than lips and sore to touch. Pustule on derma of upper lip, arising from a painful red, shining pimple. Dry and viscid; lips, mouth, tongue and fauces parched night and morning.

Jaws.—Shooting over r. ramus. Bruised pain in r. lower. Drawing in r. lower.

Mouth.—Teeth. Exfoliation of a r. lower molar, causing ulcerative pain and a vacillating sensation. Stitches in lower; in r. molars, lower, then upper. Sudden tearing in morning when washing mouth with cold water. *Aching;* in l.; in r. molars; < *chewing, eating sour things and putting cold things into mouth, with grumbling and digging, especially in l. lower teeth.* Raging in a carious l. lower molar. *Sensitiveness to cold water* (*Calc. c.*). Drawing in r. upper; in molars; in r. lower molars; in lower T., also at 9 P.M.; through lower incisors, with sensation as if lifted.

Gums.—*Loose, bleeding readily.* Inflamed and standing off from teeth in the shape of white indentations, especially painful when touched. *Tender and disposed to bleed* (Merc., Zinc.).

Tongue.—**Red tip, with pain** *and prominent papillæ. White;* and slimy. Dirty brown. Dark-bluish spots. Yellowish-gray. Yellow coat at base and dry feeling though it was moist. Swelling, with ulcerative pain. Prominence of papillæ of l. side; prominence and soreness of papillæ. Roughness. Stitches deep in; in tip. Burning; in fore part; in tip at 10 P.M., with bitter taste; warmth in tip, then in œsophagus; warmth in tip alternating with warmth in pharynx. Pain as if burnt, with papillæ of l. margin becoming erect and forming reddish, painful pimples. *Dryness;* morning; evening; with slimy mouth.

Mucus in mouth and fauces in morning, obliging him to hawk and spit (Nit. ac.); watery, and in posterior nares. Ulcerated crusts on mucous membrane, especially of l. cheek. Astringent sensation, and in tongue and region of lips. Tension in palate, with prickling, then a swelling with a wart-shaped excrescence on middle of soft palate, impeding deglutition. Dryness; of palate and fauces. Warmth. *Salivation;* thin, with a taste bitter or like soap-suds; drooling in sleep (Merc.). *Fetor* in morning (Merc.).

Taste.—Inky. Metallic; and astringent, < by warm tea. Sweetish. Astringent, with watery saliva; bitter, metallic; as of verdigris, with nausea. Bitter; with warmth on tip of tongue and then in pharynx; pappy, with viscid mouth; sweetish. Clayish; morning after rising, the tip of tongue being white and the root yellow. Pappy, chalklike, with mucous coat on the reddish-white tongue.

Throat.—*Redness of velum palati, posterior nares and isthmus;* pharynx; **dark R. of uvula and fauces.** Congestion, especially posteriorly, with heat; with burning soreness on r. side. White patch at back of pharynx; on posterior pillars of fauces. Palate white, swollen and sore. **Mucus** in morning fasting, and in posterior nares, sinking deeper into throat and forming lumps, which cause retching and hawking (Nit. ac.); **thick, tenacious M.,** *obliging him to hawk; causing hawking and hoarseness; in posterior nares, obliging him to hawk* (Nit. ac.), also *in forenoon.* Hawking up yellow-brown, bloody mucus. Cramps and choking.

Pricking, making r. eye water. Pain suddenly at night in bed, with short dry cough; burning pain in region of velum palati and posterior nares. Ulcerative pain in spot of velum pendulum palati; in posterior wall of pharynx, changing to an aching pain when inspiring deeply and yawning; *in r. side, with drawing and tension upward and downward,* **sensation of a splinter when swallowing** (Nit. ac.), *eructating, stretching and moving neck, and sometimes undulating jerking and pulsating.* **Rawness and soreness. Roughness;** at night, with dryness and ulcerative pain (Merc.); causing hawking. *Scraping; causing hawking and cough.* Cauterized feeling in uvula. Soreness morning on waking (Hydrastis); at night on waking; when drinking cold water and during empty swallowing; when swallowing, as from a swelling or splinter (Nit. ac.). Swollen feeling in velum pendulum palati when moving tongue and swallowing. *Burning. Dryness;* at night, with strangulation and shortness of breath. Tickling causing cough; evening and morning; several days before dinner; in throat and palate at noon, causing lachrymation and fatiguing hacking cough; as from a feather, obliging hawking. Catarrhal feeling, and in larynx. Styptic sensation.

Œsophagus.—*Cramp* at 10.30 A.M. Feeling in Œ. and stomach as if full of food. Soreness and burning.

Clinical.—Acute and chronic sore throat, with much thick mucus and a feeling of a splinter lodged in the throat (Nit. ac.), sometimes with burning and dryness, generally with dark redness of all internal parts of throat. Catarrh of smokers, with sensation of a hair causing cough, > again by smoking.

Stomach.—Appetite increased; *irresistible for sugar* in evening; insatiable in morning and evening; desire for acrid cheese; diminished; lost for breakfast; lost, with a strawlike taste to food. Aversion to food. Thirst increased. *Eructations;* in morning; with most of the gastric derangements; in morning after rising, with sick feeling and pain in abdomen; **violent;** insipid; tasting of ingesta.

Nausea; *after each meal, < during and after dinner* and in evening; > eating; *with troublesome efforts to vomit;* with warmth in stomach, both > eating; with burning and pain in stomach; with gnawing in stomach; with heaviness in S.; with pressure in S.; with gurgling in abdomen; with discomfort and emptiness in abdomen; with stiffness of legs, chilliness and shuddering; *faintish N. in afternoon, with palpitation;* resembling hunger. **Retching. Vomiting;** *with diarrhœa and colic;* with anxiety in præcordial region; V. *substances which tinge the clothes black;* violent.

Shifting of flatus and twisting, with eructations. **Painful swelling of pit,** *with anxiety. Fulness in pit* (Nit. d. s.); in epigastric region at noon after bread and milk. Cramp at 4.30 A.M.; before breakfast. **Pain;** afternoon; > towards evening; > diarrhœa; in attacks; in pit at 8.30 A.M.; on r. side near pit, < deep inspiration; at r. of epigastrium, with tenderness; *ulcerative P.* after dinner; *stinging ulcerative P. below l. short ribs, < touch and deep inspiration. Griping, with burning. Inflammation; gastro-enteritis. Gnawing on l. side;* wild G., a sort of hunger, with nausea. *Cardialgia;* before breakfast, with nausea; before breakfast, with internal chilliness and bad appearance; *waking her at night, with twisting in stomach, which extends into abdomen. Burning;* and on chest; ascending from S.; with nausea; with rumbling in intestines and emission of flatus. Coolness. Compression, aggravated periodically, > diarrhœa. *Constriction; periodical.*

Feeling as if it would burst after yawning, with sensation as if œsophagus were spasmodically closed, hence ineffectual effort to eructate, with strangulation, pressing pain in S., faintish nausea, salivation and inability to stir, all > by empty eructations. Tension and pressure causing anxiety and sensation as if filled unto bursting. *Sensation of a lump in pit, waking her at midnight, vomiting of glairy mucus, which can be drawn into threads,* in morning, then nausea in forenoon, *with tremulous weakness and* **sensation as if head were in a vise.** Oppression; from food and dragging downward. Heaviness and dragged-down sensation. *Trembling and throbbing.* Warmth in epigastrium.

Clinical.—Great craving for sweets. Well-marked gastritis characterized by enormous distention, or therewith free eructations of gas. For the gastritis of drunkards it is unrivalled. Ulceration of the stomach; the pain extends from the stomach to the chest and shoulders and down to abdomen; the greatest distress from water or food, often associated with enlargement of the liver and cutting pain in the region of the liver. Sometimes severe cardialgia as from a stone in stomach, with ineffectual efforts to eructate, becomes strangulated, face becomes purple, followed by almost unconsciousness. Disordered stomachs of children from sweets, with distention, nausea, eructations, violent cramps in bowels, tongue thickly coated white, dark redness of the face, headache, etc.

Abdomen.—*Distention* (Carbo v.); *after supper, with heaviness, anxiety* and impeded respiration; with oppression. *Flatulence. Emission of flatus;* after dinner. Shifting of flatus in morning, then diarrhœa; in morning, waking him, with rumbling and urging to stool. Rumbling; at night. **Pain; at night, waking from uneasy slumber, then sixteen evacuations of greenish fetid mucus, with noisy emissions of flatus;** P. before diarrhœa. Cramp after catarrh. Sore pain, with hunger, > eating, then trembling in that place. Feeling of a ball rising into throat (Ign.). Tension, < towards evening; painful T. and pressure as if sore and ulcerated. Uneasiness. Coldness in A., with painful irritation. Feeling of looseness, with pain in hypogastrium.

Feeling below umbilicus as if distended, or as if a weight were on it, > emission of flatus. Pain around umbilicus. *Stitches like electric sparks through l. side, < sudden transition from rest to motion.* Stitches in spleen evenings; intermittent S. in spleen. *Pain in hypochondria;* l. Drawing down l. side when standing, with heaviness.

Liver.—Stitches; beginning with a jerk; periodical, in anterior surface. Cutting. Painful fulness, with occasional drawing and stinging, < walking, often reaching into chest.

Lower A.—Flatulent distention, > emissions of flatus, with heaviness. Intermittent pressure in transversalis muscle, near crest of ilium, as from a foreign body. Aching, in groins, < touch; in groin when walking, and below and in front of l. trochanter, causing bending of knees. Drawing in one or other groin, with pressure; oppressive painful D. down to groin, with tension, as in ascites. Dragging and weight, at times amounting to burning pain, > micturition. Oppression.

Rectum.—Stitches. Urging during diarrhœa; *sudden, waking at* 6 A.M., *with copious half-liquid yellow stool,* then ineffectual urging. Burning spot on anterior wall, about an inch above sphincter, unaffected by stool, < micturition and at night. Discharge of ascarides; of tænia. *Itching in anus* (Æsc. h., Sulph., Zinc.); in perineum. Creeping in anus, with burning.

Stool.—Liquid, with mucus. *Brown, liquid, fetid. Copious, fluid, then vomiting.* Diarrhœa; after breakfast; in evening; with pain in abdomen; with retching and vomiting of mucus; **scanty, watery about midnight, with flatulent colic and noisy flatulence during stool** (Jatro.), *after eating sugar in evening.* Pasty. *Hard. Constipation;* or diarrhœa. Dark. **Of green mucus, with retching, vomiting of mucus,** *pain in stomach, drawing pain in abdomen and* **intolerance of lacing around hypochondria. Bloody**; with debility; *of bloody mucus frequently* towards morning. Small, with discharge of mucus. Frequent; with pain in abdomen; with pain in hypogastrium; of a peculiar odor, of a greenish semi-solid mass made up of lumps of undigested food and mucus, passed with flatus. Slowness and diminution of fecal and urinary discharges.

Clinical—Diarrhœa of green mucus, like chopped spinach, usually with great flatulence. Evacuations of shreds of mucus or of undigested food, with enormous distention of abdomen, emissions of much flatus, stools excessively offensive. Green, fetid, mucous stools. Dysentery, with bloody slimy stools, with symptoms of ulceration of the rectum. Chronic dysentery. Diarrhœa immediately after drinking. Diarrhœa caused by the least excitement; many cases of chronic diarrhœa, the result of shocks, have been cured by this drug, especially with the chronic flatulence so characteristic of it.

Urinary Organs.—Urging to urinate; at 4 and 6 A.M., with scanty dark urine; waking at night; *quick, with copious clear urine;* frequent at night, with scanty urine; frequent, with much yellow urine, then cutting in end of urethra. Micturition. Difficult; at 7 A.M., with burning and discharge of white pellicles, shreds of epithelium from mucous membrane. Accelerated. *Rare, urine scanty and dark.* Frequent; at night; and copious, also in forenoon. *Inability to pass urine in a projecting stream* (Caust., Gels.). Divided stream (Canth., Thuja). Larger stream. Of a few drops after he had done, with feeling as if interior of urethra were swollen.

Urethra.—*Oozing of mucus; thick white,* at night, then thinner. *Stitches in extremity* (Nit. ac.). *Cutting from posterior part to anus when emitting last drop of urine* (Thuja). *Ulcerative pain between acts of micturition* (Prun. sp.); *during micturition, then ineffectual urging; in middle, as from a splinter.* **Inflammation, with pain** (Cannab. s., Cubeb, Thuja, Merc. c.), **increased gonorrhœa, priapism, dysuria, bloody urine and fever** (Petrosel.). Dragging pain during micturition. Drawing through end. Painful pushing. **Burning** *in urethra during micturition* (Cannab.), with constricted sensation in fore part; *during micturition, with swollen feeling and difficulty in passing last part of urine; during and after micturition, at times amounting to a stabbing pain* (Nit. ac.); *after micturition; in morning on urinating, with itching and tickling;* especially at meatus and below scrotum; *with increased gonorrhœa, burning during micturition, painful tension during erections, chordee, bleeding from urethra, and shootings in same from behind forward. Sensitiveness near orifice. Soreness, even after micturition; sore and swollen feeling.* Sensation as if swollen, hard and knotty. *Pain as if swollen and ulcerated.* Peculiar sensation in orifice. Feeling as if a fluid ran along. Feeling as if a burning drop ran along, after urinating (K. bi.).

Urine.—Copious; at night; pale and frequent. *Scanty, concentrated, with disappearance of uric acid;* in evening. Dark; and acid. Cloudy at noon, from mucus, with a light red sediment covering vessel as far as the urine reaches. Strong smelling. Inorganic salts increased. Silicic acid abundant.

Clinical.—With the gastro-intestinal troubles the urine is generally very scanty; with the nervous symptoms it may be profuse; in paralytic troubles there may be incontinence. Very valuable in the early purulent stage of gonorrhœa, with most profuse discharge and terrible cutting pains, urine bloody, of great value, given internally. Profuse purulent leucorrhœa, with great soreness and bleeding of the vagina, ulcerations of the cervix, which bleed (compare with Arg. met.).

Sexual Organs.—Pain on coition, with stretched feeling in urethra and absence of pleasure. Chancrelike ulcers on prepuce with pus at their tips, then diffusion of the ulcers through a spacious depression, with a tallowlike coating. Enlargement of r. testicle, with hardness. Pain extending into and along course of spermatic cord. Pain as if from pins and needles in testes and scrotum, < r. side. Spasmodic contraction of cremaster muscle, drawing testicle high up into scrotum, with a drawing pain extending into testes. *Desire wanting, with shrivelling of genitals.* Emissions at night; with lascivious dreams; frequent and copious at night.

Female.—Uterus, hæmorrhages; congestions; excitement of capillaries. *Orgasms at night.* Menses copious, with cutting in small of back and groin and contractive sensation in latter; suppression of menses, miscarriage and metrorrhagia.

Respiratory Organs.—Larynx. Whizzing and whistling as regular as the pulse, caused by movement of blood when lying on l. ear after dinner. Balls of soaplike mucus, causing cough. *Soreness, < morning, and in pit of throat.* Scratching, causing hawking and cough. Irritation and tickling, then accumulation of mucus, causing rattling and whizzing breathing until the mucus is thrown off in lumps. Tickling at 2 P.M.; at 3 P.M., with lessened inspiration, then short, dry, shaking cough, > sitting; dry T. in daytime, causing cough. **Hoarseness** at night, with dry cough and expectoration of blood-tinged mucus mixed with saliva; with roughness in throat.

Cough; *in evening, < tobacco smoke;* at night; at night from tickling in larynx; at night, with sweat; several days before dinner from tickling in throat; from tickling in throat; from scraping in throat, with hawking. *Suffocative* at noon for several days; impeding speech, after dinner. Violent, short, dry, at night in bed, from sudden pressure in throat. Fatiguing hacking, at noon, with lachrymation, from tickling in throat and palate. Dry, fatiguing evening and morning from tickling in throat; dry, paroxysmal, at night, sometimes causing vomiting; dry and hacking.

Dyspnœa. Suffocative respiration. Sighing from oppression of chest.

Clinical.—Chronic inflammation of larynx in singers (compare with Arg. met.). Threatening paralysis of the lungs, the patient could scarcely breathe, fear of suffocation, distress in stomach, great accumulation of gases.

Chest.—Mucus. Stitches in l. side; in breasts; longitudinally in sides; superficially about centre of eighth rib. Pinching moving about in pleura costalis and pulmonaris, with oppression of chest. Pain at night; externally in l. in evening when drawing on boots, then sore pain in pectoral muscles, < stretching arms, especially near l. nipple; externally on touch; caused by walking, with need of deep inspiration, > walking; *tensive, internally in spots;* as if it would burst, in middle of upper part after ascending stairs; ulcerative, in r. mamma, towards axilla, < touch, and when stretching arm and turning trunk speedily to one side an oblong protrusion is felt; almost in heart, causing uneasiness in chest, forcing him to walk. Pressure outward from r. nipple. **Burning**; warmth between scapulæ and sternum, changing to pressure in epigastric region, also with eructations; warmth between scapulæ and sternum, changing to pinching and pressure in epigastric region. Stuffed sensation. Oppression; with wandering clawing. Fulness, with anxiety and disposition to sigh. **Heaviness,** with disposition to sigh; as from a stone in middle. Aggravation of symptoms from lying, especially evenings.

Clinical.—Threatening paralysis, with feeling of a bar around chest. Angina pectoris, intense pain, can hardly breathe.

Heart.—Pressure when walking, with necessity to breathe deeper. Pain in præcordial region. **Anxiety**; paroxysmal; in præcordia after dinner, also with sighing and feeling of disease. Fulness in præcordial region. Faintness in præcordial region. Feeling as if beating once or twice stronger when walking. *Irregular action, intermitting sometimes, with discomfort in chest, also with increase of irregularity from attention to it, > motion in open air.* **Palpitation**; *in afternoon, with faintish nausea;* towards evening on motion; at night; *from sudden muscular exertion or excitement;* from rapid motion; > lying and in evening in bed; with restless sensation in heart; like a sudden falling from above towards middle, with pain in middle of upper part of chest as if it would burst. Trembling when walking rapidly.

Neck.—Rhythmical bounding pulsations in l. carotid. Clawing like a cramp in r. anterior cervical muscles. Drawing in r. side, with pressure. Muscles of r. side sore and stiff.

Back.—Tensive clawing pain. *Pain at night;* P. in middle; in centre at r. of spine. Pressure between shoulders, penetrating deeply in morning on waking, especially at angle of r. shoulder; on spots in dorsal muscles. Pain at back of r. scapula on motion, with tenderness of muscles.

Loins.—Cutting and in abdomen; on touch. Digging, < bending. *Pain;* in kidneys; > *standing or walking;* passing off into flatus; as from a band. Sprained feeling in morning when sitting; in morning, < rising, and preventing walking, except crooked. Bruised feeling. Rigid and stretched feeling. Weakness; in lower lumbar and sacral regions and in gastrocnemii. Heaviness, < sitting; with drawing in the same, with trembling of lower limbs and debility; paralytic H. in l. extending into hip-joint.

Sacrum.—Pain; in afternoon on standing, and in thigh; in r. sacro-sciatic notch, where the nerve passes out, on rising, < blowing and sneezing. **Heaviness** *in os, extending along pelvis, with painful drawing, as before menses; H., with paralytic sensation, preventing long sitting and obliging him when walking to stretch the dorsal spine;* extending along pelvis and hips, with stiffness and paralytic pain.

Extremities.—*Chorealike motions. Trembling, with general debility.* Stitches in last phalanx of l. index, then in first r. toes; in knuckle of r. third finger and on dorsum of foot. Pain in spots of joints and soft parts of arms and legs. Boring in l. outer malleolus at 5.30 A.M. in bed, and in l. shoulder; in spots in ankles and in soft parts of limbs. Drawing internally in centre of r. upper arm after rising, then in flesh of r. thigh, below and internally. Weariness, with heaviness. Sensation as if they would go to sleep or become rigid. *Paralysis.*

Upper Extremities.—Paralytic drawing in r. Pain in r. axilla as if sprained or torn, and upon raising the shoulder the pain extended along arm to hand, where there was a prickling. Tension in glands of r. axilla.

Shoulder.—Pressure in l.; in spot on r.; on top; on top of l. while resting arm; in l. joint. Boring; l. in morning in bed; r. at 4 P.M.; l. joint, < motion. Drawing in l.; in top of l., with pressure. Skin of r. tender, irritated by brace.

Arm.—Pain in r. on motion, < at shoulder, with tenderness; P. through whole r., at times more violent on back of hand or in upper arm; in muscles of l. side at 6 P.M., while walking, towards lower part of thorax, into muscles of loins, < inspiration and walking. Stitching about r. olecranon, < resting the joint. Tearing internally on r. elbow. Pressure in elbows, extending to forearms. Boring in r. elbow. Pain in ulna at night. Drawing in r. forearm; r. or l., with pressure; in lower part of l. forearm; paralytic, in bones of forearm.

Wrist.—Pressure; in r.; in l.; in l., always at 10.30 P.M. Boring in l. at 8 A.M. Sprained pain in l., waking at night, with heat and uneasiness in hand, then in morning a pustule on a red hard base, with stinging pain in it, near joint. Tension and stiffness of l. on bending and on leaning on it, > towards morning, with a deep-seated pain. Stitches in knuckles of r. hand. Drawing in l. hand; on dorsum of r.

Fingers.—Spasmodic contraction; of adductors.

Cramp in ring, when seizing anything. Sticking in tip of l. little. Tearing in first phalanx of l. index at 6 A.M. in bed; rheumatic, in thumb where the phalanx joins the metacarpus. Pain through joints of l. index at 9 P.M., < bending, when there is a stiffness as from swelling, which lasts till morning. Boring in several joints; in spots on fingers, with tearing. Constriction in tip of l. index, with stinging and throbbing. Drawing in r.; in l. little; in l. thumb; r. thumb; in single joints; in second joint of l. index. Tenderness of tendons of back of r. index and l. middle, with hyperæsthesia of skin over them extending to outer condyle, spreading during the day over dorsum of r. hand to ulnar side, up back of forearm, outer side of upper arm, shoulder and r. side of face, finger-joints became tender and stiff, outer side of head of ulna and olecranon tender to touch, shooting through metacarpal joint of index and at elbow, increased sensitiveness of skin, with diminished power of distinguishing sensations, afterwards spread to r. side of body, metacarpal joints of l. third and fourth fingers tender.

Lower Extremities.—*Starting up, especially of knees, waking him at night.* Staggering in open air. Vacillating gait, with discomfort in whole body and crawling in limbs, as in incipient fever. Weakness; especially of legs, with at times feeling as if they would suddenly fail him; *in forenoon, with sick feeling, dread of labor, drowsiness, chilliness and sickly appearance; with vertigo as from intoxication;* paralytic, with emaciation. *Paralytic heaviness and debility, so that he did not know where to put them.*

Thigh.—Pressure above r. patella when sitting. Drawing through r. T.; sticking, from hip to tarsal-joint; paroxysmal nervous ("cramplike"), in hips, along ischias antica, to knees; paralytic painful, as if bruised, in rectus cruris muscle above l. patella.

Knee.—Tearing, raging, digging-up pain under patella, l. then r. Drawing tearing, extending into legs; drawing T. on l. side of patella and near it; internal T. in l., then r. Pressure when sitting; when walking, < on stepping; in r.; r. when walking; r. when sitting and walking, and on dorsum of l. foot; in r. anteriorly, l. anteriorly. Boring on r., and in spot on outer side of r. calf. Drawing; r.; internally in l. when sitting and walking. Throbbing, with weariness.

Leg.—Drawn up to abdomen by muscular contraction. Tearing on r. anteriorly; on r. tibia. Pressure on anteriorly; anteriorly in r. leg, afterwards in l. knee; internally in a spot, then on l. inner malleolus. Boring in spots, with tearing. Compressive sensation in whole l. when walking. Drawing through l. when sitting; through whole r. on sitting; with pressure; anteriorly on l.; anteriorly when walking; anteriorly in lower half of tibia, with scraping. Weariness; in morning.

Calf.—Cramp at night. Cramplike pain in l. when walking. Sensation like a stitching or hot fluid running over skin of l. when walking. Pain in a spot on outside of l. when walking, causing bending of knees, also on standing. Drawing when ascending stairs. *Weariness; with rigidity.*

Ankle.—Stinging in r. outer. Tearing in l.; below l. inner malleolus when sitting at 1 P.M., > walking rapidly, with stitching. Pressure in r. when sitting; in l.; l., with drawing. Painful drawing below l. inner malleolus, beginning and passing off when walking. Boring in r. malleolus; l. outer malleolus in morning in bed; internally behind and below l. malleolus when walking. Bends easily.

Foot.—Tearing in bend of r.; on dorsum of r. Pressure on spot on dorsum of l., > walking. Boring on sides of l. tendo-achillis; on dorsum of r. foot, drawing from without inward, when sitting. Drawing on outer margin of r.; on dorsum of l.; in bend of l. when sitting at 7 A.M.; arthritic, in r. Prickling in r. sole when sitting. Tenderness of under part of r. heel on treading.

Toes.—Stitches in r., with drawing. Drawing in r. at 11 P.M.; in l. at 11 P.M., shifting to other parts.

Skin.—*Discoloration (argyria) from blue-gray, violet or bronze to black.* Brownish on lower limbs; brown spots on upper chest and on hands; *brown, tense and hard.* Blotches on border of nape of neck, etc.; irregularly-shaped B. on border of nape and scalp, with itching, soreness when scratched, and after scratching inflammation and moisture; red, on dorsum of r. hand and index, changing to yellow blisters on a red base.

Pimple, painful, inflamed, in l. corner of mouth, forming a pock-shaped pustule, which after efflorescence passed into a hard pimple; itching, blotched shaped, on lower limbs; hard, on lower limbs and in bend of knee, with itching at night and burning after scratching; itch, covered after scratching with bleeding scurfs.

Pustules in l. canthus; on chin and cheek. Pustulous ecthyma preceded by itching and pain. Itch-like eruption, especially on back. Itching vesicles on back, the itching < evening; itching V., resembling itch stigmata, especially on chest and back, towards shoulders. Elevation with red base, looking like a blister, but only semi-fluid, under l. eye, with burning, later a similar spot on margin of r. lower lid, afterwards below lashes on both lower lids. Irritable urticarious spot on back of r. shoulder.

Stitches alternately above and at sides of r. knee when walking at 7 P.M. Boring in skin of tip of nose, with crawling in skin of l. side of nose. Drawing in cheeks; on l. forehead and l. cheek as from a spider's web. Crawling on l. cheek. Itching of chest and axillæ; in various parts at night, also prickling; stinging, especially around l. nipple. Itching smarting when getting warm in night, especially in thighs, hypochondria, chest and axillæ.

Sleep.—Yawning at 10 A.M. and in afternoon *long and deep;* Y. in forenoon, with sleepiness; Y. at 5 P.M., with drowsiness; *Y., with chilliness.* Sleepiness; in evening; while sitting in evening; in evening, but sleeplessness till midnight from thinking, then monstrous dreams, which seemed an extension of his mental condition when awake, for through the day he was disinclined to talk, but took a morbid delight in building air-castles; desire for sleep, in night, with tossing about, but no sleep; S. when sitting.

Sleeplessness *from fancies before his imagination,* then in the first part of the night fantastic half slumber, full of dreams; S., with tossing about. *Restless sleep;* with talking; with dreams and frequent waking; with headache and stupefaction; *and stupefied, with horrible dreams.*

Dreams; of snakes; of putrid water, fishes and *serpents, filling him with horror* and waking him; that an insect burrowed deeply into his heel; in morning *that he is hungry, which wakes him, when he has spasm of stomach, with hunger, nausea, pain in back and flatulence;* lascivious; L. in morning, during which he would have had an emission of semen if he had not awakened; restless, in early part of night, of long dim passages, with a *succession of strangely dressed figures,* who retreated when approached but followed when he went on; fantastic; heavy; confused, of places where he had been and of persons he had seen.

Fever.—Chilliness in forenoon, with headache, also loss of appetite at noon, nausea, and at 4 P.M. tumult and beating in head, heat in head, creeping chills, dry hot skin, nausea, desire for something salt, weakness, increase of the desire for something acrid and sour, so that at 7 P.M. she ate pot-cheese, which improved the symptoms, but the febrile condition lasted all night. Chilliness in evening; every day at 6 P.M., then heat, the chill lasting longer and returning on uncovering, even during the heat, perceptible pulsation of l. temporal artery during the heat, both stages *without thirst;* after rising, with nausea; after eating, with weakness, nervousness and obtuse feeling in head. C., with pale, almost yellowish countenance, nausea and empty eructations.

Shuddering forenoons, at the same hour, passing into a chill, with gooseflesh and coldness, hot head, cold hands and nausea, > warm soup. Chill up back and across shoulders, < after eating and on coming in from open air; running along spine at noon, with heat and flushing of face and limbs; in spine close to occiput, extending to end of coccyx, from noon till 5 P.M., with heat and lethargy, heat of head, hands and feet, chills > by warmth, then sleepiness, but lack of sleep, caused by vivid imagination, till 10 P.M., then restlessness, heat, aching of legs and back, feeling as if brain were too large for skull, sweat in palms, on lower part of abdomen and inner sides of thighs, then sleep about midnight, afterwards recurrence of chills for eight days, beginning at noon and lasting four or five hours. Feet cold in afternoon and evening.

Heat.—Fever every day at 6 P.M.; feverish, sick feeling in afternoon, with weakness. Heat, with heaviness. Burning spot on one or other hand; on inner condyle of knee; on back of arms after dinner.

Sweat in morning; from 4 to 6 A.M., after a restless sleep disturbed by cough; *at night;* as soon as he got warm in bed, with chilliness; on chest at night. Profuse, at night.

Arnica.

Arnica, montana, L., belongs to the Compositæ. A tincture is prepared from the root, leaves and flowers, mixed.

General Action.—The most pronounced effects of Arnica are *on the blood,* general anæmia, with sharp neuralgias, tendency to hæmorrhages; depression of temperature; malnutrition, with disordered digestion, involuntary diarrhœa. Rheumatic and cutaneous symptoms are marked. The soreness of flesh is quite characteristic.

Allied Drugs.—Bry., Rhus t., Ruta, *Bapt., Bov.,* Sec. c., *Elaps, Phos.,* Nit. ac., *Hyper.,* Symphyt., Carbo v.

Generalities.—Agitation increasing to tetanus of r. side. Convulsions. Twitchings; of single muscles, especially in limbs. Fibrillar contractions of isolated muscular fasciculæ, especially in region of jaws. Trembling of whole body alternating with convulsive movements of limbs. **Stitches**; in almost every part, especially nose, eyebrows, eyelids, even in hands and fingers; in whole body, with itching; burning, in different parts. Intermittent tearing in almost every part, especially in limbs, for the most part rising from below upward, in lower limbs, < sitting.

Pain in periosteum of all bones, resembling almost a drawing in all limbs, as in fever and ague; *formicating or dull pain in a contused part;* twitching, in affected parts; in whole body on lying, as if it were on pebbles. **Sensitiveness of whole body** (Plat.); *of all joints on motion and of skin.* **Bruised pain over whole body.** Sudden illness when pressing on dorsal vertebræ, with jerks in muscles of nape and of back, with throwing back of the head while the trunk is upright, the illness < on pressing on last dorsal vertebra, when there is a pain in waist, radiating to epigastrium, with suffocation and weight on chest. Orgasms of blood in evening, with pulsations in whole body and vertigo. Sensation as if everything on his body were tied too tight. Uneasiness of whole body, becoming a trembling. Faintness; when walking, > standing; from heat of sun, with nausea.

Weakness; on rising; on retiring at 10, but restlessness and wakefulness until midnight; early in bed, with relaxed testicles, as if he had had an emission, which was not the case; when walking, as if suddenly blighted with old age; **with a bruised sensation** (Bap.); *with sluggishness; with sleepiness;* with tremulous uneasiness; with a desire to sit down.

Feeling when walking in open air as if whole r. side, especially shoulder, were heavy and hanging down paralyzed. Aggravation from speaking, blowing nose, *motion* and almost every noise. Amelioration from a long walk in cold weather.

Clinical.—Extremely valuable when the body feels bruised and sore; results of injuries (rather of cuts than of bruises). Excessive prostration, with anæmia, sticking pains, or after low fevers. Hæmorrhages of venous blood, passive; general tendency to blood disorganization. Thromboses. Hæmatocele. Paralysis (r. side). Pernicious anæmia. Tendency to degeneration of tissue, with foul odors, boils and abscesses which do not mature well or do not granulate. In septicæmia, burrowing abscesses, enlarged veins, which are sore; muscular pains from overexertion; bedsores; affects of contusions and sprains; stings of insects, etc.

Mind.—*Memory wanting* (Lach., Phos.). Absent-minded; with wandering of thoughts. Reveries. *Inability to perform continuous active work.* Aversion to work; any work requiring perseverance. Indisposed to think or talk after walking in open air. (Inclination to perform greater literary work than can be accomplished without injury to health.) Uneasiness of body and mind, feeling as if prevented from doing something necessary, with indisposition for any kind of work. *Indifference to work, to everything* (Phos.). *Fright;* from unexpected trifles, with starting. Horror of instant death. *Hopelessness.* Anxiety; *hypochondriac.* Apprehension of future evils. Weeping; after supper, with peevishness, will listen to nobody. Depression of spirits.

Sensitiveness, sometimes without physical sensitiveness, sometimes in alternation, sometimes simultaneously with it. Excitability, she could easily laugh when there was no occasion for it, and when something disagreeable was told her she got angry and howled. **Sullen.** Sullen insolence and imperiousness. Quarrelsome. Obstinate and headstrong resistance to other people's opinions. Contradictory, opinionative, nothing suits him. **Morose and does not speak a word**; morose, desires all sorts of things and then repels them.

Clinical.—Valuable in mania, delirium tremens, especially with involuntary discharges of a putrid odor, nosebleed of dark blood. Affections of head or mind, which appear slowly long after an injury. Delirium of low malarial fevers. Delirium of low malarial fever, muttering or complete stupor. In apoplexy, with stertorous respiration (paralysis < on l. side), or with involuntary stools, with no cerebral excitement, but a heavy stupor, with foul breath; or if the patient should be somewhat conscious he complains of aching soreness over the whole body, fear especially of persons coming towards him, as if they would strike him; this condition of fear is an extremely well-marked mental symptom of Arnica in gout.

Head.—**Stinging** from 3 to 8 P.M., now more in forehead, now more in occiput. Stitches when coughing; extending upward, renewed on coughing and moving head, > resting head on painful side. Jerking lancinating when stooping, as if everything would come out of forehead, with nausea. Twitching tearing, < stooping and coughing. *Aching; morning on waking*, < 8 A.M., *on walking in open air, when there was vertigo*, > 10 A.M.; in forenoon; (A., > lying); with weight in eyes and sensation of oppression and drooping in lids; then throbbing aching in temples; *as if a knife were drawn transversely through head from l. side, then internal coldness of head*, causing hair to stand on end; *distending*, seeming to arise from something soft in vertex, with drawing in occiput and tearing towards temples; distending, when walking in open air; distending, with burning; rheumatic, with vertigo (commonly one-sided); stupefying, in morning.

Emptiness. Obscuration, with confusion in sides of head and contraction of pupils. **Confusion**; *with pressure in r. half, especially over r. brow*; < artificial vomiting, with vertigo and anguish; with fulness; with sleepiness; changing to r.-sided headache; so that she feared falling over while sitting, with frontal headache. **Heaviness**; so that it hangs on one side; heavy and so movable on account of weakness of muscles of neck that it inclines to all sides. Blood rushes to brain, with aching in forehead. Vertigo; during rest; when walking; when reading too long, *with nausea*; > *sitting and bending head, but on righting head or moving it feeling as if everything turned with her*; sudden V. at dinner, as if he would fall forward.

Forehead.—**Stitches**; in sinciput on coughing; in sinciput and occiput, morning on waking, lasting all day; in l. eminence, *with sensation of extravasation of blood*; < raising eyes, with heat in face and thirst; jerking. **Aching**; in morning, changing to confusion of whole head, > afternoon; < *walking*, ascending stairs, reflecting or reading; in l. half in evening; in r. forehead, temple and r. eye; then stitching and twitching stitching, with chilliness; *over eyes, extending towards temples, with sensation as if integuments of forehead were spasmodically contracted; as if brain were rolled up into a lump*, < *near stove*; pressing out in spots in afternoon; as if conjested; stupefying, more externally; twitching, in fore part of head; in r. half of bone, then sneezing, then it extended into l., afterwards into r. ear. **Bruised** pain in l. side after sneezing. Crawling in. Heaviness. Vertigo as if everything turned around with her, < walking.

Temples.—*Stitches*; extending inward; extending towards forehead; jerking, in l. *Intermittent tearing in l.; with stitches.* Aching; in l.; on coughing; *as if a nail were thrust in*, with general sweat about midnight, then exhaustion. Constriction.

Vertex.—Aching externally; in r. side, impeding work. Tender and sore feeling in brain.

Sides.—Intermittent sticking and tearing in l. **Aching** on r.; on l.; in parietal region and in orbits; under parietal bone and in region of lachrymal fossa.

Occiput.—Twitching tearing in l. half in forenoon. Aching in r. half at 11 A.M., < 1 P.M., extending to r. half of forehead at 2 P.M., > evening; in spots as if hair were pulled out, or as from electric shocks.

Scalp.—Immovable almost as far as eyebrows. Stinging itching. Formication over orbits; on vertex.

Clinical.—Neuralgias, sharp (as from a nail or knife), all pains worse on motion. Neuralgias following injuries to nerves; intermittent, with a malarial basis, with coldness, no fever. Apoplexy. Hot head with cold body. It has been found useful in meningitis or meningeal irritation as a result of concussion. It is particularly indicated in a severe headache as if the head were being distended, with extreme sensitiveness of the brain internally, or sometimes sharp knifelike pains.

Eyes.—*Sunken*, glassy, with dilated insensible pupils. Protrusion of r. Staring, denoting anguish. Aching in l. Burning. Itching. Tension and sensitiveness to pressure. Burning lachrymation. Ball, aching in inner half of r. and in corresponding part of forehead; drawing A. in r.; *pinching in inner half of r.*, also > motion in open air. *Pupils contracted; dilated. Pain as if too dry and sore in margin of upper lid along contact with ball when the ball is moved.* Stitches in inner canthus. Itching in canthi. Intermittent pressure on margin of l. orbit. Cramplike tearing in l. eyebrow. Vision of sparks. Blurred V. Diplopia, hallucinations of V., could not judge of distances and saw only half of an object, saw a bright light with l. eye, which disappeared on closing that eye but reappeared on closing both.

Clinical.—Useful to hasten absorption of hæmorrhages in conjunctiva or retina, paralysis of the muscles from a blow.

Ears.—Stitches; behind; through r., then l., then through eyes, with feeling as if the eyes were forcibly turned upward; extending inward through middle ear; then tearing. *Bruised pain internally in cartilage of l.* Painful drawing extending into l. half of skull. Pressure in; intermittent P. in region of tympanum. Hearing more acute; *less acute. Humming.* Roaring. Ringing in l. Singing in r.

Clinical.—Meniere's disease, with vertigo (inclined to fall to the left) and salivation, deafness, vomiting and coldness in the occiput.

Nose.—Twitching on bone under l. eye, extending over eyeball. Sticking tearing. *Bruised pain from above downward.* Cramplike pain at root. Pressure on bone, with benumbing. Ulcerated feeling in nostrils. Sneezing; frequent. *Blown frequently, with traces of blood.* Coryza; evening on going to sleep, then catarrh on chest in morning on waking. Bleeding (Ham., Sec. c., Carbo v.); morning on blowing; at night (Nit. ac.).

Clinical.—The nosebleed of Arnica is characterized by dark fluid blood; especially during low forms of fever or in whooping cough (compare Carbo veg.).

Face.—Pale. Flushed and swollen. *Sunken.* Twitchings (intermittent tearings) in muscles of ramus of lower jaw. Twitching throbbing in l. cheek. Cramplike pain in cheek when yawning. Creeping over l. cheek, like a shivering without coldness, extending to side of occiput. (Bruised pain in r. articulation of jaw on moving jaw to and fro.) Incipient paralysis of lower jaw.

Lips.—Trembling of lower. Swelling. *Chapped;* external margin, especially of upper lip. Hydroa. Pimple on both sides of upper; in groove of upper, with redness all around and tensive pain. Vesicles in middle of lower. Ulceration in corners, with burning pain, < motion of parts. Dryness. Formication as if asleep. Itching of upper, with burning if rubbed.

Clinical.—The face of the Arnica patient is usually cold and pale; in apoplexy paralyzed; in low fevers a dusky red.

Mouth.—Teeth. Covered with mucus (Bov.). Wabbling and elongation. Tearing in l. upper molars when eating. **Aching** in l. lower molar; in teeth as if roots were scraped; (as if teeth had been bitten out, were dislocated, wabbling, throbbing, with feeling as if pressed outward by blood, the pain then < by touch). Gums, pain as if ulcerated when chewing, especially under the tongue; as from a leaden bullet on lower and internal G.; formication in G. as if asleep.

Tongue.—*Coated white* (Bry.). White and yellow, with want of appetite. *Biting;* stinging, at root. Burning, and in palate; in anterior third, and in soft palate. Burning scraping from root through œsophagus into stomach. Sore feeling. Dry feeling in tip and in palate and lips, with shivering over arms and thighs.

Aching in hard palate. *Dry mouth* (Bry.); in morning without thirst, but with foul taste; without thirst; *with thirst.* Burning in palate. Puckered feeling in palate. Scraping, especially at the root of the tongue and in œsophagus; *burning scraping, and in œsophagus.* Cool, with thirst, desire for strong drink. *Salivation;* thin, with nausea. **Breath fetid** (Nit. ac., Sec. c.). *Taste of rotten eggs between meals; putrid, slimy T.; bitter;* bitter morning on waking; sour; (sour to everything).

Clinical.—Serviceable for toothache after filling. Persistent hæmorrhage after drawing teeth. The tongue, in fever, is dry and *sore,* sometimes blackish.

Throat.—Swelling of submaxillary glands; with pain, < raising or turning head and on touch. Mucus, tasting bitter when hawked up. Subdued whistling. Noise when swallowing. Stinging in back part when not swallowing. Pain as if something hard or rough had lodged in fauces in afternoon when lying, > rising. Scraping. Soreness. Constriction. Swollen feeling. Dryness. Swallowing difficult; *prevented by nausea, as if food would not go down.* Burning when swallowing; in back part, with feeling of internal heat, or rather that sort of anguish that originates in heat, without external heat; with scraping causing shuddering and nausea, afterwards the burning and scraping extended down œsophagus to stomach, causing nausea, fulness and pressure, with warmth over whole body and sweat; in palate and pharynx, changing into scratching; extending gradually to stomach, and ending in mouth and œsophagus; *scraping burning, extending to stomach, becoming a pressure in stomach;* scraping burning in uvula and œsophagus.

Œsophagus.—Pressure on l. side, extending upward, sometimes with stitches. Scraping; burning scraping. Burning. Dryness.

Stomach.—Hunger increased; in evening, then after eating repletion, with coliclike pressure in places in abdomen, especially in sides; H., with decreased appetite; ravenous, which could not be satisfied on account of want of appetite and a certain aversion to food; desire for vinegar. *Appetite lost;* in evening; at dinner; with nausea. *Repugnance to food; to meat and broth;* to tobacco; (to milk).

Thirst; at night; during the yawning before the fever, with much drinking, afterwards during the hot stage, but little drinking; *without external heat, the pupils being little capable of dilatation;* desire to drink constantly, but she knows not what, because everything is offensive to her.

Eructations; **bitter and like bad eggs** (Elaps., Phos.); **like rotten eggs,** in morning; of bitter mucus; *empty;* of salt water. Imperfect hiccough after dinner. Nausea; in morning; forenoon, *with general relaxation;* on opening eyes during siesta, > closing eyes; from the usual tobacco; with eructations; *with burning scratching in throat;* with distended feeling in stomach; with pressure in stomach. Retching; violent; *empty; empty at night,* with weight as from a lump in pit of stomach. *Vomiting;* caused by cough; of bitter yellow bile; inclination to, without nausea.

Digging movements in epigastric region, > after dinner, with pain in forehead. Grumbling, unpleasant motions; grumbling, with colic. Cramps. Griping, with sticking and frequent gagging; *pinching, spasmodic griping. Pinching; pinching and pressure, extending through small intestines as a constriction, with many movements.* **Pain**; in upper and anterior part; in epigastrium; in epigastrium, < pressure; especially at posterior wall and extending to spine; with heaviness on anterior wall of chest; transversely across above pit, with dyspnœa; in pit as from pressure of a hand, gradually ascending to throat, where there was nausea, with salivation, > lying, leaving pressure in abdomen; as from a stone; contractive; *spasmodically contractive, also > eating; spasmodic contraction moving up and down in stomach, causing general pain, especially in posterior wall of stomach, with sensation as if wall of S. would be pressed against spine and spine would be made painful; as if posterior wall were pressed against spine;* flying pain in epigastrium and in r. hypochondrium; intermittent; in region of cardia; as if xiphoid process were pressed inward. *Digging pain* in pit, with sensation as if something were rolling up like a ball. Burrowing in pit, with sensation as if something were knotting itself up. Drawing in epigastric region. Cardialgia. *Emptiness;* after a meal, as if she had not eaten enough, but feeling as if she had drunk much, with a swashing feeling in abdomen.

Fulness; in pit after eating, with pressure in a spot deep in hypogastrium behind pubis, < standing, and almost urging to micturition; with pressure and with burning pain in upper part. *Repletion, with loathing.* Satiety even though stomach was empty, with frequent acidity in mouth. *Heaviness.* Oppression. Tension; in lower part of epigastric region morning in bed.

Abdomen.—*Distention;* before diarrhœa; after supper, especially in lower part, with tension and with pressure, especially in side of abdomen, lasting all night, with heat of limbs, fatiguing dreams, hourly waking and with emissions of flatus; *with frequent urging to stool,* also with emission of flatus; *with fre-*

quent urging to stool, though more than ever constipated; tympanitic. Flatulence. Flatus, with pressure in stomach; fermenting; frequent emissions, also night and morning; **offensive** (Sulph.); *smelling like rotten eggs* (Sulph.). Movings. Rumbling; grunting, from flatus. Gurgling. Grunting, then tenesmus, with emission of flatus; as from emptiness. Twitchings under stomach. Tearing in muscles. *Cutting,* then tenesmus, then lumpy stool, with flatus; C. as after a cold. Pain; after a light meal, with tenesmus; flatulent; flying.

Upper Abdomen.—*Stitches below last ribs; below r. ribs* (Merc. s., Chel.); **under l. false ribs when standing, intercepting breathing** (Bry., Seneg., Zinc.). *Pressure below last ribs. Constriction at level of attachments of diaphragm.* Clawing throbbing in l. side between pit of stomach and umbilicus; pinching throbbing in same place. Pinching in splenic region.

Umbilical Region.—Stitches, apparently in small intestines. Tearing over. Cutting in small intestines; over umbilicus, < breathing deeply and at every step, > before and during stool. Pinching over umbilicus. Aching in spot on r. side of U., with sensitiveness to touch, as from accumulation of flatus.

Sides.—Distention of r. every day from morning till 2 P.M., at rest, > emission of flatus, with pain as from an internal wound, and with pain as if shaken, torn or cut when coughing, blowing nose or setting down foot, and with pain as if cutting into a wound when touched. *Stitches during cough;* in spleen, shooting upward when walking. *Thrusts from one side to the other.* Cutting in l., darting like a stitch to vertex. Sudden bruised pain in r. when walking. Pressure in liver region; as from a stone when lying on l. side during inspiration and expiration. Intermittent aching, seemingly in liver or duodenum.

Hypogastrium.—Fermenting flatus below umbilical region. Stitches in muscles, leaving an itching, > scratching. *Intermittent tearing in l. half of pubic eminence. Deep-seated digging within hips on both sides, as in dysentery, with nausea and drowsiness.*

Rectum.—Rumbling. Squeezing and pressing when standing. Aching. Straining. *Tenesmus; then copious, thin or paplike sour-smelling stool, with relief;* every half hour with passage of only mucus. Sudden urging as before diarrhœa, but only a few fæces. Ineffectual urging; frequent. Swelling of hæmorrhoidal vessel (Ham.). Burning in anus, with shooting (Sulph.).

Clinical.—Diffuse, subacute gastroenteritis of a low type, the above symptoms especially, offensive gases passed upward and downward, and general soreness as if bruised.

Stool.—Thinner and darker. *Diarrhœa; at night,* with flatulent colic; *with cutting in intestines;* with tenesmus; **like brown yeast** (Kali. bi.); choleraic; white; sometimes scanty and tough stool, with flatus. Increased, soft, with blood from hæmorrhoids. Brown, paplike, with grumbling in abdomen. *Constipation.* Hard, difficult, with pressure in abdomen; hard and less frequent. *Undigested.* **Involuntary at night in sleep** (Hyosc., Bry., Con.). Frequent, *with necessity to lie down after every stool; small, consisting of mucus.*

Clinical.—The diarrhœa, as above, is associated with great prostration. Involuntary, putrid stools in typhoid. Hæmorrhage from bowels in typhoid, dark, venous. Dysentery (with tenesmus) of a low type. Prolapsus ani.

Urinary Organs.—*Tenesmus of bladder, with involuntary dropping of urine; tenesmus of neck, with ineffectual urging.* Desire to urinate, with biting burning, < after urinating; frequent, also with copious urine; frequent, with scanty yellow-red urine. Urging, with copious watery urine. Frequent micturition; with watery urine; with scanty white watery urine, with difficult emission of last drops. *Urine retained, with aching and pressing in bladder.* Has to stand a long time before urine is emitted.

Urethra.—Stitches; after micturition. Cutting in orifice, at end of micturition. Itching in anterior part, in region of glans, when not urinating.

Urine.—Copious and dark; copious, with inability to retain it long, especially at night; in morning, flowing slowly, as if urethra were constricted. Scanty; and red. *Brown,* clear, becoming whitish and turbid; *dark brown. Brown, with brick-red sediment.* Sulphur-colored, turbid, frothy, with neutral reaction, depositing a sediment. Watery. Earthy phosphates increased. Acid; and dark, of high specific gravity, opalescent on boiling, but clear on adding Nitric acid. Sediment contains crystals of phosphoric acid, ammonia, magnesia and urates, the latter adhering to sides of glass.

Clinical.—Pain as from knives in the region of kidneys. Hæmaturia. The bladder symptoms, above, have been found associated with the dysenteric symptoms, with paralytic conditions or as the result of injuries.

Sexual Organs.—Stitches through glans; in afternoon. Itching of glans or itching stitches. Erections after waking, without amorous thoughts or desires. Stitches in scrotum. Testes hard, swollen and tender. Desire, with continued erections. Little desire. Emission by day during a caress; several in one night, with voluptuous dreams.

Clinical.—Uterine hæmorrhage resulting from a mechanical injury. Uterine disorders from injuries, with easy bleeding; prolapsus; hæmorrhage after coition. After parturition excessive soreness and lameness, especially useful after instrumental delivery. Sore nipples. Mastitis from injury.

Respiratory Organs.—Larynx sore. Swollen sensation in larynx, causing cough and hawking, which brings up nothing or only a little thick mucus, without relief. Hoarseness in morning. Voice low, muttering. Agreeable cooling in trachea on expiration, as if walls were too thin. (Crackling sense in trachea when walking and in evening when lying down.)

Cough; at night in sleep; **in children caused by weeping and lamenting;** *in children caused by cries, with anger and tossing about; during siesta, from itching in upper part of larynx;* on yawning; irritation (with expectoration, which seems to come from posterior nares). *Dry, from tickling in lowest part of trachea; short, hacking, dry, also every morning after rising, from tickling deep in trachea; constant, shaking the whole frame. Hæmoptysis. Expectoration bloody* (Bry., Phos., Sec. c., Nit. ac.); of glairy mucus, with blackish points.

Suffocation. *Short, panting respiration. Dyspnœa; quick inspirations and expirations.* (Difficult quick inspirations, with slow expirations.) Frequent, slow, deep breathing, with pressure below chest. Loud, blowing B. in sleep. Breathes with open mouth at night and mouth is dry on waking. Desires open air; open country air.

Clinical.—Spasmodic cough (whooping cough), with nosebleed, hæmorrhage into conjunctiva, etc. Bloody expectoration in chronic cases; too weak to spit it out, must be swallowed.

Chest.—*Stitches;* in sides (Bry., Sulph., Ran. b.); r., near ribs; l. side; *in middle of l.;* under sternum; in sternum, < walking; in l. near sternum during deep inspiration; *in one side, with short cough, which aggravates the pain, and with tightness of chest;* in sternum, extending into chest; as from flatulence, in sides under ribs. *Pain; in spot in r. side;* on sternum over pit; lower part of sternum, < deep inspiration; cutting outward, on both sides, < inspiration; twitching, in l.; (drawing, with anxiety). *Bruised feeling in ribs from coughing; bruised pain in joints of bones and cartilages during motion and breathing. Sprained pain in connections of parts of chest with back. Raw feeling,* < walking, with bloody sputa; (pain as if raw, with clawing in larynx during cough). Soreness of walls.

Anguish across, with nausea. Suffocative oppression (Nat. arsen.). *Tightness, with difficult breathing* (Phos.). (Tension across, as far as neck, > lying on back, < walking and standing.) Weight on; on upper part; in chest in morning on waking, > exercise. Painless constriction in middle of l., which tightens breathing, with pain on touch in pit of stomach, which arrests breathing. Blood seems to have accumulated in morning, > exercise. Coldness internally.

Clinical.—Soreness of the walls of the chest, as if bruised, with sharp pains like neuralgia, serves to indicate this drug in rheumatoid affections of the pectoral muscles.

Heart.—*Stitches* in region; *from l. to r. side* of heart. *Squeezing pain or pain as from shock.* Anguish (præcordial), with feeble and intermittent cardiac contractions and feeling as if heart stopped. Palpitation. Action stronger; jerking; rapid, then suddenly slow. Rhythm irregular. **Pulse.**—*Feeble, rapid and irregular* (Apoc., Dig.). Rapid; and strong. Thready. Irregular; in evening. Small and slow.

Clinical.—Bruised pain about the region of the heart and stitches, with other symptoms, have led to its use in affections of the cardiac muscle, hypertrophy and fatty degeneration (compare Baryta c.). Angina pectoris. Palpitation and pain about the heart, as the result of excessive straining.

Neck.—Swelling of glands, with pain, < moving neck or speaking. *Pain in last cervical vertebra on bending head, with tension; on spinal processes of last cervical and first dorsal vertebræ, with tension;* in nucha on standing; in muscles as if cravat were too tight; where r. external carotid emerges from sterno-cleido mastoid muscle, as if a lymphatic gland were swollen, < suddenly turning head to left, by forcible pressure and by severe throbbing in arteries of neck; cramplike, in muscles of nape, with stitches extending inward; cramplike tensive pain in muscles of nape when sneezing or yawning. Lameness of muscles. Rough drawing in l. muscles, with bruised pain.

Back.—*Pains, as from long stooping at hard work, in morning on rising from bed* (Caust.). Arthritic pain, and in limbs. Burning pain when walking in open air. *Bruised pain. Pain; in middle of spine when sitting; in spine as if it could not carry the body.* Crawling in spine.

Scapulæ.—Twitching tearing in fascia supinator of l. in forenoon, often > motion; drawing tearing, extending downward from l. in evening. Cutting thrusts between when walking, extending into chest. Pinching on lower angle of l.; in muscles between lower angle of r. and spine, < stretching the parts (had been noticed in former years). *Pain between;* in l. and in acromion; *seeming to extend from posterior wall of stomach, with pressure near spine;* superficial pain between, afterwards more below r.; in spine between scapulæ, with cramp in stomach. *Bruised pain in r. towards back.* Feeling almost under shoulders as if a lump lodged there, which caused stitches on motion.

Stitches in r. side from last ribs to axilla at every inspiration. Pain in dorsal vertebræ as after sudden rising from long stooping, this cramplike pain was internal.

Loins.—Stitches; when coughing, breathing deeply or walking (Bry.). Pain as if something inside had been torn. Cutting inward, < stooping (Berb.). Pain (Æsc. h.). *Bruised pain* (Berb., Rhus t., Sul.). Fulness, with pressure. Weight across lower part, with feeling as if a cord were drawn tightly across. Bruised pain in sacrum (Berb.).

Extremities.—Twitchings, especially of feet and shoulders, with heat of feet. Convulsive movements alternating with trembling of whole body. Stitches here and there. Pain, arthritic, and in back; drawing P. in spots on hands and r. foot; *tingling, when body is shaken (e. g., in a carriage) or when treading. Bruised pain;* **paralytic, in all joints during motion** (Calc. c.). Weakness; of feet and arms when walking in open air. Falling asleep of those on which he rests. Heaviness; in muscles under joints when walking in open air, with pressure.

Clinical.—Rheumatoid affections of the muscles, with bruised feelings, sharp pains, great loss of power or even paralysis. Gouty inflammation of the joints, *with great fear of being approached.* Sciatica during pregnancy. Varicose veins; with ulcers.

Upper Extremities.—Stitches inward below axilla. *Twitching pain from l. shoulder-joint to middle finger.* Drawing aching in l. shoulder when standing erect. Rheumatic pains in shoulders. Shoulders lame. Smarting sore sensation below shoulder. Tearing in arms and hands. *Bruised pain on anterior surface of arm. Arm weary as if bruised,* so that he could not bend his fingers inward.

Upper Arm.—Twitching in muscles; in l. as if a nerve were twinged. Stitches; like shocks in upper part. Tearing, apparently in bone, from lower part of l. to elbow.

Forearm.—Stitches in l. in morning in bed, with pain as if arm were broken; Burning S.; below elbows. Tearing along ulna from elbow to ring and little fingers. Tension of flexor muscles when bending arm, with tensive pain on extending those muscles again.

Wrist.—*Cracking of r.* on moving hand, *with dislocated feeling.* Stitches, < motion. Tearing in l., < writing, the pain is felt especially in dorsum of hand, > letting arm hang down; sticking T., < l. *Sprained feeling;* l. Aching in l. W. and palm, with itching. Weakness of l., with feeling generally as if he could not use his arms.

Hand.—Distended veins, with full, strong pulse. Trembling. Tearing; on back between ring and little fingers; *drawing T. on ulnar side of back of r.; twitching T.* on ulnar side of back of r. during rest. Pressure on back. *Drawing in outer half of back of r.* Feel swollen and sore. Weakness, < seizing something.

Fingers.—*Cramp in l.* Stitches in bend of middle joint of index; in both middle; in distal joint of middle; itching, in tip of middle; burning, on end of l. third; twitching S. *Tearing in tips of two last l.; in ulnar side of ungual phalanx of r. ring. Aching in joints of r. ring and little; in ungual phalanx of r. ring;* in first phalanges of three last l. *Bruised pain in balls of thumbs. Crushed pain on pressure,* in ungual phalanx of r. ring finger. Drawing cramplike pain in shafts of bones of fingers and forearms, extending backward and upward. Drawing *in r. thumb;* in r. third finger in evening, especially in ungual phalanx, with tearing, also at times in little finger and along ulnar edge of forearm.

Lower Extremities.—Trembling. Tearing. Pain at night when laid across one another. Standing is painful.

Thigh.—Twitching of l. recti muscles (common); pinching, in l. thigh near scrotum; feeling of T. of muscles. Stitches above knee; itching, on inner side above knee, < rubbing. Tearing in l. upper (very common). Pinching on outer side. Thrusts in hips. Pain when rising and stepping; *drawing, in l. hip-joint when sitting with thigh extended;* drawing cramplike, in muscles when sitting. *Sprained pain in hips. Bruised pain when walking;* in adductors of r. in afternoon when walking. Tension in l. buttock and in knee.

Knee.—Tottering when standing. Bending suddenly when walking; while feet are insensible. Stitches; *when touched.* Tearing (not uncommon); in region of l., > violent friction. Aching in r. Bruised pain when ascending stairs. (Cramplike pain, and in leg.) Weariness, < rest, and in r. fibular joint.

Leg.—Twitching lancinating pain extending upward in tibia. Tearing below l. knee; in l. calf like boring and digging from above downward, afterwards extending into thigh, thence crossing behind os coccygis and ending in r. iliac bone. Aching in l.; A., with soreness when walking. Bruised pain in tibia when walking; *over r. calf, with weakness of legs.* Gurgling feeling from below upward in lower part at rest. *Burning* spot on outside of l. tibia. Tension in muscles of calf, from below upward, with drawing when standing.

Ankle.—Tearing in malleoli; *on r. outer malleolus and on dorsum of foot;* undulating (almost dull stitching), in A. *Sprained pain in tarsal joint.* Weakness, with weight on insteps.

Foot.—Cramp in muscles of soles. Stitches extending through big toe; in r. tendo-achillis when extending tarsal joint, not when walking; in soles when walking, as if in a corn; crawling, in soles. Tearing in l. sole in evening; in heel. *Arthritic pain,* with fever towards evening. Pain as from internal uneasiness and as if lying too hard, in evening. (Aching in the paralyzed F.) *Crawling in outer half of l.,* as if a nerve were pulled, *when walking, on raising l. foot and bending l. ankle. Drawing in outer half of back of l.* Tired after walking in open air, with bending of knees, sleepiness, sleep and dreams.

Toes.—Cramp in l. Shocks in big. Stitches when walking; in big; in r. big. *Tearing in l. little;* sticking, in under surface of big T. when lying down for siesta, and when setting down foot. Pain, throbbing, in one; (numb) trembling P. in one. *Arthritic pain, as if sprained in joint of big T. towards evening, with redness.*

Skin.—Pallor. *Livid color of thighs, with blue and yellowish marks. Redness; with heat and œdema;* red patches, with swelling and burning; points and vesicles with red areola, smarting and itching; erysipelatous, with turgescence, heat and papular elevations, which on touch itch and are tipped with a vesicle; *over front of feet, with puffing and infiltration of cellular tissue, causing the hard caked feeling of true erysipelas, with soreness, the latter > walking.*

Swelling of nose, also erysipelatous and vesicated; under l. eye; of face, with smarting pain, especially under eyes, heat of face, blotches on cheeks and forehead; *hot, red, shining, stiff, of l. cheek; red, of r. cheek, with throbbing and pinching pain, swollen lips,* **heat in head, cold body** and sometimes hot feeling in feet; S. of cheek, with throbbing and pinching as if two hammers beat against each other, crushing the flesh; of arm, with papules, then vesicles, then excoriations, with redness, itching, burning; of ankle, extending to thigh, with heat and pain, afterwards blackness of whole limb, with feeling as if a weight were attached to it, then skin began to peel off, and the blackness changed to purple, l. then r.; sudden S. of (sick) foot.

Inflammation of hand, then redness and erysipelas; *erysipelatous, l. hand* **dark blue** *and covered with vesicles,* giving the appearance of a rhinoceros hide, then pustules; erythematous I., with œdema of face and whole body, becoming vesicular and scaling. *Erysipelas; over l. cheek, from under border of lower maxilla to scalp, with irritation and constitutional disturbance.* Erythema of face, less about margins of hair, worse on lids, with redness and swelling of cheeks, upper lip and nose, and concha, especially its margin, lids œdematous, œdematous sacs hanging from lower lids, with heat of face and biting (itching).

Eruption, with burning and smarting; over malarbone; like pin-heads, with red skin; on palms, causing exfoliation, with scaly look of hands and cracking of skin in folds. Eczema, with crowded bullæ and pain; on back and down to knees, on abdomen and genitals, with general hyperæmia, papules, vesicles, excoriating and exuding surface and crusts, itching, stinging and burning. Rash coming and going on face, especially on forehead. Nettle-rash, erythematous and vesicular rash, then bullous, but on nose it was inclined to be pustular, forming crusts, when the bullæ burst much serum exuded and vesicles appeared in the places over which the serum ran.

Pimples (on scrotum); itching, on prepuce; on side of neck, with stinging and ulcerative pain on touch, itching; between thumb and index, with *sticking when touched;* painful, on margin of beard. *Pustules;* on side of forehead; in and under nose, with biting pain; acne under r. labial commissure, with burning pain. Eruption like smallpox on cheeks, especially under eyes. (Abscess of psoas muscles.) Vesicles, with itching; V., with heat and irritation; then erysipelatous patch; acuminated, on an inflamed base; exuding.

Stitches; as from fleas, on chest and inner surfaces of arms after suddenly becoming heated; (burning and itching S. here and there when lying down for siesta, > scratching). Tearing at different times and on different parts. Pain, *drawing on dorsum of l. little finger;* tensive P. (at place of application), with burning, afterwards when washing, the hair-follicles look like prominent crimson grains, which later are red flat spots; burning, at times in this, at times in that part; cold, now here, now there.

Sensitiveness, and of all joints on motion. Formication over orbits; near nose; of forearms; of feet; itching F. on side of nose, > rubbing. *Itching;* in morning on waking; l. outer thigh and foot; of toes; of whole body, with stitching; red spot on glans; crawling I. in l. side of chest; stinging, in sides of chest and in back; pricking, on scapula; stinging, on inner side of thigh like soreness, > touch; pricking I. on proximal joints of fingers, > scratching.

Clinical.—Erysipelatous inflammation, with tendency to ecchymoses, great prostration, tendency to boils, especially in diabetes. Gangrenous appearance in contused wounds. Bed-sores.

Sleep.—Yawning; frequent; *frequent in evening, without sleepiness;* with stretching, and with dilatation of pupils, without sleepiness. *Sleepiness;* in forenoon; *in evening;* after a long walk in open air, with disinclination to think or speak. Sleeps much. Sleeps two hours in evening, then sleepless till 5 A.M., then sleep till 9 A.M. *Sleepless;* till 2 or 3 A.M., with anguish as if owing to heat; till 2 or 3 A.M., with stinging, biting itching here and there. Falls asleep late in evening, but sleeps long in morning. Sleep restless; and diminished. Unrefreshing S. Disturbed sleep after going to bed exhausted, waking frequently, each time from a dream that he was dying and that his bed was surrounded by friends. Talking loud and unintelligibly. Lamenting in sleep. Starting up in fright; when falling asleep; starting and jerking backward of head. Waking early; frequently from dreams; frequently with emissions of semen.

Dreams. Of lightning striking, of graves, etc. Frightful, with screams, which wake him; that men are flayed; of large black dogs and cats in evening immediately on falling asleep. Anxious; about visions in previous dreams. That she is scolded and reproached (about immoral conduct). Vivid towards morning, and waked by his own talking; V. but unremembered. The dreamer showing much irresolution, while half asleep. Agreeable.

Fever.—Chilliness; *beginning in morning in bed,* lasting the whole forenoon; in morning, then heat; C., < evening. External and internal C. Internal; on waking by day or at night. Shaking C. without thirst. *Shivering* when gaping; when walking. **Shivering C. over whole body and head, with heat in head, redness and heat in face, coolness of hands and bruised feeling in back, hips and anterior surface of arms.** *General shaking chill, with internal heat, hands and feet being cold. Cold spot on forehead as if touched with a cold thumb. Cold nose towards evening, with dry heat of face as far as behind ears, without thirst (Apis.);* C. externally in nose, with internal heat. Chills in back, in morning, and in anterior part of thighs. Cold feeling in r. side when lying on it in morning. Cold dry skin. *Shivering* of limbs; over arms and thighs, with dry feeling in tip of tongue, in palate and lips.

Heat when lying quietly for some time, especially on head, which he must move constantly. *Dry H. over whole body in morning after waking; in bed, with thirst, but chilliness on uncovering or making slightest motion.* Flying H. over whole body, with anguish. Internal H., especially in head, with heaviness of head, without thirst. Itching burning of skin. *Burning in brain while the rest of body is cool, or at least not hot;* burning on top of head and neck externally; heat in head at night, waking him, then anxiety, with fears of apoplexy; in flushes over head, with sweat on face; internally and externally in head. Heat in lobule of ear; externally on l. ear and cheek; internally in ear, but not externally. (Burning about border of nostrils, with desire to sneeze.) *Heat of one cheek, with redness,* body otherwise cool, or at any rate not hot; (H. of one cheek at noon during dinner); in face, with itching; flushing over face, also in evening; *of lips;* in back, in paroxysmal flushes. Burning in feet; on external edge of l. foot, with biting; heat of feet, with twitching of limbs, especially feet and shoulders.

Sweat; at night, with anguish; on waking. *Sour; at night.* Cold. Intermittent at night, with anguish. On face; forehead; chest and inner surfaces of arms; on soles of feet and toes. Red, on chest.

Clinical.—Arnica is indicated in a low type of fever, generally of a malarial nature (typhoid or typho-malarial). Bed-sores develop, hæmorrhages are frequent from internal parts, the lower extremities cold while the upper part of the body is hot. In fever stupid, secretions foul.

Arsenicum Album.

Arsenious acid is triturated with sugar of milk for the lower attenuations.

General Sphere of Action.—Arsenic is, above all, a tissue drug, ranking with Phosphorus and Antimony. An irritant poison, it produces most violent gastro-enteritis, with destructive action. It suspends and destroys the glycogenic function of the liver (Phos., Ant.), and causes acute and chronic inflammation of the kidneys (Phos., Merc., Plumb.). It irritates the air passages, increases, at first, the secretions and finally paralyzes the pneumogastric. It irritates the heart and finally produces vaso-motor paralysis. The skin is irritated, and violent itching and burning are followed by eruptions and finally ulceration. Glandular action is excited, then diminished. It produces intense irritation of the spine, affects chiefly the gray matter of the chord, and causes persistent hyperæmia and softening, with consequent paralysis. It has a special affinity for the blood-corpuscles, which may be destroyed. It causes general fatty degeneration (Phosphorus). It produces well-marked intermittent fever, with incomplete resolution.

General Peculiarities.—The general key is irritability (skin intolerant of scratching, the stomach intolerant of water, though the patient is thirsty). Aggravation shortly after midnight. Profound exhaustion; excessive restlessness. General relief from warmth (Camph.)

Allied Drugs.—Antimon., Phos., Merc., Plumb., (Zinc.), *Rhus tox.*, Secale c., *Camph.*, Thea, Colch., Verat., Tabac., *Silicea.*

Antidotes.—Ferrum, China.

Generalities.—Body crouched. Lies crouched in bed, moaning and groaning. Gathers himself together in bed, can scarcely move his limbs and is with difficulty awakened from his delirious sopor. Lies on his back, touching the region of coccyx with his heel, while knees are raised and widely apart, suddenly he turns around and takes a different position. Lies on back during sleep with his l. hand under occiput. *Screaming frequently from pain. General swelling.* Weight increased, with dyspepsia, foul breath and general malaise. Weight increased, then emaciation. *Emaciation; with weakness; with excessive sweats; with clay-colored face, blue margins around eyes, weakness of limbs and inclination to rest;* complexion pale bluish-gray, abdominal walls olive-green, back ecchymosed, mouth and nose covered with scabs, and nearly all the hair fell out; progressive, without loss of appetite. *Consumption.* Fatal marasmus. Jaundice.

Convulsions; caused by pain in soles; with foam at mouth; with cramps in legs; with horrible distortions of limbs; with unconsciousness, vomiting and colic; then renewed violent vomiting; then dysenteric stools; then violent sweat, then sleep; seemingly from external causes, especially from vexation or other violent mental agitation, an hour before their appearance drawings in limbs, longing to lie down, without finding sleep, when the convulsions came on a sudden jerk through whole body, or coldness running from head down back like lightning, and at the same moment unconsciousness, stretching and writhing, then drawing together of limbs, especially of arms, at times also convulsive distortion of facial muscles and tetanus, with injury and bleeding of under lip or tongue, but more frequently the spasm rages in the abdomen, which rises and falls rapidly, with rumbling, the attack is generally repeated before return to consciousness, when she calls for water, which renews the convulsions; felt a dart go through her, then became insensible, with lividity of face, foaming at mouth and moaning; on regaining consciousness did not recollect what had happened during her fit; found prone on the floor, body arched in that curve which evinces spasmodic contractions of muscular coat of stomach and intestines, or of diaphragm and anterior abdominal muscles, or of both, convulsions every fifteen or twenty minutes, lasting each time thirty to forty seconds, with wild, staring, bloodshot eyes, imprecations, fearful ravings, between the convulsions prostration, irregular, intermittent and accelerated pulse, during and between the convulsions intense suffering in stomach and abdomen, evinced by pressure on abdomen, forward inclination and anxiety of countenance; arms jerked outward, then unconsciousness, lying like one dead, pale but warm, clenched thumbs, twisted fists, drew up her arms slowly, then lowered them slowly, after ten minutes worked her jaws, breathing imperceptible, in a quarter of an hour the fit ended in a jerk through the whole body, a sort of starting forward of arms and lower limbs, consciousness returned at once, but there was great weakness.

Tetanic spasms; body bent backward and chest distended high up, with miserable wailing. Rigid spasms, with body bent backward. Convulsions in rapid succession, with such stiffness that no joint could be moved, and teeth clenched so as to scarcely permit the escape of the froth and contents of mouth and stomach. *Epileptic convulsions* in the night, preceded by palpitation, with the fits peculiar trembling of r. arm and lower limb, symptomatic fever, insatiable thirst, white but moist tongue, face flushed, respiration hurried, pulse rapid, irregular, contracted, frequent gripings in bowels, twitchings of chest and abdomen, fits repeated following nights, no sound sleep, if he dozed he woke suddenly and much agitated, pulse rapid, twitches, tremor of r. arm and lower limb, headache, eyes painfully affected by light, and vertigo, which was < sitting up in bed or by exertion, afterwards a fit every day about 8 P.M.; on recovering from each fit he looked wild, forgot where he was, talked incoherently, then complained of languor. Fell down senseless, was convulsed, had cramp in limbs and was cold, afterwards limbs cold and bathed in sweat, skin blue and corrugated, feeling as if parboiled, pulse imperceptible at wrist, pulsation of carotids rapid and fluttering, eyeballs retracted, face livid, voice husky and guttural, thirst, distress at epigastrium, frequent vomiting, appearance as in malignant cholera, then cramps and coldness of limbs increased, vision failed, voice faltered, throat became dry, tongue swollen, hiccough, delirium and death.

Hysteria; tossing her arms about, unconscious and unable to speak. Hysterical spasms, then exhaustion. Raises herself anxiously, stares, attempts to throw off all the clothing, jumps out of bed, throws about her clenched hands, then sinks down unconscious, with convulsions of arms and legs, toes flexed. While rolling about in bed he screams "I am suffocating," throws off the cover, opens his mouth wide as if to draw breath, and remains fixed in this condition several seconds.

Twitching; of body and limbs; T. of chest, abdomen and limbs. Inclination to start. Convulsive startings all over body; in sleep. *Startings like concussive shocks in the affected part in evening on falling asleep, excited by a slight trouble in a remote part, such as tearing, itching, etc.* (Nux vom.). *Trembling;* in morning; with formication; with sweat on face, convulsive, with coldness and faintness. Grasping head and throat.

Cramps; in legs and stomach, muscles of former spasmodically contracted, abdomen rigid and tender, in intervals of pain eyes half-closed, tongue covered with creamy fur, breath soon became more rapid and difficult, with increasing lividity of face. When on the stool sudden difficulty in breathing, with *cramp* in chest, hands and arms, then cramp in calves, cold all over body, stiff and helpless, violent vomiting, prostration, countenance anxious and restless, skin cold and clammy, pulse feeble and frequent, eyes sunken, with dark borders, lip and tongue parched, thirst, breathing slow and oppressed, sometimes sighing, burning pain in stomach, < pressure, nausea, limbs cold, vomiting, with griping and purging, the cramp came on almost every fifteen minutes, the slightest movement seemed to excite the spasm (Nux vom.), vomiting of greenish-yellow fluid at intervals, brandy and all warm drinks were rejected, but a little cold water was retained.

Stitches over whole body. Tearing in bones. The burning, stitching tearings, especially in extremities, affected the patient more as the energy of body decreased and sensibility increased. Pain through the whole system; *felt at night during sleep; of the affected part waked him from time to time at night, < before midnight;* at night can only be endured while walking. worse when lying quietly than when sitting; P. < evening; < after dinner, especially when sitting; < being talked to; < easy breathing or slight motion; P. > *external warmth;* > by pressure; in joints. *The paroxysm of pain is frequently accompanied by other minor symptoms.* Pain in the joints; in various parts, especially across shoulders, down spine and limbs, also in joints, which were often stiff and swollen; in whole trunk, mostly in small of back, and back, < after riding on horseback (in a practised rider). *Pain seems intolerable* and drives the patient mad. Sharp pains all over body, especially in genitals. Sharp pains all over body mornings on waking, with aching across shoulders and back of neck.

Neuralgia; came with throes of violence over l. eyebrow, into bones of face, crept up the spine and settled in vertex, making her feel as if she could go mad or rush out anywhere, with intolerance of noise. **Burning pain, especially in inner organs** (Sec. c.), **skin and ulcers.** *Pains generally burning,* at times, also stitching, then again gouty tearing, with which at times rapid twitching and pulling appeared at one spot, and in general the affected limb was constantly twitching. Pains all over body as if he lay on fire or needles. **The pain and uneasiness return at regular hours, as in fever and ague** (China?). Ulcerative pain in affected part, as if it had passed into suppuration and were about to open, when sitting. Pain in affected part when sitting as if the bone were swollen and excoriated. Numb pain in whole side of body.

Prickling in various parts, < eyes, with tingling and with lachrymation. Anxiety in whole body, with cold sweat. He felt thick. Feeling as if he would burst before the diarrhœa. Whole body feels œdematous, especially hands, with heat. General soreness. Sensation as if the whole l. half of the body were drawn together. Malaise; morning on rising; during forenoon; with necessity to go to bed early and inability to get warm; then vomiting. Wretched in morning on waking. Unusual lightness. Great muscular activity and aptitude for walking.

Restlessness (Sec. c., Camph.); at night (Sulph.); **throwing himself from side to side;** *changing from one bed to another;* especially of arms and legs; **with anxiety** (Camph., Rhus t., Sec. c., Sulph.); tossing about the bed in a sort of anguish; **and unquenchable thirst;** threw herself about the bed and tightly clasped a bystander in her anxiety and oppression; with hypochondriac anxiety, as from continued sitting in a room, as if coming from upper part of chest; with contraction of body; the child is restless, moans and is fretful; dejected restlessness when sitting occupied, obliging her to walk about.

Collapse; with cold extremities, purple lips and dusky face (Camph., Sec. c.). **Faintness; in morning, with anxiety and weakness;** *when discouraged; with anxiety,* inability to control her thoughts and reeling; with coldness over whole body; with burning and nausea. **Weakness** (China, Phos., Merc. cy., Mur. ac., etc.); in morning; in evening; **after a meal** (Mur. ac., China, Ph. ac.); on movement or unusual mental exertion; *on slight exertion, with pallor;* after dinner, with excessive yawning; after drinking milk or vomiting, then tossing about of arms and legs, with pain and sickness, ending in vomiting and prostration as before; **after vomiting** (Verat.); **from diarrhœa** (Sec. c.), so that he felt faint, could not get into bed, legs trembled, the weakness > by white wine; W. < night, especially affecting the heart; with irritability; with vertigo and headache, so that he fell after rising; **obliging him to lie down with the slightest paroxysm of pain** (Plumb.); **so that he could scarcely walk, he feels as if he would fall over;** almost losing the use of l. side; cannot speak without effort; so that he could not hold an object; as from want of food. *Muscles lax.* Could not sit upright, stand nor walk, but when lying could make every motion. **Nervous prostration. Typhoid state;** sleepiness, numbness, stupid appearance, ringing in ears, no pains, redness of cheeks, slight ophthalmia, dorsal decubitus, paralysis of limbs and trunk, emaciation, moist skin, violent beating of heart, pulse rapid, abdomen retracted, hollow gurgling in abdomen, no diarrhœa, and involuntary micturition.

Senses morbidly acute. Sensitiveness, so that a draught of air caused cramp and convulsions; the gentle opening and shutting of a door or the touch of the bed clothes caused her to start, and the careless closing of the door drew tears and gave her pain. *Electro-muscular contractility diminished.* Stiffness, with inability to move, is only able to stand; muscular S. < in morning and extends to arm and forearm, which pain on motion.

Feeling as if pressed by a heavy body. Leaden heaviness. Heaviness and formication, which soon attacked upper limbs. Oppression. Tingling, beginning in l. arm, five days afterwards numbness of thighs and calves, the eleventh day anæsthesia of fingers and partial paralysis of flexor of forearm, then the same in lower limbs, with pain in both, in five weeks skin of whole body had desquamated, most on hands, in six weeks the paralysis of flexors of both extremities was unabated and accompanied by soreness on pressure, in two months and a half he was still unable to stand, in eight months the paralysis of sensation and motion and soreness on pressure continued, though they were less (compare Plumb.). Affection of tactile sensation. *Numbness;* and tingling; N. extending down r. side to foot. Cannot move. Immobility of eye and limbs. *Paralysis;* of motion and sensation; incomplete; of lower half of body; local P., preceded by numbness or tingling in fingers and toes. *Many symptoms occur only in the evening after lying down,* **several occur two hours after midnight,** not a few in the morning after rising.

Aggravation at night; while sitting and lying, and amelioration while standing and moving; she was glad if she was not required to move or speak (on account of the pain); aggravation during heat and damp. Felt better after eating.

Clinical.—It is adapted to a condition of profound prostration, rapid exhaustion or even collapse. Paralysis, especially of lower extremities. Hysterical paralysis. Spinal paralysis from myelitis. General dropsy, with weak heart. Dropsy from kidney disease. General anæmia. Pyæmia, with œdema, erysipelas, gangrenous ulcers and purulent expectoration.

Mind.—Delirium; *at night; with carphology;* with attempts to escape (Bell.); with restlessness; < **at night, with restlessness;** with tetanic convulsions; every morning when sleeping by himself, as if he heard wild beasts gnashing their teeth around his bed. Sees vermin crawling about the bed, from which he wants to escape, and throws away handfuls of them (Stram.). Motioning as if measuring with a rule, so that his ravings mostly related to his business. *Delirium,* rose to visit his absent daughter and could with difficulty be quieted, but spoke rationally. Runs through the house at night in search of thieves. Sees thieves in the room and hides under the bed. Imagines the house and space under it are full of thieves, which causes fright and anxious cold sweat. Suspected that people were about the house plotting against his life, jumped out of bed, reached after imaginary objects, stared wildly and suspiciously around him and at every one who made the slightest noise or stirred, and talked incoherently. Attacks of madness and sorrow. *Anxiety and fear,* he sees an absent acquaintance dead upon the sofa and has great dread of him. Furiously mad when offered something to eat, without appetite.

Alternating lively phantasies. Delusions alternating with half-confused sleep. Feeling as if she would lose her senses when thinking long about anything. Foolish answers. Loud wailing. Piercing lamentations interrupted by attacks of weakness. Cried and howled and spoke little and abruptly. Crying at trifles, with quarrelsome inclination. Sobbing, with childish spells of crying.

Her desire exceeds her need, *she eats and drinks more than is good for her, and she walks farther than she needs to do* or can endure. **Anguish; with tossing about the bed** (Acon.); **with despair driving him from place to place for relief;** *with oppression of chest and difficult breathing; with trembling* and with tearing in the abdomen; with cold sweat on face and trembling; *as if everything became constricted, with anxiety in pit of stomach;* so that he fainted; from the heart, interrupted by attacks of weakness; as if he had not done his duty. **Despairs and weeps, imagines that he must die** (Laches.); **is cold and chilly, and then weak. Fear; and anguish,** *sees ghosts day and night; with jumping out of bed and hiding; of solitude and death, rage from slightest cause, especially if one spoke of her recovery, which she considered impossible, with at times indescribable melancholy. Dread of death* (Acon., Sec. c., Plat.); **sudden, when alone** *or on going to bed.*

Anxiety; at 3 A.M., now with hot feeling, now with nausea; after 3 A.M., after waking; *in evening after lying down; and heat did not permit sleep before midnight* for many days; *and restlessness of whole body; and restlessness,* with cries of "kill me or relieve my pains!" *with impatience;* with excitement; with cold sweat; *deathly;* as regards some persons; in evening, lest some evil had befallen his relatives; periodical. *Sadness;* after eating, with headache; *and crying at slightest provocation;* with want of interest in anything. Despondent about his condition. **Disposition to suicide** (Plumb.); *after midnight,* by stabbing his heart through and through. *Indifference to life. Indignation* alternating with mildness, in her indignation she looks at nobody and does not want to hear anything, she also cries; morning in bed, pushed the pillows about indignantly, uncovered himself, saw no one and did not want to be spoken to.

Fretfulness and fault-finding at everything, every conversation, noise, even the light was disagreeable (Sulph.); *fretful, indignant, capricious, every word angered her. Vexed at trifles and talking constantly about other people's faults.* Quarrelsome. Dislike and indifference to those around him. Discontented, has no desire for anything. Dissatisfied all day and vexed with himself, believes he has not done enough and reproaches himself.

Sullen and silent. Silent and turned away his head when spoken to. Indisposed to reply to questions. Returns short answers. Answers slowly. Talks but little, complains only of anguish. Seriousness. When alone thinks about disease and similar things, from which it is difficult to free his mind. Irresolution. Impulsiveness. Inclination to jest in a malicious manner. Agitation; mental and physical. Excitement; towards morning, hindering sleep, though he was drowsy. *Sensitiveness; to least noise.* Easily made to laugh or cry. Indisposition to amuse himself like other children, with sensitiveness and precocity. Laughing fits, irritability and tendency to tears. Good humor, he likes to converse. Lively and combative. Mind energetic and fresh, inclined to gayety. *Laziness.*

Inability for mental work, fear of his fellow-men, irritability, passion *and such down-heartedness from sleeplessness that he committed suicide. Ideas crowd upon him and he is too weak to repel them in order to dwell upon one alone.* Confusion of mind. Absence of mind. He scarcely knew what he said or did. Absence of understanding and of external and internal senses, and when one shouted into his ears he looked at those present like one intoxicated waking from a deep sleep. Stupor; after vomiting and diarrhœa; with staring eyes; with sleepiness. Coma; with paralysis, tetanic convulsions, or spasm in muscles of extremities. *Unconsciousness;* with pallor. Memory lost; of recent acts, with frequent vertigo, drowsiness and feeling as if she were "losing her mind."

Clinical.—Melancholia, with suicidal tendency, great restlessness, constant change of place, wringing of her hands, < last part of the night. Insanity, with self-mutilation. Excessive fear of death, yet despair of life. Nearly all the mental disorders are characterized by extreme anxiety, fear and restlessness.

Head.—Palsied shaking. Felt swollen to an enormous size. Bent on one side and pain on raising it as from rheumatism in sterno-mastoid. *Lancinations,* > cold wet towel *or open air on affected part. Tearing,* and at same time in r. eye; with heaviness and with drowsy faintness in the daytime; pain as if brain were being torn out.

Aching; morning on waking, > rising; in morning on rising, < l. side; from 6 to 8 P.M., with sweat, anguish and loss of appetite; growing worse all day, with constriction at temples, as from intoxication; < 11 P.M., with cold hands and face; < at night; < *light and noise* (Bap., Sil.); < vomiting; < in a warm room; > applying cold water; *with vertigo; and in face,* < *on l. side,* preventing leaning or resting on that side and obliging her to sit up all night and keep the head erect; and across eyes; and in breast and belly, with vomiting and thirst; with soreness of scalp and itching.

Throbbing pain when raising himself in bed, especially in forehead, with nausea; tearing throbbing pain, < night; tearing throbbing, in attacks, sometimes on one side and extending over whole head. *Stupefying* aching; especially in forehead, when walking and standing, > sitting, with fine stitches in l. temporal region near canthus; especially over r. eyebrow, with sore pain when knitting the brow. Tensive aching. Contractive pain. Aching as if the brain were pressed by a hundred-weight. *Burning pain. Periodical pain.* Intermittent pain all day. Headache alternating with pain in stomach. Drawing and throbbing. Throbbing, and in all limbs. Throbbing like a hacking at 2 A.M., as if the skull were pressed asunder, with sweat. *Confusion;* evening; with noise; with somnolence. Stupidity towards noon, with weakness of head; from 11 A.M. till 6 P.M., as if he had not slept enough; *as if he had done much work in great haste, with internal uneasiness;* as in violent coryza, and when out of humor, with confusion and vertigo.

Heaviness; > **open air, but returns on entering room** (Tab., Zinc.), *with humming in ears;* with stupefaction; in morning after rising, as if the brain were oppressed by a load, with humming in ears; as after sexual excess (China). Irritability of brain. Weakness from much pain, with weakness and nausea in pit of stomach. "Aching tired sensation" at base of brain. Congestion. *Sensation as if brain moved and beat against skull during motion* (China, Sulph.). *Brain seems to flap when moving head while walking* (Rhus t.), *with pressure upon it.* Wavering sensation in brain, < moving head.

Vertigo; every evening, she has to hold on to something when closing her eyes, on studying or reading; when sitting; on rising; after sleep; on going into open air, < on re-entering room (Tab., Plat.); on walking in open air, with a stupid sensation in head, especially in forehead, so that he staggered; when vomiting; with vanishing of thought when rising up; *with stupidity* and inability to think; with dulness of head; with obscuration of sight; with nausea when lying; with rush of blood to heart; with inability to keep erect; with trembling; when walking, as if he would fall to the right; sudden, with qualmishness.

Forehead.—**Aching,** *with vertigo;* over brows; (over l. eye, < evening and night); during sleep, he complains of headache, now in forehead, now in occiput. Neuralgia in F. and face. Pricking pain over r. eye. *Drawing pain in r. side. Throbbing pain during motion. Throbbing pain over root of nose.* Constrictive pain above eyes and in temples. *Bruised or sore pain in F.; and over nose,* > *rubbing.* Inflammation of sinuses, with aggravation at same hour each day. Heaviness, < evening, with pulsations more painful in forehead and temples.

Temples, swelling of superficial veins; stitch in l., also > touch; tearing stitches in l.; pain; *pain in r.;* neuralgia in l. on waking; painful hammering at noon and midnight, after which her body feels paralyzed. *Vertex,* pain; in morning and in occiput; pain in V. as from a weight; burning pain in V., with sore pain in scalp when touched; now a pressing confusing, now a throbbing, or a burning pain in V., > rubbing; drawing pain under coronal suture every afternoon. (*Hemicrania.*) *Neuralgia on l. side;* then paralyzed feeling. *Dull beating pain in one-half of head, as far as above eye.* Aching on l. side. Tearing in l. side. When walking, sensation of two marbles striking each other over ear. Bruised pain in one side in morning when rising. *Aching in occiput.* Tearing in occiput. Occasional shooting in O.

Hair falls out; on l. side; thick only on middle of skull, and the skin desquamated; with hairs sticking together in places like felt; matted on l. side; the H. which had come out grew again, was stiff, brittle and gray, but gave place to healthy hair. Scurfy eruption on occiput. Pimples over whole scalp, painful on touch as if ecchymosed or ulcerated, with the same pain in whole scalp; (very red pimples); pimple on l. side, covered with scurf, obliging scratching, and painful when rubbed as if ulcerated. Hard pustules; (P., with burning pain, and on face). Moist discharge. Herpetic eruption behind r. ear, with red base, burning, twitching and stitching, then itching. (Corroding ulcers.) (Ulcerated crusts; as far as middle of forehead.) Sensation as if hair stood on end and were pulled up by the roots. Pain on touch; as if ulcerated. Soreness of scalp; with pain at vertex and sensitiveness of the hair when touched at the points. Bruised pain in external head, < touch. (Burning pain in scalp.) Formication every other night. Creeping on occiput, as if roots of hair were moving. Itching; corrosive; painful as of an ulcer, with pain as if ecchymosed, especially in region of occiput; (gnawing); (*burning*).

Clinical.—Neuralgic headache, with extreme prostration, burning in stomach, retching, thirst, etc. The pains are burning, shooting, like needles, with soreness in the painful part. Dandruff, head dry and scaly, soreness, rarely eczema and still more rarely pustular eruptions.

Eyes.—Blue circles around. Yellow as in jaundice. *Injected;* glistening; and vessels of cornea injected. Sunken; with pale face. *Protruding;* and red; and watery. *Staring.* Distorted. Turned upward and squinting. Rigid; and turned upward. Suffused, languid; with lividity of inner part of under lids. *Tearing;* in l.; in r. and at same time in head. Stitches, with burning. Pain in l.; in l. at night; deep-seated in r., with stitches when turning it; drawing, with twitching in lids; burning, with photophobia. Heavy pressure. *Feeling of sand* in l.; *in eyes in evening.* Burning pain. **Burning;** during the day; *in evening,* < lying down, with pricking; *B., with smarting. Pulsative throbbing after midnight, and at every pulsation a stitch.* Jerking in l. Soreness; with inflamed look. Sensitiveness. Distended feeling, then conjunctival inflammation. Prickling.

Nightly itching; biting, gnawing. Feeling as if there were a boil below each. Feeling as if full of tears, but without lachrymation. Feel worse when moving them or looking steadily. *Lachrymation;* in morning, with fluent coryza; of r.; *L. and itching,* with pus in eyes in morning; with dazzled sensation in eyes; with half-open and red eyes; **corrossive L., making cheeks sore, also lids** (Merc. cor.). *Blue spots in white of eye,* and on abdomen and genitals. White of eye yellow. Icteric flush in albuginea and at edge of the reddened cheeks. *Eyeballs hot and burning sore. Pupils dilated; contracted;* alternately contracted and dilated, < in night and by a lighted candle or moving finger to and fro; insensible to light.

Lids.—Agglutination; in morning; at external canthi in morning. Gum in the morning. **Œdema** (Rhus t., Apis) **often closing eyes;** of l.; of upper, with redness, *Swelling; and redness;* redness and excoriation, of upper. then of lower l., then of forehead, head and neck, without pain and without secretion of mucus; with tendency to eversion and with redness along edges and at angles, and painful vision. Blue. Red and half-shut; *edges red; inner surface red,* with uneasy sensation rather than pain, obliging rubbing. Desquamation, with redness and with line of excoriation at outer canthi. Lower lid externally excoriated where the burning was most severe. *Blepharadenitis, cil; and ulcerosa* (Graph., Merc.). Inflammation; of l. upper. Not closed during sleep. Spasmodic closure. Spasms; and of jaws, etc. *Trembling of upper, with lachrymation.* Aching over l. lid, < raising eyes, and in upper half of ball; sudden, in lids at 1 P.M., with pricking and lachrymation. Smarting as from smoke.

Pain in margins during motion, as if they were dry and rubbed against the balls. Dry when reading by candle light, as if eyes were rubbed by them. Burning in margin of upper. Itching about lashes. Stiffness; as if he had smoked all night. Could not open them at night without lifting them with her finger; l. cannot be opened.

Conjunctiva.—*Red;* or sore. *Minutely injected, with diffused pale redness.* Yellow. Bluish-white. *Inflammation.* Conjunctivitis of tarsal portions; *with suffusion of eyes and photophobia;* with itching and depreciation of vision; with sparkling eyes, anasarca simulating increased fat, ending in a hide-bound skeleton slowly sinking to the tomb; as from external irritation.

Suborbital pain on l. side, with stitches. Aching under r. eye at night, causing so much anguish that she could not remain in bed. Pinching over eyes. Vision lost; dim; as through white gauze; impaired, with pain in eyes if used. *Photophobia.* Flickering; and dark; and when eyes were closed shining particles floated backward and forward. Dazzled by snow, with lachrymation. Vision yellow during nausea (Dig.); of sparks; of white spots or points; of bluish sparks.

Clinical.–Ophthalmia, which is extremely painful, with very great sensitiveness of the eyes to light, burning, swelling of the lids. In all the external inflammations of the eyeball it is characterized by extreme painfulness (burning), hot and excoriating lachrymation, swelling of the lids, great photophobia; with these symptoms it has been found useful, not only in ophthalmias, but in inflammations of the cornea, with or without ulceration, and also in internal inflammation, with accumulation of pus in the anterior chamber (keratitis). In ciliary neuralgia, with fine, burning pains. Disseminated choroiditis. Retinitis albuminurica.

Ears.—Stitches in morning; *outward in l. meatus auditorius at night.* Tearing in middle; *sticking T. outward through l. meatus auditorius, < towards evening;* drawing T. in l. lobule; drawing T. behind ear, extending along neck to shoulder. *Otalgia.* Cramp, pain in outer. Deep-seated agreeable creeping. Voluptuous tickling in r. meatus, causing rubbing. Sensation as if l. meatus were stopped from without. Closure from within while swallowing, like deafness. Deafness. Sensitiveness to sound; to noise. Sounds, and in whole head. Ringing; in r. when sitting. *Roaring; at every paroxysm of pain;* in l. Rushing noise as of a near waterfall.

Clinical.—Otorrhœa, with thin excoriating discharge, sometimes fetid. The skin within the ear becomes raw and burning, and the discharge becomes ichorous and very offensive (compare Mercury).

Nose.—*Swollen and pouring forth a watery discharge.* Pointed. Tip violet and cold. (*Ulceration of upper part of inner, secreting a fetid, bitter ichor*); U. of inner surface. *Soreness of mucous membrane.* Stitches in bones. *Pain in bone, at root.* Burning pain. *Burning;* in l. nostril in evening, with peculiar dryness in back part of mouth. Itching internally. *Dryness. Stoppage as from catarrh; distressing S. under bridge,* which occasionally altered his speech (Lyc.). *Sneezing;* without coryza; *violent, waking at night, with a copious watery discharge. Coryza;* every morning on waking, with sneezing; *with hoarseness and sleeplessness; fluent and dry together; fluent, with frequent sneezing;* fluent, with lachrymation in morning. Running from nose; with itching. *Discharge every day, beginning at 5 A.M., > hot weather, < morning* (Euphras.), **went off in open air; excoriating** (All. cep.); **watery and excoriating** (All. cep.); watery excoriating from l. nostril; profuse, thick, yellow. *Nosebleed;* after wine; during ill humor; when vomiting. Offensive smells. Smells of pitch and sulphur alternately.

Clinical.—Fluent coryza, with watery, burning, acrid discharge and sneezing. As a rule there is no ulceration or stoppage as in Nux vom., though they may occasionally happen. The discharge is always burning, excoriating. Extreme sensitiveness of smell, cannot bear even the smell of food.

Face.— **Swollen** (Apis, Rhus t., Merc. c.); especially about eyes, *and red;* with fixed redness, more or less under eyes and on cheek-bones; red and covered with cold sweat; dark and hot; with erysipelatous redness and blisters, which soon discharge and look gangrenous; of r. cheek, with pain in that side of face and smooth, shining, scarlet skin over swelling; with fainting fits and vertigo. Pinched, with sunken eyes (Sec. c., Verat.); and livid. **Sunken;** *and pale and covered with cold sweat* (Verat., Tab.); and leaden-hued. **Deathly color when vomiting** (Verat., Tab., Cocc.). **Pale, yellow, cachectic.** *Pale; corpse-like and convulsively distorted;* except a flush on each cheek. Pale-gray and swollen. Leaden-gray. Bluish-gray. Dusky. *Livid; and lurid;* livid and sunken. (Clayey, lead-colored, with blue and green streaks and spots.) Complexion by gaslight, dark greenish. *Yellowish;* with sunken eyes; greenish Y; grayish Y. Black around mouth. *Red;* spot on r. cheek; in spots and covered with sweat; especially upper parts of cheeks; and distorted; with yellowish tinge about nostrils. *Hippocratic. Appearance is best compared with that of a cholera patient in the algid stage* (Camph., Verat.). **Expression of agony.** *Wild look;* look of vague anxiety and desperation, as well as an expression of deep trouble. Expression of apprehension. *Stupid.* Frequent smiling. *Distorted, as if dissatisfied; distorted drawn lines;* distorted by convulsions and pain. Convulsions. *Twitching of muscles.*

Tearing of a quotidian type; in l. half. Pain, and in teeth and gums; < by touching painless side. Sensation as if an eruption would appear all over it. Throbbing, and in head, as if the boils would burst. Stiff feeling. *Lancinations along r. inferior maxillary nerve,* repeated while lying, with headache. Jaw, abscesses; clenched; tonic cramp in J. and throat; convulsive motions, so as to almost break the glass, when drinking (Merc. v.); pressure in l. upper J.

Lips.—Spotted *black. Livid. Bluish;* and cold. White-powdered. *Swollen; and cracked;* with a blister discharging lymph on r. edge of upper, and a blister discharging pus on l. edge of lower. Desquamation. Brown strip of shrivelled epidermis through middle of vermilion border of lower. Painful blotches in upper. *Corrosive ulcer* (Merc.), painful in evening after lying down, and waking at night, tearing and smarting in day on motion, the pain < touch and exposure to air. Superficial ulcers on inner surface, with swelling of lips and pain < eating or speaking, afterwards with ptyalism. *Sore, with ulcers in mouth.* Eruption similar to herpes labialis. Eruption on lower, with a thick crust and lardaceous base. Painless E. on margin of vermilion border. Bleeding of lower after eating. Distorted as in risus sardonicus; mouth drawn in all directions. *Pricking twitching in one side of upper, < when going to sleep.* Lower burning, hanging down, everted, painful, and cannot be approximated to upper lip, preventing speech. Itching of upper, as if pricked with red-hot needles, extending as far as under nose, next day swelling of upper lip above vermilion border. Dry; and pale red; and covered with herpes.

Clinical.—Face is apt to be pale and puffy, even in fever, especially with all gastro-enteric troubles; sometimes pinched and drawn, hippocratic, cold or covered with cold sweat. Facial neuralgia, with burning tearing pains.

Mouth.—Teeth. Yellowish-earthy, with little lustre. Sordes. Tartar at base. Progressive caries, with aching. *Grinding; in sleep.* Falling out of all. *Looseness and prominence of one in morning, with pain in gum on touch,* and pain in outside of cheek over the tooth, *the tooth not painful when biting teeth together.* The r. upper began to loosen and were removed with the fingers. *Loose, seemed longer, was sensitive to pressure and cold water* (Merc.). Painful looseness, with soreness, < chewing, likewise the gums are painful on touch and the cheek swollen (Phos., Merc.). Stitches. Tearing recurring regularly at night; tearing in teeth and head before menses, driving her almost to frenzy, and she strikes her head with her fist. Aching; in l. upper; in all l.; and in gums and face; on rising, < afterwards, with salivation; in r. molars in evening, < lower; waking at night; in upper on biting on them; extending to all teeth of that side; *jerking continuous A., extending to temple, > sitting up; as if loose, not < by chewing.* Loose sensation. Dull, as if she could not chew with them.

A large portion of the alveolar process of superior maxilla was detached (Phos.). Abscess over r. upper canine tooth, discharging sanious pus (Phos.). Gingivolabial groove much injected. Gums crimson line; *swollen, bleeding, painful to touch* and spotted white; swollen and covered with a network of white false membrane; spongy; aphthous ulceration of G. and tonsils; tender and shining; burning in G.; stitches in G. in morning; nightly tearing in G. of incisors, < lying on affected side, > *warmth of stove,* next morning the nose is swollen and painful to touch; pain.

Tongue.—Swollen; and grayish; and foul. Large, indented, with silvery-white fur, through which the dark red papillæ project. Protruding papillæ, at end scarlet. *Bluish. Red;* and smooth and dry (Verat v.). *White* (Ant. c., Bry., Tarax.); *and dry;* and moist; W., with red tip; whitish in centre; upper surface white, not coated, but thickened. **Brown** *and dry* (Plumb.). Dryish, coffee-brown color, changing to an inky color. Black and dry, and the ecchymosed spots on the skin became dry and black. *Tongue coated; sometimes with red edges;* patchy (Tarax.), *with a red streak in middle* **and redness of tip** (*Verat. v.*, Phos.); **brown** (Plumb.) **and dry**; white, with red margins and pain; white, with scattered red papillæ, as in scarlatina; *yellowish-white;* tongue, roof of mouth, gums and fauces covered with white velvety coat, growing dryer and harder until fourteenth day, then began to detach itself and was discharged by the bowels, having the fetor of putrid animal matter, leaving mouth, throat, stomach and bowels tender; green; yellow at base and red at tip and edges; (*Merc. i. f.*). Tongue inflamed, dry, cracked, with a brownish coat in centre, gums dry and angry, mouth feeling as if lined with flannel. **Tongue dry**; *D. morbidly red, with papillæ at tip;* D. and coated towards back; D. and excoriated. *Superficial ulcers on edges.* Stitches in root, as from a fish-bone, when swallowing or turning head. Boring in r. border in a sort of half sleep. Pain on side of tip as if corroded. Sensation of blisters on it. *Pain as if covered with burning painful vesicles.* Scalded feeling. *Burning; and in pharynx and stomach;* and in palate and throat. Coldness. Seemed thick. Drawn together, as from alum. Weakness and pain. Insensibility as if burnt and dead, and no taste.

Mouth in general.—Lost the power of speech. *Speech* monosyllabic, tremulous. *Aphthæ;* and in tongue; A., white then becoming black. *Painful blisters, and on tongue* (Borax, Sul. ac., Merc.). Mucous membrane abraded. Hæmorrhage, and from rectum (Phos., Crotal., Sec. c.). White pointed prominences on palate and uvula, seemingly the membrane covering palate, bones and velum pendulum detached at the parts by a whitish liquid. Slimy M. and throat. Stinging, and in pharynx. Pain beginning at l. side, then affecting all gums. Burning pain. **Burning in mouth, along pharynx and in a pit of stomach** (Arum t., Nit. ac., Mag.). **Dry feeling in M.; with thirst, but he drinks little at a time.** Roughness of hard palate. Imagines he has sand in M. M., lips and tongue sore and appeared scalded in patches. Tenderness, and in throat. Salivation; *must spit often. Bloody saliva* (Merc., Sec. c., Zinc.). Bitter saliva. *Frothy S. expectorated.* Breath has a peculiar offensive, pungent odor. Fetor of breath (Arn., Merc., Nit. ac.); with superficial ulceration of gums and throat.

Taste.—*Bitter;* (mornings); after eating; after eating and drinking; with yellow diarrhœa. *Sweetish and in throat. Putrid;* mornings. Nauseous. Metallic. Burning, astringent. Dry, as of wood. Sooty. Disgusting, sour. Sour; to food. Flat T. to beer. Salt T. to food. Food tastes as if not salted enough.

Clinical.—Neuralgia of the teeth, burning tearing; > heat of the stove, < after midnight, with great prostration; teeth feel long and very sore. Gums unhealthy, bleeding easily, with a general cachectic condition. Tongue ulcerated. Canker sores on tongue. Epithelioma of tongue. Neuralgia of tongue, with burning pain. In fevers the tongue may be red and dry, or it may be brown and black, smooth, as if varnished, generally very sore mouth; gangrenous sloughs of tongue (cancerous). Ulceration of mouth, with great dryness and burning heat. Gangrenous sore mouth of children (compare with Chloride of Potash).

Throat.—Submaxillary glands swollen, with aching and contusive pain; swelling of l., < evening; (S., with pain on pressure); of parotid and submaxillary glands. Swelling of l. carotid when stooping. Swelling of thyroid gland, especially on r. side; of fauces, with redness; of uvula, with redness; of tonsils, with false membrane. *Diphtheritis.* Redness, with aphthous ulceration. *Ulceration;* with inflammation resembling diphtheria and quinsy; spotted with white ulcers, next day soreness descending gullet into chest, with an excoriation on each side of uvula, a white ulcer on l. tonsil, and redness and tenderness of rest of throat and back of palate, swallowing a liquid caused gasping, hurried cough and pain. At base of each pillar aphtha surrounded by red areola, with redness of pharynx. Obstinate follicular soreness. Superficial excoriation. *Inflammation and swelling internally and externally about root of tongue.* Tonsillitis, with dry tongue and mouth. Constant spitting of saliva and mucus from fauces. Hawks up gray mucus. Spasm. Cramp. Tearing. Pain; in evening; when talking; from vomiting, and in chest; with inflammation; on l. side as far as pectoralis muscle. Nausea, with accumulation of water in mouth.

Strangling. Feels closed, and nothing can pass through it. *Constriction;* as if swollen; suffocative C.; spasmodic C. Sensation as of a hair in it. Scraping; as of rancid grease, in morning on swallowing first mouthful; behind velum pendulum palati between acts of deglutition. Roughness; morning, with hoarseness. Husky feeling. Soreness; capricious. *Dryness; with soreness, scraping and burning;* with thirst. *Burning;* in pharynx; *and in œsophagus; and in region of stomach;* and in chest; with lancinations; with uneasiness and hoarseness; with oppression as if suffocating. Uneasiness. Sensation of a lump of mucus, which tastes of blood. Bitterness after a meal, the food having a natural taste every other day (like a tertian fever). Sweetish taste. Globus hystericus. *Paralytic condition of pharynx and œsophagus, the bread fell with difficulty and a rumbling noise. Swallowing difficult; and painful;* impossible. Constant desire to swallow saliva.

Œsophagus.—Burning pain; and in stomach, with nausea and vomiting. *Burning.* Soreness. Constriction. Spasmodic contraction.

Clinical.—Arsenic is not so often indicated in ulcerations of the throat as many other drugs, rarely in the early stage of diphtheria; it is valuable in the later stages with profound prostration, especially if the membrane of the throat becomes dry, with burning thirst, irritable stomach, profound prostration or with albuminuria and dropsy. Inflammation of the œsophagus, with spasmodic stricture on swallowing food, burning.

Stomach.—Appetite increased. Constant craving for food. Desire for acids and acid fruit. Inclination for lard. Inclination to eat, but everything is repugnant. Capricious. *Lost;* for dinner; lost, with pressing in region of stomach; *lost, still he relishes the food he eats;* lost or else craving. **Loathing of food;** *of butter;* of animal food.

Thirst; frequent in evening, seldom during the day; at night, from dryness of throat; < evening; > night; **but drinking did not refresh him; he drinks much, but little at a time;** *with dryness of mouth and a peculiar thick, white saliva;* with anxiety. *Burning T;* without especial desire to drink. **Constant T. for cold water, the smallest quantity of which could not be retained.** Desire for coffee; for milk, which was usually repulsive; for malt beer; (for brandy). Thirst absent; *during the chill* (Gels., Op.).

Eructations; < drinking; with nausea; with hiccough. *Unsuccessful.* Empty; after every attack of vomiting. Of foul-smelling gases. Tasting of ingesta. Sour after dinner. Bitter after eating, with gulping up of bitter greenish mucus. Acrid fluid rises into mouth. *Waterbrash* after 4 P.M.; when coughing violently. *Hiccough;* at night; at night when rising, with a scraping repulsive taste in mouth; *after eating,* then eructations; *long-lasting* **at the hour when the fever ought to come;** convulsive.

Nausea; *at* 11 A.M. *and* 3 P.M.; in forenoon, *obliging him to lie down,* with tearing around knuckles and on dorsum of foot; often about 10 P.M. and nearly always on waking, but not at night unless she happened to be up; from drinking; after eating, with vomiting; before a meal, and after eating or drinking distention, or pressure and cutting in abdomen; before and after dinner, with imperfect waterbrash; in open air; when sitting, with waterbrash, the N. > walking in open air, then profuse papescent stools; when sitting up in bed, and frequently sudden vomiting; in open air; after the heat; > *brandy;* in pharynx and stomach; *with rare vomiting, but frequent retching, which increased periodically, with oppression.* Ineffectual inclination to vomit and purge, *with cramp in stomach and abdomen, and he imagined he had cholera. Nausea, with anguish; with faintness, tremor, heat all over and shuddering;* with copious flow of tenacious saliva; with flow of viscid saliva from mouth, heat in fauces, stupor and small, frequent pulse; *with failure of vision, pallor* and difficult breathing; with headache and diarrhœa; with sweetish taste in mouth; constricting, then vomiting; as high up as chest in morning on waking, then vomiting of white mucus and a bitter taste in mouth; with distended feeling in stomach, pain as from a fire within, burning in mouth, then vomiting of a greenish fluid, then burning in throat and along œsophagus, tenesmus, slight discharge of mucus, excoriation of anus, then bloody vomiting.

Retching; violent; violent, with vomiting, griping in abdomen and pain; ineffectual; tendency to R. from crying or coughing; as soon as he had taken a few spoonfuls of soup, with vomiting; and vomiting, nearly approaching convulsions; with violent vomiting of much greenish liquid, and two stools consisting of food eaten the previous day, almost undigested; constant, and sometimes vomiting, with spasms of stomach and bowels, weak and quick pulse, frequent dark bloody diarrhœa, frequent coldness of limbs, then soreness of stomach.

Vomiting; all night, with diarrhœa; **every time after drinking** (Eup. per.), *also with pain in abdomen and pharynx; after eating* (Tab.), also without nausea; *on raising head;* whenever he drank, with shivering (Caps.); an hour after getting up; waking her from sleep; < night, > towards morning, when diarrhœa appeared; > water (cold, *Cupr.*); **of all nourishment as soon as it touches the stomach;** *of food; then mucus and green bile;* of food mixed with a tenacious mass; of food mixed with a reddish brown liquid; of food, mucus and a fluid partly acid, partly bitter; of food and white mucus; fragments of food, then water, with relief; of food, then repeated diarrhœa, with relief; sudden V. of food mixed with bile. Incessant vomiting of the milk, with roaring like a wild animal on account of pain.

Difficult V. of the beverage and of yellow-green mucus and water, with bitter taste in mouth, which remained a long time. **Violent vomiting; excited by any substance taken into stomach;** *with sensation as if it would tear out his stomach and intestines;* violent, with frequent unconsciousness, then trembling, abdominal pain and repeated stools; violent, with violent nosebleed; *violent, of a brown turbid matter mixed with mucus and sometimes streaked* with blood; violent, of mucus and bile, also of frothy masses; violent, with internal burning, thirst and heat. *Vomiting of blood; and mucus;* of blood, and evacuation of blood (with burning pain in anus). Evacuation upward and downward of much blood, mixed with bilious matter, with relief; with cutting in stomach. *Bilious V.;* on getting up; of bile and mucus; bilious and watery; bloody and slimy, of green insoluble bile; of green bilious matter and ropy mucus. Vomiting of greenish matter, streaked with blood. Of green matter at night and of whitish stuff next morning. *Bitter; bitter green-yellow liquid;* greenish bitter. Green; on drinking. Grass-green. Yellowish, greenish, stercoraceous. Pinkish. Reddish. Brown and green substances. Brownish fluid, which became green on standing. Of an alternately thin or thick *brownish dark substance, with exertion and increase of pain in stomach.* Discharge of a reddish-black matter through mouth and anus. Vomiting of a yellow fluid; yellow, mixed with frothy saliva or streaks of blood; of a thin, bluish, dirty yellow substance, then debility; of a yellowish fluid, streaked with green. White fluid. Frothy fluid. Watery. Glairy fluid in morning. Glairy substance, tinged with blood. Mucus in morning, with increased saliva; of white mucus; of yellow mucus; of tenacious mucus and a brownish mass. Sour. Of a substance which causes constriction in throat.

Vomiting brings no relief. V., with apprehensions of death; with anxiety, prostration and tightness at throat; *with diarrhœa;* with diarrhœa of greenish bloody water; with diarrhœa, then collapse; with purging and unbearable odor; with pains in abdomen and legs; *with thirst, also with burning in abdomen;* with palpitation; with prostration; with horrid cries. Sudden vomiting, ending in abortion, alternating with diarrhœa, then constipation. Periodic, more a retching. Paroxysmal. Symptoms like cholera, except that the vomited matter was like thin coffee grounds. Attack like sporadic cholera, incessant vomiting, diarrhœa, cramp in calves, livid appearance and evacuation of liquids, showing no signs of blood.

Pressed hand on epigastric region, lamented, groaned and screamed. Distention; and hardness; D., with greater warmth than in rest of body. Fulness; in morning. Repletion in evening, with aversion to food and pain after eating; in epigastric region, with pinching in abdomen. Spasms, with colic, diarrhœa and fainting fits; spasmodic jerks from pit to rectum.

Stomach seemed to jump, then pain with vomiting of fluid, apparently the water he had drunk, which relieved the pains, but they returned and were acute over the whole body. Cramp in S. and abdomen. Stitches as with a thousand red-hot needles; in pit when coughing. Tearing, and in abdomen; transversely across in afternoon when walking; spasmodic. Spasmodic cutting in S., abdomen and chest. Pinching stitching cutting in pit during menses, extending to hypogastrium, and in back and sides of abdomen, so that she had to bend double when standing or sitting, with loud eructations, moaning and weeping. *Tearing boring in S. and intestines, with spasm.* Pinching in pit, towards r. side of abdomen, causing her to stoop. Gnawing and pricking in pit (acute and fine beating), with tense feeling. Gnawing, corrosive pain. Cardialgia.

Pain; in epigastric region; across epigastric region; in epigastric and umbilical regions; in epigastrium and chest; in gastric region; *in pit; in pit, arresting breathing;* in evening; at exterior wall when talking; from eating; when she drank; after breakfast and dinner, with empty eructations and nauseating relaxation of body; after eating, so that he could not stand up; in epigastrium after evening meal, with nausea and indifferent appetite; at orifice after eating, and in fauces as if food remained high up, then empty eructations; *from violent retching; on pressure; in pit; in pit, with heat;* epigastrium and upper abdomen; *and navel region;* and abdomen, more at large end of S. Pain on touch; in epigastrium; and abdomen; and bladder; then more in regions of liver and abdomen; > *sweet milk;* with constantly increasing anxiety and cries for help; with headache; with cramp, vomitings and waterbrash in S. and lower part of chest, with heat; in epigastrium, with heat; in epigastrium, with tension, alternating with headache. Intermittent pain.

Pain in epigastrium as if cut off from hypogastrium, with anguish and lamentations about his pains. Pain as if S. would be distended and torn to pieces. Pain as if full of flatus, < after vomiting and diarrhœa. Paroxysmal P.; in epigastric region. Spasmodic, with writhing, moaning and making strange faces; periodic spasmodic P., and in abdomen. Throbbing pain in epigastrium, preventing sleep. Painful drawing, with shivering. *Drawing pain in pit in evening when sitting, extending around lower border of l. ribs,* as if something were torn loose. Smarting P.

Burning pain (Ox. ac.); *and in abdomen; < pressure;* in epigastrium and upper abdomen, < pressure; extending to pharynx. **Burning; in pit; in region;** *in epigastrium;* in cardiac portion; < motion of child in *uteri;* > vomiting; with uneasiness; with pressure as of a load; with pain in S. and liver, < touch; *with thirst; with anxiety and retching;* with tenderness of epigastrium and cramps, with aching; in epigastrium and throat, with constriction in latter; in S. and chest, with oppression; extending from pylorus to throat; from pit to throat, where it is most violent, causes scraping and hinders swallowing. Heat rises from S.

Internal chilliness in epigastric region, and he is never clad warm enough, though the parts feel warm to touch. Coldness; in pit. **Anxiety in pit** (Arg. n.); *at night rising high up.* Indescribable anguish in pit, without distention or colic. Constriction in epigastric region. Contraction in S. and pharynx, with painful burning. Strangulating feeling, with sensitiveness to touch. *Gastritis* (Arg. n., Phos., K. bi., etc.). Gastrodynia. Inflammation of alimentary mucous membrane. Dreadful suffering in epigastrium. Distress; then nausea and vomiting. *Soreness in pit when talking, drawing breath or moving about* (Bry.); when coughing. Tensive sensation in epigastric region. *Could not bear any wine. Digestion weak,* with dislike to meat. Inability to digest food, especially meat. Indigestion in various forms. Acidity. *Weight after eating, as from a stone* (Bry.). Heaviness; with anorexia. Weakness of epigastrium after micturition, so that she trembled. Sinking.

Clinical.—Most violent gastro-enteritis, even ulceration, and various diseases of the stomach (cancerous, etc.), are cured by Arsenic, always with a few characteristic indications, extreme thirst, with extreme irritability of the stomach, which will retain but little, if anything, extreme soreness, with burning heat. In less serious conditions it is frequently useful, for instance, persistent deathly nausea of pregnancy, chronic catarrh of the stomach; the whole inner portion of the stomach seems raw; constrictive pain when the stomach is empty. Severe gastralgia brought on by the slightest food or drink, the patient thinks that she shall die, with profound prostration, the pain is burning hot and extends up sides and over abdomen.

Abdomen.—Inclined to lie on. **Swollen; and painful**; and tympanitic; every morning, then emission of flatus; after stool. Distention after eating, > leaning his back against something. Softness. Retraction; with feeling as in lead colic, and little sensitiveness to pressure. Walls contracted and almost touch spinal column, recti muscles stretched like a rope. *Tension;* of muscles, outline distinct, with pain in r. hypochondrium on firm pressure. Unevenness from epigastric region to pubis and to hypochondria, caused by spasmodic contractions of abdominal muscles and of viscera, with faintness, sickness and purgings of bright green color like paint. Spasms in evening after lying down, with pinching and with sweat, then emission of flatus and thin stool. Gurgling. Rumbling; morning on waking; then twisting and cutting, then diarrhœic stools. Flatulence; after eating; putrid smelling flatus. Increased peristaltic action. Hæmorrhage.

Cramp; beginning in abdomen. *Stitches, extending into vagina. Tearing;* with nausea and vomiting.

(Lancinating tearing and gnawing, and in stomach.) *Cutting;* and tearing, with coldness of hands and feet and with cold sweat on face; before diarrhœa, with twisting; with vomiting; clawing, in evening after lying down and in morning after rising, sometimes darting through abdominal ring (as if a hernia would protrude) into spermatic cord and perineum, then rumbling and grumbling. Pinching as if diarrhœa would occur. Griping; and free movement of bowels.

Pain; in afternoon, with diarrhœa and chilliness, the pain continuing after the diarrhœa; at night; at midnight, especially in hypogastrium, then burning in stomach; on touch; < touch of bed-covers, with tension; < pressure; > *after stool;* **with unbearable anxiety**; with tense and heavy sensation in r. epigastric and hypogastric regions; with urging to stool, then diarrhœa; with diarrhœa and vomiting; with constipation; with heat in face; and in legs; *so that he rolled about the floor and despaired of his life;* so violent that she had to hold on to the houses to prevent falling; causing screams. Twisting pain and griping; twisting before and during stool, with pinching and rumbling. Deep-seated. Pain moving, with diarrhœa and pains in anus. Pain becomes seated in l. side. Intermittent, smarting. Sore. Bruised, as if crushed, during cough. Drawing pain, which moved to the head, where there was a beating and still more a jerking, then it extended to the l. side, where sudden jerking stitches were felt.

Burning pain; noon and afternoon, > after stool; *increased to sharp pain on pressure;* especially in side. *Burning;* < stretching feet, with constriction; *with heat and thirst;* and in throat and chest. *Anxiety, with pain so violent that he grasped bystanders and again pushed them from him, frequently jumped out of bed and sat on the chamber or ran about;* A., with fever and thirst. Piteous complaints that *an unpleasant sensation in A. and* **anguish** *took away his breath* and forced him to bend double in this or that direction or to rise and walk about. Discomfort. Intestines feel as if drawn together. Drawing and pressure, as from incarcerated flatus. Uneasiness when at rest. Pulsation extending deep inwardly. Weakness of muscles.

Pain in upper abdomen. Tendency to inflammation of duodenum, with pain. Digging in r. side of A., with pressure. Pain in r. side. Rheumatic pain in l. side. *Liver,* congestion and torpidity, with various symptoms resulting therefrom, and bilious and feverish attacks; *pain over region of liver, also < pressure;* pain in liver when walking in open air; tenderness in region, > diarrhœa; irritation of L., with yellowish or sickly pale look.

Spleen hypertrophied. Stitches under short ribs, < lying on that side. Lancinations under l. short ribs in evening after lying down. Cutting below last ribs, < touch. Hypochondria tense and shaken by convulsions; increased tension of H. during paroxysm of fever, and he is almost unable to lie on that side. Pain in r. hypochondrium; and in adjoining lumbar region, extending through side of scrotum, sometimes into r. groin and side of abdomen, like renal colic. Drawing stitching under l. H. when clearing throat, extending into chest.

Umbilicus.—*Pain about, causing him to bend forward, < touch, attempting to raise himself or to lie on back;* drawing pain in region; pains which were in the stomach at first passed down into intestines, he pressed with his r. hand on the navel and *cried that his intestines were burning.* Pains below U.

Hypogastrium.—*Pinching increasing to cutting, in morning, before, during and after diarrhœa.* Cutting. Slow stitches in groins. Pain on pressure. Pain in inguinal and iliac regions, < pressure. Sprained pain in groin and r. lumbar region when stooping. Contractive pain in l. groin during micturition. Sensation of a bar around flanks. Burning in groin.

Clinical.—Metro-peritonitis, nausea, vomiting, profound prostration, cold sweat, brown tongue, burning pain, etc. Catarrhal enteritis. Ulceration of the bowels. Enlarged spleen, with paroxysms of violent pain. Enlarged liver. Inflammations of the liver, associated with inflammations of the kidneys. A great variety of inflammatory disorders of the abdominal viscera, characterized by extreme sensitiveness, tendency to collapse and general Arsenic symptoms. Dropsy of abdomen.

Rectum.—*Painful spasmodic protrusion of;* remains protruded after hæmorrhage. *Hæmorrhage.* Stitches during menses, extending to anus and pudendum; deep in, with itching. Prickling; as if passing sand. *Burning; after stool* (Æsc. h.), *with weakness and trembling in all limbs.* Peculiar feeling of smarting and pain at end, with inclination to evacuate, but not tenesmus. *Urging to stool;* driving out of bed; constant U.; *ineffectual. Tenesmus; as in dysentery, with burning, pain and pressure in rectum and anus* (Sulph., Nit. ac.); with mucous stools; with stools tinged with blood.

Anus.—*Hæmorrhoids; blind, painful, with slow hot prickings;* bleeding and protruding; with pricking when walking and sitting, not at stool. Twitching. *Hæmorrhoidal tenesmus, causing burning pain,* < at night, preventing sleep, < in day and increasing to stitches, < walking. Soreness when touched. *Burning;* > hard, knotty stool; with itching. Itching; and in privates, with soreness and sometimes *sharp* pain. Itching scraping or smarting. Corrosive itching in perineum.

Clinical.—Hæmorrhoids, with burning like fire, > heat.

Stool.—*Watery;* and offensive; and painful; and frequent; profuse; profuse, with relief; *only of blood and water;* white, curdy; ash-colored, like dirty water, with yellow mucus, without pain or tenesmus; yellow, scanty, then tenesmus and colic around umbilicus; frequent yellowish, after pinching in lower abdomen, with thirst; *contained acrid water. Greenish,* watery, involuntary; G. watery, painless; G. bloody water, with vomiting; watery, mixed with lumps of green mucus. *Violent, watery. Black fluid,* **burning the anus,** *after uneasiness and pain in abdomen.*

Diarrhœa; in afternoon; from fruit or fresh vegetables (China.); < night, **with coldness of extremities** (Sec. c., Verat.); **with vomiting** (Verat.); **with prostration**; with tenesmus; with much rumbling; *with abdominal pain,* also with grasping of hands towards head and drawing of the legs up high; with itching and soreness of anus; *with tearing and cutting in abdomen;* with anxiety and cutting in abdomen and exhaustion; difficult; *dark, bloody-colored; black mucous, with persistent vomiting;* chronic, dark, muddy, offensive, forcible and sudden, and he turns pale at the same time; *frequent, violent, offensive, black; yellow, with tenesmus and burning pain in rectum and anus* (Aloe); yellow, with bitter mouth; olive-green; inodorous, also unhealthy; inodorous as after indigestion. *Dysentery-like. Slimy,* morning and forenoon, preceded by griping and followed by straining; S., having a hacked appearance. Containing grumous particles. Bilious. (Greenish dark brown, smelling like a putrid ulcer.) Profuse, first white, then yellowish half-liquid, involuntary, while standing, as if one suddenly opened the pipe of a vessel containing liquid. Scybalous passages of clayey color. Diarrhœa alternating with constipation.

Constipation; *with pain in abdomen.* Hard stool, with vomiting; scanty; black; black at first, afterwards stools covered with bilious mucus. (Knotty, unsatisfactory.) At first thick stools, at last diarrhœic, green.

Stools black, acrid, putrid. *Black;* containing black matter and worms. Discharge of a reddish-black matter through mouth and anus. *Blackish-brown bilious, with griping.* Brownish, mixed with mucus. Yellowish-brown. *Dark, offensive, frequent,* and at same time vomiting of a clear mucous odorless liquid. Green; streaked with green and offensive. Bloody; with tenesmus; contained bloody mucus. *Watery blood with and surrounding S.* Evacuation upward and downward of much blood mixed with bilious matter, with relief, covered with a mass which appeared combined of jelly and bile. *Expulsion of pieces of mucus, with tenesmus and cutting in anus, as from blind hæmorrhoids.* Stools unhealthy, pale, with constant passing of mucus and rarely of blood; of white tenacious mucus, similar to rinsings of intestines, which masses formed lumps of the size of a fist.

Stools excoriated skin about anus. Contained a ball, seemingly of undigested fat mixed with tendinous parts. Profuse S. *Small S. after colic, with tenesmus, first of dark-green fæces, then of dark-green mucus.* Frequent calls, with scanty discharges of brick-red fluid. *Involuntary; and micturition;* and copious, painless; copious at every act of vomiting; serous, corroding, as if there were fire at anus. *While fully conscious she discharges stool and urine unawares;* supposing it to be flatus. Frequent; in afternoon; but not effectual; mixed with slimy, fatty masses. Retarded. No stool.

Clinical.—Diarrhœas generally dark, scanty, watery or mucous, sometimes bloody. Stools may be brown or black, burning, putrid, brought on by eating or drinking, or < after midnight, preceded by most violent burning and cutting pains and followed by extreme exhaustion; the general Arsenic symptoms are usually present. Constipation rare, abdomen painful.

Urinary Organs.—Urethra. *Burning;* **on urinating** (Sulph.); in anterior part in morning at beginning of micturition. Urethritis. Deep-seated tearings. Biting pain. Urging to urinate; *frequent,* with copious urine; frequent, which at times is accomplished only with difficulty; constant urging, with burning in bladder; constant urging, with hot and dark urine; *desire which he cannot satisfy,* and with a catheter only a few spoonfuls of clear urine are discharged.

Micturition involuntary (Caust.); *of scanty urine.* Frequent at night, with a large quantity each time. Difficult; spasmodic difficulties. Strangury; with red urine. Ischuria; with pain in bladder. *Urine retained;* in spite of all internal exertions to pass it; *as if bladder were paralyzed.*

Urine copious; and dark brown (Benz. ac.); *burning hot.* **Scanty; and burning** (Canth., Merc. c.); *passed with difficulty;* and dark yellow, and depositing lithate of ammonia; drawn by catheter, and giving the characteristic reaction of *glycosuria.* Almost colorless. Red. Dark, wine-yellow, with pressure. (Greenish, dark brown, turbid when emitted, looking like cow-dung stirred up with water, and forming no sediment.) *Hæmaturia* (Phos., Tereb.). Turbid U. Red sand and pain in passing it. Much sediment. Brick-dust sediment.

Clinical.—Acute and chronic inflammation of the kidneys, either idiopathic or associated with various diseases, the urine is scanty, hot, there are generally great œdema and dropsy, very irritable stomach and bowels, great thirst. Inflammation of the bladder, with extreme burning on urinating. The urine is usually very scanty with all diseases, suppressed (in Asiatic cholera or in dropsy), thick, sometimes fetid. Diabetes has been cured.

Sexual Organs.—*Painful swelling.* Sharp pain. Sphacelus of male. *Penis swollen* (Merc. c., Rhus t.); *blue-red and cracked;* and burning; painful, with violent efforts to urinate. Pain in penis, bladder and kidneys. Itching on glans; corrosive, on posterior part. Stitching itching on tip of prepuce. Discharge of prostatic juice, with diarrhœic stool. Erections in morning; with burning in anterior part of prepuce; rare and incomplete. Frequent priapism. Scrotum swollen; all the reddened part covered with small vesicles discharging slightly and reddening in dessication; cuticle peeled off leaving *cutis vera* exposed, inflamed and bleeding, both testes were enlarged and could not be touched. Loss of power. Strong desire. Emission, with sexual dreams; without dreams, then continued erection.

Female.—Itching. Tenderness of labia. *Sudden profuse discharge of dark blood from vagina.* Discharge of bloody mucus after menses (Zinc.). *Leucorrhœa;* while standing and emitting flatus; *copious, yellowish, thick and corrosive* (Sep.); yellow, offensive, watery after menses, with discharges from rectum of blood and purulent mucus, with burning pain. Uterine suffering. Uterine weakness, with abdominal pain and nervous prostration. Active fœtal movements during the attack (she was seven months advanced in pregnancy). Premature delivery. Difficult and distressing delivery of a stillborn fœtus, apparently between fifth and sixth month, and great weakness, though there was no flooding. *Amenorrhœa* (Puls.). *Constant exhausting menorrhagia* (Phos., Sec. c.). *Menses too early* (Calc. c.). *Menses profuse* (Calc. c.); pale (Phos.); and scanty (Sulph.); suppressed; and, in their stead, stitches in gluteal region and in shoulders. Furor, and if not satisfied spontaneous orgasm.

Clinical.—Hydrocele in a child. It has been found valuable in inflammations of the pelvic viscera, pelvic cellulitis, uterine enlargement and tumors, ulcerations and cancer of the uterus, uterine hæmorrhage; in all these diseases the indications are lancinating burning pains, etc. Leucorrhœa acrid, burning, offensive, thin, or sometimes thick and yellow, with general anæmia, etc. Burning pain in r. ovary, amenorrhœa, instead of menses profuse, excoriating leucorrhœa. Granulations on inner surface of uterus, with pains as from red-hot wires.

Respiratory Organs.—*Air passages seem constricted. Larnyx dry.* Spasm of glottis (Chlorine.). *Hoarseness;* on waking, *with pain in chest;* toneless voice. Husky and guttural. Voice hollow, speech unintelligible. *Voice trembling;* and speech monosyllabic; *uneven, now strong, now weak.* Feeble, whispering, thick and rough. Aphonia. Bronchitis; obstinate.

Cough; evenings directly after lying down (Dro.)*; evening after lying down, she has to sit up, then contractive pain in epigastric region and pit of stomach, this pain continued the cough, which made her weak; evenings before sleep, from a* *smoky sensation in larnyx, as from sulphur fumes;* C. in evening, with nausea and retching; *at night, he has to sit up as soon as it begins* (Con., Hyosc.); *fits of C. wake him at night, as if he would suffocate, and the throat becomes swollen* (Lach.); *when going into cold open air* (Phos., Kali. c., *Dulc.*); when moving the body, frequently putting him out of breath suddenly; on drawing a deep breath or moving about; when he drinks without thirst; *from tickling in larnyx* (Brom.); *from a constrictive sensation in upper part of larnyx, as from sulphur fumes;* from irritation in air passages; < *after drinking* (Phos.); < morning, with expectoration of slimy purulent masses; < night, from tickling in throat, < speaking, causing pain in abdomen, with green expectoration.

Cough, with yellowish expectoration, and bronchitic râles in chest; with muco-crepitant râles (without dulness), in posterior part of lungs. Violent in morning. *Spasmodic;* lasted till heat of summer, with tendency to vomit; waking in middle of night, the coughing fits ending in bringing up a little clear phlegm; *with spasmodic asthma*, bronchitis and congestion of lungs. *Asthmatic* (Iod., Ip.). Short cough; in morning after the (usual) tea-drinking. *Dry C. in evening, with dyspnœa; deep, dry, short C., increasing, after midnight.* Frequent, short, dry, from a suffocative sensation in larnyx, as from sulphur fumes. Dry, choking C., with short, labored breathing and sore pain as if ulcerated, extending from pit of stomach to middle of chest. Irritation to cough, with sore sensation in larnyx.

Spitting of blood; with such nervous irritability that a current of air causes convulsions. The mucus coughed up is streaked with blood (Phos., Sulph.). Discharge of mucus streaked with blood, then nausea. Expectoration painful; thick yellow; green bitter, in morning; difficult to loosen.

Breath lost in evening on getting into bed, with constriction of trachea and wheezing in it like the sound of a fine string. Threatened with suffocation, he puts out his tongue. Imagines she will suffocate, being so weak that she cannot take a deep breath. (*Sudden catarrh at night, threatening suffocation.*) *Suffocative sensation when walking in open air, obliging him to cough;* when ascending stairs (Calc. c.). **Asthma at midnight, making him spring up**; in sleep; when fatigued, as from anguish; beginning with running from nose, then rapid exhaustion, then bronchitis and congestion of lungs (Iod., Aralia r.); spasmodic (Ip.); *the breathing becoming weaker and shorter, until she can only breathe and talk very low by bending chest forward.* **Short anxious breathing.** *Short breathing;* < walking; *as if chest were contracted, after cough;* and irregular; *S., accelerated, moaning.* **Breathing difficult, with anguish**; in sleep; when vexed; when reclining (Ac. ac.); with pain in r. chest and shoulder. Distressed, ending in asphyxia. *Heavy breathing;* as if chest were oppressed, during pain in abdomen. *Painful* breathing; from tender state of abdomen; inspiration painful. Hurried. Slow; and imperfect. Moaning; *spends the night in moaning and groaning.* Sighing.

Clinical.—Laryngeal catarrh, with dryness, burning, sensitiveness. Bronchitis, cough in the night, with rawness behind the larynx. Paroxysmal cough, with suffocation, < cold air. Capillary bronchitis, with extreme anxiety, puffiness of the face, etc. Emphysema, with excessive dyspnœa, suffocative cough, cold perspiration, etc. Asthmatic attacks coming on after midnight, suffocative, with cold sweat, burning in chest, extreme anguish. Asthma especially < cold changes of temperature, feeling of great constriction in air passages and gasping. Dyspnœa from œdema of lungs in Bright's disease, consumption; consolidation of the lungs, with extreme prostration, fever, sweat, etc. Valuable for the cachexia which leads to chronic disease of the lungs. In all pulmonary troubles the cough is < after midnight, < lying on back, expectoration is very scanty, with general Arsenic symptoms. Angina pectoris.

Chest.—Muscles wasted, peculiar sunken appearance. Hollow between his chest and belly, into which "she could have laid her arm." *Suffocative catarrh;* catarrh and oppression of chest, with phlegm; wheezing, with bruised pain between shoulders. Cramp. Twitching.

Stitches; when stooping; *in l. during deep inspiration, obliging to cough;* in side under short ribs, she cannot lie on that side; when coughing in side of chest, then in side of abdomen; under ribs when coughing, and increased headache, as if heat were in it; upward on sides from talking; *upward in sternum when coughing.* Stitching-tearing in region of r. upper ribs. Stitching-tearing, tensive pressing and burning pain. *Pain;* in r. clavicle; at junction of upper and lower sternal regions; in r. side; in lower, on full inspiration; internally in upper part; in r. upper, ending in stitches, < breathing; tensive, < sitting; smarting pain along sternum.

Oppression; evening; wakes at night with O. or spasm in chest and anxiety; *in region of sternum, making respiration difficult;* **when walking fast,** *coughing or ascending stairs;* after eating, with prickling of skin, restlessness and desire for fresh air; with anxiety; sudden while walking, threatening suffocation, with weakness. *Tightness;* as soon as he walked a little; with dryness; as if bound by a hoop; he feels as if he must burst. *Constriction evenings, with anxiety and restlessness;* C. with heaviness; with short and hacking cough; so that he could scarcely speak and came near fainting. Heaviness on sternum. Weight on. Compressive sensation when eating.

Pneumonia of posterior lobes of lungs and partial consolidation of lower lobes of both sides. Inflammation of lungs. Congestion of lungs. Shock in apex of r. lung, with higher percussion sounds than in l., increased auscultation, vesicular murmur and large and fine moist râles. Soreness in chest, with rawness. *Burning internally;* with excruciating pain; extending below diaphragm; in r., extending to groin, where it is a pressure. *Chilliness internally*, in evening and after supper. Creeping internally. *Lassitude when walking, with oppression of breathing.*

Heart.—Sounds, especially the "choc," violent, not agreeing with the small pulse. Decided *bruit de souffle. Cramp.* Pain in region; burning P. in region, with tumultuous beating of heart and feeling as if it were turning inside out and everything were spilling out of it. Præcordial anxiety. Oppression in region. Sensation as if pressed down. Inflammation, and its results, dilatation and œdema of feet.

Irritable. Palpitation (Spig., Thea); *at night* (Sulph.); **after stool, with tremulous weakness, so that he has to lie down; irregular, but so violent at 3 A.M. that he imagines he hears it, with anguish;** *visible and audible, at night;* visible in carotid, causing beads of sweat on face; with profuse sweat; with vomiting; *with small irregular pulse.* Tumultuous beating, but no pulse. Violent action, and one hears a violent blowing sound, with full rapid pulse. Irregularity of heart's action and breathing. Beats faster and stronger when lying on back. Quick and faltering; and feeble, also with no pulse at wrist. Slow, with weak pulse. *Weak; and irregular;* almost imperceptible, small, irregular.

Clinical.—Very valuable in weak heart, which is irritable, rapid action on the slightest provocation. Tumultuous action of heart, palpitation. Irritable heart of smokers or of tea-drinkers. Occasionally indicated in inflammatory affections of the heart, endocarditis, hypertrophy, dropsy about the heart.

Pulse.—Rapid; weak and irregular (Dig.); *weak and unequal, with occasional indication of fluttering;* soft and jerking; full and hard; sharp, but easily compressible; hard, irregularly accelerated; full and compressible, then fluttering, then weak. Slow and hardish. Tense; and small. Full and strong. *Feeble; and small.* Small, contracted and intermitting. Restless, small, increased after repeated vomiting. *Pulseless;* with frequent, irritated beating of heart.

Neck.—Drawn by spasms to l. side and backward. Distortion of muscles. Painless swelling. Swelling of an artery on l. side when stooping. Neuralgia on l. side, then paralyzed feeling. Pain in morning on waking, across nape and shoulders; P. in vertebræ on pressure; cramplike P. on l. side. Stiffness; of nape; *of nape as if bruised or sprained,* night and morning, and a similar pain over hips. Lost the use of muscles of nape.

Back.—Pain; with uneasiness and anxiety; with weakness and inclination to lie down, which did not relieve; with painful drawing on external surface of extremities. Beating, drawing and stitching pain at night in back, small of back and thighs. Bruised pain; and across scapulæ. Burning pain, < sitting up. Drawing pain in forenoon. Drawing up and down. Gurgling movements in muscles of l. side when lying on r. side. *Weakness.*

Spine.—Unmistakable alteration of cord, which may manifest itself as myelitis centralis acuta or poliomyelitis acuta, in more chronic cases inflammation may result, not only of the gray substance, but of the white also, constituting a diffuse myelitis (comp. Phos.). Tearing in lower part. Acute pain in lower part. Neuralgia at top, extending to vertex. *Stiffness beginning in region of os coccygis.* Weakness, with coldness and tenderness.

Pain across scapulæ, extending down arms. Drawing pain between *scapulæ, obliging him to lie down.* Pain in region of two last dorsal vertebræ. Stitches in region of kidneys when inspiring and sneezing. Loins, tensive tearing, especially below curve of l. rib, where it is sensitive to touch; pain; pain after vomiting; periodical pain; *bruised pain; drawing pain from loins to shoulders,* with stitches in sides and flatus moving about in abdomen and pressing up, > eructations; painful contraction over anus, towards loins; **weakness**; painful stiffness. *Drawing from sacrum to nape,* causing trunk to bend backward.

Extremities.—*Nails* lost; badly colored; altered color and peeled off; livid, violet; dirty yellowish brown, with longitudinal furrows and cracks; changed color nearly every month, at first fiery red, then black, as if suffused with blood, then new nails, which were thin and transparent. Swelling. Atrophy of muscles. Hands and feet as if mummified, so that the skin hung in folds about the bones, which protruded. Hands and feet wasted, so that joints protruded, and so paralyzed that nothing could be held firmly, the feet would not permit him to rise, on stepping he always planted the flat sole and on walking dragged his feet like weights.

Convulsions; with rigidity and pain. Distortion. *Twitching;* with painful drawings starting from back. *Startings on falling asleep.* Stretching from time to time and remaining in that condition several moments on account of relaxation, then vomiting with renewed violence. *Contractions;* in knees and elbows; drawing together of upper and lower. Toes and fingers continually flexed, > after profuse loss of blood by vomiting and from anus, after being bent straight they appeared dead, but, after a warm bath, life returned to hands and feet, and the toes and fingers again remained bent. Contraction of flexors of four last fingers of both hands and of all toes, the two last phalanges flexed upon the first and the balls of fingers and toes rested on palms and soles, so that walking was difficult. Cramp; with rigor and numbness; in legs and arms. *Trembling;* after a moderate walk; after vomiting; with jerking; of r. arm and lower extremity; in hands and feet, with prickling. Hands and feet constantly agitated.

Stitches in hands and feet. Tearing; in long bones; *in arms and lower limbs, < lying on affected side, > motion of affected part;* sudden tearing jerking or stitching in thumb or big toe in morning in bed, changing to a burning. Gnawing in legs and arms; as of rats, or like the boring of a gimlet into bones. Neuralgia in arms and legs. Pain; with stiffness; with dread of moving them; with feeling of sickness; occasional, in joints, as shoulder and knee. Wandering pain; especially in arms, which were weak. Arthritic pain in shoulders and hips. Drawing pain; > by exercise; in joints of knees, feet and hands; in evening in foot and middle finger. Sensitiveness of muscles. Uneasiness before retiring, > lying down.

Weakness (Phos., Merc., Plumb., Verat., Mur. ac.); < r. side; paralytic, at a certain hour every day; with stiffness, so that it was difficult to hold anything and his gait became stumbling; especially from knees to toes, with crawling; of wrists and ankles, with stiffness and pain; in joints in forenoon, < sitting, with pain; of hands and feet, with trembling feeling in morning; of fingers and toes as the gastro-enteritis got better, slowly extending to knees and wrists, with numbness.

Heaviness. Stiffness; of fingers and toes; < l., with diminished sensibility (of all joints, with inability to stretch himself because of tension in whole body, and with stiffness and coldness of knees, so that he tied handkerchiefs around them, otherwise they were painful and disturbed sleep). Tingling; in hands and feet, with burning. Creeping as if asleep. Falling asleep, with insensibility; of r. arm and foot. Numbness; in arms and legs, also with pain; in arms and legs, with prickling and weight, like being asleep, arms > raising them in an upright position; of hands and feet, also with pains day and night, preventing sleep; in hands and feet, with paralysis; of finger-tips, and in feet, where there was occasional cutting; of soles, and diminished sensation in hands; of limbs, with pain across shoulders, extending down arms. Diminished sensibility; in finger-tips, spreading over hands and arms, then in toes, spreading over feet and legs.

Ataxia of muscles, with gait as in excessive chorea, and the hands could hardly be held up. Lost the use of hands and feet, legs and arms, there was little sensation below instep, with soreness in arch of r. foot on motion and pressure, cramps in all muscles of lower limbs at once, especially in plantaris of r. leg, with neuralgic pain in forearm and legs below hips, the pains increasing to a climax, then gradually diminishing, < cold air or water and between 9.30 P.M. and 8 A.M., the paralysis was both of sensation and motion, though the paralyzed parts were sensitive to cold. Paralysis; with anæsthesia and violent pains; sometimes general and affects both upper and lower limbs; of feet, hands and arms; of arms and legs, with pain in muscles and in bowels; of l. arm and leg, with sensibility of skin and coldness in limbs.

Paresis, with crampy pains in feet, calves, hands and abdomen, no use of arms or legs, great muscular atrophy, tremor, no patellar reflex, but slight hyperæsthesia, later hand and feet felt numb and prickling, itching over body and limbs, formication of feet, sensation of a tight cord around waist, "throat felt as if gone at times," legs flexed and contracted, extension caused pain in flexor muscles and tendons, muscæ volitantes, dropping of wrists and ankles. Faradic reactions of nerves and muscles of limbs lost, daily a fainting spell, with dyspnœa, cardiac sounds feeble, later lower limbs œdematous, difficulty in flexing fingers into palms, tabetic gait, two apparent gastric crises of locomoter ataxia, diarrhœa, nausea, colic, trembling, etc.

Upper Extremities.—Weakness, with retraction of flexors of fingers. Axilla, (glandular swelling); tearing sticking in r.; soreness in; tingling in. Shoulder, cramplike sensation in l.; neuralgia, afterwards extending to groins, thorax and back, abdomen became tympanitic and muscular paraplegia slowly ensued; neuralgic pain extending to fingers, with numbness; unbearable pain in l.; drawing pain.

Arm.—Painful swelling of r., and hand. Constant motion as if picking at something above the head. Tearing at night in bed, especially in elbow and wrist. Sudden peculiar neuralgia in l. after meals; N. of l., then paralyzed feeling. *Pain in A., of that side on which he lies at night;* P. < l., which was weak; in l. ulnar nerves; drawing. Weakness. Going to sleep of r. if he lies on r. side. Immobility of l. Pain in elbows and fingers; rheumatic P. in r. elbow. Swelling of r. forearm, with pain. Drawing pain in styloid processes every evening. Weakness of wrists, and the fingers could neither grasp nor hold anything smaller than the crutches, which they could hold a little, though there was no sensation in finger-tips even when injured.

Hand.—Swollen. Deep furrows in interosseous spaces in dorsa, the H. looking like skeletons, the palms forming deep concavities. Never recovered their fulness and strength, and the "nævus" almost disappeared. Contractions. Cramp when moving it. *Trembling* (Merc.). Drawing tearing in metacarpal bones in morning. Tearing sticking in bones of H. and of little finger. Pain on extension. Drawing in l., with cramps. Sensitiveness of palms, yet he does not know whether he has taken hold of an object. Weakness. Stiffness and insensibility. Neither extension nor flexion was complete. Motion less impaired than in arm and forearm, especially the ability to bend forearm on arm is almost lost. Numbness, with swelling. Paralysis, beginning with heaviness, without wasting.

Fingers.—(Hard swelling, with pain in bones of fingers.) Ungual phalanges wasted and nails hard, brittle, clawlike. Clenched. Flexed; half-flexed. Two last phalanges of all F. are bent on the first; and the tips touch the palm. F. and hands moved in sleep. Trembling, with occasional creepings in hands and feet. Tonic spasms, cramps, < night in bed; of r. on attempting to stretch them. Painful cramp in lowest joints of all; in tips from morning till noon. Pain in joints when moved. Drawing pain in middle. *Drawing from tips into shoulders, with jerking and tearing.* Could not be moved; could be bent, but not extended. Fuzziness extending up arm, ending in loss of sensation. Sensation blunted as far as wrists. Insensibility; of l. fourth and fifth; as if everything stagnated. Tingling creeping to shoulders, with burning.

Lower Extremities.—*Œdema* (Apis., Merc., Plumb.). Painful swelling. Wasting. Retracted to abdomen. Twitching. Trembling. *Unsteadiness when walking across an open place, with vertigo.* Tottering; and stumbling, as if stiff, with slipping outward of feet. Gait heavy, "slumpy," and it is difficult to raise himself after eating. Painful shocks. Painful cramps. *Tearing; from top to bottom, with inability to tread, sit or lie, had to shake the limb to and fro day and night, or else limp about and had no rest, < night;* on motion, especially in knee and tarsal joint. *Tearing sticking, apparently in periosteum, down to tip of big toe* (Nit. ac.). *Pain;* especially in joints; drawing. **Uneasiness, he cannot be still at night and has to move his feet all the time or walk, to get relief** (Rhus t.). Weakness; with heaviness. *Sensation as if they would break down when descending stairs.* Can walk only a few minutes very slowly. Hyperæsthesia. Wooden sensation. Asleep. Stiffness. Can scarcely be rotated. Immobility; with tearing. *Paralysis;* with insensibility (Phos.); partial P. and desquamation of cuticle.

Muscles of thigh feeble and soft, calf flabby, foot extended so that the back of it formed a line with the spine of the tibia, while the inner margin of the foot was turned inward and upward and the plantar surface looked inward and backward, the instep formed an angle with the tibia directed inward and forward, the joints of ankle and foot were weak, on flexing the leg the foot could be moved in a loose manner, toes flexed and motion restricted.

Thigh.—Convulsions, and of legs. Jerking in hip, then cough, which it seems to incite. Painful cramplike contractions of bundles of muscles of T. and calves in evening in bed, toes being drawn inward, then he became very weak. Paroxysmal cramp-pain of single parts of muscles of T. and legs, and when feeling the parts a jerking as of something alive. Pricking in r. hip. *Drawing tearing in hips and l. foot in morning after a sleepless night.* Drawing tearing from anterior surface of thigh to knee and tarsal joint when walking. *Sciatica.* Intermittent pain extending along crural nerve as far as heel and toes. Pain in anterior and inner part of T. on rising in morning. Soreness between T., with itching. Stiffness as after a long walk, with the headache; S. over hips as if bruised or sprained, night and morning, and a similar pain in nape.

Knee.—Starting as from an electric shock after dreaming directly after lying down that he is going to knock his foot against a stone. Pain. Bruised pain in side when touched and when sitting, sensation as if the flesh were detached. Bruised or sprained pain in l., < rising from a seat. Sensation as if bandaged tightly. Tension in bend when sitting and standing, as if tendons were too short, > walking. Weakness; r. unable to support body. *Stiffness, especially of K. and feet, alternating with tearing;* S., and in ankles. Paralysis.

Leg.—*Swelling;* and of feet; to above calves, preceded by tearing in calves, which went off by application of warm cloths. Dwindling. Calf is hard and as if pressed flat, with cramp-pain, the whole leg cold, insensible and stiff, then tension in calf and a sort of paralysis of leg. Convulsions; and of knees. Twitching; in afternoon when sitting. Contractions of extensors. Convulsive contractions in calves; in legs, with bending up under thigh. Strange nervous affection, with pain and stiffness. *Cramp;* till 11 P.M.; with diarrhœa; and of feet. *Cramp in calves* (Cupr.); when walking; < night in bed. Cramp-pain in leg in morning, ending in humming or buzzing. *Tearing during the shuddering;* T. in tibia; in r. calf when sitting; drawing, from bend of knee to heel, as if sprained. Tearing sticking in lower part. Boring in r. tibia. Drawing, tearing and jerking from ankles to knees. Tearing drawing in tibia. Pain; and in feet; on touch; when stretched; in calves; especially in joints; *drawing P. when resting perpendicularly upon floor while sitting;* pulsating, in head of l. tibia; (jerking from upper to lower part). Muscular soreness. Clucking. Weakness. Heaviness; with weariness; with weariness and drawing, < morning, with bending, unsteadiness and weakness in knees. Feeling as of a weight hanging from them. When he turns on l. side he can easily move the whole r. leg inward or outward, the toes still point towards l. leg, but in l. leg these motions are impossible, and the voluntary extension of feet is impossible. *Stiffness;* of the swollen legs and feet during and after the fever, with pain. *Numbness of legs and feet; with tingling* (Phos.). Prick of a pin had no effect on l., and a hard pinch was requisite to excite motion in r. Paralysis.

Ankle.—Swelling without redness but with tearing, which can be > application of warmth. Tearing; around ankles and on dorsum of feet when lying down, with nausea. Pain on touch.

Foot.—*Œdematous; with exhaustion. Swelling;* then weakness, then heaviness of them; with numbness and creeping in lower limbs; hard, red-blue, green-yellow and painful; shining hot, extending above ankles, with round red spots, causing burning pain. Drawing, so that he cannot hold it still and can step only cautiously. Trembling. Dragged loosely when walking, when lying they lie relaxed and fallen down. Steps flat with the whole sole when walking. Cramps; and in legs to knees, > warm applications and friction. *Stitches* in outer border; in soles; in bottom of l. heel when treading, extending to posterior surface of thigh. Tearing in heels; in metatarsal articulations, with stitches, and with stitches in joints when treading or walking, as if feet were sprained, and ankles feel sore and painful when touched; prickling T. in a corn at night in bed. *Pain;* < motion; < on appearance of menses; in soles on stepping. *Sprained-pain* when in unnatural position and on a misstep; in joints, on top of instep, when stepping. Pain in heels as if they had lain in a hard place, in morning on waking. Prickling pains from soles to about two inches above knees, with sensation lost in l. leg and impaired in r. and loss of motion in both. Numb pain in r., with inability to raise it when sitting except with the hand. *Weakness;* on great exertion; gave way beneath him. Fuzziness, extending a hand's breadth above ankle, with falling asleep and coldness; in soles, with formication and pain; the numbness and pain gradually extending up calves and thighs, with cutting. Soles feel as if made of wood and do not feel the ground. *Numbness,* with stiffness, insensibility and occasional swelling and pain. *Stiffness,* with weakness. Could be moved only when lying. *Paralysis;* preceded by vomiting.

Toes.—Drawn downward (Cupr.). Contracted so that the tips touch the soles, walking is difficult and standing upright causes pain. Flexed, can be extended a little by exertion of the will, but easily with the hand, and her gait is difficult and awkward. Weakness. (Stiffness so that she could not walk.) Numbness to knees (Phos.). Paralysis of extensors and flexors.

Clinical.—**Sciatica coming on at night, > heat, burning pains, anguish.**

Skin.—*White and pasty-looking; W. as in infants, then yellow and scaly, producing an irritating eruption all over body,* with a strong and peculiar smell. *Blue; in spots on abdomen, genitals and in white of eye;* in spots anteriorly on thighs, not removed by pressure. Blue, corrugated and feeling as if parboiled. Yellow on neck; *yellow spots on chest;* upper part of chest; and brown, with rare perspiration; then dusky brown. Livid on arms; on anterior part of chest and neck; *dark and L. on hands and lower half of forearm,* as in malignant cholera. Smutty, mottled, especially on limbs. Smutty brown, especially on uncovered parts. Red over whole body, with moisture; R. spots over whole body; redness of hand, with red points extending half way up forearm. Spots of purpura on neck. Anæmic, lustreless, parchment-like and could be raised in thin folds from the underlying tissues, especially as all fat had disappeared. Hard and horny on toes, especially little toes, which pained like a burning and made walking difficult. *Dry; and rough;* and cracked, *also scaly, very sore,* with a strong and peculiar smell. *Petechiæ* (Phos., Sec. c.); on trunk and thighs; purple, on chest and neck; *red,* circumscribed, in evening, *painful, moist, and burning after scratching.*

Eruptions; **around mouth** (Rhus t.), **burning and painful**; over whole body; chiefly on hands, forearms, scrotum and thighs; on forehead; colorless, biting, around whole neck, on shoulders and on sides; rough cracked, dirty, brownish-red on neck, bosom and shoulder, with burning and itching, which were always < during coryza; reddish-brown, rough in patches on chest anteriorly; itching, dry brownish-red in irregular patches on waist and bosom; *painful black. Rash* red, scorbutic; over whole body, *falling off in scales* (Hydrocotyle); with such pains all over that he could not turn in bed; red anteriorly on body, spreading to whole body except face, skin red, swollen, covered with fine blisters, with itching and burning, disturbing sleep, then desquamation. *Miliary eruption;* on forehead, wrists and feet; with amelioration of all symptoms and re-establishment of urinary discharge, then mealy scales. Nettle-rash; especially on abdomen. *Blotches* on forehead; on hands, with pimples; small white, and the skin colored, smarting and painful, the pain generally < at night; large red blotches, and partially in wheals, on face and neck, spreading over whole body.

Swelling of all parts around orbits; painless under l. eye, soft, partly closing eye (Rhus t.); like a nut on each frontal eminence, < evening; of ears, with erysipelatous redness and blisters, which soon discharge and become gangrenous looking; of l. hand, forearm and axillary glands, with inflammation of hand, and purple patches gradually covering arm and side. *Œdema of head, face, eyes, neck and chest.* General erysipelas, with sensation of a devouring fire.

Desquamation; from head to foot; of whole body except head; of the cuticle and skin of tongue; scaling and irritating eruptions, which nothing relieves but Turkish baths. Eruption on face dried into scabs, and nose and lids scaled. Eruption on face dries, here and there scabs fall off, and on l. concha new blisters form.

Pimples on hands, chest and forehead; on thumb; around mouth; *burning, causing anguish;* red, conical, over hands and fingers, with *itching*, **which is < by scratching**; painful nodes on r. arm; small, on several parts, *causing burning pain*, but not much itching; pointed, with itching, > scratching in region of l. temple, exuding bloody water when scratched and painful and sore when rubbed; itching, between eyebrows, exuding bloody water and then filled with pus; whitish pointed, the tips filled with watery fluid, *with burning itching*, on hands, between fingers and on abdomen, the fluid flows out on scratching and the itching disappears. Inflamed spot on l. side of face, by the parotids, red, solid, painful, appearing yellow on pressure. Inflammation of lower part of abdomen, penis, scrotum and upper part of thighs, with ulcerations in some places, burning pain and constitutional derangement.

Deep gangrene (Sec. c.). Whitlow. Abscesses on hands, then pain in wrists and arms; on posterior side of arm above wrist, on opening it copious discharge of thick yellow pus, with denudation of surface of ulna. Boils; which refuse to heal; on back; digging burning pain in the boil in groin when touched. Sores on head and neck. *Pustules;* on forehead; face; l. cheek; about angles of mouth; on chest; on neck and arms, especially painful at night; pale red, between thumb and index, with pain < in evening; itchlike, then desquamation and itching; as in varioloid, on face and upper part of body; partly confluent, easily torn open, changed to thick crusts and left scars, on forehead, about eyes, on cheek-bones, shoulders, upper part of arm and chest.

Blistering of feet. *Vesicles* covering face; about mouth; *black, causing burning;* on face, with itching; coalescing, surrounded by a red base, over ear and on nose; over whole body except limbs, with inflamed appearance of skin between them; containing clear watery liquid, on inner side of thumbs; filled with yellow fluid, on the red inflamed part of face, the redness and inflammation spreading about nose and mouth. Discrete papulo-vesicular eruption on trunk and upper limbs, with itching < at night. *Shingles.* (Ran. b., Rhus t.). Eczema. Herpes-like spot on side of neck, and upon face, with *itching and burning*, l. then r.; *red herpetic skin around mouth.* (Itchlike eruption, especially in bends of knees.)

Ulcers on face; which did not yield to treatment; around lips; cancerous, ulcer necessitating amputation of the limb; *on leg, with gray crust and surrounded by an inflamed border*, **it is burning and painful**; with very high edges; *much coagulated blood comes out;* on heels, discharging ichorous matter. **Burning pain in ulcers.** *Burning in border of ulcer and itcing in U. itself;* **around ulcer,** *which is fetid and suppurates, with faintness and drowsiness in daytime.* Tearing in U. Painful ulcers, < morning, with dark-brown, thin, bloody pus under a thin scurf, with single stitches while sitting, the stitches > standing and still more walking. Suppuration and swelling around the spreading U., especially on abdomen, genitals and inside of thighs. Fleshy excrescences spring up from U. on fingers, they soon become decayed, blue and green, with viscid ichor, spreading an intolerable odor. Painful sensitiveness of old U. previously painless.

Stitches; *slow, hot, here and there.* Pain; burning P. < walking, in the horny skin on toes, especially little toes. Prickling over whole body; after eating, with restlessness, oppression of chest and desire for fresh air. Tickling in l. palm. Sensibility or irritation, with vesicles, sometimes nettle-rash or the eruption of scarlet fever. Smarting and itching disturbing him at night, forcing him to apply cold water compresses, he got a little sleep about 4 A.M. *Formication, with trembling* (Phos.); F. on r. arm and forearm; hands and feet; hands at night; fingers and toes toward evening; *in lower limbs. Habit of picking fingers and lips till they bled* (Arum tri.).

Itching over whole body; with exhalation of back all night; with blotches and rawness; under r. ear, with pimples; on backs of fingers, with pointed papulæ between fingers; at inner surface of thighs, afterwards becoming seated on l. side of scrotum, with redness of that side only and of posterior part of penis, and with heat. Tickling I. in r. middle finger. Creeping I. in thighs as far as abdomen and in loins and nates; tickling creeping I. of r. big toe, as in a healing wound. **Burning I.**; *with pain after scratching;* around eyes and temples as if pricked with red-hot needles. Biting I. on forearm near wrist; of thighs; r. thigh near groin.

Clinical.—Eruptions on face. The skin diseases requiring Arsenic are, as a rule, dry, scaly, with soreness, intense itching and burning. In unhealthy states of the skin and in low fevers we may have ulcerations and even gangrenous sloughs. It is sometimes, but rarely, indicated in vesicular and even pustular eruptions, when the general symptoms of the patient correspond. It has cured a great number of indurations and tumors even after the ulcerative stage has been reached. In all these (numerous) diseases the general indications must be followed.

Sleep.—Yawning; after eating, with weakness; with stretching. *Sleepiness;* in daytime when sitting; sleepiness, but no sleep. Sleepiness alternating with restlessness. Slumber and slight delirium. Sleep between acts of vomiting. Heavy sleep; with tendency to walk in sleep. Sleep at night alternates with raving and different visions. *Drowsiness interrupted by uneasy dreams and anxiety.*

Sleeplessness; till 3 A.M.; *with restlessness, and moaning;* with creeping in abdomen; with fainting fits. **Startings of various kinds in evening when falling asleep; tossing about, sleeps only at times after 3 A.M.** *Restless; and disturbed by dreams; and disturbed till* 1.30

A.M. *by attacks of cough*, anxiety and heat; with feeling as if a chill were coming on; tries to uncover, jumps out of bed, with a fixed stare, and tears her clothes off. General sick feeling in sleep. He hears every sound during the morning slumber, yet dreams. Moaning in sleep in evening; M. < about 3 A.M., with tossing about. Talking and quarreling. Loud talking and indistinct murmuring with half-closed eyes. He complains in sleep of headache, now in forehead, now in occiput. Light sleep, with muttering delirium. *Feeling in morning as if she had not slept enough; with weary eyes and inability to get out of bed.*

Dreams, uninterrupted, about thunderstorms, fire, black water and darkness; full of care, sorrow and fear, disturbing sleep; full of care and danger, he wakes with a cry and when asleep dreams of something else; full of care, he wakes and then continues his dream. Anxious; while falling asleep, he wants to cry out, but cannot, and is suddenly waked by that cry, which he hears yet. D. and nightmare, and the dreams hovered before his mind even during the day, disquieting him. Frightful. Full of threats, apprehension or repentance. Vivid, vexatious. *About death*, catalepsy, did not know where she was on waking. Sexual, with emissions.

Fever.—Chilliness; in daytime, then thirst, in evening heat in face; *in afternoon, with shuddering about head, stretching and drawing in limbs, then chilliness and gooseflesh, from 8 till 9* P.M., *heat over body, especially face, without sweat, with cold hands and feet; towards evening; then heat;* towards evening, then sweat without heat; towards evening, with drowsiness, general sick feeling, as after a paroxysm of fever, after midnight sweat on thighs, *the attack returning at same hour two days afterwards;* evening in bed; in evening and in morning on waking; every day at 3 P.M., with hunger; > after a meal; at night in bed; on waking, or fever; on entering house, then hiccough, then general sweat, then again hiccough; when talking or moving about, with ill humor and flushes of heat, then redness of face, with chilliness; before vomiting, then heat of skin, which is cold to touch; *after the heat.*

Coldness, with chattering of teeth, distortion of facial muscles and trembling; *of body and dryness of skin alternating with cold sweat;* general C., with profuse sweat; with cold feet, yet he began to sweat; with dryness of whole body, especially hands and feet; with chattering teeth, but red and hot forehead; with internal heat like fulness or fire in vessels; then dry heat of skin; alternating with heat; with alternating burning pain in stomach and anxiety. *Internal C. in afternoon, with external heat and red cheeks.* Internal C., but not external, or else heat internal, but not external, except perhaps in palm.

Shivering; in morning, alternating with heat; in forenoon without thirst, with spasms in chest, pain in whole body and a kind of inability to use one's senses, then heat, with thirst, then sweat and roaring in ears; every day at 5 P.M.; every evening before retiring; **when walking in open air**; *after dinner; after drinking;* from slightest chill from dampness or sitting in a cold church, with abdominal pain, diarrhœa, rapid loss of strength and distressed countenance; during the pains, then thirst; > after dinner (rare alternate effect); **without thirst**; with shaking of head; with heat of external ear, anguish and gnawing in pit of stomach and nausea; general, with hot forehead, warm face and cold hands, or with warm forehead, hot cheeks and cold hands; *is apt to be accompanied with other ailments;* after drinking, as from disgust. Feverish S.; every evening.

Ague, quotidian, sometimes tertian. Chilliness every other day at 6 P.M., with weariness of thighs and bruised feeling, on third day at 5 P.M. inclination to lie down, then chilliness over whole body without thirst, then heat without thirst, and oppressive aching in forehead. *Intermittent fever, chilly between* 8.30 *and* 9 A.M., *after getting out of bed, till* 1 P.M., *with chattering of teeth, nails and lips blue, sometimes sickness on waking, bad taste, desire for much cold drink, pulse feeble, wants to lie down, be quiet and wrapped up, breath offensive, tongue brown, then fever till* 4 *or* 5 P.M., *with full pulse, frontal pain, not much thirst, especially hot to touch on abdomen, with pain there, feet and hands cold objectively, cannot bear draught of air, breath offensive, tongue brown, then well till* 6 P.M., *when there is slight chill lasting till* 8 P.M., *then heat again, bad dreams, sleeplessness after* 3 A.M. Coldness and numbness of whole r. side, especially of arm and hand, with frequent exhaustion. Coldness of nose and ears; tip of nose, and pinched; face; face in afternoon; face, with blue nose and lips; face and hands, with cold sweat on them; l. side of face colder than r.; sensation as if cold water were poured down back; of trunk and limbs. **Cold limbs,** *with the diarrhœa;* limbs in afternoon; and pulseless; limbs cold, with pain in abdomen; C. limbs bedewed with clammy sweat; l. arm colder than r.; C. forearms. Cold hands and feet; in evening, and about abdomen. *Coldness of lower limbs* (Sec. c.); with stiffness and without power of motion; especially of knees and feet, covered with cold sweat; from calves to feet in evening. Cold feet; with fever; with contracted pulse; soles cold.

Heat; at 2 A. M., *warmth over whole body, sweat on face and feet, tension in hypochondria and epigastrium, causing colic and anxiety;* heat at sunrise, in bed, with sweat on face and dryness of forepart of mouth, without thirst; in afternoon with thirst; *every evening;* from 4 to 6 o'clock, with sweat; at 10 P.M., with redness of whole body, then sweat; *at night, without thirst or sweat; H. at night, with restlessness and with pulsations in limbs, hindering sleep;* < evening; > morning and < night. **Heat, with thirst**; H. with delirium; with rapid, hard pulse; with restlessness; with sore throat and rash; with headache and sensitiveness in region of stomach; with pain in shoulders and nape; with vertigo, flashes of light and apparent motion of stationary objects, twitching of limbs and intermittent pulse; *with diarrhœa, slight hypertrophy of spleen*, spasm of glottis, anorexia, nausea and headache, after three weeks the *fever* and intestinal symptoms ceased, but appetite did not return, tongue furred, blepharitis, after some days *seized every evening by chills, followed by heat.*

Anxious heat. **Internal heat; after midnight, with anxiety** *and inclination to uncover; while vomiting, with thirst;* after diarrhœa, with thirst, and external, as from too much wine, with thirst for beer. Heat alternating with chill. **Typhus-like fever, with restlessness,** *alternating with stupor. Tertian intermittent fever. Fever at same hour for several days. Remittent fever*, only flushing heat, chiefly felt in præcordial region and forehead, sometimes ending in partial or general sweats, but usually there is only *heat beginning in stomach and præcordial region, passing to rest of body,* especially felt in forehead and eyebrows. Hectic fever. *Irritative fever*, with weakness, fainting and vomiting of bile. Unpleasant sensation through body like a sort of fever, and when lying the head is hot, especially ears, but knees are cold. *Feeling as if blood in arteries were boiling hot. Burning in all veins on the frequent waking at night. Sensation as if the blood coursed through the veins too rapidly or were too hot, with small, rapid pulse. Burning flush over whole body.* Heat over whole body except hands.

Heat in head when coughing; in head on waking, with colic; on vertex, with disposition to lie with hands over head; H. on scalp of vertex; in outer ear in evening. Heat in face at 7 P.M.; in face and body at beginning of pains; with redness; with flushes and anxiety; with itching, during which the pain in face diminishes; with pain in abdomen. Heat in hands and feet. Feeling as if hot water ran down calf, from knee to ankle, *l. then r.* Burning in soles, in toes, gradually rising above ankle. **Hot skin; and dry.** Burning in skin of finger. Hot skin and flushed face, with occasional vomiting and shuddering, when the paroxysm of pain and nausea came on relief only on sitting up, bending forward and pressing on stomach, relief after vomiting.

Sweat; in morning, till he rises; in forenoon, with heaviness of head, roaring in ears and trembling; nights; *in bed, causing faintness; when beginning to sleep, > after a little sleep;* on least exertion; after vomiting; *after the fever; with desire to drink all the time;* with diuresis; with griping in bowels, then loose stool, then keen appetite and excitement. Moist skin, with cold limbs. Sweat on face; mornings on waking; on hands and thighs at beginning of sleep, > after a little sleep; *about lower limbs at night, especially about knees;* on legs in morning; on legs at night. *Sweat copious; offensive; over whole body; on feet. Cold;* returning towards evening and disappearing rapidly. *Cold, on forehead,* also after exercise; **cold on face,** also on limbs; over whole body, especially hands and feet. **Cold, clammy.** Clammy.

Clinical.—Malarial fevers of various sorts, with profound prostration. A great variety of intermittent fevers, with the general indication of inequality between the three stages; the febrile stage is generally greatly prolonged; either the cold or sweating stage, or both, may be suppressed, with the general Arsenic symptoms of great restlessness, prostration, thirst, irritability of stomach and bowels, etc. In low types of typhoid fevers, with the Arsenic characteristics frequently enumerated. In typhus fever; in blood poisoning; hectic fever; yellow fever; in short, in a great variety of low types of fever, with tendency to disorganization of the blood and other tissues. Eruptive fevers, sometimes in scarlet fever. In hæmorrhagic measles.

Arsenicum hydrogen.

The gas may be passed into distilled water and kept in a cold dark place; it rapidly decomposes.

General Action, like Arsenic, but much more violent. Compare Ars., *Phos.*, Carb. ac., *K. clc.*

Generalities.—Pale blood exuded from the mucous membrane and from the prepuce. Anæmia, with systolic *bruit de souffle* at apex, in consequence of retention of poison in the body, from lack of urinary secretion, as well as fatty degeneration of heart and paralysis of that organ, finally anguish, pain in region of liver, cold limbs and nettle-rash. Epilepsy, has become nearly imbecile. Twitching of muscles of forearms, then contractions of facial muscles, > warm bath. Malaise; indefinable. Difficulty of motion. Restlessness. Syncope. Weakness; on waking; sudden, indescribable W., with nausea. Hands as far as middle of forearm, feet as far as near knees, nose, eyebrows, became dead, pulse ceased, and every sign of life left these parts, though they could be moved. All hair on "deadened parts" became snowy white, and the white brows formed a strange contrast to the dark-brown face. Crawling in the deadened limbs (as they became restored), especially in nose.

Mind.—Delirium, with desire to escape from bed; slight D., but he answers all questions clearly after some hesitation. *Anxiety; while vomiting, with belief that death is near and despair of being better.* Disinclination to work. Sopor.

Head.—Aching; < during chill; with dulness of head; sudden, then pain in epigastric region, with renewed vomiting, pale tongue, great thirst, features again altered, sclerotic yellow, prostration. Vertigo; on ascending stairs, so that he staggered against the sides of the stairs; with cephalalgia, nausea and vomiting; with pain in stomach, prostration, cerebral congestion, fever, dim sight, indigestion, nausea and griping; with weakness; sudden, with fainting and vomiting. Aching in forehead; after eating, < at night, with weakness.

Eyes, Nose and Face.—Eyes sunken, lustreless, conjunctiva bulbi red; E. yellow, sunken, with blue circles about them; sclerotic injected with blood of a yellow color; E. watery. Violent sneezing, with coldness of nose. Nose and lips excoriated. Face yellowish; pale; bronzed; features drawn; expression as in cholera; hippocratic. Lips colorless.

Mouth and Throat.—Gums pale, discolored, bleeding easily. Fuligo on tongue and gums. Tongue yellow; red and foul; dry and coated; dry, whitish. Mouth dry and sticky. Blood oozed from mucous membrane of mouth and accumulated on anterior pillars of palate, exhaling a nauseous odor. Taste sweetish; bitter. Constriction of throat; with burning. Dysphagia.

Stomach.—Appetite lost. Great thirst. Eructations; spasmodic, of much gas, without relief of the pain in the abdomen that causes moaning. Nausea and vomiting. Incessant retching and vomiting. Vomiting; of food; of everything taken into stomach; greenish; of bitter green mucus, with the colic. Pain; in epigastrium, also on pressure of hand; in epigastric region during chill. Cutting in epigastric region and below it. Heat. Distress about heart and stomach, then profuse vomiting. *Irritation,* with acrid burning from pharynx to lower end of alimentary canal, vomiting of food, then of bile, ultimately of coffee-grounds-looking matter, consisting of broken-down blood corpuscles and epithelium of stomach and lower part of œsophagus, constipation, three or four pints of bloody urine, fever, full, hard, frequent pulse, dry, hot skin, burning pain in alimentary canal, deep-seated pain in lumbar region, restlessness, anxiety, pale, anxious face and prostration.

Abdomen and Stool.—Spleen and liver at first diminished in volume, later hypertrophied. Tympanitic A. Distention during chill. Colic. Heat in A., with cold extremities. Intestinal hæmorrhage. Desire for stool. Bloody stool; frequent blackish S.; bilious. Diarrhœa. Obstinate constipation.

Urinary and Sexual Organs.—Strangury. Ischuria and bloody urine. Dysuria and hæmaturia, with arsenic in urine, and disorganized cells of blood, abundant desquamation of epithelium from renal canaliculi, with small proportion of albumen and hæmoglobuline, uric acid during convalescence. Urine suppressed. Scanty and bloody; and black. *Hæmaturia* (Canth., Phos., Ter., Senec.). Almost black (Ph., K. clc., Carb. ac.); reddish black, forming a thick clot of blood. Copious, black urine, with sensitiveness of renal region to pressure, enlargement of liver and spleen, hæmoglobinuria, jaundice, afterwards urine decreased from day to day and was lighter in color, at last total anuria. *Foreskin and glans covered with pustules, leaving round superficial ulcers, sixty-five on outside of foreskin alone.*

Clinical.—Sudden suppression of menses, with internal chills for three days, followed by tearing pains in hands and feet, confused head, ringing in ears, loss of appetite, thirst, with vomiting of everything, rumbling in bowels, sleeplessness, diarrhœa of red mucus, tongue dry, red, cracked, expectoration of viscid dark mucus, cough at night caused retching and vomiting; Ars. failed, but Ars. hydrog. cured immediately.

Respiratory Organs and Chest.—Voice whispering. Respiration difficult; anxious, frequent moaning, rapid. Ronchi in lungs. Oppression of chest during chill; O., with weakness. Constriction at suprasternal notch; at base of lung with quick breathing.

Pulse, Neck and Back.—Pulse rapid; and small; R. and weak. Tearing in neck during chill. Pain in kidney region; with urging to urinate. Unpleasant pressive feeling in kidney region, which rapidly increased and spread up back to between shoulders. Pain in lumbar region.

Extremities. — Trembling. Painful contractions. Pain. Weakness. Tearing in upper, during chill. A kind of stiffening of upper, which afterwards extended to lower and caused pricking. Pain in elbows and upper arms; in lower limbs, < r. Rheumatic tearing in knees. Walked with difficulty.

Skin and Sleep.—Yellow skin and sclerotic (Phos.); skin deep-yellow, pseudoicteric, then grayish-yellow, then cadaver-like, with excessive itching; *dark-brown skin* (Ph., K. clc.). Violet eruption. Papules on abdomen, face and loins. Somnolence. Profound sleep. Sleeplessness.

Fever.—*Chill*; while walking; < 10 P.M. on undressing; from 3 to 5 P.M., when the headache was usually worse, C. beginning with yawning, discomfort, anxiety, oppression of chest, pain in neck, drawing in upper limbs, increased frontal headache, then heat till 8 P.M., with hot, dry mouth, only little thirst, then sweat and sleep, with at first frequent startings during the unrefreshing sleep, but after midnight he became quiet, next day slight paroxysm of fever, the following day a severe paroxysm, then fever every day; with pain in head and in renal region and vomiting. Cold body; extremities; skin. Heat; in evening. Burning in head. Sweat; profuse.

Arsenicum Iodatum.

For use the pure substance is triturated with sugar of milk.

Affinities; with Arsenic and Iodine.

Generalities.—Feeling in the morning as if he had taken a cold. *Nervous system very irritable*, with wakefulness (Ars.). *Weariness of whole body, with heaviness of limbs* (Ars.).

Clinical.—Threatening pyæmia; blood-poisoning, with debilitating sweats. Enlarged scrofulous glands. Eruptions and ulcerations in syphilitic patients. Enlarged mesenteric glands, with diarrhœa and cholera infantum.

Head.—Aching all over head; preventing sleep. Seemed large and heavy, with pain. Dull heavy aching morning on waking and lasting all day, < motion, stooping or studying, with pressing outward. Dulness the entire morning, with dull pain in l. malar-bone and occasional frontal headache. Bad feeling in evening, like a cold. Aching in forehead, with dulness of whole head during forenoon, with stiffness and soreness of l. side of neck, < moving head. Sharp pain in forehead and in ears, < l. ear, when riding in a sharp cold wind. Pain in r. temple.

Eyes.—Weakness, with burning pain and feeling as if lachrymation would set in.

Clinical.—Scrofulous opthalmia and tendency to ulceration of lower lid. Parenchymatous keratitis.

Ears.—Clinical.—Otitis, with fetid corrosive discharge. Catarrhal inflammation of the throat, nose and middle ear; swelling of the tissues within the nose; hypertrophied condition of the opening of the Eustachian tube and increasing deafness. Chronic irritability of the middle ear following scarlet fever; thickening of tympanum.

Nose.—Dryness.

Clinical.—Coryzas, burning, acrid. Hay fever. Catarrh, burning sensation, tubercular diathesis.

Mouth.—Intermittent pain in first r. upper molar.

Clinical.—Epithelioma.

Throat.—In morning after moving about hawking up thick mucus, mixed with clotted blood, which seemed to come from the head and relieved the pain.

Clinical.—Later stage of diphtheria, with evidence of putrefactive degeneration. Diphtheritic croup.

Stomach.—Appetite increased at first (Iod.); lost. Pyrosis. Pain, < rising after sitting; in afternoon, with raising of wind and greasy fluid similar to that after eating salt pork; at epigastrium, with thirst, dry throat, fever and sometimes diarrhœa and tenesmus.

Abdomen.—*Hardness and distention from flatus*, which was discharged constantly. Cutting as if he would have a stool, > emission of flatus and warm applications; C. embracing the whole abdomen and obliging him to bend almost double, > large soft stool, evacuated with straining.

Anus and Stool.—Aching in anus, with seeming inability to keep the sphincter closed, amounting to dysenteric straining at stool. Urging to stool in morning on rising, with scanty stool, small in size, as if anus were contracted, *mushy*, with small scybalæ, and of peculiar black color, resembling fæces of an ox, with straining as in dysentery. *Mushy stool*, almost black, with straining and tenesmus. **Diarrhœa**, five to ten stools each day, *not at night*, **but the urging began on moving about in morning**. Painless diarrhœa every night at midnight.

Urine.—Increased in quantity.

Genital Organs.—Clinical.—Leucorrhœa, bloody, yellow, with hard swelling of the labia, followed by indurations in the axilla. Mammary abscess. Mammary tumor, with retracted nipple, sensitive.

Cough.—*Hacking*, with dryness and stoppage of nostrils.

Chest.—Clinical.—Pulmonary tuberculosis, with cavities in lungs, hectic fever, etc. Chronic catarrhal pneumonia, with muco-purulent expectoration, dyspnœa, night-sweat, etc. Chronic pneumonia, with abscess in the lung, hectic fever. Acute catarrhal pneumonia, with caseous degeneration and fibrosis. Fibroid degeneration of the lung, with inflammation and hæmorrhage; commencing cavity. In general, many cases of pulmonary disease, pneumonia, subacute and chronic, and various forms of phthisis pulmonaris have been cured, the special indications being great debility, night-sweats either after the cavity is formed or when a cavity threatens to form, with a decidedly cachectic condition of the patient. It seems probable that in the Iodide of Arsenic we have found a remedy most closely allied to manifestations of tuberculosis; it will be indicated by a profound prostration, rapid, irritable pulse, recurring fever and sweats, emaciation, tendency to diarrhœa, etc. It is especially valuable in nontubercular phthisis.

Heart.—Clinical.—A number of cases of weakness of the heart have been reported as relieved, and it undoubtedly acts similarly to Arsenic in such cases; unfortunately nearly all the cases reported have been treated with a combination of other drugs with this one, so that perhaps as much credit should be given to the other drugs as to the Arsen. iod.

Pulse.—*Irregular, rapid.*

Back.—Soreness as if beaten, and especially of back of neck.

Extremities.—Heaviness, with weariness of whole body. Rheumatic pain, as if in shaft of bone, in upper third of r. humerus while writing, suddenly shifting to r. metacarpal bones, then to l. femur. Laming pain in l. calf, afterwards embracing entire leg, > motion, returning at rest. Dull heavy soreness of l. calf. Weary feeling in calves while kneeling. Formicating prickings on external l. ankle, then on inner r. ankle.

Skin.—Dryness. Painful formication on external border of l. foot, then burning pain on l. instep. Itching on various parts; on back; on back of l. hand, then stinging itching on back of r. hand.

Clinical.—Eczema of the beard, watery oozing, great itching, < washing.

Sleep.—Constant yawning, with early sleepiness. *Restless night*, with little sleep.

Fever.—Peculiar chilliness of l. thigh, beginning on posterior surface and noticed more there, then formication and weight in l. foot, the latter extending up leg, the clothes when touching the limb feel cold, the formication and weight afterwards extended to r. foot and were partially > by walking, the chilliness > application of warmth. Fever, pulse 80, strong. Heat in lumbar region as if clothes were on fire.

Clinical.—Night-sweats of phthisis and of many other debilitating diseases.

Arsenicum Metallicum.

Pure Metallic Arsenic is triturated with sugar of milk for use.

Action and Affinities. See Arsenicum alb.

Generalities.—Emaciation. Pulsation over whole body; especially under sternum; especially in r. hip-joint, < morning, > evening. *Weakness.* Disinclination to rising in morning after sound sleep. Recurrence of symptoms after two weeks. Aggravation in morning; after brandy. Appearance of symptoms on r., then l. side.

Mind.—Stupor in morning after sound sleep all night. Despondency. Depression of spirits. Indifference.

Head.—Aching, < when laughing. Swollen feeling morning on waking. Sensation as from fumes of whisky. Heaviness like vertigo. Swollen feeling in forehead, with immovable skin. Heaviness in forehead, with dull feeling. Aching in l. side of head, extending to l. ear and eye, with nausea. Soreness of scalp when pulling even one hair.

Eyes.—Pain so that he could not read much. Heaviness. Lids swollen and inflamed.

Nose.—Coryza; with hoarseness, then with angina faucium; fluent. Discharge of scalding water, which excoriates nostrils.

Face.—Bloated; feeling as if. Ulcer on l. inner side of lower lip; on r. inner side of lower lip, with soreness on touch of tongue.

Mouth.—Gums swollen and painful to touch; gums swollen and feeling as if scalded, with salivation. Tongue coated white and covered with mucus; coated white and showing imprint of teeth. Dryness.

Stomach.—Aversion to wines and liquors. Eructations of hot bile. Nausea.

Abdomen.—Bloated. Lancinating griping after waking at 6 A.M., > sharp, burning, watery stool, then debility, sleeping in his chair, loss of appetite and full pulse. Tension and sensation of swelling. Pulsation in umbilicus. Painful swelling in r. groin, where a bubo had suppurated twenty-four years before, < extending leg, the pain goes to hip, < sitting, when the leg goes to sleep, > walking.

Anus, etc.—Sore feeling in A. Bleeding varices; V. on r. side, painful after stool (not bleeding). Constipation. Red, sandy sediment in urine. Pain in region of heart; P. in l. muscles of chest.

Pulse.—Full and hard; at 9 A.M., and rapid. Rapid; in morning; in morning, but slow in evening. Slow after midnight, rapid in morning, after rising.

Back.—Lumbago. Numbness in r. lumbar region from vertebræ to crest of ilium, and inside of r. thigh down to knee.

Limbs.—Cracking of finger-joints. Swollen feeling in hands, fingers and feet, with feeling as if he could not close hand. In lower limb sensation as if he could not use it, but he could walk well after using it. Hip-joint, lame feeling in r.; numbness in r., extending to pubes; paralyzed feeling in r. hip-joint extending to pubic symphysis and down inside of thigh to knee. Dry feeling in r. knee. Pulsation in r. anterior tibial artery at superior extremity of its inferior third.

Skin.—Scales. Itching of forehead; on face, > pinching; on face, > pressure, but not by scratching; on lower part of face, with burning, as before eruption; on face, < night, > bathing with cold water, with burning, stinging and swelling, then desquamation in small scales; in r. groin, extending to knee.

Sleep.—Very sound at night. Sleepiness in morning after rising; in daytime and evening; afternoon when walking in street; S., with little sleep. Restless sleep; with fulness in head, which was < on waking in night. Sensation in sleep as if he would have headache in morning on waking. Dreams of danger, especially by water, that he is in danger of drowning, etc.

Fever.—Dry heat in palms of hands. Burning of hands and feet. Heat of feet, with a bloated feeling; dry heat of feet, also at night. Sweat of feet; offensive S. on genitals.

Arsenicum Sulfuratum Flavum.

Triturate with Sacch. lach. for use.

Cramps, grips, vomiting, diarrhœa, with thirst and fever. Falling down in spasms. Faintness. Weakness. Anxiety and fear. Apprehension. Confusion of head, too many thoughts crowd upon him. Vertigo on walking in open air, feeling through head as from drunkenness. Stitches externally in r. frontal region; throbbing stitches in r. frontal region. Gum in canthi. Tensive feeling behind r. ear, as if something stuck there and pressed the ear forward, on brushing hair on occiput. Teeth pain as if loose on chewing food. Tongue white; T. swollen, afterwards dry; stiff, immovable. Taste bitter. Mouth and throat dry.

Disgust for all nourishment. Thirst. Nausea after dinner, at noon. Nausea and vomiting. Vomiting offensive bile, then feeling better. Cramp in stomach, with faintness, griping, diarrhœa and vomiting. Abdomen distended, soft, painless. Colic as from a cold, morning on waking. Tenesmus. Liquid, profuse stool on touching abdomen.

Respiration difficult. Stitches extending outward in r. chest. Pulse frequent, hard, afterwards small, thready; slow, suppressed, afterwards rapid, scarcely to be felt. Pains in l. knee. Fright on falling asleep in evening, as if he fell out of bed. Cold forehead. Cold, stiff body.

Arum Dracunculus.

Preparation, General Action and Relationship same as Arum tri.

Taste styptic and metallic, with bitterness in back of mouth. Hand feels as if plunged among nettles. Fingers feel as if stings were driven perpendicularly into them when rubbed together. Prickings as of thorns in r. fingers. Pricking in fingers, with itching. Pain in r. index as if pulled.

Arum Dracontium.

Preparation, General Action and Relationship same as Arum tri.

Generalities.—Occasional shooting pain in r. malar region, then in r. external malleolus, then in thenal eminence of r. thumb, then in l. malar region. The pains are mostly transient in any one part, course along the extremities, sometimes in one direction, sometimes in the opposite one, are not very sharp, are generally intermediate between aching and shooting, those in nervous trunks are more of the shooting character, but always leave an aching, at first the pains are confined to r. side, afterwards chiefly to the l. Prostration. Languor and depression of spirits.

Head.—Aching pain over l. eye. Head feels heavy and aches in occipital and r. parietal regions in morning on waking. Aching in l. occipital region, then in l. temporal, then in l. frontal region.

Eyes.—Conjunctivæ injected on waking at 6 A.M., lids dry, stiff, agglutinated, and burning and smarting of edges of lids. Heat of eyelids, with dryness and smarting.

Ears.—Shooting pain in l; in r.; in r., leaving fulness and aching in middle ear. Warmth and fulness in l. middle, then in r., afterwards in one or the other when swallowing, seldom in both at the same time, caused by mucus in Eustachian tube. Aching pain behind r.

Face.—Aching in r. malar region in morning on waking.

Mouth.—Aphthous ulcer on tongue. Soreness of mouth and throat. Peculiar acrid sensation in mouth and throat. In the morning tongue and mouth coated with a foul slimy mucus, having a putrid taste.

Throat.—Uneasiness, with disposition to cough. Soreness in muscles when swallowing. Loose cough, with soreness of throat, < swallowing, simulating catarrhal angina, with dryness and smarting in throat, rawness and fulness, causing continual disposition to clear the throat by swallowing, coughing or hawking. Raw feeling, morning on waking, with rattling of mucus in larynx at every full *expiration*, > after rising and moving about. Mucus, the raising of which by cough produces a rattling in larynx, with disposition to swallow arising from excess of mucus.

Stomach.—Eructations of flatus. Sinking at pit.

Abdomen.—Pain caused by incarceration of flatus. Escape of flatus from stomach and bowels.

Stool.—Copious, semi-fluid, with much flatus. Three, copious, bilious, with aching in abdomen and burning in rectum. Bilious diarrhœa, with borborygmus and emission of flatus. At one time slightly constipated, at another somewhat loose. Late and insufficient.

Urinary Organs.—Tenderness and smarting or burning at orifice of urethra, < during micturition. Burning in urethra after micturition. Irresistible desire to pass urine, which is diminished in quantity, high-colored and causes burning or smarting in urethra. Frequent copious emissions of limpid urine.

Sexual Organs.—Fine shooting in course of l. spermatic cord. Desire diminished and most of the time absent, with flaccid and relaxed penis.

Respiratory Organs.—Rattling of mucus in larnyx at 7 A.M. if expirations are prolonged. Soreness of larnyx, with disposition to cough. Hoarseness; at 6 A.M on waking, with expectoration of mucus, rawness and tenderness of throat, rattling in larnyx on *expiration*, > by rising, except when expirations were prolonged. Cough; all night; from laryngeal irritation, < night and lying down. *Expectoration of thick heavy, yellowish-white pus;* of mucus by coughing in morning. Asthmatic attacks nightly; waking about midnight, leaving rattling of mucus in larnyx and upper part of trachea, followed by bad sleep. Dyspnœa in paroxysms, with aching in chest and secretion of mucus in larnyx and trachea.

Chest.—Dull heavy aching. Shooting and aching pain in l. brachial plexus of nerves.

Heart and Pulse.—Aching pain in præcordial region and down l. arm. Heart beat so violently as to shake walls of chest. Pulse rapid, hard and jerking; rapid, small and irregular, the artery seems to roll under the finger, and it requires considerable pressure to be counted correctly.

Neck and Back.—Shooting in l. anterior inferior triangle of neck, near clavicle. Aching along spine, especially between scapulæ and in lumbar region, with weakness across loins.

Extremities.—Aching pain along outer aspect of l. foot, then in corresponding part of l. hand. Tingling or slight stinging in fingers and toes, as when circulation is impeded. Fine tingling or pricking in hands and feet, < r.; in r. foot, then in r. hand, then in l. foot, then in l. hand. Aching pain in r. shoulder; r. humerus. Occasional shooting and aching pain along r. humerus and r. thumb. Aching pain in r. forearm; l. forearm, l. hand and r. humerus. Sharp shooting pain in styloid process of r. ulna. Fine tingling all over r. hand, which is warmer and redder than the l. and swollen. Shooting down r. thigh.

Skin.—Flushing of hands and face. Pimples, a species of lichen, on nose, and urticaria near r. elbow.

Fever.—Heat in palms. Burning in soles. Sweat on neck and breast at 8 P.M.

Arum Italicum.

Preparation, General Action and Relationship same as Arum tri.

General malaise. Debility; and emaciation. Aggravation from pure wine, coffee and brandy. Mental uneasiness. Intellectual incapacity. Headache in damp weather, especially in occiput. Contusive aching in anterior lobes of brain. Aching in brain from least mental exertion, < stormy weather. Acute enterocolitis. Colic after eating, then diarrhœa; C., with pain in vesical region and urging to urinate; contractive twisting, < before stool. Sensitiveness of abdomen, with heat. Smarting and tearing in rectum during stool. Stools generally liquid or very soft, scanty, yellowish or dark, with emission of flatus and towards the last mixed with frothy mucus; S. more frequent from 3 to 6 A.M.; frequent, preceded by colic, mostly in umbilical region, and renewed with each urging to stool.

Hoarseness suddenly < about 9 P.M.; < evening, with tickling in larynx and cough, < after sleep. Shocks of dry cough and constant hawking of thick, tenacious, gray or brown mucus, often blood-streaked. Contusive pains in l. chest, sometimes in front, below clavicle, sometimes behind, below spine of scapula and near its inner border. Heat behind sternum and anterior part of chest. Dull pain behind l. scapula. Pricking in finger-tips, with formication. Skin of fingers red, as from wine-lees, with sensitiveness and pain as if burnt, < pressure. Last two phalanges of fingers covered with almost invisible elevations, with itching, < after bathing, then desquamation. Itching, < about 6 A.M.

Drowsiness every morning. Chills in daytime at slightest draught. Coldness and shivering in afternoon, especially down back, in evening redness of face, general heat, rapid pulse, at night sweat, especially on chest, having an odor resembling that of Hedera helix when rubbed between the fingers. Heat of skin and hands at night in bed, with rapid pulse. Night-sweats.

Arum Maculatum.

A tincture is prepared from the fresh root and kept in a cool, dark place.

General Action and Relationships same as Arum tri.

Horrible convulsions. Weakness; with inability to speak, raising hands frequently to its mouth and throat, uttering at intervals a sharp cry and starting up as if suffocated. Torpor, then violent febrile reaction. Taciturnity, with sleepiness after eating. Pressure in l. temple; below ears, behind lower jaw. Gums bleed (on kissing). Tongue, *stitches; with burning; swollen;* feeling as if swollen. Burning pain in mouth and lips. Caustic effects over lips, mouth and as far as could be seen. Salivation. Throat; swollen so that a probe could not be introduced into œsophagus; stinging in T. and œsophagus. Pain on l. side below larynx, near trachea, on pressure; P., provoking swallowing, which is difficult, as from a swelling on l. side above larynx. Tickling in throat, becoming a burning. Swallowing impossible; difficult, as if the "palate were down."

Appetite lost. Vomiting; *of blood.* Cramp in stomach. Cardialgia. Pain in stomach on pressure Constriction in abdomen as in anxiety and fear, then it ascended over whole chest, with hot breath, then it rose into throat, first like a pressure inward in the back part of palate above larynx, provoking swallowing, which is difficult, afterwards it feels too narrow. Emptiness in abdomen as after vomiting, mornings after eating. Pressure on a spot between navel and top of hip, < standing, or lying on side or back, most on filling chest full or making abdominal muscles tense, with pain on pressure.

Diarrhœa. Bleeding from urethra. Urine copious. Urine watery, smelling almost like burnt horn, becoming cloudy in middle on standing. Hoarseness. *Bloody sputa. Sleepiness,* < *after dinner and sleep, with red face.* Sweat.

Arum Triphyllum.

A tincture is prepared from the fresh root of this plant ("the Jack-in-the-pulpit"), and kept in a cool, dark place.

General Action.—An irritant poison causing inflammation of mucous surfaces and destruction of tissue, together with a low type of fever.

Allied Drugs.—Kali bi., Ail., Nat. ars., Ant. cr., Canth., Graph.

Generalties and Mind.—Weakness. Forgetfulness. Low spirits. Irritable disposition.

Clinical.—Tendency to great depression of the vital forces. In low types of scarlet fever, diphtheria, typhoid fever, with carphology, especially boring into the nose and picking the lips until they bleed. Delirium in scarlet fever, with boring into the nose.

Head.—*Aching;* > after breakfast; > after dinner; < after drinking hot coffee. Dulness; morning. Fulness. Heaviness; morning; at night. Obstructed feeling, as if full of mucus, and in chest. Vertigo; with fulness of head and absence of mind. Feels better after dinner. Worse at night.

Forehead.—Stitches over l. eye; in evening, suddenly repeated. Tearing in r. side, in r. temple and ear. *Aching;* and on r. side of head; in r.; terrible A. in both sides, with heaviness of eyelids. Heaviness and dulness in morning.

Stitches in l. temple; at 10 P.M.; in r., extending towards submaxillary bone. Aching in temples; in vertex, sometimes with cold feeling as if cranium were open; in scalp of vertex, with soreness on touch. Boring in r. side of head in morning on waking. Shooting in occiput when turning eyes upward.

Eyes.—Cloudiness. Aching in r. Smarting. Sensation as after shedding many tears. Sleepiness. Heaviness. Much water in eyes from morning till evening, especially in outer canthus, with swelling of margins of lids. Tension in lower lids in evening, as if swollen. Vision dim.

Ears.—Tearing in l.

Nose.—**Soreness of nostrils** (Graph., K. bi., Aur.). **Nose, lips and face feel chapped** (Ant. cr.), **as if he walked in a cold wind. Obstruction, must breathe through mouth**; *l. nostril obstructed;* in morning. Dryness. Sneezing; *much in afternoon, with feeling as if he had taken cold, and chills over whole body, beginning at vertex;* much at night. Moisture in afternoon, with obstruction.

Coryza; fluent, also profuse; **fluent afternoons, with heat in face and head. Continual discharge from l. nostril.** *Discharge in morning, with streaks of blood and hardened mucus; yellow and thick D. during the day;* watery; watery at 4 P.M., with sneezing; *watery, and at the same time obstruction, < in morning;* profuse watery, with obstruction of r. side; tough, yellowish, with sensation of approaching swelling in soft palate and pressure.

Clinical.—Violent coryzas, fluent, acrid, ichorous; nostrils very sore, with constant desire to bore into the nose and to pick it. Nose completely stopped, with fluent acrid discharge. In hay fever, with terrific pain over root of nose; nose and throat feel raw. In scarlet fever and in diphtheria the nose becomes ulcerated, with an offensive excoriating discharge; the patient is constantly working at the nose.

Face.—**Lips chapped; thick and burning;** dry; *scalded feeling in morning. Sprained pain in l. articulation of jaw when swallowing.*

Clinical.—Lips chapped and burning; the patient constantly picks at the lips until they bleed; the corners cracked, bloody; with this the submaxillary glands are often swollen, the tongue red and the whole mouth raw.

Mouth.—Tearing in l. teeth. Aching in l. lower decayed teeth towards evening. *Tongue cracked, painful and burning* (Ail.); **raw feeling at root and at palate;** *burning at root and in throat;* pain on l. margin; smarting at upper anterior part. **Mouth, lips and soft palate sore and burning** (Ars.) *in morning. Palate sore, with pain when eating and drinking. Dryness of mouth* (K. bi.). *Salivation.*

Throat.—**Swelling of l. submaxillary glands** (Bar. c., Merc. i. r.). Internal swelling in region of larynx, < r. side. *Mucus;* tenacious; much M., with tickling, compelling to cough. Stitches in l. side. *Pain,* < night; < when coughing; *burning.* Scratching, > after drinking hot coffee; *constant, with burning* and desire to swallow. *Soreness* at 5 A.M.; 4 P.M.; *burning* (Canth.). *Burning;* morning in bed, > after rising; at 10 P.M., and in lungs; before midnight, *with dryness,* then much mucus, which goes deeper and deeper down by swallowing. *Constriction;* at night. *Swollen feeling in soft palate in morning when swallowing.* Constant desire to swallow; with stitches in throat, which is painful to pressure. Swallowing difficult; in morning. Amelioration during morning till after dinner; A. after breakfast.

Clinical.—Throat raw. Occasionally useful in diphtheria with the characteristic nose and lips. Sore throat from speaking. Sore throat, with hay fever, violent coryza, rawness and soreness, constant hawking.

Stomach.—No appetite. Thirst to drink a little at a time.

Abdomen.—Intermittent distention from noon till evening. Rolling in morning, with frequent painful urging to stool. Cutting. Pain in hepatic region, first in front, then in back.

Stool, Urinary and Sexual Organs.—Burning in anus (Caps.). Urging to stool driving from bed, stool watery, dark brown. Diarrhœa frequent, from 3 to 8 A.M.; diarrhœa like mustard till noon, afterwards no stool for two days; *watery, brown* (K. bi.), *with eructations of food.* Stool soft; with much tenesmus; thin, yellow, in morning. Micturition frequent. *Urine copious; and pale.* Sudden tearing in r. testicle, repeatedly from noon till evening. Cutting in region of l. ovary. Menses darker.

Respiratory Organs.—Internal swelling in trachea, r., then l. side, and when pressing against it soreness of l. parotid. **Hoarseness** (K. bi.). Cough from tickling in throat, with much mucus; frequent C., also at 6 A.M. after waking; much at 5 A.M.; spasmodic. *Expectoration of much mucus; scanty but constant discharge of tough mucus from mouth* (K. bi.).

Clinical.—Laryngitis, with great hoarseness, the result of talking; hawking and clearing the voice.

Chest.—Stitches in r. lung and under r. scapula. *Soreness of lungs* (Ail., Pho.). Burning pain in lungs (Ail.) when coughing. Burning, extending from lungs to pit of stomach. Full feeling, with soreness in l. lung and l. upper arm and pain in forehead.

Neck and Back.—Neck stiff. Pain in region of atlas and dentoid vertebra, extending to r. side; P. over hips.

Extremities.—Heaviness, especially of lower. Aching in r. shoulder and between scapulæ. Swelling and stiffness of hands, > about 6 P.M. Pain in r. hip under trochanter. Cramp in r. leg in morning on waking. Pain in middle of l. tibia, where there has been a discolored spot for years. Stinging in soles. Tickling itching in centre of r. sole.

Sleep.—Yawning in afternoon; at same hour on two days, with coldness running over body; Y. < in afternoon, with stretching and sleepiness. Sleepiness at 11 A.M., also with yawning and heaviness of eyes; S. in evening. Sleeps in his chair after supper. Sleep restless at night, with heaviness of head.

Fever.—Chills running over body at night. Flushes of heat at night; flushes from 4 to 9 P.M. with burning face. *Heat of face;* r. ear.

Asafœtida.

A tincture (solution) is made of the gum-resin obtained from Narthex Asafœtida, Falc., a plant of the natural order Umbelliferæ.

General Action.—Most marked on the nervous system, producing effects like hysteria and chorea. Especially valuable in globus hystericus and flatulence.

Affinities.—Con., Puls., Croc., Mezer., Cinnab., Nit. ac.

Generalities.—Hæmorrhages. Trembling over whole body, with cold skin and small, weak pulse. Stitches; in tips of toes, in skin of r. axilla, on r. cheek; fine, superficial here and there, so that he must rub. A good night's sleep was followed in morning by oppression of chest, quick breathing and beating of pulse and heart, distention of abdomen, then aching in stomach, *all > stools partly solid, partly papescent, dark brownish and blackish, smelling of the drug,* also the rheumatic pains in back of head extending to arms and drawing, rending pain back of neck, were > after the stools.

Pain in l. chest, in elbows, below l. scapula, in hands, shoulders. Pressing in joints of r. hand and in r. temple at 6 A.M. on waking, with pressing in nape of neck. After rising pressure in forehead, drawing in muscles of r. forearm, in muscles of l. cheek, pressure in r. tibia and l. calf, and drawing and pressing in different places in forehead. Pains return frequently and jump from one place to another. Drawing aching below edge of l. ribs when walking and in muscles of scapulæ. Drawing in muscles of scapulæ, thighs, fingers and in r. cheek. Drawing in spots in skull, in feet, forearms, quickly jumping from one place to another, in wrists, on soles, in calves and temples (Puls.).

Restlessness. Heaviness in whole body. Weakness (in evening, then very sound sleep); in evening, with sleepiness; on motion; with limbs sinking down heavy and relaxed and vertigo. Pains appeared when walking, but were < when sitting. Pains > towards 9 P.M. Pains appear less frequently towards evening. Symptoms disappear in evening, except distention of abdomen. Relieved by emission of offensive flatus.

Clinical.—It has been found useful in various forms of destructive syphilitic processes, deep ulcerations, caries of the bones, especially of the tibia; in these cases the characteristic indications are the terrible throbbing pains at night, with extreme sensitiveness of the affected part. It has been used for various forms of hysteria, with extreme sensitiveness to external impressions. Hysterical spasms, with suppression of habitual discharges. Hystero-epilepsy.

Mind.—Ill humor and dislike for work. *Irritable*, yet indifferent to everything. Fretful and apprehensive mood, which seems to arise from abdomen.

Head.—Stitches. Aching; in brain; in joints and bones during night when waking and in morning; on small places; with heaviness; with heat and confusion when sitting and reading; alternately increasing and decreasing; extending to eyes and nose; A. like an emptiness. Vertigo. Drawing in skull. Heaviness; with fulness and confusion, then aching over whole brain. Fulness; after waking, which gradually changed to periodical pains, lasting into next night. Rush of blood, with warmth of face and headache. Tension in brain; stupefying tension in head, < l. side. Confusion; with stitches in forehead and temples; with pressure in temples; with aching and sensation as if a string were drawn across brain; changing gradually to a pain as if the whole brain were compressed, with vertigo, heat of skin and quickness of pulse; making thought difficult. Weakness.

Forehead.—Stitches in l. eminence; in middle and below bone, with aching and burning in sternum and inclination to cough; burning externally, near eminence, > touch, and pain as if ulcerated; extending to occiput, then confusion in head; *sudden, deeply penetrating under l. eminence, like shocks, then sensitiveness* (Ign.). Tearing. *Boring above eyebrow*, r. then l. *Aching;* l.; in bones above; with heaviness; with weakness of whole body; on different spots on bones, at times with sticking and burning pains. *Drawing wave-like pressure through l. half, ending in dull pressure on eminence.* **Pressive pain from within outward**; r., also intermitting. Pressure externally. Aching in l. side, extending over head; A. over eyes as from sleepiness. Drawing. Swashing and gurgling sensation in brain beneath upper part of bone. Heaviness in sinciput; in sinciput and forehead, with pressure and with external warmth of cheeks and ears, chill in back and sticking in tongue. Tensive confusion and burdensome heaviness.

Temples.—Stitches deep in l.; slow in l. Tearing in r. Pressure; *r.;* sudden in r.; asunder in both; *outward in l.; sudden, inward, as from a pointed plug;* intermitting in l., almost like a pushing inward.

Vertex.—Superficial stitches on r. side. Pressure on; and over r. eye; starting from l. half, changing gradually to pressure in direction of eyes, increasing and decreasing alternately.

Parietals.—Aching in r. side of head; *in l. side of head, extending to eyes* and changing to intermitting fulness of brain; *in r. bone as from a deeply penetrating plug* (Mez.); sudden in l. side of head as from a dull tool pressed in, rapidly increasing and suddenly disappearing. *Pressure outward in l. side. Drawing above r. ear, which changes into stitching.*

Occiput.—Tearing. Drawing and tearing pains, extending through nape to upper arms and feeling like rheumatic pains. Drawing pain. Drawing. Pain, extending over head, as if brain were compressed by a cloth. Wandering pain. Pressure on l.

Eyes.—Burning stinging in l. *Dryness. Periodical burning, with pressing together of lids as if overcome by sleep.* Pressure. *Itching of r. Burning in r. ball; in l. ball, as from within outward;* tensive, in r. ball. Burning stinging in r. ball. Sensation of sand between balls and lids; and as if a cold air blew upon bulbi. Pupils dilated. Lid, twitching of upper; of l. upper; stitching and itching, also in edges; itching, sticking and burning, < r.; burning in r., also edges of r. Burning in r. inner canthus. Pressure in middle of upper lid.

Pressure on external margin of l. orbit. Pinching drawing across supraorbital region (Cinnab.). Muscæ volitantes. Vision dim; when writing, > blinking.

Clinical.—Orbital neuralgia, severe boring pains above orbits, throbbing at night, > pressure and rest. A most valuable remedy for a similar pain, which occurs in severe cases of iritis and for intraocular inflammations, permitting the case to progress rapidly towards recovery.

Ears.—Aching in r.; l. Drawing and stitches around l. Drawing behind l.; on outer rim of r. concha; in meatus auditorius. Dull sensibility, especially dull hearing, in forenoon. Ringing before.

Nose.—Pressure as if it would burst, especially in r. wing. Sneezing. Coryza.

Face.—Pressure in l. cheek; in bones of face; on zygomatic bone; outward in r. side. Drawing in l. cheek; r. cheek. *Painless tension in various places, on malar-bone* (Con., Verbasc.), *nasal bones, with a kind of numb sensation.* Swelling of lower lip, with burning sticking, then similar swelling in l. corner of mouth. Numb pressure in l. angle of chin, extending into tooth above it.

Jaw.—Pinching in ramus of lower. Pressure in lower; in l. corner; angle of l. lower; in joints. Drawing in l. lower; r. lower, then in r. forehead; from angles into muscles of nape; in joints, changing into pain, which returned late in evening.

Mouth.—Severe drawing in lower incisors. Teeth blunt. Gums sore. Tongue, stitches in tip; burning in tip; biting burning pain in tip. Burning in mouth, throat and stomach. Mouth dry; dry sensation, though there is moisture enough. Sensation as if upper skin of anterior walls of mouth were loosened, as in incipient cancrum oris. Salivation. Taste fatty, rancid; taste insipid and acrid; insipid, changing to that of onions.

Throat.—Drawing down l. side on motion. **Hysterical rising, as if a ball or large body ascended from stomach to œsophagus** (Nit. ac.), *or pharynx, in evening* (Senec.), *obliging him to swallow, which relieved* (Ign.), but the sensation returned. Scraping. Constriction, with pressure in chest. Dryness, and while swallowing tension.

Œsophagus.—*Spasms* (Stram.); *like hysteria. Sensation as if peristaltic motions were reversed, and, in œsophagus, were driven from stomach towards throat.* Rising in, afterwards with nausea and scraping in pharynx; hysteric rising. Aching and burning, and in throat, like heartburn, as after fat food. Soreness, and of stomach. Dryness, without thirst.

Stomach.—Appetite increased; with nausea; with desire for something relishing and nourishing; poor; lost. Wine was not relished as usual. Aversion to beer, which tastes slimy. Eructations of air; also tasting of garlic; with garlicky smell; offensive; warm; with salivation; then nausea, as from emptiness of stomach and disgust for food. Nausea. Feeling as if disordered by fat. *Distention of stomach and bowels* (Lyc., Croc.) *with feeling as if peristaltic motions were reversed* (Elaps.), *with spasmodic working in œsophagus. Perceptible pulsation in pit* (Puls.). *Sensation as if beaten in epigastric region and abdomen, with fulness in former and eructations.*

Pain; in l. side; in epigastric region after eating, also with debility; when sitting, extending towards liver; intermittent, and in abdomen; and warmth towards l. side, and more up into œsophagus, like *globus hystericus.* Aching and distending pain, as from flatulence, and, in œsophagus, beginning in cardiac region, extending more towards spleen than liver, and rising into œsophagus. Pressure, with sensation as if incarcerated flatus were pressed about in intestines. Pressure changing to tensive pain, extending to both sides, < pressure downward of diaphragm and on touching stomach. Pain in epigastric region, < touch, afterwards drawing, at last tensive. Sickly sensation in pit, like pressure, not exactly painful. Burning; in epigastric region and diaphragm, also cutting. Peculiar movements, and in mouth.

Clinical.—Violent gastralgia, with distention of abdomen, belching of wind and regurgitation of liquid. Flatulence of hysteria.

Abdomen.—Rumbling; with pain. Emissions of flatus; with retained stool; easy; offensive. Flatus retained, passing off in morning, with half diarrhœic stool. *Distention;* after a hard, dark, offensive stool, causing pain in rectum; with discharges of flatus; with constipation and tenesmus. *Griping, with emission of flatus.* Pain, with movements and rumbling. Flatulent pain when walking after dinner. Cutting; when walking or sitting. Pinching. Cutting, pinching. Pinching drawing across, when sitting, with stitches in l. side of abdomen extending outward. Burning. Heaviness; from drinking, with chilling sensation. Sensation of illness, with heaviness and pressure in sides. Tension after eating.

Upper.—*Pain as from taking cold and as if diarrhœa would ensue, with ravenous hunger. Intermittent griping.*

Umbilicus.—Stitches; burning; crawling, in region. Cutting in region, < sitting and retracting abdomen. Griping (*into a ball*) below U. when standing. Aching extending outward.

Sides.—Stitches in l. when walking; in l. externally, > rubbing; extending outward, while sitting after eating, > pressure; outward in l., also with flatulence; sudden, jerklike, outward in r.; gurgling, in l. Sticking, griping in l. *Aching in flanks on drawing in abdominal muscles.*

Lower.—Stitching. Sticking and drawing in l., extending along inner side of ilium, when sitting. Attacks of griping.

Rectum.—Tenesmus. Constant dysenteric feeling as if stool would occur. Persistent, ineffectual urging to stool. *Pain in perineum as if something dull pressed out there.*

Stool.—Watery; with discharge of flatus, which does not relieve distention of abdomen; with pressing down on rectum. Diarrhœa; with pain in abdomen, also frequent. *Profuse, thick, papescent, brown, offensive, relieving symptoms.* Thick, papescent, light yellow. Pasty and yellow, containing a little bile. Mushy, with flatulence, without pain, but with fulness and heaviness in abdomen. Constipation. Solid, dark, offensive. Profuse, hard, preceded by pressure and dragging. Two knotty stools in forenoon. Small, partly hard, partly mushy. Difficult, hard. Frequent. Two painless stools, with rumbling, then heaviness and distention of abdomen.

Clinical.—Diarrhœa, extremely offensive, with meteorismus, which rises, and regurgitations of food; it seems as if the peristaltic action of the bowels were reversed.

Urinary Organs.—Stitches in urethra. Stitching and burning in extremity of urethra, but not when urinating. Urine dark brown, easily discharged; brownish-yellow, also ammoniacal; scanty and dark; smells of drug; acrid, pungent and light-colored.

Sexual Organs.—Pressing towards, with pain in testicles, < touch and motion. Stitches in mons veneris close to penis. Stitches externally on penis. Drawing pain in glans penis before and on urinating. Drawing in penis while urinating. Swelling of scrotum. Desire increased.

Female.—*Swelling.* Labor-like cutting and forcing pain in region of uterus. Intermittent labor-like pain in region of uterus. Menses too early, scanty for three days, then natural. Nymphomania in a plethoric woman.

Respiratory Organs.—Cough, hoarse hacking, from smothering in air passages; dry, irritative, from tickling in larynx; frequent, with slimy expectoration from trachea. Respiration quickened; and interrupted by coughing and yawning.

Chest.—Breasts swelled and a milky discharge escaped. Weak movements of l. intercostal muscles.

Stitches after hawking, when standing and sitting; when lying, with pressure and difficult sighing, sobbing inspiration, > pressure or sitting up; in l. cavity; in cavity when sitting and standing, extending to fauces; in intercostal muscles when sitting; in l. ribs; r. ribs; on r. lower ribs, extending into r. flank; in region of last true ribs after eating, with oppression of chest; in region of diaphragm, on r. side; outward, at sternum; burrowing, from diaphragm out to l. ribs; boring outward in l. cavity; drawing, in l.; pinching, in inner side of r. ribs; tensive, in l. intercostal muscles; pressive, in r. cavity, then fine S., with pressive pain in ribs near spine.

Pressure on, with constriction of throat; P. here and there, and in muscles of back; under front edges of l. ribs; behind in region of l. short ribs, also when stooping; in sternum, also on r. side of it; in sternum, >inspiration and expiration, returning on writing; on lower part of sternum on bending chest forward; on lower part of sternum on compressing abdomen, with nausea and fulness at pit of stomach. *Pressure outward in r. side; in l. intercostal muscles*, also < *inspiration and expiration.* Aching at scapular end of clavicle when sitting; in middle of sternum, with nausea rising from chest; in sternum, with burning, inclination to cough and stitches in middle of and below frontal bone; drawing, with contraction; *peculiar, changing into mucous expectoration.*

Spasmodic tightness, as if lungs could not be expanded fully (Bell.). Oppression; < l. side; when lying after eating, with pressure and throbbing; spasmodic; *preventing respiration and driving patient about in a restless manner.* Spasmodic contraction, so that pulse became small, irregular and slow. Jerklike constriction around across back, in region of short ribs; constriction as from a weight on sternum. Drawing in cavity; burning, in r. intercostal muscles. Pressive throbbing extending to fauces, on standing and sitting.

Heart and Pulse.—Aching and drawing pain in cardiac region, extending towards spleen, afterwards towards liver, < full inspiration. Pain in region of heart as from overfilling. Aching in præcordial region as from distention of heart, with small pulse, then loose stool. *Palpitation more like a tremor, when sitting. Heart's beat and pulse small, quick and irregular.* Pulse quick; and full; small and quick; small and slow.

Neck.—Twitching in r. side. Stitches in r. side of nape. Drawing pain in muscles of r. side. Drawing in nape; in muscles of nape; down l. side on motion.

Back.—Stitches in r. side. Pain; r. side; in attacks, < below scapula; *preventing work.*

Scapulæ.—Stitches under l. when stooping; in muscles, < motion; externally in l.; *fine burning in and behind r., extending towards ribs.* Cutting below r. Aching in r. Drawing in muscles; l. muscles. Clucking in muscles of l.

Stitch in latissimus dorsi, near upper arm. Tensive stitching upward in l. dorsal muscles. Pressure in some dorsal vertebræ. Drawing aching along the four to five last dorsal and first lumbar vertebræ, as if internally along bodies of vertebræ. Aching in region of short ribs, on both sides of the spinal column, sometimes < motion of trunk. Twitching in lower half of back when sitting.

Loins.—Fine stitches around l.; extending from r. towards ribs; boring outward, in l. towards ribs, with anxiety; boring, in l., > inspiration and expiration; tensive, in l., > walking. Dull pressure. Tearing in small of back when sitting. Aching in small of back, < bending upper part of body forward and backward. Stitch down sacrum extending to anus.

Extremities.—Tearing in r. shoulder after waking and in l. tibia, and after rising in joint of l. foot, in toes and in finger-joints. Bruised pain in muscles of upper arm, in joints of hands and feet, and paroxysmally in some places. Pressure in single joints of toes and in shoulder-joints and elbows. Aching in r. knee, ankle and elbow. Wandering rheumatic pain, especially in joints and scapulæ. Drawing in joints of fingers, on dorsum of hands and feet. Pressive drawing in bones of hands and tarsus on motion. Drawing and stitching in calves, in muscles of arms, here and there, more in the bends. Cramplike drawings in many places on, like a twitching.

Axilla.—Superficial fine stitches below l. Pressure inward beneath l.; intermittent P. inward below r., towards the front.

Shoulder.—Twitching in l.; *in l. joint extending inward;* in l. joint towards outer side. Stitches in l.; in joints, < motion; outward in l. joint; fine tensive, inward in joint. Bruised sensation in shoulder and elbow-joints. Aching in joints. Pressure in; < in r. Drawing pain. Drawing paralytic pain along l. at rest, and down upper arm.

Arm.—Drawing and pressure in muscles. Pressure on muscles of r.

Upper Arm.—Twitching of deltoid; twitching on outer side of l. upper arm. Twitching sensation in inner muscles of l. Sticking on inner side of l.; outward on inner surface of r.; boring, in inner surface of r.; burning, on outer side of r.; tensive, in r. from upper part outward towards inner side. Pressing in muscles of r. Intermittent cramplike pressure in l., not far from shoulder. Tensive drawing on inner side of l. Drawing pain around head of humerus on holding arm still, with trembling irritability (as from fatigue) of muscles, so that he must move them constantly.

Elbow.—*Fine sticking.* Fine long stitch extending into bend.

Forearm.—Cramplike twitching extending down, with feeling as if hand would stiffen. Tearing up, on moving finger; up along on bending fingers. Sticking on middle of r.; tearing up r. during rest, then burning. Pressure on outside of l.; boring P. outward on inner side of l. Intermittent cramplike drawing along inner surface of l.

Wrist.—Scraping on inner condyle. Bruised pain in bones, at rest. Pressure; in muscles. Aching extending from r., into r. index; intermittent, in external condyle of l., and in side of thumb.

Hand.—*Cramplike twitching in metacarpal bone of l. thumb.* Sticking on back of r. Pressure on joints. Pain in r. palm as from a pressive body, with sensation as if hand would stiffen. Numblike pain on metacarpal bone of l. middle finger, as from a weight. Cramplike aching in flesh between metacarpal bones of l. thumb and index. Drawing.

Fingers.—Stitches in joints; paroxysmal, in joints of little, < motion of joint; S. outward in thumb towards back of hand. Pressure at roots of r. middle and index, continuing on various motions; on inner side of thumb; in joints of thumbs; joint of l. thumb, afterwards also in joints of other fingers; drawing P. on back of finger on lying and in rest, with jerks from forearm to elbow. Drawing. Drawing pain in joints of all fingers. Cramplike pain in r. thumb, then l.

Lower Extremities.—Drawing when walking, with pressure.

Thigh.—Twitchings in r.; l.; r. gluteals; l. gluteals; on anterior side of r.; on upper half anteriorly; superficial, on inner side of l.; intermittent, on inner surface of upper; wavelike, on anterior surface of l., not far from knee. Tearing around hip-joint on walking; in l. femur when sitting. Stitches in r. gluteals; drawing fine, in r. hip-joint, extending into intestines; regularly beating, on outer surface of l. thigh below hip-joint. Pain in flesh of r. as if a pointed body stuck therein. Aching of muscles of inside of r. when sitting and walking, and in joints of feet. Drawing; in muscles of r.; in muscles above knee; in muscles of r., running down to knee and foot, where pressure is felt, also jumping to knee when sitting; here and there in muscles of r., with pressure; twitching, in l.; tensive, on inside of r. Paralytic drawing pain on outer side when sitting. Restlessness (trembling) of thigh and leg, like a pulsation of arteries, when sitting after walk.

Knee.—*Twitching on inner side of r.;* on outer side of l. Stitches near patella on sitting, with pain in patella when touched as if sore and ulcerated; burning, in r. patella; fine, in l. knee when sitting; wandering, when sitting, and in joints of feet. Bruised feeling when sitting, and in ankles, changing at times to pressive sensation. Pain; when sitting, < r.; when sitting, and above them; when walking, and in ankles; l. knee and l. ankle, < walking; behind l. patella. Burning aching in upper part, sometimes changing to burning throbbing. Drawing in bones. Drawing aching in hamstrings on making them tense. Stitching drawing pain in and above r., < walking. Clucking on inner side of l.

Leg.—Twitching in muscles of upper half of r. tibia. Tearing in whole r., > walking. Stitches in r. calf when sitting, later when walking; in r. calf and like pinching, when sitting, then in muscles above r. knee; itching, in forepart of l. tibia below knee, > walking; outward in r. tibia; (running down l. tibia, towards inside). Bruised feeling when sitting, especially in knees. Pressure in muscles; in l. tibia, > motion; in calves, with drawing. Aching below r. calf, > walking. Drawing in muscles; l. tibia; calves; l. calf. Intermittent drawing pain in joints. Goes to sleep if slightly compressed.

Ankle.—Twitching in r., extending downward. Stitches towards inner side of l.; itching, below r. inner malleolus, > rubbing. Pressure when sitting; l. when walking; r. when walking, and towards calf. Aching in r. when walking, then in l. foot when sitting, < walking. Drawing in r.

Foot.—Twitching in l. sole towards toes. Stitches in dorsum of r., > walking. Aching on dorsum of l. when sitting; in r. sole when sitting. Burrowing on inner side of l. Sensation in ball of l. sole as if he had stood a long time. Intermittent tension in r. instep as from a tight boot. Intermittent throbbing on inner side of l. Sensation in lower part of l. as if it would stiffen when riding over the other and hanging down.

Toes.—Twitching in r. great. Sticking, < motion; S. in tips; burning, in l. little; fine, in r. third, on walking. *Intermittent throbbing in l. great; painful throbbing in tip of great.* Pain in l. great, sometimes throbbing. Pressure on joint of r. great, above r. carpus and on its back; burning P. at root of l. great. Drawing; in bones. Drawing pain in r.

Skin.—Stitches in forehead and r. thigh; l. cheek, then r.; r. forearm; external side of l. thigh; itching, in r. side of lower abdomen. Crawling on back. Drawing on external surface of l. leg. Itching in r. cheek; below navel; on r. scapula; inner side of r. knee; l. patella, not > by scratching; on dorsum of foot, continues when sitting and walking; crawling I. on lower surface of r. great toe.

Sleep.—Yawning, with discomfort, restlessness and debility. Sleepiness. Night restless. Sleep disturbed. Waking frequently and tossing about. Merry dreams of company and feasting. Sleep full of dreams of things of which he had previously spoken or of what he had done, and the dream became a true continuation, which was afterwards realized.

Fever.—Chilliness till after 9 A.M.; at 8.45 A.M., with the pains, especially in ankles, knees and elbows; at 6 P.M., with warmth of hands. *Running over body from time to time.* Cold, dry skin.

Shivering from last dorsal vertebra to second lumbar vertebra. Chills in back when walking in room, with cold feet and hands and blue nails; in back and loins; back and hands, also with slow pulse; in back, with heaviness and pressure in sinciput and forehead, external warmth of cheeks and ears, and sticking in tongue; in back while face, head, ears and hands were hot, heat in eyes, < r. and in cheeks, and itching, sticking and burning in lids; running down back, with hot hands and heat in face and ears; in back running through limbs, cold hands, creeping chill through whole body, nails bluish, salivation and asafœtida eructations. C. in back and hands, alternating with heat, heaviness and pressure in head, the chilliness < slight motion in a warm room. Cold hands and feet, 8.30 to 9 A.M., with chills in back and *heat in face.* Coldness of hands at 9 A.M., with chilliness in back, heat in head and face and wandering pains, also at another time, with blue nails, twitches in r. lower eyelid, stitches in tip of tongue and pressure in sternum.

Heat.—Fever, > 5.30 P.M., and only sensation of heat remains. Feverish after eating, with heat in face without external heat, without thirst, but with anxiety and sleepiness. External heat. Heat in sinciput and face, with chills in back, and cold hands off and on. Burning in l. eyebrow. Heat of face; and ears; of cheeks, also in afternoon in flushes; of cheeks and forehead, with heaviness; stinging burning in l. cheek; of ears, with redness; in neck and occiput; along back. Burning in vertebræ, < l. side; on outer side of r. elbow. Sticking burning at tip of l. index. Burning on anterior surface of thigh when sitting; in skin externally on l. leg; tensive B. in l. calf.

Cold sweat on forehead and limbs.

Asarum.

The Asarabacca (Asarum Europæum, L.) is a native of Europe and closely allied to the American wild ginger, Asarum Canadense. It grows close to the ground and has a creeping, knotty root; the whole plant is used for a tincture.

General Action.—Its chief action seems to be upon the nervous system; general and excessive erethism, neuralgic pains and spasmodic muscular actions predominate. Great loss of energy accompanies the general symptoms.

Allies.—(Group for study.) Piper methysticum and ingrum, Nux moschata, Moschus.

Generalities.—Sensibility of all nerves, when merely imagining (which he is constantly obliged to do) that

some one is scratching even slightly on linen, or some similar substance, with finger-tips or nails, a disagreeable sensation thrills through him, arresting thoughts and functions. Ebullitions of blood evenings in bed, preventing sleep. General discomfort, with nausea. *Laziness, with slowness. Weakness every afternoon, with constant yawning;* such weakness in evening as soon as he rises from a seat, with nausea, that he felt as if he would die; weakness after dinner; *weariness, sometimes as if bruised all over* (Arnica).

Clinical.—Very valuable in certain forms of irritable nerves (anæmia) with the above peculiar sensitiveness, associated with asthenopia, nervous deafness, loss of appetite, flatulence and nervous hacking cough.

Mind.—Imagines that he is hovering in air when walking, like a spirit. Thoughts so overstrained that they vanish. *Mental faculties fail,* > vomiting. *Thoughts vanish when attempting to reflect, with drawing pressure in forehead. Ideas gradually vanish, as when falling asleep.* Stupidity, with increase of headache and nausea when trying to reflect. Gayety alternating with calmness or even sadness. Angry and cross before the cough. Weeping, sadness and anxiety. Melancholy, fretful.

Head.—Aching (> vomiting); with heat of cheeks, both > walking in open air; in different places in brain, mingled with various sensations when bending head to left, pain as if a bundle of muscular fibres had been displaced by violent exertion, the pain extending over l. temple and behind ear towards l. shoulder, increasing and decreasing synchronously with the pulse; drawing, as if it would extend into temples, at noon, > open air and lying down. Pressure inward over a greater part of the brain; pressure in brain, mostly forward.

Drawing (stupefying) here and there in brain, in ear and in nape of neck. Stupid feeling, with indisposition to do anything. Weight as if some wabbling body were in it, which lets its weight be felt when head is turned forward or backward; weight and confusion, with pressure on sagittal suture, as if intoxicated. Confusion and stupidity, with tension in region of ears; confusion > walking, with pressure outward as with a dull point in eyes, especially below r. lid; painful tensive confusion. Vertigo morning on rising, with aching in l. forehead; > washing face with cold water, with headache, both returning on drying face; in evening, as if not standing securely; as from intoxication, when rising from a seat and walking.

Forehead.—Tearing after stooping and raising head again; pulsative tearing. Aching above root of nose; A. causing a stupid feeling, as after being waked too early; drawing, in brain below forehead, < when retching; *pressing upon eyes,* which then water; throbbing, morning on rising; throbbing, from stooping. *Pressure downward;* as from a stone in brain.

Temples.—Tearing in l. Aching, < l.; in l., with confusion, then below parietal bones, then in occiput; *compressive, in l. and behind ears,* < walking or shaking head, > sitting.

Headache along coronal suture in attacks, with qualmishness in abdomen. Pressure outward in sides of head. Pressure in l. occiput, extending to side of head. Feels pulsations in arteries of occiput, then in whole body. *Tension of scalp, making hair painful.*

Eyes.—Tearing in interior of l. synchronous with pulse. Pressure in l.; as soon as he reads sensation as if pressed asunder. Warmth and pressure in, with diminished lustre. *Painful feeling of dryness interiorly.* Feeling of dryness and drawing. Lids, *swelling of l. upper, with inability to endure much reading:* twitching of r. lower; paroxysmal twitching sensation in l. upper, when holding lid still, > raising lid; crawling under upper, < l.; dry burning in lids and inner *canthi* (Sulph.), < *l.;* feeling in r. outer canthus as from a cold breath. Vision obscured. Does not perceive objects around him.

Ears.—Pinching like earache in external and middle. *Pain in meatus auditorius owing to pressive tension.* Pressure behind and below l. Tension and pressure on r. meatus auditorius, afterwards extending to r. lower jaw, when violent, with cold salivation on r. side. Feeling in outer and inner side of l. as if cartilages were contracted. Stopped feeling in front; as if pasted up. Imagines a membrane stretched across r. meatus auditorius, also with warmth in that region, also < during the chill, with tensive pressure in it; imagines a membrane stretched across meatus auditorius, with a compressed sensation. Hearing worse in r. than l. Diminished hearing in l. as if closed by the hand, with feeling as if the walls of the meatus drew nearer one another, or as if ears were stopped with cotton. Distant roaring as of a wind in l., with shrill singing in r.

Nose.—Tickling, as from the copper pole of a galvanic battery, causing sneezing, after many unsuccessful attempts, and discharge of clear fluid. (Violent sneezing.) Discharge of bloody mucus. (Dry coryza, with stoppage of l. nostril.)

Face.—Burning stinging in l. cheek. Fine stinging in r. cheek. Contractive pain in l. cheek, with thrusts, and with drawing pain in third molar. Dryness of inner side of lower lip. Cutting cramp-pain in articulation of jaw.

Mouth.—Feeling in upper incisors as from a cool breath; l. teeth feel as if hollow. Tongue coated white. Smarting of tongue and gums. Burning across middle of tongue, then burning and dryness in whole mouth, the burning > by washing face in cold water, but returning on drying face. Sweetish, insipid mucus. Contractive sensation, causing watery salivation. Saliva hot when discharged; saliva and breath feel hot, without dry feeling in mouth. Saliva tenacious. Cool salivation. Taste as from a foul stomach. Bitter taste to bread; to dry bread in evening; to tobacco when smoking. Smoking tobacco gives no pleasure.

Throat.—Scraping. Nausea in fauces. Tough mucus, which he cannot hawk up. *Dryness, with stinging.* Swallowing difficult, as if cervical glands were swollen.

Stomach.—Hunger in morning. Eructations frequent, empty; reaching only upper part of chest. Rising of air from stomach when walking in open air, with yawning twice, then eructations and emission of flatus. Hiccough. *Nausea;* with loathing and shuddering; with pressure in forehead and salivation; with disclination to attend to business, laziness and want of thinking power. Retching increases in violence in proportion as it becomes more frequent, with lachrymation; empty R., with water collecting in mouth. *During the retching all symptoms increase, only the stupid feeling in head decreases.*

Vomiting, with anguish; V., with diarrhœa; with exertion of stomach and compression in epigastrium and head; sourish water, with great exertion, pressure on stomach and arrest of breath; scanty, greenish, sourish juice in paroxysms, with great exertion, and with every paroxysm a sensation as if head in region of ears would burst. Cutting in epigastric region, also in places, > emission of flatus. Pinching; in or above it. Pressure in region and pit; in region during inspiration; as from a dull point; in pit, so that he cannot decide whether he is hungry or not. Fulness, with hunger.

Clinical.—Nausea, eructations and vomiting, especially during pregnancy, with the peculiar and excessive sensitiveness of the drug. Desire for alcoholic drinks is said to be controlled by Asarum. "Strings of odorless mucus pass from the bowels;" whether this drug will prove curative in catarrh of the bowels remains to be proven, many of the symptoms point to its homœopathicity to that condition.

Abdomen.—Painless movement of flatus. Breaking of the flatus not emitted. Cutting in morning before stool, with stitches downward in rectum. Pain; l. during motion, with painful pressing; with vomiting; single painful sensations in l. side, in an oblique direction below umbilicus; raging, in l. groin, darting through urethra into glands and causing sore smarting, contractive pain in the same. Constrictive sensation in region of diaphragm. Fulness, with hunger. Qualmishness, with attacks of headache along coronal suture.

Stool.—Urging to, an hour and a half after a stool, *with cutting in abdomen and rectum before and during the stool*, which is softer than the former. Diarrhœa; like resin and consisting of tough mucus, for six days shaggy masses of mucus, with ascarides. Whitish-gray and ash-colored, with bloody mucus on top. In small hard pieces. Morning stool delayed, *scanty, yellow* like an egg (*mucous*) *and in a thin string.*

Urinary Organs.—Pressure upon bladder during and after micturition. (Drawing in urethra.) Constant desire to urinate.

Respiratory Organs.—Stitches and constriction in larynx, making respiration short and jerking, the constriction > by hacking cough. Cough from irritation in throat caused by inspiration. Cough from mucus in chest, which rises into throat and causes difficult breathing, then cough with expectoration. Expectoration by hawking and cough. Respiration short at night; short, with constricted feeling in throat and hacking cough. (Whistling when beginning to cough.)

Chest.—Twitchings in region of clavicle. Stitches during respiration; stitch on l. side near pit of stomach. Pressure on; in r. side, at regular intervals; in region of last ribs, as with the back of a knife. Painful stretchings in l. side. Burning in r. half, more external than internal. Lungs, *stitches during inspiration;* on deep inspiration; *in r. during inspiration;* deep-seated in l., at every inspiration, arresting breathing; pain as if constricted with a sharp wire; l., or as if cut into by the wire.

Neck.—Spasmodic contractions of l. cervical muscles, with bending of head towards l. side, the contractions > by washing face with cold water, but returning on drying face. *Pain in l. side of nape as if a bundle of muscular fibres had been displaced by violent exertion, afterwards extending over head and shoulders. Paralytic pain as if bruised in muscles of nape when moving them.* Sensation in muscles of nape as if the cravat were too tight, or as if parts were pressed by a blunt edge. Weight about neck and sensation as if muscles were compressed by a cravat.

Back.—Stitches below scapulæ. Pain across the spinal column from one crista ilii to the other as if the flesh were torn or pulled towards the outer side, in tearing jerks, when walking. *Bruised pain;* along inner border of r. scapula on touching or moving it inward. *Paralytic pain as if bruised when standing or sitting, > lying.* Burning pain in small of back while sitting, with stitches.

Extremities.—*Lightness,* he is not aware of having a body. Occasional twitching and tearing pains. Bruised feeling.

Upper Extremities.—Axilla, pressure in l., as with a rough piece of board; sudden aching in axillary glands. Shoulders, tearing stitches; sprained pain when moving arm. Arm, tearing in l.; contractive tensive pain in deltoid when laying hand on table, or when it lies there; discomfort and exhaustion of arm when lying on table; paralytic weakness. Wrist, drawing paralytic pain in l.; sudden drawing and burning pain extending from wrist through thumb and index. Fingers, drawing, evening in bed.

Lower Extremities.—Weakness when ascending stairs; weakness as if not rested by sleep.

Thigh.—Spasmodic contractions near r. knee, > extending limb. Lancinating tearing in l. Sudden digging in upper muscles of l. Pain in hip; *r. hip;* in hip-joint and middle of thigh on touching or walking; in hip-joint and middle of thigh when stepping, with paralyzed feeling in the limb; drawing, in hips when walking; drawing and tensive, in head of l. and further on, < walking. Pressure above bend of r. knee as from something hard and blunt. Sensation from r. hip-joint to knee as if it would go to sleep. Weariness and bruised feeling in thighs and knees as in a fit of ague.

Knee.—Tearing stitches. Drawing; in tendons of hollows, evenings in bed. (Clucking in hollow.) Uneasiness in l., causing one to move about. *Weakness, with staggering if not very careful,* > washing face with cold water, but returning after drying face. Twitching in calf. Bruised feeling in l. tibia. L. leg feels asleep and foot is insensible as when very cold, and as if dead. Sudden stitches in sole. (Toes painful as if frozen.) Drawings in toes, evening in bed.

Skin.—Itching below l. temple, beginning with fine stinging. Itching as from a flea-bite in front, below r. axilla.

Sleep.—Frequent yawning. Drowsiness by day; drowsy and out of humor, > walking in open air. Sleep restless every other night, cannot easily fall asleep. Nightly vexing dreams about insults received.

Fever.—Chilliness when drinking. Shaking over whole body. Chilliness and shivering, without thirst. C., with gooseskin, cold hands, cold and blue face. Shaking chills in evening, with faintness, especially in knees and small of back, without thirst, with cold hands and hot forehead. Shuddering, with disgust and nausea. Shivering, with heat in face. C. after the hot feeling, the heat in head and face remaining, with shivering on slightest motion. C. when seated and not well covered, or when moving, but heat as soon as he covers himself, sometimes with rigors. C. all day, when sitting or lying still and keeping covered he feels only pain in eyes and forehead and pressure on pit of stomach, and sometimes external heat, but during exercise in room or exposure to open air he feels chilly, with scarcely any thirst, but when walking fast or entering warm room from open air, or when becoming heated by animated talking in room, or after dinner, or when in warm bed he feels better. Fever all day, chilliness in forenoon, then after midday nap hot feeling externally, with internal rigor and thirst. Feeling as if a cold wind blew on him, with coldness to touch, gooseskin, then heat (in afternoon), with slimy mouth, dryness in throat and thirst, then coldness as before, then in evening heat, continuing in bed, with necessity to uncover his hands and with dryness of palate. Cold feeling above l. ear. Rigor in back (suddenly, from biting on a hard crust). Coldness of hands, with warmth of arms and rest of body, still they are covered with gooseflesh, and he has violent chills.

Heat; as if sweat would break out. Heat after chills, especially in face and palm, with return of the symptoms in ears. Heat of forehead and scalp, with shivering and chilliness, no thirst, pulse strong and quick. R. external ear hot to touch; warmth in region of r. external meatus auditorius, with sensation as if a membrane were stretched across it. *Warm feeling in cheeks; l. cheek.*

Sweat in evening immediately after lying down; at night; when sitting still; easily; on upper part of body and upper extremities.

Asclepias Cornuti (Syriaca).

This species of milk-weed is quite common in the United States, growing on roadsides. A tincture is prepared from the root.

Group for comparison.—Apocynum c.

Appeared dull and stupid. Headache; morning on waking, with disagreeable feeling in stomach; principally between eyes. Vertigo. Constriction across forehead. Tongue covered with thick fur. *Tickling* in fauces. Burning and tickling in fauces and throat. Appetite increased. Food little relished. *Nausea.* Vomiting; violent, with retching; then rawness in stomach and pain, cold skin, feeble pulse and *feeling as if a sharp instrument were thrust through from one temple to the other.* Pain in stomach; and rawness. Uneasiness in stomach. Increased secretion of bile. Excoriation of anus. Stool, *slight inclination to;* soft and yellow; fluid, copious, yellowish, with griping; soft, copious, brown, with pain in bowels; frequent. Ardor urinæ. *Urine increased;* in morning; with increase of specific gravity and solid matter; and pale, of lighter specific gravity. Increase of water in urine. Tickling at end of penis. *Increase of bronchial secretions.*

Heart's action increased. Pulse quick and full; quick and feeble after vomiting. Drowsiness and sleep. "Slept rather hard" during the night. Sweat profuse.

Clinical.—Has relieved persons suffering from dropsy dependent on disease of the kidneys and heart; it appears to increase the quantity of urine and perspiration. Nervous headaches after suppressed perspiration, followed by profuse flow of urine. Dropsy following scarlet fever, or from heart disease. Rheumatism of large joints. Intermittent, pressing uterine pains, threatening miscarriage in pregnant women, have been removed.

Asclepias Tuberosa.

The butterfly-weed has bright orange-red flowers and a large fleshy root; from the root a tincture is prepared.

General Action.—A marked cathartic; muscles, especially of chest, painful (Bry., Coloc., Kali c.).

Generalities. — Pandiculations. Emaciation. It seemed when walking as if he leaned forward and to the left. Sharp bone-pains from time to time in different parts. Pain in joints. Oppression from dinner till evening. Distress and general weakness after walking a short distance and smoking a cigar, with aversion to all movement. Pulsations in muscles, in arms, back and various parts. Numbness of whole body. Feeling as if recovering from a long and severe illness. Weakness; morning; morning, especially in legs; > evening; so that walking is difficult; with disinclination to work; of body and mind all day, with dulness.

Mind.—Elevation of spirits towards evening. Low spirits. Fretfulness. Thought difficult. Memory weak.

Head.—Aching; morning on getting up, also obliging him to lie down again in consequence of debility; > foot-bath. Heaviness; with pain, < l. side; with drowsiness; with uneasiness; and of eyes. Confusion; when getting up, with heaviness. Intoxicated feeling after smoking a little, vertigo, dim vision and general debility. Vertigo, with dulness behind forehead. Aching in forehead; *forehead and vertex, < motion and > lying.* Aching in r. side of head at noon. Headache presses deeply on base of skull and is similar to Ipec. headache. Alopecia. Pain in scalp of l. occiput, with pain on touch, as if there were a pimple there.

Eyes.—Dull, and he looks as after several weeks' sickness. Ophthalmia. Blepharophthalmy, heaviness of eyes and itching in r. ball. Blepharitis. Feeling as from sand. Pain from gas-light. Fatigued; and heavy. Ulcerative sensation in lower lids. Pain in l. inner canthus, with itching in globe, and on shutting lids a noise like the sucker of a pump-box. Itching in r. inner canthus at 6 P.M., in lower lid and all over face, with stitches in forehead and several parts of body. Pain in l. orbit. Vision disturbed. Vision of black spots.

Nose.—Pimple on septum in r. nostril and at r. side of root, with itching. Pricking in like a flea-bite. Itching; in l. nostril; in root on both sides. Sneezing; desire for, in l. nostril. Coryza in morning in open air; dry C.; fluent. Blows blood from l. nostril.

Face.—Hippocratic. Yellow complexion. Lips inflamed and full of pimples.

Mouth.—Teeth yellow. Pain in r. lower molars. Gums and buccal membrane pale, inclining to yellow. Gums bleeding; of r. upper canine tooth. Tongue has yellow sticky coat. Breath fetid, even smelling of pepper. Taste putrid; taste of blood.

Throat.—Constriction, with pricking in larynx. Angina.

Stomach.—Appetite depraved; deficient; anorexia in morning; insatiable hunger at noon. Thirst. Eructations; till evening; prolonged, smelling of medicine. Nausea morning on getting up. Cramps. Pain; with rumbling in bowels; in pit, with burning in stomach; nervous. Gastralgia; after supper, and it seems as if the cough would shatter the stomach. Burning in stomach and intestines, with noisy borborygmi and slight pain. Weight.

Abdomen.—Rumbling; at 3 A.M., with cutting pain, which wakes him; at 6 A.M. on waking, with soreness of peritoneum; and uneasiness, with heat in umbilical region. Flatus emitted till evening; emitted, with rumbling in region of transverse colon; smelling intolerably of medicine. Pain; forenoon; 11 A.M.; after dinner; on ascending stairs; on pressure; continues long after a stool, with smarting in rectum; with emission of fetid flatus. Wind colic after breakfast; flatulent pain and stool of intolerable smell, with sharp pain in hypogastrium as if rotten, with soreness on pressure and as if it would all come out; wind colic while walking, pain as if everything would fall down. Pain at 1 A.M. as if intestines would fall out, with painful and large stool, then at 1.30 and 2 A.M. small and painful stools with increasing pains. R. hypochondrium, pain; grumblings in evening after being magnetized. Throbbing in l. hypochondrium.

Rectum and Anus.—Urging to stool. Blind hæmorrhoids.

Stool.—Dysentery, with threadlike pulse. Liquid (after salad); liquid causing smarting; *soft and fetid, preceded by rumbling.* Of intolerable smell. Like moss and suspended in water, at 4.30 A.M. Entirely albuminous. Sticky green, smelling like rotten eggs. Yellow, like tincture of turmeric, with yellow and green flocks. Frequent, painful, with colic, of bistre color and slimy, the last containing false membranes, looking as if intestines had been scraped, also yellow spots as from grease and feeling like a stream of fire. Always accompanied by colic. Insufficient.

Urinary Organs.—Lancinations in urethra, with excoriations of glans penis and beginning of a sanious and purulent secretion, the excoriation > bathing with urine. Shooting in orific of urethra. Urine red; and after standing there rise to surface small red, almost black spots, the sediment is deep-colored and thick, in the form of clouds and masses of moss, while the surface (beneath the spots) is clear and as if decomposed.

Sexual Organs.—Sweat and insipid smell. Flabbiness and insipid smell. Weakness. Chancre on r. side of prepuce, was washed with urine and passed to l. side. Erection without desire; prolonged erection in morning.

Respiratory Organs.—Pain in bronchi. Asthmatic paroxysm. Inspiration noisy and forcible, and the lungs seem to be dilated more fully. Forcible inspirations at 4 P.M. *Respiration painful, especially at base of l. lung. Cough dry; with constriction in throat; dry and harsh, causing pain in forehead and abdomen* (Bry.); *dry and hacking* (Bry.), though a little mucus is raised with effort; dry and spasmodic.

Chest.—L. lung dull on percussion. *Shooting downward from l. nipple, with stiffness of l. side of neck. Pain moves up to behind sternum and becomes sharper and cutting, < long breath and motion of hands, as in triturating* (Bry.). Acute pain on r. side, seemingly in pleura. Pain < singing or loud speaking; P. in region of diaphragm on motion; beneath l. nipple, with palpitation; *in lungs, > bending forward* (Coloc.); in l. lung, then weariness, the pain returning on coughing or drawing a deep breath. *Spaces between ribs close to sternum tender on pressure, and darting pain shoots over to r. side.* Oppression after smoking; after the forcible inspirations; with difficulty in breathing. Warmth internally, with dull pain at base of lungs and with feeling of tightness. Weak and sore feeling. Paralysis of r. lung in forenoon, with violent pain.

Clinical.—Pleurodynia or acute pleurisy.

Heart and Pulse.—Lancinating pain near heart; lancinations in heart and r. intercostal muscles at 6 P.M. Pain as from the prick of a pin. Constrictive pain. Pulse disturbed after dinner. Rapid and small.

Neck and Back.—Torticollis on waking. Lancinating pain between shoulders. Pain in back and between shoulders; between shoulders, < on r. side; between shoulders, a little to left, in afternoon. Rheumatic pain in r. scapula and in l. wrist. Pain in loins near sacrum, lumbago.

Extremities.—Bone pain in r. arm and r. leg. Pains are always felt crosswise, when r. leg is affected the l. arm is equally so, and when it is r. arm it is also l. thigh. Pain in r. shoulder and l. leg; r. shoulder and l. knee; l. thigh and r. shoulder; l. wrist, r. arm and l. knee; r. arm near wrist and in l. leg near malleoli; l. knee and r. forearm; r. knee and leg and l. elbow; l. knee and r. elbow; above l. knee and in l. arm.

Upper Extremities.—Shoulder, pain shooting up to l., which was painful on motion; sharp shooting pain in r. Pain in shoulders and in r. breast; in r. shoulder after dinner; in l., and in r. forearm near wrist; in l. after getting up.

Arm.—Bruised pain in l. Pain in r.; l.; rheumatic, in l. Arthritic pain in r. elbow. Pain in l. arm near wrist. Pain near r. wrist at 3 P.M. Hand, pain in l. at 9.30 P.M.; rheumatic, in r.; neuralgic, in r. palm; numbness of l. hand.

Lower Extremities.—Thigh, pain in r.; in l. near knee at 6.30 P.M.; rheumatic, close to l. knee; coxalgic, in l.; coxalgic, in r. hip.

Knee.—Sharp and lancinating pain as far as thigh; lancinating pain in l. at 2 P.M., and when walking pain in r. hip-joint. Pain in l.; pain in l. when walking; in r. when walking, and in l. when sitting; aching, in knees and driving P. in thighs; rheumatic, in l. knee and r. thigh; rheumatic, in l., also morning on getting up, also at 8.30 P.M.; rheumatic, in r. at 1.30 P.M., extending into femur.

Leg.—Rheumatic pains. Sharp pain in r. tibia near knee at 6.30 P.M., with sore pain on pressure. Weakness of legs in morning. Sharp bone pain near l. malleoli. Pain in l. tarsus; rheumatic pain in r. tarsus. Pain in l. foot. Sprained feeling in l. foot. Lancinating pain in l. metatarsus. Painful corns on foot and a callosity on each fourth toe; corns painful in bed, < touch of bed-clothes. Rheumatic pains in l. fourth and little toes.

Skin.—Red erythematous tetter on r. thigh below ilium (after dinner), with pain and itching, less inflamed in evening, then another of lighter color, but sore to touch, behind it, the first followed by a dark-colored spot for several months. Pimples; on l. temporal region and on back; below upper lip, on r. side; small red, in a thick cluster beneath l. labial commissure, with crawling and gnawing itching; on lip, then below angle of mouth, becoming pustular, and one on eyebrow, which is painful (r. side); on l. side of nose, filled with serum; itching, on nose, thighs and back; red, on stomach; on nape of neck; on back, itching at night and towards morning; on l wrist; on l. middle finger; on thighs; red, on r. thigh. Itch-pustules on l. hand, with itching. Variolous pustule on bend of l. arm. Blister as from a bug-bite between sacrum and r. ilium.

Itching of lobe of r. ear, of face, nose, and especially

lips. At root of nose on both sides. Around body like a girdle, evening when lying; of waist and at top of l. thigh; thighs; nates; r. thigh in evening, then l.; hips and l. thigh; l. ham; arms at night; forearms at night; wrists at night; l. hand and r. side; l. hand between middle and little fingers; last l. fingers, then in r.

Sleep.—Drowsiness; > open air; irresistible. Somnolence till evening. Sleeplessness. Slumbers tardy; with drowsiness in morning. Night restless; sleep restless during first part of night, with frightful dreams.

Dreams gloomy and frightful; frightful, all night, waking him at 5 A.M. Tiresome, of duels, flight, etc.; fatiguing, of reckless boasting, of trying to sing political songs in a loud voice in spite of the presence of spies. Extraordinary, of political affairs. Of churches, of horses and of troublesome things. Of supernatural things. Of the country, and other dreams. Complicated, but containing its own explanation, as if it had happened the night before.

Fever.—Chilliness, with cold feet. Fever, with adipsia and rapid pulse. Warmth of skin.

Asimina Triloba.

The Papaw, a small tree growing in the South and Southwest of the United States, ripens a fleshy fruit, which is edible when ripe. A tincture is prepared from the crushed seeds. The cutaneous disturbance (and fever) were caused by eating the skin of the fruit.

Compare Anacardium, Rhus t., Cocculus.

Languid and pale. Discomfort all day. Did not care to converse, even with his best friends. Headache; morning on waking; became general through frontal region after walking in open air and somewhat relieved. Aching in temples; morning on rising, involving eye, with occasional sharp pain over it, which was < by a single cough. Throat sore, but not so much so as the hoarseness would indicate. Stomach felt increased in size; soreness on pressure. Colic. Rumbling pain in abdomen in evening, with desire for stool, then a pappy, insufficient stool. Soreness in abdomen, < pressure. Pain in l. hypochondrium. Rectum and bowels inactive. Insufficient stool.

Hoarseness; with unusual difficulty in talking, seeming as if mucous membrane were thickened, and organs slow to respond to efforts of speech. Cough slight and dry. Aching pain in upper part of chest, < l. side; in upper part of l. lung. Lower end of sternum sore on pressure. Pain in l. shoulder, involving pectoral muscles. Sharp pain in l. hip-joint at 10.30 A.M., 1.30 P.M., and in evening.

Eyes red, burning and smarting, lids swollen, and face covered with pale red eruption, with some swelling of integument and with much smarting and burning, if allowed to run its course watery vesicles form, which coalesce, burst and form large dark crusts, but on this occasion, after Rhus tox. 3d, the eruption did not form crusts and subsided in a few days, when the stomach became tender to touch, as if "sore inside," for three days, with bloating, then > by appearance of dry, papular eruption in patches over body and extremities, with now and then a watery vesicle, and with intense itching and burning, < scratching and heat, > cold air and cold water, the eruption beginning with a red, itching, burning point, after scratching and rubbing a blotch like hives, the itching < from early in evening till after rising in morning, the poisoning has followed this course several times, it began this time on l. cheek.

Waking about daylight, unrefreshed, with headache. Did not rest well at night, turned and moved all night, could not dismiss from my thoughts what had occurred during the day, and got up unrefreshed. Fever, with vomiting of ingesta, scarlet eruption, pulse rapid, full and steady, fauces red and swollen, tonsils and submaxillary glands enlarged, yellowish diarrhœa, frontal headache, soreness of throat and nausea, afterwards desquamation of cuticle and a carbuncle on anterior aspect of thigh, the eruption, fever and diarrhœa being much like some cases of scarlet fever, and the diarrhœa lasting much longer than the other symptoms, all the other children had the eruption on neck and upper limbs.

Asparagus.

Asparagus officinalis, the well-known garden perennial, contains an active principle (Asparagine), which also occurs in Convallaria, Paris, Robinia, etc. A tincture is prepared from the young sprouts.

General Action.—This substance is a marked diuretic and sometimes an emetic; it depresses the heart, produces profuse mucous secretions, nasal and bronchial, and causes weakness. Its allies are Convallaria, Squills, Paris, Digitalis, Apocynum, etc.

Generalities.—Most symptoms < on motion. Pains > throwing chest forward and head backward.

Mind.—Serenity. Peculiar anxiety, with palpitation and ill humor.

Head.—Confusion and vertiginous staggering. Forehead, aching, with confusion; aching in brain near eyes; confusion; heaviness in sinciput; stupefaction in sinciput, then aching in temples, < l.; vertigo in sinciput. Temples, pressing pain, < pressure.

Eyes.—Stitches and crawling. Vision acute.

Nose.—Sneezing; irritation to. *Coryza, with profuse thin whitish fluid* from l. nostril, then from r.; C., with aching extending from root of nose over forehead to fore part of head; C., with beginning dryness and swelling of internal nostrils, then impeded entrance of air; dry C. Smell lost.

Face.—Pale.

Mouth.—Painless cavity and exfoliation of a carious molar. Saliva diminished; increased; sweetish, as if mixed with blood. Talking through nose. Taste coppery; T. sweetish, insipid.

Throat.—Hawking almost constantly, with rough feeling in throat; inclination to hawk and cough, rising from deep in throat; and inclination to cough, the mucus is not readily loosened, but is brought up by paroxysms of cough; H. of mucus. Copious tenacious mucus from throat.

Stomach.—Thirst. Eructations. Retching while coughing. Nausea on waking before 5 A.M., and vomiting of the food eaten in the evening, with bile and mucus, then fecal bilious diarrhœa, then frequent vomiting with increased effort. Wind.

Abdomen.—Discharge of much wind. Distention. Colic, with bilious diarrhœa. Griping in region of navel, which is painful on touch. Pinching below navel in evening. Drawing pain in groins.

Anus and Stool.—Burning and soreness at anus.

(Itching in anus.) Peculiar desire for stool and somewhat difficult hardish stool.

Urinary Organs.—Burning in urethra; and cutting; burning after urinating, with sensation as if there were more urine to pass. Urging to urinate. *Urinating frequently, with fine stitches in orifice of urethra.* Frequent scanty discharge of urine, preceded by sticking in urethra, with burning. Urine scanty and cloudy; decreased, beer-brown, without sediment; a little straw-colored urine, becomes turbid immediately. Diuresis; with thirst and increase of appetite. Urine of peculiar odor. Turbid urine after dinner; turbid when passed, but became clear and formed a white, flocculent sediment. Fatty coating on sides of glass after the urine was shaken out and the glass well washed. Urine kept over night formed a reddish deposit on sides of vessel.

Clinical.—Cystitis, pus and mucus, tenesmus, weak bladder, enlarged prostate or inflammation of the neck of the bladder from cold, with pus and mucus.

Sexual Organs.—Swelling of penis, with erections and urging to urinate. Stitching on r. side of glans. Excitement of sexual passions. Menses one day longer than usual.

Respiratory Organs.—Tickling and inclination to cough. Cough towards evening; remitted after breakfast; straining, with inclination to vomit, and also forcing tears into eyes; distressing, with oppression of chest and copious mucus. Expectoration difficult. Mucus is more readily loosened upon each turn of coughing. Breathing difficult when moving or ascending stairs. Is obliged to sit up in bed to relieve the breathing.

Chest.—Stitches in l. on inspiration; in various parts on inspiration, especially about l. scapula. Pressure in, after breakfast. Sudden darting pain through r. at 10 A.M. Oppression. Constriction; < writing. Tension when taking a deep breath; tensive sensation on inspiration, as if hollow. Hollow sensation, with external heaviness.

Heart and Pulse.—Stitching in region of heart after eating. *Palpitation*, < after motion and ascending stairs, with anxious restlessness; *with oppression of chest;* while sitting, so that the leaves of the book he held trembled. Pulsation of heart perceptible to touch and hearing; on moderate motion. Irregular, quick, twofold stroke of heart. Heart's beat hardly perceptible. Pulse small, compressible. Pulse accelerated; when sitting.

Clinical.—Cardiac affections of people with weak pulse, pain about the left shoulder. Palpitations and pains about the heart, with troubles in the bladder.

Back.—Rheumatic pain between scapulæ. Pain in small of back, at beginning of lumbar vertebræ. Shooting pains through loins, in region of lumbar vertebræ while sitting.

Upper Extremities.—Shoulder. Pain in region of, on touch. Rheumatic pain in region of r.

Lower Extremities.—Thigh. Pain as from dislocation in neck of r. bone while walking; in forenoon while walking, preventing rapid motion and sometimes causing limping. Bruised pain in muscles in middle, making it difficult to walk, < descending stairs, with sore pain on touch. Sore pain in upper surface on touch and on bending hip and knee-joints, making it difficult to walk. Stitching above r. knee, then below l. side of knee, evening when sitting. Indications of cramp in calves. Cramplike pain in l. calf while stretching on waking, > rubbing. R. foot more painful than l. R. foot weaker than l. Drawing in l. toe, which he had cut with an axe when a boy, at 10 P.M. before sleep.

Sleep.—Drowsiness and yawning; in morning.

Fever.—Shivering, with weary sleepiness. Warmth increased. Febrile excitement at 3 P.M., with weariness. Heat of face. Burning of cheeks.

Asterias Rubens.

The red star-fish is found on the seacoast of Europe and America; for medicinal use a tincture is prepared from the live animal, which is cut in pieces and macerated in Alcohol.

General Action.—Experiments hitherto made developed chiefly nervous phenomena. Hysterical and neuralgic symptoms predominate. Notice particularly the neuralgia of the left breast and arm.

Generalities—Desire for open air, anxiety and impatience in the house. Difficulty in keeping still. Scarcely able to work. Malaise, lassitude > after eating; malaise after evening meal, with heat of skin, frequency and fulness of pulse. Lassitude under influence of heat, especially warmth of bed. Symptoms increase in intensity in the second part of the day, especially in the evening.

Clinical.—**Is reported to have cured a case of chorea, quiet only when the hands were in the pockets; at other times trembling of arms and legs, could scarcely walk.**

Mind.—Uncommon cheerfulness in evening. Inclination to bite. Irritation from noon till 2 P.M., with anger and inclination to pick a quarrel with some one. Melancholy alternating with cerebral excitement, with inclination to give herself up to mental or bodily work, to walk or engage in violent exercise, species of moral intoxication. Weeping, with despair, then calmness. Sensitiveness prompting him to weep from least emotion. Anguish from noon till 3 P.M., as if a misfortune were impending or he were going to hear bad news, and he then feels as if he should give way to tears. Disturbance of understanding, with general debility.

Head.—Distress in brain. Headache stopped at noon. Aching, < at close of day, more severe at back of head than at forehead, the head aches all night. Whole skull painful during the severe pains. Pain in skull as if being crushed. Vertigo; when walking. Shocks in brain as from an electric battery, waking him in the night, with light feeling in head, consciousness almost lost, fear of apoplexy, and on coming to himself hard quick pulse and violent throbbing in r. carotid, this fever lasted till close of next day. Rush of blood; with fulness, heat and feeling as if about to burst. Throbbing; when ascending or walking. Twitches in brain; during first half of night, when blowing nose. Heaviness; with heat, throbbing in head and flushed face.

Forehead.—Boring above l. eye, coming on and ceasing suddenly, causing contraction of brows, with misty vision. Aching above eyes; in sinciput in morning, hardly ceasing in daytime by walking in open air; with fulness, contraction of muscles and compression above eyes; seeming to crush eyes by a heavy weight. Twitchings in forehead, at temples, especially occiput.

Pressure at temples. Lancinating pain in r. temple. Pain in vertex as if skull were bruised. Agitation, spasms, feeling of uneasiness in upper part of brain, < exercising memory or understanding, a sensation similar to the weariness of a limb after great exertion. Flying pain in r. half of head. Sudden pain in r. side. Fulness of head, seeming to disturb it laterally. Occipital aching after breakfast, going and coming suddenly; at r. side, < walking.

Eyes.—Bloodshot. Fatigued look. Pain from within outward. Heat. Balls drawn backward. Winking, with redness of edges of lids. Fatigued by light. Can hardly be used in evening.

Ears.—Lancinating pain, which is felt in auditory meatus, is concentrated at occiput and there ceases, returns in the course of the day, but more feebly. Hard hearing, < r. ear; hard hearing, with sounds as of a river, of waves. Sudden loud noise in both ears.

Nose.—Sneezing in morning on waking, with coryza. Epistaxis.

Face.—*Red;* and swollen. Expression of dulness, a kind of stupidity in posture and look.

Mouth.—Tongue swollen. Drawing pain in tongue. Tongue troubles her, with repugnance to talking. Saliva increased.

Throat.—Dryness. Irritation; with heat. Soreness in morning on waking, with constriction. Dull pain extending along œsophagus.

Stomach.—Appetite wanting, with loss of taste. Aversion to meat. Capricious appetite, with desire for highly seasoned dishes, strong cheese, liquors, coffee, tea. Loud and frequent eructations in morning. Nausea. Lassitude of stomach in morning, after many loud eructations, with heat in this organ.

Abdomen.—Alternately swollen and lessened in size. Colic, with shivering alternating with flushes of heat in face; colic, then diarrhœa. Drawing in walls. Flatulence very troublesome after each meal, because it does not pass off either above or below. Dull pain in shocks in r. side and near navel.

Rectum and Stool.—Hæmorrhoidal swelling. Hæmorrhoidal flux. Heat in rectum. Stool liquid, brown, gushing. Frequent, soft stools. Difficult, firm stool. Constipation, ineffectual urging.

Urinary Organs.—Frequent urging to urinate, and more abundant urine. Frequent emission of watery urine. Thick viscid urine, with heat in urethra on urinating.

Sexual Organs.—Erections in morning; frequent in sleep. Pressure in lower organs of abdomen (womb ?), walking is troublesome. Anguish in womb as if something protruded. Jerking in uterus. Unusual moisture in vagina, which affords relief. General sensation as before menses. Menses delayed eight days, during which the colic and other sufferings which usually accompany them are present, but they cease after appearance of the flow, which is more abundant than usual. She is harassed by sexual desire every morning in bed.

Chest.—Breasts swell, as before menses. Lancinating pain in anterior inferior portion, to r. and l. of sternum, > throwing back upper chest and shoulders. Pain under sternum; P. in whole l. side, < movement; dull, in muscles of præcordial region. L. breast feels as if pulled inward. Drawing pain in breasts; *towards inner portion of chest, from before backward, under the l. breast this pain extends over inner portion of arm to end of little finger.* Compression in præcordial region. Fulness, making him fearful of syncope. Undulating pulsations at night causing anxiety.

Heart.—Anxiety during the night and in morning. Palpitation; leaping, and when strong extending to epigastrium, with a tightening sensation. Beats scarcely preceptible and prolonged.

Back.—Drawing pain; in sacrum.

Extremities.—Uneasiness especially in bends o arms, and she can hardly bear the arms covered. Diminished sensibility, especially in legs and thighs. Pain in r. shoulder; l. elbow; flexor tendons of l. wrist; extending from thumb-joint to shoulder. Numbness of hands and fingers; of l. hand, extending to arm; of hypothenar eminence and of l. finger.

Lower Extremities.—Bruised pain. Restlessness in a close room, with need of fresh air. Lassitude.

Thigh.—Lancinations in anterior part; on anterior surface; burning, in l. great trochanter and hip-joint, darting to outer side of ham. Aching in l. hip-joint in morning. Pain in r. hip and in whole l. side as far as scapula, causing fever. Pulling pain at outer side of l. Drawing in r. hip as if leg were too long and were pulled downward.

Pain in l. knee. Lancinating pain in a sore made on leg by scratching. Legs weak when standing. Pain in r. ankle; in l., < walking. Foot, pain in l., and in muscles of leg; in joints of l.; gouty, in l., < movement, it centres at articulation of great toe with the metatarsal bone and continues there all day. Painful drawing in soles and toes.

Toes.—Cutting in l. great, with soreness of l. sole and pain in toes. Lancinating pain, especially in l. great, with heat and soreness, which prevented wearing a shoe, < after sunset and in a close room, with redness, which was < by heat, the pain > cold air or cold water, renewed by warmth of bed, but ceased in early part of night, and returned several evenings.

Skin.—Eruption between breasts. Redness on chest, with branlike efflorescence; red spot over l. olecranon process, with a dry, branny, friable coating, and a similar spot on anterior part of same arm; red blotch on chest, with itching. Formication in lower limbs. Itching around l. thumb-nail; of thighs and legs, > towards 6 P.M. in open air.

Sleep.—Sleepy when reading. Sleep from 2 A.M. till middle of day. Sleep, with restlessness. Vivid dreams about persons and events.

Fever.—Shivering, with drowsiness, heat of skin and restlessness at night; S. during the colic, alternating with flushes of heat in face. Coldness of l. arm as from a cold wind. Heat. Antipathy to everything which causes heat, with extreme desire to bathe in cold water. *Heat in head; as if surrounded by hot air;* in head, then in whole body, with desire to drink cold water and cool herself internally and externally; of feet; of skin, fever at close of day, shivering, heat followed by cold; of skin after evening meal, with malaise, frequency and fulness of pulse.

Astragalus Menziesii.

A tincture is prepared from the plant. Natural order, Leguminosæ. Compare Oxytropis, to which Astragalus is closely related.

Weak feeling, with a feeling in arms as if trembling; weak feeling, with emptiness in stomach, the latter >

a light supper. Feeling as if all nerves were trembling. Vertigo in occasional attacks, with fulness in head. Aching in temples. Fulness in r. temple and superior maxillary bone, with nausea, shivering and chilliness. Pain in l. superior bone, then pressure. Aching in r. superior bone, with pressure in both bones. Pain in masseter muscles. Burning in pharynx, œsophagus and stomach. Stool loose, like diarrhœa, at 7.15 A.M., an unusual hour, with burning and tenesmus, at 8 A.M. burning at anus, recurring occasionally, and at 9.15 A.M. occasional tenesmus. Sleep restless after midnight, frequently disturbed, with dreams of quarreling.

Atropinum.

Atropine and its salts, obtained from Belladonna, are prepared for use by trituration.

Physiological Action similar to Belladonna.

Allied Drugs.—Bell., Hyosc., Stram., Sulphur, (Secale c.).

Antidote.—Morphine, Nicotine, each in part.

Generalities.—Appears dull and stupid. Convulsions; especially of limbs; beginning in neck and face. Clonic spasms of biceps flexor cubiti and of muscles of jaw, < by disturbing the patient. Clonic cramp in face and limbs (moves arms forward in front of chest). Staggering, then falling, with convulsive movements of limbs, then pupils much dilated, heart beating rapidly, tongue curled to roof of mouth, lips, mouth and throat dry, convulsions about once in five minutes, glossopharyngeal not responsive to tickling. *Twitching* in head and arms, with vomiting, face red, then pale, pleasant delirium, head thrown from side to side, fingers closed, arms flexed, convulsions of upper limbs, looking as if deeply drunk, after three hours clonic spasms over whole body, passing into toxic ones, pupils dilated, no reaction, difficult deglutition, voice hoarse and thick, skin insensible, dry, bluish-white, no fever, pulse small, frequent, soft, irregular, intermittent, respiration accelerated, superficial.

Jerkings; especially in legs, arms and face, when attempting to drink the arm contracted suddenly and the water was spilled, and when walking one or both legs contracted, throwing one to the ground. Hands tremulous and eyes closed, but she became quiet and drowsy, then kicking and throwing her arms about, limbs weak, unable to stand, face flushed, then meddlesome and pleasant delirium, picked at her clothes, tried to get out of bed, imagined she was sewing, nursing her child or shopping with her sister, then repeated sighing and yawning, then unconsciousness and stupor, eyes closed, pupils dilated, muscular system relaxed, except trismus, deglutition almost impossible, respiration labored and like that of an intoxicated person, lids closed, conjunctivæ injected, eyes brilliant and staring, tongue, hard and soft palates glazed and parched. Face flushed, pulse full, strong, hard and bounding, respiration almost stertorous, somnolency, impairment of senses, when aroused and raised up he would look around wildly, and when addressed in a loud voice muttered incoherent words, tremor, weakness, especially of lower limbs, so that he was unable to stand, though there was considerable strength in his arms, involuntary micturition. Convulsive trembling of one or another muscle.

Startings in women; S. at any sudden noise; at night when nearly asleep, as if frightened (Bell., Sul.). Busy with his hands, pulling the bed-clothes about. Restlessness; in morning on rising, and unrefreshed; with agitation of body and mind; with sleeplessness; with haste, becoming a desire to fight. Impossible to keep him in bed and difficult to keep him from walking about. Sensitiveness; to sounds and objects at night, with symptoms akin to early stage of meningitis, in morning rapid pulse, furred tongue and hot, dry skin. General discomfort. Weakness; morning on rising; in morning, lay in a half-dreamy sleep and after dressing great desire to lie down again; *in open air;* during stool, with nervousness, general discomfort and sweat; and trembling all over. Faintness and need of fresh air. Anæmia.

Motion difficult, and when I raised my arms they fell as if made of lead. Heaviness, drowsiness or actual sleep, with tendency to dreamy delirium. Numb or crawling sensation, formication, down back, on arms and backs of hands. Torpor and paralytic trembling. Anæsthesia (Abs., Acon., Bell., Sec. c.); and water glides over skin without moistening it or producing sensation. Lost the power to estimate distances either by eye or touch, touching an object produces no sensation. Better sitting or standing than lying.

Clinical.—It has been used homœopathically for neuralgias; supraorbital, < emotion; earache; neuralgia under the knee, > warm wraps, etc. It has sometimes been prescribed for the symptoms of Bell., especially in meningitis, spinal irritation.

Mind.—*Delirium,* with restlessness; < at night, with agitation; with drowsiness; followed by or alternating with stupor. Meddlesome D. Frightful phantasies. Spectral illusions at night. Struggling to rise from bed (Bell.). Jumping out of bed and insisting on dressing himself. Resists being undressed, saying continually that he shall lose the train. Restless and unmanageable, refusing to answer, swallow or to be examined, and appeared profoundly intoxicated. Delirious and restless, talking constantly about his affairs. Talked almost unintelligible nonsense in morning on waking. Attempts to reason. Insisted that her blood did not circulate, and that her feet must be put into hot water or she would die. Answers imaginary questions. Talked and laughed wildly, but answered questions readily, fancying that they were at home and attempting to arrange furniture. Returned answers when addressed, whose beginning showed that he understood, but which passed into irrelevant, senseless talk. Incoherent quarreling. Delirium after a chill, resembling the subdelirium of certain typhoid fevers. Busied with subjects which at other times occupy his mind, politics and struggles consequent on his relations in life. On closing eyes after retiring, mind filled with strange ideas, rambling, incoherent speech, spectral illusions, with fits of wild, uncontrollable laughter, the delirium lasting all night, fancied that I was afflicted with epilepsy and afraid others would discover my condition, nearly oblivious of all that transpired the latter part of the night, but know from bruises and pains from contact with a stove, chair or some solid body that it was passed in the wildest delirium.

Delirium, resembling delirium tremens; incessant rambling, restlessness, grasping at imaginary objects and screaming from fright, terror was depicted on his face, and he clung to his nurse's neck or he threw himself in different directions to escape the frightful objects (Stram.), later the delusions were pleasurable, of playing with toys, drawing, eating, etc. Pleasing illusions, meddling with everything, picking at and handling imaginary objects, with muttering and smiling, or with loud chattering interrupted by subdued laughter. Hallucinations, grasping at imaginary objects, with staggering, rapid, full and strong pulse, drowsy, stupid, answered in an indistinct tone but rationally, afterwards coma increased, head hung upon his shoulders in a limp state, unconscious, respiration ceased and artificial respiration was resorted to. Picking at specks and at the air, on lying in bed. Picking at bed-clothes, as if searching for something at night, with confused mutterings (Hyos.). Incoherent quarreling. Frenzied with excitement. At times when it seemed to him as if he were fully conscious he saw persons at the bedside, and slowly reached out to grasp them, or saw books and newspapers which receded, or the hand would come in contact with them and feel nothing. Felt a wet cloth on my head, but supposed I had been out in the rain without a hat, etc., etc.

Delirious, but not wholly unconscious, starting from a brief repose, and screaming with pain or terror and clutching, flexor muscles of limbs, especially upper, were principally affected, muscles of spine occasionally contracted so as to jerk head backward, pupils dilated, pulse rapid and weak, skin dry, hot and covered with scarlatinoid redness. Violent delirium, tongue dry and brown, respiration labored and quick, with flapping of cheeks, twitching of arms and legs, catching at imaginary objects. Excitement, with congested skin, face, hands and whole body swollen, delirium, sensibility suspended, clonic spasms at times of limbs, pupils dilated, thirst, speech thick and clogged, tongue and throat swollen. Delirium, with absurd hallucinations, pulse rapid and feeble, skin flushed and dry, tongue dry and brown, thirst, throat dry.

Motion unpleasant, and if feet were lifted in walking the floor seemed to recede before they were put down again, a sliding of the feet seemed the only safe way of locomotion, with dizziness and fear of falling, great thirst, but only a little water could be drunk at a time because swallowing was unpleasant, languid feeling, a semi-recumbent position was assumed, and whether sleep with wild dreams or waking hallucinations followed it was impossible to tell, but they were the opposite of those produced by Cannabis indica, for all the imaginations and conversations were of the long past, whether there was total blindness or imagination of blindness could not be remembered, but all the images were very distinct, the actions were performed by embodied spirits of those long since departed, and lengthy pleasant conversations were held with Plato, Alcibiades, Aspasia and others, sound sleep must have followed, for consciousness did not return till sixteen hours after taking the Atropia, then sudden waking, with nothing abnormal but languor and disturbed vision. Loud cries without pain.

Fretful. Desire to scold and quarrel, alternating with internal anxiety and fear, changing at last to anguish. Morose, quarrelsome, angry at trifles. Sudden fear of death, with nervous excitement and formication all over body. Apprehension after his internal restlessness, soon amounting to anxiety. Sadness; with anxiety, restlessness and fear of misfortune, or angry and inclined to be alone, seldom lively. Cheerful to an exaggerated degree. Indolence of mind; then vertigo, then beginning intoxication. Want of memory. Memory wrong, thinks what happened in the night of the 11th took place in the night of the 10th. Attention difficult to fix. Absent-minded; and forgetful, after partly finishing a sentence was obliged to inquire what I had been saying. Feels as if awakened from a dream. Confusion of mind when he closes his eyes, and all sorts of spectres. Dull and not inclined to move about or converse; *when spoken to often turns his head to the wrong side. Unconsciousness;* with incoherent talking; and irritability, striking his mother when she took him from the nurse. Comatose; and insensible, with dilated pupils and flushed and swollen face; with cyanotic and cool skin, pale face, livid lips, relaxed limbs, jaw hanging down, mouth and tongue dry, pupils dilated, insensible, respiration slow, pulse 90.

Head and face flushed and hot, with full, bounding, irregular pulse. *Sticking in base of skull and especially over eyes on every motion and < stepping. Feeling as if screwed up, and walking caused sticking.* Aching; with vertigo, pain in back and nausea; with vertigo on sudden motion; sick headache, with pain in r. eye and r. temple. Fulness and discomfort; skull feels too small for brain, pain in vertex and over eyes, pain in all that part of head above eyes, head feels as if it would burst. Dull feeling, with feeling as if hair were matted into a thick felt. *Confusion* in morning as after a disturbed night, > open air; dizzy, evenings, alternating with vivid phantasies, with general fatigue and at times ringing in ears. Intoxicated feeling, afraid to walk, must concentrate the mind to keep from falling, staggering.

Vertigo; in morning on rising, so that it became dark before his eyes; on waking; on waking, < rising, with confusion of head; on waking, with staggering towards objects for support; on turning head quickly; when attempting to walk; with wanderings of vision; with weight on vertex and over eyes; with pressure in temples, with little or no pain; with strange feeling in head, so that he could not see, throat deep red, sore, with inability to swallow; with heaviness, drowsiness or sleep, tendency to dreamy delirium and in women startings; intermittent; intermittent in forenoon.

Forehead.—*Intermittent fine drawing stitches accross F. and temples.* Aching; >closing eyes; headache beginning in middle of F.; in anterio-superior cerebral region; with vertigo on moving suddenly. Fulness, with heat of head; in anterior part of brain; in front part of head, with dilatation of pupils.

Temples.—*Stiching in l. in morning on waking, extending behind ear, scarcely permitting him to open l. eye, < moving about in open air.* Aching; and in eyes; *intermittent,* like a deep heavy pressure, and at other times tension in anterior cerebral region, as if brain pressed out in all directions. Pressure from without, < r. Bruised feeling. Fulness; in T. and forehead, with pain and with vertigo so that one can scarcely walk. Throbbing.

Pressure under parietal bones. Throbbing in vertex.

Eyes.—Restless. Projecting from sockets. Congested; and glassy. Fixed and glassy. *Aching;* and in head; and in temples; with lachrymation; in back part; with fulness and pressure in anterior part of head, making me restless, with sleeplessness till near morning. Swollen feeling, and the pain in eyes and temples < with each pulsation of the heart. Eyes and lids sore to touch. Dryness. Intolerance of light. Weariness.

Pain in l. ball. Pressure from without in every direction in ball. Pupils immovable; and dilated; dilated, with diplopia; dilated, with clouded vision, images confused, with a reddish tinge. Lids swollen; red and excoriated skin of lids; erysipelas of lids spreading to face and head; inflammatory swelling of mucous membrane of eyes, with muco-purulent secretion, often with swelling of lachrymal sac, occasionally with less swelling but more marked hyperæmia and lachrymation; *lids heavy and difficult to keep open about* 9 P.M., without sleepiness; lids ache; lids feel sore and are red. Glaucoma of r. Congestion; with dryness of the conjunctiva and aching in ball; erysipelatous inflammation and swelling of conjunctiva and lids; conjunctivitis. *Sharp pain under r. eye, with aching in temples. Intermittent neuralgic pain under l. orbit running back to ear.*

Vision and hearing morbidly sensitive; at night. Difficult vision with r. eye; D., of small, near objects. When talking with persons they suddenly vanish. After looking at objects a few minutes they become indistinct and fade away. Letters run together after reading a little. Eyes lost control of distance, print held at usual distance was blurred, at a long distance letters could be distinguished but words soon ran into confusion, distant objects were plainer than natural, but near objects soon became indistinct and light caused pain deep in balls. Partial blindness, with one pupil twice as large as the other. Partial color-blindness. Cannot estimate distances correctly. Staggering, catching at distant objects which appeared near and often stumbling over objects which appeared distant. Quick rotation and duplication of objects. Dim V.; with golden circles dancing before eyes. During the increasing dimness illusions of gigantic figures, whirls, double images, enlarged appearance of all objects and laughable or frightful appearances of all kinds. *Diplopia.* The large figures on the carpet seemed to be constantly and successively rising to her face (perpendicular diplopia, the apparent object below the real one). Round or oval objects seem elongated; the vertical diameter of the human face seemed equal to the rest of the body, especially prominent were the nose and chin, with their margins enveloped in mist, next day pupils large and sluggish. Eyes of attendant seemed very large. Letters of a newspaper seemed to expand and contract with each pulsation of heart. Objects appear enveloped in a white vapor. Vision of many white flies on the door, which was was white, at night, continued till next noon, on closing eyes. Bright spots and stars and a brilliant glow around letters. Bright flashes at night on closing eyes. V. of a black bug, with veritable legs, below a black door knob. V. in morning of a thousand-legged brown worm on carpet, the predominating color of which was brown.

Ears.—Hearing sensitive, with frequent illusions. Roaring. Hears tinkling bells. Ringing.

Nose.—Mucous membrane dry. Sneezing caused by glaring light; and rubbing nose frequently.

Face.—*Red; and hot;* with white spots; afterwards pale. Pale; and sweaty. *Expression of mania;* of anxiety. Twitching, especially around mouth and lids. Mouth opens but little, masticator muscles are rigid. Lips swollen and hanging down; L. parched, and no relief from water.

Mouth.—Teeth and lips dry and covered with sordes. Teeth feel "on edge." Tongue trembles when protruded; with light redness of tip and edges. Tongue coated dirty gray; white; whitish on margins and yellow in middle; T. thick, cannot articulate distinctly. Tongue dry; and coated; mucous layer dry, brown and hard; anterior part or whole of dorsum, except a wide margin, dry, brown and rough; dorsum of T., roof of mouth and velum palati dry and glazed; feeling as "dry as a chip," though moist to sight and touch, and the throat seemed almost as if its sides were stuck together; and hard and soft palates, extending down pharynx and larynx, making voice husky and often inducing dry cough and difficult deglutition. Tongue and mouth dry and feverish and throat dry, > for only a short time by water, the dryness of throat increased, causing at first frequent deglutition, afterwards strong effort to avoid swallowing, which had become painful. Tongue partially paralyzed. T. difficult to protrude and cannot be moved about in mouth at will. T. and other muscles assisting in speech difficult to move. Stuttering, especially at words difficult to pronounce. Slowness and embarrassment of articulation. Articulation indistinct, rapid and chattering. Speech thick, probably from dryness of mouth and throat.

Mucous membrane red. Hard and soft palates completely glazed. Thick, viscid or slimy mucus. Coating of viscid, slimy, white mucus. Mouth and throat feel as if she could not swallow, but she drank with avidity warm water, though it seemed difficult at first. Formication on palate. Buccal cavity feels hot. Dryness; at night, especially along median line and on each side of it. Hard and soft palates and back of œsophagus as dry and glazed as a piece of paper. Dryness; of M. and throat, with sensation of burning and choking and difficult swallowing; D. suddenly > by a viscid acid secretion, of offensive odor, like sweat of feet, the mouth becomes foul and clammy, with a bitter coppery taste; but no thirst, and inability to feel passage of water through mouth and throat. No sensation in M. and throat when drinking water except slight coldness. Loss of sensation in buccal cavity, with loss of taste.

Salivation. Taste slimy; sour; sweetish; to food lost; salt, to everything.

Throat.—Mucous membrane dark and mottled. Fauces and uvula red. Drops of white mucus stick to uvula. Hawking of clinkers from posterior nares. Throat feels raw and irritated. Soreness; with pain on swallowing; increasing till hoarse. Burning; and in stomach. Dryness; > towards morning; and especially in gullet, so that he could not swallow bread and butter unless he took water; with pressure in anterior and superior cerebral regions; with constriction and desire for something sour and juicy, the D. and C. < by a sour apple; extending to lower passage of nares; causing constant inclination to swallow; causing inclination to cough, > swallowing water. Constriction. Fulness. Choking, then inability to swallow, with feeling as if seized by the throat. Throbbing or heaving sensation in carotids. *Swallowing produced spasms of suffocation; swallowing appeared to give pain, manifested by grimaces and increased facial spasms.*

Stomach.—Hunger, < eating; H. for salt food; constant but soon satisfied, food tasteless. Appetite lost. Aversion to meat and beer, the beer aggravated the empty feeling in stomach and caused painful pressure. Thirst; with dry mouth and throat, perversion of sensation, everything tasting very acid; *no T. in spite of dryness of throat.* Eructations, empty; tasting like the yolk of eggs.

Nausea; in morning, with vomiting. Ineffectual retching. *Vomiting* after warm drinks; after milk; of food after dinner; profuse V. of colorless mucus, then of green, bitter fluid after the morning vertigo. Nervous and wakeful for three hours, hurried from bed and vomited profusely a watery fluid, bitter at first, nearly tasteless, afterwards with sticking in umbilical region. Constrictive pain caused by beer, < walking, with eructations of air and nausea. Distress in epigastric region. Feeling in night as if the stomach had got a grip of the apple eaten in the evening and would hold it as in a vise. Sensitiveness to strong pressure. *Soreness of pit.* Discomfort. Burning. Uneasiness, with empty eructations, then with nausea and retching, increasing to a pressing sticking and contractive pain, with pallor and sweat of face, singing in ears and aching in forehead.

Abdomen.—Tympanitis and tenderness. Tension; and swelling but not tympanitis. Pain in umbilical region, > copious watery, gushing stool.

Rectum.—Urging to stool. Paralysis of sphincters of R. and bladder.

Stool.—Diarrhœa of yellow bile. Frequent watery, gushing. In the stool, fluid seemed mixed with urine. No stool for five days and then induced artificially.

Urinary Organs.—Tenesmus and frequent desire to urinate; ineffectual desire; frequent desire with only a moderate quantity. Micturition prevented by spasmodic stricture, after long waiting void half a teacupful, stream no larger than a knitting-needle (stream ordinarily extra large), inability to empty bladder, then only in drops, then complete stricture, the catheter drawing off a pint of normal looking urine. Micturition only after some trouble; difficult and in drops. Urine passed slowly and increased in quantity; U. retained. Incontinence of U.; and involuntary stool. Frequent micturition at night; and profuse almost colorless urine. Dysuria. Urine profuse; scanty; high-colored, turbid; acid, dark, brownish, without sediment and containing *atropine.*

Respiratory Organs.—Voice husky; lost; weak. Cough; paroxysmal, from mucus in throat, with difficult expectoration of thick tough mucus, after the cough burning in throat; periodic dry tickling, from speaking or smoking, with sore feeling in throat and pressure on chest. Scanty, thick, frothy, white sputa. Choking. Rattling inspiration. Rapid respiration.

Chest.—Râles about base, pain over r. side of, cough, with rust-colored and scanty expectoration, dulness of chest as far as spine of scalpulæ on r. side behind, tubular breathing and bronchophony, rough breathing over l. lung posteriorly. Warmth.

Heart.—Fluttering sensation in cardiac region. Palpitation; at night, with great debility and distress. Action accelerated and pressure of blood increased by weak doses, the reverse from poisonous doses. Action irregular and apparently obstructed. Labored heavily and to my feeling at the rate of about fifty per minute, with sore feeling over base of heart.

Pulse.—Rapid; with increased force of cardiac contractions and of arterial tone; with increased tone but diminished volume; increased in volume and power, often with vertigo; full and soft; in morning on rising, and small and irregular, with lassitude; irregular, generally full but varying much; small and compressible; small and weak; with heat. Slow; afterwards rapid; S., afterwards small and rapid. Weak.

Extremities.—Movements are unsteady, as from loss of control over limbs. Trembling. Sudden stretchings, always waking him. Spasms, clonic. Weakness; especially of lower. Heaviness and inactivity, especially of lower; H. and numbness. Tingling in ends of fingers and toes. Numbness, with formication in arms. Partial paralysis of arms and legs.

Upper Extremities.—Arms, hands and fingers thrown about constantly, as in delirium. Hands feel dry and glossy; numbness of H. extending to finger-tips, with prickling, afterwards insensibility. Fingers numb, with feeling as if holding a book, which he fears will drop, and on taking a small object, as a pin, it appears as if there were five or six; insensibility of tips.

Lower Extremities.—Gait weak. Staggering; or inability to walk. "Limbs felt like sticks," thought she could not walk across the room, but with aid did so with difficulty. **Stiffness of l. knee, l. leg and in r. great toe.** Dragged legs when walking. Jerkings of legs; waking at night. Kicking, waking at night.

Skin.—Hands and fingers suddenly swelled and became stiff while the face was scarlet-red and eyelids swollen. *Redness; like scarlet fever, over face and upper half of body, skin hot and dry. Feeling as if turgid and swollen, afterwards covered with a rash similar to that of scarlatina.* Formication; preventing sleep.

Sleep.—Yawning often. Sleepiness, with disinclination to speak or move; S. with vertigo; with perversion of ideas; with sometimes flushing of face. Waking late in morning, with heaviness and confusion of head. Sleepiness early, but inability to fall asleep, heard every noise, but could not open his eyes, wearied by diversified dreams, that he was in a forest followed by serpents, tried to flee, but could only move with difficulty, the serpents wound themselves about him or crept into his clothes, or a common play-ball lying on the table increased in size, so that the room could no longer contain it and it threatened to choke him, or he thought the masonry work was going to yield on all sides and the house was going to fall, afterwards covered only with a shirt he came to a place deserted by people, saw several persons come up to him, tried to flee but could not because he was lame, these endeavors to escape from danger exhausted him, and he was glad to be free from this condition when awakened by a loud cry.

Sleeplessness; till 1 A.M., then dreams of people moving about disfigured in such a way that the perpendicular diameter of the face almost equalled in size the rest of the body, especially the nose and chin and the contours appeared misty; with delirium. Unintelligible talking in sleep. Short restless naps. Restless sleep, with dreams of running horses, of playing baseball, of amputating a man's arm, of shadowy forms sitting or standing by the bedside or moving in the air.

Dreams and startings, a fancied noise is a common cause of waking, and at these times the patient generally manifests a little delirium. Frightful dreams waking him, disconnected, of being murdered, of falling from a height, of being attacked by large dogs, etc. Pleasant D., of flying, etc.

Fever.—Chilliness and cramp, with tingling of extremities. Internal C., < towards 6 P.M., with external heat, apprehension and restlessness, palpitation, anxiety as if he had committed a crime and sleeplessness till towards 11 P.M. Frequent rigors and loss of muscular power, being unable to walk, or, as he expressed it, "to feel his legs." Chill alternating with heat, with tension of chest, dyspnœa and feeble pulse. C. over back alternating with heat (cold predominating). Cold sensation along spine. Cold extremities. Cold hands. Cool skin on forehead and head.

Heat; of head; subjective H. of head; H. of face, with redness. Hot and dry hands. Hot skin; and pungent, also with face flushed, veins of forehead turgid and head burning; hot, pungent and dry skin covered with a rash resembling that of scarlatina, which the child frequently scratched; hot, dry skin, with biting and tickling; hot, dry, red skin, with itching; hot, dry skin and lips covered with mucus. Dry skin. Sweat in sleep.

Aurum.

For use triturate the precipitated metal with sugar of milk.

General Action.—A general destructive action on tissues, especially on connective tissue in parenchymatous organs; on bones, etc.

Relationships.—Mercury, Nit. ac., Plat., Iod., Phos., Rhod., Puls., Ign.

Generalities.—Tremulous agitation of nerves, as in joyous hope. Trembling when he cannot express his anger. (Makes small motions without knowing it when thinking of a motion.) Cannot lie on either side at night. Simple pain or bruised pain in morning in bed, in all joints, especially in small of back and knees, < lying still, > rising. *Bruised pain* in head and *all limbs* morning in bed, < rest, > rising; B. pain in all joints in morning and forenoon. Painful drawing in veins in afternoon, with weakness. Sensitiveness of whole body, when thinking of pain he imagines that he already feels it, and everything is disagreeable to him. All sensations fine and acute.

General indisposition, as before an illness. Sensation in joints and muscles as after unwonted exercise, feel very strong, going up stairs I involuntarily take two steps at a time and run in and out of houses. Constant inclination to be in motion. Internal emptiness and weakness of whole body. Weakness in morning on waking; in morning, with aching in legs, so that she desired to lie down immediately; in evening but inability to sleep; from mental labor; with no inclination for rest or sleep; with causeless vexation; sudden, in afternoon when sitting or reading, > sleep. Feels well in open air.

Clinical.—A remedy frequently indicated in secondary syphilis and effects of mercurial poisoning, by its mental symptoms, nocturnal aggravation of pains, etc. It is always to be thought of in interstitial changes of heart, liver and kidneys and in gouty diathesis. Especially suited to old people.

Great oppression of heart, cardiac difficulty in breathing, weak pulse and great depression of spirits; the skin showed large brown patches and again patches like albugo. Severe attacks of oppression at heart at night, with palpitation and with great debility.

Mind.—Awoke at 3 A.M. and said rapidly in a strong voice and with red face, "Mother, thou art my jewel of a daughter! What sort of a dog is that? What sort of a head is that on the wall? What is running about there in the room?" and asked many other such foolish questions. Says something absurd in a reverie. Religious excitement. *Howls and screams and imagines herself lost.*

Disgust for life, suicidal tendency (Arsen., Nit. ac.). **Anguish, increasing unto self-destruction,** with spasmodic contraction of abdomen; *A. with palpitation,* weariness of limbs and sleepiness; with weakness and appearance as if near death (Arsen.). **Peevish and vehement wrath at least contradiction** (Bry.). Silent peevishness alternating with cheerfulness. Sullen mood and taciturnity. If left alone he sits still in a corner, taciturn, melancholy, but the slightest contradiction excites his wrath, which he manifests by disputing and talking much, afterwards by a few detached words. *Anger and vehemence;* when thinking of absent persons. *Quarrelsome* (Verat., Plat.); and abusive. Impatience. Some persons are offensive to him. **Melancholy** (Cimicif., Sulph., Plat.); *imagines that he is unfit for this world and longs for death, which he contemplates with delight; imagines he can succeed in nothing; and he seeks solitude* (Con., Nat. m.). *Weeping; because he imagines he has lost the affections of his friends* (Puls.); alternating with laughter, as if unconscious of herself (Ign., Plat.).

Discouraged at least trifle; and out of humor with himself. Dissatisfied with everything, imagines obstacles everywhere, partly occasioned by adverse fate, partly by himself, the latter making him morbidly depressed. *Apprehension, anxiety from a noise at the door, gnd fear lest some one would come in, anthropophobia* (Nat. m.). Anxiety > while eating (Mez.). Timidity. Uneasiness; he imagines that he neglects something and deserves reproaches, which deprives him of energy and perseverance. Cheerful, with constant desire to converse. Anxious to reflect deeply about this or that subject, but this makes her weak, tremulous, cold and damp over whole body. Intellectual faculties more active and memory more faithful (reaction). Memory sharp, afterwards bad; impaired.

Clinical.—Settled melancholy, with suicidal mania, (it has not proved so valuable for suicidal mania as might have been expected from its symptomatology; in nonsyphilitic cases Arsenic seems more efficacious). Most valuable for the melancholy of syphilitics, with longing for death, disgust for life, but without attempts to commit suicide. Melancholy, with weeping. Religious melancholia, with weeping and crying. Mental derangements, with constant rapid questioning, without waiting for replies.

Head.—Shaking sideways and up and down (Merc. v.). Tearing here and there, especially in forehead, with vertigo. Aching from mental effort (Phos.); before lying down in evening, then shivering and chills after lying down; stunning, as from a violent wind; as from an incipient cold; bruised, ever since morning, < reflecting, reading, talking or writing, when the ideas are confused, > 7 P.M.; as from a contusion, sometimes like a pressure in one part of the brain, sometimes like a tearing, < since morning, > 3 P.M.; *in bones on lying down, as if broken, so that all his vital energy seemed affected.*

Confusion; morning on rising, with heaviness in occiput. *Hypochondriacal intoxication,* head feels full of compressed air, especially towards nape. *Rush of blood;* while stooping. *Vertigo* when standing; *when stooping* (Sulph.), *as if turning in a circle, > raising head; as if he would fall to the left when walking in open air, forcing him to lie down, but returning even then on slightest motion.*

Forehead.—Stitch in centre where hair begins; externally; in bone like a slow drawing. Tearing; in l., < during motion; deep-seated in F. and temples, > open air. Aching in l.; externally. Tingling in forepart of head. *Bony tumor on upper part of l. side* (Sarsap.).

Tearings in l. temple. Aching in temples; on l., < touch; on l. temple externally. Tearing in r. vertex; in l.; l., < during motion; cutting T. in r. vertex. *Bony tumor on r. vertex, with boring pain,* < touch.

Megrim returning every three or four days, with stitching, *burning* and beating in one side of forehead, heartburn, nausea and bilious vomiting. One-sided throbbing, hacking headache. Boring in r. side. Grinding, boring and throbbing in one side in morning after waking, < cough and bending head backward. Tearing in r. occiput; *through brain to forehead, also < during motion* (Bry.). One-sided drawing in occiput. White pimples all over hairy scalp, with heat and itching.

Clinical.—Most violent pain in the head, with symptoms of exostosis of the cranial bones, pains < night, pressure outward, roaring in the head, sparks before the eyes, longing for death.

Eyes.—*Protruding.* Red sclerotica. *Tension making vision difficult; < fixing eyes, > closing them, with diminished vision. Feeling of sand.* Pressure as from a foreign body; P. inward upon l. *Heat; when looking, as if blood pressed upon optic nerve. Feeling of weakness and pressure. Constant lachrymation.* Ball, *pressive pain from above downward in r.; pressive pain inward in r., < during motion;* pressing out in internal and superior angle of l. ball.

Lids agglutinated in morning; lids red at approach of menses; lower lids swollen; *burning* in lids, with stitching and itching; biting pain in l. upper lid. Inner canthi bluish; stitches in l. inner canthus and lid; *burning in inner canthi, with stitching, drawing and itching;* itching in r. canthus, with burning. Stitch outward in lower part of l. orbit; tearing in r. O. close to external canthus; spasmodic pressure in posterior segment of l. O.

Vision double (Gels., Nit. ac., Con.), *and one object is seen mixed with another, with tension in eyes. Half-sighted, as* **if the upper half of vision were covered with a dark body** (Gels.), *can only see lower objects with the inferior half,* **upper objects invisible.** Fiery sparks. *V. indistinct, as through a black veil.* Momentary loss.

Clinical.—A most valuable remedy for very acute inflammations, particularly characterized by tendency to ulceration of the cornea; *extreme photophobia,* the patient very sensitive. In iritis, with intolerable pain in the bones, extending down into the face and nose, with great sorenesss all about the eye (Asaf.).

Ears.—Tearing in l. meatus auditorius externus. Burning, with stitches. Tension. Hardness of hearing. Crackling in l. Roaring in morning in bed. Raging and roaring as if close to roaring water. Humming, with whistling and ringing; H. before l.

Nose.—Nostrils ulcerated, agglutinated (Nit. ac., Thuya, Phos.), **painful,** *so that he cannot breathe through the nose. Swelling of r. nostril and beneath it, with redness. Swelling* in house after walking in open air; *S., with redness.* Shootings downward in septum. **Sore feeling internally,** < *touch* (Graph.). **R. bone and adjoining part of upper jaw painful to touch** (Merc.), especially where infraorbital nerve comes out. *Appears obstructed though air passes through it. Burning in* (Nit. ac.), *with itching, sticking and smarting.* Biting pain in lower part; so that tears came into his eyes, as when desiring to sneeze, excited by strong sunlight, or exalted, pious grief or highest degree of pity. Itching in nostrils. Itching titillation in wings, as in a cold, sometimes with a desire to scratch. Sneezing. Coryza; fluent; with thick discharge like the white of an egg. *Crusts in; in r. nostril, as from ulcers* (K. bi.), yellowish, almost painless and dry. *Smell acute* (Graph.), the smoke of the lamp is offensive; *putrid S. in nose when blowing it* (K. bi.); sweetish; smell of brandy in nose, with dyspnœa.

Clinical.—Inflammation of the nose, with deep-seated destruction of the tissues, caries of the nasal bones, which are very sore to touch, fetid discharge, purulent, bloody; boring pains < night.

Face.—Red; and blue spots. Pale; with a worn look. Swelling of cheeks, lips and nose, in morning; *of one cheek, with drawing and tearing in jaws* and hacking and grumbling pain in teeth, which appear too long. Bloated, shining as from sweat, with protruding eyes. Stitches in one cheek; *burning, in zygoma;* itching, on r. side. *Tearing in zygoma* (Arg., Kali iod.); in r. half of chin; *drawing tearing in l. side of face.* Tension in malar-bone and ear. Tearing in r. lower jaw, > pressure. Intermittent stitches in external border of lower jaw. Pain in a gland of lower jaw as if swollen. Burning vesicle on vermilion border of lower lip. Pimples on lips, with stitching and itching.

Clinical.—Diseases of the bones of the face, involving the mastoid, with horrible odor from the nose and mouth.

Mouth.—Teeth. Looseness, even of anterior, in sudden paroxysms. Stitches; in upper. Tearing in two r. upper posterior molars, excited by touch and eating, with painful swelling of gums (Merc.). *Aching caused by drawing air into mouth;* in upper incisors when chewing; hacking and grumbling A., with swelling of cheeks. Dull sensation in molars; *sudden painful dulness in one upper molar when chewing.* Gums, painful pustules, as if a fistula dentalis would form; ulcer, with swelling of cheeks (Merc.); redness, with swelling; swelling of G. of r. upper molars, with soreness on touch and when eating; bleed easily.

Tongue coated brownish. Mouth blistered inside. Aphthæ. Pressure in region of palate. Heat, with smarting. Difficulty in eating. Accumulation of agreeably sweetish saliva. *Putrid smell. Fetid odor* in evening and night, unperceived by himself. Smell as from old cheese. *Taste putrid, as of spoiled game, between meals; bitter,* with dry sensation in mouth; astringent metallic; sweet, on anterior part of tongue; sourish; agreeable milky; insipid.

Throat.—*Pain in a gland below angle of jaw* (Merc.). Pain in parotid glands; *bruised pain in P. gland on touch* (Merc.). Mucus; which can be hawked up, but prevents full inspiration. *Stitches; when swallowing* (Ign.). Burning, < swallowing, with stitching and itching. Drawing, with scraping. Attacks of distention, as in vomiting, but without nausea. Lumpy, wakes at night and desires to moisten it. Painful obstacle to deglutition in l. side.

Clinical.—Sometimes useful in syphilitic sore throat.

Stomach.—Appetite not appeased by eating. Is forced to eat hastily, especially at the beginning of a meal. Appetite lost, can eat only bread and milk. Repugnance to meat. Thirst; for cold drinks; for coffee; for spirituous liquors. Eructations tasting of the drink (beer); watery; regurgitations, as if the person would vomit, with pressure in abdomen. Hiccough. Nausea; after eating and sometimes while eating; in stomach and throat; with discomfort from stomach and in abdomen; mental labor causes nausea, which affects his whole being. *Pressure in region at noon; on l. side, near pit,* below cartilages of upper false ribs, < during expiration. Pain as from hunger. Burning, with hot eructations; B. with drawing and cutting.

Abdomen.—*Rumbling.* Emission of much flatus; of fetid. Pinching here and there; with cutting, then diarrhœa, then distention of abdomen. Pain; labor-like, as if menses would appear; flatulent, at night, especially in l. hypochondrium; flatulent, after midnight, with squeezing and anxiety in abdomen; flatulent, after lightest meals; twisting, before and during stool; tensive, in abdomen and lumbar region, with desire for stool. Painful feeling of contraction. Tender to touch. Heat, with drawing. Discomfort, with urging to stool, < after dinner. Heaviness, with cold hands and feet.

Tensive pressure just below navel and on both sides in lumbar region, with fulness. Tearings in r. side, extending to below ribs, when sitting, as if everything were shattered, forcing him to bend crooked.

Hypochondria.—Stitches in l.; like stitches in spleen. *Burning in r., with cutting.* Pressure as from flatus, < food and drink, often < motion and walking, goes off with flatus. *Flatus becomes incarcerated under l. ribs, with lancinating pain.*

Hypogastrium.—Rumbling. Pinching in inner side of ischiatic bones. Jerking twinges in l. side of pelvis. Bruised pain in r. iliac region when sitting, > rising and drawing up the thigh. Heat, with sensitiveness. Burning pain in abdominal ring. Pressing in ring when sitting and stretching body, as if a hernia would protrude, > rising. Weight on pubis (Lil. t.).

Groins.—Inguinal hernia protrudes, with cramp-like pain, and flatus seems to get into the hernia. Cutting thrusts, forcing him to draw the abdomen in and the feet up. Pain as from a swollen gland. Painful stiffness in bends when walking or spreading legs, as after a long walk, and in tendons of lumbar muscles. Drawing, extending into thighs. Weakness.

Clinical.—Enlarged liver, fatty degeneration.

Rectum and Anus.—Stitches. External hæmorrhoids, bleeding during stool. Border of anus painfully swollen. Cutting in A., with heat and scraping. Burning in A., with tearing. Heat in perineum, with dull pain.

Stool.—Soft every morning, with pinching. Diarrhœa; green; < night, grayish-yellow; nightly, with burning in rectum. *Hard, knotty.* Constipation. (White-yellowish.) Copious; in evening. Large and difficult.

Urinary Organs.—Stitches in side of bladder when breathing. Constant desire to urinate, with scanty but natural urine. Infrequent micturition, with scanty yellowish urine. Dysuria. Stinging tearing in urethra. Burning in canal of urethra, with stitching and smarting. *Diuresis.* Urine more copious than corresponds to the quantity he drinks. Diminished; *turbid, like buttermilk,* with much mucous sediment. Thick, with a strong ammoniacal odor and decomposing rapidly. Hot, red, containing sand.

Clinical.—Chronic inflammation of the kidney, associated with cardiac and hepatic disease.

Sexual Organs.—Discharge of prostatic fluid, with relaxed penis. Moisture around glans. Painful twitchings from before backward in penis. Prickings at end of glans, every pricking followed by a similar one above the navel, towards pit of stomach. Tearing stitches at glans when obliged to urinate. Erections many nights in succession; *nightly, with pollutions;* at night, without pollutions; painful. *Itching of scrotum.* **Swelling of r. testicle,** *several days at* 6 P.M., > *towards* 11 P.M., *with aching when touched or rubbed. Testes swollen and hard* (Rhod., Puls.). **Tensive pain in r. testicle,** *as if bruised.* Desire; morning after rising, with violent erections. Lewd fancies at night, with small and relaxed penis. Pollutions at night; with voluptuous dreams.

Drawing pain in mons veneris. Redness of labia majora, with swelling. Burning in vagina, with pricking. Heat in vulva, with pricking and smarting. Thick, white leucorrhœa. Menses retarded.

Clinical.—Testes on the verge of atrophy, in boys, with pining condition, low spirits, lifelessness, bad memories; tongue commonly coated at the back; appetite for plain food bad. Chronic enlargement of testicles, with induration and severe pains at night, dependent on chronic inflammation. Hydrocele. Enlarged and prolapsed uterus. Chronic metritis. Great sensitiveness of the vagina, with the preceding symptoms. Sterility, with lowered vitality of the parts; especially called for when want of children has resulted in depression of spirits. Vaginismus, with hysterical spasms, hysterical paralysis, palpitation, ovarian pains, etc.

Respiratory Organs.—Larynx, tickling when sitting and writing, then dry cough, almost causing retching; adhesive mucus; deep-seated mucus, which he cannot hawk up. Voice husky. Cough; at night, on account of want of breath; short dry; racking; splitting, at night. Difficulty in raising mucus.

Suffocative sensation after eating. *Dyspnœa; at night;* when walking in open air; when laughing or walking fast, as if the chest were too tight for breathing and too flat in front; *with stitches in chest when inspiring; he constantly takes deep breath and cannot inspire air enough. Frequent deep breathing.*

Chest.—Dry catarrh in morning on waking, and difficult expectoration of mucus after rising. Râles in upper part during expiration, descending into abdomen and groin, then quick beating of heart, with weakness and apprehension, then slumber. Mucus deep in lungs which is easily thrown up, then free and expansive breathing, whereas he was generally asthmatic.

Stitches in sternum; near sternum, under last r. true ribs, with lancinations; in sides, < inspiration, with heat in chest and dyspnœa; over heart; in l. when breathing; under l. ribs when coughing; under ribs when breathing deeply and yawning, > going to bed; under cartilages of first three r. ribs, sometimes they continue as a sensation of a plug, sometimes they are intermittent, > walking, with external redness; tearing S. on right side near lumbar vertebræ, > pressure.

Cutting on l., near sternum, < during inspiration. *Pressure* in l. wall; on r. side, with anguish; on sternum, with drawing tearings towards shoulders; on sternum, with busy demeanor, as if something agreeable were about to happen. Tightness, with anxiety. Oppression when coughing, and in abdomen. Sensation of narrowing in the direction of the sides, with feeling of a movement anteriorly. Burning, with stitches. Shuddering in r. when yawning.

Heart.—Swelling of præcordial region and of upper abdomen, with stitches when pressed upon or laced tightly. *Attacks of anguish, with tremulous fearfulness; anguish coming from præcordial region and driving one from place to place.* Drawings, with cutting. Heat, with itching. Seemed to shake as if loose, when walking. *Palpitation;* at night; when lying on back. Strong irregular beating. Sometimes a single violent beat.

Clinical.—A remedy of considerable value in hypertrophy of the heart, with tendency to fatty degeneration, wandering pains, sometimes with palpitation and irregular pulse, feeling as if the heart would cease beating, with hypochondriasis, etc. Rheumatic endocarditis in the course of rheumatic fever.

Neck.—Tearing near r. clavicle. Jerking tearing stitches in l. external muscles. Tension as if a muscle were too short, < stooping. Difficulty in turning head, as in torticollis.

Back.—Stitches below r. scapula, near spine. Tearing on inner side of scapula when bending body backward and to the left, and below it. Pain in spine in the morning so that he could not move a limb. Pain at lower part of spine. Loins, piercing pain in r. during inspiration; cutting over loins when sitting; bruised pain; pain, as from fatigue. Pressure on l. side near lumbar vertebræ and on upper border of os innominatum. Heat starting from kidneys and extending to bladder.

Extremities.—Shooting in arms and legs, with drawing pain. Arms and legs go to sleep in morning on waking, < lying, with numbness and insensibility. Tearing tension under axilla. Shoulder, stitches; soreness; pressure in l. S. when walking. Arms, drawing pain down l. on bone, > motion; fatigue; difficult movement. Upper arm, tearings in l., < uncovering it; tearing in anterior surface of both; pressure in l. near periosteum; pressure on under surface and in middle of r.

Cramplike tearing in r. elbow. Bone pains in r. elbow. Forearm, intermittent tearing on inner side of l.; pressure on anterior surface of r.; pressure on external side of r.; heavy feeling during rest. Tearing in bones of wrist; *cramplike*, deep-seated, from upper to lower row of carpus, < at night. Metacarpal bones, tearing; cramplike pain in l., especially of thumb. Pecking, almost stitching, between thumb and index. Fingers, tearing in r.; tearing in lowest joints of r.; tearing in last joint of l. little; tearing in joints, often spreading into phalanges; pain in joints; boring in knuckles of r. at 3 P.M.; drawing in joints. Tearing in anterior joint of r. thumb.

Lower Extremities.—*All the blood seemed to rush from her head into the lower limbs* with a paralyzed feeling in them and necessity to sit down. Cramplike pain in region of hip, on inner brim of pelvis, < rubbing. Paralytic pain in hip-joint when rising from a seat and walking. Stitches in gluteal muscles, winding downward.

Thigh.—Twitching of r. posterior muscles when sitting or laying l. limb across r. Tearing during motion, as from growing. Tensive pain in muscles of l. when walking in open air, > sitting, but not when standing or walking or by touch. Pain in r. femur as if broken, on laying r. thigh across l. Cramplike drawing in tendon of psoas muscle down into thigh when sitting. Sore place on external surface of l. when lying at night. Weakness when walking. Thigh feels paralyzed and tendon of lumbar muscles so painfully stiff that the thigh cannot be raised.

Knee.—Tottering. Pain in r. when walking; in r. when sitting; *as if bandaged* when sitting and walking. Boring in l. Weakness of r. when walking, so that a drawing pain is felt when walking and setting the foot upon the floor. Stiffness and paralyzed feeling. Hard red swelling from malleolus to calf from rubbing of boots, > rest. Pressure on l. tibia when stretching leg. Gnawing pain on both sides of legs over malleoli, > motion, with stitches in tendo-achillis. Tensive pressure near r. internal malleolus. Weary pain in r. tarsal bones, shooting towards knee, in morning in bed.

Swelling of feet, so that walking is difficult. Stitches on dorsum of foot, behind toes. Tearing posteriorly in r. sole. Pressure as from something hard in hollow of sole. Heels painful as from ulceration or extravasation of blood. Drawing pain in feet. Drawing in heels in evening when going to sleep. Paralytic drawing in metatarsal bones of great toe, as far as tip. Toes, tearing in r.; bruised or sprained pain in last joint of great T. when walking; drawing in joints; paralytic drawing in r. T.

Clinical.—Dropsy of lower limbs, which were painful, pitting on pressure, < night, > morning, with profound melancholia, difficulty in breathing, pulse and heart feeble, discharge from nose, at times bloody.

Skin.—Redness of toes, with burning. Brownish-red elevations on nose, which ache upon touch. Elevations on leg and below knee, changing when rubbed to nodosities under skin. Elevations on legs and calves, < in open air, looking like blotches from the stinging of nettles, burning and feeling like knots, of a dirty yellowish color. Wheals under skin on leg, over heel and behind knees, with itching, < walking. Lump in the groove between nose and cheek, it irritates, gets picked, scabs over and persists. Smooth pimple on border of r. lower lid. Red pimples on nose; on face. *Pustules on face;* on neck and chest. Moisture behind ears.

Stitches below r. scapula, near spine. Grinding pain in an old chilblain. Formication here and there. Itching, < walking; here and there, and burning shootings, almost like stitches; *in inner third of r. groin*, with a wheal made tender by rubbing, the tenderness remained after the wheal had disappeared.

Sleep.—Sleepiness; by day. Slumber by day when sitting, with weakness of head. Slept after dinner and his mind was thronged with ideas. *Sleeplessness all night without pain, nevertheless no sleepiness nor lassitude in the morning.* Sleeplessness, with nightly restlessness. Sleeps badly after 4 A.M., with turning from side to side and tired feeling in the hand on which he lies. Wakeful in evening; with great mental activity.

Sobs aloud in sleep. Sleep uneasy, during which he feels the pains. Sleep unrefreshing. Waking frequently at night as from fright.

Dreams towards morning; every night, with constant erection. *Frightful;* at night; *about thieves, with loud screams while asleep.* That he would fall from a height. Troublesome, fatiguing. Full of disputes. Of death. Of the dead and of corpses. *Vivid, unremembered.* Erotic at night. Agreeable and sensible, but unremembered. In evening while half awake, that some one was talking to her.

Fever.—*Sensitiveness to cold.* General horripilation in evening, with dry coryza, without heat or subsequent thirst. *Shivering* through whole body, with gooseflesh on thighs and shaking of brain against frontal bone. General *coldness* in morning, especially of arms and hands, beginning at shoulders, with blue nails, without fever; general chills in evening, with coldness of hands, warmth of face and forehead, without thirst. Chilliness in evening in bed; lasting all night, with coldness of legs as far as knees, sleeps only half an hour at a time, anxious but remembered dreams. *Coldness,* with blue nails, insipid taste and nausea, then increased warmth but without fever. C. especially of hands and feet; in back; between scapulæ; of hands and in evening in bed; of soles of feet and patellæ as soon as he gets into bed in the evening. C. alternates with heat.

Orgasm as if the blood were boiling in all the veins. Heat on vertex; of head, worse at occiput. Burning behind ears, with pricking and itching. Burning on exterior of nose, with itching. Heat in cheeks; in face, with cold hands and feet; in axillæ; in nape of neck, extending to head and cheeks; in back, with pricking and itching; in loins. Burning in arms, with stitches. General sweat in morning. Slight perspiration at night, only between the thighs was there real sweat.

Aurum Muriaticum.

For use one part of the crystals is dissolved in nine parts of distilled water.

Clinical Application.—This soluble salt of gold has been preferred by some to triturations of the metal; the indications for its use do not vary essentially from those of the metal, and we may refer in a general way to the different clinical paragraphs under Aurum met.

Generalities and Mind.—Drawing tearing in various parts, especially in limbs. General erethism. Aversion to work. Weariness. Excitement. Disgust for life, inclination to suicide. *Sadness;* with frequent weeping; as if a misfortune impended. Unreasonable contrariety. Excessive cheerfulness, carelessness. Indisposition for mental work. Memory weak.

Head.—Shaking frequently. Aching on rising after a restless night; throbbing A., with heavy dreams. Confusion. Heaviness. Vertigo; on every motion, with whirling before eyes and tearing over eyes, < stooping, > open air and on going to bed at night. Pressure on brain along sagittal suture. Tearing beginning above l. eye and extending towards r. ear, > lying down. Pain in l. frontal eminence, like a toothache, extending towards supraorbital foramen, next day in r. side. Drawing pain in forehead. Beating in l. forehead. Tearing in r. temple; in l.; in l. all day, extending to r., > in bed; from l. towards ear, with vertigo and tearing over eye. Drawing pain in l. temple, extending to vertex. Throbbing pain in l. temple after rising, > applying cold water, returning in afternoon.

Eyes.—Tearing in l. Pressure in open air, with tearing and blindness. Burning, with pricking and itching. Dryness. Symptoms appear periodically. Symptoms > covering eyes with hands. Lids red and swollen; lids agglutinated in morning; difficult to keep shut; burning, with sticking and smarting. Biting in r. external canthus, with itching. Burning of conjunctiva. Vision weak. The paper appeared white, as if not printed, when reading by candlelight.

Ears.—Sticking in l. Drawing pain in r. Sensation of a plug in l. Ringing. Deafness after the ringing in ears, as if the ears were wide internally and hollow, and so nothing could be heard distinctly.

Nose.—Redness, with swelling; with itching inflammation, then desquamation. *Red swelliug of l. side, the cavity is ulcerated deep in, with dry, yellowish scurf and sense of obstruction,* though air passes through it. Red swelling in and beneath r. nostril, with a crust of ulcers internally and sense of obstruction, though air passes through it. Burning and itching pain externally on upper part. Burning, with itching. Crawling internally. Sneezing, then tearing in l. nasal bone towards eye, with heat of eye, injection of conjunctiva and spurting lachrymation. Coryza, with tickling in throat; fluent, nights; fluent, with sore throat and irritation to cough; thick, yellow. *Offensive watery discharge,* irritating to lip. Discharge of yellow-greenish matter. Crusts in nose, with inclination to pick at them.

Face and Mouth.—Face red. Pimples on lips, with smarting and itching. Twitches in r. upper jaw. Jerking toothache in anterior and upper teeth; jerking partly on one side, partly in upper incisors. Gums red, < at night, and swollen. Aphthæ all over mouth. Burning in mouth, with itching and smarting. Taste flat, > at night in bed, with nausea. Taste metallic, with salivation, frequent desire to swallow and sensation of a plug in throat.

Throat.—Painful swelling of submaxillary glands. Sore throat, with red fauces. Scratching, with pricking. Swallowing difficult.

Stomach.—Appetite lost. Thirst. Putrid eructations. *Nausea* in morning, < after breakfast; after eating; with vomiting of the water drunk and a trace of clear blood. Vomiting, with violent retching, foul eructasions, then cutting colic and four watery stools. Digestion slow. Gastritis. Distress after eating. Burning, with stitching, gnawing and cutting. Eruptions. Painful paroxysmal drawing in pit, extending to middle of sternum, as if a hard body were pressed into cavity, < stooping, eating and drinking.

Abdomen.—Distention. Rumbling and gurgling. Emission of flatus. Flatulence, with colic and fluid stool. Colic; constrictive, obliging her to bend up, > in bed. Tenderness on touch. Drawing. Drawing pain in small intestines, intermittent, > fluid stools, eating, drinking and motion. Redness at umbilicus, with heat, itching and smarting. Hypochondrium, stitch in l. as from running too fast; disagreeable feeling in r.; burning in r. Heat in hypogastrium, with pricking.

Rectum and Stool.—*Hæmorrhoids, with discharge of blood during stool.* Continual urging, with rumbling, but no satisfactory stool. *Diarrhœa;* < at night, gray-whitish; frequent, with burning at anus; frequent, with tenesmus. Watery stools.

Urinary Organs.—Constant desire to urinate. Urethra, sticking through whole length on standing; burning while urinating, with smarting; heat, with ischuria, and the urine feels hot; heat in canal of urethra, with itching. Urine increased; scanty, red, thick, containing sand; burning and acrid; decomposes rapidly.

Sexual Organs.—Itching on penis wakes at night. Exhausting erections. Swelling of testicles, with tension. Paroxysmal painful drawing in l. testicle, extending towards inguinal ring. Drawing along spermatic cords. Labia red and swollen. Red pimples on labia majora before menses. Itching of pudenda. *Heat in vagina* (Merc. c.), *with itching* (Kre.). *Burning in vulva, with itching. Constant running from vulva. Light-yellow leucorrhœa, < in morning. Leucorrhœa returned*, acrid, with itching of genitals (Puls., Kre.). Menses too early, profuse and acrid, preceded by leucorrhœa, which she formerly had had after menses. Menses too early, short, blood bright.

Respiratory Organs.—Speech difficult, rough, hoarse voice. Tickling in trachea, with dry cough as from inspired dust. Cough loud; short, dry, paroxysmal, < at night, then heat in throat; frequent C., < at night; frequent, hard, with white expectoration mingled with threads of blood; constant thick, with thick yellow expectoration. Sense of suffocation. Suffocative attacks at night. Heavy deep breathing on standing, as if a stone lay on chest. Breathing short, with apparent obstruction in larynx. Breathing difficult.

Chest.—Sticking in r. pectoral muscles, < deep inspiration and motion of upper part of body. Tearing in r., from middle of sternum towards r. shoulder-joint, < every inspiration. Sticking tearing in intercostal muscles, r. then l. Sprained feeling in r. side on standing up, with pain in pectoral muscles on touch. Burning pains in l. clavicle. Drawing pains in both sides. Spasmodic drawing between sixth and seventh ribs, with sensation as if some one attempted to stretch out the heart. Oppression.

Heart.—Stitches immediately over; in region, extending towards middle of sternum, < motion and deep inspiration. Sticking boring at point of impulse of apex, waking at night, > hard pressure on præcordial region, then lancinations extending from this place to l. hypochondrium, > deep inspiration. Burning, with pricking. Drawing and cutting pain. Oppression, compelling deep breathing, which relieves. Palpitation.

Neck and Back.—Stiffness of neck. Burning in back, with pricking, cutting and tensive pain. Pricking in loins. Bruised pain in loins, < stooping. Fatigue in loins.

Extremities.—Bruised feeling. Weakness. Shoulder, tearing in l., then sensitiveness to touch; drawing pain in r. joint; lame feeling in l. after rising; pain in S. and arms. Arms, shocks; sprained feeling in l.; stiffness; burning and lancination in A. and forearms. Drawing in middle of r. upper arm, with boring. Intermittent drawing in elbows, as if in a tendon. Tearing in r. forearm from elbow to tip of little finger. Drawing in balls of r. hand. Hands difficult to clench. Finger-joints stiff. Tearing in middle finger after dinner.

Lower Extremities.—Drawing tearing in muscles of hips. Paroxysmal lancinations in front and middle of thighs, extending towards patellæ. Tension in thighs and legs. Knees swollen. Spasmodic tearing below hollow of knee, extending to middle of calf. Bruised feeling in lower third of r. leg, < walking, with limping and feeling as if the pain tended more and more to the great toe and would go off the end of it. Burning pain on anterior side of l. leg. Feet swollen. Tearing in l. metatarsus. Tearing in r. great toe and on inner side of r. knee. Cutting in toes when walking. Intermittent drawing burning pain in l. great toe, < walking.

Skin.—Redness of toes. Swelling in wrist, with tensive pain on bending hand backward, and stitches in wrist on seizing anything. Red pimples above pubis. Boils on buttocks and thighs. Petechiæ-like exanthema on legs, with a pimple in centre. Crusts behind the ears. Tickling itching of forehead.

Sleep.—Yawning after eating; > after eating, but it returns. Sleepiness in daytime. Deep sleep. Waking, with a start. Sleeplessness. Restless sleep, with frightful dreams. Heavy dreams of impending unhappiness. Troublesome dreams.

Fever.—Chilliness, with gooseflesh. Cool sensation on vertex. *Violent fever. Burning* in forehead; in occiput, with stitching; behind ears, < at night, with itching; in hands, with itching. Heat in knees, with pricking and lancination. Burning of feet. Sweat increased.

Aurum Muriaticum Natronatum.

Triturate with sugar of milk for use.

General Action and Relationship.—See *Aurum* and *Natrum mur.*

Generalities.—Increase of secretions from stomach, intestines and kidneys. Boring in those parts which are at rest. Circulation accelerated. Weakness; in morning on rising. Symptoms are most frequent during rest.

Clinical.—Hysterical spasms, with unconsciousness for several hours, beginning with coldness starting from abdomen, sometimes with pulsation in occiput, with inflamed uterus filling the whole pelvis, interfering with the action of the bowels and bladder, entirely cured.

Head.—Tearing diagonally over H. Aching. Deep-seated drawing, and in face.

Forehead.—Tearing in bone. Sticking in bone. Boring in bone; in bone above eyes; in l. bone, extending into eye; in bone, with cutting. Pain; wandering; wandering, in bone. Drawing in l. side; in bone; in bone when sitting; above eyes, with pressure and heaviness; on r. bone, mostly with a bruised feeling. Heaviness; in sinciput; in sinciput when sitting; in sinciput, with heat; in sinciput, with pressure.

Boring in temple; in l. as with a wedge. Distensive pressure in temples. Throbbing in temples. Vertex, cutting shooting across l. side; tearing across to l. side; boring in r. side; drawing diagonally across. Side, tearing in l.; cutting in l. above forehead, when sitting; cutting in a spot in r.; drawing in l. Occiput, boring in side; B. in r. side when sitting; drawing; D. in bones; D. in l.; heaviness and heat. Frequent tearing on various parts of skull. Cutting in a spot on scalp of r. side of vertex.

Eyes.—Boring in r. Stitches in l.; in ball; in

margins of lids, with burning; in r. inner canthus; l. outer canthus. Burning in edges of lids. Boring in bones below eyes; above eyes; above r. eye; in bone over l. eye; in orbit above r. when walking.

Ears.—Stitches in r.; deep in l.; in bone in front of l. Boring in depth of r.; behind ear; in bone behind r.; deep-seated in neighborhood of r. Pressure in bone before r.; in bone above ear. Tingling deep in l.

Nose.—Boring in bones; close to r. bone; along l. side; in r. side, with cutting. Pressure in l. side of bone. Drawing from tip upward, also on sides, with sensation as if it and adjacent parts were thickened; D. in r. nostril and in skin of cheek on l. side of nose, with biting pain. Air passes with unusual freedom. Sneezing.

Face.—Twitching about chin, towards lip. Stitching in skin of l. cheek; in skin of cheek, then heat. Tearing in l. cheek. Cutting in a spot in skin of r. cheek. Boring deep in l. cheek; in l. zygoma. Drawing pain downward in l. cheek. Drawing in chin; in l. cheek; in r. cheek when sitting. Lip, crack in middle of lower, with biting, burning, and pain on touch; stitches in l. side of lower; stitches in vermilion border of lower; pulsation in lower, with sensation as if its centre were thickened. Jaw, boring in l. side; in r. side of upper.

Mouth.—Boring in roots of r. teeth; when sitting, alternating with stitches; B. in lower incisors, extending towards knees, with cutting. Drawing in lower incisors. Tension in roots of l. teeth. Stitches in tip of tongue; below tongue, with scraping. Biting on tip of tongue. Burning in tip; on under surface of tongue and below tongue; deep-seated below tongue, on sides of frænum. Redness behind upper incisors, with swelling and with pain, < motion and warm or salt food, the inflamed spot is like a yellow blister, with a red edge, the redness extending towards l. palate, afterwards it is rose-red, painful to touch and feels rough and swollen. Mouth and throat dry. Salivation; with scraping in fauces; with taste partly sweetish, partly metallic. Taste coppery after milk-soup, which was salted only a little, with smarting pain and with dulness of teeth; coppery, with constriction of salivary glands, clear saliva and dulness of teeth, > eating, but returning.

Clinical.—Indurations of tongue.

Stomach.—Nausea. Gastric irritation. Pressure in epigastric region.

Anus and Stool.—Hæmorrhoid painful, protruding. Stitches in anus. Constipation or diarrhœa.

Urinary Organs.—Stitches in end of urethra. Cutting in end of urethra, also on urinating. Frequent urination. Diuresis.

Sexual Organs.—**Clinical.**—Obstinate leucorrhœa, with spasmodic contractions of muscles of vagina. Chronic metritis and prolapsus. Induration of vaginal portion of uterus. Enlargement of uterus for fourteen years, twice its natural size, entirely cured, uterus replaced itself. Induration of ovaries, reaching as far as umbilicus. Cases of ovarian dropsy. Ulcerations of neck of womb and vagina, resulting from inflammations and indurations. Cases of subinvolution, anteversion and prolapsus, with greenish-yellow discharge. All these cases were cured by internal use of the remedy, generally 3d trit., it usually caused increase of appetite.

Respiratory Organs.—Tickling in larynx and somewhat deeper; in larynx, with dry cough. Cough spasmodic; short dry, with scraping in larynx; short dry, even to retching. Difficult respiration, with anxiety.

Chest.—Stitches in wall below l. axilla; in wall, now r., now l., when walking; in wall below l. nipple, unaffected by respiration. Tearing between ribs, below l. nipple, when walking. Boring in wall above l. nipple. Wandering pain in l. wall during rest. Drawing pain above l. clavicle, towards shoulder and nape, when sitting. Pressure between sternum and r. nipple; behind sternum, extending into back, when walking; outward from r. nipple, unaffected by respiration.

Heart.—Violent beats, with pressure while standing. Beats rapid, irregular when stooping; rapid, small, irregular, on slight motion, with oppression. Irregular beating, with anxiety and difficulty in breathing, afterwards arrest of breath. Palpitation irregular, anxious, when walking; palpitation irregular when sitting, with inclination to inspire deeply; palpitation small, rapid, when standing and sitting, with necessity to inspire deeply.

Neck.—Cracking in cervical vertebræ on bending head. Sticking in l. side, with burning. Tearing in l. side. Pain in l. side; burning, in skin of nape. Drawing in skin on l. side; in l. side, with burning. Tension in l. muscles as far as clavicle, < bending head to r., with pressure, at times unbearable during rest.

Back.—Boring in l. scapula. Drawing in dorsal vertebræ; in muscles on l. side, with pressure. Pressure on r. scapula; in muscles on side of l. scapula.

Upper Extremities.—Stitches in r. axilla during rest. Shoulder, boring; pressure in r.; pressure in l. when walking; frequent P. in joints; drawing. Upper arm, sticking above inner condyle of l.; pinching above inner condyle of r.; boring above r. elbow; pressure above r. elbow; pressure in r. deltoid, with warmth, which extends into fingers; drawing; drawing in skin of r.

Elbow.—Tearing in l., > motion. Boring on r.; in l. during rest. Bruised pain in r. Pressure; during rest; in bend of l. when walking; inward in l. E. and forearm during rest. Drawing; in l. during rest.

Forearm.—Boring in lower part of l. Bruised pain in r. during rest. Pain as from weariness in lower part of l.; in r., with warmth. Burning pain in skin of dorsal side of l. Pressure in r.; below l. elbow; when lying quiet; when sitting, and in elbow; in l., < rest.

Wrist.—Boring. Bruised pain during rest, and in joints of arms. Pressure; in l., then r.; r. then l. when sitting; during rest; in r., < rest. Drawing in bones of r. hand, with bruised sensation.

Fingers.—Stitches in roots of l.; tip of r. little; several joints. Tearing in roots; in second joint of r. thumb. Boring in roots; in joints of r.; first joint of l. index during rest. Pressure in roots of l.; joints of r. little; second joint of r. thumb. Stretching sensation in r. when walking; in roots of l., then in l. wrist, when sitting. Drawing in roots; on back of second phalanx of r. thumb; in roots of l. when sitting and walking; painful, in r. when sitting. Tension in roots; in roots of r.

Lower Extremities.—Sticking in skin above knee; in flesh on inner side of l. thigh; in flesh above r. knee, on inner side. Tearing in skin above l. knee. Cutting in skin above l. knee. Boring above r. knee. Pressing in l. hip-joint when sitting.

Knee.—Stitches in l.; in l. when sitting; in l. when walking. Boring; in r.; when sitting; r. when sitting; l. when standing. Pressure; in r. when walking; l. during rest; r., then l., when sitting; r. knee and foot, > motion, with drawing; in r., as if bruised. Drawing in l.; r. when sitting.

Leg.—Sticking in skin of l. calf when sitting. Boring below r. knee; in sides of r. tendo-achillis when sitting, afterwards when walking. Pain as from weariness, > motion. Drawing in shins.

Tibia.—Tearing; on l. Boring; in l.; lower part; r., then l.; l. when sitting. Pressure on r.; in lower part of l.; in lower part of l., extending through foot and toes, extending again in a turning motion to the tibia, when sitting. Drawing in r.; in lower part; in centre of l., extending into ankle.

Ankle.—Painless crepitus, as from rubbing dry leather, below inner bone of r. when lying still, afterwards rhythmical, slower than the pulse. Sticking above inner malleolus. Boring; in r. when standing; in l. outer malleolus extending to tibia, during rest. Pressure in l.; P. when sitting; in l. when sitting; in r. during rest. Drawing on r. outer malleolus; in l. when lying. Quick pulsation about l. inner malleolus extending to great toe, when standing.

Foot.—Stitches in ball; on ball of l.; in ball of r., with burning; in the usually painless corn. Tearing in r. sole. Boring on dorsum; in dorsum of r.; in os calcis; in bone on r. sole; on r. sole when standing; on dorsum of l., extending to toes. Pressure on dorsum of l.; on r. when sitting. Drawing in ball of l.; in l. heel; in inner edge of l., then r., in evening when sitting; in r. sole to tips of toes when sitting.

Toes.—Stitches; in tip of great; in back of r. great; in tips; in tips when sitting. Sticking cutting in tips of r. when sitting. Boring in l.; r. great; l. great when sitting; posterior surface of r. great during rest; l. great, with cutting. Stretching-apart sensation in r. Drawing; in l.; roots of r.; in r. during rest; in r. when walking; deep-seated in l. great, < rest; in roots of l., mostly with a bruised feeling. Tension in roots.

Fever.—Cold hands, blue nails, with heat in face and ears. Coldness in back. Internal warmth. Heat in head and face; ears. Burning in l. wing of nose; skin on l. side of nose; cheeks; skin of l. cheek; cheeks, < stooping; lower lip; edge of upper lip; on skin on r. side of neck; skin of r. axilla; inner side of r. arm; skin on back of r. hand; tip of l. little finger; skin of r. hip; in skin above l. knee, then above r.; skin of r. knee; in knees when sitting; skin of l. calf; drawing, in nape.

Badiaga.

The fresh-water sponge (Spongilla lacustris, Link.) is not uncommon in ponds and slow-flowing streams. It belongs to the section Protozoa of the animal kingdom. A tincture is made from the dried sponge; or it is triturated.

Related Remedies.—Iodine, Spongia.

Generalities and Mind.—Pains in various parts in afternoon, < motion, with stitches in the sides, especially in posterior part of r. side. *Soreness of muscles and integuments*, especially the integuments, < motion and friction of clothes, afterwards with sensitiveness to cold. Soreness of muscles and whole body, causing a restless and sleepless night. More inclined to mental activity in spite of headache.

Head.—Aching from between 1 and 2 till between 6 and 7 P.M.; *from 2 to 7 P.M., with pain in posterior part of eyeballs and in temples;* < from 1 till 7 P.M., with pain in *posterior part of eyeballs*, < l.; A., < 7 to 10 P.M., on a rainy day, with soreness of body. *Aching* in forehead in forenoon, < moving eyes, worse in temples and *extending into posterior part of l. eyeball;* in forehead, extending through l. temple and eye, < afternoon and evening; in forehead, extending to eyeballs, < afternoon and by motion, with heat in forehead and aching in temples; in forehead in afternoon, < 7 P.M., with heat and congestion. Scalp sore to touch, with tetter on forehead and dull, dizzy feeling of head in forenoon. Itching of scalp, with dandruff like tetter; and dryness of hair.

Eyes.—Irritation and inflammation of r. Scrofulous inflammation, with hardening of Meibomian glands. *Intermittent pain in posterior part of r. ball* at 3 P.M., the same next day, < afternoon, and in temple. *Pain in balls, extending into temples, < turning them in either direction.* Pain in l. ball and temple, extending to l. side of head and forehead. *Soreness of l. ball, even on closing it tightly. Bluish-purple margins of lids and blueness under eyes.* Twitching of l. upper lid.

Clinical.—Intermittent neuralgia of r. eyeball, extending to forehead and temple, < afternoon.

Ears, Nose and Face.—*Hears slight shocks as of distant artillery in afternoon and evening.* Sneezing, with coryza and cough (Iod.), < afternoon. Sneezing, < afternoon and evening, with coryza, most on l. side, with occasional stoppage of nose; S., with fluent coryza and occasional stoppage of nose. Discharge from l. nostril; thick yellowish mucus, < afternoon, it is also hawked up. *Face pale, ashy or lead-colored.* L. cheek and malar-bone sore to touch.

Clinical.—Hay fever, sneezing and watery discharge, with asthmatic breathing (Iod.), paroxysms of suffocative cough, during the cough the mucus flies out of the mouth and nostrils.

Mouth and Throat.—Scalded feeling in mouth and tongue. *Mouth and breath hot in afternoon and feverish, with thirst for large quantities of water at a time. Hawked up a viscid solid lump of bloody mucus in the morning. Throat inflamed and sore, < swallowing.*

Stomach and Abdomen.—Appetite bad, with bad taste. Lancinations at pit of stomach at 8 A.M., extending to the vertebra opposite and to r. scapula, and at times to r. side, resulting there in a pleuritic pain, with pleuritic pain in l. side, the pleuritic pains < by contortions of body and on full inspiration. Lancinations in region of liver, with a bounding movement. Constipation.

Clinical.—Indurated buboes (Iod.).

Urinary Organs.—Lancinations in orifice of urethra and near it, at noon. Urine reddish; high-colored.

Genital Organs.—**Clinical.**—Uterine hæmorrhage, < night, with feeling of enlargement of the head.

Respiratory Organs.—Cough, > in warm room. Cough, with yellowish mucous expectoration. *Spasmodic cough from tickling in larynx as if sugar were dissolved in the throat*, < afternoon, *ejecting viscid mucus from bronchial tubes, which at times flew forcibly out of the mouth*, next day similar paroxysms, < after 1 P.M., causing sneezing, with coryza most from l. nostril.

Clinical.—Whooping cough, with thick yellow expectoration, it flies out of the mouth half across the room.

Chest.—Lancinations in r. supraclavicular region, in or near subclavian artery, in evening, afterwards drawing lancinations in evening. Stitches in sides, < r., from seventh to eighth rib, < motion. Pleuritic stitches, < afternoon and evening, with soreness of whole body, especially the chest. Pleuritic pains in sides in afternoon, < motion or full inspiration, with stitches. Pain in r. side on contortions of body.

Heart.—Is heard and felt to pulsate from chest up to neck at night while lying on r. side. Pulsations felt and heard while lying, extending up to neck on slightest emotion or thought. Vibrating palpitation on least elation or other emotion. Vibrating palpitation at midnight in bed, then while lying on r. side sensation as if lower lobe of l. lung were settling down or collapsing, > changing position.

Neck and Back.—*Stitches in nape, < bending head back and forth, with soreness and lameness.* Stitches in nape, < flexing head back and forth, with stiffness. Intermittent drawing pain in nape. *Stitches below r. scapula, < throwing shoulders back and chest forward or by contortions of body,* at times causing a moan or shriek. Pain in or near head of r. scapula. Painful drawing downward from l. scapula to near spine, a similar sensation in forehead, and slightly in a decayed molar. Pain in small of back, hips and lower limbs. Pain in r. kidney in afternoon.

Extremities.—Pain in lower limbs; in r. knee at 2 P.M.; in l. knee on going up or down-stairs; running from anterior of r. leg to posterior of r. thigh between 12 o'clock and 1 P.M.; intermittent, in muscles of lower posterior third of r. leg, with a sore, contracted, clumsy, bruised feeling of anterior muscles of lower third of r. leg, < by flexing foot and ascending stairs, when the toes tend to drop, as if the foot were asleep, though without a sensation as if asleep. Anterior muscles of r. leg sore as if beaten, with a contracted feeling, sore upon ascending stairs or walking, with a numb feeling while sitting or lying, afterwards the sore numb feeling < ascending stairs or flexing foot. Stinging in posterior part of r. heel, < pressure.

Skin, etc.—Itching of l. wing of nose. Awoke at 3 A.M., with frightful dreams and crampy pains in metatarsal bones. Palms dry; and hot.

Baptisia.

The wild Indigo of America, Baptisia tinctoria, R. Br., is a perennial herb belonging to the Leguminosæ. A tincture is prepared from the fresh root.

General Action.—It produces profound depression, with a tendency to disorganization of the blood; low type of fever and conditions simulating malarial poisoning (dysentery and typhoid fever).

Compare Rhus, Arnica, Gelsem., (Apis, Bry., Phyto., etc.). Paralytic symptoms, Lathyrus, Oxytropis, Physostigma.

Generalities.—*Intolerance of pressure on all parts, could not rest back against chair without pain, obliged to change sitting posture often, even the feet were painful from resting on floor* (Arn., Bry.). *Pain in all parts on which he lay, each time after waking from nightmare, especially in sacral region and hips, inducing the conviction that the position would soon cause bed-sores, obliged to lie on his face to relieve the back and hips* (Arn.). Rheumatic pains in r. side. Erratic pains in various parts.

Indescribable sick feeling over whole body. Feeling as if he had taken cold, soreness of throat and sneezing. General feeling of having slept too long and too hard, with bloated feeling in eyes. **Restlessness** (Rhus); **does not sleep quietly,** *wants to get up, yet does not want to; R. in evening.* Faintness; with trembling of legs and aching in them. *Weakness;* after a light dinner at 3 P.M., with sleepiness; *especially in lower limbs, with weak knees and vertigo* (Gelsem.); *in all parts, with bruised and sick feeling, yet does not feel very badly; with tremulous feeling, as if recovering from a fit of sickness and as yet incapable of vigorous mental or physical exertion,* > walking in open air, which causes lachrymation; with flashes of heat from small of back in all directions. *Indisposition to move* (Bry.). *Feeling of inability to make physical or mental exertion, on going to bed. Weariness* of whole l. side of body; in back and lower limbs, especially r., after walking, and in r. shoulder and arm. Stiffness and soreness over whole body, with dread of motion; stiffness of all joints as if strained. *Paralysis of whole l. side,* l. arm and hand numb and powerless. Aggravation of all symptoms after a glass of beer (Rhus.).

Clinical.—Weary bruised feeling over the whole body, especially in the limbs. Hysteria, with great physical prostration, with numbness and fear of paralysis, wanted to die, rubbed her hands all the time, restless. It is indicated in low types of disease, tendency to disorganization of the blood, with restlessness and generally with delirium or stupor. It may be useful in low typhoid states of a great variety of diseases, all the eruptive and malarial diseases. All the secretions are offensive, even the sweat and urine, with frequent attacks of faintness and exhaustion.

Mind.—Excitement; of brain like the beginning of delirium. Disposition to talk. Low spirits. *Mind cannot be confined, a wild, wandering feeling. Indisposition to think and inability to think.* Memory weak. Stupid feeling after breakfast. Weakness rather than confusion. Very distinct recollection of what he had been reading.

Clinical.—Delirium, with low fever, ideas confused, wandering, muttering, seems to be endeavoring to get pieces of the body together; incoherent muttering. Brain fag, the head feels very heavy, is averse to any mental effort and lacks the power to think.

Head.—Aching, < noise; < motion (Bry.); with bruised feeling in forehead; with pain in loins; causing a sensation of wildness. Heaviness; in morning after rising, with pain; with pain in occiput; as if he could not sit up. Feeling as if large; and heavy. *Soreness of brain, < stooping.* Confusion; especially in occiput, where there were pain and fulness. Stupid feeling, with pain at occiput. Numbness of brain, with stitches or shocks in various parts of head. *Vertigo; with weak feeling of whole body, especially of lower limbs, with weak knees.* Swimming sensation, as before operation of an emetic.

Forehead.—Aching; in morning; in evening, with smarting of eyes and drawing pain down nose*; with pressure at root of nose;* with fulness of whole head; with pain in abdomen all the evening; then passing to occiput; in anterior lobes of brain in afternoon, and in r. frontal sinus; in sinuses, < r.; in r. sinus; over r. eye; sharp over r.; then l. eye. Feeling as if it would be pressed in. Tightness across, with pain over r. eye. Soreness in front part of head in evening on moving eyes or turning them upward.

Pain in temples; *in r.; sharp pains in T. by spells.* Pain at base of brain, with lameness and drawing pain in cervical muscles; heavy P. at base of brain (Petrol.).

Pressure in occiput in morning; P. in occiput from ear to ear and from vertex to nape. Fulness of external vessels of head and face. Soreness of scalp.

Clinical.—Feeling of great tightness of skin of forehead, it seemed to be drawn to the back of the head, the head felt too large, heavy and numb (in fever).

Eyes.—Shining. Congestion of vessels, with redness and inflammation. Smarting and aching. Feeling as if pressed into head, with confusion of sight, cannot place anything until he looks at it a few seconds, everything appears to move. Swollen feeling, with burning and lachrymation. Lachrymation on going into open air. *Soreness of balls* (Eup. perf.); *with lame feeling on moving them* (Agar.). Partial paralysis of lids, it is difficult to keep them open (Gelsem., Rhus.).

Ears, Nose and Face.—Dulness of hearing. Pain at root of nose. Soreness extends to posterior nares. Sneezing and feeling as after taking a severe cold. Catarrh. Thick mucous discharge from nose. Face sallow.

Mouth.—Teeth and gums sore, and much blood oozes from gum when pressed with the finger (Merc.). *Tongue coated yellow; along centre;* coated yellow, with flat bitter taste; *coated first white, with reddish papillæ here and there, then a yellowish-brown coat in centre, the edges being red and shining,* and tongue feeling thick; coated white in morning and congested; feels scraped; *dry on waking* (*Rhus t.*), *and feeling burnt;* numb pricking sensation. *Ulcers. Salivation;* in evening; then sore throat, with scraping and burning; then pain in r. lung; *viscid and flat-tasting;* sweetish bitter, then a dryish or glutinous substance, and the lips stick together. *Taste flat, bitter;* filthy, with salivation; of food not quite natural.

Clinical.—The gums, mouth and throat are sore, ulcerated breath fetid, salivation, ulcerations, with red areola. Useful in the sore mouths of nursing infants and of nursing women. Stomatitis of phthisis.

Throat.—*Redness of tonsils and soft palate.* Congestion; *of tonsils and soft palate; of tonsils, with frequent inclination to swallow, which causes pain at root of tongue* (Phyto.). Angina, throat feels swollen or full, with oppressed respiration and sharp pains in chest when taking a long breath. Pricking in upper part. Scraped sensation extending through it. *Soreness, with a contracted feeling;* S. extending to posterior nares. Rawness, with much viscid mucus. *Constriction, causing frequent efforts to swallow* (Apis., Lyc.). Dryness, extending to nares, with roughness and stringent sensation, then increased secretion, especially from pharynx. Tickling, provoking cough.

Clinical.—Diphtheria, the patient semi-comatose or delirious, could swallow only liquids; the face is dark red, and there is a horrible odor from the mouth. Contraction of œsophagus, with great difficulty in getting food into stomach, could swallow only liquids.

Stomach.—*Appetite lost.* Thirst. Constant desire for water. Eructations of air. Feeling as if it would be a relief to vomit. *Nausea;* in evening; with heat. Feelas if he would vomit, but no nausea, with shooting in l. kidney and l. side of umbilicus.

Stitches in cardiac extremity. Cramp in evening. *Pain;* in epigastric region; in epigastric region all night; in S. and liver; in S. and in r. hypochondriac and umbilical regions; in S. and in r. hypochondriac region, the pain in r. side very severe when walking; in epigastric region at night, < turning over, which he had to do constantly; with belching of much wind; with feeling as if a hard substance were in it; in pit, with constriction of diaphragm. Intermittent pain in cardiac portion. Pain in S. and r. hypochondrium, extending to spine, < motion; in S., abdomen and r. hypochondrium, passing down to r. iliac region; in S. and liver, sharp at times. Drawing pain in epigastric and r. hypochondriac regions, < walking. Heavy pain in S. and liver, with heat in those parts. *Distress* all the forenoon, and in abdomen, with desire to vomit; D. in epigastric and umbilical regions, with rumbling; in S. and umbilical region, with pain in region of gall-bladder; burning, in epigastrium, with colic in umbilical and especially in hypogastric region, rumbling in abdomen and desire to vomit, but no nausea. Empty feeling.

Abdomen.—*Distention. Rumbling;* with desire for stool; with mushy stool. Shooting pains all through. *Pain* on pressure. Distress. *Pain* in r. hypochondriac region (Bry.); *in region of gall-bladder, also < walking* (Diosc.); in liver, stomach and umbilical region; *in liver, extending from r. lateral ligament to gall-bladder; in liver* and stomach, which caused a numb feeling to pass all over the body. Soreness in region of liver. *Pain* in umbilical region (Diosc.); < full inspiration; with rumbling in abdomen; in umbilical and hypogastric regions, very sharp in hypogastrium by spells. Swelling of glands in l. groin, very painful when walking. Cutting in hypogastric region at 1 A.M., waking him, with rumbling, then *restlessness.* Drawing pain in r. groin; and in r. testicle and r. foot.

Clinical.—It has been found useful when there is great soreness over the region of the gall-bladder, especially in diarrhœa.

Rectum and Stool.—Rectum felt as if the drawings were upward instead of downward. Inactivity of lower bowels and rectum, stool natural but slow. *Diarrhœa; in morning. Papescent stool, with much mucus, but no real pain. Constipation;* with hæmorrhoids in afternoon; with *fulness of abdomen,* flatulence, pain in hypogastrium, and soreness of abdominal muscles as from cold or coughing severely.

Clinical.—Diarrhœa in low types of malarial fever, evacuations horribly offensive, thin, fecal, usually dark. Dysentery, discharges bloody, some tenesmus, but not painful.

Urinary and Sexual Organs.—*Burning when urinating, urine not very copious but dark red.* Urine high-colored. Urine whitish, has no effect on blue litmus nor on red paper. Shrivelling and relaxation of genitals, with dragging pain in r. testicle and spermatic cord, the same next day, with absence of sexual desire and with seminal losses from relaxation and inertia of sexual organs, afterwards the aching in spermatic cord was very annoying at night.

Respiratory Organs.—Epiglottis swollen in morning. Hoarseness. *Breathing difficult* (on waking from a dream of hard labor in snow, which caused great heat, and finally of being smothered in the snow), *the lungs felt compressed,* obliged to open the window, heat of surface, dryness of tongue, increased pulsations of heart, rapid pulse and excitement of brain (as in beginning of delirium), then chilly horripilations over lower limbs and back. *Breathing difficult* on lying down, from a feeling of weakness of respiratory apparatus, such as he had only felt during fever, *obliging him to rise, with fear of going to sleep lest he should have* *nightmare and suffocate* (Lach.). Breathing oppressed at 6 P.M., with cough, *soreness of r. lung*, sneezing, increased secretion from bronchial tubes and fauces and expectoration of mucus. Constant want to take a full breath.

Chest, Heart and Pulse.—Pain through l. chest; in sternum; in r. lung, less in l., with soreness. Constriction of chest, with oppression. Tightness of chest, with desire to inspire deeply. Oppression in præcordial region in afternoon, with a feeling of unsatisfied breathing. Feeling of increased compass and frequency of pulsations of heart, the pulsations seem to fill the chest. Audible throbbing of the heart. Pulse rapid at 2 P.M.; and full, soft; then faint; slow and weak; slow, round and full.

Neck.—Pain, unbearable on moving head. Soreness of muscles. *Stiffness of muscles, with lameness.*

Back.—Twitching of l. latissimus dorsi. *Pain*; < walking; extending to sacrum. Lameness of muscles of B. and chest, < moving head. *Stiffness of B. and hips, with pain. Pain* in lumbar region; < walking; heavy, in lumbar region at night on going to bed. *Pain in sacrum compounded of a feeling as from pressure and fatigue from long stooping, soon extending around hips and down r. leg.*

Extremities.—*Aching; drawing, in arms and legs*; at times drawing, in r. wrist and l. ankle; wandering, with vertigo. Prickling of hands and feet, < motion, with numbness. Thrilling through hands and feet, somewhat like going to sleep or want of circulation.

Upper Extremities.—Constant twitching of l. deltoid. Pain in l. shoulder and arm; in l. shoulder, extending down arm; drawing, in shoulder and arms, < l. Sore and stiff feeling in shoulders and chest, the jar of the buggy is painful. Numb prickling pain in hand and arm, < movement, with sharp darting pain through fingers. Hands felt large and were tremulous. *Numbness of l. hand* and forearm, with prickling.

Lower Extremities.—Feel weak and vacillating on walking. Pain in hips and legs, with numbness. Drawing pain in l. hip; in r. hip and in both calves. Soreness in anterior part of thighs, < after sitting. Darting pain in l. knee and l. malleolus. Cramp in calves whenever he moves them. Drawing pain in calves; in legs. Pain in legs. *Numbness of l. foot, with prickling.* Prickling of foot and leg, they can be moved but little.

Skin.—*Livid spots all over body and limbs, thickest on body.* Feeling on forehead as if it would be pulled to the back part of the head, with numbness in forehead and face. Contracted feeling in forehead. Tight feeling in forehead, with pain over r. eye; T. feeling in forehead, with pain in temples.

Sleep.—Yawning while conversing with people. Sleepiness; all day; after breakfast; with stupidity and weariness; with desire to have eyes half closed. Sleep unusually sound; deep till 3 A.M. *Slept well till 2 A.M., then restless till morning.* Fell asleep while sitting and writing; in a carriage. *Restless night; with frightful dreams. Sleeplessness*; after midnight; after 2 A.M.; *after* 3 A.M., *with restlessness.* Nightmare, feeling on waking as if the room were insufferably hot and close; N., then anxiety after waking. *Frightful dreams.* Dreams of being bound down with a chain across the mouth; of fighting and disputations, but always comes off best; of triumphing over all opposition; continual.

Fever.—Chill about 11 A.M.; in evening on going into open air; all day, with fever at night and rheumatic pains and soreness all over body; of surface; over back in forenoon while sitting by a hot stove; over back in evening; in lower limbs and back.

Heat after going to bed. Hot sensation over whole body, then sweat, vomiting and *diarrhœa, stools dark.* Heat in flashes on waking at 3 A.M., with feeling as if sweat would break out. Heat in forehead; on top of head, with soreness of scalp; of face; cheeks; of face in flashes; *of face, with redness*; in l. side *of face and head*, with prickling; of lower limbs at night; in feet, with pulsation; external H. of limbs, except feet, which are cool. Heat of whole surface, especially of face, the tongue dry on rubbing it against roof of mouth, smarting and feeling sore as if burnt, compelled to move to cool part of bed and finally to rise, open a window and wash his hands and face, with a peculiar feeling in head which is never felt except during fever. Dry heat of whole surface, with occasional chills, principally up and down back.

Clinical.—Typhoid fever, with great sensitiveness of the r. iliac region and soreness of the abdomen generally. Generally useful in the early stage of typhoid fever, restlessness, with muttering delirium, fetor of breath and body, face dusky, etc.

Baryta Acetica.

Dissolve the acetate of Barium in distilled water for use (one to nine).

Action and Affinities, as Bar. carb., except the modifications by Acetic acid.

Generalities.—Lies on his back, deprived of voluntary motion. Discoloration of tissues, with emaciation. Bruised feeling in whole body, with weariness and heaviness of lower limbs; B. pain in spots, slowly increasing and decreasing. Drawing in whole body, now here, now there, especially in joints. Indescribable malaise. Inability to cough, to expectorate, to articulate words of more than two syllables (owing to failure in expiration), or to lift head from the pillow.

Weakness (Acet. ac.); after eating, with depression, discomfort, constant desire for stool, and anxiety in lumbar region, as in dysentery; with constant desire to lie or sit; with giving way of knees when standing, pain in spine, especially in lumbar region, as after a long ride, discomfort in whole body and constant desire to sit, or rather lie, would rather walk than stand. Paralysis extends rapidly downward, affecting first the abdominal muscles, then those which have their insertions in chest, then those of neck, lastly sphincters of bladder and rectum. The symptoms (tearing, drawing, throbbing) in head and limbs appear more on l. side.

Mind.—*Wavering long between opposite resolutions. Resolved during the day that she will undertake a certain matter in the evening, but scarcely has the time come when she repents and is undecided whether to do it or not.* He proposes a short journey, but as soon as he makes preparations he is inclined to remain at home. Self-confidence has disappeared. Anthropophobia. Sadness. Grief at every trifle. Sudden fearful suspicion, for example, that a friend was taken suddenly deathly ill. Solicitude; with fear, the slightest noise in the street seems like a fire alarm, and he is so frightened that he starts in every limb. Dread, when walking in the street she imagines that people are judging her wrongly, which causes anxiety, so that she will, not look up and sweats over the whole body. Fretfulness; with disinclination to work. Sudden but transient anger. Obstinacy, irritation and excitement about trifles. *Forgetful of the word he was about to speak; of a common word in the midst of a speech* (Bar. c.).

Head.—Pressing as if it would burst, especially in frontal eminences and over orbits. Dulness; with tensive confusion in forehead and eyes, especially in inner canthi. Confusion, with heaviness; C., extending to temple and forehead. Light feeling as if empty. Vertigo; on moving body.

Stitch outward in r. frontal eminence. Burrowing in forehead and temples. Pressure over r. eye; stupefying, over root of nose. Pain pressing outward in forehead, < raising head, > stooping, especially in orbits. Deep-seated twitching in l. temple, orbit and ear. Thrust outward in l. temple. Aching in l. temple. Burrowing in top and front of head almost every morning after rising, > afternoon, with loose sensation in brain on shaking it.

Pressing-asunder stitch in l. side, traversing l. occiput and ending in cervical vertebræ. Aching in r. half of brain, from neck to frontal protuberance. Sudden drawing in occiput, extending over r. ear and lower jaw. Heaviness in occiput, especially close to neck, with tension. Scalp painful on touch. Stitches here and there on scalp, compelling scratching. Creeping, as if hair stood on end. Formication, with pricking under scalp and under skin of face. Head and face feel as if covered with parchment.

Eyes.—Aching, with fatigue. Pressure in l. after a twinging pain in l. temple and orbit, with sensation as if eye would water and weakness compelling her to close the lids, afterwards same sensation in r. eye; deep-seated pressure, < looking at one point or upward or sideways, > winking or looking downward. Pressure on balls. Rapid alternations of dilatation and contraction of pupil, whereby it has obtuse angles. *Vision misty if she closes the eyes and presses the balls, with aching in balls.*

Ears.—Stitches below r. near ramus of jaw; drawing, in l. mastoid process, aggravated at intervals, then pain in the spot, < touching it or turning head.

Clinical.—Neuralgia behind r. ear.

Face.—Pallor, with drawn features and drooping eyebrows; cadaverous P. Feeling as if much swollen, but is only slightly so. *Feeling as if covered with cobwebs* (Graph.). Sensation as if something were drawn tightly over F. and scalp, especially in temporal region, with cold sensation in face. Tension, which draws down eyelids, with inclination to expectorate saliva; T., with nausea and diarrhœa.

Lips.—Pustules in r. corner, with pain on touch. Broad wheals under skin of upper, with pain on touch. Upper feels swollen, with sensation on inner surface and on palate as if burnt or numb.

Mouth.—Painful swelling of gums of r. upper back tooth, with redness and a dark-red border around tooth, pain in tooth from cold drinks and sensitiveness in its vicinity. Tongue cold and somewhat black. Utterance imperfect. Constant spitting of saliva without nausea. Taste detestable; bitter, but natural to food; pungent in throat on smoking tobacco.

Stomach.—Appetite great, but if satisfied then discomfort and heaviness. Aversion to eating, yet hunger. Satiety. Little appetite, food will not go down, it is repugnant and eating gives discomfort. Appetite satisfied if she eats a little, with heaviness in stomach as from a stone and gnawing, the pain transiently > by stretching up or bending backward, < sitting bent. Thirst.

Empty eructations; with insipid taste and salivation; with sensation in epigastric region as if it would force itself through, which causes soreness, then tasteless eructations. Nausea; when walking, < touching epigastric region; then sudden and copious vomiting of bile and brownish substance (probably the chocolate taken in the morning). Retching. Vomiting almost every hour; copious V.

Sticking below pit, near ensiform cartilage, continuing as a simple pain. *Writhing pain when food passes into it, as if it forced its way against sore places.* Pain; in epigastric region, < slightest food, with pressure of breath and sensation as if on deep breathing the breath were arrested there, with a rough voice, which is only transiently > by frequent hawking. Intermittent sudden drawing pain in pit. *Sensitiveness in pit, pain on every hard step. Sore pain in pit* on pressure and on breathing; sore pain, even when fasting; < standing, walking and sitting bent, with gnawing, but when lying on back, bending forward or pressing on stomach she feels only the pain, not the gnawing. Heaviness in morning fasting, > breakfast, with nausea; in pit, making respiration difficult, > deep breathing, < carrying a slight weight. Heartburn after eructations.

Abdomen.—Borborygmi; with grumbling. Gurgling; in afternoon on moving it, with sensation of much fluid in it though she had drunk nothing. Griping extending downward. Pain as from diarrhœa, drawing to and fro, > transiently by rumbling. Sensation as before diarrhœa, with chilliness. Sensation in upper as before vomiting. Sudden stitches in r., making her cry out. Aching spot in r. hypochondriac region, only on inspiration (< deep breathing), with pain on pressure. Pinching in a spot below l. hypochondrium, < pressure of finger; sudden, in region of transverse colon, as if flatus pressed through it. Sudden stitch from r. groin into abdomen. Sudden constrictive pain above pubes, worse by paroxysms.

Rectum and Stool.—*Frequent urging to stool, with pain in lumbar region* and creeping coldness over head and along thighs, *as in dysentery, then soft stool at intervals,* then continuing pain in loins and *renewed urging.* Urging with pain as if the intestines were spread out, then soft stool with renewed urging. Frequent desire, but she goes no oftener than usual, and the passage then is natural. Stool half liquid, then constipation. Stool soft, finally like diarrhœa; soft, granular. Involuntary stools.

Urinary and Sexual Organs.—Necessity to pass clear watery urine frequently, though little at a time. Frequent and copious micturition in morning before eating or drinking. Almost complete incontinence of urine and fæces. Urine increased; and clear. Much mucus in urine. Sweat on scrotum. The formerly-swollen epididymus swells anew violently. Desire diminished.

Respiratory Organs and Chest.—Pressure just below larnyx. Voice extinct. Voice rough on account of tough mucus in throat and larnyx, on hawking he raises but little and makes his voice clear for but a short time. Respiration imperfect; and frequent, respiratory sound almost imperceptible. Stitch between r. sixth and seventh ribs. Heaviness across chest, < inspiration, which causes sticking beneath upper end of sternum.

Heart and Pulse.—Heart sounds dull, deep. Pulse rapid and small; slow; irregular.

Neck.—Aching extending from cervical vertebræ to behind r. ear, obliquely to parietal bone, at 4 P.M. and afterwards, on two days. Tensive pain on l. side.

Back.—Relaxation of posterior muscles of trunk after vomiting. Stitch on l. scapula and on outer side of r. thigh. Sudden pinching on l. scapula. *Anxiety in lumbar region, with discomfort and restlessness, like urging to stool,* > passage of flatus or empty eructations, then frequent soft stools. Throbbing, grumbling sensation in lower part of small of back.

Extremities.—Muscular relaxation, he was scarcely able to sit in an arm-chair. Digging in l. shoulder-bone. Bruised pain in middle of l. humerus. Sensitive pain in a spot in humerus. Drawing in all long bones of r. arm. Heaviness of l. arm, with difficult motion of it, the shoulder alone seems to act, the hand and forearm are paralyzed. Bruised pain on back of forearm, as if in bone, worse by paroxysms. Painful drawing in l. forearm, as if in bone. Twitching in inner condyle of wrist in slow, wavelike paroxysms in morning in bed; rhythmical T. in outer condyle of wrist. Tearing in wrist, extending to tips of fingers. Cramplike pain in r. wrist, extending outward. Stitches in lowest joint of l. index.

Lower Extremities.—Tearing down leg, most painful and lasts longest in knees, and also in other joints, nates, hips and ankles; intermittent, downward in r. nates; in external and anterior side of thigh, extending downward under skin, as far as knee when walking.

Knee.—Tearing extending downward under skin, while walking. Stitches through l. on ascending stairs, leaving painful paralysis; sudden S. on inner side of l. Aching on inner side of l. on raising it and putting leg forward in walking. Pain in l. when sitting, more towards inner side, on extending foot it becomes a dull pressive sensation.

Drawing pain down whole l. leg. Sensitive drawing in small spot in l. tibia. Legs dragged, < ascending steps, on account of lame sensation in middle of thigh. Giving way of r., then l. leg. Weariness of legs when sitting, with jerks in foot and aching in posterior surface of thigh, which is < by stepping and extends to foot. Drawing pain in l. sole.

Skin.—Acne pimples on chest. Pustules on l. middle finger, with sore pain on touch. Red, eroded, moist, burning spot between scrotum and thigh. Fine stitches here and there. *Crawling here and there, with burning stitches,* often sudden in a spot, *not* > by scratching and rubbing; C. in palm, with biting; in whole body nights, especially on back, hips, legs, ankles, back of feet and fingers, waking him, with constant scratching, which only transiently relieves; burning, on back of hand and fingers, only transiently > scratching. Itching on chest.

Sleep.—Yawning, with stretching and sleepiness; Y., with suffusion of eyes. Wearied with sleep in forenoon. Overpowering sleepiness. Sleep in afternoon and continual nodding. Frequent waking, with heat, throwing off of covering, and with aching of feet as after long standing, > walking. The first sleep uneasy, with frequent waking, though he was tired and sleepy on going to bed. Sleep unsound and unrefreshing. Unrefreshed in morning on waking, > rising, with bruised feeling in limbs. Dreams of dead persons (which did not frighten him), with murmurings in sleep. Vivid, strange dreams. Confused dreams; with restless sleep, frequent waking and fatigue, so that he soon fell asleep again.

Fever.—Chilliness in forenoon, coldness rising in pit of stomach, with pressure, so that it seems as if the hairs were drawn together, it then extends slowly down arms and legs into feet. C. in attacks extends down through whole body, with coldness of hands; C. in attacks, especially in arms, with gooseflesh and yawning. Shivering chilliness in head, with tension in malar-bones as if there would be gooseflesh in face and as if the hair stood on end. Shivering in attacks, with flashes of heat, mostly in back, the chilliness extends from the face, in which there is tension. Skin cold; and covered with sweat. Feeling of a cold air along leg as far as condyles. Chilliness extends from pit of stomach, then warmth of whole body except feet, then chilliness again.

Flushes of heat over whole body, then exhaustion, so that the hands sink down, face and hands hot, the rest of the body almost cool. Hot sensation on back; in face, without redness.

Baryta Carbonica.

Pure Carbonate of Barium is triturated for use.

Action.—A profound tissue remedy affecting glandular structures especially; indicated in general degenerative changes.

Affinities.—*Lycop.*, Merc. i. rub., Mag., Nat., Calc., Kali.

Generalities—Stitches in joints. Tearing in whole body, now here, now there. Pinching in several places. Bruised feeling over whole body in morning on waking, with weakness. Tense feeling in whole body, with anxiety in forenoon. Beating through whole body in morning on rising. Drawing alternately in r. shoulder, in lower extremities, arms, occiput and eyes, with heaviness of occiput, great indolence and sleepiness causing dizziness.

General sick feeling. Sensitiveness of all senses. Faint feeling at night, with profuse vomiting, next day nausea. Walking in open air is difficult, but the farther he walks the easier it becomes. Weakness at 8 P.M., so that he almost sinks down; W. from a short walk, then necessity to sleep; when lying, which generally seems a kind of heaviness. Relaxed condition of joints. Indolence after dinner. Paralysis extending from below upward, so that he could only nod his head, with red face, difficult speech, sensation intact, reflex irritation increased, respiration rapid, with tracheal râles. Several symptoms decrease during dinner. Many symptoms arise when sitting, are better when standing, and disappear on motion. Many symptoms disappear in open air.

Clinical.—It is useful in conditions of malnutrition in children when there is imperfect development of mind or in diseases that have a tendency to slow degenerative changes, like scrofulous glandular indurations of various sorts. It is an extremely valuable remedy in degenerative changes in coats of arteries, aneurism, arterial fibrosis, in apoplexy as the result of senility, etc. *Fatty tumors*, particularly about neck and back. Paralysis of old people.

Mind.—Delirium at night, with stupefaction, as in fever. Anxiety evenings in bed, with necessity to open her clothes. Fear and cowardice. Sadness and fear for his future, in the evening, he thinks that he is lost. Despondency, with crying and the belief that she must die. Lachrymose mood at night. Dejection, with disinclination to speak. Ennui and ill humor. Peevish and quarrelsome. Good humor becomes mischievousness. Stupid feeling in the morning on waking. *Want of memory; so that he does not know what he has just spoken* (Anac., Dig.).

Clinical.—In children mental weakness, approaching idiocy. Mental impairment, as a result of masturbation, irresolute, memory lost, no confidence in himself. Senile dementia, with loss of memory.

Head.—Stitches, from warmth of stove; in brain, with heat and crawling in head; increasing and decreasing. Shattering in brain on stamping. *Aching* in evening, < noise, especially the human voice; from walking. Heaviness in morning on waking, after rising heat in it, with coldness of hands and feet. *Confusion;* in morning on waking and the whole forenoon; in evening, with heaviness in it, sleepiness, constant falling forward of head, fretfulness and fatigue; when sitting, > open air. Humming as of boiling water. Rush of blood, with feeling as if the blood stagnated there. Loose feeling in brain, it seems to fall here and there when moving head.

Vertigo in morning after rising; and everything turns around, with a faint nauseous feeling; on rising from stooping; with headache on stooping; with nausea on stooping; so that he must cling to a support, with nausea; so that everything turns around suddenly, on raising arm; so that he does not know where he is when walking along a little path.

Stitches in l. frontal eminence on stooping when washing. Pressive pain outward in forehead. Throbbing in F. deep in brain, on stooping. Heaviness in r. side of F., with pressure. Sensation in F. on stooping as if everything would fall forward. Stitches above r. temple in morning when yawning; burning S. in r. temple. Pulsation in temples. Vertex, *stitches when standing in sun, extending through head;* tearing; pressure in brain on waking, extending towards occiput, with stiffness of neck.

Sides.—Stitches; after dinner and in evening, when they are most severe in l.; in l., extending from occiput to frontal eminence, or alternately here and there. Tearing in spot deep in r. parietal bone; deep-seated, in brain beneath r. ear, renewed by touch, with intermittent twitching. Painful screwing together from both, then tearing in a spot on l. parietal bone, afterwards in l. side of occiput. Throbbing in l., with sticking. Tension on l. parietal bone, with burning in a small spot.

Tearing in l. side of occiput, > bending head backward. Rheumatic pain in occiput, with swelling of glands in neck. Throbbing in occiput in evening, extending to frontal eminence. Hair falls out when combing. An old tumor on scalp hitherto painless becomes larger, and when touched pains as if ulcerating. Pimples on sides. Pain in scalp as if the hair were pulled in a spot on r. parietal bone. Formication in evening. *Itching, with biting,* and on temples; creeping I. here and there, > scratching.

Clinical.—Apoplexy of old people. Wens. Crusta lactea, with moist crusts, falling of the hair, especially with swelling of the glands.

Eyes.—Swelling in morning. Redness of white, with white pimple upon eye near corner; of white, with lachrymation. Tearing. Pain in l., extending over temple into ear. Pressure, with itching as from dust. *Itching;* with burning pressure, soreness and dryness. Burning on exerting vision. Dry heat and pressure. Pain in balls.

Lids.—Swelling in morning. Inflamed redness internally. Agglutination; at external canthi, at night. Matter on externally, < in morning. Closed in twilight. Difficult to open in morning. Stitch through l. upper; twitching, in external canthus. Twitching tearing in r. upper. Pressure in external canthus as from sand. Burning in inner canthi, with lachrymation. Itching on border of upper.

Sharp drawing over l. in evening, extending from nose towards temple. Sensation as if a burning spark passed from upper margin of r. orbit to root of nose. Vision obscured; *gauze before eyes in morning and after a meal;* double; of a black spot; of sparks in the dark; of sparks, with tearing in eyes; halo of rainbow colors around candle-light.

Clinical.—Cataracts.

Ears.—Gland below r. swollen and painful to touch (Merc. i. rub.). Stitches; deep in l. *Tearing* behind r.; in l., extending outward; *in bones in front of r., with boring and drawing.* Boring in r., causing cries. Crawling pain in bones in front of r. *Drawing pain, a kind of twinging.* Drawings at night. *Throbbing* in front of l. when lying upon it; deep-seated, after midnight when lying upon it, r. then l., with pressure; in l. like a pulse, when lying upon it at night. Crawling in l., with twitching. *Itching internally;* in l. Sensation as of hard hearing.

Hardness of hearing. Reverberation on blowing nose violently. Sound like a sounding-board, even when breathing. Stunning noise. Roaring before, with buzzing. Ringing. *Buzzing in evening like a ringing of bells and a violent wind. Cracking* when swallowing; *in one on swallowing, as if it were breaking;* when walking fast, swallowing, sneezing, etc. Crashings at night. Crackling in l. if he lies upon it, extending to r., preventing sleep.

Clinical.—Deafness, the result of impairment of the auditory nerve, especially in old people. Suppurative inflammations of the middle ear, especially in connection with suppurating tonsils.

Nose.—Dryness (Kali bi., Lyc.). Seems swollen and internally agglutinated. *Sneezing* in rapid succession in evening; so violent that it shakes the brain, then vertigo. Stoppage. Frequent inclination to blow, with discharge of thick mucus, then dryness. *Discharge of thick yellow mucus.* Profuse mucous discharge. Fluent catarrh, which rapidly appears and soon disappears; F. catarrh, > night, with hollow deep voice and dry cough. Catarrh, with stopped sensation. Frequent but transient catarrh. *Frequent bleeding;* and profuse; bright red in morning in bed; easily when blowing and cleaning nose. Smell very sensitive.

Clinical.—Coryza, with great swelling of upper lip.

Face.—*Pallor;* with peculiar tensive sensation in skin. Redness in evening; with purple-red color of lips and congestion of blood. *Puffiness;* of l. cheek and region behind ear, with pain in temple. Twitching in l. side. Stitch. Sensation of swelling. Pressure under chin, < touch and motion of jaw. Lip, cracking of lower; vesicle on lower; swelling of upper, with burning pain; upper feels swollen; burning spot on red part of lower; burning smarting of lower; dryness in morning after rising; dry sensation in lips and gums, not > by drinking. Jaw, stitch in middle of lower; tearing in r. lower; *pain in articulation on closing;* pain in glands on under J.; gnawing in l. side of lower.

Mouth.—Teeth. *Frequent and profuse bleeding.* (One becomes hollow rapidly.) Looseness, with pain while eating and afterwards. Tearing in back. Tensive and sticking pain in all r. Boring as if they would be rent asunder if he takes anything cold or warm into mouth. Gnawing in roots and gum of molars. Aching in evening in bed; burning, in l., now upper, now lower, with salivation, and if he lies on l. side the side of the head feels pressed in and there is throbbing in l. ear; sore pain, < touch. Throbbing pain in a lower back tooth in morning after rising, with sensitiveness; drawing, jerking, throbbing toothache, as if something were seated under teeth, extending into ear and r. temple. Grumbling in a molar. Crawling in tips of teeth in evening. Crawling-burning in l. lower T. Gum bleeds and retracts.

Tongue.—Coated. Vesicle under; burning V. at tip; pointed, in middle. A tear on l. border, which smarts and pains as if sore. Hard spot in middle, with burning when touched. *Smarting burning pain in tip.* Pain in side as from vesicles. Rawness in morning on waking, with feeling when it touches the palate as if it were a grating-iron. Dryness in morning, with swollen sensation in throat when swallowing.

Mouth filled with inflamed vesicles, especially palate and inside of cheeks. Much thick mucus in mouth. Stitches in palate. Stickiness. Dryness in morning after rising. Numbness in morning. Continual spitting of saliva; saliva runs out during morning sleep. Intolerable odor, which he does not perceive himself. *Taste foul every morning,* with coated tongue; taste and smell foul and bitter. Bitter taste, with slimy mouth and coated tongue. Sweet T. behind root of tongue. *Sour* taste in morning after rising; in evening; before eating. Salt T. in mouth and throat in afternoon. Loss of T.

Clinical.—Paralysis of tongue in old people.

Throat.—Submaxillary glands swollen (Calc., Merc. i. r.). *Takes cold easily and has inflammation of T. in consequence. Inflammation (after a bruised feeling in all limbs, chilliness and heat), with swelling of palate and tonsils, which suppurate* (Merc. cor.), *on account of which he cannot open jaws, speak nor swallow, with dark-brown urine and loss of sleep.* Swelling of l. tonsil. *Stitches; in evening, < swallowing, with dryness;* on swallowing; on swallowing after taking cold. **Smarting pain when swallowing, < empty swallowing,** *with pain externally on sides of throat when touched. Rawness after night-sweat,* **worse during empty swallowing than when swallowing (soft) food,** *with smarting;* < after swallowing, with scraping; then paroxysms of cough (Argent.). Pain when swallowing.

Constriction, < afternoon, with sensation on swallowing as if a plug were in region of larynx. Choking in attacks after dinner when sitting and writing, with sensation as if the thyroid gland were pressed inward, thereby impeding respiration; C. during dinner, with arrest of breathing, so that he must open his clothes. Scratching, then feeling as if a plug or morsel lodged there. *Sensation as if a fine leaf lay before posterior nares in morning after waking.* Sensation in upper part when sneezing, as if a piece of flesh were loosened, with burning. Feeling of mucus, with desire to drink to relieve the sensation. Swollen feeling internally in morning when swallowing, with dryness of tongue. Dryness in l. back part when swallowing, with sticking and pressure as from swelling. Tickling, causing constant hawking.

Clinical.—Submaxillary glands swollen, indurated, especially those glands posterior to parotids. Quinsy (it seems to remove the predisposition to quinsy). For suppurating tonsils from every cold; indicated when the tonsils are inflamed with swollen veins, in persons who have habitual sweat of the feet.

Stomach.—*Hunger but no appetite;* H. even in morning on rising. Insatiable appetite. (Desire for dainties.) Appetite lost; slight. Aversion to fruit, especially to plums. *Thirst,* with dryness of mouth; T. almost every day at 6 P.M.

Eructations; from afternoon till far into night, preventing sleep; forcible, with pressure in stomach, as if a stone rose and fell; suppressed, after dinner, then spasmodic constrictive pain in stomach; empty, in morning, waking him; empty, in morning, with sensation as if a lump the size of a hazel-nut rose with them; empty, in afternoon; empty, after a (natural) stool; rancid; sour, after eating; bitter; sweetish, after dinner, or of bitter water. Water rises from stomach and fills mouth constantly. *Hiccough;* violent in forenoon and after eating. *Nausea* in morning fasting, with palpitation and anxiety; in morning as from foul stomach. *Vomiting,* with diarrhœa; frequent V. of mucus; of fluid, water and chalk, forming a sediment.

Stitches extending into spine. Drawing-tearing in pit on becoming erect after stooping, with sensation of a heavy body there. *Pressure* after bread, not after cooked food, with nausea and salivation; in r. side from morning till afternoon, extending into chest, with retching, as if a hard body pressed upward with difficulty; *as from a stone, > eructations.* Ulcerative pain on pressure. Constrictive pain in afternoon. Tension in pit, with heaviness, as from flatulence and palpitation. Feeling of repletion. Fulness after eating, as if he had eaten too much (Lyc). Throbbing in pit, extending into l. chest, with stitches. Burning in region in afternoon. Cold and empty feeling. *Weak feeling, > after eating* (Sep.).

Abdomen.—Hardness and tension (Calc. c.). *Distention* (Carb. v., Lyc., Mag. c.); *painful.* Offensive flatus. Many troubles from flatulence, whereby hæmorrhoids protrude, with pain when sitting. Cutting in evening, especially around navel; at night; wakes about midnight; during menses, with griping. Pinching, with nausea. Pain at night preventing sleep, renewed on slightest motion; after a customary walk, then exhausting night-sweat; > partly by eructations and partly by warm poultices; in evening so violent that the umbilicus is retracted and he is obliged to crouch. Tension, with sensitiveness to touch. Feeling as if something were swollen.

Aching in forepart as if in muscles, < evening and when walking and on motion, > sitting and lying. Stitching in l. hypochondrium; short, below r. H., without effecting respiration. Drawing-cutting in l. upper abdomen, extending upward. Aching in region of liver, < motion and touch. Feeling of contraction in a spot in l. upper abdomen. Stitches in r. side and in small of back; in r. side when hiccoughing, turning body, yawning and breathing deeply, not when walking. Pressure in r. side morning in bed, > rising. Pinching around umbilicus on slightest motion when lying down at night and when sitting by day, > passage of flatus and ceased when walking; P. around umbilicus, more when sitting than when moving. Sudden stitches below umbilicus.

Hypogastrium.—(Inflammation of a hernial ring.) Pinching on urinating. Cutting at night when lying outstretched, with pressure towards rectum, rending pain in intestines, fulness above pubes as if everything were stopped and the abdomen would burst, the pains > by a stool, which at first was hard and knotty, then liquid, with pressure, after the stool burning in anus. Deep-seated drawing pain, down along r. groin, as from a string. Pressure above pubes in morning when lying on back; outward in abdominal ring on motion and during stool. Heaviness over pubes during menses.

Clinical.—Habitual colic of children who do not thrive, who seem hungry but refuse food. Enlarged mesenteric glands, the abdomen is hard and swollen, the swallowing of food is painful, in scrofulous children (Calc. c.).

Rectum and Anus.—Stitches in rectum all day, and hard stool. Frequent desire for stool. Urging to stool, she cannot retain the stool because it is forced out rapidly. Hæmorrhoids, with smarting and sticking; moist, after stool. (*Passage of round worms;* in stool.) Frequent passage of blood, with distention of abdomen. Painful soreness around anus, as from excoriation (Nat. m.); sore pain around A. towards evening, with burning. Burning in anus; with the (natural) stool. Crawling in anus. Biting in anus (Alum.).

Stool.—Diarrhœa; mixed with blood (in a child). Soft, with urging (previously there had been a hard one), then burning and pressing-asunder in rectum. Hard, with burning in anus (Sulph.); H. and difficult, with pain in rectum and *bloody mucus.* Tough. Light-colored.

Clinical.—Constipation, with hard knotty stools (Mag. m.); hæmorrhoids, burning and soreness.

Urinary Organs.—Renewed desire after urinating, then when walking a few drops of urine pass. Urging to urinate after dinner. Urging, she cannot retain the urine, it passes so quickly. Frequent micturition every other day; twice every night, with much urine each time. Micturition rare and scanty, with burning in urethra. Burning in urethra on urinating (Sulph.). Yellow sediment (Lyc., Sepia).

Sexual Organs.—Numbness. Sudden erection in evening, with shivering and great desire; slow E. Itching on r. side of scrotum. Burning in l. testicle. Desire disappears. Falls asleep during coition, without emission. Emissions in an old man, then feeling of dryness in whole body; E. in close succession, then exhaustion; profuse shortly after coition.

Painful drawings in pudenda in evening, like tearings by jerks. Discharge of bloody mucus from vagina, with anxious palpitation, restlessness of body, pain in small of back and faintness. Menses too early; and too profuse. Menses scanty; and short.

Clinical.—Diminished sexual desire and premature impotency. Enlarged prostate.

Respiratory Organs.—*Sensation in larynx as if he inspired only smoke.* Stitches in trachea. Hoarseness; or rather loss of voice. Cough after midnight; from continued speaking (Caust.); from incessant irritation, with mucous expectoration. Suffocative cough (Ip.). Dry cough in morning after rising, then sensation as if a hard body fell in chest; D. cough from a tickling in trachea and in præcordial region, > at night and sometimes after dinner; short, in evening; violent, in evening, then weakness in head.

Clinical.—Chronic aphonia in scrofulous patients. Capillary bronchitis, suffocative catarrh of old people.

Chest.—Stitches in l.; on every respiration; in l. on lifting a heavy weight with both hands; in r. in evening, causing her to cry out; deep under sternum, then bruised pain; extending to shoulder; sudden, deep in l. in evening, with burning. Tearing externally in breasts, with sticking (Con., Sep.). Pain; > partly by eructations and partly by dry, warm applications; beneath r. ribs, with coldness of hands and feet and heat and redness of cheeks. Soreness when coughing; sore pain in and on externally. Fulness, with bruised pain in l. side; F. < ascending, with short breath and with stitches, < inspiration. Sensation of palpitation in forepart. Burning in l. side (Senega, Ran. b.).

Heart and Pulse.—Palpitation; when lying on l. side (Puls.); renewed when thinking of it, for then it makes her anxious, < noon. Pulse full, hard, 80.

Clinical.—Palpitation and distress in region of heart, etc. See Bar. mur.

Neck.—**Swollen glands in nape and occiput** (Sil., Sulph.). Swelling in nape, extending over head, with redness and ulcerative pain in skin and *great swelling of all glands of this region.* Boring bone-pain. Stiffness on waking from midday sleep.

Back.—Pain in r. side on lying down; backache as if he had lain too hard; tensive pain under r. ribs when rising from a seat and when stooping far forward (to lift something), extending forward. Pulsation, < rest and after excitement. Stitches through l. scapula to front of chest; burning S. on outer border of scapula. Bruised pain between scapulæ. Dislocating pain in l. scapula. Weakness of spine, with clumsiness, it falls together when sitting a long time.

Loins.—Stitches; worse when sitting than on motion. Pain; *tensive,* < evening, so that he could not rise from a seat nor bend backward. Bruised pain during menses. Sore pain, extending around abdomen externally. Painful drawing, as if a heavy body dragged downward. Heaviness as from taking cold. Burning, extending through abdomen.

Extremities.—Weakness in afternoon, sweat towards evening, vomiting at night, all reappearing (according to a three-day type). Feet, arms, etc., go to sleep when lying upon them.

Upper Extremities.—*Pain in axillary glands* (Merc. s.). Audible cracking in l. shoulder-joint on every motion of arm. Throbbing alternating with tearing, now on l. shoulder, now between scapulæ; at night. Swelling of r. arm, with pain in axillary glands. Tension here and there in arms. Heaviness of arms, with trembling. Falling asleep of l. arm; of arms when lying on the table. Ulcerative pain in humerus. Pain as from a blow above l. elbow.

Twitching in bend of l. elbow, almost like shuddering, extending to middle of upper and forearm.

Twitching-tearing in bend of r. elbow. Bruised pain in elbow. Tearing extending from middle of l. forearm to wrist. Paralytic pain in forearm in morning, > motion, returning during rest.

Stitches in l. wrist, > motion. Sudden tearing in wrist. Drawing in l. wrist, extending to middle of upper arm. Tension in wrist and other parts of r. arm, or drawing. Distended veins on hands, with redness. Trembling of hands when writing. Pinching in hand. Wrenching pain in back of hands.

Fingers.—Ulcerated nail on l. fourth. Cracking in joints of thumb and little F. on motion. Stitch in first joint of thumb and suddenly in tip. Tearing under thumb-nail; T. in first joint of thumb and in fourth finger, so violent that it seems as if the finger would be torn off. Drawing pain in first joint of thumb. Drawing in index as if paralyzed, with sensation on touching and bending as if pithy, especially at tip. Throbbing in middle joint of middle finger.

Lower Extremities.—Tearing, extending into heels, > when walking, with tension. Pain at night, as after a long walk or much dancing. Tension, > walking, with tearing; extending up to hips, as if all tendons were too short, < when standing, > when lying. Stitches in nates. Drawing pain in r. nates as if flesh were drawn downward.

Thigh.—Twitching above r. knee. Sticking in r., so that he could scarcely walk; sudden, on inner surface; sudden, in hip-joint, as if it would be wrenched out, with pain on walking as if it would break to pieces. Tearing in r. in morning after rising, > warmth of bed. Pinching in r. hip-joint, as if stiff or screwed up, extending down front of thigh. Pain in r. hip-joint on walking in open air. Pressing inward in bend of r. thigh. Bruised pain in middle of r.; extending over whole leg and lasting from afternoon till towards midnight. Blow above r. knee when standing, so that he believed he would fall forward. Drawing down front, as if in bone, > when walking.

Knee.—*Stitches.* Tearing on inside, extending to middle of tibia, > when walking, returning when sitting. Intermittent cutting in r., making leg lame. Cutting burning in r. knee-pan. Pain, and in legs.

Leg.—Cramp; in calves; in calf on stretching leg. Twitching in r. calf. Paralytic pain, > elevating leg, as, for example, on a sofa, especially in r. tibia. Drawing pain, as if in bones, in evening when sitting, obliging him to stand and walk. Tension in tibiæ on descending a mountain; in tendons of calf, as if too short. Crawling in l. calf when sitting, as if going to sleep. Weakness in morning, so that he sinks down.

Sprained pain in ankle; and on back of foot, with stitches on motion. Trembling of feet when standing, so that he must hold on to something. Stitches in heel; deep in ball of r. foot; burning S. in a corn. Tearing in feet, extending to knee, < motion. Pinching in corns. Pain in tough skin of sole like a corn, when walking. Ulcerative pain in ball of foot on stepping, < morning after rising. Drawing pain in feet when walking. Cramplike pain in soles. Uneasiness in feet; when sitting, with constant necessity to move the leg in order to relieve the tension in thigh and the burning in pubic region.

Toes.—Corns. Cramp on stretching foot. Tearing in r. great, towards tip; in l. great, by the nail, with stitches, sensitiveness of the place and fretfulness. Drawing pain.

Skin.—Eruption on ears; on r. eyebrow, with stitches when touched. Desquamation on backs of hands. Chaps on tips of fingers, and desquamation. Dryness of hands, like parchment. Roughness and dryness on back of hands; in a spot on r. cheek. Rash (tetter-like) on upper part of forehead, with a sensation that is more burning than itching. Boils on forehead; on nates; on face, but without sensation. Pimples on arms; hips, nose, upper lip, forehead, etc.; itching, in nape close to scalp; itching, on wrist; itching, in a cluster, with a red base, below l. corner of mouth. A small wound easily becomes unhealthy, for example, the wound would not heal after removal of a splinter from a finger, it ulcerated, throbbed and prevented sleep at night.

Stitches. *Tensive feeling in face;* tension in forehead after a meal. Crawling in l. cheek; on both sides of nose; in hands, then they fall asleep. Itching in hernial ring; on back; evenings in bed, now in face, now in back, now in hands; *in thighs*, even at night; here and there, partially > scratching; *here and there, then pain after scratching;* on l. scapula, then pimples after scratching; on back, with eruption; over whole body, preventing sleep for several hours; burning, here and there; sticking, in nates.

Sleep.—Yawning; every morning. Sleepiness every day after dinner; in evening, with involuntary closure of eyes. The thought which she had had all day that she would sleep very well prevented sleep all night. Sleeplessness; on account of heat. Falls asleep late, then restless sleep, with dreams. Starting in evening on falling asleep, so that the whole body rises. Waking every hour. The child wakes frequently and calls for its parents. Unrefreshing sleep in afternoon, then heaviness, bruised feeling, painful confusion of head and constant yawning. *Dreams nearly every night; anxious, nearly every night*, with restless sleep; A. at night, then heaviness of head in morning; frightful; of fire and the like; so that she wakes in sweat; confused, several nights, so that in the morning on rising it is some time before she collects her mind.

Fever.—Sensitiveness to cold. Chill in forenoon, then sudden heat in evening, with pulsations of blood in head; C. in afternoon, with thirst; towards evening, alternating, with heat; general, at 8 P.M., with shivering beginning in feet and with bristling of hair; alternating with heat all night; on entering house; as if dashed with cold water, < afternoon; sudden, in forenoon, with gooseflesh, external coldness and bristling of hair. Shivering in arms in afternoon, > warmth of stove, < least draught. Coldness of hands, then itching; C. of r. foot when walking in open air, with tension in calf; of feet from afternoon till evening, then general heat after lying down. Cold sensation in r. side of head, and at same a burning; burning cold sensation in forehead in forenoon.

Heat all night, with anxiety; H. when eating or drinking; after dinner, with discomfort and with pressure in r. side above stomach. Orgasm of blood and palpitation, preventing lying on l. side, with sore feeling in heart and anxiety. Alternations of heat. Dry H. all night, with sleeplessness, but if she puts her hand out of bed, chilliness and thirst. Hot and dry skin. Burning, now here, now there, on skin. Burning in upper part of r. scapula; in nates. Heat in head in morning on rising, and sticking as with knives; H. in head, with sweat on it, then thirst in evening; frequently rising in head; H. and redness of one cheek, with coldness of the other; dry, of face in afternoon; on back of nose, as from a drop of hot fat. Burning externally in whole breast, with redness; B. spots on l. side of lumbar vertebræ and lower part of l. scapula, < rising from a seat, > walking, occurring also at night, so that he can lie only on one side; in bend of thigh when sitting, as if in bone; in soles all night, yet he cannot bear anything cool on them.

Sweat after midnight; exhausting, at night; on inner surface of hands and fingers in afternoon; profuse, on l. side, especially on head.

Clinical.—Tendency to sweat of the feet.

Baryta Muriatica.

For use dissolve one part of Barium chloride in nine parts of distilled water.

General Action and Affinities.—See Baryta carb.

Trembling. Convulsions. Weakness; with laxity of muscles. Heaviness so that he cannot keep up. Immobility. Paralysis. Anxiety; with retching. Headache. Head affected. Heaviness of head, so that he can scarcely sit up. Vertigo. Eyes sunken. Eyes stiff so that he cannot move them. Paralysis of l. lid. Catarrh of eyes, ears and nose. Deafness. Face red. Face pale, with anxious expression. Sensitive drawing in facial muscles.

Clinical.—Whizzing and buzzing in ears. Noises in ears on chewing and swallowing.

Teeth loose. Toothache, first sticking, then (twitching) throbbing, < after sleeping and after midnight, which compels him to sit up in bed. Tongue coated. Mouth and tongue dry. *Swelling of salivary glands;* of palate. Salivation. Offensive breath, as from mercury. Taste bad, even to food. Swallowing difficult.

Clinical.—Chronic hypertrophy of the tonsils. Valuable in loss of power, paresis of the pharynx and Eustachian tube, with clacking sounds on swallowing or sneezing; air is forced into the tympanum too easily.

Appetite lost. Nausea. Retching. Vomiting in morning; V., with pain in abdomen; of everything taken, with stringy mucus; of small portions of nauseous-looking and tasting substance; violent; violent, with anxiety. Stomach troubles; cramp; pain; warmth going to chest and head. Pain in abdomen; burning. Burning in abdomen. Pinching in pelvic cavity. Diarrhœa; painful; profuse, without pain in abdomen. Stool liquid; S. greenish and chopped; coated with mucus. Micturition painful; constant M.; involuntary. Urine increased; U. has a white sediment. Frequent emissions at night. Menstruation induced. Voice weak. Cough. Dyspnœa. Oppression of chest. Internal heat in upper part of chest.

Heart beats irregularly, pulse scarcely perceptible. Pulse rapid, full. Pulse soft and irregular.

Clinical.—Some remarkable cases of aneurism have been reported cured by this drug; one particularly of the descending aorta, in which death seemed inevitable, entirely cured in six months by the 1st dec.; there were persistent palpitation, fulness and painfulness in the chest, swelling of the thorax close to the sternum, etc.

Pain in back. Swelling of hands and feet. Trembling of extremities, with faintness and twitchings. Weariness of muscles of extremities. Hands and feet paralyzed. (Extremities paralyzed, cold.) Twitching of arm, < night. Tension in legs. Cramp in toes. Skin inflamed. Eruptions, small; itchlike, on body and throat; itching, on neck; scurflike on abdomen and thighs. Scurf, profusely suppurating, on scalp. Red pimple on side of tip of nose, with biting, tickling, sore sensation, with fine stitches on touching and rubbing it. Suppurating glands discharge more. Biting pain in skin. Tearing-burning in denuded spots. Cold surface; C. extremities. Fever, with thirst. Tertian fever. Dry heat day and night. Sweat.

Belladonna.

The entire fresh plant of Atropa Belladonna (Solanaceæ) is used for a tincture.

General Action.—Action on the heart is complex, stimulating the accelerator centres and paralyzing the pneumogastric; heart's action rapid, pulse full, peripheral vessels dilated; wild delirium, ending in stupor; convulsions, with dilated pupils. Suppresses secretion of glands, of mucous membrane and skin. Intense scarlet redness of skin. Urine first increased, then suppressed. Fever.

Affinities.—Hyos., Stram., Verat. vir., Duboisia, Hydrocy. ac., Sulphur.

Generalities.—Falling down, without ability to raise himself. Lying on his belly, with head bent backward and chin resting on hand, not noticing what was said or done in the room. (*Walking round and round in a circle.*) Swelling of whole body, with redness and heat. Distention of veins over whole body; of bloodvessels of limbs, especially arteries of neck pulsate, so that when lower jaw is opened it strikes against the upper at every beat, causing chattering of teeth, with internal and external warmth, < head.

Convulsions; when forced to swallow liquids; *especially of flexor muscles;* C., with gnashing of teeth; with ludicrous gestures, whistling, singing and crying all together; **epileptic**; *epileptic, then apoplectic condition;* after a vexation, which compel him to run to the wall; of muscles of limbs, trunk and face. Subsultus tendinum; with carphology. Incessant movements, especially of arms. Movements as in chorea. Jerks, with loud raving. Constant motion of muscles, partly alternate contractions of single muscles, partly automatic motions, startings of limbs, biting motion, carphology. Jumping, as if alarmed, when touched. Intermittent cramps. Want of muscular co-ordination. Trembling; with convulsive shivering. Unsteadiness in all her motions. Haste in all motions.

Irritability and acuteness of sense, of taste, smell, touch, sight, hearing, and the mind is easily moved and thoughts are more active (Nux vom.). *His senses deceive him.* Stitch in affected part on every second or third step, extending to head. Tearing in a part of the muscles, especially in volar side of ulna, just above wrist. Gnawing in affected parts. Boring in glands. *Cramplike pain, < in sleep, in one side of chest, one side of abdomen and one loin, so that she bends the painful part inward.* Pain in evening, preventing her from stretching. Pain disappeared suddenly when it had reached its height and instantly a pain arose in some other place. Pain in all joints, extending as far as tips of fingers and toes, with a cold sensation.

(Tenderness to touch where the shootings had been.) Bad feeling in whole system on turning in bed. Trembling sensation in all muscles. *Pulsation of all arteries in morning on waking;* P., like a pendulum, alternating between head and chest; perceptible through whole body. *Restlessness; at night, with grinding of the teeth and now and then convulsions;* **every moment he wished to get out of bed** (Hyos.), *but then would fall back in prostration;* **the boy wished to escape** *and was strong far beyond his age; especially of hands and feet* (Acon.); body thrown now to one side, now to other, now chest is raised, now abdomen; occasionally raising his feet, as if ascending stairs, moving his mouth as if talking, but the sounds were inarticulate.

Weakness; in morning, with vertigo; in evening; < evening, with short breath; with tottering gait and feeling as if knees would give way; in frequent attacks, feeling too heavy and as if drawn down; of l. side, numbness of l. side of face and of l. arm and prickling in same parts. Desire to lie down. Faintness. Stiffness of whole body; with head drawn backward and body agitated by single jerks. Anæsthesia of whole body. Insensibility, with rattling respiration and twitchings of hands and feet. Paralyzed feeling on getting up and attempting to stand. Aggravation in afternoon, especially about 3 or 4 P.M.; (A. in l. half of body); (in flexor surface and fibrous membranes).

Clinical.—Violent convulsions, with great rush of blood to head, face red and hot. Epilepsy. Chorea. A valuable remedy for taking cold from a slight draft of air, especially after having the hair cut. Particularly useful for plethoric persons. Hysterical spasms, with red face and wild actions. Effects of sunstroke. Scarlatina. Measles. Acute inflammation of glands.

Mind.—**Delirium**; > after a meal; > after sleep, with quick movements; **with heat; with springing out of bed, laughing** (Hyosc., Stram.) **and constant talking; violent D., with livid face, injected and protruding eyes, dilated pupils, strong pulsation in carotids, full, hard, frequent pulse and inability to swallow. Fury** (Hyosc.); **pulling at the hair of bystanders. Inclination to bite bystanders** (Hcy. ac.). **Inclination to tear everything to pieces. Attempted to bite and strike, broke into fits of laughter and gnashed her teeth, head hot, face red, look wild and fierce. Fury, with heat of body, staring eyes and continually spitting at those about her.**

Delirium, with picking at bed-clothes and throwing them off (*Hyosc.*)*; threw herself from a height in D.; with violent motion of arms and legs. Running into the street naked* (Hyosc.), *gesticulating, dancing, laughing, uttering and doing many absurd things. Paroxysmal D.* D. alternating with lethargy. Fury, at the forcible administration of liquids. **Abhorrence of liquids**; *liquid poured out makes her furious,* resembling delirium tremens; almost hysterical. Grasping for imaginary objects. The patients thought they were pursuing their ordinary occupations. *Persisting that there were horrid monsters all over the room staring at her.* Carphology. Suspicious D.; refusing food, also drink. Speech loud, disconnected. Delirium, at one time expressive of great joy, at another of great terror. Talking about mice and other *dark-colored* animals that he saw (Stram.). Imagined that he was swimming in his bed evenings on lying down. He dreads decaying with a living body. Beautiful images. Imagined that he was rich. Muttering like one asleep.

Garrulity (Hyosc.); *using absurd language, at which he often laughed, turning to the speaker when addressed but not answering correspondingly;* with squinting and stupid expression. Laughter; involuntary; violent spasmodic. Singing (Stram.); inclination in evening to sing and whistle; alternations of singing and scolding, with constant motion of limbs. Mirth; after supper, with increase of vital powers, then drowsiness.

Taciturnity; with desire for solitude and quiet. Weeping; on waking, with ill humor. Despondency. **Anxiety; with desire to flee.** Fear that death was near. Anguish; tearful while walking in open air, with weariness of life and inclination to drown herself. Timid mistrust. Starting in affright, < at approach of any one. Anger. *Quarrelsome mood* (Verat. v.); with disposition to laugh in annoying manner. Howling; about trifles, < soothing words. Losing her temper soon, then weeping. Ill humor; silent; whining, with headache as if a stone were pressing forehead. Apathy. Aversion to work and to movement.

Disorderly, so that speech did not correspond to thought, nor thought to sense, nor sense to objects present. Confusion, with flickering before eyes; C., so that he did not know whether he was dreaming or awake; with general trembling. Manner of expression incomplete, speech difficult. Speech slow and confused; S. loud and disconnected. Answers hasty; and laconic and dry. Passing quickly from one idea to another.

Absence of mind. Thoughts disappear during headache. Memory diminished; lost. Forgot how to do the simplest thing. Stupor; with cramp of extremities; interrupted by shrill screams; compelling sleep in forenoon, after waking hunger, with heat and dryness of mouth without thirst, then hacking cough, with offensive breath as of human fæces. *Coma; with rattling in throat, red face, dilated pupils, convulsions of upper limbs, heat of skin, red spots on neck and chest and feverish pulse;* C., with small, weak, unequal pulse. Unconsciousness; with stiffness of lower limbs, distention of superficial bloodvessels, red, swollen face, full, rapid pulse and sweat.

Clinical.—The general character of the delirium is one of great activity, tendency to run about, to escape from the room *or bed;* in general with great excitement, hot head and face, sometimes with fury, sometimes excessive fear.

Head. — *Drawn backward* (Hcy. ac.), *boring deep into pillow. Thrown hither and thither, even to shaking,* then again convulsive bending forward of head and trunk. *Swelling.* Distention of brain. *Stabbing in evening, as with a double-edged knife.* Shootings; through brain from all sides. Tearing; here and there; *as if sutures of skull would be torn open;* cutting T. extending from one part to another. Boring during the day, with pain, in the evening shooting. **Aching**; on waking, with lassitude; *stooping and motion* (Bry.); > after leeches, *with feeling as if enormously large,* **with intolerance of light and noise** (Ferr.); *and in eyeballs, which felt as if starting from their sockets;* with swelling of lids, heat in face and lachrymation.

Jerking pain, < walking quickly or ascending stairs rapidly, with at every step a jolt downward as if a weight were in occiput. *Drawing and expansive pain as if something in it rocked in a jerking manner.* Drawing pain. Pain as if screwed together on both sides. Throbbing pain, with heat; T. pain, with pressure at vertex. Pain as if brain were numb. *Throbbing;* **in**

brain, from before backward and towards sides, ending at surface in shooting. Pressure now here, now there, in large areas; especially above nose, < stepping; *deep in brain during and after walking in open air;* outward, as if bursting, also in open air, < **coughing.** Heaviness; morning on rising.

Spasm of brain, generally when standing or walking, *seldom when standing or sitting with back against something*, a sudden drawing and giving way, as if nerves were in motion, when all upon which he looked appeared to move in one direction and then back to their former position, with feeling as if he would fall, without giddiness, with sensation in pit of stomach corresponding to the feeling in the brain. **Confusion,** < *movement;* in evening, with garrulity; < walking; with warmth rising from stomach; with swelling of glands and neck; *as if intoxicated.* Dulness > open air, < in room, with turning in head. Uneasy sensation. Weariness, with inability to raise it after stooping.

Rush of blood, with pulsation in cerebral arteries and throbbing in head (Glon., Ferr.); *and sensation as from a ligature around neck;* R. of blood when leaning head backward; on stooping, with heaviness as if giddy. Apoplectic condition (after epileptic convulsions); A. condition alternating with paroxysms of rapid automatic movement, with convulsive laughter, and during the brief intervals of sleep subsultus of face and limbs; a kind of apoplexy, causing her to fall down insensible. Intoxication; after eating; after least quantity of beer; with disturbed vision and difficult speech, he imagines that he cannot move his tongue.

Vertigo; in morning, with weakness; while sitting; < *movement;* < walking, with turning in pit of stomach; > after sleep, with headache and drowsiness; *with rush of blood to head, roaring in ears and misty vision; with pulsation in head, dilated pupils and nausea;* V., with vision of snow-flakes, etc.; *as if objects swayed to and fro; as if everything turned in a circle.* Affection of head and eyes, > coffee.

Forehead.—*Three stabs extending to occiput,* **whereupon sudden disappearance of all previous headache.** Sticking; in r. eminence, < bending forward, > pressure; outward in eminences; tearing, over r. orbit. Tearing; externally; in sinciput; T. over eyebrows; burning, in l. eminence. *Boring under r. eminence in morning after waking.* Gnawing externally in eminences. Crampy pain in eminence, extending over zygoma to lower jaw. **Aching; so severe during motion that it caused him to close the eyes,** > *sitting and lying, returning on rising, but on going into open air the forehead seemed pressed in by a heavy stone,* > while sitting in a room; on l. side; behind and above eyebrows; under eminences on rising; *in orbital region, with redness of eyes and face;* below r. eminence, soon occupying the whole forehead, decreasing at intervals only to return in greater violence. **Pain as if brain rose and fell with every step, > strong pressure.** Shooting burning pain in l. eminence. *Pain as if a stone were pressing it, > laying head down and stooping, with dilated pupils and whining ill humor; P. on stooping as if everything would come out; as if brain were pressed towards forehead, > bending head backward; as if brain would be pressed out above orbits, preventing opening of eyes and obliging him to lie down;* outward in l. eminence. *Pain as from a board before it. Pain above orbits as if brain were compressed, so that he must close his eyes.* Weight at top, causing vertigo and sense as if intoxicated. Pain above eyes like a weight in head, felt on touching eye. *Tensive pressure in r.* Pain in morning as if something over brows sank down and hindered opening of eyes. *Drawing pain in bone and in nape.* Drawing; in head towards forehead, as if brain would dilate. Contracted sensation in muscles of F. and eyes. Dulness. Confusion, with periodical attacks of vertigo. Cloudiness as if an oppressive cloud moved to and fro, especially under bone. Cold sensation in middle of brain. Pulsation in bloodvessels and pain as if bones were lifted up. Rush of blood on stooping.

Temple.—**Stabbing from one to other.** *Shooting in r.;* S. outward; outward in l. Darting pain in r., affecting eye. Tearing; in r. and in vertex, extending in various directions. Cutting outward, spreading through brain and there passing into strong throbbing. Pain through T.; in l. at 3 P.M.; in r., *which on supporting head with hand increases to a sense of bursting and extends into r. frontal eminence.* Pressure inward in l., spreading over anterior half of brain, on that side where the head is supported by the hand. Weight from centre of brain towards T., with diminished hearing. Drawing pain extending to over r. orbit. *Drawing down in temples and in r. orbit.* Beatings.

Vertex.—*Tearing in r.,* < movement. *Twisting pain, sometimes also digging, sometimes tearing, the pain < pressure, and the skull seemed thin, as if it could be pressed through.* Pain; crampy, in r. Pressing in r., then l., then r. again. **Tensive pressure in l. and in forehead.**

Side.—*Stabbing in r. as with a two-edged knife, then in front of head, then in vertex, then in occiput, so that she cannot lie on either side. Cutting in r. from frontal to occipital region, becoming general, at last setting in l. parietal bone.* Darting pain under l. parietal bone. Boring in r., < motion, with throbbing. Gnawing in r. upper part, down to ear, caused by gnawing in a hollow tooth. **Pain;** in r. after rising and moving briskly; in l. parietal bone, extending to temples; in. l. parietal bone, extending to r. temple; throbbing, in parietal region; drawing, in r. at rest after dinner, and in r. arm. Pressure outward in l. half of brain, < forehead.

Occiput.—Lightning-like stabs behind ear in evening. Shoots in l. Cutting to l. of protuberance. Pain. Throbbing pressure in l. *Weight.*

Scalp.—Hair falls out. Hair which was previously naturally electric is no longer so. **Sensitiveness, even pressure of hair causes pain** (Sulph.). Soreness of roots of hair. Pain as after strong pulling at hair. Sensation as if hair on top were pulled. Frequent unconscious scratching of head and rubbing of nose.

Clinical.—Terrific headaches; the head feels full of blood; violent at base of brain, head drawn backward; violent throbbing in carotids, with red face. The headaches are almost universally aggravated by the slightest noise or light Headache so violent that he seems to get blind and then becomes unconscious. Headaches greatly aggravated by bending forward the head is generally drawn backward. Meningitis. Meningitis from erysipelas. Apoplexy, in the early stage.

Eyes.—Staring. Projecting; and sparkling. *Glassy. Animated, with dilated pupils. Squinting.* Sunken. *Spasms. Inflammation and a wild expression.* Conjunctiva covered with red vessels, with shooting and lachrymation; and cornea dim, lids swollen, afterwards pus in anterior chambers. Puffy appearance about. Swelling, with lachrymation. Trembling mucus before.

Shooting inward. Pain; and once hot prickling in r.; crawling, as if full of sand; drawing from, below upward under l. Smarting. Feeling as if protruding. Feeling as if too large. Pressure, < morning, with lachrymation; P. as if hard spring water were in them. *Sensitiveness.* **Dryness, on motion dry and stiff sensation**; *burning*, more violent alternately in one or other. **Heat**, *as if in hot vapor;* H. afternoons while walking in open air, with sticking and drowsiness; < coffee, and sensation as if swimming in tears; > pressing them upward, with itching. *Insensibility to light.* Tickling. Soon tired on reading. Feeling as if he could see nothing, yet he saw when he strained his eyes.

Lachrymation; salt. *Optic disk deepened in tint and retinal arteries and veins enlarged. Balls in constant motion;* alternately fixed and very movable. Balls turned upward; and outward. Pain in balls; deep in, on closing eyes. Dryness of surface of ball.

Pupils.—**Dilated**; < r.; **and immovable**, and eye devoid of expression; < l., with flickering before l.; l., with a white scale in it; r., with necessity to close that eye on writing in order to see the lines plainly. *Contracted;* with headache. *Insensible to light.*

Lids.—Lead-colored spots. Redness; of margins. Swelling; of lower; of upper, with paralysis and redness of palpebræ of l. eye, with prolapsus of upper lids as in ptosis. Mucous membrane of eyes and lids injected and swollen. *Agglutination in morning. Wide open.* Closed; in morning on waking; half closed. Twitching. Quivering of l. upper; r. upper. Throbbing pain in lower, towards inner canthus, with inflammatory swelling and lachrymation. Heaviness; < r.; with feeling as of a sticky mass between them and ball, compelling rubbing.

Canthi.—Dirty redness of internal, as if washed out. Swelling of l. punctum lachrymal. With suppurative inflammation, at first with burning, then with pressing pain. Itching shoots in internal. Tearing in inner, extending into eyes. Pain in l. internal, even on slight touch.

Conjunctiva.—Full of blue-red vessels. Red streaks in morning, with pain. Red vessels at l. external canthus in morning, with twitching of eye. Yellow color.

Orbit.—Darting pain in and near l. Pain, often feeling as if eyes were being torn out, sometimes as if pressed into head, with pain pressing from forehead into eyes. Pressing pain in upper part. Confused pressure, alternately in r. and in forehead. Pain in l. supraorbital ridge, with weak vision of r. eye on writing, whereby the letters swam, and oppressive sensation as if r. lid hung down paralyzed.

Vision dim; > strong effort of will, < afterwards, sometimes with double vision and undulating motion of objects. Distinct only for distant objects and completely parallel rays, as those of a star in the heavens. Weaker while walking in open air and in bright light. *Photophobia.* Blindness; in morning; in l. eye, the lid of which is drooping, inflamed and painful when touched; for near objects, double V. for distant ones. Amaurosis. *Diplopia;* and objects appear far off; and objects appear to revolve and run backward. Vision of r. eye became clearer, l. more impaired, upper lid more tumefied and prolapsed, conjunctiva more vascular and raised above margin of the transparent cornea, which in a few days became opaque and a little puriform fluid accumulated in anterior chamber. **Vision of sparks. Of halo around candle-light, partly colored, the red predominating, at times the light seemed broken into rays.** *Of occasional flashes of light.* Of flames when leaning hand upon her swollen cheek, and the air seems like a mist. *Chromopsia.* Letters swim while reading. Lines jumped hither and thither when reading by lamp-light. Saw nothing when reading but the white margin which surrounded the black letters transformed into rings. All objects seemed bordered with yellow. Objects appeared white; during the delirium. All colors appeared reversed. Vision of a large white star in the ceiling and across it from l. to r. silvery clouds seem passing. Of black points and stripes at 10.30 A.M., on going out. Letters seemed larger than usual, and vision sharper in l. eye than in r. On seeing himself in the glass he asserted that he squinted badly, and that both eyeballs were turned towards nose. Faces looked large, broad and out of proportion, a speck as large as a fly and the head of a nail appeared like a spider with its legs in constant motion, and for months afterwards there was a sort of glimmer upon all objects, like the motion of heated air rising from the roof or sides of a building, and the figures on a carpet seemed to blend.

Clinical.—Great congestion of eyes, but not often useful in inflammatory affections of the external parts of the eye. Neuritis of optic nerve, hæmorrhages from the retina from suppressed menses, congestion of the head, sudden heat of head, suppressed eruptions. Pains of acute glaucoma. (Bell. must be given only occasionally in glaucoma, and the use of Atropine is absolutely forbidden; it brings on aggravation of acute glaucoma, though it will not cure the chronic disorder.) Ciliary neuralgia, with great heat and throbbing pain. Spasms of the lids and muscles. Squinting. Exophthalmic goitre.

Ear.—Purulent exudation. Shootings to chin; in external meatus; in middle during eructation tasting of the ingesta; in middle, with hard hearing on that side. *Thrusts in middle, with pinching;* T. through mastoid process below ear. **Tearing downward in middle and external**; T. behind r.; in lower half of r. cartilage; on posterior side of l. cartilage; in r. external and in r. side of face downward; from before backward externally in r.; feeling in r. as if it would be torn out of head; pain in ears and temples as if alternately torn out and pressed in, alternating with a similar pain in orbits. Cutting behind ears. Pinching after hiccough, r. then l. Boring close to r. Pain; l.; drawing, extending into nape. Pressure on mastoid process below ear; on muscles behind l. and on muscles of forehead; on external meatus; in meatus as if one bored in with a finger. Tingling.

Sensitiveness to loud tones (Sil.). *Noises. Ringing. Roaring;* with flickering before eyes, < l., and twitching of l. upper lid. Singing. Din as of trumpets and drums and a roaring, then a humming and buzzing, < sitting, > standing and lying, still better when walking. What was said to him sounded like a humming. Fluttering and bubbling before ears in morning after waking. Hard hearing. Deafness as if a skin were drawn over ears. Hearing lost.

Clinical.—Acute inflammation of the ears, terrific pain, rolling of the head, screaming, loss of hearing. Acute inflammation of the parotid gland, erysipelatous swelling.

Nose.—*Sudden redness of tip, with burning;* R. of Schneiderian membrane. Ulcers in nostrils; painful, on side of nostrils where they unite with lip. Stitches in tip in evening and night; S. below nose. Cramp at root. Pain in l. nostril in morning and stoppage by matter; pressing P. in bones; bruised internally above wings on external touch. Painful drawing over l. half. Crawling on tip, > rubbing. They frequently bored into their noses. *Dryness;* with redness; *of Schneiderian membrane, also of eyes, with burning in them and in lids;* of nostrils, with frontal headache. Sneezing; *frequent dry, with tickling, especially in l. nostril; prolonged fits.*

Catarrh or cough, with coryza. *Blowing out of mucus mixed with blood.* Watery mucus. Mucus dries to crusts. Fluent coryza from one nostril only. Coryza, with smell in nose as of herring-pickle, < when blowing nose. Moisture in l. nostril, then sneezing and collection of mucus in nose, throat and air passages. Stuffing alternating with flow of water (Nux v.). Stoppage of r. nostril, then sneezing, then coryza. Bleeding; in morning; at night. **Smell sensitive,** *the smell of tobacco* and soot is *intolerable;* S. of camphor is loathsome; of rotten eggs before nose; bread smells and tastes sour; loss of smell.

Clinical.—Acute inflammation internally and externally. Hæmorrhage from nose. Nose swollen, red and hot.

Face.—**Swelling;** of cheek, with burning pain; **and redness; and R. especially about eyes. Redness and heat** (Bry., Stram., Verat. v.); **without sweat; and heat, with swelling of face, neck and chest; glowing, with headache;** *and neck, then desquamation; with general warmth and restlessness,* then pallor and lassitude; with heat of face and coldness of limbs; R. of cheeks. Bluish redness. Dirty redness. Purple redness of cheeks. Red irregular spots, < l. cheek, with heat. Bluish-red spot on l. cheek in morning on waking, increasing until it occupies the whole cheek, with burning and sticking in the spot and boring and throbbing in whole cheek, < movement, afterwards swelling of other cheek. Pale; and cold. Sunken and covered with cold, clammy sweat. Expression anxious and vacant; vacant; alternately anxious and joyful; joyful and astonished; stupid; E. of stupid astonishment.

Spasms; with ridiculous motions of all parts; with grinding of teeth and at times stretching and extension of limbs; convulsive motion of muscles of l. side, especially of l. canthus; remarkable mobility of muscles. Distortion. Disfigured and on expiration the boy puffed as if hot. Risus sardonicus. Shootings in chin. *Tearing below r. zygoma, with drawing.* Pinching on l. zygoma. Sharp pains in cheek. *Pressing below r. zygoma.* Swollen feeling. Nestling, spasmodic sensation in chin. Numbness.

Lips.—**Swelling of upper, with stiff feeling on opening mouth. Redness and swelling** (Bry., Apis); **dark R., and of tongue and gum, with dryness of throat and difficult swallowing.** Crack in middle, < upper, on sneezing and coughing. Desquamation. Pimple beneath externally and to the side, with biting corroding pain; P. on upper, with creeping while untouched, but itching shooting when touched; pale-red P. in corners; on margin, changing to an ulcer covered with a scab and paining as if inflamed; on upper, near r. wing of nose, covered with a scab, another beneath margin of lower lip and on inner skin of lower lip, both with biting pain, as from salt water. Pustules on borders, with smarting pain. Ulcer, with red edges and corrosive itching, in corner; U. in corner, also with tearing. Sore feeling at corners, as if they would ulcerate. Burning pain at lower outer edge, with vesicles. Drawing in upper, then red swelling. Heat; *and of mucous membrane of mouth, fauces and nose, with dryness. Dryness,* and of tongue, skin of cheeks and throat, with constriction of pharynx, difficult speech, incomplete phrases.

Jaws.—*Trismus. Tetanic closure on attempting to pour down liquid, and regurgitation of liquid.* Spasms. *Twitching.* Convulsive chewing, with foam from mouth. Shooting in socket; on lower margin of r. lower; *from upper into internal ear; in direction of ears, with tension;* in r. joint on chewing, extending into ear, then twitching. **Tearing on inner surface of corner of l. lower, < during deglutition, and in and behind l. tonsil.** Pain (a jerking drawing?) in lower (in glands?), shooting inward. Lower feels as if drawn backward, with pain on advancing it and on biting. Clucking along under edge of lower.

Clinical.—Erysipelas of the face. Facial neuralgia, with flushed face, etc. Lockjaw.

Mouth.—Teeth. Grinding. Bleeding of hollow on sucking them. Shooting in an upper hollow molar, then swelling of cheek. Tearing (?), waking after midnight; T. in a hollow lower T. and in an adjoining sound molar, < contact with air or food. Feeling as if they would be forced out. (Digging.) **Drawing in r. upper all night,** with swelling, burning pain, external heat, sometimes painful jerkings; D. in r. upper anterior molars. Pain drawing from ear to upper hollow teeth, where the pain becomes a boring, > while eating, < afterwards, < at night, becoming after drinking coffee jerking and boring. Pain rather drawing than shooting. Toothache in a child. Pain running through upper middle incisors. Toothache after eating, increasing gradually and as gradually diminishing; T., with drawing in ear. Painful jerkings in nerves of fangs, or throbbings. Pain when biting anything, as if roots were ulcerated and would break. Pain in roots in evening after lying down and during mental occupation, like the pain of excoriation, and when worse like a cutting; like a soreness, on admission of open air. Incisors feel too long.

Gum.—Vesicle below an incisor, with pain as if burnt. Bleeding near a hollow tooth. Pain on touch, as if ulcerated. Heat, with itching and throbbing. Itching, with pain in throat.

Tongue.—**Deep redness;** *of papillæ, with swelling.* Vessels beneath T. bluish and injected with blood. Pallor. Swollen; and pressed close behind lower incisors. *Cracked;* and white-coated, with salivation. Coated; yellowish; white; white and moist; white, with smarting in middle, as from a vesicle; white tenacious coat, which comes off in shreds. *Trembling* (Lach., *Merc.*). Sticking to throat on attempting to spit. Cramps at base. Pain, < touch. Feeling as if there were a vesicle at tip, which caused burning pain on touch. Swollen feeling. Feeling as if lying deep in mouth and so the buccal cavity was larger. Cold feeling in anterior half, with dryness of it. **Dry; and D. throat, interfering with speech** (Verat. v.); *and retracted; hanging from the child's mouth, and swollen; D. and cracked; and difficult to move;* and yellow-brown; with thick frothy mucus adhering to its sides; as if covered with a crust; D. sensation, < drinking water. Paralyzed feeling.

Speech.—Stammering. Interrupted. Slow and impeded. Rapid, interrupted. Difficult. Indistinct. Speechlessness. Paralytic weakness of organs.

Mouth slimy in morning on waking, with headache; S. in morning, > after eating; with feeling as if a bad taste came from it. Mucus < morning after rising, sometimes of putrid taste. Foam; bloody. Drawn to one side by spasms. *Deep crimson color from posterior third of palate as far down as could be seen, with enlargement of tonsils.* Redness, and of gullet, with heat and dryness.

Scraping, and in throat, extending into stomach, with constriction; S. on palate. Pain beneath hard palate, about the middle, when eating rolls and milk, extending through fauces to nasal cavity. Rawness of palate, < touch of tongue and chewing, with soreness. Soreness on inside of cheek, with erosion of mouth of salivary duct. **Dryness** (Acon., Bry., Verat. v.); *at night, with thirst; of lining of cheeks, lips, tongue, which look burnt, roof of mouth and pharynx;* dry sensation though tongue was moist; though moist, with stickiness and great thirst. Aridity as if mucous membrane had been removed by some pungent or corrosive substance. *Heat* in hard palate. Unctuous clammy state, < drinking water. (*Paralytic weakness of internal parts.*) Salivation; in evening. Saliva flows from mouth. Saliva has a spoiled taste; S. in throat was thick, white, clinging to tongue like glue. Constant spitting without ejecting saliva. *Breath hot;* offensive B. in morning on waking.

Taste.—Disgusting, with clean tongue. Metallic. Coppery. Like copperas. Nauseous, with empty eructations. Sickish-sweetish. Putrid; after eating; rising from fauces even when eating and drinking, though food and drink have their proper taste. Aromatic. Like wine. Salt-sourish. Sour to bread; to the last part of the bread and butter, every evening, then heartburn; to the broth that had been taken, then scratching in throat. Salt to food. Natural to food when beginning to eat, then suddenly taste partly as if too salt, partly insipid, with feeling in pit of throat as if she would vomit what she had taken. (Bitter to bread and apples in evening.) Clammy. Pasty. Insipid. Lost; to food.

Clinical.—Difficult dentition (acute symptoms). Stammering. Paralytic weakness of the organs of speech. Inflammation of mouth and throat, all the parts are red, hot and dry, < r. side.

Throat.—*Shooting in r. parotid, extending into external ear, where it becomes cramplike, repeated at same hour next day.* Strong pulsation in carotid. Swelling; around T. and jaws; of tonsils. Inflammation; *of tonsils;* aphthous. Aphthæ. Redness; with burning along alimentary canal; of uvula and velum palati. Tenacious mucus. *Great expectoration of light mucus as soon as the throat began to feel sore.* Frequent E. of mucus. Hawking of mucus from upper part. Mucus in upper part, with general sensation as before catarrh of throat, with swelling and inflammation of arches of palate, tonsils and posterior wall of pharynx. Spasm; spasmodic action of muscles at every attempt to swallow. Cramp extending from r. tonsil to top of pharynx.

Shootings on swallowing and breathing; in pharynx on swallowing, turning head and feeling side of neck, with pain as from internal swelling; in l. side; in pit. *Scraping; from dry hawking;* in soft palate when swallowing. Pain; in region of tonsils; in posterior part on swallowing; as if swollen during deglutition and expectoration, < l. side. *Soreness;* after reading aloud; when swallowing; *with redness about tonsils and palate, extending to ears* (Gelsem.), also in morning. *Constriction; extending to stomach.* **Feeling as if too narrow when swallowing**; painful narrowing of pharynx, with stretched sensation when preparing to swallow. **Dryness; with difficult swallowing** (Duboisia); *hindering swallowing and altering voice; causing constant attempts to swallow, then at every attempt suffocative spasms of fauces and glottis;* and of lips without real thirst. *Burning;* (with natural moisture in mouth), *not > drinking, transiently > sugar;* intermittent, in upper part, with frequent necessity to swallow. Tickling. Paralysis.

Swallowing.—**Difficult**; *of water; of solid food possible only by constantly taking liquids; and painful; only a few drops, the rest being forced out by spasmodic action of muscles of deglutition* (Lach.). Inability to drink; to swallow solid food; painless I. to swallow. Constant urging to swallow.

Œsophagus.—*Intermittent contraction, when swallowing,* **followed each time by scraping in region of epiglottis as if latter were raw and sore.** Dryness.

Clinical.—Adapted to the early stage of a great variety of inflammatory diseases of the throat, characterized by the above symptoms; and especially by intense hyperæmia, with dryness and tendency to spasmodic contraction of the pharyngeal muscles.

Stomach.—Longing for food and greedy swallowing of it. Hunger but no inclination for any kind of food. Desire for this or that, but no relish if he eats it. Appetite diminished; especially for animal food. Appetite lost; for breakfast; for dinner, yet he ate with relish, and the hunger was < after eating; lost, with feeling of emptiness and hunger, but if he begins to eat relish; lost after smoking tobacco; lost for everything but water, soup and bread and butter. Aversion to food; A. to acids.

Thirst; in morning; in evening, with watery taste, though all liquids are loathsome. Violent every noon; after midnight and in morning. *Unquenchable;* with slow pulse. Burning, with heat in all parts, craving for drink, but repelling it when offered. *For cold water.* Desire for beverages without appetite for drinking. Absence of T. Repugnance to beer; to coffee; to milk, which appears to have a loathsome smell and (bitter, sourish) taste, which disappear after continuing to drink.

Eructations; with flatulence in bowels and stitches in l. breast; *incomplete;* bitter; bitter, after a meal; tasting of ingesta; of burning sour moisture, with a kind of retching; hiccough-like. Something midway between eructations and hiccough. Hiccough; which jerked her up, then deafness until the next attack.

Nausea; in frequent attacks in forenoon; after breakfast; in evening, in throat (not in scrobiculus cordis,) with occasional bitter eructations; when walking in open air; < when he would eat; with efforts to vomit; with inability to vomit; changing to burning, with full sensation in throat. Empty retching. *Vomiting; after eating and drinking;* after drinking, with large swallows; after milk, then slight amelioration; then sleep; of food; of undigested food eaten twelve hours before; difficult to excite.

Distention; and tension; of epigastrium in evening in bed, with tensive pain in stomach. Spasm always during midday meal; S. like cramp. (During cough turning, as if vomiting would come on, even when empty.) Cramp; and in abdomen. Shootings in pit. *Shooting cutting in pit, forcing him to bend backward and hold his breath.* Pinching across epigastrium and downward, as if in colon. Squeezing in pit while walking, obliging deep breathing. Acute pain. Pain; after drinking; *about pit; periodical, in pit at night, with tremor. Hard pressure < after eating;* painful P. in pit when walking, forcing him to move slowly; P. in pit, in part gnawing. Oppression in pit, so that she could not breathe properly, alternating with nausea.

Contractive sensation after a little food; C. pain in pit. *Burning;* in region. Burning pain at orifice. Heartburn when smoking, then scraping, burning, smarting at beginning of gullet, and chiefly at upper part of larynx. *Sensitiveness to touch in region.* Distress; as from indigestion. Sensation as if something were in pit, making him cough. Feeling in pit as of accumulation of flatus. Emptiness. Painless throbbing in pit.

Clinical.—Vomiting, cannot keep any food in the stomach. Soreness and distention in the region of the stomach. Neuralgia of the stomach, of the most violent character, with extreme tenderness. Gastritis, with violent vomiting, even of food. Nausea and vomiting are among the most persistent effects of this drug; these symptoms are more frequently associated with other Bell. symptoms than is generally supposed.

Abdomen.—*Tumefaction;* **with tenderness to touch,** constipation and weak pulse; with rolling or grumbling in l. side. Meteorism; with constipation, in one case subsiding and recurring with the delirium. Retraction; while lying, with pain. Rumbling; with pinching. Emission of flatus; of inodorous.

Pricking at 11.30 A.M. (Shooting after drinking milk); S. outward and in chest. (Cutting in evening.) *Pain in a spot as if seized with nails, a griping, clutching, clawing.* Pinching; in evening before soft stool; deep, < retracting abdomen and on bending upper part of body to the left; obliging him to bend double, with ineffectual urging to diarrhœa, then vomiting. Cramplike pain extending to spine, occasional sharp pain in hypochondriac region. Pain; with urging to stool. **Pain as if sore and raw. Tenderness on pressure,** especially in ovarian region. Constrictive pain, obliging her to bend up. Pain as from a heavy weight when walking and standing. Drawing pain, with cold feet. Drawing as from flatus.

Feeling of distention, with constrictive pain below umbilicus, the latter coming in jerks and obliging bending double. Full feeling in evening, with griping and rumbling; F. feeling < after stool. Something seems to rise and to press on throat, with retching, but without nausea or vomiting. Feeling as before diarrhœa, when straining at stool, with internal heat in abdomen. *Heat* **(with anxiety)**, *and in chest and face,* with obstruction of nose; H. rising into chest.

Upper and Side.—Distention in region of stomach. Pain in upper. Cutting in l. side in morning while lying on that side. Griping in r. side while walking, with shootings thence to r. axilla. Pressing-out pain in side when pressing upon pit of stomach.

Hypochondria.—Bile increased. Fulness below short ribs, and when stooping fulness at pit of stomach and darkness before eyes. Shootings near last r. ribs. Pinching in hepatic region, < rising from a seat. Sharp pain in splenic region. Pain in hypochondria, as if pressed out when pressing on epigastrium. Tension round ribs.

Umbilical Region.—Sticking; itching, in navel, > rubbing. Stabs as with a knife in l. side below navel; between r. hip and navel; shooting, extending round l. hip to lumbar vertebræ. Clawing-together pain coming from sides into navel. Pinching; immediately under wall below navel after eating. Griping; transversely across below navel, then emission of flatus, with rumbling; as if he would be obliged to go to stool, > emission of flatus. Squeezing, < noon and afternoon; S. and clawing, obliging him to bend forward. Pain. Constriction; as if a ball were forming. Tensive sensation below navel after stool.

Hypogastrium.—Distention, > emission of flatus, with griping and with nausea. Shooting in inguinal glands; S. in l. groin. **Cutting, now here, now there;** C. < l. side; outward in crests of ilia on rising from a seat. *Tensive pain in morning on getting out of bed, especially in region of os pubis, with feeling as if hypogastrium (rarely epigastrium) were spasmodically constricted, sometimes as if distended (although not really so), pains gradually increasing and decreasing. Feeling immediately below umbilicus as if intestines pressed outward, < standing. Pressure in morning as if everthing would be forced out towards organs of generation, with distention of abdomen, then contraction of abdomen, then discharge of white mucus from vagina.* Feeling in r. groin as if a hard body pressed outward when sitting bent forward. Drawing pain in whole circumference of pelvis, alternately in sacrum and os pubis; flatulent D. on r. side, over horizontal ramus of pubis. Congested feeling in pelvic region, with *excited sexual desire.*

Clinical.—Peritonitis. Metroperitonitis. In abdominal affections characterized by extreme sensitiveness to touch, intolerance of even the clothing, with great heat. Acute inflammation of liver. Gall-stone colic cured. Jaundice.

Rectum.—Shootings during motion. *Squeezing, constrictive pain in lowermost intestines, alternately with shoots or jerks in direction of perineum.* Contractive pain, then sore pain in upper abdomen, then rapid evacuation of mucous diarrhœa, lastly empty straining. Voluptuous tickling in lower part. Itching in lower part; sudden I., and in anus. Sense of constipation. Inability to press during stool. *Tenesmus, a constant pressing and urging towards anus and genitals, alternating with painful contractions of anus. Straining to stool, then scanty diarrhœa, then increased straining.* Constant desire for stool. *Urging to stool, which is thin; frequent but ineffectual, or with a scanty, hard stool;* ineffectual, then vomiting.

Anus.—Bleeding. Hæmorrhoidal flow. Itching, with constriction; I. externally when walking in open air. Itching in perineum, with moisture.

Clinical.—Bleeding piles, with great forcing and great sensitiveness. In dysentery the mucous membrane of the anus is swollen and everted, with excessive tenderness.

Stool.—Watery, scanty, with tenesmus; W. copious, greenish. Diarrhœa-like; greenish; offensive, greenish; dark, at night; scanty, with stitches above umbilicus; frequent, with tenesmus; then frequent desire, with no stool or a scanty one. Granular, yellow, somewhat mucous. Pappy, mixed with mucus. Constipation. Hard and scanty. Green, fæces enveloped in reddish mucus. (Sour smelling.) Small; and rapid, involuntary. Slight, with colic. *Involuntary.* Frequent. *Retarded.* Slow and dry. Suppressed; also urine, with profuse sweat.

Clinical.—Diarrhœa of green mucus and blood. Dysentery, especially in children.

Urinary Organs.—Discharge of prostatic juice from relaxed penis. Irritation, especially of neck of bladder, with strangury, bloody urine, with heat, redness of whole body, palate and pharynx. *Pressure in vesical region at night.* Pain in region of bladder; with desire to urinate, but evacuation of only a few drops by the catheter. Twisting as of a worm in bladder. Bladder half paralyzed. *Tenesmus.* Urging to urinate, with bloody urine; U., with scanty, dark urine; with ability to pass only a few drops of colorless urine; with difficult micturition in a small stream. *Frequent urging; with scanty urine;* but urine passed after great effort and *guttatim.* No inclination to urinate.

Urine retained, passed by drops. *Involuntary micturition; during deep sleep in daytime;* while in a stupor; in children. Dysuria. Painful micturition. Strangury; with bloody urine. Urine suppressed. Frequent, copious micturition. Bladder full, urine flowing slowly through catheter. A stitch from bulb of urethra to orifice when walking. Shootings behind glans between acts of micturition, < movement. Burning in urethra, with ineffectual urging to urinate.

Urine.—Copious; with strangury at neck of bladder; pale and watery; now C., now scanty. *Scanty;* and passed with exertion; strongly ammoniacal, evacuated by a catheter. Dark. Bloody. *Deep red,* with light sediment. *Yellow, turbid.* Whitish. Scalding. Containing vesical mucus. *Turbid like yeast, with reddish sediment.* Thick, white sediment.

Clinical.—Acute cystitis. Dysuria, especially of children and excitable women. Acute inflammation of the kidney.

Sexual Organs.—Irritation in boys, manifested by constant erections and by seizing the member with the hands. Weakness and relaxation, sweat at night. Tearing upward in l. spermatic cord in evening before sleep. Drawing in spermatic cord during micturition. Soft, painless pimple on glans. Prepuce retracted behind glans, causing disagreeable feeling in glans. Smarting in outer edge of prepuce after micturition. Itching, as from a flea-bite, on forepart of glans. Frequent erections. Scrotum blistered. Shootings in the testicles, which are drawn upward. Sexual indifference. Emission at night during relaxation of penis; at night without lascivious dreams; twice in one night.

Female.—*Shootings in internal organs at every step.* **Urging as if everything would fall out,** < *sitting bent and walking,* > *lying and sitting erect.* Dryness of vagina, with burning, stinging. **Badly smelling hæmorrhage from uterus. Menses too soon;** *M. inordinate, sudden.* **Metrorrhagia, the blood having a bad smell.**

Clinical.—Inflammation of pelvic viscera. Prolapsus of uterus; inflammation of uterus; inflamed ovaries, < r.; all with heavy dragging and forcing pain, as if the uterus were heavy with hot blood; suppression of menses with these symptoms. Ovarian tumor, with forcing pain. Dysmenorrhœa. Uterine hæmorrhage. Threatened miscarriage. Rigid os during labor. Post partum hæmorrhage. Fibroid tumor of uterus. Retained placenta, with *hot* gushes of blood. Metrorrhagia, very offensive. Inflammation of mammary gland, which was extremely sensitive and hot. Violent cerebral symptoms (see mind and head) from suppressed menstruation.

Respiratory Organs.—Noise and rattling in bronchial tubes. Pain under larynx after eating, with hiccough. Pressing in l. side of larynx, < external pressure. *Constriction of larynx.* **Painful dryness of larynx,** *with aversion to all drinks; D. of larynx, making voice husky and often inducing dry cough.*

Hoarseness; especially when crying; *with dryness in larynx, with frequent cough, and frequent necessity for empty swallowing, and when swallowing pain in larynx extending to l. ear* (Lach.); *hoarse and weak voice. Aphonia; or confused sounds uttered with pain.* Weak voice. Piping voice with difficulty in speaking (Stram.). Sharp and clear voice.

Cough beginning about 10 P.M., *recurring every quarter of an hour or oftener, in three or four fits at a time;* C., waking her at night; from rawness and dryness in upper part of larynx; *preceded by crying* (Arn.) (*in a child*)*; with bloody taste in mouth;* with much straining and fretting (in a child); with prickings under l. ribs; in attacks which end in sneezing; croupy, hollow and scraping; *violent C. in sleep with grinding of teeth. Dry cough from scraping in larynx;* D. at every inspiration; from tightness of chest like dry catarrh; *short, in evening in bed, from itching tickling in back of larynx;* violent, in forenoon, as if a foreign body had lodged in larynx, with coryza. Cough, with bloody expectoration in morning; with expectoration of thick white mucus, preceded by angina, followed by rawness and dryness in upper part of larynx; C. as he had inhaled dust, waking him at night, with mucous expectoration. Coughing up a substance resembling old catarrhal mucus, of purulent appearance, from upper part of trachea in morning.

Expectoration of mucus from air passages by coughing and hawking; E. of blackish thick mucus.

Respiration.—*Difficult. Short, after coffee in afternoon.* Anxious, with the brazen stridulous sound of croup. Violent, short, hurried, anxious. Groaning; at every expiration; < morning; alternating with jumping and dancing. Sighing. Moaning. Deep, at times yawning; D., as in croup. Jerking. Irregular. Intermittent; at night, inspiration and expiration together lasting only half as long as the pause before the next inspiration, expiration by starts and louder than inspiration, inspiration only a little longer than expiration. *Rapid; and oppressed;* and irregular; and sighing, shallow. Retarded, at times whistling. Stertorous; with râles in anterior part of chest. Vesicular murmur, without rattling. Appearance at times as if he had drawn his last breath.

Clinical.—Acute laryngitis, with great hoarseness or loss of voice, the larynx feels dry and is painfully sore or feels swollen, with suffocation. Spasmodic croup. Spasm of glottis. Whooping cough, with hot face and head, and nosebleed. Chronic laryngitis, with cough like the barking of a dog, without fever and without soreness. Catarrhal croup in the first stage, the child gasps for air and tosses about wildly (Acon.).

Chest.—Milk runs out of mamma, in a woman not pregnant. Inflammation of the lungs. Stabs as with a knife below last two ribs, close to xiphoid cartilage and above false ribs. Stitches in l.; in mamma; (under l. ribs); here and there below skin of r. side; at 3 P.M., and just below r. axilla; under r. arm towards evening, hindering breathing; in sternum when coughing and yawning; in l. side from sternum towards axilla, < motion; deeply penetrating, in r.; backward below clavicle when walking; in cartilage of l. ribs, < expiration, when it changes into an almost burning sensation.

Intermittent cutting in r. Shooting pinching on both sides of upper part of sternum. Gnawing beneath cartilages of last r. ribs. Squeezing in l. and r. sides. Acute pain in sternum above xiphoid cartilage. Cramping pain below end of sternum, gradually extending to pit of stomach and upward to sternum and over cardiac region. *Pain, and between shoulders;* when sitting and walking, with short breath; at sternal end of fifth rib; below r. nipple; beating, under sternum, above scorbiculus cordis. Pressing in r. causing anxiety; P. outward in region of sixth true rib.

Oppression; in evening in bed, causing difficulty in breathing, as from mucus in windpipe, with burning in chest. *Tightness.* Constriction as if pressed inward from both sides; spasmodic C., and in throat, with sense of suffocation. *Spasmodic tension, extending to deep in abdomen,* < motion. Drawing in l., with stitches. *Burning in r.* Inquietude and beating. Air seems to have collected beneath sternum, disappearing with rumbling in abdomen, whereupon the nausea is worse.

Clinical.—Pleurisy. Rarely, in inflammatory diseases of thoracic organs.

Heart.—Stitches. Pressure; arresting breath and causing anxiety. Anxiety. Violent beating. Clucking on ascending stairs, a sort of palpitation. Palpitation; when exercising, *with labored breathing;* with pulsation in carotids and temporal arteries, heat and redness of face, congestion to head and fever; (during rest, with feeling as if the concussion extended to throat, < movement, with difficult slow, respiration.) Action feeble; but frequent. Action and pulse smaller and contracted. Trembling.

Pulse.—Full, frequent. Increased in force and frequency (Acon., etc.). Frequent and small; F., irregular and uneven; contracted, often intermitting; and feeble. Sometimes frequent, sometimes slow. Strong, hard. Irregular; one strong beat being followed by four or five weak ones. Slow and full, and large; S. and weak; and small; slow, radial artery full, hard, firm to touch, with insensibility, a vein in the arm being opened the blood, which flowed slowly, was dark and thick. Small, intermittent. Feeble. Scarcely perceptible. Imperceptible.

Neck.—*Swelling of glands on l. side,* with burning pain; *S. of glands of nape,* with cloudiness of head; of glands, with pain at night. **Shootings in a gland at side;** S. in region of second and third cervical vertebræ on carrying head erect. *Pain in nape as if it would break, when coughing.* Sharp pain between last cervical and first dorsal vertebræ. Pain externally when bearing head backward and on touch; pressing, in nape close to occiput; drawing, in r. muscles. Drawing in muscles. Cramplike tension in l. muscles. Stiffness; so that he could not lay the head on the side; of nape.

Clinical.—Stiff-neck from taking cold. Torticollis, r. muscles contracted. Acute inflammation of glands (compare Iod., Calc. c., etc.).

Back.—Cramplike tearing now here, now there, now in arms, during menses. Pain as if dislocated in r. side and in spinal column. Pressive pain at l. of spine, under false ribs. Stiffness of muscles of B. and lower limbs, preventing sitting up in bed or raising himself upright, if supported he can stand, but is unable to move his feet or to walk.

Spine.—Stabbings inward in vertebræ. Shooting and gnawing. *Gnawing, with cough.* Cramplike pressive sensation in middle, becoming tensive if he attempts to straighten the back. *Rigidity.*

Scapula.—Shootings in r.; electric, from l. to r. Darting pain at vertebral end of eighth rib. Drawing cutting behind r. Pain under l., more towards outer side. Cramplike pain between r. and spinal column, almost like pinching. Strained pain between S. Drawing pressure between r. and spinal column. Drawing between S. in evening, extending down spine. Painful stiffness between S. and nape in morning when turning neck to and fro.

Lumbar Region.—Cutting in r. and in lower end of sternum. Spasmodic sensation in l. Sharp pain in r., above ischium. Pain; in l. kidney; in kidney region in morning, > pressure. Sacrum and coccyx, cramplike pain, with ability to sit for only a short time, while sitting he becomes stiff and unable to rise again for pain, he cannot lie well, it often wakes him at night and he has to turn on to the other side, with violent pain, he cannot lie on the back, > standing and walking slowly, but he cannot walk fast.

Clinical.—Spinal irritability, pressure upon the dorsal vertebræ causes screams and distress in stomach, or violent cough and flushed face. Hyperæmia of spine, with difficulty in walking, loss of co-ordination when walking. Lumbago, with pain in hips and thighs, cramps in legs, etc.

Extremities.—*Moved slowly upward, then with greater force thrown downward. Twitchings. Convulsive movements. Convulsive extension on waking.* Movements now simulating chorea, now hysteria, then tetanus, changing to opisthotonus. Distortions alternating with immobility. Involuntary performance of the motions peculiar to the daily duties. Constant motion all night. Trembling; with inability to walk, and if lifted they fell powerless.

Stitches in shoulder region and in feet. Tearing in flexor surface of l. forearm and in palm and sole; shooting T. through l. knee, with crawling on l. sole, tearing in volar side of l. hand and in upper third of metacarpal bone of little finger. Gnawing as of ants in bones of arm and thigh, creeping downward. Pain in all. Drawing pain. (Soreness in bends of joints.) Uneasiness. Weakness; in morning, with restlessness of them on account of pain; with indisposition to work; paralytic, of all muscles. Numbness. *Heaviness of hands and feet.* Stiffness. Immobility.

Upper Extremities.—Affection as in chorea. **Sense of stretching and twisting.** Heaviness and paralytic feeling, especially in l. arm. Painful swelling of one of l. axillary glands. Tearing under and in r. axilla. **Shooting pressure on top of l. shoulder.** Stitches in region of shoulder and in region of l. false ribs.

Arm.—Continual contortions, and of hands. Stretching, and of hands, as if she would seize something. Convulsive shaking. Trembling on slightest motion. Contractions and twitchings, the fingers clenched and elbows rigid. *Painful twitching;* < r. When eating he often put his hand instead of the spoon into the soup, and often he was unable to find his mouth with his spoon. Weakness, still more in hands, as if she must let them hang down. Heaviness. Stiffness of r. (upon which she had not lain) at 3 A.M., with feeling as if shorter than the other and with tearing.

Upper Arm.—Stabbing outward below head of humerus. Tearing in humerus. **Paralytic tearing pressure in anterior surface of l. Paralytic pressure in l., with paralytic feeling and weakness of whole l. arm. Paralytic drawing pressure, and in forearm, with weakness.** Bruised pain. Drawing pain in inside of l.; in l. near insertion of deltoid, > pressure.

Drawing downward in muscles of r., which when it reached region of elbow twitched upward again to axilla. Paralytic weakness of r., then also of forearm.

Elbow.—Shootings externally in l. Cutting in interior of l. when walking. (Pain as if burnt when moving or touching it.) Paralytic drawing pain; and in l. fingers. Rumbling in bend of l., as if water or some heavy liquid were running through veins.

Forearm.—Twitching of tendons and muscles on inner side. Shootings in l.; in middle of inner. Cutting tearing in lower muscles of l.; in lower muscles of r. during rest. Aching in muscles. Throbbing pain along r. radial nerve at 11.30 A.M. Burning throbbing near olecranon and posterior ridge of radius often during the day, < touch and pressure, at 6 P.M. a similar pain at base of scapula, near angle, < pressure, with warmth in this spot.

Wrist. — Shooting along ulnar nerve to elbow. Paralytic tearing in carpal bones. Inability to turn hand easily, he can do it only by jerks, as from deficiency of synovial fluid.

Hand.—Swelling; with dryness and dropping of anything he takes hold of. Constant motion, and of fingers. Twitchings. Trembling; with periodical twitchings of rest of body. Shooting in metacarpal bones of thumbs. Tearing pressure in metacarpal bones and in distal joint of l. index; shooting T. in l. metacarpal bones. Soreness; on pressure. Dry sensation in palms, with smooth feeling. Stiffness of r. and of fingers.

Fingers.—Easy dislocation. Shootings out at tips during general chill, < when grasping. **Paralytic tearing in middle joint of r. index.** Tearing-cutting in muscles of r. little. **Painful drawing in proximal joint of l. middle, as if in periosteum.** Pain in tip of middle as if a foreign body had lodged and caused ulceration, < touch. Pain in tips of l. as if they had been jammed. Tingling. Stiffness of anterior joint of middle, with pain on bending, a simple pain (? sore).

Lower Extremities.—Stumbling. Staggering; in morning on rising; with vertigo, headache and drowsiness. Sensation in joints as if they would give way, particularly in knee, < walking and descending stairs. Weakness, with nausea, trembling, anxiety and vertigo. Little control over, with weakness and dragging. Paralysis; *temporary, and of neck of bladder and of sphincter ani.*

Hip.—Shoots in r. Pain in l. when lying on r. Paralytic tension in joints when walking, as if dislocated.

Thigh.—**Cutting shoots in external muscles above knee only when sitting.** Knife-stab in middle, more towards posterior side, after eating. Cutting twitching-tearing in posterior muscles of l. when sitting. *Pain in T. and* **legs as if bruised and as if brittle, with shooting and gnawing towards shafts of bones, tearing in joints, the pain gradually rising from tarsal joints to hips, obliging him while sitting to continually move feet, > when walking** (comp. Rhus. t.). Cramp pain in gluteals on bending forward, with tension. Fluctuating throbbing pain in upper and inner part of l. Sore pain on inner side. Feeling as if there were no flesh on ischia, but more comfort on a hard than on a soft seat. Pain drawing outwards on a spot on inner side of l. Hard pressure in middle of anterior surface of r. Rheumatic drawing in a spot between l. knee and trochanter at night, changing to burning throbbing next day, with erysipelatous redness. Paralytic drawing in r. T. and leg. Heaviness while sitting; while walking, with stiffness; of T. and legs while walking, with stiffness of knee.

Knee.—Twitching in bend of r.; in bend extending into muscles of thigh. Shooting in bend of l.; in r. patella while sitting. Pain. Cramplike pain in r., near patella, towards outer side, when sitting; especially about patellæ, preventing him from ascending stairs. Squeezing pain in bend of r. Feeling when walking as if outer hamstrings were too short, alternately with a similiar sensation in inner hamstring, but it is more intense in outer. Tingling-quivering sensation over r. when sitting. Bubbling in forepart of l., as of water.

Leg.—Trembling; with tottering gait, raising of one leg as if he had to ascend a hill, whereupon he falls and cannot rise without aid. Cramp in calf in evening in bed on bending leg, > stretching leg. Shootings in l. calf coming up from lower part. Prickings below l. patella when sitting. **Tearing pressure in middle of inside.** Tearing; in tibia; frequent, in l. calf; burning-tearing upward through inner surface of popliteal space; drawing, in r. tibia, with sensation of pressing-asunder. "Growing pain" in r., a feeling of stiffness, with heaviness. Sensation as if jammed, < night, > letting leg hang down, with commotion (dull tearing) and stir therein. Pressure in forepart of l. tibia when standing. Sensation drawing upward, as of crawling externally, but internally as of shootings. Drawing on l. tibia near knee. Tension in muscles, especially in calf, where there is crawling. Feeling in calf as if he would have cramp. Necessity to extend them. Weakness; paralytic; paralytic, when ascending stairs, especially of calves. Painful heaviness of r. when laying it over l.; drawing H.; tremulous. Numbness; crawling over them after lying a short time, in r. then l. Loss of control.

Tendo-achillis.—Boring or tearing shoots. Tension in r. tarsal joint when walking in open air.

Foot.—Swollen. Raised when walking as if stepping over a high obstacle. Cramp in sole in evening in bed when drawing up knees. Shootings in soles; S. from l. to knee when stepping upon it; in dorsum of l. when sitting. Tearing in metatarsal bone of great toe; T. in l. sole while walking, with occasional shooting. Boring digging in soles; digging in soles, with burning. Sharp pain at base of first metatarsal bone of r. Pain in metatarsal bones as if dislocated while walking or bending foot. Bruised pain in ball of heel when treading on it. Drawing pain in hollow of r.; D. pain extending to scapulæ and thence into fingers, at last into teeth, which then seem on edge and become loose; cutting, in a spot, extending through legs and thighs, then through small of back to shoulders; painless, or creeping from heels around ankles to toes. Tension in r. sole in region of heel, changing to tensive pressure, > pressure. Bubbling as from the dropping of water. Creeping from below upward in feet. Lassitude, with drawing pain. Numbness. Inability to stir l.

Clinical.—Sciatic nerves extremely sensitive, as if uncovered, cannot bear to have anything press upon the affected part. Acute inflammation of hip-joint, with heat, etc. (Symptoms of neuritis, see also arm.)

Skin.—Distention of veins. Gray spots on chest. White like a statue; W., except face, which is red and swollen. **Redness as in scarlatina;** *R. suddenly spreading over body, especially in face and legs, with heat and exaltation of all faculties; red spots* (which itch?); in spots over whole body, especially on chest; in spots on backs of hands; sharply defined uniform R. on face, neck, arms, trunk and thighs; on face, chest and limbs; then roughness and desquamation.

Appearance in color, and to a certain extent in thickness, like scarlet flannel. *Scarlet eruption;* on arms and legs. *Eruption like scarlatina; on face, upper limbs and trunk, ending abruptly at wrists and flexure of thighs, with hot and dry skin;* like scarlatina, covering skin with occasional livid spots. Scarlet rash on neck, upper part of chest, on hand and forehead. *Red, scaly eruption on lower parts of body as far as abdomen.* Red elevated spots on chest and belly, frequently disappearing and suddenly appearing, with general redness of skin. Red elevations at root of nose, and when touched pain as if ulcerated. Red elevations similar to nettle-rash, gradually coalescing, covering face and front of neck, around the spots a white border, also around mouth.

Erythema. Inflammation. Cold, painful, long-lasting nodosities and swellings (apparently secondary effect). Boil upon shoulder; painful, on temple; red, hard B. at angle of lower jaw, with stinging when pressed. Pimples on chin; on face, and boils; rash-like on chin, with burning on touch; on side of chin, with itching sticking, or rather stitches than itching, > scratching; on l. mamma, with crawling itching, > rubbing; beneath r. elbow, with stinging on touch; red exuding bloody serum when scratched, on temple, at r. corner of mouth and on chin. Pimply exanthema on face, suppurating slowly.

Pustules; **on cheek and nose, rapidly filling with pus, becoming covered with a crust,** also on nape and arms; between lips and chin, with burning smarting, pain < night; white-tipped, under l. wing of nose; red, on back, especially in scapular region, the whole skin is red and smarts when touched, but in tips of pustules there is shooting. Erysipelatous fever, with inflamed swellings passing into gangrene. Gangrene, hot and cold. Ulcers; exude only bloody matter; (become covered with black scabs); cutting in U. during rest, and tearing on moving the part; sore pain around U.; painful, on side of nostrils where they unite with lip; become painful to touch, almost a burning pain; pain in U. almost only at night (from 6 P.M. to 6 A.M.), burning as if something would press outward, and the part seems paralyzed and stiff; itching of U.

Sensitiveness to touch; S. to the free air. Pleasant prickling as of warmth out of all pores. Creeping upwards on l. arm. Itching prickings here and there in evening in bed. Itching stinging on r. scapula. Scratching of various parts, especially of neck and chest. Itching; of feet; shooting, on scapulæ, > scratching; tearing, here and there, < night in bed, after rubbing only tearing pain remains; scraping, on forehead; biting, on feet and their dorsa; crawling, now here, now there; creeping, on legs and back; (titillating, on l. scapula).

Clinical.—Early stage of erysipelas. Early stage of boils.

Sleep.—Yawning; frequent, in afternoon, with stretching and filling of eyes with water; frequent, in evening, then chills along skin; like that of an intoxicated person. *Sleepiness;* on waking; in morning after rising; from 5 to 9 P.M., with desire to stretch; towards evening, with yawning, but in morning feeling as if he had not slept enough; with dulness of intellect; with inability to sleep because of itching, scratching causes erythema; full of inquietude. Sleep in afternoon. *Somnolency, with subsultus tendinum, pale cold face and hard, small, rapid pulse.* Deep sleep. Heavy disturbed sleep, with stertor. Profound, late S., with headache and languor on waking and no appetite for breakfast. Inability to rouse himself in morning, and on waking ill humor. Stupefied sleep; with opening of eyes, looking about him wildly, then stertorous slumber. Soporous condition, with convulsions of face and limbs. Sopor, coma or lethargy after the delirium, and sometimes the delirium returns as the sopor goes off.

Ineffectual efforts to obtain sleep. Sleeplessness; after midnight, with sweat; except from 1 to 6.30, then unrefreshed on rising; from anguish, also with drawing pains in all limbs; from a fancy that he has some pressing business; with relief of pains at night. **Restless sleep;** *before midnight,* **the child tosses about, kicks and quarrels in sleep** (Hyosc.); **with irrational talking and difficulty in keeping them in bed;** *with active dreams.* **Starting in otherwise quiet sleep, feeling as if falling deep down, which caused shuddering. Starting and waking when falling asleep; in evening,** *the feet are jerked upward and the head forward.* Suffocative snoring only on inspiration. Croaking and moaning. Singing and loud talking.

Awoke from noon sleep with restlessness, screamed and stamped. Waking three times about midnight, with ineffectual retching and cold sweat as from anguish. Frequent waking with restlessness; F. waking as if he had slept enough. *Waked constantly by fearful dreams and twitchings. Waking in night full of fear, it appeared as if there were something under her bed which made a noise, dry heat on waking.* Sleep intolerable on account of increased pains and frightful dreams.

Dreams immediately on falling asleep. *Frightful D.* Wakened by D. of danger from fire. Anxious D. about murderers and street-robbers, he heard himself shouting, but did not come to his senses. Fatiguing D. Vivid but unremembered. Unremembered. About household affairs. That she was occupied with many people, and she wished to get away, but did not go so far as that. Pleasant; provoking laughter, after the delirium.

Clinical.—In children a kind of restless sleep, with sudden starting, twitching of arms, with half-closed eyes, hot head, fright, dilated pupils, etc.

Fever.—Chill over body in evening on undressing, then heat in whole l. side of body; C. after bathing; after eating; after dinner, with chattering of teeth, and when lying trembling of limbs as in cold stage of intermittent fever; on undressing, especially in arms, with gooseflesh and with redness and heat of ears and nose; with shuddering and gooseskin. (Chill, then felt quite well, then sweat on face, hands (?) and feet (?) before the heat, no sleep during the heat, scarcely any thirst during the chill, none during the heat and sweat, headache during the sweat on face, none during the chill or heat.)

Chilliness internal and external in sleep and on waking. External C., with internal heat. Shivering; during stool; as soon as cold air blows on her, in other respects better in open air; then in afternoon flushes of heat; convulsive, towards evening, then heat and general sweat. Thrills of chill running over whole body, then internal and external heat, especially in face. *Chill alternating with heat; without thirst, and mostly with confusion of head;* suddenly, with sleepiness in the daytime.

Shivering over abdomen; intermittent, down back. Chill in back, or pit of stomach, or in arms, spreading thence all over body; in sacrum in evening in bed, spreading over back and lower limbs, then heat. Shivering over one arm. Coldness of hands; in morning, with dulness of head and weeping; of lower limbs, with rigidity; in r. hip-joint; C. of legs; *of feet;* of feet in evening, with heat within ear; of feet, with bloated red face and flow of blood to head. Everything he touched seemed very cold, < the *longer he held it.*

Heat; in morning; at night, < towards morning, yet he does not dare to uncover, for the uncovered part is painful as from a chill; on slight motion; after attack of cough, *with distention of superficial veins, insatiable thirst, anxiety and trembling; with furious delirium;* with bluish redness of skin; with phantasies, the boy talked of animals which he seemed to see, and hearing seemed dull; with palpitation; with general sweat when hands are in bed, but general chill when they are put out of bed; from below upward, breaking out of sweat as of anguish, then nausea, with anxiety, the nausea descending lower and lower.

Heat internal or external. Internal H. after beer. **Internal and external, especially in face, which was red and covered with sweat, with confusion of head. Hot and scarlet skin,** especially on face and interior half of trunk. **Dry, hot and scarlet skin, especially on face and ears.** Hot and dry skin, with small, wiry, hard and rapid pulse. Dry heat in attacks. **Heat and redness of head; H. of head,** *with coldness of rest of body;* internal and external H. of head. **Hot and puffy face;** H. sensation in face, with cold feet. Internal heat in face, without redness; afterwards redness and swelling. Creeping H. under skin of face. Heat in evening on hands and feet. Dry H. in extremities of hands and feet, with thirstlessness and pallor of face. Heat of feet. Warm feeling along back of r. forearm as of approaching numbness, with paralytic feeling along anterior tibial nerve.

Sweat; in sleep during the day; about 2 or 3 A.M., after waking, on covering arms, > uncovering them; in evening in bed on covered parts; at night; after midnight in sleep; as soon as he covers himself in bed, especially on upper parts; on least exertion, mostly on face, down nose; when walking in wind, with colic, as if he had got cold; suddenly occurring and as quickly disappearing; on upper parts; on face only; on forehead and at pit of stomach, on waking from frightful dreams; intermittent, in morning rising from feet into face, which especially sweats, then coldness; S. on feet when sitting, without warmth. Cold sweat on forehead; on limbs; on hands; on feet. Dryness of skin; and insensibility.

Clinical.—Scarlet fever, throat red, hot and dry, nausea and vomiting, with hot head or delirium, etc. Typhoid fever rarely. Occasionally indicated in typhus. Worm fever. Fever of dentition, etc. Very rarely, as an intercurrent, in any form of malarial fever.

Benzoic Acid.

Dissolve the pure crystals in Alcohol (1 to 9) for use.

General Action.—Produces symptoms of a uric-acid diathesis; pains in joints and tendons; great change in the quality of the urine.

Affinities.—Carbol. ac., Berb., Arn., Led., Viola t., Rhod., Sulph.

Generalities.—Emaciation. Trembling, with palpitation. *Tearing and stitching, especially in metatarsal joints of r. great toe* (Sulph., Berb.). Pains change their place incessantly and suddenly, but are most constant in region of heart. Pain passes from the r. hand and appears in l. arm, extends downward into elbow, then appears in region of heart, later in r. thigh and ankle. *Weariness;* after menses.

Mind.—Hilarity, preventing sleep. Sadness. Anxiety while sweating. Activity of mind while at work, afterwards anxiety. Omits words every moment while writing.

Head.—Aching after mental emotions. Confusion; with sleepiness. Sensation as if there were air in it. Excitement in morning when sneezing, with lightness. Sensation of shaking in it. Vertigo, making him fearful of falling sideways, < afternoon. Tired feeling as from night-watching. Symptoms easily produced on uncovering or on exposure to a draught, and in morning on waking, and < during rest. Symptoms return periodically and are often accompanied by pains in stomach, nausea, gagging and coldness of hands. Symptoms are generally accompanied by depression, lassitude and loss of appetite.

Hard throbbing in temporal arteries. Pain in l. temple; hammering P. in temples, obliging him to lie down. Tearing in vertex. Pressure in vertex and spinal column forenoons while sitting, as if pressed by an elastic body, causing stretching, bending forward and anxiety. Pain in sides internally, with bruised sensation. Rheumatic pain on outside. Itching of hairy scalp.

Eyes.—Burning. Distress as from want of sleep. Symptoms easily appeared in open air when walking, and when reading by candle-light. Throbbing in balls. Burning in lids. Itching in canthi; r. outer, then in r. inner.

Ears.—Swelling behind, which seemed to reach periosteum. Intermittent shooting in r. Itching in l. Starting. Puffing from pulsation of temporal arteries. Noises when swallowing. Sound as of confused voices, < swallowing or walking in open air.

Nose.—Redness at angles. Pain in bones. Pressure at root. Sensitiveness. Itching of septum. Irritation in l. nostril as before sneezing, with inability to sneeze. Sneezing, with hoarseness. Coryza from exposure to cold, renewed every day. Epistaxis. Smell dull. Smell as of dust, cabbage or something stinking. Symptoms appear especially in evening.

Face.—Circumscribed redness. Pressive sensation. Tension in one side. Numb feeling. Symptoms > heat, pressure or rubbing. Trembling of lips. Lower lip bitten involuntarily two successive days at dinner.

Mouth.—Stitches in a r. lower hollow molar. Cutting pain in teeth. Darting pain in carious molars. Slow jerking in a r. upper molar. Tongue bluish. Velvety coat on tongue; white mucous coat on T. in morning. Soreness at back part of tongue, < swallowing; at root of T. and on palate, with rawness.

Acid mucus in M. Taste of blood; bitter taste on drinking coffee or milk; B., with pressure at stomach and eructations; flat, soapy, after drinking water; salt, to food; smoky, to bread; after-taste of food. Symptoms of M. and throat > after eating.

Throat.—Thyroid gland feels swollen. Sensation of swelling or contraction. Sensation of lumps in pit, as if food stuck there. Scratching. Heat, with sensation of stretching. Mucus. Swallowing difficult; S. incomplete. Heat in œsophagus, as from acid eructations.

Stomach.—Appetite increased in evening; lost morning. Thirst in evening, with sleepiness. Singultus. Nausea mornings; N., with malaise; with gagging and disturbances about head. Vomiting of a salt substance; bitter V. Gastric disturbances when ascending a height (in pregnant women). Pressure, with eructations. Burning. Fatigued by pressure of clothes on epigastrium. Symptoms < walking.

Abdomen.—Discharge of flatus in afternoon and evening. Tearing. Heat; spreading over body, with rapid pulse, increased sweat and excretion of phlegm, indigestion and confusion of head. Pain below l. short ribs. Superficial stitching midway in upper part of liver. Cutting about umbilicus, > stool. Tensive pain in groins.

Rectum, Anus and Stool.—Stitches in rectum; contraction of extremity of R. Urging to stool, with ineffectual straining. Stitches in anus in evening; formication in A. Bowels opened freely, with extraordinary pressure to stool. *Stool frothy;* S. putrid, bloody; insufficient.

Clinical.—Diarrhœa, offensive, light-colored, of a pungent, urinous odor; stools like soap-suds, very copious, odor is similar to that of the urine, which is dark and of very strong odor.

Urine.—**Of repulsive odor** (Rhod., Viola t., Sul., Sep.), **changeable color, brownish** (Carbol. ac., Nit. ac., Arn.), *cloudy, alkaline* (Carb. ac.), *effervescing with hydrochloric acid, immediately after micturition white flocculent sediment of phosphate and carbonate of lime, without uric acid,* with pallor, weakness in loins and languor. *Fetid, with prolapsus uteri.* Aromatic. Bloody. Thick. Copious, turbid, with traces of urea, mere traces of hippuric acid. At first increased in quantity, not in frequency, afterwards frequent micturition, with strong pressing, urine aromatic odor (Carb. ac.), long retained, saline, the urinary symptoms < in forenoon. Decreased. Acid; and irritant; with copious hippuric acid, with a base. Abundant hippuric acid after adding hydrochloric acid, but no uric acid. Disappearance of urea, but not uric acid.

Clinical.—Valuable especially for catarrh of the bladder, with offensive brown urine. Cystitis, with extremely offensive odor. Nocturnal eneuresis, dark offensive urine. Kidney colic. Offensive, acid urine in rheumatism.

Sexual Organs.—Pain; raw. Smarting of frænum preputii. Thrilling, almost painful sensation, on l. side of glans penis, extending into urethra, ending in tickling and itching. Itching of glans; in sulcus behind corona glandis. Menses too early; M. retarded. Lochia too long-lasting.

Respiratory Organs.—Irritation. Hoarseness in morning, with sneezing and pleasant excitement and freedom of head. Copious mucus in bronchi. Respiration whistling. Difficult breathing on waking. Cough; after a slight cold; excited by inspiration; from sensation of something rough or dry in chest; then expectoration of greenish mucus; hacking, after rising.

Clinical.—Asthma, especially in rheumatic persons. Inflammation of bronchi and lungs, with great tenderness of the chest, cough < night, lying on r. side.

Chest.—Stitches in middle; in evening; in evening in bed, < deep breathing; in r. side. Cutting. Pain in l.; about sixth rib, < deep inspiration and by bending to either side; on sides; about r. third rib, midway between sternum and side; deep penetrating, posteriorly in l. side, about sixth rib. Painful starting. Agitation. Rough sensation. Swollen sensation; in mammary gland. Burning in nipples. Can scarcely bear pressure of clothing.

Heart and Pulse.—*Pain in region of H.* Constriction of H. Weak feeling in region. Palpitation, waking after midnight and every night at 2 A.M., with heat and hard pulse, sleep prevented by throbbing of temporal arteries; P. while sitting and after drinking; with trembling. Intermittent beats. Undulating beating. Pulse accelerated; slow; full.

Clinical.—Has been prescribed in valvular diseases of the heart.

Neck and Back.—Pressure in nape. Stiffness on one side of neck. Pressure on spinal column. Pain in r. side between tenth dorsal vertebra and side; in region of kidneys; starting in loins. Trunk symptoms < on motion after long sitting, at night on going to bed and on blowing nose.

Extremities.—Knicking in joints and cracking on motion. Tearing in various parts, with stitches; T. in r. toes, especially in their middle joints, then in r. knee, last joint of metacarpal bone and of l. thumb, in lower part of r. radius, etc.

Clinical.—Gout and rheumatism, with swelling of joints, with the peculiar urinary symptoms. Valuable in rheumatic gout of the fingers, nodes very painful, with the urinary symptoms (Arnica). Gouty deposits in wrists. Swellings of the wrist (ganglion). Gout of great toe.

Upper Extremities.—Sensation of swelling under axillæ. Stitches on outer surface of r. arm in evening, then on inner surface of l. Tearing in bones of arm; at outer surface of wrists, as if in bones. Fingers swollen; with tearing and stitching in various parts of limbs, especially in front at metatarsal joint of r. great toe. Tearing in metacarpal joint of l. thumb; deep in upper joints of l. index. Pain in joints of r. fingers; paralytic pain in fingers.

Lower Extremities.—Sensation as if bandaged. Lassitude; in r. hip. Tearing in posterior surface of thigh. Pain in gastrocnemii; in r. hip; in l. hip, then in thigh, next in knees, then in toes; in l. hip, in knee and worse in toes, leaving the toes it seats itself in muscles of calf and then in knee, leaving these parts it appears in r. thigh and ankle. *Cracking of knee. Pain in both knees; in r.;* in l.; drawing P. in knees after drinking wine. *Dry sensation in knee.* Pain in r. tendo-achillis, and at the same time in region of heart, then in l. tendo-achillis; in l. tendo-achillis, close to os calcis, while supporting a slight part of weight of body. Sharp pain in l. ankle during the time it supports the body while walking.

Toes.—Stitch perpendicularly upward through r. great, in morning while lying, then burning, which increases gradually to a stitch, then in l. great toe, from which it vanishes with a thrill. Deep sticking tearing in lowest joint of great (Led., Sulph.). Pain; raw P. between. Numbness.

Skin.—Red spots on fingers; on nose. Formication in forehead. Itching on various parts, then an agreeable feeling of being scratched, leaving burning; I. on chin; I. in nape; I. in r. palm in evening, with deep tearing in metacarpal joints of little and ring fingers.

Sleep.—Sleepiness, with dulness of head. Deep sleep. Starting up from S. Disturbed by dreams.

Fever.—Horripilation before stool. Coldness, with feeling of heat; C., then heat and sweat. Cold sensation in head. Coldness of back; at sacrum; of hands; feet; knees; of knees, as from a cold wind; of hands, with head symptoms. Heat during the coryza; H., with sweat. Internal H. on waking; *internal H. wakes every night at 2 A.M. with a hard-bounding*, but not quickened pulse, so that he must lie on his back because the pulsations of temporal arteries sound like puffing in ears and prevent sleep. Heat of face; on one half of F.; around mouth. Sweat; morning in bed, especially on face, with moderate heat; at night; while eating; while walking; on disappearance of other symptoms; with anxiety; with itching; of feet; with aromatic odor. Cold sweat on head; on face; on feet. Exhalation from skin diminished.

Berberis.

Berberis vulgaris. The common Barberry. A tincture is prepared from the bark of the fresh root.

General Action.—The most numerous and decided effects are the shooting pains in almost every part of the body. The pains in the region of the kidneys are most marked and have been frequently verified clinically. It also exerts a marked action on the liver, promoting the flow of bile.

Affinities—It is interesting to note the close resemblance of the neuralgic symptoms to the botanical relatives in the Ranunculaceæ, Cimicif., Clem., Puls., and even Aconite; the hepatic symptoms similar to its allies Pod., Chel., as well as Iris and Aloes. Also see *Diosc.*, Agaric., Silicea and Zinc.

Generalities.—Bruised feeling (Cimicif., Arn., Sil.), after long stooping, with feeling as if unable to do anything; B. feeling, as after great fatigue, especially in lower limbs. Weakness; of body and mind in morning on waking; in evening and after supper; in evening, with early falling asleep; from continued occupation, with sweat; < walking or long standing; even to trembling, so that she feared her knees would break down, with vertigo on rising from stooping; faintlike, when walking, standing or rising from a seat, with vertigo. Attacks of faintness after a walk, with sudden orgasms of blood, and shortly before going to bed sweat and heat in upper part of body, cold, pale, sunken face and oppression of chest, on lying down in bed shivering, difficult falling asleep and restless sleep, with heavy dreams. Condition near faintness after a drive followed by a short walk.

Mind.—Anxiety from 4 P.M. till going to bed, with fright, and in the twilight some children and dogs appeared twice as large as natural; A. if she moves, stands long, rises from a seat, even in morning when rising in bed and on getting out of it. Ill-will, intrepidity. Peevishness, becoming a loathing of life. Melancholy and disinclination to speak, with quiet, not conscious longing. Satisfaction with nothing. Apathy; with dizziness and disinclination to work. Easy disturbance from external causes during mental work, with fretfulness and necessity to cease work. Thought difficult; < morning. Memory weak.

Head.—Sticking. *Tearing now here, now there in whole H., in forehead and temples.* Aching; < morning, with heaviness and confusion; as if skull would burst, and on stooping sensation as if something shook in H. and as if everything would come out at forehead; as if pressed asunder or pressed down by a heavy weight, especially in forehead; heavy, with prostration. Heaviness; and on stooping sensation as if head were drawn down by a heavy weight. Fulness, especially in forehead. Tension. *Puffy sensation. Feeling as if becoming larger* (Cimicif.).

Emptiness and gloominess. Confusion; from morning after waking till after noon, with heaviness of head, pressure in forehead, prostration, fretfulness, chilliness, sometimes with heat between the chills, then heat, especially in head, with symptoms of impending coryza, especially moisture of nose and sneezing, which go no farther, repetition of these attacks, with which aggravations always begin; as from a cap and as if it would be drawn downward from behind. Intoxicated feeling. *Vertigo;* on stooping; on walking, with faintish weakness; so that she must turn from l. to r. and forward (during hard work, with frequent stooping and exertion of arms), with attacks of faintness, frontal headache, then chilliness in back and occiput. Symptoms generally > open air.

Forehead.—Stitches in sinciput; S. and jerking in F., and in vertex when stooping; in r. extending outward to side; in spots above margin of l. orbit, extending outward and upward, or twitching or rolling pain; paroxysmal, especially suddenly through supra-orbital region; paroxysmal in F. and temples, generally ceasing suddenly; tensive, over r. orbit. Tearing; in l. eminence, with pain on touch; sticking, and in temples. Pain in r. upper part; now over eyes, now in frontal eminences, now in temples, now in other places in forehead; extending towards vertex; twinging tensive, caused and < by stooping, > open air; tensive, in F., temples and eyes; in F. and eyes on stooping, as if brain were heavy and fell forward; outward-pressing, and in temples. Stupid sensation.

Temples.—Stitches; inward in r.; jerking, in r., extending into r. eye, then shooting into vertex. Tearing; in r. and in r. cheek; intermittent twitching. Pain in r., extending to eye, as if in bone, with stitches into sinciput; P. in r. as if it were thick or would be pressed out, < touch; tensive in l.

Stitches in l. parietal region. Tearing in l. occipital region. Tensive pain in occiput as if scalp were too small and brain too large.

Scalp.—Pimples on head and face, most frequently on occiput, temples and forehead, especially near hair, with burning stitches as from fleas in same spots. Scalp and skin of face feel puffy and tense; with difficult motion of scalp. Tensive numb sensation in S. and in skin of face. Smarting or corrosive sensation, now here, now there, in S. and in skin of face, < rubbing, then sometimes red spots. Corrosive itching or sticking on spots, in scalp and skin of face. Itching below hair, chiefly in occipital region, either simple or biting, or burning, < evening, the itching > by scratching, but appearing in other places, with stitches, often with warm sensation in skin.

Eyes.—Sunken, surrounded by blue or dirty gray rings. Red. Inflamed, < afternoon. Stitches; outward into forehead; usually sudden, mostly coming from other parts, as from forehead or from temples into eyes, or rising in eyes and spreading into forehead; digging, in r., then l., beginning deep in and extending obliquely across middle of orbital margin upward and outward into forehead. Tearing. *Pain;* on beginning to read by candle-light; after crying; < motion of eye; as if he had wept long. Sensation as if forced out. Throbbing in l. Bubbling in l.; in evening; in r. Coldness, as on going into cold air, with lachrymation on closing them. *Burning;* in morning after rising, *with dryness,* dim look, redness of conjunctiva of lids and misty vision; from 12 o'clock; at 3 P.M., < till she went to sleep, < l., with sensation of sand in them; *with dryness and redness* and with matter in canthi. *Dryness; with biting or burning,* sometimes with itching, often with feeling as of sand between lid and eye, at times with redness of conjunctiva of lid and even of ball. Stiff feeling, with dragging. Troubles < afternoon and evening; < in open air. Intermittent tearing in l. ball, extending obliquely downward and outward.

Lids.—Inflammation, < l., with swelling. Redness of margin and of sclerotic; of inner surface, and margin covered with white frothy fluid. White crusts on the dry margins in morning after rising. Agglutination of l. in morning. Twitching when reading by candle-light, seldom by daylight. Sticking on border of l. upper, towards outer part, then burning. Tearing in upper; in l. lower; pinching. Tearing drawings and twinges. Sensation as of a foreign body in l. internal canthus, with inflammation of lachrymal caruncle and dryness of conjunctiva in internal canthus. Biting beneath r. lower; crawling B. on margin of r. lower, becoming a twitching bubbling in lid. Itching, at times burning, biting or sticking, seldom smarting; I. in canthi, at times biting or sticking. Burning in spots or biting. Dry sensation if closed. Feeling as of drops of cold water between margins of lids or between lids and balls. Heaviness on motion. Sticky sensation in margin in morning after rising.

Orbits.—Twitching in region of r. upper. Stitches from l. margin to r. frontal eminence; biting S. and itching pain in margins, in skin, especially in inner canthus. Tearing in outer side of l., with tendency to lachrymation; T. in upper margin of l., extending towards forehead; in inner angle of r., extending towards nose and forehead; in bone on margin, especially lower, often extending into orbital cavity, at times it only begins to pain on touch.

Vision.—Dim, < for far objects; D., with sleepiness. Everything seems to run together when sewing. Sensitiveness to bright sunlight. Daylight blinded her more than lamp-light. If she looks at anything fine she must hold her hand before her eyes to shield them from the daylight and still more from lamp-light, which blinds her. Blackness on exertion in sewing.

Ears.—Stitches in l.; in r.; in r. at 5 P.M.; tearing, in middle, alternating with the same symptom in other parts of head; tensive, inward in r.; tensive, in r. in evening, as if something were digging in it; bubbling inward in l., then continued S., then pressure, then stopped sensation; drawing upward, deep in r.; in slow jerks deep in r., then tearing in antitragus; jerklike in r., as if it came out through the drum, when at work while sitting, as if a nail were forced through, or as from a stinging animal, with digging S. between the pains, with sensation as if ear were full and dragged downward. Tearing in external; in one or other middle; in bone behind l. Drawing pain often during the day, ending in stitches. Painless throbbing and whizzing in l., seldom in r., in rapid shocks, as if the air or the wing of a bird struck against the drum, with dryness and coldness in ear. Ringing in r., beginning deep, then becoming higher.

Clinical.—Gouty concretions in the auricle, becoming very painful, with tearing stinging pains.

Nose.—Biting gnawing in tip. Crawling in nostrils, biting or itching; C. in l. nostril as before sneezing. *Dryness of mucous membrane;* with sensation as before catarrh, with sneezing. Moisture of N. and eyes as before coryza. Fluent catarrh; of l. nostril, involving frontal and maxillary sinuses, a yellow, burnt-smelling water, afterwards purulent, sometimes whitish, at times yellowish or greenish mucus, of burnt smell and taste, was blown from nose and hawked up, < in morning. Bleeding from l. nostril in morning on rising; from l. at 6 A.M., preceded by pain in l. temple extending to eye.

Face.—*Pale, dirty-grayish, sunken cheeks, deeply-seated eyes, surrounded by bluish or blackish-gray circles, and sickly expression.* Tearing sticking in cheek-bones. Burning stitch in l. side of chin. Tearing in l. cheek, especially in malar fossa; chilly, in a spot on l. cheek; posteriorly in l. cheek-bone, in jerks upward. Aching jerk in r. cheek, as from a box on ear. Sticking cold sensation in a spot on l. cheek.

Lips.—Bluish-red color on inner side of lower. Red, bluish spots on inner side of lower, towards angle. Pimples; painful inflamed, with deep suppurating points in centre, on mucous membrane of L. and cheeks. Vesicles on r. inner side of lower. Epidermis becomes sticky and scales off, and a thin brownish flat scurf appears on its inner margin. Stitches in margins, sometimes itching, sometimes burning. Tearing in l. side of upper, with burning and tingling. Pinching in r. half of lower. Twitching bubbling in l. side of upper, as if some one were pricking it. *Dryness.* Painless throbbing in upper, just over r. corner of mouth. Burning spots in upper; B. in outer margin, as from pepper or as if swollen; in upper, in r. corner, as from pepper, with bubbling and drawing-downward feeling. Cold sensation in l. corner. Sticky feeling on margin in morning after rising and during the day. Formication on r. side of upper. Itching, > rubbing, but returning, sometimes biting or burning.

Jaws.—Sticking, especially in lower, < night; jerking, in angle of l. lower, digging, biting, extending into lower and back teeth, as if the gum were loosened from the teeth, or as if they were raised; tearing, in r., shooting by jerks into temples. Tearing in r. upper, extending from angle in front of ear into temple. Aching in l. upper, alternating with tearing; A. as if squeezed, on margin of horizontal ramus of r. lower, about middle; bruised, on touch, in lower margin of l. lower, near and in front of angle.

Mouth.—Teeth. Stitches in two anterior r. lower

molars, then sensation as if too long; S. in r. lower as if carious, in afternoon and night, with sensation as if teeth were too large and on edge, with sensitiveness to cold air, especially with tearing and sticking in lower jaw. Tearing in l. upper back; in the second l. upper molar, extending to other parts of face; in l. upper canine, extending to superior maxillary bone. Scraping-gnawing in all l. lower molars, as if in roots or necks. Slow digging in root of r. upper canine, as if denuded from gum. Aching in next to last l. upper molar as if too long. Drawing, bubbling pain pressing downward in first l. upper hollow incisor, with sensitiveness to touch, as if too long and on edge, or as if something heavy hung upon it, afterwards a boil in gum over it.

Gum.—Dirty red scum on several upper incisors, less on lower jaw and on molars. White nodes on upper. Gumboils (pustules) becoming ulcers, above second l. upper back tooth. Bleeding.

Tongue.—Red pimples on r. side of tip, with stinging, < touch, with stiffness and thickness of forepart of tongue. Painful white vesicle in r. side of tip. Stitches, < r. side. Sticking burning in spots on l. side, with pain of tongue on touch and motion.

Sticky feeling, pasty and as if burnt, in mouth and throat. Smarting-burning on mouth and chin, sometimes like formication. Dryness and sticky sensation; D. still more in fauces, < morning after rising, > eating and drinking, with sticky sensation, rawness of mucous membrane, white tongue, diminished saliva or a *sticky frothy saliva like cotton*, seldom with thirst and heat, taste lost or impaired, but sour after eating. Sticky saliva. Bad metallic smell.

Taste.—Lost. Bloody, < morning and afternoon. Bitter; at 8 A.M.; after eating; and sour. Scraping-burning in M. and throat, like heartburn. Insipid, nauseous, rising from stomach like heartburn.

Throat.—Inflammation of arches of palate, uvula, tonsils and œsophagus. Sticking in side, passing behind jaw and shooting out of ear, < l. side; digging S. just below r. angle of jaw, extending into ear and out again. Pain in l. tonsil caused and < by speaking and swallowing, with sensation as if the seed of fruit were sticking in throat, with redness and sensitiveness to pressure in l. arch of palate and sensitiveness of neighboring parts of throat to motion. Pressure in back part of palate and pharynx, with dryness. Smarting, < r. side, < scratching, which causes a red, hot spot. Scraping; in morning; in morning on waking, > moistening; in evening, extending into stomach and trachea; > drinking water; < mornings after rising, sometimes with pain in one side of it; obliging hawking and raising.

Stomach.—Appetite increased; in evening. Hunger without appetite. Appetite lost; with a bilious, bitter taste; lost, with almost no taste for food. Thirst, < afternoon, with dry mouth; T. waking her at night. *Eructations; without bad taste or smell;* with griping in abdomen; alternating with yawning; bilious. Hiccough. Nausea; after dinner; N. > after breakfast. *Heartburn.* Peculiar sticking burning, more violent than heartburn, extending into pharynx. Stitches in region. Pressure in region. Sensation in epigastric region as if it would burst, in evening after eating till 9 P.M. Writhings in region. Chilliness in region.

Abdomen.—Rumbling. Fermentation, especially in region of colon, with motions. Movements, as before stool. Emission of flatus; seldom offensive, preceded by painless gripings, at times with warmth in anus. Cutting sticking. Wandering tearing in muscles, or tearing sticking. Sticking cutting. Cutting as before diarrhœa, in afternoon till next day, when there was diarrhœa in morning and afternoon. Griping. Twinging in walls, with constriction. Writhing. Pain; morning in bed; in region of l. descending colon; burning, in l. side, in a spot under skin and extending into it. Constriction. Drawings. Urging before stool, with moving.

Upper.—Stitches extending across in region of stomach. Sticking tearing from 10.30 to 11.30 P.M., on going to sleep, extending into stomach and l. hypochondrium, mostly corresponding to a place in front of kidneys, < breathing, motion and touch, with short respiration, distention and hardness of abdomen, the pains returning next morning on rising and afterwards.

Hypochondria.—*Stitches in region of gall-bladder < pressure* (Diosc.); *in l. hepatic region, near border of false ribs, about three inches from linea alba, < pressure, extending into region of stomach,* appearing when walking; tearing, in l., in front; tearing, in l., extending through l. lower and outer part of chest towards back, and shooting back and forth; burning, on border of r. false ribs, about two inches and a half from linea alba. Drawing tearing below tips of false ribs on inspiration, with feeling as if something were torn loose. Twinging, constrictive sensation in l. upper part of abdomen, especially in l. H., across towards umbilicus. Pressure in hepatic region, on margin of false ribs, about three inches from linea alba; in forepart of r., extending inward into border of false ribs; in l., extending backward or downward. Bubbling sensation below tip of false ribs, in r. forepart.

Umbilicus.—Stitches above to r.; deep at l. of; superficial tearing, in l. side. *Pain to side of, corresponding to a place in front of kidneys and rather to side, mostly sticking,* or burning or gnawing, usually only on one side, generally in a small spot, for the most part < only by deep pressure, *often extending to lumbar region or to groins, liver, spleen or stomach.* Cutting drawing in l. side, extending deep inward. Cutting jerking pain an inch above U., an inch and a half from linea alba, extending in slow drawings outward across l. lumbar region. Griping around U. (Diosc.). Twisting pain in region (Aloes). Twinging around and above U. (Chel.), in l. side of abdomen. Intermittent pain pressing outward, to l. of U., as from something living. Colic below U. (Diosc.).

Inguinal Region.—*Varicose veins, near r. ring,* extending to thigh, preceded by pressing. Stitches in one or other, and above Poupart's ligament; paroxysmal throbbing, in r., shooting suddenly into thigh; dragging, and above and in Poupart's ligament, especially in ring, < walking and standing, with pulselike stitches, sometimes with painless bubbling, they extend into testicles and upper anterior part of thigh and upward in region of kidneys, at times beginning in this last place, with stitches in front of region which corresponds to kidneys posteriorly. Tearing extending to mons veneris. Cutting constriction in l. ring, extending inward, as if it were going to deepen. Pain in ring; itching burning, in region of l. glands; in r. glands on touch, as if they would swell, with aching in region. *Burning smarting in r.*

fold, with tension on motion. Dragging in l. Tension in one or other ring, as if a hernia would appear, < standing and walking. Sensation above and to outer side of r. ring as if something would protrude, extending to thigh. Peculiar cold feeling in region of r. ring, becoming more like a burning.

Poupart's Ligament.—*Stitches at its origin at l. ilium, extending down it, then shooting outward into l. side of female urethra;* dragging, above l., extending outward and upward; above middle of r., extending inward and becoming a twinging; tensive, above middle of r. Twinging in and especially above them, extending outward and into inguinal rings. Drawing pain above one or other, extending towards thigh.

Ilium.—*Sticking deep in one or other* (Agar. m.), *an inch or an inch and a half from the spine, extending obliquely inward towards small of back,* sometimes with bubbling, deeply penetrating stitches; dragging S. from anterior inferior spinous process of l. and above it, towards inguinal region and thigh; drawing or cutting, above anterior border of l., down Poupart's ligament. Tearing-sticking above l. crest in morning on waking; in anterior region of one or other crest, extending up towards abdomen; in crest, to region of anterior spinous process and farther backward, sometimes inward and upward into walls of abdomen, mostly towards Poupart's ligament and region above it, at times into thigh; across from spine into crest, at times extending into pelvis or upward into muscles. *Tearing posteriorly in crest, usually only on one side, extending into gluteal muscles or into bones;* from posterior border downward and inward; sticking, about middle of outer posterior surface of l., deep in bone, extending inward, in morning on waking; dragging, anteriorly in crest, extending into one or other side of abdomen. Gnawing, tearing, ulcerative pain. Smarting in region of crest of r., extending into hip. Drawing pain in anterior region of pelvic bone, extending outward into muscles of thigh.

Clinical.—Very valuable for hepatic diseases; with indigestion, eructations, salivation, heartburn, vomiting of food, etc., after eating. Soreness in the region of the liver. Bilious colic; colic from gall-stones, with jaundice.

Rectum.—*Long-continued sensation after stool, as if one had just been to stool or had just recovered from a pain in anus.* Sensation of relief after stool. *Urging to stool; constant;* before stool, especially in colon, extending into small of back; after stool, also with perceptible movement in intestines; tensive, in small of back and in anus.

Anus.—Hæmorrhoids, *with burning pain after stool* (Sulph.), the stool frequently hard and of a dirty blood color externally; H., with itching and burning. Stitches; *burning, during, before and after stool* (Sil.). *Tearings extending around A. Smarting.* Pressing. Throbbing pain. **Burning pain as if parts around it were sore** (Sil., Sulph.). Warmth in region. Fulness. Itching. Crawling as from ascarides. *Crawling, burning, itching in and about it.*

Perineum.—Digging sticking, with jerking stitches, extending deep into l. side of uterus. Pain in front of anus.

Stool.—Diarrhœa; painless, watery, clay-colored, offensive, < daytime; frequent, pasty, yellowish, with rumbling, emission of flatus, at times nausea, thirst, heat in face and confusion of head, with increased appetite in evening; frequent, with cutting. Soft, profuse, also at an unusual time; soft, profuse, then pressive tensive sensation in small of back and in rectum. Copious, thick, pasty. *Constipation.* Hard stool; then soft; like sheep-dung, with much, frequently ineffectual, urging. Scanty, hard; S., thin-formed, not hard; and hard or soft, thin-formed, delayed. Painful, in morning, with pressure. Omitted.

Clinical.—Diarrhœa, painless, clay-colored, with burning and smarting in anus, sallow complexion, tenderness over region of liver and pain extending around back and abdomen.

Urinary Organs.—Bladder. Stitches in region (Clem., Sulph.); **drawing, in one or other side, extending into female urethra, often arising in lumbar region and extending along ureter;** tearing, in region, < l. side, just above symphysis and extending into it, then passing into l. side of penis or returning higher up; pulse-like, above symphysis, becoming a slight sticking, returning next day when the bladder is not very full; compelling micturition. **Cuttings in l. side of region, extending into urethra, coming from l. kidney along ureter.** *Cutting tensive pain deep in l. side, becoming a sticking obliquely in female urethra, as if in orifice. Cutting constriction.* Pinching constriction in region. Pinching in one or other side of region, sometimes on pressure upon it burning in whole urethra. **Burning pains** (Canth.), *sometimes when full, sometimes when empty, even after urinating and in morning before urinating.* Burning-itching, biting-smarting in region. Aching in region when filled, when empty and after urinating. *Sensation as if some urine remained after urinating.* Urging to urinate; < morning on rising.

Urethra.—*Stitches* (Sulph.); in female; *in female beginning in bladder,* sometimes in the middle, sometimes on one side; extending into bladder; jerking, in female, with spasmodic constriction. *Cutting;* < one side. Smarting during coition, once pain during ejaculation of semen; S. in U. and glans, < towards forepart and on one side, or extending into bladder, the pains in urethra caused or < motion; extending to l. anterior part of penis. Smarting biting, often with soreness, < when not urinating, chiefly in forepart, sometimes extending into bladder or rectum, often more pain on one side. Constriction posteriorly; smarting C. Pressure when urinating. *Burning pain in female, during and after urinating* (Sulph.), but more at other times. *Burning;* especially anteriorly or sometimes more posteriorly, *or along the whole length,* more on one side, < when not urinating; smarting, in l. side, with intercurrent bubbling shocks. Bubbling posteriorly when sitting. Itching; crawling I. pain when not urinating, when bladder is not full. Crawling posteriorly in male.

Urine.—Sometimes increased, sometimes diminished, when increased it is clear, light-colored, with slight mucous sediment, when scanty it usually has a sediment, this is the case in the beginning and during aggravations, the other during the reaction, but at times intercurrent conditions arise. *Blood-red,* **soon becomes turbid and deposits a thick mucous and bright red mealy sediment** (Sep.), *slowly becoming clear, with pain in bladder. Pale yellow,* **either with slight transparent gelatinous sediment, which does not deposit, or a turbid flocculent, claylike, copious mucous sediment mixed with white or whitish-gray, and later a reddish mealy sediment** (Agar. m.). Clear, saturated, yellowish, thick, flocculent, or like mealy water, *depositing a* *copious mucous and mealy sediment, with white-grayish, white, or dirty reddish or red granular sediment* ,with yellowish-red crystals upon bottom or sides of glass. *Bright gellow, with profuse mucous sediment. Inflammatory red.* Dirty wine-yellow, depositing a copious sediment or only gelatinous flakes. Greenish, turbid. Seems warmer than usual when urinating. The first passed in the morning cloudy. *Sediment clear, mucous.*

Clinical.—Renal calculi and renal colic, pain extending from kidneys along ureters to bladder, with burning in urethra, bladder, etc.

Genital Organs.—Most of the pains of external G. are caused and < by motion. Weakness in external male; W. after coition. Mons veneris, twinging-tearing; in one or other side; pinching constriction in region of mons veneris and bladder, sometimes only on one side, sometimes when full, sometimes after emptying bladder; pinching constriction extending along dorsum of penis; smarting itching pain; burning, itching or biting, also smarting.

Spermatic Cord.—*Soft pulpy swelling of l., especially of lower part, when walking, with at times drawing, burning or smarting, or tearing pain, at times when sitting, with pain extending into testicles* (Clem. r.), *especially into epididymis* (Senecio). Stitches. Twinging in one or other, only at abdominal ring, or extending to testicles. *Drawing pain, extending into testicles* (Pul.) *or into abdominal ring. Smarting burning pain, now in one, now in other* (Clem. r.; Berb. l.), *with stitches.* Smarting pain in one or other, at one time in region of abdominal ring, at another behind it, at another more beneath it, often extending into testicles.

Penis.—Shrivelling and retraction. Stitches; in forepart. Smarting in l. side, more externally, chiefly in forepart of mucous membrane and in part behind this spot, when walking and afterwards and after coition. Smarting burning in l. side; in r. upper part; on corona glandis. Smarting-burning itching pain in prepuce. Dryness of mucous membrane. Coldness of prepuce and glans, with numbness. Frequent erections.

Scrotum.—Sore pain, < sides, most often on l. Smarting constriction in l. lower part when walking. Itching, simple, or burning, or with stitches, at times smarting or crawling. Coldness in r. side, with tearings.

Testicles.—Stitches; in one or other (Rhod.); cutting; cutting in one. Pain; in one; constrictive, and in spermatic cord, with contraction of scrotum, as if it would be drawn up against abdomen, coldness and shrivelling of scrotum and pain in testicles. Drawing pain, sometimes extending up spermatic cord. Burning pain, as if they would swell. Crawling pain, usually in only one. Smarting or smarting-burning pain; in one.

Desire diminished in both sexes, the ejaculation of semen during coition too soon, the desire weak and transient, in women orgasm is delayed, sometimes associated with cutting or sticking. Emission at night.

Vagina.—Stitches outward in side, < l., twinging, or burning, twisting or long-drawn, often sudden, leaving pain, at times ending in urethra, with sensitiveness to touch. **Burning and soreness** (Kreo., Puls.), *especially anteriorly, even extending to labia,* sometimes only on one side, but often in region of orifice of urethra. Smarting, usually on one side.

Menstruation too soon, *discharge of grayish mucus, then bloody, scanty,* the fifth day it omitted, the sixth day watery, bloody, *then till eighth day grayish mucus, for some days previous tearing in limbs, with pain in small of back,* at times only on one side, with bruised feeling, as if suppurating, almost like labor-pains, < lying upon it and at night, with sometimes pain in one hip-bone, dragging pain in thighs, extending into calves, especially in veins of legs, which are injected with blood, pain in lumbar region, and once in evening in bed *sticking on l. side of navel, extending into l. side of vagina,* fretful, tired of life, **smarting in vagina, burning, pain and soreness in anus,** tensive pain in upper arm and shoulder extending into nape. Short-lasting; and *scanty,* at first pale, expedited by foot-bath, like bloody water, at beginning chilliness and pain in small of back, tearing in whole body, especially on l. side, painful distention of abdomen, *pain in kidneys,* stitches in chest, sickly look, and during the first days bursting headache. Ceases the third day, returns on the fifth, but more like bloody water, followed by weakness and tearing sticking headache. Like bloody water on the second day, some drops of dark blood on the third day, discolored mucus on the fourth, then nothing more, during the first days dragging in genitals, pain in small of back, dragging spliting headache on r. side, with faintness.

Clinical.—Neuralgia of spermatic cords and testicles (Clem., Cimicif., Puls.). Uterine symptoms, with leucorrhœa, associated with painful symptoms in urinary organs. Dysmenorrhœa, with pains radiating in every direction, down thighs, into abdomen, etc. (Cimicif., Berb.). Vaginismus, with inflamed kidneys, etc.

Voice.—Hoarseness, with pain or inflammation of tonsils.

Clinical.—Polypus in larynx cured.

Chest.—Stitches in r. clavicle; in l. mamma; below l. mamma, towards heart; in l. side externally and in lower part; deep in anterior middle part, < deep breathing, with short dry cough; inward in r.; here and there, extending inward; outward in r.; pulse-like, in r. clavicle; lightning-like, in r. clavicle, shooting up r. side of neck; long-drawing in region of false ribs, leaving pain extending downward in region of l. false ribs; deep, near l. mamma, outward and downward through the gland. Burning stitches near l. nipple; in region of r. clavicle, as from wasps; deep below r. clavicle, crossing horizontally into first ribs. Intermittent jerking stitches in l. almost as from electric shocks. Sticking jerking pain, like electric shocks, extending into forepart of l. hypochondrium and then backward, with pain in whole lower part of l. chest and abdomen. Tearing stitches, extending around r. side in forepart; near r. scapula, extending into arm and seating itself in muscles of inner side of upper arm.

Tearing in l. side; in wall below l. scapula; on both sides of C. and spine; in r. side, chiefly in forepart, and sometimes in scapula, also between it and spine, with oppression of chest; in l. pectoral muscles, extending towards their insertion in arm; drawing, in sides, chiefly in l., more towards back, and in scapulæ; drawing, in walls, sometimes caused by stretching or exerting muscles; pulsating at last pressive and tensive, tearing below l. axilla, extending to ribs.

Sudden cutting constrictive pain in front of middle

part, extending to abdomen, obliging her to bend double. Pain between l. mamma and wall of C., most severe behind nipple, extending outward into mamma, so that the middle of the sensation is in the nipple, with feeling as if mamma were swollen. Tensive drawing pain in l. side, more towards back. Tearing burning pain in lower border of l. pectoralis major, extending towards arm. Bubbling pain in region of l. pectoralis major in evening in bed, coming from deep in chest, with tension in this region and impeded respiration. Bubbling in r. side below middle. Oppression, < night, with fluent coryza. Scraping; with rawness and soreness. Rawness, as in catarrh, with increase of the habitual expectoration. Peculiar coldness in r.

Heart.—Twinging stitches, extending outward and downward in region. Palpitation. Pulse slow and weak.

Neck.—Sudden stitches shooting from l. side to muscles on inner side of upper arm; tearing stitches in l. side and posteriorly, in slow jerks, extending to occiput. Tearing in l. side; in l. upper part; in cords, < l.; on r. side, once with pain on pressure; in N. and nape, extending to l. occipital region and drawing down again; shooting cutting, on l. side in muscles, near axis, with painful stiffness of neck; rheumatic, in l. side; superficial tensive, on r. Drawing pain in nape on stooping, as if muscles were tense. Tensive pain in nape, with stiffness. Tensive stiffness in one or another place on nape or side.

Back.—Scapulæ. Stitches between, < respiration; from lower part of vertebra, extending through chest and arresting breath; tensive, in region of lower dorsal vertebra, extending towards loins; burning, between; digging pulsating, in region of tip of l., extending upward and outward below shoulder, chiefly along its inner margin; tearing, in r., across back, as if ulcerated. Tearing in tip of r.; between; between, in spine; between, extending towards loins; below spine of r., extending out to a spot, first noticed on touch at 10 P.M. and lasting next day; in l., extending to shoulder, l. upper and anterior pectoral region, along expansion of pectoral muscles and over forearm and hand. Digging sticking tearing in tip of l. Tensive tearing in r., externally, or rather superiorly, towards shoulder, extending into flesh of upper arm and into l. clavicle and pectoral muscles, in the latter it is irritating, as if muscular fibres were torn, with painful movement of arm. Rheumatic pain just below l., extending into loins. Sudden deep-seated pain at tip of r. when leaning against arm of chair, and along its outer border, extending towards axilla, involving whole shoulder-joint and extending down inner side of arm to elbow, the parts seemed bruised, swollen or suppurating, and the shoulder-joint sprained, on raising the arm the sensation extends into chest and arrests breathing, the pain often extends from r. side of neck, the pain > during rest, < pressure on motion, pain in humerus as if there were something living in it, next day chilliness in affected part, extending into region of kidneys, with goose-flesh. Pain on outer lower margin of r. and in ribs, externally pain when grasped, as if swollen or injected with blood, suppurating. Drawing, and in sides of chest, in region of pectoral muscles. Bubbling on border of r., near axilla, as if a bottle of water were shaken or as if air were forced into the flesh.

Loins.—*Sticking, now in a small spot, now in a larger place, when it is chiefly pressing, either exactly in region of kidneys or extending above or below, but* **especially outward, so that it extends around abdomen in front, or to region of hips,** *sometimes in spine and extending to small of back* **and region of bladder and groins** (Canth.), *the sticking at times extends from region of kidneys straight forward into abdomen, at times with* **numb, paralyzed, bruised sensation. Stitches from kidneys into bladder** (Coc. c.), < severe pressure; *burning, in kidney region; inward in one or other, at times as from a nail and arresting breathing;* in region of r. kidney shooting quickly into outer side of scapula; twinging, obliquely inward and downward in l., in morning on waking, with pressure; pulse-like extending inward in one or other; beginning in lumbar part of spine and extending outward across l. loin. Tearing or tearing sticking, at times only on one side; *T. or tearing sticking, usually more on one side,* **often as if crushed or bruised, with stiffness, making it difficult to rise from a seat,** *so that the hands must assist rising, sometimes involving hip, nates and upper and posterior part of limbs,* **at times with numbness.** *Tearing in morning immediately after rising, extending sideways, forward, upward and downward, affecting whole back between thorax and pelvis, with stiffness in lower part of back if she stooped and difficulty on standing up on account of this stiffness, the tearing when sitting more severe than when standing, > afternoon;* T. anteriorly in region of l. ischium; in r. ischium when sitting, extending to r. side of genitals; superficial, frequently upon only one side. *Tearing, pulsating pain in kidney.* **Pressive or tensive pain** (Rhus t.), **sometimes on one, sometimes on both, or often across small of back, at times extending into posterior part of pelvis, of thighs,** *and even to calves,* **with stiffness and lameness** *or swelling of back and lower limbs,* and warmth in affected parts, at times numbness in them. *Tensive or pressing sensation deep internally, when severe with a feeling as if bone would be pressed asunder,* often with heaviness, warmth, numbness or tingling, < morning on waking and **when sitting and lying** (*Rhus t.*), at times > stool or passage of flatus, sometimes only on one side, < stooping. Pressure before stool, and in anus. Pain, with the morbid urine; P. during menses, and in back; extending to nates and upper posterior part of thigh. Digging or tearing sticking; D. in one or other, or gnawing, as if ulcerating; **sticking, in one or other, or digging tearing,** *as if suppurating, < deep pressure.* Burning itching and burning-digging in one or other, seldom in both, sometimes in region of small of back, generally superficial, or at times deeper, but then sticking or gnawing, *often moving about abdomen.* Tearing dragging, with dragging in anus. Twinging, with desire for stool. Bruised and paralyzed feeling, as after long stooping, often in morning on waking, mostly worse when sitting and lying than when walking. Burning pain, mostly with tension and pressure. Burning tensive pain. Drawing pain in l.; usually one-sided, or pressing, or tearing, or alternating therewith. Drawing in one or other, from nates into thigh. Bubbling, usually only on one side, < lying and rising from a seat; in l., extending across into abdomen and into bladder; below l. ischium, extending inward and downward, as if a worm as large as the finger were forcing its way downward. Tensive stiff feeling, sometimes in morning on waking when lying on back, with numbness of it and with lameness of body. Symptoms worse when stooping and when becoming erect, in sitting and in lying than when standing, though not always.

Clinical.—In lumbago one of our most valuable remedies; pains extend from back around body and down leg, with red and mucous sediment in the urine, etc.

Upper Extremities.—Axilla. Bubbling digging in forepart of r., external to and below head of humerus, with a living movement. Painless bubbling in r., chiefly in forepart, as if something living would bore its way out.

Shoulder.—Tearing sticking; along border of r., then extending quickly down outer side of arm and ending in a stitch in tip of little finger; burning S. in region of r. acromion, extending into it. Tearing in joint, especially in forepart; in l., extending across scapula and down back, < motion; along border of l., extending up side of neck and nape to l. occipital region, where it becomes seated; superficial tensive. *Rheumatic paralytic pain in r.* (Puls., Rhod.), *with stitches over l. eye.* Pain in r. as if it would suppurate. Strained pain externally and posteriorly in l. Pain in l. as if swollen, especially deep in joint in front, as if in head of humerus, < moving arms backward, always noticed on pressure. Corrosive smarting on l.

Arm.—Aching, especially in thick muscles of shoulders, in inner muscles and on inner sides of upper arm, less in forearm. Drawing tension, at times with tearing, often with heaviness and weakness. Weakness, with paralyzed sensation, painful on exertion after violent exercise of arms, with pain in muscles, < motion and pressure.

Upper Arm.—Stitches in thick flesh in front of l.; on inner side just below r. axilla, with burning between the stitches and afterwards; on inner side just below l. axilla, as if a fine splinter were thrust into bone, ending in a long-drawn stitch; twitching, above r. elbow, extending upward; burning, in middle of r.; burning, in thick flesh of r. Tearing in muscles of inner side of r.; on anterior part of l.; in upper and inner part of l., with burning; under skin in outer side of l., extending to middle; in outer middle part of r., extending to bone; in outer part, extending to elbow; deep in l. humerus, extending from inner and anterior part to the elbow, and in radius to wrist and inner side of back of metacarpus, while at work, obliging her to hang the arm down and incline it to the left, with feeling of heaviness and swelling in arm. Forcing tearing inward in l. humerus, behind belly of biceps. Drawing sticking-tearing in flesh below r. shoulder. Drawing tearing at insertion of l. pectoral muscles. Jerking digging tearing in a spot deep in humerus, anteriorly, just below shoulder. Bubbling tearing extending outward, in muscles of inner side of l. Pain in middle and on outer anterior side of l., in vicinity of bone, with heaviness, so that the arm must hang down. Burning pain on inner side of l. below joint, superficial, with intermittent pressure, whereby the arm becomes worse. Drawing pain in outer side of l. Tensive pain in muscles of r.; in l., about middle of forepart and inward on bone, as if something would be pressed loose, so that it is sore as far as the bone. Bubbling anteriorly in r. below shoulder; externally between muscles and bone, below r. joint; externally in muscles in middle of r.; in thick flesh of r. on going to bed; as if muscles were alive.

Elbow.—Crawling sticking in l. Tearing sticking in forepart of r., especially in tendons of muscles, < motion. Tearing in r., extending outward; extending down muscles of flexor surface of radius; in r., extending slowly along outer border of ulna, as if something scraped the bone, and as it were distended, with lameness and heaviness of forearm; drawing, in r., extending to lower part of forearm. Pain in tendon of biceps at bend after lifting or moving arm, < extending it, reaching deep into joint and along radial side of forearm for a way and along outer and posterior surface of upper arm. Burning pain in outer anterior part of l.; as from nettles in r., between olecranon and inner condyle of humerus. Smarting pain; in r. Drawing tensive pain in outer part of l. Tension on flexor surface of l., a few inches on forearm, extending forward, < extending arm.

Forearm.—Lymphatic swelling in flexor tendons on lower and inner border of l. ulna, not very painful on touch, not at all on motion, covered with petechial spots, with burning pain in skin. Stitches in muscles below middle of l. ulna; above r. wrist, extending deep through joint into middle of hand, decreasing and returning; below each other on inner side of r., in muscles and tendons of ulna, extending lengthwise from about the middle anteriorly; lengthwise in muscles of l., slowly penetrating inward along radius; boring, in inner side of r., four inches above wrist, as if a nail were forced into the bone; burning, on dorsal side above wrist; burning, in r. radius, above wrist, extending inward to bone. Tearing, along inner side of r. radius; under skin in flexor surface; inward in l.; in r., chiefly in ulnar part, from elbow into wrist and back again, nearly all night, and the next morning, at the same time extending into posterior lower part of muscles of upper arm, with heaviness and weakness of arm; tensive, aggravated by paroxysms, from l. elbow to ulna, especially in its lower part, deep as if in bone, in evening and next morning, extending to dorsum of hand and metacarpal joints of fingers, with heaviness and weakness of arm, as if it were swollen. Pinching constrictive pain in lower external part of l. Pinching painlike cramp in flexor surface above r. wrist. Pain in extensor surface of r.; in a spot in flexor surface above r. wrist, as if it extended into bones. Drawing pain in l., outward external, in flexor surface, after exertion, and on continued grasping with r. hand pain in flexor muscles and heaviness of hand and forearm. Burning pain in outer side of l.; on outer side of l. radius, some inches below elbow; biting, in middle of outer side of l., then pressive numbness; biting, tearing, in ulnar side of r. Smarting on back, behind l. wrist, < rubbing; or smarting burning pain, in spots, especially on outer side, < rubbing, at times a red spot appears after it. Numb paralyzed pain in extensor surface above l. wrist, deep between long bones, extending into wrist and on motion to elbow, < letting arm hang down, and then the forearm feels as if asleep. Cold sensation like a tearing on anterior margin of r. radius.

Wrist.—Stitch posteriorly in middle of l., extending deep to middle of palm, after exerting hand; burning, in l. external bone, then burning; itching-burning or biting. Tearing; on inner side of l., extending to flexor surface of ring finger, penetrating deep into joint of hand and then a jerking sticking; alternating with T. in hands and fingers; corrosive, on dorsum of r., extending from metacarpal bone of index to its last joint. Gnawing in r. Pain after exertion of hand. Sprained pain in r., chiefly on outer side, extending into hand. Burning pain; on back of l., as from nettles, < rubbing, once extending between metacarpal bones of little and ring fingers.

Hand.—Stitches in outer border of r.; burning, in inner side of metacarpal bone of r. index; burning, in inner side of metacarpal bone of l. little finger; burning, extending inward on back of l., between metacarpal bones of index and middle finger, then burning; sudden, in l. palm, cutting into it from the outer side, shooting back and forth; tearing tensive, in r. palm, in region of metacarpal bone of little finger extending deep towards little finger. Tearing in outer ball of l. palm; along metacarpal bone of l. little finger; in metacarpal bone of l. ring finger, < pressure; along side of metacarpal bone of r. little finger, with heaviness and weakness in outer part of hand; along metacarpal bone of l. index, with pulselike stitches inward in bone; in r. middle metacarpal bone, with pulsations, returning in single tearings; on external margin of r., extending to little finger, affecting the whole hand; in metacarpal bone of r. thumb, backward towards wrist, changing to stitches; wandering, in dorsum, often extending into extensor surface of finger, often ending in stitches in finger-tips; in dorsum, in region of l. fourth and fifth metacarpal bones, changing to gnawing; tingling, in l. as if distended and heavy. Tearing pulsating pain deep in l. palm, in region of metacarpal bone of middle finger. Digging and tingling pain on dorsum of r., beginning in region of first joint of fingers at 9 P.M., > next morning, with heaviness in fingers, so that she must let them hang down. Pain in metacarpal bone of r. little finger; on motion and pressure, extending to neighboring extensor tendons, with swelling of joint of first phalanx. Gnawing smarting on dorsum of l., < rubbing. Smarting burning pain in region between fourth and fifth r. metacarpal bones, < slight touch. Burning pain in dorsum of r.; between metacarpal bones of r. second and third fingers; along metacarpal bone of r. middle finger, with stitches as from insects, the pain spreads on rubbing.

Fingers.—Stitches on dorsum of first phalanx of index; in flexor surface of first joint of l. index; in flexor surface of first part of index; in tips of index and ring F., at times involving other fingers; in ball of first joint of l. little; in ball of r. thumb; in inner surface of r. thumb, sometimes from pressure; inward in middle of flexor surface of first phalanx of l. index. Twitching-cutting stitch extending across from first joint of little F., into palm. Burning stitches on outer side of second joint of r. index; on inner side of second joint of l. index; on inner side of third joint of l. index; in second and third joints of l. little. Biting sticking in ulnar side of second phalanx of r. middle. Itching stitches in region of first joint of l. index, on inner side. Pulselike stitches in tip of r. index. Bubbling stitches in inner side of tip of r. thumb, under nail, as if shooting out from bone. Tearing in joints; in tips, especially of index; on dorsum, now here, now there, chiefly in joints; in second and third joints of r. index; in inner side of joint of l. index; on inner surface of first joint of r. index; in balls of thumbs; along inner surface of r. thumb; especially on dorsum, often with stiffness, especially in index and ring F., often changing to stitches outward in tips of F.; in outer side of l. thumb, as deep as the bone, < pressure, with pulselike stitches inward near joint; from second joint of r. middle, along tendons of wrist; inward under l. thumb-nail; on inside of r. index, as if the flesh were torn from the bone, so that she almost trembled; as if sprained, in first phalanx of r. middle, chiefly in the first joint, < motion and touch, with swelling about the joints, mostly on dorsum and in sides, and in phalanx itself, with cracking of joints on motion; drawing, in second joint of r. index and near it, on the back; tingling, in l. thumb, with feeling as if heavy and distended; burning, in volar surface of first joint of r. thumb; smarting, in outer surface of l. index, < rubbing, and changing to a burning pain. Smarting on dorsa. Pain in second joint of l. index, < bending, with stiffness; in second joint of r. middle, in morning on waking, < at first by pressure, with stiffness; in bone in region of first joint of l. thumb, extending into second joint. Suppurating pain in tip of l. index, < rubbing, most severe under nail, where it seems as if the flesh would be torn loose, with hot sensation and with pain in second joint. Burning pain on dorsum of r. index; in inner side of dorsal surface of r. index; in first joint of l. index, < rubbing, afterwards red pimples; gnawing, as from nettles, in first joint of l. middle, < rubbing; jerking, in outer surface of r. middle, from second joint into nail, as if in bone. Tingling pain in outer side of third phalanx of r. middle; in tip of l. index, as if it would suppurate. Bubbling in ball of r. thumb.

Clinical.—Neuralgia under finger-nails, with swelling of finger-joints.

Lower Extremities.—Bruised pain, so that he cannot rise from a seat without assistance of his hands, with paralyzed feeling in knees, suffering especially along posterior surface from loins and downward, and bruised feeling in calves, the pains < pressure, motion and stooping, at last the pain extends into feet. Drawing-tensive sensation, < rising after prolonged sitting, with superficial tearings and a heavy or stiff paralyzed feeling. Feeling as if becoming emaciated, which really seemed to be the case. Weakness, with bruised sensation, sometimes with stiffness and paralyzed feeling, as after a long march, or as if strained, as if muscles were too thick, usually in soft parts, with pain easily excited by motion. Weakness while walking, so that he scarcely felt them, as if numb. Heaviness, < ascending stairs, especially in thighs, with bruised feeling and lassitude.

Nates.—Sticking; in l. when standing, extending deep into muscles. Tearing; in r. or l. when walking, extending deep into ischium. Burning pain in l.

Thigh.—Tensive contractions of muscles, especially in posterior surface and in calves, < when walking. Stitches inward in middle of posterior or anterior region; inward in posterior and inner side of l., six inches above knee; long-drawn-out S. inward in inner posterior and middle part, in flesh, when walking; long-drawn, in inner posterior side of middle of l. when walking; pulsating inward, in muscles of posterior part of l. when walking and sitting; outward through l., in forepart above middle; externally in middle of l., extending upward; in forepart of l. five inches above knee, extending into flesh, afterwards S. near knee; on inner side of r. above knee, extending obliquely downward to opposite side, <

stepping, when sitting at rest paroxysmal, less sensitive S. Biting stitch in lower and inner part of l. Bubbling stitches above l. knee; in middle of posterior part of l., whereby he thinks he feels a throbbing with the fingers, touch causes continued pain. Burning stitches anteriorly above l. knee; in outer upper side of r.; in outer anterior part of r., below the middle; pulselike, extending downward from r. trochanter, deep inwardly; pulselike, in posterior lower part of r., with pulsation perceptible to finger; tearing, in outer middle region of r., penetrating deep into bone. Tearing in hip-bones of one side near spine; below l. trochanter; on inner side; in thick flesh of l., about middle of forepart; under skin on outer side of l.; in forepart and down over knee; in l. from trochanter to knee when sitting, aggravated by paroxysms; in lower external and anterior part of r. or l. when walking, at last changing to tension; in lower outer side of r. extending across knee into lower part of leg and calf; intermittent, in outer side, sometimes spreading over thigh, < after motion; biting, in inner, upper and anterior part of l. when walking; on outer or inner side, or tearing drawing; in extensor muscles, often after motion, or tearing sticking; in posterior muscles, chiefly about middle, or tearing sticking, or drawing tearing. Pinching in muscles, especially in flexors and in calves; in muscles on violent motion. Pinching-grasping in upper anterior part of r. when standing and walking. Smarting in outer side of r., then in middle of forepart. Gnawing on outer upper part of l.; on posterior surface of l. above hollow of knee; on outer lower part of r., < walking and rubbing; biting, in outer side of l. above knee. Gnawing biting on outer anterior side of l., about middle. Burning pain in region of l. trochanter; in inner anterior side of upper part of r.; on inner side of lower part of l., < touch. Sore pain in bends; in outer anterior side of r. Tension in muscles in upper and anterior part when walking, often changing into pain; T. in thighs and nates from hips downward, with numbness and at times heat; drawing, in posterior muscles. Tensive pain as if muscles were too short, and in calves and knees; in one or other bend when walking, as if tendons were too short; drawing, in tendons when walking, extending over knee-cap; drawing, in muscles of outer side of r., outward and backward, as if cramp would come on. Drawing pain in region of r. trochanter; extending from region of trochanter into thigh; in muscles of r., above knee. Drawing on inner side or drawing tensive sensation or pain. Bubbling anteriorly above r. knee; below nates, slowly working and digging; in muscles of forepart of r., moving here and there, as from something living; anteriorly in r., evenings in bed, extending along thigh, as if a stream of water or blood forced its way through the flesh; painless, in lower part of r., as if a stream of air or a worm as large as a finger forced itself through the flesh. Workings like crawlings or drawings on outer side of l. at night on falling asleep, extending over knee, then cramp in calf, with tingling in it and in the outstretched foot.

Knee.—Swelling of veins near, and in outer posterior upper part of calves. Cramp in l. popliteal space when stepping or stamping, extending into middle of calf and into thigh while standing, when she does not step hard it is less, with tingling and heaviness, as if the parts were enlarged. Stitches through; in l. at night; above patella; above margin of patella on ascending stairs; below margin of l. patella when walking, then burning pain, extending into joint; now in one place, now in another, especially on inner side; backward through r., beneath patella, when walking; in inner side of r. extending outward into tendons; just above patella, deep inwardly, as from a nail, when descending stairs in morning, afterwards a pressure; inward, as from a nail, near lower margin of r. patella on motion, with heaviness in calves; drawing, in hollow of l., extending into upper part of leg, the same pain superficially in inner side of r.; bubbling long-drawn, in tendons of outer side of l. popliteal space when walking and standing. Pain as if inflamed or swollen on inner side of l., near patella, shooting backward into knee, from 4 till 11 A.M., when bending knee, > during rest in an extended position, and through joint beneath patella. Tearing; in r. patella from motion, and in ligament beneath it; in tendons when walking and standing, especially in posterior muscles; superficial, extending down outer side of l. calf; most frequently in inner side, often extending into neighboring parts, or tearing sticking. Pinching in r. popliteal space and in calf when sitting down in evening and when lying, after a moderate walk. Gnawing on outer side of l. knee-pan. Smarting in forepart near patella.

Aching in hollow of l., extending through joint to patella, < bending and extending knee, with feeling as if knee were stiff and swollen and as if tendons were too short. Drawing pain in patella, extending into anterior upper part of leg, < walking. Tensive pain in r. patella after walking, and in ligaments and tendons behind it. Tension, < motion and stretching, now in sides, now in forepart, especially in region of patella, now posteriorly, chiefly in tendons, as if too short, often with sensation of heaviness or paralysis. Drawing burning pain in hollow of r. Weakness during and after walking and on rising after long sitting, with bruised and paralyzed feeling.

Leg.—Sticking near lower part of r. tibia when walking; below r. knee when walking, shooting obliquely upward beneath patella; biting, in middle of outer part of r., < walking and standing; burning, inward externally near l. tibia, a few inches above ankle; intermittent burning, on outer side near middle of l. tibia; tearing, on side between l. tibia and fibula, in extensor muscles, especially in tendons, above joint, extending into external malleolus and outer side of back of foot. Tearing along whole outer side of r., into external malleolus and over outer side of dorsum of foot, then upward along outer side of thigh; intermittent tensive, in outer part of l., a few inches above external malleolus, between tibia and fibula. Corrosive pain on outer side of l.

Tibia.—Stitches in r.; in inner side of l. about middle; inward when walking and standing, seldom when sitting, especially in middle; corrosive, in middle of crest; burning, in lower part of l., in skin on outer side, close to the ridge of the bone, as if it pierced the bone; sudden burning, inward in outer side of l.; burning-itching, on outer side near middle of r.; tearing, outward near middle of l.; tearing, in intermittent twinging jerks, in the middle, as if periosteum would be torn loose. Tearing; in sides; superficial, on side; in places, most frequent in middle, often extending into knee and ankle; down its inner surface when walking, standing and sitting, at times tearing sticking, with pressive, heavy, or bruised or burning sensation, as if the bone would be pressed asunder; tingling, in r., a few inches from joint, extending upward, < pressure. Burning gnawing on inner anterior side below r. knee when walking, < rubbing. Burning smarting in middle of r., < rubbing and motion, changing to sore pain. Tensive aching or pain, with burning or numb sensation, as if bone would be distended, with bruised and heavy sensation in leg, at times bubbling, at times alternating with tearing or sticking or associated with them, and at times on rubbing burning in skin of tibia. Tearing tensive pain in middle, extending to knee.

Calf.—Stitches; now slight, now severe, chiefly in middle, often penetrating deeply; outward above middle of r.; cutting, in outer part of r., near tibia; in upper inner part of l., changing to bubbling, as if a bloodvessel were throbbing under skin; drawing, outward to middle of r.; burning, in middle of l.; burning corrosive, on outer and posterior part of middle of r.; tearing, especially in middle. Tearing in l., extending as far as bones; in places, especially in middle, sometimes extending into tendo-achillis or knee; tensive cramplike, in upper and lower part of r., < walking and standing. Cramplike pain in l. in evening when going to sleep; in upper part of l. evenings on ascending stairs; in r. when walking, with stitches; in l. when sitting, as if muscles were bruised. Biting on outer and anterior part of l. when walking. Smarting burning pain in upper part of r., externally below knee, extending backward and downward over calf, with bruised sensation. Drawing or drawing pain, now here, now there, at times with a feeling as if asleep, heaviness or stiffness. Tensive pain when walking, < rising from a seat. Bruised pain. Bubbling deep in muscles of l.; in outer part of middle of l. in morning in bed. Tingling as from being asleep.

Tendo-achillis.—Lymphatic swelling of l., dusky, pale red, then dusky red spots along tendons, at first violent pain on raising foot, less when stepping upon it, then returning periodically, with sensation as if a weight hung upon foot, > horizontal position, when stretching foot it extended into calf and hollow of knee, with bruised sensation, often with tensive pain, cramp in sole if the foot hangs down, at first flexion almost impossible on account of pain, with sometimes bubbling or tearing or itching, < rubbing, with burning in affected parts, desquamation of skin, chilliness in evening, swelling of affected part of foot after motion and swelling of heel, with burning in it and cramp in foot. Stitches; intermittent, in l. when sitting and hanging foot; paroxysmal, in l. when walking, more posteriorly; burning, in l. Tearing, sometimes extending into foot; sometimes extending into calf, when standing, walking and sitting; sticking, in one or other. Smarting on inner side while sitting, extending to calf. Pain as if strained. Drawing pain or drawing tearing, when standing and walking and afterwards, seldom when at rest. Tensive pain when standing and walking and afterwards, seldom when at rest.

Ankle.—Stitches in anterior region of r. when driving; in inner side of l. on bending joint outward; inward in r. when standing; sudden, in l. when running; burning, in outer anterior part of r., then itching. Tearing extending now upward, now downward; T. in forepart of l., across to inner malleolus and down to sole; in outer anterior part of l., extending into leg and dorsum of foot; tensive, in forepart of l. Gnawing on forepart of r. Smarting. Smarting itching pain in forepart and sides of l.

Malleolus.—Bubbling twitches from l. internal, across over joint, as from something living. Stitches in r. inner, < stepping; on r. external when walking, extending into joint; backward across r. internal; biting, on anterior and outer side of l.; burning, below and in front of l. internal; burning, on l. external, changing to burning-sticking; pulselike inward in l. external, in morning when waking, then single stitches; bubbling, in l. internal, preceded by simple sticking, at last changing to bruised numb pain, with hot sensation on inner side of leg. Tearing in l. external, extending upward into tendons; in l. internal, extending into heel; in l. external, in evening when going to sleep, extending into little toe, with digging, so that he could not move the foot; in l. internal, with sticking inward; in l. internal, changing to burning; almost sticking, from l. upward into neighboring tendons; drawing, in l. external, extending forward and downward; or tearing-tensive or sticking pain. Scraping at external, extending up inner side of r. tibia. Gnawing on r. external; in region above and behind l. external, with sticking. Aching in r. inner; below l. internal when walking, with swelling of ligaments and tendons of this region, extending to inner part of foot, as far as great toe; on touch, in tendons and neighboring parts of bone, in front and above, especially in l., < uncovering, > motion. Burning pain in l. external; above l. external.

Foot.—Stitches in balls; on outer side of dorsum of r. when sitting, leaving pain; inward in middle of outer border of r., repeated on stepping; in middle and outer part of l., as if foot would be nailed down; between l. fourth and fifth metatarsal bones when standing, as if a nail were forced through; pulselike, in r. balls. Tearing in inner border of l.; in middle of dorsum of r. when sitting, extending to middle toes; in balls, mostly of great toe, < stepping; jerklike, in outer border of r., involving the whole metatarsal bone of little toe, while sitting after a walk; at one time drawing, at another tensive, at another sticking-tearing on dorsum, drawing back and forth, at times more severe, often ending in a stitch in tips of toes. Pain in forepart on stretching it. Pain as from chilblains, especially in toes. Corrosive pain anteriorly on inner border of l.; on outer side of dorsum of l. Burning pain on outer side of dorsum of r.; as from nettles on outer border. Tensive pain on dorsum of r., across behind first joint of four outer toes in morning on rising, becoming a sticking on stepping. Sensation in hollow of l., as if tendons were too short, like a cramp, when walking and sitting. Bubbles on dorsum of l., extending towards little toe.

Heel.—Stitches, especially in lower part; from anterior outer part of margin of l. when stepping after a walk; inward across r. when standing; mostly in lower surface, extending deep into bones, < motion and stepping; slow cutting through l.; burning, in inner side of l.; pulselike, inward, especially in lower surface of heel, often changing to stitches; tearing, when walking, < stepping, extending deep into bones, > sitting; tingling-tearing in r., extending deep into bones, as from something alive. Tearing, < stepping. Suppurating sensation, < after long standing.

Sole.—Stitch on inner side of r.; inward at first joint of r. middle toe when standing; in l. behind second toe, changing to bubbling; pulsating inward deep in l., not far from heel; crawling, and on back of first joint of l. middle toes; burning inward in r., behind joint of first toe. Tearing on outer border of r.; in l., and in metatarsal joints of toes; now here, now there, often with crawling motions and heat. Pain in a corn in r. Bruised pain in middle of l., rather externally. Sticking burning pain. Burning sore pain in inner side of l.

Toes.—Stitches in tips, especially of great; in a corn on l. great; in under surface of r. great, when walking; penetrating deeply first joint of l. fourth; on back of metatarsal joint of l. fourth while standing, extending into the toe; in ball of l. great, extending into toe; downward through metatarsal joint of little; inward as from a nail, in ball of r. great; inward and backward in great, a stitch with every step, continuing while at rest; in tips, chiefly of great toes, sometimes inward, sometimes outward. Crawling sticking in r. great. Burning stitches in l. great, extending from ball; or smarting S. on dorsum of second joint of r. second. Twinging, drawing, sticking in r. fourth, extending along dorsum into foot. Jerklike sticking in single; in metatarsal joint of r. great; inward in r. great, < when driving. Pulselike stitches upward in region of first joint of l. third, when sitting; at times inward, at times outward, in great toes. Tearings especially in joints; in all r. when sitting; in ball of r. fourth; in metatarsal joints of single; sticking, in r. great, from second joint to tip, while sitting after a walk; sometimes drawing, sometimes sticking, some burning, in joints on surface and in tips; jerking, in first joint of r. fourth; burning, in ball of little. Tearing-wrenching in r. third and fourth, sometimes with stitches. Digging in r. great, as if it would become inflamed; tearing sticking, in tip of r. great; tingling, in r. great. Suppurating pain in l. second. Intermittent, ulcerative or bruised pain in r. second and third. Bruised sensation in tips of great, at times only on pressure. Sprained pain in metatarsal joints of r., extending into middle of foot, < taking hold of it, with swollen sensation. Tingling pain in r. great, as if it would swell. Burning pain in tip of l. great. Burning, corrosive, or sore pain, especially in two last and great toes, even after a short walk, < tight boots, with redness, as after slight freezing, sometimes the outer border of foot suffers, skin between toes painful to touch, alternating with itching tearing between toes.

Skin.—Swelling of a cutaneous gland below and behind r. ear. Redness of tip of finger and of dorsum of two first phalanges, with itching, as after freezing. Red spots on sides of forehead; dusky, punctiform, mottled, on forepart of l. shoulder, at times smarting; dusky, on forepart of r. shoulder and when grasped pain as after a bruise or like "vibices;" dusky, near external condyle of l. humerus, at times burning and itching as if congested, in the middle of a nettle-rash-like welt; dusky red petechial spots, at times itching or burning, on forearm, at times on dorsum of hand near wrist; smarting, on inner side of l. thigh, the pain < rubbing; painful, in r. cheek in afternoon, then cold sensation, the spot extending over whole face, with heat.

Semi-transparent warts in ball of r. hand; itching wart on outer surface of third phalanx of r. middle finger. Nettle-rash above l. elbow; on dorsum of l. hand, in forepart, between second and third metacarpal bones; on l. arm, just beneath shoulder, then desquamation. Pimples on outer ears; on nose; chin; throat; chest, most on scapulæ; nape, especially near hair; back; shoulders; dorsa of fingers; radial side of r. ring finger; nates; thigh; painful to touch in skin of l. external ear, near head; on tip of r. elbow, much inflamed by rubbing; on dorsum of first phalanx of r. index, as if a wart would form. Pustules, sticking, red, burning-itching or sticking, or gnawing, sensitive to pressure, usually with a red areola, changing to liver spots.

Stitch on posterior, external and upper part of l. upper arm; in inner surface of anterior phalanx of l. index; sudden biting, in flexor surface of l. forearm above wrist; biting-itching, in middle of flexor surface of r. forearm, on radius, becoming a biting-itching. Burning stitch to left of navel; then itching; in middle of r. thigh externally and posteriorly; burning-itching S. on l. heel; itching, now here, now there, on limbs and trunk, waking at night. *Raw feeling around anus, with burning, pain on touch and sensitiveness when sitting*, then a thin scurf on border of anus. Soreness after a long walk. Gnawing, burning, sore pain in r. popliteal space when walking. Pain in a spot in middle of outer and anterior side of r. thigh, then biting stitches. Burning pain in front above middle of r. upper arm; on and near metacarpal bone of l. middle finger; of r. thumb inward; sticking B. pain to right of umbilicus and above it.

Smarting here and there on chest; posteriorly on lower and outer side of r. thigh. Corrosive sensation in region of l. lower orbital margin. Gnawing in upper part of r. side of chest; in a spot above middle of forepart of l. thigh; in upper anterior part of r. thigh; G. in wrists, < rubbing; in calves, < walking. Biting spot on inner and upper side of l. thigh. Biting itching pain on inner anterior part of l. tibia; smarting itching pain on r. upper arm, in middle of outer part, < rubbing; burning, about middle of r. arm, anteriorly and externally. Crawling in first phalanges of four outer l. toes; on toes, with burning, sometimes with stitches.

Itching on chin; in region of one or other inguinal ring; in fossa above l. clavicle; on neck; externally above r. elbow; on flexor surface of l. forearm; on flexor surface, from r. elbow to middle of forearm; in heels; on external surface of lids and on temples and forehead; momentarily > by scratching, which causes redness in region of eye; on knee and thigh in afternoon, > scratching, but returning; on wrists, or biting-itching; in region of tendo-achillis, sometimes burning. Simple I. or biting or burning I. on face, forehead, temples, cheeks, ears, lips and chin; on neck, > scratching but returning; on legs, rapidly changing places. Simple I. or biting, or burning or sticking I. in lumbar region; in calves; in soles; in and around elbow, more on outer side; in various places in thighs, > rubbing, but easily returning; on chest, now in front, now in sides or axillæ, chiefly on scapulæ, > scratching, but returning; on outer ears, with stitches and warm sensation, at times with pimples; in skin of nose, with fine burning or itching stitches and with pimples. Simple I. or burning or biting or crawling or sticking I. in region of shoulder, chiefly on anterior or posterior border of axilla, and in axilla, on dorsum of hand or in palms, > rubbing, soon returning in same or another place. Stitching itching on and behind l. external knuckle; in fingers, or burning sticking I. Biting I. in middle of r. leg externally, near crest of ilium, caused and < by walking; externally in region of elbow, especially above it, > scratching, which causes redness of skin; or burning I. on flexor surface of l. forearm, not far from wrist. Burning itching in lower part of back; on knee, now in front, now behind, now on one side, or I., with stitches. Itching, burning or sticking or biting, on ankles and malleoli, sometimes extending to dorsa and sides of feet. Smarting burning I. on dorsum of l. foot in bed before sleep and during the day when sitting, < scratching, obliging her to seek cold places in the bed for the feet. Itching, either burning, or biting, or sticking, on small of back; on dorsa of feet; in eyebrows, sometimes with burning or burning-itching stitches. Itching on toes, either burning, crawling, biting or burning, or with stitches. Burning scraping I. on r. cheek, in front of ear, down to lower jaw.

Sleep.—Yawning alternating with eructations. Sleepiness during the day, < morning and after dinner. Sleep unusually long, till after 7 A.M., with a weary and bruised sensation and with pain in head and small of back. Difficult waking in the morning, when she cannot collect her thoughts.

Sleeplessness till 2 A.M. Restless sleep, disturbed by dreams; disturbed by itching burning or by anxious dreams. Frequent waking in an unusual position on l. side; frequent and easy W. about 2 to 4 A.M., with inability to sleep again although tired, or if he falls asleep he wakes again, with tension in head, rush of blood to it and excitement. Condition between sleep and waking at night, in which she is tormented by a system of education, which at times assumes the form of a tree, at another some other wonderful form, she tries in vain to get rid of the image, to rouse herself from slumber, to open the eyes, and is fretful about it.

Fever.—Chilliness in morning from 11 o'clock; in evening, then heat, with thirst; before dinner; < before dinner, with cold feet, dryness and stickiness in mouth, without thirst, with pain in region of l. tonsil. Shivering C., then heat. Creeping C., < going into cold air; even shivering in various parts, < forenoon and evening, especially beginning in face and arms and extending over back and chest, then heat, with anxiety and oppression of chest.

Peculiar cold sensation in r. temple. Frequent C. in head in morning, with cold feet, confusion of head, headache as before coryza, frequent heat of head, the hands being cool. Coolness in cheeks, with heat in head. Cold spot in l. side of neck, becoming a burning. Chilliness in back; in upper part of r. side of B., with painless tearing; alternately on back, outer side of arms and in calves, in forenoon, in afternoon burning stitches, < at night, with vertigo, sticking in head and angina, then sweat of a urinous odor. Intermittent, in back in evening before sleep, and posteriorly on arms, extending to hips, after the second attack swelling of l. tendo-achillis. C. in hands, feet and whole body from 11 o'clock on, with heat in face and warm feeling in hands. C., almost tearing, on front of r. tibia. Cold sensation behind l. external malleolus, with painless tearing. Cold spot on skin below r. nates; on upper outer part of l. leg; above l. internal malleolus.

Feeling as if spattered with cold water on face on going into open air; on dorsum of hand on going into open air; in inner anterior part of l. thigh; below l. calf; on posterior lower part of r. thigh while walking, or as if touched by cold metal. Sensation as if ice-water touched outer side of l. leg not far from knee. Sensation as if posterior part of l. thigh, about five inches from joint, were touched by something cold in morning after rising and next day at noon. Creeping coldness on outer side of thigh as from quicksilver running on or beneath skin, < standing, seldom when sitting, sometimes with tension in muscles or a stitching, though painless, at times ending in burning. Sudden sensation in upper and forepart of r. thigh as if a cold animal, aboul the size of a lizard, lay on the skin.

Heat; in afternoon, with tendency to sweat; at 6 P.M., then cool sensation; < evening and night, with tendency to sweat; with sweat breaking out on motion, standing, etc., then about 6 P.M. chilliness; in head; face; on outer part of l. thigh; on posterior upper part of thigh; in head and hands in afternoon; H. in head excited by touch; in head after eating and afternoons, the head sweats easily on exertion, stooping, standing, etc.; on dorsum of first joint of l. great toe while sitting; H. in soles, < evening. Heat in face, with redness; in cheeks, with redness; in face, with coldness of other parts; in face, more subjective than objective, with redness of cheeks; in l. outer ear, then coldness of same and of temples. *Warmth in lower part of back and in small of back, as if loins were distended or asleep, extending into small of back, hips and posterior part of thighs.*

Burning in outer anterior part of l. elbow, in skin and deep in flesh and extending outward; in styloid process of r. radius, with a red spot, becoming larger on rubbing; between r. thumb and index, then a red spot after rubbing. Warmth in palms, often with itching and crawling, as in chilblains; W. on posterior lower part of l. thigh, extending into upper part of calf. Cold burning on l. side of chin. Tensive burning in l. upper part of neck, with stiffness. Biting burning on inner side of r. knee. Corrosive burning on outer anterior side of dorsum of l. foot. Burning as from nettles on dorsum of second joint of r. ring finger; in second joint of l. index, < bending, with stiffness. Tingling warmth in feet; in legs, as after rubbing with woolen cloths, < sitting; T. in soles, at times crawling, often at the same time in toes and on back of foot; as in frozen feet.

Sweat after midnight, waking her frequently; on exertion, < afternoon, with anxiety; cold, on face.

Bismuth.

The precipitated subnitrate is triturated with Sacch. lac. for use.

General Action.—The chief action of Bismuth is manifested in the alimentary canal, causing irritation and catarrhal inflammation.

Affinities.—Puls., (Arsen. in part), Colch.

Generalities.—Swelling of face, hands, tongue and abdomen. Lying upon his back at night. Spasmodic contraction of voluntary muscles, especially of lower limbs. Faintness. *Weakness.* Some relief from loose stools.

Mind.—Delirium. *Morose, discontented and complaining about his condition.* Ill-humored all day, > in evening, and will not talk. Solitude unendurable. Restless peevishness. Begins one thing, then another, but keeps to one thing only a short time.

Head.—Aching; burning contractive, especially in forehead and eyes. *Pressive drawing now here, now there;* < motion. *Confusion;* on rising. Heaviness. Vertigo; in morning; on violent motion; *in attacks, as if anterior half of brain were turning in a circle;* as if brain were turning in a circle.

Forehead.—Tearing above r. inner canthus and in back part of orbit. *Cutting above r. orbit, extending to occiput.* Digging and boring in F., eyes and in nose down to tip, an alternately contracting and distending sensation. Boring-outward pain in eminences, at times in r., at times in l., sometimes in both. *Pain; < motion, with heaviness; heavy,* when sitting, especially above root of nose and in temples.

Tearing in r. temple, especially externally, < pressure. Pressure outward in temples. Twitching-tearing in whole l. occipital bone, more violent close to parietal bone. *Pressure in occiput, < motion, with heaviness.*

Clinical.—Violent neuralgic headaches which alternate with gastralgia, the pains in the head involve the face and teeth, < eating, > cold, feeling as if the parts were torn by pincers (Puls.).

Eyes.—Redness, with dim vision; R. of conjunctiva. *Pressure backward and upward on r. eyeball. Mucus in canthi.*

Ears and Nose.—Tearing in external cartilage of E. > pressure. Drawing pressure in l. external meatus. Roaring in E. Dryness of nose.

Face.—Pallor, with coldness of whole body. Earthy-colored, with blue rings around eyes and features changed as if he had been sick. Pressure in r. malar-bone at regular intervals.

Mouth.—Drawing pressure in back teeth, extending into front teeth, with drawing pain in cheeks. Gums swollen, sore and painful, with soreness of whole interior of mouth; blackish-blue seam on gums. Tongue coated; white; *coated white in evening without heat or thirst* (Puls.); under surface, tip and borders discolored. Salivation. Taste offensive; *nauseous metallic* (Puls.); *metallic, sweetish-sour, on back of tongue; bitter;* bloody, in morning, and the mucus hawked up is colored with blood.

Throat.—Uvula, palate, arches of fauces and inside of cheeks discolored. Inflammation, with pain and inability to swallow; I. of fauces and uvula, with burning in throat, difficult swallowing and thirst. Gangrene of œsophagus, epiglottis and larynx.

Stomach.—Appetite lost. Thirst; *for cold drinks in evening without heat* (Puls.). *Eructations of wind; after drinking water;* **frequently empty, with discomfort in stomach** (Puls.), then liquid stool, but not bilious; violent E., with griping in bowels and sudden bilious vomiting; acid and bitter. Hiccough. *Nausea; < after eating; with pressure in stomach;* with bilious vomiting. Vomiting; with diarrhœa, retching and burning in throat; violent, of brownish matter, with profuse diarrhœa. *Pressure; < after eating* (Ars.); *in region; in region, with burning* (Ars., Colch.); *changing to burning. Discomfort.* Tenderness of epigastrium (Ars.). *Gastro-enteritis* (Ars.). Oppression of epigastrium, with constriction.

Clinical.—Gastric catarrh, with terrible gastralgia, the pain extending from the stomach through the body to the spine. The gastric disorders requiring Bismuth vary, but usually are burning, with a feeling of a load or hard lump in stomach (compare with Abies); vomiting of food and of mucus; gastric symptoms > cold drinks (Puls.). Very valuable for inflammation of the stomach occurring during the progress of chronic diseases, for instance, scirrhus. A marked indication for Bismuth is that while taking cold drinks there is relief, yet when the stomach becomes full there is vomiting of enormous quantities.

Abdomen.—Rumbling, with eructations; R. in r. side when standing; in lower. *Frequent passage of flatus;* passage of much F., then thin bilious stool. Griping, then two liquid bilious stools. Colic. *Pinching in lower, with rumbling and urging to stool; P. now here, now there, in lower, also with rumbling and grumbling.* Burning and shooting pain in various parts. Discomfort now here, now there, in lower, with pressure.

Stool and Urinary and Sexual Organs.—Ineffectual straining at stool in evening. Liquid, bilious stools; L. frequent, with griping. *Micturition frequent, with copious watery urine.* No urine was passed, and the region of the bladder was not distended. Urine contained albumen and casts. Aching in r. testicle, < touch. Emission of semen at night, without voluptuous dreams.

Clinical.—Painless diarrhœa, with great thirst. Cholera infantum, with tongue thickly coated white, vomiting, etc.

Respiratory Organs.—Difficult breathing. Cough disturbing him in sleep at night, with profuse expectoration, and cough by day.

Chest.—Stitches in middle of sternum; (pinching, in region of both nipples); tearing, in region of nipples (apparently superficial in lungs and at the same time in pectoral muscles), at times < when inspiring or expiring. Tearing around and near l. nipple; sticking; in region of last ribs. **Pinching in region of diaphragm, extending transversely through chest,** *when walking.* Pain in spot in r. side near sternun, more severe at times; *in C. and back, a burning and boring;* near upper, extending inward towards sternum. Oppression. Burning contraction, so that it is difficult to breathe or speak.

Heart and Pulse.—Severe beating of H. Pulse rapid; at midnight, and spasmodic; and hard, small; and contracted; and small, tense; and hard, full. Pulse spasmodic; and tense; and tense, small. Pulse small; and intermittent.

Neck and Back.—Tensive pressure on r. side, in cervical vertebræ. Twitching sensation in muscles of r. side of N. Sharp pressure on upper border of r. scapula and clavicle. Pain in l. side of back when sitting, as after long stooping. Intermittent stitches on lowest l. ribs at their union with dorsal vertebræ.

Extremities.—Spasms. Cramps in hands and feet. Tearing in r. shoulder-joint. (Spasmodic) contractive tearing in muscles of r. arm. *Paralytic weakness of r. arm.* Paralytic pressure in forepart of r. upper arm. Spasmodic contractive pain in anterior muscles of l. upper arm during complete rest of body.

Forearm.—*Paralytic tearing in r., especially in bones of wrist; in r., towards outer side, at times more in upper part,* at times more in lower part, > motion and touch. Cutting tearing in muscles of lower part of r. Pressure on l., more in lower and outer part. Grumbling pain in bones of l. as if bruised.

Tearing in bones of l. wrist; in bones of r., > motion; upon and around r. styloid process, extending into muscles of hands, more violent in the process itself; *in metacarpal bones of r. index and middle fingers;* itching, in inner processes of both hands. Trembling of hands when eating. Weakness of hand, with trembling. *Tearing in tips of r. fingers, especially under nails;* in tips of r. fourth and fifth fingers; in last joints of l. fingers; intermittent, in ball of l. thumb.

Lower Extremities.—Intermitting pressure above l. knee, towards outer side. Drawing in middle of calf and in anterior part of l. leg, down into foot. Drawing in r. external malleolus, > on motion. Tearing below r. external malleolus, terminating every time in tendo-achillis; in l. heel; on r. heel near and on tendo-achillis; between two last l. metatarsal bones, close to toes, while sitting; in last phalanges of l. toes; in tip of l. great toe.

Skin.—*Itching erosion near tibia and backs of feet near joints, < scratching.*

Sleep.—*Sleepiness mornings a few hours after rising, but inability after eating to take his accustomed nap;* S. in forenoon during work, he reads without knowing what, falls asleep and has vivid and confused dreams. *Restless sleep; on account of voluptuous dreams, without, but oftener with, emission of semen. Frequent waking, with weariness; frequent W. as from fright.* Startings in evening slumber as if he fell. Vivid, anxious dreams.

Fever.—Cold limbs. Heat; in flushes through whole body, in morning after rising, especially on head and over chest; of head, with confusion of it. Sweat < at night, with burning in skin.

Boracicum Acidum.

For internal use a solution of the crystals may be made (1 to 99), or a trituration for the first decimal.

General discomfort, > walking. Confusion of head in morning on waking. Gastric headache. Much cold saliva. Hawking. Nausea, > walking in open air, with heaviness in stomach. Retching, with vomiting of tough mucus and alkaline fluid. Heaviness and restlessness in stomach till dinner. Rumbling in abdomen in afternoon and two scanty, pasty stools. Pasty stool. *Pain in region of ureters. Frequent urging to urinate.* Copious urine. On r. thigh vesicles, which continually extended and became covered with crusts, in middle, a spot surrounded by new vesicles, which were moist when broken, afterwards this eruption extended to r. leg, then passed over to l. leg.

Clinical.—A solution of Boracic acid is frequently used as an injection in chronic cystitis, with marked benefit.

Borax.

Dilutions are made from a solution composed of one part dissolved in ninety-nine parts of distilled water.

General Action.—A tissue remedy, allied to the Potashes and to Silicea. Its action on mucous membranes is marked by a tendency to aphthous ulceration (compare Mercury). The peculiar nervous phenomena are very characteristic and unlike any other remedy.

Study in close relationship *Silicea.*

Generalities.—*The infant becomes pale and nearly earthy-colored, flesh soft and flabby, cries much, refuses the breast and screams out anxiously in sleep.* General trembling, especially in hands, while meditating at his work, with nausea and weakness of knees. Restlessness; while eating, > stretching backward, with nausea; after animated conversation, with nausea, stupefaction and vertigo.

Weakness; with heaviness of feet; with indolence, fretfulness, thirst after the midday sleep, heat when walking in open air, sweat on head and face, confusion of head, pressure in forehead and eyes, which pain on touch as if sore, inclination to breathe deeply, and when doing so sticking in intercostal muscles, with hard, quick pulse; of joints; especially in abdomen and limbs.

Mind.—Violence; with scolding and swearing at trifles. *Fretfulness;* every day at 4 P.M.; *in afternoon before the easy stool, with indolence and discontent, after it liveliness, contentment and cheerfulness in regard to the future;* F., with whining and crying. Irritability during important business. Crying violently at intervals (in a child).

Anxiety increased till 11 P.M., *with sleepiness,* then vertigo and sleep; *A.* (*in a child*) *when dancing and if rocked in the arms* **anxious expression of face during the downward motion;** *on riding down hill, feeling as if it would take away his breath;* with rumbling in abdomen. *Fright, with starting at a distant shot; with starting in every limb on hearing an anxious cry; (in a baby) at hawking and sneezing; on waking, the rustling of a paper or dress or the slamming of a door would cause the child to start, scream and seem badly frightened,* **when laying her down she would start and throw up her hands as if afraid of falling,** *and some nights they could not put her down at all.* Fear of contagion.

Idling through the afternoon, changing from one business to another and from one room to another. Disinclination to work. Earnestness. Liveliness in forenoon, with affectionate mood and desire for work. Voluptuous mood. Vanishing of thoughts. Obliged to reflect long before he can remember what he has done through the day, and for a long time is uncertain whether he was at a place yesterday or to-day.

Clinical.—Extreme anxiety, especially in children, especially from motions which have a downward direction, rocking, being carried down-stairs or laid down, there is starting as in great fright; this dread of a downward motion is extremely characteristic of the drug.

Head.—Aching in morning, especially in forehead; *at* 10 A.M., *with nausea and trembling in whole body;* evenings, with confusion of head and sticking in l. ear. Throbbing during menses, with roaring in ears. Lightness, clearness. Confusion on waking. Heaviness. Fulness in morning, > after walking in open air, with lack of clear ideas, of presence of mind and of desire for mental work, leaving weakness in feet and joints; F. on ascending a mountain or steps; with pressure about eyes as if held fast, so that he can scarcely move them; with pressure in small of back when sitting and with sleepiness in eyes. Vertigo in morning in bed; in morning, with full feeling in forehead, so that he lost his good humor; in evening when walking, as if some one had pushed him from r. side towards l.; in attacks, with loss of presence of mind.

Forehead.—Sticking over eyes and in temples, alternating with heat and coldness, so that one time the hands were hot, at another blue, with sticking in the swollen glands of the neck, which afterwards became softer and smaller. Aching; in evening, with sticking in l. ear and in a l. lower hollow molar; above eyes, > walking in open air; intermittent, above eyes. Drawing pain extending towards eyes; above eyes and towards root of nose, at times extending into nape, and on stooping pressure in frontal bone, when reading and writing the pain becomes more violent, with pressure in region of spleen. Twitching pain in afternoon, with nausea and tearing in eyeballs. Throbbing.

Temples.—Sticking in r.; from r. T. to l. half of forehead; rhythmical, in r. Throbbing; throbbing pain, < r.

Vertex.—Stitches in l., then in genitals, and the next night lascivious disgusting dreams (in a married woman). Tearing in forenoon, with roaring in ears. Boring in a small spot near V. Pain in evening, and in forehead.

Stitches deep in r. side, with discharge of pus from r. ear and tickling in l. ear as before a discharge, then acute hearing. Throbbing pain in occiput as if suppurating, with general shivering. Pulsating rush of blood to occiput. *Hairs tangled at tips, so that they cannot be separated* (*in a child*), *as in Plica Polonica, and if these bunches are cut off they form again.*

Eyes.—Stitches in l. in evening. Sensation as if something were penetrating them, > rubbing. Cutting lengthwise in l., coming and going suddenly. Pain as if it would be pressed into the orbit, in morning. Itching, with sensation of sand in them. Pressive burning in r. in afternoon. Burning as soon as he put on the glasses, with contraction. Lachrymation. Stitches in ball, with contraction of upper lid. Tearing in balls, with twitching in forehead and nausea in afternoon.

Lids.—*Lashes turn inward towards eye and inflame it, especially at outer canthus, where the margins of lids are very sore.* Great redness around eyes when crying (in an infant). Agglutination in morning, and lachrymation; A. at night, with hard mucus, which irritates the eyes like sand. Inflammation of margin in an infant, he rubs them, and at night they are agglutinated. Aching in upper on opening. Sensation in r. when sitting as if something pressed outward from between the skin coming from temples, then pressure around eyes. Difficulty in closing in evening and difficulty in opening in morning.

Canthi.—*Inflammation of r. outer, with irregularity of lashes, and at night agglutination of eyes; I. of l. inner,* with nightly agglutination. Soreness in outer. Itching in inner.

Sensitiveness to candle-light in evening. Vision obscured in l. eye in evening. *Vision of bright waves moving now from r. to l., and now from above downward, mornings when writing.*

Clinical.—Inflammation of the edges of the eyelids, which turn inward towards the ball, so that the lids rub against the ball, entropium.

Ears.—Purulent discharge preceded by itching in occiput; P. discharge, with sticking headache; with hot inflamed swelling. *Stitches; in l.;* in l. on waking unusually early; in morning when washing in cold water. Pain internally, with pressure behind r.; sore pain on boring in with finger. Itching in l. in evening when walking, and sore pain after removing earwax, and at same time sticking in l. side of neck. Sudden sensation as if enveloped or stopped. Difficult hearing in l. (in a child). *Roaring* and difficult hearing; R. in r., with ringing. Ringing in r., with piping, changing to roaring. Rushing in l. as from a storm. Drumming in l. as over a subterranean vault. Crackling in l. in evening, as if thick wax stopped the ear, which then opened again.

Nose.—(*Red and shining swelling, with throbbing and tensive sensation.*) *Ulceration superiorly in l. nostril towards tip, with sore pain and swelling of tip* (Aur., Kali). Itching internally, with crawling. The infant rubs his nose vigorously, then his eyes. Sneezing, with great pain, causing stitches in r. side of chest; S., with fluent coryza. *Dry crusts in nose constantly.* Fluent coryza, with crawling in nose. Discharge of much greenish thick mucus. Bleeding; in morning, and pulsating headache in evening; on blowing nose, preceded by itching in nose.

Face.—*Pale, earthy* (*in an infant*), *with suffering expression.* Flushed. Expression of fear or suffering whenever lifted up or put down in bed. Swollen, with pimples on nose and lips; S., hot and red, with tearing in malar-bone, and pain in the swelling when laughing. Twitching of muscles near r. corner of mouth. Feeling of cobwebs on r. side by the mouth.

Lips.—Red inflamed swelling on lower, with burning soreness when touched. Large herpetic spots upon mouth, and after burning heat the upper lip became scurfy. Pain in corners as if they would ulcerate. Burning pain in lower in evening. Burning below l. nostril in morning in bed. Crawling as from beetles.

Clinical.—Erysipelas of face, with feeling of cobwebs on it.

Mouth.—Teeth. A piece broke out of a hollow one. Sticking in a l. lower hollow back tooth in evening, with sticking in l. ear and pain in forehead; intermittent, mostly in a l. lower hollow back T. Tearing in upper hollow, with griping and sensation as if enlarged, so that she cannot bite nor clench the teeth, with inflammation and swelling of gum, as if a gumboil would form, in the evening the pain extends into lower teeth, > going to sleep; T. in hollow, extending into l. half of head; from hollow into half of head if touched with the tongue or if cold water is taken into mouth; in hollow, extending into l. cheek, with pressure in forehead and eyeballs. *Griping in hollow, in rainy weather;* constrictive, in hollow. Aching in hollow, in bad weather; in upper hollow, with swelling of cheek, which pains as if tense when touched; drawing. Boring in hollow in cool evening air. Digging after every supper and breakfast, > tobacco-smoking. Elongated sensation. Crawling in upper and lower incisors, with tickling, then salivation.

Gums.—*Painful gumboil on outer side, with pain in a hollow tooth, and with swelling of cheek and whole l. side of face, as far as below eye, where there was an œdematous swelling* (the pain > smelling of chamomilla). Swelling, with pressure in hollow teeth in bad weather. Bleeding of upper.

Tongue.—*Aphthæ. Red blisters, as if skin were eroded, with pain on every motion of tongue and on touch of anything salt or sour.* Dryness in afternoon. Cramp, as if stiff and asleep, so that breathing is impeded.

Palate (of an infant) *wrinkled,* and **frequent crying when nursing.** *Mucous membrane of forepart of palate shrivelled, as if burnt, with pain, < chewing. Aphthæ on inside of cheek; bleeding when eating.* Membrane of hard palate pinched and dry, with a few small erosions. **Mouth of an infant very hot** (Kali, Sil.). Slimy mouth. Copious, cold saliva. Taste, *bitter, if she eats anything or swallows saliva everything tastes bitter; insipid;*

lost, to food; lost, to soup, at dinner, and the soup causes sweat.

Clinical.—Aphthous sore mouth, the ulcers bleed on eating or on touch; mouth very tender in nursing children; mouth is very hot, with thirst and vomiting.

Throat.—Mucus, which he must expectorate. Hawking of lumps of mucus in morning. *Tough, whitish mucus, difficult to loosen.* Tough mucus, difficult to loosen; causing vomiting. Hawking of green, loose mucus. Hawking of a piece of blood-streaked mucus. Roughness; in morning. Rawness in pit, > hawking up mucus, with drawing stitches when coughing and sneezing. Dryness. Burning, causing him to swallow saliva, which is painful.

Stomach.—Appetite increased for breakfast; in evening. Hunger, without real appetite. Little appetite; in evening; especially for supper. Appetite lost for dinner; evenings, with nausea, drawings from vertex to temples and drawings from abdomen towards groin. No desire for tobacco. Thirst in morning, he must drink much. Longing for sour drinks.

Hiccough after eating; H. (in an infant); which makes the throat raw. Nausea; in morning, > after dinner; in morning, with faintness; at noon, at the thought of food, with coldness, drawing headache and pain in abdomen, > diarrhœa; in afternoon, with faintness; every day from 3 P.M. till evening, with pain in sternum; while eating; after waking, and on drinking water difficult, copious vomiting of mucus and some bitter substance; periodical. Vomiting when riding; V. of a tough fluid; of mucus, with heat and rapid, feverish pulse; of sour mucus after breakfast (of coca).

Distention after eating, > in evening on going into open air, *with discomfort, sick feeling and ill humor.* Sticking in pit, with oppression of chest, which impels him to take a deep breath, but he cannot do it on account of pinching in r. side of chest. *Pain in region after lifting something heavy* (before menses), *the pain goes into small of back, where it becomes sticking, so that she cannot turn without pain the whole night, > in morning;* P. as from bad digestion, on external pressure on pit. Pressure after every meal; in pit after eating pears, especially in morning or forenoon, with discomfort; in pit, > walking.

Constriction in pit; in region every day from 4 A.M. till noon, a kind of winding-up sensation, which extends to spine, where it causes sticking. Tightness in pit when sitting stooped, extending into chest, impeding respiration and causing sticking in lung. Fulness after eating apples and mutton, with ill humor and with fulness in head, as if the blood forcibly pressed into it. Heaviness, > walking in open air.

Abdomen.—Distention after supper; D., especially in epigastric region; *flatulent, after every meal.* Flatulence. Rumbling; at night, > passing flatus upward and downward; after dinner, with diarrhœa. Emission of flatus. *Pinching; with diarrhœa.* Griping, with shivering and gooseflesh. *Pain as if diarrhœa would result;* after eating, > after midday nap. Weakness.

Hypochondria.—Cutting in r. after breakfast, extending downward across through abdomen, then sudden diarrhœa; C. in l. on walking rapidly, as if a hard, sharp, movable piece were there, with sensation in abdomen as if only hard pieces were in it much mixed up. Pressure in l.; from lowest ribs to hipbone, after midday sleep till evening, < external pressure; in l., sometimes with a burning and with a sensation on deep breathing as if something rose into chest, which sank down again on expiration; in l. as with hands, when riding in a carriage without springs; in l. as from a stone, when dancing, > continued dancing.

Pressure as from a stone in r. flank (after menses), extending to scapula, from which place it extends spasmodically into stomach and small of back, then vomiting. Pinching constrictive pain above navel every morning, obliging her to bend double, then it ceases. Spasmodic dragging in hypogastric region during menses, with shooting.

Rectum.—Stitches in evening. Contraction, with itching. Desire for stool in morning, stool at first hard, then diarrhœa-like, with burning in anus; frequent desire, with rumbling in abdomen and diarrhœa; frequent desire, with pinching in abdomen and easy pasty stool. Feeling as if diarrhœa would come on, after smoking.

Anus.—A swollen vein as large as a quill, painless, soft to touch. Brown mucus after stool. Boring-sticking, and in small of back. Itching in evening; I. as from hæmorrhoidal mucus.

Stool.—Soft, light yellow, *three times a day, with weakness. Diarrhœa; six times from morning till* 2 P.M., *without pain;* in morning, then usual stool in evening; immediately after eating, with weakness in joints and legs, which is > by walking; with rumbling in abdomen; then no stool for several days, afterwards a hard stool daily; sudden, with rumbling and grumbling in abdomen. Slimy stool every hour. Like yellow water. Watery, greenish, with some mucus, crying out during each evacuation. Constipation, with fæces like sheep-dung. Hard in morning, then diarrhœa in afternoon, with much wind; H., with straining. Two scanty, pasty. *Green (in an infant), preceded by crying. Frequent; and easy;* F. diarrhœa after breakfast. Pale mucus passes four times, with the stool once involuntarily. Reddish liquid mucus with the stool. Tenacious, glutinous, yellowish mucus with the stool. Passage of blood and mucus from anus, after diarrhœa. Passage of round worms.

Clinical.—Diarrhœa in nursing infants, offensive, preceded by colic, stools mucous, with aphthous sore mouth, screaming before urinating, etc.

Urinary Organs.—*Urging to urinate; several times at night;* after an emission, and on urinating cutting in urethra; *ineffectual,* with cutting in genitals and distention in hips. *Frequent micturition; (in an infant)* **often with cries before the urine passes** (Nux v.).

Urethra.—Dark blue spots at orifice, as if skin were off, with biting pain on urinating. Orifice seems agglutinated. *Smarting after urinating;* < touch. Cutting during involuntary emission of such thin semen that he thought he urinated. *Pain in orifice as if sore, after urinating.* Burning tension after urinating.

Urine hot, in an infant (Canth.). *Pungent smell to urine* (Benz. ac.).

Clinical.—Children are afraid to urinate, almost have convulsions when the desire to urinate comes.

Sexual Organs.—Sticking sore pain on penis at margin of place where a chancre formerly existed, < touch. Tensive erection in morning on waking. Excitement, without desire for coition. Sensual sensations while resting his hands in a kind way on a sick woman, without desire for coition. Indifference to coition. Rapid emission, with dream of coition, waking him. Emission very soon on coition and continual irritation in genitals. Obliged to wait long during coition for discharge of semen.

Easy conception. Sensation of distention in clitoris at night, with sticking. **Leucorrhœa like the white of an egg, with sensation as if warm water were flowing**; *as thick as paste and white* (Aur.); white, like mucus, fourteen days after menses. Sticking in region of uterus. *Menses too soon;* and *very profuse, with griping in abdomen, nausea and pain in stomach extending into small of back,* which lasted till midnight, then sweat; and preceded in evening and morning by heaviness on chest, with difficult breathing and roaring in ears. M. delayed, pale at first, redder in afternoon and more profuse, ceased on third day in the night and returned on the fourth. M. very scanty for two days, then profuse and pale red from third to sixth day, with weakness, M. omitted in second month, but after dose of Borax in the sixth week appeared next day, with pinchings in abdomen.

Clinical.—Dysmenorrhœa, extreme pain during the menses; membranous dysmenorrhœa (Acetic ac.). Leucorrhœa preceding and following the menses, albuminous and acrid. Very valuable for inflammation of mucous membrane of the vagina and uterus, endocervitis.

Respiratory Organs.—Tearing in larynx in evening; in larynx, extending into chest, provoking cough. Cough at night; C., with scraping in throat and pressure in chest. Dry cough from tickling in throat; from scraping in throat. Dry hacking in a child. *Dry cachectic cough, as in old people, < morning on rising and evening on lying down, with sticking in r. side of chest and r. flank* (Kali c.), *the pains < wine, > washing chest in cold water. Hacking and violent cough* in evening, *and with every paroxysm of cough expectoration of* **mouldy taste and smell** *from chest.* Cough, with difficult expectoration of white *mucus streaked with blood.* C., < morning, with expectoration of mucus and with pain in liver, which continues, but without cough, till noon.

Necessity every three or four minutes to take a quick deep breath, which is every time followed by a stitch in r. side of chest, with a subdued painful sigh and slow expiration. Arrest of breath when lying, he is obliged to jump up and catch for breath which causes a stitch in r. side of chest (Kali c.). Respiration short after ascending steps, so that he cannot speak, and every time he speaks a **stitch in r. side of chest** (Kali c., Merc. s.), the same on running or on any other exertion which heats him. Difficult R.; with necessity to breathe deeply, which he cannot do on account of stitches in chest.

Chest.—Milk increased. Milk flows, so that the bed is wet; M. which flows from the breast is curdled. **Stitches with every cough** (Merc. s.) **and deep inspiration** (Kali. c.); *S. when yawning; in region of r. nipple in evening with every paroxysm of cough; between r. ribs, < lying on r. side, with drawing and obstruction of breathing;* on sternum after dinner, < deep inspiration; in r. side if he raises the arm, with drawing; in l. ribs, with soreness internally in chest; as from incarcerated flatus; in l. on every inspiration, as with a knife; drawing, in r. intercostal muscles, waking him as soon as he turns upon r. side, obliging him to sleep on l. side; drawing, in r., extending into r. flank, where it is < by hiccoughing, sneezing, coughing and yawning.

Griping in l. breast, sometimes with stitches, and when the child has nursed, necessity to compress the breast because it aches on account of being empty. Pain; *in r. when coughing, > pressure, and in r. flank;* > walking slowly about the room; in side, > holding it with the hand; at night in pectoralis major, as from a hard bed, with soreness on touch. Drawing pain in r. intercostal muscles if he bends forward and to the right; in a spot in intercostal muscles, which changes on bending to the left into a pain as from a blow. *Contractive pains in l. breast when the child nurses the r.* Contraction at every attempt to breathe.

Oppression in evening in bed. Heaviness preventing breathing. Tightness, with constrictive oppression of breath on ascending steps, he is then obliged to take a deep breath, which is accompanied every time by a drawing stitch in r. side of chest. Feeling as if the heart were on the r. side and were squeezed. Weakness, with dryness in throat. Feeling better when lying quietly stretched out on back.

Clinical.—Pleurodynia or true pleurisy in upper part of r. chest, with cough, expectoration of a mouldy smell.

Neck.—Rheumatic drawing pain in nape in evening when walking in open air, extending into l. shoulder and then into scapula.

Back.—Stitches in evening, extending into chest. Pressive pain on both shoulders. Stitches in r. lumbar region, < in morning by stooping while walking, > sitting. Pain in small of back; when stooping; when walking; with mucous discharge with the stool; when sitting and stooping, as from pressure. Pressure in kidney region, < turning, with sticking.

Upper Extremities.—Stitches in r. shoulder. Drawing and tearing in shoulder and between shoulders, so that he cannot stoop. Burning pain in upper arm a hand's breadth around the whole arm. Sticking in palm in evening, with feeling in whole hand, extending above wrist, as if asleep. Tearing in forepart of r. hand, with breaking sensation, as if rheumatic. Feeling as of a cobweb upon hands. Throbbing pain in tip of thumb day and night, waking frequently at night.

Lower Extremities.—Burning pain on l. thigh, a hand's breadth around the limb. Tearing in r. femur, extending from the middle downward and up again, from morning till noon and in evening. Numbness of l. leg, with heat. *Stitches in sole;* in corns, < rainy weather; boring S. in corns, > pressure. Pain in heel as if sore from walking. Pain in joints aud toes of l. foot on stepping as if something pressed them. Heaviness of feet in evening on ascending steps. Burning pain in great toes, especially in balls, < when walking.

Skin.—Inflammation of balls of little toes, with itching, as from freezing. *Erysipelas in face.* Erysipelatous inflammation of leg, with coldness, shivering, thirst, vomiting of food and bile, then heaviness in head and throbbing in temples, with restless slumbering at night, afterwards nosebleed. Erysipelatous inflammation and swelling of l. leg and foot after violent dancing, with tearing tension and burning in it and increased burning pain when touched, on pressure of finger the redness disappeared for a moment, afterwards tension on back of foot, so that standing was difficult. Wartlike inundations on inner surface of hands after beating something with a stick.

Herpetic eruption on nates of a child. Psoriasis on limbs and trunk. Pimples on face; red, on cheeks and around chin (in an infant); inflamed, on back of little toe, which pains like a corn; whitish, with red areola on chest and throat as far as nape. Pustule with red areola on r. middle finger, with swelling and stiffness of finger, which continued to suppurate and pain long after the pustule opened. *Unhealthy*, slight injuries suppurate and ulcerate. Old wounds and ulcers are inclined to suppurate. Long-continued suppuration under thumb-nail where she had stuck a needle, with pain on touch. Suppurating spot in heel, that had been rubbed by a shoe. Ulcer in l. axilla. Corroding blister upon nates.

Formication of feet, > open air, with trembling of feet, nausea and tendency to faintness. *Itching on back of finger-joints*; here and there on backs of hands, as if bitten by fleas; on malleolus; on os coccygis, with crawling, and after scratching discharge of mucus from anus.

Sleep.—*The child at the breast sleeps more than usual, but wakes frequently.* Sleepiness at noon and deep sleep for two hours. Sleepy in evening and tired. Sleep early in evening and long sleep in morning. Sleepiness in the twilight, but disappearance of sleep when he went to bed. Feeling in the morning as if he had not slept enough.

Falls asleep late and wakes early. Wide awake in evening. *Wakes at* 3 A.M. *and* **cannot sleep again for two hours on account of general heat, especially in head**, *with sweat on thighs.* Wakes before midnight and cannot sleep till 2 o'clock; W. at 1 A.M., and cannot sleep till 4 on account of much thinking. Wide awake at 4 A.M., so that he goes to work cheerfully.

Restless sleep; on account of rush of blood to head, restlessness of body, rumbling in abdomen and diarrhœa; with thirst and coldness; with frequent waking, crying out in fear, and during sleep muscular twitching and starting at a slight noise. *The child tosses about, cries till* 4 A.M., *frequently out of its sleep, and in the morning is in a whining mood.* **An infant cries out of sleep and anxiously grasps its mother, as if frightened by a dream.** Dream of sore throat and other diseases. Vexatious D. Voluptuous D. She dreams of coition, but without pleasurable sensation.

Fever.—Chill from 2 to 4 A.M., with trembling, vomiting of food, tearing in thighs and pain in their bones as if they would be broken, followed after sleep by heat and thirst, then at 8.30 bitter vomiting, then sweat, with diminished thirst. C. from 2 to 6 P.M. (after thirst in forenoon), then till going to sleep heat, with pain in l. hypochondrium. Coldness every second afternoon, with thirst and sleep, on waking heat with aching in inguinal ring. C. after eating, with more thirst than appetite for dinner, tensive drawing backward around hypochondria, heat suddenly rising into head on deep breathing, then heat at 6 P.M., during which he must lie down till 10, then sweat, then thirst.

Coldness, with headache and subsequent heat, without thirst, > walking in open air. C. alternating with heat, often with sweat in face, during which coldness runs down back, with stretching of limbs, weariness and sleepiness so that he must lie down in afternoon, but inability to sleep, when walking he drags the feet and is fretful and taciturn. General shivering, with throbbing pain in occiput as from suppuration. Coldness, especially in back, without thirst, with flat taste, rawness of larynx, stitches in chest when breathing, weakness, stretching of limbs, contracted, quick pulse, heat, heaviness and stupefaction in head and burning of eyes, with sensitiveness to light. Sensitiveness of external head to cold and to change of weather.

Heat; in evening in bed, with sweat, but chilliness as soon as he rises; if she puts her hands under the bed-covers, but coldness as soon as she puts them out again. Flushes of H. in morning, with nausea. *H. of head*, mouth and palms, *in an infant;* in head in evening when writing, with thirst and sensation as if sweat would break out; of l. cheek, with redness. Burning in small of back while sitting. H. of fingers, even from slight cold, with redness, as after freezing; in r. thigh near pudenda, < cough and laying hand upon it; of toes, with redness and some coldness, as after freezing.

Sweat at night; during morning sleep, and when dressing cold sensation, dry cough and rawness in chest, as after taking cold.

Bovista.

A tincture is made of the entire puff-ball (Lycoperdon bovista, L.).

General Action.—Its most marked action seems to be upon circulation predisposing to hæmorrhages (compare Ergot, Ustilago and other allied fungi).

Relations.—Carbo veg. (and the Carbons), Aloes, Magnes. c., Secale, Phosph.

Generalities.—*Awkwardness, everything falls from his hands.* Sretching without sleepiness. Fell down and remained motionless, with despair. Fell down in a swoon when trying to walk, and her limbs and body became stiff.

Bruised feeling in whole body on motion and touch, especially in joints of arms and in abdominal muscles. (Sensation as if intoxicated with wine.) General anxiety and weakness of body, eructations, nausea, distention of abdomen, passage of flatus, yawning, stretching of limbs and irresistible sleepiness. Restlessness; with anxiety, unpleasant warmth, heaviness in abdomen and alternating sensations of coldness through body. Sudden attack like faintness at noon when sitting down, as if objects turned bottom upward. Weariness; in morning on rising later than usual, especially in limbs; in evening after eating; after a walk; during and after dinner; after dinner, obliging her to sleep.

Mind.—*Sensitiveness*, offense at everything. Ill humor; in morning after rising; in afternoon during headache; with indifference to life; with apprehension and confusion of head. Apprehension, with fretfulness and disinclination to work. Anguish, sensation as if enveloped in black vapor. Melancholy; and towards evening weariness; then alternating moods. Life seemed very charming to him at one time, at another very hateful. Liveliness in company, but when alone sadness and indifference to everything. Exhilaration in morning, but peevishness in evening.

Indifference to external objects. Aversion to everything after dinner. Courage, vigor and desire to fight with everybody. Talkative. Open-hearted, she spoke of her own failings. Stupid feeling. Thoughts confused. Absent-minded, writes several words entirely wrong and omits syllables; A., with vacant look; so that she could not remember what she had been told or ordered. Memory weak.

Head.—Tearing, with heaviness and bruised sensation. Aching in morning; in open air, with heaviness, mostly in occiput, the A. > at night, returned in morning on going into open air, < in room; at night, < raising it, > towards morning; with weariness; with heaviness, which makes him ill-humored and unable to think continuously, the pain < lying and on waking from midday nap, with pulsations in head, the pain chiefly over nose, which is stopped; intermittent.

Raging pain in brain, as if suppurating, at 8 A.M., beginning in cold air and continuing in the room. Aching on waking at 3 A.M., as if the head would burst, with which he feels every pulsation, > sweat, especially on head. A. after waking, as from too much sleep. Stupefying A., especially in forehead. All the pains are felt deep in brain. Brain feels as if screwed together in morning, > open air, with heaviness. Contractive sensation > after breakfast, with dulness. Drawing around, without pain.

Enlarged sensation with the headache. Heaviness. Stupidity in evening, with heaviness and bruised feeling. Confusion; on stooping, mostly in l. temple, with pain; after coition, with vertigo and sleeplessness; < in morning, with emptiness and drawing; with inability to think correctly and with heaviness and pressure in forehead.

Vertigo; in morning; in morning on rising, with stupefaction so that he nearly fell; after rising from stooping, with stupidity; while standing, with heaviness of head, then sudden jerking backward of head; with sensation as if all his senses would leave him; *in sudden attacks on standing after headache in morning, with stupidity in head and unconsciousness;* which drew him backward; even to falling forward towards evening; the room seemed to turn about with him; as if everything turned in a circle with her, in morning on rising.

Forehead.—Stitches; over l. eye; over l. eye after dinner, with redness of cheek, without external heat; in r. side; in r. eminence; in r. eminence, extending towards r. ear, with tearing; in middle, rather externally, in evening; deep in, in evening. Tearing on stooping, with heaviness in head and burning in r. eye; T. in middle rather externally in morning; extending to l. side of occiput, then back to forehead and becoming seated in l. temple; in sinciput, especially above orbits, extending into root of nose. Pain; above r. eye, extending towards temple; deep in l. side in morning on moving about, with heaviness and pressing upon eye, with cloud before l. eye, which disappeared by frequent wiping; intermittent twitching, in brain above r. eminence at 2 P.M., with peevishness; heavy, especially on temples. Painful contraction at root of nose, extending outward behind l. frontal eminence, with stitches, as if the eminence would be screwed together, and lachrymation of l. eye, then sensitiveness of the place above l. eye to pressure, after the pain ceased general heat and feeling as if sweat would break out during dinner. Boring outward in l. side at 8 P.M. Sudden turning when sitting or sensation of a sudden current of air above l. eye, above root of nose.

Temples.—Sticking in l., with jerking. Tearing in l., extending towards ear; intermittent, in r., and in r. half of forehead; raging or digging, deep in brain in afternoon. Aching in r. in morning, with throbbing and fretfulness, the A. extending to neck; compressive, starting from temples. Heaviness.

Vertex.—Stitches on l. side in evening, with pain on touch; S. in afternoon, extending over whole head. Tearing in morning, with bruised pain on touch and with tearing on margin of r. concha. Pressure. Stupefying pain, with heat in eyes. Bruised pain on l. side. Drawings in whole top of head.

Sides.—Stitches in r. at 7 A.M.; on r., near vertex; in l. parietal bone; sudden, like boring, deep in r. side, with dulness. Tearing in r. Pressure in both; in l.; in both in evening on entering house, with throbbing. Pain in brain as if it would be pressed from both sides in afternoon; compressive P. in both, on entering room after walking in cold air; bruised, in whole r. at 10 A.M., affecting eye; almost a throbbing, in a spot on l., at 1 P.M. Painful throbbing in r., as in an ulcer. Beating in r. at 7 A.M., on entering room from cold air, with raging. Painful heaviness in r.

Occiput.—Stitches in l. side at 7 A.M.; in l. side, with tearing; boring, in afternoon in a warm room, extending to forehead over l. eye. Tearing, and at same time in lower jaw. Pain, with tension in temples; P. in forenoon, extending over vertex to forehead; on both sides in afternoon, till evening, extending to forehead, with feeling in O. as if everything would protrude; as if a wedge were pressed in. Confusion, < bright light in evening, with heaviness, with inclination of eyelids to fall, feeling as if eyes would be drawn backward, and with anxiety and uneasiness of body.

Scalp.—Hair falls out. Reddish blisters, with itching. Pimples and itching. Sore spots, with itching. Itching, < morning; *I. extending to nape, < becoming warm, not > scratching, so that he must scratch the forehead sore.* Sensitiveness to touch.

Eyes.—Inflammation of l. Weakness, without lustre or snap. Tearing deep in r., extending above it to forehead. Pain, so that he had to keep them shut; P. as if something were in them, with redness of l.; as if something were in r., with lachrymation. Heat in r., with painful contractive sensation, then in both, and such heat in cheeks that she thought they would burst. Lachrymation in morning.

Redness of canthi. Agglutination of lids in morning; of l. Involuntary closure of lids, with redness of eyes. Difficult opening in morning. Irritation of lids. Tension in l. brow. Sticking in r. orbit. Pressure deep in r. orbit during menses, with whirling and sensitiveness to pressure. It seems as if there were a veil before E. in morning on rising. Vision distorted, it seems as if some scissors with which a person was cutting paper two steps away were close to her eyes.

Ears.—Ulcer in r., with pain on swallowing. Twitching in both external E., with pain in r. on swallowing. Stitches; in r. Tearings in l. in afternoon; in front of r. after dinner; deep in r., with tensive sensation on border of concha. Picking in l. as if something were in it. Drawing. Itching, and in eyes; > boring in with finger; with difficult hearing. Tingling in l., with diminished hearing. Indistinct hearing, misunderstanding and mistakes in speaking. (Noises like rain, < r.).

Nose.—*Scabby nostrils.* Scab in nostril frequently renewed, after removal burning of the sore place. Redness where septum unites with upper lip, with soreness. Contraction over N., with heaviness and pressure, as if the skin were too short. Burning in nostrils as if sore. Itching in upper part of r. nostril, with ineffectual attempts to sneeze. Sensation of coryza, with swelling of it.

Stoppage at night; S., with pressure in temples; of l. nostril, with flow of a few drops of water; troubling her in talking. Coryza; in morning after rising, with frequent sneezing and ability to draw air only through r. nostril; stopped; fluent, also with confusion of head. Discharge of thin water; of thin mucus. Frequent need of blowing, but slight discharge. Sneezing; in morning after waking. **Bleeding** *in morning; a few drops every time on blowing* (Carbo v.).

Face.—*Pallor mornings after rising;* at one time, at another redness. Boring in malar-bones, with digging. *Eruption at corners of lips.* Tensive pimples on both lips. Cracked lips. Stitches in lower L. Burning on inner border of l. side of lower L., as in a cut. Tearing in l. side of lower jaw and in one of its teeth. Throbbing on l. side below lower jaw, with sensation as if a gland were swollen.

Mouth.—Teeth. Mucous coating. T., gums and lips filled with clotted blood in morning on waking. Gnashing now and then in evening, as in a chill. Stitches, < at night, with easy bleeding of gum, the pain > sucking blood out of teeth; S. extending into eyes. Aching in evening in bed, > only by warmth; > going into open air; then pale swelling of upper lip and sweat all night, especially profuse on head; in upper incisors, < touch and chewing, > after upper lip began to swell, the lip being far over the lower one and was even with nose, after this swelling began to subside the l. cheek began to swell, pain on touch in all swollen parts; as if the exposed nerves were rubbed; jerking. *Drawing* toothache waking before midnight three successive nights; D. in hollow tooth; in a right lower hollow T. in evening; in l. lower hollow molar *evenings in bed till morning,* during menses; as if the roots would be torn out, in evening. Digging in a hollow tooth in morning and evening; tearing, in a hollow tooth in evening in bed, extending into temple. Boring in evening; digging, in a hollow T., < cold, with drawing pain in r. side of head and stitches in ears. Elongated feeling in a hollow T.

Gums.—*Bleeding on sucking* (Carbo v.), *with pain.* Oozing of clear blood. Retraction. Swelling and pain. Ulcer exuding blood on pressure. Inflamed spot over a decayed tooth, with ulcerative pain < touch, and throbbing and feeling as if the root were too long.

Tongue.—Yellow coat in morning. Depressed ulcer on r. margin, sore and painful to touch. Red spot painful to pressure near l. ligament of T., where it is united to tongue. *Cutting.* Burning in tip every morning after waking, with numbness on posterior part of tongue and over whole mouth. **Stammering**; when reading.

(Swelling internally on l. cheek, then externally a burning blister filled with yellow fluid.) Stitches in palate extending to chin. Dryness of mouth towards evening, in the evening satiety; D. as from sand, with thirst. Heat in mouth. Painful tension in r. cheek. Numbness of M. and tongue in morning after waking, > after eating; in morning on waking, with sensation as if burnt and with bitter slimy taste and with soreness of throat. *Salivation* (Merc. s.). Offensive breath. Taste bitter; T. of blood; bad, with much mucus in mouth.

Throat.—Pain. Soreness in evening, pain on swallowing saliva as if something were sticking in T. and difficulty in swallowing food. Rawness mornings after rising and evenings. Scraping mornings, with mucus; S., with irritation to cough; and burning, as if he had eaten something too hot; as if sore, extending into chest, with tough mucus in chest, which threatens to suffocate her, this mucus is difficult to raise and tastes salt; interrupting sleep, with necessity to hawk up mucus. Irritation. *Burning.* Dryness on waking, > rising and eating, with sticking on swallowing and with numbness in mouth; D. in morning on waking, so that the tongue seemed almost like wood.

Stomach.—(Hunger in afternoon); towards evening; excessive. Appetite without real hunger. Appetite lost; for cooked food, only for bread; lost, in a child, with heat of whole body, puffy, scarlet face, it lies and vomits mucus and food, then sweat all night, mostly on head, with nosebleed twice in sleep. Thirst; in afternoon and evening; during chill; < evening; for cold water; for wine and water; for milk in morning; unquenchable; lost.

Empty eructations; mornings fasting; eructations all the forenoon, tasting of the breakfast. Hiccough at 1 P.M.; after dinner; inclination to H. in forenoon, amounting to only half a hiccough. *Nausea in morning, > after breakfast, with vomiting of water;* in morning, with febrile chilliness, then vertigo, which relieved the headache; in morning, with chilliness and sticking tearing toothache, < l. side, the pains > cold water; in forenoon, also with coldness; during chilliness, < motion, with palpitation; as from prolonged fasting.

Distention of epigastric region, > passage of offensive flatus at 8 A.M., with twinges. Gurgling in morning, > after eating; on l. side, near pit of stomach, in evening. Pressure in pit after eating, extending into chest, > walking, < sitting, with drawing tearing in l. side of head; P. as if overloaded, after eating, with good appetite. Feeling as if one had fasted, even after eating. Coldness as if a lump of ice lay in it. Foul sensation mornings on rising, with nauseous taste.

Abdomen.—Distention increasing till midnight, > passage of flatus; > passage of flatus in morning (Carbo v.), with rumbling; with pain. Rumbling, with gurgling and constipation; R. and noises as before diarrhœa, but diarrhœa only after several hours; as from a purge, > passage of flatus. Violent motions in evening, > passage of flatus, with urging to stool. Trembling, > at 10 A.M., by passage of flatus, with cutting as before diarrhœa. Emission of flatus (Carbo v.); copious, in bed; loud, at 5 A.M., then distention of abdomen and cutting; offensive, < morning and evening; offensive, in evening, with rumbling (Carbo v.).

Stitches; on stooping; with discomfort. Cutting, extending towards stomach, intermitting in evening, renewed next morning and till noon, > emission of flatus. Colic in afternoon, with urging to stool; C. night and morning, with diarrhœa; (always after dinner, with chilliness); with trembling and gnashing of teeth on account of chillliness, < after stool, the pain <

morning on waking, with distention of l. side and urging to stool, the side > walking or pressure on abdomen, < during rest, the pain > stool, which was first hard, then fluid.

Cramplike pain, < inspiration and on retraction of abdomen. Twisting pain. Suppurative pain on last day of mensturation, with tearing, diarrhœa and exhaustion. Colic obliging him to bend double, with high-colored urine and much thirst. Colic in morning on waking, as if he should go to stool. Pain as if everything were dried, in evening in bed. Sensitiveness internally and externally, with intolerance of touch and necessity to walk bent. Creeping coldness.

Stitches in l. hypochondrium and at same time in l. elbow; in r. H. near back; in r. H., with indescribable pain; burning, in l. H. when sitting bent. Twinges in r. hypochondrium after dinner. Pain in sides of abdomen, almost like burning, after dinner. Tension in upper part, with sticking. Cutting in forepart in morning, > after eating.

Stitches about umbilicus; S. below U. Cutting in umbilical region after eating. Pinching about umbilicus. Burning internally about U. at 11 A.M. Stitches in r. groin; alternating with stitches below r. ribs. Suppurative pain extending from l. to r. side of hypogastrium. Pinching in r. groin. Constriction in r. groin, > stretching body.

Rectum.—Pain deep in, extending forward, after diarrhœa. Itching as from worms, on riding. Urging to stool, then a scanty, thin, yellowish stool, then burning in anus; U. then three attacks of diarrhœa, then tenesmus and burning in anus, with general prostration; frequent, and after exertion, with twisting in abdomen, a stool, first hard, then soft; ineffectual, at 6 A.M., with emission of flatus. Feeling after an ordinary stool as if diarrhœa would come on. Burning in anus after a watery stool. Stitches through perineum towards rectum and genitals.

Stool.—Diarrhœa frequently before and during menstuation (Aloes); D. in morning; in morning, with pain and feeling as if abdomen were suppurating; in evening, with colic; at night, with tearing in abdomen and tenesmus in rectum; with cutting in abdomen; profuse, morning and evening. Liquid, in afternoon, after a normal S. in morning; two L. every day, mostly in forenoon; frequent, with tenesmus and burning in anus. Irregular, at an unusual time and too hard. Soft in morning and hard in evening. Constipation.

Urinary Organs.—Frequent urging to urinate; with profuse discharge. Frequent urging, with scanty discharge; after micturition. Frequent micturition in afternoon and much each time; (frequent M., with sudden urging). Frequent intermission when urinating. Urethra, stitches; pain on urinating as if urine passed over a sore place; burning on urinating; burning always after urinating; burning when not urinating; itching when not urinating; orifice inflamed and agglutinated. Urine copious in afternoon; in night. Urine turbid, like gruel, with violet sediment. Yellowish-green U., afterwards turbid. Very yellow U., with a slowly forming cloud.

Genital Organs.—Red, hard, painful nodule, which suppurated, on penis. Burning. Emissions two nights in succession, once with voluptuous dreams.

Voluptuous sensation in female. *Leucorrhœa; after mensturation; profuse, yellowish-green, acrid L.; mucous, tenacious, when walking; thick, like the white of an egg when walking* (Borax). Soreness of pubes during menstruation. *Traces of menses between menstruation* (Carbo v.). **Menstruation too soon; and copious,** *then leucorrhœa.* Menstruation too late; and beginning in evening on lying down, then *after midnight painful urging towards genitals, with heaviness in small of back, > next day with discharye of blood. M. most profuse in morning, but scanty during the day and night.* M. did not last as long as usual and **flowed for the most part only at night** (Mag. c.). M. less than usual and did not continue so long. M. watery, with weariness of thighs.

Clinical.—Metrorrhagia, blood flows at night or early in morning, easily from a little overexertion between the menses, blood dark; can bear nothing tight around the body; menses preceded and followed by diarrhœa. Leucorrhœa follows the menses, acrid, corrosive; discharge only at night. Cyst in the broad ligament.

Respiratory Organs.—Catarrhal voice in morning, with roughness in throat. Hoarseness every morning. Cough in morning on entering house from the cold air, from tickling in chest; every evening and morning after rising, from tickling in trachea; at 5 P.M. from tickling in throat; from irritation in larynx; spasmodic, > opening window, with deep, anxious respiration and calls for help in feeble tones; dry, evening and morning; dry, from scraping and burning in throat; (irritation to C. from tickling in larynx, with difficult expectoration of tough mucus). Respiration anxious; R. deep, noisy; short on every exertion of hands.

Chest.—Stitches in l. side; in l. lower part; in r. side and at same time in r. great toe; in middle, then in r. hypochondrium, then in l. H., in middle of sternum; beneath r. axilla in morning; in r. lowest rib in morning; in r. side in forenoon, with constant stretching; in sternum in evening, or boring; in lower forepart after dinner when standing stooped; during dinner, extending backwards, < deep breathing; in forepart of l. lowest rib, extending up into chest; below r. ribs alternating with stitches in r. groin; as with an awl in upper part of l. mamma, extending through to back; burning, on last l. rib.

Pressure beneath sternum and in stomach; spasmodic, beneath sternum, as if stomach were overloaded. Oppression in middle, with stitches on inspiration; O., with necessity to sigh, intolerance of anything on chest and sensation as if his large waistband were too small; with heat, the latter rising into head. Heaviness, with difficulty in inspiring deeply. Constriction below sternum. Burning on sternum, with visible pulsation, especially in pit of stomach; cutting, in middle, more externally. Visible pulsation above r. mamma, near clavicle.

Heart.—Pressure in præcordial region and on sternum, with tension in temples. Sharp pain in præcordia. Fulness in præcordial region, with anxiety. *Palpitation;* with general trembling and uneasiness; with vertigo and headache; with congestion to head, heat, thirst and itching in r. eye.

Neck.—Swelling of cervical glands; with tension and drawing pain. Stitches in nape in evening; on l. side extending into ear. Tearing in tendon of l. side. Tension in nape, with bruised pain on pressure; painful, on r. side on moving head, with twitches in l. ear. Stiffness in nape in morning on rising.

Back.—Stitches on inner border of r. scapula, >

sitting bent and rising up, with tearing and feeling as if a piece would be torn off; on inner border of l. S., deep in bone, with tearings; as with a knife between scapulæ in afternoon; in lumbar region, < turning body. Pain in region of kidneys.

Extremities.—*Weariness of hands and feet;* sudden, in afternoon. Increase of a previously-existing onion-like smell in axillæ. Shoulder-joint, tearing; piercing T. in r. in afternoon; tension, also as if too short, on bending arms backward; weakness of r., with difficulty in raising arm; W. of r., with pain in arm if she took hold of anything.

Arm.—Swelling of r., with soreness to touch and with pressure in shoulders. Weariness, especially in shoulder-joints; in l. Paralyzed feeling in l., < movement. > morning by sweat, with a sprained feeling.

Upper Arm.—Tearing on inside of l., as if in bone; as if in bone in outer side of l. in afternoon. Pain on inner side of l. as if it would break, in morning. Bruised pain in r. humerus in morning, > firm pressure.

Stitches in elbow in evening, r. then l. Tearing in morning in l. elbow; in r.; in tip of r. E. Stitches on inner side of l. forearm, with tearing; boring, on maring of radius, beneath elbow,extending to fingers, which became paralyzed on account of it. Tearing a hand's breadth above wrist and extending into wrist in morning. Pain on inner side of wrist near thumb, as if tendons were torn, and the same pain on outer side of other arm, in direction of index. Paralytic and itching sensation in radial arteries.

Wrist.—Stitches in r.; < taking hold of anything, especially bringing thumb and index together, then in l. Tearing in r. in evening, with throbbing. Suppurating pain in a spot on back of r., on bending hand and pressing upon it. Sprained and ulcerated pain in middle of upper surface of l. on touch and on bending hand upward and downward. Spasmodic drawing in tendons of l. Numbness of l.

Trembling of hands, with palpitation and anxiety. Heaviness of l. hand; of r., with bruised pain at place where pulse is felt and with intolerance of touch. Stiffness of hands, with weakness of fingers. *Weakness of hands; < r., allowing the slightest objects to fall.* Stitches in joints of r. index while working. Tearing in l. thumb.

Lower Extremities.—Stitches in middle of l. thigh on sitting down; in l. T. and leg and in chest. Intermittent pain in r. hip on stooping, as if small of back were broken. Bruised sensation above knee-cap. Sore feeling in bend of thigh during menses; in bend of r. thigh, and on walking feeling as if something woolen rubbed against it. Stitches in l. knee, < rising from a seat; in l. K. in forenoon; on inner side of r., as if in bone. Stiffness of l. knee and pain if he tries to stretch it after it has been bent some time. Weariness in hollows of K.

Cramp in l. leg; in calves towards morning, in bed, pain till evening as if legs were too short. Stitches in middle of l. tibia. Raging or beating pain in r. fibula in afternoon, with tearing extending to knee. Weary pain in r. leg during menstruation. Whole l. leg so sleepy, with formication, that she cannot stand upon it; r. leg asleep in afternoon. *Stitches in r. external malleolus,* with pain in internal malleolus.

Stitches in corns. Tearing breaking-drawing pain in foot which had been sprained in childhood, as if joint had been broken, with swelling. Pain in corns; P. in forepart of l. sole when walking. Drawing in r. foot, with tearing. Heaviness of feet. Stitches in great toes in evening, extending into ankles.

Skin.—Fingers unusually dented by instruments, with which she was working (Carbons.) (**shears or knives.**) Roughness over body, with itching. Painful eruption on temple. Reddish hard swelling like a boil on r. leg. Pimples on forehead; on l. side of face near mouth; on back of hand and between middle and ring fingers; *dry, reddish, covering hands;* on tibia, with sensation as if burnt; itching, over whole body, on temples, above knee; itching P. on neck; itching, on forepart of neck, the I. < after scratching; hard, red, itching and burning, on chest, l. hand and l. foot, the itching < after scratching; red, rash-like, on feet and half way up calves, with itching-burning pain.

Raw spot below r. side of chin, with itching, like tetter, the itching not > scratching. Maturating eruption in l. corner of mouth, on chin and forehead. Itching maturating eruption on forehead. (Panaritium from a slight prick of a needle); (P. on one finger after another.) A previously existing wart developed a red point, suppurated and burst. Longish, flattened pustules under nose, on which a scab remained for more than fourteen days. Vesicles containing water about l. corner of mouth; white, on r. hand, with red areola and itching; red, sore and painful, on backs of feet and at roots of toes. Formication on back at night. Biting on hips and abdomen, as from fleas.

Itching on inner side of l. forearm; on head, lower jaw, l. side, extending to behind ear, on l. side of neck, on abdomen, r. arm, inner margin of r. foot, heel, over whole body, especially on hands and head; over whole body in evening, then tetter; on arms always at evening, then after washing biting and burning; on arms every day, < evening and morning after washing, with biting; < scratching, near nose, beneath lower jaw, below r. hip. Itching > scratching on r. knee; above forehead, r. side of nose, r. shoulder, l. hip, inner side of r. knee, hollow of knees and in r. sole. I. not > by scratching, on forepart of nose; on l. side of head, on nose, chest, abdomen, inside of r. upper arm, inside of l. forearm, on r. hip, inside of thigh, here and there in limbs; I. not > scratching on inside of r. forearm, then itching pimples. Itching always returning after scratching, on forepart of scalp, on inside of r. upper arm and on l. shoulder. I. on various parts, with red pimples. *I. in coccyx so that he scratched it sore, then a crust;* on chest, then after scratching itching pimples; on r. forearm, then after scratching redness and burning for a long time; on l. side of chest, then fine eruption. Burning I. on forearms, in region of pulse, in evening, not > by scratching.

Clinical.—Urticaria, itching on getting warm. Eczema of external ear. Red eczema, burning and itching disturbing sleep. Eczema, moist, formation of thick crusts.

Sleep.—Yawning at 5 P.M., with sleepiness; Y. in evening. *Sleepiness early in evening;* during dinner; after dinner. Sleep after eating. On waking at night from a sound sleep he did not seem to know where he was. Little sleep. Restless sleep; with waking every hour.

Sleep full of dreams. Frightful dreams, that she was in a cellar, the walls of which had fallen in, and she could not get out, etc.; vexatious, with waking every moment. Tiresome; of the past and future; in a sound sleep, of subjects of previous conversations; unremembered.

Fever.—Chilliness; every day at 5 A.M. in bed; every day from 6 to 9 A.M., with external coldness and with griping in abdomen; in evening; *all night. Intermitting fever, chill every day from* 7 *to* 10 P.M., beginning with shivering in back, the first days with thirst, without subsequent heat or sweat, every time with drawing pain in abdomen. Shivering in evening on lying down; during supper; with glowing heat of face; with thirst, sticking in chest and tension and stitches in throat, so that she could not turn her head easily. Coldness of hands and feet; of feet at night; on uncovered parts, on neck and chest, and necessity to bind cloths about them, even at night.

Heat in afternoon; in evening, with sweat; > uncovering, with oppression of chest; with thirst; with anxiety and restlessness; in flushes. Orgasm of blood, with thirst. Orgasm and heat rise into face. Heat extending from r. ear down to angle of lower jaw. Burning above knee; in l. sole; externally in pit of stomach after dinner, with stitches in it. Sweat every day from 5 to 6 A.M., especially on chest; profuse, under arms when walking slowly in a cold temperature.

Brachyglottis.

The fresh leaves and flowers of the Brachyglottis repens, Forst. (Nat order Compositæ), are used for a tincture.

General Action.—Information is yet too meagre to say. See symptoms of kidneys and bladder in the clinical reports.

Relatives.—Liluim tig., Crocus, Merc. c., Arnica, *Apoc. c.*, Canth., Dig., Kalmia.

Generalities.—Appearance of general illness. Loss of flesh. Pains at first nervous, afterwards muscular. Spine and nerves more affected than muscles, the pains are transitory, and except in the spine, where the pain is not constant, it seems as if the action could be traced along anterior branches of the saphenic nerves, and perhaps along saphenic vein. Soreness to touch (Arn.). Inclination to stretch. Heaviness, with sleepiness. Weakness. Symptoms ceased in afternoon, except weakness of limbs.

Mind and Head.—Irritable mood. Headache; with faceache, preventing sleep at night. Confusion of H. Desire to bend H. Vertigo, with flushed face. Pain in forehead; in evening; in l.; headache, concentrated about l. eye; throbbing pain in F. (Apoc. c., Merc.). Throbbing in l. temple (Dig.); sudden throbs in l. side of head (Kalm.).

Ears and Nose.—Pricking in E.; with itching. Pain in E.; l. in evening. Tingling in E.; with secretions. Soreness in nostrils exteriorly. Irritation in nostrils, with repeated sneezing; I. in l. nostril, with feeling as if the air were too sharp. Itching in nose; with burning.

Face.—Twitches in l. side in evening. Sudden lancinating pain in r. side. Pain in l. submaxillary glands; extending to upper part of face. Pain in l. lower jaw; and in face. Soreness of r. zygomatic process; l.; in corners of mouth, relieved by swelling of lips.

Mouth and Throat.—Toothache; r., extending to ears. Tongue sore. Pricking in tongue in evening, with numbness. Heat in mouth. Scraping in throat. Rawness of throat; with dryness; in evening, with soreness. Soreness of throat.

Stomach.—Appetite lost. Nausea; in evening; in evening, with eructation tasting of ingesta. Pain and soreness. Soreness in evening after tea, with throbbing in r. side of S. and bowels. *Fluttering.*

Abdomen.—**Fluttering sensation** (Crocus.). Colic, with desire for stool. *Pain in groin; l.* (Dios.); in groins, with weariness of lower limbs. Soreness in groins, as if in spermatic cords, with thrilling through penis and testes. Throbbing in r. hypochondrium (Apoc. c.); in l. groin; in l. groin in morning; sudden T. pain in l. groin.

Anus and Stool.—Prostration about anus. Ineffectual urging to stool. Diarrhœa in evening. Small, soft stool, with pain and constriction in anus. Dry S., with sore constrictive pain in anus. S. like balls, knotty and painful.

Urinary Organs.—Pain in bladder during micturition, with soreness in urethra and feeling as if the urine could not be retained; **pain in B. after evacuation** (Canth., Merc. c.), *and in urethra, with stinging in penis.* **Pressure in neck of bladder; with soreness.** Irritation of bladder in evening; I. during micturition. *Urging to urinate.* Stinging pain in urethra (Arn., Merc. c.). Throbbing in penis, with desire to urinate and pressure in bladder. Urine abundant, pale; and specific gravity decreased, full of mucous corpuscles and epithelium, afterwards urine scanty, full of mucus, dark-colored, two days afterwards pale, containing albumen, then dark, containing transparent waxy casts, afterwards a mass of epithelial cells adhering to each other (phosphates, oxalate of lime), afterwards dark, containing mucous cells and triple phosphates, specific gravity slightly increased, white mucous sediment, containing epithelium, triple phosphates and mucous casts from kidneys.

Clinical.—Bright's disease, the result of overwork.

Genital Organs.—**Clinical.**—Dysmenorrhœa, with chronic basic peritonitis and fluttering in abdomen; the fluttering in the abdomen and fluttering in r. ovary are the keynotes to its use.

Respiratory Organs and Chest.—Breathing oppressed in evening, > sighing; as if pectoral muscles were contracting and a stretching would relieve, with the same sensation in dorsal muscles and in r. scapula. Shooting in pectoral muscles in region of heart. Pain in region of heart in evening; in r. side; in chest (œsophagus?). Painful soreness in sterno-mastoid process. Throbbing in sternum, with pain in pectoral muscles. Painful throbbings about shoulder and collar-bone.

Neck.—Pain prominently affecting upper part of trapeze muscle and extending to shoulders. Pain on moving head from one side to the other, with soreness in region of attachments of sterno-mastoid muscles, pain in neck continues in the evening. Stiffness.

Back.—Pain; < evening, and in region of kidneys; with weariness; with weariness in limbs; isolated throbbing, in r. side. Uneasiness, with prostration. Whole B. feels as if it would contract backward, and the muscles of the neck were affected. First dorsal vertebræ sore to touch. Sudden pain about fourth and fifth dorsal vertebræ in evening, extending to r. side of chest and shoulders.

Loins.—Gnawing pain in region of kidneys. Pain across; after riding, extending to pectoral muscles and arms. Soreness; in lower part of spine, almost traceable to sciatic nerve. Weakness after walking, with pain. Weariness in back from coccyx upward, and dull pain in region of kidneys.

Extremities.—Inclination to stretch, especially arms, to relieve the weariness between scapulæ and trapeze muscle. Weakness; in morning; < afternoon.

Upper Extremities.—Pain under r. axilla; extending to pectoral muscles. Painful soreness under arms. Cracking in l. shoulder. Soreness in shoulders and neck. Cracking in joints of l. arm. Isolated throbbing or shooting in arms. Isolated sore throbs in r. arm and under r. axilla. Weakness of arms; in evening; of r. arm from writing; of arms and wrists. Pain in deltoid of l. arm in evening; running along l. upper arm, becoming stationary; weary, in upper arm. Weakness in biceps, with soreness. Pain in l. elbow in morning. Throbbing and shooting pain in wrist. Soreness of l. wrist; with pain; of r. wrist, extending to elbow, as if in flexor carpi ulnaris; in fingers and thumb, with weakness of hands when writing.

Lower Extremities.—Cracking in joints when walking. Weakness from walking. Pain in thighs from walking; short sudden pains in thighs. Weakness extending from hip to knee. Sharp throbbings or shootings in knees, with cramplike contractions in muscles of thighs. Rheumatic moving aching in l. knee. Sore throbbing pains in knees; r. knee. Knees weak in evening. Throbbing sore pain in legs. Pain in lower part of legs. Weakness of legs in morning, more in l. than in r. thigh, with soreness in lower part of spine. Soreness on soles.

Skin, etc.—Itching; in face. Painful itching burning under big toes from walking, with itching of r. sole. Sleepiness; during the day, with constant yawning. Inability to fall asleep after waking. Restless sleep. Restless and sleepless night. Talking in sleep. Sleep full of dreams. Confused dreams. Chilliness; with shivering; and pulse 50; with heat in face. Cold sensation and tightness about scalp. Cold hands and feet.

Bromium.

Dilutions are prepared from a solution of one part of Bromine in ninety-nine of distilled water.

General Action.—The phenomena known as *Bromism*, produced by the bromides generally, is partially shadowed by our provings of pure Bromine; but our exact knowedge is imperfect. In *Bromism* we find intellectual weakness and melancholia; anæsthesia of mucous membranes, especially in throat and eyes, loss of sexual power, acne on the face, general paralysis. The effects of Bromine upon the larynx and trachea furnish most useful guides to its use in disease.

Affinities.—Iodine, Kali bi., Puls., Ant. crud., etc.

Generalities.—Embonpoint increased (Iod., emaciation). Cracking in joints in morning after rising. Clonic cramps in muscles of eyes, in face and limbs. Trembling. If introduced into a cut it becomes unhealthy-looking and green decay forms about it, with an offensive odor. Jerklike tearings through l. thumb at 6 P.M., in frontal bone, through r. great toe, in lower part of r. leg, in r. knee, with bruised pain when sitting in evening. Flesh feels loose and bruised on touch, especially on l. side of chest. Pressure in single joints and in pectoral and dorsal muscles. Indisposition; mental and physical.

Sensation of fasting, with heaviness in head and stiffness in muscles of neck. Restlessness. Weakness; all the afternoon and evening, with sleepiness, when walking; trembling, at night on waking; after breakfast, as if bruised. Stiffness of throat in afternoon, and of neck, arms and legs, with pain extending from occiput towards forehead, shooting and dragging as if everything would press out in forepart of head. Aggravation from evening till midnight (Iod.); *in warm room* (Iod.) and when sitting; on r. side; on l. side. Amelioration after eating (*Iod.*); during motion; on walking; when riding horseback and driving; from ammonia-gas and vapor of spirits of wine.

Clinical.—For scrofulous children with enlarged parotids.

Mind.—Illusions of fantasy, it seemed as if strange persons were looking over his shoulder. Obliged to look about him in evening when alone, and it seemed as if he would see an apparition. Anxiety. Apprehension in evening, with oppression of heart and headache. Fretfulness. Quarrelsome disposition. Taciturnity. Apathy, with weakness. Activity in buisness. Desire for mental labor. Aversion to his business. Indisposition for mental work. Disinclination to read. Disconcerted, with heat in head. Difficulty in fixing thoughts. Loss of ideas. Forgetfulness.

Head.—Aching; at 3 or 4 P.M., on appearance of menses; with here and there vertigo; in bones in damp weather, mostly in forehead and occiput; especially in forehead, alternating with pain in small of back; bursting pain, more on l. side; dizzy, in morning on waking, with general itching, especially on chest and between shoulders. Confusion; with heaviness; especially in sinciput, with pressure on brows and root of nose, often affecting a spot above eyes, alternately in one or other side; as if a hoop were about it, causing vertigo. Sensation in brain soon after dinner (that was eaten with little appetite), as if apoplexy were imminent, a feeling as if he would loose his senses and have vertigo. Vertigo; as soon as he steps over running water, also with involuntary drawing of foot in direction of stream; < evening on lying down, with confusion of head; < damp weather; with feeling as if one would fall to the ground and flushes of heat; with nausea; with bleeding at nose, then headache; with tendency to fall backward.

Forehead.—Necessity to keep wrinkled. Stitching to lower jaw, thence into a hollow tooth, with throbbing in it. Tearing in bones. Boring in l. bone. Gnawing in bone. Raging over eyes. Pain; after dinner; on accession and during menstruation, with feeling on stooping as if eyes would fall out; in sinciput, < cough; in bones; in r., then l. bone; in bone in evening, with stitches in larynx; in bone, > open air; above eyes; deep in eyes, with sensitiveness of eyes when reading; over r. eye, with photophobia; with heaviness and heat; in morning affecting eyes; over l. eye, extending into sinciput, with heat and oppressive benumbing pain; in r. eminence; in r. anterior lobe of brain and in r. side of nasal bone; ranging from sinus to base of brain; intermittent; in sinciput in forenoon, as if everything would press outward; hot, in sinciput, extending inward at 9 A.M., throbbing and extending to maxillary bone; stupefied,

< during rest, > riding; stupefied, over l. eye. Confusion. Heaviness; in sinciput *in heat of sun.*

Pressure in l. temporal bone; in l. temple, with vertigo in head; on vertex. Tearing in r. cranial bones. Stitches through r. side. Pain in l. side; extending to l. eye; from l. ear to l. temple, < stooping; throbbing, in l. side after *drinking milk,* > lying on r. side, with arms over his head. Drawing in l. side. Crawling beneath skin of occiput; tickling C. in l. half of head in afternoon, and on l. cheek. Tickling in r. side.

Clinical.—Migraine of left side, < stooping, especially after drinking milk.

Eyes.—Sunken. Inflammation; of r., with dimness and lachrymation. Stitches; *through l.* Pain in and above r., with inflammation of conjunctiva; paroxysmal, and in root of nose, as if extending from interior of brain towards vertex. Burning, with spasmodic closing of orbicularis and lachrymation. Lachrymation; *of r. eye.*

Conjunctiva dull and wrinkled. Distended tortuous vessels in conjunctiva bulbi, with stitches in lids. Biting in conjunctiva palpebrarum. Lids close as if sleepy. Increased moisture in canthi. Stitches in canthi; in r. inner; in l. lids when reading. Cutting in r. inner canthus, then in outer; in r. inner canthus, next day in l. inner. Biting in margins of lids. Heaviness of lids, with coldness of them. Sticking about orbits. Tickling in l. arcus superciliaris in afternoon.

Photophobia; with pressure on moving eyes. Vanishing of vision in evening when sitting and reading, as if caused by a wind. Vision of lightnings. A gray point before r. eye moving up and down with movement of the eye. Illusions as if all sorts of things jumped up on the ground before her.

Ear.—Stitches in r.; deep in; deep in r., with heat in ear and sensitiveness of head to cold air; behind l. Pain deep in r.; in r. in afternoon, with tickling on r. cheek; as if internal around ear in evening before sleep, in l., then r. Pressure above l. in morning as from a plug, then sticking in tip of tongue. Throbbing. Tickling in r. lavator auris, > scratching, and behind r. ear, on lobule of l.; on margin of r. Ringing in r. as if full of bells. Roaring, < l.; and in morning closed sensation in r. Rushing in r.; noise of distant R.

Nose.—Inflammatory affection, and of fauces and respiratory organs. Swelling in l. side and on pressure pain as if a boil were forming. Ulceration in l. nostril like a crust, with tickling under it. *Soreness internally, with crusts; S., with swelling of wings, a scurf forms in it, with pain and bleeding on wiping it;* and swollen feeling around lamilla and then in wings, then crusts. Twitching in r. side. Pain on r. side of tip; in l. compressor nasi on pressure. Pressure on nasal and superior maxillary bones and in various places in frontal bones. Smarting beneath r. nostril. It seemed to him as if coryza would appear, with soreness in r. nostril as if he had pulled out some hairs, with dim eyes, pain in r. ribs and little appetite. Itching inside, with continued smell of Bromine. Tickling inside; in l., then in r. nostril; in l. side of tip. Stopped sensation; stoppage, with fluent coryza and lachrymation of r. eye.

Stopped by mucus. **Obstinate coryza, with soreness beneath nose and on margin of nose** (Iod.); *C., with stoppage and soreness of r. nostril. Fluent coryza* (Iod.), *in which r. nostril is more affected and more stopped, then l.; fluent C.,* with *violent sneezing and corrosive soreness under nose and on margin of nose* (Iod.); with discharge from r. nostril and at same time stoppage of it. Much mucus, especially in posterior nares; much M. in afternoon, sometimes with streaks of blood; watery mucus streaked with blood, at other times dryness in nose; frequent blowing of thick M. Much tough white mucus, < r. nostril, at times pieces of tough yellow M. in both nostrils. Yellowish mucus, with yellowish expectoration. Crusts in morning; C. < r. nostril; in r. nostril, with bleeding after removal. Sneezing; shattering S., then stoppage. Bleeding on blowing; from l. nostril; from r.; from r. in morning; bleeding, with relief of chest and eye symptoms.

Clinical.—Coryza, with pressure at root of nose, internal soreness, watery, excoriating discharges, nose seems stopped.

Face.—Haggard. Pallor. Pain in l. zygoma, with stitches in ear, then same pain in r. side; in l. zygoma in evening, then stitches in l. ear, then pain in r. zygoma. Hot unpleasant sensation, especially below nose, tickling smarting *as from cobwebs, especially on moving nose,* with fluent coryza and lachrymation of r. eye. Tension in l. cheek, extending to lower jaw, at times with pain extending into l. ear. Sensation of heat in cheeks, < r., then in l.

Lip.—Soreness of upper, with desquamation and coryza. Pain in upper as if it had burst, with yellowish spots beneath epithelium, containing yellowish fluid and extending almost to r. corner of mouth. Stretched feeling in middle of upper, and in neighboring part of nose. Burning in upper, with very smooth feeling. Tickling in r. corner in afternoon; T. in upper part of r. side of upper, > scratching, but returning.

Jaw.—Boring in r. lower. Pressure as from a dull body in front of l. joint, but deep in, extending towards lowest fossa of l. nostril, as if in Eustachian tube, on swallowing the motion of the superior muscles of the pharynx changes this sensation for a moment. Peculiar sensation of beginning pain in l. upper.

Mouth.—Teeth. Pain; in l.; in hollow; in r. hollow tooth and in l. upper eye tooth; in l. lower hollow tooth from blowing coals; > pressure; painful sensation in l. upper hollow T. as if toothache would develop; especially in a l. lower hollow tooth, and the anterior half of the hollow T. pains as if sore when touched and seems to be loose. Sensitiveness of a hollow T. to cold water. Elongated sensation in a hollow T. when biting. Throbbing beneath hollow T. Drawings in hollow T. Bluntness. Pain in gum.

Tongue.—Inflammation. Pimples posteriorly on r. side. Stitches in tip; then suddenly disappearing tickling. Dry sensation. Burning on under surface, with stitches; B. under, as from pepper; acrid, extending to stomach, causing nausea, salivation and difficult, painful respiration. Inability to protrude.

Inflammation of buccal cavity. Dryness. Sensation as after a glass of rum, and in pharynx. Smarting on arches of palate, with sore pain. Heat; to stomach, with internal dryness in larynx; and in pharynx and stomach, with increased secretion of mucus, nausea, eructations and colic. Salivation; with constrictive sensation in orifice of salivary glands; with increased mucus in mouth and nose; thin.

Taste.—Scraping. Disagreeable. Nauseous, offensive. Bitter at tip of tongue. Burning. Peculiarly puckered, burning and offensive. Sour. Sweetish. Salt on tip of tongue; S. to water in morning fasting.

Throat.—Pain in submaxillary glands; in l. Redness of fauces and uvula; of fauces, tonsils covered with mucus, scraping-sticking rawness, swelling of tonsils. Inflammation of fauces and uvula, < morning, with dry cough caused by irritation of elongated uvula, with yellow thick nasal mucus streaked with blood, without sneezing or blowing nose. Spasms of muscles of deglutition and respiration.

Stitches; with lachrymation and flow of saliva; S. in glands at side of frænum of tongue; near frænum of tongue, with secretion of thin saliva, then coldness in tip of tongue, with salivation; deep, with scratching. Feeling as if a small body were in fauces, causing hawking. Scraping; towards evening, with dryness; *with a rough, deep voice;* with frequent hawking of scanty mucus; causing hawking. Soreness. Rawness; in pharynx; in evening, with stitches and tickling in larynx, lachrymation and feeling as if larynx were laced together. Burning from pharynx into stomach; in pharynx, with scraping, so violent that there were twitchings in face and hands, with nausea and forcible empty retchings. Puckering. Nauseating puckered sensation; then burning and sore sensation. Swallowing painful, < morning, with dark redness of œsophagus.

Clinical.—Diphtheria and enlarged parotids, which finally suppurate. In diphtheria, symptoms of the disease invading the larynx. Goitre.

Stomach.—Desire for acids, which aggravate symptoms (Ant. cr.) and cause diarrhœa. Appetite diminished; lost. Aversion to the customary tobacco-smoking, it causes nausea and vertigo. Thirst; in afternoon. Aversion to drinking cold water. Eructations; with vomiting of much mucus; with rumbling in abdomen; empty; like foul eggs. Hiccough. Nausea; towards evening, > after eating, without ability to vomit; with eructations, rawness in throat, salivation, slow pulse and congestion of chest; in epigastric region.

Inflammation, with suggillations like ulceration. Sticking in pit from 8 to 11 A.M., extending to navel, < deep pressure and it generally seems deeper than stomach. Contractive cramp at 11.30 A.M., > after eating. Pain; < pressure; in epigastric region, < pressure, > bending forward, with distended abdomen and flushes of heat starting from back; with rumbling in abdomen; and in r. hypochondrium, with full sensation; extending to navel and below short ribs; rising into œsophagus; intermittent; burning; as before diarrhœa, then liquid stool, with urging. Pressure as with a stone; with internal heat. Heaviness. Emptiness; > after eating, for which he had no longings. Warmth; with confusion in forehead; W., with salivation.

Abdomen.—*Tympanitic distention and passage of much wind.* Rumbling. Sounds of gas, and in œsophagus. Sticking before menstruation, > lying bent. Griping. Pinching after tobacco-smoking, > pressure, < sudden motion, when sitting bent and pressing upon it he noticed the pain only during expiration. Pain; gradually moving downward; as during menstruation, *and in small of back, with passage of much flatus,* as was the case during menstruation. Warmth, with accelerated pulse.

Hypochondria.—Stitches; in l.; deep in l.; from r. to l.; from liver towards navel. Cutting deep in both, < pressure, especially on l. side, with diarrhœa. Painful pressure upon H. Pain in l.; in region of spleen, extending towards spinal column; in liver; in region of liver, < pressure and riding, with distention and hardness of r., and feeling as if a hard body were sinking down there. Sensation of a ball in l. Sensitiveness to pressure, and in epigastric region, with flow of saliva. Pulsation in r. in evening. Pain in region of gall-bladder, < pressure and < a few hours after eating, afterwards > pressure, stooping and fasting, sometimes with painful breathing and distention of abdomen by gas, it extends on deep breathing to navel.

Cutting in umbilical region after eating, < pressure. Pain in U. region, < retracting abdomen. Twitching in l. side. Sticking on l. side of umbilicus, on inner surface of wall of abdomen, morning and evening, < pressure, and in evening cutting deep in region of umbilicus, < pressure, with stitches extending towards rectum, to neck of bladder and along r. spermatic cord. Twitching in l. side. Pain in l. side; deep in l. side of umbilicus, < pressure; in l. side, becoming a dragging towards inguinal ring.

Swelling of r. inguinal glands (Iod.). Stitches in anterior spine of crest of l. ilium. Boring posteriorly in crest of l. ilium. Pain in crest of r. ilium; in l. inguinal ring; in l. inguinal canal, < walking, pressure and cough.

Rectum.—Tenesmus during stool. Urging to stool at 2 P.M. after the natural morning stool, with passage of much more wind than fæces; frequent U., with passage of flatus and stitches in anus.

Anus.—*Hæmorrhoids.* Stitches. Ineffectual tenesmus. Tickling. Itching-crawling, as from something living.

Clinical.—Intensely painful hæmorrhoids.

Stool.—Fluid. Thin and frequent. Diarrhœa, > black coffee; bright yellow, preceded by cutting and rumbling; mucous, with much wind. Hard. Like sheep-dung, brown and glistening; like sheep-dung, with pressure in stomach and abdomen. Constipated, then two each day, thinner and more copious than usual. Frequent; at night.

Urinary Organs.—Pain in region of bladder and in its sides, with desire to urinate. Desire to urinate, with tickling in tip of urethra. Frequent calls to urinate. Very little desire to urinate. Pressure in prostate gland when walking. Dribbling after urinating. A drop of burning urine after urinating.

Urethra.—Discharge of drops of clear mucus. Stitches; in orifice; extending towards its orifice. Burning after urinating. Pulsation behind testicles.

Urine increased. Scanty; and dark; dark and turbid, with red sediment; dark and turbid, with whitish sediment adhering to vessel. Contains large flakes of white mucus. Becomes cloudy after an hour and ammoniacal.

Sexual Organs.—Stitches in glans; in tip; in sides and root of penis, extending through penis to glans. Pinching in penis in evening, more on r. side. Erections in morning; from 3 to 8 o'clock. Stitches in l. spermatic cord. Pressure in r. spermatic cord.

Swelling of l. testicle, with sore pain. Increased firmness of testicles. Coldness of l. testicle. Desire increased. Emissions at night; E. early during coition. *Loud passage of flatus from vagina.* Sore pain in pudenda. Clear blood with menses. Menstruation too early; and too profuse; delayed. Membranous dysmenorrhœa.

Clinical.—Membranous dysmenorrhœa; spasmodic contractions. Loud emissions of flatus from the vagina, with dysmenorrhœa. Chronic inflammation of the ovaries. Tumors in mammary gland.

Respiratory Organs.—Larynx. Mucus, causing hawking. Stitches; at night, with itching; *posteriorly on swallowing saliva, with feeling of contraction;* with pressure; with lachrymation. **Scraping in evening, provoking dry cough** (Puls.); **and rawness, provoking hawking.** Scratching. Pain in l. side as if crushed. *Constriction; sticking.* **Cold sensation, with a cold feeling when inspiring,** after breakfast, > after shaving. *Tickling, then cough; T., with irritation to cough, constriction deep in throat, dry cough,* coppery taste on arch of palate, spasmodic sensation, extending downward from throat, dry cough in evening, and scraping in throat. *Spasmodic closure of glottis. Contracted sensation in trachea,* **or feeling as if pit of throat were pressed against trachea.** *Tickling in trachea on inspiration, causing cough.* Dryness of trachea. **Hoarseness; loss of voice,** *voice weak and soft* in evening, *with raw feeling in throat; < in afternoon, then in forenoon.*

Cough on deep inspiration; C. < during the day; **with paroxysms of suffocation suddenly** (Ipec.) **on swallowing;** racking, preventing speech; violent, with sensation of sulphur fumes, then confusion of head and headache; rough, and hollow and dry, with fatigue; hacking. Dry cough, in morning; from tickling rawness in throat; with pain in l. side of chest; with stitches extending from l. nipple into l. side of chest. Short C., without expectoration, with sore pain in chest.

Respiration.—*Oppressed* (Ipec.). *Difficult; he cannot inspire sufficient air,* > walking, even rapidly, and in evening and night, < morning. *Short, obliged to catch for breath* (Kali cyan.); S. and quick; and difficult, with prolonged inspiration and mucous râle. *Deep forcible inspirations necessary from time to time.* Spasmodic. Frequent, deep. Deep breathing becomes a yawning; D. expirations now and then; frequent D. expirations when sitting. Impeded by pressure in pit of stomach, as from pressure on lower end of sternum; inspiration as from impediment in middle of chest.

Clinical.—Croup, diphtheritic; croup idiopathic. In croup Brom. is rarely indicated in the early stage; but when the febrile symptoms have subsided, the patient is weak, perspiring, has a hard, tight cough, which is spasmodic, with suffocative attacks and sometimes rattling of mucus in larynx; the element of spasm generally indicates the drug. It follows well after Iodine. The choice is generally between Kali bich., Ipec. and Brom.; these are adapted to the same stage of the disease. Spasmodic croup symptoms, starting up as if choked, > drinking; every inspiration provokes cough. Asthma in suffocative attacks, it seems as if the breathing were hindered by spasmodic constriction. In pneumonia, for suffocative attacks, cannot expectorate. Asthma > at sea.

Chest.—Swelling of mamma. Stitches; here and there in wall; *in r. side,* < rapid walking; in r. side between sixth and seventh ribs at 6 P.M.; in r. side beneath fourth rib, with palpitation; in l.; in l., below ribs; in l., extending towards arm; in upper part, with difficult breathing and sensation of distention; in lungs on attempt to breathe deeply, with cough, pulse full and hard, in beginning slow, afterwards rapid. Tearing in l. clavicle. Pressure upon; on deep inspiration; in r.; in l. pectoral muscles; in wall below r. nipple; in upper part; below l. clavicle; in sternum, with lassitude; intermittent, outward in spots in r. wall in evening, < motion of thorax.

Pain during cough; P. under ribs, < pressure, more in r. side; in l. side; in l. by fourth rib; under l. ribs, < lying bent and in night; in l. side during cough, extending inward from nipple; in l. lung; in r. lung; in r. wall on waking; in r. side beneath ribs, < pressure; in r. between seventh and ninth ribs, < motion; in r. side, gradually extending towards back; in r. side, < morning and evening, lifting a light weight with r. hand and by walking, on account of increased motion of pectoral muscles, < moving thorax after rest, and on waking, afterwards less when walking than when sitting, at times changing to r. dorsal muscles and then < by expiration; wandering, in l. on waking, < bending shoulders forward, with slight flexion of upper part of chest, or by turning thorax on its axis, thus seeming to be in muscles, then extending to r. side of chest, then leaving l. and continuing in r. Paralytic drawing pain through l. towards scapula and into l. arm.

Anxiety, with difficult breathing. Constriction, impeding respiration, with dry tickling cough. Tension. Fulness increasing till noon, continuing till evening, and in throat, with feeling as if a soft substance were between lungs and sternum. Congestion. Burning, then ineffectual retching. Tickling in region of r. eighth rib; in r. side, in region sixth rib, in afternoon. Peculiar exhaustion.

Heart.—Severe beats when standing, > deep inspiration. Palpitation; in evening, < lying on l. side; when walking; on rising from a chair; with forcible inspiration; with oppression around heart, sensation as if the inspired air were cold, and with tendency to yawn.

Clinical.—Hypertrophy of heart, palpitation, suffocation.

Pulse.—Rapid; and tense. Slow and hard; and full then rapid. Full.

Neck.—Swollen gland on each side. Stiffness in morning; on l. side and pain on turning head.

Back.—Twitching in l. latissimus dorsi. Pain before menstruation, with weakness and want of appetite. Creepings down. Sticking tickling in spine, more towards r. side. Boring in spinous processes of dorsal vertebræ. Pressure in l. dorsal muscles. Wandering pressive pain in dorsal muscles below scapulæ. Tension in r. lumbar and dorsal muscles, < moving these parts. Sore pain in small of B.

Extremities.—Pains; alternating with chilliness and heat. Compression in upper arm and in forepart of both knees. Stiffness at 11 A.M., > in afternoon.

Upper Extremities.—Constriction. Stitches in r. axilla; burning, on top of r. shoulder-joint. Pain in r. shoulder; in joint; below S.; in l. shoulder-joint, with weariness; bruised, in l. S. then in r. elbow; rheumatic constricting, in r. S. when walking in street, extending into arm; painful paralytic sensation in l. S., then in r. S. joint.

Arm.—Tearing in evening, especially in hands and fingers. Restlessness and jactitation. Weakness; of l. Paralyzed feeling in l.; as after a blow, in afternoon on holding it bent while walking, with ill humor.

Cracking in l. elbow. Sticking in inner condyle of r. elbow. Sensation from wrists to a little below elbows as if in a vise, then sticking in fingers, which extends towards head. Pressure in l. forearm; in l. wrist. Trembling of hands. Pain in r. hand, once shooting into middle finger, with throbbing pain. Pressure in metacarpal bone of r. index.

Fingers.—Stitches; on back of joint between first and second phalanges of l. fourth all the forenoon; on back of r. little, with red spots; burning, in tip of l. index. Tearing; in first phalanges of r. fourth and fifth; through l. fourth and in r. third and fourth; in middle joint of l. middle obliging extension of fingers; T. asunder pain between metacarpus and first phalanx of r. thumb. Pressure in roots of l.; on back of joint between first and second phalanges of r. fourth. Compression at bases of l. fourth and fifth. Dead pain in all joints of l., extending to elbow and shoulder, with pain in upper and lower part of arm. Stiffness of r. so that she is afraid of letting the dish fall which she is holding.

Lower Extremities.—Knee. Twitching in inner side of r. Pain; in bone of r.; in bend of r.; in r. and downward, with heaviness in r. leg; in l.; in forepart of l.; in l. in morning, < motion, and in l. hip; rheumatic, in l.; burning, in l. Throbbing in forepart of r. while sitting.

Leg.—Gnawing in tibiæ; sudden G. in forepart of leg, extending to r. side, or sawing pain. Boring in r. tibia; in l. T.; in lower part of l. T. Pressure in r. tibia; in head of r. T.; deep in l. leg; deep in l. leg, extending into foot, with weariness. Pain deep in leg while sitting, l. then r. Throbbing pain in evening on going out, especially in r., with stiffness as far as foot, and with stiffness and pain in r. great toe and in middle toes. Fatiguing pain in bones of l. Weakness of l. Paralytic sensation in r.

Ankle.—Pressure in r.; in l. and anteriorly in bones of r. tarsus and bones on back of r. foot; in r. internal malleolus.

Foot.—Tearing in tendons on back of r. Pressure on back of l. Pain in middle of ball of l. in evening, as from stepping on a hard body, with paralyzed feeling in knee and hip, then aching in l. side of throat near thyroid cartilage. Drawing in tendons on back of r. Tension in tendons on back of r. on bending ankle while walking.

Toes.—Cutting in flesh near nail of great; on back of l. fourth. Pain in r.; in r. fourth in evening; in tip of r. fourth, with tickling on forehead and pain on inner side of r. knee; in a corn on r. little, with rapid growth. Burning and pain in a corn on r. fourth and beneath its ball.

Skin.—Yellow. Bluish in many parts. Red spots on back of l. hand, more towards thumb and index, disappearing and reappearing, sometimes itching, sometimes changing to vesicles, which leave red spots. Destruction, with burning, then inflammation. *Boils on arms* and face. Pimples on nose and posteriorly on r. side of tongue; about r. inner canthus, with pain on touch and watery discharge when pricked; in suture before anus, with pain on pressure and < rubbing; on r. ring finger, on lower part of ulnar side of third phalanx.

Stitches on malar-bone; on larynx. Pricking changing to burning and dryness. Cutting on ball of r. great toe. Sensation of something living, especially in arms and legs. Crawling below l. nostril, then on r. cheek; of l. great toe, with coldness in it, waking at night; in fingers and short twitches in muscles of foot and in region of knee; tickling, in l. cheek, also in middle of l. cheek. Tickling, > scratching; T. on r. side of forehead and on l. side of occiput; on l. cheek and l. side of head; on l. malar-bone in afternoon; on r. cheek, > scratching; on r. shoulder; on lower limbs; on outer side of l. thigh in afternoon; below r. knee-cap, > scratching. Itching, > scratching; above r. external canthus; between fingers; in various places, but reappearing; I. now here, now there, mostly on r. side of face; tickling, in spots, now on r. side, now on l.

Clinical.—Foul ulcers.

Sleep.—Yawning; in morning; *all day, with difficult breathing;* on full inspiration; with heat in face and nose. *Sleepiness;* in evening when reading, with inability to sleep; in evening when writing, with confusion of head, sensation as if scalp were too tight or as if a band were around head, and pain in shoulder; with weakness and great inclination to sit down, yet he feels better when moving about. Sleep very sound. Prolonged, unrefreshing sleep in morning; prolonged, in morning, as if stupid, then sluggishness. Light sleep. Sleeplessness. Sleeps with her mouth open. Starting in sleep; and twitchings. Restless, dreamy sleep.

Dreams of nothing but dying, coffins and funerals. Vivid D. and wide awake on waking; V., of journeyings, climbings, quarrels and fights, with distinct recollection on waking; of ascending a height; of descending a steep place, with leaving the bed, but waking when his feet touched the cold floor.

Fever.—Chilliness; on motion in evening; with confusion of head and headache extending into l. eye. *Shivering; with yawning and stretching,* as in intermittent fever, with confusion of head, drawing in l. tibia down to ankle, whereby the foot becomes cold, this is *repeated every other day, as a chilliness, with cold feet.* Cold, unpleasant drawing through whole body, with rapid alternations of warmth, at first in l. hand and side. Sensitiveness to cold air; with coldness running through back into legs, < walking. Coldness in back at 3 P.M., and in limbs; in back when sitting; over back now and then, with cold hands and feet; creeping over back; drawing down back; shivering drawing down back. *Cold and moist hands.* Cold finger-tips. Cold sensation in l. great toe.

Burning internally at 9 A.M., then it seems between skin and flesh; in whole body during moderate manual labor, then clammy sweat in evening; internal, in forenoon, as if in a hot vapor, yet without sweat. Heat rising into head now and then; H. in forehead and chest; in occiput; in face; in nose and on l. cheek; in l. ear, as from a coal or hot water, in evening. Heat in back, extending over body; in back, extending into head and face; in forepart of r. shoulder-joint; in hands; in hands and head, with coldness in rest of body; of r. hand, with fulness as if distended; in feet; in feet, with coldness of rest of body.

Sweat on slight movement; S. in palms; cold and clammy.

Bryonia.

A tincture is prepared from the fresh root of Bryonia alba, L.

General Action.—In large doses a violent hydragogue cathartic. It also (like its botanical ally, Colocynth) produces sharp pains. It causes inflammation of various organs, particularly of serous membranes and lungs, and gives rise to a fever of a rather low type. Its marked peculiarity is a disinclination to make any effort and great aggravations from motion of any sort.

Analogues.—Iodine, Bell., Verat. v., Colch., Led., Coloc., Lyc., Arn., Phos., Carbo v., Sulph.

Generalities.—*Unsteadiness of all parts of body when walking, < after rising from a seat and on beginning to walk, > continued walking.* Trembling of the part on disappearance of the pain, with coldness of face. Anxious tossing about of hands and feet until 1 A.M., she lies as if unconscious, with cold sweat on forehead, with sighing, then weakness. Convulsions, with tonic contractions of extremities, opisthotonos, immobility of thorax and on inspiration remarkable depression of pit of stomach.

Stitches; **in joints on motion and on touch**; over whole body; *in affected parts upon pressure;* here and there, especially in r. eye and l. arm; *jerking, here and there,* on vertex, wrists and elbows, *especially in places on forehead, with sensitiveness of teeth;* in evening in anterior and posterior direction through middle of chest and above navel. *Tearing across forehead, then in cervical muscles, then in r. arm;* in head and limbs, afterwards in chest and abdomen; in r. shoulder, in knees and toes; in various parts, especially in toes and r. shoulder, with feeling as if motion were difficult. *Bruised or suppurating pain in whole body when taken hold of* (Arn.), *especially in pit of stomach, and < morning;* B. feeling in morning, especially in r. hip, with lame feeling.

Pressing in whole body, especially on chest. Pains in every part, *< on r. side;* in teeth and limbs, < lying down and last till sleep; in joints, < after walking; in several parts, in metacarpus, metatarsus, ribs and clavicles; *here and there in body when walking, and in l. knee, l. hip and in loins;* during rest, are > after motion, **others arise during motion and are < during rest**; wandering, gradually becoming seated in l. shoulder; over whole body, as if the flesh were too loose.

Drawing pains here and there; especially in sinewy expansions; at 10 P.M. in bed, wandering through all limbs and joints, especially in l. middle ribs, where it caused stitches, impeding respiration; in periosteum of all bones in forenoon, causing apprehension, as in onset of ague. *In almost all limbs and joints, with tension,* the pain most sensitive in l. wrist, now in knees, now ankles and neck, remaining longest in l. shoulder-joint, with sensation of paralysis (during motion), afterwards the same pains also in neck, with drawing scraping in long bones, combined with stitches. *Drawing rheumatic pains in various parts at different times during the day, especially at insertion of l. ligamentum patellæ, anteriorly on r. leg and in nape.* Drawing in lumbar region and in temporal bones, < after eating, with pressing; in temporal muscles, and in muscles of upper arm and here and there in body; painless, back and forth in affected parts.

(Painful throbbing in all vessels.) Anxiety in morning, which seemed to rise from abdomen, as if a purge had been taken and as if the breathing were too short. Attack as if the ailment rose up and took away breath and speech. General sick feeling. Discomfort, with weariness, so that even the clothes were oppressive. Lameness; with desire to keep quiet. Soreness of old bruises; in morning of every part on which he lies. Sensibility < in evening. Necessity to bend forward when walking. Restlessness; of affected part.

Weariness; in morning; **on rising, < in forenoon while walking** (Phos.), **so that he drags himself about,** *with weakness in knees and legs on ascending stairs;* in morning on waking, > rising and dressing; in morning after rising, with heaviness; in forenoon; *in afternoon;* in afternoon, then two liquid stools without tenesmus; towards evening; *on slightest exertion,* also *with general sweat;* on waking; when sitting, > walking; when walking; when walking in a room, > walking in open air; walking in open air, < ascending steps; > a hearty supper; *with aching in arms and legs, with sinking down of arms if she works, and with difficulty in ascending steps;* with anxiety; as if quickly cooled by a rain after a fatiguing, heated walk, at 4 P.M., in the house, on approach of a storm, with chilliness, bruised sensation and wandering pains, as after taking a similar cold.

Faintness on rising from bed, *with cold sweat and rumbling in abdomen.* Does not like open air as well as formerly. Aggravation on every motion; A. after waking from midday sleep, with ill humor. Amelioration in evening from emission of flatus; A. while lying. *Disappearance of symptoms after a short rest in bed, except the weakness and depressed mood.*

Mind.—Delirious; talking about his business; prattling about business to be attended to (Op.), *at daybreak,* > when the pain begins; *D. talk at night;* talking on waking. Furious delirium, then coma, with occasional subsultus tendinum. Delirious, frightful fantasy at 10 P.M. of soldiers cutting him down, he was on the point of escaping, with heat and sweat (without thirst), the delirium > uncovering and getting cool. Attempts to escape from bed (Bell.). Mental illusion, her head seems too heavy. Nervous excitement; at noon.

Anxiety, apprehension for the future; anxiety in evening on lying down, from constriction of chest; > *open air; in whole body, forcing him to do something constantly.* **Ill humor** (Rhus t.), **with needless anxiety. Everything puts him out of humor.** Ill humor during and after a meal; after a meal, with discomfort. *Irritable, weeping mood;* (and desire to be alone). Fretful, she imagines that she cannot accomplish her work, constantly takes up the wrong piece, is inclined to take another, then aching in forehead. *Angry at contradiction. Quarrelsome. Inclined to scold. Taciturn. Hesitating.* Discontented. *Despondent; (and disinclined to think, with exhausted mental power);* afterwards cheerful. Over-busy. Indolent.

Weakness of mind; so that his ideas disappear, as if he would faint, < standing, *with heat in face. Imagination sluggish, it is impossible to make plans for the future,* but the judgment is unimpaired. Thoughts vanish suddenly on attentive reading. Want of memory, with loss of reflective powers. Unconsciousness of what she is doing (in a room), < when lying; of what she is doing (in a room), everything falls from her hands.

Head.—*Stitches through on stepping hard, mostly from before backward;* through H. when coughing. It goes through the head when coughing. *Pressure on coughing;* (on stepping). Aching; in morning; **beginning in morning on first opening and moving eyes**; in morning on waking, also especially in upper part of forehead, extending after rising to supraorbital region, > afternoon; in forenoon, especially in forehead and vertex; in afternoon, more on one side, with pain in eye of same side; towards evening, with incipient coryza; after eating, and on walking pressing outward in forehead; < touch, mostly in forepart; < riding; on waking, especially over l. eye, after rising the pain extended towards vertex and occiput; **in morning after rising,** *a twitching drawing in malar and maxillary bones;* more a twitching than a throbbing, with hot face; *as from a weight in head, as if he would incline it to either side, with pressure outward in brain and desire to lie down; as if brain were too full and pressed asunder,* < *sitting; as if something pressed skull asunder,* pulsating; *as from compression, before daylight,* < *raising eyes, with heaviness and stitches in it and inability to rise;* pressing together, with jerks in brain like pulsation; throbbing, more rapid on motion, she thinks she hears it, affecting eyes so that she cannot see well; oppressive, in afternoon; stupefying, in evening.

Confusion; in morning; *in morning on waking, with aching, as after intoxication, with disinclination to rise;* in forenoon; *after rising from bed; before sleep, with drawing in occiput extending into neck;* while riding over a rough road; after eating, with heaviness; < walking, > sitting quietly; > moving in open air; > empty eructations; till sleep; with pain in forehead; and pain in temples; with pain in various places, now in temples, now in occiput, now in forehead; sudden; as if in a vise; dizzy; increasing to aching, especially in l. temple, the pain < at 5 P.M., accompanied then by nauseous vomiting, sensitiveness of smell and hissing in l. ear as of boiling water, all > riding in a wagon.

Stupefaction. Dulness, with difficulty in reflecting. Fulness, < turning head. *Heaviness; with pressure forward of whole brain;* dizzy, on sitting (stooping) and reading, > raising head. Lightness, with wabbling in ears. *Rush of blood;* then pressing together of temples. Felt as if drunk and would lie down.

Vertigo; in morning on waking, with weakness; in forenoon; *on raising head* (Phos.), *from inclining it forward;* on turning head; after eating; while walking, with reeling of all objects and prostration; with fulness of head; *with weakness in limbs;* **in morning on rising, as if head were turning in a circle; on rising from a chair,** *everything turns,* > *after walking; in afternoon as if brain were turning around; like a whirling if she sits up in bed, with nausea in middle of chest as if faintness would ensue* (Phos.); *when standing, as if everything whirled about; so that he nearly fell backward* at 8 P.M. *on standing;* as from drunkenness and as from rush of blood to head; in attacks while walking in open air, > sitting down; sudden, towards noon; sudden, after having a tooth extracted.

Forehead.—*Stitches; to occiput;* above r. brow; in forepart, with confusion of head; itching, in r. muscles. *Digging in forepart of brain,* < *stooping and rapid walking, with fatigue from walking. Pain;* in forenoon; in evening; after continued reading; < **stooping**; < *motion, and in occiput;* after motion, especially towards brows; **above l. eye, then in occipital protuberances, spreading thence over whole body, the pain becoming so severe on quick motion and after eating that it seemed like a pulsation in head.** Pain in l. side and in occiput, with tension in r. side of neck below mastoid process at 4 P.M. **Pain as if everything would press out; on stooping, as if everything would fall out;** *as if pressing outward from above downward,* < evening *on stooping, and in l. eyeball.* Pressure outward on stooping, with stitches; outward over l. orbit, extending into brain, changing to a pressure on eyeball from above inward. Constrictive pain in afternoon after a nap, > washing with cold water, with heaviness in head. Drawing pain, with confusion of head; D. pain in sinciput and pressure in occiput; above r. eyebrow; over r. eye, then in diseased r. eyetooth, then the headache returned and spread over forehead; in r. eminence at 6 P.M., with tension and posteriorly on r. parietal bone, then alternating with the same pain in same places on l. side; in l. side in morning; in l. half above eyebrow, with tension, also as if a bud slowly unfolded in forehead; intermittent, over l. eyebrow. Drawing distending pain in l. half of F. and occiput while walking about room. Throbbing pain, so that he must lie down; hollow, and in occiput. Pain as from a burn over l. eye, > pressure, and on l. side of nose. Compression above eyes. Pressive sensation in sinciput without pain. *Confusion.* Tension in muscles under skin on moving eyes. Whirling in r. side, with a stitch in l. side of it.

Temples.—Stitches through, on walking in open air; sudden, to forehead; twitching, sometimes extending over l. parietal region. Tearing; sometimes extending to occiput, sometimes to petrous portion of temporal bones, and frequently changing its position. Pain; and in frontal region, alternating with pain in finger and wrist-joints, and with griping in abdomen; in r.; r. then l. Pressing-out pain; l.; from both T. towards forehead. Pressing together in bones, alternating with drawing pain in occipital protuberances. Throbbing outward pain towards T. on going to bed. Pain as if pulled by the hair. Intermittent drawing pain near l. eye. **Drawing in bones towards zygoma,** < *l.,* afterwards this returned and extended to l. jaw; *in both towards malar-bones;* in l., with pressing; then copious pasty stools. *Tensive twisting pain in single muscle fibres of r.* Gurgling.

Vertex.—Increase of pain under V., with soreness of scalp over the same, and bruised soreness of vertex. *Throbbing pain in morning on waking.* Beating, with beating and fulness in cerebellum. Burning pain in a spot. Weight. Dull motions, and in forehead, causing vertigo and cessation of ideas.

Sides.—Throbbing in r., perceptible to hand. *Stitch deep in l. side of brain on coughing.* Tearing; l.; in r. parietal bone as by a sharp hook. Digging in a spot in r. half of brain, extending down along both jawbones, or tearing, with pain in a submaxillary gland. Pain above and behind l. ear; throbbing-drawing pulsating, in parietal bone, extending to forehead; sudden drawing-throbbing, in r. parietal eminence in forenoon, > pressure; pressing-together, on both. Sensation as if pressed together from both ears.

Occiput.—Pain; in l. lower part at 4 P.M., < touch; > **towards noon, with drawing down into neck,** but in afternoon pressure in temporal bones and frequently in forehead and occiput; sharp P. in l. protuberance, coming and going suddenly; tensive, in both sides.

Pain like a heaviness which pressed upon a sore spot in morning when lying on back, extending to shoulders. Pressure in both sides; on l. side, with sticking in l. heel. Soreness to touch on one side. Numbness, with enlarged feeling.

Scalp.—*Hair seems fatty in morning and hands become fatty while combing.* Drawn tightly and sensitive. *Sensitive towards evening.* Sensation as if posterior half were spasmodically contracted, which caused tension in anterior half. Smarting erosion on occiput at night. Crawling on both sides of ears, with creeping. Itching; while combing.

Clinical.—The headaches of Bryonia are all aggravated by motion, even of eyeballs. The pains either begin in the occiput or finally become seated in the occiput, frequently associated with dryness of the mouth, thirst and coated tongue; the headaches are rarely neuralgic, but are generally sympathetic with gastric disorders or with inflammatory affections. Meningitis from suppressed eruptions.

Eyes.—Sudden swelling of one, with pain, discharge of pus, and the conjunctiva is dark red and swollen. Aching all about r. in evening in open air, especially on lower margin of orbit. Pain as if burnt, extending outward into l. Pressure; with burning itching in lids; painful, < r., with redness and swelling of lids; as from a hand or as from a room full of smoke, in morning on waking. Sensation as of sand in r., in afternoon. Biting as of sand (?), which causes rubbing. *Burning of r., with lachrymation.*

Lachrymation; in open air; with redness of white of eye and agglutination of external canthus; with itching of lids. *Intermittent pain in l. ball,* < **moving ball,** *with feeling as if the eye became smaller and were retracted within orbit.* Pressure on ball, more from above downward. Throbbing in r. ball. Pupils dilated.

Lids.—*Swelling of r. upper;* of lower, with pain; in morning, with *agglutination;* < r., with redness; with redness and pressure. Redness of lower, with inflammation of it and twitching of upper. *Twitching drawing together in l. upper, with heaviness.* Twitching of r. upper; of upper and of r. eye. Agglutination in morning; with burning biting in r. canthi; in morning, and after forcible opening vision as through a veil. Feel agglutinated in morning, red and swollen, and feel as if rubbed and heated. Pressure above lids towards evening. Burning of r. Itching on border of l. upper, with burning and tearing; sticking, on margin of r., > scratching; sticking, below r. upper, as from a stiff hair, > rubbing.

Canthi.—Sore pain in l. internal, with smarting. Burning in external, on touch. Itching in r. inner, < by rubbing, which causes lachrymation; in l. external, not > rubbing, with biting. Itching-biting in l. external; in l. internal, as from sand, at 3 P.M.

Orbits.—Stitches in brows; in upper border of r. O., with heaviness in eye and itching on lid. Drawing pinching in r. brow, with itching in l. brow. Aching in l., with pulsation; A. deep in r., < pressure on ball; in supraorbital ridge in a spot of the size of a needle; in r. supraorbital region, extending to l. side; contractive, in muscles of r. brow.

Vision misty; in l. eye. Weak in morning, letters run together if she attempts to read. Presbyopia. Flickering before r. eye on looking out of the window after a moderate dinner, *then every object seemed covered with rainbow colors,* on closing the eye appearance of a jagged, broken iridescent stripe, which on keeping the eye closed a long time became of a blinding white color, then weakness of eye, then *photophobia* and confusion of head.

Clinical.—Congestion and soreness of the eye (sympathetic). Inflammation of the eye, especially of internal parts, iritis, choroiditis, glaucoma, etc., the eyeball very painful, full feeling, pains extending to back of head.

Ears.—Discharge of blood. Stitches; now in one, now in other, on going into open air and on entering house; in r. meatus auditorius; (on convex surface of r. when touched). Pressure on cartilage of r.; in r. concha. Sensation as if a finger were pressed into external meatus, < stooping to read. Pain about l.; drawing, in r.; constrictive, in meatus auditorius, at first > removing wax, but always returning with difficult hearing; as if burnt, extending out at l. ear. Stopped sensation. (Sensitiveness of whole union with skull); and of border of ear.

(Sensitiveness extends from convex to concave surface, with redness of latter, heat of ear, swelling of external meatus, pain in convex surface, stitches piercing deep into ear, diminished hearing, ringing, difficulty in chewing, pain in bony parts about ear, inability to lie on r. side at night, next day noise before ear as of boiling water, pressure upon ear and warmth were pleasant, cracking in ear upon blowing nose, restlessness at night, next day stitches, < every step, the pain < cold air, stoppage of ear, the swelling and pain extending over a part of parotid gland to zygoma, stitches extending into head and external part of neck, chilliness in evening, with acceleration of the otherwise small pulse, the lower tones of music seeming incorrect and reversed, inability to find any place to lay his head. without tension of the skin over parotid, which caused sleeplessness, sensitiveness of parotid to touch of steel bows of spectacles, which also caused burning, with tearing in two lower teeth, continued swelling of ear, redness, towards evening creeping shivering over back, external ear standing out from base of ear, the skin, especially on margin, thickened, dry, white, with scales, insensible to touch but itching, contraction of meatus, thickening of antitragus, cracking in internal ear when blowing nose, hawking, etc., the swelling extending to lower eyelids and r. side of neck, pain like electric shocks in first r. lower molar [> for a time by drinking cold water], next morning chill in back and limbs, with small, rapid, depressed pulse.)

(Sensitiveness of parotid, with swelling and stitches, then stitch in middle ear, with warmth in ear and sensation as if an abscess were bursting, then ringing in ears and itching in concave surfaces of ears, afterwards stitches, especially in region of articulation of jaw, on swallowing sensation of swelling in throat, with stitches and noises in r. ear, pain in forehead, pasty taste, stools irregular, in afternoon stitches in the hitherto healthy l. ear.)

Hearing difficult in l., as if stopped. Ringing, with difficult hearing; R. as of small bells in front of l. Chirping in head, as of locusts. Humming; before r. *Roaring;* < r.; with rapid pulse; in l. like water pouring over a dam. Sudden noise in l., then in r., as of a distant windmill.

Nose.—*Swelling, with bleeding; S. of l. side of tip, with twitching pain in it, and on touch feeling as if it would ulcerate.* Ulcer within r. nostril, with biting pain. Crawling in septum, < blowing it, with tickling.

Coryza, > in open air; C. with stitches in head and sensation as if everything pressed out at forehead (< stooping); stopped; sudden, stopped, with roaring in l. ear and sensation as if something were before it, which diminishes hearing. Closure of r. nostril, with opening of l. and tendency to watery discharge. *Fluent coryza;* with chilliness in skin, stretching of limbs and frequent yawning; with greenish discharge. Thin discharge from l. nostril; thin light-colored discharge from r. nostril. *Profuse coryza.* Severe C., with pain in forehead. Profuse fluent C., with much sneezing; so that he speaks through the nose, with chilliness; causing a restless night. Discharge of consistent whitish-yellow mucus, smelling like bread. Much mucus in nose and bronchi.

Sneezing; < stroking hand across forehead; *twice when coughing.* Frequent S.; in forenoon; in afternoon; in evening; at 10 P.M. Violent S.; in morning; in morning, with yawning. Bleeding; **for a quarter of an hour in morning after rising** (Carbo v., Phos.); *daily;* at 3 A.M., waking him; from r. nostril; from r. after vertigo; from l. nostril in morning; then ulcerated nostrils.

Clinical.—Catarrh, with dryness, sudden suppression of the discharge and headache. Bleeding from suppressed menstruation, occurring regularly every day.

Face.—Red, hot(Bell., Op.), **soft puffiness; red, round, hot spot on malar-bone.** Swelling of upper half, especially under eyes and over root of nose, with swelling of lids and inability to open l. eye; of r. cheek close by ear, with burning pain; of l. side, more along nose, within it (with diarrhœa). Red spots, and on neck. *Yellow.* Pale. Sickly, jaundiced look. (Painful throbbing in all parts, perceptible to touch.) Tearing in l. cheek; *twitching, externally in malar-bone, extending to r. temple, < touch. Painful pressure under r. cheek, > pressure.* Drawing pain in l. cheek. Drawing in muscles. Stiffness of muscles, whereby it seemed as if any desired expression could be given to the face by pushing the muscles. Feeling as if gauze were over it.

Lips.—*Swelling of upper* (Bell.), *with redness and heat, as in beginning erysipelas, and in expansion of nose,* then sensitiveness of lip to touch. *Crack in lower.* Eruption outside border of lower, with itching biting as from salt. Suppurating fissures on lower, with burning pain on touch. Aphthous erosion on mucous membrane of upper. Bleeding aphthæ on inner surface. Bleeding pimple on r. corner of lower. Vesicle on vermilion border of lower, with burning pain; burning, in middle of upper, looking like hydroa. Trembling of lower, then insensibility in it, then it is drawn to l. side. Twitching in corners, so that he cannot hold a cigar; sticking T. between lower lip and gum in morning in bed, like cancer of lip. Sticking together. *Dryness* (Verat. v.), *and of tongue and hard palate* (Verat. v.), *while tip of tongue was moist;* on inner side of upper and on upper teeth. Burning in lower.

Jaw.—*Pinching in articular cavity of r., < motion.* Drawing tearing in l., as from drawing toothache. Feeling in lower as if there were a node on the bone, with pain on touch and on turning head.

Clinical.—Neuralgia of one side of the face, cannot even speak or eat, because it is so much aggravated by motion.

Mouth.—Teeth. (Yellow coating, with some smell from mouth.) Looseness. *Tearing-sticking on eating, extending into muscles of neck, < warmth.* Sticking and twitching pain extending towards ear, which compels lying down. Tearing in l.; alternating with drawing pain every day towards evening. Sharp pain. *Aching on taking anything warm into mouth;* on opening mouth; during rest, < in bed, > chewing; in back T. on chewing; *about* 3 A.M. *as if an exposed nerve were paining from cold air,* < **lying on painless side,** > **lying on painful cheek;** *as if screwed in and then pulled out at night till* 6 A.M., > **momentarily by cold water** (Coff., Puls.), *better on walking in open air, with tearing in cheeks and pinching in ears;* sudden intermittent, in l. lower second bicuspid, somewhat as if being pulled out, < morning and evening and on pulling with the fingers (in evening), sometimes shootings in the tooth, sometimes the pain ends in a shoot; *jerking in evening in bed, now in upper, now in lower back, when in upper and they are pressed with the finger the pain changes to the corresponding lower teeth;* jerking, when smoking; *drawing, at times jerking, in l. upper back T. during and after eating, when the teeth seem too long and wabble back and forth;* drawing, in back T.; periodic drawing and tearing; throbbing drawing, in roots of r. lower incisors, when > by pressure a similar pain in upper middle incisors, then in last r. upper molars, the pain causing a waving sensation; drawing-tensive, in two r. upper molars, > pressure with tongue or biting teeth together; sore, during cold drinks. Grumbling in a hollow T. Sensation as if too long; in molars in morning after waking, with looseness and when trying to bite pain as if they fell out. Sensitiveness of l. lower hollow T. to touch of tongue, and in gum about it.

Gums.—Spongy. *Pain as if sore and raw, with painful loose teeth.* Aching, now jumping, now mild, in r. upper alveoli.

Tongue.—**White coat** (Tarax., Ant. cr.). Yellow coat, with sunken raphe. *Aphthæ on tip.* Painful blister in middle of l. margin; biting and burning blisters on anterior margin. Pricking in anterior third. Burning caused by smoking tobacco. Burning pain in middle in evening, then a hard lump. Dryness, with sensation of prominent papillæ; D. of tip, the filiform papillæ are much elevated and prickle.

Something bitter rises into mouth without eructations, with nausea. **Dryness** (Verat. v., Phos., etc.), *> for a moment by drinking, then <; so that tongue sticks to palate;* dry sensation in morning; in evening, palate, tongue and lips almost stick together, so that speech is difficult; *without thirst;* of whole mouth except tip of tongue. Dryness of palate; after eating; of palate at night as if tough mucus were on uvula and could not be loosened. (Sensitiveness, but not followed by aphthæ as formerly.) *Salivation;* after smoking tobacco. *Soapy, frothy salivation.* Saliva mixed with blood. Saliva runs out of mouth involuntarily. Much spitting. Offensive breath; with hawking of offensive tough mucus, in which were cheesy lumps, sometimes round, sometimes lentil-shaped.

Taste.—**Bitter** (Chel., Sulph.); in evening after lying down; > **frequent drinking of cold water, with nausea; offensive,** *after drinking beer; nauseous, in morning; pasty, in forenoon; on posterior part of palate after dinner;* in a spot on tip of tongue; *to everything, with inability to swallow food;* to soup, with nausea, then after warm water (which tasted bitter) vomiting of yellowish-green fluid, with remnants of food, then relief. *Sweetish;* salt, sweetish, after cherry brandy. *Flat; and* *nauseous.* *Pasty;* offensive, especially at root of tongue. Clayey. Nauseous, with bitter salivation; acrid, with bitter eructations. Acrid dry, after eating, with dryness of forepart of mouth without thirst, the lips being dry and cracked. Unpleasant towards evening, with nausea. Offensive to beer; causing nausea and shivering over back. Bad to tobacco, with salivation on attempting to smoke; to meat. As of bad meat or bad teeth in morning fasting. *Lost for food, bitter when not eating.*

Clinical.—Dryness of lips, mouth and throat. Tongue dry, rough (in low fevers). Tongue heavily coated white (in gastric derangements).

Throat.—Strong pulsations of carotids. Sharp rheumatic pain in tendon of l. trapezius on turning head to l. Stitch on r. side, above sternal end of cavity. Simple pain in submaxillary gland, or swelling. Redness of fauces and uvula. Posterior nares closed by swelling. Slimy in evening, with thirst. *Tough mucus loosened by hawking;* tough M. in posterior nares. Foul-smelling mucus, as after eating crabs or fish. Pseudo-membranous catarrh, and in palate. Hawking of yellow mucus; H. of offensive mucus and cheesy lumps, easily raised, < in morning.

Angina tonsillaris. *Stitching when swallowing;* on coughing; internally on pressure and on turning head. Sensation as if a foreign body were sticking in it; alternating with a sensation as if a worm were moving in it. *Soreness, < in warm room, > drinking, but returning, with dryness and rawness, on empty swallowing;* in evening, with redness and difficult swallowing. Pain in back part on motion; especially in r. tonsil only on empty swallowing, with stitches shooting into r. ear; in l. tonsil in morning on waking, with full sensation in loins. (Swollen sensation when swallowing, or as if full of mucus); in back part, with feeling as of severe coryza, which hinders talking. Scraping; as after strong rum. Rawness; scraping.

Constriction; in pharynx, as from a broad band, with frequent yawning. Drawing extending into ear, with pressure. Tickling and warmth. Dry sensation, with much mucus in it; D. sensation in posterior and upper part in evening; in pharynx, with smarting behind pomum adami. Rancid, smoky taste late in evening; bad T., > eating, with taste in mouth like the smell of decaying meat, with a tolerably clean tongue. Constant disposition to swallow, with stinging externally on r. side, on a line with the promontory of larynx.

Inability to swallow food and drink, they cause choking. Pain in œsophagus as if contracted, more in lower part. Pressure in œsophagus as from an overloaded stomach; P. in O. as if he had swallowed a hard angular body.

Stomach.—*Ravenous hunger* (Iod., China); in morning, with thirst and flushes of heat; ravenous H. continued into night. Ravenous hunger without appetite; in morning fasting. *Desire for acids* (Verat. alb.) (fruit). Craving for oysters and strong coffee. Longing for things not at hand. Longing for many things which he cannot eat. *Desires things immediately, but when offered does not wish for them* (China). Food smells good but when he begins to eat the appetite disappears. Appetite diminished; for dinner. Appetite lost; for breakfast, which almost nauseates him; *lost for milk, but if he takes it he begins to relish it.* Aversion to food; and even a glass of beer before eating is repugnant, with longing for warm broth, and after taking it urging to stool, with three painless greenish-brown liquid stools, discharged as from a tube, then burning pain in rectum and on nates. Aversion to tobacco, with salivation on swallowing.

Thirst excessive (Iod., Chin.); **she must drink much at once,** *and the drink does not distress her;* **with necessity to drink much cold water,** *with internal but not external heat;* in morning on rising; about 3 A.M., then sweetish-sour sweat, before this ceased drawing headache, which after rising changed to confusion of head; on waking at 11 P.M., with feverish excitement, pulse accelerated, hearing sensitive, even the swinging of the pendulum of a small clock affected him unpleasantly, he tried to sleep again, but lay long in a dreamy half-sleep; necessity to drink several times at night; great after eating; < drinking beer; *for very clear, cold water. Longing for coffee. Desire for wine;* the moderate use of which relieves nausea. Thirst, then loss of thirst, with coldness of hands and feet. Loss of thirst. Aversion to beer in evening.

Eructations (Carb. v., Phos.) *after eating* (Carb. v.), but not after drinking; (with burnt taste in mouth and mucus in throat); severe, after eating, from morning till evening. *Bitter* (Arn.); after eating. *Sourish after eating;* with sourish salivation. Of food; tasting of food. Of contents of stomach. Of mucus in morning. Of water and mucus, like waterbrash, which rises into chest at 6 P.M., with general coldness. (Burning, which makes the mouth raw and prevents the tasting of food.) Empty; after eating, with dizzy confusion of head and drawing pain in l. half of forehead; with confusion of head; with rumbling on l. side near stomach; suppressed.

Hiccough; *after eating, and on every shock caused by it, pressure in forehead, as if the brain shook from behind forward;* after vomiting; after eructations.

Nausea; in morning on waking (Lyc.), *with vomiting;* in morning after anxious dreams, without ability to vomit, with empty eructations; every morning, two hours after rising, with salivation; all the forenoon; in afternoon after drinking; in evening before sleep; in evening, then flow of much water from mouth; before midnight; on waking after midnight, with necessity to vomit food and bile; *on slightest motion, even to vomiting;* after a breakfast of coffee; after eating, with vomiting; on walking in open air, > in house, returning in open air, with weakness in limbs and head, so that he expected to fall, he gasped and warmth came into chest and extended into head; from tobacco; < smoking; even to vomiting, < lying on r. side, then easy empty eructations alternating with salivation; with much salivation; with dizzy confusion of head and frequent yawning; with creeping chills; with shuddering and convulsive contraction of abdominal muscles, especially on each side of epigastrium; causing shivering, with involuntary shaking of head and closure of lids; then ravenous hunger; intermittent, all the forenoon, even to vomiting; anxious, during dinner; suddenly, then vomiting at intervals of half an hour, the last time with violent retching and constriction of stomach, the matter seeming like chocolate, water and mucus, with taste of the medicine (he had taken chocolate for breakfast), then difficult vomiting of saffron-yellow, tough, bitter fluid; suddenly after dinner, then paroxysmal and difficult vomiting of much more than had been eaten, with a few drops of bright blood from r. nostril; sudden intermittent, at 9 P.M. in bed, then salivation, with rancid and scraping sensation in stomach. Heaving, as if he would vomit when coughing, without nausea.

Vomiting, incessant, *of solid food* (Lyc., Verat. a.), *but not of drinks;* of food on coughing; sour in morning of the fish eaten the previous evening; of bitter thick fluid, tasting of food; of bitter, musty and putrid liquid, which leaves a similar taste, about 6 A.M.; of mucus in evening; frequent, of yellow and green mucus; (of blood, with lying down).

Distention (Lyc.); *with sensitiveness to pressure* (Phos.); of epigastric region; feeling of D., as from flatus which pressed forward towards stomach and caused pain, soon pressing backward, all < bending forward, > walking and bending backward. *Swollen feeling in pit* (Lyc.); below pit. Stitches on deep inspiration; with every eructation; in pit, < walking about room and deep inspiration. *Cutting in pit;* attacks of sticking, in pit. Griping in epigastric region, < motion and standing, with cutting, then passage of flatus. Pinching, changing to colic in abdomen; P. in pit. Digging extending to abdomen, with tension.

Sensation as if a stone lay in it, after eating (Abies nig. in part); **making him fretful; sensation of a stone in it, with pain in epigastric region on touch;** continuing after breakfast, then rumbling and griping in intestines, with constriction of chest and tension in pectoral muscles. Pressure at 4 and 5 P.M., with constriction; *P. while eating;* after eating; when walking; *in pit;* in pit when walking after supper, then pressure on bladder and perineum, > while sitting; < moving arm, with tension and burning in r. side of chest; in pit, oppressing the chest. *Pain;* **in epigastric region on pressure**; *with anxiety;* after drinking wine and water, < deep inspiration and pressure. *Soreness in pit when coughing.* Burning twisting pain. Twisting in pit, waking her in evening, causing nausea and threatening to suffocate her, so that she must sit up. Tension, and in bowels.

Contractive pain after eating; then cutting in and above pit, eructations, rising heat, nausea and vomiting of food. Intermittent burning constriction, obliging bending forward, < deep inspiration, with salivation, during its greatest severity pain in axillæ and on r. hip, confusion in head, then pain in intestines and desire for stool. Constrictive pain as if rolled into a ball, which he believed he could feel with the hand, so that he could not straighten up, > in bed, *by drawing legs up against abdomen* (Coloc.), then pain in l. side of chest, which impeded breathing, with sensation as if l. lobe of lung were enlarged, then sweat and sleep. Constrictive pain in epigastric region, extending over chest, < towards evening, so that he could not stand upright, > rubbing, he lay in bed, took a cup of warm soup, covered stomach with warm clothing, and drew legs up to abdomen, scarcely was this pain relieved when there was urging to stool, rumbling, and frequent offensive, yellowish diarrhœa, causing burning in rectum.

Burning; in afternoon; from a glass of wine in evening; in pit, < during every inspiration; in region of pit, with thirst, but without dryness of throat; in epigastric region, causing shortness of breath, with pain; paroxysmal burning and pressure; burning pain. Scraping. Scraping, rancid feeling, as of beginning heartburn, with tensive pain in r. hypochondrium. Sensation as of something sharply rancid. Emptiness; in afternoon; with distention of abdomen. Discomfort, with flatulent distention of abdomen; in epigastric region, with distention of abdomen. Weakness of digestion.

Clinical.—An extremely valuable remedy for catarrhal inflammation of the stomach (dyspepsia), with thirst, white-coated tongue, nausea and vomiting, < warm drinks, which are vomited; feeling of a hard lump, which makes the stomach sore. Gastric derangements, which recur often in persons who have been in the habit of taking mercury, the attacks frequently preceded by great hunger and apparently caused by overeating; the patient becomes very irritable, tongue thickly coated, etc. In all gastric derangements there are usually great sensitiveness of epigastrium to touch and vomiting of food.

Abdomen.—Retraction. *Distention;* towards evening; sensation of D. at 6, 7 and 8 P.M., with weight and sensation of hypertrophy; *after eating,* also with discomfort; > emission of offensive flatus; *with motions and colic, then continued constipation and feeling as if something lay in abdomen;* with uneasiness in it and pinching, as before menstruation; with dragging. Sudden dropsy, with inability to breathe and necessity to sit up.

Rumbling; after eating, with tension; < in forenoon; < in evening in bed; with sensation as before diarrhœa; with urging to stool, which was soft; with griping in l. side, then emission of flatus; then three liquid stools. Wandering gurgling at 3 P.M., then pasty stool and emission of flatus. Constant motions as before stool. Emission of flatus in night, preceded by loud rumbling and grumbling; E., with urging to stool like a pressure, heat, weight, and powerlessness of sphincter ani and rectum; **of offensive flatus** (Sul.); frequent short, of offensive flatus; loud.

Cutting stitches upward into stomach (after drinking warm milk in afternoon), obliging him to bend double, > stool. Tearing, < motion, with drawing, then stitches, < during stool and in evening. Cutting, with gurgling and rumbling, then watery stool; *sudden C., > profuse pasty stools, with digging, compelling him to bend double* (Coloc.); in forenoon, as before dysentery. *Griping;* while walking before a meal, then a liquid stool, as if poured from a tube, after the meal a similar stool, then burning in anus; *with constriction,* with rumbling and ineffectual urging to stool; intermittent, > emission of flatus; in places. Pinching; < open air; > by emission of flatus; with motions, then watery stool with passage of flatus, the P. occurring frequently in afternoon, with *soreness and dragging downward and outward,* then two profuse watery stools, then burning in anus (Sulph.).

Pain; on rising and through forenoon; during and after dinner; after dinner, then emission of flatus, then pasty stool; on urinating; > walking, with anxiety and difficult breathing; *as before diarrhœa,* and in anus; as from a purge, or as if hæmorrhoids would come on; spasmodic, after dinner; flatulent, after supper, with pressure in cæcum; wind colic, disturbing night's rest; as if one would vomit.

Sensitiveness. Tension; < afternoon, after eating, with distention; > after a long walk; > towards morning by emission of offensive flatus, with distention, and in epigastric region; with dragging and digging; painful tympanic tension, > two pasty stools. Sensation of looseness of bowels, < towards noon, with emptiness in stomach. Qualmishness preceded by watery stool and alternating with pinching. Heaviness; while sitting, especially in lower, as if it hung down upon thighs.

Rumbling in upper. Throbbing twitching in or just beneath wall, to left of epigastrium. *Twitching in l. side between navel and l. flank, as if in muscles of wall, then sticking deep in l. side of back.* Convulsive movements of r. muscles. Tearing in l. side. Pinching in l., then emission of flatus. Pain in sides like pleuritic stitches.

Hypochondrium.—Wandering gurgling in l. Stitches in r., then in epigastrium; *in r., with sensitiveness, the latter < hard pressure and deep inspiration;* deep in r.; beneath wall of r., extending towards epigastrium; long-drawn, in liver while sitting; in l. flank. Griping in hepatic region, extending to spleen, with nausea. Pain in flanks. *Tensive pain in hepatic region; in r. below false ribs, < deep inspiration;* in r., disappearing with rumbling in upper abdomen. Burning pain in hepatic region. Bruised sensation at ends of l. false ribs, extending to navel. Sensitiveness of hepatic region.

Umbilical Region.—Hard swelling, and beneath hypochondria. *Griping, with pinching, as after taking cold,* then profuse thin stool; G., waking at night; after dinner, starting the sweat on forehead, > passage of offensive flatus; periodical; frequent, above umbilicus. Pinching when walking and standing, with pressure; P. above navel in afternoon, while riding in a very jolting wagon, extending towards spleen; sudden sticking, in r. side below navel, then passage of flatus. Twisting, with nausea; painful T., with stitches. Digging. Boring; with chilliness; beneath navel. Pain, waking at 6 A.M., with urging to stool; before eating; after dinner, > passage of flatus; > walking in open air, but lasting in a slight degree till 5 P.M.; below navel, towards noon; below navel, then emission of flatus after eating. Pressure every time on waking, with urging to stool, but he soon sank into a half-sleep, in which he was busy with fancies, in morning pungent, fluid, difficult stool, then several similar stools during the day. Pressure on navel as from a button when walking in open air. Burning below navel. Heaviness below navel.

Hypogastrium.—Sudden stitches from l. to r. during dinner, then two stitches through chest from l. to r.; in r. inguinal region. Deep cutting; crampy, in r. < inspiration, with heat in it. Pressure, with pinching. Pain in l. inguinal ring every morning; towards inguinal ring on sitting down. (Sensation of a lump low down in abdomen.) Soreness in iliac region, in overhanging folds.

Clinical.—Symptoms of inflammation of the liver, which seems swollen, very sore to touch, pains sharp, greatly < motion, > warmth and pressure, *typhlitis, peritonitis,* gastro-enteritis; a frequently indicated remedy for these diseases, characterized by extreme soreness, thirst, fever, coated tongue, etc.

Rectum.—Pulselike jerking. Stitches as often as flatus passed, it seemed to press towards rectum. *Burning, with evacuation of stool and urine* (Sulph.); B. after hard stool. Pressing towards anus. Inclination to diarrhœa from slightest draft of air. Dragging-like urging to stool, without real need of it, with pain in anus. Much straining to finish stool, *stools dry and large.* Urging to stool; at 6 A.M., then frequent acrid fluid stools, with compact portions; from slightest tightening of clothes, without pain in abdomen, stool soft; *then copious pasty stools, with relief of all symptoms except the confusion of head;* then soft stool; then scanty firm stool; U. after a crumbly stool. Ineffectual U.; in afternoon; with rumbling and emission of flatus.

Anus.—Protruding hæmorrhoids. Retraction. Discharge of mucus. Itching, jerking stitches extending into rectum. Feeling of a plug; at 6 A.M. Pressure in hæmorrhoidal vessels; with dragging and with stitches through perineum into urethra; P. in hæmorrhoids, with burning. Aching in hæmorrhoidal vessels, < sitting. Burning pain before a meal; B. pain, with a soft stool. Burning after a natural stool; B. in hæmorrhoidal vessels in evening; with itching.

Perineum.—Tearing sticking in evening, extending to bladder and especially to bulbus urethræ, whereby micturition was momentarily prevented.

Stool.—*Pasty,* soon after waking, *with burning in anus* (Sulph.); soon after eating; **offensive; two offensive, in afternoon, then burning in anus;** *with much flatus, then hard portions, then again soft, so that he believed he would scarcely finish the evacuation;* brownish; copious, also only after long exertion.

Diarrhœa; in morning; evening and morning; after dinner, then in an hour stool with little fæces but much mucus, *then burning in anus; < at night and burning in anus with every stool; preceded by cutting in abdomen; then prickling and burning in anus* (Sulph.); **smelling like old cheese;** *bilious acrid, with soreness in anus;* greenish, frequent brown (in an infant); painless, also after eating; painless and frequent, with offensive flatus; frequent, and so sudden that he could not retain it; frequent, then constipation; causing weakness; bloody.

Liquid, after every meal; after a meal, then pain in small of back; and profuse, also with tenesmus and burning in anus; frequent, then burning in anus; *and offensive;* painless, of greenish-brown liquid after dinner, then pinching extending from r. hypochondrium towards stomach; of slimy fluid after eating; of green slimy fluid, then loud passage of flatus. Two mucous stools in evening and a third at night.

Obstinate constipation; C., with painful swelling of hæmorrhoidal vessels (Sulph.). **Dry and difficult;** (Op., Lyc.); *with confusion of head* (Iris); dry and difficult, only every other day; hard and difficult, at first hard portions, then softer. Hard, with inclinations to eructations; H., with pressing out of rectum, then diarrhœa, with fermenting in abdomen; with drawing and pressure in small of back: then drawing and heaviness in sacrum; two unsatisfactory, preceded by cutting in abdomen; *and large,* also dark.

Dark. *Offensive, profuse,* preceded by cutting in abdomen. Scanty; and delayed. Difficult; from inactivity of rectum; and thick-formed. Sluggish; with twitching and sticking in anus. *Unsatisfactory, after much straining, which caused rush of blood to head and contusion of head;* U. or omitted, then frequent, copious, almost like diarrhœa. Involuntary at night in sleep. Frequent; then constipation. Retained.

Clinical.—Diarrhœa in summer, brought on by cold drinks or from vegetables or being overheated, movements in the morning on moving around; diarrhœa from suppressed eruptions; during typhoid fever (of putrid odor), brown. Constipation, stool large and hard.

Urinary Organs.—Heaviness in region of bladder after micturition, with cramplike motions in it. Contraction of bladder after urinating, with feeling as if there were more urine to pass. Feeling in bladder on urinating as if he had not finished, and a few drops pass involuntarily. Sudden urging to urinate, even when bladder is not full. Involuntary micturition of a few hot drops when moving about. Frequent M.; at night; at night, with scanty hot urine; when walking in open air; with burning in urethra and sensation as if some urine remained; with profuse urine; with hot urine. Rare micturition, with scanty urine.

Urethra.—Red, sensitive, burning spots around orifice and on glans and on inner lamella of prepuce, the secreting gland of prepuce became swollen and secreted a profuse yellowish smegma, with painful micturition and with itching and biting on prepuce and glans, all < when walking. Inability to retain urine long, and if he does not urinate immediately on urging there is a feeling as if the urine passed involuntary, though this does not happen. Stitches; in anterior part in evening. Drawing tearing in forepart when not urinating. (Pain.) Feeling as if too narrow when urinating. Burning; before the urine passes, with cutting; itching, in forepart when not urinating, with sticking.

Urine.—Copious; < night, and pale; with sudden desire; sometimes clear, sometimes high-colored. *Scanty; and dark;* and red; and hot. **Red** (Ocim.). **Almost brown**; *brown* (Benz. ac.) *like beer* (Asp., Coloc.). *Reddish yellow at night, with white sediment.* Burning. Containing a thick brown cloud.

Sexual Organs.—Red itching rash covering glans. Stitches in r. spermatic cord. Sticking, burning itching on border of prepuce. Stitches in testicles when sitting. Painful tension from r. testicle along spermatic cord into groin. Increased desire; with emission in night after coition and in morning almost painful erections. Emission at night and in morning, with strong erections.

Swelling of l. labia majora, on which a black, hard pustule rises, like a button, without inflammation or pain. (Increase of leucorrhœa.) Pain in region of r. ovary as if a sore spot caused irritation and dragging, while at rest, < touch, extending to thighs. Menses too early.

Clinical.—Suppression of menses, with the characteristic gastric derangements, or with periodical discharge of blood elsewhere, nose, throat, etc. Inflamed ovaries. Puerperal fever in the early stage, with headache, pains in limbs, weakness. Suppressed lochia. Pelvic peritonitis. Inflammation of mammary glands, breasts much swollen, hot, sharp pains.

Respiratory Organs.—Larynx. Hawking of mucus. Sensation as if an apple-seed cell lodged in upper part or rima glottidis. Sudden scraping at 7 P.M. while sitting, with dry cough. Tickling, with dry hacking cough; T., with violent shaking cough. *Hoarseness;* on walking in open air, with only one tone of voice; with inclination to sweat. Voice lost at times. Voice higher than usual.

Trachea.—*Tough mucus, loosened only after frequent hacking. Sensation of a vapor, on going from a warm room into open air, causing cough, with feeling as if he could not inspire enough air.* Scraping causing dry cough; in lower part in morning, provoking dry cough; at bifurcation of bronchi, causing dry cough.

Cough; (caused by nausea); (< after eating). *Irritation to C., as from mucus in trachea, and after coughing pain, pressure and soreness in trachea, the pain < while talking and smoking.* **Dry cough**; in morning, with coryza; < morning, with waterbrash; *with sticking under sternum;* in attacks; **as if from stomach** (Sepia), *preceded by crawling and tickling in pit of stomach* (Sang.); *hacking, striking against upper part of trachea, which seems covered with dry, tough mucus, even from tobacco-smoking.* Scraping, painful, hacking cough, in throat, in evening in bed, as from rawness and dryness in larynx. Hacking cough, with sensation of soreness and swelling in throat and trachea in morning, and difficult expectoration of mucus. Dry, violent cough on waking after a restless night, > next night, with soreness in chest and thin greenish mucous expectoration. Cough, with expectoration; forenoons; in morning, expectoration of gelatinous mucus; *C. from crawling upward in throat, then expectoration of mucus;* severe C. in morning in bed, with profuse mucous expectoration; sudden C., as from irritation in abdomen, with yellowish-green mucous expectoration. Coughing up clots of blood.

Frequent expectoration; of thick mucus; F. and easy expectoration of thick mucus in morning. E. of transparent, tough, salt mucus. E. of thick mucus, almost without cough, which nearly causes vomiting.

Dyspnœa so that he could not speak. Oppressed breathing; in forenoon, so that the whole chest could not be expanded, with rapid breathing; from distention of abdomen; > walking; in middle of upper half of sternum on every movement of trunk, *with stitching in anterior wall of chest.* Short breath. Gasping before a paroxysm of cough, as if the child could not catch the breath and on this account could not cough, < after midnight, a suffocative attack, then cough. Frequent sighing. Rapid breathing while walking, with sensation as if upper part of chest were too narrow.

Clinical.—Laryngitis and bronchitis (the cough in these diseases is generally dry, hacking, with soreness of abdominal muscles, < night and motion, < coming into a warm room, < after eating or drinking, > heat).

Chest.—Swelling of anterior outer part. *Stitches at 6 P.M., with oppression; S. in sides;* in l.; in middle of l.; in r. ribs; in region of fifth and sixth ribs, on r. side of sternum; in l. clavicle, then simple pain; at insertion of deltoid muscle and in l. side, mostly superficial in l. intercostals. **Stitches in sternum on coughing, with necessity to hold the chest with the hand,** *even pressure upon it caused sticking; in last rib on coughing; between r. third and fourth ribs while sitting;* **in side on which he does not lie,** on turning in bed; below l. nipple, and on deep inspiration or bending towards the right; in pit of stomach; *beneath sternum, < motion and deep inspiration,* with pressure; in r. lower part, with pulselike throbbing; *through chest; in upper part, through shoulders, on inspiration;* outward; *outward below r. nipple on expiration;* in r. side of sternum, extending to navel, < sneezing, so that he must bend double; *tearing in l., extending forward; > during rest, < motion and deep inspiration;* **in r. side, so that he must hold his breath in order not to cry out;** below scapulæ, then below pectoral muscles, almost arresting breath and causing him to sit upright, then S. in vertex; under l. lowest ribs, alternating with S. in r. loin, > 9 P.M.; jerklike, in ribs on deep breathing, > open air; drawing, between r. tenth and eleventh ribs; wandering, in r. side of C., in pit of stomach and in umbilical region, some of the S. piercing r. half of chest like lightning and seeming like cuttings; as in an ulcer, in a spot below sternum, in morning during inspiration, < raising r. arm, with ulcerative pain on touch.

Pleuritic pain in r. breast, to r. of and in intercostal space, two ribs above nipple, < during inspiration, > during expiration. Sharp pain in l. inframammary region, < during inspiration. Tearings between r. sixth and seventh ribs, near sternum, afterwards they approached pleuritic stitches, with throbbing pain in r. clavicle; pain as if ribs were torn from their union. Griping near sternum. Pinching behind sternum, < inspiration and expiration; just about pit of stomach, < sitting and bending forward, or in bed, lying upon the side.

Pain; at 9 P.M., > emission of flatus, with oppression; in various parts; posteriorly in lower part; at bend of r. lower ribs; in middle of sternum, also during respiration, with cold feet; in l. intercostal muscles at 11 P.M., while sitting; in a spot below r. axilla, < touch; in pectoral muscles when writing, with tightness of thorax; throbbing, in a spot between r. tenth and eleventh ribs, > touch; in l. side, *extending forward,* and in region of lower angle of scapula, causing deep breathing; intermittent, at noon on walking; in ensiform cartilage as if injected with blood, in evening on touch; drawing, externally; drawing, in r. muscles. Drawing in pectoral muscles; with tension.

Burning pain in r. side; in a spot in r. ribs at 9 A.M.; along anterior insertion of diaphragm; extending backward from inner surface of sternum. Bruised pain in pectoral muscles on touch; *on r. second rib, extending to sternum.* Sore pain beneath sternum; in whole length of sternum; on inner surface of sternum; on inner surface of upper part of sternum, < breathing; in a spot between l. seventh and ninth ribs, rather externally, < touch. *Sensitiveness all forenoon, with stitches in l. side on inspiration;* S. of anterior muscles; of pectoral muscles on moving hands and on pressure; of pectoral muscles and of pleura, so that inspiration is difficult.

Pressure over whole; in r. wall; in region of r. nipple, < expiration; on r. border of sternum, < in open air; in region of false ribs, impeding respiration, with stitches in region of nipple; as from mucus, and on inspiration stitches in sternum, > eating; as from a hand on upper part of sternum, and she believes that she cannot walk in open air without pain there. Heaviness, > on eating, with heaviness in body; *beneath sternum, extending towards r. shoulder, impeding respiration, with oppression of r. side of chest, and stitches in r. axillary glands.* Sensation as if too narrow on going to sleep, with sensitiveness. Pectoral muscles do not seem free, < on deep inspiration.

Constriction, with necessity to breathe deeply (as if chest were stopped) and on attempting to breathe deeply, pain as if something were being distended which could not be distended completely; C., with heaviness in sternum; after riding over a rough road, compelling to get out of the wagon, with sore pain in inner surface of sternum, bruised feeling in pectoral muscles, and pain on every movement of arms; in upper part; in lower part. Oppression; in morning, with feeling as if clogged by tenacious mucus; in forenoon while sitting and talking; frequent, in forenoon while walking; of r. side, impeding inspiration and especially deep breathing. Fulness. Tension when walking; T. (across short ribs); on both sides externally, < deep inspiration; tensive pain in angles of ribs towards back on inspiration, increasing to a stitch on deeper inspiration, especially below scapulæ, < when stooping. Sensation as if contents were loose and fell into abdomen. *Internal heat;* at every inspiration, < l. side.

Clinical.—Pneumonia in the early stage; Bryonia follows immediately after Aconite, high fever, sharp pains, > lying on the affected side, thirst, profuse sweat, headache, etc. In pleurisy it is most frequently required (the Bryonia patient sweats easily and freely), extremely sharp pain, > pressure and warmth, cannot tolerate the slightest motion. Sometimes useful in pleuritic exudation, when the sharp pains continue.

Heart.—*Stitches. Aching.* Oppression at 6 A.M. Cramp; with rapid pulse. *Beating rapidly and violently.* Palpitation.

Clinical.—Pericarditis, endocarditis (very frequently called for). Great oppression over the region of the heart.

Pulse.—*Full, hard and rapid;* F., large and quick, two hours after breakfast. Rapid. Feeble. Imperceptible at wrist.

Neck.—Tearing in muscles of l. side, down to shoulder. Pain on moving it; *in nape as after taking cold; where nape joins occiput, like a pain and weakness together, as if head were weak;* sharp rheumatic pain in tendon of l. trapezius on turning head to left; sore on motion, in l. side of nape and neck and muscles of face, and mastication renders turning the head or chewing difficult. Pressure on l. side of nape. *Drawing in muscles of r. side, with stiffness.* Tension in nape on moving head. *Stiffness towards r. shoulder;* of l. side; of muscles, with rawness in throat when swallowing; rheumatic, in side towards nape.

Back.—Sticking twitches on both sides near spine when sitting, < morning and evening. Stitches at night, and in loins; *extending through chest* in forenoon; on l. side in afternoon, < moving trunk or bending l. arm backward, and especially in l. chest and l. nipple. Tearing, < bending and standing, > lying, and in lumbar vertebræ. Constrictive pain across, as if bound with bands, almost like cramp, from 4 to 8 P.M. *Drawing down* when sitting, > motion. Tension in forenoon, and in loins. Stiffness on rising, > after walking.

Scapulæ.—Stitches in r.; intermittent lightning-like, in region of lower angle of r. in evening, < in bed; between S., *extending forward,* in afternoon when lying; scraping, in a spot between on motion. Pains alternately dull and sharp at lower angle of r. Spasmodic pain between, almost like shivering. Rheumatic pain between inferior angles. Pressure between S. when sitting, > when walking, and opposite in forepart of chest. Tension between. Drawing between S.; < on r. side; between S. on moving trunk, with stitches. Discomfort between S., more internally towards posterior mediasternum, causing frequent motion of shoulders and trunk.

Dorsal Region.—Stitches in spot between tenth and eleventh ribs. *Twitching and tearing pain in region of last dorsal vertebra and sacrum.* Drawing tensive pain in first dorsal vertebra (where he had suffered fourteen years previously from distortion of spine) *extending through chest to lower part of sternum,* with difficult respiration.

Lumbar Region.—Stitches in vertebræ; on r. side of lowest part of back; from third to fourth vertebra, extending on both sides of chest, < on breathing; drawing, deep in upper part of r. loin. *Drawing tearing at union of r. ilium with sacrum in evening. Pain;* in r.; < *walking; in muscles;* in vertebræ in forenoon; with fulness; waking him at 1 A.M., with P. in occiput and chilliness in skin, *preventing lying outstretched,* < *sitting up, lifting or turning leg, putting on trousers, walking and ascending stairs,* > *at rest, with body bent forward, with exhaustion while walking,* afterwards in bed the pain extended along spine and down legs, < attempting to raise or stretch legs or to raise body upright and slightest touch of spine, especially in sacral region, with copious, yellowish-red urine, moderate fever, and full, hard pulse and numbness of thighs, < r. Jerklike pain, like a cramp, when sitting and lying. Intermittent suppurative pain in region of r. kidney in morning in bed. Coliclike pain extending over hypogastrium. Pain in r. as after long stooping. Tensive pain in r.; T. pain on walking, throbbing, intermittent, above r. ilium. Tension. Rheumatic pain, < by exercise, and in limbs; in r. sacro-iliac region, a drawing lameness, and at centre of r. deltoid. Bruised pain; *when lying on it;* when sitting, < lying, > motion; and in thigh. *Drawing pain, waking him,* < *turning;* D. pain in afternoon, with moderate fever; after a meal. Drawing in both, gradually changing to burning on r. side, afterwards extending over inner surface of r. thigh. Sensation of a bladder filled with air in l. supra-iliac region, lying beneath walls of abdomen and pressing outward, when lying on abdomen, > lying on back. Sensitiveness of muscles to touch. Pressure; in muscles, with drawing. Heaviness, with dragging in hæmorrhoidal vessels. Weariness on r. side of sacrum, < walking. Paralyzed feeling. Loss of sensation in forenoon while walking, so that muscles acted automatically.

Coccyx.—Sticking-drawing while walking.

Clinical.—**Severe muscular pains in back, lumbago, etc.**

Extremities.—*Swelling on elbow as far as middle of upper and forearm, and on soles.* Stretching in afternoon. Jerking in arms and feet while sitting during the day. *In r. elbow sensation as if arm were broken, with paralytic pain, then drawing pain, extending to shoulder-joint,* and a similar pain in r. thigh. Stitches in l. knee when walking, and in first joint of r. thumb; sudden, in bones, now in l. upper arm, now in r. leg; drawing, in r. great toe and r. thumb; tearing, in r. knee after warm covering, then S. in l. shoulder-joint. Tearing in elbows and in r. middle toes; in tibiæ, with swelling of feet and heaviness of arms; jerklike, in first joint of r. thumb and in lowest joint of r. great toe; drawing, now in upper, now in lower, now in ligaments, now in tendinous sheaths of muscles, at first on motion, then also during rest.

Pinching in thumbs, with sticking in r. great toe. Scraping in long bones, < riding; tearing, and in joints; drawing-tearing, in l. little finger and in l. great toe. Pain; in every joint; while riding, > cider; growing constantly worse till towards noon, < r.; now in fingers, now in wrist, extending to axilla and shifting to knee, then alternating back and forth, with stitches, so that walking is difficult. Rheumatic pains in tops of both shoulders and in l. knee. Bruised pain; when sitting, in knees, legs, arms and single joints of fingers and legs; in arms and legs even when lying, worse when sitting than when walking, with restlessness of limbs while lying; *and paralyzed feeling* in evening, as if he had lain upon a hard bed.

Drawing pain in r. upper arm and in r. leg; in thumbs and great toes; in r. great toe, extending over back of foot and to middle of tibia, and a similar pain at same time in l. forearm; alternately in lower third of r. ulna and in l. knee; wandering, alternately in both hips and in r. shoulder. *Drawing; in sheaths of muscles;* in r. fingers and on l. instep; alternately in knees, hips, and especially in l. shoulder; in long bones, with scraping; in upper arms and thighs, with tension; in joints of forearm and metatarsus, with tearing; tearing, in l. knee, l. middle toes, both elbows and on flexor surface of thighs, all > during rest.

Weariness, with heaviness, *the feet can scarcely carry her on account of heaviness; W., especially of lower, with stiffness;* with shivering in face. Feeling in afternoon in upper arm and thigh as after violent exertion. *Leaden heaviness.* Numbness. (Hands and feet felt dead at night, sleepy and cold.)

Clinical.—**Acute inflammation of numerous joints, especially of the large joints, characterized by swelling, heat, *shiny* redness, > warm wraps, intolerance of slightest motion, etc. Sciatica > lying on the affected side. Muscular rheumatism. In all forms of rheumatism, acute, chronic, muscular or articular, there is generally the additional indication of easy, profuse perspiration.**

Upper Extremities.—Stitches in axilla towards noon; S. across shoulder to arm. Tearing in r. shoulder and upper arm, at 6 A.M., < moving upper arm, > after rising, returning at 11 A.M., while walking in open air and alternating with similar pain in r. hip, at noon in the house the pain was only in shoulder-joint, but the arm could scarcely be moved, afterwards creeping along ulnar nerve, with feeling of coldness and inflation in all limbs. Tearing in r. shoulder, with uneasiness of arm, the arm nearly painless in afternoon in open air, pain renewed on entering house, with sensation bordering on paralysis, inability to hold anything firmly, the pain in S. < writing, and on rubbing hands together the r. seemed thicker than l.

Shoulder.—*Pressure on top of r.,* > *touch, becoming on deep breathing a sticking, which extends downward and outward to shoulder-joint;* P., with fulness and heaviness. Sprained pain in region of acromion on raising arm. *Tension in r. during rest, with pressure.* Sticking tensive pain in ligaments of l. joint at 11 A.M., > during rest, but on motion pain as if wrenched. Drawing pain in r.; tensive-drawing, in joints, with sticking and tearing, and on raising arm feeling of paralysis, tension and heaviness on top of shoulder and at insertion of deltoid in arm. Drawing in r., extending into upper arm, > motion, < rest, with tearing. Discomfort in joints, obliging movement of S. Paralytic feeling in l., whereby motion of arm becomes difficult.

Arm.—(Sticking in l., with crawling.) Nervous tearing down inner part. Pain in r. in forenoon, > at noon, intermittent in afternoon. Drawing pain in r. Drawing through shafts of bones, as from a thread, extending to finger-tips. Falling asleep in evening when writing, then heaviness.

Upper Arm.—Swelling of r. as far as elbow. Stitches, < raising it; (in deltoid, with jerking); deep in l. deltoid, extending towards surface. Tearing in l.; tensive drawing, and along r. ulna. Pressure in humeri, preventing sleep in evening. Rheumatic pain in r. Drawing pain below insertion of r. deltoid; in middle of r., in l. arm and in l. chest. Drawing paralytic pain in r., with feeling as of lead. Drawing on inner side of r. Seeming too thick in evening, with diminished sensation in it and itching on skin. Heaviness of r., with drawing.

Elbow.—*Swelling of r.* Stitches in tips, with drawing in tendons down to hands, the S. < bending elbows.

Drawing in l.; in r., extending to wrist, with tearing. Aching in r.

Forearm.—Tearing, < r.; with pressure and gnawing; *on inner surface, in a line from elbow to wrist.* Pressing in r. in morning, with drawing, then in l. hand and r. fingers. Pain in r. ulnar nerve. Drawing while riding, with scraping.

Wrist.—*Stitches if hands were warm and during rest, not > motion.* Pain, and in thumbs. *Sprained pain on every motion.*

Hand.—Trembling, with distention of veins. Sticking in joints, with heaviness in them. Jerking-tearing in r. metacarpal bones while writing. Pain from long-continued holding of pen or strong pressure upon any object. Inability to grasp anything tightly. Stiffness of r. and of fingers; of r. < motion; of l. and of forearm, as if in ligaments and aponeuroses. Numbness of palms, with stiff sensation.

Fingers.—Involuntary jerking on motion. *Sticking when writing;* S. in joints of l. little; (in balls of thumbs, with cramp). Tearing in joints of l.; jerklike, in joints between metacarpus and fingers on motion, or in last joints of F. Pain in last phalanx of r. index during rest; in root of little F. as if pus were in it. *Swollen sensation in joints on writing or taking hold of anything, with pain on exertion and on touch.* Sensitiveness of phalanges to pressure, with swollen sensation in articular surfaces, impeding motion. Drawing in ball of l., then r. Stiffness of r. joints, < bending them; in middle joint of r. middle, < bending, > rubbing. Paralytic feeling. Sudden refusal of r. third to work while writing. (Falling asleep, and of hands.)

Lower Extremities.—Staggering in morning; to both sides when walking; when walking, as if he would fall backward. Tottering to one side after moving when standing. Unsteadiness, and when descending stairs tottering. Pain in whole l. on sitting, especially in leg and ankle, compelling motion of foot, > walking. Heaviness; *while walking. Weakness.*

Hip.—Stitches; *when walking bent, extending into knee;* in trochanter at every false step, during rest throbbing in it and sensitiveness to touch; *as with knives.* Pain in l.; *in head of femur, extending along anterior surface of thigh to knee,* especially about middle, > night, < motion, when it is drawing tearing, and during rest a paralytic sensation; in r. acromion; in l. joint, < motion, afterwards extending to r. hip, then suddenly leaving l. hip and attacking l. inguinal region, especially tendinous fibres which form inguinal ring, then sensitiveness of both hips. Pain like a jerk or shock in joints when sitting or lying, > when walking. Cramplike bruised pain in r. trochanter, < every motion, and in gluteal region. Drawing pain in l.; in hips and gluteal muscles; paralytic, in head of l. joint on walking, > pressure of hand, and on every step cracking in joints. Drawing, and in knees. Painful tension in l. Feeling in joints which makes rising from a seat difficult, > on walking.

Thigh.—Tottering, < ascending and descending stairs. Stitches in forenoon, now here, now there; S. in upper anterior part. Tearing in r. on motion. Clawing across l. Bruised pain in middle, and when sitting throbbing. Drawing anteriorly on l. and posteriorly on r.; D. in l., extending towards hip; as before menstruation. Tension in tendinous expansion while walking; painful T. and drawing on anterior surface below r. Poupart's ligament, > rest but returning; tensive pain on anterior surface below r. Poupart's ligament. Stiffness in morning in bed, like a cramp. Weariness; < *ascending stairs,* > *descending stairs.*

Knee.—*Tottering and bending under him when walking.* Cramp when sitting and at night when lying, and in sole. Stitches; *when walking;* on ascending steps; only on motion; in r. on motion; in r. and in r. external malleolus; in hollow in afternoon when walking; tearing, in l. in morning, > after rising; jerking, on inner side of l. Tearing after eating, < riding one leg over the other; in l. extending along tibia to ankle; and burning in r. Pain; in r. at 3 P.M. on walking, and in lower leg; < morning; in l. < walking; at inner condyle of r. femur; in caps on descending stairs, as if they would break; in caps as if beaten loose. Drawing in l., with sticking, and in calf. *Tension in bend, then changing to dragging and tearing along crest of fibula. Tension and pain in r.,* < *evening on walking,* > *next morning in bed, but returning after being up awhile, with pain on touch on inner side of K.* **Tensive, painful stiffness.** *Feeling in r. cap as if he had knelt long.* Weakness; of r. in forenoon when walking, with paralyzed feeling; in evening, < ascending stairs; < walking, > rest, with lameness; extending into middle of thighs.

Leg.—Swelling; of lower part, except feet; sudden. Twitching at night, during the day twitching like an electric shock. Cramp in l. calf in morning; in calves while lying; of calves (contractive tension) at night, > motion. *Pinching tearing in r. calf* while sitting after a meal. Tearing-twitching pain in upper half of tibia. Pain in tibia only when walking, and in hollow of knee; as after walking the previous day. Bruised sensation in evening; in l. while sitting; *on outer side of l. calf on moving and turning foot and on touch, during rest a numb sensation in this place.* Drawing pain in shafts of long bones; in muscles, < rest; in l. calf, > walking; especially in calf, then sweat in that place. Drawing; < l. leg and around r. knee, with tearing, and on touch pain in r. knee; in whole r., with tearing, the weariness disappearing after walking an hour; sticking, along outer border of tibia. Tension in r.; pinching, in l. calf; drawing tensive pain in r. tibia, > walking. Heaviness of r.; with tension, also in afternoon. *Weakness on beginning to walk and on standing;* on ascending stairs.

Ankle.—Dreamed that pain prevented walking and on waking found that he had sticking and scraping in outer malleolus, when it ceased pains spread over body, alternately attacking limbs and joints, after midnight restless sleep, interrupted by fatiguing dreams, only towards morning quiet sleep, and on rising remnants of the wandering pains. Pain; in r.; and in r. great toe; in l. when sitting. *Tension on motion.* Immobility of r. when walking.

Foot.—**Hot swelling; of instep, with bruised pain on stretching foot, tension in foot on stepping and suppurative pain in foot on touch.** Swollen and damp. Cramp in dorsum at night in bed, and in heels; in r. heel; in plantar muscles, sometimes at night. *Stitches;* in hollows on stepping; on inner side of r. heel; in heels in morning in bed; in balls towards evening, with heat and necessity to take off shoes; burning, in l. heel, at insertion of tendo-achillis; burning, in a corn only on slight touch, > severe pressure; in soles, preventing stepping, with tension in ankles, the stitches and tension preventing lying; as with a knife in l.

sole; as with a hook in heel nights on lying down. Tearing on ridge of r.; on dorsum of r. at night; on inner side of r. heel; stitchlike, extending into hollow of knees, > rest; sudden, in r. metatarsal bones in forenoon when walking, > standing still. Pinching in r. sole while sitting. Sharp pain in r. F. and toes when walking. Pain in r.; in a corn, < stepping; deep in r. between bones, < walking, with itching and roughness of the skin, the metatarsal bones seeming swollen and dislocated; intermittent, in metatarsal bones in afternoon. *Sprained pain.* Pain in hollow when stepping as if numb and tense. Pain in corns as if sore on slight touch, even of bed. Sore feeling near middle of tarsal bone of l. great toe, < walking, sprained feeling in ligaments, then in corresponding place in r. foot, then bruised pain, extending higher up tendon, with tenderness to touch from an inch above joint of toe to bend of ankle, then sprained pain in large joint of great toe when standing or walking, sometimes when stepping on that foot feeling as if joints were *giving way or spreading apart*, afterwards the pain extends to metatarsal joints of all toes except little toe, afterwards skin over tarsal bone of great toe is swollen and inflamed, the soreness appearing to be in sheath of tendon, but *principally in periosteum and ligaments, the pain always < motion*, swelling of top of foot, then sprained pain in corresponding joint of next, stitches in knee, tender sensation at bottom of heel on pressure, pain in toes extending up metatarsal bone, then soreness along top of metatarsal bone of great toe, with swelling, redness and engorgement of veins, at last swelling of skin in a spot high up on instep, with tenderness of part beneath. Drawing pain; along l., after rising; with stiffness in joints; in r. heel; on dorsum of l., with difficulty in walking and with pain in sole. Pressure on inner margin of l. sole. *Tension in evening, with swelling; tensive pain on dorsum, even when sitting.* Heaviness in forenoon; on rising after eating; with numb sensation as if swollen. Stiffness on rising after long sitting. Weariness; as after long running.

Toes.—Stitches beneath nail of l. little; on lower surface of r. third and fourth in afternoon; in balls of great, with pressure and pain as if frozen; in ball of r., < sitting, > walking; through tip of l. great; extending into toes. Pain in l. second, in afternoon when walking. *Sudden pain in balls of great* (Ledum), it seemed as if he could not stretch out the toes. Bruised pain in balls of l. Burning pain in second l. Drawing pain in corn on l. little. Sore pain in l. little. Sensitiveness of l., with itching.

Skin.—*Yellow.* Livid. Redness of knee-caps; red round spots on arm; red spots on arms and feet, paining like burning nettles, the spots momentarily disappearing on pressure. Inflammation of dorsum of hand about midnight, with burning pain. Swelling of r. third finger, especially of joint between first and second phalanges, with pain on pressure, < motion, next day r. fifth finger similarly affected; *hot, pale S. in last joint of little finger, with sticking in it on moving finger and on pressure.*

Red elevated rash over whole body; red rash on neck; on upper part of forearm. Rash on arms, front of chest and above knees, becoming red in evening, with itching and burning, the itching and rash > warmth of bed. Red eruption in hollow of knees, with itching in evening and with biting after scratching. Eruption below l. corner of mouth, with smarting. *Itching eruption over whole body, especially on back as far as throat;* biting, around throat, < after sweating. Biting and smarting eruption in forepart of night and in morning, on abdomen, on back as far as neck, and on forearms. Tetter on r. cheek.

Pimples.—Red. Painful on thigh. Painful on touch; on l. lower lid. Stinging on touch, between r. thumb and index; (on chin). Inflamed, on back and face, especially on forehead, with pain on strong pressure, then soreness. Burning and itching, on abdomen and hips, with smarting when scratched. Rashlike, pointed, with white semi-transparent vesicles, in groups on small of back, extending over back, abdomen, chest and forearm, becoming confluent, itching on active motion, then desquamation, then redness.

Hard boil behind ear, frequently changing its size. Soft boil in l. inner canthus, with flow of matter. Boil-like swelling before ear, discharging and then becoming a yellowish scurf. Pustule under knee, with pain and sticking on touch; (white, on foot, with pain as in an ulcer, redness of foot and inability to walk on account of the pain). Cracks, with thin crusts. Excoriation of hollow of knee. (Exuding eruption on legs.) (Itchlike eruption on inner surface of wrists, in bends of elbows, externally on condyles of elbows, externally on knee and in hollow of knee). (Ulcerated cartilage of ear.) (The discharge from an ulcer stains the linen blackish.)

Itching stitches on neck, < walking rapidly, > scratching. Tearing in an ulcer. Intermittent burning pain on outer margin of l. knee-cap. Sticking throbbing near crust of an ulcer after dinner. Sensitiveness. Tension on face when moving muscles. Paroxysmal drawing under r. lower jaw, on inner side of l. thigh, from flank to knee. Crawling on both sides of ears; as of a mouse from axilla to hip; (in hands as if asleep). Biting in region of scab of an ulcer in morning after rising, < standing, > sitting and moderate motion.

Itching on face; on scalp and about anus; chest; hands; at union of first and second phalanges of l. fingers; on hips and thighs; r. knee; on legs, about knees and on thighs, with digging, after scratching or rubbing red elevated pimples, with burning pain, the itching > when the pimples arise; in hollow of knee at night, as if something were healing, with sweat in that place; sticking, here and there; burning pain as from nettles on r. side of first dorsal vertebræ; burning, in various parts in evening in bed, with stitches; sudden sticking (itching) burning over whole body, as in nettle-rash, during slight excitement (in laughing), when thinking of it and when heated; tearing, on soft parts of body, before sleep, during day or in evening, or digging burning-itching stitches; tickling, during the day, on arms, hands and feet, with rashlike pimples,

Sleep.—*Frequent yawning;* towards noon; constant, before dinner, with thirst. *Sleepiness;* in morning on waking; during the day, with great inclination to a midday sleep, on waking all the limbs were asleep; *during the day when alone;* in afternoon; after eating. Sleeps all day, with dry heat, without eating or drinking, with twitching in face and with six involuntary, brown and offensive stools. Sound sleep at night, sleepiness all next day, uneasy sleep next night, and wide awake the following day. Difficult waking in morning. Desire to lie long in morning (without weakness).

Sleeplessness; in evening, in a child; *before midnight*, also with frequent micturition; *before midnight on account of frequent shivering over one arm and leg, then sweat; till 12 o'clock, with warmth and anxiety in blood;* after midnight, with weariness, which increased in legs after rising; till 1 A.M., on account of anxious heat, but without external heat; till 2 A.M., with turning back and forth, then sleepiness in morning after waking; till 4 A.M., then dreams of dead persons; S. till towards morning; *from uneasiness in blood*, with tossing about; from *uneasiness in blood and anxiety*, with necessity to rise from bed and with thoughts crowding upon one another; on account of heat, but coldness on uncovering; (though tired, with loss of breath when he tries to sleep). Late falling asleep, then restless, unsound sleep.

Waking at midnight, with frightful dreams and crick in back, sour stomach and much itching kept me awake some time; suddenly before 3 A.M., then sweat till morning, wherewith he lay comfortably on the back and slumbered a little, with dryness of forepart of mouth and lips, without thirst. Waking early in night. Waking every hour, with vivid remembered dreams. Frequent waking from dreams; from unpleasant dreams, with necessity to urinate; from restless dreams or from involuntary motion of legs which caused pain; always with chilliness in toes.

Restless sleep, could scarcely sleep for half an hour, and **during his slumber was busy with what he had read the previous evening**; R. sleep, with sweat; with confused dreams. *Starting up in fright in evening before sleep; from an anxious dream and screaming out;* which wake her. Moaning in sleep about 3 A.M. (Motions of the mouth in sleep, as if chewing.) Towards evening while asleep, she drew her mouth back and forth, opened her eyes, distorted them and spoke distinctly but hastily, and as if entirely different persons were about her, looked freely about, talked with strange children and desired to go home. Consciousness that he was sleeping, causing anguish, since consciousness became weaker and at last threatened to be lost as in faintness, and from this anguish arose an internal struggle, which caused complete consciousness, after waking the arm on which he was lying was senseless and stiff. Somnambulistic condition. Arose from bed at night and went to the door as if she would go out. Found himself lying upon the floor in the corner of the room opposite his bed, with the bed-covers under him.

Dreams.—**That he was busy about his household affairs.** *Of dispute and vexation. Frightful, with frequent waking. Vivid; all night, of anxiety about his business;* after midnight, and remembered; after eating, and after waking, stitches and pressure near sternum, in region of fifth rib. Anxious, with crying out in sleep about three o'clock. Confused, in which he was very active; C. and anxious. Heavy, with cries and groans. Indistinct, of battles, in which he took part. Restless. Pleasant. While awake, that he tried to break someone's window. On waking he could not free himself from his dream and he continued to dream waking.

Fever.—*Chilliness; after midday nap, with confusion of head;* in afternoon, while walking, with heat; towards evening; in evening before lying down; *in evening in bed; all over in evening, with gooseflesh, thirst and with hot and red cheeks;* on lying down, with yawning and nausea, then sweat from 10 P.M. till 10 A.M., without thirst; on waking; in open air, also with dread of it; on moving; after walking in open air; while ascending a mountain, then sweat and weariness; with weakness; with sudden heat; then heat; frequent, while walking on a hot day; creeping.

Shivering; in afternoon, then heat in head, with pulselike pain in temples (< in evening), warmth in arms and hands, and with chill on chest and arms, all without thirst; in evening; with nausea and aversion to tobacco-smoking; peculiar, while washing. Shaking chill, compelling her to lie down, with sticking above l. hip as if a suppurating ulcer would break. Sudden shivering caused by a draft of air from turning in bed, with jerking up in bed, twitching of dorsal, pectoral and abdominal muscles, trembling of limbs, the chill concentrating itself in the interior of chest, reappearing on moving body or putting a limb out of bed. Sudden shaking chill, then heat, with debility of limbs.

Chilliness over whole skin. Coldness down whole r. side. Chilliness in face; on arms; in feet; in an ulcer, with pain as from too great cold. Cold sensation over back after eating, extending forward, with pressure in pit of stomach, then the cold sensation extends over shoulders and forearms; along spine, > motion, with drawing pressure in back and lumbar muscles and necessity to suddenly straighten up; along spine, next day heat, with hot sensitive skin and transpiration on slightest motion. Shivering in back; with involuntary closure of eyelids; from nape down spine. Creeping chill down back; in lower limbs in evening in bed, especially in thighs, even the skin felt cool; over l. leg; in l. thigh in evening.

Heat; in forenoon, with thirst, chilliness in afternoon without thirst, but with redness of face and headache; without thirst; in flushes; *in interior of body*, especially in abdomen; internal, with unquenchable thirst; **internal,** *the blood seeming to burn in the veins; internal and external on lying down in evening, lasting all night, without thirst, with turning from side to side, and on uncovering any part, griping-sticking or sticking-griping in abdomen, as from spasmodic movements of flatus, with sleeplessness from crowding thoughts.*

Dry heat in morning; *at night;* sudden; on every motion and at every noise; internal, extending over whole body, with dryness of tongue, lips and palate, and with loss of thirst, weakness, especially of limbs, pulse full and rapid, skin dry and rough; especially of hands, feet, face, with rapid pulse, confusion of head, pressing-out pain in occiput and neck, roaring in l. ear, coryza, stoppage of l. nostril, discharge of watery substance from r. angina tonsillaris, loss of thirst and appetite, stitches below l. nipple, as in pleura costalis, pain in loins, continued erection of penis without desire, stitches in l. testicle, burning in region of lower third of r. ulna, quiet sleep, all symptoms > about midnight, by copious sweat.

Heat in head in morning, with external warmth of it; H. in head in forenoon, with feeling as if it would come out at forehead; in head at 3 P.M., with pressure in frontal eminence; *in head*, with nausea; **in face, with redness and thirst**; in face towards evening; in face, and after light work sweat of face; in flushes over face; lobules of ears; in external ear in evening, then shivering in thighs. Burning in throat externally, with tension;

B. in back; below and between scapulæ. Heat in palm and forearms, forcing her to lie out of bed, then cold sensation in them; frequently in lower limbs, as if she stepped into hot water. Burning on inner side of thigh towards evening; externally on knee; on anterior surface of r. tibia; feet as far as malleoli, as if in hot water, with stitches in heels and corns, and with stiffness of lower limbs and nape. Burning in an excoriated painless spot.

Sweat in morning; towards morning, after waking; towards morning, especially on feet; at night; all night, with sleep only from 12 till 3 o'clock; on waking; while eating; *all over body when walking in cold air;* **after slightest exertion;** after moderate exercise in open air, and after changing the linen it streamed from face and whole body, with such rapid breathing that he could only speak in broken and jerklike words; while eating; of whole body and head in bed; *profuse after* 3 A.M. every night; necessity to go to bed at 9 A.M., then copious S., then disappearance of the symptoms in the same order in which they appeared, only vertigo continued longer; **sour** (sometimes towards midnight); *sour, during a good night's sleep.* Cold. Anxious, preventing sleep. Sweat which seems like oil when wiping; S. on whole body, even dropping from hair; streaming from face while walking; in axillæ; in palms. Transpiration suppressed.

Clinical.—It is frequently indicated in scarlet fever, when the eruption does not develop well and the general symptoms of the drug are present; the same is true of measles. In typhoid fever it is very frequently indicated in the early stage with the occipital headache, furred tongue, thirst, abdominal soreness, etc. In a great variety of fevers not eruptive. For febrile states, which are the accompaniment of inflammatory processes in various organs and tissues, always with headache, thirst and intolerance of motion (closely allied to Iod.).

Bufo.

The poison of the toad (Rana Bufo) is triturated with sugar of milk.

General Action.—Our knowledge of this substance is too meagre and the symptomatology too indefinite to enable one to form conclusions concerning its properties.

Generalities.—Progressive emaciation, even to consumption and death. Swelling of whole body. *Convulsions.* Jactitations of tendons. Constant shaking of head and arms. Pandiculations. Disposition to lie on l. side, feels better so than when on r. side. Intoxicated feeling. Inability to answer or move, though he hears what is said. Gradual failure of strength. Prostration in the midst of a meal, with inability to speak or move, with dim vision and distress at heart. Faintness; now and then; after breakfast; as from hunger, in morning and during the day, before a meal.

Clinical.—Epilepsy ushered in by a cry, livid face. Epilepsy, the result of sexual excitement. Epilepsy coming on at the time of the menses.

Mind.—Propensity to bite. The child runs like mad. Choleric disposition. Nervousness, great irritability. Howling, constant crying. Alternate complaining and crying in a child. Impatience. Little disposition to work. Apathy. Coma. Stupor, with inability to speak; S. obliging him to seek a support, after the dizziness.

Head.—Aching two days on waking at 3 A.M.; in afternoon and at night, preventing sleep; towards 5 P.M., obliging him to lie down; after breakfast, continuing into the night and preventing sleep; during work while sitting; > at night and by lying; > epistaxis; with fatigue, nausea and cold feet; increasing for three or four minutes, then diminishing during the same time; shifting about, during menses. The beating of the head increases the headache and corresponds with it. Heaviness. Vertigo; only in morning, < after eating; < in morning, with weakness as from loss of blood; then face flushes, heart feels compressed and chest seems squeezed in a vise; the head feels as if carried along by the motion of waltzing. Symptoms < movement.

Forehead.—Aching after a hard and curled stool (with protrusion of hæmorrhoids), with heaviness in eyelids and nausea; and vertex, with soreness on touch, the soreness < towards 4 or 5 P.M. Weight, and in eyelids, with disturbed vision, sparks before eyes, pain at heart, cold sweat on head and in hair, coldness of body, especially of feet, such piercing colic as to almost cause faintness, burning thirst, vomiting after drinking, vomiting of food, then of bitter and acrid matter, the least movement aggravates the headache and brings on nausea and vomiting.

Clawing-digging in l. temple when walking. Pain in l. temple and vertex on waking towards 3 A.M., with soreness to touch. Hemicrania of r. side, > nosebleed. Hair falls out.

Eyes.—Frightful and squinting look. Bloodshot. Itching, with redness, swelling, dimness of vision, lancinating pain, stinging (local effects). Lids opened wider. Inability to keep lids open. Vision dim. Appearance as of a veil before eyes at 3 or 4 P.M., with smarting in eyes and lachrymation. Vision lost.

Nose.—Burning in nostrils. Much sneezing in evening on going to bed; in evening, with obstruction and with heaviness in head and eyelids. Coryza in morning, with sneezing; C. > after sweat in morning in bed. Blowing out of clear water. Crusts after coryza. Mucous secretion, which is dry or soft and very fetid. Offensive mucus. Mucus descends from nasal fossæ into throat. Bleeding. Blowing out of blood.

Face.—Expression altered. Flushed, with heat every now and then. Herpetic pimples on upper lip after coryza.

Mouth.—Teeth fall out. Boring in teeth. Hard swelling on gum, with feeling as if forcing out the back teeth, which seemed too long, with salivation at night, the symptoms preventing sleep, the pain transiently > by putting warm hand on cheek. Pain in gums as if burned. Tongue black. Loose, pasty yellowish coat on tongue. Tongue difficult to move. Stammering. Pain in palate and in r. margin of tongue, with aversion to tobacco. Scraping dry sensation on palate and back of mouth, painful on empty swallowing.

Saliva abundant, frothy. Breath offensive. Taste bitter (not of food); biting B. at back of mouth, as from radishes. Nauseous, sweetish taste in morning in bed, with clammy mouth. Taste of tobacco not as good as usual, after long smoking nausea and vomiting, smoking in forenoon causes overpowering sleepiness.

Throat.—Painful swelling of r. submaxillary glands. Something seems to come from head. Dryness in morning; D., with inflammation, and in œsophagus.

Stomach.—Desire for pastry and dainties. Appetite

irregular, ceasing after first mouthful. Aversion to food; and to drink. Slight thirst during a meal, while the cough continues. Urgent thirst for cold sugared water. Eructations during the day, with some acidity; fetid; tasting like spoiled eggs, after eating fresh bread and pastry. Hiccough. Nausea; after meals. Vomiting of food after drinking, during the headache, then bitter and acid vomitings; violent V. Cramp; after breakfast. Drawing as from hunger, but without appetite, with strong beating of heart, then headache.

Abdomen.—Flatulence; < after meals, with eructations. Emission of flatus in morning, preceded by borborygmi, with empty feeling in stomach; fetid flatus. Lancinations, nearly causing faintness, with burning thirst, cold sweat in hair, then four stools, increasingly liquid. Digging-cutting, after the ulcers on finger and tibia had healed, especially in morning, and after drinking milk and from smoking tobacco. Pain; intermittent, after meals, with borborygmi. Colic in hypogastrium. Incurable obstruction of liver, with enlargement.

Rectum and Stool.—A jet of blood from a hæmorrhoid when straining at stool, then fatigue. Frequent urging to stool, but only one scanty evacuation daily, afterwards four daily stools, with colic and flatulence. Stool towards 2 or 3 A.M. Dysentery. Liquid, yellowish S. Semi-liquid, after meals, afterwards an obstinate hæmorrhoid outside margin of anus, preceded by smarting of anus. Sometimes hard, sometimes soft S., sometimes both together. Whitish, as in icterus. Lumbrici in a child's S. Frequent, yellowish, soft, but consistent; F. and copious; S. every two days. Suppressed, with coldness of whole body except head, which is hot.

Urine.—Copious and frequent emission. Suppressed. Scanty, during constipation, and thick, yellowish, of strong ammoniacal odor, depositing a sediment; S. of a yellow-ochre color, with yellowish sediment, with pain in loins, after the pain in loins the urine is clearer and more abundant, micturition four times in a night. Red. Brown, smelling like fishbrine. Clear, with liquid stools.

Sexual Organs.—He applies his hands to genitals. Involuntary discharge of semen. Impotence. Leucorrhœa without smell, as clear as water. Menstruation too early.

Respiratory Organs.—Hoarseness. Suffocation towards 3 A.M., with restlessness of limbs, trembling of hands, legs, and head, sensation as if everything, even in head, were unsteady. Panting. Breath lost when ascending stairs. Breathing difficult. Cough every night at 3 or 4 o'clock, from pricking in larynx; from stinging in larynx, following coryza; before a meal and in the house, > at night. After cold feet, pricking in larynx, exciting cough all day, < evening, the C. continues all night. Motion increases the frequency of cough, although it is equally troublesome during rest. Dry hacking C., > more frequent stools.

Chest.—Stitches piercing the deep pectoral muscles and mammary gland, mostly on r. breast, impeding respiration. Pain in a spot, now here, now there, when walking. Smarting in upper third of sternum. Oppression. Compression afternoons, and of heart. Sensation as if there were two swellings at upper part of sternum, appearing to grow larger in bed, impeding respiration and causing pain on swallowing.

Clinical.—Indurations in the mammary gland.

Heart.—Pain every two hours (four days after getting chilled), with retching, cough and expectoration tinged with blood. Palpitation at intervals; after a meal, with an interval, during which he felt as if going to be ill.

Neck and Back.—The headache affects the nape, which feels compressed. Pain in loins as if pierced by a red-hot iron two mornings, < movement, arresting the breath and nearly causing faintness, next day pain as if strained, preventing him from straightening himself or stooping, during the pain in loins the urine is scanty, of yellow-ochre color, thick, with yellowish sediment. Pain in loins, then trembling of legs in morning and giving way of them from weakness.

Extremities.—Pinching-digging in middle of long bones, wandering about as if in periosteum. Falling asleep of upper E. when lying upon them lightly, afterwards of the lower ones. Burning of arm after the poison has touched the r. hand, with swelling and a yellow color on a black ground. Digging pinching in r. deltoid on raising arm. Digging, throbbing, periodic pain on inner surface of tip of r. elbow.

Lower Extremities.—Weariness of thighs when walking. Legs drawn up so as to touch the buttocks, in a child. Cramp of legs towards 4 or 5 A.M., drawing up with a start. Crampy pain in calf (during the weakness), < motion, > at rest. Pain as from a blow in middle of r. tibia when standing. Stiffness of r. leg, beginning above knee, where it is most marked. Weakness of legs, even to falling. Digging pain in ungual phalanges of three last toes, and on inner malleolus, with corrosive itching on inner border of r. foot.

Skin.—Yellow. Pale and swollen, as in dropsy. Pimples (local effects). Whitish crust over eyebrows. Vesicles in palms and soles, with yellow excoriating fluid. Burning-itching vesicle, surrounded by erythematous blush, near l. wrist, discharging a little serum, then a boil, with fever and with lancinations to axilla; corrosive painful V. on inner surface of proximal phalanx of r. index finger, then desquamation; corrosive painful, in middle of r. tibia, with red areola, then a whitish-gray, thick, fatty scurf, from which new exudations enlarged, 'till of the size of a quarter of a dollar, with corrosive pain and red areola, afterwards desquamation, leaving a reddish-brown spot, with shiny, scaling skin.

Pustules covering the whole body, like a bad case of scabies. Suppuration from every slight injury, even the prick of a needle, with corrosive pain. After a slight bruise, pain in r. little finger, with suppuration, then inflammation of finger, causing tearing-drawing pain along whole arm and redness of finger along lymphatics, extending to axilla, in which granular swellings appeared and were painful, especially on motion and touch, the inflamed lymphatics became swollen, the arm heavy and painful, Hepar sulph. > the lymphatic inflammation and the corrosive pain in ulcer of little finger and ulcer under thumb-nail.

Swelling, hot, bluish-red, painful to touch, on inner lower border of l. thumb-nail, then suppuration involving half the nail, with throbbing-digging pain, extending into joint of index and metacarpal bones, then gnawing, then scaling of skin several times. Itching, > friction of body-linen, then smarting, especially when it has been thus allayed; I. on whole outer surface of thighs and legs every day towards 4 or 5 P.M.; corrosive, on l. leg and knee-cap.

Clinical.—Bullæ, which open and leave a raw surface, exuding an ichorous fluid.

Sleep.—Invincible sleepiness after a meal. Waking at 3 or 4 A.M. Waking every few moments. During sleep sense of fatigue and of numbness in every limb, obliging frequent change of position. Dreams of travel, of projects and of greatness.

Fever.—Shivering after stool, < evening. Chilliness in calves, then cramplike pain in them. Quartan fever, with intense heat and violent delirium. The heat of the fire is distressing. Heat rising into face; H. of limbs; of hands; of feet; except in feet, which are cold. Sweat in morning in bed; S. mostly on hams; copious, on hairy scalp; cold.

Cactus.

A tincture is prepared from the fresh flowers and youngest twigs of Cactus grandiflorus L. (Cereus grand., Dec.).

General Action.—Particularly a "heart remedy," most of the symptoms being the outcome of cardiac disturbance. A malarial feature is marked and valuable, and in this respect (only) it is to be compared with *Gelsem.*

Affinities.—Dig., Crotalus, Phos., Amyl nit., Spigel., Gelsem.

Generalities.—Muscles did not obey the will accurately, owing to defective vision or to other causes. Restlessness when sitting, legs thrown here and there involuntarily; R., with haste in his actions, he seemed never to be in time, with agitation at heart and feeling of oppression. Jerking-tearing in forehead and in limbs. Pain now and then during the day, in muscles of r. upper arm, of chest, of calves, of soles. General discomfort. General malaise. *Weakness;* with sadness and bad humor; so that he does not venture to speak; so that he does not venture to walk. *Inspiration of fresh air is very reviving.*

Clinical.—Intermittent neuralgia, < fasting.

Mind.—*Hypochondriasis. Fear of death, belief that his disease is incurable* (Dig.). *Sadness, taciturnity and weeping mood. Love of solitude.* Anxiety, returning in evening. Passion at slightest contrariety. Feeling of having done violence to myself. Semi-remorse at having done something wrong. Disposition to do deliberately whatever was undertaken. Impulse to do something facetious; something bordering on the grotesque; to swallow large and unwholesome portions of medicine. Repugnance to the taking of more medicine. Talking nonsense in sleep at night and talking disconnectedly on waking. Difficulty in arriving at conclusions.

Head.—Aching from congestion; A., with weariness; causing anxiety, so that he cannot stay in bed; with weight on vertex, pressing in temples, pulsating in temples, ears and eyes, as if they would burst outward, weakness of vision and intolerance of light and sound. Empty feeling. Fulness as from congestion. Sensation at night as if brain had grown fast to skull. Vertigo; from congestion to head; causing staggering.

Aching in forehead; in l. side in evening and on waking in night; in F., < bright light, loud voices or noises; intermittent, in F., < in house. Pulsating pain in temples, < at night. Pulsations in temples, as if skull would burst; in T. and ears, causing hypochondriasis. Weight in r. temple, > pressure, and on r. eyebrow. **Pain like a weight on vertex;** > *pressure;* < *sound of talking and by any noise.* Tensive pain in vertex every two days.

Pressure on r. parietal bone; in l. Pain in l. parietal-bone in morning after rising; in l., in forenoon, more externally; in r. side of head, < raising head from pillow; in r. side, < sound of talking and by bright light; *pulsating, in r. side of head, with weight,* Aching in cerebellum; in occiput, > quick exercise or mental activity; in O., < motion of head, with drawing. Painful drawing in aponeurotic covering of occiput, > bending head backward. Heaviness in posterior part of brain on retiring, < touch of pillow, > lying on side, with pain.

Clinical.—Congestive headaches. Threatening apoplexy. Neuralgic headaches, especially in r. side and on vertex, periodical.

Eyes and Ears.—Vision weak; periodically; lost momentarily; lost, with circles of *red light.* Pulsations in ears. Hearing diminished by buzzing in ears. Noise all night like the running of a river.

Nose and Face.—Dry coryza, with necessity at night to breathe, with the mouth open; fluent and acrid C. *Profuse nosebleed. Face pale,* with emaciation; flushed; bloated (acceso) and red, with pulsating pain in head.

Mouth and Throat.—Tongue dry and coated, with slime in nares and throat. Sensation in mouth of having swallowed something unpleasant. Scraping in palate. Breath fetid in morning. Taste soapy; T. slimy, weedy. Scraping on soft palate. Felt in throat an accumulation of mucus, which was expectorated. Constriction in throat, causing frequent swallowing of saliva; C. in œsophagus, preventing swallowing, he must drink much water to force anything into stomach.

Stomach.—Appetite better than usual; at breakfast; great, but digestion slow and weak; *lost;* lost, with nausea; lost, with loss of taste of food. Thirst; satisfied with a small quantity of water at one time. Acrid, acid rising in throat and mouth and making all food *taste acid.* Nausea; with retching and copious discharge of mucus. *Copious vomiting of blood.*

Gastro-enteritis. Pain; terrible, with pressure inward, *constriction* of scrobiculus, extending to hypochondria and to fifth rib, as from a hot-iron cincture having involuted edges of an inch in size, pressing more and more till respiration was distressing. *Pulsation; in pit;* in cœliac artery after dinner, corresponding with pulsation of r. temporal artery. *Heaviness.* Oppression and weight. Stricture about S. and chest. Constriction in scrobiculus, extending to hypochondria and impeding respiration. Burning. Empty feeling. Sensation of something disagreeable in it. Uneasiness as from difficult digestion. Digestion bad, all food causes weight in S. and so much suffering that he prefers to fast. Digestion slow, even after eight or ten hours the taste of food rises in throat.

Clinical.—Dyspepsia, with heart symptoms, palpitation, constriction, etc.

Abdomen.—Borborygmi before stool. Pain; almost causing faintness. Distress here and there as if a serpent were turning around. Soreness, with distention. Burning internally. External heat in parieties. Cutting in umbilicus after stool; in lower umbilical and hypogastric regions. Wandering periodical pains in umbilical region. Constriction in groins, extending around pelvis.

Anus.—*Copious hæmorrhage* (Crotal., Phos.). Bleeding of hæmorrhoids after stool. Swollen painful varices outside. Pricking, > slight friction. *Sensation of great weight and urging to evacuate a great quantity, but nothing passes.* Sensation as if rectum were swollen, causing scraping during stool and prickling. Itching.

Clinical.—Hæmorrhage from the bowels in malarial fevers and with heart symptoms.

Stool.—Soft, then pain in hypogastrium. Frequent diarrhœa from 6 to 12 A.M., preceded by great pain, no stool in afternoon; frequent bilious, always preceded by pain; bilious, with pain in abdomen; frequent mucous, preceded by drawing pain; copious watery, the morning stools always preceded by pains and borborygmus. Hard, difficult, then discharge of blood from anus. Constipation; as from hæmorrhoidal congestion.

Urinary Organs.—Constriction of neck of bladder. *Frequent urging at night, with a copious flow each time.* Ineffectual urging. Micturition by drops, with much burning. Involuntary M. in sleep at 5 A.M. *Frequent and copious M. Irritation in urethra as if he should urinate constantly.* Redness of orifice of urethra. Heat in urethra, gradually increasing. Urine copious; after a long endeavor to pass it; and *reddish, turbid;* and *straw-colored.* Urine scanty. U. of the odor of freshly-drawn green tea. U. deposits a red sand.

Clinical.—Hæmorrhage from the bladder.

Sexual Organs.—Tendency to congestion to urino-genital system. Priapisms towards evening; just before retiring. Great desire, with priapisms. Copious emission about 12 M., after strong desire.

Pain in uterus and its ligaments every evening, increasing gradually till 11 P.M. Pulsating pain in uterus and ovarian region, like an internal tumor suppurating, at the same hour every day, extending to thighs. (Constriction in uterine region, gradually extending to stomach, causing sensation of a great flow in veins and eliciting cries, then passing off rapidly.) *Painful menstruation, causing loud cries;* painful, with prostration. *Menses eight days too soon.* Black, pitchy, rather abundant M. *Scanty M., ceasing while lying.*

Clinical.—Inflammation of the ovaries, with constriction. Vaginismus. Dysmenorrhœa, pains occur periodically, menses cease on lying down, with heart symptoms.

Respiratory Organs.—Cough, which aggravated the suffering, with mucous expectoration; C., with thick expectoration like boiled starch and yellow; *catarrhal, with much viscid expectoration; spasmodic, with copious mucous expectoration;* obstinate, stertorous, < night; dry at night, from itching in larynx.

Hæmoptysis (Phos.). **Difficult breathing, with oppression and uneasiness as if chest were constricted by an iron band** (Dig. in part.). *Periodical suffocation, with fainting, cold sweat on face and loss of pulse* (Dig.). Congestive asthma. Oppressed breathing when walking; < open air; with anxiety; *as from weight on chest* (Phos.). Short inspiration; short breathing when walking and when ascending stairs, with palpitation.

Clinical.—Bronchitis, with rattling of mucus, great distress for breath, etc. Hæmorrhage from the lungs, with violent action of the heart, oppressed respiration (compare Aconite).

Chest.—Stitches in r. upper. Pain; in upper part of r. side; at night in nerves running from l. axilla to adjoining pectoral region; in l. breast, < touch, > gently raising it; < walking and ascending stairs, causing deep breathing, with palpitation; between l. second and third ribs when sitting quietly, causing deep breathing; sharp wandering, in cavity, worse in scapular region. Painful drawings in l. muscles extending to shoulder-joint and impeding respiration and use of arm. *Constriction as if bound;* **as from a tight cord around false ribs, with obstruction of breath; in middle of sternum, as with iron pincers,** < *motion, with oppression of breathing;* preventing free speech, when forced to speak the voice is weak and hoarse; in upper part, hindering respiration. Oppression, with loss of breath; O. in l. subclavian region. **Congestion,** preventing lying in bed.

Clinical.—Inflammation of diaphragm, with feeling of pain and soreness marking the attachments of the diaphragm.

Heart.—*Pricking pain,* impeding respiration and motion of body. *Acute pain, with stitches, causing loud cries* (Spig.), *with obstruction of breath. Heavy pain,* < pressure. Heaviness and pressure. **Constriction as by an iron band** (Amyl. n.). Sensation as if a reptile were moving backward, < by day. Drawing.

Increased action all forenoon, and on walking pulsation in chest, with anxiety; beating, < lying on side at night, with pulsation in chest, and with anxiety and restlessness. *Rapid, short, irregular beats on rapid motion. Violent irregular beats, with pressure and heaviness;* violent irregular beats towards evening, from a sudden movement while sitting; on slow walking, rising from a chair, turning suddenly. Single irregular beats, with necessity to inspire deeply. Small, quick, irregular pulsations in morning on moving in bed. Violent beat on slow walking in the room, with tightness of chest and deep breathing.

Palpitation (Spig., etc.), < *walking, and at night when lying on l. side;* on sitting and lying in evening, < lying on back, with oppression at heart; at night in bed, with pulsation in upper part of chest; on standing and sitting, with anxiety at heart; at beginning of any motion, with anxiety in chest rising into throat, but continued walking does not bring on P.; from rapid motion, such as suddenly stooping or rising from a seat, and from excitement, not from rapid walking; *in small, irregular beats from slight excitement or deep thought, with necessity for deep inspiration.* Nervous palpitation, augmented gradually at occurrence of catamenia. Heart symptoms felt on waking at night and changing position, as in daytime. Symptoms so violent when beginning to walk that he must stand still and inspire deeply, the same occurred on ascending and descending stairs.

Clinical.—Cardiac dropsy, with labored breathing, œdematous extremities, inability to lie down. Nosebleed, with hard, violent action of the heart and constriction. Acute inflammation of heart, pericardium and endocardium. Hypertrophy of heart. Violent palpitation. Angina pectoris. In all these diseases there is present the characteristic feeling as if an iron hand prevented the normal action of the heart, with suffocation, cold sweat, etc.

Pulse.—Irregular. Hard and sudden, but not rapid.

Back.—Pain in spine, worse in lumbar region, pressing down gluteal muscles to inferior extremities. In muscles of lower r. side, extending into gluteals, in morning before rising, lasting all day.

Extremities.—Tearing in joints, now in shoulder, now in elbows, now in fingers, < r. side. Pain towards evening; P. in various joints. Drawing in fingers, toes, knees and ankles. Drawing pain in axilla and in neighboring part of chest anteriorly, affecting the nerves, in bed, before sleep. Tearing in l. shoulder-joint; in shoulders and arms, at first worse in joints, afterwards worse in long bones. Constriction of shoulders, so that he could not move them. Tearing through l. arm; drawing, in r. arm in morning on waking, lasting through forenoon, after rising it extends into r. wrist. Numbness of l. arm at night, with pricking in little finger. Weariness of arms, with heaviness. Œdema of hands, < l.

Lower Extremities.—Pain in knees; waking him at night, extending from r. knee-cap to outer side of leg, < slightest motion of leg. Weariness of legs in morning after rising, with heaviness in them and with sleepiness. (Œdema of legs up to knees, the skin shines and pressure with fingers leaves an impression for a long time); (O. of feet up to inferior third of legs). Cramplike pain in r. sole when walking.

Skin.—Dry, scaly herpes (Ars.) at outside of elbows, r., then l.; on internal malleoli, l., then r. Formication of arms, < l., with weight and difficulty in raising them. Itching on lower part of tibia; on ankles; on abdomen in evening on undressing, and on calves; like stings of insects, on chest and abdomen every evening, > in bed on going to sleep, afterwards it appeared during the day, > at evening.

Sleep.—Sleepiness, lay down early and slept well all night with his clothes on; S. as after severe illness. Sleeplessness; in evening and night from arterial pulsations in pit of stomach and in r. ear; the forepart of the night on account of rush of ideas, then restless sleep; the first hours in the evening, then sudden waking; with pulsations in both ears. Restless sleep. Interrupted sleep, and the next morning fatigue as if he had not slept at all. Delirium at night, ceasing on waking, but returning as soon as he goes to sleep. Voluptuous dreams, with painful erections; V. dreams, with emission of semen.

Fever.—Shivering, which passes off quickly towards 2 P.M. Chilliness towards 10 P.M.; at night; with chattering of teeth. *Fever every day at the same hour* (Cedron), chill at 1 P.M., then heat, dyspnœa, pulsating pain in uterine region, ending in sweat, then from 11 P.M. till 12 A.M. complete apyrexia. Chill, then fever and headache, ending at 4 P.M. in sweat; C., then heat, which causes shortness of breath and madness, so that he cannot remain quiet in bed. *Coldness in back and icy-cold hands*, although he took warm soup and his face and hands became hot. Heat at night, with headache, dyspnœa and inability to remain lying; H. in head and face, causing madness and anxiety. Copious sweat after the hot stage.

Clinical.—Intermittent fever, paroxysms about midday (11 A.M.), the paroxysms may be incomplete in their stages, accompanied by hæmorrhages, especially from the bowels; coldness predominates, not > heat; it may be followed immediately by cold sweat, with terrible anguish; in one case (a child) the paroxysm was accompanied by convulsions and hæmorrhage from the bowels.

Cadmium Sulfuratum.

This salt is triturated with sugar of milk for use.

General Action.—Our knowledge of its action is too meagre to enable one to generalize. It seems, however, to be analagous to Zincum.

Generalities.—Lying with the head low and the hands under it. Jactitations, startings of limbs (Zinc.). Cutting in joints. Restlessness. Weakness after vomiting; W. of affected parts, with horripilation. Aggravation of symptoms in morning, before noon, after grief, after drunkenness, by hunger, when lying and sitting; after sleep, on walking in open air, from a draught of air, from reflection, in air, in sunshine, when staring at an object, when ascending steps, when walking, after running, when lying, finally they may compel lying down; during deglutition and after vexation. Amelioration when sitting; when eating.

Mind and Head.—Horror of solitude; of work. Anxiety; before going to stool. Apprehension at approach of anybody. Irritability. Head, lancinations. Hammering in H. Inflammation of brain. Tingling in head, with digging and twitching. Tension and sensation as if in a vise. Apoplexy. Pressure above eyes. Pain in vertex. Pulsation in temples.

Eyes.—Hollow. Surrounded by blue circles. Lancinations extending outward. Rending pain. Burning lachrymation. Dilatation of one pupil with contraction of other. Tension in brows. Inability to read small type. Hemeralopia (Lyc.). Aggravation of symptoms in the dark, at night, on looking at a white object and when walking.

Clinical.—Opacities of cornea, with sluggish inflammation (scrofulous).

Ears.—Lancinations. Lacerating pain. Pressure behind. Clucking. Abnormal hearing alternating with abnormal vision. Sounds echo in head.

Nose.—Obstruction by swelling. Lacerating pain. Tension. Tightness at root. Numbness. Epistaxis. Smell ulcerative. Smell cancerous. (Caries of bones and ulcerations?)

Face, Mouth and Œsophagus.—Face grayish. Countenance gloomy. Looked vexed. Trembling of jaw. Lips swollen; aphthæ on lips; spasmodic motion of upper lip. Mouth symptoms < during deglutition. Salivation. Taste pitchy; salt T. Constriction of œsophagus.

Clinical.—Facial paralysis from cold.

Stomach.—Thirst; at night in bed, with heat. Rancid eructations, < noon. Nausea; at chest, in mouth, in abdomen, generally with red face and trismus. Gagging and retching up of tough mucus every few minutes. Vomiting; of food, bile and mucus; of acid matter, of black or yellowish matter, with cold sweat on face and griping (Phos., Zinc.). Cutting. Pain, and at umbilicus, with urging to stool; burning. Aggravation of symptoms in forenoon; during pregnancy; in drunkards (Arg. nit.); after cramps in stomach; after drinking beer; walking or carrying burdens, and symptoms in hypochondria.

Clinical.—Black vomit of yellow fever or of other diseases. Persistent vomiting of drunkards.

Abdomen.—Lancinations; in l. hypochondrium. Griping in lower. Stretching pain. Bruised pain. Pressure in sides. Compressed feeling. Pulsations. Inertia.

Respiratory Organs and Chest.—Breathing interrupted during sleep. Want of air on waking. Cough, with unconsciousness, agitation, red face, pain in stomach or vomiting of bile. External chest swollen. Inflammation of mammary glands. Painful blows in chest. Rheumatic pain in external C. Drawing in external C. Lungs feel as if adherent to chest. Contraction of C. Feeling of dilatation in C. Tingling in C. Beating near heart. Weakness of C. Symptoms of C. < squatting posture.

Neck and Back.—Pain in muscles of neck, as from efforts to vomit. Griping in region of kidneys.

Upper Extremities.—Stretching of arms. Swelling of bones of arms. Swollen sensation in arms. Tension in forearm. Gnawing in hands. Jerking of fingers. Tearing in metacarpal joints.

Lower Extremities.—Lancinations in joints and in heels. Digging. Sprained pain. Boring. Rheumatism. Numbness of thighs. Cramp in legs, with trembling of knees. Pressure in knee. Tearing in legs. Cramp in calf. Feet agitated by shocks while asleep. Heaviness of feet.

Skin.—Blue. Red spots on limbs. Brown spots on elbow; on chest. Yellow spots on cheeks and nose. Yellow eruption. Eruption on forehead, nose and around mouth. Chilblains. Erysipelatous inflammation of nose. Erysipelas of mammæ. Herpes on temples. Scaly, tearing, damp, suppurating herpes. Boils on nose; on buttocks. Suppuration of axillary glands. Crawling in face. Itching at night in bed; I. when touched and during cold; > scratching, which excites a voluptuous feeling.

Sleep.—Sleepiness in forenoon; S. when sitting. Sleeps with his eyes open. Moaning and smiling in sleep. Somnolence, with revery. Nightmare on falling asleep, with startings.

Fever.—Coldness; after sleeping and after waking; with heat of hands. Horripilation after drinking; H., with hot hands. Fever before midnight. Sweat in axillæ; in palms.

Cainca.

A tincture is prepared from the dried bark of the root of Chiococca racemosa, Jag.

General Action indefinite, except that the urinary symptoms seem pronounced and similar to Sarsap., Apocyn., and probably will be found allied to Galium.

Generalities and Mind.—Precipitancy in all actions. Uneasiness. Weakness; after dinner forcing him to lie down. Symptoms < in daytime and especially from 4 to 6 P.M. Violence in evening, with anger. Ennui, forgetfulness. Indisposition for mental labor.

Head.—Aching; especially in occiput, forbidding reading and every mental exertion. Heaviness. Vertigo; on ascending stairs; with vomiturition. Lancinating shocks in l. frontal eminence. Tearing in middle of forehead. Supraorbital pain alternately on r. and l. side. Sinciput, darting pain in r. half; pressure; pressure downward; embarrassment, with pressure, then weight; uneasiness, with pressure and heaviness. Piercing pain in r. temple. Lancination in l. temple and r. side of chest. Weight in temples and occiput; in occiput, with pressure.

Eyes.—Pain, with impaired vision and œdema of upper lids. Increased sensibility. Burning. Pressure in balls, with œdema of l. upper lid, which was afterwards red and wrinkled and itched; P. downward and upward in balls, with sensation as if the balls were pressed upward, and the light fell only from above, with troubled vision. Œdema of r. lower lid, then minute pustular point. Pressure in orbital bones, then pressure downward in upper half of r. orbital margin, pressive drawing along supraorbital nerve, with vomiturition and uneasiness in abdomen, afterwards the same on l. side. Photophobia. Vision misty after sleeping in afternoon; cloudy before r. eye, before twelve o'clock.

Ear and Nose.—Hissing in E. Roaring and buzzing as from a swarm of insects. Catarrh, < in daytime, of thin mucus, excoriating nose.

Mouth.—Pasty mucus on teeth in afternoon; much paplike mucus on T. after dinner. Tearing in upper teeth in evening. Tongue coated white; coated with mucus; dry, with a dirty white coat. Irritation of buccal membrane as far as larynx, with increased saliva. Salivation; thick abundant saliva. Saliva seemed no longer to be secreted. Offensive breath on waking.

Throat.—Ulcers extending up to the Eustachian tube. Inflammation, with foul-smelling saliva. Scraping; causing cough; on uvula, with pressure in stomach mounting into œsophagus, not > by eructations, and with vomiturition, then borborygmi as before diarrhœa; in throat and œsophagus, with itching. Grating. Roughness. Rawness, with peppery taste in it. Irritation in upper part, obliging hawking. Burning and grating pain. Burning, at first with sensation as from pepper, with hoarseness and rawness and dryness of throat, requiring frequent clearing. Dryness. Dysphagia, beginning at upper and back part of T. Cold feeling down œsophagus.

Stomach.—Appetite lost; for supper; less at dinner. Thirst. Eructations; tasteless, with dryness of throat and trembling of hands. Nausea. *Vomiturition;* with shivering; *then borborygmi, several liquid stools, copious urine and continual desire to urinate;* < by spitting. Violent vomiting. Copious vomiting of saliva, bile, chyme and fæcal matters, then several stools enveloped in viscous mucus. Peculiar indefinable sensation in epigastrium and in umbilical region, with increased urine, > pappy stool. Coldness, then on whole anterior part of chest, forcing him to button his coat, then pressure in S. and throat as from a foreign body, changing into burning; C. in epigastric region.

Abdomen.—Fulness; after stool; with nausea and turgescence at upper part, < clearing throat. Inflation and discomfort, with tenderness to touch, especially under umbilicus. Gurgling. Rumbling; with pain under umbilicus and desire to go to stool. Perceptible pulsation in aorta during rest after eating. Cutting; after breakfast and dinner; C. before stool; C., with calls to urinate. Pinching. Pain; with rumbling, then liquid stool; then diarrhœa mixed with air-bubbles; tractive, all around A., with continual borborygmi and eructations, he is obliged to go to bed in apprehension of inflammation of the liver, > diarrhœa. Tenderness on touching it and bending backward. Uneasiness and fulness, not > by eructations.

Stitches in and through spleen. Pressure in r. and l. lobes of liver, extending into r. inferior pulmonary lobe. Warmth about umbilicus, colic, with borborygmus, then eructations as from small doses of tartar emetic. Pressive and lancinating pain in middle of ascending colon, not > by eructations. Hypogastrium distended; but soft.

Rectum and Anus.—Inclination for stool, with pressure at anus. Frequent calls to stool, with escape of nothing but air, and with anxiety and warmth in lower abdomen. Burning in anus. Tickling in anus in evening on lying down, obliging scratching.

Stool.—Soft after dinner. *Copious;* and soft and frequent, followed by short colicky pains returning periodically; frequent, semi-fluid, yellow, preceded by cutting in abdomen. Two in the day, soft, dark. Frequent in forenoon, first hard, then paplike and less highly-colored. Scanty, then itching at anus. Delayed, containing partially digested food.

Urinary Organs.—Constant desire to urinate (Apoc. c., Equis.). Micturition, with erection of penis, urine fiery and causing burning pain in urethra (Sarsap., Apoc. c.); difficult M. in morning, afterwards with burning in glandular portion of urethra, at noon, with burning at orifice of urethra and constant desire to urinate. Frequent micturition, but urine not increased; with copious urine. Burning in glandular portion of urethra. Drawing pain in urethra, causing desire to urinate. Copious urine; frequent and dark; and colorless. Scanty dingy-brown urine, burning the urethra, almost with strangury. Darker urine. Urine through the day strongly saline with an animal smell, not unlike sausage-soup.

Sexual Organs.—Drawing in testicles and spermatic cord, in evening, with flaccidity of scrotum and feeling as if it were enlarged, afterwards with pain, the pain < during passage of pungent-smelling urine. Desire increased.

Respiratory Organs.—Hoarseness; with vomiturition and colic, all > by diarrhœa; voice hoarse and hollow, with dry heat in pharynx. Aphonia. Easily detached mucus in trachea. Heat in trachea. Tickling cough, waking him at 3 A.M., with tough, greenish-gray expectoration. Inclination to cough.

Chest.—Peculiar shooting over trunk, with beating pain. Isolated pains in trunk, lancinating and bruising. Dartings in middle third of r. side. Piercing pain in middle of r. Pricking in lower third of r., with feeling of weight there. Oppression in inferior third, with embarrassed respiration on ascending steps, beginning in sternum. Constriction; with pressure.

Heart and Pulse.—Tension in præcordia. *Pulse agitated.* Rapid P., < after siesta. Small P., a little accelerated. Full P. Slow P.; and small. Carotids beat more violently.

Back and Extremities.—Pain in small of back, as if in kidneys, > lying bent backward. Pain in l. arm as if broken. Pricking pain in l. hand. Lower extremities, stretching; heaviness; depression in lower limbs, with drawing in muscles of calf, in femoro-tibial articulation, with rheumatic pain in shoulder and back on r. side, in l. intercostal muscles of second and third spaces and in upper lumbar vertebræ, the pain in the second intercostal space extends to sternum and lasts till evening. Breaking pain in knee, with feeling as if the lower end of the femur would escape from the patella (?). Tearing in feet after dinner. Pressure in lower third of under part of r. foot. Weakness in soles; in feet after eating. Pricking under nail of great toe.

Sleep.—*Yawning;* with stretching of limbs and cramplike feeling in lower limbs. Sleepiness; in morning. Sleepless all night. Restless sleep, with lascivious dreams. Frequent waking and disturbing dreams, as, for instance, that he was about to fall. Wakes in fright and with cries, from painful dreams. Lascivious dreams, with erections, restlessness, and was awakened towards morning by an emission.

Fever.—Chill, with trembling, then weight in head, heat in face and roaring and tingling in ears. Heat; dry, < towards evening, without thirst; H. of face. Sweat; in evening on least motion and in cold air.

Cajuputum.

The Oil of Cajuput, obtained from the leaves of Melaleuca leucadendron, L (Myrtaceæ), is diluted with Alcohol for use.

Generalities.—Trembling, with sensation as if *a good deal larger all over.* Sensation as if larger all over. Feeling all the afternoon as if just getting over a drunken spree. I feel and walk as if I had taken too much lager. General feeling as if poisoned. Weakness; in morning; with sleepiness. General heavy dull feeling after going to bed. Numbness, especially in face. Amelioration after supper; A. on lying down.

Mind.—Sad, as if I could cry, do not want to be spoken to, feel better in society of ladies. Do not want any one to speak to me but like to see people and hear them talk. Want to walk in a slow and very dignified manner, and prefer to walk alone. Felt at 10 P.M. as if I could not get myself together and could not find my clothes, although they were quite near, felt better in open air. Dull and stupid feeling at 8.30 A.M., with no energy. Stupefied and intoxicated feeling all the afternoon. Cannot think of anything, cannot bear to work or study. Can think of a thousand things in a minute.

Head.—Aching on waking at 5 A.M., with neuralgia in malar-bones and stiff dry feeling in jaws; A. on rising at 5 A.M., suddenly > at breakfast, with prosopalgia; at sunset and lasting all night, after riding in afternoon and evening, with pain in face. Neuralgia almost every day and every other night, suddenly > on eating, and in face. Dull heavy feeling; in morning on rising, > after moving around; full and dull heavy feeling, afterwards settling in occipital region. Dull feeling. Feeling as if as large as a half-bushel. Vertigo when walking, can hardly walk straight, feeling as if I should stumble over my own legs. Sticking above orbital arches, > pressure of hand, < removing hand. Frontal headache, especially in eyes, < bending forward. Pain over l. eye.

Eyes.—Look about E. as if he had taken too much liquor. Dull look. Pain in r.; pungent, with lachrymation. Heaviness without sleepiness. Upper lids feel as heavy and thick as shoe leather. Burning in l. inner canthus. Inability to see at midnight on going out of doors, rubbed his eyes to bring sight.

Ears, Nose and Face.—Redness of lobules of ears; *sudden,* clearly defined, of alæ of nose. Nose is most prominent, on looking down it looks large and as if extending out from face. Face yellow. Rough feeling in F. Puffed-up feeling in F. Insensibility to pinching in F. Pain through l. malar-bone.

Mouth.—Aching in unsound bicuspids when biting anything. Tongue white and rough, looking like a calf's, with feeling as if scalded and as if the skin would peel off. Feeling as if the tongue filled the mouth. Speech thick and slow. Salivation. Taste as of lye; T. between sour and bitter; sweetish now (always had been salt); acrid, in pharynx and œsophagus.

Throat.—Constant inclination to spit and hawk up much tough white mucus, which I could feel drawn through nares. Burning in lower part; B. down to stomach.

Œsophagus.—Sensation as if lye from wood ashes had been swallowed. Soreness in morning, < thinking about eating. Seemed to close and prevent swallowing. Feeling during breakfast as if solid food lodged until forced down by more food, after breakfast pain as if swollen and constricted and as if something were trying to force through it, < after dinner and supper, and on attempting to swallow solid food.

Stomach.—Appetite good, but unnatural feeling while eating, the eating seeming to be performed mechanically; A. disappeared when I got what I had desired; lost. Thirst; then salt taste; no T. Nausea; from smoking tobacco; on rising from a seat.

Clinical.—Has proved valuable in obstinate hiccough on the slightest provocation, talking, laughing, eating or any motion.

Abdomen, Anus and Stool.—Griping on riding. Ineffectual urging to stool, with paralyzed feeling in rectum. Itching around anus. Watery, frequent yellowish diarrhœa, < *at night.* Stools frequent, bright yellow, afterwards delayed. Stool small in morning on rising.

Urinary and Sexual Organs.—Micturition delayed, urine dark red, smelling like that of cats. Diminished urine; and sparkling; with milky appearance and smelling like that of cats. Erections, with great desire; E. all night and long after rising, but without desire, penis soon becoming shrivelled and not half its usual size. Desire gone.

Respiratory Organs and Chest.—Hoarseness. Warmth down trachea into lungs. Cough, with strangulation; C. almost causing vomiting. Pain across chest; in r. side below ribs; in r. lung; sharp, through superior part of lungs; occasional sharp, through lungs; sharp, from before backward through superior and internal parts of r. lung. Soreness across chest, with pain in l. shoulder. Lungs felt loose while riding and as if I must hold them together by pressing on them.

Pulse, Neck and Back.—Pulse rapid; full and strong; P. weak. Sensitiveness of cervical muscles to pressure. Pain in dorsal surface of l. scapula. Stitches through r. lumbar region when stooping.

Extremities.—Almost complete loss of sensibility on outer side of thighs and dorsal surfaces of forearms and hands, with sensitiveness to pinching on inside of thighs and palmar surface of hands. Enlarged feeling in joints, with some pain; in shoulder-joints. Pain on pressure on inside of shoulder, < l.

Arm.—Dislocated feeling in l., with pain on raising it. Tired in morning on rising, and heavy. Feeling as if tied to body, < l.; and l. particularly numb, with feeling as if they would tremble if I would let them. Feeling like soaked wood hanging to me, after breakfast. When raised, feeling as if they would drop in spite of me. Weakness of elbows, with lame feeling. Laming sensation in carpal bones of wrist.

Knee.—Stitches through at midnight on rising in bed. Pain. Weakness when walking; with pain, so that walking was difficult.

Skin.—Eruption as thick as measles all over arms and body and upper part of legs. Itching, < scratching.

Sleep.—Gaping and stretching. Desire to sleep with arms locked under his head. Sleep unsound. Amorous dreams without emissions; unpleasant D., and in the latter part of the dreams disposition to swear and act like a rowdy.

Fever.—Cold feeling, with cold sweat. Burning in face. Profuse and weakening sweat.

Caladium.

A tincture is prepared from the fresh root of Caladium seguinum (Arum seg., L).

General Action.—Very marked on whole mucous membrane, especially of alimentary canal, and on skin. *Compare* Arum (species), Sulph., Rhus t., Graph., Hepar s., etc.

Generalities.—Nervous trembling. Purring feeling along aorta as low as abdomen. Discomfort in evening after eating pickled fish, > by walking, < by driving, with distention of abdomen. Restlessness in forenoon, inclination for nothing, afterwards very busy and forgetful. Dread of motion, with necessity to lie all the time, though there is strength enough when he makes an effort. Necessity to lie down and close the eyes, when it seems as if he were rocked. Weariness. Faintness after writing, when reflecting, lying and on rising. Aggravation from 3 or 4 P.M. till midnight. Amelioration from a short sleep during the day; A. from sweat; motion and open air.

Mind.—Delirium. Excitement. Cries about a vexation, with inconsiderate prattlings. Apprehension before sleep; A. about his health and everything, after fever. Fear of cutting himself while shaving. Anger. Ill humor; and despondency; when his appetite is hardly satisfied at breakfast, with discomfort, confusion of head and sleepiness. Wants something, but does not know what. Forgetfulness of what he has done during the day. Confusion, inability to concentrate mind. Occasional tendency to stupor, from which he would arouse, cry, talk incoherently and perhaps drop into stupor again.

Head.—Drawing tearing, extending to head. Aching; after midday sleep or after lying on side, > when sitting; with nausea; throbbing; tensive; bursting, < in forehead. Feeling as of too much blood. Confusion, with whirlings. Vertigo in morning, with nausea and with stitches in pit of stomach; V. after running; on rising. Forehead, vessels prominent; boring; aching, also in eyes; tension as from a plaster; dulness in sinciput, with heaviness. Temple, stitches in r., < in r. eye; stitches in l., > by pressure, with boring; cutting. Pain in temples; from r. to occiput; throbbing; stupefying, in r. on waking. Numbness of r. side. Drawing in occiput. Pimples sensitive to touch, on hairy scalp behind ear. Stitches in skin of sinciput. Itching.

Eyes.—Red; and watery. Stitches in l. Sensation of sand. Sensation of a hair. Pain on looking at distant objects; stupefying P. when smoking tobacco, and in forehead, with heat in face and restlessness, then hawking of mucus, slimy vomiting and urging to stool. Burning. Hot lachrymation. Sclerotica yellow. Balls, stitches; aching; aching posteriorly; sore to touch. Lids red and inflamed (Rhus t.), eyes smarting and burning (Apis., Sulph.); styes on lower (Graph.). Bright spots before eye, and flickering.

Ears.—Sticking in middle. Pain during fever; shock of P. in r. Throbbing in r., with sensation as if warm water flowed about it in a circle. Tickling in r. evenings, with itching. Sensation of something before them, even in a deaf person. Sensitive to noise, especially if he wishes to sleep; S. to the folding of paper, which wakes him when going to sleep. Twittering. Roaring. "Tic-tac" sounds in r., like two drops of water falling.

Nose.—Painful pimples in r. nostril, on septum. Smarting from the air. Sudden burning in upper part in evening, then irritation to sneeze, short sneezing, then fluent coryza. Stoppage. Dry, as if lined with white of egg. Fluent coryza. Discharge of scanty yellow, glairy mucus.

Face.—Scarlet. Pale, sickly, with black rings around eyes. Biting-burning stitches in cheek. Chapped feeling. Lips swollen; dry and scaly; sore (Arum t.); under sore and swollen; smarting of upper.

Mouth.—Toothache; mornings and evenings; as if elongated; boring, with stitches in ears; drawing downward through l. molars. Teeth seem too long after vomiting, with insipid, herbaceous taste on tongue and scratching in throat. Tongue white; dark purple; dark brown streak down centre (Bap.); yellowish red on edges, dirty yellow at base; cracked, yellow down centre (Bap.); "strawberry"; swollen, feels too large for mouth; rough; sore on margin; pricking in tip; tip feels burnt; feels greasy; tender, feels raw. Articulation difficult, as if mouth were full of mush.

Mucous membrane red, curtains of palate very red, uvula swollen. Inflammation of mucous membrane of M. and fauces, with salivation, choking sensation and desire to swallow, which was difficult. Slime. Burning, and in fauces. Sensation as if burnt with creosote. Dryness. Sticky and herby. Saliva sticky; streaked with blood as it poured from mouth. Taste slimy; bitter; sweet; metallic; of petroleum; foul; sour to milk, which was repugnant.

Throat.—Hawking of yellow mucus from posterior nares. Inflammation, with pain on swallowing. Pricking in r. side. Pain in soft palate on swallowing. Scratching, with dry sensation and hawking of mucus (Arum t.). Dryness, not in mouth, without thirst, *with aversion to cold water;* D., with irritation and roughness; of posterior nares, with rawness and roughness; of fauces and base of tongue, with stiffness. Tickling, with cough. "Wanted to shut up," with stitches towards ears and with burning and pain in stomach.

Stomach.—Hunger; in evening, but he eats nothing, then nausea in morning while half asleep, like faintness, as if he had overeaten and must vomit, > when fully awake; desire for sour things, pickles. Appetite lost; he eats only because the stomach is hollow, without hunger, but hastily, and is immediately satisfied. Great desire to smoke and uncommon relish for it. Thirst; waking him at night, with dryness of lips. Longing for beer without decided thirst, with inability to drink water. Drinks nothing all day.

Eructations of air; as if stomach were full of dry food; acid E.; incomplete, because hindered by burning pressure in abdomen. Hiccough. Nausea; on rising; when smoking his accustomed tobacco and afterwards; with confusion of head; sudden, when smoking a cigar, with urging to stool, but necessity to strain to get rid of a pappy yellow stool.

Swollen and tender to touch. Stitches in pit, < by sitting, causing weakness and nausea, with retraction of pit at every stitch; S. deep in pit. Cuttings in pit and in l. flank, preventing sleep after midnight; C. across pit as with glass. Pressure and gnawing; P. in pit, impeding respiration and causing cough. Deep-seated pain in pit on pressure. Burning pain, with frequent ineffectual retching (Ars.). Burning; all the evening after tea and chocolate; and in upper abdomen, becoming a pressure that extends under breast, and then gnawing in orifice of stomach, which prevents deep breathing and eructations. Heaviness in pit, preventing cough. Fluttering as of a bird, from morning till afternoon, causing nausea. Throbbing in pit, tiring him, after walking. Dryness after eating, different from thirst. Weak, gone feeling.

Clinical.—Inflammation of stomach, with fluttering as of a bird, tolerates only warm drinks, stomach feels full of dry food, with acrid vomiting.

Abdomen.—Distention, hardness and pain on pressure; D. and intolerance of weight of clothes. Fetid flatus. Cramps, could not walk nor sit straight. Sudden twisting pain in evening. If the burning extends into A. it leaves a pressure. Pain on touch, < in region of bladder. Drawing in forenoon after a sour plum, then nausea from smoking a few whiffs of a cigar, then corrosive acid vomiting, with mucus and part of some cocoa, then hunger. Throbbing after internal heat, with prostration; T. < on r. side above umbilicus.

Stitches in region of spleen, with jerkings and pressure. Pain in region of liver. Soreness under margins of r. ribs after much writing. Pulsation in upper A. Spasmodic cutting at umbilicus, with necessity to bend himself double. Boring about umbilicus. Pain in hypogastrium, > by emission of flatus; paroxysm of sharp P. in l. H. when lying. Sensation as if a long worm were writhing in region of transverse colon or transverse duodenum.

Rectum and Anus.—Stitches in R.; after stool; as with knives. Urging in morning on rising; mornings, noisy flatus, then straining to eject a pappy stool; frequent desire for a pasty yellow stool. Burning in A. after stool (Sulph.). Discharge of thin red blood after stool; D. of mucus after stool, then of fluid.

Stool.—Frequent, watery, then thicker. Diarrhœa, with tenesmus. Soft, large, yellow; soft, yellow, frequent; S. sour, offensive, yellowish-brown; S., then passage of flatus, later moving about and burning in abdomen, then hæmorrhoidal symptoms after a second stool and passage of blood. *Scanty, pasty.* Mushy, dark. Lumpy. Constipation. Nearly white. Clay-colored, difficult (Hepar s.). Omitted, with feeling of diarrhœa in evening.

Urinary Organs.—Region of bladder painful to touch, bladder seems full, without desire to urinate, then moderate micturition. Spasmodic drawing at side of bladder towards penis, or deep behind or near bladder. Stitches in urethra in evening. Burning in urethra. Urine pale; high-colored, smells strong; turbid, pinkish, with pellicle; gelatinous precipitate.

Sexual Organs.—Seem larger, as if puffed, relaxed and sweating, and skin of scrotum seems thick. Glans covered with red points, with dryness, causing desire to rub it, prepuce swollen along its margin, sore and painful. Burrowing in penis. Retraction of prepuce after coition, with pain and swelling. Swelling of prepuce, soreness on its margin, with biting on urinating, compelling rubbing. Sore corrosive pain on prepuce. Erections mornings when half-awake, > when fully awake; in morning without desire; in morning, and cohabited, but suddenly his desire ceased and he did not know whether there was an emission or not; painful, without desire, changing one morning to desire with relaxation of penis; incomplete, it seems as if broken, with too early emission; no E., even after amorous caresses. Sweat on scrotum. Impotency, relaxation of penis during excitement and desire. Desire increased; diminished. Emission after micturition; in dreams; no E. during embrace, and no orgasm, penis less hard than usual.

Female.—*Pruritis vulvæ* (Amb., Rhus t., Sulph., Graph.). *Cramp pains in uterus after midnight.*

Clinical.—The most efficient remedy in pruritis of the vulva and vagina.

Respiratory Organs.—Epiglottis and adjacent parts swollen and painful to pressure. *Constriction of larynx and trachea* (Brom.), *impeding deep breathing, the attacks of cough seem to originate above larynx.* Hoarse. Inability to speak, apparently from swelling of vocal cords or from cough. Cough, < by attempts to speak; hoarse C.; in weak paroxysms, with expectoration of lumps of mucus, also chest seems hollow afterwards, weak, toneless, at night, preventing sleep and recurring next morning. Constant desire to take a deep breath, cannot get air enough. Difficult respiration, with grasping at his throat; D., irregular and accelerated. Incomplete respiration, inspiration catching, with sinking in pit of stomach on inspiration.

Chest.—Cracking below last ribs on straightening up, as if they had been dislocated and snapped back again. Stitches; in evening; l. side near sternum; r. side, evenings in bed, < by lying on l. side, > lying on r., with oppression; deep-seated between l. nipple and shoulder. Cutting in r. side, < during respiration and by pressure. Aching in r. side; in twinges on r. side over fifth rib. Tightness. Oppression; with burning in stomach. Peculiar throbbing below heart, not palpitation, only perceptible to hand.

Heart and Pulse.—Heart, cutting in region; constriction; action irregular; action slow. Throbbing of all arteries on lying down, < carotids, the thud of heart-beats rises into ears. Pulse rapid, weak; P. hard, full, jerking.

Back.—Stitches in forenoon, as from incarcerated flatus. Pain in spine. Bruised feeling in morning on rising. Stiffness, and in neck. Loins, boring and burrowing, and in anus; pain in l.; pain in morning, a kind of weakness, with stitches on certain movements, < walking.

Extremities.—Jactitation. Drawing pinching between bones of forearm and behind tendo-achillis. Pain; cramplike, in flexors of l. arm and l. calf, then of r. Crampy tingling running up from feet, and then in l. arm. Loss of power.

Upper Extremities.—Pain in muscles of l. forearm. Stiffness of r. forearm. Veins stand out on back of hand. Feeling in palms towards evening like pins and needles, similar to what is felt when ulnar nerve is struck, or by some persons when looking down from a height, > sleep. Fingers felt large, like sausages, with inability to use them well and feeling as if they would be paralyzed.

Lower Extremities.—Sharp pains, > moving about. Leg, sticking in l.; tired when walking. Knee, sudden pain in l. as if it would be torn asunder, with cracking on stepping, preventing walking; weakness when standing, with trembling. Pinching in soles at night. Sticking in a corn; in a corn on l. foot, and S. in l. eye; in a corn on l. little toe.

Skin.—Dry and rough; D. on forehead, and harsh. Red inflamed spot on bridge of nose. Rash on wrist, forearm and bend of elbow, with white vesicles and itching at night in heat and internal burning after scratching; itching, on chest. Nettle-rash on chest, alternating with asthma; N. of red pimples, which itch and burn, on inner side of forearm, *with oppression of chest, so that he could scarcely breathe, as if mucus would suffocate him,* < after eating and after midday nap. Pimples on mons veneris and l. ear; painful, red, on r. ear. White pustules here and there, with red areola, itching and soreness to touch. Blisters at l. corner of mouth and on cheeks. Mosquito-bites pain greatly, then itch and burn. Tingling. Crawling as of a fly, < on face. Itching of various parts; at base of r. index; l. elbow; shin; in a point on l. calf; fingers, < when lying at night.

Sleep.—Sleepiness; at 7 A.M., with fretfulness and desire to return to bed; in morning after rising, with closure of eyes while walking in open air, with nausea like emptiness, weakness and prostration in knees; evening; before dinner, so that eyes close, with tension in temples. Necessity to lie down during the day, but inability to sleep, with shivering and vertigo. Sleepless; till 1 A.M. *Anxious groans and moans in sleep.* Starting in sleep. Sleep unrefreshing. Restless sleep, with confused dreams; R. sleep, with heat, then excessive erections at 4 A.M., without desire, then deep sleep towards 6 A.M., so that he could not rouse himself, with vivid dreams of persons he had not seen for years. Everything troubles him in sleep.

Dreams.—Restless, anxious. Vivid; of dead persons, of events of past years, after waking he falls asleep again directly and continues to dream of them. Of fighting and murder. Confused sleep, during which everything comes to his mind which he had forgotten while awake.

Fever.—Chilliness; in evening, coldness extending from abdomen to feet, with coldness of fingers; in limbs; feet and legs, with hot face, head and hands; l. hand and arm as if ligatured; over back and whole body, with drawing pains in l. little finger, which feels as if full and gone to sleep, and stretched sensation in whole body. Shaking, < of lower jaw.

Heat; during the day, then in evening till midnight coldness, thirst, wheezing in chest, sleepiness, fever wakes him again about midnight and then disappears with throbbing in chest and coryza; after midday sleep, then sweat, then chill in open air; every day between 4 and 5 P.M.; in evening till midnight, and again waking him, with thirst; before midnight, chill after midnight; with fulness and heaviness over orbits; with thirst, pain in ear, swelling of submaxillary glands and constipation; internal, > sleep; internal, with exhausting sweat. Hot and dry skin. Hot hands and feet. Heat in flushes over head, face and chest; H. ascends into head; H. of feet every day between 4 and 5 P.M.; hands, face and abdomen, with coldness of feet before midnight, after midnight coldness of abdomen and heat of feet, without thirst. Burning on external upper margin of ear, without redness or heat; sudden corrosive B. in spots on skin, on cheeks, nose, toes, etc., obliging touching, always on r. side.

Sweat over whole body in forenoon; towards evening, with prostration, yawning and sleepiness; after heat, alluring the flies; cold, clammy on face.

Calcarea Acetica.

To follow the symptomatology use the drug as prepared by Hahnemann, a solution of clean broken oyster-shells in dilute Acetic acid.

General Action.—Compare Calcarea carb. and Acetic acid; but note the brilliant clinical results in inflammations of mucous membranes characterized by a membranous exudation, (uterus, bronchi, etc.).

Generalities.—Weary from want of sleep during the day, but unable to sleep.

Clinical.—A valuable remedy for inflammation of mucous membranes; see under Respiratory and Genital Organs.

Mind.—Anxiety as if he had committed a crime or feared reproaches, with constant inclination to work; A. about the present and future, with deep thought and with indifference to anything not concerned with himself, though not without inclination to work; intermittent, in evening before sleep, > emission of flatus, with which objects seemed like different objects and with dread of darkness; the first part of the day, liveliness and contentment the last part. Apprehensive, sad mood, as if awaiting depressing news. Sadness, almost to weeping, with solicitous care for the present and future.

Fretfulness as soon as he left the open air, where he felt better, with disinclination to talk and with increased headache; F. as soon as he was quiet and thoughtful, with sleepiness and aversion to everything; with indifference to most important objects, he did all his work with aversion; all day, but good humor and talkativeness in the evening. Disinclination to talk, without moroseness. Liveliness and desire to be with people and to talk. Loss of will power though he feels strong.

Head.—Aching, especially in temples; A. while standing after stooping, with heaviness in head and with pressure outward in forehead, especially over l. eye; drawing and at times tearing, now in forehead, now in occiput, now in temples, > pressure or on exerting mind. Shattering in brain on stepping, like an echo in the head. Heaviness on stooping, > rising. with jerks in temples and with pain in whole head, Stupid feeling from 3 A.M. till 4 P.M., as if he had turned in a circle. Vertigo; *on walking in open air;* on walking in open air, as if he would fall to the right; stupefying, the head inclines forward to the left; as if his body did not stand firmly,

Forehead.—Stitches on walking, which especially affect l. side of forehead, > continuing to walk; intermittent, in l.; boring, in l. when sitting, > walking, standing and touch; boring, in middle, extending into brain. Aching on walking in open air, especially above l. eyebrow; in r. eminence, extending to r. eye and compelling him to close it; *stupefying*, with confusion of senses and obscuration of head *while reading*, and he did not know where he was; stupefying, in r., < stooping; stupefying in morning after rising, as if he had not slept enough or had been dissipating; drawing, above r. eye on exerting mind, and in occiput; drawing and pressive A. in l. supraorbital region or in temporal bone.

Temples.—Stitches penetrating T.; digging, near l. eyebrow on moving jaw; rhythmical, intermittent, boring outward, extending upward into l., > touch and when sitting. *Drawing aching in r. muscle*, also in evening, at times with pressure on upper teeth, on pressing upon the temple the pain changes into aching in the forehead; the drawing aching always < after eating and even while eating, with sensitiveness of teeth while chewing, as if they were loose and would be bent over. Cramplike pain in r.; in l. Pressure as from something hard, close to r. eye; in l. bone as if it would be pressed in, internally and externally; outward in l., and on whole l. side of head and on r. occiput.

Stitches in vertex externally. Pressure on V., extending into eye. Throbbing in V. as in an artery, with cutting shocks extending outward. Jerking stitches in r. half of brain, which often return and leave a pressive bursting sensation. Pulsating stitches in l. parietal bone. Feeling in r. side of head on stooping as if headache would begin.

Pain suddenly shooting through occiput; sore pain in O. on touch, as if suppurating; drawing pain in l. side of O., with stiff feeling in neck; jerklike pressing-outward in l. side of O., extending into neck; feeling as if O. would be pressed asunder. Whole scalp sensitive on moving frontal muscles back and forth; crawling and itching on S. not > rubbing; tickling-itching on S., with pain at roots of hair on touch.

Eyes.—Inflammation, the white entirely red, with much matter in eyes, especially in external canthi, and ulceration of external canthi. Tearing-stitching in r., as if inflamed. Itching. Pupils dilated, then contracted. Agglutination in morning on waking. Stickiness of lids on moving them, with pressure in canthi, especially external one. Burning in l. upper lid, extending to internal canthus. Hardened matter in canthi. Sticking in canthi; itching, in inner, > rubbing. Itching in canthi; tickling, in r. external canthus. Boring-stitching on upper margin of orbit. Twitching on upper margin of orbit, extending to nose. Far-sightedness in one naturally near-sighted.

Ears.—Twitching in cartilage. Cramplike feeling on back of concha. Stitches. Feeling as if something were before r. drum, without diminished hearing. Sensitiveness to noise in evening on falling asleep. Whizzing, with confusion of head.

Nose.—Pimples in nostrils, with scabs. Gnawing pain in root. Frequent sneezing without coryza. Coryza, with sensitiveness of nose and internal heat in head; fluent, with headache; fluent, with much sneezing; stopped, with frequent sneezing.

Face.—Yellow. Pain in muscles of l. cheek. Tension in r. cheek as if swollen. Throbbing on cheekbones. Tearing in r. upper jaw. Aching in r. upper jaw when chewing. Moist scurf below r. angle of mouth. Roughness of lips, especially of upper, with dryness, as if they would crack. Itching-crawling on upper lip, which, after rubbing, appears on another spot near by.

Mouth.—Stitches in teeth. Gnawing pain in r. upper molars, as if they would be hollow. Throbbing toothache, with sensitiveness of teeth to touch and with swelling of gum, which pained when touched. Stitches in upper gum. Boring in r. upper gum, then swelling, with pressive drawing in r. temporal muscles. Blisters on tongue, with burning pain and heat in mouth. Rawness on tongue, with soreness and white coat; R. on back of tongue, with scraping, provoking cough. Dry sensation on tongue. Dryness in mouth as from chalk. Mucus, which he could not swallow fast enough. Milk tastes sour, and he is averse to it. Little taste to food, especially to meat.

Throat.—Submaxillary glands swollen, with a pressive sensation in them. Throat hoarse and rough. Sensation of much mucus in fauces on swallowing, with dryness in mouth. Sticking on r. upper part of œsophagus when not swallowing.

Stomach.—Thirst in morning; T., with dryness of throat; for cold drinks, especially for water. *Eructations sour; and offensive;* empty E. Hiccough. Woke at midnight from nausea, cough and a kind of heartburn. Nausea, with eructations, accumulation of water in mouth and a kind of vertigo; N. after drinking milk in morning, as from a sour stomach. Pinching-retching just below pit. Anxiety at pit. Anxiety as if it arose from the pit, when sitting, > walking or standing, with burning in abdomen.

Abdomen.—Rumbling and gurgling, as from emptiness; R. in r. side, as before diarrhœa; audible, and crawling in r. side, extending outward, as from flatus, which is passed. Tearing in muscles, < inspiration. Cutting every morning, and in evening and night, > after eating, leaving a gurgling. Pinching, almost cramplike pain in walls, in r. groin, in a spot, when speaking, with pain on pressure.

Griping in hypochondriac region, below pit of stomach, with chilliness over whole body. Tensive pinching in hypochondrium and in pit of stomach. Pinching in H. and in chest, which here and there ends in stitches. Griping-twinging in H., extending to beneath sternum, where it becomes sticking and causes eructations. Griping in a spot below umbilicus, which becomes a gurgling, on rubbing; frequent in region of bladder, always with emission of flatus. Pressure in hypogastrium, causing confusion of head. Pinching on crest of ilium. Swelling of glands of l. groin. Tearing in inguinal glands when sitting and walking. Sore pain in groins as if glands would swell, < walking, with slight swelling of glands. Pressive tension in region of l. groin.

Rectum and Stool.—Twinging in end of R. when at stool, with rumbling and gurgling in abdomen. *Itching in anus.* Pressure in anus. Frequent diarrhœa. Frequent stools, first solid, afterwards pasty, then thin, with difficulty, then constipation. Constipation. No stool.

Urinary and Sexual Organs.—Frequent urgings to urinate, with profuse discharge; frequent desire, with scanty discharge. Urine turbid, like gruel, after standing. Tickling itching at end of glans; tickling I. on prepuce. L. testicle spasmodically drawn up to abdomen, with pain on touch and with pain in l. groin. Emissions at night; with voluptuous dreams; without voluptuous dreams; frequent. Itching of pudenda. Discharge of blood from uterus in the last quarter of the moon, in a woman who had not menstruated for years.

Clinical.—Membranous dysmenorrhœa in persons of a Calcarea habit.

Respiratory Organs.—Rattling on expiration, as from mucus in chest. Tickling, which provokes cough. The cough becomes loose, with expectoration of large pieces like purulent matter. Breathing difficult, > bending shoulders backward.

Clinical.—A most brilliant cure was made of an obstinate membranous bronchitis, which for months had resisted all other treatment; the paroxysms recurred every two or three weeks; each time it seemed as if the patient would die, until extensive casts of the membrane of the bronchi were expectorated; entirely cured by this drug.

Chest.—Stitches beneath r. ribs; broad, in muscles at every beat of the heart; outward in r. side; outward beneath l. axilla, < inspiration; out through spine, between scapulæ; itching, < expiration, > rubbing. Cutting outward in lowest ribs, < inspiration. Anxiety, as if too narrow, < sitting, with short breath, with aching in chest, < inspiration, the heart beating anxiously and trembling. Constrictive, anxious sensation, as if there were not room enough to breathe, with stoppage of nose. Anxious constriction and difficult breathing, like a tension in lower chest, almost suffocation on motion and when sitting.

Heart and Back.—Sticking-drawing pain in præcordial region. Jerks from posterior wall of chest to between scapulæ, synchronous with beat of heart, with anxiety. Stitches on inner side of scapula; in middle of spine on walking in open air, > when standing; in a spot above small of back on touch; jerking, in sacrum and at same time above ankle. Cutting, pressing-out pain in r. loin, transiently > touch.

Upper Extremities.—Pain in shoulders. Stitches in axillæ. Upper arm, jerking in l.; tearing-jerking; tearing-stitching in muscles of l. when sitting; pinching (with tearing) in muscles on walking in open air. Tearing in muscles of l. forearm; with boring stitches; cramplike tearing in muscles of l. forearm. Cramplike pain in forearm, in front of elbow; in outer side of F. near l. wrist. Sprained pain just above wrist, < rest. Stitches in outer condyles of wrists. Crawling and sticking in wrist.

Lower Extremities.—Soreness between nates when walking. Pinching-jerking on posterior side of hip-joint, < rest. Stitches on outer side above l. knee; on inner side of l. thigh when sitting; cramplike, in muscles of r. thigh when standing and walking, > sitting; tearing, on inner side above knee when sitting. Tearing on inner side of thigh on motion; in hip-joint and about anterior crest of ilium on motion, extending into groin. Cutting in socket of hip-joint when sitting. Bruised pain in muscles of thigh when walking. Drawing, sprained pain in hip-joint when walking.

Stitches in r. knee. Pain in knees when turning or touching them; in l. knee, even during rest; drawing cramplike, on knee-cap; sprained, in l. knee-cap when sitting, > walking and standing. Tearing-jerking in forepart, below knee during rest. Aching in l. tibia near ankle when walking in open air; intermittent, in calf. Cramplike pain close to fibula when sitting. Bruised pain in leg when lying, especially in lower leg; below patella on walking in open air; in leg, as if weary, he was obliged to change frequently from one place to another. Drawings in legs extending to tips of toes.

Swelling of l. external malleolus. Cramp in soles

and toes at night, and on drawing on the boots during the day; in soles after walking, > continuing to walk, and ceased when sitting. Cramplike pain in l. sole. Stitches in last joint of great toe during rest; in l. little toe, as if outside of it; intermitting cramplike, in r. toe when sitting and standing, > walking.

Skin.—Inflamed swelling below patella. Pimple beneath lobule of ear, causing tensive pain in joint of jaw on chewing; P. in middle of cheek, that became moist after scratching, then greenish crusts. Pustule above l. eyebrow. Ulcer on cheek, with sticking. Crawling beneath eye and on side of nose. *Itching below calves;* on a spot where there was a tetter years previous; tickling, on index finger. Itching-tickling on border of l. hand; itching-sticking tickling in r. palm.

Sleep.—Frequent yawning, as if he had not slept enough. Sleepiness in morning, with fretfulness and pain in forehead; S. in evening, with fretfulness. Sleeplessness nearly all night, with tossing about and general sweat. Restless sleep, with talking and frequent waking. Frequent waking as if he had slept enough; as from some disturbance; on account of tossing about, and he thought he was lying turned around in bed.

Dreams.—Frightful, shuddering. Of sick people, and of dead people, with violent weeping in sleep. Vivid, full of strife and anger; V., confused, unremembered; of previous transactions, with long, deep morning sleep.

Fever.—Frequent chilliness, with yellow color of skin. Shivering, with frequent yawning; S. over back; over whole body, with warmth or heat of forehead and face and cold hands. External heat, even on lying down, with internal chilliness. Heat and redness of face, with hot forehead, cold hands and thirst. *Sweat every morning;* exhausting, day and night.

Calcarea Carbonica.

Triturations of the pure white middle layer of the oyster-shell are used (Hahnemann).

General Action.—A general nutrition (tissue) remedy. It seems to produce a well-marked cachexia which may develop tuberculosis, epilepsy or other chronic disorders. The functions of various organs are disturbed, but the lymphatics are most prominently affected.

Allies.—Baryta c., Magnes. c., Kali c., Sulph., Phos., Lyc., Sepia, etc.

Generalities.—Restless motion of whole body on account of suppressed eructations. *Trembling;* in morning; in body on waking, with twitches of various muscles in thigh and arm; < in open air; with weakness. Anxious, with weakness. *Twitching of muscles.* **Epileptic attacks,** *while standing he suddenly fell to the ground sideways and on returning to consciousness found himself lying with outstretched arms, then heat and sweat.* Starting from slight prick of a needle in finger, so that she became nauseated, *tongue, lips and hands became white and cold, with coldness of forehead and face,* obscuration of vision, uneasiness, flushes of heat, trembling and necessity to lie down, all > mesmerizing.

Congestions of blood. Rushing of blood in all veins in morning on waking from a restless sleep, with swollen veins and with bruised sensation in whole body. Pulsation in vessels after dinner, especially in chest, with rapid pulse. Stitches in various joints and muscles; in upper arm, beneath arms, in back and limbs. The pain was intense, but disappeared quickly. *Strained easily* (Con.), *pain in small of back from lifting anything heavy* (Sil.). *Taking cold easily* (Kali c.). Painful tension over whole body. Drawing in whole body when walking, extending into head, obliging her to sit down.

Sick feeling in whole body, with necessity to spit much and dread of open air; S. feeling after a walk, with hoarseness and oppression of chest. Great indisposition, > motion, *with coldness of hands and feet,* paleness of face and palpitation. Indisposition, as in previous pregnancy. Discomfort in evening as before an attack of ague. Greatly affected by noise. *Inclination to stretch in morning.* Uneasiness; in evening, especially in limbs; in evening, after nausea in afternoon, with absent-mindedness; with orgasm of blood. Attack of general depression, with confusion of head, vertigo, pain in small of back and general chilliness.

Inability to go up-stairs *and exhaustion from it* (Ars., Baryta, Spong.). *Weakness; in morning, also on waking from deep sleep, so that the confused and sleepy condition continued after rising;* in evening; **on walking,** *especially in limbs, with exhausting sweat; after walking,* even to feverishness, attack of chilliness and thirst; *from speaking; for several days after coition, with sickness;* after dinner; after stool; the day before menstruation, with fright at a trifle; > walking; > fresh open air, with oppression and anxiety; *all day, with sleepiness;* with yawning; with attacks of convulsive laughter. Faintness; in evening, with blackness before eyes when sitting; with sweat on face; in attacks, with coldness and indistinct vision. *Heaviness of body.* Parts on which he has lain during afternoon nap go to sleep. The chronic troubles are better every other day.

Clinical.—Very frequently indicated in affections caused by working in water. In chronic inflammations of joints; swellings, without inflammations. Pains < change of weather, especially in damp weather. Muscular rheumatism. Glandular enlargement, with suppuration, with fistulous ulcers. Various phases of scrofula. It is generally indicated in persons of a fair complexion, who are very sluggish and inclined to be fat (fair, fat and flabby). The child is not able to walk, is very backward. ***Epilepsy;*** **very frequently indicated in the cachexia, which leads to the development of epileptiform spasms, and it will sometimes radically cure the disease. Marasmus. A general condition of mal-nutrition, the patient is flabby, weak, sluggish, has profuse sweats, profuse discharges generally, and cold extremities.**

Mind.—Much crying in an infant. Lachrymose; in evening. Cries and complaints about long-past offenses. Weeping when remonstrated with. Eccentric fancies as soon as she closes her eyes in the evening. Despair, with dread of disease and suffering and forebodings of sad events; D. of her own life, with sadness, weeping and sudden attack of heat as if dashed with hot water. Hypochondriac, she thinks she is deadly sick, but can complain of nothing.

Anxiety, with palpitation; A. in afternoon, with headache, after nausea in forenoon; at night after waking from a frightful dream, with trembling; *at night,* as if she were or would become insane, then shuddering chilliness and sensation as if body were dashed to pieces; with busy mood, but accomplishing nothing, then exhaustion. *Fear that people would observe her confusion of mind; F. that she would lose her reason* (Cannab. ind.); *that some misfortune were about to* *happen to himself or some one else* (Chin. s.), *which he could not overcome; and restlessness, as if he expected bad news;* at every near sound, < morning. Dread of the future, with fear of consumption. *Despondency,* with a kind of anguish. Sadness from every walk in open air, with necessity to weep. Melancholy about heart, not exactly a sad feeling, with voluptuous trembling of body. Loneliness is oppressive, with coldness of face, hands and feet.

Anger at everything in morning before stool; A. at thought of former vexation. *Peevishness* in morning after a little work, with weakness and despondency; P. evenings; after taking cold, < morning; with spitting of saliva; about trifles, so that she was dizzy all the evening and went to bed early, but could not sleep. Restless disposition, with gloominess and anxiety. Obstinacy. Impatience. Sullen mood. Indifference and taciturnity. Disgust for most persons. *Desire to be mesmerized. Disinclination for every kind of labor.*

Misplaces words and easily chooses a wrong expression. Forgetfulness. It seemed as if she did not know where she was on stooping or on moving head. Vanishing of thoughts. Weakness of imagination, during a slight effort in speaking it seemed as if the brain were paralyzed, especially in occiput, he could not think nor remember what had been said, with confusion of head. Stupefaction like an unconsciousness of external objects, with waving tingling in upper part of head. Unconsciousness in evening when walking, and she would have fallen if one had not caught her; U., with illusions as regards place, the room seeming like a bower; with anxious oppression of stomach, from which she was suddenly awakened as by a fright.

Clinical.—Melancholia, fear of becoming insane or that something dreadful is going to happen. Imbecility. Enfeebled memory. Dull intellect. Obstinacy, especially in children who are inclined to get fat. From slight mental effort the head gets very hot.

Head.—*Stitches;* in evening, and in limbs; during cough; if she rises from lying on her back and after stooping; here and there; in brain, also with empty feeling in head; through head, with chilliness; extending outward at eyes; like tearings, during cough. Stitchlike throbbing when walking rapidly. Tearing on H. every day from 3 or 4 till 9 or 10 P.M., and in eyes, with redness of face. Jerks; or shocks through H. Shattering in brain on shaking head and on every step, especially in r. side of occiput; in brain on severe motion, with tearing; during every cough, as if head would burst.

Aching every morning on waking, with vertigo; in forenoon, which continually increased, with rapid sinking of strength, heat in forehead and hands, thirst for acids, then after lying down coldness of hands, with rapid pulse; A. the day before menstruation; < open air, mostly in forehead; with nausea. Throbbing pain in middle of brain every morning and lasting all day. Burning headache. Pain as if skin were detached, extending upon neck. Pressure extending to eyes, nose, teeth and cheeks, with digging, and with sensitiveness to noise and attacks of faintness. *H. easily becomes cold, which causes pain as if a board lay upon it, and general chilliness.* Dragging outward, with feeling as if the brain would be pressed together.

Fulness. Tension. Dulness every morning on rising. *Confusion;* in morning on waking, also with trembling through whole body and rush of blood to head; after midday nap; *as if too full;* painful, so that she did not understand what she had read nor comprehend what was spoken. Confused trembling condition. Heaviness in morning on waking; < moving head and raising it, with heat in it; almost only in forehead, with heat. Stupefaction all afternoon, like vertigo; S. at night, waking him, increasing until it almost amounted to faintness, then trembling of limbs and weakness, so that he could not sleep again. Insensibility, with bluntness, as in severe coryza. Great affection the day after coition. Feeling as from intoxication. **Rush of blood,** *during menstruation,* **with heat in it** (Sulph.); *R.* after a meal, with heat in face; with discharge of blood from anus. Congestion of blood, and to chest, preceded by painful stiffness of spine.

Vertigo in morning after rising, with nausea, roaring in ears and feeling as if he would fall unconscious; V. in morning when rising, < walking and standing, with painful turning of head, as if in a circle, chilliness and stitches in l. side of head; in forenoon, so that everything seemed in a half dream; at night, lasting till noon, with flickering before eyes; **on suddenly turning head** *and during rest; on walking in open air, as if he would fall,* < **suddenly turning head;** *after walking when standing and looking, as if everything were turning around with her;* during menstruation, on stooping and rising again; even to falling, after stooping, when walking and standing; when stooping, then nausea and headache; from vexation; < sitting, > standing, and still less when walking; with loss of sense; even to falling, with weakness; as if he were raised up and pushed forward.

Forehead.—Stitches; in l. side at 11 A.M.; in one-half, > when lying; in l. eminence on waking, so that she believed the bone was being pressed out. Tearing in l. eminence; stitching; drawing, in l. nerve. Pinching. Boring externally in l. side after walking in open air. Digging in r. eminence, causing nausea, with redness of r. ear. Sharp tensive pains. Pain; then in occiput; in morning on waking, with confusion of head and dry coated tongue; at noon over nose; in middle; *stupefying,* as in vertigo; throbbing; sticking throbbing, on r. eminence; spasmodic (after taking cold), extending to vertex; drawing, in nerve (nervous P.); burning, and posteriorly; burning P., with chilliness; as if too thick. *Painful pressure, extending into nose* in evening. Pressing out, > pressure of cold hand and walking in cold air, causing vertigo. Painful full sensation, with throbbing in temples. *Heaviness, < reading and writing.*

Temple.—Stitches; in l; in l. nervous profundis; penetrating l. and coming out through r. Tearing, and in orbital bones and cheeks, with swelling; upward in l.; throbbing, in nerve. Pinching-drawing pain in l., towards parietal bone, with heat of face. Jerking pain in r. Pain in morning on waking, with empty eructations. Pressure.

Vertex.—Aching; waking him every day at 5 A.M., and lasting an hour; during menstruation; when walking in open air, > sleep. Drawing pain; beneath V. and in temples, seeming to come from back. Spasmodic drawing beneath V., with stitches in temples and heat in ears. Tension. Pressure after dinner, and in forehead; now in V., now in temples; outward, almost sticking, while stooping; stupefying, as after rapidly turning in a circle.

Side.—*Stitches in l.*, above temple; in both, with nausea, but inability to bring up anything; on r., extending into eye; on upper part of r., extending into r. eye. Pinching on l. *Frequent one-sided aching, always with empty eructations;* A. in bones; in side on which he had just been lying (a burning?); sudden, in l. bone as if hacked to pieces, with general shivering; drawing, in whole r., and in zygoma and in jaw. Paroxysmal tension in r., with pressure as if blunt instrument pressed downward through head.

Occiput.—Crackling audible to himself towards noon, then warmth in neck. Stitches in r. side. Cutting, < walking and pressure of hand and in forehead. Gnawing. Pain; whenever she ties anything tight about head; drawing P., always towards the side to which he moved the head, > after sneezing. Tensive pressure on bone. Heaviness, with pressure.

Scalp.—Hair falls out on combing. Swelling on r. side; in r. temple; below l. temple. Eruption; with swelling of glands of neck. Scales on vertex. Thin moist scurf. Pain in places on touch. Formication on l. temple. *Itching; every night on waking;* when walking in open air; on occiput; burning; burning, in evening before sleep, with crawling, and on lower part of face. Numb spot on r. side.

Clinical.—Headaches in school children. Congestive headaches, with violent surging of blood in the head, which feels hot and heavy, with pale face and cold feet. Chronic headaches, with vertigo, < ascending stairs; in anæmic women who have profuse menses, leucorrhœa, etc. Hydrocephalus. Eczema on head. In children the bones of the head do not develop well, fontanelles remain open, with enlarged glands.

Eyes.—Inflammation of r., with agglutination of lids. Purulent mucus. Paroxysmal twitching and throbbing. Stitches; during menstruation, and in head; as from a foreign body in l., in r. between lower lid and ball. Tearing in l. *Sensation as if sand were under upper lid;* as if sand were in l. eye. *Sensation as of a foreign body.* Sensation as if something painless were moving in r. Sensation as if fat were in them. Pressure; *in evening.* Pain as if they would be pressed in; so that she must close them, with feeling as if she ought to press them in. Biting. *Itching;* in evening, with pressure in morning. Burning; on closing lids; with heaviness of upper lids; burning, and on head and in throat. Cold feeling.

Lachrymation; in morning; on writing; of r. eye; of r., with burning; biting, from l. eye, which is red. Ball, injection; pressive pain in r.; stiffness of l. in morning after rising. *Pupils dilated.*

Lids.—*Swelling, with redness and nightly agglutination, during the day they are full of gum, with heat, smarting pain and lachrymation* (Sulph); S. of lower in morning after rising. Redness of margins. Dry matter on margins and in canthi. *Agglutination;* in morning; *in morning, eyes watery,* with pain if he looks at the light; in morning in various places; during menstruation, with lachrymation, heaviness of head, inability to fix the thoughts. Spasmodic trembling of lower; l. lower spasmodically moved downward towards internal canthus. Twitching of r.; of r. lower; *of upper,* with sensation as if the eye were moving of itself. Necessity to wink when reading, with redness of eyes and lachrymation. Smarting pain in lower. *Itching on margins* (Sep.).

Canthus.—Inflammation and swelling of l. and of lower lid, with sticking and throbbing pain and itching all about. *Stitches in inner* (Zinc.), with alternating stitches and throbbing in eyes, then frequent blowing of nose. *Burning in inner,* with stitches. *Itching; in r. inner.*

Redness of white of eye; with oozing of blood. Tension in muscles on turning them and on exertion in reading. Stitches in r. supraorbital nerve in evening; in supraorbital margin and nervous supraorbital and supratrochlear. Pain in supraorbital nerve as if pressed, and in supratrochlear. Drawing-tearing in suborbital nerve.

Far-sighted. Could scarcely see any near object in forenoon on waking from a nap. Dim vision after getting the head cold; D., with need to close the eyes without being sleepy. It seemed like a veil before inner canthi, which disappeared with lachrymation. Small objects seem more distinct than large ones. Sensitiveness to sunlight, with headache; to glare of candle, with headache. The light blinds her. Blackness at times; sudden, after dinner, > sleep, with anxious sweat, nausea, and a bright light before eyes. Flickering vision; of letters; in morning on waking, with sparks of fire. Vision as if a shadow passed before eyes with dilated pupils, *so that she saw only one side of objects,* for example, only one eye in a person. Vision of black spots during physical exertion; black spot before l. eye; black floating spots before l.; a black point accompanying letters when reading. Dark objects like spider's webs on waking from noon nap. Feathers before eyes. Electric sparks in the dark. Halo around the light and around the moon. Frightful visions on closing eyes.

Clinical.—Scrofulous ophthalmias; parenchymatous inflammation of cornea; spots on cornea; ulcers on cornea; pannus of cornea. Inflamed eyes from working in water. Lachrymal ducts are closed, in scrofulous people. Asthenopia. Easy fatigue of eyes, feet sweaty and cold.

Ears.—Swelling of r.; of l., with itching; of inner and of r. side of face, with profuse earwax. Purulent discharge. Trickling of water from one, with difficult hearing in other. Twitching in r., with hissing, so violent that sometimes the whole body twitched with it. Stitches; when sneezing; in r., with pain; in l.; in l., > rest, with closed eyes, and in temples; behind l. in morning; in posterior auricular nerve; tearing, in r. Tearing in l.; behind l. *Crushing when swallowing.* Sticking throbbing pain in l. Cramplike pain. Drawing pains. Burning pain around. Pressure. Bones behind l. seem swollen, with itching, with pain on touch as if suppurating. *Pulsation.* Flapping, as if a piece of skin were loose. Sensation of fanning before l. *Heat within,* like hot blood; H. streams out of l. Crawling in r. Burning itching. On blowing nose hard something comes before the ear so that she cannot hear well, > swallowing.

Sensitiveness to a shrill sound. Hearing bad. Noises in l. and in head. *Cracking when chewing* (Nit. ac., Nat. m.). *Singing* (Kali c.), *then crackling; S. and roaring;* in l. at one time, at another cracking. Roaring in morning, with difficult hearing. Humming in l. Ringing before ears. Grunting when swallowing.

Clinical.—Deafness from working in water. Scrofulous inflammations of the ear, with muco-purulent otorrhœa, enlarged glands, etc. Chronic inflammation of ear, thickening of the drum. Polypi, which bleed easily.

Nose.—*Intermittent swelling, especially at root;* of r. wing, with pain on motion. Inflammation of forepart, with redness and swelling. Pimple in r. nostril, painful on moving muscles of face and nose, the wing of the nose is red and itches internally and externally; painful P. in l. nostril, with itching-stinging. *Sore ulcerated nostril, preceded by frequent sneezing* (N. ac.). Sore, painful, swollen, erysepelatous-looking, hard to touch, with frontal headache and fluent coryza. Soreness of r. nostril.

Twitching in external muscles. The almost sore nostril stings and pains on touch. Sore pain on border and especially in septum. Tensive pressure above bones as if swollen. Dryness; *at night*, with moisture during the day. Itching internally and externally. *Sneezing;* in morning; *without coryza.* Stoppage; *in morning on rising.*

Coryza; with headache and oppression of chest; with heat in head and cough; with pain in hypogastrium; which changed to colic; affecting every limb. *Stopped; with sneezing;* with headache. *Fluent;* with ulceration of l. nostril; with weariness; after ineffectual sneezing. Profuse mucous discharge while nose is stopped. Bleeding; in morning; at night; almost to faintness. Blackish blood is blown out. Smell blunted; very sensitive. *Offensive smell in nose. Smell before nose as of bad eggs or of gunpowder.*

Clinical.—Coryza, clear, watery secretion or chronic ozæna, with a thick purulent, fetid discharge, with swelling at root of nose and ulceration. Nasal polypi. Inclination to nosebleed in fat children.

Face.—*Yellow. Pale, lean, with deep-seated eyes surrounded by dark rings; P.,* with blue rings around eyes. Red and hot; and swollen. Swelling, with stitches here and there; of cheeks in morning on rising; of r. side, which was covered with pimples. Twitching of muscles; r. cheek drawn spasmodically sideways, with pinching, contractive pain. Stitches in r. cheek. Tearing in bones of F. and head; in l. cheek-bones. Pain, then swelling of cheeks. Prickling, and in neck. Swollen feeling, especially under eyes and around nose, without visible swelling. Sensation in various parts as if a spider's web or delicate substance were lying on skin.

Lips.—*Swelling of upper in morning* (Phos.). Eruption in red portion of lower. Pimples on upper; *scurfy P. on border of red portion of lower.* Cracked, with a cracked, smarting tongue; upper C. Ulcerated corner; r., and paining as if sore. Drawn together spasmodically, so that she could not open them. Drawing in lower, then white color, numbness and feeling as if it would be thick and would hang down. Stitching-itching about upper and lower.

Jaws.—Swelling on l. side of lower, with drawing pains. Tearing in lower.

Mouth.—Teeth. *Offensive smell.* Protrusion, with pain when biting. Looseness of an old stump, with swollen gum and with soreness and sticking when touched. *Inclination to gnash, as in a chill.* Stitches; in last back after eating, then boring, > eating; in all, < *entrance of cold air*, waking him at night; only during the day, extending to r. eye and r. temple, with inclination to touch the tooth with the tongue, which always causes a stitchlike jerk in the tooth, so that she starts and it shakes her; boring, extending to eye and ear, < riding in a wagon. Tearing; in first l. upper molar; extending to head, to temples, < night; in hollow ones at half-hour intervals, < taking anything warm, and at night T. through cheek; as if roots would be torn out. Drawing-cutting. *Gnawing*, < evening. Boring, with stitches extending to nasal bones, and swelling of gum and cheek; B. in hollow T. during menstruation, becoming a pulsation on stooping. Toothache in evening as soon as she lay the head down; **when cold air or drinks enter the mouth**; from heat and cold, < *current of air*, with running of saliva from mouth and sticking from out ears and eyes, preventing sleep at night; while eating; on slight touch; during menstruation; < noise. Jerking toothache; in l. and in l. side of head. Throbbing toothache in incisor when eating. Toothache nights on lying down, more like a pressure or rush of blood. Biting. Tickling pain in hollow tooth. *Toothache after menstruation*, drawing and sticking (Amm. c.), < inclining head to r. or l., or backward, preventing sleep or waking her. Boring-drawing pain in most molars at night. Paroxysmal drawing pain in incisors. Drawing; in first l. upper. Feeling as if too long; in hollow back. Thrust as from a fist.

Gum.—*Bleeding*, even at night; of teeth on slightest hawking. *Swelling* near a hollow tooth; (and of jaw), and especially near a broken tooth a pimple swells, from which pain extends into ear; painful S. without toothache, with swelling of cheek, which is painful to touch. Pustules above molar, like a dental fistula (after taking cold?). Ulcer. Tearing at night and on biting feeling as if teeth were loose. Soreness, with pain in roots of teeth. Pulsation; in the swollen G. Itching.

Tongue.—*Coated white;* and thick, with feeling as if raw and sore. Swelling of one side, impeding swallowing. Blisters impeding eating. Sticking in evening. *Pain beneath T. when swallowing, on l. side behind hyoid bone;* along side and on its lower surface, < chewing, swallowing or spitting. *Burning pain in tip as from soreness, < taking anything warm into mouth.* Dryness in morning on waking. Burning, and in whole mouth. Difficulty of motion. Speech difficult. Mouth moved as if he would speak or scream, but he could not utter a word.

Thick nodule inside r. cheek, with drawing-tearing every evening. Blisters inside cheek where teeth touch it; B. (after anger?) (also after taking cold?) which open and form ulcers. Swelling of palate, with inflammation of it while the uvula is dark red and full of blisters. *Slimy;* in morning, not > rinsing S., with dry sensation. Sticking in palate. Dryness; and of tongue, with a raw sticking sensation; dry sensation in palate, forcing him to hawk up mucus. Salivation; in forenoon, with nausea. Constant spitting of sour saliva. Hot breath, with heat in mouth without thirst.

Taste.—*Offensive* in morning, as from foul stomach. *Sour;* with much tough saliva; to all food. Sweet, as of sugar. Salt, with much thirst. Bitter; in morning after rising; in back part of throat. Inky in morning on rising. Of iron. Of lead in morning. Fæcal, and in fauces. Unsalted, to everything. Flat, watery, and the taste of food very sensitive. Blunted.

Clinical.—Delayed dentition. Toothache in pregnant women, excited by cold or a draft of air. Epulis above upper incisors.

Throat.—**Swelling of submaxillary glands** (Bar. c.); **as large as hen's eggs, and hard,** with *painful tension* *when chewing and sticking when touched; of tonsils, with elongation of uvula and feeling when swallowing as if throat were too narrow*, with soreness and stitches; of uvula and dark redness. Whitish-yellow ulcers on r. tonsil. Mucus which tastes like iron; hawking of M. in morning. *Spasmodic contraction of pharynx.*

Stitches when swallowing, with inability to swallow bread; S. on swallowing, with pressure; when swallowing, extending to ear, < speaking. Tearing. Gnawing, as of a worm from 4 P.M. till she goes to bed. Pain on swallowing; *as from internal swelling, extending to ears;* as if uvula prevented swallowing, even on empty swallowing, > speaking, none when lying. *Feeling in pharynx in afternoon as if food stuck in it, with nausea* (Zinc.). Feeling of a foreign body in pharynx, which obliged him to swallow constantly. Feeling as if something were sticking, as in globus hystericus, and in œsophagus and cardiac orifice of stomach. Sensation as if something rose up and stuck. Obstruction on swallowing as from a pressing substance. Pressure in pharynx after swallowing.

Soreness; with difficulty in swallowing; of uvula on swallowing; in pharynx on swallowing during menstruation, and on uvula and behind it; when swallowing, as from a lump. Rawness; and of uvula, with soreness of them; R., with burning and sensation as if whole œsophagus were raw and sore. Dryness, < morning, with bitterness. Burning during menstruation, with hoarseness; B. after meals, with and without eructations. Swallowing difficult, as if tongue were swollen posteriorly. Inclination in œsophagus to choke, with waterbrash, without nausea.

Clinical.—Many cases of goitre.

Stomach.—**Ravenous hunger** (Iod., Lyc., Nat. m., etc.), with weak stomach; *R. in morning.* Great appetite in evening, with great weakness; great A. for salt things. Relishes milk. *Loss of appetite; but when he began to eat he relished food.* Daintiness. Slight appetite; with acidity in stomach. She will eat nothing cooked. No relish for his accustomed tobacco, smoking causing headache and nausea. *Thirst;* in afternoon; for wine; for beer. Eructations in morning, even on waking; at night on waking; at night when lying, > rising; after eating. Empty. *Tasting of food* (Ant. cr.); after every meal. *Of food* (Lyc.). Tasting of bile in afternoon. Bitter; of bitter, acrid fluid. Rancid, with scraping heartburn. Sour; in morning; in evening; of the milk taken in the morning; of brownish sour fluid, with burning extending upward from pit of stomach. *Of tasteless fluid* in evening (Puls.). Waterbrash after milk; W., with colic. Hiccough-like. Hiccough all day till evening.

Nausea; *in morning; in morning fasting, with shuddering; in pit of stomach in morning fasting, with blackness before eyes, so that he must sit down;* in forenoon; at 11 A.M.; in pit of stomach in afternoon, as from emptiness of S.; at 6.30 P.M.; in evening till going to bed; in evening, with heat and restless sleep; *caused by milk; when he had eaten almost enough, > if he once ceased eating;* at dinner when scarcely half-satisfied, with rising of food, nauseous taste and eructations; before stool; during menstruation, with ineffectual urging to stool; *with flow of sour water into mouth;* with salivation; with anxiety; with vomiting of food, weakness, faintness and loss of consciousness; faintish.

Vomiting in morning, then nausea all day, with digging in abdomen; **V. of sour water** *at night;* black (Phos.).

Swelling of epigastric region, towards l. side. Stitches in pit in forenoon on breathing; in epigastric region after dinner; in pit on pressure, < after morning stool; transversely through epigastric region. Cutting, with constricting cramp, and in abdomen. Griping in pit. Spasmodic pinching in region of cardiac orifice after dinner, < pressure. Gnawing and sensation of jerks. Jerks in pit, with anxiety. Cramp in afternoon till general sweat broke out; C. at night waking him; obliging her to rise from bed; with nauseous eructations and yawning. Spasmodic pressure after supper, then feeling in intestines as before diarrhœa.

Pain; *in epigastric region on touch;* sore pain; sudden pain as if it would be distended. *Pressure; in pit* in forenoon, when pressing upon it and after stool; at night; when fasting; after eating; in pit, with oppression; with salivation; *as if a lump were in it, after a moderate supper; transversely across;* in evening before lying down, like a retching; in pit, extending into abdomen. Fulness in afternoon. Stuffed feeling in evening after fluid stool, with spasmodic pressing. Constriction. *Warm streaming of blood from pit into head.* Heartburn. *Burning extending into throat, after every meal,* < after hard, dry food; B. as from an acrid fluid.

Clinical.—Chronic dyspepsia, repugnance to hot or warm food, thirst, bloated abdomen. Ravenous hunger and great thirst, particularly longing for eggs and for indigestible things, chalk, coal, etc. Acid fermentation in stomach, everything turns sour, sour risings.

Abdomen.—**Distention** (Lyc., Sulph., Mag. c.); on walking in open air; after eating and drinking a little, and in stomach; after dinner; < after eating; **and hardness,** also after dinner; with colic; with constriction of rectum, which retains the flatus; in evening so that he could scarcely move, with colic. *Rumbling;* on inspiration and expiration. Passage of offensive flatus. Fermentation. Accumulation of much flatus nights. Incarceration of flatus, with pain in small of back; I., with vertigo. Twitching of muscles during stool.

Stitches; < inspiration; extending through back, with impeded respiration. Tearing extending towards genitals. Cutting in morning on waking; twisting C. *Cramp, < evening and night, with coldness in thighs.* Griping; during menstruation when the discharge ceased for some hours; frequent G., then nausea. Pinching after breakfast, then thin stool; with diarrhœa; after supper, as from flatus or as before diarrhœa, then pasty stool containing the undigested dinner. Twisting. Griping crawling, extending towards uterus, with passage of bloody mucus with the stool.

Colic at night; after supper; in attacks after disappearance of coryza, suddenly > cold bath, with weariness and sickly look. Drawing pain, now here, now there during menstruation, and in other parts, with stitches and with uneasiness amounting to faintness. *Drawing* in morning on waking, with uneasiness in it. Constriction, and in stomach, with appetite at times great, at times small; C. in morning, extending to chest; extending to small of back. *Tension;* in afternoon, > passing flatus, with distention, without sensation of flatus; when sitting and after exertion. Burning.

Constrictive pain in upper, so that she must walk bent, < deep breathing. Tension in muscles of upper when leaning backward, with pain in upper when stroked as if skin were sore. Sticking in region of ascending colon. Pain in small intestines, with rumbling in them, pain in small of back and dragging towards rectum, as if a stool would follow.

Sides.—Gurgling in l., with uneasiness. Stitches in l., extending to small of back, < evening, turning body or stooping. Cutting in l., > soft stool. Jerklike tearings down sides.

Hypochondria.—Rumbling in l. Stitches outward in muscles below ribs, < inspiration. Griping in l. **Intolerance of tight clothing.** *Feeling below H. as if laced, with trembling and throbbing in epigastric region.* Attacks of pressive throbbing in l. Tension.

Hepatic Region.—Enlargement on r. side of abdomen (hepatic region?), with pressure, < sitting, heaviness, inability to lie upon this side and incarceration of flatus. Stitches in r. hypochondrium in forenoon; in evening, extending to back; *during and after stooping;* extending into chest, causing shuddering; smarting S. in last rib. *Pressure on every step.* Pain, < at night, with hardness; raw; jerking; *drawing, in posterior part, extending towards back, like tearings; drawing, in r. hypochondrium, extending towards symphysis pubis. Tensive pain. Tension and pressure as if enlarged, even to bursting.*

Umbilical Region.—Rumbling above navel when eating. Stitches transversely through abdomen below navel on inspiration. Pinching below navel after supper, < when walking, with dragging, then distention. Griping in abdomen extending from navel during dinner. Spasmodic twisting and griping. Pressure inward below navel in morning after rising, with constipation. Burning pain below navel in afternoon; now a burning, now a sticking pain below navel, extending into groin, which is distended, < l. side. Soreness in middle of abdomen from nausea, without inclination to vomit.

Hypogastrium.—**Swelling of inguinal glands** (Merc. s.); with pain. Stitches; in l. inguinal region all forenoon, < at noon; in inguinal region, as if a hernia would protrude; in upper part of l. inguinal region, as if in peritoneum. Tearing in l. pelvic bones. Cutting in groin above pubes. Griping; deep in region of bladder, with pain on every step as if internal parts were dragged down. Smarting in r. inguinal region; cutting, in groin, extending into testicles. Twitching pain in r. groin when sitting. *Pressure on physical exertion;* P., with hard stool; with sticking in pit of stomach extending downward. Pain even when walking a few steps, with general heat; P., with nausea; above hips when walking and breathing. Sore pain, with painful tension on holding oneself erect or bending backward; in groins as from being shaken. Sensation as if inguinal glands were swollen. Tension, with cutting; T. in inguinal glands when sitting. Dragging in the groin, in the hernia, in rectum and back, with stitches in chest. Heaviness in groin, with drawing pain. Pulsation in pelvis along course of rectum.

Clinical.—Enlargement of liver, which is sore (Merc. s.), with jaundice. Gall-stone colic, terrible darting pain, profuse sweat, intolerance of garments about the waist. Tendency to great increase of fat in the abdomen and flatulent distention, enlarged mesenteric glands; abdominal dropsy. Umbilical hernia.

Rectum.—*Protrusion. Gurgling. Cramp all the forenoon, a griping and sticky, with anxiety, so that she must walk about.* Stitches towards R. Pain as if torn during a stool that is not hard. Twisting, almost a dragging-down pain, after eating. Tensive-twitching pain in evening. Pressure; in evening when sitting; after stool, with oppression of breathing; as in diarrhœa. *Heaviness in lower part* (Aloes). Drawing after a natural stool, with cutting and heat in it. Twitching. *Crawling as from pin-worms.* Troubles from pin-worms. *Burning* (Sulph.); *in morning after a copious stool.* Constant desire for stool; then a scanty difficult stool; urging as in diarrhœa, though with a natural stool; ineffectual urging.

Anus.—Hæmorrhoids, with itching in anus and constipation (Sulph.); H. protrude, also with pain, < walking, > during stool; *swollen H. protrude and cause pain during a stool which is not hard;* swollen; with pain when sitting and discharge of blood; sudden swelling. Inflamed, burning, painful, grapelike eruption. *Hæmorrhage;* in evening during stool; with severe coryza. Oozing of moisture smelling like herring-brine. Discharge of pin-worms; during stool. Stitches after coition. Sticking sore pain externally in region. Drawing cuttings in and about A. after stool. Smarting. Soreness, and between thighs. Twistings, with dragging in rectum. Crawling. *Burning* (Sulph.); during midday nap; *during stool;* with dry sensation. Burning itching after stool.

Stool.—Diarrhœa; **undigested**; in morning, yellow, sour, looking as if membranes were in it; thin at first, then crumbling; profuse, yellow, watery. Pasty after dinner. *Constipation. Hard* (Ammon. m., Mag. m., Nat. m., Nit. ac., Sulph., etc.), *undigested, intermitting; frequent, at first hard, then pasty, then liquid;* H. and black; with mucus, burning when passing. *Perfectly white;* W., streaked with blood, with ill humor and pain in liver caused by breathing and touch. *Offensive, like bad eggs* (Sulph.). Thick-formed. Scanty; mixed with blood. Omitted, with constant urging and with confusion of head.

Clinical.—Diarrhœa of undigested stools; of sour odor, large in quantity, sometimes fetid. Ascarides and chronic diarrhœa, with great appetite and distention of stomach, which is sore to touch. Cholera infantum, with vomiting of sour food or curdled lumps, ravenous appetite.

Urinary Organs.—Pain in urinary passages after wetting feet; in bladder through night, with cutting on urinating. Sensation as if he could not finish micturition, as if some urine remained in bladder. Flow of prostatic fluid after micturition; and after stool. Urging to urinate; < when walking; in a child, without urine following immediately, at another time involuntary discharge of a few drops; frequent, soon after micturition, with scanty discharge.

Frequent micturition; in forenoon and afternoon, with copious urine; *at night.* Micturition at night, with burning in orifice of urethra. Involuntary M. on every motion during menstruation. Trickling of urine after micturition.

Urethra.—Stitches through female; cutting, with ineffectual urging; tickling, through. Cutting when urinating. Burning before and after micturition; *when urinating;* when urinating, with sore pain; and constant desire to urinate after urinating.

Urine.—Copious, watery. *Dark-colored, without sediment. Offensive, dark brown, with white sediment. Sour-smelling at night.* Pungent odor; and offensive, clear and pale. Much mucus passes with the urine, like leucorrhœa. Turbid soon, with whitish flaky sediment, fatty pellicle on surface, and with a fatty smell. White mealy sediment in evening.

Clinical.—Inflammation of bladder; irritable bladder, the urine of a sour, disagreeable odor, sometimes abundant and fetid.

Sexual Organs.—Penis. Smarting, oblong transverse ulcer on lower surface, which burns, with hæmorrhoidal sweat on scrotum and perineum. Twitching in bed in morning and evening. Stitches. Cutting in tip. Burning in tip. Tickling in forepart during coition. Itching in forepart, < after urinating. Inflamed and red prepuce, with burning pain on urinating and on touch. Erections in morning after rising, with inclination for coition; frequent E. at night; incomplete at night.

Pain in spermatic cord as if contracted. Scrotum hangs down relaxed. Sore spot on scrotum. Itching on scrotum. Stitches in testicles (previously indurated). Crushing pain in testicles; pressive pain in r.; pressive or bruised pain in l. *Desire increased;* in evening; < in forenoon when walking; *caused by lascivious fancies, erection only induced by rubbing, scarcely had coition taken place when the semen was emitted, then weakness, excitability of nerves, discontent, anger and giving way of knees.* Emissions at night, then improved condition; *frequent;* incomplete, at night; late, during coition; omitted at the orgasm during coition, but a slow discharge afterwards; the usual E. during coition, but no thrill of enjoyment.

Female.—Burning-sore pain. Burning-biting, with soreness. Itching, with sticking. Voluptuous sensation in afternoon, with orgasm, then weariness. Pudenda of a little girl inflamed, red, swollen and purulent discharge when urinating. Moisture in fold between pudenda and thigh, with biting. Sore pain in pudenda after urinating. Stinging burning pimple on border of labia. Burning in labia before menstruation. Itching on internal and external labiæ. Discharge of bloody water from vagina of an old woman, with pain in small of back as if menses would appear. Discharge of blood nine days before menstruation. **Leucorrhœa like milk** (Sepia); usually during micturition; like mucus. **Menstruation too early** (the other alkalies, Kali, Magn., Natr., are "too late"); next time too late; *too early and lasting eight days;* reappearing in a woman of fifty-two years, in whom it had long ceased; profuse, twice in succession, bringing with it a small fœtus, with labor-like pain, urging to stool and cutting and pressure in hypogastrium.

Clinical.—Hydrocele in children. Profuse menstruation is the rule in women who require Calcarea. General weakness of women, with exaggerated desires. Membranous dysmenorrhœa, with cold, sweaty extremities and sensitiveness to cold air (see Calc. acet.). Endocervitis. Often indicated in girls whose menses do not come on, but in place there are congestion of the head, dyspnœa, palpitation, hæmorrhage from the lungs, night cough, general anæmia, unnatural appetite, etc. Constant aching in vagina. Leucorrhœa like milk, very profuse, with general Calcarea symptoms. Excessive flow of milk in nursing women; it is thin and does not satisfy the child; with itching of vulva, with swollen veins or sometimes glandular swellings. The milk of a nursing woman is disagreeable to the child, who refuses it and does not thrive on it, though the secretion be very great.

Respiratory Organs.—Larynx. *Whistling in evening after lying down.* Mucus loosened by hawking. *Roughness,* < morning. Rawness, with pain on swallowing. **Painless hoarseness,** *so that she was unable to speak,* < *morning.*

Cough at night; on waking; at night without waking; *caused by eating; from playing on a piano; from inspiration; from a sensation as if a plug stuck in throat and moved up and down;* from tickling in throat as if a small object were there; < in sleep, with stopped, then fluent coryza; *tickling as from a feather in throat* (Phos.); in single hacks; spasmodic, in evening; forcible scraping, after the first waking (about 10 P.M.). *Dry cough after midnight* (Arsen.), *so that heart and arteries throb;* < *night; hacking, in evening,* < *in bed. Violent cough, with pain as if something had been torn loose from larynx, first dry, then with profuse salt expectoration.* Hacking, hoarse cough, which to the sound was not obstructed by mucus; hacking C. when moving rapidly, with expectoration of blood; vertigo and unsteadiness of thighs.

Cough, with expectoration; > *night;* with mucous E.; **with sweetish-mucous E.** (Stan.); *in morning, with yellowish E.* (Phos. ac.); in bed morning and evening, with tough E.; at night, with thick mucous E.; in evening after lying down and at night, with mucous E., but during the day only a little dry C.; violent, in morning after he had choked himself, with E. of blood, then stitches in palate; *violent in evening, with sweet E.*

Expectoration of blood when coughing and hawking, with a rough and sore sensation in chest (Phos.). Mucous E. in morning, with hacking; at night, with scraping in throat.

Respiration.—**Short on going up slightest ascent** (Coca); worse when sitting than when moving; almost sobbing, in sleep after previous weeping. Difficult; with stitches in chest; when walking, loud and through nose. *Urging to take a deep breath;* with distention and contraction of abdomen and pain in abdomen and chest; *necessity to breathe deeply, which caused sticking now in r., now in l. side of chest or hypochondrium.* Desire to hold the breath. Loss of breath on lying down, then whistling R.; loss when walking in wind, the oppression of chest continuing in the room; < walking a few steps.

Clinical.—Chronic inflammation of larynx and bronchi and hoarseness, chronic cough. Extreme dyspnœa on going up the slightest ascent (one of the most marked indications for the drug). Chronic inflammation of the larynx, especially in the upper part. Asthmatic attacks in children, from suppressed eruptions. Ulcers in the lungs, with purulent expectoration. Hæmorrhage from the lungs. Calcarea is very frequently indicated in the general cachexia leading to various forms of consumption; the cough is usually troublesome at night and dry, with very free expectoration in the morning; the patient perspires easily and frequently has enormous appetite, though the emaciation is rapid.

Chest.—Swelling of r., with external heat; S. of l. mamma, with inflammation and stitches; glandular, of r. breast, with pain on touch. *Mucus* without cough. Disappearance of milk in a nursing woman.

Stitches in r.; around whole, in region of fourth and fifth ribs; in region of l. fifth to seventh ribs; in region of l. seventh and eighth ribs; *in evening on breathing;* deep in r. side in evening, < breathing; in l. on breathing and on moving; *in l.* on almost every respiration, usually > rubbing; in l., < evening; in various parts, with oppression; from l. to r. side, with feeling of contraction, the S. < breathing; beneath sternum, from anterior to posterior part; extending to throat; in l. side, extending to l. submaxillary gland, with drawing; jerking, < l. side.

Tearing under l. ribs; beneath r. arm; wandering, in r. *Cutting on inspiration.* Gnawing in l., as if externally on ribs and sternum, < inspiration. Gnawing-griping, extending into stomach and abdomen. Cramp in l. intercostals, > suddenly bending to left. Pain; in r. ribs; changing to stitches; in sternum as if pressed; *in mammary glands as if suppurating,* < *touch.* **Sore pain,** < *inspiration; in r. mamma on slightest touch;* **sensitiveness to touch and on inspiration.** *Raw pain* evening and nights *during cough;* after much speaking and walking and on coughing.

Pressure on l.; on r.; especially below r. nipple; paroxysmal, in r. side after motion. *Anxiety. Tightness;* in morning after rising and inability to walk; in forenoon on walking in open air; *as if filled with blood.* Oppression after stool; O. of forepart; in region of r. fifth and sixth ribs, with stitches; *with tension.* Fulness in morning on rising, as if he could not sufficiently expand the chest, > expectoration. Tension in ribs of both sides, extending across to pit of stomach. Weakness after loud speaking.

Clinical.—The chest is very sore externally to percussion or pressure, sharp pains shoot through it from front to back.

Heart.—Stitches, which prevent breathing and leave aching. Painful pressure. Spasmodic contraction in region, impeding respiration, then shocks. Anxiety. *Palpitation;* waking from his midday sleep while sitting; in evening in bed before sleep, *with anxiety;* at night, with restless sleep; after eating; after dinner; during a walk, with pain in chest; with anxious dread that he might have organic disease of heart; with anguish and restless oppression of chest, pain in back, a loud sound as if on every inspiration breath would leave the body, coldness of body and cold sweat; with irregular pulse.

Pulse.—Rapid.

Neck.—*Swelling of glands on margin of hair* (Bar. c.); of glands on l. side, with sticking in throat on swallowing; *hard, of glands;* of lowest cervical vertebræ, with pain. Sticking in nape; and in scapulæ, with confusion of head. Tearing in muscles; in r. side; in nape. *Pain in glands;* P., with stiffness; *on turning head as if a tumor or boil would protrude;* sudden sprained, on turning head; drawing, extending into head. Tension so that she could not turn the head. Stiffness; in side; on stooping; from taking cold, with stitches in neck and head, over eyes, and cough; in nape and throat.

Back.—Stitches. Pain; bruised, and in chest; in both sides as if wrenched. Painful jerks in r. side on breathing, with chilliness and cold creepings. Pain in spine on bending backward. Painful stiffness of spine in morning on waking and after rising, with indolence and heaviness in legs. Stitches in upper part during inspiration.

Scapulæ.—Twitching in both, and on chest. Stitches between S.; in l., in præcordial region; in r. at 9 A.M.; burning, between S. (as in phthisis); itching, in r. Tearing between S.; drawing T. between S. Cutting between S. during rest. Aching beneath S., and in middle of back; in spine between S., with short breath and < by breathing, with pain in vertebræ on touch. *Drawing pain between S. Pressure between S.; which on motion impedes respiration;* beneath r., extending upward. Pinching constriction between S.

Lumbar Region.—Sticking in l. side of sacrum while walking. Tearing. *Pain;* in morning when rising; when riding; from lifting a heavy weight; < motion; *so that he could scarcely rise from a seat;* so that she could neither sit nor lie. Jerking pain extending from l. side to anus. Pain as from straining; in spine on stretching. Pain as if menstruation would come on, and in iliac bones. Drawing pain when sitting. Drawing. Dragging towards rectum.

Coccyx.—Sticking. Drawing.

Clinical.—Useful in disease of the bone and curvature of the spine, tabes dorsalis. Muscular rheumatism.

Extremities.—Twitching of single E. during the day; T. at night, and drawing up, waking him; in r. thigh, l. shoulder and l. arm. Shootings through, with imagination that he would have rheumatic fever, *swelling of finger-joints,* fever, chattering of teeth and chilliness. Sticking in joints; on great exertion; tearing, in various joints; wandering S. in joints.

Tearing; in small spots in arms and legs; in forepart of l. foot and in fingers. *Paralytic bruised pain in long bones on motion and in joints of limbs and small of back, even when sitting and standing the small of the back pains as if beaten, and the muscles of legs are sore to touch.* Drawing pressure in joints. Painless drawings in afternoon. *Weariness* in evening; till going to bed, especially in feet; of arms and feet at night. Falling asleep of hands and feet.

Upper Extremities.—Shoulder. Stitches in r. after dinner; under l.; in r. joint; *in l. joint all day.* Tearing; in l. joint and in elbow, also with stiffness of arm. Pain in joints in evening and night; in r. joint during rest; as after great fatigue, and in elbows. Pressure. The joints disturb him at night, at beginning of sleep, obliging him to lay arm above head.

Arm.—*Cramp of the whole of one or other.* Tearing in l.; in r.; below r.; downward in r.; drawing, in r. from shoulder to hand; sticking. *Bruised pain on moving them or taking hold of them.* Twitching or sticking pain at night, and in wrist, preventing sleep. Jerking pain in r. in evening. Wrenching pain in l. on moving it. Burning paralytic pain in r., from finger-joints to shoulder. Uneasiness and anxiety in joints and in wrist. *Weakness of l., with a kind of paralysis, difficulty in moving or raising it and falling of itself. Falling asleep if he lies upon it, with pain.*

Upper Arm.—Sticking in r. humerus, then trembling of arm, with stitches in various muscles. Tearing in middle; in r.; sticking; sticking, in l. Pain just below shoulder-joint so that he cannot raise it high nor put it across back. Pain in middle as if flesh were tightly adherent to bone. Drawing pain in l. when sitting (and sewing). Partially paralyzed condition of muscles.

Elbow.—Sticking in r. Tearing; in r. Drawing pain, extending from bend to wrist, < during rest.

Forearm.—Swelling, and of back of hand, with tension on motion. Stitches in l., with weakness. Tearing in r.; in l.; *spasmodic, on outer side,* extending from elbow to wrist, as soon as he takes hold of anything. Drawing pain in l. Painful pressure in muscles when walking, > touch, standing and sitting.

Wrist.—Stitches in l.; in r., like tearing. Tearing; in r.; in l.; sticking. Jerking shocks. *Sprained feeling in r.;* on motion, with sticking and tearing. Drawing pain, and in metacarpus. Jerklike drawings and thence up arm, even in morning in bed.

Hand.—Distention of veins, with burning on backs of hands. Twitching in muscles of l. *Trembling* in afternoon. *Cramp* all night; in l. Sticking in l.

bones; in palms in morning in bed. Tearing in r.; in l.; in l. metacarpus; in palms. Pain in morning, with relaxation; cramplike, between r. third and fourth fingers; drawing.

Fingers.—*The three middle are white, cold and senseless, preceded by drawing in them. Swelling of joints.* Spasmodic contraction. Cramp, without being drawn inward. Twitching of l. thumb. Stitching through r. middle; in last phalanx of r. middle; in l. joints; in first phalanx of r. index; in first joint of l. index. Tearing in l. index; in r. middle; in r. and l. ring; in l. thumb; in tips; in joints; in first joint of l. index; in second joint of l. index; in first joint of l. ring; in second joint of l. ring; in first joint of little; in second joint of l. little; in first joint of l. thumb; in second joint of l. thumb; sticking, in r. thumb when lying. *Pain in joints as if swollen on waking in evening, without swelling.* Pain in knuckles as if cauterized. Jerking pain. Cramplike pain in last joint of index. They seem tense and bent inward, as if stuck together, on stretching them. Drawing in second joint of l. index. Fuzziness in l. little and ring. *Deadness.*

Clinical.—Rheumatoid arthritis of fingers.

Lower Extremities.—Dizzy tottering in evening when walking in open air. *Weariness* at noon, especially in ankles; *of legs, especially above and below knees, after coition, with trembling of them; as after a long walk, especially of thighs.*

Hip-joint.—Stitches on stooping; when walking and running; in l., < motion; in l., extending in direction of psoas major, < running; above r. hip. Tearing; in l.; from hips to ankles. Suppurating pain when walking in room. Wrenching pain in l. Tension in evening when walking, with drawing in hip-bones. Numbness on r. hip and thigh, with feeling as if brittle, short and small.

Nates.—Painful muscular twitches when sitting and standing. Drawing spasmodic pain on r., extending towards anus. Pain on touch as if suppurating, less when sitting than when walking.

Thigh.—Painful twitches in a spot in r. Stitches only at night, and in knee and heel. Tearing. Cutting in upper part of l., as from distention of muscles, < motion. Bruised pain in muscles of r. when at rest after walking. *Weariness in anterior muscles in morning on beginning to walk, with stiffness;* W. when walking, and in groin.

Knee.—**Swelling.** *Stitches;* in l.; in l. in morning, more when sitting than when walking, with throbbing pain, obliging him to limp; at noon when riding; *in patella on stepping when beginning to walk,* extending into hip-joint; *tearing,* in l.; tearing, in the stiff patella (formerly broken); drawing, in patella. *Tearing;* in r., with tension, and in r. hip-joint; on inside on rising from a seat, with tension; stitchlike, in l. Pain in patella; in patella on rising from a seat. Sprained pain in r. Bruised pain. Drawing pain about, just above hollow. Tension. Feeling as if she could not stretch the leg enough. Weariness; at night; after a warm bath, and in ankles. Numbness during afternoon nap.

Leg.—Twitchings, and around pelvis. Jerking upward; suddenly in r., from a stitching jerk. Cramp in r., with drawing inward and bending of foot; C. in muscles near tibia at night. Tearing in l.; in l. tibia; in r. tibia. Cuttings over tibia. Aching in muscles near tibiæ when walking. Sprained pain in anterior tibial muscles when walking. Bruised pain in bones. Drawing pain in muscles in evening, and on back of thighs and in calves. Drawing and crushed pain in tibiæ. Tension below knee on kneeling; T. from foot to knee, as if bone had gone to sleep, with pressive cramp in stomach. Uneasiness, with many eructations. Heaviness. Weariness, especially in joints, with bruised feeling. Numbness of l. *Falling asleep in evening when sitting.*

Calf.—Twitching in muscles of r. *Cramp at night; on stretching legs* (when drawing on boot) *and in hollows of knees,* > bending leg, returning on stretching it again; if he moves much, with stitches, and in foot. Stitches, with weakness. Tearing; in l.; in muscles of r.; sticking, and in tibiæ. Tearing drawing. *Pain on stepping,* on touch and on bending foot. Tension; in r.

Ankle.—Tearing; in r.; in l., < motion. Pain in l. as if tightly bound. Pain as if broken, when walking, < afternoon. Pain in r. malleolus when stepping, as if foot would be dislocated. Tension in inner malleoli. Weariness; < standing.

Foot.—Swelling. *Cramp in l. sole.* Stitches in a corn. Tearing; in anterior part of l.; in soles; in r. sole; in tendo-achillis; in l. tendo-achillis; in r. metatarsal joints. Cutting on outer side of r. sole in evening and all night. Suppurative pain in soles. Sprained pain in l. Rheumatic pain in l. Drawing pain at night, waking her. Sore burning pain in corns. Sensitiveness of the soles, even in the room, as if softened by hot water, with pain when walking. Heaviness. *Weariness, as if they could not bear the body and knees would bend;* as if they would break to pieces, from 7 P.M. till going to bed.

Toes.—Twitching of l. great, in evening in bed. *Cramp.* Stitches in great. Tearing; in great; in l. great. Pain on tip of r. great. Pain as from a tight boot. Burning pressure beneath nails.

Clinical.—Inflammation of hip-joint, the joint is painfully sore to pressure. Sciatica from working in water. White swelling of knee-joint, of a sluggish character. Cramp in calves. Gout in knees.

Skin.—Nose seems covered with oil. Hang-nails. White spots on face, with itching; W. spots on wrists, backs of hands, thighs, legs and ankles, with red patches and irritation. Red spot on tip of nose; on legs, with itching and swelling; elevated, mostly on cheeks and elbows, with heat, thirst and little appetite, leaving spots, as if congested with blood. Swelling under l. eye; *in front of l. ear, which pains like a boil when touched;* on l. side of neck, with pain on touch or on turning head, with internal soreness of throat; inflammatory, on back of l. foot, with burning pain and itching all around.

Warts here and there; wart in bend of elbow inflames, pains like a boil, then dries up and disappears; wartlike growths (behind ears) inflame and ulcerate. Easy inflammation or suppuration from injuries. Scurfy spots on leg, with burning during the day. Rash in face, about eyes and on nose; on chin and neck, with itching. *Nettle-rash,* > in cold air; *in red stripes on tibia, with itching and burning after rubbing.* Eruption on nose; *behind r. ear, which becomes moist; on feet, itching, biting, bleeding when scratched and changing to nettle-rash in its vicinity.*

Erysipelas on cheeks (which become thick). Erysipelatous inflammation of leg, with swelling and with general chilliness. *Pimples on forehead;* all over face; around mouth and in its corners; beneath r. corner of mouth; in middle of chin; on small of back and on nates; on thighs; on lower part of chest, with smarting on rubbing; itching, on malar-bones; itching, over whole face; itching, on forehead, with itching all over face.

Pustules on back. Suppuration around nail of r. index; around nail of middle finger. Boil on margin of hair on forehead; on back of l. hand, with sticking on touch; *painless, on last phalanx of fourth finger.* Blisters on l. heel when walking, which became a kind of large boils, with sticking and itching pain. *Itching vesicles,* over whole body, especially over hips; filled with clear fluid, in a group on back of hand, a dark point forms at tip, they gradually dry and the skin desquamates, if the vesicles are scratched they enlarge and seem like nettle-rash, the itching > cold (the prover had suffered for two years during great heat in summer from insignificant vesicular eruption on back of hand). Ulcers on legs. *Skin unhealthy, ulcerating, even small wounds suppurate* and do not heal again. Old ulcer on thigh becomes painful, throbbing, with tearing about it and begins to be offensive like bad eggs.

Damp open air does not agree with her, the skin is immediately affected by it. Stitches. Sensitiveness to touch, mostly in feet. Stitching crawling on leg.

Itching; over whole body; *all over face;* on chin, about mouth, on nose and nates; in concha; on chest; *on thighs;* r. thigh; *on leg and foot;* about ankle and below calf; on malleolus of diseased foot; on sweating parts, especially between scapulæ; on back in evening in bed, and on pit of stomach, neck, chin, l. eye, scalp, mons veneris and scrotum; on lower part of thighs at night; behind ear, with vertigo after scratching; on back, with itching pimples; about chest, back, neck, shoulders and calves, with reddish rash all over back and chest. Sticking itching on thighs; in a spot on l. thigh. Itching of the dry, hot skin as if sprinkled with salt and ashes. Burning itching on l. fingers; on nates; on r. tibia; from morning till evening on l. arm; on l. thigh; on r. malleoli. Tickling itching on margin of r. lower jaw.

Clinical.—Warts, rhagades, eczema, offensive scabby eruptions, urticaria.

Sleep.—Yawning; almost endless, then shattering throbbing in head, abdomen and chest, with heat of face. Sleepiness; in morning; in morning, with weariness; *during the day, with weariness,* and with sleep several times in forenoon; during the day, with weariness, chilliness and headache; *early in evening;* after dinner, with nodding; *after supper. Difficulty in arousing himself in morning. Weary sleepiness in all limbs in evening, with chilliness* and continual waking, next morning sweat, with dryness in throat without thirst. Long sleep at noon. Overpowering sleep after eating, then chill and tickling cough. Frequent sudden falling into sweet sleep from 7 till 9 P.M., with nausea and blackness before eyes, which continued while lying.

Difficult falling asleep on account of many involuntary thoughts. Late falling asleep in evening; with inability to free himself from lascivious or vexatious thoughts, which followed him in the morning after waking. *Sleeplessness when she went to bed late, with feeling as if her rest were disturbed.* Sleeplessness before midnight on account of mental activity; after midnight, with tossing about; till 2 or 3 A.M.; except from 11 till 2 or 3 o'clock. Sleep short in evening on account of heat. Frequent waking; and anxious, caused by anxious dreams. Anxious waking after midnight, with difficulty in breathing. Uneasy waking in evening, full of frightful fantasies. Restless sleep; with screaming; with sweat; towards morning; restless, half-asleep at night, with dry heat and confusion in head and constant waking, as in fever. Unrefreshing sleep.

Snoring all night in a stupid sleep, from which he could not be wakened, with tossing about, sweat on face before sleep. In sleep she laid the arms above the head. Starting up in evening till she was wide awake. Jerking of upper part of body on going to sleep in evening, with jerking extending into head, then roaring and hissing in ears. He often chews in sleep and then swallows. The child rises in bed after midnight, calls out, begins to cry and tries to spring up, the more one talks to him the worse his cries and resistance, he rolls upon the floor and will not be touched. Soon after falling asleep at night he rose up in bed and worked with the hands, with open eyes, without consciousness.

Dreams; with talking; with confused talking, restlessness and heat. Vivid. *Anxious; and frightful, from which he could not free himself on waking;* and confused; half-waking in evening, soon after falling asleep; with crying out and starting; towards morning of fire and murder; that he would be bitten by a dog, which woke him, then several equally anxious dreams. *Frightful;* as if he would fall or be thrown down. Voluptuous; with an (extremely rare) emission; the night before menstruation. Of dead people and smell of corpses. Illusions when going to sleep as if she heard noises and clattering about her bed, which caused shuddering.

Clinical.—Insomnia, starts at every noise, fear that she will go crazy.

Fever.—Gooseflesh on thighs and legs from slightest contact of cold air. Sensitiveness to cold air, with deadness of feet in evening. *Chill in forenoon, alternating with heat; C. in evening;* in evening in bed; on getting out of bed; after supper, before menstruation, then colic all night; with thirst; with pale, sickly look, alternating with heat, obliging her to lie down. Shaking chill at night. *Internal chill,* with cold hands but warm feet; I., with restlessness and trembling anguish. External C. in evening, with internal heat and thirst, even in bed. Chill, with sweat, at last profuse sweat. *Chill in and on head;* frequent external, on ears; on side of back on which he had lain in midday sleep, with numbness; cold feet after eating. Shivering over face, with bristling of hair, then general S. with chilliness.

Heat in morning after rising; from morning till noon or afternoon, with at first tearing in joints and heaviness in head, then with weariness, with heaviness of limbs, stretching, sensation as if she would sweat, and trembling and uneasiness in all limbs; several days from 6 to 7 P.M.; in evening in bed and sweat all night; with thirst. Dry heat at night; towards morning. Internal heat; *at night, especially in hands and feet* (Sulph.), *with dry tongue in morning,* without thirst, with external heat of head; and external, before menstruation, every day at 11 A.M., without thirst, with red face, then anxiety and sweat, especially on hands, feet and face. Intermittent heat; and anxious, < in face and hands, while sitting, with sweat of face and hands. At first causing weariness and anxiety, lasting till sweat broke out. Orgasm of blood mornings on waking after a restless sleep; *at night, with many dreams; at night,* < *during menstruation, with restless sleep.*

Heat in head, with orgasm of blood; H. in l. side of head; about head in evening; H. in head and chest all day, with chilliness of rest of body. Burning in face; in palms; *in soles;* in soles at night; in sole, with formication; in feet in evening; in tip of great toe; sudden, on back of l. foot and on leg, as from a hot wind. Burning in skin, with itching over half of back, on nates and posterior surface of thighs; itching sticking, in neck and between shoulders, with heartburn.

Sweat mornings; *through the day when walking*, and at night in bed; during the day in cold air; **during the day on slightest exertion**; *at night*, < before midnight, with cold hands; *frequent S. through the day;* anxious, with nausea, on head and back during noon nap; on face at supper; on back at night; *on palms* on slightest exertion; on knees; *on feet; on feet towards evening*; clammy, on limbs at night.

Clinical.—Scarlatina in scrofulous children, undeveloped, rash. Hectic fever, alternating thirst and fever, with night-sweats, particularly about head; cold hands and feet. Chronic form of intermittent fever.

Calcarea Fluorata.

The finest crystals of Fluor spar are triturated for use.

Generalities, Etc.—Fatigue. Depression of spirits; with anxiety about money matters. Indecision. Headache, with faintish nausea all the afternoon, > evening. Vision blurred after writing some time, with aching in eyeballs; > closing eyes and pressing lightly upon them. Sneezing. Blowing of much mucus from nose, with ineffectual desire to sneeze. Cold sore at l. corner of mouth.

Throat.—Hawking of mucus in morning caused an attack of hiccough, which was weakening and recurred frequently all day. Prickling, burning, suffocative sensation, < in latter part of day, at night and by cold drinks, > transiently by warm drinks.

Stomach and Abdomen.—Thirst. Paroxysms of lancinations in r. hypochondrium, under eleventh rib, waking about midnight, < lying on painful side, so as to cause a bursting sensation, > lying on painless side and doubling up, with restlessness. Frequent attacks of lancinating pains in hepatic region at 8 A.M., < sitting, > walking. Much wind in lower bowels, < riding and towards evening, > after lying down at night.

Stool and Urine.—Urging to stool, the first part of the stool natural, the last part loose. Itching in anus as from pin-worms, waking at night. Constipation, with vertigo and dull headache. Frequent urging to urinate, urine causes smarting along urethra, particularly at external orifice, urine has a pungent odor. Micturition twice at night, with profuse urine. Urine copious from 8 A.M till 3 P.M., pale and watery. Urine copious and pale, afterwards scanty, high-colored and turbid.

Respiratory Organs.—Larynx. Oppression, with tickling. Tickling in forenoon, with desire to clear it and with hawking. T. extending about three inches down trachea, as from a foreign body, after dinner, causing paroxysmal hacking cough, not > by cough, a desire to swallow from the same cause, but without relief. Itching tickling, > hawking mucus from that spot; at night, forcing a spasmodic cough, > hawking mucus. Tickling itching, < from 3 to 4 P.M., inducing hacking cough. Dryness of larynx; towards night, with desire to clear it and with horseness. Hoarseness; in evening after reading aloud, with desire to clear the throat; after laughing. Cough at 4 P.M., with hoarseness. Respiration oppressed, as from taking cold, increased after a few days so that it seemed as if the epiglottis were nearly closed or as if he breathed through a thick substance.

Back.—Tired aching, with restlessness; in lower part in afternoon.

Sleep.—Unrefreshing, on account of indistinct dreams of unsuccessful efforts to do various things, leaving an unpleasant impression on waking. Dreamed constantly, jumped from bed and tried to get out of the window, which woke him. Unremembered dreams. D. of the death of his daughter and of great grief and weeping. Vivid and distinct D. of the death of a relative, causing grief and weeping; of new scenes, places, books, etc.; of new scenes and places, not unpleasant, but with a sense of impending danger. Distinct and apparently long-continued D. of cutting a woman to pieces, as an animal for salting.

Clinical.—In biochemical therapeutics it has been especially recommended for varicose and enlarged veins, indurated glands of stony hardness. Mal-nutrition of bones, especially of teeth. Many cases of cataract. Chronic synovitis of knee-joint. Exostosis after injuries.

Calcarea Iodata.

The pure iodide of lime is triturated for use.

Mind.—Easy, indolent feeling. Indifferent to everything which may happen.

Head.—Aching at night and in morning on waking; A., with heaviness over eyes and nose; giddy. Fulness. Lightness. "Sensation as if it wasn't, yet was." Frontal aching in morning on waking and aching on r. side of face and in first r. upper molar; over forehead while riding against cold wind, and in temples; in forehead and temples, < r. temple; in forehead and sides of face, < r. temple; in forehead, afterwards < l. temple; over eyes; heavy, in forehead. Fulness in forehead, < stooping. Aching in temples; < l. and over root of nose; sharp piercing pain in r.

Ears and Mouth.—Numbness in ears, with ringing. Dry, furred feeling on lips and tongue. Burning in mouth and gums. Taste sweetish, then astringent and metallic; astringent, like alum; bitter, but not disagreeable, like myrrh; bitter, partially > tobacco.

Stomach, etc.—Inclination to belch wind. Hiccough. Nausea. Constant emission of much flatus; emission of much F. after rising. Rumbling in abdomen, with discharge of wind. Pain in abdomen. Desire for stool at 7 A.M., with discharge of much wind. Pulse regular, soft, 80. Stiffness of neck; of nape. Heavy lameness in posterior surface of r. arm. Laming pain in external surface of r. arm, with numbness of hands and fingers. Tired feeling in lower limbs, especially in calves, and weariness of whole body. Pain across anterior surface of upper third of thighs as if beaten. Itching in various parts, disappearing and reappearing in other parts, > much scratching; I. on r. elbow, then on l. knee.

Clinical.—Inflamed submaxillary glands. Tubercular meningitis. Polypus in ear. Uterine fibroid. Chronic cough day and night, with night-sweat, hectic fever, green, purulent expectoration.

Calcarea Phosphorica.

Precipitated phosphate of lime, obtained by dropping dilute phosphoric acid into lime water, is triturated for use.

General Action.—A tissue remedy. Compare Calcarea carb., Phosphorus, etc.

Generalities.—Convulsive starts when the child lies on his back. Stretching. Trembling and weakness. Rachitis, fontanelles open, diarrhœa, emaciation. Phosphatic diathesis. Sharp pains in tendons. Pains in various parts, often shooting along muscles into joints; pains in bones, especially in shin-bones; in bones or joints, in bed; in joints, then in bones; caused by every cold, in joints and *where bones form sutures or symphyses.* Rheumatism in cold weather; rheumatic pains in shoulders, chest and other parts after getting wet in rain.

Sensitiveness to touch; of places hurt by a shock. Soreness of tendons when stretching and bending. Trembling feeling, then toothache and uterine pain. Restlessness, spasmodic motion of limbs, < lying on back, > lying on side. Discomfort. Ailments from grief, disappointed love. Weakness; *on ascending stairs;* with flushes of heat in head. Stiffness in morning in bed.

Sensations mostly in small spots. Small of back, knees and thumbs especially affected. *Right to left* sutures of frontal and lateral bones, *earache*, ears stopped, cold feeling, jugular bones ache, upper jaw pains, toothache, pain in abdomen, aching in groins, above os pubis, mammæ, neck, chest, back, armpits, arms, elbows, forearms, hands, fingers, buttocks, thighs, above knees, shin-bones, calves, heels, big toes, toes.

Last half of day stands to first half like 5 : 7; sunny half to the dark like 5 : 3. Aggravation in morning; evening; *after taking light cold, rheumatic pains and displaced uterus;* in changeable weather, especially when snow melts, with east winds; when thinking about the symptoms; of some symptoms when sitting or lying; of head, chest, abdomen, limbs on pressure; pains after great exertions, when lying; during motion of single limbs. Amelioration by lying; on abdomen during restless night.

Clinical.—Valuable in diseases of mal-nutrition, especially with predisposition to diseases of the bones. In children the osseous tissue is badly developed; the child grows slowly, does not learn to walk rapidly, is emaciated, has symptoms of indigestion, colic, vomiting of undigested food, green, mucous stools, fetid flatulence, etc. General lack of vital heat. General symptoms of Calcarea, particularly the aggravation from wet, the tendency to perspiration, glandular enlargement, etc., but there is less enlargement of the abdomen and perhaps less obstinate disposition, the child is rather stupid. Generally valuable in promoting the development and healing of bones. Grauvogl advises that if a woman has scrofulous children, with a tendency to hydrocephalus, she should be given Calc. phos. and Sul. at intervals, when pregnant again.

Mind.—Screaming, grasping in agony towards his mother, cold sweat, especially in face, whole body cold. Easily excited. Beside himself at unpleasant news, with sweat, inclination to indignation and anger. Fear of bad news. Feeling as if she had been frightened. Anxiety; in children; with palpitation, Ill humor; *in children.* Likes to be alone. Restlessness. Depression as if lame, after vexation, cannot work, can hardly walk, looseness of bowels. Indisposition to work, also to mental work. Obtuse. Stupid indifference, cretinism. Writes wrong words or the same word twice. Memory lost.

Clinical.—Children are weak and fretful.

Head.—Every step is felt in head and sacrum. Aching; in morning; in morning, with sore throat; before menses; after meals, < after dinner, or drowsiness, weariness, itching, etc.; < exertion; < on going into open air, > scratching head; >lying; >going out; with hot head and face, ill humor and indolence; with flatulence; with gastric symptoms; with uterine complaints; throbbing, during menses; like confusion on inner side of skull. Painful confusion in morning on waking, as if close to bone, from within and without, especially on vertex, < bodily exertion, > mental exertion and washing with cold water. Painful pressure of brain against skull, especially at vertex, < every ten seconds, < motion, stooping, moving while sitting, sitting up after lying, also rising from seat, when there is vertigo; > lying still and after stooping. Confusion. Fulness and pressure < pressure of hat.

Vertigo towards noon, and nausea; V. at dinner, and loss of memory; on motion; on stooping, with rush of blood to head and headache; on getting up or rising from seat; while walking, with running from nose, aching in bones of pelvis, hip-joint, thigh, knees, and ankle; before menses, with leucorrhœa; during menses, with throbbing in forehead, rush of blood to head, throbbing headache, pressure over os pubis, want of appetite, pain in abdomen, diarrhœa, shooting in back, weariness in lower limbs, fatigue, stiff feeling all over on ascending stairs; in old people, with constipation; with headache, nausea; with complaints in eyes; < windy weather.

Forehead.—Pain; to nose, < change of weather, and from temples to jaws, with rheumatic feeling from collar-bone to wrists. Pressure above and towards eyes.

Vertex.—Pain, and behind ears, with drawing in muscles of neck to nape and occiput. *Crawling* **as if ice were on upper part of occiput,** *head is hot, with smarting of roots of hairs.*

Sides.—Stitches in l., sleepiness during the day; in l. before menses. Throbbing pain, < quick motion. Pressure towards back in afternoon, transiently > after supper, with dread of labor.

Drawing pain around lateral protuberances of occiput. Skull, sore pain, drawing, rending, tearing, especially along sutures, chiefly between frontal and parietal, or around temporal bones. Scalp sore, creeping, numbness, cold crawls, coldness on occiput. Tight feeling in scalp; tension in scalp of forehead. Itching evenings.

Clinical.—Valuable for the headaches of school children, especially of girls who are maturing and who are anæmic. Headaches on the top of the head particularly. Chronic hydrocephalus, pain in head extending down spine, weakness, vomiting, very large head, separated bones. In chronic irritation of the brain resembling hydrocephalus, following exhausting diseases, like cholera infantum. Bald spots on the head.

Eyes.—Red streaks from corners to cornea. Feeling as if something were in them, *renewed when it is mentioned;* frequent sensation as if something were in l., seeming to move about, < inner canthus and in upper part of ball, in morning matter in inner canthus, afterwards swelling and redness in upper part of inner canthus. Itching. Worse in air. Lachrymation, most with gaping.

Squinting, distortion of balls as from pressure, balls protruding. Pain in ball as if beaten. Biting in l. lid, towards external canthus, in afternoon, compelling rubbing, which causes pain. Hot feeling on lids and sweat of brows and lids. *Inability to read, light hurts, especially candle-light.* Using by gaslight hurts. Veil over eyes. Glimmering, fiery circles. Letters change to black points or small round gray spots, or as if a little bird flew from right to left.

Clinical.—Scrofulous keratitis, with photophobia, large tonsils, etc.

Ears.—Inner and outer swollen, red, sore, itching. Excoriating discharge. Shooting outward in bones behind and around. Pressing, tearing, rending in and around, < behind or below. Tearing, shutting, jerking pains in alternation or with other rheumatic complaints. Burning pain in spot over r., with sensitiveness to touch; burning pain in spot over r. when scratching, with sensitiveness to touch. Soreness in and around. Cold and aching; coldness, then throbbing, heat, hard hearing. Hot and aching; heat of middle and outer. Difficult hearing. Singing and other noises, < r.

Nose.—Sensation of a foreign body. Biting-stinging in anterior angle of l. nostril, then in r. nostril, sneezing and lachrymation. Tickling. Itching and soreness in r. angle near tip. Violent sneezing, with running from nose and salivation; sudden sneezing and soreness on margins of wings of nose and fluent coryza in afternoon; sudden sneezing in evening, with relief of headache, then sore sensation in nostrils. Coryza < in air, hoarseness and cough; fluent, in cold room, stopped in warm air and out of doors. Streaks of bright blood on nasal mucus while sneezing. *Bleeding in afternoon.*

Face.—Pale, sallow, yellowish, earthen. *Pain, < upper jaw-bone, from r. to l., extends from other parts to face or from face to other parts;* pain in zygomatic process. *Upper lip swollen, painful, hard, burning.*

Clinical.—Valuable for acne of girls (Calc. pic. more frequently for boys).

Mouth.—(Backward in teething and in closing of fontanelles); (slow in teething, with cold tremors and emaciation.) Shooting in molars. Sensation as if something were sticking into lower incisors, like painful swelling of gum. Toothache, with other complaints; pain in eye and stomach teeth. Teeth cannot bear chewing. (Carious teeth cannot bear fresh air.)

Tongue white, furred on root, < morning; *tip sore, burning, little blisters;* burning on back part, then in larynx; on swallowing, pain in tongue, fauces, pharynx, chest and pit of stomach. Sore spot inside r. cheek. Dryness of mouth and tongue into choanæ, with salivation, with or without thirst. Running of saliva, with fluent coryza; copious and acid saliva.

Taste bitter in morning, with headache; bitter at beginning of menses; especially wheat bread tastes bitter. Flabby sweetish. Foul taste and smell; bad taste in morning; disgusting when waking, < hawking.

Throat.—External glands hurt. Hawking up phlegm in evening, night and morning, with gagging; constant hemming and hawking when talking. Fauces and uvula red and swollen. Soreness in morning on waking, < r. side, low down, < towards back, < swallowing, > after rising and at breakfast; in evening, < in bed, with tickling cough. *Sore aching, < swallowing;* sore pain in region of parotid. Pains from other parts towards T., *and burning;* pain in r. tonsil (after mustard); pain on sides, aching on pressure up to ear, or from ear to shoulder, < turning neck and swallowing. Contraction as after much weeping or after running. Sensation of weakness or emptiness. Dryness at night. Burning in pit. Saliva hurts to swallow, not food.

Stomach.—*Unusual hunger;* 4 P.M.; appetite diminished at noon, with headache in afternoon, more appetite in evening, when headache was relieved; no A. from noon to noon, but if thinking about it she wants to eat; no A. before or during menses. Desire for tobacco-smoking. Thirst in after part of day, with dryness of mouth and tongue.

Belching all the forenoon, with nausea; after breakfast, with hawking and gagging; sour. Nausea from smoking or coffee; after coffee, with incipient heartburn and unpleasant sensation, confusion of head, headache and ill humor; with vertigo and headache < stooping, with confusion of head and confusion of thought; rising from pit of stomach when moving, then headache and lassitude. Vomiturition from hawking phlegm. Vomiting, with trembling of hands; *easy in children.*

Cutting or cramplike pain, with headache. Sharp pain. Pain at every attempt to eat; after dinner, with soreness on pressure; < lying; with watery, burning stools. Pressure > rest. *Burning and waterbrash; in epigastrium; in epigastrium after belching.* Heartburn after dinner; H. up into throat, with soreness in r. groin and kicking-quivering over os pubis. Anxiety in pit. *Expanded feeling. Sinking sensation in epigastrium.* Flabbiness. Uneasiness in region.

Clinical.—Dyspepsia, after eating thirst, pain > for a short time by raising wind, when fasting the pain goes to the spine, feeling as if one ought to raise flatus and could not. Dyspepsia, with indescribable distress in region of stomach, only temporarily > eating.

Abdomen.—Meteorism and pain > stool. Flatulence and rumbling > thin stool, with confusion of head increasing to dull pain, the stool preceded by pain. *Fetid flatus;* difficult emission of flatus. Cutting after drinking cold water; *cutting, pinching, then diarrhœa.* Pinching, stitches, running, kicking. Griping before menses; with rumbling and leucorrhœa. *Pain on every attempt to eat;* from ice-cream in evening, then vomiting in morning; > lying; > emission of wind, stool or after leucorrhœa; with flatulence and frequent stools; with headache, earache, hot face, pain in groins, diarrhœa, weary legs, crawls, or in alternation with headache, burning in throat, uterine pains, lassitude. Pressure, with urging to urinate. Burning rising into throat. Motion as of something alive.

Numbness of wall, with quivering, aching, etc. Stitches in hepatic region on deep breathing. Sharp pain in region of spleen. Throbbing in r. hypochondrium, > belching or passing wind. Pain in region of transverse colon at 3 P.M. Hardness in r. side, with soreness and pressure. Stitch in l. side while breathing. Pressure in l. side, with soreness. Moving in l. side.

Soreness and pain around navel, > emission of fetid flatus. Pain from N. and from other parts drawing to vagina. Drawing-aching in region of navel, extending to sacral region, < forenoon. Emptiness around navel or in whole abdomen. Burning in navel region. Feeling when walking as if sacro-symphysis were separated. In lower abdomen throbbing, stinging, tickling, sore-aching, pressing, drawing upward in symphysis, downward in thighs. Aching soreness, cutting drawing in l., then r. groin. Drawing pain over os pubis, from r. to l., passing of blood, then earache from l. to r. (female). Warm feeling in groin, burning pain.

Rectum.—Stitches in evening; S. towards anus or shooting in anus. Pressure after supper, with stool, the first hard, the last thin. Urging to stool, with costiveness or after looseness.

Anus.—Protruding piles after buzzing in ears; protruding P., aching, itching sore, oozing of yellow moisture. Bleeding after stool or with a soft stool, followed by mucus. *Sore feeling, worse outside, with stitching, burning, throbbing;* sore aching morning on rising. Burning, pulsating, bearing down towards anus. *Itching,* < evening. Shooting through perineum into penis.

Clinical.—Fistula ani.

Stool.—Diarrhœa; *from juicy fruit or cider; during first dentition, with much wind;* after *vexation; containing white points or flakes, like pus; offensive;* watery day and night, with urging after stool. Scanty, *with much flatulence.* Stool morning and evening.

Clinical.—Cholera infantum, great desire for indigestible things, like ham, smoked meat, etc., abdomen sunken, flabby, emaciation, stools green, undigested, offensive, forcibly expelled.

Urinary Organs.—Weakness of male; after urinating, Bladder, shooting in mouth; cutting before urinating. pressing down, cutting in urethra; pressing and cutting in female B., deep into l. after urinating; pressing pain, < r. side; pain and in neighboring parts; pain in neck as when stream is stopped suddenly; sore aching, < after micturition; drawing upward in female B. while urinating. Frequent urging to urinate. Frequent and copious micturition, with weakness and weariness. Cutting in urethra; in male U. after micturition, and burning; burning in male U. while urinating, and hardness. *Urine copious; with weariness;* copious, with flocculent sediment; dark in afternoon; dark, warm and of penetrating odor; smelling like strong tea. Diaper reddish-yellow.

Sexual Organs.—Weak feeling in male. Affection of genito-urinary organs after stool and micturition. Shooting in root of penis and in bladder. Cutting drawing pain in glans when sitting, extending towards tip. Erection while riding in a carriage, without desire; painful E. in evening, with burning in urethra and tension in penis. Desire increased in some, in others decreased; D. towards morning, with unusual orgasm.

Female.—Swelling of external parts when awaking, and of vagina. Clitoris erect after micturition, with desire. *Pressure upward over mons veneris,* a throbbing or other sensation. Pressive-drawing and sore feeling as if menses would appear, pressure in uterus and vagina, in loins, flushes of heat, fatigue from ascending stairs, pain from r. groin into l. hip. Sore aching in labia, warm feeling between externals, stitching in inner labia. Pain in vagina, with flushes and faintness. Burning in vagina, with pain on both sides of bladder and uterus, burning up into chest. Aching in vagina after nosebleed. Leucorrhœa before menses; two weeks after menses or from one term to another; *like white of eggs,* < *morning* after rising, and of sweetish odor; creamlike, in afternoon.

Cutting from uterus through to sacrum. *Aching in uterus* in morning; pressing in U., desire, aching in neck of bladder, prostration. *Weakness in region of uterus, < stool and micturition, with distress and uterine displacement.* Menses too early and bright-colored; every two weeks, black, clotted, menorrhagia; too late and dark; too late and first bright, then dark, at last lochia-like and fetid. Nymphomania, < before menses; desire, then copious menses. Voluptuous feeling as if all parts were full of blood, with pulsation in all parts and increased desire.

Clinical.—It has been used for nymphomania with heat and weight on vertex, melancholia, flushed face, etc., the symptoms always worse before menses. Uterine spasms, sometimes after stool or micturition, < change of weather. Menstruation too early, with faint feeling in stomach, etc. Dysmenorrhœa. Leucorrhœa. After prolonged nursing, cough, weakness of voice, pain between shoulders, etc.

Respiratory Organs.—*Hoarseness.* Dry cough, with hoarseness, soreness and dryness in throat. Suffocative fits when lifting the child from cradle; S. fits in child after nursing, < after crying, and after being taken out of cradle, head turns backward, face blue, fighting with hands and feet, after attacks relaxed. *Frequent, short and difficult breathing.* Difficult breathing in evening, > in bed, < next morning. *Sighing;* desire to sigh, with pain in chest and shooting in liver.

Clinical.—Chronic cough, short, dry (with chronic inflammation of lungs, which even may become tubercular), with night-sweats, etc. Suffocative cough of children, > lying down, < sitting up.

Chest.—Tumor like a walnut in l. mamma. Hardness of l. mamma, with soreness to pressure (in a man). Creaking on l. side of sternum like cracking in joints. Milk acid; changeable, from alkali to neutral or to acid; watery, neutral.

Shooting during inspiration and expiration, < deep breathing; in l., with inhalation, and in r. temple; in l., through shoulder. Tearing in sternum, with pressing and shooting. Pressing in mamma, with tearing, rending, drawing, contraction, pinching, shooting, burning. Pain; especially below and upward; in a spot from coughing; where ribs and cartilages meet; intermittent, sharp in region of r. sixth rib, then on l. fourth and fifth rib, during the day, taking away the breath, < deep breathing; as if an instrument passed through end of sternum, during the day. Sore pain on sternum; nipples; r. mamma, then l. Soreness of l. clavicle, then r.; cutting, over clavicle. Soreness to touch; *of mammæ. Contraction till* 10 P.M., *> on lying down, < when getting up, with difficult breathing.* Painless gnawing, with quivering, jerking, heat and fear. Burning into throat, sometimes downward. Beating on spot on l.

Heart.—Cutting, shooting in region, interrupting respiration. Sharp pain in region during inspiration, interfering with respiration. Pain in morning. Beating. Pulse frequent, but not quick.

Neck.—**Rheumatic pain after draught of air, with stiffness and dulness of head.** *Cramplike pain in one side, then in other.* Muscles hurt up to occiput, r., then l. Pulsation in nape when sitting, and in l. chest.

Back.—Pain in morning; P. > after motion, and in lower limbs; *backache and uterine pains;* sudden jerking pain, with inhalation; jerking, rending, cutting, shooting pain. Drawing, < evening and morning, getting awake, moving, and in limbs, with gaping, stretching, bending backward. Throbbing, jerking pain in, near, between and < *below scapulæ.* Tensive pain below r. scapula, extending forward. Sharp pain in sacrum, and lameness. *Pain in kidney region when lifting and when blowing nose;* in kidney region when digging; P. above sacrum and in hips. *Soreness in sacro-iliac union as if separated.* Sore aching in l. loin. Numbness and lameness in sacrum. Pain, soreness, pressive, tearing and shooting in os coccygis.

Clinical.—Potts' disease, spinal curvature, lumbar abscess.

Extremities.—Trembling of arms and hands; with other complaints, especially uterine. *Pain, with weariness; flying, in all parts of rump and limbs after getting wet in rain;* P. in all joints, < l., then and less in r.; rheumatic, in all joints after taking cold. Lame feeling in flexors, sudden aching in extensors. Weariness; during pregnancy. Extensors more affected then flexors.

Clinical.—Chronic rheumatism (compare with Calc. carb.).

Upper Extremities.—Shooting from shoulder-joint along arm, with tearing. Pain in shoulder and scapulæ. Sore, bruised pain in shoulder or down arm. Pain from clavicle to wrist; from shoulder to fingers, l. then r.; in all bones of arm, especially of thumb; in l. arm in afternoon, with numbness; rheumatic pain in arm near shoulder-joint, cannot lift arm. Soreness under arms, with burning, itching. Paralysis of l. arm.

Shooting through elbows, usually l., then r. Pain from l. elbow to shoulder-joint; in elbow as after a blow. Cramplike pain in forearm, sore bruised feeling, tearing. Sudden pain in wrists, < l.; P. in wrist, with lameness as if beaten, cramplike and other pains on moving it. Trembling of hands. Tearing in hands and arms, < wrists and r. middle finger. Hands asleep. Paralysis of l. hand and arm. Thumbs moved spasmodically. Pain in single fingers; in r. in evening when writing; in ball of thumb; in joints of r. thumb as if sprained; *ulcerative, in roots of r. finger-nails, < in middle finger;* around nails as if ulcerated. Soreness of points of finger and thumb. Paralysis of all finger-joints.

Lower Extremities.—Stepping motion. Staggering in old people, on rising from a seat. Pain in damp, cold weather; P. during menses. *Asleep, also abdomen and sacrum, cannot rise from seat; asleep, with anxious feeling, has to jump out of carriage, also at night.* Child cannot stand. Lame feeling, tired, heavy.

Nates.—All kinds of pains, with soreness, after a storm, most from r. to l., but alternating most on r. side. Sore aching, heat, itching, oozing pimples, itching scurfs. Bruised feeling after snow-storm, with lameness. Asleep, also back, with uneasiness.

Thigh.—Stitches up and down hip-bone, < from ischium down, jerking, drawing, with warm feeling; S. through l. thigh to knee, stirring above, down to ankle-bone, toes too thick. Tearing, shooting, drawing in hip-bone. *Pains above knees.* Pain and soreness; afterwards extending into l. knee, then sensitiveness of knee. Sharp pain in tendons on inside, < walking. Labor-pain during sixth month of nursing a child, with involuntary stool and passing of blood.

Knee.—Tearing in l., to feet, and crusty tetters covering leg. Boring in r., < stretching and at night. Sharp pain; in afternoon when walking. Pain < walking, l. then r.; in l. extending to sole; on inner side of r. as from a blow, < bending, with soreness; sprained pain, sore when walking. Tendons in hollow feel too short.

Leg.—*Cramp in spot inside of calves when walking.* Cramp pain in calves, drawing, rending, shooting, warm feeling. Tearing in calves. Pain in calf in morning, < raising leg; below hollow of knee, < taking off boots; beneath hollow of knee when it is strongly bent, making use of limbs uncertain; P. in head of l. tibia, caused by a kick, returned every night, with intolerance of touch, formation of exostosis. Drawing pain in shin-bone. Feels blood run from knee to feet. *Weak, restless, crawling, tingling.*

Rending, tearing, shooting in ankle. Pain in ankle as if dislocated. Cramplike pain in feet, < ankle. Twitching of big toes, little toe drawn inward. Pain in r. great toe, < walking; old (gouty) pain in l. great toe, with inclination to crack joints.

Skin.—Dark brown, yellow. Red after foot-bath, with prickling like nettles. Tetter on place burnt twenty-three years ago; scaling T. on legs. Furuncle between r. eyebrow and lid, eye inflamed, lids falling or closed, < morning; to r. of anus, with pain, inability to sit, discharging blood and pus, remaining a painless fistula. Pimples on ears; in region of joints; on back of hand, on wrist; inside of forearm. Ulcers above and around ears and in region of parotid; in old scars; scrofulous, lax and lazy. Formication; on abdomen. Stinging spots on buttocks, itching, burning, sore spots, oozing scurfs. Itching on point of nose; biting, < on places years before affected; burning, of outer ear in warm room; and burning.

Clinical.—**Fistulous ulcers on ankles. Varicose veins. Caries of hip-joint and heel, with offensive pus.**

Sleep.—*Gaping, with irresistible drowsiness all the forenoon.* Sleepiness by day; before menses; all forenoon, before and at dinner; with gloomy mood, inability to think, headache, singing in ears, sweat in face, prostration in limbs. Sleep all the evening. Falls asleep while eating dinner, deep sleep after dinner. Sound sleep in evening, early waking. *Inability to get awake in morning.* Early waking. Starting in sleep. Disturbed, < before midnight. Sleepless till 2 or 3 o'clock. Dreams, with thoughts about many events; of fire; of fire, but without many flames; of danger, but without fear; of traveling; vivid, most from late events or last readings.

Fever.—Chill in morning after dressing, with cough and coryza; C. when going into cold air; with uterine pains; shaking, out of doors; shivering, with hot face and colic; *creeping shivering,* with motion of scrotum not like that after urinating; cool feeling towards eyes; behind eyes; cold ears; outer ears; point of nose; lower parts, with hot face.

Warm room is oppressive. Heat, with other complaints; dry H. in evening, hot breath, beating of heart, mouth and tongue dry without thirst, gaping, stretching, etc.; running from head to toes; running from vertex to toes; in face in evening; in face, with chill or other complaints; external in mamma, towards l. arm. Sweat at night; *on parts, waking at night; on single parts,* towards and in morning; on palms; cold, on face, body cold. Dry skin, moisture on hands.

Clinical.—Night-sweats in phthisis.

Calendula.

A tincture is made from the flowers, buds and leaves of fresh plants of the common Marigold.

Compare Arnica.

Generalities.—Rheumatic drawing pain during motion. Nervous exhaustion. Feeling best when walking or when lying quite still.

Clinical.—Useful for open wounds, with great soreness and pain, the parts will not heal, tend to inflame and suppurate. In phlegmonous erysipelas it seems to be a valuable topical application; it is also useful as a local application in bad ulcers of os uteri, offensive leucorrhœa.

Mind and Head.—Anxiety during chill, with taciturnity and solicitude. Fretfulness, with a sleepy, dreamy condition. Irritability, then despair and anguish. Dull sensation in head, especially in upper part of occiput. Confusion of head as after a night's debauch, in morning heaviness of H. as after a long illness. Pain in forehead after eating, with heat in it; P. in occiput. Disagreeable sensation in occiput; extending to back of neck. Itching of scalp.

Eyes.—Inflammation of white of eye, with headache while lying, now in forehead, now in temples. Dilatation of pupils. Swelling of lids. Dryness of margins of lids, with biting as from smoke.

Face and Mouth.—Prickling pain in face, then in forehead, then in face again. Drawing tensive pain in glands before l. ramus of lower jaw on moving head. Vesicles in l. corner of lower lip. Swollen sensation in lips, spreading to sides of nose, then to eyes and forehead, with burning stinging, speech scarcely recognizable. Salivation.

Throat.—Submaxillary glands swollen and painful to touch as if suppurating; painful on touch in afternoon as if swollen, at times causing tensive pain, which, especially on swallowing, becomes a pressure in throat. Pain in front, beneath chin, on motion and pressure, and at union of clavicle with sternum. Scraping and accumulation of mucus. Bitter taste of mucus before eating.

Stomach and Abdomen.—Appetite diminished for dinner, though he relishes food when he eats. Hiccough after smoking. Threatenings of nausea in forenoon. Disordered digestion. Boring-digging deep in umbilical region when walking. Stitches in middle of r. side of abdomen on motion.

Stool and Urinary and Sexual Organs.—Stool in morning preceded by griping and anxiety in abdomen and accompanied by chill. Soft stool covered with mucus. Tearings in urethra at times during a chill. Frequent micturition, urine as white as water and burning. Emission of semen.

Respiratory Organs, Chest and Pulse.—Deep inspiration, with heat in chest and face. Great efforts to inflate lower lobes of lungs, only successful when sitting up. Pressure in l. side of chest in evening in bed, with oppression. Drawing pressure in l. side of chest when standing while taking drug; drawing P. in l. side of C. and on sternum, with stitches in r. side of chest. Pulse irregular and diminishing rapidly.

Neck and Back.—Rheumatic drawing pain in r. side of neck, extending to shoulder, < bending neck to r. side and on raising r. arm. Tearing between scapulæ. Aching beneath lower tip of r. scapula in afternoon, with sensation as if everything were suppurating and bruised; A. in l. lumbar region, then in both lumbar regions.

Extremities.—Axillary glands painful to touch. Drawing pressive tension in wrists and ankles during rest. Weariness of lower limbs. Bruised pain in outer side of knees while sitting. Burning tearing in upper part of calf while sitting. Drawing pinching on inner border of sole while sitting.

Skin and Sleep.—A wound becomes raw and inflames anew. Sticking in the wound during feverheat, with redness of surrounding parts. Bruised pain in a wound in morning, with smarting and throbbing as if it would suppurate. Itching. Restlessness at night, with continual waking, frequent micturition and much drinking.

Fever.—Chilliness all the morning, with sensitiveness to air; C. at beginning of almost all symptoms. Shivering, with gooseflesh, while skin is warm to touch; S. in back, with pressure in l. last true ribs and movements in epigastric region and abdomen as if he would faint. Cold hands and feet; all the forenoon, with drawing, rheumatic pains through whole body, and after sitting for some time, aching in ribs as if squeezed together and bruised. Heat all the forenoon, with sweat, weakness in chest and heat in axillæ; in afternoon, with creeping chills and thirst, but drinking always causes a shaking chill. Heat in evening in bed; with sweat, especially burning and sweat of feet. Heat, but cold drinks cause shivering, H. abates after 5 P.M. without shivering, even in open air, the head feels freer, breathing is easier, voice stronger and deeper; internal, towards evening while sitting, with external coldness, creeping chills and almost dread of drinking; flushes, in forehead in evening; H. in face after dinner, and in hands and feet, then thirst.

Calotropis.

A tincture is made from the bark of the root of Calotropis gigantea R. Br. (Asclepiadaceæ), which grows in India.

Depressed, tired feeling, which came on gradually when walking, with nausea and faint feeling, great coldness, dizziness, frequent micturition, constant eructations, went to bed at 5 P.M., body cold, frequent chills passing up spinal cord, head and temples hot, cheeks burning, after a time, with rugs on the bed, heat and perspiration, pulse quickened, but he was too ill to count it, heat and cold alternately, with nausea until he sipped strong coffee, then vomiting of about a wine-glassful of yellow bile, vomited a lesser quantity an hour later, oppression of chest, short respiration, lips and throat dry, head painful, with throbbing and confusion, sipped coffee all night, little sleep, tossed from side to side, two days before, when moving, had felt pain inside of r. thigh just below crotch, now back of r. thigh was very sore, red and hard, so that turning over in bed was difficult, next morning the thigh was so sore, swollen and painful that the leg could not be bent in walking and every step was painful, with lameness, again chills towards bedtime and in bed, beginning in feet and running up spinal cord, occasional movement of feet in bed seemed to bring on the chills, fits of perspiration alternating with the chills, restless, head and face hot, breath foul, sleepless, pulse weak and thready, urine dark red, with strong smell, cramplike pains in centre of r. palm on grasping anything, lasting many days, pain, but less in degree, in wrist on moving it, soreness and swelling of r. palate, giving pain on moving jaws in eating, next day diffused red blotches on thigh, elevated and papular, veins on hand, which are usually full, seemed thinner, took several doses of Camp. rub., tingling-burning pain in thigh on standing up.

Dull aching in occiput at 11 A.M., gradually increasing till bedtime, 12 P.M., very bad at times in evening, next morning lightness of head, > after breakfast.

Pain in tarsal bones of l. foot on movement or on bearing weight on foot, < Hepar sul., at night intermittent cramplike pain while foot rested on the bed, restlessness, kept moving the foot about the bed, drank coffee and pain ceased when at rest, instep red and swollen, could not let the foot touch the ground, yet by putting the foot down very gradually and by degrees bringing the weight upon it he could stand without pain, which returned as soon as he took off the weight, coffee as a lotion sent the redness in and made the foot worse, before trying the coffee lotion slight pain in r. foot, which afterwards became affected like l.

Clinical.—It has been used in tubercular leprosy. In lupus of face. Violent pain in both legs, with swelling of knees and stiffness, cannot walk.

Camphor.

A tincture is prepared by dissolving one part of camphor gum in nine parts of Alcohol.

General Action.—It produces violent convulsions, hysterical and epileptiform, delirium, and various phases of nervous excitement. It also produces coldness of the body and profound collapse, with feeble pulse.

Allies.—*Cupr.*, *Tereb.*, *Secale c.*, Ars., Verat. a., Carbo v., Op., Hyosc., Stram., Alcohol.

Generalities.—Emaciation. Distention of veins. Inflammations. Drunken appearance. Symptoms like delirium tremens, optical delusions, fright, screams, hideous sights, and burying his head in pillow (Stramon., Hyosc.). Hysterical. Falling down insensible. Convulsions; in children; with loss of consciousness; with disordered expression of face and livid aspect; violent, especially of hands and feet. Clonic convulsive movements. *Convulsive circular motion (rotation of arms).*

Subsultus tendinum (Ars., Cupr., Op., Tereb., Verat., Alcohol) and insensibility. Epileptic fit; in which his tongue was badly bitten. Several times the body curled itself up into a ball and projected itself out again with great activity. Froth oozing from mouth, constant chewing motions, twitching of head, cold sweat on face, which was bluish or purple, cadaverous and distorted, twitching of occipito-frontalis muscle, orbicularis oris rigidly drawn to left, masseter so contracted that the jaw could not be depressed.

Flung himself back on the bed, with dreadful shrieks, fell into strong convulsions, foamed at the mouth, stared wildly, endeavored to lay hold of and tear everything in his reach, then a calm similar to fainting with this difference only, the skin was florid, lost all remembrance of past actions and knowledge of present objects, then slowly began to recover both, though in a manner so amazing that his business connections and everything of the same nature which he had entirely forgotten, at their first occurrence startled his mind as if he had never been acquainted with them before, but after he knew all the family he did not recollect the use of the furniture in the room, and every object appeared as strange as if he had only that moment begun his existence.

He rubs his forehead, head, chest and other parts, leans against something, senses leave him, he slides and falls, stretched out stiff, shoulders bent backward, arms at first bent, hands bent outward and somewhat clenched, fingers spread apart, then stiffness of all parts, with head bent to one side, lower jaw open, stiff, lips drawn inward, gnashing of teeth, eyes closed, twitching of facial muscles, cold all over, without breathing. Giddy, lost self-control, talked incoherently and excitedly, ran up-stairs and fell on the floor in convulsions, face and neck dusky, foam flying from his mouth, pulse full and pupils dilated.

Convulsions in which opisthotonos was considerable, whole surface red, eyeballs injected and prominent for an instant, then eyes forcibly closed, loud moaning, grinding of teeth and blowing of bloody saliva through closed teeth, then after half an hour the opisthotonos gave place to rapid rolling over and over, now this way, now that, sometimes burying face in bed so that breathing was difficult.

Opisthotonos (Tereb., Cupr.), head thrown back, rotated to left, jaws locked, mouth drawn to left, with twitchings. Stiffness and early stage of opisthotonos. Cataleptic rigidity, with unconsciousness, then relaxed sinking down so that he could scarcely be held upright, then vomiting, then return of consciousness. Trembling (Stram., Cupr.); > cold bathing of face and hands. *Easily startled when awake, with throbbings.*

Tearing stitches here and there, in joints. Rheumatic stitches in all muscles, especially between shoulders. Pain in periosteum of all bones. Nervous drawings, with something like shivering. General oppression. Soreness and rigidity over whole body as after severe exercise or exposure to cold. Trembling sensation. Dry feeling in and over body, especially on head and in bronchial tubes. *General discomfort.* **Restlessness**; at night (Ars.); constant walking about the room. Excitement of nervous system, especially in skin and muscles. Feeling at night as if he could fly or as if he were drawn into the air in spite of himself. Increase of muscular strength.

Relaxation of whole body, with heaviness; paralytic R. of muscles. *Weakness;* after stool, with general sweat; on waking from a sound sleep; after sweat during sleep; compared to the stillness of the wind, with heaviness. Listlessness. Faintness; on rising to walk; with shivering and numbness. Deathlike sensation. Susceptibility to external impressions diminished in skin and muscles. Partial paralysis. Insensibility to touch. Aggravation of pains in evening; A. during motion. Most of the pains at first only during partial attention (so tearing in various parts only when falling asleep) >, especially the headache, by paying attention to them, afterwards aggravation when paying strict attention to himself. Amelioration of symptoms from profuse sweat.

Clinical.—It may be given to new-born children who have been asphyxiated and who have spasms in consequence. Great coldness of the surface of the body, rapid sinking of strength, sometimes with delirium or convulsions. General feeling of soreness as if beaten. Spasms, especially in children. Effects of shocks

from injuries, coldness of surface of body, etc. Consequences of suppressed eruptions in scarlet fever, and especially in measles; the skin is blue and cold. It may be used as an antidote to irritant poisons; for the effects of poisonous insects, tobacco, mushrooms, etc. It is used, as a rule, in prostration occurring suddenly and increasing rapidly.

Mind.—Delirium; at night; with somnolency and small languishing pulse; but when spoken to gave rational answers; active; furious, being with difficulty restrained in bed. Stripped himself, danced wildly and tried to jump out of the window (*Hyosc.*). Felt as if he ought to kill someone (not any of his own family) when in the street. Strange and wild gestures and conversation. Wild talk, constant repetition of same sentence. Talked irrationally and undertook absurd things. Incoherent muttering.

Exact ideas of time were lost, everything seemed new, thought he was higher than the houses and suffered at the thought of the disadvantages of his height, felt better by striking himself on the head, finally fell into a mechanical state of existence, was contented with everything, would talk and realize what was said, but had no interest or continued memory of events, on greeting his family on his return from the asylum he was thrown into a trance, in which he could not talk or act, but fully realized what was said or done about him, afterwards from excitement he had another trance and came out of it weak and trembling, for a long time he was conscious of an unstable brain, which seemed balanced on a slight point, likely at any moment to be turned over, fragments of conversation whirled through his mind, and at times his surroundings were all perverted, he would walk about and not know what he was doing or where he was, he was somnambulistic.

Screaming loudly "I shan't faint, for if I do I will have fits and never come out of them." Howled, leaped from bed, apparently in great agony and bent on something desperate. The child creeps into a corner, howls, cries and thinks he has been insulted and scolded. Crying for he knew not what when at work and when walking.

Anxiety. Fear, < in the dark. *Dread of being alone in the dark* (Stram.). Dread of being drawn upward. Fear of the mirrors in the room, lest he should see himself in them, he would have gotten up and broken them only he was more afraid to get up alone in the dark. Vague sense of impending danger, > walking rapidly until he perspired. Cheerful talk relieved him, vexed by want of sympathy, afraid to be alone a moment (Ars.), wanted to think he was well, always asking his father about it, wanted to be with his father, fearing death. Imagined he would get yellow-fever, etc. *Indescribable wretchedness. Agitation. Haste.* Sadness, ill humor. Irritability; in children. Fretfulness at night, with anxiety and frightful visions. Desirous to dispute and self-willed. Jealousy. Aversion to all external objects. Indolence; during the chill, with depressed disposition. Indifference. Exhiliration.

Thoughts quickly followed one another, but he could not fix attention upon any of them, and he lost consciousness of his personality, after vomiting consciousness returned, but distraction, forgetfulness and crowding of ideas returned, time seemed very long and full of events which he could not remember, impressions received by sight were evanescent, finally oppressive warmth spread through head and body, he lost consciousness and fell down, face flushed, slow breathing, convulsive movements, on waking he had to make persistent efforts to recover consciousness of his personality and knowledge of his surroundings.

Intellectual powers increased. Dulness of intellect. Confusion of ideas. A tumult of crude ideas floated through his mind. Stupefaction of senses like faintness. Memory lost. Coma. Unconsciousness; with howls and falling down; semi-unconscious, eyes partly closed, and if placed in a sitting posture, her head and body inclined to fall forward and to the side, but if roused and spoken to loudly, she made an attempt to sit upright, lifted her eyelids for a moment, responded rationally, but in the unformed halting accents of a drunken person.

Clinical.—**With the collapse extreme anxiety and restlessness in some cases, in some great lethargy, can scarcely be aroused, in others loss of consciousness or even delirium.**

Head.—Thrown back. Drawn spasmodically towards the shoulder. Tearing; especially in forehead. Aching; mornings after rising; with drawings in r. side; and through temples, with sensation of sinking and exhaustion, as if her breath were leaving her; with burning pain in stomach, eructations, thirst and formication in limbs; sudden; *as from constriction of brain; as if brain were compressed from all sides,* > thinking about it; throbbing; as if bruised or as if brain were sore. *Contractive pain at base of brain, especially in occiput* and above nose, < stooping low, lying or pressure, with leaning of head to one or other side, coldness of hands and feet, heat of forehead and waking slumber. Pressure outward. Intermittent drawings all around head as if nerves were drawn up. Throbbing. *Heaviness;* especially in vertex; *with vertigo and sinking backward of head; dizzy.* Confusion; especially in anterior part; with noise in ears; approaching vertigo. Stupefying feeling, like effects of laudanum. Lightness. *Congestion.* Intoxication.

Vertigo; when sitting; < *stooping, with heaviness of head;* with dim vision; in attacks, also after nausea; so severe that knees knocked together and he nearly fell; with flushing of face, then pallor, eyes turned to right, upward and backward, head the same, r. arm extended above head as if catching something, bubbling of watery fluid from mouth, *limbs cold and cramped,* pulse feeble, mind wandering, talking, shouting, crying and laughing by turns, convulsions, indications of a relapse if patient were silent; while studying, the book seemed to go round "with the sun," could hardly keep his seat, felt as if falling towards his right and as if going into sleep or unconsciousness, but not drowsy, as if going off and rousing up again, thought he was going to die, felt bad whenever he thought of it, could not speak from words seeming to choke him in larynx, as with persons disappointed or grieved, all > in open air, but next day in school on thinking of it felt it again. Sickening sensation of swinging when in bed.

Forehead.—Veins distended and tortuous. Throbbing-stinging through night, with general dry heat. Tearing sticking in F., with pressure on upper part of frontal bone. Tearing in l. side, with pressure outward; T. in l. side of F. and l. side of occiput; in l. side of F. and in l. cheek. Cutting jerks from F. and temples to middle of brain on lying down. Aching; in middle; on r. side; in l. side; in l. eye in evening; in sinciput, with intermittent stitches starting in temporal bones; *above frontal bone, with nausea;* extending to occiput; extending to temples, < evening, > in afternoon by a walk in open air, often with stitches in temples and orbits; alternately in F. and eyes; throbbing. Pressive but not painful sensation in sinciput, changing to confusion of head. Drawing above eyes; in l. side. Heaviness; in sinciput; in sinciput, < walking, with heat. Pressure in upper, with heaviness; P. on various places in sinciput.

Temples.—Tearing in r.; and in forehead. Boring daily, < during morning nap, > after waking, then toothache, B. in r. in morning on waking, ending with a stitch, which extends into eye and tooth, returning. Pressure in r.; throbbing. Throbbing of arteries and distended jugular veins.

Pressure in vertex; on r. side of V. Stitches in r. half of brain. Pressure by jerks over l. ear. Cutting from l. side of occiput to forehead. Pressure in occiput. Uneasiness in occiput. *Throbbing in cerebellum.*

Clinical.—It has been used after sunstroke, especially with beating pain in cerebellum. The predominating head symptoms are throbbing, or constrictive as if knotted up, with general coldness.

Eyes.—*Hollow.* Surrounded by blue circles. *Staring; distorted.* Inflamed. Suffused with blood. Brilliant. Twitching, turned upward, pupils dilated, eyes sometimes turned to r., *but generally to l., lachrymation.* Soreness or tense, stiff feeling of E. and lids. Tension. Lachrymation in open air. Balls turned upward. Pressing-out pain in r. ball on moving it. Sensation in l. ball as from pushing upon it from behind. *Pupils contracted;* then dilated; dilated; insensible.

Lids.—Covered with red spots. Constantly agitated and half-closed, showing balls turned upward and outward. Twitching; of upper; T. in external canthus. Smarting. Biting and sticking. Biting of edges; in external canthus. Biting-itching. Burning; in l.; in edges.

Conjunctiva injected. Red spots on white of r. Pressure on muscles of r. brow. Photophobia. Occasional loss of vision. Dimness of V.; for objects farther off than arm's length; with ocular hallucinations. *Glittering of objects.* Flickering. Letters ran together on reading script in forenoon, after ceasing to read a bright circle before eyes. Objects appeared encircled by a cloud. Hallucinations. Wonderful forms float before eyes. Black floating spots. Sparks and fiery wheels.

Ears.—*Red ulcer in l. external meatus, with sticking on pressure. Lobules red;* and hot. Sticking; from a draught of air or wind; deep in l. Tearing above and behind; in l. Roaring. Ringing. Singing; in l. Buzzing.

Nose.—Stitching from root almost to tip, or crawling; S. in anterior corner of nostril, as if ulcerated and sore. Sudden boring in r. side, near nose. Drawing in l. side. Itching internally; in l. nostril. *Air of room breathed through the nose seemed cooler when walking.* Obstruction in r. side, then secretion of thin mucus. Stoppage or running or bleeding. *Sneezing. Coryza; stopped.* Discharge of thin mucus in morning on rising (and evenings on going to sleep?) without real coryza. Bleeding; at 7 A.M.

Clinical.—The first stages of violent coryza, generally dry, with sneezing and flatulence. A palliative in many forms of fluent coryza, especially hay fever.

Face.—Pale and anxious (Ars., Carbo v., Sec. c., Verat.); *P., distorted and sunken* (Ars., Sec. c., Verat.); *and livid;* alternately P. and livid, with incessant spasmodic movements; with fixed and stupid look. *Red;* and puffy; with a wild expression; *cheeks and lobules of ears. Bluish* (Cupr.). Black. Vacant expression; and eyes wandering about room, speechless and powerless. Twitching. Spasmodic distortion, with froth from mouth. Stitching in l. cheek. Boring in r. zygoma. Distortion of mouth. Lips everted as in bleating. Trismus. Tensive pain in masticators. Drawing in angle of r. lower jaw. Stitching in chin.

Clinical.—Collapsed expression, with cold sweat, blue lips, etc. (Cupr.).

Mouth.—Teeth. Looseness. *Seemed too long, with toothache, which seemed to originate from the swelling of submaxillary gland.* Stitch extending into eye, on going into cold or windy air, with the toothache. Cutting shootings through gum to roots of incisors and canines. Gnawing and boring in nearly all back teeth, especially in hollow T., < coffee or alcoholic drinks and touch of soft bread, > drinking cold water but < rinsing with cold water and by cold air, with longing for beer, which relieved, as also tobacco-smoking. Toothache now in one, now in another tooth; T. ceases during coition, after which he sleeps quietly for the first time. Drawing in hollow lower back T.; in decayed upper incisors when walking. Gums loosened, of a livid color.

Tongue.—Thick, spongy, fissured, covered with tough yellow mucus. *Cold* (Cupr., Verat.), flabby, trembling; C. at tip. Feeling as if swollen and numb (Acon.). Biting in end as from pepper (Acon.). Burning on edge and on hard palate. Dry at night; D. or covered with aphthæ; D. sensation on back part, like a scraping, with much saliva. *Speech feeble, broken* (Stram.), *hoarse.* Loss of speech. Difficulty of speech; and of thought.

Stitches in palate. Dry scraping on palate. Swollen sensation in whole interior of mouth, tongue, gums and palate. Burning on palate, extending into œsophagus, not > by drinking. Heat in mouth and stomach. Sensation in M. and stomach as after peppermint lozenges. Cold sensation rises into mouth and to palate. Coolness, changing to sharpness and burning. Dryness. Froth; about teeth, which were clenched. Salivation; *at times slimy and tenacious;* watery.

Taste.—*Increased to all food.* Bitter to food, to meat more than to bread; to everything, even to the customary tobacco. Bad. Offensive breath in morning.

Clinical.—Tongue cold, mouth cold, breath cold.

Throat.—Stitches at back of pharynx and towards l. side. Hysterical choking sensation. Scraping. Soreness at night, < swallowing, with feeling as if gullet were sore and excoriated and sensation in throat as if she had eaten rancid substances. Heat; *in pharynx and in stomach;* in œsophagus and stomach, extending over whole body.

Stomach.—Hunger. Loss of appetite. Aversion to the accustomed tobacco-smoking, without its tasting badly, the aversion amounting to vomiting. *Thirst;* at night. Pleasure in drinks, without thirst. Loss of thirst. Eructations; *after eating;* of contents of stomach. Nausea; from drinking; < mornings, with vomiting; > eructations; with salivation; without inclination to vomit. Retching. Vomiting;

from drinking coffee; yellow, liquid; black-streaked; bilious, colored with blood.

Stitches. Pain; *in pit or anterior part of liver;* in epigastrium, radiating over belly and into limbs, with uterine tenesmus; gradually increasing pain in epigastrium, loins and abdomen, with strangury and vomiting. Oppression of pit, with warmth in it. Sensation in pit as if distended and bruised, with fulness in abdomen; sensation in pit as if abdomen were distended at this point and the diaphragm thereby pressed upward, with oppression of breathing. *Coldness;* in pit. Heat; peculiar, in region of pit; warmth in epigastric region, extending forward over whole body, with exalted condition of brain, rush of blood to head and warmth of face, especially of cheeks. Heartburn.

Abdomen.—Retraction. Distention by gas. Flatulence. Rumbling. Movements and in afternoon frequent emission of offensive flatus, and next night, from 1 till 2 o'clock, pain in cœliac ganglia, with anxiety and sweat. Emission of flatus; when walking. Cutting at night. Pain; drawing bruised, more internally, < inspiration, extending into region of liver and into chest. Feeling as before diarrhœa. Pressure in morning as of distention from flatus. Burning; and distention.

Heat in upper and lower (Ars., Cupr.). *Coldness in upper and lower* (Sec. c.). *Constrictive pain below short ribs, extending into lumbar veretebræ.* Pressure beneath diaphragm extending upward and downward, with tension, changing to pain in region of cœliac ganglia. Pain in hypochondria; region of cœliac ganglia, causing in evening anxious sweat, it seemed as inflammation would attack organs of abdomen, this irritability extended to lungs and caused cough, with pain on inner surface of spine, extending upward from diaphragm.

Scraping acrid sensation now on r., now on l. side, sometimes posteriorly, sometimes anteriorly, approaching a burning and changing to a grumbling pain in region of cœliac ganglia. Cutting in umbilical region, then emission of flatus, inclination to stool and urging to urinate. Pressure above umbilicus, with burning. Sensation of hardness above umbilicus, with heaviness.

Hypogastrium.—Burning-sticking below anterior crest of ilium, extending to groin. Pinching in lower abdomen, especially in umbilical region. Sticking-drawing heaviness in r. side on pressure. Pain. Pressure in l. side. Pressure outward in groins at root of penis, as if a hernia would protrude. Drawing in l. side, with a tensive bruised sensation. Heat.

Clinical.—Colic, insatiable thirst. Vomiting, with cold sweat, great exhaustion. Internal burning in abdomen, with external coldness.

Rectum.—Smarting. Contracted sensation on passing flatus, with swollen feeling and pain. Urging to stool; with scanty stool, then violent U. and a more scanty discharge; and in abdominal cavity, in urinary and genital organs, the U. to urinate beginning in kidneys, extending along ureters to bladder, with dragging along spermatic cords to testicles and general feeling of turgescence in this part of the body.

Stool.—Thin, dark brown, scanty. Hard and retarded. Constipation. Sour. Increased, afterwards difficult, and difficult emission of flatus, usually before the stool. Difficult, as if peristaltic motion were diminished and as if rectum were contracted. Sluggish and incomplete. Two the first day, preceded by griping, next day none, the third day a hard difficult one.

Clinical.—In cholera infantum, vomiting and diarrhœa suddenly, pains, with coldness of body, etc. In Asiatic cholera, in the early stage, when the stools are loose and contain fecal matter, in a later stage with coldness, but, as a rule, with dryness of the surface of the body, with sudden suppression of the discharges and collapse (the remedy should be stopped when the patient perspires).

Urinary Organs.—Diminished power of bladder, slow micturition. *Strangury. Micturition painful;* M. in a thin stream; dribbling; frequent and difficult; frequent, with profuse, colorless urine; almost involuntary, then pain in urethra as from a contraction from before backward; *retention of urine; with full bladder* (Op.). Urging to urinate, then involuntary micturition; frequent U., also with pain in course of spermatic vessels; ineffectual U. Burning in urethra; sticking B. in urethra on urinating. Biting in posterior part of urethra when urinating, then pressure in region of bladder. *Urine scanty;* U. red; dark yellow, very saturated; brown; yellowish-green, turbid, of musty odor; turbid, whitish-green; pale, odorless, containing sugar and mucus, but without sediment; *burning;* saturated, of pungent odor. Sediment red or white.

Clinical.—Excessive strangury, retention of urine (in Asiatic cholera, sometimes in poisoning by Cantharis).

Sexual Organs.—Excitement. Weakness, with want of desire. Impotence. Painful priapism, > by urinating (Canth., Tereb., Phos.). Pressure in l. side of root of penis, in groin, when standing. Sticking-itching on inner surface of prepuce. Laxity of scrotum, want of erection and want of desire, then violent erections. (Contractive sensation in testicles.) Incomplete erection, with weak desire. Desire increased; with delusions respecting the object of embrace. Nightly emissions. Slight discharge of blood from vagina. Os uteri enlarged and hot. Abortion. Menses ceased; M. too profuse. **Desire increased.**

Clinical.—Chordee, effects of sudden suppression of gonorrhœal discharge, coldness, strangury, etc. Sexual excitement in women. Puerperal mania, with suppressed discharges, dryness of the surface, etc.

Respiratory Organs.—Contractive sensation in larynx, as from sulphur fumes. *Mucus in windpipe,* making the voice husky and not removed by hacking or clearing throat. Pain in trachea and bronchi, < coughing, hacking and clearing throat. *Suffocative dyspnœa, as if from pressure in pit of stomach.* Choking. Hurried respiration and labored. Short and snoring. (Inspiration in sleep shorter than expiration.) Oppressed, anxious, panting. Slow and shallow. Deep and slow. Heavy, slow and difficult. *Almost arrested.* Impeded and feeble, apparently due to spasmodic contraction of circular fibres of trachea, whole body livid, cold, and skin feeling tensive to touch. *External, laborious, without assistance of abdominal muscles. Short cough from scraping in throat. Dry, hacking cough;* < forenoon.

Clinical.—Asthmatic attacks, with great suffocation. Violent dry cough, especially in measles, with suppressed eruption, with congestion of lungs, etc. In pleuro-pneumonia, emphysema of lungs.

Chest.—Stitches; *in l. when walking;* in nipples; < l., often extending to spine; with hacking cough, as if caused by a cutting cold sensation deep in trachea. Tearing near r. nipple, extending towards pelvis. Pressure on sternum when standing; internally under sternum, with difficult inspiration and a cold sensation which rises from chest into mouth; in upper part of sternum as from a load. Oppression. Contraction. Internal trembling of l. side when lying upon that side, and of l. arm.

Heart.—Anxiety. Cramplike stitches when lying on l. side, with oppression of chest. *Indefinable distress, coldness, with sleepiness. Palpitation;* as if heart turned forward and over, with stoppage of breath and gasping. Impulse hard; heard and felt after eating. Trembling. *Slow and intermittent beats.*

Pulse.—Rapid; and *full;* and small, irregular; and small, weak; and undulatory, weak; and scarcely perceptible. Slow; small and hard. *Weak* (Ars.); and thready. Irritable in evening. Hard and full.

Neck.—Swelling of cervical glands. Stitches near r. shoulder on motion. Tearing in nape on bending head forward. Pressure in nape when walking. Tensive pain in nape, < every motion and on turning neck, and in posterior cervical muscles. Drawing on l. side of nape towards shoulder; painful D. and stiff sensation in side of neck and down nape when walking in open air; painless, in cervical vertebræ on motion. Stiffness of nape.

Back.—*Drawing stitches through and between scapulæ on moving arm, extending into chest.* Tearing on anterior margin of scapula, < motion of arm; along medulla spinalis. Pain; in spine; on stooping; in small of back, < motion of head, > pressure of hand, especially in region of fifth, sixth and seventh dorsal vertebræ. Pressure in small of back. Movements in region of kidneys. Tired feeling in small of B. when walking.

Extremities.—Stretching. Cramps. Trembling. Tetanic stiffness, then convulsive agitation. Rigid but straight, upper ones spasmodically drawn and flexed at intervals, partially rotated. Drawn in or flexed upon body and muscles relaxed, then suddenly and violently extended till the joints cracked. Tearing in back of l. foot, in l. elbow and r. tibia. Aching. Pressure on inner side of legs, extending to ankles, and still more on inside of arms, > motion, with drawing. Bruised pain in l. elbow when sitting, and in r. knee. Sensitiveness. Lightness, all movements easy, in walking legs were raised beyond ordinary height. Heaviness. *Difficulty of motion. Numbness; with tingling* **and coldness** *of them,* at times preventing walking, and with feeling as if they did not belong to him.

Upper Extremities.—Shoulder. Tearing on l. Pressure on top; of r.; P. in r.; P. in l., < when raising arm. Bruised pain. Drawing pain in l. Tired feeling in l., > motion of arm, extending into wrist.

Arm.—More convulsed than lower limbs. Tearing on inside of l., at times passing into thumb and index. Pain during rest. Pressure on inside of both, > moving them, with drawing. Bruised pain in l., especially in shoulder-joint; in l. arm towards evening, especially in l. elbow, with heaviness. Heaviness of l.; H. of arms and hands. Fatigue of l.

Upper Arm.—Tearing in middle of posterior part of r.; jerking, from middle of inner surface of l. to middle of forearm. Pressure in muscles on inside of l.; in muscles above r. elbow. Drawing in muscles of l. when walking.

Elbow.—*Pressure in r., < leaning upon it, when it extends into hand.* Bruised pain in r., and in wrist and fingers. Tired feeling from l. into hand.

Forearm.—Tearing in forenoon, sometimes only in forearm and sometimes only in fingers; T. pressure on inner surface of l.; T. pressure on l. radius above wrist. Stitches. Bruised pain in lower part of l. Pressure in r.; painful; on inner surface of l.

Wrist.—Pressure in l. Pain in flexor margin of l. Heaviness in r., with drawing in thumb and stiffness of fingers.

Hand.—*Pale. Bluish,* fingers distorted and flexed. Trembling, especially noticed when writing. Hands in constant motion. Tearing in r. Drawing in l. palm; between fingers; in ball of l. thumb. Drawing-stitching in second joint of l. index. Sprained pain in distal joint of thumb on motion.

Lower Extremities.—*Staggering as if drunk.* Tottering, with weariness and heaviness; uncertain gait, and on looking down upon grass it seemed as if all objects were commingled. *Cracking and creaking in hip-joints, in knees and ankles.*

Thigh.—Tearing; anteriorly in muscles of r.; anteriorly in soft part of l. Pressure deep in r.; in r. hip-joint. Pain, even when walking, and in ankles. Drawing bruised pain after walking; *in r. and on inner side near and below patella, he fears that the leg will bend forward suddenly.* Pain as after a long walk, posteriorly above hollow of knee. Drawing in gluteus maximus at its attachment to crest of ilium, as if it would make the extremity lame. Difficulty of motion and weariness. Stiffness in outer side of r. when walking.

Knee.—Tearing below patella, < when walking. Stitches in r. patella while sitting. Pressing in l. Pain in r.; when walking; in r. as if fatigued. Pressive drawing on inner side below patella. Feeling as if they would bend forward, and as if beaten. Heaviness; when sitting, with pressure; in r. when walking.

Leg.—Stitches beneath l. knee; in calves; in l. calf. Pressure; on l. tibia; in middle of inner surface of l; in middle of l. calf when walking and sitting; above l. malleolus and posteriorly. Pain in r. even when sitting and walking, especially in knee. Drawing on l. tibia; *in muscles of l. calf when sitting, extending into foot.* Tired when sitting, especially knees. Heaviness; of whole r. when walking; as from a weight dragging from knee. Pricking when sitting, as from numbness. Goes to sleep when sitting and bending knee, with cold sensation. Numbness of r.

Ankle.—Pressure; on r. externally; in l. and above l. knee; when walking, when sitting it is more in knees. Sprained pain in morning on rising and walking. Drawing pain between r. malleolus and tendo-achillis when standing, becoming a tearing on moving foot. Drawing about l.

Foot.—Trembling. Tremulous tottering. Stitches in ball of l.; on both sides of tendo-achillis when walking. Tearing on dorsum of r.; T. on dorsum when sitting; in forepart of l. when walking, in tips of toes and under nails. *Tearing cramp pain on dorsum, extending along outer side of calf to thigh. Drawing cramp pain on dorsa, < motion* (Cupr.). Pressure on l. sole. Drawing in r.; in r. sole; on margin of l.; on dorsum of r. when walking. Weariness when walking, with tension and stiffness of thighs. Numbness in r.

Toes.—Sore pain in knuckles and in corns. Pressure; in r.; in r. great T. in evening. Drawing; in l., and in ball of r. foot. Pricking in tips of l., then of r. Numbness of r.

Clinical.—Cramps in calves.

Skin.—Pale, moist and cold. Shrivelled, relaxed. Loose, leathery, dry and burning. Dry. Erysipelas. Erysipelatous inflammation. Vesicles on neck and chest. Stitches on side of last joint of r. fourth finger. Drawing pain on nape and beneath zygoma. Drawing above and below l. clavicle. Creeping on neck above l. clavicle. Itching-crawling in r. groin, > rubbing. Itching; here and there in evening in bed; in palms; on knuckles and between them; on backs of hands and knuckles, > scratching, with sticking.

Sleep.—Yawning; when walking, without sleepiness. *Sleepiness;* towards noon, with confusion of head. Deep prolonged sleep. Stupid slumber, with pinching headache, heat, distended veins, rapid breathing and bruised pain in back. Deep sleep, then difficult waking in morning, next night waking at midnight with inability to sleep again, but in morning inability to rouse himself on account of sleepiness. Sleeplessness. Restless sleep; with continual waking on account of thirst. Starting in sleep; and crying out. Murmuring and sighing. Talking in a low tone. Snoring.

Dreams; fearful; confused, afterwards jealous and later anxious, of thefts, etc.; of projected occupations; about circumstances which had been the subject of conversation the day previous, especially in morning; amorous, with erections and pollutions. On closing eyes, while slumbering, fanciful objects appear, which sometimes seem too thick, sometimes too thin, changing as rapidly as the pulse goes.

Fever.—**Coldness**; after eating, with drawing through whole body *and with cold arms, hands and feet.* (Chill, with gnashing of teeth and much thirst, then sleep, with frequent wakings.) C., then heat. *Sensitiveness to cold air; in evening, with headache as from constriction of brain* and with pressure over root of nose. *Takes cold easily*, from which either a cold results or cutting in abdomen, with blackish-brown or black diarrhœa like coffee-grounds. Shivering chill; in evening when lying down; *with chattering of teeth; with gooseflesh, also with sensitiveness of skin to slightest touch;* with pale face. S. of limbs and abdomen, with heat in head and sensation as if sweat would break out. *Chill of skin;* with insensibility of it. *Internal coldness*, < walking; on r. side, then on l., as if a cold liquid flowed downward from head. *Coldness of forehead, cheeks and hands;* agreeable, through upper part of body, especially in stomach and œsophagus.

Chilliness in back; as from a cold wind. Internal chill beneath scapulæ; in lumbar region, < walking. C. over back mingled with warmth, as if sweat would break out. Alternate C. and heat in small of back when walking. Sticking coldness in sacral region, passing with lightning-like velocity along side of vertebræ to nape of neck and over whole body, alternating with heat. *Cold limbs; hands and feet; fingers; hands*, when walking; hands, with hot face. *Internal coldness in r. thigh as from a cold wind;* I. coldness, extending from knee into foot, when sitting. *Cold sensation in r. leg and toes; in r. leg as from a cold wind; in l. ankle as if a cold wind blew downward through calf, on foot a similar sensation when standing. C. of feet, with heat of head.*

Heat; when sitting, with internal quaking proceeding from nape and between scapulæ, and extending as a pressure in limbs, with heat and sweat of forehead; H. < walking; with redness of face; with rush of blood to head; with rapid throbbing of heart; H., with trembling. Dry H.; then easy sweat. Heat of skin; as if sweat would break out. Heat of head; in forehead; in vertex; in occiput; of scalp, also on forehead and temples; in head, with tearing headache, > pressure; in skin, vertex, and heaviness of head alternating with internal coldness in lumbar region. Burning in ears; in lobules of ears; in face; rising from nape into head, alternating with a cold sensation, but skin is warm and moist; H. in back. Creeping H. in back and lower limbs. H. in hands; in r. knee; of feet; in r. sole, with stitches.

Sweat; at night, then weakness in morning; in sleep; inclination to S. on slightest exertion in cool, rainy weather. *Cold;* when beginning to vomit, especially on face. Clammy; on forehead; and cold. Smelling of camphor. Sweat on forehead; when sitting; cold, on head; cold, on forehead and chest. Sweat on face; on nape when walking; on back, when sitting; on hands; on palms.

Clinical.—Feeling as if a cold wind were blowing over the body. Congestive chill, icy coldness over whole surface of body.

Camphor Bromide.

The monobromide of Camphor may be dissolved in Alcohol for dilutions.

Restlessness at night. Dull headache all over head in afternoon; heavy headache extending to occiput. Appearance all day of fine snowflakes falling straight down before eyes. Sharp aching in jaws. Discomfort about jaws, waking at night. Sore and stiff feeling in jaws and throat. Sharp shooting in teeth. Dryness of mouth and throat, with bitter taste. Sudden violent vomiting, with little nausea. Burning in stomach, then diarrhœa. Catharsis at 5 A.M. and about every hour all the forenoon, and about every fifteen minutes from 2 P.M. till midnight. *Suppression of milk.* Respiration and pulse slower. Temperature fell one degree. Heat.

Doziness, but not sleep in the natural acceptation of the word, rather a species of trance, eyes open and senses as acute as ever, perhaps more so, but the points of compass seemed reversed, at first these trances lasted five or ten minutes, finally four days, with ghastly dreams at night, in the day vision of large black flies coursing to and fro in swarms, lances of pain shot from temple to temple, and at base of brain a dull benumbing pressure extending towards coronal region, fell into an uneasy drowse about midnight and slumbered for several hours without real rest.

Canchalagua.

A tincture is prepared from the whole plant of Erythræa Chironioides, Griesb. (Gentianaceæ).

Sore all over body, especially in lower limbs. That kind of pain in head and fingers which accompanies attacks of intermittent fever. Head feels congested. Pain in forehead. Fulness, tightness of scalp, it feels as if drawn together by india-rubber. Burning in l. eye, then in r. Stitches in ears. Pain in ears. Increased buzzing and roaring in ears. Spitting of white mucus, with trembling and nervousness. Appetite increased. Regurgitations. Waterbrash. Ructus. Flatus. Pain in abdomen, > pressure. Loose stools, several a day. *Constipation.* Morning stool hard, knotty. Chills repeatedly down spine and all over body, < in bed, at night. Sleeplessness. Heat in whole body, and after the proving I could bear better the cool trade wind, usually setting in, in San Francisco, in afternoon.

Clinical.—Most severe types of intermittent in hot countries, with a general sore and bruised feeling, nausea and retching, the skin becomes wrinkled like a washerwoman's. Alleviated a catarrh produced by influenza.

Cannabis Indica.

A tincture is prepared from the dried tops of the herb (gathered in India), Cannabis Sativa var. Indica, L.

General Action.—The chief effect is on the mind; an abnormal exhilaration and excitation of thought. Ideas crowd upon each other with extreme rapidity so that time seems infinite, space immense. The sense of duality is also pronounced. Convulsions are sometimes induced.

Generalities.—Dropsy. Determination of blood to surface. Creeps on hands or knees in the open air. Unconsciously walks sideways in the street. Cannot avoid running against people in the street. Did things automatically. During the intoxication, when the spells of laughter came on, he stamped and raised his body up and down on the sofa in a violent manner. Closed his eyes and tried to think of something solemn, suddenly felt as if he were a marble statue, unable to move, general chill. Shaking of whole body. Trembling on moving hands or feet. Twitchings. Spasms. Catalepsy. Tetanus at the moment that water was taken, others frothed at the mouth.

Stitches in chest and limbs. Aching in nape, r. shoulder and r. ear. Pressing pain on different spots of cranial bones, in l. wrist and ankle, and violent pain in muscles below l. scapula. Thrilling; through whole frame to finger-ends and through brain, then terror; agreeable, through body and limbs. Enlarged feeling in single parts; E. feeling in r. side of body. Light feeling on motion. The first sensations are physically extreme lightness and mentally keen perception of the ludicrous. Feeling as if raised from the ground and as if he could fly. Nervous feeling. Uneasiness; vague. Excitation as from quick circulation of blood, as if streams of it poured towards the head, which felt dull, eyes glistened, and on walking he could scarcely find his way, everything seemed dark and perverted, on reaching home great cheerfulness and serenity, as if an unseen power lifted him into a higher region, everything seemed too small and dark, frequent protestations that he saw something unearthly and could accomplish great things, he saw spirits dancing around him as happy as himself, hearing very acute, thirst, cataleptic and epileptic attacks.

Sudden oppression, everything seemed too narrow, with distortion of features, pallor, the oppression increasing to anxiety, with feeling as if boiling blood mounted to his head. Heaviness after going to bed, or drowsiness, could hardly lift his arms or legs. *Desire to lie down in daytime.* Disinclination to physical labor. Indolence in morning; luxurious I., with erotic delirium. **Weakness; from a short walk;** < about knees; *so that he could hardly speak, and soon deep sleep;* of whole body, arms heavy, a kind of fainting, as after loss of blood; limbs rigid, and he became cataleptic, feet cold and insensible to hot applications, subsequently the anæsthesia extended over the whole body, with rapid automatic movements of hands, at times portions of the head and whole body seemed petrified, so that he could not move these parts, then they relaxed, the brain seemed suddenly changed to marble, eyes semed as hard as marble.

Felt as if under the influence of an opiate. Felt drunk. Rigidity. Torpidity. Numbness; creeping through body and limbs. Paralytic feeling of whole body caused by candle-light, with stupefaction of senses, compression of brain, and everything appears without color. Collapse. Syncope as soon as he closes his eyes. It affects most the nervous and sanguine temperaments, the bilious nearly as much, but the lymphatic only slightly. Aggravation on r. side. Amelioration from rest; from washing in cold water.

Clinical.—Cataleptic spasm of muscles of neck. Tetanic spasms about the jaws.

Mind.—Lunacy. **Imagines that he hears music, shuts his eyes and is lost in delicious thought.** *Imagined that he was gradually swelling.* Extreme exaggeration of the duration of time and extent of space, a few seconds seemed ages, the utterance of a word as long as a drama, a few rods seemed a distance so great that it could never be passed, things in the room seemed to recede to a vast distance, the ceiling was raised, and the adjoining room seemed an enormous depth below him though on the same floor.

Ridiculous speculative ideas; or he imagines that he hears sublime music or sees magnificent architecture or beautiful landscapes. Imagined that he was a huge saw darting up and down, cutting off planks, that he was a bottle of soda-water, running to and fro, then a huge hippopotamus, then a giraffe, then a huge fan, surrounded by clouds of music and prefume, that his leg was a tin case filled with stair-rods that rattled as he walked, or that the other leg extended hundreds of feet into the air, on which he was compelled to hop as he walked. Imagined that he was a pump-log, through which a stream of hot water was playing, that he was an inkstand and that the ink might spill over the bed, that he could open and shut his cover, could see and feel the ink splash against his sides.

He seemed transparent, fire seemed to shine through him and warm the marrow in his bones, was conscious of the blood coursing through his veins, and everything within him trembled with pleasure. Could trace the circulation of the blood along every inch, knew when every valve opened and shut, the beating of the heart was so audible that he wondered why others did not hear it. He seemed possessed of a dual nature, one of which watched the other from a height while it passed through various phases of delirium, or one seemed thinking of something while he laughed at it. He seemed a third person looking at himself and his friend. The soul seemed separated from the body. His voice seemed as if not his own. Imagines that he is possessed of infinite knowledge and power of vision, that he has creative power, that he is very eloquent, that he possesses the wealth of the world and has a benevolence equal to his wealth.

Excitement; in afternoon, with irritation; with dancing, laughing, talking nonsense, knew that he was talking nonsense, but could not stop without an effort of the will, which he did not care to make. Sees dancing satyrs and mandarins. Dancing before a looking-glass, with laughing and singing. Sings and extemporizes both words and music. Shouts, leaps into the air and claps his hands for joy. Whistles and wishes to hug every one. Delightful ecstasy was converted into horrors, which were < by darkness. Ecstasies of pleasure, of agonies, of terror and pain are constantly followed by more gentle forms of delirious excitement or hallucinations.

Sees diabolical imps, who terrify him or make him laugh at their grotesque grimaces. All around and within seems a mystery, and is terrifying. Imagines that men are bribed to kill him. Idea that he was about to die; and be dissected. Looks under beds and tables, unlocks and relocks doors, for he fancies that he hears strange noises, and that thieves are in the house. Melancholic delirium. Thinks that every one he meets has some secret sorrow and wishes to sympathize with him. The most familiar objects seem strange. Did not know where he was, or whether men generally existed, or for what purpose he existed. Difficulty in refraining from saying and doing unusual things. Speaks uncontrollably loud now and then, and then corrects himself. Sensations exalted and magnified, the pulse seems strong, ideas flow rapidly, pictures seem larger. There seems to be no possible freak of the imagination that is not aroused by this drug.

Exaltation of spirits. Loquacity. Incoherent talk. Uncontrollable laughter, until the face is purple and back aches; *immoderate L., full of fun and mischief;* immoderate, and he accents the last syllable in all words; spasmodic, < flatus rising in throat, threatening to choke him and make him vomit, without nausea. Tendency to make puns and to talk about grammatical questions. *Constant theorizing.* **Anguish > open air, with oppression**; *A. and despair.* Despair and fear of being eternally lost, the name of God seemed terrible, demons clutched him, he seemed walking in a vast arena, encircled by tremendous walls. **Fear that he should become insane**; *F. of darkness;* of approaching death; of spectres; of the coal-scuttle; at the sight of bright objects, asked for water, carried it convulsively to his mouth, but was unable to swallow; of things real and unreal, alternating with delight. Dread of congestion, apoplexy, hæmorrhage, and a multiplicity of deaths.

Depression of spirits; and disinclination to study; from which he could arouse himself only by imitating the movements and follies of others. *Crying and moaning.* Weeping, the tears seem blood. Passionate. Intolerant of contradiction. Sarcastic. Tendency to blaspheme. Reckless feeling. Suspicious. Lonely. Taciturn. Indifference to the world and to the dictates of conscience. No power of will.

Capable of great effort. Ideas quick and sensations pleasant. *Thoughts crowded upon each other so that he could not recall any thought or event.* Remembered the events and ideas of his childhood. **Ideas fixed. Absent-minded.** Writes one word for another. Repeats words and sentences when writing. Unable to collect his thoughts. *Forgetful; of what he intended to write or speak, so that he cannot finish a sentence; of his last words and ideas, and spoke in a low tone and thick voice, as if tired. Inability to read, partly from dreamy spells and partly because he had not full power of vision.* Stupidity. Deathly stupor in the reaction. Cataleptic state. Lethargy in attacks, with unconsciousness.

Unconsciousness every few minutes; U. caused by the candle-light; when listening to the piano, is seemingly gently raised to a great height, when the music becomes celestial, on regaining consciousness his head is bent forward, neck stiff, with ringing in ears; at night, alternating with delirium and semi-consciousness; of the centre of gravity, and seeming on the point of falling.

Clinical.—Delirium tremens, with misapprehensions concerning time and space. Delirium, with great exaltation of mind, great flow of language, very exalted ideas and florid notions. Delirium, he laughs at trifles, is inclined to be very foolish.

Head.—Frequent involuntary shaking. Jerking extending to l. outer canthus. Aching; on waking; in the sunlight; > coffee; < vertex, with beating; *heavy throbbing through it,* with sensation of a blow on occiput and nape. Bruised feeling. Gradual expansive feeling in brain, as if I were apart from myself and dwelling in a new world, within the cavity of the skull. Crisping sensation in brain on falling asleep or on waking; seething or C. of blood in brain like sheet-lightning. Confusion. Fulness; with drowsiness and flushes in face; with sharp intermittent pain under r. parietal bone. Tension. Compression of brain in a warm room, with paralytic feelings. Constriction, with inability to think; C. as from an iron skull-cap. Swollen sensation. *Heaviness; with unconsciousness and falling;* with wandering of mind and apprehension that he was going to faint; *on brain, forcing him to stoop.* **Shocks through brain on regaining consciousness.** Felt light, mind very active, yet apparently sluggish. **Vertigo**; *on rising; on rising, with stunning pain in occiput, and he falls;* on bending forward or walking; with backward inclination of head.

Forehead.—*Jerking in r. side and towards interior and back part of head. Pain; throbbing; drawing; < over eyes;* heavy; heavy, in brain, < l. side. Heaviness in sinciput, with confusion; H. in sinciput, with heat; H., with fulness and with pressure at root of nose and over eyes, headache over l. eye, pain in vertex and l. side of occiput. Pressure on F. and vertex, which seemed to cause his slowness of speech and action; outward over eye in afternoon. Fulness as if it would burst.

Temples.—*Sticking in r.; gradually changing to pressive pain. Pain; < r.;* burning; darting, throbbing, in r., and from occiput to forehead; throbbing, extending anteriorly in r., with warmth about head, cheeks red and hot, nausea, increased during the warmth, vomiting of mucus and bitter-tasting water, with scratching in throat, afterwards dulness in occiput, sick feeling in the whole body, necessity to go to bed on account of weariness and heaviness in limbs.

Sides.—*Pain in r.;* intermittent, near anterior-inferior angle of l. parietal bone. Feeling as if something were going around from before backward in r. Boring in r. parietal protuberance at 11 A.M.

Occiput.—Pain; before the convulsive movements, which changed into heat, then coldness, in consequence of which his hands were carried automatically to that spot and held there, as if it were difficult to detach them. Surging towards forehead. Fulness in r. side of cerebellum, < shaking head, with pain.

Scalp.—Sore to touch. Feeling as if tightly stretched, and in skin of forehead. Crawling on vertex.

Clinical.—Migraine as if the head were opening and shutting, cannot realize her identity. Uræmic headache, feeling as if head were opening and shutting.

Eyes.—Fixed. Staring wildly, and he seemed to have awakened suddenly. Wild-looking. Brilliant. Injected. Swollen and inflamed; S. and dull. Divergent squint. Has an expression of cunning and merriment. Appeared small and drunken on looking at himself in the mirror. Pressure on r. Heaviness. Heat; and smarting. Weakness.

Lachrymation. Pupils contracted; and insensible; dilated. Pain at back of ball. Distended feeling in balls, as if starting out of head, they ached on trying to read. Lids, twinkling; drooping, then coma; contractions; distention of bloodvessels of upper, with heat; prickling in margins; soreness of upper; heaviness; burning of edges, with itching. *Jerking in external canthus and in lid.* Cool burning-stinging in l. inner canthus and in adjacent side of nose. Sharp pain in r. inner canthus, extending up side of head, back, and out. Inflammation of caruncula lachrymalis, with swelling. **Injected vessels in conjunctiva;** *in a triangular patch from each internal canthus to cornea, < night;* with heat, greater in eyes than in lids. Conjunctivitis. Pain from bottom of orbit through brain, and in ear; P. as from a blow over r. orbit.

Vision.—**Letters run together when reading.** *Twinkling, trembling and glimmering.* A large spot hovers above vision of l. eye. Violet spots on the paper when reading. Pea-green circles around the candle-light. Ugly faces assume a pleasing expression. Clairvoyance; on waking suddenly at midnight, although the room was dark he could see everything about him and could read the titles of books twelve or fifteen feet off, this passed off as soon as he had urinated. Photopsia. Sensitiveness of r. eye to light, with lachrymation. Confused. Weak. Lost, except a small spot where he looks.

Ears.—Jerking or electric shocks. Stinging in l. Tearing in r., > pressure. Boring in r.; above r. and back of it. *Aching;* in l., with singing. **Throbbing and fulness.** Stuffed feeling in r. Burning. **Buzzing;** in r.; **and ringing.** *Noise like boiling water. Singing;* in l.; when lying and dozing, > rising; *periodical, always renewed during the dreamy spells.* Music is intensely agreeable. His own voice sounded a long way off. Hearing acute. Hearing difficult.

Nose.—Pain at root; with fulness. Dry, feverish feeling in l. nostril. Sneezing. Blew coagulated blood from r. nostril.

Face.—Expression drowsy and stupid. *Wearied expression.* He thinks his expression must be altered, as people look at him more than usual. Intoxicated look. Red; from mounting stairs. Pale; and anxious; as in faintness, > fresh air. Stinging on r. side as if stuck with pins, on scratching it changes to another part of the body. Pressure about posterior borders of both malar-bones. Warm tingling over l. side. Skin, especially on forehead and chin, felt drawn tight. Insensible, but to the hand (which was moved with difficulty) it felt hard. Drawing in muscles of mastication. Jaws, constriction; sensation as if muscles were drawn tight; desire to forcibly compress them; immovable before falling asleep. **Lips glued together;** trembling; jerking of lower.

Mouth.—Teeth. *Grinding in sleep.* Boring in r. lower molars, > pressure, < grinding them together. Aching in r. lower molars; at root of first r. upper molar; in upper T., with feeling as if loose. Felt no pain while conscious that the toothache was present. Heavy throbbing at roots. Soreness at union of incisors and gums, < inside, with sensitiveness to touch of tongue. Clenched feeling in r.

Tongue.—White and sickly-looking. Coated white; in morning, with bad taste, as if he had been intoxicated over night. Viscid mucus on its upper surface. Covered with dry mucus. Thick mucus before rising, with dry feeling as if scalded. Felt as if covered with pepper. Stinging-burning as from a blister, at r. anterior pillar of fauces. Sensation in T. and throat as if covered with a dry, soft body. Dryness. Metallic sensation on r. half. *Stammering and stuttering.* Lips failed of utterance, as if paralyzed.

Mouth dry; and lips; all night, with thirst; with thirst;. without thirst; with froth; radiating from back of throat, *without thirst;* and in fauces, so that he can hardly speak or swallow. **Saliva white, thick, frothy and sticky.** Foam. Thick, tasteless salivation. Breath hot. *All food is extremely palatable.* Taste metallic; with dry sensation and exudation of gummy mucus; coppery.

Throat.—In morning hawks up glairy lumps, with a spot of blood in each. Pressure in tonsils. Sensation of a fleshy body at pit, impeding deglutition. Sensation of a plug rising in it, choking him. **Dryness; with thirst for cold water;** in open air, with rawness, so that he could not smoke a cigar; and roughness. Burning; on inspiration; in pharynx and œsophagus.

Stomach.—Appetite increased; at dinner; great for bread; ravenous at tea; little; lost. Thirst for water, and yet dread of it. Eructations; when moving; of tasteless gas. Nausea; after eating, with efforts to vomit; with scraping in pharynx and eructations; with heaviness and pressure over eyes.

Cutting griping. Agonizing clutching.. Crampy pain. **Pain at cardiac orifice,** > pressure; in epigastrium, > eructations of tasteless gas; in pit, then pricking, > eating; in pit, nervous grumbling sensation in stomach every few minutes, extending into thorax. *Swollen feeling when eating, with oppression of chest, as if he would suffocate, forcing him to loosen his clothes.* Weight. Burning; changing to aching, with oppression of chest. Cold feeling. Sinking.

Abdomen.—Distention; > belching wind. Rumbling on lying down. Stitches above symphysis pubis; in r. hypochondrium when breathing.

Rectum and Stool.—Tenesmus. *Sensation in anus as if he were sitting on a ball, as if anus and part of urethra were filled with a hard ball.* Liquid stools besides frequent ineffectual urging. Painless, yellow diarrhœa; frequently, and heat in abdomen. Constipation. Stool omitted.

Urinary Organs.—*Urging after micturition; U., with much straining;* with copious discharge; with contracted sensation in genito-urinary organs and strangury; *ineffectual;* constant; no desire to urinate the first day, constant desire the next day. **Dribbling after the stream ceases.** *He has to wait some time before the urine flows.* He has to force out the last drops with his hands. *Frequent micturition; in evening, with burning pain;* at night, urine copious; at night, urine dark; *but in small quantities;* and urine copious; with difficulty at the beginning. The stream suddenly stops and then flows again. Could not voluntarily retain the urine.

Urethra.—Excessive discharge of prostatic fluid at night, during a hard evacuation. Inflammation of orifice. **Stitches; before, during and after micturition;** in end; in end in evening and night; and in anus; *sending a thrill to cheeks and hands.* **Burning before, during and after micturition;** *during micturition, with pain; at orifice during and after micturition;* < evening. *Feeling as if there were a gonorrhœal discharge. Uneasiness; in U. and penis, with burning and frequent calls to urinate.*

Urine.—**Copious, colorless;** *C. and clear, light-colored;* and clear; at times, and again in small quantities, with burning and biting. Scanty and dark. Thick, red.

Genital Organs.—Oozing of white glairy mucus on squeezing glans. *Penis relaxed and shrunken.* Sticking-burning soreness of glans. *Itching of glans. Chordee. Erections when riding, walking and sitting still, not caused by amorous thoughts;* painful E. after coition. Itching of scrotum, with burning. **Satyriasis.** Thrill prolonged, with more than a dozen ejaculations of semen; thrill consists of intense burning, with no ejaculation of semen. During coition scarcely any emission or sensation, but afterwards acute pain in loins. *Menstruation profuse, lasting five days.* Nymphomania. It excites desire in women, but causes sterility.

Clinical.—Chordee during gonorrhœa. Uterine colic, with great nervous agitation.

Respiratory Organs.—Voice high; low; unable to measure the compass and volume of the voice when speaking. **Cough rough, scratching the sternum;** C. dry, hard; dry, becoming almost like a bark. Breathing stertorous. Suffocation from least pressure on stomach. Dyspnœa. *It required a great effort to inspire deeply.* Respiration rapid; slow. Desire for open air.

Chest.—Stitches extending from both nipples through chest. Cutting behind sternum, < swallowing. Pain. Anxiety, with rapid, irregular, small beats of heart. Constriction; on a line with heart, when ascending steps quickly. *Oppression;* < *mounting stairs; with deep labored breathing, he feels suffocated and has to be fanned;* with tightness in pit of stomach. Heaviness when walking. Burning.

Heart.—*Stitches, with oppression, the latter* > *deep breathing;* S. in small spots; *as with the prongs of a fork;* intermittent, on surface. *Pain; all night, with dyspnœa.* Auguish. Weight in region. Oppression of præcordium; O. until he went to bed about 3 A.M., with sick feeling at heart, the beats embarrassed, sharp and quick, weak and small, its contractions jerky. Sick feeling. Feeling as if it rubbed against the ribs on breathing. *Palpitation; waking him.* Beats intense and rapid; small, uneven and anxious, when sitting or stooping. Impulse weak.

Pulse.—Rapid; and full, bounding; and irregular, small; and irregular, afterwards small, contracted; but feeble. **Slow;** and small, with long intermissions; in carotids and temporal arteries, and weak. Strong. Full and bounding. Feeble; and intermittent, afterwards rapid. Tracings showed irregularlities in tension and frequency, with increase in prominence of waves. Oscillations singularly marked in tracing, tension increased, amplitude and frequency diminished, later increased cardiac excitement at beginning of systole, with some obstruction, later diminished tension and oscillation of cerebro-spinal implication.

Neck.—Surging like waves into head, seeming to try to press it forward. Beating in nape. Rigidity of nape.

Back.—Feeling as if a stream of warm water gradually stole up it to the brain. Reflex movements of spine, a wavelike motion beginning at dorsal region and extending to pelvis, alternately raising and depressing first the dorsum, afterwards the pelvis. Stunning pain between scapulæ. *Stitches in kidneys. Pain in kidneys when laughing; in kidneys, keeping him awake at night.* Burning in kidneys. Sensation in sacrum as if a red-hot iron rod passed up spine to the atlas, around occiput, over eyes from r. side stopping at l. ear, leaving a charred feeling, taking six hours to perform the passage.

Extremities.—Gesticulatory convulsions of arms and legs, and by degrees his symptoms assumed the appearance of hydrophobia. Contractions of arms and legs. Shuddering through all, with weight in occiput and tetanic intermittent contractions of muscles of nape. Pains in joints; in wrists and ankles. Feel very large. Leaden feeling, as if he could not move them. Heaviness of forearms and feet. Weariness in r.; W., with disposition to go to bed; *almost amounting to paralysis,* < *l.* Stiff sensation. Pleasant numbness. **Paralysis of lower and of r. arm.**

Upper Extremities.—Shoulder. Shooting pain from l. to tip of middle finger, producing in the finger soreness as in neuralgic pains, the pain at one time concentrated itself in the pulpy part of the ungual phalanx, at another in the upper part of the axillary border of the scapula, whence it radiated like the spokes of a wheel, for two inches. **Pain across S. and spine, forcing him to stoop;** P. in outer edge of trapezius, at 4 P.M. Lameness; as if beaten, < l.

Arm.—Trembling; and hands. Pain in front of arm and back of elbow. **Agreeable thrilling, and in hands.** Heaviness in l. arm and hand, with swollen feeling, at other times pain as if the parts were pressed apart by blood. Inability to raise r., with coldness of r. hand.

Sudden pain in r. upper arm, with constriction, numbness and tingling, as if electrified, extending down arm and to axilla, gradually passing to feet and then to head, chiefly felt in arm and axilla, it came on and off like a wave, it stopped at the mesial line (the r. side was next the fire). Pain as from fatigue in bend of r. elbow at 7 A.M. Weight in forearms so that he cannot raise his hands. Pain in l. wrist. Constant rubbing of hands. Hands shake so that he cannot write. Hands feel monstrously large. Fingers suddenly red, with burning and prickling in joints; sticking in F.; aching in joints.

Lower Extremities.—Gait stumbling; balancing; unsteady, as of one who tried to keep down, for he felt as if there were springs in his knees. Incoördination of movements. Lameness of r., with drawings in calves. Unable to support him; r. suddenly gives out and he falls. Numbness of l. and of foot. *Paralyzed feeling in r. when walking.* **Paralysis**; *preventing him from ascending stairs, with stiffness and tired aching in knees.*

Pain in r. hip; l. femur; above l. knee, with itching; laming, in r. knee, with drawing and aching. Tearing in l. knee. Patellæ feel as if dragged down. R. leg frequently shot to the left, missing the plank on which he was walking. Cramp in calves, preventing movement of legs, or causing them to be distended, or to take a sudden jump. Pain in l. leg near external malleolus when lying on back. **Agreeable thrilling from knees down, with sensation as if a bird's claws were clasping knees.** Weakness of l. leg; painful W. of legs. Pain in r. ankle in evening.

Dragged the feet when walking. Contractions of tendons of feet. Sticking in soles. *Pains in soles as if he trod on spikes, extending to hips, on attempting to walk < r., with drawing pains in calves,* the pains forced him to limp and to cry out. Bone pains in metatarso-phalangeal joints of r. foot. *Numb feeling in l. sole, then in foot, extending to the whole limb;* in joints of feet. Feet go to sleep. *Sticking in joints of l. toes, < great toe; in ball of l. great toe, with aching; in joints of l. great toe, with aching.* Pain in joints of r. great toe in forenoon and evening.

Skin.—Formication. Itching of nose; sole; face, shoulder, abdomen and feet, > scratching. Insensibility.

Sleep.—Sleepiness; *in daytime;* in afternoon; in evening; on going to bed, he imagined that his finger-nails were of the size of plates, very curved, and on opening and shutting fingers they seemed to slide over one another like a fan, and tapping them on a hard substance caused a delicious sensation; with feeling as of a cold wind on occiput and nape; with alternate sleeping and waking, but the waking was a pleasant dreamy state; but inability to sleep, the mind wandered rapidly from one subject to another, he seemed to be dreaming with open eyes, for he noticed everything around him, then headache till late at night. Alternations of dozing and waking; in afternoon; after dinner, > coffee. **Sound sleep**; *with melancholy dreams.* Prolonged sleep. Slept in his chair. When asleep he looked stiff, as if dead, with lower jaw down. Indisposition to rise in morning.

Sleeplessness. Waking in night; before midnight in semi-consciousness, with inability to move, palpitation, breathing slow, deep, labored and intermittent, and feeling as if dying; before midnight, imagines that he is going to be choked, cries and groans, for some time, when objects appear their respective sizes, then sleep; after midnight, with thirst; at 6 A.M., with fulness of head and heaviness of body; frequent, with mild, pleasant dreams. *Talking in sleep. Starting of limbs in sleep, which woke him, when he feared that he would have a fit.* Screaming in sleep.

Nightmare every night as soon as he fell asleep. Dreams, with open eyes; *D. of danger; vexatious; prophetic; voluptuous, with erections and emissions;* vivid, sometimes ecstatic; ugly; *of dead bodies;* wild, shapeless, waking him in agitation and perspiration; various, delightful. *Dreamy attacks periodically in the daytime.* Dreamless sleep.

Fever.—*Coldness;* and shivering, with external heat. Shuddering. Shaking chill, with chattering of teeth, coldness of body and limbs, cold sweat, tired feeling in limbs, aching in joints, dry mouth, with thick, white, sticky saliva, thirst, drinking of large quantities of water, staggering and falling on attempting to walk, thumping in head and heart, inability to rise from stooping on account of weight on cerebellum, neck and shoulder, blindness, except at a small point immediately where he looks, pulse very slow and full, seeming descent of the ceiling to crush him, belief that he is dying, but inability to cry for help, falling to the floor, and lying unconscious, then sleep for three nights and three days afterwards.

Coldness of surface. *Coldness of face, nose and hands after dinner;* hands and feet after dinner, < nose, with shivering; across root of nose at 9 A.M. when leaning forward writing, > moving; in small of back and between shoulders; limbs; limbs, with at times trembling; *r. hand,* with stiffness and numbness of r. thumb.

Heat; when lying. Fever boiled in my blood and every heart-beat was like the stroke of a colossal engine. Burning in skin; and dryness. Heat in forehead; over front of body and arms; face; in a line from l. side of lip to chin; in soles; moist, in palms. Cool burning in l. side of border of lip and point of nose. Pleasant warmth beginning in spine and extending through body.

Sweat; < on front of body; **sticky, in drops on forehead**; none.

Cannabis Sativa.

A tincture of the tops of the fresh herb of Cannabis Sativa L. (grown in Europe or America) is used.

General Action.—As compared with Cannabis indica we see much less mental disturbance (less of the peculiar gum "Hashish" in the plant used) and more effects due to the other constituents of the plant, etherial oil and *Nitrate of Potash* (the latter is found in an unusual amount in the plant).

Allies.—Cannab. ind., Nux vom.

Generalities.—Secretions greatly increased. She spun around on one foot and began to walk. Gesticulations. Spasmodic gestures. Seemed affected with chorea when walking. Jerking as if in blood of head, chest and stomach. Tearing constrictive pressure in l. knee, in forehead and over all parts of body. Tearing pushes and tearing, deeply-penetrating stitches in many parts, especially in limbs. Pinching superficially here and there in flesh. Sick feeling in whole body, with necessity to lie down on account of weariness and heaviness in limbs. General discomfort an hour after breakfast, especially in abdomen, as if inflated, with sticking cutting there and with general chilliness. Uneasiness, with sudden forgetfulness of what he wished to write. Indolent sensation in whole body. Indolence, with weariness, yawning and stretching. Weakness; greater in morning after an almost unbroken sleep than on lying down the previous evening; after slight motion; after eating, with indolence, everything affected him, even talking and writing; with sleepiness; with giving way of knees and aching in them; sudden, especially of lower limbs, with staggering on slightest motion of body, but more steady when walking. General stiffness.

Mind.—About 4.30 P.M. took a large dose of the extract, about 7 P.M. while writing a prescription he became oblivious of surrounding objects, but went on writing, when the receipt was finished he suddenly recollected where he was and apologized for remaining so long, but was assured he had been only a few minutes, about 7.30 he returned home, now he was greatly excited, the hilarity rapidly increased, it was a feeling of inner joyousness, the system felt as if fatigue were forever banished, the mind gladly ran riot, was disposed to laugh, to make comic gestures, a frequently recurring fancy was to imitate with the arms the motions of a fiddler, and with the lips the tunes he was supposed to be playing, he knew that he was acting foolishly, but could not control himself, once he raised his head and exclaimed, "Oh, the mountains, the mountains!" about 8 numbness in limbs began, with general uneasiness and fear lest he had taken an overdose, he walked constantly about the house, the whole surface felt flushed and warm, mouth and throat were dry, legs felt as if not a part of the body, pulse 120, full and strong, fear as of impending death, legs felt as if waxen pillars and to his hand felt very firm, as if the muscles were in a state of tonic contraction, then began marked "spells," when all connection seemed severed between himself and the external world, but on coming out of them it was not a void on which he looked back, but a period of active, though aimless life, a chaos of disjointed ideas, these spells lasted from a few seconds to one or two minutes, but seconds seemed hours and hours seemed infinite, was perfectly conscious between the paroxysms, would look at his watch, and then after an hour or two, as he thought, would look again and find that scarcely five minutes had elapsed, when most lucid there was a duplex action in regard to time, he would think it was so long since a certain event and then reason would say No, it had been only a few minutes, your thoughts are caused by the hemp, but he was never able to shake off this sense of the prolongation of time even for a minute, an exaggeration of distance was noticed only once, and that was when standing in the door watching the approach of the doctor in the street, limbs grew cold, on attempting to walk up-stairs the lower half of the legs seemed made of lead, felt as if an evil spirit had control of the whole of him except the will-power and was in conflict with that, felt as if his only chance was to struggle against the paroxysms, hopeless anguish and utter weariness, once or twice nightmare sensation, felt himself mounting upward, expanding, dissolving into space, overwhelmed by unutterable despair, then with tremendous effort he shook this off and started up with the shuddering thought, Next time you will not be able to throw this off, and what then? after an emetic vomited freely, without nausea and without much relief, about midnight went up-stairs to bed, legs and feet were so heavy that he could scarcely move them, did not recollect being undressed, went to sleep immediately, on waking early in the morning the mind was at first clear, but the paroxysms soon returned and recurred until late in afternoon, all day anæsthesia of skin, urine increased. (Compare Cann. ind.).

Agitation. Excitement after drinking wine and water, with cheerfulness, afterwards the former nausea and discomfort returned; E., then sensation of ease and comfort, with pleasing languor, then inebriation. Unsteadiness of mood. He became almost violent, when he assumed a sad, preoccupied air. Anxiety. Anger at trifles, with frenzy. Fretfulness, < afternoon. Pleasure in nothing, indifference to everything. Fear at slightest noise; of the bed, in which he afterwards lay down. Sadness; in forenoon, liveliness in afternoon. Desire, especially at dinner, for wine to enliven his depressed mood. Gayety, as from intoxication. Disposition to laugh (Cannab. ind., Nux mos., Nux vom.). Constant laughter mingled with tears. Animation, with congestion of face, great loquacity, and inclination of head to r. and l. Loquacity. Constant murmuring of unintelligible words. Whistling and singing.

Mistakes in writing. Confusion of thought in afternoon and evening, with forgetfulness, heat and congestion of head, but coldness on going into open air. Wavering and uncertainty of mind, overwhelming vividness of ideas. Ideas remain stationary after fixing his mind long upon a subject. Ideas seem to stand still, with staring and absorption in higher thoughts, but is unconscious of them, with pain in parietal bones. Absent-minded. Wanting in reflective power, deficient in imagination, spiritless. Coma. Unconsciousness of the existence of the limbs, a sensation compared to that when under the influences of chloroform, without complete unconsciousness.

Head.—Aching; on moving head, and in nape of neck; piercing pain. Confusion; with heaviness and with pain in forehead and on eyes, so that his lids threaten to close. Heaviness. Tension. Throbbing, *with heat in it* and fever; T., with pain. Congestion when writing. Rush of blood; causing heat and flushes; causing pleasant warmth in it, with pain in temples. Intoxication. Vertigo; *when standing; when walking, with tendency to fall sideways* (Nux v.); as if head moved from one side to other; as if everything would turn around with her. Head seemed to describe a circular movement, which extended to the whole body, so that he fell. Dreamy in head for several days as if the room turned around with her.

Frontal pain; *beneath eminence, extending to occiput;* drawing, through forehead. Throbbing outward beneath l. frontal eminence, then stupefying pressure. *Compression from margin of orbits to temples.* Heaviness in sinciput till evening, with heat in it. Constriction in sinciput. Visible throbbing in r. temporal artery in morning. *Pressure in temples;* throbbing headache extending forward into r. T., with warmth about head, red and hot cheeks, with nausea < in the warmth. Tickling spasm in T. Compression in T. Pain in vertex; as from a stone upon it. Pressure internally in side of head when leaning the other side of head against a wall. Pain in r. occipital bone; drawing, in occiput, extending to ears. Tension in O., then in sinciput, *lastly in temples.* Painful pimples, sensitive to touch, and on nape and behind ears. Crawling on scalp.

Eyes.—Injected; and brilliant. Cornea obscured. *Pressure from behind the eyes forward. Sensation of spasmodic drawing.* Sensation of sand in r. in evening, with necessity to rub it. Burning evenings. Weak sensation with indistinct sensation. Pupils dilated; alternately D. and contracted. Tearing in upper lid. Pressure on lids, that makes them difficult to open, with sticking in orbits. Heat in external canthi, with prickling. Sensation as if eyebrows were pressed down. On attempting to write found that the characters made with the pen were very fine. Vision of a flame playing before eyes; of a circle of white flaming zigzags on r. side near field of vision, so that only a portion of objects is seen indistinctly; of vertical shining, white points, that move in lines from one eye to the other, mornings on waking, then flickering before eyes, and light and dark dots floating in different directions.

Ears.—Inflamed pimple, painful to touch, in r., with swelling of meatus, afterwards discharge of pus mixed with blood. Stitches in mastoid process; in external meatus while chewing; outward in l.; at 10 A.M., with pain in throat, then cold and heat alternating with headache, < notion or stooping, > supporting herself on r. side, with feeling as if head were shaken, stitches in l. side of head, near skull and opposite to it, S. behind r. ear very violent, the condition lasting at night in sleep, so that she groaned, complained and often awoke. Pain behind r. as if pushed with a blunt instrument; in external as if drawn out of head; jerking, in r. tympanum, extending to shoulder. Smarting in external cartilage, which may have been pressed upon at night in bed. Throbbing. Throbbing dragging, extending almost to cheeks, > stooping, returning on becoming erect. Sensation as if membrane were stretched before them. Roaring before E. Ringing. Loud singing. Sound in l. as if the string of an instrument were struck.

Nose.—Itching-swelling on wing. Stupefying pressure on root as with a dull point. *Dryness;* with heat. Warmth, as if it would bleed. Sneezing, with sensation of stopped coryza, although air passed through the nose. Bleeding; in spurts till faintness.

Face.—Pale; and sunken; and he fell prostrated. Red; l. cheek, but not hot, r. pale, with pain in r. tooth. Grimaces as in chorea. Contraction of muscles. Efforts to laugh. Stupid expression. Drawing pressure in l. malar-bone. Stupefying compressive pain in l. side of chin, affecting l. teeth. Pulsations in various parts, especially in l. buccinator. Eruption on red part of lips and in corner of mouth. Spasmodic contraction of jaws. Pricking in l. ramus of lower jaw, then drawing.

Mouth.—Teeth. Crumbling of a hollow one and the pieces were like hard leather. Shooting in several at the same time. Cramplike pain in l. lower. Drawing pain in a hollow one, < evenings, with swelling of gums; D. in a hollow one after a vexation, changing after trying to suck air from it to sticking. Drawing in a hollow one, < touch of anything acid. Dulness, as after acids. Painful bunch on r. upper jaw, on side of palate, as from an ulcerated tooth. The gum around a hollow broken tooth is inflamed, swollen and painful, with drawing in root.

Tongue coated. Inability to speak as usual, at times he missed a word, at another he lost his voice, towards evening at one time a torrent of words, at another faltering, so that he spoke the same word ten times in the same breath, at times his idea was anxiously repeated and he was angry if he could not repeat it in the same words. Dryness; and of lips and throat; < evening, with sticky saliva, loss of thirst and heat of hands; of mouth, with tenacious mucus in throat; of palate in morning. Taste lost.

Throat.—Difficult hawking of mucus. Rising of water, which gets into trachea, so that he is obliged to swallow. Pain as if sore, < mornings in bed, > after rising by discharge of a lump of mucus, with dryness. Dryness. Swallowing difficult on account of absence of saliva, with inability to eat.

Stomach.—Eating like a glutton, and after the meal appearance of astonishment. Appetite increased evenings, with discomfort after much eating. A. lost. Cocoa relished tolerably at breakfast, but he can take only a little and feels neither hungry nor satisfied, with growling and rumbling in abdomen, cramp in stomach, when he thinks of what he could eat he has no desire for anything and yet his stomach feels empty.

Eructations of air; of bitter, sour, acrid fluid; of a bitter sour fluid; with taste of bread after breakfast. Hiccough in morning. Nausea; in morning on waking, < lying on r. side, > lying on l. side; on waking, < thinking of what he has eaten; > drinking coffee, with inclination to hawk mucus and with vomiting; with discomfort, weakness, empty eructations, fulness in abdomen, no appetite, but tolerable relish when he eats; rising into throat, when nearly satisfied with food that he relished. Retching; rising from pit of stomach into throat. Choking suddenly rising into throat, as from acidity of stomach. Vomiting profusely; of tough acid mucus after coffee; difficult, of mucus, bitterish at first, then flat, which left the teeth dull, then hunger and eating with relish; V. of slimy, bitter water, with scraping in throat, then dulness and confusion in occiput; (green bilious vomiting).

Stitches in front near pit, just below ribs, > bending trunk forward or backward, soon returning. Cutting across upper part after stooping; in pit. Cramp; mornings. Pinching in pit. Ulcerating pain on touch, > on eating. *Anxiety in pit, with oppression of breath, palpitation,* rising of something warm into throat, with arrest of breath, as if something lodged in trachea, and flushes of heat. Heartburn. Feeling as if he had taken cold, < forenoon, with movings in abdomen and griping. Discomfort all the morning, sleepy yawning, indolence and disinclination to everything. Heaviness in epigastrium.

Abdomen.—Emission of almost odorless flatus every morning; noisy emission in morning. Incarceration of flatus till evening, with pain. Movings, then stitches in l. side, extending to ear. Shaking of intestines on violent motion of arms. Fulness, compelling deep breathing. Pinching stitches. Cutting, > drinking cold water. Pinching as if to stool. Griping. Pain before stool; as before menses. Bruised pain. *Painful jerks, as from something living, moving from one place to another* (Crocus), *with drawing from l. hip-bone across to r. and thence into knee, still the pain remained in hip, where it was a tearing, pushing pain.* Shivering as if cold water moved in it. Complete loss of tone of intestines, not overcome by the strongest cathartics.

Pain in upper, then diarrhœa and smarting in anus. Anxious throbbing in upper. *Sticking in l. side, just below ribs;* in both sides in evening in bed, extending up back to between scapulæ and again down sides of A. Pinching on l. side near umbilicus and posteriorly near spine. Shocks in sides below ribs. Beating as with a hammer in l. side below ribs, extending towards back. Griping above umbilicus after eating. Pain in r. side near umbilicus like a beating outward. Sensation below U. as if he had taken cold, mornings from 8 till 10 o'clock, with movings in abdomen. Stretching outward in sides. Griping in hypogastrium, with cutting in loins. Pain in abdominal ring, with pressing outward, as if suppurating. Shocks above l. groin; jerking, in bend of groin, then distended sensation in region of abdominal ring and sensation as if ring were pressed outward. Tickling in parietes of hypogastrium.

Rectum.—Sticking, < walking, with contraction of sphincter. *Pain in R. and in sacral region while sitting, as if intestines would be pressed out.* Woke at 6 A.M., with desire for stool, but emission of only noisy flatus, urging to stool and micturition continued, after drinking coffee and smoking a hard stool, then nausea, that was only > keeping quiet. Urging to stool after dinner, then itching in R., with stitches; U., tenesmus and urinating continued so that he could hardly walk, after coffee and a pipe of tobacco crumbling stool and decrease of symptoms, but vomiting of coffee mixed with mucus.

Anus and Perineum.—*Constrictive pain in anus, with sensation as if thighs were drawn together, so that she must close them.* Sensation as if something cold trickled out of A. Itching of perineum.

Stool.—Thin and yellowish, she thought it was flatus, but it spurted away. Sometimes like diarrhœa, sometimes hard. Scanty, crumbling, with flatus. Suppressed. At irregular times, only a little is evacuated by straining, and tenesmus remains after it, sometimes sudden urging and a forcible pappy or liquid tool, with relief.

Urinary Organs.—*Urging to urinate, with pain;* frequent U., occasionally some burning, when the urine, especially in morning, is wheyey and turbid. *Micturition in a split stream.* Micturition difficult, profuse. Frequent M., with copious watery urine.

Urethra.—Orifice agglutinated by moisture which could be pressed out. Orifice inflamed, painful and hard to touch. Painless mucous discharge; and transparent; watery mucous discharge. *Stitches along when not urinating;* in end, > when urinating; anteriorly in orifice when not urinating; *jerking, posteriorly while standing;* burning, posteriorly while urinating; itching-tickling, in forepart. *Zigzag tearing in fibres.* Cutting in forepart when urinating. **Inflamed sensation, with soreness to touch, and with tensive pain during erection. Burning-biting pain, extending backward from orifice while urinating, posteriorly more sticking**; sticking-biting on urinating, biting when not urinating. *Pressure to urinate, especially in forepart of U., when not urinating.* **Burning while urinating** (Nux vom.), < **just after urinating**; < in evening; in orifice while urinating; in forepart while urinating; *at beginning and end of micturition;* from glans backward while urinating, biting after urinating. *Burning pain in forepart when not urinating* (Sulph.), *compelling him to urinate almost constantly, even when there is no more urine to pass* (Nux v.). Itching. Urine scanty. Red and turbid. White and turbid. Full of fibres, as of mucus, with pus.

Clinical.—In urethritis, with burning biting pain extending backward towards bladder when urinating, with frequent urging to urinate, the urine is scalding, with spasmodic closure of the sphincter of the bladder, cystitis in consequence of gonorrhœa, with bloody urine; gonorrhœa, great swelling of prepuce, etc. This drug is useful in gonorrhœa immediately following Aconite, provided Aconite has been indicated in the first few hours of the disease; cases which require Cannab. have less profuse discharges than those requiring Arg. nit., and usually there is much less swelling and inflammation about the glans penis, though the excessive swelling of the prepuce has proved a valuable indication in some cases. Many physicians are in the habit of using Cannab. sat. through the whole course of gonorrhœa, claiming that by its use the disease usually does not last more than ten days.

Sexual Organs.—Coldness, with warmth of rest of body. Stitch in r. side of mons veneris. Tensive pain in spermatic cord, and contraction of scrotum, with contractive sensation in it when standing. Swelling of prostate gland. Moisture about corona glandis. *Glans as dark red as the prepuce; G., covered with red spots. Penis painful as if excoriated or burnt when walking (with necessity to have it suspended).* Pain on r. side near penis like piercing shocks. *Penis swollen, without marked erections;* S. of glans and penis, a kind of insensible erection. Erections while coughing, then pain in urethra; *frequent E., then stitches in urethra;* frequent, during the day, only when sitting; excessive, mornings in bed, without desire, with cutting-sticking in orifice of urethra; excessive and painful, waking him at night after an embrace in evening without desire; no proper E. during an embrace in morning, especially towards the last, scarcely perceives the ejaculation.

Prepuce.—Swelling of r. side and lower part; of frænum and P., especially where it unites with frænum. Dark redness, heat and inflammation. Soreness on border and inner side. Burning, and in glans, applications of cold water cause soreness; corrrosive, in P. and urethra, in region of corona glandis, with sticking. Excoriation of margin. Itching beneath prepuce and on frænum, with redness and moisture behind corona glandis; agreeable, on border of prepuce and in orifice of urethra; disagreeable, on r. side near anterior margin, more internally, becoming agreeable during and after scratching.

Dragging in testicles when standing. Strangling pain in l. testicle in afternoon while walking, the epididymis and spermatic cord seem to swell and divide into lumps like soft beans and to fill out the upper part of the somewhat drooping scrotum. *Desire excited.* Indifference during the day, but after an embrace in evening excessive erections in morning and frequently during the day, < in forenoon. Aversion to coition.

Female.—Itching-sticking in vagina, and much leucorrhœa after an embrace. Miscarriage at the eighth month, with frightful convulsions. Profuse menses. Desire during morning sleep, but no pleasure during an embrace. Much pleasure during an embrace. Excitement without desire, then out of sorts, with aversion to sexual intercourse.

Respiratory Organs.—Voice frequently inaudible. Voice raised, with anxiety and complaint of pain in back. Voice changed, more like a clangor than the human voice. *Tough mucus in lower part of trachea in morning, with ability to loosen only a little, which he must swallow, after hawking and coughing scraping in trachea as if raw and sore, finally the mucus loosens itself, and he is obliged to hawk it up repeatedly.* Bronchial irritation, with repeated attacks of pulmonary congestion and inflammation, emaciation, premature decrepitude of frame, organic affection of lungs, then phthisis ending the existence.

Breathing oppressed; from tensive-pressive pains in middle of sternum, which was sore to touch, with sleepiness; < after dinner, > sitting down, with anxiety in chest and stitches between scapulæ; with pain over whole chest; with weight upon chest. Breathed with great force, with sensation of heat. Breathing rapid. Cough; *hacking, from pit of throat, with which a cold salt fluid is felt deep in throat;* in violent paroxysms; dry, violent.

Clinical.—Asthma, with mucous râles, extreme dyspnœa.

Chest.—Inflammation of male nipple, with itching and pain on touch, and beside the nipple a pustule which heals without opening. (Inflammation of chest, and lungs); of lungs, with incoherent talk. Stitches in external parietes; burning, in l. side, near ensiform cartilage. Cutting across external parietes. Pinching in lower part, under sternum, > bending backward, < bending forward, when it was worse on inspiration. *Digging beneath upper part of sternum, without oppression of breath.* Drawing pain in l. lowest ribs. *Oppression, with apprehension in throat and necessity to breathe deeply;* tensive O. in l. half, with jerkings, palpitation and anxiety. Scraping as from salt in morning, with necessity to loosen and swallow something. Roughness, scratching and dryness. Pushings or beatings in both sides, arresting breathing, most painful in region of heart; P. as with intermitting, dull stitches, a kind of pressing inward in l. side, without oppression of breathing. Throbbing against ribs of l. side. Hammering outward beneath one of the cartilages of ribs, near sternum.

Heart and Pulse.—Cardiac oppression. *H. beats as if it would fall out on moving body and on stooping, with warm sensation about it.* Palpitation. Pulse rapid; and irregular; and small; small and irregular; slow, scarcely perceptible.

Neck.—Stitches in lowest part, as with a knife. Pinching in muscles above gullet. Drawing, extending upward in cervical vertebræ; externally to ear, more like a pinching. Beating in nape.

Back.—Pain, arresting breath. Itching stitch near r. scapula, > scratching. Burning beneath r. scapula. Pinching in middle, extending towards abdomen. Slow intermittent stitches in l. side, beneath lowest ribs. Pain in loins, < after slightest exertion, obliging him to sit down and rest; at base of spine, extending along sciatic nerve and in hip-joint; on coccyx, as from a dull point; on l. side, near coccyx, in bone, as if pressed forcibly by a hard body. *Drawing pain in kidney region, extending into inguinal glands, with anxious nausea in pit of stomach.* Pain in kidney region as if ulcerated.

Extremities.—Contractions, as in chorea. Rheumatic drawing in all long bones on motion, as if bruised. Weariness; > when walking; after eating, with tearing in l. side, beneath short ribs, and the spot is painful to pressure. Heaviness. Stiffness.

Upper Extremities.—Intermittent tearing upon top of shoulder. Pain on pressure between end of clavicle and head of humerus, which extends into fingers. Bruised sensation in shoulder on stretching arm. Sticking in upper arm and in bones of little finger. (Dead feeling in wrist, with inability to use it.) Cramplike contraction of metacarpal bones; intermitting cramplike C. of r. hand. Stitch in hollow of hand, over carpal bones. Heaviness of r. hand, > motion, for instance writing, with falling asleep of it. Sudden lameness of hand, with inability to hold the fork with the fingers while eating, trembling of hand on taking hold of anything and painful loss of power. Cramp in joints of thumb while writing. Stitches in tip of r. third finger. Crawling in tips of fingers as if they had begun to go to sleep and were numb.

Lower Extremities.—Cramp in buttocks always on stooping. Pain in r. buttock on sitting, as from strong pressure, with going to sleep of r. foot. Pinching, jerking-strangling pain in r. hip. Stitches in flesh of thigh near groin. Pressure in middle of forepart of T. when sitting. Painless cramplike sensation posteriorly in r. T., as if a muscle would begin to twitch. Patella snaps when ascending stairs. Drawing cramp in hollow of knee when walking, extending along inner muscles of thigh. Intermittent prickling-burning in l. knee. Cramp in calf when walking. Bruised pain externally in flesh near l. tibia, then sticking in whole l. extremity. Burning in r. tibia when standing. Sticking in l. ankle, > washing with cold water with sore pain. Cramp in r. heel. Painful throbbing on dorsa of feet. Painful tensive stretching in instep. Drawing in heel when sitting, with pressure. Heaviness of feet after eating; of feet when ascending stairs, so that he feels them as he lifts them. Sticking in l. little toe, where he formerly had a corn. Drawing in ball of r. great toe; to and fro from l. toes to ankle. Prickling under l. great toe as when a severe cold settles under the nails.

Skin.—Pimples on nose, surrounded by red swelling, like acne rosaceæ; itching P. on neck, nape and breast; itching, on arms; itching and painful, on chest and back. Papulous eruption on nates and thigh, small white vesicles, with large red, smooth border, burning like fire, < lying upon them and touching them, leaving brownish-red spots, which are painful to touch. Vesicles filled with white serum, burning on touch, surrounded by red areola, on head and chest. Pustule on nape, painful at night.

Sticking over whole body at night in bed when he became sweaty from warm coverings, beginning in a few places, when he scratched them it suddenly changed and extended to other places, > uncovering, with anxiety of heart and sensation as if hot water were thrown over him repeatedly. Crawling itching-biting on face, as from salt. Itching here and there on face; on chin and tip of nose; around knee; on hands and fingers; stinging, in ball of l. great toe; painful, almost sore, about umbilicus, which pained as if sore and was sensitive after rubbing. Vague tingling like the beginning of anæsthesia.

Sleep.—Frequent yawning. Sleepiness; during the day; after dinner; overpowering, in forenoon. Sleeplessness after midnight. Uneasy sleep; and frequent waking, with confused and at times anxious dreams, emissions, then sleep of exhaustion. *Waking at night with frightful dreams, without knowing where he was. Disagreeable and frightful dreams, he is disappointed in everything and filled with anxiety.* Vivid, agreeable D.; horrid vivid, which, however, did not make him anxious, but he always retained a kind of presence of mind. D. of mishaps to others. Confused D. every night, which were remembered after waking.

Fever.—Chilliness; in afternoon, with thirst; in evening, with yawning, stretching, indolence and going to bed early without real sleepiness. Coldness of whole body, but the face becomes warmer and warmer. Shaking C., with thirst, shuddering after drinking, cold hands, knees and feet, with hurry, trembling, distortion of face, at one time weeping, at another joyous, at another raging mood, anger at everything, during the chill some warmth in back and feet, which prespired but were not warm to touch. Shivering in r. thigh as if gooseflesh would form. Creeping shivering in thighs; over whole body, reaching head and seeming to draw hairs together; frequently upward over legs; intermittent, over trunk, with discomfort. Coldness of extremities; under finger-nails in afternoon; of limbs to touch, with general trembling from chilliness; internal and external, in hands; *as from a drop of water on parietal bone, then in other places on head.*

Heat; at night and sweat towards morning; with warm sensation in face; with glowing in face, but coldness at every motion, with pain in throat, which was swollen inside and outside, difficult swallowing, prostration, necessity to lie all day and stitches in head. Orgasm of blood. Heat of head; especially of feet, hands, abdomen and in palms, then itching all night and next morning. Sweat on forehead and neck at night.

Cantharis.

A tincture is prepared by digesting one part of the pulverized dried Spanish flies (Cantharis vesicatoria) in five parts of Alcohol.

General Action.—Spanish flies applied to the skin produce blisters (vesication, with inflammation and even sloughing). It produces (taken internally) the most violent inflammation of the whole gastro-intestinal canal, especially of the lower bowel. It is eliminated by the kidneys, and causes acute inflammation of that organ, and of the entire urinary tract. In some cases it produces sexual excitement. Delirium and convulsions occasionally result from large doses.

Allies.—Merc. cor., Terebinth., Caps., Ars., Apis, Nit. ac.

Generalities.—*Marasmus.* Emaciation. Bent almost double, with arms folded across hypogastrium. Increased plasticity of blood drawn from veins. Trembling. Throwing herself about as if on fire. Twitching of tendons; intermittent, painful twitching, now on r. side of occiput, now on external surface of l. knee. Catalepsy. Epilepsy; complicated with hysterical symptoms. Convulsions; with horror of liquids; in paroxysms, with priapism.

Convulsions almost constantly, sometimes he tossed about in despair, sometimes he got up, rushed like a madman to another bed in the same room, bent the curtain rods like reeds, screamed, eight men could scarcely hold him, sometimes emprosthotonos, sometimes opisthotonos, sometimes mouth open, sometimes trismus, with grinding of teeth, running of frothy, at times blood-streaked saliva, face expressive of fright and despair, in the convulsions the hair bristled, the gaze fixed, eyes sparkled, then rolled frightfully, pulse full and slow, abdominal muscles contracted when pressing on umbilical region, that part of abdomen seemed glued to spine, especially recti, which were like tightened cords (Plumbum), then spasms became general and head was thrown back, on attempting to make applications to most painful part of abdomen, he broke away like a madman, frothing at the mouth more than ever, eyes became fiercer, the constriction of throat almost choked him, *howled like the barking of a dog, then general convulsions, which ended in fainting and stupor*, renewal of these attacks on pressure upon painful places in hypogastrium and at sight of liquids.

Stitches over whole body; now here, now there in body, in afternoon; now here, now there, with tearing; all extend inward; are generally combined with tearing; in l. lower ribs, then tearing near r. wrist, then S. in l. upper arm; in afternoon, in r. side of chest, then tearing between scapulæ, then S. in r. shoulder, then in r. hypochondrium, then in r. scapula, whence it passes into r. hypochondrium. Tearing in affected parts, for example, in ulcers; in forehead, then in region of r. ear, then in lower jaw, then on ear again. Violent pains. *Raw and sore pain internally and externally. Crushed feeling, with sensitiveness of every part, internally and externally, and weakness.*

General tension, with dryness in mouth, thirst, anxiety and pains in limbs. Pulsation in whole body, so that the limbs tremble. Restlessness; with heat in head; walking the room screaming; seeming to originate in stomach, with prostration, shiverings and nausea. Feeling as if dying. Indefinable illness. General discomfort. *Weakness;* in morning after sweat at night; in morning after emission, then restless, unrefreshing sleep, > wine, with emptiness in stomach and hunger; *progressive (> drinking freely of alcoholic liquors, which produced no intoxication);* as in beginning of nervous fever; restless, at night; so that muscles were almost unable to contract; < on r. side of body; so that she could hold nothing in her hands; W., especially in legs. *Faintness.*

Stiffness, with open mouth, showing the teeth; stiff feeling in whole body, with heaviness, ascending steps is very troublesome, legs feel as if filled with lead. Paraplegia, with cramps and itching. Reappearance every seven days of attacks, excepting urinary symptoms. Aggravation sometimes from coffee. Amelioration in morning in bed; in evening, of all other symptoms when the urinary difficulties appear; at night of all pains except in abdomen; from eructations; after emission of flatus; when lying; from warm applications; from warmth; from severe motion, even to perspiration.

Clinical.—Violent spasms reproduced by touching larynx.

Mind.—Screaming, with legs drawn upon thighs; S., with frequent loss of consciousness. Delirium; in evening; at night; with convulsions; *furious;* talking disconnectedly of his business and of people who long had been dead. Frenzy. Excitement; they rose from bed, ran about the room, racked by vomiting and copious stools. *Insolent and contradictory mood in afternoon.* Anger. Instability.

Alarm and agitation. Fright at night, with dreams of falling. Despondency, saying that she must die. Distrust of himself in afternoon, like a hypochondriac. Melancholy after dinner, with anxiety. Anxiety; with general trembling, the latter continuing while walking in open air; in morning, as if he expected something important; as if he had committed murder, seeming to arise from stomach. Discontented; and absorbed in thought. Morose, anxious and lachrymose mood in forenoon. Churlish mood. Fretful; in morning when rising; in evening during the pains. Brawling, nobody does anything to suit her. Cheerful, talkative; C., merry, feeling as if newly born, and the room and all objects appeared clearer and more pleasant. Apathetic as if stupefied. Indolent, indifferent, pensive.

Confusion. Distraction in forenoon and many ideas of various kinds running through his mind, which he cannot keep away. Depression of powers in morning. Dulness of perception, then stupidity and loss of reflecting faculty. Loss of thoughts as soon as he wishes to think of anything, gaze fixed in silence on one object (which he scarcely notices), and trouble in recollecting himself in order to express a few words coherently. Forgetful. Comatose. Unconscious.

Clinical.—Acute mania, generally of a sexual type, amorous frenzy, fiery desire for sexual intercourse, with persistent painful erections, paroxysms of rage, crying and barking, even convulsions. Acute mania after erysipelas. (Mania in a woman, with occasional spasms, attempts to bite, with strangury, which seemed to have resulted from applying turpentine to the feet, immediately > Canthar.)

Head.—Sinking in every direction, from heaviness. Stitches in forenoon and evening, > walking; with soreness and sensation as if the pains would extend through eyes; cutting, waking him. Dragging and tearing, only on motion, on stooping and turning head a sensation starting from neck and pressing head forward, with feeling as if everything would press out at forehead. Boring, with drawing, tearing throbbing and pressing pain. Aching; > breakfast; sometimes with delirium; with vertigo; with internal and external heat in forehead; with shivering; with dull heavy feeling around eyes; with trembling and universal spasms, then coma; as if sore internally. Oppression. Confusion; in morning, with pulsation in forehead; with heaviness in vertex. Heaviness; < motion, with aching. Congestion of brain. *Vertigo;* on walking in open air, with unconsciousness and fog before eyes; with weakness in head; with staggering; with faintness.

Forehead.—Stitches in r.; in l. eminence on standing; above root of nose. Tearing; and in nape; in sinciput. Aching; and in supraorbital regions; above nose; extending to temples; pressing out, waking him at night, > sitting up in bed; like a heaviness. Deep-seated heaviness, with dulness and sensation as if head were pressed forward. Confusion, with pain and drawing.

Temple.—Stitches in l.; in r. in afternoon; in r., becoming a painful throbbing, > rubbing. Shooting-darting pain in r., and in r. eye. Tearing; in r.; in r. after a meal. Gnawing in periosteum of r. bone. Throbbing externally in r., with painful drawing in bone. Compression towards each other. Forcing-out pain in r., passing towards teeth.

Vertex.—Tearings in forenoon, with sensation as if a lock of hair were drawn upward. Pressing on V. and in temples, with stitches in temple, < r.; P. alternating with throbbing, at 8 P.M., < every motion.

Sides.—Stitches in l. in morning; in r. in afternoon; in r. in evening when sitting and standing, with throbbing; in l. parietal bone, then boring in l. ear; in l. parietal bone after dinner, with tearing in l. jaw while speaking; in upper part of r. parietal bone. Tearing in r., with stitches; T. in r. parietal bone; in l. side, < touch. Aching in l. half; sudden, in r. side, with chilliness, trembling and spasms, then coma, then alternately lethargy, coma, rational condition and convulsions; drawing, in l. and in forehead. Painful throbbing deep internally in r.

Occiput.—Stitches in evening on lying down; in l. after dinner; in afternoon, extending into sinciput; deep into brain on r. bone in afternoon, more in upper part; in upper part, from both sides inward, with tearing. Tearing from l. side into l. side of forehead, with vertigo, which lasted longer than the pain. Painful twitching externally in r. bone.

Scalp.—Hair falls out on combing. Stitches in r. side of occiput, then tearings in l. parietal bone. Head and hair feel stiff to him.

Clinical.—Neuralgia of head and face from taking cold, with loud screams and jerking of muscles.

Eyes.—Turned towards nose. Protruding. Sunken; and surrounded by blue rings. Red and lustrous. Inflamed; causing blindness. Lustreless. Sticking in l., with itching. Tearing in r. Cutting while writing. Pressing; in afternoon, so that lids close. Pain on writing; on exertion; as after excessive weeping. Smarting in r. in afternoon; S. as from salt. Itching in r. in afternoon. Heat.

Lachrymation; in open air, with necessity to close lids, if he opened them pain as if margins were sore, like raw flesh; with tension of upper lids. Painful drawing in r. ball before dinner. Pupils dilated; with dim vision; contracted. Lids closed more than usual, eyes looking small. Twitching of lid; of l. lower; of r. upper at 2 P.M.; of r. lower, with stitching. Smarting of lids on closing; of lids and around balls, with burning. Conjunctiva suffused. Spasmodic stitches in brows, drawing down to chin, with heat in palate as from eating something burning. Pain in l. orbital arch as if pressed by a blunt instrument.

Vision dim; (on writing, then headache). Inability to distinguish an object until he nearly closes the lids and shakes the head two or three times. Vision yellow in morning. The letters on the paper are green and yellow.

Clinical.—Acute inflammation of eyes, with biting and smarting as from a burn.

Ears.—Stitches; in l. Tearing externally in r. meatus, then in l. shoulder; deep in r. ear, with tickling in l. Tearing in r. mastoid process; in evening, with stitching; sudden, in r. mastoid process, extending into lobule of ear, with stitching in ears, < rubbing; in r. mastoid process below ear, as with a knife, even at night, with headache in forehead like a heaviness. Painful drawing in r. mastoid process. Pressing behind r. ear. Hot vapor issues from either alternately. Drumming. Roaring after supper. Ringing before, with humming.

Nose.—Swelling, with internal redness and soreness; with redness and sensation as if it would fester, especially internally, the pain < touch and talking. Redness, with heat and a pustule. Inflammation, with spots, sore pain and pimples; I. of tip; on edge of r. wing, especially towards end, appearing at irregular intervals red and shining, with swelling and pain. Pimple in l. nostril, burning on touch.

Stitches in nostrils; outward in l. wing. Pain, with tension, throbbing, swollen sensation and pain on touch. Pain on top at 3 A.M. as if he had pressed it, then tension and erysipelatous inflammation and swelling from back of nose down sides into cheeks, < r., like redness of cheeks, becoming white under pressure of finger, then rapidly again red, hard to touch, afterwards desquamation, then similar inflammation, especially on r. upper lip, sides and tip of nose. Soreness of nostrils. Drawing in r. nostril, with tickling and ineffectual irritation to sneeze. Itching in nostrils, uvula and throat.

Sneezing; then sticking in l. wing; violent in morning. Catarrh, with much tenacious mucus from nose, hoarseness, painful hawking of tough mucus from chest and nightly dry, cutting stitching along trachea. Mucus mixed with blood. Bleeding. Constant stench before nose, passing down throat.

Face.—*Deathly look during and after pains* in afternoon. *Suffering expression. Sallow and puffy.* Yellow, also eyes. Hippocratic. Pinched. Cyanotic. Pale; in afternoon during and after pains; during the chill; and covered with sweat; sunken and expressive of terror; with flushes. Sickly, with dim eyes surrounded by dark rings. Anxious countenance. Red; on stooping, blood shooting forcibly into head, even head becoming hot when sitting, not when walking; in spots. Glowing of r. side while l. is waxy yellow. Swollen; r. half; r. side, and tense; r. cheek S. and inflamed, with drawing pain in upper teeth. Disfigured. Animated expression. Sore pain in bones, extending into ear, < r. side.

Lips.—Swollen. Eruption in corners. Pimples on margin of upper in evening. Inflammation and blisters on lips, tongue, palate and pharynx. Desquamation; and of mouth. Cutting in middle of margin of lower, ending behind r. ear. Soreness, and tongue loosened from its upper skin and arch of palate dark brown. Burning, and of tongue and palate. *Dryness, without thirst* (Apis); D. during and after the pains, with thirst.

Jaws.—Mouth wide open, with chewing motions of jaws. Twitching in middle of l. lower while speaking. Stitching in upper in afternoon, somewhat on r. side. Tearing in r. lower in morning while walking; in l. lower, in afternoon, extending backward; in middle of r. lower, and in a tooth there. Gnawing in middle of r. lower; in middle of lower, spreading to teeth. Sore pain on inner margin of lower, where there is an itching tetter, the pain < speaking and touch.

Clinical.—Erysipelas of face, with burning biting heat and urinary symptoms.

Mouth.—Teeth. Looseness. Rising up of the root of a r. lower, and it can be drawn out easily, when the tearing ceases. Tearings in r. lower molars; in r. lower carious molar. Drawing pain in upper in afternoon, < eating. Drawing, then sticking, < evening after lying down, preventing sleep.

Gum.—Swelling, and of mucous membrane of cheeks; with redness. Red spot above carious root of upper incisor, painful, if pressed discharging pus from an opening in centre. Red spot above l. upper incisor, painful, becoming elevated, inflamed, yellow-reddish, sore, the pain < external pressure, with swelling of upper lip. Blister, with red points, with swelling of upper lip. Sudden tearing, and in l. lower incisor. Pain. Painful drawing in r., extending outward on r. upper incisor, with sensation as if something were drawing across lip. Quivering in G. of l. upper eyetooth.

Tongue.—*Swollen and coated. Sublingual glands swollen. Coated, red at edges.* Coated white; down centre. White, with bitter taste, nausea and aversion to everything. Bleached along sides and tip, blackish-brown in centre and swollen. Red at edges, with yellow coat on its anterior two-thirds. Bluish-red, covered with white blisters, containing bile-like fluid. *Painful blister along centre. Part of T. and back of mouth excoriated, part covered with blisters.* Festering, and of throat and gum. Aphthæ covering margin and gums (Tarent.). Trembling. Stitch in tip, as if she had bitten it. Burning, and on palate. Dryness in morning and mucous coat; D. and pallor. Tickling on tip.

Mucous membrane red and covered with blisters (Borax, Sul. ac.). Back of mouth swollen and red, the tissues crossed by enlarged veins. Purple swelling near last lower molar, discharging clotted blood. Inflammation and ulceration; I. and swelling of mucous membrane, with salivation. Excoriation; of mucous membrane from mouth to anus. Blisters, and in pharynx; *white, on palate, gum and tongue.* Slimy in morning, with white tongue; S. in morning, and bitter; at night on waking. Much tough mucus drawn into M. through posterior nares. Mucus and blood from M. and nose. A clot of blood comes into M. towards morning.

Biting pain in palate, < after eating. Sensation on r. side of M. as if its membrane were raised by a needle. M. and tongue seemed deprived of mucous membrane. Tension, with dryness, thirst and pains in limbs. *Burning pain, and in throat and stomach* (Arsen., Arum t.). *Burning, and in pharynx and stomach. Dryness;* and of nose. *Salivation;* in morning; with redness of gums; with mucus from mouth; with constant spitting of mingled mucus and dark saliva; so that he must lie on his side; *without coppery taste;* disgusting, sweet. Offensive breath. Breath like cedar pitch. Taste as of cedar pitch; nauseous; foul on rising; foul afternoons; bloody; bitter; insipid, as of sweet cheese; sour; unsalted, to food; lost.

Throat. — *Swelling,* with erysipelatous flush and turgid veins across fauces; S. of tonsils. Redness, with pressing, which on swallowing changes to sticking. *Inflammation and covering of plastic lymph;* I. of tonsils. *Aphthous ulcer at back part, covered with a whitish adherent crust, and a similar one on side of r. tonsil* (Merc. cor.). Abrasion, with blisters. Relaxation of uvula.

Pain in pharynx during hunger; burning, and constriction. *Burning soreness, with inflammation.* Scraping, with necessity to hawk up mucus after meals; burning S. in pharynx, with sweetish, disgusting taste on tongue and in mouth as far as pharynx. Roughness; in forenoon, with hoarseness. *Constriction at back part, with pain;* C., even to suffocation. **Burning**; in pharynx on swallowing; < pressure, and in pit of stomach; especially at entrance of œsophagus, extending to epigastrium. Dryness in afternoon, without thirst; D. in pharynx, with occasional sticking. *Swallowing difficult;* impossible.

Œsophagus. — Constriction. Burning; < while drinking.

Clinical.—Inflammation of throat, which feels on fire (Arsen.). Aphthous ulceration of throat, regurgitation of drink, etc. Diphtheritic inflammation of throat, with constriction amounting almost to suffocative dyspnœa, etc.

Stomach.—Appetite increased. Hunger, waking at night; H. after relief of pains. *Appetite diminished.* Lost; evening and morning; for supper; lost after coffee. *Disgust for food;* in evening during the paroxysm, at seeing food or hearing about it; for tobacco. *Thirst;* at 8 P.M., after the shaking chill; at night, with fever; during dinner; during the coldness; after the chill; when not in pain; *with burning pain in throat and stomach* (Arsen.); with frothy and bloody sputa; but liquids can hardly be swallowed and are at once vomited; loss of T., and water does not taste good.

Eructations; *frothy and sour; of frothy, sour mucus, tinged bright red;* tasting of food after dinner; hot, with heartburn, no thirst, the burning in pharynx < drinking water; empty; incomplete, almost like hiccough, also passing backward from pharynx towards stomach, before dinner. Hiccough; in afternoon.

Nausea; in morning, with coldness, in afternoon heat; in morning, even to vomiting; towards evening; when eating; on walking and standing; with disgust for everything; with salivation; with trembling of feet; intermittent; in epigastric region on stooping or on inspiration; like a weakness in stomach, after coffee in forenoon. Retching.

Vomiting; with pressing in stomach, then cutting; with pain in hypogastrium and bearing down, urging to urinate, with heat and smarting and ineffectual urging to stool; with strangury, then inflammation of kidney. Of blood; with strangulation. Of greenish, offensive matter. Of mucus; frothy M.; bloody; frothy, bloody; of glairy, tenacious; of tenacious, taking the form of the gullet; of mucus and ingesta, without exertion. Of bile; and ingesta. Of everything. Of ingesta. Of herby-tasting food, with stool. Of the water he drinks, with blood. Of membrane; of membranous flakes (morbid secretion of alimentary canal). Of a cylinder mass, apparently inner membrane of gullet.

Lancinations. Cutting; intermittent, in pit and about umbilicus. Pinching in r. epigastric region in morning, with stitching. Gnawing in region, extending into back between shoulders. Cramp; with free emesis. *Acute pain in region of S. and bladder, with such sensibility that pressure caused convulsions.* Pain; in epigastrium; in epigastric region and in groin; in epigastrium, < pressure, and in umbilicus. Pressing, < when empty; P. extending backward from both sides into spine, where it seems screwed together. Pressure in pit in afternoon. Drawing pain. Burning pain in region.

Inflammation. Cardialgia, < drinking, with sour eructations. Burning; all forenoon, with taste of wine in mouth; at orifice; in epigastric region, with pain. Sensation before dinner as if screwed together. Crushing in pit, > as soon as she takes anything warm or drinks anything cold. Heaviness in epigastrium and umbilicus, with heat and smarting. Fulness, with pressure, as if he would eructate; F. in epigastric region, with anxiety and restlessness. Sensitiveness internally in afternoon, with good appetite; S. internally in epigastric region and externally. Distress, with nausea after eating, feeling as if a load oppressed him; D., with nausea, then vomiting of the water he had drunk, gasping and general chilliness. Indescribable sensation in epigastric region, she feels hungry without really being so. Weakness.

Abdomen.—*Distended; and tympanitic* (Terebinth); *and tender;* with movements as if flatus would pass. Retracted and sensitive to pressure, especially hypogastrium. Rumbling; while sitting; with rattling. Growling, more on r. side of hypogastrium, passing backward; G., with rumbling and shaking. Rolling, with sensation as before diarrhœa. Movements of flatus in evening, with pinching, the pain extending into chest; M., causing lumps, as if a child were there. Movements, with yawning. Emission of flatus; noisy, in evening.

Tearing, with pinching; T., with diarrhœa and pain in anus. *Cutting; towards evening, during stool, after the stool shivering* (Caps.); from 5 P.M. till morning, with necessity to roll about; with boring in knees, after coffee vomiting of bitter stuff, then bitter taste. Pinching during stool, after the stool shivering. Griping; at 3 A.M.; then liquid stool; extending upward and becoming stitches, then stitching backward on both sides, hindering respiration. Sensation as after a drastic purge. Inflammation; of whole alimentary canal, ureters, kidneys and internal sexual organs.

Pain; after coffee; from coughing; before diarrhœa; < pressure; < pressure, worse over hypogastrium and scrobiculus cordis; < during stool, which is increased thereby, with pain in anus; > diarrhœa; with nausea and vomiting of ingesta; with urging to stool; in intestinal canal, changing to inflammation and gangrene. Sensation after midnight, as if menses would appear. Bearing-down pains. Dragging pains to genitals in afternoon. Sensitiveness to touch. *Burning along alimentary canal;* < morning, > several stools, with twisting; internally and externally in morning; as after strong wine.

Cutting in upper. Pain in upper. Cutting in r. side. Pinching in l. side. Sudden gripings in sides when standing, rather externally.

Hypochondria.—*Incarceration of flatus under short ribs* (as of offensive flatus). Stitches in l., and in centre of sternum. Aching below ribs. (Inflammation of liver, with erosion of intestines.) Sensation as if something held her together below r. false ribs.

Umbilical Region.—Pinching. Griping below navel before and during stool. Burning pain above navel on coughing, sneezing and blowing nose, whereby the abdomen seems very hot, with yellow spots externally in region of this pain, which spots when touched are more stinging than burning.

Hypogastrium.—Fermenting. Sticking in r. groin in morning; in l. groin, extending downward; cutting, in groin, and burning, with cutting when urinating. Cutting in groins, > sitting and standing, < walking; intermittent wandering C. in H. Gnawing. Griping from morning till 1 P.M., with pressing towards genitals. Pain; extending into lumbar region, most intense just above pubes, with nausea; above symphysis pubis and down ureters. Drawing in pubic region, with tearing. Tension along inguinal canal and testicles, around pelvic region. Compression on sides, but farther downward in l. Heat in pelvis, with constant desire to urinate, then some drops of urine.

Clinical—Intestinal inflammation, with burning heat, tympanitic distention (Tereb.).

Rectum.—Cutting at 8 P.M., > emission of flatus while standing and walking, but return of the pain with urging to stool, the pain > soft stool. Burning. Crawling. *Tenesmus* (Caps., Merc. c.). Urging, then copious soft stool; to a hard stool, soon afterwards liquid stool preceded by colic. Frequent urging; with scanty stool. Ineffectual urging; after first stool; during micturition.

Anus.—*Passage of pure blood, and from urethra;* after violent efforts (Merc. c.). *Burning after diarrhœa* (Merc. c., Nit. ac.); after stool, with stitches. *Pain in perineum; seeming to arise from neck of bladder rather than from root of penis.* Itching in perineum, with tenesmus at anus.

Stool.—Dysentery. *Diarrhœa; with burning in anus;* with irritation in rectum; **consisting of blood and mucus** (Caps., Merc. c., etc.); mucous; of green mucus after three days' constipation; frothy; watery; of brown liquid in morning; two liquid yellow stools during the day, with cutting in abdomen after each and biting pain in anus; frequent, with colic.

Constipation. Hard in morning, afterwards soft, with colic; H., with protrusion of rectum; then twinging in anus; and delayed; and difficult. *Red, slimy. White tough mucus with the stool, like scrapings from intestines, with streaks of blood* (Nit. ac.), seven times in one night. *Copious.* Scanty, black and tarry-looking. Slight, somewhat hard, difficult, with cutting in rectum. Painful. Difficult and insufficient. Frequent; two in morning, with tenesmus. Omitted; but emission of flatus.

Clinical.—Diarrhœa like scrapings of intestines, reddish, mucous or bloody, flaky; during stool extreme burning at anus, dysenteric bloody stools, with intolerable burning tenesmus, with chill as if water were poured over one (Caps.). Acute dysentery, with unquenchable thirst, even the lips, mouth and throat feel raw and burning, with canker, tendency to collapse, cold hands and feet.

Urinary Organs.—Inflammation, with bleeding. *Irritation, so that he can bear scarcely more than a spoonful of urine in bladder without urging to urinate* (Nux vom., Ars.). *Cutting in ureters, extending towards penis, > pressure on glans, with contracting pain, the pains at times passing from without inward.* Inflammation of kidneys, ureters, bladder and urethra.

Bladder.—Ulceration; and of urethra. Gangrene of lining. Discharge of dirty purulent matter. *Spasm.* **Pain; with frequent urging, intolerable tenesmus** (Merc. cor.); over B. and over uterus and kidneys, and especially over hypogastrium. Pressure downward towards B. Inflammation. *Burning; before micturition, < as the water left the bladder, continual urging, micturition by drops, urine often bloody* (Tereb.), sometimes in clots, causing so much agony when passing urethra that he nearly fainted, about the same time several loose stools, with, as the last fæces left the rectum, pain and straining, which soon extended to bladder, causing tenesmus, which was little relieved when one or two drops of bloody urine passed (compare Merc. cor.), afterwards intermittent tearing-boring over region of r. kidney, following direction of ureters, with pain when lying in any position but more comfortable when back was bent, micturition most painful as the last drops passed the sphincter vesicæ.

Neck of Bladder.—Sticking; *in forepart during urging, then micturition of a few drops.* Tearing. **Burning-cutting,** *extending to navicular fossa* (comp. Berberis), < before and after micturition. Pain. Paralysis.

Tenesmus (Merc. c., Prunus sp., etc.). **Urging,** waking at 3.30 A.M., *after discharge of some urine burning in urethra changing into all the torments of gonorrhœa, > sitting,* painful micturition every three or four minutes, the pain > after drinking three glasses of water by copious micturition; *< standing and walking; > lying quietly on back;* **with burning in urethra;** with copious urine, priapism, pain in stomach and dysuria; with discharge of two spoonfuls of dirty tenacious mucus with cutting. **Frequent U.;** always preceded by pain at penis, urine scalding, turbid, tinged with blood; with scanty urine and towards end of micturition pressing pain in base of urethra, extending to orifice. **Constant urging, micturition painful, in drops;** *C. urging, and always but one spoonful, also in morning; with passage of a few drops, causing smarting and burning along urethra, especially near fossa navicularis, finally, after long straining to pass a few drops of bloody and albuminous urine, a convulsive tremor of all limbs, cold sweat on forehead and chest, sinking back in bed half-exhausted, no rest on account of immediate return of these sufferings. Ineffectual urging; then several drops, with bloody streaks and pain.*

Dysuria. Painful micturition; towards the close, > when there is much urine; *with scanty and bloody urine* (Tereb.); *with pain in kidneys;* with constant urging; and continual; as if cut with knives, with frequent urging, *but always emission of only a few drops; as if a red-hot iron passed along urethra, with a few drops of bloody urine,* the pain worse at membranous portion of canal and in meatus urinarius; as if it were impossible to evacuate the urine, with pressure in region of bladder. *Strangury; and urine passed in small quantities;* with pain in back; with disagreeable smell in nostrils. *Micturition by drops; with cutting; by drops, urine reddish, sometimes mixed with blood;* painful dribbling of albuminous urine, with membranous pieces, which are rolled up, grayish-red, covered with blood-streaked mucus, and large pieces, white on one side, red on the other, firm and elastic.

Micturition in a thin, divided stream and difficult, < 9 A.M. *Ischuria. Urine retained;* on account of too great fulness of bladder; *retained, causing pain.* Micturition rarer, but urine increased. Involuntary micturition; and dribbling. *Frequent micturition;* at night; *with copious urine;* but urine not increased; of scanty watery urine, at first with pain and towards the end with cutting, at last by drops or in a weak, intermitting stream.

Urethra.—Swollen internally. *Contracted internally, hence micturition in a thin stream. Passage of blood; bright, with urging to urinate and cutting burning pains through whole urethra;* a few drops of watery B. after the urine. Bloody gonorrhœa; yellowish G., staining linen yellow. Discharge of pasty colorless liquid. Urinary flatulence. Sticking, with *burning during micturition.* **Cutting before, during and after micturition** in afternoon, *so that she must double herself up; burning, at end of scanty micturition.* Pain; with the gonorrhœal discharge; in base towards end of micturition, extending to external meatus. Twitching and burning pain on urinating. *Burning;* at night, with passage of a few drops of blood; **urine scalds him and is passed drop by drop;** (before, and during micturition); *during micturition;* during micturition before menses, with white sediment in urine; *after micturition;* with constriction at prostate. Soreness; on urinating. Biting pain while urinating. Smarting while urinating. Tensive sensation in morning on urinating, as if urine were checked in its course. Tickling, with voluptuous warmth. Itching; after urinating, with crawling.

Orifice of urethra, agglutination; inflammation; stitches, also in evening and night, extending to anus; itching, at times almost a cutting. Burning in and near orifice; during micturition; *B. in excretory ducts of vesiculæ seminales during and after coition;* B. in forepart, as if a drop of urine remained there. Sensation in forepart, at tip of glans, on urinating as if the urine were retained at that point, with aching there, but the urine passes freely.

Urine. *Increased.* Scanty; in morning; with cutting in urethra, especially in forepart; and high-colored; and bloody; *and turbid.* Suppressed. *Dark. Red as if mixed with blood.* White. Pale yellow; during the chill, with pain in evening. Acrid. *Albuminuria* (Apis., Merc. c., etc.). Mucus in urine; floating threads of M. **Bloody urine** (Tereb.); passed with pain and in drops; and hot; urine contained coagulated blood; urine contained bloody filaments, then blackish, coagulated masses of blood, at last much mucus. Urine contained blood-corpuscles mixed with mucus, pus-corpuscles, epithelia of bladder and kidneys, spheroidal cells from tubuli uriniferi and pelvis of kidney, considerable sediment after standing, reaction alkaline, after some days mucus mixed with large quantities of urates and some crystals of carbonate of ammonia, afterwards cloudiness, < towards noon. Specific gravity high. Turbid when discharged; immediately, *frequently depositing a fine white sediment adhering to glass*, sometimes an iridescent film; *during the night, like mealy water, with white sediment.* Loaded with sediment and fibrinous matter.

Clinical.—Most violent cystitis, with intense tenesmus, constant desire to urinate, the urine is bloody, scanty, etc. The cystitis calling for Cantharis is of a most highly inflammatory character, it may be associated with general fever, chill, always with most terrible distress in the neck of the bladder. Acute nephritis, with extreme distress in the bladder, urine scanty, bloody, albuminous, etc. (compare Tereb.). In renal calculi, with the acute bladder symptoms of the drug, hæmaturia, etc. Gravel in children, constant pulling at the penis. In gonorrhœa, with most intense suffering, sexual excitement, chordee, with constant distress in bladder, discharge of blood.

Sexual Organs. — Inflammation. Weak feeling. Itching. Heat; with itching. Sweat. *Drawing pain in spermatic cord while urinating.* Brown cheesy accumulation about corona glandis in morning. Absence of the usual smegma preputii.

Penis.—*Gangrene.* Inflammation. Swelling; *with pain even to external pressure;* with heat, without erection and without desire; of frænum of prepuce; red, hot and diaphanous swelling of prepuce, with phimosis and discharge of purulent secretion from beneath it. Discharge of blood from the rigid penis and from the anus. Pain; *before micturition;* drawing, and in back and thighs, > passing flatus upward and downward; burning, especially at tip of glans, with frequent urging to urinate. Pruritus. Lax; and drooping. **Priapism** (Tereb., Copaib.); with swollen genitals; with pain about bladder and wild delirium. Erections; every morning on rising; with emission; painful erection; *severe, at night, with contraction and sore pain in whole of urethra; strong, persistent, painless, without voluptuous sensation.*

Swelling of scrotum; painful, of r. testicle. Satyriasis. *Desire disturbing sleep;* absence of D. Emission in morning while awake in bed, from relaxed penis, almost without sensation; E. at night. Blood flows instead of semen (Tarent.).

Female.—*Swelling of vulva, with irritation.* Vagina; itching; burning; burning, with a thick white discharge; bloody mucous discharge after menses. Swelling of neck of uterus, with tenesmus; S. of neck of uterus, with burning in bladder, abdominal pains, vomiting and fever. Pregnancy. *Miscarriage;* after irritation of bowels and urinary organs. Menstruation, too early, with nausea and colic; too early, but scanty; M. which had ceased one day reappeared in forenoon, with pain, and lasted till noon; too late; short; profuse; profuse and painful.

Clinical.—Constant discharge from uterus, < false step, with discharge from bladder. Inflammation of the ovaries, with burning pain, especially worse during menstruation, ovaries extremely sensitive. Puerperal metritis, especially mania of a sexual character, with inflamed bladder, etc. Pruritis of vagina. Menstruation too early and dark, with great soreness of breasts, etc.

Respiratory Organs.—Pain in larynx. Burning in larynx. Hawking of tenacious mucus from larynx. Inability to speak. Hoarseness. Voice feeble. *Voice low, with sensation of weakness of vocal organs.* On deep respiration and on speaking she dares not exert herself on account of weakness of respiratory organs, hence a weak, frightened tone. Contraction of trachea.

Cough; caused by tickling; hacking; paroxysms of dry, from irritation in larynx, with rapid respiration and tightness in chest; in morning on rising, with difficult expectoration. Expectoration bloody, after short cough. Bloody and frothy sputa. Expectoration of pink mucus.

Respiration.—Threatened with suffocation. Gets out of breath on ascending a mountain, with catching in chest and nausea. Difficult; partly on account of contraction of larynx and trachea, partly on account of dryness of nose; and hurried. Groaning. Hurried. Irregular and imperfect; sometimes quick, sometimes slow and at great intervals.

Clinical.—Acute inflammation of larynx, with extreme heat and burning. Occasionally useful in croup in children, with swelling, expression of great agony, loss of voice.

Chest.—(Drawn together at times when coughing, the lungs themselves are contracted.) Pneumonia. *Stitches;* in centre of sternum; in lower part of sternum; in sternum, then in last r. false rib; (in sides); *in r. side;* in r. false ribs; in middle of r. clavicle; in l. side; in l. side, then below r.; in l., more externally on ribs; below l. axilla; in region of l. axilla in morning; in sternum in afternoon; in r. lower ribs in afternoon; in r. costal region below arm in afternoon; deep in l. lower ribs in afternoon; at midnight on inspiration, preventing her from lying on l. side; in r. side on each inspiration after midnight and next day; in l. after dinner; in r. after dinner, more in upper part, then in l.; in r. costal region after dinner; in r. lower false ribs while yawning; in forepart, < inspiration; *from one side to the other; from front towards back, impeding respiration;* in l. lowest ribs, extending towards back; *in r. lower part, extending towards middle of sternum; in r. forepart, passing downward into r. lower ribs;* under r. arm, extending into chest; under l. arm, extending to middle of sternum; below r. chest on inspiration, extending into r. shoulder; inward below l. breast, extending under axilla; below l. arm on sudden turning of body and on inspiration, extending through body, as if pierced by a spear, with a jerk, arresting breath, the same once on r. side, > rest, not at all on respiration and motion.

Tearing, especially in region of heart. Inflammation of side of diaphragm. Pain on both sides beneath ribs. Pressure; on sternum; in side in morning in bed, > rising; deep internally on r. side of sternum, with stitching outward. Sensation as if something beneath r. false ribs were pressed together. Squeezing in forepart from 11 A.M. till 8 P.M., > lying, but returning, with impeded respiration and stitching in whole chest. Fulness after coffee, and in stomach and abdomen. Sensitiveness to touch. Dryness internally. Burning; in morning, with a clot of blood in mouth; with stitches externally and internally, as if in bones; on chest, with pinching in abdomen and constipation; on sternum. Amelioration of symptoms by empty eructation.

Clinical.—Extreme heat and burning in chest. Pleurisy. Has proved valuable in the exudative stage of pleurisy, with the characteristic burning sensation.

Heart.—Stitches; then crawling. Pressure from H. towards sternum towards evening, < speaking and deep respiration. Pain; drawing. Anxiety; in afternoon. Jerking, running to head. Palpitation; towards evening.

Pulse.—*Diminished.* Scarcely perceptible. Imperceptible. Thready. Irregular and intermittent. Small, hard and intermittent. Slow and full; S., small and intermittent. Rapid; and small; and weak, trembling. Hard and full, as in inflammatory fevers. Full and bounding at wrist, with congestion of vessels of head and neck.

Neck.—Thickness. Swelling of glands, with pain on touch. Twitching of l. muscles. Stitches in l. muscles in afternoon. Tearing in l. muscles on walking, with headache like a heaviness; T. in afternoon, extending towards vertex; in nape on moving head, extending into upper part of head, with stitches in r. cervical muscles. Drawing pain in a narrow line extending downward, deep in r. muscles. Stiffness, with tensive pain on stooping.

Back.—Tearing; < morning. Cutting in B. and abdomen, extending through urethra; sticking C. through B. and abdomen. Dragging as before menstruation. Pain; and in limbs; in spine.

Scapulæ.—Stitches in upper part of l. in afternoon, with burning in skin on same place; S. in r. in evening; inward below r.; between S., on every motion, as if sprained. Tearing; in upper part of r., with stitches; T. between S. Pain between S. Intermittent throbbing on r. side of spine, near eleventh and twelfth dorsal vertebræ at 11 P.M., < every motion, extending by single jerks to r. thigh.

Kidney Region.—Twitching in r., with throbbing. Stitches in r. Paroxysmal cutting and burning pains, *with sensitiveness to slightest touch, alternating with pain and burning in tip of penis, urging to urinate and painful micturition, by drops, of bloody urine, at times passage of pure blood, with clots. Pain; late in evening; with urging to urinate; and in ureters, extending to bladder;* in r.; in l., with tenderness on pressure and sympathetic fever.

Lumbar Region.—Stitches after rising from a seat or on walking; extending into r.; in r., then tearing in l. hypochondrium; pointed, in l., with cutting in abdomen; on r. side of sacrum, as if in bone, with gnawing. Tearing, with stitches. Cuttting, < sitting; in afternoon, extending to beneath shoulders, where it becomes stitching. Boring. Gnawing; in sacrum in evening. Biting. Pain; < pressure, and in hypochondria; *with incessant desire to urinate, with scanty discharge;* P. extending to perineum; on motion as if he had injured himself; heavy, < pressure. Weariness while sitting, with peculiar pressing pain in back, in region of last rib.

Coccyx.—Stitching, with tearing.

Clinical.—Lumbago, or great pain in loins, region of kidneys, etc., incessant desire to urinate, moaning and screaming. Pain in os coccygis, lancinating and tearing.

Extremities.—Convulsions. Unconscious tossing about. Trembling; of hands and feet in evening during chill. Stiffness as in tetanus. Tearing in middle of r. forearm and in calves in evening and next day. Pain, with stiffness. Bruised feeling in forearms and legs. Contracting, almost paralytic pain. Drawing, almost paralytic pain. Painful drawing on external surface of l. thigh, a hand's breadth above knee, to below knee, and from r. elbow to middle of forearm, on inner surface. Drawings. Dry feeling in joints of arms and limbs. Weakness; in morning; of hands and feet. Numbness of arms and legs. Collapse.

Upper Extremities.—*Stitch in r. axilla, extending into chest.* Tearing in A. Stitching-tingling in A. Stitches through and through bones of r. shoulder in afternoon. Drawing pain in l. shoulder-joint.

Upper Arm.—Tearing in middle of r. in afternoon; from middle of r. to middle of forearm, > rubbing; on inner surface of r. humerus during breakfast, > pressure. Boring in middle. Gnawing in middle, of r.; in middle, on external surface; in middle of r. humerus, with stitching farther up. Bruised pain in r. Drawing in r., as if in bone, after dinner, with stitches.

Elbow.—Tearing in bend of r.; from bend of r. into shoulder; in bend after dinner, passing on rubbing into outer side of upper arm. Drawing pain in r. Sensation in r., as if she were holding something fast.

Tearing from middle of l. forearm to middle of upper arm. Stitching from r. wrist towards elbow in afternoon, and with each stitch a blow. Hand. Tearing in l.; on back of r., with stitching extending into l. upper arm; on inner margin of r., towards little finger, > rubbing. Painful drawing from r. into fingers, with tension. Drawing pain in bones of H. and of forearm. Tearing in l. thumb; in l. finger in afternoon. Pain in little finger, with tension.

Lower Extremities.—Tottering as if dizzy. Inability to stand or walk. Paralysis; with weakness of arm.

Thigh.—Twitching in flesh in middle, in afternoon, with itching. Stitches in r. hip in afternoon. Tearing in posterior part of l., with stitches; T. from middle of r. into hollow of knee in afternoon; from r. nates down posterior surface to knee; from r. hip down posterior surface to knee; from l. hip-bone into knee. Gnawing on external surface of bone from middle of r. into calf. Weight in muscles. Falling asleep of one or other.

Knee.—Tottering on ascending steps. Stitches deep into r.; on inner surface of l. penetrating the knee. Tearing about r.; in r., > rubbing; on external surface of l., and after sitting down sensation like falling asleep; in r. extending to middle of leg; boring, now in both, now in r. only, extending backward and downward into feet, upward into r. hip and thence into l. hip, > warm dry applications, with sticking. (Cutting while walking.) Boring, so that legs were drawn together. Pains on bringing them together; P. causing lamenting and whining; as if swollen, impeding walking, lasting longest in r. Drawing pain in hollows. Sensitiveness to touch, and in legs. Tension on r. Weariness, and of legs.

Leg.—Trembling on motion. Tearing in l. calf after dinner; in calves worse while walking than while sitting; in calves at 10 A.M.; as if flesh were torn away. Pain > violent rubbing; P. in calves, > afternoon by walking violently till she sweated. Bruised feeling in forenoon when walking. Feeling in tibia, just above ankle, as if skin and flesh were loosened from bone, > touch. Tension in r. calf after dinner. Weariness.

Foot.—Tearing on back of r. in afternoon; from r. instep to middle of thigh, with stitching. *Ulcerative pain in soles, preventing stepping.* Drawing on inner surface of r. Lassitude, so that she can scarcely go upstairs.

Toes.—Tearing in r. towards tips, > rubbing, then in r. external malleolus, > rubbing; in second l., with stitches.

Skin.—Pale. Yellow spot near umbilicus and another on inside of l. thigh. Brownish-yellow. Red, inflamed; red spots on first joint of l. thumb at 2 P.M., as if a pimple would form. Swelling on back of l. foot, with burning, the burning > rubbing; itching S. on last phalanx of finger. Eruption on knee, with pain, < touch and impeding motion; E. on breastbone, paining on touch like an ulcer; burning, on l. buttock.

Pimple on r. upper eyelid; on backs of hands; on back of r. hand, between fourth and fifth fingers; on external surface of r. little finger, with sticking on pressure; between r. thumb and index, with red areola; on side of neck, with burning pain; on cheek near corner of mouth, feeling tense, but when touched causing burning pain; on nates, with burning pain on touch. Pimples burning on touch, on forehead and cheeks; on r. mastoid process; between r. thumb and index (preceded by tickling). P. deep in cheek, itching when touched. Itching P., covering inner surface of arms and middle of chest, with burning after scratching. Pellucid P. between chin and lip, from one angle of mouth to the other in afternoon.

Pustule on chin, burning on touch. Psoriasis. Eczema. Vesicles; on r. palm; *burning on touch*, between chin and lips and on forehead; itching, on r. cheek in evening, with burning after scratching; itching-burning upon nose. Ulcers on lower limbs.

Twitching on inner surface of l. knee. Stitches on abdomen; below r. breast; on neck. Burning pain. Dryness. Formication in r. foot, then dead feeling. Tickling on outer side of l. upper arm, > rubbing, with biting. Itching; with sticking; on forehead; on coccyx above anus; on chest under r. arm in afternoon; at night, now in hands, now in feet, with twitching; in an ulcer, with tearing; here and there as from lice; crawling in bends of elbows.

Clinical.—Vesicular eruptions, with burning and itching. Effects of burns. Erysipelas, especially of the face, of a vesicular type, with great restlessness, burning pain. Eczema on backs of feet and hands or between fingers, > cold, < warmth.

Sleep.—Yawning after dinner; Y., with stretching; without sleepiness. Sleepiness; in morning, with depression; in afternoon, with lassitude; after dinner; < eating. Fell asleep while spinning, her eyes closed involuntarily, then smarting in eyes. *Sleeplessness;* in evening from excitement, then vivid, confused dreams; after midnight, also with restlessness. Late falling asleep. Frequent waking. Little sleep. Half-sleep. Light sleep before midnight. Restlessness at night; with late falling asleep on account of anxiety, then nightmare after a short sleep. Starting in morning sleep.

Dreams. *Anxious.* Unremembered. Confused. Voluptuous. Of business. Of cooking, etc. Of quarrels. Vivid, of deer, of walks in woods. Visions at midnight when half-awake, she hears soft steps in the room, then knocking under the bed, and the bed is raised. Visions at midnight while half-awake and lying with r. hand on l. shoulder, something took hold of her hand and bent it up and down, then it seemed as if icy hands took hold of her throat.

Fever.—Gooseflesh during chill. Chill; waking at 2 A.M. and preventing further sleep; after rising at 3 A.M., > lying down; from 11 till 3 P.M., when she took camphor, with pains in knees and calves, which continued till lying down; at 1 P.M., somewhat later each day for three days; slight, till 1.30 P.M., then shaking C. till 11 A.M., > hot stove, with creeping in hands and feet; at 5 P.M.; from 5 to 7 P.M.; towards evening, after stool, with sensation as if dashed with ice-water and with internal warmth; for three hours in evening; in bed at 10 o'clock; at night, also preventing sleep; on putting a limb out of bed and on rising; on rising from bed, then heat.

Chill, with external warmth of forehead; C. mixed with heat, with heaviness of feet, paralytic immobility of limbs, loss of appetite, pain in eyes and necessity to lie in bed; C. irregularly alternating with heat and sweat. Frequent creeping C. Shivering chill from 11 till 1 o'clock; from 3 to 4 P.M., > warming with cloths; from 3 P.M. till 3 A.M., then warmth without thirst; from 4 to 4.30 P.M.; about 6.30 P.M., and tossing about, as from electricity, then sticking in scapula; with weakness; universal S., with chills down spine.

Coldness of skin; with imperceptible pulse. Cold face; cold sensation in a spot on l. side of lumbar vertebræ, < evening while sitting, as from getting cold or like gooseflesh, with formication. Shivering up back in afternoon; from 2 till 8 P.M., beginning in back, then heat, then shivering again. *Cold limbs;* and covered with cold sweat. Cold hands and feet, with pain in urethra; C. hands, which look yellowish; hands, with burning soles.

Heat; at night, especially in anus and genitals; after violent motion; after coldness; < afternoon; with rapid pulse; H., with thirst, also with dryness in mouth, anxiety, restlessness and pain in limbs; with scanty and painful emission of blackish urine, then urine increased to four-fold the amount of liquids taken, with thirst and desire for meat, afterwards urine lost its blackish color and tasted rather like salt water. Heat in afternoon, as after much walking on a hot day, with red face and increased sweat; suddenly rising in evening, with redness of face and thirst. External heat; from 10 to 3 P.M. for three days; at night; at night, with thirst. Burning here and there in skin, with some itching-tearing; B. in the spot where he had bruised himself.

Hot head; anxious heat rising into head; H. rises into head after dinner, with burning, sweaty hands; in forehead in evening, with cold sensation in body. Glowing of ears and chin. Heat in face; internally, in afternoon. Hot abdomen. Burning of palms; of tips of fingers; in soles in bed; in all cavities of body, as if raw and sore.

Sweat; towards morning; before midnight; at night on waking; when walking; on violent motion while lying, but warmth relieved the pains; cold; cold and viscid; on external pelvic region in morning, and in groins; on chest at night on waking. *Cold, on hands and feet;* cold, on forehead.

Clinical.—During typhoid fever, with tympanitis, dysuria, etc. In a late stage of yellow fever, with suppression of urine, hæmorrhage from the bowels, cold sweat.

Capsicum.

A tincture is prepared from the dried fruit of Capsicum Annuum L. (the red pepper).

General Action.—It produces inflammation of mucous membranes, with bloody mucous discharges (bowels, bladder, throat, etc.). It produces well-marked chill and fever, neuralgias and phlegmonous inflammations, with threatening, deep-seated abscess (lungs, ear).

Compare Bell., Canth., Merc. cor., Rhus t., Nat. m., and probably also Oleander.

Generalities.—Cramp in l. arm, then in whole body, with stiffness of arms so that they could not be straightened, stiffness of feet on rising after sitting, with crawling and sensation as if asleep. General trembling while caressing. Superficial stitches between scapulæ when breathing, and in epigastric region, side of abdomen, in ensiform cartilage and sternum. Aching, now in one part, now in another. Drawing pain here and there in limbs, back, nape, scapulæ and hands, excited by motion. Painless sensation in body, moving upward and downward, with redness of cheeks. (Clucking sensation, with sudden throbbing in some large veins.) *He shuns all motion.* Weariness; < morning; not inviting sleep. Sensation as if all parts would fall asleep, > sulphur-fumes.

Clinical.—Most useful in older persons who have become debilitated by disease and who react badly, not so useful in young people. Often adapted to people who have exhausted their vitality, especially by mental work, and whose vital heat is diminished, who do not react, especially from chill, muscles are weary and painful, fear of the slightest draft of either warm or cold air; sometimes indicated in persons who abstain from their accustomed alcoholic stimulants. The pains in general are burning in character and are accompanied by chilliness. Many of the sensations are those of constriction, about the throat, chest, bladder, rectum, etc.

Mind.—*Disposition to start. Taciturn, absorbed in himself; T., sullen and obstinate. Contented, jocose and singing, but angry from slightest causes.* Capricious, at one time laughing constantly, soon again crying. Obstinacy without cries. Reproaches and anger at the faults of others, offense at trifles and fault-finding. Anxiety; forcing him to take a deep breath. Busy, uneasy mood. Repugnance and fretfulness. Indifference to everything. Jokes and witticisms. Indisposition to work or think. Comatose all day.

Clinical.—Homesick, cries all the time, with chilliness and hot face.

Head.—Stitches. *Headache more sticking than tearing, < rest, > motion.* (Tearing.) **Aching as if the skull would burst** (Bell.), **on coughing** (Nat. m., Phos.); *on moving head and on walking; bursting headache or feeling as if head were too full.* Throbbing pain. *Confusion;* on waking; on waking, so that he did not recognize himself. Emptiness. *Intoxication.* Vertigo in morning on waking; and dulness in head, like a heedlessness and awkwardness, so that she knocked against everything, with chilliness and anxiety; with staggering from side to side.

Forehead.—*Drawing tearing in bone, < r. side. Aching above root of nose* (Canth., Prunus sp., Ign., etc.), *with stitches through ear and over eye. Throbbing pain* (Glon.). *Aching* as if it pressed from occiput outward to forehead, with cutting from occiput to forehead. Bursting pain (Ferr.). Drawing pain.

Aching in temples; throbbing, in one or other T. Deeply-penetrating stitches in vertex. Sudden stitches from vertex to forehead. *Drawing-tearing in l. side of head.* One-sided sticking, like a hysterical migraine, < raising eyes and head or stooping, with forgetfulness and nausea. Corrosive itching, and after scratching soreness as if the hair had been pulled.

Clinical.—The bursting headache is often associated with severe cough or is the accompaniment of malarial fever.

Eyes.—Protrusion, with pallor of face. Inflammation. Stinging. Burning in morning, with redness and lachrymation. *Pain as from a foreign body.* Pressure on, so that he could not open them sufficiently. Pupils dilated. Painful twitching beneath r. lid. Vision almost lost. All objects seem black. Dim vision in morning, as from a foreign body floating over cornea, > for a moment by rubbing.

Ears.—**Swelling on bone behind E., painful to touch.** *Tearing behind l.; in concha. Pain, deeply seated; deep-seated itching; with every cough, as if an ulcer would open;* beneath E.

Clinical.—Valuable remedy in chronic suppuration of the ears, with bursting headache, chilliness, etc.; suppuration of the middle ear, with perforation of the drum and discharge of yellow pus. Particularly in mastoid disease, with great tenderness over the petrous bone, threatening to involve the meninges of the brain.

Nose.—Constrictive jerking pain on l. side, extending to above l. eye. Burning-tensive sensation on l. nostril, as if a pimple would form. *Crawling-tickling, as in stopped coryza.* Burning-crawling, with violent sneezing and discharge of mucus. (Itching internally, with stitches.) Racking sneezing, with discharge of thin mucus. *Stopped coryza.* Discharge of bloody mucus. *Nosebleed* in morning in bed and blowing of blood from nose.

Face.—Redness of cheeks; of face, then pale, suffering expression. Now pallor, now redness, with red lobules of ears, with internal but not external heat. *Pain, partly like bone-pains, from external touch, partly like fine pains piercing the nerves, which are tormenting when falling asleep.* Pain in l. side of lower jaw, as from a boil or ulcer. *Lips swollen; chaps on L.* (Arum t.), *fissures* (Nat. m., Rh. t.); scaly; ulcerating eruption on L. (not in corners), painful only on motion; burning.

Mouth.—Drawing toothache. Teeth seem too long, and raised up and on edge. Swollen gum. Drawing pain in gum. Pimples on tip of tongue, with stinging and pain when touched. Dry sensation on forepart of tongue in morning, without thirst. Pimples on inner surface of cheeks. Palate pains as if pressed or pinched, < at first when not swallowing, then < when swallowing. Mouth dry. *Tough mucus.* Salivation. *Taste watery, flat, then heartburn;* as of bad water; flat, disagreeable, earthy (for example, of butter); sour; sour to broth; astringent, sour.

Clinical.—Stomatitis, burning ulcers.

Throat.—*Spasmodic contraction.* Stitches in region of epiglottis, causing dry cough. *Pain on swallowing as if inflamed, but when not swallowing drawing pain.* Pain when coughing; *as from a swelling; during a paroxysm of cough, as if an ulcer would break.* Pain in upper part when not swallowing, as if sore, with spasmodic contraction, as in waterbrash. Pain externally. Rawness.

Clinical.—Sore throat of smokers and drinkers, with inflammation, burning, relaxed uvula, sometimes dry, in other cases with tough mucus difficult to dislodge. Diphtheria, with gangrenous sloughs extending to roof of mouth, with excessive burning, spasmodic constriction, chilliness, etc. (compare Canth.).

Stomach.—Desire for coffee. Appetite lost. Thirst lost. Eructations only when walking, and with every E. a stitch in side; odorless, afterwards they had a peppery taste. *Nausea;* in pit in morning and afternoon; caused by cough; after drinking coffee, with spitting of saliva. Vomiting, with purging.

Stitches in pit when breathing deeply and suddenly, talking or on touch; sudden S. in pit. Pinching boring-outward in pit, < sitting bent. Pressure in pit during menses, with nausea; in pit, < pressure; in pit, with nausea; beneath short ribs and in pit. Burning; above pit after eating at noon and in evening; warmth in epigastrium, then nausea and general sick feeling; warmth extending to fauces, then burning eructations; after breakfast, extending into mouth. Feeling as if cold water were in it, then sensation as if he were trembling.

Abdomen.—Distention after eating, then shooting headache towards occiput and sweat; D. and hardness, with intolerance of tight clothing. Rumbling; with inclination to stool, > emission of flatus; extending upward and downward. Flatulence. Flatus moves about painfully. *Feeling as if distended even to bursting, causing suffocation.* Pinching after eating, with incarcerated flatus.

Colic, with cutting twisting about navel and passage of tough mucus, like diarrhœa, at times mixed with black blood, **after every stool thirst, and after every drink shivering** (Ars., Verat.). *Drawing, with twisting,* with and without diarrhœa. Pain deep in, rather burning than sticking, on motion, < stooping and walking, with cutting in umbilical region, ill humor about the pain, discontent and whining about inanimate objects (not about men or moral subjects), apprehension and sweat on face.

Pressure here and there. *Tension, especially in epigastric region, between pit of stomach and navel, < motion, with tension in lower part of back. Tensive pain, extending to chest, as from distention of abdomen.* Strong pulsations in bloodvessels. Warmth in intestinal canal. Pinching in upper part of abdomen. A hernia, consisting of wind, protrudes forcibly and painfully from abdominal ring. Pain, almost sticking, in a spot on l. side of hypogastrium. Pain in hypogastrium as from flatus.

Rectum and Anus.—**Tenesmus.** *Urging to stool after drinking, but only a little mucus passed. Feeling as if he would have diarrhœa as soon as he drank anything* (Crot. tig.), *but only a little passed every time.* Urging, with pain in intestines and constipation. *Hæmorrhoids, itching at times;* blind, paining severely during stool. Discharge of blood. *Burning in anus* (Berb., Sulph., etc.); **burning pain.** *Biting-stinging in anus, with diarrhœa-like stool.* Itching in anus.

Clinical.—Hæmorrhoids, with excessive burning as from pepper, throbbing, soreness, with drawing pain in back, etc. (Æscul.).

Stool.—Immediately after eating (at noon), with redness of cheeks. **Small frequent passages, consisting of mucus, at times mingled with blood and causing tenesmus** (Merc. c., Canth.), *preceded by flatulent colic in hypogastrium. Diarrhœa, then empty tenesmus; mucous D., with tenesmus. Small S., consisting of only mucus.* Soft and glimmering, then burning in anus. Constipation, as from too much heat in abdomen.

Clinical.—Dysentery, stools bloody, tenacious, mucous, with excessive burning and tenesmus, also associated with tenesmus of the bladder (Canth. and Merc. cor.); also particularly characterized by excessive thirst, with shivering from drinking (Arsen.) and by severe pain in back after the stool (Nux. vom.).

Urinary Organs.—*Tenesmus, strangury, frequent, almost ineffectual urging to urinate* (Merc. c., Canth.). *Pressure towards bladder while coughing and afterwards, with stitches extending outward in region of bladder.* Frequent desire to urinate, < sitting, not when walking. Intermittent spasmodic contraction of neck of bladder in morning in bed, > micturition, with cutting, without urging to urinate. Micturition difficult and in drops.

Urethra.—Stitches after urinating; *in forepart when not urinating; in orifice when not urinating.* Cutting extending backward, when not urinating. Pain, < in forenoon; P. on touch. *Burning-biting pain after urinating. Burning in orifice just before, during and after urinating* (Canth.). Gonorrhœa; a purulent discharge.

Urine copious, and she could not wholly control micturition. Scanty, light-colored U. *Burning U.* White sediment in urine.

Sexual Organs.—Pressure in glans, < morning and evening, with bruised sensation. Itching-stinging on glans, as from insects. Erections in morning in bed without sexual thoughts; E. in forenoon, afternoon and evening; violent, in morning on rising, only > cold water. Drawing pain in spermatic cord while urinating and afterwards, with pinching in testicle. *Coldness of scrotum in morning on waking; C. of scrotum,* with impotency (Agnus. c.). Loss of sensibility in testicles, with softening and dwindling, not noticed till reduced to the size of a bean, insensible, hard, drawn up close to abdominal ring and suspended by a shrivelled spermatic cord. Emission at night.

Clinical.—Gonorrhœa, with chordee, excessive burning (Canth.), pain in prostate. Impotency, with coldness of scrotum, tendency to atrophy of testicles (Agn. cast.).

Respiratory Organs.—*Hoarseness. Crawling in larynx and trachea in evening after lying down, with dry hacking cough.* Tickling in trachea, causing violent sneezing. Mucus in upper part of trachea, expectorated from time to time by hawking and voluntary hacking cough. *Cough,* < *5 to 9* P.M.; < drinking coffee; *painful; frequent, dry, hacking;* paroxysm about 5 P.M., causing nausea and vomiting. **Cough expels an offensive breath from lungs.** *The exhalation from the lungs on coughing causes a strange offensive taste in mouth.*

Asthma, fulness in chest. *Dyspnœa;* when walking; even during rest, with stiffness of back, which hurt when stooping, with deep sighing from time to time and dry cough; with redness of face, eructations and sensation as if chest were distended; *which seems to rise from stomach.* Only able to inspire with the body erect, orthopnœa. Frequent necessity to take deep inspirations, whereby all his troubles were relieved. A voluntary strong expiration. Breathing deep, almost sighing.

Clinical.—Violent cough, with feeling as if the chest would fly to pieces, pains shoot to all parts of body, cough explosive. Threatening gangrene of lung. The odor from coughing is putrid.

Chest.—Stitches between l. second and third ribs; between l. third and fourth ribs; between l. fifth and sixth ribs; in side of C. and back when coughing; between l. third and fourth ribs on inspiration; in side on breathing while walking, > sitting; in l., arresting breathing.

Drawing-tearing, extending from r. clavicle along arm to tips of fingers. Pain on ribs on inspiration, and on sternum; in side on which she lies; beneath r. arm, if he feels the spot or raises the arm; (in a spot in one rib, < touch); *throbbing;* drawing, in side on coughing, extending to throat; like a pressure on C., on deep breathing and on turning body.

Constriction, < *slight motion, arresting breathing. Pain when sitting as if too full.* Fulness after eating, with anxiety, then sour eructations or heartburn, at last thin stool.

Heart and Pulse.—Stitches in region of heart. Pulse rapid.

Neck and Back.—*Jerking-tearing in r. cervical glands.* Jerking pain in nape. Stiffness of neck on motion; > motion. Weak sensation in neck, as if loaded. *Drawing-tearing in and near spine.* Sudden drawing-sticking in middle of spine. Pain in back on stooping. Drawing pain in back. Pain in small of back, drawing-downward, when standing and moving, with bruised pain.

Extremities.—Cracking and creaking in joints of knees and fingers. Convulsive jerks and twitches, now in thigh, now in forearm. Pain shoots into one or another limb when coughing and sneezing. Joints pain as if dislocated and feel swollen. Joints feel crushed in morning on rising, with a paralytic stiff pain on beginning to move, especially in knees and ankles, > continued motion. Joints become stiff after lying down, then crushed feeling in them on rising in morning, especially the lameness of knees and ankles < rest; stiffness of joints, < beginning to move, > continued motion, with pain in them and catarrh and tough mucus in trachea. Weariness, < rest and sitting; with heaviness, then trembling of upper limbs and knees, and the hands refused their service when writing; as if bruised.

Upper Extremities.—Shoulder-joint pains as if dislocated. (Drawing paralytic pain above and below elbow.) Stitches in l. elbow, extending into hand, with flushes of heat, from which the arm felt as if asleep. Grumbling pain in l. forearm. Twitching pain in hollow of l. hand. Deep-seated stitches in ball of l. little finger. Contractive pain in l. index.

Lower Extremities.—Thigh. Drawing digging-sticking in middle of posterior surface of l., > motion. *Sticking-tearing from hip-joints to feet,* < *coughing.* Tearing on inner side of l. *Drawing pain in hip-joint (pain like a stiff neck),* < *touch and bending trunk backward.* Pain in muscles like a pressure and a sprain. Sprained pain in r., < stretching out thigh. Bruised pain in r., > walking, returning during rest. Deep, pressing-inward pain in side, on coughing, extending into knee.

Tensive pain in knee. Tension in calves when walking. Internal drawing-sticking in l. leg. (Paroxysmal bruised pain in bones of heels, at times becoming tearing.) Trembling weakness of feet. Stitches extending to tips of toes; S. in r. great toe, > stamping.

Skin.—Red points on face, and on forehead a tetter with corrosive itching; (red round spots on abdomen and thighs). Painful pimples beneath nostrils; (pimples on l. side of face, with bitting as from salt.) Pimples from neck to knees, with itching and burning, < at night, afterwards P. became filled with erythematous redness, then vesicles formed, most abundant where perspiration was most confined, as in folds of axillary region, under bindings of skirts, etc., the eruption spread to scalp and soles, with swelling, a bagging of cheeks and neck, l. side of face and l. ear being more affected then r., and where the perspiration was confined the skin was raised and broken, as if scalded.

Sticking on wrist. Crawling here and there; in arms and legs, from feet upward to throat. (Itching only after touch); I. in hair of head, > scratching, and in spots on rest of body; here and there, mostly in face and nose; sticking burning, especially on chest and face.

Sleep.—*Yawning;* after eating. Sleepiness all day; after the heat; < eating. Snoring, as if he could not inspire through the nose. *He becomes wide awake in the night and cannot sleep again;* wide awake after midnight and also later. Frequent waking after midnight. Sleep interrupted by crying and starting as if he fell from a high place. *Sleep full of dreams.* Dreams full of difficulties. Sad dreams, of past experiences, and on waking he did not know whether it was real or not.

Fever.—Aversion to cold air, especially a draught. *General coldness.* Chill in afternoon, then the skin burned and itched more than before; C. in evening; in evening after lying down, then coryza; (in evening, with thirst (without heat, yawning or stretching), with weariness, short breath, sleepiness, fretfulness, and shivering on slightest motion, without internal or external coldness, and yet he was not too warm in a hot room). Chill at night, general sweat the following nights; C. from a little air in bed. Coldness increasing, with increase of ill humor and of contraction of pupils. Gradual diminution of warmth.

Trembling on account of shivering. **Shivering after every drink, with chilliness** (Ars., Verat., Chin., Asar.); S. over hairy part of head, then burning-itching on scalp, which was > by scratching, but returned with increased severity. Coldness of feet as far as ankles in morning. Shivering and coldness in back in evening, then sweat without heat or thirst. Sensation in thighs as if covered with cold sweat, when walking in open air (as if a cold wind blew against sweaty parts), but the thighs did not sweat.

Heat over whole body after pressure in stomach, with increased redness of face. Heat, with shivering and thirst; H. and sweat without thirst, then shivering at 6 P.M., with chattering of teeth, thirst, anxiety, uneasiness, loss of senses and intolerance of noise, next day at 7 P.M. similar shivering, with coldness and thirst. (Internal heat, with cold sweat on forehead). *Heat of ears towards evening, with hot, red tip of nose;* H. of hands; *of hands,* < *morning on washing in cold water;* of face, with redness of it and trembling of limbs; glowing hot cheeks two days at noon after eating, with coldness of hands and feet; (burning hands, feet and cheeks, the latter swollen). Burning on skin, with itching, Corrosive burning on tender portions (lips, mouth, nose, tip of nose, wings of nose, eyelids, etc.).

General sweat in morning. Sweat so acrid that it caused the hands of any person who touched the patient to burn and tingle. Sweat on forehead; under shoulders; cool, on hands.

Clinical.—Intermittent fever, chill begins in the back (Eup purp.), > heat, thirst, but chill after drinking, with the chill excruciating pain in back and limbs, heat and sweat often commingled; generally less thirst during the fever and sweat than during the chill; the thirst begins even before the chill (Eup. per., China, Nat. mur.). In scarlet fever, with corrosive discharge from nose, great fetor of breath, general tendency to coldness. Sometimes indicated in typhoid fever. Occasionally in pyæmia, with high temperature and profuse sweat, easily chilled, < drinking.

Carbo Animalis.

Animal charcoal, obtained from charred ox-hide, is triturated for use.

General Action.—A tissue remedy, like all the Carbons.

Compare Carbo veg., Aurum, Caps., Carbon. s.

Generalities.—Spasm, vertigo, she screamed, opened her mouth and bent backward to the right side and threw up her hands. She came near falling, opened the mouth and raised her eyes, with heat over whole body, sweat on face and whining mood. Stitches in the scar of a burn. Aching in joints and muscles. All joints feel bruised, pulled apart and powerless. Throbbing in whole body, < evening. Orgasm of blood, without heat. Uneasiness, with haste. Indolence.

Weakness in morning on waking after a good sleep; in morning on rising, with such sadness that she could have cried; in morning, especially in lower limbs, with bruised feeling; in forenoon, even to sinking down; from eating; while walking; from walking, especially in hypochondrium; after walking, with sleepiness; < afternoon, with apprehension and melancholy; *with want of energy and confusion of head; so that she could scarcely speak after appearance of menses, with yawning and stretching;* at night as if bruised; of mind and body after an emission, with apprehension. Weaker every day, although he eats and drinks.

Clinical.—Especially suited to old people. Sometimes indicated after debilitating disease. Veins distended, skin blue, especially on hands and feet. Indurations of the glands. Indolent tumors, especially with burning pain.

Mind.—Desire to be alone, she is sad and reflective and avoids conversation (Aur.). Frightful images in evening before sleep. Fear; in evening, causing shuddering and weeping; and shyness. Apprehension in afternoon, with heaviness in body, so that walking was difficult. *Anxiety at night, with orgasm of blood, so that she was obliged to sit up;* A. < evening and night, with depression, the A. preventing sleep, she felt best in the morning; so that he was constantly obliged to rock back and forth on his chair. *Homesick* (Caps.). Feeling in morning as if abandoned and homesick. Thoughts of death. Hopelessness. Lachrymose; at times, foolishly jovial at other times; he cannot weep enough. Discouragement and sadness, everything seems so sad and lonely that she desires to weep. Melancholy; in morning on waking, with anxiety; with feeling as if abandoned.

Anger. Ill humor; in morning on waking; ill humor, with aversion to talking. Sullen mood and ill humor about the present and past, with weeping. Obstinate, and no one could do anything to suit him. Indifference, then irritability for passionate impressions. Jovial. Involuntary jolly whistling.

Stupidity in forenoon, < after dinner, with drowsiness. Stupefaction while sitting eating, with lightness of head and dread lest he should fall down unconscious; sudden S. when moving head and on walking; sudden, he did not hear, nor see and had no thoughts. Inability to write a letter and to express his thoughts. Forgot the word he was about to speak.

Head.—Stitches, especially in temples. Tearing after dinner, > pressure, with throbbing, and in orbits, ears, l. side of face, cheek-bones and lower jaw, then swelling of cheek. Drawing-boring, < cold, especially towards the ears, with tearings. Aching in morning on waking, as after intoxication; at night as if asleep and sprained, and in neck; which presses down the eyebrows. Pressure after dinner till evening, with confusion. Everything on H. pressed upon it, even the neck-cloth was uncomfortable. *Heaviness; in morning, with dim vision and watery eyes; at night, with weariness in feet, which she could scarcely lift; especially in occiput* and of l. temple, with confusion. *Confusion in morning, he did not know whether he had been asleep or awake; C. in morning,* and she was vexed with everything she looked at; in morning, and feeling as in a confused dream. Discomfort from 10 A.M. till 4 P.M., as if confused in head and uncertain on her feet, with pale face, nausea and blue rings around eyes. Tension almost daily. Feeling of painful looseness of brain, on motion. *Rush of blood, with confusion.*

Vertigo in morning, with feeling as if he had not slept enough; V. about 7 P.M., if she raised her head everything seemed to turn around, she was obliged to sit bent, on rising staggering, with confusion of head and feeling as if all objects moved, the V. > on lying down at night, returning in morning on rising; *on rising after stooping, with nausea;* while walking, with fog before her eyes, forcing her to walk rapidly and to the right; with nausea and a sudden watery mist before eyes; with blackness before eyes; when sitting, as if she would fall backward from her chair, with stupidity; as if moving head back and forth; V. to the r. side.

Forehead.—Pricking pain on l. in morning after rising, > open air. Sticking over l. eye, extending into lid and upper half of ball. Stupefying pain while spinning, > after dinner. *Sensation as if something lay above eyes, so that she could not look up. Heaviness on stooping, with sensation as if brain would fall forward, then vertigo on rising, so that she nearly fell.* Sensation of something heavy in it or as if a board pressed upon it, a sensation as when going from very cold air to in front of a hot stove. Drawing above eyebrows.

Stitches in temples, with contractive pain or twinges. Pinching in lower part of temples. Aching in T. Boring in temporal bone, extending into zygoma. Stitches in vertex in evening. Pain in vertex, with a sensitive spot externally, on stooping it changes to the forehead; *pain in V. as if skull had been split or torn asunder, so that she held her head with her hands from fear lest it should fall asunder, also at night, < wet weather;* throbbing pain in V. when walking, with stitches as if head would crack. *Tearing on r. side;* T. in r. side. Pressure daily in a spot on parietal bones near vertex, < forenoon and dampness of soiled clothes, > open air. Splashing in l. half of brain when walking rapidly.

Occiput.—Twitching tearings shoot back and forth in l. in evening. Tearing in r. in evening, with sticking. Aching; in a spot; during menses, > open air, extending to vertex anteriorly, with heaviness; intermitting in l.; headache in neck when writing. Painful, heavy sensation. *Throbbing*, with stitches.

Falling off of hair. Tearing on external parts. Pain in l. side externally, as if suppurating. Anxious tension and drawing up in skin of forehead and vertex. Itching, not > scratching.

Eyes.—Stitches. Aching in evening by a light; during menses, extending to forehead, vertex and into l. ear, with heaviness. Sensation of a foreign body in l. preventing vision, with constant necessity to wipe the eye, with extreme dilatation of pupil and far-sightedness. Twitching of r., with feeling as if something were moving in it, which blinded her, and drawing downward in upper lid, > rubbing, but returning, leaving sensitiveness to touch in margin of upper lid.

Sticking-burning after itching and rubbing of them, with watering. Itching during the day, with pressure; biting I., with burning after rubbing. Lachrymation in morning on rising. Eyes seemed loose in their sockets, and he could not see distinctly, which made him anxious. Agglutination of l. lids in forenoon. Twitching of upper lid. Itching of upper lid, > scratching. Sticking in l. internal canthus in morning after rising, > rubbing, with biting. Pressure in internal canthus. Smarting-burning in external canthus.

Weakness; in evening she could do nothing requiring vision. Photophobia in evening. *Vision of a net swimming before the eyes;* of black and yellow points in regular rows, by candle-light. Objects upon the street seem altered, for example, farther apart and brighter than usual, as if the city were empty and deserted. V. as through a mist. V. obscure.

Ears.—Swelling of periosteum behind r. every day after 7 P.M., with sticking in it. Stitches. Tearing in l.; in lobule of r., and boring in the ear. Pinching within l.; in l. extending into pharynx, making swallowing difficult. Drawing; in external ear and in l. cheek-bone. *Hearing weak; and confused, commingling of sounds, he cannot tell from which side they come, and they seem to come from another world.* Ringing all night; in r. while walking in open air. Whistling on blowing nose.

Clinical.—Deafness, with confused hearing, cannot tell the direction of sound.

Nose.—*Redness of tip, with pain on touch;* of tip during menses, with cracks, burning and tensive pain; with swelling and internal soreness. Swelling, and of mouth; S., with pimples internally and externally, which form a long-lasting scurf. Tensive boil in nostril. Blisters in r. nostril. Tearing in side. Bruised pain above and in root; when touched. Sensation of beginning coryza after eating, < evening. Stoppage of l. nostril in forenoon.

Coryza, catarrh and scraping in throat, < evening and night, and swallowing. Coryza, with rawness of throat. *Fluent C.;* in evening; with loss of smell, yawning and sneezing; of much watery mucus. Stopped C. in morning on waking, > after rising; from forenoon till evening; no air can get through nose. Frequent passage of mucus, with stopped coryza. **Bleeding mornings** (Carbo v.), **preceded by vertigo;** *B. in morning when sitting*, and in afternoon; at night; *preceded by pressure and confusion of head.* Blowing out of blood.

Face.—Yellow. Tearing in l. malar-bone, extending towards temples; in r. jaw, now upper, now lower. Lips swollen and burning; corner of lip ulcerated, with burning pain; blisters on lips; cracks; bleeding of lips; dryness in morning, as from too great heat.

Mouth.—Teeth. *Looseness* (Carbo v.), so that chewing the softest food was painful; L. < evening in bed, with tearing; of lower, with pain in gum. She frequently bites the inside of the mouth. Tearing, especially in hollow teeth, even at night, disturbing sleep. Griping in l., < open air. Throbbing from cold drinks, then looseness; T. < pressure, and in evening. Drawing, with flushes of heat in face; D. back and forth, even in incisors; in a l. lower back tooth as often as she woke at night; in l. back teeth, < afternoon; sudden and sticking pains in back T. while eating bread. Nerves sensitive to touch of crowns. A hollow tooth becomes sensitive and feels prominent, it pains on biting, and still more in the evening, in bed, with salivation. Teeth too long and loose; r. upper. *Gums red, swollen and painful.* Gums pale and painful as if suppurating.

Blisters on tongue, with pain as if burnt (Caps.); blisters on margin of T. *Burning on tip of T., with rawness of mouth* (Caps.); B. on side of tongue as if sore. Mouth swollen. *Blisters in mouth*, which cause burning. Mucus in M. in morning, > rising. M. and tongue seem immovable, with difficult drawling or very low speech. Dryness of M. and throat, without thirst. Flow of saliva during sleep. Frothy saliva. Breath offensive.

Taste.—*Bitter every morning;* in morning, > rising; *at times.* Sour; bitter sour; slimy sour in morning after waking. Foul in morning; bitter foul. Nauseous in morning.

Throat.—Parotids swollen; r. *Much mucus, with frequent hawking and raising.* Feeling as of mucus in morning on waking, compelling hawking, > noon. Scraping-sticking. Pressure, with dryness of tongue; P. extending to stomach. Sore pain and burning like heartburn, extending to stomach, < towards evening, night and morning, > rising, eating and drinking. *Rawness almost every morning, > breakfast; extending to pit of stomach, not < swallowing.* Scraping, with salivation. *Burning* (Caps.). Acidity, but not in mouth. *Swallowing painful;* as if a blister were in throat. Soreness when swallowing, with ulcerative pain. Rising into œsophagus and throat, with choking, pressure and rawness.

Stomach.—Appetite increased. Hunger in morning; two hours after a large dinner and again towards evening, then thirst; but he does not relish food. Longing for sour and refreshing things. Appetite for raw sauerkraut, no appetite for other things. Little A., but it returns while eating; soon disappears while eating. *Aversion to food; to fat.* Thirst even in morning; especially for cold water, with dryness and heat in throat. Aversion to cold drinks.

Eructations.—Tasting of food eaten a long time previous. Empty, every time after eating; E., changing to hiccough. Hiccough-like, during dinner. Foul, almost constant; foul, fishy. Inclination to waterbrash at night, with nausea. Waterbrash, with salt water rising from stomach and running from mouth, with retching and spasmodic sensation in jaws, then violent empty eructations, with cold feet, then hiccough.

Nausea in morning after rising, with heat, anxiety, eructations of sour water and weariness; *N. from smoking tobacco and aversion to it;* when he sits down after walking much; *long-continued, after eating meat,* with empty eructations. Gurgling; in morning on waking. Constrictive cramp. Fulness after eating a little, with good appetite. Stitches; in r. side near pit, even on inspiration, > walking; tearing, from pit into chest, on rising after stooping. Boring as after fasting, extending to abdomen. Pressure in evening after lying down, > pressure on epigastric region; P. after eating; even when fasting; with heaviness, fulness and inclination to waterbrash; and in chest and sometimes in abdomen. Sudden pressive pain in pit on deep inspiration. Bruised feeling in pit, as after a violent cough. *Heartburn rising from S.;* scraping heartburn.

Abdomen.—*Distention;* during menses; after a moderate dinner; *with motions and passage of offensive flatus.* Protrusion here and there, like a hernia. Rumbling; as from flatus which could find no outlet; in colon, rising to beneath stomach, then passing down again, with gurgling. Fermenting; and gurgling. Motions, with ineffectual urging to stool; M. of flatus, with sensation as if something were moving, as if torn and bruised. Frequent passage of offensive flatus in forenoon; much offensive F. when walking after supper. *Much trouble from flatulence* (Carbo v.).

Cutting in forenoon; from morning till noon, with frequent urging to stool and tenesmus, but emission of only flatus. Partly cutting, partly sticking. Griping after stool. G., with uneasiness. Pain as if ulcerating. Pain as before diarrhœa. Painful tension, with pain beneath ribs on touch as if suppurating. Constriction when fasting, with sensation of emptiness, though without hunger and without appetite. Heaviness like a lump, even when fasting. Qualmishness towards evening, with flushes of heat. Heat; when walking. Weakness of intestines after a stool, with pain as if they would be screwed together.

Pinching in r. side of upper when sitting, with stitches; sticking, in upper every morning, < in bed. Digging in upper, with twisting. Pressure in liver, even when lying. Pain in liver, almost like cutting, and soreness of region to touch. Boring in r. after eating. Aching in l. side. Stitching pinching above umbilicus and in pit of stomach every morning in bed, as from flatulence, > passage of flatus, of stool and of urine, though it also disappeared of itself and was less noticed when walking. Griping in umbilical region; with feeling as if stool would follow.

Hypogastrium.—Rumbling and grumbling in r. after drinking warm milk, now in upper, now in lower part, with ineffectual effort to pass flatus. *Tearing transversely across pubes and then through pudenda as far as anus.* Cutting deep-seated; C. in r. flank, > walking and on deep breathing. Deep-seated pinching constriction. *Pain in r. as if something would be squeezed through.* Pain as if sore from coughing. Bruised pain in crest of l. ilium, < evening, with pressure, so that she must bend double, and on external pressure pain as if ulcerated.

Groins.—*Sticking;* at night waking her; as from flatus, with a hard stool. *Feeling after sitting down as if a large heavy body were lying there, > after pressure by passage of flatus.* Dragging at times, like a burning in strangury. Pressing during menses, and in small of back and in thighs, with ineffectual attempts at eructations, chilliness and yawning. Tension and contraction, preventing stretching of legs.

Rectum.—Large hæmorrhoids appear, with burning pain. *Hæmorrhoids swell very much, with burning pain on walking.* Cutting in hæmorrhoids during stool. Protrusion, with pain on walking, on motion and on touch. Gurgling. *Burning* in evening. Scratching after a stool. Frequent but ineffectual urging to stool in lower part. Pressing as for stool, but only flatus passed and the pressure returned. Much urging to stool, which is passed with difficulty; and is hard and streaked with blood.

Anus.—Boil. *Oozing of sticky odorless moisture.* Sticking during stool; *S., with soreness. Soreness in evening, with moisture in it.* Painful contraction. Drawing, extending through pudenda before stool; cutting, extending through coccyx, between stools. *Burning.*

Perineum.—*Sticky odorless moisture, behind scrotum.* Pinching-biting pain.

Stool.—After midnight. Liquid, followed by straining. *Soft,* preceded by dragging in pubis; S., green, preceded and accompanied by pains in abdomen; with mucus like coagulated albumen. Diarrhœa, with burning in anus, preceded by griping in abdomen.

Hard, then a soft one, with burning in anus; H., preceded by shivering in head as if dashed with cold water; first part hard and difficult, with feeling as if there were more which the rectum could not evacuate; and crumbling, in evening, difficult as from inactivity of abdominal muscles, with oppression of breath; and scanty, in small pieces. *Scanty and delayed;* S. and light-colored. Frequent, preceded by pain in abdomen. *Passage of blood during stool.* Portion of a tape-worm passed with a hard stool.

Urinary Organs.—Pain in bladder at night. Urging to urinate after stool (urine very red), then weariness and early sleepiness without ability to sleep, after lying down immediate jumping up, ringing in ears, feeling as if she would faint and a shaking chill; urging, and after urinating voluptuous tickling in urethra; sudden desire. Urine passes on slight pressure, almost against his will. The passage is much more forcible. The stream is interrupted. Frequent micturition; *at night;* at night, with profuse urine. *Burning in urethra while urinating;* after urinating; *burning sore pain in urethra while urinating* (Caps.). Spasmodic pain along urethra, especially its posterior part, in morning on waking, after an emission. Urine profuse in morning after waking; P. after a night fever. Scanty U.; at night, and burning. Yellow U., with a speedy loose sediment. Turbid, orange-colored. Turbid when passed and soon depositing a turbid sediment.

Sexual Organs.—Relaxation and weak feeling. Itching. Lack of the usual morning erection. Sticking on both sides of scrotum. Desire wanting, even on provocation. Emissions at 4 P.M.; E., with voluptuous dream, without erection; frequent; frequent at night.

Tearing from pudenda into abdomen, with stool. Leucorrhœa; *coloring the linen yellow;* watery, when standing and walking. *Menses profuse. Menses scanty the first day, more copious than usual the second, the blood dark.* M. too early, preceded by headache; too early, with pain in sacrum and groins. M. shorter than usual and late. M. lasting longer than usual and flowing only in the morning.

Clinical.—Chronic metritis, with induration of the neck of the uterus. True scirrhus of the uterus; painful induration in the mammary gland, with stinging pain. Induration of r. ovary, which feels like a heavy ball. Sometimes indicated in disorders following suppression of the menses, with feeling of goneness, desire to be alone, etc. (compare Sepia). The pains in the sexual organs are generally burning or sometimes tearing, with heaviness and pressure. Sometimes indicated in syphilis, with copper-colored eruptions or with buboes, which have a blue look (Tarent. cub.). Old buboes which will not heal, but which secrete an offensive ichor. Scirrhous nodule in mammary gland, skin looks bluish and mottled, axillary glands involved, with burning, drawing pains.

Respiratory Organs.—Pain as after much coughing. Tickling in trachea, > after eating, with cough. *Hoarseness in morning after rising, with rawness* and dry cough; *H. < evening;* during the day, then loss of voice at night, awoke with coldness, swelling of pit of stomach, violent cough, difficult expiration, anxious sweat and inability to get her breath.

Cough, which impedes the breath. Suffocative, in evening after going to sleep. Rough, with pain in throat as if sore. *Tickling; with constriction of larynx and chest.* Hacking, in evening, < in bed; from tickling in larynx. *Dry,* day and night; *in morning on rising and nearly all day, shaking abdomen as if everything would fall out, she is obliged to hold the bowels with the hands and sit down, loose râles in chest until something is coughed up;* in evening, from tickling in larynx; *only at night* when lying on r. side. Cough in morning from dryness of throat, > expectoration of mucus. The former dry C. becomes loose. C., with expectoration; purulent expectoration. Cough arising from a small spot in r. side of chest, with greenish, purulent expectoration. Greenish, purulent expectoration after dry cough. Thick, greenish, purulent expectoration from a vomica which formed in r. thorax. Whitish-yellow mucous expectoration.

Fear of suffocating in evening while lying with closed eyes, > sitting up and opening eyes, it prevented sleep all night, with mucus in throat. Dyspnœa after eating. Breath seems arrested in chest. Catching of breath on inspiration, with oppression of chest.

Chest.—Rattling in evening in bed, with piping. Trembling, like a crying. Stitches in side from coughing; S. in r. cavity; in r. lower, extending into axilla; under l. ribs; in upper part of l. side and sometimes in r. side; in morning, now in lower portion of l. chest, now in r. shoulder-joint, now in r. flank, < dry cough, with oppression of breathing; in lower portion of female breast, < pressure, arresting breath; below r. breast, so that she could not sit still, when sitting and writing, > after rising; in r. side on every breath, as from something sore there; (burning) in l. side, even when sitting; in sternum as with knives, < motion.

Digging-pinching in upper part, with tension. Pain in side ceases after a dry cough. Pain as if it would burst, with sore pain in it. Painful twisting in and beneath it. Anxiety in morning; A. after eating. Oppression in middle; with oppression of breathing. Compression in morning when sitting, with arrest of breathing. Constriction; in morning in bed, with suffocation, she thought she would die, with stitches in heart on speaking and sensation on moving arm as if heart and chest would be torn to pieces; with feeling as if whole chest were oppressed or over-fatigued; sudden on deep breathing. *Burning, with pressive pain;* B. especially r. side. Cold feeling. Speedy fatigue while eating, and of organs of mastication.

Clinical.—Pneumonia in a late stage, with ulceration of the lung, suffocating, hoarse cough, the expectoration purulent, extremely offensive (Cap.) and feeling of coldness in chest.

Heart.—Pressure almost like pinching. Palpitation in morning on waking and necessity to lie still without opening eyes and without speaking; P. in evening without anxiety; after eating; when singing in church; and every beat of the heart is felt in the head.

Neck.—Cervical glands swollen. Stiffness; of l. side. Tension. Feeling as if skin were raised in a spot.

Back.—Anxiety and uneasiness after eating. Pain on l. side nights so that she cannot lie on it. Stitches between scapulæ. Sprained pain between scapulæ, and in forepart of chest on moving arm. Painful tension between S., > rubbing. Sticking tension in r. S. Stitch in sacrum. *Pain in sacrum during stool,* with distention of abdomen extending into chest. Pain in lower part. Pain as from an ulcer under skin, on lowest end of spine, < sitting and lying.

Stitches just above loins on deep breathing; in loins, extending into thigh, with every breath; alternating S. above r. hip. Sticking-picking in region of kidneys. *Pain in loins;* on rising after sitting some time; in region of kidneys when walking; in loins when sitting, as before menses. *Drawing pain in loins when walking, standing and lying, and feeling as if broken. Drawing across loins, < every step.* Stiffness of loins. Jerks in coccyx towards bladder, compelling her to urinate. *Dragging bruised pain in coccyx. Pain in coccyx, on touch it became a burning.*

Clinical.—The pain in the coccyx has led to the successful employment of this drug for injuries of the coccyx and for neuralgia of the coccyx.

Extremities.—Cracking of joints. Internal trembling on going to sleep in evening, with twitching of knees, legs and feet and necessity to draw them up. Joints are easily sprained. Joints feel broken. Pinching pain here and there. Pain in joints at night; in ligaments of elbows and knees when lying. *Bruised pain,* < motion. Tearing-drawing pain in fingers and toes. Pain as from pressure of a finger on arms and limbs. Numb sensation, especially also in head. Heaviness; in morning; of legs and arms, with trembling. Stiffness after sitting. Frequent sensation in arms and feet as if they would go to sleep. Arm goes to sleep when resting upon it and the leg when riding it over the other; now r. arm goes to sleep in evening in bed, and now r. foot.

Upper Extremities.—Tearing in shoulder, > motion and rubbing. Shoulders are heavy and tired. Shoulders and chest seem oppressed and loaded on walking. Tearing in r. upper arm on raising arm; in middle of r. upper arm after midnight when lying on that side, preventing sleep; in r. humerus towards elbow. Burrowing in arms, extending down bones, > lying on arm. Drawing pain in arms and hands.

Drawing-sticking in tip of elbow, the skin is painful as if sore on slight touch, but not when grasped tightly. Burning and twinging pain in r. elbow in evening. Sticking below bend of l. elbow, extending to palm. Burning in l. forearm, sometimes extending into shoulder, with stinging, only transiently > rubbing. Boring in condyles of wrists. *Sprained pain in wrist.* Tensive pain in wrist on moving it.

Hand.—Tearing. Stitches in l. palm and in ball of r. hand. Drawing stitches in outer margin, where the skin is painful on slight touch as if sore, but not on pinching. Numbness of l. in morning in bed, > rising. *Falling asleep* daily; falling asleep during rest. Chilblains on little finger. Stitches in fingers; in tips; in tip of index like the sting of a wasp. Tearing on back of fingers and in bones, > rubbing. The middle finger-joints pain on motion. Tension in first joint of middle F. on motion. Falling asleep of F., then of whole hand.

Lower Extremities.—Tottering, as if caused by some external power. Cramp in thighs and legs at night. *Stitches in l. hip when sitting;* burning, here and there in thighs and loins; tearing, in middle of r. thigh, on inner side, in evening when standing. Tearing below hips from morning till evening, < forenoon and when sitting; above knees, as if in bones, only transiently > rubbing; in outer side of thigh at night, > rising; in l. thigh, as if in marrow, while standing during menses, > sitting. Pinching in r. hip when walking. Boring in upper part of r. femur after a restless night, with drawing. Twitching pain in thighs. Drawing in muscles of thighs, with tearing. Weariness of thighs before and during menses.

Knee.—Cramp in r. when walking. Stitches in hollow of l. while walking; tearing and crawling, in r., that after rubbing extend into tibia, only transiently > rubbing. Tearing at night, > rising. Pain in r. when standing in evening, as if screwed together, with sensation as if leg would bend together. Sore pain on bending; sore pain in r., < walking. Painless drawing in r., which bends it up, it pains when stretched, > continued motion. Sensation in bend of r. while walking as if tendons were too short, > sitting.

Leg.—*Cramp in forepart near tibia when walking;* in calves mornings; in calves disturbing sleep at night; painful, after walking. Jerklike drawing in tibia. Stitches in r., when rising after kneeling, shooting through whole body. Tearing in r., especially in knee and ankle; in lower part of l. tibia and outer surface of r. leg, then in great toes. Pain in tibiæ at night; in tibia while walking. Intermittent bruised pain in tibia while walking, with tension in calves. Sudden pain as if broken, in leg, on waking at night and turning it in bed, then leaden heaviness. Painless drawing up l. leg at night. *Tension in calves when walking. Falling asleep of legs as far as calves during the day* (Carbon. s.); r. leg, as far as toes, goes to sleep at night when lying on r. side, with feeling as if leg were longer than natural. Stiffness of ankle in morning on rising. **Weakness of ankle when walking** (Carbon. s.), so that it turned over.

Foot.—*Corns appear, which are painful on touch* (Sil.). Swelling, with tension; inflammatory S., beginning on one toe. Stinging in a corn. Stitches penetrating l. sole. Pain in heels as if suppurating. Drawing in tendon of r. heel, with tearing. Painful contraction of tendo-achillis in evening. Tension of back of foot as if tendons were too short, next day soreness to touch. Stitchlike crawling in morning, as if going to sleep. Giving out while walking, as from weakness of joints.

Toes.—Cramp during the day, while walking over an uneven path it seems as if they would give out. Swelling of ball of great T. in morning, with heat and pain as if it had been frozen and ulcerated. Tearing in r. great T. Sprained pain in last joints while walking and on every motion. Cutting-burning, especially in little T. Soreness between T.

Skin.—*Red eruption on cheeks.* Coppery eruption on face. Hard, itching elevations on forearm near wrist. Painful nodules in breasts. *Pimples on face;* red on chin, with yellowish tip; itching, on wrist, neck and on back of foot, with burning-itching after scratching; white, itching, on backs of hands, with burning and redness after scratching. Hard boil on forehead. Pustules on l. cheek and forehead. Excoriation of nates from riding, then blisters. Dryness of tip of nose, with desquamation.

Pain in face after shaving, especially on cheeks and about mouth and chin. Tension on limbs, with a feeling of burning or icy-coldness. Biting as from flea bites, changing to another place after scratching. Itching, spreading over whole body, < evening in bed; on tip of nose, not > by scratching; in r. axilla; on inner surface of r. forearm, then itching eruption there; on backs of hands and fingers; in warts on fingers; of the toes that had been frozen.

Sleep.—*Sleepiness the whole forenoon, with frequent yawning;* S. in evening, with photophobia. He seems as if in a slumber all day, and on account of it, indolent, hard of hearing, with obscured vision, fretful and gloomy. Unable to sleep in the evening and had generally only very light sleep. Sleeplessness at night on account of heat and restlessness; S. till 2 A.M., with excitement; after 2.30 A.M., on account of internal uneasiness; till 5 A.M., but was refreshed after two hours' sleep. Restless night; with anxiety and frequent waking. Starting on going to sleep, as if she would fall; frequent starting up on falling asleep in evening. Groaning in sleep. Loud talking in sleep. Crying in sleep at night and sobbing on waking.

Dreams vivid; and frightful; about scientific subjects, he made literary compositions and spoke aloud. D. of murders. Anxious, with screaming and crying, then sad, then voluptuous, with emissions. Fanciful and confused, so that he scarcely slept at all.

Fever.—*Chilliness; during the day;* he was scarcely able to get warm in the morning; in afternoon, with cold creeping and with trembling as from within outward, without thirst, then thirst, burning in skin and in eyes; from 5 till 8 P.M., with gooseflesh, waking at 11 P.M., with sweat which lasted till 2 A.M., during which she could not tolerate the bed-covering; in evening in bed, then sweat during sleep; in evening without thirst, then heat, > lying down; at 9 P.M., then after lying down heat, during which she fell asleep but was frequently awakened by thirst, sweat towards morning; *febrile, woke her at night;* in bed; immediately on being uncovered during febrile stage; when a little air entered the room; after dinner; internal, on beginning to eat.

Shivering in evening after stool; every other day towards evening, with thirst, then dry heat, so that she believed that fiery sparks darted before her eyes, then sweat at night; down back, which seemed to begin in chest, every afternoon. Cold limbs during the day. Cold hands and feet in evening. *Cold feet;* from 9 A.M. till 3 P.M.; in forenoon while walking; in evening in bed.

Easily heated. Heat at night, with thirst; H. at night, with moisture of skin; frequent rising, in evening, with redness and burning of cheeks; anxious, before menses. Hot feet. Burning of lobule of r. ear. Heat in head in evening in bed, > rising, with anxiety; of head and upper part of body at night in bed, with coldness of legs, then chilliness towards morning; in forehead in forenoon, with heaviness and external coldness of it; face and head in afternoon; in face during dinner, with sweat. Flushes of heat in cheeks, with redness. Heat in palms in morning; in hand in evening as he went into the open air and sat down; of feet while walking and swelling of them while sitting.

Sweat in morning after waking; *at night;* as soon as he closes the eyes; when eating; when eating warm food; when walking; when walking in open air. **Offensive sweat at night. S. which colors the linen yellow. Exhausting, at night.** On head at night. Much moisture in axillæ. Sweat of feet; in hollows of knees on waking after midnight, with swelling of fingers.

Carbo Vegetabilis.

The finest birch (or beech) charcoal is triturated for use.

General Action.—A tissue remedy. It seems to have a marked effect on the digestion and in a general way acts as a tonic in conditions of great prostration. It seems also to control hæmorrhages, especially in older persons.

Compare The Carbons, Lycopod., Phosph., Sepia, Sec. c.

Generalities.—A wound from a stab began to bleed again at various times. Trembling every afternoon from uneasiness and anxiety, with feeling as if he had committed a great crime, ending in violent weeping, even in the street; T. from uneasiness and anxiety, with inability to remain in any place; with prostration. Starting at night on account of noises, with shivering in back. Stitches over whole body in warmth of bed; itching, in the side on which he was lying in evening. *Tearing in varions places* at night in bed; *in various places, with drawing pain;* in morning on waking, in l. shoulder, then in r. hand, then in r. upper incisors; here and there, in l. side of occiput, l. half of face, l. shoulder, l. thigh, etc., with pressure in arms and legs.

Rheumatic drawings in whole body, with coldness of hands and feet. Rheumatic pains and lameness, worse in arms and thighs. Drawing pain in most parts, especially below breast, in neck and arms. Every member of the body hurts, also the back, with headache and weakness. Anguish in all vital organs. *Uneasiness;* in evening; at night, with drawing pains in limbs; *preventing sleep.* Inability to rest in any other position than with limbs drawn up against abdomen. Disinclination for physical exertion. Indolence in morning, with weariness, trembling in all limbs and sweating easily; I. in evening, with sleepiness and indisposition. Sick and weary, as if he had just risen from a serious illness.

Weakness; in morning in bed; in morning in bed, especially in joints, > rising; in morning on rising; in morning, with trembling of limbs and feeling about stomach as after too much wine; *in morning, with stretching of limbs;* towards noon, with inclination to lean head against something and to rest, empty feeling in head and hunger; in evening; after breakfast; after dinner; after stool; after the pains; *after a short walk in open air;* < morning, with faintness; < *walking,* > *sitting, mostly in arms when writing;* sudden, when walking in open air; *sudden attacks of faintlike;* in forenoon, as from stupefaction; in evening, as after great loss of blood; tremulous, after stool; especially in limbs. Attacks of faintness, even to sinking down, with vertigo, then griping in abdomen as in diarrhœa, though he had an ordinary stool. Numbness of all external parts. Most symptoms appear when walking in open air.

Clinical.—Tendency to hæmorrhage in low types of disease, as in pernicious anæmia, purpura, typhoid fever, etc. Tendency to putrid decomposition. Sometimes indicated after excesses. Faints readily, especially as the result of debilitating diseases. In the collapsed stage of various diseases the *patient wants to be fanned constantly,* with general fetid odors, bluish appearance of the skin. Senile gangrene, humid leg; varicose ulcers burn at night, offensive discharge, purple all around. The veins are swollen and livid.

Mind.—Excitement in evening, with distended veins. Anguish, < evening. Anxiety during and after eating; after stool, with sensation of trembling and involuntary movements; during the pains, with heat; increasing in evening, with heat in face; *in evening so that he could scarcely remain lying;* as in fever, with coldness of hands and trembling; inexpressible, from 4 to 6 every afternoon; trembling, in morning on waking; *as if oppressed;* in evening after lying down, as from oppression of chest, with heat in head and hands, sweat on forehead, inability to remain in bed on account of a sensation as if the heart would be pressed downward, objects seem to become constantly narrower and smaller, and when the room was dark horrible visions. Discouragement and fear. Weeping mood; with desire to shoot himself; lachrymose, afraid of everything, and he seemed to despair. Unhappiness with every little pain.

Violent mood; in forenoon. *Irritability;* after eating; with mental exhaustion; with hurry in business; with confusion of head. *Anger;* in involuntary outbreaks. Impatience; with desperation and desire to shoot himself. *Indifference;* to music, of which he is fond. Cried easily over sad events and laughed over trifles till tears came. Easily excited to foolish mirth, and, when laughing, muscles of arms and hands became relaxed. Immoderately jovial, but easily put out of humor.

Ideas flow slowly, they constantly turn about one object, with sensation as if head were bound; ideas slow, confused, with periodical loss of memory. Disinclination to think. Peculiar mental weakness, with confusion. *Periodic want of memory;* sudden loss of memory.

Head.—*Stitches through H. when coughing;* S. in evening in bed, extending into occiput; here and there, extending into H., with general painfulness of surface of brain. Tearing in frequent attacks, extending to r. temple; T., sometimes starting from limbs and ending in head. Aching; at night; after eating; from sudden change from warmth to cold; with heaviness in forehead; and on stooping it seems to press outward in occiput and forehead. *Throbbing headache; during respiration,* and in teeth; in afternoon; in evening in bed, with difficult breathing. Headache in attacks, in several places, associated with flatulence. Jerkingaching. Paroxysmal aching, with drawing. Drawing aching here and there, especially in forehead, extending to above root of nose; here and there externally. Pain as if too full. Contracting pain; < motion; headache which contracts the eyes, during menses. Pain as in beginning of coryza. Burning pain, evenings in bed, especially on vertex, and extending to forehead.

The hat pressed upon the head like a heavy weight, and the sensation continued even after taking it off, as if the head were bound up with a cloth (Phos. in part). *Heaviness; leaden.* Tension in brain, more like a confusion than a pain; spasmodic tension of brain. *Confusion; in morning after rising, > lying down, with inability to think easily and necessity to make a great exertion as if rousing him from a dream;* after midday nap; in evening after walking; after dinner; with pressure in forehead; *which makes thought difficult.*

Buzzing, as from bees. Noise from reading. *Rush of blood;* with hot forehead and confusion of head. Sensation as of rush of blood several times on waking in night, with bristling of hair, anxiety, shivering, sensation as if some one stroked the body, a kind of formication on every movement, and such acute hearing that the slightest noises re-echoed in ears. Pulsation as if he would have apoplexy, waking several times at night, with anxiety, soon after waking he came to his senses and felt that it was an illusion, for the pulsation had disappeared, as he looked for further development of this symptom while in a state of slumber the limbs and knees were drawn involuntarily upward and the back was bent, and he felt that if he had longer postponed waking he would have fainted.

Vertigo; in forenoon, with nausea, obscuration of vision, ringing in ears, trembling, general sweat, which stood in drops on forehead, the attack preceded by nosebleed; in evening after sleeping while sitting, with trembling and faintness on rising from the seat, which continued after lying down; on slightest motion; on slightest motion of head; when walking or sitting; in bed after waking; on stooping, on turning in bed and on gargling; with staggering; *so that he was obliged to hold on to something; when stooping, as if head reeled to and fro;* when sitting, as if head reeled to and fro. Sickening, on looking out of the window, with falling down unconscious, on recovering consciousness it seemed as if he could scarcely rouse himself from a deep sleep, after waking nausea, which obliged him to lie down and returned on rising, afterwards he was lachrymose and despondent.

Forehead.—Stitches above r. eye; above r. external canthus. *Tearing in spot near temples.* Boring. *Aching, especially over eyes,* in afternoon, with soreness of eyes on motion; A. over eyes, extending into them; in a spot formerly wounded, in r. side; pulsating, after eating, with pressure in occiput, heat in head and eructations; oppressive, above eyes, with nausea; intermittent. Drawing through head above r. eye. Tearing-drawing in upper anterior part of head.

Temples.—Tearing, extending to back teeth; T. over l. Boring beneath l. Pressure outward in l. *Pain in both* and on vertex; in l.; in l., afterwards extended over top and sides of head and was almost unbearable. Throbbing after long, deep sleep in afternoon, with fulness of brain. Tension and pressure in T. and forehead, with inability to hold the lids open.

Vertex.—Stitches; from reading; extending to temples. Paroxysmal tearing, and in temples. Pain in morning in bed, with painfulness of hair to touch; P. every afternoon; then drawing about whole head, though more pain on l. side; *with soreness of hair to touch;* as if something were lying on it, or as if integuments of head were too tight, extending to forehead.

Parietals.—Tearing in l. half of head; with drawing in l. arm. Deep-seated, intermittent tearing stitches in one side of brain, as if a nail were driven into it. Pinching above and behind l. ear, with cutting. (Pain in r. side when shaking head); in whole r. side of head and face, with chill, coldness and trembling of body and jaws; biting, in r. half, on which he lay, and in occiput, like the sensation in the nose from a suppressed sneeze, in morning on waking, > raising head and disappearing on rising.

Occiput.—Crackling while sitting. Burning-sticking in spot on. Tearing in r. side; T. in a spot, extending through the head. Pinching. **Aching**; at night, with boring in forehead, sweat, pale face, cold, trembling hands and nausea; < after supper; *in and on lower part;* in upper part of r. side, with pressure in eyes. Headache first in neck, then in forehead, then lachrymation, with closure of lids. Intermittent aching; throbbing A., as if suppurating, from morning till evening; short drawing, in r. *Drawing in l. side; with tearing;* D. affecting whole head. Confusion like a tension from within; C. as after intoxication. Vertigo as after intoxication, spreading forward, < evening, and involving whole head, < walking.

Tearing in skull. *Hair falls out.* Ulcer on fontanelle exuded a corrosive moisture. Tearing in an old scar on vertex. *Headache as from contraction of scalp;* < after supper. Crawling as if the hair moved.

Clinical.—Falling of hair, especially after pregnancy (Sepia).

Eyes.—Swelling of l. Inflammation of r. Stitches. Tearing pressure on l. Pain as if it would be torn out, with headache. Aching in l.; A. in evening after lying down; with confusion of head; as from sand in r., with sore feeling in canthi; as from sand, with sore pain, especially in canthi; with biting in r. eye. *A heavy weight seemed to lie upon E., so that he must make a great exertion when reading and writing to distinguish letters. Burning.* Itching in r.; with great dryness of lid; of l., with biting in it after rubbing, especially in internal canthus; with smarting and burning; biting, especially in r. external canthus. Lachrymation, with biting in r. eye. Pressure downward in r. ball.

Lids.—Twitching; of l. Trembling of upper. Inability to open at night, even when unable to sleep. Agglutination in morning; l. seemed agglutinated, but were not. Pressure in upper, on motion in open air, and in upper half of balls; biting, in r. external canthus. Drawing in r. *Itching on margins;* in l. internal canthus. Biting, with redness of margins; B. in l. canthus.

Muscles painful when looking up. Shortsighted; after exerting eyes. **Vision of black floating spots** (Lyc.). Flickering in morning on rising. Vision of rings surrounding a brighter field.

Clinical.—Asthenopia from overwork, floating black spots.

Ears.—*Discharge of thick flesh-colored, offensive moisture from r.* A thick brown substance comes out of r. Stitches extending inward in l. meatus. Tearing in r.; in fossa behind r. Tearing jerks in r. external meatus, or stitches. Twinges in l.; in r. in evening; coming out of both. Pinching in l. Tearing-burning pain in lobule of l. *Something heavy seems to lie in front of them; and they seemed stopped*, but without diminution of hearing.

Pulsations. Itching, with inclination to relieve it by swallowing; crawling, after boring in with finger. Sensitiveness to loud talking. *Roaring. Ringing;* in l. in afternoon; in l., with whirling vertigo; with humming and pressure. Humming before E. Chirping as of crickets. Crackling as of straw, on every motion of jaws during breakfast. Illusions of hearing, he thought he heard some one step up to his bed, and he woke with anxiety.

Clinical.—Offensive otorrhœa. Usually in mal-secretion of cerumen, with exfoliation of epidermoid cells. Deafness after exanthematous diseases.

Nose.—Trembling in skin and muscles of r. side of root. Tearing in l. half, extending to l. half of head. *Drawing in root.* Pressing in root and bones, as in severe coryza. Sensation in root as of commencing coryza. Heaviness. Crawling internally; in l. side in evening. Itching internally, with increased moisture.

Sneezing; with stitches in abdomen; with burning over a large part of r. side of abdomen; with lachrymation of l. eye, then biting in inner canthus; then biting pain when blowing nose; continual, at night. *Frequent* sneezing; at night in bed, *with crawling and tickling in nose* and catarrhal roughness in it and in upper part of chest; without coryza. Violent sneezing, then biting pain above and in nose, with lachrymation, outbreak of violent coryza, also same pain on blowing nose. *Ineffectual attempts to sneeze; with crawling in l. nostril*, which became moist, and after blowing nose the r. nostril was stopped, with catarrhal crawling and biting in l. side of palate.

Stoppage of l. nostril; after sneezing. Catarrhal irritation on waking nights and mornings, > during the day, except occasional sneezing. *Coryza;* with hoarseness and rawness in chest; so that he could scarcely speak aloud; *dry;* dry, with scraping in throat; fluent; fluent, every evening; fluent, with sneezing. Increased moisture preceded by stoppage. Watery discharge. Discharge of mucus, with crawling in l. nostril, then sneezing, lachrymation of r. eye and coryza; D. of green mucus. **Bleeding several times daily, preceded and accompanied by pallor of face** (Phos., Sec. c.); B. morning in bed, then pain in chest; every forenoon; *at night*, with orgasm of blood; that could scarcely be stopped.

Clinical.—Recurring nosebleed in persons who have been overtaxed with anxiety, especially in elderly people. Varicose veins on nose.

Face.—**Pale** (Sec. c., Sep.). *Grayish-yellow.* Swollen cheeks; about chin. Tearing stitches in r. cheek. Tearing; *in l. cheek;* drawing, in bones; *jerklike, in l. zygoma, in front of ear, evening in bed.* Intermittent boring-burning pain in l. cheek. Twitching pain in several parts. Twitching-drawing pain in cheeks and in jaw. Drawing pain in cheeks.

Lips.—*Swelling; of upper, and of cheek, with jerking pain;* dry and cracked. Ulceration of r. corner. Burning pustules below red portion of upper. Painful eruption on upper, the red portion is full of pimples. Itching tetter in l. corner. *Twitching in upper.* Tearing in l. corner, extending to cheeks. Drawing from r. corner to chin.

Jaws.—Tearing-jerking in l. lower. *Jerklike tearing in upper* r. side. *Soreness of bones. Drawing pain* on both sides, with drawing and confusion in head. Cramplike pain in lower.

Mouth.—Teeth. *Bleeding when cleaned;* and of gums, when sucking them with the tongue. Sticking, then in abdomen; tickling, in first upper l. back, with drawing. *Drawing tearing in all molars.* Drawing and tearing pain, with chronic looseness and with soreness of gums. Pinching in r. lower back. Drawing-jerking in a hollow back tooth. Sudden throbbing while eating. Aching at root; in anterior incisors; in l. upper back; with dry lips; as from acids, especially in gum, as often as she ate anything salt. Gnawing and drawing pain in a hollow tooth, with swelling of gum. Drawing pain; in upper incisor; in hollow T.; in hollow molars; intermittent; in r. molars, with jerking; biting, in incisors, more in gum. Sore pain in first l. upper back, with drawing. T. seem to protrude, with ulcerative pain when touched by the tongue and when eating.

Gums.—Swollen about a hollow tooth. *Pustule. Bleeding* (Lyc.); *after sucking. When sucking the gum pure blood flows into mouth, at the same hour several forenoons. Retracted from lower incisors* (Sep.); *from incisors. Lossened from teeth, and sensitive.* **Sensitive when chewing** (Sep.). *Sore pain during the day.* Drawing pain. Heat.

Tongue.—*Coated white. Yellowish-brown mucous coat.* Fissure, with vesicles around edges, that smart as if burned. Stitches. Tearing in r. side. Cramplike pain on l. side of root. *Sensitiveness, with rawness.* Soreness; of r. side, with sticking. Heat of tip, with dryness. Heaviness and stiffness, so that speech was difficult.

Blister in upper part of palate. Mouth filled with mucus by eructations always only a few hours after dinner. Bitter mucus in morning. *Aching on posterior part of palate. Heat, with rawness and dryness of tip of tongue; H.*, especially in upper lip. Sensation in M. and tongue as after drinking wine freely in the evening. Dryness in morning; in morning on waking; without thirst. *Salivation.* Breath offensive. Breath cold, with coldness in throat, mouth and teeth.

Taste bitter; before and after eating; B., with eructations; *B. on palate, with dryness of tongue.* Salt. Sour after eating. Flat, watery, offensive.

Clinical.—Spongy condition of gums, which retract and bleed easily, with tendency to nosebleed, fainting fits. Teeth decay rapidly, gums retracted. Tongue dry and black in late stage of typhoid fever. Tongue cold in the collapse of cholera, yellow, fissured, with cold breath. Offensive odor from mouth in persons who are debilitated, or during fevers.

Throat.—Swelling of parotid gland as far as angle of jaw. Inflammation, with stitches and sensation as if something were sticking in it; I. of uvula, with swelling and with sticking in throat. *Much hawking of mucus.* Much tenacious mucus, which he must raise; M. of unpleasant taste and odor; much M. constantly passes from posterior nares.

Tearing in muscles; in back part and in l. side o root of tongue. Aching; in r. muscles; when coughing; just behind palate; extending into stomach, with fulness, almost like heartburn. *Sore pain on swallowing, coughing or blowing nose, and in posterior nares;* sore, when eating. Sore, as from swelling on palate, with painful swallowing. Roughness in back part. *Scraping;* evening and morning, provoking dry cough; transiently > by hawking, with crawling; *with rawness;* with cough, which causes lachrymation, especially of l. eye.

Contracted sensation; deep-seated; sensation of constriction and internal swelling. *Burning in upper part;* in back part, as in coryza. Frequent sensation in forenoon as if something hot and sharp rose. Coldness low down. Dryness, and in posterior nares; D. when swallowing. Biting posteriorly, more acrid than in beginning of coryza; frequent B. and burning, and in palate. Crawling, transiently > hawking, with salivation. Swallowing difficult; *of food, throat seems constricted with spasms, but painless;* painless impediment when swallowing, the saliva was swallowed only gradually.

Stomach.—Longing for sweet and salt things. Hunger, with aversion to the usually agreeable food. *Aversion to meat,* with loss of appetite; *A. to fat meat; to milk, which makes her flatulent;* to butter. Loss of appetite; morning and evening; with coated tongue and weariness; with eructations and confusion of head; with weakness of muscles of limbs; for coffee. Soon full and satisfied at a moderate breakfast. Little appetite towards noon, with nausea; L. at noon, with cutting in abdomen; with no taste, as in catarrh; with heat in mouth and rawness and dryness on tip of tongue; with aching in pit of stomach and emptiness in stomach.

Eructations (Phos.); *after eating and drinking;* < afternoon; *violent, almost constant. Empty,* < afternoon (Lyc.); after soup and every time after drinking; and accompanied, especially in afternoon, with flatulence. Sweet. Bitter scraping. Sour in open air, towards evening; after milk; with burning in stomach; sour, bitter. *Waterbrash.* Hiccough after a moderate dinner; H. < every motion; inclination to H. from slightest cause; painful, after eating.

Nausea; in morning; every day from 10 to 11 A.M.; at night; caused by every meal; with every meal; after eating, with pressure in stomach, then dragging-down pain about umbilicus; even when fasting, < eating, with loss of appetite, anxiety, vertigo, obscuration before eyes, white tongue and necessity to lie down towards evening, without sleepiness; with trembling feeling; *without vomiting;* without appetite and without stool; even to retching, before dinner; in attacks.

Cramp, with incessant acid eructations; C. in a nursing woman, with cardialgia; **contractive, at night, extending into chest, with distention of abdomen,** *paroxysmal, arresting breath, obliging her to bend double,* < *lying. Griping in pit, as from flatulence.* Gnawing in morning, fasting. Clawing, extending to throat, like heartburn. Pain beneath pit; *in pit* in evening, *with sensitiveness to touch,* nausea and aversion, even at thought of eating; in pit and in upper abdomen, as if in stomach, after 7 P.M.; beneath S. at night, with uneasy sleep and anxious dreams; when standing and walking, with feeling as if heavy and hanging down; after rumbling in abdomen; in region, > emission of flatus, with rumbling; which rises into head and destroys her senses; as from something sore, < touch; anxious, in pit. **The simplest food distresses.**

Contractive sensation beneath S.; beneath pit, < pressure of finger; near pit on r. side, morning and afternoon. Tension above S., extending from ribs, with pressure; *T. and fulness. Oppression and fulness* (Lyc.). Fulness after a moderate breakfast, with eructations and general heaviness, writing is slow and difficult. Hard sensation, as if something were there that ought not to be, > sour, bitter eructations. On stooping it seems as if sausages were lying on sides near S. Heaviness, with trembling sensation in it. *Sensitiveness of epigastric region* (Phos.). Feeling of goneness (Sep.). *Acidity when lying on back and when walking. Burning;* with acidity constantly rising into mouth. Throbbing in pit.

Clinical.—Flatulent dyspepsia, with sour eructations, stomach is swollen like a drum, the distress comes on half an hour or an hour after eating; every sort of food disagrees, the stomach seems to be suffering from inertia, is unable to digest the simplest article. Acid dyspepsia, with heartburn, coldness of the surface of the body, feeble pulse, etc. Gastralgia of nursing women, with excessive flatulence, sour and rancid belching, vomiting of food. The sensitiveness in the stomach or burning sometimes extends into the small of the back (Bismuth), with excessive distention by gas.

Abdomen.—Distention after dinner; after eating a little, *with rumbling; by flatus* in afternoon; like an induration, after stool. *Rumbling; with griping; moving about slowly.* Incessant noise, without urging to stool. *Motions;* with frequent passage of loud or noiseless or moist flatus; with stitches here and there, especially in l. side, towards ribs. Fermentation, then diarrhœic stool, with offensive flatus. *Flatulence and distention from things which usually digested easily;* F. in afternoon, with rumbling and loud movings; sudden, in afternoon, which passes without difficulty. **Offensive flatus;** *and at last moist flatus, with dragging towards sacrum and thence towards abdomen.* Much odorless flatus; in morning on waking.

Pinching-sticking extending upward. Pinching, < r. side. Cutting; in evening; C. shooting through A. like lightning. *Dragging or griping after stool.* Griping almost only in afternoon and evening, > emission of flatus; G. during and after eating; when sitting bent; with natural stool; then empty eructations; in various places.

Pain before stool; during diminished flow of menses, with bruised pain in back and all bones; > passage of hot flatus, with urging to stool; > passage of moist, warm, odorless flatus, with rumbling; in a small spot; obliging her to hold it with the hands; drawing across A. before stool; *paralytic drawing, extending into l. leg; as after taking cold,* < before emission of flatus and continues after it; *as from lifting or a sprain, as soon as she lies on side, especially in l. side of A.;* as from lifting a heavy weight, on touch and when slightly raising arm to work with the hand; bruised, in muscles; extending to small of back and bladder, almost as after rhubarb, after a stool; flatulent, with passage of odorless flatus; cramplike, from morning till evening, before menses.

Feeling as if it would burst if he eats or drinks. Tension; in afternoon from accumulated flatus, but it passed copiously and easily. Tensive and pressive pain over nearly whole A., with uneasiness and weeping, as from despair. Pain over whole A. as far as pubes as if muscular fibres were tense or hardened, causing anxiety. Constrictive sensation. Anxiety. Fulness as if overloaded, with eructations. *Heaviness; sensa-*

tion as if it hung down heavily, obliging her to walk bent. Emptiness after stool, < walking. Burning.

Upper.—*Accumulation of flatus in l., more towards back, with pinching; here and there, under short ribs, in hypogastrium,* causing pinching and pressure, and gradually passing into rectum, with heat. Sticking in region of liver. Tearing in liver, causing cries; sticking T. in hypochondria, starting from a point just below pit of stomach and extending to both sides. Pinching. Pain in r. hypochondrium; in l. H.; *in hypochondria on touch;* P. beneath short ribs after breakfast; *in liver region on touch;* in liver when walking in open air. *Bruised pain in liver;* in hypochondria. Drawing pain beneath l. ribs. Tensive and pressive pain in r. upper A., extending across stomach. *Tension in liver region as if it were too short there, on waking from midday nap. Hypochondrium oppressed by clothing, which was unendurable.* Feeling of a band around waist, > 8 o'clock, with discharge of offensive flatus.

Umbilical Region.—Rumbling. Griping about, after a little harmless food, > eructations or passage of wind; G. about extending into stomach, < standing erect, preventing sleep at night, with chilliness and diarrhœa, the last < night. Pain; sore, in a spot below umbilicus; intermittent burning, in skin. Burning.

Sides.—Sticking in l. side of A. and chest, < breathing. Pinching on l. side of spine while sitting bent. Pain in l.

Hypogastrium.—Gurgling in l. Deep-seated movings. Deep-seated crawling creeping-sticking. Pinching stitches in l. after a hard scanty stool, with ineffectual urging to stool like a pressure upon rectum. Tearing stitches, extending to umbilicus. Tearing near l. hip, extending to back. Cutting during menses. *Pinching;* deep in r., extending towards hips; labor-like colic, which pressed upon sacrum (and bladder) on waking at 3 A.M. from uneasy sleep and anxious dreams, with rumbling in abdomen. Griping in l., with stitches; G. in r. inguinal region. *Pain;* in r. inguinal region; with cramp; sore, externally, even on touch; drawing, extending into small of back, before menses.

Clinical.—Colic, < riding in the cars or carriage, > emission of flatus.

Rectum.—*Stitches during stool.* Pinching when not at stool. *Gnawing when not at stool. Crawling and complaints of ascarides. Tenesmus.* Urging to stool after breakfast, which though not hard is difficult; U. > by loud emission of flatus; with burning in anus and emission of flatus; to stool which is scanty and difficult; sudden, as from fulness in rectum. *Ineffectual urging; only wind passes, with pressure in rectum;* from a sensation in abdomen and small of back; I. U., with crawling in anus, intermittent pressure in bladder towards small of back, like hæmorrhoidal colic, labor-like pain in hypogastrium, in front and back, burning in anus, and sensation as in diarrhœa, pains > a scanty, soft, difficult stool.

Anus.—Swollen, painful hæmorrhoids; tickling itching in H. Passage of ascarides. *Bleeding during stool* (Sulp.); B., with tearing in rectum. *Glutinous musty exudation at night. Acrid, corrosive moisture;* moisture, with tenesmus when urinating. *Passage of mucus; with urging;* mucus precedes the stool, followed by hard, then soft fæces, with cutting colic. *Stitches towards A.;* S. in evening. Cutting during stool; during hard stool. Aching. *Soreness.* Rush of blood. *Burning after stool;* during stool, which consists of small, hard fæcal masses; with sticking; with dryness; in r. side. Biting. Itching, < scratching, then burning; morning, in bed; also on waking from a long sleep.

Perineum.—*Soreness, with painful itching when touched; S. at night, with itching and moisture.* Stitches near anus.

Stool.—Diarrhœa; with urging. Pasty, with burning in rectum. Hard; and rare; and delayed, difficult. *Enveloped by filamentous yellowish mucus, this mucus is entirely bloody in last portions of fæces.* The child cries aloud every six or seven minutes, while bloody mucus passes instead of stool. Much mucus, with S. Discharge of blood with every S. Acrid, with coated tongue. Tenacious, scanty, not cohering properly, with inactivity of rectum. Frequent. Delayed, with rumbling. Omitted one day, two stools next day. Constipation; but with soft stool.

Clinical.—Diarrhœa, brown, yellow or slimy, of a putrid odor, often involuntary. The diarrhœa is generally the accompaniment of low types of fever, associated with tendency to coldness in the extremities, cold tongue, lips, etc., tendency to collapse, desire to be fanned, pulse weak, voice lost.

Urinary Organs.—Aching in bladder; during micturition. Urging to urinate waking in morning; nearly every hour; frequent, though urine passes slowly; with copious pale urine; with copious pale urine and with constipation. Frequent micturition at night.

Urethra.—Tearing in morning after urinating, with drawing; T. when urinating, the last drops consist of mucus and are painful to pass. Pinching. Contraction every morning. Burning when urinating; with twinging. Urine copious; after drinking a little; scanty; U. diminished, with frequent urging. *Red U., as if mixed with blood; dark red,* with roughness of throat; *reddish, turbid.* Dark U. Offensive. Thick, milky, at close of micturition. Deposit of gravel. *Red sediment* (Lyc.).

Clinical.—Suppression of urine in cholera. Hæmaturia (Tereb.).

Sexual Organs.—Contraction. Vesicle on inner side of prepuce, with itching soreness. Itching of prepuce, with soreness. Constant erections at night, without voluptuous sensations or fancies; frequent E.; every hour on waking. Swelling of scrotum, with hardness. Crawling in testicles and on scrotum. Desire increased; lost in morning. Discharge of prostatic fluid when straining at stool. Emissions without dreams; too soon on coition, then roaring of blood in head; frequent, without much sensation; excessive, which painfully shake the nerves, then burning in forepart of urethra, with cutting and burning when urinating and renewed on pressure.

Pudenda.—*Aphthæ. Red sore places, looking like ulcers,* with itching and leucorrhœa. Sticking when urinating. *Soreness during leucorrhœa, with rawness;* S. towards forepart in evening. Smarting pain, with leucorrhœa for two days, then appearance of menses which had been suppressed for many months, menses black, then leucorrhœa. Burning; with redness. *Itching, and in anus;* on urinating.

Bloody mucus from vagina. White mucus from vagina. Leucorrhœa after urinating; *milky, excoriating L.; copious, thin, only in morning on rising;* thick, yellowish-white; greenish. *Menses too thick* **and of strong odor**; *M. too soon;* too late, causing biting and soreness; M. delayed or very slight for three or four days, then unusual pain and profuse flow, next time they lasted a shorter time than usual.

Clinical.—Useful in the effects of sexual excesses (China). Varicose veins in female sexual organs, with hæmorrhages. Menorrhagia, passive flow. Menstruation too early, profuse, thick, corrosive, offensive, preceded by violent itching. Corrosive leucorrhœa.

Respiratory Organs.—Larynx. **Roughness, with deep rough voice which failed if he exerted it, but without pain in throat** (Phos., Mangan.). *Rawness in evening from frequent clearing of throat, with soreness. Pain as if ulcerated when coughing, and in region of thyroid cartilage.* Crawling, with itching and with whistling when breathing, and in evening after lying down tightness of chest and dry cough. *Hoarseness in evening; H., with roughness, so that speaking aloud was difficult* (Phos.); with distortion of eyes (as if something were sticking in them) when he wished to speak, and lachrymation, then redness of cheeks, pain on swallowing, loud breathing in sleep, cough, vomiting of milk, obstinacy and frequent screaming; sudden, in evening when walking in open air, with dyspnœa. Voice rough, as if constricted or fatigued by speaking. *Voice almost lost in morning.*

Trachea.—*Dryness, not > hawking.* Pressure on inspiration. Crawling in upper part as if something were tightly seated there, provoking cough.

Cough after the slightest cold, in morning on rising, or if she goes from a warm room into a cold one; *in evening in bed; in evening on going to sleep and in morning after rising,* from *itching in larynx, with tenacious salt expectoration;* in evening, causing vomiting and retching; as soon as he has eaten sufficiently; from irritation in upper part of chest, with roughness and scraping in throat; with yellowish purulent expectoration and sticking in l. hypochondrium on breathing, then stitches in upper part of l. chest. *Spasmodic cough; in evening* (from walking too rapidly); at night; from irritation and crawling in throat, the C. causing pain in chest as if pressed in; repeated at the same hour on the third day. *Cough partly voluntary, rough, from roughness and crawling in throat. Hacking C., causing expectoration of mucus from larynx.* Short C. in evening. Fatiguing C., with dyspnœa and burning in chest. Tickling C. in morning after waking, with whitish expectoration. Rough, dry C. Dry C. in evening after every expiration, causing warmth and sweat. *Irritation to C. frequently returning,* in back of throat, with short C.; I. to cough in evening, with chilliness and drawing in cheeks; as from sulphur fumes, with retching. *Expectoration of pieces of green mucus.*

Breath stopped; immediately on falling asleep, with increased vertigo. Gets out of breath on turning over in bed. *Dyspnœa, <* towards evening, with *fulness of chest, and palpitation on slightest motion;* D. in evening when lying, with throbbing in head; from oppression of chest; < sitting; obliging her to walk slowly. Short breath, with anxiety on chest and necessity to walk about. Desire to breathe deeply, with moaning. He was obliged to fetch a deep breath, with exertion of chest, abdomen, back, neck and head, with lifting of the feet.

Clinical.—Aphonia from relaxation of vocal cords. Chronic laryngeal catarrh, with rawness and soreness in larynx, particularly in old people. Has been prescribed in the last stage of membranous croup. Chronic bronchial catarrh of old people, burning in the chest, choking when coughing, > heat. Cough, generally spasmodic, suffocative. Asthma, particularly in old people who are debilitated, with flatulence, etc., especially with blue color of the skin. Hæmorrhage from the lungs, with burning pain in chest, oppression, desire to be fanned all the time, cold skin. Sometimes useful in a late stage of pneumonia, with excessive dyspnœa and tendency to collapse.

Chest.—Stitches beneath l. breast; preventing sleep and walking, they continue while sitting; *in l. side, extending into short ribs;* in r. side of C. and abdomen, < inspiration; deep in r., during deep breathing; beneath l. ribs in morning in bed, extending into abdomen, pit of stomach and chest, with pressure upon larynx, < by breathing, renewed by pressure upon abdomen; on going to sleep, impeding respiration; outward like shocks deep in r. lower part; constrictive, below l. breast, impeding respiration.

Tearing in r.; *oppressive, in l.;* in morning in bed, extending into back, arms and l. ear, with internal heat, especially in head. Pinching in a spot, caused by flatus. Pressure on l. Pain on expanding it; P. in r.; in l., then r., < expiration; in upper, with rough cough; *in r. upper,* extending to r. scapula; externally on l. breast when touched, like a pressure and tension; in a spot on sternum, above pit of stomach, as if caused by stooping or touch; as from incarcerated flatus.

Rheumatic pain in r. short ribs; extending from l. ribs into hip; drawing, in r. short ribs. Painful drawing in C. (shoulder and arms), < l. side, with hot sensation and rush of blood to head and coldness of skin to touch. If the tearing-drawing, burning pains attack the external chest they are accompanied by oppression of breathing. Pain when coughing as if flesh were raw. Lungs and throat feel scraped. Roughness, with frequent irritation to cough. *Oppression; on waking, with weakness of it; after disappearance of coryza, with wheezing and rattling, inability to remain in bed on account of want of air and the cough, which caused vomiting and was difficult to loosen;* > eructations; of lungs and heart; with short breath, as from flatus pressing upward; spasmodic O. and contraction; as if coming from abdomen, and caused by flatulence.

Compression in morning after rising, and in shoulders. Tightness in morning after rising, like a catarrh, with hard cough, which caused shooting through head. Constriction in attacks, with impeded respiration; hot C., causing dyspnœa, and short dry cough. **Burning, as from glowing coals**; B. in l. chest and in r. side near pit of stomach. Rush of blood in morning on waking, with coated tongue; R., with burning in it; warm, with anxiety caused by flatus in abdomen; it seemed as if blood were rushing to it, with chilliness within the body. Pulsation, with uneasiness and anxiety. **Weariness**; *on waking.* Itching internally.

Heart and Pulse.—Sticking in præcordial region; ending with rumbling in l. side like the escape of flatus. Pain in præcordial region, burning rather than sticking. *Palpitation;* in evening on going to sleep, with intermittent pulse; after eating; < sitting; with rapid beats. *Pulse weak;* P. rapid. Throbbing in all pulses if she spoke in the presence of others, with puffiness and bluish-redness of the usually pale face.

Clinical.—Useful in weak heart from fatty degeneration with cold sweat, desire to be fanned, tendency to hæmorrhages.

Neck.—*Cervical glands swollen, especially posterior ones, near nape.* Paroxysmal shaking and trembling of neck and head. *Tearing in muscles;* l. muscles; in l. muscles, < motion. Pain in muscles; *drawing, in nape, extending to head, with nausea and rush of water from mouth;* burning, in muscles; tensive, in vertebræ. Stiffness, and of spine.

Back.—Twitches in muscles of l. side. Pinchings near spine. Bruised pain in side. *Drawing pain,* < sitting; D. pain evening. *Rheumatic drawing,* < *stooping.* Drawing only when sitting, and in feet. Weakness. Heaviness, with oppression of chest; H. at night as if weary, and in limbs. Stiffness in morning on rising. Sticking between scapulæ at night, arresting breathing. Tearing in l. scapula on bending arm back. Rheumatic sensation in l. scapula when writing; R. pain in upper part of l. S. after the usual bath.

Loins.—Tearing; near sacrum; which sometimes extends to hips. *Pinching near lowest part of spine.* Pain near lowest part of back; above r. loin, arresting breath; *as from a plug, with inability to sit and necessity to put a pillow under it;* tensive, with stiffness. Drawing pain, extending into coccyx; D. pain, and in abdomen and l. side of back, causing l. side to be bent over. *Sore pain beneath coccyx.* Hot stitch extending from coccyx through rectum and anus.

Extremities.—Twitching of arms and legs evenings, preventing sleep. *Drawing pains;* in hands and feet. Drawing and tearing pains, then burning pain. *Bruised feeling;* in joints in morning after waking, > stretching limbs and rising. Tension in knees and l. hand, as if overworked. Uneasiness in evening in bed, with necessity to stretch them frequently. Heaviness and stiffness on rising after long sitting, > walking; H. of l. arm and leg, as if paralyzed. *Going to sleep; of that on which he lies.*

Upper Extremities.—Drawing pain beneath r. axilla, < motion. Shoulder, stitches in r.; tearing in joint; T. in r. joint, < motion, with drawings in humerus; frequent paralytic T. in r. joint; burning pain on r. S.; drawings in joints; drawing pain in l. joint; rheumatic drawings in r. S.; paralytic weakness of r. S. and r. arm.

Arm.—Cramp. Bruised pain in r. *Drawing pain when lying on it at night.* Drawing in r. Heaviness, with drawings in back; H. on motion, and exhaustion; A. and hands go to sleep, < night. Upper A., tearing in r., < motion; T. in l.; paroxysmal T. in l.; drawing pain, with burning; drawing pain from above downward in r.; drawing on inner side of l.; heaviness. *Bruised pain in elbows* in morning in bed. Tearing in r. forearm; *drawing, from l. elbow to hand;* drawing, in upper side of l., near elbow, with pain on pressure upon bone; drawing, in l. radius; drawing pain extending down ulna towards wrist; drawing extending down F. to fingers, < motion, with tearing. *Wrist,* stitches, extending into ball of thumb; *tearing in r. or l.; W. feel too short,* numb and go sleep; sensation in l. on certain motions as if tendons were too short; drawing pain; drawings in W., elbow and shoulder-joints in morning, < wind, > motion; paralytic pain in W. on motion.

Hand.—Spasmodic contraction. Stitches in evening, then second and third fingers were drawn spasmodically across each other and caused the others to stand far apart. Tearing in inner part of l., extending into base of little finger. Pain in back; throbbing, in metacarpal bone of middle finger; bruised, in back of l.; sprained, in r. H. and wrist. Drawings in r. metacarpal bones. Weak sensation, < when writing. He could write only slowly and with difficulty. Inclination to numbness. Going to sleep; sensation as if they would go to sleep in morning on washing.

Fingers.—Swelling of ungual phalanx of l. middle, with drawing pain in it. Stitches when rising from a seat; in ungual phalanx of fourth; in metacarpal joint of l. middle; sudden deep, in first joint of r. middle; tearing, in middle joint. *Tearing in l.;* in r.; in evening; in two r. middle; in tip and beneath nail of l. fourth; in r. little, < motion; in joints of two last; in middle joint of r. index; in last joint of l. index; under thumb-nail; in thumb, as if in bone; burning, in tip of r. thumb. Boring in metacarpal joints of middle, and of thumb; in middle joint of l. index when at rest, but stitches on motion or bending. Slow throbbing pain in ungual phalanx of thumb. Gouty pain in last joint of thumb. Drawing in r. index, extending towards tip. Pulsation on back of thumb. Paralysis of r. when grasping anything, with weakness of them.

Lower Extremities.—Tearing in upper and lower leg. Legs pain, especially lower legs, when sitting or lying, so that he did not know where to rest them. Drawing in evening in bed; in legs, especially in lower legs. Weariness and paralytic sensation. Joints seem unable to sustain the body.

Thigh.—Twitches on posterior part of l. in morning in bed. Stitches in upper part; down through T. when walking. Tearing frequently in middle; in r. hip; *frequently near l. hip,* extending to back and sacrum; paroxysmal, in hips; down r. thigh through leg. Cramplike pain in outer lower part of l. when walking, < raising thigh and ascending steps, with pain on touch. *Drawing pain in hip-joints, extending down thighs,* < *when walking.* Contractive pain when walking, extending to knee, so that she has to bend the knee inward. Rheumatic drawing in l., evening in bed, > lying upon it. Tension above knees in morning on rising; in hip-joints and knees in morning on waking; and drawing as if paralyzed or sprained. Uneasiness in r. T. and leg. Numbness when walking. Paralyzed sensation in l. caused by flatulence.

Knee.—Tearing, and in lower legs. Stitches in cap after rising from a seat, with sensation as if knee were swollen. Soreness of bone from a moderate blow. Pain when ascending stairs; burning, in inner side of l.; paralytic, when sitting or rising from a seat and when lying at night, if she turns over or stretches the knee; drawing, when standing. Drawing extending down leg. Tension, and in ankles; in hollow, as from weariness. Weariness, with stiffness; W. when walking or standing, with sensation of unsteadiness. Stiffness and falling asleep. Paralyzed sensation after walking.

Leg.—Cramp at night in bed, especially in soles; when walking in open air, especially in soles. Tearing in r.; in bone above l. malleolus; < great accumulation of flatus; in calf, extending into inner malleolus. Drawing in l., with uneasiness; D. with jerkings and necessity to stretch them at one time and at another to draw them up; rheumatic, in both, extending to metatarsal bones. Tickling restlessness in evening. Relaxation from noon till evening, so that he could not raise them. *Heaviness. Stiffness after evening nap, so that the gait was unsteady until he had walked a little* (Phos.). Numbness. Going to sleep. *Paralyzed sensation in l.* (Phos.).

Stitches in l. ankle as if sprained. Feet swollen and tender. *Cramp in soles* in evening after lying down, making toes crooked. Pain in corns at night in bed; in metatarsal bones as if they would be torn on stepping; in soles while walking, as if too soft. Drawings in feet, < sitting. Uneasiness of l. foot. Heaviness of feet after every dinner. *Numbness of feet.*

Toes.—Swelling. Stitch through r. great; in a corn on little. Tearing in r. middle; in r., < when walking; under nails from evening till into night, extending into soles. Pain in great; in joint of great; under nail of great.

Skin.—Red uneven spots on neck in evening, with itching. Scurf on tip of nose. Nettle-rash; on calves. Eruption in angle of wings of nose; on chin, with ulcers beneath jaw and in front of ear; *fine itching, on hands;* itching, on neck and between shoulders, before menses. Swelling on flexor surface of wrist; S. painful to touch on calf. Pimples on forehead; and face; temples; neck; red smooth, here and there on forehead; red, painful on touch, on forehead near hair; red, itching, with blackish tip, close to anus; white, on temples; white, on lower part of cheek; white, like glands, on forehead; white, itching, about nose.

Boil on upper arm, surrounded by itching pimples. *Pus from ulcer offensive, like asafœtida.* Ulcer that had healed broke out afresh and discharged lymph mingled with blood instead of pus, and the place was hard and painful to touch. Itching vesicles on knee. A place which had been rubbed sore and which was nearly covered with skin again began to be denuded anew and was moist.

Stitches on r. index, renewed by bending arm; S. in a node on calf. *Burning pain in various places.* Tension about an ulcer (on leg), with pressure. Formication over whole body. Itching over whole body; *about eyes;* behind ear; about nostrils; on mons veneris; in r. axilla; on outer side of l. thumb; in palms at night; in a tetter before menses; *on thigh near scrotum,* with moisture; in axillæ, with moisture and soreness; in upper part of outer ear, then heat; on back, chest, navel, thighs, etc., with burning; burning, on forearm near elbow; on arms, hands and between fingers, preventing sleep at night; sticking, in several parts; sticking, in region of coccyx in evening in bed; sticking, on throat and neck, with red spots; biting, on lower inner side of l. upper arm, transiently > scratching.

Clinical.—Useful in low types of ulcers, with ichorous corrosive discharge, offensive, with burning pain, < night. Tendency of carbuncles to become gangrenous. Purpura hæmorrhagica.

Sleep.—*Yawning; and stretching; and stretching, which seemed to do good. Sleepiness in forenoon while sitting and reading, > motion;* S. in daytime, with late falling asleep at night, frequent starting in sleep, with strange fancies, etc., early in evening; after supper, with red heat of face; after dinner, without ability to sleep. *Sleepiness during the day, he was obliged to sleep before and after noon, at night his sleep was full of fancies.* Overpowered by sleep in evening; O. after eating; after dinner, with burning of eyelids on closing them.

Sleeplessness at night, with inability to open eyes; S. at night, though the eyes seemed full of sleep. Half-awake all night, and awoke in morning feeling tired, cross, sleepy, feeling in mouth as if painted or covered with something, and taste as in measles. *Falls asleep late,* not till 1 o'clock. Waking about 4 A.M. Frequent waking, with heat and thirst; *F. waking, with coldness of limbs and knees.* Uneasy sleep, with frequent waking; then in morning in bed headache, with burning here and there in body; uneasy, unrefreshing sleep, then sweat in morning; uneasy for hours after eating, on account of anxious dreams. Starting up in fright on falling asleep. Much coherent talking in sleep wakens him, when he remembers the dreams. *Many dreams;* frightful D.; tormenting; anxious, with uneasy sleep; vivid; vivid but unremembered; lascivious; causing restlessness.

Fever.—Chilliness from morning till afternoon, with thirst, chattering, and *blue finger-nails,* then in evening heat and sweat without thirst; C. several days at 11 A.M., and heat at 6 P.M.; in evening; towards evening, with heat; < night; *with thirst;* with flashes of heat. Shivering; *in evening* before sleep, *with weariness* and flushes of heat. Coldness of hands; *of hands and feet in evening;* of feet in bed till 1 A.M.; of l. arm and l. leg; of tips of fingers, with sweat; in small of back, with numbness and tension.

Heat in evening, with anxiety and external coldness; H. in evening, with weariness and fantasies at night; at night in bed; from a little wine; with cold feet. Orgasm of blood; with congestion to chest, hoarseness and hawking. Heat in blood at night, preventing sleep.

Burning in forehead; upper part of l. side of back; *on r. scapula; on r. shoulder;* on shoulder-joint; on upper part of upper arm; on r. elbow; externally on r. hip; on r. knee; in upper part of outer side of thigh; in skin; *in various places in skin* at night in bed; *of l. ear every evening, with redness;* in both limbs in evening in bed; in thigh at night in bed; in hands and soles during menses; in soles after standing; in soles when sitting and walking. Heat in forehead and mouth, with pain in eyes. Spot on head hot to touch, with headache. Glowing heat of cheeks after sitting a short time. Warmth in spine rising to throat. Burning on skin as from a mustard plaster, here and there, on back, sides, r. side of abdomen, etc. Cold burning in metacarpal joints of r. middle and ring fingers.

Sweat; in morning; before midnight, even of head; after a moderate breakfast; in morning on waking. Sour. Offensive at night. Sweat on face; balls of hands; feet; feet, when walking; on forehead while eating. Sweat easily on upper part of body in a warm room, and then became just as easily chilled.

Clinical.—Valuable in low types of fever, with putrid discharges, hæmorrhage, offensive odor of the body. Hectic fever, long-lasting suppuration. Cold extremities, especially cold knees. The third stage of yellow fever, with hæmorrhages.

Carbolic Acid.

The pure crystals may be dissolved in Alcohol, and the solution diluted for use.

General Action.—A powerful protoplasmic poison. It destroys life by producing paralysis of heart and respiration; preceded by vertigo, roaring in ears, profuse sweat, contracted pupil and collapse. It sometimes produces convulsions. The blood is disorganized, and hæmoglobinuria results (black urine). It produces an inflammation of mucous membranes, characterized by hard, shrivelled membranous patches of exudation. Applied to the skin, anæsthesia results. The stomach is sometimes paralyzed, so that one cannot vomit.

Allies.—Pic. ac., Petrol., Phos., Ars. hyd., Kali chl.

Generalities.—Blood black, thick, without shimmer, of peculiar brown color by transmitted light, smelling of the acid, the clot soft, without air, diffluent, had not contracted by next day. Swelling of the body. Fell to the ground; insensible. Uttered an exclamation, became unconscious, with tremor of limbs, pallor of skin, clammy sweat, intermittent laborious respiration, imperceptible pulse, etc. Convulsions; with falling to the ground, delirium and unconsciousness; C. with trismus and biting of tongue, so that it bled. Twitching of facial muscles and trembling of limbs. Trembling; inward. Relaxation of muscles; except of chewing muscles, which showed tonic trismus, then becoming clonic occasionally.

Pricking, like needles, all over her body. Sensation of electric sparks at l. wing of nose, with desire to rub the part, afterwards at sternal end of r. clavicle, then on l. middle finger, then on vertex, the sensation changing slowly to pricking-itching, > rubbing the part. Pains affect first r. side, then same parts of l.; only r. side; most frequently on l. side, coming and going suddenly, generally affecting muscles and joints, but not bones. Soreness and stiffness of all muscles prominently used; general soreness, as if he had taken cold, worse in back, abdomen and chest. Feeling if he had taken a bad cold. Uneasiness. Physical and mental exhilaration.

Prostration; at night, and *not at all amiable; from a short walk;* with sleepiness. Languor, with disinclination to work; and with drowsiness, fulness in head, and intermittent pain in forehead, or r. or l. temple. Loss of involuntary motion and speech. Collapse. Faintness; especially at stomach; causing *sweat* and nausea, *the heart seeming to almost stop.* Sensibility almost lost. Anæsthesia; of skin and eyeballs; with reflex action of muscles, closed eyelids, pupils dilated and inactive, skin cold and clammy, with sweat running down face, temperature lowered, respiration feeble and shallow, pulse at wrist imperceptible, heart's action feeble and intermittent. Reflex paralysis. All symptoms go from head downward. *Aggravation by reading, especially of the pressing at occiput, unfitting him for study;* A from jarring of carriage. Amelioration of all symptoms from a cup of tea; A. after a hearty lunch, except of frontal headache; in fresh air, riding lulls to sleep, and walking is an exertion.

Clinical.—Profound prostration, collapse, cold sweat. Putrid discharges. Malignant types of disease, especially when there is tendency to destruction of tissues.

Mind.—Delirium; like intoxication; vivacious; violent. *Irritability;* and less brilliancy in conversation than usual. Affection bestowed seemed distasteful. Sadness; with disposition to sigh and yawn. As soon as he went to bed, fear of impending sickness. Happiness. Unusual cheerfulness in evening. Agitation. Delightful ideas, which came faster than he could give them shape in words. Activity, with desire for intellectual work, though mental labor caused confusion and pain in head. *Disinclination for mental work; and for physical labor* (Pic. ac., Phos.); to think or speak. Dulness; > after breakfast. Inability to concentrate mind; when reading. Absent-minded condition, from which he started when addressed, with nervous tremor when spoken to suddenly. Stupefaction. Loss of memory.

Unconsciousness; with stertorous breathing; with sudden falling, as if in a fit; with livid face, staring eyes, slow and noisy breathing, foaming at mouth and nose; motory and sensory U., if a limb is raised it falls lifeless. Coma; with relaxed limbs; with livid face, dilated pupils, sweat, cold hands, pulse imperceptible, muscles of soft palate and tongue so relaxed that the tongue must be kept extended with catch-forceps, afterwards pain in tongue, prostration and gastric catarrh.

Head.—Aching; especially over r. eye, with fulness; with nausea, a cup of green tea relieved the pain, but not the sense of smell; < bending head forward; > after breakfast; > smoking after tea; > moving about, but the eructations become more frequent; as if a sword were jagged in and out all around head, < noise and light, with difficulty in keeping eyes open and desire to have head bandaged; intermittent, with fulness as from suppressed catarrh. Expansive pains, with swimming before eyes, difficulty in writing. Pressure as from a band, especially at temples. Constricting pain at 7.30 A.M., < till noon, continued till falling asleep at night, > intermittent pressure, < continuous pressure, with sensation as if head were swollen and were radiating heat. Hot, constricted feeling, from 6.30 A.M. till late at night (> pressure), especially in forehead.

Bruised and sore feeling. Soreness when moving it; as after aching. Sensation as after headache. Oppression and dulness, as if intoxicated. Heaviness; when leaning forward. Confusion; with pain over r. eye. Sensation as after a large dose of opium, < walking. Fulness; in brain. Feeling as if inflated like a ball, especially at temples, < shaking head, the sensation so peculiar on rising from a seat as to cause laughter, afterwards, on standing, loss of all feeling, except in head, which seemed ten times its natural size, on walking loss of all realization of a body, the head seeming to float in the air, > lying, then vertigo.

Vertigo; from slightest motion; on going up and down-stairs; easier in afternoon on exposure to wind, which cooled the brain, but V. returned on entering house; > walking fast in open air, < as soon as he sat down, so that he had to hold on to something to prevent falling; with fulness or peculiar feeling in head; with cold clammy sweat and feeble pulse; with sensation as if staggering; with trembling; and things look as if moving backward and forward, with inability to see across the room; speedily passing into profound coma.

Forehead.—Intermittent. Cutting through F. and temples. Pain; in morning on waking, with burning in throat; < hot room; > fresh air; *in centre; over r. eyebrow;* over r. eye, > open air; over r. eye, extending to temple, with soreness of eyeball; in l. side; with general lassitude; with chilliness; with oppression of chest, beginning on l. side and going over to r.; **as from a rubber band** (Phos.); as from a band, at night and in morning. Neuralgia. Pain running to occiput.

Burning pain; in brain over brows. Heavy pain running to occiput. *Tightness above frontal sinuses.* Fulness; in frontal lobe of cerebrum, increasing to pain.

Temples.—Pain in l.; when stooping, and in occiput; P., < reading, with feeling in head similar to an "asleep" sensation in a limb; *sharp;* neuralgic, in l.; heavy, in l. during the day; burning, in r., and in vertex. **Tightness as if a rubber band were stretched from one to the other**; bandlike constrictions from one to the other, then heavy headache, < walking in open air.

Headache in upper half of head in morning on waking, > after breakfast; burning pain in vertex. Sensation in vertex as if brain were swashing about. *Headache in r. side;* l. side; neuralgic pain in l. side; N. pain changing from one side to the other, and affecting eye of painful side so that it was difficult to keep the eye open; beating pain in r. side.

Pain in occiput (Pic. ac.); and in r. side of head and in temple; in O., and in muscles of nape and especially behind ears. Sore feeling in occiput. Distention of superficial veins of head. *Pustulous vesicle to l. of vertex.* It hurt to comb or brush the hair. *Itching;* of r. then l. side. Desire to rub head and eyes.

Eyes.—Fixed; insensible to light and pupils dilated. Burning pain, < l. Heaviness. Neuralgic twitching in balls and through temples. Anæsthesia of conjunctiva. Pupils contracted; and insensible to light; dilated; D. and inactive. Lids closed; half-shut; opened, and eyes turned upward. Conjunctiva insensible. *Orbital neuralgia over r. eye.* Piercing pain in a spot in l. supraorbital ridge, > on rising, leaving soreness to touch. Sensitiveness to light. Swimming before eyes. Letters blurred. Dark spot before l. eye. Circles before eyes. Loss of vision, opthalmoscope showed very indistinct outline of papilla, especially r., the r. eye recovering more slowly than l.

Ears.—Crowded feeling. Intermittent aching in l. Beating pain, with a humming sound. Humming-buzzing. Roaring. Ringing, when stooping, with pulsations.

Nose.—Sensation of coryza, r. nostril plugged up and r. eye watery. Nostrils plugged up. Tickling in r. nostril, with sneezing. Discharge of bloody mucus and bright blood when blowing. Watery discharge in open air, > in house, returning on entering cold room. Exudation of froth. Smell very acute; and the odor of food satisfied the appetite.

Face.—*Pale;* and pinched; and covered with sweat; and covered with cold sweat; with weakness and cachectic condition. Pinched and anxious. Flushed and burning. Red, then pale, then red, with a trace of cyanotic color. Cyanosed. Dusky. Leaden-hued and covered with cold sweat. Livid; with cold clammy sweat; with clammy sweat. Idiotic expression. Pain. Drawing in r. zygoma. Sensitiveness to touch. Trismus. Drawing pain in r. jaw. Mouth open and filled with mucus. Lips and finger-tips livid. Lips, gums and pharynx coated with a white membrane, and white membranes were ejected from the mouth. Lips, mouth and throat white; grayish-white. Bloody foam before the bluish-red, closed lips. Burning in lips, mouth and œsophagus, with heat rising from stomach.

Mouth.—Pain in r. upper teeth. Tongue retracted. Tongue foul. Biting on tongue. Burning on tongue, especially at tip; on tongue, with tingling, stinging and with sharp taste. Swelling on inner side of l. cheek, with soreness. Mucous membrane livid; and in throat. White and corroded, and tongue and fauces. Corroded and painful, and tongue, afterwards mucous membrane came off in great flakes. Pain; burning, and in throat and pit of stomach. Burning. Soreness, and of throat. Frothing. Mucus continually ejected, and from nose. Exuding bloody slime. Constant discharge of saliva. Filled with thick saliva. Bluish-white, frothy, copious saliva. Tarry odor to the breath. Taste nasty; T. horrid, pungent and metallic, making him feel sick and squally all over; coppery, on tongue and upper palate; sweetish.

Throat.—*Spasm of carotid* (common, left) while walking rapidly after dinner. *Fauces red and covered with mucous exudation. Uvula whitened and shrivelled.* Soft palate relaxed, making breathing noisy. Much mucus. Hawking of clear white mucus while in open air; of much white mucus, and from posterior nares. Choking, with disposition to hawk up mucus. Intermittent stitches. Pain; on swallowing; burning. Burning; pricking, as if she had eaten something strong. Soreness; on r. side in evening; on swallowing; on empty swallowing; < r. side, when swallowing and on pressure on upper larynx; with hoarseness. Sensitiveness to pressure, > smoking after tea. Dryness in morning on waking, and in posterior nares. Irritation. Nausea. Swallowing difficult; impossible.

Œsophagus.—Spasmodic contraction; just behind pomum Adami while drinking ice-water, with pain. Burning.

Clinical.—In diphtheria, especially with tendency to involve the nose and inside of mouth, extremely fetid breath, regurgitation on swallowing liquids, urine highly albuminous, face dusky red, white about the mouth and nose, rapid sinking of vital forces.

Stomach.—*Appetite lost;* for supper; diminished; D. for dinner; unusual A. for supper; voracious, with thirst, then colic and call to stool. Wanted to smoke a cigar and thought that would relieve him. *Felt as if a little more whisky would do him good.* Thirst. Eructations; after a light breakfast; *empty;* tasting like buttermilk and cabbage (after drinking milk at dinner). Hiccough after dinner.

Nausea; most of the morning; *while eating a little breakfast;* after tea, till next noon, < sherry; from cold water; > drinking much water; > after tea, but she was drowsy; with shuddering, shaking of head, wry faces and *frequent spitting;* with desire to eructate; with prostration. Retching. Vomiting; on getting up; bilious; of a white creamy substance, smelling of carbolic acid; of blood and oily matter, next day of greenish watery matter.

Dyspepsia. Gastritis. Gastric catarrh. Pain; in pit; in epigastrium; and in r. side, with inability to eat any dinner; with dragging feeling, and low down in abdomen; burning; burning, in epigastrium. Burning; with heat rising up œsophagus; with sore feeling to touch; as from a corrosive acid, with good appetite and good digestion. Burning, ulcerating feeling after smoking a pipe, and in œsophagus, with nausea. Distress < lying on either side, > lying on back with legs drawn up; D. as from indigestion.

Feeling as if he had eaten too much. Fulness after a hearty lunch, with rising of heat tasting of carbolic acid; F. as if filled with wind, then eructations, afterwards distention impeding respiration. Wind is very troublesome, > raising a sweetish-sour liquid. Heaviness in epigastrium as from flatulence, with inclination to relieve himself by fruitless efforts at eructation or by pressing hand into pit of stomach. Food lies heavily. Empty, gone feeling (instead of hunger at meals), with fulness in throat and constant desire to swallow. Tenderness on pressure, and over cæcum. Dull, uneasy feeling. Irritation. Spasm of diaphragm.

Clinical.—Vomiting of drunkards; vomiting of pregnant women, with violent, frontal headache. Has been found useful in cancer of the stomach.

Abdomen.—*Distention*, with emissions of fetid flatus; D. especially in epigastric region, but neither hard, tense nor sensitive; flatulent, also with soreness of abdominal muscles. *Rumbling and rolling*, with sense of distention; rumbling, and after walking feeling as if diarrhœa would come on. Emission of much flatus all the evening; E. of much putrid flatus; of fetid flatus. Bloated feeling, with soreness. Feeling as if gas were incarcerated; with inability to discharge any. Feeling of goneness, with heaviness about stomach, ineffectual disposition to rift up and constriction about middle of œsophagus. Discomfort from jolting while riding, with heat and soreness. Soreness on walking; S. of muscles.

Pain in hypochondria; *in r. and in both iliac regions;* over H. and along back; over region of liver and across fifth, sixth and seventh dorsal vertebræ. Soreness in hypochondria, < motion. Pain and soreness in r. side and iliac regions. Crampy stitch in l. inguinal region while sitting. Pain in hypogastrium; burning.

Clinical.—Great flatulent distention of abdomen and accumulation of flatus, with belching of wind and desire for stimulants (compare Arg. nit.).

Rectum and Anus.—Desire for stool all day after a natural stool in morning. Urging, stool loose, with much flatus. Itching in anus, with feeling as if skin were rubbed off.

Stool.—Thin, blood-streaked. Watery, frequent, with pain and nausea. Dark. In thin strips, like tape, appearing as if composed of thick glue and mixed with currant seeds, though he had eaten nothing of the kind, with flatulence. Copious and consistent, but almost inodorous. Insufficient and sluggish. Constipation. Involuntary, and I. micturition. Frequent; and involuntary, at night in sleep, small and in strips like tape, next morning symptoms of bad diarrhœa, burning in rectum, but no stool, and feeling, especially in head, as after a large dose of opium; at first black, then dark brown.

Clinical.—Dysentery, of bloody mucus, like scrapings of the intestines, often involuntary diarrhœa, putrid, dark, with vomiting of dark green substances.

Urinary Organs.—Acute nephritis, with uræmia. Urging at 5 A.M., and copious urine. Micturition frequent; at night; and copious; involuntary, giving the linen the color of red wine; straining at, then discomfort; ineffectual attempts at. Urine copious; at night, and pale; and of strong odor; and limpid, colorless, with a peculiar odor. Urine scanty; and high-colored; and blackish, not containing urea. *Urine almost black* (Ars. hyd., Phos., Kali chl., Merc. c.). *Dark;* and offensive, depositing urate of ammonia and sometimes phosphates, but no albumen. Dark brown, alkaline. *Dark smoky color, alkaline* (Benz. ac., K. carb.), with sediment of granular urate of ammonia, and with a mixture of different-colored pigments, which apparently came from the coloring matter of the dissolved blood-corpuscles. Smoky and of aromatic odor, the addition of strong sulphuric acid causing a purple color, changing rapidly to blue, without odor of drug and without albumen.

Urine greenish, with disappearance of all deposits of lithates; dark G., acid, albuminous, with thick sediment of pus; dark olive green, without odor. Of the color of blood, the microscope showed no red corpuscles, but the spectroscope showed bands of oxyhæmoglobin, afterwards the urine had to be drawn off, no more hæmoglobin, but some albumen, granular casts, some red globules and renal epithelium, afterwards hyaline casts. Hæmoglobinuria, as determined by the spectroscope, but no red corpuscles were detected. Contained whitish flocculi, but on standing it turned a dirty brown color. Acid.

Clinical.—Diabetes.

Sexual Organs.—Burning-itching. Relaxed, weakened state during the day, and every night lascivious dreams, with emissions, which caused weakness and horror. Prickling pains through glans and in urethra. Excitement, waking at night. Appetite decreased. *Pain in region of l. ovary when walking in open air.* Menses profuse; and later; and dark, then headache and nervous irritability.

Clinical.—Ulcers of the cervix uteri, with fetid, acrid discharge from the vagina. It nearly cured epithelioma which involved the labia and extended to other organs; it was prescribed from the indication of the eruption on the skin of vesicles and pustules which contained a bloody matter, with offensive discharge. Leucorrhœa in children.

Respiratory Organs.—Vocal cords red and swollen and mucous membrane of larynx injected. Soreness of larynx and of bronchial membrane, with hoarseness; S. of l. side of larynx on pressure. Râles in trachea. Hoarseness. Bronchitis.

Cough; after slight exercise, with palpitation; with expectoration; without expectoration; *hacking, with tickling in throat;* hacking, from irritation in throat; hacking, from tickling in upper part of trachea and in fauces; croupy, at night. Constant inclination to cough. Expectoration rusty; E. of much thick, whitish mucus.

Respiration stertorous; and rapid. Difficult; and jerky; with large vesicular râles fully covering the sounds of breathing; irregular, noisy during inspiration. Panting; and tracheal. Gasping and inability to lie down. Groaning. Rapid; and irregular. Slow and irregular. Irregular. Feeble and shallow. Free and deep, inclination to take a deep breath.

Clinical.—Whooping cough, with frontal headache. Palliative in offensive, purulent expectoration in tuberculosis of lungs.

Chest.—Full of large mucous râles. Dulness and bronchial breathing on r. side of back, below angle of scapula; absolute D. on back, right from angle of scapula to lower limits of lung, with loud bronchial breathing and râles. Pneumonia; circumscribed, at base of r. lung. Pain < on r. side; under l. clavicle; through upper lobes of lungs; under sternum in region of sixth rib; in whole l. side of chest and abdomen, running around to scapulæ; uneasy, in r. lung. *Narrow feeling, as if diaphragm oppressed lungs.* Tight feeling in lungs, especially in centre of chest. Compressed feeling across lower end of sternum. Oppression; as from a load in front (Phos.). Feeling of expansion (of lightness) in lungs and nasal passages while walking in open air.

Heart.—Sounds scarcely audible. Stitches. Palpitation when quiet. Action irregular. Action weak, free from murmur; W. and intermittent.

Clinical.—Great palpitation or violent beating of heart at night.

Pulse.—Rapid; and full; and weak; and weak, trembling; and intermittent, weak; and intermittent, small; and irregular, undulating; and sometimes extinct during inspiration. Slow; and small. Small, intermittent. Compressible and occasionally intermittent. Weak; and fluttering; and uncountable. Irregular. Imperceptible. Intermittent.

Neck.—Livid color. Stitches in r. side in morning, increasing during the day, afterwards with intermittent twinges. Pain. Sense of weight, with tenderness even to touch over seventh cervical vertebra. Soreness of muscles (*splenitis capitis*). Drawing in muscles of r. side, seemingly in *splenitis capitis*. Lameness and stiffness; L. of nape while smoking after tea, and of shoulder.

Back.—Pain; and in r. side; in spine, extending down posterior muscles of thigh. *Soreness of muscles of back and limbs.* Weakness and soreness. *Pain in loins; < straightening himself and by jolting while riding;* > pressure of hand; and in lower limbs. Boring in loins. Sore or bruised feeling in loins and in abdomen. Tired in renal region.

Extremities.—Twitchings. Relaxation. Flaccidity, except convulsions of r. arm. Occasional pains; in hips and shoulders. Pain in hip, then in l. shoulder-joint. Bruised pain beneath l. tendo-achillis, close to posterior part of tibia, then sharp pain in middle joint of l. large finger, then in leg again. Difficulty of motion, and when raised they dropped like those of one dead drunk, as indeed she was. Numb feeling.

Upper Extremities.—Pain in r. shoulder-joint; in r. shoulder when bending forward. Lameness of r. shoulder when walking, with soreness. Atonic spasm of r. arm. Pain in l. arm and in r. wrist; drawing, from l. shoulder to elbow; burning, in arm waking him, elbow, lower third of arm and upper third of forearm swollen, tissue tense, dark red and hot, vesicles filled with yellowish watery fluid around elbow, skin could be detached by gently rubbing finger over it, temp. 102 4-5 (from application to axillary abscess), in another case the inflammation was not confined to the elbow, but extended slightly behind scapula. *Soreness of muscles of r. arm. Tired, heavy feeling in l. arm.* Weakness of arms, so that he could not write. *Pain in l. forearm.*

Hand.—Swelling so that he could not write. Trembling. Contracting pain in r. palm. Numbness of r. when trying to write. with inability to close it tightly. Stiffness, with discomfort (pricking), the discomfort remaining on middle finger until night, and in one spot until a pimple formed, which increased until it became a sore resembling a carbuncle, suppurating until a probe could be passed nearly through the finger, with pain which prevented sleep. Pain in second phalangeal joint of r. middle finger.

Lower Extremities.—Staggering. Draggy sensation, causing unsteadiness in walking. *Leaden heaviness.* Tingling. Pain in hips; in r.; in r. hip and in l. knee; in r. hip-joint when walking; in r. hip like sciatica, moving along that nerve, and at night in bend of knee. Bruised or sore feeling in hips.

Thigh.—Pain in muscles of r.; deep-seated in muscles on inside of upper third of l., almost making him lame. Bruised feeling in r.; B. feeling, with weakness and lameness of back; deep-seated, in middle of anterior part of r. about 7 P.M. while walking Drawing in r. Faint feeling, spreading all over body.

Pain on inside of l. knee; at night; bruised P. in r. knee. Cramp in calves. *Pain under r. patella; to the left of middle of l. shin-bone; sharp pain in l. shin. Aching soreness beneath l. patella all day till* 4 P.M., *feeling as if it would be stiff and sore if moved, but > during motion.* Weakness of legs. Pain in r. ankle; most of the morning, and in l. knee; P. in l. outer malleolus.

Stinging through corns. Bruised feeling in feet; in r. foot. Heaviness of feet. Feeling in feet as though they could not support the body, though he was lying on his back. Pain in l. great toe; in under surface; in r. great toe as if pressed upon. Tingling in l. great toe, then feeling as if pressed upon.

Skin.—Pallor. Cyanosis. *Lividity.* Horripilation. Pustules on r. side of face. Vesicles all over body; **on hands and all over body, with itching, > rubbing, but leaving a burning pain**; on centre of nose, changing to a pustule. Nettle-rash.

Hands, especially fingers, rough and scaly, afterwards erythematous blush over hands, with eruption on fingers of small, round, hard elevations, close together, giving a bossy appearance, not red nor inflamed, with itching, which was < at night, gradually the fingers became rougher and rougher and large scales peeled off, leaving reddened patches of varying size, then deep, bleeding, tender fissures, mainly in folds around knuckles on dorsal surface (palmar surface of fingers never being affected), and about this time a boil on neck, afterwards on renewed use of the solution the erythema and nightly itching reappeared, with itching over whole body, beginning one night in feet and during succeeding nights progressing up legs and trunk, then down arms, till it centered, with increased virulence,in hands, with burning smarting when rubbed, and with red wheals on trunk and arms, painful abscesses upon fingers, some upon phalanges and some under nails, boil on neck, painful pimples on face, the former scaly, and fissured condition of fingers, the hands presenting appearance of eczema.

Sensitiveness to touch. Numbness, on hands. Formication in limbs. Itching; of face; r. cheek; r. ear; nose; nape; l. elbow; l. shoulder; r. forefinger; hypogastrium about l. hip; outside of thigh and genitals; r. thigh, buttocks, back, shin, etc., inner side of l. knee; ankles, arms, calf and other parts; of inner part of thigh and scrotum, > scratching, but returning; tingling, of r., then l. little finger.

Clinical.—It seemed to cure epithelioma in cheek and nose, with hæmorrhages. Prairie itch. Ulcers following burns. Chronic ulcers on the feet. Vesicular eruptions over the body, which became bloody, with burning pain, fetid sweat.

Sleep.—Yawning; with long inspirations. Sleepiness; in afternoon, with inability to fall into sound sleep; with desire to stretch; with chilliness; with heaviness, but perplexing dreams on lying down and waking unrefreshed, with coated tongue and nausea. Heavy sleep, and on waking general soreness, especially in legs (gluteals), back, chest and arms.

Sleeplessness; after midnight, the smell of carbolic acid seemed to keep her awake. Waking frequently; W. early; wide awake in an instant at 6 A.M. after a sound sleep. Unrefreshing sleep, with many unremembered dreams. Restless sleep; with busy dreams.

Dreams.—Frightful, waking her several times. Vivid of fire, waking him, when he found that he was feverish, though the room was cold. Many, some amorous, others unremembered. Of traveling. Of great mental activity, and awoke with clear intellect. That she could not get to sleep on account of thinking about the body I had embalmed, that she tossed about, that she pulled me out of bed to wake me, but I was bathed in perspiration, face pale, and she thought I was dead, awakened by the fright she found herself lying on her back, with mouth open, apparently paralyzed with fear, she aroused me, whined for something to make her sleep and could not be persuaded at first that she had been asleep.

Fever.—Chilliness; at 9 A.M.; at breakfast; in open air; with great nervousness and distress, although externally warm, pulse unsteady, weak and irregular, vertigo and impending convulsions. Temperature lower, then higher. Shuddering. Coldness of surface; especially of limbs. Coldness of limbs; with insensibility of them; hands and feet; feet all the afternoon; on skin just below knee, as if touched with ice; in one spot on stooping, as when the nerve of a tooth is touched, then clammy sweat. Chill running from face downward, in a hot room. Shivering chills along spine, with pulse 80, full and strong, head hot and dry, hand cold, inward trembling, could feel heart beat. Creeping shuddering or horripilation in l. forearm, running upward.

Heat; with flurry and rapid pulse. Room feels close and hot, with rush of blood to head, flushing of face, then chilliness. Heat of head; hot feeling in forehead, > pressure of cold hand; of face and forehead, especially of l. side, with pressure in l. temple, seemingly on surface of brain; of face, with sweat on it. Burning in skin.

Sweat; on waking in middle of night. Clammy; on forehead. Cold; on head on least exertion. Cold and clammy; on face and hands.

Carboneum Sulfuratum.

The pure bi-sulphide of Carbon is dissolved in Alcohol (1 to 99).

General Action.—It produces paralysis, with symptoms of intense congestion of nerve centres. Cerebral excitement followed by depression. General hyperæsthesia, then anæsthesia, etc. (Abdominal symptoms of Sulphur.)

Allies.—*Plumb.*, all the Carbons, Phos., Ars., Absinth., Gels., Rhus t., Carbol. ac., etc.

Generalities.—Emaciation, < arms and legs. Awkwardness. Falling; with loss of consciousness. Epileptic attack, then paralysis of limbs. Twitching of muscles. Cramp in muscles. Trembling. Muscular contraction inefficient and tremulous, the fingers could not be closed forcibly, and on extending arm there was trembling of muscular fibres (all the Carbons). Nervous attacks analogous to hysteria, with convulsions of face and involuntary laughter.

Sticking or itching pains in various parts. Itching sticking in various parts all the forenoon; in various parts, especially in tuber ischii and at point of insertion of gracilis and sartorius at knee. Jerking stitches in various parts at 10.30 P.M.; in various parts, especially in muscles of r. eye; peculiar jerking S. at times till after dinner, now in hollow of r. knee, now in abdomen towards spermatic cord. General pains, especially acute in knees. Fulgurating pains and sensations as of girdles about limbs and body. Jerking pain, now in forehead, now in joints of feet, now in joints of arms. Erratic pains. Rheumatic pains in all parts, especially in muscles of fingers and toes and in l. hand; in l. upper arm, occiput and nape; wandering. Biting, as of leeches.

Symptoms of cerebral congestion, motor troubles, hyperæsthesia of skin, with finally complete paraplegia, the powers of co-ordination being almost absent while the perversion of sensibility reached a remarkable degree, the sexual apparatus lost its functional activity (Phos.), with darting pains in almost all regions, but chiefly in cardiac zone, where mitral insufficiency was found. Indisposition in evening on going to bed, with discharge of warm flatus. General sick feeling all the afternoon, with nausea, colic, aversion to beer, etc. Wretchedness > the gas of the factory. She seemed to herself as if swollen over her whole body (Rhus t.). Throbbing and trembling after disappearance of anæsthesia. Excitement of whole body. Restlessness (Rhus t.). Hyperæsthesia.

Weakness; in morning, also on waking; on slightest exertion; especially in back, loins and joints of feet, with bruised sensation; muscular, with inco-ordination of movement, like motor ataxia. Sinking on her knees if raised from bed and gradually sliding to the ground. Relaxation of muscles. Faintness; then inability to walk or remember anything of her condition, was confused, even demented, on attempting to speak she stuck out her tongue like a child, stretched the lower jaw far forward and gnashed it against the upper one and stared at her hands and fingers with a vacant look. Partial syncope, with convulsive movements of limbs (Absinth.).

Rigidity of muscles. Anæsthesia of various parts of skin (Absinth., all Carbons, Plumb.) and of mucous membrane of mouth, eyes, ears and nose. Paralysis; progressive multiple neuritis, most resembling that of alcohol, without the hyperæsthesia of alcohol. Loss of motion and sensibility of whole r. side (Plumb.). Hemiplegia, sensibility of r. side very slight (Ars., Phos.), muscular contractility lost, but contraction, especially of arm, with pain on attempting to extend it. Paraplegia, so that the limbs could not support the body (Ars.). Skin, patellar and other tendon reflexes could not be elicited, could not rise from a chair without the aid of his arms, could not rise to his legs from the floor, the steps were very short, the sole brought flat to the ground while the knee, after giving way slightly, was extended, with a jerk before each step, hands very weak, < r., could not place his hand behind his head or shave himself, on raising a tumbler of water much fibrillary tremor of muscles of forearm, but the vessel was carried up steadily, although the hand was unsteady in the descent. Senses blunted. Aggravation from tobacco; from wine and beer (Nux v.).

Mind.—Delirium; with incoherent talking (Hyosc.). Raging (in a child), with attempts to bite his father; jumped from the window and hid under shavings. Imagination that he is surrounded by enemies at night, heard imaginary voices and saw strange objects (Stram.). Excitement; at night; so that he was put in a strait-jacket. Depressing and disagreeable visions. Fancied that he was surrounded by cats. Hallucinations of vision and hearing, splendid spectacles of carriages, with magnificent objects, talking of the emperor, of money, of grandeur, often incoherently. Violence. Beating his wife. Anger. Revengefulness. Impatience. Intolerance of contradiction. Irritability. Screaming. Weeping mood. Sadness; with obstinacy; with preoccupation.

Changeable mood, sometimes extravagant gayety, sometimes unreasonable anger, smashing everything about him. Gayety; changing to sadness and indifference. Desire to laugh and prattle without cause. Loquacity (Hyosc.); with inability to think of the words he wants to use and with stammering. Lack of energy. Disinclination for all work, with sleepiness and pressure upon eyes. Listlessness, would not talk nor be talked to, at times nervous and easily agitated, at others half stupid, losing memory and thinking he was about to lose his reason.

Activity of mind. Peculiar idiocy and childishness (Carbons, Plumb.). Replied by monosyllables or signs with the hands, intellect impaired, he sought solitude, like a child was occupied by objects immediately about him, when not amused was inactive, seemed distrait. Inability to fix the attention. Distraction; when reading. Loss of all desire for study, with absurd reveries. Stupidity. Memory impaired; especially for recent events. Memory lost (Anac.). Often at a loss for words. Frequently she did not know what to do with the things she held in her hands. Unconsciousness. Coma.

Head.—Aching; beginning about 9 A.M., with confusion of head and difficulty of thought; in forenoon; all. forenoon, especially in forehead and over eyes; after breakfast, with confusion; towards 10 P.M.; when reading; < towards evening; < towards evening, with throbbing at temples; > afternoon, returning in evening; intermittent, and in frontal region. Throbbing pain all day, < moving head. Aching on brushing hair, as if sore, especially on vertex. Constrictive aching. A. as from a tight cap (Gelsem.). Sensation as from an iron band. Compressible A., especially in root of nose and in temples, with stiffness of neck, coldness of neck, especially over posterior part, pain on turning head, vertigo, with the pain in neck.

Confusion; > noon, by sweat from constant walking, with pain, as in catarrho-rheumatic headaches; with stitches here and there in forehead and intermittent jerking pain in it; as from spirituous drinks. Heaviness. Vertigo; in afternoon while sitting; in attacks while sitting; with partial loss of consciousness; with loss of smell, vision affected so that objects appeared larger than they were. So that he could not stand.

Forehead.—Stitches here and there, sometimes with twitching pain. Tearing, extending to temples, > afternoon. Digging. Aching; in a spot, and between eyes; on waking; < evening, with vertigo and ringing in ears; < reading and stooping; with heat; in sinciput; in eminence, extending to l. temple, with tearings in that direction; soon extending to l. parietal bone; from root of nose round head to occipital protuberance. Intermittent, extending towards eyes; intermittent, < evening, with vertigo and ringing in ears; flitting, gradually extending to l. temple. Ulcerative pain; with burning in eyes. Confused aching; with nausea. Drawing pain, extending to temples, > open air and during rest, with tearing. Tensive pain at 10 P.M.; T. pain, with eructations. Pressure, with sleepiness, and in temples; P. extending to orbits and temples. Confusion; with constriction in cerebral hemisphere. Vertigo; in sinciput, even to falling forward (Petrol.).

Temples.—Stitches in l., extending to occiput. Tearing; in l.; in r. when stooping. Aching; < r. Drawing pain; in l. Reeling pain in afternoon, < shaking head or stepping hard. Pulsating pain (migraine) at 6 A.M. on waking, so that he could not lie quietly, > breakfast at 7.30 A.M. Compressing pain; and in occiput; from one to the other, with vertigo and agitation; through T., < walking, so that each step caused a painful shock in head. Pressure; at insertion of muscles; inward, afterwards extending to vertex.

Pain in vertex. Semilateral headache, returned when walking, with dulness and confusion of head; pain in r. side. Pain in r. parietal bone as if pressed by a hard body. Fulness in occiput in evening and night, with a humming noise there. Pimples on scalp, painful to touch. Itching of scalp.

Eyes.—Sunken, surrounded by gray rings. Congestion of optic. Inflammation of r., kerato-iritis. Fixed, without expression, pupils dilated, < l., but sluggish, could not see with the r. as with l., ophthalmoscope showed in r. eye slender retinal veins, extravasations of blood into vitreous, filaments and points floating in vitreous. Paleness of internal segment of optic nerves, with marked excavation of papillæ (Phos., Plumb.), which were less transparent than normal, and appearance of optic nerve like smoked glass. Progressive atropy of papillæ of l. Neuritis, disc pale and hazy, the haze extending a disc's breadth into retina, veins engorged, arteries too small, central scotoma for red, not for white. Stitches in r.; when reading; jerking, in r., in region of superior rectus muscle. Pressure upon eyes; with inclination to close them; itching, with burning on upper lids and an itching pustule, and with whitish-yellow mucus in eye. Heat and pricking. Lachrymation; while reading.

Pressure on l. ball, with heat in it. Itching of ball. Pupils dilated; contracted. Cornea insensible (Gels.).

Lids.—Twitching. Heaviness. Burning in margin, with redness. Biting in r. lower. Itching. Bruised pain in r. lower, near outer angle, in afternoon, first observed on touch, then in upper, over region of lachrymal gland, and in upper and inner part of globe, all < by movement of eye or lid and by pressure, r. lids feel swollen but are not, redness of outer margin of lower lid, with sensation as if a stye would begin, next day r. lower lid hot, painful, sore, swollen, red near outer canthus, the following day stye on r. lower lid, hot and painful.

Paroxysmal jerking stitching alternately in various

muscles of r. eye. Sore pain in l. orbicularis, towards external canthus, < moving lids. Pressure in orbits.

Photophobia. Vision misty; in r. eye; for everything beyond a certain distance. Double vision. Trembling of all objects (Plumb.); of letters when reading. Objects seemed confluent. Loss of vision; in r. eye. Obscuration of a part of the field, so that he did not see the concluding letters. Field restricted (Physos.), especially for colors; especially for white and blue. Loss of power of distinguishing objects and bluish-green appearance to everything, as if seen through a green veil, ability to distinguish only large objects quite close, inability to distinguish type of newspaper from the white margin, both alike appearing greenish (Osm.), glasses did not improve vision. Inability to read, all objects appeared yellow, ophthalmoscopic examination revealed nothing abnormal, usual field showed a central scotoma for red and green.

Ears.—Stitches; in r.; in r. in afternoon; in r. after dinner, at intervals of a quarter of an hour; in r., < towards evening; in l.; in l. in evening; in l., waking him at night, with griping pain in it; in l. as from an insect at 9 P.M; in external meatus auditorius; jerking, in l. Boring in r. Pain in l., with stopped sensation; intermittent P. in r. as if a dull instrument were thrust into tympanum. Feeling of deafness in l. as if obstructed by a thick substance, during and after dinner.

Deafness. Hearing lost in l. ear. Hearing impaired; as if something were stuffed into ears. Ringing; before ears. Tinkling. Humming in l.; < eating; in l. like a distant wind, obliging him to raise his voice. Buzzing and singing of wind in r., like an æolian harp, in morning when walking.

Nose.—Pain in nasal fossæ as from fumes of sulphuric acid. Prickling in tip like an irritation to sneeze. Burning in root, and in throat. Stoppage. Sneezing; with traces of blood in nasal mucus. Bleeding. Smell impaired; everything smelled of the vapors of the factory.

Face.—Pale; and covered with clammy sweat, lips blue and moist, with saliva and frothy mucus. Red, then pale; R. and puffy. Sudden congestion, with anxious, uncertain expression. Sad expression. Aspect of astonishment, with hesitancy of speech and loss of memory. Convulsive movements of lips; in corners. Dry lips. Burning of lips, tongue and throat. Stiff lips. Drawing pain in l. lower jaw. Compressive feeling in muscles of under jaw, especially alongside larynx.

Mouth.—Teeth. Stitches in r. lower molar extending from crown to root; in r. upper carious T.; jerking, in carious T. at 9 A.M.; drawing, in upper back carious at 6 A.M., and in lower one opposite to it, lasting in first till after rising. Tearing reappeared in afternoon, < cold, > after midnight, with drawing. Toothache from cleansing mouth, with cold water in morning; T. < night; in r. lower molar; with an ulcer about the tooth, extending towards palate, with itching, tension and impeded chewing; throbbing, in l. back teeth in evening and all night, with burning in it. Blunt feeling.

Tongue.—Coating. Pricking on tip. Coldness, changing to sticking-burning, then sensation as from an acrid and astringent substance. Burning; in papillæ; at tip and in throat; at root; sticking; as from oil of peppermint, with garlicky taste. Stiffness. Paralysis (Plumb.). Speech difficult.

Burning in mouth; with pain, and in pharynx. Irritability in mouth and pharynx, with constriction in larynx provoking cough, which amounts to retching, with expectoration of mucus. Clamminess. Anæsthesia of mucus membrane of M. and throat. Salivation; with nausea. Constant spitting. Glutinous saliva. Sweetish saliva. Fetid breath. Hot breath.

Taste.—Metallic. Sulphur-like. Saltish-sourish all forenoon. Sweetish, offensive. Bitter; on waking, > after breakfast. Bitter sour in morning. Repulsive, acrid and scraping, with burning in throat and along œsophagus on swallowing. Pasty; and nauseous. Unusual, to beer between 5 and 6 P.M. Impaired. Blunted, frequently herby. Lost, except for salt and sugar.

Throat.—Hawking, with inclination to vomit; H. of salt mucus. Oniony taste and smell. Intermittent sticking constriction near beginning of œsophagus, as if a bone were sticking there. (Pains caused by cold wet weather, with burning and with catarrh.) Scraping; with burning, and in œsophagus. Rawness; scraping, (as from a foreign body) in l. side, extending on swallowing to l. ear. Scraping roughness; with stitches. Acridity. Sensation of a hair. Burning; extending to stomach; in soft palate. Burning pain. Dryness. Difficulty in swallowing.

Stomach.—Appetite increased; and digestion difficult, irregular, with colic, vomiting and congestion. Ravenous A. Desire for food, with salivation. Irregular appetite. Hunger, with aversion to eating; H., with aversion to the food set before him, but it had real relish. Little appetite; especially for meat. Loss of A.; for supper. Aversion to all food, it smelled and tasted of the drug. Thirst; especially for beer.

Eructations; in morning on waking, with emissions of flatus; with nausea. Insufficient. Loud; in afternoon, with fetid flatus. Empty; and of acrid smell and taste; as after eating radishes. Of milk that had been eaten, without nausea and vomiting. Of bitter fluid at 10 P.M. Of nauseating fluid. Sour; at 8 A.M. after drinking coffee; burning; burning, corrosive, in afternoon after eating; corrosive fluid.

Nausea; on stooping; < entering a room or going into open air; > eructations; > vomiting; with frontal headache; with pressure and coldness in stomach; in attacks, with movements in hypogastrium; intermittent, > after dinner, with salivation; faintlike. Vomiting; violent, on eating; vomiting of food and glairy mucus. Inability to retain water long. Vomiting of scanty, bitter water. Greenish vomiting; and bilious, with nausea, cold sweat and prostration.

Inflation. Stitching through to back when resting epigastrium on window-sill and inspiring deeply; S. in epigastric region; radiating from a single point in pit into cardiac region, > noisy eructations. Tearing. Pinching in region. Cramp. Pain; after breakfast, < deep breathing; in region; in epigastric region. Sensitiveness to pressure. Constriction, with good appetite. Pressure; beneath pit; after breakfast; after breakfast, > eructations of air; after dinner, with constriction and sticking in chest; after dinner, stretching into abdomen; from all food and drink, even from beer and sugar; after beer, with eructations of air; after stool, then headache and cramplike sticking in ears; and in abdomen, with pain in loins.

Heaviness; extending all over epigastric region. Fulness; extending all over epigastric region, with vertigo. Emptiness. Discomfort; in epigastric region, with nausea and eructations of air having the taste and smell of the drug. Indigestion. Heartburn all day, < forenoon and at every eructation; H. < after smoking. Burning, < pressure, and in region of liver; B. in forenoon, extending through œsophagus; spreading through hypogastrium, with increasing warmth in chest and in the perspiring face and palms; in pit. Warmth in pit spreading through chest to head and downward to umbilicus.

Abdomen.—Distention; after eating; with soreness. Rumbling. Movements. Emission of flatus; when walking, with eructations; with itching in rectum; noisy; fetid. Increase of peristaltic motion. Flatulence. Stitches here and there. Tearing; here and there. Cutting in evening after salad, then urgent, knotty stool. Griping, > stool; G., with rumbling and rolling, as before diarrhœa; here and there, with emission of flatus. Flatulent twinges. Feeling as before diarrhœa; at 10 P.M.

Pain; at 4 A.M., with wandering swellings as from flatus, the pain increasing to sticking on inspiration, the pressure becoming seated in cœcal region, the pain < turning from one side to the other or doubling up; on pressure; after eating; after dinner; before soft stool; before insufficient liquid stool; > stool; while sitting and writing, > open air, seeming to cause attacks of nausea; with diarrhœa; intermittent jerking, in muscles in afternoon. Soreness of walls (Sulph.). Constriction, with discharge of flatus upward and downward. Tension. Discomfort after coffee; D., with nausea in it, then soft fecal stool; paroxysmal, also after stool.

Discomfort in upper, with salivation and paroxysms of nausea. Griping in small intestines, with emission of flatus. Stitches in l. side; pinching S. in r. side.

Hypochondria.—Sticking after long sitting; jerking, at 9 A.M. in r., then in l.; paroxysmal, in region of small lobe of liver before stool. Stitchlike jerkings in l. Paroxysmal cutting by r. false ribs at 6 A.M. Pain in region of l. lobe of liver.

Umbilical Region.—Stitches in r., extending into cœcal region, in morning in bed, with emission of flatus; itching S. on r. side below navel, before a semi-fluid stool. Tearings from r. side to bladder, returning till dinner. Cuttings after dinner, with nausea. Griping, with urging to stool, then nausea and salivation. Pinching twinges in a spot to r. of navel.

Cœcal Region.—Jerking sticking; itching sticking; pinching sticking; pinching sticking in cœcum after stool.

Hypogastrium.—Sticking on pressure. Stitchlike twinges in l. Cutting; after drinking coffee, then partly softish, partly crumbly stool. Pain as before diarrhœa, at 10 A.M. Acute pain in groin. Discomfort, < stooping or motion, with paroxysms of nausea.

Rectum.—Stitches. Urging to stool; at 5.30 A.M. on waking, with copious, thin, yellowish stool, then burning at anus as from acridity (Sulph.); at 8 P.M., stool pappy, accompanied and followed by a feeling of weakness and tremulousness.

Anus—Burning, with itching; in anterior commissure in afternoon after stool, with soreness to touch (Sulph.).

Stool.—Diarrhœa; after breakfast; frequent, with smarting in anus; sudden, after dinner, repeated twice in afternoon, with colic; fetid; fetid, alternating with constipation (Sulph.); slimy, in afternoon; semi-fluid; watery; of yellow, frothy, sour-smelling fluid nights, with pain in abdomen, especially in umbilical region, with retraction of umbilicus and tenesmus; profuse. Pappy; with discharge of blood; and involuntary in afternoon during micturition; in part, crumbly in part, then soon a fluid one. Stool with mucus and discharge of cherry-red blood (with the headache).

Constipation; alternating with diarrhœa. Dry. Solid at first, then liquid, with burning in anus, then pasty, with burning in anus; S. at first, then soft, then rumbling as if another stool would occur. Scanty and pappy; S. and soft; and hard, with urging; in evening, small and even if fluid still difficult from inactivity of rectum. Frequent. No stool; for three days, then soft, with discharge of cherry-red blood.

Urinary Organs.—Sticking crampy pain in bladder and neck of bladder at midnight during micturition, after a glass of wine, extending into urethra, with similar pain in anus and rectum. Urging to urinate; with emission of two or three drops at a time, also with burning in urethra and tenesmus of neck of bladder. Sudden desire to urinate arising from fossa navicularis, without real urging or necessity to urinate. Inability to retain urine any length of time, passed with pain and difficulty; inability to retain urine above an hour, micturition often attended by scalding and followed by a discharge that stained the linen. Micturition involuntary (Ars.). Painful and slow micturition; P., with burning pain (Ars.); with tenesmus and frequent desire to urinate, and bloody urine (Ars.).

Urethra.—Cutting during micturition. Smarting during micturition. Burning during micturition (Ars.). Irritation of mucous membrane. Tickling in forepart, with sensation as if something would run out

Urine.—Increased. Highly colored. Red, containing abundance of carbonate and phosphate of lime. Albuminous, red and turbid (Ars., Phos., Plumb., etc.). Turbid; and pale. Smelling of sulphur. Increase of carbonates and sulphates.

Sexual Organs.—Relaxed. Chilled. Stitches in l. spermatic cord in evening. Sticking-burning pain in spermatic cord, running deep into abdomen; evening in bed. Shrivelled penis. Erections, with nightly emissions; difficult erections; violent erections, with burning in urethra. Shrunken and painful scrotum. Itching on scrotum. Testicles small; with diminished sensation on pressure. Swelling of l. testicle and epididymis; of l. testicle, with hardness and pain. Jerking sticking in l. testicle. Uneasiness in tumor testiculi. Impotency; with atrophied testicles.

Excitement; with loss of power; with rare erections, coition too long, ejaculation short and incomplete; with constant fatiguing erections, speedily changing to impotency (Pic. ac.). Desire increased (in both sexes); increased, then diminished till lost, at times an incomplete erection resulted in indefinite coition without emission, or at times difficult but profuse ejaculation. Loss of desire; and of power (Phos.). Emission copious; at night (Phos.).

Miscarriage. Uterine catarrh. Ovaries almost obliterated. Menstruation too early; profuse M.; irregular M. Sexual sensation disappeared (in a woman).

Respiratory Organs.—Irritability of larynx. Heat of larynx. Hoarseness; at noon, as from catarrh; with irritation to hawk, especially on posterior wall of larynx, seldom provoking cough. Voice feeble. Voice altered in tone. Voice deep bass.

Cough; from scraping in throat; caused by heart-burn; tormenting, with irritation in bronchi. Dry C.; and hard, after lying down, from tickling in posterior part of palate; convulsive, at 10.30 P.M. on lying down, from tickling as if snuff had lodged upon uvula, straining chest and making it sore. Inclination to C.; arising from bifurcation of bronchi.

Respiration.—Rattling (after respiration). Difficult on ascending stairs. Oppressed after much exercise; O., with pressure on sternum (Phos.). Gets out of breath easily. Accelerated. Expiration prolonged; over posterior part of lungs. Inspiration deep and slow. Almost stertorous.

Chest.—Emphysema of lungs. Congestion of upper lobes of lungs (Ars., Iod.). Stitches, and below l. short ribs; near l. side of sternum after coffee; under middle of sternum, extending upward like lightning; periodical, in l. half; paroxysmal, in region of last r. ribs at 5 P.M.; jerking, in lower r. side; itching, in r. nipple. Aching in r. side; tensive A. in chest, stomach and abdomen. Pressure under sternum. Oppression; < impure air and unventilated room, when it is associated with anxiety. Fulness and oppression of breathing seem to arise from anterior part of r. side of diaphragm. Constriction, as if expiration were impeded, > deep respirations in open air. Sensitiveness of anterior wall in evening, when sneezing. Warmth. Periodical burning in l. half beneath sternum. Symptoms, < ascending steps.

Heart.—Anæmic murmur. Murmur of first sound extended along the great vessels. With the first sound there was a prolonged murmur, which extended along vessels of neck. Accelerated action. Palpitation (Ars.).

Pulse.—Rapid; and hard; and weak. Slow. Feeble, compressible.

Neck.—Peculiar venous murmur in vessels. Intermittent *bruit de souffle* in vessels. Itching sticking in r. sterno-cleido-mastoid. Drawing pain in r. sterno-cleido-mastoid. Pain in nape, with tension, then anthrax, which was arrested by crucial incision, then profuse suppuration, then cure of the paralysis and general condition. Stiffness; < turning to the left; of nape.

Back.—Pain. Feeling at noon while walking as if a weight were lying across shoulders, weighing him down, so that his head sank forward.

Lumbar Region.—Jerking stitches in r. at 7 P.M. Tearing, with pressure. Pain; > morning; in morning on waking, and in sacrum; in kidneys; over base of sacrum; in r. tuber ischii in afternoon when riding, and in flexor side of foot; obliging him to lie down; hæmorrhoidal; dislocated, in r. at 10 P.M. Drawing in afternoon. Tension, < ascending steps, with occasional jerks extending towards hip-joints.

Extremities.—Emaciation; of extensors, with paralysis; < in legs and forearms, with weakness of triceps of upper arm, extensors of lower limbs, toes and feet, abductors of leg, muscles on back of thigh, difficulty in standing erect, has to stand with feet wide apart or else he sways from side to side, has a high-stepping gait, cannot flex the foot on leg, hence in stepping has to raise the thigh on the trunk, the paralysis of lower extremities is very similar to that of pseudo-hypertrophic paralysis, the sole is directed backward and somewhat outward because the tibialis anticus is completely paralyzed, numbness and tingling in toes, feet and tips of fingers. Cramps; with sometimes involuntary contractions; in r. leg and arm. Trembling; < r. Intermittent sticking (sensitive twitching in single muscle-fibrillæ) in spots on inner side of upper arm and thigh.

Jerking sticking in several joints; on back of l. foot and in r. wrist. Prickling sticking in fingers, < l., at noon, and in feet. Lightning-like pains, < pressure, with cramps. Acute pains, especially in thick muscular parts, with cramps, especially in lower limbs and in feet. Pain; in muscles; in joints, with rigidity; deep-seated, apparently in bones and muscles; like chronic rheumatism, with formication and general prickling. Peculiar prickling; prickling (*formicatio*) through feet, as from electric currents, at 5.30 P.M., while sitting on a soft sofa, afterwards in arms.

Desire to stretch. Tremulous feeling. Weakness; < legs; with paralyzed feeling in l. leg, numbness and coldness of feet and legs, cramp in calves, dilated veins of r. leg. Walking difficult, standing upon r. leg impossible, while in bed movements of lower limbs slow but perfect, fingers in a state of semi-flexion, with contraction but stiffness on extending them, pain on attempting to grasp anything.

Stiffness; of tips of fingers and toes, with insensibility. Difficulty in holding hands extended, they, with feet and toes, dropped easily (Plumb.), great toes flexed on soles, but little toes were extended more than normal. Numbness; with pain in joints and along limbs, < by movement; in hands and feet, with tingling, legs heavy and feeble, wrists weak (Plumb.). Sensibility impaired, and in hands, forearms and arms, especially at insertion of deltoid (Plumb.).

Upper Extremities.—Trembling. Pain, < night; acute, especially in shoulder-joints. Weakness. Anæsthesia, extending into thorax. Stitches in shoulder-joints, extending to wrists; jerking, in r. shoulder-joint; paroxysmal itching, in l. deltoid.

Arm.—Itching sticking in spots on inside of r. Pain in r.; rheumatic, in r. in forenoon, and in shoulder; rheumatic, in l. to the bones, in evening; paralytic, in l. at 10 P.M., from holding a newspaper to read in bed. Prickling and tingling. Weakness of l. in morning. Diminished sensibility, and of hands. Anæsthesia; and of hands. Falling asleep of l., with pain and weariness in it. Jerking stitches in upper A. and shoulder-joint.

Elbow.—Jerking in region. Frequent stitches in r., along extensors to wrist. Tearing in l. elbow and shoulder. Rheumatic pain in l. in evening, > when quiet.

Forearm.—Trembling in l., with sticking, especially about wrist. Paroxysmal jerking sticking at tendinous insertion of biceps in afternoon and night. Pain; in l., < when touching it or leaning upon it.

Wrist.—Sticking in l. Pain in l.; jerking, now in l., now in r.

Hand.—Trembling; < by attempting to grasp anything. Semi-flexed while lying in bed and could not be fully extended. Pronated and hanging down, on account of greater weakness of extensors, though the flexors were enfeebled. Cramps or contractions of extensors, preventing bending of fingers, with the weakness. Piercing pains in l. metacarpal bones when in bed. Pain from washing in cold water, with pricking. Prickling, with numbness. Weakness. Sensation on back very obtuse, hands feeling as if covered with gloves, < r. Diminished motility and sensibility of r. Insensibility. Rigidity; and contraction; with pain and awkwardness.

Fingers.—Swelling, insensibility and difficulty in bending. Atrophy of thenar eminence of thumb and interossei muscles. Sticking in metacarpal joint of l. index; through r. middle and ring, at noon; jerking, in various joints; jerking, in metacarpal joint of index; jerking, in joints of l. thumb; intermittent jerking, in third joint of l. fourth. Weakness. Rigidity and insensibility; and awkwardness, inability to take hold of small objects. Index partially paralyzed, with cramps.

Lower Extremities.—Gait hesitating; unsteady; insecure, < the dark or closing eyes; tottering from general weakness of extremities. Trembling. Pain; on going to bed, causing restlessness of legs. Prickling. Weakness; < l. Difficulty in walking. Heaviness. Difficulty in moving, especially l., > while lying. Rigidity. Insensibility.

Thigh.—Cramp; and in feet; and in soles. Jerking stitch in middle of r.; in middle like a pain in a nerve, repeated next forenoon, in afternoon the same pain between tibia and fibula after dinner. Muscular pain, especially in ankle, < walking. Pain in r. as if dislocated, in forenoon while walking, and in l. foot near tibia. Rheumatic pain in muscles after rising. Drawing pain in l. while walking. Drawing from l. hip to knee.

Knee.—Stitches from inner side of l. to great toe; itching S. on external tendon of l. popliteal space; itching S. in hollows at insertion of tendons of the gracilis and sartorius muscles and in r. ischium. Tearing in r. in afternoon, and in ankle. Pain in hollow; dislocated P. in forenoon when walking, and in sole; repeated dislocated, in r. Sprained sensation in l. Tensive pain in r. popliteal space when walking or stretching foot. Drawing pain. Rigidity.

Leg.—Cramp; at night; in calves; in calves and toes. Contractions of muscles of calves, < r., with pain. Rheumatoid pain in l. tibia. Insensible spot on upper part of l. leg, with impaired sensibility of whole limb.

Ankle.—Œdema (Ars.). Frequent jerking pains. Pain as from long walking. Lassitude at 10 P.M.; and in soles.

Foot.—Cramp in r. sole, > stepping firmly. Sticking in metatarsal bones in forenoon when walking, extending into toes; jerking, in heel at insertion of l. tendo-achillis. Tearing in l., especially in tarsal bones. Pain in l. heel; in os calcis at insertion of tendo-achillis on ascending steps. Burning and digging pain in joints. Pain in joints as if dislocated in morning in bed, with trouble in walking at first, > walking. Pain in l. metatarsal bones when walking, as if they would be dislocated by a false step. Weakness; in soles after dinner. Insensibility, so that he did not know when they touched the ground.

Toes.—Jerking stitches, and in muscles of thighs; in balls of r. Tingling.

Skin.—Eruption on face after shaving in morning; on face, < after beer at noon, end of nose red, burning and sore, next day scales on cheeks; red, raised, on cheeks and across nose and on alæ nasi at 2 P.M. after shaving, resembling acne potatorum or the soreness of nose accompanying catarrh, with burning of nose and lips, face as if bloated, afterwards scales on parts where eruption had been. Pimples on r. forearm, itching when touched; itching (like nettle-rash) on back of r. forearm. Boils; on l. thigh.

Stitching all over, < hands and feet; itching, in various parts. Hyperæsthesia, except on fingers and toes. Formication; of limbs; from l. elbow to tips of fingers (excepting thumb); over hands and feet, with prickling; along forearms alternating with stitches; all over r. arm, with sensation as if arm would go to sleep. *Itching on various parts.* Itching, with itching stitches. Itching over chest, thighs and especially on scrotum, with smarting; I. on hands, especially between fingers, with stinging, with vesicles filled with lymph between fingers; in a spot on r. forearm, then pimples; in morning after waking, < scratching, on chest, r. side of back as far up as region of kidneys and on r. forearm, with colorless pimples, becoming red after scratching, then pointed, at last itchlike, after scratching burning and easy bleeding.

Sleep.—Yawning. Sleepiness; all day; during the day, with sleeplessness during the night; in morning after 2 o'clock; after 3 P.M., with late falling asleep in evening; in afternoon, with late falling asleep in evening, then uneasy sleep, interrupted by vivid dreams; in evening; in evening after wine, but late falling asleep, with heaviness of upper lids, which would fall; alternating with wakefulness. Sleep heavy. Sleep prolonged and deep.

Sleeplessness; from heat. Difficult falling asleep. Sleep late in evening, restless and interrupted at night by stitches extending from inner side of l. knee to great toe. Restless night; except the first part; especially throwing the head about; with frequent waking alternating with dreams. Unrefreshing sleep. Interrupted sleep after midnight, and full of unpleasant dreams. Disturbed by startings; and constant waking, in morning he was difficult to rouse. Startings from sleep in fright, then prostration during the day. Sudden waking from bad dreams or nervous starting. Early waking, with many dreams.

Dreams; towards morning. Restless. Distressing. Sad; and fatiguing, with a hallucination that she was swollen. Unpleasant, with weeping; with loud shouting, starting up in terror and wild throwing about of arms. Horrid, that he was surrounded by cats and other animals. Of what he had read about in the evening.

Fever.—Horripilation. Chilliness; at 7 P.M.; at night, then heat and sweat; with coldness from within outward; then weariness as if beaten or as from a forced march. Sensitiveness to cold. Cold trembling all over. Shivering with the nightly restlessness, then heat and sweat. Felt a cold band around head from forehead to occipital protuberance. Coldness in cheeks during complaints in abdomen; C. of limbs, with numbness; of hands, forearms, feet and legs, with numbness or tingling; fingers, with rigidity of them and little sensibility; lower limbs; feet; forepart of foot; skin, then burning pain; skin of legs from knee downward.

Heat towards 5 A.M., then prostration, then sleep; H. < night; with headache and full pulse; with dryness of skin, preventing sleep, then restless sleep, with heaviness of head. Orgasm of blood, with rapid pulse. Heat of skin, with burning like nettles in various parts; H. of upper part of body; head and face; forehead; on forehead, with aching and desire to rub forehead; cheeks; face; face in afternoon, especially of cheeks; hands, especially of palms; hands and face, which are red and hot to touch, on putting hands into cold water they became livid, numb and cold and looked as if they had been frost-bitten, face less affected by cold water.

Sweat; on waking from frightful dreams; cold; checked.

Carduus Marianus.

A tincture is prepared from the seeds of St. Mary's Thistle, Carduus Marianus, L.

General Action.—Its chief (and only prominent) action is on the liver, causing soreness, pain, jaundice, etc.

Allies.—Chel., Iod., Merc.

Generalities.—Discomfort, with drawing pain in r. scapula and l. side of chest. Weariness; in morning on waking, with sweat and erection; at 7 A.M., with yawning; at 4 P.M., with sleep for ten minutes; at 5 P.M., with sleep for some minutes; after dinner.

Clinical.—Diseases of miners associated with asthma, despondency, sallow skin, orange urine, yellow stools (disturbed function of liver). Numerous cases of varicose veins have been cured.

Mind.—Sadness, with inclination to weep. Forgetfulness.

Head.—Aching before dinner, > dinner, with empty feeling in stomach; A. like commencing catarrh. Heaviness. *Dulness;* all day; in forenoon, with disposition to anger; with tensive pain in suture of l. parietal bone. Frontal pain; above orbits; over l. eye; in sinciput; before dinner, > eating (Chel.), with pain in eyes and occiput and sweat on forehead and back; and pain in eyeballs; intermittent, and temporal. Contractive feeling above brows. Drawing pain in lambdoidal suture. Tensive pain in sagittal suture as if something contracted around skull. Pain in temples; r. temple; on inner surface of skull at coronal suture; in l. parietal bone; in occiput.

Eyes.—Pain in r.; as if balls would be pressed into orbits. Burning in balls; lids; edges of upper lids; pressive, in lids in morning, with swelling and weight of them, < l. eye, which is difficult to open. Lids heavy.

Ears and Nose.—Pain in r. concha around orifice. Tickling in l. nostril; then r.; in outer orifice of nostrils. Burning in l. nostril; with watery discharge; B. at 3.15 A.M. Fluid in nose towards external orifice; watery discharge in morning on waking.

Mouth.—Carious tooth aches on touch of tongue. Drawing pain in carious tooth. Tongue coated white in middle, red at tip and edges. Tongue feels rough. Dry feeling in lips and palate. *Salivation* (Iod., Merc.); after coffee and milk. Taste bitter; astringent, metallic, on palate and fauces, with smooth feeling as if greased; flat to moderately salt soup, good taste to well-salted soup, but repugnance to salted meat.

Throat.—Pain in region of os hyoides on l. side, when speaking and swallowing, with swollen feeling, < pressure. Roughness in fauces, but palate feels smooth and greasy; R. in palate and fauces, with dryness, causing dry cough. Scraping causing cough; S. in œsophagus. Burning pain; in pharynx.

Stomach.—*Appetite small;* lost; ravenous, with pressure in hepatic region (Iod.). Empty eructations, with burning in œsophagus like heartburn; E., with burning in mouth of stomach, as from acidity; tasting of food taken against the inclination. *Nausea;* with eructation; with flow of water into mouth; ending in an inflated feeling in stomach, a horseback ride in afternoon increased the inflated feeling in abdomen. Retching and vomiting of acid, green fluid. Shooting on l. side, < inspiration. Griping, with pain in bowels, here and there. Pain; externally in pit; < by bread and milk; drawing, through pit and epigastrium from l. to r. Burning, as from acidity. Uneasiness in epigastric region. Empty feeling; at 3.15 A.M.

Abdomen.—Discharge of flatus. Feeling as if bowels moved on expiration. *Inflated feeling, < r. side, with pain in hepatic region on pressure* (Merc., Chel.). *Shooting in hepatic region, with moist skin* (Merc.). *Pain in r. hypochondrium* (Chel., Merc.); *between r. ribs and hip when driving; in hepatic and gastric regions, < pressure;* occasionally in liver and sacrum; *tensive, in r. hypochondrium. Full feeling in hypochondrium,* > after stool, still obliging me to draw a long breath. *Tension in liver when lying on l. side, with pressure.* Crawling, as if a body of the size of a pea moved in a narrow channel on posterior side of liver, from r. to l., in pit of stomach, at the level of edge of ribs, three times after a minute's pause, each time lasting three seconds. Shooting a hand's breadth from r. hip. Pinching on l. side. Pain in r. side; r. side, < pressure, lasting till sleep; r. side when body is stretched out, with hot feeling. Drawing in r. side when urinating. Drawing pain between navel and pit of stomach, in peritoneum, from r. to l., then burning pain, with hot feeling in a spot midway between navel and l. groin. Sensation for a hand's breadth around navel, as if bowels moved when breathing. Ilium, flatulent distention; rumbling; stitches > pressure; pressure in l.; pain near r. os ilii on waking and on walking in open air. Drawing pain through hypogastrium; through r. groin. Burning pain in hypogastrium.

Clinical.—Hyperæmia of the liver, with sluggish action of that organ, with jaundice, constipation, heavy, stupid head, foul tongue, fulness and soreness over the region of the liver, sometimes with cough (Chel., etc.); the tongue is usually furred, there are usually nausea and vomiting of green fluid.

Rectum and Anus.—Burning in A. at 3.15 A.M. Itching in A. Urging, as from diarrhœa, after a glass of small beer, stool normal; ineffectual U., with pressure on bladder, causing urine to dribble.

Stool.—Pappy, loamy, destitute of bilious coloring. *Hard,* unsatisfactory; *and difficult, brown, knotty,* after dinner; H. and lumpy; and difficult; and scanty at 10 A.M., at 11 a copious, pappy one, of chocolate color, preceded by rumbling and pain in abdomen. Delayed. *Omitted;* but inclination to one.

Clinical.—Constipation alternates with diarrhœa.

Urinary Organs.—Drawing pain in bladder and testicles when sitting; D. pain in bladder, with burning. Call to urinate, with burning in urethra and rectum, preventing her sitting. Burning in urethra; in orifice at 2 A.M., after micturition; with swollen feeling. *Urine cloudy, without sediment, golden, acid.* Urine wheyey, yellowish-brown, diminished in quantity, acid, also depositing a sediment consisting chiefly of salt and lime, and with traces of coloring matter of bile. Scanty, brownish, containing coloring matter of bile (Chel.). Copious, with drawing in sides of hypogastrium.

Sexual Organs.—Pressure in urethral part of glans. Contractive pain in vagina.

Respiratory Organs.—Dry feeling in larynx, with irritation to cough in back of larynx. Cough in morning on waking, from irritation in fauces, with burning in palate; C. from roughness in larynx; roughness in fauces and œsophagus; from raw feeling in pharynx. Short dry cough; from irritation in pit of throat. Frequent urging to deep breathing, then undefined pain in abdomen.

Chest.—Stitches behind l. short ribs; to r. of and downward from l. nipple; a hand's breadth above r. nipple on bending backward and on raising r. arm; anteriorly in lower borders of ribs at every inspiration; in r. sixth rib between linea mammalis and axillaris when inspiring; anteriorly in region of r. seventh rib on deep inspiration; in region of fifth rib during expiration after supper, with drawing; in a spot on sixth l. rib, in linea axillaris, with continual drawing pain in that line, afterwards the S. affected the breathing and gradually forged forward, later S. only during expiration and deep inspiration; *in region of seventh r. rib when stooping, afterwards the pains spread all over front of chest and made movement of arms, walking and stooping almost impossible* (Chel.). Pain in r. pectoralis muscle; in C. and abdomen on sudden and violent motion of body; as from flatulence under border of l. ribs, then on r. side spreading to the right and backward, when the pressure on l. side goes backward.

Drawing pain in l.; through l. pectoralis muscle, also in l. intercostal muscles below axilla; through r. pectoralis and on inner border of r. scapula; in borders of ribs, with stitches on breathing, < expiration; from l. side of C. to back, then towards l. pectoralis; in l. side up to axilla when driving. Tightness in l.; in l., < deep inspiration, with pain.

Heart and Pulse.—Stitches in cardiac region. Pressure in præcordium. Drawing pain in cardiac region at 2 A.M.; D. pain, with tightness on deep breathing. Pulse slow.

Neck.—Pressure in nape. Pain in nape at a level with mastoid process, l., soon afterwards in r.; rheumatic, extending to shoulders.

Back.—Burning pain. Drawing pain; through B. and hypogastrium; in morning on waking; on inside of l. scapula; in inner border of r. scapula; from r. scapula down back when driving; from r. scapula to loin, changing from one place to another after one minute, also on outer border of l. scapula and through muscles of r. or l. radius. Shooting in inner border of l. scapula. Tearing in l. scapula and upper arm. Burning sore pain in l. scapula when inspiring, < pressure and leaning. Pressure on back below scapula. Drawing pain in lumbar muscles.

Extremities.—Daily periodic cramp-pain in r. calf, r. sole and in extensor tendons of three middle fingers. Bruised feeling in arms and legs. Prostration in arms and legs in morning after rising.

Upper Extremities.—Pain in shoulders and wrists; in r. shoulder-joint on raising arm (Chel.). Drawing pain in r. deltoid; and muscles of r. radius; in r. upper arm at 2 A.M. Periodical pains in r. upper arm. Cramp-pain in muscles about radius and in l. fingers. Drawing pain in muscles covering l. radius at 3.15 A.M. Burning pain in skin on inner side of lower half of l. forearm, also on outer aspect of l. index. Cramp-like drawing pain in inner side of r. hand extending to two first joints of fourth finger. Cramp in r. second, third and fourth fingers. Drawing pain on outer side of r. fourth finger. Rheumatic drawing in first joint of l. fourth finger; in first joint of r. index.

Lower Extremities.—Bruised pain in nates. Pain in hip-joints in morning, spreading through nates, making rising difficult, < stooping; in houghs when walking, < l. Drawing pain in l. knee; in skin on outer side of l. knee; from l. down leg; from outer side to external ankle. Stiff feeling in patellæ and tendons of houghs when walking, with paralyzed feeling in legs and staggering. Cramp-pain in calf. Drawing pain on inner side of r. leg to internal ankle. Paralytic pain in l. tibia, with drawing pain in cutaneous nerves on outer side below patella. Feeling of a band around calf a hand's breadth below knee when walking. Sudden cramp in muscles of r. sole flexing toes, then itching in sole in front of heel. Pain in r. instep; in lower part of r. heel, < treading; in sole in front of heel, < moving ankle.

Skin.—Itching after lying down in bed.

Sleep.—Yawning. Sleepiness. Waking at 11.30 P.M., with chilliness and urging to urinate, passed about two tablespoonfuls of urine; W. at midnight, with cough from irritation at back of larynx; at 2 A.M., with pressure in stomach and burning in eyelids and anus; at 3 A.M. from pain in r. loin and in urethra; at 3 A.M., with erection, rheumatic pain in r. deltoid and in muscles covering r. radius. Restless, dreamy night; R., frequent waking, and when lying on back nightmare.

Fever.—Rigor; with quick pulse; with pulsation in abdomen. Shivering. Cold feeling in knees; in soles; toes. Hot feeling in face.

Caulophyllum.

A tincture is prepared from the fresh root of Caulophyllum thalictroides, Mx. (the blue Cohosh).

General Action.—Two general effects are prominent: (1) on the uterus, causing labor-like pains; (2) on the small joints, causing pain, soreness and swelling.

Allies.—Cimicif., Puls.

Weakness and nervousness. Headache. Dulness of head. Frequent vertigo. Aching in forehead; with sensation as if needles were stuck into it; with contracted feeling in skin of forehead. Drawing pain over l. eye. Intermittent pain in temples as if crushed together. Aching in eyes, with feeling of something under lids. Lachrymation. Drawing pain in nose. All the teeth seem sore and elongated. Tongue coated white. Distress in fauces, causing frequent inclination to swallow. Canine hunger. Desire to drink a great deal of water. Eructations of sour, bitter fluid; empty E. Frequent pain in stomach and umbilicus. Distress in stomach; and in umbilicus; and in small intestines; and in bowels, with drawing pains in r. hypochondrium; burning.

Rumbling in abdomen, waking at 1 A.M., with urging to stool, copious, painless stool of water running in a stream. Drawing pains in r. side over liver. Pain in umbilicus, > emissions of flatus; when moving, > emissions of flatus; intermittent. Stool soft, very white. Stool dark. Stool hard, afterwards a soft one, followed by pain in umbilicus. Intermittent stinging in glans penis. Drawing pain in sterno-cleido mastoid, that draws the head to l. side. Pain in back; in lumbar region.

Pain in fingers, ankles, feet and toes, causing a restless night; flying P. in arms and legs, first in one part, then in another. Drawing pains in fingers, ankles, feet, especially in toes; in hips, knees, wrists; elbows; legs; in joints of arms and legs. *Aching in wrists and joints of fingers;* in elbows. Cutting in second joints of all fingers on closing hand, with stiffness. Pain in finger-joints, with redness and stiffness, and on closing hand pain in them. *Stiffness of fingers.* Cracking of joints of lower limbs when walking or turning. Drawing pain in inside of l. thigh; in thighs, *knees,* legs and *ankles;* in knees and toes, very sharp by spells. Sharp pain inside of l. knee. Weakness of knees when walking. Drawing pain in legs and more in feet. Pain in l. ankle and l. toes; in feet; in metatarsal bones, from walking. *Drawing pain in toes.* Restless night; after 3 A.M. Skin hot and dry.

Clinical.—Labor pains are weak, do not press downward, but pass off with a kind of shivering. Inefficient labor pains which do not press downward, but fly in all directions. Useful in false annoying pains a few weeks before the time for labor. Rigid os during labor, pains sharp, pricking. Threatening miscarriage, with uterine cramp, hæmorrhage. Prolapsus of uterus. Retroversion of uterus, with dysmenorrhœa, profuse leucorrhœa, etc. Subinvolution of uterus after child-birth, with general debility and loss of power in lower extremities. Aphthæ in vagina, with dysmenorrhœa. Dysmenorrhœa. Leucorrhœa in a child. Hysterical convulsions during dysmenorrhœa, with pain shooting to various parts of body, great debility. Whooping cough, with vomiting and nosebleed. Rheumatism in small joints, especially of the hands, with cutting pains on closing hands, especially in women with suppressed menses.

Causticum.

A clear liquid, distilled from a mixture of Caustic Lime and bisulphate of Potash (see Hahnemann's direction for preparing it), is mixed with an equal part of Alcohol. Chemically and pathogenetically it is doubtless a solution of Potassium hydrate.

General Effects.—The general key to the action of Causticum is the same as that to all the Potashes, namely, paralysis, slow pulse, low temperature, etc. Diuresis is a general concomitant.

Allies.—Kali in general, Rhus t., Zinc., Sulph., Sep., etc.

Generalities.—Spasm, when slumbering in evening he felt that he could not move the tongue well, rose, cried out, but fell back again, stretched arms and legs, then moved them, eyes were distorted, gnashed his teeth, saliva flowed from mouth, with icy coldness, consciousness returned after half an hour, with anxiety, transient thoughts, lolling tongue, all > a swallow of cold water. Spasm, in morning in bed heat, after rising cold sensation in the arm in which he had at first a jerk, with twitchings in upper part of body, in trunk and in arms, with full consciousness but with apprehension. Spasm in evening, vertigo as if turning involuntarily hither and thither, > open air, with apprehension, stupid expression of face and heat over whole body.

Falling suddenly without consciousness while walking in open air, but immediately rising again. Twitching here and there; T. in r. side of body and in various other parts of skin. Starting up frequently at night. *Trembling;* in morning on waking; after supper, with apprehension; anxious T. in morning and forenoon, with sleepy confusion of head, heavy pressure in occiput and forehead, with heaviness of limbs, pain in joints and muscles of fingers, arms, shoulders, knees and feet.

Sticking in nearly all parts; now here, now there (after menstruation), or contractive pain. *Tearings, especially in joints, or from them through various bones, sometimes in several at once.* Pinching here and there; and in various parts of skin. Drawing pain, especially above knees. Drawings in several parts, increasing to tearings. *Soreness as if bruised or pressed in the side, hip and thigh on which he lay at night, with frequent necessity to turn over. Bruised pain in every part when touched* (Arn.); general B. pain when sitting, > working and in open air, especially in arms; B. feeling in whole r. side. Sensation of internal trembling.

Inability to lie still a moment at night (Rhus t.). *Uneasiness of body while sitting, with anxiety about heart;* U. at night in bed, with anxious weeping and indistinct talking; when rising from a seat and when walking; in blood, with anxiety of mind and sudden sickness and weakness, so that she must lie down; especially of head, like a painless burrowing.

Weariness in morning on rising, and lack of cheerfulness; all forenoon, with feeling as if crushed; at noon, > walking in open air; in evening, with sleeplessness till 1 A.M. and with heavy pain in legs; after copious micturition; after slight effort; after walking in open air, with disinclination to work; < evening, with general sick feeling, as if a severe illness were imminent; with sweat on beginning to walk; with anxiety; with sleepiness; *faintlike;* in morning in bed, as if he would fall asleep again, > rising; after a short walk, so that he could not move his legs; tremulous, after a stool, with palpitation. Sensation as if he would fall, without vertigo. Attacks of faintness after going to bed. Stiffness of joints if she did not move for a quarter of an hour. Numbness and deadness of all soft parts on l. side, even in foot and head, as if there were no blood in the skin. Aggravation when walking in open air and in evening; A. in open air; A. from coffee. Amelioration in the room of the symptoms which originated in the open air, except of the pain in forehead. Sees only terrible visions and distorted human faces when she closes the eyes.

Clinical.—Children are slow in learning to walk. Cracking in joints. The pains, neuralgic or rheumatic, make the patient very restless, but are not > motion. Chorea, especially affecting the muscles of the r. side and eyeballs. Epileptiform spasms or chorea-like spasms, especially at the time of puberty. Patients requiring Caust. are always weak, anæmic, have no desire and scarcely the ability to make an effort. General tendency to paralytic affections (like all the Potashes). Paralysis resulting from rheumatism, *after diphtheria, etc.*

Mind.—**Peevish;** during menstruation, with weariness; and weeping mood; and self-absorbed; takes no pleasure in music. *Morose silence; persistent silence.* Taciturn in forenoon and indifferent. Sullen. Sensitiveness and inclination to anger, chilliness and on motion easily heated. Irritability, so that her knees sink under her at the slightest vexation. Sensitive, hot-headed and vehement. Furiously opinionated and quarrelsome. Violent after midday sleep, with despondency. *Melancholy; before menstruation; M., with prostration.* Sad weeping mood, full of care. Inclination to scold; and make a disturbance, without being peevish. Discontented with herself, with gloomy looks. Whining at every trifle (in a child). Sympathetic, beside herself with weeping and sobbing, and cannot be contented when hearing of hardships.

Anxiety; in morning on waking; *in evening, with unwillingness to go to bed; at night, with uneasiness, preventing sleep; after stool,* also with heat in face and inclination to sweat; *with uneasiness as if something unpleasant impended;* with sweat; as if stupefied; as if he had done something bad or apprehended it, or as if he had been unfortunate. *Apprehension whenever anything happens;* A. of evil, with urging to stool. *Frightful ideas in evening.* Fear; at night; and anxiety, so that she did not wish to live; of a dog near by, so that she trembled, apprehension at every noise in the street and when she saw boys climbing. Thoughts of death, with uneasiness and solicitude. *Disinclination to work.* Mirth alternating with depression. Joy alternating with peevishness. Good humor in forenoon, with talkativeness.

Inattention and distraction. Absentminded, with loss of ideas. Cloudiness. Weakness of thought, slow succession of ideas. Mispronunciation of words and confusion of syllables and letters (*e. g.*, "cluent foryza"). *Weakness of memory.* Coma.

Head.—Involuntary nodding while writing, as if pressed down. Stitches in morning on waking and almost all day; S., especially in orbits, all night, > during the day; S., with warmth in it. Tearing. Jerking-pinching through H. Screwings, > open air, with heaviness. Aching caused by hunger; A. in whole brain on shaking head; with nausea; from all sides, with pinching in ears and boring toothache; deep-seated, with heaviness at night as from an ulcer; compressive; throbbing, with painful throbbing in cerebral arteries. Jerkings and beatings. | *Painless digging in whole H.*

Confusion in morning, with coryza; C., with heat in it; painful tensive, almost like a throbbing headache, > after eating; all day, as if in a damp room where clothes were washed and dried, < stooping, not > by walking in open air, but on returning to the room. Dulness all day after an emission; D., with a screwed-together feeling, also > in open air; with intoxicated feeling and with redness of face. Feeling of stupefaction and drunkenness. Rush of blood in evening; R. after short walk in open air, and to face, with dim vision; > open air, with sensation as if intoxicated; with heat in it. Sensation as if brain were loose and shaken when walking in open air.

Vertigo; in morning on rising; in morning on stooping, > rising; in morning on waking, with painful confusion of head; *at night on rising in bed and lying down again; during menstruation, < stooping, > afternoon; on fixing vision;* on looking up (to a high tower), so that he fell; while standing; while standing and sitting, with heaviness of head; while sitting, as if he would stagger; in open air, everything turned about with her and persons seemed larger than usual; > *open air;* with anxiety of whole body; with weakness of head; with falling down; *forward and sideways; as from compression of head;* as from spirituous drinks; almost like loss of consciousness, after walking, he nearly fell while sitting.

Forehead.—Tensive stitching from lower part of F. to upper part of head; shifting slow S. above l. eye. Tearing in middle, during the day in a heated room and in tobacco-smoke, < night, when it prevented sleep, and in cervical vertebræ; sticking, extending to r. side through the whole head. Cutting in upper part of bone on violent motion of arms while stooping. *Pain in r. eminence;* sharp, in l. side; sharp, after large flow of urine; extending to eyes; twitching, in r. side of F. and head; burning, as if forepart of brain were inflamed, after entering the house; as if something were forced in between frontal bone and cerebrum, or as if the place behind frontal bone were hollow; constrictive, in open air, < fast walking, suddenly > stooping low; stupefying, when sitting and reading, not > walking or standing; tensive and drawing, between eyes. Drawing in l. side; between eyes, with pressure; painful, in forepart. Slow pressure above r. orbit. Tension and warmth in F. and nose, with intermittent drawing in eyes. Throbbing, < afternoon, with tension in neck; painful, in arteries above orbits; painful, as with a dull point. Sensation as if everything in head would come out in front on stooping.

Temples.—*Stitches;* in l. bone, spreading in a circle. Tearing in r.; in l. at 4 P.M. Pain in r.; on upper margin of bone; pressing-out, with nausea and vomiting; throbbing, in r. on motion, when quiet it is only a pressive pain; drawing, gradually increasing to its highest and then disappearing. Tension in r. as if paralyzed, and in eye.

Vertex.—Sticking-tearing on l. side. Pain as if brain were torn or shattered, < morning on waking. Pain on pressure or touch. *Bruised pain in a spot on touch.* Sudden pressure in region of coronal suture as from a sharp stone falling on it. *Paroxysmal throbbing mingled with stitches;* T. as if everything would be forced out, in morning after rising. Frequent drawing in l. side.

Sides.—Stitch in r.; in l. evenings. Tearing in l.; in l., especially in forehead and temple, beginning in evening and constantly increasing, with swelling of painful side. Pain in r., extending into eye; in r. parietal bone and in both temples. Tension in l.

Occiput.—Stitches. Sudden pain in bone while sitting, as if something in muscles had been displaced. Throbbing pain on r. side, which on rubbing extends towards vertex, where it pains as if beaten. Drawing pain; in r. side; beginning in open air, < rapid walking, and in muscles of r. side of neck. Sensation in bone as if numb, pithy and dead.

Scalp.—Hair falls out. Movements towards forehead. *Tension.* Pain when rubbed. Sensation of trembling or shaking in skin of r. temple till lying down. Creeping sensation on vertex. *Itching;* stinging, on various parts, in parietal bones, on forehead, r. cheek, behind l. zygoma, extending towards ear and upward to temporal bone; on r. side, transiently > scratching; on r. temple, > scratching.

Eyes.—Inflammation, with burning and pain; I., with pressure in them during the day and agglutination in morning. Tearing and pressure. *Pain < touch.* Pressure in morning before he can open them, > closing them again; **as from sand** (Nat. m.); in l. as if it would be pressed out; as if they were pressed inward and tried to come out; internal, as if it would be distended; in r. as from swelling of lids, which are really red, with lachrymation. *Rubbing as of sand. Burning* (Zn.); from 4 P.M. till evening, *with dryness;*

from 6 to 8 P.M.; *with stinging,* **dryness and photophobia.** *Dryness; in morning* (Zn.), *with stiffness,* then lychrymation. *Biting, with pressure and heaviness and with redness of lids;* B. as from salt. *Itching, especially of lids;* in l., > rubbing; of r., > rubbing, then lachrymation. Weakness. *Lachrymation; < open air.*

Distending pain in r. ball. Itching of r. ball in morning. Pupils dilated; contracted, then dilated.

Lids.—**Involuntary closure** (Rhus t., Sep.). Agglutination in morning. Inflammation, with hard matter between lashes. *Twitching,* and of l. brow. Swollen sensation, < morning. Pressure in upper as if a stye would appear. Burning in l.; B. pain on margins, as from burning with gunpowder. Smarting in l. Biting. *Itching on lower and on its inner surface, with burning as soon as he touches the eye or moves it.* **Heaviness of upper, as if he could not raise it easily** (Rhus t.), *or as if it were agglutinated to lower and could not be easily loosened. Sensation as if they would close from weakness* (Rhus t., Gelsem.). *Difficulty in opening,* < morning, with swollen sensation.

Canthi.—Dry matter. Drawing in r. outer, extending into wing of nose. *Burning in inner.* Itching sore pain in r. inner in morning after waking, as from salt, < rubbing, so that lachrymation is produced. Itching in l. inner, > rubbing; in r. inner, with lachrymation; *in l. inner like flea-bites;* voluptuous, in r.

Twitching in l. brow. Drawing in arch of r. brow. Pressure in orbits and behind eyes; over r. eye as if upper lid would be pressed down.

Photophobia, with constant necessity to wink; P., with pain on motion. Far-sighted. Blackness before eyes. Some letters become invisible while reading. *Dimness of vision; on blowing nose;* < wiping and rubbing; < looking at a light; with sensation as if something came from head into l. eye, and the light looked as if there were many points of light in a black circle; when standing, *as from a veil; as from a cloud* in morning after waking, > washing; as if a membrane were drawn over eyes; as if a membrane were drawn from inner canthus over half the pupil, in morning when blowing nose. Vision flickering; and confused on looking long at an object, then pain in eyes; *as from swarms of insects;* like a veil. *V. of sparks if he winks, even in daylight;* V. of sparks in daylight. Small, round objects pass before his vision while lying.

Clinical.—Blepharitis, > open air. Paralysis of muscles of the eye, especially of upper lid. Weakness of the muscles of the eyeball, causing asthenopia, amounting even to paralysis, especially with feeling of sand in eyes. Has arrested cataract in some cases. Frequent sudden loss of sight as from a mist (muscular asthenopia). Double vision from paralysis of the ocular muscles; vision worse on turning eyes to the right. Ptosis after catching cold (Rhus).

Ears.—Swelling of external, with contractive pains; S. of meatus, with twinging earache and discharge of bloody matter. Suppuration and discharge from within, with offensive odor. Stitches on outer margin, < evening in bed, with burning pain; boring knifelike, externally behind l., with sudden general sweat; paroxysmal, *in r.;* intermittent, in r. mastoid process; tearing, with roaring, as from a storm of wind.

Tearings in l.; beneath l. at 4 P.M.; in drum, with tensive confusion of head. Sensation as if everything were dragging outward and as if they would burst, like a tearing mingled with itching. Twinging. Boring in r.; in fossa below r., then on pressure bruised pain; behind l. at one time, at another pulsating-throbbing. Pain in mastoid process; in r. meatus in evening; in meatus on cleaning, as if sore and ulcerated.

Sensation internally of jerking outward. Tension behind. Sensation of contraction in l. and in whole side of head in evening when lying, with inability to sleep upon that side, and when touched (but > pressure) sensation as if flesh had been separated from bone. Crawling in l., with itching-biting. Itching in l.; sticking, in front of r. meatus. Sensation as if cold wind were blowing into r. meatus. Air rushes in during eructations. Stopped sensation mornings; S. sensation in r.

Re-echoing of her own words and steps; *of sounds, with difficult hearing;* every morning. *Roaring before E.;* in r.; in each alternately in evening before sleep. Rushing sound as of a waterfall, with difficult hearing. Thundering tones in r. Ringing in l.; in front of r. in evening. Singing as of distant crickets, then throbbing, then singing again. Whistling in l.

Clinical.—Chronic inflammation of the middle ear. Buzzing, roaring in ears, with re-echoing of sounds (in Meniere's disease), (compare with Nat. sul.). Burning heat of ears after a frost-bite and rheumatism. Unnatural accumulation of wax in ears.

Nose.—Hairs in nostrils fall out. Swelling in morning, > evening. Cutting tearing through r. wing. Soreness internally. Septum painful to touch. Sore pain in lower part, as in severe coryza. Burning in nostrils, as in coryza. Itching internally; as before coryza. Tickling in l. nostril, > external pressure. *Frequent sneezing; in morning;* ineffectual attempts at S.

Coryza, with inability to speak aloud; C., with cough and scraping in larynx; with cough, pains in chest, drawings in limbs, frequent waking at night and chilliness; *stopped;* stopped, when lying, with nightly dryness of throat; stopped and fluent, with rawness in throat and smarting in chest caused by cough; fluent, in morning, with agglutination of eyes; fluent, with painful cough at night and headache. Discharge of offensive mucus, with sneezing. Watering after drinking. *Bleeding;* from l. nostril; blows out blood every morning. Loss of smell, with stoppage.

Clinical.—Dry catarrh, with stoppage. Fluent coryza, with acute inflammation of larynx and trachea. Ulcers and crusts in tip of nose.

Face.—Pale, with suffering expression. *Yellow;* during menstruation. Discolored, yellowish about temples, pale bluish lips. Sickly look. Swelling of cheeks, with throbbing pain. Stickings in cheek, over lower jaw. Tearing in l. cheek-bone; T. in cheeks, with sticking. *Drawing pain in r. cheek, then in ear.* Burning pain in cheeks, in front of ears, as if an eruption would appear. Throbbing in cheeks, with twitching of their muscles.

Lips.—Swelling of lower, and papulous eruption, with sticking and crawling in it. Papules in l. corner, with crawling sticking. Tetter on lower. Ulcer on inside of upper, with burning pain. Vesicles in r. corner, painful when eating. Soreness of l. corner. Pain as if sore. Tearings. Spasmodic sensation.

Jaws.—**Tension and pain, so that they were difficult**

to open, with difficulty in eating because a tooth seemed too long. *Difficulty in opening*, with sensation as if throat below jaw were swollen or tense. Tearing in r. lower. Prickling-digging in lower. Pain in r. joint (in "Hahnemann's Mat. Med. Pura" it is l.); *rheumatic in lower;* burning, in lower. Drawing first from r., then from l. ramus towards the chin and thence back again in direction of angle of mouth.

Chin.—Tearing in middle of bone; T. on lower part. Burning-cutting in r. side, as if a piece of glass were cutting outward. Tensive drawing pain in lower part.

Clinical.—Facial neuralgia at every change of weather. Paralysis of face from taking cold, with hemiplegia. Acne rosacea. Rheumatism in the articulation of the lower jaw.

Mouth.—Teeth. Looseness of some; of incisors; *painful L. of incisors. Stitches; on biting on them;* on opening mouth; *in upper back, extending upward; in lower back, extending downward. Tearing in diseased root of a l. lower;* T. in last l. upper back, at 2 P.M., < open air; *in both r. rows, extending into zygoma, with bruised pain in both r. jaws on pressure and on chewing;* extending into head and l. eye; in all in forenoon, as if they would fall out; intermittent, in roots of lower in morning. *Boring in a lower molar,* **extending to nose and eyes.** *Prickling-digging in lower back, extending to ear.* Pain; with much spitting of saliva; in a r. back; in a sound one on drawing in cold air; consisting of pressing-tearing and sticking combined, with erysipelatous swelling of cheek and a swollen suppurating pimple on gum; jerking; *throbbing*, with painful gum, so that he could not chew; throbbing, in a diseased back T. Toothache as if ulcerating, at night and during the day when she moves the mouth. Pain as if sore, in morning, then throbbing, the pain > bleeding of gum. Drawing toothache; in l. lower, from articulation to chin, in afternoon; with itching between teeth; in r. second molar, more in external surface, and extending into temples. Burning pain in hollow T. while eating and drinking. Pressure from without in roots of both anterior upper molars. Sensitiveness to touch; S. of T. and gums in morning. Peculiar sensation in roots, so that he must gnash the teeth.

Gums.—*Swelling;* in front and behind, with pain; of l. side, with sensitiveness while eating and with spasmodic pain in evening; with excoriation of pudenda on urinating. Bleeding. Drawing pain in lower. *Sensitiveness without pain in teeth.*

Tongue.—Vesicles on margin; painful V.; *painful on tip.* T. and back part of mouth threw off a thick and tough membrane. Sore pain on and beneath T. and on palate. Pain on l. side as if bitten. Pain as if burnt on tip and margin. Scraping, then roughness of mouth as if covered with a skin; burning S. on tip, as if burnt, with salivation and burnt taste. Burning on tip. Dryness, with thirst.

Epidermal coating of mouth and fauces abraded; in morning, but partly hanging in large pieces, the mucous membrane itself swollen and loose, tongue scarlet, papillæ swollen, arch of palate and uvula swollen and dark red, in mouth and fauces sensation of glowing coals, with constant pressure to swallow and hawk, which increased the pain, discharge of much saliva and mucus, voice hoarse and nasal, disposition bordering on desperation, with febrile symptoms, rapid pulse and unquenchable thirst.

Sore, painful spot on hard palate. Swelling of inside of cheek, which he bites when chewing. Mouth open at night, causing dryness. Stitches in l. side of palate. Pain in mouth, œsophagus and epigastric region; anteriorly on palate, as if suppurating, when touched with tongue. Burning scraping. Burning on palate, with soreness. Crawling posteriorly on palate, with burning pricking. Dryness at night; all forenoon, without thirst; and on lips, without thirst; with thirst; burning. Salivation; when walking after eating, with moisture in nose; rancid; watery, in forenoon, with nausea.

Taste of food remains long after eating; T. for food diminished. *Fatty.* Bitter. Offensive; afternoons, as from a disordered stomach. Viscid, glutinous.

Clinical.—Violent toothache from taking cold, even in sound teeth, from cold air. Painful looseness and elongation of teeth. Gums bleed easily, and are swollen. Dental fistula.

Throat.—Painful swelling of l. submaxillary gland. Distention of l. side, with suffocative sensation and necessity to loosen the neck-band. Audible cracking, deep-seated. Mucus after eating; clots of M.; after dinner *which he cannot loosen by hawking,* **but he is obliged to swallow it.** *Hawking of mucus;* in morning; from 5 P.M. till night, with soreness and burning in throat; every half hour of mucus, which immediately accumulates again; *with pain in pit of throat.*

Torn sensation, not on swallowing, but on making an exertion with head and on lifting or carrying anything. Pressure behind palate and on epiglottis; in pit on deep breathing; as if under sternum, as from swallowing too large a morsel; choking, in morning on waking, as from swallowing a large crust. Sensation after eating as if food stuck. Frequent contractive sensation. *Tension in r. side of T. and chest, drawing the body towards r. side.* Sensation as if swollen and too narrow; as if swollen and raw. Sensation of tightness and suffocation, obliging him to loosen the neck-band. *Rawness, with tickling and with dry cough and expectoration only after long coughing;* R., with heartburn; with hoarseness and sore pain; with oppression of chest and febrile coldness; and, when breathing, sensation as if he had inspired too little air. Scraping, < evening and swallowing; S., with clawing and with heartburn. Scraping-clawing, with sensation on swallowing as of a lump. Burning.

Soreness; behind palate; from morning till afternoon, > dinner, with stitches, so that he could scarcely swallow; as if attachments of tongue had grown fast; as from a lump, with sticking; burning-sticking, < swallowing, and on uvula. Dryness in morning; *D. when swallowing, then scraping down throat; of back part;* in forenoon, with dry hacking cough; without thirst; now D., now moisture. Coldness, rapidly passing over palate, with salivation. Nauseous sensation. Itching, extending along Eustachian tube into ear. Constant inclination to swallow. Dysphagia, with stricture five inches and a half from incisors.

Œsophagus.—Ejection of mucous membrane in a perfect cylinder. Pain.

Clinical.—Acute sore throat, with laryngitis. Paralysis of muscles of pharynx.

Stomach.—Eats with too much haste. Hunger early; ravenous H.; causing headache, > eating; but food is not relished. Appetite, but without having aversion to food it seemed as if she did not dare to eat. Little appetite, but food is relished; little A. but much thirst, < eating. Satiety, then hunger; speedy S. if she attempted to eat without being hungry. Appetite disappeared when beginning to eat; A., but when eating aversion to food. Aversion to food, even when beginning to eat; A. to sweets. Can eat only smoked meats, vomiting on eating fresh meat. *Thirst;* mornings; for beer; for something cold from forenoon till 3 P.M.

Eructations; with choking in œsophagus, impeding breath. Suppressed in middle of throat. Loud, explosive; violent, with a sour taste. *Of air.* It seems as if lime were dissolving in stomach, causing a bubbling, with a continual rolling eructation of much air. *Hot, in afternoon and evening. Of food* five hours after eating; *E. as when undigested food remains in stomach;* E. tasting of the soup eaten at breakfast; E. having the odor of the food. With the odor of musk. Pleasant-tasting, almost like almonds. Gulping of water, with soreness of anus. Eructations of tasteless water, or rising of it into mouth, with nausea, which disappears after the eructations. Acrid fluid rises into mouth. Cool waterbrash in evening on lying down, with constant spitting. Salt waterbrash in forenoon; slimy salt W. after the third stool that day. Hiccough.

Nausea; every morning; in afternoon; in afternoon, then hunger; on waking from evening sleep; in evening when beginning to eat; before eating, with hunger; while eating; after supper, which had been eaten with good appetite; after stool; with frequent gulping of water, which causes constant spitting; with emptiness in stomach and acid taste; with weakness of stomach and with alternations of chill and heat; with anxiety. Vomiting; sour, then sour eructations; of clotted blood at night. Movements extending to throat.

Stitches; in pit; in pit, seeming to contract heart. Cutting in pit after eating, extending to abdomen, with taste of food in mouth, eructations tasting of food, confusion of head, diarrhœa, chilliness and necessity to lie down. Cramp; like a pressure and contraction, in morning on waking from a frightful dream, with nausea and salivation. Clawing in pit; *pinching, in pit on deep breathing. Pressure in pit;* in epigastric region; in region of S. and in diaphragm; in morning after rising, only when sitting; in morning after rising, < sudden motion, with heat in r. side of head and necessity to lie down, and the pain seemed now in stomach and now in chest; in morning fasting, then contractive sensation in abdomen; at night on waking; after breakfast; in orfice, < leaning against edge of table, reading aloud, talking much, lying upon back and when cold air strikes abdomen. *Pressure, > lying down;* > dinner, with uprising; in and above S. and below navel, with diarrhœa three times at night, with periodic stitches from back forward to r. side of abdomen, arresting breathing.

Bruised pain; on pressure. Rhythmical chilling pressure in pit, as from ice. Tensive pain in pit. Contractive sensation in epigastric region. The tightness of clothes about stomach and hips is very oppressive. Heartburn after supper; H. in mouth; burning rising from stomach, as if he had eaten pepper. *Sensation as if disordered,* with distention of abdomen. It seems as if she would constantly eructate, which does not happen, but all manner of trouble is caused thereby. Sensation of fasting. Emptiness at 4 P.M. Crawling in epigastric region. Pleasant warmth, and in abdomen. Weakness.

Clinical.—Acid dyspepsia, sour vomiting and sour eructations. Gastralgia, colic and distention of abdomen.

Abdomen.—Jerking at night, with uneasiness, preventing sleep until midnight. Twitching contraction at noon. Distention all afternoon, with frequent loud emissions of flatus, which relieved only for a short time; D. in evening, also with hardness; after eating; after eating and drinking, with uneasiness and drawing in it; < evening; with cramps; with internal pressure, < deep breathing. Rumbling after eating, with distention; then frequent emissions of flatus; and croaking, as of frogs; when sitting, as from emptiness. Moving about, > soft, brown stool, with cutting. Accumulation of flatus, with hard stool; A. of much F. after a slight meal, on account of which the hæmorrhords protrude, are painful and moist. Emissions of flatus; after breakfast; upward and downward; *loud, all the afternoon; offensive.*

Sticking in whole A. at 4 P.M.; S. preventing sitting. Pain during menstruation, as if everything were torn apart, with bruised pain in sacrum and discharge of large clots. Cutting in morning, then three soft stools, and all day sensation in abdomen as of diarrhœa; *C. on appearance of menses, < motion, with tearing in back and small of back; during menstruation, with diarrhœa;* with emission of flatus on inspiration. Pinching, with paleness of face; P., with cutting and with yawning; with soft stool; cutting, even while eating, > emission of flatus. *Pain in morning;* in morning after rising, with shortness of breath; every afternoon; in evening, extending into throat; twisting, before stool; drawing back and forth just before menstruation, and on first day of it; when breathing, as if constricted by a string.

Tension at 7 P.M., with distention, causing difficult breathing, with frequent passage of flatus; contractive T., and in stomach. Emptiness, > pressure. Electric shocks, extending to fingers and bending the fingers. Pulsations. Crawling, with moving about, as after a purgative. Coldness internally, with cracking and crackling; becomes cold easily, if air touches it he has pressure in stomach and diarrhœa.

Upper.—Cutting in a streak, > dinner, with soft stool at 11 A.M. Frequent griping. Burning pain about epigastric region, waking him. Contractive sensation. Tension, with pressure.

Hypochondria.—Distention of l. Stitches in l.; beneath last r. true ribs; below r. ribs in evening; *in hepatic region in afternoon;* in a spot in hepatic region when riding, and touch caused a stinging, with sleepiness and general weariness. Tearing in liver in evening. Tensive pain in liver when lying on back. Burning pain in l.

Umbilicus.—Swelling, with pain about it when touched. Griping, in morning, > rising. Crawling, with sensation as before diarrhœa.

Sides.—Distention in l., extending into groin. Stitches in l.; *in r.* in evening; in r. when lying; in r., then bruised pain in l. lower ribs, also noticed upon pressure; in r., extending through and through bowels and out at small of back. Cutting in r.; with pinching, as in diarrhœa. Griping in r., below navel, after eating. Bruised pain in r.; then sticking outward through pudenda. Sticking burning in r., with sensation as if something would be loosened. Tension in r.

Hypogastrium.—Twitchings in l. side when sitting bent. Stitches below last false ribs, above ilium; above l. hip, extending to l. false ribs; in r. groin, extending downward, as if a hernia would appear, after breakfast; as with an awl in r. groin, > rubbing. Deep-seated pain, at last with fever, heat, anxiety and restlessness, so that he could not sleep at night nor lie, and pain on touch, as in inflammation of abdomen; *P. above l. hip as if it would burst there on coughing;* as from a weight. Bruised pain in l. groin at 2 P.M. when walking; in r. groin, at first > then < pressure, with stitches. Dragging in inguinal regions, extending forward, while sitting, with ineffectual urging to urinate.

Rectum. — *Frequent, sudden pressing-piercing pain.* Sticking during stool. Cramp, obliging her to sit still. Sensation of something hard in it, like a kernel of fruit. *Pressure all day;* < after stool, and in anus. Dragging, as if fæces should be expelled. Urging to stool, with rumbling in abdomen; U. after dinner, stool hard and difficult; but spasmodic contraction of anus, so that no stool passes; frequent, with emission of only flatus; *frequent, ineffectual,* with pain, anxiety and redness of face. Crawling. *Itching, and in genitals; I., with sticking.*

Anus.—*Hæmorrhoids, with sore pain,* **unendurable on walking** *or reflecting; swollen H., with itching-sticking and much moisture; hard H., stinging-burning, painful when touched* (Æsc. h.), *when walking,* standing or sitting, > stool; *impeding stool;* painful. Stitching before a meal. Spasmodic drawing pain after coition. Sore pain, with moisture. Biting pain after stool. Burning during stool; *after stool,* with depressed pulse and palpitation; after stool, making him powerless. *Itching* (Æsc. h., Sulph.); after dinner; crawling. *Pain in perineum,* with pulsation.

Clinical.—Hæmorrhoids, intolerably painful, < walking. Partial paralysis of rectum, stool passed better when standing. Pruritis of anus and fistula.

Stool.—Watery; with stomachache. Semi-fluid; at 5 A.M. *Diarrhœa* in evening; at night; from taking cold in abdomen; with tenesmus and burning in anus; with passage of blood; with passage of flatus. Constipation. Solid S.; with passage of a round worm. Nodular, with mucus and clear blood, without trace of hæmorrhoids; N., then contraction of rectum, then soft stool, then in form like a goose-quill. First hard, then soft, then dyspnœa, then distention of hypochondria, < r., with pinching on every step. Black, after the sweat. Bloody, with burning and soreness in rectum; painless passage of blood, with a soft stool. With white mucus. *Passes better when standing.* Passes with sensation as if only flatus passed.

Urinary Organs.—Pain in bladder, with inability to pass urine, but if a few drops pass he has pain in urinary passages, with constipation and cramp in rectum. **Micturition so easy that he is not sensible of the stream, and can scarcely believe in the dark that he is urinating until he makes sure with the hand. Involuntary M. while coughing or blowing nose** (Zn.); *I. at night in sleep. Intermittent M. in evening. Delay of last drops of urine.* Enuresis, with violent erections without desire. Frequent micturition; at night; at night, and copious, with diarrhœa, which was repeated in morning; and copious; *and copious* (K. c.), soon depositing a sediment like yeast; F. and scanty.

Urethra.—*Discharge of blood, with the ejaculation of semen during coition.* Cutting. Pain in evening after urinating, with aching in vertex. Burning; *when urinating;* after an emission; when urinating, or at root of urethra; in region of frænum when urinating; *sudden, at night.* Itching in orifice.

Urging to urinate after a walk; *U., with necessity to wait long, then scanty urine, then renewed urging. Frequent urging;* at night, waking her; *with involuntary dribbling of urine;* then shivering in open air. *Frequent, ineffectual U., then while sitting involuntary micturition. Ineffectual attempts at micturition, after passing a few drops pain in bladder and (after much walking in order to relieve it) cramps in rectum.*

Urine.—Copious; then scanty; and slightly acid. Scanty, with great thirst. *Often dark brown. Turbid on standing.* Reddish. Clear, like water. Containing much tenacious mucus.

Clinical.—Weakness of bladder. Paralysis of bladder, the urine is expelled very slowly and sometimes is even retained. Weakness of the sphincter of bladder, especially in children, the urine passes involuntarily, especially during the first sleep at night, also involuntarily from the slightest excitement during the day. Paralysis of bladder after labor, the urine is retained.

Sexual Organs.—Cutting in mons veneris, < walking. Increased smegma, much on corona glandis. Red spots on penis. Herpetic redness of penis, with oozing on frænum of glans. Vesicles under prepuce, becoming suppurating ulcers. Burning pain in penis. Itching scurf on inside of prepuce. Itching of frænum; on inner surface of prepuce, at one time tickling, at another biting; voluptuous, of penis, with incomplete erection. Erection in morning, with desire; E. all the forenoon; frequent, incomplete, in morning after coition. Impotence. Itching cutting in septum of scrotum. *Itching of scrotum* and on skin of penis; of scrotum and sweating. *Stitches in r. testicle.* Tearing in testicles. *Pain in testicles* at noon; *in r. T. as if crushed.* Desire; with disinclination to work; very little. Discharge of prostatic fluid after stool. Irritation to emission. Frequent emissions at night and next forenoon, with constant excessive erections; frequent E. in an old man; E. every night and during afternoon nap in one who was impotent.

Female.—Burning. *Biting in pudenda as from salt during and after micturition. Leucorrhœa flowing like menses and of same color* (Zn.); L. at night (Nat. m.). Uterine spasm, > application of warm stones, pain now in hypogastrium, now in stomach, now in chest, now in small of back, obliging her to bend forward, with intolerance of clothing on epigastric region, pain in abdomen and stomach from even the most digestible food, fulness as if abdomen would burst and ineffectual desire to eructate. *Menstruation delayed;* too soon; *no discharge at night* (Puls.); *offensive and causing itching in pudenda;* copious. Intermittent traces of bloody discharge for many days after menstruation had ceased.

Clinical.—Uterine inertia during labor (K. carb.). Post-partum hæmorrhage from inertia of uterus. Leucorrhœa especially < night, with great weakness.

Respiratory Organs.—*Dryness; of larynx. Pain in larynx on blowing nose.* Drawing in larynx. *Frequent need to clear something out of L.* Irritation in L. as in beginning of cold, with general febrile excitement. **Muscles of L. do not perform their function and inability to speak a loud word.** *Hoarseness* (Kali bi.); < *morning and* **evening, with scraping in throat;** *in morning, with rawness in throat.* Stoppage of voice every morning, as if there were a wedge in larynx which should be expectorated.

Cough in forenoon, with rawness in throat; C. in forenoon, with rattling on every inspiration as from mucus in r. side of chest; *wakes her in evening and morning, > during the day;* only at night; every night at 2 A.M., > during the day, with much expectoration; *always caused by speaking; caused by crawling in larynx or by stooping to pick up anything;* caused by incessant crawling; on becoming warm after being cold; < after eating, with expectoration of mucus. *Tickling cough.* Paroxysmal C., caused by tickling of mucus in throat. Violent C., even at night; *at times dry, with pain in r. side of abdomen. Hollow C., < night and morning, with adherent mucus in chest, in which there is sticking, soreness and ulceration, with and without coughing, with stopped coryza. Dry hollow C., in paroxysms,* **with a sore streak down trachea, where it pains on every paroxysm of cough** *and almost prevents breathing.* Dry cough at night, disturbing sleep; C., with scraping in throat, without expectoration; causing burning in chest; racking, in morning on waking and preventing him from sleeping again. Hacking C., with difficult breathing; dry H. cough and only seldom some expectoration of mucus. Hoarse C., < morning and evening, > night. *Irritation to cough, even in morning in bed; I., with every expiration.* Expectoration of tough mucus, at first difficult, then easy to loosen.

Suffocation in attacks during inspiration while sitting, as if some one grasped the trachea. *Arrest of breath while speaking or walking rapidly, with necessity to suddenly catch for breath;* sudden A. when hunting, with rapid palpitation, necessity to kneel, general sweat, shortness of breath, rush of blood to head, bluish-red color of face, as if he would have apoplexy. Want of breath, with weakness of thighs. Dyspnœa after lying down; < sitting; spasmodic. Inspiration difficult and deep. *Short breath* in morning, with pain in abdomen; S. when walking in open air; with oppression of chest; *then paroxysms of cough.*

Clinical.—Acute laryngitis, loss of voice and rawness and soreness in larynx and trachea (Bell. and Benzoin.). Sudden aphonia after taking cold. Paralysis of vocal cords. Loss of voice in singers and speakers. Cough, < warmth of bed, > *sips of cold water.* Cough, with sensation as if he "could not get under the mucus" to raise it. Constant hacking cough, with involuntary micturition. Expectoration as a rule scanty, must be swallowed, excessive rawness in chest on coughing, especially under sternum.

Chest.—*Rattling when coughing* (Ant. t.). *Stitches on walking in open air;* S. beneath skin; in region of r. clavicle; in l. breast below nipple; in l. side opposite ensiform cartilage; in l. side, on a level with pit of stomach; in first l. false ribs; below l. female breast at 5 P.M., > rubbing; deep in C. in forenoon on deep respiration; beneath l. breast during menstruation; above heart on motion; in l. after eating; in l. when coughing; in r. side on inspiration; *in sternum on deep breathing and on lifting;* in sternum on physical exertion; below sternum on inspiration and expiration, then stitch in sternum, lasting all the forenoon, with alternating severity, < expiration, with stitches in l. shoulder-joint; on two last false ribs, > rubbing; *below arms,* extending to pit of stomach, with apprehensiveness, then rumbling in abdomen, and griping extending into chest, > passage of flatus; deep in C., out to back; near nipple, extending suddenly towards navel, < inspiration; as with a nail; knife-like, anteriorly in l. side, piercing through to back, at night, with anxiety, restlessness and sleeplessness.

Tearing in forepart, < open air; sticking, in l. side. Cutting in morning, with burning. Pressure; above pit of stomach; by l. lowest rib; on r. side; on r. side in evening; with difficult or short breathing; in intercostal muscles, transversely across chest, on stooping; in upper part of ensiform cartilage, extending upward; sharp, after dinner, < walking. Pain in r. side as if lung were loosened from pleura, even when lying; rheumatic P., and in abdomen. Bruised pain in muscles, < pressure; B. pain below r. mamma, not affected by breathing. Sprained pain in l. lower muscles on moving l. arm. Burning pain, and sometimes stitches. Drawing pain internally in upper part after immoderate running or singing, with heaviness. *Sore pain when coughing.*

Scraping. Rawness in morning. *Anxiety* in evening *after stool,* with distention of abdomen. *Tightness; with frequent necessity to take a deep breath. Sensation as if clothes were too tight. Painful compression from both sides towards sternum, with oppression of breath and weakness of voice.* Constriction, with hoarseness and rawness of throat. Oppression in afternoon, > dancing; O. (bronchi) after eating; of both sides as if pressed together. Rushing in region of heart mornings, until rising, > motion, returning when lying. Heat internally; rising into throat.

Clinical.—Nipples sore and cracked.

Heart and Pulse.—Oppression of H., with melancholy. Palpitation in morning, with irregular pulse and pain in back; P. in evening, with anxiety, which made the breath short; with weariness; anxious, with rhythmical constriction of abdomen. Pulse small (almost thready) and slow.

Neck.—Jerking motion, near head. Stitches at night when lying. Pinching in r. side. Bruised pain. Tensive pain, extending to head. Tension of muscles on becoming suddenly erect or on turning head. Tensive sensation in nape as if drawn backward by both ears. *Stiff pain in r. side. Stiffness, so that he could not move head* (Zinc.); *S. of N. and throat, with pain in occiput, and bound feeling in muscles, so that he could not move the head;* of r. side, with tensive pain.

Back.—Stitches; when sitting; then pain. Sticking piercing-jerking, and in sacrum, arresting breath. Tearing in a spot. *Pain during menstruation.* Pain like a drawn and beaten sensation, then extending into small of B. and thence into abdomen, where there is flatulence, with pain, then discharge of flatus and leucorrhœa. Crawling. Pulsation in middle.

Scapulæ.—Stitches in l.; near r. when swallowing and hawking and on exerting voice. Tearing in r.; between scapulæ at 4 P.M.; in vertebræ between S. extending into r. scapula, then into l. Pain on border of r., extending to back, < bending r. upper arm and head backward, and at last on every motion of body, even if the part be only shaken, < turning head towards the l., with tearing. Stiff pain between. Tensive pain in upper part on motion. Drawing; in l.

Loins.—*Stitches in l. by last false ribs;* above r. ilium,

like electric sparks, extending to ribs; itching. Tearings. Pinching in region of kidneys. Pain; on every motion; when sitting; after copious micturition; the two last days before menstruation, with anxious dreams; *cramplike, while sitting;* pinching cramplike, and in nates; so that he must bend over, with pain in hypogastrium. Sore pain, then pressing in hypogastrium, as if everything would come out of rectum and pudenda, like flatulent colic (from straining). Bruised pain towards evening, with passage of leucorrhœa; B. pain when walking, > sitting. Sprained pain on motion. Tensive pain. Pain as if squeezed. Stiffness of lumbo-sacral joint.

Coccyx.—*Bruised pain. Drawing pain in region.* Jerking pain.

Clinical.—Lumbago, painful stiffness of back and sacrum, < attempting to rise.

Extremities.—Twitchings in evening. Stitches in joints after taking cold. *Tearing now in one, now in another, at one time severe, at another slight; T. < joints and extending thence into long bones.* Pain in arms and thighs. *Gouty pains.* Drawing pain in r. index finger and in l. second toe. Drawings here and there; D. in fingers, soles and toes. *Uneasiness in morning in bed; in evening.* Sensation as after great exertion, after rising from a seat. *Weakness and trembling; paralytic W.;* so that he can scarcely walk and the hands must lie outstretched. Crawling in arms and legs, as if they would go to sleep. Heaviness at night, preventing sleep.

Clinical.—Rheumatic paralysis of arm, < r. Unsteadiness of the muscles of forearm and hand. Numbness, loss of sensation in hands. Contracted tendons in palms of hands. Sciatica; on r. side, < motion, especially < easterly storms. Rheumatoid arthritis, especially in persons who suffer from great weakness of the limbs, < east wind, limbs become distorted. The hamstrings under the knee seem too short, in chronic rheumatism. Weakness of ankles.

Upper Extremities. — Axilla. Glands swollen. Stitches near, extending towards breast.

Shoulder.—Stitches on top; in l.; tearing, in r., extending into hand. Tearing in joint of l.; in r. at 6 P.M. if she moves r. arm or turns head to r., with bruised pain on inner border of r. scapula, but if she turns to the l. the place feels tense. *Pressure upon.* Pain on moving r. arm; in l. as if dislocated, from morning till evening; in joint and in elbow as if asleep, at night, waking her frequently, < morning after waking; paralytic, in l. Goutlike drawings here and there, < motion, and in elbow and wrist. Stiffness.

Arm.—Spasmodic flexion of l. at times. Convulsions up and down l. (which is weaker) after exertion, then heaviness of arm, then rumbling down muscles, extending into bone, as from crawling of a mouse, with which the twitches disappear. Trembling of r. if he holds anything at arm's length. Inclination of r. to cramp, waking before midnight, with crawling as if asleep. Stitches, extending into l. side of chest. Tearing, and in hand; extending into back; in l., and in shoulder-joint. Pain in r. Drawing pain in muscles; in bones at night, preventing sleep. Drawing in r., with paralytic heaviness. Weakness of r., with crawling in front of both shoulders; W. of r., almost like paralysis, < writing, with stiffness. Heaviness, with weakness; H. of r., as from a blow upon thick part of forearm. Stiffness of l. when holding it upright for a long time, with sensation as if the blood flowed back into it, with pain in r. side of chest as from contraction of muscles; inclination of l. to become stiff, waking him at night.

Upper Arm.—Stitches in r. on raising arm; S. near l. shoulder; on inner margin of r.; in upper part of r., > rubbing; in r. at night in bed, preventing motion; in deltoids if she carries anything; outward in l. humerus, near its head. Tearing just below shoulder-joints; T. at night in warmth of bed, especially in shoulder-joint; in l. humerus, extending to elbow, in which it is most painful. Drawing cutting in r. deltoid. Pinching in deltoid, with coldness that ends in burning. Bruised pain in flesh. Drawing pain in l. humerus; now in one, now in other deltoid, extending to clavicle.

Elbow.—Quivering externally when leaning upon arm. Boring in tip of l. at 4 P.M., with sensation as if it would force him to bend the arm. Bruised pain; in bend, < pressure. Drawing pain, and in forearms. Pain in bend of l. on stretching arm, as if a tendon were too short.

Forearm.—Swelling, as if on periosteum, painful when pressed. Trembling of r. while writing, with twitching. Stitches along tendons on inner surface of r.; drawing, in muscles in lower part of r. Tearings; in tendons of r.; in l., from elbow downward; throbbing, in l. Boring in a spot below r. elbow as if in bone, at 4 P.M., with tearing. Drawing pain in muscles of lower part of l. Contractive pain in muscles of lower part of l. Paralytic pain in r. ulna. Paralysis, with difficulty in raising it on account of heaviness and stiffness.

Wrist.—Sticking in r. as if sprained, when at work; crawling sticking in r., and in second and third fingers. Tearing in r.; on back of r., extending into middle finger, with pinching. Pain in r. as if sprained or dislocated. Drawing pain; from r. into fingers; in bones, through metacarpal bones into little finger, where it is worse in tip, < stretching hand, when fingers are involuntarily drawn together, then the drawing extends from bones of wrist into the other fingers and they all become bent; drawing pain in l., from within outward.

Hand.—Swelling at night, with crawling in them. *Trembling.* Stitches in l. palm, with crawling in fingers; jerking, in muscles of l., transversely across dorsum, on moving arm. Tearings, and in fingers; on dorsum, now of one, now of other; in metacarpal bones of thumbs; in inner margin of r., extending towards little finger, as if in bone. Spasmodic sensation. Tensive pain transversely across l., as if sprained, on moving it. Fulness in inner part of l. when grasping anything. Weakness in a hot room; spasmodic W. in morning on waking. Heaviness of r. Paralytic sensation in r. Going to sleep, with crawling in it.

Fingers.—Twitchings when writing; drawing, in l. *Stitches in little,* then extending upward like knife-stitches, with apprehension and aching about heart. Tearing; in l. index; in joints of r. index, with pain on pressure; in l. middle, at 3 P.M., with pinching; in tips of all, with trembling of hands. Pain under nails when touched. *Drawing pain in joints;* l. Burning pain under nails, but when touched pain as if suppurating; shooting-burning pain in joints. Crushed pain in tip of r. little; in tips, as if they would burst, now of one hand, now of other. Throbbing pain as from an ulcer in proximal joint of r. thumb. Tension in knuckles of last joints on bending in forenoon. Numbness, with loss of sensation and with tension. Deadness, < morning; seem dead, icy-cold, white and without sensation.

Lower Extremities.—Tottering from side to side when walking, with sensation as if he staggered more than he really did, without vertigo. Stitches, first from hip-joint and then from patella downward, < rest. Weariness from afternoon till evening, especially in legs and knees. Numb or bruised pain in nates when sitting.

Hip.—Stitches in joint every two minutes, extending towards abdomen; in l. as if in bone. Tearing in joint; when sitting and walking, and down whole leg; in l. as if in bone, and on pressure bruised pain. Pinching in region; above joint, with twinging and with coldness that ends in burning. Pain above joint; paroxysmal, in l. joint, as if sprained or dislocated, causing lameness; drawing pain when sitting and walking; prickling-burning in region.

Thigh.—Twitchings above knee. Stitches in l.; in bend of r.; on outer surface of r., just above knee; in l. in evening when walking, extending into chest. Tearing in middle of l., > rising from a seat; scraping, in l.; paralytic T. on outer surface of r. *Bruised pain in morning in bed, and in legs.* Jerking pain from nates downward. Trembling or throbbing sensation in flesh, like a painful tingling. Tension in bend of r. in morning on rising, and on bending knee. Beatings in tendons above bend of l. knee. Weariness when walking, and in leg; W., with want of breath; in upper part, from without inward, < rest. Paralyzed feeling when sitting and walking.

Knee.—*Cracking when walking;* painful, when walking, as if it would be broken or sprained. Jerking in l. in afternoon. Stitching when at work. Tearing in r.; on outer side of l.; in patella at night, preventing sleep; in l., extending through toes; with stitches, so that he could not step and could not sleep at night; drawing, in evening, extending into ankles. Boring in r., with bruised pain on pressure. Pain externally, as from an ulcer, extending to thigh. Sore pain. Drawing pain, then jerking pain. Drawing and jerking pain in l. patella; D. pain, as if weary from walking, worse when extending knees than when bending them. Drawings. *Tension in hollows when sitting or beginning to walk, > continued walking. Tensive pain in hollow when walking, with stiffness.* Weariness after walking, with heaviness of foot; W. < ascending steps; so that they knock under. *Stiffness of l. when walking* (Led.); stiff pain in patella when rising. Tingling, gone-to-sleep sensation in morning, and in legs.

Leg.—Varices. Twitchings. Trembling on beginning to ascend (*e. g.*, on a ladder), > standing still and working; as from a chill when walking or standing in open air. Tearing down outer side of l. from knee when sitting, the pain extends into hip-joint on rising from a seat, with bruised pain in hip when walking and on pressure, not > when sitting; burning, in tibia. Pain after copious micturition; P. at night, extending into groins; down tibia. Sprained or paralyzed pain in muscles in afternoon and evening. Pain as from a blow on r. tibia. Drawing pain; as if in bones. Drawing in r. in evening, with pain in throat; cramplike, down outer side of r. when sitting or standing. Uneasiness in evening; in l. at night. Weariness in morning on waking, > after rising. Heaviness; at night in bed, and of feet. Falling asleep.

Calf.—*Cramp in morning in bed;* at night. Intermittent stitches in l. *Tearing in tendons beneath r.;* down l.; and on dorsum of foot; from outer part of r. to outer margin of foot, < moving foot or toes. Bruised pain in r. all the forenoon, extending into and above knee. Contraction of r. Tension as if some one forcibly contracted the skin, from 7 to 8 P.M. Drawing when rising from a seat and when walking, with sensation as if r. leg were too short. Crawling in l., with prickling, as if it would go to sleep.

Ankle.—Tearing stitch, extending to knee and thence to hip-joint, but not in the knee itself. Tearing in outer malleolus in evening. Pain when walking as if sprained or as if it would be broken; S. pain on a misstep or on bending it from side to side, with cracking in joint. Pain as if weary or crushed when sitting after walking, > walking again. Drawing pain when sitting, with sensation on sitting as if leg would bend under. Drawing. *Stiffness.*

Foot.—Swelling, especially of anterior part, in evening, with heat and internal itching, as if frozen, and on pressure pain as if suppurating. *Cramp;* on stretching it; in r. sole and tendo-achillis on stretching them. Tearing in dorsum of l.; in ball behind great toe; in inner margin of r.; in inner margin, even in morning in bed; in l. tendo-achillis when sitting; sudden, in r. heel. Boring and burning pain in a corn. Pressure on dorsum. Aching in soles like a nervous disease. Drawing in r. in evening; in tendons of r. instep, extending into great toe, where it is only felt on motion. Tension in heel and tendo-achillis. Weakness in morning so that he can hardly stand. Going to sleep when sitting or lying. Numbness of heel when sitting, with pithiness.

Toes.—Stitches in great; in ball of great; in a corn on little toe; *burning in ball of great;* burning, beneath nail of l. great. Tearing in great; in l. great towards tip; on outer margin of r. little; on margin of little, extending towards tip; burning in second little; burning, behind nails of first and second. *Pain on posterior joint of great;* in great as if suppurating; as from inflammation behind nail of great; in great as if burnt. Drawing during a storm, extending into thigh, with tearing. Crawling in l. great, with sticking, as if it would go to sleep; crawling falling asleep of r. big toe in afternoon.

Skin.—Spotted on thighs and legs, full of dark red veins. Red spot above upper lip, which seems cracked and causes a burning pain; painful red spot on tibia, extending along length of leg, with itching when healing. Inflammatory swelling beneath chin, as if an abscess would form, with burning pain. Old liver-spots become elevated, with corrosive itching. *Eruption in face;* more felt than seen. Nettle-rash, especially just above knees; on neck, between scapulæ and on back. Itching tetter on dorsum of ring finger; on nates; *on neck, with moisture.* Eruption of the size of pin-heads, with hollow tip, without moisture, on forehead, neck, scapulæ, arms, hypogastrium, especially on thighs and in hollows of knees, with itching, especially in warmth of bed, with burning after scratching, when not warm scarcely noticeable, whitish, prominent on scratching, after scratching a red spot with large areola.

Pimples on tip of nose; at root of nose; between eyebrows; near upper lip; beneath l. corner of mouth; on r. thumb; behind r. thumb; on index, becoming a wart; tensive, on neck; under skin on r. side of body, on chest, arm, back and bend of elbow, with stitching on touch and sore pain on hard pressure, afterwards with pain and stinging when not touched. Itching P. on l. cheek; on forearms; P. on various parts, with corrosive itching, and after scratching burning. Transparent crystalline P., rounded at apex, itching, on hands, the second day, with red areola and filled with milky liquid, the third day discharging pus and ulcerating, the fourth day some dessicated, others ulcerated and coalesced and left a red spot.

Eruption like chicken-pox (in an infant). Red pustules on l. side of forehead, l. temple, on nose and on middle of chin, with stinging when touched and when healing covered with scurf. Boil behind ear; on back; on chin, near lower lip, with red areola; near anus, painful, discharging pus and blood. Suppuration of l. great toe-nail, with burrowing burning pain and proud flesh. Soreness between thighs; painful, between female thighs; on thigh, near scrotum, as if excoriated, with itching, and after rubbing smarting. Vesicles on feet from rubbing; on chest and back, with anxiety of chest, and fever consisting of chill, heat and sweat; painful, on l. side of chest and back, which burst, with fever, heat, sweat and anxiety; on calf, discharging water and healing without suppuration; burning, in face, exuding corrosive water when touched, afterwards drying into a scurf; corrosive V. on heels, with itching; itching, covering inner surface of r. forearm, the itching only transiently > scratching. Ulcer on tip of thumb; on heel; on leg, with red, hard, inflamed areola, discharging more blood than pus, of offensive odor, causing sleeplessness. Ulceration again of cutaneous wounds that had almost healed.

Formication. Crawling in thighs, legs and feet; in l. calf, extending to knee; *in soles;* in ball of great toe; on r. forearm, > rubbing; between first and second phalanges of l. ring finger, with twitching in inner side of upper arm; in r. heel, > scratching, with itching, as if it would go to sleep; tingling burning, in soles. Tickling in r. sole, so that she could not scratch it enough; in toes, as if they had been frozen.

Itching over whole body; in various parts; on head; forehead; above eyes; *in face; tip and wings of nose;* on nose, chin and throat, below ears; about mouth; about breasts; *on back; on arms;* in hands; of palms; on dorsum of l. hand; on last and middle joints of l. fingers; between fingers; on nates and back of thighs; on thighs; hips; in hollow of r. knee; of patella; legs; calves; *dorsum of foot;* on r. heel; over whole body at night, with dry heat; on thighs, perineum and scrotum, < night in bed and in morning. Itching, > scratching; behind r. ear; on eyebrows, l. malar-bone, temples and ears; in middle of l. scapula; on back; upper sternum; r. shoulder; l. axilla; bend of l. elbow; l. forearm; behind l. ring and little fingers; in bend of r. knee, then on tibia; on r. tibia. Itching over whole body, not > scratching, with redness like scarlet-rash and many vesicles. I. on back, with sweat. Itching on lower part of forearms, burning after scratching, I. soon reappears, and new vesicles constantly appear; I. in palms and after scratching itching vesicles; I. in hollow of l. hand, and after scratching many itching vesicles containing water; I. between first and second phalanges of l. index, and after scratching burning itching pimples; I. on forearms (sometimes with burning after scratching), with itching pimples and vesicles; I. on outer margin of l. knee, then burning after scratching. Sticking itching over skin; on index; on r. nates; on thigh towards outer part; as from fleas, on back, shoulders, arms and thighs, especially on dorsum of fingers. Corrosive itching on face, with rush of blood to it, with heat and redness, then many red pimples. Burning itching near nose. Itching on lobule of ear as from a tetter. Voluptuous itching of last joint of great toe.

Clinical.—General tendency to soreness in folds of skin, back of ears, between thighs, etc. (Sul.). Small flat warts. Warts on fingers, especially on tips and about nails. Horny warts. Horny growth on tip of nose.

Sleep.—*Yawning and stretching of limbs; < night;* Y. in forenoon and afternoon; excessive, from 11 A.M. to 3 P.M., after intermittent hiccough; excessive, all the evening, without sleepiness. Sleepiness in morning; in afternoon; *even when busy, with necessity to lie down;* when walking, < when sitting; but sleep was unrefreshing. Sleep after dinner; and is sleepy early in evening. Falls asleep while conversing. Long sleep in morning. Difficult waking in morning.

Sleeplessness on account of dry heat; every night after midnight on account of general bruised pain; every night after 2 o'clock. Woke at 4 o'clock every night (in winter) and could hardly ever sleep again. Falls asleep late on account of heat. Frequent waking; with general sweat, which increased on waking. *Frequent starting up in fright from sleep;* starting up in fright on going to sleep. *Motions of arms and legs in sleep. Uneasiness all night, after a short sleep she was awakened by anxiety and uneasiness, then necessity to sit up, with involuntary turning of head from one side to other, until, being exhausted, she fell asleep again* (Rhus t., Sul.); U. at night, then sweat in morning; every night, with occasional crying in sleep. Whining, "come here, come here," after midnight in sleep. Loud laughing in sleep.

Dreams, many. Anxious. Frightful, waking her and causing anxiety so that she cannot sleep again. *Fretful;* and vivid. Full of strife, with uneasy sleep. Sad, of dead acquaintances. Confused. Merry at first, then confused, historical. Lewd; of beautiful girls, with emissions.

Fever.—Chilliness; at 4 P.M., with creeping in legs up into back and weariness, then sweat without heat or thirst; the first half of the night, then heat, and towards morning moist skin, after which the first rest and sleep; in sleep towards morning; after eating, also with hot face; in open air after dinner. Sensitiveness to free air; to cold air; to a draught, which causes pain. Takes cold easily, with general chilliness from a slight draught. Chilliness, with yawning. C., then heat in forehead. C., then rising of heat in head, with sweat in palms in a room. Internal C. every day; frequent internal C., with cold hands and feet; internal C. about midnight, especially in arms and legs, with cutting in back, then general sweat, with tingling and heaviness in head and necessity to lie until noon. C., alternating with sweat; C., alternating with heat in face.

Shivering chill; at 7 P.M. in open air, > in room.

Shivering always on waking at night; in a room; always on going into open air, with gooseflesh; general, as often as he lays down the l. hand after motion; during pain in stomach. Shivering chill, with gooseflesh; and with urging to stool, which is soft, accompanied by pinching in whole abdomen, then general chill, with external coldness, then in the room internal warmth in head.

Chilliness of various parts. Whole l. side of body cold; and gone to sleep. Coldness of r. forearm and fingers, with stiffness; C. of hands, extending up l. arm to elbow; of hands; *of feet;* of soles. In spine between scapulæ, as from a wind. Sensation as if cold water ran from r. clavicle across chest to toes. Shivering over whole r. side of body; S. from r. temple through forehead, where it becomes a throbbing; from face over back to knee; in neck in evening, extending into brain; along back; in back in attacks, extending nearly all over abdomen; now in arm, now in leg, now general; sudden from face over chest to knee.

Heat every day from 6 to 8 P.M.;. H. causing late falling asleep in evening; after a short walk in open air, with excitement; general, without moisture and without thirst, then gradual coolness, with yawning and stretching of arms. H. in flushes after walking, with discomfort. Orgasm of blood. Burning wherever she takes hold of herself; B. in vertex; in r. temple and side of forehead; on r. malar-bone in evening; in middle of r. scapula; on outer surface of l. upper arm; transversely across forearm, close to wrist; in finger-tips; in soles; in a spot on r. side of neck, with redness. Heat in face after eating, and in eyes; in face after eating, with redness. Internal H. in head after dinner; I. heat in head without external heat; in forehead and back, as if sweat would break out; sudden, in l. thigh. Sticking-burning in axilla. Tearing burning in scalp in front of vertex in evening. Cool burning on malar-bone; frequently in front of vertex. *Crawling B. in ball of great toe.*

Sweat; in morning in bed; waking him at 4 A.M.; in afternoon when walking, with weariness; *at night;* every night; at night, with uneasy sleep; *profuse, when walking in open air;* in attacks; *general sour, at night;* on back and abdomen after walking.

Ceanothus.

A tincture is prepared from the fresh leaves of Ceanothus Americanus, Linn.

Clinical.—Enlarged spleen, with pain in the whole l. side. Chronic hypertrophy and inflammation of spleen, painful at times, with extreme dyspnœa, has to fight for her breath. Persistent pain in l. hypochondrium, profuse menses and yellow leucorrhœa. It has cured yellow leucorrhœa, with pain under l. ribs.

Cedron.

A tincture is prepared from the dry-powdered seeds of Simaba Cedron, Planchon.

General Action.—Too little is positively known to enable one to judge of its general sphere of action, but it seems to produce well-marked symptoms of intermittent neuralgia, and indeed of regularly recurring febrile attacks. It has proved curative in marsh malaria characterized by severe pains recurring periodically. It may be compared (remotely) with Arsenic.

Generalities.—Neuralgic pains, then general numbness, with smarting and burning in nose. Sharp pain in occiput, then, in abdomen, then in lower limbs. Sharp flying pains in all parts on getting warm in bed, keeping him awake most of the night (Merc., Sulph.), in limbs the pains seemed to be in cartilages of joints, < first joint of great toe and streaking *up* bones, in abdomen the pain was < in region of ascending colon, liver and spleen, the pains of head were dull, except in occiput and in facial and optic nerves. Contused feeling. Restlessness; and anguish; and nervousness. Malaise. Weakness; of body and mind after waking. Dulness of senses. **Periodicity, often clocklike,** *is a characteristic of Cedron.* Aggravation in provers of voluptuous disposition and of nervous temperament, < in women.

Clinical.—It is often found curative in acute malarial poisoning, with enlarged spleen and liver, general anæmia and dropsy. It has cured puerperal convulsions recurring at regular intervals, beginning with severe pains in l. temple, with albuminuria. Hysterical spasms recurring regularly night and morning. Recurring attacks of chorea in a woman after coition.

Mind.—Excitement. Weeping mood. Gloomy. Dread of friends, especially in women. Torpor, with uneasiness. Symptoms mostly repeated in morning and < night.

Head.—Bending backward, with pressure on occiput and parietal regions as if those parts would burst. Headache < open air; < deep in orbits, obliging him to shut his eyes, and extending to occiput. Dulness in morning, with heaviness. Distensive headache, < night. *Swollen feeling;* < r. side, and heavy. Vertigo at 11 A.M.; on rising from bed, could not see to light a candle, could not tell when it was lighted, did not know her acquaintances. **Shooting over l. eye** (Arum tr.). Pain above eyes as from a band.

Temples.—Arteries enlarged. Pain; *from T. to T. across eyes;* passing from one side to the other; throbbing, extending around forehead. Pressure at r., causing dull pain in whole r. side of head, > towards noon. Throbbing; 10 A.M.; increasing to pain, extending around and over eyes; increasing to pain and extending over ears. Pulsating sensation, with twisting pain behind r. ear, changing to dull pain and extending to temples.

Aching in vertex at 10 P.M.; 10 A.M.; on waking; on late waking after sound sleep. Pressure at vertex, < when the shivering begins. Sharp pain in occiput; sharp jerking pain at 10.30 A.M. Pain in occiput and forehead. Pressure in occiput in morning.

Eyes.—Redness, with itching of inner and outer surfaces of lids; R. and protrusion, with aching extending to forehead. Smarting during fever, < closing them; S. and burning, with lachrymation. Alternate dryness and smarting, with moisture. Swollen feeling. Itching. Lachrymation; acrid. Redness of white at 11 A.M., with dry feeling in eye when exposed to air. Pupils dilated; and fixed. Enlargement of Meibomian glands and conjunctiva. Redness of lid, with pain on pressure. Twitching of levator palpebræ superioris. L. lid seems dried to ball, conjunctiva is inflamed and dry. Burning of lids. Vision misty. Objects seem red; at night, yellowish during the day.

Clinical.—Ciliary neuralgia. Neuralgia of the supraorbital nerve and also in the whole r. side of the face, coming on every day, generally about 9 A.M., and lasting a few hours. Numerous cases of chills and fever characterized by the regular recurrence of

supraorbital neuralgia are reported cured, also many cases of supraorbital neuralgia without malarial symptoms. Severe pain in eyeball, with radiating pains all around eye, shooting into nose, causing flow of scalding water from eyes and nose, the pain in head, across forehead caused a crazy feeling, coming suddenly after working on black.

Ears.—Pain over. Hard hearing at night. Buzzing towards noon. Singing as of crickets.

Nose.—Discharge of much glassy mucus; of much clear, thin, acrid mucus.

Face.—Puffy. Red; cheeks red and burning at night, pale and cold in morning. Pressing or tearing pain in one or both cheeks, with shooting under orbits. Lips dry.

Mouth.—Pain in a decayed tooth. Tongue coated yellow; in morning on rising; at back; pricking in morning, > after eating; P. at 5.30 P.M.; pricking-itching at 5 P.M. Smarting, and in fauces. Tingling as from shock of galvanic battery. Burning, and in throat and stomach; with scraping and profuse, thin saliva; as if *raw*, and in fauces, œsophagus and stomach. Dryness, with thick, viscid saliva; D., with viscid saliva when talking. Saliva sour at night; white and thick after talking; profuse, metallic tasting. Taste metallic; of iron, causing acid salivation; sour; sickish, bitter; slimy; bad.

Throat.—Prickling in fauces, extending down œsophagus, with tingling. Swallowing difficult.

Stomach.—Appetite lost. Thirst; at night and during febrile symptoms; for cold water at noon and for warm at night; for only warm drinks during fever; no T. during chill. Aversion to cold water in evening. Gulping up of bitter wind in morning on rising; in morning before rising, with pains in temples. Nausea. Distention and nausea, generally < rest, > walking and eating. Sensation of a stone on. Rolling pain. Heat and fulness.

Abdomen.—Distention; towards evening, and hardness. Flatulence in morning, with colic and fetid flatus. Pain during dinner; flatulent, in morning, with fetid flatus; P. in small intestines, also with cramps. Borborygmi in l. side. Sharp pain at noon, alternating in cæcum, liver and spleen, running from one to other. Stitches in spleen and liver. Pain in hepatic region on rising; griping-cutting in lower.

Stool.—Ineffectual urging. Loose, yellowish. Whitish, mixed with fragments like clotted milk. Copious; with *tenesmus*. Constipation.

Urinary Organs.—*Frequent ineffectual urging.* Frequent micturition of much pale urine. Discharge like gonorrhœa; thin, gleety D., with formication over body. Feeling as if a drop of urine were in urethra or a constant dropping from it. Pain in urethra when not urinating, with burning. Burning in urethra; and along ureters. Urine profuse; and light-colored; with numb, uneasy feeling in urethra; scanty; scanty, and deep-colored; red; dark, with sediment; high-colored, with branlike sediment.

Sexual Organs.—Erections in morning; all night, with frequent waking from dreams of pleasant social interviews with female acquaintances; E., with desire. Excitement at daybreak, with discharge like leucorrhœa, and swollen mammæ, with pain.

Respiratory Organs.—Larynx constricted and tender. Much clear, thin mucus in bronchi. Difficult respiration, with partial loss of voice.

Chest.—Darting-cutting under ribs. Pain under floating ribs and under r. scapula; in r. side; oppressive, extending now and then to back, with inclination to sigh and draw a deep breath. Oppression.

Heart.—Throbbing. Palpitation during fever, with hurried breathing and headache. Pulse rapid; in morning; increased, firm, full.

Back.—Pain in morning on rising, and in loins; P. under scapula and in pelvis. Pain in kidneys; with profuse urine, smarting and burning in urethra; then profuse micturition of clear urine; with burning, and along ureters, as if boiling water were poured through them. Uneasy feeling in lumbar region, with sensation as if a drop of urine were in penis.

Extremities.—Lancinations in joints, < r. elbow. Sharp flying pains in all joints at 10 P.M., < feet, < first great toe-joint. Rheumatic pains in all joints. Rheumatic flying pains, < night, < feet and hands, some in elbows, more in knees and hips, most troublesome in first joint of great toes, pains > motion and cold before soreness came on, when they were < by motion and cold. Pains (when not febrile concomitants) > friction. Numbness of hands, arms and legs.

Upper Extremities.—Weariness in shoulders. Cutting in elbows. Pain towards noon in elbows and forearms, with cold sensation, extending to hands. Bruised feeling in elbow and r. forearm. Numbness of r. hand and forearm, and dead feeling.

Clinical.—Sudden acute pain in ball of r. thumb, extending up arm to shoulder; 2d dil. cured like magic.

Lower Extremities.—Lancinations in knees. Twitching of tendons of legs, tendo-achillis and r. foot. Contracting pain in legs as from contusion in evening. Legs feel enlarged. Numbness of r. leg. Sharp lame pain in r. ankle. Swelling of feet, with pain in all joints. Pain in heel as if ulcerating in forenoon while walking.

Clinical.—Sudden acute pain in ball of r. foot caused her to drop to the floor, afterwards pain extended to above knee.

Skin.—Yellow.

Clinical.—In shingles the radiating pains have been relieved.

Sleep.—Yawning at 7 P.M., with stretching. Sleepiness. Profound sleep. Frequent waking. Sleeplessness; and restlessness. Restless sleep. Waking dreams; confused D.; D. of quarrelling with dead sister and other dead friends, cried about it, woke with nightmare, with sensation of stone in stomach.

Fever.—Chilliness towards 6 P.M., *then frontal headache extending into parietal regions, red eyes*, itching of lids internally and externally, rapid pulse, coldness of hands and *tip of nose*, even during fever when the rest of face was red and hot, similar attack next day at 5.30 P.M.; at 6 P.M., after dinner, with shivering in back, cold feet, burning hands, feeling in eyes as after much weeping; at 6 P.M., with heat of face, pale hands, feet and tip of nose cold; at 9 P.M.; all the evening; with congestion of head, coldness of hands, feet and nose. Shivering; at 3 o'clock, with malaise and inclination to lie down, the S. renewed by movement, coldness of hands, feet and nose, flushes of heat in face, towards 6 P.M. face constantly hot, lively expression, smarting in eyes, < closing them. Cold feet; forehead in morning, with empty feeling; back and legs at 6.30 P.M. after dinner, pale hands, red face, heavy head.

Heat; 11 A.M., rapid pulse; 6 P.M., with itching of eyes; in evening; with full, strong pulse; quotidian; tertian, towards 8 P.M., preceded by depressed spirits, dulness of senses and headache at noon, cramps, then contracting and *tearing pains in limbs*, cold sensations in hands and feet, mouth dry, desire for cold water, shivering, palpitation, hurried breathing, weak pulse, then sensation of dry heat, then profuse sweat, full and quick pulse, with animated, red face, cold and pale in the apyrexia, thirst for warm drinks. Flushes. Dry at night. Flying in face towards evening, alternating with chills, with bloated appearance.

Sweat.

Clinical.—Recurring chills, with left-sided headache, numbness of the limbs, etc. In chills and fever the whole body feels numb with the headache.

Cereum Oxalate.

Triturations with sugar of milk are used for low dilutions.

Clinical.—Vomiting of pregnancy. Whooping cough, with nosebleed and vomiting. Nervous reflex vomiting from intestinal or cerebral irritation, almost always spasmodic. Dysmenorrhœa in fleshy, robust women, with scanty discharge, > thorough establishment of the menses; 5 grains every hour.

Chamomilla.

A tincture is prepared from the whole fresh plant of Matricaria Chamomilla, Linn., when in flower.

General Action.—It belongs to the catarrhal group, affecting all mucous membranes. Its rheumatoid or neuralgic pains are noteworthy (compare its botanical relatives, Arnica and Gnaphalium). Its action on the emotional sphere is, however, most characteristic and serves to indicate the remedy in a greater number of complaints than its general symptomatology might suggest.

Allies.—Puls., Sulph., Acon., Nat. m.; also Arnica, Gnaphal. and Tanacet.

Generalities.—Sitting stiff like a statue, noticing nothing; *the child becomes stiff, bends backward, stamps on the nurse's arm, screams and throws everything off. Convulsions in children, now one leg, now the other is moved up and down, grasping for something, mouth drawn back and forth, eyes staring* (Tanacet.). Twitching of limbs and eyelids; of limbs and head in morning nap. *Tossing about, with heat and redness of cheeks, confused talk and open eyes.* Starting. Stretching. The child will neither stand nor walk, and cries piteously; will always lie, does not wish to be carried.

Stitches in various parts, < joints; *jumping from place to place* (Puls.), *< knees and ankles, > motion;* in joints, along bones and in muscles, in latter with jerking and tearing; or drawing pains, in r. then l. leg, extending into ankles and dorsa of feet, then again in r. shoulder, on hips or l. half of head. Tearing here and there; T. in attacks in evening. **Pains seem intolerable.** *Pains < eructation;* at night, > warm compresses; (at night, > sitting up in bed); < neck, throat and occiput, when standing long and keeping body in one position; composed of itching and sticking, in spots, now in one part, now in another, < scratching. Bruised pain in stormy weather. Drawing pain in all bones, even in occiput; in head, now in shoulder-joint and hip-joint, now in lower limbs; in scapulæ, chest and hands, as from taking cold. Oppression; on moving; in morning, with irritability. Feeling of impending illness. *Uneasiness; anxiety, agonizing tossing about, with tearing in abdomen* (Acon.); cannot remain in bed.

Weakness; in morning; during rest; when the pain begins; > motion, with inability for earnest thought; *in attacks, < limbs;* sudden, while sitting and walking, < knees, with cracking of knees; faintlike; faintlike, after breakfast; paralytic, of painful parts, > walking, the pains < sitting or lying, < parts at rest or tensely drawn, for instance, in wrist when writing. *Faintness; and sickness, sinking about heart, sudden paralyzed feeling in legs, pain in all limbs as if beaten* (compare Tanac.). Paralyzed feeling in parts where pains had ceased; the paralytic feeling in any part is always accompanied by drawing or tearing pain, and the drawing or tearing pains rarely occur without the paralytic or numb sensation in the part (see Tanacet.). Stiffness. Aggravation on r. side; of all symptoms by walking. Amelioration when walking; during midday heat; by sweat.

Clinical.—Rheumatism and rheumatoid pains, the pains make the patient wild and walk about in distress. Convulsions in children brought on by excitement, especially with one cheek red and the other pale, and hot sweat.

Mind.—Whining restlessness, the child wants this and that, but when given it he will not have it or pushes it away. Piteous moaning of a child because he cannot have what he wants. The child can only be quiet when carried on the arm. *Moans on account of trifling, even imaginary insults; moans with heat of face.* Weeping and wailing. Talking strangely at night while awake and sitting up in bed. **Peevishness** (Puls., Ant. cr.); **about everything**, *with dyspnœa;* **about pains,** especially those which involved joints and extended along bones, as paralytic and drawing pains; in morning on rising, with disinclination to mental labor; on *appearance of menses, with obstinacy even to quarreling;* after dinner; the hypochondriac whims and peevishness seem to him to depend upon stupidity and heaviness of head and constipation. **Impatience** (Ign.); *everything goes too slowly. Intolerance of being spoken to or interrupted, < after rising from sleep,* with sluggish pupils. Reserved. Taciturn; and earnest, reconciled to his fate, about which he is deeply affected (later action). Talks with aversion, in a short, abrupt way. Cannot stop talking about old vexations. Quarrelsome. Suspicious that he may have been insulted. Inclined to scold. Gloomy. *Anxiety* (Acon.); in bed, with rapidly changing pupils; while urinating, without mechanical hindrance; *with ineffectual urging to urinate, without much urine in bladder; and dissatisfaction with everything that she undertakes, irresolution, with flushes of heat in face and cool sweat in palms; with uneasiness;* with trembling and palpitation; as if he must go to stool. Apprehension. *Dread of wind;* of work. (Conscientious scruples about everything.)

Excitement; and confusion. Joyless dulness of senses, with ineffectual desire to sleep. Waking stupefied slumber or inability to open eyes, quick expiration, tearing in forehead and nausea. Omission of words when writing or speaking. Stammering, mistakes in speaking. Vanishing of thought; in afternoon. Inattention. Ideas fixed (later action). Stupefaction, with vertigo; with compression of brain. Comprehends nothing aright, as if deaf or in a waking dream. Misunderstands questions, answers incorrectly, with a subdued voice, as if delirious. Exhaustion; in evening. Indolence; in morning. *At night it seems as if he heard voices of absent persons.* Mistakes a familiar person for a different (larger) one, while overpowered with sleep. *Unconsciousness in a child, frequent changes in face, distortion of eyes, contraction of facial muscles, rattling in chest, cough, yawning and stretching.*

Clinical.—The great indication for the use of Chamomilla is to be found in the mental condition of the patient; children are extremely restless and impatient, they want to be petted constantly and carried about, and they cry piteously if they cannot have everything they want; older people are peevish and impatient, extremely sensitive to pain, even the slightest twinge is intolerable, they are always complaining. It is not infrequently indicated in people who have been in the habit of taking opium, bromide of potash, etc. These mental symptoms will call for the drug in a great variety of neuralgias, painful diseases, hysterical symptoms, etc., even if indications other than the preceding are wanting; it, at least, changes the aspect of the case and makes it more amenable to treatment.

Head.—Wagging backward and forward. *Inclination to bend backward.* Inability to hold erect, necessity to bend far forward or far backward. Stitches; as if eyes would fall out. Tearing at night. Burrowing, < forehead and temples. *Pressure increasing and decreasing, < half of forehead and in r. temple, where there are stitches, which sometimes extend to occiput like electric sparks.*

Aching; in morning, > when fully awake; in evening; in afternoon, with heaviness and with stitches in temples, < r.; after eating; after sitting a long time after mental exertion, with vertigo; even in sleep; after waking, < mental effort, especially the pressure in vertex extending to forehead and temples, with sensation as if temples were pressed by thumbs; on waking, < motion, earnest thought, reading, < in forehead, with inability to fix attention; < evening, with weakness of head; with pressure as from a finger, sometimes in temples, sometimes in lower part of forehead and in frontal eminences, with inclination to bend head backward; with pain in eyeballs and sensation in r. half of head, < r. temple, as from an angle pressing into head; mostly one-sided frontal, > dinner and eructations, with warmth of head and vertigo; throbbing, as if it would burst, on waking; consisting of heaviness and bruised sensation; confused, when sitting and reflecting; paroxysmal, in morning; periodical, stupefying, in afternoon, beginning with pressure upon vertex, then extending to forehead and temples. Brain feels constricted by meninges; by dura mater, > appearance of heat in head and sweat.

Confusion; 5 A.M. on waking, and stupefaction; morning on waking; morning after waking; in morning, with sticking and boring, < r. temple; *afternoon, with pressure on eyes;* afternoon, with paroxysmal pressure; < lying; > nosebleed, with abnormal sensations in nose; with disinclination to mental labor, which aggravated the headache. Stupefaction; 7 P.M., with vertigo, < closing eyes. Fulness. Pulsation. Heaviness; morning on waking; 6 P.M., with pressure and burrowing in temples, < r. Congestion; 5 A.M.; < mental work, with pressure on vertex. Rush of blood; at noon during the heat, > in evening while walking in cool air, with pain; 3 P.M., > 7 P.M. by nosebleed, with stitches; and to nose, with full sensation; and to chest; and to chest, on earnest thinking, with stitches in r. chest. Vertigo (Tanac.); in morning; forenoon; *after eating* (Petrol.); after coffee; on rising after long sitting; while sitting erect; after long stooping and some cough; (on stooping); (after lying down, with dim vision and heat in face); < when talking; *staggering, in morning on rising; in attacks, with tendency to faint;* as if head were top-heavy, when walking after eating; in evening, as if unable to collect his senses; even to faintness.

Forehead.—Stitches; in r. eminence. (Tearing while sitting or turning in bed, with sensation as if a lump were falling forward); paroxysmal T.; sticking, extending into chest. Digging; and in r. temple, changing to sensation of a sharp corner pressing inward. Pressure; forenoon; above eyes; over r., eye towards noon, with pressure on r. ball; in protuberances, < sitting and studying, > walking; now r., now l. eminence, with digging; in sagittal suture, with aching and heaviness. Pain; < moving head; in bones; over r., with pressure upon eyes and stitches in r. temple; jerking, < eating. Constriction as with a broad band. Heaviness and dulness.

Temples.—Swelling of l., with pain on touch. Stitches in r.; l.; now r., now l.; > cooling rain, with pressure and rush of blood to head; boring, in r., with heaviness and digging in head. Tearing in one; *extending outward, with sticking.* Digging; < r., with pressure. *Pressure as with a finger,* also < mental work; and in vertex, with sticking, > midday heat, with stitches in l. temple. Pain; l.; l. then heat in forehead, with pain in it; *wandering, always < at the beginning. Compression; forenoon.* Painful pulsation in arteries towards noon, with compressive pain in r. temple.

Vertex.—Stitches extending to pharynx. Pressure; forenoon; < r. side, extending to forehead and temples; *extending over forehead and temples, <* **directing attention to it,** *and sudden stooping and mental exertion;* extending to temples and occiput, with sensation as if head were pressed from all sides; extending to neighboring parts, < forehead and temples, < r. side, with pressure often on r. eyeball in region of superior oblique muscle; extending over head, the head seems pressed from all sides, < r. temple; in upper part of brain, extending as a compression over skull. Pain; in r. side at noon; extending over forehead and temples. Biting.

Sides.—Stitches in r.; in r. bone; in region of parietal eminences; in one half of brain, < r.; in one half, as after taking cold. Pain, with warmth in head and vertigo. *Throbbing in attacks* **in one half of brain.** *Drawing pain.* Cracking in l. half of brain, with grating.

Occiput.—Stitches; jerking in l.; pain in l. Heaviness; and confusion. Fulness.

Scalp.—Stitches, < vertex, as if seated in bone.

Eyes.—*Swollen in morning and agglutinated, with purulent mucus.* Inflamed in morning and full of gum. Stitches. Pressure. Heat; with feeling as if their surfaces were dry and rough; then lachrymation, then heat about eyes. Lachrymation; of r. Sensation as if ball were drawn backward. Pupils contracted; and immovable; dilated. Lids swollen, bluish-red, l. then r., cannot open them; half-open in morning, eyes turned downward, pupils dilated, stupid drowsiness; trembling of r. lower; agglutination after sleep; inner surface and ball covered with yellowish, purulent mucus and bloody fluid, pressure on lids brings out blood or pus, oozing of blood on screaming and coughing; dried pus in canthi and on margins; canthi full of matter in morning; pain beneath upper on moving eyes and on shaking head; sore feeling in outer canthi, with denuded sore lips. Dryness of Meibomian glands. Congestion in white of r. inner canthus.

Conjunctiva swollen and dark red. Stitches in orbital region; r.; after waking, and in eyes, with pain as if pressed with fingers; in upper and inner part, through nasal canal into nose. Pressure in orbital region; *pressure in orbital region, sensation as if ball were compressed from all sides and obscuration of vision* (Nat. m.). Sensitiveness to light. Weakness in morning, by the light it seemed as if rays of light passed from the eyes to the flame. Blackness before eyes. Vision dim; with chilliness; obscured at side if vision is fixed upon a white object. Flickering.

Clinical.—Various forms of inflammation, ophthalmia neonatorum (purulent ophthalmia), keratitis, especially of the pustular variety.

Ears.—*Stitches, < stooping, with ill humor about trifles; from tragus into meatus; in region of r. tragus and spasmodic sensation, sometimes extending into auditory canal;* above l.; in meatus; in r. meatus; from tragus into external meatus, with contraction; in r. mastoid process. Tearing; (in r. lobule). Pressure in middle on stooping, as from a blow. Sensation as if stopped, and as if a bird were rustling and scratching in them. Dulness before ears in evening. Intolerance of music. *Ringing* in r., with stitches in r. tragus, extending into meatus. Roaring; afternoon; in r., with ringing; *as from rushing of water.*

Clinical.—Earache, with soreness, swelling and heat, driving the patient frantic.

Nose.—Ulceration of nostrils. Pressive stitches in bones. Dryness; in morning and stoppage, tension and heaviness; and pain on border of l. wing on touch, as if a pustule would form. Heat, > bleeding, with dryness. Fulness. Stoppage, with heat in it; stoppage, with mucous discharge; with rush of blood to it; with sensation as if he would have nosebleed. *Crawling; with lachrymation;* in r. nostril at 10 A.M., as before coryza; in forenoon, with fulness. *Irritation to sneeze, with crawling, dry heat, stopped sensation, feeling as if coryza would appear, also with pressure in forehead.* Sneezing; in evening. *Coryza;* thin, fluent. Bleeding; in afternoon; from r. nostril, with increase of inflammation of l. wing. *Sensitiveness to all smells* (Acon.). Offensive smell to beer.

Clinical.—Nasal catarrh, with inability to sleep.

Face.—**One cheek red** (Acon.) *in paroxysms.* Puffy, and hands. *Lips crack* (Nat. m.) *and peel* (Puls.); *crack in middle of lower* (Nat. c.); scabby ulceration on borders; dry; dry at night and sticking together, without thirst. *Stitches in jaw, extending into inner ear; in r. joint, extending into upper back teeth;* pain on opening as if masseters were cramped, extending into teeth; heaviness, with burrowing in alveoli; heaviness of lower at 1 P.M. Weak feeling in muscles of mastication, with inclination to hold mouth open and with salivation.

Mouth.—Teeth. Covering of mucus. Looseness. Stitches in lower, in morning; in roots of l. upper molars; in r. lower back, with pressure and with heaviness of lower alveoli; intermittent, back and forth, extending to eye, < drinking cold water, with swelling of cheek and salivation; jerking through roots of hollow back, with digging, and with heaviness of upper alveoli. Tearing evenings, < tea, with restlessness and heat in face; towards ear, with swelling of cheek. Digging in back, < lower, with pressure; in roots of lower back. Boring in morning on waking, with digging; in roots of back, with digging; in roots, < hollow ones, momentarily > cold water, then <, with digging. Aching in second and third back in afternoon; *A. after eating and drinking; while eating; after warm food; in l. upper after warm food* (Puls.); in diseased l. upper back during breakfast; (in warm room); < **after warm drink** (Puls.), < *coffee;* < night, when *they drive one to the borders of distraction,* with thirst and redness of one cheek *and hot sweat on head* (Acon.); of l. lower canine and incisor next to it, < touch of tongue; in l. upper hollow back, > dinner, < supper; with swelling of cheek; *as from exposure to cold air when sweating;* as if something scratched the nerve, from 3 to 7 A.M., then jerklike stitches; pressing-asunder; throbbing, in second and third r. lower molars, < pressure, > cold water. Drawing pain; *after eating and drinking; in indefinite teeth, > eating, < night, with feeling as if teeth were too long;* in lower, towards the front; grumbling. Grumbling in upper, with crawling. *Sensitiveness to touch; < hollow back;* < hollow upper; in l. canine and first molar of both jaws. Throbbing in roots of back, < r. upper. Sensation in upper back as if they were heavy and dragged downward. Distended sensation in roots of upper back, in morning, with heaviness.

Gum.—Swelling; of second and third r. molar, with redness, easy bleeding and pain on pressure; *sensation of swelling about some of the molars.*

Alveoli.—Stitches. *Burrowing in some molars, with heaviness,* **seeming intolerable and making him peevish.** *Fulness and heaviness of first and second molars, with burrowing and boring in their roots and sensation as if the alveoli formed hard, tense swelling.* Pain in r. upper; of upper second and molar; intermittent, of second and third upper molars, < r., extending into malar-bone, with feeling as if distended by wind. Pressure; of second and third upper molars, extending to beneath eyes; at 6 P.M., < lower, where it seemed to start from anterior foramen (mental foramen); of upper back teeth. Tensive pressing-asunder in upper, < second and third molars. Throbbing and heat in A. and gum of upper back teeth at 9 A.M., then about lower jaw, with boring and digging in roots of teeth, momentarily > cold water. Heaviness; in upper, < r.; of lower, < in last molars.

Tongue coated; yellow; dirty white; with slime; *blisters on and beneath it, with stinging;* red; smarting on back and on palate; *dry;* with thirst for water, loss of appetite, flushes of heat, sweat of face and palpitation, then unnatural hunger. Jerking from posterior end of hard palate to scalp. Spasmodic drawing pain in palate towards fauces. Scraping-burning in back part towards noon. Tickling in hard palate. Dryness in morning, with bitter-tasting mucus; in morning, then distention of abdomen and imperfect stool. Stitches in salivary glands. Pressure in salivary glands. *Salivation; of sweetish, metallic taste,* also after supper; tough. Foul breath after dinner. Taste bitter; *in morning;* bitter, aromatic; fatty; *like rancid fat, to everything;* sour; sour to bread; slimy; (putrid at night).

Clinical.—Various toothaches and neuralgias of the face. Extremely valuable in the distress of teething children.

Throat.—Spasmodic contraction of external pterygoid muscle; l. Sticking in parotid; r., with pressure. Pressure in parotid, with tension and salivation. (Throbbing pain in submaxillary glands.) Tough mucus, causing hawking. Hawking of mucus and blood; offensive taste to what he hawks up. Stitches in tonsils; r.; with sensitiveness to touch. *Pain; in l. side of fauces on swallowing, redness of velum and pain in fauces on pressure under angle of jaw;* in back part, < moving throat and swallowing; burning pain in soft palate, with irritation to cough. Pressure in pharynx, obliging frequent swallowing; P. in soft palate, with stitches. *Constriction of pharynx;* in morning and towards noon; afternoon; with stitches extending to base of skull; with pressure on hard palate; *spasmodic.* Tension in soft palate, then spasmodic contraction in it; tension and pressure, with pressure upon uvula. Oppression.

Soreness, with swelling of parotid; on swallowing, as from a plug. Rawness. Throbbing in back part. Swollen sensation in tonsils; in morning, with difficult swallowing; with feeling of hardness and heaviness. Food at supper seems to remain in pit, with fulness, nausea and eructations. Uvula feels too long. Tickling in soft palate at noon. Feeling in œsophagus as if a ball filled with air were raised into throat by contraction of œsophagus, with anxiety.

Stomach.—Appetite diminished; with pressure and tension in stomach and nausea, which was > by eating; lost; lost, but returned on eating. Disgust at food. Shuddering when food is set before him. Aversion to animal food; (to broth). Unnatural hunger in evening. (Desire for sauerkraut.) *Thirst;* in evening; with febrile heat and redness of cheeks; unquenchable (Acon.). *Eructations* (Puls.); after breakfast; after supper, with pain in abdomen, near l. anterior superior spinous process of ilium; *of gas smelling like bad eggs* (Sulph.); sour; almost sour, after eating; as after radishes; of burnt-tasting, salt fluid, in afternoon; of food. Hiccough. Nausea; in morning; *after morning coffee, with attacks of suffocation;* 8 A.M.; after eating; after breakfast; with salivation; with tension in stomach; faintlike; faintlike in pit of stomach, > eating. Vomiting; bilious; *sour* (sour smell from mouth); of food, caused at first by fulness of abdomen, then by nausea.

Rumbling. Stitches; in l. side near pit; in pit. Griping in pit, inclined to extend to chest, in morning on getting out of bed, > pressure, warmth and *bending double.* Pain; on r. side near pit; in pit on pressure; *and beneath short ribs, impeding breathing,* < *coffee. Pressure after eating a little;* at cardiac orifice in afternoon, not seldom extending to œsophagus; < cardiac orifice, with spasmodic constriction; anxious cries about pain at pit as if it were pressed down, with sweat; *as from a stone.*

Constriction. Oppression; in pit, with pressure downward. Tension; and in œsophagus; and in umbilical region; spasmodic, and above navel; spasmodic, and about navel; spasmodic, extending along œsophagus to throat, with apprehension and nausea from profuse sweetish saliva. Drawing, with pain and heaviness as if distended by a hard body. Heaviness. Fulness; after eating; while eating, with nausea after eating; extending into pharynx, with heaviness and tension, and with heartburn. Heartburn. Burning; in epigastrium, with fulness. Coldness in epigastric region. Sinking at pit, he is beside himself with anxiety, moans and sweats. Indigestion.

Clinical.—Gastralgia.

Abdomen.—Distention; in evening on going to sleep, with hardness; *after eating;* with tension; with hardness. Tympanitis in afternoon. Rumbling; < below navel; with feeling as before diarrhœa; with cutting as before diarrhœa, > pressure and rubbing; with pain and sensation as before diarrhœa, > emission of flatus which has the odor of sulphuretted hydrogen. *Emission of flatus.*

Sticking; and in anus; on walking, > pressure; while walking or breathing deeply, < in hepatic region; after dinner, with urging to stool, and stool; with urging to stool and passage of flatus; transversely across; before midnight, extending into chest, with thirst; into chest after starting as in fright; *as from flatulence, extending into middle of chest. Cutting rather than sticking, with salivation; C. before menses, with drawing in thighs;* C. in afternoon, extending downward into bladder, > emission of flatus and rubbing; on waking, extending deep into pelvis. Pinching. Griping; after a glass of water, with rumbling.

Pain; in morning in bed, > doubling up; with rumbling, urging to stool, which consisted of dissolved fæces, with rushing wind, the pain causing nausea and sweat, < on face; intolerable at sunrise; *intermittent, with flatulence in hypochondria and stitches through chest;* flatulent; flatulent, with motions of flatus as if it would push through muscles, rumbling and grumbling, pushing especially on abdominal rings, then emission of flatus; compressive; drawing. Troubles as in constipation. Tension, < above navel, with nausea. Sensation as if hollow, with constant motion in it (with blue rings around eyes), when the attack occurs in the evening it is associated with anxiety. Coldness, < region of kidneys, extending over back, lasting between scapulæ, with stitches in r. frontal eminence.

Upper painfully distended in morning. Nausea in upper/in morning on rising, causing anxiety, restlessness and peevishness. *Griping-tearing in region of navel and lower down on sides, with pain in small of back as if broken;* cutting above navel after dinner. Pain above navel. Gurgling in side extending into abdomen. Sticking in r. side; l. while walking. Tearing in side as if parts were rolled into a ball. Stitches in r. hypochondria; < walking and standing; in l. on walking, > pressure and retracting abdomen. Tensive pain in hypochondriac region, with tension around brain and dry catarrh in chest. Pressure in hypochondria and stomach after eating. Pushing outward of flatus in hypochondria. Sensation as if a hernia would protrude in hepatic region while walking; while sitting, > pressure and rubbing; below anterior margin of liver while walking at noon, > pressure and rubbing.

Stitches above pubis; in r. inguinal region, with sensation as if something would protrude; near r. ilium after violent running; near ilium, < l., when walking, < after eating, > pressure or bending far forward while walking. Cutting deep in pelvis, > emission of odorless flatus; spasmodic, in lowest part of abdomen in morning. Pain above pubis after dinner; near r. and l. anterior-superior spinous process after breakfast. Bruised pain in lower muscles. Dragging towards ring as if a hernia would appear. Uneasiness along crest of ilium on motion, with pain.

Clinical.—Flatulent colic. Colic, especially after anger, with red cheeks and hot perspiration. Indigestion produced by anger.

Rectum.—Sticking after stool. Urging to stool in morning on rising; after eating. *Blind hæmorrhoids; tendency to; bleeding* (Puls.). *Itching pain in anus.*

Stool.—*Diarrhœa; nightly, with colic so that she must bend double;* **hot, smelling like rotten eggs; green, watery** (Puls., Grat., Mag.), *painless, consisting of fæces and mucus; white, slimy, with colic;* watery, also with colic; painful at night, with nausea; with pain and passage of wind. Hard; and sluggish. Constipation; from inactivity of rectum. Diminished. Dark. Light-colored, with griping. Fæces coated with mucus, with mucus between the fæces (Graph.). (Undigested.) Like those of a healthy baby, bile increased.

Clinical.—Diarrhœa, green, slimy, mucous; chopped, white and yellow mucus; often of a changeable color; often undigested; often like chopped eggs and spinach; nearly always of foul odor, especially in children during teething or after taking cold; associated with colic, often with soreness of the anus.

Urinary Organs.—Sticking in neck of bladder when not urinating. *Burning in neck of bladder when urinating.* Micturition in a weak stream; involuntary M. Biting pain in urethra when urinating. Urine increased.

Sexual Organs.—Stitches in "bulbo-cavernous" muscles; itching, on margin of prepuce. Itching of prepuce and glans. Soreness on margin of prepuce. Erections; in morning in bed; violent; violent in afternoon. Itching of scrotum. Desire (later action). Emissions nightly.

Female. — Smarting-burning in vagina. *Acrid, watery discharge after dinner; yellow, biting leucorrhœa.* Discharge of dark blood from a newly-born girl. **Drawing from anterior part of small of back, griping and pinching in uterus, then discharge of large clots of blood.** *Dragging towards uterus like labor pains, with frequent urging to urinate.* **Profuse discharge of clotted blood, with labor pains in uterus** *and tearing in veins of legs.* Metrorrhagia; even in old people. Suppression of menses, with swelling of pit of stomach and pain as if it would be pressed down, swollen abdomen, labor pains and anasarca.

Clinical.—A very valuable remedy for uterine hæmorrhages, the flow is irregular, dark and clotted; sometimes there is constant oozing of dark, foul blood, with occasional bright gushes (Bell.). Membranous dysmenorrhœa. Menstrual colic, especially the result of anger. Severe pains following labor, especially if they extend down thighs, with great nervous excitement. Threatening miscarriage from fits of anger. During labor the patient is intolerant of the pain, the os is rigid and the pains extend into the thighs. Puerperal convulsions after anger, one cheek hot, the other pale. Suppression of milk from anger. Inflamed breasts.

Respiratory Organs.—Tickling in afternoon, with irritation to hacking cough. *Larynx raw; and scraping;* oppression in region, with constriction; tickling in morning, with hacking cough and expectoration of clear blood; irritation to cough, with sweetish mucus, which rises from trachea into larynx, but is involuntarily swallowed; feeling as if a fluid would rise out of it; burning. Hoarseness; *on account of tough mucus in larynx, which is only detached by violent hawking; catarrhal, of trachea, with dryness of eyelids. Trachea, whistling, wheezing and rattling when breathing;* mucus, with rattling respiration; *rawness in upper part; pressure, with irritation to cough* (Acon.).

Cough at night from irritation low in trachea; in a paroxysm at midnight, with which something seems to rise into throat, as if she would suffocate; on account of rattling mucus in upper part of trachea, with pain in place from which the mucus was detached (when the child is angry); dry; *dry in sleep;* dry on account of itching and tickling in trachea behind pit of throat. Expectoration of blood after tickling in larynx and trachea. Moaning and groaning. Short breath after a short, rapid walk, with palpitation and small, hard, rapid pulse; and croaking; and deep, with heaviness of chest. Rapid breathing.

Clinical.—Catarrhal laryngitis, with hoarseness and rawness in larynx. Catarrhal croup in children, with suffocative attacks. Bronchitis, with free expectoration of mucus, especially in children. Irritable dry cough from tickling in larynx. Expectoration only occasionally. (All cough symptoms to be compared with Puls.)

Chest.—Scirrhous hardness of mammæ. Rattling in r. in night on waking, > hawking of clear blood. Jerking in l. pectoralis major. *Stitches;* in r.; in inner part of r.; r., about nipple; in r., near sternum; near r. side of ensiform process; in r. nipple; anteriorly in region of r. fifth rib, also in evening, < deep breathing; in cartilages of r. sixth and seventh ribs; in streaks along l. ribs, above nipple and around it, then above heart, and in anterior half of seventh and eighth ribs; above l. nipple; below l. nipple; in l. lower part; anteriorly on l. lower part; in cartilages of l. sixth rib; to l. of middle of sternum; beneath ensiform cartilage, somewhat to l.; above heart; deep above heart during the day, < morning; in r. half at 11 A.M.; r. half in forenoon; beneath ribs and scapulæ when breathing; through chest on every respiration; from middle towards r. side after every expiration; between l. nipple and sternum on inspiration.

Tearing in clavicle and neck. Pinching transversely across upper in evening. Pain beneath sternum; under l. clavicle after long sitting; on r. side after long stooping, then in l., then farther backward; beneath sternum, impeding breathing; drawing, in r. or feeling as if repeatedly drawn inward; tensive, across chest on inspiration; burning, from beneath sternum to mouth. Pressure above r. nipple; below r. clavicle, and sticking in small of back. Constriction; on level with nipples; *in upper part, which hurts on coughing. Suffocative tightness, constriction of larynx, in region of pit of throat, irritation to cough* (Puls., Sulph.). Oppression; in morning; at 11 A.M., while sitting, pain while walking; as from flatus in upper abdomen, with pain, and with pain in stomach as in beginning of heartburn, then burning in spine. Contraction. Internal soreness, as if bruised. *Irritation to cough beneath upper part of sternum, without cough.* Burning, with dulness of head, as if he did not know where he was, with anxiety. Rush of blood.

Heart.—Stitches; above r. ventricle; during motion, arresting breathing; flying, in cardiac region and extending, now shooting, now drawing, now r., now l., down legs to dorsum of feet and ankles, then back to r. shoulder or hip or l. side of head. Nausea. Sinking about. Rush of blood. *Palpitation.*

Pulse.—Rapid; and irregular; and small and tense. Hard and full in morning on waking. At one time strong, at another small and weak, also irregular as to frequency. Small and soft; small in morning and easily compressible.

Neck.—Stitches near ear. Pain behind l. ear; rheumatic pain in muscles. (Tensive stiffness of muscles.)

Back.—Stitches; forenoon; towards evening; on inspiration; on l. side. Tearing; drawing. Pain; afternoon; 11 P.M.; on long sitting; *drawing. Bruised sensation in muscles of back and loins;* B. pain in morning on waking; on lying down to sleep, with drawing along nerves, extending into pelvis and parietes of abdomen; < stooping. Fulness after eating, with anxiety and tearing, afterwards extending to abdomen.

Contractive sensation in spine. Stitches in r. scapula; in region of r.; between r. and spine; in r. cucullaris muscle; jerking, in region of r. scapula in evening. Pain in r. scapula while stooping; in r. acromion. Bruised sensation in rhomboid muscles of scapulæ; B. pain between scapulæ, < stooping, and in intercostal muscles.

Lumbar Region.—Stitches; r. Pain in afternoon after sitting; pain after stooping, with bruised feeling and stitches; *in sacral region, < night;* unbearable, at night if he lies on opposite side, and in hip-joint; (labor pain); drawing paralytic pain extending into thigh. Feeling in bed as if it would be broken, with dragging and drawing pains extending from hepatic region over abdomen deep into pelvis. *Bruised feeling,* also after stooping; on lying down to sleep, with drawing along nerves extending into pelvis and parietes of abdomen; with drawing and pressure extending into walls of abdomen; extending with drawing over walls of abdomen to inguinal region. Drawing pain when stretching on walking. Stiff pain after sitting. Weakness.

Extremities.—*Cracking of joints, < lower, with bruised pain in joints.* Jerking on falling asleep. Trembling of legs and hands. Stitches around joints, < shoulders and ankles; around joints, < r. knee; in joints, extending into bones; in ankles, knees and wrists, extending outward and downward into long bones; deep in joints, usually with paralytic feeling; in arms and legs, following the nerves, with weakness; paralytic, from joints along long bones, > rising; wandering, in joints, extending into long bones, with feeling as if pain in bones would appear. Tearing; > tossing about in bed; in joints, < of arms; wandering; < arms and legs, now in lower, now in upper half of fibula, then along tibia, now in metacarpal, now in metatarsal bones and < along outer side of radius, then pain in knees and elbows, along flexor surface, in tendons and in bellies of flexors, < stretching joints. Drawing-tearing jerks in shafts of bones or in tendons.

Pain; in knees and elbows; l. forearm and r. leg; *in periosteum, with paralytic weakness;* wandering, < at the beginning; in joints on motion, as if they were stiff and would break; rheumatic, in bends of knees and elbows. Drawing pain now in fibula, now in ulna, extending from joint above; the drawing pains and stitches about joint seem intolerable and make him peevish; paralytic D. pain in various joints, in elbows, wrists, knees, extending thence along bones, then weakness. Drawing in articular ends of long bones, with digging; D. in joints, jumping from one to another, in morning; D. and tearng, < along r. forearm into wrist, with feeling in forearm as from pressure on nerves. *Soreness of all joints as if bruised and tired out* (Arn.), *no power in hands and feet, though without ordinary weariness.* Bruised feeling; in joints at 7 P.M., < r. wrist; even in bones, with stitches in ulna and tibia, which seem to start from joints; preventing sleep. Paralytic pains in volar surface of metatarsus or dorsal surface of metacarpus or lower half of bones of forearm and leg, < on their dorsal surface.

Weakness; sudden; of joints; in forenoon, < rest, > motion and going into open air, with heaviness and with drawing pain in shoulders and ankles, and especially weakness and restlessness of arms. Heaviness; in forenoon, with wandering tearing in r. upper arm, l. leg, back, temporal muscles, finally seated in l. teeth; on waking, with general weakness; with yawning and sleepiness. Numbness of hands and feet as if they would freeze.

Upper Extremities.—Stitches beneath r. axilla; like electric sparks in l. shoulder, extending into muscles of nape. Pain in r. shoulder-joint in afternoon, and at times in its vicinity,

Arm.—Stitches through r. into shoulder; along bones, < in forearms and in metacarpal bones, < r. Tearing in muscles in morning after waking, < in flexors of forearm; along nerves; < cool evening air; crawling, in shafts of bones,as if numb and asleep, extending into fingers. Drawing or tearing in articular ligaments and periosteum, from shoulders to fingers, after midnight, < later in night, > lying on painful arm. Paralytic pain along nerves to finger-tips; in muscles, < flexors, and extending along nerves into hands, alternately in both arms, at one time in median, at another in ulnar or radial nerve. *Stiffness as if it would go to sleep when grasping anything.* Going to sleep of l.; *going to sleep on grasping anything firmly.* Pricking, numb feeling, waking at night.

Upper Arm.—Pain in r. and in shoulder-joint. Bruised pain in r. biceps and brachialis, < pressure.

Elbow.—Stitches in r.; l.; l. at noon; on outer side of l. in afternoon; in r. in forenoon, with jerking-biting, and along ulnar side of forearm. Pain in r.; below internal condyle, as if ulner nerve were compressed; as after carrying arms bent, < extending arms. Drawing and paralytic pains and in hands. Paralytic feeling in region of head of radius and of tendon of biceps, extending into middle of upper arm; in r., as from pressure on ulnar nerve. Paralytic drawing extending along nerves, with sticking.

Forearm.—Stitches on outer side of upper half of r.; through middle of dorsal surface of r.; along ulna, with drawing. Pain in l. above wrist; drawing, internally from elbow to finger-tips late in evening; bruised, in muscles, < l. Paralytic pain along r. radial nerve, < lower half; in ulna, extending to tip of little finger; as from pressure upon radial nerves, also extending to middle of hands. Feeling as if too short, and on bending hand backward pain in arteries on flexor surface, < below styloid process. Arteries feel too short, < radial, with spasmodic pain; ulnar, with pain in arteries on bending hand backward. Spasmodic feeling in l. flexors as if asleep.

Wrist.—Stitches in vicinity; in l.; from r. to middle of forearm, with paralytic pain; drawing, extending in part along metacarpal bones into hands, in part along inner surface of radius. Pain; drawing.

Hand.—Swelling of veins on dorsum. Stitches in ball of l., also at 10 P.M.; on inner margin of l.; in dorsal surface of r.; on dorsal surface of l., then r.; on dorsal surface, between l. thumb and index; in metacarpal bone of thumb; in metacarpal bones, < r. and < dorsal surface of fourth and fifth, with paralytic feeling. Pain in l.; burning, in afternoon. Drawing in metacarpal bones, < interosseous surface, with stitching.

Fingers.—Stitches in r. index; in third joint of r. index; third phalanx of r. index; in little; on dorsal surface of l. little; in thumb; in first joint of r. thumb; about first joint of r. thumb in afternoon; in flexor surface of second phalanx of r. thumb; in first phalanx of r. thumb, extending forward from upper joint. Sticking-jerking in first joint of r. thumb. Pain in tip of l. ring; sprained, in thumb and index on motion. Going to sleep in morning.

Lower Extremities.—Drawing and tension in joints, < knees. Weakness; and heaviness.

Thigh.—Stitches above r. gluteus maximus; in r. nates; deep in l. nates; along l.; lower half of r.; in outer side below nates; on outer side of lower half of r., also on bending leg; on outer side of l. in evening, with difficulty in walking; in forepart of lower half of l.; upward in l. Tearing, and in legs. Pain; on posterior surface of r. when walking; on posterior part of r. while extending leg in walking, < inner side; in hips; indescribable, on rising from a seat and when lying if stretched out; in hip-joint as if dislocated, in evening on walking after sitting; bruised; bruised, on anterior surface on walking, with weakness; tensive, in r. while bearing weight upon leg with knee bent; paralytic, on outer side of r. Paralytic stiffness, with weariness like a bruise. (Compare hip and thigh with Gnaphalium.)

Knee.—Creaking on motion, with cracking. Giving way at 7 P.M. on walking. Spasmodic contraction in muscles, as after a fatiguing walk. Stitches; r., then l.; r., and in hip; r., and in l. ankle; on inner side of r.; outer side of r.; outer side of l., and in neighboring parts of thigh; near patella; deep under patella; in l. patella; in inner side of patella and in several places in joints; now l., now r., now both, with pain in popliteal artery as if too short; on outer side of r. in morning; in anterior surface of r. on bending it. Feeling on inner side of patella as if a blunt plug had been forced under it, < r. side. Drawing tearing extending to ankle. Pain; tensive, in hollow on stretching; drawing, extending through leg late in evening; spasmodic contracting, in r. popliteal artery, as after a fatiguing march. Feeling as if articular surfaces were separated; r., then l.; on walking. Tension. Feeling as if popliteal artery were too short while sitting. Sensation in hollow as if an artery were swollen and painful. Weakness.

Leg.—*Cramp in calves;* night in bed when stretching out feet, > bending knee. Stitches below head of fibula; r.; in middle of forepart of r. leg; on outer side below l. knee on walking; on outer side of r. calf, extending downward into leg. Pain below head of fibula at 5 P.M., as from pressure on ulnar nerve at elbow, extending downward, < lower half of r. leg; pain in peroneus tertius (?) as after ascending a mountain, with pain along extensors of l. foot, then pain along nerve peroneus extending to middle of thigh, < at lower part of interosseous ligament, with stitches in metatarsal bone of l. great toe, which feels asleep, and constriction above ankle. Pressure below head of fibula; as from pressure on a nerve; upon peroneal nerve below head of fibula; along peroneal nerve, with crawling. Bruised pain in muscles; peroneal. Feeling as of a broad bandage, < sitting, with heaviness. Tension in calves. Paralytic pain on anterior and inner side; in peroneal muscles, with bruised feeling; P. feeling beneath head of r. fibula, extending downward. Pain as after an exhausting climb; feeling as after a long march, > motion. Necessity to stretch to get rested. Weakness; in muscles of calves in morning; with inclination to stretch them. *Crawling in calves, with heaviness;* in l. calf, with weakness of it and of knees; C., gone-to-sleep feeling in l. calf. Prickling in calf, with stitches, weariness and heaviness in muscles. Heaviness in muscles of calves while sitting, with tingling-crawling. Falling asleep while sitting; feeling as if they would fall asleep.

Ankle.—Stitches in l. Tearing during rest. Sprained sensation. Constriction as of a band; of extensors above malleoli.

Foot.—Sudden swelling of one and of one sole. Spasmodic contraction of soles. Stitches on outer margin of l.; in soles along metatarsal bones; l. sole along first and second metatarsal bones. Tearing, with intolerance of bed-covers. Pain in middle of l. sole; in heel, as after long standing and as if os calcis would push through skin. Sprained pain in bones; in soles while lying. Itching pain internally in side of heel. Necessity to draw up on account of pain in calves and knees, on stretching out they fell asleep. Spasmodic sensation in muscles of soles. Drawing in l. sole. Weakness; nightly paralytic, with drawing pain in legs and ankles and pithy sensation in soles. Paralyzed sensation. Going to sleep; while sitting; l. while sitting.

Toes.—Spasmodic contraction, with tearing in limbs. Stitches in l. second. Bruised sensation in bellies of long flexors, as from a long walk. Sensation while sitting as if they would bend under and go to sleep, < great toe.

Skin.—Wrinkles in forehead above nose. Hard node beneath nipple, painful to touch, with at times drawing tearing. Eruption, slightly elevated, on nape, with biting, compelling scratching. Red spots covered with miliary pimples (Arnica). *Red rash on cheeks;* and on forehead. *Œdematous, unhealthy, injuries tend to suppurate.* Pimples; red, on back; red, crowded into a red spot on lumbar vertebræ and on side of abdomen, they itch, < night, with smarting and with shuddering about the spot, < evening. Inflamed pustule on margin of ala nasi; pustules on face, itching on touch. Ulcer surrounded by red areola and itching; *burning and biting pain in an ulcer at night, with crawling and hyperæsthesia to touch* (Sulph.); jerking and sticking pain in an U.; (previously existing U. became painful); (on foot, with redness around it, swelling and bruised pain). Sticking, > scratching, with prickling. Biting on various parts. *Itching of sweating parts;* I. of forehead; nates; sole.

Sleep.—Yawning; in forenoon, with desire to stretch; without sleepiness, with gay activity; incomplete. On waking always found himself lying on r. side, with hand under head; on r. side, with legs drawn up or on r. half of back; on back or r. side. Sleepiness; *during the day if he sits down, but inability to sleep if he* *lies down;* while eating. Difficult and late waking; from an unpleasant and dreamy sleep. Late falling asleep on account of unpleasant thoughts. Sleeplessness and attacks of anxiety, with vivid fancies; *S. till* 2 A.M. *on account of painful weakness in limbs, heat and restlessness.* Frequent waking in sweat, which ceases on waking. *Weeping and wailing. Starting up, crying out, tossing about and talking.* Talking unintelligibly, directing that obstacles be removed. *Moaning.* Groaning, with hot, clammy sweat on forehead. Snoring inspirations; which are shorter than expirations, with open mouth and hot, clammy sweat on forehead. Restless, with frequent waking and difficult falling asleep again. Oppressive, his face looks fretful and sad. Unrefreshing. Dreams; towards morning, with emission; frightful; anxious; quarrelsome, vexatious; fantastic; vivid.

Clinical.—Sleeplessness in children.

Fever.—Chilliness; at 4 P.M., during which he said things which he would not have said, with nausea in abdomen lasting till 11 P.M., then throbbing-sticking in forehead, < lying; in evening on lying down, with which sounds seem to come from a distance, nausea, uneasiness, tossing about, stupefaction of head and dead feeling in skin when scratched; in evening, at night sweat and thirst; on uncovering; on going to sleep; (after eating, then heat in cheeks); *over whole body, with heat of face,* **which comes out of eyes like fire**; (with necessity to lie down, thirst during chill but not during heat, after heat sweat with sticking in l. half of brain, next morning bitter taste); alternating with heat; (internal, without external coldness, except cold feet, with thirst, then heat and sweat, but if she puts an arm out of bed chill, and if she covers it in bed sweat, with tearing in forehead).

Chill on anterior part of body. C. in various parts, alternating with heat, at one time hands cold at another warm, at one time forearm at another upper arm cold, at another warm, at one time forehead cold and cheeks hot, etc. (Acon.). *Cold limbs, with heat of face and eyes and hot breath;* cheeks, hand and feet, with heat on forehead, neck, chest, then heat and redness of r. cheek; in dorsal vertebræ, whence shivering extends over body; in region of kidneys, with attacks of shivering; creeping, in back at 11 A.M.; internal, in lumbar region, with general shivering; internal, in lumbar vertebræ, extending over abdomen, with shivering along spine. Hands, with cold sweat on palms; hands, with paralytic stiffness in them, confusion of head and sensitiveness to open air; *fingers, and they are inclined to fall asleep;* feet, evening on going to sleep.

Shaking chill in afternoon, with flow of saliva from mouth, bruised pain in back and side and pain in forehead, then heat at night, thirst and sleeplessness. *Shivering in cold air;* S. if he uncovers; *with internal heat;* with external heat; creeping over whole body, extending into limbs, with increased urine, weak and rapid pulse, then warmth in whole body, beginning in head, with shivering in body and external coldness, then sweat; *on posterior part of body, of arms, of thighs and of back, in paroxysms, with external and internal dry heat, < forehead and face; in some parts, in face, then on arm, with and without external coldness*; on single parts which are not cold, with sleepiness. In back; at 7 P.M., with bruised feeling in peroneal muscles; *creeping over back and abdomen, alternating with heat;* in thrills from back to abdomen; between scapulæ; in morning on waking till 9 o'clock, < lumbar vertebræ.

Heat; *in morning after coffee, with sweat, vomiting of bitter mucus, then bitter taste, weakness in head and nausea* from 9 A.M. till noon; at night, with sleeplessness; at night, with restlessness; at night, with unquenchable thirst, dry tongue and stupefaction; before midnight when lying on back trying to sleep, with sweat; *even in lightly covered parts, those not covered almost cold;* dry; internal; *sensation of external* without external heat; external, with intolerance of bed-covers; flushes over whole body. In head; with confusion; with heaviness, < occiput; *head and face; rushing over head and face;* in head and face, with rush of blood and feeling as if sweat would break out while the skin remained very dry; flushes of dry, over head and trunk; burning in forehead. *Of face;* 6 P.M.; *after eating and drinking, with sweat;* with redness of cheeks; dry, with redness; in r. cheek; rising into cheeks; *in cheeks in evening, with flying shivering.* Of ears. Of hands. In l. foot, with sweat, then general sweat; *burning in soles at night* (Sulph.); burning and itching in feet as after freezing.

Sweat; in morning; (in morning, with biting in skin); at night from 10 to 3, without sleep; on slightest motion, with weariness; sour; *on covered parts;* < below temples; on face, neck and hands; on palms.

Chelidonium.

A tincture is prepared from the fresh plant of Chelidonium Majus, Linn.

General Action.—The most prominent action of Chelidonium is upon the liver. Symptoms of inflammation, of jaundice, of disturbed function of the bowels and kidneys and sympathetic affections of the right lung are numerous, and well marked. See also the symptoms in joints, skin, etc.

Allies.—Caulophyll., Podophyll., Mercur., Bry., China, Mag. c., Bap., Phos., Lyc., Puls.

Generalities.—Emaciation. Reeling as if she would fall forward, without vertigo. Trembling of whole body. Stretching. Twitching; now and then on various spots; in head, clavicle and limbs; of arms and legs, and in head on moving arm; on inner side of thigh, in feet and in back. Rising in anxiety and tearing clothing from neck and chest. Crying as soon as l. leg is moved or l. side is touched.

Stitches here and there; in afternoon; in pit of stomach, then in back, then in l. cheek-bone, then r., extending to temple; beneath r. scapula, then in perineum and testicles, and again in r. shoulder. Tearing and sticking here and there, extending downward, < in r. leg. Pain < afternoon, when it is spasmodic. Wandering pains in all parts; in upper limbs, in forehead, sides of nose and in upper jaw. Burning pain in spots on shoulders, trunk and arms. Bruised pain on moving about; B. as after a long march. Rheumatic or bruised pain in morning on waking, at nape and anterior part of neck, in shoulders and arms; R. pain now in r., now in l. upper part of body; drawing R. pain now here, now there, and in r. upper half of body, in shoulders, arms and wrists. Drawing pain from l. upper jaw to l. nostril, l. eye, l. meatus, l. temple, l. half of neck, l. scapula and l. ankle; in whole body, with fluent coryza. Drawing through whole body; towards noon; in head, teeth, jaws and shoulders.

General sick feeling. Affection as after a severe illness. General sensation as in influenza. Discomfort; *without knowing what is the matter*, necessity to lie down, inability to sleep and discontentment with everything. Excitement of whole body; from 10 to 11.30 P.M. Internal uneasiness; muscular U. in evening, alternating with pains in head and chest. Must be carried constantly.

Horror of movement. Inclination to lie down (China). *Weakness* (China), in morning; in morning after uneasy sleep; in morning on waking, also with sleepiness; in afternoon; at 2. P.M., with indolence and yawning; at night, with pain in kidneys; after dinner; when walking; when walking in open air; when sitting, with sleepiness; with inability to sleep. *Indolence, > open air, with prostration and sleepiness; I., with sleepiness without yawning;* of whole body, with uneasiness. Faintness; in evening on undressing, with anxiety in chest, trembling and short cough; on rising from bed. Heaviness; after eating, with disinclination for work and sleepiness. Numbness, with drowsiness; *N. in muscles of hepatic region and in r. side of neck, face and head;* (and insensibility, as from apoplexy, with trembling). Symptoms generally return at noon after eating (except the chill, instead of which there was internal heat, with internal burning between chest and shoulders). Amelioration from eructations; from a light-colored, pasty stool.

Clinical.—Great lethargy, debility, weariness and indisposition to make any effort (China).

Mind.—Weeping mood; about the present and future; crying at night when taken up and carried; crying all night, < when taken hold of. Hypochondriac mood. Sadness; thinks she has ruined her health by the proving. Fear at slightest noise, as if he had not a good conscience, or fear that pneumonia is coming. Fretfulness; in afternoon; on waking, with red spots alternately on both cheeks; about every trifle; without knowing what is the matter. Dissatisfaction.

Anxiety; in morning, with uneasiness; on waking at 4 A.M.; at 6 P.M., with trembling of limbs; in evening; at night, with fear of death, and with ineffectual desire to eructate; at night about death and being a soldier; after rising; till evening; > open air, with trembling, vertigo and heat of head; at every slight noise; with trembling of hands; with twitching of limbs; with uneasiness and palpitation; with oppression; with constriction of chest; trembling; sudden, with palpitation; in attacks, with nausea and retching; in attacks in room, with sensation as if sweat would break out on forehead; as if she had committed a crime, on account of which she must run away. Uneasiness; with willingness to die.

Anger; outbreaks of, feeling as if she could beat the children, and trembling from rage because she has no reason for doing it. Quarrelsome mood. Obstinacy. Silent mood. Inclination to talk too much. Excitement. *Apathy.* Absence of mind. Forgetful as to what she had done or was to do. Stupefaction; at night; with vertigo. Difficulty in thinking; and it seemed as if she would lose her reason. Confusion of ideas, as when half asleep, > towards 3 o'clock, then pain in lumbar region till night. Unconsciousness at night on frequent waking, with heaviness of occiput, which seems fastened to pillow if she attempts to rise; > rubbing soles.

Clinical.—Low form of delirium, quiet in character, with the peculiar pneumonia of the drug. There have been some cures of melancholia associated with enlarged liver and jaundice. The mental condition is generally heavy, lethargic, disinclined to mental effort; convulsions associated with disturbances of digestion. Patients often feel as if they had committed a crime, or that they will go crazy, or they become very forgetful, etc.

Head.—Trembling. Inability to raise it in evening on lying down, and necessity to lift it with the hands. Sticking; when coughing. Tearing; sticking, here and there. Aching; on waking after 4 A.M.; on rising, also > breakfast; in forenoon on entering house; towards noon; in afternoon; towards evening, with chilliness; in evening; at night, with pain in l. temple; on rising; < afternoon, and extending to occiput; > evening by a nap; > closing eyes; > rubbing soles; with throbbing in temples; with throbbing in r. temple synchronous with pulse, as if overdistended with blood; with twitches here and there in it; as after intoxication; contractive; rheumatic. Pressure towards middle; P. in brain after breakfast; outward, < towards forehead, < open air, coughing, blowing nose or stooping, but not while eating. Feeling in morning as if surrounded by a band, with internal heaviness.

Dulness from 3 to 3.30 P.M., with rapid pulse. *Confusion;* in afternoon, with vertigo; on waking from nap after dinner, with heat in head; < towards evening, with sensation of a lump in brain; < l. side of forehead, extending to occipital protuberance; > after shivering; with heavy pain about forehead; as after alcoholic stimulants. Heaviness; in morning; on waking; in brain; in middle; *extending to r. side of head, whence rheumatic drawing extends into r. side of neck,* then through arm into wrist, affecting injured fingers, and rheumatic drawing in flesh of r. side of chest; as if tightly bound; confused, in morning.

Violent throbbing in arteries, with pain extending over head from one ear to other and photophobia. Rush of blood; and to throat and upper part of chest. Intoxication. *Vertigo;* in morning after rising, with confusion; at 6.30 P.M., after dinner; on sitting up in bed (Bry.); on rising, with nausea and salivation; before menses; with nausea; with faintness; even to falling forward on rising from bed; as if everything were turning in a circle on closing eyes; as if turning in a circle, with shivering in upper part of body and unconsciousness; as from drunkenness, from 6 to 9 P.M., with nausea, warm sweat on face and internal and external heat of throat and chest; as if it moved forward while the occiput remained lying held firmly by the neck, when raising head in night on waking. Waving sensation in brain; after drinking white beer, with heaviness in forehead and top of head extending to temples; < moving eyes.

Forehead.—Sticking; in middle; in r.; above l. eye; in bone above l. eye, then in l. side of occiput; above l. eye, with twitching of lids; under skin; itching, in middle; transversely across; between eyebrows, extending into r. eye and l. temple and above l. ear; tearing, in l. eminence. Tearing in afternoon; T. above r. eye; above l. eye; above l. eye, extending into eye and lid and root of nose; between brows, which tends to press lids together, > eating; suddenly over l. eyebrow, extending over r.; in middle, extending over vertex, at noon after dinner, > pressure. *Neuralgic pain above eye* (Nat. m.), < reading in evening by artificial light; N. pain over l. eyebrow. Aching; in morning, < root of nose; at 4 A.M., and in occiput; towards evening, and in occiput; towards evening, with sticking in l. side of forehead; **in r. side;** over r. eye (Cedron); over l. eye (Bry.); in l. side from afternoon till going to sleep in evening; in upper part of bone; in direction of parietal bone in evening; in sinciput; > walking in open air; *extending to orbits, which on moving eyes are painful as if sore;* extending into nasal bones; over r. eye, extending to occiput; in l. side extending to l. temple; extending towards both temples, then to occiput also; and in temples, extending to neck. Pain as from a hard stool. Pain in r. side as from a blow. Pain as if brain would fall out in afternoon on stooping. Sensation as if screwed together from both sides. *Pain as from a band* (Carbol. ac.); after rising till towards noon; > *closing eyes;* lasting till noon, returning at 7 P.M., and in temples; *above eyes;* about anterior lobes of cerebrum. Drawing pain over l. eye. Drawing beneath bones. Dragging in cerebrum as if there were not room enough for it in the skull and it would press out through the ear, in which there is a noise as of a distant waterfall. Confusion. Heaviness; about 4.30 P.M.; periodical; dizzy; as if brain would fall out there.

Temples.—Twitches in l. Sticking in r. in bed, > lying on affected side, reappearing when he turns on other side; S. in l., with jerking pain; in l. after a sensation as if blood suddenly stagnated; twitching. Tearing; in r., < touch; in r., then l.; in r. and in eye, then in l. eye extending to l. temple. Neuralgic pain in r. Pain; in evening; *in bone behind ear* (Caps.); *in posterior part of r. bone;* in squamous part of l.; *in r., r. parietal bone, then over r. eye;* < l.; in r., with stoppage of r. nostril; in r., extending into r. half of forehead; in r., extending to vertex; extending upward; throbbing; drawing, in l.; drawing, so that the whole head is confused. Drawing. Tension in r., extending into r. half of forehead. Compression. Throbbing; in arteries, with headache; synchronous with pulse at night in bed before sleep, with sensation as if blood were rushing to throat and top of chest.

Vertex.—Jerks in a spot, with sticking and pain on touch. Sticking, with boring and with twitching of lids; intermittent S. in l.; paroxysmal, < rapid walking. Tearing transversely across. Pain; anteriorly in bone after supper; *extending back and forth to neck, whereby the shoulders are drawn upward;* so severe that she could not think, and in l. temple. Drawing pain to r. temple; occasionally to nape, with involuntary shrugging of shoulders, closure of eyes and when walking necessity to tread softly. Bruised sensation, and in occiput. Confusion. Pressure upon; extending to r. side of forehead and to l. side of occiput. Dizzy heaviness in morning and sensation of a band around head; tensive H. in upper half of head, extending to occipital protuberance, with sensation as of a band about head. Vertigo in upper part of head, < vertex, < reflecting, with tension and with soreness to touch on vertex.

Parietal Bones.—Sticking in r.; in l.; in upper part of l. in afternoon; paralytic, in l. Drawing pressure in l.

Occiput.—Sticking in r. side; *drawing, extending from l. side to forehead;* pinching, in r.; pinching, externally in l. Tearing in r., with stitches extending forward; close to l. ear, extending forward. Pain; from morning till noon; at 11 P.M.; at night; at night, waking her, with chilliness; at 6 P.M. extending around to forehead; in upper part; with sensation as if head would be drawn backward; with drawing pain in muscles of l. side of occiput, extending towards neck. Pain in evening on touch as if broken loose from skull. Drawing pain; with anxiety in chest, without appetite for dinner; *on l. side* and above l. mastoid process; in r. side. Drawing through l. Rheumatic symptoms when lying in bed with forehead raised. *Tension in r. side.* **Heaviness;** *with drawings downward in nape* (Bry.); *at night, as if it could not be raised from pillow.* Congestion of blood.

Scalp.—Hair falls out; on occiput. Hair matted and dry for four inches above r. ear. Pain in roots of hair; as if ulcerating, on combing. Sensitiveness; of vertex. Soreness of upper part, with heat on top. Sensation above forehead and on occiput as if hair stood up. Crawling on r. side; > rubbing; in upper part of l. at 2 P.M., not > scratching; > scratching. Itching on occiput; scratching, returning at 1 P.M.; on r. side of occiput at 5 P.M., > scratching.

Clinical.—The vertigo is very marked, associated with jaundice or with general hepatic and gastric disturbances. With the vertigo inclination to fall forward. Right-sided headaches extending down behind the ears and generally to the r. shoulder-blade, where it becomes seated. Violent neuralgia in r. side of head and especially over r. ear or r. cheek-bone, as a rule more or less associated with hepatic symptoms; with the neuralgia over the r. eye there is frequently profuse lachrymation; pains are cutting and extend upward and downward and may involve the r. ear, etc.

Eyes.—Swelling in morning on waking, with agglutination of lids. Sticking in r.; suddenly in l., with sensation as if eye were torn out. *Tearing in l.; and above it;* intermittent, in l. and in l. temple. Sensation of sand in them; in forenoon, with lachrymation; at 7 P.M.; > closing eyes. Pain < lamplight. Spasmodic pain in r. Burning pain in l. in morning on waking, > on rising. Pain as if lids were forced downward. Pressure; in l.; in r., then l.; < moving eyes, and in orbits, with sleepiness. Heaviness. Burning; in morning on waking, and in cheeks; on closing them; in r.; in l., with sticking in inner canthus. Itching; of r. at 5 P.M., > rubbing; in l., > rubbing; as after drinking liquor. Lachrymation; in open air.

Dirty yellow color of whites (China). Balls painful; *on moving eyes* (Eup. perp., Bap.); in middle of l., > evening on closing lids, with sensation as if so large that the upper lid could not cover it; in upper part, as they would be pressed inward, < l., > closing eyes; *sore sensation on looking up;* (tickling-itching). Pupils contracted.

Lids.—Redness; of margins; of conjunctiva of lower; of margin of lower, with swelling. Dry mucus on r. Agglutination; in morning, < l.; in morning, with foggy vision. Blinking. Trembling of r. upper. Twitching; of l. Clonic spasms, forcible closure on attempting to hold them open. Closing when writing. Sticking in l.; inner side of l. lower; in inner side of r.; sudden, in r. upper; in l. inner canthus, and burning, as from sand, with redness and inflammation, then weakness and lachrymation; itching, in l. inner canthus; jerking, in r. inner canthus, > rubbing. Pressure; on r. upper; in l. upper; in upper in morning;

at night on waking. Rubbing against ball; of upper in morning on moving lid or ball. Swollen sensation. Difficulty in opening; as if upper were drawn downward, lasting till towards noon. Inclination to close; and to lie down, as after intoxicating drinks. Heaviness. Burning; in lower; in l. upper; in margin of l. upper; in morning after rising, < l., with pain in balls as if they would be pressed into head; after slight rubbing, and about eyes; in l., lasting till sleep; sticking, in l. outer canthus. Itching of margins; of l. inner canthus; of l. upper, > scratching; burning, in morning on waking.

Orbits painful just above l. lid; P. < moving eyes; *pain above l. eye which seems to press down upper lid;* stupefying pressure in r., extending inward.

Vision dim; in morning on waking, < r. eye; when writing; with illusions. Letters run together when writing; and can be seen more easily at a great distance; when reading. Flickering; before diarrhœa; with vertigo; in a bright point during anxiety. Glare before r. eye so that she can hardly read. Glittering points, then blackness. *Blinding spot before eyes, and if he looks at it lachrymation.* Blackness before eyes, with sensation as if she would faint.

Ears.—Whitish wax, like mush. Sticking; *in r. external;* in l.; in l. meatus; in r. meatus; in r. meatus and in upper part of forehead; in r. external meatus; in l., with noise in it; in l., with difficult hearing; in l., extending to throat; in r., extending to vertex, then into l. ear. Tearing in l.; behind r.; in r. meatus and in temporal bones; in r. inner meatus; below l. lobule; above r. in evening; down behind r.; in middle, then on boring in with finger ringing; *from r. into r. teeth in afternoon;* intermittent, in r. inner meatus. Boring in r.

Pain; *behind r.;* above, < r.; above and beneath r.; in l. meatus; in r. meatus; above l., extending through l. upper back teeth. Painful pressing out of r., with tickling in it. Bruised pain behind l.; in lobule of l., then burning in r. lobule. Drawing pain from l. into l. upper teeth; behind and above l. when in bed. Drawing in l. and in l. back teeth; in l. meatus; from l. meatus into l. temple. Hammering sensation. Feeling as if too full. *Stopped sensation;* l.; with ringing before them. *Sensation as if a wind were streaming out of them, > putting finger into ear.* Heat in r. meatus. Itching in l.; now in one, now in other meatus.

Hearing vanishes when coughing, as if a hand were held over r. ear. Noises. Ringing; in r.; before l.; in l.; in l. when walking; with burning in cheeks. Singing on closing eyes, with ringing. Whistling before ears. Buzzing. Humming. Sounds as of distant cannonading. Roaring; in r.; with difficult hearing; *as of a distant wind;* before ears, as of a wind; before l. like a wind, from 8 P.M. till going to bed.

Nose.—Tip swollen and red. Tip trembling and twitching. Sticking in tip. Tearing in nostrils, < l. Pain in bones; in tip; in cartilage; in root. Soreness in nose. Tension in r. side in afternoon. Beating near nose, as if a tooth would ulcerate (she formerly had an ulcerated tooth in this place). Stoppage; of l. nostril. Dryness; in l. nostril, with itching. Sensation as of a cold wind through it on inspiration. Burning in nostrils; in l.; in mucous membrane towards tip, as in catarrh. Crawling in tip. Itching of tip; I. in l. nostril; in l. side, > scratching; in r. nostril, > scratching, then in l. nostril and zygomatic arch and across l. temple, > scratching. Sensation of catarrh.

Sneezing. Stopped coryza; in morning on waking; in morning, < warmth. Fluent coryza; on rising from stooping, with cough; with much sneezing; with heat; with hawking up of mucus. Mucous discharge. Watery discharge; in drops, < l. nostril, with burning on outer margin of nostrils. Bleeding of l. nostril; black blood from nose in morning on waking, with nasal mucus. Illusions of smell; as of black soap.

Face.—Yellow (Fer., China, etc.), **< nose and cheeks; the usual redness of the cheeks has a mixture of dark yellow;** grayish-yellow. *Redness, with flushes of heat;* R. at 5 P.M., with distended veins of hands, without external heat; of l. cheek; of cheeks, with heat. Red spots on chin; on cheeks; on l. cheek; on r. cheek, gradually involving whole cheek; on l. cheek, gradually becoming larger from 2 to 6 P.M.; on r. cheek, gradually becoming larger from 2 to 5 P.M., with burning. Pallor. Suffering expression. Sunken. Sickly look; with sunken eyes surrounded by blue rings.

Sticking in cheek-bone; in l., with boring, alternating with pain in l. upper eye-tooth; prickling, in l. Jerking in l. malar-bone, as if it would be torn to pieces. *Tearing from r. cheek-bone to ears and around ears, then to upper part of occiput along suture of parietal bone* (Bry. to temple). *Pain in r. cheek-bone and in upper part of occiput;* in l. cheek-bone; in l. side in chilly, windy weather, < touch and from 6 to 8 P.M., > magnetic passes, next day sensation as if swollen and ulcerated, but no perceptible swelling; in r. cheek-bone at 10 P.M., extending to r. ear. Painful spot in cheek as if swollen and suppurating. *Swollen sensation in r. cheek-bone* (Mag. c.). Drawing pain in r. malar-bone. Pain in l. cheek-bone as from a blow. Burning pain in cheek-bones, extending into eyelids. Pressive drawing in l. bones. Tension in cheeks between eyes and mouth; in l. malar-bone when lying, with drawing.

Lips.—Swollen in evening, with peeling of skin. Dry, hard and crusty; dry in morning. Papular exanthema with red base, on upper lip and on r. cheek. Vesicle filled with limpid serum, in mucous membrane of lower. Sticking in l. side of lower. Burning; of upper. Itching in r. corner of mouth, > scratching.

Jaws.—Sticking through l. upper. *Burrowing tearing in antrum maxillare.* Pain in upper; waking at night; in r. upper in bed; in l. side of both, extending to eye, near nose, and throbbing pain in temples. Burning pain in r. upper and lower, extending into cheek and r. half of both lips, < in evening in bed, with intermittent stitches back and forth. Drawing pain in l. upper and in cheek-bone, extending to eye, with heat in cheek. Drawing through upper jaw and upper teeth.

Mouth.—Teeth. Sticking in l. back; in r. hollow back; S., with boring; in r., with tearing, then in l. Tearing here and there; T. in l. in afternoon, extending into l. meatus; in l. lower, < chewing. Jerkings; in upper incisors. Aching; in l. upper; in l. lower; in r. upper eye-tooth; in r. upper in evening in bed; at night; in l. back at night; in l. back, waking at night; in all when speaking, and in both jaws; in l. lower on touch, with looseness; in three last l. upper when chewing or pressing on gum; < towards evening; in two last l. upper, < chewing; < every motion of mouth; in r., > in evening; in two last l. upper, with pain on touch; extending to r. temple; in upper, extending to eyes; at night, extending over l. cheek, then in r. side; in back and l. upper jaw, extending to l. meatus and l. eye, waking towards midnight; involving whole r. side of face, after going to sleep; involving whole r. side of face, jaws, lips and cheek, < warmth, momentarily > cold air or cold water; now l., now r., alternating with sticking in l. side of chest. Intermittent aching in l. Periodic aching; < at night, destroying appetite, extending to l. side of forehead, temple and ear, with heat in forehead; < warm food, < r., preventing sleep at night, with frequent tearing in l. ear and l. arm. Drawing pain; in upper; in upper incisors; in l. upper; in r., then l.; in l. back; in l. back and in cheek-bones; through r. upper back and through two middle lower incisors; through lower middle incisors in morning; extending into eyes; in l. upper incisors, extending into l. upper and lower teeth. Dragging. Elongated sensation; < chewing; in l. lower, with loose feeling. Heat.

Gum.—Boil, with thick yellow discharge; above l. eye-tooth, discharging blood. Redness and swelling of l. upper, and of l. half of hard palate. Bleeding in forenoon. Sensitiveness of l. upper to touch.

Tongue.—Coated; **yellow,** *with red margin showing imprint of teeth* (Merc.); *yellow; white;* gray, rough. White. *Slimy.* Sticking on l. side of tip. Sensitiveness. Inability to stretch it out or to open mouth as wide as usual. *Dryness.* Burning; on tip; as after vinegar. Difficulty in speaking.

Vesicles in mouth and lips. Mucus; full of stringy. Pain in palate, < motion of body, and in gum. Scratching, with burning, and in gullet and stomach. Burning; to throat. Dryness; in morning; at 4 P.M., with thirst. Watery sensation. *Salivation* (Merc.); *collection of bitter water, obliging constant expectoration.* Saliva tough and slimy; saliva sulphur-yellow. Hot breath, with dry mouth and lips.

Taste.—**Bitter** (Bry.); > *when eating and drinking;* spirituous; nauseating, sweetish-bitter; sourish or saltish; bitter. Sour; metallic. Sweetish; of blood in morning; offensive, of blood, with blood-streaked mucus in throat. *Pasty* (Bry.). Insipid; and nauseous, as after elder-flower tea. Bad to the dinner in evening.

Clinical.—With the disturbances of digestion and of the function of the liver, the tongue is yellow and shows the print of the teeth around the margin. There are frequently bad taste, bad odor in the mouth and accumulation of tough mucus.

Throat.—Skin yellow. Stiffness in l. side. Twitching, and in region of larynx. Mucus; thin; hawking of lumps. Choking; and in region of larynx; *as after suddenly swallowing too large a morsel;* and in trachea, as after strong cigars or lager beer, < breathing. Sticking; on empty swallowing; in region of larynx; in tonsils on empty swallowing, as from a fishbone. Pain in night, < swallowing; in l. side when swallowing; > swallowing, < pressing tongue against l. side of palate while swallowing; in forepart, extending to temples. Soreness in morning on waking; in region of larynx on swallowing food and drink, < empty swallowing; as from a cold. Scraping. Rawness; > swallowing. Irritation in morning on waking; towards evening, with scraping in larynx exciting fits of cough; > swallowing.

Constriction; *internally and externally, above larynx, only the gullet was contracted.* Compression; below chin. Sensation in pharynx of contractive cramp. Sensation as if a body rose, forced her to swallow and went down again. Sensation as if uvula had fallen into it in morning, with involuntary snoring when awake. Throbbing at night, and in top of chest, then griping in hypogastrium. Bubbling or trembling motion above larynx without pain. Sensation of dust in pit and in upper part of sternum; not > coughing. Dryness; on waking from midday nap, < empty swallowing; on swallowing; of back part and of palate; with sensation of dust in it; with constriction, obliging swallowing. Sensation on inspiration as if cold air were streaming through nose into fauces. Burning; in morning; in gullet; itching, below pit before sleep. Swallowing difficult. Œsophagus feels swollen and contracted, with bubbling, choking and scraping.

Stomach.—Appetite increased; morning and noon; for milk; longing for acids in morning; longing for vinegar and other sour things, and vinegar tastes less sour than usual. *Diminished;* for breakfast. Lost; for supper. Aversion to cheese; to cooked food.

Thirst; in evening; for cold water; longing for wine. Diminished. Aversion to coffee; to cold things at dinner, so that she would not drink though thirsty.

Eructations; in afternoon, at one time with heartburn; till evening; empty; *tasting of juniper berries;* tasting of breakfast; tasting of food, at 1 P.M.; sourish or saltish-bitter or bitter; bitter in night, causing shivering, then bitter taste. Hiccough. Nausea; on attempting to eat broth; > eructations; > lying down; > eating bread, with emptiness in stomach; with salivation (Merc.); with heat of whole body; rising from stomach, with griping and warmth in epigastric region; as if she would faint. *Vomiting;* of mucus; of tough mucus; of curdled milk during cough; of potatoes eaten yesterday, with a sharp, sour taste and scraping in throat.

Distention of epigastric region. Gurgling as if air bubbles burst and afforded relief. *Sticking in pit* at 5.30 P.M., **extending through body to back** (Bism.); S. in pit; in epigastric region; in r. side; in l. side near pit in afternoon when writing, during inspiration and on making body erect. Cutting; at 1 P.M. when yawning; in epigastric and umbilical regions, < pressure. Pinching in and below pit, < touch. Twinging now in r., now in l. epigastric region after dinner, then tension in it. Gnawing, > eating. Digging; in epigastric region, > eating. Pain; in epigastric region; in pit; in pit and opposite in back; < external pressure; > eructations; > emissions of flatus; > lying on l. side with legs drawn up, together with eructations; in pit towards evening, with oppression of chest and difficult breathing; with gas in it; paroxysmal; spasmodic, in pit; spasmodic, in r. side of pit; alternating with pain extending from nape to forehead and temples; as from a dull body, < external pressure.

Anxiety. Contraction; below epigastric region; in pit in bed. *Oppression;* on front of; in upper part of pit; > eructations; extending to clavicle. Distended sensation in pit. Tension; in pit; in pit on deep inspiration. Spasmodic pressure on. Heaviness from drinking water, with pressure. Cramplike throbbing in pit, causing anxious respiration. Ineffectual desire to eructate. Hollow sensation; with exhaustion when walking. Coldness (Colch.); in pit; with distention, as if cramp of stomach would follow. Heartburn.

Burning; in pit (Merc.); in epigastric region (Colch.); on l. side below ribs, on level with pit.

Clinical.—Generally the gastric disturbances are relieved temporarily by eating (Puls.); prefers hot drinks and hot food; sometimes very hot water relieves the vomiting temporarily. Gastric catarrh, with nausea, thickly-coated tongue (Bry., Ant. c.), etc. Violent pain in region of stomach goes through to back and r. shoulder-blade or over towards the liver.

Abdomen.—*Distention* (Mag. c., Merc., Lyc.); by gas. *Tension and hardness.* Rumbling; with colic; moving downward across umbilicus. Gurgling. Movings at 1.30 P.M., with twinging here and there; M. after stool, with sensation of a foul stomach. Emission of flatus; in evening; at night; with stool. Contraction of muscles, with pain about umbilicus. Increased peristaltic motion. Trembling, with diarrhœa.

Sticking through. Intestines feel as if torn out of body, on which account she lost her senses. Cutting; *after eating* (Coloc.); *jerklike,* not > soft stool; in evening so that she was doubled together; sudden, before diarrhœa. Griping; in morning, then three thin stools; at night, with emission of much flatus; as before stool. Digging, with nausea. Twinging and moving about whole, the pain in l. side extending into præcordial region, where it became sticking. Pain; in afternoon, with coldness; with urging to stool; with distended sensation; extending to chest; drawing through; *contractive, with every cough.* Fulness. Tension. Discomfort, > wine, with colic; as after a purge, then a stool. Coldness; in afternoon on drinking water; on drinking water. Heaviness.

Cutting through upper. Tension across upper. Pain in r., then l.; in l. walls in evening, < retracting abdomen. Drawing pain in walls at night.

Hypochondria.—Sticking in l.; in liver; in liver at 10 P.M. (Lyc.). *Pain through,* **and in r. scapula**; *in region of liver and spleen;* in liver (Lyc.), about an inch from stomach; between l. ribs and hip; between pit of stomach and umbilicus, and in sternum, with burning; *in hepatic region* (Bap., Merc., etc.), *in margins of ribs,* in afternoon, < pressure of clothes; *in hepatic region on pressure* (Phos.); **in hepatic region,** *extending downward and across umbilical region, as if constricted by a string;* cramplike pain in hepatic region on lying down; spasmodic pain between pit of stomach and navel; burning pain below l. short ribs. *Sense of distention in r.* (Phos.).

Umbilical Region.—*Spasmodic retraction, with nausea.* Rumbling above navel, passing downward, before and after diarrhœa. Painful collection of wind, > slimy diarrhœa. Sticking above navel; below navel, so that he must bend double, recurring when standing. Cutting; above navel. *Griping* (Sulph.), *then cutting in abdomen and across r. lumbar region, extending to back;* G. above navel. Pinching, then discharge of flatus. Twinging, with tension or contraction about stomach; T. below navel at 5.30 P.M., with coldness of body. Twisting above navel. Pain; in l.; above navel; to l. above navel; from 3 to 4 P.M.; above navel, extending to l. chest; spasmodic; burning; drawing, above navel. **Constriction transversely across as by a string** (Coloc.), *in afternoon till* 6; *above navel,* then griping in abdomen and six watery stools; *C. transversely above navel;* spasmodic C. Burning in intestines; below navel; B. in l. region and in l. hypochondria.

Hypogastrium.—Griping. Pinching in l. inguinal region. Aching deep in; above pubis; in l. iliac region; above pubis in evening; in inguinal region preventing walking, also at 4 P.M.; in r. wall, < inspiration; *cramplike, above pubis in afternoon, with frequent urging to urinate.* Drawing pain; *tensive spasmodic, in inguinal regions, extending from upper and outer part downward and inward;* spasmodic drawing pain downward in iliac and inguinal regions, extending into pelvic region; drawing spasmodic pain in inguinal region, preventing walking and causing difficulty in raising r. leg. Spasmodic drawing in inguinal region. Drawing dragging in inguinal region. *Constriction before passage of turbid urine.* Pressure on crest of ilium, < l. Tension in ilium, with pressure; T. in iliac fossæ.

Clinical.—Enlargment of the liver, pain under angle of r. shoulder-blade, or with jaundice, yellow tongue, bitter taste, etc. In jaundice, sometimes with clear urine, tongue white, stools dark, urine offensive. Distention of abdomen, enlarged liver. In all the hepatic and intestinal affections the pains are worse on r. side and generally are seated under the angle of r. scapula.

Rectum.—*Burning* (Sulph.) *and cutting, with constriction of anus, alternating with itching in anus. Itching; and crawling* (Sulph.). Sensation as if protruding, with spasmodic constriction of anus and rectum. Drawing towards. *Urging;* on rising; then three watery stools in quick succession, then relief of colic in evening; frequent, then hard stool, with pressure. Ineffectual urging; periodic, in afternoon; every half hour in forenoon, with griping in abdomen and constriction in rectum.

Anus.—External pimples. Mucous discharge. Sticking. Pain, and in perineum; *pain caused by stool;* > standing bent over; sore, also < lying on back or sitting. Drawing in evening. *Contracted feeling during stool.* Spasmodic constriction after stool. Swollen feeling during stool and soreness after stool. Crawling. Itching. Itching in perineum. Tension in perineum, with pressure. Crawling in perineum.

Stool.—Diarrhœa; with urging, then cutting in anus; *slimy;* frequent, in afternoon; frequent, in night; frequent, yellow, mucous, with blood at close; and insufficient; greenish, with cutting in rectum and higher up. Watery; *on rising,* **bright yellow**, *copious, with much mucus* (Pod.); and brown; and dark yellow; and frequent; frequent, copious, whitish, with nausea at night. **Pasty; and bright yellow** (Aloe, Pod.); *and light gray;* and dark brown; and frequent; with mucus; with pain in intestines; then pinching in abdomen extending to back and chest, > emission of offensive flatus.

Constipation. Hard; with pain; and dark brown; whitish-red; at first then easier to pass; and delayed. Nodular, difficult, with smarting in anus; N., difficult, with cutting in anus and rectum. Like sheep-dung. Dark; *dark yellow.* Light-colored; and ribbon-shaped. Whitish-red. Light red, painful. Mixed with blood; followed by blood. Slenderly-formed (Phos.), preceded by griping. Increased. Diminished; with itching in anus. Difficult, with pain in rectum. Frequent; the second after dinner. At unusual time. Delayed; and difficult; and whiter than usual. Omitted.

Clinical.—Diarrhœa, thin, bright yellow or white, pasty stools, or alternations of diarrhœa and constipation; in general, either with jaundice, pain over the region of the liver, especially under the r. scapula, or with symptoms of general intestinal catarrh.

Urinary Organs.—Sticking in region of bladder,

with frequent urging to urinate. *Dragging in bladder; with spasmodic trembling pains in inguinal region.* Pressure on bladder; with frequent and scanty micturition. Urging to urinate; with cramplike pain in urethra; with groaning and pressing to urinate; all day, with scanty passage; sudden; continual; frequent; frequent, ineffectual. Micturition in a vigorous stream; dribbling; delayed. Frequent micturition; but scanty each time; and copious, pale urine.

Urethra.—Discharge of a drop of fluid. Sticking when urinating and on motion of body, with cutting; S. in tip; in meatus. Cutting when urinating and afterwards. Pain when urinating, then pain in urethra and drawings in l. testicle. Burning; before micturition; during micturition; in orifice; near glans penis. Itching at orifice, with smarting as from urging to urinate, which, however, does not exist.

Urine copious; and whitish, foamy; and pale, at 6 P.M. then twinging; at another time scanty. **Urine dark yellow**; *and clear;* **turbid when passed, dark brownish-red, like brown beer** (Benz. ac.), frothing at edge of vessel, in afternoon; *stains diaper reddish-brown; red and turbid as soon as passed; lemon-yellow, turbid;* reddish; dark; foamy; of resinous odor; of acrid, sour odor. Urine pale; and scanty. Sediment in urine reddish, flocculent; grayish-yellow, flocculent, the vessel covered with reddish-yellow crystals of uric acid.

Sexual Organs.—Pain. Penis, sticking; pinching in a spot on r. side; pain; pain and anxiety as after a violent erection; pressure in lower part and at orifice of urethra; dragging towards root; itching; frequent erections. Scrotum covered with dry, red, cracked, thin scurf; red, hot and swollen; red, hot, with yellowish, fluid-like, flat blisters, painful to touch; vesicles flattened towards evening and raw, with raw, red, swollen and moist skin; itching; itching and crawling, with frequent desire to urinate. Testicles, sticking; pain; pain in r.; drawing pain; drawing pain in r.; drawing tensive pain, and in spermatic cord; drawing; D. in r.; D. from l. to hip; D. in l., with pain. Spermatic cord, drawing pain along; drawing.

Itching of vulva. Burning in vagina. Leucorrhœa; slimy, staining linen yellow; tenacious, slimy, whitish, staining linen yellow, after menses. Menses profuse; and too early; and too late, continually increasing for three days, with pain.

Respiratory Organs.—Larynx. Spasmodic movements of glottis before sleep, without cough. Sticking; through, extending outward and inward into throat. Pain; in region towards evening; on coughing; in cartilage, with sensation as if throat were swollen externally in region of larynx; burning. Constriction. *Sensation as if pressed from without against œsophagus, impeding swallowing but not breathing.* Swollen feeling; < r. side; at night, and in trachea, with tickling in larynx and short dry cough after waking; with oppression in larynx and trachea; and feeling as if the swelling hindered breathing; and choking gurgling in it.

Hoarseness; in morning; with dry cough and expectoration of lumps of mucus. Bronchial catarrh returned in evening. Heat in bronchi.

Cough; after waking and on rising, with sensation of dust under sternum; from tickling in larynx; from irritation in larynx. *Paroxysmal;* towards evening; from scraping in larynx, < *night, with pain behind sternum* (Sang.); < open air, with spasm of glottis during expiration; without expectoration and without previous irritation; *as in incipient whooping cough;* and short. *Racking, as in consumption, < morning, with much expectoration from deep in lungs, difficult to loosen, the rattling in chest < changing position after waking.* Hollow. Dry; in *paroxysm* at 4 P.M., and short; and short, from irritation in larynx. Short; at night waking her, also with pain in back and itching on occiput. With expectoration of mucus. Irritation to cough in evening, causing lachrymation; with dry cough, which relieved the spasmodic attacks; in short paroxysms. Expectoration of mucus.

Asthmatic attack at 11 P.M. when urinating, then nausea, > empty eructations, with difficult breathing even in bed. *Dyspnœa;* at 2 o'clock; at 6.30 P.M., with full pulse. *Breath short; and difficult, with oppression and anxiety of chest* (Phos.); *with constriction of chest;* during fever, and rapid. Heavy. Difficult; after dinner, with sticking in l. pectoral region extending backward; < walking. Rapid, > eructations. Obstructed as by a foreign body in bronchi. Necessity to breathe deeply. Longing for fresh air in order to breathe more easily. Inability to breathe deeply on account of stitches.

Clinical.—Cough loose and rattling, the expectoration raised with difficulty (Tartar emetic). Frequently useful in the bronchitis of children, with dusky red face, oppressed breathing, etc. Cough, with pain in r. side of thorax, either with severe bronchitis or with pneumonia. Numerous cases of pneumonia in r. lung have been cured when associated with symptoms of hepatic derangement, distressing pain under r. scapula. (R.-sided pneumonia, also Lyc., Sang., Iod.)

Chest.—Yellow color of skin. Stitches; here and there; **beneath r. ribs**; in r. ribs; in r. side behind ribs; along margins of l. ribs; in borders of ribs about præcordial region; below heart; in l.; l., then r.; r.; l. nipple; upper part; in l. clavicle; below clavicle; in upper part of sternum; in lower part of l. lung; in l. at 4 A.M.; in side at 4 A.M., preventing deep breathing; *in r. lower side at 2 P.M. on inspiration, < motion and cough;* in r. from 2 to 6 P.M., < inspiration, obliging her to speak softly; in r. ribs on inspiration; in region of r. nipple when sitting, not < breathing, then in l. side; in l. when sitting; in r., < deep breathing; with stoppage of breath; in r. side beneath breast, then extending into præcordial region; *anteriorly in lower part extending into intestines below umbilicus;* l. extending to back, with burning; in l., extending towards scapula; externally from l. to r. side, on inspiration; jerking, in l. clavicle.

Sticking jerking pain to r. of lower part of sternum, extending straight through to back, < motion and inspiration, the pain in back < bending backward, in chest < bending forward and > eructations, with restlessness. Jerking in sternum; in l. clavicle.

Pain; and in back; in l.; in l. ribs; r.; r., then l.; forepart; in upper part; in sternum, just above pit of stomach; between ribs and l. hypochondrium; in morning, < till 9 A.M.; in morning, obliging her to sit upright, < motion; in morning, > short and rapid breathing, and in back; in forepart in morning, preventing deep inspiration; in afternoon on inspiration, < motion; *between r. sixth and seventh ribs on bending to l.;* in sternum on every inspiration; on inspiration, < short, dry cough; in ribs of r. and l. sides on bending to that side; when walking, but not

< thereby; in r. side, in region of seventh and eighth ribs after sudden cessation of headache, < inspiration and motion, then pressure in brain again; *behind sternum, < inspiration; deep-seated in r. and in r. shoulder, < at axilla and beneath scapula, not much < by moving arms, preventing deep breathing, at times with throbbing in chest;* > eructations; in ribs, > supper; *in lower part of r. wall, extending into side, < inspiration;* and in back, extending to between shoulders; in l., extending to back, < motion; sudden, in r.; wandering, and in limbs; wavelike, in l.; intermittent, beneath l. ribs, then below r.

Pain as from an abscess deep-seated in r. at 1.30 P.M.; P. as if ulcerated in ribs, preventing deep breathing. Bruised pain in l., < motion, and in l. hypochondrium. Burning pain in sternal region, then a red spot, as of herpes. Drawing pain in afternoon; D. pain, and in pit of stomach; in muscles of C. and back; in forepart, waking at midnight, with dyspnœa; in sides, extending into abdomen; in forepart, extending to umbilicus; in lower part of sternum, extending towards r. side of spine; through muscles, extending to umbilical région, now more, now less severe; intermittent, in l. and in back. Drawing; in lower part, with difficult breathing and compression of chest; downward in r.

Soreness in r. lowest ribs; in l. lung; behind sternum; behind upper part of sternum on coughing; r. ribs on touch; seventh and eighth ribs on touch, < r., with injured feeling on inspiration; ribs on touch, < afternoon, when the cold sensation, pressure in stomach and difficult breathing return; r. lower half, < touch of clothes; l. lung, < coughing and sneezing. Anxiety. Uneasiness, making breathing difficult.

Oppression; of l. (Phos.); 4 A.M.; 6 P.M., with cough and expectoration; evening in bed; waking after midnight, with dyspnœa; on expiration; when walking; *as if clothes were too tight.* Constriction, as from a coat of mail; C. below arms. Compression in region of bodies of vertebræ, < stooping, not affecting respiration, afterwards felt after rapid walking, violent blowing of nose, sneezing or when stooping, and is more externally along spinous processes of dorsal vertebræ. Pressure upon l.; on sternum; over forepart in morning, with difficult breathing; P. in morning on waking, cannot get air enough on inspiration, > several deep inspirations; upon sternum on waking at 4 A.M., > sweat; *on inspiration after dinner;* beneath l. clavicle, extending into throat; *spasmodic, in a spot behind sternum, waking at night, extending into bronchi, with constriction in them.* Tension; in sides; on forepart; about base of inner side on deep breathing; intermittent, in evening; in muscles from upper part of l. towards throat. Burning in lower part; heat rising into larynx. Rush of blood; sensation of. Pulsation at base of r. lung and in liver; under top of sternum at 1.30 P.M., isochronous with pulse. Numbness in r.

Heart.—Sticking in præcordial region, with dry cough; in præcordial region, with palpitation, anxiety and uneasiness; in region of heart, obliging short and quick inspirations. Action imperceptible, also pulse. Beats loud and strong. Palpitation; afternoon, with anxiety; towards evening after sitting, during fatigue from unusual exertion; when walking in street and in evening in bed; periodic, at 11 P.M.

Pulse.—Feverish. Rapid; in evening; and full; and small, compressible. Large, full. Hard. Slow; and irregular.

Neck.—Swelling of l. side and of l. cheek, painful on touch. Cracking in vertebræ on motion, with pain in muscles of nape. Sticking in nape. Sensation as if bones of N. and scapulæ would be torn from their places. Broken feeling on motion. Pain; *in r. muscles and in region of r. clavicle;* in l. muscles; in nape; in muscles of nape; in upper vertebræ in afternoon on turning head; in r. muscles on moving head; in nape, < afternoon, and in l. shoulder and l. arm; in first cervical vertebra, < motion of head and pressure; < turning head to one side or bending it backward; at night in upper vertebræ, < motion, extending to vertex in a spot in which are jerks and sticking. Throbbing pain extending to forehead and occiput.

Drawing pain in nape; intermittent, in neck, over shoulder into wrist, < using arm, especially in writing; rheumatic, in nape, < turning head to r. or l. Drawing in muscles; D. in l. side and in l. meatus auditorius; *in nape; in nape down back;* paralytic; paralytic, in nape. *Tension in r. side, as if in tendons, extending towards shoulder, in afternoon when sitting.* Constriction of muscles as by a band; C. in muscles as if head were drawn backward. Heaviness in nape; *in muscles of nape; with tension, and in occiput.* **Stiffness;** *of nape;* of l. side; *of r. muscles on waking; on moving head, with pain on deep breathing; with cracking of vertebræ on moving neck; with paralyzed pain.* Paralyzed feeling in sides.

Back.—Pain; afternoon, and in small of back; < rising from a seat and from stooping; when sitting bent, extending to shoulders, > becoming erect; wandering, as far as between shoulders; pain as after immoderate exertion, in morning when turning in bed. Bruised pain on motion. Drawing pain; afternoon; extending into sides of chest; into forepart of chest and thence into walls of abdomen as far as navel. Drawing; on waking after 4 A.M.; evening; at night, preventing sleep, with headache. Oppression extending around to ribs. Tension, < stooping, with pain and with drawing around to chest. *Stiffness, and between shoulders.*

Scapulæ.—**Sticking beneath r.;** below l.; between; between in afternoon when sitting; below r. on every inspiration; from lower angle of l. through chest. *Pinching cramplike pain on inner margin of r., preventing motion of arm.* **Pain beneath r.;** in l.; below l.; in l. near lower angle; on outer margin of l.; in spine between; **in r.** *on waking at 4 A.M., < inspiration and motion of r. arm, extending after rising around r. side of chest and causing oppression of chest, the pains > after dinner till 2 P.M., then < till evening;* about lower angle in morning on every inspiration; in l. in evening; below l. on motion, and in l. side of ribs; *in r. extending through chest to sternum, with oppression; in r. suddenly extending into shoulder-joint,* with inability to move arm because it causes a sensation as if the arm were broken, the pain extending to wrist, > in forenoon, with coldness and stiffness of arm; sudden pain in lower angle of l. at 9 A.M., < touch. Sprained sensation, preventing motion. Bruised pain extending from r. down back. Drawing pain in l.; on outer margin of l.; in l. extending into l. chest; from l. into upper arm, then painful drawing in dorsum of l. hand; between, extending to small of back. Drawing on outer margin of l.; between, in afternoon; between, towards evening, < in r., and extending to r. side, with pressure. Oppression between. Tensive pressure below l.

Sticking in middle, near spine. Pain in vertebræ; as if sore, < motion and pressure on spinal processes. Pain as from a blow on l. side of spine where ribs cease, then on r. side of spine, then in r. tuber ischii.

Lumbar Region.—Sticking in l., < towards back; in region of kidneys in morning on rising; in l. kidney on deep breathing; < l. side, < walking; in region of kidneys, < motion. *Tearing in lowest vertebræ, as if they would be separated, on bending forward, or if he bent backward, extending forward to near ilium*, even felt on walking. Pain in last vertebræ, as if they would be broken; in vertebræ on motion. Labor pains in vertebræ, extending over hips and into abdomen. Pain; in sacrum; in vertebræ; in last vertebræ; in kidneys; in morning on motion; in last vertebræ at 8 P.M.; in last vertebræ in evening, on motion in bed; in l., waking at night; in kidney region from bands of clothes; in lowest vertebræ on pressure, and in scapulæ; in sacrum, < motion; in kidneys, < lying on back, > lying on stomach; > bending forward; in sacrum and region of kidneys, with sensitiveness to pressure; in a spot in liver and along bend of ribs, in linæ mammalis; in vertebræ in morning, extending into chest; in sacrum, from 6 to 10 P.M., extending to below scapulæ; *spasmodic, in r. kidney and in liver*, < 4 to 9 P.M., with sweat on forehead and hands; in last vertebræ, < motion, alternating with pain in scapulæ; in kidneys, at times pulsating. Sore pain in vertebræ; in lumbar and five lower vertebræ, < pressure and motion, some pain extending into the five lower r. ribs towards evening. Bruised pain on motion. Drawing pain in vertebræ, extending across hips down abdomen. Pulsations. Weakness, she cannot stand upright.

Extremities.—Trembling. Jerkings in arms and legs. Sticking, now in arms, now in legs; S. and drawing in l. index, on lower side of l. great toe, and on lower end of l. ulna, with pain in skin on these places as if burnt; rheumatic S. till 10 P.M. in l. hip, l. knee and r. elbow. Uneasiness. Lameness. Weakness; after rising; with bruised sensation. Paralytic sensation; in arms and legs. Paralytic drawing in joints of knees, hands and feet.

Clinical.—Rheumatic symptoms in upper limbs; pain in shoulders, arms, tips of fingers, the whole flesh is sore to touch; sweat without relief; all symptoms associated with hepatic derangements. Rheumatic pains in hips, thighs, etc., < r. side and r. knee, and œdema of ankles, with stiffness, feeling as if r. leg were paralyzed. Rheumatic and neuralgic pain in lower extremities. (Compare Caulophyllum).

Upper Extremities.—Trembling. Sticking in l. axilla when sitting. Tearing in l. axilla and farther forward towards nipple.

Shoulder.—Jerking in r. Sticking; in r.; in r. joint in afternoon during rest; in l. joint; in r., extending into neck. Tearing; in r.; in r. in afternoon. Pain in l. as if it would be broken or strained. Pain; *in r.;* in l.; in r. on moving arm; in r., < when arm is at rest; in l., < touching arm, and in l. scapula; in l., extending down outer side of arm; in l., extending into deltoid; in afternoon, and in nape, extending to wrists, < l. side. Rheumatic pain from l. to elbow. Pain in r. as after taking cold. Bruised pain in r. Pain in l., as if he had lain too long upon it. Drawing pain in r.; l.; from joint into fourth finger; from l. to fourth finger. Drawings; in r.; l.; paralytic, in r. Paralytic pain in r.; in l. and in l. arm.

Arm.—Twitching of r. Tearing in l.; in r.; in r., with loss of power in it. Pain; < l.; in l. deltoid and biceps in morning on motion; drawing through l. Paralytic drawing in l. Weakness; intermittent, in r. Heaviness. Numb and paralyzed feeling in r. in morning, > rubbing, with internal and external coldness. Paralytic sensation; in r.

Upper Arm.—Sticking in l.; anteriorly in r.; rheumatic, in l. Tearing in l.; in muscles of r.; in flesh below l. shoulder in forenoon; in middle of r., as if in marrow. Pain above l. elbow; on outer side of l. above elbow in morning on rising; in r., extending along inner side to fingers; above l. elbow, then in r. shoulder, in l. side, in r. forearm, extending from one part to another; on inner side of r., extending into forearm, then pain on inner side of l. forearm; paralytic, in l. Paralysis of muscles on moving them.

Elbow.—Sticking in region on inner side of l. arm. Cramplike pain in l., < bending. Burning pain at tip of l.

Forearm.—Swelling, and of hands. Round red spots on palmar surface, with burning pain. Sticking in r.; above l. wrist; through inner side of l.; extending into l. wrist. Pain in r.; P. on touch; drawing, in l.; rheumatic, in r. Drawing in l., extending thence into palm, in which there was twitching. Relaxation of muscles of r., with pain on motion and on grasping anything. Paralytic sensation in l.

Wrist.—Trembling. Sticking in r. Tearing in carpal and metacarpal bones of r. thumb; T. from l. to tips of two smaller fingers, > rubbing. Pain in outer side of l.; rheumatic, in r. Stiffness of r.; of l. in evening.

Hand.— *Yellow color. Veins swollen.* Dryness. Trembling; when writing. Sticking in l.; tearing, in bones of r. metacarpus, < pressure. Pinching tearing on dorsum of r.; paralytic T. in metacarpal bones of l. thumb and index and in their proximal joints. Swollen feeling in l.; > rubbing, with numbness, paralyzed feeling and inability to bend it. Drawing in l.; D. pain on dorsum of l. Helplessness when writing. Heaviness of l. on raising it. Numbness.

Fingers.—*Distal phalanges of r. yellow, cold and as if dead, with blue nails.* Trembling. Twitching of l. Cramp in l.; tonic C. in flexor tendons after waking, so that the hand was difficult to open. *Sticking in l. index;* in third joint of r. index, then in second joint; in r. middle; in index and middle finger (which had been injured eight weeks previous by a blow), with heat. Tearing in tips of r.; frequently in distal phalanx of r. little. Pain in r. little; in l. index; in r. thumb; as from a blow in second phalanx of l. ring. Drawing pain in l. index; in l. middle; in r. fourth; on inner side of r. fourth. Drawing in joints of l. thumb in forenoon; on l. side of l. middle, from middle to last joint. Falling asleep of third and fourth of each hand (compare finger symptoms with Caulophyllum).

Lower Extremities.—Tottering. Stumbling. Wandering pains in joints, < l., < rest. Bruised feeling. Drawing pain in r. Weariness. Paralyzed and dead feeling.

Thigh.—Sticking; in r. hip; l. hip; on inner side of r.; on inner side of l. Tearing. Pain in lower part;

in middle of r., in rectus femoris; on touch; in r. on rising from a chair; in hip on walking, extending to knee, so that the whole limb felt out of joint; P. in l. hip as if dislocated, < walking. Bruised pain in middle of r.; above hollow of l. knee; extending into calves, < walking and touch. Drawing pain in inner side of r.; in hips; in hips in afternoon; in l. hip, extending to foot; in lower part of rectus femoris, extending into knees, sometimes into patella; paralytic, from r. hip-bone to toes, relieved suddenly. Tensive pains midway between hip and knee. Pain as from exertion; in middle of r., also > rest. Numb pain in r. hip and knee. Paralytic pain above knees; in middle of r., then in l., then in l. leg, then in l. foot. Pressure on upper part of l. Swollen sensation above l. hip; midway between hip and knee. Weakness; when walking; r. thigh and leg, with stiffness and coldness. Falling asleep of anterior surface, with sticking and smarting. *Paralysis of l. when treading, and of knee.*

Knee.—Bending under when walking and standing. *Trembling.* Twitching. Sticking in l.; in r. popliteal space, also when sitting. Boring in r. and in forepart of ankle. Pain in r. as if it would break. Pain; *in r.;* in inner side of r.; in r. patella; *in l.;* in hollow of l.; in hollow when walking; in patella when walking; in l. on extending leg; in r., < motion; sudden, in evening, < stepping. Pain as after a long march; in evening, < on posterior surface of patella, < when walking. Pain in articular surfaces as if injured. Soreness, < pressure; in lower articular surface of l., < bending knee. Drawing in l.; in forepart of r., < bending; extending to great toe; to feet, with tearing; paralytic. Weariness, with bruised sensation. Heaviness, and in legs. Stiffness; stiff sensation in l., with burning.

Leg.—Swelling in afternoon, < about malleoli and calves. Twitching of calves. Cramp of calves. Sticking in l.; in r. tibia, above ankle; in l. calf, extending to foot; flying, in r. Boring in bones of r.; sticking, in l. tibia. *Pain below r. patella; below l. patella, < inner side;* l.; calves; on touch; paralytic, in evening, < walking. Drawing pain in calves; through l. leg; on inner side of l. in evening; through r. tibia to back of foot; drawing-down pain in l. calf. Drawing; in calves; in calves, extending to knees and thighs; paralytic. Tension; in r. calf in evening; in calves when bent, with sticking. Difficulty in moving when walking. Lameness. Weakness; when walking; when sitting. Heaviness; with stiffness. Paralytic sensation in l.; P. sensation till evening, with coldness.

Ankle.—Sticking in r. internal malleolus. Pain in l.; r.; r. when sitting; l., < walking. Sprained pain, < r.; in tibio-tarsal joint; < when walking. Weariness, with bruised sensation. (Stiffness as if sprained.)

Foot.—Cramp of r. sole, which, together with toes, is bent under, the toes seem dead, the cramp > grasping calf, < stepping. Sticking; in r., then in inner, then in outer malleolus; in a corn on r.; below r. inner malleolus; in r. heel; under l. heel; in l. instep at 3 P.M. on walking in open air; burning, on r. metatarsal bones and bones of toes. Pain on dorsum of l.; below r. inner malleolus; under l. heel on every step, and under r. inner malleolus; in r., extending into toes; as if dislocated; in lower part of l. metatarsus as from a blow; bubbling, in dorsum of l.; drawing, in inner side of r. tendo-achillis. Drawing in dorsum of l. Shoes seemed too narrow; pain in heels as if hurt by shoes, also in r. heel, < walking. Painful pressure below r. outer malleolus. Tingling as after a long walk. Paralyzed feeling; insensible to rubbing of soles.

Toes.—Sticking in great; r. great; r. third; r. fourth and fifth. Pain in r. third; r. fourth and fifth; two smaller l. in evening in bed, as from a blow. Drawing in l. great.

Skin.—Dark, as if sunburned, < on face. Red spot between breasts, with burning itching; R. spots, with rough points in centre, in upper part of r. cheek, with a circumscribed red spot on l. cheek; round R. spots close together around r. cheek, with painful pimples in their centres; R. spots, mostly confluent, with pimple in middle, on whole face except forehead, in morning, > evening, with burning on touch; red elevation on l. cheek, from 2 to 4 P.M., after relief of pains in cervical vertebræ, with heat in it; inflamed red E. in centre of forehead, with pimple in middle. Redness of l. half of face, with burning, swelling and tension, as in erysipelas, involving l. ear, the redness > after rising. A red areola around a scab on nates reappears and becomes dark red. Scabs here and there on cheeks.

Pimples on face; on back and loins; on r. cheek near angle of mouth, sensitive to pressure; near r. angle of mouth, with red areola; on margin of l. upper eyelid, where a white vesicle forms, which after opening has a burning pain; in groups on face, < temporal and frontal regions, on cheeks, ala nasi and upper lip, < l. side, with pustules; like chicken-pox, with red areola, on r. nates; indolent, on thick part of lower lip; red, on wings of nose; red, indolent, on shoulders and arms, on thighs and nates.

Pustules on forehead; on breasts; on cartilage of l. upper eyelid, with pain on touch and on closing eyes; with red areola, on l. side of neck, l. scapula and l. hand; red, with white tips, on thighs, with corrosive itching; on r. cheek, similar to chicken-pox; stinging, in various places. Furuncle about middle of r. under jaw. Vesicles on lips and wings of nose, then scabs; V., with red areola on r. cheek near corner of mouth; yellow, burning V. on r. wing of nose and l. side of lower lip, next day yellow scurf in these places.

Dryness of chest and neck, and as if contused. Sticking in afternoon, and in various parts of body; here and there in evening; here and there, with coldness, < in hands and feet; now here, now there, < on back, arms and legs. Itching biting of r. cheek, after rubbing it appears in l. cheek. Pain above l. eyebrow on touch. Burning pain in cheek near ear; above l. corner of mouth; in a spot below l. clavicle; in spots above tendo-achillis, with sticking in middle of them, the pain < scratching. Tingling on arms; on feet, with creeping. Crawling; on forehead; in r. hand; in last joints of r. toes; in perineum and penis, then on toes, tip of nose, then in perineum again; intermittent, in frontal eminences.

Itching; over whole body; here and there; here and there, < back, arms and legs; in various portions of upper part of body; of r. ear; in r. concha; face; abdomen; chest and along l. ribs; back; coccyx; in l. palm; on dorsum of r. hand, near joint of third finger; second joint of l. middle finger; ungual phalanx of r. middle finger, in bend of joint; legs; r. leg; calves and tibiæ; dorsum of l. foot; r. sole; r. ankle, then l.; l. toes; here and there on face in afternoon, only when sitting; now here, now there, on face and head, at 2 P.M., seldom > scratching; on inner side of r. calf at 5 P.M., not > scratching; on l. tibia at 6.30 P.M., then burning after scratching; of calves, < afternoon, and on tibiæ, back, forearms and sides, from hips to lower part of arms, on ribs. Itching > by scratching, on l. frontal eminence; in middle of forehead; on r. temple; above l. eye; of outer ear; r. side of neck; r. nipple, then on zygoma, then l. nipple, then above l. temple; outer side of r. upper arm; in palm and on r. thumb, but returning; outer side of l. leg; at base of l. toes; on r. frontal eminence after supper, and above upper lip. Itching > by rubbing, on ball of last phalanx of l. middle finger when walking in open air. Itching below ball of l. foot, with sticking beneath little toe. Sticking I. on outer side of l. arm above wrist. Corrosive, on arms and legs. Burning, in r. cheek near ear; anteriorly, on l. hip-joint; on hand that had been scratched by a thorn. As if sweat would break out on hips when walking in cool air.

Clinical.—Yellow skin, jaundice. Violent itching, with jaundice. Painful red pimples and pustules on various parts of the body. Old spreading ulcers which are offensive.

Sleep.—Yawning; in evening, with pain in throat as in catarrh, after which the pain in forehead was relieved; with stretching; with pain in sternum just above pit of stomach. *Sleepiness;* at 10 A.M.; in afternoon; at 2 P.M.; in evening; *when walking in open air;* after dinner. Desire to lie down after eating, with inability to sleep, with starting up from this slumber, and as he rose from it the headache was worse. Sleeps more than usual. Sleep from 7 to 9 P.M. when sitting; S. when sitting during the fever; sound, towards evening if she sits quietly; stupefying.

Sleeplessness; till after 11 o'clock; till midnight. Late falling asleep. Restless sleep; in forepart of night; before midnight and waking in sweat at 5 A.M.; disturbed by symptoms in throat and irritation to cough; and full of dreams. Frequent crying out in night; without waking. Frequent sudden stretching. Snoring, rapid, whistling respiration during a dream that I was in a dissecting-room with a corpse which sprang from the table and seized my throat. Waking frequently; before midnight; with confusion of mind; W. early, with twitching in muscles; W. suddenly, with sweat during and after sleep.

Dreams; lively; unremembered; disconnected; fancies without sense or connection in evening in a half sleep; of the occupations of the day; of journeys; vivid, of a journey; voluptuous; of a procession with music, so that he woke from the sound of kettle-drums; of great lice upon her shoulder and thinking long about whence they came. Anxious; of being a soldier, with weeping; of being killed. Of being buried alive; of dying, of a funeral and of a wedding; of corpses; of falling and bloody wounds.

Fever.—Chill; in morning on waking, with cold feet; at 4 o'clock, then heat, < of head, with coldness of legs; at 4 P.M., with general sick feeling; at 5 P.M.; towards 6 P.M.; about 7 and 8 P.M., with chattering of teeth; at 8 P.M.; in evening; towards evening, with chattering of teeth, cold hands and feet; in bed; < at 10.30 P.M. in bed, with chattering of teeth; with headache, cramplike constriction of chest and nausea; with nausea and oppression of chest. Sudden. Internal, < hands and feet; at 1 P.M.; I. and external; but not external. External; with heat, mostly in soles, where she sweats. Alternating with heat; towards evening, with thirst for *Weiss Bier;* C. at 2 P.M. as if dashed with cold water, alternating with dry heat, < in face, with constantly cold feet. Shivering; from 10 o'clock till noon; in afternoon; at 4 P.M., then heat; 6 P.M., with chattering of teeth, then heat, < in head; in evening; in evening on lying down; in evening in bed, with gooseflesh but external warmth, then sweat lasting all night; at night on waking, with trembling and heaviness in knees; before supper; after drinking water; in open air in summer; with nausea; with unchanged warmth; as if dashed with cold water.

Coldness of face, with pale cheeks; below umbilical region; of back; limbs; upper arm; hands; tips of fingers; lower extremities; knees; legs; calves and soles; *feet;* feet, < l.; toes; hands in morning; feet in morning; feet towards evening; lower extremities in evening, with stiffness, preventing sleep; arms and legs, < towards evening; from spine along seventh and eighth ribs to sternum, < r. side; of r. ear, with burning of l.; of tip of nose, with burning in tips of ears; of feet, then burning of them; in face, alternating with heat in it; in different limbs, alternating with heat; rising from neck into occiput; internal and external of r. leg, with swelling of veins of hands and arms; on inner side of r. calf, extending into popliteal space, a feeling as if the place were laid bare. Creepings in back; between shoulders. Shivering down back; in back; in back, with heat in head; from neck down back in afternoon; in hands, which are warmer than usual.

Heat. In morning on waking, with anxiety; from 5 to 7 A.M., with anxiety; in afternoon, with full pulse; every afternoon at the same hour; in evening in bed, without thirst; at night; with uneasiness; with oppression; with sensation as if hair stood on end; with restlessness and weakness of legs. *Dry; at* 4 P.M., *with rapid pulse and cold ears;* at night; D., with full and hard pulse. External. Internal at 4 P.M., with moist forehead; I., with internal burning between chest and scapulæ; I. at 1 P.M., not external; except in lower limbs, without external heat.

Heat in head; forehead; forepart of forehead; in skin of temple near l. eye; upper part of head; l. side of head; on scalp; ears; tips of ears; nose; tip of nose; face; cheeks; l. cheek; cheek-bones; back; in spot on upper part of l. scapula; in l. lumbar region and region of hips; hands; on dorsum of hand; in palms; in ball of r. thumb; muscles of r. thumb; l. leg; soles; in face in morning; cheeks in morning, with redness; cheeks in morning, with circumscribed redness; face at 4 A.M.; at 9 A.M. above eyebrow, extending to temple, then to forehead and vertex, < towards evening, with pressure deep in brain; in lower part of l. calf in afternoon when sitting; between shoulders at 1. P.M.; in cheeks towards 4 P.M.; at 5 P.M. in whole body, spreading from palms, not in feet; face in evening; of head, < after beer; forehead, with headache; forehead, with sweat on it; face, with redness; cheeks, with red swollen face; hands, with swelling; in head only internally; extending from l. ear over l. half of head; rising into head, with general warmth and distention of veins of hands. In flushes in face; at 2 P.M.; in head at 6 P.M., without external heat. Here and there in face as if blisters would appear. As from nettles in whole face except forehead, in evening.

Sweat; in morning; in morning sleep; towards morning; in morning on waking; in morning on waking after anxious dreams; at 4 A.M.; 4 A.M. on waking; *at night, < towards morning;* on waking; on lying down; on appearance of pains; in axillæ; palms; upper part of body from morning till afternoon; on forehead at night. Dry skin; and cool.

Chenopodium Anthelminticum.

A tincture is prepared from the fresh herb, in flower.

General Action.—Attention is called to the cerebral symptoms, especially in connection with those of the ear. Comparison is to be made with Santonine.

Convulsions, with insensibility and foaming at mouth, on recovery no remembrance of taking the poison. Convulsive movements of r. half of body, breathing heavy, stertorous, with a peculiar rattle, as if a ball were rolling loose in the trachea, pulse small, weak, frequent, eyes insensible to light or external objects, extremities cold, any attempt at deglutition threatened instant suffocation.

Disagreeable eructations, nausea, staggering, progressive deafness to the voice but great sensitiveness to the sounds of passing vehicles, each one of which sounded like the roaring of immense cannon right into his ear, the same sensitiveness to other sounds, for example, the tea-bell, also buzzing in ears, he would scarcely light a cigar before he would lay it down, so that the mantel-piece was strewn with cigars only slightly used, no disposition to engage in conversation, aphasia, at which he laughed heartily, whatever he did he repeated many times, he sat down at the wrong place at the tea-table, while grasping a piece of bread there was a spasm of r. forearm and hand, fingers were firmly clenched and hand firmly flexed on forearm, he was assisted to his room, his walk being natural, when being placed in bed he showed resistance by striking at me, he began to groan, draw himself up and toss from side to side, soon became unconscious, paralyzed in r. arm, next day impaired motion and sensation in r. side, r. eyeball insensible to touch, during the third day twitchings and stiffness of r. limbs, on fourth day unilateral convulsion, copious involuntary micturition, the heavy breathing, with flopping of cheeks, of apoplexy, yellow, frothy regurgitation from mouth, which, like the evacuation from his skin, smelled of wormseed, at times so profuse that it embarrassed respiration, during an attack of dyspnœa and while in a drenching sweat he was gently turned in bed, when there was a general opisthotonic convulsion, icterus, on the fifth day death in coma, with high temperature in axilla. (These symptoms retained though turpentine was mixed with the Chenopodium, T. F. A.)

Neuralgia in head and eyes. Pains through breast, under r. scapula and in r. shoulder. *Slight dull pain a little lower than inferior angle of r. scapula, but nearer the spine.*

Clinical.—Intense pain below lower angle of r. shoulder-blade, through to chest. Aurists have found in this drug a valuable remedy for torpor of the auditory nerve, as well as for inflammatory states of the middle and internal ear with the peculiar disturbances of hearing above noted.

Chimaphila.

A tincture is prepared from the entire fresh plant of Chimaphila umbellata, Nutt.

General Action.—The clinical record of this drug seems to point to its special action on the bladder, and, perhaps, kidneys and liver also.

Allies.—Uva ursi, Apocyn., Spiræa, Equiset., etc.

Pain in all bones. Weakness. Faint feeling. Melancholy. Nervous, cannot bear anything, hot, irritable, restless, thinks diseased state of blood irritates the skin, as before eruption of erysipelas, scarlet fever or measles, with itching. Stupidity and sleepiness. Partial unconsciousness, faint feeling, as if brain were paralyzed, mind gone. Headache; with pain in bowels; sharp, with internal heat in head, unfitting him for exertion. Desire to have head pressed. Heaviness of head, feeling as if he would fall down on it. Vertigo. Pain in forehead and above it; over r. eye; dull, heavy, over whole front and top of head. Weight in brain along brow. Burning in eyes, with sore feeling in lids. Running from nose.

Aching in hollow teeth. Tongue feels stiff and thick in the middle, cannot raise it. Mouth dry. Gnawing hunger. Nausea. Burning in stomach. Feels drunk, as if stomach were burnt up with liquor, as if it were hard, tough and dry. Hardness of abdomen, with swelling, pain, feeling as in dropsy of abdomen. Pain in abdomen; then diarrhœa. Uneasiness in abomen. Sharp pain in r. hypochondrium. Liver feels enlarged. R. side of abdomen feels sore and swollen. Colic between pubes and navel.

Urging to urinate, waking constantly. Urine increased, of a greenish color.

Clinical.—Catarrh of the bladder both acute and chronic, especially indicated when the urine is offensive, turbid, containing ropy or bloody mucus and depositing a copious sediment, with burning and scalding during micturition, and straining afterwards; it is very difficult to begin to urinate, the patient strains a great deal, urine sometimes fetid, concomitants of chronic cystitis. Sometimes useful in suppression of urine in infants. Urine very scanty. Acute prostatitis, with retention of urine and a feeling of a ball in perineum when sitting.

Excitement of sexual system. Stinging in labia, as in boils. Swollen sensation in labia. Pain in vagina, as if labia were inflamed. Pulse full and hard; F., then weak. Neck feels too small and tired. *Fluttering sensation in kidney region, sometimes in one side, sometimes in other, without pain or uneasiness.* Needle-like pains in sacrum. Full sensation in extremities, as if distended. Weakness of arms and legs. Pain from axillæ to scapulæ. Swollen sensation in axillæ. Paralyzed feeling in r. arm. Pain in bones of index. Needle-like pains in hip-bone. Inflammation of skin, with itching, then desquamation, different from the vesication of cantharides, the cuticle being little raised with water, the inflammation extending farther around the part, and next day the blister was circumscribed by an eruption, which continued to increase, appearing like a ringworm. Drowsiness, with weak feeling in head. General chill, with quivering of flesh. Blood feels as if on fire; with dry skin; blood feels heated, with prickling. Hot flashes. Burning of feet.

China.

A tincture is made of the dried bark of Cinchona Calisaya, Weddell.

General Action.—For general physiol. action, see Chininum.

Allies.—*Cedron*, Ferr., Ars., Nat. m., Nux v., Lyc., etc.

Generalities.—Dropsy. Erysipelatous swelling of whole body. Stretching. Jerkings. Trembling. Stitches when sitting, now in tibia, now in back, now in chest. **Pain all over,** *in joints, bones and periosteum, as if sprained, like drawing tearing, < spine, small of back, knees and thighs* (Eupat. perf.). *Pain in joints when sitting and lying, with restlessness of limbs;* **P. as after fatigue from a journey or exhaustion from bleeding or profuse loss of semen.** *Tensive drawing pain in almost all bones, now in one, now in another, > for a moment by lying, then more violent than ever* (Cimicif.). Bruised pain in all joints during morning nap, < the longer he lies, > motion and when fully awake; in joints of ribs, of limbs, shoulders and scapulæ, on touch or motion. Rheumatic pains; wandering, alternating with pains in interior of body, without swelling or fever. Drawing in bones.

Sensitiveness of all nerves, with general weakness (Ars.); S., *sight, smell, hearing and taste too acute, internal sensibility offended and disposition unpleasantly affected;* nerves affected by customary tobacco-smoking. *Dread of open air. Uneasiness.* Lightness of all movements as if he had no body. *Oppression of all parts as if clothes were too tight, after a walk in open air. Heaviness. Weight on joints in morning in bed, > rising;* on joints when sitting. *Aversion to mental or physical exertion.* **Weakness** (Ars., Fer., Nat. m.); in morning; on waking; *after dinner; after eating* (Ars.), *with sleepiness; after supper, with sleepiness; on rising from a seat; < walking;* in open air, with faintness about stomach and chest, but he has abundance of strength for walking; with loss of senses; of joints, alternating with extreme vigor. Inclination to rest, with mirth. Inclination to lie down. *Faintness.* Stiffness on remaining erect, with pallor and loss of consciousness; of joints on rising from midday nap. Internal sensation of impending disease. Complaints from a slight draught of air. Aggravation after mental exertion (Ign., Nux v., Nat. m.). Comfort in evening. Amelioration from hot tea.

Clinical.—Anæmia, with extreme debility from nursing or from loss of blood. Rapid emaciation, with indigestion, voracious appetite, undigested stools, copious night-sweats. Purpura hæmorrhagica after nursing, with roaring in ears, cold, clammy skin, painless diarrhœa, which may be bloody. Leucocythemia.

Mind.—*Sudden screaming and tossing about during cheerful mood.* Piteous, subdued whining and crying out. Weeping mood (Nat. m.). *Excitability* (Nux v.); *with pusillanimity and intolerance of noise.* Despair; with tossing about the bed. No desire to live. *Solicitude about trifles. Discouragement. Discontented; and thinks he is hindered and tormented by every one.. Absence of the usual lively mood, with desire to be alone. Anxiety; in morning on waking* (Nux v.); about 8 P.M. and 2 A.M., he springs out of bed and wishes to take his own life, but is afraid to go near the open window or take a knife, with heat of body; on waking from frightful dreams. *Ill-humored; and easily angered;* when excited (Nux v.); at other times stupid, perplexed, embarrassed; < caresses; with sighing. *What formerly seemed joyous now seems unworthy and shallow* (Nat. m.). Despondency (Nat. m.). Inconsolable. Taciturn. Earnest mood. Wrath so that he could have stabbed one. *Quarrelsome* (Nux v.). Disobedience. Want of docility. Despising everything. Irresolute and disobliging. Absorbed in himself. Indifferent to external impressions and disinclined to talk. Liveliness all the evening, with staring eyes. *Cheerfulness alternating with gloom. Many plans for the future;* in evening; grand.

Disinclination for mental labor (Nux v.); *with sleepiness. Inability to arrange his thoughts, mistakes when writing or speaking, reverses words, disturbed by the talking of others;* inability to collect his senses if he wakes at night. *Slow flow of ideas.* Slow perception, with aversion to motion. Periodic stoppage of thought.

Clinical.—Sometimes it has been found useful in confused delirium in anæmic persons or as a result of great loss of fluids. Rarely in nymphomania. Occasionally in melancholia during pregnancy or in chronic malaria. There is generally disinclination to any mental effort; general apathetic condition and indifference to what goes on about him; low-spirited and gloomy; or extreme irritability, with weakness.

Head.—Sticking, < l. frontal eminence. Tearing in many places, < walking or motion of head; sticking, in many places, < moving head; *jerking, in places, < motion and walk, > lying.* Aching; at night, alternating with frightful dreams; after dinner, lasting till bedtime; < *in open air;* with weariness, then coldness; now in one part of brain, now in another; *deep in brain, < walking, with constriction, < r. side of forehead and in occiput;* **as if skull would burst, brain beats in waves against skull** (Acon.); *pulsating,* with heat, coldness of hands and feet and repugnance to food (Fer.); *as if brain were pressing together from both sides and out at forehead, < walking in open air;* pressure towards forehead as if everything would be pressed out, > strong pressure with hand (Nat. m.); like a jerking towards forehead, < till evening, when it disappeared; as if brain were kneaded together, with excitement, uneasiness, too rapid attention and overstrained fantasies; as if brain were sore, < touch, fixed attention, deep thought or talking; bruised, on walking in open air; burning, with hot sweat on forehead; stupefying, in morning on waking.

Confusion; *with tensive pain in forehead and orbits;* with emptiness of head and indolence of body, as from night-watching; *in morning as after intoxication, with dry mouth;* like dizziness from dancing; like catarrh. *Stupefaction, with pressure in forehead.* Oppression, with sweat on forehead. Heaviness; in morning on waking, with weariness in limbs; < *turning eyes, with heat in it and jerking pain in temples. Rising of blood, with hot forehead and cold limbs* (Ferr.). Brain seems pressed by much blood. Intoxication; with inclination to be jolly. *Vertigo;* rising into head at noon; *at night on waking, so that he is afraid to sit upright; with inclination of head to sink backward, < motion and walking, > lying,* with faintness and staggering; with nausea, then heat.

Forehead.—Sticking when sitting; S. and in one temple; between F. and l. temple, > touch, when he feels severe throbbing in temporal arteries; between F. and r. temple, with violent pulsation in temporal artery; above nose and on cheeks; in r. eminence, < touch; externally on l. eminence, with vertigo and nausea in throat; burning, between F. and vertex. Jerking tearing in eminences. Digging in l. side when sitting unoccupied or occupied with something for which he has no inclination. Aching; in r. side; over l. orbit; above orbits in forenoon, < walking, > dinner; in middle in afternoon; *when sitting, changing to temples on bending backward;* when walking, then in temples; extending over head; moving back and forth on touch; drawing; tensive, and in orbits; itching, above orbits. Confusion. Fulness above eyes. Weight in morning, > noon.

Temples.—Sticking in r.; l. Tearing in l.; jerking, in r.; as if bones would be pressed out. Cutting, and in occiput, extending to orbits, < stooping and motion. Hammering, extending towards T. Aching; in evening; like dry coryza; *jerking, extending to upper jaw. Pressure on l.;* pressing together.

Spasmodic pain in vertex, then bruised sensation in side of head, < motion. Contractive pain in a circle in middle of vertex. Digging in l. side of head when sitting. Headache in side to which he inclines himself. Throbbing pain in l. parietal bone. Jerking from parietal bones along neck.

Occiput.—Tearing from r. bone to r. frontal eminence. Aching; as if cerebellum would be pressed out. Drawing pain when sitting; painful drawing on r. side; upon bone; drawing pain in l., > bending head backward; in articulation of O. and atlas, obliging him to bend head backward; to forehead, as if whole forehead were drawn together, ending in temples as a throbbing, > walking, returning when sitting or standing, > pressure. Dulness in lower part, as when waking. Vertigo while sitting.

Scalp.—Stitches in l. side. *Contractive pain on l. side of occiput; as if drawn to one point.* Contraction on forehead as if it would be drawn together in centre. Pain on upper part of head as if grasped. *Sensitiveness to touch, < at roots of hair.* Sticking itching.

Clinical.—The headache is generally intense, throbbing pain, with great sensitiveness of the head, it seems as if the skull would burst; this throbbing headache is usually worse in the temples, or it may be only in the temples; this temporal pulsation is often noticed as a precursor of malarial paroxysms; with the headaches the external head is usually extremely sensitive to the slightest touch. Violent anæmic headaches as a result of sexual excesses or after loss of blood, pulsating, even hammering, with flickering before eyes, > hard pressure, < slightest touch; sometimes a feeling as if the brain were moving back and forth and hitting against the sides of the skull.

Eyes.—Redness in afternoon, with burning pain and heat. *Pain on motion, with sensation of mechanical hindrance.* Biting in one, then other, with lachrymation; B. as from salt, with necessity to rub them. Sensation in night on waking as if swimming in water. Painless pressure as from weakness and loss of sleep. Sensation as in general weakness, as if sunken. *Lachrymation, with crawling pain in eyes and on inner surface of lids. Pupils dilated;* and almost immovable, with myopia; *contracted.*

Lids.—Gum in external canthi after sleep. Twitching of r. upper; l. upper; twitching, blinking, trembling. Closure from weakness and sleepiness. Tearing in l. external canthus. Pain; in external canthi. Dry sensation between lids and ball, with rubbing pain on moving lids. Tickling. Itching on l.

Pressure on brows, more externally, < motion of frontal muscles. Photophobia. Darkness before eyes. Vision of black floating points. Room lighted by a candle appeared in a blinding sulphur-yellow light, then all surroundings were of a shimmering rosy-red (this appeared as the headache suddenly disappeared during a sluggish stool, with tenesmus).

Clinical.—Retinal asthenopia, with transient blindness or with flickering before the eyes (after sexual excesses). Hemeralopia. Neuralgia about the eyes; ciliary neuralgia, supraorbital neuralgia (Ced.); the neuralgia < slightest touch. The weakness of vision and the neuralgia about the eyes are frequently associated with spinal irritation and great soreness of the spine, extending into the occiput and even into the eyes; the pains frequently < at night when lying down, but not always.

Ears.—Sticking from middle upward through brain; here and there in parotids. Tearing in lobules; in cartilage and external meatus. (Pain in middle); in l. on touch; drawing, behind ear, extending to mastoid process. Tickling. Throbbing, then ringing. Hearing difficult. *Deafness as if something were before the ear internally.* **Ringing** (Cannab. ind.); *with pain in temples;* in r., with tickling crawling as of an insect. *Roaring. Ticking as of a distant watch.*

Clinical.—Ringing and roaring in the ears, loss of hearing. Frequent neuralgic pains in ears, < touch. Hearing extremely sensitive to noises. External ear very sensitive to touch, sometimes inflamed.

Nose.—Redness and heat. Stitches in cartilage of septum. Tearing in back. *Pain in root* (Ign.) (*after heat of cheek had disappeared*), *extending to side.* Pressure across root, extending upward, and on eyebrow, > touch, with tension of skin of l. wing of nose. Sudden biting deep in l. nostril in evening, < compression of nose, sticking on every inspiration, then itching externally on back of nose. *Sneezing;* at beginning of fever; with coryza. Catarrh, with sensitiveness of nose and pimples on margin of nostrils and septum, which are painful to touch; *fluent C., with sneezing and lachrymation; trickling from nose; watery discharge, with stoppage; attacks of stopped C. Bleeding;* between 6 and 7 A.M., after rising; after violent blowing.

Clinical.—Smell very acute. Nosebleed in anæmic persons, with ringing in ears, or relieving headache.

Face.—Red; and swollen; *cheeks and lobules of ears. Pale; and sunken, pinched, sickly.* Hippocratic (pointed nose, hollow eyes with blue rings), with indifference, insensibility. Earthy. Changing color frequently. Sticking in l. side; in r. cheek, > pressure. Pain in r. side; picking, in zygoma and r. back tooth. Pressure across, < near nose and cheek, with contraction of lids as if upper and lower lids were drawn towards each other. Lip (cracked); in middle of lower when sneezing; (shrivelled); inner surface of lower sore and excoriated; *dry,* without thirst; lower painful near l. corner as from a corroding ulcer; sore sensation in r. upper, near corner, as after much wiping in coryza. Jaw, jerking, sticking in r. side of lower; tearing in l. side of lower; T. in r. before midnight; cutting-burning pain in upper when standing.

Clinical.—Facial neuralgia. Occasionally useful in erysipelas of the face, of the vesicular variety, with low delirium. Facial erysipelas in an infant, with hot, swollen extremities (Acon.).

Mouth.—Teeth. *Looseness* (Merc.)*; and pain on chewing.* Sticking extending outward in incisors; S. in r. upper back on inhaling cold air, with tearing. *Jerking tearing in l. upper back;* drawing tearing upward and backward in upper, then faintness. *Digging in upper back, > for a moment by biting teeth together and pressing upon them.* Pain; in crowns of r. back when biting teeth together; throbbing; picking, in upper back; in lower incisors as if they had been knocked against something. Drawing pain in l. lower; D. pain in incisors in morning; in upper back in morning, with numbness; in open air and in draft; in l. upper back, with feeling as if gum or inner part of cheek were swollen. Gum and lip swollen.

Tongue coated, < afternoon; on waking; white in morning; *yellow; dirty white crust;* (yellowish, not coated); whitish; *painful swelling posteriorly on side;* vesicle beneath, painful when tongue is moved; *burning stitches;* sticking in tip; biting in middle as if sore or burnt; biting on tip as from pepper, then accumulation of saliva at this place; sensation as if dry and covered with mucus. Swelling of velum palati and uvula. Bright blood suddenly came into mouth after an agreeable surprise. Mucus in mouth; in morning after waking and after exertion, and he believes there is an offensive odor from his throat. Scraping on palate. Sensation as if he had smelled too strong vinegar, causing coagulation of mucus. Sensation as of an offensive exhalation. *Dryness* (Ars.); of palate in evening after fever, with thirst. Contractive sensation in salivary glands. *Salivation* (Merc.); with nausea. Offensive breath towards morning, > eating.

Taste bitter (Chel., Bry.), *even to tobacco-smoke;* B. in morning (Nat. m.); when drinking coffee; *to everything, > after eating; to bread on swallowing, although it tasted good while chewing;* to food, < wheat cakes; to beer and the beer mounts to the head; in throat, obliging him to swallow saliva constantly. *Slimy* (Merc.), *which disgusts him with butter;* bitter slimy. Sweetish; to tobacco-smoke; *S., then sour.* Sour; to coffee; to black bread; as if stomach had been disordered by fruit. Salt; to food, then bitter; sweetish salt; bitter, salt to bread and butter. Watery and flat. *Flat, qualmish* after drinking. Nauseous, at times bitter, < morning, with unpleasant taste to food; N. as after cheese. Acrid in posterior part of palate from tobacco-smoking, with biting. Little to supper. Lost when smoking tobacco; after smoking tobacco.

Clinical.—Neuralgic toothache > clenching teeth tightly, yet < slightly touching teeth, in anæmic persons. Chronic salivation, the effect of mercurial poisoning.

Throat.—Submaxillary glands painful, < touch and motion of neck. Choking in r. submaxillary gland, < touch and motion of neck, with pinching. Choking and contraction in gullet. Sticking in evening when breathing after lying down, > swallowing; in r. side on swallowing; from a draught of air. Scraping, < on margin of larynx, as after rancid eructations or heartburn. Roughness. Contractive sensation. Swollen sensation internally and when swallowing sticking on l. side of tongue, with pain in that spot on talking or breathing. Sensation as if food remained in upper part. Sensation in pit as if it would become sore, sensation when swallowing like a sore throat although swallowing does not hurt it. Tension in gullet on bending head backward. Empty feeling in pharynx and œsophagus. Dryness, with cool breath. Swallowing painful, with swollen submaxillary glands and pain in them on swallowing; difficult on account of narrow feeling. Contraction of muscles of œsophagus.

Stomach.—*Appetite increased;* at 8 A.M. without knowing what he wishes to eat; in afternoon; *for various things but does not know exactly what;* for sour cherries; ravenous, with nausea; ravenous, with insipid taste; *hunger but want of appetite, food tastes natural yet is disagreeable in mouth;* relishes supper, but is immediately satiated (Lyc.); **indifference to eating and drinking,** *only while eating appetite and natural taste to food return;* little appetite at noon; dinner is eaten without relish; does not relish tobacco-smoking. Anorexia; before and after noon, with ineffectual desire to vomit.

Thirst; *in evening after fever, with hunger, then after eating coldness and rumbling in abdomen; after shivering through skin; after chill;* (during chill); *during sweat on back and forehead after fever;* < morning; then heat over body, with throbbing in all bloodvessels, burning in ears and forehead, internal sensation in cheeks, hands and feet as if too hot; for cold water, with chill and heat, < morning after waking; for wine; little; none when eating. *Aversion to coffee* (Nux v.); to beer (Nux v.); to water, with longing for beer (Nux v.).

Eructations; after eating; *empty;* as from nausea, also with colic; bitter, also after eating; bitter, sourish, after bread and butter; tasting of food; of badly tasting mucus; hot, then taste of China beginning at root of tongue and spreading through mouth; incomplete, sourish, after milk; something half way between E. and sobbing. Nausea; when he hears not unpleasant things spoken of, with aversion to labor, sleepiness by day and yellow color of eyeballs; > eating, with flushes of heat and orgasm of blood; in region of pit of throat after eating. Vomiting; at 11.15 A.M., principally of water, of sour taste, of penetrating odor, like the bark.

Spasm in cardiac region. Sticking here and there, and in abdomen; S. in pit; in pit during inspiration; in pit extending to sternum; jerking. Clawing. *Soreness in pit mornings, with pain as from pressure on a sore place.* Pressure; *after eating a little;* after eating vegetables, then flatulence, then vomiting, then burning extending half way up chest; > while eating; in region, > rising from a seat; below pit as if everything were excoriated, then violent diarrhœa. Constriction in morning when lying on side, > lying on back. Compression in pit, impeding respiration. Oppression. Fulness; after eating; *as full for a long time after a meal as when he had just eaten, the food seems to stick high up* (Lyc.). Sensation as if he had eaten, drunk and smoked to satiety (Lyc.). Weight. *Emptiness, with nausea.* Nauseous anxiety when sitting after a moderate meal followed by a walk, together with hunger. Coldness. Agreeable warmth from region to navel, with tasteless eructation. (Indigestion); of supper. *Disordered by milk* (Nit. ac., Nux v., Sulph.); by too much food.

Clinical.—Dyspepsia, constant satiety, with coldness in stomach, craving for pungent spices and sour things and stimulants; digestion extremely slow; after eating he feels full, drowsy, taste of the food rises, with dyspnœa, etc. Dyspepsia, with painful pressure and distention in region of stomach after eating and drinking a little. Appetite entirely lost, and after eating a little loud belching and inability to work. Acid dyspepsia, heartburn even after milk, constant satiety, no relief from belching gas. After hæmorrhage from the stomach, with great sensitiveness of the stomach and great prostration, etc., the abdomen sensitive over the region of the liver, which is sometimes swollen (compare gastric symptoms with *Lyc.*).

Abdomen.—*Distention; after eating; after a moderate supper* (Lyc.), *with griping and here and there sharp pain;* in morning without flatulence; until eructations; with colic and diarrhœa; *as from flatulent food and much drink.* **Fermentation from fruit** (Ars., Bry., Puls.) (cherries). *Flatulence. Rumbling; between 6 and 10 P.M., with movement of flatus and aching, then emission of flatus.* Rattling. Commotion. *Emission of flatus; offensive* (compare Carbo veg.)

Sticking when sitting, extending downward on inspiration; griping S. Cutting at noon; during and after passage of whitish, turbid urine, with pressure; shooting in all directions before passage of flatus. *Griping;* towards evening when walking; after drinking, as after a purge; > rising from a seat; *with pain on passage of flatus;* with hunger and weariness. Pain like a pinching and drawing, < sitting. Cold, colicky cramp, then diarrhœa. Sharp pain. *Colic before stool; before passage of flatus;* during digestion; *with thirst; flatulent;* pain in evening when sitting, as before diarrhœa; spasmodic, composed of pressure and constriction; bruised, in muscles; contractive, in evening when sitting. Contracted sensation, with rumbling in lower. Drawing, with emission of flatus and hard, difficult stool. Heaviness. Warmth.

Sides.—Crackling downward and backward in l., as if in ascending colon. Drawing-jerking pain when eating. Drawing pain in r. on walking. Pressure in both sides as if stool should follow but could not. Beating in r.

Upper.—Rumbling. *Swelling of liver* (Chel., Merc., Lyc.). Sticking in several parts in morning in bed; in spleen (*Cedron*), on walking; in hepatic region, beneath ribs; in hepatic region on expiration, extending outward; below l. ribs, extending outward, < inspiration; pinching, in l. hypochondrium; pinching, below region of stomach in evening, as before diarrhœa. Cutting as if spleen were hardened. Pinching, > bending double, alternating with nausea, urging to stool and shaking chill all over, then pressure in upper abdomen. *Intermitting pressure in hepatic region while standing, > bending forward, with pain on touch as if suppurating. Fulness after eating, the food remains long.* Constriction. *Internal coldness after every swallow of drink, renewed on every inspiration* (compare Ars.).

Umbilical Region.—*Sticking on l. side below umbilicus on walking rapidly and afterwards;* in r. side above umbilicus, < touch; in l. side and at same time below r. nipple, extending inward. Tearing; below umbilicus, with rumbling; on r. side, extending into hypogastrium, > bending backward. Cutting, with cold sweat on forehead; attacks of C. Griping externally below r. side of umbilicus in evening when sitting. Pinching in evening in bed; above umbilicus, noon and evening after moderate eating, < motion, > rest; above umbilicus on rising after stooping, with constriction. Colicky spasms. *Colic, with shivering.* Pain on sides below umbilicus after eating. Pressure. Contraction in r. side below umbilicus when sitting, as from an induration. Heat.

Lower.—Painful distention. Gurgling. Increased peristaltic motion, with pressure. Sticking in l., in region of kidney; in bend of groin, on mons veneris, < walking. Tearing on l. side near mons veneris. Griping drawing back and forth above mons veneris as before diarrhœa, when sitting, with short passages of flatus. Pressure in l. Pain during chill; in region of cæcum when sitting; paroxysmal cramplike, in groin when standing; flatulent, with constriction and tension, the flatus endeavored in vain to expel itself, with tension under short ribs and anxiety; sore, in ring, with sensation as if a hernia would protrude through the ring. Drawing in bend of groin when sitting, < tendon (of psoric muscle).

Clinical.—Gastro-duodenal catarrh, especially with yellow tongue, oppressive headache at night, loathing of food and yet canine hunger. Enlarged spleen, which is painful (especially in chronic malarial poisoning) (compare Ceanothus, Cedron); the pains in the spleen are acute and sticking. General distention of abdomen, with desire to eructate gas, which affords no relief. The fermentation which results from the acid dyspepsia involves the whole abdomen and there are a great deal of rumbling and pains of different sorts. Gall-stone colic (Dr. Thayer declares that China 6th will permanently cure a tendency to gall-stone colic, with all the attendant symptoms). Jaundice in nursing children, abdomen tympanitic, spleen and liver enlarged.

Rectum.—Sticking in lower part, < in sphincter; during stool, then sticking drawing. Tearing when in bed, with tearing jerks. *Pressure.* Contractive pain, < sitting; spasmodic, extending through urethra to glans penis and through testicles, in evening. Burning pain after midday nap. Crawling as from ascarides and discharge of many of them; C. as from ascarides after stool. Urging to stool; in morning soon after rising; to thin stool; (ineffectual, with emission of flatus).

Anus.—Hæmorrhoids, painful; H. bleeding. Sticking during a stool, mixed with blood; when not at stool, and in rectum. Sensation of an acrid substance during stool. Burning, with burning-itching. Crawling. Crawling-creeping, and in urethra, with burning in glans. Sticking in perineum, < sitting.

Stool.—*After eating. Diarrhœa;* with urging; with burning pain in anus; **of undigested fæces** (Ferr.), *also passed in several pieces, then ineffectual urging;* and nodular, yellow; (frequent, blackish); *and frequent, with biting-burning pain in anus, and colic before and after every stool.* Pappy; but difficult, then ineffectual urging with pain. Hard. Difficult, painful, after long urging. Constipation; with accumulation of hard fæces in rectum; with accumulation of fæces in intestines, heat in head, and dizziness. *White, with dark urine.* Bilious. Two in morning. Intermitted for two days.

Clinical.—Painless diarrhœa, with bloated abdomen, stools containing undigested food, < at night, with great fermentation in bowels, general desire for acids and relishes of various sorts. Stools, sometimes involuntary, of cadaverous odor. Diarrhœa from eating fruit. Diarrhœa, recurring after meals (Crot. tig.). Diarrhœa occurring in the course of debilitating diseases. Dysentery, rarely.

Urinary Organs.—*Pressure in bladder after frequent and almost ineffectual efforts to urinate.* Micturition frequent; two calls at night; involuntary; in a feeble, slow stream. Urethra, sticking when urinating; sensitiveness also when sitting and rising up, with stiffness of penis; burning in orifice; burning pain in orifice during and after micturition; burning-biting in forepart in evening, when urinating; bubbling sensation in region of bulb. *Urine dark; with brick-red sediment* (Lyc.); *copious;* increased, with burning in orifice of urethra; whitish, turbid, with white sediment; pale, depositing a cloud; pale, depositing a dirty yellow, flocculent sediment; scanty and dark; scanty, with brick-red sediment.

Sexual Organs.—Swelling of spermatic cord, painful to touch, and of scrotum, < epididymis. Sticking in frænum of glans, < touch, with tension. Pain in glans before urinating; jerking pain between glans and prepuce when walking; itching of glans in evening, in bed. Sore sensation on margin of prepuce, < rubbing of clothes. Frequent erections; at night. Scrotum hangs down; sticking itching of scrotum; itching crawling on scrotum in evening in bed. Tearing in l. testicle and in l. side of prepuce in evening in bed;

drawing pain in testicles. Desire increased. Emissions nightly; at 3 A.M.

Metrorrhagia, with black clots. Suppression of menses.

Clinical.—Impotency resulting from sexual excesses; nocturnal emissions, very debilitating; in general, frequently useful for symptoms resulting from sexual excesses. Uterine hæmorrhages, especially after labor, with atony of uterus, discharge of large quantities of blood, cold skin, fainting, convulsive jerks, etc. Menstruation too early and profuse, with dark clots, distention of abdomen, etc. Leucorrhœa that comes on instead of the menses; bloody, fetid, purulent, great weakness, etc. Metritis. Ovaritis from sexual excesses or following hæmorrhages, all the parts are very sensitive to the slightest touch. General anæmia resulting from prolonged nursing. Hæmorrhage from the lungs while nursing.

Respiratory Organs.—Tickling in evening provoking cough, which, however, he can suppress. *Whistling and wheezing in trachea on breathing.* Collection of mucus in larynx; which he constantly loosens and which causes hoarseness; *something is adherent to larynx, so that the voice is deep and rough.* Stitches in larynx, with roughness. Pain in trachea and sternum on coughing. Drawing in trachea below larynx, then cough in one impulse. Hoarseness.

Cough caused by laughing (Phos., Stan.); *C. after eating* (Nux v., Ars.); waking after midnight, with sticking in both sides of chest at every paroxysm of cough; *irritation to hacking, as from sulphur fumes, whereby nothing could be loosened, mornings;* suffocative (a kind of whooping cough), at 2 and 4 A.M., with screaming on account of it after coughing a few times; (coughing up bloody mucus). *Suffocative attack as if larynx were full of mucus, < towards evening and at night on waking.* Inspiration difficult and painful, expiration quick. Dyspnœa, < walking, with difficult, at times rattling expiration and with roughness of chest. Inclination before dinner to breathe deeply.

Clinical.—Asthmatic attacks. Nervous cough, dry and hacking, with pain in spleen, palpitation, intolerance of tight clothing, dyspnœa, etc. Bronchorrhœa, with great prostration, simulating the last stage of phthisis, intolerance of the slightest pressure over chest, which is extremely sensitive; loud râles through the chest, and extreme debility. Hæmoptysis, with anæmia, œdema of the extremities. Phthisis from excessive loss of fluids and vitality, night-sweats (compare Acet. ac.).

Chest.—Twitching here and there in muscles. Stick- in l.; in forepart beneath last ribs, without relation to respiration; between l. seventh and eighth ribs; *in cartilages of l. third and fourth false ribs;* in morning; in side at night, but during the day only on motion and touch; in side when sitting and reading; *in a spot below last r. ribs on pressure and on walking; above præcordial region when at rest, < reading;* in l. on expiration when sitting; on l. side near ensiform cartilage on expiration, and in pit of stomach; in side when eating and drinking, and in back, with nausea; when walking rapidly; in sides, with heat, hard pulse and staring eyes; from sternum through to back, after drinking; below r. arm, in region of fourth rib, as if in pleura, > pressure and stooping; beneath last ribs on inspiration, arresting breathing; compelling inspiration; *outward near r. nipple;* outward in region of sixth and seventh true ribs, without affecting respiration; rhythmical, outward; inward in sternum at attachment of ribs, without affecting respiration; tickling, in l., extending towards præcordial region. Tearing below last true ribs, on l. side of ensiform cartilage. Tearing drawing beneath last rib when standing. Intermittent cutting across when sitting bent.

Pain; in region of r. fourth and fifth ribs; when coughing, with soreness in larynx; in side, impeding breathing; *in side as if beaten; drawing across lower when sitting, causing anxiety, > standing and walking;* drawing, behind sternum; in joints of ribs as if bruised, on inspiration; contractive, in middle of r. side, so that he must expel the breath suddenly; contractive, beneath last ribs when walking, and a bruised sensation; tensive, in morning, < external muscles. Pressure upon chest; on l. side near ensiform cartilage; over anterior part at night when lying upon back; in sternum after eating, < sitting bent and raising arm; externally upon middle of sternum when upper part of body is bent and when standing, > pressure; externally upon sternum when sitting bent, causing anxiety and insufficient inspiration; (sharp, with crawling in one side); outward in region of last ribs; burning, inward; drawing, on r. when sitting. *Oppression;* in evening, > sighing, with uneasiness, weak pulse and anxious, impatient mood; at night, with whistling and rattling, and with wheezing and râles in trachea; *in region of pit of stomach as if something were burrowing there.* Agreeable fulness as from satiety, with sweetish saliva. Burning; extending from upper part to stomach, then agreeable warmth. (Throbbing in sternum in morning and evening.) (Crawling in one breast.)

Heart.—Dilatation of r. side. Sticking in præcordial region after drinking. *Palpitation;* waking at 3 A.M., < lying on l. side, returning at 9 A.M., < motion; after dinner, < movement, > quiet; after slight exercise, with oppressed breathing; *with rush of blood to face, which was hot and red, and with cold hands; with intermitting pulse,* intermission of every ninth beat, then three or four rapid beats; with depressed pulse and cold skin; with anxiety; then chill.

Pulse.—Rapid; and irregular; and hard, with flushes of heat alternating with chilliness of back, which is covered with cold sweat and cold sweat on forehead. Full and hard. Slow and weak. Thin and irregular.

Neck.—Sticking, then stiffness; slow drawing sticking in anterior muscles when at rest. Pain on motion; *pain in nape* as if glands were swollen, on turning head, extending after a walk to throat, < touch, when it is a bruised sensation. *Drawing pain; on r. lower part of nape* when standing, > stooping.

Back.—*Sticking in l. side* when sitting; throbbing sticking. Bruised pain on motion. Sticking in middle of spine; across r. scapula and in l. chest. Tearing in region of l. scapula on inspiration; drawing tearing in l. scapula. Pain in scapula as from dislocation. Contractive pain between S. when standing. Jerking across sacrum; painful. Sticking in lumbar region; in region of r. kidney, < bending. Jerking tearing in l. side of small of back. Aching in sacral region, extending down thighs, with languor, distention of abdomen and ineffectual desire for stool; sticking drawing, in middle of sacrum, extending towards lumbar vertebræ; **tensive, in sacrum, as from a heavy load or after long stooping; in small of back as from cramp or as if bruised and crushed,** *with sudden crying out on motion.*

Clinical.—Spinal irritation; the spine is extremely sensitive to touch, pain shooting into head, etc. Many symptoms of tabes have been relieved (see under **Extremities.**).

Extremities.—Cracking in joints. Trembling from a chill and creeping shivering over thighs in open, not cold air. Twitching. *Jerking tearing, < touch, < hands and soles. Sensible, but invisible trembling, with a cooling sensation. Laxity of all and trembling of hands; trembling weakness. Heaviness, as if lead were hanging to them* (Phos.), *< thighs. Numbness and stiffness. Paralytic stiffness in all joints on rising from sleep in morning and from midday nap, causing mental depression. Falling asleep of those upon which he lies.*

Upper Extremities.—*Paralytic jerking-tearing in long bones, < touch;* paralytic tearing, extending into all parts, < more by touch than by motion. Tearing in l. axilla and on anterior and inner border of scapula. Intermittent drawing pain on margin of r. axilla, near forepart. *Paralytic jerking-tearing on top of shoulder, with sensitiveness to touch, the pain renewed by touch, even of coat.*

Arm.—Tearing if she stands by the window, with drawing. Tension, and in hands. Weakness noticed when clenching hands. Sticking in upper, > motion. Tearing in l. upper, then in r.; jerking tearing in humerus, towards upper and inner part; *paralytic jerking-T., extending from head of humerus along muscles and bones to phalanges, where it is painless, the pain < touch, with weakness of whole arm. Paralytic pain in head of humerus, losing itself in hand as a tearing, with general warmth, < forehead.*

Elbow.—Tearing through l.; in l., < motion. Sticking in l. Painful drawing in bend of l., on cronoid process of ulna, < touch; drawing pains in bones to fingers in evening.

Forearm.—Tearing, > rubbing, with drawing back and forth, now r., now l.; T. in shafts of ulnæ, < touch. Drawing pain, as if periosteum were scraped with a dull knife. Falling asleep on bending, for example, on writing, with sticking in tips of fingers. Drawing sticking across wrist in evening. Jerking tearing in wrist and metacarpal bones.

Hand.—Swelling of l., with pain across dorsum on motion. *Trembling when writing.* Sticking in l.; in metacarpal bone of r. index. Tearing where metacarpal bones unite with bones of wrist; jerking T. in metacarpal bones and fingers, < touch; jerking T. in metacarpal bone of r. little finger. Cramplike drawing pain on taking hold of anything; drawing pain in palm across roots of fingers. Swelling of knuckle of middle finger, with stiffness and pain on motion. *Tearing in bones of r. distal phalanges, < joints;* sticking T. in distal joint of r. thumb; jerking T. in phalanges. Jerking pain in l. little finger. Drawing in thumb, middle and index fingers of l. hand, extending upward.

Lower Extremities.—Tottering. Pain like a sticking and burning on several places. Painful drawing in long bones. Weakness when walking. Falling asleep when sitting.

Thigh.—Hard swelling, at times extending to beginning of feet, becoming thinner in lower part, reddish and painful to touch. Jerking in middle of l. Sticking on posterior part of r. when standing, extending upward. Jerking-tearing; *on anterior part of l.; on anterior and outer parts on touch.* Paroxysmal tearing downward in femora. Pressure in upper part of flesh of r. nates, on pelvic bone, when sitting, increasing in a pulselike manner. Bruised pain in posterior muscles when sitting. Cramplike paralytic pain in r. on rising after sitting some time and on walking, and in knee. *Drawing pain in bones as if periosteum had been scraped with a dull knife.* Drawing in nates and knees when standing; painful D. in skin on inner side of l.; painful D. downward in shaft of femora in afternoon, < sitting; tearing, in l. nates when sitting; cramplike (sticking), and in legs. Sensation in l. when standing, as of a hard pimple in flesh, with drawing pain in it. Tension in anterior muscles when walking. Burning and crawling on rising from a seat, as if asleep, < in hollow of knee, < standing. Weakness; as from heaviness and paralysis; of hip-joint and knee in morning, with unsteadiness, changing on motion to a bruised pain in thigh, then < legs.

Knee.—*Hot swelling of r.*, with drawing-tearing, waking at midnight. Trembling on rising from a seat, > walking. Giving way; when walking; < ascending steps. Sticking in l. *Tearing to thigh, with weakness; paralytic T. in r., extending now to thigh, now to leg, < more by touch than by motion, with weakness;* jerking T. on inner side of patella. Pain on bending, preventing sleep, with nodes in its skin; pain on side of patella when touched; *jerking P.;* bruised, on motion; drawing, in r. in afternoon on rising from a seat and on walking > sitting. Drawing when sitting, and in inguinal joint; jerklike, synchronous with pulse, in tendons of flexors of hollows; spasmodic, in hollow of r. in evening when sitting, > standing and walking, extending into thigh (with pressure), as if leg would be drawn up.

Leg.—Painful cramp in l. calf at night on stretching and bending up foot. *Sticking in tibiæ when walking;* sudden, in upper part of calf when walking in open air. Tearing in calf. Bruised pain in bones on stepping, < touch, and if she feels of it shivering of foot and chilliness of it as if she put it into cold water; pain in lower half as if periosteum were bruised and swollen, on standing, but on touch sore pain as if excoriated. Drawing pain on tibia in evening when sitting, > standing and walking; in r. tibia near heel when sitting, then in foot; on inner part of l. tibia, below patella, when stretching leg while sitting, > bending leg. **Sensation as if garters were too tight and leg would go to sleep and be numb** (compare Coccul. and *Cedron*). Burning tension above tendo-achillis. Restlessness, obliging him to extend and draw them up. Weakness.

Foot.—Hard swelling, spotted red; *soft swelling of soles.* Sticking in l.; (in scar on l.); tearing, in sole when sitting and walking. *Jerking tearing in metatarsal bones and toes; in metatarsal bones and phalanges of toes, < touch, < joints; in tarsal and metatarsal bones;* at union of metatarsal and ankle bones. Sticking tearing in sole, in region of heel, when sitting and walking. Contractive pinching on outer side of r. sole. Drawing pain in r. metatarsal bones. Drawing on dorsum when standing, with sore pain, > sitting; sticking, in heels; cramplike, on inner side of l. when sitting. Sticking burning in upper part, close to tibia when sitting. *Weakness as if bruised.* Boring sticking in tips of toes. Sticking crawling as after freezing, from great toe to dorsum of foot in evening when sitting, > standing and walking.

Clinical.—Occasionally useful in hip disease, the effects of prolonged suppuration, with sweats, diarrhœa, etc. Chronic synovitis of knee. Sensation as if cords were tied about the leg. Anasarca of lower extremities, always < towards night, with general anæmia and general sensitiveness of the surface of the body to the slightest touch.

Skin.—Turgor of veins. Eruption in concha; (red miliary, on forepart of throat). Boil on cheek; on pectoral muscles. Urticaria of face, forearms and hands, afterwards with vesicles like varicella. Watery vesicles behind ears. (Ulcer discharges offensive ichor, with burning and aching in it, he cannot let the foot hang down and the foot is painful when standing); boring in U.; throbbing pain on moving part; (sticking throbbing pain, even during rest); sensitiveness; sticking-itching pain.

Sticking in various places. Digging in a wound. Tugging as if a hair were pulled, < on abdomen. **Sensitiveness** (Ars.), *even of palms;* on thighs, to rubbing of clothes, as if rough and covered with pimples. Sensation on elbow as if infiltrated with blood. (Creeping on forehead.) Itching at night; I., with oozing of blood on scratching; followed after scratching by vesicles as from burning nettles; on arms, loins and chest, < evening, and after scratching pimples; on r. sole when walking and sitting, > scratching; crawling, on coccyx, > for a short time by rubbing; burning, under knees and on inside of arms when warm and at night in bed, with watery blisters, which disappear in cold air; biting, almost only on those parts on which he lies, > scratching and lying on other side; biting, during midday nap, almost only on those parts upon which he does not lie and which are turned upward.

Sleep.—Yawning; with stretching of limbs; with chilliness; without sleepiness. Sleepiness during the day; at 8.30 P.M.; *after eating;* after dinner; with palpitation; then wakefulness. Sleep during the day; S. when sitting; as soon as she sits down during the day, with nodding, but if she lies down she is wide awake at the slightest noise; with one eye open, the other half-closed, with balls turned upward as in a dying person; on his back, head thrown backward, arms stretched above head, with slow expiration and strong, rapid pulse; sound, as of a drunken person, then in morning confusion of head as if he had not slept enough, with pressure in temples on shaking head.

Sleeplessness all night; with vivid disagreeable thoughts crowding upon each other; till midnight, with headache; after midnight, though sleepy, with activity of thought and frequent changes in his position; till 2 A.M.; except from 3 to 5 A.M.; on account of thoughts crowding upon him, also with warmth towards morning, but inability to have less covering; with restlessness. Falling asleep late, then unsound sleep and exhaustion in morning on rising. Frequent waking; with sweat on scalp and forehead and chilliness over back. Early waking. *Snoring inspiration* (through nose); *inspiration and expiration;* inspiration at one time, at another *a puffing expiration; S. in a child, with moaning.* Starting out of sleep; with inability to collect himself; starting on falling asleep. Uneasy sleep; interrupted by four or five erections; with general sweat after waking in night; full of dreams and crying out; with uncovering, worrying dreams of former occurrences, and in the morning he cannot get awake on account of confusion and stupidity in head, in morning out of sorts and unrefreshed.

Dreams.—*Heavy, making him anxious after waking.* Anxious, whereupon he woke half conscious and remained frightened; that he is descending a precipice, waking him and remaining vivid before his fancy, < closing eyes, and he cannot quiet himself. Frightful; just as he is falling asleep, waking him; waking him without his being able to come to his senses; of falling from a height, with waking full of uneasiness and inability to collect himself. Confused, on falling asleep, on account of which he woke; C. and senseless; *C. and senseless after midnight,* with half conscious waking. Of nasty things on closing her eyes to sleep. Voluptuous, with emissions.

Fever.—Chilliness; at 5 A.M., with weakness of feet; after dinner, then heat; < drinking; with pressure in abdomen. Alternating with heat all the forenoon; in afternoon, together with weakness of lower limbs, all < walking in open air; with some thirst for cold water during the heat; C. and sweat all day, A. with heat and redness of face, with thirst. *Intermittent all day, < forehead, where there is cold sweat, thirst after the first chill;* I., with weakness of knees and tibiæ when walking and standing, > sitting. Internal; without external; without external, then cutting in head extending into orbits; periodically, with shivering; and external, < at times in marrow of bones of feet, which are colder than hands. As from a cold wind, < walking, seldom with shivering, it only comes when sitting, over arms, loins and thighs.

Shivering in morning; in morning and forenoon, with cold hands, nausea and rapid pulse; at 5 P.M. when walking in open air, > in room, with coldness, then heat, < face, < motion and walking, then thirst; (in evening on lying down); *after every swallow of drink, or chilliness, with gooseflesh* (Caps.); on entering warm room from open air; in open, not cold air, > in room; in open air, with gooseflesh; with gooseflesh; with cold hands and dulness of mind; *general; general, without thirst* (Ars., Phos.), *also with internal chill* (Ars.); general, less on limbs.

Coldness, except of face, which was red, with sometimes internal coldness on the warm forehead; C., except of face, which is warm, then coldness of forehead with internal warmth in rest of body. Cold cheeks and feet, with cold sweat on forehead, internal heat of face, trunk and thighs. Cold nose. Back; when walking in open air, then heat in back with sweat, then again chill. Limbs internally and externally, with general internal and external heat and slight thirst for cold water. Arms and abdomen, with redness and heat of cheeks and lobules of ears; arms, with nausea, then cold limbs, with shivering and recurrent nausea. **Hands,** < r.; < l.; in morning, and feet, with shivering over thighs, < walking; in evening, with hot cheeks; in open air, with external chilliness as if dashed with cold water, and chattering of teeth, > in room except the coldness of hands; alternately, with warm; internally, and in arms; internally in l., though not externally colder than r. Lower limbs. Knees; from l. knee to sole. **Feet**; in evening; < l.; with general internal heat and distended veins; with redness and internal heat of cheeks.

Shivering above elbows and knees; over chest and arms when walking in open air.

Heat in forenoon before a meal, then when walking in open air cold sensation on ankles and coldness of rest of body; in afternoon, with redness and heat of face, great hunger, burning of lips if they touch each other and burning sticking in skin about lips; towards evening, with rapid pulse; after midnight, with dry lips but no thirst; *with distended veins and easily dilating pupils, without thirst;* almost with inability to uncover hands without difficulty. **General, with**

sticking in skin (Merc. cor.), < **on neck,** with *thirst for cold water;* with swelling of veins of arms and hands, without sweat or thirst; **from 5 to 7 P.M.,** < **walking in open air,** which caused sweat on forehead, with hunger preceding and lasting into beginning of heat and returning after the fever, and on walking sensation of hot water running down (a creeping of heat over abdomen and down thighs), with red cheeks, without thirst. *Dry,* all day. In flashes, with thirst for cold water. Internal, with red cheeks, heat of trunk and arms and moisture of forehead. *Internal and external, with sticking in several places in skin and thirst for cold water;* I. and E., as from wine, with redness of face.

Burning in various parts during the day, with crawling and itching. Heat of head towards morning, with oppression of chest; of head, with swollen veins of hands; of head and face, with congestion, swelling of veins. External ear. Face; at 3 P.M., with red cheeks and dry sticky lips, without thirst; on coming from open air into a room that was not warm; and chest; then shivering and chilliness and general coldness; one or other cheek and lobule of ear, with redness, and before this disappears chill over body, then over lower limbs. (Anteriorly on upper part of thigh.) *Skin not sensitive to air in morning after night-sweat.*

Sweat; in morning sleep; at night; **in sleep** (Ferr.); **general, as soon as he is covered,** *with such sleepiness that he cannot get up;* general, when walking in open air. Cold. Oily in morning. *Of body after waking at 3 A.M., with thirst, without sweat on feet or head,* **except where he lies upon cheek.** In hair of head; when walking in open air. *On face and hands;* on face in morning on rising; cold, on face, with thirst. On nape and back on slightest motion.

Clinical.—Intermittent fever, *without* constitutional cachexia, except general weakness and anæmia; the paroxysm is fully developed, the three stages of chill, fever and sweat are fully marked; preceding the chill there is violent thirst, often violent temporal headache; there is an interval between the chill and fever, but rarely any gastric disturbance; during the fever there is generally thirst, sometimes unnatural hunger; an interval between the fever and sweat; the sweat is profuse, debilitating, with thirst; during the apyrexia great debility, ringing in the ears, feeling of emptiness in stomach, soreness over the spleen and liver, with many symptoms characteristic of the drug.

Chininum Arsenicum.

The arsenate of "Quinia" is triturated for use.

General Action and Allies.—See Chininum sulph. and Arsenic.

Tired feeling. Head feels too full or as if it would burst. Painful pressure in forehead and temples. Confused pain in forehead and occipital protuberance. Dull, heavy aching in forehead and occiput; in cerebellum on motion. Sudden throbbings in temporal arteries after 1 P.M. Taste metallic, bitter. Throat dry. Loss of appetite, with weak feeling. Hiccough. Belching, then urging to stool. Nausea; during stool, with retching. Burning in stomach. Pressure behind stomach, not > dinner, which was relished; in solar plexus extending towards back, where it changed to pinching, spine sensitive to touch at this point. Emission of flatus. Colic; below umbilicus, with urging to stool. Intermittent sore pain in a spot below and to right of umbilicus. Sudden violent urging to stool. Diarrhœa four times; urgent D., containing jellylike lumps; watery, blackish, immediately after dinner; watery, brown, painless; fæcal stool, with mucus and blood, tenesmus before and after the stool.

Respiration very free, as if chest were hollow, in afternoon. Stitching in front of r. lower part of chest, < inspiration. Pain below and to left of l. nipple, not affected by breathing; coming and going quickly in lower part of l. lung, with pressure as from flatulence. *Palpitation* on leaning against back. Sensation as if heart stopped after 1 P.M., beating imperceptible. Trembling of heart, with a rumbling noise, I was unable to distinguish the pulsations, this lasted an hour, then beating of heart and pulse (the latter imperceptible on l. side) became irregular and numbered 200. Pulse 200.

Momentary pain in joint of l. great toe, in l. little finger and in region of l. olecranon. Weariness in shoulder and elbow-joints. Tired pain in biceps of l. arm. Sore aching in l. forearm, in muscular mass composed of supinator longus and brevis and flexor longus pollicis; in flexors of l. forearm, < radial side near elbow, same pain below l. knee; in first phalanx of l., then r. thumb. Pain in first joint of l. ring finger. Palms dry and hot. Weariness of lower limbs. Pain along front of lower two-thirds of l. tibia; intermittent sore, in r. biceps midway between hip and knee and in calf; fleeting sore, in sole at root of l. little toe. Sleep interrupted.

Clinical.—It has been prescribed in malignant sore throat (diphtheria), with great prostration, especially in the latter stages or when the disease is very prolonged and shows no tendency towards convalescence. Angina pectoris, with burning pain and great prostration, occurring in periodical paroxysms. Asthmatic attacks or suffocative attacks, recurring every day at the same hour, during phthisis, with icy-cold skin and great anxiety, wants the open air. In marsh malaria it has been used when after the paroxysms there are cold sweat, prostration, great irritability, brown diarrhœa, etc.

Chininum Sulfuricum.

Pure sulphate of "Quinia" is triturated for use.

General Action.—Quinine is, above all, a protoplasmic poison, devitalizing the blood and tissues; it particularly retards the elimination of nitrogenous waste (urea and uric acid), and causes the retention and accumulation of effete products in the system (though, for a time the diminished waste gives a sense of "tone" to the system, the ultimate result is deplorable). It causes congestion of the brain, and, in large doses, abolishes the cerebral functions. It is an irritant to serous membranes and to the skin; it causes deafness and serous inflammation of the internal ear; blindness, ischæmia of the retina and optic neuritis; it produces stupor, delirium and even convulsions. (Epilepsy is intensely aggravated by it.) Quinine, however, arrests the development of low forms of vegetable life, and especially of the poison of marsh malaria, but it rarely antidotes the effects of the poison on the system.

Allies.—(See China).

Generalities.—Emaciation. Pandiculation, with frequent yawning. Falling suddenly in the street; falling to the ground senseless. Convulsions. Twitchings in evening. Trembling. Wandering symptoms.

Neuralgia, > warmth; wandering N. Shocks or pricks like neuralgia or rheumatism in divers places, as l. supraorbital nerve, r. ear, r. elbow, r. knuckle, etc. Twinges in various places in afternoon; in lower half of r. scapula in afternoon, then in r. lower jaw, then in upper, in malar region, frequently recurring in some places. Catching or sprained pains on sudden motion, *e. g.*, in outer fibres of deltoid tendon on raising arms, in tendons in front of l. ankle when flexing joint suddenly.

Quivering sensation internally through body at the middle, in afternoon, then eructations. General sensitiveness. Restlessness; in forenoon, after writing a letter; at 5 P.M., with coldness; at night; and discomfort. Excitement of arterial system, as from strong wine. Increase of physical powers. *Weakness;* in morning; in morning, on waking, with dulness of head; on waking from afternoon nap, with dulness; with sleepiness and desire for solitude in some dark corner. Old and "wooden" feelings, with deliberate motions and speech. Faintness. Heaviness; in forenoon, with drowsiness. Amelioration from sleep; from sweat, after walking in open air.

Mind.—Disturbance, or rather emptiness. Insanity. Excitement. **Feeling of impending evil** in afternoon; > specific trust in the Almighty. *Despondency.* Anxiety; at night, with little sleep; at night, obliging him to leave the bed; as if he had committed a crime. Fretfulness. Anger after sleep, even about a draught on legs. Resolute in evening, but shrinking from taking much trouble about matters. Positive in insisting on professional orders in forenoon, but self-restrained and deliberate. Buoyancy; in evening. Lively mood returned at 9 P.M., after a walk in open air, with activity. Quietness. Apathy. Indolence. Disinclination for mental labor. Thought difficult when writing. Memory "muddled." Mistakes in writing, "left" for "right," and *vice versa.* Loss of power to name substances, mistakes in adding figures, perception of quantities impaired. Vacancy of ideas.

Head.—Swelling in morning, with difficulty in opening mouth. Chronic disturbance of brain. Aching; in morning on rising, < stooping or moving; at 3 A.M., > rising, with pain in occiput; in forenoon, < l. side, with pulsations in temples and excitement in whole body; in afternoon, after a long walk in the sun; in afternoon, extending to temples, > evening; with vertigo and loss of memory; < towards evening, with pulsation in head, as if it would be torn to pieces, heat of face, vertigo, at times ringing and roaring in ears; > sweat on walking in open air, with fever.

Fulness in forenoon when writing, with coldness of feet and inner calves, < l.; sudden, in forenoon after writing, when leaning it to the left, < l. side and top. Heaviness; in forenoon, > putting cold hand on top, with fulness and dry heat, and with coldness of fingers and feet; in evening, < top. Confusion. Emptiness; in morning. Stupefaction. Throbbing on rising and bending over table, and in shoulders. Rush of blood; towards evening. Intoxicated sensation, though his mental powers were perfect; I. sensation, preventing walking; changing to heaviness of head. **Whirling in head like a mill-wheel.** Vertigo; at night, < sitting up in bed or getting up on his feet; on stooping; with palpitation; increasing to faintness.

Forehead.—Sticking; boring, in l. centre in evening. Pricking, with confusion of head. Tearing and drawing. Neuralgia from r. supraorbital foramen in a narrow line to vertex, at night when bent forward reading, > sitting upright. Pain; in morning on rising, < l. side, then confusion of head, then frontal pain, < at 5 P.M.; at 9 A.M., < l. side, with vertigo, ringing in ears and weakness; towards noon, < till evening, and in temples, with visible pulsation in temporal arteries, heat in head and ringing in ears; in afternoon; from 1 to 4 P.M.; 4 P.M.; between 5 and 6 P.M.; 7 P.M., at last extending to occiput; on waking; after dinner; < towards evening; < moving eyes or head, and in orbits. Pulsation in arteries at 4 P.M., with heat of face and redness, < about eyes.

Temples.—Twitching of muscles above l. zygoma in afternoon. Neuralgia shooting up l. anterior when sitting at the table, leaning to r. Tearing in l., with drawing. Pain; towards evening; in l.; in afternoon, extending to middle of forehead; in l., extending to eyebrow, obliging him to seek a cool place on the sofa to relieve the pain; drawing, to middle of forehead; in l. T. and supraorbital region in morning on rising, > by a walk, returned on following days, sleep poor on account of toothache on l. side next night toothache on both sides, < by bringing teeth together and biting, with anxiety and sharp pain in l. temporal and supraorbital regions, < under l. ear, where it extended deeply inward, sometimes cutting in l. external auditory meatus, face puffed and red, pain in both temples > walking, with tensive drawing in skin which made work impossible, the toothache was transiently > by pricking gums and rinsing mouth with cold water, later this neuralgia appeared every night at 3 A.M., and lasted till 6 A.M. Fulness of arteries in evening; bounding in artery in afternoon.

Parietals.—Stitch in l. upper on rising suddenly; in l. upper, when standing holding head down, extending to l. side of root of nose. Neuralgia in l. in evening, then in r. vertex; in and behind l. protuberance in afternoon on going out, with the head down; in r. side of head in evening on walking in open air, lasting some time in r. upper temple. Pain in r. side of head when writing, extending as neuralgia to r. outer brow, then to mastoid process, returning to brow and r. temporal ridge, again in r. ear, then back to brow, later a catch in middle of r. sterno-mastoid muscle on turning head that way after midnight. Pain in l. side of head in morning on writing with head inclined to l., extending to l. side of neck and throat, r. mastoid process, then to vertex, then to occiput, then shifting to brows (varying with the position of head), now in temples, extending over coronal suture.

Occiput.—Shock across lower in evening on holding head suddenly to r. Pain, waking at 3 A.M., > rising; threatening of pain in l. in evening. Dull twinges in l. protuberance in afternoon, becoming a steady ache.

Scalp.—Dandruff, and in beard on chin, < l. side. Itching, intermittent in evening; itching on l. side of vertex and occiput; above edge of frontal hair, r. and l. sides, when writing, then below r. zygoma, then on r. side of vertex, then l. vertex, r. side of chin, l. post-mastoid surface, l. inner eyebrow, etc.

Clinical.—Intermittent neuralgia in head and face, with intense pulsation, vertigo, etc. Vertigo, twitching of eyelids.

Eyes.—Surrounded by gray rings. Red, with swelling of lids and appearance of pimples. Lustreless. Restless. Dry; > walking in wind in evening, when there was lachrymation of r. eye. Easily tired when reading. Sleepy feeling in afternoon when sitting.

Heaviness in forenoon, and in forehead. Retrobullar optic-neritis, with sudden loss of vision. Lachrymation at 5 P.M. in the full light; L. in open air. *Disc and retina anæmic,* disc looked *dry,* with the vessels running over it smaller than usual. Disc papery white. Ball pale. Dirty color to the white of the eye. *Pupils dilated.* R. upper lid red and swollen. Twitching of l. lids; in afternoon; in afternoon, < lower; in evening; of l. outer canthus. Closure of lids from weakness when writing. Feeling as if something pressed lids down, making vision indistinct.

Brow.—Sticking in l. in evening; at l. inner in evening when writing. Neuralgia in r. inner; deep in r. outer; in r. inner in morning on bending forward; in r. outer in morning on raising brows, extending up side of head, then twinge in outer end of l.; in l. supraorbital nerve in forenoon; in r. supraorbital nerve in evening in street-car, then in l.; in l. supraorbital nerve, near foramen, in evening when writing; from r. to lamboidal suture in evening when sitting; in r. outer at 11.30 P.M.; in outer half of r. after midnight; alternately in each at night; in r. supraorbital nerve, near foramen, when sitting in church; from r. outer to lamboidal suture when standing. Twinges about r. outer in afternoon. Flashings in branches of l. infraorbital nerve in afternoon. Pain in r. outer supraorbital region in morning; in l. infraorbital nerve at 1.30 A.M.; in outer half of l. orbit, above it, below it, in evening when sitting, and in eyeball.

Vision lost; with pain in forehead as if head would burst; *dim. Photophobia, with lachrymation in full glare. Bright lights and sparks.*

Clinical.—Intermittent strabismus.

Ears.—Sticking in l. in forenoon; r. at noon; r. in evening; l. on retracting chin, involving throat; in l. meatus in afternoon after going down-stairs. Pain above r. ear and mastoid process in evening; in r. between 1 and 2 A.M.; suddenly in l. when walking; in open air. Tension in parotids, with flow of saliva; in afternoon; in r. when walking after supper, after a jar; in r. at 11.30 P.M., also in r. submaxillary, then in l. glands. Tingling. Feeling as if stuffed with cotton.

Ringing, < l.; with sensation as if plugged up; intermittent; sudden, in r. like a bell in E., when walking in open air; causing deafness. Hissing. Buzzing; in r. extending over head, after coffee; intermittent. Resonance in r. in morning. Roaring; causing deafness. Sensation as if a horse railroad had its course through the brain, < on alternate days. Deafness; in l. Hearing lost. Hearing difficult. Intolerance of noise.

Nose.—Sore pimple on r. side, at end of nasal bone. Twitching in afternoon. Neuralgia at end of l. bone in evening (head held obliquely down in writing). Tingling anteriorly in nostrils in evening when sitting; in *l.* side after supper on going from one room to another, with sneezing and flow from *r.* side. Titillation in r. upper nostril in afternoon, then sneezing, then snuffling and flow of water. Sensation of coryza, with sneezing. Stoppage when in a greenhouse after riding in wind. Moisture in evening, < r. side. Fluent coryza in r. side.

Sneezing in morning when dressing, with discharge of mucus; at noon when waiting on doorsteps; afternoon on entering house; at 2 P.M. when standing in a cool shady alley, then blowing of mucus from r. nostril; in evening when sitting in shirt-sleeves; at night when resting back against cool wall; on walking in open air; < getting feet cold. Hæmorrhage.

Face.—*Pale; and suffering.* Red. Earthy color. Sickly expression; and hollow-eyed. Œdema; and of limbs, with erythematous rash, and feeling as if arms would burst. Twitching of l. zygomatic muscles. Pain below l. zygoma between 1 and 2 A.M.; *about l. malar-bone in evening;* in l. infraorbital and superior maxillary nerves, < cold air, with boring, at times involving eye, swelling adjacent to upper molars; *suddenly above l. zygoma when writing, with head bent to l., also at temporal ridge;* varying from l. supra-zygomatic region to ear, throat, upper molars, in evening when riding in street-car, with head inclined reading, > holding head up. Rheumatic (or neuralgic) pain in zygoma, malar and nasal bones, extending to side of head, in afternoon, from cool wind on r. side of face, with tingling in nose, as before sneezing. Dull twinge above root of r. zygoma in afternoon.

Cracking in joints of jaw; every time mouth is opened. Cutting in l. lower jaw in night. Neuralgia in r. joint of jaw in morning; in l. lower jaw in a cool room. Lips livid; and cool. Eruption on lower lip, l., then r. side.

Mouth.—Teeth. Clenched after midnight. Tartar increased; soft T. on upper front, after removal of which soreness of gum on touch of lip; the secretion about upper molars seems to putrese and irritate. Sticking in incisors in afternoon, < l.; in l. upper second and third molars in evening. Cutting downward and outward from l. lower amalgam-filled molar. Neuralgia in last l. upper molars in afternoon, extending to zygoma; in molars in afternoon, extending into l. jaw, < in lower and in ear; in l. molars filled with amalgam, extending to jaws; in l. upper molars filled with amalgam, in afternoon, then in middle upper and lower molars. Aching; between amalgam-filled molars, < cold air, > application of warm hand. Pressure as from a knife-blade, in first l. lower molar, downward and forward into l. jaw, in afternoon. Rough feeling in morning. Soreness of sockets, with inflammation of gums.

Tongue.—Coated yellow; and dry; at root; except tip, which is red; with slimy yellowish froth; with slimy fur, yellow posteriorly; yellowish white; coated with white mucus. White; in centre, pale on margins; with yellow coat at root. Pale, covered with tenacious mucus. Flabby in morning, and whitish. Twitching of middle of r. lingualis muscle in afternoon; of end of l. lingualis in afternoon when writing. *Articulation impaired.* Speech difficult; lost.

Mouth.—Cavity pale. Full of mucus at night, with hunger; tenacious coat of mucus on back part of palate in afternoon, causing efforts to swallow it. Dry. Salivation. Offensive breath. Expired air cool. Taste bitter; to bread; bad on rising, with bad breath; pasty; brassy after breakfast; acrid, > motion of tongue.

Throat.—Swelling, impeding respiration and causing hoarseness. Sudden starting from sleep at 2 A.M., throat swollen, inspiration difficult, necessity to rise, difficult coughing up of mucus, respiration > coughing, with sweat, < back and legs, general heat, respiration became rattling and gasping. Catarrhal clogging of upper pharynx in morning; of upper part in afternoon, the mucus detached by repeated swallowing. Tough mucus; at night, waking and obliging him to cough it up. Pain < swallowing; < moving neck; > evening; till night, with rough voice; in both sides, afterwards extending into larynx, > towards evening, with sensitiveness to pressure. Constriction. Sensation as if something had lodged. Scraping in afternoon, with irritation to cough and slimy expectoration difficult to loosen. Dryness. Irritation to cough. Tickling. Itching of r. side of velum palati in afternoon.

Stomach.—Appetite great; at 9 A.M. after eating; in afternoon; at 2 P.M., with eructations; at 2 P.M., with drowsiness when in street-car; in evening; after supper, then nausea; for acid food; ravenous at night; ravenous after eating, changing to nausea; canine, satiated by a small quantity of food, which took away all appetite for the next meal. Diminished. More frequent desire to eat though the appetite was not increased. Lost; with sensation of fasting; lost for breakfast, with increased hunger; lost, but drawing in stomach as from need of food; lost, but sensation indicating that one has some loss to make up, < retracting stomach. Aversion to food; to beer and tobacco, which act as if used for the first time. Thirst; in afternoon; in evening; < morning; < night.

Eructations; bitter; tasting of food; tasting of breakfast; tasting of tea taken at supper; tasting of supper; at midnight when sitting, tasting of supper; at 1.30 A.M. when crouching, tasting of supper, with flatus and yawning; tasting of supper, with fulness and uneasiness in stomach; E. of ingesta in evening when sitting bent; of half-digested matters at 1 A.M. when sitting, causing me to loosen the clothes, pyrosis; like hiccough, at 1 A.M. on starting out of the room, with sticking in r. lumbar region. Hiccough and retching.

Nausea; in morning, > eructation; during a meal, with vomiting; with weakness and shivering; sudden, forcing her to bed; sudden, after moderate eating of pork and vegetables, with vomiting, heartburn, constriction of stomach and distention of abdomen; threatening, when walking after eating, > loosening waistband. Vomiting; of insipid taste in afternoon.

Pain; in epigastric region, extending towards umbilicus, < pressure. *Pressure after eating, then cutting in upper and middle abdomen; P. from the slightest food, with return of the usual symptoms.* Fulness; in afternoon; > eructations; in epigastrium. Oppression when sitting, > evening by loosening waist-bands and eructations; in epigastrium, waking towards morning, > turning over; in epigastrium and hypochondrium, < l. side, with emissions of offensive flatus. Pulling, and in œsophagus. All the symptoms of a continued fast. Emptiness, > drinking cold water and eating, with drowsiness.

Sudden gnawing at 10.30 P.M., before supper, on ascending stairs, then crampy gastralgia, > standing up straight, then shuddering of head, > eructations. Cardialgia. Pyrosis in evening. Heat; starting from cardiac orifice and extending to abdomen and sometimes to chest. Heartburn; at midnight when standing bent over table, after eating dry bread. Coldness after ice-cream, > loosening clothes, with uneasiness. Indigestion from eating two apples late at night. Acidity, with distress in epigastrium. Trembling. Gastric catarrh.

Abdomen.—Distention; in afternoon; before diarrhœa. Tense. Rumbling; with tension, sensitiveness to pressure and discharge of flatus. Commotion as before diarrhœa, then emission of flatus. Emission of flatus; on rising, then irritability around anus; offensive; offensive, in evening; offensive, on moving about after midnight; offensive, after micturition. Flatus goes into rectum with a shock, when leaning back in chair, then presses on anus and escapes, then similar movements in l. colon and intermittent twinges of colic, the colic > emission of flatus. Tearing. Pain during the day; on rising, > stool of cadaverous odor, at first mushy; at noon, < sudden standing up, > emission of offensive flatus; with diarrhœa; sudden, at 2 P.M., with emission of flatus.

Hypochondrium.—*Sticking in l. side below short ribs;* from region of gall-bladder to r. rectus muscle; moving from edge of liver to outside of and below r. nipple, in evening on entering house; subcutaneous cutting S. in l. hypochondrium in afternoon. Suppurative sensation in region of liver. *Pain in region of spleen; > pressure; in liver region before going to bed;* in liver region in morning, > pressure of hand. Crampy feeling in l. rectus; in l. border of l. upper rectus at 1 A.M. when walking, < sitting; in l. border of upper l. rectus in evening.

Cutting in upper; < pressure of hand; transversely across upper and umbilical regions, with twisting. Discomfort in upper after 2 P.M., with tension and distention of abdomen towards evening, with pain on pressure, and oppression of chest. Pain to l. of and above umbilicus in afternoon when sitting, extending to sigmoid flexure and rectum. Cramp to l. of and above umbilicus when sitting in street-car. Rasping pain from umbilicus up to chest before copious menstruation, with dragging towards genitals. Pain in l. side in evening when sitting bent to l. Wandering pain in small intestines, with cutting, then diarrhœa. Warmth in duodenum.

Hypogastrium.—Subcutaneous cutting stitch in l. outer groin in afternoon when sitting. Cramp in l. inguinal region in morning when standing. Dragging towards genitals.

Colon.—Commotion in l. in evening, including l. lumbar region. Sticking in transverse, in evening. Pinching in transverse and l. in afternoon when walking in the house and when in street-car. Pain in transverse and l.; in afternoon; in transverse in afternoon, going to rectum as if for stool; in r. superior angle in evening when writing; in transverse and sigmoid in evening, > emission of flatus; in transverse when sitting. Grumbling; colicky, in l. at noon when sitting after motion.

Rectum.—Commotion in evening; when sitting. Itching. Tenesmus; with griping in abdomen; with a difficult, small, soft stool; ineffectual.

Anus.—Hæmorrhoidal trouble increased. Discharge of bright blood. Sticking in l. side of inner sphincter in afternoon; to r. of anus in evening when walking, with itching; sudden crampy or cutting stitch in inner sphincter when standing. Uneasiness > by gently forcing down rectum. Itching in perineum.

Stool.—Liquid, frequent. Dissolved, dark brown. *Pappy, frothy, frequent, with much wind.* First half jelly-like, with much wind. Diarrhœa; with pain across abdomen; with drawing and cutting in abdomen; light-colored; slow in coming away, with much wind. Soft, but impeded by painful contraction of inner sphincter, which feels like a firm rim. Mushy at first, then like diarrhœa, preceded by offensive flatus. With yellow, clear mucus. Constipation. Hard; and crumbling; at first, then liquid; at first, then thin. Profuse; rather hard. Scanty after postponement. Sluggish and scanty. Difficult; and painful; but not hard, with a peculiar sensation from r. hand to shoulder. Omitted; and abdomen distended.

Urinary Organs.—*Hæmorrhage.* Catarrhal inflammation of bladder. Flow of residue of urine after replacement of clothing. Micturition slow, with turbid urine. Urging to urinate; early in morning; in afternoon when walking about the room, with colic in transverse colon; frequent, without increased secretion. Constrictive biting in orifice of urethra at 9 P.M. after urinating.

Urine.—Copious; preceded by distention of upper and lower abdomen and by oppressed respiration; and pale; and bloody; and bright-colored; and high-colored, turbid. Scanty, cloudy, contained urates. Jumentous. Frothy. Dark; of strong odor and acid; and scanty, with sediment; with sediment of yellowish-red crystals; with powdery yellowish-white sediment. Of strong odor. Watery, does not redden litmus-paper. As clear as water, containing four-sided prisms, with four-sided pointed ends, the crystals enveloped in tough mucus. Turbid; with chocolate-colored sediment. Uric acid decreased. Phosphoric acid increased.

Sediment.—Light-colored, mealy. Yellowish-white, adherent, of strong odor. Red. Gravelly. Brick-dust. Fatty, with slimy flakes in urine. *Straw-yellow, granular*, with glittering transparent colorless crystals. Like candied sugar, consisting of urate and purpurate of ammonia, with phosphates. Of brown granules; kidney-shaped, one of which showed bright concentric layers. Of crystals; orange-colored; orange-colored, right-angled prisms, with rhomboidal fragments; brown, starlike; rhomboidal and pillar-like; prisms and fragments of three-sided pointed pyramids; sediment rose-red, of rhomboidal flat crystals, with here and there double pyramids, with only traces of uric acid, consisting almost wholly of phosphates.

Sexual Organs.—Eruption. Itching on l. side of scrotum in afternoon. Aching in r. spermatic cord in afternoon, with relaxation of scrotum. Relaxation of r. testis in evening, with aching. Function decreased; lost. Emission in morning without sensation; at night without waking. Uterine hæmorrhage. Abortion. Labor pains.

Respiratory Organs.—Contractive feeling in a weak spot on l. side of hyolaryngeal space in morning. Scraping soreness in larynx and trachea when swallowing in morning on rising, > coughing up mucus, which caused rawness in l. bronchus and l. lung, afterwards the cough caused rending in fauces. Tickling in larynx; in evening, with cough and expectoration of mucus; after midnight; at bifurcation of trachea in evening, with cough and raising and swallowing of mucus. Hoarseness at 4 P.M.; H. > swallowing mucus. Loss of voice.

Cough towards morning, caused by a painful spot in throat; at 12.30 A.M., with tickling in windpipe; in evening when dressing, with sticking in l. upper lung (?) and rheumatic pain in l. trapezius, near posterior edge of scapula; when in open air without overcoat; when sitting in street-car, < towards morning, with anginose condition. Cough, with expectoration of mucus; in morning, once the mucus struck the roof of the mouth; in forenoon; in afternoon when walking in open air; in evening when standing in open air, with threatened irritability in l. bronchi; at night, with necessity to sit up in bed to get his breath; after midnight, with swallowing of mucus; when walking in open air; cough > expectoration from very low down; cough, with gelatinous expectoration from lowest part of bronchi. Loose cough. Short cough in afternoon, with swallowing of mucus.

Expectoration of mucus from r. side of glottis in morning, afterwards from posterior part; E. in forenoon of opaque, white globose mass of mucus, another of exfoliated epithelium, these surrounded by three times their quantity of transparent secretion stretching out between fingers to more than an inch; of lumps of thick sea-green mucus, which sank in water, in morning on rising, then soreness of chest.

Respiration increased. Oppressed in steam-cars; O. as from a hoop about chest. Short. Superficial and irregular. Slow; and irregular. Sighing. Long weary inspiration in evening when eating, then loud sighing, heaving, groaning expiration. Arrested by contraction of throat on rising suddenly from a seat and attempting to swallow at the same time.

Chest.—Hæmorrhage from lungs (probably). Sticking in l.; in r.; in r. half in afternoon, extending to shoulder, impeding respiration, > bending forward; in l., preventing deep respiration. Pain below sternum, almost sticking, < deep breathing or sudden motion. Pain in r.; in morning on rising, > noon; in l. half at 7 P.M., extending to back, < deep inspiration and forcibly throwing l. arm backward, > leaning upon l. forearm with body bent forward (as when writing); on rising; in l. clavicle; transversely through chest at night, from racking cough. Crampy feeling at ends of r. false ribs in morning on bending forward to urinate; at angles of r. true ribs in afternoon; outside of and below r. nipple when in street-car. *Oppression.* Feeling behind middle of sternum (œsophagus?) as if food stuck; feeling as of something indigestible behind lower sternum in evening, > eructations; feeling to l. of sternum in morning as of spasmodic condition of œsophagus from indigestion. Tickling in l. in evening.

Clinical.—**Pneumonia, with great oppression, weakness, deafness and whizzing in ears, or rushing like a storm in ears, or ringing of bells, must lie on the back (Sang).**

Heart.—Sticking in region of apex. Pressure in præcordial region, with passage of flatus. Tension in præcordial region, < l. side below short ribs, with necessity to loosen bands of clothing. Præcordial anxiety. Præcordial uneasiness. Palpitation; in morning on waking, lying on l. side, > lying on heart; in morning caused by indignation, > lying on heart; in afternoon; when roused suddenly, had to lie on heart and support it with the hand; when lying on r. side, > lying on abdomen. Action accelerated in forenoon. Strong beating at 10 A.M., after excitement. Action subjectly preceptible in forenoon when sitting partially doubled up; in l. chest and abdomen in forenoon after straining at stool; in l. chest in afternoon after going up-stairs; through much of chest on being awakened from a nap, > lying still; in forenoon when sitting after an incomplete stool, extending to head; after breakfast, sitting at stool with elbows on knees, felt through chest, down back to sacrum and through abdomen. Feeble movements.

Pulse.—Rapid; and full; and irregular and intermittent; and small and irritable. Slow; in morning and afternoon; and strong, afterwards rapid and weak; and scarcely preceptible. Scarcely perceptible. Small, almost imperceptible.

Neck.—Swelling along r. sterno-cleido-mastoid muscle. Sprained feeling in upper r. sterno-mastoid muscle in afternoon in street-car on suddenly turning head to r., with sticking in r. ear. Crampy feeling in l. sterno-mastoid muscle in morning, then in l. levator anguli scapulæ. Rheumatic feeling from cool wind, extending to l. ear.

Back.—Pain. **Sensitiveness of last cervical and first dorsal vertebræ to pressure**; *of dorsal vertebræ; first and second dorsal vertebræ; third dorsal vertebræ pain on touch*, **with oppression of chest** (Phos.); pain in second and < first, on pressure in afternoon; dorsal vertebræ more painful to pressure during the chill than the cervical or lumbar vertebræ. Sticking around lower angle of r. scapula. Rheumatic feeling at inner border of l. scapula; in l. upper and inner scapular muscles in afternoon after sitting in a draught; at l. inner scapular border at midnight when writing, > supporting arm. Crampy feeling at inner border of r. scapula in afternoon.

Lumbar Region.—Pleurosthotonic cramp in l. on exertion. Subcutaneous sticking in r. when walking, later when straightening himself, running up l. side. Pain; in middle of l. costo-pelvic muscular region in afternoon; in afternoon when walking, after raw, condimented oysters; in l. in afternoon when walking, then in r., then when sitting in l. again; in l. kidney region in afternoon when sitting bent to r. side; in l. in evening; in l. lower in evening when writing; in l. about lower end of kidney after dinner when sitting bent forward in street-car, then indications of pain on r. side; when sitting bent up in street-car; in l. kidney on bending over table; in l. when walking; in l. kidney, < by positions, etc., which cause compression. Crampy pain in l. renal region in evening. Crampy lumbago when standing in street without overcoat, > external support and adjusting position. Uneasiness in l. Feeling in forenoon, not having defecated, as if a firm mass pressed against sacrum, hips and lower lumbar region.

Clinical.—In spinal irritation, with great sensitiveness of the spine in the region of the first dorsal vertebræ, the pain extending towards the head and apt to recur periodically.

Extremities.—Livid and cool. *Trembling; and control over them much hampered;* even on slight exertion, with numbness; with coldness. Tearings and drawings in hands and feet. Neuralgic twinges in r. index and r. little toe in afternoon on using them. Bruised feeling. *Weakness;* of arms and legs.

Upper Extremities.—Sticking in r. axillary folds. (Rheumatico-neuralgic ache in r. posterior axillary fold in afternoon when pressing scapulæ against chair.)

Shoulder.—Cracking of joints on raising arms. Cramp in anterior half of l. deltoid after 1 A.M., before going to bed, on some motions of arm. Sticking above r. external condyle of humerus in evening. Pain. Rheumatism in r. acromion in cool wind, with false position; in l. deltoid region, near acromion, in cool, humid, windy day, > warmth. Rheumatic feeling in r. deltoid at 2.20 A.M. (after sleeping); > change of position; in tendons of both deltoids and of l. biceps in afternoon, from muscular effort; in one or other deltoid when arm was in malposition, extending half way down outer arm. Rheumatic pain in l. at noon.

Arm.—Swollen and covered with pustules, also hands. Neuralgia in tendon of l. biceps at noon on holding forearm flexed and pronated, hand on edge of table. Rheumatic pain in r. (outer origin of brachialis anticus); rheumatic threatening in r. arm when sitting with arm in malposition in afternoon, then in course of musculo-spiral nerve to back of forearm and hand when resting palm on car-seat, and in ulnar nerve adjoining pisiform bone. Pain in middle third of ulnar nerve from below l. axilla to below elbow, in afternoon when writing. Bruised feeling. Lack of control over muscles in afternoon.

Upper Arm.—Twinge in superficial nerves, in inner and outer aspects in evening when writing. Pain in r. outer in evening.

Elbow.—Pain in front of, in afternoon when pulling a door. Sprained feeling at biceps tendon on forcibly flexing r. forearm.

Forearm.—Twitching of l. ulnar flexor; of tendons in front of r. ulna. Cramp in flexors of l. in morning on feeling for levator anguli scapulæ. Sticking in dorsum of r. lower, in nerves; in dorsum of r. at noon on putting hand behind me; in dorsum of r. in afternoon when holding a weight; in dorsum of r. in evening when sitting. Neuralgia in dorsum of r., over belly of supinator longus, in forenoon; in r. ulna in morning when writing; in afternoon in dorsal branches of radial nerves, then suddenly in digital nerves of adjacent sides of middle phalanges of first and second l. fingers. Neuralgico-rheumatic sensations in dorsum of r. in afternoon when walking, extending as a hard ache to middle of ulna. Rheumatic pain in r. ulna in morning on waking, the arm being uncovered, > warm sponge-bath; in extensor tendons of r. in afternoon when riding in cool wind, > motion. Carrying medicine-case in r. hand in afternoon, compression of ulnar nerve against body, pain to termini of nerve in little finger; pain in lower end of l. ulna in evening when holding paper to write on; pain on inner edge of r. ulna when writing, then in its upper dorsum, then anteriorly in same, < when ulnar nerve is on the stretch, > relaxing it or removing compression.

Wrist.—Sticking in dorsum of r. in forenoon when writing. Rheumatic pain around r. carpus in afternoon after writing.

Hand.—Fulness of veins in evening. Seem puffy when closing them. Sticking in l. between bases of first and second metacarpal bones in forenoon after vigorous use of hands; in r. palm between first and second metacarpus in evening. Neuralgia in space between first and second r. metacarpus after midnight, extending along digital nerve, inner aspect of first phalanx of first finger. Crampy, then rheumatic pain in r. third knuckle and above it, in afternoon when writing. Sensation in r. during every stool as if drops of fluid passed thence to the shoulder. Refused their service, also the arms.

Fingers.—Livid. Nails unusually tough. After morning sponge-bath, inflammation of l. index (on which there is a slight cut). Neuralgia in inner digital nerve of l. second; in ball of r. thumb in evening;

in l. index when holding papers in l. hand and writing on them. Pain in r. finger and thumb. Soreness of last joint of r. little to pressure, with swelling and redness; proximal palmar portion of last phalanx of r. thumb sensitive to pressure, as in incipient felon.

Lower Extremities.—When walking the tendons seem to catch and pain. "Wooden feeling" in evening when walking. Inability to walk. Disposition to aid walking by gravitation in afternoon, walking bent forward to supplement muscular inertia, especially in calves.

Thigh.—Sticking behind l. trochanter in afternoon on walking; in r. gluteus medius on walking. Stitch-like catching in anterior superior part of l. gluteus maximus in afternoon on walking. Cutting across lower half of l. rectus femoris at every step in afternoon after jumping from car; transversely in inner and lower part of r. rectus femoris in forenoon when at stool; crampy, across, in afternoon on entering house and in lower half of rectus muscle, then on walking out in l. thigh on same level. Crampy pain in lower border of r. gluteus maximus in evening. Neuralgic twinge behind r. trochanter, afterwards felt when walking. Rheumatic twinge behind r. trochanter in evening when walking. Rheumatic pain in exterior of l. thigh and upper fibula in afternoon when sitting with limb suddenly doubled up, by leaning far forward; along inner border of l. rectus femoris when walking. Rheumatic feeling behind r. trochanter in afternoon when walking; in lower half of r. vastus externus in afternoon when walking; in part of l. gluteus maximus on standing bent over. Myalgia along exterior aspect of r. rectus femoris, on standing bent forward with r. foot advanced. Tension in rectus muscles in evening on walking, > standing still. Rigid feeling in rectus muscles on walking, then similar sensation posteriorly. Hips feel old, inert and stiff in morning on walking. Tired feeling in upper front, in afternoon on walking; in l. rectus femoris in evening when sitting; when walking, and knees are ready to give way; in hips before going to bed, < l., almost a stiff feeling. Loss of power.

Knee.—Trembling. Sticking in upper part of l. in evening. Feeling as if bones at inner half of r. did not fit when walking, increasing to a drawing at inner part of popliteal space and up inner hamstring muscles, with awkward gait, he shook the limb to relieve the tension. Contractive sensation down inner side of r. in afternoon. Weakness; in afternoon on walking.

Leg.—The disease at first confined to neck, face and arms, afterwards covered the legs, one of which was swollen and covered with a scaly eruption, like a kind of elephantiasis. Neuralgia in lower half of l., in course of anterior tibial nerve, in morning; in front of lower end of r. fibula in evening. Twinges in middle of r. tibial nerve, anteriorly, in evening. Rheumatic feeling about lower head of r. fibula in afternoon on rising from a seat. Aching over lower inner part of r. tibia in evening. Pricking in r. inner calf in afternoon when resting l. knee on r.

Ankle.—Sticking in l. posterior tibial artery, near malleolus, in forenoon; below r. inner malleolus in morning on rising; below r. inner malleolus when walking. Feeling as if injured. Sprained feeling about l.; in front of l. in afternoon during forced flexion when sitting, then in both sides of astragulus down to attachments of internal lateral ligament when walking, then under inside of l. instep; of flexor tendons under l. inner, when standing, the same in front of malleolus when walking; intermittent, under and about l. inner malleolus when walking, and in tendo-achillis.

Foot.—Trembling, with aching in malleoli. Vertical stitch back of r. heel. Cramp in outer part of hollow of r. Crampy feeling in hollow of l., inside. Crampy aching in hollow of l., in inner muscles, < sitting, > standing; in outer muscles of r. sole in morning when sitting; in muscles of outer part of r. sole in evening when resting it on its inner side. Pain at l. inner calcaneal spaces in afternoon when walking, then in r. when standing. Strained pain in hollow of r. in afternoon; in inner part of hollow of r. in afternoon, in street-car. Dull twinge at inner side of l. instep. Soreness like a "stone-bruise" anteriorly in ball of l., causing limping. Insteps hurt by boots at 10 P.M. Swollen feeling in r. in evening when putting on boots. *Weakness;* on walking, with numbness.

Toes.—Sprained feeling in l. middle on rising from bed and standing. Gouty (?) pain in r. great joint on pressing foot to floor. Rending pain in joint of r. great, when walking indoors, on pressing foot to floor. Twinge in corn on l. little in evening from pressure of slipper, > changing its position.

Skin.—Soft. Retains the folds when pinched. Eruptions; purpuric. Wheals, with local redness over neck, chest and arms. Erythema of face and limbs, with swelling of r. arm. Rash, with œdema, then desquamation; R. as vivid as scarlatina, with itching, then exfoliation. Urticaria over whole body U., with puffiness of eyelids, face and sometimes of limbs, which does not appear to be dropsical. Flat, lymphy, itching papules in patches on dorsa of hands, < radial side. Sore pimple to l. of bridge of nose; in beard on r. upper part of chin, with watery discharge. Pimples over whole body, with a discharge thicker than serum, but thinner than pus, with itching, then squamous scabs. Pustules resembling an itchlike crust. Offensive suppuration. Furuncle on r. upper lid.

Vesicular exanthema, with itching, redness and swelling of skin, first on genitals and thighs, then on face, hands and arms, moist but usually drying with a fine crust, sometimes causing cracks and ending in desquamation of thick scales, with febrile symptoms and gastric disturbances.

Pricking at night, then sweat, < of face; sudden pricking on back, chest and thighs in evening when walking in open air, then sweat on chest and back. Itching on chest, back and arms; in sides of chin and on head, etc., in morning; of r. alar crease of nose in afternoon; of anterior wall of concha of l. ear in evening, > scratching, which yields whitish scales; in external meatus of each ear, with crawling; on r. side of back about midnight, voluntary friction by clothing caused chilly creeping round from back to sides and front of chest.

Sleep.—Yawning; towards evening; in evening in the street. Sleepiness; during the day; in forenoon when standing; at noon when sitting, with downward pressure in forehead extending to upper eyelids; in afternoon when conversing, the lids seem to contract spasmodically, < glare on white wall; in afternoon in car and church; in evening in close railroad car; in street-car, and after getting out laggy gait; in warm rooms when conversing; during conversation before and after dinner; like a warmth about eyes and down to throat in afternoon when sitting. Dozing in chair before dinner. Sleep profound but unrefreshing. Difficult waking.

Sleeplessness; from heat and thirst; except for a few hours in the morning. Frequent waking; towards daylight, sleep almost semi-conscious. Early waking from an uneasy sleep. Restless sleep; with much cough; full of dreams; interrupted by wonderful dreams. Crying in sleep at midnight, waking him, with necessity to get out of bed.

Dreams; frightful, with restless sleep; indistinct, in morning; vivid towards morning.

Fever.—Chill; in forenoon; at 11 A.M., with pallor of face, pain in forehead and temples and ringing in ears; in afternoon; in afternoon when at work; towards evening, with rapid pulse, dry mouth and thirst; with accelerated pulse. Shaking; then fever; at 3 P.M., then heat of face from 6.30 to 9 P.M., chill with trembling of limbs, then in bed heat with yawning and sneezing, then sweat. Alternating with effervescence of blood causing pulsation.

Chill from occiput over trapezius muscle and to upper arms in afternoon in open air; creeping, in r., side of occiput in afternoon, then in l. Creeping over trapezius in forenoon, then from spines of scapulæ to shoulders, then on taking off hat in the house from trapezius over occiput to vertex and behind ears; creeping over trapezius in afternoon, with soreness in r. lower bicuspid. In back, with pain in one of the middle dorsal vertebræ; in scapular and mammary regions; in sacrum on lying down before breakfast, and in l. leg. In limbs; in afternoon, and in hands, feet, chin, nose and ears. Creeping over l. shoulder, scapula and l. side of neck on moving arms, then after sitting down in a warm room warmth about face, shoulders and downward and backward, becoming general, with throbbing of heart and of arteries to feet and hands. Of l. arm in evening when writing in shirt-sleeves, with sneezing, tingling of nose and snuffling, stoppage alternating with sneezing. Of l. hand in afternoon when writing; of backs of hands and fingers in afternoon. Of fingers in morning, and of toes and soles. Of knees; in forenoon if uncovered by wrapper, < l. Of feet in forenoon in a draught of air, with sneezing; l. in forenoon when sitting; l. at noon; at noon when sitting, < l.; l. in afternoon, with flushing; in afternoon, and of hands, < l. foot and tendo-achillis; in afternoon when writing; in afternoon, then of knees and above boots, < l. Of soles, < l., with sneezing, then of anterior half of foot.

Heat; in afternoon, < forehead, then in face; towards evening when quiet, then sweat; when walking, with tingling or stinging on front of thighs. Dry, during a sleepless night. Of skin; towards evening. Intermittent fever in the cycle of an ordinary tertian. Symptoms resembling scarlet fever, chill, with præcordial anxiety, nausea, vomiting, headache, fever, then erythema on face, spreading over body, with burning, itching and with œdema of face, injection of conjunctiva, the color > for a moment by pressure, angina in posterior wall of pharynx, prostration, then desquamation.

Heat in head; then sweat; with a strong rapid pulse, then sweat; of forehead, with pain in it. Of face; down l. side of face in afternoon; towards evening; towards evening when writing; at 4 P.M. in flushes, with thirst; as after coffee; dry H. of face and hands at 1.30 A.M. when writing. Extending down to external chest, subjectively, in afternoon. Feeling as if sweat would break out about neck and face in evening; from r. scapula to l. face and hand, forehead and nape and down back in evening, with general sweat. Of hands in forenoon when sitting writing.

Sweat; in morning sleep; in evening when in a crowd; in evening on parts pressed by the clothing, as dorsal, axillary and perineal regions; in sleep.

Clinical.—Intermittent fever, the paroxysms recurring with great regularity at the same hour, especially indicated by the extreme sensitiveness of the dorsal vertebræ, with pain on pressure, in other respects very much like China. Intermittent fever is sometimes certainly cured completely and permanently by this drug, but only a small proportion of the cases are thus cured. Quinine possesses the curious property of preventing in a measure the development of marsh-malarial poisoning in the system in a way similar to that in which mercury prevents the development of syphilis, but when once developed China will only occasionally cure the disease.

Chloralum.

For homœopathic use 1 part of Chloral hydrate is dissolved in 9 parts of Alcohol.

General Action.—Chloral is a powerful hypnotic, as well as a depressant of the heart; it also causes vasomotor paralysis, feeble and slow respiration and muscular weakness. It produces a decided erythema, particularly aggravated by alcoholic stimulants; ecchymoses, and destruction of tissue in consequence.

Affinities.—Op., Bell., Nux v., the *Carbons*, Plumb.

Generalities.—Uncertainty of movement, with tendency to fall forward. Almost jumping and springing, he changed from one bed to another. Agility. Appearance as if intoxicated; by brandy. Resemblance to a living skeleton, a maudlin, semi-narcotized condition, when aroused by loud and repeated questionings her answers were incoherent, her manner wild and uncertain, evincing a state bordering on idiocy. The blood contained garnet-colored amorphous particles, a number of dark red globules (double the diameter of white corpuscles, and many smaller), some of these dark red. Epileptiform convulsions. Ataxic symptoms, with numbness and burning. Muscular pains, < upper limbs. Pains as sometimes from chronic alcoholism, < about joints, *encircling* the limb, finger, etc., just above or below the joint, < moist and cold weather. Restlessness. Weakness; and limbs extended, head low, and at times aspect of impending dissolution. Lipothymia. Inaptitude for exertion. Anæsthesia.

Mind.—Delirium; hurled a hot-water bottle at an imaginary figure which stood at the foot of the bed menacing her; wandering about in the upper stories of the building. Delirium tremens. Muttering and talking about dead friends; M. of a religious character; unable to resist uttering what he knew to be nonsense, though conscious of everything going on around him (Stram.). Pleasant excitation, with rapid pulse. Excitability as from champagne, with pleasant feeling, smiling and dancing. Lively mood, with loud laughter and witty remarks. Talkative. Listless, peevish, childish, begging for chloral. Perversion of moral sense. Morose, deceitful and imbecile in intellect, memory and will. Terror, with weakness. Melancholia; and irresolution.

Stupefaction. Inability to concentrate thought. Confusion; feeling now as if in one county, now as if in another, with anxiety to get home. Almost idiotic. Memory impaired. Insensibility; with quiet but incoherent talking; with screams now and then, restlessness, retching, foaming at the mouth, pallor, dilated pupils, l. leg spasmodically stretched, r. relaxed.

Head.—Bent upon chest. Aching; on waking; in morning on waking, lasting all day; < sudden motion. Discomfort. Dulness. Fulness at 8 A.M., and constriction. Veins filled to bursting, and in neck. Heaviness. Intoxication; on waking; feeling as if he had been intoxicated by wine (Glon., Nux v., Valer.). Vertigo.

Pain in forehead; extending to occiput; over r. supraorbital ridge, < movement; over eyes, running down in eyes, < l. side, with constriction of eyes. Heavy pain over eyes, < l., during supper. Fulness over eyes, < over l. eye, with nausea and sour eructations of liquid, supposed to be what had been eaten for breakfast. Feeling as if a hot band were drawn from temple to temple, directly over eyes, with sensation of a burning ring around each eye. Pain about cerebellum after any alcoholic stimulant, with red face and suffused eyes (Nux v.). Weight and soreness in occiput and over eyes, inside skull, < moving about and lying down, slightly > in open air. Hair woolly, with a dry and fluffy feel.

Clinical.—Has cured morning frontal headaches, with great sensitiveness to motion, laughing, etc., and better in open air.

Eyes.—*Bloodshot and watering;* B. and as if starting from sockets. Staring wildly. Glistening. Inflammation and photophobia; I., with weakness and burning lachrymation. Lachrymation. Capillary congestion of l. disc. Disc transparent, like white wax, retina pale, the central artery and vein and their branches dark and prominent. Haziness of fundus. Throbbing pain in l. ball at 11.20 A.M., < leaning forward.

Pupils dilated; with sensitiveness to light. Pupils contracted; and insensible to light; C., < r., then dilated, then alternations of myosis and mydriasis. Pupils elliptical, then almost angular contraction of l., at first directed downward and outward, afterwards outward and upward, and at the same time dull notches in an outward direction in middle of r. Pupils more sensitive to light. *Conjunctiva congested;* or yellow; and lids red and swollen. Ptosis. Lids closed and difficult to open. *Vision dim;* lost. Diplopia, then muscæ volitantes. Colored objects look white.

Clinical.—Retinal asthenopia, with circles of light, black spots, etc. (Coca?).

Ears.—Tinnitus aurium.

Face.—Pale; and anxious; and hippocratic, veins sunken. Purple. Dusky. Red; and anxious. Cheeks and lips livid. Wistful and haggard. Swollen; < below eyes. Rush of blood, with heat. Jaws firmly closed. Lips and mucous membrane of mouth excoriated, afterwards lips covered with crusts.

Mouth.—Gums spongy. Tongue coated; white. Tongue blistered and ulcerated. T. dry, brown. Tongue thick, speech indistinct. Speech broken as if partially drunk. Mucous membrane livid. Frothy mucus flowed from mouth, and it seemed filled with a membranous substance, not unlike membranous croup. Fetid breath.

Throat.—Pharyngeal congestion, with rash resembling that of scarlet fever. Spasm involving epiglottis and almost strangling him. Catarrhal soreness, with pain in fauces. Sensation of a cold in head on waking at 7 A.M., with sensitiveness, rawness and burning in throat and posterior nares. Burning in fauces and stomach. Swallowing difficult, the act not beginning till he strangled and coughed. *Partial paralysis of œsophagus* (Op.), with nervous disinclination to eat or drink, and interfering with nutrition; partial paralysis, not spasmodic stricture (Plumb.).

Stomach and Abdomen.—Longing for food. Little appetite for dinner. Appetite lost; capricious. Thirst; in morning on waking, with dryness of tongue and fauces, headache, vertigo, nausea and nervous sensibility. Eructations, > eating; sour E. of food. Nausea; > supper, but returning in evening, with oppression of stomach, without inclination to vomit. Retching. Vomiting (Nux v.). Pain in pit of stomach; in epigastrium on waking; in stomach and abdomen, with difficult breathing; sharp, in epigastric region. Epigastric tenderness. Burning in stomach. Sinking at stomach-pit, with oppression. Colic.

Clinical.—Seasickness.

Stool.—Diarrhœa; twice in afternoon; containing gelatinous matter. Soft, with pain in rectum; soft, light-yellowish; with sharp pain in rectum. Constipation. Pale and hard. Frequent.

Urinary and Sexual Organs.—*Copious micturition in bed without knowing it* (Op.). Frequent and profuse micturition; frequent in afternoon and night. Urine albuminous. Seminal emissions at night; copious. Menses reappeared in seven or eight days.

Respiratory Organs.—Redness and swelling of epiglottis and of false vocal cords. Suffocating sensation and oppression of chest in front and at its base. Dyspnœa; increasing to asphyxia, with swelling of face, paralysis of facial muscles and all the signs of cerebral effusion. Respiration stertorous; and slow (Op.). Panting. Gasping. Respiration rapid; and shallow and stertorous. Respiration intermittent (Plumb.). R. deep, at times imperceptible.

Clinical.—Asthmatic attacks, with sleeplessness, delirium, etc.

Chest.—Oppression after eating, < ascending stairs, interfering with speech. Pain.

Heart and Pulse.—Heart's sounds indistinct. Cardiac debility. Action increased and arterial tension. Heart's action rapid but feeble. Failure of l. ventricle. Strong pulsation in arteries after a glass of beer, with swollen red face. Pulse rapid; and bounding; and hard, tense; and weak and wavy; and weak, irregular in force and rhythm and frequently intermittent (Dig.). Pulse weak; and slow and intermittent; could hardly be felt in carotids. Pulse of r. arm (she had lain on that side) not perceptible, that of l. small and thready.

Neck.—Veins full. A "singing sensation" comes from nape or medulla oblongata.

Extremities.—Jactitation. Tingling, and weight as if asleep. Blood settles under finger-nails and purple spots appear on side on which she had lain. Staggering. Lower limbs, acute wandering pains, < in calves; crampy pains, < through knees and ankles; weakness.

Leg.—Cramp; and inability to co-ordinate movements of lower limbs. Giving away suddenly in morning on rising, inability to stand or walk, then nervous depression, general weakness, vacuity of mind and inability to concentrate the attention. Pain in calves, at times running down into feet, with sense of fulness in skin and throbbing, then steady legache. Feeling "as if in a mash," "as if he could not clearly distinguish between one part and another," in morning on putting feet to the ground. Feeling as if asleep. Weakness and want of co-ordinative power. Paralysis from knees downward on waking at 10 A.M.; P. of motion and sensation.

Skin.—*Red blotches on arms, legs and face, then over whole body, gradually coalescing, till they resembled measles.* Red spots becoming confluent, with fever and rapid pulse, then swelling of face, cheeks, lids and ears, with now impetiginous, now moist, now scaly eczema and ichthyoses, desquamation in great sheaths, then falling of hair and nails of all fingers and toes, with this skin disease watery diarrhœa and then similar affection of conjunctiva and bronchi, abscesses on arms, over shoulders and arm-pits. Redness on chest and shoulders, next day extending over whole trunk and limbs, livid spots and red patches alternating, afterwards the spots on chest and abdomen were yellowish, with white patches between them, then general desquamation, and fissures over sacrum and near joints. Scarlet color of face from roots of hair down to ramus of jaw, < over cheek-bones, and shading in different directions, ears of same color and red blotches over neck and chest down to centre of sternum, all > paroxysm of sneezing, with contraction of pupils, injection of conjunctiva and excitement of circulation. Redness of face, forehead and whole head to neck. Smooth scarlet eruption over whole body.

Diffuse inflammatory redness. Erythematous redness over head and neck, with twitching of facial muscles. Scarlatinal rash over whole body, with fever and tenderness of skin, then desquamation. *Erythema of head and neck*, with dark areola, < *wine, beer or spirits, with palpitation*, the hyperæmia disappearing last from forehead. Erythema of head in spots, then more diffuse, the vessels being dilated, in pronounced forms extending to trunk and becoming general, following by preference the larger trunk nerves. Petechial and purpuric eruptions, which may run into a species of pyæmic condition, with ulceration of gums and prostration, as in scurvy, with abscesses and deep ulcers. Erysipelatous inflammation of fingers, with desquamation of skin and ulceration around borders of nails. Erysipelatous eruption on face, face so swollen that she could not see. Papular rash on arms, with red bases. Nettle-rash; *on arms and legs. Anæsthesia.* Itching preventing sleep at night.

Clinical.—Has been prescribed for erythema and urticaria.

Sleep.—Gaping. Sleepiness; in evening, retired early, unrefreshed on waking in morning; S. but remained awake till 1 A.M. Prolonged sleep. Deep sleep; from 1 to 5 P.M., with loud snoring; with red face, fulness of veins of neck, deep respiration and rapid pulse. Snoring. Woke with a scream, jumped out of bed, sat on the edge of it, semi-conscious (Bell.).

Fever.—Coldness. Cool skin. Cold limbs. Fever. Sweat; in beads on forehead; cold. Singular dryness of skin.

Chlorum.

A solution, freshly prepared, of Chlorine Gas in cold water, is diluted for internal use.

General Action.—From the few observations hitherto made, it would seem that spasm of the glottis is the marked feature of the action of the drug on the organs of respiration. Compare *Bromine;* other symptoms may be compared with *Iodine.*

Generalities.—Old appearance. Loss of fat. Quantity of chlorides in blood increased, while the carbonates and other salts were lessened. Consumption. Sensation at 3 A.M., as before severe sickness. Inclination to lie down; during the headache. Disinclination to rise in morning, and ill humor. Restlessness. Nervous sensibility. Sensibility diminished. *Exercise in open air agreed with him.*

Mind.—Anxiety; he could not speak. Fear of becoming insane, with loss of memory, everything seems confused. Irritability; in morning. The difficulty in recalling names is worse, and of recollecting persons when he sees their names.

Head.—Aching during coryza; A., < after dinner; threatened; in l. side before the shuddering, < after dinner, at 2 P.M., with necessity to lie down, > walking back and forth, a lighter attack next day at the same hour. Crawling shuddering at 11 A.M., < at the back, < sitting with the back to the sun, then fever. Disagreeable sensation when shuddering. Vertigo and stupefaction. *Painful wearing sensation in vertex and down l. side, with inclination to lie down.* Pressure in occipital protuberance, with burning.

Eyes.—Protruding. Lachrymation; on waking; during coryza. Dim during fever. Fantastic images suddenly floated before the eyes and disappeared with lightning-like rapidity.

Ears.—Ringing in r. (and dulness in l., which had been deaf for forty years).

Nose.—Sticking. Burning pain, with tension and dryness, and in eyes. Eroded sensation in corners. Dryness; with irritation in windpipe to cough, and pressure on chest. Sneezing. Stoppage of l. nostril. Coryza in evening, next morning violent sneezing; C. in evening, < lying, sudden dropping of corrosive water, with lachrymation and dryness of tongue, palate and fauces, without thirst, but cold water is agreeable, with stoppage of nose while it flows; C., with headache and fever; with copious yellow discharge. Discharge of mucus; of corroding water; dropping of water from l. nostril; flow from r. nostril, his l. is always stopped. Smell lost.

Face.—Pale, often greenish. Heightened color. Bloated.

Mouth.—Sensation of fulness in teeth. Tongue dry and red. Articulation difficult. Increased vascularity and minute ulcerations in mouth and throat. Mouth, fauces and œsophagus sore, as if the tongue had been burnt, as if he had eaten vegetable acids, or as if his teeth had been injured by acids. Much mucus. Dryness. Salivation. Saliva altered in quantity and character; acid. Taste febrile in morning, > rinsing mouth; not good to tobacco, smoking bites the tongue and causes dryness in mouth.

Throat.—Choking sensation. Soreness from uvula to bronchi; S., and in chest, with hoarseness. Inability to swallow.

Stomach.—Appetite less evenings. Desire for wine increased. Nausea. Vomiting. Acidity. Inflammation. Warmth. Sensitiveness of epigastrium to pressure.

Abdomen and Stool.—Bile altered; increased. Colic. Weakness of abdomen mornings. Diarrhœa; in morning; twice in forenoon.

Urinary and Sexual Organs.—Frequent desire to urinate, but the urine is passed only in moderate quantities. Urine increased. Urine possesses bleaching properties; loses the power to redden litmus-paper. Sudden impotence, even sexual aversion.

Respiratory Organs.—*Spasms of glottis; of vocal cords.* Irritation of epiglottis; of larnynx and bronchi. *Constriction, with suffocation.* Inflammation, and of lungs; of bronchial mucous membrane. Bronchial catarrh. Warmth. Loss of voice; from damp air.

Clinical.—Some brilliant cures of laryngismus stridulous have been cured by the internal administration of a dilute solution of Chlorine Gas.

Cough; irritation to. Violent. Spasmodic. Paroxysms evenings as if he would have a cough, as if the pharynx were raw or becoming so. Whistling-wheezing. Dry, with at each cough soreness in a spot in region of r. bronchus. In exhausting fits, with expectoration. With spitting of blood. With expectoration of thick, white, frothy mucus. Constant, with sensation as if bronchi were filled with thick, tenacious mucus, no relief from expectoration, with sweat on forehead, it seemed as if the effort to raise the mucus would empty the stomach, yet no nausea is felt. Expectoration; of mucus.

Sudden dyspnœa from spasm of vocal cords, *with staring eyes, blue face, cold sweat covering body, pulse small and soft, temperature sinking;* D., with sensation of a band around lower third of chest. *Suffocation; in paroxysms, often followed by catarrh;* with violent cough, sensation of cramp in muscular fibres of bronchi, increased mucus, often with spitting of blood. **Inspiration comparatively free but crowing, with obstructed expiration,** *livid face, convulsions of limbs and partial coma;* **inspiration unimpeded, but expiration impossible** from closure of rima glottidis, inspiration crowing, *the lungs becoming inflated to a painful degree, it seemed as if air might pass through walls of chest more readily than by larynx,* face turgid and livid, partial coma; *inspiration easy but insufficient, with short, rattling-crackling râle, expiration difficult, prolonged, insufficient, with prolonged, loud, whistling râles* (a combination of many sounds), and each pulsation of heart gives a crescendo diminuendo effect to them; *inspiration difficult and attended with râles.* Whistling râles, which are quite loud on forced expiration. Anxious respiration. Respiration and heart's action increased.

Chest.—Hæmoptysis; and consumption. Pain. Contraction. Oppression, not > in open air; O. of lungs, < l. Affection of lungs, < r. Inflammation of lungs and air-passages. Sensation in lower and inner third of r. lung as if ruptured, a feeling as if the air escaped into the pleural cavity at each inspiration, at each inspiration a râle at the quasi-ruptured place. Soreness internally, > cough.

Pulse.—Frequent. Diminished.

Neck and Spine.—Jerking of muscles, drawing head backward.

Extremities.—Stiffness. Weakness of lower.

Skin.—*Cutis anserina;* and dry, yellow and shrivelled. Red and painful, becoming swollen and thickened as in facial erysipelas; with bruised sensation, then itching and desquamation. Accumulation of blood in capillaries, with heat. Determination of blood, with papillæ close together, which suppurate and vesicate or desquamate, < on back, loins, breast, abdomen and arms. Tetters. Inflammation and ulceration. Desquamation. Urticaria febrilis. Nettle-rash, white wheals in clusters, surrounded by diffuse redness. Minute vesicles all over skin, on the shoulders their bases nearly touch, then red and livid spots. *Sensitiveness.* Smarting. Sticking. Stinging, then symptoms as from cantharides, then soreness and bruised sensation, then itching and cuticle coming off in thick scales, as in psoriasis. Stinging as of nettles. Stinging as of insects, with sweat, rush of blood to skin, sometimes pimples or vesicles; intermittent S. as of insects here and there, on arm, back, abdomen and lower limbs. Itching; with increased sensibility.

Sleep.—Late falling asleep after every excitement, the following days early sleepiness.

Fever.—Shivering; in evening in a warm room. Cold shudders over anterior surface of arms from 10 or 11 A.M. to 2 P.M., and over back and thighs, with dimness before eyes, then fever. Heat; when eating and afterwards, with irritability while drinking wine and coffee; of skin. Sweat; in sleep at night; critical.

Clinical.—In typhus the diluted Chlorine water has been given, especially when the tongue was extremely dry; it seems to relieve the profound prostration, the subsultus tendinum and extreme dryness of the tongue.

Chromicum Acidum.

A solution of pure Chromic Acid in distilled water (1 to 9) may be diluted for use.

Generalities.—Pain, < draught of air; < l. side; < cold water. Amelioration from quick walking. Heaviness, dulness, stupidity. Weakness.

Mind.—Confusion. Memory affected so that when writing he was at a loss to make several letters.

Head.—Pain over l. eye. Heavy pain along coronal suture from 10 A.M. till 4 P.M., extending backward over parietal region. Throbbing in forepart, with fulness, with emptiness in chest, soreness on pressure and cold feet. Fulness; at night, with lightness at heart and vertigo on descending stairs; in vertex and frontal region at 5 A.M., on waking. Lightness like vertigo at 10 P.M., with heat in face. Vertigo at 10 A.M. when walking, inclining him to the right.

Eyes.—Sore and feeling heavy, as if inflamed. Pain at noon from r. ball into interior of brain, with soreness of orb to touch. Vision diminished.

Ears, Nose and Face.—Sudden intermittent feeling of water in r. ear, disappearing suddenly. Sensation when eating as if expired air smelt putrid, almost causing nausea. Features contracted, face leaden, eyes sunken. Lips dry and disposed to crack.

Mouth.—Toothache in l. lower jaw in morning after the usual rinsing with cold water; repeated, < r. lower, with violent beating of corresponding artery;

sudden, in l. sound teeth in night, < lower, with violent beating of corresponding arteries; intermittent, in r. at 10 P.M. in bed, extending into forehead, with uneasiness, teeth seemed too long, with relief of pain between head, l. scapula and shoulder, then uneasiness in limbs, next morning r. teeth felt too long and cold water caused pain.

Throat.—*Tough mucus, with inclination to swallow it, as it could not be easily hawked up; white mucus, < morning, causing hawking.*

Stomach.—No appetite for breakfast. Nausea from 2 till 4 P.M., after dinner; after a simple supper, with sensation as if stool would follow; < when stomach is empty. Vomiting profuse, first of contents of stomach, then of much bile, then of blood; frequent V. of food, then of bile, with sweat, much retching, the nausea which precedes each vomiting > quick walking, between the attacks of vomiting pressure and fulness in stomach so that he must loosen the clothes, after the last vomiting sleep, then pressure or heaviness in stomach. Burning pain.

Abdomen.—Cutting in hypogastrium and ascending colon at 6 P.M., > profuse diarrhœa. Pain in l. hypochondrium; in colon in morning on waking, > rising, with rumbling. Uneasiness in morning in bed, as before diarrhœa, > rising; in lower, waking at 4 A.M., with soreness to touch, < along colon, with nausea, eructations and retching, throwing off white mucus.

Anus and Stool.—Hæmorrhoids internal and bleeding; painful, externally on l. side of anus. Hæmorrhoidal discharge during stool; with weakness in small of back. *Diarrhœa; watery, with nausea and vertigo. Frequent copious stools.* Small stool of mucus and knotty fæces.

Urinary Organs.—Strangury in morning on waking after a dream of it.

Chest, Heart and Pulse.—Pain in l. lung, with throbbing. Rawness or soreness in chest, with hacking cough. Pulsation through chest at noon. Weakness of chest. Sudden stitch in region of heart. Stricture in region of heart at 10 A.M. Throbbing from region of heart to l. eye and l. side of head at 10 A.M., with fulness in frontal region. Pulse rapid; and full; slow; irregular in frequency.

Neck and Back.—Stiffness of muscles on l. side of neck at 10 A.M. Pain deep-seated in l. shoulder, scapula and l. side of nape up to occiput, with stiffness, < rising from lying or turning head to l. or backward, and draught of air, > standing and walking, at times the pain extended into l. olecranon, to muscles on chest below l. shoulder and spine, all muscles connected with scapula painful to touch, use of l. arm impeded, on drawing a long breath a stitch in chest near l. shoulder, on coughing pain over whole l. upper chest, deep coughing was impossible, pressure on chest, the pain moved from l. scapula to pelvis, lumbar region sensitive. Shooting from small of back into l. hip-bone at 3 P.M.; from lumbar vertebræ to crest of r. ilium at 6 P.M. when sitting. Pain in lumbar region at 9 A.M.; at 4 P.M., and weakness.

Extremities.—Pain on top of l. shoulder as from fatigue from 10 A.M. till noon. Growing pain anteriorly in middle of l. brachium, and lameness as from a blow. Arms easily fall asleep. Pain in elbows. Drawing pain anteriorly in upper half of l. femur, extending to hip-joint. Rheumatic feeling in r. knee in afternoon and evening. Hitching in l. knee on walking. Weakness of l. knee at 8 P.M. when walking, with knocking. Paralyzed sensation in r. leg at 10 A.M.

Skin.—Prickling and itching here and there, > evening, with uneasiness in limbs.

Sleep.—Sleepiness in evening; in the daytime, but if he lies down inability to sleep. Late falling asleep, restlessness during the night and anxious dreams. Waking at 5 A.M., and restlessness; waking at early dawn and inability to sleep again though sleepy and not excited. Night restless, with swollen sensation in eyeballs, which continued after waking. Dreams unpleasant, unremembered; distressing, that he is about to be put to death by poison and at the same time is innocent of crime; of crossing a stream on horseback, the stream and the water on him freeze.

Fever.—Coldness; in nape at 10 A.M.; of feet; of feet at noon, even when walking.

Clinical.—Diphtheritic sore throat. Post-nasal tumors. Epithelioma of tongue. Watery diarrhœa, with vertigo. Foul-smelling lochia, bloody.

Cicuta Virosa.

A tincture is prepared of the fresh root of Cicuta Virosa, L.

General Action.—The Cicutæ are most prominently convulsants, producing the most terrific convulsions, with loss of consciousness.

Allies.—Œnanthe, Conium, Absinth., Hydrocy. ac., Cupr.

Generalities.—Veins very prominent. Lying as if dead, with clenched jaws. Falling to the ground; unconscious; and rolling about; on stooping it seems as if he would fall forward. Catalepsy, limbs hung down relaxed as if dead, without breathing. *Tetanus.* **Convulsions, with wonderful distortions of limbs, head turned backward, back bent as in opisthotonos; frightful distortions,** *with unconsciousness; spasms of all the muscles; spasms, with dark redness of face, blue lips and bloody froth from mouth. Epilepsy; with swelling of stomach, as from spasm of diaphragm.* **Hiccough, screaming, redness of face, trismus, unconsciousness and distortion of limbs**; with wonderful convulsions of limbs, head and upper part of body, and clenched jaws; with wonderful distortions of limbs, upper part of body and head, blue face, interrupted breath and froth from mouth, afterwards unconsciousness; frequent E. at night. Restlessness, tossing about, the pallor of face changed to cyanosis, twitching of face, of muscles of eyes and neck, a peculiar scream, finally tetanus of whole body, head bored into pillow, the spine forming a concave arc backward, froth before mouth, teeth clenched, limbs drawn up towards abdomen, unconsciousness, insensibility, micturition in a full stream, breath stopped at the height of the convulsions, no action of heart during the spasm. Fell to the ground, urinated with great force, violent convulsions, mouth could not be opened, gnashed the teeth, distorted his eyes, blood spurted from the ears and much swelling was felt in præcordial region. Tonic spasms so that the fingers could not be straightened, neither could the limbs be bent or straightened. Twitchings; on back, forehead and l. toes. Cramplike stiffness of whole body, with coldness. Rigidity in a child, and sleeplessness. (Symptoms of spasms, compare Œnanthe, Cupr., Absinth., etc.

Swollen sensation in whole body when in bed and

frequent starting as if he would fall out of bed. *Weakness; after standing a short time, < in knees and in muscles of back;* on rising. Faintness.

Clinical.—Convulsions from various causes, injuries, after opium, chorea-like, epileptiform, tetanic, puerperal, from worms, from indigestion, *with insensibility*, staring eyes, with jerking of eyeball, muscles of the face and whole body, face red, hot, sweaty; or with the convulsions violent opisthotonos, tetanic rigidity of the whole body, eyes fixed at one point, and frothing at the mouth, with spasmodic breathing; spasms brought on by the slightest jar, etc.

Mind.—*Delirium; singing, dancing grotesquely, shouting* (Hyosc.); after an unusual sleep heat of body, she sprang out of bed, laughed, did foolish things, drank much wine, jumped about, clapped her hands and grew red in the face. Constantly screaming the name of his sister. It seemed as if he were a child and objects were as attractive to him as toys to a child. Belief that he was not living under ordinary relations, everything seemed strange and almost fearful, it seemed as if he had awakened from a fever and saw all kinds of visions, without physical sick feeling. *Weeping, moaning and howling.* Laughing and biting.

Excitement and apprehension about the future. Anxiety, much affected by sad stories; (A. at noon, and sweat on face, trembling of hands and faintness at heart). Fear, with stitches in l. side of head from fright at every opening of the door and at every word. Belief that he would die. Sadness. Occupied with tormenting ideas of human conditions. Misanthrophy; he went into solitude and reflected upon people's errors and about himself. Likes to be alone, is disinclined to speak and is irresolute. Suspicious. Disinclined to work and morose. Indifferent and doubtful if he really were in the condition in which he found himself. *Stupefaction. Loss of ideas. Mental torpor. Unconsciousness.* Confusion of ideas and rapid change of thoughts, often of a depressing nature; confusion of the present with the past.

Clinical.—Delirium, with funny gestures, red face, confounds the present with the past. Melancholia, with indifference. Sadness and concussion of brain. Great apprehension; very mistrustful. Hallucinations, with convulsions after typhoid fever.

Head.—*Jerking.* Sinking gradually when sitting quietly, while her eyes stare at the same point, then a kind of internal jerk with sudden return to consciousness, then similar insensibility, wherefrom she was aroused from time to time by internal shivering. Sticking. Pain; > passage of flatus; > sitting upright; in places deep in brain; in morning on waking, as if brain were loose, and shaking on walking; compressive, from both sides. Anxiety. Heaviness; when sitting; and stupefaction. Fulness. Confusion in morning after rising. Dulness, with shaking chill, stiffness of neck and sensation as if muscles were too short. Strange feeling. Intoxication; intoxicated feeling when sitting, standing and walking. *Vertigo; and reeling; and falling to the ground;* on walking, as if he would fall forward to the left.

Forehead.—Sticking in bone. Tearing in upper part, beneath bones, extending to vertex. Pain; beneath l. eminence; in l. bone; in sinciput; in places in sinciput, beneath bones; with fulness, and in r. temple, then in l.; *stupefying pain externally, < rest;* hammering, in afternoon. Pulsation in sinciput, with heat and violent action of heart. Confusion; in sinciput. Heaviness; in sinciput; in sinciput, and heat; with pressure deep in brain.

Tearing in l. temple. Pain in r. temple, between skin and bone. Strong pulsation in temporal arteries. Tearing beneath bones on r. side of head; in bones of l. side, with internal pulsation and confusion deep in brain; backward through l. side, < towards top of skull. Pressure beneath l. bones; one-sided P., rather external. Tearing in bones of r. side of occiput. *Pain in O.* like a pressure and as with coryza. Sensation in O. when sitting as on lying down after a fatiguing walk, extending through back and along posterior surface of legs. Heaviness in O.; deep in O. Distention of skin of sinciput. Eruption, and on face.

Clinical.—Vertigo, with gastralgia, vomiting, with muscular spasms and tendency to convulsions. Sudden violent shocks through head and whole body, with jerking, premonitory of spasms. Suppurating eruptions and pustules larger than the head of a pin, which became confluent, with infiltration, etc. Basilar meningitis. Cerebro-spinal meningitis, with convulsions, many cases. Effects of concussion of the brain, especially convulsions.

Eyes.—Protruding. *Staring;* whereby everything looked like black cloth; with a gray fog before eyes; *without ability to help it* and without entire control of senses, she must be much excited to answer correctly, on attempting to turn her head loss of consciousness and blackness before eyes. Pressure on reading; P., with sensitiveness to light, at times gray spots before eyes. **Pupils dilated and insensible** (Bell., Hyosc., etc.); contracted; *contracted, then dilated; sometimes contracted, sometimes dilated.* Sticking in lids; in l. Tearing in r. lids. Pressure upon lids. Pressure in r. inner canthus, > pressing lids together. Twitching of orbicularis beneath lower lid. Stitches along brows. Pain in bone beneath l. brow, extending towards temple and zygoma.

Sensitiveness to light. Everything seems very distinct and brighter than usual. Everything seems shining. *When attempting to stand objects seem now to approach, now to recede.* Objects seem to move, everything blinds her; objects seem to move from side to side; seem to move in a circle, < sitting. Everything runs together on fixing vision. *Objects seem double at one time* (Con., Gels.), and black, at another time she hears with difficulty. Vision obscured; by black points when reading and afterwards. Vision of bright spots; and stripes; bright point floating before r. eye, mingled with dark streaks and specks. Blinded by the white snow, and on looking at a dark wall a gray curtain seems to cover the l. part of vision.

Clinical.—Commencing strabismus, periodic, spasmodic, or after convulsions.

Ears.—Flow of blood. Sore pain behind l.; as from a bruise; bruised pain behind r. Bursting in r. on swallowing. *Difficult hearing* (Con.). Ringing; in l. Roaring; before ears, < in the house.

Clinical.—Hæmorrhage from the ears in cerebral troubles. Deafness of old people, with sudden detonations in ears, especially on swallowing (compare Con.).

Nose.—Bruised pain in r. wing. Dryness as if stopped. Stopped; with much mucus in it. Yellow discharge. Sneezing without coryza. Bright blood from r. nostril; bleeding from r. on touch.

Face.—*Red. Pale; and drawn; cadaverous paleness;* pale, < around lips. Swollen. Anxious expression. Muscular movements. Pressure beneath r. malar-bone. *Lockjaw;* with froth from mouth. Burning-itching vesicle on vermilion border of l. side of upper lip.

Mouth.—Gnashing of teeth. Pain in lower teeth. *Whitish sore on margin of tongue, with pain on touch.* Tongue immovable. Dumbness. Five or six words articulated without hesitation, then jerking backward of head and jerking of arms so that he draws backward and swallows a syllable and articulates almost as in hiccough. Dryness. Froth. Flow of water tinged with blood. Salivation.

Clinical.—Eruptions about corners of the mouth, beginning like honey-colored crusts, with burning and itching, the crusts extended to the chin, became thick and "fatty," sometimes with swollen glands.

Throat.—Sticking. Scraping; burning, extending into epigastric region. Feeling as if grown together, with bruised pain externally, < moving or taking hold of it, with eructations in afternoon. Sensation in throat and chest as if something as large as a fist lodged and were pressing throat asunder, impeding respiration, worse when sitting than when walking. *Dryness.* Irritation. Inability to swallow.

Clinical.—Spasm of œsophagus from worms, the child cannot swallow, strangling on attempting to swallow.

Stomach.—Appetite great; less evenings; lost; at noon, at first mouthful; lost on account of dryness in mouth, with incomplete taste to food. *Longing for coal, he swallowed it. Thirst;* for cold water in afternoon. Desire for wine increased. Did not relish his breakfast, it filled up his abdomen as if he had eaten too much. Waterbrash, with nausea and general heat. Eructations of bitter yellow fluid in afternoon, while stooping in open air, causing burning in throat. *Hiccough;* loud. Nausea; in morning, with sticking-tearing headache; when eating; with sticking in forehead. Vomiting; copious; difficult, then relief; of blood.

Gastritis. Sticking in pit, and burning. Sudden tearing in epigastric region. Scraping. Shock in region of pit as with a finger, causing staring, then return to his senses. Pressure in pit after eating, compelling deep breathing, with inclination to eructate. *Burning. Burning pressure.* Sensation as if hot water were in it. Anxiety in pit; with tightness and constant desire to go out and cool himself. *Throbbing in pit; which was raised up to the size of a fist.*

Clinical.—Desire for unnatural things, like coal. Violent hiccough, with loud sound and with spasms of the chest.

Abdomen.—Distention. Flatulence. *Rumbling and roaring.* Emission of flatus. Tearing deep in A., < pressure. Pain; on pressure; after eating, with sleepiness. Sick feeling in morning, > afternoon, then sticking in r. side of head extending from r. eye and nose to occiput, then running from nose and discharge of yellow mucus. Chilliness. Heat. Sudden stitches from navel to neck of bladder. Hypogastrium distended and painful. Cutting in H. after eating. Sensation in r. groin when sitting as if an ulcer would break through. Sore pain in r. pelvic region, in margin of ilium, a pulsating drawing sensation.

Rectum.—Protrusion, with thin stool. Sensation as of a liquid stool. Sudden urging, with bruised pain in small of back and general loss of strength, sudden stool, then urging, with frequent desire to urinate. Itching just above anus, after walking, when standing still and during stool, and after rubbing pain as if burnt, the pain causing shuddering.

Anus.—Sensation on r. side as from hæmorrhoids, whereby the orifice is contracted, with annoyance during stool. Burning, with soft stool.

Stool.—Diarrhœa; *at 2 and 5 A.M., with irresistible urging to urinate;* brown; slimy, frequent, with urging and copious urine. Frequent, of black asafœtida-like mucus, in small portions, with urging at 2 P.M. Constipation. In single hard lumps.

Urinary Organs.—Sticking in urethra; in navicular fossa. Tickling in navicular fossa and frequent erections. Urging to urinate; frequent. *Involuntary micturition* (Cupr.). Frequent M. *Spurting of urine.* Retention of urine (Nux v.). Difficult micturition at night. Urine copious; scanty and dark.

Sexual Organs.—Sore drawing pain beneath penis, extending to glans, compelling him to urinate. Erection without desire. Testicles drawn up against abdomen. Sudden pressure in skin of r. testicle. Emission without voluptuous dreams; in morning; three E. in the night. Menstruation delayed.

Respiratory Organs.—Pressure below larynx when sitting. Hoarseness. Cough, < during the day, and much expectoration. *Want of breath. Oppressed respiration.* Respiration stertorous; and frequent; and uneven, interrupted by hiccough. Respiration deep; when sitting; deep and difficult. Slow, difficult R. Feeble and rattling R. Scarcely perceptible R.

Chest.—Sticking beneath last l. false ribs on inspiration and expiration, > standing and walking. Tugging about pit of stomach. Pain in r. pectoral muscles; in r. pectoralis major when walking slowly, then in l. pectoral and intercostal muscles, not affecting respiration. Pressure on lower end of sternum as after a blow, when walking, with a sore sensation. *Tightness so that she could scarcely breathe.* Heaviness. Heat.

Clinical.—Spasms of pectoral muscles, sometimes with violent hiccough or with great difficulty in breathing.

Heart and Pulse.—Sticking in præcordial region and burning pain. Pain in præcordial region. Sudden sensation when walking as if heart stopped. Heart's action intermittent. Pulse rapid; slow and full; slow and small; small and soft; imperceptible at radius.

Clinical.—Palpitation, sometimes the heart felt as if it stopped beating.

Neck.—Swollen. A kind of cramp in muscles, if he looks around he cannot bring the head back again, the muscles do not yield, and when he attempts to force them it hurts very much. Tearing in muscles of r. side. Drawing pain in l. side. Tension in muscles; sore, in l. on bending head backward.

Clinical.—Spasms and cramps in muscles of the nape of neck and spasmodic drawing backward of head.

Back.—**Bent backward like an arch** (Œnanth., Cupr., Abs., Nux v., etc.). Painful stiffness on stooping. Sticking in muscles on r. scapula; in muscles in region of eleventh and twelfth dorsal vertebræ, < deep inspiration. Shock in dorsal vertebræ. Sensation as if there were an ulcer on r. scapula. *Pain on inner surface of scapulæ;* in dorsal muscles. Painful tension above r. scapula. Pain in lumbar muscles. *Tearing-jerking in coccyx.*

Clinical.—Neuralgia of the coccyx during menstruation.

Extremities.—**Spasmodic distortion** (Hydrocyanic ac.,

etc.), *throwing himself to the distance of two feet. Trembling.* Tossing about. Tearing in extensor of l. forearm and at base of three last r. toes. Pain in l. knee, l. external malleolus, r. forearm, radial side of r. wrist and dorsal surface of hand at base of r. fingers. Alternating painful pressure in various muscles, < legs, with prickling in toes. Bruised sensation in forearms and legs; alternately in arms and legs, with heat streaming through them and difficult motion. *Weakness of arms and legs* after slight exertion; of legs when sitting and standing, less in arms, > walking; now in r. shoulder, now in one or other knee or in ankle. Paralysis; sensation benumbed but not lost, incomplete paralysis of arms.

Upper Extremities.—Shoulder. Twitching in l. Tearing in muscles of l. Cracking sensation in joint. Sore pain in r. joint as from a blow.

Arm.—**Jerking and sticking, and in fingers** (lower limbs and head); J. in l., so that the whole body is jerked. Tearing in l. as far as fingers. Pain in muscles of r.; beneath r. Drawings in l. Tension. Heaviness on raising it, with sticking in shoulder, so that she cannot raise the arm to the head without crying aloud, and cannot move the fingers. Weakness, and of fingers; of l. arm, with sticking tearing. Numb feeling and weak motions.

Tearing in inner side of lower part of r. upper arm. Pressure in muscles of l. upper arm. Painful weakness in muscles of lower part of l. upper arm; suddenly in muscles of r. upper arm when writing. Pain in l. elbow, with heaviness. Sticking tearing in muscles of r. forearm when writing, > rest. Sore pain in l. forearm, as from a bruise. Pain in ulnar side of l. wrist. Sensation of cracking in wrist. Veins of hands distended. Drawing on dorsal surface of l. hand, at base of fingers. Pulsation on hand when supporting oneself on a chair. *Nails blue* (Nux v.). Twitching together of r. thumb and fingers. Drawing in tendons of dorsal surface of l. fingers. Deadness of fingers (going to sleep, numbness, coldness).

Lower Extremities.—*Jerking.* Reeling. Tottering when walking. Pressure in various muscles. Painful stiffness. Numbness and paralysis. *Trembling of one thigh.* Burning sticking in l. hip-bone. Tearing in thighs when walking, with heaviness; T. in thighs after rising from a seat, with aching in knees as if beaten, the pain in thighs < when walking, like a deep-seated stiffness. Pressure on r. trochanter major. Drawing in muscles on inner surface of r. thigh. Tension in fascia of anterior upper and outer part of l. thigh when walking, and in hollow of r. knee and to its side. Painful pressure in r. knee. Bruised sensation in knees. Feeling in knees when sitting as after a long walk.

Leg.—Trembling of l. Tearing in r. peroneal muscles; in lower part of extensor of l.; suddenly in lower part of r. calf, extending to tendo-achillis. Pressure; in calves; in l. calf. Bruised sensation and heaviness alternately through each, becoming seated in knee. Jerklike drawing on posterior and lower part of r., extending into heel. Compression in all muscles of l. when walking, as if the whole leg were contracted. Tension in calves; in lower part; in l. on walking. Prickling in muscles. Prickling pulsation in r. calf. *Refusal to carry him and staggering.* Weakness; sudden, in l. on rising; painful, streaming through both when sitting, also in knees. Stiffness in r. calf.

Tearing about l. malleoli. Soles turned inward when walking. Sticking in r. sole; in l. sole, with tingling; in heels when sitting. Tearing in sides of r. tendo-achillis; in l. sole; deep in inner margin of l. sole; in tendon on back of l. foot; in tendon on back of l. foot when standing and walking. Sudden pulling in r. sole. Drawing on back of r. foot, rather towards inner side; in tendons on back of l. foot; in tendons on back of r. foot and in l. sole. Stiffness of tendo-achillis when walking slowly, with painful pressure in muscles of posterior part of l. thigh. Twitches in l. toes. Sticking in corns when sitting. Tearing in l. toes; on inner side of r. great toe. Drawing-jerking pains in toes. Prickling in l. great toe.

Skin.—**Elevations over face** (*and on hands*), **with burning pain on touch,** *afterwards confluent,* dark red, then desquamation; *E. on hands, even on balls of fingers, in which there is burning pain on touch, afterwards confluent,* dark red, moist; (swelling on inside of l. elbow as if an ulcer would form, and on motion pain as from pressure on an ulcer). Red spot on back of l. hand, more in the direction of metacarpal bone of thumb; cluster of red spots on back of l. hand, smooth, > pressure. Black spots. Most of chest darker than the rest of the body. Eruption on ears. Painful pustules below and in front of ears. *Red vesicle on r. scapula, painful to touch;* V., with red areola on back of l. hand, between first and second fingers; itching V. on back of r. hand.

Drawing beneath skin on outer side of r. thigh; beneath skin just above l. tendo-achillis. Formication on forehead; beneath skin on back of r. foot; beneath skin of l. upper arm; beneath skin of thighs and legs when sitting, and < soles, as if the leg would go to sleep; in soles, with pressure in various places in legs; in l. toes. Itching over whole body; on r. side of chest, with heat; burning; burning, on r. thigh, > scratching.

Sleep.—Yawning. Sleepiness; in morning; so that the eyes closed; if she looks long at one place, with feeling as if the head were pressed down, she does not recognize letters, with staring eyes. Sleeplessness. *Frequent waking, with general sweat every time, from which he, however, feels refreshed;* frequent W. at night, with sensation as if he had slept enough; W. every quarter of an hour, with painful heaviness in head. *Dreams vivid but unremembered; vivid, of the events of the previous day;* confused, full of disquietude; voluptuous, with emissions and drawing pain in navicular fossa.

Fever.—*Coldness.* Shivering; through back; through back from 2 to 3.30 P.M. Coldness of surface. Coldness of ears; of limbs; of arms and feet, with stiffness; streaming through legs, < r., with tearing in toes; creeping down thighs, then coldness in arms (the coldness seems to come more from the chest), then greater inclination to stare at one point; creeping through legs and arms, with alternations of heaviness and lightness in those parts.

Heat; < by the accustomed smoking, *with special heat in chest.* In head, with heaviness; in sinciput, with heaviness; in forehead, with heaviness, puffy skin and throbbing in temporal arteries; from low down in occiput to crown; deep in occiput to vertex and to one side of head (always deep in head). About eyes. Internally and externally in ears. In face, with redness; in flushes, < towards upper part.

About nipple. Over back in flushes; creeping over back into head and feet, when sitting, as from hot water, and in upper arm and sensation of hot water in chest, then pain in muscles on posterior part of r. thigh. In legs. Of skin, with dryness. *Sweat on abdomen at night.*

Cimicifuga.

A tincture is prepared from the fresh root of the black-snake root, Cimicifuga racemosa, Ell. (Actæa racem., L.).

General Action.—It seems to exert a marked action on the spinal nerves especially at the upper part, symptoms of meningeal irritation and inflammation, neuritis, neuralgia, muscular spasms and tremors, etc. Clinically it has been found to control a large variety of troubles of the uterus and ovaries, neuralgias and even inflammations.

Allies.—Aconite, Ranunculus, Pæonia, Clematis, *China*, Gels., Silicea.

Generalities.—**Tremors over whole body** (Arg. n., Gels., Stram.). **Nervous shuddering** *through upper and back part of body. Jerking after going to bed, obliging change of position*, beginning in side on which he was lying as a perceptible twitching in l. foot. Continual stretching and yawning. **Bruised feeling** (Arn., Sil.). *Soreness of whole body, with stiffness*, as after hard labor. Lameness in morning, with many unenviable feelings. Feeling as after a "spree." *General feeling of intoxication.* Peculiar tingling in muscles, then aching in limbs, from above downward. Feeling of illness; > by supper; with weakness and trembling, believes the condition to be but one remove from mania-â-potu.

Restlessness; *in forenoon;* in afternoon; at night; latter part of the night; *nervous, in afternoon, with indisposition to fix the attention on any subject;* in all parts, hardly amounting to pain, < r. side. Nervous all day, full of work and doing it fast. Sensation as from severe muscular exertion, < small of back. Desire to lie down and close the eyes. Weakness; in morning, with trembling; caused by great discharge of clear urine; with trembling, sinking feeling and nausea; nervous, in afternoon. *Aggravation on l. side;* A. by motion.

Clinical.—Reflex neuralgias in various parts of the body, especially in women, dependent on ovarian and uterine troubles. Muscular rheumatism affecting the fleshy parts of the muscles, < motion, but great restlessness. Chorea, especially in muscles of l. side.

Mind.—A sort of delirium, with inclination to run over the subject on which he was reading. *Symptoms as in delirium tremens.* **Grieved, troubled and sighing**, next day tremulous joy, playfulness and clear intellect. *Miserable, dejected feeling;* in afternoon, and dulness. Anxiety.

Clinical.—Delirium, with excessive restlessness, twitching of tendons, starting up suddenly. Delirium, wild imaginings of rats, etc. (Stram.), with crazy feeling about head, talking continually, changing the subject and moving about. Puerperal mania, she is very suspicious, talking of a great variety of things, constantly changing the subject, sometimes sees vermin, speech is often disconnected. Insanity in the form of melancholia, is very apprehensive, talks of becoming crazy, she is suspicious or talks incessantly, constantly changing the subject. Delirium tremens, is frightened, trembles, cannot remain in one place. Puerperal melancholia, with sleeplessness, sighing and moaning all the while. The two marked characteristics of the delirium or insanity of this drug are the mental and physical restlessness, the patient cannot remain in one place, and when talking constantly changes the subject.

Head.—*Pain;* in morning on getting up; *in forenoon and part of the afternoon,* **especially in occiput** (Gels., Sil.), **extending to vertex**; at 10 A.M., < forehead, extending over vertex to occiput; in evening; on waking, with vertigo, flushed face, dilated pupils and rapid pulse; *indoors,* **especially in occiput**, *< afternoon and evening,* > 9 P.M. *after walking in open air; always > in open air;* partly > by throwing head backward; with heat in head and face; with sleepiness and coldness, then warmth; paroxysmal, in forehead, occiput, vertex, etc., > open air; heavy, at 9 A.M., < l. temple. Heaviness. Dulness; *as after a "spree;"* and of eyelids, with heaviness, as from a cold. Fulness; in brain. Feeling as if too large; brain feels too large for the cranium. *Vertigo;* **with fulness and aching in vertex** *and impaired vision;* with half-intoxicated feeling.

Forehead.—**Pressure outward and upward in upper part of cerebrum as if there were not room enough.** Shooting over l. eye. Boring over l. superciliary ridge. Pain; over eyes; over r. eye; over l. eye, > open air; deep in; before breakfast; in afternoon; waking at 2 A.M., extending to temples, with coldness of forehead; at 6 A.M. extending over vertex to occiput, with heaviness; at 10 P.M., and between eyeball and orbital plate of frontal bone, with dryness in pharynx; in front part of head and in eyes; with heat in face and sweat; occasional, over r. eye; intermittent, in l. side after a hearty dinner, also after sleep, < when walking in open air; over l. eye, extending along base of brain to occiput.

Temple.—Cutting in r. Pain in l.; pain as if head would burst; pain in r., extending in burning lines to forehead, afterwards with fulness, drowsiness and heat. Occasional compression.

Vertex.—Tearing in centre. *Pain in afternoon and evening; paroxysmal, < morning, and in occiput;* and soreness, finally passing to forehead, lasting all night and preventing sleep. Fulness in evening; F. in upper part of brain, and dulness.

Shooting about sides of head. Pain in l. side. Fulness in l. side. **Soreness in occiput** *caused by the pain through the whole brain, < motion.* Pain in occiput.

Clinical.—In general the headaches affect the base of the occiput or the headaches begin at that point, frequently they are extremely violent and shoot up to vertex or down spine, and bending the head forward seems to pull upon the spine; sometimes it seems as if a bolt would be driven from the neck to the vertex with every beat of the heart; sometimes the whole neck is very lame from distress on moving the head. These headaches of Cimicifuga may be neuralgic, associated in women with uterine disturbances, or they may be associated with symptoms of inflammation of the meninges of the brain and spine. Neuralgic headaches, feeling as if the top of the head would fly off.

Eyes.—*Congestion during the headache.* Aching; at 10 A.M.; *extending to vertex*, as if nerves were excited to too much action. Swollen feeling. Heaviness as from a cold. Pupils dilated. **Pain in balls** (Ran. b., r.); in forenoon; in evening on going up-stairs; in r. at night in bed; *in centre and between ball and orbital plate of frontal bone,* < morning; occasional; at night, extending from r. through to r. side of occiput, slightly affecting ear. Lids inflamed; and stinging. Swelling of r. lid, and heat in it. Pain in r. lid in afternoon on closing it. Vision dim; distorted; *V. of black specks.* Increase of myopia.

Clinical.—Ciliary neuralgia, eyeballs feel enlarged and the pain shoots into the head, sometimes associated with photophobia and extreme asthenopia.

Ears and Nose.—Pain in ears. Stitch to outside of r. wing of nose. Stinging in nose in evening. Sneezing. Dry, stuffed condition of nose, then open, moist condition and sensitiveness to cold air as if the base of the brain were bare and every inhalation brought cold air in contact with it. Roaring in ears. Coryza, with sore throat and gradual extension of the disease to the bronchial mucous membrane, and hacking cough; fluent C., with tickling in nares, exciting sneezing; profuse, greenish, sanguineous C.

Face. — Redness; and of eyes. Pain; more in lower jaw, articulation of jaw and in lower teeth. Feeling of lateral expansion and pressure outward in malar-bones and forehead at 10 A.M. Upper lip swollen and inflamed, skin cracked and came off. Ulcer on inner surface of lower lip. Lips dry; and sore. Pain in l. jaw; in r. upper jaw and in teeth.

Clinical.—Facial neuralgia, either of rheumatic origin or associated with uterine disturbances, pain > at night, reappears next day.

Mouth.—Thick mucus on teeth. Uneasiness in teeth in afternoon, a desire to chew or pick at them. Swelling of back part of tongue; and of fauces. Redness and inflammation of palate and uvula. Dryness; in morning. Salivation. Thick saliva, sticking to mouth and throat. *Offensive breath.* Taste unpleasant; bitter.

Throat. — Thick, viscid mucus. Roughness and scraping; R., with dryness and thirst. Rawness; with difficulty in swallowing, hoarseness, which is < towards night. *Soreness;* on swallowing; on swallowing and on pressure, < on l. side, with dryness; in evening on swallowing, with full sensation high up in throat. Fulness of pharynx; with inclination to swallow; of throat and vertex, with stiffness of neck. Sensation as far as top of sternum as if partly filled. Constriction of pharynx, with increased mucus. Dryness of pharynx; at 4 P.M.; at night and inclination to swallow. Empty aching along œsophagus in afternoon.

Stomach.—Appetite lost. Repugnance to food at supper. Desire for tobacco lessened. Thirst, but no desire to drink. Eructations; violent. *Nausea;* in women, with vomiting and much gastric irritation; with general tremors; with weak, trembling feeling; then freer expectoration, relaxation of surface, nervous tremors and vertigo. Violent retching. *Vomiting.*

Distention, and of upper abdomen. Darting pain in epigastrium after a light supper. Pain and heat, the pain > eructations, with warmth and dryness in the whole alimentary canal; pain in epigastrium before breakfast, extending to l. hypochondrium, with emptiness. *Faintness;* in epigastrium before breakfast, then repletion after eating; in epigastrium in forenoon; in epigastrium, with repugnance to food. Feeling as if too much had been eaten; in forenoon. Uneasiness; in epigastrium, with oppression. Oppression. Tremor; after breakfast. Burning.

Clinical.—Nausea and efforts to vomit, in uterine affections or with spinal irritation. Nausea and vomiting caused by pressure on the spine and cervical region, with palpitation, suppression of menses.

Abdomen.—Flatulence. Nausea through A., then loose stool, with sharp pain in abdomen and downward pressure in rectum. Pain; in morning, with thin, light brown diarrhœa; wandering; heavy; periodic, > stool, with inclination to bend forward. Fulness; full sensation at 10 P.M., caused by flatulence. Soreness of muscles on full inspiration. Pain in hepatic region; in l. hypochondrium, < motion and deep inspiration; sickening P. in duodenum. Rumbling below umbilicus at 10 P.M. Cutting in umbilical region; in afternoon. Griping from U. down. Griping-twisting in U. region, < towards l. Pain below U., with weight and pain in lumbar and sacral regions.

Hypogastrium.—Rumbling; at 10 A.M. Fulness. Cutting, waking at 3 A.M., with uneasiness in it and urging to stool, stool thin, partly undigested, uneasiness in abdomen all the forenoon, with desire for stool, next morning waking at 3, with thin, undigested stool, pain low down in bowels, diarrhœa once in four or five hours. Pain in evening, with fulness in abdomen and sensation as before diarrhœa; P. in l. iliac region.

Rectum and Stool.—Urging to stool, inclined to diarrhœa. Disposition to diarrhœa; after rising; in evening. Scanty diarrhœa, with tenesmus. Copious papescent stool; with general indisposition; two, in morning. Constipation; *alternating with disposition to diarrhœa.* Hard and dry stool.

Urinary Organs.—Sticking in urethra in morning. Frequent micturition; with increased urine; after retention of urine. *Increased urine;* and pale. Scanty and high-colored urine. Copious urea. Specific gravity decreased at first, afterwards it rose, after standing the urine was acid, cloudy, contained fibrinous casts of uniferous tubes (!), with minute lozenge-shaped crystals of uric acid adhering to their sides. Sediment of uric acid like yellow sand, in the nucleated form of crystals, with the obtuse angles rounded so as to make an elliptical figure, while above this floated a cloud of mucus and urate of ammonia, and above this floated yellowish sand, which seemed to be gradually settling to the bottom, the urine appearing like a mixture of ginger and water.

Sexual Organs.—Pain in testicles, with tenderness. Pain in r. spermatic cord, and retraction; drawing pain along r. spermatic cord. Bruised feeling in vagina. *Bearing down pain during menstruation.* Menorrhagia. Suppression of menses.

Clinical.—Neuralgia of the ovaries and uterus, with great tenderness and bearing down, the pains shooting up the sides and across the lower part of the abdomen. Menstruation painful, irregular or suppressed, with hysterical symptoms or epileptiform spasms at the period. Menorrhagia, menses too profuse and early, dark, clotted, with severe pain in back extending through hips and down thighs. Endocervicitis, with general nervous hysterical symptoms, uterus engorged, cervix hypertrophied, all the organs very sensitive, especially the ovaries. During parturition the pains do not force downward but extend across the abdomen and upward into the sides (false pains). Threatening miscarriage, the pains fly about, with fainting spells. After-pains, with great sensitiveness, the patient feels that she cannot tolerate the pain (Cham.). During parturition the os is rigid. Ovarian neuralgia, especially of l. ovary, pains extend up and down l. side, with great tenderness.

Respiratory Organs.—*Tickling in larynx causing dry cough; in evening, causing short dry cough; T. < speaking, causing inclination to cough.* Hoarseness; after rising; < towards night. Contraction of bronchial tubes after full inspiration, impeding expiration. Hacking cough. Respiration quick on waking. R. difficult after slight exertion, with general ill feeling.

Clinical.—Nervous cough excited by every attempt to speak.

Chest.—Lancinations along cartilages of false ribs, <

inspiration; < long inspiration, occurring after waking at 3 A.M. and in bed between 10 and 11 P.M. Pain; in l.; in r. lung, from apex to base, to r. of sternum, < inspiration. Soreness. Prickling in mammæ (female) during the day, with cold chills.

Clinical.—Neuralgia of the diaphragm. Pleurodynia on either side; in women with uterine trouble, in the l. inframammary region.

Heart and Pulse.—Stitches at heart; with slight twitching or pulsation of external muscles in that region. *Catching pain* on bending forward, and when sitting still at dinner and after dinner. *Pain in region of H., then palpitation.* Palpitation and faintness. Pulse quick; and weak; and small; and full, hard, *irregular. Irregular.* Feeble pulse; in morning, with weakness and trembling; with general lassitude, with heat and smarting of face. Slow pulse; and intermitting at every third or fourth beat.

Clinical.—Angina pectoris, numbness of l. arm, irregular trembling pulse, tremulous motions of the heart. In women catching pain about the heart preventing respiration, with palpitation and faintness.

Neck.—**Rheumatic pains in muscles of N. and back, with stiffness and contraction** (China, Dulc., Clem.); heavy rheumatic pains in upper posterior part. Cramping in muscles of l. then r. side, on moving head. Stiffness; in evening.

Back.—Trembling and weakness. *Pain;* > pressure;. wandering, during menstruation, and around through hips, inside; as of boils, and in small of back and in limbs. Stitches below r. scapula and spine. **Drawing-tensive pain at points of spinous processes of three upper dorsal vertebræ** (Chin., Sulph.), *in morning on bending neck forward.* Drawing pain in a single muscle between r. scapula and spine. Pain below l. scapula; behind r.; in region of lower dorsal and upper lumbar vertebræ; occasionally in scapulæ and shoulders.

Small of Back.—Aching both sides of spine in morning; heavy A. extending towards sacrum; heavy, in region of r. kidney, < motion; weak, trembling A. Weight; *in lumbar and sacral region, and pain,* sometimes extending all around the body, somewhat below crest of ilium. Lame, tired feeling extending from region of kidneys to sacrum, > rest, < motion.

Clinical—Spinal irritation, the cervical and upper dorsal vertebræ particularly sensitive to pressure.

Extremities.—*Twitching of fingers and toes* (China.). *Trembling, scarcely able to walk. Pain;* in l. external malleolus and l. forearm; in r. arm, elbow, wrist, and in knee, extending to ankle; in shoulder passing down arm, with numbness as if a nerve had been compressed, then in forearm, sometimes causing a cramping sensation, similar pains in legs, < in upper part of thigh, about hip-joint and inguinal region. Rheumatic pains all day. Drawing rheumatic pains in muscles of arms and legs. Pains as of boils. *Uneasiness, almost an ache;* restless, drawing sensations. Tired. Feeling in joints in morning on motion as after hard labor, stiffness.

Upper Extremities.—Pain deep in muscles of r. shoulder, extending to wrist; *in muscles from shoulders to wrists.* Laming pain in l. elbow anteriorly. Lameness of l. wrist. Weakness and trembling of hands and forearms, inability to grasp anything firmly. *Trembling of fingers when writing.* Second l. finger lame, and cannot be flexed.

Lower Extremities.—Pain in muscles, < in anterior part of thighs, on walking out into open air, as from great fatigue. Weakness. Jerking in muscles of l. thigh, < in region of inferior third. Constriction of l. sartorius muscle. Rheumatic pain in r. knee; in l. leg. Lameness in r. leg, < bending forward, soreness and stiffness, moving forward to inside of ankle. Sharp wandering pains in l. ankle and scapula. *Pain in l. tendo-achillis when walking in open air, and a shortening sensation. Soreness in region of tendo-achillis* towards evening, < walking, with aching and stiffness. Feeling in foot as if it had been compressed. Stinging in l. great toe in afternoon, on lower surface, then on upper. *Pain in r. great toe. Burning pain in second joint of r. great toe; extending up limb,* from 8 to 9 P.M., same the next evening, but not extending up the limb.

Skin.—Red papillæ, becoming a diffused redness. Eruption like mosquito-bites; < hands and wrists. Pustules on back of hand; back of l. Inflamed and bleeding ulcer near centre of each cheek. Itching on back of hand and wrist; on back of hand, with redness, also in afternoon, < evening; I. on back of l. hand and wrist in evening, < back of thumb, then red papulæ, becoming, after slight irritation, a diffused redness, the redness could be reproduced by slight irritation.

Sleep.—Yawning. Sleepiness; in afternoon; after dinner; in forepart of the evening, but restless sleep after 3 A.M.; in evening, with creeping chills upon back, then frequent waking in night and desire to throw off the bed-clothes, although the thermometer was below zero. Falling asleep on attempting to read. Sleeplessness. *Restless sleep;* after sleeping well for three or four hours, *and dreams of being in trouble;* from 3 to 5 A.M., and unrefreshing, with disposition to fold the arms over the head. Imperfect sleep, waking at midnight. Frequent waking at night. *Troublesome dreams.* Dreams of accidents, seeing limbs broken, great suffering, etc.

Fever.—Chill; in bed before rising; in forenoon; afternoon; with prickling in female mammæ; with pricklings in breasts. Occasional. Sensitiveness to cold air. General internal nervous chilly feeling, less over back. Cold arms and feet; hands and feet; back, in afternoon; l. thigh and leg, as from a cold breeze; surface in morning after waking; whole surface at 3 A.M., with cold sweat and lancinations along cartilages of l. false ribs, < long inspirations; surface of body and of face and hands cool and dry.

Symptoms of catarrhal fever. Heat in front part of head; hot and dry forehead. H. in cheeks in flashes; H. in l. side of face, with general lassitude; of face, with slight inclination to sweat, and full, rapid pulse; in region of kidneys, with pain and weariness; of feet, then weakness of knees. Hot and dry skin. Burning in skin in morning after rising, with itching.

Disposition to sweat at night; at 3 A.M., beginning while asleep, > soon after waking, the first week with coldness of surface, afterwards with heat. Sweat, with headache similar to morning sickness during pregnancy. Cold S.; on hands and feet.

Cina.

A tincture is prepared from the dried flowers of Artemisia Cina Berg. (wormseed).

General Action.—From our present knowledge this drug acts similarly to Absinth. and other allied plants, producing increased reflex irritability and spasms. Its symptoms particularly simulate worm affections or peculiar forms of indigestion.

Allies.—Absinth., Chenopod., Cham., Arn., China, Nux v., Ign., Calc. c., Ferrum.

Generalities.—The child raises herself suddenly before coughing, looks wildly about, becomes stiff, loses consciousness, as if she would have epilepsy, then coughs. *Convulsions; epileptic-like, with consciousness;* with distortions of limbs in all directions, except that fingers and toes were unaffected, head and trunk were drawn now backward, now forward, now to one side, while arms and legs were thrown about, then shocks through whole body, with motion downward, like stamping of feet, jerking of head upward and backward, the shocks were felt by the hand, < lower part of chest and upper abdomen, face pale, then livid, at last blue, eyeballs turned convulsively upward, then directed staringly forward, pupil insensible, tongue at times contracted to a cylinder and spasmodically protruded. Paralytic jerking in various parts, < in limbs. Spasmodic stretching at 4 P.M., then trembling, with blue lips and weeping complaints about pain in chest, neck and limbs. *Trembling, with shivering when yawning. Tossing about even when awake (in a child).* (Convulsive symptoms to be compared with Absinth., Chenopod., etc.).

Sticking here and there in body; here and there on trunk when sitting, < on abdomen; *S. sometimes like a squeezing, sometimes like a pressure, sometimes like a blow or jerk, sometimes like an itching, now here, now there, in body, now in limbs, arms, feet, toes, now in side or back, now in nasal bones, < on posterior part of crest of ilium, on hip, the places pain on pressure as if bruised;* cramplike contractive S. in muscles, now of r., now of l. thigh, now in muscles of r., now of l. upper arm, now down small of back, when sitting, > walking in open air. Tearing, in part cutting, in limbs, head and jaws; tensive T. in scapulæ, after eating, < touch, and in upper arm, head and nape. Uneasiness; at night, tossing about on account of discomfort. *Weak; and pale;* in morning on rising, and nauseated. Aggravation morning and evening; A. after eating.

Mind.—*Delirium and crying out.* Talking nonsense. **Cannot be quieted by any persuasions; proof against all caresses** (Nux v.). *Piteous cries if one attempted to touch or lead him. Lachrymose and complaining (in a child). Earnest and sensitive, offended at the slightest joke* (Nux v.). Refuses everything, even the things of which he is usually fond. Indifferent. Grunting, croaking and groaning in afternoon. Anxiety and anguish about heart when walking in open air, as if he had committed a crime. *Unconscious and frothing at the mouth.*

Clinical.—Great mental excitement, children wake in fright and scream and tremble. Children become very fretful, cannot be pleased, and though very weak when sick they are very cross and obstinate and strike everybody (Nux v., Sulph.).

Head.—Leaning to one side (in a child). Sticking in brain, < l. side of vertex. Tearing, extending into malar-bone. Aching; *in morning, with affection of eyes;* < reading and reflecting; with general discomfort; *internal stupefying, on walking in open air, < in sinciput, then also in occiput;* as if screwed in, with numbness; drawing, after eating, < reading and mental labor. Vertigo; *on rising from bed, > lying down, with blackness before eyes, faintness and tottering.*

Forehead.—*Sticking above orbital margin extending deep into brain;* in bone above r. temple, extending deep into head and threatening to stupefy him. Paralytic tearing in l., then r. eminence, with stupefaction of head. Pain in evening; pressing downward externally; as if upper bones were pressed together from both sides; stupefying, externally, when sitting, and in temples, at last involving whole head. Pressure in bone, with internal beating as of waves; drawing P. in l. side of sinciput. *Drawing from l. eminence to root of nose, causing confusion of head.*

Tearing in l. temporal region, > moving head; tensive T. in r. temple. Pressing-out pain in temples after sneezing. Cramplike drawing in temples, < pressure. *Intermittent weight in middle of vertex, as if brain were pressed down* (Calc. ph.), *> pressure.* Drawing tearing in whole l. side of head. Pressing-out pain in r. parietal bone on waking, and in r. side of forehead. A spot on r. parietal bone feels numb and asleep.

Clinical.—Cerebral symptoms of meningeal irritability, especially in those suffering from worms, particularly with swollen, hot abdomen.

Eyes.—Sickly look about, with pallor of face. Pain during reading and mental labor. Pressure internally. Dryness when reading, with drawing pain on exerting them. Weakness in morning, upper lids so weak all the forenoon that he could scarcely open them. *Pupils dilated;* contracted. (Inner canthi agglutinated in morning after rising.) Burning pain in outer canthus, with itching on margin of upper lid. (Burning in lids in evening by the light, < inner canthus.) Dryness of lids in evening by the light, with sensation of sand in them. Crawling in lids. Tickling itching in r. inner canthus; in l. outer canthus. *Pulsation of superciliary muscles, a kind of convulsion.* Pressure on lower margin of orbit, < pressure. Vision dim when reading, > rubbing eyes; in evening. Blue seems green, carmine-red fawn-colored, madder-red bronze, and white seems yellow (Santonine).

Clinical.—Asthenopia, vision becomes blurred on attempting to read. Strabismus from worms.

Ears and Nose.—*Sticking below mastoid process, like a pinching, and on pressure a bruised feeling. Cramplike jerking in external ear.* **The child bores into the nose until the blood comes** (compare Arum tri.). *Violent sneezing.* Burning deep in l. nostril as if blood would come or as after snuffing up brandy. Burning aching on septum of l. nostril, as if one had picked off a scab, < external touch. Fluent coryza; in forenoon, then stoppage of nose in evening. Nose constantly full of loose mucus in morning, necessity to blow it frequently. Purulent discharge from nose.

Cinical.—The child constantly picks its nose, is very restless, cries and wets the bed.

Face.—Pale and cold. White and bluish about the mouth. *Red.* Bluish, puffy. *Pain in malar-bones as if seized by pincers and pressed together, < pressure* (Verbasc.). Periodic, wandering tensive-tearing in malar-bone, < pressure. Cramplike jerking in malar-bone, renewed by strong pressure, then cramplike or paralytic pain. Sticking in l. lower jaw, < pressure; in r. ramus, < pressure. Jerking pain in l. lower jaw.

Clinical.—Twitching of muscles of the face and about the eyes, especially with disordered stomach and bowels. Pallor around nose and mouth particularly marked, with worms, sometimes one cheek is hot and the other pale, sometimes the whole face is burning hot; the symptoms vary rapidly (Cham.). Neuralgia of the malar-bone as if pinched with pincers, < pressure (Verbasc.).

Mouth and Throat.—(Round worms come through the child's mouth.) Toothache from cold drinks and inspiration of air; T. as from soreness. Dryness of mouth, and rawness, < palate, with uneasy qualmishness. Pain in submaxillary glands. Mucus in back of throat and in larynx in morning, causing hawking and hacking. *Inability to swallow.*

Stomach.—**Great hunger soon after a meal** (China, Calc. c., Nux v.). **Desires many and different things.** No appetite. *Thirst.* Empty eructations in morning fasting. Eructations tasting of food after eating. E. of a bitter, acrid fluid after eating. Frequent hiccough. Nausea, with emptiness in head; N. in pit of stomach, with creeping shivers. *Vomiting of mucus only; of food, then general chill, then heat, with great thirst; violent;* repeated, violent, of yellow water. Sticking in l. side beneath pit, < pressure, > deep inspiration. Twisting, digging in epigastric region, as from a bruise. Pain in pit, impeding respiration. (Pressure at night.)

Clinical.—Unnatural hunger, the child wants a great variety of things, refuses ordinary food. Vomiting of mucus.

Abdomen.—Crackling of flatus and inaudible motions. Griping; cutting, > stool. Pain; alternating with headache; labor-like, as before menstruation. Emptiness, with silent passage of flatus. Heat becoming a griping. *Pinching or cramplike pressure transversely across, in region of pit of stomach, after eating.* Intermittent sticking in l. side when sitting; suddenly in l. side near navel towards evening, < inspiration and always associated with stitches on inner side of scapula. *Twisting about navel* and pain on pressure upon navel. Boring above navel, > pressure. Pain at navel after eating and on pressure; pain in region as from pressure inward of navel or as from a blow, afterwards < inspiration. Cutting in ilium in morning. Pulsation internally above mons veneris.

Clinical.—Distended, hard, sore. Abdomen swollen, hot, very sore above the navel, where there is a great deal of colic, sometimes > pressure (Pod.).

Rectum and Stool.—Single stitches in lower part on passage of flatus. *Watery diarrhœa.*

Clinical.—Diarrhœa of white mucus in little pieces like popcorn. Passes worms, both round and thread-worms.

Urinary and Sexual Organs.—*Frequent urging to urinate and much urine. Turbid urine.* Saffron-yellow urine, containing flakes of mucus. Hæmorrhage from uterus (in a girl of ten years).

Clinical.—Involuntary micturition (Ferr.). Frequent desire to urinate all day.

Respiratory Organs.—*Mucus hangs in larynx in morning after rising, soon collecting again after expectoration.* Loud whistling whooping on inspiration, not on expiration. Tickling irritation to cough in trachea beneath sternum, with whitish mucous expectoration. Dryness of trachea in morning, a catarrhal sensation.

Cough, then the child cries au! au! **A gurgling going downward is heard,** *she is anxious, catches her breath, and is pale.* **Hoarse, hacking C. in morning after rising,** *the irritation thereto (as from dust) renewed by inspiration; hoarse, hacking, in shocks in evening; violent, paroxysmal;* in morning, so violent in order to loosen the mucus that tears came into his eyes; hollow, in morning after rising, in violent shocks against upper part of air-passages, with difficult loosening of mucus. Disposition to cough caused by deep breathing. Expectoration of mucus from larynx.

Respiration short, **with omission of some inspirations.** Short, rattling; on walking in open air, as from much mucus in chest. Dyspnœa when standing, with anxiety and sweat on chest. Difficult, loud R.

Clinical.—Capillary bronchitis in children, screams when approached (Arn.), swallows after coughing, screams and talks in sleep. Whooping cough.

Chest.—Stitches; beneath l. clavicle, near sternum, on deep inspiration, with pain on pressure; on one of the cartilages of the ribs, near sternum, < pressure, > inspiration; jerking, in r. side, between sixth and eighth ribs, not affected by respiration; sudden jerking, in l., between fifth and sixth ribs; boring, in middle of r. side below ribs, > pressure; intermittent prickling, burning, in side, on one of the true ribs; pinching, in l. Pinching in l., between second and third ribs; in l., < inspiration; on sternum when running; on clavicle, like the pressure of a dull point.

Digging beneath upper part of sternum; cramplike, beneath sternum, as if chest would be pressed asunder. Feeling as if it would burst out at both sides when sneezing, then pain, < r. side. Pressing-out pain alternately in l. chest and in small of back, the latter seems as from much stooping, < expiration. Aching anteriorly under sternum; beneath upper part of sternum during morning cough, then, after difficult loosening of something, soreness and burning; sudden oppressive, in l. Sternum seems to press on lungs. Cramplike contraction in l. half. Tightness on inspiration.

Heart and Pulse.—Trembling of heart. Pulse small, contracted.

Neck and Back.—Boring sticking in r. cervical muscles, rhythmical with beat of pulse, > moving neck. Paralytic sensation in nape. Sticking in middle of spine, > motion. *Tearing sticking in middle of spine;* in upper part of spine, extending to r. scapula. *Drawing tearing down spine.* Spine feels as if broken when lying on back; in evening when lying on side. Sticking on outer margin of r. scapula. Aching in scapulæ if he moves them. *Bruised pain in small of back. Pain in loins as if he had stood long* (Arn.). Pain in loins and spine as if weary, on bending backward or to one side. Pain in lumbar region after eating, as from a band just above hip. Paralytic drawing in loins.

Extremities.—**Twitching.** Convulsions. Cramplike tearing in muscles now of r., now of l. leg, now of r., now of l. forearm, > walking in open air. Paralytic pain in arms and legs. Sensitiveness on motion and touch.

Upper Extremities.—Sticking in front of l. shoulder; on top of l. Pinching on top of shoulder. Tensive tearing in arms, with paralytic pain, and on taking hold of them bruised pain. Paralytic pain in arm, so that it must hang down; P. drawing pain through r. arm, < hanging down or resting on anything, < on anything hard. Paralytic sensation in r. arm, like a stiffness of the joints, so that he cannot move it.

Upper Arm.—Drawing tearing in r., > pressure. Pinching in r., > motion; *boring, in l.* Paralytic drawing from upper part down to middle, < motion, and bruised pain on pressure. Bruised pain above elbow.

Elbow.—Tearing in r. when at rest. Intermittent paralytic pain externally in bend, like a jerking.

Forearm.—Paralytic jerking downward on lower surface, < at the point where it begins. Drawing tearing in r. Contractive tearing like a cramp in muscles of l., close to wrist, > motion. Drawing digging in l. Cramplike pain in muscles on bending; C. pain on violent stretching of arm in morning after rising, < from elbow downward, and in wrists on bending hands back and forth when arms are outstretched.

Wrist.—Pinching boring in r. Feeling as if dislocated. Drawing pain.

Hand.—Intermittent cramplike contraction. *Jerking sticking, now l., now r.* Sticking in l., extending to little finger; in upper end of metacarpal bone of ring finger, and on pressure bruised pain. Jerking tearing in hollow of l., < stretching out hand.

Fingers.—Cramplike jerking; sudden jerking inward of r. Spasmodic contraction inward of r. middle, with cramplike pain. Cramplike pain in muscles of outer side of l. little, < motion. Bruised pain in ball of thumb on pressure and on moving metacarpus of thumb towards hollow of hand. Drawings; paralytic, in ring. Burning pain in proximal joint of middle. Crawling in tip of thumb as if asleep; C. in last joint of thumb almost as after being asleep.

Lower Extremities.—Thigh. Tearing in l. hip and nates; drawing, in anterior side of r. thigh, > violent motion. Boring outward below gluteals when sitting, > pressure and motion. Pain in great trochanter when walking as if he had fallen upon it. Pain in nates when sitting, as if wearied by long sitting. Cramplike pain in anterior muscles of l. when standing. Paralytic pain in l. not far from knee.

Knee.—Intermittent sticking; single stitches in patella.

Leg.—Spasmodic stretching (in a child). Paralytic twitching in forepart, between tibia and fibula. Intermittent sticking as with a fork in l. tibia, just below knee. Tearing in middle of l. calf when sitting. Digging in l. tibia below knee. Cramplike pain in muscles, now of r., now of l., on walking in open air, > standing and sitting.

Foot.—Spasmodic motion of l., at last immobility, abduction far from body (in a child). Twitching-tearing in interior of l. Sticking in ball of r. Tearing sticking in l. heel when sitting.

Toes.—Cutting in l. as if loosened from the feet.

Skin.—Miliary rash. Red itching pimples. Boil surrounded by an induration, on cheek. Burning sticking here and there, > scratching. Prickling, itching crawling, > scratching. Itching tickling on border of r. hand near thumb and index. Itching here and there at night; I. on back of l. hand, > scratching; *voluptuous, in front of anus.*

Sleep.—Yawning. Sleepiness all day; in afternoon; overpowering, in evening; when sitting, he must lie down. *Sleeps when erect with head leaned backward or to right. Tossing about in sleep, with lamentations and cries about colic.* Sleepless. Waking with weeping complaints, groaning, hiccough and restless motions. Frequent waking from unpleasant or busy dreams. Dreams anxious; tiresome; absurd.

Fever.—Chill; *daily at the same hour, then heat, without thirst* (Ign.). *Shivering over whole body; with hot cheeks, without thirst* (Ign.); *S. creeping over trunk, so that it trembled;* over upper part of body, extending to head, as if the hair would stand up; creeping over thigh. Cold cheeks. Cold face, with warm hands. Cold hands in morning and creeping chills. Cool skin.

Heat; in evening and night; every afternoon, then increased sweat and deep sleep; *daily at the same hour, with short breath;* daily in afternoon, from 1 P.M. onward, then several attacks of chill with thirst, coldness in hands and feet, then heat of the pale face, < heat of hands and feet, with cutting colic; with vomiting and diarrhœa; (with redness of face, then sweat, without thirst). *H. mostly in head during fever, with yellow color of face and blue rings around eyes.* **Rising H. and redness of cheeks** *after sleep, without thirst* (Ign., Cham.); *H. over face, with redness of cheeks and thirst for cold drinks.* H. creeping over knees, with sensation as if a glowing coal were near the knee. Internal H., with heat and redness of face.

Sweat; *cold on forehead, nose and hands.* Dry skin.

Cinnabaris.

The pure Mercuric sulphide (Cinnabar) is triturated for use.

General Action and Allies.—See Mercurius.

Generalities.—Nervous thrill through the whole frame, < in joints. Excitement of nervous system. Sensation as before typhoid fever. Sensation of having taken cold. Discomfort after eating as if the body were distended, oppression across chest and abdomen. Restlessness. Weakness; in morning; in morning after restless sleep and many dreams; on going to bed, with confusion of mind; on any extraordinary mental or physical exertion, so that he must lie down, with palpitation, which was < lying on l. side or with head low, pain in head from front to back and down spinal cord to below scapulæ, if the exertion was continued there followed nausea, vomiting, diarrhœa and pain in r. hypochondrium. Heaviness, with sleepiness during the day. Aggravation in forenoon; evening; of pains and fever in evening and cold; at night in bed, of all symptoms except sweat. Amelioration in afternoon and evening; in open air and after dinner; after eating and sleep; of pains generally by continuous rest, warm bathing, galvanism and heat.

Mind.—Illusion, he considers himself well. Sense of elevation on walking in open air. Exhilaration, with fulness extending from all sides of chest towards stomach and heart, with or followed by similar sensations in all joints. Cross and sullen in afternoon. Dissatisfied with himself; and every one else. Irritable; about noon, and nervous. Troubled by every noise. Nervous, uneasy, desirous of improving spiritually, but disconsolate. Melancholy, cynical. Indisposed to mental labor. Difficult to fix the attention, > in open air.

Head.—Occasional darting inwardly through; from out in front and front to back. Aching; < sleep, in eyes; > external pressure; deep in centre; stupefying, < thinking, reading and pressure. Fulness; in forenoon; > open air, with pressure as after taking cold, and pain in region of benevolence; with heaviness and with strong pulsations in temporal arteries. Heaviness; and dulness, can scarcely lift it from the pillow. Dulness in evening, < in forehead just over eyes. Weariness as from long mental application. Congested sensation, < in forehead. Sensation as of rush of blood; < morning, with vertigo and weakness. Vertigo, with lightness of head; V., with weakness in head and staggering when walking; V. on rising at 7 A.M., > breakfast, with pain in forehead and soreness in eyeballs.

Forehead.—Shooting, with heaviness. Sharp pain < r. orbital region; in supraorbital region, shooting to ear and side of neck, < warm room and moving eyes and scalp. Aching; in sinciput; in organ of tune; region of causality; in morning after waking, < lying on l. side and back, > lying on r. side and pressing head into pillow, also > rising and washing, and in crown; in r. in afternoon, < evening; over eyes in afternoon, < evening and on motion; all night; with coldness of it, > warm hand; heavy; throbbing, on waking, > pressing head on pillow. Fulness and pressure.

Temples.—Shooting in upper part of l., along ridge, in evening; flashes of pain backward in r. (organ of mirthfulness). Pain in r. Fulness and weight across, < motion, with sometimes throbbing over r. temple. Beating burning. Throbbing.

Vertex.—Sore pain at 9 A.M., lasting all day, extending to organ of veneration, with sensitiveness to touch and sometimes throbbing. Drawing pain extending to occiput, inclining to r., before going to bed.

Parietals.—Sticking over secretive region, becoming a numb pain, extending to r. temple (time and locality), with warmth on r. side, pain extending from r. temple to l., across os frontis, mild in forehead, but violent in organs of time and locality, night and day and on rising in morning. Darting through sides and temples, near outer edge of r. orbit, more frequent on r. side, the pain going from temples to occiput. Pain in r. side; in l. side at 11.40 o'clock and in temple and supraorbital ridge. Throbbing pain in organ of conscientiousness in morning on waking, extending to forehead over eye.

Occiput.—Shooting from l. side to forehead. Pain; in l. (organ of amativeness). Fulness after rising, > at noon, with pressure, and in nape. Rush of blood, with itching and heat extending to ears, and behind l. ear three hard lumps.

Scalp.—Protrusion only during the day. Sore to touch. Skull sensitive to touch, even the hairs pain.

Eyes.—Surrounded by livid circles. Red, painful, feeling as of sand in them, conjunctiva of lower lid injected and covered with small granulations. (Inflammation of r., itching, pressure and sticking in inner canthus and in lower lid, lachrymation on looking at anything, with fluent coryza.) Sensation as if something were in them. Numb pressing pain. Aching soreness, < evening. Sensitiveness to cold open air. Sensation of a cold breeze in afternoon when sitting in the house. Weak about noon and sleepy; weak sensation in l. Watery sensation in l. Lachrymation; and dulness, with sticking in l. inner canthus as from a sharp stick in lower lid.

Lids.—Sticking about punctum lachrymale, next day a transparent vesicle, sore to touch, on inner edge of lid near where the pain had been. Shooting in r. inner canthus, with burning itching. *Pain from r. lachrymal duct around eye to temple;* **from l. inner canthus across brows.** *Drawing from r. inner canthus across malar-bone to ear.* Puffed feeling on looking up to the wall, as if muscles were too short. Itching; of inner canthus; outer canthus from 9 to 12 o'clock, with stiffness of upper lids; inner and outer canthi, with sticking.

Clinical.—Inflammatory affections of the eyes, blepharitis, kerato-iritis, ulcers of the cornea, etc., inflammations mostly superficial or characterized by severe pain in the bones of the orbit, especially by a pain running from the inner to the outer canthus, in the bone.

Ears.—Aching; in l. meatus, with fulness. Soreness from r. into middle of posterior cervical region, as if glands were affected, < evening. Sensation as of a foreign body; of water in l. Noises after eating. Roaring after dinner and in evening before sleep, causing vertigo. Rushing sound and deafness.

Nose.—Itching pimples at r. nostril and dark blood from nose after blowing. *Sensation on bridge as if touched with a metal. Uneasy creeping and pressive sensation about ossa nasi, as from heavy spectacles* (compare Kali bi.). Epistaxis. Coryza. Discharge of much mucus (Merc.); flow of mucus from r. nostril. Symptoms of a cold, with much mucus in dirty yellow lumps from posterior nares and lameness in thighs.

Clinical.—Nasal catarrh, subacute and chronic, with pain about the root of the nose, extending into the bones on each side.

Face.—Flushing of l. cheek. Pain in l. side and in teeth, sores on inside of lower lip; towards the l.

Mouth. — Aching soreness of teeth. Pain in r. molar. Tongue white; white fur; white fur in morning; sore spot on tip; sore on r. side of tip, and one on each lip; soreness on l. side of root on swallowing, with roughness and stiffness through the night; itching spot on l. side. Pricking in mouth and fauces. *Mouth and throat dry, must rinse the mouth every time he wakes;* with heat in them and sticking posteriorly under tongue. Peculiar drawing in M. after rising till breakfast. Contractive burning in palate. Sore; on roof; soreness of roof. Salivation. Great fetor. Taste metallic after tea; M. from 8 A.M. till 2 P.M., modified by continual tendency to hawk and spit, with salivation and much mucus; bitter M.; T. as of tobacco, coffee; T. bad, with mucus in mouth and ptyalism.

Throat. — Sore. Contractive pain on swallowing saliva. Dry at 8 A.M., on waking.

Clinical.—Angina faucium, with accumulation of stringy mucus passing through posterior nares into throat (Nit. ac., etc.).

Stomach.—Appetite great; capricious; impaired in morning; lost; aversion to food. Thirst; on waking at 8 A.M. Empty eructation. Nausea; with uneasiness in stomach; with occasional throbbing in l. hypochondrium; with bitter and sour vomiting. The mucus thrown up tastes like old tallow mixed with coffee. Soreness, with tightness in temples. Tenderness of epigastric region. Emptiness two hours after a hearty breakfast. Heat rising into throat and head at night in bed, > sitting up. Sensation as if secretions were flowing from S. and from all mucous surfaces, as well as from salivary glands.

Abdomen.—Distention; with desire to have everything loose about it. Rumbling, with pain passing from epigastric to pubic region. Intermittent shooting. Griping; > two soft stools. Pain; before stool. Soreness. Uneasy, indescribable feeling. Sensation in evening as before diarrhœa. Flashes of heat, with flatulence.

Hypochondrium.—Swelling of r., with heat in it. Pain; in r.; sharp P. in front of l., < moving and in open air, soon extending round lower border of ribs behind, and to l. kidney, where it is dull and oppressive, soon afterwards in front of r. H., extending round to back and r. kidney, where it is dull, then the dull pain is felt alternately in each kidney, the pain in hypochondria > bending forward. Burning pain in liver and soreness, with at times suppression of bile; B. pain in r. lobe of liver, with soreness and heaviness there. Throbbing; in region of spleen.

Rumbling below transverse colon. Hot feeling below transverse colon. Constriction in umbilical region at 11 A.M. Soreness in U. region, obliging him to turn. Pain in hypogastrium after eating boiled cabbage, with diarrhœa and flatulence.

Rectum, Anus and Stool.—Weight in lower part of rectum after dinner, with aching. Bleeding piles. Itching in anus, < night in bed. Two stools daily; two in afternoon, the last with straining. Diarrhœa at night. Constipation. Stools hard and too large; hard and copious, or sudden diarrhœa, consisting of white or dark passages.

Urinary Organs.—Soreness of urethra on urinating. Sensation of a raw spot in centre of urethra, waking at night. Urging to urinate. Urine increased; and frequent micturition, with sediment at first whitish, later reddish. Turbid urine.

Sexual Organs.—Red spots on penis; as if pimples would form; on each side of glans, secreting much lardaceous matter. Redness of prepuce, with swelling and itching pain. (Warts on prepuce, bleeding on touch.) Penis swollen. Jerking in penis. Tearing stitches in glans. Itching pain in fossa behind penis, and pus of a nauseous sweetish odor oozes. Itching of corona glandis, > by rubbing, then <, with much pus; burning sticking-itching in evening, > by rubbing, then returning more violent. Violent erection in evening; in bed. Excitement on least provocation. Loss of desire. *Leucorrhœa, the discharge of which caused pressure in vagina.*

Clinical.—Indurated buboes, condylomata on prepuce, which bleed easily. Enlarged testicle resulting from gonorrhœa; chronic gonorrhœa.

Respiratory Organs.—Œdema of epiglottis. Irritation of larynx. Hoarseness; in morning; and loss of voice; (in evening, with crouplike cough). Cough; < night, expectoration at first clear, then opaque, afterwards gray, puslike, occasionally blood-streaked sputa, smelling very offensive in morning; (C. in single dry shocks on lying down, > sitting up). Suffocation on swallowing.

Chest.—Sticking beneath sternum. Pain beneath sternum; on l. chest; in middle of l. breast, in front; in upper part of lungs; in a spot on seventh rib of each side, < l.; occasionally in l. side between cartilages of fifth and sixth ribs; from seventh rib on r. side running near ensiform cartilage diagonally through to chest; from cartilage of seventh rib at its junction with the sternum, to r. hypochondrium under inferior border of tenth rib, from 4 to 5 P.M.; under lower end of sternum, extending to l. side under short ribs; extending from region of short ribs to r. kidney and l. hypochondrium; in upper part of r. lung and in cardiac region, extending into l. arm, which often feels numb; wandering pain in forenoon.

Soreness under r. breast, near last true rib, < drawing breath; in a spot on r., on one rib, when touched, with occasionally sore pain in and around it; internally over heart, extending along l. arm on taking a long breath. Pulselike throbbing here and there beneath short ribs, < walking, > sitting and lying, with sticking. Warmth under sternum.

Heart and Pulse.—Cutting at H., impeding breathing. Pain at H., < lying on l. side. Palpitation during frightful dreams. Pulse rapid; in evening; and intermittent, strong, then tremulously weak; slow, then rapid; lowered in forenoon and irregular.

Neck.—Muscles of nape seem contracted. Pain on r. side below sterno-cleido-mastoid muscle on turning head; in nape when head is thrown back, extending to occiput; in vertebræ as if dislocated.

Back.—Tearing in side, < night on motion in bed, > warmth of stove, with sensation as if everything would separate. Pain down to loins, < drawing a long breath; P. in lower dorsal spine. Sticking in region of l. side of fifth and sixth dorsal vertebræ in evening, next day the same pain occasionally on r. side of same vertebræ.

Lumbar Region.—Sticking in region of l. kidney, waking at 4 A.M., then tossing about and sleeplessness. Sharp pain in region of kidneys as if a nail had been driven in on each side of vertebræ. Pain, and in legs; P. in morning, and in limbs; in kidneys; l. kidney. Aching and drawing pain from kidneys to sacrum and in thighs and legs, > drawing up legs. Bruised pain. Sore feeling, extending around both sides over ossa illia, < pressure.

Extremities.—Aching; in bones of forearms and legs; in all joints, with lameness. Lame feeling in all, < mornings, with fatigue. Weakness in morning. Paralytic sensation, with general heaviness and sleepiness. Numbness of arms, knees and legs at 8 P.M., with heavy aching.

Upper Extremities.—Lame sensation in r. shoulder-joint in evening. Œdema of r. arm. Stitches in arm. Tearing in arm when writing, > warmth of the stove, with sensation as if everything would separate. Pain along l. arm, < in little finger, third finger and thumb, on supinating forearm the pain is worse at elbow, it feels as if the crazy bone were struck. Heavy deep-seated pain in r. humerus, beginning at centre, extending to elbow and along radius to its lower end, causing lameness and difficulty in moving arm.

Cracking in elbow and shoulder at the least twitch. Pain in l. arm-joint on turning and straightening arm and when writing. Numb feeling in elbows as if ulnar nerve were compressed. Numbness of l. forearm from elbow to end of little finger; > using arm. Occasional shooting and prickling pain in two l. middle fingers, > firm pressure upon thumb. Darting pain from first phalanx of r. ring finger to middle of forearm and from lower end of l. radius to elbow. Pain in r. little finger.

Lower Extremities.—Lameness and stitches on walking, < inner side of knee. Drawing in all muscles, on under surface. Tired feeling in joints, > rising and walking. Shooting on posterior side of r. thigh, from hip-joint to middle of femur, on straining at stool. Pain in thighs; in r. hip, then l., with tired feeling. Drawing pain in thighs from hip-joints nearly down to condyles, < motion, with lameness on getting up and attempting to walk, > walking a short distance.

Sticking in back part of l. knee in forenoon; in r. knee in afternoon, with creeping in bone above and below it. Pain in knees; < at noon on walking; in l. knee, near inner side of tibia. Numbness of knees. Painful jerking in leg, waking in evening. Sore feeling in ankle, with heat and itching over whole leg. Pain in tendo-achillis and os calcis after walking. Pressive sensation in foot as if it would go to sleep. (Rheumatic pain in great toe.)

Skin.—Redness like chronic eruption. Eruption on nape; on inner and lower part of thigh, with itching. Scurvy tetter exedens on r. middle finger and palm. (The margins of ulcers become painful and tense.) Itching during the day; at night, < on inside of thighs; l. side of face; r. palm; on inside of thighs and legs, < knees, < at night; inner side of knee, < night and morning before getting up, with pricking; in various parts when walking in open air; sticking I. on forepart of throat, forepart of chest, with swollen cervical glands, then round red spots with hard pimples, with itching and burning, < scratching, at last the spots are painful.

Sleep.—Sleepiness; during the day; during the day, but restlessness at night; at 11 A.M. when listening to a lecture; *in warm room, with weakness*; on going to bed, but inability to sleep on account of nervous sensation, which caused tossing about; with nightly sleeplessness, hears the clock strike every hour; with heaviness over eyes.

Sleeplessness; during the day; till 2 A.M.; for over an hour after retiring, tossing about, nervous and vexed; forepart of the night, then tossing about, with anxious, unremembered dreams; and restlessness from constant flow of ideas, changing from one subject to another; S., but in the morning he feels strengthened. Restless; and dreamy sleep, seemed to dream before getting to sleep; R. sleep, with continual dreaming and waking; with vivid unremembered dreams. Waking suddenly as from a dream; after midnight, and he has no breath, like a nightmare. Waking and starting up several times without a purpose. Unrefreshed on waking at 8 A.M.

Dreams, with restlessness and talking in sleep. Many, with frequent waking. Vivid but unremembered; V., sensual; V. of the lectures, < the anatomical; V. of studies and business. Anxious. Troublesome. That there is a lump in his throat and r. ear.

Fever.—Coldness; in a spot above and between supraorbital regions, sensation as if pressed by a cold metallic body, with heat within the cranium beneath the spot; in joints, with shivering and drawing in arms and legs; cold hands; C. hands and feet mornings, but heat of them nights, with heat of skin in evening, and heat at night in bed, fetid sweat between thighs at night.

Heat; at night; occasionally, with fulness in forehead; in head, from front to back, < over r. eye and temple; front of head hot; glow through legs, then aching above l. elbow and occasional darting pain in lower limbs; then copious, sticky, stinking sweat, as thick as mucus. Sweat at noon; between thighs, < about noon; offensive, corrosive, between thighs when walking. Cool sweat.

Cinnamomum.

A tincture is made of Cinnamon bark (Laurus Cinnamomum, L.).

Excitement of vascular system and respiratory organs. She imagines that the l. side of the brain is shrunken; l. side of head seems smaller; she thinks that the l. side of the face is smaller; l. eye seems smaller; l. leg feels shorter, < when walking. Numbness all over; l. side. Amelioration of symptoms after breakfast. Crossness. Headache. Head stupefied. Eyes sunken. Sunken, sickly look to face. *Nosebleed in frequent attacks.* Blisters all over mouth. Tongue dry after eating, without thirst. Soreness of mouth and tongue, preventing eating. Rawness and soreness of mouth and tongue returned after rinsing mouth with cold water. Loss of appetite in evening.

Feeling as if everything in abdomen were suppurating. Abdomen sore to touch. Tension in abdomen in morning, in both ovarian regions, as if a thread were drawn in that direction. *Bright red and clear hæmorrhage from bowels, < after physical exertion.* Diarrhœa. Urine increased. *Bearing down in genitals.* Scanty yellow discharge from vagina. *Menstruation early, profuse and prolonged, so that soon she was but comparatively few days in the month free from the hæmorrhage, at times the flow would be unattended by other symptoms, again she would be quite hysterical.* Backache. Fingers seem swollen. Sleepiness, no desire for anything; drowsiness in morning, with heaviness.

Clinical.—Uterine hæmorrhages; post-partum hæmorrhagias; hæmorrhages from the bowels, menorrhagia, menses early and profuse, bright red; hæmoptysis (compare Millefol., Erig., Sabin., etc.).

Cistus.

A tincture is prepared from the fresh plant of Cistus Canadense, L.

Generalities and Mind.—Trembling with the fever. Bad effects from vexation. Aggravation from mental excitement. Amelioration after discharging mucus from throat. Cheerfulness after supper, till bedtime.

Clinical.—Has been used for swollen glands in general, which become inflamed, indurated or ulcerated. Herpetic eruptions, scrofulous ophthalmia, offensive discharges. All the cases are extremely sensitive to cold.

Head.—Aching, < *towards evening*, and lasting all night; oppressive, all day; A. in sinciput after being kept waiting for dinner, > after eating. Pressure above eyes. Weight above eyes. Aching in r. side, with piercing pain in eye.

Eyes.—Stitches in l. Feeling as if something were passing around in it, with stitches. Pressure in glabella. Spasmodic piercing pain in middle of upper rim of r. socket, with headache on that side.

Ears, Nose and Face.—Inner swelling in ears; with discharge. Discharge from ears of water and bad-smelling pus. Swelling of parotid glands. Tip of nose painful. L. side of nose painfully inflamed and swollen. Burning in l. nostril. *Sneezing*, without cold in head. Facial muscles feel as if they would be drawn to one side.

Mouth.—Twitching stitching in a decayed l. upper molar. Gums scorbutic, swollen, separating from teeth, bleeding easily, putrid, disgusting. Tongue sore, as if raw. Tongue and roof of mouth dry. Breath impure.

Throat.—Swelling of glands. Hawking of mucus; of mucus which is lodged at head of windpipe. Inflammation and dryness, without dry feeling, with hawking, < morning, of tough, gumlike, thick, tasteless mucus. Tearing when coughing. Stitches whenever mentally agitated, causing cough. Pain on inhaling cold air; sore, in morning, with dryness of tongue. Feeling of sand. Feeling of softness. Dryness, < at night; > eating; with heat. Tickling, with soreness. Periodical itching.

Clinical.—It has been used for sore throat, mostly subacute, with intolerable dryness, <cold air, > swallowing liquids, great swelling of uvula and tonsils. Sore throat, with a small dry spot, has to rise at night to sip water, feeling as if it were glazed with strips of tough mucus.

Stomach.—(Inclination for acid food.) (Desire for cheese.) Thirst with the fever. Eructation, with feeling as if it would relieve; cool E. Nausea. Pain after eating. Cold feeling before and after eating.

Abdomen.—Puffed up, with flatulency in evening. Flatulence towards evening; at night; with discomfort. Emissions of flatus; in evening, as when air-bubbles rise in water. Internal coldness. Much flatulence in hypochondria, with pain. Stitches in l. hypochondrium. Bruised feeling under hypochondria in morning, with flatulence.

Stool and Sexual Organs.—Urging to stool, stool pappy. Diarrhœa; in morning; *after fruit;* after drinking coffee; *thin, till daybreak, squirting, grayish-yellow, then three more discharges before noon;* (thin, hot). Itching of scrotum.

Clinical.—Diarrhœa from coffee, thin, yellow, urgent, < early in morning. Dysentery.

Respiratory Organs.—Itching in larynx at night, with scratching, and with anxious dreams. Pain in windpipe. Cough, < mental anguish. Expectoration of bitter mucus.

Clinical. The windpipe feels narrow, has to open the window to breathe fresh air, < lying down, a kind of asthmatic attack.

Chest.—Pressure on. Pain, and in throat; P., and in shoulder. Fulness. Rawness, extending into throat; in upper part, extending into throat.

Clinical.—Induration of the mammary gland.

Back and Extremities.—Burning bruised pain in os coccygis. Pain in all joints. Bruised pain in all limbs, as from fatigue. Drawing in joints, especially in knees and fingers, with tearing; involuntary D. in muscular parts of hands and lower limbs, with trembling feeling in them and with pain in wrists, fingers and knees.

Upper Extremities.—Pain in front of r. shoulder; in l. S. in evening, and in chest, with feeling as if an eructation would relieve the pain. Piercing drawing pain in arm, extending periodically to tip of little finger, so as to draw up the finger. Sensitiveness to touch on r. arm and dorsum of hand. Sprained pain in wrist, drawing, scraping. Pain in hand; in r. in evening, and in l. shoulder; in r. H. in afternoon, so that he cannot use it. Drawing trembling feelings in H. Tearing in finger-joints. Pain in r. fingers when writing; in joints. Sensitiveness of finger-tips to cold, the pain < cold.

Lower Extremities.—Drawing, trembling feeling. Pain in l. buttock as from a blow or shock, extending down inside of femur, distinctly felt in knee, with spasmodic drawing together of calf. Pain in r. thigh while walking. Pain in knees; in evening; when walking and sitting, and in r. thigh. Piercing pain in r. great toe in evening.

Clinical.—Has cured white swelling of the knee.

Skin.—Swelling, beginning at ear and extending half way up cheek. Inflamed spot below r. scapula, extending round to front of body, with soreness to touch, then burning pimples, then rheumatic pain extending to l. hip and into groin, the pain < motion. *Eruptions like zoster on back.* Vesicular erysipelas in face. Formication evenings after lying down, > rising and opening window, with anxious, difficult breathing, both returning on lying down again. Itching all over body; on outside of throat near larynx; of abdomen and umbilicus; on back.

Sleep.—Restlessness at night; with pain from flatulency, he could move the wind with his hands and hear it. Anxious dreams.

Fever.—Chill, then heat; with trembling and with quick swelling and redness of glands below ear and in throat. Coolness especially in throat; on forehead; in nose. Cold feet. Heat, with thirst; in facial bones; in face in flushes. Moisture of skin in a warm room, with internal and external coolness in forehead.

Citric Acid.

Pure Citric acid is triturated with sugar of milk for use.

Allies.—Organic acids generally, which as a class produce conditions of malnutrition and anæmia.

A case of scurvy was brought on by its excessive use as a preventive against yellow fever.

Clinical.—Seemed beneficial in a number of cases of diphtheria. Checks excessive menstruation.

Clematis.

A tincture is prepared from the fresh plant of Clematis erecta, L.

General Action.—A remedy full of pains, swelling of glands, inflammations, etc.; remarkably similar to several of its botanical allies.

Allies.—*Puls.*, Aconit., Cimicif., Ran. b., Berb., Rhod.

Generalities.—Emaciation, < lower limbs. Swelling of lymphatic glands, < r. inguinal glands. Twitching of all fleshy parts. Jerking as of electric shocks in whole body, with fright from a sensation as if he suddenly fell. Trembling after lying down, < r. side, upon which he lay. Perceptible pulsations of blood-vessels, < heart. Running about the street, with lightness and rapidity, more like a kind of floating, then no sensation in any part, no will power, no power to think, then weariness in all parts, with sticking beating pain in head extending outward and sensation as if it would burst, feet felt heavy and fastened to the ground, walking painful and unsteady.

Sticking in joints, forearms, thighs and genitals, then itching spots, and after scratching urticaria. Numerous pains in various parts, lasting till falling asleep at 2 A.M. Wandering pains, mostly pressive, worse when sitting than when walking (Puls., Cimicif.), in legs, skull, r. scapula, forepart of r. shoulder-joint, toes, knees, l. lower jaw, tarsal bones. Bruised sensation; wandering, in joints, skull and other parts. Drawing in various parts, < feet. Drawing pains in teeth, nasal bones, in small of back, toes and tibiæ. Heaviness. Discomfort. Inclination for open air (Puls.). No desire to go out. Restlessness and dry heat, obliging him to rise at 4 A.M.; R. in evening, with oppression. Tossing about in bed, with anxiety and sweat on forehead. Sensitiveness to external impressions, they cause irritability and anxiety; S. of painful parts to touch. Sensation in body in morning as after emission, or as if one had been suppressed.

Disinclination to exertion; rising from bed difficult. No desire for his accustomed evening walk. Weakness; in morning; in morning, with sweat; in morning on waking from unrefreshing sleep, with sleepiness; in morning on waking, as if he had danced all night; at noon, with little appetite; in evening; in evening when with many people, then clammy sweat; on rising; on waking; on walking, and chest easily oppressed; after half an hour's exercise in open air; after stool; after eating, with sleepiness so that he must lie down, with quickened pulsations in blood-vessels, when called he was not bright and fell into a slumber; with cracking of knees; with stiffness of joints (Cimicif.) and cracking in them on motion; trembling. Aggravation on walking; after black coffee; after a restless night, > open air (Puls.).

Clinical.—It is a very valuable remedy for a rheumatic constitution, especially in a patient who occasionally suffers from herpetic eruptions; whose herpetic eruptions sometimes become pustular, especially about the occiput; eczema impetiginoides.

Mind.—Raving in evening during exacerbations. Seemed oppressed by grief or insults or shadow of impending misfortune (Cimicif.). Uneasy as if an evil would befall him. Dread of misfortune. Discontented. Anxious. Sad; > nap; with thoughts of suicide. Loss of "moral strength" so that he shed tears, then sleep (Puls.). Morose; in morning; on waking from afternoon sleep. Taciturn; > evening. Angry, fretful, avoiding every one, shunning his usually agreeable occupations, dreaded being alone, tired of living, full of thoughts of death, with fear that it would be speedy, but longing for the repose of death, then apprehension, weeping, homesickness, at last trembling and weeping till he was exhausted. Indifferent, quiet, almost without thought.

Excitement. Exhilaration, with desire for mental work, sweat and itching, then exhaustion, anxiety, depression of spirits, fretfulness and loss of desire for mental work. Busy and lively mood from 10 A.M. to 2 P.M., then sleepiness and disinclination to work. Lively mood from 10 A.M. to 4 P.M., then sudden disinclination for work, morose mood and lassitude in limbs. Excited, lively, stronger and more disposed to read and think than usual, then mentally exhausted and condition generally like intoxication. Desire for mental work and power of thinking increased, then sweat when sitting quietly, with mental exhaustion and heaviness of whole body. Aversion to mental work. Distraction. Confusion in morning, with bruised feeling; in morning, with prostration. Lost in thought without knowing what he was thinking about. Memory weak.

Clinical.—It has been used for the effects of homesickness, with restless, dreamy sleep and vibratory sensations throughout the body.

Head.—Obliged to carry it forward and hanging down. Aching; in morning on waking, with sleepiness; after walking in open air; < night on closing eyes in bed, with raging, digging and vertigo, all > 3 A.M. at the open window, then, on the outbreak of sweat, sleep; increasing from morning till 2 P.M., < occiput, causing nausea and vertigo, > sweat (with cold body and face); as if it would burst, in evening; as from a band about it; tensive, after eating, < forehead and temples; drawing, with pressure in sides of vertex.

Sensation as if skull were too small for the brain. Screwed-together sensation. Raging and beating, < forehead, preventing reading and writing. Hammering in evening when lying. Shocks in brain, extending forward. Dulness. Emptiness. Confusion; in morning; in morning on waking; in morning on rising, with heaviness; > open air; as after intoxicating drinks; as from coryza, > 1.30 P.M. Stupidity. Heaviness; in morning; in morning on rising, and in chest, with deep expiration; with sinking down; with external heat. Congestion. Almost intoxicated condition. Vertigo; till 2 P.M., with sleepiness; on holding head erect or turning it; on carrying head forward, > carrying it backward; with tottering on walking in open air; > open air, with trembling of whole body, gait unsteady and rapid, as in slight intoxication. Aggravation by the accustomed cigar.

Forehead.—Tearing in frontal and parietal bones. Aching; in morning, < 10 A.M.; < pressure; > evening; > pressure, < cold, on l. side extending into orbit; in eminences; in eminences in morning; in one side; in sinciput; with external heat; tensive, in forepart of brain, worse when walking than when sitting, with heaviness of head; drawing, in l. side. Drawing in bones. Pressure on eminences. Tension. Heaviness in sinciput; and fulness. Sensation as if lead were in it. Confusion; with emptiness and tendency to vertigo.

Temple.—Pain. Boring in l. Burrowing in r. and frontal and zygomatic regions, with pressure. Tension. Pulsation in l. in evening in bed, preventing reading. Heaviness in r., with pressure in it.

Pain in vertex. Frequent sudden tearing, now in r., now in l. side of head. Burrowing in r. half of brain when walking; in sides of head, extending to occiput. Tensive pain in r. side of head, rather in bones than in brain. Drawing in side, < turning head. Pain in occiput; as after moderate use of spirituous drinks, daily after midnight, waking several times, extending to nape and forward, sometimes with a feeling as after lying in an uncomfortable position. Tearing in skull. Boring in skull. Pressure in skull; here and there.

Scalp.—*Itching crusts and stitches* (Ran. bulb.). Painful pimple under skin of occiput. Pressure. Sensitiveness in circumscribed spots over forepart, afterwards with itching and fine scurf. *Itching* on l. side of vertex; on forepart.

Clinical.—Eruption like eczema on occiput, itching < warmth of the bed, with stinging, crawling and tickling.

Eyes.—Staring. *Red; and glittering, hot and dry* (Acon.). Yellow color of the white. *Inflammation of white, with lachrymation.* Pressure; on optic nerves. *Burning; as if fire streamed out of them* (Acon., Rhod.). *Biting burning pain* (Acon.). Biting; < closing, then on opening them photophobia. *Sensitiveness to air* (Acon.). *Dryness; and heat, compelling him to close the lids* (Acon.). Itching. *Sensation of a veil before them. Lachrymation* (Puls., Acon.). *Pupils contracted. Pain in middle of l. ball* (Cimicif.).

Yellowish crust in inner canthus. Inflammation of inner canthus, with weak vision. Sticking in inner canthus; l. Burning in lids. Burning pain in r. upper lid; in l. inner canthus. Biting on margins of lids. Itching in r. inner canthus, next day extending to l. inner, with burning. *Pressure in orbits on moving eyes.* Blackness before eyes. *Vision indistinct;* in r. Flickering. Letters run together when writing, at times double vision and flickering; letters run together when reading, with frequent blackness before eyes. Illusions in l. in evening.

Clinical.—Especially useful in inflammation of the iris from cold, with pressing pain, great photophobia, lachrymation and heat in eyes and great sensitiveness to cold air; also useful in pustular conjunctivitis. Chronic syphilitic iritis, aggravation at night, with adhesions (Iod., Aur.).

Ears.—Biting sticking in r. *Burning pain in external, with internal and external heat of it;* B. pain in l. external. Drawing in region of r. ear, cheek and side of neck towards evening, with stitches. Difficult hearing; at 7.30 A.M.; in morning, with ringing in l. Ringing before ears; periodical ringing in r. Roaring, < r.

Nose.—Tip red and swollen and at root a red, painful pimple. Dry and hot (Acon.); dry in morning. Stoppage. Sneezing in morning; repeated S., with increase of nasal discharge; violent, after breakfast, then clear water from l. nostril; frequent violent, in morning, with watery discharge. Mucus streaked with blood. Fluent coryza, with frequent sneezing (Puls.).

Face.—Yellow; and sickly. Red. Sudden flush, with yellowish redness of cheeks. Swelling of r. cheek in morning, with sensitiveness to touch. Weary look. Drawing stitches in l. side of upper jaw, rhythmical with pulse, extending upward. Painful pimples on upper lip. Itching vesicles just beneath vermilion border of lower lip, discharging water, then covered with a tough skin, itching somewhat (compare Ranunculus). Burning cutting stitch through l. side of lower lip.

Mouth.—Teeth. Sticking in carious, with throbbing. Jerking sticking in l. upper; sticking extending upward into whole l. side of face, a drawing and jerking pain, rhythmical with pulse, with jerklike twinges into ear and pain in eye on moving it; jerking stitches, extending across cheek-bone to ear, a drawing jerking in ear, extending to eye, which is painful so that he cannot endure motion or light, and eyeball is painful to touch. Tearing jerking in all upper. Sudden drawing jerking-tearing in l. lower canine at 7 P.M., with sticking, soon extending through whole jaw backward and upward, > cold water in mouth. Jerking pain in r. upper hollow molar, > rinsing mouth with cold water. Jerking sticking-drawing pain now in one, now in another l. upper. Jerking drawing pain, < smoking tobacco, > firm pressure with a cloth. Burrowing in r. back in evening.

Toothache in hollow teeth; *toothache during the day, < as soon as he lies down in bed,* > lying quietly; in hollow, at 10 P.M., after reading in bed, sleepless till 1 o'clock; at night, next day elongated sensation, gum loose, swollen and pale, the pain extending on both sides to eye-teeth and preventing chewing; all night, driving him to despair, with tossing about, weakness in limbs and anxious sweat, so that he cannot endure the covers; in last hollow molar, < *getting bread into it; in hollow, transiently* > *cold water, also* > *expiration,* which causes a stitch as if something pressed upward into the tooth; unfitting him for work, especially for thinking; extending over temple to vertex. Sensation in last upper hollow molar as if it would ache. Elongated feeling in hollow, with pain on touch and running of much water from mouth. (Compare face-pains with Aconite.)

Gum.—Tearing jerking pain where l. upper wisdom tooth was drawn seven years ago, waking at 11 P.M., lasting till 2 o'clock, and again at 4 o'clock, extending to zygoma and temple. Sore pain, < chewing hard food; l. lower back, < when eating. Sensitive on chewing, and teeth.

Tongue.—Coated; on waking; white. Vesicles on surface and r. margin, with wartlike elevations on lower surface and sides of frænum. Boring sticking at root. Dry; in morning on waking; on waking, and rough; and rough and acid. Speech weak.

Painful cracks across r. arch of palate and on r. margin of tongue, next day those on tongue were surrounded by hard margins. Aphthæ in mouth. Sticking in r. arch of palate, impeding motion of tongue. Tension in soft palate. Dry mouth. Mouth cold, < inspiration of cold air. Bloody saliva. Salivation. Taste sour on tip of tongue; < touching incisors and when stomach is empty; bitter T.; pasty; flat; like melon-seeds; bad, to cigar.

Throat.—Swelling of thyroid gland; in r. upper trapezius, just under jaw, with salivation; of submaxillary glands; of submaxillary glands, with tension and throbbing, as if they would suppurate, with pain on touch and causing pain in teeth; of submaxillary glands, < in r. triangle of r. side of neck, painful, < motion of head. Sticking, < on swallowing. Burning; with redness, vesicles and ulcers. Rawness; with hoarseness and constant spitting of watery saliva. Dryness. Uvula sensitive. Uvula feels too long.

Clinical.—Violent toothache in back teeth, transiently > holding cold water in the mouth or drawing in cold air, greatly < at night on lying down, warmth of bed and tobacco; with the toothache there are often free salivation and soreness of gums, teeth feel too long (compare with Merc.).

Stomach.—Appetite increased; for dinner; towards evening; ravenous towards 2 P.M., then discomfort after eating; with hurried eating; then diminished; little for supper; lost; lost at breakfast; lost at noon; lost at noon on account of weakness. Does not relish the accustomed tobacco. Thirst; in afternoon; in evening; with longing for ice, which does not refresh him.

Eructations; empty; tasting like melon-seeds. Nausea; towards 11 A.M.; when smoking; after smoking, causing weakness of lower limbs, so that they seem to totter; with general sick feeling. Vomiting from smoking the accustomed cigars.

Distention, and of abdomen. Pain; after dinner; in epigastric region after dinner. Pressure on after dinner; P. in epigastric region, with tension over abdomen. Constriction, then also in abdomen, which was tense and hard, then difficult vomiting of a bitter fluid more watery than slimy, with streaks of pale blood. Oppression. Tensive sensation in epigastric region. Heaviness in pit. Satiety, relishes the dinner, but immediately feels that he has eaten too much. Faintness, with yawning. Coldness.

Abdomen.—Distention, with rumbling. Rumbling in afternoon; R., as if empty; extending into hernia. Flatulence. Emission of flatus. Sticking up into chest on urinating, < inspiration. Cutting. Cutting contractive pain. Griping. Drawing pain, < umbilical region, < pressure. Fulness in afternoon; F. and tension; F. and T. at 4 P.M., < till 9 P.M. Tension in muscles on attempting to walk in the room, < coughing; painful T. in parietes, < touch. Contractive cutting in r. abdominal and kidney region on walking.

Hypochondria.—Sticking; in l.; in liver and spleen; in spleen, < pressure, with tensive sensation in fundus of stomach; with tension, impeding respiration; periodical, in liver and spleen; intermittent, in hepatic region, < certain motions and positions. Pain in hepatic region, < pressure; alternately in region of liver and spleen on certain motions. Bruised pain in liver when touched, and on stooping (Acon.).

Hypogastrium.—**Swelling of inguinal glands,** < r., *when at rest after continued walking;* **swelling of I. glands,** *with sensitiveness on walking, the r. glands become more swollen, with prickling pain in them, < walking and in bed, afterwards with tension in them, < walking; S. in r. inguinal region, painful to touch.* Periodical sticking in inguinal region; intermittent burning S. in l. inguinal ring, with swelling of glands. Pain, then diarrhœa; P. extending into penis; *in r. inguinal glands;* in l. inguinal region. Jerking pain in inguinal glands. Pressing-out pain in r. ring, as if a hernia would protrude. Dragging towards r. inguinal canal, with protrusion of a hernia (which he had always had). *Sensitiveness of inguinal region* (Ran. b.). Prickling in r. inguinal glands. *Sensation in ring and inguinal glands as if a swelling would form.* Tension in l. inguinal glands; *in inguinal region when walking, with swelling of glands,* afterwards especially l. glands swollen; T. in l. inguinal region, extending into thighs, < on walking; T. in inguinal glands and rings, with pain.

Clinical.—Swelling of inguinal glands, which are sore on walking and are painful at night (Merc.).

Rectum and Anus.—Burning in rectum; and in genitals; during and after stool; sudden, then urging to stool. Urging to stool, which was pasty and accompanied by flatulence; U. after eating, stool profuse and thin, with burning in anus; ineffectual U. Hæmorrhoids swollen and covered with mucus. Itching of hæmorrhoids in evening, with discharge of mucus; I. of anus. Burning in anus during stool and swelling of hæmorrhoids; B. after stool, with itching.

Stool.—Diarrhœa; copious; frequent. Pasty; with burning in rectum; and increased. *Constipation;* then diarrhœa. Solid; after much urging; with exertion; and scanty. Knotty and scanty. Blood with the stool. Stool every three days. Twice daily. Omitted.

Urinary Organs.—Sticking in bladder. Frequent tense pain in prostate during the day. Urging to urinate; frequent, at night, then burning in orifice of urethra; frequent, with slight discharge, urine clear, reddish. *Inability to evacuate all the urine at once,* it frequently stops, the remainder trickles, during the stoppage there is jerklike tearing in forepart of urethra. *Micturition slow and in a thin stream* (Puls.); *as if urethra were constricted,* then burning in urethra and tickling, itching and sticking in orifice. Frequent micturition; at night; then prickling burning in orifice.

Urethra.—Mucous discharge. Sticking; in orifice; in navicular fossa. Twinging in evening on standing, > sitting and at night in bed; in evening. Painful to touch. *Constriction,* micturition only in drops (Canth.). *Burning on urinating; B., < beginning to urinate, with biting and with sticking on urinating* (Cannab.), and when not urinating irritation in forepart of penis; in navicular fossa (Petros.) in morning on urinating; anteriorly, then urging to urinate, with hot tickling in orifice, after micturition itching tickling, which after half an hour gave way to the former condition, to be renewed after micturition, thus alternating till 1 A.M. Burning pain in orifice on passing the last drops of urine. Coldness. Tickling; < navicular fossa. Itching in navicular fossa.

Urine.—Copious; and red; and turbid; then diminished. Scanty; and dark red; and thickish, of peculiar odor; saturated, offensive. Hot; and saturated, smelling of violets. Red; dark. Odor like Russia leather. Milky, with floating flocks of mucus and thick froth. Deposit of many crystals of urate of soda.

Clinical.—Inflammation of the neck of the bladder, great pain on beginning to urinate, feeling as if the urethra were contracted, has to strain to pass a few drops, dribbling after micturition. Stricture.

Sexual Organs.—Pressing. Formication. Burning sticking in frænum preputii after a warm bath, with soreness, and in orifice of urethra, with burning pain on urinating. Stitches at base of penis. Burning pain in penis on emission during coition. Burning, irritable sensation during emission. Erections frequent; strong E., with sticking in urethra; long-continued E., with aversion to coition. **Swelling of r. half of scrotum** (Puls.), *which is thickened and hangs down with r. testicle.* Scrotum drawn up. Scrotum feels as if contracted by cold. Prickling in scrotum, and itching.

Sensitiveness of r. spermatic cord, with drawing up of r. testicle. *Pain in r. spermatic cord.* Painful drawing in spermatic cord on urinating, extending into abdomen. Drawing pain in l. S. cord. *Tension in r. S. cord.*

Testicles.—**Swelling** (Rhod., Puls.). Hanging down, heavy, sensitive. **Sensitive**; in morning in bed, *and in spermatic cord; on walking, enlarged and hanging down,* < l. *Pinching, with pain on slightest touch* (Spo.). *Bruised pain on touch* (Rhod.), *with drawing and tension in inguinal region, l. thigh and scrotum, in which there is pinching when touched and on walking. Drawing-upward pain, and in spermatic cords* (Berb.). *Pain* in morning in bed, *and in spermatic cords.* Pressure in r., then in both. Intermittent burrowing in r., then in both. Heaviness in l. at 11 A.M.

Excitement; when talking with women. Desire, more of a mental nature, without erections or emissions. Dread of desire, even during an erection, as if satisfied to excess. Emissions at night and during midday nap.

Menses profuse; and early; early, lasting two days, on second day about noon griping below umbilicus, then pasty stool and emission of much flatus, after two days return of menses.

Clinical.—Inflammation of testicles, pain greatly < at night by warmth of bed; with the swollen testicles there are numerous symptoms of distress in urinating; see above. Orchitis from suppressed gonorrhœa. Corrosive leucorrhœa and shooting pains in the breasts, < when urinating. Indurations and tumors in mammary glands (scirrhus?), very painful to touch.

Respiratory Organs.—Tickling in larynx and irritation to cough. Dryness of trachea, < smoking, motion and in open air, with burning. Cough during the accustomed tobacco-smoking; violent C., with respiration sometimes rapid, sometimes slow; dry; rough, barking, leaving burning along inner surface of sternum and sticking in lungs; irritation to C.; irritable C., with scanty expectoration; with mucous expectoration. Expectoration frequent; mucous E. Inclination to sigh. Expiration weak. Breath almost arrested at 1 P.M. on slowly ascending a little hill, with heat in chest and sensation as if he would spit blood, which afterwards was only a white frothy saliva, the same next day after walking over an uneven road.

Chest.—Hardened gland below nipple, painful on touch. Sticking shocks in l. chest and l. side of abdomen, so that he must cry out. Sticking in lungs; in r. chest during inspiration and expiration; < respiration; < inspiration; in r., < inspiration; in l. intercostal muscles, with cramplike sensation; sudden, in l., beneath ribs, so that he must hold his breath, bend to l. and press against the place. Sticking, jerking, contractive pinching in l. intercostal muscles at 7 P.M. Tearing externally above heart. Drawing, tearing, prickling over l.

Pain in r. intercostal muscles; P. in chest not affected by breathing; in upper part of l. half on inspiration; in l. upper part, < inspiration, extending on deep breathing through whole l. side of chest to the scapula, preventing full inspiration and causing involuntary crying, the pain < violent motion upward or backward of l. arm, pressing l. scapula against anything, bending body to l. and walking in open air, > sitting quietly and breathing superficially. Tensive pain across, < at 10 P.M. to a cramplike pain. Constriction of C., with pains in lungs, making him uneasy. Oppression; in evening; with deep respiration; in præcordial region. Heaviness. Sensitiveness of breasts; with sticking at times and on touch sensation as if they would suppurate, and sensation as if fuller and heavier. (Compare intercostal pains with Ranunculus).

Heart.—Sticking outward in præcordial region. Intermittent oppression now at base, now at apex, till 2 A.M., when he fell asleep exhausted. Palpitation preventing lying on l. side. Pulse rapid; and strong and full; and full and irregular; and small and soft.

Neck.—Tearing in nape, with drawing. Drawing in side, with pain on touch and turning head or bending body backward, and below knee. Tension in glands and muscles. Sensitiveness of glands. Pain in glands (previously indurated).

Back.—Bruised feeling, and in arms and thighs. Sticking behind and beneath tip of r. scapula, impeding respiration. Pain in l. scapula, < raising arm; between scapulæ and in lower part of chest.

Lumbar Region.—Sticking in r. when not breathing. Sticking constriction alternating with burning, itching drawing pain, and in shoulders and upper arms, more in bellies of muscles. Pain in l. kidney. Pressure, < stooping, with tension, and in kidneys; frequent P., extending higher. Drawing pain in vertebræ, extending around lower part of chest. Bruised pain, and in kidneys; above kidneys, extending to gluteals and thighs, < motion and touch, especially stooping. Heaviness, with painful swelling of hæmorrhoids. Painful weariness.

Extremities.—Stretching even on rising. Sticking in palms and soles. Tearing in l. arm and l. ankle; in bones of leg and in l. elbow. Boring in joints, with pain and weakness. Pain in joints of hands and feet; in joints, making motion difficult; rheumatic, in knees, ankles, elbows and wrists. Sensation in ankles, toes, knees, shoulders, elbows and upper arms as if twisted or drawn asunder. Drawing and tension; in joints. Drawing in joints of hands and knees; in wrist and tarsal joints; tearing, in r. arm and knee, both ankles and r. toes. Sensitiveness of ankles and wrists. Weakness; < morning, > motion in open air, with bruised sensation. Heaviness; during the day; in morning on waking; on walking and ascending stairs.

Upper Extremities.—Pain in r. axilla. Drawing pain from shoulder to elbow. Weariness in muscles of shoulders and upper arms, afterwards involving pectoral muscles. Bruised pain in arms; after eating. Heaviness of r. arm, with pressure through it. Twitching of r. upper arm. Tearing in l. upper arm in evening. Burrowing in l. upper arm, < shoulder, hindering motion. Oppressive pain in upper arm.

Tensive sticking in elbows and wrists. Pain in bend of elbow on stretching out upper arm. Bruised pain on outer side of l. elbow, < pressure and motion. Pressure and boring in r. elbow and above and below it. Sudden sticking below l. elbow. Drawing stitches in l. forearm. Tearing in l. forearm. Pressure in r. forearm. Drawing pain on r. side of forearm, extending from elbow downward, with impeded motion. Drawing sticking in wrist on walking in open air. Rheumatic pains in metacarpal bones and fingers. Hands feel too thick, dry and hot. Sticking in joints of r. thumb. Tearing in r. finger-joints, < sudden or rapid motion. Drawing tearing in r. thumb.

Lower Extremities.—Drawing downward towards soles. Heaviness even in bed; H. in evening after waking, with weakness in them. Tearing in r. thigh when sitting and lying; in hip-joint, with sticking; intermittent T. in l. hip-joint and in bones of small of back. Pain in hip; on anterior surface of thigh. Burning tensive pain posteriorly in thigh. Sticking drawing in r. hip and hip-joint, extending into r. inguinal region. Drawing and tension in r. thigh, sometimes extending in painful jerks deep into penis. All muscles in gluteal region affected. Weariness of thighs and knees.

Knee.—Tearing; in r., with sticking, and in ankle;

in r. patella, waking, seating itself after rising in r. leg, < tibia. Drawing like a tearing after walking, and in thigh. Pain in r. on walking; P., with heaviness as if asleep, preventing walking, ending with circumscribed sweat; rheumatic, in l. outer and in hollow, with difficult walking. Weak and knocking together after walking. Stiffness of r.

Leg.—Dark red soft swellings near inner margin of r. tibia, the uppermost showing fluctuation at the centre. Decrease of size. Periodical cramp, compelling rubbing. Sticking in l. calf when sitting. Drawing tearing, now in r., now in l., extending along tibia to ankle. Boring in l. tibia in morning after rising and frequently through the day. Burrowing in tibia. Pain in l.; in tibia during the day; in r. tibia, < walking. Bruised sensation; in calves; in calves after eating. Drawing in bones. Weariness, and in back on slight motion of arms. Heaviness and weariness; with swellings on legs and on calves, prominent and closely anastomosing cutaneous veins, with varicosities between them. Heaviness, with pain and tottering gait.

Tensive sticking in region of r. malleolus. Sticking tearing on inner side of r. ankle. Boring in malleoli; B. in l. ankle. Pressure in ankles and ankle-bones. Pulselike sticking in sole in evening after going to sleep and at 3 A.M. Pain in r. heel; in afternoon. Bruised pain in ball of r. heel; in feet and legs, as after fatigue. Drawing and tension on walking, in foot (on which there is an ulcer). Weakness of feet; on walking. Crawling in forepart of r. sole as from being asleep. Burrowing in ball of r. great toe. Sore pain towards inner side of l. great toe, < rest. Pressure in l. toes.

Skin.—Redness, vesicles and ulcers. Pimples on forehead; painful; painful, < forehead, with sticking and pain on touch; itching, above r. eyebrow; red, on l. thigh, surrounded by red areola, some of the glands of l. thigh suppurate and discharge thin pus. Pustules painful to touch above eyebrows, at root of nose, on chin and tip of nose; about loins. Suppuration of cutaneous glands in face and limbs. Boil on thigh. Vesicles removed by shaving, again filling with clear serum; itching V. on nape; itching V. on thighs, with warmth.

Sticking on washing; lightning-like S. here and there. Pulselike stinging thrusts in a wound in evening after going to sleep and at 3 A.M. Prickling in many parts, with itching; P. beneath skin (like formication), with dryness, then towards noon moisture and softness. Burning cutting in l. side of forehead, < when skin is drawn smooth. Throbbing pain in an ulcer in morning. Crawling and throbbing in ulcers, with stinging in their margins on touch. Burning pain in l. cheek. Sensitiveness of nerves to cool temperature and rubbing with clothes.

Burning-itching pain in r. cheek and on wing of nose, waking him, a circumscribed redness, with elevations, towards evening vesicles on lower lip, corners of mouth and wings of nose, with burning. Itching over whole body; in various parts, < those covered with hair; on back, chest and outer part of lower limbs; on toes in evening after lying down, with sweat between toes; > full bath; on forearms and upper abdomen, after scratching burning, then red nettle-rash; then pimples thickest about umbilicus, where there were several vesicles filled with lymph, the itching pain changing to burning, with fine scurf and itching.

Clinical.—Eczema on various parts, said to be worse during the increasing moon, with corrosive secretion, itching always < warmth of bed at night. The eczema is prone to appear on the occiput, sometimes moist (during the increasing moon), sometimes dry (during the waning moon). Eczematous eruption following suppressed gonorrhœa. Chronic eczema of hands.

Sleep.—Yawning; when sitting, with sleepiness; > open air, with sleepiness. Sleepiness; in morning on waking; at noon, with weariness; every afternoon; in evening, but late and difficult falling asleep; after dinner; after dinner, without ability to sleep; after eating. Irresistible sleepiness from 2 to 5 P.M.; after eating; after supper. Sleep after eating more than usual at noon. Must go to bed early, but fell asleep only after long tossing about, with internal heat and headache, then confused dreams till 3 A.M., when he awoke with a sudden start and could not sleep again. Difficult waking in morning from a semi-slumber. Unrefreshed in morning on waking, with sweat, sleepiness and intolerance of being uncovered on account of coldness.

Sleeplessness; in evening; all night, with closed eyes, fatigue and internal dry heat; with sleepiness and tossing from side to side till midnight. Waking early; at 3 A.M., having slept enough, though he went to bed at 12 o'clock. Waking twice at night; frequent W. by confused dreams; with difficult motion and dry heat. Uneasy sleep; full of dreams; with groaning; disturbed by desire to urinate and by dryness and pain in mouth; with heavy dreams, frequent waking and starting from sleep; with constant waking from anxious dreams and sensation as if bed and ground were moving; jerking of body now to r., now to l. by electric shocks. Frequent starting from sleep, then anxiety and sweat, < on forehead. Tossing about from midnight till 2 A.M., towards morning light sleep, with confused, anxious dreams.

Dreams.—Vivid. Uneasy. Heavy, confused, then confusion of head in morning on waking. Lewd; with erections. Anxious. Of misfortune. Of danger, from fire, for instance. That he was arrested and wrongfully accused of a crime. Frightful; with tossing about so that unconsciously his head exchanged places with his feet, with frequent waking and dry heat.

Fever.—Cold in evening. Cool cheeks. Shivering after slight uncovering; S., with creepings of heat and coldness; < back; across shoulders after 6 P.M. on walking in open air, then heat; across shoulders and back at 7.30 P.M.

Heat in morning; every day, beginning between 3 and 4 P.M., with headache, thirst, rapid pulse, scanty and dark urine, uneasy night, > copious sweat at night and emission of urine loaded with chlorides; towards evening; in evening, with anxiety in chest; on urinating; of whole body after a glass of liquor, with confusion of head; of whole body, with fulness and heat of face; of whole body, then general coldness while the head remained hot. In flushes; with red cheeks. Orgasm of blood, towards evening, with sexual excitement. In various parts, or burning pain. Of skin. Of forehead. Of head and chest after eating and after midday nap; in head and chest, with sighing; creeping H. of external head, with pressure upon it; sudden H. streaming outward through head, face.

and ears, which last were burning hot. Of nose, with fluid discharge. Of cheeks, with redness. In face; with circumscribed redness of cheeks, external heat in small of back, extending from centre to periphery, as from a warm moist bandage. In back, extending upward on l. side, across lowest ribs to scapula; in small of back, involving whole r. side of back and r. shoulder; over back and chest in flushes; on back and chest, < region of sternum, with itching. Of hands and feet at 3 A.M.; in soles. (Compare febrile symptoms with Aconite.)

Sweat during sleep; at night; on slightest motion. Sudden, on affected parts at 2.30 P.M., giving general relief. On head; giving relief, and at the same time on small of back but without relief. Sour-smelling. Of a peculiar odor towards morning. Transpiration suppressed.

Cobaltum.

The pure precipitated metal is triturated for use.

Generalities.—Lying in sleep on l. side, with head on arm (usually sleeps on r. side). Aching when sitting; A. in bones. General soreness in morning, with bruised pain and indisposition to move. Restlessness, with late falling asleep, then lewd dreams, and waking at 4 A.M., with emission. Weakness; in evening, with aching in knees; with disposition to lie down, and flushes of heat along legs. Suffering < by all mental excitement. General relief after discharging mucus from throat. Remarkable feeling of being unusually well.

Mind.—Condemned, mean feeling, as if guilty of some deed of which others knew, as if he could not look one in the face. Low spirits, thinking too little of himself. Exhilaration. Vivacity; with rapid flow of thought. Desire for study. Indisposition for mental or physical labor. Dulness, with weakness, aversion to mental exercise and necessity to lie down.

Head.—Aching on waking and during the day; < in a room; two mornings till 10 o'clock and again in afternoon; in morning when rising; in morning, with beating and sore aching all over; all forenoon; at noon, especially in occiput; at noon, with nausea and languor; in afternoon; on walking; increasing from 1 to 8 P.M., mostly in forehead; caused by unrefreshing sleep from dreams; < bending forward, especially in occiput; > open air; especially in forehead, with sensation of undigested food in stomach. Dulness in forenoon, < motion, with pain in temples; D., especially in forehead and temples, in morning, with fulness and bruised pain. Feeling as if it grew large during stool, with dizziness and weakness, headache continues after the stool. Sensation when stepping as if brain went up and down.

Pain in forehead; after rising; < stooping; in F. and in back part of eyes; in F., with fulness in stomach as if filled with air. Tearing in r. temple, near orbit, in forenoon. Pain in temples; in l. during the morning, with languor, nausea and sensation as if diarrhœa would set in, but it did not.

Pain in vertex when rising from a seat, with prickling pain in stomach. Top of head feels as if it would come off at every jar. Pain in occiput; in morning; from morning till 3 P.M., < open air; beginning at noon. Sore pimples in edge of hair on occiput. Itching of scalp at night; of scalp and in beard under chin, with burning when scratched.

Eyes.—Dartings at 2.30 P.M. on entering bright sunlight; when writing, with a feeling when opening lids as if strings were holding them together and were snapping; on going into out-door light. Pain when coming into the light; when writing. Smarting in light; when writing, with almost loss of vision; in l. corner of l. eye as from hot water, with pain in vertex. Burning, especially in upper lids. Lachrymation in cold air, with pain in eyes; L. in open air, with water from nose. Pain in upper lid as soon as he looks at anything steadily, with smarting. Smarting in lids; in evening; as soon as he begins to use them; on inner side of upper. Muscæ volitantes, with dim vision, and while reading blurring of letters.

Ears, Nose and Lips.—Aching in l. ear; in evening; beating in l. in evening; in l. (like a slight humming). Humming in l. ear. Stitches in l. angle of nose, with burning on scratching. Feeling as of a cold in head, headache, with thin nasal discharge and sneezing. Nose feels obstructed with mucus. N. feels dry and filled with dry scales, with itching, especially of l. nostril. Itching in l. nostril in evening. Sensitiveness at end of nasal cartilage on pressure. Putrid, sickish smell before nose. Peeling of lips, with soreness and easy bleeding.

Mouth.—*Pain in a hollow tooth, with feeling as if too long;* P. in first l. lower molar (hollow), < inhaling cold air, with swelling of gums, tenderness around it and feeling as if it would ulcerate; paroxysmal, in a hollow T. *Tongue coated white;* with cracks across middle; white mucus, with flat mucous taste; white. Sore on l. side of mouth, opposite stomach tooth. Pricking in roof; extending through to l. ear. Salivation; with frequent swallowing. Taste flat; with rising of sour water, which had an acrid feeling in throat; nauseous, in morning; and mucous. Bad T. in morning, with belching of wind. Sweet T., of mucus, with expectoration of thick, white, frothy mucus, with lumps in it.

Throat.—Drawing pain in l. submaxillary gland. Filled with white mucus; with mucus in morning. Soreness in morning when hawking; when hawking, as if raw. Sensation of something sticking in it, causing him to hawk. Rising of heat, as if from stomach. Dryness in morning on rising; with soreness on swallowing, feeling as if something dry had collected in it; with soreness and rawness. Discomfort, with pain on empty swallowing and gaping. Hawking of mucus in morning in lumps; afterwards thinner; H. and spitting of thick white mucus.

Stomach.—Appetite lost; *for supper;* diminished. Eructations of wind; of sour water; of sour bitter water; of bitter water an hour after dinner; of bitter water, with pain in stomach, then dryness of throat; of hot bitter water in afternoon. Hiccough after dinner; till 6 P.M., renewed after supper; with shooting in forehead till midnight. Nausea, with pain in forehead. Sourness, < at 11 P.M., with bursting headache, and after supper necessity to lie down, at midnight watery diarrhœa with tenesmus, then till sleep sour taste and nausea.

Pain; in morning after rising, with headache; after eating; after dinner; after dinner, with pain in abdomen, < pressure, and with uneasiness; in S. and in abdomen, with sensation as before diarrhœa; as from wind; as from hunger, before dinner, partially > by eating. Soreness in region in morning on inspiring deeply; in pit caused by constant hiccough. Sense of fulness and hardness, as if filled with wind.

Abdomen.—Rumbling; with feeling as if diarrhœa would come on. Cutting before stool. Pain at 4 A.M., > after a watery stool, having had no stool for two days; on waking at 5 A.M., then watery stool, with tenesmus; in evening and at night; during stool; as from fulness, after a light dinner. Strange but not unpleasant sensation, as after diarrhœa. Stitching from liver region to thigh at 3 P.M. Pain in l. hypochondrium, with sour eructations. Sharp pain in region of spleen, < deep inspiration. Feeling in l. side above spleen as if it would drop down, < walking, > sitting still. Pain in umbilical region an hour after eating, < contracting walls of abdomen. Feeling of emptiness at umbilicus. Pain in hypogastrium; in evening; in l. groin and in small of back.

Rectum and Anus.—Burning in R. during stool and long afterwards. Pressing in R.; towards anus, < till stool. Urging to stool while walking, < standing still, with cutting, stool profuse, watery, spouting, in an hour another stool. Stinging during and after stool.

Stool.—*Large, thin,* with tenesmus and pain in lower part of abdomen as if the bowels would protrude, with pain in sphincter ani continuing after stool and tenesmus. Diarrhœa, with tenesmus and colic. Soft, with stinging during and afterwards. Small and hard; at 9 A.M., small, soft and painless at 9 P.M.; having had none for two days; with scratching in rectum; and lumpy. Small, with tenesmus. Scanty. Twice a day.

Urinary Organs.—Frequent micturition and in small quantities; with flocculent sediment and *pungent smell;* with necessity to urinate at night, urine yellow. Pain in urethra, with emissions; P. in urethra while standing, with bruised feeling in back and loins towards latter part of day. Burning in urethra during micturition. Smarting in end of urethra during micturition. Frequent desire to urinate; after drinking coffee, < forenoon, with copious pale urine. Urine scanty; and light-colored; and more saturated. Greasy pellicle on urine; with yellow flocculent sediment. Deep red urine, with a flocculent red sediment. Sediment of yellow-red flocks.

Sexual Organs.—Pain in r. testicle, > after micturition at 10 A.M. *Emissions without erections;* emission during evening nap, lying on his back, with a vivid dream; E. at night, with headache; in sleep, with partial erections. Impotence. Desire in morning.

Respiratory Organs and Chest.—Stitching in front of larynx in forenoon, next day at 9.30 A.M., with general warm sensation, flushes of heat and sweat. Cough, with soreness of throat and rawness when hawking; hacking C., with expectoration of blood, which according to the sensation comes from the larynx.

Expectoration of mucus in morning, < open air; of white mucus in morning, with bubbles of air in it, < in open air; of frothy white mucus about 9 A.M., with lumps in it; of thick, tough mucus mixed with blood in morning, with scratching as if something had lodged in throat, inducing swallowing; of thick, tough mucus mixed with blood, in morning, with fulness and pain in larynx, < pressure, empty deglutition and cold water, with scratching, rawness, occasional burning pains and disposition to keep jaws tightly closed.

Sighing. Deep stitches in lower part of chest on inspiring deeply, mostly on l. side.

Back.—*Pain while sitting, > walking or lying;* on sitting down after rising; < all the morning; < *sitting;* with seminal emissions; as if he could not straighten himself; on either side of dorsal spine similar to that felt in chest when it is said "the food has lodged;" between scapulæ and in lumbar region. Pain in small of B.; at 6 P.M., with headache; in evening; after dinner, with pain in and below knees; *always while sitting;* while sitting, < rising, walking or lying; partially > lying, not by standing.

Clinical.—Backache in lumbar region following seminal emissions, with weakness in legs, etc.

Extremities.—Trembling; especially legs. Jerks when falling asleep. Stitches here and there in arms, legs, etc. Bruised pain in morning, especially in joints; B. pain in all, in afternoon. Weakness; from walking. Aching in wrists, with occasional stitches. Bruised pain in l. hip, in region of trochanter, in morning, < motion, > rest. Aching anteriorly in middle of thighs (in muscles); in knees and lower limbs; in knees, with itching on external side. Weakness of knees; after exercise. Tired feeling in legs.

Skin.—Yellow-brown spots on abdomen, about genitals. Pimples on back of l. ear, near top; painless, on nose; on shoulders, pit of stomach and buttocks, bleeding easily when scratched. Vesicles on r. side of neck, containing watery lymph, sore to touch, with inflamed base, leaving tenderness. Itching on l. side of nose; on shoulders; general I. when getting warm in bed.

Sleep.—Yawning; after dinner, with languor. *Distressing drowsiness in evening.* Can do with less sleep. Difficult falling asleep; *disturbed by lewd dreams* and frequent copious emissions, with partial erections. Frequent waking with fright. Waking with a wide-awake feeling; at 6.30 A.M., earlier than usual. *Sleep unrefreshing.* Falls into a light sleep about 1 A.M., with tossing about. Sleep disturbed; by dreams. Dreams of having the *back part* of the hair cut. Lewd dreams, with pollutions, waking at 6 A.M., with pain in end of urethra.

Fever.—Chilliness from 11 to 12 A.M.; general C., with yawning. General warm sensation, with flushes of heat and sweat; fever from 12 to 2 P.M., with sweat. Sour sweat of feet, with an odor like sole leather, like what he had years before, reappears and is most between toes.

Coca.

A tincture is prepared from the dried leaves of Erythroxylon Coca, Lam.

General Action.—In moderate doses it acts as a general stimulant, like its allies tea and coffee, but its remote effects are disastrous. Its alkaloid applied to mucous membranes produces complete anæsthesia.

Generalities.—Emaciation. General consumption. Weight increased one-eighth of a pound. Waste of tissues prevented. Œdematous swelling, then ascites. Jaundice, with headache, weakness, can take little food, emaciation, then leuchæmia, a leaden hue and sleeplessness. Becoming old early and imbecility in old age. Tottering gait, with trembling of lips, disconnected speech and apathy.

Hurried and impatient movements. Agility in walking. Involuntary rapid walking with head bent forward, vertigo and dread of falling (> bouillon). *Great lightness when climbing a mountain, without respiratory troubles* (Kali chlor.). *Great vigor and endurance in spite of slight nourishment and light sleep.* Bouyancy on walking in a chilling fog. Freedom of chest and whole body, with vigor and desire to walk rapidly and a long distance, though it is warm and sunny. Nervous excitement, as from a mixture of coffee and brandy; unpleasant E. Aptitude for work increases. Power of muscles increased. Peculiar comfort, with pleasant warmth starting from stomach.

Restlessness. Endeavors to get into the open air. Tossing about in bed, the child often puts the arms under the head, indistinct speech. Turning about in bed incessantly, sometimes afraid of losing my balance and fancy myself carried off into space, I walk the room with great strides and feel as if I could run a long time, feel buoyant and flexible all over, then heaviness of head, drowsiness and desire for rest and quiet, with disinclination, not inability to move.

Discomfort. Weakness; in morning, > during a walk after breakfast; in afternoon; in evening; after a moderate walk. No desire for work; nor skill at it. Torpor. Numbness; with feeling of serenity and desire to make no motions, then sleep with strange, quickly changing dreams, which could last all day, without lassitude or restlessness. Aggravation by rest. Amelioration in open air; riding on horseback, walking or manual labor.

Clinical.—Mountain sickness; useful in a variety of complaints arising from climbing mountains, weak heart, dyspnœa, fainting fits, etc. Useful for old people who get out of breath easily. Angina pectoris from climbing (Kali. chlor.). Nervous erethism, with restlessness, especially after abuse of tobacco.

Mind.—Madness. Hallucinations. Fancies now beautiful, joyful, now frightful. Imagination excited, with increased desire for bodily exercise, trembling of hands and legs, shivering in back and inability to keep still. Excitement; pleasant, then sleeplessness. Elated. Animated and contented. Lively and inclined for mental work. Felt something like expectation. Apathy. Passion for solitude. Sensation of isolation from the world, with inclination to feats of strength, so that he sprang upon the table without overthrowing the things there. Changeable mood, mostly morose, irresolute, false, suspicious, malicious. Wayward. Irritable. Sad; in evening, and weary. Apprehension; with palpitation. Faculties blunted. Slow in finding words to express himself. Averse to concentration of thought. Lazy at 9 P.M. and sleepy. Desire for work from 7 to 10 A.M., then frontal headache.

Head.—Aching; at 10 A.M., > walking in open air, returning on going in-doors; at 1 P.M., in-doors; in afternoon, > evening; (in-doors in afternoon, then after beginning to walk in open air pain in upper part of forehead from heat of weather); after rising; < 7 P.M., < over r. eye, with burning of eyes; > dinner; > eating, then returning, > at sunset; with shivering; (as if catarrhal) in afternoon, with cold feet and urging to stool. Symptoms as after exhaustion. Pillows felt hard to head and neck, though sleepy, turning all night and dreams of great activity, awoke tired and heavy next day, with aching shoulders. Heaviness. Dulness; dull feeling in brain; as after intoxication. Fulness at 4 P.M., as from wine. Confusion; in morning, > washing and drinking coffee; at 5 or 6 P.M. in the house, with vertigo in forehead, sleepiness, want of appetite and low spirits. Intoxication; like that of Cannabis. Vertigo; at 7 P.M., after dinner, with dulness in forehead; on moving in open air; when walking, with sensation as if the body were drawn to r.; on rapidly ascending steep steps, then diarrhœa; when sitting still and afterwards when rising from a seat; > rest and wine.

Forehead.—Boring over r. eye. Aching; in morning; 9 A.M., > walking a mile, returning on entering house, with heaviness of eyelids; in afternoon in the house, sometimes in r. half, sometimes in l., sometimes in the whole forehead; (in afternoon on walking in hot open air, < at every step); > at sunset, then exhilaration; in sinciput; < over r. eye; just above eyes; just above eyes, < elevating head and turning up eyes. Beating over eyes. Pressing asunder deep in l. side on coughing or on pressing at stool. Sensation as if a band were stretched from one temple to the other. Fulness; although sitting near an open window, < towards 9 P.M., with pain; with swimming of letters on reading and heaviness of eyes.

Temples.—Shooting in r.; in a straight line to vertex, sharp on rising and all day on looking up, leaving a sore feeling, pain through this place on coughing. Pain in r. as if a nail were driven into it. Pain over l.; in l.; headache in afternoon when walking in rain, now in r. temple, now in forehead, > standing still; (at 12.50 P.M. on quick walking in hot sun, > standing still, after entering the house pain in crown, then on shaking head from side to side, pain in r. temple, then when lying down in anterior part of crown and other parts); sudden in l., the same at 10.45 A.M. and 9.30 P.M.

Sides.—Constriction. Sudden pain over anterior part of r. at 9.50 P.M. on blowing nose.

Occiput.—Pain; (at 6.10 P.M. at every step on running, from hot weather, then when walking); headache in fresh air changed to occiput, *as if it were held from ear to ear in a vise;* in lowest part on yawning. Drawings extending to temples, on attempting to read after midday nap. Vertigo at 7.30 P.M. when head was bent forward in writing, extending forward on l. side.

Clinical.—Peculiar shocks, which come from the occiput, with vertigo, so that he staggers about the street. Nervous sick headaches.

Eyes.—Brilliant. Dull; and hollow, surrounded by violet-brown rings. Staring, fixed upon the ground, with automatic motions of hands and groaning. Discharge of mucus. Pain. Lachrymation of r. in morning, with redness of conjunctiva and lids at inner canthus. Pupils dilated. Widens pupils and lessens sensitiveness to light. Lids heavy; upper lids disposed to fall without sleepiness. Vision disturbed. *Photophobia; with dilated pupils.* Blackness on ascending stairs. Flickering. Letters swim. Flickering black points at 4 P.M. when reading. White spots on reading so that the book seemed mottled white; white spots on going out after eating, with glittering, tortuous lines and with great weakness. Vision of colors and floating of sparks from before downward. Fiery points flit before eyes; downward. Flames similar to distant heat-lightning; in evening. It seems as if he were writing with two pens.

Ears.—Excess of wax in r. Aching in r. middle at 1 P.M. in-doors; at 7.20 P.M.; in church; and in r. mastoid process. Sensation as if something in them caused deafness, but everything is heard as usual. During loud reading in the room sensation as if the tympana were pressed outward by the tones or as if the tones first entered the ears through a thicker medium. Pulsation in forenoon, and dull roaring; audible P. Hearing painfully acute in evening. Singing in l. Cracking on empty swallowing. Ringing; distant, repeated in evening; of a middle-toned bell; does not hear a knocking at the door, and when one speaks it seems as if the voice came from a great distance. Roaring.

Clinical.—Chronic deafness, with noises in the head.

Nose.—Sensation at midnight on going to bed as if swollen and stuffed, as in incipient catarrh. Heat internally in nostrils in evening in-doors, as from catching cold. Heat and irritation, as from catarrh in r. nostril in morning in bed; before and after rising, < l. nostril. Irritation, as from taking cold in evening, awakened at 9 P.M. by running from nose. Sneezing; after rising and in evening; in-doors. Mucus increased; in morning; in-doors in morning, with heat in nose. Flow of clear water and occasional sneezing, without real coryza; F. of clear water from 6 A.M. till 5 P.M., when in a draught, with occasional sneezing and sore feeling in l. nostril; of clear water, with specks of blood on blowing nose.

Face.—Pallor. Burning redness of l. cheek, then of r., with white spots in centre of latter. Yellow tinge about corners of mouth. A kind of chlorosis, the bilious color first noticed gives way to a leaden hue. Animated expression. Pain in r. malar-bone. Soreness of l. lower jaw, just above submaxillary gland, < talking and chewing solid food on that side. Black spots in corners of mouth. Lips pale; and gums, with green, blunted teeth. Swelling inside r. lower lip, then one inside l. cheek, nearly opposite first upper molar, painful on eating, then flattened on two sides with a thin border, red, with whitish tip. Burning on l. upper lip where the moustache grows, at 10.45 A.M.

Mouth.—Teeth stained bright yellow; greenish and stumpy. Pain in a hollow tooth. Tongue coated. Appearance towards r. side of tip of tongue of a vesicle that had broken, with a red circle around it, the place feels sore, as scalded by tea, when eating, touching it, and at other times, then sore as from a sore place. Offensive blackish froth around corners of mouth. Swollen sensation in arches of palate, impeding swallowing, at times with tickling, causing cough. *Dryness; on waking;* and of lips, > breakfast. Burning; night and morning, and of palate; and in throat, with thirst; with fulness, and in stomach. Coolness in mucous membrane of M. and throat, verging on numbness. Salivation; bitterish, then aromatic. Disgusting breath.

Taste bad; in morning, and not the usual appetite; > drinking cold water. Slimy. Bitter in morning; on waking, then unusual flow of water from nose. Salt at tip of tongue. Salt, anteriorly on r. side of tongue in morning; at 9 P.M.; > supper; > gingerbread. Herring-like to butter. Burnt to water.

Throat.—*Hawking up transparent lumps of mucus, < morning.* Uvula long and red. Uvula swollen and swallowing difficult; in morning on waking. Pain. Scraping, with swollen uvula, causing hawking and expectoration of mucus. Soreness from cough; at back on rising; in morning at back, with obstruction, not > hawking and coughing, with hoarseness; on r. side of uvula on swallowing, with a swollen sensation. Swollen sensation in morning on swallowing. Feeling as if mucus were at back of pharynx, not < by coughing or hawking. Irritation to cough. Tickling at l. side of pharynx at 8.45 A.M., on talking; in pharynx on talking, or soreness; at back of pharynx, towards l. side, on talking; at back on rising. Dryness; and heat.

Stomach.—Appetite increased; sudden voracious, especially for animal food; great, dinner was eaten at 11 A.M. with appetite, but less was eaten than on the preceding day when he had no special hunger; longing for food though the epigastric region was distended. Morbid hunger, even to swallowing human excrements. Irregular appetite, the aversion to all food is often suddenly followed by insatiable craving, especially animal food. *Little need of nourishment, even during heavy work, with remarkable vigor. Great satiety for a long time.* Little appetite, especially for meat. No appetite; with weak digestion, nervous irritation and headache; for dinner, in spite of which much is eaten with relish. Aversion to food. Thirst; at 8 P.M.; for brandy.

Eructations; after his usual coffee; after dinner; with heaviness in stomach and constant desire to eructate; empty, every quarter of an hour; loud; slimy; of the dinner. Hiccough after sandwiches at noon; after a tepid shower-bath taken after supper, > lying down in bed. Nausea; after breakfast; sick feeling before supper, > by it; with disorders of stomach which may be compared to seasickness. Violent vomiting of slimy water at 6 P.M.

Distention returning after dinner and lasting till evening, with gulping and constant desire to eructate. Pricking about cardiac end at 7 P.M. when sitting in-doors. Gnawing, hungry sensation at pit. Pain about cardiac end on walking, would have amounted to a cutting, > standing at 4 P.M., returning during a walk. Painful contracted sensation, with pain in l. side like a splenetic stitch. Dyspepsia. Increase of digestive powers. *Emptiness;* in morning before rising; 8.30 A.M., renewed by breakfast; after rising, > before breakfast; after rising, > breakfast, for which he had not much appetite; after breakfast; after a long walk. Fulness; and heaviness; in epigastric and mesogastric regions. Uneasiness of digestive organs. Comfort in epigastrium, somewhat as from a glass of wine, radiating over whole body, an agreeable heat.

Abdomen.—Distention; in evening; tense, tympanitic. Rumbling; with emission of flatus. Gurgling, with emptiness. Constant urging of flatus without emission. Emission of flatus, with urging to stool; E. of flatus, with the smell of burnt gunpowder at 8 A.M. Pain renewed after a cup of chocolate; P. < coffee, > 5 P.M, after cold beer; > emission of flatus, with rumbling. Emptiness. Pain in region of liver, with gall-stones. Cutting-drawing digging in small intestines in morning, < 9 A.M., lasting till 11 o'clock, > rapid walking and eating something, but returning, excessive in jejum and ilium, > pressure in gastric region. Gurgling in ilium, extending to ascending and descending colon.

Clinical.—Violent palpitation caused by incarcerated flatus, which rises with violence and great noise, as if it would split the œsophagus (Thea.).

Rectum.—Urging to stool; all day, with sulphuretted hydrogen flatus; waking at night, stool copious, solid; then diarrhœa; then evacuation of scanty, clear, watery mucus, with small brownish flocks swimming in it; then hard scanty stool, with sensation as if sphincter were paralyzed; ineffectual, waking at midnight. No desire for stool at usual time in morning, no stool all day, but awakened at 11 P.M. by urging, then abundant firm stool.

Stool.—Thin; then continued urging; and copious, having more smell; with urging, more smell than usual and soreness in anus during its passage; and difficult, smelling more, with sensation of looseness in bowels as before diarrhœa and with griping; copious diarrhœa, with frequent copious micturition, urinating three times at night. A teaspoonful of mushy diarrhœa. Constipation. Hard, delayed, knotty. Last part like walnuts. Irregular, dryer than usual, partly in lumps and inodorous. Dark. Gradually lost their stercoral odor but had the odor of Coca. With urging. Scanty; and dark and in small pieces; and dark, and after dinner another scanty one; and difficult, at first in small pieces, with straining in r. spermatic cord or testis. Frequent. Delayed; and difficult, though soft enough and well formed, rectum seemed dry during evacuation.

Clinical.—Chronic atonic constipation, with dyspnœa, palpitation, eructations of gas, which are offensive.

Urinary Organs.—Sticking in female urethra before urinating. Frequent desire, with increased urine. Micturition at night, < after midnight, towards morning or early in morning. Urine scanty; and dark brown. Urine dark. Thin. Acid, smelling like sweat. Film on its surface, iridescent in certain lights, with fissures mapping it out, and a pale flocculent sediment floating at the bottom. Turbid when passed, with dusky red, adherent sediment, and after standing an oily-looking film on surface. Yellowish-red, adherent sediment and flocculent precipitate. Urine passed at night soon formed a cloud, which by morning gathered into bits like crumbs of bread, swimming at the bottom of the vessel. Urine passed at night has a pale orange, flocculent sediment, chiefly collected in one spot. Increase of phosphoric acid. Abundance of octahedral crystals of oxalate of lime, of all sizes. Decrease of urea, of chloride of sodium, of sulphuric acid and of free acid.

Sexual Organs.—Weakness beginning as an indefinite sick feeling. Emission at night, with voluptuous dreams, sleep restless and broken. Menses delayed, profuse at night, *in gushes, waking from sound sleep*, with pain in lower abdomen.

Respiratory Organs.—Irritation in larynx in afternoon when sitting quietly in the room, exciting cough. Tickling in larynx when smoking, causing short dry cough. Tickling in larynx and trachea at 2 P.M. and irritation to cough. Hoarse; in morning; in evening; with tickling in upper part of trachea and cough.

Cough in morning; C. in-doors; from tickling at back of throat; *tickling, causing tingling;* paroxysmal, at 4 P.M. when walking in hot sun; paroxysmal, in evening, in cool wind, then frequent cough, usually preceded by tickling at back of pharynx, sometimes followed by soreness there and loosening of mucus, with fluent coryza in r. nostril; dry, in evening in bed, as from catarrh of air-passages; *in morning, with expectoration of tenacious thick, whitish-yellow mucus, as in chronic catarrh*, with dryness of mouth and throat and thirst; at 11 P.M., with expectoration, which was swallowed; at 8.20 P.M., loosening mucus from back of pharynx, which was swallowed; coughing up green mucus.

Groaning (in a child) in evening when writing, with irregular and difficult breathing. Dyspnœa, a pressure on whole chest and constant desire to take a deep breath. Difficult breathing continuing even in bed, with palpitation and not unpleasant weariness. Short breath on ascending a height, with oppression. No want of breath on climbing a hill.

Clinical.—Nervous dyspnœa, with weak heart. Asthma, with nervous exhaustion, restlessness and sleeplessness. Weakness of vocal cords, with hoarse voice, < after talking.

Chest.—Stitches near sternum, about r. fourth rib; S. under l. clavicle at noon; under r. clavicle at 4 P.M.; in l. lung, between third and sixth ribs, < deep inspiration. Pain below clavicles; beneath first and second false ribs of l. side when walking. Compression in region of short ribs. Oppression. Fulness in afternoon, and of stomach and abdomen. Soreness of upper lobes of lungs. Heaviness in forenoon when walking, with dyspnœa, sometimes painful pressure on chest; H. in evening when walking slowly, with short breath; continuing when sitting still after walking, with constant need to take a deep breath and sensation as if lungs were too much distended; on walking or ascending steps, obliging him to take a deep breath frequently. Heat in r. about middle of sternum indoors at 1 P.M. and afterwards.

Heart and Pulse.—Palpitation. Heart's beats nearly quadrupled. Pulse rapid; and strong; till night, and weak; with peculiar noise in ears. Pulse slow; and small, with increased tension.

Neck and Back.—Pain at upper part of nape on bending neck down forward. Sprained pain in muscles of l. side of nape at 10 P.M. on bending head backward or forward. Sudden sharp pain in r. lumbar region in morning, during forcible expiration when standing.

Extremities.—Pain, > outbreak of boils. Warm indistinct pain in l. shoulder-joint at 12.30 P.M. Pain about insertion of deltoid in morning on moving r. arm by that muscle; in arm about insertion of r. deltoid at 4 P.M. on raising or lowering arm after having raised it; occasionally in l. deltoid. Sprained pain in l. deltoid at 10 P.M. on raising or lowering arm and during the night when lying on r. side; suddenly in lower part of r. deltoid in morning on lowering arms, often on holding arms clasped above head and afterwards on raising or lowering arm by that muscle; suddenly in r. deltoid at 9 A.M. on using it.

Pain in bones of l. forearm as if broken, < raising or stretching out the arm, so that he could scarcely use it or take hold of anything with l. hand. Pain in muscles of forearm and along border of radius as from a blow, on moving it and on pressing on it. Lame pain on borders of hand.

Fingers.—Painful lameness of r. fourth and fifth, < stretching fingers or grasping anything, without external pain, next day this lameness was more in abductor of little finger and consisted of pressure with pain deep in flesh, as after a blow or great exertion. Deadness of r. little, in morning and on waking from siesta; of l. little, on waking, with enlarged sensation.

Lower Extremities.—Staggering; to l. Sudden pain in r. buttock at 5 P.M. on walking in open air, preventing movement. Sticking on r. hip, with weakness in walking; S. on r. hip, running towards bowels; occasionally in muscles at back of l. inner side, above knee, at 5 P.M. Pain in l. thigh from hip-joint to knee. Bruised pain in region of r. hip-joint when walking. Aching anteriorly in r. knee, shooting down tibia to foot, after getting warm in bed, lasting till sleep.

Cramp in r. calf in night, with pain on pressure and on walking during the day, afterwards at 4 P.M. or while lying on back with leg extended, suddenly in l., afterwards in evening when sitting with knees bent, next morning when stepping with l. foot on descending stairs. Occasional pain in l. calf as after cramp, on walking, descending stairs or using muscles of calf. Weak, trembling sensation in legs.

Sudden painless feeling in r. ankle as if it had given way or become loose, at 1.45 P.M., on lifting r. leg when running gently. Sudden weakness of l. ankle as if it had given way, at 4 P.M. on running gently in open air. Pain in l. instep on walking as if dislocated. Strained sensation in l. instep in morning on rising in warm weather, and later on walking or sitting. Feet heavy. Feet fatigued.

Skin.—Yellow; and tense. Leaden. Hæmorrhage from people with thin skin and fair complexion. Ecchymoses on contiguous sides of first phalanges of r. ring and little fingers, on r. palm and on ulnar side of palmar aspect of first phalanx of l. little finger, near the base, and on radial side of first phalanx of r. little finger, some of them > washing. Lump tender on pressure and sometimes when walking, in loose skin between l. thigh and scrotum posteriorly. Pimples in hollows of knees; red, on inner surface of thighs, itching at night. Circumscribed erythema. Exanthema resembling herpes, around eyelids. Swelling on r. cheek, close to ala nasi, hard, resembling one he had on perineum, movable in the integuments, afterwards on pressure discharge of pus and blood from a hole just below it. Nettle-rash on several parts or limited to lips, causing scabs, bleeding and insupportable pains.

Soreness in l. groin and region of abdominal ring (where he had a glandular suppuration several years ago, from cold and fever), at 8 or 9 P.M., when writing, with smarting and tenderness to touch. Tingling in hands in evening and morning during expiration after deep inspiration, when very warm, > when cooler, < in l. palm, once in palm and back of r. hand and once down r. palm towards fingers. Itching at junction of r. thigh muscles with gluteas maximus at 2.20 P.M., renewed after scratching; on front of throat at 8 and 10 P.M., not > scratching, with feeling as if rash were coming out; fearful, on scratched spots.

Sleep.—Yawning; all the forenoon without weariness; after supper; when sitting, with sleepiness. Sleepiness; at 4 P.M.; at 5.30 P.M., > coffee; after dinner; early in evening but wide awake in bed, with heat and throbbing of temporal arteries till midnight; when sitting reading or studying; then wakefulness till 4 A.M.; but can do with only four hours sleep in the twenty-four without overfatigue. *Slept later than usual in morning.* Slept after dinner; at 1 P.M., and sleepy till 4 P.M. Long in recovering herself when awakened in the night, and staring with widely-dilated pupils.

Sleeplessness; in evening; till 2 A.M., with pressive pain in eyes when working, then quiet sleep; till 2 A.M., with shivering, vertigo, fever, rush of ideas and anxiety, then sweat and quiet sleep; with flow of ideas; passed the night in reading and writing and felt no fatigue nor hunger in the morning. Sudden jerking in the usual afternoon nap, and waking. Sleep disturbed; with frequent waking, unpleasant dreams and constant sweat. Restless sleep, with dreams of being hurried; R., with frequent waking. *Waking on back;* after many dreams; in the midst of a dream; or inclined to l. side. Rose more than an hour before the usual time, then read, then slept in the chair.

Dreams, many; heavy, with sweat; active, troubled; incoherent, unremembered. That something was adherent to fauces at posterior nares, which he was trying to detach, woke at 8 A.M. in the effort, and there was mucus to detach, then smarting soreness; at 3 A.M. that he was trying to remove mucus from pharynx by hawking, on waking found himself trying to do so, but could not succeed by coughing or hawking, with hoarseness. Vivid, partly suggested by what he had lately read; V., of fighting, suggested by reading the "Fire Worshipers" a few days ago; V., that the medicine had loosened the teeth and a piece of the jaw; V., that he held a large beetle by the upper part of the body in the agony of death, firmly grasped between index and thumb, and wondered at the power it exercised to get loose and bite him. That he saw a recently-deceased friend hanging dead by his legs for hours. Of fighting with six or seven black generals who garroted him, binding him with ropes, causing great agony of mind.

Clinical.—Insomnia, inclined to sleep, but cannot.

Fever.—Chilliness; at 10 P.M. when sitting with a window behind my back open, then shivering, the S. continuing in open air, > quick motion in open air; at night; with headache on r. side and in occiput and less on r. side of forehead, and vertigo; in head; of limbs. Fever, with heat of skin; fever in afternoon, > wine, with prostration; heat up back in flashes and burning across abdomen in flashes. Sweat; in evening; unpleasant. Secretion of skin diminished.

Cocaine.

An alkaloid ($C_{17}H_{21}NO_4$) obtained from the leaves of Erythroxylon Coca, Lam. Solutions in Alcohol may be diluted for internal administration.

Allies.—Theine.

Generalities.—The body has a pendulum-like motion laterally, with closed eyes and toes together. Body inclined to one side, at angle of forty-five degrees, resting on his elbow, head on his breast, lids tightly closed, mouth half open, pupils not larger than a pin's head, breathing slow, pulse feeble, fluttering, not to be counted, face congested and whitish-gray, lips and hands blue, body bathed in cold sweat, could not be aroused by shaking and pinching. Movements diminished from want of co-ordination.

Pleasant tremors shooting through body. Twitching of various muscles; T. of face (after having a tooth pulled), then faintness, everything turned black, the voice of the dentist sounded as if in the distance, lips and face so numb that she tried some time before she could speak, icy coldness, general numbness, with weight on chest, gasping, sensation as if every breath would be the last, inability to swallow, then feeling as if sailing around the room a little way from the floor (gum did not bleed until then), feet and limbs cold and numb as far as knees and feeling as if asleep, gait like a drunken man's, feet remained cold all day, with headache, remained weak several days. Convulsive movements. Convulsions, with difficult breathing, unconsciousness and livid face; then rising in frenzy and striking about violently, the gasping suggestive of obstruction about larynx, after the paroxysm of pain in l. arm; tetanic C.

Muscular power enhanced. Tottering gait, difficult speech, confusion of mind and restlessness. Nervousness. Malaise. Sinking sensation. Weakness. Faint, asked repeatedly for drinks and was covered with cold sweat. Hyperæsthesia. Anæsthesia (local); and anæmia, afterwards swelling and hyperæsthesia. Amelioration from the vomiting of clear mucus.

Mind.—Talkative, repeats the same idea over and over, because words fail to express the delightful sensation, afterwards is sober, but feels foolish. Every breath seems stimulating. Constant desire to undertake vast feats of strength, feels like haranguing, gesticulations and strides around the room are irresistible, feels as if nothing he could see or hear would depress him. Feeling "very good, similar to that after a big drink of whisky," on walking about the room feels light, face flushed, after walking the feeling of exhilaration passes off, after half a grain more he feels "glorious all over the body, with stimulating waves running through the limbs," says he is intoxicated. Cerebral activity, mounting at intervals into the region of delirium, the latter tendency subservient to a powerful effort of the will, the reflective faculties seemed stimulated. Apathy. Semi-comatose condition, from which she could be aroused easily, but answered questions with difficulty.

Head.—Aching; throbbing. Hemicrania. Throbbing and bursting sensation. Heaviness; and fulness. Agreeable lightness, ideas flowed with facility and fantastic images followed each rapidly, then drowsiness, in resisting which there were oppression of head and confusion of thought. Vertigo on waking; V., with dark vision, sinking sensation and weakness, then semi-comatose condition, from which she was easily aroused, and when so aroused her mind was clear, heat, skin hot and dry, radial pulse rapid and scarcely perceptible, pupils dilated, deglutition difficult, dyspnœa, dryness of fauces, bitter taste, cold shivers though the temperature was above the normal, chattering of teeth, then drowsiness, eyes closed, muscles of face affected, weakness, inability to support the head, and nausea.

Eyes.—Sunken. Panophthalmitis from local use during operation, the superior part of the conjunctiva being as much swollen as the inferior. Burning from local application, cornea and conjunctiva soon became anæsthetic, feeling of tension in lids, eye seemed protruded, as in Graves' disease, conjunctiva pale, these symptoms lasted about ten minutes and gradually disappeared, in ten to fifteen minutes pupil began to dilate and there was slight paresis of accommodation, mydriasis lasted some hours after anæsthesia disappeared.

Pupils dilated; < r.; at intervals; contracted. If the drug reaches the upper lid Græfe's symptom is often marked, the lid halting on looking down. Pallor of inner surface of lid on which the Cocaine had been dropped. Peculiar stiffness of lids (from application to ball) and diminished sensibility of eye increasing to insensibility, pupil widely dilated, Jæger No. 1 could not be read inside of five and a half inches with this eye, while with the other No. 1 print could be easily read at four inches, and on looking steadily with both eyes at an object a few feet off there was an indistinct second image to the left but in close contact, and the dot-and-line test with vertical displacement by prisms proved negative, and the ball looked rather paler. The range of accommodation is shortened by the moving of the near point from the eye, the far point not being influenced (from application to eye). Astigmatism, the letters appearing to slant from l. to r. (the l. eye being "cocainized,"), in one case the slanting was more perceptible in near vision, in the other case in distant vision. Amaurosis.

Ears and Face.—Ringing in ears. Deafness. Pallor. Cyanosis; and puffiness of face. Flushes in face; coming and going; and clammy skin. Facial muscles affected.

Mouth and Throat.—Tongue dry and anæmic; *T. numb.* Speech incoherent. Dryness; dry, leathery feeling in mouth. Burning pain in palate. Taste bitter; lost. Fauces dry. Warmth in pharynx. Deglutition and articulation difficult.

Stomach.—Loss of appetite. Nausea. Retching. Vomiting. Cramps; on eating. Gripings. Pressure in epigastrium. Warmth. Vacant feeling.

Stool and Urinary Organs.—Constipation. Secretion of urine ceased, also sexual function. Burning on micturition (from injection into urethra).

Respiratory Organs.—Dyspnœa. Respiration rapid. Breathing very easy; and principally thoracic, very superficial; with frequent inclination to sigh. Disposed to sigh and unable to draw a deep breath.

Heart and Pulse.—Suffocative feeling in cardiac region. Heart's action retarded; slightly increased; the beat was felt and blood rushed to head, then dulness and roaring in head and noises in ears, confusion of thought, impairment of volition, general uneasiness, twitching in fingers and toes, with numbness, nausea and pressure in epigastrium, after the acme of the paroxysm face pale and covered with cold sweat. Pulse rapid; and stronger, while the breath was slower, but deeper and fuller; and weak. Pulse intermittent every fifth beat. Pulse feeble.

Extremities.—Fleshy parts of arms and legs insensible to pinching, etc. Heaviness. Tingling in hands, with numbness; T. in fingers, < r., with numbness. Hands and lips blue. Tremors of fingers when outstretched. Prickings in finger-tips. Cramps in legs and feet, < dorsal aspect of r. foot. Legs weak. Lost the use of legs. Queer feeling, extending from toes over whole body.

Sleep.—Sleepiness; giving way to a feeling of great

energy. Wakeful feeling, with weakness of legs in walking. Sleep for thirteen hours.

Fever.—Coldness. Hands cold and clammy. Subjective heat. Rise of temperature; with cold shivers and chattering of teeth. Skin hot and dry. Sweat; then prostration, shivering, feeling of impending death; cold; on face or neck; clammy, on forehead.

Coccinella.

A tincture is prepared by digesting the live insects, Coccinella Septempunctata (L.), (the common "lady-bug"), in Alcohol.

Tensive pressure in head. Vertigo. Tearing sticking in one side of forepart of head. Aching in temples and occiput as if brain would become enlarged or distended. Redness of cheeks, < r., with heat. Rushes of blood to face like flushes of heat. Tearing rhythmical with pulse, extending from r. upper jaw to lobule of ear. Jerking and tearing in one and tearing in the other teeth, with stitches extending towards occiput and warmth through the whole head. Pulselike jerking in molars. Throbbing pain in upper molars. Knitting pain in molars. Pain in molars as if hollow and as if air were forced into them. Drawing in upper molars, extending towards r. ear, when sitting; rhythmical D. in teeth when eating. Paroxysmal drawing or tearing, as if a tooth would be torn out; in teeth, with hacking in them. Cold sensation in all teeth; pleasant, in one tooth on touch of finger. Gum swollen. Tobacco bites the tongue severely. Coldness in mouth.

Clinical.—Neuralgic headaches, beginning in forehead over r. eye, which is very sensitive to touch (red); neuralgia of teeth, etc. Effects of cold in the region of the kidneys, pain in loins. Hiccough and burning in stomach, but particularly pain in region of kidneys (compare with Doryphora and Canth.).

Cocculus.

A tincture is made from the dried fruit of Anamirta Cocculus, W. and A.

General Action.—It produces violent convulsions and loss of control over muscles; excessive vertigo and nausea. Paralysis of muscles.

Allies.—Rhus tox, Zinc., *Nux v.*, Plumb., Phos., Arg. nit.

Generalities.—*Starts easily. Inclination to tremble.* Fell to the ground, trembled, vomited and became senseless. Convulsions; tetanic; clonic, in upper limbs, then general, with frothing at the mouth; tonic and clonic, with severe contortions and shocks of limbs and danger of suffocation, trismus, biting of the protruding tongue, bloody foam from mouth and nose at every expiration, tetanic stiffness of whole body alternating with convulsive shocks, with cold sweat, dilated pupils, fixed look, unconsciousness, convulsive shocks when the skin was pinched.

Epileptic attack, intoxicated feeling on sitting down, then staring without answering questions, then fell unconscious, bent himself together with unintelligible cries, passed urine involuntarily, general convulsions, the outstretched hands clenched, with paroxysmal choking in throat, mouth half open as if he would vomit, bubbling foam at the mouth, hands cold, face covered with cold sweat and spasmodically distorted, eyes glassy, protruding, then he stood up, but did not answer questions, showed his teeth and bellowed at those who spoke, endeavored to strike the bystanders, face expressed rage, then groaning and grunting, after recovery aversion to all nourishment. Twitching of various parts of muscles (Zinc.), < lower limbs, as after a long walk. Hæmorrhages. (Compare convulsions with Cicuta and Nux v.).

Sticking in cold swollen glands, at least on touch, with heat; S. in parts previously inflamed, if touched with fingers; burning S. here and there. (Tearing in hard swollen glands.) Drawing pain in limbs and abdominal muscles, as from taking cold. Paralytic drawing in side of neck and in other places, at times almost like an intermittent paralytic pressure. Alternation of diarrhœa, vomiting, sopor and delirium.

Indolence; with taciturnity, also in morning after waking. Inclination to lie down. Avoids the open air. *Restless.* Want of vital energy. Weakness; general, several days at 9 A.M., with heaviness of limbs, so that she must sleep; *from slightest exertion, with exhausting sweat;* from slightest loss of sleep; when walking; < sitting; **attacks of paralytic, with pain in back** (Rhus t.); *so that it is difficult to stand firmly* (Rhus t.). *Faintness; on motion, with distortions of facial muscles. Hemiplegia on l. side.* Immobility. Aggravation from cold air (Rhus t.); from coffee (Nux v.); smoking tobacco (Nux v.); *drinking, eating, sleeping and speaking aggravate head symptoms.*

Clinical.—General tendency to paralysis, heaviness and sluggishness of the whole body, numbness; sometimes trembling and jerking of various groups of muscles; at times unconquerable drowsiness. Spasmodic affections; epilepsy characterized by cold extremities and numbness; chorea, the patient is exhausted; hysteria, especially menstrual, complaints of numbness and weakness of the extremities; particularly useful in complaints resulting from loss of sleep. General hyperæsthesia of all senses, intolerance of the least excitement. Symptoms of emptiness and hollowness in thoracic or abdominal cavities are frequently associated with the symptoms of weakness of paralysis. General bad effects of prolonged insomnia. Nervous exhaustion, with profound weakness of extremities, aching in thighs, falling asleep of limbs, weak, empty feeling in chest or abdomen.

Mind.—*Mania, irresistible inclination to sing and tra la.* Weeping. Despair. *Sad; as if he had suffered an insult. Sensitive; everything offends him* (Nux v.). Offended at trifles, often to weeping, with contraction of pupils, after weeping loss of appetite. Angry; and peevish, after a few hours lively and jocose. Dissatisfied with himself. Earnest, then breaking into complaints; earnest, little concerned as to his own health, anxious about others' sickness. *Thoughts directed to an unpleasant object, absorbed in herself. Dread of every surprise.* Fear. Hypochondriac, < afternoon. Anxiety; *sudden; as if she had committed a crime;* in morning, about the incurability of a slight complaint; like a dream, preventing sleep. Discouraged. Intolerance of interruption or noise. No desire to do anything and pleasure in nothing. Time passes too rapidly. *Memory lost* (Anac.). *Sits in deep thought.* Stupidly dumb. Stupefied; when awake, as from sleep. Unconscious.

Clinical.—It is especially adapted to cases which present a mental condition of stupidity, slow of comprehension or cannot think of words with which to express themselves, the mind feels benumbed, especially with vertigo, nausea, etc. Mental derangements resulting from suppression of menses. Melancholy, is wrapped in profound sadness, with apprehension, desire to escape, etc.

Head.—*Convulsive trembling* (Cicuta v.). **Aching, with nausea**; A. < cold air; *as if bound up;* as if brain were bound together by a band; *brain feels as if rolled up or compressed into a smaller bulk* (Rhus t.). Pressure through whole, < forehead, in forenoon, < reading and reflecting, until there is loss of ideas; P. downward in whole, < forehead, < walking. Aching composed of constriction, burning, tearing, digging and boring. Much affected by thinking. **Confusion, < eating and drinking; C. and stupefaction;** C. in morning, with humming in it as after a debauch. *Dulness; and confusion, < reading, so that he must read a passage several times in order to understand it;* with cold sweat on forehead and hands and aversion to food. Heaviness; with confusion, as after intoxication; sensation as if something heavy were lying on it. (Painful shaking of brain when walking, moving head or speaking.) **Vertigo; on rising up in bed** (Bry., Phos.), **with nausea, compelling him to lie down; as from intoxication, with dulness in forehead as if a board were across forehead;** when sitting, as from intoxication.

Forehead.—Sticking above r. eye; intermittent boring S. in r. side. *Headache as if the eyes would be torn out; aching as if something forcibly closed the eyes.* Tearing throbbing pain from 7 to 9 P.M. Intermittent pain in l. eminence consisting of raging, throbbing, sticking, afterwards extending as a crawling to r. frontal eminence. Aching in sinciput. Compression in r. half; wavelike, in l. half.

Stitches in l. temple; crawling S. in temples. Cramplike pain in l. temporal muscle. Pain in temples as if head were screwed in. Inward-pressure in l. temple; in r., as if a dull instrument slowly pressed deep into brain. Pain in vertex. Stitches in r. side of brain. Shuddering in l. side of occiput as if hair would stand on end.

Clinical.—Vertigo as if intoxicated is an almost constant concomitant of Cocculus symptoms, generally associated with a feeling of stupefaction of head and numbness and unsteadiness of extremities. Sick headaches, pain, especially seated in occiput, extending down spine, extremely sensitive to external impressions, with constant nausea and vertigo (Petrol.). Sick headaches, especially brought on by reading in cars and carriages (Petrol., seasickness).

Eyes.—Turned upward. Surrounded by blue rings. (Swelling of one and of half of nose in morning after headache through the night.) Stitches from within outward. *Bruised pain at night, with inability to open lids* (Rhus. t.). Pain, with inability to open lids at night; P. as from dust. Pupils contracted; to their smallest diameter, then as the spasm abated dilated to their fullest extent, and again contracted as the spasm returned, the spasm produced by touching lids. Lids dry. Pressure in outer margin of orbit. *Dim vision.* Dark spots and objects like flies float before the eyes. Vision of a black object that receded from her, turning with her, but she saw everything clearly.

Ears.—Sensation alternately in ears as if closed and deaf. (Heat in r. outer and middle, in morning in bed.) *Sound of rushing water, with difficult hearing.* Rushing as when listening at a tube. Cracking on forcible yawning. Hard hearing in r.

Nose.—Swelling of r. half. Pain in anterior angle of nostril, < touch; in l. nostril as from an ulcer. Sneezing. Inability to sneeze when walking in open air. Coryza. (Blows bloody mucus from nose.)

Face.—*Earthy, and painful expression. Red cheeks* in a cold room, *with heat in face.* Cyanosis. Expression rigid and irritable. Cramp in malar-bone, in masseter muscles. Cramplike pain in masseter muscles, < opening jaws. Pressive sensation in l. malar-bone, rather benumbing than painful. Tearing digging in lower jaw.

Clinical.—Paralysis of facial nerve, involving the lids of one eye and side of face (Caust., Rhus t.).

Mouth.—Incisors seemed raised up and heavy as if they would fall out. A decayed, loose tooth feels elongated and the gum about it is swollen. Pain in hollow tooth only on chewing, as if loose, no pain on biting teeth together when not eating. Biting in back teeth as after using much salt, causing a pleasant sensation on biting together. (Gum sensitive and sore.) *Tongue coated white, and dry at edges. Tongue dry, with a yellowish coat, without thirst.* Pain posteriorly in tongue as if beaten if he protrudes it far. Tongue rough in morning.

Filled with aphthæ, becoming gangrenous, so that the soft parts of mouth were destroyed and the teeth fell out. (Contraction when speaking, and she must speak slowly.) Sensation as if there were a smell from it. Burning in palate. *Dryness* in night, without thirst; D. sensation, with frothy saliva and thirst. Sensation as if water collected in it. Salivation. **Metallic taste, with loss of appetite** (Nux v.); *M. at root of tongue.* Bitter taste; *at root of tongue;* to tobacco when smoking. Coppery T. Salt T. anteriorly on r. side of tongue, > gingerbread. Sour T. after eating; S. on coughing. Slimy T. though food has a natural taste. Nauseous T. T. as if he had fasted long. Food tasteless and seems unsalted.

Throat.—Swollen glands beneath chin; beneath lower jaw, and hard, with nodes on forearm, which are painful on passing hand over them; S. of parotid gland. Violent beating of carotids. Sticking in outer parts. *Choking contraction in upper part of pharynx, impeding breathing and causing cough. Sensation in pit as if something arrested the breathing, constriction of glottis.* Scraping, > swallowing. Sensitiveness, food seems as sharp as if excessively salted and peppered. Pain in tonsils worse on swallowing saliva than on swallowing food; P. in upper part of pharynx, with sensation of swelling at root of tongue, which makes swallowing painful. Heat, and in stomach; afterwards extending over abdomen; H. in evening, extending into palate, with shivering about head. *Dryness;* in upper and back part, as if it and the tongue were rough; in fauces and œsophagus, < swallowing, with roughness, without thirst. Paralysis (Rhus t.).

Stomach.—Aversion to food (Nux v., Rhus t.), *even the smell of food causes it* (Colch.), *but hunger;* averse to eating and drinking; to sour things, bread tastes sour. Appetite lost, food has no taste; A. lost for breakfast, he feels full. Hunger in pit of stomach, little > eating. Thirst, < eating; T. for cold drinks, especially *beer;* unquenchable. Eructations; *bitter* (Nux v.); *putrid* (Nux v.), in forenoon; *empty;* empty, leaving bitter taste in mouth and throat; of musty air; tasting of food; sharp scraping, < evening; *incomplete, ineffectual, instead of which there is hiccough.* Hiccough (Nux v.); *inclination to.* Nausea; *in morning so that she can scarcely rise* (Nux v.); *in afternoon after every drink, mostly in mouth;* **when riding in a wagon** (compare Sepia); *if he became cold or took cold, causing salivation;* on eating; *with headache and bruised sensation in abdomen;* as from overloading stomach. Vomiting; during the accustomed smoking; frequent; frequent, of greenish fluid; (of food and mucus towards midnight, with bitter and sour taste in throat, and attacks of suffocation).

Gurgling beneath pit. Pricking beneath pit, with gnawing. *Griping. Pinching. Constrictive pain*, preventing sleep. Squeezing in pit when walking, and tension. Pain in pit; *beneath S., after eating;* in S. after eating; several hours after a meal, or at night in bed, and in pit and hypochondria; on attempting to eructate; almost a stitching in pit on eructation; on touch; in pit, impeding breathing. Bruised pain in pit on eructation. *Sensation as if a worm were moving in it.* Sensation as if he had not eaten for a long time and the hunger had passed away. Burning, and in abdomen, < about navel.

Clinical.—Nausea and even vomiting are almost constant concomitants of a Cocculus condition. Nausea and vomiting from riding in the cars. Extreme aversion to food, with persistent, slightly qualmish, bitter taste, metallic taste, putrid taste. Nausea associated with vertigo, < taking anything into the stomach, with faintness, etc. Nausea and vomiting of pregnancy.

Abdomen.—Distention; by flatulence, waking about midnight, causing oppressive pain here and there, some flatus passed without remarkable relief, new flatus collected for hours, > lying on one side and the other; with heat and pain. Emission of hot flatus before diarrhœa. Flatus presses upward; moves here and there after supper, and is passed with difficulty. Stitches through to lower part of back, morning in bed; S. in several parts on stooping. Tearing. Cutting when walking after dinner, with chilly sensation and vertigo. Pinching. Drawing pain. Constrictive pain, with pressure towards female genitals, nausea in pit of stomach and inclination to waterbrash. Empty feeling, as if she had no intestines. Burning. (Compare flatulence with Nux v., Carbo v., Cham., Lyc. and Plumb.).

Griping in upper (epigastrium), taking away the breath. *Pinching constriction in upper, after eating, extending to l. side of abdomen and chest.* Pain in upper; beneath last true ribs of r. side, < bending forward, coughing or inspiration. Bruised pain in hypochondria. Stitches in r. side; l. side; intermittent, in l. side near navel. Twinges in r. side above navel. Pinching in l. muscles. Drawing pain from r. to l. side. Nausea extending from r. side towards navel, without inclination to vomit.

Hypogastrium.—Rumbling. Stitches in r. inguinal region. Cutting, extending to upper, > standing. **Painful inclination to inguinal hernia,** < *rising from a seat.* R. ring dilated, a hernia inclines to protrude, and sore pain. *Internal feeling in groins as if stuffed,* < *stepping forward, when it seems as if the thickness pushed forward and everything would fall out. Paralytic pain in r. ring as if something would force its way through* (Nux v.), *when sitting,* > *rising.* Drawing pain in groins as before menstruation.

Clinical.—Flatulent colic only slightly > evacuating gas, attacks come at night, associated with feeling of emptiness, nausea, vertigo, etc. Gastralgia from suppression of menses. Excessive flatulent distention of abdomen and dysmenorrhœa. A valuable remedy in hernias, both umbilical and inguinal; is particularly indicated when the abdominal muscles are weak and it seems as if a hernia would easily take place. Flatulent colic in pregnancy, etc.

Rectum and Anus.—Urging to stool, with offensive diarrhœa; U. to stool and to pass flatus at the same time, then frequent, sudden diarrhœa, in small portions, with emission of flatus; U. after stool, causing faintness; desire for stool, but the stool is delayed by want of peristaltic motion in upper abdomen; ineffectual U., with constipation for three days, then hard, difficult stool (Plumb.). Crawling and itching in rectum, as from ascarides. *Contractive pain in anus* (Plumb.) *in afternoon, preventing sitting.* Burning itching in anus.

Stool.—*Thin. Fluid, frequent, whitish-yellow.* Soft. (Slimy). Constipation. Hard, difficult, only every other day. Putrid. Frequent, small; (frequent and pale).

Clinical.—Diarrhœa brought on by riding in cars or carriage, < drinking cold water, with flatulent distention, colic, feeling as of sharp stones rubbing together in abdomen, numbness of legs, vertigo, nausea, etc.

Urinary Organs.—Sticking in urethra. Pain in urethra on urging to urinate. Tensive pain in orifice of urethra when not urinating. Sticking-itching in forepart of urethra. Frequent urging to urinate, with scanty discharge; (constant U., with frequent copious discharge of watery urine). (Retention of urine for ten minutes.) *Urine watery.* Urine red, without sediment.

Sexual Organs.—Relaxation in night, with retraction of prepuce behind glans. Sensitiveness. Sticking in end of prepuce; in one testicle. *Itching of scrotum.* Itching-burning of scrotum. Bruised pain in testicles, < touch. Drawing pain in testicles. Excitement, with desire. Emissions at night.

Menstruation too early, with distention of abdomen and cutting-contracting pain in abdomen on every motion and every breath (Cham., Nux v.), *with contraction of rectum* (Nux v.); *M. too early, with distention of abdomen and pain in upper abdomen on every motion and when sitting, as from sharp pressure of a stone, with pain on touch* as from an internal ulcer. (Metrorrhagia.) Leucorrhœa.

Clinical.—Menses too profuse, gushing, very exhausting, with menstrual colic as from sharp stones rubbing together, flatulent distention and dysmenorrhœa and suppressed menstruation, with numbness, remote symptoms, vertigo, nausea, flatulent colic, numbness of extremities, etc. Suppression of menses, with purulent gushing leucorrhœa and flatulent abdomen.

Respiratory Organs.—Tough mucus hangs in larynx and obliges hacking and hawking. Irritation to cough high up in larynx; I. to cough posteriorly in larynx in evening in bed, the cough always in two paroxysms. Cough every fourth night, waking at 12 and 2 o'clock, with dryness of mouth, and on coughing sensation as if the glottis were not wide enough; C., with great exertion on account of oppression of chest, which only appears on coughing. Suffocative sensation provoking cough. Dyspnœa. Whistling-snoring, threatening suffocation, < inspiration, slow breathing alternates with suppressed breathing, with face distended as in apoplexy. Breathing quick; and difficult. Short breath.

Clinical.—Dyspnœa as from constriction of stomach and hysteria.

Chest.—Rumbling in l. side as from emptiness, < walking. Sticking in r.; in l.; in nipples; in l., near pit of stomach, in evening; through l. into back when walking; in sternum when walking; internally when sitting, rhythmical with pulse; paroxysmal, in l. on inspiration; intermittent, in r. false ribs, in front.

Pain in middle of sternum, with anxiety, then sticking in sternum; in middle of sternum as from pressure with a blunt instrument. Pressure on chest on eructating; sudden P. against sternum as with a fist. Drawing pain in r. side on bending body to r. while sitting or standing; in side towards back when talking, walking or stooping, < for a few minutes when lying, then >. *Tensive constriction in r., impeding breathing. Oppression,* < upper part of sternum, impeding breathing. Affected by reading aloud. (Raw and sore.)

Heart and Pulse.—*Palpitation.* Pulse rapid. Pulse small; and hard.

Neck.—Painful cracking of vertebræ on moving head. Sticking in nape on moving head forward or backward; S. externally in r. side; pulsating, externally in l. *Stiff pain in muscles on moving neck and on yawning* (Zinc., Cimic.). **Weakness of muscles, with heaviness of head,** *necessity to lay head now here, now there, else the muscles are painful,* > *leaning backward.*

Back.—*Trembling.* Tearing. Boring. Pain in spine as if it would break. Piercing pain in all joints of vertebræ as if sprained or spasmodically drawn together, < motion. Pain on standing as if fatigued or strained. Pain when sitting, < l. side. Drawing pain. Stiffness on moving shoulders, with pain.

Sticking in scapulæ, extending from r. to l. Tearing between scapulæ in evening before lying down, and in spine. *Pressure in scapulæ and nape.* Intermittent paralytic pain beneath l. scapula during rest. Drawing pain below l. scapula when standing and lying, < morning. Sharp pressure in loins and region of kidneys in morning in bed, > rising. *Paralytic pain in small of back; with spasmodic drawing across hips, preventing walking, with anxiety and fear.* Bruised pain in bones of small of back.

Clinical.—Great weakness of cervical and dorsal muscles, then severe paralysis; in spinal irritation, with great hyperæsthesia of all senses.

Extremities.—*Trembling;* < *evening, with chilliness.* Cracking in joints; when walking. Burrowing in bones. A slight noise shoots through all limbs. Pain on motion as if they would be crushed or broken. Pain in muscles on touch; P. internally, < touch and pressure. Drawing pain in l. Seem paralyzed. *Paralytic drawing, constant and paroxysmal, here and there in bones. Paralytic feeling in arms and legs, she could scarcely rise from her seat* (Arg. n., Phos.), *with loss of appetite.* Paralytic and stiff, with drawing pains in bones and back. Paralytic immobility, with drawing pains in bones. *Painful stiffness of all joints;* now in hands and fingers, now in knees and ankles. **Feet and hands alternately asleep.**

Clinical.—Paralysis of extremities, with numbness, symptoms preceded by convulsive movements of groups of muscles.

Upper Extremities.—*Sticking in shoulder-joint and muscles of upper arm during rest.* Pain in shoulder-joint, consisting of a broken, tearing and sticking sensation, > motion, with heaviness and dread of moving arm, and in elbow, shafts of bones and between them. Drawing pain in shoulder-joint and shafts of bones on raising arm after eating, with bruised pain on touch.

Arm.—Convulsions, with closing of thumb in fist. Pain as if beaten in the one on which he lies. Paroxysmal burning pain in l. Pain when eating, and on attempting to raise it heaviness and tired feeling. Paralytic pain on violent motion, as if bones were broken. *Asleep and a crawling sensation* (Rhus t.); feel asleep and paralyzed during and after a meal. Paralysis when writing, can scarcely hold his pen.

Upper Arm.—Jerking in muscles of l.; pulselike, visible J. just above elbows. *Sticking in r.;* like shocks on outer side, below its head. Digging (wavelike drawing) in shaft of l. humerus, bruised pain. Pain as if broken on raising it. Drawing in upper part of humerus, with bruised pain. Humeri above elbow seem beaten and paralyzed on motion.

Sticking in l. elbow. Sudden paralytic pain in bend of r. elbow. Sticking in outer side of l. forearm, extending into little finger. Pain in r. forearm. Pain in radius as if dislocated. Intermitting, almost tearing, paralytic pressure in anterior muscles of forearm, < rest. *Forearm asleep and sensation as if the hand were swollen* (Rhus t.), constrictive pain in muscles and cold fingers. **Trembling of hands when eating,** < *the higher it is raised.* Redness of l. hand, with drawing in little finger. Cramplike pain on outer side of r. hand and in the four fingers, with heat of hand. **Now one hand, now the other insensible and asleep.** Cramplike contraction of finger. Painful paralytic jerking through fingers. Cramplike sticking from behind forward in r. index. Cramplike pain in r. little finger when writing. Tearing, boring, drawing pain in fingers.

Lower Extremities.—Paralytic immobility. Jerking in muscles about r. hip-joint. Cracking in l. hip-joint on turning thigh, < walking, with pain. (Trembling of thighs when kneeling.) Twinging in r. nates when sitting, then shocks. Sticking on outer part of l. hip-joint; in l. hip-joint on walking; in r. femur when walking; pulsating, on outer side of l. thigh when sitting, causing involuntary motion. Pain in thighs on raising them, as if broken. Bruised pain in thighs if he raises the leg while sitting; on beginning to walk after sitting; in inner side of l. if he walks in a circle to the left; intermittent, in middle of l.; with a paralyzed feeling. Painless constriction of thigh, descending into muscle below hollow of knee, with sensation as if thigh would become stiff. Intermittent paralytic pain in l. hip-joint. Paralytic drawing in thighs, with weakness of knees as if they would bend under him. Paralytic feeling in l. thigh, < rest. Intermittent paralytic stiff sensation piercing l. leg from middle of thigh downward. Numbness of thigh extending over knee.

Knees crack on motion. Sticking in knee; l.; outer part when walking. Drawing tearing in patella. Drawing pain in knee on rising after sitting. **Knees threaten to sink from weakness, he totters when walking and threatens to fall to one side.** Cramp of calves at night when bending knees. Tensive pain in calves on motion. Constriction on outer side of l. leg, more numb than painful. Sensation below l. knee as if too tightly bound with the garter. Wavelike paralytic pain down outer side of l. leg. Sprained pain in ankle on motion.

Foot.—Swelling in evening. Boring. Tearing. Tearing jerks in a corn in evening during rest, with tearings. Bruised pain in bone of heel; on dorsum of foot on bending up foot and on touch. Drawing pain. **Falling asleep when sitting** (Secale c.); *of l. when walking after sitting, and sticking as from pins.*

Tearing in great toe even during rest. Corrosive pain in toes. Pain in metatarsal joint of great toe as if a chilblain or boil would form, with pain on touch. Drawing pain in r. toes.

Skin.—Red spots on chest, sides of neck, behind ears. Eruption resembling scarlatina on body and arms. Pimple beneath shoulder, itching under bed-clothes; red miliary P. on face, back and chest, itching when warm; hard, on limbs, wrists and backs of fingers, with itching burning pain, itching, and red areola. Pustules above nose, on temples and chest and between scapulæ; below r. corner of mouth, with red areola, painful, tense to touch. Boil on inner side of thigh. Vesicle at night on side of hand where little finger ends, discharging next day.

Sticking externally in skin and muscles of face; S. in l. side of epigastric region, > rubbing; on l. knee when sitting, so that he must move the leg at every stitch; itching, in l. axilla, as from a flea; burning itching, here and there, as from fleas. Crawling below r. shoulder, extending to fingers, with throbbing and burning. Itching of ankles; on back in evening on undressing, with red pimples; in various parts at night, then pain after scratching; at night, sometimes from pit of stomach to throat, sometimes on tibia and beneath shoulders, and after scratching oozing of serum; < in evening on undressing; under the feather-bed, changing to tickling after scratching; in hollow of l. knee when walking, > standing still, and on calf and ankle; here and there, < inner part of thighs, with burning, as from nettles, and pimples, with stinging on touch; biting, as after profuse sweat, on undressing; piercing tickling, in ball of thumb, not > scratching.

Clinical.—Abscesses at root of the toe-nail, as from a hot iron, with Cocculus symptoms.

Sleep.—*Yawning constantly in bed, with stretching;* Y. towards evening; forcible; interrupted, with inability to take a full breath. Sleepiness; *in morning, and constant yawning;* but must open his eyes as soon as he closes them on account of a frightful sensation in his brain like that produced by the most dreadful dreams. Sleeps late in morning. Sleeps with one arm under the head; (upon the stomach). Sopor.

Sleepiness from thoughts of the business of the day for an hour and sleepless after 1 A.M. Waking as if he feared ghosts. Frequent waking; and starting up; with heat; *as in fright.* Night restless, with sticking and biting here and there. Cried out anxiously in sleep, called her mother and sisters, anxious rapid breathing, clutched about the bed, struck out with the hands, with open distorted eyes, without being awake, constant motion of head, < towards the left.

Dreams vivid, frightful; vivid, unremembered. That he had done something wrong. That his knees were swollen and painful. Of dying and death.

Fever.—Coldness; in evening; in open air; with colic; general, with bluish hands; of whole body, with glowing of cheeks; (gradually increasing, with little or no thirst, with warm forehead, cold cheeks, cold nose and hands, then heat with anxiety as if he could not breathe, nausea and thirst, then cold sweat, < on head and hands, with continued anxiety). Internal, so that he trembled, but not external, in evening, with longing for stimulating nourishment. Shaking, at 8 A.M.; in afternoon. Creeping shivering; frequent shivering, then flushes of heat in head; S. over lower parts; recurrent S., < through lower limbs; S. across breasts; in back in evening. Chills alternating with heat; now in one hand, now in the other; the heat rising from feet through whole body, with sensation as if blood rushed into face, but she was pale, then coldness creeping from head to feet. Internal coldness in shoulders. C. of back; here and there as if touched with ice; creeping over back. Hands seem cold when held to the face, but seem warm to each other. Cold feet, but hot cheeks. *Intolerance of both cold and warm air;* of open air, with heat and redness of cheeks.

Heat; in flashes; internal, with rapid pulse; (external, without internal, and without thirst). H. in forehead; and sticky sweat on it. H. of face, with redness of it and thirst; of cheeks, with redness of them, but intolerance of open air; in cheeks, in flushes; in face, in flushes after drinking. Of hands at 6 P.M., with sensation of general dry heat and sleeplessness till 4 A.M., then shivering and cold hands all day. Of feet, with swelling and corrosive itching. Frequent thrill as when one warms himself by a fire in cold weather, then heat and weakness so that he must lie down, all without thirst or sweat.

Sweat; on body from evening till morning, with cold sweat on face; in morning, < on chest and affected parts; on hands. Cold, on forehead and hands; now on one hand, now on the other; on feet. Dry skin.

Clinical.—**Intermittent fever, chill associated with flatulent colic, nausea, disgust at the smell of food, vertigo, etc.; chill, frequently partial, with coldness of lower extremities and heat of head, the chill mingles with the heat and the febrile stage seems to be imperfectly developed; the sweat is general, cold only on the face; the attack followed by extreme debility and by numerous Cocculus symptoms. Low types of malarial fevers, typhoid, rheumatic, relapsing, etc., with intense headache at base of occiput, vertigo, nausea, extreme faintness, numbness, great difficulty in collecting ideas.**

Coccus Cacti.

A tincture is made of the dried insects, Coccinella Indica (Coccus Cacti, L.); Cochineal.

General Action.—The most marked (verified) action of this substance is on the fauces and larynx, great irritability, with profuse secretion of ropy mucus, and on the urinary organs.

Allies.—Iodine, Kali bi., Kali iod., Canth.

Generalities.—Sticking alternately in finger-tips, temples and soles. Tearing or drawing sticking, < warm bed, in evening and night at rest, sometimes from slight exercise of certain muscles, for example, holding a book caused them in upper arm. Sticking tearing here and there in muscles, < r. hip-joint, < rising or sudden motion. Drawings and tearings here and there, < neck, between shoulders and in forearms. Drawing spasmodic pain in r. calf, shoulder, foot, etc.

Fulness of whole body, with heaviness, as if stuffed. Swollen sensation in whole body when half awake at night, sensation as if the body were adherent to a woolen sack, everything he touched seemed thicker than natural. Sudden sensation as if something were distending within me, with sticking in rectum (?), after the distended feeling increased warmth extended over the whole abdomen. Uneasiness, > open air. General excitement in morning on waking, the pulses beating so violently that it seemed as if he heard them; mental and physical E., then half-stupid condition. Indolence. Disinclination to rise and after rising weariness. Weakness; in morning, with sleepiness; in afternoon; in evening, with yawning; after a nap after dinner, with irritability; after a moderate walk; with yawning. Aggravation in afternoon. Amelioration of head and chest symptoms in forenoon, after lying down; A. of headache, symptoms of chest and cough after a drive.

Mind.—Joyous. Lively in evening; L. and clear in mind. Talkative. Excitement after beer, > walking, with heat and sensation as if pulses beat violently. Apprehensive; in evening. Anxious and uneasy. Irritable; morning and evening; then in evening lively. Gloomy. Less active than usual.

Head.—Stitches through brain. Aching; in morning on waking, frequently returning; in forenoon, < violent motion of it; in evening; from his accustomed beer; < stepping hard; in brain, < at bridge of nose; with such weakness that she must sit down frequently during a hurried walk; in morning after waking, as from drinking too much, > rising; as from a disordered stomach; consisting of fulness, with heat and stupefaction. Painful fulness. Swollen sensation. Confusion; in morning, with vertigo; in evening; in evening when walking, < in vertex; in evening and lasting into the night, with pain in vertex and burning in skin of forehead; after breakfast; as after drinking too much; as before violent coryza, > in open air; dizzy C.; dizzy C. in morning on waking. Intoxicated obscuration; in morning on waking. Rush of blood; in forenoon on entering warm room after a walk. Vertigo; after eating, as after intoxication.

Forehead.—Tearing in bones. Burrowing. Pain; at breakfast, which was eaten without remarkable appetite; above r. eye in morning on waking; above arch of nose and in frontal sinuses; in r. side, sometimes extending to occiput; indefinite, after supper, < shaking or turning head or moving hands. Confusion in morning on rising, with heaviness and dulness; C., with pain extending across l. eminence, involving a small part of l. half of forehead, parietal bone and temple, extending to zygomatic part of r. jaw, leaving in all those parts tearing or cutting.

Temples.—Sticking; in l., > during pressure. Pain; in r.; in l. after rising, lasting all day, frequently extending to l. eye; extending towards vertex, > washing with cold water; throbbing and pressive, often alternating with heat and redness of face. Sensation as if too narrow.

Pressure in vertex in morning on waking, with burning pain. Confusion of vertex. Sensitiveness of vertex. Sticking near r. coronal suture. Paroxysmal burrowing in posterior part of r. parietal bone in morning in bed.

Occiput.—Stitches as from the bite of a leech, waking and causing scratching. Boring in l. towards ear. Pressing pain extending to l. cheek and side of nose, with sensation as if scalp were swollen. Pressure in it at 6 P.M. in a warm room, with warmth in it. Sensation as if a hot constricting band extended from one mastoid process to the other, at last affecting the whole scalp, and it seemed as if the bones were drawn closer and closer together. Indefinite drawing and pressing, and in temples and r. eye.

Scalp.—Painful elevation on vertex. Feeling as if drawn tightly over skull. Crawling pain in morning on waking, obliging scratching. Creeping at roots of hair and bristling of hair.

Eyes.—Inclination to stare. Tearing from l. into forehead in evening after lying down. Raging pain in r., extending along squamous bone, on its inner side to the occiput, it seems as if a fluid were injected paroxysmally into a small bloodvessel. Pressure upon l., < inner canthus. Sensation of a foreign body between lids and balls. Smarting as if a hair were between ball and lid; morning on waking. Burning in evening. Consistent tears, < open air. Pressure in l. ball. Agglutination of lids. Jerking of l. lower lid. Margins of lids feel swollen. Burning in margins of lids. Pain in orbital regions; in superciliary ridges. Vision weak.

Ears.—Sticking in l.; in r.; then aching in r. upper back teeth; deep in front of l., between antitragus and zygoma; above and behind l., increasing to burrowing congestion that seldom remitted, and when worst extended to l. side of neck and clavicular region, last l. lower molar and l. side of occiput. Biting sticking in l. antitragus; in r. meatus and r. temple. Drawing tearing above and behind l. then roaring in it. Drawing twinging in l. Pain in region of r. parotid, then in submaxillary glands and salivation; suddenly in r. Eustachian tube before dinner, < turning head to right and on swallowing, suddenly > warm soup. Tensive pain in mastoid process; in bones above and behind l. ear, < mastoid process, with salivation. Drawing pain in r.; at times becoming sticking, with roaring in l.; on convex surface of l. concha, < touch; cramplike, in r. Drawings; in r. meatus in evening. Throbbing pain in l.; in l. mastoid process, at times increasing to a burrowing outward, before midnight in bed, when most severe it extends into l. ear, l. occipital region and nape, last l. lower molar and along sterno-cleido-mastoid muscle to l. claviculo-pectoral region, and on touch pain in the parts as if suppurating. Rhythmical throbbing in ear upon which he was lying.

Stoppage, with pressure in meatus; stopped feeling in l. so that hearing is indistinct; S. feeling in external passages on snapping fingers in front of r.; internal S. feeling in l., < lying upon ear, with sensation as if fluid wax were pushing outward, tensive pain in l. mastoid process, extending to l. clavicle and last lower molar. Tickling from external canal through inner ear to mouth, with voluptuous itching; in l. meatus, with itching, afterwards becoming a pressure in concha. Itching in l.; with roaring; in l. external meatus; in r. external meatus; in r. external concha and external meatus; < going from cold air into a warm room.

Ringing in l., with bruised sensation about l. external ear, < mastoid process, the pain extending down l. side of neck to clavicular and pectoral regions. Cracking in l. on empty swallowing; in l. on spitting, and sensation as if wax would flow from it. Roaring in l.; periodical; seething, in l.; as of a storm in a forest. Impaired hearing; as if ears were stopped with cotton.

Nose.—Redness of nostrils, with soreness in them. Crusts on outer margin of nostrils. *Yellowish pulverulent substance on margin of nostrils.* Dryness; and of throat, > water; of posterior nares, so that he drew water through nostrils, then blew out hard masses of mucus. Stopped; sensation, but watery discharge. Itching internally, then violent sneezing. Sneezing; in evening; with cough and expectoration; violent; violent, in morning, with discharge of mucus; in violent paroxysms, with burning in mucous membrane of nose and on margins of wings. Coryza, with sticking in temples and rawness and soreness of throat. Much mucus; thin, white.

Face.—Crawling in malar-bones; in l., extending across back of nose to r. cheek; extending across back of nose to l. cheek in evening; in l. side of face and nose, corresponding to plexus anserinus, with drawing, resembling prosopalgia. Pain in l. articulation of jaw on chewing, with cracking in it on empty swallowing. Longish bluish-red spot on upper lip. Cracks in lips, which seem covered with meal. Dry lips. Skin of lower lip feels contracted. Sensation in lower lip as if drawn from both sides towards the middle, often alternating with pulsating beats of heart.

Mouth.—Teeth. Tearing in a r. hollow molar interrupting the morning sleep. Burrowing in r. upper posterior molars in morning on waking. Pain in last l. lower; in hollow roots of third l. upper molar (which was broken a year before), with sensitiveness to touch. Jerking pain in l. lower canine after smoking; J. toothache in morning after waking, < l. upper incisors and canine, with sensation of a cold wind on teeth, increasing next day, < inspiration or holding a pipe between teeth, next day teeth very painful on biting them firmly together. Drawing in l.; in r. back; in r. lower incisors; in l. back, in forenoon; sudden; sudden, in incisors and in r. meatus auditorius. Sensation as if a lateral incisor were grasped by a cold finger and forcibly drawn upward. Sore pain in l. teeth and gum waking him when lying on l. side, > changing the position, with sensitiveness to touch. Sensitiveness of lower, with sensation as if too long; S. to cold things; to cold air; to cold water; to cold water in morning.

Gums bleed longer than usual after removing old roots, and the cavities ache for some time. Biting sticking in gum of r. anterior incisor, with dryness of mouth and frequent itching in l. external meatus auditorius. Soreness in toothless places in lower jaw. Heaviness in l. upper jaw as if teeth were pressed out of their sockets.

Tongue.—White coat. Vesicles. Biting anteriorly as from pepper. Biting sticking in l. side of tip, with salivation. Dryness; in morning on waking, with a brown coat; with roughness.

Redness of arches of palate; of velum palati and fauces, with pustules on r. arch of palate. Sticking and burning in palate and tongue. Scraping in arches of palate. Pain in soft palate, < talking or swallowing. Tensive pain in arches of palate on swallowing, > water. Tension in arches of palate. Rawness. *Sensitiveness of mouth and fauces, so that rinsing mouth caused cough and vomiting of thick masses of mucus. Irritability of arches of palate, so that loud talking and brushing of the teeth caused cough and vomiting.* Tickling irritation in palate to vomit in morning, increasing to vomiting of mucus on rinsing mouth with cold water. Burning. Dryness; of palate; behind arches of palate; of M. and throat in morning on waking, > cold water, with heat in them and stiffness of tongue. M. and fauces feel as if covered with velvet. *Constant desire to spit, and metallic taste* (Iod.). Salivation. Hot breath. Odor as from a disordered stomach. Sourish odor.

Taste.—*Metallic, with salivation* (Iod.); *sweetish metallic* (Iod.); M., < smoking; M. at tip of tongue. Sweetish; and bitter, aromatic; and offensive, resinous, < at root of tongue, after a glass of water. Bitter; and nauseous; offensive, bitter, sour, at root of tongue and entrance to fauces in forenoon; sharp, bitter, sour, towards root of tongue, provoking vomiting. Pasty; in morning. Nauseous, flat. Unpleasant to coffee and water. Food at dinner distasteful.

Throat.—Redness; of pharynx, with difficult swallowing; of r. tonsil, with swelling. Swelling of r. tonsil. Tonsils pale and distended. Hawking of mucus; in afternoon; with tickling of larynx, then paroxysms of cough. Scraping sticking and constriction. Sensation as if a hair stuck in it, causing hawking of various-colored mucus. Sensation as if a crumb stuck behind larynx; the sensation of crumbs frequently descends towards stomach and then rises again. *Scraping;* from morning till noon, > after dinner; *with expectoration of mucus; causing paroxysms of cough, with expectoration of mucus;* causing nausea. Rawness, > at night in warmth of bed, with roughness and hoarseness; with scraping, as after highly-seasoned food; causing violent cough; causing frequent hawking of mucus. Roughness; in morning. Constriction. Choking, with constriction beginning in stomach and extending to throat. Sensation as if a thread were hanging down, and constant hawking of mucus. *Sensation as if uvula were elongated, causing constant hawking.*

Pressive sensation; in pharynx, < empty swallowing. Almost a burning pain from smoking. Soreness; without difficulty in swallowing. Feeling of beginning inflammation. Burning; on soft palate; in œsophagus; in fauces every morning; on soft palate in morning on waking; when smoking, and on lips; somewhat > cold water; like heartburn, and on palate. Sensation as if a piece of ice had slipped down. Peculiar coolness extending up œsophagus to mouth. Dryness; of posterior wall of pharynx; with much mucus on uvula; with painful tension on r. side on swallowing; < palate, with scraping, disturbing sleep; waking him, > cold water; of pharynx, causing cough; as if full of dust, < till evening, when it was accompanied by burning in arch of palate.

Tickling; on uvula extending over velum palati, < cold water, when there was irritation to cough; < uvula, soft palate and posterior wall of pharynx, in morning, preventing lying, causing violent paroxysms of dry cough, only after warm drinks the mucus was expectorated in large loose masses, then through the forenoon hawking and expectorating of loose mucus; in fauces as with a feather; T. irritation to vomit. Frequent swallowing, with sensation as if a ball were sticking in the throat. Inability to drink water. Swallowing difficult in evening, with swollen sensation in larynx and difficult speech. Sensation on swallowing liquids as if they were forced down by a spasm. *Aggravation of symptoms in warmth, especially in bed* (Iod., Merc.).

Clinical.—Coryza, inflammation of fauces, with accumulation of thick viscid mucus, which is expectorated with the greatest difficulty, even with retching and vomiting (Kali bi.).

Stomach.—Appetite at 6 P.M., an unusual time; even after eating. Ravenous; for supper; soon passing away. Great for dinner, which was eaten without relish and with speedy satiety, the food though light caused discomfort and pressure in stomach and eructations, stomach somewhat > by uprisings of food. Variable. Little at noon. Satiety soon after dinner; S. from water, with aversion to drinking. Lost, with increased thirst; at breakfast, but afterwards ravenous hunger; at noon. Aversion to food and drink. No relish for smoking.

Thirst; in evening; in evening, with longing for beer, after a glass of which there were headache and weakness so that he could not sleep until midnight; after eating, then chilliness from much cold water; < morning; < eating. Aversion to coffee and water.

Eructations; tasteless; loud, spasmodic, empty, in evening. Nausea; in morning; in morning on waking; from constant rising towards stomach; < after a violent paroxysm of cough, which brings tears to the eyes; > weak wine; with empty eructations; with cramp in stomach, and hunger; in paroxysms, with rabid hunger. Retching; in morning on waking, with nausea and salivation.

Distention; after rising, with retching rising to throat; flatulent, after eating; with pressure upward and choking as far as fauces; and sensation as if vomiting would relieve it. Sticking in afternoon on lying down, obliging sitting up; S. in fundus, then in cœcal region; in pit at every inspiration, > expiration; and griping. Intermittent griping extending to cœcal region. Pinching. Gnawing after drinking. Cramp. Pain; in epigastric region; in pit and l. hypochondrium; with sensation of a ball in it; in attacks, with beginning nausea. Pressure as from indigestion; P. as if overloaded, after a light dinner, extending to fauces, lasting till sleep; as after mineral water, with nausea, then heat of stomach, repeated for hours, then sensation as from drinking too much water, which lasted all the forenoon.

Heaviness; as if a stone were in it. Sensitiveness to pressure; in pit; to touch in epigastric region. Burning. Heartburn in afternoon, with tensive pain in throat; H. at night; two hours after eating; when walking after smoking; after wine, with pressure in stomach; with eructations of almost corrosive fluid. Sensation as if region of stomach and ilium were bathed in warm water. Sensation as if a cold air blew into it. Coldness and discomfort. Discomfort, < breakfast, with inflated feeling in abdomen. Emptiness. Weakness.

Abdomen.—Distention; in morning; after dinner; as if he had eaten too much; flatulent. Flatulence; after dinner; after dinner, with discomfort in whole body. Gurgling. Rumbling; after eating; preventing midday nap, > when walking about the room by short passages of flatus; < lying on l. side; with pain in loins. Noises and movements of flatus, > short passages of flatus. Emission of flatus; odorless. Sticking here and there, extending more towards hypochondriac region (apparently to bladder). Cutting. Pinching after dinner. Griping in morning on waking, then diarrhœa; G. in morning, then liquid stools repeated three times during the day; on waking, > stool; after eating; after dinner, then liquid stool; with pasty stool; with ineffectual urging to stool; with headache. Pain, then pasty stool, with shivering; P., as if many spots were ulcerating. Sensitiveness to pressure. Warmth.

Hypochondria.—Rumbling beneath r. short ribs. Sticking in region of spleen; in l. H., extending to l. side of chest in forenoon, when walking; periodically in spleen, gradually changing to fulness and benumbed aching in l. hypochondrium. *Pain in l. as from incarcerated flatus, extending to l. side of back and lumbar vertebræ. Burning drawing in region of spleen,* extending into l. side of chest, with jerking stitches; *burning, drawing in l.,* waking at night, > application of warm hand. Burrowing, tensive, dragging and drawing pain, and in pubic and inguinal regions. Dragging, and in pubic region, with discharge from vagina. Fulness in region of bladder.

Umbilicus.—Cutting, < motion. Griping in region; then soft stool. Digging about. Pain, and deep in cœcal region; in region, at times extending towards ilium.

Hypogastrium.—Audible movement towards genitals, then sticking from bladder along urethra to glans when sitting. Sticking in l. groin; in r. flank extending from border of false ribs to r. side of back, < pressure, > passage of flatus; drawing S. extending from l. flank along l. hip. Cutting, with passage of much odorless flatus. Griping above pelvic region as from incarcerated flatus, > emission. Sticking drawing and dragging pain in inguinal, hypochondriac and pubic regions. Dragging downward, as during menstruation, with frequent micturition. Sensitiveness of tuber ischii when sitting long or on pressure.

Rectum.—Sticking; with every stool; < walking, with exertion to stool; jerking and boring S., constantly jumping to neck of bladder and along ureters to kidneys. Burning pain after stool. Urging to stool, then hard fæces; U. as if to diarrhœa, then pasty stool, with much flatulence. Ineffectual urging; frequently, then three stools relieving the pain in lumbar and sacral regions.

Anus.—Much moisture in fissure between A. and nates. Sticking extending through urethra. Twinges after moderate exercise. Burning. Crawling. Itching.

Stool.—Diarrhœa. Soft and frequent; and copious; soft, mingled with hard lumps. Constipation, then after eating profuse pasty stool, with much flatulence. Hard; and scanty. Fæces enveloped in mucus, with straining, with burning and protrusion of hæmorrhoids. Delayed, difficult and clayey. Like kneaded clay, with straining, then spasmodic pain in rectum just at lower end of sacrum. Irregular. Copious, pasty; C. after walking. Omitted.

Urinary Organs.—Bladder. Cutting in region, with heat in face. Twisting pain in neck. Constant alternation of cramp, heat and coldness in region. Pain in region; waking him at night, with ineffectual urging to urinate. Pressure on; and constant urging, > after micturition. Heaviness, < in forepart, towards urethra, with constant urging to urinate and frequent discharge of normal color, acid in forenoon. Tension and fulness without leading to micturition, the tension remaining after micturition. Painful drawing in region of l. ureter.

Urging to urinate; in morning; but necessity to wait long before the urine passed, also waking twice at night. Frequent urging; suddenly; with urine as clear as water. Frequent ineffectual urging at night. Strangury in evening. Spurting micturition. Strong stream of pale urine. Frequent micturition; in afternoon; < at midnight and 4 P.M.; of copious urine; of saturated urine; of pale, odorless urine; of urine as clear as water, but it seems heavy and as thick as oil. Infrequent micturition. Waits long for the stream of urine. Retention of urine until there is great urging, when a little is passed slowly and painfully, sometimes sticking jerking on urinating extending into the sore pudenda.

Urethra.—Sticking in forepart of glans at 11 P.M.; in orifice, with tickling; in region of navicular fossa, with pain; in forepart, < in glans, with jerking. Pain on urinating as from obstruction. Burning pain on urinating, with sensation of a stone in urethra. Burning during micturition; B., > micturition, with at times prickling at its orifice, the latter during the day before much micturition. Tickling in forepart before micturition, as if dull needles were suddenly forced into it. Itching in orifice; in evening; in evening, with biting.

Urine.—Copious; and as clear as water, then in afternoon dark urine with sticking along urethra, < near glans. Scanty; at night, and red; and dark, very ammoniacal and concentrated. Dark, turbid, of putrid odor. At first straw-yellow, afterwards lemon-yellow, afterwards light brown, then reddish-brown and finally red. Acrid, burning. Thick and hot. Acid. Began to decompose in half an hour. Turbid. Contained mucus forming in part flakes, clouds and threads, mixed largely with the sediment. Brick-red sand after standing long; brick-red sediment easily mixing with the fluid on shaking the vessel.

Clinical.—Urinary calculi, with violent colic, hæmaturia, large deposit of uric acid and of urates, pains lancinating, extending from kidneys into bladder.

Sexual Organs.—Pustule in middle of penis. Throbbing in glans, with tickling in urethra. Heat in glans and l. testicle. Itching of glans; and of prepuce, with biting. Biting stitches in prepuce. Erections towards morning greater than usual, and emission; frequent erections. Itching of scrotum in morning on rising. Drawing sticking in r. testicle, extending into inguinal region. Desire; in morning, with erections; in morning, with lascivious actions, without erections; at night, and voluptuous dreams; on waking. Emission in morning; at 5 A.M.; at night, without dreams; at night, with diminished desire.

Pudenda swollen, < towards the front, and sensitiveness, with cramp, which contracts the orifice of the urethra so that the urine flows slowly over the sore parts, often with burning, with frequent painful thin discharge, which does not seem to be leucorrhœa, next day the swelling was hard and hot. Shooting in pudenda like electric shocks. Sudden burning in pudenda, with throbbing and sensitiveness. Swollen sensation in pudenda. Discharge of mucus from vagina preceded by drawing-dragging in inguinal and pubic regions and region of bladder. Menses too early, profuse, black and thick; too early and too long, with towards the close tension, then constriction in abdomen rising towards stomach, as if she would vomit water (which sensation usually occurred at the beginning).

Clinical.—Menorrhagia; discharge of large dark clots, with dysuria. Intermittent menstruation, flows only in evening or night when lying down.

Respiratory Organs.—*Mucus.* Catarrh of larynx and trachea. Sticking in larynx; with hoarseness. Scraping and irritation to cough; S. in larynx and trachea; *in larynx, causing paroxysms of cough and expectoration of balls of mucus. Rawness in trachea, obliging coughing.* Pain in larynx after speaking a short time, and rawness. Roughness during and after speaking. *Sensation as if crumb stuck behind larynx, obliging constant swallowing.* Choking. **Tickling in larynx, waking at 11.30 P.M., causing cough, with expectoration of much tenacious mucus** (Calc. acet.°); T., then hacking cough. Burning after cough; B. behind larynx as from a corrosive fluid. Irritation in larynx to cough in evening and disturbing sleep at night. *Fatigue of vocal organs, even after speaking, without exertion, with hoarseness and labored breathing* (Phos.). *Hoarseness;* in morning; in morning, with violent hawking of tenacious mucus; in morning, > rinsing mouth with tepid water or taking warm fluids, with paroxysms of cough and hawking of mucus; in afternoon; evening; at first, after not speaking for some time. Voice husky and deep on going into open air.

Cough; waking at 1 A.M., then sleeplessness, partly from the cough, partly from a burning soreness in lungs, partly from headache, then uneasy sleep from 6 to 7 A.M., the headache > waking; after dinner from the ordinary smoking; in hot room, preventing speaking; from irritation in bronchi and larynx, which made the soft palate so painful that swallowing was difficult; < 10 to 11 A.M.; < evening, with soreness and subsequent burning in chest; > evening and night. *Violent, from brushing teeth, then vomiting of slimy fluid.* Paroxysmal; in forenoon; frequent P. in warmth of bed, lasting from 2 to 2.30, leaving aching in throat as if fatigued, with heat and sore burning; short; frequent, as from tickling in larynx and pharynx. Painful, fatiguing, on waking, from irritation in larynx and trachea.

Dry cough; in morning; in morning, causing vomiting of mucus; waking at night; from the accustomed smoking; at night from tickling in air-passages, in morning looser, with easy expectoration; with pain, < apices of lungs; D. and violent in morning after waking; D., racking and painful; short and D.; short and D. in forenoon from irritation in trachea; D., rarely loosening yellow mucus of nauseating sweetish taste; at times D., at times expectoration of thick mucus. *Barking, clear, dry, waking at 6 A.M., afterwards with expectoration of mucus, the hawking of which provoked vomiting* (K. bi.), with sore throat and frontal headache, the cough and heat in throat > by rinsing mouth with cold water and drinking a few swallows, the heat in throat returned after a cup of warm milk, the cough returned on entering a hot room.

Cough, with expectoration; towards evening; at night; **of much viscid albuminous mucus** (K. bi.); *tenacious E. at 6 A.M., through the day and at 3 P.M. (an hour after eating), > vomiting;* E. of lumpy mucus; mucous E.; easy, slimy E., mingled with tenacious threads; yellow E.; difficult E. of greenish-yellow sweet mucus. *Paroxysmal cough before going to bed, with easy expectoration of globules of mucus;* P. cough, with expectoration of greenish lumps (K. iod.); P. cough, with expectoration of round masses of grayish mucus; P. cough, with grayish, gelatinous, lumpy mucus; *paroxysm of tickling cough, ending with expectoration of mucus.* Cough, with tickling about bifurcation of bronchi, caused by a feeling as if a plug of mucus were moving in chest, in spite of profuse expectoration.

of mucus. Fatiguing cough, then expectoration of mucus.

Expectoration alternating with dry hacking. Expectoration of mucus; easy; lumpy; yellow, sour; yellow, lumpy after slight hawking; greenish-yellow, and sweat; of white lumps of the size of peas from larynx, with dry sensation in mouth, extending into fauces; of whitish-gray masses; tough and sweet, next day lumpy and grayish-blue and looser; yellow, with a tinge of red, tasting sourish-sweet; thick; thick and nauseous.

Breathing difficult; in afternoon, < towards evening by periodical sticking in l. upper chest; when walking. Dyspnœa, with oppression of lower part of chest. Short and oppressed breathing after rising. Inspiration deep when walking, > by yawning.

Clinical.—Laryngitis with most violent cough, difficult expectoration of very tenacious mucus. Suffocative catarrh of the bronchi, with tough white mucus which strangles, cough < first waking. Whooping cough, with vomiting of ropy albuminous mucus, < morning, the attacks ending with vomiting of this ropy mucus.

Chest.—Sticking in upper part; in lower part; in r., along sternum; near l. nipple; in region of bend of fifth and sixth ribs; between sixth and seventh ribs, l. then r.; now l., now r.; lungs feel as if affected by S. behind sternum; in lower part of r. lung in morning after rising, < deep inspiration; in l. lower chest in forenoon when walking in the street, and in the evening; r. lower lung at 4 P.M. on deep inspiration; in a spot in middle of first l. false rib in the street, > when quiet in the room; in walls on uncovering abdomen, < epigastric region; in greatest curvature of last l. true ribs, also when sewing, < walking and ascending steps but not by deep breathing, > rest; in a spot in l., < walking, not by breathing; in l., < rapid walking; in region of l. nipple, > paying attention to it; between l. fifth and seventh ribs, > deep inspiration, returning on expiration; in a spot in ribs and præcordial region, with pain in the spot as if suppurating; in l. extending forward towards sternum, with pain on chest; deeply piercing, near l. clavicle, then ulcerative pains, similar to commencing tuberculosis; biting, on margin of l. false ribs between stomach and flank (deeply-seated).

Pinching in middle. Pain; in lungs on sneezing. Bruised pain in region of l. clavicle in morning on waking; in region of l. clavicle on moving head or l. arm or lying on l. shoulder, with sprained pain; in region of l. clavicle, < moving arm and changing when lying to sprained pain in l. shoulder. Drawing pain in region of l. clavicle, < lying upon l. shoulder. Tensive pain in region of clavicle; l., < day and moving l. arm; in l. upper chest. Pressure in evening, then ulcerative pain in præcordial region; P. beneath sternum, < towards stomach, with burning; P. upon chest, with hoarseness; with weakness and bruised sensation; in middle of sternum extending to scapulæ; painful, in middle of sternum in forenoon when walking, extending backward, with a similar pain between scapulæ extending forward. Suffocative sensation, as if too narrow, < drinking beer. Oppression; in forenoon when speaking; on ascending a hill, with soreness of apices of lungs, a feeling as if he had run too violently; > warm breakfast; paroxysmal, with external soreness.

Soreness beneath sternum, with pressure; S. in apices of lungs when walking in warm weather, with chilliness; after the heat, with pressure and tension and with throbbing, < in apices of lungs; beneath clavicles, with much affection of air-passages; in apex of l. lung, with at times pulsation that constantly alternated with contraction of lower lip (like a cramp in skin); in lungs, becoming at times sticking or boring and sometimes seated in pleura and pericardium, at another time deep in lungs and heart, with stronger beats of heart; becoming burning, frequently changing its seat, but affecting most the heart and apices of lungs, with irritation to breathe deeply and to cough. Sensitiveness about l. nipple.

Pulsations in lungs; now in heart, now in middle of chest, now in apices of lungs, consisting of several beats in rapid succession, then after five to ten minutes appearing in another place. Heat beneath sternum; in lungs when walking; < præcordial region and r. lower chest; deep, < præcordial region; between fifth and seventh ribs, l. then r., with sticking; in lungs, with feeling as if the expired air were warmer than usual. Increased vigor of organs.

Heart.—Sticking through it in morning, with throbbing, which seemed to be audible but was not perceptible to hand. Burrowing on rising and when driving, > leaving the carriage. Soreness from morning till noon. Pressure in præcordial region. Pain in præcordial region at night, with palpitation; indefinite P. at heart interrupted by beating of the pulse; throbbing, towards evening, with at times pulsations on its upper surface. Sensation when walking as if an artery were pulsating rapidly on its upper surface. Sensation as if something were forced towards it. *Rapid, irregular beating after dinner, causing anxiety.* Tumultuous action when lying after dinner. Palpitation waking at night; sudden P. as from a fright, waking at midnight, and shaking of whole body, recurring with constantly decreasing severity; causing anxiety.

Pulse.—Rapid; and tremulous.

Neck.—Sticking in nape; in l. cervical muscles on turning head. Pain between second and third vertebræ. Tension in l. muscles in morning on waking, > rising.

Back.—Pain; with sensation as if several places were hard. Drawing. Sticking in scapulæ; between S. extending in rays; in region of l. scapula, extending into l. elbow, < moving arm, with sticking in l. side. Tearing from r. scapula across outer surface of r. upper arm. Pressure between S., after a while extending to small of back and becoming seated in region of kidneys.

Lumbar Region.—Sticking ending in cœcal region; from kidney along ureters to bladder; digging, in r., in region of kidney, in evening in bed, then sticking making him jump. Dragging pain; in sacral region, extending downward and forward towards bladder. Twisting pain in l. side of spine, whether in kidneys or uterus (?). Pain; in sacrum; in region of kidneys; region of r. kidney; in afternoon; in evening and < night; in kidneys in evening; when eating; in kidneys, < r., < pressure or motion of upper part of body, > towards evening, next day alternating with drawing pain from kidneys to bladder, > frequent emission of flatus. Bruised pain in l.; and in sacral and hip regions; in l. sacro-iliac region in morning on waking. Oppressive pain in region of kidneys. Drawing pain; in r. kidney, extending along ureter to bladder, waking at 5 A.M.; spasmodic, in region of kidneys, streaming out from both sides, in afternoon when sitting, to be compared to the cramplike pain after an injury to the testicles, > emission of flatus. Drawing, with dragging, and in joints and hips. Tension in muscles; T. extending towards rectum, with drawing. Soreness in region of kidneys, gradually extending to bladder, < into sphincter, with frequent urging to urinate and increased dark urine. Sensitiveness of tuber ischii on long sitting and on pressure.

Extremities.—Sticking now beneath nail of l. great toe, now in tips of fingers and beneath nails of thumbs and of r. index. Tearing; here and there in long bones; in knees and elbow; along anterior inner surface of r. thigh, then in outer side of r. upper arm, then painful drawing in metacarpal bone of r. thumb and sticking in r. inner malleolus. Tensive pain, now in l. shoulder, now in l. fingers and in r. hip, > evening. Weakness; in morning after rising. Paralytic sensation in legs and l. shoulder, waking at night.

Upper Extremities.—Shoulder. Tearing, and in small of back, extending in evening to forearm. Pain at night, > lying on it and pressing firmly against the bed. Drawing in r. extending to forearm and index, with tearing; D. in l., gradually changing to heaviness and in evening changing to painful paralysis, as from taking cold in a draught when heated. Tension in r., with drawing and tearing. Heaviness like a pressure on r., extending down back to region of kidneys; tensive H., and in lower part of nape.

Sticking in middle of r. upper arm at night. Sticking tearing in fleshy part of l. upper arm, in anterior and inner surface; drawing tearing in anterior surface of muscles of r. upper arm during rest. Drawing in r. deltoid, making motion of upper arm difficult, < raising it. Sticking in tip of l. elbow; in muscles of bend of r. elbow during rest; as from a leech in bend of l. elbow. Scraping in elbows. Pain near l. elbow. Burning drawing in condyles and joint of l. elbow, waking at night.

Tearing in tendinous expansion of forearms. Drawing pain in muscles of r. forearm. Paralytic pain in r. wrist. Biting sticking on back of r. hand. Tearing in r. little finger, < motion. Sudden drawing in l. thumb. Swelling of l. thumb, with pain when moved or pressed.

Lower Extremities.—Bruised pain, < calves. Weariness; < calves. Tearing sticking in anterior inner muscles of thigh; in l. sciatic nerve, extending from gluteal muscle to outer and posterior side during rest; throbbing sticking in thighs in forenoon. Bruised pain behind r. trochanter, > walking. Aching in thighs as after a long walk. Drawing pain on upper and outer side of l. thigh during rest. Drawing down thighs and calves, with weariness in calves; sudden D. anteriorly above r. knee.

Knee.—Sticking in r. patella; in evening, as from an electric spark; in margin of l., as from an electric spark; deeply piercing S. in hollow of knee, extending along l. tendo-achillis and in back of r. foot; in knee, with tearing. Sudden sticking tensive pain in bend of r. in afternoon when walking, < stretching foot. Pain in side of l. patella; in r. patella, < on its inner margin, < motion and pressure, so that in the evening walking was impossible, in the night knees and toes were swollen and hot to touch, the pain was pressive and prevented motion.

Leg.—Sticking near r. ankle after eating; throbbing S. in legs; tearing, along muscles of r. calf. Sticking tearing on inner side of r. tibia. Scraping in tibiæ. Pain; in r.; along large vessels and nerves; in lower half of l. tibia in forenoon when sitting, extending upward and downward; in tendo-achillis on walking, < in street, obliged to turn the foot outward and stop, < next day, < ascending steps, the tendon sensitive to pressure, afterwards cracking in tendon on moving foot up and down and inability to stretch foot completely. Burning pain in r. Drawing pain in l. tendo-achillis when stretching foot while walking. Spasmodic drawing in r. calf. Sore sensation on r. tibia. Weakness in evening and night.

Sticking in l. inner malleolus. Bruised pain in malleoli on bending foot, and on inner surface of heel. Sticking in l. sole near toes. Pain in forepart of l. foot on walking, it seemed as if the mobility of the joints were impeded by swelling of articular surfaces. Pain in soles, mostly burning, < forepart, even after a moderate walk, becoming after sitting a hot sensation. Weariness of feet in evening after a short walk; of feet, < sitting quietly in the house, > going out.

Toes.—Cramp of r.; three last r. on lying down at night. Sticking on lower surface of l. great and in its tip; beneath nail of l. great, at 4 A.M. Tearing in l. great. Pain in l. great, < evening, so that he could not step upon that foot, then chilliness, which lasted after going to bed; in great, with swelling and redness, preventing walking, almost like gouty inflammation; in a corn on r. little, so that he limped. Sudden drawing in r. great.

Skin.—Redness of face and hands, with distention and throbbing of vessels; red spots here and there, and itching pimples. Pimples on r. side of forehead; on tip of nose and to right of sternum; on malleoli; on back, with discharge on pressure. Boils on l. wing of nose.

Biting sticking on r. pectoral muscles and r. groin; in various places, scalp, concha, r. side of neck and throat, on margin of rami of jaws, near nipples, in back, pit of stomach, axillæ, inguinal regions, all > by leaving the warm bed. Pricking on anterior surface of thigh when walking, sensation as if warmth were streaming through skin; P. on internal surface of thigh, as on taking sparks from an electrical machine, alternating with heat in chest, with palpitation. Biting in various places before sleep; above malleoli, extending in afternoon to knee, then returning to other places. Sticking biting on various parts; in region of r. clavicle; in spots on abdominal walls, with sensation as if leeches were drawing at these spots, afterwards similar sensation at r. nipple and on prepuce. Itching biting now in r., now l. antitragus. Itching biting-drawing in inguinal and pubic region, on prepuce and penis, back, feet and toes; on and between toes. Itching; l. upper arm; extensor surface of limbs, abdomen and back; lower limbs; legs; fold beneath l. great toe; r. leg, with burning; legs and l. fingers, in afternoon.

Sleep.—Inclination to yawn and stretch, with tensive pain in small of back. Sleepiness; in morning after a good night's sleep; in afternoon; evening; after eating, then general prostration. Sleeplessness; from internal heat; for an hour and a half after midnight; with restlessness; sleep only after midnight, restless and light, waking at slightest noise and palpitation as from fright. Restless sleep on account of previous vexations; disturbed by pains; interrupted by cough, throbbing headache and throbbing of heart; with sexual desire without complete erections. Disturbed by noises in abdomen, < lying on r. side. Groaning in sleep. Frequent waking; with excitement as from coffee. Early waking; with inclination to yawn and stretch.

Dreams.—Many; of many people and full of care. Of many men, large palaces, churches and frolicking with girls. Vivid; and fretful; of syphilitic formations. Unremembered. Affectionate, with reminiscences of his youthful loves.

Fever.—Chill; all day; when lying at 10 A.M., then headache and cough from rawness in air-passages; in afternoon; in afternoon, with thirst; in evening; in evening, with dull throbbing in heart and soreness in chest; > open air. Creeping over whole body. Shivering; between 3 and 5 P.M.; 9 P.M., with rapid pulse; after dinner; on going to bed, < back, with thirst, then dry heat of head and redness of face, with chilliness of rest of body, then the dry heat became general and lasted till midnight, then sweat on upper part of body till 5 A.M.; before sleep, with heat in head, then general dry heat, > sweat; in attacks; across scapula extending down arm, after dinner, > moving in open air, with sensation as if the skin would be loosened from the flesh. Coldness of occiput as if in a draught; C. of limbs; of back; creeping along spine; frequently in skin on r. shoulder and across r. side of back; of feet in morning, with sweat on upper part of body.

Heat; towards evening; in evening in bed; in evening in bed, as if there were a tumult in the whole body; on entering room, with confusion of head, which increased till evening to a moderate headache, > open air; at night, then sweat. Dry, at 3 A.M., with uneasiness. Hot and dry skin, the heat > in morning by cold water. Heat on vertex; in l. ear, with ringing; in cheeks in morning on waking; in cheeks at 5 P.M.; prickling, in cheeks in evening without redness; in chest, abdomen and thighs, with prickling in thighs on walking. Burning in legs; in r., with itching; in soles.

Sweat; in morning; on rapid walking, with weakness; at night on back, sacrum and coccyx; on r. leg; in morning on legs and feet.

Codeinum.

Pure Codeia (one of the alkaloids of Opium) is prepared for use by trituration.

General Action.—This alkaloid, similar in a general way to Morphia, seems to possess convulsant properties in a higher degree than the other alkaloids of Opium.

Generalities.—*Trembling of whole body.* Convulsive motions; of different parts; of muscles of chest, neck, arms and legs, then (in one case) soreness of the parts and weakness. Inflammation if placed in contact with the cellular tissues. Circulation and respiration rapid, then depressed. Prickling in various parts, with numbness. Restlessness. Constant inclination to sit and close eyes. Weakness. Nervous sensibility increased, then depressed. Heaviness. Sensation and power of motion impaired. Paralysis, < lower limbs; state of mixed P. and spasm, both tonic and clonic.

Mind.—Delirious at night. Bewildered. Excited as after spirituous drinks. Gay. Exhilarated. Depressed spirits and headache; D., with sleepiness, frightful dreams, and on waking in morning dull headache. Tranquil. Listless. Increased capacity. Stupor; in afternoon and evening, with disinclination for exertion. Sluggish association of ideas. Inability to concentrate mind; or to remain quiet in the house.

Head.—*Aching in morning after rising, < l. side; in morning, > noon;* with dry lips. Confusion; and heat. Strong pulsations, and in carotids. Vertigo; in afternoon; on blowing nose; on blowing nose, with sparks before eyes wherever he looks; as if the room went round with him; objects appear to turn around on closing eyes. Pressure in temporal and frontal regions. Pulsating pain in r. temple in afternoon. Neuralgic pain in occiput extending to nape. Itching of head extending over whole body.

Eyes and Ears.—Eyes injected; sclerotic injected. Eyes glassy and immovable. Burning in eyes, < l. Pupils dilated; contracted. Vision weak; did not see the letters distinctly on beginning to write; failed suddenly. V. of floating sparks on stooping. Stoppage of ears. Ringing in ears.

Clinical.—Twitching of eyelids (Agar., Croc.).

Nose and Face.—Nasal discharge, with irritation of Schneiderian membrane. Loss of smell. Face animated, rosy and gay, or dull and stupid. Terrified look. Pallor. Lips dry.

Mouth and Throat.—Dryness of anterior part of tongue and hard palate; of mouth, with thirst for beer. Inability to speak. Salivation. Tickling in throat in afternoon and evening.

Stomach.—Loss of appetite. Thirst; with desire for bitter substances. Eructations. *Nausea.* Violent retching on attempting to move. Vomiting. *Pain;* paroxysms of neuralgic, and in abdomen; acute, and in chest, extending through to back, between shoulders, < r. side of spine. Tenderness, with violent pulsations of heart and arteries.

Abdomen and Stool.—A. distended with flatus. Peristaltic action diminished. Pain in transverse colon, > gentle pressure; P. in A., with pulsations and rapid circulation and respiration. Tenderness of A. in morning extending to epigastrium and lungs; of hypogastrium in morning. Uncommon sense of tonicity in A. Purging. Constipation, tenderness of bowels, < transverse and descending colon, and flatulence.

Urinary and Sexual Organs.—Diminished power of retention of urine and semi-paralysis of neck of bladder. Urine increased and light-colored, then scanty. Lascivious thoughts, causing frequent erections, day and night; excitement at night, with pollutions. Sexual power increased, then diminished.

Clinical.—Diabetes.

Respiratory Organs and Chest.—Tickling in larynx causing cough. Voice reduced to a whisper. Cough in morning, with soreness and sticking; *short and irritating C., < night; C., with copious mucous and sometimes purulent expectoration.* Sticking in l. lung on breathing. Sharp pain in r. lung on inspiration. Pain in chest and shoulder on motion. Sore feeling in sternal region. Fulness and oppression of chest. Drooping sensation below l. clavicle.

Clinical.—Dry, teasing cough, with phthisis.

Heart and Pulse.—Drawing pain around H., with loud and full beats of it, causing uneasiness. Uneasiness about H. Painful pulsations of H. on attempting to study or write. Fluttering of H. and oppression in its region, with great desire to walk in the open air. Pulse rapid; and full and strong; slow; small; small and weak; scarcely perceptible at wrist.

Neck and Back.—Convulsions of muscles of neck; of nape. Painful twitchings of muscles of neck. Painful pulsations in l. side of neck. Sharp pain below l. scapula on inspiration. Drawing pain below scapula on inspiration. Acute pain in kidney region. Heaviness and fatigue of lumbar muscles.

Extremities.—Paralytic weakness of arms and legs. Numbness of hands and feet; of hands and arms. *Twitching of arms.* Pain in deltoids; r.; l. in morning on dressing, > rest. Pulsating pain in l. upper arm. Feeling in upper arm as after a blow. Jerking pain in arm on attempting to remove the handkerchief from breast pocket. Twitching of lower. Weakness of lower. Paralytic sensations of lower. Knees give way when walking. Sudden pain in l. knee preventing walking and ceasing suddenly. Sprained pain in morning; S. feeling compelling him to stop abruptly when walking. Painful pulsations in soles, < resting them against a hard object.

Skin.—Eczema. Soreness after neuralgia. Sensitiveness to touch. Sensation as if a fly were crawling on chest, not > rubbing or scratching. Itching; over whole body; on face and head, gradually extending over body, with heat.

Sleep.—Sleepiness; with heaviness and gaping; with inability to sleep. Sleeplessness. Frequent waking, with the covers thrown off. Sleep unrefreshing. Dreams; unpleasant, of dead persons, etc.; pleasant; ridiculous.

Fever.—Cold skin; and moist; and clammy. Cold limbs. Agreeable warmth. General warmth, with itching, < between shoulders. Heat in head. Sweat in large beads on forehead.

Coffea Cruda.

A tincture is prepared (in a special manner) from the unroasted beans of Coffea Arabica, L.

General Action.—A general stimulant of cerebral activity.

Allies.—Opium, Nux v., Hyosc., Plat., Zinc.

Generalities.—Excitement, with lightness of all movements. Lightness of head and of all movements, increased sense of health and vigor. Pain in whole body so that he had little rest. Affected by walking in open air, it forces water from his eyes and he becomes weary. Aversion to open air. Disinclination for business (Nux v.). Inclination to lie down and close the eyes without ability or desire to sleep. *Mental and physical exhaustion* (Op.). Weariness on ascending steps. Dulness of internal sensibility on account of supernatural speculations. Aggravation when walking in open air.

Clinical.—Neuralgias of various parts of the body, face, abdomen, extremities, etc., always with great nervous excitability, intolerance of pain. Bad effects of stimulants, alcohol, tea, etc.

Mind.—Irrational talking during the heat, with open eyes, wishing this or that brought to her. Lively; in evening; *lively fancies, full of plans for the future,* charmed with the beauties of nature of which he reads. Ill humor; > open air, with sadness and crying aloud; and disinclination to speak; he could throw everything away from him; full of care, lachrymose mood. Sad on walking in open air, lachrymose, disinclined to all business. Anxiety and unsteadiness; A., with trembling and inability to hold the pen still. Vivid flow of ideas. **Unusual activity of mind and body till midnight** (Op. in part), then sleep. Disappearance of thoughts for a moment. Inattention and loss of memory. Inability to think clearly. Does not know what he is reading or has read, without being conscious of foreign thoughts, when he does not read he is beset by a thousand thoughts and remembers the most remote events.

Clinical.—Delirium tremens, with trembling of hands, fears, thinks that he is not at home, restlessness, etc. Extreme activity of mind, the patient is sleepless, great flow of thought, with great acuteness of all senses. Mental excitability resulting from pleasurable emotions. Recurring attacks of weeping, with hysterical excitability, tremulousness, etc.

Head.—Feeling as if the brain were torn or crushed when walking in open air, > in room. *Aching, < eating, > open air, soon returning in the room;* A. as if brain were too full and crushed, after midday nap, < occiput; drawing, caused by reflection, with pressure in upper part of forehead. Tension in brain in morning on waking, he avoided opening eyes, it seems on stooping as if the brain fell forward and pressed against temples and forehead. Confusion; *dizzy.* Heaviness, with heat in face; H. and dizziness, with general anxiety, she believes she will fall. Rush of blood, < talking; rush of blood, with anxious heat and redness of face. Vertigo on stooping, with blackness before eyes.

On reading, brain feels torn and crushed at frontal eminence, then behind frontal bone. Compressive pain in forehead in evening. Confusion in forehead, < walking in open air, changing in r. temple into sticking-drawing pain. Pain in temples when walking in cold air, extending to occiput, > sitting in the house, again first <, then > going into open air. Pain in upper part of vertex. Crackling heard and felt in vertex when sitting still. Crackling in region of ear, rhythmical with pulse. *Pain as if a nail were driven into one of the parietal bones* (Ign. nearly). Rheumatic drawing in l. side of occiput. Itching of scalp.

Clinical.—Extremely violent neuralgic headaches, it seems as if the brain were being torn to pieces, the patient is unable to bear the pain; it seems as if a nail were being driven into the head, etc.

Eyes and Ears.—Boring in r. eye, with dim vision. Hardened mucus in canthi in forenoon. *In the open air he sees more clearly than before.* Music sounds too loud and shrill, he can bear only the lowest tones of the instrument.

Nose and Face.—Pain in anterior angle of l. nostril; almost burning sore P. in l. nostril. Warmth in l. nostril like a coryza, < hawking. Sneezing; in evening in bed and on waking. Stoppage of nose. Stopped coryza, with scanty discharge. Fluent coryza evenings, with sneezing. Frequent, sudden, watery discharge from nose. Nosebleed; in morning on rising and at 6 P.M., with heaviness of head and ill humor. Cheeks red and hot (in an infant), with uneasy sleep. Drawing in l. malar-bone, alternating with tearing in a tooth.

Mouth.—Sticking jerking from above downward into nerves of roots of teeth. Pain in a back tooth when biting on it; in front teeth on touch and on chewing, as if loose. Drawing in a hollow l. upper back tooth as after taking cold; (D. pain across l. upper back teeth, > biting jaws together). Tongue dry in forepart and burning, without thirst. Mouth dry in morning in bed, without thirst. Pain at margin of arches of palate, < by swallowing. Salivation. Taste bitter; in morning; in mouth all day, but food does not taste bitter; to water; excessively B. to bitter things. T. as after hazel-nuts. T. as after sweet almonds. T. especially pleasant to tobacco. Good, but too strong T. to food and tobacco, so that he cannot eat much or smoke much.

Clinical.—Neuralgic toothache with intolerance of the pain, > only by holding ice-water in the mouth (Pul.).

Throat.—Soreness, swelling of arches of palate, which seems like an accumulation of tough mucus. Sensation of catarrh in back part in morning after rising, flow of mucus from nose without sensation of catarrh in nose or frontal sinuses. Heat rises into throat.

Stomach.—*Great hunger before dinner and hasty eating. Appetite diminished,* the supper tasted good, but he was not hungry. Aversion to food, drink and tobacco, with nausea and salt taste in mouth, although food has no unusual taste. Aversion to coffee. Thirst, without dryness of tongue or heat; T. at night, frequent waking to drink. Short eructations of air; E. tasting of food from noon till evening. *Hiccough.* Nausea; in morning; at 5 P.M., with weakness; from 8 to 9 P.M., like a faintness and vertigo, with necessity to sit and lie down, weariness of limbs and chilliness; while eating palatable food; in upper part of throat. Vomiting. Easy contraction of gastric and abdominal muscles. Sticking in pit, with pressure, then painless distention of pit. Pressure in pit, she was obliged to loosen the clothes; P. in epigastric region when eating bread after a moderate meal, and afterwards. Tension, and in hypochondria. Unpleasant sensation beneath stomach, then distention and pain.

Abdomen.—Fulness after supper, with griping; F. after walking in open air. Fermentation and passage of much flatus; fermentation, then repeated vomiting, then waterbrash. Movings, as if necessitating a stool. Frequent and easy passage of flatus, then difficult, scanty, short, interrupted emission of flatus and constant urging to pass it; frequent, profuse, almost odorless F. Pain and diarrhœa; P. as if it would burst; P. as from incarcerated flatus; (cramplike pain, and in abdomen, with outward manifestation of labor pains, complaints as if intestines would be cut to pieces, with convulsions, body bent up, feet drawn up towards her head, frightful cries, grinding of teeth, became cold and stiff, piteous cries, holding her breath). Sticking extending out at ring, as in inguinal hernia; jerking S. in sides with every expiration. Painful pressure in sides in morning, temporarily > emission of flatus, extending into rings, as if a hernia would protrude.

Stool.—Urging to stool, stool soft, but difficult. Two, the first consistent, the second liquid. Frequent, hard.

Urinary Organs.—Pressure upon bladder, obliging him to urinate. Frequent urging in morning, but micturition scanty and in drops. Frequent micturition. Burning tearing in forepart of urethra. Urine copious; about midnight, with relaxation of genitals. Urine scanty. Urine blood-red.

Sexual Organs.—Relaxed, and desire diminished. Erections and emissions. Itching in forepart of penis; voluptuous I. on tip of penis in morning; I. on r. side of scrotum. Sore pain on scrotum on slightest rubbing of clothes. Relaxation of scrotum, with excitement of inner genitals, yet with cold fantasies. Digging-smarting in one testicle. Nightly emissions. Desire, then general dry heat without emission. Impotency and sluggish desire.

Clinical.—Uterine hæmorrhage, extreme sensitiveness of genitals, flow dark, clotted (Plat.). Useful in after-pains, which are extremely difficult to tolerate.

Respiratory Organs.—*Roughness in larynx in morning on waking, with hoarseness* (Nux v.). Irritation to cough about midnight. He must restrain the cough, eyes obscured, faint and feeling as if he were whirling around. Cough in evening in bed and on waking; short, frequent, scraping C. Dry cough (in a child) in evening after falling asleep. Hacking cough frequently, as from irritation of throat; H. cough in sudden paroxysms, as from spasmodic constriction in larynx, which seemed covered with dry mucus.

Clinical.—Nervous cough, with anxiety, sleeplessness.

Chest.—Pain in side on coughing, almost like sticking. Oppression; (after disappearance of heat of face), with necessity to take short breaths, the chest raised visibly by respiration. Warmth, and in abdomen.

Heart.—**Clinical.**—Palpitation caused by excitement, surprise, etc.

Back.—Trembling, with warmth in back and between shoulders. Pain in small of; when walking; paralytic, in small of, when sitting and standing.

Extremities.—Lightness. Sticking-jerking through one or another. Bruised pain in all joints in morning in bed, > rising, < those that had been bent. Weakness after 4 P.M., the knees knock together, warmth internally and externally, with chilliness. Tearing in l. arm, < motion. Spasmodic drawing up arms after holding them bent, almost twitches. Weakness of arms and of whole body. Rheumatic bruised pain in l. upper arm. *Trembling of hands if he tries to hold anything* (Zinc.). Cramplike contraction of one or another finger, in the morning he cannot straighten the little finger. Drawing in soft parts of fingers or tearing downward. Pain in a burnt finger that had been painless before the drug was taken. Numbness of fingers.

Lower Extremities.—Bruised pain in nates, from ischium to thigh, when sitting and walking, obliging him to limp. Sore feeling on inner side of thigh from slightest rubbing of woolen clothes. Knees tremble when descending steps. Cramp of calf on drawing up knee. Jerking on r. tibia, with corroding and smarting and with bruised sensation and heat of femur. Pain in legs after every walk, obliging her to lie down. Drawing pain beneath r. knee. Jerking-sticking beneath r. inner malleolus on stepping upon heel or bending foot backward or touching part. Feet tremble. Cramp of sole on putting out the foot.

Weariness of feet after walking in open air, extending half way up thighs. Sticking in balls of great toes at 4 P.M.

Skin.—Eruption and itching over the whole body. *The itching of the eruption changed into burning.*

Sleep.—Yawning. *Weary with sleep.* Overpowered with sleep, he dreaded apoplexy. Sound sleep. **Sleepless on account of mental and physical excitement** (Hyosc.). *Sleep till* 3 A.M., *then only dozing and on waking he did not come to his senses* (Nux v.). Sleepless from 2 to 7 A.M., with colic-like incarceration of flatus under ribs, which causes anxiety and heat over whole body and sweat under nose. Little sleep. Uneasy; so that he was lying turned about in bed. Talking immediately on falling asleep. Waking with a start. Frequent waking towards morning; frequent W. as from fright. *Dreams long, vivid.* Light D. His fancy is occupied with one thought when slumbering, from which he cannot free himself and which prevents sound sleep.

Clinical.—A most valuable remedy for sleeplessness with nervous excitability, extreme sensitiveness to external impressions and flow of ideas, the patient cannot sleep on account of mental activity.

Fever.—Chilliness; in bed at 5 A.M. and at 1 P.M.; < motion; < moving body, with warm skin, and on rising from the chair creeping chill with pale face; over whole body, cold creepings down back, then redness and heat of face, with cold hands, which are hot on inner surface while externally they are cold; then heat. Sensitiveness to cold. Open air seemed very cutting. Shivering, with redness and heat of one cheek; internal S., even in chest, with chilliness and with heat in head and sweat in face, without thirst. Chill, with heat, on both cheeks. C. in back, with shivering, but usual warmth of rest of body; C. in back with sensation of heat, especially warmth in middle of back and across lower abdomen, as if sweat would break out. Cold hands, then C. feet; C. feet after 4 P.M., with headache and rush of blood to head, > in open air.

Heat in morning in bed, but dislike to being uncovered; general H. at 3 P.M., with redness of face and thirst, then general sweat, thirst during the first hours of the sweat; general, at 8 P.M., externally perceptible, with dryness of mouth, shivering in back and down posterior part of body, then hands and feet cold, then in bed at one time heat, then coldness till after midnight, in morning headache as if beaten, so that every step is painful; H. in evening after lying down, everything seems too close, and at night sweat, < back; H. with red face. General dry heat waking at night and obliging her to turn around, with hot breath, but without thirst or dryness of mouth. H. in face, with red cheeks; *after eating;* dry H. of face. Hot feet.

Sweat towards morning; S. of hands when writing; of feet, with soreness of toes.

Coffea Tosta.

The effects of a hot infusion of roasted coffee having been observed, a *fluid extract* should be used as the basis of the pharmaceutical preparations.

Generalities.—Increase of solid constituents of blood; of fat in serum and of fibrin in blood. Hæmorrhages from nose, lungs, uterus and rectum. She walks uneasily up and down the room, with an anxious expression. Trembling; and muscular shiverings. Jerking (secondary effect). Reflex contractions in nearly every part alternately. Painful cramps in thighs, legs, feet, walls of chest and muscles of hyoid region at night. Restless. Feels strong enough to do anything. *Weak.* Peculiar sensation, somewhat like faintness. *Aversion to open air, which aggravates symptoms* (secondary effect). Left side generally affected. Amelioration from moderate outdoor exercise.

Mind.—Delirium tremens; (after a rheumatic attack, with great weakness). Excitement; agreeable, with sweat; agreeable, causing wakefulness. Loquacity. *Fear. Timidity and fear of sudden death,* causing trembling. Anxiety. Love for family. Veneration for Supreme Being. Desire to perform good deeds intensified.

Imagination and memory stimulated. Power of judgment increased. Attention more alive. Impelled to push things, wants to keep going ahead and doing something. Brain clear and very active. Creative activity, vivacity of thought, versatility and ardor of desire, more favorable to the exaggerated expression of ideas previously formed than to the quiet examination of new conceptions. Mental energy taken away by sudden symptoms. Sensorium not clear, and next day obscure recollection of what had occurred, plain or connected answers were not obtainable, it was difficult to engage her attention, she repeated incessantly the same phrases in the most dolorous tone. Somewhat unconscious.

Head.—Aching; < noon and evening; twice a week, usually lasting two days, commencing with neck beginning to grow stiff *always on l. side,* spreading over l. side of head and down over outside of humerus, across biceps, diagonally to elbow, > quiet, rubbing with ice or cold compresses and transiently by lying down, < jar in moving, with tight feeling in head and pressure outward in *occiput behind l. ear,* throbbing up and down in l. occipital region, when headache is severe l. side of breast is red and mottled in fine points, white and red, skin on l. side red-hot, moist and swollen, irritable mood, intolerance of noise, must have perfect rest, after the headache weak feeling in head and inability for mental labor. Rush of blood. Vertigo; < thinking, partially > change of position, with burning in stomach and faint feeling (secondary effects). Sensation as if everything in head were going in slow circles, now in one direction, now in another, with noises in ears.

Neuralgia in supraorbital nerve, extending through eye into malar-bone, first r., then extending to l., < r., > mental distraction and by sleep, pain at first dull, becoming sharp. Heaviness over eyes (secondary effect). Sensation as if a piece of lead were nailed to parietal bones, < motion of head. Stinging in locality of amativeness on l. side. Numbness in occiput, with aching and throbbing.

Eyes.—Surrounded by blue rings. Conjunctiva of lids slightly red, < towards margin, and C. of bulb slightly red in canthi and corners. Pupils enlarged; but sensitive. Sensation of a fog. Intolerance of candle-light, it seems surrounded by a dim broad halo, causing pressure in brows. Muscæ volitantes. Aggravation of myopia.

Ears.—Every step and every loud word is painfully felt in ears. Ringing. Sounds of pounding or ringing in the distance. Roaring, buzzing and singing. Incessant noises.

Face.—*Pale; and anxious; waxy.* Puffy, as if dropsical, waxy, pale yellow. Flushed. Lips and tongue pale and dry.

Mouth and Throat.—*Pain in r. lower teeth (sound), driving him nearly crazy, > cold water in mouth, returning as soon as the water became warm.* Tongue dry. Spasmodic contraction of throat.

Stomach.—Loss of appetite. Aversion to food, she can take only small quantities of water. Nausea, with faintness; N., with ineffectual retching. Vomiting with difficulty. *Fulness in epigastrium and partial loss of appetite* (secondary effects). Tympanitic distention of epigastric region, very sensitive to touch, less so to pressure. Cramp, with nausea. Anxiety in epigastrium. *Tension so that she must loosen her clothes.* Distress in epigastrium and l. chest, < cold water and cold food (secondary effect). Heaviness in cardiac region (secondary effect). Sinking and emptiness.

Abdomen.—Painful tympanitic distention. Swollen and hard, < region of bladder, which was sensitive to touch. Rumbling; causing warmth, painful, forcing her to bend up and press with hands. Sticking. Warmth and coldness moving about alternately. Pain in hypochondria; just below spleen. Hepatic region sensitive. Ebullition in hypochondria.

Anus and Stool.—Hæmorrhoids. Discharge of bright blood every morning with the regular stool. Pruritus ani. Frequent diarrhœa. Copious stools, later constipation. Frequent stools; with tenesmus. Stool omitted.

Urinary Organs.—Ineffectual urging. Micturition frequent, copious, sp. gr. 1014; frequent, of scanty pale urine. Ischuria, with burning and pressure in region of bladder. Milky discharge (probably prostatic) at close of micturition, with smarting or burning at orifice of urethra, then cutting in sphincter vesicæ or region of prostate (secondary effect). Tickling in urethra. Urine increased and colorless; increased, with diminished sp. gr.; U. increased, but urea, phosphoric acid and sodium chloride diminished; and urea and phosphoric acid diminished, sodium chloride increased. Solid constituents of urine, except earthy phosphates, diminished. Urea diminished, it was not a diuretic though there was frequent micturition.

Genital Organs.—Power lost; weakened in men. Spasmodic sensation deep in uterine region, it seemed as if something tried to press outward and could not because it caused spasms. Menstruation increased and prolonged. Pruritus vulvæ.

Respiration.—Asthma, with oppression of chest. Dyspnœa, with quick breathing. Rattling. Painful, short, rapid. Complained of want of air, and compression of chest and clung convulsively to the furniture or persons, but sank down powerless. Diminution of expired water; of expired carbonic acid.

Chest.—Constriction.

Heart.—Præcordial symptoms. Increased, vigor of action. *Palpitation;* and the impulse seems almost to raise chest. Diminished action. Fluttering.

Pulse.—Rapid; and tense; and full; and together with heart losing one beat to every four. Slow. Variable, often almost imperceptible, sometimes intermittent (secondary effect). Decreases according to the tracings, with diminished extent of oscillation and consequent increase of arterial tension, but when the tracings are taken a few moments after an infusion of black coffee, especially when well roasted and of a strong aromatic odor, the peculiarities are directly the opposite.

Extremities.—*Trembling;* of arms and legs. Chorea-like movements; < hands. Gait tottering.

Skin.—Itching.

Sleep.—Restless on account of unpleasant and confused dreams. On going to sleep starting up in fright, with groans and fear of falling or of impending danger (secondary effect). Sleeplessness; from rush of all kinds of thoughts; with ecstatic excitement, intermittent, with dreams. Vivid dreams of magnificence. Dream that the sky is spanned with rainbows from horizon to zenith, visions of enchantment, beautiful landscapes, view of Paradise, later dreams of the death of friends, which do not abate the exhilaration, but he looks at all with supernatural indifference.

Fever.—Cold feeling. Shaking chills ascending from fingers and toes to nape and thence to vertex, *with general shaking and chattering of teeth.* Cayenne pepper taken internally produces warmth and makes him fearless (secondary effect). *Shivering (on account of easy sweat) from least exposure to cold air* (secondary effect). Shivering in lumbar region. Cold forehead; *C. skin and limbs; feet and hands* (secondary effect). Orgasm of blood. Heat; in flushes alternating with cold currents down back; in cheeks, with hot flushes in face, with scarcely noticeable redness. Sweat; cool; *cold, clammy, < palms* (secondary effect).

Coffeinum.

An alkaloid found in coffee, Thea, Guarana, etc., but usually prepared from tea leaves. There is some reason to believe that the alkaloids of coffee and tea, though chemically similar, are physiologically different.

Trembling. Uneasiness; and inability to keep erect. Faintness. Collapse; and pulse hardly perceptible, irregular, 120, skin cold and clammy. Numbness. Delirium. Excitement; so that he was unable to fix his mind; of nervous and vascular systems. Confusion of ideas. Visions. Head, aching; heavy and confused; marked pulsation in arteries of H. and temples. Peculiar intoxicated condition. Vertigo. Vision of sparks. Roaring in ears. Features expressive of anxiety. Grating of teeth. Tongue dry. Burning in throat and gullet. Constriction of throat and neck every fifteen minutes.

Thirst. Nausea. Vomiting, with relief of all symptoms; V. of digested matters and violent purging, on leaving the closet he could hardly walk. Pain and tenderness in stomach and abdomen. Abdominal pulsation. Constant urging to urinate, with scanty discharge. Increase of urine; with decrease of urea, phosphoric acid and sodium chloride; with decrease of urea and phosphoric acid and increase of sodium chloride. Urea increased; decreased. Erections. Oppression of chest. Præcordial anxiety. Palpitation. Pulse rapid; and full, hard; and irregular, often intermittent. Trembling of limbs. Sleep very sound at last. Sleepless.

Colchicum.

A tincture is prepared from the fresh bulbs of Colchicum autumnale, L.

General Action.—It produces violent inflammation

of the gastro-intestinal canal, with profound depression of the heart and of the temperature. It produces also acute inflammation of the kidneys. It is specially interesting to note that it produces symptoms of the acute manifestations of gout, quite apart from any direct modifications of the excretion of urea or uric acid. Its relief of acute gout seems to be purely a homœopathic action.

Allies. — Verat. alb., Merc. cor., Arnica, Rhus t., China.

Generalities. — Solid constituents of defibrinated blood diminished, also the absolute amount of blood-corpuscles and of plasma. Appearance of being in the advanced stage of typhoid fever. Stretching. Trembling. Convulsions; of l. side and muscles of face; involving neck and face, jaws clenched, froth from mouth, eyes distorted; limbs spasmodically flexed, fingers and toes flexed, eyes convulsively rotated, l. hand, which kept hold of penis, trembled, C. became more frequent, extended to muscles of neck, jaws clenched, frothing at the mouth; r. arm could not be extended, the l. could not be flexed, feet were drawn upward, soles formed a half circle and toes were spasmodically drawn inward. Tearing jerks, < l. side; suddenly through one half of body.

Stitches above eyes, in shoulders, elbows and wrists. Tearings here and there. Cutting or pinching in spots, now in r. anterior and lower part of chest, now deep in hepatic region, now in region of spleen. Pinching and crawling in some toes, in ball of r. foot, in fingers, ears and in spots of skin of face, in evening, as after freezing or change of weather. Drawing, jerking and tearing in incisors, facial muscles and other muscles here and there. Tearing tension here and there, for example, below pit of stomach, in ribs of l. side, below axilla, in r. popliteal space. "Aching all over." Sufferings seem intolerable; in evening. Anguish and agitation. Symptoms similar to rheumatic fever; rheumatic pain in whole body in evening, < in back, upper arms and shoulders. Tremulous sensation in whole body as from fasting, in afternoon, < after dinner. *Sensitiveness to slightest touch* (Arn., China, Bell., etc.).

Confused sensations. Malaise, with formication. Much affected by work, < reading or writing. Discomfort; prickling. Restlessness (Rhus t.); in morning, constantly turning head from l. to r.; could not lie on l. side. Disinclination to work. No inclination to leave the bed. **Exhaustion** (China, Rhus t., Verat., etc.). *Weakness;* all day, > in evening; in morning; in morning on waking; in morning on rising; in evening; on ascending steps; after stool, with indolence, sleepiness, prostration of limbs; when sitting quietly, > moving (Rhus t.), especially in open air, returning on sitting down, with nausea in throat and confusion in head; with restlessness (Rhus t.); with paralyzed feeling, < in arms; sudden W. Faintness; after a copious stool. Muscles seem paralyzed, < limbs; paralysis of r. side, with only slight sensation, the toes on slightest touch drawn towards sole. Aggravation from mental exertion; from coffee; of all pains at beginning of night and at daybreak. Amelioration from rubbing; A. for a short time after every attack of vomiting; after stools, except pains in pelvic organs, which become worse.

Clinical.—There are always extreme prostration and tendency to collapse, with internal coldness (Verat.).

Mind.—Delirium; at night; in evening. Muttering and raving at times. *Beside himself at external impressions, for example, a bright light,* **strong odors,** *contact, rudeness of others.* Complained there was something in the bed, generally a piece of soap. Carphologia. Excitement, with disinclination to mental activity. Exhilaration. Sadness; with weariness, painfulness and sensitiveness of whole body, so that he could scarcely refrain from weeping. Apprehension. Anxiety; causing sighing. Irritability. Indifference. Great flow of thoughts at night disturbing sleep. Absent-minded. Inability to write connectedly; to think connectedly; to fix thoughts, with tension of forehead. Weakness. Consciousness of logical connection destroyed, and perception impaired by slightest interruption. Memory weak; so that he forgets the word he was about to speak. Unconsciousness.

Head.—Falls backward. Moved from side to side. Sticking in brain. Tearing, < in forehead. Pinching here and there. Burrowing, < on r. side and vertex. *Aching;* in evening; night; on entering room after walking in open air, > sleep; feeling in morning after rising as if the previous pain would return, < shaking head, after washing pain in outer posterior part, < towards evening; deep, extending across through head, between ears and posteriorly. Feeling as if tightly bound. Confusion; in morning; in morning, like vertigo. Emptiness. Seems thick. Congestion. Perceptible pulsation. Vertigo; on rising; even to falling, when sitting after walking; with stupefaction of head; with confusion in middle of forehead; on looking fixedly at an object, objects appear to whirl and change color, they generally appear yellow and sometimes with iridescent borders.

Forehead.—Sticking above r. eye; in brain beneath coronal suture; deeply piercing, above l. brow, with occasional feeling as if drawn upward. Pinching above eyes. Boring, < over r. eye. Neuralgic pain in r. eminence, > pressure and cold, with dull pain in r. occipital protuberance. Aching; r. then l.; above eyes; above r. eye; near coronal suture; and in eye; in a spot on r. side in morning on waking; on washing; above l. eye after eating, > open air, < in the room; in bone over l. eye on every motion, < afternoon and by noise, in the same place next day, < motion of head, next day in r. side of occiput, < bending head backward or raising eyes, next day pain at 6 P.M. above l. eye extending over l. side of head, > supper, next day in l. side of occiput extending to l. eye and into face; < above brows and extending into dorsum of nose; in middle, with hyperæsthesia of cranial nerves; extending towards occiput towards evening, becoming a drawing pain. Oppressive pain above eyes in afternoon. Pressure as if everything would be pressed outward. Tearing tension in a spot on l., as if an abscess would form. Constriction above eyes. Confusion; < walking in the wind, > in the room.

Sticking in r. temple, < evening. Tearing in r. temple; jerking T. in temples. Painful drawing in l. temple. Pain in r. temple in evening, > when quiet in bed. Boring in skull of vertex, moving along sagittal suture. Pain in vertex. Oppression of vertex.

Tearing in l. half of head, extending to vertex; crawling boring T. in a spot on r. upper part of head, then in l. side; drawing T. in l. half of head, mostly beginning in l. eyeball and extending towards occiput. Pain in r. parietal eminence; in a spot on upper

r. side of head. Drawing in upper part of l. side extending into nose.

Tearing in a spot on r. side of occiput; in spot on l. side of O. Pain in occiput; in r.; then in upper part of sinciput, > warmth and rest in bed; deep in cerebellum from slightest literary occupation. Confusion in head posteriorly and superiorly. Heaviness in O., < motion or bending forward. Hair falls out. Tearings in scalp. Feeling as if scalp were drawn forward to top of skull. Crawling in forehead.

Clinical.—Intense neuralgic headaches, with frequent ineffectual efforts to sneeze, the pains are usually throbbing and shooting, < waking in morning.

Eyes.—Red and watery, pupils dilated. *Conjunctiva inflamed and congested.* Sunken. Surrounded by dark rings. Dim. Staring. Distorted. Rolling convulsively. Tearing in and around r. Pain; in r. Biting in r., < external canthus, with lachrymation and feeling as if lids were agglutinated. Heaviness as if he had not slept enough, with injected vessels. Dryness. Lachrymation in open air. Pupils contracted; l.; dilated; uneasy. Drawing digging deep in balls. Pain in l. ball. Compression in r. ball. Ulceration of Meibomian glands of l. lower lid, with swelling of lid and irritability of nerves generally. Lids in constant motion. Twitching of r. upper lid. Redness and burning of margins of lids, as in blepharitis. Drawing (similar to twitching) in l. lower lid, towards inner canthus. Pressure in brows. Vision very acute. Flickering before eyes. Blackness before eyes on attempting to stand. Hallucinations, fatiguing.

Clinical.—Kerato-iritis, with pus in anterior chamber of eye. Occasional attacks of rheumatic inflammation of iris (see Clematis); ulcerations of cornea and opacities of cornea. (The symptoms of destructive inflammation within the eyeball observed but once, in a boy, have been omitted.)

Ears.—Sticking; in l.; twinging S. in l. Tearing in r. meatus; behind r., in region of articulation of jaw, with pain on touch. Pinching. Digging in r. Pain, then sticking deep in them; P. behind r. as if a gland were swollen. Waving sensation in r. Stopped feeling in r.; S. feeling if he takes a few steps, with roaring in them. Itching deep in them, with dryness, boring does not reach the itching painful spot. Roaring; in r. Tinnitus aurium. Distressing noises. Noises cause disagreeable sensations, with starting. Hearing acute; difficult.

Clinical.—It has been used for discharges from ears after measles.

Nose.—Pinching in upper part. Sore pain in r. nostril, in septum, < touch and on moving nose. Pressure in bones; and facial bones; in nostrils, with tearing. Weight in bones. Sensation in mucous membrane as in beginning coryza. Nostrils dry and blackish. Crawling; in tip; with sneezing; with warmth, as in nosebleed. Sneezing. Bleeding in evening. Coryza; fluent; with discharge of much tough mucus. Catarrh, and in fauces. *Smell very acute; the odor of a freshly-poached egg makes him almost faint.* Smell as of smoked ham.

Clinical.—Extremely acute smell, especially for the odors of cooking, the smell of food being prepared causes nausea and disgust for food, indeed all strong odors are oppressive; this symptom occurs in the course of many diseases, gout, dysentery, etc.

Face.—Red. Cheeks red; and hot. Cheeks, lips and eyelids purple; cheeks, lips, r. eyelids purple. Bluish. Hippocratic. Bluish-white. Pale; and sunken; cheeks and chin alternately pale and red. Sunken; about mouth and in front of ears. Drawn; and pinched, the lips, nose and lobes of ears blue. Anxious; and haggard. Suffering expression. Sticking in l. cheek. Tearing in l. side, extending to ear and head, with tension. Pain near r. temple; near r. articulation of jaw, or twinges in ear. Bruised pain in l. cheek. Jerking-drawing pain in muscles extending into bones. Sensation in cheeks as if drawn asunder; sensation in bones as if widely drawn asunder, with drawing jerkings in them.

Lips cracked. Lips appeared as if they had been seared with a hot iron. Round ulcer on vermilion margin of lips. Hydroa on upper lip. Lips pale; and tender, and cracking of lower on motion of mouth. Lips bluish; and dry, also tongue. Cutting tearing in vermilion border of l. upper lip. Sudden sticking in l. lower jaw; sticking pressure beneath l. lower jaw. Tearing in r. jaws, with sensation as if teeth were too long. Pinching in r. articulation of jaw. Drawing in r. upper jaw, extending to margin of orbit, alternating with irritation in throat. Tension in articulation of jaw, so that he must lay aside the cigar. Masseter muscles seem increased in breadth, allowing him to open the mouth only a little, and pain.

Mouth.—Teeth. Sordes. Grinding. Sticking in r. Tearing in roots of l. lower. Pain in l. lower back; (in decayed T. when chewing). Drawing pain on taking anything cold after something warm; D. in lower incisors, with cold sensation in them. Soreness from pain; S. so that he could not bite on them. Grumbling in upper back. Seem too long. Blunt feeling, with pain, especially drawing extending from tips of upper teeth into jaw-bone. Follicular inflammation of gum about a r. incisor. Follicular ulcer in commissure of upper lip and gum, with burning pain. Tearing in r. lower gum; in gum of l. lower incisors; in r.; in the gap of a r. upper tooth. Pain in gums.

Tongue.—White. Pale blue and cold. Yellow. Red, covered with mucus; bright red, coated only at root. Coated; in morning; white; white patches on under part; white, with velvety sensation; yellow; brown. Dry; on dorsum, and brownish; and brown in centre, red along edges. Sticking in middle; S. and burning. Tearing posteriorly in l. side. Sharp pain about root on moving it and on swallowing. Burning; prickling, on margin. Enlarged feeling, as if stretched out across teeth. Biting, and in throat. Cold; and breath. Heavy; then stiff, then insensible; and difficult to find the right word and to articulate it when found. Speech difficult.

Working her mouth and spitting, as if trying to spit out a hair. Mucous membranes secrete a viscid substance. Greenish mucus involuntarily thrown out when sneezing. Scraping in mouth, with pasty taste and great hunger. Scraping crawling in posterior part of palate as in coryza. Agreeable prickling as after champagne, with salivation. Dryness. Heat. Blunted sensibility, especially of root of tongue. Salivation; of agreeable taste; watery; watery, with nausea, fulness and discomfort in abdomen; watery, with dryness in throat; bad-tasting; flat-tasting, causing nausea. Saliva salt, piquant-tasting. Taste bitter; and flat; pasty; pasty in morning; like vinegar; improper to water. Strongly-tasting food causes a sensation as if chewing old linen.

Throat.—Perceptible pulsation in carotids. Drawing in external half of r. side. Much greenish mucus. Frequent hawking of scanty mucus. Inflammation. Tearing far back, < l. side. Pinching posteriorly as in beginning angina, with dryness in throat and impeded swallowing. Uvula painful and red. Scraping. Rawness in morning and hoarseness. Constriction; of pharynx. Crawling provoking cough and hawking of mucus; C., with loosening of thin mucus, which must be frequently expectorated; biting C. in back. Fulness at night disturbing sleep. Burning in pharynx; and along œsophagus; in uvula, then profuse pale urine. Dryness; with redness of uvula and arches of palate; posteriorly, very painful on swallowing, as in beginning of quinsy; scraping; scraping, with tickling cough. Swallowing difficult; with pain along œsophagus; S. painful. Sensation at beginning of œsophagus on swallowing as of a round swelling.

Stomach.—*Great appetite* (China); at noon; in afternoon; evening; for dinner; gnawing, almost a throbbing in stomach; *A. for different things, but as soon as he sees them,* **or still more smells them** (Nux v.), *he shudders from nausea and cannot eat.* A. diminished; for breakfast, but great at noon. *A. lost;* lost for breakfast; lost at noon. Aversion to food and drink. *Thirst;* in afternoon; *unquenchable;* for cold drinks; with pain in stomach and bowels.

Eructations; with burning in stomach; empty; empty in forenoon; of water. Hiccough. Nausea; in morning on waking, with rumbling in abdomen, painful contractions, gripings and urging and sensation of loose bowels; at times during dinner; after dinner, at which he could eat but little; after eating; if he swallows the saliva; on becoming erect; on motion of head, with faintness; < raising oneself in bed, and vomiting of bitter bilious fluid; > small swallows of cold water, which she desires constantly; in throat caused by pressure below; in throat as after vomiting. Retching; long, then violent vomiting of a large mass of yellowish, bitter mucus, leaving a bitter bilious taste in throat.

Vomiting; with watery diarrhœa (Verat. a.); symptoms of cholera morbus; attack similar to cholera, with constant rice-water vomiting and similar stools, which were forcible and accompanied by tenesmus. *Violent, unless he bent himself up and lay still;* violent, with trembling and cramps; with diarrhœa; violent, of all food eaten three hours before; violent, of a brown substance; violent, of greenish water, then of contents of stomach; of yellowish-green fluid, so violent that he could not retain the slightest food or drink. Frightful on motion, > lying on r. side; F. of food mingled with a bitter brown powder, then of water, partly bitter, partly flat-tasting mucus. Constant. Frequent, but scanty; F. of colorless and inodorous fluid; F. of bile, with griping in abdomen, then bitterness in mouth and throat. Copious and easy, then appetite. Of food immediately; of the breakfast; of food and pale greenish mucus; of undigested food and a yellow liquid, then diarrhæa; of food eaten the night before, then of much thick, yellow bile, then thinner and less yellow, at last of pale straw color containing many white shreds. Of drinks tinged with bile. Of bile; then like rice-water; of tenacious bile. Of everything taken into stomach. Thin and slimy. Of profuse yellow fluid. Of much yellowish-green water. Of green fluid. Of whitish-gray fluid. Of a quart of thick whitish substance in morning, of tenacious greenish matter at 11 A.M., soon repeated, V. of brandy and water at 3 P.M. Of viscid, tasteless fluid. Of mucus.

Spasmodic contraction on touch. Rumbling and moving. Gastritis. Gastralgia. Tearing on beginning to vomit and purge. Cramp; and in abdomen and legs. Pinching in epigastrium. Pain; in morning; in evening when walking; after a light meal; in epigastrium; in epigastric region, with swollen feeling in stomach without real swelling, with intolerance of pressure; extending into l. side of abdomen; in region, extending over abdomen, with tenderness; in region, gradually extending over abdomen, with nausea and vomiting; and in abdomen, causing her to bend double. Soreness. Sensitiveness of epigastric region to pressure. Constriction; in epigastric region. Oppression in pit; with pressure; in epigastric region. Fulness; in epigastric region, < when walking, with pressure and oppression; as if sensitive to pressure of clothes. Desire to hiccough. Disordered feeling, with eructations tasting of undigested food. Tension. **Burning** *in epigastrium;* with drawing; *in stomach, with pain;* before stool; in epigastric region, with fulness; in S., with heaviness; warmth in S. at night; B. extending upward along sternum. Heartburn. *Coldness* (Verat.). Uneasiness. Discomfort; extending to spine; in epigastric region. Crawling; on becoming erect, as in vomiting. Weakness in pit, with oppression. Faintness, even after breakfast.

Clinical.—One of the most characteristic indications for Colchicum is craving for various things, but when they are brought to him, especially if he smells them, he is seized with extreme aversion and becomes nauseated, and may even vomit. It is indicated in the most violent attacks of gastralgia, with retching and vomiting of food and bile, from the repression of gout.

Abdomen.—Bile increased. Sunken. Doughy and painful on slightest pressure. *Distention;* after supper; after eating, > copious thin stool; and tension and hardness; and in rectum; *as if she had eaten too much,* < light food. Tympanitis. Rumbling; then soft stool; after stool; then hunger; with urging to stool. Movings as before diarrhœa. Emission of flatus; offensive, forcible; much offensive; *offensive, in evening;* of odorless. Painful flatulence. Cramps in muscles and in flexors of limbs.

Sticking transversely through; S., < r. side, beneath liver, inguinal region and in pit of stomach. Cutting. Enteritis. Pinching, then soft stool. Tormina. *Griping;* with unsatisfactory stool; then pasty stool. Gnawing. Pain; at night, and frequent vomiting; after rising, with diarrhœa; before thin stool; > rubbing, then tasteless eructations and passage of flatus; temporarily > watery stools; < colon, with lumbar pain and pressure about pelvis, stools at first of usual appearance, then soft, yellowish, of pitchlike stickiness, fetid, causing heat of anus, then pain, then tenesmus, later they diminish in frequency, become watery and colorless; with vomiting and diarrhœa; extending to chest, with anxiety and heat, < head; as from incarcerated flatus. Spasmodic constriction before vomiting. Tenderness, with intermittent pain, as in peritonitis. Soreness and discomfort. Drawing as before colic. Uneasiness; with movings and urging to stool. Burning here and there becoming griping.

Chilliness, < stomach, with pain and weakness. Pulsation in morning, and in chest, like a great rush of blood to chest. Weak sensation becoming hunger. Paralysis of intestines and change of inflammation to gangrene.

Upper.—Sticking in r. hypochondrium; in spleen in evening. Tearing in l. hypochondrium; cutting, in hepatic region; cutting, in r. upper. Cutting cramplike pain in evening, extending to navel. Pinching in l., extending to region of hip, > eructations. Pain in morning on waking; on pressure; as from incarcerated flatus anteriorly beneath r. short ribs; in spleen on pressure, as from the pressure of a fold, preventing sleep on account of inability to lie on l. side according to custom. Pressing-out pain beneath pit of stomach, > eructations. Tension, extending to r. hypochondrium; T. transversely across hypochondria. Warmth in middle, and fulness; when walking.

Sticking in umbilical region; here and there below U. region. Pinching in l. side of A. and near r. hip. Sharp pressing-outward pain above and to l. of navel. Pressure in thin intestines, on l. side of navel; in l. side of navel as from incarcerated flatus, with sensitiveness to pressure. Pain in umbilical region before and at beginning of noon meal, with flatulence. Internal soreness between l. hip and ribs, even on touch. Burning below umbilicus, with dragging towards small of back.

Lower.—Rumbling in transverse colon. Sticking in l. part of transverse colon. Tearing to l. of r. hip. Cutting in r., then in upper l. side, but not in intestines. Sudden pain, with slimy, watery, almost involuntary stools. Pressure in ilium to l. of navel; in region of transverse colon, with discomfort. Dragging in descending colon, with moving. Irritation of pelvic organs; I. as from diarrhœa, and in anus, and urging to stool, with aching in abdomen. Warmth just above anus, with sensation of a live worm there, itching and burning on the corresponding spot on skin, sensitiveness to slight touch, but not to hard touch, > scratching, with redness.

Clinical.—In typhlitis; in extreme distention of abdomen, with icy coldness in stomach, colic, occasional attacks of nausea and vomiting. Ascites with the characteristic gastric symptoms.

Rectum.—Prolapsus. Throbbing. Throbbing smarting. Sensation of diarrhœa, preceded by cutting, without thin stool. **Tenesmus**; *with only a little fæces at first, then* **transparent, bilious, membranous mucus, with relief of colic**; > *frequent passage of flatus; urging to stool, which is unsatisfactory;* after stool; with passage of flatus; with scanty fæces; urging, then painful stool, as if sphincter would be torn asunder; then difficult, soft stool, then pain in small of back; sudden urging, with copious stool and griping, afterwards much motion in colon, then six copious, watery, yellow stools; frequent urging, with hard stool or none, with pain in anus. Ineffectual urging; though the fæces were felt in rectum; frequent, preceded by colic.

Anus.—*Spasms of sphincter, with chilliness running up back, then urging to stool, and insufficient stool.* Sticking, and anteriorly in urethra and in l. hip. Sticking tearing. Pain; in sphincter, as if it would be torn, with hard stool. Sensation as in diarrhœa, copious, not thin stools, then in rectum sensation of diarrhœa and sore biting in anus. Crawling and jerking. Sudden itching. Burning; intermittent; with prickling.

Stool.—Contained many white shreds. *Dysentery, stools slimy and bloody, with tenesmus.* Watery; and frequent; and frequent, without sensation; and frequent, with griping; and frequent and large, with griping at each discharge; and frequent, copious, colored with bile; and painless; *and copious, yellowish; and offensive, containing pieces of white membrane; and frequent, offensive, orange-yellow, slimy, with bright yellow flakes, without fæces;* like rice-water, copious, frothy, slimy, compared to clean soapsuds; and frothy, painless; and slimy, brownish-black, of a turpentine look, putrid, as if mixed with fresh bile or blood; and slimy, greenish-black, smelling like fresh bile or fresh blood that has stood some minutes in a water-bath. Thin, profuse, dark brown; T., yellow and bloody; T., yellow, copious, preceded and followed by pain, rumbling and motions in abdomen, then ineffectual tenesmus; T., yellow; T., yellow, forcible, with discomfort, almost pain in abdomen during and after stool. Soft, difficult, partly returning into anus. Pasty; and profuse; after dinner, with flatulence, then emission of offensive flatus. Slimy, with tenesmus.

Constipation; with full sensation in rectum; then scanty stool. Hard stool; scanty and sluggish. Copious; and offensive. Scanty, difficult, not hard. Difficult, but not hard. Easy. Involuntary; at night; and black, offensive; and involuntary micturition. Bloody. Frequent; at night; alternating with vomiting. Offensive, containing lumps looking like sponge.

Clinical.—Dysentery, great tenesmus, discharges jellylike or bloody, mucous or changeable in character, but with great tenesmus, with or without stool, with tympanitis, colic, inability to stretch out the legs; at times the dysenteric discharges are reddish, mucous, like scrapings of intestines, sometimes there is even protrusion of the lower bowels (Pod.). Especially indicated in autumnal dysentery (compare Aloes and Mercurius).

Urinary Organs.—Strangury. Urging to urinate. Symptoms as from Cantharides, often muddy sediment, consisting of epithelium of vesical mucous membrane. Frequent micturition; day and night; every half hour, of diabetic urine; of deep yellow, copious urine. Retention of urine. Cutting in urethra on micturition; C. in forepart. Drawing pain in urethra. Drawing in urethra; posteriorly; with tearing. Tickling in navicular fossa after urinating. Burning in urethra; then profuse discharge of pale urine; B. on urinating, with contraction of neck of bladder; B. as if sore, on urinating; crawling B. in morning after urinating, with sensation as if more urine would pass, and burning when passing a few drops.

Urine.—Copious; with urging; and hot; and pale; and dark; and golden, clear, then with white floating clouds, and turbid. *Scanty;* and red and burning. *Dark; dark brown. Bloody, with strangury.* Turbid, then clear and yellow; T., mucous. Like lime-water, the turbidity caused by urate of ammonia.

Clinical.—Nephritis with extreme pain in the region of the kidneys, in some cases < stretching out legs, as from pressure on the kidneys, in the abdominal cavity, urine bloody or dark albuminous; in some cases there are symptoms of inflammation of the neck of bladder, with terrible pain after urinating (Canth.). Inflamed kidneys, with pain in back and sacrum, hot, burning urine, constant chilliness and cold extremities, with coldness in stomach.

Sexual Organs.—Tearing in glans; in l. spermatic

cord. Erections and exhausting emissions. Pain in l. testicle as if crushed, when stepping on l. foot. Great desire; at night; after eating. Menses too early; M. that had just appeared disappeared.

Respiratory Organs.—Pain in larynx, with croupous expectoration from it; in muscles somewhat to l., internally and externally above larynx. Scraping in larynx. Tickling in larynx. Crawling in trachea and chest, with cough. Hoarse; and husky voice, with pain in speaking. Voice hollow and deep. Voice lost, as in cholera. Cough and deep respiration; severe C. at regular intervals; almost voluntary coughing up of starchlike lumps of mucus; (C. alternating with coryza.) Bloody sputa. *Difficult breathing;* and short; and anxiety. Dyspnœa; and contraction of chest. Rapid breathing; and heavy, almost stertorous. Desire to take frequent deep inspirations. Respiration irregular; intermittent. Moaning and clutching at heart.

Clinical.—Dyspnœa, with œdema of extremities, chronic troubles with the kidneys and heart.

Chest.—Twitching of r. pectoral muscles. Increase of carbonic acid from lungs. Sticking in r.; near r. arm; in r. lower side, in lung; beneath l. clavicle; in l. upper part; in l., near eighth rib; in l. in morning in bed on and after exertion; in l. on coughing and on inspiration; in muscles on moving chest; deep in l. side on complete expiration, not on inspiration, afterwards only on inspiration; here and there, not affecting respiration; < breathing, with cutting; from anterior wall to posterior wall; S. outward in r.; burning, externally on r. Sticking, rheumatic pain in r. wall.

Tearing near r. axilla, becoming soreness, even on touch and motion; sticking, deep in r., where it is difficult to say whether it is more in the back, whence it extends, or more in chest; cutting, across. Cutting in l., not affecting respiration; C. in l. lower forepart, on blowing nose; in r., almost taking away the breath, then in chest, not deep and not affecting the less sensitive parts; pinching, here and there, in l. anterior and lower part. Pinching. Boring in l., < 10 P.M., with difficult breathing and anxiety; drawing B. from middle of sternum to l. nipple, > deep inspiration, the pain less severe in r. side of chest, it afterwards extended over whole chest and caused constriction as from a weight.

Pain; around r. side, preventing writing; on sitting a long time, extending to scapulæ. Intermittent pressure in r., now upper, now lower. Sore pain deep in a spot in region of l. nipple, < inspiration, > rising from bed. Anxiety, < l. Sternum and spine feel as if screwed together, the pressure beginning on sternum. *Oppression;* when walking; alternating; anxious. Constriction; with necessity to breathe deeply; with sticking and boring through chest, < beneath l. nipple; sudden C. in r., causing starting. Spasmodic compression of l., with difficult respiration. Tension. Fulness; with pulsations in abdomen. Orgasm, < evening after eating, with sensation as if something alive were working in it.

Heart.—*Trembling in præcordial region, with sticking.* Sticking; in præcordial region. Tearing in P. region. *Pressure in P. region;* in afternoon; after coffee, > walking, with oppression and sensation as if he would have apoplexy. *Anxiety in P. region, provoking sighing. Oppression; extending into l. side of chest, obliging deep inspiration; in P. region; in P. region, with trembling of heart. Fulness at night when lying on l. side, with oppression, as from stagnation of blood. Sensitiveness of P. region to pressure. Palpitation;* in afternoon; at night; on waking; on going to sleep; periodic, *with oppression of heart. Dull, irregular, suppressed beats, with indescribable sensation in chest.* Scarcely perceptible beat, with perceptible pulsation in abdomen. *Impulse not felt, and even heard with difficulty, a blowing sound, like a heart heard at a great distance, or through a stone wall,* both sounds lapsing into one.

Clinical.—Chronic or subacute pericarditis, with exudation of water in pericardium, with severe pain about heart, oppression and dyspnœa as if the chest were squeezed with a tight band (Cact.); in these cases the heart's action is weak and indistinct, the pulse may even be threadlike; in many cases there is chronic feeling of icy coldness at pit of stomach.

Pulse.—*Rapid; and small; and weak; weak; and irregular; and weak, thready;* and contracted, spasmodic; and large, hard, full; and strong. Slow; during the nausea, and weak; and thready; and weak, afterwards rapid. *Weak, irritable, at times rapid, at times slow. Weak, small and irregular. Intermittent; scarcely perceptible.* Small; and tense. Imperceptible, then thready and tremulous.

Neck.—Visible throbbing of arteries, < sitting still. Pain in nape; beneath ear, near joint of jaw, with soreness to touch; in neck and occiput, and stiffness; drawing P. from nape across occiput to ears; tensive P. in r. muscles externally and on swallowing. Rheumatism in nape, < r. trapezius, < wrong movement of neck. Stiffness of nape and occiput, and pain, < moving head. Paralysis of muscles, so that when the child was raised the head fell backward, with the mouth wide open.

Back.—Sticking in dorsal muscles; S. between and beneath scapulæ; on superior l. angle of r. scapula. Tearing to l. of spine; behind r. axilla. Pain; acute, along back and to heels; between shoulders; tensive, in tip of l. scapula, towards spine, < motion of arm. Rheumatic pain in l. scapula and in nape, mostly tensive and pressive, < turning neck to l. or far backward; periodic R. pain, more in scapulæ than in nape.

Lumbar Region.—Sticking; and in coccyx; burning, in sacrum. Sticking tearing. *Pinching and in urinary passages,* with constant desire to urinate. Pain; on both side of vertebræ; deep in sacrum in afternoon; in sacrum, waking frequently at night; in a spot in sacrum, as if suppurating, < touch; *bruised,* in morning. Drawing pain; when lying quietly, > by moving. Drawing on waking; D., < motion. Tension in region of kidneys. Heaviness, with sensation as if rectum were stuffed.

Extremities.—L. elbow and knee swollen, hot, painful, while r. side was partially paralyzed and almost insensible. Twitching. Toes and fingers painfully flexed. Trembling increasing to convulsive movements, a similar attack afterwards ending in two attacks of vomiting; T., becoming convulsive, with flow of whitish froth from mouth, becoming similar to opisthotonos, repeated after a quiet sleep from 11 to 2 at night. Drawing, now sticking, now jerking, < morning, now in muscles of shoulder, now in r. hip. *Pain; in joints of fingers, toes, wrists and ankles; in shoulder-joints and knees during rest, with uneasiness; rheumatic,* *in hands and feet, so that she could not bear to have her finger-joints pressed or extended from their semi-flexed condition.* Uneasiness at night. Weariness; of arms and legs; in morning. Numbness of hands and feet, then prickling as if they had been asleep. Paralysis of r. foot and l. arm. *Joints stiff and feverish.*

Clinical.—Gouty diathesis, soreness of the flesh, of the joints, extreme irritability, intolerance of touch, with gastric symptoms. Articular rheumatism, with tearing jerking pains, cardiac complications, gastric symptoms. Shifting rheumatism, pains < towards night, the patient is very irritable, etc. It is generally indicated when the smaller joints are affected; the pains are violent, often paralytic, so that the patient can hold nothing in the hands, or when the feet are affected they become swollen, œdematous, it is difficult to lift the feet. Rheumatism or gout in heel, which is extremely sore, with tearing pains. Inflammation of the joint of great toe, with acute pain as from sharp sticking, cannot bear to have it touched or to have any one come near him (Arn.).

Upper Extremities.—Tearing, now in r. axilla, now in l. Pain as after a blow in a spot beneath and almost in r. axilla. Bubbling sensation in l. axilla, even perceptible externally. Sticking in r. shoulder. Tearing in r. shoulder and forearm; in r. shoulder-joint; anteriorly in l. shoulder-joint. Pinching on l. shoulder. Pain in shoulder-joint; in l. shoulder, < lying on l. side.

Arm.—Tearing, with paralyzed sensation; cutting T. in l. Pain. **Paralytic pain so that he cannot hold the lightest thing firmly.** Weakness of r. at noon. L. felt lame and weak. Heaviness. Numbness; with pain and at times sensation as if she had no hands, hands and feet warm, legs and arms cold. Paralyzed feeling in l. Paralysis of r. arm and hand, with thumb drawn inward and the fingers spasmodically closed over it. Pressure above l. elbow, < moving and raising it, preventing his putting on his coat alone, > rest and at night. Burning pain on inner side, near l. axilla. Bubbling sensation on outer side of l. upper arm.

Forearm.—Tearing near wrist; in r. forearm, < on outer side of muscles; on outer side of l., as if in fascia; in flexor surface of l., extending to elbow; in extensor surface of l., extending into some of the fingers; on extensor surface, extending into fingers, as from electric shocks; intermittent, on extensor surface, as if some nerves were torn. Pain; with sensitiveness to touch. Numbness.

Elbow and Wrist.—Sticking at night; S. in l. elbow; in l. elbow, then sensitiveness to touch. Tearing on inner side of elbows, extending to upper arms; jerk-like, from r. elbow into wrist, then from wrist into fingers. Sticking on volar side of wrist, with heat, l. then r. Tearing in r. wrist. Pain in r. wrist.

Hand.—Spasmodic contraction so that the fingers were stretched out and the ball of thumb turned into palm. Trembling; of r., almost preventing writing. Tearing in metacarpal bones of r. middle and ring fingers; on back of r. hand; in r. and beneath last phalanx of little finger; sticking, in lower part of r. Pain in l. metacarpus, < between third and fourth fingers, on motion, < flexion of hand. Drawing extending into fingers. Weakness.

Fingers.—Nails blue; and tips. Spasmodically flexed, but in constant motion. Third and fourth drawn inward. Cramps; < second. Sticking on volar surface of tips; in l. thumb; in metacarpal joint of r. thumb. Tearing in l. little; in joints of r. fingers; beneath nail of l. index; in middle phalanges of l. little and ring; sticking T. in ligaments of joints of r. little. Drawings from l. thumb up radial surface of forearm; in posterior part and ball of r. thumb; rheumatic, in metacarpal joint of l. thumb. Numbness under thumb-nails.

Lower Extremities.—Tottering gait, partly on account of weakness and partly on account of sudden sticking-tearing jerks through periosteum, with sensation of paralysis and actual paralysis. They seem to have lost their power on attempting to walk.

Thigh.—Abducted. Snapping in l. hip. Sticking in hips, < l.; tearing, from l. hip-joint to leg. Tearing in upper part of l.; high up on inner side of r.; in region of hip; in middle of l. in evening in bed; above l. knee in evening in bed; deep in nates towards anus; extending towards hip; in r. hip-joint, extending to knee; drawing, in ligaments of l. hip, < night; jerking, in upper part of r. Pinching in l. like cramp, as if asleep; P. on and above r. hip. Pain in hips and loins. Pressure upon femora, < in middle. Drawing pain in hip-bone on moving about at night; in hip when sitting, > motion; in l. femur, at times worse, as from fatigue or like growing pain; sudden sticking, beneath l. nates, extending into perineum. Drawing deep in muscles; in r. hip-joint; paralytic, in r. in evening in bed. Sensation as of something living in l. hip. Stiffness of l., making walking difficult.

Knee.—Snapping on l. surface of r. Sticking; in l.; and in ankles. Tearing in l. Pain; in l.; in inner side of r.; in r. in evening in bed, with lame sensation; in bend of r. during a long walk, extending down calf. Broken feeling (weariness) on ascending stairs. Weakness so that they give way, < by raising leg to step over a high object.

Leg.—*Cramp;* of calves. Tearing below patella; posteriorly beneath patella; in l. side of l. calf; in lower part of r. calf; pinching, at insertion of r. tendo-achillis; tensive, on l. lower half of l. tibia. Pain; in calves and feet; in forepart, as from chilliness, < tibia, with coldness of legs, even in bed; in forepart of tibiæ, like a chilliness in bones, not > warmth; in forepart of tibia, as if the bone were chilled or like growing pain. Drawing in lower part of r. calf; in both calves and in r. metatarsus. Heaviness extending into feet.

Tearing in l. tarsal joints. Pressure in r. external malleolus at 8 P.M., as from fatigue. *Cramp of feet; painful,* < l.; painful, in soles. Tearing through l. foot; on back of l.; in r. heel, near sole; in a spot in forepart of r. foot, near sole; in l. sole, in a spot in metatarsus; in l. sole, not far from toes; on inner curvature of r. foot, between ball of great toe and heel; in feet as if lame; drawing, in l. sole; drawing, on r. instep. Weariness of feet.

Toes.—Jerking in metatarsal joints. Sticking in l. big. Boring sticking across top of r. great. Tearing on inner side of metatarsal joints; sticking, in ball of r. great, near its lower side. Sticking drawing in r. great. Drawing pain in l. great, then also in r., then in l. middle toes, < lower surfaces of toes. Pain in l. great as if the nail would enter the flesh.

Skin.—Pale. Scarlet. Livid, dry and hot. Eruption. (Wartlike pimples on nape.) Pityriasis on inner surface of l. thigh and on corresponding part of scrotum. Pustules on face and lower limbs, resembling poisoned wounds. Sticking, so that it jerks through the whole body; jerking S. as from flea-bites, > scratching. Crawling on inner surface of r. great, second and third toes, as if asleep. Itching over whole body; in various parts; on hands; on face, with eruption; on ulnar side of forearm, with redness; over whole body, as from nettles; sticking, here and there; burning, here and there, after scratching redness, and the itching changes to another place; burning-sticking, here and there, driven to another part by scratching.

Clinical.—Generally indicated in sequelæ of eruptive diseases, scarlet fever, typhoid fever, etc., suppression of urine, accumulation of water in thorax, abdomen and extremities.

Sleep.—Yawning; after dinner, with rumbling in abdomen, then copious stool. Sleepiness; during the day; in afternoon; in evening; after supper; till midnight, then waking with oppression in stomach, then wide awake for two hours; with disinclination to work and confusion of head; soporous condition in a child, lying on its back, with half-open eyes and loud, rapid respiration. Deep sleep, with vivid dreams and grinding of teeth.

Sleeplessness; from sticking jerks, sometimes only in skin, sometimes deep in soft parts of head and face. Late falling asleep. Restless sleep; in afternoon, on the sofa, only slightly refreshing; and exhausting; with anxious dreams; with heavy dreams. Unrefreshing S. in afternoon. Frequent waking in fright, with the idea that there were mice in the bed. Many dreams; D. in a half-waking condition. Confused, always of the same objects. Heavy, full of solicitude. Of snakes. Anxious, and erections at night. Lascivious, towards morning, with erections.

Fever.—*General coldness* (Verat. a.); all day, > at 7 P.M.; in afternoon; in afternoon, after dinner; in afternoon, in open air; in evening, with chattering of teeth on going to bed, > by lying still, but threatened to return on motion; at night, with heat of head; in the room; in the room, then vertigo; and pulseless at wrist, respiration slight, nose, feet and hands cold, stiff and blue, blue under eyes and about mouth, then unconsciousness. Alternating with heat. Progressive. Shivering; in back; down back; through limbs. Creeping chill in scalp. Cold forehead; nose, cheeks and soles; **limbs**; fingers; fingers, and numb; hands and feet; knees; feet, in afternoon; feet, limbs, hands and arms, while the rest of the body had a clammy feel, but was below the normal temperature; skin; skin of hands and legs, even in bed; whole body cold and clammy.

Heat at night; H., with gastric disturbances and soporous condition. Passing into headache. In flushes in afternoon. Orgasm of blood. Dry; at night. Hot skin; and dry; dry and lead-colored. H. in bed like rush of blood through skin of chest and head. In anterior part of head; in face; externally on r. side of nape; externally on r. side, near pit of stomach; in small of back, extending into rectum; on side, in small of back, when sitting, with throbbing; in palms. In flushes in head; in face; in hands and feet; up spine, in a warm room.

Sweat; at night; towards morning; on waking after midnight. Easy on walking; E. and profuse. Sour; at night. Clammy, with blue spots on skin, < along spine; C. and cold, as in cholera. On face; on neck. Cold on forehead; on arms and legs, with heat over abdomen. Clammy on forehead. Suppressed.

Clinical.—Occasionally indicated in typhoid fever, tympanitis, coldness in stomach, cold breath, nausea and vomiting, cold sweat, albuminous urine. Effects of sudden suppression of perspiration in gastralgia, etc.

Collinsonia.

A tincture is prepared from the fresh root of Collinsonia Canadensis, L.

General Action.— From our scanty information it seems to act upon the "hæmorrhoidal sphere" similarly to Aloes, Sulphur, etc.

Generalities. — Warmth spreading along internal mucous surfaces of lips, deepening into a feeling of largeness, with sensation of needles darting back and forth, the same numbness or needle-like darting to and fro in face, cheeks, forehead, hairy parts under chin, from ear to ear, while inner surface of lips and whole buccal cavity were excited, the face seemed to grow broader and broader, with exhilaration of mind, then r. forearm to finger-tips felt numb, a weary heaviness, then l. arm and fingers, balls of thumbs more numb than fingers, nausea, lips seemed growing larger and mouth seemed to stand open like a huge catfish's, lips dry, mouth tingling and burning, face flushing and pricking, whole head "growing," forearms to finger-tips asleep, hands feel broad and heavy, desire to lie with head high to get more air, uneasiness, head seemed growing bigger while straining to get boots on, staggering, faintness, symptoms < swallowing hot things, in the cool open air feet and limbs felt strangely light, loss of personal identity in lower limbs, then a glow from umbilicus to toes, sense of increasing largeness and numbness from hip to hip, while r. thigh was thus affected the l. was skipped, calves seemed elephantine and asleep. Weakness; in morning, with faintness; with sleepiness.

Head.—Aching on waking; tensive, at point of emergence of l. supraorbital nerve. Forehead, aching while sitting, with tearing in knees, passing down inside of legs to feet; A., with frequent flying pains in legs; with frequent rheumatic pains in arms, hands and legs; over eyes and in r. temple.

Nose, Face and Tongue. — Dryness of nostrils, with frequent sharp pains in r. temple and aching distress in stomach and bowels. Face yellow around eyes in morning. Neuralgia in superior maxillary bone in open air. Tongue coated yellow along centre and base in morning, with rough, bitter taste.

Stomach.—Nausea; while sitting, with intermittent cutting in hypogastrium; with distress in stomach and bowels; with cutting in hypogastrium and emissions of flatus. Cutting while sitting.

Abdomen.—Pain at umbilicus at 10 P.M. Distress at umbilicus, with eructations of air. Pain in hypogastrium in morning, with desire for stool. Cutting in hypogastrium twice on waking in the night, and with urging to stool at 4 A.M., first part of stool hard and lumpy, last part running out as thin as milk, with pain in hypogastrium, straining, nausea and faintness, pain continued fifteen minutes, then copious watery stool, after sleeping an hour woke with pain in hypogastrium and desire for stool, stool of bile, mucus and yellow matter, with tensemus, then cutting in bowels, then *intermittent cutting in hypogastrium, compelling him to sit down and causing faintness, stool of yellow fæcal matter, mucus and blood, with tensemus, then cutting in hypogastrium*, at 10 A.M. small stool of mucus and blood, *preceded and followed by cutting in hypogastrium*, at 12 M. stool of bilious matter, mucus and blood, with same symptoms as last, then dull distress in hypochondrium, then at 2 P.M. *cutting in hypogastrium, with stool of bilious matter, mucus streaked with blood, and tensemus, then intermittent cutting in hypogastrium* all afternoon and evening.

Clinical.—It has been prescribed in ascites, both from cardiac trouble and especially from hepatic disease.

Rectum.—Clinical. Hæmorrhoid, sharp sticking in rectum, constipation, etc. Hæmorrhoids, bleeding almost incessantly, especially with sensation of sharp sticks in rectum; general aggravation late at night.

Stool.—*Light-colored, lumpy, with straining, then aching in anus and hypogastrium.* Papescent at 7 P.M., preceded by pain in small intestines. Mushy at 8 A.M., then no stool for three days. *Constipation* for two days, with languor. Omitted. *In form of balls.*

Clinical.—Most obstinate constipation, with protruding hæmorrhoids.

Urine.—High-colored and scanty. Urinated several times.

Genital Organs.—Clinical. Dysmenorrhœa, with hæmorrhoidal troubles; membranous dysmenorrhœa. Pruritus of vulva and prolapsus uteri, hæmorrhoids, constipation, etc. In all these pelvic troubles Collinsonia reminds us of Aloes, though obstinate constipation is the rule with Coll., looseness of the bowels with Aloes. Pruritus during pregnancy, swelling and dark redness of genitals, cannot even sit down.

Lung.—Gurgling suddenly low down in l. while lying, then desire to cough, which was restrained as he had had hæmoptysis from that side, the breathing and pulse varying while lying on l. side, the pulse under the finger would withdraw and then return with increased volume.

Colocynthis.

A tincture is made of the dried fruit (deprived of its rind and seed) of Cucumis colocynthis, L. (Citrullus colo. Shrader).

General Action.—A violent hydragogue cathartic, producing also terrible colic. It also causes violent pains in nearly all the nerves of the body, almost always relieved by pressure.

Allies.—Bry., Magnesia, Cupr., Diosc., Berb., Puls.

Generalities.—Increased secretion of mucus. *Inclination to painful cramp in muscles of all parts* (Cupr.). Spasms. Sticking in various parts; with drawings, itching, burning, biting; tearing S. lengthwise in whole body, head, back, abdomen and limbs. Pressure in different parts, < posterior joint of r. middle finger and r. great toe. Anguish. Pains frequently repeated at 5 P.M. Pains jump from one part to another (Puls.); and change quickly from one kind to another; wandering P. < sitting. Paroxysmal pressure and drawing in posterior joint of r. great toe, in ankles, knees and bones of l. pelvis, < walking. Drawing pain on outside of r. thigh, with pain in l. upper molars. Drawing in posterior joint of l. thumb, r. great toe, in r. knee and on l. side of neck, < turning head; in l. trochanter in forenoon, then drawing pressing in l. metatarsus, then drawing in teeth; after rising, quickly changing its location, in legs, ankles, shoulders, forehead, muscles of thighs, in wrists and knees; sticking, now here, now there, in morning after waking. Sensation of general contusion, < walking, with tired feeling. Internal oppression towards evening.

Sensitiveness to damp weather. Pulsation in whole body, < in back and l. side of chest; in whole body when lying still. Discomfort in evening, < in lower limbs, with weakness; D., he demands much. Uneasiness in afternoon, < digestive organs. Lazy, gloomy, listless, almost pusillanimous. *Weakness;* in afternoon; at 5 P.M., with shivering, thirst and rapid pulse; in evening; in evening before sleep and waking next morning, > moving about; in evening when walking; on going out; when at rest; from slight exertion in walking, with sweat which made his limbs weak, but if he stood still the air, though not raw, struck through him like a cold creeping; from watery diarrhœa, with pallor; *general W., with bruised sensation in small of back.* Faintness; > holding hands before eyes; with external coldness.

Some pains appear only when walking, for example, the painful drawing in muscles of calves and thighs, preventing motion. Symptoms appear in groups, < evening and rest. Aggravation when sitting; symptoms more severe in evening than in morning. Amelioration when sitting; when walking, but symptoms are always felt in evening after considerable exertion and are connected with weariness in lower limbs; A. from black coffee after dinner.

Clinical.—It is a valuable neuralgic remedy, not simply for colic but for neuralgic pains in various parts of the body; the pains are usually sharp cutting or boring, nearly always > pressure (Bry.).

Mind.—He could not find his way about the room and it was difficult to get rid of the idea that he was not in his own room. *Anxiety. Disinclination to talk. Morose, offended at everything.* Irritable; he asks for many things. Impatient. Despondent. Absent-minded. Confused by the beer drunk in the evening. Could not pursue any train of thought. Not inclined to search after and grasp objects of interest. Indolent in morning, woke late and disliked to get up. Memory weak.

Head.—*Tearing digging through brain, < moving upper lid. Tearing in brain,* < moving lids, becoming a pressure outward in forehead. Aching; in morning in bed; daily from 8 A.M. till afternoon, with pains in knees and foot, then soft stool; in evening; < *bending forward, with pain in eyes* (Bry.); < stooping or turning head, < forehead, with incapacity for mental exertion; < after beer; as from a draught of air, > walking in open air; paroxysmal, here and there; as from pressure in region of middle of linea semi-circularis. Tearing drawing-pressing in different parts, especially boring behind r. ear and on r. side of head. Drawing when walking, with boring. *Sensitiveness* as if compressed, < bending forward, > open air, < *sinciput* and temples, with pain in eyeballs.

Heaviness. Dulness in morning, < in frontal region, returning in forenoon when walking; D., with vertigo and colic. Stupefied feeling after dinner. Confusion; in afternoon, *with pressure in orbits;* after eating; < dinner, > towards evening; with dulness, as after a debauch; with heaviness and feeling as if catarrh were coming on. Intoxicated feeling after a bottle of Bavarian beer. Vertigo; in evening; when walking rapidly after breakfast; suddenly in evening on sitting down, with darkness before eyes; *intimations of V. and nausea;* almost giddy after dinner.

Forehead.—*Sudden sticking* towards nose; sticking externally in morning after rising; S. above r. eye, with itching of scalp. *Tearing;* r. side; l. side; in evening; in different parts in morning. Boring; *r. side; r. side, with drawing;* l. side; above nose; in day and evening, with tearing; tearing, during a walk; B., and above eyes, with pressure. *Boring-burning pain on r. side.* Pain; *in l. side;* in nervus frontalis sinister; and in eyeballs; in forenoon when walking; < *stooping and lying on back;* along sagittal suture, < moving or shaking head and on stooping; at 1 P.M. in the arch which defines the lateral and superior boundaries of l. sinus, sometimes vibrating; and at root of nose, as before catarrh; throbbing P., > sitting up and moving head, but confusion of head all the forenoon. Drawing pain; in l. side. Drawing; in r. *Heaviness in sinciput, with stupefaction;* H. in forehead towards evening, with pressure; in l. side on waking after midnight, while lying on r. side. *Confusion;* r. side; in sinciput.

Temples.—*Boring sticking in r., > touch.* Tearing; in r.; in r. and above it; in r., with pressure. Boring; in r.; in l. at 2 P.M.; in l. as from a plug, in evening. Digging in l. Screwing. *Pain; early; in l. in afternoon,* > sitting, < standing and walking, but especially when urinating; in r., < stepping, with gloomy mood; first <, then > open air; tensive, in r. *Pressing and drawing pain in r. Pressing in l., with throbbing, becoming cutting,* with similar sensation about l. shoulder-joint; P. towards nose, with dryness of latter. Vertigo on suddenly turning head, as if arising in l. temple, it seems as if he would fall, with tottering of knees.

Pinching in upper part of brain. Tearing in r. side of vertex. Pain in vertex and l. eye, as of a nervous pressure. Tearing in l. side of head; towards forehead. Boring in different parts of r. side. One-sided drawing pain. *Confusion of l. side, with pressing burning pain in l. orbit, temple, nose, dorsum of nose and upper teeth,* it seems as if eye and nose were swelling; C. in r. side, < temple. Boring in r. side of occiput. Pressure in lateral occipital protuberances; in occiput, < inferior lateral protuberances, with tension. Boring in skull, < r. side. Roots of hair painful. Burning pain in skin above eyes. Drawing in scalp. Vertex sore as if the hair were pulled upward, > towards evening; with drawing pain in occiput. Itching; on l. side, with crawling. Biting burning on l. side of scalp.

Clinical.—Violent neuralgic headaches, cutting or boring, > firm pressure.

Eyes.—*Smarting, with pain in balls.* Dryness in evening. Sticking as with knives in r. ball, extending to root of nose. *Cutting in r. ball. Pain in balls, < stooping;* P. in ball, extending upward and outward, in evening, < rubbing, with hardness; as from a pressure downward upon balls. Burning pain in r. ball. Itching of r. ball. Sticking in l. conjunctiva palpebrarum, then inflammation, then ulceration. *Twitching of r. upper.* Stye on l. Burning cutting in r. lower lid during rest. Smarting of lids. Pressing in r. lid. Burning of r. upper lid; sticking, on edge of l. upper lid; biting, beneath upper lid; prickling, in r. inner canthus. L. lid lay thick and heavy upon ball, which felt squeezed anteriorly and superiorly. Heaviness of lids without sleepiness. Sticking in l. orbit, with drawing and aching. Pressing in orbits towards root of nose. Vision obscured; of r. eye in morning. Flickering before r. eye in the shape of a circle, with rays, at 10 A.M., after writing. A bright white light at side of and below r. eye, > turning eyes rapidly sideways.

Clinical.—It has been found useful as a palliative of the pain of glaucoma and iritis, the pain extending into head, > pressure.

Ears.—Itching sticking extending from Eustachian tube to tympanum, > boring in with finger. Cutting sticking in lower fossa of r. external, > boring in with finger. Boring in r.; behind r. Twinges in r. Pressure behind l. Drawing above r.; behind l.; painful behind l. Crawling within, > boring in with the finger. Obstruction before l. Ringing; in r. *Roaring, < l., with throbbing;* R., with every sound; rhythmical, in l., with obstruction, the R. changing to ringing.

Nose.—*Throbbing burrowing* from l. side to root. Feeling as in incipient catarrh. Itching in l. nostril in evening, with irritation as in coryza. Sneezing; with dryness of nose. *Fluent coryza;* in morning; with frequent sneezing; (constant dropping from nose, < in open air).

Face.—Twitching of muscles of chin during rest of the parts. Muscles relaxed and pale, and eyes sunken. *Tearing in cheeks. Constriction in l. malar-bone, extending into l. eye, with pressing.* Pain in l. cheek; r. malar-bone and eye. Burrowing burning pain in cheek, < rest. Painful drawing. Tension in l. side, extending to ear and into head, with tearing. Prickling as if an eruption would appear in region of r. cheek-bone. *Sticking in upper jaw.* Boring in r. lower jaw; in lower at 10 A.M.; in r. joint in evening. Drawing in lower jaw. Pustule on l. corner of mouth. (Bleeding of a liver-spot on upper lip). Burning of under lip; with swollen feeling. Burning pain in r. corner of mouth.

Clinical.—Facial neuralgia about eye, < l. side, great soreness and yet relief from pressure (Magnesia m.).

Mouth. — Painful looseness of a lower incisor. Toothache in r. teeth; l.; all upper; a hollow tooth; upper hollow; in lower teeth as if nerves were torn or stretched; twitching from l. lower molars to l. elbow; sticking throbbing, in r. lower back teeth, as from beating with a wire. Drawing toothache in lower incisors; in all teeth in afternoon; D., with tearing; in r. upper teeth, with swollen feeling in upper lip. Incisors sensitive. Teeth feel as if on edge in evening and next day. Heat in roots of r. lower teeth, with swollen feeling.

Tongue red; coated white, with rawness as from too much smoking; rough as if sandy; sticking in tip when sitting; *scalded sensation. Burning on anterior surface of tongue; on tip of T.;* on apex at the beginning of every exacerbation of symptoms. Biting in middle of tip as if sore. Border of tongue sensitive when eating. Scraping in palate. Biting in r. cheek and on side of tongue. Burning, < hard palate. Salivation. *Taste bitter;* after drinking beer; to beer at noon; and disgusting; T. metallic, astringent, on upper part of tip of tongue; insipid T. after dinner; nauseous T., more in throat than in mouth.

Throat.—Constant hawking; H. up of salt mucus; of bitter mucus. Angina. Sticking as from a bristle on upper part of arch of palate; biting S. in fauces, > swallowing. Scraping; and on hard palate, with burning; in region of uvula, with redness of whole throat and difficult swallowing. Pain. Rawness. Roughness; in pharynx and soft palate, > afternoon, with burning. Sensation of a foreign body, as if he had to swallow over a lump. Sensation of a ball as large as a fist rising in pharynx, with oppressed sensation. Dryness; and of hard palate, as if the parts stuck together.

Stomach.—*Canine hunger;* especially for bread and beer; then heartburn in throat; at noon. Appetite diminished; at noon; for dinner. Appetite lost; in evening. Aversion to food towards evening before eating, with nausea. *Thirst;* unquenchable. Desire to drink without thirst, the mouth is watery, drink is relished, but there is a flat taste after every drink.

Eructations; on rising from stool, mostly empty; *violent;* violent after eating; sobbing; sour; bitter; of the breakfast; of bilious substances; of a bitter, white, frothy liquid after breakfast. *Empty eructations;* in morning; on rising up; with burning in pharynx; causing palpitation and spasm in throat, with desire to retch and vomit. Hiccough. *Nausea;* towards noon; after eating, with malaise, as from indigestion; till sleep at night, returning in morning on waking; with scraping in throat, the N. > a glass of water; *rising from stomach. Vomiting of a yellow, bitter, serous fluid;* V. of food without nausea; profuse V.

Rumbling. *Griping in epigastric region after every meal, < towards evening; G. in E. region, with movements, then soft stool;* paroxysmal G. in stomach from beer (after 11 A.M.), > dinner. *Pinching in pit, preventing sleep, with constriction of stomach, and sensitiveness of S. so that it could bear no covering;* P. in epigastric region. *Intermittent compression in epigastrium, changing to pinching, with confusion of sinciput. Cramp at night, > eructations;* C. at night, rising along œsophagus into throat.

Pain; in pit; l. epigastrium; after dinner; in epigastric region, < eating, with hunger, which was not > repeated eating; with flatulence and headache; with headache and diarrhœa; always with pains in face and teeth; in pit, with constriction in larynx, obliging frequent swallowing; in pit, with sticking, obliging rapid breathing, it seems as if the lungs could not be sufficiently inflated; *burning,* even when eating; spasmodic, rising into throat, in morning; contractive, in pit at 10 P.M., during a walk after supper. Pressure as from a stone. Sore feeling in pit. *Full feeling in epigastric region* in forenoon. Sensation of a ball in S. and pharynx. *Emptiness.* Heat; in epigastrium. Coldness. Dyspepsia.

Abdomen.—Distention and pain (Magnes. c.); towards noon, when walking; after supper, with heaviness; with tension and sensitiveness to touch, the pain > by two watery stools; *D., with tension.* Collapsed. *Croaking as of frogs. Rumbling;* early in bed; towards 9 A.M.; in forenoon, with griping; after dinner; *with deep-seated pulsations;* with excitement as before diarrhœa, but discharge of only fetid flatus; as from bursting of bubbles. Gurgling; then light-yellow, fluid stool. *Movements;* towards noon, *then two brown, almost watery, painless stools;* in evening, then pappy stool; *after dinner, then copious soft stool, then griping, < vesical region, > thin stool;* in afternoon, as if he had fasted; in various parts, as from the breaking of bubbles. *Discharge of flatus;* offensive; *offensive after dinner, > after stool, with movements in hypogastrium;* noisy, in morning; noisy, when walking, causing rectum to vibrate; long, rapid and smooth discharges of bubbles of inodorous gas; ineffectual desire to pass flatus, then profuse discharge. *Incarcerated flatus* (Diosc.). *Flatulence, with tension.*

Sticking deep into abdomen. Drawing tearing in whole A. **Pinching; as if bowels were pressed inward, > by pressure and bending inward, with cutting extending towards pubic region, so severe below navel that facial muscles were distorted and eyes drawn together; as if squeezed between stones,** *and threatened to burst outward,* at times with rush of blood to head and face and sweat on them, which on relief of pain seemed blown upon by a cool wind; threatening of P., < forenoon, with insipidity. **Griping; < below navel, obliging him to bend over,** > *pappy stool;* < walking; > *thin stool, with discharge of flatus upward and downward; so that he could not lie nor sit, and could only walk bent over, > violent motion and rolling about;* waking in morning, with tenesmus, then normal stool. the G. > black coffee, but returning in forenoon with rumbling and movement; ending above mons veneris. *Gnawing after moving about* in forenoon, > towards noon; *G. < after dinner, with boring, obliging him to sit down or lie and bend forward, tenesmus, copious, pappy, offensive stools, then watery, scanty and almost inodorous stools,* the colic > black coffee at 4 P.M., < supper, then with confusion of head *and aching in sinciput, < bending forward.* **Cutting;** in afternoon, > evening in warmth of bed, with tenesmus; after eating; after dinner and supper; from flatus which cannot be passed, with sticking, waking him; *like an electric shock through whole A. to anus, towards noon.* Cramplike pain, preventing sitting quietly, lying or walking, with empty urging after eating. Pain as from taking cold or from improper food.

Pain; in morning on waking, with tenesmus; at noon and evening after eating; in evening, with heat in stomach, the pain > 9 P.M. by diarrhœa; at night; at night, with discharge of flatus; *when walking a few steps; when walking* at noon, > standing still; after eating a potato, with sudden stool; when lying, with rumbling, urging to stool and general shivering; before and during a light-yellow, fluid stool; in integuments, < walking; > diarrhœa; > diarrhœa, with uneasiness; > a cup of coffee, but then he must go to stool; > by smoking, which left a sensation in abdomen as if he had taken cold; *with urging to stool,* which was subject to control; with feeling of gnawing diarrhœa; with general uneasiness, and shivering in cheeks, which seems to rise from abdomen; **paroxysmal, obliging him to bend forward,** > *soft stool.*

Flatulent pain after midnight from sudden incarcerated flatus here and there. Bruised pain combined with pressure. Tensive pain, > pressure; T. pain as if intestines were gathered into a ball, had fallen down and were lying like a heavy weight in hypogastrium, it seems as if the anterior parietes of A. were wanting and the intestines were in danger of falling out. Pressure outward in r. side. *Sensitiveness;* in afternoon, with griping and commotion; with constipation. Constriction of viscera, > *pressure* (Magnes. m.). Feeling of looseness. Coldness. Heat; rising towards chest; pleasant warmth ending in griping, > walking, with sweat on chest and abdomen. Emptiness; < eating, stooping forward when sitting and in evening; as after copious diarrhœa.

Upper Abdomen.—Flatulent distention, > emission of flatus, with pulsation in small of back. Rumbling in l. hypochondriac and umbilical regions, with cutting. *Sticking in hepatic region;* after dinner, and in sacrum; in hepatic region, causing a restless night; beneath last ribs. *Cutting;* on inspiration, as from flatulence. Griping; with two pappy stools. Pinching after taking anything, < towards evening. Sudden thrust forward through hepatic region and then in a straight line through head. Pain towards noon after violent exercise; P. rose towards chest and became constrictive, < a shock, hawking or the like; in r. hypochondrium, at arch of diaphragm, oppressing respiration. Throbbing in l. hypochondrium, at arch of diaphragm. Drawing in l. hypochondrium.

Umbilical Region.—Swelling, with confusion in forehead and temples. *Sticking in a spot obliging him to bend up, < lifting;* S. on r. side beneath navel, then on l. side of navel, only when walking on a level, > standing still and even on violent agitation (as in descending stairs); *twitching S. extending towards loins and spine.* Burrowing tearing, < expiration or loud laughter. *Cutting after eating, with tenesmus.* **Griping**; < **eating fruit**; < *stool,* **with cutting** *and general chill;* < dinner; < pressure, with sensitiveness of abdominal integuments; with discharge of flatus; below navel; (*drawing hither and thither*), *changing into cutting as if a chisel were thrust deep into upper abdomen, passing in a curve backward into pelvis, then cutting upward again, at* 4 P.M., *at* 4.30 *the cutting in the hypogastrium was forward and upward, < forcible discharge of flatus and by straining and consequent expulsion of a long train of slippery bubbles of wind, with scanty bland mucus, returning at intervals, finally after* 5 P.M. *a painful expulsive pressure, then involuntary thin bland stool of fæces and much mucus, then relief of all pain in abdomen.* Pinching; with cutting. Gnawing, < morning fasting. Repeated sensation below navel when walking as after taking cold, with urging to stool as if the sphincter had no resisting power, stools thin, orange-colored and pappy, afterwards drawing-cutting darting repeatedly from behind forward and upward in a curve to navel, < urging to stool, which ran out in a watery stream and contained undigested soup, the sphincter seemed paralyzed, then ineffectual urging, which when repressed by voluntary muscles caused tension in lowest abdominal parietes and pressure at inferior angle of r. scapula, with tensive pain extending thence forward, then free protracted stool, the sphincter standing wide open. *Acute pain, < walking.* **Pain emanating from navel** (Diosc.), > **by frequent discharge of flatus,** *preventing sleep;* P. in evening; *at night;* after rising, with eructations; > night-sweat and flesh-colored urine, with the difficulties in the head; in spot below navel, extending after the night-sweat through whole abdomen. *Bruised pain in a spot, < walking, > eructations.* Constriction; waking at 3 A.M.; in evening; **after dinner.** Compression at times, < towards morning, with sensation of a ball, increasing to a twisting or cutting pain. *Sensitiveness. Sense of inflation, after dinner* (Mag. c.), *with compression in throat and nausea.* Bubbling in a spot below navel.

Lower Abdomen.—Gurgling in groin. Movements after dinner, > a soft stool. Sticking in pubic region; in r. flank; in l. groin; deep in l. groin; in flank, interrupting respiration; **single S., now in r., now in l. groin, apparently connected with ovaries.** Cutting; so that he must walk bent over, with general weakness, which makes walking difficult, with dread of work; after dinner, forcing him to a fluid stool; smarting, when walking, < every step. Griping, with rumbling and inflated sensation, going off with a stitch towards l. pubic region; G. in l. groin. Boring in l. groin close to pelvic bones. Pain after dinner, > discharge of fetid flatus and a stool; P. in pubic region; *in groin as if a hernia would protrude and on pressure pain as if a hernia were going inward,* in afternoon. Bruised pain, < walking and sitting bent over. Constriction about pubic region. Dragging from both sides to middle of hypogastrium, as from flatus which will not pass, but provokes emission of serum. Drawing pain in both groins, going all around pelvis. Tensive pain in r. groin, < pressure. *Tension in region of l. anterior superior spine of ilium in evening,* changing next day into *drawing, extending from spine of ilium to inguinal region and upper third of inner surface of thigh.*

Clinical.—Colic of the most violent character, < hard pressure, sometimes with nausea and vomiting, sometimes with diarrhœa, sometimes with discharge of great quantities of gas; pains often extend into chest and pelvis, and may be caused by suppressed perspiration, as from drinking ice-water when heated, or it may be brought on by fits of anger; the patient always doubles up with the colic (compare Diosc., Magnesia, etc.).

Rectum.—Stitches. Pain in lower part; as from swollen hæmorrhoids, when sitting, walking and at stool. Tickling after a pappy stool. *Urging to stool; with sensation in anus and lower part of rectum as if weakened by diarrhœa; U. to a copious, yellowish-brown, partly thin, sourish, offensive stool, then transient relief of colic; then two abundant stools in quick succession, first pappy, then fluid, with ulcerative pain in bowels, > by bending forward, < upright position; sudden, then copious, pappy stool, then griping,* coldness in abdomen, sleepiness and disinclination to study; *frequent;* which was under control. *Ineffectual urging; frequent; then stool in single stony pieces.*

Anus.—Hæmorrhoids; painful; blind. *Discharge of blood; daily, with sticking and burning in small of back and in anus.* Moisture, and at perineum. Oozing of moisture in afternoon instead of the expected flatus. Twitching in anus and rectum in afternoon, with burning. Itching sticking; and in rectum. Pressing as before stool, but escape of only dissolving mucus; P., > escape of slightest quantity of wind or mucus. Sensitiveness around A., with frequent urging to an *unsatisfactory diarrhœic,* but painless stool. Sensation as if successive slippery bubbles were escaping. Prickling and oozing. Itching; and in orifice of urethra. Burning; after stool; during insufficient stool, with sticking; as after diarrhœa, with excoriated pain and moisture; B. and jerking in anus and rectum.

Stool.—**Fluid; after eating,** *with discharge of flatus, with colic all the afternoon, > warmth of bed;* with tenesmus; with griping, then tenesmus; and frequent; frequent, mucous, painless; and slimy, then bilious, at last bloody; and feculent at first, later almost of pure blood, with tenesmus and passage of pieces of mucous membrane; and light yellow in morning, F. and dark green at 6 P.M.; and rapidly discharged after gentle pressure and passage of slippery flatus at noon; almost F., frequent, yellowish; semi-fluid, with a storm of flatus, then considerable flatus; half watery, half solid. Dysentery; with passage of blood, with burning pain in sacral region. *Thin, frothy, saffron-yellow, musty, smelling almost like burnt blotting-paper.* Diarrhœa; after dinner; with tenesmus; with nausea without ability to vomit; then flatulence and weakness; *copious, with discharge of much mucus;* frequent; yellow, after dinner; greenish-yellow, with feeling as if he had taken cold. Soft, frequent, brown; soft, frequent, mixed with lumpy fæces and flatulency; soft, light-colored, mixed with hard knots; soft, dark green; soft, slippery, with tensive pressure over forehead, at 11 A.M., and again in afternoon, then pressure alternately upon bladder and anus; soft, scanty, viscid, every three days. Pappy after dinner; with shivering over head and back; P. after eating, then burning at anus; with burning at anus; then intermittent griping and feeling of having taken cold in umbilical region, and rumbling in bowels; *and frequent;* and frequent, with discharge of flatus; frequent, yellow, painless; with much mucus, then burning in anus.

Constipation. *Hard, only occurring once in two or three days; H. as if he were passing stones;* and dark, small (Bry.); dark green; and unsatisfactory in morning and after dinner; hard, lumpy, with much flatus. Partly dry and knotty, partly diarrhœic. Consistent, brown, often blackish-brown. *Bloody.* Scanty, mixed with mucus; S., slimy, tenacious. A second stool after dinner. Several small stools. Sluggish, occurring every other day. *Delayed, and either diarrhœic or hard and unsatisfactory.*

Clinical.—Diarrhœa as the result of anger, or from fruit, with colic, the evacuation preceded by the characteristic colic of Coloc. as an important indication. Dysentery, bloody and mucous, stools always after eating or drinking, preceded by colic.

Urinary Organs.—Sticking in bladder; alternating with sticking in rectum, > discharge of flatus. *Sudden pressure upon bladder, which was full, suddenly > rapid expulsion of flatus, which drove before it some mucus, these flatulent attacks often alternated with other symptoms.* **Frequent urging to urinate,** *with scanty emission; with copious, clear, watery urine,* in forenoon; urging, with pressure in pubic region; ineffectual U. *Frequent micturition;* and copious; of clear, watery urine. Urine retained, with painful retraction of testes and priapism.

Sticking along urethra. Sticklike tearing through urethra. Pain in tip, as if crushed, after urinating. Prickling in orifice in urethra after urinating. Burning in urethra after urinating; on passage of last drops. *Urine like brown beer* (Bry.), *becoming turbid as soon as cold, with copious sediment. Urine of faint flesh-color, depositing a light brown, flocky, unequal, translucent sediment, with hard, solid, reddish crystals, adherent to the vessel,* the urine passed during the day lighter-colored than towards evening, night and morning. *Copious;* in evening and night, and yellow. Scanty; and clear, dark orange-colored, sp. gr. increased, reaction acid, "urophain" and uric acid increased, chlorides diminished, epithelium increased. Dark. Deep wine-colored, with transparent cloud.

Clinical.—Pains from kidney calculus (comp. Berberis).

Sexual Organs.—Prepuce always drawn back and constricted behind glans at night. Impotence, the foreskin drawn behind glans, without aversion. Tearing in glans. Prickling sticking like an electric spark from tip of glans towards l. flank. Prickling in end of glans. Frequent erections. Painful twinges in r. testicle. Drawing pain in l. testicle. Desire increased; diminished. Pollution two nights in succession. Swelling of labiæ during pregnancy, with dragging and warmth in vagina.

Clinical.—Suppressed menses with the characteristic colic. Dysmenorrhœa, with violent pain, > hard pressure. Ovarian tumor. Cysts in the broad ligament. Many cases of cystic tumors in the ovaries or broad ligament have been cured by Coloc., especially if the tumors are round and small, associated with pain or with general discomfort, > pressure; the patient always wants the abdomen supported by a bandage, or has periodical attacks of severe pain. Inflammation of ovaries, with great soreness, ovarian colic, etc. Chyluria, urine is white like milk, coagulates in cold.

Respiratory Organs.—Scraping in a spot in larynx provoking cough. Constriction of larynx, > open air. Sensitiveness of larynx towards evening, with hoarseness. Tickling in larynx, with dry cough; T. in larynx, < night, waking him, with short, dry cough. Dryness of air-passages, then fatigue. Cough; less frequent during the day and as the articular pains increase; frequent teasing, day and night; hacking, in evening on smoking. *Tickling cough at night;* and during the day; in evening and night without expectoration; during the day, with choking and vomituri-tion; sudden dry, during the day, with nausea and retching. Dyspnœa at night, with slow breath, provoking cough. Breathing rapid.

Chest.—Whistling in morning on inspiration. Twitching in region of l. fifth and sixth ribs; in r. intercostal muscles, > becoming erect. Sticking in l.; under l. pectoralis; here and there and under ribs; in r. in forenoon; in l. towards evening, cutting short the breath; S. on inspiration and pressure on expiration; backward in r. in afternoon. Griping in r. intercostal muscles. Pain in places towards evening, and in hepatic region and over heart, impeding respiration. Tensive and pressing pain in both sides where diaphragm is attached. Frequent pressure in afternoon, with oppression and with sticking in chest and sides. Pressure in middle of sternum as if something were lying upon lungs. *Oppression;* in evening; before midnight, preventing sleep; after eating; on inspiration, with sticking; of r. side on breathing, with sticking; of r. ribs, on arch of diaphragm, arresting breath. Constriction, < walking, with sticking; C., then sticking in l. upper part, < walking. Compression on sides, < stooping forward, when sitting and in evening. Tension in chest and forehead before a soft and smoothly-passed stool. Bruised pain in spots anteriorly. Burning in a spot on r. side towards 11 o'clock.

Heart and Pulse.—Sticking in cardiac region on going to bed. Oppression towards 8 P.M. Palpitation; when sitting. Pulse rapid and small; slow and full.

Neck.—Tearing in l. side of nape. *Drawing pain in l. muscles, < motion;* D. pain in nape even during rest, then painful stiffness of neck, < on moving head; in l. large muscles, on motion it extends backward and disappears; as if nerves were torn and stretched, or as if bruised, extending from r. side across scapulæ. *Drawing in nape;* D. and boring in all muscles of neck, on different parts of occiput and of r. side of head, < evening. *Pressure in l. side of nape as in rheumatism, < turning.* Weight, extending towards occipital protuberance. *Stiffness of nape on moving head* (Bry.); S. on l. side, painful on motion.

Back.—Sticking. Drawing in dorsal muscles. Sticking beneath r. scapula on inspiration; tensive, between scapulæ, < walking, so that he must walk bent over.

Drawing pain in region of r. scapula as if nerves and vessels were tense. Drawings in scapulæ. Sore pain in l. scapula during rest. Stitches in sacrum; *tensive, in r. loin on inspiration,* < *lying on back.* Periodic cutting from region of l. kidney to abdomen, spasmodically drawing thigh up to abdomen so that he must bend over. *Pain in small of back;* as after a forced march, and in lower limbs; *in region of l. sacro-iliac articulation, with crawling in whole l. side as if asleep;* in sacrum, > movement; above hips, with nausea and chilliness. Pressing inward in r. loin when sitting, with throbbing. *Bruised pain in small of B. and in lower limbs in evening;* B. pain in sacrum; in lower part of back, with pressure in pit of stomach. Weariness in small of B. Heaviness in small of B.

Extremities.—Contraction of all so that he resembled a hedgehog. Twitching of different parts of muscles. Drawing sticking in joints of feet all day, < wine and coffee, with boring in lower limbs, in afternoon upper limbs similarly affected. Tearing in joints of arms and legs, < rest, > night. Boring in joints of toes, then in shoulders; in joints of toes and fingers at 9 P.M., with pressing; in muscles of limbs and buttocks, with burning pain; in finger-joints, shoulders, knees, shin-bones and ankles, with drawing; drawing B. in wrist, fingers, knees and muscles of thighs, in morning after rising and in evening. Pain in joints; P. in l. little finger about 6 P.M., < towards middle, then in all r. toe-joints except those of great toe; when sitting, in knees, wrists and thighs; in joints of hands and feet after rising; in joints of fingers and toes, < during rest; migrating, in joints of fingers and feet.

Rheumatic pains, and in joints; sometimes in joints, sometimes in bones of limbs. Drawing towards evening; *D. in external condyle of r. femur,* in elbow, fingers and toes, on motion, < knees; in different parts when walking; in joints, > motion, < fingers and toes; in all joints < sitting, with pressing; *tearing, in thighs, and in l. arm down to finger-joints;* tearing drawing-pressing in different joints. Pressing drawing pain, a tired sensation, < towards evening when sitting, < knees, feet and shoulder-joints. Bruised feeling; in knees, arms and shoulder-joints when sitting. Some of the joints feel as if compressed by rings. Constriction in dorsum and ankle of l. foot and in r. upper arm. Disagreeable feeling in all on mental exertion. Weakness of joints; W. in limbs on walking in open air, with heaviness and trembling of legs, < r., so that sweat broke out over the whole body; from diffusion of a genial warmth.

Upper Extremities.—Drawing and pressing pain in joints of hands, fingers and shoulders. Axillary glands swollen and painful. Drawing in l. axillary muscles extending down arm, with burning, then in r. shoulder. Tearing in shoulders. Boring in shoulder; in r. Pressing in shoulders when sitting. Drawing pain in shoulders in afternoon. Drawing in r. shoulder; at night in bed; in r. joint, with tearing all day; in shoulders and joints of hands, with boring. Tension in r. shoulder on waking, < using arms.

Arm.—Intermittent sticking now here, now there. Pain in l. Sprained pain behind r. scapula. Drawing pain in long bones during rest, < below head of humerus and across wrist, where it seems as if in periosteum on raising arm. Intermittent paralytic bruised pain. Paralytic pressing in l. Swollen sensation. Pulsation in l. Weakness.

Upper Arm.—Sticking in humeri in evening. Tearing in l. Pressing in joints. Throbbing, finally twitching pain in periosteum, in region of insertion of r. deltoid, extending through shoulder to upper teeth and to temples and vertex, then sore pain in muscular parts of arm on pressure. Prickling burning pain in r. on motion. Drawing in r.; < dinner, > walking in open air.

Elbow.—Sticking in r., and in forearm; itching S. in bend of r. during rest. Tearing in r., with burning pain. Boring. Pressure. Drawing in r.; l. Weakness.

Forearm.—Drawing sticking in periosteum. Boring and pressing, and in wrists. Crampy pain in l. Occasional pains in r. in morning. Drawing pain in l., persisting at elbow. Tensive pain in r. Pressing drawing. Stiffness of r., with pain in extensors. Falling asleep of r.

Wrist.—Boring. Drawing pain when sitting. Pressing; and in forearm.

Hand.—*Sticking in r. metacarpus* at 7 P.M. when writing, *hindering opening of the hand and stretching of fingers,* repeated at 8 P.M. when reading and afterwards at different times. *Tearing in joints of l.* Pain in joints; in palmar joints; cramplike, in palms, so that the fingers were difficult to open, < during rest; contractive pain in r. hand, < until a similar pain occurred in malar-bone, the pain in hand then spread over forearm as the facial pain decreased and grew milder, when the facial pain and colic occurred. Drawing in hands and fingers; with pinching; in r. hand and wrist, then in r. elbow. Stiff feeling.

Fingers.—Sticking in joints. *Drawing tearing in joints of l.* Drawing pain in ball of r. thumb, as if in a tendon, disappearing at the tip. Drawing; in ball of thumb. Pressure in r. *Tensive pain in thumb, impeding its motion.* Bruised pain in r. middle, at noon. Burning pain in one point in r. middle.

Lower Extremities.—Pain < till noon and when walking; P. > drinking beer. Boring in joints, < towards evening and when sitting. *Heaviness.*

Thigh.—*Cramp on middle of l. Drawing twitching in region of l. hip, with throbbing, and in r. loin over crest of ilium, towards buttock.* Sticking in muscles above knees; on inner side of l., from ischiatic tuberosity towards knee, in forenoon when walking; in flesh, with drawing; *in region of r. hip, suddenly appearing and disappearing when walking, > sitting, but instead of S. there was weight in lumbo-dorsal region, > lying on l. side, with heat and* **sensibility of the part,** *> on rising and walking, when the sticking returned, the pain > night in warmth of bed, but it woke him at 4 A.M., when it was throbbing and boring,* **the trouble lay in the sacral region, corresponding to the position of the plexus ischiadicus, extended through the incisura ischiadica major towards the hip-joint, down posterior part of thigh into fossa poplitea** (compare Gnaphalium). Sticking tearing when sitting and standing. Boring in muscles; in spots in muscles of l. when sitting; in r. hip-joint. Pressure in middle of l.; P. in muscles; above knees when walking; in muscles when sitting. *Pain in r. upper when walking, as if psoas muscle were too short.* Bruised and weary pain in hips and knees in morning. Burning pain in muscles of r., making walking difficult. *Drawing pain in r. as far as knee;*

D. pain in muscles. *Drawing in inner side of l. as far as flank; in l. side of l. all the afternoon;* in T. and calf; in muscles of T. and calves when walking, so that flexure of lower limbs was painful; in muscles, with burning; cramplike, along inside of r. at 7 P.M. when walking. Drawing tension in r. Clucking in l. buttock. Stiffness of hip-joint. Weariness, < ascending stairs.

Knee.—Sticking; in l.; in r. patella when walking, > continuing to walk; in hollow on motion, at last itching S. Boring in l., then r.; in r. at 6 P.M.; when sitting, with pressing; with drawing. Cramp pain, and in calves. Pain, and in ankles; frequent P. in r. in evening; *in l., impeding walking.* Bruised sensation when sitting; and when walking. Paralytic pain when walking, as if bound. Drawing pain; when sitting; when sitting, with bruised sensation and general malaise. Drawing and pressing, and in shins; in l. knee as if pinched; intermittent D. in inner part of r. towards noon when walking, with tension and empty feeling; D. in l. popliteal space on getting out of bed, as if tendons were too short; in r. in forenoon, *then in r. thigh;* D. and stiffness alternately in r. and l. Tension in l. on rising from bed, with stiffness; T. in l. patella in evening, < next day, so that walking was painful, with heat and swelling and pulsation in the swelling. Pulsation in l. popliteal space. Weariness; < sitting; when sitting at 9 A.M., extending into legs and ankles. Stiffness in l. when sitting, > walking. Heaviness of both in evening, > walking, with tearing in l.

Leg.—*Cramp;* in muscles near tibia towards morning, < by bending knee. Sticking in l.; drawing, on outer side when sitting; itching, in r., even on motion; itching, in r. tibia, < during rest. Tearing in sides of tendo-achillis; in l. tibia and ankle, on waking at midnight. Boring above ankles when sitting; B. on tendo-achillis. Pain in the hitherto painless varices. Throbbing pain in upper inner part of r. when sitting and walking, extending to posterior side of thigh towards ischium. Bruised sensation. Pressing together in r. when sitting. Cramplike squeezing around middle of l., as from a narrow ribbon. Tensive pain in tibiæ when sitting. Drawing, and in ankles; in tibia; in tendo-achillis; in tendo-achillis when sitting; in legs when walking and sitting; in r. when sitting; on tibia, < l., < sitting, and in calves; *sticking D. along l. tibia into ankle-bones,* in evening, *with burning pressure in l. eye.* Weakness. Asleep.

Calf.—Twitching in r., > motion. *Cramp in l.;* C., < coition. Sticking; itching, in r. *Tearing in l. as far as heel;* T. at times when sitting and standing. Cutting on inner side of l. during rest. Boring pinching in muscles. Pressing. Drawing when standing, with pressing; cramplike D. in r. *Feeling as if asleep* longitudinally along outer side of r., as if in tract of a nerve, then increased in extent, as if the nerve were swollen in its periphery, gradually passing into constriction, and then the same feeling on dorsum of first joint of r. great toe, then under nail of l. great toe.

Ankle.—Sticking; and in dorsum of r. foot and in l. great toe; tearing, about r. inner malleolus. Boring when walking and sitting; when walking, with drawing, and in dorsum of foot; in malleoli. Pressing in l.; in r., with drawing; when sitting, with tearing. Pain when walking in the street as from a misstep, > rest. Drawing in r.; towards inner malleolus.

Foot.—*Increased in size,* so that the boots were too small in the instep. Trembling; as from fright, with shaking chill. Sticking along external border of l. sole; itching-boring, in dorsum of r., < during rest. Tearing on dorsa; on dorsum of l.; in periosteum of heel; in r. metatarsus, towards great toe-joint in evening; in r. sole, < during rest. Sticking cutting in r. as if a nail were driven through it. Boring in l. sole. Gnawing in inner ball of l. in evening. Cramplike pain *on dorsum of r.,* in scaphoid and internal cuneiform bones, as if in periosteum, *with soft, pale, painless, circumscribed swelling like a lymphatic tumor, on r. edge of tarsus, lasting six months, the same pain in l. foot* and sometimes in second joint of great toe, without swelling. *Painful pressure on dorsum of r.,* < l. side towards great toe, > walking, *with falling asleep of r. leg.* Twitching pain in dorsa towards tibiæ when walking in street. *Drawing aching in l.* Drawing in soles. Heaviness in morning in bed, > rising and walking. *Falling asleep of l., then r.; of l.,* even during rest; when stooping in evening, *and knees;* of l., with swelling and heat, gradually extending to whole leg, with itching and tickling; sensation as if l. would go to sleep in evening when sitting.

Toes.—Sticking in tips and below nails of l.; in tips of r., with boring. Tearing under nail of l. great. Boring in r.; in ball of great; in joints of r. great. Cramp pain in r. second, extending towards sole; sudden C. pain in r. great in evening, extending towards sole, then swelling of whole r. foot, < sole, in night and next day, with pain when stepping on it or making strong pressure; threatening of cramp pain and stiffness alternately in r. second toe and both knees. Sprained pain in l. in evening on ascending steps. Pressure in posterior joint of r. great, in evening when moving about; P. on r. great, < during rest; in some, in afternoon, and in calves; in posterior joint of l. great, as if the boot were too tight, > walking, with throbbing and with heaviness of feet, < forenoon, and sensation in feet when sitting, < l., as if falling asleep. Intermittent pain in r. second, and in knees. Drawing extending to dorsum of foot and to ankles; D. in r. Stiffness of l. great.

Clinical.—Sciatica, pain extremely violent, tearing, shooting, boring, < heat, pressure and by flexing leg on abdomen.

Skin.—Desquamation over whole body. Pimple on l. cheek, with biting on touch, and after scratching watery oozing; white pimples on face, < between eye and ear, on forehead and chin, with twinging, and when touched biting. Boil on face, then one on back; on l. side of neck, with burning pain, and one on lower angle of l. scapula; on ulnar side of both hands. Ulcers, with itching and burning. Vesicle filled with pus on l. upper arm, with red-hot border, with pain on motion, then with drawing in whole arm, the pain sometimes extending to axilla and fingers, preventing sleep at night, then discharge of pus.

Sticking on calves; on dorsum of hand. Prickling on different parts, with crawling. Crawling on l. side of chest and abdomen. Itching on various parts; causing restlessness; on various spots, < l. side of body, which smart like burning points; I. of face; in umbilical region in evening; in hollow of l. knee, then biting after scratching; biting I. here and there in evening in bed, only transiently > scratching, then uneasiness so that the limbs must be moved constantly, and sleepleesness; (I. of whole body, < chest and abdomen in morning, as after profuse sweat). Tickling itching in l. gluteal muscles when sitting; tickling I. on r. arm, > scratching; on thigh, face, shoulders, flanks and on tip of glans penis, with urging to urinate.

Sleep.—Yawning; spasmodic. Sleepiness at noon; early when reading an interesting work; with disinclination to mental labor; with inclination to lie down and during sleep uneasiness of limbs, < legs. Sleeps on his back, with one hand under the occiput and the other arm over the head. Sleeplessness; all night, thoughts and plans about his occupation keep him quiet and dispassionate. Restless at night. Restless sleep; before midnight, with voluptuous dream and a pollution, during which he awoke; after midnight, with vivid, troublesome dreams; with horrible, exciting dreams; with vivid, senseless dreams; with vivid dreams, frequent waking from pain in umbilical region; interrupted by vivid dreams, sweat every time on waking. Frequent waking. Interrupted by vivid dreams and frequent calls to urinate. Heavy, full of dreams. Many and various dreams. Dreams full of difficult thought. Vivid, anxious D.; vivid, with frequent waking, always on his back. Voluptuous dreams; when lying on back, with emissions without erections; with intractable erections without emissions; with emissions.

Fever.—Chilliness; *in whole body;* in whole body, then heat. Shivering through whole body in morning after rising, with cold hands, heat of face and rest of body, without thirst; S. after eating, < upper arms. Cold limbs; knees; hands and tips of fingers in morning after rising, with warm face; hands in evening, with warm feet; upper arms in evening. Internal coldness, but not external, in knees; in soles. C. alternating with heat and intermittent sweat.

Heat; < upper part of body; on waking in night, < lower limbs. Internal and external. In flushes, without thirst; F. < in face, with sweat on forehead. In head; in r. ear; nape; in l. foot and along tibia when walking; in skin of calves, < r.; in pin-scratches on fingers, also in face and head.

Sweat over whole body towards morning; S. at night; general S. on walking, with weakness; over face; on legs in morning on waking; greasy, on forehead and chest; of urinous odor on head, hands, legs and feet, at night.

Comocladia.

A tincture is made of the fresh bark of Comocladia dentata, Jacq.

General Action.—Almost exactly similar to *Rhus tox.*, *Anacardium*, Ailanthus and other botanical allies.

Generalities.—Swelling of whole body; *then redness all over like scarlet fever* (Rhus t.), afterwards color of skin like a mulatto's. Aching in both sides and upper arms, in forenoon, < r. side. General malaise, fever and headache. Weakness in afternoon, with heat and perspiration on face and neck. Symptoms < l. side. Symptoms disappear when moving in open air (Rhus t.).

Mind.—Cheerfulness in morning; in forenoon. Combative, vindictive disposition, with contempt for opponents. (Self-complacent thoughts and contempt for others?)

Head.—Aching, stupefying, throbbing; indescribable A. Confusion. Heaviness in morning; H., with enlarged feeling. Catarrhal symptoms, with soreness of eyes from 4 or 5 P.M. through the evening, and lachrymation. Symptoms worse near stove and when stooping, > open air. Aching in os frontis and in orbital bones; deep in brain over r. eye; deep in anterior part of brain on sitting down; above l. eyebrow at 4.12 P.M.; in forehead in afternoon, and on moving head sense of fulness, rigidity and lameness of muscles of neck. Heaviness in forehead and eyes.

Temples.—Pain; in r.; in r. at 1 P.M.; in r. at 6 P.M., and in r. orbital bones; in r. at 11.30 P.M. while lying on r. side, then pain and sense of fulness in r. side of face; in r. bone, beginning in temporal ridge at 4 P.M. and extending to occiput, with pain in whole base of brain on moving head and in mastoideus and trapezius muscles; sharp, at 2.35 P.M. passing down r. temporal ridge and external angular process, then sharp pain in r. supraorbital ridge, close to supraorbital notch.

Intermittent pain in r. side. Constriction in sides. Sharp pain in occiput, extending down neck. Itching of scalp; mostly in superior l. parietal region.

Eyes.—Look dull and glassy, vessels congested, lids red, swollen and inflamed. **Pain in r. at 3 or 4 P.M., with feeling as if larger and more protruded than l.**; *P., < near a stove*, with lachrymation when stooping, and with soreness of eyeballs, < r.; from posterior part of r. through head to occipital protuberance, with soreness of eyeball, lachrymation and feeling as if the eye were as large as two eyes, next morning sore feeling in eye. *Feeling heavy, larger, painful, pressing out of head, as from a pressure on top of eyeballs moving them downward and outward* (Rhus t.). Symptoms < l. towards and during evening; S. < r. during the day; < moving head, reading, looking at a lighted candle and bright objects. Symptoms > sitting quietly before a wood fire on the hearth. Lachrymation from looking at a lighted candle, with increase of pain in eyes; L. < in open air.

Balls.—Intermittent pain from posterior part of both through head to below occipital protuberance, with pressure on superior surface of balls, seeming to move eyes downward and outward. Soreness in evening; *of r.* at 6 A.M., < *moving eye;* aching, from 4 or 5 P.M. till 10, < evening, by candle-light and by motion, sometimes causing vertigo, and stooping or motion caused flow of tears. *Feeling worse on moving them.*

Lids.—Inflammation of Meibomian glands of r. upper. Stitches upward in l. external canthus about 8.30 P.M. Itching at r. external canthus, then at lower border of l. eye.

Clinical.—*Ciliary neuralgia from asthenopia and pain from other causes, especially if the eye feels large and protruding.*

Ears.—Pain extending to lower jaw. Heat internally in r. at 1 P.M., with fulness. Ringing, with vertigo.

Nose.—Itching internally and externally over all that part inferior to bridge, until going to sleep at night, momentarily > by rubbing.

Face.—*Swollen, with eyes projecting from their sockets and ability to see only a faint glimmer of light with the l.* (Rhus t.); S. around eyes at 6 A.M., much puffed below superior tarsal cartilage in afternoon. Aching at base of r. antrum of highmore at 10.30 P.M., then at base of l. Sensation as if skin were drawn up from face and about nose, causing vertigo.

Jaw.—Aching in ramus of r. at 9 A.M.; in l. articulation at 5.10 P.M. after light exercise in open air, leaving a sense of fulness, then aching in r. articulation ending in sharp pain; in r. articulation, involving whole r. side of head, at 5.22 P.M. on entering a warm room after a walk in open air.

Lips.—Dry and chapped; and often bleeding. Sensation as of a scabby eruption on median line of lower, close to vermilion border. Corrosive burning on l. side of lower at 10 A.M. while at rest.

Mouth.—Molar. Aching in body of last r. lower, at 1 P.M., after dinner; in r. upper, at 5.30 P.M., < cold air, and in gum; sore pulsating, in body of r. upper middle, at 6.30 P.M., > holding r. side of face to the stove; in a r. upper middle (the molar below it is carious), < at 12 M. and becoming twitching, that is, a sensation as if the tooth were drawn out of the socket, putting the nerve on the stretch, and suddenly pressed into the socket again, the pain shooting into temple, lasting till 3 P.M., < holding cold water in mouth, > pressure of hand and holding affected side close to hot stove, with elongated sensation. Loose sensation in r. at 4.30 P.M.

Aching in lower incisors at 3 P.M. while reading, passing to r. cuspid and bicuspid teeth; A. in lower incisors at 4.30 P.M., leaving them sensitive to pressure of upper teeth. Intermittent aching in bodies of all teeth. Swelling of the gum of a carious tooth. Cutting in gum of first l. lower molar at 1 P.M. Aching in gum and root of r. middle lower molar (which is hollow and loose) till going to sleep at 9.30 P.M., > holding r. side of face to the fire; sore, in gum of r. upper molars at 5.30 P.M., while at rest in a warm room.

Tongue.—Dryness at night, and of mouth; like a chip, with burning and swelling of lower lip, which remains chapped. Burning; in forenoon, with redness and dryness, especially of anterior part. Burnt feeling; and smoother and redder at tip than usual.

Throat.—Attacks of inflammation. Hawking up of mucus. Roughness, with scraping. Difficulty in empty deglutition. Sense of expansion in œsophagus at 3.30 P.M. while at rest, as of air slowly ascending from stomach.

Stomach.—Appetite for dinner less than usual; no A. for dinner. Eructations; with relief; frequent, at 9 A.M.; of air at 11 A.M.; of air at 4.30 P.M.; of air tasting of the drug at 10.15 A.M., while at rest; of sour acrid water at 2.5 P.M.; acrid, producing momentary strangulation, at 10.10 A.M., after walking in open air. Hiçcough at 3 P.M., then gaping. Nausea. Stitches in every direction in pit while lying on l. side at night < inspiration. Pain in epigastrium at 10 P.M., as from flatus. Expansive distress in epigastric region, like heartburn, extending through posterior border of l. scapula, about 11 P.M., while lying on l. side, > lying on r. side. Acrid, rancid sensation at 3.30 P.M., while walking in open air.

Abdomen.—Flatulence, with noisy eructations and discharge of flatus. Discharge of flatus, with desire for stool; of odorless flatus while walking in open air after breakfast. Full feeling, with pain. Pain in evening; P. < eating; with distention, rumbling and discharge of flatus; in various parts, sometimes mounting to axilla; in attacks, < r. side, and < sitting in-doors. Tensive feeling, as from flatus. Uneasiness; with pain.

Stinging in hypochondrium at 11 A.M. Aching in l. side at floating ribs at 7.15 A.M.; in l. side and rumbling of flatus, extending over abdomen; in r. side, extending down course of rectus muscle, at 3.40 P.M.; wandering, in r. side at 10 P.M. Pains around umbilicus at 8.30 P.M., extending to epigastrium. Sore pain extending across umbilicus at 9.30 P.M., affecting respiration, with bubbling in abdomen as of wind, and with emission of hot flatus. Pain in r. ilio-cœcal region, coming on like a thrust.

Hypogastrium.—Bubbling at 6.25 A.M., while sitting after a walk in open air. Pain at night, with gurgling, uneasiness and emission of odorless flatus. Flatulent pain; at 4.30 P.M., with emission of flatus, then pain in abdomen, at 6 P.M. flatulent pain in abdomen, preceding and during diarrhœa, then weakness and perspiration on face and neck. Shifting pains at 9 P.M. in bed. Throbbing in l. posterior side of abdomen, between spleen and kidneys, from twitching of tendons.

Stool and Urine.—Stool loose; and urgent, with aching at anus. Stool omitted. Urine covered with a pellicle and containing a cloud of mucus suspended in it, next day urine scanty.

Scrotum.—Numb tensive pain at 10 P.M., extending to inner condyle of thigh. Itching; when sitting and standing; about noon, and on lower part of penis, extending to prostate gland, and on inner surface of prepuce; tingling I. at night.

Respiratory Organs.—Itching in r. side of trachea at 7.15 P.M., after walking in open air, producing a dry, hacking cough, then itching in l. side of trachea, causing dry, hacking cough. Cough at night in bed, from irritation.

Chest.—Stitches just below apex of heart; beneath sternum, < towards r. side; inward in cartilages of sixth and seventh ribs, at 10.50 A.M., while walking in open air. Prickling in costal cartilages of eighth, ninth and tenth r. ribs. Aching in anterior wall during the day; in r. anterior wall, near axilla, at 3.40 P.M.; in r. anterior wall at 5 P.M., extending through to scapula; at posterior aspect of middle of sternum at 3.15 P.M.; in lower third of sternum at 11 P.M., while lying on l. side; in l. mamma, above nipple, at 3.30 P.M., while sitting in-doors, sometimes like a throbbing sore pain, sometimes as from pressure of the edge of a knife, > walking and deep inspiration, < expiration, with bruised feeling in ribs beneath when pressed by the hand, a return of the pain at 5 P.M., after supper, after leaving the mamma it passes down the side as low as the spleen, at 6.30 a return of the pain in the mamma, after leaving mamma lancinating pain passing down r. side of chest and inner side of r. upper arm, then to elbow, down forearm and along dorsal surfaces of second and third fingers, then pain in l. carpus, the pain returning at 7.25 and 9.20.

Sharp pain in upper part, apparently in pleura, at night in bed, on deep inspiration. Pulsating raw pain near sternal border of l. mamma, seemingly in cartilage of fifth rib, at 5 P.M. Sore aching in anterior wall while in bed. Sore spot below l. ribs at 7.30 P.M., then worse below r. ribs. Soreness in l. lung, as during convalescence from pneumonia, at 5.30 P.M. while at rest.

Drawing in r. anterior wall soon after 3.50 P.M.; at 1.30 P.M. while writing, and in r. arm, passing down arm to elbow. Drawing crampy sensation at outer border of r. mamma, extending to axilla and arm, at

2.30 P.M.; in r. anterior wall of chest and axilla at 3.25 P.M., extending to fingers and ending in jerking of little finger. Feeling of fulness and tightness across lower part of chest and upper part of abdomen, as if nothing could move, with swelling, and with difficulty of breathing, the last < morning in bed, > moving about and in open air.

Heart and Pulse.—Palpitation in morning on slight exercise. Pulse accelerated every day at 9 A.M. Arterial excitement at night.

Back.—Scapula. Pain under lower part of l. at 3.50 P.M.; crampy, below r. at 9.45 P.M.; sore, at r. at 9.50 P.M.; sharp broad, from lower angle of r. to locality of serrations of serratus magnus muscles, at 2.35 P.M., then pulsating pain at posterior aspect of coccyx. Aching in dorsal region at 10 P.M.; in coccyx while in bed. Pulsating pain in periosteum of l. pubic bone at 3.40 P.M., generally > walking, sometimes felt when walking, with sensitiveness to pressure. Pulsating pain in l. sacro-iliac articulation at 2.18 P.M.; in r. at 3.05 P.M., leaving a lameness, which is felt when walking. Intermittent pressing-outward pain at l. sacro-iliac articulation at 3.20 P.M., > walking, with sensitiveness to pressure, then lameness and soreness.

Extremities.—Aching in r. ankle at 11.30 P.M., then in r. forearm, then deep pulsating pain in r. gluteal region near tuber ischii. Drawing in muscles of r. upper arm at 6 P.M., in dorsum of r. foot, then in plantar region of r. foot, shifting rapidly from place to place.

Drawing in upper part of r. forearm at 11 P.M., while lying on l. side, with aching, then pulsating deep pain in r. gluteal region, just above tuber ischii, seemingly in periosteum, then sharp pain above crest of r. ilium, then return of the pain in r. gluteal region, then sharp pain above crest of l. ilium, then drawing and aching in r. foot, then in anterior muscles of r. forearm, then pulsating, deep pain in r. gluteal region, sensitiveness to pressure, then drawing and aching in anterior muscles of l. forearm, drawing in outer side of l. foot, extending to plantar aspect, as if the foot would cramp, then drawing and aching in l. leg, lame aching and drawing in r. forearm, near elbow, then return of the pain near r. tuber ischii, then aching in r. leg, then pulsating deep pain in r. thigh, at inner border of sartorius muscle.

Upper Extremities.—Axilla. Drawing or cramplike pain in r. Heavy drawing pain in l., extending towards shoulder, with sensation as if shoulder would be drawn towards neck. Sudden drawing at 4.15 P.M., while at rest, moving down inner side of arm to elbow, with aching.

Sharp pain through r. shoulder to scapula, at 3.08 P.M. while at rest. Trembling of l. arm and l. shoulder when reclining and supporting body with l. hand. Aching in muscles of r. arm while in bed. R. arm more painful, but in l. more tremulous sensation (and loss of power?). Pain at internal condyle of r. arm at 4.30 P.M., while standing in open air, at the same time and while arm is resting on a support drawing at inner side of l. upper arm.

Upper Arm.—Pain extending from a little above elbow down posterior part of arm, dorsum of hand, to ends of fingers, > exercising arm, with numbness of arm while holding anything with hand. Lame pain in r. at 2.30 P.M., while at rest. Drawing in r. at 7.15 P.M.; in muscles of r. at 7 P.M. while riding on horseback. Drawing crampy sensation in muscles of r. at 3.45 P.M., then in r. elbow.

Sticking in r. elbow at 2.45 P.M. Aching in l. forearm at 9.30 P.M.; in r. at 3.40 P.M., beginning in belly of flexor carpi radialis, extending through arm, with sensitiveness of arm to pressure. Pulsating pain in interosseous tissue of palmar aspect of l. forearm, near wrist, at 4.30 P.M., extending to little finger, where it becomes a drawing, crampy pain, then a drawing sensation, extending up forearm from wrist.

Numb tensive pain in forearm at 6 P.M., with rheumatic stiffness of shoulders and elbows. Drawing in r. forearm at 3.45 P.M., extending to metacarpus. Numbness of forearm, especially along ulnar nerve to end of last two fingers, and prickling when resting on elbow.

Carpus.—Pain suddenly piercing palmar surface of l. at 9.25 P.M., after a walk in open air, traversing dorsum of first and second fingers, becoming a drawing pain in its progress to metacarpo-phalangeal joints of those fingers, then involving all the r. metacarpo-phalangeal joints, drawing the fingers closer together and the thumb towards the palm, and the whole hand is numb, looks and feels swollen, with heat in it, the drawing > continued motion. Drawing pain through r. at 10 A.M., leaving lameness. Drawing, crampy sensation in l. at 6 P.M., then in anterior muscles of r. upper arm. Crampy aching in r. wrist at 9.45 P.M.

Hand.—Trembling of l. and of forearm. Sudden dancing pain in r. metacarpus at 1.30 P.M. while writing, ending in lame aching and drawing in metacarpal region of thumb and index. Drawing pain in dorsal aspect of metacarpal region of r. thumb at 3.30 P.M. Drawing crampy pain in middle of r. palm, extending to tips of fingers (not thumb), as if fingers would be drawn towards palm. Painful weakness of r., especially the two last fingers are inclined to numbness when writing. Numbness of l. at 9.30 P.M., with pain in dorsum of first phalanx of r. index, shooting to joint of first and second phalanges of index.

Fingers.—Stinging on dorsum of first phalanx of r. second, at 4.15 P.M. Pain in palmar surface of last phalanx of third, at 3 and 7 P.M.; in r. little while reading. Crampy sensation in first phalanges of r., at 3.47 P.M., increasing to aching, > motion of fingers; drawing C. sensation in first phalanx of r. ring, and sensation as if the finger would be flexed on palm, this drawing seemed to move towards metacarpo-phalangeal joint, appearing next day in first phalanx of r. ring finger, then in first phalanx of r. index.

Lower Extremities.—Twitching of tendons of r. buttock at 8.30 P.M. Aching in outer hamstring of r. leg in afternoon, with drawing; A. in upper and posterior part of l. thigh at 2.35 P.M. while writing; along outer side of r. thigh at 3.27 P.M., while at rest; near r. tuber ischii at 10 A.M. while standing before a stove.

Pulsating pain in neck of r. femur; in capsular ligament, at 4.10 P.M., > walking, returning during rest; pulsating P. in gluteal region, near r. tuber ischii, at 5 P.M., with sensitiveness to pressure. Pulsating, deep pain in posterior and upper part of thigh at 4.50 P.M.; at inner border of r. ilio-femoral ligament, at 1 P.M., > walking. Lame aching at inner side, just above r. knee, at 9.50 P.M., then wiry or threadlike pain in r. instep. (Tensive pain in anterior and lower part of thighs at 8 P.M., < r., with bruised feeling in periosteum on pressure.)

Knee.—Stitches in every direction in l. popliteal space, then smarting as if burnt. Intermittent pressing-outward pain in r. at 12.30 A.M., in bed, > motion. Lame pain in r. at 3 P.M. Crampy aching in l. at 9.20 P.M., while sitting in a warm room, not > motion. Drawing pain in r. at 3.50 P.M., extending into anterior muscles of thigh.

Leg.—Aching in r. at 12 M.; above r. ankle at 9 P.M., while sitting, > walking, returning on sitting down; intermittent, in r. tibia at 9 P.M. Pulsating pain in head of r. tibia at 3.20 P.M., > motion; in head of r. tibia at 5.30 P.M., while at rest, with sensitiveness of tibia to pressure; pulsating, near upper and outer side of r. fibula at 6.30 P.M., then in r. thigh. Numb aching passing down outer side of r. to foot at 2.50 P.M., then aching and drawing in outer hamstring. Crampy lameness in r. leg, just above instep, at 3.30 P.M., while the leg is resting on a table, > walking, then while at rest drawing crampy sensation in hollow of r. foot, passing up outer ankle and along outer border of gastrocnemius muscle to knee, > walking, returning while sitting with feet resting on floor, passing slowly from outer ankle to knee, then in tibia, where it becomes a numb aching, then in tarsus, where it causes drawing aching, as if foot would cramp, > continued motion.

Ankle.—Pain passing upward over l. inner, at 4.30 P.M., while at rest in a warm room. Sudden lameness in l. at 8.30 A.M., while walking in open air, with loss of strength.

Foot.—Threadlike pain below r. outer ankle at 4.30 P.M., ending in aching. Drawing crampy sensation at dorsum of r., in region of external cuneiform bone, at 5.45 P.M. (while at rest in a warm room, the air being moist), spreading outward and over cuboid bone and over metatarsal bone of little toe, then moving to region of anterior ligament, where it becomes a bruised aching, extending to external malleolus, sometimes up tibia and fibula, causing a full feeling in those bones, with lameness when walking, next day at 3 P.M., while at rest, return of the aching in r. ankle.

Instep.—Pain in r.; crampy, in r. at 12.30 A.M., > motion. Numb drawing in l., extending to knee, while at rest, then sensation as of warm air, like an aura, ascending half way to knee, the numbness and drawing then concentrated at instep, and again the aura ascended slowly to knee, at same time aching in tibia and fibula, with heat and fulness in leg, then the numb drawing moved over dorsum of foot to toes, where it ended in prickling, > motion, returning when motion ceased.

Toes.—Sticking in metatarsal joint of great, at plantar aspect. Drawing in r. great, at 6 P.M., as if it would cramp.

Skin.—Pale redness on lower part of r. hypochondrium, down to crest of r. ilium, and extending two-thirds across abdomen, with papillæ, next morning similar appearance (though less marked) on l. side. Red and white streaks (the former broader) on back and r. half of abdomen, outer part of r. thigh, and as high as scapula, at 9 P.M., the redness > pressure, but returning immediately. Burning eruptions occasionally.

Pimples (some of them white at apex) on back part of neck, shoulders, scapulæ and lower down on back; red, hard, on l. side of sacrum, with pain on touch; round, dull, red, on r. scapula, anterior and upper half of l. forearm, in same region of r. arm, but more numerous on l., and on outer and upper part of l. calf, those on l. half and l. arm looking dry and scaly. Inflammation of the part, with deep, hard-edged ulcers, which discharge a thick, fetid, purulent, greenish-yellow matter, the parts becoming in appearance similar to raw, decayed meat, while the surrounding skin is covered with shining scales.

Itching on various parts; in afternoon; in evening; at r. eyebrow; on face; on face, most about mouth; on abdomen; on scrotum; on extremities; on dorsum of l. hand, on l. scapula and inner side of thighs; on upper part of calves; on various parts of lower extremities in forepart of day, and in evening; below r. elbow at 7.30 P.M., > rubbing, with sensation as if it would return if I ceased rubbing; of palm, > getting up and moving around, with warmth in it; on inner side of l. thigh at 10 A.M., then above r. eye, then on scalp, at 10.15 at inner border of l. gastrocnemius, > rubbing, then tingling I. on r. side of upper lip, then crawling itching on r. malar region, then I. moving downward from r. commissure of mouth, then I. on palmar aspect of r. carpus, moving towards palm, then on r. angle of jaw.

Stinging itching on r. scapula at 2.45 P.M.; between metacarpal bones of r. thumb and index at 3.30 P.M., and itching on lower part of l. scapula, with sensation as if there were pimples there, then on r. scapula. Biting-corrosive itching on r. forearm, over belly of palmaris longus muscle at 11.40 A.M., then itching near r. angle of jaw, then itching on posterior aspect of r. forearm, then on dorsal aspect of first phalanx of r. index. *Burning itching* on whole body; on r. ear and surrounding tissue, extending into whiskers. Itching of nose, burning in open air, < in warm room. Burning tingling itching on lower extremities.

Tingling itching on lower part of sternum, then on whole chest; on ankle; along lower extremities, changing its position, > scratching; on various parts, mostly extremities, < the longer it lasts, > rubbing, scratching, in open air and on motion, < warmth and rest, in forepart of the day worse on upper extremities, in the after part worse on lower extremities; on l. side of scrotum at 8 P.M., while sitting, shifting to inner side and lower half of l. thigh; then on inner side below knee, then on upper extremities, the l. first, then on r. lower extremity, the itching changing places rapidly, > rubbing or scratching, < warmth and rest, for the most part proceeding from above downward, especially on lower limbs, and generally of a tingling character.

Clinical.—In erysipelas of face.

Sleep.—Night restless till 2 A.M., no sleep, with heat of hands and head, full, heavy and accelerated pulse, cold feet and hands. Dreamy and refreshing, seeming more like a clairvoyant state, after midnight dream of birds singing, which woke me and caused me to listen. Light, dreamy and refreshing, after midnight dream of entering a beautiful garden, from which I passed into a low woodland, in the eastern border of which was a sluggish, broad, shallow stream of water, and to cross dryshod required some exercise of mind.

Fever.—Heat; over superior maxillary bone at 10 A.M., while at rest, with sense of fulness, and with sensation as of a pimple over r. antrum. *Burning on face and arms*, especially about *eyes*, warmth with *painful weakness*, extending from shoulders to hands, and remaining there, more in palm and wrist, afterwards pain in r. hand grows severe and extends to elbow, > getting up and moving around. Burning in finger-tips, < r., with aching.

Conium.

A tincture is made of the entire fresh plant of Conium maculatum, L.

General Action.—It produces paralysis of voluntary motion, then of respiration. The brain is benumbed, vertigo, dilated pupils, and even convulsions follow.

Allies.—Phos., Gels., Lyc., Hyosc., Curare, Arg. nit.

Generalities.—Concealed caries, especially in middle of long bones, with burning gnawing. Haste in all his actions. Clumsy movements. Walking about as if half asleep. Lay as one intoxicated, could not speak nor raise himself. *Trembling* (Gels.); < of arms, with throbbing motion of whole body. Starting at every sound; jerklike S., as in fright. Constant tossing about and violent screams. Subsultus tendinum (Hyosc.). *Convulsions; with danger of suffocation;* with uneasiness and wild fancies; of upper part of body, with paralysis of lower limbs; of facial muscles, so that there was a frightful expression, with frequent contractions of other muscles, < extensors of back and flexors of limbs, with motion of thumb and index as if unwinding a skein of thread. Epilepsy, distortion of eyes, flow of blood from ears, jaws could not be opened, ineffectual retching, singultus. Epileptiform attack, with contraction of all muscles. Hysterical attack, with spasmodic motions.

Sticking in whole body; in swollen glands; now in cardiac region, now in hands, head and legs, with tearings; smarting S. about swollen glands; tearing now here, now there, as if to the bones. Tearings through various parts; wandering, in arms, legs and teeth. Cutting around glands. Paroxysm, < after eating, beginning with yawning, sticking in sternum and pressure in pit of stomach, even on touch, whence it extended to the back and became a sticking in region of kidneys. Cramplike pain in various parts, chest, jaws, etc. Pain in affected parts became intolerable. Pain in a place injured several years previously. Bruised sensation. Contractive sensation in inner parts, with salivation. Fulness in chest, head and hypochondria, mornings on waking. *Easily overstrained. Liability to take cold;* even in the room when sitting after a walk, during which he had perspired. Uneasiness; of blood in the whole body. Pulsation in whole body. Feeling as if the whole body were inclined to the right.

Disinclination to work. Standing is very irksome. Every step was irksome on returning from a walk, with ill humor and impatience for the time when he could rest in solitude. Nervous prostration. *Relaxation of muscles and limbs, then difficulty in walking and inability to control movements, necessity to lie down.* Weakness; morning and evening; morning on waking, > rising; morning after waking, as after a fever; morning fasting, with aversion to food; morning in bed, and sickness, with ill humor, sleepiness and pain in stomach; on waking from midday nap; after eating; *on walking* (Ars., Phos.), *with tendency to fall forward on knees, heaviness over eyes and giddiness;* after a walk, with paralyzed feeling and fretful, hypochondriac mood; from walking in open air, and affected by the air; with desire to lie down; with chilliness, palpitation and headache; with chilliness, so that he must lie down, next day occiput felt as if pierced by a knife at every beat of the pulse, and palpitation, heart throbbing violently at times, at times beating rapidly, at times wavering; of head and whole body, with loss of appetite; **tremulous weakness after stool** (Arg. n., Ars.), > *open air. Faintness.* Heaviness; in afternoon, with unsteadiness. *Dulness of all senses.* Stiffness, movement of limbs, neck, etc., caused unpleasant sensation. Paralysis; of all muscles (Gels.), those of deglutition being the first, and those of respiration the last to fail. *Aggravation at night*, waking him; A. during rest; when sitting; in the house. Amelioration at night.

Clinical.—Indurated glands (occasionally hard), usually with sharp knifelike pains, but not always painful. Useful for weakness following exhaustive diseases. Paralytic affections (after diphtheria). General physical and mental debility, *tremulous weakness*, sudden attacks of faintness, especially with vertigo.

Mind.—*Delirium;* running wildly about the house, knocking against the walls; during which he at first took to walking about; with stupidity, they threw themselves into the water, thinking they were geese, and partly paralytic, with much pain; violent, interrupted by crying out from pain; mirthful, going out of the house; intermittent; in a man who had been somewhat addicted to the use of liquors, he saw all sorts of animals dancing upon the bed and "picked straws;" partly delirious and partly foolish. Fantasies in morning. Illusion at night that some one had come in at the door. Vision of her brother and child who had died, she saw persons in the room, she knew that it was an illusion and tried to get it out of her mind, but saw them coming in at the door.

Superstitious. *Aversion to being near people and to the talk of those passing him, inclination to seize hold of and abuse them.* Dread of the approach of men, yet dread of being alone. *Everything makes an unpleasant sensation upon him.* Fretfulness; in morning after eating, with confusion in forehead and anxiety; *every day from 5 to 6 P.M., as if a great guilt weighed upon him, with paralyzed feeling in all limbs and indifference;* time passes too slowly. Discontent. Easily aroused to anger. Anxiety; with palpitation and nosebleed; impelling them from place to place; waking at night, then long wakefulness. Fear; at night after waking; after midnight when half awake; of thieves. Sadness; without speaking. Hypochondriac and indifferent mood when walking in open air. Lachrymose mood; when alone in the house, on giving way to it it changed to hiccough, then flickering before eyes and indistinct vision, so that she must steady herself in walking, then exhaustion of limbs and headache; and faint-hearted; and smiling. Frequent thoughts of death. Hurried mood. Lively excitement. Constant mirth. Tendency to laugh, with loss of energy; tendency to laugh as if coming from r. hypochondrium and stomach, during exhaustion. Without sympathy. Apathy. *Disinclination for business.*

Inability to sustain mental effort (Phos., Op.). *Stupefaction, difficulty in understanding what he is reading.* Mistakes in speaking. Sunk in deep thought, apprehension and desire to be alone. *Loss of memory* (Anac., Hyosc.); after waking from midnight sleep. Coma;

at beginning of general paralysis, or collapse, or a condition between coma and collapse, with foam from mouth; with unconsciousness and difficult breathing. Unconsciousness; eyelids firmly closed, pupils dilated, respiration weak, pulse small, rapid, skin cold, spasmodic movements of upper limbs and facial muscles.

Clinical.—Melancholy, quiet, sad, picks his fingers, makes short answers, or this condition alternates with excessive gayety. Hypochondriasis, especially resulting from excessive venery. Averse to people, yet dislikes to be alone. Melancholia resulting from suppression of menses, aversion to members of her own family. General mental weakness, inability to get the mind fixed on his business or to stand any prolonged mental effort.

Head.—Inability to keep it erect (Tabac.). Sticking; on coughing. *Aching in morning on waking, as if brain were too full and would burst;* A. in morning as if head were beaten or as if it would be pressed asunder. Aching in morning on waking, as in epidemic fever, as if brain were torn, < towards occiput. Aching; at night in bed, with nausea; on waking, with weakness from broken rest, and diarrhœa during the early morning; from scanty but frequent stools, with urging; on walking in open air, even in morning, lasting till breakfast; on entering house after a walk, with pressure in r. eye; on going into open air, he must rub the forehead; on stepping, she felt every step in the head; with diminished appetite; with nausea and vomiting of mucus; with muscæ volitantes, diplopia, languor and sleepiness; extending to jaws and thence to l. side of chest, with sticking.

Drawing on going into open air, > *closing eyes;* D. > after eating, with going to sleep of brain. Tension after every meal, with compression from temples, necessity to rest forehead on table. Cerebral oppression. Fulness; at breakfast, from a ligature around neck, with vertigo. Stupefaction, with sleepiness. Dulness after drinking. Confusion; on waking from sound sleep, with heaviness. *Heaviness;* of brain, and pressure deep in it. Intoxication; *from the slightest spirituous drink. Vertigo; in morning on rising* (Lyc., Phos.); *on walking;* on descending stairs; < lying, as if the bed turned in a circle; with weight at orbits; tendency to, with sensation as if eyes were swollen and protruding; so that everything turns in a circle; as if turning in a circle, on rising from a seat; as if head would burst, on rising after stooping; sudden, with such weakness of legs that he must lie down. Apoplexy.

Forehead.—Sticking; *outward, at noon;* extending out of, in morning after rising; extending out of, in forenoon, with inclination to lie down; jerklike, < in the house. Digging and griping, as if from the stomach, with such sensitiveness of brain that it was painfully shattered by noises and by speaking. Pain; in various places; externally; in sinciput; r. side and in l. side of occiput and in l. parietal eminence; and in eyes, with burning lachrymation as from salt water in eyes; above eyes, extending into eyes; externally, causing stupefaction; alternately severe and slight, in sinciput, then heaviness, then the same sensation in occiput. Pain on shaking head as if something were loose, extending to occiput. Pain in upper part as from external contraction, > stooping or leaning it on hand, with chilliness, vertigo and fretful loss of memory. Pressive aching outward over eyes. Pain as from a stone on upper part of bone. Pressure as from a band, then in occiput; above eyes, then in occiput, with heat in occiput, then in forehead and cheeks. Drawing pain above brows; in brain just behind forehead; wandering, and in r. temple. Throbbing. *Confusion in region of brows and root of nose.* Heaviness; in sinciput.

Temples.—Tearing in r., and in r. ear; through temples in morning; when eating; after eating, with pressure in forehead. Pressure. Pain from one to the other. Drawing pain in bones; D. pain on touch. Drawing in r. muscles, < walking.

Vertex.—Pain and heaviness, and in occiput. Squeezing pain, then it went to sides of jaws, then to below l. breast, with choking feeling and inability to draw a breath. Pressure deep in; P. on, then around forehead; P. on, with feeling as if one would fall. Nipping at every step, without pain.

Parietals.—Sticking in bones, in forehead and cervical muscles, with vertigo; tearing S. from l. bone to frontal region. *Sensation in r. half of brain as of a large foreign body.* Pain in r. half of brain, extending backward. Bruised pain in side of head, < by moving eyes towards affected side, with sensation of something heavy pressing downward. Pulsation in r. side of head in evening in bed. Confusion in l. half of head as from coldness or as if the brain did not fill the skull. *One side of head numb and cold.*

Occiput.—Tearing in l. on walking; T. and in nape and especially in orbits, with nausea so that she must lie in bed. *Pain as if pierced with a knife at every beat of the pulse.* Pressure on l. side; as with a plug in r. side. Fulness and confusion. Intermittent heaviness on sitting bent.

Boring tearing in various parts of skull, with pressure. Falling of hair. Sharp pressure in a spot on scalp. Itching.

Clinical.—Vertigo is a common accompaniment of the Conium condition, especially < motion, as turning over in bed or rising up; this vertigo is sometimes accompanied by partial paralysis of the muscles of the eye, or objects seem to be unsteady; especially indicated in vertigo of old people; vertigo resulting from excessive use of tobacco. With the head symptoms the brain is frequently extremely sensitive, with feeling of a hard lump in the brain, or with feeling of numbness or coldness in head or one side of the head.

Eyes.—Red. Staring. Protruding. Weak look. Wild and piercing look. Trembling look, as if eyes trembled. Movements as if pressed outward. Mucus in morning. Drawing pain, with redness. Pressure, < reading; P. if she closes them to sleep in evening; as from a grain of sand, < in forenoon, with inflammation and redness of white and biting lachrymation. *Burning;* towards evening, with pressure in orbits; heat shooting through them in afternoon and evening. Irritability. Discomfort so that he brushed them frequently to clear apparent obstructions from lids.

Lachrymation. *Pupils dilated;* alternately D. and contracted. *Yellow whites.* Pressure and sticking in r. conjunctiva bulbi, in inner canthus, with fine vessels closely aggregated at inner margin of cornea. Inflamed lids and styes and frequent blinking. Lids drooping, almost ptosis (Gels.), with difficulty in walking. Lids drawn together in morning. Twitching of upper lid; l. lid. Inability to open lids; difficulty in opening (Gels.). Sticking in margins of lids and in canthi; in inner canthus, with agglutination of lids in morning; itching, in inner canthus, not > by rubbing. *Lids seem pressed down, and sleepiness.* Pressure as from sand in external canthi. *Burning on inner surface of lids.* Biting in inner canthus, with lachrymation. Itching of margins of lids. Contractive power of muscle orbicularis weakened. Pain across eyebrows and misty vision. Pain in orbits, < with the headache; P. in bones above r. eye late in evening, and in nose and malar-bone.

Vision.—**Weak; with dazzling, vertigo and general debility, < arms and legs, so that he staggered.** Fatigue from reading. Sensitiveness to light. *Sluggishness of adaptation*, dim vision when an uneven object was put in motion, causing vertigo. *Double;* with sensation as if squinting; and the images slowly receding from each other to the apparent distance of six inches, here they generally became stationary, but at times alternately approached and receded from each other; and triple, with rings before eyes. On looking at near print the lines moved up and down. Flickering on moving eyes, with sudden vertigo, nausea and staggering, all > closing eyes, then general paresis, and even when eyes were shut any motion involving the balance of the body was attended with uncertainty and falling short of the desired effect and fresh rush of the seasickness, all > shutting eyes and sitting still with every muscle relaxed. Confused on raising eyes from the object on which they had been fixed to a distant one, with vertigo, then heaviness of lids. Imperfect, > sleep. Greater short-sightedness than usual. Dim; on walking in open air; < rising from breakfast-table, with vertigo; and flickering; with bright points quickly moving in the distance and light feeling in head. Lost; after sleeping in heat of sun; or objects tinged with all colors. Of black points and stripes. Of a large dark spot with white margins. Of sparks; on walking in open air. Clouds and light spots. Bright spots on walking in open air. White spots, with glittering stars, on looking at different things in the room. Fiery zigzags moving through each other, on closing eyes at night. Of a thread swimming before r. eye. Of a transparent vapor floating before eyes.

Clinical.—Valuable for partial or complete paralysis of the ocular muscles, especially of the internal rectus; the attempt to fix the eyes upon any object becomes painful and may even cause vertigo, hence many symptoms, of letters running together, vanishing of vision, etc. This drug is very valuable in numerous forms of scrofulous ophthalmia, in a general way indicated by extreme photophobia, greater than the apparent inflammation would warrant. There is general aggravation at night on lying down, especially of ulcers of the cornea. Appearing adapted to old people, it has proved beneficial in cataract when the above symptoms were present.

Ears.—*Blood-red wax.* Sticking; behind, < mastoid process, then dull pain at this place; pinching, on drinking. Sharp shocks shooting out of, < swallowing. Sudden sharp pressure, almost like twinges. Pain as if middle would be torn asunder. Pain in external, partly drawing, partly tearing. Drawings within l. Throbbing of blood. Itching in outer. *Stopped feeling before ears on blowing nose.* Intolerance of noise. Sensitive hearing, so that noise frightened him. Bubbling and humming; in r. Ringing; in r., with dull hearing. Roaring in r.; in l., < eating, with difficult hearing; like a wind, < dinner, lasting till sleep, and on exerting head when sitting, < in bed, even at night on waking. Noise in r. as of a waterfall. Noises as if blood were rushing through brain. Buzzing. Surring at noon when walking in the street, with darkness before the eyes, nearly unconscious, with some strong beats of heart, passing off quickly.

Clinical.—Much wax accumulates and hardens in the ear, with greater or less loss of hearing, or the hearing may be extremely sensitive with the head symptoms.

Nose.—Tip thick, red, hot, painful, < l. side, painful swelling in l. nostril, afterwards at l. tip a yellow blister, full of pus. Twitching; at root. Sticking in skin of lower part of septum. Sticking sore pain in septum on pressure, as if a pimple were there. Tearing in bones. Stuffed. Itching in nose; sticking, in r. side, as from a foreign body. Itching crawling in nose. Burning on nostrils. Frequent sneezing; without coryza. *Bleeding;* at night, then vertigo in morning on rising; when sneezing. Dropping of water. Blowing out of watery fluid. Frequent discharge of mucus. Acute smell. Tarry smell at back of nose, which he also tastes.

Clinical.—The patient is inclined to pick at his nose, which bleeds easily and becomes sore (in melancholia). It has been prescribed for polypus of the nose.

Face.—Blue; and turgid with blood. Livid. Red, looking like erysipelas. Pale; in morning; and sickly. Swelling on malar-bone and upper gum, with tensive pain. Risus sardonicus. Twitching of l. cheek. Expression calm, but like a figure of wax. Sticking through r. side about malar-bone; through r. cheek, extending to corner of mouth; in chin, extending upward through jaw; tearing, in front of ear in evening. Pain at night. Feeling of a cobweb on r. cheek. Drawing on zygoma, with tearing; D. on r. zygoma; painless, through chin towards ears and to head after drinking. Pressure in masseter muscles. Falling of jaw. Stiffness of r. masseter muscles. Trismus; and next day aching soreness in jaws. Lips cyanotic; eruption on lips after slight fever; vesicles on vermilion border of upper, with smarting; sticking in lips and tongue; drawing pain in an old wart on upper; dry lips and tongue; itching of upper; burning of lips and tongue; burning on inner surface of lower; burning and redness of upper, l. then r. side.

Mouth.—Teeth. Looseness of back. Boring sticking between l. on moving jaw. Drawing boring in l. back. Jerking and gnawing. Aching; on chewing, as if loose (tearing?); on eating, extending to ear, eye and cheek-bone. Sensation as if lower incisors were pushed up. *Drawings in hollow T. from cold food (not cold drinks)*, extending through temples; D. through r. lower T. into malar-bone. Bleeding of gum; of back. Swollen, bluish-red gum. Painful burning of gum.

Tongue red, mottled; T. covered on upper surface, and large part of lower surface with dirty mucus, and dry; sticking on tip; S. on tip, with biting; S. in l. side of tip, with burning; boring at night; pain; stiff, swollen, painful; feeling as if sticking to roof of mouth, and inability to move it; dry; dry and reddish; burning on, and in hands; burning at tip. *Speech difficult.* Inability to articulate. Burning on inner surface of l. cheek; with biting. Dry mouth; with sour sensation. Salivation; sour after eating. *Taste bitter in throat;* and mouth; bitter-sour T. after breakfast; sour; sour after eating; salt, < hawking up mucus; metallic on tip of tongue; coppery, with sensation as if tip of tongue had just been touched with copper; bad when eating and on swallowing; peculiar to food; of coryza from posterior nares to mouth.

Throat.—Spasm. Drawing in muscles of T. and chest. Frequent hawking of mucus. Sticking, < empty swallowing. Shooting drawing pain in tonsils. Pain. Soreness on swallowing. Scraping; with cough at night. Constriction; on bowing, with choking, a sensation as if neck-band were too tight, so that she must grasp the throat, with blackness before the eyes and dark redness of face. Fulness. Catarrhal obstruction in T. and head in morning on waking. Feeling as if something were coming up to choke her. Sensation as if a large body were in it. Constant desire to hawk. Dryness; in fauces, with constriction on larynx; alternating with salivation, with the latter dry sensation in fauces. *Itching, with irritation to hacking cough.* Tickling when sitting, with provocation to dry cough. Obliged to swallow much if she goes into the wind. Inability to swallow; water. Difficulty in swallowing (Op.). Heat in gullet.

Stomach.—Appetite increased; with nausea as if she had eaten to satiety. Longing for salt and salt things; for acids. Appetite diminished; for food and tobacco-smoking. *Appetite lost;* with weakness in stomach. *Thirst;* every afternoon; unquenchable; for coffee. Eructations; < towards evening. *Empty E.;* < in morning. *Sour E. after eating;* sour in evening; S., with burning in stomach. *Offensive E.* E. tasting of food. Incomplete E. after breakfast; I., then pain in stomach. Hiccough; on beginning supper. *Nausea;* in morning, > stool; in evening, with weakness, so that speaking is disagreeable; on trying to rise; after every meal; after eating, then hiccough, with the usual taste and good appetite; after dinner, with pain in nape, vertex and forehead; with vertigo; with satiety after eating. Retching; ineffectual. Vomiting; *violent;* profuse; of mucus in afternoon, with headache, nausea and then eructations.

Flatulent distention. Sticking in pit; in epigastric region towards evening. Intermittent sore tearing from epigastric region into sides of abdomen, as if everything were torn out of abdomen, mornings. Sudden thrusts deep in pit. Sudden cutting on eating a light meal. Cramplike pain. Spasmodic pinching. Griping between 1 and 2 A.M., with constriction; G. which contracts chest, with griping in back and eructations, waking her; G., then becoming dull in intestines. Contractive pain, with coldness in it and in back, waking her in morning. Gastralgia in evening. Drawing pain in pit in morning after rising and after stool, extending to throat, with short, difficult respiration. Pain in pit as if suppurating mornings when lying and turning in bed. Pressure, then heat; *P. in epigastric region, gradually extending to l. side of abdomen, with nausea; in pit, extending to throat, as if a ball rose* (Ign.); in pit, as if something moved about, even in morning, then sticking in side of chest. Fulness in pit, < inspiration and motion, with sticking. Tightness in pit on leaning backward, with choking of respiration and speech. Soreness and rawness. Uneasiness in pit, with haste in all his actions and difficult breathing. Cardialgia. *Heartburn;* in evening; rancid. Heat; in region; in epigastrium; after eating, extending through arms to fingers, whereupon the fingers became pale and dead. Acidity, with flat and bad taste. Indigestion at the least excess.

Clinical. — Gastralgia, especially with spasmodic cough (stomach cough). Sometimes spasmodic constriction of stomach and œsophagus, as if a round body ascended from the stomach (globus hystericus). The symptoms of pain, of vomiting, etc., have led to the use of Conium in cancer of the stomach and liver.

Abdomen.—*Swelling;* of mesenteric glands; in afternoon; after midday nap; in evening, after eating, with hardness of abdomen and protrusion of navel, which made sleep uneasy; flatulent, after milk; like flatulent colic in evening, with coldness of one foot. Rumbling; which passed into griping or pressure in epigastrium. Gurgling; l. side. Flatus passed easily; F. emitted with stool, with dragging and cutting in rectum; violent emissions of much; emission of cold; offensive. Flatulence after eating, which then passed with noise and relief. *Trembling.* Pulselike jerks, and in small of back.

Sticking; in l.; and through glans; deep in l., waking at night, then deep in r. side of chest when lying on l. side, impeding respiration, then boring in ball of l. great toe, which continued on waking in morning. Sticking digging in l. Cutting in morning after chilliness, with headache and nausea; *C. before emission of flatus;* before stool, < r. side; with diarrhœa; deep; in l. side as if a bunch would protrude. Griping; *before discharge of leucorrhœa;* as in diarrhœa. Shocks against muscles, as from a child in pregnancy. Pain; in morning after eating, with fulness of stomach and chest all day; when laughing; when coughing; in sides when coughing. Drawing bruised pain. Drawing pain when walking. Drawing after drinking. Tension in r. side on deep breathing; T. in abdomen, with jerking contraction, extending towards chest, with griping. Oppression. Burning pressure. Weariness of muscles after breakfast.

Upper.—Venous vessels of liver and sinuses of dura mater gorged. Distention after eating, with pressure in stomach, which causes anxious respiration. Sharp drawing jerking under r. ribs. *Sticking in hepatic region* (Lyc.); in l. hypochondrium; beneath margins of ribs on r. side; in morning on waking, < motion; in l. hypochondrium in morning in bed, > rising, with oppressed breathing; beneath border of l. ribs when sitting; in hepatic region before menstruation, < night when lying, and especially on inspiration; *intermittent, in hepatic region;* in hepatic region, impeding respiration. *Tearing in hepatic region.* Pain in liver when walking; tensive, in l. hypochondrium, extending to side of lower abdomen. *Constriction of hypochondria as from a band* (Lyc.). Sharp drawing in anterior lobe of liver. Feeling as from fright, caused by the noise of opening a door, a feeling as before diarrhœa. Pulsation on l. side, between eighth and ninth ribs, then sticking.

Umbilical Region.—Sticking upward in muscles on l. side below navel. Tearing in a spot below navel. Deep cutting; C. to l. of navel. Pinching in muscles above navel on bending forward. Bruised pain after supper. Drawing pain in morning after rising; D. pain after eating.

Lower.—Cramp. Sticking; in groin on rising from a chair; in r. groin when walking. Tearing above pubis, extending to ring. Deep griping after every meal. Pain, then fermentation; P., < by pressure; above hips when walking; in r. groin as if swollen, and on touch pain as if suppurating. Contractive pain after appearance of menses, > walking in open air; *C. pain like after-pains, with urging to stool.* Distending pain in a place where there is a hernia. Constricted spot in colon. Dragging towards the place of a previous inguinal hernia, without protrusion of a hernia; D. outward in the place of a hernia; D. outward in r. groin. Drawing pain when sitting after dinner. Drawing pressing towards upper, in morning when sitting. Heaviness when not eating.

Clinical.—Hard swellings of the liver have been cured (note the sticking, tearing pains in the hepatic region). Enlarged mesenteric glands and tumors in the abdomen have been treated successfully (note the great sensitiveness of the abdomen, the swelling and the character of the pain, knifelike).

Rectum.—Sticking. Heat, and in anus; *in lower part of R.; in R. during stool.* Itching after itching in chest and abdomen. Urging, with diarrhœa three times; frequent U., with scanty soft fæces, then still more distended abdomen; frequent, with scanty stools; constant, with two thin stools; ineffectual; constant, ineffectual. Straining at stool.

Anus.—*Sticking when not at stool.* Dragging towards A. and abdomen; towards A. and sacrum. Heat. Itching; and on nates, perineum and near scrotum, so that he must frequently rise.

Stool.—*Diarrhœa. Watery, frequent, with many empty eructations and copious urine; W., mixed with hard parts,* with colic and loud emissions of flatus; and frequent, with undigested portions, with griping in stomach, extending through abdomen; and urgent, then sweat. Soft. Pasty, twice daily, with burning in rectum. Constipation. Solid, every second day, with pressure; every second day, the first part with pressure. *Involuntary in sleep* (Phos., Hyosc.). Undigested. Passage of offensive mucus. Passage of blood with the morning stool. Scanty. Frequent.

Clinical.—Chronic diarrhœa of old people, with tremulous weakness, discharges sometimes involuntary; specially indicated by the symptom that the flow of urine is intermittent. In obstinate constipation, especially if it sometimes alternates with diarrhœa, the stool followed by tremulous weakness.

Urinary Organs.—Lancinations in neck of bladder. Pressure upon bladder; cramplike, in neck after urinating, < walking, with sticking. Frequent urging; with scanty urine every time; constant U. like labor pains, with burning pain at neck of bladder and along urethra, and frequent, scanty micturition. *Frequent micturition at night;* frequent M. without ability to retain urine. Painful M. Strangury; biting, after micturition. Ischuria. Discharge of a few drops after micturition, they cannot be retained nor forcibly expelled. *Involuntary micturition. Dribbling after micturition.* Necessity to urinate at 2 A.M. several nights. Could not urinate.

Urethra.—Discharge of pus preceded by itching; of mucus from male U., even after urinating. Sticking; in orifice; extending to orifice; at times increasing with every beat of the heart; jerking, in posterior part. Cutting during micturition; in orifice. Burning; *in morning after urinating; when urinating;* with tickling. Pain on passing urine, which is mixed with tenacious turbid mucus.

Urine.—Frequent hæmaturia, with dyspnœa. A few drops of bright red blood with first part of urine. Red. Turbid, with red sediment; and frothy. Copious. Scanty, dark, frothy, depositing a red sediment.

Clinical.—Partial paralysis of bladder, *the urine flows by fits and starts,* though urinating better when standing.

Sexual Organs.—Increased sweat. Inflammation of prepuce. Sticking in glans. Cutting in glans. Tearing through penis when not urinating. Compression at root of penis. Itching of penis, prepuce and glans, not > by rubbing. Painful stiffness of penis in evening before sleep. Many erections at night. Drawings in spermatic cord; l. Scrotum seems swollen. Cutting through middle of scrotum, between testicles, backward to above root of penis. Sticking on outer side of l. testicle, then burning. Griping in testicles in evening, with tearing. Pain in l. testicle; in testicles, < after erections; drawing, in l. Testes heavy and sore. Desire; **desire without erections** (Phos.); at night, coitus attended by spasmodic respirations and musklike odor from axilla, then exhaustion; no D. **Emission even when frolicking with a woman** (Phos.); *E. without dreams at night* (Phos.); E. at night; three nights in succession, then awakening of desire. *Discharge of prostatic fluid at every excitement, without voluptuous thoughts, with itching of prepuce;* D. on pressing at stool.

Female.—Cutting between labiæ during micturition. Sticking in pudenda. Itching in pudenda, < after menstruation, and in vagina, and on rubbing it pressing downward in uterus. *Itching deep in vagina* (Kreo.). *Leucorrhœa; ten days after menstruation, with colic before discharge; with weakness and paralyzed sensation in small of back before the discharge, then weakness; of white, acrid, burning mucus* (Phos., Kreo.); *thick, milky, with contractive, laborlike colic coming from both sides;* profuse; profuse, then hoarseness, with cough and expectoration; bloody mucus instead of L. False pains for several days before delivery, preventing sleep and exhausting her. Pressure upon uterus during micturition, with cutting. *Menses suppressed;* which had scarcely appeared, then drawing pain down back into sacrum; M. delayed; M. on seventeenth day; discharge of brownish blood instead of menstruation. Tearing in mons veneris when sitting. Papules on mons veneris, painful on touch.

Clinical.—Useful in the bad effects following excessive venery, sexual weakness or impotence, flow of prostatic fluid with constipated stool or on the slightest motion. Enlarged testicles, which are very hard, especially following injuries. It also has been found useful for the sexual nervousness of strong, healthy men who are unable to have an erection. In both sexes useful for the effects of suppressed sexual appetite, for instance, collapse, hysteria, melancholia, etc. Uterine polypi. Uterine hæmorrhages, with pain in the uterine region running down thighs, etc. Dysmenorrhœa, menstruation too scanty and too early. Numerous accompaniments of the menses, gastric or mental symptoms. Cancer of uterus. Pruritus of the vagina and pudenda following the menses, excessive hyperæsthesia of the genital organs, especially in suppression of menses (compare with Plat.). Useful in various indurations and tumors in sexual organs, especially in the cervix, particularly with burning, stinging or knifelike pains. Leucorrhœa following the menses, excoriating and burning; sometimes bland in children. Mammary glands indurated, with sharp, knifelike pain. (It certainly has cured tumors said to be scirrhous; it is well followed by Silicea.) Numerous symptoms of the mammary glands preceding the menses, viz.: swelling, sharp pain; aggravation of the tumors at the menstrual period.

Respiratory Organs.—Dry spot in larynx, where there is crawling with almost constant irritation to dry cough. *Scraping in larynx, with irritation to cough, and dry cough in evening;* S. in larynx during the day, with tickling and dry cough. Tickling in larynx, with dry cough. Hoarse. Cough at night; C. **almost only on first lying down, during the day**

or evening, he must sit up and cough it out, after which he has rest (Hyosc.); < *lying, shocks in the beginning as if he would vomit; constant, before going to bed;* forcible whooping, with dyspnœa; whooping, every night; whooping, with expectoration of bloody mucus; short, racking, caused by deep inspiration; dry; dry, in morning; dry, from acid and salt things; as from tickling in middle of sternum, with and without expectoration; *whereby something is loosened, but cannot be expectorated* until afterwards, when it comes up with an easy cough, with coryza; loose, without ability to loosen anything. Yellowish expectoration tasting like bad eggs.

Suffocative attack as if mucus collected in throat; S. attack as if something collected in upper part of larynx. Dyspnœa. Difficult respiration; on stooping; in evening in bed, and slow; with pain in chest; as if chest could not be sufficiently distended; as if something rose in larynx and threatened to suffocate her, and noisy. Groaning. Short respiration. Slow respiration; with pain in chest. Subdued respiration.

Clinical.—Very valuable for tormenting night cough of old people; it is usually dry, they can expectorate a little only after coughing a long time; the cough is caused by a dry spot in the larynx, < lying down at night, is accompanied by suffocative attacks; the usual indication is that the patient is unable to expectorate the little mucus which seems to be loosened, it must be swallowed. Asthma in old people. Stomach cough; it seems as if the cough came from the abdomen, he must hold the body tight. Occasionally whooping cough.

Chest.—Hardness of r. breast, with pain on touch and nightly sticking in it. (Inflammation of mammary scirrhus.) Atrophy of mammæ. Caries of sternum. Rattling in evening on lying down, then much cough on sitting up. Tremor at base of clavicle and in muscles across chest, just above sternum. **Sticking in l. mamma** (compare Sil., which follows well?); beneath ribs; beneath l. axilla; behind cartilages of eighth and ninth ribs; between cartilages of l. ninth and tenth ribs; in side; *about r. nipple on every inspiration when walking, > hard pressure;* above heart on deep inspiration, then on every motion; beneath ribs of l. side when sitting, obliging him to press on them; in r. side on walking in open air; in nipples and vicinity in bed, and on inner surface of l. cheek; in both sides, < lying on front of chest; < inspiration and when sitting; behind sternum, extending to axillæ; in l. side on coughing, waking her and then causing uneasy sleep; sudden, between r. nipple and sternum when sitting, < slight inspiration; throbbing, in l. upper part, more towards middle.

Sharp thrusts through sternum to spine when sitting. Tearing; through whole in evening when lying on one side, with drawing and with oppressed breathing and pressure upon upper part of sternum, which on inspiration takes away the breath; cramplike, in r. Cutting on both sides, < inspiration. Scraping, with crawling and irritation to dry, almost constant cough. Pain; in female breasts; under l. breast; in ribs; in r. side of C. and abdomen, < inspiration; in various parts, not < by respiration; behind sternum and desire to breathe deeply; behind sternum when sitting, not < inspiration, and in l. side of chest; on sternum, now with tearing, now with sticking about breasts and nipples, with frequent oppression and shortness of breath; upon sternum, with difficult breathing when standing; with cough; as if sternum were pressed inward; sudden, when sitting, in C. and to l. of sternum. Bruised pain in forepart and in back; on inner surface of sternum. Oppression on sternum after eating, with external pressure; O. of r. upper part, with sensation of incarcerated flatus. Tension across on inspiration, with pressure. Fulness, on coughing nothing will loosen, then sticking in sternum. *Clothes lie like a weight on C. and shoulders.* Stiffness of sternum on physical exertion. Itching interiorly.

Heart.—Frequent shocks. Anxiety; with rapid action. Pressure in præcordial region at times, as if H. would be pressed down, with oppressed breathing. Palpitation; *after drinking; after stool, with intermittent beats of heart;* on rising; anxious, on being awakened by a loud noise. Weak impulse.

Pulse.—Rapid; from excitement; and tense; and weak. Slow; and weak; and small, hard; and small, soft; and large and between these, but without regularity, several small rapid beats. Small and hard; small and weak. Soft and feeble. Lowered, and the temperature. Lost; sometimes losing a beat.

Neck.—Apparent thickening. Sticking in muscles of nape, with pressure; S. in muscles of r. side of nape. Tensive pain in nape during rest, with dryness in throat. Drawings in nape on walking in open air; in r. side of neck during rest, extending to shoulder-joint; throbbing, on nape, extending to r. shoulder.

Back.—Cramp, with drawing and aching. Sprained pain in l. side. Crawling in spine as if asleep. Sticking between scapulæ; and in lumbar region, region of short ribs and in hypochondria. *Pain between scapulæ* and in lumbar region; beneath r. scapula on every motion of arms. Painful tension in muscles beneath scapulæ during rest, < raising arms. Drawing pain in r. scapula. Drawings beneath r. scapula. *Sticking in small of B. when standing, with drawings through lumbar vertebræ;* S. in lumbar muscles, with painful stiffness on moving back when sitting. Pain in small of B.; r.; l. and beneath margin of l. ribs; on bending backward; on walking, then nausea and exhaustion; in ischia on rising from a seat. Drawing through lumbar vertebræ when standing. Lumbar region feels disjointed on exercising.

Extremities.—Swelling of knees and elbows. *Trembling.* Tearing in one or another in evening in bed; T. in all, almost as from a sprain. Cutting in flesh below l. thumb-nail and on r. great toe, with burning. Pressure in joints of arms, legs, fingers and toes, with tearing. Pain in joints of hands, feet, fingers and toes in humerus and femur in morning, compelling him to sleep; in joints after exposure to cold and wet, with swelling and numbness; weary, in joints. Bruised sensation in all; in arms and legs; in joints during rest, > motion. Dragging sensation. Drawings; in l. elbow and r. heel; r. fingers, r. great toe, and in evening anteriorly on r. lower leg, and in l. toes in evening in bed. Sensation of grasping in joints of arms and legs.

Gritty sensation in joints when moved, with partial loss of power, inability to raise her hands to head or extend her legs. Buzzing, with tingling. All affected before menstruation, with weeping mood, restlessness and anxious solicitude about trifles. Heaviness in lower and feeling as if she could not move them, the same in arms, with weakness in limbs distinct from the sensation of paralysis, the latter affecting the whole body. *Difficulty in using, so that he cannot walk.* Inability to move arms or legs. Dropped an inkstand and could not walk. Numbness of fingers and toes, with coldness; N. of lower, with inability to move them, then similar state of upper, and with the numb feeling, stiffness in limbs, the numb, powerless sensation extending over whole body. Asleep. Paralysis, with unconsciousness; *P. of lower, then of upper,* or the reverse; temporary, once or twice loss of sensation.

Upper Extremities.—Sticking in r. axilla; l.; in l. along inner side of upper arm. Tickling in axillæ excites no motion of arms. Arms when lifted fall like inert masses and are immovable. Drawing pain up and down arm, < on moving it. Pain in r. arm as if bound. Weakness of arms; r.

Upper Arm.—Sticking on inner side and in axillæ. Tearing through them in evening in bed; T. during rest, alternating with sticking, transiently > motion. Drawing on inner side of r.; in posterior surface of l. Paralytic drawing pain during rest. Pain as from fatigue in soft parts of outer and upper parts of r., so that it is difficult to raise it. Weariness in lower part of biceps brachii, with disposition to flex and extend forearm.

Elbow.—Cracking, < evening. Sticking in l.; S., with heaviness. Tearing on walking in open air. Cutting outward in bend of l. during rest. Pressure. Bruised pain in r.; l.

Forearm.—Sticking on dorsal surface of r., with sensitiveness to touch. Cramplike pain in muscles, < resting arm. Pressing in flexor tendon above l. wrist; P. deep in l., extending to fingers. Bruised pain in extensor muscles of r.; on outer side of l., < touch. Drawing in l.; on lower part of r.; in extensors of r.; in muscles on outer and inner side of l.; < during rest; with pressing.

Cracking in wrist, < evening. Sticking in wrist; at articulation of metacarpal joint of l. thumb with wrist, as if sprained, < bending it inward. Paralytic drawing pain in wrist during rest. Boring in palm at the point where the line around ball of l. thumb meets that of the third finger. Deadness of l. hand, < of palm.

Fingers.—Nails yellow. Twitching in ball of l. little; in ball of l. thumb, which draws the thumb and metacarpal bone back and forth, visible under the skin when the thumb is forcibly kept straight. Cramp in r. third prevents writing easily. Spasmodically stiff and cramped on cutting with shears. Sticking in tips; beneath nails; beneath r. nails; in metacarpal joints during rest. Cutting shocks in metacarpal joint of thumb. Pain under nail of r. index as if it were torn and nail pushed up. Pain in r. fourth, with stiff feeling, then pressure on upper and outer part of l. upper arm. Burning pain on flexor surface of index, then a hard lump. Drawings; in l. thumb; in first phalanx of l. little, with stiff feeling; sharp, in one or other. Numbness. Numb prickling, gradually extending to elbows, causing stiffness of muscles and making it difficult to move forearm and hand.

Lower Extremities.—*Reeling* (Gels.); when standing; and dragging his legs after him; with tendency of knees to fall forward. Sensation when walking as if his steps were impeded, but he walked very rapidly. Weakness. Sticking near trochanter; deep at superior attachment of gluteus maximus; in muscles of l. thigh when sitting; in hamstring on walking in open air. Tearing in forepart of thigh when walking. Cramplike pain in anterior muscles of r. thigh on walking in open air. Pinching over l. hip. Sprained pain in r. hip in evening on walking. Drawing in r. gluteal muscles, < on walking; D. in r. thigh during rest, > motion. *Weakness of r. thigh on walking, even to trembling.* Hip-joints almost immovable. Paralysis of hamstring.

Knee.—Crackling (in patella?) on becoming erect. Sticking; in outer tendon of flexor muscle of hollow when walking in open air. Tearing about; about patella when sitting. Pain on stepping; l.; rheumatic P.; sprained, in r.; bruised or broken feeling in l. patella when walking and standing in open air, with general anxious heat on exertion in walking; paralytic, in hollow, as in dropsy of knee. Drawing beneath r. patella. Weakness; on ascending stairs; after ascending stairs. Stiffness in tendons under l., on beginning to walk, with pain.

Leg.—Occasional movements of l. Jerking at night, with uneasiness, then shivering. Sticking in l. calf. Tearing on tibiæ in evening in bed; cramplike, in tibiæ on walking in open air. Bruised pain in tibiæ. A place that had been bruised and remained painful became blue and mottled, with cutting on motion and bruised feeling on walking or on touch. Pressure in r. calf. Tensive stiff pain in calves. Oppression in anterior surface of r. in bed, extending to foot, with weakness, then the same in l. lower, > by walking. Tingling pressure on tibiæ on stretching out limbs when sitting. Drawing on outer side of r.; in r. tibia; in muscles of r. as far as toes; in l., with tearing and uneasiness; in r. calf; on inner side of l. calf and on back of r. foot; in l. calf and in back of foot; in lower part of l. calf and in sole. Weakness; < of knees, with heaviness and trembling. Going to sleep when sitting.

Ankle.—Sticking in r. malleoli day and night, waking him, at last extending into calves, > sitting, < walking. Tearing from noon till evening, < sitting and walking; T. in external malleolus in open air, extending along leg. Pain; bruised, in l., with tension and stiff feeling on moving it.

Foot.—Swelling, with burning pain; painful S. Trembling in morning on rising. Sticking in r. heel on walking and standing; burning and throbbing S. in bend of foot. Tearing on dorsum in evening in bed; T. in inner side extending up leg, in open air; in soles on walking. Burning pain beneath heel on stepping, with redness and swelling. Crawling pain in soles when stepping upon them, but stitches when walking. Sharp drawing beneath heel. Heavy clogging sensation in heels. Numbness; of heels when sitting, with prickling. Numb prickling creeping to upper part of thigh.

Toes.—Sticking under nail of l. great, when sitting; in tip of l. great, with burning; pulsating, in little, with pain on walking. Tearing in ball of great in morning when standing and sitting; burning, in metacarpal joint of great, on waking. Cutting at tips of l. Pain in tips as if suppurating. Burning pain beneath, when sitting. Pressure in ball of r. great. Drawing; in l.; in lower surface of l. great. Prickling.

Skin.—Whole body blue; and covered with cold sweat. Yellow spots on fingers. Inflammation of whole body, with pain and burning. Fine eruption on face, back and rest of body, with itching like creeping under skin. Petechiæ. Erysipelatous tumor in neck. Pimple in an old liver spot on cheek; on forehead, with tensive drawing pain; on forehead, with tensive pain, which during and after itching becomes tearing in their vicinity; painful on touch on forehead, also on chest. Pustule in fold near r. wing of nose; on feet. Ulcers with inflammation around finger-nails and throbbing, suppurating, burning pain; margins of U. became black, with discharge of offensive ichor; cold gangrene in a portion of an U. Vesicles filled with colored fluid, with bright red areola; V., with bright areola near knuckle of l. little finger; on back of r. hand, between thumb and index, with red areola and itching, which is < after scratching; itching, on back of ball of l. thumb.

Sticking on l. zygoma; itching, on posterior surface of thigh, < when sitting; itching, as from fleas, here and there in rapid succession, always singly; itching-biting burning, here and there. Smarting of face as if sore, after washing and drying. Painful tension behind ears and on mastoid process. Sensitiveness on dorsum of hands. Crawling in affected parts; on back of nose; posterior surface of thigh; in toes; under skin of r. cheek, extending to corner of mouth; in glands, with agreeable itching; itching, on tip of nose and in nostrils; itching, in forearm, only transiently > rubbing.

Itching; here and there in all parts; on r. half of body; around l. eye; on nose; about chin; on abdomen; small of back; limbs; in various places on wrist; on flexor surface of r. wrist; ball of l. hand; *backs of fingers;* of l. thumb and little finger; in fossa between nates; thighs and arms; r. patella; backs of toes and fingers; hairy parts, < scrotum, then erection without desire or other cause; on pit of stomach when walking; on soles, with itching pimples; on legs and feet and l. palm, with sticking; sides of third and fourth fingers, transiently > rubbing; on back of balls of thumbs, next day vesicles; on forepart of r. leg, then burning sore pain, then redness, next day the burning had extended and was < touch, then a bright red spot, with burning in it and sensitiveness in and around it; of breasts, on rubbing redness, roughness and burning; agreeable, but violent, in nipples; sticking, on chest, transiently > by scratching; sticking, in cheek and r. side of face, > repeated scratching; corroding, on forehead, transiently > rubbing; corroding, on r. half of body in evening in bed, < lying upon it, always beginning with sticking, > scratching, but reappearing in another place, with uneasiness in limbs.

Clinical.—The skin is very frequently pale yellow. Papular eruptions, with burning and itching.

Sleep.—Frequent yawning. Sleepiness; during the day, he cannot keep awake when reading; during the day, with inability to sleep; feeling in morning as if he had not slept enough; in morning on rising; morning on waking, with weariness; in afternoon, with necessity to lie down and sleep; in evening, and disinclination for occupation. Inability to rouse himself at the usual time and sleepiness for a long time afterwards. Slumbering all day and prostration. Dozing even when walking in open air. Stupid, too sound sleep, then aggravation of the headache.

Sleeplessness; on account of uneasiness and heat, with tossing about the bed. *Falls asleep only after midnight.* Waking early; at midnight, with sweat; anxious half-waking from a sound sleep. Sleep interrupted. Uncovers his arms in sleep. Twitching in arms and hands at night in sleep preceded by ill humor, the eyes are open, staring and turned here and there. Weeping in S. Growling in sleep at night.

Dreams.—*Frightful at night and towards morning;* F. and easily remembered. Anxious before menstruation; A. and hostile; and full of threatening dangers; and vivid. Full of vexation and fighting. Full of shame. Of wretched diseases. Of physical mutilation. Of dead people and of the death of those living. Horrid, from which he woke in fright about 3 or 4 A.M., with distended feeling in stomach, > lying on it, nervous feeling and palpitation, like nightmare. Nightmare. Bad, frequently interrupting sleep. Vivid, voluptuous. Confused; with uneasy sleep.

Fever.—Chilliness; in morning, with headache and nausea; in morning, with dizzy constriction of brain, indifference and depression; waking him at 4 A.M., with bruised pain in head and scapulæ on turning body, with pain in abdominal muscles of epigastric region on deep inspiration, which took away his breath; after midday nap; from 3 to 5 P.M.; at end of evening meal; with every stool; with sadness; with cold hands, hot face and nausea; with trembling in all limbs, so that he must constantly go into the sun. Internal, with numbness extending from thigh to foot; I., waking at 5 A.M. (almost without thirst), with cold hands and soles and hot face, lasting eight hours, then heat in face and weakness. Shivering; every day at 8 A.M.; on motion; in afternoon, with coldness, then after five or six hours creeping of heat over all limbs, when the confusion of head and the indifference with sadness disappeared, and the most active participation in every occurrence took place; in back, usually about 10 A.M., with cold hands and blue nails, sometimes the coldness extends up into arms; itching, from nape to head. Cold skin; coldness through back, with cold hands and blue nails; C. limbs; limbs, with heat in head.

Heat; through whole body, with thirst; daily; at night in bed, necessity to pass the night upon the sofa; the child desires to go to bed early, is then very hot and sweats, with uneasy sleep, trembling, short, rattling, snoring respiration; after a cup of tea with two spoonfuls of wine, and sweat; with sweat, thirst, loss of appetite, diarrhœa and vomiting. Dry H. of whole body before menstruation, without thirst. Sudden H., with vertigo and pain, which spread over whole head. In flushes; in afternoon, without thirst. Orgasm of blood; with jerking in heart. Tertian bilious fever. Catarrhal fever, with inflammation of throat and loss of appetite. Insidious fever, with loss of appetite. Internal H., < face, with redness, without thirst. Internal and external H. after sleep; I. and E., with dry sticky lips, aversion to drink, insipid saliva, noise, bright objects and every motion affect him, he desires to sit alone with closed eyes. H. of skin seems greater than it is. More internal than external, in face and sinciput. H. in head; occiput, then in forehead and cheeks; in skin of r. temple, then in side of tip of l. thumb-nail; skin on r. side of forehead; on upper part of l. concha; down back in morning on waking; of head, with confusion and heaviness; of face, with rush of blood to head and sensation of coryza in nose; hot flashes in occiput, then in forehead, frequently repeated when sitting and reading. H., with sensitiveness on scalp, above r. frontal eminence; above l. knee; on back of forearm, < l.; on side of l. little finger, with redness.

Sweat; over whole body in morning on waking; inclination to S. in morning on and after waking, even on the cold legs; in evening when sitting, with heat of face; at night; on waking at midnight; after midnight; on eating and drinking; as soon as the eyes are closed, even on beginning to sleep, and during the day on dozing when sitting; < forehead, with redness of whole body, without remarkable heat. Intermittent. Cold, alternately on different parts; C., like death-sweat, on forehead and hair. Sweat on forehead; on hands; on perineum; on legs at night. Offensive, in axilla.

Clinical.—Sweat immediately on falling asleep.

Convallaria.

A tincture is made of the entire fresh plant of Convallaria Majalis, L.

General Action.—In large doses it causes irregularity of heart's action, vomiting and collapse; in somewhat smaller doses it diminishes the rate of the pulse and promotes the flow of urine. In small doses it acts as a cardiac tonic and dissipates dropsical effusions of cardiac origin.

Ally.—Digitalis.

Generalities.—Feeling as if I had taken cold. General sick feeling. Sensation as if she were getting fat internally and filling up. Restlessness. Tired, bruised feeling all over body. Weakness; in morning after rising; in evening; during the laborlike pains, with sleepiness; with staggering; and feeling as if recovering from a long sickness. Faint upon having the gums lightly touched with the point of a knife; faint, dizzy feeling, like morning sickness, on raising head from the pillow in morning, nausea > vomiting a clear substance tasting like phlegm. Aggravation from 2 to 5 P.M. Amelioration from eating; after dinner; in open air.

Mind.—Depression. Grieve very easily. Irritable feeling when asked a question. Nervous feeling, with trembling of hand. Do not feel like talking. No desire to get up in the morning. Time passed very slowly. Intellect dull. Wandering from the subject when reading, sees small words before the beginning of sentences, and the letter P is substituted for other letters.

Head.—Aching on ascending stairs; < ascending a hill; < hawking; < stepping heavily or jarring head, gradually passing away after supper; < r. temple; with sleepiness; as from too sound sleep, in morning, > lying down again, also < motion; heavy, < vertex; heavy, after a short walk, < motion. Dulness; and heaviness. Feels weak. Vertigo.

Forehead.—Pricking as from nettles at times during the day, < warmth. Aching in morning on waking, with soreness of eyeballs on motion, dizziness; A. on jarring head; in F. and nape when walking, < jar or ascending a hill; headache beginning in F.; in fronto-temporal region, < r. Heavy aching; over eyes, with sleepiness.

Vertex.—Pain; extending to temples at 8 P.M., > walking in open air. Dulness in r. side.

Eyes.—Dark lines under them. Smarting of r. at noon. Pain every fifteen minutes from r. over top of head and down r. side of neck; heavy P. in r. eye and temple. Heaviness, wanted to keep the lids closed, but if I closed them while walking I staggered. Dry feeling from walking in morning till 10 A.M., with sensation as if inner part of lids were rough. Upper lids feel heavy on looking up. All letters looked alike when reading. Saw gray spots about three inches square in different parts of the room on entering the house after a walk.

Ears and Nose.—Pulsating pain in l. ear, with heat in it; sharp pulsating pain in r. middle ear, and when swallowing the r. tympanum seemed to bulge, > pressing on temporal artery in front of ear. Hydroa on inner edge of l. nostril, with feeling as if the flesh had been torn. Epistaxis at 2 A.M., waking me.

Face.—Pinched; and sallow. Of a smoked color after exercising enough to cause free perspiration. Lips covered with sore hydroa, < l. side.

Mouth and Throat.—Grating on teeth in morning on waking. Tongue coated yellow at base, tip and sides dotted red, tip feels sore, as if scalded. Collection of tough, clammy mucus in mouth. Taste coppery. Suffocating sensation in throat; at 6 P.M., with dryness.

Stomach.—Appetite diminished; lost. Could not eat breakfast. Food does not seem clean or fit to eat. Thirst, < evening. Frequent drinking of large quantities. Desire for lemonade or something acid. Eructations of fat all the afternoon; of fat after dinner; of gas tasting of food; after supper, tasting of food eaten four hours before; after eating cucumbers, tasting of the cucumbers. Nausea; with cold sweat about waist (Verat.); after exercising for about ten minutes immediately after eating, with faint feeling and vomiting twice of mucus which looked and tasted like the slime from oysters. Vomiting. Weak feeling in region after dinner.

Abdomen.—Pain; at 6.30 P.M. when eating, causing me to hold my breath, < beginning to eat, < sitting up straight or leaning back, causes sleepiness; paroxysmal, causing desire for stool, > stool, four stools of natural consistency between 2 and 5 P.M.; grumbling, as if bowels would move, sensation as if flatus would surely pass, but can retain it. Soreness, < coughing or being in a warm room, > open air or exercising; S. on pressure, clothes feel tight. Sensation as if filling up, causing dyspnœa, desire to breathe deeply when sitting down, abdomen distended, but sensation as if larger than it really was. Uneasiness, and on going into open air pain, < walking; U., then colic, causing desire for stool, stool scanty, with tenesmus. Weak feeling.

Pain in r. side going to l.; P. in hypochondria on deep inspiration or gaping; in region of gall-bladder on deep breathing or raising arms. Gurgling in umbilical region. Umbilical pain in l. part after a short walk; in r. side, which comes quickly and passes off slowly; extending to l. groin during dinner.

Hypogastrium.—Pain in morning before rising, > stool; P. every time he woke all night till after 5.30 A.M.; < r. side, with fulness and with desire for stool, the pain continued after the stool; > stool, with fulness; > stool, with dulness in head; in l. iliac region, > micturition; intermittent, when eating. Sore pain on coughing and breathing deeply; S. pain in middle at 7 P.M. after eating, it came on gradually and passed off suddenly, < sitting up straight; causing me to hold my breath, passing into a dull ache. Soreness all the afternoon, < between 5 and 6 P.M.; S. when eating, with intermittent pain. Bruised sensation in r. side on laughing or coughing. Uneasiness, with colic, then urging to stool, stool rather thin, light, smelling like decayed meat, relieving the colic, tenesmus after the stool, these symptoms occurred four times in afternoon.

Sacro-iliac Synchondrosis.—Laborlike pains, with bearing down extending across pelvis, < at sides, < sitting down, especially sitting straight or leaning back, > standing or leaning forward while sitting, went to sleep between the pains; laborlike pains, < r. side, extending down inner side of r. thigh, with sleepiness, as if tired, also pains ran down leg, < motion, sitting up straight or leaning back, pain beginning in anterior part of abdomen, on the r. side it was the same as in the second stage of labor, but extended higher up, the pains returned afterwards, < sitting, extended up back and caused nausea and faint, sick feeling, with hunger, when lying on back the pains were relieved, but there was a sensation as if a fœtus at eight months were kicking, < being on the feet. Sensation as if a large cord extended to inguinal region and this cord were pulled down by the pelvic organs, < r. side, sensation as if uterus descended and retroverted, the fundus of the uterus pressing on rectum caused pain in anus and rectum, sensation as if rectum were full of gas, not > passing flatus.

Clinical.—In pelvic congestion, with sore aching pain in lower part of abdomen, especially after miscarriages or operations. Feeling as if uterus had descended and pressed upon rectum, causing cutting in rectum and anus, dull aching soreness in lumbar region, great prostration, pain > lying on back.

Rectum and Anus.—Sore, burning sensation in anus during stool. Tensemus during stool, with inactivity of rectum. Ineffectual desire, with soreness of anus as if raw, on straining.

Stool.—Thin; and brown, offensive, with tensemus and heat at anus after stool; and offensive, twice a day, each one preceded by uneasiness in epigastrium. Offensive. Scanty, after prolonged tensemus, which continues after the stool. Twice a day.

Urinary Organs.—After micturition, aching in bladder as if over-distended, with aching and lame feeling in back after lying down. Frequent desire, but only a little urine was passed, which seemed scalding hot, but left no smarting. Frequent micturition, urine light brown, after standing over night it smells like fresh fish, slight mucous sediment. Urine dark; and strong-smelling; and offensive, acid. Copious urine; and light-colored. Urine contained an excess of earthy phosphates; and sugar.

Sexual Organs.—Itching at orifice of vagina, extending to meatus of urethra, then gradually all over labia, with hyperæmia, almost unbearable at 8 P.M., < slightest motion of legs, > cold water.

Respiratory Organs.—*Paroxysms of hot suffocating sensation, with general perspiration. Dyspnœa on ascending a hill. Breath short when walking.*

Clinical.—Dyspnœa with pulmonary status and hydrothorax, relieved so that she could lie flat on her back; it also caused profuse micturition.

Chest.—Stinging beneath sternum, at about third rib, radiating in all directions for a circumference of about four inches, at 8 P.M. Sudden transient shooting in l. nipple, leaving soreness. Sharp pain in nipple; in l. side, with every breath; in r. nipple, leaving soreness. Intermittent pain in r. nipple, beginning slowly each time, increasing to a sharp pain, then gradually passing off. Sensation as if milk were coming into r. breast, then stitches which centre in nipple, from 3 to 4 P.M.

Heart.—Sounds feeble; with anæmic murmur over jugular veins. Pain in præcordial region; in region of apex. Discomfort in region in afternoon. Uneasy feeling. Fluttering when exercising, then redness of face and sensation as if heart stopped beating and started up again suddenly, causing faint, sick feeling. Beating not as hard as normal.

Clinical.—It benefits valvular disease of heart, with scanty urine and dropsy, great dyspnœa, sometimes produces bloody urine. In several cases of heart diseases it relieved œdema, so that the patient could lie down. In a case of very feeble, irregular action of the heart, soft, irregular pulse, doses of 10 drops of 1st dec. dil. relieved the dyspnœa and palpitation. It relieved dyspnœa, on ascending stairs or walking, in a woman without organic disease. Heart irregular, urine suppressed, dropsy, dyspnœa, mitral disease, after Conval. the heart's action was regular, and the dropsy disappeared.

Pulse.—Rapid; when standing, and soft; and weak; and temperature high. Slow when lying, rapid on moving about the room. Changeable; in frequency (Dig.). Full, compressible and intermittent, < motion, > lying (Dig.); F., compressible and imperceptible, with hand extended above head. Weak and easily compressed; W., and when holding my arm above my head it was imperceptible, hand turned pale, became numb and soon went to sleep. Dicrotic when hand was extended above head.

Back.—Aching after leaning over, with lame and weak feeling in dorsal region; A. as if bruised or broken; lame; A. under lower angle of r. scapula; under point of l. scapula on lifting arm; sudden, under lower angle of r. scapula, passing off gradually, > bending shoulders backward, constant yawning after the pain; sore, between lower angles of scapulæ, afterwards it extended up and down spine. Pain in lumbar region; as if muscles were bruised; across region of kidneys from 2 till 4. P.M.; < in r. loin, after a short walk, < motion, deep breathing or sitting up straight; sharp, in post-sacral region; sharp, in region of r. kidney, leaving soreness; sore, in lumbar region from 5 to 10 A.M.

Extremities.—Pain in wrists and ankles, < after sleep, afterwards extending about four inches up legs. Rheumatic pain in l. elbow after going to bed, < motion. Trembling of hands. A small aneurism on l. index, after pricking it it bled profusely and was difficult to stop, the bleeding caused a faint feeling. Cramp on inner side of r. thigh, it would come quickly and go away gradually, when riding, > straightening leg and pressing foot against something; C. in l. calf when walking; below r. knee when sitting, > standing, returning on sitting down. Knees felt sore when walking. Legs ache; < r., and below knee. Feet numb on first bearing weight on them, then they seemed as if filled with needles (or as if asleep). Aching of r. great toe.

Sleep.—Sleepiness; after breakfast, with dulness; at 2 P.M. after entering a warm room; between 3 and

5 P.M., also with weakness; at 6 P.M. when sitting; after dinner; when sitting; with laziness. Woke between 12 and 1 A.M., was restless for two hours, with burning all over body; woke at 2 A.M., was restless for some time, and after a short sleep woke again very restless; woke between 2 and 3 A.M. and was restless the remainder of the night. Restless sleep; towards morning. Troublous dreams.

Skin.—Rough when washing after perspiring. Blotches like mosquito-bites on anterior part of thigh and foot, and sides of back; on body, with itching on undressing, so that she scratched the skin off, the itching continued after getting into bed. Feels sore over whole body on waking and after rising. Itching on anterior part of thigh.

Fever.—Temperature lowered. Chill whenever I felt a little cold, with nervous feeling so that hands trembled; C. all night, with waking twice, before rising pain in forehead and temples, < r. side, < motion, chills running along back on moving any part, nausea, on getting out of bed shaking chill all over body, ends of fingers pale, the rest of the hand mottled purple and white, lips purple and sore, covered with hydroa, hair sensitive to touch, chill > heat of stove or warm coverings, water tasted bitter, no appetite, tongue felt as if scalded when drinking warm coffee, thick, clammy saliva, aching in lumbar region and legs, nausea, inability to sleep, at 10.30 A.M. chilly from a draught of air or when lying on a cold sofa, at 2 P.M. high temperature; C. from 8 to 9 A.M., beginning in back, soon extending all over body, > warm wraps, chill < in back, when walking in the street chattering of teeth, ends of fingers white, first joint of r. index numb, fever from 9 to 11.30 A.M., then slight sweat, not much headache during chill or fever; C. between shoulders running down back to legs, at 1 P.M., at dinner, when sitting in a draught of chilly and damp air, ends of fingers pale and cold, C. > heavy wraps and sitting in a room where there was no draught, at 2 P.M. the C. is noticed the more the harder it rains, touching any part with anything cold will cause a C. to begin between scapulæ and pass down legs, aching at anus, with desire for stool, but only flatus passes, raw feeling posteriorly in pharynx when inspiring, > for a moment by hacking cough, dulness and sleepiness, with desire to go to bed, at 2.20 P.M. fever beginning in a spot between scapulæ, then extending to r. side of head, then all over head and down back, the fever passes away in the reverse order from which it came, sensation as if bladder were overdistended, but micturition scanty, stool followed by tenesmus, not much thirst during chill or fever, at 4 P.M. slight sweat.

Fever without thirst; towards night; F. from 8.15 until 11 A.M., with heavy aching in forehead, aching in lumbar region as if back had been pounded, I went to bed but could not sleep, aching in legs, difficulty in hearing, ears seemed stopped, could feel the heart beating throughout chest, general chilliness on moving any part, the headache < motion, but > after moving around and talking, at 11 A.M. sweat, fever returned at 4.30 P.M., with headache, < jarring or moving head, thirst during the first part of the fever, trembling of hands or legs during the fever, < draught of air, coppery taste, rapid pulse, heat in chest and hypochondria, weak, empty feeling in pharynx extending to stomach, dyspnœa, with desire to breathe deeply, backache, tired after walking, with aching in legs and back and aggravation of headache, urine scanty, dark and smelling like cows' urine, appetite poor, sleepiness, at 7 P.M. chills running down spine from a draught of air or drink of cold water, water felt cold all the way down œsophagus, sensation as of bubbles of air passing through water from symphysis pubis to r. side of hypogastrium, pain across umbilical region.

Warm sweat all over body.

Copaiva.

A tincture is prepared by dissolving 1 part of the balsam, from Copaifera Langsdorffii, Desf., in 99 parts of alcohol.

General Action.—It is an irritant to all mucous membranes, particularly to the urinary tract, for which it has special affinity; it is also diuretic and laxative. It produces an urticaria-like eruption on the skin, or, at times, an eruption like pemphigus.

Allies.—Canth., Apis.

Generalities.—Spasmodic paroxysms and other hysterical symptoms. *Uneasiness, then chill, then heat and circumscribed lenticular patches, with itching and pricking like measles, but without catarrhal symptoms, then mottled appearance, no desquamation.* Pulling in all muscles, < evening and night. Pulsations here and there. Weakness; with anxious sadness. Sensitiveness to coldness and dampness; S. so that noise makes him tremble and angers him. Sensibility diminished.

Mind.—Disgust with life, but fear of death. Dislike for his usual employment. Sadness in morning after waking, > during a walk, returning in evening; S. in morning during menstruation, with pain in loins and nervous excitement; periodical, in afternoon, with weeping, coldness of limbs and hot flushes in face. Bursting into tears at the sound of a piano. Anxiety about his health. Peevishness, with ebullition of blood, heat of head and trembling of limbs from least contradiction. Absurd recriminations about long-past trifles. Misanthropy. Unfit for study, head empty, ideas confused, and pain in forehead when striving against it. Defective memory, which vexed, then discouraged him.

Head.—Aching; in forenoon; with nausea. Heaviness, < occiput, > pressing it against coat-collar. Rush of blood to head and face during and *after eating.* Vertigo, with aching; V. in forenoon when riding on horseback; in attacks when sitting, working, walking, < standing and when motionless. Pressure at forehead. Sticking in temples and behind ears; sudden S. in temples in morning on washing face with cool water. Tearing in temples, < l., > gentle pressure. Bruised pain in r. temple in evening and night, > pressing against pillow. Pulsating sticking in vertex. Boring in l. side, with coldness of the part, weeping and moaning (in a man disposed to hypochondriasis). Sticking in r. occipital protuberance; in l. O. protuberance in morning, with occasional shocks in head; deep-seated pulsating S. in occiput. Pain in occiput. Falling of hair. Sensitiveness of scalp, and even of hair.

Eyes.—Redness of l. Pupils contracted. Lids agglutinated in morning. Involuntary contraction of orbicularis muscle in morning. Spasm of r. upper lid, with pain in eye. Formication in canthi. Sensitiveness to light. Vision obscured. Objects look paler when seen with l. than with r. eye. Black points hover before eyes.

Ears.—Sticking in l. at night, then purulent discharge. Formication. Hearing sensitive, < to sharp sounds, so that the report of a pistol caused pain, not from the detonation of the powder, but from the impact of the ball against a metallic disk. Painful reverberation of every sound, > walking. Humming. Roaring.

Nose and Face.—Frequent sneezing. Stoppage of nose mornings. Coryza, with headache, pain at root of nose and itching in eyes. Face bloated. Face pale and sickly. Tearing in l. cheek. Red, humid tetter on upper lip, with swelling and pain on touch. Lips and tongue red.

Mouth.—Teeth loose; unpleasant smell from T.; gnawing in carious, < cold air or cold drinks, with throbbing pain; elongated feeling; on edge; sense of coldness. Excoriating pain in gums, palate and pharynx. *Tongue coated white*, green at base; T. at sides and tip red and smarting. Tenacious phlegm, which is constantly reproduced in M. and throat. Dryness; < night and in morning. Salivation; evening, night and morning; sudden, intermittent, sweetish. Foul breath in morning. Taste bitter; T. too salt to all food.

Throat.—Parotid glands sensitive, submaxillary glands swollen, with bruised pain in latter. Swelling of tonsils, < r. Pain; in pharynx. Constriction. Sensation of a foreign body in pharynx. Heat, with stinging.

Stomach.—Hunger in evening on going to bed; excessive H., then loss of appetite. Appetite lost. Loathing of food all day. Thirst, with diminished appetite. Eructations; after eating; bitter; sour; foul; tasting of ingesta. Hiccough after eating. Nausea; in morning; with diarrhœa. Vomiting and weakness of stomach; V. and cardialgia. Spasm. Epigastric region tensive and painful to touch. Gastro-enteritis. Paroxysmal sticking. Pain during menstruation. Burning pain. Pressure at pit, even before breakfast. Beating at pit after eating, then palpitation and obnubilation on leaving the table. Faintness, without real appetite. Digestion retarded and painfully increased by sensitiveness and pains in epigastrium. Heat.

Abdomen.—Rumbling; with flatulence and threatening of colic. Emission of fetid flatus in morning in bed and after rising. Griping. Pinching. Cutting, after a cup of *cafe au lait* (as usual), then diarrhœa. *Colic; and looseness.* Coldness. Sticking in hypochondria. Pressive, at times pulsating pain in hepatic region. Swelling of lower. Swelling of inguinal glands; with sensitiveness. Inguinal glands painful to touch. Pressure in lower as from a stone. Beatings in lower.

Rectum and Anus.—Spasms of R. Sticking in R. Urging to stool; frequent ineffectual. Bleeding piles. Oozing of serous or purulent fluid. Burning itching in anus.

Stool.—Two liquid. Thin, frequent, without pain or urging, with increased mucus. Diarrhœa; in morning; with exudation from skin; frightful; involuntary; frequent at night, with spasms of stomach, coldness of limbs and cramp in calves; whitish, < morning, with coldness and drawing tearing in abdomen, obliging him to bend double, before and after the stool; alternating with constipation. Soft, frequent, then prostration, < morning. Constipation. Dry and formed at first, ending in diarrhœa. Like sheep-dung. Whitish, sour, with discharge of ascarides. Insufficient. Copious. Frequent, at first shaped, then pasty, at last mucous and mixed with blood (Canth.).

Clinical.—Catarrh of the intestines, mucus comes away in masses or the stools are coated with mucus, especially in morning, with colic and chilliness (compare Canth.). Dysentery, with intolerable burning at anus, tenesmus and blood (Canth., Caps.).

Urinary Organs.—Pain in bladder. *Burning in neck of bladder and in urethra* (Canth.). Pressure on bladder; with frequent ineffectual urging and micturition by drops. Constant urging; frequent urging after urinating. Micturition frequent and copious; at night, and urine light; frequent, mostly in small quantities. Micturition by drops (Canth.). Micturition painful; with milky, acrid discharge (Canth.). Retention of urine.

Urethra.—Inflammation and swelling, with pains along penis; I., with retention of urine, phlegmasia of bladder, of prostate, anus and rectum; I. of urinary passages and adjacent parts. Discharge was inversely as that of skin; D. of mucus; purulent blennorrhagia; profuse milky D. Pain at orifice as if wounded; pulsating pain in U. when not urinating, the orifice gaping, tumid, inflated. Drawings. Burning on urinating; B. and itching in U. and vagina. Itching before and after micturition, with biting. Tickling in orifice (compare "urethra" with Cantharis).

Urine. — Bloody; with strangury and ischuria (Canth.). Copious; and smelling of the balsam; and acid, smelling of violets. Had a strong odor of Copaiba, frothed much, dark yellow, acid. Bitter-tasting. Albuminuria (Canth.).

Clinical.—Catarrh of the bladder, with great dysuria, especially if it follows gonorrhœa, has to make a great effort to pass a little water. Inflammation of urethra, with great burning far back on urinating, swelling of the orifice of the urethra. Constant desire to urinate. Hæmaturia. Urine smells of violets, especially in gonorrhœa, discharge yellow and purulent.

Sexual Organs.—Excoriation of glans and prepuce. Tickling of glans. Itching at tip of glans. Excessive erections, with lascivious thoughts and desires; violent E. night and morning, with or without lascivious thoughts; no E. Redness and oozing between scrotum and thigh. Burning in skin of scrotum. Swelling of l. testicle, with sensitiveness to touch. Heavy pain in testicles. Pressive drawing in testicles. Desire; without erections.

Female.—*Itching of vulva.* Burning of vulva and red spots. Sticking in vagina and neck of uterus. Leucorrhœa after menstruation; acrid L.; milky L. Spasms of uterus. Pulling pains in suspensory ligaments of uterus; dragging on uterus and bladder; pressure on U. as if prolapsus would set in; drawings in uterus, orifice of urethra and vagina. Throbbing in ovarian region with pain; T. in r. ovarian region when standing. Menses too early; menses reappear after they had ceased for several days. Menses pale and scanty. Metrorrhagia.

Clinical.—Swelling and induration of testicles from suppressed gonorrhœa. Gonorrhœa in women, with throbbing in region of r. ovary.

Respiratory Organs.—Excoriating pain in larynx. Dryness and roughness of larynx. Tightness of larynx during menses, with hoarseness in morning and dry cough morning and evening. Hoarseness, < morning, with excoriating pain in larynx on talking. Voice loses its compass, the higher notes cause excoriating pain, which finally makes their rendering impossible. Bronchial mucous membrane excited. Cough from tickling in larynx, trachea and bronchi; dry C. morning and evening; rough C., with difficult expectoration of greenish mucus; C., with profuse whitish expectoration, sometimes saltish, sometimes flat and nauseous. Respiration slow.

Clinical.—Bronchial catarrh, with profuse purulent expectoration. Catarrh of larynx, dryness, painful cough, hoarseness in morning.

Chest.—Sticking in r. Pressure on sternum. Burning. Fulness, obliging sighing. Distress when working in a stooping position, as when digging, with labored breathing.

Heart and Pulse.—Frequent and feeble pulsations of heart. Palpitation; during work. Pulse frequent; slow.

Neck and Back.—Rheumatic pain in nape and l. side of neck. Stiffness of back, > walking. Burning pain in dorsal spine. Sticking in l. scapula; between scapulæ, cutting short the respiration. Pulling in scapulæ. Lumbar pains; spasmodic.

Extremities.—Trembling; during rest. Sticking in l. axilla, extending into chest. Axillary glands sensitive to touch. Pain in l. shoulder at night, next evening in r. elbow; acute, in l. shoulder-joint; P. of dislocation in r. shoulder. Numbness of arm on which he lies at night. Pullings in forearms. Pain in l. wrist. Trembling of hands. Stiffness of fingers.

Lower Extremities.—Uneasiness. Cramplike pain in hips, < r. Bruised pain in r. hip when lying on it; in r. hip on walking and on touch. Rheumatic pains (as from fatigue) in l. hip and knee during menstruation, with spasms of uterus. Constrictive pain in hollow of femur before the griping. Cracking of knees on stretching legs. Pain in knees; l., when walking. Numbness of legs when sitting. Pain anteriorly in r. ankle; P. in r. ankle when walking; in l. when walking. Swelling of feet; of l. foot. Pain on dorsum of foot during the cold stage. Sprained pain in feet on beginning to walk, > walking.

Skin.—Irregular, itching, yellow spots on r. cheek in morning and evening. Hæmorrhage and red spots on whole body, < on face. Erythema (Vespa); rosy "pumiceous," as if bitten by insects. Confluent scarlet elevations on hands and feet. Red blotches over whole body, < on face; *large red blotches, with constipation and fever* (Apis). Red itching spots on l. elbow; at sternal region and r. axilla. Red miliary eruption, sometimes confluent, preceded by headache, vertigo and loathing. Red miliary E., preceded by cardialgia, vertigo and nausea, the E. may be slow in developing and locate upon wrists, hands, knees, ankles and feet, at other times it develops rapidly and covers the whole skin and is accompanied by febrile phenomena, it is characterized by red spots, disappearing under pressure, the spots round or with uneven edges and separated by healthy skin, or they unite and form large red spots, with itching, if the medicine is continued the spots become papules, in rare cases the region becomes tumefied, painful and impeded in its movements. Eruption resembling roseola, but the spots are larger and more elevated, confluent on parts of chest and arms, and look like petechiæ. Redness and swelling of face, with thirst, nausea, vomiting, anorexia and restlessness, then arms and legs, and finally whole body, red and swollen, face dusky yellowish-red, œdema, < about eyelids, which could not be opened, sticky discharge at margins of lids, elevations on face and neck like measles, < next the hair and at lower parts of neck, over whole body dark red smooth eruption studded with points of a deeper color, hands and feet somewhat resembling face, throat inflamed and dusky red, with œdema of uvula, no difficulty in swallowing, sleeplessness, tossing about all night, thick, yellowish-white fur on tongue, no stool for two days, heat, pulse rapid, small, thready, vertigo, sore throat, ineffectual retching after food. Elevations as from wasp-stings, confluent on ears and backs of hands becoming after a few days brownish-yellow like liver spots, with mealy desquamation on ears, even after four weeks burning spots could be seen. Furfuraceous tetter on l. concha, with burning pain on touch.

Nettle-rash; or like scarlet fever, first on face, < on forehead, then on backs of hands, finally in other parts, with burning of skin, also with sore throat (without swelling), then sweat, no fever or thirst, elevations like bug-bites, confluent on ears and backs of hands, then the spots become brown without desquamation, except on ears. Red itching pimples on upper part of forehead, on hairy scalp, above ears and on occiput. Boils on pubis. Pustules like the itch between fingers and on forearms. Eruptive fever, with heat and headache, purple eruption like variola, in twelve hours it spreads, sinks down and each pustule becomes depressed, soon forms a petechial blotch, which becomes confluent with adjacent blotches. Modified pemphigus over whole body, beginning at flexure of joints, the bullæ aborted where the skin was thin, the discharge excessive, offensive, viscid, then general desquamation. White miliary vesicles on a red base on l. wing and tip of nose. Itching of cheeks, here and there, in nostrils and on chin. (Compare skin symptoms with Apis and Vespa.)

Clinical.—Urticaria, dry, hot, biting, with violent itching.

Sleep.—*Drowsiness in daytime* (Apis). *Restless sleep.* Sleeplessness and restlessness all night after an embrace. Frequent waking. Early waking and inability to sleep again. Dreams frightful or lascivious.

Fever.—Shivering in morning; and in afternoon heat and thirst. Cold hands; feet from morning till noon; feet, knees and thighs at night; feet and knees during menses. Heat; in face in morning on waking; in flushes in face and head after eating, with sweat in hollow of hands, anxiety and indigestion. Sweat; in morning; sour at night; with the odor of Copaiba. Sensation as if sweat would break out, which afterwards took place in bed.

Corallium Rubrum.

A trituration is made of the red coral, Corallium rubrum, Lam.

Allies.—Coccus cacti, Dros., Merc.

Mind and Head.—Full of pains, he uses bad language and curses. Peevish. *Head feels very large.* H. feels empty. Immediate stupefaction from wine.

Confusion of H. as after intoxication. All the blood seems to rise to H. and face on stooping. Dizziness after eating, as if intoxicated. *Pressing-out pain at forehead, obliging him to move the head from side to side, but it is not > thereby nor by sitting, but transiently > almost complete uncovering of the hot body.* Pain in forehead so that she cannot keep the eyes open, > walking and moving about in open air. Pressure at F. sinuses, > open air, with increased secretion of nasal mucus; P. in forehead and temples, whereby the sinciput seems flattened. Pain in temporal muscles on swallowing. *Pain in parietal bones as if forced asunder, < by stooping. Sensation as of a wind through skull on rapid motion or on shaking head.*

Eyes.—Redness in evening, with pressure as from sand. Pain in l. as if hot and dry. Sore pain on moving balls or lids. Pain as if pressed into orbits. Burning in candle-light; heat on closing lids, with sensation as if swimming in tears. *Drawing pain in external wall of l. orbit, extending along nervus malaris to beneath cheek-bone* (compare Cinnab.).

Ears and Nose.—Hearing less distinct than usual. Painful swelling in r. nostril and on inner side of wing of nose, with pain in nasal bones as if pressed asunder, the pain extending partly into frontal sinuses, partly towards eyes and to temples, with thirst, r. side of nose swollen, hot and pulsating, disturbing night's rest. Dryness of nose and throat. Frequent sneezing, preceded by tickling in nose. Epistaxis at night; E. now from r., now from l. nostril. Stopped coryza, could get no air through l. nostril; stopped C., then dropping of mucus like melted tallow. (Profuse secretion of mucus through posterior nares, obliging constant hawking.)

Clinical.—Painful ulcer in r. nostril, sensation as if nose were pressed asunder. Profuse nasal catarrh, the inspired air feels cold.

Face, Mouth and Throat.—*Bruised pain in l. zygoma, < by touch. Sprained pain in l. joint of jaw on drawing jaw far downward and on biting and yawning.* Lips cracked, painful. On pressing on fossa canina ulcerative pain in corresponding teeth. L. teeth feel blunted and as if too near each other, or as if a tough substance were sticking between them. Taste of food like sawdust; like straw to farinaceous food; sweet to beer. *L. submaxillary glands swollen and painful, < on swallowing or bending head forward* (Merc.). Throat dry, sore on swallowing.

Clinical.—Hawking of profuse mucus, throat very sensitive, especially to air (Merc.).

Stomach, Abdomen, Stool and Urine.—Longing for acids; for salted meat. Appetite lost. Thirst; during chill, with normal temperature of skin and pain in forehead. Nausea, with dry tongue; N., < sitting up, with headache. Pressure in pit of stomach, < coughing, swallowing and deep inspiration. Rumbling in abdomen. Constipation for six days, then a large, pasty stool. Burning micturition. Urine clay-colored, with similar sediment.

Sexual Organs.—Sweat. *Red flat ulcer on glans and inner surface of prepuce, with yellowish discharge. Glans and inner surface of prepuce secrete a yellowish-green offensive matter, with sensitiveness, redness and swelling* (compare Merc.). Swelling of prepuce, with sore pain in its border where it rubs against the clothing. Pain in frænum preputii as from needles. Emission at night and another next afternoon during a nap, the latter with relaxed penis and without dreams.

Clinical.—Ulcerations on glans penis and prepuce, with sensitiveness and exudation of thin offensive moisture. Venereal ulcers, very sensitive, bleeding easily.

Respiratory Organs.—*Feeling as if cold air were streaming through air-passages in morning on deep inspiration, with provocation to cough and with difficult hawking of bronchial mucus.* Expectoration of yellow purulent mucus. During cough pain in cavities of pleura as from a stone pressing downward and causing pain beneath sternum, extending thence to scapula.

Clinical.—Most violent spasmodic cough (whooping cough), often preceded by sensation of smothering, followed by exhaustion; the attacks are extremely violent, the patient becomes purple in the face, followed by exhaustion or vomiting of quantities of tough mucus. Indicated in whooping cough by the extreme violence of the paroxysms, even with expectoration of blood.

Neck, Back and Extremities.—Stiffness of cervical muscles. Pain in scapulæ, < coughing. Bruised pain in small of back. Pain in sacral region, as from pressure with a dull instrument. Weariness of extremities in evening after exercise in open air. Pain as if head of the humerus would be forced out of the joint, l., then r., then both together. Pain at insertion of deltoid and in middle of r. forearm, as if pressed with the ends of the fingers. Pain in wrists as after much rapid writing. Sudden shooting through r. tibia. Tearing in r. tibia when walking, with tickling in hollow of knee so that knees crack. Pain in knee, tibia and ankle as after a fatiguing walk.

Skin, Sleep and Fever.—Flat spots, coral-red, then dark red, then copper-red, on palms and some fingers. Painful pimple on lip close to orifice of r. nostril. Frequent excessive yawning, with pain in joints of jaws. Sleepiness so that she fell asleep when standing. Sleeplessness till midnight; with tossing about and coldness if uncovered, but heat if covered. Tossing about and uncovering in sleep. Uneasy, dreamy sleep. Starting up from anxious dreams as soon as she falls asleep. Chilliness in hot parts on uncovering. Cold feet after eating, with hot forehead and cheeks. Internal and external heat, with full, hard pulse. Dry heat, without thirst. Heat of face, < bending forward; dry H. of face in morning, with cold shuddering creeping over her on putting her hand to her face. Symptoms of heat and cold, > artificial heat.

Cornus Circinata.

A tincture is made of the fresh bark of Cornus circinata, L'Her.

General Action.—Not sufficiently known, but seems to exert a marked action on the liver and intestinal secretions.

Allies.—Cinchona, Alstonia, Chel.

Generalities and Mind.—*Weakness; in morning on waking; in morning on rising, with apathy. Indolence and loss of physical energy. Disinclination to read, think or work. Depression of spirits.* Peevishness. Indifference. *Inability to concentrate thoughts.* Confusion of ideas; towards night, with increase of stupid, sleepy sensation. Forgetful of little things.

Clinical.—Chronic malarial troubles, with jaundice, tendency to diarrhœa or dysentery, enlarged spleen, etc. General debility, with drowsiness and depression of spirits, unrefreshing sleep, etc.

Head.—Shooting through the whole brain. Aching; deep in brain, under centre of skull; on waking at 6 A.M., with distention and pain in abdomen, urging to stool, pains more acute during the stool, which was thin, dark green, offensive, with tenesmus and offensive flatus; tensive. Heavy pain; < walking, stooping or shaking head. Heaviness. Fulness; in brain in morning on rising; > copious, thin, bilious stool, after the stool tenesmus and burning at anus. Confusion; in morning on rising. Lightness. Congestion of blood to H. and face. Giddiness; on shaking head or stooping.

Pain in forehead; and vertex; with rumbling in abdomen; over r. brow; over r. supraorbital ridge. Pulsations from front to back part of head. Pain in temples and vertex; in T. in afternoon and evening. Throbbing pain in temples; and sides of head; gradually passing off in afternoon and night; in vertex. Heavy confused feeling in vertex, with drowsiness. Pain in occiput; deep-seated, pulsatory, and in sides of head; drawing, and in nape. Drawing sensation from occiput to nose. Scalp sore. Aggravation of an habitual scurfy eruption.

Eyes.—Sunken. Surrounded by dark circles. Dull and heavy, as after a debauch. Contracting feeling around them. Heavy sensation around them. Conjunctiva yellow. Balls painful; B. sore; dull feeling over them. Lids heavy.

Clinical.—Scrofulous ophthalmia and herpes of the conjunctiva, with chronic diarrhœa.

Nose and Mouth.—Prickling in nasal cavity. Symptoms of coryza in morning. Face sallow; yellow. Dull and sickly expression.

Mouth.—Smarting, and in throat. Dryness; and in throat. Tongue furred; white; yellowish. Taste bad; bitter; pungent; clammy; insipid.

Clinical.—Nursing sore mouth. Aphthous stomatitis of children.

Stomach.—Appetite impaired; small; lost. Aversion to food; and to drink; to meat and bread. Desire for sour drinks. Eructations; empty; bitter. Nausea; at 10 A.M.; at 1 P.M. Flatulent distention of S. and abdomen. *Pain in pit during dinner, with distention of abdomen from wind, both > immediately after dinner by loose, windy, dark, bilious stool.* Occasional drawing pains extending to hypogastrium. Gnawing, faint feeling. Fulness and oppression, and in abdomen. Burning; and in abdomen. Heavy pulsation. Empty feeling. Faint sensation, and in abdomen. Weakness.

Abdomen.—Rumbling. Offensive flatus. Constant working, as if all the contents were in motion. Griping, with distention; G. at 2 P.M., with ineffectual urging to stool; with rumbling, the G. < in umbilical region; occasional. Pain. Uneasiness; with vague pains; with fulness. Pain in umbilical region. Rumbling in hypogastrium; at 11 A.M., with griping and offensive flatus. Weight in hypogastrium.

Clinical.—Chronic inflammation of liver, jaundice, face yellow, sunken.

Rectum and Stool.—*Urging to stool; at 5 A.M., with bearing-down pain in abdomen; early in morning, not > discharge of a few slimy lumps, with pressing and smarting at anus; on rising; but discharge of only scanty, dark and slimy fluid and offensive flatus. Loose stool, copious, with pressing-down pain in rectum; L., large, dark, with griping and tenesmus; and dark, with tenesmus and burning in anus; and bilious, offensive, five hours later another less loose and less offensive; and scanty, with burning pain in rectum; and scanty, with offensive flatus and burning at anus, also with tenesmus; and scanty, with tenesmus, griping in umbilical region, rumbling and offensive flatus; and scanty, with pressing pain in rectum, smarting at anus after the discharge, dull feeling in head, drowsiness and lassitude. Scanty, bilious, slimy, with flatus and tenesmus, during and after the stool burning pain at anus and a short distance within rectum. Scanty, with burning at anus; S. and dark, with burning pain at anus; and hard, with pressing in rectum. Dark, copious, with pressing down in rectum.*

Clinical.—Diarrhœa, dark, bilious, very offensive, with sallow complexion and sunken face. Dysentery, with burning in anus and rectum and great debility. It is to be compared with Chelidonium in its hepatic symptoms and diarrhœa.

Urinary and Genital Organs.—Urine scanty and red; and passed often. Strong and persistent erections frequently during the night.

Chest.—Stitches, and in back; in C. and under r. scapula; intermittent griping, from centre (apparently in muscles), down to hypogastrium. Bruised feeling in morning on rising, and in back. Choking sensation in upper part. Dragging down each side.

Heart.—Accelerated pulsation.

Back and Extremities.—Pains in back; and knees; in small of back; in lower part of back and abdomen; sore, in lumbar region, < bending forward. Legs weak; on walking or ascending stairs; and trembling.

Skin.—Scarlet rash on breast, with itching. Prickling on arms and legs. Itching all over body; on different parts; on head and legs and nasal mucous membrane; legs, thighs and around labia; scalp, legs and feet, < rubbing or scratching, burning after scratching; in paroxysms, on back, legs and feet, generally in evening.

Clinical.—Vesicular eruptions.

Sleep.—Sleepiness; by day; at 1 P.M.; > strong coffee, with headache; with stupid feeling; with disinclination to make any effort. Sound sleep, with frightful dreams; S. and prolonged; but unrefreshing. Restless sleep. Dreams unpleasant; frightful, waking him, with profuse perspiration.

Fever.—*Coldness, then flushes of heat; and sweat; C. and flushes of heat in alternation, followed by cold sweat.* Cold hands and feet, but hot head. *Flushes of heat; then sweat; to head and face. Heat of head and face; in morning on rising; on vertex;* face and hands, also feet; face in morning on rising, without redness of cheeks. Sweat on slight exertion; clammy S., then chilliness.

Cornus Florida.

A tincture is made of the fresh bark of Cornus florida, L.

Headache. Face flushed. Nausea. Heat in stomach. Pulse accelerated and bounding; and tense; and full, strong; and full, afterwards soft, but full; and irregular, afterwards slower and smaller. Pulse full, afterwards slower and smaller.

Clinical.—Intermittent fever, with dulness, drowsiness, dull headache, great exhaustion, during the intervals between the paroxysms very weak, with diarrhœa, general clammy sweat, etc. (compare with Cornus cir. and Alstonia). It seems to be adapted to chronic malaria; the paroxysms sometimes begin with heat, followed by oppression, with heat beginning in the back, the patient feels weak and miserable in the apyrexia, and especially has diarrhœa and jaundiced skin.

Crocus.

A tincture is made of Saffron, the dried stigmas of Crocus sativus, L.

General Action.—It seems to produce marked hysterical symptoms, with tendency to hæmorrhages of dark blood.

Allies.—Plat., Ign., Zinc.

Generalities.—Distended veins, with internal heat but not much increase of temperature. Lying as if in apoplexy. Anxious trembling of whole body. Spasms every evening, with delirium, alternating with tender mood, wildness and outbreaks of rage, with inclination to bite. **Sensation of something living and jumping about in pit of stomach, abdomen, arms and other parts.** Uneasiness of blood, with palpitation. *Weakness in evening after a moderate meal, > literary occupation, with sleepiness, pressure on egelids and feeling as if they were swollen;* W. in morning, > open air, < in the house, with yawning; with indolence and sleepiness; with sensation as if general sweat would break out and desire to sit or lie; even to sinking down, with sensation as if general sweat would break out, and rapid pulse; of whole body, hands and feet. Faintness. Aggravation in morning. Amelioration in open air.

Clinical.—Chorea, with repeated nosebleed of the Crocus charactèr. Hysteria and nervous prostration, with the peculiar abdominal symptoms or chorea-like twitchings, etc.

Mind.—Silly dementia. *Anger at everything and sudden repentance at having injured others. Vehement, peevish, quarrelsome, an hour later talkative, lively, laughing, singing* (compare Plat.). *Vacillating mood towards evening, anger at the behavior of her relatives and friends and she is at the point of breaking into a passion, but at this moment she feels calm, the next moment this calmness seems a weakness, then vexation with herself and greater anger than ever. Joy alternating with sadness;* with pallor. Affectionate mood alternating with rage and inclination to bite. Peevishness alternating with desire to embrace others. Ill humor at what would usually make her laugh, so that she loses consciousness, then astonishment at the outbreak; I. at the slightest thing, then she does not know what she is doing, with anxiety and general trembling. *Sadness; with anxiety and uneasiness;* sudden S. so that he could not fix his mind upon an interesting lecture. (Alternating moods, see Plat., Ign., Zinc., etc.).

Inclination to sing; *involuntary singing if she hears a single note sung, then she must laugh at herself, but soon sings again in spite of her determination to stop* (Tarent.); quiet repetition of a lively melody, even when out of humor. Gayety; bordering on delirium, with pallor, headache and obscuration of vision; and witty, jocose and talkative mood (Tarent.). Laughter; immoderate, as if he would die; sardonic, with attacks of morbid jollity; and joking, with prostration and dilated pupils. Longing for he knows not what, with apprehension and joy. Indifference. Thoughtlessness from the least thing which affects her. Sudden vivid recollection of a concert, then inability to recall the music. Forgetfulness; and absence of mind, does not recognize an old acquaintance. *Loss of ideas on attempting to write down anything.* It suddenly seems as if thoughts would vanish. Confusion. Mistakes about the time or objects though they were distinctly visible. Senses easily lost, with blackness before eyes. Disinclination for every work.

Head.—Sticking, with stopped coryza. Tearings, and in r. eye and a l. hollow tooth, with dimness before l. eye and feeling as of a cold wind in it. Aching; rising from stomach; on moving, with sensation as if brain fell back and forth. Stupidity, with painful confusion of occiput. Intoxicated feeling, with confused vision and warmth of face. Vertigo; in night after rising, with staggering and general heat; with confusion of head; with confusion of head and pain in eyes.

Forehead.—*Thrusts extending deep into brain above l. eminence, then painful confusion, > pressure* (Ign.). Pain; above eyes, < r., < towards evening, with burning and pressure, compelling rubbing; beneath l. eminence as if a dull point were pressing inward, then intermittent paroxysms of the same pain; drawing P. in a line down middle; painful drawing, with nausea. Painful cramplike drawing from l. eminence to l. side of bony parts of nose. Tension in l. eminence. Confusion; tensive, as if intoxicated, then in whole head. Stupefaction of forepart of head as if drunken and reeling, > open air.

Sudden thrust in r. temple, extending deep into brain. Pressure on vertex in morning after waking, with heaviness of whole head so that he could scarcely hold it up. Pain on r. side; in l. side; in l. side, extending into r. temple as a contractive drawing pain, then to ear and throat, where it is < swallowing; intermittent drawing pain in r. side like a painful vessel, rather externally, extending forward. Rhythmical pulsation in whole l. half of head and face. Drawing pressure in r. half of occiput. Hair falls from temples and sides of head.

Clinical.—Headaches during the climacteric, frequent, pulsating, sometimes in one side, sometimes in the other, the pain involves the eye.

Eyes.—Weak, glassy, with sleepiness. *Feeling of biting smoke. Pain, with sore burning after reading, with dimness so that he must frequently wink. Feeling as if she had wept much;* with corresponding expression of face. Burning. Dryness. Feeling as if smaller than usual. *Feeling as if water were coming into eyes, > open air.* Running of much water from the dim eyes when reading letters. *Pupils dilated,* then contracted. Sticking at one point in r. ball in morning. Pain in balls, with great running of water, then dimness of eyes; P. in balls as after looking through too powerful glasses, without dim vision. Crawling in brows.

Lids.—*Twitching* (Plat.), *with sensation as if something must be wiped from r. eye; T. of upper, with itching;* sudden T., with crawling in l. brow and sensation as if something were in the eye which he must wipe away. *Frequent necessity to wink and wipe eyes as if a film of mucus were over them* (Euphras.). *Inclination to press them tightly together.* Drawing together, with running of water from eyes. Sticking in l. lower. Burning pinching beneath l. lower. Sore sensation in evening by the light, with inclination to press them together and wipe the eyes. Burning; < closing them. Itching extending towards outer side, r., then both; sticking I. in l. upper in evening. Heaviness of upper, with dim vision. Inability to open on waking at night, as from a weight, if she forcibly opens them tension and pressure, and they are only incompletely opened after much rubbing and pressing.

Vision.—Dim; intermittent: *as if there were a veil between eyes and the light;* on reading in evening by a bright light, with dryness of eyes and frequent necessity to wink; as if a veil were before eyes on reading, > frequent winking, with pressure on balls, which became a pressure on closing lids, but returned after opening them. Darkness before eyes, then bright stars dancing before eyes; frequent D. Lightnings like electric sparks during the day. When reading the white paper seemed pale red.

Clinical.—Ciliary neuralgia, the pain goes from the eyes to the top of the head, with feeling as if a cold wind were blowing against the eye. Asthenopia, pain extending from the eye to the top of the head. Affections of the eye in near-sighted people, posterior sclero-chorioditis. Asthenopia with extreme photophobia, cannot read without a gush of tears. Spasmodic affections of eyelids, as if he had to wink all the while.

Ear, Nose and Face.—Cramplike pain in and behind r. ear. Cramplike drawing in concha and auditory canals. Distant ringing in l. ear in evening in bed, > forcibly fixing his thoughts away from it. Roaring and noises in ears; R. as from a storm of wind. *Violent sneezing;* S. at 7 P.M., then shaking extending from back to feet, < posterior half of body. **Epistaxis of tenacious, thick, black blood,** *with drops of cold sweat on forehead.* Stopped coryza, with cold hands and feet and hot face, < eating; r. nostril completely stopped. Circumscribed redness and burning of face. Lips dry, inclined to crack. Smarting of lips.

Mouth.—Throbbing pain as if blood were pumped too quickly through the first l. upper incisor, extending to all l. upper teeth (all decayed), < by any one walking across the room or by opening mouth, > quiet, it caused throbbing in forehead and vertex, the toothache lasting all day, being bad for an hour, generally alternating with watery diarrhœa, the latter usually from 4 A.M. to 1 or 2 P.M., and before and during the stool cutting from sides of abdomen to centre, > bending forward. Tongue coated white, moist, with prominent papillæ; coated white and dry in morning, clean after breakfast. Speech refuses its service when angry at reproaches and desirous of justifying herself. Dryness and scraping; D., with burning on one side of upper part of tip of tongue as if a blister would appear, very painful on talking or touching tongue. Heat. Salivation, with biting as from salt on tip of tongue, with sweetish salt taste. *Offensive, sickly breath.* Offensive, sweetish-sour taste in morning after rising, > rinsing mouth. Sweetish taste in back of throat. Bitter taste in back of throat.

Throat.—Hawking on account of tough mucus, which makes the voice rough and scrapy. Feeling on empty swallowing as if a husk were sticking in it, < morning after rising, with frequent necessity to hawk. Sensation during inspiration as of sulphur fumes. Scraping before and after coughing; *S. and roughness;* S. as after fat food; in back part, which compels hawking. *Feeling as if uvula had fallen down.* Sensation as if a stopper were forced into it after eating, more on empty swallowing than on swallowing food, with elongated sensation in uvula and pressive sensation when not swallowing. Sudden drawing internally and externally in l. side, extending into ear.

Stomach.—Canine hunger in afternoon and evening. *Thirst for cold drinks* in afternoon. Eructations; empty, in morning fasting. Nausea; > open air, with weakness in pit of stomach; in chest and throat; and discomfort, extending from pit of stomach into abdomen, where they moved about as if griping would appear. Frequent vomiting in one gush, from tickling in beginning of trachea during respiration. *Distention, and of abdomen.* Rumbling in pit, with fermentation. Sticking in pit. Sinking pain in pit. Contractive pain in pit and beneath sternum. Drawing back and forth and up and down in pit. Sensitiveness as after taking cold. Fulness after a little food, with loss of appetite. Burning. Heartburn rising into throat, < a meal, which was eaten with relish.

Abdomen.—Rumbling in morning in bed; R. on yawning. Moving in whole when standing, with griping and intermittent urging to stool. **Sensation internally in sides as if something living were jumping about** (compare Thuja), *with nausea and shivering.* Shocks in l. side at night when fully awake, like the movements of a child at the end of pregnancy. Griping jerking after an ordinary drink of water. Sticking in side, arresting breathing. Aching, in a child, he bends forward. Pain as from taking cold; drawing P. as if menses would appear; P. as from pressure on a sore spot, now l., now r. side. Fulness and pressure in A. and chest as if she had eaten too much and too rapidly, though not after eating. Distended sensation in forenoon, with empty stomach. Emptiness, with loss of appetite. Tickling rising upward through A.

Rumbling in upper, with discomfort. Painless shock in upper as if something jumped upward. Painless pinching as from a broad, hard body in r. hypochondrium, on every inspiration. Drawing in upper, then in region of uterus. Griping in a spot to l. of navel; G. above navel in morning. *Sensation as if something living were moving about deep in lower* (Thuja) towards evening. Bubbling in lower. Pressure in pubic region as in menstruation. Heaviness in pubic region.

Anus.—Sticking extending through sacral region and into l. inguinal region, where it remains as an aching, < inspiration; S. on r. side above A.; *intermittent S. near l. side of A. Cringing. Crawling as of thread-worms* (Ign.). Itching in evening.

Stool and Urine.—Blood with the stool. Stool tinged with the drug. Stool earlier than usual, but difficult. Desire to urinate, waking at night, with bruised pain and numbness in l. humerus, upon which he was lying, sweat on lower part of body, and on rising vertigo, staggering, sensation as of a cold wind upon the sweaty parts and feeling as if cold sweat trickled down feet.

Sexual Organs.—Sudden intermittent sticking extending up into r. hypochondrium, piercing farther each time. Itching on r. side of scrotum in evening. *Desire. Sensation as if menses would appear, with colic and pressure towards genitals.* **Metrorrhagia on slightest movement.** Fatal hæmorrhage from uterus, especially after parturition.

Clinical.—It is not only useful in uterine hæmorrhages of thick dark blood, but it has removed the disposition to miscarriage associated with an unnatural sensation of worms in the abdomen, or of something dead and heavy.

Respiratory Organs.—Hoarseness in morning, with cough. Sticking in trachea, < posteriorly. *Cough; attack of exhausting dry, > laying hand on pit of stomach;* paroxysm of dry C. as from irritation in trachea; C., with easy expectoration of large masses of mucus. Rattling inspiration, then mucus in throat and hoarseness, the mucus > hawking. Dyspnœa. Choking during inspiration from tickling in upper part of trachea.

Chest.—*Sticking in l.;* r.; beneath heart, <inspiration; in sides, rather externally, afterwards extending farther forward and becoming burning, not affecting respiration or motion. Aching in the whole; sudden, in lower part and in pit of stomach, with nausea. *Jumping as of something living in r. lower part, beneath ribs.* Shocks beneath r. short ribs, near pit of stomach, and on inspiration soreness as if the pain were caused by breathing; jerklike S. in l. side, as if they would take away the breath. Jerking pain internally in l. side, as if drawn at intervals towards the back by a thread. Oppression; impeding yawning. *Heaviness frequently obliging deep breathing.*

Heart.—Drawing in præcordial region, extending to stomach, like colic. Emptiness in præcordial region. Warmth about heart, > frequent yawning, with anxiety and oppression of breath and inclination to breathe deeply. Palpitation; with anxiety at heart, with weakness extending through whole body to soles, as if the body were sinking down.

Neck and Back.—External swelling of neck. Painful stiffness of neck. Tearing in small of back, < breathing. Pain in small of back on motion in bed, in morning and at night.

Extremities.—Cracking in joints, with pain on motion. Weakness, with bruised sensation on motion, < hip-joint. Falling asleep of an arm, hand and foot.

Upper Extremities.—Shoulder. Twitching on top in morning in bed. Shocks in a spot on back of. Cracking in joint on sudden motion, with pain as if arm would be dislocated. *Pain on motion as if humerus were lying loosely in joint and would be easily dislocated;* feeling in l. joint as if humerus were lying loosely in it and would be easily dislocated. Bruised sensation. Tensive aching in joint, with cracking in it on moving arm outward.

Arm.—Pain in l., with sensation of paralysis. Bruised sensation on motion. Heaviness and bruised sensation, < forearms. Falling asleep; at night in sleep, and of hands, the crawling pain wakens her; with immobility, and of hands. Sudden tearing in r. elbow. Pain in r. forearm, extending obliquely to thumb; P. in forearm, in a spot near l. elbow, whereby the elbow is spasmodically thrown upward. Intermittent drawing in forearm, so that every intermission causes burrowing in a spot, < resting forearm on anything, whereby benumbing warmth spreads over hand.

Hand.—Pain in r. Tensive drawing in l. metacarpal joints. Sticking in l. index. Sudden burning-crawling motion in finger-tips, as if asleep, on entering house after a walk in raw air, with sensation as if bound so that the blood could not circulate freely, the sensation > bending fingers into a fist.

Lower Extremities.—Sudden shuddering in nates when sitting, as after a violent fall. Cracking in r. hip-joint on stretching thigh and on moving it forward. Aching on lower surface of thigh after long sitting. Weariness of thighs, <sitting; of femora in evening, > during motion, < after motion, > by rest, with painful tingling extending from above downward.

Knee.—Cracking, even when standing. Noise on stooping, with pain. Tearing extending to malleoli, where it continues aching and drawing back and forth, so that she must often move the feet at night. Painful tension on sitting down, on rising it becomes a pain as if dry and as if they would creak on motion. Intermittent painful drawing in the bent knee. Weariness, even to sinking.

Leg.—Intermittent pain in a spot above malleolus, as if in periosteum. Bruised sensation; in calves, as if he would stumble over his own legs. Smarting in calves, then tearing. Sensation of paralysis on walking and standing, < knees and ankles.

Tensive drawing in l. ankle. Smarting of l. sole when sitting. Aching of soles after standing; A. of soles as after a long walk, with necessity to move them. Burning and crawling in feet, < soles, as after walking in tight shoes. Weakness of feet; < standing and walking; even when sitting, with heaviness as after a long walk; of feet and calves as if she had walked too far, < walking. Sticking in ball of l. great toe.

Skin.—Scarlet redness of whole body. Suppuration of an old indurated bruise on finger, with pain and soreness. Crawling here and there, > scratching; C. in r. index. Itching on several parts; intermittent painful, on l. frontal eminence.

Sleep.—Yawning, with chilliness, burning of lids and thirst for cold drinks, without drinking much, after supper; frequent Y.; excessive Y., with sleepiness. *Sleepiness;* after dinner, with creeping chills. Waking early and thinking that it is late; waking early and then more wide awake than usual. Frequent waking; with uneasy sleep and vivid dreams. Singing in sleep. Laughing in a dream. *Confused and frightful dreams of what had been spoken or done during the day, of fires and the like.* Dream that she hurries for a distant place, but cannot reach it.

Fever.—Chilliness; all the afternoon, with thirst; at 9 P.M., increasing to a shaking chill, with pale face and cold hands. Sudden cooling sensation on l. parietal bone as if a drop of water fell upon it from a height. Coldness in back; l. side, as if he had been dashed with cold water; creeping along back, across shoulders and then down arms, with gooseskin and frequent yawning. Cooling of hands, sensation of a wind extending up arm.

Heat towards evening, < in head, with redness of face and thirst, without dryness of mouth. Internal H., with prickling in skin as if sweat would break out, but almost cold temperature. H. creeping rapidly over body; H. so that it seems to crawl in the skin. Orgasm of blood as if everything were moving in the body, without much noticeable heat. Heat of face in morning after waking; H. of face without marked redness.

Crotalus Horridus.

The venom of the rattlesnake is received on sugar of milk and triturated.

General Action.—It produces a general disorganization of the blood, with hæmatogenous jaundice, hæmorrhages, etc.

Allies.—The serpent poisons, also Canth., Phos., Carbo veg.

Generalities.—Lying on back, with limbs flexed and head hanging slightly towards r. shoulder. Turning about much in bed. Motionless, eyes and ears inaccessible to any impressions. *Bleeding from all orifices; suddenly, from eyes, ears, nose, gums and beneath nails.* General dropsy. *Swelling of whole body;* < head; yearly, with fever and maculæ. General trembling. Nervous agitation. Twitching. Convulsions; in morning, with trembling of limbs (compare snake venoms and Phosphorus !).

Pricking all over body. Pain, universal; P. in muscles and joints; in wounded part after recovery, or twitchings in it; pains alternating rapidly with each other; burning pain in trunk, < touch, with sensibility; burning P. in trunk, < lower part, < touch. Soreness. Bruised pain in morning after waking, is scarcely able to rise; in all bones in morning on waking, > rising. Restlessness. *Weakness;* **tired by slight exertion** (Phos.); by standing; in morning; in morning, with disinclination to rising and to taking his usual cold bath; *and the muscles refuse their service;* with head hanging upon his chest; *trembling, as from apprehension;* sudden. Faintness; with imperceptible pulse and nausea. Paralysis of one side. Symptoms chiefly in bones.

Clinical.—Palsy has been relieved. Chronic rheumatism. Tetanus was cured by the injection of the poison, though the patient was greatly prostrated thereby. Gonorrhœal rheumatism. General exhaustion, with numbness of extremities, vertigo, cold hands and feet, backs of hands mottled. Purpura hæmorrhagica.

Mind.—*Delirium; at night;* with plaintive and feeble moans; with swollen face and besotted expression, pupils dilated, vision lost, asked frequently if it was not raining hard, though the night was calm and clear. Excitement and loquacity; E., for example, when reading Humboldt's lecture to naturalists in Berlin he was moved to tears. Ecstasy. Buoyancy. Anxiety; with restless heat. Apprehension. Dread of selecting remedies, which is usually an agreeable occupation. Peevishness and relaxation. Annoyed by the least noise. Depression. Melancholy was quickly changed into gay anticipations, then general dropsy. Misanthropic and indifferent mood, with sudden weakness, headache, heartache and excessive diarrhœa. Indifference, seems only half alive. Indolence and dulness, so that he cannot express himself properly. Inability to think, comprehend or remember distinctly. Mistakes in writing, inability to spell correctly; though thinking of the proper letters. *Memory weak.* Speech confused. *Answers disconnected, skin cold, pulse rapid;* incoherent answers. Senses lost.

Clinical.—Incipient senile dementia, forgetful of figures, names and places, or he imagines himself surrounded by foes or hideous animals, antipathy to his family. Delirium of typhus and delirium tremens.

Head.—Aching; before going to sleep, < undressing, > sleep; from rush of blood and constipation; with melancholy; gradually increasing and decreasing; *extending into eyes;* extending into l. teeth; paroxysmal, < above r. eye, with vertigo and nausea on moving; neuralgic, and in neck. Singing, as after taking chloroform. Confusion. Lightness, with pressure in temples, < l., which makes him bite the teeth together. Heaviness. Rush of blood; with convulsions. Feeling in morning on waking as if brain were contracted and fell about on moving head, with sensitiveness and grasping pain, synchronous with pulse. Feeling of intoxication. Vertigo; when sitting, > resting head and keeping quiet, but recurring on slightest movement, with heaviness of head, as if the cervical muscles were too weak to support it, both vertigo and heaviness > lying down; V. > walking in open air, with pain above eyes and in temples, < r., nausea, vomiting of bile, constipation and necessity to lie down; with nausea; with sopor; before eyes, even to falling, with dilated pupils, earthy paleness of face and blue rings around eyes; sudden, when writing.

Forehead.—Stinging above l. eye. Tearing in brain above root of nose, < coughing and sneezing, with confusion. Pain; in front part of head; above eyes; in r. side and under r. orbit; over l. eye in morning on waking; > towards evening; above r. eye, with nausea and vertigo; *above eyes, with oppression;* then nausea; grasping, over back part of l. orbital plate; pulsative, behind l. orbit; heavy, across middle, > sleep; in whole front part of brain, as if congested, also in morning on waking, < under surface of l. frontal lobe, with sharp pain in centre of l. occiput. Full, congested feeling in front of brain. Tension of muscles, and in nape. Confusion in front part of brain.

Muscular twitches in temples. Sticking in temples; l., and in l. side of head; pain in temple; l. Drawing pinching in r. temple. Painless pulsations in temples. Pain in vertex in afternoon, till night, for three days. then in forenoon, with heat and flushing of face, Downward-pulling in a spot in r. side of vertex. Drawing pain from vertex into r. eye in evening. Shaking and wavering in l. upper part of head, < ascending steps or walking rapidly. Feeling as if there would be a violent pain in r. side of head. Alternations of different kinds of pains in l. side, drawing, pressure, pinching, tension and bruised pains, extending into orbits and teeth. Clawing pain in l. side of cerebellum. *Pain in occiput;* as from a blow, < lying down again after rising (felt years previously). Falling of all the hair. *Itching;* with much dandruff.

Clinical.—Vertigo; with faintness and weakness. Occipital headache recurring several times a day. Has relieved the extreme headache in diphtheria and frequent headache in dysmenorrhœa. Soreness of back of head, everything looks yellow, aching in liver, numbness of extremities and coldness, skin dark. Cerebrospinal meningitis, with red tongue, nosebleed, delirium, offensive bloody stools, offensive breath, etc.

Eyes.—Yellow (Phos., Vip.). Red and watery. Looking as if shooting from the sockets. Sunken. Muddy and heavy; in morning. Dry. Lachrymation; < damp weather, with momentary loss of vision. Conjunctiva injected. Pain in ball on moving eye like a pressure and as if eye were too dry internally. Pupils contracted. Half open and staring. Dark redness of l. upper lid, with dryness and burning within eyes and redness of canthi. Lids swollen. Lids almost closed; closed, upper lid and superior recti being paralyzed, pupils slightly dilated and insensible to light, vision apparently lost, eyes looking straight forward, but when the lids are forcibly opened the eyes were directed outward to escape the light. Quivering of l. lower lid. Itching of canthi. Heavy pain in back of orbit and at l. brow. Pressure deep in orbits, behind ears and in nasal bones, obliging him to bite the teeth together. *Vision dim;* < for distant objects; when reading, and double. Vision lost; when reading; in r. eye, with paralysis of levator muscle, injection of conjunctiva, < r., red zone around corner, < r., pupils contracted, *aqueous humor cloudy,* vision in l. as through a film, l. pupil grayish.

Clinical.—Ciliary neuralgia as from a cut around the eye, pain tearing, boring, photophobia, especially felt at the menstrual period. Hæmorrhage in the retina, especially in Bright's disease. Keratitis, cutting pains around eyes, swollen lids, especial aggravation at the menstrual period.

Ears.—Bruised feeling in lobules. Drawing behind r. and down neck; in r., with pain in l. side of head and paralyzed feeling in l. jaw. Tickling deep in r. meatus; hot tickling as from wax. Stoppage; in r. and drawing in both ears, painful in r., with heat and sensation as if wax would run into mouth. Dull hearing.

Clinical.—Otorrhœa with scarlatina, offensive and bloody, with deafness.

Nose.—Drawing-downward pain on r. side, near canthus, then changing to bruised pain. Stinging about nostrils. Coryza. Frequent sneezing and much catarrhal irritation; violent S., with sticking in chest near r. shoulder-joint, then pain in sternum.

Clinical.—Syphilitic ozæna.

Face.—*Yellow. Leaden-colored.* Dark. Red. Discolored. Swollen; in morning; and black. Pale. Anxious. Drawn. Convulsed. Drawing pains in bones, first in r. maxilla and zygoma, then in l., then in both together. Jaws, spasmodic contraction; cramp; locked; pain in lower and in direction of submaxillary nerve; bruised pain in lower, and in teeth. Lips swollen. Trembling of lips; with weakness and faintness; of lower, near l. corner of mouth. Lips covered with foam. Dryness of lips and throat without thirst.

Clinical.—Erysipelas. Acne. Papular eruption on the chin, associated with delayed menstruation.

Mouth.—Teeth loose. Shooting downward, almost like a blow, in an upper back tooth; sudden S. up and down in r. lower back teeth. Toothache. Teeth and jaws seem bruised. Inclination to press the tongue against the lower incisors, with crumbling of them on the inside. *Gums bleed* (Lach., Carbo v.); *white G.;* swollen; painful, with red margins around the teeth. **Tongue swollen**; *and mouth inflamed;* and out of mouth; so that it closes the throat, and brown; with indistinct articulation. Tongue brown. *T. red and sore.* T. coated; white. T. dry. Loss of speech; from constriction of tongue and throat; and motionless, with trembling pulse. Pain in salivary glands and in different branches of nerves of face and teeth. Tickling of palate and fauces. Salivation obliging him to swallow. Taste bitter. Taste sourish after the usual breakfast. There was no taste of salt in a glass of salt and water.

Clinical.—Grinding of teeth at night, so terrible that she has broken her molars, on waking face distorted, drawn towards the left (in an epileptic family), with delayed scanty menstruation.

Throat.—Swelling of parts under jaw and about throat. Angina tonsillaris. Pricking in fauces when reading, with constriction. Neuralgic drawing in fauces, < l. side about root of tongue, waking at 2 A.M. and almost producing choking. Sore pain about uvula on swallowing; sudden soreness in evening, > next morning, with bronchial catarrh, returning at night; sudden S. in the night, as of swelling of uvula and velum, with dryness of mouth. Feeling as if velum was stiff and too long and as if fauces were lined with mucus, afterwards mucus must be hawked up or swallowed. Painful rawness. Constriction. Tickling in pharynx. *Dryness; and thirst.* Frequent swallowing of saliva, with compression of throat without dyspnœa. Difficult swallowing; of liquids. Mucus in œsophagus. Scraping rancid sensation in œsophagus, extending to stomach, with pressure in pit of stomach.

Clinical.—Diphtheria, fauces swollen and dark red, frightful headache. Diphtheria, with oozing of blood from anus, mouth, etc. Chronic spasm of œsophagus, cannot swallow any solid substance. Hysterical spasms of œsophagus.

Stomach.—Appetite bad; lost. Craving for stimulants, < wine. Thirst; during the fever; *unquenchable.* Eructations tasting of food; rancid E. all the afternoon; of sour acrid fluid after eating white bread. Nausea; > vomiting; with inability to vomit; with sensation as if something rose in œsophagus and remained in upper part of chest; with coldness; with cold skin; with rigors, pulse rapid, threadlike; with syncope on becoming upright; paroxysmal, till noon, > sitting, < walking or standing. Vomiting; on least exertion; with vertigo; sudden; violent; *stomach unable to retain anything; V. of food; violent V. of food;* of everything but jellies, brandy and coffee; undigested food mixed with a greenish fluid, then thick viscid mucus like the white of egg stained yellow; *green;* green fluid, with pain in chest; green fetid matter every half hour; yellowish-green and fetid; bitter bile; blood.

Sticking in pit. Pain; after breakfast and dinner; *in pit;* in epigastrium. Pressure, with discomfort in S. and region of pit, as if he had eaten too much, a sensation as before fainting. *Intolerance of clothing in epigastric region and beneath hypochondria* (Lach.). Soreness in morning on rising; < food; S. in epigastrium, extending upward under sternum. Throbbing in pit, with rancid sensation in stomach. Quivering sensation in epigastrium, with nausea. Weight, and on chest. The breakfast lies heavy all day. Burning pain in epigastrium, > stool. Heartburn all day, < afternoon, with feeling as if œsophagus were full of rancid food and eructations tasting of food; H. at 4 P.M., lasting all the evening; after the usual light supper. Faint, sinking sensation in epigastrium.

Clinical.—Bilious vomiting, inability to lie on r. side, with instant dark green vomiting. Vomiting of blood, with ulceration of stomach. Gastritis in chronic alcoholism, with constant nausea and vomiting. Atonic dyspepsia, with continual throbbing, occipital headache and trembling, fluttering feeling below the epigastrium towards the umbilicus, tongue very red and small, feels swollen.

Abdomen.—*Swelling.* Flatulency. Inflammation of viscera. Burning pain; with sensitiveness, < touch. Tension. Pain in l. side like cuttings through spleen after violent running, < deep inspiration. Burning pain in umbilical region. Pain in middle, beneath umbilicus, as if too full. Inguinal glands on one side enlarged; l. Pain in course of colon; at 11.30 A.M. Burning pain in hypogastrium extending to sacrum, waking at night.

Clinical.—Abdominal troubles, with extreme tenderness, cannot bear the touch of her clothes, perityphlitis with high fever, great tenderness over the appendix and hardness; after Crot. 6th dark offensive evacuation and rapid improvement. Jaundice, with hæmorrhage from the nose, dusky flushes of face, tenderness of the liver, dark scanty urine, the result of a wasp-sting on the upper lid, immediate relief from Crot. 6th. The liver is painfully sore, with jaundice, sensitiveness of abdomen, etc. Chronic hæmorrhage from the bowels, dark, fluid, continual oozing, with great debility, faintness and depression of spirits (Phos.).

Rectum and Stool.—Tenesmus. Passed blood with mucus from the anus. Diarrhœa; in afternoon; with nausea, anxiety and thirst; then constipation and hard stools; frequent, with pain in rectum; frequent, with colic extending downward from umbilicus; watery, with colic and tenesmus. Pasty stool. Constipation. *Bloody S.* Frequent S.; two in evening. Involuntary S.; in morning, of dark bilious color.

Clinical.—Diarrhœa during bilious, remittent and other adynamic fevers.

Urinary Organs.—Strangury (Canth.). Involuntary micturition; every few minutes. Micturition frequent and copious; copious, afterwards small quantities of pale urine. Micturition rare and urine scanty and high-colored. *Hæmorrhage from urethra. Urine looks like that in jaundice.* Urine increased; and reddish-yellow; scanty and red.

Clinical.—Inflamed kidney, dark bloody urine. Hæmorrhage from the kidney after scarlet fever. Hæmaturia with bronchitis (Phos.). Hæmaturia with disorganization of blood in low fevers.

Sexual Organs.—Cutting in glans. Erections at night. Excitement; during the day, with apparent impotence. Intermittent shooting, rather burning pain from l. side of uterus, passing to region of transverse colon and there shooting or cutting across, as if from both sides towards centre, thence passing up l. side of trunk to face and temple as a cutting, intermittent, neuralgic pain. Menstruation too soon, free, preceded by weight in head and ears, accompanied by pains in abdomen and back and cold feet, *lasting longer than usual* and going off after two days, with frontal headache, which lasts from 10 P.M. till 1 A.M.

Clinical.—Dysmenorrhœa preceded by pain in uterine region extending down thighs, which continued for two days during the flow; during the flow aching in region of heart, extending through l. arm, cold feet, etc.

Respiratory Organs.—Pain in larynx extending into teeth. Larynx painful to touch. Paroxysmal bruised pain in larynx, shooting into chin and at times into lower teeth, sharper in larynx than in chin. *Voice weak; and hoarse.* Tickling in trachea provoking dry cough, afterwards tickling without cough. Cough, with sticking in side and bloody expectoration; dry C. at night, with tickling in throat; *C., with expectoration of bloody mucus. Spitting of blood* (Phos.). Expectoration of florid color. Every appearance of suffocation. Said his blood was suffocating him. Dyspnœa, with symptoms of inflammation of lungs and intestines. *Difficult respiration* (Phos.); in evening in bed, with tightness of chest. Easily out of breath on ascending a hill. Respiration labored; and rapid; and slow. Singultus. Stertor.

Clinical.—Whooping cough, with great debility, cardiac weakness, blueness of face, after the attack gets its color slowly, or when the face is puffy, nosebleed, etc.

Chest.—The milk of the mother became deadly poison to her 5-months' child. Sticking in r. side, near sternum; in r. side on sneezing; in forepart, extending into bones of l. shoulder. Pleurisy, with remittent fever. Pain; l. then r. side; below r., then l. arm; beneath l. arm, extending into l. side of chest, with great pain on deep inspiration; with vomiting of green fluid; in lower part or at pit of stomach, with stricture; sudden P. above l. nipple, as from a blow. Soreness, with cough in morning; along cartilages of ribs in epigastrium; sore pain in bones, in the middle, somewhat to r. side, < touch but not on deep inspiration, with sticking. Oppression; with evident inflammation of lungs and bowels; when sitting, almost amounting to faintness.

Heart.—Sudden digging. Pain. Soreness as if in pericardium. Tenderness in morning when lying on l. side. Weak sensation about; and on exertion rapid beats. Rapid beating on slight exertion, with deep-seated aching at point of l. scapula. Irregular action; and trembling and scarcely perceptible. Feeble action. *Palpitation, with sensation as if the heart tumbled about.*

Pulse.—Rapid, weak; and intermittent; R. in evening, and small; R., then slow, small, compressible; R. and hard, then weak and slow. Slow and small. Strong and full after formation of an abscess. Hard, then weak. Irregular. Low. Weak alternating with rapid. Tremulous; and scarcely perceptible. Almost imperceptible and thread-like next morning. Imperceptible; at wrist; at wrist, but action of heart rapid and feeble, with remarkable shortness of systo-diastolic interval.

Neck and Back.—Gouty drawing on l. side of nape, extending to shoulder. Visible twitching of lumbar muscles. Inflammation of r. side towards lumbar region, with pain and extravasation of blood. Pain in kidneys.

Clinical.—Softening of the spinal cord has been arrested (Phos.).

Extremities.—Swelling and pain. Convulsive movements. Tearing yearly or at times. Rheumatic pain in wrists, elbows and ankles. Numb pain in toes and anterior part of fingers, as after cramp. Heaviness of arms and legs, as if the bones were made of heavy wood. Painful paralytic sensation in bones of fingers, arms and legs when sitting in evening. Paralysis, < upper, particularly below elbows, ineffectual attempts to stand, as soon as he got on his elbows and knees or into a kneeling position he fell back helplessly on his side.

Upper Extremities.—Glands in axilla swollen and tender. Paroxysmal bruised pain in bones of shoulder, extending backward, < bending arm backward. Tensive pain in shoulder, extending to neck, < on moving arm; drawing tensive pain in r. shoulder, extending up neck, as if some one were pulling on a tendon extending from shoulder to neck and drawn tense under skin, < moving arm, especially backward, and by pressure.

Arm.—Swelling and heaviness; S., with discoloration; with inflammation and gangrene. Pain in morning when moved; drawing pain in bones of r., extending into thumb and little finger. Numbness in morning. R. could not be used with freedom (from bite on l. hand). Bruised, cramplike sensation in both upper. Pain above r. elbow; in r. elbow, < by touch and moving arm up and down, with throbbing, bruised pain in ribs beneath r. arm. Swelling and pain of forearm and hands; S. of forearms, of l., extending up arm, of r. only to elbow, with pain, < l. Drawing pain in r. wrist, waking in morning.

Hand.—Swelling (of the bitten H.), and of the fingers, fingers semi-flexed on palm and rigid, the hand flexed on forearm and forearm on arm, all livid, black and blue and cold. Cold swelling of H. and arm, with pain on pressure. Contraction of some flexors. *Trembling* (Phos.); during rest. Pain in l. palm as from a bee-sting, but more spasmodic, < moving middle finger, in the last joint of which the pain is first felt. Paralytic weakness of r. and of fingers.

Fingers.—Swollen and insensible. Shooting into l. ring, with pulsation. Bruised pain through metatarsal joints of r.; in two last phalanges of l. little, with pulsation in tip. Pain in l. ring, and in last phalanges of r. little and of l. middle, as when a very cold hand is suddenly brought near the fire. Paralytic pain at times in bones, < r. index. Drawing pains in bones of l. thumb.

Clinical.—Symptoms of paralysis of l. hand, it feels dead when sewing, also l. leg.

Lower Extremities.—Tottering. Feeling in r. as if a tendon were drawn from sole through femur and the foot were thereby drawn up. Insensibility. Sticking backward across r. hip-bone, < motion. Sudden pain in head of femur, with throbbing perceptible to the hand. Pain in thighs, < l., as if deep-seated muscles were tender, afterwards as if suppurating, < resting thigh on edge of chair and on walking. Bruised pain in thighs as after skating too much, < walking and touch. Sore pain in thighs, < touch and walking. Tensive drawing bone pain from l. hip to foot, with bubbling sensation in calf. Weary and cramplike pain in femora, extending to abdomen and backward, as after much skating, it seemed as if the flesh would be drawn up, which aggravated the pain. Sudden drawing in l. hip, in evening on walking, extending to foot.

Knee.—Drawing pain as if through marrow of bone from l. to sole. Goutlike drawings through r. and down leg, < standing on r. foot; in r. patella and tibia on walking, then pain in hand and jaw; sudden, in r. when walking and sitting still. Rheumatic drawing in hollow of r., between tendons.

Leg.—(Bitten) became the color of the snake, the flesh decayed and fell off in pieces. Dropsical. Distended and threatened mortification, the skin shining, black on outside, with black and yellow spots on inside. Lower part and foot so swollen as to rupture skin from toe to ankle, and black. Cramp; in calf; disposition to, in morning. Pain in r. tibia; sore, in l. calf, < touch; burning (in bitten leg), with swelling and heat. Bubbling in calves, with pains in bones. Weariness; aching. Feeling as if the whole r. were only half alive, and, on stretching the muscles, which he is involuntarily inclined to do, shivering through upper part of body, with shaking of head and tension of forehead and muscles of nape. Going to sleep after riding one over the other; going to sleep when sitting, and tingling.

Bruised pain in malleoli on walking; B. pain in tendon behind l. malleolus, < moving foot and touch. Swelling of feet; every evening; and ugly ulcers. Shooting from the bitten foot up inside of leg to knee. Sticking in r. sole, with burning and with heaviness of foot. Pain in l. foot; in foot on stepping; sore, in sole; in sole, in front of heel, as from stepping on something sharp with the bare foot; pinching drawing P. in heels, < bones, extending to malleoli. Cramplike sensation beneath l. little toe, as if some one turned it around. Weariness of toes.

Skin.—Yellow color of whole body; in spots; Y. and dark spots reappearing, with swelling of hands and feet the next year at the same time. Blue and yellow spots next year, with swelling; yearly with fever and pain; green, yellow and bluish spots after the swelling had ceased. Whole arm livid as if putrefaction had begun. Black spots. Jet black elevation on r. hip (after bite on l. ring finger), with soreness, afterwards the discoloration extended to level of umbilicus, around body and down to limbs, gradually disappearing from above downward, leaving toes last. R. side of neck and body down to loins inflamed, painful and mottled.

Swelling of hand, forearm, arm and shoulder, with a dark ecchymosed line from root of finger almost to shoulder-joint, the inside of the bitten finger, as far as the second joint, covered with blisters filled with dark fluid blood. Swollen, hot, tense, painful, with cold arm and hand, then an abscess forms, which becomes gangrenous.

Glands of axilla sore and painful (after a bite on l. index), with restlessness and sleeplessness, next morning a line of inflammation along arm to axilla, on attempting to walk nausea and vomiting, the pain > resting arm on an inclined plane, then soreness of back, then the swelling extended down side of hip, on removal of the blistered skin of the finger discharge of watery sanguineous fluid, without smell, the nail loose, the red line following the lymphatics was filled with yellow serum, then palmar surface of the first and second joints of the finger was gangrenous, the granulations rough and appearing as if sprinkled with ochre, then the nail was removed, a slough formed and on coming away left the bone exposed, this afterwards exfoliated and had to be removed, the finger was left deformed and its circulation imperfect, the finger susceptible to cold.

Eruptions of various kinds. Soft lumps under skin in forepart of shoulder-joint, above axilla, with sticking, < bending arm backward. Pimples; red, small, with large ones on and between scapulæ. Hard itching tubercles in the skin of calves, < l., gradually coming to the surface and scaling with the scratching. Pustule near l. wing of nose, with tensive pains extending into cheek, then redness and hardness in this place. Boils on arm as far as the swelling had extended, in all about eighty at one time.

Vesicles; on the swollen arm; passing into ulcers; with a red spot under each vesicle; with red areola, on inner side of arm, beneath shoulder and near elbow; (at the place of the bite), on being opened the water that filled it scalded the parts it passed over; over metacarpal bone of r. thumb every three months, with contraction of flexors and inability to extend the hand, the first time with beating pain; filled with dark, bloody serum. Abscess on outer side of elbow, with discharge of reddish-brown matter and membranous parts of cellular tissue, with diarrhœa and chills, then extension of the ulceration, then gangrene near shoulder. Gangrene of bitten part, extending over body. Ulcers; on r. thigh. Old scars break out again.

Oozing of blood in the form of sweat. Tension. Itching; whole body in morning on waking; about bend of arm; on middle joints of all fingers; sticking, alternately in all parts, < on scapulæ.

Clinical.—Chilblains, especially when threatened with gangrene, in patients with very low vitality. Felons. Pustular eruptions about the wrists. A little tubercle, resulting from the sting of an insect many years since, was cured by the daily local application of the 6th. Petechiæ and varicose ulcers on the lower

extremities, and very languid circulation. Petechial spots over the whole body, especially the lower extremities, with faintness, irregular action of heart, dizziness. Erysipelas after vaccination, the pustule filled with dark lymph, the whole extremity became inflamed, this extended even to the trunk, eruption even on the lower extremities. After vaccination, pustular eruptions on back of arm, across shoulders, over the breasts. Lymphangitis and septicæmia from dissecting wounds. Gangrenous inflammation of skin and cellular tissues. Abscesses, pustules, boils, carbuncles, etc., the parts look bluish and unhealthy, with great prostration, etc. Erysipelatous inflammations following bites of insects.

Sleep.—Yawning. Sleepiness; at noon; early in evening; in evening, with heaviness; with cold skin. Coma. Lethargic state, requiring to be spoken to in a loud tone. Starting in sleep. Sleeplessness. Dreams, many, not unpleasant; D. that he was traveling in all parts of the world; anxious; of strife and anger, that he had fallen out with his father, who would not recognize his son because he had embraced homœopathy; of horrid places on earth only, often of rolling amongst rocks, sometimes that he was a white hawk cut into pieces, and frequently his feet would grow into two hickories.

Fever.—Coldness; with rapid pulse and nausea. Shivering; with diarrhœa; in head; creeping over scalp, so that the hair stands up. Cold skin; with rapid, weak pulse; with nausea; with hot swelling of arm. Coldness of limbs; in morning; with insensibility; of hands and feet; of fingers.

Heat; even in cases where the pulse sank; with thirst, hiccough, vomiting of bile, palpitation, weak, rapid pulse and exhaustion. Dry; and exhausting, with dry tongue and thirst. Fever resembling yellow-fever in its initiatory stage, nothing was wanting, expression of countenance, pain in loins, headache, symptoms of gums. Burning in the wound, extending over body, even to top of head. Heat of ears; in r.; with sensation as if wax were running down throat. Heat of feet; in l. anterior foot, and gnawing, with drawing in bones of r. arm, extending into thumb and little finger; of palms, with itching and general flushes of heat.

Sweat, cold; and viscous. S. in axillæ stained a reddish-orange. Dry skin; in palms, with stiffness and heat.

Clinical.—**Extremely valuable in fevers of a malignant type, especially malignant scarlatina, and in all fevers which present a hæmorrhagic or putrescent character. Malignant scarlet fever, great weakness, tremulousness, torpor, unconsciousness, efforts to vomit anything taken into the stomach, when vomiting blood oozed from the gangrenous fauces, respiration sighing, intermittent. Malignant scarlatina with epistaxis, extreme prostration, tonsils dark red, tumid. Hæmorrhagic measles, dark confluent eruption, œdema of face, etc. Malignant remittent fevers of the South. Bilious remittent, eyes sunken, tongue dry, nausea, black pasty stools, drowsiness, extreme prostration. Bilious fever, with yellow color of face, gnawing aching pain in liver, bloody evacuation, r. lung hepatized. Low type of bilious fever, tongue dry, cracked, brown in centre, edges deep red, cold, clammy perspiration, skin yellow, unconsciousness, urine dark. It is the most homœopathic remedy for yellow fever with symptoms of blood-poisoning, vertigo, pain all over the body and tenderness of liver, or with swollen parotids, nosebleed, face dusky, hands nearly black, dry tongue, vertigo as if falling over a precipice, or with yellow face, nearly black urine. Yellow fever, stools dark, bloody, generally offensive, sometimes involuntary, with great debility, tendency to collapse, suppression of urine, etc.**

Croton Tiglium.

One part of Croton Oil (expressed from the seeds of Croton tiglium, L.) is dissolved in 99 parts of alcohol, and diluted for use. (Much of the commercial "croton oil" is obtained from the seeds of Jatropha curcas.)

General Action.—A powerful drastic purge. When applied to the skin it producсs an eruption of small pustules with inflamed areolæ.

Allies.—Jatropha, Gamboge.

Generalities.—Sudden emaciation. Generally lying quietly on belly, but occasionally tossing about. Tossing about convulsively. Trembling of whole body. Sticking, with sweat on forehead. Nauseating pain, < lying. Malaise; < bread and butter, she must lie down. Discomfort after dinner. Dulness of whole body. Uneasiness. Lay in a lethargic state, sometimes drawing himself up as if in pain. Collapse. Faintness; during and after vomiting. Disinclination for every exertion. *Weakness;* in morning on waking, with weakness of limbs; in morning on rising, with trembling of hands and feet; after stool, with pain in abdomen; with nausea; with ill humor.

Mind.—Sadness. Anxiety. Dissatisfaction. Disinclination to speak. Disinclination to work, would rather play than attend to his business. Fretfulness. Thought difficult. Memory lost.

Head.—Jerkings; sticking. Sticking extending to vertex. Aching; when walking, > taking off his hat; < the middle of the day and a few hours after dinner; as from a disordered stomach; burning. Confusion; on rising; in morning on waking, with heaviness and dulness; all night; on going into open air; till supper, with vertigo; < bread and beer, with pain, throbbing, tension and pressure outward in sinciput; < r. side, with pressure downward from vertex, so that sometimes sticking extends below ear, with impaired hearing in r. ear; with dulness and pressure in forehead; with heaviness of head and crawling in eyes; with pain, then general heat and sweat; with pressure towards forehead and nausea; with vomiting and loss of appetite. Fulness. Heaviness. Feeling as after intoxicants. Vertigo; in the room, with vanishing of vision; < open air, with nausea, pallor and weakness; < r. side, with pressure in r. eye; and falling down insensible; with roaring in ears and inability to stand from fear of falling; so that she could scarcely remain sitting, < looking up; threatened, when walking in open air.

Forehead.—Sticking in brain above r. eye; in sinciput, on walking. Pain; r. side and temple; l. half of sinciput; > keeping quiet; with tearing extending to r. temple, where it remains as a sticking; confusing P. in anterior and upper part of head. Tensive pain in sinciput, with pressure and sticking; T. pain above r. orbit, with pressure in r. side of occiput. Dragging in sinciput. Fulness and pressure. Confusion; in sinciput; with pressure and heaviness. Vertigo in sinciput.

Sticking in l. temple. Pain in temples; twinging; in l., as if burnt. Tearing towards vertex. Pain in occiput. Confusion of l. half of occiput, as if held tight. Confusion in occiput. Crawling on occiput. Prickling in scalp of vertex.

Eyes.—Brilliant. Inflammation (local effects); of one and side of face. Sticking in middle of l., then indications of it in r.; S. in l. ball. Pain, then swelling of eye and side of face (local effect). Heaviness and weakness. *Lachrymation;* with running of water from nose. Pupils dilated. Redness of l. conjunctiva. Red swelling of a gland in r. lower lid. Twitching of lids. Jerking sticking in r. external canthus, with contraction and twitching of whole eye. Cramplike pain in r. lids, < towards external canthus. Itching of r. lower lid; of l. upper. Fog before r. eye, then weakness of it. Vision dim; as from smoke in the room. Vision impaired, with staring, glittering eyes. Vision easily vanishes.

Clinical.—Pustules and vesicles on the eyeball. Ciliary neuralgia, and feeling as if a string were pulling the eyeballs back into the head. The pustules and ulcers in the eye are characterized by excessive photophobia, superciliary pain, and often by eruption about the eyes, on the lids and face.

Ears.—Sticking beneath l. Twinging in l.; *spasmodic deep within l.* Dragging towards orifices of both; with twisting. Roaring.

Nose.—Red eruption on r. side of septum, with pain in morning when washing, then an elevated crust, which desquamated, the epidermis continued red and tender and again desquamated. Drawing pain extending through to root and thence into brain. Dryness, and of throat. Burning, and in mouth; in r. nostril, obliging him to rub it. Irritation, and of conjunctiva. Respiration through nose stopped. Mucus. Coryza, with slight discharge. Smell in the room as after an offensive stool.

Face.—Pale and sunken; P. and cold. Jaundice-colored. Cyanotic. Swollen; and red and covered with vesicles, also eyelids. Expression of distress; of debility; of confusion, with brilliant staring eyes. Lips swollen and sore (local effects); vesicles (local effects); burning in angle, with swelling on outward border; dry and cracked; dry in evening, and tense; tension in corner.

Mouth.—Tearing in r. lower eye-tooth. Sore pain in last l. lower molar on chewing. Swelling on l. inner alveolar margin of gum; painful, on inner side of r. upper gum. Easy bleeding of gum in morning on washing. Tongue swollen and numb; T. white, showing impress of teeth; coated white; furred and dry; red, smooth, glistening and dry in centre; eruption on root and on soft palate and posterior wall of pharynx; burning and contraction, and in throat; tickling pain at tip; feeling at tip as if electrically sensitive, with sweetish bitter taste; feeling as if too large and numb, without change in its appearance.

Pustules, with burning in mouth and throat. Vesicles on hard palate. Swelling of palate. Inflammation of M., lips and pharynx. Burning scraping extending low down into œsophagus. Burning, and in throat; gradually and successively increasing on palate, uvula, isthmus faucium, pharynx, tongue and lips. Burnt feeling. Dryness; with scraping in throat; without thirst. Salivation; with profuse mucus; sour. Taste flat; and nauseous; flat and nauseous to water, which causes emptiness; pasty; as after almonds; bitter; sweetish, then bitter and burning; like chocolate, then burning; sometimes burning, sometimes scraping; scraping-burning, with salivation; acrid-burning, and in throat.

Throat.—Swelling of submaxillary glands, with pain on touch; S. of tonsils, with pain on external pressure. Redness and soreness; R. and smarting; R. of uvula, with elongation. Hawking of mucus tasting like vinegar. Jerking and shooting through T. Sensation of a morsel which he was unable to swallow. Pain. Rawness. Scraping; < expiration; > cold water, with warmth at back of mouth; in fauces, then burning, then tickling in larynx; causing frequent hawking; burning. Scraping tingling. Acrid sensation; and down œsophagus. Tickling of r. tonsil; where hard and soft palates unite, then scraping, then burning.

Complaints that his throat was swelling. Fulness extending up T., with pressure in pharynx. Burning; in pharynx, > drinking water; in fauces, > inspiration, < expiration; and in œsophagus; sometimes extending to pit of stomach; with contraction, and in tongue. Burning pain. Dryness; with irritation in pharynx. Inclination to swallow, with pain as if a ball were pressing out of l. side of œsophagus, > by cold water; frequent inclination to swallow, which causes pain as if a ball were pressing through l. wall of œsophagus. Swallowing difficult. Pain in œsophagus. Prickling at entrance of œsophagus. Burning extending up œsophagus; above entrance, with acrid taste at back of mouth.

Stomach.—*Hunger, with rumbling in abdomen;* unnatural H.; great, after the pains had ceased; H. without appetite. Appetite diminished; at lunch, and repletion after eating a little. A. lost; with dull feeling, yet he eats his usual allowance at lunch. Loathing of his usual breakfast. Thirst; slight. Aversion to beer. Eructations; with nausea and weakness; empty, < afternoon; empty, then nausea; sharp sour; acrid and burning; bilious in evening; of water. Hiccough and yawning.

Nausea; after milk; after every drink, with eructations; with sour salivation; with salivation and chill; with anxiety and oppression, and pressure in epigastric region; with inflation of abdomen and borborygmi in epigastric region; so that he lost hearing and vision; disturbing sleep after midnight, then sudden vomiting of copious sour, strong-smelling fluid, then diarrhœa, with sensation as if fluid were swashing about in abdomen. Retching; with vomiting of food and water; with vomiting, rumbling in abdomen and diarrhœa; spasmodic, > by pressing against the washstand; violent, with difficult vomiting of yellowish water, of oily smell and sweetish-bitter oily taste.

Vomiting; especially in women; then diarrhœa; of bile; of bitter mucus; of light and glairy matter; of much strongly-smelling fluid; of water, mucus and food, after eating. Violent vomiting; and copious; of matter containing streaks of a white, shiny, emulsion-like substance, mixed with clear glairy fluid; and frequent, sudden, of whitish-yellow, frothy liquid.

Rumbling, with heaviness on chest. Gastro-enteritis. Cramp, and in upper abdomen. Cutting beneath stomach. Severe turning, then cutting below stomach, then tearing in r. side near ilium. Burning pain. Pressure; in forenoon; in pit; in epigastric region; with anxiety; with tickling, nausea and spasmodic motions as if one would vomit; with discomfort in abdomen; in S. and chest, with fulness; in epigastric region, with fulness; in epigastric region, with constriction; changing into nausea, with salivation. Epigastric region sensitive to touch. Scraping, then nausea; burning S., extending into S. and along intestinal tract.

Constriction; in upper part. Oppression at midnight, with fulness, then nausea, then easy vomiting of the supper, then sweat on face and comfort, after half an hour bitter vomiting, then good sleep till morning. Tension in epigastric region; in region of S. and upper abdomen, with pressure, anxiety and oppression. Weight and heat in epigastrium as after strong spirits, then the heat radiates in every direction, then extends to cardia, > barley-water. Repletion; impeding respiration. Indigestion. *Emptiness. Sinking, with weakness.* Relaxed sensation, with pain on pressure. Burning; and in bowels; in pit. Heartburn; after dinner, with nausea. Epigastrium felt hot and tense.

Abdomen.—*Distention,* < sitting, with tension, tenesmus and emission of offensive flatus; with griping; *with griping* above umbilicus; with tension and rumbling; flatulent, with heaviness. **Swashing as of water.** *Gurgling, < l. side. Rumbling;* on l. side; on rising and when writing, with emission of offensive flatus; after supper, > emission of flatus, with pain and feeling as before diarrhœa. Movements, with griping. *Flatulence; then urging,* **stool sudden,** *thin, small, with flatus* (Jat.); with intermittent pain. Emission of much flatus in evening; easy E. when walking, with urging to stool; difficult, noisy E.; offensive. Urging to pass flatus when sitting.

Cutting, and about umbilicus; C., with emission of fetid flatus; then frequent diarrhœa; then a stool, at first pultaceous, then liquid mingled with mucus and bile, then three greenish-yellow diarrhœic stools. Tearing when eating. Twinging; < in colon, with cutting; spasmodic, when walking, and about umbilicus. Griping after dinner; G., < touch; with pressure towards anus. Pain; in morning after rising, with much offensive flatus; during stool, then pain in rectum; after eating; when walking; < dinner; > gruel; in walls, especially deep, < pressure or deep inspiration; with tenesmus; with loud emission of offensive flatus; flatulent, in evening; flatulent, disturbing sleep, > noisy emission of flatus. Sensation as before diarrhœa. Soreness; on coughing; < pressure. Heaviness and confusion, with retracted parietes. Uneasiness, with griping and twinging. He felt the medicine working downward, causing gurgling, and as it approached the umbilicus twinging. Congestion rising to head, with warmth of skin and sweat. Burning; creeping warmth in parietes; febrile excitement across A. Coldness.

Upper.—Rumbling, with gurgling and griping, then emission of offensive flatus. Sticking in spleen in evening. Griping. Dragging, movements and retractions, and in umbilical region, then stool; spasmodic D., < sitting, then tensive pain. Pain in region of spleen. Tensive pain. Tension between umbilicus and pit of stomach. Throbbing in region of spleen. Heaviness.

Umbilical Region.—Gurgling, with vermicular movements. Painful movements, with increased pain on touch or pressure. Sticking, > two pasty stools; S. to l. of umbilicus. Tearing after dinner. Cutting; so that she could scarcely breathe, extending to stomach, causing her to bend double, extending thence to l. side of abdomen; as if two knives were cutting towards each other, > two stools, then a watery stool. Twinging on going out, with tension and pressure upward to epigastric region and sudden nausea; T. above umbilicus, with pressure. Twisting, then tearing in l. side of abdomen. Pain; below umbilicus in evening, with distention of abdomen, then urging to stool; on touch, with rumbling and gurgling; **on pressure on umbilicus pain is felt down to anus, where there is constant protrusion;** spasmodic, < sitting bent over. *Griping;* extending to l. side of abdomen, with pinching. Tension when lying, with movement and pressure towards anus.

Lower.—Sticking in cæcum. Tearing in transverse colon; from l. groin up to r. nipple. Griping in transverse colon before every stool. Pinching and cutting in thick intestines. Pain; and in bladder; above posterior superior spine of l. ilium; undefined, in l. inguinal region; tensive, in inguinal regions.

Clinical.—Gurgling and swashing, as if there were nothing but water in the intestines.

Rectum.—Feeling as before purging. Tenesmus; after lunch, scanty stool, mixed with mucus. Urging in morning in bed, on rising soft, light-brown stool, then soreness of anus; U. and stool soft, dark brown, offensive, with spasmodic griping; **constant U., then sudden pasty, dirty green, offensive, forcible stool;** U., with fulness in abdomen and rectum, stool scanty and difficult; sudden U., he was unable to reach the closet, but was obliged to sit long; frequent, ineffectual U.

Anus.—Swelling, extending to anus, with burning. *Pain, as if a plug were forced outward. Dragging as before diarrhœa.* Pulsation, sticking and burning. Sore pain after moving about, with burning. Painful soreness after stool, with feeling as if rectum were swollen and would protrude, urging to stool, compression of abdomen, causing pain, extending into genitals and ending in glans as a sticking, so that he was anxious and oppressed, sweat on forehead, nausea, vanishing of sight and hearing, the pain < bending over, > quiet, on walking sore pain on outer part of anus, then prostration, ill humor and loss of appetite. Scraping after stool. Scratching on l. posterior wall during thin stool. Constriction on walking, with sticking at times. Itching. *Burning;* during pasty stool; so that he can scarcely sit.

Stool.—*Watery; and yellowish,* **forcible** (Jat.); *and painless;* with emission of flatus; and frequent; frequent, shooting away (Jat., Gamb., etc.); and choleraic, copious, every few minutes; at first fæcal stool, then watery, with sticking in abdomen. Diarrhœa; with urging; with colic; frequent; frequent scanty; frequent yellowish; light yellow, *with sweat,* crawling in occiput, pressure upon larynx, < l. side; grayish-brown, evacuated at three different times and forcibly, with tenesmus, then prostration and colic; involuntary, with streaks of white, shiny, emulsion-like substance mixed with much clear, glairy fluid. *Pasty, light brown, after urging, then rumbling and gurgling in l. side of abdomen, after an hour a second soft, mucous, urgent, grayish-green and dirty brown,* **forcible** *stool.* Soft; slimy, frequent, with tenesmus; delayed, sluggish, unsatisfactory. Semi-fluid, semi-solid, dirty brown. Half soft, half solid, after the morning stool.

Constipation. Crumbly, difficult. Nodular, mixed with white points (larvæ of worms), the second contains long white thread-worms, the other nine stools offensive and bilious, or slimy, and at last watery. Dirty yellow, clayey. Tenacious. Large. Scanty, by efforts of abdominal muscles, without peristaltic action of bowels. Slimy, with tenesmus. With pinching. With rumbling and pain in epigastric and hypochondriac regions. Frequent; the first feculent, the others yellow and green; with sweat, < forehead. Copious, with rumbling in abdomen; C., mucous, frequent, with colic.

Clinical.—A very valuable remedy in diarrhœa, with the general character of sudden expulsion and great aggravation from taking anything into the stomach, stool occurs immediately after

eating or drinking, generally very watery and yellow, passed with gush, sometimes associated with nausea and vomiting, sometimes with pain following the colon down to the rectum.

Urinary Organs.—Burning in urethra on urinating. Urging to urinate; immediately after micturition. Frequent micturition. Copious urine; and yellow; and turbid. Pale frothy U. Foaming U. in morning. Turbid. Brown U., soon becoming turbid, and a copious brown sediment. Fiery red at night and in morning, with oily pellicle and flocculent turbid sediment; almost blood-red after standing through the night, with a thick mucous sediment. Pale orange yellow U. after standing over night, with turbid sediment, which is at first flocculent. Pale U., with white sediment. Cloudy sediment, which gradually disappears, and brownish crystals float where the clouds had been and adhere to the walls of the glass.

Sexual Organs.—Inflammation of inner surface of prepuce, with irritation and some secretion. Pain in penis, with redness of glans and sticking coming out of urethra. Burning in glans when urinating. Constant painful erections. No erection in morning, contrary to custom. Retraction of l. testicle, relaxation of r. Drawing in l. spermatic cord, hindering walking. *Scrotum shrivelled and itching, disturbing sleep, > scratching, which caused a voluptuous sensation.* **Vesicles on scrotum** *and penis.* Inflammation of scrotum and penis (local effects). Herpetic eruption on scrotum. Phlyctænæ on scrotum, with pustules on penis, penis partly denuded, pain at end of penis on urinating, urine dark (local effects). Itching of scrotum. **Corrosive itching of scrotum and glans; of scrotum,** < *walking, with redness;* of scrotum, and a moist, offensive spot on thigh, then desquamation of these places; of scrotum, disturbing sleep, > rubbing, which caused erections. Menstruation too soon and scanty.

Clinical.—Valuable in eczema of scrotum and penis.

Respiratory Organs.—Laryngeal catarrh. Mucus in larynx; with tickling and irritation; rattling of M. in evening. Mucus in bronchials, which he cannot remove. Mucus in trachea, provoking cough. Speech low. Voice hoarse. Voice hollow; with constant hawking. Cough and frequent hawking; constant C.; C. in morning, with expectoration; in evening, with white mucous expectoration and oppression of chest; with difficult yellowish expectoration and spitting of blood. Expectoration of much tenacious, sour-tasting mucus. **Sensation as if he could not get air enough into air-cells.** Dyspnœa, < ascending stairs. Difficult respiration; and anxious; with constriction of chest. Short breath after stool; S. and hurried. Slow respiration; and powerless.

Chest.—Catarrh. Sticking in l.; through middle of l. in afternoon; in r. lower third during inspiration. Tearing along edges of ribs, extending backward and to small of back. Pain; on touch; and in l. chest, l. hypochondrium; in l., with oppression. Pressure over sternum; deep within at middle of chest. *Fulness, with burning sticking in l. chest and towards scapulæ;* F., with pressure and burning; F. impeding respiration. Oppression; in evening; on deep inspiration; with anxiety. Feeling of mucus in lungs, which could not be removed by hawking, with difficult breathing and whistling on deep breathing. Throbbing-bubbling in r., between sixth and seventh ribs. Throbbing in r. posterior part; sudden, in region of aorta. Hollow feeling. Burning. Malaise, and in abdomen; forcing him to stretch and yawn.

Clinical.—**Nipples very sore, with excruciating pain running through to scapulæ on nursing.**

Heart and Pulse.—Sticking in præcordial region; on expiration. Jerking in l. side. Palpitation; in afternoon; after dinner, < lying. Pulse rapid; and weak; and small. Pulse full. Pulse feeble. P. small; and weak, then strong and full.

Neck and Back.—Sticking between nape and occiput. Pain in muscles of l. side of nape on nodding. Pressure and drawing in cervical vertebræ. Tension in r. side of neck. Sticking in l. renal region; in afternoon, impeding breathing. Pain in small of back; in back and lumbar region, in the space between lumbar vertebræ, false ribs and ilium.

Extremities.—Trembling of hands and feet. Pain. Weariness; *of arms and legs.* Tearing in r. shoulder. Sticking in l. shoulder-joint. Pain in r. shoulder-joint. Tearing in r. arm, extending to upper arm, then to fingers. Heaviness of arms, with weariness. Tearing in r. upper arm, then in r. shoulder-joint; sudden, in l. upper arm, < deltoid. Rheumatic pain in l. upper arm, waking him. Pain on inner side of l. upper arm. Tension, weary pain in upper arm; in r. extending to hand. Heaviness of upper arm, with lameness. Boring in l. elbow at noon. Tearing in l. forearm. Drawing in r. forearm; above r. wrist in evening. Swelling of hands. Jerking of l. middle and r. ring fingers. Tearing in r. finger-joints. Drawing in l. middle finger, with tearings.

Lower Extremities.—Swelling of nates where they approximate by the anus, after moving about, with burning. Tearing in l. thigh. Pain in thighs; sore, between l. thigh and scrotum; tensive, in l. hip-joint, < by rising from a seat. Weariness of thighs, with tensive feeling. Heaviness of thighs on waking after midnight. Paralyzed feeling in l. thigh. Cramplike pain in r. knee. (Tearing in knee, with crawling.) Pain in legs and feet. Sticking on r. outer malleolus; extending to forepart of foot. Heaviness of ankles in evening, with pressure. Cramp of l. sole and inner side of foot. Jerking in l. foot when sitting; J. in l. sole, with tearing. Sticking in l. heel when sitting, as if sprained; on margin of l. foot. Sprained pain in l. foot. Rheumatic tearing in l. foot. Nervous weakness of feet. Feet failed him on ascending stairs. Sticking in lower part of great toe, l. then r. When walking sticking and tearing as if sprained, < in metatarsal bone of l. great toe, so that he could not step fairly upon it. Rheumatic tearing in r. great toe. Prickling in r. great toe, where the nail enters the flesh, with sticking.

Skin.—Face, hands and toes cyanotic. Pimples on face; red P., with corrosive itching and sore pain when touched or rubbed; on a red base, hard, burning itching, about neck. Erythema of face, often symmetrical. Erysipelas; erysipelatous phlyctenulæ on face, ending in desquamation. Redness; with coldness, then warmth. *Red spot on l. thigh opposite scrotum, with offensive exudation, painfully sore on touch or walking, which also causes biting.*

Redness of affected part, with smarting, heat and white, glossy, tense pustules, then desiccation, leaving a yellowish spot or crust, then *intra-epidermic* pustules, then *dermic* or *sanguino-purulent* pustules and *a two-*

story pustule, when the scabs fell off from the scratched pustules they were succeeded by pits, while the others were still elevated, so that the hand perceived a roughness, brownish discoloration after the scabs, pustules and inflammation of walls of abdomen, then desquamation.

Redness, then burning, next morning when lying on l. side throbbing, tension and jerking in l. upper arm, extending to fingers, red-pointed and roundish pustules, the itching and burning < touch, motion or rubbing, heaviness of arm and shoulder, redness and roughness of whole skin, the small pustules disappeared as whitish, shiny elevations, the whole skin became whitish, the large pustules red, then whitish desquamation only noticed on rubbing, itching continued, and also an alternating heaviness and tension of upper arm.

Tingling, with red points, then little pustules in apices, many formed patches filled with white opaque fluid, the eruption died away like smallpox. Pustules; on scrotum and face, those on side of scrotum were flattened and became suppurating ulcers, the other pustules dried and desquamated; with red areola, on abdomen, itching began in the night and disturbed the sleep, the P. became pale and disappeared without crust or desquamation, then pale red spots; dark red, with itching and burning on movement, < touch or uncovering, with roughness of the whole spot, elevations after the small pustules had disappeared.

Vesicles on labial commissures, r. upper lid and l. buttock (local effects); itching, on chin, which coalesce and form a crust, which is moist on pressure, then desquamation, then a red spot. Brick color, < face, scalp, larynx and chest, in the order enumerated, > abdomen, more on muscular parts of arms and legs than where the bones are more superficial, then swelling, then vesicles, differing in size and shape, some confluent, at first containing limpid serum, then pus, and ending in scabs (local effect).

Prickling in first r. toes; in lower third of l. leg. Formication on face; in lumbar region; knees; r. little toe; jerking, in r. great toe. Itching, then painful burning; I., or rather smarting, as of vermin, on pubic region and on glans; prickling, on r. sole, with burning.

Clinical.—Vesicular and pustular eruptions, with painful burning and redness extremely like herpes and especially like herpes zoster.

Sleep.—Yawning; in forenoon. Sleepiness; towards noon, but on lying down after dinner inability to sleep, with palpitation; with weakness. Easy falling asleep, then chill across back. Sleeping on the back and sudden waking after an emission. Deep sleep after vomiting. Sleeplessness, with anxious tossing about. Difficult falling asleep. Frequent waking. Sudden waking. Twitching of thighs during midday nap. Uneasy sleep; with many dreams. Light sleep, disturbed by many dreams. Dreams; anxious; anxious, interrupted; in afternoon nap, about the occurrences of the day; heavy, till 1 A.M., then sudden waking from headache.

Fever.—Chilliness; with shivering; with weakness; in afternoon, obliging him to go to bed. Easily chilled. Chilliness extending, < over back. Cold skin. Coldness, < lower limbs, so that she seemed covered with gooseskin, > in bed. Cold limbs. Sudden C. and pallor of hands, with shrivelling of fingers. *Cold feet and legs; as far as calves.* Cool skin, then hot, then sweaty.

Heat; with sweat and rapid pulse; with salivation; with the pustules; with anxiety, so that he sought for a chair; general, then coldness in abdominal vertebræ; in flushes; prickling. Heat of face; r. half, starting from r. corner of mouth; in cheeks. Warmth starting from lumbar vertebræ. Heat of skin, < hands, with swollen veins. Itching burning in middle of l. thigh; in lower third of r. tibia.

Sweat; cold, clammy; on forehead; on forehead in drops, with nausea.

Cubeba.

A tincture is made from the dried berries of the Piper Cubeba, L.

General Action.—A marked affinity for the urethra, bladder and vagina, where it produces violent inflammation. The mucous membranes of throat and air-passages are also involved, as well as the skin.

Allies.—Copaiba, Canth.

Generalities.—Emaciation. Peculiar odor to evacuations, sweat and saliva. Face red and swollen, lips dark purple, saliva viscid, frothy, tongue dry, chapped in centre, brown sordes on teeth, veins of forehead and temples turgid, eyes turned upward, injected, pupils contracted to a point, clammy sweat, pulse slow, dispersed by least pressure, gasping, he was aroused for a moment by shaking, uttered an incoherent expression and sank back into a comatose sleep. Convulsions. Restlessness. Weakness. Partial paralysis.

Mind and Head.—Mind weak. Memory lost. Headache; deep-seated. Dulness of head.

Eyes, Nose and Face.—Eyes turgid and watery. Full feeling in eyes. Coryza. Face swollen; and occasionally flushed. Face flushed. Lips puffed, dry and shining. Lips twisted to one side on attempting to speak or smile.

Clinical.—Obstinate otorrhœa, offensive discharges. Nasal catarrh, with fetid odor, and catarrh of the throat, with greenish-yellow expectoration of fetid odor. In catarrh of the throat the mucus trickles from the nose into the throat, is greenish-yellow, with rawness of throat and hoarseness (compare Sinapis).

Mouth and Stomach.—Tongue white. Tongue furred and moist. Appetite increased. Intense thirst; slight T., with burning in throat. Eructations, with warmth in epigastric region; acid E., with uneasiness, heat at pit of stomach and fever. *Nausea.* Vomiting. Gastric irritation. Disordered stomach. Burning pain in stomach. Burning in epigastric and umbilical regions, with pressure.

Abdomen, Rectum and Stool.—Flatulence. Griping, with diarrhœa. Colic. Burning in abdomen; in rectum. Hæmorrhoids. Diarrhœa; copious; distressing, with headache.

Clinical.—Dysentery, stools colorless, transparent, mingled with white particles like rice, with unquenchable thirst, distended sensitive abdomen, < fruit, acids, etc.

Urinary Organs.—*Inflammation of urethra. Mucus from urethra much increased. Cutting after micturition, with constriction. Irritation of passages.* Urine copious, dark. Urine frothy. *Hæmaturia* (Tereb.).

Clinical.—Chronic inflammation of bladder. with cutting and constriction during micturition. Hæmorrhage from the bladder.

Inflammation of bladder and urethra in women, necessity to urinate every ten or fifteen minutes, with smarting, tenesmus and ropy mucus.

Sexual Organs.—*Prostatitis* (Cop., Elat.), the gland feels enlarged to finger in rectum, perineum tender, last drops of urine passed with pain, after micturition sensation as if bladder still contained water. (Hernia femoralis.) Testicles swollen (Cop.). Excitement. No inclination for coition, with weakness of sexual organs.

Clinical.—Inflamed prostate, with thick yellow gonorrhœal discharge; especially useful in the chronic form, sometimes with swollen testicles. Leucorrhœa, profuse, acrid, offensive, yellow or green, with pruritus, intense sexual desire, uterus swollen and painful, etc. Acrid leucorrhœa in girls. Catarrhal leucorrhœa, offensive, yellow.

Respiration and Pulse.—Respiration hurried and difficult. Pulse rapid; and full; and small. Pulse intermittent and sometimes slow, sometimes rapid.

Clinical.—Dyspnœa, with deposit of a false membrane in the larynx and danger of suffocation; also useful in bronchitis, in which the cough seems to tear the bronchi, expectoration difficult, sometimes streaked with blood.

Extremities.—Numbness of fingers and toes. Acute deep-seated pain in wrists, then redness and swelling of them. Wrists stiff and thickened. Hands swollen and so stiff that the fingers could not be bent. Pricking in soles.

Skin.—Eruption from head to foot, with fever. Urticaria (Cop.); febrilis. Redness, afterwards eruption from head to foot, which in some parts could not be distinguished from urticaria febrilis, while in others it appeared more like lichen in its papular stage, but with more inflammation around base of papulæ than is common in that disease. Itching.

Fever.—Heat; with thirst; fever, with heat at pit of stomach; internal and external, with tingling over whole body; hot skin; heat at times in palms and soles; in hands and feet, with numbness of them; in flushes upon face, soles and palm.

Cucurbita.

A tincture is made of the fresh stems of the pumpkin, Cucurbita Pepo, L. An emulsion of the seeds is given for tape-worm.

Clinical.—A tincture of the vines and of the seeds has been prescribed with alleged benefit in vomiting of pregnancy, and it also has cured vomiting of food and salivation in non-pregnant women. The seeds have been used very extensively for tape-worm.

Cundurango.

A tincture is made of the dried bark of Gonolobus Cundurango, Triana.

Generalities and Mind.—Weight increased. Did not feel well; when walking. Miserable feeling. Soreness all over body, like rheumatism, < through l. shoulder and under l. scapula. Languid when awake in the night. Stiffness of the muscles. Confusion of mind.

Clinical.—Tumors of the breast, very hard, painful, associated with ulcers in the corners of the mouth; this soreness and cracking in the corners of the mouth seem to be very characteristic of the drug. It seems also to have cured stricture of the œsophagus with burning pain behind the œsophagus, where the food seems to stick. Vomiting of food and indurations in l. hypochondrium, with constant burning pain.

Head.—Aching; in morning, < l. upper part of forehead, with feeling as if bigger. Vertigo; on stooping or turning head; with slight pain across top of forehead. Frontal headache; all day; at top; all day along top of brow and hairy scalp, > early in evening. Dulness in forehead. Forehead feels as if very broad and high. Heaviness in l. half of forehead. Pain in l. temple spreading over upper part of brain to r. side of head, feeling as if some one were pulling up the upper part of the skull, with one-half of brain, at 10 A.M., increasing till 6 P.M. Pimple on scalp.

Eyes.—Pain in l. ball. Vision dim. Vision of black serpents jumping in all directions before r. eye, on closing l. eye I seemed looking through a dense fog, afterwards the appearance before the eye was like two black horns, with large black balls on the upper ends, and a mound of crystal between them, their tops tapering off and tipped with black, afterwards the obstruction appeared in the shape of a pear, with the large end up, red on looking towards the light, purple on looking from the light, later appearance of curled hair in front of r. eye and a blur before l., retina congested, inability to recognize any one in the street with l. eye closed.

Nose.—Stiffness. Discomfort. Stuffed up. Full feeling in bridge. Ability to pronounce the French nasal sounds with great perfection. Discharge of much glairy mucus alternating with a dry feeling.

Face.—I do not look well. *Painful crack in r. corner of lips.* Lips unusually red; lower.

Mouth and Throat.—Tongue unusually clear and red; coated brown; painful pustule on r. upper side of tip, next day pain in r. side of tip; pain in l. half; feels burnt, also acrid. Sore throat, with enlargement of tonsils. Aching in throat extending to stomach, with burning in stomach.

Stomach and Abdomen.—Anorexia. Nausea; arising from r. hypochondrium. Cardialgia. Pain in S.; < *at cul de sac.* Fulness in S. Flatulence. Emission of flatus; painful, foul-smelling, in afternoon. Pain in r. hypochondrium. Uneasiness in abdomen; in iliac region, not quite a pain, at 8 A.M.

Stool, Urinary and Genital Organs.—Stool papescent, small, with mucus, without sense of aid from sphincter muscles. Constipation. Stool dry and scanty. Frequent micturition; at night, with urging in renal ducts; and at times copious. Urine scanty; U. thick; high-colored and loaded with phosphates; almost colorless, emitted without effort, urging in renal ducts after bladder is emptied. Sexual appetite depressed.

Heart and Pulse.—Sharp pain in H. in morning on rising, then passage of flatus. Constrictive pain in H. Pulse accelerated, afterwards slow; slow and small.

Back.—Pain in l. scapula; then in r.; under apex of l. scapula; across lumbar region; about fourth dorsal vertebra; heavy, in l. scapula; as if in the bone, in r. scapular region; weary, in l. kidney; in occasional darts through kidneys.

Extremities.—Sharp pain posteriorly in l. shoulder in morning when driving. Creeping pain along periosteum of r. humerus. Tingling in l. fingers when writing. Apparent increase of strength in legs when walking.

Skin.—Brown. Some congenital, warty excrescences look red, fresh and unusually large. Blotches on upper arms, < l., after growing nearly invisible they again become red, and there is a new one below elbow, one on wrist, one on clavicle; erythematous, on face.

Pimples on thighs; on front of l. thigh; indolent, on chest, one on l. side of nose. Small pustule between eyebrows and one on r. side of nose, afterwards pustule on border of tip of tongue to right of mesial line, one on r. cheek, two on abdomen, to right of mesial line, and still farther to the right tiny papules, a large pustule that did not ripen near acromion. Itching on scapulæ and legs; along anterior and outer tibial regions; shoulders and sternum.

Sleep.—Sleep as if narcotized. Sound, dreamy. Transient. Intermittent. Restless; and dreamy; but felt rested in morning. Had a bad night; < towards morning; and snored. Dreams.

Fever.—Rigors.

Cuprum.

Pure precipitated metallic Copper is triturated with sugar of milk. Solutions of the salts of Copper are used.

Allies.—Plumbum, Arsenic.

Generalities.—Stretched upon the floor without sense, lay constantly with legs drawn up; constant dorsal decubitus; on back, with head bent backward; the child lay upon its stomach, with jerking upward of pelvis; lay still and apathetic, looking straight ahead, with dim eyes and stupid expression. Emaciation. Violent struggles. Writhing of whole frame under the pain. *Trembling;* < hands. Cramps.

Convulsions; from pressure on stomach; *general; with stiffness of limbs and body, jaws clenched;* in sleep, twitching of fingers, arms and hands backward and inward towards body, drawing back of feet, at one time opening and distorting eyes, at another closing them and distorting mouth; after pain in last dorsal vertebræ, the pain extending suddenly into l. arm, to wrist, arm was spasmodically flexed and extended, then loss of power, these attacks returning the two next days; with constant vomiting and pain in abdomen, gradually passing into paralysis; C., < abdomen and limbs, when attacked they croaked like frogs or howled, were crazy, looked frightened, attempted to escape, eyes glistened and seemed to start from their sockets, if one was attacked the others on hearing his cries were likewise attacked. Epileptic fits; *epileptiform convulsions, trembling, staggering, falling down unconscious, without crying; epileptiform attacks, with frothing at mouth,* trunk bent outward, limbs forcibly thrust outward and mouth open.

Shooting through body; < r. side, causing shuddering. Painful jerks or thrusts in various parts. Pains all over; in muscles; in bones in morning, with headache and nausea; in bones during remissions of delirium and convulsions, with headache; neuralgic P. in various parts, stomach, intestines, hips and lower limbs; rheumatic. Jaundice, with vomiting, eructations, heaviness in head, difficult hearing, grayish stools, thirst, dark, turbid urine, with yellowish sediment. Sensitiveness to changes of weather. Sensibility of paralyzed parts.

Agitation. *Uneasiness; with tossing about* (Ars.); with piercing cries; with anxiety (Ars.); with jerking of limbs. Weakness (Ars.); after walking, so that limbs trembled; with increase of corpulence. Faintness; on slightest motion. Heaviness. *Paralysis.* Trunk and limbs stiff, jaws clenched. Aggravation from lying down. Amelioration after stool; and micturition; A. of pains and of hardness of abdomen after diarrhœa, then nervous symptoms.

Clinical.—Spasmodic contractions of flexor muscles, especially of the fingers, toes and thumbs. Epilepsy characterized by the most violent spasms, with cold sweat, blue surface, etc. Chorea brought on by fright. Chorea of the most violent character, with spasmodic vomiting, cold sweat, etc. Chorea, with violent hysterical symptoms, laughing or violent weeping. Chorea during pregnancy. Uræmic convulsions following cholera. Convulsions preceding the outbreak of eruption in measles, scarlet fever, or in repression of the eruption. Convulsions from worms. Neuritis, with lightning-like pains, < touch. Paralysis of flexor muscles. (Plumb., extensors).

Mind.—*Delirium; with disconnected talking; in attacks, with full, rapid, hard pulse, inflamed eyes, wild look and disconnected talking, ending in sweat;* attack of surly; in attacks, he fancies that he is a captain in the army, fancies that he is selling green vegetables or that he is repairing old chairs, merry singing, spitting in faces of attendants and laughing at it; quiet, unintelligible murmuring interrupted by lamentations; furious. Rage in attacks, they tried to bite bystanders. *Talking all the time. Crying like a child;* C. out frequently. Howling in unexpected paroxysms. Spasmodic laughter; immoderate L. in evening.

Anxiety; with tossing about (Arsen.); *deathly, in attacks, without heat;* that is peculiar to pain in pit of stomach. Fear; it seems as if he must tread lightly to avoid injuring himself or disturbing his companions. Melancholy; with desire to be alone and anxiety about her death, which she supposes imminent. Fretfulness, with irresolution and dissatisfaction with everything; intermittent F., he does not know what he wishes, he desires to be alone. Apathy. Disinclination to work; yet idling is irksome. Aversion to everything. Taciturnity. Loss of sensitiveness and moping in a corner. *Obliged to think a long time before they can answer.* Loss of ideas, weakness of memory. Lethargic stupefaction. Coma. Semi-conscious, voice faint, eyes half open, fixed, glassy, insensible to light, pulse weak, in some quick, in others slow, difficult to arouse, when aroused complaining of cold and of pain in abdomen. Senseless, he seems in a half-waking dream. Unconscious; and fell down in sudden convulsions.

Clinical.—In mania, biting and tearing, foolish gestures of mimicry, or the patient shrinks with fear and tries to get away from every one, with general chilliness, not > heat, etc.

Head.—Drawn backward; D. obliquely. Inflammation of brain. Lancinations, < turning it to either side, it felt as if fastened to shoulders by a long peg. *Aching;* in evening; < motion; with nausea; then vomiting and purging; *bruised, in brain and eyes on turning eye;* beating; compressive, in different parts; drawing, in many parts, with vertigo and general sick feeling. *Confusion;* with beating. *Heaviness;* with sticking in l. shoulder on moving it from side to side. Dulness. Congestion. Apoplexy. *Vertigo; on looking up* (Plumb.), *with vanishing of vision as from a veil before eyes;* on reading; on rising from bed, even to falling; < moving, > lying, with weakness, head sinking forward; > stool, with stupefaction; preventing sitting up in bed; *in attacks;* as if it were turning around in head and he would fall forward.

Forehead.—*Intermittent lancinations, sometimes in F., sometimes in vertex, sometimes in temples or occiput,* < *pressure.* Burning sticking in l. side. Pain; over eyes; as if brain were pressed outward, < stooping, with confusion of head.

Temples.—Veins swollen. Burning sticking in l. and on vertex. Tearing, < touch. Pain in r., < touch; P. in temples, frontal eminences, occiput and in brain, < motion and touch, with vertigo; drawing P. in l., < touch. Painful throbbing in arteries.

Pain in vertex. Cutting jerking in l. side of head. Pain on r., then l. side; (P. in parietal bone, < touch). Drawing in l. side, extending to face, ear, behind ear and to l. side of neck. Burning tearing in occiput at attachment of cervical muscles on moving head forward. Heaviness in occiput. Hair colored green; from white. *Crawling on vertex.* Prickling tickling on vertex. Soreness; on touching hair.

Clinical.—Meningitis from suppressed eruptions, with convulsions, loud screams, clenched thumbs, lips blue, etc. Valuable in extremely violent continued headache, with sensation as if cold water were poured over the head. Violent headaches, with vomiting of all food and drink, sunken eyes, etc. Extremely violent headache over frontal sinuses in nasal catarrh (compare Kali iod.).

Eyes.—Sunken; and staring; and dim; and glazed. Surrounded by blue rings; and sunken; and looking weary. Prominent. Fixed; upward. Wandering. Sparkling. Dim, inclined to close from weakness. Pain as from night-watching; burning P.; sore burning P. now in one, now in other. *Itching towards evening.* Pupils dilated; contracted; insensible. Conjunctiva injected; C. greenish-yellow. Itching of balls. Lids red; and swollen. Pressure in lids on opening and closing them, < touch. Pain in orbits; *bruised, on turning eyes.* Photophobia. Blackness before eyes, flickering vision of sparks.

Ears.—Sticking in r. Tearing in cartilage of l. Pain in ears, tearing in r. Boring in and behind E. Pressure in r. concha as from something hard. Itching. *Distant drumming in ear on which he lay in morning, > raising himself.* Roaring and ringing. Fluttering in l. Deafness.

Nose.—Red and swollen. *Sensation of rush of blood.* Itching internally. Stopped coryza, with sleepy yawning; fluent C., with lachrymation and smarting of eyes; profuse C. Bleeding; with petechiæ. Frequent sneezing. *Loss of smell.*

Face.—*Pale;* dirty, shining color; and thin; and collapsed; with expression of prostration or stupidity. *Bluish, with blue lips;* B. over cheek-bones. Red; and swollen; and swollen and hot; with heat and sometimes coldness running over body. Icteric. Pale-yellow coppery color. Sallow, almost clay-colored; dark S. Greenish-yellow. Lead-colored. Sunken; and yellow. Swollen; and discolored; and pasty. Look confused. Heavy. Sad. Anxious. Suffering expression. Expressive of pain. Wild. Distorted; spasmodically, also with staring, retracted eyes. Sticking in r. side. Pain in l. side as from a thrust. Pain in front of ear. Drawing inward beneath chin, < touch. Spasmodic contraction of jaws; tetanic C., with spasm of pharynx, preventing speech. Sticking inward in l. lower jaw, < touch, and in l. tonsil. Pressure in l. ramus of J., < touch; drawing P. on r. side of lower, < touch. Lips pale; livid; swollen; dry; soreness within upper.

Clinical.—Neuralgia of the face, burning stinging pains, < touch (Ars.).

Mouth.—Teeth green; T. coated with sulphuret of copper; dark greenish-blue line on T.; T. fell out, < upper, without salivation. Black line on gums; purple line; G. lax and spongy; soft, with purplish-red patches at their juncture with cheeks; retracted; ulcerated; swollen and ulcerated at their edges.

Tongue.—Coated; white; yellowish; light brown, except on edges and tip, which were clean and pale red, whole T. moist; and clammy. Pale, with thin whitish coat. Green. White; in middle, red at edges. Red, with enlarged papillæ; and dry. Cracked and brownish. Swollen and pale. Moist and flabby. Roundish ulcers, with yellow base, on tip and margins. Epithelium came off and mucous membrane of mouth loosened in large flakes. Dry; and foul. Loss of speech.

Mucous membrane pale inside of lower lip and part of upper, mostly where the teeth had made an impression, dark blue, teeth slate-colored, < edge. Froth. Much mucus in morning; thick bloody mucus in mouth and throat. Spitting of blood, < morning on rising. Soreness, with blisters on mucous membrane. Sharp pain in M. and pharynx. Dryness; and of throat; without thirst. Tingling of M. and teeth as from a galvanic current, from acids of any sort, fruit, etc. Saliva flowing from mouth. Salivation; with swelling of tongue and of salivary glands; viscid.

Taste.—*Bitter.* Nauseous. Sourish all the afternoon as if the tongue had been held against iron. Salt, sour in morning. Bad. Coppery; with burning in throat; in œsophagus. Sweetish; and metallic, also with saliva running from mouth, dryness of throat and *constriction when swallowing.* Flat. Food tastes like water. Lost.

Clinical.—Paralysis of tongue associated with general paralysis. Speech stuttering.

Throat.—*Audible gurgling of drink.* Spasms preventing speaking. Redness of velum, with croupous exudation on tonsils; spotted R. of fauces; velum palati and posterior wall of pharynx brownish-red and dry, with difficulty in swallowing and rough voice. Inflammation, preventing swallowing. Swelling; and hardness, with inability to swallow. Sticking. Pain; in thyroid cartilage. Constriction (Zinc.); of pharynx; of gullet; of fauces, with nausea. Compression of pharynx as from a foreign body at anterior surface of throat. Soreness. Dryness, with thirst. Burning. Swallowing difficult.

Clinical.—Spasms of the œsophagus (Zinc.), paroxysmal cough, intense pain behind sternum on attempting to swallow.

Stomach.—Eats hastily. Desire for cold rather than warm food. *Appetite lost;* in evening; but empty feeling in stomach; A. diminished. Aversion to food. Thirst; for cold water; unquenchable; drinking only a little at a time. Desire for acids. *Eructations;* in afternoon and evening; of mucus mixed with green lumps; bitter and sourish, as from heartburn, spasmodically constricting throat and preventing swallowing. Hiccough; with spasmodic contractions of pharynx; then eructations of sourish bitter water; then vomiting of offensive odor, tasting like copper.

Nausea; on attempting to swallow animal food; as if associated with intoxication; in upper part of throat, then vomiting of bitter, greenish mucus and pain in stomach; in almost whole abdomen, extending into throat, < pit of stomach, with putrid taste; sudden, then vomiting of fluid arterial blood, next day vomiting of dark fluid, then sensation of something passing into stomach and thence into bowels, next day hæmorrhage again, then sudden collapse. Retching; *ineffectual; ineffectual, with constriction of œsophagus and across chest in direction of diaphragm;* violent.

Vomiting; with burning nausea rising to throat; with colic; > *drinking cold water* (Ars. in part). *Forcible.* Constant, with purging; C., with colic. *Frequent; after drinking* (Ars.); at night; with colic and diarrhœa, as in cholera. Of breakfast; of every kind of food; of contents of stomach and bile, then dry retching. Of water, with lachrymation. Frothy fluid mixed with blood. Bloody matter; of blood and mucus; bloody, with bloody diarrhœa, little colic, but much cramping in limbs; of B. without cough, with deep stitches in l. side of chest. Bilious fluid. Greenish; *and yellowish; and liquid;* liquid, with blood; *violent, sudden, of water, with copious greenish diarrhœa and colic* (compare Verat.); violent, bilious, with frequent liquid stools; and yellow-green bile, with cramps; bitter, slimy, at one time of sweetish, clear, tenacious saliva; viscid, glairy, tinged with blood. Frequent, almost brownish-yellow, in part greenish.

Distention in region, with soreness to touch; in epigastric region. **Cramps and pains, and in bowels. Griping and pressure, then vomiting.** Sticking near l. side of pit, not affecting respiration; gnawing S. in stomach. Tearing; in pit. Pinching, extending at times into throat and at times into abdomen. **Pressure, with intermittent, contractive pains.** *Pain;* in region; *epigastric region;* in pit, < pressure; in pit, as from something hard, < touch. Cardialgia. Heartburn in afternoon, then bitter mucus in throat. Burning, rising into throat and mouth. Distress after eating; D. in S. and abdomen, < vomiting. Occasional weight in epigastric region, rather towards r. side, with uneasiness, and after meals sense of distention; W. in epigastric region, with weakness and oppression. Epigastric pulsation. Internal heat in epigastric region. Sensation of something bitter in it. Sensitiveness to touch; epigastric region. Weakness. Irritability, < eating. Impatient of everything but the most bland and simple milk diet. Disposition to remove some offending substances, without nausea.

Clinical.—Obstinate vomiting always on waking in morning, on the slightest movement. Cramp in the region of the stomach and abdomen, or very violent cutting pain going through to back as if transfixed and preventing the slightest motion.

Abdomen.—Tense, hot and tender to touch (Bell.). *Stretched like a board* (Plumb.). Distended, hard, painful to touch; D., with paroxysmal soreness and with falling out of teeth, < upper, without salivation, trembling of limbs, after a third attack perfect lameness, paralysis of r. hand. Tympanitic. Rumbling in sleep. **Spasmodic motions of muscles;** S. motions of A. and stomach. *Contracted; and sore to touch;* almost to spine, but not sensitive to pressure (Plumb.).

Acute enteritis. Cramp at 6 A.M., as if drawn together with a fist, and ineffectual urging to diarrhœa; occasional C. Shooting across A. and under ensiform cartilage; corroding S. and internal ulcers. Cutting; and tearing; and constriction. Chronic gastro-enteritis. Griping; after warm milk in morning; on walking after eating green vegetables, > rest and lying down, then weakness. Sudden pain as if struck when sitting reading, > pressure. **Colic;** during digestion; < pressure; < fatigue; > stools; with constipation; with almost constant urging to stool; with vomiting and purging of green matter; **intermittent C.**; intermittent, > bending double; paroxysmal, with hot sweat; causing anxiety; extending transversely across A., remitting at times but not intermitting; as from something hard, < touch; spasmodic; intermittent drawing. Feeling as if intestines were drawn into knots, in some paroxysmal, with inclination to draw knees up and press hard upon bowels. Pressing together of intestines every forenoon, < walking or pressure, with pressure from upper and posterior part towards l. lower part. Constriction. Tension. Sensitiveness so that she could bear no covering. Internal heat. Inclination to waterbrash.

Colic in upper and middle, < pressure. Griping in l. side. Drawing in r.; l., from below false ribs to bend of thigh. Feeling in l. as if bubbles formed and broke. Swelling of liver. Sticking in hepatic region, in axillary line through to pit of stomach. Griping in l. hypochondrium, extending to hip. Pain in hypochondria; in r., extending to r. shoulder; drawing P. from l. H. to hip. Sensitiveness of H.; l. Cramplike pain in middle and one side, < l. Pain in umbilical region; l. Hypogastrium dull on pressure. Pressure downward in lower A. as from a stone; drawing P. as from something hard, < touch. Pain in l. iliac region, < pressure.

Clinical.—Most horrible colics, with tendency to collapse, convulsive vomiting, hiccough, etc. Neuralgia of the abdominal viscera.

Rectum and Anus.—R. inflamed and sensitive. Heaviness of R. after stool, with uneasiness. Tickling as from pin-worms. Tenesmus; after stool; with scanty, dark, pulpy stools; with burning in R. close to anus. Frequent urging; ineffectual U. Sticking above anus. Smarting in A. after stool.

Stool.—*Diarrhœa; violent;* bloody; slimy, brown, then greenish, with streaks of blood; profuse, with tenesmus and prostration; alternating with constipation. Liquid; and involuntary, also green and offensive; and involuntary, copious, waking him at 2 A.M., when lying on abdomen; and frequent, with bright red blood and shreds of membrane, sometimes scanty, sometimes containing fragments of solid fæces. Like frothy molasses. *Constipation;* with tenesmus; with intermittent drawing pain about umbilicus and flank. Green. Grayish. Bloody; of bloody mucus; of almost clear bright red blood; bright blood from bowels. Scanty, mucous, brownish, afterwards greenish, next day streaked with blood; S. mucous, greenish, preceded and followed by griping, and tenesmus after stool. Copious. Difficult. *Painful, green, with cutting and tenesmus.* Involuntary. Frequent; and small, bilious, with burning and tenesmus; offensive, copious, green, relieving symptoms somewhat; slimy, tinged with blood, and on straining shreds of lymph and frothy ash-colored secretions were forced out, aggravating the sufferings. Omitted.

Clinical.—Cholera or choleraic stools, not copious, with desire for warm food and drinks, which are swallowed with a gurgling sound, the attacks are characterized by the most horrible cramps in stomach and abdomen and piercing screams, cramps in extremities, especially of the flexor muscles, with intense coldness and paleness of the surface, thumbs clenched across the palms.

Urinary Organs.—Urging, with scanty discharge and burning sticking or cutting, < meatus urinarius. Painful inability to urinate, requiring considerable time and effort to relieve bladder. Frequent micturition; and scanty, with smarting as from soreness of urethra. Involuntary M. M. rarer and scantier than usual. *Urine suppressed* (Plumb.). Burning sticking in meatus. Burning during micturition. Urine scanty; and scalding. Tinged with blood. Turbid and jumentous; T., dark red, with yellowish sediment; T., brownish, with sediment.

Sexual Organs.—Penis swollen, glans inflamed. Menses delayed, dark and painful.

Clinical.—Violent pains after labor. Puerperal convulsions.

Respiratory Organs.—*Hoarseness so that he cannot speak;* H. on breathing cold dry air. Voice trembling, stammering. Cough; **with interrupted, almost suppressed respiration;** *fatiguing, with blowing of blood from nose;* paroxysmal, without signs of lung disease; violent, at night, then chilliness and hoarseness from morning till evening; short; short, dry, straining; *violent dry, at night between* 11 *and* 1, < *sitting, with tearing in head and return of the anxiety and pressure in chest;* dry, preventing speech; hard, dry, with night-sweats; in morning, with offensive-tasting expectoration; with mucous E.; with bloody E.; with purulent E. Much expectoration. Purulent dark expectoration.

Respiration difficult. *Suffocative loss of breath;* sense of suffocation, < walking, fatigue and in damp weather. *Spasmodic dyspnœa, with constriction of chest, then spasmodic vomiting.* Short R. Rapid R.; with rattling in bronchi. Vesicular murmur weak, absent or replaced by a subcrepitant râle.

Clinical.—Whooping cough. Laryngismus stridulous, with thumbs clenched in the palms. Spasmodic asthma, with blueness of the face and constriction of the throat, intense dyspnœa, retching and vomiting. Violent spasmodic cough and whooping cough, face became purple, vomiting, the paroxyms > drinking water. Occasionally useful in pneumonia when there is want of reaction with coldness of the surface and cold sweat, excessive dyspnœa.

Chest.—Rattling when awake; R., ceasing during epileptic attack, with bloody mucus from nose and mouth. Spasms; cramping, after vomiting. Diminished elasticity posteriorly on both sides. Sticking beneath heart; S. in side, preceded and followed by screaming, which interrupted sleep. Pinching in l. side, extending to hip. Pain on r. side; sharp drawing P. in cartilage of sixth rib. Pressure as from something hard on cartilage of third rib, < touch. Constriction; *spasmodic, impeding respiration and increasing the anxiety.* Feeling as if blood accumulated. Coldness along sternum, with coldness of limbs and internal heat in abdomen.

Heart.—Dulness in præcordial region on percussion. Boring in præcordial region. Anxiety. Interval between first and second sound shortened by one-half, "*bruit de rappel.*" Palpitation. Rapid action after a light supper. Contractions weaker.

Clinical.—Chronic aortitis, with distress behind sternum, etc. (see Baryta).

Pulse.—Rapid; and hard and full, also with red face and dry skin; and irregular; and weak; and thready; and small; and small, spasmodic; and small, intermittent; and small, weak; and small, wiry; and small, weak and thready. Slow, large and intermittent; S. hard and small; S. and small; S and weak. Hard; and full; and contracted; and small, spasmodic. Contracted; and small; and small, weak, hard. Soft. Weak and small.

Neck.—Swelling of r. glands, with pain on touch; S. of r. glands, with induration. Lacinations in nape on bending head backward. Intermittent sticking tearing in muscles. Resisting pain in muscles where neck and back unite on moving head backward. Tensive pain in nape.

Back.—Pain; < rest, > motion. Cutting drawing in l. side. Sticking in l. scapula on moving head; S. beneath l. scapula near spine, not affecting respiration. Pain between scapula; P. beneath r. scapula changing on respiration to sticking. Sticking transversely across small of B. Lancinations in loins, sacrum, navel and in iliac region. Pain in loins; < rest, > motion.

Clinical.—Spinal irritation, with violent paroxysmal pain, extreme senstiveness of the whole length of the spine.

Extremities.—*Cramps; convulsive movements.* Rigidity between convulsions. *Periodic painful contractions of fingers and toes, often so that fingers could not be extended by any force.* Painful jerkings alternately in flexor and extensor tendons of hands and feet, extending into upper arms and legs, with cramps in calves. Trembling. Pain; < rest, > motion. Bruised and paralyzed sensation in E. and small of back, so that it was difficult to use E., with tearing. *Drawing and tension, often with shuddering and chilliness though skin was not cold.* Sick feeling as before coryza. *Weakness;* with pain at elbows, in bends of knees. Numbness; of different parts and under certain circumstances prickings in various parts of body. Difficult to move.

Upper Extremities.—Tearing. Paralysis as from lead. Drawing pain in shoulders. *Jerking of arms and hands.* Arms painful during rest, < r. Arms weak. Thrust or jerk in l. upper arm. Pain in upper arm; as if broken or bruised. Sensation as if bubbles of air issued from upper arm. Tearing in ulna, < wrist, < touch; jerking T. in ulna. Pain in l. forearm as if something were broken. Drawing pain in forearm, extending to thumb, r. then l.

Hand.—Swelling and inflammation, and of arm, with pain, fever, quick pulse, thirst, furred tongue, then abscesses on H. and arm, afterwards fingers and back of hands were œdematous and contained transparent fluid, finally it was necessary to make an incision from middle of forearm along wrist, over tendons, into palm. Twitching in morning on rising. Jerking tearing in metacarpal bones and first joint of thumb, < touch. *Constriction of different parts of r. H. and forearm and sensation as if increased in size, motions not fully under control of his will.* Pain in ball as if something were thrust through it. Lameness of r., forearm in constant pronation, hand bent at r. angle to arm, thumb drawn into palm, fingers flexed, extension of hand, especially of finger-joints impossible, flexion only partial, upper limbs emaciated, < r., r. hand nothing but skin and bone. Weakness; and paralysis. Numbness.

Fingers.—Nails white. Tearing in tips. Bruised pain beneath thumb-joints. Pain in thumb-joints as if dislocated. Tensive pain in balls of thumbs. Numbness and shrivelling.

Lower Extremities.—Cramps, < calves. Reeling from side to side. Drawing pain in nates. Sticking down from l. hip at noon, < joints of knee and foot.

Pain in muscles on anterior surface of thighs. Pain above knee as if bruised or broken. Drawing pain in r. thigh. Pain in knee as if broken. *Knees weak, and painful drawing on walking or standing, they give way.* Œdema of legs. *Cramp from ankle into calf;* C. in calves; in calves on attempting to walk; paroxysmal, in calves, drawing one limb sideways and backward, > rubbing. Tensive-drawing cramplike pain in calf. Tearing below knee. Burrowing in and below calf. Pain in legs; in calves, < quiet; in lower part of calf as from a thrust or jerk; drawing P. in lower part of calf. Legs weak. Legs fall asleep. Legs feel heavy and dead.

Painful heaviness of ankles. Pain in ankles when tired. Jerking tearing in sole and on back of foot. Pain on inner margin of l. sole; P. in metatarsal bones, < touch; sprained P. in l. sole. Drawing pain in feet; in metatarsal joints, at root of great toe; in l. sole, < walking. Great toes drawn tetanically downward and pain in soles. Pain in toes. Sensation as if wind issued from toes.

Clinical.—Paralysis of lower extremities, attacks of suffocation, internal heat, external cold, with anxiety and anguish, the results of fright.

Skin.—Yellow; light, < face and conjunctiva; and pale, earthy. Red spots on arms, with burning itching, < night. Flabby. Dry and lifeless. Contracted on limbs. Rash on chest and hands. *Eruptions;* from back of r. hand to elbow and on l. hand, with irritation, < night in bed and near fire, and occasional oozing. Petechial spots on neck and arms. Tetter on bend of elbow, causing yellow desquamation, itching, < evening. Eruption similar to leprosy; < hair of head, the largest spots white and scaly, with moist base, appearing as if something acrimonious had been secreted under the cuticle, which thickened and separated from cutis. Vesicles exuding water, on tips of fingers. Sticking outward in various parts. Formication of hands, < finger-tips. Itching on soles.

Sleep.—Yawning much in evening; frequent Y. without sleep; Y., with sleepiness, but inability to sleep on account of a crowd of ideas. Sleepiness; especially in children; with weakness. Lethargic sleep after vomiting. Deep sleep after colic; D., after the weakness; D., with twitching of limbs. Sleeplessness. Restless S., interrupted by dreams; R. and unrefreshing. Twitching in sleep. Raving in S. Difficult falling asleep, then sleep full of dreams, with frequent waking. Sleep frequently interrupted by dreams. Anxious dreams waking her.

Fever.—*Coldness; with cramps in limbs;* internal, with external heat and at night burning skin. Shivering. *Cold limbs;* and covered with cold sweat; *legs, hands and feet.* Cold skin. *Fever;* with full, hard, frequent, variable pulse; hectic; continuous, almost typhous; hot face without sensation of heat; pungent heat of skin; hot and dry skin. Sweat; at night; profuse, at night; profuse, on forehead; green; bluish-green; light green between toes and under nails; cold, clammy during the collapse, < forehead, with moaning, cheeks and eyes sunken, face bluish, jaw hanging down; skin clammy, pale and doughy. Dry skin, then moist, and (< during great prostration) profuse sweat.

Clinical.—Intermittent fever, with icy coldness of the whole body, predominating cramps in the limbs, blue surface, collapse, suppression of urine.

Curare.

The arrow-poison of S. America is triturated for use.

Generalities. — Loss of four pounds in weight. Tremors in afternoon and evening. Pains sharp, wandering, in all parts; needle-like through various parts, < l. temple; needle-like at intervals through various parts during the day; fleeting, first under sternum, then in abdomen, wandering, in evening, with pain under r. scapula. Pulsations in all parts except feet. Restless feeling. Inclined to physical but not mental exertion in morning. Unusual feeling of well-being, as from out-door life.

Weakness; all day, with weakness of back; on waking, lasting all day, with headache and malaise; on waking, with stupidity, the stupidity > afternoon, hurried feeling in evening; < arms and legs; > towards evening; with trembling feeling; with trembling on trying to walk; with vertigo on trying to hold head up; with malaise and stupidity. Faintness. Numbness in all parts, < r. arm and wrist, and in cervical region, with tingling. Discomfort, as from a combination of numbness and tingling in superficial muscles, < r. arm, beginning in r. arm and becoming general, always with pain in basilar region. Symptoms gradually > towards middle of forenoon, then < again about noon, and continue severe the remainder of the day.

Clinical.—It seems to have arrested the paroxysms of hydrophobia when injected under the skin. Catalepsy. Threatened paralysis of respiration, the breath stops on falling asleep, sometimes palliative. Nervous debility, especially in old people, arms and hands weak, as after long-continued sickness, numbness as if a heavy weight hung to the arms, soreness of muscles of the arms, < attempting to lift anything. Nervous debility, with leaden heaviness of the arms, difficulty in using the muscles, especially of the wrists and hands. Paralysis following epileptic attacks.

Mind.—Laughed a great deal through the day. Changeable disposition, jesting and laughing, then shedding tears. Sensitive, the least annoyance brings tears. All feelings intensified, have to guard myself to prevent showing affection towards those I like, and irritability towards those I do not like. Energetic feeling all day; and hurried. Nervous, hurried feeling all day. Discouraged and cross; and sick of living, tired of everything. Depression of spirits; and feeling like crying, desire to be alone. Inability for mental work, from heaviness on vertex; I. for mental or physical work, wish to keep quiet. Laziness. Inability to fix the thoughts, overcome by the will. Do not wish to talk or have any one talk to me. Intellect dull. Stupid, confused feeling; transiently > nap. Forgetful.

Head.—Aching; through the day, < immediately after eating, sometimes nausea; on waking, lasting all day, with irritability; on waking, < after breakfast, by walking, stooping and quick movements, < afternoon, when there was pain in occiput; after waking, < an hour after breakfast, varied during the day and evening, at times in occiput, shooting into neck, at other times pain in vertex, always in temples; before breakfast, and in early part of day, but gradually wore away; at base of brain and passing upward, beginning at breakfast, < chewing; in evening; in brain after eating; in steam-cars, with nausea, the A. > night's sleep; during menstruation, with dragging pain in pelvic organs, leaving weariness for several days after flow has ceased; < noon; < eating, motion, light, noise and at night, > pressure and quiet; > open air; forcing her to lie down before breakfast; with tingling, prickling and nausea; with malaise; sudden, with weakness and trembling of all limbs, confused feeling and tension of head, pain indescribable at first, but soon became definable, sharp pain in forehead and l. temple, with occasional pains in vertex and r. temple, pains < stooping and motion, sensation as if ears were filled with compressed air, tingling pain along malar-bones and zygomatic processes to temples, the headache reached its climax at 11 A.M., then gradually diminished, < 4 P.M., pain through entire brain, confusion of thought, weakness of joints, pulsations through whole body, inability to study or think, stupidity and sleepiness; neuralgic, extending down spine; radiating from base of brain to vertex and outward to ears, during the day, < eating; wandering; wandering, all day, < motion and eating, located in occiput after tea; tired, on waking, increasing till 8 P.M.; tired, heavy, < forehead and temples; heavy, all day, with occasional sharp pains through temples and lower part of occiput.

Feeling as if about to ache on waking, lasting till middle of afternoon. Soreness in every fibre of brain, < motion. Confusion; > lying, with heaviness, dulness, difficulty in holding head up, weight on vertex; with enlarged feeling and with darting pain through r. temple to base of brain; with enlarged feeling and with darting through temples, < r., coughing causes a shattered, torn feeling, so that she must hold on to temples, the same sensation on motion of head unless moved very gently; preventing study. Heaviness; with weak, tired feeling. Dulness and stupidity. Feels large. Must hold on to it to keep the parts together. Empty feeling, it is a great effort to talk. Lightness. Rush of blood, with aching. Congested feeling. Throbbing in all vessels. Vertigo; on looking at near objects or at water, while walking briskly to avert the headache. Symptoms < stooping.

Forehead.—Sharp darting pain over r. eye, severe at times, leaving confusion; over r. eye, extending to vertex, after eating, disappearing suddenly. Sharp pain in F. and temples in morning on rising, < motion, > lying, with dull pain in other parts of brain, < towards occiput, drawing pain from occiput to between scapulæ, with nausea, faintness and weakness. Pain; all day, and in temples; along infraorbital ridge, through temples and about ears; over r. eye, < eating and at night; all day, beginning after breakfast, in central and upper part of F. and in anterior part of vertex preventing thought, < vigorous exercise and stooping; in l. side after waking, afterwards in entire F.; and in temples and occiput, extending to ears; and in vertex, in occiput running to nape and outward to ears, also in every bone of face, < through zygomatic arch.

Temples.—Neuralgic pains during the day; when walking in the wind; through l.; intermittent, through them during the day; in r., running through head to spine. Sharp pains through T. and r. side after retiring. Aching; through l.; and in zygoma, malar and nasal bones; beginning after breakfast, and in upper part of forehead, but at times in the whole brain; vague, in r.; through r. running down spine; through r., extending to occiput, with heat on vertex; occasional, when of brief duration neuralgic, when longer lasting, a dull ache which gradually wore away; heavy, beginning over r., gradually spreading over whole r. side, with weight on vertex, it hurts to move the head, shattered, confused feeling in head, congested feeling, as if all the blood were in the head and face, at times shooting from temple to temple.

Vertex.—Pain; in morning, < motion, walking or stooping, > eating, sharp pain at a central point within brain, also through forehead and temples, with dragging and at times sharp pain in occiput extending to between inferior angles of scapulæ. Weight; at 12.30 P.M.; as if skull rested on brain; preventing sitting.

Sides.—Pain in l.; now in l., then in r., then in forehead, in afternoon and evening, finally confined to a space in front of l. parietal eminence; tired, in base of brain on l. in afternoon; half dizzy, in r. after eating.

Occiput.—Pain. Pulsations at 3 P.M., with strong throbbing in carotids and dazed feeling in head.

Scalp.—Sore to touch. Itching.

Clinical.—Neuralgic headaches beginning over r. eye and extending through r. side of head.

Eyes.—Dull, and pupils contracted. Feeling as if full of sticks. Strained feeling. Feel hot, sore, it hurts to move them. Feel weak. Feel badly, desire to keep them closed. Tears roll down cheeks. Heaviness, no power over upper lids. Sensitive to light.

Ears and Nose.—Ears felt as if filled with compressed air. Dryness of nasal mucous membrane every evening; at night, with chapping of epidermis; and of cuticle. Constant flow of nasal mucus. Sneezing; violent, at 8 P.M.

Clinical.—Post-nasal catarrh, constant hawking, trickling of mucus down throat.

Face.—Pale, sallow; pale all day, with dark circles under eyes. Red, with dark circles under eyes; r. cheek red, l. pale, with dark circles under eyes; with congestion of blood to head. Feels tired. Tingling in zygoma, then dull pain creeping through it, then pain in temples, finally pain in occiput, vertex and upper part of forehead, and this lasted through the day. Tingling numbness in zygoma.

Mouth.—Arterial pulsation in r. teeth on ascending stairs. Tongue white; coated white, taste bitter; coated yellow; coated yellow at base, papillæ raised and bright pink anteriorly, also with bitter or bloody taste. Salivation. Taste bitter; in afternoon; later unclean; T. foul after eating an apple in forenoon, lasting all day; T. bad; insipid.

Throat.—Tough white mucus, hard to remove, feeling as if throat were full, and would suffocate unless mucus were removed. Stinging from swallowing the drug. Smarting, sore feeling. Tingling.

Stomach.—Excessive hunger; but satisfied with a reasonable amount of food; almost to faintness, sometimes before meals, especially dinner; sudden H. before meals. Appetite lost; for breakfast; but stomach feels empty, craves acids. Aversion to bread. No thirst; with the fever. Nausea. Pain in S. and upper part of abdomen in evening, > pressure. Pressure in epigastrium, with needle-like pains. Empty feeling about 10 A.M., then faint feeling. Feels collapsed. Symptoms > after breakfast, still hardly able to hold head up or to sit up.

Clinical.—Persistent bilious vomiting, preceded by a chill, associated with vertigo. In a case of cirrhotic liver it relieved the vomiting, etc.

Abdomen.—Bloated around the waist, < r. side. Rumbling and uneasiness. Occasional shooting through A. and chest; through A. during the day. Sharp fleeting pains through A. and chest; at intervals; through A. during the day. Pain every few minutes all night, with restlessness, tired feeling, a long night; P. for a few minutes at a time, causing a faint, sinking feeling; sudden fleeting in A. and chest during the day. Bruised feeling and trembling; B. feeling, must hold on to it when walking or coughing. Pain in side opposite to the one lain upon, > pressure; in l. hypochondrium when walking, also stitches at night in bed; fleeting, in hypogastrium, with pressure and fulness in vagina; sharp fleeting, through hypogastrium, < region of ovaries and uterus, with heavy, pressing feeling in vagina.

Anus and Stool.—Itching at anus, with smarting. Diarrhœa early in morning. Frequent diarrhœa all day, with pain; F. at night; at night, with faintness during and after stools; painless. Stools milky-white, sometimes like half-beaten eggs; and before the stool pain more in large intestines, but at times radiating to every part, causing a faint sinking sensation, diarrhœa < after 1 P.M. Constipation.

Urinary Organs.—Frequent anxious desire to urinate. Urine copious; scanty, with brick-dust sediment; thick.

Sexual Organs.—Fulness in vagina when standing; when walking. Weight in vagina, > continued motion. Menses too early; and profuse; every three weeks, preceded by weak feeling, bearing-down pain in pelvic organs, with frequent micturition, flow lasted three days, dark, scanty, with bearing-down pains, with occasional griping in r. ovary, weakness, restlessness, tired feeling, head symptoms and depression of mind, in another proving the same, with severe pain in lumbar and sacral spine, running down thighs, with weight on vertex, loss of appetite, nausea, giddiness.

Clinical.—Ulceration of the uterus, the discharge ichorous, corroding, fetid, with hæmorrhoidal fissures and general appearance of scirrhous cachexia, with aching in all limbs and numerous symptoms.

Respiratory Organs.—Hoarseness, almost aphonia. Smarting way down in bronchia. Bronchial tubes sore, inflamed. Cough in afternoon and evening; C. jarring the head; dry, hard; dry, hacking, causing shattered sensation in head; dry, harsh, hollow, shaking the whole body, < head, < after 3 P.M. till midnight, and lungs feel dry; dry, harsh, hollow, paroxysmal, from irritation at base of lungs, causing a shattered, torn feeling in head and redness of face, no expectoration; paroxysmal, in afternoon and evening, causing shattered, torn feeling in head. Dyspnœa, with pain about heart; D. from exercise, with distress, almost amounting to pain, in præcordial region. Difficulty in breathing after ascending stairs. Short breath; on slight exertion. *Sighing.*

Clinical.—Dyspnœa of emphysema, exceedingly distressing.

Chest.—Stitches through middle of C. and about heart in morning after waking; S. on ascending a hill, with palpitation and breathlessness; about middle and lower part of sternum, later from behind sternum through whole lower part of chest. Darting pains through it; in evening, now through base, then through apex; through lungs. Sharp pain two inches to left of sternum, extending from second to fifth intercostal space, at night. Pain through r. lower side in afternoon; at base before breakfast, with pressure; P. when walking fast; when ascending stairs, stooping or leaning forward, with difficulty in breathing. Lungs feel raw. Lungs feel sore. Constriction; of lungs. Fluttering several times during the day. Lungs feel dry. Lungs feel as if I had taken cold.

Heart.—Sudden intermittent sharp pain in region. Strange sensation, not real pain, yet causing faint feeling, after retiring. Semi-conscious of action, also of arterial pulsations in r. middle ear and in other places, in evening, only needed to think of any point to be conscious of pulsations there. Palpitation; from a little excitement; on walking; when walking a little hurriedly; when walking in the street and on first going into open air; on ascending stairs; on ascending stairs, with difficulty in breathing.

Pulse.—Rapid; and temperature high. Strong. Slow and almost imperceptible; S., weak and lagging; some beats not as full as others; and intermittent; and I could count two beats, then a pause, three beats, then a pause, eight beats and a pause, then two and a pause, etc.

Neck and Back.—Pain in region of seventh cervical vertebra after a walk; drawing, in nape. Sensation as if atlas and axis had been pried apart, on rising to the feet it changed to a sharp pain. Pulsation extending from neck along spine to lumbar region in afternoon when sitting. Weakness of back; all day; all day, with lameness of it and aching at lower third of scapulæ; of B. and hips all day, with lameness; when stooping, with lameness. Pain extending down spine; P. between scapulæ. Bruised feeling in l. loin.

Extremities.—Unsteady feeling on walking, gait as if intoxicated. Weakness, and in joints; W., < lower; with heaviness; with inability to walk straight, giddiness, knees feel weak. Go to sleep. Arms weak; < r.; in evening, with tingling; r., with numbness. Heavy, nervous, uneasy feeling in arms, with weakness of wrists. Sore spots in flexors of l. forearm, preventing a firm grasp. Lame spots in flexors of l. forearm in afternoon and evening. Lower limbs have no strength when walking, with trembling feeling; weak feeling in muscles on ascending stairs. Bruised feeling in muscles of l. thigh. Sore spot in flexors of r. thigh all day; muscles of l. thigh sore to touch; l. knee sore to touch in afternoon and evening. Legs lame when stepping up or down. Tenderness of feet in evening; T. of callosities of feet; of callosities of l. foot. Feet feel nervous. L. foot and limb go to sleep when sitting still.

Skin.—Rhagades above ankles. Chapped; above ankles. Itching; on various parts; < night; on head and back; arms; arms and thighs, extending over abdomen; arms and thighs, < after waking in morning and after 3 P.M.; lower limbs; thighs; sole.

Clinical.—Liver spots.

Sleep.—Yawning. Sleepiness; nearly all day, with stupidity, head feels tired and dull; slept in a chair at 9 A.M. while trying to study; at 1 P.M., inability to keep eyes open, yawning; had to take a nap at 2 P.M.; at 3 P.M., and deep sleep for two hours. Shortly after retiring the thoughts were suddenly interrupted by a rush of disconnected ideas, which could not be controlled by the will. Sleepless the first part of the night; and waking every morning about 4 A.M.; till midnight, and waking at 4 A.M.; till after midnight, and waking every morning at 3 or 4 A.M. Frequent waking, with a disturbed feeling; F. waking, feeling as if some one were trying to rouse me. Woke in morning unrefreshed. Restless sleep; after midnight; and head felt hot and confused. Uneasy dreams all night; laborious dreams.

Fever.—Chilliness, chills running up back, chattering of teeth, then heat and congestion of blood to head; C. of feet at 6.30 P.M., chattering of teeth, chills running up back and then extending to extremities, chill came on after eating, lasted half an hour, then high fever, face almost purple, eyes red, cannot keep them open, lids hot, eyes sensitive to light. Cold hands and feet, all the blood seems to be in the head. Fever until nearly midnight. Heat in cervical region; between scapulæ. Burning on l. thigh, then itching in evening; B. in a spot on ball of each foot; in a spot in each sole, < l.; in a spot on l. sole in morning; in a spot on each sole when shoes were removed; in feet on removing shoes, with itching. Sweat over the whole body.

Clinical.—Pernicious fevers, with continued chilliness.

Cyclamen.

A tincture is made from the fresh root of Cyclamen Europæum, L.

General Action.—The symptoms seem to group themselves about the functions of digestion and menstruation.

Allies.—Lyc., Puls., Carbo v., Cham., Coccul.

Generalities.—Drawing or tearing pains, < motion, in various parts where the bones are immediately covered by skin, as, for example, on tibiæ and calves. Boring in r. metatarsal bones and in r. temple, then extending into r. upper teeth, and, after leaning on l. temple, extending into this also. Paralytic pressure on chest when sitting still and in upper arm and tibia. General discomfort. *Uneasiness at night.* Constant desire to lie down, in a child.

Weakness; in morning; on waking; in evening; in evening, with sleepiness and frequent yawning; in evening, with shortness of breath; in evening, but on rising after a nap bruised and stiff feeling in limbs and drawing pains in thighs and knees; *on waking, also with clammy mouth and irritable mood;* on waking, with fretfulness, confusion of head and pasty taste; after eating; after dinner, after midday nap, with tension in abdomen, passage of flatus up and down, profuse micturition, with dragging in bladder and rectum, heat in head and shivering in back; when moving, but on sitting itching and other symptoms towards evening; *with pallor, sunken eyes and rapid pulse;* with profuse sweat; with disinclination to work. General depression, with weariness of feet, sleepiness and frequent yawning. Sudden faintness as if everything turned in a circle, with blackness before eyes, then violent vomiting. Heaviness of body and weariness of knees; H. of body in morning on waking, with pasty mouth, hot head, pressure in stomach and passage of flatus upward and downward.

Mind.—*Ill humor;* with sleepiness of mind and weakness of body, the latter > on moving about; with disinclination to speak and little feeling in the body; with sadness, no desire to work and anxiety as if some misfortune were impending; then sudden joy, which he expresses by quivering of joints; alternating with liveliness. Anxiety. Apprehension. Sadness as if he had committed some evil and had not done his duty. Melancholy, complaints about her weeping mood (Puls.). Profound reflection concerning, the present and future, almost to weeping. Sudden joy towards evening. Absorbed in himself and disinclined to talk; A. in thought, desires to be alone and thinks especially about his future state. Paroxysmal disinclination to talk. *Disinclination to work,* lasting till evening; D. to work, alternating with great desire therefor. Dulness. Stupefaction, inability to rejoice or to be sad, although he feels as if he had just been afflicted, his mind is only somewhat clearer when he is excited, and he then acts as if just awakened, having only half understood what was going on. Memory weak; he easily misplaces words; alternating with great activity.

Clinical.—Symptoms of depression, with weeping and desire to be alone, in suppressed menstruation.

Head.—Sticking, > appearance of menses, with weakness; S. in brain on stooping. *Aching;* in morning; **in morning on rising, with flickering before eyes**; in afternoon, with vertigo; in evening; in evening on going to sleep; all night; with nausea; with weakness and nauseous taste; stupefying. *Oppressive stupefaction, with obscuration of vision and sensation as if eyes were about to close. Confusion; in evening, with vertigo,* as if objects were wavering, stupidity, heat of head, red cheeks, glistening eyes, alternations of heat and chill, full, hard, rapid pulse, finally nausea and watery diarrhœa preceded by rumbling and colic; after breakfast, with salivation, eructations and pressure in stomach; > cold applications to forehead, with other symptoms of head; *with obscured vision;* with roaring in ears; with warmth.

Emptiness changing to prickling in scalp and skin of face. Feeling as if bound. Heaviness. Dizzy fulness, with heat of it. Pulsations in brain in evening in bed, with late falling asleep. Congestion. *Rush of blood,* with headache, anxiety and dim vision. **Vertigo**; all the afternoon; towards evening; *towards evening, with pain in forehead;* < walking; with dim vision; periodic, with general sick feeling, disordered appetite and fulness in stomach; as if descending a mountain; as if objects wavered; as if all objects turned in a circle, and on lying down frequent eructations; as if objects were turning in a circle, < motion in open air, > in the room and when sitting; as if the brain were moving in the head or as if he were riding in a wagon with his eyes closed, on leaning against anything when standing. Sensation as if the body were turning around, and darkness before eyes.

Forehead.—Contraction of muscles as in anger. Sticking; in r. and in temple; in forepart of brain on stooping; jerking, in r., extending to face, < motion. Sudden tearing in r. bone. *Pain;* making night uneasy; drawing from r. side to l., then back into r. side, then in l. temple, > after touch. Stupefying pain, in r., then nausea and eructations. Confusion; of l. gradually extending over whole head, with prickling in scalp; in sinciput, with heat of it; in sinciput, with itching of scalp.

Temples.—Sticking in r.; in l., then in sinciput, with vertigo, then pressure in forehead; outward in bones; jerking, in l., then r.; drawing, in l., > touch. Pain; in l.; in l., with heat of head, then confusion of r. side of head; contractive, and emptiness; jerking and drawing pain towards vertex, with confusion of head, < forehead, and stiffness of nape.

Sticking on sides, < along coronal sutures. Sudden boring in l. parietal bone. Sticking in coronal suture; with pulsations in temporal arteries; in r., preceded by pressure. Pain in middle of vertex, at times causing vertigo; in vertex as if the brain were bound with a cloth and as if he were thereby deprived of his senses. Pain in occiput; painful drawing in brain, in a line from l. side of occiput through l. temple. Tearing externally. Pimples on occiput. *Itching sticking, changing its place on scratching.* Itching.

Clinical.—In menstrual derangements, vertigo, with headache, nausea and vomiting. Vertigo in gastric derangements, things turn in a circle, > in the room, < open air (Coccul., Nux v.), (the opposite of Pul.). Periodic headache on one side, with debility, in an anæmic patient. The headaches of Cyclamen are apt to be associated with menstrual disturbances, or with anæmia, indigestion, etc.

Eyes.—Sunken and dull-looking; S. and surrounded by blue rings. Glittering. Burning, < reading; *on reading in evening in bed, with flickering of the light*; of r. Sticking itching of E. and lids. *Pupils dilated;* < r.; alternately D. and contracted, finally contracted; alternately D. and contracted, dependent on respiration, occurring after inspiration or expiration, prover seemed able to see the fibres of the iris as through a magnifying-glass. Pupils contracted. Sticking in r. ball and lid. Vessels visible in whites, < l.

Lids.—*Swelling of upper.* Contraction as from a strong light. Blinking; on slightest pressure or rubbing; of r. upper. Vibration of r. upper on rubbing eye or forehead. Pressure upon, on frequent waking at night; P. as if agglutinated; P. in l. canthus; l. inner canthus. Dryness and pressure as if swollen, with itching sticking in them and in balls. Itching; in r. inner canthus.

Vision dim; < on waking, with spots before eyes; *in afternoon, so that she could not knit.* **Flickering,** *of various colors, glittering needles, vision of smoke* (comp. Lyc.); *F., with confusion of head;* beginning with headache, < r. eye, but lasting longer in l., with inability to read, the light appeared like a luminous ball, also with open as well as closed eyes, vision of a dark disc frequently pierced by lightnings, afterwards he saw with l. eye as through a dark blue glass. More acute than usual. *Double.* Rings around the light, so that she must stop embroidering on white. *Vision of colors;* yellow, at other times green; at times yellow, at times black.

Clinical.—The visual disturbances of flickering obscuration, etc., particularly associated with disturbances of the female functions and of digestion. Convergent strabismus.

Ears.—Tearing in inner passages of l. *Drawing pain in inner passages of r.*, hearing less distinct in this ear. Itching, with removal of much wax. Stopped feeling in r. Ringing; < night, with sticking and headache. *Roaring;* on walking a long time.

Nose.—Pain across bones in evening. Dryness. Coryza, with frequent sneezing; fluent C.; sudden fluent C., causing febrile excitement; sudden discharge of much watery mucus several times at night, without sneezing. Frequent slight bleeding. *Sneezing;* violent, with itching of ear and much ear-wax. *Smell diminished.*

Face.—Red cheeks. Itching sticking in r. cheek, then burning. Biting together of jaws. Tearing in l. joint of jaw; T. in r. upper jaw and in crown of r. eye-tooth. Lips numb or feeling as if indurated. Dry lips without thirst.

Mouth.—Sticking in last upper hollow molar. Tearing in l. upper teeth; in three l. back T., as if they would be torn out. Jerking through upper T.; tearing, sticking J. in two first r. upper molars. Pain in r. lower T.; sore P. in r. upper incisors, < crowns, extending into walls of mouth. Tongue white; yellowish-white; T. coated; coated white; tip red, burning, covered with yellow blisters; tip red, burning, covered with blisters, with pain on speaking or chewing, and with salivation; sticking; burning in l. side, with sticking; burning in tip in evening. Pale M. and fauces in morning. Much mucus. Rough, slimy sensation. Palate feels swollen. Dryness of palate in evening, with thirst and hunger. **Saliva has a salt taste, which is communicated to all he takes.** *Salivation; with pasty taste;* with frequent hawking; frequent S., with incomplete eructations tasting of food. **Salt taste to food;** T. flat; *flat to food and almost wanting;* bitter T.; nauseous T.; sudden nauseous.

Throat.—Drawing pain in submaxillary glands on bending neck forward. Fauces red; and painful on swallowing, with much tough mucus. Uvula and tonsils contracted and white. Much hawking. Scraping in fauces; frequently, with pain on swallowing; burning S. Sudden sore pain. Drawing-bruised pain deep in muscles, extending internally down œsophagus and causing tension in it. Jerks in evening, with pain. Constriction. Burning.

Stomach.—Appetite great; alternating with loss of A.; unnatural, then at times lost; *diminished;* D. at dinner, then constant empty eructations; *lost; L.* especially *for breakfast and supper, at these times satiety, as soon as he begins to eat. Aversion to bread and butter*, warm food goes down more easily. Thirst; at night; after eating; great during dinner; **no T. all day,** *but it occurs in evening as face and hands become warm; absent,* then greater at times than in health. Aversion to beer.

Eructations; after breakfast, which consisted of a cup of coffee; in evening after eating, always ending in hiccough, wherewith rancid fluid rises into throat; *sour;* empty after eating; empty, burning and rancid; of a fatty smell; *with oppression of stomach.* Hiccough; *after eating; when eating and afterwards, or hiccough-like eructations.*

Nausea; towards morning; at night; in morning after the accustomed smoke, with fulness of chest and unusual hunger; in afternoon; towards evening, with vertigo, weakness and ill humor; after a cup of coffee in evening that was not relished, with sour eructations; after the breakfast that was not relished, with vomiting; *after dinner and supper, with uneasiness and qualmishness in epigastric region as after eating too much fat* (Puls.); *in throat and palate on eating a little;* caused by everything but lemonade; with waterbrash; with headache; with diarrhœa.

Vomiting; at night, with diarrhœa; then vertigo, dim vision and frontal headache; violent, then sleepiness; of a greenish liquid; of mucus; of food and mucus, with vertigo; of mucus, then uneasy sleep interrupted by starting up and unpleasant dreams; of watery mucus, then vertigo, so that she must lie down. Distention; with rumbling in hepatic region; and of abdomen, with eructations, especially D., like a ball beneath liver, with crawling as from something living in abdomen, on rubbing the crawling changed into the breast, and it felt as if air streamed out of nipples. Fulness as if overloaded, and six hours after eating incomplete eructations tasting of food. Sticking; in epigastric region. Pain; in epigastric region; in pit; in pit, and fulness as if overloaded; ending in eructations.

Clinical.—A general aggravation from fat food, like Puls., and many other symptoms similar to that drug, from which it is differentiated by its peculiar conditions.

Abdomen.—Distention (Lyc.); at night, with full feeling; by gas. Rumbling, with griping; R. after breakfast, with movings, then pain. Flatulence. Frequent emissions of flatus. Sticking; through A. on moving. Cutting, with pain in small of back. Griping at night; G., then diarrhœa twice. Gnawing as from a tape-worm, with sensation as from something living in it. Cramplike pain; in evening; with headache, < in forehead; sudden intermittent. Pain; in afternoon and night; on touch. Dragging, with increased warmth.

Sticking in hepatic region; beneath hepatic region. *Tearing, piercing through-and-through sticking beneath stomach, on moving about.* Griping in upper as before diarrhœa, then yellow soft stool, then griping, then constipation. Throbbing in upper. Paralytic pressive sensation in upper, as if part of the intestines were loose, with tensive sensation in neighboring parts. Tension in flanks. Sticking in umbilical region. Frequent griping in U. region, waking him at night, > pressure upon abdomen, disappearing after stool. Deceptive distended sensation in r. side beneath umbilicus.

Lower.—*Rumbling after eating* (Lyc.); R. after emission of flatus. Sticking in l. inguinal canal in evening. Jerking cutting along inguinal canal; sudden intermittent pinching cutting in lower A. Pinching; and pressure inward. Pain on touch, with sometimes pressive, sometimes griping pain, at other times a mixture of the two. Tension in inguinal region after midday nap. *Discomfort, with nausea in it.*

Rectum and Anus.—Sticking in R.; in A. in evening. Drawing pain in and about anus and in perineum, as if suppurating, when walking and sitting. Heat in R., with pressure and with swelling of hæmorrhoidal vessels. Urging to stool; which was thin, with burning and straining, then streaks of blood; ineffectual, after a normal stool.

Stool.—Fluid, with frequent rumbling and passage of flatus. Thin, light yellow. Diarrhœa; *after every cup of coffee;* sudden. Slimy, which afterwards is passed unnoticed. Pasty. Hard and frequent; in hard masses; compact, with burning in rectum. Constipated. Odorless, brownish-yellow and mixed with mucus. Shooting out, at first crumbly, then soft, with palpitation. With great urging and drops of blood. Delayed. Twice a day. Absent.

Urinary Organs.—Pain going from bladder to urethra in evening when urinating. Pressure on bladder and rectum after midday nap, with frequent urging to urinate, much urine and emission of much flatus; P. on bladder and rectum without frequent micturition or stool. Urging, with pressure in anus. Frequent urging; with scanty discharge. Frequent micturition after dinner; F., with dragging; F., with urging in bladder and rectum, with passage of flatus upward and downward; of much clear urine, also at night; of watery urine. Rare micturition; and urine scanty. Sticking in urethra; in forepart when urinating; with urging. Urine increased; and passing in a large stream; diminished; light, containing epithelial cells; dark, containing floating flakes; dark, reddish-yellow, discharged as if shot out all at once; much sediment, reaction acid, chlorides abundant.

Sexual Organs.—Prepuce retracted in open air. Frequent erections at night without dreams to cause them. Sore sensation in glans and prepuce in evening after slight rubbing. **Menses profuse, black and clotted** (Cham.), with labor pains and distention of abdomen, so that she could scarcely stoop; **black, clotted** *and membranous;* M. **too early** (Cham., Carbo v.), *relieving somewhat the heaviness of feet and melancholy;* M. preceded by pain in abdomen; omitted the second day.

Clinical.—Profuse frequent menstruation, which comes on too early, with labor-like pains extending from back to pubis. Suppressed menstruation with a great variety of symptoms of the head, eyes, stomach, anæmia, etc. (general dread of fresh air or with constant chilliness). Chlorosis, with scanty and suppressed menses, great dread of fresh air. Membranous dysmenorrhœa, with profuse flow.

Respiratory Organs.—Pain in larynx. Scraping in trachea in open air, with dryness, causing suffocative cough; sudden S. in larynx. Tickling in larynx, with scraping and with dry cough, lachrymation and watery salivation; T. in larynx, with dry cough; frequent sudden T. in larynx, with paroxysms of cough. Voice rough. Voice weak when reading, with hiccough *Cough, < during sleep, never caused by talking or walking, even against a cold wind; violent at night, with tickling in larynx; violent at night, with scraping in larynx, pain in fauces and thick mucus;* hacking. Much expectoration; E. in yellowish-white consistent lumps. Suffocation.

Chest.—Sticking in r. side; l.; about l. nipple at 4 P.M. when walking; in r. side above sixth rib in evening; l. side, < by inspiration; intermittent, in upper part of sternum; tearing, with dyspnœa and short breath; tearing, on last true ribs on bending forward. Pressure on sternum; in middle of S. in evening; in l. side, < about heart, as from too much blood, with palpitation. Tightness in morning. Oppression, with difficult respiration. Fluttering in l. side. Burning in l. Mammæ feel larger than usual, sticking and tensive pains in them, glands hard and painful, flow of watery milk from nipples, the milk left a starchlike spot on the linen, as this fluid appeared the symptoms of the breast disappeared. Feeling as if air streamed out of breasts, with swelling and painfulness of them and discharge of watery, milky fluid.

Heart and Pulse.—Sticking in præcordial region at night on waking; S. in region of apex. Heart's action excited, fluttering in region. *Palpitation* in evening. Heart's beat and pulse scarcely perceptible. Pulse full. Pulse rapid and respiration somewhat accelerated; P. rapid, but respiration quiet; R., hard and full; R., scarcely perceptible.

Neck.—Rheumatic drawing in l. side on bending head backward. Drawing rheumatic pain in l. side in evening on moving head, with heat in muscles of neck and in l. ear. Paralytic pain in nape, > on bending head backward. Smarting sore sensation internally and externally in nape.

Back.—Drawings down spine, > throwing shoulders backward, < throwing shoulders forward. Tearing across scapulæ, with sticking and paralytic pain in arm. Sore pain in region of l. acromium, < taking off overcoat. Sticking in region of l. false ribs when sitting, > touch. Periodic deeply-piercing, griping sticking on r. side near spine, between os innominatum and last rib, < during inspiration, which is impeded by the pain. Pressure in region of lumbar vertebræ, at times < stooping, at times < pressure. Drawing on small of; D. pain. Tension in lumbar region.

Extremities.—Stretching as before paroxysms of fever. Trembling of hands and feet. Pain in joints on motion. Fatigue as if their mobility were impaired. Heaviness, < arms and hands, so that objects easily drop.

Upper Extremities.—Heaviness. Sprained pain in shoulder-joint. *Paralyzed, hard pressure in r. upper arm and forearm, in periosteum and deep in muscles, extending to fingers and preventing writing.* Drawing in l. arm, extending into fingers. Tearing in elbow and wrist. Bruised pain in l. elbow; B. pain across outer side of elbow, < moving arm and on touch. Pain in r. elbow, > morning after rising, returned in forenoon, gradually extended to shoulder and fingers, < forearm, > moving arm or changing position, returned on keeping arm quiet, the pain returned on going to bed.

Sticking in muscles of r. forearm. Tearing in l. forearm; in periosteum of l. radius near to and in wrist. *Paralytic, hard pressure extending to fingers, where it is so violent that writing is difficult. Painful drawings in inner surface of shaft of ulna, and in wrist.* Bruised pain in r. forearm, extending from elbow to fingers, painful on motion, waking him, > towards morning. Swelling of veins on back of hands in evening. Aching on back of l. hand. Feeling as if everything would fall from hands. Numbness of r. hand. Cramplike, slow flexion of r. thumb and index, the tips approach each other and have to be forcibly extended. Tearing in periosteum of little, middle and ring fingers.

Lower Extremities.—Tearing on outer side of r. thigh in evening. *Cramplike pain above r. popliteus.* Rheumatic drawings in l. gluteus maximus, along its attachment to ilium, towards sacrum, when sitting, > standing. Weakness of thighs and legs, on long standing they sway to and fro. Sprained pain in l. knee-cap. Bruised pain in l. knee; when walking, or fatigued pain; B. pain, now in one, now in other knee, > on motion. Drawing pain in l. knee-cap; in r. knee, in acromium and cap; in bends when standing; in bend of r., becoming a drawing; in flexor muscles, extending to tips of toes, < l. leg. Tensive drawing in tendons of knees when sitting and standing. Weakness of knees. Twitching internally beneath l. knee. Sticking in muscles of r. calf. Tearing in l. leg. Tearing paralytic pain in tibiæ on motion, with weakness and unsteadiness of knees. Drawing in l. leg. Drawing pressure in tibiæ, appearing when sitting, and disappearing when walking, or *vice versa*, but more painful when sitting.

Sprained pain in ankle on stepping; when walking and standing, > sitting down. Cutting behind l. inner malleolus when walking. *Sprained pain* in l. foot; *in r.*, > touch and when walking; in foot when walking; when sitting and standing, < walking, < near heel and in ankles. Drawing pressure on back of foot when sitting, > standing. Sore pain in heels, preventing walking; burning sore P. in heels, < walking in open air. Weakness of feet. Heaviness of feet; paralytic, making walking difficult. Dead feeling in feet at toes after walking, and when walking sore pain, < jumping. Pulsating tearing on lower surface of r. toes. Pressure on l. great T.; drawing P. on great; drawing P. outward in periosteum of l. little. Drawing in l. great T.; D. inward where the l. great T. unites with metatarsal bone.

Skin.—Red spots on thighs like burns; R. spots on face, < forehead, with pustules. The almost imperceptible scars of smallpox became distinct and dark red, and the forehead was covered with similar spots. Pimples on forehead; on scalp, face and rest of skin; heat P. on r. chest; itching P. on parotid gland; speedily filling with white lymph, on face, also with whitish-yellow lymph. Sensation as if a large animal were running over her body. Prickling and sticking in evening in bed, causing scratching.

Itching on lower jaw; scalp, neck, shoulders and below axillæ; in region of l. inguinal canal; on elbows; on calf; on r. calf in morning, with swelling of veins extending to foot, so that he scratches till it bleeds; of r. calf in evening, so that he scratches till it bleeds, which causes burning pain; in evening, not only in skin, but apparently in bones of l. toes; on back of r. great toe, after scratching itching white pustules, the I. > rubbing until the toe is sore; on middle joint of l. little finger, then red vesicles; then a red pimple on metacarpal joint of ring finger, soon becoming white as from a blister, surrounded by a red areola. Sticking itching in all parts in evening in bed; sudden S. itching between fingers; sudden S. itching above ankles and on toes, now better, now worse, then warmth alternating with numbness of skin; stitching itching in various parts in forenoon, changing to drawing and tearing pain; sudden throbbing S. itching in various parts, then numbness. Itching gnawing in various parts, > for a time by scratching.

Sleep.—Yawning; frequent. Sleepiness in forenoon; at noon after eating, with weariness; in afternoon, with fretfulness; in evening, with deep sleep at night and lascivious dreams (after a cup of tea, with four teaspoonfuls of rum); after eating; when sitting; irresistible in evening, also with chilliness. Early sleep and confused dreams. *Sleeps longer than usual in morning.* Sound sleep, with indistinct, frightful dreams; S. sleep, with confused, unremembered dreams.

Sleeplessness; with thirst, heat and headache. Late falling asleep and frequent waking; late falling asleep, much dreaming and frequent sudden waking, fully awake at 4 A.M., but sleep again about 6.30, with no desire to rise. Starting from sleep. *Restless sleep; interrupted by dreams;* with frequent crying out; with frequent starting in fright, caused by dreams, then weariness in morning on waking; with dreams of money; with confused dreams, though he went to bed after midnight; and disturbed by frequent attacks of anxiety and nausea. Frequent waking. Waking early, with inability to sleep again, and when he wishes to rise inability to do so from weakness and sleepiness. Sleep interrupted and towards morning many dreams, with an emission. Unpleasant dreams; frightful, in evening. Nightmare in evening as soon as he fell asleep, inability to cry out though he woke.

Fever.—Coldness; all the forenoon, after the usual warmth begins the nose is still cold, but as this becomes warm the hands become cold; general, after midday nap, with heat in head, tension about flanks, pressure and heat in rectum, with swelling of hæmorrhoidal vessels, flatulence, prostration and ill humor; towards evening, with sensitiveness to cold, then heat in different parts, on backs of hands and on nape, but not on face; towards evening, without thirst, with sensitiveness to cold, which causes sudden shuddering, then heat of certain parts, with anxiety as if some evil were impending; after eating; after dinner, with congestion to brain; after a feverish attack and paroxysms of heat and throbbing in head; then general heat, < of face, with redness that was < after eating, without thirst.

Coldness of cheeks, with internal and external heat of hands and swelling of veins. Coldness in back after midday nap, with tension of abdomen, passage of flatus up and down; C. over back after midday nap, with heat in head and eyes, frequent urging to urinate and pressure in rectum; C. over back after eating, with pressure upon bladder. Cold hands in morning; C. limbs till midnight, with heat in face, causing restless sleep. Chill alternating with heat; then profuse sweat. General shivering in morning, with yawning, but without coldness or gooseflesh; shivering in open air; sudden S. in evening; sudden shaking chill at 8.30 P.M., then a sleepless night, with heat, fever lasted next day, with headache through afternoon, in evening again fever lasting till 2 A.M., when he first fell asleep.

Heat; at night, preventing sleep; during restless sleep, also with sweat. Internal; in morning. In head; in morning on waking, with pressure in forehead; in morning, < forehead, with pressure in temporal region; towards evening; with confusion; in r. side, with fulness; and in abdomen; rising into head in bed, with sensation as if head were turning about; rising into head and lasting till evening; rising into H., with sweat; and towards evening cold shivering, then palpitation. In various parts, hands, nape, neck below jaw, and after an hour dryness of palate with thirst. In whole l. leg in evening, with drawing pain in it when sitting. Sweat at night; every time on waking; S. on waking, burning in face, without redness; offensive S. between l. toes.

Datura Ferox.

Datura ferox, from India. Symptoms from numerous cases of poisoning. Compare Stramonium.

Symptoms on an average continued twenty-four hours, then usually recovery with the return of mental sensibility, on the second day contraction of pupil and in many cases an attack of fever, but in the fatal cases the tympanitis of abdomen increased, coma set in with stertorous breathing, pulse weak, at last imperceptible, cold perspiration over whole body, death. Distressed appearance and did not like to be touched.

Raving. Out of her mind, dizzy and sleepy, at last sleep, in which the eyes were more or less open, if disturbed she sprang up raving and uttered unintelligible words, and if one sang she began to dance in the Japanese fashion. Delirium, characterized by incoherent talk and by peculiar movements of hands, as if to pick up something from the ground or moving away from an imaginary thing in the air. Tried to escape whenever held, and shouted loudly and attempted to strike and kick when caught. If left alone they lay on the ground curled up, with legs drawn up on abdomen and chest bent forward, groaned incessantly but did not speak nor answer. Whenever they said anything it was with reluctance. In boys a tendency to run away. Considerable strength, eight or ten persons were required to hold a patient when the stomach pump was used. Two brothers of 50 and 55 years wrestled with each other when alone in a room.

Pupils always dilated and insensible to light, and in extreme cases ball insensible to touch. Conjunctivæ clear or pale bluish for the first twelve hours, became bloodshot afterwards and remained so for nearly twenty-four hours. Sight could not be fixed on any object and lids were mostly kept closed. In almost all cases the lips, inside of mouth, and throat were dry. Tongue dry, with thick fur, causing difficulty in swallowing and hoarseness. Stomach and bowels generally found loaded. Sour smell from mouth due to undigested food in stomach. Vomiting took place of itself in one case only. Tympanitis. In one case, which died on the seventh day, symptoms of enteritis, fever and constant discharge of muco-sanguineous stool, peculiar, hoarse, feeble and hesitating speech, though answers were rational and senses perfect, rapid loss of flesh, no appetite, the day before death tetanic spasms, mostly in legs. Bowels in general costive, and they took a long time to move, even with purgatives, in a few cases looseness of bowels followed after they were once opened, and one man died of enteritis, discharging blood and mucus. Answers in an undertone when recovering; answers shortly and quickly and suddenly appears to lose the string of thought, looks in another direction and wanders away as if thinking of something else. Pulse slow and full.

Digitalis.

A tincture is made of the leaves (of the second year) of Digitalis purpurea, L.

General Action.—The chief interest centres in its action on the circulation, which it seems to affect through the vaso-motor centres. It slows the pulse, increasing arterial tension and causing contraction of arterioles. Its action on the heart is remarkable in that it produces vigorous systolic contractions which become very irregular, one portion of the ventricle dilating while another remains in a state of contraction; finally the heart stops in systole. Its actions on the urinary secretion is uncertain and variable, but it is a valuable remedy (at least a palliative) in some forms of dropsy, with a weak heart.

Allies.—Apocynum c., Tabac., Hell., China, Ferr Bry., the Alkalies (Calc., Kali, Bar.), Zinc.

Generalities.—Lay on back prostrated, scarcely able to move a limb; lay supine in morning, *cold, pale and covered with profuse sweat. Could not bear the upright position.* Falling senseless. Tense white swelling of whole body, with pain on touch, afterwards becoming soft and changing to anasarca. Wasting of body in proportion to recuperation of mind. *Convulsions.* Epileptic attack. Cramps. Stiffening of body; painful S. of trunk and limbs, < thighs. Universal and partial trembling. Symptoms of inflammation of gastro-intestinal mucous membrane as well as of brain. Tearing burning and itching sticking in various parts. Feeling as if electrized on every inspiration. Bruised feeling. Malaise. *Restlessness.* Lightness of body. Relaxation of all muscles, with sensation as if he had not slept enough. **Weakness**; *in morning on waking* (Calc. c.), < **rising** (China); with trembling of muscles; *sudden, with sweat;* sudden, after dinner, as if he would lose consciousness, with heat and sweat. **Faintness**; between attacks of nausea; and nausea on motion. Heaviness.

Clinical.—Post-scarlatinal dropsy, urine frequently scanty and dark, extremities œdematous, dyspnœa, œdema of lungs, etc.

Mind.—Delirium; at night, with agitation; violent, at night; secretive insanity, with disobedience, obstinacy and attempts to escape. Lively fancies. Gayety bordering on intoxication, with debility. **Anxiety** (Calc. c., Ars., Bry., etc.); < *about* 6 P.M., *with dread of the future,* > weeping; as if he had committed a crime or expected to be reproved. *Fear of death. Apprehension;* < *music, with depression;* with sighing; as if rising from upper abdomen. Anger at everything. Ill humor. Sadness; and weeping about disappointments; and all objects appear as to one sick with fever. Continual complaints. Disinclination to talk. Desire to be alone. Indifference; as if he had not slept enough, without sleepiness. Great desire to work. Increased energy, especially of imagination. Weakness. Intellect destroyed. *Thought difficult, forgetfulness of everything,* with internal and external heat of head. Incapacity for study. Confusion of ideas. Inability to connect ideas. Dulness, < evening, with indifference; D. in evening, with uneasiness in various parts of head and weakness of forearms. Stupor. Coma; interrupted by convulsive attacks of vomiting. Unconsciousness in morning, then falling down in syncope.

Head.—*Falls backward when sitting and walking, as if anterior cervical muscles were paralyzed* (Tabac.). *Sudden cracking sound during midday nap, with starting up. Aching;* in morning; in morning on waking; in morning on waking, < afternoon and evening, unfitting him for work; in morning on stooping immediately after rising; in various bones; with heaviness as from rush of blood; with nausea; with cutting in abdomen, then warmth over whole body and pressure towards bladder. Drawing in bones. Weight: > forenoon by nosebleed. Pressure on spots. *Heaviness and confusion as if full;* H., < forehead, < walking, stooping or overheating, with confusion and pain. Dulness as if hypochondriac. *Confusion;* like intoxication; causing difficulty in thinking, gradually changing into pain; gradually becoming a pain, extending from vertex over whole head; changing into intermittent pressure in occiput, lasting till noon, with false vision.

Tension in evening, < forehead and l. temple. Congestion, with ringing and roaring in ears. Apoplexy. Sensation on bending head forward as if something in it fell forward. Intoxication. **Vertigo**; in morning, with heaviness; *when standing leaning against a chair, with anxiety as before faintness; on rising from a seat, with weakness of limbs;* after rising from a seat or bed (Bry., Phos., Cocc., Apoc. c.); so that he must fix his eyes upon some object; with inability to think; with dim vision, preventing descent of stairs.

Forehead.—Sticking in l.; externally. Sharp pain in spot over r. eye. Aching; in morning on waking, with nausea; in r. side in forenoon; in evening, with pressure on temples; < movement; in sinciput; over r. orbit; with fulness; with frequent uneasiness in region of heart; *throbbing,* or at bottom of orbits; contractive, in forepart and in temples, < thought. Weight; in middle of upper part on mental exertion; in sinciput, with heat. Confusion in sinciput. Tension on turning eyes to one side; T. in forepart.

Temples.—Sticking now in r., now in l.; in l., shooting through whole brain, in evening and at night in sleep; tearing, in l. Tearing in r. close to ear. Pain in r.; jerklike, now in temples, now in whole head.

Pain in vertex. Heaviness in vertex. Tearing in l. side of head. Stitchlike tension in a spot in parietal part of brain on stooping, extending into a l. upper tooth, > rising. Pressure in sides; with tension; jerklike P. in r.; one-sided P. like an internal itching; like the beating of waves against sides of skull, also < standing or bending backward, > lying or stooping. Drawing in sides causing vertigo. Sticking in occiput and vertex. Pain in occiput; l. half; extending from r. to l. side and from occiput to vertex, with confusion of head and incipient vertigo; in protuberance, as from a blow.

Clinical.—Cerebral meningitis, state of effusions, albuminous urine, slow or feeble and irregular pulse, cold sweat, etc. (differs from Hellebore only in the character of the pulse). A sudden crashing noise in the head, with frightened starting up, has led to the use of Dig. in periodical attacks of this sort occurring in the course of general nervous prostration or in threatening epilepsy.

Eyes.—Inflammation. Redness and sensitiveness to light; R., < in evening, with pain. Dimness and weakness. Both inclined to turn to l., with pain on turning them to r., when vision is double and triple, with puffy face (compare Gelsem.). Burning of r., then a pustule, with areola of inflamed vessels in periphery of cornea towards inner canthus. Lachrymation; < in the room, eyes dim, hot, full of red vessels, with pain and hardened mucus in canthi; biting. Pain in balls; on touch; sudden intermittent, in r. Conjunctiva anæmic; C. inflamed. *Pupils dilated;* < r.; *and insensible;* contracted; C., with stronger, clearer vision; alternately D. and C., *pupils only slightly sensitive.* Inflammation of Meibomian glands. Lids red. Swelling of lower lid. Agglutination in morning, then weakness of eyes. Sore pain in margins of lids in evening in bed on closing eyes. Scratching in inner canthus. Smarting burning in external canthi. Heaviness of lids in morning, with inability to hold them open. Sudden intermittent sticking tearing extending from r. brow into r. frontal region, at 1 P.M. Pain in r. superciliary ridge extending towards external canthus; burning pain in r. S. ridge, with dim vision. Throbbing pain in orbits.

Vision dim; and his own hands and another's face looked blue. Distorted in afternoon, with anxiety and pressure as from a finger upon eyes. Amblyopia or diplopia. Flickering (China); and double; before l. eye in morning and also in r. towards noon, so that he saw three varieties of figures, closing eye and rubbing it slowly caused clouds of phosphorescence, the eye sensitive to light, the form of the rose was the type of the flickering, in the first experiment there were round spots in the field of vision, the space circumscribed, four deep oval lines forming four convex indentations, and the waves of light and shade surrounding this showed the same form only less indented, the next two days the flickering figures were surrounded by curved lines with five indentations, but more superficial, which were again surrounded by enlarging waves of light and shade, with superficial indentations, afterwards when the flickering decreased there were only fragments with the rose formation on the side, like a segment of the larger and more superficially indented circle; F. before l. eye on winking and on looking from light to dark portion of field of vision, afterwards < before r. eye, there was in the middle of the field of vision an alternately appearing and disappearing roundish spot of light, and about this concentric waves of light and shade in similar motion, at last F. only on entering house after moderate exercise, on walking or ascending stairs. Hallucinations. Sparks; like lightning before r. eye at noon. Spots, stripes, white surfaces, waving before eyes. White spots and black rings waving before eyes. Vision of colors, red, green, yellow, like a shimmering light in the twilight. Objects seem green or yellow. The flame of a coal fire appeared blue. All objects appeared covered with snow in morning on waking. Blindness; sudden, as from going suddenly from the dark into the light, with vertigo, then floating sparks.

Clinical.—Detachment of the retina. Amaurotic symptoms and illusions seeming to result from disturbed circulation. Anæmia of retina and optic nerve.

Ears.—Painful swelling of glands behind E. Sticking behind E. Jerking in outer and middle. Drawing pain beneath r. mastoid process, > pressure. Tension in l. Constriction internally, he hears the pulse in them. Intermittent fulness as if suddenly stopped, < excitement, with flush of heat over face. Sudden obstruction of hearing, with ringing in ear. *Hissing, as of boiling water.* Ringing. Noises. Buzzing.

Nose.—Much sneezing without coryza; violent S., which seemed to start from orifice of stomach and rise as a nauseous sensation till it affected the nerves of sneezing, waking at night. Stopped coryza in morning; in evening and night, fluent during the day; fluent C., with much sneezing, then stoppage of nose; (C., with loss of smell, with catarrh of larynx and trachea and expectoration of greenish mucus without cough, sometimes with fever). Bright blood from both nostrils.

Face.—**Pale**; with greenish, livid tinge. Livid. Red and hot. Swelling of cheek from ear to corner of mouth, painful to touch, with eruption on it. *Sickly expression.* Convulsions of l. side. Cramp beneath r. zygoma on moving jaw, which on biting is drawn upward spasmodically. Cramplike drawing pain in zygoma, > pressure. Paralytic drawing beneath l. zygoma, in front of ear. Sticking in lower jaw. Lips anæmic. Eruption on upper lip. Swelling on inside of lower lip. Lips dry.

Mouth.—Pain in incisors; pulsating P. in l. lower eye-tooth in evening in bed. Gums anæmic. *Tongue white;* pale; moist T., with grayish-white coat; T. coated; coated white and swollen; coated white in morning; coated yellow and swollen; swollen. Full of mucus. Sticking posteriorly in palate and in beginning of throat, > swallowing. Palate rough after much smoking. Scraping raw feeling in palate. Soreness, and of fauces and œsophagus. Feeling as if covered with velvet. Dryness; of palate and pharynx, with nausea. Moist and thick. *Salivation;* with soreness of mouth, tongue and gums; with ecphysesis and nausea on swallowing the saliva; as after vinegar; sweetish; intermittent, watery, sweetish, then salt. Fetid breath. Taste bitter (Bry.), to bread, with good appetite; flat, slimy T.; T. as of sweet almonds, after smoking.

Throat.— Tenacious mucus loosened by cough. Sticking. Scraping in pharynx; in œsophagus; in fauces, with dryness. Scraping and burning in pharynx; in œsophagus. Rawness in pharynx, with burning. Dryness. Spasmodic constriction. Constrictive pain, and along œsophagus. Sensation as if walls of pharynx were swollen or as if constricted by swelling of tonsils. Choking sensation. Sore pain on swallowing; soreness in fauces and posterior nares, < morning and evening. Swallowing difficult.

Stomach.—Painful hunger; at intervals. Longing for bitter food. Appetite diminished; for dinner; **lost**; lost, with emptiness of stomach; no relish for food and indigestion when it was eaten. **Thirst** (Bry., China); unquenchable; for cold drinks; for sour drinks. Eructations; after dinner, with violent hunger; of tasteless liquid; sour, after eating; of a sour fluid; of an acrid fluid, then acidity in mouth like vinegar. Hiccough; in paroxysms, not quite rising to throat.

Nausea; in morning, in a woman; in middle of night, beginning with a noise in throat, then suffocative convulsions, in which he wakes in great distress, then general convulsions, then delirium and ungovernable mood, biting of his tongue, full pulse, noise in head, the fits often preceded by frequent but ineffectual desire to urinate; after eating; on going to bed; with pain at stomach; with uneasiness and weight at stomach; with relish for food; with headache and flashes of light before eyes; occasional; in epigastric region.

Retching. *Vomiting;* every day at 5 or 6 P.M., with retching, nausea, anguish in pit of stomach and external heat mingled with shivering, then sweat, with chilliness; renewed by drinking, after meals when seized with fit of coughing, violent, also with *irregular feeble pulse* (compare Tabac.); violent, then cold sweat (Tabac., Coccul.); of blood; bilious; bilious, and diarrhœa; greenish; of greenish fluid; of much mucus; frequent, of mucus, then of bile; in evening, of much saliva, mucus and acid food; of ingesta, then greenish liquid; of ingesta, then liquid, then greenish-yellow; with purging and colic.

Distention after dinner, with pain; D. in S. and upper abdomen after eating, with heaviness and disinclination to work. Fulness as if the breakfast would be eructated; F. as if food remained in upper part of œsophagus. Pinching stitches in pit, < touch only when standing, not when sitting. Cutting; in pit, with nausea in it. Paroxysmal pinching. Gastritis, with weakness and double vision. *Pain;* in pit < pressure; in epigastric region; epigastric and umbilical regions; in epigastrium, then vomiting and stool of dark yellow color and offensive odor; in epigastrium, extending to abdomen; spasmodic; sickening, rising up line of sternum to throat. Bruised pain in epigastrium and over sternum after dinner, >

by weak tea, with languor and feeling of indigestion. *Anxiety in epigastrium.* Soreness; *in epigastrium, also causing frequent deep sighs.* Constriction across epigastric region towards liver. The food presses in pit when sitting, > standing. Weight on straightening up body. Uneasiness; after moderate eating. Difficult digestion. Unpleasant sensation in epigastric region. Heartburn; towards evening. Burning; extending up œsophagus, also in afternoon; in epigastric region, with pressure. **Faintness as if dying** (Tabac.). Frequent emptiness before sleep.

Clinical.—Nausea and vomiting of pregnancy.

Abdomen.—Contracted, hot, dry and rough to touch. *Fulness.* Hardness. Noises. Rumbling; with gurgling and pain; with gurgling and feeling as if bubbles of air moved along colon. Flatulence; causing tension. Emission of flatus; profuse, in afternoon. Moving, with colic, then the pain extended into pubic region, changed into pressure and dragging, extending into testicles, then frequent urging to urinate, with itching of penis. Sticking in whole. Tearing on bending forward; cutting T. in evening as after taking cold, < rising from a seat, with pain in vertex; pain more tearing than sticking, in morning in bed, then diarrhœa and tenesmus. Cutting; with urging to stool; by jerks; almost causing nausea. Griping; with sticking and attacks of nausea. Tormina after going to bed, till 3 A.M. Pain; in morning; towards evening, then sudden liquid stools; before and after diarrhœa; > vomiting of food enveloped in white tasteless mucus; now pressive, now cutting, > diarrhœa of fæces mixed with mucus; ulcerative, on moving but not on touch. Constriction; pinching, as from a cold, when sitting.

Sticking in l. hypochondrium, with sensation as if parts thereabouts were asleep. Pain in a spot beneath third l. false rib as if everything internally were torn. Anxiety in hypochondria, with tension and constriction. Pressure in l. hypochondrium; in upper A.; paroxysmal and cramplike, in upper A. Sticking in r. side during expiration while standing and walking; S. in l. side, < expiration. Boring in forepart of l. side, with dragging downward. Feeling in l. side as if something were forcing itself through. Sticking in umbilicus; above region of U., with burrowing; dull, almost pinching S. in r. side above U. when eating. Tearing about U. in morning; sticking T. in region when walking. Movings about lower A., with gurgling and pressure. Jerklike tearing from mons veneris towards l. groin when leaning backward. Griping in lower A. as from a purge. Frequent gnawing in lower. Sore pain in l. ring as if a hernia would protrude. Dragging in pelvis, extending into testicles, with pressure.

Clinical.—Jaundice, with vomiting, soreness over the region of the liver, irregular pulse. Enlargement of the liver frequently associated with a jaundiced hue, when calling for Dig., is generally accompanied or caused by disease of the heart, stools may be white and urine high-colored (compare Myrica). Ascites, with attacks of faintness, etc., especially associated with hepatic diseases. Incarcerated hernia has been relieved.

Stool.—Urging to S. *Diarrhœa; violent; ash-colored;* painful; sudden; frequent; then urging. Thin, frequent, next morning constipation. Liquid and profuse (Bry., Apoc. c.); L. and frequent. Bilious and mucous; B. and frequent. *Constipation.* Dry and indolent; D., difficult and copious, at 11 P.M. *Grayish-white, nearly white,* with liver symptoms (China). Containing many thread-worms. Copious; and containing much bile. Frequent. Involuntary. Scanty; and green. Retained, then yellowish-white.

Clinical.—Stools, clay-colored. Diarrhœa associated with dropsy, intermittent pulse, cold sweat, etc.

Urinary Organs.—Contractive pain in bladder when urinating, with difficult micturition. *Dragging in bladder as if distended, not > frequent micturition.* Urging; at 3 A.M. and scanty urine; *U., but difficult M. as if there were almost no urine in bladder, after M. pressure in bladder and burning in urethra* (Apoc. c.). *Frequent urging;* with dribbling of reddish urine, with burning in urethra and glans. *Constant urging at night,* also vertigo on rising in consequence; C. urging, with large amount of urine though not much at a time. Ineffectual efforts to urinate. Involuntary micturition. Frequent micturition of watery urine; and copious; F. at night and copious. Rare micturition, urine scanty, then frequent M., with cutting drawing in bladder. Painful micturition of scanty red urine. Urine retained, with distention of bladder, which could be felt above pubis. *Function of kidneys suspended.* Pressing burning in middle of urethra as if too narrow, when urinating, > even while urinating.

Urine.—Copious; in afternoon; with constant urging; with urging and inability to retain it; with exhaustion; then retained, with *nausea,* vomiting and diarrhœa; and pale, passed every hour; and watery; and watery, it did not collect in large quantities, but provoked constant micturition; and pale straw-yellow, feeble acid reaction, sp. gr. diminished, organic and inorganic solids diminished, and deep-colored. *Scanty; and dark;* and of high sp. gr.; and red; and clear and pale. Dark. Brownish, offensive. Red and burning; *R., depositing a sediment.* Acid. Neutral; in afternoon, acid at other times; in evening, not after dinner. Thick, with dense white sediment. Turbid in morning and afternoon and depositing a thick, white sediment. Thin brownish sediment. Free deposit of lithates.

Clinical.—Nephritis after scarlatina. Cystitis. Inflammation of neck of bladder, after passing a few drops the desire to urinate is increased and the patient walks about in great distress, associated with tenesmus of rectum; these symptoms have indicated the use of the drug for the relief of acute inflammation in chronic enlargement of the prostate. In inflammation of the kidneys of the chronic form it is sometimes of temporary value when there is threatened failure of the heart, or very scanty or suppressed urine, with œdema of the lungs, etc.

Sexual Organs.—Flaccidity, with loss of desire. Irritation. Itching of glans. Erections in morning; continued, in morning on rising; almost chordee-like, waking at night, with urging to urinate, but scanty urine; almost painful, disturbing sleep. Bruised pain in r. testicle. Frequent sensation at night as if an emission would occur without one, in morning glutinous moisture at orifice of urethra. Emissions, then pain in penis; E. at night without dreams and without waking; almost every fourth night with voluptuous dreams; at night, then exhaustion next day and erections on and after rising; *copious, at night;* copious, at 1 A.M. and on waking smarting in urethra. Lascivious fancies, with frequent erections. Desire, with frequent erections during the day. Power diminished, the propensities disappear, liquor seminis diminishes and may at last cease. Menorrhagia. Uterine hæmorrhage. Discharge of menstrual blood.

Clinical.—Gonorrhœa, with strangury, inflammation of prostate, upper portion of the urethra and neck of the bladder. Weakness of sexual organs in men, seminal emissions with general Dig. symptoms of the heart, faintness, weakness of the extremities, etc. Hydrocele, especially with suppressed or scanty urine and albuminuria. Suppression of menses, with hæmorrhage from the lungs, associated with cardiac disease.

Respiratory Organs.—Mucus in larynx in morning, easily loosened, but he is obliged to swallow it. Tenacious mucus in larynx, loosened by hacking cough (Kali). Rawness of air-passages. Hoarseness in morning; on waking (Iod.); after night-sweat so that he cannot speak; *frequent painless H.* (Calc. c.). Cough; at midnight, with sweat; irritation to C. as far up as arch of palate; with catarrh so that he could scarcely speak; so violent after eating that he vomits the food; sympathetic with affection of stomach; C. from tickling in trachea without expectoration. Dry cough in morning after rising, with dyspnœa (Ferr.); D., with tensive pain in arm and shoulder; D. spasmodic, after much talking; D. and short, from itching in larynx. C., < long sitting, with expectoration and peculiar weakness in chest. Expectoration of grayish, sweetish, offensive-tasting mucus (Stann.); E. of mucus in morning by involuntary hawking; *of blood.*

Respiration.—**Irregular and performed by frequent deep sighs** (K. cy.). *Difficult, slow and deep. Dyspnœa* (Ferr.), < sitting, with necessity to breathe deeply. *Constant desire to breathe deeply* (Ferr.), < evening, *but on attempting to do so it seemed as if the chest could be only half filled or as if there were an impediment deep in chest, with dry cough, < deep inspiration,* with rare expectoration of hard lumpy mucus, the expectoration freer in morning than in afternoon and evening, everything about body seemed too tight, the shortness of breath > evening in bed, returned in morning on rising with painful weariness and general affection of chest and frequent dry cough, the difficulty in breathing < afternoon and evening, especially when writing, < next day in afternoon and evening, when it was accompanied by palpitation. Short. Short gasping. Sighs; and groans. Rapid. *Feeble murmur.*

Chest.—*Œdema of lungs.* Sticking in r. above pit of stomach. Pinching sticking in ribs beneath r. axilla. Itching sticking rhythmical with pulse, in l. on a line with pit of stomach. Cutting externally in front, in region of third rib, on violent motion of opposite arm. Rawness, with stitches. Pain on coughing. Pulsating pain in l. lower part, more in walls, in afternoon, unaffected by breathing; P. pain in region of r. nipple when walking slowly, causing oppressed breathing. Drawing pain deep in lower part of r. in evening, preventing sleep; D. pain in middle of sternum when walking. Bruised pain over sternum and epigastrium in evening. Soreness to touch from ensiform cartilage upward. Oppressive pain beneath ensiform cartilage.

Contractive pain in sternum, < bending forward head and upper part of body. *Suffocative constriction as if internal parts were grown together* (Ferr.), < morning on waking, obliging him to sit upright. Tension, with pressure in pit of stomach, obliging deep breathing; T. in l. on becoming erect. Pressive drawing on coughing. Pressure in l. upper muscles, with boring; P. on lower part when sitting bent, with shortness of breath; outward in C. and epigastrium towards evening, > beating on chest. Uneasiness in mammary region, < l., and extending to l. shoulder and upper part of arm. Pulsations in r. Peculiar relaxed sensation, < long sitting. Weariness across to l. side.

Clinical.—Pneumonia, especially in old people, with prune-juice expectoration, cold extremities, cyanotic face, feeble pulse. Œdema of the lungs and effusion into the pleura, with weak heart.

Heart.—"Heart-worm," with intermittent pulse and congestion to head, < occiput, somewhat to l., and nausea. Pain; shifting. Oppression; with need to inspire deeply. **Sudden sensation as if it stood still** at 9 P.M., **with anxiety**; after dinner, *with anxiety and necessity to hold the breath;* S. as if it stood still, violent slow beats, with sudden pain in occiput, unconsciousness and cold sweat on forehead (compare Apoc. c.). Uneasiness; in afternoon; with cold sweat; *in various parts of region in evening, with weakness of forearm.* Confusion, < moving, with weakness of wrists and forearms. Disagreeable sensation.

Palpitation; at night, starting him from commencing sleep; from a slight ascent (Calc. c.); from moderate exercise, with uneasiness at heart. Beats accompanied by gentle "*bruit de souffle.*" Action rapid, < the systole, heart dilated slowly and on each movement palpitation. Oppressive, contractive action, with anxiety and spasmodic pain in sternum and beneath ribs. Violent, slow action when sitting; V., with anxiety and contractive pain beneath sternum. Strong action; at night, so that he must rise, walk about and open the window, with orgasm of blood, palpitation, strong, rapid pulse; when walking in the room, with palpitation; and difficult; extending over entire l. side, the first sound dull and prolonged, the second clear, beats intermittent and irregular. Irregular action. **Action feeble, frequent, intermittent and irregular** (Apoc. c., Hydrocy. ac.); **action and pulse feeble and small;** *F., with palpitation.*

Clinical.—Pericarditis, with effusion; fluttering of heart. Cardiac dropsies. In all forms of disease of the heart in which Dig. is indicated there is feeble, irregular or fluttering pulse, feeling as if the heart stood still, with anxiety and oppression; sometimes there is a cyanotic hue of the face, general desire to take a deep breath, which only partially relieves the sense of suffocation.

Pulse.—**Irregular**; after walking; **and small**; and weak. Strong and full; when sitting; S. and hard; *S. from twelve to twenty times, then very weak for four or five times.* Rapid; after gentle exercise; after exercise, and weak and irregular; when standing, slower on sitting, very slow when lying; *on slightest motion, and on slowly sitting upright from reclining it became jerky, small and weak;* on standing, and weak; and strong and full; and strong and wiry; and irregular; and irregular and full; and hard and small; and small and weak; and small, weak, irregular, with strong beat of heart; and soft, feeble, arteries dilated, irregular; *three or four rapid, small beats, then several slow, strong and full beats;* suddenly R. for a few beats, then slow again, or it loses a whole beat. Full.

Slow; **slow, thready, intermittent**; *and irregular, also small;* and irregular, always a full hard beat after every three or four soft ones; and a peculiar explosive shock with each of the three or four feeble beats, then intermissions of several; and small, intermittent; but strong; and full; and strong, irregular and intermittent; and full and large, soon rapid and small; but accelerated on slighest exertion; and strong, full, their shocks rapid and separated by considerable intervals when at rest, but on slight exertion rapid, irregular and less full; and *frequently intermittent*, with every intermission oppression as if the heart were slowly grasped. Intermittent. Irritable. Undulating at noon. Small; and soft; and weak; *and weak and jerky on slowly sitting up after reclining in a chair;* when standing, and weak, irregular in rate and strength. Feeble. Almost pulseless.

Neck.—Sticking in muscles on moving neck; S. in nape on motion, with tearing. Cutting in nape, with numbness, obliging him to draw the head backward, which seems hindered by a soft, dead substance compressed between the joints. Pain in muscles as from a band. Bruised pain in nape between shoulders, extending over anterior part of chest, where there was pain on pressure, < over sternum, with frontal headache, bruised pain in epigastrium and distended feeling in stomach. Pressive drawing in nape at occiput, at point of insertion of cervical muscles on bending head backward. Painful stiffness of neck and throat, < motion, with tension.

Back.—Tearing on motion, with sticking. Drawing in B., limbs and fingers as after taking cold. Stiffness of B. and sides of neck, with thrustlike pain; S. in muscles of r. side, < bending head, with pain. Thrust in first dorsal vertebra. Sore pain in joint of last cervical and first dorsal vertebræ on bending neck forward. Sticking between scapulæ. Tearing beneath r. scapula. Sticking in region of kidneys; l. when sitting. Drawing cutting in l. side in region of lumbar vertebræ, > pressure. Pain in small of B. on stooping. Pressure on both sides of spine in lumbar region after stool. Bruised pain in small of B. on blowing nose; B. pain on beginning to move after lying down. Drawings above nates.

Clinical.—Spinal anæmia resulting from seminal emissions (China).

Extremities.—Tense painful swelling of legs, then also of forearms and hands. Burning sticking in tips of fingers and toes. Piercing pain in joints. Pain in all joints after midday nap, as if crushed. Pressure in r. shoulder and l. knee. Drawings in elbows and knees. Weakness of arms and legs. Heaviness, with sluggishness; H., with helplessness.

Upper Extremities.—Pain in l. shoulder and in elbows, at night, with semi-conscious sleep, lying upon back, with l. arm over head. (Muscular rheumatism in r. shoulder, allowing but little sleep.) Tensive pain in muscles of arm and shoulder on moving arm. Paralytic weakness of l. arm, so that he can hardly raise it, and cannot clinch the fingers without pain. Heaviness of l. arm. Upper arm, sticking in lower part; burning S. in l.; tearing S. in r. when walking; painful itching throbbing in flesh. Pressure in r. elbow; pain in elbows on touch as if the nerve were pressed, or as if the arm would go to sleep.

Sticking in muscles of r. forearm. Tearing in r. forearm. Pinching on back of ulna above wrist, with sticking pinching. Paralytic pain in middle of ulna on stretching arm or when it lies outstretched. Boring in r. wrist towards thumb. Paralytic tearing in bones of wrist; in r. metacarpal bones. Swelling of r. hand and fingers at night. Jerking and drawing outward of l. index. Cramplike sticking in ball of l. thumb; burning S. in l. thumb above nail, < pressure. Paralytic tearing in finger-joints; jerking paralytic T. in r. index. Drawing in fingers. Frequent sudden stiffness of fingers. Falling asleep of F. Numbness of three last F. and of one side of ball of r. hand.

Lower Extremities.—*Staggering. Infiltration.* Stiffness of joints after sitting in a wagon, > walking. Nates fall asleep in evening when sitting, and feel dead.

Thigh.—Drawing cramp in forepart of bend of r., < motion of lumbar muscles, when it becomes a bubbling and continues even when sitting. Spasmodic movements of muscles. Sticking in bend when walking; S. above l. knee, towards l. side. Cutting on laying one leg over the other, > separating legs. Bruised pain on beginning to move after lying down, and in legs. Pain anteriorly, pressive rather than drawing. Tension in tendons of lumbar muscles in bends of T., < motion, but almost only when walking, on pressure there is pain, as from pressure of a hard body under skin. Drawing in anterior muscles; D. in inner side when sitting; cramplike, in muscles above popliteus when sitting, > after walking. Painful itching throbbing in flesh.

Pressure in l. knee and in bones of foot. Tension in hollows of K. Fatigue of K. on ascending steps. Stiffness of external condyles of K. as from internal swelling, with coldness. Jerking of muscles below hollow of l. K. rhythmical with pulse, > touch. Sticking on outer side of tibiæ below knees. Pain in calves. Smarting pain in l. leg when standing, as if crushed. Drawing in l. fibula as if a part were torn out; painful D. in leg when sitting, < thigh, then in r. knee and r. ankle. *Weakness of legs;* with trembling; with necessity to stretch them; paralytic; *and of knees;* of tibiæ and knees when walking. Heaviness in l. tibia impeding walking. Pressure in l. ankle. Sprained pain in ankle on stretching it. Sticking in r. sole in evening, so that the whole leg jerks. Pressure in toes. Drawing in toes.

Skin.—Pale, ashy-gray and parchment-like. Rash on backs of hands. Desquamation of whole. Erysipelatoid affection of face resulting in ragged desquamation. Red round spots on body, supinator surfaces of forearms and backs of hands, > pressure, uniting in large elevations, next day desquamation on face, new eruptions on upper arms and neck, later desquamation. Itching eruption on cheeks and chin, which desquamates and leaves red spots. Pimples on back; beneath l. nostril, with biting pain; red, on middle of forehead, with burning biting, < touch. Comedones on face, which suppurate and ulcerate. Painful furuncle on nape. Cluster of vesicles on chin. Tension of abdomen on becoming erect. Itching on back of hand, < night, also on back of r. foot; on cheek and chin, < night, with biting; voluptuous, in axillæ. Corrosive itching in l. loin; of upper and anterior part of thigh; on leg above external malleolus; in various parts, returning after scratching; < when he does not scratch, becoming intermittent, burning, sticking.

Sleep.—Frequent yawning and stretching, with chilliness. Sleepiness; till evening, with incapacity for study; early in evening, with indolence and dulness of mind; after eating, with frequent yawning after dinner; on going to bed, but unsound sleep. Deep sleep; from noon till midnight. Lethargic sleep.

Sleeplessness; at night, leaving his bed every moment and conversing with persons not present; with restlessness, palpitation, and at 1 A.M. an almost jerking pulse; with palpitation and uneasiness, < lying on l. side, and pulsations in ears, < l. Little sleep, with restlessness of mind; little sleep, disturbed by dreams. Slumbering instead of falling asleep, complete consciousness without ability to sleep. Difficult falling asleep; though at times in a stupor. Starting in sleep. *Frequent waking as from anxiety* and as if it were time to rise; *F. waking in fright*, from dreams of falling from a height or into water. *Restless and unrefreshing sleep;* R., with frequent waking, also with dreams; with frequent waking and internal and external heat of face; with frequent waking, always lying on back, with emissions; and waking in semi-consciousness; and he lies only on the back; with merry dreams. Many dreams, not unpleasant; unpleasant D. full of unsuccessful projects; anxious, confused D.; confused, vivid.

Clinical—Deep sleep.

Fever.—Sensitiveness to cold. Chilliness; before stool; after vomiting, then heat and redness of skin, then pain in lower limbs, < calves and knees; then frequent general warmth, but cold sweat on forehead; and pale and covered with sweat. *Internal coldness;* with external heat; and external. External C. of whole body, with warmth of face, also with redness of face. Shivering; in afternoon, then sweat at night, even of head; then heat; then heat of skin; over back; in back, cold hands and creeping coldness through limbs. **Cold skin**; and alternately hot. Coldness in back; in the room after eating, with burning of head, face and ears and redness of cheeks, and l. eye is smaller than r.; **C. of limbs**; of arms and hands, then of whole body; of one hand, with warmth of the other; of fingers, then of palms and soles, then of whole body, < limbs.

Disease similar to typhoid fever, with affection of gastric viscera. Heat at night, with restlessness; general H., with swollen veins and rapid pulse; sudden general H., then general weakness. Heat in head; internal and external; in flushes; in forehead and vertex, with heaviness; in face; in back, then creeping coldness, with cold hands and shuddering through back; of hands; burning in r. calf on resting one leg over the other; sorelike B. of r. arm; externally in chest, then coolness. Hot skin; in evening, < towards head; with dryness and roughness. Sweat; in morning on waking; at night in sleep; in palms; *copious;* cold.

Dioscorea.

A tincture is made of the fresh root of Dioscorea villosa, L.

General Action.—The most prominent effect of the drug is its pain. Pain in every part of the body shooting and cramplike, these pains usually resemble the neuralgias of the various preparations of *Magnesia* and Pulsat., they are generally relieved by motion in the open air. Most useful in practice hitherto have been the abdominal pains, here again comparison may be made with the Magnesias and Colocynth.

Allies.—Magnes., Puls., Berb., Colo., Bry.

Generalities.—Trembling, with faintness at stomach. Sharp pains in various parts at 4 P.M.; darting from one part to another in evening; darting cramping pains in limbs and various parts in morning. Cramping pains after going to bed, in stomach, abdomen, arms and legs. Occasional pains in bones. Feeling in forenoon as if he had taken a bad cold, pains in bones, head, r. temple and r. lung, with chilliness, in afternoon and evening pain in occiput, the throat feels sore but is not on swallowing, pain in r. lung, in back, hips and legs, < r. side, sharp pain in l. hand and fingers, chilliness, yet easy sweat, dryness of mouth, at night restlessness and chilliness, then sweat but no fever or thirst, and sharp pain in heart. Nervous, easily troubled. Great desire for the open air at 5 P.M. Restlessness; at 4 P.M.; 4 P.M., > walking; at night.

Weakness; in morning after a restless night; on waking, with disinclination for mental exertion; in evening; < ascending stairs, with pain at head of tibia; with trembling of hands and legs; with restlessness; but relief of pains on moving. Desire to lie down and keep still. Faintness; at 3 A.M.; after going to bed; at night on waking, with numbness, the faintness < sitting up in bed, the numbness < lying down and > lying on back and pulling the hair in front of the ears; at stool. Aggravation on lying down. Amelioration in open air, and especially when *moving in open air* (Puls., Magnes.); of all pains in morning, except the headache, by motion; of symptoms, except those of the abdomen, by riding or walking.

Mind.—Irritability; with dulness and desire to be alone, usually am fond of the society of ladies, but now they seem repulsive. Conversation is troublesome. *Call things by the wrong names* in evening, write r. for l. Stupidity; in afternoon.

Head.—Aching; in morning; in morning on waking; at 5 A.M., with vertigo; in forenoon, < through temples; at night in bed; after dinner, < occiput; with nausea; deep in centre. Confusion; during stool. Dulness; with heaviness and occasional quick pain through it. Fulness. Tightness as if squeezed after breakfast. Heaviness; at 8 P.M., with pain between eyes and on side of head near top of ears; at 9 P.M., with feeling as if it would be crushed when it rested on the hand. Bad feeling till after dinner. Discomfort as from a cold. Vertigo; in morning; 7 A.M., with rumbling in abdomen; in evening, with headache; when eating; with inclination to go to the right; sudden, in afternoon and evening, with heat of head.

Forehead.—Intermittent cutting along r. side at 9.30 A.M., shooting to ear, < pressure and cold air. Darting pain over l. eye at 10.30 P.M., > motion. Boring in morning, extending to occiput. Sharp pain in morning; over l. eye; over eyes in morning; over r. eye in morning; over r. eye at 1 P.M., extending to occiput; over r. eye at 2 P.M.; over l. eye at 10.30 P.M. *Pain;* in morning; in evening, and in l. side of head; at 9 P.M.; at night; at 11 P.M., occasionally sharp, and in vertex; extending into nose, with nausea and symptoms of a cold and fluent coryza; at 8 P.M., extending to occiput, as if he would lose consciousness, with inclination of head to fall backward; over eyes; over eyes, sometimes one, sometimes the other; over r. eye in morning; over r. eye at 2 and 5 P.M.; over l. eye at 7 P.M.; over r. eye to occiput; between eyes and over r., < afternoon. Pain as if lifted up, and in temples. Heavy pain over r. eye at 1 P.M., extending to temple.

Temples.—Darting in l.; at 5 P.M. Digging cutting in l. at noon. Digging in l. at 10 A.M. Sharp pain; in r.; l.; l. at 6 A.M.; l. at 8.30 A.M.; r. in morning;

in afternoon; in l. in evening; at 10 P.M.; in l., with nausea and chills beginning on back, < over l. scapula; in sudden shocks in l. in evening; occasionally in r.; in r. and over r. eye, in morning, occasionally darting to l. temple. Twisting pain in r.; l. Grinding pain in l. Squeezing pain at 5 A.M., with nausea, chills and dryness of mouth, but no thirst; S. pain in r. in morning, extending to angle of jaw, sometimes sharp; sharp, in r. at 9 P.M. Pain; l.; < r.; in morning; l. in morning; at 7 A.M., < l.; r. at 7 A.M., then l., at 9 A.M. in both, < stooping or walking; in forenoon; r. in forenoon; at noon, < r.; r. at 5 P.M.; in evening; r. in evening; after dinner; > pressure; in l., > pressure, which causes heat in l. nostril, pressure after the pain; in r., over a large surface externally, but concentrated to a point internally. Stupefying pain; at 1 P.M., > during pressure. Unpleasant feeling through temples.

Sides.—Pain in l.; pain in morning; 7 A.M.; before and behind ears at 3 A.M.; before and behind l. ear at 11 A.M.; above and before ears at 5 P.M.; as from a band at 6 A.M., with coldness of head.

Occiput.—Sharp pain in l. in afternoon; suddenly in l. protuberance at 5 P.M., > pressure. Sharp twisting pain in l. at 7 A.M., > rubbing. Intermittent cramping pain in r. in evening. Pain; in morning; in l. in morning; forenoon, < r.; afternoon and evening; 2 P.M., extending through to front of head; deep-seated in l. Pulling pain; at 7 A.M.; in l. in morning; in l. causing a stupid sensation. Heavy pain in afternoon, and in shoulders.

Eyes.—Redness in morning. *Smarting;* < r.; in morning, with stiffness of lids; in morning, < r., < on edge of upper lid; at 10 A.M., with weakness so that he could not read coarse print; in evening; after going to bed, as if hot air came out of them and passed over face. Sharp pain in r. at 8.30 A.M.; in l. at 2 P.M., > pressure, with necessity to close it. Aching in l. in evening. Feeling as if sticks were in them; at 10 P.M. Feeling as if a large smooth substance were in them; at 8 P.M. Feeling as if dust or eyelashes were in them. Feeling in l. at 7 P.M. as if dirt were in it. Feeling in forenoon as if a foreign body were in them, < r. Soreness; r.; morning, < l.; r. in morning, < lower lid; in morning, with agglutination of lids; l. at 8.30 A.M., extending to l. temple; afternoon; r. in evening; in evening, with smarting and with smarting lachrymation of r. so that it must be kept closed; at 10 P.M.; in night. Itching; in morning; evening; r. at 2 P.M. Weakness in morning; at 4.20 P.M.; 9 P.M., with soreness and smarting; 10 P.M.

Lachrymation from r.; lachrymation in open air. Sharp pain in r. ball at 7.30 P.M. Stye on r. lower lid. Smarting at inner angles, < r. Pain over inner angle of r.; below outer angle of r. at 11 P.M. Soreness of r. lid; at 7 A.M., but they do not look sore. Lids feel stiff. Desire to keep lids closed. Itching of l. inner canthus in evening. Vision blurred.

Ears.—Balls of wax fall out of r. Darting behind l. in evening; in morning, extending in front of ear and to angle of jaw. Sharp pain behind l.; behind r. in morning; in front and behind both in morning; behind l. at 7 P.M.; in l. at 9 P.M.; over r. at 9 P.M.; deep-seated behind r. Twisting pain in front of l. at 11 P.M., causing a numb sensation in head. Squeezing pain of front of both, extending to angles of jaws. Pain in l.; in l. in afternoon, from blowing nose; r. in evening; in front of both; in front of r.; in front of r. after going to bed. Pulling pain in front of both as before vomiting. Soreness internally in l. in afternoon; internally on touch at 8 P.M. Itching in evening; l. internally; internally in l. at 1 P.M.; internally at 10.30 P.M. Stopped feeling; suddenly at 8 P.M. Buzzing in morning. Ringing at 4 P.M., < r.

Nose.—Pain from nose and forehead to occiput at 9 P.M. Smarting inside nostrils; at 6 P.M. Soreness on l. side, afterwards on top and r. side and swelling of r. side; soreness inside nostrils at 9 P.M.; inside at 7 P.M., with dryness. Dryness at 11 P.M., with bad smell in it. Irritation in passages. Itching in r. nostril at 3 P.M. Sneezing; violent, with vertigo. Stoppage; inclination to, at 7 A.M. Watery discharge from l. nostril; constantly at 9 P.M. Discharge of bright blood in morning, with spitting of blood; bright blood from l. nostril at 11 A.M.; bright blood from l. nostril, then a dark clot and spitting of blood. *Bad smell;* at 7 P.M. Smell as of bilious fever in morning; at 10 P.M. Smell as of bilious fæces; in morning.

Face.—Sharp pain in l. cheek or in lower part of temple, then dry cough. Lips sore at 9 P.M.; l. corner of lip sore. Lips burn at 9. P.M. Spasmodic action of jaw in evening. Spasmodic closure of jaws, with biting of tongue. Jumping, darting pain at r. angle of jaw at 7. P.M. Grinding pain at l. angle at 6.30 A.M.; in l. lower jaw, between teeth and angle, at 7 P.M. Digging at l. angle at 5 P.M. Sharp pain in l. angle of lower jaw at 10 A.M. Pain in jaw near teeth in afternoon; at angle at 6 P.M.; pain at r. angle of lower. Drawing pain at angle of jaw. Sore pain at l. angle of jaw in morning.

Mouth.—Teeth. Jumping pain in l. upper in morning; in a r. upper in afternoon, as from touching a bare nerve. Sharp pain in upper incisors in morning; in a r. upper molar in afternoon. Pain in incisors; lower, at 3 P.M.; upper at 6 P.M.; lower, with soreness; in l. lower molars at 6 P.M., extending to angle of jaw and parotid. Soreness of l. Swelling of inside of gums of upper incisors. Soreness of gums and roof of mouth in afternoon; at 9 P.M.

Tongue.—Coated in morning; brown in morning; brown in morning and sore at tip; yellow; white; yellowish-white. Sticking to roof of mouth in morning. Bitten often in evening when neither talking nor chewing. Biting stinging in tip at 4 P.M. Soreness of tip; when eating; soreness on l. side at 7 A.M.; S. in evening; r. side in evening; l. side at 6 P.M.; near last molar, < by talking. Burnt feeling in morning; on sides. Dryness in morning, with stiffness; of sides; dryness in morning, with bitterness and soreness.

Mouth in General.—Soreness in morning; evening; of roof; of roof in morning; of roof in evening. Very smooth feeling. Slimy in morning after eating, and sore. Sticky, nasty in morning. Burning, and in fauces. Burnt feeling in morning. Clammy in morning. *Dryness in morning* (*Puls.*)*;* with bitterness and roughness; < eating, with bitterness; but full of sticky mucous; at 1 A.M., with bitterness and soreness; at 3.30 A.M., with bitterness and soreness, and in tongue; in forenoon, with soreness; at 8 P.M., with bitterness. Salivation; with peculiar prickling at end of tongue as if burnt by hot drink. Saliva runs from mouth in sleep; in morning.

Taste.—Bitter; *in morning, also mouth clammy* (Puls.); in afternoon on waking; in evening. Rough, flat.

Sweetish; in morning on waking. Bloody. Sickening, with whitish coat on tongue. Bad in morning on rising. Of food ten hours after eating.

Throat.—Pain in l. parotid; in parotids in afternoon. Sharp wringing pain in l. parotid at 10 P.M. Soreness of parotids in evening, with pain extending to throat. Congestion of tonsils. Stinging in fauces; at 9 P.M.; sudden, in r. tonsil at 2.30 P.M. Smarting of fauces; posteriorly, and dryness. Pain at 11 A.M. and in r. ear; below r. tonsil at 11 A.M. extending to ear; in back and r. side of throat, causing choking. Pulling pain in l. tonsil in evening. Soreness in morning; with hoarseness; it seems sore in morning but is not; in afternoon and evening; posterior fauces; of fauces, with smarting and appearance as if the skin had peeled off; of posterior fauces, with dryness and difficult swallowing.

Dryness; of fauces; of posterior fauces at 8.30 P.M.; with roughness and frequent inclination to swallow. Burning of fauces; l. tonsil and l. side of throat; l. tonsil, then itching. Tickling low down at 6.30 A.M., causing deep cough. Irritation in morning; of l. side, in morning, extending to ear and down pharynx, causing cough; in fauces in evening; in fauces in evening, with inclination to cough; at 10 P.M., with inclination to cough; < evening. Constant desire to swallow in morning, but it causes nausea.

Stomach.—Appetite increased; at 7 A.M.; lost for breakfast. Empty eructations; at 7 P.M.; with sensation as if temples were in a vise; but the wind is stopped by dryness of throat; *sour;* in evening, with bitterness, < on sides and back of tongue; bitter; bitter, with shuddering; sour, bitter, with shuddering; bitter sour in evening, also with pain in epigastrium and l. hypochondrium; acrid, at 5 P.M. Eructations of sour water. Eructations tasting of rotten eggs. Eructations tasting like bile. Hiccough; after a light supper, with emission of flatus, and shuddering. *Nausea;* in morning after eating; in morning, on swallowing, with shuddering; in morning, with chills; in morning, with sharp spasmodic pain in umbilical and r. iliac regions, with rumbling on pressure; with disgust for food; with rumbling in cardiac part of stomach.

Cutting tearing in epigastrium and region of gall-bladder, at times spasmodic. Cutting and in region of gall-bladder; in epigastrium; in morning; frequent sinking, cramping, in epigastrium and upper abdomen, > standing erect or by pressure, almost preventing walking and breathing. *Cramping pain in pit, then eructations of wind, then hiccough and emissions of flatus;* C. pain across epigastrium at noon, holding me still; in epigastrium at 10.30 P.M., > motion; and in abdomen and legs; cutting, in epigastrium occasionally in forenoon, < afternoon, with faintness extending nearly to umbilicus, as before diarrhœa. *Sharp pain in epigastrium;* at 2.30 A.M., extending to l. hypochondrium; *in stomach at* 7 A.M.; in E. at 7 A.M., < by stooping, > standing erect; at 7 A.M. in E. and l. hypochondrium, > eructations, which leave soreness; in E. at 9 A.M., causing bending over; r. side of E. at 10 A.M.; stomach at 3 P.M.; E. at 6 P.M., > sitting erect; in E. and l. hypochondrium in evening; in E. in evening, extending to l. nipple; in E, > eating. Sharp, sore pain in epigastrium. Frequent sharp, prickly pain. Twisting pain in epigastrium. Grinding pain at 7 P.M., with bad smell in nose.

Pain; in region; epigastrium; in morning, and in abdomen; in morning in epigastrium and l. hypochondrium; in E. in morning, with soreness; in E. before breakfast; in E. at 9 A.M.; in E. in afternoon, with fulness; in E. at 6 P.M., and in l. hypochondrium; in E. at 7 P.M.; in E. at 9 P.M., and in r. hypochondrium; in E. at 10 P.M., and at lungs, < deep inspiration and < behind sternum; in evening, when eating light food after fasting nearly twenty-four hours, > while eating; in E. on going to bed, extending into abdomen; in E. at night and in hypochondria; on touch; *in E.,* > *eructations of sour bitter wind.* Pulling pain at 3 P.M. *Distress;* in morning, and in liver; *in morning, and with burning;* at 7 A.M., with occasional sharp pains and heat in it; after eating a little; > *empty eructations; had to unfasten the clothes;* at times cutting, < stooping, < sitting down after riding or walking, at times necessity to walk around the room to get the breath.

Heaviness in morning, as of undigested food; H. in epigastrium. Fulness in evening; and in abdomen, with pain; in E. Bad feeling; in morning; in epigastrium, as from undigested food; at 1 P.M., with rawness. Sourness; in evening, with burning; in evening, at times extending to roof of mouth, with burning; after eating, with burning. *Burning;* in epigastrium; waking at 2 A.M.; in morning; in epigastrium in morning and in l. hypochondrium, and across dorsal region; at 7 A.M.; 2 P.M.; 5 P.M., with smarting and soreness; in evening, with smarting; in evening, with smarting in throat; in evening, extending over chest; sour, at 8 A.M.; sour, at 3 P.M. Uneasiness; in epigastrium in morning on waking. Ineffectual inclination to eructate in evening. Faintness; in morning; in morning, with soreness; in epigastrium in evening; in night; in epigastrium, partially > eructations. Faint pain in epigastrium in morning, extending to umbilicus, > standing, < stooping. Weakness in epigastrium at 6 P.M., > supper, with desire to sit down, sinking in abdomen and stirred-up feeling in abdomen.

Clinical.—Dyspepsia of a flatulent character, resulting from tea. Flatulent dyspepsia, with belching of large quantities of offensive gas, partially relieving the pain in stomach and abdomen. Neuralgia of the stomach most severe, pain even along sternum and extending into both arms, with cold, clammy sweat, etc. (compare Puls. and Magnes.).

Abdomen.—**Rumbling** (Puls., Mag.); in evening, **with emission of much flatus;** with urging to stool. *Emission of much flatus; offensive* (Sulph.); of coppery odor; frequent E., with rumbling in l. side; frequent E., with pain, < hypogastrium and desire for stool. Incarcerated flatus. **Griping** (Colo., Puls., Sul.); in morning. *Cutting all through; C. in morning;* in evening, < *walking. Twisting in all parts,* < *lower, constantly changing,* at 3.30 A.M., > a soft yellow stool. Grinding at 7 A.M., with desire for stool. Sharp pain in afternoon. Griping drawing pain on sitting down, with pain in legs, the colic > lying down and by pressure. *Pain;* in morning on waking, > rubbing, with desire for stool; in forenoon; on going to bed; on lying down, > rising and walking, renewed on lying down, with pain in r. leg and urging to stool; in evening, with *emission of much flatus; with frequent cutting in stomach and small intestines;* frequent, at 9 A.M.; intermittent, at 6 P.M.; paroxysmal; spasmodic, with burning in the intermissions and with soreness.

Pressure from front and sides. Distress; in morning, with full feeling; with desire for stool; with deep-yellow diarrhœa; heavy in morning. Heaviness. Sensation as before diarrhœa. Stirred-up feeling. Soreness in morning, with weakness; S., < walking; *S. on pressure, with eructations.* Burning. Unpleasant feeling at 4 P.M. Gurgling sensation. Constant desire to pass flatus. Faintness; at noon, with hollow feeling, without hunger, > dinner, with pain around navel.

Hypochondria.—Pricking in l. at 7 P.M. Darting in l. at 11 P.M. Cutting at 8 A.M. *Sharp pain in l.;* at angle of ribs; in morning preventing walking or deep inspiration; in hypochondria in morning, with urging to stool; in region of gall-bladder at 11 A.M.; in region of gall-bladder in evening; in l. at 7 P.M.; in l., with stabbing, then aching in l. temple. Cramping pain in l. part of l. and r. side of r.; in l. at 3 P.M.; in l. in evening; frequent cramping pain. Twisting pain in l. at 8 A.M.; in l. in evening; in region of gall-bladder at 2 P.M.; wringing, in l. Wringing pain in l., then in epigastrium. Twisting-sinking pain in region of gall-bladder in morning. Digging in l. at 5 P.M. Pain; *in l.; in region of gall-bladder* at 7 A.M. (Berb.); in l. in morning; in l. at 1 P.M.; l. at 8 P.M.; l. at 9 P.M., when lying on l. side; l. at 10.30 P.M., > motion; at night; l. on lying down, < lying on r. side; l., with faintness of stomach, chills in back, pain in r. temple, sharp pain in middle of l. tibia, empty acrid eructations and shuddering. Lame pain in l. in morning, < motion. Soreness of l. in morning. Distress in l. at 6 A.M.

Liver.—Stabbing in evening. Darting through liver. *Cutting;* in r. lobe. Sharp pain in morning; extending to nipple; S. pain at noon; frequent, in afternoon; through to back. *Heavy grinding in region, < evening.* Squezing pain at 8.30 A.M. Twisting pain in region at 2.30 P.M. Painless twisting sensation at 10 P.M. Pain; in morning; in morning, < inhalation, > exhalation; in forenoon; at 5 P.M.; at night in bed; < by lying on r. side; with chilliness. Heavy distress in r. lobe; in region of gall-bladder when lying on r. side.

Umbilical Region.—Bloated and sore on pressure. **Griping**; at 8.30 A.M; at 9 A.M.; *below umbilicus* after supper. Cutting, waking at night; frequent, < walking. *Cramping pain above umbilicus* at 3 P.M. Sharp pain; at 5 A.M.; at 7 A.M., and in lower abdomen, with inclination to stoop, the pain > standing erect, which causes a faint chilly sensation; between epigastrium and umbilical region, > standing erect. *Pain; in morning;* at l. of umbilicus and below r. hypochondrium in morning; and in hypogastrium, waking at 5 A.M., with urging to stool, *profuse, thin, yellow stool, not relieving the pain,* another thin deep yellow stool relieving the pain, then faintness of stomach, not > eating; < doubling up, > pressure and motion; *with frequent cutting through all small intestines.* Pain as if a finger-tip were pressed upward and backward on umbilicus. Faint pain at 8.30 A.M., extending to epigastrium. Distress; with desire for stool; **distress, and in hypogastric regions, with intermittent cutting in stomach and small intestines** (Colo., Gamb.). Uneasiness.

Hypogastrium.—Swelling of l. inguinal glands, with soreness and pain. Intermittent shooting down into iliac region, < r. Drawing darting in l. inguinal region at 9 P.M.; sore D. in l. inguinal region at 9 P.M. Neuralgia in l. groin in evening. **Griping** in morning; at 7 A.M., then in epigastrium; in morning as before diarrhœa, > emissions of flatus. Cutting in morning; across in evening; in l. inguinal region in evening. Sharp pain at 4 A.M., > emission of flatus, then urging to stool; in l. inguinal region in evening; in l. inguinal region, extending down leg. Frequent wringing pain in l. inguinal region at 1 P.M. Wringing twisting pain in morning. Pain at 3 A.M., > urinating; P. in morning; *in l. inguinal region;* l. then r. inguinal region; in inguinal regions in evening; l. inguinal region and glands in evening, with soreness; inguinal region, in evening, with chills; *inguinal regions, extending to testicles;* r. groin, extending down inside of leg, making me lame. Pulling pain in l. inguinal region in morning. Heavy pain in l. inguinal region, with soreness Soreness at 7 A.M.; in l. inguinal region in morning, extending down spermatic cord, with nausea; l. groin in night, with pain. Faintness at noon.

Clinical.—Most violent flatulent colic, generally > walking about, <lying down at night, the pains are generally cutting, twisting, > pressure (like Coloc.), but they generally radiate from the abdomen to the back, into chest and arms, etc. Colic from the passage of gall-stones, pain shooting into chest and arms, with terrible eructations. Colic from passage of gravel from kidneys, pains shoot up into kidneys and down into testicles and legs, with cold, clammy sweat, etc. (Berb.).

Rectum.—Darting. Sudden pricking at 5 P.M. Occasional pulling twisting pain. Pain in morning; afternoon; evening. Itching; in evening; of l. side. Urging to stool, during breakfast and dinner; with faint burning pain in rectum; with cutting extending from umbilical region to rectum, with shuddering during stool and chill after stool; and small bilious stools and pain in abdomen during stool. Sudden urging, with small stools and much flatulence; S. at midnight when urinating, and loose stool driving out of bed in morning; driving out of bed, stool loose, in twenty minutes ineffectual straining, then in half an hour a soft dark stool. Constant desire. Frequent desire; beginning with pain in upper part of sacrum, extending to rectum, then to region of bladder, causing a sick, faint sensation, then pain in rectum and distress at umbilicus. Ineffectual desire.

Anus.—*Hæmorrhoids like red cherries protrude after stool, with pain in anus,* afterwards one is dark livid blue (Sulph.); H. partially prolapsed; H. sore; sore at 2 P.M., and itching; sore in evening, preventing sitting still. Oozing of moisture; in evening. Involuntary discharge of mucus. Sharp pain from the hæmorrhoid to region of liver at 5 P.M. Pain. Bearing-down, prolapsed feeling.

Clinical.—Hæmorrhoids, with darting pain shooting to liver; hæmorrhoids look like bunches of grapes, with great pain and distress.

Stool.—Diarrhœa; with pain in epigastrium and cutting in rectum; frequent. Loose, with straining and protrusion of hæmorrhoid; L. and offensive. Soft, with pain; S., very yellow, then a weak, faint feeling. Watery, with shuddering. Last part thin, in an hour a small soft stool, with urging, transiently > stool. Slimy; and light-colored; and light-colored, loose, frequent; and almost white; white, like the white of an egg, but lumpy, with straining and burning in rectum and sensation as if fæces were hot; and dark, offensive; with straining in rectum, each stool smaller than the preceding.

Dry and lumpy; and black; then prolapsus of anus, with pain in hæmorrhoids. Slightly costive, dark, bilious. First part dry and black, the last part mushy and white. First part lumpy, then diarrhœa. Almost white. Dark; and frequent, small, offensive. Offensive; and bilious. Forcible at 4 A.M., then straining; at 6.30 A.M., then straining and pain in hæmorrhoid. Small; with straining and shuddering. Large and difficult. At an unusual time. Driving out of bed at 2 A.M. Delayed. Frequent; with straining and burning in rectum and with one stool shuddering; and each smaller than the preceding one but more slimy, with less pain before the stool but more pain after the stool.

Clinical.—Diarrhœa, with violent twisting colic, paroxysmal in character; stools most frequent in the morning, generally yellow, thin, followed by exhaustion (Colo., Gamboge).

Sexual Organs.—*Relaxation and coldness* (Agnus c., Carbon) in evening. Coldness and almost insensibility. Inaction. Pain in penis and l. testicle in afternoon. No erections for many days. *Strong-smelling sweat on scrotum and pubes* (Sil., Thuja). Scrotum cold and moist, penis cold. Cramping pain in l. spermatic cord in morning, extending to testicles. *Excitement, with frequent erections. Desire diminished;* in evening. **Emission in sleep** (Dig.).

Clinical.—Seminal emissions from sexual atony. Uterine colic (dysmenorrhœa), pains shooting in different directions from the uterus.

Respiratory Organs.—Constriction of glottis. Irritation of larynx, with inclination to cough. Cough from irritation of r. side of throat; deep C.; dry in morning and deep; hacking; *hacking, from tickling deep in throat;* violent, at 8 A.M., from tickling deep in throat, can but just breathe, cannot walk, frothy expectoration seems to come from the head, during the cough pain at the lower end of the sternum so that he can hardly move, then pain in front of r., then in both ears, as if the head would burst. Inclination to cough in morning; at 2 P.M. from irritation deep in throat; at 9 P.M. from tickling in throat.

Chest.—Darting below l. nipple at 10.30 A.M., arresting motion, but > motion; D. in lower part of l. lung at 7 P.M.; in lower part of r. lung, from back to front; twisting, beneath axilla at 8 P.M., extending to nipple and about ninth rib and deep into lung, almost arresting breathing. Cutting in l. lung. Cramping pain in r. lung below nipple, at 6 P.M., arresting motion and respiration; twisting, below l. axilla at 9 P.M.

Sharp pain below l. nipple at 6 P.M.; in l. chest in evening; in middle of l. eighth rib, hindering deep inspiration; through l., above nipple and towards sternum, at 9 P.M., arresting respiration; deep below l. axilla in morning, arresting breathing. Sharp pain in r. lung at 9 A.M.; 10 A.M.; 5 P.M.; evening; at night; lower part also at 9 A.M.; posterior part in morning; in centre; in centre at 10 A.M.; through centre in morning; through centre at 4 P.M.; in centre at 9 P.M.; at side of nipple; below nipple in morning; below nipple at 7 A.M. and in l. lung below axilla; below and to right of nipple at 4 P.M.; opposite or at side of nipple, > pressure; in region of nipple, hindering breathing. Sharp pain in l. lung in evening; in lower part at 7 A.M.; lower part at 9 P.M.; in back part and in scapula, extending down inside of arm; in centre in morning; in region of nipple; outside and parallel with nipple; through l. lung near nipple at 7 A.M.; through lung above nipple; below and to l. of nipple; suddenly at back near centre at 7 P.M. Sharp pulsating pain at top of sternum.

Pain below l. nipple at 10 P.M.; behind top of sternum at 8 P.M.; in middle of sternum at 9 P.M.; in lungs. Pain in r. lung; in morning, then in l.; at 3 A.M.; at 5 P.M.; through r. at 6 P.M.; through top at 9 P.M.; in centre in the morning; in centre in evening; back central part at 10 P.M.; above nipple at 8 P.M.; below nipple at 8 P.M., with feeling as if it would arrest the breath, not < deep inspiration, but causing inclination to cough; through lung below nipple at 9 P.M. as if it would arrest the breath, but by > deep inspiration. Pain in l. lung in morning; through top at 4 P.M.; in upper part at 2 P.M., then in upper part of r. at 4 P.M.; upper posterior part at noon; back part in morning; back part at 5 P.M.; back part near lower part of scapula at 2 P.M.; in centre posteriorly at 9.30 P.M.; back lower part in morning; parallel with and at side of nipple; above nipple in morning; frequent pain through l. lung at 9 P.M.

Flying pain in chest and back (cervical part). Drawing pain in r. lung at 7 A.M. Sore pain in centre of r. lung; S. pain in upper part of both lungs in evening and in back part of l. Burning pain behind top of sternum at 7 A.M. Dragging below l. axilla at 2 P.M. Distress in l. lung near heart at noon; D. across chest and in upper part, causing difficult breathing, > deep inspiration. Tightness across upper part at 11 P.M. Burning in l. lung in region of nipple at 2 P.M. Cold sensation extending from end of sternum to navel, about an inch in width, with almost burning around navel.

Heart.—Sticking; in evening. Darting at 4 P.M., arresting breath. Catching pain in evening. Sharp pain; and to left of it; at 7 P.M., with faint feeling in it; arresting motion in morning and in forenoon; frequent, in morning. Pain in morning; with faint feeling. Faint distressing sensation. The beating can be heard after walking a little. Hard, slow beating, shaking the chest and waking suddenly.

Pulse.—Pulse 80.

Nape and Neck.—Sharp twisting pain at 3.30 A.M. in l., then r. side. Pain in morning; evening; pain extending to occiput and shoulders, < l. Pulling pain in morning, < l. side; P. pain in vertebræ at 1 P.M.

Back.—Pain; at noon, and in middle of r. lung. *Lameness* (Berb.); in morning. Weakness of spine, with soreness. Tearing through scapula and lung. Cutting in l. scapula. Sharp pain at lower part of l. scapula at 1 P.M.; at 3 P.M., extending through lung; deep, in morning, then through middle of r. lung. Pain in l. scapula and through lung; at 7 A.M.; at 5 P.M.; through r. scapula and lung. Drawing pain between scapulæ. External soreness over r. scapula at 9 P.M. Sharp pain in dorsal region. Pain in dorsal region. Lameness of dorsal region at 6 A.M.; in morning, > motion. Sudden sharp pain in l. side at tenth rib, in afternoon.

Lumbar Region.—Darting in r. Cutting on bending spine. Cramping pain at 5 P.M.; C. pain in r. sacral region. Sharp pain in r. in morning; S. pain in muscles in morning; in l. at 9 A.M., < stooping, hindering motion; in r. at 3 P.M.; in evening; in morning, extending to testicles; in r. in afternoon, pulling me over backward and to the right, and in l., pulling me over backward and to the left. Sharp drawing pain in l. at 7 A.M.; at 7 P.M. Pain; r.; in region of liver in morning; in r. in morning, with soreness; at 6 A.M.; in r. at 9.30 A.M.; in l. at 5 P.M.; in evening; in evening, with lameness; in upper part on bending spine; < bending spine; < walking or stooping; < stooping, and in hips. Heavy pain, < stooping. Pulling pain in l. at 10.30 P.M., > motion. Lame pain, hindering motion; L. pain in afternoon, extending to legs. Lameness; in morning; in morning, < r. side, with pain; at 1 P.M.; 2 P.M., with pain; 6 P.M.; 9 P.M., with stiffness; 9.30 P.M.; 10 P.M., < stooping; 11 P.M., with pain in l. inguinal region; < by stooping or pulling (holding a horse); in region of liver in morning, so that turning in bed was almost impossible, > walking. Soreness in morning. Weakness, > standing and walking.

Extremities. — Nails of fingers and toes brittle. Aching in wrists, hands, fingers, ankles, feet and toes; with stiffness; A. in hands and feet; in elbows and knees; in r. elbow, then in r. knee; in morning, in r. knee, r. ankle and r. elbow; in morning, in l. arm, l. leg and l. foot; in hands, fingers, ankles, feet and toes, > exercise, with stiffness of them. Frequent pains in joints; in morning; at 6 P.M., in knees and elbows; in evening, in elbows and knees. Lame pain in l. elbow at 1 P.M., alternating with pains in knees. Stiffness of hands and feet.

Upper Extremities.—Axilla. Sticking in l. at 9 P.M. Sharp twisting pain below l. at 10.30 P.M., > motion. Sharp pulling pain below l. at 4 P.M. Sharp sore pain in r. Pain in l.; with soreness; in r., extending down arm, < walking, with soreness.

Shoulder.—Sharp pain in r.; l. joint; frequent, in r.; on top of l. in morning. Sharp jerking pain in l. *Pain in l.;* in r; in top of l.; in morning, < l.; on top of l. in afternoon; on top of l. at 1 P.M.; in l. at 7 P.M., > motion, with lameness; in top of l. at 7 P.M., extending into neck; in l. at 11 P.M. Frequent pain on top of l.; F. pain in l. in forenoon; occasional pain in joints in forenoon. Pulling pain in r.; through shoulders in morning; on top of l., extending to neck and head, < at attachment of sterno-cleido-mastoideus muscle; sharp, in r. at 7 A.M., extending to back part of lung; frequent, in l. and in neck. Weight on top of r. at 4 P.M.

Arm.—Pain in l. at 3 A.M.; P. in l. arm and elbow, passing into forearm. Numbness, and of hands. Weakness, < elbows. Cutting in l. above elbow at 5 P.M. Sharp pain in middle of l. humerus. Pain in middle of l. humerus in evening; in r. upper arm at 3 P.M.

Elbow.—Sharp pain in r.; in l. in morning; in r. in forenoon; in r. at 7 P.M. Sharp cramping pain in r. at 7 A.M. Grinding pain in morning; in l. at 8 A.M.; in r. in evening; l. at 7 P.M.; at 9 P.M.; l., as if out of joint. Pain; in morning; l. in morning; 6 A.M.; r. at 1 P.M.; r. at 4 P.M.; r. at 8 P.M.; l. at 9.30 P.M.; r. at night. Drawing pain in l. at 9 P.M.; D. pain in elbows, wrists and fingers, at times very sharp in fingers; sharp, on inside of r. at 7 P.M. Numb pain extending from l. down ulna towards wrist, at 7 A.M. Lameness of l. in morning, with stiffness.

Forearm.—Sharp pain in middle of l. radius. Grinding pain in middle of l. Pain in r.; below l. elbow; in middle; in bones; in middle of l. ulna; in middle of l., between ulna and radius; in morning; middle of bones in morning; under side of l. at 2.30 and 5 A.M.; bones of l. at 10 A.M.; in middle of r. at 10 A.M.; l. at 2.30 P.M.; r. at 3 P.M.; bones of l. in evening; l. at 10 P.M.; middle of l. ulna at 10 P.M.; in ulnar side of lower third of l., extending to little finger; intermittent, in middle of r. in evening. Drawing pain, and in wrists.

Wrist.—Sharp pain in r. in evening. Sprained pain in l. Pain in l.; at 9 A.M. and lameness; in r. at 9 P.M.

Hand.—Sharp pain in r. Darting sprained pain in r. in evening. Cramping pain in r. at 3 P.M. Grinding pain in r. at 9 P.M. Pain; *in r.;* l.; in bones in morning, < l.; in night; frequent, between third and fourth metacarpal bones of l. in afternoon. Drawing pain; in l. in morning; sharp, in l. in morning. Weakness in morning; 1 P.M.; r.; r. in evening. Numbness of l. at 7 A.M. with pricking in index; N. at 7 P.M., < l.; of l. hand and forearm as if asleep, < little finger.

Fingers.—Sensation of a briar in middle, l. then r., with throbbing pain, darting stinging next to the bones, and tenderness on pressure. Cutting tearing. Cutting in r. index. Sharp pain in l. little; l. thumb; r. thumb; r. thumb at 7 P.M.; in bones of one, then of another in afternoon. Grinding pain in first joint of r. thumb; at 10 A.M. Twisting pain in first joint of r. thumb in morning. Pain; in a spot on back of l. thumb, between first and second joint; in first joint of l. thumb; first joint of r. thumb in morning; r. thumb at 5 P.M.; l. little, at 6 P.M.; first joint of r. thumb at 8 P.M.; l. thumb in evening; l. index in evening. Stiffness. Numbness of r. in morning, with tingling.

Lower Extremities.—Occasional cramping pains in back sides of legs at 1 P.M., < above knees. Pain in whole length of r. leg, < buttock and heel. Difficulty in getting out of a chair at 2 P.M. and in walking. Tearing in r. hip, hindering walking. Sharp pain in r. hip-joint. Pain in r. hip; in morning; in l. hip in evening; in r. hip in evening, extending down front of thigh nearly to knee, causing limping; in l. hip, heel and sole in morning. Lameness of r. hip as if gluteals were too short, < walking, > rest.

Thigh.—Cramping pain midway between hip and knee, l. then r.; C. pain posteriorly in r. as if muscles were too short, < walking. Pain like an electric shock from l. to vertex when lying in afternoon after dinner. Pain in r.; in l. in morning; above l. knee in morning; in r. femur above knee at 7 A.M.; above r. popliteal space at 4 P.M.; above r. knee in evening. Drawing pain on inner and back side; D. pain above r. popliteal space at 10 P.M.

Knee.—Tearing in l.; r. at 1 P.M. Cramping pain; in morning; on back side in morning, also extending down back of r. leg; in l. at 10 A.M.; r. at 11 A.M., < by ascending stairs; r. at 3 P.M.; in posterior side of l. at 11 P.M. Sharp pain; in morning; on inside of l. at 9 A.M.; forenoon; in outside of l. in afternoon; l. popliteal space at 1 P.M.; in front of l. at 5 P.M.; r. in evening; on inside of r. in evening; in night; on inside of l. when walking, after walking a little way on inside of r. at head of tibia; r. popliteal space, hindering walking. Twisting pain in l. at 10 P.M. Grinding pain in r.; on inside of l. at 8 P.M.; at 9 P.M.; at lower part of l. patella at 10 P.M. *Pain; l.;* r.; on inside; at head of r. tibia; in l. popliteal space, then in r. knee; then in r. popliteal space; < inner and posterior side of r.; in morning; in morning on ascending stairs; at head of r. tibia in morning; on inside of l. at 7 A.M.; at head of l. fibula at 9 A.M.; in r. in forenoon; at noon; in afternoon; in r. at 6 P.M., when walking; evening; at night; < ascending stairs, < r.; at head of r. tibia, > motion; in l. popliteal space, hindering walking; in l. at 9 A.M., extending up thigh; in l., extending into foot; < l., extending into legs, > when rubbing, but appearing in feet and returning in knees on ceasing to rub, the pain > motion, which is difficult on account of a dry, grating sensation; alternately in each, beginning at back and extending to front, at 7 A.M. Pain in l. as if out of joint, > motion. Bruised pain at 10.30 A.M. Drawing pain; in r. in morning; r. popliteal space at 6 P.M.; in r. at 9 P.M. Soreness at 1 P.M., < walking. Sore pain in r. popliteal space; S. pain on inside of l. in afternoon. Lameness of r.; with weakness; with stiffness; in morning, with pain and weakness; at 8 A.M., with soreness; in evening; of l. in evening. *Weakness; in morning;* l. in morning; in afternoon; evening; at 9 P.M., < l.; in evening when walking; in evening from standing a short time; < descending stairs, with pain at head of tibia; r., < walking; > continued walking, with trembling.

Leg.—Cramping pain at head of l. fibula at 9 A.M., < walking; in evening; C. pain posteriorly in r. leg in morning; in r. tendo-achillis at 11 A.M.; < near r. knee. Sharp pain in r.; in l. at 9 A.M., hindering walking; in l. tendo-achillis at 3 P.M.; in middle of r. fibula at night; in l. tibia near ankle, causing limping, then in r. tibia, then in r. hand. Grinding pain in upper part of r. tibia at 9 P.M. Pain; in middle of r. tibia; at middle of l. fibula; below r. knee, < on back side. Pain in morning in r. tendo-achillis; in r. calf; at head of r. tibia; below r. knee; in bones below knee; on both sides below r. knee on waking. Pain in bones at 1.30 A.M.; P. below l. knee at 3 A.M.; posteriorly near r. knee at 11 A.M.; in upper part of l. fibula at 1 P.M.; in middle of r. tibia at 4.45 P.M. when walking, with soreness, then the pain extended to l. side of knee, at edge of patella, causing lameness, then the pain moved to lower part of fibula; in l. fibula in evening; at middle of l. fibula in evening; in bones below l. knee at 7 P.M.; in r. calf at 9 P.M.; in r. tibia when walking at 10.30 P.M., > touch, with soreness; > motion; > elevating feet; at head of r. tibia, extending into knee; at head of l. fibula, extending into knee; frequent P. in l. tendo-achillis. Drawing pain in calves; in upper part of l. fibula at 7 P.M. Lame pain in upper part of l. tibia at 2 P.M.; at head of r. fibula at night. Lameness of r. at 3 A.M. Sore lame feeling below r. knee and in front at 6.45 P.M. Weakness; of r. in morning, with numbness; on rising, > walking. Heaviness. Numbness and heaviness of r. as if asleep; of l. at 9 P.M. Numbness of legs and feet at 7 P.M.

Ankle.—Stinging on outside of l. at 5 P.M. Sharp pain in l.; on inside. Pain; < r.; r. in morning; in morning, with lameness; in afternoon; in r. at 2 P.M., with lameness; in evening; in l. in evening when sitting; in l., with lameness; in l., with inability to sit still. Drawing pain. Weakness of l.

Foot.—Cutting in soles and bottom of toes. Darting pain in r. heel at 2 A.M., darting to the body, leaving pain in r. knee. Sharp pain in l. heel in morning; sudden sharp pain in outside of r. foot at 10 P.M., then in leg up to knee. Pain; < r.; running into soles. Drawing pain.

Toes.—Sticking on under side of r. great at 10 P.M.; in a corn on l. second in evening; biting, in same corn in evening. Cutting tearing. Jumping darting pain in corns on both second toes at night. Sharp pain in r. little, > pressure; S. pain in a corn on l. second. Grinding pain in r. metatarsal joint at 4 P.M., then on top of foot and leg, half way to knee. Boring in r. little. Pain in l. great; at base of r. second, > motion but returning; in corns on both second, with soreness; in corn on l. second in evening; in same corn P., with soreness.

Clinical.—Sciatica, pain shooting the whole length of the extremity, in the r. side, > lying perfectly still (Bry.).

Skin.—Sudden stinging in various parts in evening. Creeping, tingling through thighs and legs, > rubbing. Itching of various parts; at 6 P.M.; on back and shoulders; over r. shoulder. Itching of scapulæ, < r.; over lower part of l.; over r. and between scapulæ, day and evening; over l. at 11 A.M., then over r.; over l. at 3 P.M.; over r. at 4 P.M.; in evening, < r.; over and between S. in evening; over lower part every evening; between r. S. and spine in evening; beginning over r. and extending over body, < arms. Itching of l. side of chest; of wrists; r. palm; r. hip, l. thigh and l. hand; hips and r. thigh at 5 P.M.; over hips in morning, extending down legs, < getting cool; on thighs and legs, < undressing or getting chilly; l. foot at 6.45 PM..; on front of l., then r. ankle; l. ankle when walking; on front of ankles when walking; on front of r. ankle when walking, extending over joint; sudden itching over r. scapula. Biting itching over r. scapula at 9.30 P.M. Stinging itching over and between scapulæ at 9 P.M.; S. itching below l. knee; suddenly over r. hip in evening. Burning itching over r. scapula at noon; over scapulæ in evening, < r.; on outside of l. leg near ankle.

Sleep.—Disposition to yawn and stretch. Sleep in afternoon; at 5 P.M., with a book in his hand. Late falling asleep; with pain in joints and bones. Sleeplessness; with restlessness. Restlessness from midnight till morning; restless night, woke at midnight with pain in r. lobe of liver and pain in l. side (eighth rib), bruised feeling in the whole of spinal cord, the pain in l. side and in liver continued next day, with pain in l. lumbar region. Sleep, with confused consciousness of the conversation around him. Confused sleep, with anxious dreams. Dreamy sleep. Dreams, with restlessness. Horrible dreams. Lascivious dreams.

Fever.— Chilliness; in forenoon; evening; after going to bed; at 1.30 A.M., with bitter mouth; over l. scapula; on back, beginning over l. scapula. Shuddering. Hot head at 7 A.M. Burning in l. lumbar region at 5 P.M.; on top of l. shoulder in evening; over scapulæ in evening, with itching; over l. scapula at 9 P.M., with itching. Hot and dry skin. Sweat during sleep; S. on forehead at 8 A.M.

Dirca Palustris.

A tincture is made of the fresh inner bark of the twigs of Dirca palustris, L.

Generalities and Mind.—Inability to sit quietly in one position. Uneasiness and sensation as if something unpleasant were to happen. Full sensation through the body, with sluggishness. Weakness; at 1.45 P.M., with desire to lie down; towards evening; at 9 P.M.; so that walking was difficult. Necessity to lie down at noon, feeling as if my senses were leaving me. Aggravation every four days, later every two days. Time passed too slowly. Expecting bad news constantly in the daytime, worried and annoyed by everything. Dulness; of mental powers and inertia; with indisposition to talk. Inability to think or study, dull and bewildered condition. Difficulty in thinking of what word to use in writing. Absent-minded, often writing the wrong words.

Head.—Aching; with sore pain in temples and vertigo. Dulness. Congestion, with fulness of head, neck and chest. Fulness, < temples and in front; fulness in morning, with heaviness; in morning, with pain in temples and in front; at night, with heaviness. Vertigo on walking, as if he would fall to the left; vertigo, with inclination to the left and with lightness of head. Sensation as if lobes of cerebrum were drawn forward towards frontal sinuses. Pain in forehead and temples in afternoon. Congestive pain in forehead, with darting inward from each temple. Sensation as if brows were corrugated and as if brain were drawn downward. Congestion to forehead in morning, with pressure. Dulness in forehead at 9.30 A.M. Sticking in r. temple, < motion. Darting pain in r. temple before noon. Sharp pain in temples, < l., extending inward. Pain in temples; at 3 P.M., extending inward, > hard pressure; at 7 P.M., extending towards centre; in l. towards evening, extending towards centre. Pain in vertex after dinner, > pressure; pain in vertex and occiput and all through head, extending into spine. Throbbing pain in l. half of head, < coughing or moving, could not have anything touch occiput, felt better with the hair down or high up on head. Intermittent pain high up in occiput, in afternoon, extending inward. Pain low down in occiput in morning on waking, < raising up or moving head, < towards noon, when it extended over vertex to forehead, where it was a congestive pain, gradually > evening, with throbbing of carotids. Scalp felt dry and tight.

Eyes, Ears and Face.—Haziness of retina. Eyes sore and painful to touch. Lids heavy. *Photophobia;* < gaslight. Roaring in one ear, then in the other. Face pale; and sunken. Face red and bloated in morning.

Mouth and Throat.—Tongue coated *white;* thicker at base; *dirty white*, thicker towards centre and far back. Tongue light and smooth. Taste sour. Throbbing of carotids. Fauces red and raw; rose-red towards evening, and dry, pain on swallowing. Acidity in throat at 9.30 P.M. Swallowing painful.

Stomach.—Appetite diminished. *No thirst.* Eructations; *empty;* of sour-tasting gas. Nausea, < afternoon. Uneasy feeling, as of a lump.

Abdomen.—Distention; and tenderness on pressure; tympanitic; tympanitic at 9 P.M., with pain. *Rumbling.* Emissions of flatus; with pain in abdomen, < about umbilicus, > bending forward and by a consistent stool, soreness and smarting of anus during stool, the smarting continuing after the stool; frequent emissions of fetid. Occasional griping at 9.20 A.M. Sharp pain about every fifteen minutes before going to bed and afterwards. Pain; on waking at 6 A.M., with urging of stool, stool dark and thin, coming but little at a time, relieving the pain, which soon returned, to be followed by another stool, after passing all that was possible, had the cramping pain every few minutes; in afternoon; at 9 P.M. *on walking* and on pressure; at 10 P.M.; with desire for stool; partly > diarrhœa.

Discomfort; in evening, with burning; like "stomach-ache" in evening, with passage of flatus. Uneasiness as before stool, but no satisfactory stool. Soreness of muscles. Lancinating pain in l. hypochondrium with tympanitis, the pain spreading over abdomen. Griping about umbilicus; below U. at 1. P.M., with aching. Biting above U., < 10 P.M. Pain above U. at 9 P.M., with flatus; sore pain in and below umbilical region. Burning about umbilicus at 7.30 P.M.; below U. at 12.30 P.M. Bearing down in lower part of abdomen as if muscles were relaxed, > when the head ached less. Aching low down in pelvis.

Anus and Stool.—Throbbing *sticking* in anus at 10 P.M., with pain in abdomen. Soreness of anus. Tenesmus and straining at stool, remained half an hour at stool. Desire for stool, but only scanty passage of mucus; but only scanty passage of frothy mucus; ineffectual desire. Violent purging, with tenesmus. Frequent and profuse diarrhœa. Diarrhœa, with flatus. Watery stool in evening, with tenesmus, only partially > by stool; W., partially relieving the colic; W., yellowish; and gushing; and bubbling, with flatus, preceded by rumbling; and mucous towards evening, with pain in abdomen; and frequent. Passage of fæcal mucus before rising, with flatus. Stool at first consistent, then thin, fæcal, slimy, with flatus. Constipation after catamenia; C. and no desire for stool. Stool small and insufficient; three times a day; and pasty; and sticky; and dry, sticky, with apparently no power to expel it. Stool scanty and soft. Stool, with colic and griping.

Urinary and Sexual Organs.—Pain in region of bladder, with soreness. Urine diminished and high-colored; diminished and with white, sometimes reddish sediment. Uterus feels as if too low and as if it would come out while at stool. Menses sooner than usual, not so profuse or long-lasting as usual.

Respiratory Organs and Chest.—Stinging from without inward in larynx, with suffocating sensation. Cough, < morning, and appearance of a cold. Expectoration of offensive *sweetish* mucus. Dyspnœa; from slightest exertion; on ascending stairs; with oppression of chest, desire to clear throat and much spitting. Out of breath on ascending a slight elevation, with palpitation, vertigo and pallor. Sharp pain in r. chest, extending into abdomen and l. shoulder. Soreness of chest as from a cold.

Heart and Pulse.—Heart's action excited by the least motion. Pulse rapid; and full and strong, then suddenly weak and irregular; then slow and weak. Pulse slow and weak; but excited by the least exertion; slow and soft. Pulse weak.

Back and Extremities.—Pain in back and loins; in small of back and in side before going to bed, running around into r. side, in the night sharp pain in the latter spot, low down in r. side, waking her three times, and a hard lump. Heavy pain in region of kidneys, with crawling sensation and occasional darting pain. Extremities weak and trembling on standing. Neuralgic pain in arm before noon; N. pain in shoulders and arms, making it difficult to keep them still. Soreness of muscles of thighs extending to knees, with stiffness, making it difficult to rise from the bed or chair. Neuralgic pain from foot to knee; N. pain extending down l. leg.

Sleep.—Sleepiness and dulness; S., but inability to sleep. But little sleep at night. Sleep delayed, restless and disturbed. Sleep full of dreams. Dream of dead bodies.

Fever.—Cold feet. Heat at night, with restlessness and inability to sleep. Feverishness on going to bed at 10 P.M., then sweat. Sweat on hands.

Dolichos Pruriens.

A tincture is made of the fuzz (hairs) of the pods of Dolichos pruriens, L.; they are scraped off and digested in alcohol for a week or more.

Pain in throat below r. angle of jaw as if a splinter were imbedded vertically, < swallowing. Pain in the gum so that she could not sleep half the night. Twitching of muscles.

Clinical.—During pregnancy intolerable itching all over body at night. It has been prescribed in jaundice with white stools, also in complaints from worms and for affections of dentition. Herpes zoster beginning on l. scapula, extending to axilla and then to sternum and backward to spine, with burning and smarting. It has been found valuable in the intense itching of jaundice; itching worse at night, and < scratching.

Drosera.

A tincture is made of the entire fresh plant of Drosera rotundifolia, L.

General Action.—The greatest interest centres about the action of the drug on the respiratory apparatus, especially its spasmodic cough, closely resembling whooping cough. It is said to have developed tuberculosis in animals.

Allies.—Hydrocy. ac., Con., Kali carb.; and compare spasmodic cough remedies.

Generalities.—Weakness in morning; on waking, so that he can scarcely open his eyes; *general W., with sunken eyes and cheeks.*

Mind.—Rage at a trifle. *Mental uneasiness when reading.* Ill humor. *Depressed by persecutions of others on all sides and discouraged and solicitous about the future.* Despondency, with anxiety and loss of appetite. Uneasy, sad, he imagined that he was deceived by spiteful, envious people. Anxiety evenings when alone; A. < about 7 or 8 P.M. as if impelled to drown himself; with restlessness and distrust; rising from region below ribs; as if his enemies allowed him no rest; as if he would hear unpleasant news, with general flushes of heat, < over face, afterwards with shivering over whole body without heat or thirst. Obstinacy in execution of matured plans. Taciturnity, with dread of hearing something unpleasant. Joyless, stupid and disinclined to physical or mental labor.

Head.—Tearing in brain, < towards forehead, < moving eyes, > resting head on hands. *Aching;* in brain, he feels every step in it. Heaviness on holding it upright, > stooping; H. and confusion. Vertigo on walking in open air; and inclination to fall to l.; with disinclination to work. Forehead, cutting stitches in r.; tearing tensive pain, < stooping; gnawing externally above brows in morning, with drawing thence into cerebellum; boring outward on stooping when writing; pain after violent motion and while walking, like the confusion of head which arises from violent talking; pain above orbits on stooping, > walking; *pain extending outward in F. and zygomatic processes;* sore pain in l. eminence. Pressure outward at r. temple. Pain above r. temple. Boring externally on vertex. Pressure externally at vertex, with at times gnawing. Drawing pain in r. half of brain, extending towards occiput; in l. brain extending towards temple. Scalp, *sore sensation in skin of r. temple;* sore pain above r. side of forehead; burning sore pain of r. side, > touch; biting burning pain on vertex; itching, < sides; itching-gnawing on forepart, > rubbing.

Eyes.—Stitches extending outward, < stooping. Cutting transversely across l. Pain more biting than pressing, on exerting vision. Tensive burning transversely across l. and lids. *Pupils dilated; contracted.* Sticking in l. ball during rest. Tearing across l. ball. Burning pain in r. ball, with sticking in l. inner ear. Agglutination. Sore pain in r. lower lid, < touch. Itching of lids. Drawing, burning pain in superciliary ridge, < towards temple. Pain in l. brow and lid as if suppurating, on pressure. Vision as through a veil, the letters run together when reading. V. obscured at 7 P.M., on entering the house from a walk, with vibrations before eyes. Presbyopia and weakness of eyes, a vibration before eyes on attempting to recognize small objects. Glistening flickerings, < about upper part and on one side, on looking at the flickering it moves out of the field of vision, disturbing him when reading.

Ears.—Sticking in l. middle, with twinging; S. in r., not wholly external; slow S. inward through l.; tensive, < externally; tickling, in innermost part of r. Tearing in front of l. meatus, with twitching pain. Gnawing beneath cartilages. Pain in r. middle as if everything would be pressed together. Drawing pain in r. lobule and part of cartilage. Pricking and burning pain externally in r., then drawing inward. Difficult hearing, with increased humming before E. Humming before E., with roaring or sound as of a distant drum.

Nose.—Prickling in l. side, with crawling in l. ear. Crawling in r., provoking sneezing. *Frequent sneezing, with or without fluent coryza;* painful S., with cough, obliging him to hold his hand upon his chest. Fluent coryza, < morning. Bleeding; morning and evening; in morning, on blowing when washing the face; on stooping. Very sensitive to sour smells.

Face.—Sudden jerking in l. cheek. Jaw, sticking tearing in l. lower, as if in periosteum; burrowing in r. joint and in adjacent bones, < opening mouth; pain in r. joint; drawing pressure on upper. Crack in middle of lower lip. Dry lips and little taste.

Mouth.—Teeth (loose); sticking in morning after warm drinks; pain; cold sensation in crown of an incisor. Tongue, whitish ulcer on tip; round, painless swelling in middle; picking sticking on dorsum; sticking biting in r. side and tip. Biting on inner side of l. cheek, as after pepper. Bitter taste to bread; B. taste in throat in morning, till dinner. No taste to food.

Throat.—Rough scraping dry sensation in fauces and soft palate, causing hacking cough, with yellow mucous expectoration and hoarseness so that he speaks with ex-

ertion in a bass voice, with oppression of chest as if the air were withheld on talking and coughing, so that the breath could not be expired. Burning rough sensation deep in T. after dinner. Crawling biting in r. side of fauces when not swallowing.

Stomach.—Ravenous hunger without appetite, returning when he thinks it is satisfied. Thirst. Acid eructations. Bitter eructations. *Waterbrash. Hiccough.* Nausea after eating; N. when coughing; (on thinking of it); with stupefying headache, < in forehead. Vomiting at night; in morning, mostly of bile; *during the chill, at last of bile;* before dinner; of water, mucus and food on coughing; of blood. Sticking in pit, with throbbing. Clawing together in pit. Pinching tension in pit as if everything would be drawn inward, < deep inspiration. Tensive pain in epigastrium before and after a soft stool, if he holds the breath, > during inspiration and expiration, < sitting and stooping.

Abdomen.—Cutting. Cutting blows in muscles of A. and chest, < sitting. Pinching, with clawing and diarrhœa; cutting P. as from incarcerated flatus. Pain; twisting. Constriction when coughing if he does not expectorate easily, with efforts to vomit. Sticking in r. side when sitting; boring S. in r. parietes; drawing S. from r. side to l. when walking, almost arresting breathing. Pain across hypochondria and lower part of chest; in H. on touch and on coughing, obliging him to press upon them when coughing. Constriction in H. on coughing; *in H., preventing cough unless he presses on pit of stomach.* Sudden contraction of lower A. as if about to vomit, on expiration in evening in bed, causing cough. Sticking in r. iliac fossa; drawing S. from l. loin into penis.

Clinical.—Constrictive pain in hypogastrium during the paroxysms of cough, so that he cannot cough on account of the pain, and so that he presses his hands on the pit of his stomach or holds his sides.

Rectum and Stool.—Pressing-out pain in R. when not at stool. Thin stool, then ineffectual urging. Stool always becomes softer as it passes. Copious, pasty. Scanty, hard, with pressing. Frequent, with cutting in abdomen. Bloody mucus, with S., then pains in abdomen and small of back.

Urinary and Sexual Organs.—*Frequent urging to urinate, with scanty urine.* Profuse urine; and frequent micturition. Watery, odorless urine, with slimy offensive stools. Itching sticking in glans.

Respiratory Organs.—*Bruised feeling in larynx when inhaling. Crawling in larynx provoking hacking cough* (Con.), *with sensation as if a soft substance were in it and with sticking extending to r. side of pharynx. Cough waking him at* 2 A.M. (Kali c.); C. in morning, with expectoration; *in evening on lying down; at night* (Hyos.); from very deep in chest; **paroxysmal, so that he could scarcely get his breath** (Hydrocy. ac.). Bitter expectoration in morning; nauseous E. in morning; (salt E. by coughing and hawking). *Dyspnœa, < talking, > walking, with constriction of throat.* Difficult respiration. Deep respiration. The breath from the lungs has a burnt odor when coughing.

Clinical.—The cough is usually < night, coming on immediately after lying down, of a spasmodic character, often ending with choking and vomiting and with cold sweat, sometimes provoked by tickling in larynx as from a feather, or from collection of mucus which must be expectorated, at other times it seems to come from the abdomen and to be associated with convulsions of the muscles of the chest and abdomen, *when he must hold his sides with his hands,* the cough generally ends with expectoration of mucus. Whooping cough, with constriction of chest and abdomen and sides, so that he must hold them with his hands, attacks < night. Whooping cough, paroxysms < after midnight, the child holds its sides with its hands, often retches and vomits. In laryngitis there is generally a rather free secretion of mucus, the cough is paroxysmal in character. In laryngeal phthisis, with great hoarseness, secretion of tough mucus, sore bruised feeling of the chest, paroxysmal cough after midnight, breaks into sweat on waking, etc. Bronchitis of old people, with severe paroxysms of cough, free expectoration. A number of cases of undoubted phthisis have been wonderfully relieved by this drug. It is often indicated in the cough of measles, especially hoarse cough in afternoon and evening and after midnight. After coughing some of the expectoration seems to remain, so that he cannot fully expire, < speaking and coughing. Whooping cough, with hæmorrhage from mouth and nose, and suffocation.

Chest.—*Hæmoptysis* (Ip.). *Sticking in muscles on coughing and breathing; near axilla through the day on coughing or breathing deeply,* > **by pressure,** with purulent bloody expectoration; in l. intercostal muscles during inspiration and expiration, almost arresting breath; hot, in muscles of r. true ribs during inspiration and expiration. Pain in and below clavicles, over a small space in lungs, when inhaling, extending round to scapulæ; P. transversely across chest, more pressive than sticking, when sitting, with pain on touch; tensive, in muscles during inspiration and expiration. *Constriction of lungs when inhaling.* Burning in middle without thirst. Crawling in l. intercostal muscles, with pain in temples, < r.

Neck and Back.—Stiffness of nape and pain on motion. Cramp in muscles of back and abdomen on turning head and body. Sticking in l. muscles of back. Sticking tearing in spine when sitting, extending to anterior spine of l. ilium. Bruised pain here and there in back. Strained pain in B. in morning. Drawing pain in B. and shoulders. Rheumatism between scapulæ on moving, extending to sacrum. Sticking in tuberosity of ischium on rising from a seat; itching S. in coccyx when sitting. Grasping pinching in l. loin on rapid walking, impeding respiration, > pressure.

Extremities.—(Jerking or jerking sensation.) *Sticking in muscles. Pain composed of gnawing and sticking in shafts of bones of arms, thighs and legs, < joints, > motion, with sticking in joints. Bruised feeling, with pain externally. Pain, with general paralyzed sensation.* Aching in those upon which he lies, as if the bed were too hard. Cramplike pressure, now in upper, now in lower. Paralyzed feeling in all.

Upper Extremities.—Sprained pain in l. axilla on walking or standing, > touch. Pressure outward in axilla during rest *Twitching in r. shoulder during rest.* Bruised pain in shoulder-joint on bending arm backward, raising, touching it or lying upon it. Pain in S.-joint as if arm would go to sleep and were tired, > continued motion. Sticking in r. arm, with pain extending from shoulder to elbow and with suppurative pain in elbow on touch. Pain in arm on motion, as if muscles would be torn from bones.

Bruised pain in region of elbow, then in shoulder. Pinching tension in bend of elbow on flexion, only slightly felt on stretching it out. Sticking through middle of l. forearm. Sudden cutting between bones above wrist, with paralytic weakness of arm. Pain in wrist at articulation of ulna and radius on bending and on touch. Bruised pain in hands, extending to elbows. Pulsation in an artery on back of l. hand, with outward pressure in forehead. Spasmodic contraction of flexors of fingers when holding anything. Now r., now l. fingers inclined to contract spasmodically, and on grasping anything joints of middle finger inclined to be stiff. Sticking extending into fingers and out of their tips. Tearing in ball of l. thumb.

Lower Extremities.—Thigh. *Intermittent cutting sticking in middle anterior part of l.* Cutting pinching in posterior part of l. (Tearing after eating, with heaviness of legs.) Pain in bones of r. thigh and leg, beginning at night in sleep, > stretching; P. in posterior muscles of l. at night, < pressure, stooping and lying upon them, > rising; *paralytic, in r. T. and hip-joint, causing limping;* in l. T. and knee as if broken.

Trembling of knees when walking, < ascending steps. Painful stiffness of knees. Sticking in shaft of fibula, extending to calf, waking at night; *cutting S. in r. calf when sitting, > walking.* Pain in leg on stretching it, with limping. (Sticking about r. ankle, < when lying at night, with throbbing.) *Tearing in r. ankle on walking, as if dislocated;* paralytic T. in ankles, < quiet. *Stiffness of ankles. Sprained pain in r. ankle.* Itching sticking in l. sole when sitting, and in balls of toes. Tearing in heel on motion. Pain drawing up and down feet, extending to calves. Weakness of feet, causing tottering on beginning to walk, > continuing to walk. Sticking in three middle toes on walking, causing limping. Tearing in a spot in ball of r. great toe during rest.

Skin.—Red elevations on back of hand and above wrist, at first painful, then itching sticking in a spot, which are < rubbing. Pimples here and there in face, with sticking on touch and pustules in centre; red P. in middle of chin, below lip, covered with white scaly skin; (painful to touch behind and beneath l. ear). Corroding ulcer on back of r. hand, with itching, which after rubbing changes to burning, then exudation of bloody moisture. Corrosion from application of the herb. Burning pain in front of r. corner of mouth. *Prickling burning pain beneath l. eyelid.*

Sleep.—Frequent yawning, with stretching. Snoring when lying on back. Sleeplessness. Frequent starting from sleep in evening. Frequent waking, always on the breaking out of sweat; F. waking as if he had slept enough; as from fright, but without anxiety on waking. Dreams vivid, partly joyous, partly anxious; vivid, vexatious, about the ill treatment of others; anxious D.; D. of thirst and of drinking and great thirst on waking.

Fever.—Chilliness; through the day and heat through the night; in afternoon, alternating with heat, with nausea; at night; creeping C. over whole body, with cold hands, hot face and nausea. Shivering; during rest; during rest, though warm to touch; *over whole body, with hot face and cold hands, without thirst,* also with warm forehead. Coldness of face, hands and nose; (cold cheeks in evening, with hot hands); (l. half of face cold after midnight and sticking in it, while the r. half was hot and dry). Quotidian fever, before 9 A.M., till noon chilliness with cold hands, blue nails and necessity to lie down, after the chilliness thirst, then heaviness of head, throbbing pain in occiput, heat of face and usual warmth of rest of body, lasting till 3 P.M., in the evening well, at night profuse sweat, < on abdomen, after the heat nausea. Febrile paroxysms, head heavy, confused, constant chilliness, no taste to food, thirst, heat of head and watery salivation. *Warmth of upper part of body towards evening. Face hot and red.* Heat of head; (on chest, thighs and hollows of knees, with sweat on these parts and thirst). Sweat; at night; after midnight; on face at night.

Duboisia.

A tincture is made of the dry leaves of Duboisia myoporoides, R. Br. These contain the alkaloid—Duboisine—from which most of the effects have been observed.

General Action.—Almost identical (as far as known) with Belladonna.

Allies.—Belladonna, Stramon.

Generalities.—Trembling. Intoxicated appearance. Restlessness; in afternoon. Ineffectual efforts to sit up in bed. Weakness; all afternoon. Faintness. Asleep sensation in legs, then in thighs, arms and other parts, afterwards patient could hardly talk or stand. Lemon-juice acted as an antidote.

Mind.—Delirium, with tendency to pick at surrounding objects, drawing up of arms, restlessness, rapid pulse, heat, attempt to get up. Hallucinations. Fidgety. Stupor, with weakness as if he had no life in him. Unable to concentrate thoughts, absent-minded, thoughts wander from one subject to another, but all are silly and nonsensical. Memory lost. Unconsciousness. Carphology, suspicious glancing beneath the bed-clothes and behind the back, incessant activity, the whole room was upset, flow of disconnected sentences, memory of things that happened years ago, an air of fun and humor, symptoms of childishness rather than of violence, imagined it was dark, afterwards unconsciousness of what had occurred.

Head.—Inability to hold it up. Aching; over eyes, in forehead and temples; over l. eye. Dulness as after interrupted sleep. Heaviness. Strange feeling. Vertigo; on rising up or walking, the legs seem unable to bear the body, staggering, but can walk straight by concentrating mind on the action and watching steps, inclination to fall backward, < ascending stairs, *almost impossible to stand with eyes shut,* constantly swaying backward and forward, obliged to be held by another when eyes are closed.

Eyes.—Pain; when reading, could read better and print looked blacker at double the usual distance, eyes feel tired, sharp pain in upper part of ball, afterwards paralysis of accommodation, could not bear to read at any distance, could not look at food when eating on account of pain. Hot and tired; hot and dry, also face, lids œdematous. Cool feeling; in evening. Lachrymation. Pupils dilated; irregularly, apparently in segments; ovoid, afterwards nearly round; dilatation grows less as paralysis of accommodation increases; pupil vertically ovoid and irregular, in response to change of light and shadow the least dilated parts show the most movement, at ten minutes it is firmly contracted everywhere, except at temporal side, and is irregularly round, at twelve minutes it is contracted evenly all around, sees horizontal lines best.

Disc very red, small vessels of disc visible, larger vessels enlarged and tortuous, outline of disc indistinct, retinal veins dilated, arteries diminished, whole fundus hyperæmic, accommodation paralyzed, could not read Jager No. 1 at any distance, but with + 36 could read it at twelve inches, any change in distance causing blur. Smarting sharp pain in upper part of ball. On looking up from book pain in upper part of balls and in forehead similar to sick headache, and eyes feel large and protruding. Lids agglutinated in morning. Palpebral orifices contracted all day.

Photophobia. Things seem elevated. Letters ran together in evening when reading. Vision misty for near objects. Accommodation paralyzed; soon and *before the pupil was fully dilated and continued when it had regained its normal size;* cannot read at any distance, can read with + 20 glasses. Cannot make out print within two feet of me, print shows blue, orange and reddish-brown, can see to read with + 20 glasses, but glass strained the eyes.

Clinical.—Neuro-retinitis. Exopthalmic goitre.

Ears, Nose and Face.—Earache in morning. L. ear felt as if water were in it, a dull feeling. Sudden ringing in ears, < r. Nose stopped; and dry. Dark flush on face. Smarting sharp pain down r. side of face.

Mouth.—Dryness; and of tongue; and throat, > lemon-juice; of M. and throat in afternoon, < lips, temporarily > water, constantly thirsty for large quantities frequently repeated; of M., throat and tongue, with stickiness, but not much desire for water. Taste bad; bitter.

Throat.—Patches of partially translucent, adherent, yellowish-white mucus in pharynx. Pain as from a splinter in l. side on swallowing, < empty S. Dryness; < back part; with burning and cough; without much thirst; pharynx dry and hyperæmic, purple-red, capillaries much engorged, here and there varicosities, follicles very prominent and configuration of spinal column readily distinguishable, a picture of pharyngitis sicca.

Stomach.—Appetite lost. Nausea; all the afternoon. Deadly, gone feeling all afternoon, as if at greater curvature, not > eating or drinking. Sick feeling, general faintness, < epigastric region, head light as if intoxicated, face feels warm but is not flushed, mouth and throat dry, saliva scanty and viscid, giddiness on walking, it seemed as if I could not control all parts of body at the same time, pain in forehead, pulse 52, full, occasionally at rate of 80 for a few beats.

Urinary Organs.—Burning in urethra during micturition. Urine increased.

Respiratory Organs.—Epiglottis hyperæmic, < vicinity of glosso-epiglottidean folds, membrane lining larynx engorged, dry, with patches of viscid, semi-translucent, adherent mucus, appearing like a pseudo-membrane, the hyperæmia < along course of ary-epiglottidean folds, the membrane covering cartilages of Wrisberg, the capitula Santorini and the interarytænoidal commissure, in the last-mentioned localities the most of the dry, translucent discharge was seen, vocal cords congested, < near posterior commissure, mucus adherent to their free borders, forming narrow bands that stretched from side to side when the cords were widely separated in deep inspiration. Hoarseness; and phonition difficult, constant desire to clear throat, generally unsuccessful; voice husky and indistinct.

Cough increased (have always had a C., but not so severe as this), next morning hard, dry, hacking, from tickling at bifurcation of trachea, cough causes soreness or rawness over lungs, < lower lobe of l. and upper lobe of r.

Pulse.—Rapid; varied from 108 to 112, but always fell to 80 when the patient was supported in a sitting posture and increased again on reclining. Slow. Intermittent; and feeble. Strong, full, regular.

Extremities.—Heaviness, < lower. Weakness of arms and legs. Jerking of muscles of arm on extending hand to grasp anything. R. hands and fingers feel as if going to sleep. Gait unsteady, occasionally feeling as if I stepped on empty space, and I would catch myself for fear of falling. R. knee sore below patella, as if strained or rheumatic. Lower limbs tingle as if asleep.

Sleep and Fever.—Gaping and sneezing all day. Drowsiness. Night restless, could not get to sleep for hours, had to get up for water every five minutes. Chilliness. Heat; < internally.

Dulcamara.

A tincture is made of the fresh plant, before flowering, of Solanum Dulcamara, L.

General Action.—The most prominent effects are those of cough, of muscular rheumatism and of urticaria. Its resemblance to other *Solaneæ* is slight, but marked. Its adaptability to conditions arising from cold-wet is very pronounced.

Allies.—Bry., Merc., Caust., Hyos.; also Rhus tox. and Nux mos.

Generalities.—Emaciation. Spasms; of facial muscles, then of whole body. Twitchings of tendons; T. of hands, lips and eyelids, < cold weather and dampness, > approach to the fire; sudden T. through whole body, seemingly from pains in abdomen, with piteous cries, then muttering. Trembling. Sticking here and there, < outward; itching pinching S. Pain as if the body would be cut off above hips, obliging him to move back and forth, but without relief. Pains in various parts as after taking cold. Restless; and could hardly be held, scratched his father. Sinking sensation, as if she would sink through the bed, she must get up at night and walk about. *Weariness;* in sudden attacks, like faintness. Necessity to lie down. Almost immovable. Aggravation towards evening; from wet-cold (Rhus tox., Nux mos.).

Clinical.—Very valuable for chronic muscular rheumatism, < cold weather, especially in cold wet weather (Rhus t.).

Mind.—Screaming as in hydrocephalus. Wakes early as if called and sees a ghost, which keeps enlarging till it disappears in an upward direction. Agitation. Picking in the air and at his clothes (Hyosc.). *Quarrelsome* in afternoon, but not vexed thereby. Restless. Ill-humored and not inclined to anything. Anxious after midnight and fearful for the future. Noticed none of his surroundings and heard nothing when spoken to. Coma.

Head.—Stitches, so that she became angry about them, < evening, > lying. Boring outward before midnight. Aching; in morning in bed, < rising; with indolence, general coldness and nausea; causing stupidity; < evening, with increasing coryza; drawing pain through brain, < evening; pressing-out towards evening on walking in open air. Pressure internally in spots as with a dull instrument. Dulness in evening; *D., with painful stupefaction;* with drawings in frontal eminences; as after intoxication, > open air. Heaviness; with boring outward in temples and forehead, as after a debauch; as if scalp were tense, < nape, where it became a crawling. *Vertigo; in morning on rising, with trembling and weakness* (Bry., Lyc.); in morning on waking, with heat of head and with obscuration of vision, which changed to flickering of black spots; at noon, when walking before eating, all objects in front of him seemed to stand still, and it became black before the eyes; with rising warmth in face.

Forehead.—Sticking deep in brain, with nausea. Boring outward above r. brow; B. outward alternately in F. and temples. Burrowing and pressure; B. deep in, in morning in bed, < rising, with gloominess and distended feeling in brain. Pain in l. frontal eminence; pressing-out P. in l eminence in evening; jerklike pressing outward, < motion; tensive, above r. eye; in F. and root of nose, as from a board in front of head. Painful throbbing in l., with vertigo. Drawing in l. eminence, < stooping; pressive D. in l. eminence; jerking, from eminences down to tip of nose. Heaviness; with sticking outward in temples.

Intermittent tearing in temples; l. Boring in r. temple. Drawings in temples, extending into head; pressive D. in l. temple in afternoon. Pressure as with a dull instrument, now in r., now in l. temple. Tearing pressing together in vertex. Drawing pain on vertex in evening when eating, extending to nasal bones, where it is a constriction. Paroxysmal pressure inward on l. vertex as with a dull instrument. Stupefying pain in l. vertex; above l. ear, as if something blunt were pressed into head. Sticking in occiput. Pain in occiput in evening in bed; P. in l. bone. Occiput feels enlarged. Heaviness in occiput.

Clinical.—Headaches during cold wet weather, heaviness of head, flickering before eyes, nausea, etc., < motion, etc. Scald head, thick brown crusts, bleeding when scratched, < cold wet weather.

Eyes.—*Inflammation.* Wide open, moist, glistening. Pressure, < reading. Feeling as if they would be pressed out of their orbits. Feeling as if fire darted out of them when walking in the sun, and in the room. Dryness and tension. *Pupils dilated;* and contracted alternately. Paralysis of upper lid. Contractive pain in border of orbit. Vision dim. V. of sparks.

Ears.—*Sticking in meatus and parotid gland;* pinching S. in l. ear, extending towards drum. Tearing in l., with sticking outward, drumming and bubbling so that he could not hear distinctly and on opening mouth cracking as if something snapped asunder. Twinging in l., with nausea; T. in r., with sticking. Prickling as if cold air were in them. *Aching all night, preventing sleep,* > suddenly in morning, except a rushing noise. Drawing in external meatus. Ringing.

Clinical.—Inflammation of middle ear, with injection of the drum, caused by exposure to cold rain, several cases.

Nose.—Pimple in inner side of l. wing, with ulcerative pain. Dryness in evening. Sneezing. Stopped coryza, with confusion of head and sneezing. Bleeding of bright red, very warm blood, with pressure in region of longitudinal sinus, which continued after the B.

Clinical.—Catarrhal troubles in cold, wet weather, with free secretion of mucus.

Face.—*Puffy, hot;* P., anxious, distorted. Tearing in cheek, with drawing. Cramplike contraction beneath l. ear, extending to ramus of lower jaw. Painless pressure upon l. malar-bone. Trismus. Pinching in lower part of chin.

Clinical.—Facial neuralgia caused by going out in the wet or < slightest exposure to cold.

Mouth.—Teeth dull and seem insensible. Gums loose and spongy. Tongue white; itching crawling on tip of T.; T. could not be protruded; swollen, stiff, paralyzed, and inability to articulate; paralyzed. Stammering, as if delirious or intoxicated. Articulation indistinct. Loss of speech; then rattling respiration, cramps, tetantic stiffness and death. Constant grasping at M. as if he would take something out of it, with constant spitting about. Pimples and ulcers on inside of upper lip and on anterior part of palate, with tearing on moving the parts. Dryness. Tenacious and soaplike saliva.

Clinical.—It has been found useful in the salivation of Mercury, which is notably worse in damp weather. It is reported to have cured gangrene of the mouth, with great swelling. Other forms of sore mouth, great swelling of mucous membrane, raw spots, heavily-coated tongue, great flow of saliva of putrid odor.

Throat.—Constant hawking of tough mucus, with scraping in pharynx. Pressure as if uvula were too long. Dryness in evening. Heat in pharynx. Inability to swallow.

Stomach.—*Aversion to food,* with shivering as if he would vomit. A., with hunger. Soon satiated when eating, with fulness and with rumbling in abdomen. Thirst but drink was immediately vomited; *unquenchable T. Eructations;* with hiccough; with scraping in œsophagus and heartburn; empty; empty, with shuddering as from nausea; of the soup when eating. Waterbrash. *Nausea;* with chilliness; with inability to bring anything up. Retching; ineffectual. *Vomiting;* of mucus in morning, preceded by warm uprisings in pharynx; of mucus, then of a thick, blackish-green liquid; of tenacious mucus. Distended feeling in pit, with emptiness in abdomen. Sticking in pit; l. side of pit. Griping, taking away the breath; G. in epigastrium in evening in bed till falling asleep. Pain in pit as from a thrust, < pressure. Tensive pain in r. side of pit, as if strained. Pressure extending into chest.

Abdomen.—Distention; after a moderate meal; when eating, with repeated griping. Rumbling; with urging to stool; with pain in l. groin and coldness in back; with pain in small of back. Emission of much flatus; F. of the odor of asafœtida. Pinching as before diarrhœa. Griping, even in morning fasting, with cutting and distention; G. here and there, with jerking cutting; in A. and chest, with cutting, as from incarcerated flatus; as if a long worm were crawling up and down, with gnawing and pinching. Burrowing, with griping, cutting and moving, as before diarrhœa. Colic; with rumbling before and after stool; **as after taking cold; as before diarrhœa;** *as before stool, with rumbling and pain in small of back;* as after a purge, moving about, always on stooping; like inclination to diarrhœa, > emitting flatus. Uneasiness, with distended feeling and frequent empty eructations. Emptiness.

Umbilicus.—*Sticking in region;* on l. side near, in evening; griping S. on r. side. Pinching in region as if he should go to stool, but without urging; P. in region and above l. hip, > hard, scanty, difficult stool and emission of flatus. Griping below U. when sitting bent; G. in a spot to l. above U. Gnawing throbbing above U. Twisting in region, with burrowing and griping (Diosc.). Forcing-out pain, as if a hernia would occur on l. side beneath U.

Sticking in r. side beneath ribs, arresting breathing; S. outward in a spot in l. side, arresting breathing, with sensation as if something would force itself out and pain on pressure; intermittent S. in l., < pressure. Sudden cutting contraction in l. side. Inguinal glands swollen and hard; l. inguinal gland S. Griping in hypogastrium in evening, with desire for stool. Burrowing above crest of l. ilium, > pressure. Pain now in l. inguinal glands, now in r. Tension in groin, in region of pubis on rising from a seat. Burning in the bubo on motion and touch, with sticking.

Rectum.—Pressing during the usual stool. *Desire for stool in evening, with griping in hypogastrium, then a large, moist, at last thin, sour stool, after which he was relieved but felt weak,* he had a hard, difficult stool in afternoon. Urging, then small hard stool; sudden U., then after some time hard sluggish stool, with pressure and griping and cutting here and there in abdomen; U., with griping, yet passes but little, with pressure; ineffectual U. all day, with nausea.

Stool.—Yellow watery diarrhœa, with tearing cutting before stool as after taking cold (Hyos., Rhus t., Thuja). *Thin, afternoons, with flatulence.* Soft; in small pieces. Infrequent, sluggish, hard, difficult. Suppressed.

Clinical.—Diarrhœa always < cold, wet weather, stools mucous, green or changeable, of sour odor, with general dry heat of skin.

Urinary Organs.—*Catarrh of bladder.* Pulsating (stitches?) outward in urethra. *Burning in meatus urinarius when urinating.* Involuntary micturition.

Clinical.—Involuntary discharge of urine, paralysis of neck of bladder. Catarrh of the bladder, the result of taking cold. Inflammation of kidneys, with suppressed urine, caused by working in water.

Sexual Organs.—Heat in female, pruritis; also desire.

Respiratory Organs.—Cough, with expectoration of tenacious mucus and sticking in sides of chest (Dros.); hacking C. as from deep inspiration. Respiration rapid.

Clinical.—Cough < cold, wet weather, sometimes dry, but more frequently with very free expectoration, caused by constant tickling in larynx, the expectoration is tough and greenish, or the cough is dry and hoarse, or even spasmodic, like whooping cough (Dros.). Very frequently useful in bronchial catarrh, with free greenish expectoration. It is a valuable remedy for the cough of old people, < change of weather to cold and wet.

Chest.—Sticking on sternum; S. in l., in region of fifth and sixth ribs; in r., in region of third rib on pressure, extending into small of back and to between shoulders, and on inspiration sticking on margin of l. scapula; suddenly coming and going in r.; pulsating. beneath l. short ribs when sitting; intermittent, in l.; stupefying, beneath r. clavicle, extending into chest; on sternum, like a thrust. Sticking tearing from middle of sternum to spine when sitting. Thrusts beneath axillæ; intermittent T. on l. side above ensiform cartilage, extending deep into chest, when sitting bent and afterwards when upright. Cutting and pinching as from incarcerated flatus; deeply C. pain beneath l. clavicle, > pressure. Pinching, < inspiration. Digging in r., > pressure; D. or strained sensation. Intermittent pressure beneath sternum. Oppression; < breathing; as after sitting bent. Intermittent squeezing in a spot beneath upper part of sternum. Drawing externally over forepart, with tension; D. beneath sternum, with jerking; intermittent surging, tearing D. through l. Tension on deep breathing. Feeling as if something would be forced out of l.

Clinical.—Suppression of milk caused by taking cold.

Heart and Pulse.—Excitement of H. Palpitation, < night; P. as if he felt the heart beating outside of the chest. Pulse rapid; and irregular; and small; P slow, intermittent; small and hard in evening.

Neck.—*Pain in nape as if head had been lying in an uncomfortable position;* drawing P. in r. cervical muscles; constrictive, in muscles of nape as if the neck would be twisted; stupefying, in nape rising to occiput; in muscles of nape as from stiffness, on turning head to one side. *Stiffness of muscles of nape* (Caust., Rhus t., Lith.).

Back.—Sticking in middle of spine on breathing; tickling, in middle of r. scapula; intermittent throbbing, in l. side near spine. Intermittent tearing thrusts on outer side of r. scapula. Drawing tearing on external margin of r. scapula. Intermittent pressure on l. side of spine near nape, when lying on back in morning. **Pain in small of B. as after long stooping** (*Bry.*). Sticking outward above l. hip on every inspiration; S. outward in loins on every inspiration when sitting bent after a short walk; burrowing S. on l. side near sacrum; burrowing, in l. loin, > walking, returning when sitting; jerklike, above r. hip, near spine. *Cutting deep in loin, transiently > pressure* (Bry.). Bruised pain above l. hip close to spine.

Clinical.—Lameness of the small of the back, or stiffness and lameness across the neck and shoulders, or severe drawing pains in muscles of the back, with fever, after getting wet or cold (myelitis).

Extremities.—Trembling. Shooting in *l. toes and thumb.* Drawing tearing in r. shoulder, above r. hip-joint and above and below r. knee. Pain; cramplike, here and there, < fingers. Bruised sensation. Weakness and heaviness. Heaviness of arms and thighs. Sudden numbness in evening, with pains in knees and elbows, increasing so that he could hardly move his limbs.

Upper Extremities.—Jerking pain in r. axilla. Pulsating pain in l. axilla, > motion. Jerkings of arm on bending it backward or forward. *Paralytic bruised pain in l. arm,* < during rest, > touch; bruised pain in r. arm, with leaden heaviness, stiffness of muscles and coldness of arm as if paralyzed, and with bruised pain in elbow when bending or touching it. Jerking in upper arm on bending it and drawing it backward, but on stretching it out stiffness of fingers so that she could not close them. Pain in upper arm in evening in bed and in morning after rising. Paralytic sensation in r. upper arm, > violent motion.

Intermittent corrosive gnawing on outer side of elbow. Drawing from l. elbow to wrist, < bending it; twisting boring D. from elbow to wrist, > during motion. Sudden jerking, pinching tearing in middle of l. forearm. Drawing pain in r. forearm. Frequent drawings in l. ulna. Weakness of l. forearm, < at elbow, with lameness. Sticking on r. wrist, > motion. Inflammatory rheumatism of l. wrist, pain beginning at pisiform bone, extending along branchings of ulnar nerve to end of little finger, and again upward along the main tract of that nerve till it was lost in the inferior origin of flexor carpi ulnaris muscles, with redness and swelling of integuments, the little finger flexed and inflamed. Redness of back of hands, and if he becomes warm by walking in open air burning pain. Frequent stretching of hands as if they would take hold of something, hands hastily carried to mouth, with motions like chewing or swallowing. Cramp in hands so that he could hold nothing firmly. Cramplike jerking in first phalanx of r. middle finger. Cramplike drawing in ball of l. thumb so that he could scarcely move the thumb.

Lower Extremities.—Staggering. Inability to stand or walk. Sticking on r. nates. Hip, drawing sticking in l. joint when walking, extending into groin, with sensation on every step as if the head of the femur would be dislocated, the pain > violent stretching of leg, which seemed to replace the femur, but bruised pain remained and caused limping; drawing pinching in r. hip; drawing tearing in l. Thigh, sticking posteriorly close to l. knee; sticking tearing in T.; drawing tearing from middle of posterior part to knee; *drawing tearing or constant pain, at one time sticking, at another pinching, > when walking, then changing to weariness and returning when sitting* (Rhus t.); pain; drawing pain on anterior part of r.; drawing here and there in muscles, with sensitiveness to touch; paralytic drawing on anterior part of r.

Tearing in knees when sitting; sticking T. from knee up thigh when walking in open air. Rhythmical undulating pressure on inner side of knee. Weariness of knees. Swelling of leg and calf towards evening, with tensive pain and weariness. Cramp in calves so that legs were drawn up against thighs; C. in l. calf when walking. Sudden sticking in l. calf, then sensation as if warm water or blood were flowing from that place. Tearing up r. tibia in morning; T. posteriorly on l. calf, > moving foot. Cramplike, almost cutting drawing through l. leg. Pain as from ripping extending down l. calf posteriorly. Pain in tibiæ as from weariness. Numbness of calves in afternoon and evening. Cramp in r. inner malleolus, waking at night, > walking. Tearing extending from outer malleolus towards forepart of foot; drawing T. near r. inner malleolus. Cutting in r. sole. Pulsating tearing in first and second l. toes.

Clinical.—Paralysis of the lower extremities from getting cold; the paralyzed limbs feel icy-cold.

Skin.—**Nettle-rash over whole body** (Rhus t., Apis); **without fever.** Dark purplish color of face and hands, with languor of circulation. Blotches on forehead, with sticking when touched. Warts covering hands. Spots like scarlet rash over whole body. White wheals, with red areola on arms and thighs, with sticking and itching and after rubbing burning. Lepra. Pimples in angles of nose; red P. in bend of elbow, noticeable morning and evening in warmth of room, and after scratching, sticking itching and burning; P. and ulcers about mouth, with tearing on moving the parts; itching, on chin; itching, on chest and abdomen.

Pricking and itching. Agreeable tickling on outer margin of r. scapula. Itching of cheeks close to wings of nose; I. on anterior part of body and thighs at night, with heat and offensive transpirations without moisture, preventing sleep; soon returning after scratching, in middle of r. forearm, also on outer side of l. leg; on outer side of r. leg, ending with itching sticking; general, < on nates, where skin was red, partly from rubbing, and where there were wheals, red spots on inner side of forearm, the swelling always renewed on going to bed, without regard to time, when there was general sweat, sleeplessness till 2 or 3 A.M., after the sixth day the eruption became general, on the tenth day shivering and heat with inclination to sweat, the eruption worse on back, back covered with red points, and sticking between and below scapulæ, on arms the eruption was in spots, where there was desquamation in small scales the red points disappeared and there was biting itching, on legs red spots and sensation as if lying in burning nettles up to hips, with copious sweat, the eruption < warmth of bed, sweat, coffee and all food, heat of body after eating, then itching, symptoms > cold. Burning itching on thighs; externally on r. upper arm, with redness and a burning pimple; sudden creeping here and there, as from vermin, < night and mostly between 12 and 3 o'clock, waking him, at first <, then > scratching.

Clinical.—Urticaria, with violent itching, especially when caused by sour stomach. Urticaria that comes on in cold weather; chronic cases always < beginning of winter; itching always on exposure to cold air, for example, undressing. Sometimes also useful in eczema, with great itching and watery discharge; and it has even been found useful for colic and diarrhœa following suppression of an eruption in cold weather. Pemphigus. Warts, large smooth warts or fleshy warts on face and hands.

Sleep.—Frequent, violent yawning. Sleepiness all day, with much yawning; S., with indolence and yawning. Snoring, with open mouth. *Uneasy sleep after* 4 A.M.; *U. sleep, tossing about in discomfort;* U. sleep, with profuse sweat and interrupted by confused dreams; tossing about all night, with dulness of head. Starting as from fright, in evening on falling asleep. A kind of waking towards morning, with closed eyes. Sleeplessness; towards morning, with weariness in all limbs and lameness, as after great heat. Inability to sleep again after being wakened early, with weariness, turning from one side to the other because the muscles of occiput were lame and he could not lie upon them. Confused dreams; frightful D., making him jump out of bed.

Fever.—Chilliness, with discomfort in limbs; cool skin in evening; chill towards evening over back, nape and occiput, with feeling as if hair stood on end; C. in back in open air, < in a draught, without thirst. Shivering as from chilliness and nausea, with internal and external coldness.

Heat of body, with sweat and redness, itching, burning and pimples, < face, so that face seemed swollen; dry H.; dry, at night; internal and external, < hands, with thirst and slow, full pulse, then chilliness; of skin; burning of feet; B. in skin of back, with sweat of face and moderate heat; intermittent sticking B. in toes. Sweat; < back; on palms; cold; profuse, in morning, < head.

Elaps.

The poison of the Coral viper, Elaps corallinus, is triturated with sugar of milk.

General Action.—Evidently on the blood, but our knowledge of its effects is too meagre to permit any generalization.

Allies.—Serpent-venom in general.

Generalities and Mind.—Rheumatic pains on moving about. Faintness on stooping. Fear, dread of being alone, as if something would happen or as if rowdies would break in. Peevishness in afternoon, even with herself, desire not to be spoken to. Aversion to work.

Head.—Sticking at 1 A.M., preventing sleep; S., extending to r. side in morning and at noon, < evening, with shaking chill. Aching; in morning on waking; from 1 to 11 A.M.; after midnight, lasting till daybreak; at 7 P.M.; on r. side; on l. side at 9 P.M.; in vertex, as if brain were loose, and at night inability to hold the head still on account of nausea. Sensation as if attacked by apoplexy, all the blood seemed to be collected in the head and to stand still, afterwards it seemed as if the blood streamed from the head or from the finger-tips into the body, > being up. Falling out of hair.

Clinical.—Violent headache in a man who was blind, first in l. then r. eye, headaches extending from forehead to occiput, vision partially restored.

Eyes and Ears.—Boring outward in eyes. Dry burning in eyes; in morning on waking. Indistinct vision in morning. The crochet-work seemed to move to and fro towards noon, the letters ran together, vision unsteady in afternoon and evening. Large red, fiery points before the eyes, becoming violet and then black on becoming erect, < reflecting on what had been read, on stooping rush of blood to head. Tearing in l. ear at 9 A.M., > 11 A.M. Diminished hearing from time to time in afternoon. *Crackling* on swallowing. Roaring in r. ear at 3 P.M.

Clinical.—Blindness. Deafness, with offensive yellowish-green discharge, buzzing in ears, headache in forehead and occiput, dull pain from nose to ears, pain goes to ears on swallowing. Chronic otorrhœa. Sudden attacks of deafness at night, with roaring and cracking in ears.

Nose.—Fluent coryza.

Clinical.—Subject to nosebleed, eruption about nose, pain in nose and forehead, skin dry and hot, but complaints of feeling cold. Stoppage and stuffiness high up in nostrils and dull aching in forehead, bad smell in nose, posterior pharynx scabby, cracked and dry, nosebleed, pain from root of nose to ears on swallowing, no smell. Another case, fetid odor from nose and throat, nose was always dry and stuffed up by yellow scales, skin always hot and dry. Sore throat; offensive discharge from nose, occasional nosebleed, posterior wall of throat covered with dry greenish-yellow membrane, stuffiness at root of nose, no smell. Old ozæna and nasal catarrh, nose always stuffed up with plugs of dry mucus, pain at root of nose (compare Lycop.).

Cheek.—Redness of r. from 1 till 6 P.M., with heat and formication in it. Pressure in r., with redness, then swelling, then general shivering. Swelling of r., with small red pimples beneath skin, then round tetterlike spots, the redness of face > next day towards noon, in afternoon swelling of face, < r. side of nose, the next day the swelling of face lasted till 10 o'clock, with increased redness and swelling under eyes, the next morning red spots on face, which was puffy.

Throat, Stomach and Abdomen.—Burning in pit of throat on swallowing, in the morning on waking, < more by heat than by cold, > towards 9 o'clock. Thirst at night, with heat and sleepiness, in the morning sweat; burning T. all the forenoon. Nausea, with vomiting. Violent vomiting of mucus in morning. Sudden cutting in abdomen towards 7 P.M., disappearing at one time, suddenly better about 10 P.M., < after midnight, > morning, return of the colic at 5 P.M., as if she would sink together, < sitting, > walking and resting the hands on the hips. Pressure downward in abdomen, preventing standing, < warm drinks, especially tea and coffee.

Clinical.—Distress in stomach from cold drinks.

Chest and Heart.—Sticking in side of chest; l. from 6 to 8 P.M., < breathing. Pain in l. side of C. at 2 P.M., > walking, with stitches in side. Oppression of C. in evening. Palpitation, with anxiety and unsteadiness of hands.

Clinical.—Cough, with expectoration of black blood and terrible pain through lungs as if they were torn out, especially in r. upper chest. Coldness in chest after drinking. (In the cold feeling in stomach and chest compare with Colch. and perhaps Lach.).

Neck and Back.—Sticking in l. side of nape, extending to head, with stiffness of l. shoulder. Rheumatic pain in neck on motion. Stiffness of r. side of neck about 5 P.M. Sticking in the whole spine. Pain in back, with chilliness, *icy-cold feet* and tenesmus vesicæ.

Extremities.—Cramplike contractive pain in l. shoulder at 6 P.M., extending to head, as after carrying something heavy in the hand. Sticking in upper arm towards evening. Rheumatic pain in l. arm at 6 P.M., then in l. leg, which was also lame. Unsteadiness of hands. Intermittent sticking, rheumatic pain in l. leg from 4 to 6 P.M., extending through the whole l. side, with mental exhaustion and indifference. Rheumatic drawing pain in l. arm and leg in afternoon.

Skin and Sleep.—Red, hot rash above r. wrist. Uneasy sleep, with frightful dreams.

Fever.—Chilliness in afternoon without thirst, then dry heat; C., then dry heat; C., then burning redness of face; at 8 P.M. alternating with heat, with the heat moisture without thirst, the C. continues on going to bed with more sweat, then good sleep, the next day the fever returned at 7 P.M. with less C., but more heat, with sweat, interrupted by heavy dreams, breathing difficult all night, good sleep towards morning, the next day fever at 7 P.M. with less chill, more heat, much thirst, but little sweat, good sleep at 10 P.M. Shaking chill as if in the bones in the evening, then heat, hot skin. with thirst, at 9 P.M. headache on l. side and boring outward in eyes, the fever lasting till 10 A.M. Shivering at 10 P.M.

Heat at 10 P.M., with thirst and mental excitement, the heat > about midnight, the next night the same dry heat after midnight, lasting till 9 A.M. Heat in flushes in evening, with redness of face and ears. Dry heat from 7 to 9 P.M., then chilliness till 10 P.M.; dry heat at midnight, but the slightest uncovering is unpleasant.

Elaterium.

A tincture is made of the green fruit of Momordica Elaterium, L. (Ecbalium E., Rich.).

General Action.—A most violent hydragogue cathartic, producing inflammation of the whole gastro-enteric canal.

Allies.—Jatro., Coloc., Grat.

Generalities, Mind and Head.—Sharp, fugitive or dull pains, now here, now there. Pains, < l. side. Weakness; on going to bed at 10 P.M. Depression of spirits. Fear of some approaching disaster. Headache in evening. Aching in forehead; in region of causality; temples; region of combativeness, r. and l. sides; headache, with constriction of temples and forehead. Dulness of head till late at night.

Clinical.—Sometimes useful in the jaundice of new-born children.

Eyes, Ears and Nose.—Sticking in l. inner canthus. Sticking near rim of cartilage of l. ear. Epistaxis.

Mouth and Throat.—Tongue coated dirty brown. Unpleasant smell to the breath. Bitter taste; with salivation. Pain in back part of throat as if scalded. Feeling as if choana and upper part of œsophagus were enlarged.

Stomach.—Loss of appetite. Eructations; empty; > sneezing, with nausea. Nausea; till after two liquid stools; with frequent vomiting, at first slimy, then colored with bile, with increase of salivation, empty eructations, flatulence, rumbling in abdomen and scraping in throat, these symptoms > warmth of bed, but replaced by pains in abomen, confusion of head and then headache. Vomiting; nearly all night; at 7 A.M. of a dark brown fluid mixed with food, with prostration and weak feeling at stomach; frequent, of scanty clear liquid, then difficult V. of copious bilious greenish substance and all the contents of the stomach; violent, and eructations of the odor of bad eggs. Pain in epigastrium; in pit of stomach, with colic. Stricture or oppression of epigastrium.

Abdomen.—Retraction. Discharge of flatus. Rumbling in cæcum and colon. *Cutting like the griping of medicine.* Griping. Pain; coming on in the warmth of the bed; in r. hypochondrium; over crest of r. ilium, round to back, extending deep into pelvis.

Rectum and Stool.—Bleeding of the hæmorrhoids. Soreness of anus. Ineffectual desire for stool. **Stool liquid, copious** (Coloc., Jatro., Grat.), frequent, at first brown, then whitish yellow; **watery, frothy S.** *Olive-green S.* Last part of S. soft. Dirty yellow S. S. of dark masses of bilious mucus. Constipation.

Clinical.—Stools watery, forcible, frothy, copious, preceded by violent cutting pains in abdomen, with chilliness, prostration, flatulent colic, etc. Stools sometimes olive-green and watery, but always gushing.

Urine.—Copious; and limpid. Scanty; after dinner, acid, pale; and high-colored, no deposit, with heat. High-colored.

Clinical.—It has been prescribed for dropsy consequent upon disease of kidney, even for dropsy of pericardium, or in jaundice with high fever of an intermittent character, with violent pain in abdomen, watery stools, dark urine, etc.

Chest and Back.—Sharp pain at lower part of sternum, passing through to spine or lower angle of r. scapula. Pain in l. sterno-cleido-mastoideus muscle near its insertion into the sternum. Pain under r. scapula; in region of l. kidney. Fugitive sticking in lumbar region, < r. side.

Extremities.—Shooting in l. axilla, near insertion of pectoralis major. Pains in r. shoulder, forearm and hand, extending to fingers; in shoulder, extending to ends of fingers and shooting back to elbow. Sticking in muscular parts of thumb; in l. fingers, out to their tips; in l. thigh, in course of sciatic nerve, extending to instep and out to tips of toes, with dull pains. Pain in r. knee, extending into instep and toes. Arthritic pain in great toe.

Sleep and Fever.—Incessant gaping; with chilliness. Fever.

Epiphegus.

A tincture is made of the fresh plant of Epiphegus Virginiana, Bart.

Languid feeling. Aggravation from walking in open air; on rising from supine position. Amelioration in morning; A. after sleep. Fears death from palpitation; F. injury to her health from the drug. When writing, could not make the desired letters. Found himself using wrong words in writing. Difficulty in thinking correctly or in selecting proper words or expressions. Sensation as if something were wrong in his head, < forepart (morning after headache).

Headache; < rising up in bed; < working in open air. Head confused. Head full; in forepart. Pain in forepart of head; in middle of forehead; sudden, transient, in middle of forehead; in r. temple; l. temple at night in bed, < rising up; l. temple till bedtime; temples, < r., leaving dull heavy pain < r.; piercing, in r. temple; flying, in temples; as from pressure of finger-ends in temporal fossæ, from 3 P.M. till evening, < l. side; pressing inward, in r. temple. Pain in occiput; pressing outward in occiput in morning on rising, increasing till 4 P.M., then declining till 6 P.M. when it disappeared, < open air, motion, rising or stooping, > warmth of the room, eating or sleeping, with nausea. Fulness in occiput, with dizziness in forehead. Scalp feels tight during headache.

Sharp pain over centre angle of r. eye. Smarting of eyes; of conjunctiva, with redness. Could not read because letters seemed blurred. Red face; cheeks, < l. Salivation; watery. Constant spitting of clear, watery saliva. Almost constant desire to expectorate. *Saliva viscid.* Taste viscid; and sticky; T. bitter (secondary). Nausea. Gnawing in stomach, < motion, > eating and quiet. Acidity in stomach, with accumulation of flatus. Weight in stomach as from a cold substance. Loose stool, with griping. Stool difficult although soft. Palpitation which makes her weak. Pain in l. shoulder; l. knee. Trembling of knees and lower limbs; of lower limbs, with weakness of them. Restless sleep, with much dreaming. Temperature lowered.

Clinical.—Several cures of "sick headache" are reported with the general characteristic of being caused by unusual excitement or fatigue, for example, visiting or shopping; some cases associated with nausea and vomiting.

Equisetum.

A tincture is made of the whole plant of Equisetum hyemale, L.

General Action.—The most prominent effects are noticed on the urinary tract, especially on the bladder.

Allies.—Cantharis.

Generalities and Mind.—Stiffness of muscles of trunk. Uneasiness in different parts; U. in evening. General malaise. Weakness. Irritability and easy fatigue.

Head.—Neuralgia at night in different parts, < l. temple. Aching all the morning; at noon, with pain in upper part of eyes or roof of orbit; with inclination to scowl; stupefying, about 4 o'clock. Heaviness; all day, with general prostration; of brain at 9 A.M., with dulness; at 10.15 A.M., with dulness and with constriction through temples and weakness from the slightest exertion; in afternoon, with inability to study; with confusion; with pain above r. temple; as if it would fall forward at 9.30 A.M. Vertigo; on moving head; with wavelike pains in head and intermittent lightness, and on walking feeling as if he would fall.

Forehead.—Aching; over r. eye; at 9.30 A.M., with tightness of scalp and pain in roof of r. orbit; across F. and upper part of eyes and through temples at 10.25 A.M.; with hot and rather flushed face; changing to occiput, then darting from l. to r. side of occiput; deep-seated, with prickling of skin on rubbing. Prickling as from electricity in evening and on rubbing. Fulness, with pain and feeling as if skin of F. *were tight*, < looking up, with heat in face, but no redness; F. as if all the brain were packed in front, at 9.30 A.M. Constriction, and in vertex; across F. and in l. temple at 10.10 A.M., as if scalp were too tight; C. in F. and through temples in afternoon, with shooting through temples, < r., the pains in temples < movement and in open air, not > quiet, but > eating. Heavy dull feeling at 11.30 A.M., and in temples.

Temples.—Sticking near l. at 9 A.M., extending in a straight line on anterior of forehead to r. temple, then darting pains extending to vertex; occasional S. in l. at 10 A.M.; S. darting from one to the other, with a heavy, drowsy sensation. Darting in each; in l. at 10.45 A.M., < in open air and extending over l. eye, in roof of orbit. Boring in l. at 11.45 A.M.; B. in l., darting to r. Sharp pains; in l. at 9.30 P.M., extending to supraorbital region, with redness and burning of face; suddenly in r. at 11.25 A.M.; intermittent, in l. at 11 A.M., extending to roof of l. orbit. Pain over r.; in r. at 9.25 A.M.; P. at 10.45 A.M., with heat in face and forehead; through T. in afternoon and evening; < l., then the pain moved in a straight line from one T. to the other. Constriction through T. at 12.45 P.M.

Vertex.—Pain. Weight. Heaviness at 12.30 P.M., with pain through temples.

Occiput.—Sticking near lambdoidal suture; S. on l. side of occipital bone, near superior curved line. Darting on sides of bones, near superior curved line. Sharp and quick pains near l. superior curved line. Boring changing from side to side. Drawing pain in evening, and in neck.

Scalp.—Tight feeling, with continual inclination to raise and wrinkle the brow, which when wrinkled requires an effort to smooth again.

Eyes.—Pain in l.; in roof of r. orbit at 10.20 A.M. Sharp pain in outer angle of r. at 4 P.M. Heavy, sleepy feeling in lids. Soreness of l. ball in evening.

Ears.—Pain at back of l. mastoid process at 12.40 P.M., with a stiff feeling. Sounds intermingle so as to be indistinguishable. Confused sounds, < l. Rumbling, with dulness and heaviness of head; R. in l., then confusion of sounds.

Face, Mouth and Throat.—Flushed face at 1.25 M.P., with hot feeling. Feeling as if blood pressed into the face, < forehead. Salivation at night, causing frequent desire to swallow. Sticking in throat at 1.30 P.M.

Stomach.—Excessive hunger. Much wind at night. Acidity. Pain in region of pyloric orifice; in epigastric and umbilical regions; heavy, after every meal. Uneasiness; in epigastric and r. hypochondriac regions. Burning over epigastric region.

Abdomen.—Emission of much flatus with the stool. Distended feeling at 11.30. A.M. Feeling as before diarrhœa. Sharp pain above crest of r. ilium at 10.45 A.M.; above crest of l. ilium at noon; in hypogastrium at 11 A.M., with sticking in anus. Pains frequently during the day, with desire for stool, three thin stools in the morning. Pain in hypogastrium at 11 A.M., with passage of flatus; at 12.50 P.M., with passage of much fetid flatus; above crest of l. ilium at 1.40 P.M., extending forward to median line of body. Heavy pain in both sides of hypogastrium and in bladder, with frequent desire to urinate, the desire not > micturition. Soreness in hypogastric region on pressure; S. in r. side of H. region in morning and in region of bladder.

Anus.—Smarting during and after stool. Aching during stool, with feeling as if rectum would protrude, and after the stool smarting in anus, with sensation as if some fæces remained.

Urinary Organs.—**Pain in bladder, not > micturition; in region of bladder pain and tenderness,** with soreness of testicles, extending up spermatic cords. **Pain in bladder as from distention;** with pricking in urethra during and after micturition. **Tenderness in region of bladder** *and in lower abdomen, extending upward from groin, < r. side,* in forenoon. **Constant desire to urinate,** not > copious discharges of clear light-colored urine. *Urging, but only a small quantity is passed each time. Frequent desire* in afternoon, with biting in urethra during and after micturition; frequent D., the urine has an ammoniacal smell; frequent D., with cramplike pain in hypogastric region, which was > by micturition. *Frequent micturition, the quantity growing less each time while the desire increases; frequent M. at night.*

Urethra.—Pricking at 10.15 A.M.; a short distance from meatus at 11.10 A.M., when urinating; during the frequent and profuse micturition, with biting. Prickling of meatus, with soreness from touch or pressure. *Cutting* at 12.35 P.M. Pain at 11 A.M., and in testicles. Smarting on urinating, extending back an inch from meatus, with prickling. Biting itching in meatus at 2.25 P.M., < scratching. *Burning* when urinating; and sharp pain in root of penis; in forepart during copious micturition.

Urine.—**Scanty and high-colored;** *S., with feeling as if he had not urinated for hours.* Copious; in morning; in morning on waking, and pale; with pressure in vesical region, heavy aching over l. kidney and sharp pain in l. hypochondrium; and specific gravity higher. *Darker.* Specific gravity diminished. Cloudy on standing a short time. *Showed great excess of mucus after standing a short time.* (Compare all urinary symptoms with Cantharis.)

Clinical.—Nocturnal enuresis. Curative even when vesical irritation is marked, especially in women (Eup. purp.), and urine contains blood and mucus. Cystitis, with tenderness over region of bladder and pain as from distention. Dysuria during pregnancy and after confinement. Dysuria, extreme and frequent urging with pain, < *just after micturition.* Incontinence of urine in old men. Weakness of bladder, dribbling, in insane people who will not attend to the bladder.

Sexual Organs.—Pain in penis on urinating; with burning. Violent erections. Sharp pain in r. testicle just before urinating. Pain in testicles and cords, < l. Soreness of testicles and spermatic cords, < l.; and the cords seem gone the whole length. No desire.

Chest.—Shooting through lungs; S. in l. breast an inch to l. and over nipple at 1.30 P.M. Pain in centre at 12.50 P.M. on any forward movement; P. in r., < evening, with pain in r. lung preventing filling it with air, < next morning, and at 9 P.M. feeling as if both lungs were becoming congested; under sternum at 10.30 A.M., on deep breathing; P. in r. lung between fourth and fifth ribs. Soreness.

Heart and Pulse.—Sharp pain at heart; at 1.50 P.M., < inspiration. Rapid pulse.

Neck.—Pain at 10.30 A.M., extending to shoulders on motion. Stiffness of muscles.

Back.—Pain in morning, > lying on back and walking, < sitting; P. in back and hips in forenoon, with soreness; P. all the afternoon, with throbbing pain in l. temple, then in r., with constriction of whole scalp; on movement; < sitting. Pain in scapulæ, < through l. Soreness in r. scapula; in l. on movement of l. arm. Lameness below lower angle of scapulæ, < motion or deep breathing.

Lumbar Region.—Pain, < r.; P. at 12.30 P.M., < sitting still; P. extending along coccyx; in two lower vertebræ; *in region of r. kidney, with urging to urinate;* in r. kidney at 9 P.M., then in l., extending down l. side of sacrum. Heavy pain in morning on waking; H. pain over r. kidney; over kidneys, preventing sleep the first part of the night. Heaviness like a lump over r. hip-joint. Rheumatic pain in region of sacro-lumbar articulation and through l. hip-joint, at 2.30 P.M. extending down outer side of l. leg, ending in front three inches above knee, > lying on back and by quiet, < beginning to move, but > continued motion, in back and hips the pains were gnawing and deep-seated, but not continuous. Soreness of kidneys; < r.

Extremities.—Sharp pain in l. shoulder at 11.15 A.M., with general shivering and heat in head. Pain in upper part of shoulders and in region of vertebra prominens from 10 A.M. till 1 P.M., < motion or touch; in r. shoulder at 10.15 A.M., extending to middle of upper arm. Occasional sharp pain through l. hip and in lumbar region at 12.45 P.M. Pain in r. hip-joint and near knee. Sharp pain in inner side of l. knee in morning on waking, > walking. Heavy pain under l. patella at 12.15 P.M. Weakness of knees on least exertion.

Skin.—Tension of forehead; at night, < opening of eyes, with confused, disconnected dreams where many persons were present.

Sleep.—Sleepiness in forenoon; at 2 P.M., heaviness of eyelids; at 5 P.M., with headache and tension of integument of forehead. Sleep unrefreshing; with headache on waking in the morning. Restless night. Intermittent sleep, constant change of position. Sleep disturbed and full of tiresome dreams of many persons, places and things. Sleep crowded with confused dreams of many people.

Fever.—Chills run up back at 12.35 P.M. Heat of face from 1 till 2 P.M., without redness. Burning in face, neck and r. ear at 1.40 P.M., without much redness.

Erigeron.

A tincture is made of the entire fresh plant of Erigeron Canadense, L.

Generalities.—Languor all day and depressed spirits; L. in morning; in afternoon and evening, and no ambition to move; with aching in all large joints. Symptoms every morning.

Head and Eyes.—Headache on waking, with aching in large joints. Pain in forehead at 9 P.M.; pain in F., with smarting of eyes; in F. and r. eye on waking. Smarting of eyes in afternoon and evening. Agglutination of lids in morning.

Nose, Mouth and Throat.—Nasal mucus increased in forenoon, with roughness in pharynx and sensation as if something had lodged in upper part of œsophagus that caused frequent inclination to swallow. Bad taste. Sore throat; all night, with frequent inclination to swallow and feeling as if something had lodged in upper part of œsophagus. Roughness of pharynx; in morning. Dryness of pharynx at 9 P.M.

Stomach and Abdomen.—Eructations of air. Nausea. Intermittent cutting in epigastric region at 2 P.M., then dull pain. Drawing pain in abdomen. Frequent rumbling pain in A., with aching in lumbar region. Rheumatic pains in abdominal muscles. Cutting in r. side of umbilicus. Pain in umbilicus; r.; frequent in l.; frequent pain in region of U., with feeling as if anus had been torn; sudden P. in region of U. when walking, with pain in lower dorsal region and singing in r. ear. Distress in U. region; frequently with aching in whole dorsal region. Pain in l. hypogastrium and umbilicus; in hypogastrium, then a dark, hard, lumpy stool; sudden, in H., then a mushy stool.

Stool and Urine.—Loose stool; at noon after a natural one in the morning. Mushy S.; next day none. Hard, lumpy S. S. omitted. Natural S., then neuralgia in anus and tenesmus. Urging to urinate, waking at 4 A.M. Urine increased and pale; and turns litmus-paper red.

Clinical.—Persistent hæmorrhages from bladder, in stone in bladder. Chronic gonorrhœa, with burning micturition, which is offensive, continual dribbling, smarting, burning, etc. Post-partum hæmorrhages. Hæmorrhages from uterus, with painful micturition (compare with Mitchella).

Back.—Distress in dorsal region at 6 P.M. Aching in dorsal region; < r. side; in afternoon and evening, and in lumbar region. Sticking in region of r. kidney; l. kidney, passing from l. to r. Pain in lumbar and sacral regions in morning on waking. Drawing pain in r. lumbar region at 9 P.M., passing to r. testicle, then dragging pain in l. hypochondrium.

Extremities.—Aching in arms and legs in afternoon and evening; A. in all joints, with despondency. Drawing pain in elbow and r. metacarpal bones in evening. Rheumatic pains in r. thumb. Pain in hips at 9 P.M., on walking. Pain in knees in evening. Drawing pain in l. ankle, < walking.

Sleep.—Frequent disposition to yawn in afternoon and evening. Restless night, but no pain.

Eryngium Aquaticum.

A tincture is made of the fresh root of Eryngium yuccæfolium, Michaux (aquaticum, L.).

Generalities.—Erratic pains in muscles during the day; E. pains in trunk and limbs. Restlessness. Erethism of nervous system. Nervous, moving about constantly; in evening. Debility. Tired, < lumbar region, after a long walk in afternoon. Faintness on rising suddenly, stepping down or turning head quickly.

Mind.—Depressed spirits. Dulness at night. Loss of energy. Inability to think steadily. Thoughts confused in afternoon, difficult to concentrate.

Head.—Shooting, < forehead, especially over l. eye, < lowering head or thinking intently, passing when sitting in a stooping posture from eye into neck and along muscles of shoulder and beneath scapula, where it remained some time. Aching; < stooping or turning head quickly, and in neck. Heavy pain in morning on rising; heavy, full P. from concentrating mind. Vertigo in evening; V. after dinner; V., with elation. Tearing or boring over l. eye. Pain in forehead on rising; P., < over l. eye; P., causing dimness of vision. Heavy pain in frontal part of brain; H. pain in forehead from reading or writing, < stooping. Expanding sensation above eyes, < stooping. Heavy pain in mastoid portion of temporal bone, passing through to opposite side, at 11 A.M., when sitting in the lecture-room. Shooting in vertex and in r. side of face from eye to teeth, in morning.

Dragging pain in occiput, neck and shoulders, disappearing in occiput about 11 A.M., but extending into eye, causing blurred vision, the pain < exercise or excitement, next day > in head, but < neck and between shoulders. Scalp sore to touch, pain on combing hair.

Eyes.—Purulent inflammation of l., congestion, redness, swelling, tenderness to pressure, pain, the latter > heat, then profuse discharge of purulent fluid, sticking the lids together, flowing on cheek from all parts of the lid, leaving the conjunctiva granulated and rough. Shooting from r. to teeth in forenoon. Burning pain, with heaviness, congestion and squinting in a strong light. Smarting burning from a strong light, with heavy pain, dull expression of eyes and sleepiness. Stiffness of muscles, with pain on turning them quickly. Sensitiveness to strong light and congestion, < looking at a strong light or walking in bright sunlight.

Ears and Nose.—Eustachian tube inflamed and l. ear swollen internally and externally, tender to pressure, painful, bleeding readily, discharging thick, white and bloody, offensive pus. Bruising-tearing as if ears were being torn from their location. Ringing, singing and cracking in l. ear. Profuse discharge of thick, yellow mucus from nose.

Mouth and Throat.—Tongue grayish, ragged. Dryness of tongue and fauces, with insipid taste. Thick, tenacious, disagreeable mucus in mouth; thick, tenacious, yellowish mucus in mouth on rising. Constant hawking up of mucus. Redness and swelling of mucous membrane of throat, with profuse, thick, whitish mucus, causing an ulcerated appearance, without bad feeling. Smarting, raw pain along l. side of throat, with dry tongue and discharge of thick yellow mucus, which increased the smarting. Smarting burning in fauces. Choking on slight pressure.

Stomach.—Appetite diminished, no desire for particular kinds of food; D., restored at the sight of food. Nausea about noon, then acrid eructations; N. between 9 and 10 P.M., with drawing, cramping pain in stomach and heavy, compressing pain between shoulders. Heavy, dragging pain; at night. Heaviness in morning. Emptiness, with heavy, dragging pain.

Abdomen and Stool.—Cramping pain in A.; in small intestines. Piercing pain in A., with bloated feeling, but not visible distention, with heaviness on walking and soreness on pressure. Pain in A. in morning on waking; P. in l. groin and testicle, < during exercise. Heaviness in groin in afternoon, perhaps due to a walk. Hard, dark brown stool, with tenesmus and with cutting in anus as the fæces passed. Stool omitted for two or three days without uneasiness, and it was more an act of the will than necessity to evacuate the bowels then.

Urinary Organs.—Sensation as if urine remained in urethra, burning smarting. Urging to urinate after rising, burning in urethra before urinating, urine scanty and high-colored; frequent desire, then micturition in drops every few minutes, with tingling near meatus; frequent desire, with stinging burning in urethra behind glans during micturition, urine at 11 A.M., scanty, lightish-red, darker before retiring, and symptoms in urethra more marked. Urine profuse, deep yellow. Urine scanty. Twenty-six ozs. of U. in twenty-four hours, acid, sp. gr. 1016, containing 382.11 gr. solid matter, U. lightish red or amber-colored when boiled, a white flocculent sediment after standing.

Sexual Organs.—*Desire suppressed, then excited, with lewd dreams* **and pollutions, discharge of prostatic fluid from slight causes.**

Clinical.—Seminal emissions without erections, day and night, after injuries. Involuntary emissions after masturbation.

Respiratory Organs, Chest and Pulse.—Mucous membrane of larynx seemed thickened, causing hacking cough and expectoration of stringy, light yellow mucus, mostly from larynx. Dyspnœa as if the clothing were too tight. Oppression of chest, with fulness, desire to take a full breath, but inability to do so, lungs seem solidified. Pulse rapid; and soft and weak.

Neck, Back and Extremities.—Rheumatic pain in nape at 11 A.M. when in the room, with stiffness of cervical muscles and soreness on motion. Soreness of muscles of neck on turning head quickly, and heavy pain on pressure. Pain in lumbar region at 2 P.M. Weakness of lumbar region, with dragging pain. Rheumatic pain in l. shoulder, l. arm, r. wrist and r. hand. Lower limbs languid and heavy, with profuse sweat on walking. L. patella and os calcis sore and painful on motion.

Sleep and Fever.—Sleepiness, < afternoon. Early waking. Wakefulness at night. Dreams disturbed, confused. Heat in flashes. Sweat of urinous odor in evening.

Eucalyptus.

A tincture is made of the fresh leaves of Eucalyptus globulus, Lab.

General Action.—It produces general vascular excitement, followed by depression and low temperature; finally muscular and sensory paralysis. Compare Absinth.

Generalities and Mind.—Rheumatic, jerking, tearing, sticking pains, < night. Pain when walking or carrying anything. Feeling as if he had taken cold. Malaise during fever. Weakness. Effects removed by a cup of coffee. General excitement and desire for exercise; pleasant excitement, with desire to move about and buoyancy. General calmness and soothing sleep. Mental depression.

Head and Eyes.—Dulness of H. Fulness of H. Cerebral congestion, with much excitement. Congestive headache. Intoxication, then mental depression and exhaustion. Vertigo and pulsation in forehead. Frontal pain. Eyes hot; and smarting. Lids heavy.

Nose, Face and Mouth.—Stiffness of nose. Coryza. Lower lip sore. Sore pain in upper incisors. Raw feeling in tongue. Increased secretion of mucus and saliva.

Clinical.—Cures chronic catarrh of nasal passages and acute coryzas.

Throat.—Posterior nares inflamed and smarting, thick, whitish discharge on hawking, frequent violent sneezing. Fulness and soreness on swallowing, and burning. Sensation of phlegm in afternoon, with expectoration of thick, white, frothy mucus and a relaxed, aphthous condition. Tickling, smarting, incessant hacking cough in evening, weak feeling in chest, expectoration scanty, transparent, mucous.

Stomach.—Appetite increased; lost. Thirst; during the fever. Eructations tasting of the drug; and burning; smelling of the drug. Digestion difficult and painful. Fulness as if he had eaten or drunk too much; F., with pressure. Weight. Tenderness and burning in S. and abdomen, with heat in rectum, then tenesmus, with discharge of mucus and prostration, purging and hæmorrhage from bowels. Burning; after dinner; in epigastric and umbilical regions, with thirst, faintness, vertigo, dimness of vision, fulness of head, frontal pain and tightness across bridge of nose as before epistaxis. Faintness after dinner, with beating sensation in abdominal aorta synchronous with heart, lasting all the afternoon and next forenoon.

Abdomen.—Burning, and in sternum. Sharp pains running through A., < morning, with thin diarrhœa; S. pain in hypogastric region after dinner; in hypogastrium in morning on getting up, with yellow watery diarrhœa. Sticking in spleen and l. inguinal region. Uneasiness in umbilical region, extending farther, with skirmishing pains in upper A., feeling as before diarrhœa.

Stool, Urinary and Sexual Organs.—Ineffectual urging to stool. Diarrhœa smelling of the drug. Irregular S. Insufficient S. Urine has a herbaceous smell; of violets. Urea increased. Urine diminished, none at night, which had not occurred for years. Sexual appetite increased.

Clinical.—Subacute cystitis.

Respiratory Organs, Heart and Pulse.—Sore pain in trachea and posterior nares during empty swallowing. Asthmatic, with crampy feeling in chest and back. Breathing quickened in fever. Painful palpitation. Rapid pulse.

Clinical.—Whooping cough. Gangrene of lungs. Bronchitis, with profuse expectoration.

Extremities.—Pricking, then aching in arms and legs, with fulness in veins and a stiff, weary sensation as if too lazy to move. Tingling in lower, as if asleep. Heels sore as from too much walking. Sticking in l. sole, near great toe.

Skin.—Swellings in different parts, one of the size of a filbert-nut below r. nipple was the seat of stabbing and darting pains; nodular S. over metacarpal and metatarsal joints. Eruptions. Herpes; and glandular enlargements, foul and indolent ulcers.

Sleep.—Sleepiness during the day, difficulty in falling asleep, sleepiness in morning as if he had not slept at all; S. (in anæmic subjects); S. and dulness. Sleeplessness.

Fever.—Temperature lowered. Chills running down back; and posterior sides of legs. Cold fingers; tips. Fever; seemed to have rheumatic; in flushes, also with sudden sweat. Burning in palms. Sweat at night; towards morning. Sweat odorous; of trimethylamine.

Clinical.—It has been prescribed in fevers, intermittent, typhoid and remittent, but without marked indications. It steadily reduced the pulse and temperature in typhoid.

Euonymus Europæus.

A tincture is made of the fresh fruit of Euonymus Europæus, L.

General Action.—Evonymin, obtained from the bark, of E. atro-purpureus has a positive action on the liver, increasing the secretion of bile. It is to be compared with Berberis, Chelidon., Podo., etc.

Generalities and Mind.—Sticking in various parts. Sticking drawing in all parts, < back. Symptoms oblige lying down, and then disappear, but reappear in other parts. Aggravation of symptoms of head, chest and abdomen after a meal. Most troubles appear on l. side. Morose. Disinclined to work. Loss of ideas; on exerting the mind and ill humor thereat.

Head.—Aching, with chilliness. Deep stitches, now low down in r. side of occiput, then in l. frontal eminence, now in r. temple, then in r. parietal bone, now in l., then in r. temporal bone, as far as mastoid process. Vertigo, < forehead, < sitting; V., with tremulous mist before eyes. Frontal headache; intermittent, between eyes; drawing. Benumbing pressure above r. orbit. Painful drawing from l. side of frontal bone to malar-bone. Tension of skin of forehead, at times a convulsive drawing back and forth. Pain in temples; in l. bone. Pressure on r. temporal bone. Stitches now in r. side, now in l., now in both. Feeling as if a nail were pressing into r. side near vertex.

Eyes and Ears.—Eyes painful. Pressure in eye, < external pressure; P. upon brows, when most violent the balls seem compressed and are painful. Vision obscured; V. of dark spots. Roaring in ears.

Face and Mouth.—Stitches in l. malar-bone; intermittent, beneath r. zygoma. Tearing in face; l. side of face, < frontal bone. Pain in malar-bone; drawing in face; paralytic, in r. malar-bone. Painful pressure on lower margin of l. malar-bone. Drawing from malar-bone to lower jaw. Tearing in teeth; r. Cutting in tongue; in muscle under tongue.

Stomach.—Nausea. Vomiting and diarrhœa. Stitches in pit; near pit, now r., now l. side.

Abdomen.—Cutting; in morning in bed, with constriction, as if A. would be cut off under the ribs. Acute pain, at one time seeming like a pressure upward of the diaphragm, at one time like constriction, at another like sticking, again a drawing about in the intestines as from flatus; frightful pain, profuse diarrhœa, then collapse, with involuntary evacuations of blood and mucus, on lifting him up tetanic convulsions, which immediately preceded death. Stitches beneath l. last ribs after eating; S. beneath navel. Pain in umbilical region; during and after eating; above navel, near pit of stomach. Stitches in middle of r. side of lower A.; in l. half of lower A. on inspiration.

Clinical.—A very efficient remedy for engorgement of liver, so-called biliousness, headache, coated tongue, bad taste, constipation. Passive congestion of liver. Constipation with hæmorrhoids, also with severe pain in back like lumbago. Diarrhœa, stool variable in color, generally very profuse. It has been found useful for gastric derangements associated with albuminuria, especially for headache and weakness or vertigo and obscuration of sight (Lyc., Sulph.).

Sexual Organs.—Cutting in penis; extending to bladder.

Respiratory Organs.—Sighing.

Chest.—Electric-like shocks towards l. side. Stitches near ensiform cartilage; above r. nipple; below or on last r. true ribs, and difficult respiration with every stitch; shattering benumbing, in region of l. nipple. Burrowing beneath sternum without actual embarrassment of respiration; B. in l. side, now beneath scapula, and near spine, now beneath arm, now beneath nipple, manifesting itself by thrusts, stitches and pressure. Pain in l. side on a line with ensiform cartilage; P. < inspiration, > expiration. Sore and bruised sensation. Painful drawing in region of l. nipple in evening before going to bed. Fulness obliging deep breathing. Tension in sternum. Compression in whole circumference of l. side, with special pain in region of l. nipple and beneath l. scapula; benumbing C. beneath l. nipple.

Heart.—Anxiety like an internal pressure, affecting even the spirits.

Back.—Stitches in first lumbar vertebra; near l. side of spine, about the middle of the body; frequent, like electric shocks in a zigzag along spine from lumbar to scapular region. Crawling, biting, itching, or paralytic pain in l. side of posterior circumference of pelvis.

Extremities.—Tearing in shoulders; l. shoulder-joint. Pain in l. humerus and shoulder-joint; in fingers; paralytic here and there in fingers; drawing, in finger-joints. Painful drawing in metacarpal joint of l. index. Sticking now in both hips, now alternating between them. Drawing pain in thighs. Intermittent drawing in upper part of l. thigh, beneath joint. Pain in forepart of knee; paralytic, in knees from walking, < standing. Paralytic drawing on inner side of r. leg when standing. Pain (pressure and sticking) beneath l. outer malleolus, < anteriorly, along outer side of foot, with soreness and pain in bed. Pain in feet; in toes.

Skin.—Pustules (reddish spots) on chest and back, without moisture. Formication on l. cheek; up and down l. half of back. Biting, itching, crawling in various parts, obliging scratching, followed by burning.

Fever.—Shivering chill over whole body.

Eupatorium Aromaticum.

A tincture of the fresh root is used.

Clinical.—Great soreness of the mouth in an infant. Vomiting of bile, pain in stomach, headache and fever.

Eupatorium Perfoliatum.

A tincture of the entire fresh plant is used.

Allies.—Bry., Ars.; and probably *Carduus ben.*

Generalities and Head.—**Soreness in bones.** Bruised feeling in every bone, preventing lying in bed and causing despair, moaning and crying out. Inability to lie on l. side. Aggravation in the morning of one day and in the afternoon of the next. *Headache, < first going into the open air, < the house and by conversation, with internal soreness.* Whirling around in brain in morning, as if placed in a coal screen and whirled around two or three times, soon repeated. Pain in forehead, extending to occiput, < l. side. Darting through temples, with sensation of blood rushing *across* head.

Clinical.—Periodical headaches, especially in occiput, throbbing, sensation of great soreness of eyeballs, soreness of scalp, etc.

Eyes, Nose and Face.—**Eyeballs sore** (Bap.). Increased lachrymation. Redness of margins of lids, with glutinous secretion from Meibomian glands. Dim vision on looking at small things. Nose dry and stopped. Redness of face; of cheeks, with dryness of skin.

Clinical.—Violent coryza or influenza, with thirst, heaviness over head, bone-pains, soreness of eyeballs, etc.

Mouth and Throat.—*Tongue coated white* (Bry.). Mucous membrane of mouth pale. Insipid taste. Throat dry.

Stomach.—Desire for ice-cream. Loss of appetite. **Thirst for cold water** (Bry.); T. for something cold at night. Belching of tasteless wind, with feeling of obstruction at pit of S. *Nausea;* from odors, the smell of cooking, etc.; with vomiting, free perspiration and copious expectoration. **Retching and vomiting of bile. Vomiting preceded by thirst** (Ars.); **V. after every draught** (Ars.); **of food.** Feeling as if something ought to come up without ability to raise it. Fulness. S. seemed contracted from side to side. Heat. Beating in epigastrium at night.

Abdomen.—Tight clothing is oppressive. Tightness in l. hypochondrium. Soreness in liver region, with fulness.

Stool and Urine.—Diarrhœa in morning. Purging, with smarting and heat in anus. Four or five watery stools in a day. Loose scanty stool, with tensemus. *Urine dark, clear.* Scanty urine; and high-colored. Urine copious, limpid.

Respiratory Organs.—*Cough, with soreness and heat in bronchi;* C., < evening; hacking, in evening.

Clinical.—Inflammation of larynx, with soreness and hoarseness, soreness extending into the bronchi and trachea, usually with bone-pain and soreness of the chest generally. The cough is generally < lying on back, > lying on face; cough hurts the head and chest, the patient holds the chest with the hands (Dros.); generally there is no expectoration, or at least very little.

Chest.—Aching under l. breast; behind sternum, with soreness, weight, inability to inspire naturally or *twist the body to r. or l. because of the soreness,* he feels best when lying on the back with his arms down and legs straight, but inability to move to r. or l., *inability to twist the body when standing, sitting or lying. Soreness on a full inspiration;* S. from coughing, > going down on his knees. Grating sensation on very deep inspiration.

Heart.—Pressure as if in too small a place.

Neck and Back.—Beating pain in nape; > *rising, and in occiput.* **Bruised pain in back.** *Trembling in back during fever. Pain and soreness in small of B. as if beaten;* deep-seated P. in loins, with soreness from touch. *Weakness of small of B.*

Extremities. — **Aching in bones, with soreness of flesh. Soreness and aching in arms and forearms; above and below elbows, as if beaten. Painful soreness of wrists as if broken or dislocated.** Stiffness of arms; of fingers, with obtuseness of touch; *of lower limbs on rising to walk, with soreness.* **Soreness of lower limbs, with aching.** Pain in r. hip when sitting; P. in l. gluteal muscles, passing round in front of trochanter major, with sensitiveness. **Calves feel as if they had been beaten.** Pricking in soles. Pain in upper part of l. foot, with soreness and with increased sensitiveness of l. great toe, the pain in foot < standing upon it. Pain in first joint of great toe, l., then suddenly moving to r.

Fever.—Intermittent, quotidian, tertian and quartan. *The paroxysm usually begins in the morning,* **thirst several hours before the chill, continuing during chill and heat;** *C. in morning, heat through the day,* **but no sweat;** *C. through the night and in the morning, with nausea from the least motion; C., with nausea and trembling;* C. alternating with flashes of heat. General shuddering proceeding from the stomach. Pungent heat at night, with sweat. Heat on vertex, with pain which is > by pressure; H. of soles in morning. Sweat at night, with chilliness from motion or uncovering.

Clinical.—The characteristic fever, intermittent fever, for which this drug should be prescribed, has thirst beginning before the chill and continuing during both chill and heat; it is extremely important to observe that vomiting is particularly apt to result from drinking or taking any nourishment, either before or after the chill and fever; this vomiting from taking water is much more characteristic of the drug than the bone-pains, especially the vomiting of bile as the chill passes off; the violent bone-pains, the violent headache, pain and soreness of the muscles, are the universal accompaniments of the intermittent fever; the patient feels as if all the bones were breaking; it is very frequently observed that these Eupatorium cases present an incomplete paroxysm, for the chill and fever are well marked, and perhaps violent, and yet the sweat is entirely wanting; while this is usually the case, it is true that the drug cures cases in which there is a decided sweating stage. Valuable for catarrhal fevers, especially if there is bilious vomiting, with soreness of the chest and muscles and bone-pains, running from eyes and nose, soreness of the eyeballs, soreness of head, etc.

Eupatorium Purpureum.

A tincture of the fresh root is used.

Allies.—Eupt. perf., Apocyn. c.

Generalities and Mind.—Neuralgia from below upward, < up l. side of back and hip. Rheumatic pain changing about always from below upward. Tired feeling; in every organ. Faintness; with the urinary symptoms; after rising, with sickness. Numbness, < in groin. Aggravation on l. side of body. Delusions; of sight and hearing. Talkative, exclamations. Depression. Homesickness though at home and surrounded by her own family. Fear of sickness.

Head.—Heavy pain, < forehead. Feeling as in a bad cold. Lightness, < morning, > at 12 o'clock; L., with sensation as if falling to the left. Sensation as if moving in all directions. Vertigo, with sensation of falling to left; V., with deep dull pain through l. temple; in which the whole body seemed to participate; as if flying round and round. Fulness in vertex, with pressing as if lifting up from adjoining parts, confusion and heaviness. Thumping pain on l. side of occipital bone. Soreness of scalp. Pleasant pricking in scalp. Itching of scalp.

Eyes and Ears.—Eyes wide open and fixed. Lachrymation. Inability to see as far as usual. Ears feel full. Reports in E. Squeaking in E. Crackling in E. like the burning of birch bark, < swallowing anything.

Nose and Face.—Copious watery discharge from nose. Constant discharge from a sore, from continued wiping of nose. Face shining as from washing with much soap. Congestion of face. Rush of blood to F. Redness, dryness and internal and external heat of F. Heat of F.

Mouth and Throat.—Gums red and hot. Stinging in end of tongue. Prickling in posterior part of tongue. Numbness of tongue as from Aconite. Salivation. Sensation in throat as after swallowing tobacco. Scalded feeling in throat. Smarting in posterior part of T.; < posterior part, with burning. Soreness of T. Roughness and dryness in T. Fulness in T., can hardly prevent crying; F., with choking, compelling frequent swallowing. Fluttering in pit of T.

Stomach.—Eructations. Nausea. Swelling, < l. side, with fulness. Crampy pain. Griping, crampy pain in pit. Gnawing.

Abdomen.—As hard as a rock. Rumbling. Fulness; with pain. Crampy, windy. Twisting pain. Pain in the whole; < l. side, with soreness; deep in ossa innominata; as in diarrhœa, without much alteration in stools.

Rectum.—Pressure all day. Ineffectual urging to stool.

Urinary Organs.—Cutting in bladder, with pressure and fulness. Pain in bladder. Smarting in bladder and urethra, with burning, so that she could not stand. Feeling of continual micturition. Constant urging to urinate, with cutting in bladder, frequent and copious micturition, the stream smaller than usual. Frequent micturition, 58 ozs. in twelve hours, once with an aromatic odor, pale, containing a white flocculent mucus, in the next twelve hours greater urging and more frequent micturition, but less urine, the next day almost constant urging but urine scanty, one-half to two ounces at each evacuation, of higher color, during the three days occasional spasmodic action of bladder. Cutting in urethra. Smarting in urethra during micturition; burning S. in U. Smarting burning in urethra during micturition. Feeling of having retained the urine long. Heavy pain in urethra.

Clinical.—It has been recommended for chronic or subacute inflammation of the bladder with dysuria, and in intermittent fever when dysuria is a prominent symptom, with constant desire to urinate, with aching in kidneys and bladder.

Sexual Organs.—Constant wet feeling externally. Jerking in and above l. ovary. Cutting two inches above l. ovary. Heavy pressure during the day above l. ovary. Leucorrhœa leaving no stain.

Respiratory Organs, Heart and Pulse.—Frequent sighing. Desire to inflate the lungs, which she did from time to time without particularly noticing that she did it. Heart and throat fluttering. Palpitation. Pulse from 80 to 100, full and bounding.

Neck and Back.—Stiff, wry neck. Lame feeling in nape; in neck, with weak feeling. Sore pain in the whole extent of the spine, from below upward. Aching in sacrum running into kidneys; deep in l. kidney; deep in kidneys, with cutting.

Clinical.—The severe pain in the back noticed in this drug sometimes seems to indicate its use for chronic or subacute inflammation of the kidneys, especially from taking cold, with suppression of urine or with more or less difficulty in urinating.

Extremities.—Gnawing pain. Weakness, with uneasiness. Cutting in l. shoulder, running to occiput. Gnawing in hip-bone. Weakness of legs, < l., with numbness of r. Feet feel as after a long walk, and as if the heels were crowding through the boots.

Clinical.—It has been used for sciatica, severe pain in the course of the l. sciatic nerve. It has also been used for rheumatism of old people, with soreness of bones, swelling of ankles, etc. It has been found useful in dropsy during Bright's disease, with œdematous swelling, scanty urine, cold extremities, etc.

Sleep.—Yawning. *Sleepiness;* with dulness, it requires a great effort to move about. Wakefulness, with staring eyes.

Fever.—Clinical.—In intermittent fever it has generally been found curative when the chill begins in the small of the back and spreads over the body. This drug, as well as Eup. perfoliatum, seems to remove the bone-pains; the other symptoms of the two remedies seem also to be similar; whether there is a marked difference in the drugs it is for future experiments to determine.

Euphorbium.

A tincture of the gum-resin of some African species is used.

General Action.—All the species of Euphorbia have an acrid, milky, juice which seems to exert a pretty constant effect; namely, most violent vomiting and purging, or if the dust of the gum be inhaled most violent irritation and inflammation of the mucous membrane of the air-passages. The juice of some species even produces vesication, like croton oil. Numerous subjective symptoms have been developed by Hahnemann's provings. See the skin symptoms and compare Anacard. and Rhus tox.

Generalities and Mind.—Starting as from an electric shock at night when awake. Relaxed and tired in the whole body. Faintness. Anxiety; as if he had taken poison. Apprehension. Quiet and earnest; Q., reflective, seeking quiet, inclined to work. Dull, listless and feeling not at all like work.

Head.—Sticking, < forehead. Pain; as if it would be pressed asunder; as from a disordered stomach. Screwed-in sensation in brain and zygomata, with toothache. Tension, < forehead and cervical muscles. Vertigo, even to falling to the left, when walking in open air; V. when standing, everything turned about and he threatened to fall to the right. Sticking in l. side of forehead. Vertiginous tearing in l. side of F. on moving head. Frontal pain; r. side; above l. orbit; externally above l. eye, with lachrymation and inability to open eye on account of pain; stupefying. Stupefying pain in forepart of r. side of head, extending into forehead. Sticking externally in temples; S. beneath r. parietal bone. Pressure in l. half of brain; P. in occiput. Bruised pain in l. occiput, preventing lying upon it.

Eyes.—Sticking extending into inner part. *Biting, with lachrymation.* Aching; as from sand. Heat and smarting. Glutinous sensation in r. Gush of tears on raising lid, which was difficult. Pupils dilated. White of eye pale red and puffy, cornea dim, pupils small, drawn upward, insensible, the inner vascular zone dark brownish-red, vision prevented by photophobia and lachrymation. Swelling of lids, with tearing above brows on opening eyes. Inflammation of lids and nightly agglutination. Agglutination of r. lids in morning on waking. Hardened mucus in r. external canthus. Pinching in l. external canthus. Lids dry and pressing on eyes. Heaviness of lids, irresistible closing and vertigo. Itching of l. lower lid; of l. external canthus, > rubbing. Tearing sticking in orbit, extending across brow and lid, both lids hot and swollen, the upper hanging down immovable. L. brow and temple swollen, red and hot, upper lid hanging down over lower, œdematous, immovable, eyes watery, with sticking in them and vision of sparks. Photophobia; and intolerance of noise. Vision dim and short. Double V. Everything seems too large, so that he lifts his legs too high. All objects appear in variegated colors.

Ears.—Aching in open air. *Ringing*, also when sneezing. Roaring at night. Chirping in r., as of crickets.

Nose.—Fluent coryza, without sneezing. Stuffed, < r. nostril. Discharge of purulent mucus; profuse discharge of mucus, with suffocative biting, extending to frontal sinuses, so that she could draw no air through nose. Increased discharge of mucus without coryza. In l. nostril ineffectual irritation to sneeze. Sneezing; with fluent coryza and full feeling in head; frequent S., without coryza.

Clinical.—It has been prescribed for influenzas with chill, headache, watery discharge from eyes and nose, with burning and cough. The juice of some species is said to be valuable for warts; it must be applied two or three times a day.

Face.—Swelling. Pale, sickly looking. Jerklike tearings in muscles of l. cheek, almost as in toothache. Tensive pain in cheek as if swollen. Sore pain in vermilion border of lower lip as if he had bitten it.

Mouth.—Sticking in last l. upper molar; in first l. lower molar. Gnawing tearing in teeth on beginning to eat, with chilliness, headache as if shattered by the toothache and a screwed-in sensation in brain and zygomata. Pain in second l. upper molar; in last l. lower molar, > biting teeth together; in next to last l. upper molar, < touch and chewing; P. in hollow tooth *as if screwed in*, with jerking as if it would be torn out; pain in tooth like a boil on touching it. Tongue covered with a thick mucus. Coated tongue and almost all the concomitants of nervous erethism. Inability to speak intelligibly. Much tenacious mucus after midday sleep. A membranous pellicle peels off upper part of palate. Burning on palate. Dry sensation without thirst. Salivation; with salt taste on l. side of tongue; with nausea and shivering. Taste bitter; and foul, < back part of tongue, after beer that he had relished; T. as if mouth were covered with rancid fat; T. flat after breakfast, with white-coated tongue.

Clinical.—It has cured toothache, with throbbing pain, sensitiveness, etc.

Throat.—Profuse discharge of mucus from posterior nares. Scraping and rawness. Burning; extending to stomach, with mucus in mouth; extending to stomach, with trembling, anxiety and heat in upper part of body, nausea, flow of water from mouth and dryness of cheeks; and in stomach, as if a flame streamed out of it, with necessity to open the mouth. Inflammation of œsophagus.

Stomach.—Great hunger, with a lax stomach, hanging down and sunken abdomen. Thirst; for cold drinks. Incessant eructations; empty E. Hiccough; frequent. Nausea during the day; in morning; N., with shuddering. Vomiting; incessant, of watery fluid; with diarrhœa. Spasmodic contractions, with empty eructations. Inflammation. Griping as if it would be compressed, then salivation and nausea; G. in l. side, with clawing, then constriction of cardiac orifice, with salt salivation and shuddering in skin. Pain in pit; spasmodic pain in S. Bruised pain in S. on touch. Pressure on l. side. Constriction from all sides towards the middle, with salivation and nausea. Burning; in pit after eating, with pressure. Agreeable warmth as after spirituous drinks.

Abdomen.—Rumbling; in l., then emission of flatus. Emission of much flatus. Griping, then a thin stool, with burning itching about rectum. Pain; with tympanites; in one spot; flatulent, > resting head upon elbows and knees, after which flatus was emitted; spasmodic flatulent, in morning in bed, accumulation of flatus in hypochondria and chest, causing spasmodic pressing asunder and constriction, > turning about, but returning on lying quietly. Uneasiness, with heat. Emptiness in morning, as from an emetic. Agreeable warmth, as after spirituous drinks. Sore pressure outward in l. flank and after micturition, also in r. Pinching on posterior part of ilium. Tearing in l. groin as from a sprain, when standing. Sprained and lame pain in l. side of pubis on stretching limb after sitting, extending to thigh. Pain in inguinal region. Anxious sore aching in lower A.

Rectum and Stool.—Burning sore pain about rectum. Fatal dysentery. Diarrhœa several times a day, with burning in anus, distention of abdomen and pain as from internal soreness; profuse D., preceded by itching in anus, with urging; profuse, with vomiting. Loose, large S., with tenesmus and sore feeling, as if dysentery were coming on. Thin S. after pressure, at last three hard lumps without difficulty. Soft S., scanty, mixed with small lumps, delayed. Pasty S.; and yellowish. S. at first natural, then fermented and watery. Clayey S., preceded by itching in rectum, with urging. Hard, difficult. Constipation.

Urinary and Sexual Organs.—Discharge of prostatic fluid from the relaxed penis. Frequent desire to urinate, with scanty discharge; urging, micturition by drops, with sticking in penis, then a natural discharge. Strangury. Itching sticking in forepart of urethra when not urinating. Much white sediment in urine. Intermittent cutting sticking in glans when standing. Erections at night without emissions or lascivious dreams; E. without cause when sitting. Voluptuous itching of prepuce, with discharge of prostatic fluid. Pinching burning pain in l. side of scrotum.

Respiratory Organs.—Irritation to short cough in upper part of trachea. Cough day and night as from dyspnœa and shortness of breath, then in morning much expectoration; C. from burning tickling in upper part of trachea; almost uninterrupted dry C.; dry hollow C. from tickling in chest during rest; hacking C. from crawling in throat. Dyspnœa as if chest were not wide enough, with tensive pain in r. pectoral muscles, < turning upper part of body to right. Deep inspiration hindered by sensation as if l. lung were adherent.

Chest.—Sticking in l. on walking in open air, so that he must stop; in sternum when sitting and standing; in l. when sitting and standing; in l. when sitting, > when walking; intermittent S. in l. when reading. Tensive pain in l., < turning upper part of body to right. Spasmodic pressing asunder in lower part. Warmth in middle as from hot food.

Pulse.—Irregular, 150; 78 in morning.

Back.—Jerking sticking. Intermittent sticking in one place in the middle when sitting. Pinching in l. scapula. Spasmodic pain in dorsal vertebræ in morning when lying on back. Pain in muscles; nightly P. in ischia; P. in small of when at rest; in l. kidney, with burning in all urinary organs.

Extremities.—Rheumatic pains. Shoulder, stiff pain in r., < stretching towards the left; tensive pain in r., preventing raising arm high; tensive pain in r., > walking, but returning with greater violence during rest; tension in joint like paralysis, in morning after rising, < motion; painful drawings in r. Internal painful drawing in arm, with weakness, < radius, humerus and wrist. Pain on outer side of arm above elbow in morning in bed. Sprained pain in r. upper arm, near elbow, on moving arm. Drawing pain in ulna. Paralytic pain in wrist on moving it. Intermittent tearing in muscles of l. hand. Pinching in muscles of r. hand near wrist, < moving it. Spasmodic drawing in r. hand on writing. Pain in ball of r. thumb, > touch and motion.

Lower Extremities.—Feeling of deadness and coldness in l. when sitting, as if it would fall asleep, not > motion, and on walking internal coldness remains, < leg and foot. Weakness on walking in open air.

Thigh.—Tearing in muscles of l. hip; in muscles about r. hip when sitting; in anterior muscles of l. thigh when sitting; in muscles of r. thigh when standing and sitting; intermittent, in muscles on outer side of r. when sitting; intermittent stitchlike, in muscles of l. hip when sitting. Pain in muscles about l. hip. Sprained pain in hip-joints; S. pain near bend of l. thigh when walking in open air, > standing. Pain as from a blow in l. gluteals on motion. Pain in forepart of hip as if crushed, only on moving body while sitting. *Burning pain at night* in bones of hip and *thigh*, waking frequently. Tensive pain on stepping forward, extending from l. gluteals to hollow of knee, as if tendons were too short. Painful lameness in r. hip-joint on stepping.

Sticking in inner knee when sitting. Tearing outward in knee. Legs, sticking in r.; hot S. in l. calf, as with a knife; tearing in l. tibia below knee when sitting; T. in forepart of l. leg when sitting; T. in muscles of r. when walking in open air; sticking T. in muscles near ankle when sitting; gnawing T. in in r. calf when sitting and standing; pain as from a blow on outer side of l. calf; frequent falling asleep to above knees, with painful crawling in them and inability to move them; weakness as if they could not support the body.

Tearing burning pain in ankles, with heat of the parts. Cramp of metatarsus, drawing the toes together. Cramplike pain in foot, < towards external malleolus, when sitting and standing, > walking. Pain in r. heel as if suppurated, when walking in open air. Sprained pain in l. heel, < walking. Frequent falling asleep of feet when sitting, with inability to move them, and painful crawling in them.

Skin.—**Erysipelatous swelling of cheek, and vesicles filled with yellow liquid.** *Red swelling on cheek, with boring, gnawing and digging from gum into ear, and with itching and crawling in cheek when the pain is relieved. Erysipelatous inflammation of face* and external head; < face and head, with great tumefaction and throbbing headache, < forehead and vertex. Erysipelas bullosum, with fever. Swelling of l. cheek, with tensive pain and on touch bruised pain. White swelling of cheeks, feeling œdematous to touch. General swelling, inflammation, cold gangrene, death. Scarlet stripes on l. forearm, which itch when touched but disappear when rubbed, with sensation as of a thin cord under skin. Reddish pimple on chin, painful on touch. Pustules above r. brow, itching, and after scratching exuding bloody water. Vesicles filled with yellowish serum, with diffused redness. Ulcerating, boil-shaped elevations. Gangrene.

Itching, with urging to stool, and stool too soon; I. on back of l. hand. Corrosive I. on l. thigh; on r. close to hip; on l. leg near knee in morning. Sticking I. on upper arm near elbow. Burning I. on middle knuckle of index; on outer side of l. forearm. Tickling I. on r. sole.

Clinical.—It seems to have cured erysipelas of the cheek, of the vesicular variety, with violent fever. Abscesses and erysipelatous inflammation. It has been found useful for old torpid ulcers and for gangrene. It is said to be a valuable topical remedy for cancers, and is said to have cured entirely epithelioma.

Sleep.—Frequent yawning. Sleepiness after mid-day meal. Irresistible sleepiness during the day. Stupid slumber in afternoon, from which he cannot arouse himself. Slept with arms stretched far above his head. Sleeplessness, with tremulous tossing about before midnight, roaring in ears and inability to close eyes. Sleep poor and tossing about two nights, afterwards heavy sleep. Frequent and easy waking; F., but immediate falling asleep again. Dreams after 3 A.M., of the transactions of two days previous. Anxious, confused D., without end. Vivid, lascivious, with emission. Vivid, anxious, causing him to cry out, whereupon he wakes.

Fever.—*Chilliness of whole body* in morning; C. when walking in warm open air; C., with sweat; with sensation as if he had not slept all night and were completely washed out, and with disappearance of veins of hands. Cold hands, with heat in face and warm forehead, without thirst. Shivering; *over upper part of body;* over back, with glowing cheeks and cold hands; frequently in skin, then salivation. Heat; with pulse at 86; all day, the clothes are burdensome, with heaviness of whole body as if he had carried a great load; of face. Sweat in morning on thighs and legs, but not on feet; on neck every morning in bed and on rising; in morning, extending from feet over the whole body, with heat, without much thirst. Cold sweat; on legs in morning.

(*Euphorbia corollata* has proved valuable in terrible attacks of deathly retching and vomiting, with a feeling of clawing in the stomach and with cold sweat, after Cocculus, etc., had failed.)

Euphrasia.

A tincture is made of the fresh plant (except the root) of Euphrasia officinalis, L.

General Action.—A "catarrhal" remedy, with special reference to the mucous membranes of the eyes and nose.

Allies.—Sulphur; Puls. > cold and open air. Compare also Allium cepa, nose and eyes.

Generalities.—Sticking here and there; in muscles; < adductors of r. thigh and last phalanx of the finger which carries the thimble and which had been bruised a few weeks previously; S. jumping about in hands, spine, arms, legs and genitals; frequent S. in l. side of head, liver and spleen (wherever there was sticking there was a sensation as if warmth penetrated); S. and burning pain in l. scapula, liver and diaphragm, in the latter, especially, renewed by deep inspiration. Pain in adductors; r. Bruised sensation in morning. Uneasiness at night, with urging to urinate.

Weariness; in morning; during the day, and sleeplessness till 2 A.M.; lasting into the night; as after fasting; obliging her to lie down towards evening, with heat of hands and rapid pulse (as she thinks), upper arms were as heavy as lead, wrists felt as if they had been squeezed, in spite of partial sleep she heard everything, and on closing eyes large heads appeared making grimaces, she woke with chilliness over the whole body, < thighs and knees, then pressure in stomach as if overloaded. Symptoms > coffee.

Mind.—Irritable. Reflective and disinclined to speak. Indolent, hypochondriac, external objects had no life for him.

Head.—Sticking. Aching in morning on waking, < forehead; A. externally, < forehead. Emptiness in morning, > riding. Confusion; on waking, > a cold sponge bath, with pain in sinciput; at 10 and 11 A.M., with emptiness; after dinner, with heaviness of head and sleepiness; in evening, with bruised pain (and fluent catarrh), so that he must lie down earlier than usual, though the headache was < lying; C. on blowing nose, with pain in nose.

Sticking in r. side of forehead. Tearing above r. eye, extending into middle of forehead and becoming a pressure. Frontal pain; at 9 A.M., > open air; and orbital, with photophobia and lachrymation; extending into eyes, > open air; intermittent, at 9 A.M., when walking in open air, extending into eyes. Sticking in r. temple; externally in l. Pain in temples, with heat in forehead. (Confusion and pressure externally in vertex.) Sticking in r. side of brain; in brain beneath r. parietal bone; in upper part of l. side of brain; in r. side of brain on stooping; in brain, more in l. than in r. side, and < in the room; in sides of head, > putting his cool hands to the temples. Headache in l. side at 9 A.M., beginning with ringing in ears, > cold applications, with heat in head and loss of appetite for dinner. Tearing sticking in l. side of occiput in afternoon.

Eyes.—**Cornea feels as if covered with mucus, it obscures vision and obliges him to press the lids together,** in morning. Vessels running through white nearly to cornea (therewith a pressure and a dark spot on cornea that had lasted a long time disappeared within two days). Sticking in r. *Biting at times,* **biting water runs from them;** *frequent burning biting, obliging winking* at noon, > increased lachrymation. *Pressure in r., then l., extending from inner canthus, with lachrymation, the lids seem smaller, pupil dimmer and eye cold;* P. in r. morning and evening, with lachrymation; in r. in bed at 11 P.M.; > the dark, with frequent winking as from twinging in eyes; when writing, on fixing eyes for a long time vision vanishes and eyes water profusely; causing frequent blinking; as if sleepy; as if some one were pressing upon them at 2 P.M., > a nap. Pain from glare of light, as from insufficient sleep. Contractive feeling on walking in open air; C. feeling in r., with lachrymation; C. from both sides, < upper lids, in evening, causing frequent winking.

Itching; of l.; *in afternoon on going out, obliging frequent winking and wiping of eyes, with increased lachrymation.* Itching tension, now in one, now in other, < upper lid, becoming a burning on scratching. *Burning* till noon, *with lachrymation;* < r., and the letters run together on exertion by reading. Dryness; so that he must close them when reading or writing; as from loss of sleep. *Lachrymation; so that he was almost blind;* in morning. Sticking in ball.

Lids.—**Burning and swelling** (Apis., Sulph.), < morning on waking, till towards 11 A.M., with misty vision, next day with redness; **B. and S. of margins. Redness and swelling** in forenoon, with burning and tension in r. ball; **R. and S. of margins** (Sulph.), < *l., with intermittent itching burning in them and increased lachrymation. Redness and dryness of margins. Swelling and sensitiveness.* **Frequent inclination to blink.** Blinking during the day as from twinging; B. in morning, twinging pain in eyes. Pressure at 11 P.M., in bed on looking at the reflection of the moon on the curtains. *Dryness. Burning in margins* (Sulph.); < forenoon, *with swollen sensation ;* < canthi, in morning on waking, with tension; alternating with itching; as from too little sleep, also with tension.

Dry mucus in canthi; in inner. Sticking in outer C., with burning, then lachrymation. Pressure in l. inner C.; in l. C., which seems protruded and cold, with sticking in ball and pressure in it. Frequent itching burning in l. C., with tension above both eyes (at noon, with migraine). Tension in outer C. Pain in upper orbital regions at 6 P.M., > lachrymation, with pinching in eyes. Vision dim on looking at a distance; when walking in open air; *D. in evening;* of r. eye, > after a sticking from forehead out of r. eye; by candle-light; sometimes the light seemed to burn brightly, sometimes dimly. Everything seemed enveloped in mist and moving. Vision bad in evening. *Sensitiveness to light; to candle-light.*

Clinical.—Conjunctivitis; the inflammation of the eyes calling for Euphras. is, above all, catarrhal in nature, subacute, characterized by free discharge of matter which seems to be acrid, making the lids somewhat sore; the margins of the lids even may become ulcerated, there may be burning lachrymation, or the discharge may be thick and yellow and somewhat acrid; one very prominent characteristic of the drug is the tendency to an accummulation of sticky mucus on the cornea, which is removed by frequent winking. It is found useful in a large number of cases of cold in the eye and nose, with acrid water from the eyes, while the discharge from the nose is generally quite bland. It is said to have cured inflammation of the cornea and even ulceration with burning, smarting tears, running from nose, etc., and various forms of superficial inflammations of the eyes and lids are treated successfully by Euphras. when there is this peculiarity to the discharge. (It is even reported to have cured iritis.)

Ears.—Sticking; in r. mastoid process. Boring outward in region of r. drum. Pain in r., with sensation as if hot water penetrated it. Tension in l. Dragging outward and a spitting noise.

Nose.—Swelling of mucous membrane of l. nostril in morning. *Dryness.* Itching in nostrils. Sneezing; (frequent, with discharge of much watery mucus); *with profuse fluent coryza,* whereby much mucus was discharged through nose and posterior nares; *irritation to sneeze all day without cause.* **Profuse fluent coryza in morning, with much cough and expectoration;** fluent C. at 5 A.M. on waking, > at 6 after a cold sponge bath, with pressure in forehead near root of nose.

Face.—Redness and heat; of cheeks. Pallor. Pain in facial nerve below eye in afternoon. Stiffness of l. cheek when speaking and chewing, with heat and sticking. Sticking in chin; with internal heat in the same place. Sticking through r. lower jaw; S. forward through l. lower jaw at noon when eating, hindering chewing; forward beneath r. lower, near throat, > touch. Drawing pain transversely across upper jaw. Drawing in r. lower jaw in afternoon, with indications of aching in r. ear. Excoriations in corners of lips.

Mouth and Throat.—Sticking in lower teeth; S. in a hollow tooth in afternoon when walking in open air, > entering warm room; also in r. lower jaw. Intermittent pain in a molar which had been sensitive several months. (Throbbing in two teeth.) Profuse bleeding of gum. (Inflamed swelling on gum near last molar, which had been loose and painful for weeks.) Pain in r. lower gum on rising, where there is an inflamed ring around incisor. Tongue coated in morning; with earthy taste. Hesitation after the periods in order to select another expression, and repetition of the first words. Dry mouth. Taste clayey. T. insipid. Unnatural T. to food at noon. Bitter T. to tobacco-smoke in morning. Isthmus faucium painful.

Stomach.—Hunger at noon without appetite. Appetite lost. Little A. for dinner; and breakfast, with pasty taste. Little relish for cigars. No relish for cigars. Thirst in evening. Eructations tasting of food; in afternoon; E. of food in afternoon. Hiccough. Nausea; on beginning to smoke; from tobacco-smoke, which has a bitter, biting taste; > a swallow of water; with emptiness in stomach; with griping in abdomen. Sticking in epigastric region; beneath pit of stomach on inspiration and expiration in evening when sitting. Gnawing at noon after eating. Pressure; as from fulness, > eructations. Pulling at noon during dinner. Tensive pain in epigastric region at noon. Heartburn, with frequent empty eructations. Distended feeling, > afternoon, with frequent eructations of food. Discomfort; increasing in the room to nausea and uprising of heat, gradually affecting the whole body.

Abdomen.—Distention before dinner, as without flatulence. Rumbling at 10.30 A.M., with hunger that was satisfied with a bit of bread; R. as from hunger and emptiness. Griping (in the morning he had had a difficult, unsatisfactory and delayed stool); G., with three soft stools and rumbling; G. waking at night, and rumbling, > emission of flatus; paroxysmal G. Pain; burning, extending transversely across. Distress. Sticking in hepatic region at 6 P.M., extending to back; S. extending sometimes to abdomen, sometimes to r. lung; in spleen in morning. Griping in umbilical region in afternoon; G., with nausea, then rumbling in abdomen. Sudden sticking drawing pain along l. inguinal canal on rising from a seat, extending into testicle.

Anus.—Swollen and tense hæmorrhoids; sticking in H. after stool, with burning; pain in H.; burning in H. in afternoon, also > cold sitz bath; itching in H.; the itching in H. becomes boring sticking. Pressure when sitting. Painful crawling in evening.

Stool.—Diarrhœa three times in a day. Pasty in part in evening, after a nodular one in the morning; P., thick, delayed, preceded by flatulence, with urging, followed by burning in anus. *Constipation.* Hard and scanty; and at an unusual time; H. and sluggish; H. and difficult; H. nodular, unsatisfactory, delayed, followed after two hours by itching in anus; H. at first, then pasty. Scanty. Profuse and formed, twice a day. Delayed. Omitted two days.

Urinary Organs.—Frequent urging at night. *Frequent micturition;* in evening, with profuse urine; at night. Urine increased; and pale. Urine scanty.

Sexual Organs.—Cramplike drawing inward in evening in bed, with pressure above pubis. Sticking on tip of glans; voluptuous itching S. on glans when sitting, painful after scratching. Voluptuous itching on margin of prepuce, and after scratching and pressure pain. Heat in glans. Testicles drawn up and crawling in them. Menstruation delayed, scanty and shorter than usual.

Respiratory Organs.—*Irritation in larynx causing cough, then tension beneath sternum.* Pressure in larynx after prolonged reading in evening, as if its calibre were diminished. *Hoarseness in morning.* Cough, < during the day; with mucus in chest which cannot be loosened; **profuse expectoration of mucus by voluntary hacking cough.** *Sudden violent C. from tickling in larynx.* Suffocation suddenly waking from midday nap (apparently from mucus in posterior nares), so that he must sit upright and cough. Breath lost when coughing, almost as in whooping cough. Respiration difficult; even in the room; *inspiration is difficult even when sitting.* Breath short; on lying down in bed, with sobbing.

Clinical.—It is sometimes indicated in acute colds with cough, associated with severe coryza and running from eyes; the cough begins in the morning on rising and continues through the day, not troubling the patient at night; in some cases the cough is dry and tickling, but usually there is a free expectoration, and in nearly all the cases the characteristic symptoms of influenza will be present.

Chest.—Sticking in r.; in r. pectoral muscles; in lungs; l. lung; in r. lung in region of nipple at 8 P.M., always renewed by deep inspiration; beneath sternum, < inspiration. Sticking pulsation in l. lung in region of nipple. *Pain beneath sternum, < forenoon, with sticking here and there in chest.* Pressure upon chest. Tension, < l. side at night, with sleeplessness till midnight.

Heart.—Sticking. Pain in afternoon, with palpitation. Palpitation on rapid walking.

Back.—Sticking along spine mornings on waking, > moving about. Cramplike pain; intermittent. Pain when sitting and walking. Rheumatic drawing from uppermost dorsal vertebra to l. clavicle in afternoon, with pain on touch. Heaviness in small of back in morning on rising, changing to sprained pain, so that he could hardly stoop forward and could not bend to right, > forenoon, extending into l. hip, where there were similar heaviness and straining, > dinner and disappearing in evening.

Extremities.—Weariness in evening; W. and generally almost febrile condition.

Upper Extremities.—Sticking in r. shoulder-joint in afternoon. Sticking in arm. Pain in r. arm in afternoon, extending to fingers. Arms asleep. Sticking in r. upper arm; benumbing S. in l. Rheumatic drawing and sticking in r. elbow, wrist and hand in evening, which latter is hotter than l., with distention of veins, the pain extending to middle finger and thumb, then suddenly jumping to larynx, < to l. side, then suddenly returning to hand. Tearing in elbow and wrist. Sticking in l. forearm close to wrist. Pain in r. forearm and hand as from being asleep. Cramplike pain in wrists. Paralyzed sensation in r. wrist, extending to elbow. Piercing pinching on back of hand. Cramplike pain in metacarpus; alternately violent and slight C. pain in l. hand, changing to fingers. Hands fall asleep. Pinching in l. fingers at 9 A.M. when sitting; P. in metacarpal phalanx of index. Cramplike pain in fingers, < l. joints. Pain in finger-joints and knuckles as from being asleep, < towards outer side. Numbness of r. index and middle finger; and thumb and parts affected by writers' cramp, on going out. Deadness of r. fingers.

Lower Extremities.—Sticking in r. natis; in l. hip-joint when walking; in anterior muscles of r. thigh when standing; posteriorly in r. thigh when standing; in fascia lata of l. thigh, with burning. Sticking drawing from upper part of thigh into groin, < sitting. Pain in adductor of r. thigh when walking, corresponding with the pain she had nine months previously, when she pushed with the foot something standing on the ground. Burning pain in r. thigh and glutei. Jerking sticking in l. knee on walking. Tension of tendons under knee when walking. Weariness of knees. Boring sticking upward in tibiæ. Pain drawing upward and downward in periosteum in front of l. tibia when sitting. Cramplike pain in calf on long standing, with heaviness. Cracking in l. external malleolus when stepping. Tension from outer malleolus, near tendo-achillis, to calf when walking and sitting. Sticking in heel in the beginning of the night; frequent S. in ball of r. foot in afternoon, becoming a burning when sitting; lancinating S. in l. os calcis at 6 P.M. when sitting. Numbness of l. foot, with an unpleasant sensation when the circulation returned. Sticking in l. great toe in evening and when walking. Tickling crawling in l. toes and after rubbing pain.

Skin.—Pustules on wings of nose. Formication beneath l. scapula in afternoon. Frequent biting and itching over whole body. (Sticking in the condylomata when sitting, < walking, with sore and burning pain when touched.) Itching sticking here and there at night, with tossing about and coldness. (Itching in condylomata.) Voluptuous itching on r. calf in evening when walking; on forepart of thigh when walking in open air, and pain after scratching.

Clinical.—Measles; very frequently indicated in the catarrhal symptoms of measles, inflammation of eyes, photophobia, cough, running from the nose, headache, etc.

Sleep.—Yawning; *when walking in open air;* with sleepiness, but inability to sleep; then nausea, > a glass of water; in short, then in long attacks; frequent, at 5 P.M.; frequent, with sleepiness, sleep only about 11 P.M.; incessant, in evening, without weariness; spasmodic, before she had completely yawned a second yawning began, without weariness, with lachrymation, humming in ears and pulsation in throat, then indistinct vision in l. eye. Desire to stretch when sitting and reading. Sleepiness during the day; in afternoon; early in evening; with activity; which begins in eyes; overpowering, in afternoon; overpowering, at 8 P.M.

Late falling asleep. Sleeplessness till midnight after going to bed early. *Frequent waking as from fright;* frequent W. from feverish dreams, with chilliness, frequent urging to urinate and copious micturition. Waking every moment after 3 A.M. for three mornings, then stupid sleep at 6 A.M., on waking from this sleep pressure on upper part of chest, heaviness of head, nausea, general sweat, vertigo, < motion, even to falling sideways, limbs weak and tremulous, on rising the upper part of the body seemed too heavy, as if the limbs could not carry it, the attack gradually diminished till noon, with depressed mood. Tossing about at night, the bed seemed harder than usual. Uneasy sleep, with many dreams and frequent urging to urinate. Sleep unrefreshing, with tossing about and frequent micturition. Sleep interrupted, then in the morning confusion of head, > cold bath, with heaviness of eyes. Dreams frightful and uneasy; frightful, of fires and conflagrations from lightning. Confused D. Disagreeable D.

Fever.—Chilliness; internal in forenoon, but in afternoon internal and external chilliness of arms. Cold skin at night. Cold hands, with flushes of heat and red face, without thirst. Heat in evening; H. of head, with pressure; H. suddenly changing to orifice of stomach and then ending in lower part of œsophagus, with spasmodic constriction. Sweat at night in sleep, > waking; of strong odor at night in sleep, < chest, on rising chilliness. Distressing dryness of skin.

Ferrum.

Pure Iron, reduced by Hydrogen, is triturated for use.

General Action.—Iron acts chiefly on the blood, producing more rapid oxydation, with rise of temperature, at first an increase of red color (or of red corpuscles), but subsequently a diminution of red corpuscles and profound anæmia. The use of the various preparations of iron for febrile and inflammatory states has been greatly neglected.

Allies.—Cinchona, Bell., Mangan., Phos., Puls., Lyc.

Generalities.—*Emaciation.* Trembling; in frequent attacks; anxious T., alternating with fatigue. Blood darker, corpuscles intensely colored, more colorless corpuscles, coagulating in a shorter time; darker, corpuscles intensely colored, sharply margined, more and larger colorless corpuscles, fewer elementary corpuscles, longer in coagulating, serum darker; corpuscles deeply colored, colorless corpuscles smaller, longer in coagulating; serum increased in one case, diminished in four, dried serum diminished, ashes of serum increased in four cases, diminished in one, coagulum increased in three cases, diminished in two, dried coagulum increased in two, diminished in three, ashes of coagulum increased, red sediment increased in three cases, diminished in two, fibrin increased in one, diminished in four, water increased, dry residue diminished, fat increased in two, diminished in two, sol. salts in ashes increased, iron in ashes increased in one case, diminished in three, calc. phos. in ashes increased in two cases, diminished in three.

Periodical pains. Wandering about at night on account of pains. Magnetized sensation on waking, irresistible sleepiness. Nervousness; after menses; for three successive monthly periods, with headache and varicose veins in l. ankle; and hysterical feeling, proneness to weep or laugh immoderately, with choking in throat as if it were swelling outwardly. Restlessness.

Weakness; all day, with sleepiness; by day, with sleepiness (little > by sleep); in afternoon; *general, from mere speaking; from walking;* walking in open air; during menses; at beginning of menses, > exercise, with mental depression, and the pain usually felt at beginning of menses disappeared; < towards evening; with falling asleep; with drowsiness and disinclination to talk or work; with aching in all limbs; periodical, then persistent (after increase of physical and mental energy), < walking. Tired aching as from lying long in one position. Inclination to lie down. Syncope; when walking, darkness before eyes, feeling as if she would have apoplexy and at every step roaring in ears; then weakness.

Aggravation in evening; A. by sitting; when standing, by motion, heat, eating, drinking water, conversation, the sight of any person, even the dearest, noise, the sound of voices. *Amelioration from gentle movement;* A. from rest, sitting, lying, cool weather, after vomiting or evacuations, silence and solitude.

Clinical.—Profound prostration, generally with restlessness and general relief from walking slowly, cannot keep quiet, but feels worse from any active effort. General oversensitiveness to pain (headache, neuralgia, etc.). General anæmia, but with tendency to flushing of the face and head and liability to violent headaches; in anæmia the extremities are generally cold, and the feet and hands often swollen.

Mind.—Wandering and discontented. *Excited by the slightest opposition. Anxiety; from slight cause, with throbbing in pit of stomach;* with alternations of trembling and weakness; as if she had done something bad, also at night, with sleeplessness and tossing about. Depression before menses; during menses, with excitement; after menses; when alone, but without complaints or weeping; (as from too loose bowels). Ill humor; after menses; with disinclination for labor; with indifference, also periodically. Sober and uncomfortable, but not gloomy. Quarrelsome, insisting that he is right. Disinclination to talk or work. Desire for solitude. Too gay one evening and sad the next. My surroundings seem large, and I am inclined to attribute great importance to trifles and am unusually earnest. Dulness and heaviness all day. Stupor, with headache; S., with vertigo. Indisposition to think and confusion of head. Memory weak.

Clinical.—Hypochondriasis or even melancholia, with profound anæmia.

Head.—Shooting before menses, with singing in ears. Intermittent tearing. Aching as if brain were torn; in morning slumber. Aching all day, < in evening, < on r. side of forehead, going down to r. nostril; in afternoon, with fever; every evening, with dulness over root of nose; in evening after a walk in the open air; *after menses;* from writing; < when walking or stooping, > when sitting; > towards evening during a foot bath, but soon returning more violent than ever; with languor and stiffness of head; with coryza; extending into nostrils; acute, then dull, > towards night, with stupor; intermittent, during the day; undulating; drawing. *Sick headache after menses, with hot head and cold feet;* sick H. a few days after menses, which, till within six months (after Veratrum), always preceded or followed menses, this time with throbbing in vertex as if a vein were too full, pulsation in stomach extending through œsophagus, as if a nerve were quivering, causing at times a sensation of suffocation as if something rose in the throat like a valve, hysterical sensations. **Hammering and beating, so that she must lie down,** for two, three or four days every two or three weeks, then aversion to eating and drinking. *Pulsations,* with sticking.

Emptiness. Heaviness; in morning on waking; with stupefaction in forehead and pressure in temples; with fulness, every pulsation is felt in temples. Fulness in afternoon; F., > sleep. Dulness in morning; on waking, as after a wakeful night, with heaviness; at 8 A.M., gradually > towards night; with heaviness of eyelids. *Confusion;* > after motion, with aching in one or other temple; as after a sleepless night. Congestion. *Rush of blood, swelling of veins of head,* **and**

flushes of heat in face (Bell.). *Beer rises to head.* Intoxication. A giddy shock in brain. Vertigo; *when walking; on descending* (see Mercurialis), as if she would fall forward; *as if everything went round with her, on looking at running water;* on sudden rising after sleep in the afternoon, with sensation as if a dark curtain were slowly let down before the eyes, nausea, prostration and lethargic dulness, then sleep from which it was difficult to rouse himself, two attacks of V. in afternoon as if balancing to and fro on water; on lying down, as if shoved forward or as if driving in a coach, > shutting eyes; with cold hands; with stupor, restlessness and inability to apply the mind. Symptoms, except the fulness, > after sleep.

Forehead.—*Sticking over l. eye;* S. inward; cutting. Prickling in l. sinus, then in r., changing to pressure, > at 3 P.M. Sharp pain over r. eye. *Pain as if it would burst. Pain all day, with cold feet;* P. waking at 1.30 A.M., with rumbling and gurgling in abdomen; over eyes; over l. eye, with lachrymation; *in eminences in morning after dressing, then extending over forehead to vertex, then changing to pressive pain from without inward, < descending stairs, transiently > pressure, decidedly > in open air*, changing at 2.15 P.M. to dull pressure, > towards 8 P.M., also lasting from 4 to 6 P.M.; in eminences, then in whole F. *Sudden* intermittent *pain over l. eye.* Pulsating, tickling pain, and in head. Drawing pain, *with hot head and cold feet;* sharp D. pain. Pain above l. brow, towards nose. Dulness and heaviness in forepart of head. Heaviness in F. and over eyes in morning.

Temples.—Sticking; *as with a penknife, waking at* 3 A.M., *extending over forehead, with chilliness, preventing sleep.* Pain, > lying quietly; P. extending over forehead. Heaviness. Pulsation.

Pain in vertex, waking at 2.15 A.M., < every change of position and preventing sleep till 4 A.M.; throbbing P. on moving suddenly or quickly ascending steps; peculiar pain in cool open air. Soreness in vertex, < r. side. *Shooting in l. side of head in afternoon;* l.-sided headache; all day; r.-sided, with itching in eyebrows and nose. Pain in occiput and neck at 8 A.M., gradually extending to forehead. Periodical beating pain in occiput and neck, gradually extending to sides and forehead, < moving or stooping. Weight from ear to ear. Heaviness in occiput in afternoon. *Falling of hair, with pain in scalp and formication.* Pain in scalp as if blood were extravasated, with pain on touching hair. Soreness of scalp; < in front. Itching.

Clinical.—So-called congestive headache, with violent throbbing, flushed face, extreme sensitiveness to all external impressions (like Bell.), the pain greatly < any sudden motion or by noise; the pain generally begins in one temple or one side of the head, and may involve the whole head, sometimes the skull feels as if it would burst open; with this very hot head there are generally cold extremities, feeble pulse, etc.

Eyes.—Redness, with burning pain. White of eye discolored; yellow. (Shooting in l.) Aching in r., with agglutination of lids at night; A. as if sleepy; *A. as if they would protrude* (Bell.), < r. Burning. Itching in evening and aching as from sand. Weakness, with lachrymation; and watery discharge from nose. Lachrymation so that he cannot read long; L. of l. eye, < open air. Pupils capable of only slight dilatation. Redness and swelling of lids, on upper a stye, the lower lids full of hard purulent mucus. Lids heavy; in morning. If he writes two hours he cannot open the lids wide, the eyes are watery as if he had not slept enough. Sticking in external corner of r. orbit. Pain in l. orbit, with heartburn. Pain in brows, extending into nose. Darkness before eyes in evening, with pain over orbits and dropping of blood from nose; D., < rising from stooping. Inability to see the stitches when sewing. Letters run into each other when reading or writing.

Clinical.—Morbus Basedowii after suppressed menstruation, with violent palpitation, extreme nervousness, etc.

Ears.—Sticking in r. in morning. Ulcerative pain in l. external. Ringing in r. Chirping before E. like crickets. Rushing, > laying head on table, with disagreeable feeling in brain.

Clinical.—Fetid discharge from l. ear.

Nose.—Numbness and stiffness. Spasmodic sneezing four times at 1 P.M. Watery discharge all day, with dull headache. *Bleeding in morning on stooping;* profuse B. in morning after rising, relieving the head; dropping from r. nostril in forenoon; B. from l. nostril.

Clinical.—Nosebleed.

Face.—*Yellow. Flushed and cheeks burning;* when riding on a cloudy day; cheeks F. Bloated; and pasty. Earthy and spotted blue. (Pale, with rumbling in abdomen, contraction of chest, congestion to head, spasmodic eructation, then heat in face, < r. cheek, and shooting on crown.) Expressions by turns melancholy and fretful. Pinched. Swollen feeling. *Lips pale;* and dry.

Clinical.—The face is generally bloodless, often puffy, but with the headache it may be flushed and hot.

Mouth.—*Toothache* all the morning. Tooth back of r. eye-tooth feels elongated and sore. Gums discolored. (Gums and cheeks swollen.) Tongue coated white; and mouth dry, taste bad; and taste slimy, without loss of appetite; T. white; T. coated yellowish-gray; T. red at tip, coated, white anteriorly, yellowish-white posteriorly; T. more natural after eating; sticking posteriorly and in centre of T., < touch of food and drink, but when not eating or drinking the part feels burnt, numb and stiff. Mouth dry in morning. *Taste dry to all solid food as if it contained neither juice nor strength,* he likes warm liquid food best; T. bitter to all food; T. like rotten eggs; putrid T. rising into mouth in afternoon, taking away his appetite; earthy; pasty; of iron constantly; (sourish in morning); bad on rising; improved in morning by drinking cold water.

Throat.—Rising of phlegm. Pain on swallowing, with heat in fauces and stiffness and pain in cervical muscles on movement. Soreness, not painful when eating; S., with dulness and heaviness all day; (with roughness and hoarseness). *Constriction.* Choking. Sensation of a lump below l. tonsil, painful during empty swallowing, > when eating and drinking. (Sensation of a plug when not swallowing.) Tickling with dry cough, then a spoonful of bright blood came up. Burning, with eructations of acrid gas. (On swallowing pain in œsophagus and soreness as after the bursting of a blister.)

Clinical.—Goitre, with protruding eyes, palpitation and nervousness.

Stomach.—*Appetite great; in evening; diminished;* little, especially for meat; *can eat only bread and butter, meat* *disagrees with him;* even when she has A. she can eat but little, she is immediately full and the food oppresses her. **Anorexia, dislike for all food** (China); *A. without bad taste or thirst; A. for he always feels full,* but drinks are relished. Thirst after the day sleep; T. after dinner, for he knows not what; T. at 3 P.M. between the chill and fever; in evening after chills and fever; in evening, then heat and sweat; unquenchable, in evening. Adipsia.

Eructations; *constant, as soon as she eats* (Ant. cr., Phos., etc.); *of food after eating, without nausea;* acrid; acrid and burning; foul. Nausea on rising; N. in forenoon; at 8 P.M., with flushes over whole body as before sweat; at night, with diarrhœa; *after eating;* before and after eating; when walking, and head inclined to right; *with vertigo;* in throat, ending in eructation. Heaving like the nausea of disgust, when eating. **Vomiting of food after midnight,** *then aversion to food and dread of open air; V. of food immediately after eating* (Lyc., Puls.); V. before midnight, < when lying, especially on l. side; on eating, having the taste of iron, or else of clear, frothy water; of mucus and water every morning and after eating, a kind of waterbrash, water runs out of her mouth and her throat feels drawn together; sour and acrid; profuse, on taking acids and beer.

Distention in regions of S. and abdomen; D. in epigastric region. Spasm. *Cramplike pain.* Pain; in pit; in pit at 2 P.M.; *after every meal;* after eating meat; after drinking; in pit on touch. Feeling as of a hard body or of undigested food, then burning and acrid eructation. *Oppression whenever she eats.* Painful contraction of everything at pit at 6 A.M. in bed, then spasmodic cough, with mucous expectoration. Tension; in epigastric region, with rumbling, becoming pressure, heaviness and griping, extending over abdomen, < morning and evening, at times with nausea. Feeling as if he would vomit, without nausea. Feeling as if something rose in it.

Heaviness in pit. Fulness; as if he would eructate after walking, > after eating. Drawing in epigastric region. Discomfort after every meal; D., > after dinner, with bitter eructations smelling like foul eggs. Occasional uneasiness in l. extremity. Heartburn; in evening after sourish beer. Burning after eating; B., > after eructations; in epigastric region, also with fulness; with indigestion; with cramplike pain in splenic region; with general unpleasant feeling, being febrile symptoms, with soreness and languor of limbs, indigestion and eructations, the heat in S. < before eating, > after eating; upward from pit during exercise, like apprehension, she must lie down. Sensation extending through œsophagus. All sensations are at the cardiac extremity and in splenic region.

Clinical.—The patients may have ravenous hunger, but the appetite sometimes vanishes and thereis absolute disgust for food; the attempt to eat brings on diarrhœa; there is frequently sinking in stomach; food cannot be taken on account of the diarrhœa which follows; there is often soreness of the walls of the abdomen.

Abdomen.—Distention; and hardness; without flatulent symptoms. Rumbling; all day, with pain in small of back and kidneys and soreness in urethra on urinating; at 1.30 A.M., with gurgling; in evening, with soreness and feeling as before stool; > after a copious stool, with griping, pasty taste, dryness of fauces and nausea; with soreness; with gurgling as before diarrhœa, but stool normal; with headache; waking, with griping, fulness and tension, > emission of flatus and copious stool, so that the colic was distressing only when sitting up. Noisy flatulence. Discharge of flatus; frequent and offensive, after rising in morning. Movement as before diarrhœa, but stool natural.

Sticking. Sharp pain; and bearing down in uterus, with aching below it. Pain; in morning after rising, < eating, > stool; after midnight, then diarrhœa; at 2.30 A.M., and urging to stool, stool free, loose, with griping, cutting and straining, nausea, disagreeable taste, > drinking cold water, at 6 A.M. another loose, brownish-yellow stool, with colic before and straining during stool; in attacks, waking him, > emission of flatus and profuse stool; flatulent, and emission of flatus; paroxysmal drawing P.; bearing down, in morning, as before menses; contractive, and in back. *Soreness as if beaten or as after purgatives, on touch and on coughing.* Distress, < in epigastric region, *increasing to a pain on touch,* > walking. Discomfort increasing to a sick feeling, with bitter foul eructations and griping, then copious, for the most part liquid stool. Tension. Warmth, < in epigastric region, > walking, with pressure, tension and griping in abdomen; heat rising from A. after sleeping an hour before midnight, mouth dry and a bad vapor and putrid taste rise into his mouth.

Sharp pain in upper A. and pit of stomach. Pressure just below stomach as soon as she eats or drinks. Flatus in r. side when riding in a carriage, soon passing off. Iron pain in l. side. Fulness in hypochondria. Shooting in l. hypochondrium. Cramplike sensation in splenic region. Pain in liver; in r. hypochondrium; in splenic region, with heaviness. Flatus in lower A., incarcerated in l. side, and copious emissions by mouth and anus. Rumbling and gurgling in transverse colon, < in cæcum. Pain in lower A. Weight in lower A., < walking.

Rectum and Anus.—Protrusion of large hæmorrhoids. Violent hæmorrhoidal flux. Ascarides are passed with the slimy stool, itching and gnawing in R. Spasm of R. Tearing in R.; in anus, with hard stool. Urging, then frothy stool, with loud flatus, then three watery, almost odorless stools, then griping in pit of stomach, but relief of the full feeling in hypochondria; frequent U., with burning in anus and pain in back on moving. Straining at stool all day; S., with and after stool.

Clinical.—Bleeding piles, with itching and gnawing. Ascarides, with itching, unnatural appetite, flushed face, etc.

Stool.—Watery, with flatulence, and frequent, more frequent after taking food or water (Coloc., Crot. t); *W. and sudden, without pain or smell;* W. and profuse, with cutting in abdomen. *Diarrhœa; frequent;* violent; with nervous spasmodic pain in abdomen, back and anus. *Constipation;* and hæmorrhoids which cause pain in going to stool; S. only every two or three days, frequent urging, S. dry, dark green. Hard and small; with pressing and tearing through anus; of small hard pieces, with straining, at first brown, then greenish or greenish-black, only once a day was there a copious soft S.; hard and delayed; hard, greenish and black, afterwards copious pasty stools; partly hard, copious, generally delayed, greenish or greenish-black; hard and soft on alternate days. Black. Yellow. Odorless. Mucus and sometimes blood with the S. Scanty.

Clinical.—Diarrhœa, especially containing undigested food, (China), as a rule painless, recurring particularly when eating or drinking, especially apt to recur at night; with the diarrhœa there is generally unnatural hunger, with easy flushing of the face, great paleness, weakness and exhausting sweats. Chronic diarrhœa, gushing, watery, painless, < night, with coldness of the body and great prostration. Diarrhœa in teething children, stools undigested, with flushed face, sometimes associated with vomiting, both diarrhœa and vomiting coming on immediately after taking nourishment.

Urinary Organs.—Pain in bladder. Urging; *constant, with pain in liver, chest and kidneys; with tickling in urethra extending to neck of bladder;* beginning with tickling in navicular fossa, obliging frequent micturition, with tenesmus recti in evening. *Involuntary micturition < by day* (Bell.); at night (Puls.); slight, when standing. Frequent micturition. (Gonorrhœa) mucous discharge from urethra after a chill. Soreness of urethra on urinating. Tickling in urethra in afternoon, < in fossa navicularis, with urging; T. in urethra on beginning to urinate, gradually extending along the whole urethra, afterwards with frequent urging without increase of urine. (Burning in urethra on urinating.) Urine copious, with prostration and nervousness; C. wine-yellow or reddish, sp. gr. rose from 1005 to 1025, reaction acid. Turbid U. Dark yellow U. Blood-red, charged with blood-corpuscles. Light-colored U., with whitish sediment. Sediment in U.; profuse, mucous.

Clinical.—Involuntary micturition, especially during the day, the child wets himself even while walking; also nocturnal enuresis.

Sexual Organs.—Tickling of glans between 8 and 9 A.M. and 6 and 7 P.M., with warmth and irresistible desire to urinate, when the urine reached the glans distressing pulsation, which continued after micturition, with increasing tenesmus vesicæ, the distress > rapidly drinking much water and compression of glans with the finger. Erections. Emissions; *nocturnal.*

Prolapsus of vagina during pregnancy. Pain in vagina during coition. Less dryness in vagina on beginning coition and more pleasure in it. A previously painless white discharge became painful as if the parts were raw. Leucorrhœa like whey, causing (at first) smarting and soreness. Discharge of stringy mucus from uterus before menses, with sensation in abdomen as during menses. Sticking shooting in uterus. Pain near mouth of uterus when lying. Abortion. Sterility without abortion. Menses delayed; one day, scanty, watery, with cutting in abdomen. Menses intermit for two or three days. Metrorrhagia. Menorrhagia, pale, increased by least movement. Menses copious.

Clinical.—Great sensitiveness of the vagina to coition (Sep., Bell., Plat.). Suppressed menses, with hæmorrhage from other parts, lungs, nose, rectum. Menses excessively profuse and prolonged, with great debility, flushed face. After severe uterine hæmorrhages, Fer. may be indicated by great coldness of the skin and bloating, by the gastric symptoms, by the prostration and headache. In anæmic women when the menses are very pale, watery and acrid, with great prostration. During anæmia or chlorosis calling for Fer. there is apt to be milky and acrid leucorrhœa.

Respiratory Organs.—Contraction of glottis in evening in bed, with rush of blood to head, burning externally on neck, and between scapulæ and on upper part of body generally, cold feet, and in the morning sweat. Pain in larynx provoking cough and hawking, < pressure, in morning on waking, but at noon giving place to a similar sensation behind upper third of sternum, and on hawking and coughing expectoration of frothy, tenacious mucus, mixed with black blood, frequently till 4 P.M. Tickling in trachea, causing frequent cough, < inspiration. *Voice almost extinct, utterance difficult and panting. Hoarseness, with rough sensation in larynx.*

Cough, < moving; C. all day and after lying down; at night. Dry cough, with sensation as if she could not get air; dry C. in evening after lying down, but expectoration on waking. *Coughing up blood in morning on rising;* at night, then increased dyspnœa; while suckling the child. *Hæmoptysis. Expectoration scanty, thin, frothy,* **with streaks of blood;** E. of bloody mucus by hacking. Copious purulent E. in morning (with putrid taste); on waking, and greenish, with sickly taste; copious, purulent, white E. after coughing, < smoking tobacco and drinking brandy.

Dyspnœa; and oppression of chest as from pressure of a hand (Chin. s., Phos.); after midnight, so that he must sit up in bed; generally < in forenoon, often > when he walked a little, sometimes < when walking in open air, with weariness of limbs; from heaviness in l. lung; and slow breathing, > by walking and talking or by constant reading or writing, < when quiet and especially when lying, particularly in evening, he must take several breaths before he can fill the lungs. Suffocation from quivering and pulsation in stomach. Asthma; anxiety in pit of stomach, impeding breathing. *Uneasy breathing from pain across chest.* Panting. Wheezing; under sternum, with slight inclination to cough at night, > after rising. Mucous râles behind manubrium sterni.

Clinical.—The very marked symptoms of Fer., of occasional oppression of chest and difficult breathing, may be compared with those of Phos.; Fer. is certainly extremely useful when the chest symptoms seem to occur from a kind of surging of blood to the chest, a not infrequent sympton in persons whose circulation is feeble, in such cases there are oppression and dyspnœa. It has been prescribed for asthma and even for pneumonia, and it is very probable that Fer. has been overlooked as a valuable remedy for inflammation of the thoracic organs, for it certainly may be indicated when there is marked febrile excitement. The cough of Fer. is usually dry, spasmodic, and may be accompanied by expectoration of blood, especially if there is the symptom of rush of blood to the chest; when blood is expectorated it is generally bright red and associated with great weakness.

Chest.—Consumption of lungs. Sticking all over; through lungs; in side under rib; in r.; r. side, with bruised feeling in neck; in sternum at night in bed; in side during exercise; wandering, in breast. Sticking cutting. Contractive cramp; *on moving, and coughing.* Pain; < full inspiration; below sternum; *superiorly under sternum, with catarrh and cough;* with sticking and tension between scapulæ and inability to move; and in liver; in r. side and in liver and kidneys, with constant desire to urinate; revival of an old P. in l. lung. Drawing pain; and around heart. Heavy pain across upper, causing uneasy breathing; heavy sore pain below l. nipple. Bruised pain. Pain in l. clavicle as if it had fallen asleep. Oppression. Tightness, with anxious asthma, < walking. Fulness. Heaviness; in upper part of l. lung, making breathing difficult, with soreness below clavicle and l. nipple, preventing a long breath. Rush of blood with hot vapor out of windpipe, sweetish taste as of blood and *hæmoptysis.* Burning at upper part of sternum after coughing. Sensation of dryness and mucus, the D. > transiently by drinking.

Heart and Pulse.—*Bruit de souffle* now and then. Tension in præcordial region. *Rapid action of heart.* Palpitation, < movement. *Pulse slow,* diminished in fulness, with rise of tonus in walls of arteries and rapid action of heart; S. and hard; S., full, tense; S. and tense; S., small, tense. Tense. *Small, weak,* sometimes intermittent, sometimes uneven pulse. Pulse scarcely perceptible.

Clinical.—Palpitation, sensation of oppression about the heart, sometimes with a full but soft pulse. In anæmia we may have anæmic murmur of the heart with palpitation.

Neck.—Chronic glandular swelling. Pain; when lying on r. side, and in shoulder. *Drawing extending from nape into head, in which there are then shooting, roaring and rushing.* Soreness as if bruised. Soreness and stiffness; and in occiput. Stiffness, with coldness of hands and feet, < hands.

Back.—Tearing when sitting and lying; between scapulæ when sitting, < when walking. Pain during menses. Sticking in scapulæ if she works a little with her hands. Tension between scapulæ and in sternum, preventing raising the arms, a kind of paralysis. Sticklike jerks in sacrum when walking, extending more towards the hips than upward, < after sitting or standing, almost as if strained. Pain in small of B.; in kidney region; on each side of sacrum at its junction with the ossa innominata; in sacrum on rising from a seat. Lumbago in l. loin; lumbago all night, > rising. Bruised pain in sacrum. Soreness in small of B. on rising, with rumbling in abdomen.

Clinical.—Rheumatism of the back; lumbago, > walking slowly, as are most of the pains of Fer.

Extremities.—*Swelling of hands and legs up to knees.* Fingers and toes drawn up with cramp and painful. Pain in joints. Pain from touch. Soreness, with languor and restlessness. Heaviness; and exhaustion; and general exhaustion. Stiffness of fingers and toes.

Upper Extremities.—Shoulder. *Creaking in r. joint, with bruised pain on touch, and shooting and tearing down through upper arm, inability to raise the arm;* C. in joint and on touch bruised feeling. *Downward-shooting, and in arms,* more severe than the shooting upward. Shooting and tearing from joint into upper arm and farther down, so that the arm cannot be raised. Boring passing down to finger-ends; in r. joint, < at irregular intervals, passing down biceps to elbow, < motion, > heat. Pain, and in neck; pain alternately in S. and elbow. Soreness in front part of r. and in r. arm; S. on touch.

Arm.—*Pinching in r. deltoid* (see Sang.). Pain, > bending them towards the chest, < motion and weight of bed-covers, with stiffness. Drawing, whereby it feels heavy and paralyzed. Lameness of r., with disinclination to move it, involuntarily assisting it with the l. hand. Irresistible desire to move them; at 2 A.M., then pain driving him out of bed. Stiffness; with pain; with soreness. Fixed in an upigrht position, with general trembling and chilliness.

Sticking in l. elbow; in l. wrist and back of hand, thumb most painful when moving it. Sprained pain in l. wrist. Swelling of hands, then desquamation. Trembling of hands in morning on trying to work; in evening, preventing sewing; T. when writing, write better when writing fast. Soreness and stiffness of hands. Numbness of hands, with swollen sensation; l. nearly numb, r. cold. Cramp in fingers, with numbness. Pain in thumb on motion; P. in fingers from shoulders; rheumatic P. in phalangeal joints of l. hand. Stiffness of r. thumb, with pain on motion.

Clinical.—It seems to have an especial affinity for the deltoid just above the insertion of the biceps, where there is pain causing inability to move the arm or fingers. Severe muscular pains about the shoulder-joint, extending to the elbow, particularly worse in l. shoulder.

Lower Extremities.—Weakness. Tonic spasm of thigh and leg. *Shooting and tearing from hip-joint down tibia, < in evening in bed, he must get up and walk, with bruised pain on touch;* a kind of paralysis, shooting and tearing from hip-joint to tibia and sole (the ball is always painful on touch as if bruised), by day he cannot step on account of pains, which, however, diminish when he walks, < in evening after lying down, so that he must get up and walk till midnight. Paralytic pain in thigh when sitting, after sitting crouched for some time she has to stretch the feet, the pain < rising from her seat, > walking. Distress in thighs during menses. Thighs feel as if asleep. Numbness of thighs.

Knee.—And ankles swollen and painful, < extending knee in bed. Contractive pain, and in ankles. Pain as if overfatigued, so that he cannot keep them still. Weariness in hollows on rising from a seat, < beginning to walk; W. so that he sinks down.

Leg.—Trembling, with bruised pain on walking. Cramp in calf in morning on rising; cramp in calves when standing, > when walking. The varicose vein in l. continued to extend downward, more painful to touch. Sensation in l. as of a swollen vein, painful on touch, sometimes inconvenient when walking. Acute pain like the moving of a screw through r. on walking. Contractive pain in tibia and calf, like cramp, on beginning to walk. Bruised pain in morning in bed, > rising. Painful drawing. Weakness of calves as if bruised.

Foot.—Swollen to ankles. Varicose veins. Cramp in r.; C. > pressing them against the footboard; *in soles; frequent, in soles and toes;* in evening, first in l., drawing up the limb. Shooting pricking in r. instep. Pain in heel; extending from r. into thigh. Soreness and stiffness. Has to take off the boots. Weariness after eating. Will not support her. Stiffness after resting from a walk.

Clinical.—Rheumatic or neuralgic pain through the whole extent of the lower limb, > moderate motion.

Skin.—Pale. Icteric around eyes, lips and nails. Dark herpetic spots on dorsum of hand inflame and suppurate. Round red itching spot on r. shoulder, which peels off like dust in the evening and night. Peeling off like dust from l. hand. (Scarlatina during desquamation corresponds to the peeling of the skin.) Burning pain when not touched, on dorsum of thumb, of toes, etc., with smarting on light touch. Itching in eyebrows; of nose; above r. knee, with sticking stabbing.

Sleep.—Yawning in morning, stretching, and eyes fill with water; frequent Y. Sleepiness; after dinner at noon, with dulness and headache over root of nose and inability to undertake mental employment; in evening, and thirst; almost impossible to keep awake when reading. Sleep in afternoon; apt to fall asleep when sitting; falls asleep when sewing, she must lie down, sleeps an hour and wakes with thirst and cramps in r. foot. Heavy sleep in morning till 9 A.M., from which he can scarcely rouse himself. Sound sleep, with unpleasant dreams.

Restless sleep; and lying awake a long time, but not tired in the morning; and dreamy, with emissions. Anxious tossing about after midnight. Light sleep. Late falling asleep. Waking every hour and light slumber; repeated W., with quiet sleep only after 2 A.M. Almost entire sleeplessness, waking in quarter of an hour bathed in sweat, with prostration, epigastric anxiety, feeling as if life were leaving her, then nervous excitement. Sleeps with half-open eyes. Sleeps on her back, cannot sleep on either side.

Dreams disturb sleep, weariness in morning on rising. Vivid D.; and anxious. Nightmare. Unpleasant D.; all night of friends and relatives deceased. D. of old friends, disturbing sleep; of meeting old schoolmates, of student life, etc. D. that he is in battle, that he has fallen into the water, etc. Confused D.

Fever.—Chilliness all day; in morning, with headache; in afternoon, so that he must go to bed; in afternoon, then fever; in afternoon, then thirst, must go to bed, then heat with sweat; between 1 and 2 P.M.; at 5 P.M., then fever; in evening in bed; then heat at 3 P.M., with sweat; all day, < afternoon, then feverish in evening, then chill after going to bed; not > sweat after rapid walking. Creeping chill at noon; C. chill beginning at 7 A.M., < in back. Rigor in evening before sleep without external coldness, chilliness all night; (R., and during the chill his face got glowing hot). Chill in back. Cold hands and feet; and numb, not > walking though there was sweat; C. and stiff hands. Cold feet; on getting into bed, lies awake some time; all night, and numb; with stiff fingers; with heat of head. Toes cold and painful.

Ebullition of blood by day and heat in evening, < hands. Heat; at 3 P.M.; after the siesta; with sweat at 8 P.M., after thirst; after beer-soup, with anxiety; > at 7 P.M.; without thirst; in flushes, as if sweat would break out; internal, with external coolness and sensation as if the face were swollen; in body, with red cheeks, but the head was free; in palms; soles; (of face in morning).

Sweat; by day when walking and sitting; mornings; in morning after rising, relieving the head; at night, with weariness; frequent, in slumber about midnight; on alternate days from daybreak till towards noon, each time preceded by headache; during digestion, with anxiety; of peculiar odor.

Clinical.—Fer. produces a decided type of fever and many symptoms of chills and fever; there is certainly general coldness, especially of the extremities, though the head may be hot and the face red; sometimes there is persistent heat of the palms and soles; there is also profuse sweat, which is very debilitating. It has been prescribed for protracted intermittent fever, especially after the abuse of quinine, with swelling of the spleen, general anæmia and dropsical swellings of the face or feet. In many cases of fever the Fer. patient feels worse while sweating (Merc.).

Ferrum Iodatum.

Fresh, pure Iodide of Iron is triturated for use.

Generalities.—Pain in and between shoulders, in nape and in joints of lower limbs. *Weakness;* all day, with weary, bruised sensation in all limbs, < legs and calves; all night, with bruised sensation; with sleepiness. Indolence in evening, with sleepiness and bruised feeling in limbs, < calves.

Head.—*Aching;* < evening; < a warm room, on stooping, shaking head, walking rapidly, reading, writing, etc., > open air, a draught, cold air and towards evening; confused, < forehead, < r. side, < putting on hat, reading, writing, etc., > open air, sitting down or standing in a draught. Confusion, < forehead; with heaviness, the aching < smoking. Drawing tearing through forehead above eyes. Pain in forehead; above and between eyes, < going to bed.

Nose.—Stopped coryza; at night, so that he must sleep with open mouth, suddenly > between 5 and 6 A.M.; > towards noon. All symptoms of coryza, profuse discharge of mucus from nose and frequent expectoration of mucus from larynx and trachea.

Mouth and Throat.—Tongue coated yellow. Tongue burns. Dryness. Taste insipid; > after breakfast; and bitter at back of mouth; pasty T.; T. of peppermint; bad in morning. Hawking of mucus, with cough and expectoration. Frequent rattling of mucus in throat and expectoration of mucus. Tickling and scraping in throat and nose, with sensation as if he would suffocate and necessity to hawk in order to raise mucus from throat. Indescribable sensation, not painful, along œsophagus.

Stomach.—Appetite diminished. Did not relish smoking. Eructations after eating; violent, after supper, with nausea; frequent E., with constant inclination to eructate. Nausea. Heat, and in intestines.

Abdomen. — Rumbling; towards morning, before stool, with gurgling; before stool; before stool, with pain. Emission of flatus smelling of iodine. Pain in evening, < after eating; P. before a small light stool; > by light yellow diarrhœa; > after a natural yellowish-brown stool mixed with black portions; with urging to stool, then a dark stool; < about middle, with flatulence and urging; usually beginning about umbilicus and extending downward about r. side. Sore pain before stool, with rumbling. Soreness; in evening, with pulsation; < after eating, with pain.

Rectum.—And in anus, sensation all day as if something turned in a circle, and something like drops of water flowed down, and as if a screw bored upward and downward. Constriction as if worms were in it, < in anus, while stool was easy and painless. Peculiar crawling and tickling all day, and < in anus. Urging, with drawing pain from above umbilicus down r. side, then a small, hard, yellowish-brown stool; ineffectual U.

Stool.—Light yellow diarrhœa morning and evening, preceded by pain. Soft, small, light brown, with much urging and pressing. Hard and small, with sticking and constriction in anus during its passage. Black. Scanty.

Urinary Organs.—Frequent and profuse micturition, urine light, of sweetish smell; F. and P. micturition, with pain in whole urethra. Pain in urethra in evening during frequent but scanty micturition; P. in urethra, on urinating, then in the whole penis; in urethra during micturition, with soreness and with frequent desire. Prickling itching in urethra, < forepart, with frequent urging, but little urine at a time. Peculiar crawling tickling all day in urethra and especially in rectum. Sensation in morning as if urine remained in fossa navicularis and could not be forced any farther. *Urine dark;* with a thick white sediment. Urine bright yellow in evening, smelling sweetish, with milky sediment.

Clinical.—It has proved wonderfully efficient in acute nephritis following the exanthemata.

Sexual Organs.—Frequent erections all night; erection waking him, with pain and burning in the whole urethra, but inability to urinate from tenesmus of neck of bladder, though there was a violent urging.

Clinical.—Uterine congestion, with great bearing down, with feeling as if something sore were being pushed up when sitting down. Uterine displacements, retroversion and prolapsus, with atony, difficulty in retaining urine. Suppression of menses.

Respiratory Organs.—Cough, with expectoration of grayish-white, tenacious mucus drawn out in threads; irritation in afternoon to cough and to expectorate, with much mucus in throat. Short breath, necessity to take a deep breath, oppression of chest and pressure beneath sternum.

Chest.—Sudden sharp sticking, extending outward from l. nipple to arm at 11 A.M., < pressure, returning frequently in afternoon and evening. Intermittent sharp pain. Pain in sides; in evening on respiration, and deep in abdomen and in region of spleen (where it was more like a stitch). Oppression, < inspiration; O., more in upper part of lungs; O., with expectoration of thick yellow mucus; with necessity to breathe deeply, which caused soreness; as from a weight. Congestion of lungs.

Pulse.—Rapid.

Back.—Pain in small of, and in kidneys; < evening; < evening, and extending farther downward; in lumbar vertebræ, extending to lower part of spine, small of back and kidneys.

Extremities.—Painful drawing in tendons on back of r. hand and l. foot. Weakness, with bruised sensation and great aversion to moving. Paralyzed and bruised sensation, < legs; in r. arm in evening, with weariness, so that he must stop writing. Rheumatic bruised sensation in upper arms, < r. Rheumatic paralyzed feeling in r. upper arm and r. shoulder. Bruised, paralytic feeling in thighs, extending to knees, which are heavy, the legs feel much lighter in proportion, in the afternoon this paralytic sensation extends into calves, even r. tibia is painful. Rheumatic pain in back of l. foot in evening, extending to pelvis.

Sleep.—Sleepiness in morning after a long sleep at night, with no desire to rise. Frequent waking, with urging to urinate and pain on micturition. Restless night, with frequent waking, many dreams and easy erections; R. sleep, with dreams of long-past events. Dream that I had grown very large and was from thirty to fifty feet high, everything about me seemed small and insignificant, the bedstead was too small and short, and waking with a paralyzed sensation, and hands and feet could not rest. Dreams of thieves and of fighting with them, waking him. D. towards morning that he met many acquaintances, each of whom complained of a different indisposition.

Fever.—Coldness from 9 to 10 A.M. and again in afternoon; C. at 10 A.M., after 12 the pulse was 84, with sleepiness and soreness in small of back and kidneys; about noon, some fever at 3 P.M., then rapid pulse, next day C. between 12 and 1 with sleepiness, at 3.30 P.M. rapid pulse with heat. Heat beginning at noon, < 3 P.M., with hot skin, > 4 P.M. and pulse decreased, skin moist and profuse, sweat only on forehead; H. in afternoon; H. without sweat.

Ferrum Phosphoricum.

The pure Phosphate of Iron is triturated for use.

Generalities.—Malaise all the evening. Weariness in morning on waking; at 1 P.M. (not having eaten since breakfast), with desire for brandy.

Mind.—Hasty, intolerant feeling in afternoon. Impetuous feeling in evening, yet obstacles cause hindrance and annoyance and trifles seem like mountains, intolerant of hindrance and annoyance. Annoyed at the conversation of fellow-passengers in street-car, < when earnest or excited, > afternoon. Shrinking and timid at hearing cross words about an absent stranger. Soothing, pleasant effect from walking in a quiet part of the city after dark, ceasing on returning to the bustle of the central streets. Inertia, indifference to ordinary matters, craving for brandy without real muscular debility. Loss of courage and hope early in evening, > sleep.

Head.—Feeling as from insufficient sleep, fell asleep at my table at 4.30 P.M. Pain all day, < r. side, < first thinking of it; P. from r. brow to r. ear when reading; in r. side. Sharp twinges of pain over whole l. side at 11 P.M.; from r. vertex to r. supraorbital foramen in afternoon. Aching dulness extending from vertex towards orbits and sides of head as a pressure, < holding head down when writing, > when walking, but when walking in the street more in occiput, and when rising, walking, etc., most in vertex, as the force of the circulation most impinges, it always seems in subcutaneous cavities. Pain in posterior part of base of skull in afternoon at every concussion (as of coughing or even sudden and hard smacking of lips).

Clinical.—Symptoms of meningitis of the brain, suffused eyes, full, soft pulse, with drowsiness and heaviness. Violent headache, throbbing, followed and > by nosebleed. Violent headaches during menstruation; the head is extremely sensitive to pain (compare Fer. met.).

Eyes and Ears.—Smarting in edges of r. lids. Neuralgia at l. inner brow and down l. side of nose, in evening when riding. Sharp aching at outer edge of l. orbit, as if in bone, at 7.30 P.M., on r. side at 8.30. Sticking in r. ear; on going to bed, extending as a headache above periosteum of that side.

Clinical.—Encysted tumor of the eyelids. Inflammation of the external ear, with muco-purulent discharge, ear red and swollen, mastoid process swollen and sore.

Nose and Face.—Lips blue after a tepid sponge bath. Grumbling in l. lower jaw, near filled molar. Smarting in r. anterior nasal passage; r. posterior nasal passage < inspiration, > expiration.

Mouth and Throat.—Increase of the usual light coat on tongue, with yellowish tint increasing towards the base. Liberation of pharyngeal, tracheal and nasal mucus. Working down of phlegm behind velum palati, also loosening from below.

Clinical.—Sore throat, catarrhal affections of the Eustachian tube and ears, especially in singers.

Stomach.—Indifferent to food on sitting down to supper, but ate heartily. Thirst for cold water and for brandy in morning; for brandy on rising in morning after studying till 2 A.M., took a teaspoonful with good effect; for ale at 1 P.M., at 3 P.M. no desire for dinner but for brandy, if he took a teaspoonful, he then ate with relish, the same desire before breakfast. Irritating, greasy eructation. Hiccough at noon after sitting bent towards the floor; H. when respiration compressed the stomach and afterwards. Nausea in morning on rising. Heartburn at 9.30 P.M. when sitting bent forward reading, with eructations causing coughing and hemming, irritation in throat and behind left of mid-sternum, later eructations of gas and of greasy fluid provoking cough (had had stewed oysters and aromatic tea at supper). Pinching in epigastrium.

Clinical.—Dyspepsia, with loss of appetite, nausea and vomiting after eating, aggravation from acids, especially with pulsating headaches, profuse menses, restlessness, etc. Persistent vomiting of food, often before eating in the morning, in women.

Abdomen.—Emission of fetid flatus when standing leaning over the table, continuing when undressing. Pain in transverse colon; at 3 P.M.; at breakfast, when bending forward, repeated when standing, using arms moderately towards the left. Threatening of diarrhœa from colon to rectum.

Stool and Urinary and Sexual Organs.—Stool soft, yellow, easy. Urine pale, copious, in cool weather; in warm weather, and limpid, less copious and darker in cooler weather; when pale there were several crystalline forms, the principal being hexagonal plates answering to cystin, and tablets answering to uric acid and chloride of sodium.

Clinical.—Hæmorrhoids. Cholera infantum, with red face, full, soft pulse; stools watery or even bloody, after checked perspiration. Hæmorrhage from the bladder. Irritable or inflamed bladder, with frequent urging. Retention of urine, with fever, in children. Ovarian neuralgia. Dysmenorrhœa, with sacral pains, headache, frequent urging to urinate, pains in l. ovary.

Chest, Heart and Pulse.—Pain in C. in morning. Oppression of l. C. and stomach from indignation. Palpitation when sitting; when sitting writing. Pulse accelerated.

Clinical.—Its action upon the respiratory organs may be clearly foreshadowed by the provings of Fer. and Phos.; like Fer., it is indicated in congestions of the respiratory organs, even when there is considerable fever, especially notice that the oppression and dyspnœa, both of which are extremely marked in Fer. and Phos., are duplicated in this chemical compound and afford good indications for its use; so, in a general way, symptoms of oppression like Phos., with the evident fever and congestion of Fer., should be treated by this drug; the cough may be short, dry and hacking, or even paroxysmal; there may be expectoration of blood, either streaked or clear.

Neck and Back.—Pain in neck in morning. Pain in l. lower lumbar region when walking bent forward; in sacro-iliac symphysis at 1 P.M. on walking in the street after standing, > pressure. The habitual aching in dorsal spine (< standing or sitting, > walking or leaning back against chair) is increased, also > change of position. Tired feeling in r. lumbar region in evening when sitting in church.

Extremities.—Rheumatic feeling in r. wrist after writing, extending downward in dorsal tendons, < rest, then the pain ebbs and flows, when writing it sometimes extends up forearm, < dorsal and ulnar aspects, on rising felt in little finger to first phalanx, > warmth and wrapping.

Clinical.—In articular rheumatism, especially of the shoulder, the pains extend to the upper part of the chest; and of the hands, which are swollen and painful, or of the knee, with severe pain, or of the ankle, with shooting pain.

Sleep and Fever.—Drowsiness at 4.30 P.M., felt much in eyes, extending up into head, necessity to take a nap. Sensitiveness to cool air; at noon; all the evening. Dry heat of palms; when sitting, and of face; D. heat of face, hands, throat and upper chest at 6 P.M.

Clinical.—There may be heat, with quick, soft pulse, thirst and sweat, which does not relieve the patient (Fer.).

Fluoricum Acidum.

For use, 1 part of the pure acid is dissolved in 99 parts of water and preserved in gutta-percha vials. This should be well diluted before taking.

General Action.—It is an irritant to mucous membranes and a profound tissue remedy. Indicated in deep destructive processes (periosteal, osseous and connective tissue generally affected.) It also seems to affect the veins and restore their tone.

Allies.—Boron (Borax and Boracic acid), Silicon (Silicic acid, Silica).

Generalities.—Writhing about in indescribable agony, Motion of hands, fingers, toes, feet, jaws, lips, eyebrows, lids, muscles of face, etc.; fond of movement of the whole body when sitting. Pain, < hand, arm to elbow and in foot, with lameness; transient P. in different parts in evening, in neck, knee, r. forearm, l. leg, r. foot, r. shoulder and l. arm, sometimes below, sometimes above elbow; erratic, in l. half of body, in arm, chest, nates, etc., with itching; jerking, in different parts, behind l. ear, on l. middle finger and in small of back; jerking burning, almost boring, in a small spot; burning, at 9 P.M. in different places, < externally, on thighs, l. upper arm, fingers, etc.

Shaking sensation in forenoon when sitting, with pressure and compression in occiput, < towards r. side, with internal numbness in l. forearm and pricking in it on stretching it. Sensation almost like rush of blood, though rather as if caused by the nerves, somewhat like numbness and confusion or burning, in r. side of forehead, then in r. sides of jaws, in posterior half of occiput, in bladder, and so on in various places. Lameness. *Lassitude;* in forenoon; at night when walking; sudden, in evening. Many symptoms worse when standing, *though better when standing than when sitting;* S. < r. side; during rest; in the room when reading or writing; as soon as she rises. *Amelioration on motion, on walking;* pains > after breakfast, except pain in head on motion of it.

Clinical.—It has been used in typhoid fever, especially for the bed-sores, and in tabes dorsalis and in other diseases where there has been tendency to decubitus. In a general way it is a remedy for an unhealthy condition of the tissues in broken-down constitutions, as in drunkards, varicose veins, bed-sores, syphilitic destruction of tissues, exostoses and bone-pains; diseases of the bones generally; also in diseases of the skin, ulcerations, varicosities, nævi, lupus-like tubercles. The symptom of necessity for energetic and rapid motion, "It seems as if she could walk forever," has been relied upon as a marked indication for the drug in numerous diseases, for example, tumors, felons, etc.

Mind.—*Satisfaction. Enjoyment of everything. Gayety next morning. Sensation as if dangers menaced him,* < during pressure in occiput, during the staggering, pain in bladder, etc., without fear. *Anxiety* so that sweat frequently breaks out. Ill humor. Discontent in evening, but joy in the morning after a restless night. Ungovernable anger when considering what might happen. Hatred, which he vents in words, but a suddenly altered view as soon as he sees the people. Dissatisfaction, with discomfort in abdomen. Aversion to his business. Disposition when alone to repulsive fantastic imagination, especially in regard to people with whom he is connected, for example, that he must get rid of all servants, children must go out of the house, a betrothal must be broken off, a marriage must be dissolved, etc. Indifference. *Mistakes r. and l. in making notes.* Writes December for August daily though memory is good. Forgets the most common things. If his ideas are interrupted by other thoughts he cannot recall the former, or only slowly and stupidly. Peculiar rush of memory every morning. Attention difficult to fix. Comprehension of philosophical works difficult, but facts appear clearer.

Head.—Aching, with nausea and vertigo. Pressure outward; P. in brain, extending upward. Contractive pain, then beneath r. scapula. Confusion. Dulness in morning till breakfast; in morning, with drawings in r. side of head; D., sensation as if brain were pressed upward. Heaviness till going to bed, he wakes with it in the morning, > 9 A.M.; H., with pain deep in middle of forehead. It seems to proceed from throat to head, feeling as if he would be struck by apoplexy, a kind of determination of blood to head and unconsciousness, he could not remember where he was. Determination of blood, with heat in forehead, increasing to pain in os frontis. Stunning sensation, < in front. A kind of shaking in forenoon, after 10, < occiput, and more towards r., at first when sitting, then < every quick, short movement, on rising, turning, during walking. Vertigo in morning on rising, lasting when walking or sitting, then eructations and nausea.

Forehead.—Shooting in l. Pain; in upper part of F. and vertex, towards r.; in morning on waking; in r. side in forenoon; over r. brow in forenoon; at noon in frontal and parietal bones, on lying down she feels it all over; in l. side in evening; in r. protuberance in evening; in r. side of sinciput and in r. eye in evening after lying down; in sinciput on stooping, with pressing on r. eye. Compressing pain in r. protuberance. Heavy pain; in upper part of sinciput in evening, < stooping, sometimes passing to upper part of temples, < to l. Heaviness above eyes, < motion, with nausea. Painful, quick determination of blood to sinciput in evening on beginning to walk after standing, not after sitting.

Pain in temples; l.; in l., proceeding from within; quick, throbbing P. in r. at 8.30 P.M. on bending head, as in stooping. *Pressure outward in temples;* in l. Pain like a contraction on vertex towards the right in forenoon, then under r. scapula.

Parietals.—Sharp, darting pain like a prolonged electric shock, or compression of ulnar nerve, from near posterior superior angle of r. bone to r. mastoid process. Shooting, undulating pain from l. side about middle of head and near sutura interparietalis to l. temple near exterior part of orbital cavity, causing an idea of impending danger, this pain shoots about for two seconds, but the undulation lasts longer. Pain in course of l. coronal suture in morning; P. in parietal bone, extending to r. mastoid process; P., a partial fulness, as if something were lying on l. bone. Dulness and painful tension towards r. side of head. Drawing in r. side of head.

Cramp deep in l. side of occiput. Pinching in lowest l. side of occiput in morning after waking. *Pressure in occiput* beneath protuberances; P. in r. side; sudden intermittent pain in l. side. *Dulness of occiput; r.* Hair tangled, unless frequently combed. Itching. Desire to scratch without itching, with great falling of hair.

Clinical.—Alopecia areata. Falling of the hair. Caries of the skull, < temporal bones.

Eyes.—Quivering externally in r., then burning shooting at bottom of orbit. Pain in r. Pressure upon r. when stooping. Burning. Itching; in l. as from a grain of sand. Affected so that he must wink and rub it. Lachrymation. Pupils contracted. Quivering above l. external canthus. *Lids feel as if forced open, and as if in a wind, then sensation like sand in balls, which felt inflamed.* Pricking in internal canthus, with burning. Itching of upper lids and inner canthi; upper lids in evening; *I. in l. internal canthus;* in r. internal C. in evening. Pain behind r. eye; deep above and behind l., occasionally in evening; behind l., extending far into upper jaw, at 1 o'clock, the same behind r. between 5 and 6 P.M.; in bone behind l., towards temple, in l. nostril and in forehead, as if something pointed were forced deep into it at 1 P.M. Throbbing in bone above and behind r. brow. Drawing around r. eye in evening.

Pleasant sensation as if lids were wider open or eyes were more prominent, *vision clearer*, and he feels a kind of luxurious enjoyment when looking at things he sees every day. Inclination in morning to go without glasses, though his shortsightedness was no better, it was very irksome to bring objects near the eyes. Vision of a large, bright ring on closing eyes firmly in evening. V. of a light crossing itself like lightning in evening in bed. V. of red sparklings crossing each other in all directions on closing eyes after going to bed, then red, flaming, trembling, > opening eyes.

Clinical.—Lachrymal fistula. Chronic inflammation of the lachrymal sac, < cold air.

Ears.—Sticking in r. Jerking behind l. Pain in r.; behind r., extending upward; about r. in forenoon, as if ringing in ear would begin; peculiar P. in l., > stirring in with finger, with itching. Itching in r., then l. Sensitiveness of hearing increased in morning.

Clinical.—Otorrhœa, with hardness of hearing.

Nose.—Pain on l. side, nose had not been sore or painful for several months; sudden P. in l. side after some emissions. Sore feeling, < towards l. side. Crawling. Feeling as from a bad cold. Sneezing in afternoon; violent S. seven times in morning, with scanty discharge of thin mucus from nose, salivation and sensation in nose as from very cold weather. Suddenly full of mucus in morning on rinsing mouth with cold water, as quickly passing over. Coryza; in frequent attacks, suddenly appearing and disappearing, coryza > excitement; fluent, and on r. side, with crawling before sneezing; fluent, at night in sleep or next morning, after drinking red wine in evening, constant dropping and stoppage of nose; sudden fluent, all day after drinking ale in evening, suddenly disappearing; sudden tickling fluent, all day after ale in evening.

Clinical—Chronic nasal catarrh and ozæna.

Face.—Appears to have become suddenly old, he sees in the glass superficial whitish, puffy folds beneath the eyes, extending towards nose, etc., without discontent thereat. Constant motion of muscles. Spasmodic sensation in zygomata at 5 P.M., drawing towards larynx. Jaw, gnawing near angles; pain in r. upper, with heat, reflected in lower; drawing pain in r. lower, towards the middle; peculiar sensation near bone of r. lower in evening, with drawing in entire r. limb; sensation in r. joint as if a spasm would occur; cramplike confusion in joints, < l.; warmth in r. upper, with confusion; burning pain on outside of r. lower, near first or second molar; numbness in r. joint, with warmth and sensation as if it would begin to pain. Lips warm; burning like a sore near inner edge of lower, towards the right.

Mouth.—Teeth. Digging in a r. lower incisor. Pain in l.; l. lower; P. in a r. tooth disappears for a moment and jumps to outer part of l. thigh above knee; P. on r. side, extending to outer part of l. thigh above knee; in r. eye-tooth in evening; in a r. upper carious incisor in evening from the cold air of the room; so that he could not bite upon the teeth. Drawing in l. lower. R. eye-tooth, which was once rough but afterwards smooth, is now rough and begins to ache, < at upper part of root, and along roots of upper teeth there is pain on pressure, < evening, temporarily > cold water. Bluntness; with sticking, contraction and tension, then the mucous membrane of mouth became whitish and peeled off. Lower incisors feel sharp, as if broken, and pain on touch of tongue. *Warm feeling*, < l. upper, especially incisor and canine, then warmth in pharynx. Acrid offensive taste coming from the roots; acrid putrid T. from root of r. upper incisor, on which an artificial tooth is fixed, in morning; like ink in evening, from a l. lower. Pain where the roots of l. teeth had been taken out. (Painful excoriation near first r. lower molar.)

Prickling of tongue, with salivation, afterwards with smarting of palate as if something acrid had been gargled, tenderness in larynx and soreness in throat on coughing to clear it. *Painful ulcer in r. angle of jaw.* Contractions, with pricklings and sour taste. Pain as from hot water, teeth so painful that he cannot chew. Sensation during a walk as if the passage to nose were wide open. Dryness in evening of l. half of palate and roof. Greasy feeling. Salivation > after headache began; and a sensation as if head were too heavy and would drop from one side to the other, a pressure outward; tenacious S. on waking at night, before diarrhœa; viscid, tasteless S. on waking at 2 A.M., with burning pinching in stomach and sensation of flatulent distention, < emission of wind, after a copious pappy stool the pains concentrate in umbilical region, the pain > after the stool but returns, a second stool with pain in umbilical region, and a pasty one at 7 A.M. Taste intolerable; T. salt in morning on waking, till breakfast; sweetish in throat at night; T. of what he has eaten, < afternoon.

Clinical.—Dental fistula, with persistent bloody, salty discharge, which keeps the mouth foul. Several cases of dental fistula and caries of the jaw-bone have been cured by this drug.

Throat.—Hawking of bloody mucus from low down. Constriction at first in afternoon, with difficult swallowing; C. in l. side; C., with pressure in stomach and fulness in epigastric region, disgusting eructations and nausea; with rumbling in abdomen, pressure and burning in stomach, eructations, retching, then constipation for two days. Soreness of pharynx, extending below larynx, swallowing bread is painful; S., with difficult swallowing, > after breakfast next morning, the same morning hawking from low down of much phlegm mixed with blood. Sensation posteriorly at entrance to œsophagus, < on l. side, as if raw, or as if an ulcer would form, in morning and forenoon, and when hawking he thought blood would come from it. Warmth; in fauces in morning. Swallowing difficult.

Clinical.—Goitre. Syphilitic ulcerations of the throat, with fetid smell, much tumefaction, throat very sensitive to cold.

Stomach.—Appetite increased; after diarrhœa; voracious. Good, but soon satisfied. *Speedy satiety.* A. diminished, he wants something "piquant." *Thirst increased;* at night. Longing for coffee. Aversion to coffee. Relishes wine no more. *Eructations;* in evening, with nausea; flat, nauseous, sour; frequent sour, in afternoon, with pyrosis and emission of flatus; sour, bitter after dinner. *Nausea; with general heat;* with vertigo and headache; with heaviness above eyes; without inclination to vomit, with dulness of head. Retching. Vomiting; difficult, several times, of clear, viscid fluid, with coagulated white pieces.

Rumbling; after eating, with urging as in diarrhœa Burning pinching before diarrhœa. Burning; with pressure; before eating, > eating, then heaviness, and again heat, < walking. Pyrosis. Weight between meals, simulating indigestion. Sensitiveness to pressure. Discomfort in forenoon. Sensation as if nausea or a kind of vertigo would set in, but it does not.

Abdomen.—Rumbling; in forenoon, with erratic pain. *Frequent emission of flatus and eructations, leaving him more comfortable and feeling as if it were the last, but everything is renewed in the same order, and so on for two or three days, only at longer intervals;* much inodorous and noisy flatus; offensive in morning; scanty, offensive, before stool; scanty, offensive, like a mixture of carburetted, sulphuretted and phosphoretted hydrogen, < forenoon, several hours before eating, and in afternoon, two hours after eating. Feeling of accumulated flatus. Pain after eating fish with vinegar; (P. after watermelon); before diarrhœa, < after emission of flatus; during diarrhœa, < in umbilical region. Warmth at night, with dragging towards bladder. Inclination to draw up muscles, with great appetite. (Unpleasant sensation after eating herring, and discontent.)

Pain in region of spleen. Pinching in region of spleen at 11 A.M.; in umbilical region at 2 A.M., and copious watery stool. Faintness in umbilical region in morning before eating, > bandaging, pressure of watch and eating, with desire to breathe deeply, in the evening it is more like a burning, when occupied he does not observe it. Shooting towards r. side in evening, as from wind. Pain in l. side; in evening. Sensation in l. side as if pain would arise and wind be discharged, but neither occurred. Jerkings in l. side of lower. Sudden acute pain above l. hip, hindering respiration. Deep-seated pain in inguinal regions. Burning in r. inguinal region in afternoon.

Clinical.—Numerous symptoms in the liver have led to its use in hepatic engorgement, and even degeneration of the liver in consequence of alcoholismus, and also in abdominal dropsies associated with hepatic disease. With the above hepatic and abdominal symptoms there is sometimes found offensive bilious diarrhœa, especially in hard drinkers, with great aversion to coffee, desire for highly-seasoned food, soreness over liver, etc.

Rectum and Anus.—Urging and soft stool, next day stool protracted and small; ineffectual desire; indefinite desire, scanty odorless wind and pappy stool, in a tertian type, one day with copious micturition, after the stool better appetite than usual. Constriction of anus on attempting to emit flatus. Feeling as if wind were retained in anus. Determination of blood to A. after drinking wine. Itching in and around A.

Stool.—Fluid, profuse at 2 A.M., with pinching. Two watery, immediately after rising in morning. Diarrhœa at 4 A.M. Loose. Large, pappy, yellowish-brown, offensive. Pappy and frequent. Free, twice a day. Hard, twice a day. *Constipation.* Scanty and delayed; S., intermittent and lumpy. (In lumps and difficult.) (Every other day and every time later.)

Urinary Organs.—Pain in region of bladder; above neck of B. after micturition; in lower part of B. before and after micturition and on pressure; in region of B., like an electric shock, extending into r. thigh; burning quick, nervous pain from region of B. extending to r. thigh, when in bed. Frequent desire to urinate. Micturition twice at night; *frequent M. of light urine, leaving him more comfortable,* and during and after micturition elasticity (in muscles?) of urinary organs, then agreeable sensation, he drinks less than usual. *Burning in urethra during and after micturition* in morning. Urine copious in evening, and of strong odor; C., with the diarrhœa; C. and of clear color; C., then more thirst. Urine diminished; evening and morning, with odor like Benzoic acid. Urine offensive; and acrid. The habitual whitish sediment is mixed with a copious purple one.

Sexual Organs.—Erections, with desire and voluptuousness; E. in morning without desire. Occasional sticking through l. testicle to abdominal ring and spermatic cord. Drawing from l. testicle to spermatic cord. Sensation of pushing towards spermatic cords, in evening. *Desire increased; with erections at night in sleep;* diminished; lost. Menstruation eight days too soon, copious, thick and coagulated, lasting five days instead of six to seven, the next time at the regular period according to the former calculation.

Respiratory Organs.—Pain in forepart of larynx, as if in cartilage, inducing him to swallow. Scraping in larynx, provoking hawking and swallowing. Soreness in larynx when coughing or hawking. Itching in larynx, causing swallowing and hawking. Breathing oppressed deep internally, not > deep breathing. Difficult B. as from an impediment in region of pit of throat and upper part of chest, with itching pimples on back and pain in chest below point of scapula. Deep B. as if the breast within and below were full, in forenoon when sitting and writing. Sighing inspiration in afternoon and evening, more observed by others than by himself, he has to bend backward in afternoon on the bed if he wants to take a full breath. Breathing continued after radial pulse had failed and even action of heart had apparently ceased.

Chest.—Stitches in side; under ribs to l. of ensiform cartilage in evening; from l. to groins, from 9 to 10 A.M., < deep respiration, < in groin and back; pain as if a stitch would appear behind heart; burning S. in l. Pain close to r. nipple; in last r. rib, near spine; in centre of sternum in afternoon, after retiring at 10 P.M. a pain in middle of chest lasting till he fell asleep; in l. side beneath skin, on moving and a similar pain in l. shoulder at 10 P.M., next morning on rising P. again in l. chest. Oppression on reclining, with trembling in lower limbs; O., with pain. Tightness as if something were fixed in upper part, more towards the front, impeding inspiration, not > deep inspiration. Soreness. Burning from l. breast to groin. Throbbing in C. and abdomen on feeling them.

Clinical.—Ascites, with great dyspnœa. Hydrothorax, with wheezing respiration, and small, frequent, irregular pulse.

Heart and Pulse.—Heart, aching; soreness; uneasiness; jerking. Pulse rapid and small.

Neck.—Cramp in some muscles of l. side and towards shoulder, in forenoon when reposing and when rising, > after exercise, the pain changing from one set of muscles to another, but is always in more than one, the omohyoideus is decidedly affected, but not the sterno-cleido-mastoideus. Pain in r. side in forenoon; P. in nape, beneath scapulæ and in l. side of chest; extending from nape through centre of head towards forehead, gradually concentrating towards the left, as if throbbing would arise there. Drawing pain along r. side; in afternoon. Constriction of l. side at 9 A.M. Soreness of l. half of nape. Stiffness.

Back.—Burning pricking in l. scapula. Pain sometimes beneath scapulæ, sometimes in kidneys; deep-seated P. below point of scapula, < towards l., < when sitting, especially when riding; in os sacrum; in the middle of tuberosities of ischia; deep in l. loin at night. Jerkings in sacrum.

Clinical.—Neuralgia of the coccyx, excessive aching.

Extremities.—Rapid growth of nails. Sensation as if shoulders and hips were being pulled out of joint. Pain in bones of r. forearm and knee; in l. arm, leg and hand; intermittent, in bones of forearms and legs, about the centre.

Clinical.—Synovitis.

Upper Extremities.—Pain extending from r. shoulder-joint into finger, as if air passed down; sudden jerking pain in bone of l. shoulder. Bruised feeling in r. shoulder and upper arm after lying on l. side, with numbness. Cramp of r. arm in morning. Frequent burning, pricking and jerking pain in l. arm as from a slow electric shock, at 2 P.M., < inside of l. little finger, with intermittent sticking outward in tip of finger. Pain in r. arm; l.; r. at 9 A.M.; l. in evening; deeply penetrating P. in arm, < about junction of the cancellated with the solid part of r., then l. humeri, then soreness, a similar pain in muscles over head of l. radius. Lameness of r. arm so that writing is difficult. Numbness of r. arm in morning on waking after lying on l. side, with heaviness; N. of l. in morning, > about noon, with jerking and lameness. R. arm falls asleep at 10 P.M. when resting on it, with paralyzed sensation and pricking.

Pinching in l. deltoid. Pain above l. elbow in morning; P. in r., then l. humerus in afternoon, extending to elbow; rheumatic, in l. humerus, from elbow to shoulder, with lameness. Pain in r. elbow; l. in evening.

Forearm.—Trembling of biceps. Jerks along l. radius to thumb, which moves involuntarily. Pinching in middle of l. in evening. Pressure in r.; P. and paralyzed sensation. Soreness in bones of l., towards the middle. Numbness of l. every forenoon, but every day later and less decided, with paralytic sensation. Numb pain extending to hands. Paralytic pain extending into hand. Asleep sensation in l. forearm and hand at 5 A.M., when lying on r. side; intermittent, in l. forearm and especially in hand, < towards medial side, more internally, < hand from the time of waking in morning till noon, several days, with prickling in ball of thumb on stretching arm and hand.

Wrist.—Pain about r. wrist and finger-joints. Drawing in r. from 8 to 11 A.M.

Hand.—Redness internally; R., < in palms, as if finely mottled, with fulness and warmth. Pain and swelling, next day fingers and especially thumb inflamed, the hot bright red skin on the tips discolored, the last phalanx almost immovable, the pain in hands extended to shoulders, and fever, towards evening of second day the pains were throbbing and finger-tips more swollen, on the third day the finger-tips were white and thumb was enveloped by a white blister, on which the nail rested, with throbbing pains, on opening the blisters a thick, brown, offensive, acid fluid was discharged, under these blisters was seen on fingers the uninjured true skin, on thumb there was underneath a second blister, upon opening which commencing suppuration was found, the thumb continued to secrete thin pus. Pain in r. metacarpus in evening after a cold from exposure to snowy air, like that formerly in r. leg. Lameness of r. Powerless sensation. Internal numbness in l., different from that produced by long pressure, extending to forearm, not > exertion. L. asleep in morning after lying on r. side, lasting all the forenoon.

Fingers.—Jerking in l. thumb in forenoon, extending to middle of forearm. Prickings; in tips of indexes, < l. and in r. thumb; outward, in tip of l. little; intermittent burning P. in fleshy part of l. thumb at 11 A.M., passing out at tip; *sensation of a splinter under thumb-nail and in cellular tissue when touched, pulsating pain in hand, < in tip of thumb, which was sore to touch, the whole hand swollen and hot* (Bor.); pricklings in tips, then violent pains, with chilliness of l. arm, then of whole body; in ball of l. thumb. *Inflammation, < thumb, with throbbing pain, then suppuration.* Pain in first joint of r. little finger as if being pulled out of joint; jerking P. in l. middle; *intermittent, in l. index as if in bone*, during the day, *the whole finger is painful internally*, < in evening; frequent throbbing, in bones of tips, like a contusion, in evening. *Soreness in l. index.* Burning about bone of r. middle, amounting to pain about first joint, with itching prickling in skin; jerking B. in tip of l. little, at 10 A.M. Paroxysmal painless sensation as if something were working its way out beneath l. nail, in forenoon. Sensation of a hair on back of l. little, in forenoon, till 2 P.M. Numbness of r. in forenoon, with rigidity.

Clinical.—Inflammation of the phalanges of the fingers, < index, like a felon; indeed most violent inflammations of the index finger, with purulent discharges and terrible pain, have been relieved. The nails become crumbled or have longitudinal furrows. In panaritiums the pain is violent and throbbing, sometimes with sharp stitches when the nail is pressed upon.

Lower Extremities. — Trembling when reclining. Sticking in r. hip-bone, spreading over nates. Burning shooting downward in r. hip, as if in a nerve, < inside of knee. Pain in r. hip; in head of l. femur; in fleshy part of l. thigh, on outside; in r. ischiatic nerve in afternoon; burning itching P. in back part of thigh. Bruised pain in muscles of thighs; B. pain in thigh, < posterior and inner part; in l. hip, < morning and on getting in and out of bed, with pain on motion. Lameness of l. hip. Numbness of r. thigh in evening when crossing legs.

Knee.—Tearing upward in r. Pain; on inside of r. in evening; in outside of l. at 8 P.M., > friction; penetrating, on outside of l.; drawing, in hollow of r. in forenoon, extending down calf to tendo-achillis. Dull feelling in r.

Leg.—Trembling. Deep-seated pain below r. knee in evening. Drawing pain in l.; and foot. (Lameness of r., with pain in femur, tibia and fibula.) Tired and heavy. L. falls asleep easily; in morning when sitting after resting it over r. leg, and the back of the foot feels like a cushion, yet motion is unimpeded; falling asleep of r. in evening on crossing it.

Ankle.—Pain in r. external in evening; drawing P. in r. during a walk in evening, spreading gradually over whole leg, causing lameness in knee and ankle, > rest. Sprained pain in l. when walking; S. lameness in afternoon, passing all around the joint, < stepping.

Foot.—Pain in l.; in r. heel; in corns of r.; in l. instep in evening; in r. instep, with burning; in l. heel, like a rush of blood, in evening. Soreness of corns, like a boil.

Toes.—Pricking in tips of r. in forenoon; burning P. under T. in morning. Pain in r. little; in first joints of r.; in all l. toes except the great one; in r. little, in forenoon; burning P. in all, so that he could hardly walk.

Skin.—Redness, with heat and pain, then desquamation in scales; R. in spots above brows; red blotches over brows, most abundant on l. side but lasting longer on r.; *cicatrices*, dating from thirty-two to two years, *are red around the edges*, and covered here and there with itching vesicles, those of more ancient date have larger vesicles, those of recent date are filled with small pimples. White and painful, forming a dense vesicle filled with matter. Roughness on forehead, in a line with its convexity upward. Desquamation in brows, with sticking.

(Painful bleeding excoriation on l. second toe.) Pimples on nose; between nose and r. eye; in r. side of face; on abdomen, < thighs and legs, the points forming a crust; here and there, and itching, < warm days; on shoulders and back, < towards l., with itching; group of red P. on l. hip, in back and lower part of region of joint and below, opening in night after scratching. Pustules. Vesicles on r. index, with itching; V. in groups on ulnar side of r. thumb and radial side of index, with itching, leaving dry scurfy spots; carmine, round, elevated blood-vesicles, the blood disappearing on strong and steady pressure, but returning immediately, near r. nipple, on r. side above navel, r. side of chest, inside of r. arm, the larger ones becoming darker, somewhat resembling nævi materni.

Soreness of warts on l. hand. Burning pain in spots on back of r. hand, angle of index and here and there on l. hand. Itching burning spot externally near r. eye. Crawling in r. sole; on r. shoulder in evening, with itching.

Itching; in eyebrows; r. brow; r. side of face; chest and r. side of nose; middle of l. scapula; back; small of back; cicatrice of an abscess on inside of l. thigh; r. shin, l. nates and forehead; l. heel; all day in different parts, < on back; every morning and evening, on l. side of nape, on top and below shoulder, and on back; in forenoon, > rubbing, almost only on back, but sometimes on throat; in scars on ball of l. thumb and joint of index in afternoon; on l. shoulder in afternoon, on back in evening, < late at night till sleep, pimples on back; *of all cicatrices* in evening, they are all on l. side, on thigh, upper arm and l. hand; on throat and chest in evening when walking; in evening, changing from the top of one shoulder to the other, with intermittent sticking; on and around r. nipple in evening, next morning the nipple is larger, redder, and areola darker and covered with a brownish crust, as of sweat and dust; < evening; in centre of perineum, < evening; in different parts, < posteriorly; sudden intermittent, above anus; burning, in r. eyebrow, > after scratching; pricking burning, near r. side of os coccygis. Sticking itching in face; r. side of face; inner side of l. finger; in spots in evening, < l. side, especially on side of chest towards back and on thigh, < 10 to 11 P.M.; crawling, in points, usually in groups.

Clinical.—Ulcerations of the legs, with varicose veins.

Sleep.—*Sleepiness;* every forenoon, or so weary that he must lie down; periodical, in afternoon. *Sleepiness early in evening;* with sound sleep and early waking; and he lay down on the bed dressed, though the window and door were open and the night cold he had taken no cold in the morning, and had not slept enough; afterwards after a walk he is wide awake and cheerful. *Sudden sleepiness* in evening; after wine he lies down and does not wish to rise, on going to bed he is wide awake and the face warm. Sleeps in the evening more than usual. Sleep long and sound; *profound S. till late in morning*, and confusion of head on waking. Irresistible sleepiness in morning, after a refreshing nap it returns every two hours till evening. Sudden falling asleep in evening, then sleep all night and long in morning. Sleepiness on going to bed, but inability to sleep on account of his thoughts.

Sleeplessness; till near morning, then short and light sleep refreshing him as if he had slept all night; with feeling as if he had slept; S. in evening. Late falling asleep, frequent waking, many dreams, yet early waking in morning and feeling better than usual. Easily awakened if called at night, but when walking weary, indifferent and relaxed. Snoring in sleep and exclamation in dreams. Restless nights, with unremembered dreams; R., with dreams easy to remember, of the occurrences of the day.

Dreams towards morning; only after midnight. Frightful; soon after falling asleep, with waking at midnight, the rest of the night many dreams of distant acquaintances. Lucid, sometimes disagreeable. Vivid, detailed, soon forgotten; of the thoughts of the day; V., that he sees his nearest relatives die. That he was dead and ordered the rapid removal of the corpse from the house; of the death of his son and of the son of a friend, he reproaches himself and weeps bitterly because he has neglected examinations and remedies.

Fever.—Chill towards evening; C. in l. arm and in whole body. Heat; in evening, < next morning, with inclination to walk about naked, cold bathing is very agreeable, < behind ears and on nape. General heat in evening after little exercise; *G. heat, with nausea;* with heaviness and lameness. Internal heat at night, but feeling better in morning than usual. Sensation as if burning vapor emanated from all pores. Heat under eyes; extending from centre of dorsal region to loins; in r. sole, in face after wine; in face, < in morning, then < in evening, with desire to wash in cold water; in r. palm in forenoon; in forehead, increasing to pain. Glowing in a spot on outer lower part of r. buttock in evening. Heat in flushes, like a warm breath, from nape to occiput. Intermittent heat in face in evening after animated conversation, with headache like a forcing deep interiorly towards the left, then passing to l. upper jaw, as if teeth ached, even where the teeth had been extracted, with inclination to bite together teeth which no longer existed.

Sweat, < face; S. from 7 to 8 P.M., and sensation of heat, < on r. upper part of body, especially along r. side of nape, almost to shoulder, as if in warm streams; S., with anxious imaginings; *profuse sour, in afternoon;* cold, clammy; glutinous, evenings, with itching here and there; dripping, glutinous, warm evenings when walking.

Formica.

Formica rufa, L. A tincture is made of the live ants, crushed.

Ally.—Apis.

Generalities.—Pink, flat, spreading swelling of the bitten part, with itching, the S. increased so that it was tender on bending wrist, then the S. went up arm, red like erysipelas, with itching, pitting on pressure, leaving a white indentation with crimson areola, aching in wrist, S. > warm bathing, the itching by Arnica. Shooting from back and hips down thighs, and in shoulders shooting to hands and fingers, with pricking in skin over region of the pain, the pain < l. side; darting S. in arm, neck and chest of r. side. Sharp, corroding, sore feeling or pain here and there, more or less all day. Aching in bones, with feverish state of system and with fulness and dulness of head; before a snowstorm. A. in aponeurosis and muscles of head, neck, shoulders and back. Discomfort.

Wretched condition, causing gaping and stretching. Indisposed in evening, forgetful, sleepy and tired, much affected on hearing of a threatening evil. Liability to take cold and bad effects from it. Lightness. Agility increased. Dulness in morning, with heaviness and bruised sensation. Indisposition to exercise muscles, they pain when exercised, < extensors of legs. Languid feeling in whole system, pain in all limbs, with chills and horripilations along spine. Weakness, with paralyzed feelings in muscles. Powders taken at night have most effect. Aggravation in open air. Symptoms all on r. side. Pains recurred after a slight cold; P. < study and sitting quietly, > smoking; P. < at 10 A.M., when sitting after a walk.

Clinical.—Articular rheumatism and gout; the rheumatism appears suddenly, with restlessness, but motion aggravates the pain, pain > pressure, r. side most affected (Hering).

Mind.—Exaltation, desire to run but soon tired, < evening; E. almost as from champagne, after pain in vertex had abated till after 9 A.M., with internal coldness as from mint. Very happy during the day, and able to study, everything seemed easy to accomplish; H. changed by trifles to transient despondency. Excitement. Sudden return of mortification and grief. Irritable and low-spirited. Morose in evening, disinclined to work and apprehensive. Very active during the day. Inability to study long at night. Confusion. Unconsciousness.

Head.—Aching all day, > combing hair; A. daily from noon till 10 P.M., < stooping; in afternoon; in afternoon, with occasional fluttering of heart; with nausea; with vertigo and occasional boring in r. temple and pain in l.; at base of cranium, extending upward, < temples; sick, in afternoon after unusual exertion in garden, with nervous shudderings and vomiting, is subject to these headaches from overfatigue, but this was more severe than usual and was accompanied by shooting neuralgia in temples, which she never had before. Confusion. Dulness, with pressure between temples and ears. Stupid feeling, with stiffness of neck. Heaviness, with sensation as if brain were too large and heavy. Congestion, and to chest. Vertigo; in morning when writing after dressing.

Frontal pain from noon till 10 P.M.; over eyes every day from 12, earlier every day and in morning; P. in r.; over l. eye; with pricking and itching; heavy; in front of head in afternoon, with occasional shooting from r. temple into head. Lancinations outward in r. temple. Pain in vertex and forehead, < through temples. Surging in upper part of brain at 10 P.M., then dim vision. Headache on l. side after dinner. Drawing headache on l. side in afternoon, > after supper. Tearing in occiput at 10 P.M. Headache in r. upper posterior part; headache in posterior upper and inner part in morning, < drinking coffee and washing with cold water.

Eyes.—Pain in morning on waking, > washing. Irritation as from sand. Fulness, and in ears, with stinging in ears. Cool burning as if snow were falling on conjunctiva and cornea. Itching of conjunctiva in morning, with burning when rubbed. Shooting in l. ball at night. Itching of r. outer canthus, with soreness, dimness of vision, sensation of sand in eyes, lachrymation and soreness of lids. Stitchlike tightening posteriorly and inwardly over l. as if a stick were pressing around something, with burning, then painful dulness of head, except upper back part. Boring in r. orbit, then pain in l. ear. Pain deep in orbits. Vision misty.

Clinical.—Rheumatic inflammation of the eyes and its sequelæ leucoma, pterygium, ulcers of the cornea, etc. (Hering).

Ears.—Swelling of all surrounding parts, with discomfort. Shooting in l.; at 10 P.M. Sharp twinges of pain in r. in morning in bed (perhaps attributable to a thin nightcap). Pain; in l., then < r.; in the deaf ear, extending into temple, with external sensitiveness. Itching deep in l., at times almost painful.

Nose.—Sneezing at 9 P.M., with fluent coryza, then sticking in l. side of vertex. Coryza; sudden transient, in evening; thin, acrid, nose sore to touch and feels stopped.

Face.—Cheeks red and burning in evening. Paralyzed feeling in l. side as if everything were hanging loosely. Lower lip dry and cracked. Lips sore at the corners.

Mouth.—Periodical tearing in r. upper incisor, with drawing, grumbling, soreness and elongated sensation. Pain in a carious tooth, with inflamed gum and swollen cheek. Tongue sore at root. Stinging in palate, < eating, smoking or touch, extending after two days to tip of tongue. Watery, offensive taste. Long aftertaste after using fresh and sweet fat with his meal, changing to a rancid taste.

Throat.—Soreness mornings on getting up, with earache; S., with huskiness. Pain in r. side of pharynx at noon during empty swallowing. Coldness, as from mint-drops. Difficult swallowing at noon, with contracted sensation in œsophagus.

Stomach.—Hunger after 9 o'clock. Thirst. Eructations of sour wind; of fluid tasting like sour food, causing smarting in mouth and throat. Nausea; after sweat, with vomiting and depression. Cramplike pain in evening, > emission of flatus. Pain in epigastrium at 10 P.M., extending from l. to r., then shifting to vertex, followed by creeping down back; P. in S. as if something had lodged at cardiac end at 6 P.M., four hours after dinner; burning P., with oppression and weight. Heat in epigastrium, extending over a large space.

Abdomen.—Forcible emission of flatus; difficult, scanty emissions in morning, then diarrhœa-like urging; fetid, almost putrid F. (had eaten at dinner only barley soup and beef). Sensation as before diarrhœa, with much yawning, then regular stool, the last part of which was thinner and of peculiar odor. Sticking in region of liver; in r. hypochondrium. Pain beneath short ribs; on deep inspiration; in region of spleen; in lower umbilical and upper hypogastric regions, > after diarrhœa, with tenesmus; in pelvis, from one acetabulum to the other; in hypogastrium, > transiently by emission of flatus, then soft stool with heat and burning irritation of anus and weak sensation in bowels; in transverse and descending colon from incarcerated flatus on waking, papescent stool, then constriction of anus, another stool at 9 A.M., with tenesmus, then constriction of anus. Bruised pain in umbilical region after drinking cold water, extending across abdomen.

Rectum and Anus.—Painful, protruding piles without constipation. Constriction of anus. Itching of anus at 10 P.M., > scratching; also about A. in afternoon, > scratching. Sensation in A. all the evening, as before diarrhœa. Pressure in rectum; < in evening and in bed.

Stool.—Scanty, painless diarrhœa twice in morning; painless D. in morning on waking, compelled to go at once, with rumbling, another stool immediately after breakfast, with urging. Pappy every morning, with inclination to sit at stool and feeling as if mucous membrane were thick and stiff. In two small balls after straining. Twice daily.

Urinary Organs.—Urine copious, even at night. Urine like saffron, passed often.

Sexual Organs.—Feeling on ascending stairs as if asleep. Hot red swelling of prepuce. Increased secretion under prepuce. Nervous fluctuations in l. half of penis, in region of prostate, with jerking pain. Erections in forenoon when riding in a carriage; strong, in morning, with increased desire; long-lasting, in morning on lying down after urinating; insufficient, during coition. Itching of scrotum. Excitability. Menses eight days too soon, scanty and pale, with bearing-down pain in back, darker next day, cramplike pain through hip-joint and pelvis the third day, next day scanty and pale again.

Respiratory Organs and Chest.—Cough from irritation in larynx, with loose expectoration during the day. Sticking in r. side of chest at 4.30 P.M., arresting breath. Pain in chest on full inspiration; P. in lower part of l. breast, then of r. at 8 P.M., with chilliness down back and lower limbs; sudden P. in l. lung, then sensation as if I were falling. Warmth in lower part of chest and in abdomen.

Heart and Pulse.—Palpitation in afternoon. Heart's action increased. Pulse 92, irregular.

Neck and Back.—Pain in neck in evening, < looking up; P. in l. side, sometimes with itching or burning; as if it would break, < l. side, when riding in a carriage. Jerks along l. side of spine, in region of ninth rib. Shooting in region of l. scapula from 11.30 to 12 P.M.; S. in l. lumbar region. Acute pain in lower part of scapula at noon. Pain in chest and dorsum of ilium at noon, extending across sacrum with traction at attachment of muscles; P. in sacrum and dorsum of ilia as if muscles were strained and about to be torn from their attachment, at 5 P.M. and after going to bed, < motion.

Extremities.—Tearing down l. arm and leg at 10 P.M., with drawing. Pain in bones, shifting about in r. arm and leg, < joints.

Upper Extremities.—Soreness, very painful in anterior part of l. axilla. Twitching in l. triceps at 9 P.M. Shooting in arms at noon, extending to elbows. L. arm and hand asleep in morning on waking; asleep sensation in arms and < hands, when riding in a carriage. Intermittent pinching in middle of l. upper arm, then on various parts of body lower down. Pain inwardly on inner side above r. elbow, < in direction of upper arm. Rheumatic pain in r. elbow. Pain in r. elbow and wrist. Shooting in forearms and hands at 1 P.M.; S. in course of l. ulnar nerve to little finger. Rheumatic pain in r. forearm and wrist; in r. wrist and course of ulna. Shooting in carpal bones at 9 P.M. when writing, extending down third and fourth finger. Burning pain in l. carpal bones at 11 P.M. Indefinable sensations in and around l. wrist. Inflammation of backs of hands, with redness and swelling, then suppuration under finger-nails, then loosening and falling of nails. Tearing in l. middle finger at noon. Burning sticking in finger-ends, first in l. and < evening, then on r. and < morning, < middle finger.

Lower Extremities.—Bruised sensation; in l. hip-joint, interfering with walking; in hips at night in bed, causing him to change from side to side. Shooting in thighs down to knees at noon; in hips, at 7 P.M., < 10 P.M., extending down thighs. Rheumatic pains from l. hip to r. Pain in hips, small of back and sacrum. Uneasy painful sensation in hips and thighs, with desire to change their position often when sitting. Lancinations in knees, waking him. Rheumatic pain in l. knee; < r., < walking. R. knee gave way in evening when walking, on account of pain below it, next day the same and hindrance in walking from a similar pain in l. middle toe. Pain below knees and in shins at 9 o'clock; P. in r. tendo-achillis. Sharp rheumatic pain in ankles, < walking. Cramp in feet at night, < under toes, and always in a small spot; C. in soles, < in forepart and under toes, < r., waking him at 3 A.M., and the same when lying on a lounge in a warm room. Stinging in l. great toe at night, with burning. Sharp intermittent pain in l. fourth toe, then burning pain behind ball of l. great toe, then pain in lower part of l. tibia.

Skin.—Creeping down back. Pricking stitches, < in region of r. nipple, then on l. side of back, then on other parts. Tingling of l. fingers. Itching on scalp, arms, abdomen and whole trunk; at r. nipple; in l. palm; in l. axilla, then soreness with a sore place inwardly, afterwards the soreness, < scratching; in r. axilla, more outwardly, mornings, instead of in the inner and anterior part of l.; intermittent, on l. scapula and l. thigh near groin, in evening, night and next day, always > scratching; burning, in bend of l. knee, < at 9.30, the same sensation, which is a union of itching, burning and pressure, here and there on body.

Sleep.—Frequent yawning at 1 P.M., with necessity to stretch the limbs. Sleepiness, with heaviness of eyelids and inability to study; sudden S. after water-soup, and falling asleep in his chair, on waking he does not feel refreshed, but goes to bed and falls asleep at once. Sleeping easily in evening; easily falls asleep at night after being disturbed. He does not feel like getting up in morning, he has scarcely aroused himself when he falls asleep again. Can do with less sleep. Went to bed at 1 after drinking beer and wine in evening, woke at 3 and felt as if he had slept enough. Sleeplessness the first twenty-four hours, then alternations of waking and sleeping. Difficult falling asleep, with frequent waking on alternate nights. Sleep disturbed, night restless. Dreams lewd, with erections some nights; vivid, lewd, with erections and emissions; D. not unpleasant; a mouldy sausage in his room caused a D. that he saw a funeral procession with a large coffin and many smaller ones, the persons had died of scarlet fever, the procession almost came up with him and stopped at the corner, as he attempted to get out of the wind which blew from the procession he woke.

Fever.—Susceptible to cold; < walking against the wind in evening. Chill at night. Cold feet. Heat; < scalp; of hand and face; of palms; pressing burning in spots on skin. Clammy sweat on waking; disagreeable S. at night; copious S. after whisky.

Gambogia.

Gum Gamboge, obtained from Garcinia Hanburii, Hook. f., is dissolved in alcohol (1 to 9) for a tincture.

General Action.—A powerful drastic cathartic, often producing nausea and vomiting.

Ally.—Aloe.

Generalities.—Sticking, < evening; burning, at times in fingers, at times in hand, also in malleoli, then over whole body; like a pinching over whole body. Pressure on head, stomach and chest. Congestion of head, chest, uterus. Feeling of ease and lightness in all movements. Faintness. *Aggravation in evening or night; A. when sitting, amelioration on motion in open air;* aggravation on r. side.

Mind.—Cheerful, talkative. Ill humor in morning on rising, with vehemence; I., with vexation, anxiety and desire to work, though the work does not advance as he would wish.

Head.—Pain in forenoon and beating in forehead towards nose; oppressive P. in afternoon, > open air, with heaviness in forehead or with general heat. Compressive pain; from both sides in forenoon. Heaviness, with inertia, drowsiness and pain in small of back. *Vertigo* in morning on rising, or in forehead when spinning (then anxiety). Heaviness in forehead in forenoon, with beating. Tearing in l. temple in afternoon. Stitches in r. side and in temples. Bruised pain in vertex in forenoon, > open air.

Eyes.—*Burning* in evening or afternoon, *photophobia*, both > walking in open air, but returning next morning. *Itching in evening*. Dryness, with redness of canthi; D. as from sleepiness, with yawning and sneezing. *Nightly agglutination, burning in morning*, photophobia through the day, and frequent stinging in eyes. Pressure in r. internal canthus as from a foreign body obliging rubbing. *Itching of inner canthi* (and in forehead), with acrid lachrymation after rubbing, > open air; I. of l. lower lid. Biting in external canthus, > rubbing. Dim vision of r. eye occasionally.

Ears.—Sticking. Deep-seated tearing in evening. Painful drawing from r. to vertex in forenoon. Throbbing pain in l. as in an abscess. Frequent ringing in morning. Frequent buzzing in afternoon and evening, > after a sensation as if a leaflet were bursting.

Nose.—Ulceration of r. nostril, with burning pain. Tearing in bones of dorsum. Itching of nostrils all night. *Sneezing;* violent chronic, only in daytime, < forenoon, < strong smells, with irritation in r. nostril, above wing of nose, *dryness of r. nostril*, the sneezing caused tearing in forehead, sticking in l. side, heaviness of lower limbs and flushes of heat all over body. Stopped coryza; then discharge of offensive mucus. Mucus smelling like pus. Hæmorrhage, and from mouth and throat; bleeding from r. nostril in evening.

Face.—Tearing in r. malar-bone in evening and in r. lower jaw frequently during the day. Burning vesicle on inside of upper lip.

Mouth.—Tearing in r. molars and in gums, with sensation as if gums were sore and swollen. Beating in a r. lower molar in cold air. *Cold feeling in tips of incisors*. Burning in tip of tongue, which feels hard; B. in anterior half of T. Sensitiveness of palate like a smarting or soreness, > cold. Dryness. Salivation. Taste sweetish in mouth and throat, then expectoration of bright red blood; taste S. in throat, with expectoration of bloody mucus. Taste bitter.

Throat.—Tearing in tendons of sides of throat, with choking, lancinating tearing in throat under l. ear, < external pressure, descending to region of larynx, with stinging in throat when swallowing. *Stinging* in r. side in evening; S. on swallowing, > eating; S. in the goitre. *Sore pain*, which is felt on external touch. Swollen feeling internally. Sore burning posteriorly in fauces when not swallowing. *Roughness* and burning, causing constant hawking.

Stomach.—Violent hunger. Increased appetite and much thirst (loss of thirst in the first days of the proving). *Aversion to food*. Thirst after dinner, and < evening; *violent T.* in evening and at night, preventing sleep. Frequent, violent, empty eructations. Hiccough in morning after rising. *Nausea;* in morning on eating soup, > bread; when walking in open air, with salivation, gulping up of sour water and movements in stomach; with stomachache; with ptyalism and roughness in throat; then pinching in umbilical region and diarrhœa. Constant heaving, > dinner. Violent vomiting; *horrid V. and purging, with faintness. Dartings. Gnawing*, with movements of flatus in abdomen. *Ulcerative pain*, > eating, then rumbling in abdomen when walking in open air, and papescent stool. Paroxysmal pressure in S. and chest at 3 and 9 P.M., impeding breathing. Pain as if sore, with sensitiveness to touch; with contraction. Constriction after dinner. Beating, < leaning against anything. *Emptiness, and in abdomen*. Weakness as after fasting, with salivation.

Abdomen.—*Rumbling. Inflation and accumulation of flatus* (Aloe); *I. and tension, with pinching in umbilical region. Frequent emission of flatus*, < evening and night. Inflammation of intestines. Cutting, with wanderings, then emissions of fetid flatus. Pinching after eating; immediately after eating, P. in abdomen or sleep; frequent P. without urging, or else succeeded by diarrhœa and burning in anus, after which the P. ceases. Flatulent sensation, < small of back, then urging. Burning and movement of flatus; painful B. in hepatic region. Pinching around umbilicus from morning till evening, with frequent urging to stool, and protrusion of rectum. Contraction at umbilicus; beneath U., with twisting and urging to stool. Gnawing in a spot beneath U. Sticking in groin, as from flatus. Sudden darting in G. when sitting. *Pinching in G.;* in r., as with a nail. Constriction deep in l. G. Tension in G.; when standing.

Anus and Stool.—Sticking in anus before stool. Ineffectual urging. **Yellow and green diarrhœa, mixed with mucus, preceded by cutting around umbilicus** (Aloe); *repeated D., with discharge of green mucus, preceded by pinching in abdomen; D., with burning pain and tenesmus of rectum, protrusion of anus, and pinching around umbilicus, sometimes with discharge of flatus; watery, profuse, with colic and tenesmus; fæcal, forcible*, with burning in anus, preceded by cutting in abdomen, waking him about midnight, > compressing abdomen, which is small, as if eviscerated, awakened again by pain in back; with cutting; frequent, with burning and tenesmus. Frequent soft S., with rumbling in abdomen, or followed by pain about umbilicus and pinching. Soft, scanty S., with sensation as if arrested by a hard body in anus. *Constipation. Hard, insufficient S., with urging and protrusion of rectum; hard*, before midnight, then burning at anus and passage of a lumbricus or with sticking in groins and emissions of flatus. Repeated S., rather hard than soft, then a hard, then a soft stool. S. late in evening, with frequent emissions of flatus, which seems to press on bladder, causing stinging, hardness and tightness in region of bladder and shortness of breath.

Clinical. — The diarrhœa of Gamboge resembles that of Aloes in respect to the suddenness of the movements, which are expelled in one gush; the evacuations are thin, yellow, generally watery, or with some mucus, associated with burning in anus and protrusion, griping below umbilicus, with sudden urging and sudden expulsion; the stool is followed by a feeling of great relief. Intense itching of the eyelids, so that children rub them frequently, is said to be a marked indication for the drug in diarrhœa.

Urinary and Sexual Organs.—*Micturition rare;* frequent, but little at a time; of one or three drops at a time, then intermitting and finally returning, with burning at orifice. Urine increased; scanty. *Leucorrhœa*. Menses too soon and too profuse.

Respiratory Organs.—Scraping in region of larynx at night, causing dry cough. Cough in afternoon, with hoarseness and hawking of mucus; C. < night, with soreness in chest; < night after lying down; violent, at night, with expectoration of loose mucus; dry, at night, forcing him to sit up; hacking and dry, in daytime.

Chest.—Sticking; in axillæ, etc.; beneath r. mammary region; *repeated S.* in forepart of sternum, in afternoon and evening; intermittent, in forepart in afternoon and evening; deep in forepart in evening, alternating with S. in r. mamma; beneath C. in evening, then pressure in middle of chest, with want of breath; under l. axilla, > rubbing; in r. side, extending from ribs towards axilla, after carrying a heavy load, arresting breath. Digging in subcostal region in evening, or gnawing. *Pain, as if everg part were sore,* even when not coughing. *Pressure in middle,* with sticking from both sides towards each other; pressure upon C., not affecting breathing. Weight at night, preventing sleep. Oppression and heaviness, with sticking in back, < subcostal regions. Tightness and heaviness, with sticking extending to back, < hypochondria. Choking sensation ascending into throat, arresting breathing.

Neck and Back.—Tearing in nape and l. shoulder; lancinating T. in side of neck. Sticking in region of l. kidney; in r. sacral region; sudden, in sacral region, > walking. Bruised pain in small of back. Gnawing in os coccygis.

Upper Extremities.—Intermittent sticking in top of r. shoulder. *Tearing in shoulders* or in axilla, in tendons of extensor muscles of fingers, in ball of thumb and index and between metacarpal bones of index and middle fingers, so that the skin is drawn backward. Pinching in r. humerus. Sticking through palm to back of hand, then burning in hand; S. in last joint of l. index; in ball of r. thumb and middle finger, with numb feeling, then S. from palm through to back of hand and extending to forearm, with heat.

Lower Extremities.—Spasmodic condition. Sticking in bend of l. thigh. Tearing in l. hip; in bend of l. thigh, with drawing. Cramp in calf, > rubbing, with tearing and with contraction of toes. Sticking in l. calf. Tearing from middle of r. tibia, extending above knee; T. in tendo-achillis, with drawing as if too short. Pain along r. tibia in afternoon and evening in bed, with stiffness and with difficult stretching of foot. Bruised pain below l. patella with ulcerative pain on touch. Pressure as with a hand above l. externus malleolus, > pressing foot to the ground, with sensation as if asleep. Spasmodic constriction in region of r. externus malleolus and great toe, when walking, causing limping. Sticking in r. sole, < rubbing. Pinching in dorsum of r. foot, towards toes. Heaviness and languor of feet. Cramp in r. great toe when walking and in evening in bed. Sticking beneath r. great toe. Spasmodic tearing in two r. smaller toes.

Skin.—Pimple above orbit, with tensive pain; P. on inside of forearms, with redness and itching in evening. Itching blister, pale, then red, on hands. Biting over whole body as from ants, < evening and at night, even walking. Itching, < evening and night, and after scratching generally a burning ulcerative pain, with swelling and redness; I. of ball of l. thumb; I. here and there on head, l. side of forehead, face, upper surface below elbow, ball of thumb, index, bend of foot, dorsum of hand; voluptuous, here and there over whole body, < evening and night, even waking, usually with burning, at times followed by redness and swelling.

Sleep.—*Sleepiness* all day. Uneasy sleep. Disturbed by anxious dreams. *Vexatious, anxious D.* D. about dancing, lice, etc.

Fever.—Chilliness all day or only in forenoon; in morning, with elongated sensation in anterior teeth; with chattering of teeth, thirst so that the lips stick together, but skin warm to touch; with empty eructations, yawning, thirst, pain in small of back, and biting as of ants over whole body (at night) or sticking in ears, in the beginning; sudden transient shaking C. waking him at night; *internal and external,* beginning at 6 to 8.15 P.M., lasting from a quarter to two hours or till 5 A.M., sometimes with thirst; shaking, from 7 P.M. till 4 A.M., proceeding from back, with external coldness, even of forehead; in l. temple in afternoon, as from a wet cloth. Remittent or intermittent, quotidian or tertian fever, rather postponing than anticipating. Heat in afternoon, with anxiety and sweat; H. in flushes; H. mounts to head, with sweat. General sweat in morning; on waking at 4 A.M.; at night.

Gaultheria.

A tincture is made of the fresh leaves of Gaultheria procumbens, L. (wintergreen).

Convulsions. Insensible, apparently in sound sleep, but could not be aroused for ten hours. Restlessness. Weakness. Hemiparesis of l. side and loss of power. Stupidity. Headache and noise in ears like the buzzing of bees. Dizziness; and drowsiness, then delirium. Contraction of pupils. Disturbance of vision when she was not delirious, with hallucinations of sight and hearing. Dulness of hearing. Tongue dry, smooth and swollen, so that speech was rather indistinct, mouth parched. Inability to speak. Beating of carotids increased in intensity. Uncontrollable appetite, notwithstanding the irritability of stomach. Vomiting; after supper of all the contents of stomach, the V. with retching continued all night whenever anything, as a cup of water, was given him; but she was nearly strangled by the contents of the stomach lodging in fauces. Gastritis. Pain in epigastrium and lower part of hypochondria, < pressure with finger. Cramp in epigastrium. Two copious stools at night. Urine contained salicylic acid. Pulse 125. Respiration labored; and quick; labored, slow, prolonged, loud but not stertorous. Sleep only prevented by strong currents of electricity. Cold limbs. Hot skin. Cold sweats.

Clinical.—The oil of wintergreen has been very largely used for both acute and subacute rheumatism. The plant itself contains salicylic acid, and to this fact may be due some of the beneficial effects of the drug. It has also proved useful in pleurodynia in the anterior part of the chest.

Gelsemium.

A tincture is made of the fresh root of Gelsemium sempervirens, Ait.

General Action.—It produces spinal convulsions and paralysis, lowering the force and rate of the heart, and finally paralyzing respiration. The paralysis of the oculo-motor nerve is noticeable, with double vision, ptosis, squint and vertigo. Consciousness is preserved to the last stage of life.

Allies.—Arg. nit., Cimicif., Nux vom., Ign., Con., Gran.

Generalities.—Lying on l. side. Trembling at noon, with general chill; *T.* in afternoon, *with weakness;* general, in afternoon, with tingling in legs; *with profuse micturition* (Arg. nit.); with anxiety. Sudden acute darting pains along single nerve branches in almost every part, at one time in quick succession down outside and front of tibia, leaving tenderness in its track. Pains fugitive or fixed, here and there; P. of a shifting character all day; erratic rheumatic (Cimicif.); drawing and aching, which seem to come from bones. Running in all nerves at noon, < fingers, and jumping as from ant-bites in finger-ends, nails blue half way to root. *Unpleasant sensation* at 10 A.M. when in a hospital, *with weakness, pallor, nausea and trembling of lower limbs*, > open air. Feeling as after "a fit of sickness;" in forenoon; feeling of general illness, as in fever.

Restlessness, with chill after breakfast. Feeling of lightness and sense of instability in whole body. Feeling of danger of stumbling or falling. Inclination to lie down. **Weakness and trembling through whole system** (Arg. n., Cimicif.); *W. in morning, with vertigo;* in afternoon; mental and physical in afternoon; in afternoon when reclining for the purpose of study, after sleeping an hour was unwilling to move, > stirring around; when reclining before a heavy shower, with drowsiness; < elevators of lower jaw and lids and muscles of arms; with emaciation; with muscular relaxation, convulsions, staggering, want of co-ordination through system; with diuresis and flaccidity and coldness of genitals; with irregular and slow breathing. *Easy fatigue;* < *lower limbs.* Sensation as if blood did not circulate. **Relaxed muscles and motor paralysis.** Paralysis; paralytic symptoms through muscular system, first in knee, then in inferior tibial region. Aggravation from any movement or touch of head or application of any fluid to lips, the dread of which nearly equalled that in hydrophobia.

Clinical.—General prostration and loss of muscular power, fear of making any effort, desire to be alone. Paralysis of various groups of muscles about the eye, throat, larynx, chest, sphincters, extremities, etc. Paralysis following diphtheria. Locomotor ataxia. Paraplegia. In general, hysterical spasms, a kind of hystero-epilepsy. Puerperal convulsions. Convulsions from suppression of menses. Catarrhal affections of various mucous membranes, with a relaxed and debilitated condition of the system, especially in women. Neuralgias of various nerves, with loss of control over the part, pain in the muscles of the back, hips and lower extremities; the pains are mostly deep-seated.

Mind.—Uncontrollable mirth. Vivacity in morning after rising. Cheerful, careless, then depressed. Irritable, impatient. Anxious. Melancholy; all day, and stupid; in afternoon, with headache. *Inability to think or fix the attention. Listlessness and languor. Dulness;* > *profuse micturition* (Nux vom.). Listless and incapable of reflection, as after ague, with headache all day and digging in r. ear all the afternoon. Mistiness of brain, not affecting lucidity of thought, but confusing the perception. Stupid, intoxicated feeling; S. and averse to study; S. and disinclined to conversation. Aroused with difficulty. Semi-comatose. *Unconsciousness.*

Clinical.—The patient has lost control of his mental faculties, his ideas flow on in a disconnected fashion, the attempt to think connectedly causes a painful feeling in the head, dizziness, heat of the face, cold feet, etc.; on falling asleep the patient is apt to be delirious. In low types of fever the patient is generally stupid, desiring to be let alone; the mental faculties are either dull or there is great depression, with fear of death. This drug is frequently indicated in bodily ailments, especially diarrhœa, uterine symptoms, etc., resulting from emotional excitement, such as sudden bad news, fright, grief, etc. It has rarely been indicated in acute mania during the progress of melancholia; if so there is wild talking or singing.

Head.—Dropped forward with chin resting on breast from paralysis of parts. He cannot hold it erect. **Bruised sensation** (Nux vom.). Pain; after dinner, lasting till evening; after breakfast, < as the day advanced, in occiput, head > dinner, but < 4 P.M. and till evening, with nausea, head > shaking it; > sitting; in head and eyes, < moving eyes, generally in forehead, < just over eyes, some call it dulness over eyes, others a heavy pain, others a giddy pain; tendency to P. during the day, < ascending stairs; band-like, around head, with shooting in jaws and parietal bones; stupefying, < forehead and temples. Sensitiveness of brain, with sensation as if every step or sudden movement of head would cause pain, but it did not.

Dulness at 11 A.M.; D., with stupor, dry mouth, coated tongue, bitter taste, full and strong pulse, intoxication, vertigo to falling. *Tightness of brain.* Fulness; with throbbing and uneasiness of occiput; and excited or feverish feeling. **Heaviness, > profuse micturition;** H. in afternoon; of brain; with fulness, increasing to pain, > copious micturition, then pleasant languor of system. Discomfort. *Lightness.* Intoxicated feeling, with painless diarrhœa. **Vertigo;** after breakfast; < *sudden movement of head and walking, with light-headedness;* < standing; **with blurred vision.** *Symptoms* < *smoking.*

Forehead.—Stinging, with pressing in eyes as if too large and with external coldness of F. Shooting in sinuses, extending to eyes and jaws, with pricking from middle of eyes to canthi, < r. eye, where the pain rolled about; S. in middle in evening on turning eyes or head and on stooping, extending as far as half the brain; intermittent S. in middle in afternoon, extending as far as half the brain; S. inward in middle at noon; S. inward in middle in afternoon. Pain in F. and vertex; after sleep both in forenoon and evening; with dim vision, roaring in ears, sensation of enlargement of head, confusion, almost amounting to delirium, the headache was heavy and alternated with *sharp laborlike pain in uterine region extending to back and hips;* in l. frontal region, waking at 2.30 A.M., extending to r. occipital region and occasionally over whole head. Pressure as if too narrow, with pressing upon eyes as if too large; P. in sinciput as if too narrow in morning on waking, > pressure of hand, necessity to close eyes. Bruised pain above and back of orbits. Fulness of sinciput. Weight over F. Drawing over eyes; r. Vertigo in brows. Contracted feeling on centre of scalp.

Pain in r. temple, with vertigo, blurred vision and nausea; P. in T., at times in occiput, at times all over head. Pain on r. side of head; at breakfast; periodical P. extending from l. parietal protuberance to mastoid process. Pain in vertex, extending to occiput, with general vertigo and headache; P. in V. in afternoon when writing, then in l. occiput, on both sides and in upper cervical region, again on vertex, then in l. side, then dragging pain, < occiput, in mastoid and upper cervical region, extending to shoulder, > sitting, resting head and shoulders on a high pillow. Drawing on r. side of vertex towards occiput.

Occiput.—Pain; at 11 A.M.; during the day, < movement, especially stooping, < towards evening; *at night, occasionally extending into os frontis* (to vertex, Cimicif.); in r. side on rising, with tendency to throbbing, previously at breakfast cutting on l. side; with sensation as if the crown were lifted off in two pieces; heavy, at night. Numbness.

Clinical.—A large proportion of the conditions indicating Gel. have more or less vertigo, which is sometimes intense and associated with loss of sight and lack of muscular steadiness, so that the patient staggers when walking (Con.). Headache as from a band around head. The pain is mostly seated in the posterior part of the head, associated with muscular soreness of the neck, pain extending to the shoulders and spine, with dizziness. Blind headaches, the head feels large, confused and dizzy. Headaches at the base of the brain extending through the head to the eyes, < heat. General nervous headache, with soreness and pain extending into face and teeth or to shoulders, with attacks of blindness and dizziness. In cerebro-spinal meningitis, with extreme tenderness of the occipital region, intolerance of slightest motion, etc. Headaches generally > discharge of profuse watery urine (Ign., Nux v.). Menstrual headaches, with blurred vision, nausea and vomiting which relieved the headache. Headaches at the climacteric period, with drowsiness, vertigo, blurred vision, > profuse menstruation.

Eyes.—Suffused. Bloodshot. Inflamed and weak, with lachrymation at intervals. Yellow. Distended. Staring; with inability to raise lids. Strabismus. Dulness in forenoon. Pains extending deep downward in l. Sore at night, sensitive to light, and lachrymation; S. in evening as if a foreign body were irritating conjunctiva. Burning, with weak vision and heaviness in forehead; B. in forenoon as if too dry. Dryness. *Heaviness* as after night-watching. *Pupils dilated;* and insensible; and muscles of accommodation paralyzed and vision weak. Sclerotic congested. Continual twitching of balls (Zinc.). Sticking outward through l. ball. Aching in balls, < moving eyes, now and then shooting, sometimes < in one ball. Pain in orbits; with fulness.

Lids.—**Drooping** (Con.); < l.; with pain on attempting to open eyes widely, > closing them. Closed; *in spite of him on looking steadily at anything; partially closed and motionless; half closed and apparent inability to move them.* Swollen. A stitch traversing r. vertically. *Difficult to open or to keep open. Heaviness;* and congestion. Paralysis of upper lid and lower jaw, overflow of saliva from corners of mouth. Burning around r. inner canthus.

Vision.—**Smoky, with pain above eyes. Dim; with vertigo;** > by profuse watery micturition; for distant objects; or glimmering. *Confused;* after the morning stool, > *by holding finger vertically before nose, or by closing either eye,* with heavy-looking eyes; after a dessertspoonful of red wine; < evening; > evening. *Blindness, with vertigo; almost B., and control over upper lid almost lost. Double;* on raising head from stooping or on looking sideways; *on inclining head to either side; controlled by effort of will;* the images sometimes above each other, sometimes on a level, in one case preceded by weight under upper lid, the constant form of diplopia occurs only in upper half of field of vision, first with objects at extreme r. or l., then nearer the middle, and at last only in a median vertical plane, then D. disappeared in the inverse order, the outer lateral image was higher and the farther the object was carried to the r. or l. the greater the horizontal and vertical distances between the images, when a colored glass was placed before either eye the outer and higher image was seen by the covered eye, when the object was high above the head the images gradually coalesced and the object looked like a thread, with well-marked D. there is impaired movement of ball, affecting the rectus, < external, the ball oscillates when carried as far as the muscles are capable, the D. often changes rapidly, thus while on one side the outer image is higher, if the object is carried to the other side the inner image is higher, or first the outer, then the inner is higher.

Clinical.—Serous inflammations within the eyeball. Iritis, with serous exudation (descemetitis); choroiditis; detachment of the retina; retinitis, with hazy vitreous or extravasations of blood; retinitis in Bright's disease; in all these interocular inflammations there are generally dull aching pain in the eyeball and neuralgia about the eye. Paralysis of the muscles of the eye; of the upper lid and of the proper muscles of the eyeball. Asthenopia from muscular weakness. Double vision from paralysis of muscles of the eye.

Ears.—Sticking in external meatus near noon when sitting. *Often affected by the pain which ascends from back to occiput.* Heaviness. Rush of blood. Humming. Sudden and temporary loss of hearing.

Clinical.—Deafness, the result of catarrh of the middle ear and Eustachian tube; several brilliant cures have been made by it. Deafness resulting from quinine has been cured.

Nose.—Pain extending from bridge to eye. Tingling in nares. Lively action in region at 6 P.M., when sewing, as of a worm or fish. Watery discharge. Bloody mucus; mucus in nose and upper part of trachea, it slips into the trachea when talking and keeps up a hacking cough. Sneezing at 9.30 P.M., with headache; S. at 11.30 P.M., then tingling and full sensation in nose.

Clinical.—Nasal catarrhs, with excoriating discharge, sore throat, associated with physical weakness. Acute nasal catarrhs, especially in the summer, with inflammation of throat and pain extending into the ear, and deafness. Disposition to take cold at the slightest change in the weather. Hay fever, with the peculiar head symptoms of the drug.

Face.—*Flushed and hot to touch.* Congested, then pale and deathlike. *Heavy, besotted appearance.* Swollen and dark. Yellow. Livid pallor. F. and lips blue and livid. Looked strange, staggered and fell. Countenance miserable, sunken, grayish-yellow, with dull dusky eyes. Contraction of muscles, < orbicularis oris, impeding respiration. Numbness. Lips livid; lips pale in forenoon; dry L. at 11.30 P.M. and heated. Jaw drooping; J. *wagging* sideways, no control over it; rigid; stiffness of muscles.

Clinical.—Neuralgia of the face, pains generally sharp, the face usually congested, of a dusky hue, associated with vertigo occipital headache and dimness of vision.

Mouth.—Foaming. Discharge of bloody brown mucus during the fits. Stinging in l. lower hollow back tooth at 6 P.M., through lower jaw to ear and zygoma, with burning. Pain in last r. molar, up towards temple. **Tongue so thick that he could hardly speak.** *Tongue coated; yellowish-white;* yellow; whitish. Tongue red, inflamed in middle; dry T. and throat; burning, soon extending over mouth and throat, then through œsophagus into stomach and abdomen, then the same burning pain passed around in all intestines, simultaneously with descent of burning pain into œsophagus, burning in chest, then a stitch in l. lower anterior side of chest, extending into l. scapula, with weakness, fluttering and irregular beat of heart; constriction at base; **numbness** (Con., Acon.); *felt thick and he could not articulate;* stiffness and thick, guttural voice; use lost and feeling like a foreign body clogging mouth. Speech muffled; S. difficult; unable to speak or move.

Dryness; and of throat, as after salt bacon, with disposi-

tion to swallow frequently. Astringent sensation. Paralysis of muscles of M. and throat. Saliva yellowish, as from blood. Fetid breath. Breath and taste foul the latter part of the day, with frequent need to rinse mouth or spit. Taste bitter; and slimy; T. mawkish; clammy T., feverish feeling.

Clinical.—Disorders of dentition in children, with fever, frightened feeling, apparent vertigo, or with drowsiness and confusion, sometimes dilated pupils, dim vision, etc. Paralysis of the tongue, it feels numb and heavy (Acon.).

Throat.—*Pain in sterno-cleido-mastoideus, back of parotid.* Hawking up of bloody matter. Soreness about root of tongue and larynx when swallowing, with mucus in upper part of trachea, causing frequent clearing of throat. Dryness, with burning; D. in fauces. Burning, with painful swallowing, the sufferings < food and drink, especially warm; B. from mouth to stomach. *Spasmodic sensations in gullet, with cramplike pains. Inability to swallow; from paralysis of muscles of T.; difficult swallowing.*

Clinical.—Various forms of sore throat, mostly catarrhal, rarely ulcerative, sometimes with difficulty in swallowing from the soreness, when the pain extends to the ears, or at other times the difficulty in swallowing may be due to paralysis of the pharyngeal muscles. A very valuable remedy for paralysis of the throat following diphtheria, a feeling as if there were a lump in the throat which could not be swallowed.

Stomach.—Hunger; appetite alternately increased and lost; want of A. in afternoon; sudden satiety after a moderate meal. Thirst during sweat. Eructations; sour; of wind and bland fluid at 11.30 P.M.; rising of tasteless semi-solid matters in œsophagus at night when sitting studying, with flatus and sensation of something lodged in œsophagus. Hiccough. Nausea; with headache. Retching. Vomiting.

Rumbling in epigastrium, > emission of flatus, with pain. Pain, with nausea and dim vision, then ineffectual retching, restlessness and general sweat; P. from pyloric end to axilla and under scapula and down r. arm to outer side of forearm, a hand's breadth from elbow, > biscuit and coffee; cramplike P. in epigastrium, leaving constriction, then burning in stomach. Gastralgia in afternoon, with colic and intoxicated feeling. Cardialgia at 11 A.M. when driving; in evening when sitting, with eructations. Heartburn at noon when riding, with pain at cardia. Oppression at breakfast, necessity to loosen waistband, then colic to l. of navel, as before stool. Sensation of something wanting in epigastric region. Empty and weak feeling in S. and bowels.

Clinical.—As a rule the Gel. cases have no thirst, and there is generally a sensation of emptiness and weakness in the stomach, or of oppression, a feeling of a heavy load. Numerous cases of hiccough, some chronic cases, < evening.

Abdomen.—Emission of flatus above and below; with rumbling. Lancinations disturbing sleep, > discharge of flatus. Griping through A. after supper, < umbilical region. Sharp pains, with pappy, cream-colored stools. Pain; in evening; at night, < towards morning. Burning towards 12 o'clock, the pain going around in intestines. Palpitation of muscles. Heaviness. Weak nauseated feeling. Tenderness of parietes.

Sharp drawing pain through l. hypochondrium. Pain in l. hypochondrium; pulsative, at 3.30 P.M. Rumbling in umbilical region. Sticking around umbilicus. Pain in U. region in morning till rising; P. in two spots on r. side of U., extending into bowels, < pressure; P. below U. in evening, extending to testes, > expulsion of flatus. R. inguinal gland swollen and tender to touch. Movement of flatus in hypogastrium at 11.30 P.M. Gnawing in region of transverse colon all afternoon. Pain in l. iliac region; P. in transverse colon, with yellow face; moving P. in hypogastrium (after chills, headache, feverish and prolonged sweat) waking him, then a large natural stool without relief, soon > bilious stool, nine hours afterwards another bilious stool without pain.

Clinical.—Gastro-intestinal catarrh, with jaundiced hue, persistent nausea, dizziness and diarrhœa. Passive congestions of the liver, with vertigo, blurred vision, etc.

Rectum and Stool.—Piles returned with raw smarting. *Urging to stool caused by exciting news, stool papescent, dark yellow.* Stool bilious; and soft, preceded by threatenings of diarrhœa, the latter renewed at noon by exciting news and afterwards when walking. Loose but difficult S., great strength in sphincter muscles. S. at first consistent, then papescent, bilious, homogeneous, preceded by flatulence. A second, consistent. S. after supper. Tea-colored; and semi-solid. Insufficient. Slow (having been put off), leaving a sensation of more to be passed and abdominal repletion. Attempt to pass stool, but only wind passed.

Clinical.—Diarrhœa, both acute and chronic, resulting from depressing emotions, such as fright or grief; stools generally painless or even involuntary, without much thirst (compare with Arg. nit., which is also indicated in diarrhœa from emotional excitement). Paralysis, more or less complete, of sphincter ani, and in some cases partial prolapsus of the rectum.

Urinary Organs.—Paralysis of bladder so that there was constant dribbling of urine, with muscular weakness, < r. side, in arm and leg. **Frequent micturition of clear limpid urine, relieving dulness and heaviness of head** (Ign.); frequent M. Urine copious at night; *C., clear and watery* (Ign.); C., watery, with chill, trembling and *alleviation of heaviness of head, dulness of mind and dimness of vision.* Urine at times clear and limpid, at times milky and turbid. Redness about orifice of urethra. *Feeling as if something remained behind when urinating, stream intermittent* (Nux v.). Agreeable sensation in urethra during micturition.

Clinical.—Loss of power of the bladder, especially in old people, or following diphtheria. Fundus of bladder paralyzed and the bladder enormously distended. In incomplete paralysis of the bladder the flow is intermittent and the patient seems not to empty the bladder (Nux v.). Dysuria from stricture.

Sexual Organs.—Irritation in spots on mucous membrane of prepuce at night with surrounding congestion; I. of r. testes in afternoon and evening, then dragging pain extending into groins and hypogastrium, > discharge of flatus. *Emission at night without erection.* **Sharp labor-like pains in uterine region, extending to back and hips** (Cimicif.). Discharge of blood from vagina from 4 to 5 P.M., next day after 6 P.M.

Clinical.—Great weakness of the sexual organs, so that men have emissions without erections. It has been prescribed for inflammation of the urethra. Inflammation of ovaries. Congestion of uterus and inflammation of ovaries, heaviness in uterine region, with melancholia. Dysmenorrhœa, with sick headache, vertigo, faintness, pains shooting up back and into legs. Suppression of menses, congestion of the head, pain extending upward and downward from the uterine region. It is sometimes valuable during labor when the os is rigid, with cutting pain in back extending upward. Inefficient labor pains, which do not force downward, but shoot upward. Threatening puerperal convulsions with stupidity, twitching of muscles, albuminuria, sharp cutting pain from the neck of the uterus upward.

Respiratory Organs.—Glottis spasmodically closed. Paralysis of glottis and difficulty in swallowing. Burning from larynx into chest under sternum. *Voice weak;* V. thick as if tongue were too large. Paroxysmal hoarseness, with dryness of throat. Food drops into trachea when eating, causing strangling. Cough from tickling and dry roughness of fauces; hacking C., with feeling as if a drop of liquid were in windpipe and with frequent clearing of throat. Expectoration of thick yellow pus. Inability to expectorate.

Respiration.—Choking, pushing his fingers into his throat as if to tear it open. Struggling for breath. Suffocative sensation, > throwing his head back; sudden S. sensation, as in hysteria. Difficult, with oppression in præcordial region, then a series of short rapid inspirations, then three or four prolonged gasps. Stertorous and imperfect. Heavy; in morning; in afternoon. Moaning. Sighing; slow, at times sobbing. Slow; and catching; and superficial, with now and then a deep inhalation; with rapid pulse; with offensive breath and slow pulse, then rapid breathing and quick, weak pulse; then spasmodic. Scarcely perceptible.

Clinical.—Paralytic aphonia, with dryness and burning in throat, < during menstruation. It has been used for spasm of the glottis in children. Occasionally in laryngitis. Cartarrhal affections of the air-passages, with relaxed, debilitated condition of the system. Dyspnœa, with distressing fulness in the chest, cold extremities, threatening suffocation, desire for fresh air, etc. Threatening paralysis of the lungs, especially in old people.

Chest.—Sticking; in anterior lower l. side in afternoon; through l. lower side into scapula, with irregular action of heart and dyspnœa; in l. lower anterior side through to l. scapula, with irregular action of heart when sitting quietly; paroxysmal, downward in upper part of r. lung on taking a long breath. Cramp in r. side at last short ribs. Pain as of a thrust with a sharp instrument under l. floating ribs at 2 P.M., when lying, changing immediately to l. temple, causing contraction of brow. Pain; behind fifth rib to l. of sternum at night, > eructation; periodical, in pectoral muscles; extending from ensiform cartilage along free ends of r. short ribs to lumbar region, as if liver were congested, < a hand's breadth from lower end of sternum; shuddering, in r. breast. Soreness when coughing. Constriction around lower.

Heaviness in afternoon. Burning in l. anterior side at 8 A.M., where she had lately had sticking, with ulcerative pain on touch and even on pressure of a loose dress, and with fulness; B. in chest at noon, going into pit of stomach and radiating over the parts covering the intestines like a tree, the stem of which is in pit of stomach, with fulness, sighing and anxiety; B. under lower part of sternum in afternoon, with heaviness of chest, drawing towards l. lower anterior side of chest, where there had been sticking, which is now repeated, ulcerative pain and tenderness to touch, chest > when the burning went to l. side. Weakness on speaking.

Heart.—Sticking. Shocks in forenoon at every exertion, with throbbing of pulse through whole body, trembling, weakness and sweat; S. at noon, with heavy breathing. *Feeling as if it would stop beating if she did not move about. Palpitation* in afternoon. *Irregular beating from noon till* 5 P.M.; in afternoon, with trembling of body. Sounds heard as if far distant.

Clinical.—Palpitation and oppression about the heart, the effects of grief. Heart's action feeble, the pulse soft and weak, extremities cold.

Pulse.—Rapid; and full; and bounding, then feeble and thready; and weak; and weak, small; and small all the afternoon; rises during the reaction after the chill as far above the normal as it has been below it. Full. Hardish at noon, and intermittent, during the intermission two quicker double strokes of heart, changing in rhythm but not in time. Irregular in afternoon; I., feeble and sometimes intermittent. Fluttering. Slow; but *arterial tension increased*, then impairment of heart's action; when the person is quiet, but subject to great variation from exercise; and full or slow and soft; and weak; 58 at noon, weak, wirey, unequal, when the first stroke is stronger than the preceding one the second one is scarcely perceptible or vanishes, irregular double action of heart, intermittent pulse, shaking of heart so that she feels it as far as neck. Weak. Scarcely perceptible; with chilliness, cold feet, heat and pain of head, etc. Pulseless at wrist and carotids.

Neck.—Aching in muscles of N. and shoulders, with soreness. Rheumatic pain in l. side on lying down. Contractive sensation in r. side at 5 P.M.

Back.—Pain as in cold stage of ague. Rheumatic pain in bones and joints of B. and limbs at night. Weakness in B. and limbs, with sleepiness. Pain under l. scapula at 7 P.M.; P. in anterior part of l. trapezius on leaving a warm room. Trapezius muscles sore on motion. Aching in loins; in lower lumbar and sacral region; in sacro-iliac and lumbar regions and lower part of l. thigh at supper-time on entering a warm room, < eating, with languor and thirst as at beginning of fever.

Extremities.—*Trembling* in afternoon; at 1.30 P.M., with chill, then stinging outward along l. lactiferous ducts, < sternal half of breast. Sensation of a galvanic current down forearm and hands and in feet, when sitting. Pain; waking at 4 A.M.; at night, < after midnight, > day; at night, < forearms and calves, also in knees and elbows; in l. elbow, wrist, knee and both ankles; deep, and in joints; in muscles; deep, in muscles, > movement; deep in muscles of upper, waking at 3 or 4 A.M., in l. arm and both calves; in bones or deep in muscles in region of humerus and in lower limbs, at 10 A.M.; in muscles of r. arm and shoulder, and sometimes in l. arm and lower limbs. Pulsative pain in l. hand and finger-joints when lying, and at same time in r. foot, < ball of great toe. Rheumatic pain.

Weakness towards 12 o'clock; *W. of hands and feet, with indisposition to move.* Heaviness. *Gradual loss of control.*

Clinical.—Loss of power in the extremities; the hands are very tired from playing on the piano; writers' cramp; loss of power in the lower extremities; gait staggering; the lower limbs feel as heavy as lead. Rheumatic symptoms in the lower extremities, the flesh feels sore. Trembling of all limbs; loss of muscular control; numbness and lack of sensibility of the extremities.

Upper Extremities.—Inability to pour coffee from a cup. Shooting from r. shoulder to dorsal vertebræ after breakfast. Spasmodic pain extending from inner condyle of r. arm to axilla. Arms insensible to pain. Aching in l. elbow at 7.30 P.M.; crampy, in bend of r. when walking after writing. Drawing about l. elbow at 3 P.M. when in a draughty church, with aching.

Sensation of a galvanic current down forearms at 6 P.M. Pain in flexor muscles of r. forearm. Pain in r. wrist, with weakness; sharp P. in r. at 6 P.M. Drawing sticking in dorsum of r. hand, running into middle and ring fingers. Sensation in hands and arms blunted, but not in proportion to the loss of motion. Flexors of hands and arms paralyzed and extensors nearly so. Shooting in last joint of r. thumb in morning. Pain in little and fourth fingers.

Lower Extremities.—*Staggering.* Pain; paroxysmal, in l. **Fatigue after slight exercise** (Arg. nit.). Feeling during and after a walk as if they could not be moved another step. Loss of voluntary motion. Jerking about middle of r. rectus muscle; of vastus externus muscle near r. knee; from r. sartorious about middle of thigh. Sticking as of drawing or cramping of single fasciculi of muscle, about origin on l. gluteus maximus, running in direction of hip-joint. Crampy pain in inner part of thigh when walking; drawing C. pain in bones and muscles of thighs, extending to toes, during the headache. Sharp drawing pain in hip-joint, extending at times to outside of thigh, < movement. Pain in l. thigh at 7 P.M.; in l. rectus femoris at 11.30 P.M., with drawing in r. calf.

Sudden twisting on inside of patella when sitting down to breakfast. Knees feel when walking as if bones did not fit. Pain under r. K. when walking; when pains are felt above K. they are not felt below, and *vice versa.* Drawing pain in l. hamstring, extending across joint to origin of gastrocnemius. Rheumatic pain in r. K. when walking. Weakness of K. Shooting in r. calf at 3 P.M.; S. midway between knee and ankle in paroxysms, each more violent. Sharp crampy pain about largest part of l. gastrocnemius. Contracting pain in l. gastrocnemius, unlike other pains in limbs, not > sitting. Soreness of gastrocnemii as if beaten. Pain in l. ankle, with spasmodic contraction of toes and drawing pain in them. Cramp in r. instep. Crampy pain in r. foot.

Skin.—Yellow in forenoon; in afternoon. Erythema on face and neck. Papules as in measles, but larger and more distinct, < on face, with little or no sensation. Sore pimple, with inflamed areola on l. side of neck, one at r. corner of os hyoides, another at l. anterior temporal ridge, a P. sore to touch on l. side of larynx. Painless vesico-pustules on inside of thighs. Sudden stinging in whole skin at 4 P.M. as before an eruption, with greenish color; then burning, then itching, with profuse sweat. Itching at 11.30 P.M. about elbows and forearms; of points on face and at edge of hair, on forehead, r. side and elsewhere on scalp.

Sleep.—Disposition to yawn, a sort of stupor, inability to keep eyes open, necessity to lie down and sleep. Sleepiness; in forenoon; with dim vision, a kind of drunken stupor; with deep respiration and general numbness; then aggravation of the habitual sleeplessness; like a lethargy, after 2 P.M., lasting all the afternoon and evening. Sleep after supper. Sleep long and sound; sound till 7 A.M., difficult, weary waking. *Restless night; < towards morning; with unpleasant dreams after midnight.* Sleepless all night; till 1 A.M., with desire to study, sound sleep the last half of night and weary waking. Late falling asleep, then nightmare woke me, N. repeated on falling asleep again, as if l. side from neck to knee were a soft muscle jerking up and down with the elasticity of jelly, the centre of this motion seemed to be in region of heart, while r. side of back, on which I lay, was quiet, with inability to stir, on waking drawing pain in lower third of l. thigh, which was repeated next day. Little inclination to sleep, and when it comes dreams much about business, etc. Dreams and early waking; D. of work and of many people; unpleasant D.

Fever.—*Chill;* during the day; all day, < morning; after breakfast; in afternoon, then cold sweat till 5 P.M.; after 2 P.M., then weakness like faintness, then cold sweat; between 2 and 4 P.M., then heat, then cold sweat, all without thirst; at 3 P.M., with cold sweat, hot running in legs and burning in soles, without thirst; at 9 P.M.; *with profuse micturition;* with chills running from loins to nape; with pains in and between bones of l. calf, inability to descend stairs without holding on to something; with tremor and sudden general cold sweat, so that drops stood on arms; with cold limbs, hot head and face and headache; then flying heat and pricking in skin, then sweat; then heat, < about head and face, with full, rapid pulse. Cold skin; and congested; and clammy, finally covered with cold sweat; in afternoon, and sweat; head cool to touch in afternoon. Chills on upper half of body, < in back and nape, at 3 P.M., when reading exciting news; *C. along spine;* cold limbs; hands and feet; feet as if standing in cold water, generally with heat of head and face and headache.

Heat in forenoon; in afternoon, as if sweat would break out, then chill down back. Heat in face, with fulness of head; with bruised pain in brain and rapid pulse; at 2.30 P.M. without external heat. Burning in zygomatic region and in eyes in afternoon whenever aroused from sleepiness; B. in l. zygoma in afternoon, then in r., drawing down to a gland at anterior r. side of neck, where it swells and pains as if an ulcer were forming (at this spot she had, twenty-two years ago, a glandular abscess, which opened internally); in l. zygoma, with swelling, and in eyes, < l., then in r. zygoma at 1 P.M.; in l. zygoma before 2 P.M., and in eyes, < l., with red swelling of zygoma. Burning running through all limbs in afternoon, with burning in first joint of l. index as if blood would come out (this joint is stiff and anchylosed from a wound). Hot and dry hands at 10 A.M.; in afternoon, < palms; palms at 11.30 P.M.

Sweat; with prostration; easy, from movement; profuse; profuse and cold during the stinging in l. breast and after the chilly tremor; sudden, profuse, cold (after pain in forehead) till 6 P.M. Dry skin.

Clinical.—Eruptive fevers, especially measles, with catarrhal symptoms of eyes, nose and throat, and cough, but with great prostration, stupor, livid eruption and lack of thirst. In malarial fevers, especially of the South, so-called bilious-remittent, it is an extremely valuable remedy; the fever is periodic, generally coming on towards evening, with stupor, dizziness, blindness, faintness, no thirst, great prostration, slight perspiration, which relieves. In pure intermittents there may be chill in the back, a prolonged low type of fever, possibly with delirium, but with soft pulse and other Gel. symptoms. Nervous chills, the effects of emotional excitement or depression. Early stage of typhoid fever, with vertigo, tired feeling in all limbs, great weakness, soft pulse, tremulousness of the extremities. Catarrhal fevers, chilliness in the back, desire to be over the fire, hot head, suffused eyes, stuffed nose, etc. Fever of erythema, or in low types of scarlet fever and mild forms of erysipelas.

Gentiana Cruciata.

A tincture is made of the fresh root of G. cruciata, L.

Generalities.—Tension of all nerves so that walking

was difficult. Uneasiness. Faintness. Amelioration in open air.

Mind.—Weeping mood, with disinclination to talk. Apprehension, with rapid and difficult breathing, swelling of temporal veins, pressure in temples, and on reading print, indistinct vision.

Head.—Constriction on prolonged sitting. Sensitiveness after dinner, < violent motion of it. Confusion. Vertigo. Pressure in forehead; in temples. Sudden stitch through l. temple towards 6 P.M. Tension in vertex, and at times jerking pain, the tension becoming an acute pressure, < exerting eyes or constant thought.

Eyes, Ears and Nose.—Pressure inward in r. eye. Eyes feel as if lying deep in orbits. Acute drawing in mastoid process. Frequent sneezing.

Face and Mouth.—Two aphthous ulcers on margin of lower lip, on either side of frænum. Saliva increased.

Throat.—Violent pulsation in carotids. Redness of posterior part of palate, of both tonsils and upper part of pharynx, at certain times of day; R. of arch of palate, uvula and posterior wall of pharynx, with difficult swallowing and anxious constriction; R., with constriction so that swallowing was difficult, and constant hawking up of tenacious mucus. Sticking in tonsils. Rawness and scraping; with constriction on swallowing; R. causing frequent hawking. Scraping, and in soft palate and half way down œsophagus. Constriction, with frequent necessity to hawk and expectorate. Difficult swallowing.

Stomach.—Appetite increased; lost. Thirst. Eructations of air tasting of the tincture; of air and of acid fluid tasting of the drug; of air relieving the tension of abdomen and the headache; acid E., then three sour, watery vomitings. Nausea; with inclination to lie down; with constriction of throat. Vomiting; violent, difficult, of mucus; difficult, of scanty, bitter, sour-smelling mucus, leaving scraping and rawness in throat. Movements, then in abdomen, > walking. Pressure; as from a stone, with nausea; inward in pit. Full sensation, with constant inclination to eructate. Burning. Sensation all day in S. and œsophagus as if he had swallowed a hot morsel, then cold water, < eating, > drinking water.

Abdomen.—Frequent passage of offensive flatus. Distention; > continued walking; with constriction; with heaviness in stomach and frequent empty eructations. Movements, with headache, then copious pasty stool. Pain. Tension; > a profuse pasty stool; with nausea. Intermittent griping, sore sensation in umbilical region, < dinner, > sitting and lying, < standing and walking, obliging him to bend forward, therewith the umbilicus seemed drawn forward. Dragging in r. inguinal region as if something would protrude, > sitting and lying, after violent sneezing sensitive protrusion the size of a hazel-nut.

Stool.—Urging, then three watery stools. Three liquid, preceded by griping. Pasty diarrhœa several times. Free, pasty, without the usual itching in anus.

Sexual Organs.—Menstruation three days earlier than usual, during which there was headache as if head were too full, with distended feeling in skull, > rest, < motion, and delaying sleep.

Respiratory Organs.—Hoarseness, the voice gave out in the middle of his speech; H. in attacks, with sensitiveness of throat. Frequent expectoration.

Neck and Back.—Drawings in cervical muscles; extending to ears, < turning head, an uneasiness so that he could not remain long in one position; D. along r. side of neck to shoulder, with jerking. Tension in lumbar region.

Extremities, etc.—Jerklike drawings in extremities. Distressing drawing in r. shoulder. Cramplike pains in soles. Creeping in evening over whole body as from fleas. Uneasy sleep.

Gentiana Lutea.

A tincture is made of the fresh root.

General Action.—In moderate doses it acts as a "tonic," increases the appetite and power of digestion, stimulates the heart and raises the temperature. Its prolonged use enfeebles digestion and depresses the heart.

Allies.—Cinchona, Erythræa.

Generalities.—Dulness; with morose mood. Weakness. Aggravation in afternoon.

Head.—Confusion; when writing, with heaviness; with heaviness, and with tensive pain in sinciput; with heaviness and fulness as if enlarged. Fulness, with throbbing pressure, especially a pressure upward towards sinciput. Feeling as after drinking liquors. Vertigo. Sticking in middle of sinciput. Pressure in sinciput after 12 o'clock; P. in forehead, with dragging; P. outward in forehead. Confusion of sinciput. Pain in temples; in occiput in afternoon.

Eyes and Nose.—Pain in eyes; at 4 P.M., with redness of conjunctiva; in balls. Sticking in l. upper lid. Vision obscured. Nose stopped. Irritability of nostrils as from coryza, then watery discharge.

Mouth and Throat.—Dryness. Saliva consistent. Taste bitter; T. earthy. Frequent hawking on account of tenacious mucus. Swelling of throat, < posterior part of palate, with sticking and constriction. Rawness of throat.

Stomach.—Appetite ravenous in evening; diminished. Eructations; violent; acid. Nausea; in evening; in attacks after the simplest meals; with lachrymation; with anxious pressure. Wind. Tension and fulness; T. in epigastric region, with pressure; T. in stomach and external epigastric region, with distention, pressure upon it causes nausea, then dragging towards anus. Heaviness, with pressure, anxiety, nausea and difficult, full respiration. Constriction. Faintness; and emptiness.

Abdomen.—Distention, with tension; and offensive flatus; and pain in lower abdomen, < about umbilicus. Rumbling and gurgling; with distention, heaviness and fulness; R., it seems as if bubbles rose. Cutting in morning, so that he must bend up, then heat extending from lumbar vertebræ; sleep delayed, waking about midnight with aggravation of the heat, cutting in A., rapid breathing, the pain prevented sleep and obliged him to toss about, > lying on back with feet drawn up, constant passage of wind upward and downward, distention of A., even above transverse colon, except epigastric region, and pain on touch, slumber after 2 A.M., the pain in A. alone disturbing sleep, weakness and desire for sleep, but inability to really sleep, next morning pain, with cutting when touched, < from pubic region to transverse colon, necessity to walk slowly because A. was painful on motion or a hard step. Twinging, then scanty, yellow diarrhœa twice in quick succession. Pain; with pressure in umbilical region and urging to stool; in walls; especially tensive pain in r. side, < posteriorly, with tension in lower A. Tension, < towards evening, with shortness of breath. General sick feeling, with dragging towards anus. Discomfort in l. hypochondrium, with pressure. Pressure in umbilical region; with tension; inward; pain like a drawing inward. Umbilical region sensitive to touch and pressure; pain below U. region on touch.

Stool and Urine.—Dragging towards anus, with tenesmus. Sudden urging, then copious stool; constant U., with frequent consistent stools. Bilious diarrhœa in afternoon. Soft stool; twice soon after rising; and light yellow, preceded by cutting. Pasty, frequent, yellow stools. Urine increased.

Voice, Chest and Pulse.—Hoarseness; in forenoon. Pressure in middle to l. of sternum; upon chest on motion. Tightness of C. Fulness of C. in morning, with pressure and with difficult breathing. Pulse rapid in evening.

Back and Extremities.—Pain in B. and abdomen, < motion, > sitting; P. in small of B., with heaviness; in r. hip near small of B.; in hips and small of B. on stooping, as from a girdle about hips. Prostration and tension in limbs. Sprained pain in l. knee. Crawling in knees. Sticking and tearing in soles on bending toes when walking.

Sleep and Fever.—Yawning. Uneasy sleep. Three times shivering spreading over back like an electric shock, then exhaustion. Heat; of head, < cheeks; of head, with confusion of it.

Ginseng.

A tincture is made of the dried root of Panax quinquefolium (wild Ginseng).

Allied botanically and somewhat symptomatically to Aralia.

Generalities.—Heaviness in all movements. Pressure and drawing alternately in forehead, r. forearm, toes, tibiæ and calves. Sensation when sitting as if the body fell backward. Malaise; after dinner, with drowsiness, internal coldness, external heat, formication in fingers, yawning, stretching, shivering, trembling, thirst, dryness of mouth, drawing in stomach, weakness of thighs and legs, as during convalescence. Uneasiness obliging him to walk. Indolence. Weakness; after a short walk; on entering the house, with heaviness in sinciput; with internal trembling feeling in limbs; < legs, with pain in various muscles; alternately in back, knees and arms; sudden, at 7 P.M., with creeping coldness, flushes of heat, cool sweat and longing to expose the body to cold air and to have something strengthening. Aggravation on r. side.

Mind.—Anxiety after dinner. Generally calm, but impatient impulses and fear of accidents, with at times disposition to weep or to be anxious about the future. Thought difficult. Not inclined to thought or business. Forgetful.

Head.—Pain; after dinner, with heaviness; deep in in brain, changing about; in longitudinal sinuses. Heaviness; constant, with pressure in forehead rhythmical with pulse, and objects have a tremulous motion rhythmical with pulse. Confusion; all day; < forehead, then vertigo, sleepiness and heaviness of upper lids. Fulness after dinner. Seemed enlarged at times and to shake in direction of sides. Vertigo; on going into open air; on ascending winding stairs, < descending; at times; ground seemed to waver when standing; with indistinct vision; with unsteadiness in walking, which seemed to start from hips, so that thighs seemed pushed outward; with obnubilation.

Forehead.—Drawing stitches extending to r. inner canthus. Lancinations; in r. eminence, extending above orbit, with heaviness of eyelid. Pain; in bone; in l. eminence; in sinciput; upper part of sinciput; with heat; with drawing transversely through it; at times. Drawing in r. bone. Heaviness. Confusion in sinciput. Vertigo.

Pressure in temples; in r., and in l. sensation as if too thick; constant P. and pulsation on exertion; on vertex. Pain on r. side of head. Pressure in sinuses of cerebellum; P. in occiput, with impending vertigo. Drawing in occiput in afternoon, on mental exertion, so that he involuntarily bent the head backward. Sudden blow upon occiput, then bruised pain. Sensation in occiput when sitting as if swaying to the sides. Reeling in O., with gray spots before eyes.

Eyes.—Sticking deep in upper half, then pressure, repeated in evening by the light; S., with lachrymation, redness of conjunctiva of bulb and inclination to close lids. Pressure inward. Pupils contracted; with sensitiveness of eyes to daylight in dim weather; large; alternately large and small. Cold sensation on surface of ball. Drooping of upper lids, < r.; lids difficult to open, with heaviness and pain. Itching of lids. Biting of margins of lids; with itching; with burning. Constriction of l. upper lid. Wearied by a bright light. Blinded by daylight. Letters run into each other when reading. Vision indistinct; distinct, but objects are not seen clearly because the eyes wander too quickly from one object to another; swimming of objects on going into open air, with unsteady gait. Vision of black floating points; of large white spots. Vision double on looking steadily.

Nose.—Dryness; with sensitiveness to air. Scanty, thick mucus in evening, next day thin and copious. Bleeding from r. nostril; at 9 A.M. on slight touch; at 9 P.M. on blowing. Frequent sneezing.

Face.—Alternately red and pale. Pressure in zygomata; in joint of jaw. Drawing in l. side of lower jaw; D. in ascending ramus of lower jaw, zygomata and upper jaw of r. side. Lips thick, covered with dry rough scales. Lips red and dry, they crack and bleed, < lower. Dryness of lips and mouth, < open air, > dinner, but returning, with scraping and soreness in fauces; D. in lips and mouth as far as pharynx, with swollen feeling in lips and nauseous odor from mouth; in lips, mouth and fauces, < talking, with rough voice and scraping in throat; in lips, mouth and fauces, < open air and talking, at the same time scraping soreness in fauces, < empty swallowing and by drawing air through nose, which is dry; of lips, teeth, mouth and throat, all parts stuck together; D. and roughness of lips, mouth, teeth, tongue and fauces as if covered with sand, in open air or on exercise, with rapid breathing.

Mouth.—Tongue red and smarting, with thirst, then white in middle; T. white, *dry*, with large glistening papillæ. Speech difficult and indistinct on account of affection of mouth. Dryness; > eating; of arch of palate; < arch of palate and tongue, then flow of saliva; < tongue, arch of palate, whole fauces, with stale odor from mouth; so that swallowing of bread and butter is difficult and leaves sticking deep in throat; alternating with salivation; dry sensation in palate, with salivation. Salivation, with nausea. Saliva almost grass-green. Mouth and throat troubles < open air, > dinner.

Throat.—Redness of uvula, fauces and posterior pharynx; of uvula and fauces, with pain on empty swallowing and swallowing of saliva. Sticking in pharynx. Scraping in fauces; in T. and fauces in afternoon; in fauces and pharynx on empty swallowing, with dryness and rawness; in fauces, < talking, also with soreness; < empty swallowing, with dryness; scraping soreness in fauces, extending into pharynx, > 1.30 P.M., after dinner. Pain on swallowing bread, which was not relished. Fauces sensitive to air of the room.

Stomach.—Appetite increased; great, at an unusual time. Thirst absent. Eructations, with relief; empty E.; bitter E. Nausea; with sore pain in r. flank, under ribs, < touch. Swelling, with throbbing, anxiety and nausea; S. from flatus. Lancination in r. side of epigastrium. Pain; with feeling as if it would burst, dyspnœa and pressure in l. frontal eminence. Constriction in region, with difficult breathing; C. in pit, like cramp, at 4 P.M., after eating. Drawings; painful, as from hunger, preceded by shivering. Oppression, the clothes feel uncomfortable. Intolerance of clothing in epigastric region.

Abdomen.—*Inflammation, with pain and borborygmi;* I., with tension and pressure in hypogastrium; I. as far as below r. ribs, with pain; from flatus, discharge of which relieved; from flatus, and pain in umbilical region, < pressure. *Tense, painful. Rumbling.* Noises from wind, it goes upward and downward. Tension. Swollen sensation. Pain, then liquid stools in evening; P. rising to region of stomach, with pain on leaning against it; vague P., and in chest; as from a bar, with digging and starting in r. hip, then internal pain; in r. side from hip to below ribs; in r. side as far as groin, with formication reaching to foot. Digging in r. side as far as groin, rising to stomach, with griping in whole hypogastrium. *Pain in r. side of hypogastrium extending to groin,* with painful formication as far as great toe, causing lancinations there; P. on r. side of H., extending to l., then rising to region of heart; in H., with pressure in groin; extending from within pelvis to thighs, as if one must sink to the ground, then four thin stools; vague, in H. Bruised pain in r. iliac region, < pressure. Heaviness of pelvic members.

Clinical.—Loud gurgling noise in ilio-cæcal region, dry tongue, delirium on going to sleep. It seems to have relieved the threatening inflammation of perityphilitis, and possibly also relieved the local symptoms of typhoid fever.

Rectum and Stool.—Sticking in rectum. Stool soft; hard; hard, difficult, then smarting at anus, tenesmus and lancinations in rectum; difficult but not hard; delayed.

Urinary Organs.—Frequent desire to urinate, with smarting. Sticking in fossa navicularis. Tickling in fossa navicularis; voluptuous T. in end of urethra, with erections. Itching in urethra, with burning pain and frequent urging to urinate. Urine scanty; and dark; and clear, in a thin stream, the bladder did not empty itself, only by pressing is a broad stream produced; abundant and clear; yellowish U., with red lateritious sediment; lemon-colored, after standing a reddish sediment.

Sexual Organs.—Erections when sitting at engrossing business; nocturnal, without pollutions. Pressure in testicles. Excitement.

Respiratory Organs.—Voice rough; and hoarse, deep. Dry cough; in afternoon; in paroxysms. Dyspnœa. Oppressed breathing; worse when sitting than when walking; slow, deep, difficult; short, anxious; deep now and then. Frequently deep, labored inspirations; when sitting; frequent deep I., with tightness of chest, anxiety and heaviness of limbs. Difficult inspiration, with sticking in r. lung.

Chest.—Sticking in r. taking away the breath; sudden, beneath l. ribs, so that he holds his breath. Tearing in anterior wall. Pain near heart, preceded by shivering, which extends to elbow. Constriction, with anxiety; C. transversely across lower part in evening. Tightness; in region of heart on deep breathing, > walking. Oppression, < sitting.

Heart.—Lancinations in præcordial region; here and there. Pain in præcordial region; at l. side of cardiac region. Tightness as if something were lying on præcordial region, with deep, labored inspirations. Palpitation. Beats increased; stronger and irregular; violent when sitting, then floundering sensation in heart, with rapid, small, indistinct pulse; sudden violent beats when sitting and lying, with anxious oppression in præcordial region. Beat not perceptible, but oppression in præcordial region.

Pulse.—Rapid; in morning; in afternoon, and irregular; < slightest cause; and full; and irregular; and small, weak; and small and soft, after coughing; and jerky; small, then slow and full, alternately rapid and slow. Jerky, sometimes like a quick trembling, that is also felt in chest. Slow and full. Irregular; and sometimes 90 when sitting; at 3 P.M., more rapid when sitting erect, slower but fuller and larger when sitting bent forward. Fluttering. Could not be felt, but it was an undulation, then small, soft beats.

Neck.—Cracking in upper vertebræ on moving head. Pain in nape; in muscles of neck and loins. Drawing in l. muscles. Pulsation in r. side. Heaviness of nape; and occiput, with stiffness of nape.

Back.—Sticking. Painful lassitude along, with bruised feeling down to sacrum. Stiffness. Pricking in scapulæ extending to l. shoulder. Lancinations between scapulæ, in shoulders and along spine to sacrum < straightening himself, with difficult breathing. Pressure in spinous processes of several dorsal vertebræ. Deep lancinations around loins. Bruised pain in sacrum. Pain in l. lumbar muscles, < bending or turning.

Extremities.—Cracking in joints on moving them. Drawing in arms and limbs as if beaten. Bruised pain in various muscles; B. pain alternately in different parts; B. pain in afternoon when walking, with weariness; alternately in l. knee, elbow and foot when sitting. Peculiar lightness and vigor in spite of much walking; peculiar lightness and flexibility in morning in spite of a bad night. Weakness; < l.

Upper Extremities.—Pain in shoulders, with cracking in them; P. in shoulder-joint; in l. upper arm. Weakness of shoulders and upper arms; of arms, with painful drawing in muscles of upper arm. Constriction of flesh of lower part of l. arm. Pain in muscles of lower part of l. forearm as from a hoop. Objects held with uncertainty, so that they easily fell, with haste in all movements. Sticking in l. hand, with insensibility of fingers. Hands feel swollen on closing them, and as if the skin were tight. Fingers feel fine and smooth, and agreeable warmth of their skin. Contraction of r. fingers, with stiffness of their joints. Drawing in side of r. index.

Lower Extremities.—Tottering; with knees bent and legs spread apart; in open air, with beginning vertigo. Sensation as if tottering in open air; always on going into open air, and sometimes real staggering, < ascending steps. Cramp-pain from r. hip-joint to tips of toes. Heaviness. Difficulty in walking, with limping; D. in ascending steps, without weakness. Cutting in r. hip, extending into abdomen and forcing him to bend over. Bruised pain in hips. Pain in muscles of l. thigh; in muscles of interior and middle parts of thighs when sitting; from l. groin to knee, with stiffness; in r. knee; in outer side of r. knee. Cracking in r. knee on motion and when sitting. Cramp in r. calf. Retraction of muscles of r. leg, with bruised pain in hip-joint. Sticking in r., then l. tibia when walking and sitting. Tearing here and there in muscles of l. leg; in l. tibia; on surface of l. leg, between tibia and fibula. Pressure in r. calf. Drawing in calves. Weakness of legs; r. Lancinating tearing in r. tibial-tarsal joint. Pain in knees and ankles, soon alternating with drawing in calves and r. joint of jaw, < walking. Tensive pain above and behind l. malleolus when the foot leaves the ground in walking and the tension is brought upon the tendo-achillis, extending to sole, < walking rapidly, so that he limped, > walking slowly. Drawing in feet when sitting, extending to back, with coldness. Weariness of feet. Lancinations alternately in both great toes. Sharp pain in l. great toe, long affected with gouty swelling which has disappeared. Pain in r. great toe and in muscles of forepart and middle of thighs. Peculiar weak pressing in r. toes. Internal trembling sensation in l. toes.

Skin.—Veins very small. Itching pimples on neck and chest. Prickling in calves. Smarting on r. cheek, chin and wing of nose, with itching and heat, then erythematous burning redness, then miliary pustules with formication, then tetter ending in desquamation. Formication along r. thigh to foot, with stiffness; F. at night along r. thigh to great toe, where there are lancinations. Itching under r. foot.

Sleep.—Yawning though he had slept all the morning. Sleepiness. Sleep deep, prolonged, quiet, towards morning. Wakes with difficulty or else with a start. Many dreams, with frequent waking, mostly with headache. Remembered dreams. Vivid, voluptuous dreams.

Fever.— Sensitiveness to cold. Coldness after a walk; C., with trembling and with numbness of hands, coldness of fingers, which are white, numb and prickly; piercing into occiput; in r. elbow and parietal eminence, with crawling; through back; in back, extending into bones of arms, with cold hands and blue nails; in back, extending into limbs, which are cold and feel bruised; in spine, > walking, with coldness in head and limbs, weakness of limbs, pressure in testicles and elbows, frequent deep breathing, oppression of chest, prickling in calves, pulse 55 to 60. Shivering through back; with warm limbs; when walking and sitting, extending into arms, with cold skin, bluish nails, weakness of r. limb, oppressed respiration, pupils contracted, and sensitive to daylight. Warmth of skin, which seems soft and fine. Heat of head; forehead; of whole body, < back, from a small glass of Malaga wine, with distention of veins; externally in tips of fingers.

Glonoine.

One part of Nitro-glycerine is dissolved in nine parts of alcohol for the tincture.

General Action.—Identical with Amyl-nitrite, paralyzing the peripheral vaso-motor nerves. Its action is more lasting than that of Amyl.

Allies.—Amyl-nit., Cactus, Mellilotus, Nitrous oxide.

Generalities.—Head fell backward, jaw dropped, stertor, pulseless at wrist. Tremor, sopor, lassitude. *Falling down unconscious, congestion to head or heart,* face sometimes pale, sometimes red; *F. down senseless, with convulsions and frothing at mouth, after alternations of palpitation and congestion to head.* Spasms after cold water was poured on head, ending in vomiting, then short relief, then return twice of pressure and throbbing in brain, each > vomiting. **Fulness in vertex, forehead,** through body, chest and abdomen. **Throbbing through whole body;** *when lying;* on moving about; wherever the body touches anything, wherever he puts his hands; with heat and sweat. Feeling as after ether; lightness, then fulness in brain, with dizziness. Discomfort. Inclination to stretch backward. Sensation as before ague. Nervousness; with clammy sweat. *Weakness;* in morning; *during headache;* with apathy; with sleepiness, inability to study, dulness when thinking, wandering of thoughts when writing. Faintness; before nausea; fell senseless on pavement, lay breathless, sighing at long intervals, face pale, conscious in two minutes, sweat, nausea, cold hands and feet, pulse feeble, *must have head elevated,* it felt full, vision indistinct, dizzy, face pale, at times flushed, at times dark livid, symptoms < motion, > hot foot baths, vomiting caused by jolting of carriage, sticking in occiput. Body seemed asleep while the mind was awake, the latter resolved to take notice of crooked, jagged objects before the closed eyes, attempted in vain to raise the body, it seemed to shrivel till completely asleep. Paralysis of all voluntary muscles, partial P. of muscles of mastication and of face and eyes. Aggravation on r. side; A. during rest; from coffee if wine has been taken. Amelioration from black coffee; A. during sweat; after each evacuation, but return of headache each time he vomited; partial A. from tea. Alternations of head and heart symptoms.

Clinical.—Epilepsy, with great rush of blood to the head and vascular excitement generally.

Mind.—Delirious, then comatose. *Familiar things seemed strange.* She felt as if she woke from a dream and she moved her arms like one waking from a dream. Animated, talkative, great flow of thought and inclination to jest. Agitation. Terror. Fear, with sensation as if chest were screwed together; F. that she had been poisoned; F. that her death was approaching. Anxiety; with headache; with inclination to run away. Depression. Recalls old grievances and determines to justify himself. *Confusion of ideas,* **so that he could not tell where he was;** *scarcely* *knew what he was about*, > effort of will; C., with weakness and with diminished power of tongue. Inability to collect the thoughts. Memory difficult. Stupor, weakness of mind and body. Partial insensibility and dislike to being aroused. *Unconsciousness.*

Clinical.—It has proved valuable for the effects of shock, which show themselves by sudden attacks of terror so that he dares not go into the street. In acute mania or insanity it has been found useful when the head was hot, full, throbbing, eyes staring, pulse very rapid, pulsation in carotids, or in other cases when there was violent maniacal excitement with hot head. It certainly has relieved the mental confusion which is characterized by the loss of the sensation of location, so that one loses his way in well-known places. Insanity caused by long-continued heat of the sun; thought he was the Lord Almighty.

Head.—*Holding it with both hands. Hands frequently raised to it. Inclination to bend backward;* to throw it backward. H. and face puffed up, blood forced upward, convulsions, frequent unconsciousness, copious urine containing much albumen. *Brain fever.* Sudden piercing pain. Sticking in morning on stooping. Darting pain in morning when stooping. Painful twitching here and there; T. at every step on ascending stairs.

Aching; from morning till 2 o'clock; in morning, with general heat and fetid flatus; in morning on rising, with pain in hypogastrium and painful copious diarrhœa, pain > stool, returning, < moving or sitting erect, soreness on l. iliac region on pressure, with shuddering and heat in anus; at noon, < sudden rising or shaking head, with soreness; returned at 1 P.M. after drinking coffee; afternoon; evenings; after eructations; when rising suddenly; from every change of position; on rising, so that he could not stand; in open air; at a concert, > during the walk home, *with fulness in vertex* and throbbing in temples; *when the period appears, with congestion and fulness; A. and pulse increase and diminish together.* Aggravation of A. *mornings and forenoons* and one afternoon; afternoon, < occiput; **shaking head**; pressure; stooping; stepping; *movement;* motion from side to side; on every motion, beginning in open air, continuing in the house, > a second walk; ascending stairs quickly; leaning forward; in open air; after dinner; reading, writing and smoking; after expelling breath, if he waits before inhaling. *Amelioration in open air;* A. in evening; throwing H. back; lying; repose; sleep; pressure; combing hair; smoking; strong tea; walking; gentle exercise, especially in open air (Ferr.). *Aching, with nausea; and with dull, heavy pain in stomach;* A. with buzzing in l. ear and redness of l. eye.

Aching deep in brain; A. in median line; *A. rising from below upward; extending to nose;* extending over shoulders and under arms; so that he walks the room all night; waking three or four times; impeding breathing; like migraine, concentrating over r. eye, with dulness about eyes and heat; drawing A., extending to occiput; racking, with faintness, intolerance of light, general distress and alarm; bursting; upward from middle; as if pressed by a band; as if brain were pressed towards centre from temples and occiput, from morning till night; *undulating*, in middle of brain; U., during fulness of heart. Throbbing pain; all night, > in morning by coffee; on stooping; after motion, < shaking head, > night; preventing lying down, obliging him to hold on to head as if to prevent rupture of skull; rising from base of skull to vertex with every throb of carotids.

Bruised sensation internally, < in forehead. *Soreness;* on moving; of brain on shaking head, with sensation as if hard and loose; < *shaking;* and **he is afraid to shake it lest it should drop to pieces;** with laced sensation and pain, < shaking head sideways. *Cracking sensation in brain*, obliging him to hold on to head on movement to prevent apparent threatened rupture of cranium. Sinking sensation, and in chest, as from working in the hot sun. Feeling as if hungry. Sensation as if he had eaten too much. Strange sensation after the pain. Disagreeable sensation, < at base of brain. Dulness; < *light shaking, not by violent shaking;* externally. Confusion. Stiffness of H. and neck; *or tension as if laced.* Heaviness; with warm sweat on forehead, skin otherwise cool; as from a weight on brain; from middle to ears. Feeling as if brain were smaller than cavity of skull.

Fulness; with full, quick pulse and red face; and throbbing, without pain; *at base of brain, with throbbing in all arteries of head and nape;* with throbbing above and behind temples and pricking on l. side of tongue near tip, afterwards the same throbbing, with almost twitching in scalp of same place, < getting up, walking across room and sitting down again; worse now and then, changing places. **Felt too large.** Feeling as if brain were distending in all directions; as if head were swelling, < stooping, with throbbing, the T. < l. side.

Shocks synchronous with every pulsation of arteries (Ferr.). **Throbbing** (Ferr.); *during motion;* < *stooping;* < *temples and over eyes,* < *motion,* > *sitting still, lying or pressure, with heat in head;* < *ascending stairs; with confusion of senses, sensation of balancing requiring constant effort to keep head erect;* < *above ears,* and in temples, with bursting sensation and choking as from a band about neck, which prevented blood from returning from head; heard and felt in brain at 8.15 P.M., after running up-stairs, and at each pulsation sensation (amounting to pain) in scalp above ears; outward; *so that pulse could be counted by it* (pulse 100). **Undulating sensation;** upward; < turning head. Feeling as if something moved inside on shaking head; and hit skull.

Sensation as if hanging with head downward, and as if there were great rush of blood in consequence. *Congestion;* till midnight; sudden; *frequently, in an old woman,* always causing coldness; and to chest; and to lungs; alternating with C. to heart. *Vertigo;* in afternoon; on shaking head; on throwing head back; on turning around; going into open air, with reeling; on rising, with blindness and nausea, also with desire to drink cold water; < moving about; *with nausea; with dim vision;* with faintness, then nausea; sudden, in afternoon, on descending from a carriage.

Forehead.—Sticking in r. from laughing. Piercing pain *outward* towards middle, more upward. Tearing near middle line, not very deep. Aching; in morning on waking; on looking long in one direction; on moving head, and in occiput; < shaking head, also evenings, > night's sleep; > when driving; in sinciput; sides of sinciput; over eyes; over r. eye; in "benevolence;" in "wonder," < r., then l.; in l. "wit," with sensitiveness to pressure, the pain > continued pressure; in "wit;" l., then r.; r. side of F. and l. side of occiput, < shaking head; over nose and in r. petrous bone; headache, beginning at root of nose; then in vertex, then in whole head;

with sensation as if eyeballs were pressed out; in sinciput, with nausea; in sinciput, with necessity to remove his hat in open air because it was too heavy; *headache from front* backward; extending to middle of brain; extending over vertex to occiput; extending to r. margo-superciliaris; over r. eye and over supraorbital ridges, across from r. to l.; and in eyes, causing winking; and in occiput, as after intoxication.

Throbbing pain; in afternoon and evening, and in temples; extending to vertex; beginning in glabella, *spreading upward and backward*, < first in front of r., then behind l., then < occiput, extending to nose and contracting eyelids; and at root of nose and in temples. Undulating pain in r., then l., then over whole head; compressing burning pain in F. and vertex, *in a spot which might be covered with the hand*, with heat, shooting and throbbing in temples, burning in malar-bone and eyes, soreness in head all day, gnawing in occiput and inability to think. Bruised sensation where the pain had been; B. sensation in l. organ of "form," then on both sides. Soreness, with bruised sensation. *Pressure downward towards eyes;* P. upward, so that he must support head; upward in F. and vertex in forenoon; as from a liquid upward from root of nose and through sinus longitudinalis, with constantly increasing force, with general sweat, redness of face and anxiety. Pain in middle as if water were trickling down inside. Dulness, > open air; D. in l. upper part; in l. and in sides, with heat in face. Drawing extending to eyes and root of nose.

Weariness like a weight over eyes, extending to temples. Heaviness; over eyes; over eyes, towards temples; between brows and across nose. *Tension over eyes and nose, extending behind ears, then choky feeling about throat like strangulation;* T. over sinus and across nose, with *fulness above and in front of ears;* with pressure at root of nose. *Fulness;* all day; in r.; over orbits; *upper part, with throbbing; in sinciput;* deep in sinciput, with throbbing. Throbbing; *in sinciput;* over eyes; in "wonder;" sinciput all afternoon; < *by every motion of head;* < rising; under bone, extending to temple; beneath bone, extending across temples. Sensation on moving head as if something were loose. Brain seemed to move in r. Sensation in F. and occiput as if something rose to vertex. Vertigo.

Temples.—Veins enlarged and face flushed. Sticking in r.; then l., causing vertigo, with sickness; from r. to l., with weakness and inability to stand or walk, without vertigo; intermittent tearing S., extending towards masseter muscles. Piercing pain externally on l.; P., < in l., after flushes of rising heat. Cutting, tending to move towards ears. Pain; through T.; in r.; in r., then in both and behind ears; r. on shaking head; on running up-stairs, with throbbing in them, nausea and vertigo; < walking, talking or reading; > open air, returned at night in bed; and when pressing on them haze before eyes; from r. to l.; extending from one to the other; to l. of T., extending inwardly to nose. Twitching pain. Throbbing pain; *at each step, obliging pressure on temporal arteries;* < moving head, > application of snow to temples. Pain moving in waves towards middle of brain, with a bursting upward and with a piercing pain on skull over l. temple. Pain undulating and raging through whole head, < at last in region of sagittal suture.

Pressure outward; < l. and towards eyes. *Tightness.* Tension in r., with occasional prickling in r. eye; T. alternately in temples, occiput and ears; changing to occiput and ears, late falling asleep, waking frequently with the same pain, > next morning. Drawing in r. Oppression, and in occiput. **Throbbing; in arteries, which felt like whipcords;** in r.; < *motion;* < standing or walking in open air; moving from T. to T.; in r., with sharp pain, then in both and behind ears; *could count the beats.* Sensation as if something were running through them. Rushing sensation as of fulness.

Vertex.—*Pain;* at night on waking; in evening; after vertigo in occiput, < evening; in region of first fontanelle, also with fulness; in region of l. coronal suture; extending to nape; intermittent in intensity, with confusion of mind. Throbbing pain; in forenoon; in region of l. coronal suture; under V., with heat and redness of face, sinking beating in aorta behind umbilicus, beating in l. parietal region, all pains < shaking head, stooping, first motion after rising, on walking, standing and turning around. Confusing pain, with languor. Burning pain. Bruised sensation in brain in V. and region of first fontanelle, < moving head; in "firmness," r., then pulsation there. Soreness just under V., < stooping or stepping, > quiet and lying down. Pain in V. and temples as if pressed together; in V. and sides of head as if pressed together. Sudden pressure inward on V., with rush of blood; P. upward as if there were not room enough, < motion, especially of head, > during rest and in open air, also across eyes. *Throbbing; upward;* with pain extending to nape; paroxysmal, and in temples and occiput. **Fulness.**

Parietals.—Twitching in r. side of head and in r. orbit at noon, then in l. side and ringing in l. ear. Pain in l., then r. side of head; l. half of head, < vertex; r. side in front and l. side behind; behind ear and up in forehead; behind ears on shaking head; in sides, extending to over eyes; intermittent, in l. P. region. Throbbing on each side near vertex and across in region of coronal suture, < motion and looking up. Fulness forward from P. protuberance, including the whole of the anterior parts, on attempting to read, increasing to pain.

Occiput.—Cataleptic state of occipito-frontalis muscle during the day, with obtuseness of brain. Sticking. Gnawing. Pain; in forenoon, gradually extending forward and upward; from congestion; > night's sleep; in lower protuberance, < r., < turning head; r. and towards ears; and in region of ears and in nape, as if in medulla oblongata, < moving head, with stiffness of neck; with fulness, heat and thumping; then in vertex; extending to vertex; *extending to eyes and temples; headache from back to front* and from below upward; extending towards vertex, < shaking head sideways and only a little on shaking it backward or forward; extending to nape. Twitching pain; in l. and in l. orbit. Drawing pain towards O. *Sore pain.* Tensive pain extending upward and downward and towards both ears, with intermittent tension above r. eye. Oppression. Dulness. Beating in head from back to front, *as if it would crowd everything out at forehead*, less frequent than pulse. Fulness; < outside; then pain extending to forehead; thumping, when sitting down, < *shaking it. Congestion, it seems as if he must lose his reason.* Vertigo; then pain in vertex. O. and neck more affected than any other part. Relief in open air, but tensive pain in O. returns at times.

Skull feels too small; and as if brain were attempting to burst skull, with violent action of heart and pulsation over whole body. Skull feels empty. Shedding of hair. Pain in wens as if pressed together by a ring. Numbness of scalp.

Clinical.—An extremely valuable remedy for most violent supraorbital congestions from a great variety of causes, in all of which there is a strong pulsation in the head with every beat of the heart, the head sometimes < pressure and cold applications, with thin lips, or sometimes purplish lips, swollen face; the pain is crushing and oppressing; the brain feels as if it surged in waves (Aconite). A most valuable remedy for the effects of sunstroke. With these terrible headaches of Glo. the patient loses all power of recalling the names of objects, becomes dizzy and loses his way. Attacks of violent hemicrania. Threatening apoplexy. Symptoms of cerebro-spinal meningitis; pains seem to rise from neck through occiput. Terrible headache and sensitiveness of the upper part of the spine, from being thrown from a carriage.

Eyes.—*Staring; and wild, protruding.* Injected; l. during headache. Bluish pallor under eyes. Lifeless, much winking, looking strangely about, blue rings under eyes. Dim and tearful. Quivering, with inability to see straight. Prickling in r. Pain at 7 P.M., then drowsiness and heaviness of lids; P. behind l. eye and ear. Pressure across E.; P. downward upon E.; P. deep in r. at 7 P.M., when walking home. Soreness when moved. Whirling sensation under r. and in bone, then above eye. Heat; with tension. Sensation as if water were running out. Lachrymation; with heat. Pupils enlarged. Burning in balls; l., with sticking. Pain in balls. Conjunctiva congested. Lids, lower swollen; lower dead, dirty looking, as if sunken, eyes unsteady; lids contracted early in evening, as by sleep; heaviness in morning, with difficult waking. Heat in r. outer canthus. Orbit, sticking in r.; pressure in r.; twitching pain in l. Pain in supraorbital ridge as if sore.

Vision dim; suddenly; with tingling in nerves of whole body. Weak in afternoon, letters seem blended and small. Confused, *dancing of objects.* He thinks he sees, with *every beat of pulse,* the blood-globules passing in eyes. Visionary objects pass before eyes. Of sparks. Lightnings so that he cannot see. Black floating spots, < *on attempting to stoop,* > driving, with vertigo so that he could not stand. Blindness; on attempting to read when standing, with faintness and nausea.

Clinical.—Supraorbital neuralgia, pulsating. Retinal congestions the result of exposure to a bright light.

Ears.—Sticking in r.; alternately in r. and l.; S. alternating with pressure in forehead. Piercing pain from region of r. towards r. eye. Throbbing pain piercing outward in r. Pain in r. as if swollen. Pain below l. mastoid process at 9 A.M. on pressure. Tensive pain behind r.; < pressure; in a spot in region of mastoid process. Stopped feeling in middle. Throbbing above E. Fulness; < r.; about E. *Ringing* and audible pulse. Rushing noise like escaping steam. Cracking in l. Buzzing. Humming. *Deafness,* with heaviness and *stopped sensation;* partial.

Nose.—Twitching in wings and prickling twitching in face. Twitching pain in r. side of root; darting T. pain in r. side of root and r. side of forehead. Pain in root. Stoppage at root. Fulness. Schneiderian membrane thick as in dry coryza. Sneezing, with running from nose; late in evening.

Face.—*Red; during headache;* < upper part of cheeks, lower lids and ears, but not forehead. Blue, then red and swollen. Pale; after sweat; and agitated; with nausea and congestion to chest; alternately P. and red; or at times flushed, at times livid. Twitching in l. malar-bone; T. pain in l. malar-bone and temples. Pain in l. malar-bone, extending over forehead to vertex. Bloated feeling and heat. Sensation as if chin were elongated to knees, chin had been injured twenty years previously. Masseter muscles contracted; tight as if lockjaw were coming on. *Gnawing in masseter muscles.* Pain in joint of jaw; P. in r. lower jaw, < about joint, with stiffness in both sides of lower jaw. Movement of jaw impeded by twitching of temporal and masseter muscles. Cyanosis of lips, with involuntary diarrhœa. Sensation as if lower lip were swollen and pendant, but it was not. Burning in lips and tip of tongue; *in various places in lips;* in lips and fauces, with smarting. Itching of lips and after rubbing swollen sensation. Numbness of lower lip, with swollen sensation.

Clinical.—Neuralgia of the face extending through the head, pulsating.

Mouth.—**Throbbing pain in all teeth** (Sul.). Drawing pain in all r. teeth as after taking cold, alternating with same in ear and lower jaw. Pain in lower molars, < r., then l. Tongue white, enlarged, indented by incisors; coated white; red specks, papillæ sore; stinging near centre and tip of T.; pricking, and in fauces; pricking, a chilling burning; pricking-biting; biting in a spot on l. side, with pricking and burning; prickling on l. side near tip; feeling swelled, raw, with twitchings; burnt feeling, and in mouth; numbness. Difficulty in conversing from diminished power of tongue and confusion of ideas.

Pimples on r. inner cheek. Soreness. Sensitiveness of hard palate. Swollen sensation in hard palate, with throbbing. Burning in hard palate. Dryness; at night, with thirst; of M. and throat at night, with choking and frequent inclination to swallow; and clamminess, and throat dry and painful during empty swallowing. Filled with thick offensive saliva in morning, during the day slimy saliva which had to be ejected as if was too disagreeable to swallow. Offensive breath. Taste fatty; and like cinnamon; T. oily; bitter; sharp and tenacious; aromatic; like pine wood; like pine roots; sweet, burning and acrid; sweet, sharp, aromatic.

Throat.—Fulness of jugular veins. Pulsation in arteries. Thick mucus. Sticking in l. tonsil. *Sensation as if swelling, with fear,* causing her to feel it constantly; swollen sensation in fauces. Choking sensation. Soreness. Roughness. Contractive sensation in soft palate. Dryness of soft palate, < towards back and downward. Heat; in pharynx. Fulness. Tingling, with increased saliva. Tickling; waking at 2 A.M., with pain as if a rough feather were drawn up his throat, causing cough, > drinking water, had the same once before. *Itching, and in soft palate.* Constant inclination to swallow. Swallowing difficult.

Stomach.—Appetite lost. Thirst. *Increased desire to smoke,* and the smoking regulates the bowels. *Eructations;* before headache; empty; empty, with pressure at pit of stomach; heavy, long, but easy; of food. *Nausea;* from fulness and heat in head; > sweat; > oysters and stout; > open air; > open air, with headache, congestion to head and chest, face pale; with *pain in stomach* and rumbling in abdomen; with pain at epigastrium; with sinking at epigastrium as from vertigo; with congestion of brain and lungs; with faintness and thirst for cold water; but inability to vomit; then headache, then repeated forcible vomiting of yellow mucus, then several thin stools, > brandy; in attacks till midnight, with congestion to chest and head. Retching. Vomiting of frothy saliva caused by coffee; repeated violent V.

Gastric catarrh. Cutting in S. and chest, > morning, with sickness, griping in abdomen and inclination to stool. Gnawing in pit and yawning. Pain in pit; P. > eructation. Soreness in pit on touch, > stooping. *Faintness in pit;* in epigastrium, with sensation of incarcerated flatus. Emptiness. Sinking in paroxysms. Uneasiness, with heat in throat; U. emanating from S. Heat in pit; in waves through bloodvessels to head, there changing to pain. Supper did not digest well.

Clinical.—Seasickness.

Abdomen.—*Rumbling*, with feeling as before diarrhœa; R. mornings, with diarrhœa. Flatulence all the evening. Emission of flatus; frequent, noisy, during stool; offensive, giving relief. Pinching before and after stool, till falling asleep, with rumbling. Pain; before stool; < motion, especially walking; waking early in morning, then at 6 A.M. copious liquid stool, similar stools at 10 P.M. Sensation as before diarrhœa. Burning. Peristaltic motion retarded. Shooting under r. ribs (region of gall-bladder), when standing, causing bending forward. Piercing pain in l. hypochondrium in morning. Pain in a spot in l. hypochondrium; half way between pit of stomach and side. Sensation as if blood rushed from l. hypochondrium through chest to head, also from r., with throbbing. Cutting under umbilicus. Pinching around U. Rumbling in transverse colon; in middle and lower A., and bursting of flatus; R. < lower A., during stool after 10 P.M., < in bed, still worse when lying on l. side, lasted till sleep.

Rectum and Anus.—(Hæmorrhoids.) Anus seems contracted during stool. The urging can easily be suppressed. Sudden urging, stool normal, full, then relief of whole condition.

Stool.—Several thin. Diarrhœa in morning; at night after eating peaches in evening; with sharp burning; D., with rumbling and emission of flatus; D., with sudden cessation of menses; copious, blackish, lumpy. Soft, copious. Copious, loose, after lunch at 2 P.M., later when driving griping in rectum and urging, resisted till 6 P.M., then loose stool, not copious, it seemed as if more were to come, but that there were an obstruction high up in rectum, before the stool sickish and faint, the urging less when driving than in warm room, after dinner another loose scanty stool, then all symptoms relieved. Constipation, with hæmorrhoids which itched and pained. Hard, at 10 P.M., an unusual time, with pinching in abdomen before and after it till sleep.

Urinary and Sexual Organs.—Urine copious, yellow, frothy; C., containing much albumen; U. high-colored, with burning in urethra during its passage. Sensation in genitals as after repeated coitus, without weakness. Prickings in pudenda. Menses ceased immediately till next morning on brisk walking.

Clinical.—Suppressed menstruation. Puerperal convulsions. Cerebral congestions during pregnancy.

Respiratory Organs.—Rattling of mucus in air-passages. Prickling in epiglottis. Constriction at top of larynx; C. in larynx, obliging swallowing; spasmodic C. in larynx and upper part of trachea. Undefined sensation in larynx and below it and in articulation of jaw. Cough from tickling in throat. Stertor. Dyspnœa; and loud mucous râles over whole chest. Breathing rapid; and the pause after it longer. Breathing oppressive and slow. Deep heavy B. Breathing superficial; with occasional deeper inspirations. Inclination to sigh; with short breath and oppression of chest. *Inclination to deep inspiration.*

Chest.—Sticking below sternum. Piercing inward above and below r. nipple. Occasional sharp catching pain under l. ribs. "Incipient headache" in l. Tension and frequent inclination to deep respiration. Oppression; causing deep, heavy respiration. *Constriction; and oppression*, with palpitation, compelling deep breathing. Tightness about lower part. Uneasiness. Sensation as if misfortune were impending. Sudden throbbing in waves from l. breast to head, < motion of head and change of position. Fulness; rising to head, throbbing in head and sensation as if skull were too small. Heat rising to face and head; with throbbing in vertex.

Heart.—Sound loud, strong and irregular. *Sticking on stooping.* Lancinations from region *to between shoulders.* Shocks, with pricking in hands and arms. *Sharp pains.* Pain, then heat; P., with contracted sensation; P. through to suprascapularis. Tension in cardiac region. Oppression, with heat in forehead. Anxiety in præcordial region; about H. evenings when lying, < lying on l. side, > lying on r. side, ceases after walking, with throbbing, a purring noise and intermittent pulse, necessity to lie with head high; A. after dinner when leaning back in chair. Heaviness and disagreeable feeling. *Fulness*, it seems as if it would rise to throat, and pulse decreased from 72 to 64. Heat. Weakness in præcordia. *Action rapid; with pulsations over whole body;* with nausea; labored A., with oppression and frequent pulse. *Palpitation; with heat in face and pulsations in tips of all fingers;* with fulness in hypochondrium. Contractions of H. and diaphragm slow.

Clinical.—Angina pectoris, with fluttering of the heart and violent beating as if it would burst the chest open, with labored breathing, pains radiating in all directions, even into the arms, with loss of power in the arm.

Pulse.—Rapid; on shaking head; *on walking; during headache;* after dinner and wine, and full; and hard; and full, throbbing; and intermittent; evening after lying down, and intermittent; and irregular, full; and full, hard, then slow; and small, compressed; and soft, small; then slow; then suddenly slow, then quick. *Full;* and jerking and soft. Bounding. Irregular; and full. Intermittent. Double. Slow; suddenly; and full; weak; then rapid, then slow again. Soft. Small and weak. Scarcely perceptible; then rapid, then small.

Neck.—*Cramp in nape*, in l. side in region of sixth and seventh cervical vertebræ, on throwing head back. Pain in nape; at night; on moving head; rising to occiput and then spreading upward; in cords of neck; tensive, extending deep into sides of neck; indescribable sensation in nape, verging on pain. *Constriction. Tightness.* Congestion. Sensation as if something moved from nape to head. Throbbing; extending to nape. Fulness in nape; in sides. Muscles weary from headache. Stiffness in nape; in l. side, with pain.

Back.—Acute pains afternoon and evenings, < region of lumbar vertebræ. Pain *down* spine; P. between shoulders; in sacrum in evening; in sacrum, with headache; in sacrum, > returning home, after supper, < going to bed, with nausea and thin stool.

Extremities.—Twitching. Pricking pains in arms and legs and cramp in r. leg. Pain > walking. Bloated feeling. Uneasiness, impelling him to rise as often as he sat down. Weariness, > towards night; W., with trembling; with heaviness; with pains in arms and tingling in fingers; in middle of arms and thighs. Falling asleep of those on which he lay at night. The feeling passed off with a whirling sensation. The first sensations went upward, then downward into arms and thence into knees.

Upper Extremities.—Stitch from l. shoulder to cardiac (?) orifice, then pain in stomach and nausea, > after eructation. Pain in l. shoulder; across shoulders, soon extending to arms, < on back of r. hand, at finger-end of third metacarpus. Drawing through shoulders. Arms drooping, could not be raised. Pain in bones of arms. Heaviness of A., with numbness; H. as if circulation were checked or as if going to sleep. Uneasiness of A. and hands. Weakness of A. and hands; l. arm, with *numbness* and with stiffness in middle joints of fingers. Pain in elbows, < r., in hollow between inner condyle of humerus and olecranon, where cubital nerve descends, l., then < r., similar pain in elbow but on exterior margin; P. in l. elbow, with weakness. Contracted sensation in r. elbow. Feeling in r. wrist as if tied up, causing lame feeling along arm. Trembling of hands, < r.; < l., with coolness; and of wrists. Prickling pain in hands and arms. Pain on inside of r. third finger, drawing to the bone, from metacarpus to first joint. Pulsation in finger-tips, causing trembling of hands and electrified sensation on taking hold of anything; P. in l. finger-tips.

Lower Extremities.—Twitching. Weariness after walking a few steps. Cracking in r. hip-joint when walking, then in r. knee; C. in r. hip and knee, then l. Thigh feels as if it would give way. Weakness of l. thigh and pain from buttocks to heel along ischiatic nerve, < calf; W. of l. thigh and leg, with numbness, which began to lessen from above downward, remained longest in foot, on lower half and outer side of tibia, at ankles and in toes. L. thigh asleep. Crackling in r. knee when walking. Sharp pain in l. knee. Pain under patella, not in tendon, but on both sides; P. under l. patella; in l. knee, with weakness; below knee; in calf; deep in l. calf. Legs go to sleep when sitting. Burning itching pain externally on r. heel, especially downward and inwardly.

Skin.—Dark blue. Rash on face after washing. Crawling on forehead; from head to tips of fingers, with sensation as from magneto-galvanic currents, then through whole body to soles. Itching on face; on back; on hands.

Sleep.—Yawning; with inclination to deep inspiration; with inclination to stretch backward; frequent. Sleepiness; at 2 P.M.; *with hot face and pallor.* Heavy sleep; in afternoon, but restless and unrefreshing. Sleep till 9 A.M. Difficult waking; and lids heavy. Early waking. Sleeplessness, waking with fear of apoplexy; S., with restlessness, thirst, heat and nausea. Restless sleep on account of pains. Dreams in morning; D. of people mowing grain and clover; D. of homesickness, moving him to tears, during the early sleep; wild, confused and unpleasant; of innumerable heads, with comical expression to the features, waking unrefreshed at 3 A.M., then after two hours sleep till morning.

Fever.—Cold sensation caused by congestion to head. Feeling as if a cold cloth were spread over brain. Feeling as if ice-water were poured over forehead near brows. Feeling as if there were cold sweat on forehead and temples, but there was not. Shuddering down back after stooping, then after continued walking flushes of heat. Cold limbs; feet.

Heat; *in flushes;* internal, with the headache. Weakly, warm sensation over whole body, < standing, > sitting, with flushes of heat to face and vertigo in forehead. *In head and face;* with headache; on top and in front, with fulness. *In head, < walking, with pain in forehead and throbbing in temples;* in head, with throbbing; *in H. in flushes, with* **pulsation in head**; rising towards H.; from above downward in H.; stinging burning in spots on head and < on neck, less on body, as from a caterpillar's hairs. In forehead; over F., with sweat; feeling as if warm water were trickling down inside of F. Of face; during palpitation; *in flushes,* with vertigo in forehead; < *about eyes;* in malar-bone and eye; r. cheek; itching, on l. cheek. From nape down back. Between shoulders. Warmth and fulness down arms, as if in cutaneous nerves, and in sciatic nerve, with warm aching in loins. Sudden glow in hands.

Sweat after sleep; S. after headache; from anxiety during headache; < *face and chest,* ameliorating symptoms; *on forehead;* on forehead during headache; on face; hands; palms; running in streams from head and limbs; clammy.

Gnaphalium.

A tincture is made of the entire fresh plant of Gnaphalium polycephalum, Michx.

Generalities.—Weak all the morning; in morning, and unrefreshed, after being awakened in the night; at night, perhaps from over-mental and physical effort during the day, with uneasiness; from diarrhœa.

Mind and Head.—Irritability after the diarrhœa. Headache from 3 to 4 P.M., with muddy feeling about head, not > smoking at 8 P.M., then night-sweat, headache, > bathing with bay rum. Morning on waking, fulness about temples like threatenings of nervous headache (which is periodic with him, usually after excessive smoking or mental effort or anxiety), > washing head with cold water. Pain in occiput. Vertigo, < rising from a recumbent position.

Eyes and Face.—Pain about r. eye in morning after rising. Intermittent shooting in eyeballs. Face bloated and expression heavy. Intermittent neuralgia in upper jaw.

Mouth.—Tongue covered with long white fur; furred and mouth dry at 7 A.M. Dryness at 2.30 A.M., and bad taste. "Furry" feeling in morning on waking, and bad taste, > washing with cold water.

Taste flat, sweetish, sickening; T. as after chewing slippery-elm bark.

Stomach and Abdomen. — Appetite diminished. Almost aversion to food after diarrhœa. Attacks of hiccough. Nausea all night, with pain in abdomen. Vomiting, with purging. Flatus in stomach, with windy eructations and nausea. Borborygmi, with frequent emission of flatus; B., with griping during the day, in the evening diarrhœic stool, with uneasiness in bowels till sleep. Pain in abdomen in morning, also with flatulence; P. in various parts of abdomen, abdomen sensitive to pressure, < region of cæcum. Weight in pelvis.

Stool.—Ineffectual attempt. Liquid, dark, offensive; L. and copious at night; three L., at night, with pain and nausea. Loose, pale. Diarrhœa, frequent; profuse D., with pain in abdomen all day; D. early in morning, again before noon, with pain and rumbling in abdomen, diminished urine, loss of appetite and taste. Early. Large, in afternoon after a good stool in morning. Constipation, preceded and followed by diarrhœa.

Urinary and Sexual Organs.—Bladder feels full and tense, even when just emptied. Urine copious, pale, inodorous, very free from sediment. Urine scanty. Frequent pain in region of prostate gland. Occasional stinging in glans. Erections mornings; waking at night, with desire. Desire increased.

Clinical.— Dysmenorrhœa, scanty menstruation, chocolate brown, with distress in pelvic region. Acne of the face, nodes under the skin, face mottled and menstruation scanty. Erythema around anus and genitals.

Chest and Back.—Pain in chest darting from side to side. Pain in kidneys. Numbness of lower part of back and lumbago.

Extremities.—Weakness of arms. Rheumatic pains in elbows; in knees and ankles. *Pain along the sciatic nerve* and its larger ramifications. *Numbness occasionally takes the place of the sciatica, and then walking is very fatiguing* (Phyto.). Cramp in calves; in feet, < in bed. Gouty pains in great toes.

Clinical.—Sciatica, intense pains extending to ramifications of the nerve, with feeling of numbness, the numbness sometimes alternating with the pains; these pains extend into the toes; Gnap. has cured rheumatoid pain confined to the toe.

Gossypium.

A tincture is made of the fresh inner bark of the root of the cotton plant, Gossypium herbaceum, L.

General Action.—It is said to be a powerful emmenagogue and commonly used by negroes at the South to produce abortion. It seems to arrest uterine hæmorrhage.

Generalities.—The pains are stinging, drawing, tearing and sometimes burning, extending from one place to another, jumping from one place to another, and from one limb to the opposite one. The pains generally take a downward direction. Uneasiness, with anxiety and sighing. Lassitude, with pains as if beaten. Amelioration after breakfast.

Head.—Aching. Stinging from forehead to vertex. Drawing pain over eyes, with stinging in pupils. Pain from temporal bones to middle of frontal bone, first drawing, then stinging. Knocking pain in r. parietal bone.

Nose, Mouth and Throat.—Nostrils swollen and inflamed, < l. Taste as of rotten eggs. Tonsils swollen, < r.

Stomach and Abdomen.—Nausea and salivation; N. before breakfast. Rotating pain in pit of stomach. Sticking in r. hypochondrium, then drawing pain from hypochondria to pit of stomach. Intermittent pains in hypochondria.

Urinary and Sexual Organs.—Frequent desire to urinate, with burning pain. Intermittent stinging in ovarian region, with drawing towards uterus. Swelling of outer part of labia, < l., the outer skin of both studded with pale, somewhat reddish granules. Menses watery and nineteen days late.

Clinical.—Valuable for retention of placenta after miscarriage. Menstrual headaches. Tumor of the breast, with hard lumps, scanty menstruation, swelling of the glands of the axilla, inflammation of the lymphatics running towards the axilla. Morning sickness of pregnancy, with sensitiveness over the uterine region, with great prostration and faintness. Suppressed menstruation. Sterility.

Back and Extremities.—Pain in back. Tearing in r. arm and hand. Heaviness of hands, > hanging down, < warmth of bed. Pain jumping from one finger to another. Twitching from hips to knees. Tearing from lower part of r. thigh to instep, then jumping over to l. leg. Drawing pain in knee-caps and from calves to ankles. Twitching changing from one leg to the other. Trembling of legs when standing, > sitting or lying. Sensation as if the marrow were being squeezed out of the bones of legs. Drawing pain from above downward in legs; in r. shin-bone from knee to ankle. Weariness of legs, < ascending stairs, > lying, with crushed feeling. Contracting pain in l. foot, < motion, > rest.

Skin. — Soft tumor between l. thigh and vulva, secreting a watery fluid, with sticking, < at night. Soreness between thighs and vulva, with watery secretion. Pale red, itching papules on backs of hands, with watery exudation after scratching. Round dark red, itching spots, with pale red circles, around knee-caps and over shin-bones, burning after scratching. Crawling in all fingers as from the moving of worms. Itching of the whole skin; I. in round spots around l. ankle.

Sleep and Fever.—Sleep a great part of the time. External coldness, with internal heat.

Granatum.

A tincture is made of the dried bark of the root of Punica Granatum, L. (Pomegranate).

General Action.—An ancient vermifuge, especially for tape-worm. The alkaloid, Pelletierine, is particularly valuable for this purpose, but large doses cause paralysis, especially of the oculo-motor nerves, with vertigo, acting similarly to Gelsemium.

Allies.—Gelsem., Verat. alb.

Generalities. — Emaciation. Laxity of muscles. Tremulousness in morning (Gelsem.). Rush of blood to upper part of body, head and chest. *Discomfort and nausea. Weakness;* in morning on rising after good sleep; with heat in hands; *could scarcely keep upright* (Gelsem.); sleepy, with confused pain in forehead, as after a night's debauch. Better after dinner.

Clinical.—Jaundiced complexion, with bloated abdomen, eructations of watery fluid and vomiting, with vertigo, waving before eyes, large pupils, feeling as of something moving in the stomach, palpitation, faintness (Gelsem.).

Mind.—Hallucination. Excited easily; excitement and weakness of mind, tranquility and persistency. Anger changing to insults. Sensitiveness. Sad. Hypochondriac. Discouraged. Inclined to criticise and blame. Dread of work, with headache. Confusion. Stupefaction.

Head.—Sticking on moving; S. through brain. Pain in whole brain when walking, < forehead; P. in brain, extending into l. occipital protuberance. Heaviness; with dread of work; with red face, rapid pulse and weakness. Confusion. Vertigo in morning on rising; V. after stool; on reading, reflecting and mental labor; with vomiting; like a dimness before eyes (Gelsem.); in attacks, with obscured vision, roaring in ears and trembling of hands. Frontal sticking; outward; beneath l. eminence. Pressure in sinciput during stool. Frontal pain, with shivering; pain in l. eminence; F. pain extending towards temples, with tearing, then becoming a tearing outward; F. pain so that she could scarcely look up; stupefying pain in frontal sinuses and upper jaw. Frontal heaviness. Tearing in r. temple; extending into r. eye. Pressure in l. temple. Heavy pain in vertex. *Tearing in r. side of head.* Tearing jerking in r. side. Pressure in occiput, with hot ears.

Eyes.—Inflamed as in catarrh. Surrounded by pale blue dirty rings. Tearing in r., which is red and swimming in tears. Dryness and burning. Yellow sclerotics. Pupils dilated; and sluggish; contracted. Opening of the lids contracted. Jerking of r. lid. Burning of canthi, with redness. Itching of inner canthi; burning I. in outer canthi. Vision dim; V. weak.

Ears.—Sticking in l.; S. outward, < l. Tearing in l.; sticking T. outward in l. at night. Cramplike pain. *Ringing;* in front of l. Roaring before ears.

Nose.—Pinching as if in mucous cavities, extending from root into r. zygomatic region. *Itching-crawling and tickling in nose.* Heat within. Dryness of mucous membrane. Catarrh alternately dry and fluent.

Face.—Red; and hot, with sparkling eyes, heaviness of forehead and oppression of chest. Earthly, sickly color. Stupid expression. Tearing in l. half. Pinching in l. side. R. cheek feels swollen. Jaw cracked painfully when chewing, as if dislocated; tearing in joints, < l., with tension and pinching; pinching in l. ramus; numbness. Lips dry; biting of lips, then burning; burning on " crown " of lower.

Mouth.—Stitches in incisors at night in bed. Drawing in incisors, then stitches. Tearing throbbing pain in upper hollow molar. Toothache in morning on rising. Incisors pain as if numb and sore. Teeth feel too long on biting anything hard. Tongue coated; white, and moist. (Moderate dryness of tongue, with feeling of " adstriction " of papillæ.) Tenacious mucus, with need of constant spitting. *Salivation;* watery. Taste altered; at one time acute, at another blunted; sweetish, flat, with salivation, nausea and pain in abdomen.

Throat.—Hawking of mucus; bloody, from choanæ. Tough mucus in choanæ, causing sensation of a lump. Tearing, extending to arms and fingers. (Contraction.)

Stomach.—*Unusual hunger* (Verat. a.); (in morning in bed). Craving for a variety of things; C. for fruit (Verat. a.); for juicy or sour things. Appetite at one time diminished, at another ravenous. *Loss of appetite.* Aversion to eating. Craving for coffee, which tastes unusually good. Thirst for water in evening, with heat of skin, and especially hot forehead. Want of thirst.

Eructations; after liquid food; < after potatoes; loud; of air; offensive, after fat food; of liquids; (of watery substances, < fasting). *Nausea; with pain in abdomen; with salivation, frequent spitting, pain in stomach and abdomen, fermenting in abdomen, frequent ineffectual urging to stool, chilliness, sickly look and ill humor* (Verat. a.); with threatenings of diarrhœa; with pain and fermentation in abdomen, then diarrhœa; with shivering, cold hands and hot forehead; with confusion of head. Loud retching. *Vomiting; with diarrhœa* (Verat. a.); with trembling; with anxiety; with weakness and sweat.

Epigastric region distended and sensitive. Fulness of pit. Sticking. Cramp in morning fasting. Contractive pain, and in small intestines. Pressure in pit and on chest; P. in pit, and sick feeling. Burning in pit and in abdomen.

Abdomen.—Distention and pain, with ravenous hunger. Emission of flatus. Frequent flatulence. Movements of flatus; M. as from diarrhœa. *Wanderings like urging to stool. Griping;* then two soft stools. Cramp before menses, with dragging from small of back to genitals. *Pain; after every meal;* < morning fasting; > drinking cold water; > external warmth and lying down; *with diarrhœa;* flatulent; crawling, which was a sticking towards præcordium. *Drawing like urging to stool.* Sensitiveness. Anxiety.

Navel distended to a ball, like umbilical hernia. Sticking to l. side of umbilicus, as from suppuration. Griping about U. Twisting in umbilical region and stomach. *Dragging in groins as if a hernia would protrude from both sides;* D. towards groins; almost painful dragging towards goins, with swelling of the parts; D. in pelvis, with heaviness. Drawing inflammatory pain in r. groin, < touch.

Rectum.—Sticking when sitting. Pressure. Sensation in R. and anus as if something alive were moving about. Itching and tickling. Heat after diarrhœa. Desire for stool. Tenesmus, with protrusion of anus during the usual stool. Ineffectual urging.

Anus.—Protrusion like a ring during stool. Hæmorrhoids protrude during stool. Sticking in evening. Proctalgia. *Itching frequently during the day, with tickling.*

Stool.—Diarrhœa; *frequent;* mucous. Liquid, two within an hour. Frequent. Profuse, with much flatulence. Delayed and insufficient (later action).

Urinary Organs.—Urethra, discharge of mucus, a kind of blennorrhœa; inflammation and swelling; cutting and sticking; cutting in evening after lying down with smarting in it and with relaxed penis; cutting, after micturition; burning drawing extending from spongy part into glans.

Sexual Organs.—Excitement. Painful dragging towards genitals and uterus. *Yellow leucorrhœa.* Menstruation too early and profuse, with griping in abdomen and dragging in small of back, extending to genitals.

Chest.—*Sticking;* in r.; l.; middle; < walking, not influenced by breathing; rheumatic drawing S. in pleura, now here, now there. Cramp in pectoralis major, stitches extending towards axilla. Pain in r.; in l. and in spine at insertion of diaphragm. *Oppression, with sighing;* O., with weakness of lower limbs on ascending steps. Heaviness like suffocation, then palpitation. Pressure upon C.; P. outward through sternum. Tension in l., beginning below ribs and gradually extending higher, with pinching and intermitting stitches. Pinching contraction in muscles about r. nipple. Feeling of catarrh.

Heart.—Sensitiveness of præcordial region. *Palpitation* on least exertion.

Neck and Back.—Rheumatic pain in nape and throat, making stooping difficult. Pain in loins; on occurrence of menstruation; as if beaten; as if sprained, < sitting. Dragging from loins to anus. Weight in loins.

Extremities.—Weariness and heaviness preventing sleep. *Bruised pain in shoulders and between them, as after a heavy load, even the clothing is oppressive;* B. pain in r. shoulder as far as axilla, < raising arm. Arms, tearing, extending forward; boring extending to fingers; rheumatic pains; paralytic drawing; *paralytic weakness; paralyzed feeling* (Gelsem.); could scarcely be raised. Tearing in ulna at wrist; in radius at wrist; cramplike T. in r. forearm. Periodic drawing in r. forearm, > external warmth. Tearing in wrists. Rheumatic pain in l. wrist. Sticking in second joint of thumb. Tearing in fingers, with stiffness; T., so that she could not hold anything; T. in last phalanges, < ring finger; in first joint of thumb. *Rheumatic pain in all finger-joints.* Paralytic stiffness of F.

Lower Extremities.—Special withering. Sticking in l. hip when walking. Pain in hips; as if injured. Sticking in l. knee. Tearing in knee; l. Paralytic drawing in knee, with heaviness, hindering walking. *Legs weak, < walking;* W., with uneasiness, leaden heaviness, he feels better sitting with legs resting upon sofa. Sticking in l. ankle. Sprained pain in l. ankle in evening, hindering walking. Pain in corns.

Skin.—Pimples on forehead and l. temple, with sore pain, they suppurate and leave nodules. Formication down arms. Itching biting between middle and ring fingers and between ring and little fingers, with red, hot hands; I. biting on balls of thumbs, they become bluish-red, hot and swollen, with distended veins, which form a bluish-mottled swelling, as after freezing. Itching on forehead and eyebrow; *in palms, with biting; in various places on face and whole body, as if pimples would break out;* on back of hands as if an eruption would break out; scraping I. on cheeks; burning I. about anus, on nates, perineum, scrotum and hairy parts of genitals, extending thence over almost the whole body, < thick parts of thighs.

Sleep.—Yawning; with filling of eyes with water; with stretching; violent, with stretching, sleepiness and creeping chills from hips to calves. Sleepy early in evening. Falls asleep late. Screaming in sleep at night. Unsound S. Uneasy S. *Night full of dreams. Numerous and varied dreams, so that she cannot remember them in the morning.* Dreams immediately if he only slumbers, cries out and awakes.

Fever.—Chilliness, < forenoon, but heat in evening; C., < arms, with sweat in palms. Shivering; about l. side; over scalp, the hair stands on end; over scalp in open air, and in lower limbs, with paralytic drawing in r. thigh; over l. hip and abdomen, with pain in l. side of forehead.

Intolerance of warmth in evening, desire for cold. Heat, with rapid, hard pulse; H., < legs, she must keep them out of bed. General heat on getting into bed, with dry tongue, without thirst. General dry heat. H. in forehead in evening. H. of face; in evening; during diarrhœa; during stool; of r. cheek, with bluish redness, also with swelling, itching, tension and crawling as if frozen. Sweat on slightest motion.

Graphites.

Purified Graphite ("Black Lead") is triturated as directed in the Pharmacopœias.

General Action.—A profound tissue remedy (like all the Carbons), showing a particular tendency to develop a cutaneous phase of internal disorders.

Allies.—Carbo v., Carb. an., Carb. sulf., Petrol., Nat. m., Sil., Nit. ac., Sep., Puls., Lyc.

Generalities. — *Emaciation.* Swelling of feet and cheeks during menstruation. Trembling in morning; T. and twitching in head, neck and r. arm. Jerking in all limbs, now in one, now in another, even in shoulder and scrotum. Constant tossing about at night without weariness. Inclination to stretch and yawn, without ability to stretch enough. Stitches here and there in whole body; S. downward through whole body. Shocks through whole body as from fright or electric shocks. Intermittent cramplike sensation in various parts, arms, neck, fingers, feet, whereupon the parts are swollen, red, indurated and sensitive to touch. Intermittent pain here and there, then soreness of the part on touch. Pain pressive rather than drawing, now here, now there, in periosteum of bones, during rest, < falling asleep. Pains return on beginning to walk. Bruised pain in whole side of body on which he lies in midday nap, and arm is asleep.

Drawing tension, < arms and trunk. *Drawing in whole body* in morning after rising, as in intermittent fever. *Oppression;* with anxiety and unpleasant sensation in stomach. Dread of open air in morning. Takes cold easily and has headache therefrom. Sensitiveness to draught of air in evening, with hoarseness, chilliness, dryness of nose and anxiety. General sick feeling; with necessity to groan without knowing for what pain. Uneasiness, > walking in open air, with no thought for his work, no inclination for anything. *Tremulous sensation through whole body. Pulsation of blood in whole body,* < heart, < motion; P. in heart, trunk and head in morning in bed. Indolence of whole body, > a long walk. **Weakness of whole body** as from catarrh; W. in forenoon and towards evening, with sleepiness and much yawning; after dinner, with falling asleep; on walking in open air; after coition; *with sleepiness; sudden;* even to sinking down during and after walking in open air, with retching and nausea; faintlike, when walking in open air, as if beginning in abdomen. Attacks of faintness. Symptoms disappear when walking in open air.

Clinical.—Chlorosis, with tendency to rush of blood to head and flushing of the face (Fer., which is contained in Grap.), menses pale, scanty and delayed, profuse leucorrhœa, pimply eruption on the face, worse at the menstrual period, constipation. A general tendency to get fat (Calc.); the obesity of Grap. is more particularly seen in older people, that of Calc. in children. Herpetic constitution, with a great variety of complaints. Paralytic symptoms, especially with suppression of menses, with numbness and coldness of arms and hands.

Mind.—Sadness, with thoughts of nothing but death (Nat. m.). **Despondency,** *she must weep.* **Apprehension and inclination to weep,** *in attacks;* A. > weeping. *It frequently seemed as if his end were near or misfortune* *impending. Grief at trifles, even to despair.* Anxiety till lying down in evening; A., with headache, vertigo and ill humor; with haste, driving him about like an evil-doer; so that she trembled; so that she cannot sit, with nausea and sweat; preventing sleep all night; in evening, as if a misfortune had happened, with heat of face and coldness of hands and feet. Weeping in evening without cause; W. at trifles; at music; in a child, with fretfulness. *Fretful;* and uneasy; and violent in morning, hypochondriac in afternoon. Hypochondriac uneasiness, discouragement, anxious sweat, loss of sleep. Easily angered, but it just as easily passed out of her mind. Would rather be alone, irritated by every disturbance. Indisposed, frightened, (nervous). *Timid. Easily excited,* hot hands even from speaking. *Hesitation.* Slowness of purpose and thought. Loss of inclination to work. Lively in morning, depressed in evening. Laughing at every trifle in forenoon, inclined to grieve and cry in evening. *Absent-minded.* Beclouded. Incapable of mental work after midday nap. Mistakes in talking and writing. Forgetful. Fancies at night. Fixed idea at night, so that he could not sleep before midnight. Thinking of all sorts of things at night, so that she slept little.

Head.—Tearing like rheumatism in morning. *Aching; every morning on waking;* in morning on waking, with vomiting, diarrhœa, cold sweat, faintness, necessity to lie two days on account of weakness, with alternation of chill and heat; on moving head; during and after eating; when riding; *during menstruation, with eructations and nausea;* during menstruation, < evening; with nausea, as from abdomen; here and there in brain, at last behind l. ear; **A. as if numb and pithy**; A. in morning as if she had not slept enough. **Constriction, < occiput,** *extending to nape, which pains as if broken on looking up,* at noon, afterwards the pain extends down back and to chest. Feeling as if screwed together and full. Bruised pain in evening, with general sick feeling. Drawing pain extending into face and to neck. Tensive pain on waking, < surface of brain, < occiput, with painful stiffness of neck, the P. < trying to sleep. Sharp drawing tension in nerves of brain.

Confusion in morning; with nausea and sour vomiting. Stupidity mornings. Weakness extending to throat. Emptiness after midday meal. Orgasm in afternoon, with compressive pain in vertex; frequent O. during the day, with heat in it and sweat. Brain feels loose. Feeling as if intoxicated. Vertigo; *in morning on waking;* in evening, with stupefaction and necessity to lie down; in evening on walking, with reeling; *during and after stooping,* even to falling forward, with nausea; on looking up; in attacks, with inclination to fall forward; inclination to V., with reeling, loss of sense, shivering and chilliness.

Forehead.—Tearing in morning on waking; in afternoon, with internal heat; pain as if torn from morning after rising till towards noon. Pain in morning after rising, < motion; in morning when half asleep, and in vertex, > when completely awake; P. extending deep into brain. Bursting pain after eating. Smarting pain on touch. Drawing pain, with pain in nape as if stiff. Drawing, then in occiput in evening; intermittent D. Pressure outward after eating. Confusion, with contractive sensation. Throbbing. Feeling as if wrinkled.

Sticking in l. temple; in temples, extending through eyes to internal canthi, if he looks intently at anything white or red. Pain in l. temple; sharp P. in the temple upon which he does not lie in morning. Sticking in sides of vertex towards middle from morning till 3 P.M. as if head would burst, > sweat in heat of sun. Tearing in r. side in evening. Painful shocks in r. side. Jerking pain in r. side. One-sided pain in morning in bed, > rising, with nausea; pain at night in side upon which he was not lying. Intermittent throbbing in r. side. *Pain in occiput;* with heaviness of head, tension and stiffness of nape, the pains < walking, > lying, disappearing at night.

Scalp.—**Scales causing itching and becoming a scurf, which disappears on washing and then is humid. Scurfy spot on vertex, with sore pain on touch. Eruption on vertex, painful to touch and humid.** *Humid eruption, with suppurative pain on touch.* Old scabs come off and have an offensive odor. **Falling of hair** (Nit. ac., Sep., Sul.). Hair becomes gray. Hair tangled (Borax.). Pain and moisture beneath scurfy spots. Sore pain. Coldness and spasmodic contraction. *Itching.*

Clinical.—Eczema of the head, glutinous moisture and moist scabs. Moist eruption on the scalp, matting the hair (Borax.). Tinea capitis, with dry eruption. Porrigo decalvans. Violent semilateral headaches during suppression of menses, with numbness, constipation, etc., or in the same trouble congestion of the head, with feeling of heat.

Eyes.—Redness; *of white, with lachrymation and photophobia;* with inflammation, drawing and pressive pain, then biting lachrymation. Hardened mucus. Maturating, with pressure in them and drawing pain extending into head. Sticking in r. *Biting.* Drawing pain. *Pain* morning and evening; P. on opening as from exertion by reading. *Weakness. Burning;* in morning; in evening light; when writing, with double vision of letters; with dim vision; with pus in canthi; with lachrymation in open air. *Lachrymation; in sunlight;* on walking in open air, with closure of eyes as from sleepiness. Pressure in r. brow, extending through eye.

Lids.—**Dry mucus on lashes. Inflammation of margins** (Sep.); **I. of external canthus.** *Stye on lower, with drawing pain before discharge of pus.* Swelling of lids and lachrymal glands. *Agglutination in morning. Dryness and pressure. Heaviness.* Inclination to draw lids together in external canthus. Paralytic pain. *Heat;* in evening on reading and in morning, with dryness. Burning biting in inner canthus. Itching of inner canthus. Twitching beneath eyes.

Vision.—*Vanishes during menstruation, l. hand becomes dead, with crawling extending up arm and with crawling in lips. Photophobia. Blinded by the light;* B. on looking at a white object, and lachrymation. Eyes affected by daylight, not by candle-light. Foggy. Short. Fiery zigzags around border of field in evening. All sorts of images on closing eyes at night.

Clinical.—Ulceration of the cornea. Pustules on the cornea and conjunctiva. In the numerous cases of pustules on the cornea and conjunctiva there is usually photophobia, a thin, rather acrid discharge from the eyes and nose, with soreness of the outer corners of the eyes, which are usually cracked. Chronic ciliary blepharitis, edges of the lids swollen, inclined to crack and ulcerate; formation of dry scurf in the lashes, with burning, dryness and itching. Tumors of the lids (compare Staph.). The tumors calling for Grap. are more apt to be situated directly in the margin of the lid.

Ears.—**Moist and sore places behind both** (see Petrol.); **M. on ears.** *Swelling of glands beneath ears, with tensive pain* (Bar. c.); S. of a gland beneath r.; S. within l. *Bloody discharge.* Redness and heat. Ulceration of l. helix. *Sticking;* in l. in evening after eating. Tearing in r. Twinging pain in middle. Frequent ulcerative pain in l. *Sensation of a hard body behind,* on turning head to l. L. feels full of water. Tightness about l. Itching in l. in evening. Sensation in r. on every step as if a valve were opening and closing. Pulsation, < stooping and after eating; P. in morning slower than pulse. Frequent sensation and report as if bubbles burst. Bubbling on stooping, with heaviness of head, on becoming erect or leaning back the B. returns as if something fell before ear and again away from it. Flapping on every eructation as if air were forced through Eustachian tube.

Screaming tone in evening in bed, shooting through all limbs. Hissing all day. Ringing in l., then roaring. *Humming. Roaring; at night* (at the full moon), with stoppage in ears at times; and rushing; then crackling, then more acute hearing. Thundering rolling. Rushing noise during coition. Creaking; *on moving jaws,* but only in morning in bed; in evening on eating; in r. on moving head; in l. on swallowing. Hardness of hearing, > riding in a wagon.

Clinical.—Eczema of the outer ear, purulent discharge; deafness, consequent upon catarrh of the middle ear, with feeling as if a membrane covered the ear, or with a sensation of valves opening and shutting, and cracking on swallowing, especially with eruptions behind the ears, which crack and ooze. Deafness after scarlet fever, with thin offensive discharge from the ears and moist eczema on the face around the ear. Eczema behind the ears, the skin cracks and bleeds.

Nose.—Redness. Black comedones. Papules in l. nostril, itching, then burning. **Soreness on blowing** (Sil., Aur.). **Pain internally;** *ulcerative P. in r. nostril.* Tension within. Stuffed and contracted sensation. Stoppage, yet discharge of clear water. Itching inside. Burning suddenly in a spot on l. side.

Catarrh; with headache and alternations of chill and heat; with tickling rawness, causing cough, with weakness and headache; *stopped, with nausea, headache and necessity to lie down;* stopped, with confusion of head, oppression of chest, heat of forehead and face, < about nose, and loss of smell. Fluent catarrh; with frequent sneezing; with nosebleed; with frequent sneezing, pain in submaxillary gland and sensitiveness of uncovered parts to open air; with headache, chill, internal dry heat and thirst; and profuse, with oppression of chest, head confused and hot, little air in nose. Scurf in nose, with pain. *Offensive, purulent discharge* (Hep., Puls.). *Offensive mucus.* Profuse mucus, at one time thin, at another thick and yellowish. Tough white mucus in l. nostril, difficult to discharge. *Blowing out of bloody mucus. Blowing out of blood* (Carbo v., Carb. an.). *Sneezing, with dry nose. Bleeding;* in morning (Carbo v.); *at* 10 P.M., *after rush of blood to head and heat of face;* evenings, with palpitation, heat and pain in back; at night. Urinous odor and exhalations from nose and mouth. **Smell acute, she cannot tolerate flowers.** Smell in nose as in old catarrh; S. in morning as from burning soot; at night as from burning hair mingled with sulphur fumes.

Clinical.—Nasal catarrh, frequently with dryness of the nose, but great soreness, with formation of scabs, a kind of ozæna, with bad odor, the nostrils externally are ulcerated, cracked in the corners and bleeding. Eczema about the nose and mouth, with cracks in the corners of the lips and wings of the nose.

Face.—*Pallor;* with blue rings around eyes; sudden, after moderate excitement, as, for example, reading. Yellow, and eyes weak, as if exhausted. Swelling of l. side in morning after rising; a kind of cystic swelling of cheek; S. of glands beneath chin. Twitching of masseter muscles. *Tearing in l. zygoma in evening in bed.* **Sensation of a cobweb** (Bar. ac.). Pain alternately in all bones. Pain in masseter muscles as if paralyzed, so that she cannot close jaws when eating. Incipient paralysis of l. side after swelling of it, and toothache, r. muscles of face suddenly distorted, mouth drawn to r. side, its motion and speech impaired, l. eye often closed involuntarily, while the r. could not be completely closed. Sticking tearing in l. lower jaw. Drawing pain in l. upper jaw.

Lips.—Eruption; **eruption in corners** (Lyc., Sep., Sul.). **Lips and nostrils sore and cracked, as from cold** (Nat. m., Puls.). *Cracking of lower* (Nat. c.). Pimples on upper, itching, then burning; white P. on upper; hard, white P. on a red base, in corners of mouth, under lips, with itching. L. corner ulcerated; scaly, painless ulcer in each corner. Vesicles on upper, with cutting; V. on vermilion border of l. lower, which rub off on washing, but form anew. Twitching of upper. Sticking through upper in evening. Sore pain in l. corner. Burning in lower, with heaviness. Dryness.

Clinical.—Erysipelas of the face, with ulcers about the nose and mouth. Moist eczema of the face.

Mouth.—Teeth. Erosion in cavities. Black, acrid blood from hollow. *Sticking;* jerking; jerking in a hollow molar on walking in open air; burning, in a l. upper molar after eating. Tearing in a root; T. in all, < warmth, renewed on lying down in bed, so that there was no rest till midnight. Aching all night; A. in all and in jaws at night, renewed during the day by chewing or biting; A. in r. molars on biting them tightly together; < *night, with heat in face,* or in evening, with sore pain on palate and swelling of cheek; < touch. *Drawing pain;* in a hollow T.; in molars when walking in wind. Sore pain on eating, < after eating. Crawling pain, and on taking cold water, sticking. Pain in lower on chewing, as from looseness. Burning pain as from looseness, now in one, now in another, < night in bed, or in evening when sitting leaning backward, with salivation, the pain < chewing.

Gum.—Offensive odor, and from mouth. *Swelling;* in evening; with dryness of mouth; painful, with swelling of cheek and general weakness; painful, over upper teeth, as if sore even when touched by cheek, with pain in corresponding back teeth, as if cheek would swell. Bleeding easily on rubbing. Pain, with sore sensation on palate and running of water from mouth. *Sore pain on inner side,* as after eating hot things; S. pain on upper incisors on touch of tongue. Ulcerative pain. Rush of blood. Itching gnawing.

Tongue.—**Burning blisters on lower side and tip** (Nat. m., N. ac., Lyc.). *Whitish, painful ulcer on under side.* Painful pimples and blisters on back, < eating and on spitting, also at times bleeding. White. Sore pain on l. side on moving or extending it. Feeling rough, raw and scraped after eating, and papillæ sensitive, as if rubbed against teeth.

Sticky mucus in morning; salt, burning mucus in morning on waking. *Saliva runs from mouth in morning on stooping. Spitting much saliva.* Running of S. from mouth, with swelling of upper-lip and painful pimples upon it, with painful gum and sore palate. Green bitter S. coming from mouth mornings after drinking or after eating. M. and throat dry at night. Offensive smell; sourish.

Taste.—*Bitter, with sour eructations* (Puls., Sep.); B. in afternoon; B., with coated tongue; B. to food. As of bad eggs in morning after rising. Salt. Sour, < eating and drinking; S. after breakfast; S., with no desire to drink. Difficult to describe, causing shuddering.

Throat.—*Glands in side down to shoulder are swollen and painful on bending neck to one side or lying upon it, as if tense or stiff* (Bar. c., Calc. c.); submaxillary glands swollen and painful on touch, and neck stiff; r. submaxillary gland inflamed and swollen, afterwards indurated and desquamating. Pain in submaxillary glands. Swelling of tonsils, with pain on swallowing. Much mucus low down; much M., which he must expectorate by hawking. Hawking of mucus, with dryness of palate from talking.

Cramp, obliging retching, as if food would not go down; C., with nausea. Sticking in morning on rising, with pressure; S. when not swallowing; on swallowing, with ulcerative pain and retching; on swallowing, with retching and dryness posteriorly in l. side of throat, on palate; sudden jerking S. low in r. side, only on moving neck, when talking, on stooping and then rising up, not on swallowing. Pinching. Feeling as if sewed together, with scraping in it. Scraping; mornings on waking, with dryness behind arch of palate, > detachment of adherent mucus; provoking dry cough. Rawness; on speaking; with scraping soreness. Pressure in region of pit as if satiated or as if he had swallowed too large a morsel. Pain as from swelling of glands. *Sensation of a lump on swallowing, with scraping in it; sensation of a lump on swallowing and < empty swallowing, constrictive retching from œsophagus up to larynx.* Feeling as of a growth or adherent mucus, so that on attempting to swallow anything small it stuck in this place. Burning as if everything were sore, preventing speaking aloud. Sensation as before coryza.

Clinical.—Chronic sore throat, with a feeling of swollen gland or swollen tonsils (Bar. c.).

Stomach.—Appetite increased; for meat at suppertime. Ravenous hunger, and after eating nausea and vertigo; R., with acidity in stomach. Little appetite for warm food. A. lost in evening. **Sweet things are disgusting and nauseous. Aversion to animal food** (Mur. ac., Petr., Sul.) *when thinking of it,* but it tastes tolerably when eating it, but bread tastes bitter; *A. to salt food;* to meat and fish. Thirst in morning; T. after eating. Desire for beer, without remarkable thirst, only desire for its internal cooling.

Many eructations, *tasting of food* (Puls., Sep., Sul.); E. all day, with nausea and loss of appetite; at night of the soup taken at noon; *ineffectual;* of mucus in morning; sour, of food. Waterbrash; at night in bed. Hiccough in morning after rising and after dinner; in evening; after every meal; after a meal, with dull head or sleepiness.

Nausea; *in morning during menstruation, with weakness and trembling during the day;* in morning after rising; mornings after rising, with dizziness as from obscuration of eyes and pallor, he thinks he will fall when walking; at noon, with aversion to beef-broth; after midday meal; in afternoon, with running of water from mouth; at night, with faintness; from food; before supper, without inclination to vomit; before, during and after eating, with tolerably good appetite, then vomiting of water and salivation; *with griping in stomach and constant spitting; as from abdomen, < morning and for several hours after eating, with contractive pain below umbilicus and much mucus in throat;* faintlike in evening, preventing sleep; faintlike as if from l. hypochondrium. Vomiting in afternoon after a walk of two hours, with great nausea, chilliness and sudden weariness; *V. of all food* (Ferr., Nux v.); V. immediately of midday meal, without nausea, with sickly aching in pit of stomach; V., with griping all day.

Sticking, and in bowels; in pit, with throbbing. **Constrictive pain.** Cramp from œsophagus to umbilicus after eating. Griping in forenoon, > eating. Gnawing before dinner; G. after eating. *Pain all day, > lying and warmth of bed, returning on rising; P. in pit all forenoon, > eructations;* in pit at night and in morning; after eating, > drinking; in pit; in r. side, > frequent eructations; *with necessity to vomit;* with oppression and anxiety; like ravenous hunger from morning till afternoon. *Insipid and spoiled sensation, with good appetite.* Heartburn; rancid; rancid, after a meal. Burning before eating, obliging him to eat; B. after eating, with heaviness of body and ill humor; B., then general heat, then sweat. Fermentation, then emission of flatus, then pressure, drawing and sticking alternating in body, then weakness of eyes. Coldness and emptiness.

Clinical.—Gastralgia, > eating (compare Petrol.), but the colic lower down in the abdomen comes on immediately after eating, < below umbilicus. Indigestion, with feeling of rancidity and heartburn. Complaints from fat food (compare Petrol. and Pul.). Gastralgia coming on some hours after eating, > warm milk, < cold drinks. Chronic gastric catarrh.

Abdomen.—**Distention** (Carb. v., Lyc., etc.); *on eating;* after eating; after eating, with sourish, astringent taste; < eating, with sensitiveness to pressure; *with heaviness; with rush of blood to head, heaviness of head, vertigo and confusion;* and in stomach, with loss of appetite and constipation; **as from incarceration of flatus,** *intolerance of anything tight about hypochondria.* Tympanites after stool, with uneasiness and griping. *Tense;* with diarrhœa. *Rumbling;* in morning; during noon meal; after drinking; with griping between umbilicus and l. hypochondrium. Croaking like frogs. Almost involuntary emission of flatus; frequent offensive flatus (Carb. v., Sul.).

Jerking. Cramplike pain at night, with absence of urine. Cutting in morning, with several stools; C. on walking in open air; C. and burning. *Griping always before emission of flatus;* G. < region of cæcum; by jerks, with thirst without appetite. Burrowing. Dragging during menstruation, with labor-pains, pain in back, anxious pain in small of back, beginning with tickling, with eructatations and then jerking-sticking toothache. Colic in morning, then diarrhœa, then consistent stool; C. after eating; after emission of flatus; one day before and two days during menstruation, with heat in abdomen; > pressure. Flatulent colic when walking; during excitement of genitals, hindering coition. Drawing pain at night, with desire for stool, but without diarrhœa. *Intolerance of anything tight after eating* (Lyc., Carb. v.).

Upper.—**Pain** *as if everything would be torn to pieces during menstruation.* Sticking in r. hypochondrium in morning after rising; in l. H. on motion; in r., extending to back; in hypochondria, obliging him to lie down; in hepatic region. Acute pain in hepatic region after breakfast so that she must lie down. Pain in region of spleen. Tension in hypochondria as from a band, with oppression of chest; T. in hypochondria, extending deep into lower abdomen. *Burning in l. H.* when sitting, > motion. Beating beneath short ribs at night on waking.

Jerking in side. Gurgling in r. side, extending into limbs, as from softly falling drops. Sticking in l. Burning in a spot in l. Constrictive griping about umbilicus, with cutting, then natural stool.

Hypogastrium.—*Sudden flatulence passing painfully towards ring;* flatus < side, with rumbling. Fulness, < evening and night, with hardness and sensation of incarcerated flatus. *Swollen glands in r. groin; S. of an inguinal gland, with sensitiveness;* inflamed gland in r. groin. Sticking jerks in pelvic muscles about r. hip when sitting. Cramplike sticking Sticking in groin. Pain in r., < every step and inspiration; burning P. in r. groin, as if intestines would protrude, which seemed to move, < stretching body, > stooping; sore P. in l. inguinal glands. L. inguinal glands feel swollen so that he cannot walk well, but they are not swollen nor painful to touch. Tension in groins when walking. Heaviness, with dragging. Nausea.

Clinical.—Induration of the liver. Relief of ascites. Chronic catarrh of the intestines and discharge of masses of mucus with the stool, with constipation, stool covered with mucus. Note the numerous abdominal symptoms, constipation, accumulation of large masses of fæces, which are covered with mucus; the anus is fissured, the cracks bleed and ulcerate.

Rectum.—*Prolapsus (with its hæmorrhoids), without urging, as if anus were paralyzed.* Discharge of blood, with sticking in it. Sticking; as if everthing were indurated. Dragging in R. and anus, with burning; D. as with hæmorrhoids. *Urging, stool not hard, but difficult on account of inactivity of R.* Tenesmus with each stool. Pressing without stool. Provocation to stool without need therefor.

Anus.—*Burning hæmorrhoids.* Swelling all about; much S. of veins. A cord like a swollen vein extending from anus towards nates, painless to touch. *Single stitches;* tearing S. extending into rectum. *Cutting* (rectum?) in morning in bed. Sore. **Smarting sore pain on wiping** (Æsc. h.). **Itching** (Sul.). Burning with the stool. Swollen feeling. Sore pain on r. side of perineum, where there are pale red, irregular pimples between the hairs, with acute pain on touch.

Stool.—Liquid, with mucus. *Diarrhœa almost without pain, then prostration;* frequent D., with burning in anus; sudden slimy, with feeling as if flatus would pass, preceded by sinking and coldness in abdomen. Soft, with blood; three S., at night, with colic; S. and sour, offensive. Pasty, dark. *Hard, with urging and* **sticking in anus** (N. ac.); H. and lumpy; H. and blackish. **Lumpy, with threads of mucus,** *and after stool there is still mucus in anus.* **Dark, half-digested, of intolerable odor** (Sulph.). *Thin, like a round worm.* Sour-smelling, with burning in rectum. *Much white mucus with stool;* reddish mucus. *Blood with stool;* after menstruation, with smarting in rectum. Round worms with stool. Passage of thread-worms, with itching in anus. Increased fæces mixed with mucus. Frequent; the first hard and thick, the others soft.

Urinary Organs.—*Urging, with dribbling after the usual discharge;* U. in morning in bed, but only a few drops passed, with cutting in urethra; sudden U., with but little urine; anxious U. at night, with cutting in abdomen, frequently forcing her to rise, though but little was passed, with cutting. Obliged to urinate early in morning; at night. *Micturition in a thin stream as if urethra were contracted. Frequent micturition;* at night; and copious. Involuntary M. Raw pressure in root of urethra, with desire to urinate. Tickling in urethra when urinating. Burning in urethra when not urinating; in orifice after urinating. *Urine clear, but after four or five hours covered with iridescent film.* Acrid, sourish odor to urine. Dark brown U., with a stitch in urethra during micturition. Dark U., depositing reddish sediment. **U. becomes turbid and deposits a white sediment** (Berb., Sep.); *becomes turbid after two hours, with reddish sediment, biting in urethra during micturition.*

Clinical.—Nocturnal enuresis associated with the eruption of Grap. Inflammation of the urethra (herpetic), with more or less soreness and with gluey, sticky discharge at the meatus.

Sexual Organs.—Tension when walking and on touch of clothing, with unpleasant sensation. Penis, *eruption;* P. covered with thick mucus; pinching; jerking pain; drawing pain; bubbling sensation during erections. Erections without lascivious thought; strong E.; strong E. after coition. *Vesicles on prepuce. Prepuce swells to a large water-blister, without pain* (see Nit. ac.). Swelling of scrotum (in coverings of testicles? Hydrocele?). **Itching and moist eruption on scrotum** (compare Nat. m.); I. within scrotum. R. testicle seems swollen. Sticking at times in r. testicle. Drawing in testicles. Jerking pain in l. spermatic cord. *Voluptuous irritability. Revival of desire.* Lascivious thoughts, so that he feared he should be insane, with running about, and with heaviness in perineum and tensive pain in penis without erections. Desire gone; afterwards aroused so that even the touch of a woman caused sexual excitement and trembling in all limbs. Emissions nearly every night. *Ejaculation does not follow coition in spite of every exertion.*

Female.—*Pressure towards;* when standing. Papules on pudenda, with itching. **Itching of pudenda before menstruation.** Soreness of pudenda. Vesicle on labia, with itching biting. Painless pimple on internal labia. Frequent sticking in labia. *Biting in vagina.* **Leucorrhœa;** < morning on rising; **profuse; profuse, of white mucus;** *profuse when walking and sitting, with weakness of back and sacrum; thin,* with distended abdomen. *Swelling of the l. indurated ovary, with stony hardness, with pain, partly on touch and partly on inspiration or hawking, when stitches shoot into it, with general sweat and sleeplessness.* **Menstruation delayed** (Nat. m., Puls., Sep., Sulph.); with heaviness in abdomen and dulness in head the first day; suppressed, with heaviness of arms and legs. M. too soon (Carbo v.) (secondary action); too soon, thin, of short duration, with pain in back, > motion.

Clinical.—It has been used for sexual debility, seminal emissions, constipation, etc. Herpes of the prepuce. Hydrocele. Moist eruptions on the scrotum. Disorders accompanying scanty or delayed menstruation or suppression of the menses, with great mental depression, weeping, vertigo, eruptions on the face and herpetic eruptions on other parts of the body. Menstruation very irregular, sometimes scanty and pale, at other times the flow is dark, associated with violent colic, at other times suppressed, with severe cutting and bearing-down pains in uterine region and hips. Particularly adapted to menstrual irregularities in women who are inclined to get fat and who have herpetic eruptions. Suppression of the menses, with induration of the ovaries. Leucorrhœa instead of menstruation, the discharge coming in gushes, with great weakness, soreness of the pudenda, ulceration. Membranous dysmenorrhœa. Profuse milky-white leucorrhœa in gushes. Diseases following laceration of the cervix, especially follicular and cystic diseases, are sometimes cured by Grap. Subacute or chronic inflammation of vagina and neck of uterus. Tumors of the pelvis, with bearing-down pains. So-called cauliflower excrescences, with severe lancinating pains, have been relieved and perhaps cured. Indurations and excrescences which bleed easily, on neck of uterus. Induration of l. ovary, very hard, with violent pain on touch or on breathing. Induration of both ovaries, which are very sore, < taking cold or getting feet wet, with tendency to cold, wet feet. Indurations form in the mammæ and become cancerous. In nursing women the nipples are sore, cracked and bleeding.

Respiratory Organs.—*Tickling in larynx, < evening in bed, causing hawking and short cough. Hoarseness every evening;* H. during menstruation, with catarrh and catarrhal fever. Scraping in trachea. Cough, with catarrh and heat in head; C. which fatigues chest in morning and during the day, > night, before and during menstruation; which fatigues chest, with pain low down in chest; dry, during menstruation, with profuse sweat; dry hacking, wakes him at night and lasts next day; C. in evening on lying down, with much expectoration. Expectoration of blood, with sensitiveness of palate and tongue. Whistling in air-passages on breathing. Suffocative sensation, waking her at night; on walking in open air. Dyspnœa in evening on lying down and cough on deep inspiration; sudden D., with difficult short breath. Difficult breathing.

Clinical.—Chronic hoarseness in persons subject to herpetic eruptions, especially if the eruptions have been suppressed, the voice breaks on attempting to sing. Spasmodic asthma, with suffocative paroxysms, which awaken from sleep, > eating. Whooping cough.

Chest.—Mucus. Sticking in l.; in forepart of l. in evening; in sides on every motion; in r. on breathing, > pressure of hand; externally in r. near sternum, < lying on r. side; in middle on ascending steps, with oppression of breathing; in r. arresting breath. Tearing in r. Pinching; in evening obliging him to stretch; on walking long in open air. Pressure on l. side, increasing to pinching and almost intolerable twinging pain, only when sitting. *Pain in nipples;* in sternum between breasts; P. in chest on ascending; when sitting; in r. ribs on touch; in lower ribs near sternum on touch; in upper part on yawning, touch or riding horseback; across from l. to r. side. *Raw pain like raw flesh.* Catarrhal rawness of C. and trachea. Tickling low down, with loose cough and salt expectoration. Intolerance of anything tight. Oppression; morning on rising, < inspiration; l. side and heart in morning. Burning pressure beneath l. axilla. Burning in middle on inspiration, with tension and sensitiveness. Burning throbbing externally in l., < inspiration. (Emptiness and coldness in C. and about heart, with sadness.)

Heart.—Sticking. Pressure on breathing. Throbbing in evening when lying on l. side, > turning over, with anxiety. Palpitation; sudden, like an electric shock from heart to throat; which moves arm and hand and causes anxiety.

Neck.—Sticking in nape; tearing; S. in sides on moving head. Smarting cutting as from an ulcer at seventh cervical vertebra. Pain in nape; and shoulders on bending head forward, preventing raising arms to head; and in shoulders when lying upon them or turning (from swollen glands on side of neck, which are not sore). Rheumatic pain in nape. Tension in nape and r. side of neck on moving head. *Stiffness of nape.*

Back.—Drawing. Scapulæ, sticking in l., with pain; pressure between; bruised pain in scapulæ; rheumatic pain in l.; contractive pain between. Cutting dragging downward from kidneys before urinating. Sticking in small of B. Griping and twisting in small of B., as from tongs, then pain in arms and feet as if they would turn outward. Pain in small of B.; in morning on rising, > motion; near spine; as after long stooping; bruised, also < touch. Throbbing in small of B. Pain in coccyx when urinating. Drawing in coccyx in evening.

Extremities.—Stretching, with weakness of them. Jerking in evening or inclination thereto; J. outward in evening, with consciousness; J. of hands and feet. Bruised sensation in all. Pain in joints as from weariness, on stooping and sitting down, so that she could not rise again from her seat. E. on which there was an ulcer began to pain on touch or slight motion, even at a distance from the ulcer. Intermittent drawing and tearing in E. on which an ulcer was healed, < open air. Uneasiness in one in evening. *Weakness.* Heaviness, with depressed mood. Stiffness; of shoulder and knee. *Arms and legs fall asleep; when sitting, on walking crawling in them,* in evening. *Paralyzed sensation.*

Clinical.—Inflammations at the roots of the nails, with tendency to exuberant granulations (Arnica). The finger-nails become rough and discolored. The toe-nails become extremely thick and hard.

Upper Extremities.—Pinching in r. axilla, with sticking. Pain in axillæ. Sticking in shoulders and elbows, even at rest, < night; *S. in l. shoulder,* taking away the breath; frequent burning S. on l. shoulder. Tearing in r. S. at night, > external warmth; *in l. joint* on moving arm. Rheumatic pain in l. S. Burning in shoulder-joint. Arm, jerking of muscles; in first sleep at night; here and there in arms in evening in bed; pinching in l., with heat in it; drawing. Falling asleep of arm when lying upon it; and hand, when sitting; F. asleep of r. arm. Sticking in upper arm, forearm and hand. Sore feeling in upper arm.

Elbow.—Twitching. Pain in condyles on touch; P. in bend, so that he cannot stretch arm; in bend, as if too short, on stretching arm. Drawing during rest, with tearing in it on raising arm and sensation as if cold water were running through bones; cutting D. in r., whereby arm felt paralyzed. Paralytic pressure in l. E. and forearm after midday nap.

Tearing in l. forearm near wrist. Gnawing in r. ulna and radius. Burning pain in r. forearm, upon which he was lying at night, with sensation of falling asleep in elbow. Spasmodic tension in a muscle of forearm. Sticking through r. wrist. Sprained pain in r. wrist. Hands wasted; tearing in r. H; *T. in hands like rheumatism;* sticking burning pain in l. palm in evening in bed, which soon passes to thumb; pain as from a blow on back of l., < pressure; numb and asleep after much using; asleep when sitting; r. asleep.

Fingers.—**Nails become thick.** Swelling of middle joint of middle, with stiffness. Spasmodic contractions; of l. index. Cross each other by a kind of spasm, but they separate when she strikes them. Sticking in tips of r., with ulcerative pain; S. in ball of thumb; beneath r. thumb-nail. Tearing in bone of first phalanx of thumb; *rheumatic T. in first joint of r. thumb*, < during rest. Feeling as if thumbs would be drawn inward when holding something in hands. Crawling in tip of index, with numbness. F. remain stiff and bent after grasping anything.

Lower Extremities.—Thigh. Sticking in spots in T. and legs; S. in l. hip; in part S. at night, disturbing sleep, in part burning. Tearing posteriorly in morning; T. now in r., now in l., extending into hip, from afternoon till evening; rheumatic, in hips. Cutting in swelling above knee. Bruised pain in middle; B. pain in femora. Drawing pain in femora; jerking D. pain towards groin, < rising from a seat. Jerking sensation in muscles. Weariness. Stiffness of r. on walking, with feeling as if bound about knee. Numbness, < sitting, with heat.

Knee.—Sticking in l.; S. in patella. Sprained pain in l. when walking. *Bruised pain* at night; in morning in bed, > rising. Drawing pain. Drawing in l., with tension; D. in l., with jerking. Tension in hollows all day, so that he could not stretch leg. Pain in hollows, as if too short, with tension in tendo-achillis, so that she could not step upon it. Fatigued pain, < knees, when stooping and sitting down, so that she could not rise again from her seat. Weakness of l., with heaviness. Stiffness; in hollows when sitting, as if held tightly by a hand. Numbness, waking at night.

Leg.—*Swelling*, even in bed; hard S., with sticking. Sticking in r. on blowing nose; S. in swollen varices; in varices, with tension. Sticking burning pain in a spot above malleolus, so that she could not step upon it, but must raise it high, because on allowing it to hang down the blood settled into it, with burning and sticking. Tearing in tibiæ; rheumatic, in both and in l. hip. Cramplike pain here and there, with heat. Pain in varices during menstruation. Rheumatic pain. Bruised pain in tibiæ; and pain as if broken; B. pain in leg and scapula on which he lies. Drawing pain on tibiæ; in tendo-achillis. Drawing from above downward; cramplike D. in varices on stretching leg. Tension when walking, with bruised pain; T. where there were swollen veins, with sticking in them. Uneasiness, preventing sleep all night. Weariness. Heaviness; r. Crawlings as if they would go to sleep. *Falling asleep; and seeming dead* on walking in open air; inclined to fall asleep at night, and peevishness. Numbness in bones of r.

Calf.—*Cramp* all day; in morning in bed; *at night;* from carrying anything, with trembling of legs; at beginning of coition, preventing coition. Jerking; *in all muscles of l.* Spasmodic drawing at night on stretching them; S. drawing on rising. Sticking when drawing on boots. Sprained pain. Throbbing in outer side every hour, always lasting about fifteen minutes.

Ankle.—Gnawing in bones of A. and heels. Pain about malleoli; on touch; in r. Sprained pain in l. on walking in open air, > in room. Pain in r. malleoli as if broken, < morning after rising, with a stitch at every step, extending to great toe, so that he must hold himself in order to avoid falling. Constriction. Stiffness.

Foot.—Swelling of the injured. Jerking in soles. Sticking in heels, with pressure; S. in heels, even when sitting. Tearing on back; in borders; in heels; in ball when walking; in r. sole, with tickling; *rheumatic, in feet and toes.* Ulcerative pain in heels; in soles. Sore pain in corns, almost without external pressure. Burning pain in a corn. Pain in corns on waking. Blood shoots into diseased F. when standing. Heaviness; with weariness. Falling asleep of l. in evening when sitting. Numbness on back when walking in open air (in June), with increased coldness. Stiffness in a sore F. after eating, with pressure and sticking.

Toes.—Swelling of T. and balls of toes. Drawn inward; with cramplike drawing up to knee. Sticking in l. great, when sitting. Tearing in l. great; in little, as if it would be drawn towards the side; *goutlike.* Pain in r. great; *in nail of great;* beneath balls, so that he limped. Constriction of ball of great, as with iron pincers.

Skin.—Hard and cracked on hands. Soreness high up between thighs *during and after a walk; between thighs, near pudenda, during menstruation; between pudendum and thigh, covered with pimples, vesicles and ulcers;* between toes, with itching; **smarting soreness between nates.** *Eruption covering chin;* **itching E. full of corrosive water, in many parts**; gritty E. on fingers. Spots like flea-bites. Red spot on thigh; R., itching spots, < calves. Erysipelas of hands; *of both sides of face, burning sticking*, then catarrh, with sticking in gum. *Red raw spot like tetter on thigh opposite scrotum, itching in morning.* Tetter becomes an inflamed swelling.

Pimples over whole body at night, > morning; **Itching P. on face, moist after scratching**; hard, painful to pressure, behind r. ear; red, itching a little, on thighs; painful to touch, on nates; deeply-seated posteriorly on thighs and legs, rapidly forming vesicles; on trunk and limbs (not unusual with me, but they assumed a peculiar appearance after three days, increased to size of a pin's head, were filled with fluid at tip and were brownish-yellow). *Red itching pimples tipped with pus, which burn after scratching.* Moist papules on nose. Unhealthy, every injury suppurates. Pustules on chin and chest; on both little toes, with sticking. Suppuration of margins of great toes. Boils on neck, back and arms; on nates. Vesicles beneath malleoli; *on little finger, itching, discharging much matter, with burning sticking;* white, on one toe. *Proud flesh in ulcers.* Ulcer on fourth toe; scaly, on tibia, with inflamed border and surrounded by swelling, so sensitive that bed-covering could not be endured. Offensive odor from an ulcer; scab of ulcer smells like herring-brine.

Tearing in ulcer. Smarting of the limbs covered with tetter; S. all over hands, on moving fingers the skin cracks. Burning pain in scars from old ulcers. Pressure in an ulcer, with sticking; itching, in an ulcer. Sensitiveness of an ulcer. Tingling of feet towards toes, like tearing. Formication on back. *Itching, general, even on face and genitals; behind ears;* on back and arms; balls of l. hand; swollen varices of legs; of all toes; r. temple, with burning after scratching; on coccyx above anus, with moisture and scurf; lobules of ears and on cheeks, after scratching lymph exudes and hardens; over whole body, after scratching pimples containing water; corrosive, here and there. Sticking itching in r. great toe; in a mole, transiently > rubbing; on thigh, as if an eruption would appear in the place of a previous boil.

Clinical.—It has removed scars; Dr. Guernsey states that he has removed by it scars after mammary abscesses. Impetigo. The itching of Grap. is generally < warmth. It seems to have removed the tendency to recurring erysipelas of the vesicular variety. Herpes zoster, with large blisters and excessive burning. Herpes zoster, if left-sided. Chronic eczema of the dorsal region of the forearm and hands, the skin becomes thick and fissured. Rhus poisoning. (Compare skin generally with Petrol.)

Sleep.—Frequent yawning. Sleepiness; *during the day;* during the day, with weariness; towards noon; *after midday meal.* Sensation in morning as from insufficient sleep, difficulty in getting out of bed. Falling asleep early in evening, with weariness. Sleepless before midnight from heat and anxiety; S. till 2 A.M.; after 3 A.M., for several hours, then waking at 7 dizzy and tired. Restless night; with sleeplessness always from 12 till 2 o'clock; with heat; with anxious warmth and anxious dreams. Anxiety at night and constant talking in sleep. Jerkings in sleep. Frequent waking; as from fright. Waking too early. Waking at 2 A.M., with restlessness, he remembered everything that could injure him and was anxious, so that he did not know where to turn; W. every night at 2 A.M., with uneasiness.

Dreams.—*Peevish;* with moaning and groaning. *Frightful;* with danger from water. Vivid; and remembered long. *Vivid, anxious. Anxious,* so that she was beside herself on waking; A., taking away her breath, she cried out and lay in sweat; A., of numberless dogs and cats, with loud talking; of drowsiness and unconsciousness, then difficult waking from deep sleep, with stiffness of cervical muscles. Full of trouble. Of unpleasant occurrences of the day, so that she woke with anxiety. *Numerous, distorted,* about everything that had happened to her during the two last days. Only of what she has seen and thought of during the day. Of fire. Of dead people. Fatiguing the head. Voluptuous.

Fever.—Chilliness all day and night, preventing sleep at night; C. during the day on lying down to sleep; *in morning in bed;* in morning and evening, then heat, then sweat; over whole body after breakfast, with shivering; before noon meal; over whole body after 5 P.M., with cold feet; from 4 P.M. till after going to bed; in evening before sleep, then itching; at night, with drawing pain in limb, waking him, then sticking above l. breast and in l. side on every inspiration; even in evening in warm bed, thirst all the evening and night, profuse sweat after midnight till morning, with the chill in evening headache and tearing in limbs and coated tongue; during menstruation; after menstruation, with cutting in abdomen, then diarrhœa; with ringing in ears; in a child for half an hour every evening; sudden, all over; as from want of blood. Daily intermittent fever, shaking chill in evening, then heat of face and coldness of feet, no sweat. Shivering; in evening, with sticking in temples, l. ear and teeth, then sweat at night; before and after eating, then anxious heat in evening; in back in forenoon, with frequent yawning and sleepiness; in back evenings; in r. limb after midday meal. Coldness above eyes; hands and feet; feet in morning; hands and feet in evening, with heat of face; suddenly in legs after coition.

Heat at night, so that he could not stay in bed; H. at night and orgasm of blood in morning; H. after coition, with sweat; from riding in a wagon; frequent, sudden, when sitting, sometimes with anxiety; dry, in evening; dry, every evening and till morning, with pain in vertex and nape till noon. Heat in head after dinner. Burning in spot on vertex; hands and soles; feet; l. sole; soles < walking; *heels, < morning in bed, with crawling;* sudden, in a spot on forearm; sudden, in a spot on r. upper arm, with cold sensation.

Sweat mornings in bed; nights, > wine; when eating; *even on slight motion;* general, from earnest conversation; even from a short walk, coloring linen yellow, with exhaustion; sour; *offensive exhalations from body;* S. on head when falling asleep; on sternum every morning. *Sweat of feet* in evening, with tearing in feet and hands; of feet, < afternoon and evening; when walking a little, making toes sore; *feet begin to smell* (Bar. c., Sil.); so that they are sore, < between toes (Sil.).

Gratiola.

A tincture is made of the entire fresh plant of Gratiola officinalis, L.

General Action.—In large doses it is a violent emetic, cathartic and diuretic, causing inflammation of the lower bowel and pelvic viscera (bladder and sexual organs), rush of blood to the head and faintness, etc.

Allies.—Magnes. c., Sulph., Colch., Iris, Sul. ac.

Generalities.—Tetanic condition when lying in afternoon, with consciousness, then deep sleep, with an emission, after waking general bruised feeling, < back and l. arm. Sticking in several parts, < lower limbs. Bruised feeling in morning in bed, > rising, but confused in head. Discomfort and ill humor (Sulph.). Pulsation through whole body, it seems seated lower than pit of stomach, < stool. Weakness; in morning on waking, with sleepiness; all the forenoon; all the forenoon, with ill humor; < open air; of body and mind. Aggravation after dinner and from 2.30 till 3 o'clock.

Mind.—Talkative and joyous. Lively and desirous to jump and dance. Excited and unable to sleep in evening. Anxiety, > open air, with general heat and weakness. Sad. Fretful; and desirous to be alone; irritated by every contradiction, angry outbreaks, misanthropic and solicitous about his own health. Earnest, reflective. Averse to everything at 1 P.M. No desire to talk or move. Disinclined to mental work. Irresolute, not persistent in work. Confused. Memory lost in afternoon, and self-absorbed. In deep thought at 2.30 P.M. and does not seem to hear what is said to her.

Head.—Aching all day, with heat in face; A. in afternoon; at 2 P.M., with nausea; < afternoon by motion of body; < 2.30 P.M. on rising from a seat; < open air; throbbing at one time >, at another <, and at another disappearing in open air. Sudden vibration internally at 10 A.M. when sitting, as if some one let go a stiff steel spring, so that hearing and sight vanished. Fulness on going into open air, with stoppage of nose; F. as if brain would be pressed outward. Heaviness on stooping and on rising again; H., with nausea and sleepiness. Brain feels contracted and as if head would become smaller, > open air, with general discomfort. Confusion; painful, > breakfast, but frequently returning after dinner. Dulness in evening; between 7 and 8 P.M., only somewhat > lying. Very light and free.

Rush of blood and intoxicated feeling in whole brain; rush of blood, < motion, especially riding, increasing to unconsciousness, > sleep, with throbbing in forehead, amounting to vertigo, with blackness before eyes. Intoxicated feeling during and after eating; she seems I., > open air. Vertigo; after rising; on rising from a seat; > open air, returning in a warm room; he stands looking long at one spot without thinking of it; in attacks, < walking rapidly; as if turned to the right, > open air; as if he would fall forward in open air, with weakness; as if head moved back and forth when reading; as if objects wavered, < l. side; as if she would turn in a circle; as if the room went round and as if she would fall, on closing eyes, > open air.

Forehead.—Sticking in morning and at 3.45 P.M., with beating; S., with warmth in it; S. in l. eminence; r. eminence; in sinciput at 2.30 P.M.; tearing. Tearing; in l.; in sinciput, with throbbing. Pain; above r. eye; in skin; in sinciput; r. side of sinciput; in sinciput, > towards noon; < r. side, with burning; drawing, in l. eminence. Beating in forepart at 3 P.M., with tearing farther back towards vertex. Screwed-together sensation in F., vertex and occiput. Tension as if drawn in folds. Feeling as if a hair hung down the middle.

Sticking in r., then l. temple. Tearing in temples in afternoon, night and morning, generally < cold and warmth, with boring, the temples become sensitive from the pain; T. in upper part of r. temple, a simple pain in this place on pressure; T. in l.; in r. muscle. Pain in temples; in l. bone on touch, as from a blow. Painful throbbing and drawing in vertex. Sticking in r. side of head and in occiput; in l. side of brain, > open air. Tearing in sides and in occiput at 2 P.M.; T. in l. side above forehead, > rubbing; in r. side, extending to ear, with bruised pain; in l. side, then sticking in l. side of forehead. Headache in r. side; as if something heavy lay upon brain, till evening. Drawing in l. side on going into open air. Heaviness in l. half.

Sticking in l. occiput; then tearing in l. side of chin. Pain in occiput in morning on waking early, > rising and lying upon abdomen; P. on l. side as from something heavy; bruised P. in l. after sneezing. Burning sticking on scalp, > scratching. Biting on r. side of occiput, not > scratching; B. in a spot on r. side after dinner, then on l., > scratching. Itching biting on vertex. Itching biting, > scratching, on vertex; above forehead; on occiput, but frequently returning. Itching > scratching, on vertex; on r. side of occiput; above l. frontal region at 2 P.M.; burning, on vertex.

Eyes.—Tearing, with mucus in lids, < inner canthi. Frequent pain all day. Pressure upon them in afternoon. Burning pain in l. Dryness and feeling as if sand were in them. Lachrymation when reading, with feeling of weakness in eyes. Pressure in balls. Twitching of l. brow. Drawing pain in l. brow. Lids closed on account of weakness; twitching of l. after dinner; agglutinated, with dry mucus, < canthi; itching; itching of r., > scratching. Canthi red, more in afternoon than in morning, and itching; sticking in r. inner, > rubbing, with itching; pressure, with inflammation of conjunctiva; tension in outer at 2 P.M. when reading; tickling in l. inner after dinner, > scratching. Vision cloudy after breakfast, with feeling as if eyes were drawn together and smaller than usual; C. at 1.30 P.M., when reading; when writing. Vision short when reading. V. better for distant than for near objects, with heat in face. All objects seem white on opening eyes. V. suddenly vanishes when writing or looking at bright objects, > closing eyes, but constantly returning.

Ears.—Sticking in l. at 1 P.M., > walking. Tearing in l.; in front of l., near eye; in a spot near l., > pressure, with drawing upward and downward. Crawling internally.

Nose.—Tearings in upper part of l. side. Pressure in l. upper region. Stoppage; when vomiting. Itching in r. nostril, > rubbing. Itching biting in r. nostril. Irritation and tickling in l. side as if one would sneeze. Tendency to sneeze. Coryza in evening, > bed. Running of water from r. nostril. Sneezing during dinner; with sticking in hypochondriac region; with sticking in l. side.

Face.—Red. Pale. Tearing in r. half; in l. side of chin. Tensive feeling like swelling. Tearing in r. lower jaw at 1 P.M. Swelling of upper lip every morning. Sticking in upper lip in morning, as if it would crack, with thirst.

Mouth.—Teeth. Sticking from r. upper molars to head. Tearings in last l. lower molars, > pressure; frequent T. in r. upper anterior molars. Intermittent boring in first l. molars in afternoon, < at night > forenoon. Pain in all, < touch and on taking cold things; P. difficult to describe in hollow eye-teeth on eating and drinking cold things and on drawing cold air into mouth. Drawing in upper incisors. Coldness in l. upper molar; in r. upper incisors. Gum of a hollow tooth inflamed.

Tongue raw. T. coated slimy, with natural taste to food and great appetite. Sticking in palate near l. side of uvula, with cutting and stiffness so that swallowing was painful. Burning in palate, with dry and raw sensation. Crawling in palate. Feeling in morning as if breath were offensive, > rising. Salivation. Taste bitter in forenoon; B. in mouth and throat, with nausea, which continues after vomiting. Taste pasty, as from meal, after morning soup.

Throat.—Sticking jerkings in forepart at 2 P.M. Jerklike drawing in forepart of neck. Mucus, which she cannot raise or swallow, provoking cough. Hawking of mucus, < morning. Sticking from afternoon till midnight; S. in pharynx at 5 P.M.; in l. side, < by swallowing; in l. side, when not swallowing it is rather a clawing. Aching as before inflammation; constrictive A. in forepart of neck; indescribable A., causing constant swallowing, which is difficult, as from constriction, but food and drinks are swallowed without difficulty, this sensation > eructations, especially if bitter fluid is evacuated. Pressure as from mucus which she could not hawk up nor swallow. Feeling of mucus, with rawness and inclination to hawk. Rancid feeling after dinner. Crawling in fauces. Rawness, with hacking cough; R., with hoarseness. Scraping in back; extending into pharynx; S. after dinner, with nausea; S. in œsophagus during and after dinner, with acidity.

Stomach.—Hunger at 7 P.M., with dread of eating, < solid food; H., but want of appetite. Appetite diminished, bread tastes best; does not relish the dinner.

Appetite lost. Aversion to food; to fat, she eats even beef without appetite; to the accustomed tobacco; with shuddering and nausea. Thirst at an unusual hour; in morning; in evening, the nausea > drinking water.

Eructations; empty; empty, after morning soup; tasting of juniper; sweet; bitter; bitter when walking in open air; tasting like bitter almonds, relieving the stomach; tasting of the food; of food while eating; of the meat; forcible, as of rancid fat, after morning soup, with feeling as if water would rise with it; nauseous fluid rises into throat; of water at 1.30 P.M.; water-brash in frequent attacks, < fasting and cold water. Inclination to eructate; with pressure extending from stomach into throat, so that it takes away the breath; changing to nausea; ineffectual.

Hiccough during dinner, with eructations tasting of the drug and heat in head; H. after dinner. Nausea; at noon; in afternoon, > eructations; at 1 P.M., with uprisings of water; at 3.30 P.M., > eructations tasting of the drug; after dinner; after dinner, with inability to vomit; after dinner, > stool, with sleepiness; after dinner, rising from lower abdomen into stomach and farther up, with salivation; during eructations; < open air; > breakfast; > dinner; > eructations; > eructations, but returning; not > vomiting; with feeling as if water would rise; with accumulation of water in mouth; *with coldness in stomach and feeling as if full of water* (Colch., Sul. ac.); with pressure on chest; obliging him to lie down, > open air, with spitting of saliva; sudden, in morning, > walking; frequent; intermittent, after dinner, with discomfort in stomach. Constant empty retching; empty R., with salivation, the nausea transiently > eating. *Vomiting; bilious; twice, of yellow, bitter sour water, without exertion.*

Rumbling in forenoon, with movings in abdomen; R. in epigastric region. Movings in S. and abdomen after dinner, with griping and feeling as before diarrhœa. Flatulence, < some hours after eating, with burrowing and with distention of epigastric region, eructations and retching, whereby bitter mucus is thrown up with exertion. Sticking in epigastric region; when walking, < inspiration; near l. side of pit after stool; tensive, in epigastrium in evening, with nausea and eructations. Cramp in morning in bed after a late supper. Cuttings in epigastrium. Twinging in epigastric region. Digging in epigastric region, with sudden nausea and shivering on scalp. *Pain with nausea and general discomfort;* P., with anxiety. Pressure in pit; < eating; as from a stone moving back and forth, < eating, with spasmodic drawings extending into chest, nausea and eructations; in epigastric region from food, with fulness; in stomach, extending into chest, with nausea, feeling as if he would eructate, the nausea > rancid eructations; P. in stomach, as from a foreign body. Contractive pain in epigastric region, which seems to come from abdomen. Sensitiveness to pressure, and in abdomen; in pit. Gnawing in pit as from hunger, > eating, but soon returning. Emptiness at 2 P.M., with loss of appetite. Full feeling; in epigastric region after every meal, < dinner, > if a little bread was eaten during the third hour after dinner. Heaviness an hour and a half after dinner; H. in pit. Tension, < inspiration. Discomfort after dinner, with fulness; D. in epigastric region. Burning; then coldness, pressure and nausea, < two pasty stools. Coldness.

Abdomen.—Distention; in morning; at 1 P.M.; after dinner, with heat in it; after dinner, obliging loosening of clothes and bending together; waking after midnight, then diarrhœa five times consisting of mucus, with tenesmus; > emission of offensive flatus (Sulph.); with hardness; flatulent, in places, then offensive flatus. Rumbling; after breakfast, with uneasiness, constant desire for stool and emission of only flatus; after dinner, with gurgling; in evening in bed; < eating, with uneasiness; with soft stool. Flatus moves about; with burning. Emission of flatus; at 2 P.M., then relief of abdomen; copious, in afternoon; offensive.

Cutting when sitting; intermittent C.; intermittent, so that she must bend up, with urging to stool; intermittent, extending around abdomen, < about umbilicus. Intermittent pinching at 4 P.M., > bending together, with nauseous pain in stomach. Griping; at 4 A.M., and at 9 two pasty stools, the G. > emission of flatus; in afternoon, with drawing and rumbling; evenings; after eating, < morning and evening; after eating, then ineffectual urging to stool; after stool, then two diarrhœa-like stools. Twinging, > emission of offensive flatus, with movings; T., with movings, then stool, which is first hard, then soft. Pain; at 9 A.M., after morning soup; on walking, after each stool, > sitting after dinner; then stool, at first soft, at last hard, with pressure; with nausea; driving heat into head; causing pallor and nausea, > pasty copious stool, sometimes with offensive flatus; as in diarrhœa after taking cold, > bending forward and by rest, with flatulence and burrowing. Feeling at 1 P.M. as of a purge, with moving about. Pressing inward after dinner, with nausea. Uneasiness; in afternoon; with desire for stool. Coldness.

Upper.—Frequent rumbling. Sticking in l.; in r. at 2.30 P.M. on sitting down; in r. after dinner, with cutting in abdomen; beneath r. false ribs at 2 P.M. and in evening; in hypochondria, > emission of flatus and stool, with fulness. Intermittent cutting; when eating. Twinging at 3.45 P.M., with ineffectual urging to stool; T. after dinner; intermittent T. and cutting at 2 P.M., so that she must bend up, then sticking beneath l. short ribs. Digging. Burning in r.; l., > walking.

Sides.—Sticking in l. on sitting down and while sitting, > walking; deep in l. at 5 P.M., which then extends to l. chest and back again. Pain in l., with movements of flatus; P. from both sides towards umbilicus, after the nausea. Contraction from both sides towards middle, with pressure. Feeling as if something heavy fell down in l. Sudden burning in r. extending into r. epigastric region, with movings.

Umbilicus.—Distention above U. Sticking about U. in afternoon, after stool; about U. before the usual stool; near r. side; in middle of abdomen. Sticking drawing pains extending from both sides of U. into inguinal glands. Cutting in region; about U., then three watery stools, then smarting in rectum; intermittent; with tearing. Twinging from 2 to 4.30 P.M.; in middle of abdomen at 4 P.M., > emission of flatus. Griping about U. after eating. Pain in region. Flatulent feeling in region, without desire to pass flatus. Crawling in region, with burrowing; C. in region, as of a worm.

Lower.—Sticking; in r.; l. groin. Cutting; at 1 P.M., with dragging downward in groins. Griping. Pinching. Twinging in sides, extending into chest, with contraction, then sticking above umbilicus and drawing inward of it. Sensation as before diarrhœa. Pain as from a blow on l. ilium, on pressure. Pressing inward, > walking and rubbing, but frequently returning; P. inward above pubis. Tension in region of l. ilium on bending trunk to that side; T. in l. abdominal ring when standing, > when sitting and by emission of flatus. Burning in r. groin at 2.30 P.M., then sticking beneath r. breast; B. above pubis, rather external, > pressure. Crawling.

Rectum.—Soreness deep in it. Burning after stool; B. at end of R. during and after stool. Tenesmus, painful contraction after stool. Urging; in evening, with discharge of blood after stool; at night and in morning, then partly soft stool, with pressure; with rumbling, as before diarrhœa, then hard stool, with pressure; as before diarrhœa, but the stool is hard; constant; ineffectual.

Anus.—Hæmorrhoids which existed sixteen years previously reappeared, with sticking biting. Spasmodic contraction of sphincter. Sticking. Prickling after usual stool. Smarting after diarrhœa. Throbbing pain. Burning at 5 P.M., after scratching it. Itching, with urging to stool and alternately hard and thin stool; I., > scratching, but returning.

Stool.—Watery fæces, yellow, frequent; diarrhœa of yellow-greenish water, *then burning in anus* (Iris v.); **forcible, of green, frothy water** (Mag. c.), *three times* after dinner; *watery fæces, frequent, with soreness in anus; bright yellow fluid fæces, twice, then chilliness* (Canth.); *three stools of yellow water*, then ineffectual urging. Semi-fluid, ochre-colored, after dinner, with emission of flatus; S. at first, then solid, with burning, in morning after rising; S., the last part more solid but scanty, and with pressure; three stools after dinner, the first part always semi-fluid, then solid, and passed with pressure. *Diarrhœa;* in morning; twice, with burning in anus. Thin, yellow; T. twice a day, next day constipation; T. and dark at 3 P.M., at 7 P.M. small, thin, dark, urgent; stool at first as usual, then copious thin stool, with pain in abdomen, then tenesmus, then pain in abdomen, then frequent liquid stools. Soft, then sore pain; S., dark, copious, also with flatulence. Pasty, with tension in abdomen; P. and offensive.

Hard; after long urging; then twinging in anus; and some hours later daily, preceded by frequent urging; and scanty, with great exertion. Copious; in evening, with griping in abdomen. Scanty, with griping in abdomen. A small part passed unnoticed. Frequent; and watery; two in afternoon; two, bilious, yellowish-green; F., with burning and pressure and pressing out of great lumps, with sticking in anus, then passage of offensive, brown, corrosive mucus, then after several attempts there pushes out a mass of pasty, dark brown, offensive fæces mixed with mucus, the last exertion evacuates only mucus like the white of an egg, then relief of irritation in anus and of pains in r. hypochondrium and abdomen. Omitted; and urine scanty. (Ascarides expelled.)

Clinical.—Diarrhœa, profuse, yellow, watery, gushing, < excessive drinking of water. The diarrhœa is generally painless, associated with *cold feeling in abdomen* (Colch.), but sometimes with cramps.

Urinary Organs.—Urging. Micturition frequent in evening; F., of watery urine; rare and less than usual. Burning in urethra during micturition; after micturition. Urine increased (apparently secondary action); *diminished; scanty and reddish*, becomes turbid on standing; contains mucus, with cloudy sediment on standing; U. like muddy water on standing; deposits a slight cloud.

Sexual Organs.—Sticking from l. spermatic cord through abdomen to chest. Drawing pain in glans. Emission in morning after a lascivious dream, then long, painful erections. Menstruation eight days earlier and three days longer than usual.

Respiratory Organs.—Scraping in larynx at 7 P.M., with paroxysms of dry cough. Scraping cough, with soreness in trachea. Dry cough in morning on rising, > walking; D. cough about midnight, with oppression of chest and chilliness; waking towards midnight; in shocks in forenoon, with pressure in abdomen beneath l. short ribs.

Chest.—Sticking; in middle; in l. fourth rib; in r. upper costal region; in region of l. short ribs; posteriorly in l.; in l. female breast; beneath r. mamma; beneath l. female breast, then twinging in whole abdomen; in r. mamma at 2.30 P.M. on bending together, > becoming erect, it is a simple pain on inspiration; in l. on inspiration; in r. lung on every inspiration; in r. < inspiration; extending from l. side to stomach, after dinner; inward beneath r. false ribs; intermittent, between short ribs during dinner; intermittent in last l. false ribs in morning on rising, after stool and after dinner. Tearing in r. female breast, with sticking in r. costal region; T. beneath cartilages of l. false ribs, with pressure. Cramp, a sensation as if contracted, < between scapulæ and beneath sternum, > eructations after rubbing the back.

Pain beneath l. short ribs after dinner. Throbbing pain in region of l. short ribs. Pressure; in r.; on upper part, not affecting respiration; in l. during inspiration and on stooping. Oppression in evening on ascending a hill; O., > eructations; O., with increased beating of heart. Heaviness during inspiration. Rawness in r., provoking cough. Burning in l. upper part; B. above pit of stomach, then in head, with redness of face and hands, but moderate warmth of skin.

Heart and Pulse.—Pressure at H. as from an impediment to its beating; with pulse rapid, once intermittent. Violent and rapid beating of H. *Palpitation* on least exertion. Pulse small; after the palpitation, and intermittent. P. slow before breakfast. Fall in the beat of P., < head.

Neck and Back.—Drawing in r. side of neck, with tearing. Nape feels as if grasped. Pressure as from a finger upon r. side of neck. Heaviness and pressure forward from nape into head. Drawing downward between scapulæ. Sticking from l. scapula across shoulder towards r. female breast, at 2.30 P.M.; in lower dorsal vertebra on l. side; in region of r. kidney. Burrowing in r. ischium in evening. Pain in coccyx after stool. Frequent pain in l. loin, < walking, > pressure. Bruised pain in loins.

Extremities.—Suppurating pain in r. hand and l. foot. Heaviness of arms and legs on moving about. Relaxed and paralyzed feeling. Weakness of arms and legs all day; W. of hands and feet when walking.

Upper Extremities.—Sticking near r. axilla; through l. shoulder-joint. Rheumatic tearing in shoulders. Arm tearing, drawing pains, < l. elbow and wrist; drawing, with tearing in all joints; weakness of r. during dinner, with trembling of r. hand; paralyzed feeling in l. in evening. Upper arm, sticking above bend of elbow; tearing in flexor muscles; T. above l. elbow; periodical T.; bruised and tired feeling in r. when moved; cramplike drawing in lower part of l. Elbow, sticking from bend of l., through arm to tip of elbow, afterwards only in bend; S. on upper surface of r. on bending; tearing in l.; T. in r. at 1 P.M.; T. from bend of r. towards index, as if in bone; tearing throbbing pain in l. Forearm, tearing on anterior surface of l. near elbow; in l. beneath elbow in afternoon. Wrist, tearing in l.; above and below r.; in l., with throbbing pain; tearing drawing in bones of r., extending to tips of fingers, at noon, lasting three hours, with itching in them. Hands, cramplike drawing in places. Sticking in first joint of l. thumb. Tearing in back of r. index in afternoon, with sticking; T. extending from two r. small fingers towards back of hand; T. between first and second phalanges of thumb in afternoon when writing, so that he could not hold the pen.

Lower Extremities.—Reeling. Thigh, sticking in bend of l.; above r. knee; in l. hip at 2.30 P.M.; tearing in r. femur below trochanter; T. from middle of l. to knee; pain extending from r. hip to hepatic region, as after long bending to the left; bruised pain after a short walk; B. pain, obliging him to sit; paralytic drawing extending to knees. Knee, sticking in inner surface of r. after dinner when walking; S. beneath r. patella on sitting down and on rising, > walking; tearing on inner margin of l. patella; painful tension in a spot in r.; drawing pain in l. when walking, > a long walk, with tearing. Legs, sticking in r. calf in afternoon; sticking tearing in middle of tibiæ when sitting, > walking, when there is sticking in r. calf, > sitting; boring in tibiæ towards evening; drawing like a pain from weariness at 7 P.M., extending to knees and into feet; laxity; weakness in forenoon, with heaviness; W. when walking in open air after dinner, with sticking in calves; l. leg and foot go to sleep when sitting, > motion, with drawing inward of toes. Malleoli and knees, tearing; boring in ankles; B. in ankles and knees only when sitting. Feet weary; F. lighter than ever before.

Skin.—Pimples with yellow tips on r. chest, burning after scratching. Boil, with pus at tip, painful on pressure. Itchlike pustule beneath l. nates, which was unconsciously scratched off at night and then burned. Two itchlike tetters anteriorly above l. elbow, scratched sore at night.

Sticking like flea-bites from l. angle of jaw to neck; in places, in nape, ankles. Tearing on tip of nose at 3 P.M., > scratching. Tension on r. side of neck after dinner, with burning. Crawling on face, < lower jaw, provoking scratching, then pustules, then desquamation. Tickling, > scratching, posteriorly on ball of r. thumb; on first joint of r. middle finger; on r. brow, but returning. Biting on r. flank; in l. ankle, > moving; at 3 P.M., > scratching, on l. eyebrow and l. side of neck; itching B. on cheeks. Itching biting, > scratching above r. temple; above r. ear; on r. lower jaw; in r. inner malleolus; on r. zygoma, then appearing above l. brow.

Itching on inner surface of l. knee at 2.30 P.M.; I. between l. thumb and index, after scratching two small itching vesicles; of r. ear at 2.30 P.M., and after rubbing burning; on l. lower margin of eye, at 3 P.M., > rubbing; on l. scapula at 2.30 P.M., > rubbing. Itching, > scratching above r. brow; on l. side of nose; in r. palm; on r. tibia above ankle; on sacrum at 2 P.M.; on l. side of chin at 2.30 P.M.; of r. external ear at 6 P.M.; on r. temple, then appearing in l.; on l. clavicle near shoulder and in nape, returning and changing to burning, then to biting. Itching not > scratching, in r. axilla; on outer margin of l. foot. Itching on r. thigh like scraping, with burning after scratching. Biting itching in a spot on l. tibia, in middle of inner side; posteriorly above bend of knee at 2 P.M.

Sleep.—Yawning, with weariness; Y. at 2.30 P.M., with indolence and sleepiness; frequent, during the day, with sleepiness, at night quiet, sound sleep; frequent at 1 P.M., without sleepiness. Sleepiness; at 2 P.M. when reading; two hours after dinner; after dinner, not > open air; after midday meal, with weakness; overpowering, in evening, and feeling every morning and evening as if she had not slept enough, > if after rising she took a short nap. Falls asleep early. Stupefying sleep, he is confused on waking. Falls asleep late. Sleepless till towards 3 A.M.; S. if he remained up longer than usual. Frequent waking after midnight, after which only half sleep. Light sleep, during which she hears everything. Dreams joyous, lively; frightful, of serpents, etc.; of the death of his relatives; foolish, disconnected.

Fever.—Chilliness; in forenoon, with shivering, < down back, with cold hands; at 3.30 P.M., on entering room; in bed, which she believed continued in sleep; on waking from a dream that she is cold; when vomiting; after stool, with shivering and hair standing on end; frequent, with cold hands; creeping. Frequent shivering; S. during dinner, with nausea; on entering room after stool; over head in evening. Head sensitive to cold. Chilliness in head; frequent, on vertex, at times painful, changing after covering with a cap to heat; externally on face at 2 P.M., with internal heat in it; creeping over back.

Heat at 1.30 P.M., with sweat of head and hands; H., < head, > open air; rising, with red face and external heat. Heat of head; after rising from stooping; in evening, with weariness and laxity of body; > open air, with redness of face; about forehead after dinner, rather external; frequent, sudden in l. frontal eminence after dinner. Burning before l. ear; behind r. ear at 4 P.M. Heat of face; after dinner, with external warmth and redness; with redness; of cheeks, with crawling and feeling of swelling; in r. zygoma, with crawling, then also in l.; sudden, in r. zygoma, which just as suddenly disappears. Heat of hands; with swelling of them. Burning in external surface of r. thigh while sitting down; in bend of r. knee when sitting after dinner, > walking; tickling, in axilla, > scratching.

Sweat; after morning soup; general; profuse, at night; profuse, towards morning; on palms.

Grindelia.

A tincture is made of the fresh herb, Grindelia squarrosa, Dunal.

Fulness of head as from quinine, then rheumatic pain and soreness in l. eyeball, running back to brain, < moving it, pupil dilated, the same pain and soreness in r. knee, then r. eye affected like l., conjunctivæ injected, eyes appearing as in congestion of brain, unbearable pain in region of liver and spleen, so that I could not lie still a moment, with rheumatic soreness in region of the pain, respiration would cease on falling asleep, and would not be resumed till awakened by the suffocation.

Clinical.—Conjunctivitis. Purulent ophthalmia. Iritis. Asthma, with profuse secretions, which are tenacious, the expectoration relieves. Paroxysmal dyspnœa, with palpitation, faintness, inability to lie down, starting up with convulsive efforts to breathe, with livid face. Cheyne-Stokes respiration, if the patient drops off to sleep he stops breathing and wakes with a start and gasps for breath (Lach., Gel., Cur.). Œdema of the lungs and bronchopneumonia in cases of fatty degeneration of the heart, can breathe only when sitting up, has to keep awake to breathe. Chronic pneumonias, with purulent expectoration, great dyspnœa, asthmatic expiration. Chronic bronchitis, with headache and purulent expectoration. Varicose ulcers on the leg, purplish-black, with profuse fetid secretions (confirmations needed).

Guaiacum.

A tincture is made of the gum from Guaiacum officinale.

General Action.—It seems to promote perspiration and the secretion of urine and to augment the menstrual flow. It has been much vaunted as a remedy for secondary syphilis, chronic rheumatism, etc.

Compare Iod., Comocladia, etc.

Generalities.—Emaciation in men of dry constitution, with hectic fever. Everything seems too tight in morning on waking, and he tosses about the bed. General discomfort. Indolence. Weakness, < thighs and upper arms. Most symptoms appear when sitting, < morning, immediately after rising, or in evening shortly before sleep, a few from 9 to 12 A.M.

Clinical.—Arthritic diathesis. Chronic rheumatism. Secondary syphilis. General tendency to emaciation. Stiffness and contraction of muscles, tendons and extremities, with rheumatic swellings of the joints. Aching in the bones and chronic inflammation and degeneration of the bones, which are very sore and cannot bear the slightest touch. Growing pains in children.

Mind.—Fretful. Morose, he speaks little. Contemptuous. Obstinate. Loss of ideas at breakfast-time, he stands in one place and looks in front of him without thought. *Memory weak.*

Head.—Sticking upward in brain. Aching at night like a pressure upward in brain; A. ending in a stitch in r. frontal eminence. Brain feels loose in morning, and as if it moved at every step. Forehead, sticking in r. eminence; tearing externally from l. bone into muscles of cheeks; drawing T. in forepart; pain transversely across; pressing in forepart; drawing pain from middle of bone into nasal bones. Temple, tearing externally in l.; pressive pain in r. as from something broad; pressure in l., without pain. Side, sticking in l. at junction of parietal and temporal bones; drawing S. from r. parietal bone into frontal eminences, where they end in a single stitch; drawing-tearing S. in r., extending towards frontal bone; tearing in whole l. Occiput, sticking in l.; tearing in r.; drawing-tearing in O. and forehead. Headache externally as if too much blood were in scalp and it were swollen, when sitting. Pulsation externally, > walking, transiently > pressure, < sitting and standing, with sticking in temples.

Clinical.—Violent rheumatic or gouty (or syphilitic) pains in bones of the head, < top and l. side, extending into the face, < night.

Eyes.—**Feeling as if swelling and protruding, the lids seem too short to cover them** (see Comocl.), with sensation of insufficient sleep, yawning and stretching all day. Pupils dilated. Hardened mucus in r. canthi.

Ears and Nose.—Tearing in l. ear; in outer margin of l. concha. *Aching in l. ear.* Frequent watery discharge from nose.

Clinical.—Persistent deafness, with recurring earaches.

Face.—Swollen, red and painful. Spasmodic drawing in muscles of r. cheek in morning on rising. Sticking in r. cheek; in r. malar-bone. Sensation as if struck with a cloth in evening on falling asleep, so that he woke in fright. Pain in l. lower jaw; drawing, ending in a stitch.

Clinical.—Facial neuralgia.

Mouth and Throat.—Tearing in l. upper molars. Pain in l. upper molars on biting them together. Taste flat.

Clinical.—Neuralgic toothache. Tonsillitis.

Stomach.—Violent hunger in afternoon and evening. Appetite lost and nausea for everything. Thirst. Eructations; *empty.* Constriction in region, with anxiety and difficulty in breathing. Frequent pressure in pit, with difficulty in breathing, oppression and anxiety.

Abdomen.—Rumbling. Gurgling as from emptiness. Pinching cutting transversely through A. on inspiration. Sticking in l. hypochondrium. Griping, which extends more and more downward, then emission of flatus; G. in l. side of umbilicus; in hypogastrium, which constantly sinks downward and backward. Trembling of inner muscles close to r. ilium. Pain in groin as from a hernia.

Stool.—Thin, mucous, preceded by griping. Soft, crumbly. Constipation. Omitted.

Urinary and Sexual Organs.—Sticking in neck of bladder after urinating. Cutting when urinating as if something biting passed. *Frequent urging to urinate;* with small discharges; constant desire, with profuse urine each time; obliged to urinate every half hour and much each time, urging immediately after micturition, when only a few drops passed. Emission at night, without lascivious dreams.

Clinical.—Ovaritis in rheumatic patients, with irregular menstruation and dysmenorrhœa. Chronic inflammation of the ovaries, with agonizing pains, irritable bladder.

Respiratory Organs and Chest.—Spasmodic inflammatory affections of trachea, < larynx, with palpitation that threatened suffocation. Mucous expectoration on hacking and hawking. Sticking from larynx to l. clavicle; S. beneath l. true ribs, < towards back; from centre of r. chest to beneath r. scapula, < inspiration. Sudden stuffed sensation in chest, in præcordial region, even at night in sleep, like arrest of breath, causing frequent dry cough until there is some expectoration.

Clinical.—Pleuritic pains in apex of lungs, especially in consumption. In consumption it relieves the extremely offensive expectoration (compare Cap.).

Neck and Back.—Pain on sides of cervical vertebræ; P. extending from l. side of neck to vertex and ending in a stitch. *Rheumatic stiffness in l. side of back from nape to sacrum, with pain on slightest motion.* Drawing down r. side of spine from axilla to lowest ribs, with tearing. *Scapulæ, sticking extending along l. side of nape to occiput;* sticking tearing on posterior margin of r.; sticking tearing on margins, then constriction in dorsal muscles; constriction between S.

Clinical.—Muscular pain and stiffness in the back.

Upper Extremities.—Stretching, with yawning. Frequent sticking on top of r. shoulder; S. in r. upper arm, < middle. Drawing tearing in l. upper arm, extending to finger, < wrist. Upper arm weak as after hard labor. Frequent drawing-tearing sticking from l. elbow to wrist. Tearing in r. forearm, extending into wrist; T. in l. wrist; drawing T. in l. wrist. Sticking in r. thumb.

Lower Extremities.—Sticking in nates when walking, < sitting, as if she sat on needles. Thigh, stickings above r. knee; S. above l. knee, which meet on both sides; jerking tearing from middle of r. to knee; drawing tearing from middle of l. to knee; growing pain in r.; bruised pain in l. on walking in open air; crawling pain from middle of r. femur to knee when sitting still; drawing pain from middle of r. to knee on stretching leg, > drawing it up and bending it; tension, < r., as if muscles were too short, when walking, < touch, > sitting, with weakness. Drawing pain in knee, which ends in a stitch. Tearing sticking from middle of l. tibia to toes; between tibia and fibula, extending to patella; tearing-drawing S. from middle of r. tibia to knee. Jerking stitches in outer side of calf. Painless constriction in r. calf. Leg seems bruised after walking, feeling as if brittle. Weariness of legs, < thighs. Sticking in r. ankle when sitting; drawing S. from r. ankle to middle of tibia. Tearing long-drawn stitches from r. tarsus to knee. Pain in a spot on back of r. foot, ending in sticking, > motion.

Skin.—Sore, painful pimple on nose; hard P., with white tip, sore on touch, on r. eyebrow. Grumbling on whole leg, with heat in it. Crawling in chest; in thighs and legs, extending to toes, when sitting, as if they would go to sleep. Itching stitches like flea-bites on thigh, < sides of knee-cap, > scratching. Burning itching, < scratching; corrosive I. on back during day.

Sleep.—Yawning all day, with stretching and sensation of insufficient sleep; Y., with stretching and comfort. Sleepiness in afternoon. Sleepless two hours in evening, and tossing about the bed. Late falling asleep in evening and early waking in morning. Frequent waking as from fright or as if falling. Unrefreshed in morning on waking. Sleep full of dreams. Dream of that she was pierced by knives. D. of fights. Vivid D. of scientific subjects. Nightmare when lying on back, and waking with cries.

Fever.—Chilliness; in forenoon and in evening before sleep, sweat in morning; internal general, in evening, then heat, < face, without thirst; in back in afternoon. Shivering in back; in breasts. Heat of face, with thirst, without redness or sweat. Sweat every morning; S. on walking in open air, < head, pearly S. on forehead; profuse S. on back at night.

Hamamelis.

A tincture is made of the fresh bark of the twigs and root of Hamamelis Virginica, L. (witch-hazel).

General Action.—Its curative power seems to extend over the venous system; it has been found useful in venous dilatations and hæmorrhages, which it controls chiefly, we presume, by virtue of the gallic acid contained in the bark.

Allies.—Arnica, Rhod., Carbo veg., Vipera.

Generalities.—Disposition to take cold easily. Takes a fresh cold on being exposed for a moment, coldness creeping over body on standing a moment in open air, chill running up leg, head stopped, pain over orbits. Inability to keep still though motion made him worse. Desire to lie down. *Weariness;* at 3 P.M.; on rising, with vertigo; when walking, instep feels strained. *Tired easily;* in evening when standing; when walking.

Clinical.—Varicose veins externally on the abdominal walls. Varicose veins on the extremities, with soreness (it lacks the bruised feeling of Arn.). Many cases of phlebitis, with soreness and swelling of the leg, even up to the hip and extending to the abdomen.

Mind.—Feeling that she ought to be reverenced by all around her and have great respect paid to her opinions. Desire to hear sublime conversation after the heat, with indisposition to talk myself. Impatient, did not care whether he attended to his practice or not. Angry, nothing suits him. Irritable; and not wanting anybody to speak to him. Gloomy; > evening; with no disposition to move. Discontented all day. Wishes to be alone, unable to settle mind on study. Quick to perceive anything out of shape. Listless, < afternoon. Dull feeling when waking; on rising; in afternoon, with stupidity. No desire to work, likes to sit and muse; no desire to study or read in evening. Inability to read or study; I. to concentrate thoughts, with restlessness and discontentment. Forgetful < words when talking; F. of what he reads.

Head.—*Aching;* all day; in morning; in morning on waking; at 7 A.M.; towards night; *on rising;* < second sleep in morning; < morning and when indoors, > thinking, reading, walking or talking; < evening; < taking cold; > evening; > out-doors; with soreness of it; with distress in pyloric portion of stomach and umbilical region; intermittent. Bursting pain on waking, < bending forward; B. pain at 7 A.M. on waking, > towards evening, with vertigo on stooping. *Fulness;* all day; in brain, < at top, after the heat; with feeling as if a bolt passed from temple to temple and were tightly screwed. Feeling as if she had taken cold. Dulness. Vertigo; at noon; when stooping; on rising after stooping, after lying down, when reading; with nausea and desire to lie down; as if drunk; as if brain were swimming around all day; as if brain were swimming around on rising.

Forehead.—Aching; in morning; across bone; over nose and eyes; over r. eye at 9 A.M.; < sitting or standing, > lying, > rubbing forehead and pressure; over r. eye, < when sitting or lying quiet, about noon, > walking in open air, returning next day at 10 P.M.; > out of doors or when busy; with burning distress in lower part of epigastrium and umbilicus; bursting, in F. and over eyes at 8.30 A.M. on rising, with empty feeling at pit of stomach, the headache > towards night; stupefying, over eyes and root of nose. *Fulness.* Sensation as if anterior lobes of brain were too large for cranium. Stopped feeling over root of nose. Dulness, < over eyes and at root of nose; root of nose all day, < 11 P.M.

Aching in temples, < morning; sharp pain in T. Mastoid portion of temples, shooting in l.; shooting when walking in wind; sore pain in r.; pain in morning; peculiar sensation. Pain in occiput. Feeling as if vermin crawled along edges of hair.

Eyes.—Blue margins around eyes; under E., < r.;

at inner canthi. Dull color of sclerotica. Sore pain. Painful weakness. Feeling as if they would be forced out of head, > pressure, < transiently after removing pressure. Swelling of balls and lids, with bloodshot appearance of r. eye. Twitching of upper lids, r., then l. Burning of lids on closing them at 4 P.M., with heat in hands. Vision dim.

Clinical.—Ecchymoses in eyes from bruises. Traumatic inflammation of iris, with hæmorrhages. Intraocular hæmorrhages (Arn.).

Ears.—Burning in r. in evening. Itching in l., and over body under the clothing. Pain in mastoid process in afternoon and evening on first going into wind.

Nose.—Swollen, inflamed, painful to touch; septum swollen and painful to touch. Pain at root, with fulness. Stoppage; > evening. Sneezing at noon; S., with running of water from nose. Coryza; only from 4 to 10 P.M.; from exposure for a moment to a draught without a hat; with hawking from throat of what should come from nostrils; fluent, burning and smarting. Tough, green plug from r. nostril. **Profuse epistaxis**, > smelling camphor; *between* 9 *and* 10 A.M., **with tightness in bridge of nose and crowding pressure in forehead between eyes,** *and numbness over os frontis.* Bad smell from N. Smell oversensitive.

Clinical.—Nosebleed, either vicarious or idiopathic. Especially indicated in diseases of the nose, pharynx and mucous membranes, generally when there is a varicose condition of the small bloodvessels, which bleed easily.

Face.—Muscles sore and stiff. Shooting along r. upper jaw to malar-bone.

Mouth.—Lancinating pain extending from molars to malar-bone and into temporal region. Pain in r. teeth. Soreness about r. upper wisdom-tooth. Gums bleed easily (Carbo v.). Tongue pale; clean, but not so red in middle as usual; coated white in morning; blisters on r. side; scalding sensation just beyond tip; pressing distress at root. Taste bad; putrid; flat, rough.

Clinical.—Gums spongy, bleeding easily.

Throat. — Pain along r. sterno-cleido-mastoid, < morning and when moving. Congestion of fauces and tonsils, with pain on swallowing. Stinging in uvula on coughing, as if it would break off. Pain; on swallowing; in pharynx. Soreness, < fauces; and every inhalation seemed to dry up their mucous membrane. Rawness; and in fauces; and in fauces in evening. Feeling all day as if something had lodged in fauces, causing constant inclination to swallow. Distress in pharynx, with roughness of fauces; D. in pharynx and œsophagus, extending to stomach. Dryness; not > by water; with thirst, causing him to drink much water frequently; with burning, uvula fallen, difficulty in talking; all night, with feeling as if something had lodged there, compelling frequent swallowing, which caused pain in tonsils, next morning very painful on swallowing food, fauces congested, tonsils swollen.

Stomach.—Thirst in afternoon; in evening; lacking. Aversion to water. Increased desire to smoke, but symptoms were < smoking. Eructations; in evening; at night, three or four hours after meals; after eating; after tea; of air; tasting of food; of unusual taste in morning; taste of food rising to pharynx three or four hours after eating. Hiccough; and spasmodic eructations; violent, at 6 P.M., four hours after eating. Nausea; at 8 P.M.; 11 P.M.; on waking, with pain in frontal bone; after eating; after dinner, with eructations, has to remain quiet, even without reading, to avoid vomiting, has even then eructations and heartburn; after pork; after pork for dinner, with eructations and violent hiccough, then burning pain in stomach and œsophagus, then cramp in stomach and chest; with vertigo, compelling him to lie down in order to avoid falling. Vomiting before midnight of plums eaten at supper.

Gastric troubles. Distended by wind. Cramp; after a hearty dinner of usual food, and in transverse colon. Burning distress in lower epigastrium and umbilicus, with ineffectual urging to stool. Throbbing. Heaviness; back of S.

Clinical.—Hæmatemesis of black blood.

Abdomen. — Discharge of flatus. Griping after breakfast. Pain; morning and evening. Distress; in morning. Pain in r. hypochondrium. Cramp in umbilical region; after rising. Griping in U. region at 7 A.M.; at 10 P.M.; before dinner. Distress at umbilicus; with natural stool. Pain in groins; drawing, passing to testicles.

Rectum and Anus.—Pulsations in rectum when he is half recumbent; P. in rectum as if piles would protrude; in R. and penis, synchronous with radial pulse. Urging to stool; with large easy stool in morning and afternoon; ineffectual. Spasmodic contraction of sphincter. *Itching in anus.*

Clinical.—Hæmorrhoidal flow. Discharge of blood from the rectum, painless, dark and thick. Intestinal hæmorrhages.

Stool.—Soft at night; at 6 A.M., covered with mucus, and with distress in bowels. Covered with mucus. Constipation.

Urinary Organs.—Urging, but little urine, in drops; frequent urging; acts upon the kidneys more when lying, compelling her to rise soon to pass much urine. Frequent micturition during the day; frequent, with constant desire. Urine copious, with frequent desire; C. and pale; C. and clear; profuse, but little at a time and light-colored; profuse, light-colored, with greasy deposit, which rises to the top on shaking and looks like laudable pus. Urine clear, saltish.

Clinical.—Hæmaturia.

Sexual Organs.—Glans, stitching; tingling; pulsations. Erections; at night; on retiring, without desire, but in morning he found he had had an emission; frequent. **Pain in spermatic cords running into testes,** at night. Sweat on scrotum at night; profuse and cold. *Frequent pain in testicles all day* (Clem., Rhod.); with distress in bowels; *drawing P. in testicles* (Rhod.). Desire increased. Emission at night without sensual dreams; and without being aware of it; E., without erection. **Active uterine hæmorrhage;** *loss of over a quart of bright, fresh blood, not coagable,* midway between two menstrual periods, her menses were usually dark and coagulated.

Clinical.—Varicocele. Varices of the labiæ. Dysmenorrhœa, with pain in ovaries. Chronic metritis. Uterine hæmorrhages, dark venous flow. Ovaritis, subacute. Orchitis.

Respiratory Organs.—Hoarse in morning on rising. Cough dry, sometimes expectoration of thick, yellowish or greenish-gray mucus. Return in evening of inflammation of diaphragm, which was caused fifteen years ago by running, now all the original symptoms, labored respiration, tightness of lower part of chest, inability to inspire deeply and fully, and on attempting to lie down inability to breathe, with fulness of blood in neck and head, and suffocation so that he was obliged to sleep that night in a chair with the neck bare, > morning, but returning, riding and walking painful.

Chest.—Sudden hæmorrhage from lungs. Spasmodic movements of diaphragm. Occasional sticking. Cramp; at 11 P.M. Pain in r. lung; at 10 A.M.

Heart and Pulse.—Pricking pain in region of H. and in veins of arms. Palpitation. H's beats can be counted by lying still and pulsations are felt in balls of fingers. Pulse rapid. Pulse irregular; full and hard, then almost imperceptible; 60, every fifth, sixth or seventh beat a little faster and stronger.

Neck and Back.—Sore pain down cervical vertebræ. Tearing across back. Backache; caused by an emission; all day, and pain in legs; along spine, back of stomach, about 4 P.M.; in loins all day; in loins in morning; in kidney region in morning on rising; in sacrum and hip all day, < walking.

Extremities.—Aching and tendency to go to sleep. Drawing pain in hands, legs and feet. Rheumatic symptoms in arms and legs through the day. Fulness in joints as if they would burst. Weariness in r.; r. arm and leg; of limbs and arms when walking. Going to sleep easily in afternoon.

Upper Extremities.—Arms, drawing pain in flexors of r.; weariness; stiffness of A. and shoulders after horseback riding; bruised pain in upper A. and shoulders, < motion, next day with drowsiness. Pain in humeri; extending to elbow and causing stiffness in elbow; sore, in head of r. in morning, extending to elbow, with stiffness of elbow. Shooting along flexors of r. forearm into palm. Pricking pain from wrist to shoulder, along course of superficial veins, < pressure. R. wrist and fingers stiff in morning. Pain in back of r. hand, extending to shoulder-joint; P. in hands and fingers in morning, with stiffness. Sore pain in r. thumb-nail after a slight knock, < night, afterwards with sensation as if growing into flesh, afterwards transiently > discharge of pus. Finger sore after rubbing off a small piece of skin. Fingers stiff at night, and sticking in first joint of r. index.

Lower Extremities.—Bruised feeling, < l. Tired; from hips to feet, inability to run fast; in r. at 6 P.M., with forcing feeling in varicose veins; in r., where there are varicose veins, > placing it on a chair, removed by walking. Sensitiveness of varices. Peculiar feeling in varices. (*Apparent diminution of varicose veins above knee.*) Sticking along l. sciatic nerve; S. in l. hip and under l. patella when walking. Soreness of femoral vessels to middle third of thigh. Sore pain in r. femur; S. pain running down thighs, < r. Weary pain in thighs; < l.; at night, < middle and lower third, and in popliteal space, with dilatation of varicose veins. Stiffness of upper part of thighs.

Pain in l. knee. Sore pain in popliteal space. Soreness of knee. Rheumatic pains in legs. Fulness in joints of legs as if they would burst, then dread of moving the limbs, with weary, stiff, full feeling. R. leg tired. Pain in feet and toes; in r. great toe; suddenly in r. great toe when running. Feet easily go to sleep when driving in cold wind. Stitching in corns on r. foot at 10 A.M., afterwards as soon as boots are put on in morning (rainy day), permanent during the day, occasionally pulsating. Sharp pain in corns on toe. Pulsations in corns on l. toes in evening; P. in corns on both feet after paring them in morning.

Skin.—Herpes on lower part of nose; on nose in afternoon, > evening. Hands chapped. Pimples between thumb and index, < r.; on face, caused by emissions, with bad feeling; on nates, sore on touch; behind ear and on body, sore on touch and pressure; fine, all over body, next day not so sensitive. Feeling as if vermin were running over body; all over hairy parts. Tingling in foot when counting femoral pulse. Itching of hands; axilla, < r.; all over body on undressing; on lower limbs on undressing; of hands in morning on waking, transiently > rubbing them together, < scratching, I. next day at 6 A.M. on waking, > rubbing and putting them into cold air, unaffected by washing in cold water.

Sleep.—Sleepiness; two hours after dinner. Less inclination to sleep than usual, slept well all night. Sleeplessness from thinking too much. Could scarcely sleep, heard the clock strike every hour. Uneasy sleep in morning; U. sleep, constant waking from thinking of the business of the day, turning over in bed, unrefreshed on waking. Restless night, whole body felt hot and dry, sexual dream, with emission, then weariness and pain in loins. Sexual dream, with an emission; without emission. Fearful D. Unpleasant D. at 5 A.M., then uneasy sleep. D. that a bat was flying in the room and fear of injury therefrom.

Fever.—Coldness; on going to bed; running up legs; in flashes over back and hips at 9 A.M., extending down limbs. Heat; then tearing across small of back and fulness in joints of legs as if they would burst, which soon extended to all joints. Hot hands; and dry; burning in palms, with dryness. Hot and dry skin. Sweat at night after lying down.

Clinical.—It has been used in low forms of typhoid or malarial fevers, with weak, rapid pulse, etc. It has been given for hæmorrhagic measles, hæmorrhagic smallpox and purpura.

Helleborus Niger.

A tincture is made of the dried root of Helleborus niger, L.

General Action.—It produces a "bluntness of sensibility" of all the special senses; also occasionally convulsions. It first produces scanty urine and dropsical symptoms.

Allies.—Puls., Colch., Apis.

Generalities.—Flesh feels soft. *Convulsions; with coldness.* Cramps and convulsive motions, with shooting in brain. General tremor. Unsteadiness in her actions. Tearing sticking in several places at once, on upper arms, chest, back, etc. Sticking boring in coverings of bones; S. boring in various parts, < cold and exertion and after eating and drinking. Feeling after the fever as if he had been sick long in bed; feeling in open air as if he had been sick long, all objects seemed new. Soreness in flesh. (Distended sensation in swollen parts, with heaviness.) Could neither sit, stand nor lie, and constantly pointed to his heart. Feeling as if blood were poor and thin, listlessness. Necessity to stretch as soon as he opened his eyes in morning, then weariness and closure of lids. *Weakness;* in forenoon, with sleepiness and yawning. Sudden relaxation of all muscles, with falling to the ground, coldness of body, cold sweat on forehead, stammering, slow pulse and contracted pupils. Faintness. Aggravation in afternoon and evening. Amelioration in open air.

Clinical.—This drug seems to be useful in a general condition of want of reaction, a semi-paralytic state of the system.

Mind.—Delirium. Vivid fancies after lying down, a hundred forms float before his eyes, suddenly coming and going. Self-confidence. Happy carelessness about everything. Mirth alternating with melancholy, desire to laugh, then desire to weep. *Anxiety; with restlessness*, apprehension of misfortune; with indifference to joy or sorrow, contented with nothing. Restless, impatient, hopeful, feeling as if circulation were increased, could accomplish great deeds, fearless, feeling as if brain were boiling. Anger at trifles. Fretfulness. Despair about his own life. Sadness; on seeing a cheerful person; on account of his condition. Homesick. Do not wish to speak, dread company; do not wish any one to speak to me or look at me. Reflective, taciturn all the afternoon. Tranquil and desirous to lie down. (Irresolute.) (Dresses himself awkwardly.) *Stupefaction, with slow answers* (Phos.); S., with vertigo. Distraction when studying. Inability to reflect. Memory weak.

Clinical.—The general mental condition characteristic of this drug is one of almost complete stupor; it is extremely difficult to arouse the patient (the Phos. ac. patient can be aroused easily). There seems to be great physical prostration, or at least loss of control of the mind over the body, possibly due to cerebral effusion (serous); this tendency to serous effusions is very marked in almost every part of the body, and in dropsical effusions everywhere Hell. is the remedy if the patient be stupid (Apis). Melancholia, fear of death, a kind of stupidity, unintelligible muttering, etc.

Head.—Tearing in various parts. Piercing pain, which on sitting upright becomes a burning in brain. Aching; all day, with heaviness in it and pain in limbs; every day from 4 to 8 P.M.; on waking, < occiput, with heaviness; in skull; deep; so that he moves constantly, > lying quietly in a half dose, with eyes closed; stupefying, all day, as from drunkenness; as if compressed all day; as if brain were pressed inward on every step in open air; as if brain would be pressed from both sides towards middle and upward. Bruised pain; now in one part of brain, now in another, < stooping, with dulness.

Brain feels too large; on waking, with paroxysmal pain in forehead, < movement, > pressure. *Confusion;* till evening, with heaviness; < stooping, with warmth; > pressure of palm; > open air, with heaviness and inclination to vertigo; with painless digging here and there; and noise hurts, sound of wind distresses. *Heaviness;* all day, < during fever, > open air, with tension and pressure inward in temples, < forehead, and with every pulse pressing drawing as if blood were forced through head; with internal heat in it, cold fingers and general chill, > wrapping up hands and keeping them warm; of brain, with sensation as if it were surrounded by a tight skin, with inability to think or remember. Stupefaction; dizzy. *Congestion of brain.*

Vertigo; all day, < walking; in morning on waking, with heaviness of head, then nausea, he feels better when sitting and bending head, but on rising return of nausea and vertigo; on stooping; on stooping and raising head again, > becoming erect; on becoming erect; on walking; with nausea and prostration; with indistinct vision, dilated pupils, roaring in ears and unsteady gait; with pleasant warmth in stomach and abdomen; stupefying, with inclination to fall forward; as if objects moved in a circle, with stupidity.

Forehead.—Muscles drawn in folds. Drawing in skin so that it is wrinkled. Sticking externally in r., then l.; boring S. transversely across. Tearing in l. eminence, involving l. eye. Boring in bone and along coronal suture; in F. and occiput, with sticking. Boring drawing pain. Aching; in l.; over eyes; in bone; in sinciput; deep in sinciput; in sinciput all day, with heat in it; in evening, with pressure in r. temple; in eminence when sitting, with vertigo; in sinciput, < evening, with tearing and heat; in r. eminence, < walking in open air; over eyes extending to temples, skin of F. feels tight, disposed to frown, head feels weak as if dazed; bursting. Pressure outward in r. Brain feels too large in front, occiput feels empty, then reverse in forehead and occiput feels as if it would fall forward, disposed to lie down and roll head from side to side, feel helpless like an infant, disposed to draw up feet like an infant. Pulsation, and in temples, with heat in face. Confusion; all day in sinciput, with heaviness and pain. Heaviness; in sinciput; in sinciput, < afternoon, with heat and pressure, then towards evening the trouble in head alternated with pressure in r. upper arm, then the headache alternated with pain in knee, r. leg, l. hand and upper arm, with these symptoms rapid pulse, cold hands, hot head and face, relief at 11 P.M., next night full of anxious dreams. Stupefaction and pressure, < eyes, as if something would fall out of F. and eyes.

Pain in temples; in r. after exerting attention, < walking; compressive; drawing, to ear; bursting sensation. Pulsation in l. temple, ending in a stitch. Drawing pain in vertex in morning in bed. Pressure upon vertex; as with a point; as if skull were pressed inward; like a clavus. Bruised pain externally in vertex and occiput, < during chill, becoming on motion, < stooping and ascending steps, a jerking in scalp, > pressure. Sticking in region of r. coronal suture, as if rising out of brain. One-sided tearing, with chill. Pressure in l. side; drawing P. in l. hemisphere of brain from behind to forehead, as if brain accumulated there. Stupefying, dizzy drawing now in one, now in other hemisphere, also in whole brain. Confusion of l. side, with change of coryza from fluent to stopped. *Pain in occiput;* extending towards nape; bruised, < stooping. Sensation as if scalp were tight over occiput.

Clinical.—Hydrocephalus, with torpidity, unconsciousness, insensibility of eyes, suppression of urine, especially with wrinkling of forehead and constant chewing motion. Hydrocephalus, with sudden screams and boring of the head into the pillow, wrinkling of forehead, automatic motions of one arm or foot. Some cases of hydrocephalus, with most violent general convulsions, distortion of the face, complete unconsciousness, suppression of urine. The sequelæ of hydrocephalus, the child is idiotic, seems to want nothing, but drinks eagerly. Effects of repressed eruptions, simulating hydrocephalus. Distortion of the eyes in hydrocephalus. Effects of concussion of the brain, after Arn. had failed.

Eyes.—Staring. Sunken and discolored about lids. Sticking as if they would lachrymate. Boring deep in r. Pressure; deep; P. upon them. Feeling as if pressed together by something heavy from above in open air, he must exert himself to open them widely. Burning biting, < inner canthus. *Pupils dilated;*

contracted. Sticking in l. ball; S. in ball and its covering in morning after waking, on pressing eyes together; S. downward. Pain in r. ball; in a spot on l. ball, between it and external and upper part of orbit. Twitching of lids; upper. Lids, half open in slumber and pupils drawn upward; (swollen, red); biting in r.; B. in margins; burning and prickling. Canthi, inner full of dry mucus in morning; soreness in l. in morning on waking, with moisture in them; pressure in r. inner, < closing eye; itching.

Orbit, sticking in upper margin of l., rather towards inner canthus, > during pressure with finger; tearing on outer side of l., as if between wall and ball, affecting ball; aching; deep A.; A. as if eyes would fall out. Twitching of brows and cheeks, with heat of face. Brow, sticking tension in l. on touch, as if a pimple would form; pain drawing back and forth, with spasmodic contraction of their muscles. Photophobia; during fever. Sensation as if everything were too clear and black. Vision dim; in morning; flickering; of floating specks; of black specks; of black specks and rings; of bright and dark spots.

Ears.—Burrowing boring-sticking in r. at night, with sticking-tearing toothache, only the earache remained in morning and during the day. Pressure; in fossa behind lobule. Drawing pain as if middle ears would burst. Roaring and ringing.

Nose.—Pain in root. Constriction as if suffocation would follow. Heat; in nostrils; about nostrils; under nose; itching, in l. wing. Biting itching beneath nose and on upper lip, as in commencing coryza. Spasmodic tickling as if it would cause sneezing, with yawning. Sneezing; in morning on rising, whereby upper lip cracks in middle; in morning fasting; with nausea. Catarrh of l. nostril; fluent C., with dizzy confusion of head; fluent C., with stupefaction of head. Smell less acute.

Face.—*Pale during heat of head; P. and features distorted; and sunken; pulse lost, icy coldness and cold sweat all over body, so that a drop is on end of every hair. Red.* Yellow. Boring in l. zygoma. Pain in l. zygoma; in r. as if in bone. A row of stitches behind ascending ramus of lower jaw, near ear. Vesicle in middle of red of upper lip in morning after waking. Ulceration in corners of lips, with itching.

Mouth.—Tearing in third molars on biting them together, extending into roots; sticking T. in r. molars in evening in bed, < warmth and cold, so that he sleeps little, the lower molars seem longer, > during the day. Hollow teeth feel as if cold air passed through them. Tongue, trembling; vesicles; pimple on tip, with sticking on touch; sticking; *dry* and white in morning on rising; stiff, insensible. Scraping posteriorly on palate; S. on arch of palate and in fauces. Dryness; all day, with scraping in throat; *of palate, with cutting scraping in it on moving mouth to swallow.* Salivation; watery. Taste bitter in throat, < eating; B. to all food; sourish T., with salivation; dry, slimy, with thirst.

Clinical.—Aphthæ of the mouth.

Throat.—Pain in cervical glands. Flapping as of mucus, like the opening and shutting of a valve on every inspiration. Sticking; low down; and in fauces and tongue, with strangury and constriction of throat and difficult swallowing, pain at epigastrium and violent sickness, swelling of tongue and other organs of deglutition, much viscid mucus from mouth. Scraping; in fauces from 10 to 1 and from 10 to 11 P.M.; in fauces, with dryness. Rawness as after acrid liquor. Pressure on swallowing, with excoriated feeling. Constriction. Burning and dryness; agreeable warmth from pharynx to stomach and over whole body, as after spirituous drinks.

Stomach.—Appetite great; in forenoon; with frequent tasteless eructations; ravenous; diminished; lost; A., but no relish to food and nausea while eating. Aversion to food; to fat meat; to green vegetables and sauerkraut. **Thirst**; none all day. Eructations; of bitter fluid; suppressed. Empty eructations; after breakfast; with nausea, but inability to vomit. Hiccough. *Nausea;* in evening; in evening, > bitter vomiting, with prostration, then helpless feeling; at night, with prostration and bitter vomiting; after eating; > breakfast, with headache; disturbing sleep; rising from pit of stomach; in whole abdomen; it often seems as if he were hungry, but food disgusts him. *Vomiting;* copious, frequent; of mucus; of food, then relief; greenish slimy; greenish-black, with colic; bitter at night.

Distention in pit and epigastric region, impeding respiration, with ulcerative pain; D. in stomach, with ravenous hunger; D., with grumbling in abdomen as of frogs. Lancinations from epigastrum to rectum. Griping. Cramp in pit and just below it, > straightening up and when walking, returning on sitting, with nausea. Pain; *in pit;* in pit at every step; ulcerative, after every meal; distending; bruised near and beneath pit and in region of pylorus, where it is painful on every step, the pain < talking loud and on touch. Soreness; < stepping and coughing. Scraping as if rubbed with woolen. Biting; in evening, with heaviness and distended feeling; during a short walk, with gnawing, ravenous hunger and prostration of lower limbs; in morning fasting, then pain in abdomen, with rumbling, then slight soft stool, then dragging in rectum. Oppression. Pit feels drawn inward. Feeling as if a fluid were poured into it. Uneasiness as before vomiting. Burning; rising through œsophagus; rising into head like nausea; and in fauces, like a streak of fire.

Abdomen.—*Distention;* in evening; with constant ineffectual urging to stool; with ulcerated sensation on pressure; painful. *Rumbling;* with uneasiness. Movements of flatus; as if bubbles rose and burst, then offensive flatus; rising of flatulence towards short ribs, with empty eructations. Offensive flatus; in morning after the customary milk; after dinner. Sticking, with tearing transversely across it. Cutting continuing in evening. Griping on ascending steps; dysentery-like C. transversely across after eating. Burrowing.

Colic; on waking at 5 A.M., with more urging to urinate than usual in morning and *scanty urine;* at night; *with pallor, sunken features and staggering, found leaning against a tree, arms hanging down relaxed, hands cold, eyes sunken, lids closed, pupils moderately dilated and scarcely sensible to light, lips bluish, face covered with clammy sweat, pulse thready,* 102, then four liquid stools, with tensemus, retching and vomiting twice of slimy, yellowish fluid (compare Colch.); as before diarrhœa; bruised pain anteriorly and laterally in walls. Loose sensation in morning, so that pressure was agreeable. Heaviness. Coldness. Discomfort, with coldness, as before diarrhœa; D., with drawing pain as before diarrhœa, then urging to stool and pasty stool.

Twisting griping in hepatic region extending downward and forward. Umbilicus, twisting about, in morning, > bending together and passage of flatus, with cutting; pain deep in region; heat deep in region; sharp pressure inward transversely across below U., < sitting. Rumbling beneath umbilicus; R. low down as if in spine. Sticking in hypogastrium, disturbing sleep. Jerking cuttings from r. iliac region (beneath and outward in umbilicus) to outer part of l. iliac region, returning in r. iliac region, which was painful to pressure. Pain in r. groin; becoming a sticking, a sensation as if a hernia would form; intermittent, in outer surface of os ilium, similar to sciatica, in afternoon. Pressure on middle of pubis.

Clinical.—Many cases of ascites have been cured. Dropsy the result of disease of the kidneys or following eruptive diseases.

Rectum.—Aching. Tenesmus after stool. Frequent inclination to stool. Sudden urging, with cutting in abdomen, then pasty stool, with disappearance of discomfort in abdomen; sudden pressing asunder urging, then a thick, dry, difficult stool, with smarting in anus during and after stool. Ineffectual urging. No desire for stool at usual time, and a sensation as if anus were closed forever, then sudden pressure and sensation of distention, at first only short emissions of flatus, then a hard, large, difficult stool, with smarting during and < after the stool.

Anus.—Inclination to hæmorrhoids. Dragging, with pressing asunder sensation, then stool difficult, frothy, mostly hard fæces in balls. Sudden pressure as from a foreign body, with desire for stool, but only flatus is passed, afterwards return of pressure and a small amount of large fæces. Feeling all day as of constipation. Burning biting after stool. Itching as from ascarides.

Stool.— **Of only clear, tenacious, colorless mucus** (Colch.). *White, gelatinous, like frog spawn, frequent, with pressure.* Liquid, twice at night. Diarrhœa; with nausea and colic; always preceded by colic, which is relieved after stool. Soft and in part thin, with feeling as if intestines had not power to evacuate it. *Constipation.* Hard, scanty, during and after which there is cutting sticking upward in rectum, as if it drew itself tightly together and something with sharp edges were sticking between its walls. Large, difficult, with burning smarting in anus, which continues after stool, < sphincter. Undigested. Frequent. Retained, next day earlier than usual, and in afternoon diarrhœa.

Clinical.—Diarrhœa, stools of jelly-like mucus, like frog spawn, generally with tenesmus (Colch.); sometimes profuse watery diarrhœa alternating with constipation, in abdominal dropsy.

Urinary Organs. — *Urging; frequent,* **with scanty discharge** (Colch.); desire and scanty discharge, with burning through urethra. *Frequent micturition.* When urinating there is no stream and no desire, as if bladder had lost its power of expulsion. Urine copious; without much urging; and watery; diminished; U. decomposes in a few minutes; U. dark yellow; passed without a stream.

Clinical.—Subacute inflammation of the kidneys, with suppression of urine in dropsical symptoms. Inflammation of the bladder and almost complete suppression of urine.

Sexual Organs.—Relaxation and no desire. Itching sticking in tip of glans. No erections even when urine has accumulated in bladder. Desire suppressed. Pain in region of r. ovary.

Clinical.—Suppression of menses.

Respiratory Organs.—Mucus, so that breathing was audible. Contracted feeling, with audible inspiration. Cough; *sudden, constant hacking, when sitting smoking tobacco as usual;* dry hacking, with painful tension in l. short ribs. Moaning. Groaning and grunting. Involuntary sighing. Breathing difficult; in evening; from tightness of chest; and he must breathe slowly and deeply; with frequent need to breathe deeply, < walking in open air. Rapid breathing. Short breath when reading or speaking. Breathes better with mouth open.

Chest.—Sticking in walls; in top of lungs; in l.; l. costal region; beneath l. ribs; in l. short ribs when walking; in last true ribs on every inspiration; in l. on every deep inspiration when lying in evening. Cutting on lowest true ribs outward through chest, < inspiration. Twinging at one time in r. anterior part, at another in region of heart. Piercing pain in l. breast near axilla. Pain in walls; in muscles; l. muscles; near r. axilla; in l. breast on leaning over; in l. breast and shoulder on moving, extending down arm to elbow. *Constriction so that he gasps for breath, with open mouth, but cannot breathe.* Tight, as if lungs were tightened, because ribs do not seem to expand. L. short ribs seem screwed to spine. Scraping in upper part of sternum. Warmth in lower part.

Clinical.—Hydrothorax, difficult respiration, necessity to sit up, with great constriction of chest and gasping for breath.

Heart and Pulse.—Pain in region of H. Heaviness in region of H. Palpitation. Violent throbbing of H. *Pulse rapid;* then slow; *slow;* varied from 30 to 50, small, at times scarcely perceptible; small; *small and tremulous;* small and feeble; strong; felt vividly through whole body, < heart.

Clinical.—Heart's action weak, pulse small and tremulous, with dropsical symptoms.

Neck.—Pain in cervical bone; P. in nape extending to vertex; in some muscles on moving neck, with stiffness. Stiffness of muscles of nape as far as occiput, during rest, < moving head; rheumatic S. of nape.

Back.—Sticking in middle of spine, with gnawing; boring S. in region of spine just below shoulders. Pain in various parts; P. under scapulæ; in l. scapula, becoming sharp on moving it; in lumbar muscles; above waist, rocking from side to side; bruised, in spine between scapulæ; bruised, in loins; P. in loins as from flatus which could not pass, towards evening when sitting; contractive, in sacrum.

Extremities.— Stretching. Unsteady, feet weak, knees tottering. Sticking in calves, shoulders and toes. Tearing in toes and fingers; T. in joints at night in bed. Boring drawing pain in fingers, forearm and knees. Pain in fingers and toes; fingers, knees and shoulders; arms, toes and knees; knees, toes and shoulders; l. knee, r. shoulder and in toes; lower part of thighs and in elbows; anterior muscles of thigh and in wrist; all day in r. knee and in legs, externally, in tibiæ, joints of fingers, wrists and ankles; r. ankle and leg, then in r. shoulder, then in r. fingers, between metacarpus and fingers; changing from one joint to another; P. and drawing alternately in l. fingers, calves, l. elbow, beneath r. shoulder, in l. cervical muscles, in r. knee, then more seldom, in toes and l. side of head; rheumatic P. in bones. Drawing in fingers and toes. Heaviness; with sensitiveness of muscles. Weariness, < standing, with bruised pain in small of back. Limbs and arms relaxed. Paralytic feeling, they feel large and heavy. Torpor, with stiffness.

Upper Extremities.—Shoulder, tearing in l.; pressure; in l., which feels higher than r. Arm, tearing in shafts of bones; pressure in muscles of A. and scapulæ. Upper arm, bruised pain; in l., with twitching of muscles; pressure. Pressure in elbows. Forearm, tearing in r.; pain in l.; drawing from middle to elbow. Wrist, sticking in l. in evening on walking in open air; pressure; pressure in r.; drawing pain from r. into index. Hand, sticking transversely across flexor tendons of l. on walking in open air; pain in bones, also in evening; pain in last r. bones; weakness; numbness of r., with prickling in it and coldness through r. arm; N. of r., with coldness through arm to tips of fingers; N. of r., with internal coldness of arm and hand.

Fingers.—Inflamed spot on nails of l. index and r. thumb, with suppurative pain on touch, next day whitish exudation, after which they heal. Jerking of l. index towards thumb during the day when walking, sitting and reading, and sometimes jerking of thumb towards fingers, sometimes sudden J. of muscles between two fingers. Tearing in l. middle, < middle joint; on backs of all l. in morning in bed; paralytic, in r. little; paralytic, in r. fourth during rest, with spasmodic stiffness. Boring in middle joints of middle and index. Painful pressure transversely across r. thumb. Tickling in l. index.

Lower Extremities.—Aching as they get warm. Hip, *sticking in l.;* pain in l. like sciatica; pain in l. all day as if rubbed sore or burnt, < touch; drawing pain in r.; burning pressure in l.; sudden paralytic stiffness of l. when walking in open air. Thigh, tearing in anterior and outer part of r. like sciatica; boring in r. T. and leg, with sticking; pain; P. in bend of r.; P. in muscles of l.; P. in anterior muscles of l.; P. in muscles above knee; compression above l. knee; weariness; stiffness of muscles, with tension; S. of hamstrings, < external, on walking in open air.

Knee, boring sticking through l., frequently in open air, when walking and standing; boring externally in r.; burrowing in r. patella; pain in l. knee and patella as after a thrust, < bending knee and by pressure; pain; P. in r.; P. in outer part of l.; P. and sticking; stiffness in hollows. Legs, frequent twitching of muscles; sticking in calves; sticking upward near r. external malleolus; pain; P. in calf; P. in r. calf; P. in tibiæ; drawing pain; weakness. Ankles, sticking extending to toes, with tearing; pressure; P. in r., above and below, in evening; sprained pain in l.; bruised pain in l. inner malleolus.

Foot, tearing in ball of l.; pain in back; P. in heels; P. in r. os calcaneum; P. in heels; P. in r. sole when sitting; prickling in l.; heaviness and weariness; numbness. Toes, sticking jerking in l. great; prickling in all; pain in r.; P. in r. great; P. in great.

Skin.—**Sudden dropsical swelling;** swellings in forehead, with bruised pain. Desquamation. Hairs of whole body and nails fall out. Pimple on l. side of forehead, with bruised pain on hard touch. Yellowish roundish tetter on arms, exuding water on scratching. Vesicles between first joints of fourth and fifth fingers, smarting on touch, moist, then scabs; moist painless V. on middle joint of r. fourth finger, with soreness of bone on pressure. Crawling in l. cheek. Itching corrosion on arms after going to sleep in evening and morning, and after scratching biting as from salt water.

Sleep.—Frequent yawning. Sleepiness in evening; S., then uneasy sleep disturbed by dreams or coma vigil, then deep sleep. Uneasy sleep towards morning, turning from side to side, with dark floating visions; U. sleep, filled with historical fancies towards morning, during which he turns from side to side. *Dreams confused, unremembered, often anxious.*

Fever.—*Coldness* (Colch.); always in evening on lying down, sweat every morning; when sitting, standing and walking, with cold hands, internal heat and dulness of head, sleepiness, heaviness and weakness of feet, stiffness in hollow of knees, and on lying down in bed heat and general sweat, all without thirst; < morning; with headache; over body without thirst, with heat in head and bruised pain in occiput; *internal, between* 5 *and* 6 P.M., < *lying down, with shivering and with heat over body,* < *head, without thirst, when he wishes to drink it becomes repugnant and he drinks only a little at a time* (Puls.); *shaking, in morning, with gooseflesh, sensitiveness of external head to touch and motion, drawing tearing in limbs, frequent sticking in joints,* < *elbows and shoulders, without thirst.* Sensitive to cold, with sticking in and about eyes and nausea. Shivering, then thirst; S. so that he desires to lie in bed, with yellow face; S. beginning in arms. Cool skin. Coldness through back; in loins during dinner, with shivering; extending up and down near l. side of spine and for a moment across l. shoulder towards front. Cold limbs, with general cold, clammy sweat; limbs, with hot head and face; *hands and feet;* hands and feet, with internal heat of head, then general sweat; backs of hands, with sweat in palms; (feet in evening.)

Heat; with rapid pulse; alternating attacks of dry H., then shivering and coldness, then concealed colic. *Heat in head; deep;* and in face, with heaviness; in forehead, with fulness; hot forehead; deep in sinciput; extending to nape and down back, with hot, red cheeks; into back and small of back in flushes. Heat in face; after dinner, with redness; with redness and rapid pulse; external, in room. H. in back; extending to small of back. Burning in l. hip. Sweat; *general towards morning, with usual warmth of body;* at night; inclination to, in afternoon by open window; in drops on forehead and back of nose; *cold; general cold clammy;* on feet towards morning.

Clinical.—Typhoid fever, with great apathy, offensive breath, feeble pulse, stupor almost resembling that of Opium (similar to Arn.), general coldness and cold sweat.

Helonias.

A tincture is made of the fresh root of Helonias dioica, Pursh.

General Action.—It produces depression, mental and physical, and is indicated in atonic conditions. It acts upon the kidneys, increasing the flow of urine and the excretion of urea.

Allies.—Sepia, Nat. ars., Nat. mur., Tereb., Cimicif.

Generalities.—"Bilious," sleepy during the day, head dull and stupid, poor appetite, no taste to food, etc. Restless. Weak at noon; W. on walking a mile. Sensations as from great fatigue, > the *work* of walking. Amelioration when moving about and when doing something which absorbs the whole attention.

Clinical.—Effects of excessive fatigue, especially in women, with tired aching in back and legs. Sometimes useful in debility following exhausting diseases, such as diphtheria.

Mind.—Despair after a feeling of general *wellness*. Discouraged. Irritability during headache; I., all conversation unpleasant, desire to be let alone.

Clinical.—Profound melancholia, intolerance of contradiction (associated with uterine derangements, "consciousness of a womb").

Head.—Darting pain. Aching, with dim vision and vertigo on sudden motion of head. Fulness, with pressure up to vertex, the latter < looking steadily at one point. Vertigo. Frontal pain extending towards vertex; P. as from a band an inch wide from temple to temple. Fulness all through forehead between temples. Pain through temples, with fulness in head and vertigo; P. in temples and forehead every day at 4 or 5 P.M. or between 8 and 9 P.M., with pressure over root of nose, feeling as if I had caught cold, internal heat and irritability; P. in vertex, < stooping. Pressure on vertex every afternoon; P. outward in vertex and occiput, > reading earnestly, concentrating attention, < turning attention from the book to my hand, with burning in scalp.

Clinical.—Headaches associated with uterine derangements, especially burning on top of head or fulness and pressure on vertex.

Eyes.—Sensation of much light; with dim vision, and on sudden motion of head almost blind. Blind from much exertion; B. from walking.

Clinical.—Inflammation of the optic nerve and retina, with albuminous urine, boring pain in lumbar region extending down the legs, feeling as if the head were bandaged.

Mouth.—Tongue and fauces dry on waking at 5 A.M. (unusually early), with bitter taste. Dryness and bitter taste.

Clinical.—Salivation of pregnant women. Nursing sore mouth.

Stomach.—Appetite not as usual. Tasteless eructations. Nausea; when at supper. Vomiting; of dinner, which was fermented. Irritability. Cramp. Pain partially > empty eructations, with tightness. Indescribable sensation in epigastrium. Indescribable distress in epigastrium. Vague distress in forenoon. Burning; griping, in epigastrium, with salivation; glow, with flashes of heat through system. Heat and cold in region.

Abdomen.—Full of flatus and each eructation caused nausea (?). "Bellyache" before stool. Feeling before stool as before diarrhœa; feeling at supper as before diarrhœa. Distended feeling in spleen, causing pain. Intermittent pain in hypogastrium. Frequent pangs of pain like electric shocks deep in r. groin when walking, causing limping, > pressure with finger-tips. Burning in lower third, as if pelvis and to midway between umbilicus and pubis were filled with warm water.

Anus and Stool.—Burning in A. after stool. Purging, with burning in bowels. S. loose and in an hour another yellow and mushlike. First half hard, dark brown, the second soft and light yellow. Two S.; and small, brown. S. in four lumps, in quick succession, sensation as if anus were distended and then a lump shaped like a Minnie bullet, the big end first, was shot out.

Urinary Organs.—Spurting of urine after micturition. Irritation of urethra. (Scalding when urine passed over the denuded mucous membrane.) Urine copious; then scanty; C. and clear, light-colored. Urine neutral, then acid (formerly faintly alkaline). Urea increased. Specific gravity lowered. (Amorphous phosphates the exception after the proving, and not, as previously, the rule.)

Clinical.—Diabetes insipidus, urine very profuse, light-colored, with great debility and emaciation. Diabetes mellitus, large quantities of sugar in the urine, with emaciation, thirst, restlessness, melancholia, etc. Constant aching and tenderness over the kidneys, which seem excessively active. Acute and chronic inflammation of the kidneys, with great restlessness, frequent micturition, weakness, etc. Albuminuria during pregnancy, urine very scanty, with soreness and pain in region of kidneys, restlessness, etc.

Sexual Organs.—Uterine hæmorrhage. (External labia and pudendum puffed, hot, red and itching, so that she scratched till the surface bled, every morning thin, transparent exfoliations, the mucous membrane of labia red, swollen, covered with a white, curdy deposit, like aphthæ, the inflammation reaching to one-third of vagina.)

Clinical.—This drug seems to have proved valuable in atonic conditions of the female organs, prolapsus with general mal-nutrition; prolapsus following parturition, this local condition being associated with general debility, mental depression and particularly with a feeling of soreness or sensitiveness of uterus, the patient "is conscious that she has a womb." Menorrhagia, atonic, < moving body. Menorrhagia, with ulceration of the cervix, dark, offensive blood, great debility. Offensive leucorrhœa, with ulceration of the cervix, which occasionally causes hæmorrhage. With the local uterine symptoms of displacement or of chronic inflammation, etc., there are generally pain in the lumbar region, dull aching, sometimes weight on the chest, pressure on head, etc. Pruritus of vulva and vagina, which are hot and swollen and exfoliate, with aphthous patches. Indurations of uterus.

Respiration and Chest.—Feeling as if respiration were about to cease. Breasts swollen, nipples tender and painful. Tired aching in chest when walking, as if front of C., and especially in a strip four inches wide down sternum, had been compressed in a vise. Sensitiveness to cold the length of sternum and as wide apart as nipples.

Pulse.—84 in evening, and full, irregular. Weak; and slow. Slow and small; and weak.

Back.—Lameness and aching. Sharp, spasmodic pain running to crest of l. ilium. Piercing drawing pain in lower part through to uterus, like inflammation. Kidney region, aching at 10 P.M.; A., then albuminuria, urine copious, with increased specific gravity; sudden A. at night on undressing, as if shot; weariness and weight, also in afternoon and evening, with general fatigue; sensation as if kidneys were two bags of hot water. Lumbar and dorsal regions, aching and burning. Lower lumbar region weak. Lower lumbar and sacral regions, aching; and lameness; A. in spine; tired A. in spine on sitting down at 3.30 P.M., with burning; tired after resting. Sacrum, aching in afternoon; at 4.45 P.M., extending into each buttock; A. in upper part and in pelvis, < night; dull feeling in morning; weakness; tired aching, and in lumbar region.

Clinical.—Effects of fatigue, with burning and heat in dorsal region.

Extremities.—Rheumatic pain in r. hip. Burning, or rather warm numbness streaming up from both tendo-achilles, < over region of gastrocnemius and in knees. Pain as if a wedge were driven into r. ankle, till sleep. Feet numb when sitting still.

Sleep.—Waking every morning at 5, an unusual hour.

Fever.—Coldness alternating with heat, < epigastric region. Chill radiating from solar plexus all over body, on motion of arms. Cold limbs. Heat in flushes on every movement in the room. Internal heat during headache. Burning in upper dorsal spine; B. in dorsal region when sitting reading at night, < between lower half of scapulæ; between scapulæ, with tired aching in lower lumbar and sacral regions; in sacral region. Heat in renal region.

Hepar Sulfuris Calcareum.

Calcium sulphide, prepared as directed by Hahnemann, is triturated for use.

General Action.—A "tissue" drug of wide action. It simulates Mercury in its action on the glandular system, especially on the liver and kidneys, Sulphur in its action on the skin and mucous membrane of the intestinal tract, Calcarea in affecting the respiratory tract, and all of the foregoing in its general action on connective tissue. Extreme sensitiveness to a draught of air, easy perspiration, profuse secretions and suppurative tendencies are marked characteristics of the drug.

Allies.—Mercury, Calcarea, Sulphur, Silicea, Nit. acid, Kali in general, Phos., Puls., Bry., Tell., etc.

Generalities.—Emaciation, with chill in back, red cheeks, sleeplessness, larynx affected, hoarse, weak voice, anxiety, apprehension and irritability, as in hectic fever. Inflammation of affected parts. Stretching. Painful throbbing here and there from slight wetting of body. **Sensitiveness to open air,** *with chill and frequent nausea.* Sensitiveness of nerves in various parts, as, for example, in septum of nose. Nervous irritability, every physical or mental impression causes a kind of inward trembling. *Weakness;* in morning, and slumbering and late rising; in morning on waking, with palpitation; in morning in bed, with uneasiness of legs and stoppage of nose; in morning on rising after good sleep, with heaviness of body; in evening, with palpitation; after eating; on walking in open air, after eating, with stretching as before ague, on walking farther cold sweat and in evening in bed heat, which prevents sleep till 2 A.M.; with sleepiness; with bruised feeling in all limbs. Sudden faintness towards evening, with slight pain. Heaviness of body. Aggravation of pain at night; during nightly fever, especially during chill. Amelioration from frequent eructations and emissions of flatus.

Clinical.—Sometimes indicated in the marasmus of children who have diarrhœa, < in the daytime and after eating, with the peculiar sour odor to the sweat and stools. Cases requiring Hep. are, as a rule, extremely sensitive to external impressions, especially to the slightest cold; for example, it has removed the effects of malarial poisoning which have been maltreated with calomel and quinine from the simple indications of profuse and easy sweat, which is offensive, and of such extreme sensitiveness to air that the patient wears an overcoat in hot weather. Hep. is generally indicated by extreme sensitivenesss of inflamed parts, as if they were about to suppurate. The pains of Hep. are almost universally splinter-like in character, even the neuralgias and toothaches are of this sort. It is indicated in threatening suppurations, with great soreness and sharp pains as if about to suppurate. General aggravation from cold dry winds.

Mind.—Irrational talking. Ghostly image of one who was dead, in morning in bed when conscious, which frightened him, and it seemed as if he saw his neighbor's house burning, which also frightened him. *Fright on slumbering,* even after eating; F. concerning sickness in the family, < walking alone in open air. Anxiety at 10 P.M. after lying down, with uneasiness in whole body and painful jerking up of lower limbs; A. in evening, belief that he would die and sadness even to suicide. *Sadness and bitter crying;* S. and apprehension; S. from stretching out on sofa. Hypochondriac. Remembers everything which has been unpleasant during her life. Everything of which she only thought was disagreeable. Violent about trifles, he could have killed some one. Irritable in morning after rising, he will not speak; I. about trifles; about his pains, and discouraged; I. and desirous to be alone; and obstinate; and impatient. Discontented with himself. Contrary, does not wish to see his own family. Desire for nothing.

Memory weak during peevishness. Mistakes when talking and writing. Sudden vanishing of thoughts when at work. Stupidity; with heaviness in forehead. Stupor, with contracted, irregular, scarcely perceptible pulse, sunken, pale face, cold skin and limbs, vomiting and diarrhœa. Unconsciousness in attacks when walking in open air.

Clinical.—Dementia, with complete stupidity, is silent and speechless. Melancholia, with paroxysms of violence, hasty speech, ("words roll out, tumbling over each other"), in patients who have taken much mercury. Hypochondriasis.

Head.—*Sticking; waking him at night, with confusion, as if skull would burst;* after deep sleep in morning, > walking in open air; on stooping, with bursting sensation, eyes close on account of the pain; on rising from stooping and on every motion, < walking in open air. Hammering. Burrowing mornings, > tight binding, with nausea. Aching; in morning on waking; in morning, > rising; every morning on any shock; *on shaking it,* with vertigo; contractive, before menstruation; contractive, grumbling, even when walking, < open air, > in the room, with pressure against skull; tensive, confused. Swashing. Vibration internally during cough. Confusion; during cough, with throbbing in forehead and temples. Vertigo in morning after rising; in evening, with nausea; on rising; during dinner, after eructations, with blackness before eyes; when riding in a wagon, so that she could not stand alone on getting out; with heaviness of head; with faintness and rigidity or vanishing of vision, as if he sat in thought; *everything turned in a circle with her* on closing eyes for midday nap.

Forehead.—Jerking of muscles in afternoon when lying. Sticking. Tearing at night, with general heat, without thirst. *Tensive pain above root of nose.* Pain like a boil from midnight onward, with sticking on stooping and on coughing, also externally pain like a boil and sticking on touch mornings. The pressure of the hat is painful. Bruised pain in morning, < moving eyes, with similar pain in abdomen.

Pulsating sticking in l. temple at 10 A.M. Boring in r. T. extending upward into head. Painful throbbing in r. T. Pressure in T. during the day, with drawing. Pain in vertex, with heat; P. in evening, with palpitation. Sticking in r. parietal region on stooping, with vanishing of senses. **Pain in one-half of brain as from a nail or plug.** Boring in spot on side. Pressure in r. hemisphere of brain, at times worse. Sticking in occiput and temples *as if a nail or plug were driven in* (Thuj., Ign.); pulselike S. in occiput and lower part of it. *Pain externally in r. side of occiput, gradually extending to nape, throat and scapulæ.* Hair falls out.

Clinical.—Headache following the abuse of mercury, of a neuralgic character, sometimes boring at the root of the nose, sometimes feeling as if a plug or nail were driven into the head (Thuj., Ign.); sometimes a feeling as if the eyes would be pulled backward into the head; the headaches generally > tightly binding the head (Merc., Iod.). Falling of the hair after mercury. Extreme sensitiveness of the scalp, could scarcely comb the hair, with painful nodes on the scalp; the bones of the skull pain at night. Eczema of the head, with great sensitiveness, tendency to ulceration, bleeding and offensive discharge.

Eyes.—*Inflammation and swelling, with redness of white.* Blue under E. Sticking. *Pain from daylight; in bright daylight if he moves them;* P. at every step; < *moving them, with redness;* frequent P. during the day, causing lachrymation; as if they would be drawn into head. *Sore, agglutinated at night, hard mucus.* Lachrymation from tickling cough. *Pain in balls, with bruised pain on touch.* Boring in upper wall of orbit. Obliged to wink after writing. *Redness of upper lid, with inflammation, swelling and pain more pressing than sticking;* R. of lids, with pressure as if sleepy. *Cannot open lids in morning on waking. Smarting in external canthus, and hard mucus.* Cutting in external canthus. Flickering; and everything looks dark, then great weakness. *Dim vision in evening by candle-light; D. when reading. Blindness on rising and standing up after sitting bent over.*

Clinical.—A great variety of scrofulous inflammations of the eyes, particularly ulcerations of the cornea involving the inner layer and accompanied by collection of pus in the anterior chamber. The cases requiring Hep. are generally of a very sluggish type, anæmic, sweat easily, < night, very sensitive to open air, and perhaps have been salivated. Kerato-iritis, involving also the ciliary body. Chronic catarrh of the conjunctiva, with very profuse muco-purulent discharges. Ulceration of the margins of the lids and inflammation of the Meibomian glands. Subacute inflammation of the lachrymal sac, with very free secretion of pus in the inner angle of the eye. Inflammation and ulceration of the margins of the lids, with collection of much dry matter in the lashes. Erysipelatous inflammation of the substance of the lids threatening suppuration. Moist, offensive eczema of the lids. Herpes following the course of the supraorbital nerve, with severe pain as if the eyes would be drawn back into the head.

Ears.—External, red, hot and itching. Wax increased. Purulent discharge. Sticking on blowing nose. Jerking pain through E. Pain in external, at night when lying on it. *Itching in E.* Cracking on blowing nose; C. as from electric sparks. Whistling on blowing nose; in r. Roaring in l. Murmuring in l.; before E. in evening after lying down till sleep, with throbbing.

Clinical.—Inflammation of the outer and middle ear; ulceration and offensive, bloody discharge (Tellur.), generally with violent pain, perforation of the drum, especially following overdosing with mercury.

Nose.—Redness and heat internally and externally, with swelling of it. Scabs in r. nostril. *Pain in bones on touch* (Merc.); ulcerative P. in nostrils; bruised P. in tip; sore P. on back on touch; drawing P. in morning, extending to eyes and becoming a biting. Crawling in l. half on blowing, as from a foreign body. Rush of blood. Contractive feeling. Burning lasting into the night. Stoppage after stool. Sneezing at night waking; S. after paroxysms of cough; S. caused by tickling; from itching in nose; frequent. Coryza, with much spitting of saliva; *C., with inflamed swelling of nose, which pains like a boil,* with cough; with scraping in throat; stopped; obliged to blow nose every moment, with too great appetite; *mucus from posterior nares mixed with blood; blowing of offensive mucus,* even without catarrh; dropping of yellow, glutinous water from one nostril. *Bleeding;* after singing; blowing of clotted blood; drops of blood exude every morning. *Smell sensitive; lost.*

Clinical.—Inflammation of the nostrils, with great soreness of the nose, which is swollen and red, with profuse greenish-yellow discharge. Ozæna, with soreness of the bones, heat, ulceration, nose very sensitive internally to air and to touch, discharge very offensive (Puls., Kali iod., Graph.). Chronic diseases of the nose resulting from abuse of mercury.

Face.—*Red cheeks;* in morning; in evening, and burning. *Yellow,* with blue margins about eyes. Pale if she becomes heated on moving about. Swelling of l. cheek; *erysipelatous S. of cheeks* in morning. Pain in bones on touch. Lip, **swelling of upper** (Calc. c.), *with tension and with pain on touch; eruption in corner, with heat;* crack in middle of lower (Puls.); crack, with pimples in red of lower and burning pain; smarting painful pimple in red of upper; ulcer in corner; twitching of l. side of upper, with trembling; pain; tension in middle of upper.

Mouth.—Teeth. Looseness (Merc.); of all, with tenderness of gums (Merc.); of hollow, with pain on biting on it. Sticking. Aching; *in all after cold drinks or opening mouth* (Merc.); < eating; in hollow, with sensation as if too long; jerklike, extending into ear; drawing, in hollow in evening, as if too much blood pressed upon nerves; drawing, in evening, in a T. which begins to be loose, < warm room, > open air, < *biting teeth together,* which causes jerking in a tooth. Gum, ulcer; inflammation on inner side of front, with swelling; swelling of back, with pain as if a new tooth would come through, < touch and biting upon it; bleeding easily; jerking.

Tip of tongue sensitive; burning pain in tip, even waking at night. *White aphthous pustules on inside of lips and cheeks and on tongue* (Kali chl.), with pain, < touch and drink. Dryness. Much mucus. Salivation. Drivelling from r. side. *Offensive odor. Bitter taste; in back of throat, with natural taste to food;* B., slimy in morning; to food. Taste metallic; and sourish; T. as of bad eggs; doughy in morning; earthy in throat, with natural taste to food; lost.

Clinical.—Abscesses at roots of teeth which have been filled. Unhealthy gums, which ulcerate and bleed, with offensive odor.

Throat.—Sticking like flea-bites externally and behind ears. Pinching near r. side of thyroid cartilage. Hawking of mucus in evening after eating; what she hawks up is mixed with blood. Mucus causing hoarseness. **Sticking as from a splinter on swallowing, extending towards ear on yawning** (compare Nit. ac.); *S. on turning head, extending to ear;* every morning, with dryness; on deep breathing; during cough, with pain as if everything would come out of forehead; *beneath larynx after supper. Fear of constriction; suffocative C.* towards evening. *Smarting,* < swallowing solids, *with rawness and scraping.* Rawness with pain on swallowing saliva. Scraping; in morning, with roughness as from burnt lard; and constantly full of water. *Feeling as of a plug of mucus or swelling at entrance* in morning; feeling as of a plug in pharynx. *Feeling as if he had to swallow over a swelling* (Phyto.); with bruised pain in external muscles of throat. Difficult swallowing of food without pain in throat. Constant sensation as if water rose after sour things. Tickling, and moist, provoking cough.

Clinical.—Tonsillitis in the suppurative stage; it is indicated after Bell. and Baryta; these three remedies may follow in succession; Bell. in the very outset, Baryta after the Bell.-dryness and fever have subsided, then if suppuration threatens Hep., the indications for which are the fetid odor of the salivation, sharp splinter-like pains on swallowing and great sensitiveness to air, or even chilliness. Sometimes indicated in follicular inflammation of the pharynx, with splinter-like pains and the general symptoms of the drug.

Stomach.—Unusual hunger in forenoon. *Appetite for only sour pungent things; A. for something at times and when he gets it he does not like it.* Appetite lost; with emptiness in abdomen. *Disgust for everything, especially fat* (Puls.). Thirst greater than hunger; T. from morning till evening; T., but she is afraid to drink much because it distends the stomach. **Desire for vinegar.** Longing for wine. No thirst.

Eructations, with burning in chest; E., with burning in throat; *E. after eating,* of sourish fluid; *frequent, without odor or taste;* constant empty, during mental exertion, with distention of stomach and abdomen; tasting of food; hot, after eating. Waterbrash, with flow of saliva from mouth two days at the same hour. Hiccough; after eating. *Nausea; in morning* when sitting and standing, > lying; at night, with vomiting; < movement; with flow of saliva from mouth; frequent; like a foreboding of faintness, in morning. *Vomiting every morning; V. of bile in morning after long violent retching;* of mucus and bile, the slightest drink caused retching and vomiting; sour, in afternoon; of mucus mixed with clotted blood; spasmodic.

Flatulent distention, with cold hands. Gastric enteritis. Pain in pit every morning on waking; *P. after eating a little;* in pit on blowing nose; *when walking, as if it hung loose;* as if lead were in it; drawing, in epigastric region and back. *Gnawing as from acids, rising into throat.* Burning during cough. Heartburn; and eructations as from too fat meat. *Tension across pit, he must loosen his clothes and cannot sit.* Uneasiness in pit during digestion, with heaviness and acidity.

Clinical.—Dyspepsia following the abuse of mercury or even quinine, indicated by the longing for highly-seasoned food or for acids.

Abdomen.—**Distended, tense** (Graph., Lyc., Carb. v., etc.); D. after stool; D., worse when walking than when sitting, with sensitiveness; D. and hard. *Rumbling.* Noisy movements. Emission of flatus; every morning, with colic, < sides; at night. Sticking; here and there many hours after meal-time, < every pulsation, with cutting and griping, as from flatulence. Cramp. *Cutting;* towards evening. Griping mornings, with soft stool; G. as after taking cold. Pain rising to pit of stomach, > emission of flatus; periodic P. during fever; drawing P.; bruised P. when walking. Constriction; before eating. Tension all day; frequent spasmodic pinching T. Empty feeling in intestines. Heat after eating.

Pressure beneath pit of stomach, with feeling as if everything in stomach were hard like a stone. Drawing pain in upper A. and across small of back. Flatulent distention of l. hypochondrium. *Sticking in hepatic region* when walking; in spleen when walking; beneath l. ribs; in r. hypochondrium in morning. Cramp in r. hypochondrium, with nausea, then ineffectual urging to stool. Pressure in r. H. as from a stone, with cramps in stomach. Painful rush of blood to H., with pain on every step. Congested feeling in H. on every step.

Fermentation above umbilicus, with eructations of hot air. *Paroxysmal clawing in umbilical region, from sides of abdomen, towards middle and sometimes to pit of stomach, causing nausea, with anxious heat of cheeks.* Twisting above U. Sore pain above U. Pressure, almost sticking, in l. side when riding in a wagon. Smarting in l. side. *Suppuration of inguinal glands, buboes* (Calc. c., Merc., Thuj., Nit. ac.). Pain in an I. gland, < on touch, with swollen sensation. Pain about hips. Fulness of lower abdomen after eating. Smarting in lower A.

Clinical.—Threatening or actual abscess of the liver.

Rectum and Anus.—Rumbling in R. Crawling in R. as from thread-worms. **Urging, but large intestines are wanting in peristaltic action and cannot expel soft fæces, only a part can be forced out by aid of abdominal muscles;** ineffectual U., with many eructations. Protrusion of hæmorrhoids. Soreness of anus, with discharge of moisture after stool. Burning in A.

Stool.—*Diarrhœa;* with colic, inclination to lie down, hot hands and cheeks; three times, with rumbling and nausea in abdomen; frequent, slight, preceded by griping, with flatulence before and after stool; of bloody mucus, with rumbling in back. Liquid, dark brown-greenish, frequent, with yellow lumps of green bloody mucus, smelling like bad eggs, with rumbling and urging so that they were frequently passed in bed, preceded by cutting tearing in abdomen, < umbilical region, extending deep into pelvis, the pain < before every stool. **Soft, difficult;** S., with blood. Thin, more frequent at night. **Difficult, scanty, not hard, with much urging;** D., of hard pieces mixed with yellow moisture. Hard and unsatisfactory, with inactivity of rectum and swelling of anus. **Clay-colored.** *Greenish.* Blood with stool. Frequent, even at night, but little is passed, with pressure, tenesmus and weakness.

Clinical.—Bowels very inactive, the soft stools are evacuated slowly and with effort. Stools may be light-colored, with enlargement of the liver. Diarrhœa white, sour, undigested, or sometimes mucous, yellow or green and of decayed odor. The sour odor of the stools and sweat is often an indication for the drug (Bry., Rheum). Chronic catarrh of the intestines, abdomen distended, tender, with fermentation or with a feeling of clawing or cutting extending towards the umbilicus.

Urinary Organs.—Discharge of prostatic fluid during stool. **Bladder weak, urine drops down vertically and he must wait before urine flows** (see Caust., Op.). **Micturition impeded, he must wait and then urine flows slowly. He can never finish urinating, some urine always seems to remain in bladder** (Helo.). Urging in morning on waking, but difficult slow micturition; frequent desire. *Meatus urinarius red and inflamed.* Urethra, sticking; cutting in female, during micturition; sore pain during micturition. *Urine acrid; and burning, making inner surface of prepuce sore and ulcer-*

ated (Merc.); *U. burning; last drops bloody; milky, even when passing, with white sediment; pale, clear, becoming on standing turbid and thick, with white sediment;* dark yellow and burning; blood-red; brownish-red; dark and scanty; copious; copious, pale, with pressure on bladder; shimmering film (Graph., Sul.); pellicular fat upon U.

Clinical.—Valuable in certain stages of inflammation of the kidneys, especially after abuse of mercury, with soreness in region of kidneys, incessant urging to urinate, sour sweat, diarrhœa, etc. Occasionally in albuminuria during diphtheria. Atony or paralysis of bladder, urine passes very slowly and without any force, the bladder does not seem to empty itself. Oily film upon the surface of the urine.

Sexual Organs.—Excitement and emission without amorous fancies or desire for women. Weakness, testicles relaxed, penis hard. Itching of glans; and frænum; on scrotum. *Ulcers externally on prepuce, similar to chancre* (Nit. ac.). Sticking in prepuce; S. in region of frænum præputii. Painful erection during caresses, with soreness and pinching in penis extending from bladder. Desire diminished. Soreness between pudenda and thighs. Itching of pudenda during menstruation. *Discharge of blood from uterus* after distention of abdomen. Menstruation delayed and diminished.

Clinical.—Venereal ulcers, with fetid discharge. Profuse secretion of an offensive odor from the glans penis. Figwarts of an offensive odor. Herpes of the prepuce, which is very sensitive and bleeds easily. Suppurating inguinal glands, with offensive moisture in the folds of the skin. Enlargement of ovaries, with great soreness, pain in back (Helo.), etc. Abscesses of the labiæ, which are very sensitive, with splinter-like pains. Extremely offensive leucorrhœa of a decayed odor. Ulceration of the uterus, with offensive discharge.

Respiratory Organs.—*Weakness of organs of speech and of chest, so that she cannot speak aloud* (Phos., Caust.). Tickling in larynx waking her about midnight and provoking cough and expectoration. Cough day and night; in morning, waking her frequently; in evening; evening and morning; < walking; < *deep breathing, so as to cause vomiting;* **paroxysmal, if slightest portion becomes cold, with sensitiveness of nervous system** (compare Nux vom.); paroxysmal, forcible, deep, painfully shocking larynx and causing retching; *almost uninterrupted, from tickling in l. upper part of throat, < from talking and stooping and till late in evening, then suddenly ceasing;* tickling at 3 P.M.; *suffocative, from tightness of breath; provoking vomiting; scraping, rough.* Dry cough; *in evening on going to sleep; and paroxysmal, in evening;* and short; *hacking, after eating;* and deep, in paroxysms on deep inspiration, from tightness of breath, with sore pain in chest. Cough, with expectoration; paroxysmal; of mucus, all day, from scraping in larynx and < throat; of mucus, and violent, from 11 till 12 in bed; of bloody mucus; bloody, preceded by sensation of a hard body in pit of stomach, offensive sweat after the cough, then weakness of head. Expectoration of acid mucus at night, almost without cough; bloody E. from chest, with peevishness and weakness. **Dyspnœa.** *Frequent deep breathing, as after running.*

Clinical.—Subacute inflammation of the larynx, with considerable secretion of mucus. In a late stage of membranous croup, with hoarseness, profuse collection of mucus, difficult respiration; Hep. should be given very cautiously even in a late stage of membranous croup; overdosing with it is apt to cause recurrence of the more acute symptoms, to lessen the secretion of mucus, rendering the cough dry and tight, and to increase the difficulty in breathing; it follows well after Spong.; Spong. should be given after Hep. only when Hep. has aggravated the cough and caused a return of the former symptoms; Hep. is never to be given when there is a hot, dry skin; the child is always sweaty and weak; it is to be carefully differentiated from Kali bi. and Bromine, neither of which is indicated when there is fever; the tenacious character of the expectoration indicates Kali bi., while Bromine is indicated by the spasmodic character of the cough and expiration, and a tendency to cyanosis. Subacute bronchitis, cough loose and rattling, < cold air, always < towards morning; (the profuse collection of mucus in the chest, which cannot be removed by coughing, with free sweating, is like Tart. emetic).

Chest.—Tenacious mucus. Suppuration on last r. rib, with sticking in it and great pain on touch. Sticking in side extending to back; S. in sternum when breathing and walking. Pain in l. side; in side on which he lies at night. Flesh of r. side and beneath r. arm sensitive on touching breast or moving arm. Oppression, with burning. Feeling as if hot water moved about in it. Heat above heart. Itching of l. nipple.

Clinical.—Late stage of pleuritis, with exudation, with the general indications of the drug. Chronic pneumonia, with profuse purulent expectoration and threatening abscess. Abscess of the lungs, when the symptoms indicate.

Heart and Pulse.—Sticking in region of heart; and in l. chest, with palpitation. Palpitation after dinner, with tightness of chest and need to breathe deeply. Pulse rapid and hard.

Neck.—Pain in muscles of nape on touch, < beneath ears. Bruised pain in muscles, with painful swallowing as from a swelling; B. pain in nape on bending head backward.

Back.—Sticking; in l. side. Tensive pain, < turning body at night. Drawing in B. and sacrum in morning, pain in whole B. after rising, so that she can scarcely move, with weakness of limbs, aversion to eating or working, shivering, chilliness and loss of thirst. Weakness of spine. Scapulæ, sticking between; S. in r. on blowing nose, hawking and deep breathing; pain between S.; sensation during micturition as if something were running internally in r. Loins, sticking, with cough; S. in l.; in region of l. kidney; pain, < walking, extending across back and backward; frequent pain; pain as if cut in two, so that she can neither stand, walk nor lie; sprained pain in loins and ischia on sitting and on turning body when walking; bruised pain on walking; bruised and sharp pain in loins and lumbar vertebræ, < articulation of sacrum, with pelvis extending into lower limbs, causing limping; pain as from fatigue, on stooping and leaning against anything when sitting.

Extremities.—Sticking in joints. *Drawing pains,* < thighs and legs, with paralytic sensations; D. pain in joints of shoulders, hips, < knees. Crawling pains, < walking and standing, which bend him up. Sick in all, as if getting cold.

Clinical.—Very valuable in run-rounds and even in felons, with sharp suppurative pains. Hip-joint disease in the suppurative stage.

Upper Extremities.—*Axillary glands suppurate.* Shoulders, tearing in l.; pain on raising arms; sprained pain; drawing pain; pain as from a weight. Arms, jerks here and there in l.; bruised pain; weariness; falling asleep of one on which he leans at night. *Bruised pain in humerus.* Drawing pain in l. upper arm. Elbows, pain in bends on stretching arms; pain or bruised feeling in tip on moving it after violent walking, > open air. Forearm, boring sore pain on inner side of F. and across back of hand after midnight, < touch, > during the day; bruised pain in a spot; painful drawing in flexor tendons; drawing tearing in extensor muscles of F. and fingers. Wrist painful. Hands tremble when writing; swelling of r. Fingers, swelling of all when lying down, with stiffness; swelling of all, with tension on moving them; swelling of joints, with gouty pains; easily put out of joint, they crack if pressed when hand is outspread; sticking in one.

Lower Extremities.— Uneasiness during the day when at rest. *Pain in nates and posterior part of thighs when sitting.* Thighs, cramp at night, extending into foot; C. in muscles of T. and pelvis if T. is drawn up; tearing in r.; T. in l. hip on undressing; T. when sitting, with numb crawling; T. as from weariness, and in legs; pain in hip when walking in open air; *bruised pain in anterior muscles;* B. pain transversely through centre; *sprained pain in hips* on walking in open air; sudden weary pain when walking. Knees, *swelling;* cramp; trembling on walking in open air, with anxiety, general heat and burning in soles; frequent sticking in r. during the day; tearing in outer side as from weariness; pain in hollow during motion; pain as if broken; bruised pain; tension in hollow of r., making walking difficult.

Cramp in calves; in morning in bed; on bending knees. Legs, tearing in tibiæ, above malleoli, at night; T. in tendo-achillis in bed, when walking a sticking in it; cramplike pain in muscles on walking; cramplike drawing pain beneath r. knee on walking; uneasiness; U. at night, with trembling; U. and necessity to keep them outstretched; weariness, < ascending; heaviness; tension at night preventing sleep; T. in back and in hollow of knees; falling asleep of l. in morning in bed, with heaviness. Ankle, cracking; pain as if suppurating; broken pain in r. on walking; paroxysmal sprained pain on walking; stiffness, with numbness and dead sensation.

Foot.—Swelling about malleoli, with difficult breathing; cramp; C. in soles and toes; C., between great toe and heel; sticking on instep; S. in heel; itching S. on back, at base of toes; tearing at night; T. in soles, with drawing; bruised pain on outer side of one on which he had lain, in evening after uneasy sleep, > touching and stroking; pressure in heel on walking, as from a stone; soles sensitive to walking over uneven stones; drawing, burning pain in evening in bed, extending to malleoli; burning pain in morning in bed, < on their backs. A hitherto painless corn begins to burn and stick on slight pressure. Toes, *sticking extending into great;* S. in hard places on little; S. in fleshy part of r. little; tearing in great, worse when walking than when standing; pain in nail of great on pressure.

Skin.—*Yellow.* Jaundice, with blood-red urine and yellow whites of eyes. **Unhealthy, slight injuries suppurate** (Silic.). *Nettle-rash on face.* Painless swellings on forehead. Chilblains on feet, so sensitive after healing that she cannot wear the shoe. Itching miliary eruption on hands and wrists. Red itching elevation on upper part of l. nates. *Red itching spot beneath lower lip, soon covered with yellow blisters, which change to scurf.* Pimples here and there; on upper lid and beneath eyes; on nape and sides of throat; on side of forehead, feeling worse in room; above anus, with feeling as if anus were swollen. Pimples like hives sore on touch, on scalp and nape; on chin, above and below lips and on throat. Itching pimples on chin; on top of l. shoulder and beneath l. patella; about knee. Warts become inflamed, with sticking in them. Erysipelas on diseased leg.

Soreness and moisture in fold between scrotum and thigh (Sulph.); *with smarting biting. Cracking and smarting of hands and feet* (Graph.). Scabby eruption on hands. Scurfy eruption beneath l. corner of mouth. Itching pustules on l. elbow; P., with sore pain on sternum. Boils; on nates; on leg, with inability to let leg hang down. Vesicles as from nettle-rash, for example, on wrist; corroding V. on last phalanx of thumb, with sticking on pressure; burning V. and ulcers on r. side of chin towards lower lip. **Ulcer bleeding on slight wiping** (Nit. ac.); sour-smelling matter from U.; sticking in U. on laughing; *corrosive pain;* itching corrosion; burning at night, with throbbing.

Sensitiveness to touch and to slightest cold (Nux. v.). Tickling in soles. Crawling in tips of fingers; in soles; toes. *Itching of nose;* on zygomata; about mouth; *in bend of elbow; in palms;* on inner side of knee; on tibiæ and backs of feet; on soles; here and there at night, < on ankles, between fingers, on wrist, back, under knees, preventing sleep; *on hands, with rough, dry, shrivelled skin;* sudden in toes; near nail of l. index, as if a paronychia would form; sticking; crawling in toes at night. Burning itching in toes; on forehead and cheeks during dinner; < morning on rising, with white vesicles after scratching, which discharge a white fluid.

Clinical.—General moist eruptions, which smell badly, suppurate and bleed. General inflammations and blisters, which threaten to suppurate, and in which there are sharp suppurative pains.

Sleep.—Yawning from morning till noon; frequent Y., causing pain in chest. *Sleepiness towards evening,* with almost convulsive yawning; sleep-weariness in evening, so that he slept from after supper till morning; sleeps in evening sitting up, with weariness. Sleep too long and dull, then confusion of head, with pressure in temples, troubles from a disordered stomach, eructations tasting of food and scraping in throat as before heartburn; sleep long and confused, with thoughts of his business passing through his head like drifting clouds. Slumbering sleep for several days, with dreams of the business of the day and many thoughts, which passed through his brain like clouds, at times he woke somewhat, not stupid, gave right answers, attended to his needs and immediately fell asleep again. Sleeps on his back.

Sleeplessness after midnight; from numerous thoughts; from midnight till 4 A.M., then sleep, sweat at 7; all night after lively conversation in evening; all night, with moaning and groaning; all night, only slumber; S., with chill; with tossing about. Difficult falling asleep and uneasy sleep. **Frequent** waking, with erections and desire to urinate. Sprang up from sleep before midnight, full of anxiety and it seemed as if he could not get his breath.

Dreams.—Anxious all night; *A., of conflagrations,* of falling from a precipice, etc.; A., with sweat on back on waking. Of flying from danger. Of danger, fright. Full of strife. Heavy, and he remained frightened after waking. Peevish. Of hearing shooting. Of expectoration of blood and pus. Of broken windows two nights in succession.

Fever.—*Chill;* every day at 6 or 7 P.M.; at 6 P.M., with weakness and slow pulse; at 8 P.M., with chattering of teeth, coldness of hands and feet, then heat, with sweat, < chest and forehead, and slight thirst; at night; *in open air* and a painful sensation presses her down so that she must walk bent over; *with frequent nausea* **and sensitiveness to open air**; alternating with heat, with photophobia. First bitter taste, then chill, with thirst, then heat, with interrupted sleep, all twice on the same day. Shaking chill; with chattering of teeth, coldness and pallor of hands and feet, pallor of face, change of expression, unconsciousness, coma, when aroused he talked irrationally or stared without expression, *then heat slight in comparison with the chill*, with dry mouth, periodic colic and liquid stools. Shivering; then heat; waking at 2 A.M., with hot, dry skin; frequent S. from nape down back and over chest, then sleep, from which he woke with sweat, pain in back, in and about hips and in abdomen and nausea; frequent S. in forenoon in open air; frequent S. extending to head, where hair is sore to touch. Chilliness in arms and legs in morning; *in feet* during the day.

Catarrhal fever, weakness, with sensitiveness of skin to touch and **to slightest cold,** *constant chill, with sore throat as if raw, pain on swallowing saliva, muscles of nape, < beneath ears, painful to touch, with dry cough, no appetite, no thirst, sleeplessness all night, with moaning and groaning;* C. fever, with internal chill and fretfulness; C. fever, with sick feeling in all limbs. Orgasm of blood preventing sleep. Heat; three nights in succession, from 4 P.M. through night, with great thirst, headache, delirium; so that sleep was bad; with violent vomiting of green acid water and tenacious mucus and nausea; dry, at night, with sweaty hands, which cannot tolerate uncovering; H. in forehead; hands; palm and wrist; *face night and morning on waking;* in soles in morning in bed; of one hand, with redness and swelling and bruised pain extending into arm on moving it; flushing, in face and head.

Constant offensive exhalations from body. *Sweat at night;* as soon as he lies down, < head, then S. in drops on face; about midnight, < back; before midnight; after midnight in bed; from midnight on, then chill in morning; **S. on slightest motion** (Merc.); S. even on writing a few lines; *frequent, without heat;* general, at night when awake. Profuse sweat; general, in morning; general, with burning of skin; *and sour-smelling at night* (Bry.); and clammy, at night; between upper part of legs; on head in morning. S. on perineum. Cold S. on hands; on feet.

Clinical.—The easy chill from exposure to air, even from putting the hand out of bed (causing cough), and the general tendency to sweat are the general indications in febrile states; there is comparatively little fever. Sour sweats.

Homarus.

The reddish, offensive liquid (the digesting fluid) contained in a sack just back of the mouth of the live lobster is triturated with sugar of milk. (This fluid mixed with warm milk solidifies it in ten minutes, making a coagulum harder than cheese-curd.)

Generalities.—Pain somewhere all day; in eyes and various parts of body and limbs after retiring. Strange feeling all over, was not dizzy, but when I tried to take hold of the door-knob I could not do it readily, but put my hand all around it, I guess I was a little scared. Felt sick, unable to move, > moving. Dull feeling. Nervous feeling; but dread of moving. Restlessness. Weakness; < walking. Amelioration after eating; after dinner.

Head.—Aching; in morning; sharp at times, mostly in temporal region, < l. Dizziness. Frontal pain; just above eyes, at times worse in l. temporal region; from over eyes to occiput, < l. side; sharp, over l. eye, had to scowl and rub the parts. Pain in temples; r.; l., and in occiput; sharp, in l.; sharp, in front part of l.

Eyes.—Aching; in r. and above l. angle of r.; in l., with soreness to touch; from l. side of r. to occiput; in l. when rising, later in r., as if something had been blown in the eye suddenly. Sharp pain in l.; over and back of l.; occasionally in r. Smarting. Sharp pain in r. ball. Aching pain in l. ball, not much affected by the light. Lids stuck together in the morning.

Ears and Nose.—Frequent stabbing through lower lobe of l. ear, had to pinch it. Stinging in nasal passages. Burning in nasal passages extending to throat after rising. Sensation of mucus in l. nostril. Nose stopped in morning. Discharge from nose; watery, from l. nostril. Sneezed often.

Throat.—Pain near l. ear; sharp, sudden, transient, in l. side, occasionally extending to ear. Smarting; and redness; < r. side, back of it looks as if covered with tough mucus, constant accumulation of mucus in fauces, next day throat sore and burning, looks mottled, arteries show very plainly, sticky mucus in mouth and T., smarting in T., < l. side, T. dry and sore on waking from a nap, T. looked granulated, expectoration salt. Irritation; of l. side. Sore and raw feeling; S. and burning, posterior fauces gray and covered with membrane or tough mucus, arteries show very plainly where there is no mucus or appearance of deposit; S. < l. side, less on r. than posterior parts, with smarting, the smarting and inclination to cough > opening mouth and inhaling very cold air; in l. side of T., ear and neck, with aching, the S. seems to be in the muscles rather than in the mucous membrane, > holding side of head with my hand. Tingling; and inclination to cough, raised white mucus. Burning; in r. side; and in œsophagus, stomach and bowels.

Stomach.—Belching of tasteless wind in morning. Pain; all the forenoon, with occasional hot flashes; sharp, after a light breakfast. Distress on waking in the night, > morning, returned in evening; before and after a light breakfast; after a plain dinner, followed by a little ice-cream; through to back; through epigastrium to back, worse near spine, several times during the day; around body at epigastric region before rising, extending down back to region of kidneys. Burning.

Abdomen and Stool.—Pain in diaphragm; in hypochondria; lower part of liver; liver and spleen; liver and spleen during the day; in liver, < evening. Sharp pain in region of liver; in liver in morning; in l. lobe of liver; region of liver, < drawing a long breath; under ends of l. floating ribs after retiring, appeared to be in the spleen, but a little higher up on the other side, may have been in lower border of liver. Frequent transient inclination to stool during the day, alternate diarrhœa and constipation, changing every three or four days.

Genital Organs.—Long-continued excitement every morning; and in night.

Respiratory Organs and Chest.—Difficult breathing after retiring. Sharp pain in back side of l. lung. Pain through chest; in sides; in r. lung; in back side of r. lung; through centre of r. lung; in centre of l. lung after retiring, and around body at diaphragm; in centre of r. lung and through to scapula. Burning distress at right of lower end of sternum; in both sides, with difficult breathing.

Pulse.—Full, rolling.

Back.—Aching; just below diaphragm; in centre of r. scapula in morning; inside of scapula, < r. Sharp pain at superior spinous process of l. ilium; suddenly at anterior superior spinous process of l. ilium; transient, sudden, in r. side near kidney, forcing me to sit down.

Extremities.—Grinding pain just above elbows. Pains in arms and legs; in l. arm in afternoon; just above elbows, < r.; just above r. elbow, seemed to be in the bone; in l. forearm; l. forearm and wrist; l. wrist in afternoon; r. thigh and leg; legs, < above knees; bones of l. leg after going to bed; knees; l. ankle; in feet, with burning. Lame pain in r. knee. Knees weak; < afternoon, < r.; and trembling. L. foot lame through metatarso-phalangeal joints at times.

Skin.—Sore pimple on l. thigh, outside. Itching in various parts frequently day and night; of various parts before and after retiring, > scratching, but appearing in another place; sudden, < night, < limbs; frequent sudden darting, on various parts, < legs.

Sleep.—Slept in a chair (unusual) after dinner. Restless at night. Sleepy after retiring, so that eyes ached, but could not sleep for a long time. Sleepless for nearly two hours after retiring, and restless, had headache, pain in back, stomach and bowels, woke at midnight, after a few minutes sleep, with hurried desire for stool, > passing much wind, after much effort passed a large, long, tenacious stool. Every night go to sleep on retiring, and in five or ten minutes wake and lie awake one or two hours. Wakefulness in the morning, but later in the proving it was both in the first and last part of the night. Woke early and could not go to sleep on account of pains all over, < epigastric region, back, arms and legs, legs lame and painful as from severe exercise and cold, expected to be very lame on rising, but felt nicely. Woke two hours earlier than usual, with dull headache, burning all over chest, seeming to be in the pleura, aching pain through lungs to scapula, aching in back part of shoulder, outside of upper portion of scapula, pain in hypochondria, extending down back, burning pain in legs and feet, mostly below knees, so that I could not go to sleep, feet so hot that I had to put them out of bed, then the pain extended to the thighs, the pain was so severe that I felt as if I trembled all over, but think I did not, I felt as if I could not move, but on moving there was no pain and I felt better by moving, could not sleep again.

Fever.—Chilliness all over so that I trembled. Feet cold; and damp; afterwards burning.

Hydrangea.

The dried root of Hydrangea arborescens is used either in the form of infusion, fluid extract or tincture.

Clinical.—This seems to be a valuable remedy for certain forms of "gravel;" particularly useful for profuse deposits of white amorphous salts in the urine. It is reported to have arrested the tendency to formation of calculus in the bladder, as well as to have relieved distress from renal calculus, with soreness over the region of the kidneys, bloody urine, etc. With these indications, it is to be compared with Berb., empirically with Bursa pastoris (Dudgeon), and with Ocimum (Mure.).

Hydrastis.

A tincture is made of the fresh root of Hydrastis Canadensis, L.

General Action.—A "catarrhal" drug, causing inflammation of all mucous membranes, with profuse discharges. It depresses the vitality, causing atonic as well as catarrhal dyspepsia, constipation and general weakness. Its action on the liver is marked; jaundice, and symptoms of inflammation resemble its near relative, Chelidonium.

Allies.—*Puls.*, Stann., Borax, Chel., etc.

Generalities.—Darting pain occasionally in long muscles. Pain at night, but too sleepy to notice where. Tendency to take cold easily. Malaise. *Languor;* in morning; at 4 P.M.; < towards evening, with headache, and giddiness, and when walking falling; and ennui. Disposition to lie down. Dulness. All symptoms except the gone feeling > dinner.

Clinical.—The hydrastis patient generally suffers from debility, constipation, atonic dyspepsia, palpitation, dyspnœa, and in a general way is subject to catarrhal discharge and ulceration of mucous membranes. Scrofulous affections, particularly marasmus in children. Malignant ulcerations (epithelioma). Retarded convalescence from typhoid fever, with loss of appetite, constipation, etc.

Mind.—Affections active. Exhilarated; and desirous to sing. Sanguine and contented. Vindictive. Spiteful, > towards evening, and disposed to hit things in general; S. and angry, and desirous to snub any one who differed from me. Angry, and desirous to curse everything and anybody who bothered me. Fretful. Despondent, > "quiz" in evening. Gloomy, taciturn. Fearful that he will become sick all over. Dislikes to go out, to read, write, do anything. Averse to mental occupation, and memory dull. Forgetful when writing. Memory deficient; and head confused.

Head.—Aching on rising; after breakfast, with sensation as if brain were pressed against frontal bones; A. till sleep; with sticking through temples; extending from centre of brain to r. parietal protuberance; bounding, throbbing; nervous, gastric, till noon. Heaviness, amounting to pressure over root of nose. Fulness after breakfast, then aching in temples, < every step or sudden movement or coughing, with bursting sensation on ascending stairs or on sudden stooping. Confusion, with heat in it and loss of memory of recent events, the heat and confusion > pressing cool hand across forehead. Brain feels partially narcotized, then cutting darting through temples. Intoxicated feeling in morning.

Forehead.—*Pain;* on rising at 6.30 A.M.; at 8.30 A.M.; in supraorbital regions at 8 A.M.; over l. eye at 9 A.M., with soreness in forehead, stoppage of r. nostril, the aching > walking in open air, when watery coryza sat in, the latter stopped again in the room; above l. eye at 10 A.M., always > laying hand on part; at night, and in temples; throbbing P. across sinuses. Bursting, almost stupefying sensation on waking at 9 A.M. > pressing skin towards middle of forehead and when in motion and when mind was engaged, < pressing skin towards temples on pressing in forehead and on wearing a light hat or loose hat drawn tightly. Heaviness, < over l. eye at 9 A.M., in a warm room, > open air, with fulness.

Temples.—Stinging, with dull pains in vertex and over eyes. Cutting through T., with dim vision. Pain over l. eye at 11 A.M.; P. at 9 P.M. from emotion, > pressure and open air; in l. at 8 A.M., extending into l. nostril; throbbing P. all day, < with all other symptoms, in warm room, when sitting and resting, especially when thinking of the symptoms, > fresh air.

Pain in r. parietal protuberance at 8.30 A.M., on ascending stairs; P. in a spot over l. parietal protuberance at noon; heavy P. in l. side of head all day. Heaviness of r. side of head, with drowsiness. Dulness in r. side. Pain in r. cerebellum, then l. Heavy pain in l. occiput, > pressure of cool hand and cool open air, with pale face, heat in head and pressure outward in region of temporal fossa.

Eyes.—Lids agglutinated in morning on waking.

Clinical.—Catarrhal ophthalmia, acute, with swollen lids, profuse secretions, smarting and burning; chronic, scrofulous, with profuse discharge, opacities of the cornea, etc. Dry catarrh of the conjunctiva. Blepharitis.

Ears.—Pain in r. at 6.30 P.M., after supper, then fulness in forehead and pain over l. eye; P. extending from l. mastoid process to scapula at 9 P.M.; tensive P. in r. in morning and afternoon. Eustachian tube partially stopped. Noises; at night on waking, with rumbling in bowels. Ringing, with pain in anus. Roaring at 9 P.M. Noise as of cogwheels at night. Whirring like a partridge on habitual waking at night.

Clinical.—Catarrhal inflammation of the middle ear and deafness, after scarlet fever. Otorrhœa, with thick mucous discharge.

Nose.—Constant snuffing through the day and occasional sneezing. Sharp excoriating feeling in nares, with constant inclination to blow nose and free discharge of mucus. Sore inside at 3.30 P.M., air felt painfully cold on inhaling, with hawking of mucus from throat and posterior nares; internal edge of r. wing sore and thickened, l. nostril stopped, r. dry and painful (in room). Sensation in r. nostril of a curtain opening and shutting during inspiration, gradually passing to l., leaving r. stopped. Tickling in back part after sneezing. Tingling down r. nostril at 3.30 P.M., then a few drops of arterial blood, stopped with cold water; T. in r. at 4.30 P.M., causing sneezing. Itching in r. nostril from 6 A.M. to 1 P.M., always > cool air. Air seemed cold to l. upper inner nostril at 9 A.M. and 2 P.M. in open air, with pain extending from posterior nares deep into head and with pressure in and over l. eye. Dryness; < r. nostril, with stoppage; and stoppage, with scabs in it. Stoppage; in morning; in r. nostril; l. nostril, with tickling in r. like a hair.

Sneezing at 7 A.M. after breakfast, from tickling in r. nostril; S. at 7. P.M.; at night, every time he woke; sudden, at 8 P.M. in a warm room, then excoriating watery discharge from nose, he goes to bed very sick; constant.

Coryza; in afternoon; < morning, > evening; in r. nostril, with constant inclination to sneeze from 7 A.M. till 1. P.M.; with dry feeling in nose in morning on walking, on going into open air discharge of water, which ceases in room, and nose feels dry and sore when breathing through it. Stopped coryza. Stuffed-up sensation in posterior nares and nasal sinuses, with discharge of thin, clear mucus; posterior nares stuffed up, smarting as from a recent cold, with increased nasal secretion. Profuse discharge from nose and bronchia. *Discharge of thick yellow matter* (Puls.); frequent D. of watery mucus on walking in cold open air; D. of thin mucus excoriating upper lip, afterwards thicker. Blowing out blood and yellow mucus. Bright red blood from nose at 2.30 P.M, after dinner.

Clinical.—Nasal discharge, watery, excoriating, with burning, rawness of the throat. Catarrh mostly in the posterior nares, which become obstructed, with headache, the discharge dropping into the throat. Hypertrophic catarrh, with yellow-greenish, offensive discharge. Ozæna, with ulceration and bloody discharge. Ulceration of the septum of the nose, bleeding easily on touch. (It has been used as a local application in diphtheria of the nose.)

Face.—Pale. Tight feeling of skin around corners of mouth, which seem drawn down. Aphthæ on under lip. Fever blisters in r. corner of lower lip.

Mouth.—Edges of teeth sensitive to draught of cold air. Tongue, large and marked by teeth; *aphthæ* (Borax), yellow coat; broad yellow stripe and bad taste. Scalded feeling in morning on rising, < smoking; scalded feeling in l. side of tip, spreading over anterior half of tongue, with smarting and with a burning painful vesicle where the scalded sensation started; dryness at root. Sticky mucus around palate, with bad taste. Sticky, with fur on tongue and aphthæ on upper lip. Smarting in l. side of palate in morning. Taste bad in morning; T. peppery; acid, peppery on forward half of tongue; strange, to food,

Clinical.—Numerous cases of aphthous sore mouth. Stomatitis in children or women. Canker in the mouth, after chlorate of potash.

Throat.—Unusual clearing when singing. *Hawking from increased mucus* (Stan.). *Sticky mucus around fauces; mucus in fauces, which cannot be swallowed* (Puls.). *Soreness;* in morning on waking; < coughing or swallowing; of r. upper part of pharynx, < dry swallowing, > swallowing fluids; < about epiglottis, with rawness and hoarseness; and dryness. *Roughness in morning on waking, < swallowing, with soreness.* Feeling of a lump in lower part of pharynx causing constant deglutition, at times the lump seems to rise, almost suffocating, the suffocative feeling > drawing long breaths through mouth. Dryness at 4 P.M., with swelling of uvula and mucus about posterior nares, throat seemed raw and swallowing scraped it. Tickling low down in pharynx at 6 P.M. after lighting a match, the fumes of which passed into mouth, > coughing and drinking.

Clinical.—Catarrhal sore throat; it is very extensively used both internally and locally by homœopathic physicians, without special characteristics, and while the indications for its use are not always plain, and it doubtless has no effect in a large number of cases, yet it seems to have a marked curative action in a certain class, probably in those characterized by hypertrophy of the mucous membrane, with rather free discharge and with burning and rawness extending into the nose and chest. Follicular pharyngitis, the mucous membrane is studded with protruding points, which are deep red and very irritable, < least exposure to cold.

Stomach.—Desire for eggs; D. for bread and tea. Appetite poor; diminished for breakfast. Dislike for meat and vegetables. Eructations of wind; loud, in afternoon. *Nausea;* at 11 A.M., with eructations of wind, empty feeling in stomach and visible sinking in region of stomach. Gurgling. Cutting in region at 3 P.M., after eating; in stomach and l. hypochondrium after dinner. *Acute pain.* Pain (Stan.); in region at noon, > empty eructations. Feeling of something twisting in it on lying upon it. Weight. Heartburn in afternoon. *Sinking in epigastrium;* in morning. Empty feeling in morning on rising, with scooped-out appearance of abdomen, nausea and heavy, white-coated tongue; E. feeling at 11 A.M., with pain.

Clinical.—Inflammation of the stomach, with frequent vomiting and loss of appetite, great soreness over the region of the stomach and burning, in a disease that had been diagnosticated as cancer. Atonic dyspepsia, with acidity, especially in old people. Ulceration of the stomach.

Abdomen.—Trembling. Rumbling as before diarrhœa. Fetid flatus. Cutting; at 10 A.M., extending to anus, > slight emission of flatus when lying; during breakfast, then desire for stool, with emission of wind before evacuation, first part of stool natural, last part soft and dark brown; after breakfast, > emission of flatus; before and after dinner, as before dysentery. Griping, with external soreness; G., with several light, acrid stools; G., with profuse light-colored, prostrating stools. Pain at 9 A.M., with passage of wind and pressure to stool. Uneasy, burning sensation.

Rumbling in l. side at noon, with gurgling; R. high up in l. side, with gurgling and pain. Cutting in hypochondria. *Intermittent acute pain in liver region, extending to scapulæ* (see Chelid.), < between 8 A.M. and 2 P.M. Pain in upper A. Soreness in upper A. in morning on rising, while inhaling. Cutting in umbilicus at 5 P.M., extending to penis. Pain in umbilical region and in anus. Cutting in sigmoid flexure of colon at 2.15 P.M.; C. from r. iliac region into r. testicle at 11 P.M., which left the parts above Poupart's ligament sore and tender, with pain extending into root of penis when pressing upon it; C. in hypogastrium before each stool, > stool, with uneasiness, frequent scanty stools, with tenesmus in rectum, which caused dragging, bruised feeling in ovarian region. Pain in r. groin at 2 P.M. when walking; P. in r. groin changed to l.

Clinical.—Gastro-duodenal catarrh, with sinking in the region of the stomach, palpitation, etc. Liver torpid, skin yellow, stools light-colored, hepatic region tender, etc. Jaundice. Gall-stone colic, with jaundice. Chronic catarrhal inflammation of the bowels, with mucous discharge, or fæces covered with mucus; fæces soft and mixed with mucus.

Rectum.—Heavy distress.

Clinical.—Ulceration of the rectum. Fissure of the anus. Prolapsus of the rectum, especially in children.

Stool.—Diarrhœa driving him out of bed at 7 A.M., and stool almost entirely of yellow water at noon; D. preceded and followed by tenesmus, before stool sensation of weakness and trembling, after stool weakness; D. preceded by tenesmus and nausea and followed by tenesmus. Three loose, greenish, with pain in bowels as after a drastic purge. Mushy, copious, light-colored. Soft and of small diameter. Of natural size, but excoriating anus, as if covered with sand. Scanty. Two mormal, in one day. Tinged with blood; covered with blood, painless. Natural, then profuse discharge of bright red arterial blood, causing anxiety, then sensation all day as if the hæmorrhage might be repeated, and was in consequence squeezing sphincter ani all the time. Constipation; no desire, passage of some flatus.

Clinical.—Chronic constipation; especially valuable after purgatives (Nux v.). Constipation in children. Obstinate constipation, with a weak feeling in stomach, sour eructations, dull frontal headache, etc. Constipation following parturition, with hæmorrhoids and headache. Constipation and hæmorrhoids in pregnancy.

Urinary Organs.—Micturition frequent, of considerable limpid urine; F., but not more copious. A little urine escapes into urethra when eructating. Tickling in urethra in evening, generally low down, once at orifice. Urine diminished and pale; D. and smelling strong; U. has an unusual odor; U. smells decomposed.

Clinical.—Catarrh of the bladder, with thick ropy mucus in the urine.

Sexual Organs.—Offensive sweat, < scrotum, and excoriating S. under prepuce. Aching in penis during and just after stool; A. at root just as flow of urine stopped. Voluptuous itching on scrotum at 8.30 A.M., > rubbing.

Clinical.—Chronic gonorrhœa. Hydrocele. Pruritus of the vulva, and hard nodular tumors of the breast, with lancinating pains. Ulceration of the cervix, with prolapsus of the uterus. Cancerous ulcerations of the uterus. Hæmorrhages from the uterus, especially with ulcerations. Yellow, tenacious leucorrhœa. The leucorrhœa is almost always tenacious, rarely with albuminuria; associated with great prostration, palpitation, or with derangements of the liver, constipation, hæmorrhoids, etc. It has been used successfully in chronic enlargement of the uterus (sub-involution). Uterine fibroids. Inflammation of the cervix, with heat and itching of the vagina. Ulceration of the neck of the womb, fungoid, leucorrhœa profuse.

Respiratory Organs.—Hoarseness; with sharp acrid feeling near epiglottis. Desire to cough increased to nausea at times. Cough from pressure of fingers on trachea; short and dry C., then loose; C., with sweetish expectoration. Breath oppressed; constant want to draw a long B.; short B.

Clinical.—Laryngeal catarrh, mucous membrane pale, vocal cords relaxed. Bronchial catarrh, yellow, tenacious mucus.

Chest.—Catarrh descended into C. causing distress and difficult breathing, constant desire to take long breaths. Stinging at 8.30 A.M. Spasmodic pain under r. clavicle in morning when laughing, extending to r. side of chest and back. Retching pain in l. lobe of lung, from front through to back, from 9 A.M. to 1 P.M., with congestive feeling and sensation as before bleeding of lungs. Pain as from excoriation under upper part of sternum at every cough, with constant desire to cough. Soreness of C. and upper abdomen on drawing a long breath, later soreness in mammary regions and disposition to stretch body backward and arms upward, with yawning. A vertical drawing streak in l. breast, half way between nipple and sternum, twelve inches long, spreading like a feather from median line, going as quickly as it came. Constriction about sternum; at middle of S. (Compare chest symptoms with Stannum.)

Heart and Pulse.—H. agitated at 5 P.M. when at a lecture. *Palpitation; in morning.* Pulse slow; and labored.

Neck and Back.—Pain from l. side of neck to shoulder, > laying hand on it; P. in nape, extending to r. shoulder, with heavy pain in r. shoulder. Soreness in muscles of neck, with harshness. Pain under l. scapula all day; sore P. in small of B. and region of kidneys all day.

Extremities.—Pain in r. shoulder, l. elbow and knees; in outer side of l. knee when walking, causing limping, with pressure in l. shoulder; stinging rheumatic P. in elbows, forearms and knees, in morning. Shoulders, stinging in r.; sharp pain, and in arms, and < l. index; deep pain, < l., with pain extending from head to shoulder; heavy pain in l. Soreness of muscles of arms on moving them. Elbows and biceps muscle, cutting; contusive lameness. Elbow, crick in r. and in l. phalanges; pain in l., with snapping in shoulder-joint on rotating arm. Drawing pain on radial side of l. wrist, extending towards elbow at 11.30 A.M. Pain in r. hip when walking, passing to knee. Rheumatic pains in thighs, < first sitting down after walking, later extending to hips and knees. Knees, pain in outer part of l. when sitting and walking; stiffness, < descending stairs. Shooting posteriorly on l. leg, down to os calcis, at 10.30 A.M. Aching in l. sole at 7 A.M.

Skin.—Yellow, < around mouth and neck. Swelling of lips, nose and mouth, pimples around mouth and chin going through the various stages of varioloid. Erysipelatoid rash covering face, neck, palms, wrists and joints of fingers, with maddening irritation and burning, after four days exfoliation, but irritation remained in a slighter form, < night. Itching of skin and pudendum, disturbing sleep after 1 A.M., > scratching; I. in spasmodic attacks in various parts during the day, < scalp.

Clinical.—It has cured lupus, epithelioma, malignant ulcers of the skin, lips and various other organs. It has benefitted varicose ulcers, especially when applied locally. Eczema, especially in the margin of the hair on the forehead, with oozing secretions. Bed-sores. Chronic ulcers, which bleed easily and smell badly.

Sleep.—Sleepy at 10 A.M., at a lecture. Sleep at 11 A.M., S. unusually sound in morning, hard to be awakened. Waking once or twice at night, thinking it was time to rise, but immediately falling asleep again. Restless sleep; waking every half hour, upon each occasion seeking a new position; and seeking cool positions; and full of dreams (had studied hard); with frightful dreams and fancies. Dreams of monsters; of being pursued by wild beasts; troubled and lascivious, with profuse emissions; vague, unremembered, lewd, disturbing sleep.

Fever.—Chill at 9 A.M.; at night on undressing; in back and thighs at 11 A.M., when walking in open air, then agreeable heat in those parts. Sensation of a draught of cold air on r. lumbar region and r. nates at 11 A.M. General heat at 10 P.M.; H., with itching in various parts; H. of skin; in flushes over face, neck and hands.

Clinical.—General tendency to profuse perspiration and unhealthy odor.

Hydrocotyle.

A tincture is made of the dry plant, Hydrocotyle Asiatica, L.

Generalities.—*Bruised feeling in all muscles;* B. feeling on waking. Wandering pains in muscles of chest and legs. Drawings in several muscles. Malaise. *Weariness; with heaviness and dulness;* and unfitness for everything.

Mind.—*Gloominess.* Misanthropy. Inclination for solitude. Ennui. Indifference.

Head.—Aching. Painful drawing in almost all cranial nerves. Heaviness. Congestion of blood. *Vertigo;* with torpor. Neuralgic pain in external frontal nerve. Pain in posterior part of skull, with swelling. Occiput sensitive, < touch. Constriction of back part of skull; C. of posterior and superior integuments of skull.

Eyes and Ears.—Look unsteady. Injection of palpebral conjunctiva. Pricking in eyes. Vision dim. Dazzling. Pain in l. internal meatus auditorius. Ear, throbbing in r.; ringing; ringing in l., with stoppage; confused noise in l.; blowing sound.

Nose.—Swelling. Tickling; < l. nostril. Feeling as before bleeding. Stoppage. Coryza; dry. Bleeding.

Face.—Intoxicated expression. Intermittent pain in l. cheek-bone.

Mouth and Throat.—Whitish spots on l. upper and under sides of tongue. Impediment in speech. Redness of velum palati, with pain on swallowing, < food. Hyperæmia of buccal mucous membrane. Saliva increased. Taste insipid or bitter. Tonsils red. Pricking in pharynx. Disorder of constrictor muscles of pharynx. Œsophagus dry and rough; burning and pricking in O.

Stomach.—*Loathing of food.* Anorexia; then strong appetite. Aversion to tobacco-smoking. Eructations frequent; **acid E.** Nausea. Swelling of S. Contraction. Cramplike pain. Sensation as if gases collected into a ball. Anxiety in region, with weight. Heat in region, spreading out like a bar.

Abdomen. — *Borborygmi in different parts. Flatus.* Violent contractions of intestines. Pain; every five minutes; < transverse colon. Constriction. Sensation as if all organs were in motion. Pain in upper part of liver. Obstruction in hepatic region. Heat in hypogastrium.

Clinical.—Cirrhosis of the liver.

Rectum and Stool.—Weight in rectum. Burning in anus. Itching in anus. Ineffectual desire. Stools dry, *dark.* Stools increased. Stools easier.

Urinary Organs.—Feeling of weight in prostate gland. Irritation of neck of bladder. Constriction of bladder. Frequent desire to urinate. Irritation of urethra. Urine increased. Urine becomes brown on cooling. U. turbid, without sediment.

Clinical. — Inflammation of the neck of the bladder in women, with inflammation, heat, etc., within the vagina and neck of the womb. Pruritis of the vagina.

Sexual Organs.—Drawing in spermatic cords, < l. Scrotum relaxed. Impotence. Indifference to intercourse. Vulva and vagina red. *Heat in bottom of vagina, at its orifice pricking and itching.* Leucorrhœa increased. Pain in ovarian region. Uterus, redness of cervix; pain, < l. side; laborlike pain in U. and appendages; heaviness.

Respiratory Organs and Chest.—Pricking in vicinity of glottis. Dryness of windpipe; of ventricles of larynx. Voice weak. Speaking soon fatigues. Irritation of air-passages. Difficult expectoration of bronchial mucus. Breath short. Oppression of chest relieved suddenly, then intermittent.

Heart and Pulse.—Cardiac spasm. Constriction of heart; with quiet and regular pulse, or with a few separate beats in certain arteries, or with hot flushes in different parts of face. Irregular beating of heart. Pulse stronger and fuller.

Neck and Back.—Renewal of old rheumatic pains in l. rhomboid, < pressure. Bruised pain in loins. Obstruction in region of kidneys, with heaviness. Formication in kidneys.

Extremities.—Contractions of forearms and legs. Irresistible inclination to stretch. Pain in all joints; < l.; P. in all muscles. Sensation as if hot water ran through marrow of bones. Weariness in all muscles of shoulders. Crampy numbness of r. forearm, hand and fingers. Pain in finger-joints. Gait unsteady. Inability to stand. Sharp pains in hips. Weariness in muscles of thighs, with crampy movements in calves.

Skin.—*Spots almost circular, with raised scaly edges. Yellowish spots on legs. Erysipelatous redness.* Red points on eyelids, l. side of neck and both hands. Red spots covered with whitish scales, on l. side of neck. Lilac-colored spot, shaped like an ear, on sole, the skin over it is depressed and walking is painful. Erythema on face, neck, back, chest, arms and thighs; E., with much itching; E., with copious sweat. Miliary eruptions on neck, back and chest. Sudamina on abdomen. *Papules on face. Pustules on chest. Pricking on different parts. Itching in several places;* I. at tip of nose (in one who had chilblain there every year).

Clinical.—It has cured lupus of suppurating variety. Lymphatic tumors. It has ameliorated cases of leprosy, seems to have arrested the destructive processes; it also has ameliorated cases of elephantiasis. Numerous cases of eruptions, for the most part dry, with great thickening of the epidermoid layer and enormous exfoliation of scales. It has cured psoriasis with the above indications, and has greatly relieved forms of dry eczema; excessive thickening and exfoliation of the epidermis is a strongly marked indication for its use (Kreos.).

Sleep.—Yawning and stretching. Sleepiness; in the daytime. Heavy, dreamless sleep.

Fever.—Shivering in afternoon. Cold hands and feet, with general condition resembling precursory stage of fever, without alteration of pulse; C. forearm, hand, l. foot and leg, > rubbing, but returning. Febrile movements. Heat of skin; H. in bones of leg; in l. tibia; in face in flushes; in different parts of face in flushes, < temporal regions. *Profuse sweat.*

Hydrocyanic Acid.

The officinal acid is diluted with an equal part of distilled water to make the first centesimal solution.

General Action.—A deadly poison, one grain of the pure acid being sufficient to cause death. It slows the heart, causes extreme dyspnœa, blurred vision, vertigo, frothing at the mouth, tetanic and epileptiform convulsions.

Generalities.—Appeared like a man suffering from excess of drink. Increased secretions from skin, glands, < salivary glands, kidneys and serous membrane. Bloodvessels injected, whole face bloated. Relaxation. Rigidity of muscles. Agitation, with trembling of whole body. Arose slowly and unsteadily. Staggered; and fell; with groaning, rapid breathing, foaming at mouth, hands clenched. Leaned forward on a table, then became insensible, fell backward and was violently convulsed. Fell insensible; and breathed deeply, slowly and forcibly. Fell suddenly; and was stretched out lifeless, without trace of pulse or respiration, limbs cold, all muscles paralyzed, but eyes glistening and full of life. Threw her hands over her head and fell. Started up, threw her hands over her head, gasped, stood for a second, then ran forward and fell with her head first to the ground, then was motionless and moaned.

Throwing herself about in a violent manner. Jerkings. Spasms; with unconsciousness; then paralysis; of limbs, < upper, and of chest; face distorted, limbs spasmodically extended, head drawn down on shoulders; so that head seemed buried between shoulders and arms nearly turned around by action of pronator muscles; beginning in toes, then distortion of eyes towards the right and upward, then general spasm, distortion of limbs, face, etc., with rigidity of body, twisting around of arms, and distention, especially of region of stomach; he drew himself up in his seat, supported behind by r. arm, contracted lower limbs and with a fierce look and fixed eye uttered three hideous groans, then twisted the body towards the left, with the face to the floor. Tetanus. Trunk spasmodically bent forward. Trembling.

Neuralgic pain in r. hip and thigh, afterwards in region of heart. Malaise. Activity of senses. Dulness of senses. Discomfort. Sensation as of impediment to touch. Standing upon feet very difficult. Movements difficult, as from loss of power of limbs. Restlessness; with dyspeptic fulness of stomach. Aversion to mental or physical exertion; with difficulty in moving and depression of spirits. *Weakness;* in afternoon; in afternoon, < feet; in evening; in evening, < lower limbs; with sleepiness; with general bruised sensation; nervous. Faintness; with sweat. Insensibility; with coldness; with coldness and pallor; and head leaning on table, r. hand hanging down, l. hand in her lap; and thighs drawn up on abdomen and rigid, upper limbs rigid, and on drawing them from the side they forcibly reverted to their former position, eyes shut, teeth clenched, face convulsed. Paralysis. Coffee removed most quickly the narcotic effects.

Clinical.—Hysteria or epileptiform convulsions, frequent, violent attacks, with feeble, irregular beating of the heart. Tetanic convulsions, with complete loss of consciousness. Tetanus, cyanosis, coldness; action of heart irregular, feeble. Hysterical attacks, when drinking the water seems to gurgle down the throat. Epileptic attack preceded by nausea, vomiting or waterbrash. Uræmic convulsions. Attacks of faintness, cyanosis, cold skin, gurgling on drinking. It has been used for the collapse of Camphor, with sudden cessation of all discharges, cyanosis and gurgling on drinking.

Mind.—*Disconnected talking.* Answered quickly, but he soon became heavy. Exclaimed "bread, bread," and sprang convulsively from his seat. *Wild delirium, with tossing from side to side, biting* at bystanders, *eyes anxious and protruding, pupils small,* heart's action *and pulse rapid. Anxiety. Fear of imaginary troubles.* Loss of courage. Could not remain in middle of road when he saw a vehicle approaching, even at a distance, but was forced to stand aside without waiting for it to come nearer. *Fretful.* Gloomy in afternoon, > open air, and ill-humored. *Thought difficult;* impossible. Memory weak. Stupefaction. *Coma;* interrupted by sudden convulsive movements. **Unconsciousness**; with weakness; sudden, with loss of sensation.

Head.—Inclined forward and unable to hold it up. *Aching; only at night; > in open air,* with confusion; *with feeling of distention;* with weight and heat in it and gastric disturbance; *violent, stupefying, on bending head the brain seemed to beat against it;* intermittent; in afternoon, now in this, now in that place; intermittent, in various parts, *always extending to forehead. Confusion;* then pressure, then pain; with acute pain in forehead and occiput, < region of r. brow; uneasy, then falling down. *Disturbance as if brain were on fire,* then falling down and debility. Feeling as if exhausted by mental exertion. *Heaviness* in evening, with pressure. A sort of *concussion. Congestion. Apoplexy.* Condition like intoxication. *Vertigo;* < motion, with obscuration of senses; with staggering and *indistinct vision;* and objects seemed to move; *feeling as if everything about him moved slowly,* with pressure in l. side of occiput extending over l. half of head to forehead, < forehead.

Forehead.—(Pain above l. eye.) Pressure; *on r. side; on r. side, extending to occiput;* outward, and in orbits, *gradually becoming sticking and boring. Heaviness and pressive sensation. Tension. Confusion;* with pain.

Pressure on vertex, not real pain, causing confusion, and extending towards forehead and orbits, where it became fixed, and *pressure extending from occiput down nape.* Pain in r. side of head; in region of crown and forehead; < frontal region, changing to region of *l. mastoid process, then to l. temple,* then to r.; intermittent P. in l. half, especially in region of forehead and vertex, at times changing to r. *Confusion of r. side,* with pressure in r. side of occiput and sinciput.

Occiput.—*Pain in open air; P. in O. and forehead,* < *r. side; P. extending to anterior surface of head; extending to frontal sinuses,* where it becomes seated; *beneath scalp.* Confusion, and in forehead; *C. and r. side extending forward* and causing pressure in forehead.

Eyes.—*Distorted.* Fixed; and prominent. Brilliant. Glassy; and prominent. Prominent and glistening, but half closed, pupils dilated and insensible. Pain deep in E. and temples, then in occiput. Balls tense and prominent. *Pupils motionless;* and dilated; and contracted. Pupils dilated; then contracted. Varicose veins in lids. *Lids open and balls fixed;* open and balls turned upward; wide open, eyes staring, injected and watery; wide open and balls difficult to move; half open; partly closed, eyes appearing as if pushed forward between them, pupils dilated and insensible; closed; closed and both eyes drawn to left. Pressure over r. inner canthus. Vision dim; with intoxicated feeling; V. of floating clouds in afternoon; V. of sparks. Blindness; with pain in forehead, pupils dilated, less sensitive to light, eyeballs tense and prominent, with injection of capillaries of lids.

Ears and Nose.—Ringing in E. Roaring in E. Buzzing in E. Difficult hearing. Pricking as if mephitic air passed over Schneiderian membrane. Sneezing.

Face.—Flushed; F. and neck red and puffy; bluish-red and swollen. Almost purple. Dusky. Blue. Gray and earthy. Almost black, then ghastly pale, swollen and covered with large drops of sweat. Pale; and sunken. Sunken. Swollen; and purple. Lines very distinct. Wild-looking and bloated. Ecstasy of features. Congested, and veins enlarged; F. and head congested and hot. Jaw fallen. *Jaws clenched in rigid spasm;* C., with corner of the sheet between teeth, along sides of sheet much thick white foam issued at each expiration; C., and lower teeth retracted within upper; C., but other muscles relaxed. Slight movement of jaw the only symptom of life. *Lips pale, bluish.* Lips distorted. Lips and tongue purplish. Lips closed.

Mouth.—Tongue white and dry; T. coated; T. protruding; irritation at root, becoming a scraping as after eating dry walnuts; feeling at root as if drawn together at both sides; coldness; numbness. Loss of speech. Unintelligible speaking. Mouth dry; before and after dinner. *Froth;* bubbles of viscid; thick, salivary, tinged with blood (from her biting her tongue). Brown tenacious matter fell on to the blankets. Spitting. Salivation, with attacks of nausea. Taste sharp, irritating; T. bitter; sweetish; insipid.

Throat.—Swelling and undulatory movements of jugular veins and quick and full beating of carotids. Gurgling. Drink rumbles through T. and intestines. Spasmodic constriction; with hawking. Pain, heat and cramp in fauces, œsophagus and stomach. Scraping; till 7 P.M.; in soft palate; pharynx; with sticking and increased mucus, which compels frequent expectoration of thin saliva; < larynx, with sticking, then feeling as if larynx were swollen and narrow and pressing against neighboring parts; with tickling extending from larynx low down air-passages and causing inclination to hacking cough, this condition of air-passages was compared to that after taking cold when hoarse or that caused by eating hips of roses when the hairs stick in throat, in the evening this changed to dryness in mouth and larynx. Soreness hindering deglutition, flow of saliva from mouth in evening. Uneasiness. Heat; in œsophagus. Inability to swallow.

Stomach.—Hunger increased, with aversion to food. Appetite diminished; and digestion; A. lost; lost, then unusually increased; lost at breakfast, a few mouthfuls cause nausea, desire for stool, oppression of chest and palpitation, at 12.30 sinking at stomach, but inability to eat. Aversion to eating. Thirst. Eructations; of gas; sour. Violent hiccough, > a cup of black coffee. Nausea after eating, with discomfort; N. and vomiting, with relief of symptoms. Vomiting; frequent; of black liquid; of black mucus. Distention of region. Heartburn after eating, with waterbrash and salivation. Feeling of a lump; gradually changing to sticking, then pressure. Sensitiveness of epigastric region. Warmth. Disturbances. Unpleasant sensation in epigastrium, with such weakness of limbs and muscles that he thought he would fall.

Clinical.—Chronic dyspepsia, with vomiting of food in evening and night (Ferr).

Abdomen and Stool.—Rumbling in A. Spleen feels enlarged. Involuntary stools. S. omitted; urgent, copious; mushy.

Urinary and Sexual Organs.—Burning in urethra during micturition. Frequent micturition, urine not increased; involuntary M. Urine and sweat copious; U. copious and saturated; copious and watery. Urine retained four days. Emissions of semen. Sexual desire increased.

Respiratory Organs.—Scraping in larynx; with rawness; with tickling, causing dry cough; as from eating too many walnuts; S. in trachea. Larynx feels enlarged. Increased mucus in trachea; expectorated in evening; increased mucus in larynx in afternoon and evening. Hoarseness. Cough; in evening; violent; in paroxysms, with expectoration of black-yellowish mucus, relieving the rattling respiration.

Suffocation, then stupefaction, and congestion and pain in chest. Dyspnœa; with contraction of sides of chest; with pressure in region of heart; with stertor and rattling respiration. Respiration difficult; caused by exercise, with nausea and sweat on face and hands; and rattling; and deep. Convulsive breathing; then regular, with snoring inspiration and moaning expiration. Gasping. Groaning. *Moans;* low. Sighs, with occasional sobs. She made a noise (Oh! oh! oh!). *Noisy and agitated breathing.* Wheezing, rattling. Irregular breathing. Anxious B. Respiration slow; and convulsive; and labored; and labored, with hissing; and stertorous; and deep; with frequent need of deep breathing; and deep, whereby the ribs were drawn back to spine; with deep, prolonged inspirations and moaning; and weak; and faint, gasping, sometimes with slight stertor. Respiration imperceptible. Respiration forcible.

Chest.—Sticking on deep breathing; S. under short ribs; S. internal to l. nipple; beneath lower end of sternum; in region of r. fifth and sixth ribs, near sternum. Acute pain, with anxiety. Pain; in r. side; between r. fifth and sixth ribs, near sternum; in region of heart, with dyspnœa; in sides, becoming a sticking. Constriction; transversely across; with sudden difficulty of breathing; obliging deep inspiration; of diaphragm, with sense of suffocation. Tightness; gradually extending into r. side of chest and becoming a pain that extends over chest and makes breathing difficult. Tension transversely across, especially in region of seventh and eighth ribs, < inspiration. Oppression.

Clinical.—Threatening paralysis of lungs and heart (compare Mur. ac.).

Heart.—Sticking. Pressure. Præcordial anxiety; alternating with vertigo, pain in same locality. Palpitation; with soft, full pulse. *Irregular action, pulse hardly to be felt; irregular,* with slow, depressed pulse; action and pulse variable, sometimes rapid, sometimes slow and intermittent, also weak. *Action weak;* and fluttering, pulse at wrist imperceptible.

Pulse.—Rapid; and weak; and weak, and action of heart could scarcely be felt when lying on back; and small; and small, feeble; and small, a weak impulse alternating with a strong one; and small, unequal; and now strong, now weak. Slow; in evening; and weak. Unequal in strength; and irritable, small; the tone of the different beats irregular. Small. Imperceptible; almost.

Neck and Back.—Neck bloated. Congestion of veins of neck and face. Cramp in back. Sudden pain in region of r. kidney, extending to epigastric region, then spreading over abdomen, causing warmth in abdomen.

Extremities.—Seemed bloodless. Flaccid; and fell lifeless when lifted. Trembling; and useless. Contractions, but no tetanus. Weak, so that he thought he would fall. Immovable and cold. Paralyzed and lay wherever placed, not rigid; hands and feet P. Arm stiff from tonic spasms. Arms bent and hands clenched. Arms relaxed, fingers contracted. Forearms stiff and inflected on arms. Trembling of r. hand. Hands partially contracted, fingers rigid and about nails of a dark lead color. Staggered. Legs dark when in a dependent position, from congestion of bloodvessels. Legs stiff; and straight.

Skin.—Pallor and coldness; P. and cyanosis. Rubescence on arms, then on legs. Yellow and livid about neck and breast. Urticaria, < upper part of body. Prickling in various parts. Formication, < epigastric region; F. on thighs, legs; limbs. Itching on neck and arms.

Sleep.—Yawning; frequent, with overpowering sleepiness, on waking confusion of head and difficulty in keeping awake. Sleepiness; towards noon. Condition between sleeping and waking, paying no attention to surroundings, on waking sensation as if he had not slept at all. Sleep prolonged and deep. Sleeplessness.

Fever.—Chill; intermittent, creeping, in afternoon; general, then general warmth; alternating with heat, with stupefaction and vertigo. Rigors, > coffee and brandy. Shivering like electric shocks; S. in paroxysms in afternoon when riding in a wagon over a rough road; creeping. Cold skin. *Cold limbs. Forehead* and face *cold and dry.* Heat; < feet. Sweat; *general;* general, clammy; clammy on forehead; cold, clammy; cold, covering face. Dry skin.

Hyoscyaminum.

The crystallizable alkaloid contained in Hyoscyamus, isomeric with Atropine, $C_{17}H_{23}NO_3$. Solutions in alcohol may be used.

Generalities.—Tetanic attacks. Muscular system flaccid, unable to sit erect in a chair, hand suddenly pronated and supinated with a jerk. Arrest of various secretions and excretions. Restlessness and tossing about bed; R. and reeling, then falling together like a drunken man. Heavy feeling. Inability to stand when she got out of bed. General numbness, with loss of power in producing ordinary movements of co-ordination.

Mind.—Delirium; violent, failed to recognize his family, saw animals about him, next day remembered nothing that had passed except the dreams of animals; wakeful, quiet and usually pleasing D., with illusions of sight or great sleepiness, and when aroused dreamy sleep, broken by occasional mutterings and jerkings of limbs. Clear when engaged in conversation, but dreamy when undisturbed, eyes wide open, he reached to an object on the table and looked about on the floor, when questioned said that he thought something had dropped from the table, and that the walls appeared to move, afterwards quiet, but meddlesome when not engaged in conversation, grasping at objects, attempting to remove them before the hand reached them, when left alone he lapsed into forgetfulness and dreamy, meddlesome delirium, picking at objects, having reached them after unsuccessful efforts he fumbled with them till he dropped them, then on attempting to pick them up lost his balance, when aroused he rubbed his hand, gaped, answered readily, a remark excited a risibility which he could not restrain, and occasionally the suppressed chuckle burst into a hearty laugh.

Dulness, heaviness. Difficulty in concentrating thoughts. Coma, with relaxation of voluntary muscles, except occasional spasmodic movements of arms and legs.

Head.—Aching. Congestion, and of face, violent throbbing of carotids with every impulse of heart. Drunkenness, nausea and vomiting. Giddiness; with staggering on rising from a seat; with staggering on walking; across forehead. Weight across forehead.

Eyes.—Suffused; sclerotic and conjunctiva. Balls restless. Pupils dilated; and insensible. Vision misty; and letters run together, can read fine print only at distance of a yard; double V.; yellow V.; V. perverted as to color and size, she thought some pills in a box were larger than the others; inability to read unless the print was within two or three inches of the nose.

Face.—Flushed; and hot; cheeks, occasionally; especially cheeks flushed and hot. Heavy look.

Mouth.—Tongue dry; and brown; at centre, and brown, also with clamminess of rest of mouth; and hard; and rough, except margins; and rough and brown, hard and soft palates dry and glazed, afterwards tongue and palates covered with a sticky, acid, offensive secretion, as after Belladonna; tongue and throat so dry that articulation was indistinct. Forepart and margins of tongue wet with acid secretion. Dryness of mouth; except gums. Clammy; and moist, exhaling an offensive odor. Suddenly moist. Sensation of mastic in it.

Throat.—Dryness; with moisture of mouth; of pharynx; with difficult swallowing.

Stomach.—Vomiting during the coma.

Urinary Organs.—Urging, dysuria and discharge in a feeble, dribbling stream, partial retention (urine contained Hyos.). Urine changed from high-colored to glaucous green. Urine changed from acid to alkaline and opalescent on boiling; and on standing a deposit of triple phosphates, the specific gravity increased. Urine pale, specific gravity decreased. Specific gravity decreased, uric acid decreased, changed from acid to neutral; sp. gr. and uric acid decreased, changed from acid to alkaline; sp. gr., chlorine, urea, sulphates, phosphates and uric acid decreased.

Respiratory Organs.—Dry, tracheal cough. Rapid respiration.

Heart and Pulse.—Heart's action excited and rapid. Pulse increased in rapidity, force and volume; then slow; then decreased in rapidity, force and volume. Pulse rapid; then slow and soft. Pulse slow; and at first increased in force and volume.

Extremities.—Jerking; occasionally, and fidgety. Inability to walk. Inability to rise from his chair or walk without assistance, and as he sat twitching now and then of the extensors of the legs, so as to advance the foot with a little jerk. Weakness of legs; of feet, so that I could only walk by fixing eyes on the ground.

Sleep.—Yawning; and sighing; and tired feeling. Sleepiness. Sleep.

Fever.—Heat; of skin, with dryness.

Hyoscyamus.

A tincture is made of the whole fresh plant of Hyoscyamus niger, L.

General Action.—It acts very similarly to Belladonna, but with less indication of congestion or fever; generally indicated in conditions of adynamia, with involuntary discharges, muttering delirium, carphology, etc.

Allies.—Stram., Bell.

Generalities.—Dropsy. Distention of veins of whole body; of neck, extremities, and < face. Clutching about her without knowing at what. If made to walk she did so with body bent backward, if she spontaneously attempted to walk she did so with feet wide apart and with involuntary motions of hands, with which she felt about her, sometimes closing them as quick as lightening. Constant change of position. Tossing about and restlessness. Tossing about the bed and screaming constantly; and rubbing his hot head with both hands constantly. In bed, at one time drew knees up, at another stretched them out, at another turned over, turned head back and forth, at another raised head and beat the bed with it, at another picked straws from his mattress, groped about him and did not speak.

Reeled, then fell; R. to the bed, fell upon it and was motionless. *Fell suddenly; with cries and convulsions; fell down unconscious, whole body cold and stiff*, face pale, eyes closed, pupils dilated, conjunctiva injected, anterior cervical muscles contracted so that it was impossible to lay head upon pillow, pulse small, thready, rapid, respiration stertorous and difficult, spasms of pectoral muscles; fell from her seat, lay immovable and slept with head upon chest, red face, deep respiration, warm skin, small, rapid pulse, eyes closed and injected.

Tremors, horripilation and rigors. Startings. *Twitchings; frequent, with violent delirium, during the remissions catching at flocks in the air or pulling at bed-clothes.* **Convulsions**; after every drink, sometimes he did not recognize his relatives; with frothing from the mouth (compare Hydrocyanic acid); with twitching of hands, feet and muscles; *C. flex the limbs, and the bent body is tossed high.* Opisthotonos, with convulsions of limbs. Epilepsy. *General rigidity as in tetanus.*

Stitches come out of finger-tips and out of all parts of body. Tearing or drawing pains in limbs and testicles. Rheumatic (tearing, jerking, gnawing) pains in outer and posterior surface of l. upper arm and in lower end of bones of l. forearm and in scapulæ. Restlessness, with confusion of speech and conduct; *R., excessive animation and hurry.* Peculiar sense of lightness and mobility. Activity, thought himself more active and vigorous then he really was. Ground seemed to give way under their feet. Oppression. Aversion to motion and work. *Weakness;* between the convulsions, with snoring; with general trembling and external coldness of limbs; with stupor and overpowering sleepiness; causing staggering; with heaviness of limbs. Inability to maintain an erect posture and reeling on attempting to stand. Faintness. *Sensibility blunted.* Insensibility; to pinching; loss of sense of touch; and he sits immovable in bed. Hemiplegia. Aggravation in evening; A. after eating.

Clinical.—Chorea, with clutching motions of the hands and numerous incoherent muscular movements. Epileptiform convulsions, especially in children or after labor. Convulsions from fright, in children. Tetanus. Hydrophobia. Paralysis agitans. During severe malaria, congestive chills.

Mind.—**Carphologia**; in nervous fever, with fumbling about his head, face and nose, and groping about the bed. **Ravings. Delirium; and restlessness, would not stay in bed** (Bell.); **with ludicrous actions like monkeys; ridiculous gestures like a dancing clown;** *ridiculous grimaces like one intoxicated;* **violent and beats people**; *bit, scratched and nipped every one who interfered with them; violent exertions to get out of bed, attempts to bite, rage,* then weeping aloud, while lying she turned the head r. and l., at times raised it and snapped as if she would take hold of something; strikes and tries to kill bystanders; attacks people with a knife; attempts to escape.

Delirium most of the time, *quick working and clutching of hands and striking his attendants, it was difficult to hold him on their laps,* afterwards talking about everything, cannot fix his attention, he cannot be held, wants to get away but cannot stand, and if he attempts to walk he falls on his face, limbs seem weak, almost paralyzed, acts as if intoxicated, *wants to fight, closes his hands and strikes at his attendants, attempts to bite, at intervals sings and at times laughs,* nervous trembling and jerking of muscles, *when anything is offered him he clinches hold of it with both hands greedily,* the slightest opposition excites him.

Lively delirium. **Foolish laughter** (Cannab. ind.). *Sings love songs and street ballads; sings constantly, talks hastily and indistinctly,* is violent and beats about her if spoken to strongly or taken hold of; merry, singing, imitating with her hands spinning; (laughable, solemn actions mingled with the raving, in an improper dress). Dancing; and laughing, running about, grasping at things, stared at bystanders, heard nothing, answered no questions, several men could not make her drink or lie down, face pale, pulse rapid, pupils dilated, capillaries of eyes injected, sleeplessness, vertigo, stupefaction.

Talking more than usual and more animatedly and hurriedly; *absurd talk; irrational, as if a man were present who was not;* T. about incoherent things; *incessant chattering without meaning,* also leaping and dancing as in chorea, did not know their own family. *Muttering to himself; absurd;* M. on being aroused, became irritable, resented attempts to make him drink, soon hallucination, in which his countenance became threatening, called on absent persons with whom he imagined himself in debate. (Prattled about things wise men would have kept to themselves.) Unintelligible answers. Excited, incoherent in speech, wandered purposelessly about the house, muttering and touching things as if suspicious of those about him, then delirious, saw policemen enter the house, heard them speaking about him in the hall, *hands in constant motion,* trying to rub his face or brush something away, was irritable, did not answer questions, but muttered a few disjointed words. In speaking used very fine language, so that the usually quiet and indolent peasant was scarcely recognized.

Frightful screams all night and tossing about. Roving about, senseless, naked, wrapped in fur in summer. Moaning and groping about, with outstretched fingers as if something should be seized suddenly. Acting as if cracking nuts; A. as if frightening away peacocks with his hands. Embraces the stove and wishes to climb upon it as on a tree. Listening to imaginary sounds and clutching at phantoms. A thousand fancies hover before his imagination. Thinks men are swine. (Considers himself a criminal.) Thought he was at home and desired to make visits. People in the room appeared grotesque, then noisy, and then quiet delirium, afterwards she sat in the corner of the room, muttered to herself, rocked her body to and fro, *now catching at the air, now pulling the bed-clothes about,* answering either not at all or incorrectly. Typhomania. Sudden intermittent excitement, with wild look.

Reproaches others and complains of a supposed injury to himself. Quarrelsome; and insulting; and tries to injure others. Uncontrollable anger. Fear; of death, becoming a monomaniac, then nervous irritation; of being devoured by animals. *Dread of drinks.* Hydrophobia. Jealousy. Anxiety; after dinner. Sad. Morose. Impatient. (Reproaches himself and has conscientious scruples.) *Quiet, reflective.* Laughter. (Lively and crochety, next day morose and quarrelsome.

Disinclination to think; or work; D. to study in afternoon. Aversion to reading. *When reading he mixes up improper words and sentences.* Disconnected words. Distraction at 6 A.M., with sleepiness, so that he must cease reading. Confusion of sense, weakness of sight and difficulty in speaking, like slight intoxication. Incapable of comprehending what was said to her. Inability to fix the attention, every attempt to overcome this was followed by confusion and headache. Ideas stand still. Ideas lost, he is troubled about everything, sleeps several hours in afternoon, often half awake. Remembrance of long-past events; easy R. of circumstances which he does not care to recollect, and remembers with difficulty occurrences which he tries to recollect. Inclined to forget himself in thoughtless staring at objects. Memory weak. Memory lost; when reading; of what she has read. Coma vigil. Sopor; after each fit. Lethargic state when left to himself. *Stupefaction.* Insensibility, but intermittent consciousness, when she spoke much, but hastily and disconnectedly. Foolishness. Amentia. Idiotic. **Unconsciousness**; on waking.

Clinical.—Delirium occurring in course of acute diseases' characterized by restlessness, is constantly busy with his hands' picking, working and clutching, and is constantly muttering or talking to himself, or is frightened; in a general way, loquacious delirium indicates the drug. Erotic delirium, refuses to be covered and talks in an obscene manner. Violent delirium, with tendency to bite, scratch or to escape (Bell.). Stupid, seems to be completely unconscious, but is picking at the clothes or catching at the air. Mania, with suspicions of his friends. Puerperal mania, with desire to be uncovered and with obscenity. With the delirium of this drug there are apt to be dry, cracked tongue, indistinct speech, involuntary evacuations and convulsive movements of the muscles generally. Acute mania, suspicious of having being poisoned or of being pursued. Delirium tremens, in which the patient is very suspicious of his friends and very loquacious.

Head.—(Sticking.) (Sticking, tearing.) *Aching;* in the room; with weight over eyes; at base of brain; when walking, as if brain were shattered; throbbing, waking him at night, with violent throbbing in carotids; stupefying, < forehead, changing to intermittent tearing; stupefying, < forehead, alternating with sticking, < l. side. Feeling as if encircled by a band. *Confusion;* at 4 P.M., with pressure in frontal region and difficult thought on going into open air; < open air, with pain in forehead and temples; with fulness, then heat; as from physical weakness, < morning. Heaviness; < sinciput, with pressure. Stupefaction. Rush of blood. Congestion of brain. Pulsation in brain. Waving in brain as from violent throbbing of arteries, < stooping, with pressure in forehead. Intoxication; after a meal. *Vertigo;* < walking, with tottering; with obscured vision; with reticulated vision, pain in r. side of forehead, then prickling in arms, then viscid sweat on them; even to faintness. Apoplectic and cramped condition. Amelioration in room; A. from a cup of coffee.

Forehead.—Sticking over r. eye when coughing. Pain; over eyes; on l. side, with amblyopia; < meninges of brain; and in occiput, less in parietals and still more seldom in encephalon; involving parietal region and occiput; so that he wrinkled the skin; paroxysmal in upper part, at times contractive, with general discomfort, at another time ease, with excited fancies. Pressure, provoking laying hand on it; P. > nosebleed, with heat. Fulness as if screwed in. Tension; and warmth. Heaviness, with burning; H. in sinciput, < stooping, with confusion. Confusion; in l.; in open air; in sinciput in morning on waking; and in occiput; with warmth; preventing thought; spreading afterwards to sight and hearing. Throbbing in eminences; l.; r., < movement and stooping, with drawing.

Aching in temples; after eating, and in whole external head; < r., < cold air, > in house; in r., forehead and upper lid, > motion in open air, with dizziness. Pressure in vertex on turning head, with drawing in nape. (Tearing in occiput.) Pain in occiput; P. concentrated itself in side of O., which felt sore, with burning, > pressure. Tension in occiput. Crawling on vertex. Gnawing on scalp, < moving or pressing it.

Eyes.—*Distorted. Squinting. Staring;* and looked larger than usual; and sunken, glistening; and looked dim, watery, pupils large, later wild look, squinting. *Red; and wild, sparkling;* and prominent. *Brilliant; and rolling about.* Lustreless, and brain obscured. Protruding, moving convulsively. Twitching. Sensation of a foreign body; pressure as from sand in them. Felt larger than usual. Felt as if he had been awake all night. Burning. Weakness; on reading. Heaviness. Insensibility, so that lids did not wink when cornea was touched. Lachrymation in open air, with sensitiveness of r. eye.

Pain in balls; r., < turning it outward and upward; in upper part, < moving them outward and upward; with heaviness of upper lids. Pressure on balls, with sensitiveness to hard pressure; P. upon r. ball, with sensitiveness to touch of upper and outer part. **Pupils dilated;** *and insensible;* l. D. and insensible; *and insensible, and albuginea red;* then contracted. Pupils contracted; < r.; < r., neither completely round; r., and angular; r., and r. ball sensitive; P. became smaller as headache grew worse; then dilated. Pupils not quite round.

Mucus in inner canthus. Lids swollen, whites reddish here and there, eyes look as after crying. Lids always half open. Biting in outer surface of l. lower lid, then r. Heaviness of upper lids; from sleepiness. Inability to open eye. Itching tearing in canthi, < external, > rubbing. (Itching in l. inner canthus.) *Conjunctiva injected;* r., and burning and lachrymation; < l., l. lids agglutinated, vessels of sclerotic injected. Pain in superciliary ridge; in r. brow. Gnawing pressure in upper margin of orbit, > touch.

Vision dim; r. eye; *and short. Short.* Uncertain. Weak. Photophobia; with lachrymation in open air. Double. Sticks the needle in the wrong place when sewing. They cry out that near objects will fall and grasp at them. Flickering; and dark points moving rapidly. When reading, letters looked like ants running together. **Small objects seem very large** (Nux mos.). Objects seem larger and brighter. All objects seem brighter and smaller, an indistinct yellowish umbra around every letter, afterwards some words seemed very large, but when viewed with r. eye they were like other words. *The flame of one light seemed smaller, that of another larger, though they were of the same size.* Everything looked like gold. Scarlet. Stars and sparks, all objects seemed cut into teeth or covered with points, all white objects surrounded by colored rings. Of stars and sparks, all white objects surrounded by rings, in which yellow predominated, if she looked into a cup the edges appeared yellow and it seemed as if small animals moved in the interior, at intervals muscæ volitantes and objects appeared strongly illuminated and to have colored edges. Blindness; and senselessness, wandering about the town; they lost in succession sight, hearing and speech. They carried the jug upside down to the mouth. They ran against all objects in their way, with open, wild eyes.

Clinical.—Spasms of the ocular muscles, eyes distorted or rolling. Illusions of vision, objects seem large, or double, or indistinct.

Ears.—Sharp stitches into ears. Tearing in cartilages, < pressure. Pain, < l.; sudden indescribable, in r. towards evening. Obstruction on hawking. Ringing. Loud noises. Roaring. Hearing weakened; **lost.**

Nose.—*Jerking downward in root. Pinching in root* and in zygomatic processes. *Dryness;* at root, with pain, mucus mixed with blood. Heat internally and externally. Sneezing; frequent, without coryza; frequent, with sensation of approaching coryza, which developed itself. Increased secretion of thick tenacious mucus mixed with blood. Bleeding; relieving head. Smell diminished. *Smell and taste lost.*

Face.—*Red; and distended; and excited;* and congested; F. and neck red, swollen and dry; dark red, with blue lips; brownish-red, swollen. *Pale;* and sunken; and covered with sweat; with blue lips. Bluish. Livid; and distorted, lurid, mouth open. Brown and turgid. Frequent changes in color. *Distorted.* Bloated, and neck. Dull, haggard look. Intoxicated look. Confused look in morning. Twitching; of cheeks. *Trismus.* Pain in upper jaw and in bone of zygoma. Chewing impeded. Risus sardonicus. Lips distorted; drawn obliquely, the drawing soon extended over face, then over whole body. Blisters on lower lip; white B. on lips; painful fever B. on lip. Lips, tongue and mouth appeared thick. Margins of lips dry.

Mouth.—Teeth. T. and all mouth covered with yellowish mucus in morning, taste disgusting. Gnashing. Grinding, with protrusion of tongues, *which were shaken to and fro with trembling movement.* Tearing in morning, with rush of blood to head as if spitting of blood were imminent; T. in gum, < entrance of cold air. Looseness, aching and tingling. Pain in upper, with swelling of l. gum; P. as if teeth would fall out, < chewing. Jerking pain in a hollow T. and on biting on the T. sensation as if too long and loose. Painful drawing here and there in a single T., as if it would become hollow.

Tongue.—Put out slowly and with difficulty, swollen, brown and dry. White coat; or yellowish; T. coated at back. Pale, dry and rough. *Dry;* T. and lips dry, burning, they look like singed leather. Heavy. Numb in middle as if burnt, < talking and drawing in breath. *Paralyzed. Speech confused; impaired; difficult and irrational;* indistinct. Muttering inarticulate sounds. *Dumb;* and wild look.

Mouth in General.—A kind of scurvy. Pain as if suppurating in soft parts behind teeth, between cheeks and gums, in evening during febrile heat. *Dryness; and of lips and fauces;* of M. and fauces in morning, without thirst; and of fauces, with warmth; with disgusting taste, tongue coated yellow. Thick feeling. Slavering. Salivation; salt. Bloody saliva, with bloody, sweetish taste. *Offensive odor;* in morning on rising. Taste bitter; in morning; nauseous B.; sharp B., causing vomiting; metallic; pasty; flat, pasty.

Throat.—Hawking of loamy, blackish mucus from fauces. *Spasm.* Angina and coryza. **Constriction** (Bell.); **impairing swallowing.** Back part affected, he points to it as if something were sticking in it. Smarting at back. Scraping; with hoarseness; with roughness; S. and roughness of throat and tongue, with moist mouth; S. in throat and fauces, with dryness and warmth; S. in throat and palate as after too much speaking. Dryness; of fauces; of soft palate; of fauces, with tickling; with contraction so that a swallow of tea threatened to suffocate him. Pressure as from a swelling. **Swallowing difficult; impossible**; I. from dryness of mouth and fauces.

Stomach.—Great appetite; *at noon;* A. diminished; lost. Aversion to food, with white coat on tongue, pasty taste and offensive breath. *Will not eat nor drink. Thirst;* from sticking dryness in throat; unquenchable. No desire or relish for water. Aversion to every beverage. Eructations; with nasty taste and nausea; empty; ineffectual efforts at. **Frequent hiccough.** *Nausea;* from external pressure on pit of stomach, > stooping; rising from abdomen at 5 A.M. Difficulty in retaining food without vomiting. Ineffectual retching. *Vomiting;* frequent; copious, after drinking coffee.

Inflammation. Gnawing. Pain in region of S. and umbilicus; flatulent P. in epigastrium, with distention of abdomen in evening after lying down. Pressure after drinking water; attacks of P. in pit, impeding respiration; paroxysmal pulsating P., returning and extending to r. side of chest. Distress in pit, rising suddenly towards sternum and up both sides of it. Heartburn; in afternoon. Burning; in pit; in epigastric region, rising towards chest. Constriction in pit. Weight. Oppression. Fulness in epigastric region in evening, with tension in abdomen. Sensitiveness of epigastric region to pressure; S. to touch in pit, with pain. Weakness.

Abdomen.—Distention; with necessity to breathe deeply, sour eructations and diminished stools. Hardness. Rumbling; < r. side, with gurgling. Discharge of flatus. Flatulence after a moderate supper, with frequent, but difficult emission of flatus. Spasmodic contractions of muscles as from something alive in them. Cutting; with drawing in small of back. *Pinching.* Griping; with soft stool. Pinching drawing, with emission of much flatus. Drawing pain. Pain; *in muscles when sitting, as if he had fallen upon them; strained P. in muscles,* in morning after waking; as if it would burst, causing screams, he thrusts his fists into his sides. *Sensitiveness of walls.* Warmth, with frequent yawning; W., then cutting, then rumbling and gurgling as before diarrhœa.

Sticking in l. side; S. in hepatic region. Burning spot in r. side in morning. Warmth in middle and upper A., > discharge of flatus. Sensation of incarcerated flatus in l. hypochondrium after dinner. *Sticking in umbilical region during inspiration;* S. beneath umbilicus when walking. Griping in umbilical region; with movings; with cutting; as from flatus; as before diarrhœa, with cutting. Pressure in umbilical region; > pressure. *Hypogastric region distended and sensitive.* **Cutting low down**; attacks of C. beneath pubes. Flatulent colic in morning on rising, a griping pressing downward like a weight in hypogastrium, with nausea and bruised pain in back; pain in hypogastrium as from incarcerated flatus, with sensitiveness to pressure.

Rectum.—(Hæmorrhoidal flux.) Heaviness as if it should be evacuated. Urging, with passage of only flatus; U. as to diarrhœa. Tenesmus and burning in anus. *Frequent desire;* constant. Desire and frequent stools alternate with delayed stools and absence of desire. Irritation of perineum.

Stool.—Liquid, frequent, with thirst, rapid, small pulse, prostration, heat of head, pain in occiput, obscuration of vision. *Diarrhœa;* day and night; after eating plums; with nausea. Soft, large; and easy; S., in small pieces; S., scanty, sluggish. Pasty, early. Mushy, copious, and scanty micturition. Hard, covered with mucus, with pain in anus during its passage; H. and insufficient; H. and delayed. Constipation; for four days, with frequent pressure in umbilical region as from fulness, frequent desire without tenesmus in rectum and anus; and impeded micturition, with urging to urinate. Scanty; but easy, next day dry and sluggish. **Involuntary, in bed** (Phos. ac., Arn.). Frequent. Delayed, next day earlier than usual.

Urinary Organs.—*Paralysis of bladder.* Spasmodic contraction in region of bladder, with frequent urging. Bladder so affected as not to discharge its contents but by partial efforts. Desire, with loss of irritability of bladder, alternations of scanty and copious urine, so that there is much desire with scanty or profuse urine, also inactivity of bladder with scanty or profuse urine may at the same time be present, still much urging with scanty urine is the chief action. Urging; (frequent, with scanty urine, next days profuse). Micturition frequent and profuse; F., but amount not increased; F. at night. Dysuria. Urine profuse; and light-colored. Urine scanty; and dark. Urine yellow, turbid when passed, afterwards a whitish-gray sediment. *Urine retained* (Nux v.); suppressed, with dragging in bladder (Stram.).

Clinical.—Paralysis of neck of bladder, with involuntary discharge of urine.

Sexual Organs.—Excitement, erections without excited fancies. Constant erections after a meal. Impotence. Tearing drawing pain in testicles. Desire diminished; then increased; increased. Soreness at entrance of vagina, with burning. *Labor-like pains in uterus before menstruation, with drawings in loins.* Menses delayed; suppressed; recurred on fourteenth day.

Clinical.—Nymphomania, sometimes of the most furious character. Metrorrhagia. Puerperal spasms. Muscular spasms during labor (threatening convulsions). Retention of urine after childbirth, seemingly no power to evacuate the bladder (Op.).

Respiratory Organs.—*Mucus in larynx and air-passages, making voice rough.* Sensation of something in air-passages which could not be discharged by coughing. Sticking in larynx, then dry cough, with sweetish taste of blood. Dryness of larynx, then sticking. Heat in larynx. Hoarseness. **Cough at night; frequent; always waking him; almost incessant cough when lying, < sitting up** (Puls.); **dry C. at night;** *dry, hacking C.; dry, tickling, hacking, seeming to come from trachea;* C., with greenish expectoration; inclination to C. Dyspnœa. Respiration rattling and difficult. Stertorous respiration, as in apoplexy; S. and irregular; S. and unequal, generally with simultaneous twitching of limbs. Constant need to sigh. Short and difficult respiration.

Clinical.—Speechless from fright. Irritable cough, < lying down and at night, from elongation of the uvula or from irritable condition of the epiglottis. Irritable cough from eating, drinking, talking or singing. Whooping cough, < night on lying down.

Chest.—Sticking; in r. Soreness beneath and somewhat to l. of l. nipple, alternating with sticking, pressure and pulling. Pressure; with sticking; upon chest, with internal sticking, < inspiration; on r. side near ensiform cartilage and last true rib, with anxiety and oppression of breath; in r. lower side and on ascending steps anxiety and dyspnœa; sudden, upon sternum, above pit of stomach after eating. Oppression, causing deep inspiration; O. like shortness of breath, with violent beating of heart. Tightness, as after too great exertion in speaking or running. Squeezing in upper part. (Burning pain in l. side in evening.)

Heart.—Sticking; causing deep respiration, alternating with yawning; tearing. Soreness and tightness in præcordial region, causing sighs. Tightness in præcordial region, causing deep inspiration, which relieved. Pain. Pressure and anxiety in præcordial region, causing deep inspiration. Oppression in præcordial region. Action violent; and irregular. Action tremulous, irregular; tremulous, small, quick, waking him.

Pulse.—Rapid; and full, strong; and full, soft; and weak; and threadlike; and small; and small, indistinct; and small, intermittent, also easily compressible. Strong. Full. Slow; and tense; and small; then rapid, small and irregular, then slight fluctuations, but constantly above the normal. Irregular; and small. Intermittent. Small, intermittent; and scarcely perceptible; S. and weak. Imperceptible at wrist.

Neck.—*Turned obliquely in attacks.* Tetanic contraction of anterior muscles so that it was impossible to lay head on pillow. Sudden sticking in region of upper insertion of r. sterno-cleido-mastoid, > pressure of thumb. Muscles stiff and tense on bending head forward. Stiff pain in nape.

Back.—(Tearing.) Sticking in scapulæ; l. Pain in loins; on stooping; on walking. Bruised pain in small of B. when sitting; in afternoon; B. pain when lying on back; when walking.

Extremities.—*Trembling.* Twitching, with flexions and tensions of fingers; *T. of hands and feet.* Convulsions; now of upper, now of lower. Distortions like chorea, the child made ill-mannered faces, between spasms eyes closed and child passive. Necessity to stretch. Sticking in joints of arms and legs. Cutting tearing in almost all joints, < motion. Drawing and tearing. Drawing pain in joints and still more in muscles near joints. Pains. Knees, feet and joints of upper limbs feel bruised and weary. Burning, prickling in hands, feet, legs, afterwards on attempting to get out of bed found her legs powerless. Stiffness as in apoplexy; tetanic S. Paralyzed sensation, < lower. Asleep.

Upper Extremities.—Tension in pectoral and dorsal muscles, at shoulder-joint, < raising arm. (Arms tremble in evening after exercise); A. convulsed; twitch at night in bed; prickling; tearing on posterior surface of l.; aching in bones of l., < posterior end of humerus. Goutlike pain in l. elbow. Pressure in bend of elbow if he holds arm bent. Sticking on flexor surface of forearm; itching S. Pain in wrists and elbows, spreading, > motion. Drawing pain about wrists and knuckles. Hands swollen; H. trembles when writing; in constant motion, she carried one, then the other to the mouth as if she had something in them which she would bite and chew; numbness; painful stupor; crawling in l. as if asleep. Thumb closed into fist during convulsions. Pain in last phalanx of r. little finger, with swelling. Drawing on inner margins of fingers on motion. Sensitiveness of second joint of r. index, with swelling.

Lower Extremities.—Gait insecure. Staggering. Weakness. Paralysis. Cramp in r. ischiatic nerve, with pain, muscles cramped if put on the stretch. Sticking in region of l. hip, S. in l. gluteal muscles, with cramplike pain. Sticking drawing in thighs, < rest. Paralytic drawing in thighs, < walking. Tensive pain transversely across middle of thighs on ascending steps, as if too short. Bruised pain in knee and ankle, with warmth. Weariness of knees on ascending steps; W., < l. when walking; W., with paralyzed feeling in lower limbs; when walking in open air, with stiffness.

Pinching in calves; sticking P. on tibiæ. Cramplike pain in calves in afternoon on moving. (Bruised pain in l. tibia when walking, < evening, and the side of calf is hot, swollen and covered with red miliary rash.) Uneasiness of legs. *Weariness of legs;* < eating. Cutting in tarsal joints when walking. Bruised pain in ankle in afternoon. Stamps one foot after the other on the ground in the convulsions. Drawing tearing in soles, < rest, > walking, returning when sitting. Pain in feet. Sensitiveness of r. metatarsus, < walking over an uneven pavement, tension and pressure as if too full of blood, < walking in street, often making him lame, like gout. *Toes spasmodically flexed as from cramp, when walking or carrying foot forward and on ascending.* Pain in a corn on r. little toe.

Skin.—Rattling like parchment. On palm seemed like stiff leather, then benumbed. Redness; of nates and feet; reddish cinnabar color after the heat, and as if inflamed. Pimples on elbow externally and sore pain when touched. Swelling of lips, then of nose, then over face and whole body, less about waist, with prickling and itching, skin of face red, shining and hard, eyes shut, no interval seen till below middle of body, where irregular patches appeared, some smaller ones looked like enlarged papillæ, with stiffness of lips and tongue so that he spoke in a thick blundering way.

Purplish rash over whole body, < about neck and face, face swollen so that she thought it would burst, scarlet, < l. cheek. Red papillary eruption covering body, > firm pressure, but returning immediately, then vesicles on various parts, resembling varicella, they dried, leaving scales, which peeled off with portions of surrounding cuticle, no desquamation of thick epidermis of hands and feet, the mucous membrane appeared somewhat as in scarlatina, but the strawberry tongue was not so well marked. Boils; small, here and there on face. Gangrenous spots, < lower limbs, with blisters. Ulcers became bloody and painful; bruised pain in ulcer on moving the part. Itching; here and there.

Sleep.—Yawning; on reading aloud; and stretching; frequent in forenoon; frequent and deep, > after sleepiness came on, then long sleep. *Sleepiness;* during the day, but restless, unrefreshing sleep at night, interrupted by dreams; from noon till 3 P.M., with inability to study and weariness; at 5 P.M., with yawning; during an interesting lecture; but wide awake after a short nap; with inability to think; with restlessness; with dreaming and occasional muttering, when aroused he rubbed his hands, gaped, answered questions readily, but dozed off with a half-finished sentence on his lips. *Deep sleep;* and long; interrupted by frightful dreams. Sleep for three days.

Sleeplessness; on account of exhilaration (Coffea); **long-continued; all night, he tried lying on one side and the other but could not get quiet,** *only towards daybreak short naps and general sweat, < about neck;* anxious S.; S., with alternate tremors and convulsive startings; S. alternates with sleepiness and sleep. Hyperæsthesia in morning like exhausted wakefulness, in afternoon sleepiness, prostration and irresolution. **Starting out of sleep.** *Woke himself with a cry. Laughing expression during sleep.* Talks of war in sleep. Suffocative snoring on inspiration. In sleep at 9 P.M. he began to weep, raised his sound arm, suddenly let it fall, then jerked the shoulder upward, then tossed head back and forth, then raised the diseased leg, then jerked the sound leg, often the sound hand was affected, when the fingers suddenly stretched out and again closed tightly, with these symptoms occasional moans. *Restless sleep;* with frequent waking, also with thoughts of business of the preceding day. Frequent waking as if disturbed or as if he had slept enough. Sleep disturbed, wakened by fluttering and agitation about centre of body. Great flow of ideas during partial sleep. Late falling asleep; and many dreams; long after midnight, yet woke early and felt lively and inclined to fantasies, active and strong.

Dreams; frightful; anxious; anxious, of furious cats springing at him, soon after falling asleep; heavy; lascivious, without emissions, but with excitement of gentials.

Clinical.—Sleeplessness, with uneasiness, cannot keep the bedclothes on, difficult breathing or difficult swallowing. Very useful in the sleeplessness of children, when they twitch, cry out, tremble and wake in fright.

Fever.—In afternoon, coldness and pain, for example, in back. (Could not get warm in bed at night.) Sudden chill in the house, < bright and warm open air. General shivering, with hot face and cold hands, without thirst. Face cold and pale. Coldness along spine; in open air; C. in back, < in house; C. runs from small of back to nape; C. in back on walking around the room, then when visiting patients heat in back, < loins. Cold limbs; hands; hands and feet. Temperature of skin diminished.

Heat; general, with distended veins; general, internal; general, external, without redness; hot and dry skin; (burning of blood in vessels); H. on walking in open air, with weakness; general, in evening, with thirst, putrid taste, much mucus in mouth and lips stick together; in flushes, with warmth of face. Prolonged burning in any place on which he has laid his warm hands for a moment. Hot head; H. deep in head; with crawling; and he often put his hands to his head with loud cries. *Heat of face; with redness;* < lobules of ears, with redness of face and dilated pupils. Along back; then sweat, < small of back and in axillæ; H. rises into back; rush of H. at spine, < loins. H. in loins; when sitting in the room; when walking in the room; in cold open air. H. in articular end of last phalanx of l. little finger, the condyle swollen, with pain, < motion, which is difficult. Feeling as if warm air were breathed on arms.

Sweat; general, < thighs and legs; on back and pit of stomach; profuse; general, profuse, clammy; cold, clammy, on palms; viscid, on arms.

Hypericum.

A tincture is made of the whole plant of Hypericum perforatum, L.

Allies.—Arnica, Calendula.

Generalities.—Starting as from fright, with rising of heat into neck. Active. Fugitive, laming pains in face, shoulders, limbs and fingers. Dull; in morning, and languid. Sensitive to cold. Disinclined to mental and physical labor. *Weak;* in morning on waking, and thirsty; in morning, > towards noon; in afternoon after a short walk, and distracted; at night; when walking, must walk slowly; and heavy; even to falling. Whole body affected as after recovery from disease. Feeling on waking at 4 A.M. as if she were not lying in bed, at another time as if lying very heavy in bed.

Clinical.—Tetanus. Tetanus of neck and jaw, < r. side, involving thorax and abdomen, from getting pins in the foot. The results of penetrating wounds from pointed instruments. Effects of gunshot wounds. Concussion of the brain and spine in a railroad accident, followed by a large number of symptoms, < between scapulæ, stiffness of extremities, nervous cough, chilliness, < damp weather, diarrhœa from slight excitement, etc., all cured by Hyper. In a general way it is indicated for the effects following injuries of nerves. In general, excessive painfulness and soreness of the affected part indicate the drug; the attacks are generally brought on by change of weather. Many cases of subacute and chronic neuritis have been apparently cured by its use.

Mind.—Talks wildly in sleep after 4 A.M., eyes distorted, red and staring, head hot, carotids throbbing, face red, puffy, pupils dilated, pulse rapid, hair of head moist, with dry heat over the rest of body, apprehensive, once she sang, then wept, screamed and gasped, after a few magnetic passes she came to herself, applying the hand to head had a soothing effect. Excited as by tea; at night. Irritable. Apprehensive. Easily frightened. Sober. Sad; at 5 P.M., in evening, and inclined to weep, which she tried to suppress. Religious thoughts, hopeful. Weakness; of memory; *memory defective, can hardly arrange ideas and cannot execute her intentions, forgets what she wanted to do. Forgets people's names. Omits letters in writing.* Mistakes in writing in evening.

Head. — Tearing stitches internally in morning. Pain, < dinner; (P. waking at night); as from hammering, in morning, < on vertex; P. of weight, generally on passage of a heavy storm-cloud. Pressing asunder sensation at 6 P.M., < vertex, a roaring sensation. Brain seems compressed; in evening. Feeling of something alive in brain at night in bed, or a tickling. Dulness; in morning in bed. Fulness; on rising; > breakfast; in morning, with low spirits, then stiffness in eyes as after tears, and strained pain in forehead. Confusion; in morning on waking. Feeling as if longer than natural; suddenly. Heaviness; in morning, with general weakness; in morning, > towards evening; in afternoon. Weak feeling; in evening. Vertigo; in morning; in morning on waking, with nausea; at 9 A.M.

Forehead.—Aching over brows after breakfast; A.

as if smashed, < night and lying down, < next day, but more towards vertex. Pressure on anterior and upper part of l. bone after breakfast. Tension as if drawn up. Feeling as if touched by cold hands in evening, then extending towards r. eye. Head heavy, tense between temples.

Temples.—Sticking in r.; in l. in evening; now r., now l. in evening; suddenly in l. when walking. Tearing in r. at 4 P.M., with general chill. Aching; in l. after breakfast. Tension. Throbbing.

Sticking in vertex at 7 P.M. Tearing in vertex in evening. Pain in V. in morning on waking, with roaring in ears, < l. *Throbbing in V. in afternoon, with heat in head.* Fulness in vertex before waking, with pain and heat in it; fugitive F. in l. half of head in morning in bed. Sticking in r. side of head on exerting eyes and head.

Shooting up l. occipital nerve in forenoon. Tearing in occiput in evening. Pain in O. on motion. Feeling in l. side of O. in evening as if violent pain, with pressure, would come on. Feeling in O. in forenoon as if bothered. Creeping feeling in r. side of O. after dinner. Falling of hair. Pain in scalp on l. side of occiput after breakfast, sometimes sharp; weakening, drawing P. in scalp over upper and anterior part of l. parietal bone. Formication on vertex. Itching at night.

Clinical.—Severe headache on vertex, as if the whole brain would burst, extending into cheeks and chin, with cramp in chin, etc.

Eyes.—Sticking through r. Tearing in r. in evening. Aching. Tension. Weariness. Pupils dilated; at 6 P.M. Lids agglutinated and tense. R. lids spasmodically closed in evening. Smarting of lids. Burning stinging in tarsi of l. lids at 9 P.M. Burning in canthi. Focal distance of vision lengthened in evening. Vision weak.

Ears.—Sticking through r. in evening. Pain at entrance to r. meatus. Drawing pain in l. towards zygoma, on touching zygoma it feels swollen. Pressure in r. in evening, with excoriated feeling in r. side of pharynx. Itching in r. meatus, > touch, but returning.

Nose.—Pain in bridge on rising. Dryness; with sneezing; of l. nostril, with crusts in it. Sneezing in morning; in a sharp fit after breakfast, with free nasal secretion. Smell very acute.

Face.—Jerking in l. zygoma in morning, with crawling. Jerking pain in cheeks. Aching; in afternoon and evening; in afternoon after eating a mulberry tart, with disturbed sleep at night, next day A. < l. side; > diet and abstinence from artificial stimulus; in brows and face, < night to distressing aching in r. half of face, < an old tooth. Pressure on malar prominences after breakfast; on malar-bone in evening. Seems puffy in evening. Tension in cheeks; in afternoon. Contraction in l. zygoma. Aching in articulations of jaws. Lips dry. Lips hot.

Clinical.—Neuralgia of the face, which had lasted for two years, following the shaving off of a cold sore, was entirely cured.

Mouth.—Toothache in forenoon; in a stump of a r. upper molar at night, keeping me awake and restless, > lying on r. cheek and keeping quiet, aching next day after a glass of beer, < night; tearing, here and there; tearing in r. at 3 A.M. on waking; drawing, in all lower after midnight; jerking pain in teeth and cheeks in afternoon. Tension in teeth in forenoon. *Tongue coated white;* coated dirty yellow; T. whitish-gray, < at base; foul T. on rising. Much mucus after eating. *Dryness.* Dry heat at 5 P.M. Taste bad, eructations. Taste of blood in throat after stool, on hawking bright red bloody expectoration.

Clinical.—Terribly inflamed tongue, resulting from a bite during an epileptic fit, inability to speak; cured in forty-eight hours.

Throat.—Hawking of tenacious mucus. Lancinations from r. submaxillary gland down neck, at 10 P.M. Raw soreness after sneezing. Feeling as if a worm were squirming in it. Rising of heat in afternoon.

Stomach.—Appetite great in morning; at noon; in evening; for pickles in evening; not great for breakfast; lost in evening; lost, with nausea and pressure as from an overloaded stomach, though he had fasted; no relish for breakfast. Aversion to eating. Speedy satiety without pressure in stomach. Tobacco is not relished. Thirst; in morning; on waking, but inability to drink on account of choking in throat and heat; with heat in mouth; for wine in afternoon.

Eructations; after breakfast; on drinking water; with pressure on chest; empty at 5 P.M. without having eaten anything; bitter; of mucus in morning, with burning and pressure in stomach. *Nausea;* so that he could hardly rise in morning, with pressure in præcordial region; at noon, with weakness; in evening, with constant eructations of wind or mucus; in evening, with distress in stomach, retching and collection of water in mouth; on waking in night; during dinner, with sleepiness and feeling as if stomach and bowels were hot and swollen; two hours after eating, with pressure and weakness; > drinking water, with retching. Retching.

Dyspepsia after plums and pickles, with bilious diarrhœa. Indigestion at night, with flatulence, woke with distention and cracking pain in hypogastrium, > morning by diarrhœa. Distention after tea-time, with flatulence. Sticking alternately in epigastric region and r. hypochondrium. Pressure after milk; P. after a small meal; after breakfast, extending towards back; P., with burning, waking, feeling as if disordered by sour wine. Weight after meat at breakfast. Oppression in evening after a little rice. Crawling in morning, with yawning, like hunger, but without appetite on account of nausea. Feeling contracted and hot in evening. Heat in morning after rising, > drinking cold water, with discomfort; H. in epigastrium and chest. Apprehension and crawling in pit and in præcordial region in evening.

Abdomen.—*Distention;* flatulent, also in evening; with cracking pain, waking at night; griping D., then soft stool. Hardness, with tension in r. hypochondrium. Emission of flatus. Flatulence through the day, with pressure and dragging. Cramp. Cutting and griping as from incarcerated flatus. Griping as from flatulence, then soft stool. After tea pinching in bowels, which became relaxed. Pain in evening after coffee, with diarrhœa. Feeling as if flatus would pass.

Sticking in r. hypochondrium. Dragging pain in liver at point of false ribs at 6 P.M.; weight and dragging in liver at 11.30 P.M., from walking. Tension in hypochondria. Cutting in umbilical region in afternoon, as if something were cooking therein. Pressure in r. iliac fossa, towards ring; in l. groin towards ring; on l. inguinal ring in morning.

Rectum.—Cutting warm pain all around, internal to sphincter in forenoon. Dryness in morning. Inclination to stool. Tenesmus with stool. Urging in morning in bed, then normal stool; U., with passage of small fæcal masses; U., with discharge of hard masses; ineffectual U. at night.

Stool.—Painless diarrhœa, then constipation. Soft; and free, bilious; and yellow, bilious, at 4 P.M., had had a firm one after breakfast, as usual. Hard; and knotty; and large; and scanty. Free. Profuse, morning and evening. Delayed. Difficult, with tenesmus so that it caused nausea.

Urinary Organs.—Warm biting in urethra in afternoon. Biting stinging in orifice of urethra. Urging; at 2 A.M., with vertigo, almost a faintness. Frequent micturition of very yellow urine. Urine clear, wine-yellow. Urine high-colored, in morning, frothy, of peculiar sweetish odor. U. profuse at night, clear yellow, with burning. Strong-smelling U. at night. Turbid.

Sexual Organs.—Tearing at night, with desire to urinate and micturition twice. Erratic ideas; in afternoon when walking, with erection. Tension in uterine region at night, as from a short band. Leucorrhœa. Menses increased, with less trouble than usual; increased, too early, preceded by pinching in abdomen, diarrhœa, cold feet, wrenching pain over eyes, > motion, and backache, during menses sickening pain in abdomen, headache and sensitive hearing; M. fourteen days too late.

Respiratory Organs.—Bronchial catarrh from night fogs. Scraping and roughness in larynx, upper part of pharynx and nares, at night, in fog. *Frequent dry, hacking cough.* Expectoration of gelatinous mucus. E. of much granular white mucus. Dyspnœa in forenoon. Short breath in evening.

Clinical.—Asthmatic breathing, apparently resulting from concussion of the brain, always < before a storm. Spasmodic asthma, with sensitiveness of the spine.

Chest.—Sticking in l., among tendons of serratus magnus; S. in l. pectoral muscles; in l. in evening; in l. breast in evening; here and there beneath r. breast in evening; through chest at 5 P.M., so that she must hold the breath; here and there below r. chest at 8 P.M.; alternately in both sides; outward through sternum and l. chest, < motion; in r. pectoral muscles, extending to back around ribs; in middle (like heartburn); (in ribs and shoulder as after taking cold). Sticking cutting in r. upper half on moving about, and in afternoon on r. side and once in l. lower part. Stinging burning pain on edge of l. pectoral muscle at noon. *Tightness;* in evening. Oppression in evening. Pressure; at 5 P.M., with burning; on r. side from seventh rib down, after breakfast; on outer third of l. clavicle after breakfast; on nipples, with warm formication. Anxiety in morning, like shortness of breath.

Heart and Pulse.—Heart feels in evening as if it would fall down. Palpitation. Pulse rapid; after breakfast; at 6 P.M.; after dinner; and hard.

Neck.—Swollen. Aching in nape and upper part of shoulders (trapezius); A. in r. trapezius in morning, > washing. Tension in nape, with pressure and sticking in middle of chest; T. in nape, motion of head is painful. Stiffness.

Back.—Stinging in scapulæ; near edge of r. scapula and near spine, in morning. Cutting under l. scapula after dinner, with pressure in stomach; C. between S., on r. side of vertebræ. Pain in l. scapula after dinner; P. on top of r. in afternoon. Sticking in loins at noon; S. in loins, with burning pain in them and coldness in back, shoulders and arms. Aching in loins; in renal region at 4 P.M. when walking; paralytic, in loins. Squeezing in l. kidney.

Clinical.—Spinal tenderness, with paroxysms of terrible pain, screaming if approached (Arn.); in other cases, great sensitiveness of cervical vertebræ to touch, with dyspnœa, short hacking cough, etc.

Extremities.—Sticking in r. middle finger as if a knife were thrust from joint along metacarpal bone to wrist, then a similar pain in great toes. Lancing pain in l. wrist and ankle at night, and along inner border of l. foot. Sawing pain in l. hand and l. inner ankle. Flying pain in r. shoulder and l. calf. Bruised feeling in all joints. Drawing in l. buttock, under tuber ischii, and in r. wrist in morning in bed, with sticking jerking on centre of back of foot. Heaviness, felt fatigue when walking before dinner. Feeling of weakness and trembling. Paralyzed feeling in r. foot and l. arm alternating with tearing.

Upper Extremities.—Sticking in l. shoulder at 2 P.M. with every inspiration. Tearing in r. shoulder and forearm. Pain in shoulder-joints in forenoon, < l.; rheumatic drawing, in point of l. shoulder in morning. Trembling of l. arm and fingers, with cramp. Sticking in arms. Tearing in arms; in l. in morning; in evening; in l. in evening, < from elbow to fingers; at night. Tension in arms. Weakness of arms; of r. behind elbow, with pain. Numbness of l. arm at night, waking her, > friction. Pressure on r. humerus at insertion of deltoid. (Neuralgic, paralytic pain in l. upper arm.)

Tearing in elbows. Pain in r. elbow; rheumatic; P. in l. elbow, then in r. forearm. Return of weakness and strained feeling in r. elbow, < lifting. Lancing pain about head of r. radius. Pain down ulnar side of l. forearm. Starting above r. wrist on going to sleep. Jerking in tendons of l. wrist on going to sleep. Sprained pain in l. wrist on motion; S. pain between l. index and thumb at 1 P.M. Lancing pain on back of l. middle metacarpal bone in morning. Pain as if suppurating on outer margin of ball of l. hand when it lies on the table. Tension in hands. Lancing pain in joints of l. fingers; in phalanges of r. middle and little fingers. Tearing in r. thumb in evening. Cutting in fleshy ends of fingers. Rheumatic pain in last joint of l. little F., with swelling and tension.

Lower Extremities.—Reeling as from vertigo. Cramp in lower part of r. gluteal muscle at 5 P.M., then flashing pain on back of l. toes. Shooting down great sciatic nerve, on back of pelvis, at night in bed. Pain running down l. median nerve in evening, then P. in front of thigh; P. on centre of front of l. thigh in afternoon; in inner condyle of r. thigh in morning in bed; intermittent, in front of l. thigh at noon. Strained feeling in r. ham at night after a walk. Bruised pain in l. thigh on walking in afternoon, muscles supplied by anterior crual nerve stiff and sore, coming and going for days. L. thigh sore and lame.

Knee.—Cramp. Sticking in l. Tearing in r.; on outside, then pressure on upper part of r. scapula. Pain in r. in morning; P. in outer and upper part, in an outward and upward direction, as from straining a tendon, in morning on walking. Tingling in knees and legs as from weariness.

Leg.—Starting of l. on going to sleep. Cramp in l. on going to sleep; (frequent C. in calves at night, r., then l.). Sudden shooting over front of l., in periosteum; sticking in inside of r. calf at 4 P.M. when walking. Tearing in r. leg and knee; T. from r. calf through foot at 6.30 P.M. Diductive pains down nerves of r. in afternoon. Drawing in r. calf; in r. tendo-achillis at breakfast; painful in r. tibialis. Flashes of weakening drawing pain all over front of l. in afternoon when walking and sitting. Pressure on l. calf as with a blunt point. Biting on l. shin; in front in evening. Tendency to tingling, < l. Heaviness. Numbness; of l.; of l. in evening.

L. ankle liable to wrench. Cramp in l. foot; at night on going to sleep. Tension in soles like a cramp. Sticking in bone in inner side of r. foot on ascending steps, as if sprained; sprained or dislocated feeling in l. foot on rising from stool at 3 P.M. Twinges of pain along outer border of l. foot after dinner. Drawing on inner border of l. foot in forenoon; cramplike D. as if feet would become dead when lying. Tingling in feet; disposition to T., in bed. Feet feel numb and sticking.

Toes.—Jerking of l. at night on falling asleep. Swelling and biting in toes and heels. Sticking in ball of great; in fold of skin internal to nail of r. great; in fourth in evening; *frequent biting S. in r.* Stinging biting in attacks in back of r. in morning. Biting on a r. Gnawing in r., then pressure and aching in middle of l. thigh, about where sartorius crosses.

Skin.—Pimple on r. side of back; on r. hip, sore under friction of clothing; on middle of r. sterno-mastoid muscle, such as had appeared before on chest. Biting eruption like nettle-rash, on hands. Cluster of itching, psora-like vesicles on root of l. thumb in forenoon, gone at night. (Ulcerating pain in a vesicle on thigh.) Biting in l. fingers in evening; on back of hand in evening; on hands, nettle-rash on backs of hands and between fingers. Fuzzy feeling in feet, with sticking in them. *Crawling in hands and feet, with fuzzy feeling in morning;* C. in r. breast up to median line. Itching in evening on undressing, < sacral region, the skin was rough and seemed full of pimples; (I. on forehead, vertex and hip); (I. on cheeks, < beard).

Sleep.—Yawning. Sleepy; at 6 P.M.; (in afternoon after eating). Heavy, exhausting sleep every night, with sweat in morning. Waking late. Lies on back at night and has emissions. Waking early, with hot sweat and uneasiness. Falls asleep late, sleep restless, wakes early. Restless sleep; and lay a good deal on back, kept jerking head backward; it seemed as if she lay very heavy; with frightful dreams, starting up and apprehension. Felt as if under the influence of tea, went to bed with brain excited, sleep unsound, dreams vivid and active, next morning found myself lying on back and digging head backward into pillow.

Dreams.—With sweat in morning. *Distressing.* Many; and waking after each. Vivid, unremembered. Confused. Busy; and confused; and indistinctly remembered. Awful, as that God was far from me, repudiated me, etc. Anxious, as if something important were left undone. Horrid, sexual; horrid, starting of legs when falling asleep, then convulsive shocks preventing sleep, erethic state of nervous system, erotic ideas and dreams. Of Mormons, horses, fights and great action, found myself lying on my back in morning, dreaming some desperate horror and half awake, saying "Why should I fear, the Lord is around and about me." Exhausting, of climbing mountains, pressure of business, etc. Of journeys, hunting, etc., indistinctly remembered.

Fever.—General chill, with nausea. General C. at 4 P.M. General shivering in evening; till midnight, when sitting, < moving about, with expectoration of mucus, nausea, > drinking cold water; S. extending from calves over thighs; (in back, extending across shoulders). Cold feet; soles; l. leg when sitting, with numbness of it. General dry heat; in evening, with anxiety. Internal heat in morning, without thirst, with sweat, preventing sleep, but coldness if he threw off the covering. Heat in face in afternoon; in face, with smarting. Hot ears on going to bed. Heat in head and feet from 3 to 5 A.M., with restlessness and desire for cool places. Sweat in morning; S. on slight exertion.

Ignatia.

A tincture (or trituration) is made of the seeds of Strychnos Ignatia, Lindl.

General Effects.—It contains a large amount of strychnia, and most of its toxic properties are due to that alkaloid, but the other elements contained in it determine marked peculiarities, especially extreme sensitiveness of the nerves, symptoms of hysteria, neuralgia and a peculiar form of fever.

Allies.—Nux vom., Cham., Silicea, Lach., Gels., Zinc., Puls., Lycopod., Staph.

Generalities.—*Trembling;* with twitching and spasms. *Twitching in various parts of muscles*, here and there after lying down. *Convulsions;* so that he could not stand, < jaws, causing risus sardonicus, without other symptoms. *Frequent change of position at night, lies now here, now there.* Constant motion of body, looks as if in a doze, it is irksome to look or to open mouth to talk, respiration light and slow.

Tearing in r. arm and on r. side of head from cold air. Deeply sticking, burning pain in various parts. Pains as if beaten in joints of neck, back and shoulders at night when lying on either side, > lying on back. Tingling pain, < head. *Pain here and there in spots on touch, as, for example, on ribs.* Pains renewed after dinner, in evening after lying down, and in morning after waking. Crawling in all bones. Weight, congestion and orgasm of blood in whole body in morning on waking, with melancholy.

Weariness in morning on waking; in afternoon, overpowering sleep at 2 P.M., unrefreshed by two hours' sleep; *in evening; on walking, it seems as if his breath would fail, is qualmish at pit of stomach, and then coughs;* from slight exertion; after dinner, < 2 to 4 P.M., with sleepiness (after stool), with yawning; as from weakness about pit of stomach, with nausea and necessity to lie down; so that he had no desire to dress himself and go out, has no pleasure in anything, but prefers to lie. Unwillingness to move, shirking of work. Stiffness of knee, ankle, thigh and sacrum in morning on rising; S. of knees and loins, motion causes pain. Faintness. Insensibility. Aggravation from coffee (Cham., Nux v.) and smoking tobacco (Nux v., Puls., Staph.).

Clinical.—The general characteristic conditions of the Ign. patient are extremely important, since they are almost always unexpected in character, for example, if the patient has fever he is not thirsty and wants to be covered, if he is cold he wants to be uncovered, the headache in the forehead is relieved by stooping, the irritation to cough increases with coughing; this "contrariness" is a general characteristic of Ign., both mentally and physically. Extreme sensitiveness to pain (Cham.). General tendency to faintness and debility, with nervous prostration and excitability. Numerous phases of hysteria and of neuralgias in various parts of the body, spasms in children from teething or from worms, or from fright. Chorea especially in children who have been frightened. Epilepsy originally caused by fright. Hysterical paralysis. In all the phases of hysteria there is a changeable mood, often flushing of one or the other cheek (Cham.), tendency to scream, or to tear, or to bite, or to cry.

Mind.—Fancies that he cannot proceed, that he cannot walk; F. at night, which fatigue the mind. Weeping. *Howls, cries and is beside herself on account of trifles; cries aloud if one hesitates to do what she wishes, remonstrates with her or tries to persuade her, or if others wish something different from what she wishes.* Cries aloud if improper things are refused. Walks about perplexed and stupid. *Unreasonable complaints about noise.* **Sensitiveness, delicate conscientiousness. Inconstant, impatient, irresolute,** *quarrelsome,* in attacks. **Changeable mood,** *alternations of joking, merry mood, with lachrymose mood.* **Anger at slight blame or contradiction, and this makes him angry with himself;** *A. at slight contradiction.* Ill humor; from headache; towards evening, and discontented, obstinate; and absorbed in himself. Thinks of vexatious things contrary to his will.

Anxiety; as if he had committed a crime; preventing talking; so that he cannot express himself clearly. *Tendency to be frightened* (Stram.). *Dread of trifles, < things coming near him. Fear of thieves on waking after midnight;* F. that she will have an ulcer in her stomach. No self-confidence. Sad towards evening; S., earnest, cannot be induced to talk or be cheerful, with flat, watery taste to food and little appetite. *Indifference to everything. Boldness.* Busy, restless; *after exerting brain, < morning, unable to do anything as rapidly as he wishes, whereupon anxious behavior, mistakes in writing and talking and awkward actions;* hurrying, with dulness of sense and rush of blood to face. Merry, jesting. Thoughts difficult to fix; from affection of head. Fixed idea, which he pursues in his thoughts or talks about with earnestness and exhaustiveness; fixed ideas in evening before and after lying down, as, for example, of music. *Memory weak.*

Clinical.—Melancholia, the result of grief, sits with a vacant stare. Many mental symptoms following depressing emotions, especially grief, such as sighing, despondency, hysterical laughing or crying.

Head.—*Inclined forward. Laid upon table.* Stitches through head. Tearing after midnight when lying on side, > lying on back. Aching; in morning, < eating (Nux v.); in morning, > rising; in afternoon and evening, with heaviness; at 2 P.M., < above eyes; *with every beat of arteries; < stooping;* < talking; < reading and paying strict attention to a speaker; *extending into l. eye, when eyes burn and water,* lids swollen, Meibomian glands secrete much mucus; extending below orbits and into cheeks; *< in r. side of forehead, extending into r. eye, sensation as if ball would be pressed out, burning in eyes, lachrymation and much mucus;* external, head sore to touch. *Jerking pain on ascending; J. pain < opening eyes. Throbbing pain. Paroxysmal pain as from pressure of something hard on surface of brain, this and all other headaches > coffee (Cham.).* Aching after midday nap, as if there were too much brain or blood in head, < reading and writing. Pain as if head would burst from talking or speaking loud, > sitting still, reading and writing. Pain as if bruised; *in brain in morning on waking, changing on rising to pain as if a nerve of a tooth were crushed, then changing to a similar pain in sacrum, the headache always renewed on thinking. Sudden pressure now in one place, now in another in evening,* and at night, next morning he was unrefreshed, the P. increased to real pain, which lasted till 3 P.M.

Confusion; in morning on waking, with discomfort of head; in morning on waking, lasting till after dinner, continued next day, changed to pain in forehead and eyes, so that movement of lids and eyeballs was painful, pain < ascending steps or any violent exertion; < thinking and speaking, with pain in r. side, < occiput; then pain in vertex, then extending into l. eye and whole head; as before coryza; like intoxication, at times becoming a pain in forehead, < r. half, so that thought was difficult. *Heaviness;* in morning on waking; as if filled with blood, with tearing in occiput, > lying on back, especially by bending head forward, < sitting erect. Seems too full of blood, nose internally sensitive to air, as before nosebleed. Hollow feeling. Intoxication; from beer; as from brandy, with burning of eyes. *Vertigo;* all day till 10 P.M., with sticking in head; with staggering; changing to pain in r. half of occiput.

Forehead.—Sticking, < above brows; S., with pain in r. side of occiput; extending outward, and in temples. Tearing in F. and behind l. ear, > lying on back, < raising head, with hot, red cheeks and hot hands. *Pain;* from towards noon till 2.30 P.M., with pressure in eyes; till sleep in evening, and around orbits; < sunlight; beneath r. bone; above r. brow; *in r. half, involving r. eye, which was sensitive to light,* < in eye by moving it, > towards evening; extending to different places in head; in r. half, afterwards extending to l. side; in r. side, extending to l., then over whole head; extending to different places in head, < evening, > night's sleep; extending downward on sides; from 2 P.M. till evening, extending at times more to r., at times more towards l. eyeball, < motion of body; in sinciput, extending into nasal cavities, and every ten minutes sensation as before violent coryza, when after ten minutes the nose was better the sensation extended to other parts of head, and so alternated; *P. above root of nose, compelling him to bend head forward, then nausea; drawing P. above r. orbit at root of nose, renewed by stooping low;* cramplike P. above root of nose, in region of inner canthus. Stupefying intermittent pressure beneath l. eminence. Digging beneath r. eminence and on r. side of frontal bone. Dulness in sinciput in forenoon, amounting at times to real pain. Throbbing above r. brow.

Sticking deep in r. temple. Pain in temples; < r.; with deep sleep; externally, extending across orbits, and when touched pain as if beaten; as if pressed outward; as if pressed outward, in morning when lying on sides, > lying on back. Contractive pain in vertex, extending to forehead, where it remained till 4 P.M. Pain in r. side in forenoon; P. in one half of brain on walking in open air, < talking or reflecting. *Pain in occiput and r. side; in r. half of O. all day,* >

night's sleep ; above mastoid process in afternoon, at times involving ear, when hearing was blunted ; in O. as if bone were pressed inward ; throbbing P. in one side of O. (Hair falls out.)

Clinical.—The headache of Ign. is usually sharp, confined to one point, as if some piercing instrument, like a nail, were being driven into the head. Supraorbital neuralgia, boring pain in a small spot. The headaches sometimes present the unexpected condition of being relieved by stooping. Hydrocephalus from sudden metastasis from the bowels to the brain during dentition, with sudden pallor, delirium, rolling the head, *difficult swallowing*, convulsions of the eyes and lids.

Eyes.—Inflammation of l. Staring in front of him without thought. (Sticking in r.). Pressure in and above them in morning on waking ; P. outward in r. as if ball were protruding. Itching internally. Irritability of r., with increased mucus in both. Pressure in balls, < looking at the light, with pressure above eyes. Itching in ball at inner canthus. Pupils contracted ; then dilated ; dilated ; cannot be dilated. Pressure beneath l. brow.

Lids. — Agglutinated in morning, with purulent mucus, on opening eyes the light is blinding ; A. in morning, pressing in eyes as from sand, on opening lids sticking in eyes. Sticking tearing in external canthus, lids agglutinated, lachrymation in forenoon. Sensation of a particle in l. external canthus, which at times presses on tissues. Pain above and behind upper ; in inner surface of upper in evening, as if too dry ; like a soreness in external canthus on closing eye. Biting in external canthi ; gnawing B. on margins of lids in morning when reading. Weariness as if they would close.

Vision.—Dim in r. after midday nap ; in one, as from tears, in evening when reading. On reading, the letters to which the eyes were directed became invisible, but those near were more distinct than ever, it seemed as if the middle of a word were marked with chalk while the beginning and end became more distinct. *Zigzag and serpentine white flickering* (Lach.), *at one side of field after dinner ;* a circle of white, glittering, flickering zigzags about point of vision, and letters at which one directed the eye invisible, but those at the side are distinct. Objects seem to move. Cannot endure candle-light.

Clinical.—Asthenopia, with spasms of the lids and neuralgic pains about the eyes. It has been used for inflammatory affections of the eyes, especially in intense photophobia and nervous excitement.

Ears.—Sticking. Pain in middle. (Throbbing.) *Itching in auditory canal. Ringing.* Roaring. Intolerance of noise. Music causes an unusual and agreeable sensation. Insensibility to music.

Nose.—Ulceration of nostrils ; sensation of U. and soreness in inner angles. Tickling. Crawling itching in nostrils. Stoppage of one nostril as by a leaf, not like dry catarrh ; (inability to draw air through N. on closing mouth). Trickling from N. then coryza. *Fluent coryza. Dry catarrh.* (Bleeding.)

Face.—Redness from slightest contradiction. Sticking in zygoma in front of l. ear ; in cheeks. Pressure in zygomata before sleep ; intermittent paralytic, in l. zygomatic process ; P. beneath rami of jaw as if flesh beneath jaw were pressed downward. Jaws closed, impeding speech. Pain in joint of jaw in morning when lying. *Lips cracked and bleeding.* Enlarged gland on inner surface of lower lip, with sore pain ; and suppuration. Ulceration of inner surface of lower lip ; U. of one corner of lips. *Sticking in lips,* < moving them ; S. in lower ; in lower on touching a hair of beard in that place. *Inner surface of lower lip painful as if raw.*

Clinical.—Distortion of the facial muscles whenever the patient attempts to speak. Neuralgia of the face.

Mouth.—Clawing digging in incisors in evening. Toothache near end of a meal, < after eating ; T. and looseness of teeth ; T. as if nerves of molars were crushed ; sore T. in anterior molars, < reading ; T. in morning as if loose ; as if an incisor were numb and loose, < touch of tongue. Inner side of gum painful as if numb, as if burnt. Glands under tongue excited, inflamed. Sticking in tip of tongue ; in frænum. Tearing in tip of tongue as if burnt or sore in morning after waking. Sharp feeling in tip as if sore. Biting on forepart from tobacco-smoke, with pain in incisors. He easily bites one side of posterior part of T. when talking or chewing. Burning of T. Front half of T. numb when talking, when eating it feels burnt or sore.

Easily bites inside of cheek near orifice of salivary duct when chewing (Nit. ac.). Painful swelling of orifice of salivary duct. Inner surface covered with offensive-smelling mucus in morning on waking. *Sticking in palate, extending to inner ear.* Inner surface sore. Palate feels excoriated (as after frequent swallowing of saliva). Palate feels as if swollen or covered with tenacious mucus. *Constantly full of mucus.* Avoids opening M. and speaking. *Salivation ;* in forenoon ; in forenoon, with nausea ; white, frothy ; frequent spitting of saliva ; spitting of frothy S. all day ; flow of S. from mouth in sleep.

Taste.—Sour, *saliva has a sour taste. Bitter, then sour, with sour eructations ;* B. to tobacco-smoke ; to beer ; B. and putrid to various articles, < beer (Puls.). Nauseous, as after fasting, with appetite and relish for food and drink. As from a disordered stomach ; flat, watery, morning and noon after eating. Insipid, as if he had eaten chalk. Flat to beer, as if spoiled. When eating, drinking and smoking, the good taste disappears as soon as the actual need is supplied, or it changes to an unpleasant taste, and one cannot take any more, though there is a kind of hunger and thirst.

Throat.—Pain in submaxillary glands ; after walking in open air ; drawing pain ; drawing, extending into jaws, then swelling of glands ; in anterior, as if compressed. Pain in glands beneath angles of jaws on motion of throat. Pain in throat on touch as if glands were swollen. Tonsils turgescent. **Sticking when not swallowing, and even somewhat when swallowing** (compare Lycopod.), **the more he swallows the more it disappears, entirely > swallowing anything solid** ; *S. when not swallowing, when swallowing sensation as if one swallowed over a bone, causing jerking ;* low down when not swallowing ; in parotid gland when not swallowing ; > *when swallowing.* Pain as if raw and sore ; when swallowing. Soreness like a lump, which is painful as if excoriated when swallowing. Pressure. Constriction in pit, causing cough. Food seems to stick high up in evening before sleep and in morning. Difficult swallowing of food and drink. *Inability to swallow bread, it seemed too dry.*

Œsophagus.—*Choking constriction in middle in evening, from a plug,* < **when not swallowing.** *Sensation as if a plug were sticking in it when not swallowing.* Sticking low down on swallowing, > *continuing to swallow, returning when not swallowing.* After dinner it seemed as if food stuck above cardiac orifice of stomach. *Crawling.*

Clinical.—Inflamed tonsils, ulcerations, with sticking pains (the general indication for Ign. in sore throat, aside from the mental state of the patient, is the relief of the throat symptoms from swallowing). Diphtheric sore throat, with sensation of a plug and with constant efforts to swallow. Some alarming cases of diphtheria are reported cured by this drug.

Stomach.—Appetite great; at 11 A.M.; at 11 A.M., but diminished when the time for eating came; ravenous, at 11 A.M., with at times nausea; A. good, but when he attempted to eat he was satiated. Desire for fruit; D. for acid things. Appetite diminished. Satiety; so that he could eat nothing in evening if he smoked in afternoon. *Appetite lost;* and desire for tobacco and drink, with frequent salivation. **Aversion to tobacco-smoking**; though it has not an unpleasant taste; as if he had smoked enough; A. to milk; to boiled milk after his necessity is satisfied; to meat, and desire for acid fruit, cranberries; to warm food and meat, desires only bread, butter and cheese; to fruit, it does not agree with him; to acids; to wine. **Thirst, with chill**; T. in afternoon and evening; at night.

Eructations, empty; bitter E. in forenoon; *of bitter fluid; of food,* and the taste of milk taken in morning cannot be removed from mouth for a long time; tasting of food; sour; musty, mouldy in evening; (ineffectual, in morning in bed, causing pain in orifice of stomach and in œsophagus to pharynx). *Hiccough from tobocco-smoking* (Puls., Staphs.); *H. after eating and drinking;* in evening after drinking. *Nausea;* towards noon; in forenoon, with loss of appetite; *from smoking,* in an old smoker. Ineffectual retching. Efforts to vomit, > eating.

Sticking; in pit. Slow sticking jerking pain in epigastric region and pit of stomach. Pinching in pit and r. hypochondrium. Cramplike pain. Spasmodic flatulent pain in epigastrium in evening on falling asleep and in morning on waking. Strained pain in epigastrium. Pain in pit on pressure as if sore internally. Pain extending to spleen, then to spine, changing to sticking, which extended into chest, then sticking and burning in region of spleen. Pressure; *in pit;* in epigastric region; in sides of epigastrium or in hypochondria; intermittent, in region of pit; alternating with pain in cæliac region, as after Camphor. Drawing as if walls would be distended, at times with pressure. Burning; B., pressive and drawing pains, and in liver and spleen. Coldness. **Feeling of flabbiness,** *S. and intestines hang down relaxed.* **Peculiar weakness in pit and epigastric region. Sensation of fasting,** *with physical exhaustion* (Sep.); feeling of F., with flat taste and weakness of limbs. Fulness alternating with emptiness, with the latter ravenous hunger. Digestion weak.

Clinical.—Indigestion, with aversion to the ordinary diet and longing for a great variety of indigestible articles; regurgitation of food, hiccough, empty retching, weak, empty feeling, has to eat at night even, especially attended with sighing; gastric symptoms generally > eating (Lach., Zinc.). Gastralgia < pressure.

Abdomen.—Distention, < umbilical region; D. after eating; flatulent D. after eating; flatulent D., with itching in neck of bladder, which causes sexual desire; anxious D. after eating in evening; pinching D. after eating, only on standing, < walking, > sitting quietly. Tense in evening after eating, mouth dry and bitter, one cheek red. *Rumbling; and noises;* in afternoon; after eating; then ineffectual urging to stool in forenoon, but in afternoon several normal stools. Gurgling. Discharge of flatus; copious, at night, even in sleep; after eating; *unsatisfactory, abrupt, offensive, not without exertion of abdominal muscles.* Wanderings. Flatulence which presses upon bladder.

Cutting sticking after eating, then meteorismus. Cutting; in evening, then diarrhœa; then diarrhœa twice. *Griping;* in open air, as before diarrhœa. (Tearing.) Pinching when walking in open air; P. after the least fruit, < standing and walking, > sitting. Flatulent pain at night; F. pain, with sticking extending to chest; F. pain here and there in evening in bed and always on waking at night. Bruised pain in morning in bed. *Drawing* two days before menstruation, *with griping in it, pressure in rectum, nausea,* **weakness in pit of stomach and pallor of face.** Oppression, with cutting. *Throbbing.* Anxiety arising from A. after breakfast.

Griping in side, then sticking. Cutting in r. Contractive pain from sides beneath ribs. Pressure in l. *Distention of hypochondria, < in sides, pit of stomach and small of back, inability to breathe on account of tension and fulness under ribs,* with anxiety and necessity to loosen clothes (Lyc.). *Intermittent pain in region of spleen and pit of stomach.* Constriction in hypochondria in morning, as in constipation, with one-sided pain as if nail were pressed into brain.

Upper.—Pain as if intestines would burst, like cardialgia, extending into throat, in morning when lying on side, > lying on back. Pain as if something pressed towards chest at 6 P.M. Tensive pain as if walls were pushed downward and diaphragm upward, pain < in region of spleen, whence it extended towards spine, alternately worse in different places, the pain returned at 3 P.M., < towards evening, when it extended into chest, where it at times became burning, which was worse in spine in region of cæliac ganglion, these attacks transiently > eructations of air.

Umbilicus.—Sticking beneath U.; *above and to l. of U.* Cutting in region. Griping in region, whereupon the pain, consisting of pinching and sticking, extended into l. side of chest. Flatulent colic above U. alternated with salivation. Pressure in region, then distention of abdomen; painful P. near l. side; painful P. near r. side, < deep breathing and voluntary distention of abdomen, > retracting U., with rumbling in abdomen. Sensation of something alive.

Hypogastrium.—Sticking in l. Cutting and contracting pains. Sticking jerking pain in l. groin in evening in bed. Pinching in region of cæcum, < walking in open air. Flatulent pain in morning, causing sticking, which extended into chest and sides. Pressure; painful in l. Sensation in l. groin as if a hernia would protrude.

Clinical.—Excessive flatulence, especially in hysterical subjects (compare Arg. nit., Zinc.).

Rectum.—Prolapsus from moderate exertion at stool (Lyc., Pod.). *Spasmodic tension all day.* **Frequent cutting deep in** (Sil.). **Sharp pain** in evening after lying down; *S. P. deep in* after stool, as from incarcerated flatus (as after a hurried stool). **Pain as from blind piles, contraction and soreness** (Sil., Lyc.), *after* *stool; P. as from piles, constrictive and smarting, as from touching a sore spot. Crawling as from thread-worms* (Sulph.); *near anus. Itching in evening in bed;* I. in perineum, < walking.

Urging, with feeling as after a purgative, then several natural stools during the day; *U. more in upper intestines* (Nux v.), *stool soft and insufficient*, the U. lasts long after stool; *anxious U., inability to evacuate fæces without danger of eversion and prolapsus of rectum* (Nux v.); sudden U., then difficult, insufficient, tenacious, clay-colored, not hard stool; frequent, almost ineffectual U., with colic, tenesmus and tendency to prolapsus; ineffectual U.; **ineffectual U. in evening, < middle abdomen, with protrusion of rectum** (Nux v.); ineffectual U., < eating, with *desire in upper intestines* (Nux v.).

Anus.—*Blind piles, with pressure and soreness in A. and rectum, painful when sitting and standing* (Æsc. hip.), **less when walking,** < *after taking fresh air.* Swelling of margin, as from a distended vein. Itching pimple, which causes pressure when sitting. Hæmorrhoidal symptoms, with soft stool. Thread-worms crawl out. (Discharge of blood, with itching of perineum and anus.) *Coarse sticking;* **extending deep into rectum. Sore pain without reference to stool** (Æsc. hip.); *pain as from blind piles* after a soft stool, **with sore pain;** after mental exertion. Contraction evenings, painful when walking, < standing, not painful when sitting, with insipid salivation. *Painless contraction.* Drawing downward towards anus. Crawling burning. Itching.

Clinical.—Fissures of the anus, without constipation, with acute pain shooting upward. Prolapsus ani, with sharp stabbing pains shooting upward. With the symptoms of the rectum and anus there is frequently spasmodic contraction of the anus, < after stool. Bleeding hæmorrhoids, with the characteristic shooting pains. Violent itching of the anus caused by swellings, which produce most violent nervous symptoms, even convulsions in children.

Stool.—*Diarrhœa; frequent. Thin, involuntary, with flatus; T., frequent, small. Soft;* after eating. Hard; then thin. Slimy. Acrid. Copious. Large and difficult; and yellowish-white. Yellowish-white. Frequent.

Clinical.—Diarrhœa from fright or emotional excitement, especially from grief, with great urging. Diarrhœa simulating dysentery, with tenesmus and great nervous excitement. Like Nux v., it is often indicated when there is almost constant desire for stool in the abdomen, but no stool follows. Painless diarrhœa, with much moving of flatus in the bowels, first brought on in a child by fright, the diarrhœa had lasted for several years and had resisted all other treatment (compare Arg. nit., Gels., etc.). Alternations of diarrhœa and constipation.

Urinary Organs.—Scraping pain in region of neck of bladder, < walking and eating, > when urinating. Sharp pressure upon bladder after supper, as from incarcerated flatus. Discharge of much prostatic fluid while urging at stool. Stitches in urethra when walking; S. in forepart after dinner, ending in tearing. Scraping in middle of urethra in evening in bed, with scratching and scratching tearing; scraping tearing in middle in evening when sitting. Biting burning in forepart of urethra when urinating. Crawling in urethra, < urinating, with burning, sometimes with stitching. Itching in forepart of urethra. **Frequent micturition; of watery urine** (Gels.). Urine burning in morning; (B. and dark). Urine lemon-colored, with white sediment. Urine turbid.

Clinical.—The urine is very much increased, not scanty, with hysterical symptoms. Retention of urine after confinement. Incontinence of urine in women and children.

Sexual Organs.—*Itching in bed about genitals and on penis, > scratching.* Penis retracted after urinating, so that it is very small. Paroxysms of pulling tearing pain in root of penis, < walking, > leaning against sacrum when standing. (Shooting into penis at every shock of cough, like sudden forcing of blood.) (Cramplike pain in penis.) Biting of gland, with itching. Urging and pressure over a large surface about penis (mons veneris), with violent erection, ending with emission. Erection; *always on going to stool.*

Retraction of prepuce. *Excoriation on margin of prepuce, with ulcerative pain and itching.* Sore pain on frænum of prepuce as if excoriated. Biting itching pain on inner surface of prepuce. Swelling of scrotum in evening. Itching sticking as from numberless fleas on scrotum, < rest. Sweat on scrotum. Strangulated sensation in testicles in evening in bed. Pressure in testicles. *Desire lost.* Impotency, with weakness of hips; I., with lasciviousnes; I., with lascivious fancies, sudden sexual excitement, weakness of genitals and external heat of body. Irresistible desire for emission, with relaxed penis. Profuse emission at night.

Leucorrhœa. Constriction of uterus like labor-pains, then purulent corrosive leucorrhœa. *Menstruation promoted;* delayed; scanty, black, offensive; discharged in clots. Lasciviousness, with prominence of clitoris, weakness and relaxtion of rest of genitals and cool temperature of body.

Clinical.—Morning sickness of pregnancy, with weak, sinking feeling in stomach, > eating. Labor-like pains during pregnancy brought on by emotional excitement. Nervous spasms amounting almost to convulsions during labor. Suppression of menses from grief, with the peculiar mental symptoms of the drug. Dysmenorrhœa, with great bearing down, menses dark. Neuralgia of the ovaries. Menorrhagia in a woman of 62 years, brought on by sudden grief.

Respiratory Organs.—Tearing in larynx, < swallowing, breathing and coughing. Scratching in upper part of larynx in evening, as from heartburn. *Provocation in larynx to hacking cough in evening after lying down* (Sang., Sil.), **not > cough, > suppressing cough.** *Inability to talk loud.* Desire to cough in evening on falling asleep. *Short, frequently dry cough, as from feathery dust in pit of throat,* **not > cough, < allowing himself to cough,** < *towards evening;* short forcible C. in evening from sudden interruption of breathing in trachea above pit of throat; hollow dry C. in morning on waking. Difficult expectoration from chest; E. from chest, yellow, of the odor and taste of old catarrh. *Inspiration impeded as from a load on chest, expiration is just so much easier.* Inspiration is slow, expiration rapid; I. slow, he must draw it from deep in abdomen. Short respiration alternates with long, light with violent. Breath fails when walking, and if he stands still, he is attacked by cough.

Clinical.—Nervous spasms of the glottis. Hysterical aphonia. Nervous, irritable cough, which becomes extremely annoying and almost constant, caused by tickling in the trachea, not > coughing, but < the more he coughs. Cough sympathetic, with remote affections especially of the uterus or ovaries, or from worms.

Chest.—Milk disappears from breasts. Catarrh, air-passages full of mucus. *Sticking in l.;* in r. when not breathing; in side in region of last rib, when not breathing, rhythmical with pulse; in nipple on deep inspiration, with flatulent movements in abdomen. Pain at both sides of sternum in morning as if ribs rubbed against each other. Pain in sternum as if beaten, even caused by touch. Pressure; in l., then r., then in ankle; in l., then sticking in r.; behind sternum in evening; in middle of sternum after eating; > deep breathing; in region of middle of sternum, as with a sharp instrument. Tensive pain across on standing upright; T. pain in forepart if when sitting he straightens up. Oppression; after midnight, impeding respiration; and oppressed respiration; with pressure in pit of stomach, < inspiration and suddenly changing to sticking in pit of stomach. Fulness. Anxiety, with pressure waking him, he must often breathe deeply and can only sleep after an hour. Throbbing in r.

Heart and Pulse.—Sticking in præcordial region on expiration. *Palpitation;* after noonday nap; during dinner; when in deep thought. Pulse accelerated; and small; slow and small in afternoon.

Neck.—Swollen glands. Sticking in nape. Sticking tearing in nape. Tearing in nape as if strained on moving neck. Sharp pain in cervical vertebræ in morning in bed. Painful pressure upon neck above l. shoulder. *Stiffness of nape* (Sil.).

Back.—Sticking in spine when walking in open air; S. near l. side of spine where true ribs are divided from false; in tip of scapula in morning. Tearing deep in middle of spine, towards l. side. Pain in scapula, < moving arm or letting it hang down. Sticking in sacrum. Pain in small of B. like a clawing, sticking, drawing and working altogether. Drawing pain in l. loin. *Pain in sacrum in morning when lying on back;* bruised P. in sacrum in morning when lying on back; (tensive P. in sacrum and chest on standing erect). Throbbing in sacrum.

Extremities.—Jerkings on falling asleep (Cham.). Tonic spasm of all, like a stiffness. Isolated twitchings. Sticking about or above joints; burning S. in external prominent parts of joints, with itching. *Sprained pain in shoulder, hip and knee-joints.* Pressure as with a hard substance, painful as a bruise, here and there in periosteum of middle of shafts of bones, < evening, by lying on side, > lying on back. Weakness; of arms and legs. *Crawling, asleep sensation.*

Upper Extremities.—Griping, pulling, kneading, in part drawing pain in shoulder-joint during rest, on motion becoming a sticking. Dislocated pain in shoulder; in joint on moving arm. *Pain in shoulder-joint on bending arm back as after violent exertion or as if bruised;* rheumatic or bruised pain in joint, when walking in open air. *Twitching of deltoid.* Drawing pain in arms. Pain in shafts of bones and joints of arm on which he lies in morning in bed, > lying on other side; in shafts of bones and joints of arm on which he does not lie in evening, > lying on painful side; in biceps on turning arm inward. Arm of side upon which he lies falls asleep. Painful drawing above r. elbow. Pulsating drawing extending from upper arm to fingers. Bruised pain in head of humerus of side upon which he lies in morning in bed, > lying on other side or upon back; B. pain in head of l. H. in evening when lying on r. side, > lying on l. side; B. pain in muscles of humerus, if arm hangs down or is raised.

Jerking in forearm as if a mouse were crawling under skin in one part of muscles, in evening after lying down. Tearing in wrist and fingers; on wrist in morning after waking. Paralytic pain on l. wrist as if sprained. Drawing in r. carpal bones. Stiffness of r. wrist and feeling as if asleep. Yellow hands. Sticking on touching a hair on hand. Cramp extending to middle finger when exerting fingers, > stroking it. Spasmodic motion back and forth of index in evening after lying down. Sticking in last joint of thumb. Tearing in joint of thumb as if sprained, in morning when slumbering. Sprained pain in metacarpal phalanx of index on motion.

Lower Extremities.—Totters when walking, falls easily and stumbles over slightest obstacles. Paralytic stiffness and jerking. Sticking in hip-joint; and knee, from 4 to 8 A.M. when walking, on moving leg. Bruised pain in posterior muscles of thigh when sitting. Intermittent deep internal pressure above l. hip; violent deep P. in middle of l. thigh. Thigh and leg fall asleep when sitting after eating. Knees crack. Knee drawn upward, preventing walking, > sitting. Knees give way from weakness. Sticking on inner side beneath l. knee. Knee stiff after ascending steps.

Cramp in calf in morning in bed on bending leg, > stretching or pressing it; C. in calf when sitting at dinner; when walking, > standing and rest. Sticking in tibia. *Tearing in backs of legs, < tendo-achillis and its muscles, as if the parts would be cut off, < standing after walking.* Grasping beating, tearing in anterior tibial muscles, < motion. Pain in tibia when walking. Paralytic pain in whole l. leg from walking, continuing when sitting. Painful drawing in whole l. leg in bed before sleep. Tension in calves on stretching legs or walking; T. in leg extending above knee, with heaviness of limb. Heaviness of legs on walking in open air, > in the room, with anxiety, then depression of spirits. Leg falls asleep when sitting after midday meal; as far as above knee in evening when sitting.

Sticking beneath malleoli on motion. Pressure in l. ankle (with internal tickling), > tremulous motion of foot; intermittent P. above r. external malleolus. Sprained pain in ankle in morning on walking. (Ankles stiff.) Attacks of cramp in muscles of foot and under toes when sitting. Sticking in heel in morning; intermittent S. on inner margin of foot; burning S. in side of foot, or a burning cutting. Tearing on back of foot. Itching jerking pain internally in ball of heel, < morning in bed. Bruised pain in ball of heel, or rather in periosteum of astralagus. Internal soreness in ball of heel, or rather in periosteum of os calcis, when walking. Burning pain in a corn when sitting; B. pain in a corn on pressure upon it; tearing burning P. in bone of heel in morning on waking. Soles sensitive when walking. Drawing in r. foot. Burning itching pain in a spot on back of foot during rest. Itching burning in heel and other parts of foot. Feet weak; at twilight, and mood quiet. Feet heavy; one foot H. Feet stiff in morning. Crawling in bones of feet, not like a going to sleep. Deadness (as if asleep) of ball of heel when walking. Pain in upper part of toes from pressure of shoe.

Clinical.—Sciatica recurring during cold weather, with intense coldness and shivering, < night, the pain is intermittent, sometimes throbbing. Violent attacks of sciatica, of a boring, tearing character, lasting about an hour, always preceded by coldness, < night, has to get up and walk about.

Skin.—Pimples about inflamed eye; painful on touch, beneath lower lip. Boil on inner part of thigh.

Burning in ulcer. Sticking here and there like flea-bites, < in bed; itching S. in thumb-joint. Outer skin and periosteum painful. Crawling in feet; sticking C. in feet (in calves) after midnight, preventing his remaining in bed. *Itching;* in umbilicus; wrist, elbow and neck; here and there at night, > scratching; here and there if heated from walking in open air.

Sleep.—Yawning even when eating; *frequent excessive Y.;* frequent, after sleep; frequent, interrupted by rigidity of chest; as if jaw would be dislocated in morning and < after midday nap; convulsive, so that eyes overflow with water, in evening before sleep and in morning after rising. Sleepiness; after sad news; when sitting, but if he lies down he is half awake; so that he went to bed at 9 o'clock and slept soundly all night, yet next morning and all day tired and apathetic. Falls asleep when reading. Deep sleep. Midday nap sound, but not refreshing; sleep sound, but not refreshing, on waking he does not believe that he has slept.

Sleeplessness. Unable to fall asleep, then waking without cause. *Light sleep, so that he hears everything. Twitching through whole body on falling asleep;* **of limbs** (Cham.). Shuddering on falling asleep on account of monstrous fantasies, which are still present after waking. Restless sleep interrupted by dreams; R., with internal restlessness and heat. Moves his mouth in sleep as if eating; muscles of open mouth moved in all directions and hands jerked inward. Suddenly starts up in moans, with piteous expression of face, stamps, kicks, face and hands pale and cold. Whimpering, prattling and tossing about. Talking as if weeping and complaining, inspiration snoring, mouth wide open, sometimes one eye, sometimes the other partly open. *Snoring inspiration.* Short inspiration, with slow expiration. Alternations of all kinds of respiration, short and slow, deep and light, intermitting and snoring. Groaning, grunting and sighing. Sleeps upon back, with palm under occiput; in morning he is lying with the outspread hand under occiput or on neck. Wakes with a friendly expression; W. with a morose look; stands up suddenly on waking, and talks disconnectedly.

Dreams in slumber before midnight, with heat. *D. all night of one thing; and the idea does not leave him on waking.* Frightful; wakes from, in morning; as, for example, of drowning, waking from afternoon nap. Of being buried alive. That he had fallen into water and cried. Sad, he wakes weeping. Full of disappointments. *With reflections and deliberations.* Full of learned excitations and scientific discussions. D. towards morning, in which thought is exerted. (D. that she was not standing firmly, that she bent herself double in order not to fall, therewith general sweat.)

Fever.—Coldness; at sunset; with one-sided headache; < *posterior parts,* > **immediately in warm room or by stove** (Nux mos., Sabad., Men.). Dread of open air. Shivering in morning on waking from light sleep; S. in afternoon, with colic, then weakness, sleep and heat of body; S. *in evening,* **with red face** (Ferr., Cham.); (after eating, at night anxiety and sweat); over body, with heat of hands and anxiety developing into weeping; constant, during apyrexia; on thighs and forearms, with gooseflesh, then on cheeks; of face and arms, with chattering of teeth and gooseflesh. Skin sensitive to draughts, feeling in abdomen as if he would take cold. *Cold nose, with hot knees* (with tickling itching of one knee). Chill in back and over arms; in arms when lying on back, < upper arms, then heat and redness of cheeks, heat of hands and feet, without thirst; *over upper arms, with heat of ears;* of hands and feet, with heat of face; *about knees, which are not cold externally;* of feet; of feet and as far as above knees; of feet in evening when eating, with distention of abdomen and hoarseness.

Heat; in morning in bed, with thirst, *but no wish to be uncovered;* in morning in bed, with palpitation; from 2 till 5 A.M. when fully awake, < on hands and feet, without thirst, sweat or feeling of dryness; at 3 A.M. on waking, with vomiting of food that had been eaten in evening; **in afternoon, without thirst** (Asaf., Nux mos., Nux vom.), *with dry sensation in skin, but sweat on face;* at night; < during sleep. **External H., with redness, without internal H.**; *external H.,* then rapid respiration; E., at 2 A.M. so that he sighs. *Flushing.* Feeling of orgasm of blood in evening, preventing sleep. Feeling as if sweat would break out; in forenoon, with partial sweat; suddenly, with partial sweat. Anxious H. at night, < lying on side, with sweat about nose, *most heat in hands and feet, which he wishes to keep covered,* with cold thighs, palpitation, short breath and lascivious dreams. *External warmth is intolerable,* then rapid respiration. Intermittent fever, with thirst during chill, but not during heat. *H. in head;* H. mounts to head, without thirst; external. H. in nape or one side of neck; *of one ear and one cheek, with redness* (Cham., Mosch.); of feet.

Sweat; in morning if he falls asleep a second time, if he then rises he is so weary that he would rather lie down again; cold; on inner surface of hands; on inner surfaces of hands and fingers; profuse on hands in evening.

Clinical.—A valuable remedy for certain types of intermittent fever, with the peculiar contrary aspects of the case, namely, thirst during the chill, but not during the fever; during the fever the patient desires to be covered; frequently there are the peculiar mental symptoms of the drug, or the onset of the paroxysms is characterized by the neuralgias of the head or extremities, which may serve to indicate it (Cedron).

Iodoform.

For internal use it is triturated with sugar of milk.

Compare Iodum.

Generalities. — Trembling. Constant convulsive movements. Neuralgic pains in various parts; N. pains flying all over him at times. Sharp pains all over body; in nerves of l. arm and back; pains sharply define the course of nerves. *Pains < thinking of them;* < touch; renewed when riding in cars; renewed in bed, in r. side of head, r. shoulder, r. arm, hands, fingers, thigh, leg, foot, toes. Strange feeling. Thinks he has taken a bad cold. Faintness. Sensations of impending death. Loss of power came on so imperceptibly that general paralysis was feared, a dreamy state, in a few days complete stupor and loss of power over sphincters, they could be aroused by great effort to take a little nourishment, but soon lapsed into unconsciousness. Paralysis of sphincters. Amelioration after sleep.

Mind.—Elated. Excitement interrupted by broken sleep; E., melancholia, hallucinations of sight and hearing. Apathetic, amnesia for recent events, nightly restlessness, did not recognize persons, weak-minded. Forgetful.

Head.—Stitching. Aching; on waking. Heaviness on attempting to rise; H., with aching in vertex; H. at night as if he could not raise it from the pillow, H. next morning after waking, with intermittent pain in skull and < l. side. Confusion, with nausea. Feeling as if he had been intoxicated the previous day. Sudden giddiness. Frontal pain; < descending stairs, with shooting in r. ear; neuralgic, < stooping. Stitching in temples. Neuralgic pains in nerves of temples, < r., extending to behind ears. Pain in temples as from a weight. Sticking in r. side of head. Itching of occiput.

Eyes.—Bloodshot and painful. Smarting and burning; S. and stinging. Bruised feeling in r. in morning. Sensitive to light. Objects appear tessellated and red, > rising. Vision double.

Ears.—Sticking in r.; S., then fulness. Feeling dry and feverish; and full. Neuralgic pain in l. Dull hearing.

Nose.—Dryness, and he complains that he cannot get any discharge from it; with fulness of membrane and constant snuffing. Constant sensation as if smelling fumes of iodine. Smell as of decaying leaves in a swamp.

Face.—Pain in malar-bones; in zygomatic muscles, < motion and bending forward. Drawing in malar-bones, with pressing. Stiffness of zygomatic muscles. Aching in r. lower jaw, increasing to pain as from a weight. Lips and throat dry; lips dry and stinging.

Mouth and Throat.—Sharp pain in upper teeth. Aching in sound teeth; in decayed, < upper and r., coming and going quickly; toothache in afternoon quickly changing to temples. Teeth feel sore and too long. Metallic taste. Stitching in r. side of throat. Dryness of throat, with bitter taste; D., with rawness on swallowing.

Stomach and Abdomen.—*Nausea;* at times. Rumbling in A. Scaphoid A. *Flatulent colic. Cutting in A.* Warmth in A. and rectum, with nausea and desire for stool. R. inguinal region, sharp pain; cutting, with desire for stool; sore pain.

Stool and Urine.—Desire for a liquid stool. Stool delayed; with feeling as if anus were drawn up into rectum. Urine very yellow; and smelling like saffron.

Respiratory Organs.—Aphonic disturbance of voice. Cough from dryness of throat; C. on going to bed, with wheezing from mucus in throat. Smothering sensation. Respiration irregular.

Chest.—Sticking in r., extending to lower angle of scapula. Pain in l.; sharp, in r.; ulcerative, in l. breast, to r. of nipple at night, then grasping at base of heart, next day aching in l. breast. Soreness on taking a long breath; S. in lungs; *sore pain in apex of r. lung, on breathing sensation as if two ulcerated surfaces were in contact. Feeling in lungs as from a heavy cold. Feeling as if a weight rested on C., preventing free expansion.*

Heart and Pulse.—Sticking through heart. Pulse rapid.

Neck and Back.—Contraction of muscles of neck. Bruised sensation in nape. Spine sore, does not wish it touched. Pain along spine; along r. side of dorsal vertebræ; in lumbar region, with weakness and straining. Sharp pain in angle of scapula.

Extremities.—Pain in l. arm and l. leg, < lower half of tibia and fibula, then extending into foot. Bruised feeling in l. arm and leg, as the pain increases the muscles feel ulcerated. Sticking in l. shoulder; and arm. Pain in median nerve of l. arm; P. in l. humerus, with bruised pain in muscles around the bone. *Rheumatic pain in r. arm; < using it.* Bruised pain in l. arm in morning on touch. Pain in l. elbow; in nerves of l. hand; sharp, in nerves of l. hand.

Lower Extremities.—Pain along l. crural nerve; P. in inside of knees; neuralgic, in l. knee. Weakness of knees on ascending stairs; W. < standing, with pain. Rheumatic pain in gastrocnemii; rheumatism of flexor muscles of legs. Legs weak. Cutting in l. ankle on walking in open air. Sticking in r. instep. Pain in l. foot, < walking.

Sleep.—Sleepiness; intermittent, ending in coma. Wakefulness. Jerks and shocks in nerves when trying to sleep. Restless sleep, full of dreams; R., < after 2 A.M. Sound sleep till 1.30 A.M., then sudden waking, restlessness and sleeplessness till 4.30, then partially conscious sleep for an hour and a half, then heavy sleep and difficult arousing. Confused dreams, of accidents, etc.

Fever.—Susceptible to hot weather. Heat at night, keeps laying off covers. Sweats easily from motion. Sweat on head.

Iodum.

A tincture is made by dissolving 1 part in 99 parts of alcohol.

General Effects.—It affects nearly every organ and tissue in the body. Acute catarrh of all mucous membranes, especially eyes and nose. Salivation; enlargement of all lymphatic glands, followed by atrophy, especially of testicles and mammæ, and general emaciation. Polyuria, nephritis and albuminuria. Skin eruptions. Neuralgia, even convulsions and paralysis. It is particularly important to observe that it controls inflammations (with high temperature) of many, if not all, parenchymatous structures, particularly the lungs, when the indications permit its exhibition.

Allies.—(Bromine), Sulph., Arsen., Merc., Nit. ac., Nat. mur., Bry.

Generalities.—Emaciation (Nat. m., Sul.); *ending in marasmus; of glandular tissues* (breasts, testicles, thyroid gland). Dropsy. *Œdematous swelling of whole body* (Arsen.). *Sitting in bed, and restless.* Indolent in all movements. A kind of catalepsy. Convulsive movements; of arms and legs, and head drawn backward; almost convulsed when the pains are intense. Cramps of arms, back and legs, with jerkings of them. Trembling; < arms from least movement, and out of breath. Restless moving about, with sleeplessness, so that she was taken to be insane. Hysteria. Nervous condition; an internal agitation, as from bad news or remorse after a quarrel, with inability to fix attention when reading or drawing, weeping and intolerance of opposition.

Rheumatic pains; in nape and upper arms; in neck, arms and body. Rush of blood to head and heart. General sensibility increased. Takes cold easily. *Restlessness* (Arsen.); in morning, with anxiety. Aversion to sitting still. *Weakness* (Arsen.); in afternoon, after a short walk, with feeling of fasting, but no hunger; after dinner, with discomfort; during menses; during the passing away of menses; after restless sleep; with craving for something reviving, temporarily > a cordial or a little nourishment, but delay in eating causes malaise, drawings and often pain in stomach; physical and mental; so that sweat breaks out on talking. Collapse, with sunken face. Inability to stand. Faintness. Paralysis of limbs, then of organs of deglutition and respiration.

Clinical.—Cases requiring Iod., when not febrile, are apt to have great appetite, but rapid emaciation. It is indicated in numerous wasting diseases in scrofulous patients. Mollities ossium. Lymphatic tumors in various parts.

Mind. — Clouded. Delirium. Excitement, with heaviness, indolence and ill humor; E. in afternoon, sleepiness in evening. Illusions of sensation. Sat all day with her head leaning on her hand, and hardly answered. *Irritability;* during digestion, from noon till evening, with sensitiveness and with oppression of throat and chest, as if about to weep. Anger. *Sad;* and taking no interest in anything, unable to fix her thoughts. Anxiety; and depression, busy with the present rather than the future. Fright; and vexation. Fear that from every trifle some misfortune would arise. Apprehension after manual labor, > sitting; A. if he does not eat every three or four hours, yet he dares not eat too much. Aversion to work. Lively and talkative. Sensitive; and easily moved to tears. Mild, scrupulous and timid, with blunted sensibilities. Thoughts fixed; troublesome and unreasonable mental impressions easily developed into fixed ideas. Sluggish, but inclined to mechanical labor. It is difficult to collect his senses, and he is irresolute. It constantly seems as if he ought to remember something, but he knows not what, he remembers nothing. Feels unfitted for anything. Stupor.

Clinical.—The mental condition of the Iod. patient is generally one of despondency, but during fevers and wasting diseases we often meet with excessive irritability and sensitiveness, much like that found under Sul.

Head.—Sticking at times. *Aching;* in forenoon; in warm air when driving far or walking rapidly; *as from a band* (Sulph.); sudden, < r. temple; intermittent, < l. side towards forehead. *Confusion, with aversion to earnest work;* C. at 9 A.M., changing at 10 to pain, > noon; with pressure in r. half of forehead; making thought difficult; becoming an intermittent pain, < temples, > evening. Heaviness. Feeling as if not right. Throbbing on every motion. Congestion, then pain. Vertigo; in morning, with weakness; on rising; on quick change of place, < quick rising from a seat; on rising from bed and walking, then unconsciousness; tending forward.

Forehead.—Tearing above l. eye and in temple; *sharp pain in l. upper part. Pain; in a spot above root of nose* (Ign.); *suborbital; above eyes towards evening; < noise and talk,* and in vertex; > sweat; with confusion of head, then violent hunger, > dinner; externally, as from suppuration. Bruised feeling in brain, with powerless and paralyzed feeling in whole body, < arms, necessity to lie down, eructations, sensitiveness of scalp to touch, next day confusion of head and painfulness of brain on motion. Throbbing.

Tearing in l., then r. temple. Stitches in vertex. Pain in vertex; on l. side. Tearing in r. side above forehead. Drawing pain in l. side, extending into teeth; D. pain in l. upper part, extending into temple. Sticking in occiput, > lying down. Pain in occiput; *before* 11 A.M., > *rest,* < *motion of body, changing at* 4 P.M. *to confusion of head,* > 7 P.M.; in under surface; in r., with occasional pain in forehead; biting sore P. in O. above r. ear, extending backward in skin. Hair falls out.

Clinical.—Persistent headaches, with vertigo on active exertion, or congestive headaches with vertigo in old people. Tubercular meningitis.

Eyes.—Red; and glistening, protruding. Whites dirty yellow, with injected vessels. Sparkling and restless. Dull-looking; and fixed, surrounded by black rings. *Inflamed; from taking cold;* with tension above r. Surrounded by black rings. Brownish discoloration under E. Sometimes fixed, sometimes wandering. Sunken and wild-looking. Ophthalmia. Jerking. Cutting stitches in l. extending towards external canthus. Tearing about r., < beneath it; T. around r., passing from inner canthus to joint of jaw. Pain; in l. and inner canthus; as from sand. Weak feeling as if sunken, < afternoon. Lachrymation. Sticking in upper part of l. ball. Pupils dilated. Lids red and swollen, and nightly agglutination; swelling and violet color of upper; leucophlegmatic S. R. lid spasmodically looped into festoons. Twitching back and forth of lower lid. Itching in canthi.

Vision.—Disturbed. Dim; and manifold. Saw nothing but the white paper when reading print, when at the end of a phrase the beginning of it was visible. Flickering; of stitches when sewing. Dark rings float down at sides and near visual axis. Of sparks. Fiery curved rays shoot sideways from visual axis, near point of vision, especially upward. By day objects seem illuminated by a flaming fiery red and almost blinding light, and artificial light in evening was intolerable.

Clinical.—A valuable remedy in inflammation of the iris, especially if of syphilitic origin.

Ears.—Tearing in fossa beneath r. and in neighboring parts of neck. Aching. Ringing. Roaring. Noises in r. as in a mill. Sensitiveness to noise. *Difficult hearing;* required some time to understand what was said to him.

Clinical.—Chronic deafness, with adhesions in the middle ear or granular enlargement; deafness, with chronic catarrh of the Eustachian tube, inflammation of the tonsils, roaring in ears, etc.

Nose.—Scab in r. nostril. More open than usual; wide open in morning and dry, almost all day stopped, smell almost lost. Itching sticking in forepart of septum. Pain in lower part on blowing, without coryza. Stoppage. *Sneezing;* without catarrh, whereby nasal mucus is thrown far out. Increased mucus; with stoppage, but without catarrh. *Blowing out of much yellow mucus* (Puls.). *Coryza; stopped, < evening, becoming fluent in open air, with much expectoration; fluent, like water; fluent, with much sneezing; sudden, violent, with lachrymation, pain in eyes, then violent cough and nausea,* **difficult, almost wheezing respiration,** *feeling as if larynx were constricted externally.* Bleeding on blowing.

Clinical.—A very valuable remedy in acute fluent coryza, the discharge is hot, the nose becomes sore, headache at root of nose and over frontal sinuses, the attack is attended with fever, sneezing, etc. (compare Ars.). In subacute and chronic catarrhs, discharge fetid, nose swollen and painful (Nat. m., Aur.).

Face.—Red; in evening. Reddish-purple. Yellow. Pale; and sunken; and drawn; with blue lines; *pale, yellowish or greenish.* Wan. Collapsed. Animated; and excited, anxious. Melancholy expression. Peculiar change in expression. Twitching. *Lips bluish, with swelling of superficial veins.* Scaling of lips. Trembling of lips as from cold. Lips painful, dry. Contraction of jaw, causing her to clench teeth. Pain in r. upper jaw.

Mouth.—*Teeth were covered with mucus in morning, became yellow and were easily blunted by vegetable acids* (Nit. ac.). Chattering of T. Toothache; now here, now there, in molars; pinching, in r. molars; pain in teeth and gum as from looseness, when eating; drawing pain in r. T., extending towards ear, with sticking; cutting drawing in roots or gum of lower incisors, now l., now r., with sore sensation. *Gums bleed* (Merc.); red G.; G. pale, swollen, painful; swollen and inflamed, causing general toothache; ulcer on G. of a hollow lower molar, with swelling of cheek to beneath eye (Merc.).

Tongue dry; in evening, white at edges, brown in centre; and hard, dark, coating apparently imbedded into mucous membrane. Tongue furred. Biting constriction of tongue, changing to burning. Stammering; and sounds other than intended, from incomplete control of tongue.

Full of mucus in morning fasting. *Aphthous eruption.* Elevations on inside of r. cheek, with inflammation in vicinity, sore pain on touch, afterwards sticking and cutting as if ulcerated, < opening mouth widely when eating or reading aloud. Irritation, and in throat. Pressure in l. half of palate. Soreness of M. and throat, with much tenacious mucus. Dryness, and of throat; causing dysphagia; walls seemed dry, but were not. **Salivation** (Merc.); after paralysis set in; with nausea. *Offensive odor* (Merc.), even in morning after rinsing it. Taste bitter; in afternoon, sweet plums tasted B.; nothing had its natural flavor but sweets and eggs, wine tasted acrid, astringent, bitter, acid; T. salt; nauseous, sweetish (Merc.); sweet, on tip of tongue.

Throat.—Post-mortem showed a thin, firm, easily detached, orange-yellow patch on uvula and arch of palate, confluent with one on posterior wall of pharynx, it extended, increasing in thickness, into œsophagus and trachea, the membrane under this was hyperæmic, epiglottis covered with a thick false membrane, mucous membrane eroded, dark, with many swollen pustules, submucous membrane œdematous, but relaxed, ventriculi Morgagnii closed by swelling and covered with a similar false membrane, mucous membrane here and there very red, a similar membrane on vocal chords and part of larynx beneath, bronchi inflamed and full of tenacious mucus, mucous membrane swollen, injected and showing points of mucus, acute emphysema between lobules of lungs, œsophagus covered with a false membrane, orange-colored, firm and detachable, with phlegmonous purulent spots in submucous connective tissue.

Redness of fauces; with denuded sensation in it, tip of tongue and part of lip. Swelling of uvula, with elongation and much spitting. Increased mucus and rough voice. Fauces relaxed and sensitive. Choking as from shreds of skin in various parts, with salivation and smarting, the latter temporarily > jelly or arrowroot. Tearing above larynx. Scraping; in pharynx as after eating hips. Biting in tonsils, < l., with twinging. Pain low down; P. in r. side, > swallowing. Constriction; in goitre. Fulness. Becomes thick when speaking loud. Heaviness extending into chest, making respiration difficult, then cough, with expectoration of mucus. Tickling crawling in region of larynx in morning in bed. Dryness. Burning; from sea-air; to stomach, with dryness; in fauces, extending to abdomen, < stomach, with pain; sharp, in pharynx, extending into trachea, with rawness; acute, in pharynx, with scraping in larynx and irritation in nostrils as from sulphurous gas; in uvula, as if consumed; biting, extending into air-passages. *Swallowing difficult;* S. of water impeded, as if throat were constricted and weak. Smarting in œsophagus, with biting, heat, constriction and roughness.

Clinical.—Acute inflammation of the tonsils, with hoarse cough and deafness, the Eustachian tube seems to be especially involved. Ulceration of the throat and mouth, syphilitic or mercurial, with swollen glands, aggravation from warmth. Very rarely indicated in any stage of diphtheria. A large number of cases of goitre have been cured by the internal administration of Iod., and many cases of goitre have been dissipated and followed by alarming pulmonary symptoms from the external application to the goitre. Valuable in mumps.

Stomach.—**Ravenous hunger.** *Appetite great;* at noon and in evening; with thirst; *diminished; lost;* lost, or else canine hunger. Aversion to food. *Thirst;* day and night; in morning; in evening; unquenchable. Eructations; empty; constant, empty. Nausea; in morning after rising, with cramp in stomach, < night; in pit of stomach, > eating, with heaviness in stomach; by paroxysms, with heartburn and feeling of disordered stomach. Retching; often, then sudden vomiting, the V. < drinking or moving about, then short relief, but nausea in the intervals. *Vomiting;* and inability to retain food or drink; < eating; and liquid stools; and yellowish liquid stools containing flocculi; incessant, with diarrhœa; serous; forcible; violent, with spasm.

Permanent contraction. Movings in S. and small intestines, with warmth and cutting; M. extending over abdomen, with cutting, once these M. extended into chest, which was constricted, then towards pubis, into bladder and towards testicles. Frequent cramp; drawing, in pit, extending into upper abdomen. Sticking in pit; upper border. Lacerating pains in epigastric region; < pressure. Cutting in region. Gnawing in upper part. Pain; in morning, > eructations; in epigastric region; in E. region, extending into abdomen, back and œsophagus; excruciating P. Painful to touch; in epigastrium. Burning pain, and in umbilical region. Heartburn. Heat; in region; in pit; epigastrium; in epigastric region, spreading over body. Heaving in epigastric region, extending towards surface, with sensation as if he would tremble or perspire. Weight in epigastric region, with universal tremors. Digestion difficult; irregular; indigestion after slightest food, with headache that often makes him senseless, without loss of appetite, with necessity to avoid relaxing, bitter or resolvent medicines, inability to drink sweet milk.

Abdomen.—Distention. Meteorism. Rumbling. Movements; gradually becoming painful, then frequent emissions of flatus of the odor of sulphuretted hydrogen and frequent desire for stool. Frequent emission of flatus. Place of a hernia inflamed from the usual truss. Heaving, with heat and determination to surface of body as if general sweat would break out. Increased peristaltic action, with frequent emissions of air and fæces; increased P. action, changing to tense feeling. Pinching. Almost cutting. Pain; < along colon; or in attachments of diaphragm; extending to spine. Heat; in morning. Irritability, < region of stomach, beginning as warmth, then cutting. Uneasiness, < night. Straining downward, then urging in rectum to evacuate gas and fæces, then relief.

Distention of upper A. lasting from dinner through digestion, with sharp pressure here and there as from flatulence. *Pain between pit of stomach and umbilicus.* Irritability in region of stomach and in small intestines, less a pain than a moving about, then tense sensation. *Inflammation of liver, with pain, hardness, swelling, constant fever, dry tongue, restlessness, little sleep, small, rapid pulse, and on rising from bed faintness. L. hypochondrium hard and acutely painful to pressure* (Ceanothus). Sticking in hepatic region; in forepart beneath r. ribs on inspiration, often recurring on deep breathing; in l. hypochondrium, as from incarcerated flatus. Pinching in hepatic region, with cutting. *Pressure in r. hypochondrium; with pain on touch;* sore P. in l. hypochondrium.

Incarceration of flatus in l. side. Sticking in sides. Cutting in umbilical region. Rumbling in site of an inguinal hernia in morning on inspiration. Sticking in l. side of hypogastrium; jerking S. above arch of pubis. Burning tearing near l. hip; bubbling tearing in r. side close to penis. Pain on r. side close to penis; P. near r. hip; in r. groin; in hypogastrium after each morning stool, which was rather hard than soft; paroxysmal, in H., < sitting, > stretching.

Clinical.—Enlargement of the spleen, with salivation. Disease of the pancreas, with salivation, vomiting and profuse watery or frothy stools; the cases reported are both acute and chronic; in the chronic form there is constipation; in some of these cases there is a depressed, irritable mood. Numerous cases of mesenteric disease, glandular enlargement, emaciation, irregular stool, enormous appetite. Jaundice, with cirrhotic liver, clay-colored stools, tenderness over the region of the liver, especially after the abuse of mercury.

Rectum and Anus.—Itching, painful hæmorrhoids; pain in H. before and after stool. Smarting in R. after a natural stool. Burning pain in R. *Burning in A. in evening* (Sul.); B. after stool. Itching in A.; as from thread-worms; frequent, with smarting and itching. Pressure in R. in evening in bed. Frequent urging and frequent liquid stools; ineffectual U., easy stool only after drinking cold milk.

Stool.—Liquid, reddish-brown, with colic and urging; of watery, frothy, whitish mucus, with griping about umbilicus and pressure on vertex. *Diarrhœa;* excessive; profuse, bloody; mucous, bloody, scanty; in violent attacks, with violent colic. Thin and copious. *Soft; frequent; whitish;* and easy; and frequent, then burning in anus. Pasty. Constipation. Hard and difficult. Difficult; and infrequent. Containing much clear blood. Of peculiar odor and early. Frequent; and copious.

Clinical. — Chronic exhausting diarrhœa, stools frothy, whitish. Fatty diarrhœa from disease of the pancreas.

Urinary Organs.—Sticking in orifice of urethra. Itching smarting in orifice of U. Cutting in orifice when not urinating. Constant desire; and constant dribbling. Polyuria. *Involuntary micturition. Frequent and copious M.;* F. and scanty each time; F., with urging; F., urine copious, bright yellow, watery. Urine suppressed. Urine dark, turbid, at times almost milky; dark yellowish-green. Urine thick, with dark sediment; and copious. Increased U. Scanty and red U.; S., dark reddish-brown, with strong odor of iodine; S. and light-colored. Biting corroding U. U. contained albumen; contained iodine.

U. amber-colored, sp. gr. 1038, acid, flocculent sediment, amorphous, acetic or nitric acid caused a copious amorphous precipitate, soluble in excess of nitric acid and from heat, on subsequent cooling a precipitate of yellow halberts of uric acid mixed with granular matter, no precipitate on boiling, no albumen, much urea, good reaction of iodine combined, not free, and of indican, next day sp. gr. 1025.

Clinical.—Diabetes, with canine hunger. Incontinence of urine in old people, with senile degeneration of the prostate.

Sexual Organs.—Irritability. Acute drawings in forepart of penis. Frequent tickling of glans; T. on and beneath glans. Itching of glans. Cutting drawing in corona glandis. Priapism. Erections without lasciviousness; violent and continual E.; feeble E.; slow E. Burning pain in a spot on r. side of scrotum. Testicles diminished in size and power; D. in size and consistency, with impotency; *double its former size;* one retracted to abdomen; vigorous activity; frequent dragging towards T. from 10 A.M. till evening. Desire increased (in men). Semen increased. Emissions, with dreams after falling asleep again, then weakness.

Activity of uterus and hæmorrhage from it. A woman became barren. Menstruation irregular; too early; too late, with vertigo and palpitation; retained; M. that was present ceased.

Clinical.—Enlargement of testicles, with pain extending to abdomen. Many cases of hydrocele have been cured by the internal administration of the drug. Amenorrhœa. Uterine hæmorrhage after every stool, with atrophy of the mammæ, aggravation from warmth. Chronic menorrhagia. Chronic excoriating leucorrhœa, with atrophy of the mammæ, goitre, induration of the cervix, etc. Chronic inflammation of the ovaries, with thick, yellow, burning leucorrhœa. Many cases of ovarian cysts. Chronic metritis, with intense pain, nervousness, constant urging to urinate, heat and dryness of the vagina, etc. Cancer of the uterus, with profuse hæmorrhages, corrosive yellow discharge, ravenous appetite, etc. A characteristic is a wedgelike pain from r. ovary to uterus.

Respiratory Organs.—Œdema of glottis. Increased mucus in trachea. Sticking in larynx; on swallowing. *Pain in larynx, with desire to cough; frequent P. in region of L. and sublingual glands, with stitches;* pressure in region of L., not exactly painful, extending to pharynx, causing swollen sensation in the parts, even in tonsils. Crawling in larynx in morning in bed, > hawking and coughing, with tickling and salivation. *Smarting in region of trachea, with frequent lancinations.* Rawness in air-passages in morning on rising, with dryness. Irritation of bronchi. Suffocative feeling. **Hoarse**; in morning. A fatiguing whisper. Voice deep; V. broken; tremulous, jerky; weak. Aphonia, want of vibration of cough.

Cough in evening; irritation to C. from tickling in throat; **croupy C.**; dry C.; dry, deep; C., with effort, so that she almost vomits, > expectoration of mucus; short, from tickling in throat, also with thick yellow expectoration and good appetite, but sickly expression. Copious bloody expectoration. Spitting of white frothy mucus, sometimes of a ropy fluid. *Respiration difficult, especially inspiration; R. tight.* Dyspnœa in afternoon; sudden D., with pain on deep inspiration, rapid and violent beating of heart, and rapid, small pulse. Oppressed respiration on slightest exertion, with palpitation and vertigo. Rapid R. Short R.; < slightest exertion. Breath lost. Inarticulate sighing.

Clinical.—In croup, inflammation of the larynx and trachea, with hard croupy cough, difficult breathing and fever indicate the drug. A large number of cases of "membranous" croup have been cured by the lower dilutions; our experience is that it is indicated in cases in the early stage with more or less fever, with dry skin and a very dry cough, great difficulty in respiration; it follows closely after Acon.; if Acon. has been given and the patient is not improving, or if Acon. has relieved only the restlessness and extreme anxiety but not the cough, the patient is still dry and hot and the cough is still croupy, then give Iod.; it is, however, rarely useful after febrile excitement has disappeared or if the patient perspires freely; (this stage, together with the attacks of suffocative cough, indicates Brom. instead of Iod.). In catarrhal laryngitis the larynx is sore to touch, the cough is dry and croupy, and there is an excoriating watery discharge from the nose (compare with Allium cepa). Whooping cough, with emaciation and with enormous appetite. Chronic laryngeal catarrh, with dry croupy cough, sawing respiration, soreness of the upper part of the chest.

Chest.—*Atrophy of breasts.* Milk diminished. Rattling of mucus, with rawness beneath sternum and heaviness on chest. Pleurisy. Sticking in middle of r. on expiration; S. in r. near pit of stomach on inspiration. Tearing in r. parietes. Burning sticking tension in parietes. Sore pain in sides when breathing and on touch. Sudden pain in r., < inspiration. Pressure deep in r.; P., > open air and hot sunlight, with sticking and frequent dry, rough cough; P. on C., at times changing to pain and often causing deep dry cough. *Constriction;* then pressure, in afternoon sticking. Tightness in middle, sometimes l., sometimes r. side, with pressure and burning. Heaviness, causing difficult respiration.

Clinical.—It is one of our most valuable remedies for pneumonia; in these cases it must be carefully differentiated on the one side from Acon. and on the other from Bry.; it lacks the anxiety of Acon. and the sticking pains of Bry., but it has the high fever of each; like Bry., it is indicated when hepatization has taken place (contraindicating Acon.) and the cough is dry; it was formerly supposed that left-sided pneumonia indicated Iod., but it is now known that it is equally useful in pneumonia of either side; it is particularly useful in the pneumonia of scrofulous subjects, especially in pneumonia at the apex. Phthisis pulmonaris, with rough voice, dry cough and night-sweats.

Heart.—Sounds weak, apex beat and pulse could not be felt. *Præcordial anxiety causing constant change of position.* Pressure in region. Squeezed sensation. **Palpitation** (Nat. m., Ars., etc.); after menstruation; till sleep; < *movement;* spasmodic, as far as umbilicus, < pit of stomach. Rapid action.

Clinical.—Valvular insufficiency, with periodical attacks of pain about the heart following typhoid, dilatation of the r. side, etc. Pericarditis complicating pneumonia. Hypertrophy of the heart.

Pulse.—Rapid; in morning, and feeble; especially < at intervals, and small; and small; and small, hard; and small, feeble; and weak. Hard, thin, carotid rapid, small, weak, *with tumultuous, irregular, at times intermittent action of heart.* Energetic in afternoon, and large, full. Small; and thready; and contracted; and slow, weak. Irritable. Tremulous. Weak; and tremulous; with long intermissions.

Neck and Back.—Tearing on r. side of neck. Rheumatic pinching in N. near l. shoulder, < touch, > eructations, but returning. Rheumatic tension in r. side of N. Constriction of N. Confusion in back extending through nape into head. Sticking in scapulæ on lifting anything; S. in small of back. Pain under l. scapula; in small of B. during menstruation; in coccyx and sacrum, now increasing, now decreasing. Drawing in region of r. kidney, with pressure.

Extremities.—Trembling; with staggering. Heaviness in morning. Numbness. Position of upper E. looked as if convulsions would come on. Stitches in shoulder-joints even during rest. Rheumatic pain in l. shoulder. (Drawing tearing in the morbidly elevated S.) Arm and part of hand swollen. Jerking of arms, hands and fingers. Twisting of arms, < r. Tearing in arms after slight manual labor. Pain in bone on outer side of arm, waking and preventing sleep again, < lying on it. Paralytic weakness of arms in morning on waking. *Tearing in l. elbow.* Pressure in bend of l. elbow. Sticking in r. wrist when lifting or grasping anything. Hands red. Hands tremble. Tearing in metacarpal bone of r. index. Pain as from a blow on metacarpal bone of index, < touch. Ulceration of nail of l. index caused by a slight prick near nail. Tearing in l. index and middle finger; in knuckle of r. little finger; in first joint of r. thumb. Tensive pain in finger-joints as if they would break on bending, with swelling and pain on pressure when stretched.

Lower Extremities.—Rheumatic drawing, < thigh and knee in evening in bed, < motion, with grumbling in bed. Lassitude as if stiff, so that he could scarcely stand. Pressure in l. nates, as if in ischium. Twitching in muscles of thighs. Thighs sore where they rub in walking (in a woman). Intermittent tearing between l. hip and articulation of thigh, < moving joint; pinching T. near head of l. femur; sticking T. in middle of l. thigh, towards inner side. Rheumatic pain in l. thigh. Tension in thighs and legs, almost like cramp, only when sitting. Tearing on l. knee; on outer side of hollow of r.

Swelling of legs. Tearing on sides above malleoli. Pain in tibia as if suppurating. Leaden heaviness of legs. Leg falls asleep easily. Cramp of ankle at night, with jerking in it. Sticking in malleoli. Rapid swelling of feet and soles, so that walking was painful. Cramp of feet. Sharp pain in inner half of r. heel. Leaden heaviness of feet. Sticking tearing beneath nail of l. great toe. Cramplike pain extending from middle toe to tarsus. Sudden pain in r. great toe, next day passing to other toes, great toe less sensitive, then cold, then black, with sudden typhoid fever, the gangrene rising to thigh, with horrid pains, leg black and cold, when the woman attempted to turn in bed the tibia and fibula broke, and then the limb dropped off.

Clinical.—Articular rheumatism, sometimes with hot shiny swelling of the joints (Bry.), with great swelling, pain, etc. Articular rheumatism complicated with pericarditis; in these cases there is generally nocturnal aggravation. Wandering rheumatism, which even seems to attack the meninges of the brain and finally attacks the heart. Subacute inflammation of the knee, with fistulous openings discharging bloody serum, nightly boring pains. Housemaid's knee. Scrofulous affections of the joints (recently treated with marked success by injections of Iodoform). Affections of the joints or of the articular extremities of the bones, following mercury or syphilis. Gonorrhœal rheumatism.

Skin.—Pale. Dingy and livid. Brown as if smoked, instead of former yellowish tint. Redness of neck and chest as if congested. Red burning spot on nose beneath eye. Scratched spots become dark brown and the ulcerated places remaining after furuncles become gangrenous. Various eruptions, from erythema to morbus maculosus. Erythema of face and inflammation. Itching elevation on nose. Itching iodine exanthem, > sweat. Round, burning, itching spot between r. thumb and index, with two whitish pellicles upon it, > rubbing. Itching papules on an old scar.

Skin of arm tight, glossy, then covered with miliary vesicles, with heat, itching and smarting, V. ruptured by any considerable motion, discharge of much water, most from inside of elbow, < bending arm. Furuncle between scapulæ, with inflammation of surrounding parts (with loss of appetite and sleeplessness), after warm poultices the F. detached itself from the skin in hard knots, leaving deep and painless ulcers, which refused to heal. Feeling over whole body like flea-bites, day and night. Itching on back above r. hip; I. of an old scar; sticking, in various parts.

Sleep.—Frequent yawning. Sleepiness. *Sleeplessness;* at night, but weariness by day; with profuse sweat; for eight days, with restlessness and delirium. Sleep broken by sudden starts. Restless sleep; with anxious dreams; with unpleasant and fatiguing dreams; then sleeplessness, on getting to sleep nightmare and hallucinations. Sleep bad, with nightmare and electric shocks, which wake her with a start. Waking early.

Nightmare. Dreams; vivid, from which he wished to wake but could not, then weakness after waking; anxious, restless; anxious, of dead people; unremembered, with sound sleep; every night, of swimming, walking in mire, that her daughter had fallen into a brook, etc.; of having unsuccessful intercourse with men, no emissions; that he was about to have connection with a man, but for some unknown reason the dream changed before the act was accomplished, no emission.

Fever.—Coldness; alternating with heat; cold nose; limbs; limbs, and trembling of them; upper limbs; hands, and clammy; feet; feet at night. Quartan fever, with constant diarrhœa on the days free from fever. Irregular febrile movements. Heat; after wine, with excitement, but feeling as if he would soon become tired; in flushes. Fever, with dry skin, weakness, rapid pulse, delirium, twitching of muscles, carphology and more coldness than heat of skin. Flushes of heat in head before menstruation, with palpitation and tension in throat, which became thick. Heat of hands; in r. scapula; flitting across r. thigh; of skin; of skin in evening, with dryness. *Sweat at night; profuse;* profuse S. on forehead; viscid S.; cold; contained iodine; general, sour, towards morning, then weakness of limbs; acrid on feet.

Ipecacuanha.

A tincture is made of the dried root of Cephaëlis Ipecacuanha, A. Richard.

General Action.—Its most marked effects are observed on the gastro-intestinal and respiratory tracts; it produces nausea and vomiting (one of its most constant effects), considerable increase of the secretions, especially in the upper portion of the intestinal canal, and also dysenteric symptoms. It greatly increases bronchial secretion, causes pulmonary engorgement, and even hepatization; it also produces emphysema. Its cough is frequently spasmodic. It produces, in some cases, violent neuralgia of the eyes and head, with intense congestion of the conjunctiva, lachrymation, etc.

Allies.—Puls., Ferr., Eupat. perf., Mag. c., Cact., Nux v., Phos.

Generalities.—Awkward and knocking against everything. Swaying to and fro of body to either side as in drunkenness, in evening when walking in open air, with stupefaction of head. Opisthotonos; symptoms of O. and emprosthotonos. **Body of the child stretched out stiff;** *then spasmodic contraction of arm.* (Sticking here and there, caused by motion, ending in burning.) Throbbing pain in head and pit of stomach after coughing. Anxiety in blood in morning on waking, as if he had been in great heat or had perspired profusely or were awakened by anxious dreams, with heaviness of head as if brain were compressed. Sensitiveness to cold and warmth. Restlessness. *Weakness;* and indolence, depression of spirits and shivering. Stiffness.

Mind.—*Cries and screams constantly (a child), sticks its fists into its mouth,* face pale, body rather cool. Whining, must be carried. *Impatient. Ill humor; scorning everything and desirous that others shall not value anything;* because his business does not proceed fast enough; and no desire to talk, inclined to weep; and quiet, retired in himself, scorning everything; and sinking of courage. Exasperated at slightest noise. Angry; often at trifles and again just as easily can be quieted. Scrupulous, fearful, thinks trifles are very important. Longing, but he knows not for what. Pleased with nothing. Averse to everything. Disinclination to work; to literary work, ideas fail him. Slow flow of ideas.

Head.—Sticking, with heaviness; paroxysmal S., then pressure. Tearing in morning after rising, > afternoon. Aching; tensive. *Bruised feeling in brain and skull, piercing throuyh skull into root of tongue, with nausea.* Drawing here and there. Feeling as if H. and forehead were compressed. Heaviness; with sleepiness. Confusion. Fulness, < cerebrum. Vertigo; on walking; only on walking, < turning around, with disappearance of thought.

Forehead.—Sticking on touch; S. above eye on stooping, with swollen sensation. Tearing, < stooping; < touch. Boring. Pain, with heaviness of eyes; P. extending to vertex; pressing outward P. in l. side, < moving head; burning P., < touch.

Pressing-out, almost boring pain alternately in temples and in a spot over orbits, > pressure and closing eyes. Pain under l. temple as if it would burst. (Constriction in l. temple and above orbit.) Pain externally on parietal bone as from a thrust with a dull point. Sticking in vertex. Feeling as of a band across the top of H. from ear to ear, with headache, < moving, and throbbing pain behind l., then r. ear. Pain in occiput and nape from moving head; tensive P. in O. and nape, extending to shoulders.

Clinical.—Neuralgic headaches. Bursting headaches or bruised feeling in the head, with symptoms of indigestion. The most characteristic indication in the head is the bruised or crushed feeling extending into the root of the tongue, with nausea and vomiting.

Eyes.—Inflammation. Tearing, < r., extending towards temple, on opening r. lids, which were swollen, copious gush of tears, conjunctiva of bulb infiltrated, tunica vaginalis swollen, cornea dim as if infiltrated, small depressions, iris congested and dull-looking, pupils contracted, reacting but little in the light, vision lost, after pounding Ip. again these symptoms appeared in l. eye, with nausea. Raging pain, < r., waking at 3 A.M., with much lachrymation and loss of vision. Biting and pressing pain, < r., < light, which blinded him, conjunctiva red and chemosed, lachrymation, vision lost, with l. eye he saw fiery rings with rainbow colors. Tensive pain waking at night, with lachrymation and loss of vision. Uneasiness, with congestion of palpebral and ocular conjunctiva. Scalding lachrymation. *Pupils dilated.* Pain in balls as if forced out of their orbits, with foggy vision. Conjunctivæ injected. *Hardened mucus in external canthi.* Lids, < r., swollen. Dryness of lids, with sleepiness.

Clinical.—Granulations of the lids are reported cured by the instillation of the dilutions. Subacute inflammation of the cornea, with intense pain and great photophobia. Extremely valuable in pustular conjunctivitis, especially in children. Inflammation of the eyes, with tearing pain and gushes of tears. Violent neuralgia of the eyeballs, shooting into the head, with gushes of tears, nausea, etc.

Ears.—Pain extending from concha into drum, then to occipital protuberance. Dull hearing with r., and pressure in it.

Nose.—Mucous membrane of N., mouth and throat irritated, dyspnœa, nostrils impervious to air, I had to sit erect and gasp for breath, yellow water ran from nostrils, soon changing to bloody serum, mouth and throat inflamed and discharging thick mucus, then free vomiting, with some relief, but for three weeks cough and tenderness of chest. Titillation in nostrils. Dryness, and in frontal sinuses. Catarrh; with drawing pain in all limbs; feeling of dry C., as if nostrils were too dry. *Sneezing; with thin mucus; violent; violent, paroxysmal, with cough and expectoration. Bleeding.*

Clinical.—Catarrh or acute coryza, with frequent hæmorrhages from the nose, associated with bronchial catarrh, loss of smell, etc.

Face.—*Pale, sunken; P. and puffed: P., with blue rings around eyes* and weakness. Red. Yellow. Anxious and livid. Biting on lips; on margins of lips and on tip and sides of tongue, with watery salivation and colic. Excoriated sensation in corners of lips when touched and on moving lips.

Mouth.—Paroxysmal pain as if teeth would be torn out; P. as if hollow tooth would be torn out on biting anything, then constant tearing. Biting on margin of tongue. Burning of tongue and upper lip. Sensation on back of tongue and on palate as from chewing liverwort or Artemesia dracunculus, which increases saliva. Burning extending down throat and bronchia, with dyspnœa. Dryness, < at top of œsophagus, with rawness. Sensitiveness. **Salivation; and obliged to swallow constantly**; with nausea; thin; saliva runs from mouth on lying down. Taste flat; to beer; nauseous T. to customary tobacco-smoke, causing vomiting; T. in throat as from rancid oil, on swallowing.

Throat.—Sensation as if he had drunk melted lead, and in stomach, causing rolling about the floor, > vomiting induced by drinking warm water, then asthma. Stitches transversely through T. into inner ear; S. in œsophagus. Soreness; of pharynx, mucous membrane of velum and pharynx injected, with many hæmorrhagic points. Spasmodic contractive sensation, and in chest. Dryness; causing inclination to cough; of fauces, with constriction of glottis; pain in œsophagus as if dry, raw and sore, transiently > swallowing saliva or drink; dry, burning sensation, almost suffocation. Swallowing painful, as from swelling at top of œsophagus; S. difficult, as from paralysis of tongue and œsophagus.

Stomach.—Loss of thirst. *Eructations; with rumbling in abdomen;* empty. **Nausea; with empty eructations and salivation** (Cupr., Puls.); **distressing**; with convulsive but ineffectual retching; (with hiccough) after customary tobacco-smoking, > several stools, the last of which was pasty; (with heaviness in abdomen); intermittent. Empty retching. **Vomiting**; on stooping, with feeling as if he would fall; frequent; of everything swallowed (Eupt. perf.); of food (Ferr., Nux v.); of food on stooping; of yellow, green and black mucus. Rumbling. Sticking in pit. Griping. *Feeling as if it hung down relaxed* (Sep.), *and appetite lost.* Sensation of emptiness and laxity (Sep.). Warmth; agreeable, with rumbling in intestines.

Clinical.—The gastric symptoms generally are indicated by persistent nausea and aversion to all food; this nausea accompanies the various hæmorrhages which call for Ipec. The vomiting is generally free, consisting largely of mucus, sometimes of blood. The nausea and vomiting are more frequently the result of nervous irritability than of inflammation of the stomach, so that the drug has often relieved the distressing symptoms of pregnancy; the nausea is a marked indication for the drug in malarial fevers, etc. Gastric catarrh from injudicious eating or drinking, with white-coated tongue, or sometimes with perfectly clean tongue. Obstinate vomiting of blood (Ferr., Phos.), extremities cold, countenance hippocratic, pulse feeble, the ejecta sometimes black, tarlike.

Abdomen.—Distention. Griping; *clawing G. as if grasped by a hand so that each outstretched finger pressed sharply upon intestines, > rest, < motion.* Pinching. (Sticking, with burning and sticking in rectum and urging to stool.) Colic; with rumbling and with warmth extending into chest, at times with sticking; flatulent; on coughing P. as if obliged to urinate and urine could not pass, as in retention of urine. Nausea, with incipient colic. Uneasiness. Tearing about umbilicus. *Cutting about umbilicus, with shivering;* C. at side of U., < touch, with white, frothy saliva and dilated pupils; C. about U. as before menstruation, with chilliness, but internal heat mounting to head. Pain in umbilical region, < pressure. Sticking in l. hypochondrium; in r. flank. *Pinching in hypochondria and region of pit of stomach.*

Anus.—Sticking; S., cutting, burning pain on margin, as in obstinate hæmorrhoids. Crawling as from thread-worms.

Stool.—Diarrhœa; *as if fermented.* Thin, frequent, with qualmishness in abdomen; (T., with burning sticking in rectum and anus.) Soft. **Frequent, of greenish mucus** (Arg. nit., Mag. c., Merc. dul., Puls.). *Bloody;* covered with bloody mucus. Offensive. (Porraceous.) (Lemon-yellow.)

Clinical.—Green, mucous diarrhœa. Dysentery, in some cases with dark, pitchlike blood. Autumnal diarrhœa, green or fermented light-yellow stools. Cholera infantum, stools light green, with nausea and vomiting. With the diarrhœa frequently flatulent colic and a distressed relaxed feeling in the abdomen, with the peculiar nausea and vomiting of the drug. Cholera infantum, with green, frothy stools, colic, hot head, etc.

Urinary Organs.—(Discharge of purulent fluid from urethra of a child, with biting pain.) Frequent desire; with scanty urine. (Frequent micturition of straw-yellow urine, with burning and urging before the discharge.) *Red, scanty urine.* Urine bloody.

Clinical.—Hæmaturia, especially from the kidneys, with nausea and cutting pains.

Sexual Organs.—Voluptuous itching when standing. Sticking in testicles when resting one thigh over the other. Twisting drawing pain in testicles. *Dragging towards uterus and anus. Menstruation fourteen days too* *soon.* The bloody discharge at close of menstruation was suppressed.

Clinical.—Menstruation very early and profuse, bright red, with colic and nausea. Threatening miscarriage, with bright red blood and cutting colic. Hæmorrhage following miscarriage or parturition, with persistent nausea, faintness and gasping for breath. Hæmorrhage in placenta prævia.

Respiratory Organs.—Rattling in bronchi during respiration. Bronchial catarrh, with exhaustion. Dryness of larynx, with burning and scraping. Hoarse. **Suffocative cough; whereby the child becomes stiff and blue in the face. Cough, causing inclination to vomit, without nausea**; *C. from constrictive tickling, extending from upper part of larynx to lowest end of bronchi; dry C., from tickling in upper part of larynx;* incessant C. after walking in cold air, and after lying down in morning and evening, caused by deep inspiration, with pain as if umbilicus would be torn out, heat in face (head) and sweat on forehead; violent and convulsive C.

Expectoration of blood (Ferr., Phos., Acon., Cact.); catarrhal E.; E. of lemon-colored viscid phlegm in balls, and traces of blood (Puls.). In morning on stirring about after a night's rest from cough, mouthfuls of mucus were thrown up, looking like a mass of nearly transparent worms, but they were real casts of bronchial tubes (see Calc. acet.).

Asthma; spasmodic, with constriction of throat and chest, **with peculiar wheezing** (Ferr.); sudden, with dyspnœa and oppression of præcordia; generally beginning with irritation of nasal membrane and rapidly extending to bronchi and all their ramifications; sudden paroxysms, with inability to lie down, preceded by tickling in nose and sneezing. *Suffocation* (Ferr.); suffocative constriction of air-passages and pharynx, with pallor and anxiety for air (Ferr.). **Dyspnœa** (Ferr., etc.); in evening; from 10 P.M. till 10 A.M.; > expectoration, **with wheezing, and weight and anxiety about præcordia** (Ferr.); *with constriction across chest, violent and convulsive cough* (Cact.), sneezing, till face became anxious and livid; D. or suffocative stricture of chest and oppression at præcordia (Cact.). Difficult breathing, with sense of suffocation and dry, hacking cough. Sudden attack of short breath, with wheezing. Breathing rapid, difficult, without aid of auxiliary muscles, and noisy, with sharp, vesicular respiration all over lungs, with loud whistling and râles. Tetanic convulsions of respiratory muscles (instead of the ordinary wheezing) like "holding the breath," with sighs at long intervals. Simultaneous imperfect efforts to breathe, cough and vomit, causing indescribable suffering, irregular spasm of all muscles of chest and abdomen, every effort to vomit interrupted by an attempt to cough, necessity to be supported in an erect position, and to have the windows open, > appearance of eruption. Thorax arrested in expiration, speech and cough impossible, in the open air he was able to inspire, sneezed and coughed without expectoration.

Clinical.—Spasm of the glottis, with rapid alternations of contraction and relaxation of the vocal cords. Spasmodic asthma. Capillary bronchitis of infants, with mucous râles, spasmodic cough, vomiting (the patient is not so prostrated and cold as when requiring tartar emetic). Bronchitis, with great accumulation of mucus, especially in the larger tubes, violent paroxysms of coughing, retching and vomiting and expectoration of large quantities of mucus. Cough, with threatening suffocation. Violent spasmodic cough, sometimes quite dry, caused by suffocative feeling as from sulphur fumes, the patient becomes blue in the face, with coughing (Cupr.). Whooping cough, with retching and vomiting (Cupr.). Whooping cough, so violent that the child seems to lose its breath entirely and has hæmorrhages from the nose or from the lungs. Hæmorrhages from the lungs in tubercular cases, with gasping for breath. Hæmorrhages from the lungs, with sensation of bubbling in the chest and expectoration of frothy mucus.

Chest. — (Griping [jerking-tearing ?] beneath r. shoulder.) Sore pain internally. Pressure. *Oppression* (Ferr.); *in forenoon, with short breath, as from dust;* after eating. *Constriction* from evening till 9 A.M., *with short and wheezing respiration, necessity to open the window and gasp, pallor, scarcely perceptible pulse and apparent danger of suffocation,* then cough, with expectoration of thick, metallic-tasting mucus. Contractive sensation beneath short ribs. Uneasiness.

Heart and Pulse.—Pricking pain in heart. Palpitation. Rapid pulse.

Back.—(Pinching between scapulæ on motion.) Cramplike pain shooting from r. kidney down r. thigh to knee.

Extremities.—Cracking of joints. Shocks through all when she wishes to sleep. *Bruised pain in all bones* (Eupt. perf.). *Pain in all joints, as if limbs were asleep.* Pressive and spasmodic pain in hollow of r. knee and in l. arm, < touch. Drawing pains in humerus and femur in evening after lying down. Spasmodic contractions of arms. Pinching in r. arm. Pain in l. arm near wrist; as if bone were bruised, then in r. Twitching of lower. Weariness of lower. Pinching in l. hip, extending from crest of ilium to great trochanter. Sprained pain in l. knee, < walking, > sitting. Pain in knee as if tendons and ligaments were wearied by a long walk. Twitching and crawling in muscles of calf, as if asleep. Sticking in r. tibia. Pinching in r. foot. Weariness of feet.

Skin.—Erysipelatous eruption covering every part, in fiery circular patches, varying from the size of a sixpence to that of the palm of hand, elevated with rounded edges, with burning. (Nettle-rash on forehead, extending into hair and to cheeks.) (Tetter on wrist and about anus, itching most in evening and after lying down, after scratching red pimples.) Papulæ and vesicles on a deep red base of irregular extent, they became flat, pustular and confluent, with external heat and tingling in the part, pustules became covered with scablike scales, which fell off and left no mark. Formication on calf.

Sleep.—Frequent yawning; Y. after eating, with stretching. Sleepiness; after vomiting; with weariness; with lassitude in all limbs. *Starts up in sleep.* Sleep with half-opened eyes. Sobbing fearfulness during sleep. Uneasy sleep; with moaning. Frequent waking and frightful dreams. Vivid unremembered dreams.

Fever.—Coldness; all night, preventing sleep; *C., then heat, then sweat; external, with internal heat;* beneath skin, < sitting in a warm place; C., feverish and thirsty. *Shivering at* 4 P.M., *then chilliness without thirst;* S., with yawning; S., with eructations; S. coldness in limbs as if startled. Coldness of one hand; of hands, with moisture; hands and feet cold and wet with cold sweat, one cheek pale, the other red, miserable in mind and weak in body, with dilated pupils.

General heat in evening; suddenly about 4 P.M., with sweat on arms and back; (external H. without internal). Heat in head, on forehead and cheeks in afternoon and evening, without thirst; H. in head and over whole body, with cold hands and feet, as heat increases to its greatest severity sweat breaks out on trunk and head, with biting and itching, < neck; H. of cheeks, even perceptible externally, without redness; (H. of face, with redness of it, without thirst). (Sweat); about midnight.

Clinical.—It has been found valuable in intermittent fever, the paroxysms characterized by persistent nausea, especially with the chill and fever, frequently with raging headache, nearly always with great thirst, but the water taken is apt to be vomited; it is to be compared with Eupatorium; Eupat., however, lacks the persistent nausea of Ipec. and Ipec. lacks the bone-pains of Eupat.; besides, the paroxysms of Eupat. are only partially developed, while those of Ipec. are perfectly developed, as a rule. (They are very similar.)

Iris Versicolor.

A tincture is made of the fresh root of Iris versicolor, L.

General Action.—It produces nausea and vomiting, is an active cathartic and diuretic, and stimulates the liver, increasing the flow of bile.

Allies.—Aloe, Sulph., Sang., Bry., Pod., Phyto.

Generalities.—Malaise with the neuralgia. Feeling as if he had taken cold, with lameness of trunk and lumbar region. Languor; in morning on rising; in afternoon, with feverishness.

Mind.—Irritable; in morning on waking. Displeased with everybody and everything, then lively and active. Depressed. Despondency, thinking that he is going to be very sick, alternating with disposition to laugh at his fears. Dulness of mind and special senses. Inability to fix mind. Memory weak.

Head.—Aching; *in morning after being in cold air and on quick motion, < forehead and vertex, as if top of head would come off, < cough; with pain in bowels; with depression of spirits and debility; nervous, gastric, in forenoon; stunning, with neuralgia; dull, stupid. Fulness. Heaviness, with dulness of eyes and pain over l. superciliary ridge. Dulness* (resembling vertigo). Feeling as if brain were partially narcotized, then cutting through temples. Intoxicated feeling at 7 A.M. Dizziness; with pressure in forehead; then lightness of head; sudden; sudden, when walking in-doors.

Forehead.—Pain; over eyes; at 6 P.M., and in posterior fontanelle; in evening, with occasional vertigo; intermittent; changing from side to side; dull, heavy (Sulph.). Tightness across. Sensation of a band across (Carbol. ac.), on attempting to laugh and preventing laughing.

Temples.—Shooting; through; from r. to l. part of occiput. Cutting through T., with dim vision. Sharp pains. Pain; in r., then it passed over vertex and behind l. ear; heavy.

Pain in vertex. Boring in r. parietal protuberance, causing him to bend head. Pain in r. parietal protuberance, becoming a hammering pain, < movement, > continued movement, returning during rest. Stitching in lower part of occiput, < r. side. Pain at posterior fontanelle. *On vertex, twenty-six pustules* tender to touch, on inflamed base, with red streaks running from one to another, and containing yellow matter. Constrictive feeling in scalp.

Clinical.—Neuralgic headaches are very frequently cured by this drug; they are generally one-sided, are associated with gastric symptoms, are, as a rule, periodic, occurring every few days, are nearly always associated with blurring of vision and frequently with vomiting; the pain usually begins over one eye.

Eyes and Ears.—Eyes sunken. Conjunctiva red. Lachrymation; with burning pain in r. inner canthus. Pressure towards and out at ears. Throbbing pain in mastoid processes in afternoon, > warmth of hand, then tingling. Tender feeling in mastoid process on moving jaws, extending half way down jaw along edge of bone.

Nose.—Sharp, raw, excoriating feeling in both nares, with constant inclination to blow nose, free discharge of mucus, constant sneezing, bronchi similarly affected. Stuffed-up feeling in nasal sinuses and posterior nares with discharge of thin clear mucus, snuffing and sneezing. *Sneezing.*

Face.—Flushed. Appearance of anguish. *Neuralgia in r. side, waking, < infraorbital nerve, with stitches in two carious teeth, next day facial neuralgia involving supra and infraorbital and superior maxillary and inferior dental nerves began after breakfast, with stupid stunning headache, next day began after breakfast, with malaise and headache, next day soreness where the neuralgia had been* (Bry.). Lips dry and cracked.

Mouth.—Toothache; in warm room. Teeth sore; and feel elongated. Elongated and sore feeling in molars, with heavy pain. Swelling of gums on inner side of l. lower molars. Tongue coated white. Tongue and gums feel greasy or slimy in morning. Feeling of a greasy coat on mouth and tongue in morning. Tongue feels thick at 7 A.M. **Mouth and tongue feel scalded** in morning; in mouth at 4 A.M., tongue rough and thick. Raw feeling on roof behind incisors, < cold or hot drinks, eating, touching with tongue, < onions or cheese, with feeling as if skin of that part hung loose, the rugæ of mouth enlarged, pale, and two on r. side excoriated, afterwards the rawness and feeling of loose skin extended to throat, afterwards rawness behind incisors after eating cherries in morning. Soreness of hard palate; < touch of tongue or solid food, with roughness, with pain in a defective filled tooth, which felt too long and was tender when used. Feeling as if on fire, and in stomach; in back part of mouth and fauces in afternoon, with flow of saliva. Burning and smarting of palate and fauces. **Profuse saliva** (Merc.); *ropy S.* (Phyto.) *drops from mouth during conversation.* Taste peppery; on forward half of tongue, and acid; acrid T.; flat; flat at 7 A.M.; bad; lost.

Throat.—Tonsils, uvula and soft palate bright red and larger vessels engorged. Rawness. Soreness, and of chest; S., < around epiglottis, with raw feeling, hoarseness, stuffed up, smarting in posterior nares, as from a recent cold, increased secretion in nose. Roughness, with running of saliva. Burning; in fauces; in fauces during expiration; in fauces, palate, tonsils and back of tongue, < expiration, > inspiration; in fauces on inspiration, extending to tip of tongue, < expiration. Heat in fauces, soft palate and tonsils, changing to smarting and burning. Smarting of soft palate, with burning and scratching, increasing to fiery heat, spreading over fauces, upward towards nares and far into œsophagus, the throat felt three times as large as usual and like a fiery cavern, the B. temporarily > drinking water, enlarged bright red vessels on uvula, palate and posterior wall of fauces. Swallowing difficult when eating, food sticks in pharynx. Spasms of œsophagus, with inability to swallow, food sticks in throat, with choking and gagging. Burning in œsophagus; with nausea.

Stomach.—Appetite increased; lost; lost at dinner. *Frequent empty eructations;* empty, with pain in stomach; empty, sour; of sour food. *Nausea;* in evening, obliging him to lie down; at 6 P.M., with empty eructations. Retching, resulting in little more than forcible eructation. Vomiting; *of sour fluid.* Rumbling, with uneasiness, lumpy, brown, offensive diarrhœa, with little pain. Pinching in pit. Pain before breakfast; P. after drinking cold water; twisting P. Heartburn, a hot cramplike sensation rising from pit. *Burning distress in epigastric region* (Sang.), cold water does not reach it; in region of pancreas in afternoon and evening. Distress; in epigastric region; in epigastric region, with restlessness and fright, with copious watery stool, then > nearly two quarts of water tinged with bile running out in a continuous stream. Fulness, > empty eructations. Uneasiness in pit, with rumbling in lower abdomen, increased till lower part of sternum seemed to protrude.

Clinical.—Nausea and vomiting of pregnancy, with tenderness over the stomach and profuse ropy saliva (see Ip.). Nausea, with profuse salivation during headaches. Dyspepsia, with severe burning distress in the stomach, vomiting of food, headache, etc. (comp. Sang.).

Abdomen.—Rumbling. Fetid flatus; in afternoon. Flatulence. Neuralgic pains. *Griping* at 6 P.M.; with soreness of surface; with several light, acrid stools; with profuse light-colored, prostrating diarrhœa. Pain; in afternoon, > night; > *discharge of flatus; in evening and night,* > *bending forward,* with loss of appetite and restlessness at night; with heat, soreness, as after cold, and premonitions of diarrhœa. Nausea like beginning of seasickness. Faintness as if intestines revolved in wrong direction.

Pain in r. hypochondrium when walking. Rumbling in umbilical region in afternoon; R. in U. and hypogastric regions, with desire for stool, soft, painless stool; R. in U. and hypogastric regions, waking at 4 A.M., with distress and desire for stool, copious watery stool, which could not be retained a moment without pain, at 8 A.M., another watery stool, with rumbling. Intermittent pain in U. region at 5 P.M. Uterine pain in shocks from U. to epigastric region, then nausea, straining, belching of wind, with commotion and rumbling above seat of pain. Pain above crests of ilia; along posterior part of r. crest; P. in r., then l. flank in afternoon, with urging to stool.

Clinical.—Flatulent colic, with constipation, especially in children. Derangements of the liver, with yellow eyes and skin, numbness of r. arm, nausea, headache, etc. Bilious colic, almost incessant vomiting of extremely acrid substances, with soreness over the liver. Soreness over the region of the liver, with cutting pains and vomiting of bile, which is very acrid and burns the œsophagus.

Rectum and Anus.—Burning in anus after stool (Aloe, Sul.). **Anus sore** *in morning, as if points were sticking in it* (Ign., Æsc.). *Distress in anus as if prolapsed.* Disposition to stool, with burning in anus. Urged to a second stool by sensation as if wind distended rectum, > discharge of a little greenish dark water, with burning in anus (see Aloe and Sulph.).

Stool.—Frequent, watery, with burning in anus (Bry.), *disposition to strain and bear down* (Sulph.), pain in epigastric and umbilical regions, rumbling in abdomen, faintness, knees weak and trembling, sometimes with blood and mucus, once with water and undigested food, at last mucous membrane of anus prolapsed and *smarting,* abdomen tender to pressure, flying pains through abdomen. *Watery, through the day.* Six dysenteric, at night, with pain and rumbling in lower abdomen (Sulph.). Diarrhœa; after breakfast, then pain in epigastrium; then pain in umbilical region; with colic; with rumbling and cutting in hypogastrium; sudden, after supper. Mushy, copious, light-colored. Papescent; with rumbling in abdomen; with pain in umbilical region; painless, with rumbling; *yellow, painless, with rumbling,* also large. *Constipation.* Hard, lumpy. Greenish-black, twice in one day.

Clinical.—Diarrhœa, with burning in anus as if on fire and burning all through the gastro-intestinal tract, the stools are generally very thin, preceded by colic. A very valuable remedy for constipation, especially with recurring sick headaches and gastric symptoms.

Urinary Organs.—Cutting in urethra at beginning of micturition; C. during micturition, with sticking and with coldness and itching of genitals, the I. < scratching. Strangury. Micturition frequent, copious, limpid; M. twice in the day. Urine high-colored. Urine thick, of strong odor, deep amber-colored (from excess of uric acid), discharged with effort, but without pain. Copious U.; and offensive. Scanty U., with burning in urethra after micturition; afterwards frequent and copious micturition; scanty and high-colored; S., red, then burning along urethra; S. and of strong odor, dark and thick in morning, passed without force and after straining.

Sexual Organs.—Glans swollen and red. Emission at night; with amorous dreams. Menses three days late and scanty.

Respiratory Organs.—Much hawking and clearing of larynx; frequent and painful H. of tough mucus from larynx. A lump of mucus rattled up and down trachea, it was expectorated with a sweetish, offensive taste at 10 A.M., obstruction and catarrhal soreness of air-passages, frequent hawking, cough, with soreness in trachea and tickling. Hoarseness; with sharp, acrid feeling near epiglottis. Short, dry cough from tickling in larynx; hacking C. in morning without expectoration, with soreness in larynx anteriorly. Expectoration of phlegm in morning. Short breath.

Chest.—Rattling of mucus not to be raised by hawking. Cramp in l. side under ribs; in l. side like a knife, then darting pain in abdomen. Pain in l.; as if ribs were pressing upon lower part of lung, inability to take a long breath for the sticking cutting in l. lung; P. in pectoralis major, < during motion and in evening. Constriction; about sternum; at middle of sternum. Soreness from nipple to nipple in morning, with tender painful spot on r. border of sternum and pain on inspiration. Tickling under top of sternum, waking at night, with cough dry and distressing, because nothing could be raised nor the tickling be reached, rattling of phlegm low in œsophagus.

Heart and Pulse.—Heart's action increased in force and frequency. Pulse rapid; and feeble. Pulse slow and labored.

Neck.—Soreness of muscles; with harshness.

Back.—Pain; < walking. Stiffness in morning, < on sitting down. Weariness. Pain behind l. scapula. Stiffness of trapezius; all forenoon, causing constant shrugging of shoulders and desire to twist head from side to side; S. of r. latissimus dorsi on motion. Tearing in lumbar region on rising, so that he can become erect only gradually. Crampy pain in r. loin in evening, causing sweat. Pain in r. kidney. Pain in lumbar region all day while sewing; P. in lumbar region, < motion; and in sacral region, so that it is almost impossible to walk; heavy P. Weakness in lower part of back.

Extremities.—Tearing in r. hip, knee and shoulders. Pain through the day; neuralgic P. like constriction around l. upper arm, forearm and thigh; rheumatic, in r. arm and r. knee, < motion; stinging, rheumatic, in elbows, forearms and knees; tensive, in all joints, mostly the smaller, shifting about rapidly, < from supper till bed-time.

Upper Extremities.—Stinging in r. shoulder; *during motion, < raising arm, with tension. Rheumatic pain in r. shoulder, < motion, especially raising arm.* Sharp pains in shoulders, arms, < l. index. Sharp pain near outside of l. arm on moving it. Lameness of upper arm, with soreness to touch, the L. soon extended to shoulders and nape, like rheumatism after taking cold, the L. and stiffness > night. Cutting in elbows and biceps, with contusive lame feeling. Heaviness of hands and elbows as after wine; H. of hands and elbows, with pains between shoulders, which settle in r. upper arm. Pain in metacarpal joints of hand and in muscles of r. arm, < motion and evening.

Fingers.—Shifting shooting in phalangeal and metacarpo-phalangeal joints, < evening and motion. Cutting in metacarpo-phalangeal joint of r. thumb. Sharp pain along l. side of first. Sharp pain along l. side of first phalanx of r. middle, then in l. middle fingers, then in l. axilla, occurring frequently. Pain; in last joint of l. middle; in r. phalanges when writing, and in end of r. index.

Lower Extremities.—Weakness and pain so that walking was almost impossible. Sciatic pain; frequent, *as if l. hip were wrenched* or forced to remain long in an awkward position; S. twinges as if hip were wrenched, then burning aching; S. twinges behind l. trochanter in morning when writing, with lameness. *Coxalgia in l. hip* in evening on walking. Pain in l. hip; when walking; in l. thigh. *Painful drawing and lameness behind l. trochanter, extending to popliteal space* in evening, causing limping. Sudden rheumatic lameness in femoral region posteriorly in morning when exercising, causing limping, then shooting posteriorly down thigh to foot on every motion, < walking, > 4 P.M., next morning pain in l. sciatic nerve only on walking, with increased soreness and with weakness of l. leg, violent exercise does not increase the pain more than moderate exertion. Pain when walking in r., then l. knee. Knees weak and trembling. Pain in calves when walking, < r. Sticking in r. foot. Sharp pain in first joint of r. great toe when walking.

Clinical. — Sciatica of the l. side, of a burning character, shooting down to the foot, greatly < motion (Bry.).

Skin.—Pimples like mosquito-bites; pimple on l. middle finger, next day the inflammation extended over hand, then great pain, it was opened but no pus found, but it afterwards formed and discharged through the opening, which penetrated as far as bone, a funguous growth around edges had taken place meanwhile, pain extended up arm, appearance of a malignant boil, disposition to a similar formation on index, sweat with the pain in finger. Boils on back, face and hand. Vesicles on r. wrist, which formed into pustules, depressed in centre, then crusts. Itching of face, < warmth from exercise.

Clinical.—Herpes zoster of r. side; psoriasis, eczema; impetigo of the head; all these symptoms associated with the gastric degrangements and other symptoms of the drug.

Sleep.—Sleepiness; with chills down back; with dulness and dizziness; in daytime, fell asleep when reading, dreamed of dissecting a woman who was hanging by the heels in my office, woke frightened, tried to get up to shut the door but could not, real nightmare. Night restless; with dreams of fighting, etc.; with awful dreams of the dead; with dreams of digging up corpses, and finally fell into a grave which woke me in fright; with dreams of snakes and everything bad; with amorous dreams and emissions. Sleep disturbed by startings. Early waking; with dry mouth and general depression. Frightful dreams. Dreams of suffocation.

Fever.—General chill at night. Heat; with itching in varions parts; general, then chill, with cold hands and feet; of skin; of head, with flushing of face; of hands all day, with dryness of them; of palms. General sweat, < in groins.

Jaborandi.

A tincture is prepared from the dried leaves and stems of Pilocarpus pinnatifolius, Lem., which contain the alkaloid Pilocarpine.

General Action.—The most remarkable property of this drug is *diaphoresis;* in a few minutes a flush of the face is followed by profuse perspiration and salivation (frequently if one of these is profuse the other is greatly lessened), which last for hours. It contracts the pupil and causes spasm of the accommodation. It stimulates the hair, making it coarse and often turning it dark.

Allies.—Agaricus, Physostigma.

Generalities.—Redness of face, throbbing of temporal arteries, then heat in mouth and on face, salivation, then sweat on forehead, cheeks and temples, incessant expectoration, sweat covering face and neck, then whole body red and moist, pleasant warmth, then general sweat, which soon runs down on all sides, then lachrymation and copious discharge from nose, increased activity of mucous glands of back of throat, trachea and bronchi, salivation so great that he can scarcely speak, salivary glands enlarged, sometimes accumulation in bronchi cleared away by cough, thirst, contracted pupils, after the sweat and salivation have ceased, prostration, drowsiness and dryness of the parts that have secreted so copiously, < mouth and back of throat, with much thirst.

Restlessness; in evening, with anxiety. Weariness; in morning, with dryness of mouth and thirst; on rising; from a short walk, with hurried breathing and palpitation; so that legs give way when walking. Faintness. Collapse.

Mind.—Confusion. Disinclination to speak.

Head.—Aching; every day about noon; about noon, with hurried breathing, pressure on chest, anxiety, palpitation and pain in region of heart; towards dinner-time (noon), not affecting appetite; < l. side, during sore throat; with suffocative feeling. Uneasiness; increasing in forenoon to pain in occiput, then extending to forehead, > late in afternoon. Empty feeling. Vertigo. Throbbing pain in vertex and front of head at 7.30 P.M.; sudden T. pain in vertex and forehead. Pain in lower part of occiput; extending over l. side of head to forehead; heavy, < l. side; pain in l. side of O. in evening.

Eyes.—Red spot near r. iris in morning, vascular appearance in both eyes as from cold or overwork. Cornea red after waking at 5.30 P.M. Lachrymation. *Pupils contracted; and tension of accommodative apparatus, with approximation of nearest and farthest points of distinct vision, amblyopic impairment of vision from diminished sensibility of retina;* P. dilated; P. sluggish. Balls sore on rolling them at 7.30 P.M. Lids stiff and heavy. Vision disturbed. V. changing constantly, becoming suddenly more, then less dim; dim, with pricking in eyes; dim, restored suddenly. *Blurred V. for distant objects.* Swimming of distant objects.. Clouds before vision. V. of snowflakes during the sweat and salivation. V. lost for distant objects.

Clinical.—Asthenopia of hypermetropia. Spasms of ciliary muscle in hypermetropia. It has relieved the asthenopia of cataracts. Convergent strabismus. Especially useful after operations for strabismus.

Nose and Face.—Nasal discharge. Redness of face; and of ears and neck; and of body; involving cheeks and ears, < when the sweat was greatest, then pallor; with heat of it and with throbbing of temporal arteries.

Mouth.—Tongue furred. Articulation difficult and indistinct. Heat. Dryness. Salivation; with profuse sweat; with dry skin; stringy, but not very viscid; *constant spitting of alkaline saliva;* alkaline saliva flows upon pillow during sleep, causing collapsed feeling in glands in cheeks. Saliva contained a notable quantity of urea.

Clinical.—Profuse salivation during pregnancy.

Throat.—Swelling of submaxillary glands (Merc., Calc.). Pain in submaxillary glands. Dryness at back; dry and inflamed feeling in forenoon, with scraping on swallowing anything, the inflammation < afternoon, with swelling of tonsils and stiffness of jaws. Soreness and smarting, with headache, < l. side, and hurried breathing.

Clinical.—Mumps, especially when there is metastasis to the testicles.

Stomach.—Appetite. Hunger disappeared and he could not eat. Urgent thirst. Eructations and vomiting. Hiccough. Nausea; sudden, and retching, often with hiccough. Vomiting; after supper; sudden, in the lad who failed to perspire; of the saliva that he had swallowed; severe, of the contents of stomach, then of bile, then continued retching. Distress, and in lower half of œsophagus, especially the latter feels constricted; heavy D. at pyloric part at dinner-time, as from an indigestible substance, > a full meal. Constrictive feeling as if rugæ were puckered (probably owing to aclohol in tincture).

Abdomen.—Empty, gone feeling. Cutting in lower.

Stool.—Watery, yellow, frequent and painless; and undigested, gushing, weakening. Yellow, gushing. Papescent and large. First part five-eighths of an inch in diameter and about five inches long, the last part papescent and dark brown. Hard. Constipation, two stools a day instead of three. At 7 A.M. and again at 7 P.M. difficult, of long, large, dark fæces.

Urinary Organs.—Sudden shooting from bladder to urethra. Burning in urethra, with urging to urinate. Urine dark. Urine increased; during the sweat; and sp. gr. diminished, urea increased. Urine decreased; and sp. gr. and urea increased. Urea diminished, next day increased. Chlorine, chlorides and uric acid diminished, next day increased.

Respiratory Organs and Chest.—Bronchial secretions increased. Loose cough. Breathing difficult. Breathing hurried. Sticking in chest. Pain in chest and around heart. Pressure on chest, with anxiety, palpitation and pain in region of heart. Anxiety in chest, with oppression, preventing sleep.

Heart.—Pain in region. Palpitation. Irregularity, weakness and rapidity of action, with nervous, restless condition and constant yawning.

Pulse.—Rapid; then slow; at beginning of sweat, the tracing becomes a little crooked, the rising line larger and more upright, the descending line more oblique, more dicrotic, at the height of the sweat the general outline very irregular, some beats shorter than others. P. rose (the reverse of temperature), returned to normal rate, with return of normal temperature, but was soft and compressible. P. and temperature increased during sweat, then lowered. Tracings showed almost complete asystolia, with diminished vascular tension during sweat.

Sleep.—Sleepiness. Fell asleep while sitting reading. Profound sleep; in daytime. Most wretched night that he ever remembers, fever, headache, malaise, *no* thirst, restlessness, moving and delirium. Did not sleep well on account of restlessness, with pressure on chest and hurried breathing. Distressing dreams towards morning. Dreams of accidents and frights, waking him twice at night.

Fever.—Temperature sank. Chilly up and down back at 7 P.M. Shivering. Temperature 98.5°, in taking which he uncovered himself, this caused coldness, with horripilation and griping, but as soon as he covered himself again profuse sweat. Heat; temperature rose, then fell; internal, in face and over body; in face; in face, then extending over body. Profuse sweat; and finger-ends shrivelled like a washerwoman's; in drops on forehead; S. on forehead, then over whole body, then chiefly on face, legs and feet; S. on forehead and over whole body, < trunk, simultaneously with the salivation; on face; on face and upper part of chest; on face, then on whole body; on chest, then on other parts, < upper extremities. S. of neutral reaction running down all over body. S. contains urea. Perspired easily before taking, but did not sweat during the proving.

Clinical.—Flushings at the climacteric period, with profuse perspiration, cold extremities, nausea and vomiting.

Jalapa.

A tincture of the dried root of Ipomœa purga, Hayne, is used.

General Action.—An active hydragogue cathartic.

Allies.—Jatropha, Rheum, Coloc.

Uneasiness, with tossing about of limbs. Weakness. Fainting fits. Headache. Humming in ears. Stinging in tongue and fauces. Nausea and vomiting. Increased motion of stomach, sometimes with nausea, succeeded by increased activity of small intestines as far as region of cæcum, where there is seated illness, then motion in colon and its flexions till there is desire for stool, which occurs without great irritation and is not succeeded by any other irritation or desire, even if there be another looser stool. Pain in small intestines as if they would be cut to pieces. Inflammation of intestines. Anus sore. The first stool is always thick, reddish and sour. *Violent, excessive stools. Bloody stools. Several watery stools, then decrease of temperature; several watery S., then weak pulse.* Pulsations slower. Pain in thighs. Febrile attacks.

Clinical.—Coryza in an infant, violent attacks of crying and intense pain, quiet during the day, but screaming all night. Chronic diarrhœa, stools six or eight times a day, dark, offensive, like gruel, with much griping and some tenesmus; it is reported to have cured a diarrhœa that had lasted twenty years, stools sudden, watery, very offensive, generally with a little blood, much gas, tongue smooth, glazed and dry.

Jatropha.

A tincture of the ripe seeds of Jatropha curcas, L., is used.

General Action.—A violent hydragogue cathartic.

Allies.—Crot. tig., Jalap, Gamb., Elat., Verat. alb.

Generalities.—*Cramps; in evening; and twitchings, "calves were twisted around to shins"* (Cupr.); of extremities, afterwards extending to muscles of abdomen and back, and occasional twitchings of those of back, as in tetanus. Pains in lumbar muscles, chest and shoulder-joints; in l. ankle, l. upper arm, l. hypochondrium and l. inguinal region; in muscles of shoulders and back, in knees and calves, with weakness; indefinite P. in hypochondria and various parts of extremities. Pressure in muscles of back and l. upper arm; painful P. in lumbar, dorsal and pectoral muscles. Bruised feeling in muscles of back and chest. More susceptible to wine than usual. Restlessness; at night on account of rush of thought and palpitation. Weakness; in evening, with rapid and weak pulse; of vital powers; of vascular system; painful, of muscles on slightest exertion. Stiffness of muscles of nape and forehead. Aggravation of symptoms in muscles when sitting. Amelioration in open air. It is said that placing the hands in cold water will stop the effects (see Jalap.).

Mind.—Delirium and insensibility. During painful diarrhœa an ecstasy as if an ideal had appeared to a poetic painter, or like that which sometimes comes to a dying person, with bright eyes directed upward, a feeling of pleasant warmth and ethereal lightness. Anxiety, with burning in stomach and coldness of body; A. at night, constricting chest and preventing sleep till towards morning. Easily disturbed by anxious events. Little inclination for anything, laconic. Forgot the events of his illness, except the earliest symptoms.

Head.—Aching. Heaviness. Confusion; and almost loss of ideas; and stupefaction. Vertigo; on raising head, with pain; with restlessness. Sticking now in r., now in l. half of forehead. Frontal pain; with heaviness; externally, and pain on r. zygoma; in muscles; pain in l. frontal and temporal muscles. Pressure in temples. Pressure inward in temples; all day when in the house; extending to crown, > open air; *returning on entering house;* with throbbing pain, afterwards extending now and then to crown. Pressure in occiput.

Eyes and Ears.—Pupils contracted; dilated. Trembling of l. lid; upper. Itching of lids; *on margins,* > rubbing, *with smarting.* Vision of black points; of bright and dark spots. Sticking in l. ear; deep. Aching in r. ear. Roaring in ears. Difficult hearing. Deafness.

Nose.—Ulcers, and in mouth. Itching in nostrils when eating. Sensitiveness on drawing in air, which seems cold though it is warm. Sneezing; with catarrh and discharge from nose. Catarrh at noon, with heat of head; sudden C., with sneezing, running from nose, frequent copious discharge of mucus, which soon became alternately yellow and white, with paroxysms of cough, with difficult expectoration, but in the intervals frequent easy hawking of large lumps of mucus, with intermittent headache here and there.

Face.—Pale and anxious; P. in afternoon, with dark rings below eyes. Aching in r. zygoma; in l. zygoma, gradually extending to r. and ending with aching in r. ear; A. in masseter muscles; contractive A. in l. masseter muscles. Lips cracked and painful. Ulceration of r. corner of mouth, with smarting and tension. Soreness of l. corner of mouth. Itching of lips in morning, with tension.

Mouth.—Sticking in a hollow tooth. Drawing in l. incisors. Rheumatic drawing in a hollow tooth. Burning pain in tongue. Numbness of tongue. Dryness at night; D. without thirst, then all night and in morning feeling as if mouth had been burnt; dry sensation, then real dryness of M. and tongue all night without thirst, then feeling as if mouth had been burnt, < night. Burning, and in throat. Salivation; thin; much spitting of saliva with the stools; frequent spitting all the morning, with metallic, bloody taste. Insipid taste, < back of throat.

Throat.—Pain along l. jugular vein. Sticking, < swallowing. Scraping; < chewing. Pain; burning. Soreness; of soft palate. *Acrid feeling gradually extending to stomach, at last causing vomiting.* Dryness; of fauces; of upper part of T. and fauces, with thirst, but dread of drinking on account of nausea, after several hours vomiting of food, with short hacking cough. Burning. Swollen feeling.

Stomach.—Appetite diminished; lost. Thirst; in evening. Less longing for wine. Eructations; of air. Nausea; after eating; > eating (Verat. v.); with salivation; with burning in stomach; intermittent; peculiar, in pit of stomach. *Dreads to drink on account of nausea* (Verat. alb.). *Vomiting; easy, of much watery albuminous substance, with watery diarrhœa;* frequent; copious; violent, also with violent diarrhœa (Verat. alb.); of all food (a few hours after Maderia wine).

Rumbling. Cramplike stitches. Cramp on stooping. Cutting in S. and abdomen, < pressure. Pain; with pyrosis; < pressure; rising into œsophagus; extending paroxysmally towards umbilicus and into œsophagus; in epigastric region; intermittent; drawing; jerking, in epigastric region; burning. Sensitiveness of epigastric region, < pressure. Anxiety in pit. Heat; with cramp rising into œsophagus; with copious easy vomiting; in S. and bowels, with nausea; extending to spine, repeated in rapid succession. Sinking in pit, with nausea; after soft stool.

Abdomen.—*Distended; and soft;* and tympanitic; and tympanitic, tense; and soft, with pain deep in umbilical region on slight pressure. *Noises as of a liquid* (Crot. tig.); < l. side. *Noise as if a full bottle were emptied in evening, continuing after a thin stool at* 10 P.M. Rumbling; all day, > going into open air, returned in warm room and lasted all the evening and night; all night; after stool; with desire for stool; with emission of flatus; with pain in transverse colon; with pain shooting through deep in abdomen. Movements. Emission of flatus. Griping. Pain; in morning, with sensation of impending diarrhœa; in forenoon, with uneasiness in it and sinking feeling in stomach, as during violent diarrhœa; with heat in it; with desire for stool; < along spine, < pressure, with distention of abdomen and desire to urinate. Sensation as before stool, which, however, occurs only next morning.

Piercing pain in l. hypochondrium extending to lumbar muscles. Tearing deep in umbilical region, < pressure. Painful thrusts from umbilicus to lumbar region. Pain in umbilical region; in morning, with rumbling, emission of flatus and desire for stool; after soft stool; deep; extending into l. hypochondrium and l. chest. Crawling about U. in forenoon. Noises low down. Gurgling low down, with rumbling. Sharp pain in transverse colon. Aching in lower part, with inclination to stool. Pressure outward in l. inguinal ring on blowing nose. Peculiar tension in inguinal region. Feeling of tension and protrusion in l. inguinal ring on coughing or blowing nose, whereby l. leg is involuntarily flexed and drawn towards abdomen.

Rectum.—Soft hæmorrhoidal swellings. Stitches; in anus. Burning after stool. Violent crawling of worms in evening. Itching in anus at night in bed. Urging; to diarrhœa-like stool in morning; *sudden, with noises as of liquids in abdomen* (Crot. tig.), < *l. side.*

Stool.—At night. **Watery, spurting from him** (Crot. t., Elat., Gamb.); W., copious, then great relief; W., copious, mucous, frequent; copious, mucous, not unlike rice-water. *Thin, preceded and followed by rumbling* **and at times noise as if a bottle were emptied.** (Crot. tig.). *Diarrhœa; violent* (Verat. alb.); violent, with tenesmus; painless, with cramplike jerkings in calves. Soft; and frequent, with nausea and much spitting of saliva; without relief of colic, which was > emission of flatus; for several days, then constipation, with pressure inward in temples. Hard; after the proving, and scanty, delayed. Delayed. Small, and in half an hour another. Frequent.

Clinical.—An extremely valuable and too little used remedy for profuse, gushing, watery diarrhœa, sometimes associated with coldness of the body and unquenchable thirst, frequently with rumbling and gurgling in abdomen, at times with vomiting of large amounts of albuminous-looking substances; it may be compared with Verat., but, as a rule, it lacks the violent pain of that drug. Cholera Asiatica.

Urinary Organs.—Spasm of neck of bladder (with every attack of nausea), with drawing pain and desire to urinate; spasm of bladder beginning with twisting pain in umbilicus, which extends to neck of B., these attacks, like the nausea, gradually > between 6 and 7 P.M., they are preceded and followed by noises of liquids in abdomen and by sour eructations. Slow oozing of clear mucus from urethra when walking and sitting. Stitches in urethra. Tickling in navicular fossa, with frequent micturition. Urging; after micturition; frequent; constant. Dysuria. Difficult micturition. Urine bright yellow; and frothy. Urine copious; in evening after exertion; and watery. Urine scanty, dark brown, clear. (Urine white.) (Blood with urine.)

Clinical.—Irritation of the bladder, most violent urging to urinate, with inflammation of the whole urethra.

Sexual Organs.—Aching, < r. testicle, with diminished urine; A. as after excessive sexual intercourse; A. in l. testicle. Drawing pain extending along inner side of r. thigh to knee.

Respiratory Organs.—Painful pressure in r. side of larynx at night, waking him, not painful on touch. Hollow cough at night. Short hacking cough. Respiration difficult. Respiration quick and panting.

Chest.—Stitches behind cartilages of l. sixth and seventh ribs; S. downward deep behind sternum; sudden S. to l. of ensiform cartilage, behind costal cartilages, arresting breath. Pain in l. clavicle; deep behind sternum; in region of l. third rib, above and inside nipple; in r. pectoral muscles; in l. clavicle in forenoon; in l. pectoral muscles, making respiration difficult. Throbbing pain in l. clavicle in morning. Constriction, with attacks of anxiety, preventing sleep. Tension in middle of sternum.

Heart.—Sinking feeling in præcordial region, with nausea, then soft stool. Violent beating; when walking slowly about the room; suddenly. Action irregular and weak. Palpitation; after moving about.

Pulse.—Rapid; and strong; and hard; throbbing; and large, full, almost jerking; and weak. Slow; and full; and full, soft. Irregular, of normal frequency. Small, thready, intermittent. *Almost pulseless.*

Neck and Back.—Stiffness of nape; of muscles of nape. Pain in muscles across back; in l. rhomboid muscle, in region of fourth and fifth ribs; in region of sixth dorsal vertebra. Stitches in lumbar muscles. Feeling of a thrust in muscles of small of back when walking. Soreness of small of back; and in rectum, as in diarrhœa. Painful stiffness of lumbar muscles. Crawling beneath skin of sacrum.

Extremities—Spasms. Cramps in arms and legs; of hands and feet. Pain in l. calf, r. knee and r. wrist; on back of r. foot, on posterior surface of l. upper arm and in flexor surface of l. forearm; P. alternately in upper arms and r. calf, only when sitting; pressive and contractive P. in various parts, < in wrists, toes and calves; drawing P. in various parts, in part seeming to be under the skin.

Upper Extremities.—Pain in shoulder-joint; in l.; in r. shoulder, extending into hand, < along ulnar nerve; rheumatic P. in r., then l. shoulder. Bruised pain in shoulder-joints; B. and stiff feeling in shoulders. Drawing in muscles of l. shoulder. Bruised pain in muscles of arm. Pressure in muscles of r. upper arm. Weariness of upper arms. Pain in elbows extending to tips of fourth and fifth fingers, with numbness and burning, causing insensibility. Gnawing in ulnar nerve. Aching along l. ulnar nerve; from elbow to tips of fourth and fifth fingers. Internal pressure in flexor muscles of l. forearm. Drawing on back of l. hand. Pain in metacarpus of r. thumb, extending to wrist and hand; P. in first joint of r. index, extending to tip; in first joint of r. thumb, extending to wrist, in morning.

Lower Extremities.—Gait tottering, body inclined to l. in walking. Tearing in l. knee and malleolus. Pain in hollows of knees; r. knee and l. calf on walking slowly in the room. Bruised pain in knees; when sitting; extending into legs and becoming seated in ankles. Cramp of legs and feet. *Cramplike pain in legs,* **and cramp in calves,** *which become knotted* (Cupr.). Scraping on inner surface of l. tibia. Painful pressure in external muscles of legs, with internal crawling. Compression in muscles of l. leg, < lower part of calf. Painful weakness of legs, < knees. Stiffness of legs when walking, with unsteadiness.

Calves.—*Cramplike jerking, with painless diarrhœa;* internal jerking and pressure in l. C. and toes, more towards inner angle of tibia and on inner surface of tibia. Sticking. Pain; in l.; in l., < towards tibia, with stiffness; when walking, with internal drawing in legs; drawing pain in outer part of r.; bruised pain in outer part of r.; bruised feeling, < when sitting. Pulsation in l. Stiffness; of l.; when walking in room; of l. and back of l. foot, with pressure.

Pain in r. ankle; rheumatic P. in l., < forenoon. Sticking in l. sole and l. calf, with pressure; S. in l. sole when sitting, with jerking. Heels sensitive when stepping on them. Drawing on back of right foot; drawing in balls of feet; rheumatic D. in l. foot, extending into ball of great toe. Rheumatic pain in ball of r. foot in morning. Twitching inward of r. toes. Sticking in l. great toe. Tearing alternately in toes and on back of l. foot. Pressure and drawing in great toe and on back of l. foot.

Skin.—Pimples on wrist and back of r. hand; hard, on middle of r. cheek; sore painful P. on nape; sore painful P. on bend of r. thigh. Prickling on back of l. hand. Crawling on legs and feet; in toes; l. great toe. Itching between r. index and middle finger and on palm; between first and second fingers in morning, > rubbing; between toes at night in bed; around mouth, > rubbing, with tension; between thumb and index, < then > rubbing; internal I. in fingers, < l.

Sleep. — Yawning, with nausea, salivation and eructations. Drowsiness; after vomiting, with heat. Dropped asleep every half minute, but was easily aroused. He is scarcely able to wake in morning and afternoon, must force himself to move, after which he feels better. Waking at 2 A.M. on account of an angry conversation which he had had in the evening, then dream of the conversation. Sleeplessness, with throbbing of pulse; all night, with tossing about. Incessant dreaming.

Fever.—*Coldness,* with shivering, clammy sweat, vomiting and diarrhœa. Shivering; with cold finger-tips; with cold hands and blue nails; with cold feeling extending through abdomen, and the palms previously dry became moist and cold. Shivering in back; in spinal marrow; in region of lumbar vertebræ; creeping; up and down back; starting from lumbar vertebræ; deep in lumbar vertebræ, with desire for stool earlier than usual; extending into upper arms. Coldness in back; at times; deep in spine; extending into upper arms. Cold hands; and blue nails. Cold limbs; in evening; C. creeping through limbs, extending to scalp.

Heat; in evening. Hot skin, with rapid pulse and dry tongue. Heat in head; < sinciput; in occiput; in occiput, with confusion of it; in ears; in face; in face, as in catarrh; across back. Sweat; during sleep; profuse, general; cold.

Juglans Cinerea.

A tincture of the fresh, young, inner bark of the root of the "Butternut," collected in the spring, is used.

Generalities.—Loss of weight. Aching in various parts. Feeling as if all internal organs were too large, < l. side. Restlessness in afternoon, with pain in region of lumbar vertebræ. Weakness; with sick feeling. Faintness, > rising and moving about. Deathlike feeling, with chills and shuddering.

Mind.—Want to be alone, want to do nothing but eat and sleep, cannot think of concentrating my mind upon any one subject. Confusion so that I could not study. Dull feeling, cannot remember anything that I read. Absent-minded, forget what I am about.

Head.—Aching; in morning on waking, with yellow coat on tongue; in forenoon; in forenoon, < r. side; in evening; and I can hardly see; heavy, in morning. Feeling as large as a barrel. Vertigo at 11 A.M., with nausea; V., with faint feeling in stomach extending to abdomen. Fulness in frontal region. Pain in forehead; *in r. temple* in forenoon; *in occiput in morning, > rising.* Itching of scalp.

Clinical.—Occipital headache is said to be a characteristic of the drug.

Eyes.—Red and swollen. Burning in afternoon. Feeling as if drawn together. Loss of vision on sudden motion, with faintlike giddiness.

Nose.—Numbness at root; in bridge, > rubbing. Dryness. Watery discharge. Bleeding.

Face. — Pallor. Erythematous redness, with dry, burning sensation.

Mouth and Throat.—Tongue coated white; coated yellow in morning. Burning and pricking in mouth and throat. Taste coppery. Swelling of submaxillary glands, < *r.* Sore throat; in forenoon, with roughness; on swallowing; with swollen feeling. Fauces dry. Burning in pharynx. Pain in *r. side* of fauces.

Stomach and Abdomen.—Ferocious appetite. Thirsty, want to drink all the time. Nausea in morning; N. < night. Burning in stomach. Stitches in hepatic region. Pain in *each hypochondria;* in umbilical region; in abdomen after dinner, then diarrhœa, with burning in anus; in region of inguinal rings, with soreness on rising from a recumbent position; flatulent, in different parts of abdomen; heavy, in umbilical region. Burning in abdomen after stool.

Stool.—Bilious, copious, frequent, painless. *Diarrhœa,* with *cutting* in abdomen; D., with burning in anus before and after stool; painless, in forenoon; yellow, frothy, with tenesmus and burning in anus after stool. A drastic purge, producing irritation and inflammation of mucous membrane of bowels. Soft, with pain and flatulence in abdomen; S. and brown; and dark, sticky. Constipation; with griping in umbilical region. Hard, and in balls; H. and dark brown; and brown, difficult; first part H. and brown, latter part diarrhœic and greenish-yellow. Small and brown. Dark brown.

Urinary Organs.—Micturition frequent and copious; frequent, with burning and smarting.

Chest.—Expectoration of dark blood. Pain in l.; in centre at times, by day and night, with foreboding feeling at night; sharp wrenching, in l. side at 6 P.M., when walking, with suffocating sensation under sternum, compelling him to stand still, which did not alleviate the pain, the attack being similar to angina pectoris. Oppression; hindering long breathing.

Clinical.—Angina pectoris, with suffocative pain behind sternum, especially < walking, has to stand still.

Pulse.—Rapid.

Neck and Back.—Neck rigid. Lame feeling in nape. Pricking up and down spine. Sticking *under* *r. scapula* on stooping. Pain between scapulæ; under scapula; *under r. scapula*, making breathing difficult; under vertical border of *r. scapula*, < moving the part and drawing a long breath; in region of lumbar vertebræ and r. sacro-iliac symphysis; in region of lumbar vertebræ in afternoon, with restlessness; in lumbar and dorsal vertebræ at night; in region of sacroiliac symphysis, < sitting, also in forenoon, and in region of lumbar vertebræ; in lumbar vertebræ, extending through lumbar region and up spine. Occasional shooting in lumbar region.

Extremities.—Pain; *in shoulder;* r. axilla in afternoon; *r. axilla*, extending down arm; l. arm; elbows and knees; wrists, extending up arms; thighs and l. knee in forenoon; r. knee on ascending stairs; ankles; sharp, rheumatic, in shoulders and wrists; occasionally sharp, in calves; cramplike, in hip at night; arms and wrists, as if sprained by hard work; numb, in r. axilla, extending down arm along nerves; numb, in arms and wrists in forenoon. Numbness of l. foot when sitting still.

Skin.—*Exanthematous eruption resembling flush of scarlatina. Eruption resembling eczema simplex on upper chest, with itching pricking when heated by overexertion. Pustules on thighs, hips and nates, with itching and burning, a few pustules on body, face and arms. Itching in spots, now here, now there; I. on arms, > scratching, with burning; head, neck and shoulders, with pricking; arms, with burning and redness.*

Clinical.—Numerous cases of scarlatina; eczema; herpes circinatus; impetigo; lichen; erysipelas; erythema nodosum; ecthyma.

Sleep.—Constant yawning, without sleepiness. Sleepiness. Sleeplessness; after 3 A.M. Sleep restless; and light. Sleep unrefreshing. Dreams vivid; frightful; frightful all night, and waking covered with sweat; troublesome; of being among Indians; ridiculous.

Fever.—Chilliness alternating with flashes of heat; C. along spine; beginning in back when near the fire, without coldness of flesh.

Juglans Regia.

A tincture of the hulls of the unripe, green fruit and of the green leaves of the European walnut is used.

General Action.—The skin symptoms of this drug and of Juglans cinerea are worthy of careful study and more extended application. Note also the marked action of both drugs on the bowels.

Generalities.—Muscles relaxed. Exhaustion and disinclination for the usual business.

Mind.—Excited in evening in bed as if intoxicated, and feeling as if the head were floating in the air. Peevish and discontented in evening. Disinclined to talk or quarrel, as was customary with him, mentally indolent.

Head.—Aching; after dinner and in evening; with flushed face. Feeling in H. and nose as in beginning of coryza. Confusion. Heaviness. Vertigo. Lancinations in forehead. Frontal pain; in l. side; above l. eye, and pain in eyes; above eyes, < motion; < shaking head or moving eyes; with yawning and sleepiness; above eyes, as if dizzy. Throbbing in temples, > going into open air, returning on entering warm room, with sharp pain in front part of head. Migraine in a spot in region of l. parietal bone preventing speaking.

Clinical.—A valuable remedy for occipital headache; sharp shooting pains.

Eyes and Ears.—Burning in eyes. Aching and fulness in r., then l. ear, then discharge of pus from both ears, external ear inflamed and two painful sores on it. Burning in l. ear, then redness and swelling, then pimple on inside, then discharge of pus from both ears, < l., with burning and redness of l. external ear and feeling as if something dropped inside of ear at every step, and soreness preventing lying on l. side of head.

Face.—Swelling of l. cheek and upper lip, with swelling on gum over l. upper incisors, without previous toothache, then a hard reddish painful swelling in l. cheek, in the middle of which was a sharply-defined, depressed, dark red, yielding circle, pus could be seen through the thin skin, the apparently sound tooth was drawn and ichorous pus was discharged through the opening, then the swelling disappeared.

Mouth and Throat.—Tearing in hollow teeth, < warmth of bed. Tongue coated white; in morning, with bitter slimy taste. Tongue covered with white mucus. Salivation. Inclination to keep mouth dry after dinner, could not make up his mind to drink wine or water as usual. Taste bitter; T. slimy in morning on waking. Hawking of much mucus.

Stomach.—Appetite increased; lost. Aversion to tobacco-smoking in evening. Thirst increased. *Eructations;* violent; loud; tasting as after eating fat. Hiccough, more violent after eating. Nausea; at 6 A.M., and after supper. Vomiting; woke suddenly, vomited food eaten four hours before, then slept without further trouble. Burning. Pain in epigastric region, with distention of abdomen.

Abdomen.—Distention; after eating; after dinner, with emission of flatus; with sudden desire for stool; so that he must loosen his clothes, with pressure in stomach; so that he could eat but little in spite of good appetite; tympanitic. Rumbling; with griping; with pain in epigastric region. Emission of flatus; < lying. Pain; > eructations; wandering; pressive and drawing, < motion, > appearance of menses (fifteen days too soon), then for eight days (instead of three as usual) copious discharge of blackish blood, often in large clots, with exhaustion and loss of appetite; drawing pain. Drawing, with pressure in region of spleen. Tension.

Sticking beneath l. lowest ribs. Pressure in region of spleen, with eructations. Pain beneath l. false ribs, < deep breathing, laughing or stooping; P. in l. side on rapid walking; P. over l. side, with wandering gripings in intestines; P. above umbilicus; P. in hypogastrium, with nausea. Sticking in hypogastrium on moving or stooping. Cutting in r. hypogastric region.

Anus.—Sticking at night, preventing sleep and obliging him to get up.

Stool.—Liquid; twice a day; preceded or accompanied by pain in abdomen. Thin. Soft, large, at last almost thin. Hard; and difficult; and difficult, scanty, delayed. Constipation. Bowels confined in morning, natural stool in afternoon. Large, then burning pain and pressure in anus. Scanty and frequent. Difficult. Omitted.

Urinary Organs.—Frequent desire from loss of tone of sphincter. Constant urging and involuntary dribbling. Obliged to urinate at night. Obliged to urinate often; and much at a time. Copious urine; but no thirst. Urine scanty; and clear. Urine dark red.

Sexual Organs.—Frequent erections. Burning in penis after coition with his wife, with abrasion where prepuce joins penis, afterwards a suppurating streak half way around between glans and prepuce, then the ulcer became larger, margins hard, base lardaceous, bleeding on slight pressure, often there was a small scab, from beneath which pus oozed and which often came off and left a suppurating ulcer, afterwards a healthy scab formed in the middle and fell off, leaving healthy skin, so that instead of one long narrow ulcer there were two small round ones, these healed and left no scar.

Clinical.—Menses early, black.

Chest.—Sticking; in lungs, not dependent on motion or respiration. Oppression.

Pulse.—Rapid; and full.

Back.—Stitches in sacral region.

Extremities.—Drawing pain as if sprained, in first phalanx and joint of l. thumb, < motion, and while in bed the same pain in r. great toe. Sticking and itching in r. leg and r. fingers. Drawing and paralyzed feeling in legs and knees, with weakness and with giving away of knees when walking, and a similar sensation in r. hand. Electric starts in forearms and hands wake him as he falls asleep. Weak feeling in r. hand. Intermittent pain in r. index. Sticking in inner condyle of knee and feeling of impediment when walking. Rheumatic pain in knee impeding walking. Pain in r. instep when walking and sensation of impediment.

Skin.—Eruption behind ears of children. Itching eruption over the whole body. Pimples on face; red P. on face, neck, shoulders and back, some containing thickish fluid; P. on nape, discharging moisture when scratched (like acne). Itching here and there; on sternum; on hands; r. hand; dorsum of r. hand, then on feet, forehead, scalp and abdomen; r. fingers in afternoon; legs, arms and abdomen at night, with tossing about and inability to sleep; here and there, causing restless sleep, with dreams and erections; on flexor surface of r. forearm, near elbow, with burning and red spot in the middle of which was a pimple, the redness disappeared, but the pimple was painful and pus formed.

Itching in r. axilla, with burning, skin sore and cracked, then red and scaly, it became moist, on margin of tetter burning vesicles, the tetter aggravated after perspiring much, the perspiration, with the secretion from the eruption, stiffened the linen and stained it greenish-yellow, the pain sometimes so great that violent motion of arms was impossible, there were always new vesicles and larger extent of redness after increased burning and itching, the same trouble in l. axilla, then a furuncle on shoulder, on coracoid process, then a painful furuncle over biceps, with circumscribed redness and induration, discharging bloody matter, then two red itching spots on r. elbow, upon which a yellow pustule formed, a furuncle, with induration and pain, between ninth and tenth ribs, with thick, bloody discharge, leaving an induration, about this time a red spot on arm near seat of second furuncle, becoming like an indurated gland, at this time on l. instep, then on r., redness, with itching and vesicles, leaving hard scurf, whereby the whole place became elevated and painful, the scabs were pressed in by the boots and rubbed off so that the part was raw, after healing the spot was bluish-red and swollen.

Clinical.—Comedones and acne of the face. Suppuration of axillary glands.

Sleep.—Yawning; in afternoon, with stretching. Sleepiness. Inability to sleep after dinner though inclined to do so earlier than usual. Restless sleep, with frightful dreams. Restless dreams.

Fever.—Cold limbs; after 9 P.M., with hot head. Alternations of coldness and heat over whole body, with heaviness of head, which after eating increased to pain, > after 3 P.M. Heat over whole body in evening; H. in flushes, with confusion of head; hot head in evening; hot hands at 9 P.M., with rapid pulse, then general sweat.

Kali Bichromicum.

Triturations of the bichromate of potash are used.

General Action.—A "tissue" drug, affecting *the skin*, papular and pustular eruptions as well as ulcers of characteristic shape; producing general catarrh of *mucous membranes* and frequently erosions or ulcerations (throat, nose, stomach, rectum); causing inflammation of the *periosteum* and of the ligamentous structures about the joints; causing also acute inflammations of the *kidney*, with albuminuria, sympathetic disturbance of the liver, etc.

Allies.—Puls., Cinnab., Merc. c., Phyto.; Kali in general, particularly K. iod., Iris, Rhus, Sin. nig., Ailanthus.

Generalities.—Anæmic appearance. Emaciation; with hectic symptoms. Cracking on moving joints of limbs and vertebræ. Cramps; in various parts, < calves and inner thighs, with gastro-intestinal inflammation; sudden, in lower limbs and nape. Stitches in different parts. Tearing here and there in body, in shoulders and hands; in r. thumb, then in l. upper arm, then along arches of l. ribs; in bones, concentrating in little toes, with crawling; in r. axilla and on posterior surface of l. thigh, with sticking. *Drawing tearing suddenly jumping from one place to another* (Puls.); *and > moving the affected parts* (Puls.); D. tearing here and there in morning on waking, < limbs, forepart of chest and between shoulders. Sharp pain in r. knee and hips, and l. breast and shoulder. Rheumatic symptoms. *Rheumatic pains in different parts;* in knee and chest.

Drawing pain in l. hand, in forearm and nape; D. pains during the day, < limbs; in small of back and in l. shoulder in morning, then drawing behind l. ear; in bones of face and of r. hand in morning; in various parts, < bones of face, in morning after rising; *in various parts, always near bones, as if in periosteum or in tendinous expansion near it, in morning on waking; in morning on waking, in hands, feet, occiput and face, then pressure and drawing between shoulders before dinner, and tension in pectoral muscles;* D. and tearing pains in l. teeth and in joints of limbs, suddenly changing their location. Drawing in zygoma and in bones of extremities; *D. here and there in sheaths of muscles, in neck, back and limbs, in morning on waking, > rising;*

in l. little and ring fingers in morning on rising, then in l. side of face and in r. knee; in r. index and in spine in evening in bed.

Discomfort in morning, with uneasiness; D. after rising, prostration, < limbs. Feeling on waking of having caught a cold. *General sick feeling; in afternoon. Indisposition, > open air, with nausea* (Puls.). Paroxysmal venous excitement in forenoon, with uneasiness. Uneasiness, rolling over, tumbling about and nervousness. Sensitiveness to touch; to cold air in afternoon. Indolence, > beginning to work. Disinclination to rise from bed and move about.

Weakness; in morning; till noon; in evening; after rising, < limbs; after slightest motion; when walking in open air, with leaden heaviness of limbs, indifference, aversion to usual business, exhausting warmth, taciturnity, inability to collect my thoughts, and I cut short conversation to avoid showing the fact, desire to be alone, feeling better in open air; with sleepiness; < region of navel; even to sinking down; so that he trembled on attempting to rise. Paralyzed feeling, < r. foot. Almost complete insensibility. Stiffness and difficulty in rising in morning. Pain more severe in winter than in summer. Amelioration towards evening; after dinner; after eating; after a short sleep; from vomiting.

Clinical.—Rheumatism or rheumatoid pains, < smaller joints, wandering from one place to another (Puls.). The rheumatism is apt to recur every spring. The pains are apt to appear and disappear suddenly and to change location rapidly, especially in chronic rheumatism. It is usually indicated in people, especially children, who are fat and sluggish.

Mind.—Good humor and inclination to laugh. Ill humor; and disinclination to business. Gloomy; in evening; during dyspeptic attacks. Anxiety rising from chest. Indifference, with distress in stomach. Discouragement amounting to ennui. Anthropophobia. Disinclination to mental work. Aversion to mental work after dinner (without physical indolence). Inability to attend to his usual business, > sleep, but ill humor, with distress and sickness, remained. Stupid, but answered questions well. Unconscious, pulseless, breathing slowly and with effort, skin cold, lower lip swollen and purple, tongue swollen.

Head.—Stitches, with chilliness; S. now in vertex, now in temples or occiput; tearing S., < temples and occiput. Tearing, < forehead and occiput, with stitches in temples. Aching; in morning on waking; in morning on waking, < forehead and occiput; in morning on waking, < vertex, > rising, then weariness and feeling as if he had not slept enough; towards noon; in afternoon, aggravated till dinner, then relieved; in evening; in evening, then feeling as if nose were stopped, with great heat of air coming through it, then nosebleed, preceded by burning in eyes and sleepiness; on waking, with thirst; after dinner, < forehead; > afternoon by nosebleed, at times with vertigo; < temples, with uneasiness of stomach and dim vision; with nausea; with prostration of limbs; with pain in eyes and frequent tearing in ears, then pain, < forehead, at times with ringing and pain in ears; *at a point;* < sides of vertex, extending towards temples; generally on one side and in a spot that may be covered with the finger; intermittent, < parietal regions; flying; nervous, in various parts after dinner; sore, with bristling of hair on vertex; burning, > warm soup, with vertigo and vision as if objects were enveloped in a yellow mist; heavy, on waking at 5 A.M.; throbbing, with sticking in a spot near crown, touching the hair at this place was painful, with nausea. Throbbing on bending forward.

Confusion; in morning during dyspeptic attacks; about noon, < forehead and vertex; < supraorbital region; sudden, about 6 P.M., with nausea, anxiety and dulness of mind, on account of the confusion and anxiety the night was almost sleepless. *Heaviness.* Fulness; < vertex, with heaviness. Feeling as if brain were too large and forced bones asunder, < temporal bones towards ears and parietal bones, the external meatus < l., sensitive and stopped. Lightness. Rush of blood. *Vertigo;* in morning on rising, < stooping, > walking, with heaviness; in evening; on rapid motion of head; when sitting writing, then sudden violent vomiting of white mucous acid fluid, pressure and burning pain in stomach, then relief, then vertigo, nausea and similar vomiting; > tea at 10 or 11 A.M., < stooping; with nausea; as if room whirled around on rising in bed, < lying down, with nausea; as if everything turned around, on rising from a seat, with pain in epigastrium. Vertigo in paroxysms; in morning on waking; in evening; sudden; sudden, when standing and walking.

Forehead.—Shooting; above r. eye in evening; across F. and in temples when walking, > rest. Darting pain, < open air; D. pain in a spot over l. eye in morning after rising, spreading over forehead, < motion. Pain; in protuberance; in bone every morning; in l. side in morning on waking; in F. and vertex in morning on waking, after rising it changed to occiput; in r. side in evening; in evening, > sleep, with pressure upon eyes; after dinner; and in occiput; then constrictive pain in vertex; extending to eyes; in arch of l. orbit, extending to l. upper jaw and causing increase of saliva; preventing sleep; sudden P. in bone along l. brow; in bone, postponing each day, in the later days a second paroxysm in evening, also postponing; in l. sinus in forenoon, as in catarrh; as after a debauch, on stooping; throbbing, in spots at angles, with dim vision. Heavy pain on r. protuberance; over l. eye in afternoon; above eyes, < cold air and motion. Heaviness. Lightness on stooping, < morning.

Temples.—Shooting; < lying. Darting pains; in l. Tearing in l.; in r. muscle, with drawing; T., with sticking; intermittent T. extending to occiput. Creeping pinching on bones in forenoon. Intermittent pressure during the day. Attacks of throbbing pain in l. bone, extending to vertex, at first only after 4 P.M., after four days in morning, with nausea. Intermittent heavy pain, < cold air and motion; frequent H. pain in r. after eating, with craving in stomach. Drawing pain in r. Drawing, and in joint of jaw; in aponeurosis of l. muscles. Tension of muscles. Compression in evening. Confusion of r.

Pain in vertex. Pressure on vertex; at noon. Constriction of vertex towards noon. Sticking in r. side of head and in whole occiput; in r. side, extending into r. ear and r. side of face. Attacks of lancinations in r. side. Stabbing and pain as if head were opening in a spot in l. parietal region, < night, then a hard lump. Darting or aching in one side. Cutting along r. parietal bone. Pulsative pain in l. parietal bone.

Tearing in r. occiput. Biting in occiput. Pain from O. to forehead (after discharge from nose stops).

Pressure in O. in forenoon. Sudden stitches through skull. Sensitiveness of bones here and there. Drawing in skull. Falling of hair. Inflamed pimples on occiput and hairy part of nape. Crawling constriction of scalp. Tension of scalp. Itching points towards nape, as from coming pimples. Itching of whole scalp, with burning and with pimples in various places.

Clinical.—Neuralgic headache confined to a small spot, with dimness of vision; (the observations of cures of "sick-headache" by this drug do not differ in any way from those cured by Iris).

Eyes.—Sunken; and glistening, with dark rings about them. Swelling in morning, with heaviness. *Inflammation; in morning, with yellow discharge and agglutination* (Puls.); with loss of vision. Opththalmia beginning with itching, then pain and heat in eyes, agglutination of lids, redness of conjunctiva. Stitches in r. Smarting; < open air. Sensation of sand in them. Sensation of a foreign body in l. Pain; in r.; < looking long at an object. *Sensitiveness; and margins of lids red, a yellow purulent substance in inner canthus in morning.* Heaviness and soreness. Biting. *Itching; with burning lachrymation and photophobia; < evening and night, with pain as from sand in them.*

Burning; in l.; in morning, with redness of l. towards outer canthus; in morning on waking, < margins of lids; in morning after rising, smoking causes burning and lachrymation; in open air in forenoon, with pressure; in evening; in r. in evening, and in skin about it; in open air in evening, with pressure; in l. in evening, with lachrymation; in evening, < margins of lids, which are sensitive to touch and motion; in E. and lids after dinner; in r. and inner surface of upper lid after dinner; on fixing them upon an object, with dim vision; *with pressure;* with running of water from nose; with indescribable discomfort in nose, though accustomed to smoke every inspiration through nose caused sensation like sulphuretted hydrogen.

Lachrymation; with burning pain in eyes. Pupils dilated; and fixed. Pain in ball. Pressure on surface of r. ball in forenoon, with burning. Soreness of caruncula. *Redness of conjunctiva;* < r.; with heat and uneasiness as when opened under water. *White granular elevations surrounded by redness, on l. conjunctiva, towards inner canthus. Pustule on l. cornea, with surrounding indolent inflammation* and with pricking pain. Leucoma on l. cornea. Brown spot in r. albuginea. Red spots and streaks in white of l. White became yellow; dirty yellow, seemed loose, with yellowish-brown dots, < l., which also showed a brown spot near inner margin of cornea, with heat of eyes and necessity to rub them.

Lids.—*Redness of margins;* towards external canthi. Swelling of r. in morning on waking, till evening; S. of upper, with redness; S., with inflammation. Mucus in canthi; dry M. in lashes in morning. *Agglutination in morning;* and white of eye reddish-yellow, with itching of eyes, eyes weak and drawing back in orbits; with pain in lids on touch and lachrymation; with lachrymation, photophobia, *itching and burning. Granular.* Twitching in r. when reading and afterwards. Stitches. Smarting of external canthus. *Raw feeling in margins. Roughness of margins, so that winking causes rubbing against balls. Inner surface felt thick and rough.* Heaviness of upper in morning on waking. *Dryness.* Itching; in canthi. *Burning pain in external angle of l. eye; B. pain in margin of r. lower lid.* Burning; and on surface of balls, with pressure in balls; on inner surface; in r. inner canthus on waking, then extending over margin of lower lid, < writing. *Burning in margins; in morning; in forenoon, with itching and on moving them sensation as if they rubbed against ball;* at noon; in afternoon; in evening, with running of water from nose, < towards outer canthus; of lower, < writing.

Pressure about orbits. A spot on r. lachrymal bone is swollen, pulsating and painful. Vision dim; in evening on walking; confused; weak; flickering; flickering at noon, muscæ volitantes, so that he could scarcely write; V. as if a black plate were before eyes at the distance of ten paces, then sensation as if a veil were drawn up and down, then the first sensation, then vertigo, then headache, < frontal and orbital regions, at times with sticking in eyes and tearing in ears, > 9 P.M. *Photophobia,* with jerking of lids, lachrymation and burning in eyes, the P. < afternoon, > towards evening.

Clinical.—An extremely valuable remedy for a variety of inflammations of the eyes; catarrhal inflammation of the conjunctiva generally of an indolent character, without much photophobia and with rather scanty exudation; it is used successfully in granulated lids with pannus; it is certainly very frequently indicated in ulcerations of the cornea, which are small and perforating, generally without much photophobia; sometimes indicated in subacute scrofulous inflammation of the cornea or cornea and iris. Subacute iritis in the later stages, especially of the syphilitic variety (compare Kali iod.).

Ears.—Inflamed swelling at entrance of l. meatus. Sticking; in l. and in parotid gland; in l. and in l. outer side of throat; in r. in forenoon; in l., extending into palate, l. side of head and l. outer cervical region, the later painful to touch and glands swollen; through external meatus, extending into r. ear, in afternoon when walking; drawing S. through r. external meatus, then roaring in head as of a distant noise. Tearing. Pain in evening; in r. Pressure outward in l. mastoid process. Drawing extending into lower jaw, with salivation; D. behind r.; D. behind l. and on l. lower jaw, with tension of l. cervical muscles. Stoppage of r., with burning in concha. Ringing. Singing. Roaring.

Clinical.—Chronic suppurative perforation of the drum and discharge of yellow tenacious pus. Eczema of the ears externally, with watery oozing. A few cases of threatening abscesses about the ear, with great swelling of the external meatus, terrible pains.

Nose.—Swelling and pain; S. of alæ. **Septum ulcerated away; in upper part, as far as its articulation with vomer and ethmoid, and purulent inflammation of whole nasal mucous membrane;** *septum dotted with minute ulcerations.* Scab in l. nostril, bleeding always on removal. Twitching in l. wing and crawling like formication, extending over side of nose to eyelids, where it caused twitching. *Shooting from root along l. orbital arch to outer angle of eye* (compare Cinnab.), every morning, < till noon, > towards evening, *with dim vision.* Pricking, with sneezing, then the membrane begins to be thrown off, septum becomes thin, perforated, then detached. *Sticking in r. side on blowing, as if two loose bones rubbed against each other, with discharge of greenish offensive masses, every portion which passed through posterior nares had a disagreeable taste, then r. nostril was filled with hard masses, ulcers in external bor-*

ders of nostrils, ulcers burn, < l. nostril, then sensitiveness of tip of nose, < r. side.

Burrowing inside root (*in ethmoid bone?*), *with beating and externally heat and throbbing rhythmical with pulse, nose swollen at root and hot, nose seemed thick and full, she spoke through it, inclined to blow it on account of a thick substance in it, but nothing was expelled, heaviness as if a weight were hanging to it.* Pain; **in root** (Ign.); **in bones** (K. iod.); in r. bone; in bones in morning; in septum, < touch, with burning. Pressive and smarting pain in margins of nostrils, with swollen feeling. Tensive drawing pain extending from r. nostril into r. auditory canal. Sore pain on r. side of septum, < touch; then a burning. *Soreness; a yellow scab on outer surface of septum*, chiefly at junction of septum with lip; of mucous membrane; in r. nostril, *and dorsum painful to touch;* as if nostrils were stiff; margins feel sore.

Sensation as if water had been drawn up violently. Burning; inside near lip; in r. side near tip; in forenoon, and in upper lip; in outer margin of r. nostril in evening; in r. nostril after dinner, < touch; in r. nostril, then trickling of bright blood. Coldness in r. nostril on drawing in air. Tickling; in l. nostril; in l. nostril, extending upward, in evening in the house; with itching and with crawling in l. side of nose and twitching in margin of l. lids. Itching; < rubbing, with tickling. *Stoppage* (Sin. nig.); in morning on waking; of l. nostril in morning on rising, with discharge of thick yellow mucus. Frequent need to blow it after dinner, though there was nothing in it. Full in morning on waking.

Dryness (Sin. nig.); r. nostril; in morning on waking; in morning on waking, then discharge; of r. nostril in morning after rising, with burning; in evening; **with pain in root,** *as in beginning of stopped catarrh, extending to temples and affecting head; with swollen sensation, the walls feel stiff and velvety* (K. iod.); with sore pain in r. nostril; with tension in wings and septum; and cavities dilated; *towards root, extending into frontal sinuses* (K. iod.); *with sore feeling and with burning, < r. nostril, extending to frontal sinuses;* of margins, which are covered with thin scales; sensation in middle of l. ala as if dry or denuded; dry and painful except in morning, when there was a watery discharge; after dinner cough forced black coffee into nose, which caused dryness and pain in nose.

Sneezing (Iod.); in morning; after eating; after dinner; on lying down in bed; with lachrymation of r. eye; with pressure in upper part of larynx, which extends through choanæ into nose; in paroxysms; violent. Coryza; sudden, < r. nostril; fluent; purulent. **Plugs.** *Clinkers, which if torn away too soon cause soreness at root of nose and intolerance of light. Always full of thick mucus. Discharge; in evening* (Puls.); with swelling; from r. nostril; from lower part; increased secretion after dinner, with sore pain on margin of nostril; *of mucus streaked with light-colored blood; scanty, acrid, causing burning on septum;* acrid, from r. nostril; thin, acrid. Thin discharge; from r. nostril; with burning in outer margin of septum as if sore. Watery discharge; in morning, causing burning of upper lip; towards noon; from r. nostril; causing corrosive pain on outer margin of septum; from r. nostril, causing burning on margin of nostril and on upper lip; with redness of nose and fetid smell; with soreness, sneezing and snuffling in speaking; unnoticed, from r. nostril; sudden, from l. nostril; from r. nostril, then dryness of nose.

Bleeding; from r. nostril, waking him in morning; in morning on washing; from r. nostril in forenoon after moderate walking; towards noon; in evening; from r., waking him at night; after eating; sudden during dinner, and in evening; bright blood from r. nostril after beer during supper; thick dark blood from r. nostril after eating, then tickling in nose extending into throat; blowing of thin blood into mouth. Smell very acute; *offensive;* imaginary putrid, with eructations and taste of rancid bacon; blunted; lost.

Clinical.—It has been used for a great variety of diseases of the nose, but a general characteristic is the peculiarly tough, adherent secretions; these may exist in subacute or chronic inflammation of the mucous membrane or there may be ulceration, but the ulcers are usually round and deep and do not spread laterally; (the ulcers of Merc. are extensive and superficial). The sensations in the nose are usually those of obstruction and swelling, especially pressure at the root, sometimes with violent pain extending into the cheek-bones or around the eyes. In a few cases it has cured catarrh with watery excoriating discharge, but in these cases there were generally adherent scabs in the nose covering ulcerated spots. The formation of "clinkers" in the nose, the detachment of which leaves very sore places or ulcers, is a strongly-marked characteristic of the drug. Nasal polypi.

Face.—Swelling; of r. cheek, < over malar-bone. Flushed; cheeks. *Pale;* and sickly; and cold; and drawn, covered with cold, clammy sweat; and cadaverous, covered with cold sweat. Ashy gray. Yellow; and earthy. Anxious. Uneasy expression. Sticking through r. zygoma towards forehead. Tearing in l. side; periodical T. in bones. Acute pain in infraorbital part of malar-bones. Pain in bones, < infraorbital region and in nasal bones; P. in side, < zygoma and towards ears, r., then l.; in cheek-bone in evening. Pressure outward in zygomatic process. *Sensitiveness of bones* (Aur.). Bruised pain in bones, < facial side of upper jaw. Sore burning in fossa between r. wing of nose and cheek. Tension of muscles; making features rigid, a sickly expression; of masseters, with drawing and salivation.

Jaws.—Tense circumscribed elevation beneath periostem of l. ramus. Stitches towards l. ear. *Sensitiveness in upper, < beneath orbit.* Burrowing in rami. Boring in l. side of lower in evening; intermittent B. in l. side of lower. Pressure below orbits after breakfast.

Lips.—Swelling under nose in forenoon, with redness; S. beneath r. nostril, with redness and blisters. Pimples on upper; on r. side of lower; itching, on upper and lower. Yellow scabby eruption over upper. *Ulceration of inner surface; U., with indurated edges and smarting.* Itching vesicles on margins, burning in evening. Itching of eruption, though it had begun to dry. Dryness in morning, with burning; D. in forenoon. Burning; beneath nose; on inner surface of upper; smoking burns lips, which are dry and tense.

Clinical.—Frequently a valuable remedy when the face is blotched, or when there is more or less indigestion and the face covered with pimples or acne.

Mouth.—Teeth. Stitches in l. molars and in an anterior upper incisor; in hollow and sound l. molars. Tearing in l. lower molars, with stitches extending into ears and l. temple; sudden drawing T. in all l. teeth, momentarily > pressure on lower jaw, lasting till towards midnight, next morning swelling of gum, which was painful near a l. lower hollow molar, at noon drawing tearing toothache on same side, with stitches in jaws extending to ear, temple and neck of same side, that side of neck sensitive to touch, cervical glands swollen, tearing in various parts of limbs, tongue coated yellow, in evening tearing sticking through head, at times cutting, with chilliness and flushes of heat in l. side of head and face, pulse rapid, next day intermittent tearing in l. lower teeth, with sensitiveness and with sticking tearing in l. ear, temple and side of neck. Burrowing in all l. after midnight. Gnawing in roots of all at noon. Boring in r. upper molars towards evening. Aching, with salivation. Sensitiveness; of upper incisors.

Gums.—Livid. Bleeding on sucking. Pain in l. upper, extending through lip to wings of nose, with inflammation, then an oblong abscess above eye-tooth, between lip and gum. Sensitiveness. Uneasy sensation in evening.

Tongue.—**Smooth, red and cracked,** during dysentery (Rhus., Merc., Ail.); *red and dry. Papillæ very long on dorsum, with a brown patch.* Coating; in morning, with dryness; thick, loose; *yellow;* yellow, except at edges; *whitish-yellow;* white; yellowish-white; yellowish-white, in morning, with nauseous taste and qualmishness; in morning on waking, a light brown, on dorsum. *Painful ulcer.* Eruptive (tetterlike?) swelling which became depressed and out of its hollow oozed blood. Stinging. Pain at back of and on velum. Burning in tip.

Apathæ. Burning pimple on inside of l. corner, next day it was a painful ulcer surrounded by hard swelling, next afternoon burning in mouth, < inner surface of lips. Rough, papular, elevated appearance of velum. Excavated cicatrix on roof, from which a slough separated, no pain till separation of slough. A stream of thin blood comes into mouth. Constriction. Burning caused by smoking. **Dryness** (Rhus t., Puls., etc.); in forenoon; in forenoon, with bitter, astringent taste; < lips, without thirst. Salivation; after smoking; till noon; with nausea; with cooling, salt, astringent, metallic and then bitter taste, with salt eructations; watery, then frothy; yellow (Phyto., Merc.); sweetish-sour; salt, bitter, tenacious (Phyto., Puls., Merc.), full of bubbles, < smoking, forcible hawking loosened large quantities, with eructations of air. Breath fetid.

Taste.—Flat. Pasty in morning. Salt in afternoon. Bad; to water; on smoking. Musty in morning. Putrid. Of rancid bacon. Of blood. Sweetish; when smoking; after soup, then pressure in stomach; S. resinous, < middle of tongue, < if it touches hard palate, when smoking. Saltish-sour; sweetish-sour and astringent, after breakfast; cool-sourish on back of tongue and in throat in morning on going out, with nausea. Astringent at root of tongue; resinous, A.; sharp, A. when smoking, extending into fauces; sweetish A., with watery salivation. Nauseous; after breakfast, < root of tongue; on putting cigar into mouth; N., sharp scraping when smoking after breakfast; N., sharp astringent when smoking after breakfast. Bitter; in morning; on smoking; to the largely watered wine; B., pasty; B., resinous; B., pungent on back of tongue. Coppery. Metallic; sudden, at root of tongue and soft palate, with nausea and eructations; sudden, at root of tongue in forenoon and evening; sweetish; sweetish, < at root of tongue and on palate, < smoking; sharp, sweetish, resinous, nauseating, < entrance of fauces, after breakfast, < a glass of water; astringent, nauseous after dinner.

Clinical.—Syphilitic ulceration of the tongue. Aphthous inflammation of the mouth.

Throat.—**On r. side of root of uvula, an excavated sore, with reddish areola containing yellow tenacious matter.** *Ulcers on tonsils and throat* (Ail., Lyc. etc.), *the surface of which was covered with an ashy slough, and the surrounding mucous membrane dark, livid and swollen. Uvula and tonsils red, swollen and painful, then ulcerated.* Redness in morning on waking, with inflammation; R. of fauces, with relaxation of uvula; R. of fauces, with elongation of uvula and sensation of a plug in throat. Erythematous blush of fauces and palate; of fauces and tonsils. Coppery color of fauces and soft palate. **Hawking of much tenacious mucus in morning; and gelatinous;** H. of thick mucus in morning, also with sensitiveness of larynx and trachea; of mucus in afternoon; of mucus and copious expectoration of thick bluish mucus; H. expectoration of white frothy saliva.

Stitches; on empty swallowing; on swallowing and speaking, < moving jaws sideways, extending into ears, with redness of anterior surface of arch of palate; in l. tonsil towards ear, > swallowing. Soreness as from a broad substance covered with prickles, impeding swallowing. Feeling as if something were sticking in it when eructating. *Feeling of adherent mucus in morning* (Kali c.). Pain; in morning on waking; at palate on waking, > open air; on swallowing, < moving jaws sideways; with red spots as if ulcers would form on anterior arch of palate. Drawing pain here and there, at first in front between lower jaw and hyoid bone, then in ethmoid bone extending to behind ears.

Sensation of a hair in fauces. Scraping; in isthmus faucium, causing vomiting; in isthmus faucium, in open air, when most severe causing cough on every inspiration. Rawness; of pharynx; in morning; in morning, with frequent hawking from larynx; in night, with burning, causing hawking cough. Raw rasping sensation. Roughness, with hawking of mucus. Constriction of fauces. Coldness, with inability to swallow saliva quickly; C. in posterior wall, gradually increasing to a dry scraping that caused painful cough. Feeling as of rush of blood. Heat; in pharynx; compelling dry hacking. *Dryness; in fauces; in morning on waking, with painful swallowing;* after midnight, < upper part of larynx, as far as hyoid bone, with scraping and burning; with pain on empty swallowing, the D. changing after washing to the usual secretion of mucus, and saliva was salt; obliging her to swallow saliva, on swallowing burning. Difficult swallowing; > evening, then rawness and scraping in fauces, with salivation.

Œsophagus.—Choking on swallowing, then a stitch through upper part of r. lung. Sensation as if food remained in it. Burning.

Clinical.—Catarrhal inflammation of the throat, with tough mucus dropping down from the posterior nares; this mucus is so tough that it is difficult to get it out of the throat. Chronic inflammation of the posterior wall of the pharynx, which is dark and glossy. Ulceration of the posterior wall of the pharynx, with well-defined edges; cheesy exudation. Follicular pharyngitis. Follicular ulceration of the tonsils. Follicular ulceration of the fauces, with tenacious exudation. Diphtheritic ulceration of the palate, tonsils and pharynx, with very tenacious exudation, fetid discharge. Numerous cases of diphtheria have been cured. In

all these cases we find profound prostration, soft pulse, tendency to perspiration, general lack of acute painful sensations, slight infiltration of the cellular tissue and very tough, adherent exudation.

Stomach.—Appetite. Increased. Ravenous on seeing food, the ill humor > eating, then shivering and chilliness, < limbs, alternating with flushes of heat and general sweat, with eructations tasting of food, nausea and salivation. Good at breakfast, soon changing to disgust, so that he had to leave the table. Hunger, with aversion after the slightest food. Diminished; for breakfast. Capricious. **Lost**; for breakfast; for dinner, but food was relished. Dislike to meat; to breakfast; to smoking all the forenoon.

Thirst; in evening; but the smallest amount of liquid causes return of nausea; burning; *for acids* and increased thirst after them; for fresh water; little. *Longing for beer;* in evening. Aversion to water; which has an unnatural taste.

Eructations; after eating; after breakfast; after breakfast, with nausea; empty; convulsive; salt; sour; offensive, sweet and of bloody taste; with taste of food; tasting of putrid fat. Hiccough; in evening. with waterbrash.

Nausea; in morning, and pituitous vomiting; at 2 A.M., but inability to vomit; in forenoon, > soup; towards noon, < evening; towards noon when smoking, with frequent spitting; during breakfast. N. after breakfast; with pressure in stomach; with sour eructations, then griping; with heaviness and tension in region of symphysis pubis and malaise; when walking in open air. N. on attempting to eat; after dinner; after coffee with milk, with salivation; after a glass of water, with pinching in abdomen; when smoking after a meal; after smoking; on moving about; from pressure on pit of stomach; < sight of food; < drinking coffee; < pressure on epigastrium or hepatic region, which caused pain; > eating; > vomiting much food and mucus, with low spirits, pallor, blunted sensibility and weakness; N. in epigastric region; N., with headache; with vertigo and confusion of head; *with hot eructations and sweetish flat salivation;* with shooting in stomach, then vomiting; with chilliness; with coldness, trembling and hunger; in attacks; intermittent, after breakfast; *sudden,* after a moderate dinner; sudden, with headache, then vomiting and purging. Retching; violent, causing cracking in abdomen.

Vomiting; with violent retching, also after breakfast; in evening after black coffee, with effort, with vertigo, burning pain in stomach, general anxious sweat and shivering, the ejecta in forenoon consisted of food but in evening of bilious fluid; *of a pinkish glairy fluid;* of clear watery fluid; resembling the rice fluid in cholera; milk is ejected (pink), with very sour smell; of white mucus containing a clot of bright blood; of mucus and blood, also violent; sour, on stooping or moving, with pain at epigastrium; of undigested food; of contents of stomach, with painful constriction of stomach, then persistent retching, then relief; sudden, forcible, of contents of stomach after breakfast; greenish V. and purging; greenish bile, then watery mucus; of a pea-green, bitter liquid, with sensation as in seasickness, bursting sensation in blood-vessels of head, smell and taste keen, the nausea < Ipecac, < Camphor, with general chill and shivering, trembling, cramps in stomach, then soreness and aching at pit of stomach; of a brownish-yellow pappy matter; light yellow, insipid fluid when walking in open air; frequent, of pure yellow bile, with mucus, preceded by nausea and retching, then hiccough; frequent, preceded by ineffectual efforts, yellow, sweetish, at last bruised pain in upper abdomen, then difficult ejection of a dark brown, bitter substance; violent, yellow, with violent purging; repeated, violent, of yellow, bitter, bilious matter, with headache, fine scorbutic eruption covering face, taste bitter and salt, thirst, external flushes of heat and internal chill; difficult, from the mildest beverage, mucous, bilious, yellow, sometimes bloody.

Distention; in evening after eating a little, also < motion, > rest, with pain on pressure and inability to bear clothes tight. Incarceration of flatus in S. and hypogastrium. Stitches after dinner in epigastrium, breast into nipple (male) and in r. hypochondrium. Cramp; alternating with griping in umbilical region, preventing sleep after midnight. Gastralgia in a spot a hand's breadth above navel after dinner, > towards evening, with anxiety in pit of stomach and sweat on upper lip. Gnawing in epigastrium in morning, with emptiness. Pain; in pit; in region; in epigastrium; in morning, with discomfort; in morning on waking; in forenoon, and in upper abdomen; in epigastric region in evening; after eating, with burning; in epigastric region after dinner; in epigastrium and abdomen, < pressure; > tobacco-smoking, but returning and lasting till going to bed; < pressure of clothes; at greater curvature, with weight; agonizing, in epigastrium, with dizziness, sparks before eyes and weakness of legs; in pit, increasing to cutting, with bruised sensation in epigastrium and retching.

Frequent sensation in epigastric region like the last stage of seasickness, a twisting and constriction, < every step, > rest, with intermittent rush of blood to head and with exhaustion and indifference. Burning constriction in anterior surface before dinner, < pressure, with nausea and salivation. Wavelike contraction at 4 P.M., extending to chest. Tightness in evening fasting, extending to chest. Oppression in pit, with smarting burning pain, then tough, light-colored sputa. Load; in pit, then pressure, with nausea, rancid eructations and griping in upper abdomen. Sore feeling in pit, with pain on pressure.

Indigestion. Disordered by meat; by anything but the mildest food; D., with general heat at night, yellow-coated tongue, gnawing at epigastrium. Discomfort in epigastric region, increasing when walking in open air to nausea, and almost faintness. Uneasiness; about greater curvature, as if overloaded; waking him, with soreness and tenderness, < a spot towards l. of xyphoid cartilage, with dry mouth, nausea, restlessness and wakefulness, heat of hands and feet, then sweat of hands, feet and legs. Heartburn; *in evening after tea; on waking in middle of night; after dinner.* **Burning pain**; *in pit. Burning; in afternoon; after dinner; with salivation; extending into throat; extendiny into mouth, or soreness, also on waking.* Coolness; and in bowels; uneasy, in epigastric region, then constriction, impeding respiration.

Anxiety; in pit; in pit at 11 P.M., with warmth, waking me, then expectoration of blood, with short paroxysms of cough and rattling in air-passages, the cough and easy expectoration of blood repeated every two hours, next day posterior wall of pharynx dark, glistening, swollen, injected with bright red vessels, and to the l. a fissure from which the blood issued, on swallowing sensation as if a dry morsel stuck in throat, frequent, sudden hoarseness and then scraping on posterior wall of curtain of palate and in choanæ, often tenacious, metallic-tasting mucus was drawn from these parts, also boring drawing pains in bones of limbs (as often as the troubles in throat were relieved, and *vice versa*). Faintness; before breakfast; but want of appetite. Feebleness in morning.

Clinical.—Dyspepsia; especially associated with nausea and vomiting; nausea and vomiting of drunkards; nausea and vomiting, with ulceration of the stomach; with soreness in a small spot in the stomach. Dyspepsia resulting from malt liquors, with flatulency, oppression after eating, nausea and vomiting of mucus. Acid dyspepsia, with sour vomiting coming on an hour or so after eating (Puls.). Gastric catarrh, with vomiting of glairy mucus, tongue thickly coated.

Abdomen.—*Distention;* after eating; after dinner, with discomfort; with sensitiveness. *Rumbling; after stool; after breakfast, with griping, then a second thin stool, then retraction of anus and nausea;* with discomfort about umbilicus; with profuse, pasty stool, then tickling in rectum. Gurgling. Movings. *Emission of flatus; offensive. Ulceration.* Gastro-intestinal inflammation, with cramps in various parts, < calves and inner part of thighs. Sudden contractions in intestines, with nausea, then pasty stool, then burning and tenesmus in anus.

Sticking; extending towards spine. Cutting; in all directions; towards noon, < parietes. *Griping; in morning, then semi-liquid stool, with rumbling;* when walking in forenoon; from a draught of air, with griping; with intermittent nausea; occasional. *Pain; with diarrhœa. Sore to pressure.* Constriction. Tension; in evening after chocolate, with heaviness in stomach. *Burning after stool.*

Rumbling in colon, < inspiration. Cutting in l. side, increasing and decreasing in paroxysms. Griping in upper; on going out after breakfast, and in middle, so that sweat stood on forehead. Spasmodic constrictions of upper. Region of sigmoid flexure tender. Sticking beneath umbilicus. Griping beneath U. Pain in umbilical region; above and to l. of umbilicus; in a spot to r. of U.; in umbilicus after breakfast, rising into throat. Weakness above umbilicus on waking at 5 A.M. Midway between umbilicus and spine of ilium, in ascending colon, a tender point, which often bulges out.

Hypochondria.—Sticking; in l.; in region of spleen, extending into lumbar region, < motion and pressure. Sticking in hepatic region; till afternoon; in evening, < pressure; sudden, when walking rapidly. Tearing shooting in r. Sticking pinching in hepatic region after dinner. Boring in l. Aching in r.; posteriorly in liver; in liver, < full inspiration and cough; heavy, in hepatic region; circumscribed in l. Intermittent soreness in r. during the day.

Hypogastrium.—Sticking in r. flank, extending to l. clavicular region and acromion process and side of neck, < stooping, causing a stretched sensation, with restlessness and depressed spirits. Pain in l. groin darting through to r. Griping as if something pierced bowels, < deep inspiration, > pressure. Pain in r. groin and r. hip; P. in groin as if a hernia would protrude. Bearing down towards r. groin. Uneasiness in r. iliac region on waking.

Clinical.—Duodenal catarrh, sometimes with jaundice, white stools dark urine, nausea, sometimes with soreness over the abdomen, with nausea and vomiting. Gastro-enteritis, catarrh, with discharges of stringy mucus. Gastro-enteritis, with bilious or bloody vomiting, prostration.

Rectum.—Urging before usual hour, urine before stool, after stool colic and debility; U., waking at 6 A.M., she could not reach the closet soon enough, a watery stool spurted from her, then tenesmus, U. and only a spoonful of liquid, but relief of discomfort in abdomen; ineffectual U. after dinner; U., but passage of only offensive flatus.

Anus.—Stitches. Dragging; after hard stool, then pressure in hæmorrhoidal vessels, then D. and pressure during dinner so that he could scarcely sit; > emission of flatus, with pressure; in hæmorrhoidal vessels after exercise, with burning. Pressure; in forenoon, with burning, desire for stool, sudden sweat, < face, disappearing suddenly, emission of only flatus; in hæmorrhoidal vessels in evening, when sitting after exercise. Painful retraction, < on days when there is no stool. *Burning pain. Burning after stool* (Iris, Sulph.); *in forenoon, with pressure.* Soreness; towards evening, < walking; after prolonged motion; with dragging in hæmorrhoidal vessels. *Sensation of a plug in afternoon when sitting. Fulness of hæmorrhoidal vessels.* Biting. Itching; when walking. Acute drawing from perineum into urethra.

Stool.—In morning on rising, then soreness in anus. *Dysenteric attacks for several successive years, frequent bloody stools, with gnawing at navel, then ineffectual straining.* **Of brown frothy water,** frequent, *with tenesmus, pain in abdomen and nausea, then sudden complete rest. Liquid, involuntary;* two L. in quick succession, *then burning in anus; semi-liquid, then griping in intestines. Diarrhœa; profuse; constant, involuntary; constant, involuntary, of mucus and blood;* greenish-yellow; partly diarrhœa-like, sudden, profuse, in evening, with griping, then tenesmus. Pasty; then feeling as if too little had passed.

Constipation; with pain across loins; every three months. *Hard, then burning and pressure in anus; H. and scanty, then burning in anus;* H. and scanty; H. and lumpy; and unsatisfactory; and unsatisfactory, difficult; and difficult, painful; and infrequent, with protrusion of rectum. *Bloody and painful.* Pale, slate-colored. Copious, relieving abdomen, but return of pain after dinner; C. and dark, with tenesmus. *Scanty, round, then burning in anus* (Iris); S., pale, clay-colored, twice a day; S., twice a day. Frequent; and dark coffee-colored; two daily, the first normal, the second diarrhœa-like.

Clinical.—Diarrhœa of brown frothy water (compare with Rheum). Dysentery, with dry, red, cracked tongue, with painful tenesmus, stools gelatinous and bloody, aggravation in the morning. Dysentery occurring periodically in the spring, with the characteristic tongue. Dysentery, with drops of blood, tenesmus, without thirst or fever, with large insular patches on the tongue. Constipation, hard, dry stools, with burning in the anus (Iris).

Urinary Organs.—Sticking in prostate gland in afternoon, preventing walking. Escape of prostatic fluid at stool. Sticking in urethra, < after urinating. Smarting in urethra during micturition. *Burning in bulbus urethræ; B. in glands of urethra when urinating and afterwards; B. in navicular fossa when urinating.* Irritation at orifice of urethra (male). Urging before the usual hour; constant U. *Some time in passing urine. Frequent micturition, with burning after urinating;* frequent M. at night, of copious, watery, strong-smelling urine.

Urine red, with pain across back. High-colored; and hot. Brownish. Turbid in afternoon, thick mucous sediment; T. at night, with copious sediment. **Milky**, contained pus, reaction acid. *Scanty; and reddish* (with pain in region of kidneys, etc.); and high-colored, with pearly-white sediment; with white film and whitish deposit. None passed. Mucous sediment.

Clinical.—Subacute or chronic inflammation of the urethra, on urinating it seems as if a drop of urine could not be expelled and it troubles the urethra for a long time; with these symptoms there is usually burning in the fossa navicularis and in the bulbous portion of the urethra after urinating.

Sexual Organs.—Itching of penis and rectum in evening; I. of hairy parts, increasing to inflammation, pustules, with itching and tearing, night restless, pustules united into an ulcer, in which paroxysmal stitches woke him at night. Pain in penis. Constriction at root of penis in morning after waking. Erections.

Clinical.—Venereal ulcers, especially true chancre, to which it seems particularly homœopathic, with the characteristic cheesy, tenacious exudation. Yellow, very tenacious leucorrhœa. Pruritus of the vulva, with great burning and excitement. Several cases of prolapsus of the uterus, particularly < hot weather.

Respiratory Organs.—*Mucus; in morning; in bronchi and nose* without real catarrh. *Bronchitis.* Dryness of bronchi; in morning on waking. *Burning in bronchi when coughing. Larynx, mucus in morning; mucus, obliging hawking; ulceration and necrosis of cartilages; ulcerative pain; intermittent scraping, with hoarseness; soreness in morning on waking; pressure, < talking, speech refused its service; roughness in morning after rising, obliging hawking; irritation in morning, causing hawking; tickling at dinner; tickling, causing cough and clearing of throat; tickling extending into mouth and ears* (preceded by pressure).

Hoarseness; *in morning, with mucus in larynx; in morning on waking, < till noon, > eating, then aggravated, with at times scraping in larynx and hawking of thick bronchial mucus all day; in morning on waking, < till late in evening, with pressure and scraping in larynx, and in evening hawking of mucus; in evening, with dry cough; > expectoration of thick, tenacious, yellowish-white mucus; sudden, in evening;* **and rough voice.**

Cough; when exercising; **after meals**; *from tickling; from irritation in trachea. Irritation to cough; sudden, then dry, difficult cough; with expectoration of thick white mucus. Hard C., with weight and soreness in chest and expectoration.* Short. Dry, in afternoon; *D., then expectoration of dark tough mucus; short D., from tickling in larynx. Hacking, in evening, with hoarseness. Dry hacking; in evening; in evening, with hoarseness; with stitches in chest. Hard, dry, then expectoration of gray mucus of the consistence of white of egg.* Dry, tickling, paroxysmal, with pressure in middle of sternum, extending to hyoid bone, when she coughed violently a taste of blood, at last with expectoration of sweetish-yellow pus from deep in lungs. Tickling C. as if an acid and acrid liquid flowed from choanæ over curtain of palate, uvula and posterior wall of pharynx, afterwards with expectoration of bright blood in paroxysms.

Cough, with expectoration of mucus; C. (with dyspnœa), *< morning,* **with E. of white mucus "as tough as pitch" and which could be drawn out in strings** (Cocc. cact., Lac. ac.); *with E. of yellowish-green tough matter; thick yellow mucus with traces of blood; dense, transparent, lumpy mucus; thick, transparent, slate-colored, in morning on waking; C. from tickling in throat, with copious expectoration of thick lumps of bluish-white mucus; C. in fits from tickling at bifurcation of bronchi, with expectoration of reddish mucus; short hacking C., with expectoration of tenacious mucus, also white; short interrupted C. in morning, which loosens lumps of tenacious mucus, then sensitiveness of larynx; "stuffing" C., with pain at chest and yellowish, heavy, tough expectoration; loud C. from "stuffing" at epigastrium, < waking in morning, he then had a fit of coughing, with expectoration of tough mucus, with lightness in head.*

Expectoration of tough mucus, so viscid that it drew in strings down to feet. *Tough light-colored E. E. of mucus;* thick; pasty; easy, white, salt.

Dyspnœa; in sleep; in morning on rising, as if mucous membrane of bronchi were thickened; < morning; with cough and difficult expectoration of black tough mucus. Stertorous breathing. Rapid breathing. Short breath, as if something tight around upper abdomen prevented deep breathing.

Clinical.—Catarrh of the larynx, subacute, generally without fever, but with very tenacious expectoration. An extremely valuable remedy in the late stage of membranous croup; (it is rarely indicated in the beginning), the pulse is soft, the child is weak, perspires; the cough is not dry, but hoarse, barking, the expectoration is very tenacious and gags the child, who sometimes tries to vomit; the constant sawing respiration, with the harsh rough voice and cool skin, is a general condition calling for this drug. Spasmodic and chronic bronchitis, with great wheezing and very tough expectoration, which must be pulled out of the mouth to prevent vomiting and choking. In bronchitis the cough is apt to be barking, croupy, it seems to come from low down in the chest, < eating. In all these cases the cough generally < morning, > warmth, sometimes > lying down, < eating.

Chest.—*Sticking in sides* (Kali c.); in inner surface of sternum in forenoon; *in region of l. nipple* in forenoon, renewed on deep inspiration; in evening; in upper part of r. lung on sneezing; through chest, < r. side; beneath one pectoralis major, at another time in an intercostal muscle; irregular, in integument; superficial, in r.; sudden, in inner surface of sternum; tearing, in whole l., from axilla to flank, as if in costal pleura, in morning on waking. *Darting pain in mamma (female)*; from middle of sternum to between shoulders, on coughing. Sharp pains. Pinching in upper part of r. lung, < violent motion to sticking, next day sticking so that he must incline to right when walking and take short inspirations.

Pain; beneath sternum; in r. mamma; in r. lowest ribs; under l. axilla; in pectoral muscles beneath axillæ; in region of clavicle; in a spot to r. of centre of sternum, next day stitches there; in a spot in upper lobe of r. lung in forenoon when sitting, then drawing internally along r. chest; in r. in evening penetrating to back; in middle of lung on waking at midnight; on pressure towards middle and to l. of sternum; on deep inspiration; in region of three last true ribs, < deep inspiration; circumscribed, in r., < inspiration; in l., in region of seventh rib, next day sensitiveness to touch; in forepart, in region of l. fifth and sixth ribs, as if in costal pleura, with burning, then in evening beneath r. axilla; so that he could scarcely turn over in bed, get up or walk on account of aggravation of pain in muscles and bones, the latter seem broken, next day these pains extended over cervical region, < turning head or lifting arm, impeding respiration.

Pain consisting of pressure and sticking, in a spot in costal pleura, in region of l. seventh rib, in evening. Burning pain in middle of sternum; sudden B. pain as from a knife-cut in centre of chest, beginning under clavicles and extending from region of lower ribs, < centre of chest, < deep breathing, but forcing him to respire deeply, > warmth. Intermittent heavy pain in r., passing through to back, then tearing. Rheumatic pain between r. seventh and eighth ribs, at angles, < raising or twisting body to l. Soreness; in evening, < region of wall; under sternum, like an ulcer under skin, causing pain on lifting arms.

Pressure, waking about midnight and preventing sleep till daybreak; frequent P. in forenoon, < beneath sternum; P., with intermittent anxiety; anxious P. at night, taking away the breath. Oppression; at night, < region of bifurcation of bronchi, compelling him to take a deep breath with the aid of pectoralis major; in lower part on deep inspiration, with sticking. Tightness; all the forenoon. Tension and constriction; T. in r. half, at insertion of pectoral muscles; T. in anterior wall on deep breathing; externally in l. in evening when walking; drawing, in r. side, < ascending stairs and deep breathing, with pain. Dryness of lungs in evening, with rawness.

Heart.—Sticking. Cramp in region. Darting pain in præcordium. Sharp irritative pain in region of apex. Pain; in evening; several hours after dinner; with palpitation and anxiety; preventing sleep; cold, heavy, in cardiac region, with tightness of chest and dyspnœa. Trembling on pressure upon region. Palpitation in bed, with pain in region of heart.

Pulse.—Rapid; and full; and full, hard; and small, sharp. Irregular, small, contracted. Slow; and filiform. Depressed and small. Weak; and fluttering. Scarcely perceptible.

Neck.—Glands swollen and sore to touch. Tearing on slightest motion. Pain in nape and l. shoulder in morning on waking. Stiffness; of nape; of nape on bending head downward.

Back.—Twitching in back and scapula as if liquid dropped on the flesh, it pulsates sharply like the key of a telegraph. Shooting. Pain from exercise; P. in different parts, > evening; running down on l. side into hip; rheumatoid pains in B. and limbs, as after taking cold. Drawing in all muscles, extending into upper arms, loins and thighs. Tension in muscular aponeurosis, < bending forward or moving arms.

Stabbing from third cervical to fifth dorsal vertebra, striking to sternum, < motion, with inability to straighten spine after stooping. Deep-seated shooting under scapulæ at night; S. at lower angle of l. scapula, then in toe. Acute pain at base of l. scapula. Pain under r. scapula; at lower angle of r.; deep-seated, at upper angle of l.; drawing P. in l. S. and l. arm, extending into hand and thumb, in the joint and bone, > moving arm. Discomfort between scapulæ. Undulating contraction of r. dorsal muscles on sitting down after exertion. Pain in r. side of spine, about ninth dorsal vertebra, with uneasiness in stomach.

Lumbar Region.—Sticking, < inspiration and cough; S. in l. side and l. groin after a meal; in l., then r., extending down thigh, < motion. Darting pain in renal region. Sudden cutting, < moving or turning, with scanty urine; C. on outer l. side of sacral bone, shooting up and down. *Pain;* in l. side between hip and last vertebra; in sacrum and coccyx in morning; in morning on waking; in coccyx in morning on waking; in coccyx in morning on waking and towards evening, < when after long sitting I rose to urinate, when it extended into urethra and obliged me to bend forward when urinating; in coccyx in morning after rising; in sacrum and coccyx in morning during coition; in coccyx at noon, with burning in anus; *in coccyx when sitting* in forenoon; in coccyx after rising; < motion; < stooping; in coccyx, < walking and touch; with scanty high-colored urine; so that he cannot straighten himself after stooping; extending to nape, striking through to sternum; extending to sacrum and down thigh, increasing to numbness, so that he could hardly rise from a chair; paroxysmal P. in forenoon when walking, afterwards at the moment of sitting down, > sitting, changing in afternoon to drawing pains in legs, in small of back again in evening; attacks of P. in region of kidneys, extending to groins, < rest, with scanty reddish urine, nausea and impaired appetite. Acute pressure in coccyx in evening. Sprained pain on motion. Pain in sacrum as from a blow at noon when sitting. Drawing and pressive pain in sacrum in morning on waking. Drawing in sacrum, < walking, with pressure.

Clinical.—Neuralgia of the coccyx, < sitting.

Extremities.—Jerking in various muscles of thighs and upper arms in evening, with drawing. Cramps. Cracking in joints. Shooting and pricking pains in morning, with general stiffness. Tearing in long bones; T. in ankles and wrists; in hands and feet; in joints; in joints, < r. wrist and r. fingers; < towards hands and feet; in r. tibia, on back of r. foot and r. ankle, in thumb, on back of hand and in several r. phalanges; in r. tibia and r. ulna in morning on waking; in r. ulna in morning on waking, then in r. tibia, > rising; in r. wrist and ankle, < motion; in r. tibia and various finger-joints, so violent in r. thumb that he could not write; in joints, now in hips, now in knees; intermittent, in hands and feet in afternoon; paroxysmal, sudden, in a single fibre of legs, feet, forearms and hands in morning on waking; wandering, in various parts; drawing and T. in periosteum of r. tibia, then in bones of r. forearm; drawing T. in various parts, < r. great toe and r. thumb.

Pain in joints; P. in shoulders and legs; in shoulders, arms, finger-joints, hips and knees. Bruised pain. Rheumatic pains in nearly all joints; R. pain in r. hip and l. elbow; R. pain, shooting and pricking, < morning. Drawing pain in l. hip and from l. shoulder-joint to elbow; in r. tibia in morning, and drawing in r. hand; in l. arm and in both lower limbs, < r. foot, and especially tearing extending into great toe; in various joints, < r. ankle; D. and boring pains in l. lower limb and in l. humerus. Tearing D. pain in r. tibia, r. ankle and wrist, in various phalanges, < thumbs, suddenly changing about. Drawing; in forearms and legs; on backs of hands and feet; in various places in long bones. Weakness in evening.

Clinical.—Syphilitic pains in limbs. Syphilitic periostitis.

Upper Extremities.—Drawing tearing in joints, suddenly changing its place. Tearing in l. shoulder; in r. S., then in l. elbow and forearm; in S. and upper arm of side not lain upon, on turning the pain went to other arm; jerking T. from r. S. to elbow; paralytic T. on top of r. S. Pain in l. shoulder, extending into l. chest, < moving arm, especially raising it; P. on moving r. as if joint were separating, < prolonged inactivity of the limb to painful stiffness, < raising arm, afterwards pain, < bending arm at elbow and drawing it backward and outward, as in putting on clothes. Rheumatic pains in shoulders, < night; R. pain in shoulder and elbow on motion, with numbness from shoulder to elbow. Spasmodic drawing in r. shoulder.

Arms swollen, painful and red. Tearing in bones of arm, < near elbow and wrist; T. and gnawing in bones of r. arm and in r. thumb and index, in forenoon, indications of same pain in l.; sudden T. in r. deltoid in evening, with jerking. Drawing in bones of arms. Arms weary. R. arm feels asleep or paralyzed at night, disturbing sleep. Sudden cramplike pain in middle of outer surface of r. upper arm, then sensitiveness. Shooting in l. elbow. Darting pain in outside of elbow. Drawing and tearing in r. elbow, extending into hand and r. leg after midnight, preventing bending up of foot. Pain in elbow; l.

Tearing in forearm; in bones of r.; pinching T. above l. wrist in evening. Pain in forearms during the day; P. in a spot on extensor surface of upper third of r. F., more in muscles and partly in upper arm, with sensitiveness to touch. Burning pain extending from middle of forearm to wrist; in lower end of l. in evening. Drawing in bones of F.; r., on radial side; D. in aponeurosis of muscles of r. F. Throbbing in l. F. Darting in r. wrist; throbbing D. in l., near pisiform bone. Hands shrivelled, wrinkled, dusky. She let things fall from her hands, with weakness and drawing in arms and distention of veins of arms. Sticking in metacarpal joints in morning on waking. Tearing on radial side of l. hand. Bruised feeling in bones of hands; hands and arms feel bruised and paralyzed. Drawing in l. hand after dinner. Hands weak.

Fingers.—Twitching of l. little. Sticking through bone of first phalanx of r. middle; in joints of r. middle towards evening. Wandering tearing in various phalanges; intermittent T. in r. thumb. Gnawing boring in bone of first phalanx of l. middle, in evening, extending towards tip, > rubbing. Pain in second joints of l.; P. in thumbs; in thumb in forenoon, extending to elbow, < motion of arm or hand, > evening, then sensitiveness of joint. Drawing pain in r. thumb. Tension in extensor surface of r. thumb, > towards noon and felt only on violent motion of thumb, and on pressure where radius articulates with metacarpal bone of thumb.

Lower Extremities.—Trembling. Drawing tearing, < in r. great toe. Whole r. leg, < hip, sensitive so that I could not lie upon r. side at night, in morning burning pain on inner side of r. lower leg, in evening after walking tensive drawing pain in whole r. leg. Tension in r. in evening after a long walk, with heaviness. Weariness.

Thigh.—Cramp, and in legs. *Darting pain down outside of l. Tearing on inner side of r. T. and leg;* T. from l. ham down leg; in muscles of anterior surface of r., with drawing; drawing T. in l. hip. Pain in r. hip; after dinner; P. in sciatic nerve; aching and jerking pain in hip only during the day. *Rheumatic pain in r.; in hip, coming on at night.* Bruised pain in middle of r.; B. pain in r. hip when sitting, so that he limps in walking. Drawing pain on inner side of r. in evening; D. pain in r. hip, extending to knee. Sudden tensive pain in middle of r. musculus sartorius, < walking, especially ascending steps, > sitting and lying, lasting till sleep. Tension on anterior surface of r. Weariness.

Knee.—Sharp pain. Sudden tearing in l. in evening, preventing motion. Rheumatic pains, and in hip; acute, in knee only on walking, with stiffness. Sprained pain in l.; on rising from prolonged sitting, lasted all the afternoon, at times with similar pain in l. ankle. Sore pain in r., < sitting down and rising. Tensive pain in r. Heaviness and tension.

Leg.—Swelling of tendo-achillis, with pain. Trembling, with necessity to sit down. Twitching in calves. Cramp of calves. *Tearing in r. tibia;* in l. tibia above malleolus in evening, with pinching; drawing T. in r. tibia. Pain in bones, preventing rapid walking, < bending ankle upward; sudden P. in middle of l. tibia, suddenly disappearing, but returning; P. in tendons of calf as if stretched, extending to ham and tendo-achillis, < walking, and causing lameness. Bruised pain in one, then other spinal tibiæ; B. or broken pain in bones, extending to ankles, < moving ankles upward, so that walking was difficult. Tension in r. in evening. Heaviness of r.; in afternoon, with burning of its skin; with tension; H. on sitting down after entering house, with burning pain in a corn. Weariness.

Hard, immovable swelling on r. inner malleolus, painful on hard pressure. Pain on r. inner malleolus. Feeling as if muscles of r. sole were cut across, hindering walking. Heels sore when walking. Pain in forepart of l. foot when walking and in a corn in hard skin of toe, > sitting still, returning in foot in afternoon after a long walk. Sudden numbness in forepart of r. foot when sitting, with crawling. Acute twinging in ball of l. great toe, then in r. Shooting in second joint of great toe at night in bed. Sore pain in r. great toe, on inner side where nail joins flesh, in evening. Pain in toes, with heat and throbbing.

Clinical.—Sciatica of l. side, > walking and bending leg, < standing, sitting, lying or pressure.

Skin.—Roughness on forehead, with burning. Elevated cicatrices on r. thumb; depressed C. covering hands. Brown spots like freckles on forepart of neck. Redness of index, with swelling and throbbing pain, then an ulcer on tip, with white overhanging edges and dark gangrenous centre. Red elevation, with a dark centre and elevated circumference, itching and painful. Red round spots on back, arms and hands, they formed pustules covered with scabs, which came off and left dry ulcers, then colorless depressed cicatrices.

Swelling of arm as high as axilla, with pain, then boil-like elevation, which turned into an ulcer with a dark centre and white overhanging edges. Swelling in seat of a scratch, ulcer covered with a scab, dry, painful on pressure, a movable knot under skin, with an ulcerated spot like a corn, this hardens and is covered with a white skin. Red, itching swelling on wrist, then pain, then matter formed and broke the skin and left a depressed cicatrix.

Eruption; on eyelids and adjacent parts of face. Rash; beginning in hot weather. Eruption like measles; < trunk and thigh, hands and face being freest, mixed with pustules, which do not break, but dry up and leave a scar. *Psoriasis diffusa* of hands, degenerating into *impetigo*. *Acne on face.* Inflammation of feet, then ulcers. *Pimples; on forearms;* on arms; r. half of face; red, on back of hand; itching, on forearm and legs. Inflamed pimples on forehead; r.; on back; painful, in r. side of nose, towards dorsum.

Sloughs on fingers and glans. If there be the smallest wound (when applied to the skin) it acts as a caustic and destroys all tissues down to bone, with sharp pains, < winter. Pustules on hands; at roots of finger-nails, < l., extending over back of hand to wrist, and on palm; on arms, with a hair in centre; P., then deep sloughs under them; P. over whole body, with a black slough in centre on an inflamed base; filled with lymph, in r. brow; painful, on back, also with bloody discharge. Pustules like smallpox on face; on calf; covering body, disappearing without bursting.

Suppuration of axillary glans, but they did not break. Boil on r. thigh; painful B. on back near last r. true rib. Ulcers on face; hands; hands and body; index; on l. scapula, with a scab; U., then elevated painless induration; deep, on wrists and arms; *painful in cold weather;* painful on touch; painful, under thumb-nail. Vesicles on a red and elevated base (itching and burning, < exposure to steam), becoming pustular and in some presenting a dark point in centre, invading hands, arms, face, back and abdomen; V. filled with serum on r. sole; abraded V. near umbilicus, with hollowed appearance, which remained after they healed.

Stinging. Itching in beard; I. on r. cheek; in various parts, lasting into night, with burning in skin; in forehead, with burning; of forearms and hands after lying down, with burning in skin; in nape, with burning in skin, then on l. shoulder, then l. upper arm and l. chest, then on back, lasting from 6 to 10 A.M., in afternoon a sudden similar I. on loins; at night in bed, with heat, then hard, reddish knots on thighs and legs, with depressed scurf in centre, surrounded by an inflamed base; I., then suppuration and ulceration of moist surface of penis; I. all over body, then pustules forming scabs, most on arms and legs, the scabs painful, smarting and burning; I. of leg, then red eruption, which ran together and formed scabs, discharging, with smarting pain, pustules on front of leg, eruption better in cold weather; I. of forearms and hands, then pain and ulcers, from which nearly solid masses of matter fell on striking arms firmly, the ulcers left clean dry cavities, then white cicatrices.

Clinical.—The ulcers are generally circumscribed, penetrating, with tenacious exudation. It has been found extremely useful in lupus of the sluggish, painless type. Lupus, with burning pains (Mezer.). It is not infrequently indicated in measles when there is little or no fever but a tendency to ulceration of the eyes, with the characteristic discharge from the nose, diarrhœa, etc. Also in measles a hoarse, croupy cough, with tenacious expectoration. A great variety of skin diseases, with the general characteristics of deep ulcerations and adherent secretions.

Sleep.—Yawning; with stretching; constant, then pain in stomach, nausea and efforts to vomit. Sleepiness; towards noon, with closure of lids, nodding, yawning and weariness of feet; in afternoon; in evening; in evening, with weariness; after dinner, with yawning; with headache. Irresistible sleepiness; after dinner; in evening, then waked by twitchings, now in upper part of body, now in single parts of muscles. Difficult waking in morning. Feeling in morning as if he had not slept enough. Sleeplessness. Difficult falling asleep. Groaning and tossing about at night. On falling asleep starting, tossing about of arms, incoherent talking and then snoring. Restless sleep; towards morning, after subsidence of headache and nausea; and interrupted by dreams, unrefreshing. Waking early; then restless sleep; then confused, heavy half sleep, in morning weariness. Waking at 1.30 A.M.; then falling asleep again. Suddenly wakened from quiet sleep by fright.

Dreams vivid; < towards morning, of various dangers and misfortunes. Disagreeable D. Frightful D. Nightmare at 4 A.M., D. that some one was lying across chest and abdomen, so that I was in danger of suffocation, groans, on waking covered with sweat, blood in a tumult, after rising weakness.

Fever.—Chilliness; in evening; when vomiting; after vomiting, with general heat; in open air, temperature 99; with nausea. External C., but not internal. Internal C. through afternoon nap, with burning in eyes, face and upper part of body; I. with cold arms, but hot face and hands. Shivering; in afternoon, < arms and shoulders; alternating with flushes of heat, sweat on back and inside of thighs; in attacks; paroxysmal S. extending from legs over whole body, with sensation as if pericranium were constricted, then heat with dry mouth and lips, next morning thirst, but no sweat. Cold skin, < limbs. Cold limbs; r. thigh; hands and feet; hands and feet, with flushed face; feet, with shivering over thighs and back.

Heat in first part of night. Febrile paroxysms night and morning. General heat; at night, with disordered stomach; with thirst; then cold sweat, then rigors, with general coldness, especially cold limbs. Heat of forehead. H. of face; at 4 P.M. without redness; in flushes at 4 P.M.; sudden, at 5 P.M. during rest. Burning of feet, < soles; on inner surface of r., on outer surface of l. leg in forenoon. Hot and dry skin. Burning in skin of forehead; in evening, with itching; in morning, < glabella; in middle of F., in nose and r. leg, in evening after entering house. B. in skin of face and head, without redness; in skin of face, < eyes; in skin of face beneath eyes, in forenoon in open air, with feeling in sides of nose as if he would have erysipelas. B. in skin of nose near lower margins of orbits. B. in skin on inner surface of r. leg; in skin of outer part of l. leg. External B. over r. trochanter major, with smarting.

Sweat; in evening when sitting quietly; on hands. Anxious, when vomiting. Cold, clammy. Cold, on forehead; on hands; on hands during vomiting.

Kali Bromatum.

The pure Bromide of Potash is dissolved in distilled water (1 to 99) for the first dilution.

General Action.—Like other potash salts it weakens the heart and lowers the temperature. Its chief interest lies in the "Bromism" caused by it, the seat of which is in the spinal cord or the nerves leading to the brain cells. Tetaniform convulsions and even opisthotonos in animals; in man, general failure of mental power, especially loss of memory and of words and melancholia, anæsthesia of the mucous membranes, especially of eyes and throat, and of the skin; acne; loss of sexual desire, imbecility, idiocy, paralysis.

Generalities.—Emaciation. Marasmus. Diminishes the retrograde metamorphosis of tissue. Diminishes mucous secretions. Capillary circulation affected, independent of heart and arteries. Threw himself down, closed his eyes, seemed above the earth, quite happy. Crouched by the fireside all day, devoid of energy and resolution. Convulsions, > appearance of eruption, papules of acne united in areas, on these areas yellowish points beneath skin, on the surface a crust, and where this was rubbed the surface became peculiarly papillated. Ataxia of limbs and tongue and impeded articulation. Restlessness. Aversion to exercise. Lazy, indifferent and sleepy. Weakness; muscular, and bruised feeling in limbs and loins; muscular, becoming paralysis. Inability to hold herself upright. Fainting. Inability to move or feel. Diminished nervous sensibility in general and especially diminution of reflex sensibility. Insensibility.

Clinical.—Convulsions, epileptiform in character, but it is doubtful whether the drug really cures true epilepsy; it certainly suppresses the convulsions for the time, in many cases, but it does not seem to remove the constitutional tendency to their recurrence; nearly all cases of epilepsy are obliged to continue taking the drug, often in increasing doses, in order to obtain its palliative effect.

Mind.—Delirium. Delusions about persecution and violence. Imagined that he was singled out for Divine vengeance, loudly deplored his fate, but at intervals fell asleep suddenly, then sound sleep, next day he walked the room, groaning and wringing his hands, said the officers were in search of him for robbing a friend. Delusion that she was deserted by her friends, hence she passed her waking moments, which were not many, in tears, another delusion that she saw her child dead, and when it was brought to her she refused to acknowledge that it was hers or resembled the one she imagined dead. Delusion that lewd women had got into his mother's house, that he was pursued by the police, that his life was threatened by members of his family, that he had gold sewed up in his clothing, his appearance and manner similar to those of a drunken man, except that he was very pale, pulse slow, skin cool, pupils contracted, manner excited and rambling, hands constantly busy, timid and suspicious, attempted to throw himself from a window and battered down a door to escape from danger. Delusions, with melancholy, imagined that she was insulted and that the weekly bills of the landlord were evidences of a conspiracy against her father, gave a loud shriek and declared that she had seen her brother fall overboard. Violent excitement, glorying in his imaginary power of mind and body, then despondent, sullen, often lachrymose, frequently even despairing. Feeling that everything felt, seen or thought had been experienced before, as in a dream. Hallucinations of sight and sound, with or without mania, precede apathy and paralysis.

Singing and dancing, saying that he was the happiest man alive, then crying bitterly. Bursting into tears without cause. Sadness; and indifference, almost disgust for life; and feeling of approaching death; and absent-minded, childish, giving way to her feelings. Anxiety. Listlessness. Confusion. Inability to concentrate thoughts, slow perception. Thinking power slow. Loss of will power on waking, with torpor. *Inability to express oneself. Weak, and in talking and writing substituted one word ending in "tion" for another.* Dull in morning, and depressed, irregular in gait, in afternoon helpless. Stupefaction; < well-educated and active people. Coma.

Memory lost; with amnesic aphasia (Cannab. ind.); *for single words, or one syllable is constantly dropped whenever that word is spoken, or two words are always interchanged; forgot certain syllables or parts of certain words and did not speak these. Writing almost unintelligible from omission of words or parts of words, words are often repeated or misplaced. Memory impaired.*

Clinical.—Acute mania, with sleeplessness and strange illusions, fear of being poisoned, of being pursued, etc. Suicidal mania, with tremulousness and twitching of muscles. Brain fag, with a numb feeling in the head, and feeling as if he would lose his reason. Loss of memory, a kind of aphasia in which words and syllables are forgotten and omitted. Profound melancholia, with irritability and weeping, or with religious delusions. Cerebral anæmia, with cold extremities, drowsiness or complete coma, dilated pupils. Night terrors in children, with shrieking in sleep, trembling, etc. (compare with Stram.).

Head.—Aching; developing a sort of dulness and giddiness, as in some forms of typhus; with heaviness and pressure on forehead and temples. Confusion; when walking; with heat. Heaviness. Vertigo; with confusion; with drowsiness and sometimes with stupor; with faintness and nausea; on standing up, < walking, as if ground gave way and the sense of resistance were lost, with staggering. Pain in forehead and occiput; in r. frontal protuberance after a simple dinner, < 9 P.M. Pityriasis of scalp.

Clinical.—It has been used for congestive headaches, with benumbed feeling in the brain, or with vertigo.

Eyes.—Hollow, fixed. Expressionless, lustreless. Hazy condition of bloodvessels. Glazed. Retinal vessels contracted. Pupils dilated; and uncontractile; contracted. Bloodvessels on fundus enlarged. Congestion of disc and retina; C. of conjunctiva. Sensibility of conjunctiva deadened. Constant closing of lids, more noticed when sitting than lying. Drooping of lids; so that they hang far over balls. Lids heavy. Vision disturbed; weak; lost.

Ears and Nose.—Roaring in ears at night in bed, synchronous with pulse. Hearing disturbed; weakened; lost. Nose full of thick mucus and yellow scabs. Nasal mucus contained the salt. Smell weakened.

Face.—Pale; ashy; and suffering. Yellow, cachectic; dirty yellow. Thin. Expression wearied; and anxious. Stupefied expression; becoming that of imbecility, then of idiocy. Looked queer in evening, next morning as if frightened.

Mouth.—Gums painful, sometimes red and swollen. Tongue red, dry and enlarged; R. and moist, then dry and brown; T. coated; T. painful and papillæ prominent, with roughness and burning through mouth and fauces; disordered action, difficult speech. Speech hesitating; stammering; slow; slow, difficult and not seconded by operations of intellect. Inability to speak. Dry mouth. Mucus increased; M. becomes sticky; ropy M. on mouth, lips and tongue. Salivation; then dryness of mouth, with thirst. Frequent spitting of viscid saliva. Saliva contained the salt. *Fetor;* becoming nauseous; *with white tongue,* with languor and sleepiness. Taste salt; T. foul; weakened; lost.

Throat.—Mucus membrane of fauces injected; palate and pharynx, and swollen, uvula swollen. Congestion of uvula and fauces, then œdema. Tickling. Irritation of T. and stomach; of fauces, with œdema and redness, sometimes with paleness of the parts. Dryness of T. and vicinity; of œsophagus. *Anæsthesia of fauces; of pharynx and larynx; of velum palati, uvula and upper part of pharynx; of mucous membrane of fauces and upper respiratory organs; in region of veil of palate, so that touch did not cause vomiting, but movements of deglutition were intact.* Swallowing difficult; in morning on waking; impossible.

Clinical.—Anæsthesia of the throat, the effect of alcohol.

Stomach.—Appetite increased; decreased; less for breakfast, lost for dinner; lost. Thirst; but inability to drink only a mouthful, as cool water is unpleasant; for cold drinks. Craving for wine. Aversion to coffee. Eructations; nauseous. Nausea; at thought of tobacco; < lying on l. side, with pain in stomach. Retchings. Vomiting; repeated, serous; of frothy mucus. Fulness in epigastric region, with heat and pressure. Habitual gastralgia. Pinching or constriction. Agony in region. Anxiety. Peculiar pressure in epigastric region. Oppression after dinner. Burning; then empty feeling, > eating. Weakness. Sore feeling.

Clinical.—Persistent hiccough.

Abdomen.—Rumbling. Flatulence. Emission of flatus. Pain; sudden, disturbing rest at night; in course of ascending colon; in umbilical region; periodical, in umbilical region, with sensitiveness to touch; flatulent, in region of duodenum at 4.30 A.M., > watery diarrhœa during the day. Warmth. Uneasiness.

Stool.—Tenesmus. Liquid; and frequent. Diarrhœa; with pain in abdomen; staining violet. Stools soft; and frequent. Constipation. Hard and infrequent. Increased. Sluggish. Diminished in weight and usually delayed.

Clinical.—Polypus of the rectum, with persistent diarrhœa and evacuation of much blood.

Urinary Organs.—Distended feeling in bladder during partial slumber, with irresistible urging. Burning at neck of bladder, with sensation of a ball forced from behind, then discharge of half an ounce of liquid like white of an egg, with mucus like milk. Desire to urinate; frequent, urine diminished. Burning in urethra, > injection of cold water, with smarting. Smarting, burning pain on urinating, with sensation as if a shot were forced from bladder along urethra, *constant copious micturition*, and just at the last drop of urine spasmodic constriction of urethra about lacuna, with sharp pain along back in bladder like forcing a large instrument into a small place, then whitish-yellow gonorrhœa, relief only from bathing the parts in ice-water.

Frequent micturition; urine copious, also pale, watery, with distress; of thin, yellowish urine; M. every half hour of about half a pint, urine pale, sp. gr. high, loaded with phosphates, of which a cloud was passed with the urine, the crystals could be seen when held up to the light, on standing the sediment filled one-quarter the whole space, heat precipitated a white sediment, which nitric acid dissolved. Urine copious; and clear, yellowish; and thin, clear; either C., thin, pale or peculiarly offensive. Urine pale and thin. Urine scanty. Uric acid increased. Acidity and coloring matter of urine increased, the phosphoric acid varied, increased by small doses, chlorides increased, save when the bromide was acting as a poison, amount of potash increased.

Clinical.—Diabetes, with impaired memory, dryness of the mouth, etc.

Sexual Organs.—Pain in l. testicle and cord, with swelling and tenderness. Excitement during partial slumber, < in bed, usually with erections and emissions, which wake him, and of which he is conscious. Appetite diminished, then lost. Debility. Impotence.

Clinical. — Effects of sexual excesses, especially loss of memory, melancholia, also with impaired co-ordination, numbness and tingling in limbs. Ovarian tumor. Several cases of cystic tumors of the ovary or broad ligament. Pruritus of female genitals. Ovarian neuralgia, with great nervous uneasiness. It seems to control an exaggerated sexual appetite in women, especially when associated with pruritus. Reflex cough in pregnant women.

Respiratory Organs.—Laryngo-bronchial weakness, sometimes with cough, sometimes with changed or whispering voice, rarely with aphonia. Hoarse. Voice faint; whispering, sinks into aphonia. *Hacking cough; dry, fatiguing C.; dry, paroxysmal C., resembling whooping cough, < night and when lying, with difficult respiration, then vomiting of mucus or food.* Vascular "*bruit de souffle.*" Sighing. Respiration difficult; R. anxious; slow.

Clinical.—Spasmodic croup, recurring every night.

Chest.—Symptoms of pulmonary catarrh. Oppression. Tightness on breathing.

Heart and Pulse.—Heart's action feeble; and slow; and intermitting; and its sounds distant and feeble; action slow and fluttering. Pulse rapid and irritable; R. and small; R., then at times slow. Pulse slow; except during the vomiting; and small; and small, intermittent; and weak. Pulse low after the fever. Small; and soft.

Back.—Pain in region of kidneys. Throbbing in lumbar region, spreading to dorsal region and down to coccyx, then half way round body, into intestines and all through him, from head to feet, < abdominal organs, then neuralgia up and down spinal marrow, > port wine, which made him eat, though he vomited his dinner.

Extremities.—Disordered action. Constant twitching of fingers. Hands and fingers in constant action. Trembling of hands; during voluntary motion. Handwriting shaky and indistinct. Inability to stand; to walk. Staggering; on beginning to walk; and his limbs shake and bend under him; with general appearance of intoxication; impaired locomotion, resembling the gait of locomotor ataxia. Weakness of lower; of knees; of extensors of legs and feet.

Skin.—Discolorations and of mucous membrane. Dead-white, < face. Affections, < sebaceous follicles and glands and in sudoriferous glands, causing inflammation, with increase of cellular elements. Erythema and swelling of nose. Hard, red patches on legs, with pains in and around them, the redness disappears momentarily on pressure, painful on pressure, movement of legs painful. Eruption beginning on limbs, extending over whole body, except face, like erythema nodosum, itching < night and getting warm, in irregular patches, cherry-red at their circumference, onion-peel color in centre, turning white on pressure or exertion of limb. On limbs and trunk, in winter, elevated, smooth patches of different shapes, of onion-peel color in centre, cherry at circumference, bases firm but elastic, as in erythema nodosum, redness momentarily > pressure, they itch at night in bed and when warm, they partially reappear when rubbed, they are preceded by itching and pain in limbs, with stiffness, they leave subcutaneous indurations, which are painful on pressure, in one case œdematous swelling of lower halves of lower limbs, in one case fever, with dry skin and rapid pulse, then sweat, in two cases only coated tongue and loss of appetite, in one case yellowish discoloration on former seat of one patch.

Patches on forearms, with pimples. Papules on forehead and scalp. Red, painful pimples and tumors on calves, with smooth, raised, shining edges, a central depression covered with a scab and having a red periphery and hard and sensitive base. Moist eczema on legs. On each leg two places covered with thick, dirty-looking, offensively-smelling scabs, these when removed by poulticing leave an uneven surface formed by vegetation and looking like the stomach of an ox, the patches red and paining like a cut.

Acne; on forehead; on forehead and cheeks. Acne pimples, with yellow tips. Acuminated itching, burning spots, similar to acne, < shoulder and region of neck. On each leg, above a dirty yellow scab of older date, is a red patch of acne-like pustules, some of which exude a creamy fluid like that from boils, between the pustules yellowish-white elevations of the size of millet-seeds, where there is no discharge the surface is cherry-red and feels doughy, the skin around the eruption light red, on r. cheek a similar eruption, but not so far advanced, vesicles and yellowish-white pustules in a circle around a cherry-red place where the skin is raised and flabby, this patch surrounded by a deep erythematous flush, the base of the patch indurated and painful.

On lower limbs, < calves, red patches, but spotted yellow, as from subcutaneous purulent infiltration, with mamillated edges, sometimes the centre also mamillated, the projections being acne-like pustules so close as to amount to a swelling, their bases indurated, the projections partially coalesce, their tips discharge a sero-purulent fluid, the centre of each pustule then presents an umbilicated depression, exuding a creamy moisture, which dries with thick yellow scabs, these make walking impossible, but the centres insensible, they have a reddish areola, with swelling, sometimes successive appearance of fresh clusters of pustules, with mamillations, in two cases the swelling on legs changed into atonic ulcers like rupia, with foul-smelling, red bases, covered with vegetation, pressure caused pain like that in cuts on fingers, they became covered with thick, dirty yellow, offensively-smelling scabs, after the eruption yellow spots covered with scabs, at first nuclei can be felt in the subcutaneous cellular tissue, and in the vicinity of these itching, even pain and cramp, the eruption more frequent in winter.

Pustules, < face, scalp and back, in successive but irregular crops, generally with heat and itching, usually disappearing without suppuration, the P. leave red points. Pustules, partly whitish, partly reddish, on forehead and limbs, which on being opened exude pus mixed with smegma, one on l. leg was covered with a tense mottled epidermis, with a red infiltrated margin, on cheeks were black crusts, which being removed showed a pale red papillary swelling, which bled easily on touch and seemed formed by stoppage of sebaceous follicles. Itching, < chest, face, shoulders, forehead and nose, then small bluish-red pustules, with red areola, becoming yellowish-white at tips, their bases hard, then suppurating, then firm nuclei and deep flush, with swelling, the eruption greatest where the skin is thick or oily, lymphatic and sanguine constitutions are especially liable to it, it is more abundant in youth and adult age.

Painful eruption like varicella on face and legs, became confluent, with many points of suppuration, a band of eruption up each side of face and across forehead, of elevated, flattened, light brown crusts, with slightly red areola, bleeding when removed, while the front and outer side of legs were covered with the eruption, the skin around the spots red, tender, hot, with burning, tingling pain, movement of legs causes pain, the smallest spots, which were the most recent, consisted of elevated conical vesicles filled with a milky semi-fluid matter, the largest spots irregularly oval, elevated, flattened, covered with flaccid moist cuticle or light brown crusts, under which were yellowish red prominences, the eruption began by a minute red, hot and tender pimple, on the summit of which quickly formed a small yellowish-white, tense, conical vesicle pierced by a hair, if the vesicle were ruptured and pressed sebaceous matter, with the root of the hair, was discharged, if let alone the vesicle enlarged and contained pus, the crusts of the older spots were partially dissolved by ether, which, on drying, left a greasy stain, while the rest of the crust consisted of epithelium and damaged blood-cells and pus-corpuscles.

Furuncles, < hairy parts of face, on forehead and neck. Vesicles on thighs and buttocks, afterwards large elevated discs, with a surrounding zone of partially desiccated vesicles, microscopic examination showed active hyperæmia of the corium, of the papillæ and sebaceous glands, especially with corpuscular and fluid exudation. Ulcers, large, elevated uniformly above skin, edges almost vertical, with no signs of cicatricial action, floors firm and grayish-red, with here and there an adherent crust, the secretions fetid, sanious and puriform, the ulcers bled on moderate touch, the tissue of these ulcers so firm that it did not look like ordinary granulation tissue, it was composed of large masses and at several points a slightly villous or rather papillomatous appearance, the U. looked like epitheliomata, but they were symmetrical and showed no evidence of malignancy, they began as papules, became boils, and after discharging degenerated into ulcers.

Sensibility diminished.

Sleep.—Yawning. Sleepiness; irresitible, after evening meal; constant dropping asleep. Sound sleep in a chair in daytime. Deep sleep; and disturbed, from which I woke with a mental struggle, not knowing at first where I was; and often broken by starts, a sort of vague nightmare, sleep prolonged, waking difficult. Sleeplessness. Half sleep. Restless sleep, frequently wakened by voluptuous dreams, with erections. Frequent dreams; and confused; D. heavy and difficult to shake off.

Fever.—Chill. Shivering. Cool skin; and clammy. Cold limbs. Heat; of head; in face. Sweat at night; copious and viscid S.

Kali Carbonicum.

Triturations of pure Carbonate of Potassium are used.

General Action.—All the salts of potash are poisonous (even though potash is necessary to the integrity of tissues). They enfeeble the heart, lower the temperature and cause anæmia. They promote tissue waste, increasing the amount of urine and its solid constituents, especially uric acid and urea. (Among the potashes in our Materia Medica are to be classed *Causticum* and *Tartar emetic.*) In studying the symptomatology special attention should be paid to the character of the secretions from mucous membranes, to the pains and the time of aggravation.

Allies.—The alkalies in general; Hep., Lyc., Nux v., Phos.

Generalities.—Emaciation, with pallor, sunken eyes and dim vision. *Twitching here and there.* Trembling; sudden; of hands and legs, and easily fatigued when walking. *Sticking is the most characteristic pain;* S. externally on head, in nape and teeth, and sticking swelling of cheek; S. and crawling within ear, with similar sensation in stomach and œsophagus. Tearing from within l. ear into external cartilage, and at the same time in bone above and beneath r. patella. Suppurating pain on pressure upon any part. Hammering pain in whole body at night. *Rheumatic pains in back, chest, shoulders and arms, < moving them. Bruised pain in all muscles.* Burning pains, < epigastric region, < pressure. Drawing pain in whole body, now here, now there. Drawing in abdomen, arms and legs, < rest, with bruised pain in upper arm. Tension within body, extending to head and eyes.

Inclined to take cold; when walking in open air in evening, then sweat at night and restlessness and heaviness in neck; after becoming heated on moving about, loss of appetite, shivering, diarrhœa, with griping, restless sleep, etc.; **symptoms of taking cold from every draught of air. Dread of open air** (Hep., Nux v.). Perceptible beating of all arteries. Pulsation over whole body, even to tips of toes; painful P. in clavicles, shoulders, sides of abdomen, etc. *Sensitiveness on touch and motion.* Hollow feeling in whole body. Agitation. Swollen feeling in all her flesh. Oppression at night if she lies on r. side, with anxiety, necessity to sit up until she has eructations. *Heaviness;* in morning in bed. A child desires to be carried constantly. Restlessness as if menses would appear, a week before menstruation.

Weariness; in morning on waking, > rising, < afternoon; after afternoon nap, with nausea; in evening; in evening, almost amounting to nausea; after eating, with sleepiness; after eating, with throbbing in pit of stomach and headache; after a moderate walk, with warmth in stomach, drops of sweat on forehead (in winter) and trembling of limbs; < small of back, with relaxation of cervical muscles and of arms and legs, with faintness about heart; *every morning as if he would faint or have vertigo;* sudden W. in evening on lying down, with aching, nausea, warmth and weakness in pit of stomach, vertigo and vanishing of ideas, two similar attacks in morning; *tremulous W. when walking,* first in knees, then trembling in abdominal muscles and in arms. *Faintness as soon as he moves a little.* Much talk affects her. **Pains recur at 2 or 3 A.M.,** so *that he cannot lie, and are worse than during the day when moving.* Pains renewed in morning after usual stool. *Aggravation in open air,* especially of febrile condition. Amelioration from emission of flatus upward and downward.

Clinical.—This drug is generally indicated in conditions of weakness, with low temperature, soft pulse and mental indifference; the pains in every part of the body are acute, sticking; there is general aggravation from cold (Nux v.), and the time of aggravation, from 3 to 4 A.M., is quite characteristic of the drug. Its action on mucous membranes is characterized by catarrh, with very scanty tenacious secretions. Muscular rheumatism of various parts of the body, with sharp lancinating pains, always < early morning. General anæmia, with great sensitiveness to cold air; with gastro-abdominal symptoms; with tendency to cough and sharp chest-pains.

Mind.—Delirium. Easily becomes violent. Easily aroused to anger; A. in morning on waking, so that he gnashes his teeth. *Fears; about her disease;* in evening in bed; and aversion to society. *Easily frightened;* < touching body lightly. *Anxiety;* in evening. Sad; presentiments. Weeping mood; in evening; after fatigue in open air; because it was constantly in her thoughts that she must die.

Fretful; in evening on falling asleep, and in morning on waking; during dinner, with drawing pain in head; < noon and evening, and every noise is unpleasant. Impatient with his children. Obstinate and does not know what he wishes. Longs for things with impetuosity, is contented with nothing, rages if everything does not go according to her wishes, and often does not know what she wishes. Uneasy. Irresolute. Alternating mood, at one time good and quiet, at another excited and angry at trifles, often hopeful, often despondent. Dread of being alone. Hurry in thought and action. Dread of work. Disinclined to everything and indifferent. Distraction. Want of presence of mind. Mistakes in speaking, could not find the right word or expression. Sensation as if thoughts vanished; and memory, with whizzing in head. Unconsciousness; as if in occiput, after much speaking, > pressing eyes together.

Head.—Jerks towards l., then stiffness of nape. Sticking; through head; externally in various parts. Jerking tearing. *Aching; mornings on waking* (Nux v.); in morning during menstruation, with heaviness; in evening, > moving about, with throbbing and sticking in knees; at night, > wrapping up head; on second day of menses; *from walking in open air;* after taking cold in head, with toothache; < forenoon, with general shivering chill; > sitting up in bed, < lying down; jerking; shattering; ulcerative, after dinner, > lying down; as if something moved in head, < moving head. Painful twisting internally. *Sensation as if something in it were loose* and twisted towards forehead. Painful throbbing when writing.

Constriction as from a band, after dinner. Fulness as if brain pressed against skull. Weakness. *Confusion;* in morning, with heaviness in region of brows; in evening; in morning after rising, as if he had not slept enough, with loss of liveliness; on waking in evening, with loss of ideas, did not know where she was, then anxiety; as after intoxication and as if ears were stopped, with nausea; intermittent, as if screwed in, with sticking in brain. Rush of blood, with orgasm in body; R. at night in bed and at times sensation as if senses would vanish; R. causing intoxicated feeling. Vertigo; *on turning around; on turning suddenly;* when sitting; when walking; when standing and walking, > open air; < morning and evening; < eating; everything turns around with him when walking and in open air; like a swaying to and fro when sitting before eating; on rising, as if head were too light; as if there were a depth behind him and would fall, on turning around after looking into a mirror and after reading.

Forehead.—Sticking; in morning; in upper part of F. and above temples on moving jaws; and at times in l. side of head, with pain in chest and coldness of limbs; in forepart of head. Tearing in l. eminence. Boring inward above l. eye. *Pain in afternoon when walking, with peevishness;* P. in evening on going to sleep, > rest, < walking, with nausea; P. in evening, with drawing; *with pressure above eyes; with photophobia;* with vomiting of mucus and acids; *extending into eyes and root of nose, with drawing tearing;* through eyes; throbbing; crawling, above F.; like confusion. Paroxysmal bursting sensation. *Drawing in forenoon and at midnight.* Pressure outward when writing; P. outward over l. eye. Digging throbbing in bone above l. eye. Intermittent throbbing in F. and especially sides of head; after dinner when walking and standing. Heaviness in sinciput, with pain. Weakness over eyes after rapid walking.

Temples.—Jerking in l.; bubbling J. in r. muscles. *Sticking;* inward in l.; outward above l. and then in middle of forehead; tearing, in l., extending into zygoma. Tearing, and in l. parietal bone; T. in r.; in l. in evening, extending into joint of jaw. *Intermittent pinching in l., also tearings.* Sharp pain externally. Pain; in r. from morning till noon; from both towards middle of head; outward in r. Beating vibration in r.

Vertex.—Pinching in whole upper part of head, < l. side. Drawing and tearing. Pain when pressing upon head; throbbing P. in upper part of l. side, more externally, becoming sticking on pressure. Pressure upon V. in evening.

Sides.—Sticking forward through r. Tearing externally on one when walking in open air. *Tearing drawing in l. half,* above, on front of and in temples. Pain in r. after taking cold, with heat in eyes; *one-sided paroxysmal P. in evening, with weakness, almost amounting to nausea.* Heaviness in l. half.

Occiput.—Stitches on surface of brain on stepping and stooping. Tearing, now in r., now in l. O. and in forehead; throbbing T. in r. side close to nape. Pain when standing, with rush of blood in head and heaviness; P. low down, with burning and with heaviness of head, even to falling forward; P. extending to nape, > open air. Drawing in O. and nape, < r. side, with stiffness. Sensation on stooping as if something sank towards forehead. Heaviness like a confusion; H., head constantly falls backward, with stiffness of nape extending to between scapulæ.

External Head.—Pain in skull extending down nape, with throbbing in head and whole body, nausea and vomiting of bile, the pain < touch and worse in paroxysms. Pressure inward on r. side of skull on rising from stooping. *Falling of hair. Hair dry.* Pimples. Painful boil on r. side as if an ulcer would form. Itching; < occiput; with sore pain when scratched.

Clinical.—Headache, with vertigo, caused by riding in a carriage.

Eyes.—Redness and heat; *R. of white, with many vessels in it.* Inflammation of whites, with burning pain. Swelling of r. Surrounded by blue rings. Staring, it is difficult to remove eyes from an object. *Sticking in middle;* S. in r.; S. and biting. Tearing in r.; in l. in evening before sleep. Pinching. Boring. *Pain;* on moving them; in l. on directing it upward; with weakness; with dry matter in lashes. Pain as if they would be pressed inward; P. at noon, and in orbits, with sleepiness; on reading. *Smarting.* Dryness; as from sand, with sleepiness of eyes. *Burning; and biting;* < open air, with dryness; hot to touch. Itching. *Lachrymation;* in evening, with rays around candle-light; < r. eye, with biting in one canthus; scalding, < at night. Stitches in ball.

Lids.—*Swelling of upper, towards nose. Inflammation of r., with pain in eyes and inability to read by the light.* Canthi maturate. Agglutination in morning. Closed forcibly. Difficult to open in morning on waking. Stitches in r. external canthus. Pulling or tearing in r. lid and above r. eye. Pressure upon lids. *Soreness of external canthus, with burning pain;* S. of l. external canthus; sore feeling in lids on waking after midnight. Coldness. Burning. Itching on margins of r.

Swelling between brows and lids, like a sac; S. of glabella between brows. Twitching in r. brow. Tearing in region of r. brow; *T. in r. orbit and eye at night.* Pain in l. brow in evening in bed, as if a boil would form.

Vision.—*Weak;* in r. eye in morning; after working in water, she sees only a small part of objects, then sticking in head above eyes, with nausea. *Photophobia.* Vanishes when writing, white stars appear, the lower lines seem above the upper, so that he rewrites on upper line. Of spots, threads and points when reading or looking into clear air. Of sparks; shooting from eyes during cough. Of white falling drops on looking at snow. Of a yellow, glistening, tremulous cloud. Of yellow and white radiant wheels, turning in a circle and becoming constantly larger, upon the paper when writing or in open air; of blue and green spots. Of black points and rings when reading; of a black floating ball. Of brilliant colors.

Clinical.—Muscular asthenopia after various diseases, especially if associated with puffiness of the upper lid or between the brow and lid, which seems to be a marked characteristic of this drug, and which has led to the use of the drug in various chronic diseases of the eyes and lids, and indeed of other organs.

Ears.—Discharge of offensive moisture. Hard swelling of parotid, with pain on touch. Inflammation and swelling within ear, with pain about it. Redness, heat and itching. Jerking above and behind ear; J. on l.; J. and trembling in r. on rising from stooping. Sticking; above and behind; in evening in bed; in l., > shaking head; outward in l.; into l. in morning. *Tearing;* in r.; in r. concha; in anterior margin of r.; in and behind; in bones in and about l.; deep in r.; now in one, now in the other; then discharge of yellow thin wax or pus. Pinching in l. outer. Gnawing internally and externally in l. Boring and pressive pain. Pain; in r.; ulcerative, in outer part of r. before midnight; drawing, in one, then in other. Pulling behind r. Hammering in r., impairing hearing. Throbbing in r. at night when lying on it. Bubbling in r., with discharge of much soft wax. *Tickling. Itching.*

Sudden stoppage of one; r., in evening when sitting, and in l. a ringing rushing so that his head wavered; stopped sensation. *Cracking;* on forcible expiration. Ringing; *in one,* with roaring in other. *Singing. Roaring.* Noises. Hearing blunted in evening; blunted, slowly increasing and decreasing.

Clinical.—Chronic inflammation of the middle ear, with sticking pains from within outward, especially behind the ear, and chronic catarrh of the nose, and soreness, with stinging pain.

Nose.—*Thick and red,* < afternoon. Swelling of tip. Red, hot and covered with white pimples. *Nostrils scurfy.* Nostrils ulcerated. Pimple in l. nostril. Pinching in nose and root of nose, < r. side. *Ulcerative pain in r. nostril. Burning;* in l. nostril; in upper part of l. nostril, extending into ethmoid bone, with biting. Itching in nose; in r. nostril. *Stoppage.*

Catarrh on second day of menses, with pain in abdomen, teeth and back, sticking in ears and restless sleep. *Stopped catarrh;* in evening in bed, with crawling in throat; with itching in nose; with much yellowish-green mucus in nose; becoming loose in afternoon on walking. *Fluent coryza;* < evening; with excessive sneezing; with much sneezing, pain in head and back. Bloody mucus from nose. *Blowing offensive matter from r. nostril.* Blowing purulent substance from r. nostril, it then becomes stopped and blowing causes sticking, constrictive pain extending to occiput. *Bleeding* (Carbo v.); *in morning;* R. nostril bloody every morning. Smell acute.

Clinical.—Dry nasal catarrh, with more or less cough and loss of voice. Catarrh, with obstruction, fetid discharge, burning, nostrils sôre and crusty. Nosebleed recurring always on washing the face or in the morning.

Face.—Swelling of cheeks, with redness and papules; S. of cheeks, with tearing and sticking; S. of lower part of r. cheek, with stitches and pain on touch; S. of cheeks developing into ulceration of gum, without previous toothache; S. of a gland beneath chin, with pain after taking cold. *Sickly color, with pale lips. Pallor;* after eating; *with weakness; < open air, and hollow-eyed, and the child looks frozen in open air.* Redness in morning, in a child, vomiting of breakfast, then pallor, then after repeated vomitings weakness; R. of cheeks in evening, then pallor of face. *Lifeless expression. Haggard and exhausted look.* Twitching in l. cheek in evening, with burning stitches and with tearing extending into l. temple. Tearing in l. zygoma, then in inner side of cheek; in l. zygoma in evening and night, preventing sleep, > pressure, with swollen sensation on cheek; pinching T. in r. zygoma extending into palate. Drawing in muscles of cheeks near lower jaw.

Jaws.—Swelling of lower and of glands, with looseness of teeth. Cramp, which also draws pharynx together. Tearing in lower and in front of ear. Pinching in r. lower, not far from joint.

Lips.—Swelling of lower, with ulceration; S. of upper, with cracks, sensitiveness to touch and easy bleeding; lips, tongue and fauces swollen, soft and red, breathing labored, with rattling in trachea and larger tubes, pulse rapid and feeble, skin cold. *Scurf on upper.* Cracked and scaling; lower. Pimples, with biting itching; pointed, itching and moist P. on lips and all around mouth. Vesicles; on red of lower, painful to touch and itching. Stitch in upper. Tearing in l. side of upper and in gum, > pressure. Cramp-like sensation. Soreness of red, with stickiness in morning on waking. Smarting sore pain in margin of red, with sensitiveness to touch. Itching about margins. Burning; of lower.

Mouth.—Teeth. Looseness of all; of one after another, with sensitiveness, or a spot on bone of face becomes painful and is sensitive, then jerking or tearing in one point by paroxysms. Offensive odor. Grinding at night in sleep. *Stitches;* in morning on waking, with frequent sneezing; here and there in incisors in evening; in incisors during supper, with feeling of bluntness; and in gum, then in cheek and swelling of cheek; burning S., < night, with internal chilliness and with swelling of lower jaw and gum; burning S. as from a hot iron, < night. Tearing in r. and r. lower jaw; T. during or soon after eating; T. in l. molar and l. zygoma, < cold, > tight binding, with griping in them. *Boring after dinner, as if something got into tooth.* Digging in a l. upper molar after dinner. Burrowing in lower from picking them. **Aching only when eating,** at noon and in evening, *as if something got into a hollow tooth,* with paroxysmal drawing extending to eye and ear; A. as if something got into a hollow tooth, transiently > cold water, with drawing behind ear and upon head, at last jerking in tooth and disappearance of pain. *Throbbing pain only when eating;* T. or picking in a r. upper incisor after dinner; T. on motion, at other times burning pain. Pain every morning on waking; P. in l. in morning in bed and all the forenoon; in roots of l. every morning after waking, < eating; *in root of last hollow molar in evening;* from contact of anything cold or warm; *only on taking food;* on taking water into mouth; after eating, extending into bones of cheek and ear, where it is a sticking; with faceache; then swelling of gums; in attacks, even from cold air entering mouth, > warmth. Constricting pain. *Drawing as soon as she gets into bed in evening;* in roots of incisors and l. molars, < evening; D. and jerking as if being eroded, usually after eating and at night. Corrosive itching pain in T. and gums. Itching after supper; in a l. upper molar after dinner, > pressure, with digging. Sensitiveness. Loose feeling in a l. upper molar.

Gums.—Swelling above upper molars, with swelling of l. tonsil and cervical glands. Red. Loosened and fell off in pieces. Ulcer; on r. lower outer. Painful inflammation of front. Tearing about first incisors. Tickling and bleeding after sucking it with the tongue. Soreness of incisors.

Tongue.—Destruction of T., gum and fauces, the cuticle appearing as if destroyed with a hot iron, while inside of cheeks, roof of mouth and velum were inflamed. Swelling, with painful blisters upon it. Painful blisters, and on gum. *Painful pimple on tip. Soreness of tip;* of frænum. Dry in morning, and white as from an acid; D. in morning on waking, and almost insensible. Burning; *on tip, as if raw or covered with blisters.*

Mouth and fauces covered with a dirty brown slough, which made the surface almost insensible, heat in fauces and gullet as soon as the slough began to separate, during the next week large portions of tough matter, sometimes firm like leather, were brought up by coughing, hawking or vomiting, then a raw surface, with burning and pain on swallowing. *Painful blisters in all parts, with burning pain* (K. chl.). *Offensive odor like old cheese every morning* (see K. brom.). *Sticking in back part of palate* in morning and evening, before outbreak of catarrh, < swallowing, *with biting*, as from dryness. Soreness. Raw feeling as from something acrid, and on tongue. Itching on hard palate. Numbness in morning after waking, as if burnt. Burning in morning, with thirst.

Dryness waking him in morning; D. in morning after rising; *in evening without thirst;* dry sticky sensation; dry sensation, with salivation. *Salivation;* every night, waking her at 3 A.M. Insipid, glutinous saliva. Offensive-tasting saliva. *Taste bad; and mouth slimy.* Bitter taste; in morning; with nausea; in throat; bitter, sour after breakfast. Taste sour; at night. T. sweetish. T. of blood in morning after waking. T. lost in morning after waking.

Clinical.—Toothache of a sticking, tearing character, extending into the head.

Throat.—Submaxillary gland painful to touch. Elongation of uvula, with stiffness of nape. **Mucus; < morning; in back, only loosened by much hawking; tenacious, in back part in morning, which can neither be completely swallowed nor hawked up** (K. bi.). *Hawking in morning, with expectoration.* **Sticking in pharynx as from a fish-bone** (Hep.), *if he becomes cold.* Anxious pressure. Sore pain; in palate on swallowing. Soreness, with difficult swallowing and difficult opening of mouth. Sensation of a plug, which is loosened by cough. Feeling of a lump; on l. side, with sticking on empty swallowing; about root of tongue, < swallowing saliva, which makes it smart, < singing in evening, > swallowing food, which makes it go lower.

Smarting on swallowing. *Scraping; with dryness and roughness. Roughness, with cough;* R., with sneezing; R. on uncovering body. *Crawling*, morning and evening, *provoking hawking and cough*, with feeling of adherent mucus. Dryness far back. **Swallowing difficult**, *food descends œsophagus very slowly;* S. painful; S. of dry or cold things impossible. Œsophagus sensitive, she can swallow only lukewarm food. Pressure and tearing in œsophagus.

Clinical.—Pharyngeal catarrh, with constant need to hawk. Catarrhal stricture of œsophagus, feeling of a lump which cannot be swallowed, or of a stick extending into the stomach. Pharyngeal catarrh, with constant clearing of the throat, sharp stinging pains, < cold (Hep.).

Stomach.—Appetite increased; longing for acids; little; little, with insipid taste, though food tastes good. Aversion to food, especially meat; to black bread. Disgust for everything. Thirst; in forenoon; in evening; at night. *Eructations; in morning; of water after midnight;* loud, with salivation; tasting of food; at night of food eaten at noon. *Sour eructations* (Nux v., Lyc., Na. c.); in morning; in afternoon, with nausea; after eating; of sour, bitter water. Waterbrash. Hiccough; at noon; before midnight.

Nausea; in morning, with violent yawning, eructations, twisting about stomach, heat and anxiety; in forenoon; at night in bed; **on every inward emotion,** *but when fasting there is only retching;* during cough; on eating fried fish, amounting to vomiting; after eating during menses, with fulness, then vomiting; before and after dinner, with vertigo, eructations, weakness of limbs and coldness of hands and feet, not without appetite; on pressing over epigastric region; < *eating;* with waterbrash; with salivation and diarrhœa; with trembling of hands and feet; with vomiting and with bruised pain in abdomen, < pressure, prostration, confusion of head, sleepiness and watery stools, then constipation. *Nausea as if to faintness;* in forenoon, > lying down.

Retching; evenings; with short breath. Vomiting; on coughing; after eating or drinking, with pain; < drinking warm water; without an overloaded or disordered stomach, next day weakness and loss of appetite; with faintlike sinking of strength; *of food and acids;* incessant; sour, at the time menses should come on but did not, with swelling of cheeks and gums and stitches in cheeks.

Rumbling; gurgling and movings. Jerking in r. side of pit. Cramp; beginning at stool, so that she doubled herself up and could not speak, micturition, nausea, eructations, vomiting of water, retching, before the vomiting shivering, during it reeling, with shaking of hands and feet, then anxiety and general heat, relief of the pain and pallor, at last the usual stool; intermittent C. in morning, > walking; jerklike, at night after falling asleep, with anxiety, groaning, coldness of tip of nose, hands and feet, then vomiting of food and acids and eructations of air.

Sticking returning after dinner; with sensation as if everything were turned about; S. extending towards l. axilla, afterwards into small of back. *Feeling as if cut to pieces in morning*, **with external sensitiveness of epigastric region**; cutting towards evening; in pit during and after breakfast. Acute pain. Digging in pit in afternoon, then eructations of bitter water; *D.*, with painful contraction and sensation as if everything would be turned about, with rising of water, all > during dinner, but returning with burning extending into throat. Digging burrowing. Spasmodic pain, with oppression at pit. Sore pain in pit during inspiration and expiration. *Epigastric region sensitive externally* to touch, eating and talking.

Pain obliging lying down. Paroxysmal screwing-together pains, < night, extending into chest and intestines, impeding respiration and speech. Painful contraction from both sides, > vomiting clear water, with fulness. Constriction extending towards pharynx; C. even at 1 A.M., in attacks till morning, extending into chest and under shoulders, where it becomes sticking, with choking in throat and oppression of breath, then anxiety, sweat and eructations, which relieved. Constrictive spasmodic pains from least food or drink, especially cold. Spasmodic contraction in pit and transversely across chest; S. C., then eructations, which often relieve, or chilliness and shivering, < hands, back and head, and the usual stool.

Feeling as if full of water. Pressure in pit; P. in morning on waking; below pit in morning and afternoon, > bending backward and after eating; P. across above S. and beneath hypochondria in evening in bed; beneath pit at night, with cough; at night, with burning; in pit and lower part of chest, > eructations, with difficult breathing and rising of heat to head; *in attacks, extending into chest*, with suffocation, nausea, prostration, necessity to lie down, trembling of hands and feet, then vomiting of bitter water with relief; as from a stone in morning in bed, > hawking. *Heaviness; after eating*, < breakfast. Oppression after bread. *Swollen feeling in epigastric region.* Fulness in pit; in epigastric region, with pressure; F. after eating, during menstruation, with nausea, then vomiting. Ineffectual desire to eructate in morning and afternoon, then spasmodic constriction.

Uneasiness in epigastric region on pressure; *U. starting from pit, then eructations of food and acids. Throbbing in epigastric region, with sensitiveness to touch; T. in pit*, < morning, whereby the pit rises visibly. *Flatulent feeling.* Drawing transversely in morning after rising, with cutting. Sudden shock, changing to eructations of air or hiccough. *Burning acidity rising from stomach, with spasmodic constriction.* Heartburn; after supper; after eating vegetables, extending into pharynx. Burning; in forenoon after eructations; as soon as fluids reach it, then vomiting; extending to mouth, with constriction. Emptiness. Milk does not agree with her.

Clinical.—The gastric symptoms indicating this drug are indigestion, with bloating, sour eructations, heartburn and a weak feeling, or a feeling of a lump in the pit of the stomach, or a feeling of pulsation; after eating there are generally pressure, belching of gas, bloating and soreness (Lyc., Carb. v.). Gastralgia, sharp cutting or sticking, < motion or eating. Dyspepsia of old people. Gastric disorders from drinking ice-water.

Abdomen.—Distention (Carb. v.); **after eating** (Lyc.); **after eating a little** (Lyc.); with dragging asunder and griping, then soft stool; with pain, fulness, weakness and disinclination for motion or mental effort; *hard, with pain in umbilical region on touch.* Rumbling, with eructations and yawning; R., then two liquid stools. Swashing, then pain in stomach, > afternoon by eructations and emission of flatus. Movings, > emission of flatus, with urging to stool; M., then cutting in stomach, with pressure extending into throat. *Emission of flatus;* at night; offensive, at night; difficult, with unsatisfactory stool. Flatulence at night; F. during menses, with bad taste and eructations of bile. *Incarcerated flatus.* Jerkings.

Cramp. Sticking at night on slightest movement in bed, with pressure as from an internal induration. **Cutting** at night (Nux v.), then in morning pain in small of back and in chest, and in afternoon bruised pain in limbs; **during menses**; *obliging him to sit bent over, pressing with both hands, or to lean far back;* with drawing like false labor-pains; *as before diarrhœa.* Griping; in morning in bed, preceded by chill, with urging to soft stool; after soup at noon and in evening and after warm cakes in morning, with uneasiness; with uneasiness and thin stool; with the usual stool, then urging till afternoon, then liquid stool; then diarrhœa, then burning in rectum; intermittent, at night, with nausea and constant eructations.

Pain; in morning, then semi-liquid stool; at night, with diarrhœa; before soft stool; after a difficult, scanty stool; during menses, with rumbling, bad taste, weakness and sleepiness; till late at night, sometimes extending towards hips; on touch; *in muscles on touch;* sore P., with pressure towards genitals, as during menses, with pain in small of back; P. like a shock during cough. Flatulent pain; after breakfast, transiently > emission of flatus; > eructations and emissions of flatus. Constriction; spasmodic, causing coldness. Painful drawings, with constipation. *Throbbing.* Uneasiness, with hard stool. *Coldness during menses, as if a cold fluid passed through intestines;* C. in evening, < r. side, with swashing. Heat in forenoon rising into stomach; H. and drawing.

Hypochondria.—Sticking in l.; *in hepatic region; in r. after dinner; in hepatic and r. inguinal regions; in a spot in hepatic region, with sore pain on touch;* in l., with pressure; and in pit of stomach, impeding respiration; *pinching, in hepatic region; in hepatic region like pleurodynia. Sticking tearing. Cutting.* Pinching in l. as from incarcerated flatus. *Pain in liver when walking; P. in liver changing to heaviness;* P. in H., with gurgling; *drawing P. in liver; sore P. in liver as after pressure; burning P. in liver. Heat in liver.*

Rumbling in upper A. before dinner, with pain. Cutting in upper as from movements of flatus, when walking, with emission of flatus. Griping in upper towards noon. Pinching in upper in morning. Pain in upper in evening. Sticking in r. side of A. when laughing; in r. side like jerkings; in r. side as after retaining urine during sleep, > emission of flatus. Tearing, at times jerking in r. side of A. or flank in evening. Pressure in l. side from stooping.

Umbilicus.—Distended feeling below, > moving about. Sticking in r. side near U.; S. above U. as from flatus. *Cutting about U.* Griping below U. during dinner and after rising from a seat, burning in r. groin, with internal and external sensitiveness and on stooping feeling as if something would fall out. Digging below U. as from incarcerated flatus, obliging him to sit bent over, < walking in open air. Painful retraction of region when sitting. Burning about U. during dinner, with griping in abdomen.

Hypogastrium.—Thickness. Painful distention of groins when sitting after dinner. Gurgling in l. side on pressure; intermittent G. pressing outward in r. groin. Flatulence presses painfully upon bladder. *Sticking;* in forenoon and evening; in groins and flanks on moving or stretching; sudden, in l. groin during stool, with swelling of glands; twinging cutting, in l., extending into anus and perineum, < retracting abdomen, > emission of flatus; drawing S. or dragging outward as if an old scar of an operation for hernia would open. Intermittent tearing near l. hip, or stitches. *Cutting as if everything would be torn to pieces, deep down, then higher up.* Griping before and after diarrhœa; G. in groins when walking, < sitting and after rising, then sticking in anus, with urging to stool. Pinching. Pain; in a spot in l. in evening; in r. groin on retracting abdomen; paroxysmal, above pubis, > emission of flatus; in r. groin, as from a swelling; in groin, as from a hernia. Pressure outward. *Dragging towards groins during stool; in groins, > emission of flatus, with sensitiveness to touch. Weight, < walking. Feeling of tension when sitting and walking, with heaviness.*

Clinical.—Symptoms of chronic inflammation of the liver, with stitches, soreness, sometimes jaundice, swelling of abdomen, etc. It has been found useful in a variety of diseases of the bowels, flatulent indigestion, colic, dropsical effusions, and even peritonitis, always with sharp pains, without fever, great aggravation from cold air and in the early morning. Sequelæ of biliary calculi. Sharp sticking in r. side, extending across the abdomen or up into the chest.

Rectum.—Discharge of white mucus before and during stool; D. of blood, then uneasiness in blood and pulsation in whole body. Stitches. *Burning and griping; B. after stool.* Tenesmus; after usual stool. Frequent urging, with scanty passage; frequent U. at night, > passage of flatus; paroxysmal U., with small, natural stool, or only flatus; U. as to diarrhœa, but hard stool, with colic; *ineffectual U., with feeling as if rectum were too weak to evacuate the stool* (Hep.).

Anus.—Pimples; ulcerative, with sticking. *Hæmorrhoids swollen, bleeding during natural stool; S.* and bleeding when urinating; *S. and protrude with a hard stool; H. protrude during diarrhœa, with stitches and burning for many hours;* protrude when urinating and discharge blood, but next day white mucus; *inflammation of H.; stitches; sore pain; pain; pain during cough; pain when walking;* crawling, as from worms. *Stitches;* in evening, with crawling; when not at stool; *with tearing and cutting. Burning cutting.* Twinging. Griping. Pinching and constriction, and in epigastric region, extending to throat. After vomiting pain as if it would burst. *Soreness.* Smarting in evening. *Biting sore sensation in and around A. after stool.* Biting pain, with diarrhœa. *Burning; after stool;* during and after stool; preventing sleep. *Crawling;* in evening, with itching; sticking, before stool. *Itching;* after supper. Burning itching in perineum at night.

Stool.—Semi-liquid (scanty), pain in bowels, then tenesmus. Thin, unnoticed, on emission of flatus. Diarrhœa day and night; in evening; every night from 3 to 4 A.M.; at night, with pain in abdomen, which lasts next day; with colic; with weariness; painless, with rumbling in abdomen; light-colored and gray, with weariness, lying down, loss of appetite and daily colic. *Soft; and insufficient;* and tenacious, dark.

Constipation; during menstruation. Like sheep-dung, painful and difficult (Mag. m.). Hard, and only every other day; H., and contained pieces of a tape-worm; H., delayed, at times with urging or followed by tenesmus; H., scanty in morning, then soft in forenoon. *Insufficient; after much pressure.* Scanty, three times in one day. Copious, brown; C., containing blackish membranes and streaks of blood, with colic. *Bloody;* then anxiety and dyspnœa. Purulent. Offensive. Tenacious, as if he could not loosen it. Containing a round worm.

Clinical.—Chronic diarrhœa, generally painless and light-colored, with chronic dyspepsia or with chronic hepatic disease. Constipation, with bleeding hæmorrhoids, accumulation of fæces in large light-colored masses, with sharp cutting pains.

Urinary Organs.—Tearing in neck of bladder when not urinating; cutting T. in neck when urinating, < pressing upon the urine. Cutting in region of bladder. *Urging; but he has to wait long and urine flows slowly* (Caust., Hep., etc.). Discharge of prostatic fluid after micturition. Tearing in urethra; pinching. Intermittent cutting in urethra when not urinating. Drawing in forepart of urethra, with tearing. Burning biting in urethra during and after urinating. *Burning in urethra when urinating;* after U.; in orifice of U. and in upper part of internal prepuce in morning in bed after urinating, with biting.

Frequent micturition; **at night**, *but often pressure upon bladder long before the urine comes;* but scanty urine each time. *She must press long before she can start the urine.* Micturition seldom, and the urine high-colored. *Discharge of a few drops after urinating.* Suddenly obliged to pass a few drops of urine while intent upon her work. Stream interrupted in afternoon.

Urine fiery, diminished; dark yellow, with a cloud; pale, scanty; pale greenish, with burning during and after micturition; turbid; like mealy water, with much sediment on standing.

Clinical.—Loss of power of the bladder to expel the urine, < night, the urine is discharged slowly.

Sexual Organs.—Strong seminal odor of male. Glans, tearing; tearing drawing; sharp drawing pain through; bubbling sensation; tension; itching, and especially at orifice of urethra, becoming tearing; sticking itching. Frequent erections; during uneasy, dreamy sleep; and painful, with spasmodic contraction of spermatic cords; E. at night without sexual excitement; impetuous E.; violent, exhausting E. after midnight, disturbing sleep; no E. Swelling of testicle and spermatic cord, with external heat. Tension of l. testicle; and of pubis. Scrotum, soreness; bruised pain; *itching;* itching preventing sleep. *Desire;* with burning; lost, with undiminished erections in morning. *Emissions, then weakness;* E., with voluptuous dreams; E. two nights in succession. Coition without emission.

Female.—*Soreness before, during and after menstruation.* Voluptuous sensation as during coition wakes her in morning before menstruation. Pinching in labia. Pudenda, burning biting pimples; sticking transversely through; burning sticking; tearing in l. side, extending through abdomen into chest; burning itching. Pinching in vagina during coition. Sore pain in vagina during coition. Discharge of clotted blood at night (after vexation) in fifth month of pregnancy, with headache and yellow color of face. Leucorrhœa; yellowish, with itching and burning on pudenda. *Menstruation too early; and more profuse, lasting longer than usual* (Calc. c.); and scanty first day, profuse second day, scanty third day, ceasing on fourth; and lasting six days, scanty the first, profuse the latter days, with weakness, sleepiness and pain in abdomen and teeth. Menstruation late, with pain in hypogastrium. Menses acrid, offensive, causing soreness of thighs, which become covered with an eruption.

Clinical.—Suppression of menses, with bloating of abdomen, sharp pains in the epigastrium, dyspeptic symptoms, nosebleed, general sensitiveness to cold, swelling of the upper lids, etc. Threatening abortion, with sharp cutting in abdomen, etc. Suppression of the lochia, with bloating of abdomen, very sharp pains, etc., without fever. Dysmenorrhœa in women who menstruate freely. Puerperal metritis, with sharp cutting. It has been prescribed for excessively profuse menstruation, with the peculiar symptoms of the drug.

Respiratory Organs.—*Easy choking when eating.* Rattling in trachea on breathing, with gurgling, then cough. Sticking in larynx, caused by cough, with fluent coryza. *Raw pain in larynx on coughing.* Drawing pain in larynx, with rawness. Constriction in larynx in open air; C. in evening on falling asleep, then sticking dryness in throat. Voice rough. *Hoarseness and loss of voice;* H., then fluent coryza; H. as if something stuck in throat, provoking desire to hawk.

Cough as early as 3 A.M., *repeated every half hour;* in evening in bed; every five minutes from 9 P.M. till morning; before midnight, > during the day; *waking him at night;* on playing the violin; after eating, from tickling; from tickling in throat; from tickling in larynx, with hoarseness (Bro.). *Tickling C. C. that affects the chest, from tickling in throat* (Phos.). *Suffocative C. at 5 A.M., as from dryness of larynx, with cramp in chest so that she could not speak, redness of face and general* *sweat.* Racking C., so that she loses her senses. Violent C. in morning fasting, > breakfast; V. in morning, *causing vomiting; V. every evening after lying some time.* Paroxysmal, C. amounting to retching, causing sore pain in vertex, then exhaustion. *Fatiguing C. in evening.* Scraping, scratching C. Hacking C. in afternoon and next forenoon; H., < night and morning, with expectoration and coryza. *Dry C. from tickling in throat; D., waking at night, with acute pain in chest on coughing, little C. during the day;* D., almost only at night, with sticking in larynx; dry, suddenly coming and going. C., with expectoration; in morning, < evening; of bloody mucus; C. loosens mucus, which cannot be expectorated.

Expectoration of small round lumps of mucus (Stan.); E. of mucus at night; E. of sourish taste.

Dyspnœa; when writing, with short breath. *Breath short in morning. He felt as if there were no air in his chest. Arrest of breath wakes him at night.* Inclination to take a deep breath.

Clinical.—Chronic or subacute catarrh of the air-passages, sometimes with dyspnœa, suffocative breathing; the cough is generally dry, or the expectoration is very scanty, regularly < 3 A.M., at times paroxysmal and suffocative. Cough, with sharp cutting or sticking in sides of chest or around the hypochondria. Asthma recurring every morning about 3 or 4 A.M., especially < sudden cold changes. Chronic pneumonia or chronic inflammation of the upper part of the lungs tending to tuberculosis, the cough regularly < 3 or 4 A.M., with sharp sticking in chest, with constant taking cold from the slightest exposure; the patients are weak, short-breathed, they have the swellings under the eyebrows and the gastric symptoms of the drug; it is almost as frequently indicated as Calc. carb., though the Kali patient is worse from cold, while the Calc. patient is worse from dampness; the chronic troubles requiring Kali should be sent to a warm climate, though moist; those requiring Calc. should be sent to a dry climate, though cold. The expectoration of this drug is scanty and difficult to raise; it is very apt to remain adherent to the pharynx or slips back when partially expectorated. It has something of the stringy character of Kali bich., but is less tenacious and less profuse. Like all the Kalis it is frequently indicated in asthma, which seems to be constitutional and hereditary, the patient wakes at 3 or 4 A.M. with dyspnœa, wheezing and sharp pain in chest on breathing; (Kali nit. is particularly indicated by burning in chest and freer secretion of mucus). Whooping cough is sometimes, but rarely, treated with it, the paroxysms occurring at 3 or 4 A.M. Chronic pleurisy, with sharp pains, dry cough, asthmatic breathing at 3 A.M., etc.

Chest.—Rattling at night when lying on back. Trembling in forepart, or twitching. Bubbling twitches in upper part of r. breast. *Sticking in r.; l.;* beneath l. short ribs; beneath r. ribs in morning; beneath breasts in afternoon after lifting a heavy weight, then griping in sides of upper abdomen, extending forward; in sternum, in front of r. breast, in evening; in r. or l. side at night; in l. breast, in region of heart, after midnight, at times extending into back, > lying on r. side, < lying on l. side, next night early waking, sticking in chest, short breath when lying on l. side, intolerable except when resting in highest possible position, > lying on r. side, reappearing third night when lying on back; **S. in l. on deep breathing; in r. on inspiration;** *in sides on inspiration;* beneath last r. ribs on inspiration; in l. during cough; between r. middle ribs when sitting; *S. beneath l. breast, at times extending from low down in chest, also in evening;* S. extending into C. below l. clavicle, in evening, transiently > pressure; intermittent *S. in r.;* beneath last r. ribs, not affecting respiration; sudden S. in sternum during eructations and on swallowing liquids; pinching S. in r. Burning sticking in r. on rising from stooping; in l. when sitting, > rising; in costal regions in afternoon. Cutting stitches beneath r. clavicle, with pain as if a thorn were sticking there. Tearing sticking in breasts; in l. costal region, taking away the breath.

Cutting in evening after lying down, she *does not know how she shall lie, < lying on r. side; C. in l. lower part, with sticking,* **the C. extending into l. hypochondrium;** in lower part, < l. side, extending into upper abdomen, leaving sticking in l. chest; *in morning,* < about pit of stomach, as from incarcerated flatus. Tearing in breasts; on last l. ribs; in sternum above l. side of pit of stomach in evening. Pinching in r.; P. in pectoral muscles. Sharp pain behind sternum on breathing, swallowing liquids and eructations. Boring deep into l.

Pain in whole l.; in r. margin of sternum in morning on rising, with pain to touch; on breathing; in ensiform cartilage on coughing and on deep inspiration; in middle and drawing downward; starting from r. breast, *extending towards liver,* with throbbing in epigastric region, which is painful to touch; intermittent, in forepart, < r. side, < inspiration, > eructations; jerking P. externally in l. lowest rib; spasmodic, > eructations. *Sore pain, < talking; in upper part on breathing, touching and lifting anything heavy.* Bruised pain. Drawing pain across C. Scraping caused by wind; tearing S., during cough. Intermittent biting now here, now there. *Oppression,* with deep moans; O., with difficult respiration; with distention of abdomen. *Throbbing in l. near pit of stomach;* sticking T. in one r. rib, opposite pit of stomach. Tension in r. or l. side at night; *T. across C. on expiration when walking.* Anxiety towards evening. Tickling in r. breast. *Weakness; from rapid walking.* Affected by loud talking.

Heart and Pulse.—Sticking in præcordial region. Pinching as if it were hanging by tightly drawn bands, < deep inspiration and cough, > motion. Anxiety preventing sleep after 2 A.M. Burning in region. *Palpitation* in forenoon, with confusion of head and nausea; *P. on least exertion;* P., with anxiety; when hungry. Intermittent beats of heart. Pulse rapid; slow.

Clinical.—The heart is weak and the pulse feeble in nearly all Kali cases. Rarely, but sometimes indicated in chronic cardiac inflammations, with sharp sticking pains and the general symptoms of the drug.

Neck.—*Swelling of glands;* with pain on turning head; with tickling, > pressure of cold hands; at angle of jaw, and hard. Seemed thicker and neck-cloth too tight. Stitches in glands; S. in nape extending into occiput. Tearing in nape; in lower part of r. side; T. in r. side in morning. Pain in muscles on motion; P. in nape on bending head backward; in glands as after taking cold; jerking P. in l. side; drawing P. in nape. Drawing in r. side. Tension in nape, < moving head. Rush of blood. *Stiffness* of nape in morning; *in morning in bed;* at night; with elongation of uvula.

Back.—Sticking in r. side, extending through chest. Aching; in spine on swallowing; drawing P.; sprained P.; *bruised P. during rest;* burning P., < walking in open air. Biting pinching on posterior parts of ribs. Contractive pain during rest after physical exertion; with necessity to lie down, then sweat all night and in morning stool of blood and mucus. Stiffness preventing stooping; S. and lameness in back and small of back. Sharp pressure on upper part.

Scapulæ.—Sticking in l.; *in r. on breathing;* between S. almost only when sitting, with oppression and anxiety in chest; near r., with tearing; in tip of l. during hard work, extending to pit of stomach; pinching; as from a sprain in l., extending into chest; tearing, under r. *Tearing in r. in morning;* cramplike, between S., then stiffness of nape, on attempting to move head it jerked backward several times. Sprained pain in l. Bruised pain between S. and on l. shoulder, > motion; sticking B. pain on motion, extending into chest. Pressure in l.; between S., then burning extending to crest of pelvis, the B. is perceptible to hand; drawing. Tensive pain behind l. on breathing; T. pressure like fatigue extending from r. along side of back into small of back, < riding in a carriage. Throbbing on upper margin of l.

Small of Back.—Sticking, ascending at times through l. side of abdomen to chest. *S. in region of kidneys;* in region of l. kidney, at first on expiration, then several times in succession, > rubbing. Tearing in region of r. kidney; *T. in lumbar muscles, impeding respiration;* T. back and forth in l. when sitting, > motion; *burning T. near r. side of spine, above small of B.*, pain as if flesh were torn away on walking, > touch. Gnawing in coccyx. *Pain in region of kidneys;* above r. kidney in morning; P. only on bending backward; after standing or walking; above small of back when sitting; with laborlike pains in abdomen and discharge from vagina; as if broken, on moving about; as from flatulent distention, > emission of flatus, with feeling as if bubbles accumulated and urging to stool; jerking, on stooping, so that he cannot stand erect; sore, in region of r. kidney; tickling weary P. above sacrum. Bruised pain, < morning on rising; B. pain in region of kidneys in afternoon when sitting. *Drawing pain.* Drawing alternating with pulsation, > lying. *Pressure inward from sides in morning; P. during menstruation, and in forepart of hypogastrium, as if everything would press out at genitals.* Pulsation. Heaviness; during menstruation. Stiffness.

Clinical.—Lumbago, with sudden sharp lancinating pains, extending up and down the back, rarely through to the front, the patient is attacked at 3 A.M. and cannot remain in bed. Lumbago, as if the small of the back were broken, pains shooting down backs of thighs.

Extremities.—Jerking. Trembling and convulsive movements. *Sticking in joints and tendons.* Tearing in fingers and toes. *Pain when he rests them on anything; in joints* of feet, knees and hands during rest; in joints, with drawing pain in long bones; drawing P. in all, with feeling as if he had been long sick, pallor and emaciation. *Uneasiness in evening in bed.* Weakness; tickling. *Heaviness,* < legs; *so that she can scarcely lift the feet.* L. arm and r. leg go to sleep at night; arm and leg on which she lies fall asleep.

Upper Extremities.—Axillæ. *Glands swollen;* and painful to touch as if suppurating. Sticking in l.; below A., with pressure and tearing; tearing, in r. in morning on raising arm when writing. Tearing in l. during rest; sore, below l., < deep respiration; T. in r., with cutting. Sensitiveness in r., with burning.

Shoulder.—Cracking in joint on moving it or raising it high. Sticking; in l., then in tendons on l. side of neck. Tearing in l.; *in l. joint;* in r. when knitting, > moving it; pinching, in r. Pinching in r. joint, < inspiration. Pain in l. on moving arm violently or making strong pressure with it. Bruised pain beneath r., < moving or touching it. Drawing pain in r. Tensive pain in l. in morning, so that he cannot raise the arm. Tension and drawing in r., with paralyzed feeling in r. arm; paralytic T. and drawing in l. in morning on waking, extending into forearm, which is inclined to fall asleep. Heaviness.

Arm.—Jerking in l.; in evening on falling asleep. Tearing in l.; down to wrist. Drawing pain in l. Tensive pain, so that he could not raise it straight. Drawing extending into hands. *Weakness;* when writing; with swelling of upper arm and hand. Asleep in morning in bed, with internal pressure as if stiff and lame, they and hands are insensible; A. and stiff in cold, they fall asleep even after violent exercise; A. on which he lies at night falls asleep. Paralyzed feeling.

Upper Arm.—Twitching in flesh of l. Sticking in r. Tearing in upper part of r. and in elbow; above bend of r. elbow in evening; in l., at times extending into shoulder; sticking, in l. Bruised pain in r., < raising arm. Throbbing pain waking at night; *intermittent, in l.* Paralytic pain, < motion. Burning tension just above r. elbow.

Sticking in bends of elbows in morning in bed; tearing, in bend of l. elbow. *Tearing in bends of elbows; in elbows, with drawing,* at times warmth. Pain in r. elbow as if stiff on stretching arm. Tearing in middle of forearms; upper part; in F. extending towards wrists; in styloid process of radius. Drawing pain in forearm; paralytic painful drawing from l. into hand in evening. Tensive pain on forearm. Stitches in l. wrist. Tearing in wrists; in r. when knitting; in l. extending to ring finger. Drawing on inner surface of l. wrist, < motion.

Hand.—Trembling in morning when writing. Restless at night. *Tearing between thumb and index;* extending from back of l. into fingers; on back of l., as if in marrow of bones. Pain on back of l.; P. in bones on grasping. Weakness. *Falling asleep* in morning on waking, with headache, which is worse on rising, with empty eructations till noon.

Fingers.—Sticking in r.; beneath nail of l. middle; in tips of r., as from suppuration; intermittent, in middle joint of r. index; in r. index; as if a needle and thread were drawn from lower part towards tip, > bending finger, renewed on stretching it out. Tearing in l. little; in l. thumb; in ball of thumb; in phalanges and joints; in middle joint of index; joints of l. middle; beneath nails; beneath thumb-nails; in lower part of r. index, extending towards tip; in l. little towards tip during motion; sticking T. beneath nail and in tip of index; drawing T. in tip of little; burning T. in tip of index. Ulcerative pain in first joint of l. thumb in evening. Sore pain in last phalanx of middle finger, < under nail, in morning. Drawing pain in metacarpal joints. Jerklike drawing back and forth in morning in bed, then numbness, difficult motion and chilliness in fingers. *Burning pain in two l.;* at insertion of nail of middle. Stiffness of thumb and index when writing, with paralytic weakness. *Falling asleep of tip,* < morning; thumb falls asleep towards morning. Paralysis of thumb from knitting. Insensibility of r. thumb.

Lower Extremities.—*Falling asleep; r. and numbness,* < leg. Ascending steps is difficult. Jerking in nates. *Tearing in and on nates not far from hip-joint;* attacks of pinching T. in nates. Pain in nates; *suppurative, from sitting, and in thighs.*

Hip.—*Sticking in l. when standing, after sitting down sticking tearing down whole leg, as if in marrow, > after rising from seat. Tearing, even when sitting, and in knees;* T. in hips or parts enveloping them, at times crawling; intermittent T. in l.; pinching T. Jerking pain in l. on turning leg. Bruised pain, with pain on motion and sneezing; B. pain in upper part of l. bone when walking and on touch; B. pain in H. and limbs, < calves, on walking, with weakness.

Thigh.—*Cramp in r. and in calf, waking him at night. Jerking;* in anterior surface of r. Soreness between. Tearing in upper and inner part; T. in l. and in tibia, during menses; close to nates, extending towards genitals. Sore pain in a spot in middle on touch. Bruised pain above r. knee as if thigh would fall off when standing, < sitting. Drawing pain; in l., extending to knee; as if it would break when ascending. *Paralytic drawing,* often increasing to tearing, < standing and in warmth of bed, often only in evening and at night. Weariness, < afternoon; W. above knees in evening. Paralysis of l., with feeling as if it would fall asleep.

Knee.—Twitching in l. *Tearing;* in hollow; in evening, with warmth in it; when walking and sitting. Pain on side when walking, < stretching leg; sprained P. on rising from a seat; drawing pain when walking, extending to thigh; tensive P. in r., then crawling, only when walking. Paralytic pain in r. when walking. Paralytic sensation when sitting. Throbbing in l. during the day. Painful falling asleep on walking fast, he cannot bend them well. Stiffness; of r., with tension and weakness, as if tightly bound.

Leg.—Twitches on anterior surface of l. when standing. Cramp in r. calf; in calf and sole at night in bed on drawing up leg. Stitches, with pain and burning; S. in fibula. Tearing in l. tibia; in tibia beneath knee; upper part of calf; on waking at night, with drawing and weariness, < ankles; in r. calf, extending deep inward on pressure and rubbing; *in tibiæ, with pain in periosteum on touch and tension when walking.* Pressure now here, now there in bones. Burning pain at night in bed. Drawing pain in r. extending to foot. *Drawing in bones, with tearing;* paralytic D. Tension in l. calf as if too short when standing; in calves on rising from a seat during the day. *Uneasiness in evening.* Weakness, they give way. Heaviness; suddenly in l., as if paralyzed, so that it is difficult to move, at night in bed and next day when sitting. Stiffness. Numbness of r. in morning after waking, as if going to sleep, then heaviness. *Falling asleep when lying;* of one, then the other, when sitting; of r., with crawling.

Ankle.—Sticking beneath malleolus; in tendons behind r. external malleolus when running; S. in malleolus and when walking feeling as if feet would break. *Tearing;* just above malleolus; about M. when feet are cold; from inner M., transversely towards tendo-achillis; spasmodic, on M., with pulsation about it extending up fibula to knee. Drawing in l. on stepping, < evening, with sticking and throbbing in it and sticking in heel, she must keep the foot suspended, it feels heavy, swollen at seat of pain and hot to touch.

Foot.—Swelling; extending to malleoli; of soles, and redness, with burning in them, < stepping. Visible twitching on back of l. in evening. Sticking; on back; beneath heel; in corns; after walking, with burning; in l., extending inward. *Tearing on inside and on sole;* on back, extending to toes; drawing, extending to toes. Pain in heel; in sole on stepping. Sensitiveness of corns. Tension. Pinching drawing as from weariness. *Heaviness; walking is irksome;* and stiffness. *Falling asleep after dinner;* of l. during dinner.

Toes.—Cramp in l. great, in evening when sitting, preventing stretching of it. Sticking in balls of great; in tips of great, with itching; tickling, in tips. *Tearing; in first phalanx of great;* in tips of great. Gnawing on outer margin of r. great. *Pain in tips on walking;* P. on side of nail of great, as if it would grow into flesh. Sprained P. in first joint of great when walking, < bending it up.

Clinical.—Sciatica, with very sharp lancinating pains. It has been indicated in hip disease of scrofulous children, with the severe pain and periodic aggravation of the drug.

Skin.—Freckles on face. Dryness and roughness of face. Hands rough and cracked. Crack in the cicatrix of an issue. Red lentil-shaped elevation above wrist. Yellow, scaly spot on upper part of forehead; scaly, itching spots on abdomen and about nipples, moist after scratching. Tetter on legs. Eruption in hollow of knee. Nettle-rash. Chilblain on ball of great toe, with sticking cutting; inflamed C. on toes, with pain; inflamed, bluish-red C. on balls of great toes, with cutting and sticking, < when in shoes.

Pimples here and there; in l. brow; *on face;* on cheek below ear; on ears; on nose; on l. thigh; above knee, with tearing; on zygomata, with burning pain; painful to touch on lip near l. nostril; red, on l. frontal eminence, painful to touch, afterwards they suppurated. Itching pimples on nape; posteriorly on l. thumb; high up on arm, with pain; on shoulders, with burning after scratching; on tibia, and vesicles with inflamed areola. Inflammation at insertion of nail of index, and on pressure oozing of thin matter. Soreness behind ears, with suppuration. Pustules on face; red, in middle of forehead. Boil in ear. Vesicle on little finger; on l. index, with watery discharge; itching, in palm. Ulcer bleeds; at night; superficial U. above l. wing of nose, painful on touch.

General sticking and gnawing; itching S. here and there; general itching S., preventing sleep after 1 A.M. Pressure in location of a former ulcer on leg, with tension. Crawling in tip of r. middle finger; in soles, extending towards toes; in limbs, < legs, when sitting, with drawing in legs making him restless; tickling C. in toes and soles.

Itching on chin; of an old wart on face; lobules of ears; abdomen and thighs; about umbilicus; of hypogastrium; on lower part of small of back; axillæ; wrist; between nates; on knee; tibia; under surfaces of toes; about ankle in morning in bed; general, in evening, > bed; palms near fingers in evening; legs in evening; feet in evening, with heat, as after freezing; general, during menstruation; general in morning and evening, < back, where small pimples appear; now here, now there, small pimples after scratching; here and there, < legs, on scratching it easily becomes bloody; on thigh near hip, which after scratching ulcerated; of arms, then after scratching white pimples; on mons veneris, about genitals and on thighs, with red papules; on r. breast, and on rubbing fine eruption; of face, preceded by twitching, burning after rubbing; *beneath great toe-nail, with pain on touch;* on back, which amounts to a pain after scratching; above r. wrist, > scratching; on pit of stomach, not > scratching; almost sticking, over whole body at night in bed. Burning itching, general, now here, now there; on face; face, back and head; sacrum and under r. patella.

Clinical.—Subacute erysipelas in old people characterized by the sac-like swellings under the eyebrows. Erysipelas resulting from a wound.

Sleep.—Yawning. *Sleepiness during the day;* she sleeps as soon as she sits down; S. in morning, and late waking; in forenoon, with yawning; in afternoon, also with yawning and suffering expression; *early in evening,* also with morose silence; *attacks of S. when eating; after eating, with chilliness and yawning;* during breakfast; after dinner, > open air; on walking in open air, with yawning; overpowering, in afternoon and evening. In morning, after a good sleep, he is obliged to lie down again, and after three hours' sleep feels well. Sleep too long, then confusion of head, lassitude, feeling of catarrh and pressure in eyes.

Sleepless after 1 or 2 A.M.; *till* 11 *or* 12 P.M.; till 1 or 2 A.M.; till midnight, after mental labor; on account of vivid thoughts after waking at night; on account of remembrance of sad events; S. or anxious dreams, in morning stupidity and hot hands. Half-waking sleep; in morning after waking, during menstruation, anxiety from hearing things, though she knows that she is dreaming, but inability to open her eyes and difficulty in arousing herself. *Restless sleep;* during menstruation, with anxious dreams; on account of pain in side on which he lies; child restless, anxious, cried, longed for this and that without taking anything.

Talking in sleep. Starting in S.; on falling asleep; S. up awake in evening, with general shivering. Jerking in limbs and snoring; J. in arm on falling asleep. Movements of whole body in sleep as in epilepsy, with jerking of arms and stamping of feet. She raised herself at night in sleep, said all sorts of senseless things to her husband, and could not collect her senses for a long time though she knew she was talking with him. Waking early; always at 4 A.M. and frequently afterwards till morning; frequent W. Late falling asleep; difficult in evening after walking in open air.

Dreams; on falling asleep; passing from one into another; fantasies at night in a waking condition, with heat in brain and general external heat, then sweat, cold limbs, shivering and starting as in fright; violent crying in a D.; horrible; of all sorts of frightful figures; that she fell from a mountain; of serpents, disease and death; that one announced his approaching death; of diseased parts of the body; of masked persons, ghosts and devils; of dead persons as if they were living and quarrelled with her; of robbers; vivid, of the business of the day. *Anxious dreams,* she cries for help; A. of danger from passing forms, some of which lay hold of her; A. that his father was about to beat him. Voluptuous dreams; after coition, with emission. Nightmare as if a stone were lying on him and his larynx were gradually constricting, with ineffectual efforts to wake.

Fever.—Chilliness; in morning in bed, then heat, after a few hours again chill; in forenoon, hot hands in evening; daily from 6 to 7 P.M., with thirst, then heat without thirst, with fluent coryza, then sweat in sleep, next morning scraping in throat, bad taste, loss of appetite, agglutination of l. eye; at 9 P.M., > lying down; evenings without thirst; towards evening with necessity to lie down, then nausea, vomiting, cramp-like pain in chest all night, with short breath, internal anxiety and sweat on head; before menstruation, with trembling of limbs and spasmodic sensation in abdomen; *after eating;* after cessation of pains; on every motion, even in bed; when riding over a stony road, without thirst, with confusion of head; with cold feet, confusion of head, faintness, swelling of lower jaw and gum, burning toothache, with stitches; with thirst, internal heat, heat of hands and aversion to food; then heat of face; alternating with heat in evening, then sweat at night; internal, at noon, with heat of hands and then general heat, all without thirst.

Shivering in forenoon, > warmth of stove, with yawning; S. in evening before lying down; in evening after lying down, with hot hands and delayed sleep; in the room; general, with chill in limbs and with fever; in back in morning in bed; about anus after stool. Chilliness on head; on vertex and over whole body in evening; cold ears in a hot room; *hands; feet* in bed; in back after menses, in evening and after midnight, waking, with cramp and coldness in stomach, which last till towards noon; arms in cold air, their sensation becomes blunted and they feel almost asleep; feet, with hot face.

Heat every day at 9 A.M. and 5 P.M., with yawning, thirst, headache and pulsation in abdomen; H. in afternoon at an open window, with burning in eyes, then chilliness in open air; in evening in bed; in evening after taking cold, towards morning sweat, with headache and after rising confusion of head; at night, with pain in zygoma; < hands, interrupting sleep at night, with vivid dreams; *before menstruation, with thirst and a restless night; in the room after taking cold in a draught of air, then heaviness of limbs, tearing in whole body and head, with roaring in ears, general coldness, during the next night sour sweat;* with sweat, then chill in a cold bed, with burning headache, heat in face, general shivering, stopped catarrh and sweat. Internal and external H. towards morning without thirst. Hot and dry skin. General dry H. in evening. *Burning in various places on skin, even under axillæ.*

Orgasm of blood and heat in head; O. in evening before sleep, with oppression and tightness of chest. Heat in head; < r. side of face; in face beneath r. eye; in lobules of ears; on l. hand; in tip of little finger; in face in morning in bed, with redness; in face, with redness of it and coldness of feet; rising H. in head in evening, > bed. Feeling as if a hot body were lying before forehead when stooping and writing, > rising. Feeling as if warmth streamed out of l. ear. Dry heat of cheeks and hands, with short breath. Crawling burning in soles, with sensitiveness.

Sweat; in morning in bed; *at night;* when walking; on every mental exertion; general, in morning in bed; cold. *Sweat in axillæ;* on feet; soles; on perineum at night; on head, neck and upper part of body during sleep.

Kali Chloricum.

A solution of pure chlorate of Potassium in distilled water (1 to 99) is taken for the first dilution.

General Action.—This, the most poisonous of all the

salts of Potassium, depresses and paralyzes the heart and lowers the temperature very rapidly. It is a violent irritant to the whole gastro-intestinal mucous membrane, producing gangrenous ulceration in the mouth and throat, ulceration of the stomach and bowels and terrible dysentery, with profound prostration. It causes at first diuresis, followed by suppression of urine and violent nephritis; on this account, particularly, it is a very dangerous drug in diphtheria, and cases have been killed by its unwise administration. Its action on the respiratory tract is marked.

Allies.—(Merc. c., Canth.).

Generalities.—Convulsions. Jerking of head and other parts. Blood taken from a vein was very viscid. Rheumatic pains in different parts. Malaise. Discomfort. Weakness; and sleepiness. Collapse. Relief from warm baths, which were always followed by profuse sweat and quiet sleep.

Mind.—Liveliness; then ill humor. Ill-humored, anxious, hypochondriac condition of the ganglionic nerve, > nosebleed. Apathy; in evening, with sadness and chilliness. Consciousness suddenly almost lost after a glass of wine.

Head.—Cutting extending into malar-bones. Aching; in evening. Confusion; on walking in open air. Congestion of brain, so that one half of head, face and nose felt paralyzed; feeling of C., with pain in forehead. Intoxication from a small glass of beer. Vertigo; after violent motion, with congestion. Forehead, jerking in upper and lower part of bone; pain; drawing; tension, then sneezing and catarrh; tension in sinciput. Temples, intermittent sticking in r.; pain; pain in l.; pain in bone extending to eye-teeth. Pain in l. side. Pain in occiput; in evening, at times extending into jaws. Confusion in occiput, with peculiar sensation in muscles of nape. Itching.

Eyes.—Redness in evening, with pain. Stitches. Cramp in l. Pressure. Rush of blood; with irritation. Feeling of strength. Detected in the tears. Twitching in canthi; inner. Pain in upper lid in evening. Appearance of light before eyes when coughing and sneezing.

Ears and Nose.—Roaring in ears, with a painful bloody stool. Drawing in root of nose. Irritation at root of N. Sneezing. Catarrh; violent; violent, with much sneezing and profuse mucus. Detected in nasal mucus. Nosebleed; at night; from r. nostril.

Face.—*Pale; bluish. Livid.* Twitching, and of eyes; of masseter muscles. Sticking in various parts. Tearing and tension. Pain in r. malar-bone, beneath margin of orbit, then tension in whole cheek and temple. Drawing pain in r. cheek till he sneezes. Drawing in r. cheek; and in gum, with cramp in muscles of r. cheek; with pain in lobule of r. ear, at one time more beneath orbits, at another more in masseter muscles; in r. half of face, with tension; cramplike, in cheeks, extending into joint of jaw, at times with tearing in upper jaw; *tensive, in l. cheek near orbital margin.* Tension, with pressure towards eyes, < r. side; T. in cheek beneath eye, extending to ear, r., then l; drawing, in r. cheek, then inclination to sneeze. Sensitiveness.

Jerking in nerves of lower jaw, at foramen maxillare posticum. Cramplike pressure in joint of jaw, with stitches in jaw and teeth, < r. side. Lips blue; swollen; pimples on r. corner; pimples on lower.

Clinical.—Neuralgia of the face, sudden electric-like pain in l. side, < talking, eating or slightest touch, followed by numbness.

Mouth.—Aching in upper teeth. Teeth blunted. Gums bright red. Gums bleed easily on brushing teeth. Tongue white; in middle. Tongue coated; at back; with diarrhœa. *Two symmetrical ulcers on sides of tongue.* Tongue cold; and throat. Sticking burning on tongue. Stomatitis; **ulcerative and follicular, mucous surface red and tumid, and gray-based ulcers in cheeks, lips, etc.** Tanned appearance, and in throat. Contracted feeling in muscles of palate. *Salivation; acid.* Taste sticking-burning, acid; T. burning, alkaline; as of blue vitriol; salt; sour; saltish, sour; bitter, sourish; bitter, > expectoration of mucus, with coldness of tongue; (like laurel-water with salt); lost.

Clinical.—Aphthous or gangrenous ulceration of the mouth. Aphthæ of the mouth. Obstinate follicular stomatitis, with extreme fetor; there is generally tough, stringy saliva. It has been found extremely useful in gangrene of the mouth in children, nearly every case having been cured (at the Five Points Hospital, New York, where it was used internally and locally). Ulceration of the mouth and throat, with extreme fetor, albuminuria, hæmaturia, cough and dyspnœa. Nursing sore mouth of infants or of mothers.

Throat.—*Submaxillary glands swollen, throat red and œdematous.* Pain, and in stomach, with inclination to eructate. *Scraping. Rawness. Dryness;* and of chest, with violent cough, as from sulphur fumes. *Swallowing difficult.*

Stomach.—Appetite increased; paroxysms of ravenous hunger, > a drink of water, then loss of appetite; diminished; lost. Thirst. Eructations; of air; sourish; violent, with alternating pains in chest and abdomen. Nausea; and shivering; and attempts to vomit, though nothing but air was ejected. Vomiting; sudden; incessant; of all food; of offensive dark green mucus.

Acute gastritis, nausea, pain in splenic region, enlargement of spleen. Cardialgia. (Gastralgia.) Pyrosis. Cutting. Pressure, with feeling of emptiness; P. in epigastric region; in pit, with apathy and chilliness. Heavy pain after a walk of an eighth of an mile, with sinking sensation. Weight in region, with distention; W. and oppression, almost amounting to pain, with cardialgia and flatulence; W. and oppression increasing to an uniform gravative pain; W. in epigastric region, > night, with fulness and twisting. Warmth.

Abdomen.—Movings, with inclination to diarrhœa. Flatulence; during the day; in afternoon; and epigastric distress, preventing sleep. Griping. Pain. Intermittent weight, tension and pain in umbilical region. Pressure in l. hypochondrium; in r., extending to umbilicus; tensive, in r., > emission of flatus. Pain in pelvic region, with diarrhœa.

Rectum.—Proctica marisca; with constipation. Pain. Urging; constant, with normal stool.

Stool.—Liquid. Thin. Diarrhœa; violent, constantly getting more liquid, at last consisting only of mucus; copious, as after a refrigerant purging salt (painful); with weakness. Hard; *and at last mixed with mucus and blood.* Constipation, but when action was solicited the matter was dark. Green. Light-colored. Indolent, delayed.

Clinical.—Dysentery, with most violent cutting pains as from knives, frequent stools, tenesmus making the patient cry out, evacuations very small, almost clear blood, great prostration (Canth., Merc. c.).

Urinary Organs.—*Nephritis. Urging* (Merc. c.); *frequent.* Twitching in urethra. Inability to empty bladder. *Could pass only a few drops of bloody urine.* Frequent micturition; and copious, with irritation about bladder and urethra. *Hæmaturia.* Urine increased in evening and night; *U. scanty; black and albuminous;* greenish-black, albuminous, containing hæmatin; five ounces of smoky U., containing albumen, casts and altered blood, drawn off by catheter; acid, and deposits urates abundantly; turbid; suppressed.

Sexual Organs.—Violent erections, with itching on scrotum; violent E., with emissions. Depression of desire, with chilliness and apathy.

Respiratory Organs and Chest.—Hoarseness. In larynx irritation to cough. Cough; violent, with catarrh. Breathing laborious. Pain in sides and loins. Painful pressure superiorly in l. costal region. Chest, tightness; constriction as from sulphur fumes; oppression, with sensation as if lungs were constricted with a fine thread; oppression, with violent beating of heart; rush of blood.

Heart and Pulse.—Præcordial anxiety without notable signs in heart or lungs. Coldness in præcordial region. Palpitation. Heart's beat distinctly perceptible to touch, with coldness in præcordial region. Violent beating of H.; with oppression of chest and cold feet. Pulse rapid; and compressible; and feeble, appearing as after a sudden and copious hæmorrhage. Pulse slow; and small, weak. P. diminished in fulness and force. P. in r. hand full and soft, intermittent, slower than beat of heart, in l. hand small, soft, compressible.

Back.—Pain in lumbar region, with weight. Heaviness in lumbar region, with dragging and increased urine.

Extremities.—Rigidity of muscles. Drawing in forearms; in wrists, with tearing. Tearing in r. wrist and along ulna. Cramp in r. index. Drawing in thigh. Sticking in r. knee. Cramp in leg.

Skin.—*Cyanosis, < lips and extremities.* Icterus. Duskiness. Congestion. Small purple maculæ on forearms. Rash, with painful pimples on l. shoulder. Inflamed hang-nails. Pimples on forehead; between lip and chin; on thigh; red P.; burning, on l. cheek; itching; itching, with vesicles on back of l. hand, > during the day, but returning next morning. Itching pustules filled with matter, surrounded by red areola, on limbs. Itching vesicles on back of r. hand. Itching over whole body; in evening in bed; in face; at night, next morning red pimples on legs and shoulders, not on joints, then pimples on face.

Clinical.—Epithelioma of face; in another case epithelioma of great toe.

Sleep—Yawning. Sleep uneasy; and interrupted by heavy dreams; and full of vexing dreams; and waking towards morning from an anxious dream, lying on back, snoring and breathing with difficulty. Dreams of occurrences of the day previous; quiet D. of prophecies of death; quiet, of death from nervous fever; voluptuous, with emissions.

Fever.—Chilliness; in afternoon; in open air; with stiffness of hands. Shivering; in evening; over back and neck, with warm feet. Cool skin. *Cold limbs;* r. arm; internally in r. forearm; feet, with palpitation. Heat; in bed; with violently throbbing pulse and heart; in face in flushes. Orgasms, < chest.

Kali Iodatum.

A first dilution is made by dissolving 1 part of Iodide of Potassium in 99 parts of water.

General Action.—The action of this salt differs from that of Iodine as shown by the depressing action of Potassium and by less tendency to febrile excitement. In the respiratory tract we find catarrhal inflammation, with freer secretions and less fever (it has produced bloody expectoration). The increased salivation and urine followed by nephritis are similar to Iodine.

Generalities.—*Emaciation* (Iod.). Marasmus resembling the third stage of phthisis. Nervous mobility. Trembling. Spasms. Subsultus tendinum. Attacks of jerking of limbs, < l. arm, and of face, < l. side, with anxiety, apprehension and palpitation, one attack ended with vomiting and headache, once violent rolling of l. eyeball, pupils contracted, facial muscles contracted, l. corner of mouth drawn downward, mouth opened and closed numberless times while uttering unintelligible words, short rapid respiration, pulse hard and full, forehead, neck and chest covered with sweat, face red, unconsciousness, after the paroxysm trembling, weeping, complaints of heaviness of l. arm, abdomen small, soft, tongue white rather than yellow, efforts to vomit, > vomiting. Continual complaints.

Sticking in l. lower jaw, in tibia, l. thigh, l. forearm, in the bones, in forenoon. Tearing here and there. Pinching here and there, < evening. Gnawing in r. upper teeth in forenoon, then in l. ear, at last in tendon of hollow of l. knee. Anguish. Agitation and nervous uneasiness. Distressing condition of nervous system. Nervous susceptibility exaggerated. Sensation of turning around. Malaise. Vague indescribable feelings in head, back and limbs. Restlessness. *Weakness.* Affects the fibrous structures, as the periosteum and capsular ligaments of joints. Most symptoms arise during rest and are > motion.

Clinical.—The use of the drug in massive doses for symptoms of secondary syphilis, such as caries of the bones, syphilitic inflammations of the eyes, etc., etc., should not be included under the proper homœopathic application of the drug (though Iodine is certainly homœopathic to some stages of syphilis).

Mind.—Half mad all night. Talkative and full of jokes. *Sadness. Anxiety.* Fright at every trifle. Apprehensive and lachrymose in evening. Irritable; especially towards his children; and excited, quarrelsome. Weeping from the slightest cause. Dreads the return of dawn, and the trivial details of life seem insupportable. Always troubled. Troublesome and unreasonable impressions easily strengthened into fixed ideas.

Head.—Aching; at 5 A.M., > rising, with heaviness of it. Heaviness; on stooping; after dinner, making her fretful; and dulness. Congestion. Intoxicated feeling. Vertigo. Forehead, *stitches on stooping; tearing or jerking S. in l. sinus; tearing in r. side in evening, transiently > pressure, with sticking; digging in l.; aching; aching in sinuses and r. ethmoid cells;* heaviness in afternoon; heaviness in l. side of sinciput in morning after rising; H. in sinciput and vertex in evening and night, with sensitiveness to touch.

Temple, sticking in l. at 6 P.M., with tearing; heaviness in r.; painful throbbing in l. in evening. Vertex, stitches in front of in evening; pinching here and there; *pain as if it would be forced asunder,* > external warmth but often returning, *with external heat in vertex,* but general chilliness; tension, with sticking in it and with tearing in l. temple extending into nape. Sticking in upper part of r. parietal bone. Screwing together from both sides in morning, > open air; S. in upper part of r. side, gradually spreading. Heaviness in sides in morning. Occiput, pain; heaviness towards evening; tension in bones, with stitches. *Pain in scalp on scratching, as if ulcerated.*

Clinical.—Frontal headaches, particularly over eyes and root of nose, associated with catarrh at root of nose and in the frontal sinuses, the pain is most violent, lancinating, pulsating, etc.

Eyes.—*Surrounded by dark rings; and sunken.* Ferrety in morning. Cellular tissue about them œdematous. Protruding. Discharge of purulent mucus in morning. Constant oscillation, inability to fix them, pupils dilated. Fixed. Dulness. Tearings beneath l. Pain waking him, with lachrymation and burning in nose and throat. Biting in r., > scratching, recurring in evening. Burning in afternoon; in evening, with purulent mucus; with redness of lids and with lachrymation of r. eye. Uneasy feeling in l. in morning on waking, external edge of periosteum of orbit tender on pressure, l. lids swollen and infiltrated, next morning r. eye similarly affected, next day a peculiar pain in a direct line from external border of one orbit to that of the other.

Lachrymation; of r. eye. Balls painful on movement. Balls felt as if in a rubber covering which kept up a constant contraction. Lids, swelling; S. of upper, < tarsal regions, which were bluish-red; purulent mucus in canthi; twitching of lower, impairing vision; stitches in l. lower; cutting in r. external canthus in evening; burning so that she cannot endure any light in the evening. *Conjunctivæ injected.* Conjunctivitis; characterized by great vascularity and chemosis. Orbital margin, gnawing on r. lower; painful drawing in r. upper. Sensitiveness to light and vision obscured by undulations. *Vision dim.* V. double. V. disturbed.

Ears.—Sticking in r. during the day; in l. in evening in bed, extending into head; extending into l. Tearing now in r., now in l.; deep in r. in forenoon; in r. in evening, making it sensitive; in front of l., extending into temple, in bones; in front of r., extending into temple, making the whole side painful. Piercing pain, < r. Gnawing within and behind l. Boring. Indescribable pain extending outward from l. in evening, and if she moves the hand towards the ear, even without touching it, it creeps over the side of the face, as if mesmerized. Feeling as if something had fallen in front of them; with tearing in them. Itching in l. Crackling in r. on attempting to swallow. Ringing; and buzzing. Sounds as of a river sweeping by. Sounds as of rain on the roof. Hearing almost gone.

Nose.—*Tearing in upper part of l. nostril. Burning; in nostrils; in upper part, with feeling as if a leaf were in front of it; and in throat. Stoppage, with running of clear water. Tingling prickling, with violent paroxysmal sneezing, alternately r. and l. nostril occluded, heat in nasal sinuses, acrid discharge from anterior nares. Sneezing; and running of clear water; ineffectual efforts at S. Coryza; with redness of mucous membrane of eyes, nose, throat and palate, with lachrymation, violent sneezing, running of water, frequent irritation to cough and swelling of upper lids; with laryngitis, conjunctivitis, œdema of lids, loss of smell, dyspnœa; stopped, in morning on waking. Running from N.; of burning water, making the skin sore; a stream of hot fluid, waking at 3 A.M., with salivation, at 7 A.M. Schneiderian membrane fully conjested, frequent and prolonged sneezing.* Discharge of thick yellow mucus. Violent bleeding. *Loss of smell.*

Clinical.—Profuse acrid coryzas, the excoriating water flows in a stream. Nasal catarrh which seems to involve the ethmoidal cells and frontal sinuses, with most terrible pains, at times with sudden suppression of the watery excoriating discharge from the nostrils. Valuable in certain forms of hay fever.

Face.—*Pale.* Red; with throbbing in superficial vessels. Yellow. More yellowish-green than dead white. Bistre-colored. Earthy. Discolored. Swelling; of l. cheek; < eyelids and submaxillary region. Distention of cheeks and submaxillary spaces, with stiffness. Emaciation, and of neck. Cheeks wrinkled, flabby. Visage lengthened. Look quick and anxious.; L. earnest, wild, uncertain; excited, sometimes depressed; sad. Countenance that of a drunkard. Sticking in l. cheek, with jerking, then sensitiveness. Tearing in l. zygoma in morning when lying on it, with sticking. Malar-bones sensitive to touch. Lost the power of moving cheeks and lips and unable to masticate.

Jaws, stitches from l. upper to parietal bone in morning in bed; tearing in l. lower and in corresponding teeth; T. in both sides of lower as if it would be torn out; gnawing in both sides of lower; excruciating pain in shocks like neuralgia, and in teeth; stiffness; stiffness and uneasiness; immobility. Lips dry and cracked; full of glutinous mucus in morning after waking; painful drawing in r. side of upper and in gum; sensitiveness of upper and of nostril, even when not touched.

Mouth.—Teeth. Jerking or shooting in r. eye-tooth, < lying down till midnight and from 4 to 5 A.M., < cold, > warmth, at one time pain as if the tooth would break or as if a worm were digging in it. Tearing in l. upper; in r. upper molars and in margin of r. orbit; in lower in evening and feeling as if a weight hung from lower jaw. Griping in a l. lower hollow molar in evening. Pain in upper and in upper jaw. Ulcerative pain in evening, night and next morning. Painful drawing in a l. lower molar. Throbbing in a hollow T. when walking in open air. Grumbling in a hollow l. lower molar. Feeling too long in evening and painful. Gum swollen and painful; r. S., with ulcerative pain; S. about a hollow tooth; stitches during the day; ulcerative pain in r. lower.

Tongue.—*Blister on tip, with burning pain.* Hypertrophied, tender, covered with nodes and fissured by deep cracks. Coated white. Spasmodic pain at root at night before sleep, extending to both sides of throat, causing fear of impending death, with sensation as if a spasm would close the pharynx. Dry in morning and stiff, coated dark brown. Burning in a spot on l. margin; *B. on tip as from a vesicle.* Speech thick and indistinct.

Hard and soft palate swollen, tender and in many places excoriated, afterwards palate painful and felt as if the tissues were stretched laterally across the posterior part of soft palate and root of tongue, pharynx and larynx dry, causing hoarseness, afterwards the secretions from mouth, nose and eyes very acrid. *Dry;* during the chill in evening, with thirst; and fuliginous; M. and throat dry and bitter. Burning as after hot food. Numb in morning after waking. *Salivation;* with nausea. Flow of mucus and saliva from M. Bloody saliva, with disgusting taste. *Offensive odor;* in morning after rising, almost as after onions. Taste bitter, < throat, > breakfast; sweetish-bitter after waking; rancid after eating and drinking; dreadful; of food lost or like that of straw.

Clinical.—Salivation of pregnancy.

Throat.—Bellows-murmur in carotids. Swelling of submaxillary region; *of thyroid gland, with sensitiveness to touch and pressure;* a small swelling became after three years a bronchocele, a ponderous tumor. (Sensitiveness of the goitre to touch.) Choking as if something stuck in it, > hawking up a piece of thick mucus. Sticking in l. side only on swallowing, < evening, with ulcerative pain; S. on swallowing, with pressure in it, even on speaking pain. Constriction. Rawness and scraping; R. in morning in bed, with dryness and hacking cough; R. and burning as in heartburn. Dryness, with cramp in it and apprehension; D. and irritation; *D. and itching, with burning at epigastrium, salivation, running from nose, injection of conjunctivæ and lachrymation. Swallowing painful and difficult, with redness and swelling of soft palate and tonsils* (< r.). Burning and uneasiness in œsophagus and stomach.

Clinical.—Painful ulcerations of the throat, with swollen glands, fever, etc., have been reported as cured.

Stomach.—Bulimy. Appetite increased, next day diminishing or disappearing; lost. Aversion to all food; to broth. *Thirst;* evenings. Eructations; hawking, of air; empty, hiccough-like. Hiccough in evening. *Nausea;* with pressure in stomach; with emptiness, not > eating. *Vomiting;* and purging at the same time; *violent, with salivation.*

Constant "cracking and crying." Pain; intermittent; like an emptiness and coldness in evening, not > soup. Painful beating in l. side of epigastric region in evening. Burning in epigastrium; externally in pit; B. during digestion; > eructation, but immediately returning, with pressure; in epigastrium, with acute pain. Constant inclination to waterbrash without its really occurring. Heaviness. Discomfort. Faintness. Indigestion.

Abdomen.—*Sudden distention as if it would burst, > by emission of flatus,* in morning after waking, then diarrhœa twice. Gurgling, < stomach. Movings and rumblings; R. as if something alive were moving in it; M. of flatus, then tension in groins. Emission of flatus. Tearing from both sides as if flesh would be torn off in afternoon, extending towards umbilicus. Griping, and in groins, with feeling as if something would come out through pudenda. Cutting burning pain, always > open air, always returning on entering house. Pain; then hard, then soft stool; in A. and stomach, > evening after lying down, returning in morning on waking. Indescribable uneasiness, < night. Irritation of bowels.

Umbilical Region.—Distention, with movings in abdomen, then two soft stools; painful D. beneath umbilicus, > stool. Sticking at l. side. Cutting in r. side; C. in attacks in afternoon, with burning and nausea, inclination to eructations, which afterwards occur, itching externally about umbilicus and inclination to emission of flatus. Griping and burning.

Hypochondria.—Sticking in l.; in r. and in l. side of chest on talking. Constriction in l. on a line with cardiac orifice of stomach. Burning externally in l., then in both groins.

Hypogastrium.—Pinching on r. side extending above both groins. Cutting in a spot in r. groin, with sticking. Bruised pain in groins and small of back during menstruation. Sudden dragging in groins so that she must bend together, after the usual cold milk in morning, with frequent yawning, weariness in thighs, griping in abdomen extending to thighs, restlessness, chilliness, gooseflesh, with anxiety and warmth in head, then eructations and rumbling in abdomen, the menstruation that had just begun, partly stopped, then nausea, pressure in stomach, < moving about, shivering in face and hands, with heat and sweat of face. Drawing in l. groin, with feeling as if something living were in it. Heat during menstruation; sudden H. in l. groin.

Stool.—Diarrhœa. *Constipation.* Hard; and difficult, of a few small fæces.

Clinical.—Dysentery, with painful tenesmus, stools of jelly-like mucus.

Urinary Organs.—Bladder irritable. Painful urging. Obliged to urinate at night. Frequent micturition of copious urine as clear as water. Urine pale and watery. Urine copious; < night, clear and transparent; and the uric acid sediments disappear gradually, while those of ammonio-phosphate of magnesia increased. Urea decreased.

Clinical.—Subacute or chronic inflammation of the kidneys, with darting pain in the region of the kidneys, chilliness, etc.

Sexual Organs.—R. testicle disappeared, the l. of the size of an almond, erection slow and long-lasting, coition painful, prolonged and no emission. Biting in pudenda, with leucorrhœa. Pressure in uterus when walking, > sitting, with dragging pain. Acrid leucorrhœa. (Leucorrhœa became thinner and more watery.) Menstruation returned in a week; M. that had been suppressed six months flowed profusely, with pain in abdomen and diarrhœa; two days later, but more profuse than usual; decreased; M. that had existed two days diminished.

Clinical.—Leucorrhœa, watery, corrosive, like washings of meat. Uterine fibroids.

Respiratory Organs.—Spasmodic croup in morning. Choking in trachea, with rawness, obliging hawking, whereby she expectorated mucus. Affection of bronchia. Provocation in larynx to dry cough. Voice altered in sound; catarrhal; short, like her answers; feeble, at times tremulous; *lost;* lost at night. Inclination to cough. *Dry cough mornings; and evenings; in evening, with soreness of larynx. Short hacking cough from rawness in throat. Respiration difficult; on waking, in night, with loss of voice. Dyspnœa on ascending stairs, with pain in region of heart. Short breath.*

Clinical.—Cough, with expectoration like soap-suds, is said to be characteristic of the drug. It is an extremely valuable remedy in asthma. Catarrh of the larynx, with raw, sore pain, as if granulated.

Chest.—Breasts diminished in size, the supply of milk was especially diminished. *Sticking deep in middle; S. in r. side; in r. costal region behind breast; in middle of sternum in afternoon, with pressure; in l. in evening; in r. lowest ribs at* 8 P.M., *with sore pain; in middle when walking; upper part of l. when sitting bent over, > becoming erect; in middle, > moving about; in middle of* *sternum, extending to shoulders. Pain as if cut to pieces in evening. Pain in l. as if sore externally, < touch. Oppression. Uneasiness about l.*

Clinical.—Hydrothorax. Emphysema of the lungs. Chronic pneumonia, with catarrhal symptoms in the nose and throat. Pleuretic exudation, with great dyspnœa, constant teasing cough. The pains in the chest are sharp, as in all the potashes. Many cases of pneumonia of pleuretic effusions and of phthisis have been reported cured by this drug, especially when associated with exhausting night-sweats, salivation, etc.; it is difficult to separate the cases requiring Iodine and those requiring Kali iod.

Heart.—Sticking when walking. All the symptoms of endocarditis, oppression, faintlike exhaustion, tumultuous, violent, intermittent and irregular action of H. and pulse, with tensive pain across chest, especially affecting r. ventricle, which gradually became dilated. Seemed unequal to the task of circulating the blood. *Palpitation;* fluttering, causing faintness and sickness and preventing sitting up.

Pulse.—Rapid; and full; and irregular; and small. Slow and weak; S. and heavy, irregular. Hard and tense. Small and soft.

Neck and Back.—*Cervical glands enlarged.* Sticking in r. side of nape when lying. Throbbing between scapulæ. Small of back, sticking when sitting; *pain as if screwed in;* pain and soreness; pain as before menstruation, with diarrhœa twice; pain so that she could not lie quietly; pain as if beaten, so that she does not know how she shall lie; pain almost as if beaten, < sitting bent. Pain in coccyx as if she had fallen upon it.

Extremities.—Tremor. Tearing above r. malleolus, in l. index and r. arm, but not in joints.

Clinical.—Subacute rheumatism, either articular or neuralgic; sometimes it seems to prevent the attacks of sciatica, articular rheumatism or acute gout; the pains in the extremities are always < night, especially towards morning, there is rarely much fever, but there is great weakness, etc. Rheumatism of the spine, with paraplegia. Rheumatism of the knee, which is swollen, with boring pains < night. Sciatica < night, like Kali carb., the patient cannot remain in bed.

Upper Extremities.—Shoulders, tearing in l.; in r., then in r. ear; pain in tendons of r. on motion and touch, like a tension and as if swollen; bruised pain in l.; paralytic pain only on moving them. Arm weak. Tearing in l. elbow, now in shoulders, now in r. elbow. Cramp in r. forearm above wrist on moving it. Pain like a tension and sticking in articular end of radius on moving r. index. Tearing in r. wrist, then itching on it, not > scratching, then an itching vesicle. Hands tremble. Bruised pain in margin of r. hand above little finger. Tearing in index from base to tip; on inner margin of r. thumb; on l. middle and ring fingers in evening; in metacarpal joints of l. fingers in evening; in inner surface of r ring, which is thereby flexed and cannot be extended; in r. thumb as if it would be torn out; jerking T. in a line on outer side of bone of l. thumb, with sticking. Pinching on metacarpal joint of l. thumb.

Lower Extremities.—Gait disturbed. Tottering. Sticking in upper part of l. thigh; now in thigh, now in tibia, in l. hip on every step, obliging her to limp. Tearing above hollow of knee, then also below it; in l. femur; posteriorly in r. thigh, with sticking; in r. thigh on and after waking at 11 P.M., extending to below knee, > lying on sound side, lying upon r. side or back was intolerable; in a spot in middle of l. thigh, with paralyzed pain as far as knee. Gnawing in hip-bones; G. in middle of r. thigh in evening when sitting with r. thigh over l. Upper part of T. seem compressed during menstruation.

Tearing twitching in r. knee. Tearing in knees at night; in periosteum of l. K. at night, with a swollen feeling; in outside of l. K. when sitting; in r. tibia; l. calf, then weakness of whole leg; l. calf, when standing, > walking, with tension; downward in tibiæ in evening. *Gnawing in periosteum of l. leg.* Painful drawing in calves when sitting. Legs give way. Painful weakness of legs. Tearing in back part of l. heel when sitting; in r. heel when standing, > walking. Ulcerative pain in heels and toes. Pain in l. instep in evening as if beaten. Tearing in great toes; in r. second toe.

Skin.—Purpura; miliary, non-pruriginous, sanguineous spots like P., in one case on thorax, in all others on legs only, more confluent anteriorly, sometimes an intermixture of petechiæ of different ages, the new being of a brighter color than the old. Erysipelas of face; and scalp, neck, etc. Erysipelatous swelling of cheeks extending towards temples, with redness, with a few spots on forehead. Itching tetter on face; and dry, on cheek. Pimples on chin and nose; sticking burning, below corner of mouth; sensitive, on nostril; sensitive, on cheek, surrounded by redness and swelling; itching, on chin and exuding water. Erythema. Eczema impetiginoides. Pustules; of acne, < face. Ulceration and yellow color of tip of l. thumb, but it does not break. Vesicles of all sizes, becoming confluent and forming bullæ, on hands, arms, groins and feet, they contained a clear serous fluid, were on a hyperæmic base, in the early stages those on the hands resemble dysidrosis, but became semi-opaque and shrivelled and dried without forming crusts. Biting on nape and forehead, then burning after scratching. Itching on r. nates, > scratching; on r. instep in evening, < scratching; on inner side of r. upper arm, after scratching a dry red spot, which itches at first.

Sleep.—Frequent yawning without sleepiness; frequent excessive Y. *Sleeplessness;* almost all night, only sleepy towards morning. Waking every hour. Cried aloud in sleep towards morning. Starting up in first sleep, but soon falling asleep again. Less sound. Restless sleep; and unrefreshing; from which he wakes with a start and distress as from some strong emotion or sense of calamity. Dreams wandering; joyous; of danger; anxious; that she would be killed; of falling in evening, and consequent violent starting up. Nightmare.

Fever.—Chill in afternoon; from afternoon till next morning; from 4 to 7 P.M., > in bed, with thirst; from 6 to 10 P.M., < lying down; at night. Shaking chill at 10 P.M.; at night on frequent waking. Shivering; of whole body in morning, except head, which felt hot. Shivering-creeping during menstruation, with coldness of hands and pressure and griping in hypogastrium. Creeping in back in evening, then coldness of whole body; chilliness from 6 to 8 P.M. creeping up back and extending over whole body, with sleepiness. Heat in afternoon; H., with dulness of head and discomfort of body; then sweat, from 1 to 3 P.M. Hot skin. Heat of head; with burning and redness of face; in forehead, eyes, nose and mouth, with anxious burning in throat extending behind sternum to ensiform cartilage; in feet. Sweat.

Kali Muriaticum.

A trituration of pure chloride (muriate) of Potassium is used.

Clinical.—The general characteristic indications for this drug seem to be connective tissue exudations; diphtheritic ulcerations; croupous exudations. Lymphatic enlargements. Ulcerations, especially at the base of the tongue, with whitish-gray exudations, etc. Epilepsy, choroiretinitis, with hazy vitreous; parenchymatous keratitis; exudative retinitis; scrofulous inflammations of the eye; kerato-iritis, with pus in the anterior chamber (Hep. sul.). In the hands of Dr. Houghton it seems to have cured a great number of obstinate cases of disease of the ear, especially proliferous inflammations of the middle ear, with obstruction of the Eustachian tube and naso-pharyngeal catarrh, retraction of drum; exfoliation of the epithelial layer of the tympanum; deafness, with earache, swelling of the glands, sore throat, etc. Nasal catarrh, sneezing and profuse secretion of mucus (Kali iod.). Naso-pharyngeal catarrh, the vault of the pharynx covered with adherent crusts (Kali bi.). Paralysis of the facial nerve of r. side beginning with faceache and facial neuralgia, with twitching and trembling of the muscles of the face, < eating, speaking or touch. Gums inflamed and bleed easily. Aphthous ulcers in the mouths of children or mothers; canker; excoriation of the mouth (Kali chlor.); epithelioma of the mouth, excessive ulceration; epithelioma of the tongue, hypertrophy and ulceration. Follicular pharyngitis, with expectoration of cheesy lumps; tonsillitis.

It is recommended by Schüssler for a great variety of abdominal troubles, especially for portal congestion, enlarged liver, constipation, hæmorrhoids or yellow diarrhœa. Dyspepsia, especially caused by fat food. Catarrh of the bladder; inflammation of the kidneys. Orchitis; gonorrhœa; gleet; soft chancre; chronic syphilis. Uterine hæmorrhage; leucorrhœa; albuminuria of pregnancy; nausea of pregnancy; puerperal fever. Asthma. Croupy cough; whooping cough, expectoration white, milky. Exudative stage of pleurisy, especially with plastic adhesions. Pericarditis. Palpitation. Swollen joints, with articular rheumatism. Chronic rheumatism. Rheumatic paralysis. Swellings. Abscesses; boils; carbuncles; a great variety of eruptions; especially eczema, erysipelas, herpes, ulcerations; warts, etc. In general, Schüssler praises it as a remedy for glandular swellings, follicular inflammations; general effects of fatty food or pastry.

Kali Nitricum.

Triturations of pure nitrate of Potassium are used.

General Action.—Like the chlorate this salt is a violent irritant to the mucous membranes, causing gastro-intestinal inflammation and ulceration and catarrh of the bronchi with asthmatic breathing. In its action on the kidneys and heart it is similar to the other salts of Potash.

Generalities.—Lying on back in collapse, with legs drawn up, as in peritonitis. Swelling of whole body, neck and legs. Twitchings; here and there; as in chorea, < l. arm and leg. Trembling of whole body; of one half of body; of all nerves, with restlessness. Stinging through whole body, causing acute pain on every inspiration. Tearing in evening after eating, high up in inner side of l. thigh (apparently in pectinæus and triceps), then in l. upper arm, then in middle of outer part of l. thigh, then on anterior surface of leg (tibialis anticus), then on and behind external malleolus, then between l. scapula and spine (in rhomboideus, serratus posticus superior); T. in r. side of chin when sitting, then beneath r. external malleolus; intermittent, day and night, transiently > rubbing. Jerking pain in occipital bone, then also in hip-bone, at last alternating with tension behind r. ear and continuing all night. (Bruised feeling became worse.) Chronic illness. Pulsations here and there after midday nap.

Weakness; in morning; in morning after mental labor; in afternoon; with pallor; with heaviness of head and stumbling over everything; with numbness of lower limbs; sudden, with sleepiness, necessity to lie down and inability to open eyes; tremulous, in morning, with frequent, hard pulse and rapid respiration; paralytic muscular. Faintness; at 10 P.M., when blowing on an instrument with tight clothes, it seemed as if everything in the room turned around, he caught himself while sinking, head at one time hot, at another cold, unsteady standing and sensation as if the attack would return; dizzy F. in morning when standing, > sitting down, then blackness before eyes, weakness, sleepiness, pain in small of back, constriction in abdomen, repeated three times in forenoon, then pain down leg to malleoli, where it remained all day, in afternoon coldness and thirst, < in bed, lasting till midnight. Collapse. Rheumatic, painful stiffness of almost whole body, < arms, neck and back, < cold, > warmth. Paralysis of organs of sense. Aggravation from smelling camphor. (Amelioration, especially of headache, by smelling sweet spirits of nitre.)

Mind.—Delirium; mild, then restlessness and wakefulness. Excitement after a glass of wine. Anxiety; frequently in afternoon; in afternoon, with sweat at pit of stomach and weakness; with general sweat; with internal coldness, then faintness. Depression of spirits; thinks she must die. Ennui, lachrymose mood. Fretfulness; in evening; with uneasiness, apprehension and sensitiveness; and perverseness, discontentment with himself and the world and disinclination to mental labor. Disinclination for work; D. to think in morning, with heat in face and forehead and exhaustion. Meditative and solicitous. Partly stupefied as in intoxication; half stupor unless aroused. Unconsciousness.

Head.—Hacking and sticking, with pressure about eyes and sleepiness. Aching; in morning, afterwards it extended to occiput, in evening increase of heat in head; towards noon, < r. side, < 1 to 4 P.M., > a nap; in afternoon; in evening; towards evening, < r. side of sinciput, with sudden stitches; on waking, with fulness of abdomen, diarrhœa and chilliness; on turning head; after dinner; < towards evening, lasting till 10 P.M., with heat; so that she could not eat; and in neck, < l. side; with stitches in forehead; preventing sleep all night and lasting in morning; in morning as after a debauch; bursting, with stitches in l. ear and clavicles, whence the pain extends into elbows; tensive, deep in head after dinner. Pressure towards middle and towards l. temple in morning. Drawing in middle from morning till evening, extending towards r. temple. Loose feeling in brain, with sticking.

Heaviness. Confusion; in morning; towards evening, with drawing in side of head and forehead; in evening, with oppression of chest; on waking; with frequent tearing drawing in parietal bones and in forehead; with drawing; with difficult thought, everything is immediately forgotten; almost like intoxication after Madeira. Stupefaction in morning, with heaviness, as after intoxication. Vertigo; with weakness of head; in morning, as after intoxication; as if he would fall forward, on stooping; in attacks, as if he would fall to the right and backward, on walking in evening (after a glass of strong beer).

Forehead.—Sticking in l. side on stooping, with pressing asunder; S. behind eyes, with rhythmical intermissions in afternoon and evening, < walking. Tearing behind r. eye in open air, extending towards occiput, > coffee, also rhythmical sticking when walking, > riding in a wagon. Aching; in sinuses; in sinciput; over r. eye; deep behind l. eye; in morning after rising, < over r. eye, and headache all day; in sinciput in morning, at times sticking; in sinciput and occiput towards noon, < towards evening; at noon, with congestion to head; in region of superciliary arch after dinner; in F. and vertex, rather to l. side, > 10 A.M., returned after dinner and lasted till evening; A., with heaviness; above root of nose, with tension in skin of forehead; in sinciput, with stitches; in sinciput, with beating in occiput and temples; in r. sinus, with stopped catarrh; in sinciput, extending to eyes. Contractive pains in F. and eyes, that unite at tip of nose, where there is digging pinching. Pressure all day, as if eyes would spring out of head and as if stones were lying about them. Drawing through F. in evening. Confusion; and throbbing; and heaviness.

Temples.—Sticking, < l.; in l. after dinner; drawing, < l. Intermittent tearing in l.; T. in r. all night, > pressure. Pain in r.; in l. and frontal region, with vertigo, staggering, anxiety and sweat. Drawing in l. and on l. eye.

Vertex.—Stitches, on l. side; S. and tearing in V. and occiput, with cutting in abdomen, then stool, at first soft, then only of mucus, at 9 and 10 P.M. Acute pain in r. side in bed, as if there would be a tearing there. Pain in r. side; P. only in morning on rising; in r. side as from a draught of air; > open air; bruised; like pulling of hair; in a spot on r. side like a contraction in scalp, in morning after rising. Sensitiveness to touch. Pressure, < laying hand on it; P. as from a stone on it. Constriction; in afternoon and night, with heaviness of head.

Sides.—Sticking deep behind r. ear. Pain in region of l. parietal bone towards midnight, > taking off the nightcap; in a spot on r. side near crown, with external heat, the P. > laying the hand on it.

Occiput.—Stitch in l. side during menstruation. Sharp, almost tearing pain in r. Drawing and tearing so that she could not move the head, with stiffness in nape, then drawing and tearing in scapulæ, with weakness, she could scarcely lift the feet, with coldness, then heat at night, all without thirst or sweat. Pain; in evening, with stitches; > binding up hair; gradually changing to rhythmical stitches, < touch; and heaviness. Compression from 11 A.M. to 4 P.M., so that everything became stiff, then pain in nape like a pulling on hairs, extending to shoulders, with tension and stitches over face and neck, impairment of swallowing, anxiety and arrest of breath. Burning throbbing on l. side in evening.

Scalp.—Profuse falling of hair. Scurfy spots, with itching. Pain on pressure. Sudden pain in r. side of sinciput when walking, soon extending to vertex, thence into occiput and temples, first felt only on shaking head, as when coughing, walking, etc., afterwards more violent and felt on turning head and during rest, with painful pulsation in occiput and temples, when worst the scalp of occiput was painful as if bruised, the pain > firm pressure and in evening. Itching, then after scratching till it bled burning and pain.

Eyes.—Staring, pupils dilated. Catarrhal inflammation, < l., in morning on waking, with pressure in them. Shooting through both after supper. Pressure; and on pressing upon balls pain in orbits; as from sand, in forenoon; drawing, obliquely through l. and in l. side of forehead. Burning in morning after rising, > washing; B. in morning after washing with cold water, with lachrymation; in morning, with lachrymation; with photophobia; with redness of canthi; with weakness as from sleepiness. Burning biting as from salt water, < l. Itching of r., with acrid lachrymation. Lachrymation of r.

Pain in r. ball; in l. ball as if grasped from both sides, so that its long axis was increased, during dinner at 3 P.M. Pressure on r. ball. Lids, redness of r., with itching; R. of r., with swelling of it and with burning and stitches in r. external canthus; agglutination in morning; A. of r. in morning; closed with the headache; sticking and burning; tearing in inner canthi; pressure as from a hair beneath l. upper; sticking itching on l. inner and r. outer angle of eye; burning biting of r.; burning in outer canthi. Compressive pain in orbits, < pressure on upper part of ball. Vision of variegated rings. Blindness.

Ears.—Inflammation of r. lobule, with swelling, burning and twitching. Sticking in r.; in evening; so that she could not lie upon it at night; then twinging; with headache; behind l. extending towards articulation of jaw. Tearing behind E.; in r. meatus. Pressure towards E. and temples. Tension in r. meatus. Tensive pain behind r. all day, with sticking behind l. Rhythmical throbbing in l. Tickling in cartilage of r. meatus in morning in bed. Itching in external meatus. Ringing; in l. in evening; clear-toned, in l. Hissing. Rushing as of water. Pulsating humming in front of l. Deafness.

Nose.—Redness as if inflamed. Inflammation of tip. Ulcer deep in r. nostril. Pain in bones, < touch; P. in tip as if a pustule would form; *sore pain in upper part of r. nostril*, with pain on pressure. *Swollen feeling in r. nostril*, with pain on pressure. Clawing about wings, with burning. Burning about nose, < touch, with clawing and burrowing, with swelling of r. nostril as if there were an eruption in it, and want of air; B. in r. nostril as if sore, on blowing nose. Itching internally in l. side of tip. Dryness, with burning of the (usually) sore place.

Stoppage; with taste as if fasting; then discharge of purulent offensive mucus, with sneezing. Sneezing; in morning without catarrh; about 10 P.M.; violent, in morning. Catarrh, with sneezing; C., with stoppage of nose, loss of smell and rough voice; stopped C., with burning externally about nose; now dry, now fluent; fluent, < open air. Dropping of water without catarrh. Bleeding; in afternoon; from l. nostril after rising, then relief of headache; from l. nostril on blowing nose; the blood acrid like vinegar; clots or small balls of blood discharge on blowing; blowing out of blood after rising.

Clinical.—Polypus filling the whole r. side of the nose was entirely cured by the 3d dil.

Face.—Pale; and sickly; and collapsed. Sunken and nose pale and cold. Pinched and anxious. Flushed, with general warmth, fulness of head and throbbing of cranial arteries. Convulsed. Jerking of muscles in a nap about 8 A.M., < eye and on r. side of neck, the first attack near r. articulation of jaw, afterwards fear that it would develop into epileptic spasm, dream during the night that he ineffectually endeavored to open his eyes during the attack and forced them open with his fingers. Sticking in l. cheek, then burning. Tearing in bones of l. side; in zygomata; sticking, between r. mastoid process and angle of lower jaw. Jerking pain in r. zygoma at night; intermittent, in zygoma, extending towards vertex. Tensive pain in cheeks, with redness and with throbbing in middle of brain.

Jaws, tearing in a streak in middle of base of r. lower; T. in l. lower in evening in bed, > pressure and lying upon it, with toothache in same row; drawing T. in l. lower and in a hollow molar of same side; gnawing in l. upper, close to wing of nose; jerking pain in upper and in zygoma; pressure in r. articulation on moving it and on swallowing, with sticking; drawing in r. side of lower. Lips distorted; pimple like "water-pock" on inner wall, not breaking; blisters on upper, with inflamed areola and tensive pain.

Mouth.—Teeth. Looseness of an upper molar, then ulcerative pain all day. Stitches in a hollow T. when touched, gum inflamed, painful and bleeding easily; S. in upper molars, now r., now l., with drawing. Tearing in a l. upper; T. in forenoon, with T. in head; shooting, in upper incisors in open air in evening and next morning. Jerking pain; in an upper molar; in a l. upper molar; in l. upper T., like ulceration. Throbbing pain, waking at 3 A.M. and midnight, < cold, unchanged by warmth; in l. upper in evening when walking in open air. Boring towards noon, > evening, with pressure in head, and at one time heat, at another coldness. Aching, < drawing in air, and extending into incisors. Ulcerative pain, in upper, < molars. Grumbling in a diseased upper molar as if air streamed in and out of it. Tight feeling in the l. lower hollow wisdom-tooth, perceptible during sleep.

Swelling of gum externally to r. upper teeth, with pain; gum on inside of upper teeth seems swollen, with throbbing in it. Tongue red; coated white; burning blister on tip; burning pimples on tip, < evening; sticking in r. half, then burning; burning at tip and anterior surface in evening, as if cut; formication. Loss of speech. Mouth coated in morning. Scorbutic condition. Painful swelling on r. side of palate. Salivary glands, < submaxillary, enlarged, hard and painful, with salivation, weakness, and heaviness and pain in head. Coldness extending to stomach. Dryness of M. and tongue in morning; of M. and tongue waking after midnight, with thirst; D. before and after dinner; > breakfast, without thirst; interrupting sleep and causing thirst. Salivation. Offensive odor. Taste sour; in morning after rising; after breakfast, as if fasting; T. as if fasting, also with hawking of mucus; T. sweetish; insipid; nauseous all day.

Throat.—Redness of uvula and tonsils towards evening, with painful swallowing of saliva, aversion to smoking and prostration. Whatever she takes, easily goes down the wrong way. Hawking in afternoon of sweetish mucus of the form and consistence of liver. Sticking in morning on rising, also externally on pressure on larynx and on eating; in middle of T. and fauces on swallowing; in l. side on swallowing and speaking, > food; < swallowing. Pain; like beginning of inflammation; sore. Soreness, with inflammation of arch of palate and uvula; S. at night, as if it would grow together and as if she could not get air through it. Rawness; evening and morning, with scraping and frequent necessity to hawk, which caused pain in chest; in choanæ as if coryza would occur. Scraping (as from acidity of stomach) after paroxysms of cough. Burning; like commencing inflammation; in pharynx, like heartburn. Tickling, with necessity to hawk, but nothing was raised. Œsophagus sore, preventing swallowing of irritating food or drink; glutinous sensation, as if covered with glutinous jelly.

Stomach.—Ravenous hunger in forenoon; between 10 and 11 A.M.; alternating with cutting in umbilical region; towards evening, without real appetite; with thirst, without real desire for food. Hunger, without real appetite, then aversion to food all the morning, with white-coated tongue, at 10 A.M. increase of appetite. Incessant desire to eat and drink. Appetite diminished. Appetite lost; and much thirst. Thirst; in afternoon, > water, with burning in throat; but no appetite for breakfast; during menstruation; lost. Eructations all day; violent E.; empty. Hiccough in morning fasting.

Nausea; in morning in bed; at 5 A.M., in bed, with pressure in stomach and aversion to food; in afternoon and evening, then eructations, retching, > eructations of bitter water; in evening after soup, with heaviness in stomach; in pit in evening; waking at night, > gulping up mucus; after supper, > eating again, with salivation; when walking after dinner, with painful retching about umbilicus; during menstruation, with salivation; with eructations of water; with shivering; with painful movements in abdomen, then diarrhœa; with general trembling, headache pressive, and as if beaten, retching, burning in eyes, weakness, as if sleepy. Retching.

Vomiting; (towards evening, after a glass of beer); constant; violent; violent and painful, with diarrhœa; of glairy fluid; of mucus and water, then of bloody mucus; of blood; of bloody, mucous fluid; ejecta mixed with dark blood; of contents of stomach, then of blood, much fluid and purplish clotted blood were ejected, afterwards grumous blood, both fluid and clotted.

Distention in epigastric region. Fulness; after dinner, then pain as from something heavy in it till evening; > towards 5 P.M., by a thin, scanty stool, with loss of appetite, then great appetite. Inflammation; and gangrene of mucous membrane. Inclination to cramp. Stitches in epigastric region; cutting, in pit and upper abdomen after breakfast. Griping. Spasmodic gnawing in pit, with burning pain, almost causing faintness. Twinging on drinking cocoa; T. after supper, with nausea and salivation.

Pain; in pit; epigastric region; at upper orifice; in cardiac extremity and base; in morning, > eructations; in pit in afternoon; in pit and epigastric region on deep breathing and on blowing nose; in l. part of epigastric region, only on walking; in posterior and upper part of epigastric region, near to and behind cartilages of ribs, only when walking, extending almost to pit of stomach, returning next day in upper part of l. half of epigastric region towards noon when walking, > afternoon; in epigastric region, with sensitiveness to touch; with soreness, flatulence and salivation; in pit, with gnawing and pain on pressure; with coldness, then sticking in whole body, with acute pain on every inspiration; extending to bowels; as if disordered. Burning pain in epigastrium, < pressure; B. pain in epigastrium, changing to boring.

Pressure in S. and chest so united that it is difficult

to tell which is the suffering part, provoking frequent inspiration, < morning and evening. Pressure inward in pit as from a knob, after dinner, with sensitiveness to pressure. Sensitiveness during menstruation, with salivation. Contraction in pit in morning on walking and standing. Feeling as if something in it were turning about in morning after rising. Heaviness in region, with fulness. Pulsation in epigastric region, towards cardiac extremity. Burning; in pit; in epigastrium. Cardialgia. Heartburn. Coldness; in morning after milk-broth; > lying down in evening, with pain on touch. *Faintlike weakness about pit.*

Abdomen.—Distention; in afternoon; in evening; > difficult, unsatisfactory, but not hard stool, much urging before the stool; with desire for stool and emission of flatus; soft, with sensitiveness to touch. Movings. Rumbling; towards noon; with griping extending into stomach, which was sensitive externally, and to l. side of abdomen, where it was a sticking, with distention, frequent emission of flatus and feeling as if diarrhœa would occur; then ineffectual desire for stool, frequent emissions of flatus. Flatulent noises and clucking. Emission of flatus; in evening; in evening, with scraping in rectum; offensive; offensive, with ordinary stool.

Inflammation of intestinal canal. Sudden stitches in various parts in evening. Tearing; in colon, soon extending to whole intestinal canal and causing cramp in stomach. Sticking, griping, as from flatulence, in morning after waking, extending to small of back, then twice urging to normal stool. Griping; here and there; in region of transverse colon; in evening, with desire for stool and two soft stools; in evening, extending to beneath l. breast, where it is sticking, with rumbling; during sleep, with flatulence; before normal stool, with cutting; in A. and small of back before the usual stool, with pain; with soft stool; with bloody diarrhœa; with frequent urging to stool, then two soft stools; with increased menses; in A. and small of back, then sticking, < morning and evening. Intermittent griping movements.

Cutting all day; mornings and evenings; before diarrhœa; in small intestines; in small intestines, as if too full of air; along tract of intestines, so that it seemed as if he could follow the action of the drug, with emission of flatus, desire for stool, heartburn and general heat, after an hour a normal stool. Excruciating pain. Pain; in forenoon and afternoon; in A. and small of back during menstruation; then emission of flatus; after veal, < r. side, ending with pain in stomach and empty feeling, afterwards cutting in abdomen all night. Burning pain when sitting bent over, extending to small of back, > rising. Burning. Drawing after supper; D. in small intestines. Urging of flatus and feeling as before diarrhœa, with the flatulence evacuation of a few drops of fluid. Empty feeling in region of transverse colon.

Hypochondria.—Sticking in l. in afternoon; S. > emission of flatus; in r. extending to back, as if behind liver. Griping in l. (descending colon) extending into epigastric region (transverse colon), < standing and walking and pressure on descending colon, > crouching. Pain in l. as after a blow, with pain in small of back, so that she could not lie, then leucorrhœa, which with pain in back ceased after menstruation.

Umbilical Region.—Cutting, with urging to stool, unaffected by the usual stool, with frequent profuse emission of urine. Griping in U. region and beneath l. short ribs in morning in bed, not entirely > emission of flatus; G. in evening, > emission of flatus; after soup; after eating, then flatulence and thin clear stool; with emission of flatus, then relief of head; beneath umbilicus, extending into chest, where it became sticking, with two soft stools; intermittent pain, almost griping, with diarrhœa. Burning pain here and there above umbilicus.

Sides.—Distention of l., > bending together, with sticking. Sudden shocks in l. as from something alive.

Hypogastrium.—Sticking in r. groin and ilium; in middle of ilia when sitting; in groins and anus before a hard stool; in l. groin when walking, extending outward through ilium; in H. and rectum, after dinner, < motion, with burning. Pain in r. groin on stooping; in pubic region on touch. Contractive pain in l. groin in evening when walking, often a sticking, almost taking away the breath, > a semi-fluid stool, with mucus. Dragging towards rings. Compression above l. ilium when walking. Burning in r. groin when sitting bent over during menstruation; tearing B. deep in pelvis and in hip-joint or in hip-bone, < during rest.

Rectum and Anus.—Discharge of blood after a hard stool. Tenesmus during normal stool; after diarrhœa. Urging in morning and diarrhœa. Frequent urging, with frequent micturition; F. urging, then hard stool; not > normal stool, with frequent but scanty micturition. Frequent sensation as before a thin stool, but next morning a hard stool. Ineffectual desire for stool. Enlargement of hæmorrhoids, with sticking in them. Burning in anus after hard stool; burning pressure in anus when not at stool. Itching in anus.

Stool.—*Diarrhœa;* with pain in abdomen; violent; bright yellow, twice, after a normal stool. Frequent diarrhœa; with emission of flatus; then constipation; then smarting in anus, once after the thin stool stopped sensation in anus, after prolonged and great urging a little is passed, feeling like hardened fæces, with relief of tenesmus. Violent, watery. Thin; and profuse; and scanty; and frequent; twice, with pressure; and sudden, then dragging and desire till a scanty hard stool passed; and small fæces, then consistent, with feeling as if something should be expelled, then soft stool preceded by urging, the stool ceased as if cut off. *Soft;* after dinner, then burning and sticking in anus so that she could not sit; and unsatisfactory; and frequent. Three pasty, with the third cutting in the whole intestinal tract, next day stool hard, not copious, third day three thin stools, fourth day four watery ones.

Hard; with discharge of blood; and frequent; and frequent, with swelling of hæmorrhoids; and difficult; with great pressure; with such exertion that rectum protrudes; with pressure and sticking in pudenda. Like sheep-dung. Straw-yellow. Slimy. Covered with mucus. *Bloody; with tenesmus. Contained membranous portions of intestines mixed with blood. With great pressure.* Frequent. Indolent.

Clinical.—Dysentery, slimy, bloody stools at night, with constant urging, pulse small and rapid, hands cold.

Urinary Organs.—Stitches in region of prostate gland when urinating. *Frequent urging, at first only a few drops, then the usual stream;* frequent U., with discharge of much offensive flatus. Stitches in orifice of urethra. Shivering and tickling in orifice. Biting in urethra during micturition. Burning in urethra when urinating; in forepart; orifice; *during scanty micturition.* Burning pain in urethra at close of micturition. Frequent and copious micturition; and the urine as clear as water; and urine brownish-yellow. Frequent micturition, with scanty discharge; frequent, urine pale and turbid; frequent, of yellow transparent urine, a few clouds forming after twenty-four hours; frequent while the stools were regular, but urine unaffected when there were several thin stools. Strangury, with bloody stools.

Urine.—Dark and depositing a brick-dust sediment. Reddish. Coffee-colored from admixture of blood. Dark yellow. Lighter than usual, without the usual sediment, decreased in quantity. Turbid, soon depositing a yellow sediment. *Diminished. Copious;* at night; at night, containing sugar; even at night, with hard stool; and dark and red, after several hours a sediment, which when disturbed rose in a cloud; with a reddish cloud; with drawing and acute pains in lumbar region in afternoon, < motion. Mucous sediment.

Sexual Organs.—Painful swelling of l. epididymus, behind and below testicle. Prickling sticking in glans; itching S. in penis in afternoon when sitting. Itching of glans. Smarting in orifice of prepuce, also smarting when urinating. Erections in morning in bed; on waking, with great desire for coition (at an unusual time), which was affected "maxima cum voluptate"; E. at noon without voluptuous thoughts. Testicles drawn up, sensitive and painful. Drawing tension in testicles and along spermatic cords into abdomen after unsatisfied desire, with pain. Desire increased; with great sexual enjoyment.

Abortion at second month. Thin, white leucorrhœa, stiffening the linen, with bruised pain in small of back. Menses thin. Menstruation too early, with pain in small of back and lower limbs; too early and profuse, lasting three days, but flowing scarcely any after the second day, blood black like ink. Menstruation prolonged and profuse. M., which was just at its close, was increased after a new dose, with pain in abdomen, small of back and thighs. M., which was slight on the fourth day, after a new dose became more profuse, thicker, with clots, next day again scanty. M. late. M. suppressed.

Respiratory Organs.—Larynx, cutting, with impeded swallowing; tensive pain when breathing; tickling causing irritation to cough. Irritation to cough at bifurcation of trachea, as from swallowing a bread-crumb; sudden I. to cough in r. bronchus near pit of throat, > slow, deep breath and by an effort of the will. *Hoarseness;* during menstruation, with cough, expectoration of mucus and stopped catarrh; with rawness in throat; and suppressed voice, with tickling provoking cough. Catarrhal voice. Voice lost.

Cough; day and night, with sore pain in chest, then catarrh, with stoppage and itching of nose; waking at 3 A.M., with stupefying headache, the C. < raising herself or moving; after entering the house, from tickling in middle of chest; < morning; with soreness in chest and pain in head and throat. Paroxysmal, < bread or cakes. Almost taking away her breath. Dry; in afternoon, with bloody expectoration; with rawness in throat and heaviness on chest; from rawness behind sternum, with tension, contraction and pressure in chest. Dry, hacking; all day, with almost audible beating of heart. Cough > expectoration. Cough, with expectoration towards morning; in morning, with pain in sternum; at night, disturbing sleep, towards morning sweat; < evening after lying down; of hard masses of bronchial mucus, that sank in water and were not dissolved by shaking; cough, with redness of face, at last a little mucous expectoration. Cough, with bloody expectoration; at the full moon; and mucous. Expectoration of clotted blood after hawking mucus (during menstruation). Sour-smelling expectoration.

Dyspnœa in region of pit of throat. *Respiration difficult;* oppressed when ascending, with sticking in chest, cough and expectoration of clear blood; accelerated, with general feverish weakness. Frequent inspiration, < morning and towards evening, from a sensation in epigastric region and oppression of chest, with confusion and drawing in head.

Clinical.—Asthma, with excessive dyspnœa, faintness and nausea, with dull stitches or with burning pain in chest, rather free expectoration.

Chest.—Inflammation. Sticking in r.; l.; beneath l. female breast; in l. side more towards back; in l. side of upper part of sternum; in anterior and farther part of l.; in middle of r. in morning; in r. between fifth and sixth ribs in afternoon; in evening, with burning; in r. at 8 P.M., with pressure; middle of upper part after dinner; l. when carrying a weight; l. on inspiration; l. near sternum on deep inspiration; r. when coughing and breathing deeply; r. lower ribs from coughing and laughing; beneath l. breast, < walking; in upper part of r., < lying on r. side and with head low; l., > walking in open air, with pain, recurring towards evening like a cutting and tearing in lungs, < deep inspiration, then chilliness and tearing from knees to toes, so that she must go to bed; in middle extending to sides and towards axillæ when walking during menstruation; in l. making breath short; periodical, in r. half; rhythmical, in l. costal region after lifting a weight.

Tearing in r. side (intercostal muscles). Cutting beneath sternum when coughing. Pain; in lowest end of sternum; behind sternum all day; beneath sternum all the forenoon; in afternoon; beneath sternum during cough, then soreness there; under sternum when coughing, with warmth and rattling, the expectoration seemed to come from low down in chest; in r. side, in region of false ribs, afterwards it extended towards pit of stomach, where it remained long like a pressure, with loud eructations and loud emissions of flatus, the pressure in stomach changed to hunger. Tensive pain across C., with stitches in l. side under ribs. Feeling when coughing as if something were loose.

Constriction in forenoon when standing, with anxious shortness of breath; *C. of lungs in morning in bed,* preventing deep breathing, extending from the back, if she attempts to breathe deeply she must gasp for air and she coughs; cramplike C., with anxiety and dread of suffocation, alternating with cramplike drawing in occiput and nape, of l. side, so that she had to hold the head backward. *Oppression; < morning. Tightness; at night from coughing; with heaviness.* Fulness beneath sternum, < deep inspiration and causing short, dry, hollow cough. Anxiety towards evening.

Need to take a deep breath in evening when sitting still, and on every inspiration a stitch in l. chest, taking away the breath. Throbbing in forepart when sitting, with heaviness in it and inclination to faint. *Burning in forepart; B. in morning extending into throat, till expectoration is loosened.* Rush of blood.

Heart.—Sticking in præcordial region. Violent beating, waking him in evening; when lying on back, waking her at midnight, she sat up full of anxiety. *Palpitation;* at midnight when lying on r. side; on sudden motion and on standing up, with heat of face and oppression of chest.

Pulse.—Rapid; in afternoon when at rest; at 4 P.M., with heat in head; in evening; towards evening, and hard; and full; and hardish; and full, hard, with condition like inflammatory irritability of whole body, < abdominal organs; and fluttering, irregular; and small; and small, with warm hands; and feeble. Increased. Slow; and weak; and small, weak. Hard, with symptoms of enteric inflammation. Weak; and small; and fluttering, unequal. Small and soft. Irregular, scarcely perceptible.

Neck.—Tearing in r. muscles, extending from shoulder to head. Sprained pain in nape like a stiffness on nodding or turning head. Tensive pain in sterno-cleido-mastoid muscle; r. on turning head. Painful throbbing in a vertebra after raising head from stooping. Stiffness of nape.

Back.—Pinching in evening. Pain; on coughing; on stooping; when fasting; > walking, < sitting and lying in bed, with burning. Paralysis of spine, with tetanus. Sticking beneath l. scapula in evening; beneath r. at night; in region of lower angle of l. on deep inspiration; between S. as with knives when lying on back, waking her and causing short breath, > lying on r. side. Tensive drawing between scapulæ at 6 P.M.

Lumbar Region.—Sticking in l. side when sitting; in kidney region, < r., in evening, < deep breathing. Pinching all day. Pain waking at 2 A.M., and preventing lying on back; P. > walking and rubbing, < cough; in region of kidneys, with frequent desire to urinate and increased thirst; in morning on waking, extending into l. hypochondrium, also obliging her to rise; at night waking him; in afternoon alternating with griping in abdomen, in evening a hard stool. Bruised pain in morning on waking; at 3 A.M., preventing turning over; in evening during menstruation. Drawing pain in region of kidneys. Paralyzed feeling in evening.

Extremities.—Jerking of arms and legs in evening in bed. Trembling; of hands and feet. Sticking in r. shoulder, then in knee; in knees, elbows and shoulder-joints, worse in afternoon than in forenoon, lasting longer in l. elbow and < motion. Pain in r. hip and l. shoulder and ankles, < walking; in r. shoulder on most motions of arm, > upward and backward motion, similar disturbances in r. ankle and hip-joint. Bruised feeling. Drawing pains; cramplike, now in r., now in l. arm, now in legs, < about knees, < rest. Drawing. Paralytic pain in r. shoulder-joint, < towards forepart, as if in head of bone, > moving arm, if the arm was turned on its axis cracking in forepart of joint, as if in tendon of biceps, there was a similar pain in first joint of r. ring finger on flexing and extending it, > next day, except when lying, when there was a similar pain in l. patella, which was > after sleep. Weakness; and lameness. Crawling in hands and feet as if asleep. Paralysis.

Upper Extremities.—Shoulder. Tearing in l.; T. waking at midnight; in r. from 2 to 5 A.M., > rising; in r., with heaviness, waking at 2 A.M., with numbness of arm, the pain afterwards extended to wrist; in r. waking at 3 A.M., with falling asleep of fingers; from r. to fingers, waking at 11 P.M., lasting till 4 A.M., with sensation as if S. were standing out farther than natural, inability to lie upon either side; drawing T. to fingers towards evening. Pain in l., on raising arm, < moving it backward at the same time; P. in l. as from weariness; rheumatic, in r.; bruised, in morning. Pressure on L.

Arm.—Jerking of muscles. Tearing in r., < shoulder, < afternoon and evening; T. in r. extending to wrist on motion, with stiffness of arm, which was > violent motion; intermittent, during menstruation, returning at night when lying upon r. side. Drawing pain if they hang down. Weakness. Falling asleep of l. when lying on back, waking her about 3 A.M. Paralysis.

Upper Arm.—Sticking in r., with throbbing. Tearing in humerus; drawing, in l. deltoid. Drawing pinching. Drawing in r. Paralytic weakness of r.

Elbow.—Tearing during the day, and in wrists, finger-joints and beneath nails; from r. to ring and middle fingers, with heaviness and numbness of the parts. Pain extending into wrists, where it is tearing and breaking, as if it would twist the bones, thence into knuckles, where it distends the spaces between them, with swelling of the parts, extending as a crushing pain thence to beneath nails, > rubbing hands, with feeling as if hands were large, heavy, numb, paralytic, with weakness of them, but only at night. Drawing in bend of l., with tension and burning; D. in r. extending up posterior surface of upper arm. Drawing pain in inner surface of r., as if starting from ulnar nerve, on strongly flexing forearm.

Forearm.—Tearing extending up dorsal surface of l.; in r. and in index and thumb, waking at night; in tendon on outer side of l., then paralytic weakness; paralytic, in l., extending to wrist. Intermittent gnawing in l. ulna, a hand's breadth above wrist, in afternoon when sitting, then paralytic feeling so that the arm must hang down, > rubbing, then frequent pressure. Paralytic weakness of r. at night.

Wrist.—Tearing; in r.; in external condyle in evening. Sprained feeling in r. when drawing a tooth. Intermittent jerking pain. Pain on inner surface of r. as if the parts would be forcibly drawn inward, with a depression externally. Drawing from r. to elbow during dinner, with throbbing and pain, afterwards in both arms.

Hand.—Trembling. Tearing stitches in bones of l. just back of little finger. Tearing in back of l., > rubbing; T. in metacarpal bone of r. index in morning; in r. in evening, with breaking pain; with shivering and thirst. Painful grabbing in ball of r. behind little finger, with gnawing. Leaden heaviness. Weakness, and of fingers, and on exertion pain in wrist.

Fingers.—Sticking beneath l. thumb-nail; jerking, in r. ring and middle fingers. Tearing in last phalanx of l. thumb; pinching, in l. thumb; cramplike, in knuckles alternating with headache. Sprained pain on holding a large object, and on stretching them, which at first he cannot do, they seem too long, and if he wishes to hold anything he must first bend them backward; S. pain in r. index and cracking in joints on every motion of hand; S. pain in r. thumb-joint on moving it backward and pain in a spot in joint on pressure; pain in r. thumb-joint as if sprained and swollen on bending it backward, with cracking. Drawing in r. little; tearing, in l. middle. Stiffness at times.

Lower Extremities.—Reeling; without vertigo. Pain in bones of r. from hip to toes from 1 to 4 A.M., > rising and walking, when there was pain only about malleoli. Weakness, with yawning. Tearing in l. nates when standing, > motion.

Hip.—Sticking in r. when standing, > motion; S. in r., with burning; S., then bruised pain in back. Tearing in r. joint in afternoon and evening. Pain in morning on waking, < after rising till noon. Intermittent sprained feeling in r. joint in morning when walking.

Thigh.—Bruised feeling in muscles. Drawing in morning. Weakness in middle of r. T. and tibia as if paralyzed three days before menstruation, > sitting and standing, afterwards < sitting. Paralyzed feeling from middle of l. to leg.

Knee.—Tearing; in evening, and down tibiæ; in r. during rest; in hollows when walking; in r., with weakness, so that she could not step properly; painless, on outer surface of r. Pain on inside of r. when walking. Sprained pain beneath r. patella when walking, > during rest. Pain in hollows as after a blow. Intermittent painful throbbing at night in bed. Drawing in evening extending to feet. Weakness extending into thigh, < walking.

Leg.—Cramp in l. calf towards evening. Spasmodic contraction of l. calf when walking. Tearing in periosteum of l. tibia in afternoon; T. in r. leg and knee during rest, > walking, with weariness; down r. tibia in evening and next morning; with drawing; drawing, in anterior surface of l. tibia. Bruised pain in l. in morning on waking, on turning over it extended into small of back and ceased, with sticking in heel. Drawing pain in r. when it lies across l. Drawing in tibiæ. Weakness; in evening, < calves; in evening during menstruation, with pain; paralytic, after a short walk.

Sprained pain in r. ankle. Burning pain at union of os calcis with external malleolus during rest, on motion it feels sprained and when touched as if suppurating. Drawing in r. outer malleolus when standing, with tearing. Sticking in upper part of r. os calcis during rest; in r. sole at night, with ulcerative pain; now in r., now in l. sole, with burning, > rubbing, but returning. Tearing on back of r. foot, about first toe-joint, in evening; in l. sole in afternoon; in ball of l. sole in evening; jerking, in soles during menstruation; ulcerative jerking, in l. sole. Ulcerative griping in r. sole in afternoon. Weakness of feet, < standing and walking.

Toes.—Painful contraction in evening when sitting. Stitches in second joint of r. little; in a spot on l. second where there had been a corn; in middle joint of r. smaller, always near dorsal surface, then on plantar surface between third and fourth last toes; through middle joint of r. second, waking at night, the next days through the same place in l. foot; jerking, in r. great at night. Tearing in l. great.

Skin.—Pale, but warm and moist. Greenish spot on l. side of thigh. Red spots on neck and l. forearm, itching on touch. A wartlike elevation on l. cheek becomes larger and itches. Bleeding of scurf on tip of nose. Pimples on nape and occiput. Itching pimples, only not on hands and feet; on r. nates after scratching; on r. forearm, exuding water after scratching; on shoulder, with sticking; on nape, forepart of nose, throat and r. elbow, with at times burning or biting. Pustule with a red base on nape; tensive painful P. on l. side of nose. Boil on lower part of thumb; on r. shoulder, with tensive pain. Vesicles which change to pustules, on face and other parts; burning V. here and there, full of yellow fluid, they burst after scratching and the burning ceases.

Stitches on motion, < chest; S., < face, then burning. Formication on hands and feet. Tickling on l. upper arm, l. ear, leg, and scrotum. Itching biting in l. knee. Itching; here and there; on upper margin of orbits; of face; l. elbow, on anterior and inner sides of r. thigh; r. side of neck, l. upper arm, l. side of forehead, r. side of chest, etc.; here and there in evening; here and there in evening after lying down, with stitches; on r. side of nose towards evening, then sticking in tip; on legs and tibiæ, with red spots here and there; in tip of nose, with crawling; on r. forearm, then pimples after scratching; on inner side of r. great toe as if frostbitten; tickling, here and there.

Sleep.—Yawning; during the day, with sleepiness; in forenoon, with sleepiness and exhaustion; with weariness and indolence; with shivering. Sleepiness; in morning after rising, with exhaustion; in afternoon, with exhaustion; after dinner, with weariness of legs on waking; between 11 and 12 A.M., irresistible during dinner at 3, sleep restless from frightful dreams and frequent waking; when walking and during rest; overpowering, at noon. Stupid sleep, with fantasies, from which she woke in fright; S. sleep as if drunken.

Sleepless till midnight; after 1 A.M. Restless sleep; on account of a throng of ideas; often only a slumber, with constant waking or wakened by pain; with many dreams and profuse sweat; from frightful dreams; disturbed by anxious dreams; with frequent waking; and full of dreams, with frequent waking in morning. Early waking. Fell asleep late, woke early and could not sleep again. Dreamy sleep, a throng of thoughts, inability to rest and anxiety.

Dreams.—Many; after midnight. Vivid, full of strife. Of quarrels, vexation and anger. Of danger from water, fire and the like. Anxious, as if she had a painful, swollen cheek or as if her child had been beaten. Of sickness or of the breaking of one of her teeth. Of the death of an acquaintance. Of journeys, yet she made no progress, which vexed her. Voluptuous. Nightmare.

Fever.—Chilliness; frequently in afternoon; at 3 P.M.; at 6 P.M. during menstruation, > lying down, returning on rising, with chattering of teeth and shivering, > lying down again, and so on frequently till 10 P.M.; at 7 P.M., with shaking and tearing in head and peevishness, then on lying down sweat with twitching of limbs; from 7 to 8 P.M.; at 8 P.M. during menstruation, > lying down; at 9 P.M., > lying down, then sweat in sleep, without thirst; towards evening in open air, heat of face in house, then general sweat; in evening, with headache, extending down vertex; in evening, > lying down, with cold creeping over back; with redness of face. Alternations of chill, heat and sweat in afternoon.

Shivering; in evening, then flushes of heat and after lying down sweat, without thirst. Shaking chill in forenoon in open air; at 3 P.M.; in afternoon, > evening by lying down, with pains and heaviness in head, then heat in bed. Cold skin; with cyanosis and general cold, clammy sweat. Coldness in occiput, with headache. C. along spine; with cold sweat on forehead and more or less on whole body. Cold limbs; hands, feet and back; hands, with hot face.

Heat in afternoon, then chilliness, in evening after lying down sweat with thirst till morning, during the chill frequent flushes of heat, and during the heat frequent chilliness, even during the sweat cold creepings as soon as she uncovered. Heat towards evening; with confusion of head and fretfulness. H. in evening, with general sweat, without thirst; in evening, with hard and rapid pulse; at night, preventing sleep, night restless; at night, with anxious, visionary dreams, frequent starting up and sweat, next morning shivering, and in forenoon thirst; at night, then sweat and a little thirst. Peculiar general H. after eating. H. in body, with rush of blood to head, vertigo and confusion of head, external heat of forehead and cheeks and coldness of hands. Hot and dry skin at night. H. in face; and head; and upper lip and hand; with redness and heat to touch, then shivering towards evening. Burning in heels and balls of feet at night in bed.

Sweat; towards morning; in morning in bed; from 3 to 6 A.M., < chest, then weakness after rising; at night on waking; with weakness on every exertion; exhausting, in afternoon, with anxiety; cold, clammy, with shivering; profuse, at night, < legs; profuse, on alternate nights, < legs.

Kalmia.

A tincture of the fresh leaves of Kalmia latifolia, L., is used.

General Action.—This remarkable drug causes tingling and numbness in various parts, neuralgic (or rheumatic) pains, which wander and cause restlessness, and, most marked of all, a slow, weak pulse.

Allies.—Aconite, Cimicif., Rhus t., Spig., the Kalis and Lithia.

Generalities.—Sticking in various parts. Tearing in r. shoulder, l. arm, r. lower jaw, and in flesh of whole l. leg downward. *Rheumatic pains all over the body; often changing their position, especially in shoulder, elbow and wrist* (Puls., Cimicif.). Pressing pains in whole body. Pains, < moving, > lying. *Bruised feeling all over body* (Arn.). *General feeling as if one had been exposed to a soaking rain. Restlessness; and frequent turning* (Rhus t.). Desire to stretch. Aversion to exercise. *Weakness; in morning; in evening; in evening, especially in limbs, so that it was almost impossible to ascend stairs; of muscles; of all muscles, < exertion, appearing first in those of mastication; could not go above three steps without being exhausted and likely to fall from weakness and dizziness* (Rhus t.). Faintness, then vertigo.

Clinical.—Rheumatoid pains in various parts, pains shifting, they go to the heart and involve the arms and shoulders, associated with stiffness and numbness (compare Lithium). In chronic or subacute articular rheumatism the pains shift from joint to joint. With the neuralgic pains of Kalmia there are generally great weakness and trembling, symptoms of paralysis. Acute inflammatory rheumatism, shifting, arms and legs feel paralyzed.

Mind.—Anxiety. Irritability towards evening and next morning. Dislike to be spoken to, do not feel like going to the office, take up a book, but cannot collect my thoughts. Do not want to study. Cannot study, restless.

Head.—*Tearing; and in neck* (Cimicif.). Pain; in morning on waking and in evening; in morning on waking, > cold water; at noon, especially on r. side; > pressure, especially in temples and forehead; with nausea; with flushed face; intermittent; wandering, in afternoon and evening, especially in parts back of forehead; internally, with sensation, when turning, of something loose diagonally across top; in all parts behind forehead. Drawing, and in eyes, < towards evening and in open air. Confusion; in evening. Dulness, with difficult hearing and pain in limbs. Dull, drowsy feeling, then raging pain in temples and occiput. Dull, full feeling on waking, for an hour after getting up did not feel like doing anything. Fulness. Surging of blood in H. and against l. cheek, with heat of l. cheek. *Vertigo;* on stooping and looking downward (from 8 to 9 A.M., and from 3 to 6 P.M.) (Puls., Anac.); on getting up after studying; < towards noon; *with pain in limbs;* with nausea and pain in head and limbs; with fugitive glow in different parts of surface and increase of sweat.

Forehead.—Shooting, extending into eye-teeth. Tearing in F. and head in morning on rising, then in hips and lower limbs to feet; across F.; in l. side, extending into temple. Pain; in evening; in morning on waking; on rising, worse afterwards; over eyes; in upper part of glabella; above r. eye about noon; < r. side; with inability to concentrate mind on book; *extending into roots of r. upper molars;* in supraorbital region, extending to occiput; in evening in F. and over eyes, moving backward and outwardly down sides of neck, then pain in l. shoulder; *sometimes shooting to eye-teeth, at one time easier in F., at another in teeth;* pulsating.

Temples.—Shootings to occiput; S. into eyes; to eyeballs at 10.30 A.M. Tearing in r., passing downward. Acute pain in l., < ascending stairs. Pain; in r.; in T., and over eyes in morning on waking, > cold water; from l. backward; heavy, in T., and especially in forehead, < mental effort, with pale face.

Shooting from vertex into temples, with feeling as if head would burst. Tearing on vertex. Pain in vertex; extending in direction of cervical vertebræ; as if bound with a cord. Pain on r. side of head; in whole l. side, with throbbing in it and with stitches in l. ear and behind r. ear; intermittent, in a spot on r. side above forehead in evening in bed. Heaviness on r. side of head, then towards evening on l. Pain in occiput; and neck; dull, in occiput, with frequent sharp darting pain in r. side of head.

Eyes.—Inflammation of l. in morning, with burning jerking pain till near noon. Sticking; towards evening; in r. in morning; under l.; in r., with pressing, the eyes feel dim and weak. Pain; in afternoon; in r.; in r. in evening; about eyes; *which makes it painful to turn them;* P., can hardly keep them open. Heaviness. Burning, < l., with pressing. Itching; in l. in afternoon, with burning; when rubbed, with stinging. Weakness. **Stiffness of muscles around eyes and of eyelids** (Rhus t.). Lids sore; at edges. Sensation in ball as if the orbit were pressing it out of its socket.

Glimmering exactly in point of vision, about 3 P.M., so that reading was difficult, with nausea. *Vision imperfect.* Dim, so that he could not read without spectacles; D. at intervals; < during paroxysms of vomiting. Almost blind when erect. Blind. Blackness about 8 or 9 A.M., when looking downward, with belching of wind and nausea. Vision affected, especially by darkness, coming before eyes every three or four minutes, and afterwards if in an erect position.

Clinical.—Inflammation of the sclera, with extreme pain on turning the eyes, and sclero-choroiditis, both anteriorly and posteriorly, sometimes with exudation into the vitreous. Retinitis albuminurica, especially during pregnancy. Paralysis of the upper lid, with feeling of stiffness (Rhus t., Caust.). Muscular asthenopia.

Ears.—Stitches; at 4 P.M.; in r. at night; in r. and behind it. Darting pains through them. Pain in r.; behind r. Ringing in afternoon. Cracking. Buzzing.

Nose.—Pain deep in l. side. Pressure on bridge, with frequent sneezing. Tickling; as before coryza. Sensation of coryza. Obstruction, < evening; O. of one nostril. Fluent coryza, with frequent sneezing and increased sense of smell.

Face.—Flushed. Pale. Sticking in bones; in l. upper jaw and zygoma; in jaws and teeth. Stinging in jaws. *Tearing in bones of r. or l. side; in r. lower jaw. Neuralgia. Darting pain in jaw. Pain between r. eye and r. side of nose in afternoon; in malar-bone, extending into r. molars and bicuspids; under angles of jaw.* Lips swollen, dry and stiff in morning.

Clinical.—Facial neuralgia, especially of r. side, with feeling of numbness and stiffness (compare Aconite), generally caused by cold; facial neuralgia following herpes zoster (Mezer.).

Mouth.—Drawing tearing in teeth. Toothache; < in incisors and eye-teeth; in upper T.; in lower incisors; in molars at 10.30 A.M.; in r. in evening; in molars for hours after 10 P.M.; as if a nerve were laid bare; neuralgic, in l. upper molars and bicuspid. Tongue white and dry. Sticking in tongue. Cutting in r. side of tongue, > biting it. Inflammation of sublingual glands. Tingling in salivary glands after eating, with sensation of fermentation in œsophagus and salivation. Salivation. Acrid, bitter taste.

Throat.—Rising of slippery mucus, with tickling in larynx. Pain in region of submaxillary gland in evening, shooting towards parotid. Scraping; exciting cough; causing desire to cough. Rawness, with scraping and pain when swallowing and with throbbing in tonsils. Pressing, with nausea. Feeling of a ball rising. Swollen feeling. Swallowing difficult; from dryness.

Stomach.—Thirst. Eructations; of air. *Nausea;* in morning; at 10.30 A.M., after stool; in afternoon when riding, with incarceration of flatus, then stool with cutting in abdomen; in evening, then dulness and aching in head; with incarcerated flatus; with loss of sight; with flickering before eyes. Retching. Vomiting, with ruminating action; V. every three or five minutes, without nausea, of bile towards the end and action like rumination.

Pain as if something were tearing the walls from their connections. Drawing tearing in epigastrium, < movement and attempting to talk. Pain in epigastrium. *Pressure in pit, > sitting erect, < sitting bent, with feeling as if something were pressed down beneath pit of stomach.* Gnawing at epigastric region at 8 A.M., with emptiness. Emptiness; with rumbling; which caused headache and nausea. Uneasiness. Distress after dinner as if overloaded. Discomfort. Contracted feeling; gradual, forcing its contents into œsophagus. Warmth; in epigastric region.

Clinical.—Gastralgia in sudden paroxysms.

Abdomen.—Cutting during stool; C. after breakfast, > loose stool. Occasional pain across A.; P. driving me to stool, diarrhœa, with tenesmus. Sensation as before a cathartic operation, but none followed. Weak feeling extending into throat; > eructations. Sticking in r. hypochondrium at 8 A.M. Pain in r. side; in liver region; in hypochondrium; about umbilicus.

Rectum and Stool.—Inclination to stool in forenoon. Burning in anus after stool. Stools soft and frequent; soft, twice in forenoon, with evacuation of wind. Pappy stool, easily discharged, as if smoothed over, then pressing in rectum. Hard, large, difficult, then burning in rectum. Too large and hard to pass in morning, passed with difficulty at 10 A.M. Constipation. Omitted, next day scanty, third day loose at noon after the morning stool.

Urinary Organs.—Burning during micturition. Urging; frequent desire. Frequent micturition of yellow copious urine; *frequent M. of small quantities of urine which feel hot.* Urine increased.

Clinical.—Subacute Bright's disease, with the peculiar pains in the back, with predominating palpitation, pains about the heart, etc. Very valuable in albuminuria of pregnancy.

Sexual Organs.—Sticking in glans. Frequent erections without desire. Pain in r. testicle in morning, in l. in afternoon. Yellowish leucorrhœa in morning, eight days after appearance of menses (during the leucorrhœa several old symptoms). Menses eight days too early, next time fourteen days too late; M. scanty and delayed, with pain in loins, back and anterior part of thighs; painful M.

Respiratory Organs.—*Tickling in trachea.* Cough day and night; in evening, with mucous expectoration; C., with expectoration of gray, smooth, unctuous matter, of a putrid, salt taste, which on being spread out separates into small pieces. Peculiar noise when breathing, as from spasmodic affection of glottis. *Oppressed breathing; with palpitation and anxiety;* and short.

Chest.—*Sticking in lower part;* S. in r. lung, under third and fourth ribs, causing dyspnœa; below breast. Tearing in whole l. side. Pressure in r. side. Sensation as if strained by lifting. Oppression.

Heart and Pulse.—**Palpitation;** *with faint feeling. Fluttering of heart; on slowly ascending stairs. Pulse irregular;* < mental effort and leaning over to write. Pulse rapid. *Pulse slow; and feeble; S., weak and creeping, the artery slowly contracted and dilated, like the action of an earthworm.* P. imperceptible.

Clinical.—Angina pectoris. Cardiac diseases of an organic nature, rheumatic endocarditis, valvular insufficiency, hypertrophy and degeneration, slow pulse, paroxysms of extreme anguish about the heart and dyspnœa, wandering pains about the heart, extending down l. arm.

Neck.—Shooting externally down sides; S. from nape into head. Sticking on l. side at night, with itching. Tearing in nape. Darting pain in upper vertebræ. Pain on both sides; in r. side; in sterno-cleido-mastoid muscle; extending down back, afterwards increased to stiffness, < seventh cervical vertebra. Shock from nape towards occiput, with heat.

Drawing in l. side in afternoon and evening, with sticking. Stiffness in morning.

Back.—*Pain; at night in bed;* during menses; *down back; in spine, sometimes < lumbar region, with heat;* extending through shoulders. Sensation as if spine would break, with anterior convexity. Sticking in lower part of l. scapula at night. Pain in scapulæ; between S.; between S., extending over head into temples. Sharp pain in three upper dorsal vertebræ, extending through shoulders. *Sticking in loins; < motion; drawing S. in sacral region and hip. Sharp pain in loins. Pain in loins; across loins, < evening; paralytic, in loins at* 10 P.M. *in bed, with dulness and pain in head. Lameness of loins in evening in bed.*

Extremities.—Sticking; in all joints; in r. index in evening, then pain in hollow of r. knee and in calf; rapidly changing their position. Pain in all joints; P. in arms, hands and legs down to feet; r. shoulder and l. arm, especially in elbow, and in lower limbs, especially knees; above l. elbow, then between elbow and hand, then alternating between the two places, then P. below knees extending to feet; l. hand and fingers and posteriorly in l. leg towards heel, with jerking of heel; bend of l. knee, then in l. index, then in r. foot; in l. shin, muscles of l. arm and in r. foot; in l. shin, shoulder and l. arm, then in r. shoulder and arm; in l. elbow, arm and knee in morning, > lying, and in both arms in afternoon; in l. arm in evening, and in both legs; in r. arm when at rest, > rising, with tearing in l. leg, it extends less severe through the whole l. side and arm; frequent, here and there; frequent, in muscles; alternate pains in shoulder, hip and knee. Sprained pain at times in feet and hands. Feeling as if they had been beaten. Weariness; as after long walking. Numbness as if asleep.

Upper Extremities.—Shoulder. Shooting in r.; in joint of r. Tearing in r.; from r. down arm; in joint. *Pain in l.;* r.; beneath l.; in l. at 10 A.M.; below l. in evening; in morning on waking, they feel as if they had been bare all night; alternately in r. S. and r. elbow, locating itself in elbow; rheumatic, in S. and scapula. Rheumatism so that the arm could not be raised.

Arm.—Sticking; under l. Tearing in l. Pain; and in hands; in r.; drawing, on inner side of l. at night. **Pressure in l.** Tired, do not feel like writing. Lancinations in middle of humerus. Pressure in upper.

Elbow.—Frequent cracking in afternoon. Sticking. Tearing, extending to index; from l. to index, which is flexed in a jerking manner. Pain in l.; extending to wrist; P. extending to wrist and causing sensation as if forearm were in a vise. Neuralgic pain in r., which alternately drew to shoulder and wrist but finally located itself in elbow. Cramplike pain to middle of forearm.

Sticking and weakness in wrist, almost preventing writing. Pain in l. wrist, so that hand seems palsied. Sticking in hands. Pains in hands; in l., < palm close to wrist; sprained. Gnawing in palms at metacarpo-phalangeal joints at 4 P.M. Paralyzed sensation in r. hand. Sticking in fingers; in index; in l. little, shooting along ulna. Tearing from knuckle of r. little finger to elbow. Pain in all l. fingers; in l. little, forcibly flexing it; in l. little, extending to wrist and along ulna to elbow; in ball of r. thumb. Drawing pain in little finger, extending along ulna.

Lower Extremities.—Tearing in l. *Pain.* Sticking in hip-bones in evening, extending from r. side; S. in thigh, extending to knee. Tearing in hip-bones, extending to feet; in hips and lower extremities, in bones down to feet. Pain in r. nates; in r. gluteus muscle; in r. thigh. *Rheumatic pain from hip down leg.* Soreness of hip. Sensation when descending stairs as if tendon of quadriceps extensor would give way and I would fall down-stairs.

Knee.—Stitches on lower part, on outside, in evening. Pain; in l.; in r. under patella; in patella; in r. near patella at night in bed and in l. ankle.

Leg.—Tearing in flesh down whole l. *Pain;* in l. tibia; in l. shin at 8 A.M.; *down to feet;* through r. to toes; in l. down to heel; below knees, extending to feet; peculiar, down outside of l., frequently. Neuralgic pain below r. knee; N. pain between ankle and knee; along tibia. *Rheumatic pain in r. in morning, extending to toes.* Rheumatism in r. Weakness below knees on standing, with feeling as if I would fall. Shins numb in afternoon.

Neuralgic pain in ankle. Aching in r. tarsal bones. Jerking in heels. Stitches in feet; in soles. Pain in feet; sprained. Pressure on l. foot. Sticking in toes; in l. great. Pain in ball of l. great toe in evening.

Skin.—Erysipelatous eruption; and itching, similar to Rhus, on hand, then spreading, with dangerous respiratory troubles, afterwards every year at the same time roughness of cheeks. Red itching spot on l., then on r. knee; on outside of l. leg below knee, then burning pain, then a second spot on outside of leg close to knee, next morning on r. knee. Red, inflamed spots in different parts like beginning of blood-boils, painful. Prickling; (such as he often felt in the spring), to be compared with nothing but the effect on mouth from peppermint, which is a coolness with pricking by minute points (compare Aconite), < scalp, with increased tendency to sweat. Itching; in bend of r. knee in afternoon; on face at night; all over body, with burning, as if bitten by mosquitoes.

Sleep.—Sleepiness; at 3 P.M.; preventing study. Sleeplessness for two hours, with tossing about and feeling as if I had worked too hard; S., with restlessness, woke at 4, could sleep only a few minutes at a time, would wake out of annoying dreams. Restless sleep, unpleasant dream, woke at 4.30 A.M. with dull headache, then could sleep only a few minutes at a time, waking from frightful dreams. Talking in sleep. Getting up and walking in sleep. Dreams fantastic; and busy. Unpleasant dreams; and wild, all night.

Fever.—Chill. *Rapid alternations of chill and heat* (Acon.). *Shivering, with coldness. Shivering, without coldness;* at 10 P.M. in bed, passing from vertex to neck, under scalp, with cracking noise and alarm, a sensation as if the body were surcharged with electricity, repeated four times in half an hour, and the whole ended with sound of a horn before ears. Cold limbs. Creeping over back; with weariness of limbs. Heat; with pain in loins; with flushed face. Hot head and flushed face; H. head in morning. Heat in l. shoulder, extending to forearm and then to finger-tips. Sweat; cold. Dry skin; and cracked lips.

Kreosotum.

One part of beechwood-tar creosote is dissolved in 99 parts of alcohol for the 1st dilution.

General Action.—An irritant poison, affecting particularly the gastro-intestinal canal, the genito-urinary organs, and the skin.

Allies.—The Carbons in general, especially Graph., Carbo v., Carbol. ac., Petrol., Secale c.

Generalities.—Loss of flesh. Twitching in muscles of all parts. Pinching here and there. Drawing in whole body. Excitement of whole body. Feeling during rest as if all parts were in motion. Pulsation in all parts when quiet; with sensation as if whole body wavered. Uneasiness; when sitting and walking, with shivering through all limbs and necessity to breathe deeply, which was impossible. Felt myself going very low. *Weakness;* after leucorrhœa; as if she had not slept enough, with warmth in eyes. Faintness if obliged to rise earlier than usual. General numbness. Insensibility; so that she did not know that a tooth was taken out. Most symptoms > open air.

Clinical.—General tendency to hæmorrhage (Arn., Carbo v.), and to decomposition of fluids or rapid decomposition of secretions. Fetid discharges and secretions. General restlessness (especially of teething children). The pains are always burning, like red-hot coals.

Mind.—Excitement; before menses, with uneasiness; with peevishness and obstinacy. Fretful in morning; F. and at the point of weeping. Despondent and wishing to cry; D. and longing for death; D. towards evening and doubtful if she would ever be well again. Music or anything else that caused excitement she took very much to heart, and she could not refrain from weeping. Thoughts vanished and she felt dazed. Memory weak and thoughts vanished. When she undertakes anything and has gone a few steps she stops and does not know what she intended to do. Stupor.

Head.—Drawing sticking extending through temples and into upper jaw, with vertigo. Tearing, with drawing in eyes; T., with heat in face and intermittent tearing in l. lower teeth, preventing sleep, with general heat, weakness, peevish and lachrymose mood. Aching; from emotional disturbances; with heat in front of forehead; with sleepiness; in middle, pressing outward; drawing, so that it closes eyes; as after intoxication; as if she had drunk too much the day previous (feeling of a board before forehead), with weak memory; tensive, < stooping. Confusion; with vertigo; intermittent, with vanishing of thoughts. Dulness, she looks straight ahead and does not know at what, hears and sees nothing and is without thought. Heaviness. Weariness. Beating. *Vertigo;* in morning in street, so that she reeled backward and forward, > in house; so that she could not bear to be lifted from the pillow; and everything looked dark blue; and everything turns around with him; if she turns suddenly she feels as if she would fall; stupefying.

Forehead.—On stooping everything shoots forward into F.; and she is near falling. Aching; in anterior lobes of brain; above root of nose; above r. eminence; above eyes, < r.; above eyes in evening; extending towards vertex, with tension; ulcerative, on r. side of sinciput; drawing, from r. sinus to middle of r. jaw, in morning, > noon, < 2 P.M. and lasting till evening; as from a plug above superciliary ridge, extending to occiput. Pressing-out pain in middle; P.-out pain, with pressure on eyes extending to vertex; P. in sinciput in morning as if everything would be pressed out at forehead. Throbbing pain; on waking at 5.30 A.M., with heat of face, weakness of limbs, crawling through thighs and feet, bitter taste, even food tastes bitter. Throbbing in middle of sinciput; T. in sinciput, with intermittent sticking in temple. Heaviness in sinciput as if something would burst out there.

Temples.—Sticking in r. bone; tearing S. anteriorly in r., extending into molars. Tearing in l.; drawing, in l., as if different parts would be torn out; drawing, in middle of sutura squamosa, extending through temple into l. side of face and l. teeth. Drawing pain in l. bone, affecting whole head. Pain in one or other; jerking, pulsating, above l. mastoid process. Pressing-out pain in lower part of l. bone; in evening. Throbbing in l. extending to vertex and to middle of lower jaw, with bubbling sensation and with twitching and contraction of eyelids and feeling as if they would become smaller.

Vertex.—Tearing in afternoon. Pressing beneath V. Hammering pain. Throbbing. Vertigo.

Sides.—Sticking anteriorly on r. in afternoon, > night's sleep, so that her ideas almost disappeared. Tearing, extending on l. through temple and into cheek, on r. side to upper jaw. Pain in r.; seeming to come from cervical muscles; intermittent jerking P. in r. upper half of brain; pressing out, beneath l. parietal bone. Confusion in l., with throbbing in it, which then involves upper molars, where it causes periodic grumbling.

Occiput.—Pain below l. bone as from suppuration. Fulness and heaviness, causing sensation as if he would fall backward.

Scalp.—Hair very gray. Falling of hair. Pain on combing hair, < combing it down towards temples. Pain in sinciput as if several hairs were grasped and slowly pulled out. Suppurative pain on vertex and sinciput when touched or hair is combed, when not touched the pain is drawing, < vertex.

Eyes.—Look as after weeping. Surrounded by blue rings. Fixed. Sticking tearing in l.; alternating with tearing sticking in r. Pressure and burning, preventing sleep till towards morning, on waking lids agglutinated; pressure, heat, lachrymation and feeling as if something were in them, after sleep agglutination. Itching, after rubbing biting, whites inflamed and pressure as from sand; I. and corrosion, then burning in eyes and frequent accumulation of fatty matter in inner canthi. Heat. Lachrymation; if she looks at a bright light; if she looks at an object for awhile; of r. eye in afternoon, with biting in it and jerking of l. lids; after rubbing eyes, they become dry, inflamed, bite and burn; hot and acrid in morning on waking; hot and acrid after rubbing eyes. *Tears are acrid, like salt water.* Conjunctiva red and burning.

Pupils dilated. Tearing in balls in afternoon as if they would be torn out, < r., then throbbing pain in r. eye towards evening. Lids red and swollen. Red, sensitive spot on r. lower lid, next day swelling of the lid, then a pimple on a whitish surface towards inner margin of lid, conjunctiva of lid very red, lid externally bluish-red, in evening sticking in the swelling. Twitching of lids. Vision obscured. Vision as if feathers hung before eyes, so that she must wipe eyes. Inability to see.

Clinical.—Chronic inflammation of the eyelids, with swelling; blepharitis, usually with scalding lachrymation in the morning.

Ears.—Sticking; drawing, in inner part of l., extending over outer part; jerking, in r. tragus, with swelling, stiffness and sticking on touch. Cramplike pain in l. Periodic pinching. Bubbling, pressing-asunder pain in r. Pressing out or sticking or ringing. Frequent bubbling in r., with twinging. Heat of l. external, with scarlet color, swelling and tensive burning pain. Ringing, humming, < before l., with difficult hearing, at times when the humming ceases ringing and hissing; humming during menses, with roaring and with pressing-out pain in head, the latter < stooping. Difficult hearing for three days before menses; during menses.

Clinical.—Moist eruption about the ear, with swollen glands on the neck.

Nose.—Sneezing; in morning; in morning, without trace of catarrh; frequent, with moisture in nose; frequent, with want of air in nose though it was not stopped. It seemed as if she had catarrh, sensation as if mucous membrane of nose would swell. Fluent catarrh, when she draws air through nose it feels too sharp in posterior nares. Catarrh stopped, then fluent, with acrid rawness beneath sternum. Obliged to blow frequently. Bleeding; thick and black; bright red in morning. Offensive smell, with loss of appetite; O. smell in morning on waking.

Clinical.—It has been used for lupus of the nose and face, with burning pain.

Face.—*Pale;* and puffy. Full and flushed. Tearing in r. angle of jaw in evening, extending into temple; in r. angle of jaw, waking her at night, extending towards ear and causing sticking. Lips dry, without thirst; dry, upper one desquamates, is hot and tense. *Upper lip feels sore and is cracked.* Tension about r. corner of mouth in evening, with burning and with feeling as if r. half of lower lip were drawn towards r. corner of mouth.

Clinical.—It has cured a tumor of lower lip, supposed to be epithelioma, with dry, cracked skin.

Mouth.—Drawing tearing in l. upper teeth on waking at 5 A.M., then involving l. muscles of face and temple, lasting till noon, therewith the teeth protrude. *Jerking pain in l. lower hollow molar, with frequent yawning. Throbbing pain in third upper molar, which is beginning to decay. Drawing toothache, diffusing itself over temple; D. in incisors; in l. lower molars, then involving upper molars, as soon as it ceases there it begins in upper incisors. Drawing pain in l. upper gum, with inflammation.*

Tongue coated white. Tongue clean, but pale and dry, with thin saliva, no appetite, much thirst and dry throat. Mouth and throat white. Burning in M., throat and stomach. Frothing. Slimy in evening, must spit much. Salivation. Bitter taste in morning; in evening, in throat, so that she could not relish food; B. to everything on swallowing. Sour T. on back of tongue, as from muriatic acid. T. like cubebs, with coldness on tongue. Flat T. T. like straw. No taste.

Clinical.—A valuable remedy for rapid decay of the teeth and bleeding of the gums; especially valuable for the premature decay of children's teeth, which become very dark and crumbly.

Throat.—(Diphtheritic appearance, the burnt parts sloughing away.) Mucus easy to loosen, provoking incessant hollow, rough-sounding cough. Scraping; with rawness; with dryness; in evening when coughing, with thick, lumpy expectoration; as after brandy containing fusel oil. Painful choking sensation low down, extending through chest behind dorsal vertebræ. Pain. Pressure on r. side on swallowing. Sore pain on l. side on swallowing, with feeling as if something hung down there and impeded swallowing. L. tonsil sore on swallowing. Sensation of mucus, which causes nausea, then expectoration of whitish, sweetish mucus. Fauces dry, they seem agglutinated all afternoon. Burning. Burning pain along œsophagus. Swallowing almost impossible.

Stomach.—Great appetite; appetite, but no relish for food, with fulness; A. lost. Desire for tobacco at an unusual time. Thirst after the chill. Eructations; *of air;* of air after dinner, then spitting of frothy saliva and scraping rawness in throat; violent; acid; of tasteless white froth before menses, if these E. do not occur mucous vomiting follows. *Nausea; with burning in mouth; with spitting of saliva and general chill, without heat or thirst. Urging to vomit, nothing but saliva results. Retching; in morning fasting;* of water and mucus, with dryness of nose, heat in forepart of head as if everything would press out at forehead, coldness of hands and feet, with thirst in morning on rising. *Vomiting; of sweetish water in morning fasting; of food.*

Pressure in epigastric region. Burning pain. Pain in pit at 3 P.M. during rest, as if a thread were drawn through it or a muscular fibre were torn out, which shoots through all limbs. Tightness in S. and pit so that she must wear the clothes loose. Gnawing if she does not breakfast, then retching, > eating. Orgasm extending from epigastric region through all parts, < motion, with throbbing in all vessels.

Clinical.—Attacks of nausea and vomiting, either of water or food, very frequently accompany the symptoms of Kre. It has been used for the vomiting of pregnancy; the nausea and vomiting are frequently associated with soreness at the pit of the stomach, and sometimes with thirst (Colch., Petrol.). Persistent vomiting of infants. Chronic irritability of the stomach, the food is not retained nor digested. The food is vomited even several hours after a meal.

Abdomen.—*Distention;* before menses; after menses; and tension. Flatus smelling like bad eggs during menses; offensive F. passed with stool. Increased peristaltic action and emission of flatus. Sticking; *like electric shocks to vagina.* Griping, > discharge of flatus. Cramp after menses, < hypogastrium. Pain; with stitches about umbilicus, as if she had eaten fruit and drunk afterwards; that cannot be described; as if suppurating, > during rest, disturbed sleep so that she must turn with frequent waking; ulcerative, on deep breathing; prickling; drawing, during menses. Painful cold sensation, with scanty urine. Thumping at 5 A.M. on third day of menses, with clawing like dull shoots, then urging to stool, with painless diarrhœa, and during the day painless diarrhœa seven times. Tension, with scanty micturition. Dragging downward after menses, as if menses would occur.

Sticking in hepatic region, not affecting inspiration. Bruised pain in upper anterior lobe of liver, causing fulness so that she must loosen the clothes. Pain in hepatic region, with gnawing beneath l. short ribs; P. in region of spleen if she sits down in morning after rising, and on slight pressure, with other symptoms, making her weak. Painless drawing in upper A., extending to small of back and there causing labor-like pain, with pressure downward towards lumbar vertebræ, as in childbirth, with flushes of heat in face, palpitation, frequent pulse, frequent ineffectual urging to urinate, which at last occurs after much pressure, is hot and scanty, then chill without thirst, these attacks associated with the eye symptoms in such a way that the eye symptoms cease when the labor-like pains set in, and when the pressure ceases a milky discharge drops from vagina.

Umbilical Region.—Zigzag sticking, then sudden shooting towards l. nipple. Grasping, extending into throat, with griping and causing nausea. Pain or feeling as if she had drunk carbonated water, with ill humor; P. as from a cold, as if diarhœa would occur; intermittent, as if diarrhœa would occur, she must crouch together. Clawing, with ulcerative pain in whole abdomen; C. before menses, > stooping, with digging, then discharge of white mucus from vagina. Painful lump as if twisted together; waking between 2 and 3 A.M.

Sticking on r. side between umbilicus and crest of ilium, during rest, arresting breath; S. in region of crest of ilium, shooting transversely through abdomen; periodic, in l. flank opposite crest of ilium, which shoots into l. thigh. Pressure in hypogastrium. Pain in l. iliac region; frequent, in r. flank, extending upward and downward and into testicle; in crests of ilia on pressure, as if she had carried something heavy or hard upon them. Tensive pain in inguinal regions when walking. Pain like a boil low down, with electric stitches in internal genitals, which caused constrictive spasmodic pains in labia externally, so that she gathered herself together when the pains came, with periodic pressure extending forward from small of back, frequent urging to urinate, scanty, clear urine, ineffectual urging to stool, general anxious restlessness so that she broke into anxious sweat, ill humor so that she quarrelled with every one and would strike them, if these attacks occurred when sitting she was obliged to walk, whereby the pains were relieved.

Rectum.—Large painful hæmorrhoids. Stitches into l. flank remaining there awhile, during menses, so that she must stand up; drawing tearing S., with ineffectual urging, afterwards > hard stool passed with pressure. Cramplike pain extending into flank, so that she must walk bent over and sit down cautiously. Frequent uneasiness, a crawling or dragging, > stool. Urging, but emission of only flatus.

Stool.—*Constipation.* Hard, nodular, with much pressure, only every three or four days. S. and flatus accumulate in rectum during menses (feels there a pressure with emission of flatus), then menses very profuse and often in clots.

Clinical.—Diarrhœa, very offensive, dark brown, undigested, generally associated with more or less nausea, sometimes with vomiting. Dysentery, with nausea and vomiting. Bloody, fetid stools during typhoid fever, with great prostration. Cholera infantum, offensive brown stools, great restlessness, with painful dentition and complaint of pain in the gums.

Urinary Organs.—*Urging, she cannot get out of bed quickly enough,* with constrictive pain in vagina. Frequent urging in evening and night; frequent, always preceded by white discharge from vagina, which colors clothes yellow. *Micturition six or seven times a day,* **always with haste and always passing much**. Frequent micturition of hot urine; F., but only a spoonful each time; F. of very little clear urine each time; *obliged to urinate every hour and each time much clear urine; every half hour from 4 A.M. till noon, each time over half a pint.* Frequent micturition at night; but scanty; and each time much hot clear urine. Strangury. Urine spurts from her during each cough (Caust., Squills, etc.). Micturition in a weak stream. Bladder and bowels not evacuated for twenty-four hours. Urine chestnut brown; reddish, depositing a red sediment; colorless, *offensive* (Benz. ac.); hot, offensive, smelling almost like cooked cedar; hot, steaming, of strong smell, red sediment; hot, causing burning between labiæ; *increased;* scanty; scanty and painful micturition; turbid, after awhile it looks like light beer yeast; sediment copious and white.

Clinical.—Nocturnal enuresis.

Sexual Organs.—Spasmodic pain in external. Burning pain in both man and woman during coition, the first impotent, the next day swelling on penis, in the woman profuse dark menses, lasting four days, then leucorrhœa staining linen gray, with swelling of external genitals, itching and corroding, burning pain.

Burning between pudenda on urinating. Soreness between labiæ, with biting pain (compare Carbo v.); **S. between labiæ and thighs, with burning biting pain. Itching between labiæ** (Graph.), **with biting,** *then burning* as from pepper on a sore place; **corrosive I. between labiæ and in vagina, then burning and swelling in labiæ. Vagina itching in evening, then smarting, external genitals swollen, hot and hard, and on urinating sore pains in V.**; *voluptuous I. deep in V.;* contractive pain in V. two days after menstruation, then whitish discharge. (Prolapsus of vagina.) *Discharge from V. white* (Graph.) *and* **of the odor of green corn**; white, painless; white, preceded by pain in small of back and heat of face; periodic white, between menses; mucous, mixed with blood, in morning on rising. Constant leucorrhœa; **yellow L. staining linen yellow, with weakness in legs** (Sep.); L. stains linen whitish-yellow, *is acrid, causes itching and biting on external genitals* (Puls.); stains linen like washings of meat and is offensive (Nit. ac.).

During coition pain as from an ulcer in neck of womb, on the neck and below there is a hard lump, in evening she has less pain in those parts than in morning. *Menses too early; and dark, profuse, lasted eight days* (Cham.); M. every three weeks, comes easily, lasts four or five days, is profuse, then discharge of bloody matter for two to four days, which has an acrid odor and causes itching and biting on genitals; omitted for one day; M. that had stopped for forty-eight hours returned, with violent pain in abdomen, discharge thin, bright red; often in pieces and profuse. Sensation of coition in morning between sleep and waking (which she had not had for years). She woke in morning with desire for coition.

Clinical.—A very valuable remedy for a variety of diseases of the female sexual organs, characterized in a general way by inflammations with ulcerations and offensive, excoriating discharges. Ulceration of the cervix, with burning pain deep in the vagina, with great heat and soreness of the mucous membrane, pressure and bearing-down pains and offensive, acrid leucorrhœa. It has been found extremely valuable (certainly as a palliative) in scirrhus of the uterus and epithelioma of the pudenda, with the peculiar burning pain as from hot coals and offensive discharge. The cases requiring Kre. are generally characterized by too early and profuse menstruation which is followed by acrid, putrid leucorrhœa; the menstrual discharge sometimes reappears after it has stopped entirely, or the flow gradually changes into an ichorous, excoriating leucorrhœa; menses often dark and offensive. Leucorrhœa of the peculiar odor of green corn. Cauliflower excrescences of the uterus, with terrible burning, as from red-hot coals, profuse discharge of offensive clots and ichorous, excoriating leucorrhœa. Valuable after parturition for offensive lochia. Pruritus of the vulva, with offensive moisture and hot swelling of the external genitals. Ichorous discharge, with retention of placenta. It has cured sterility caused by profuse acrid leucorrhœa and irregular menstruation.

Respiratory Organs.—Secretion in larynx provokes cough. Crawling below larynx, provoking cough; in upper bronchial tubes towards evening, provoking cough. Hoarseness in morning, > sneezing; voice raw, hoarse, with scraping in throat. Cough from sensation of adherent mucus in middle of chest; incessant C., with sleepiness, chill, then dry heat, during which the child continued to sleep (influenza); C., with retching; with efforts to vomit but discharge of only saliva; whistling, dry; dry, with scraping in throat and soreness in chest; difficult to loosen; (whooping); with expectoration of firm gelatinous mucus; with white mucous expectoration easily loosened, and scraping in throat. *Short breath*, tightness of lower part of chest. Often obliged to breathe deeply. Anxious, difficult respiration. Difficult R., as if chest were compressed, so that she must constantly breathe deeply.

Clinical.—Diphtheria, with a most putrid odor from the mouth, vomiting of food, swelling of glands. Violent laryngeal cough, with hoarseness and soreness of the lungs, and bloody or greenish-yellow expectoration. Winter cough of old people.

Chest.—Sticking in l.; r. lower; in l. on inspiration, then it seats itself in r. side; externally in l. during rest, not affecting respiration; in l. lower when menses came on, with cutting above umbilicus; *in l.*, < turning over in bed; in r., often < inspiration and expiration; in middle, < inspiration, spreading over r. shoulder and extending with paralyzed sensation to elbow, the pain in S. < raising arm; *above heart* in afternoon, impeding respiration, > pressure; internally in r., arresting breath; beneath l. breast, extending upward across r., with S. beneath r. scapula preventing breathing; in r. chest and beneath r. scapula at 3 P.M., so that it took away the breath and she thought she would fall; transversely across middle in morning on rising, < towards noon; forward beneath l. breast in afternoon, thence transversely across pit of stomach towards r. breast, down into r. side of abdomen, into leg, ending in ankle; in middle of r., an inch from nipple towards sternum, extending through chest and felt on inner margin of scapula; periodic, in various places between ribs. Drawing sticking in r. side near sternum, between second and third ribs; beneath l. short ribs towards evening.

Scrapy raw sensation beneath sternum, obliging cough, the C. > expectoration of gray mucus. Raw pain in lower part. Bruised pain in middle on inspiration, with short breath; B. pain internally on inspiration, preventing deep breathing. Pain from 12 till 1 o'clock; throbbing, in a spot behind pectoralis minor; throbbing constrictive, in r. side till sleep. Pain as from pressure on sternum; more during expiration than inspiration; in centre, also felt on inspiration, extending to clavicles and muscles of nape and throat; as from pressure inward internally, not affecting respiration. Contractive pain on deep inspiration. Heaviness, with sticking; H. often causing deep inspiration; in lower part, so that expiration was difficult; in middle, it seemed as if she could not get the breath out of the chest; in middle, with short breath, so that she must frequently breathe deeply. Fulness and oppression, provoking deep breathing; sudden O., with sticking in middle of l. side of chest.

Periodic drawing from outer side of female breast towards nipple. **Burning**; wanted water to quench B. in lungs; from middle into throat, as if she had drunk brandy, tongue painful as if burnt, face hot, red and tense. Crawling in middle in morning, with tickling, provoking dry spasmodic cough till retching follows. Breasts feel as if milk came into them, but they are withered.

Clinical.—Chronic pneumonia or phthisis, with violent burning pain like red-hot coals in chest (Carb. an.). Gangrene of lungs (Cap.).. When inhaled it has proved valuable in cases of phthisis when there were no cavities.

Heart and Pulse.—Sticking in heart; not affecting breathing. Heart's action slow and weak. Pulse 80, rather full. Pulse slow; and labored; and weak. P. small and compressed.

Nape.—Rheumatic stiffness; in afternoon.

Back.—Pain; at night, extending over l. hip, becoming seated in flank and involving l. inguinal region, so that she could scarcely become erect, the pain in back < during rest. Intermittent sticking between scapulæ. Pain behind l. scapula; two inches beneath r.; behind r., with feeling of a plug, at times throbbing; as if scapulæ had been beaten. Drawing tension between scapulæ. Drawing pain posteriorly in r. upper ribs, extending forward and causing sticking above r. mamma.

Lumbar Region.—Sticking in external muscles in region of l. kidney. Pain extending upward, with heat in palms and soles; P. in morning as she woke, < rising, when sitting and walking, > lying down, extending to abdomen, causing pressure outward in genitals, extending into thighs, causing general anxiety and trembling and internal chill; almost making her sick, < rest, > motion; if she presses during stool, spasmodic P. in vertebræ passing to r. inguinal region and into r. hip, making walking difficult; as if broken, extending to between scapulæ, so that she could not move arms without pain (as if a band were between shoulders), < stooping. Suppurative pain in vertebræ during menses, with pressure towards rectum as if flatus would pass, before this the pains in back were > motion; P. as if a vertebra were suppurating or as if flesh were torn from it, causing sensation on standing up as if something would fall out there. Pain in vertebræ and iliac crests as after long running or as if bruised, extending into thighs and down calves, where it ended like an electric shock, then stiffness in lumbar vertebræ in morning. Pain as after much stooping, < motion and stooping. Pain in vertebræ as before menses. Labor-like pain causing ineffectual urging to stool, with distention of abdomen. Cramplike drawing, labor-like, in vertebræ, extending forward and down thigh, with general uneasiness. Drawing pain extending along sacrum into rectum and vagina, causing spasmodic contractive pain, with stitches, the pains intermittent and > standing up, after these attacks leucorrhœa like milk and water, flowing by paroxysms. Spasmodic drawing in vertebræ, extending into genitals. Burrowing as if something would come out.

Extremities.—Jerking and pinching pains in all joints. Aching in all as if beaten. Sick feeling as before catarrh. Heaviness and weariness as from sleep.

Clinical.—Rheumatoid pains in joints, with numbness.

Upper Extremities. — Shoulders. Sticking in r.; from top of r. into lower part of ear; in posterior part of joint, extending to fingers, in F. it causes sensation as if asleep, with loss of sensation and power, so that she cannot hold anything tightly, when there is no sticking there is jerking in hands with crawling and heat in them. Pain in r. on motion; P. as if they had been uncovered at night; as if pressed against sharp corners. Acute drawing posteriorly.

Dull, almost gnawing pain in r. humerus. Upper arm, bruised pain on inner and lower part when touched; pinching in inner side of l.; paralytic heaviness of r. Elbows, periodic pains as if ligaments were too short; spasmodic bubbling pain on inner and lower part of l. in afternoon; cramplike sensation in tip of r. when writing. Cramplike pain in region of lower part of radius extending into fingers. Painful drawing along l. ulna; intermittent, in lower part of muscles of r. radius, extending towards fingers, so that she cannot grasp anything as usual, and causing paralytic sensation. Drawing pain in l. forearm, extending to fingers. Drawing in l. forearm.

Sticking on back of l. hand, between thumb and index. Paralytic pain shooting towards l. hand, so that she lets everything fall. **Sprained and stiff pain in l. thumb**; *sprained pain in second joint of l. thumb.* Pain in ball of l. index as if something had been stuck into it and it would suppurate. Drawing pain in r. ring finger; in tips of l. fingers, with swollen feeling. Paralytic pain in l. index, > motion. All the two first phalanges go to sleep in morning, with crawling, they look white, must put r. index into water because sensation will not return. Deadness of all first phalanges, they look white.

Lower Extremities.—Intermittent drawing tearing and sticking, now in r. calf, now above r. knee, now in region of hip. Thigh, piercing jerking in middle of l. during rest; jerking pain in fleshy part above l. knee during rest; pain on motion from middle of l. to middle of leg as if there had been tearing in them and they were stiff; P. in l. hip as if dislocated, if he stands on r. foot there is a sensation as if l. foot were too long; gnawing pain on outer side of l. T. and leg, < sitting; bruised pain in muscles of middle of l., < sitting; painful drawing, < r., extending to sole, < motion, with stitches; drawing pain from head of r. femur into knee, so that she can scarcely ascend steps, > rest; drawing pain from tuberosity of r. ischium into middle of thigh, on outer side, with shivering; pain in muscles above hollow of l. knee as if too short, < stooping and walking; tensive pain in muscles above knee, < r., and on pressure pain as if flesh had been beaten loose, > rest; tensive pain posteriorly, as after a long walk, < walking and stooping; tension in l. fascia lata.

Knee.—(Tearing, boring, sticking in l. patella in evening and night, with chilliness.) Jerking tearing in r. during rest. Sharp pain beneath r. patella. Sprained pain in l., so that he could not stand on l. leg alone, with sensation as if it would give way. Throbbing like a boil, extending to toes, < soles. Weakness so that they gave way during motion.

Leg.—Jerking through l., throwing foot upward. Contractive pain like cramp, in r. calf, extending to malleoli. Sprained pain in l. tendo-achillis. Paralytic drawing through l. Painful tension during motion, < calves. Heaviness in morning during motion. Tingling and whirring. Weariness; of l.

Ankle.—Sticking in r., extending through whole foot to toes; S. in r., < motion. Tearing extending to knees and causing tension in calves. Pain twisting outward in r. external malleolus during rest. Burning in malleoli in forenoon, extending through soles of feet and toes, < soles, with drawing and sticking.

Foot.—Swelling of l.; (œdematous S.); white, œdematous, from calves to toes, < l., with coldness and heaviness of feet. Sticking in heel on moving it so that she started and was obliged to stand. Feeling of suppuration in soles. Drawing pain in r. Tearing drawing in heels in evening, till sleep, extending through soles to toes, with sticking, next morning on stepping the soles felt like balls. Working in soles as after a long walk, with weakness, the weakness < l. Heaviness when walking.

Skin.—Blue spots on thighs, as from pinching. Redness in hollows of knees, with scales. White, then dry and epidermis scales off. Stiffness on hands, with cracks. Urticaria-like nodes. Pimples covering forehead, sometimes causing sticking; P. more felt than seen, covering r. hand, with itching, the I. < towards evening and in evening in bed; P. in l. upper concha, so that whole external ear is swollen, inflamed, hot to touch, with burning pain, l. side of neck stiff, with tensive pain, inability to turn head well towards the left, the pain extends through shoulder into middle of arm, with internal shivering through all limbs, heat in forehead and pressure above eyes; on spine of r. scapula, painful to pressure of clothes, becoming covered with a crust; "fatty," on chin and r. cheek, forming yellow honey-like crusts; ("fatty," itching, covering body, with swollen and stiff feet). Pustule in r. wing of nose; large and "fatty" (like smallpox) covering body. Hydroa beneath nose, without coryza. Vesicular eruption (as from bite of a bug) covering body except calves, chest and face, the itching < between 5 and 7 P.M. and in night.

Crawling beneath chin, not > rubbing. *Itching in evening, so that she was almost crazy;* general I., > scratching, then burning on arms and limbs; in ears and on soles; on eyelids and about mouth, < rubbing, with biting, then redness, then desquamation; agreeable, in r. palm, between thumb and index, not > rubbing; *burning, on soles; burning, at night in bed, preventing sleep.*

Clinical.—Urticaria after menstruation. Senile gangrene of a horrible odor and terrible burning (Sec. c.). Tendency to gangrenous degeneration of ulcers.

Sleep.—Yawning, with stretching, as before ague. Frequent yawning in morning; all day, with lachrymation; with chill; with pain in forehead, and weariness. Sleepiness; in morning, with paralyzed feeling in limbs; with much yawning, bad taste and little appetite.

Sleeplessness in evening from general restlessness; S. from 9 P.M. till 2 A.M., with tossing about, on account of pain in small of back, internal chill and pulsation in head; till midnight, on account of weariness, with pain in all limbs; till 1 or 2 o'clock, then many dreams, on waking at 7 arms as far as elbows were asleep; with weariness and tossing about till 4 A.M., then regular menstruation set in, then sleep for an hour; with restlessness, in morning on rising weariness, and on slightest exertion sweat ran down all over her, obliged to sit down to rest, when standing she sank down. Restless sleep; after 3 A.M. Bad sleep, she cannot lie to suit her, in morning eyes are agglutinated. Frequent waking; yet in morning she had slept enough. Sudden waking at 2 A.M., as if called, menses had come on. Shocks in whole body in sleep. Starting up in fright from sleep.

Laughed in her dream after midnight, as she woke she knew nothing more of it, and was lying uncovered and cold, without chill. Anxious dreams on falling asleep; all night; of a bright fire, which woke her; that she saw a small object that constantly became larger; that it snowed, and she was in the open air with her little child; that something had happened to her children, so that she wept, and on waking was wet with sweat; that large men followed her and wished to violate her, without sexual excitement. Dream of falling from a height. Dream of dirty, disgusting linen. Dream that she had taken poison and was emaciated in consequence. D. of stoppage of throat. D. of erections, and that as he wished to urinate the glans broke off.

Fever.—Chilled easily; general C. as soon as she became quiet; C. during menses, without heat or thirst; general C., skin seemed dead, general feeling as if she had revelled all night, in morning shivering C., with heat in face, red cheeks, cold feet and heaviness from shoulders to elbows, so that she was unable to carry arms to head, the pain > rest, with fretfulness from 10 A.M. to 10 P.M. Internal C., with red cheeks. Shivering; in morning on rising, with bright blood from nose; all afternoon; over whole skin; for five hours, then heat of face and hands, cold feet, with shivering, from 2 till 11 P.M.; with flushes of heat, without thirst, drawing and sticking pains in forepart of temporal bones, pressure in eyeballs, dim vision so that she must rub her eyes, then hot and acrid tears, and inflammation of white of eyes. Alternations of chill and heat, with much thirst, weakness of limbs, constant cough, partly dry, painful and racking, caused by irritation in lower part of chest and by crawling from middle of chest into throat, epigastric region much shaken by cough, with pain in middle of vertex, < touch.

Chill between shoulders during menses, extending down back; between S., extending to middle of small of back, then pain in small of back, so that she must walk constantly, which relieved pain in small of back, but then new pains appeared in hips, which extended to middle of thighs and did not allow her to lie quietly, > warm applications, the pain in hip < external air. Cold hands. Cold feet; at 9 P.M., then chill in back, head and arms to fingers, without external coldness; from back of F. to above knees; with hot and red ears.

Heat; on waking after midnight, but coldness if she put feet out of bed; with good appetite; general flashing; in periodic flushes, with sharply defined redness of cheeks; general dry, without thirst, cheeks seemed painted, then warm sweat, then drawing and sticking pains in small of back, preventing sleep all night, and making turning over difficult. Heat in face, with feeling as if it would perspire, but it was dry; H. in face during midday rest, with throbbing in cheeks and forehead, face brownish-red, heat of face > rest; in face, with short breath in warm room and necessity to go into open air, else she became faint. Agreeable warmth in palms, then sweat. Heat of feet; of soles every day from 2 P.M. till 2 or 3 A.M.

Sweat on chest and back on fifth night of menstruation; on feet at times.

Lachesis.

The venom of the Trigonocephalus Lachesis, L., is triturated.

General Action.—Like all the serpent-venoms its action is directly upon the blood, destroying its vitality and inducing a great variety of disorders characterized by disintegration of tissue. The nervous phenomena of Lachesis are peculiar and characteristic. Note particularly the universal distress which increases during sleep and wakes the sufferer in agony and fright, also the extreme sensitiveness of affected parts (out of proportion to the severity of the disease).

It is not to be compared with any other substance, except, in a very general way, with the serpent-poisons.

Generalities.—*Emaciation, with suffering and weakness.* Audible beating of carotids and feeling of throbbing in chest and abdomen. Stretching after breakfast. *Trembling as from anxiety, without anxiety* (Arg. nit., Cimicif., Gels.); *sensation of faintlike T. Jerking; sudden, of whole body when sitting, starting from below.* Limbs stiffly outstretched, head bent back, eyes distorted. Fell unconscious to the ground as if struck by lightning, had an involuntary stool and vomited.

Stitches in various parts; S. over whole body, loins, face, < night; deep in flesh, extending outward through skin; in neck, back, r. arm, with feeling as if r. arm were asleep and itching of arms, hips and lower limbs. Tearing in flesh, now here, now there, afterwards here and there in body. Sharp pains, < forenoon, in temples, jaws and eyes, with sticking from head towards eyes, nose and temples, eyes swollen, < afternoon, running of cold water from l. eye and nostril, redness of l. eye, *the swelling gradually extended over the whole face so that the eyes were closed* (Apis), face pale and itching, also head and whole body, < afternoon and evening, > night.

In evening on lying down alternations of headache, hoarseness, tickling in throat and violent cough, with frequent pains in limbs and other parts. Pain in l. shoulder and in forepart of l. foot, then in l. knee, wrist and shoulder, then in r. limb, arm and teeth; in l. arm and elbow, side and hand, next day in r. side, in neck, elbow, lower extremity and shoulder; in evening when sitting, above l. knee, then below it, extending to foot, then in r. arm and r. ear; here and there when coughing. Pressure on r. eye and on r. side of forehead, then in l. temple, then on r. side of face, as if in an upper tooth, then in l. leg and foot in the evening. *Rheumatic pain in l. side, then in r.*, and frequently alternating, at times from r. to l. and back again, always in different places, in shoulder, arm, wrist, hand, lower limbs, knee, calf, foot and teeth. Bruised feeling all day; in morning after waking; after midday nap, also with pains in loins, between shoulders and in spine; always after sleep, with stiffness.

Drawing, jerking tension in bones of skull and cheeks and lower jaw. **Intolerance of slightest touch, it almost puts him into a rage.** *Longing to get into the open air. Restlessness driving him into the open air. Necessity to do everything very rapidly,* he bolts his food and afterwards cannot remain sitting. *Inclination to lie down;* in morning and forenoon; < *eating.* Indolence after eating. *Feeling as if the body were overwhelmed by a disintegrating tendency, with sinking of all forces.* Aversion to motion.

Weakness; **in morning on rising,** < *arms and feet; in morning in sleep, on waking general sick feeling, vertigo, feeling of lead in occiput, can hardlg raise it, sprained feeling in all joints,* pressure in small of back and fulness in abdomen; in morning after rising, < arms and feet, less exhausted after bad sleep than after good; in morning, > lying down, with sadness, disinclination to work, indifference, as after a debauch; in forenoon; in forenoon, with bruised feeling as after a debauch, with mental depression; in evening; in evening on walking; in evening, with sleepiness, but inability to sleep; after breakfast; after supper; when walking at meal-time; from motion; after emissions; after nightly attack of vomiting; > eating, < back and legs, with heaviness; intermittent, during the day; with bruised feeling, catarrh, cough, sore throat, morning-nausea, rumbling in upper abdomen, etc., *as in the spring;* sudden, towards evening, with insatiable thirst, dry mouth, pallor, distress, as before violent fever. **He would constantly sink down from weakness. Physical and mental weakness,** < *morning;* mental and physical W. after an ecstasy the day previous; *W. every morning* in the beginning physical, then inclining him to sleep, afterwards mental.

Faintness during breakfast, with nausea; and vertigo, falling down and vanishing of sight, and during the day frequent attacks as if it would return; when waiting for a meal, with spasmodic yawning; with coldness so that all limbs became stiff and he sank down powerless. Paralyzed lameness in almost all bones, with intermittent pains. Paralyzed feeling, < knees, > walking; P. feeling, inability to bend feet or close hands, at times only on l. side. Stiffness after sleep, > rubbing and stroking by another person. Wine has less effect upon him than usual. (*Acids disturb the curative action.*) Aggravation in afternoon; after every sleep; during rest; a few hours after eating; smoking tobacco; from wine. **Amelioration from opening clothes,** *with faintness; A. from eructations;* after coffee; in open air during the pains in abdomen.

Clinical.—The blood is dark-colored and does not coagulate. It is often indicated in persons of a phlegmatic constitution, with disposition to melancholia and indolence. It is probably most frequently indicated for persons with dark eyes and dark complexions. Phlebitis following pregnancy. Cures of epilepsy have been reported. General dropsy, with blackish offensive urine and dark purplish or bluish skin; especially valuable in the ascites of drunkards Very valuable in suppurating wounds or in abscesses which threaten to become gangrenous. Valuable in all typhoid types of disease when the indications of the drug permit, especially when there is tendency to loquacity, to offensive discharges or exhalations, and a dry, red tongue. Valuable for the effects of sunstroke, especially if the person is in the habit of using alcoholic stimulants, particularly if the face is dark red and limbs cold. Extreme prostration, with tendency to disorganization of the blood. The complaints of Lach. are mostly on l. side, nearly always < sleep, so that the patient is awakened by distress.

Mind.—Lively; and wide awake for a long time *in the evening.* The more cause for fretfulness the greater the inclination for humor, jest and satire. Animation the whole morning. Quiet and firm during vexatious and exciting causes. Excitement, with physical exhaustion; E. in evening, with liveliness in spite of sticking beneath scapulæ. Fanciful imaginings during the evening fever. It seems to him during the day that he has dreamed everything that has happened, only somewhat different. Ecstasy as after sublime impressions or excessive joy, with desire to talk and do much. **Loquacity;** *in evening; in evening during the fever; in evening, with animation;* in evening, with physical laxity, sleepiness without ability to sleep, he goes from one story to another, mixes and distorts everything, corrects himself, but makes the same mistakes again; *with vivid imagination and impatience of tedious things.* Longing for amusement, with lively fancies, about which he laughs. Weeping from joy at soothing poetry.

Rage about trifles. Anger. Quarrelsome mood. Impatience, desire for positive answers when it is impracticable. Crazy jealousy towards evening. Irritability; during the fever; in an infant, it cries, will not lie down, then heat, with eructations, vomiting of milk, frequent stools and external heat. Obstinacy. Sadness; in morning. Anxiety. Apprehension when riding in the open air. Easily frightened in evening; easily F. and brain sensitive. Mistrustful. *Indifference* and forgetfulness; I. in forenoon and disinclination to work. Ennui, with trembling. Dilatory. Inability to perform anything in an orderly manner.

Fond of sitting quietly and meditating. Indolence; and disinclination for study and business; *disinclination for his own proper work.* Objects to reading long at a time though the subject interests him. *Sitting up late at work, with great activity.* Increased power of originality and increased activity of fancy. *Ideas crowd upon him when writing so that he cannot finish the record.* Wishes to do a great deal, begins many things. Sudden doubts in afternoon about truths of which hitherto he had been convinced. *Confusion as to time. Mistakes in writing.* Mistakes in spelling. Loss of ideas. Inability for abstract thought, no persistence. *Memory weak;* lost, hears and understands nothing said to him. Unconsciousness, with vomiting and purging; U., with weakness and with disppearance of pulse; with irregular motions of limbs, cold, clammy sweat, pulse small, slow, almost imperceptible; > when the feet became warm; as before apoplexy.

Clinical.—Mental alienation; thinks that she is not at home, or thinks that there are robbers in the house and tries to escape, great aggravation from alcoholic drinks. Dementia, with extraordinary loquacity. Religious melancholia. Delirium tremens, loquacity, suffocative feeling about the throat. Muttering delirium. Insane jealousy.

Head.—And face swollen so that eyes were closed. Sticking; *extending into eyes;* extending to eyes, nose and temples, with sharp pains < forenoon, in temples, jaws and eyes, swelling of eyes, face, etc.; deep. Tearing. *Aching* in evening, with vertigo; at night after vomiting; after pollutions, with weakness; before menstruation; in a round spot in centre; *with nausea;* with vomiting of food; with sleepiness; with nasal catarrh and fever; with nasal catarrh and full, hard pulse; with tension in shoulder and cervical pulse; **extending into nose;** *extending into root of nose; dizzy;* internally; internally and externally. Aching as before coryza; *with flickering before eyes.* Intermittent pain beneath skull as after taking cold, < stooping, with nausea, the pain alternating with heat. Tensive pain, > open air and by pressure, with an indolent hard stool; T. pain > pressure, a roaring in it, it feels hot, sneezing, fluent catarrh and hard stool; T. pain as if a string were drawn from nape above ear internally to eyes, on coughing.

Beating on stooping, with erysipelas of face. Heaviness in morning, then pain in vicinity of r. eye; H. at 11 A.M.; after wine, with nauseous vertigo; in a spot in middle, moving hither and thither on moving head. Fulness; during the fever. Confusion; in morning; in morning, in afternoon pain on r. side of head; in morning, with heaviness and blowing of blood from nose, with headache in forenoon and congestion in afternoon; then heat and congestion till afternoon. Dulness in afternoon, with nausea; D. during fever, with roaring in ears and vertigo.

Congestion; in morning, with pain; with pain above l. eye; with aching and with burning on scalp after scratching; with blowing of blood from nose; with flickering before eyes in angular jagged figures, then headache. *Rush of blood;* in forenoon on stooping, with headache on r. side extending towards occiput; in forenoon, < stooping, preceded by headache above r. eye; in afternoon on stooping; to H. and face during cough; before and after headache, with flickering before eyes; after a satisfactory pasty stool, with vertigo; < stooping and walking and in afternoon, preceded by headache, blowing of blood from nose in morning; *with heat in head;* with painful pressure under skull and he was conscious of all diseased teeth, though they were not painful, blowing of bright blood from nose, drawing in nose and frontal sinuses and under whole skull as if water had been injected into it; with beating roaring in ear; with drumming growling in ears; with hæmorrhoidal troubles.

Lightness, with swimming sensation, then pain in occiput and sensation as if hair were tied too tight. Intoxication. *Vertigo;* **in morning on waking**; in morning when standing, > sitting; in morning after rising, with reeling towards the left; in morning, with general illness; at 11 A.M., < **closing eyes**; in evening; evenings, with reeling and attacks of unconsciousness as if he would have apoplexy; at night, then violent vomiting; after rising; on going into the street; on sitting down; when sitting after walking; during fever, with dulness of head and roaring in ears; before faintness; < stooping; with pressure in eyes.

Forehead.—Sudden shooting. Tearing sticking across above eyes. Tearing above brows in morning, also as if in bones; T. above orbits, with pain in face and vomiting; from r. upper part to nose. Writhing above r. eye. Pain; in sinciput; deep in F. and l. temple; above eyes; near r. eye; above l. eye in forenoon; above eyes after weeping; **above eyes extending to root of nose** (Ign.); *deep in l. eminence* in morning, as if connected with ear, with bruised pain externally on pressure; becoming more concentrated towards l. sinus; headache externally near l. eye, then blowing of blood from nose in morning; headache externally near r. eye, with blowing of blood from nose, then congestion in afternoon and evening, < walking; intermittent; P. in l. sinus as if sore; *throbbing, above r. eye,* with nausea, bad taste and heartburn. Throbbing above l. eye. Pressure inward in evening, > open air and on moving about, returning when sitting still in the house. Drawing in sinuses, beneath whole skull and in nose. Heaviness; so that he cannot open the eyes, lasting into the night, with pain in hip and thigh.

Temples.—Stitches in l. and in side of head. Pain; in l. in forenoon; extending into eyes; extending to ears; *as if swollen in angle in front of styloid process,* < *pressure;* pulsating, in r. extending into r. orbit. Drawing from l. to forehead. Throbbing in morning on waking; constant T. for ten days before menstruation.

Vertex.—*Sticking; with boring;* and in temples, extending through whole head, with catarrh and stiffness of nape. Pain internally as if beaten, < pressure.

Sides.—Sticking in r.; starting from a scar on that side; from smelling coffee, with drawing. Feeling in afternoon as if some one cut a piece from r. parietal bone. Pain in whole l.; *in r. extending to neck and shoulders, with tension in muscles;* sudden, in l. side in forenoon. Intermittent painful drawing above r. ear after eating, extending to vertex. Constriction above ears and pressure in temples towards ears. *Numbness on l. in evening and morning, with crawling.*

Occiput.—Pain extending into eyes. Tensive pain in r., extending to orbits and into nasal bones. *Leaden heaviness in morning on waking, can hardly raise it, with vertigo.*

Scalp.—Tearing in an old scar. *Sensitiveness in l. temple from vertex down, and in l. half of face on touch or moving muscles, as in laughing, chewing, etc., a sensation as if sunburnt.* Pain on touch. Tension in a scar above r. ear at night on sudden and sharp changes in weather, then drawing pain. Itching; as from ants.

Clinical.—Headache always < rising in morning. Neuralgic headaches which concentrate at the root of the nose or extend into the face and eyes, or even to shoulders. Meningitis, pain in vertex, spreading over the whole head. Terrible neuralgic headaches, with tearing, < l. side, > warm applications. Headaches from exposure to cold (Glon.). Chronic neuralgic headaches, always < r. side, pulsating, extending into neck, which became stiff and swollen. Neuralgic headaches starting in vertex and spreading over the head. Threatening apoplexy, especially in drunkards.

Eyes.—Blue rings under in morning. Inflammation, with dulness and sticking; I. of l., with weakness so that he could not read. Seem thicker (swollen?) even to others in evening, they look as after weeping. Eruption. Sticking; extending to vertex; burning. *Sticking drawing pain in r.* in afternoon, *extending to vertex.* Pain, *near;* about r.; < l.; external to l.; in l., then r.; on reading; in and above eyes, with pain in skin of forehead on touch; about E., < stooping, on r. side extending towards occiput, or general, with heaviness, confusion and congestion. Pressure on l. in morning; P. as if orbits were too small, < moving eyes. Feeling as if dust were in them. Sudden smarting of r. causing lachrymation. Burning pain. Burning; in l.; aching. Itching; in l.; in l., > coffee, with pressure in both eyes and dizziness; in and about E. in afternoon and evening, with heat in them. Dryness; and sensitiveness to light in evening. Stiff feeling.

Watery, with nasal catarrh. Running of cold water from l. eye and l. nostril, with swelling of lids and face. Feeling as if something were in ball, with pain in r. orbit. Sticking from brows down into lashes; hot, in l., then r. Pain in r. orbit on moving lid. Lids, swelling of l. like an incipient stye; inflammation of r. upper in evening as if a stye would form; inflammation, < r., with burning pain, the pain < reading;

inability to open, with heaviness in forehead; sticking in r. upper; sticking in r. down to lashes; pain in inner canthi; itching pains; drawing itching pains.

Vision.—**Dim** after much reading, **with black flickering,** *it often makes reading difficult;* D., < r. eye; for near objects, < evening, and on reading flickering; with vertigo, necessity to wipe eyes; of r. by candle-light, as if dust were on the ball; *in evening, with a bluish-gray ring around the light. Sensitiveness to light. Flickering;* in evening when reading, with weariness of eyes; *of r. eye,* > moving about in open air, *with jerking in it and congestion to head; as from threads or rays of sunlight; in peculiar zigzags, with congestion to head and headache. A blue ring about the light, that was filled with fiery rays. A fiery ring about the light, with fiery rays.*

Clinical.—Neuralgia of the orbit, < l., the eye feels as if it had been squeezed. It is particularly useful for affections of the optic nerve and retina, rarely indicated in external inflammatory diseases. Particularly valuable for hæmorrhages of the optic nerve and retina, with consequent dimness of vision; this apoplexy may occur in persons who have no albuminuria. Retinitis hæmorrhagica (idiopathic). Cellulitis of orbit (compare with Rhus t.). Asthenopia following diphtheria, a paralysis of accommodation, necessity to wear far-sighted glasses (Gels.).

Ears.—The white cerumen is changed and becomes like paste. Tearing extending to temples. Cutting in upper part of l. outer in evening, < night and on touch. Pain in r.; deep in l. in evening when walking, or between ear and throat, < putting temporal and masseter muscles on tension; in a spot in petrous bone behind E. on touch; **P., with sore throat**; with nasal catarrh; with headache; (with sticking). Constrictive pain deep in l., on inserting earspoon it is painful as if swollen. Throbbing in bones behind r. Intolerance of wind. Biting in lobule, then a pimple. Itching; sticking. Numbness of concha, and on pressure it is also felt in inner parts, then generally painful pressure and heat.

Whizzing as of insects; extending back into head; with ringing and tearing. Singing in r., then feeling as if closed. Cracking in front of E.; (in ears, with poor hearing). Roaring with the pains; R. with cold feet. Thundering in both. Growling in l.; drumming, in attacks in r. (the hearing ear) in morning after waking, > shaking finger in ear, but returning, < evening. Sensitive to noises, frightened. *Hearing diminished;* lost during catarrh.

Clinical.—Pain in ears, generally extending from the throat and zygoma into the ear; it has been found useful for inspissated cerumen, in deafness with great sensitiveness; these symptoms are usually associated with diseases of the throat or of other parts of the body.

Nose.—(Inflammation of mucous follicles in outer skin.) L. nostril internally swollen and painful, then scab on the spot. A bleeding sore spot beneath N. Soreness in inner angle at tip after catarrh, with redness. Spot beneath l. wing painful to touch. (Drawing pain in bones about union of cartilages at night, sticking on pressure, stoppage of nose and discharge of dry mucus and watery pus.) Drawing in bones. Tensive burrowing beneath r. nostril, then biting across under nose. Feeling as in fluent catarrh, with red, sore margins of nostrils and lachrymation, without coryza. Itching in N. in evening; I. on eating; on sitting down to eat. Dryness. Stoppage in morning, > blowing out membranous pieces, < 10 A.M., > evening. Sneezing, with mucus in throat; violent S.

Influenza, with fever. *Catarrh;* > morning on waking, *with soreness of nose;* with red, sore and erysipelatous margins of nostrils; with burning of upper lip; *with sticking in head and stiffness of nape;* with crawling in tip of nose; with full and hard pulse, headache and drawing in legs; with cough, easily loosened expectoration, heat of head and hands, dim eyes, palpitation, rash over whole body in small spots without being elevated, restless sleep at night and sweat; incomplete. Stopped catarrh; beginning in evening; in evening, > morning on waking, with burning in upper lip; with cough and sneezing; at one time stopped, at another only on one side, then fluent, with sneezing. Fluent catarrh morning and evening, relieving the headache, lachrymation and stoppage of nose; F. late in evening, with sneezing; suddenly in evening, with crawling in tip of nose, lachrymation and pressure in inner canthi. Discharge of mucus when coughing; D. of thin water in morning; painful D. of watery clots, sometimes a scab. Catarrh, with dropping of water, margins and tip of nose inflamed, > morning, returning with fever, pain in head, ears and teeth. *Many symptoms end with catarrh.*

Bleeding; of thick, dark blood; discharge of blood and matter, with plug in trachea. *Dropping of blood;* from l. nostril after boring in with finger. *Trickling of blood on blowing.* Blowing out of blood in evening; B. of blood and pus in afternoon; B. of blood and bloody streaks in mucus.

Clinical.—Coryza and ozæna, when the general symptoms indicate the drug. Sometimes in low forms of typhoid indicating Lach. there may be dark hæmorrhage, also dark hæmorrhage in amenorrhœa. With the sore throat there may be obstruction of the posterior nares and discharge of bloody matter from the nostrils, and often soreness of the nostrils and lips.

Face.—*Swelling; with heat and redness; of cheeks, with redness of face; erysipelatous, r. eye almost closed;* (bluish-red, of cheek, with sticking and throbbing and toothache, it discharges matter). *Earthy, gray, with abdominal troubles.* Pale. Yellow during the fever. Bad color and general discomfort. Expression of pain, with coma. Suffering look, sunken and as if he had been up all night. Distortion, with jerks in small of back. **Tearing in zygoma, extending into ear.** Screwing in r. zygoma and in flesh, with burrowing. Burrowing beneath l. ear, near angle of jaw and in sterno-cleido-mastoid, as in erysipelas, in evening, then on the other side. Pain on r. malar-bone, more towards eye; in side of F., upper jaw and head. Burning pain. Drawing in bones of cheek and lower jaw; in bones and in teeth during fever.

Lips; eruption on l. side of upper. Pimples, with white pus on upper and on face. Swelling of upper and gum. (Thickness of upper.) Dryness. Heat.

Clinical.—Facial erysipelas, with great swelling and purplish appearance. Neuralgia of the face. Flushes of heat, especially at the climacteric.

Mouth.—Teeth. Crumbling of hollow. A piece breaks off a hollow molar. Sticking in incisors. *Raging in roots of lower,* **periodic, always after waking, after eating and from warm and cold drinks, often extending through upper jaw to ear,** *with jerking, tearing, sticking.* Pain in r. upper and in l. limbs, next day in l. lower teeth and in limbs, < r.; P., with swelling of cheek; with catarrh; with cold ear; *extending through jaw to ear.* Drawing in some; in sound second r.

upper molar; itching, in some of l. *Feeling as if too long when biting them together;* in last, partly broken molar, with boring extending into jaw, < after eating, the gum around it is swollen and painful down into throat, the pain > discharge of pus from tooth. Crawling in a r. upper.

Gums.—*Bleeding. Swollen; and spongy;* bluish-red, swollen and painful; painful swelling of anterior lower incisors; swelling of G. of upper incisors, with throbbing pain and burning; G. of lower incisors swollen internally and externally, as if it would be loosened, in r. molars feeling as if something were between them, a piece of the gum is grown out, the whole gum bleeds on rubbing. Swollen feeling. Pain, with toothache; P. from warmth in mouth; in G. of the two l. lower molars.

Tongue.—Coated. Swelling of l. half, feeling as of the effects of mercury, soon after rheumatic pains; (thick in forepart, with disgusting taste). Sticking and tearing, and on palate, with ulcerated fauces. Prickling. Constriction on l. side of root. Feeling as of pepper-dust, with salivation. Burning on l. side; B. from water, then hoarseness and rawness in throat. Speech stronger and more distinct than usual.

Tearing and sticking in palate. *Burning pain and rawness, then aphthous and denuded spots.* Pain on curtain of palate when yawning. Pressure on palate, as if it came from stomach. Burning on palate after acids, with dryness and thirst; B. and throbbing pain in mouth. *Soreness and dryness,* mucous membrane cracked and bleeding, *tongue swollen and covered with blisters on each side. Dryness and thirst;* D. and constriction. Scraping burning posteriorly on palate. Rawness. Salivation; when thinking about the sensation in throat; with burning in throat; with stretching; with biting on tongue; as if it came from stomach. Water runs from M. during violent cough.

Taste sweetish; in back of throat and to mucus. Salt, like Glauber's salts. Nauseating; with headache, nausea and hawking of mucus; as from stale fat. Coppery, causing nausea, making teeth dull, < forepart of tongue, which seems thicker there, < during eructations (in a hysterical woman). Like meal or paste.

Clinical.—Toothache, with swollen bleeding gums; gums sometimes dark purplish. The tongue is usually red, dry and tremulous, or the tip is red and the centre brown, sometimes there is a red stripe through the centre (Verat. v.). It is often indicated in canker sores on the tongue and in aphthæ of the mouth. Gangrene of the mouth. Paralysis of tongue, it cannot be protruded, it catches in the teeth.

Throat.—External. **Sensitiveness to external pressure; in evening on lying down, with suffocative sensation; even to touch of the linen,** during evening fever; *sometimes with nausea;* **and neck,** *no position is comfortable; extending to nape, with sticking on swallowing and scraping on swallowing bread, as if everything were raw, dryness of throat, without actual dryness of tongue;* (of an aneurism of r. carotid, the sensation extending to pit of stomach). Throbbing in glands, afterwards extending into malar-bones, which feel stiff.

Ulceration, with soreness and difficult swallowing (tonsillitis); U., with hawking of mucus, ecpyesis and cough. Swelling. (Inflammation.) Mucus; with hoarseness, then stopped catarrh, then yellow mucus from nose and throat; tenacious; in back part, mostly sweetish, then in nose. **Hawking of mucus after a nap in daytime, with rawness in throat;** H. of mucus only in evening after tea instead of in the morning, as if an abscess had broken; of mucus more from fauces, less from larynx; tasting like saltpetre; salt.

Sensation as if a crumb stuck; *obliging her to swallow,* > hawking. Feeling as if closed by something sticking in pharynx after supper, lasting all night and next day, with difficult swallowing of saliva, but not of food and drink. Intermittent pinching in a spot on r. side of pharynx, < pressure, < evening, when it affects larynx. Twisting in pit. *Ulcerated feeling on swallowing.*

Pain; (on turning it); on r. side; *posteriorly at side of larynx;* in r. side, < pressure; > *eating,* which caused an agreeable tickling; in r. side, extending to ear; extending to root of tongue and into hyoid bone; *in pit, extending to root of tongue and into hyoid bone and to l. tragus, behind which it shoots out, with pain on touch; in l. side, extending to tongue, jaw and into ear,* < breakfast, *tongue sore on l. side, with sticking here and there,* gum inflamed, all teeth painful, **L. side of face and lower jaw swollen and sensitive to touch,** with sticking in spots in thighs and legs, disagreeable taste, loss of appetite and bad sleep. Pressure on both sides; intermittent P.; as from something astringent; in r. side as from external pressure; as from a plug (after acids); low down, causing salivation if he thinks of it.

Soreness; in pit; on both sides in morning; < *evening,* **with pain in l. side;** *in children, with tossing about and moaning;* with fever, much spitting, tossing about at night, groaning, and eyes surrounded by brown rings; **with feeling in pit as if something were swollen and would suffocate him, it cannot be swallowed. Feeling of a painful lump** *on swallowing;* painful lump in pit, > hawking mucus. **Swollen feeling** *on swallowing;* **on empty swallowing, > when eating.** It seemed as if something should be hawked up which could not be loosened.

Rawness; (on deep breathing); *with swelling, painful on swallowing, < drinking;* as after exerting it. Feeling as if tendons were drawing it up to palate, with pressure as after astringent pears. *Dryness;* **at night on waking, without thirst,** *with suffocative sticking.* Burning in l. side and pit; B., with hoarseness. *Crawling in the ulcer, causing hacking cough;* C. in morning (in a pregnant woman) causing nausea, then prickling and sticking and vomiting; at night, causing hacking cough, during the day aggravation of the soreness. Bubbling above r. clavicle. Swallowing difficult; **more of liquids than of solids;** *of saliva, not of food;* with feeling as if something in it obliged swallowing; of food and drink, as from a hindrance in region of cardiac orifice. *Pain on empty swallowing, not on swallowing food.* Troubles on alternate days. T. and chest troubles < after rising, lasting till noon.

Œsophagus.—(Feeling as if a morsel of food stuck in it, the sensation extending in afternoon to stomach, causing pressure, > lying down, inability to sleep in evening, at one time it extended up to r. side across chest to shoulders, then towards umbilicus, with burning, in morning sensation in abdomen as before violent diarrhœa, in evening violent cough, with horribly tasting expectoration, next day again the sensation about umbilicus.)

Clinical.—Swelling of submaxillary and salivary glands. One of the most frequent uses of Lach. is for sore throat; in all the ulcers and diseases of the throat requiring this remedy there is extreme sensitiveness externally to the slightest touch, which causes a feeling of suffocation, all bands around the throat must be loosened; internally the throat is swollen and suffocation threatens. A feeling of a lump in the throat wakens out of sleep. There is great difficulty in swallowing, especially when not swallowing food; liquids are apt to regurgitate through the nose. The l. side of the throat is chiefly affected, or the trouble has extended from l. to r. It is called for in various phases of disease from simple tonsillitis and pharyngitis to the most terrible and destructive diphtheritic process; in the latter disease, and indeed in nearly all cases requiring the drug, the throat is purple (not bright red and œdematous like Apis). It is not only indicated in diphtheritic and ulcerative diseases, but in certain phases of scarlet fever, with gangrenous throat; it has also proved useful in syphilitic ulceration of the throat. In all the diseases of the throat indicating Lach. there is usually pain, sometimes sharp, which is apt to extend from throat into the ear, on l. side. Elongation of uvula, with constant efforts to clear the throat.

Stomach.—*Appetite increased; at one time good, at another lost. Longing for oysters* evenings; L. for wine; for something he knew not what, at last he took a swallow of water. Food is relished without real hunger, it is swallowed hastily. Feeling as when obliged to wait for food, without real hunger. Hunger, with aversion to food. Appetite lost in morning; in evening, with discomfort in abdomen; with discomfort in abdomen at meal-time; for bread; for rolls, the usual milk causes nausea; for food, wine and tobacco. Thirst; in evening after beer, with loss of appetite; before the chill; before the fever; *with dry tongue and skin;* insatiable. Eructations; after eating; during fever, in an infant; *amounting to vomiting;* of food after eating; of sour water after dinner; sour and bitter after meat fried in butter; violent, evenings, with cramp in stomach. Empty eructations; when fasting; after dinner; dry, burning. Hiccough in evening after smoking tobacco.

Nausea, waking at 2 A.M., with oppression of chest and pressure in stomach, at 3 violent vomiting, then colic, then spasmodic vomiting, at last vomiting of bile, with vertigo and profuse sweat, then diarrhœa four times between 6 and 9, burning on urinating, then weakness and headache; N. in morning; *in forenoon;* in afternoon, with feeling as if poisoned; at night on waking, with vomiting and diarrhœa; *from anything tight on throat;* after dinner; after dinner and in afternoon; on swallowing; after milk; from smoking tobacco; (from drinking water); < thinking about it; (> open air?), with aversion to food and headache; with pain in stomach; with pain in pit of stomach and also with diarrhœa; with risings in œsophagus, but only mucus is expectorated, with dyspnœa; with anxiety and oppression of chest; with faintness; with aching in abdomen and stomach as if he would faint, *necessity to loosen his clothes;* as if in a single place in stomach, from the sight or thought of sugar of milk; sudden, in afternoon after drinking tea, with hiccough and eructations, at last amounting to vomiting air; paroxysmal, in forenoon and afternoon.

Retching every evening, with vomiting and cramp in stomach; R., with vomiting of mucus and cramp in stomach; constant R., with commotion and anxiety in chest.

Vomiting; at night, then diarrhœa; in nightly attacks, with oppression of chest; in nightly attacks, with pressure in stomach; in nightly attacks, with diarrhœa, then burning in urethra when urinating; of blood; spasmodic, bilious; of food; forcible, of all food, with pain in head and abdomen.

Sticking extending to chest; to vicinity of breasts. Cramp every day at 6 A.M., with violent eructations, retching, vomiting of mucus. Burrowing as from a worm; B. in forepart of r. side, extending towards l. side, then a stitch upward between flesh and bones in middle of chest to the vicinity of breasts. Pain in pit on pressure; P. in l. side near pit in spring; P. causing faint feeling; flatulent, in pit, extending into chest.

Pressure; at night and in morning so that he must stand up, > emissions of flatus; in pit in morning; *after eating;* in pit when lying, > moving; in pit, < touch, with drawing towards umbilicus and warmth in chest; *with weakness in knees;* then clawing in anus extending inward; extending towards heart; in epigastric region, extending towards heart; as of a load, > eructations and emissions of flatus. Drawing pressure from pit to umbilicus. Feeling in S. and intestines as if something were drawn up into a ball. Tension beneath pit in afternoon, extending towards umbilicus. *Painless gnawing, then gnawing in sides, extending across under ribs deep in abdomen.* (Sensitiveness and feeling as if something were turning about in it, with heart troubles.) Throbbing in pit; jumping, extending up under ribs, then sensation as if something pressed from pit towards heart.

Coldness; in pit alternating with heat; alternations of C. and heat, with want of breath. Feeling as if heartburn would occur. Heartburn in evening after smoking; H., with headache. Burning in S. and hepatic region, distention of stomach, itching in epigastric region, abdomen distended and hard, when walking necessity to stand still, feeling as if a stone pressed downward in upper abdomen and in pit of stomach and would break away, so that he must step carefully, feet swollen when sitting and cold though burning, with offensive odor from mouth. Emptiness in afternoon; at night.

Clinical.—Cardialgia and indigestion, great soreness of the pit of the stomach to touch, and intolerance of the clothes. It has been found useful at the period of black vomit in yellow fever, and sometimes in the vomiting of pregnancy. It is a valuable remedy for the gastritis of drunkards, and for weakened digestion after Mercury.

Abdomen.—*Distention* in morning on waking; at night; after eating; *with sensation as if the inner parts or ligaments from stomach were stretched,* **so that she must wear the clothes, < about stomach, very loose, even in bed she must pull up the night dress, she dares not lay the arm across the abdomen;** *with hardness;* with tearing and chilliness. Rumbling and gurgling; R. in evening after eating, with colic and emission of flatus. Flatulence; and tension, preventing her from walking far. Loud flatus; therewith the anus seemed closed, so that she must press it out. Short violent emissions of offensive flatus.

Sticking through chest to shoulder. Cutting before menstruation; for ten days before menstruation, with beating in temples and headache, so that she expected the menses every moment; C., with urging to stool, then burning discharges from anus; C., with burning pain and with pressure on bladder. Cramps during menstruation as if a knife were thrust through it; C. so that she cannot straighten herself, with diarrhœa. Pain in afternoon; after vomiting at night; from the shock of cough; in attacks after confinement, with return of other symptoms. Contraction. *Emptiness.* Eviscerated feeling. Heat. (Feeling in morning as for diarrhœa.)

Hypochondria.—Sticking; in l.; from r. to l.; from hepatic region through urethra. Deep-seated gnawing. Acute pain as if on short ribs, < inspiration. Pain in r., then l.; in hepatic region; in splenic region only when riding in a wagon, > stretching out straight. Clothes are very annoying.

Sides.—Sticking in l., extending into chest, making breath difficult; S. outward in l. in evening. *Tearing in r.;* deep from sides towards middle. Griping in l., then r. and in loins, < walking, then in hypogastrium and loins, sometimes shooting, with occasional desire for stool, > emission of flatus, and once with borborygmi, till stool. Pain in l. Tension in l.

Umbilical Region.—Pain transversely across in morning after rising; P. all day as before diarrhœa. (Burning.)

Hypogastrium.—Flatulence in a hernia. Sticking in forepart; in groins during cough; near r. ilium, extending through abdomen and chest into l. shoulder and on the other side from the l. below to the r. above. Tearing in r. side. Intermittent gnawing in lower part of l. groin, near the bone. Intermittent pain. Feeling as if a hernia would protrude.

Clinical.—Valuable in inflammation of the liver, threatening to develop an abscess. Sometimes in the distress from gallstones; the liver swollen and very painful, with dirty yellow color of the face and numerous other symptoms. Note particularly the intolerance of clothing over the hypochondriac and epigastric regions. It is extremely valuable in typhlitis and in the late stage of peritonitis, with aggravation from sleep and intoleranee of clothing. It may be noted here that the r. side of the abdomen presents numerous symptoms of this drug, while in the throat most symptoms are on the l. side. The abdominal symptoms have pointed to its use in metritis and peritonitis, in dysentery, in dysmenorrhœa, in inflammation of the ovaries, in short, in a great variety of diseases of the abdominal and pelvic viscera, usually of an adynamic type, with the characteristic symptoms of the remedy. Hæmorrhage from the bowels in typhoid fever, sometimes with nosebleed, the hæmorrhages consisting of decomposed blood.

Rectum.—Discharge of blood; on pressing after a copious stool; painful D. of acrid mucus, with voluntary pressure. *Protrusion after stool; P., then painful constriction of anus;* P., with swelling, then spasmodic contraction of anus. *Stool lies close to anus without passing and without urging;* S. lies close to anus, but only flatus passes. *Pain in evening, then diarrhœa,* **then throbbing as with hammers in anus.** Urging with the fever; U. after vinegar, then a soft stool; ineffectual U. during the first period.

Anus.—Hæmorrhoidal troubles. Hæmorrhoids, with determination of blood to anus, diarrhœa and increased itching in anus. **Beatings as with hammers.** Jerkings. Clawing alternating with oppression of chest. *Spasmodic pain before and after stool;* before a natural stool, and in rectum. Pain; with a hard stool; as if it would be torn out on coughing; and pressure, both extending inward. Pressure both painful and painless. Soreness after a strong-smelling stool. Drawing now in one, now in the other side; D. during fever, extending into r. side of chest; during fever, extending into chest and even head; painful hæmorrhoidal, to umbilicus. *Burning during and after stool;* after the usual stool, with biting. Throbbing, and in small of back. *Closed feeling.* Constant feeling of flatus, but he only presses out small short emissions from time to time. Itching in morning.

Clinical.—Fistula in the anus, with sensation of beating as of little hammers. Hæmorrhoids which are painful and strangulated with sticking or feeling of a plug in the anus or throbbing. **Strangulated piles, with great constriction of the anus, which makes straining extremely painful.**

Stool.—*Watery, frequent, with burning in anus;* only a watery evacuation. Diarrhœa in morning; D. after a natural stool; after acids, even fruits; with straining; *sudden, about midnight, with urging, very offensive, ammoniacal;* frequent. Thin, alternating with normal ones. *Soft; and bright yellow. Pasty;* and later every day; *and scanty,* delayed, occurring only after smoking; and scanty, then omitting one day. Constipation. Nodular. Hard, and urine burning. *Bright yellow. Of the odor of putrefying snakes.* Copious. Scanty, smooth, claylike. Frequent during the heat (in a nursing infant); two in morning, then weakness and ineffectual urging. Later every day. Delayed, after pressing only a scanty, unsatisfactory one. *Omitted three days;* then ineffectual urging, then scanty stool, with pressure and pain as if the sphincter would be forced asunder; S. and urine omitted seven days; omitted several days, with good appetite, so that abdomen became distended and hard.

Clinical.—The stools of Lach. are generally very offensive or putrid, and sometimes, in low types of disease, involuntary. Diarrhœa, especially in hot weather or in the relaxing weather of spring; D. in drunkards; during the climacteric, symptoms always < sleep; there is generally sensitiveness of the abdomen and desire to loosen the clothing, with more or less tenderness in l. side.

Urinary Organs.—Troubles return when riding in a wagon (after wine). Urging; at night, with cutting in urethra and pressure downward in testicles as if a hernia would protrude; with emission of milky semen (or prostatic fluid); with peculiar discomfort in bladder and slimy sediment in urine; constant; frequent; frequent, without much discharge, drawing pains in small of back extending to hips. Milky gleet returns after micturition. Urethra, sticking; cutting; *sticking cutting in forepart; sore pain in forepart;* pressure; burning on urinating.

Frequent micturition; and dribbling; and urine copious, frothy; and urine dark and frothy; twice at night. Micturition with urging. Urine of the color of a new copper coin, staining linen yellow and depositing a cloudy sediment; U. reddish-yellow, increased; U. of a strong odor; contained dirty mucus before and after menses, urine clear at first, then depositing a sediment like beaten egg, with discomfort in bladder and urging; red sediment.

Clinical.—Subacute inflammation of the bladder, with very offensive dark brown urine and frequent urging. After diphtheria or scarlet fever the urine is very dark or blackish, with a sediment like coffee-grounds (of decomposed blood), albuminous.

Sexual Organs.—Red pimple beneath margin of glans, with itching. Red spots on glans, the margin congested in two places; (red spot on prepuce). Profuse secretion beneath prepuce. Jerks in penis. Strong erections in morning; forenoon; after midday nap and towards evening; at night. Erections in morning when half awake; unusual E. during the day. Pain in r. side of scrotum in morning. Testicles hard and scrotum relaxed. Dragging upon testicles in evening; pressure upon T. from above as if a hernia would protrude. Amorous thoughts; during the day, with lascivious or quarrelsome dreams at night; in morning, with relaxed penis; in morning on waking, with pain in loins and prostration; in morning after waking, with pain in loins and bruised feeling; after midday nap. Desire; without amorousness, when controlled it caused great inclination for mental labor. Desire wanting; and inability for coition or late emission, erections feeble. Semen of penetrating odor. Emission during the midday nap; evenings, then weakness and headache; at night; at night, and profuse sweat; at night, with vivid and disagreeable dreams, with complete waking, then weakness; unconscious, at night; difficult.

Tickling itching from thighs into genitals, which swelled, with desire and tickling, then cramplike contraction in uterus, extending into r. side of abdomen, thence into breast (in a circular direction), with heat and apprehension, with these symptoms tickling in anus extending into region of kidneys, thence to between shoulders, as if between skin and flesh (she had had a similar sensation years before). Menses recurred after three weeks.

Clinical.—It has been found useful in venereal ulcers (chancroid), when the sore tends to become gangrenous, with the general peculiarities of the drug. Membranous dysmenorrhœa < alcoholic stimulants, with great pain in l. ovary darting upward. A valuable remedy for inflammation of the ovaries, < l., with violent pain and sensitiveness to weight of clothes, especially if the menstrual flow is offensive, sometimes general relief on the free appearance of the menses. Puerperal metritis, metro-peritonitis and fetid lochia. Valuable for a great variety of troubles at the climacteric, especially for metrorrhagia, fainting turns, hot flushes, hot vertex, flatulent distention, pain in ovaries, exhaustion from sleep, etc. The most frequent indications for Lach. in all diseases of the uterus and ovaries are the intolerance of the weight of the clothing and the tendency of the disease to extend from l. to r., with these conditions it has cured almost every pathological condition of the female organs, tumors, inflammations, displacements, indurations, neuralgias, etc.

Respiratory Organs.—Larynx. *Swollen, raw, scraping, with necessity to swallow.* Paroxysmal rattling low down at night in sleep. **Painful to touch; and whole throat. Painful on bending head backward, and throat.** Pressure. Seems tensively swollen, and swallowing difficult. Feels obstructed by a foreign substance. Feeling as of a plug moving up and down, with short cough, inability to lie down, blowing of bloody and purulent matter from nose. (Peculiar spasmodic sensation extending downward.) Dryness in epiglottis and vicinity, with scraping.

Hoarseness; with cough; and constant necessity to hawk; the voice will not come because something in larynx prevents, which cannot be hawked loose, though mucus is brought up; with much mucus in back of throat and sweetish taste, afterwards mucus is loosened and there is a discharge from nose, < morning, next morning almost stopped catarrh, afterwards whitish-yellow mucus in nose and throat.

Trachea.—Stitching through it, with irritation to cough, and dry cough. Feeling of an inflamed, painful lump by sternum, > violent hawking of mucus. Seemed narrowed, no mucus could be loosened as usual.

Cough; in evening; **from pressure on larynx;** during sleep; *during sleep, of which the patient knows nothing; from increased fluid in larynx;* from tickling in chest; (during or after drinking); < **after sleep.** *Dry cough;* in evening and always with the first irritation to cough a stitch through trachea; violent, in evening, with pain in trachea and horrible taste to the expectoration, as after eating salt fish. **Dry, hacking from touching throat, also in morning,** *and from smoking*, with stopped catarrh, with much blowing of nose and sneezing. *Cough without expectoration in a child in evening on lying down and in sleep, sometimes awakened thereby*, sometimes causing vomiting. *Hacking C.;* at night from crawling in throat; when riding in a wagon, from pain in chest and tickling in larynx; *and violent, from crawling in the ulcer in throat;* and fatiguing (in phthisis mucosa) only during the day, < after sleep, walking and talking (as the throat thereby becomes dry), < eating fish and in damp weather, sometimes causing vomiting, expectoration scanty, difficult, mingled with harder, heavier lumps of mucus, and with pain in pit of stomach, so that he must hold it. Racking C. if lungs are irritated (as, for example, by tobacco-smoke) and all the blood is driven to head and face. Fluttering, nervous C. every evening, from about 9 o'clock, from tickling in larynx, > going to sleep. *Tickling C.*, the tickling at one time in larynx, at another in chest, at another in cardiac orifice of stomach, the mucus at one time round and gray, at another tenacious and yellow, at another watery, rarely at night, always with nasal mucus; *violent tickling, from contact with open air; with expectoration of mucus.*

Expectoration of blood; difficult E. becomes loose; (E. of lumps of gray mucus on coughing and on sneezing).

Suffocative sensation if anything reaches larynx; S. sensation, with the throat troubles; when coughing. Inability to breathe, with necessity to sit up, then rattling of mucus like peas boiling, with alternations of cold and heat in stomach, general chill and flushes of heat, risings into œsophagus, with nausea, whereby only mucus is raised. *Respiration difficult;* in evening after eating a little; **constantly obliged to take a deep breath,** < *sitting.* Sighing during fever, with pressure in chest. Short breath; with depression of spirits. Paroxysmal rattling at night in sleep.

Clinical.—Various forms of laryngitis, aphonia, catarrhal or paralytic; laryngitis, catarrhal, croupous or diphtheritic; in all these forms of disease there is extreme sensitiveness of the larynx to external touch, and especially a feeling of suffocation and constriction, so that the patient cannot bear anything tight about the throat; the cough is spasmodic, suffocative and wakens from sleep, the pain extending from l. side of larynx into ear. In diphtheritic croup there is a purplish hue of the face, with suffocation, extreme fetor of the exhalations, albuminuria, great prostration, etc. Whooping cough, the fits repeatedly awaken the child out of sleep. Asthmatic attacks preventing sleep, intolerance of the least pressure about the neck or chest, > expectoration. The chest symptoms point to the use of the drug in bronchial catarrh and pneumonia of the subacute or chronic form; in these diseases the cough is suffocative and wakens from sleep. In pneumonia when there is threatening abscess, with muttering delirium. In threatening paralysis of the lungs, with albuminuria, the patient is unable to sleep on account of great distress for breath, or if he falls asleep he is immediately awakened by the necessity to breathe. Dyspnœa so great that the patient has to sit up, cannot lie down on account of suffocative fulness in chest, and cannot bear anything tight about neck or chest. Frequently indicated in coughs of nervous or reflex origin, for instance, from inflammation of ovaries or of pelvic viscera, or nervous cough at the climacteric without symptoms of local inflammation. Emphysema. Hydrothorax.

Chest.—Jerks. Sticking; in l.; in l. nipple; through C. on coughing; in l., < coughing and breathing, with sticking in l. knee, drawing in fibula and down into foot, and sticking in r. ankle; through l. breast, not much < inspiration and cough; in lower forepart, extending inward; making respiration difficult. Feeling as if labor-pains extended into breasts. *Pain; in l.; in sternum; beneath l. breast; beneath breast and drawing extending upward;* all the afternoon, and in night, in evening frequent, pulse; *in sternum at night; with burning in chest;* beneath short ribs on breathing; extending inward in lower part of ribs. *Pain at night, so that he could not touch it;* with a swollen feeling. Soreness; extending to between shoulders, < eating.

Pressure upon it as if full of wind. Feeling as if wind rose into it and became fixed, > eructations. Heavy pressure in the whole. Tightness; suffocative, in evening after lying down. *Oppression* in evening; *O. in sleep;* on becoming heated; after getting feet cold; suddenly disappearing; alternating with clawing in anus. Throbbing; and in abdomen. Bubbling. Orgasm. Heat externally; H. in r. lower part, afterwards extending to axilla, with pressure in pit of stomach. Stiffness and pain on pressure at insertion of sterno-cleido-mastoid. Affections at night.

Clinical.—Inflammation of breasts, with suppuration and bluish appearance, extreme sensitiveness of the nipples.

Heart and Pulse.—Cramplike pain in præcordial region, causing palpitation, with anxiety. Pressure about heart during fever. *Constriction of heart. Palpitation; causing anxiety. She feels the beat of the heart, with weakness, even to sinking down.* Pulse rapid and small, and skin hot; P. increased in evening after moderate exercise, full and hard, with profuse sweat.

Clinical.—It is not infrequently indicated in all the inflammatory diseases of the heart, with the symptoms of palpitation, suffocation, intolerance of pressure about the heart, with pain and numbness in l. arm, and a feeling as if the heart were growing up and suffocating him; it is extremely useful in atheromatous arteries and in chronic aortitis, with terrible dyspnœa. Nervous affections of the heart, palpitations; feeling as if the heart turned over, and very irregular action of the heart. Hypertrophy of the heart. Angina pectoris.

Neck.—Swelling of r. muscles, painful when taken hold of. Jerking in glands, and pulling. Sticking in nape and back. Tearing in vertebræ. Pain in nape, extending into eyes; P. in l. muscles, < sterno-cleido-mastoid, extending around head like a headache. *Nape sensitive to pressure.* Wandering about in glands. *Stiffness of nape, with catarrh; S. of glands, extending to malar-bone;* of atlas-joint, with pain on pressure.

Clinical.—The pains in the neck are most severe in the cervical region.

Back.—Sticking extending upward; S. in upper part. Sprained pain during fever. Drawing, < ischia; *D. extending into hips, with urging to urinate.* After stooping he could with difficulty become erect. Sticking between scapulæ; near point of r. scapula, towards spine, deep in back, < sitting, < by paroxysms, obliging one to bend backward and take a deep breath, not affected by breathing. Tearing in scapulæ, < r.; T. between S. Pain between scapulæ and on chest; in l. S.

Small of Back.—Sticking to liver (perhaps also to kidneys) and thence to urethra; S. (jerks) on every motion. Sprained pain extending into abdomen; S. pain, with jerks, taking away the breath; S. pain, < r. side, preventing most motions, with a clumsy gait, then troubles in anus. Pain in ischia; sacrum and coccyx; P. after midday nap; after acids, with yawning and stretching as in fever; with numbness of fingers, crawling in calves and toes, pain in l. knee and elbow, feeling as after exhaustion in muscles of r. leg near outer side of tibia and frequent sprained feeling in knee; extending to abdomen; *as if lame and weak;* as after great exertion, spreading upward like a fan. *Drawing pain. Drawing extending up back; extending into legs in evening, < ischia;* across region of kidneys, with warmth during the fever. Throbbing, and in anus, with drawing in all limbs.

Clinical.—Neuralgic affections of the spine and spinal nerves. Myelitis and neuritis. Neuralgia of the coccyx, < rising up, must sit perfectly still.

Extremities.—Stretching of all. Jerking in hands and legs; in arms and legs, with creeping from l. shoulder to head. Tearing in all; in arms and legs; in arms and legs, with cramp. Gnawing in all. Sprained pain in elbow and knee; l. Pain; in r. upper arm, then in r. calf; after profuse catarrh; in l. arm and below l. knee, < ankle; in r. upper arm as if in flesh, then also in tendons and bones, then pain in r. calf; as if pressed from without in arms, hands, legs and feet; on motion, as if beaten; weary, in all on waking, beginning in knees and elbows. Drawing from l. hip to knee, then from r. shoulder to elbow; painful, in knee and elbow, extending downward. Weakness; *in morning.* Heaviness. Inability to close hands or bend knees, as if paralyzed, sometimes only l.

Upper Extremities.—Shoulders. Sticking near and beneath r., < midday nap. Tearing; in l. in morning, extending to tips of fingers. Aching extending through them and arms, with heaviness, but less than in legs. Drawing pain in joint in evening. Rheumatic pain in r. and in wrist; in r. in evening and in both wrists. Pressure on r. in morning. Paralysis of l., < morning on dressing and on bending arm backward. Axilla, sticking externally beneath r.; a turning about in muscular margins as in erysipelas, < r.

Arm.—Sticking, with feeling as if asleep; in r. Tearing through, < r.; downward through A.; in humerus and outward through flesh after acids. Pain in bones after acids; paroxysmal, in r. like a pressing in bones. Tension extending to middle fingers as if tendons were too short; in l. on stretching it out. Weakness in fever; *W. so that she cannot raise them, they fall down again;* sinking down after trifling exertion.

Sensation in l. elbow on touch as if glass were sticking in it. Bruised pain in elbow; in nerve. Pain in elbow extending to hand; l. Rheumatic pain in elbow, then l. hand. Swelling of muscles of forearm, painful on grasping anything, > night. Tearing in forearm; along ulnar side of r. carpus and metacarpus, extending to tips of outer fingers, < l. side; intermittent, in bones of r. wrist, on side of little finger. Sprained pain in r. wrist in evening on exerting it. Pain in wrist extending to elbow; sore, in bones.

Hand.—Jerking in l. in afternoon when sitting. Cramp between metacarpal bones of fourth and fifth fingers. Sticking; l.; in bones and cartilages of hands, which were bent by contraction of tendons if she attempted to sew, and in wrist, with paroxysmal crawling in them. Tearing in joints of r.; T. in l., extending into upper arm; in r. like a forcible extension of muscles, it refuses its service on attempting to hold anything. Pain from the bitten H. into chest. Rheumatic pain along l. on side of little finger, often extending to elbow. Drawing pain in r. metacarpus. Pain as after violent exertion in all joints of l. on waking. Disagreeable dryness. Dead feeling on rubbing them (on backs?), also on washing them rapidly after eating.

Fingers.—White. Visible pulsation in ball of l. thumb, then recurrent jerking in whole thumb. Sticking in tips; sudden. Gnawing in bones and flesh of r. third and fourth, with crawling, also under nail, beginning in tips and extending to second and third phalanges, it seems as if something were boring from backs of fingers through and through and upward, but without pain. Sprained pain in metacarpal joint of l. little. Pain in ball of r. thumb. Numbness of tips of r., then l., < morning.

Lower Extremities.—Stumbling gait, with stiffness of joints, then movements rapid and active, often uncertain and clumsy. Thighs, jerking at times in l., afterwards with painful drawing downward in l. leg; tearing downward in l.; tearing in femora extending to knees; pain posteriorly; rheumatic pain posteriorly; bruised pain in muscles of r. after wine; pain posteriorly as if swollen, < towards knee, knee is swollen, with pain, < in hollow, < touch, and there is tension, stretching of leg is difficult; paralyzed feeling in recti muscles, disappearing over night, with swollen feeling.

Knee.—Creaking in l. Cramp on waking. Thick, painful on rising, he can scarcely walk, > after walking awhile. Stitches; when walking. *Sprained pain in r.;* S. pain during fever. Pain on r., < towards inner side; P. in r. extending inward; crawling P. in r., down forepart of tibia to back of foot and to toes. Bruised feeling in evening. Drawing pain to tarsal bones; D. pain as from swelling, a sticking; gouty D. pain in l. when sitting. Tension, stretching was difficult. *Weakness after eating.*

Leg.—*Swelling of l. and of foot.* Jerking in l. in afternoon when sitting. Cramp in calves waking him at night and towards morning. Sticking, with changes of wind and weather. Tearing here and there; T. up legs, with uneasiness in knees. Pain in l.; at night in bed, < about knees, returning about 8 A.M., with heaviness of legs; reappearance of old P. in calves; above l. external malleolus, < stretching the contiguous muscles in stepping. *Burning pain in spots on tibia, with itching, after rubbing a sensitive spot with dark bluish-red margin and dry scurf.* Bruised feeling in bed, with sleeplessness because he cannot get the right position, everything causes pressure on neck. Drawing; in l. to ankle; in l. as if in bone, extending to ankle; downward; extending upward; in fibula and foot. Necessity to move feet, otherwise the legs jerked upward, then drawing extending up leg like a crawling; N. to move feet up and down, otherwise the legs jerked up and caused uneasiness in whole body, with tearing up leg. *Weakness.* Feeling in r. calf as if asleep, then in whole leg.

Ankle.—Stitches in r. malleolus. Pain in l. external malleolus, < stretching contiguous muscles in stepping. Pain; in tarsal bones.

Foot.—Redness, then swelling, with fever, similar to elephantiasis. Swelling of r., < walking. (Boots were too tight.) Cramp in forepart; C. which draws up toes. (Corns grow rapidly, but are not painful.) Tearing in r.; T., < evening, with heat in them. Aching in a corn on r.; A. in forepart as if pressed between boards. (Sensitiveness of balls on stepping.) Tension in tendons beginning at heel (before a snowstorm). Bubbling in r. near great toe.

Toes.—Stretching extending through whole body to fingers. Stitches in l. great; S. extending upward. Painful surging back and forth in them. Feeling as if something were digging beneath r. nails and pushing them up. Pain sometimes in r., sometimes in l.; P. in a corn on r. little. Drawing extending upward from toes. Numbness in r., with crawling.

Clinical.—It has cured sciatica of r. side, with the characteristic indications of the drug.

Skin.—Red spots covering chest, arm of diseased side and shoulder; R. itching spots here and there on fingers; R. burning spot on thumb, then a hard vesicle; R. spot on l. shoulder exuding moisture, vesicles suppurate and break. Inflamed spot, with sticking burning, on a r. toe that had been pressed. Group of flat warts on outer side of thumb. Desquamation of face and scalp; of forehead, with biting itching. Nettle-rash covering face. Hives on back; shoulders; legs.

Soft nodes about an ulcer. Tubercles on r. forearm, gradually spreading over body, except face, chest and abdomen, itching at night in bed, afterwards the eruption was partly like hives, partly, after scratching, like scarlatina or roseola or prickly heat. Pimples; here and there; on face; forehead and cheeks; hairy part of genitals; arm; l. arm; r. forearm, afterwards over whole body; outer part of r. thigh, with pain around it; not unlike vesicles of scabies, on face; itching, on elbow; red, on forehead not far from root of nose; red, here and there, at times with tickling, which is < in bed, scratching causes pain, sleepless on account of the biting itching.

Erysipelatous eruption beneath l. eye, itching at night, she was awakened by fright about trifles, in the morning the skin began to redden and swell, < midday nap, next morning very thick and red, with itching, lower lid swollen, red and itching, preceded and followed by beating headache on stooping. Transverse crack on outer side of little toe in fold of joint, with itching (near where a sand-flea had been taken out). Profuse bleeding of a small wound beneath nose. **Sore spots become fungoid, dark red to brownish,** *with whitish spots, burning on wiping.* Gangrene at place of the bite, hands and fingers swollen and insensible, the inflammation extended to the arm, the swelling to the shoulder, here and there gangrenous blisters.

Pustules on r. brow and face; on face, then beneath nose, on brows and chest, then on other parts; < thighs, with red areola. *Boils near spine, with burning throbbing pain,* not suppurating; B. on heel caused by slight rubbing of shoe, with shaking chill on formation of matter. Vesicles on l. nostril; (on tip of l. second toe, breaks and is moist); clear V. on r. fourth finger; on hands and fingers, with itching burning. Itching vesicles on backs of feet; on outer margin of r. hand, with voluptuous burning after scratching; on back of l. middle finger, then a warty elevation leaving a scar. Itch-vesicles here and there on fingers; deep hard, in groups on r. hand.

Ulceration of nail after a bruise. Ulcers on elbow. *The brownish-red areola about the ulcer became blackish-blue. Old red ulcer-scars reopened,* suppuration after a blow, then vesicles and epidermis loosened about them, *the open spots were dark red, looking like a flat sponge,* here and there whitish, burning after rubbing. Bleeding of U., which then became cleaner; (profuse B. of the opening of a cancerous U., the base bluish); (a cancerous U. had on its base streaks of coagulated, almost black blood). (U. became cleaner and the areola painful to pressure.) (Burning in U. at night.)

(Panaritium on a finger in which there had been jerking and pain, so that she could not bear the arm under the covering, shooting sometimes upward, sometimes down into the arm, which was weak.)

Sticking deep in skin extending outward through it. Pain in and about a scar of a fistula on thigh; P. on forehead on touch; unusual, from a sand-flea, the wound remaining after removing it will not heal, and near by are *cracks between toes;* between temple and outer canthus as if a pimple would form. Tense feeling about ulcers on legs. Crawling from l. shoulder to head; on r. shoulder, upper arm and beneath shoulder; fingers and calves; l. toes, with prickling; l. calf, with cold feet and ankle; from anus to head, with the fever; arms and legs in fever, with jerking in flesh; in l. hand, < toes, at times in l. side from vertex to toes, with prickling. Biting in various places as from ants.

Itching; *over whole body; of face;* near l. eye; loins; arms, hips and lower limbs; l. arm; upper arm; hands; bend of fourth finger; between fingers and on knees; thighs; leg; from morning till evening, in face about eyes and on cheeks, > scratching; in various places in evening, < legs and loins; on sides and on short ribs towards umbilicus (where there are red spots like bug-bites) in morning, < evening by walking and in bed, with white hives on l. scapula and whole back, next morning the hives were red; on r. heel, then on both heels, then on r. hand and fingers, on top of foot and on toes, always worse and burning after scratching, *then hard, white, deeply-seated vesicles;* on legs, then red wheals; in spots between fingers, then after scratching hard, shiny elevations, then vesicles, with burning and tension; on back of middle finger, then a round, red, hard bunch, a deep point of pus slowly formed, of which a little exuded, sticking on hanging down the hand, six weeks later after a blow on the bunch (which had almost disappeared) it bled profusely; *preventing sleep;* as from ants, < loins; burning, on l. thumb and index, then two pimples, with burning after scratching.

Sticking itching in various parts; of face and body in afternoon; S. itching on hands and feet in afternoon and in r. ear; in a point in instep as if an insect pierced the skin; as from ants over body, face and scalp in afternoon, < night, with burning pain, lasting till next forenoon, but then without the burning.

Clinical.—Purpura hæmorrhagica, the whole body is swollen and extremely sore, intolerant of clothing. Tendency to ecchymoses, to bed-sores. Indolent ulcers, with bluish-purple color. Carbuncles. Varicose ulcers. Various forms of pustular eruptions, which suppurate and become bluish-black. Pemphigus, the bullæ containing decomposed serum, with bubbles of gas. Erysipelas; of infants. It is not infrequently called for in scarlatina. Fungus hæmatodes. A valuable palliative in congenital cyanosis.

Sleep.—Yawning; towards evening; with stretching; spasmodic, in morning. Sleepiness in forenoon; with weakness in all limbs; after walking in open air, dreams for hours of very important things, but everything was forgotten on waking; at noon; in afternoon; evening; after breakfast; after breakfast, with prostration, stretching and much spitting of saliva; before dinner, at times irresistible; *after dinner, with weakness;* after supper; after supper, with weariness; she could sleep when standing and walking; *without ability to sleep.* Overpowering sleepiness in evening; O. before eating; after eating; after dinner, *afterwards the troubles in abdomen were worse.* Sleep in forenoon. Early falling asleep in evening. Stupefied slumber after the pains have passed off. Waking late.

Sleeplessness; before midnight; one evening, overpowering sleepiness next evening; *from internal restlessness, abdomen and chest seem swollen, with pain in chest so that he could not have anything touch it.* Late falling asleep; and next morning early waking. Early waking. **Waking in fright at a trifle.** *Restless sleep; in children, with groaning and moaning;* with dreams of his home and anxiety as if he had done wrong. Light sleep, then sleeplessness after 1 or 2 A.M., with peevishness, distrust and no appetite for bread. Partial sleep full of dreams.

Dreams in forenoon; *constant D., with frequent waking; amorous; with meditation;* vivid; constant and fatiguing, with frequent waking; joyous, humorous in afternoon nap; with mental activity and of the many occurrences of the day; all night of the occurrences and business of the day; poetic, full of inventions in midday nap; that he possessed an intriguing character; of being accused of a theft and that he had knives ready to take vengeance on a haughty earl when he should come and show himself insolent; that a person dear to him had died, he woke weeping and looked about convinced that he should see his ghost, without fear; (anxious, so that she was weary in the morning); of his home, with anxiety as if he had done wrong.

Fever.—*Coldness; in evening, with chattering of teeth and feeling as in trismus;* in evening, with thirst and pain in forehead; with prostration; general, with tearing and distention in abdomen; internal, every evening, with external heat, loss of appetite and headache. *Shivering during the heat; paroxysmal S.;* after thirst, then creeping heat without thirst, but with desire to be covered, several attacks during the day, < evening, at times sweat; over back. **Chill in back beginning in small of back;** C. in one side of head. Internal C. in side of head and in ear (with toothache); l. Cold knees; and calves, at times only on l. side r. ankle. *Cold feet; with oppression of chest;* then hot; then hot, with pain in some toes as after walking all day.

Heat beginning at 3 A.M. (after vinegar), with drawing from toes upward and urging to stool, with frequent soft stools, then drawing in r. side and in anus, extending into chest and across region of kidneys, with warmth, with pressure in chest, sighing (pressure about heart lasted several days), then chilliness and stretching, with thirst, in open air shaking chill, then creeping from anus into head, with dulness, dizziness, roaring in ears, dazzling before eyes, weakness of arms, crawling and twitching in flesh, even in legs, and yellow color of face. Heat in evening; and all night; > the rubbing of other people, with hot palms and hot nape; agreeable warmth in evening as after a cold bath or as after coition. H. at night, with restless sleep; H. after vinegar and salt things. H., with dry skin, dry mouth and thirst. H., with fulness of head, drawing in some teeth and bones of face, eyes glistening, indicating exhaustion, sprained pain in knees, next day the same symptoms, with irritability, sprained feeling in small of back, restlessness, discomfort, symptoms as in influenza, during the attack the habitual expectoration of tenacious gray mucus did not occur, next day catarrh without fever.

Heat as from orgasm of blood, with necessity to loosen clothes about neck, there is a sensation as if they hindered the circulation of blood, with suffocative feeling. Orgasm of blood caused by disagreeable news; O., with restlessness, anxiety, pressure on chest, violent, quarrelsome, morose mood, he involuntarily speaks louder and more distinctly than usual, thinks clearly and expresses himself well, but has no memory, does not hear or understand what is said to him.

Heat in face; ears; nape; hands and feet < evening, with tearing in feet; toes of one foot, with crawling; palms and soles; palms, soles and abdomen in evening, with sleepiness without ability to sleep, fanciful imaginings, sensitiveness of throat, intolerance of bed-covers or shirt; between skin and flesh, as if it came from small of back (after acids). Heat in skin after acids; (in various places in skin, < afternoon); *with dryness* and dry coated tongue, thirst, small, rapid pulse, weak eyes. Sticking burning in small of back extending upward; S. burning everywhere in skin, worse up from small of back.

Sweat; in evening after moderate exercise, with increased, full, hard pulse; *at night*, with catarrh and cough; between the paroxysms of fever; on back staining the shirt sulphur-yellow; strong-smelling in axillæ; in axillæ smelling of garlic; *on feet;* on toes in morning in bed. Disagreeable dryness of hands.

Clinical.—Chronic intermittents, a tendency to recur in the spring when the weather becomes debilitating, with the general characteristics of the drug.

Lactuca.

A tincture of the fresh plant of Lactuca virosa, L., is used.

Clinical.—It has been found useful for incessant spasmodic cough, with great irritation of the larynx; the cough threatens to burst the chest, is associated with a sense of suffocation, and is followed by copious expectoration. It is to be compared with Dros.

Lappa.

A tincture of the fresh root of Arctium Lappa, L., is used.

Generalities.—*Trembling and excitement.* Sore pain in r. shoulder, above l. elbow and under l. scapula, near axilla. Aching next day after walking and driving in wet and cold, with stiffness and soreness; numb, in shoulders extending to wrists, and in small of back extending down posterior surface of thighs. Lameness. Inability to work. Tired; at 11 A.M.; 4 P.M.; at night; by a short walk; and stupid feeling; mentally and physically. Faint feeling in church. Aggravation from 4, 6 and 8 P.M.; A. from motion; after eating, except morning headache; of pain for an hour or two after going to bed. Amelioration in open air.

Mind.—Worried as if something were going to happen. Nervous, excitable. Unusually bright and active. Confused.

Head.—Aching; on waking; on waking, > breakfast; from 1 P.M. till he goes to sleep at night; at bedtime and next day till 5 P.M., > sarsaparilla soda-water and supper; throbbing, with "stretchy," sleepy feeling, pain in small of back. Confused, heavy feeling. Lightness, with dulness. Dizziness; as if she would fall; as if she would fall, not unpleasant, as if going to sleep, < lying, > towards noon, afterwards > open air and walking. Shooting over l. eye, sometimes extending over top of head. Frontal headache; over l. eye all the forenoon, over r. temple in afternoon; at night and next morning; after supper; headache (in forehead?) when awake, on top in afternoon; sometimes subsiding, then returning with stitches and gradually settling down into its former heavy ache. Pain over temple; sharp, over r.; heavy, over r. in afternoon; sore, above l. Pain in vertex; in morning. Heaviness in vertex and occiput. Shooting from base of occipital bone up into head; at times S., stunning pain as if struck with a hammer at base of bone behind ear. Pain in occiput; extending from nape to forehead, with feeling as if she would faint and heavy aching in upper surface of eyeballs as if eyes were tired by reading, eyes > closing.

Eyes, Ears and Nose.—Sensation of a hair in r. eye and inclination to rub eye; began about 8 P.M. in the dark, > bright light. Earache. Nostrils feel dry and stopped up. Great sneezing the day after having his hair cut.

Mouth and Throat.—Tongue coated white in morning; T. thick and flabby. Taste bitter. Aching in r. side of throat; A. in muscles of throat and inclination to tie something around throat. Soreness of r. side of T., with cough.

Stomach.—Appetite increased; hungry, but after eating a little seemed oppressed; poor in hot weather; lost; variable, wanting at one meal, ravenous at the next. Thirst; in evening, not > soda-water. Nausea; all the morning; after eating, with pain in abdomen. Pains, at times sharp, extending to r. side below ribs. Gone feeling, < dinner and breakfast, > open air, with empty eructations.

Abdomen.—Pain; in evening, causing dizziness; acute, and in hepatic region; bearing down, before stool. Uneasiness, with rumbling and rolling; U. under umbilicus. Pain in hepatic region, and soreness to touch in lower r. chest anteriorly; P. in hypogastric region; in l. groin in afternoon; sharp, above pubes after dinner; heavy laming, in r groin.

Stool and Urine.—Stool loose, griping; natural, with feeling of approaching diarrhœa. Urine high-colored and offensive.

Sexual Organs.—Emission during afternoon nap. Pain during menses, < back; more pain than usual in back and hypogastrium during menses, < 10 A.M. till 1 P.M.

Clinical.—It has been used with some success in displacements of the uterus, particularly in prolapsus associated with sore, bruised feeling, great relaxation, all symptoms < standing or walking.

Respiratory Organs.—Sharp, choking cough in larynx. Breath short; B. oppressed at 10 P.M., with heat.

Chest.—Pain in r. side below ribs; through middle, extending through to back; intermittent, in middle of r., > open air; intermittent twitching, in muscles. Sore aching in and above r. nipple; along l. lower ribs, with pain on touch. Tenderness. Sensitiveness to taking cold. Heaviness across middle and constant desire to press upon chest. Congested feeling in lungs in evening.

Heart.—Fluttering; all the morning, with uneasiness about it. Violent beating after dinner, and at 7 P.M. Palpitation.

Back.—Aching on waking, > getting up, with disinclination to move; A. in middle, with flashes of heat; under l. scapula after supper, < sitting; sharp, under l. scapula, near axilla; intermittent, under l. scapula during the day, < morning. Pain low down. Pain in small of B.; < lying on back; > rest.

Extremities.—Pains in hands and knees, extending to ends of toes; gnawing, extending from l. wrist to finger-tips, also intermittent gnawing P. in knee, these pains > motion, returning during rest, next day the same pain in r. hand.

Upper Extremities.—Sticking in shoulder, extending along clavicle and sterno-cleido-mastoid. Darting pain in shoulder. Pain in l. shoulder; through l. S. in afternoon, < raising arm; in arms, < exercise. Sharp, constrictive pain in and above elbow. Shooting in elbows, extending to hands; intermittent S. in r. elbow; in r. wrist. Pain in l. wrist; r. wrist in evening; metacarpal bone of r. thumb, with soreness to touch. Numbness of r. hand; l. hand on waking. Sticking in r. thumb.

Lower Extremities.—Pain down l. hip, in region of sciatic nerve, in evening; P. just above knees, also < motion; in calves; in calves, with numbness and burning; calves, with tired feeling; tired, in legs; intermittent, in feet and hip-joints, similar to those in other places. Knees weak. Legs and feet tired and numb. Tingling in dorsum of l. foot, next day with numbness.

Skin.—Clinical.—Some cases of infantile eczema, with yellow scabs, have been reported cured.

Sleep.—Sleepiness; all the time; at noon; in afternoon, with dulness and laziness; < towards evening, and in-doors. Sleeplessness; and restlessness, without pain. Sleep restless; and sleeplessness after 5 A.M.; and awake most of the time, mind overactive; and late falling asleep, then frequent waking. Waking early and feeling refreshed, after going to bed late. Dreams; troublesome; of great exertion; of being murdered in afternoon nap, and waking in fright.

Fever.—Coldness. Cold sweat.

Laurocerasus.

A tincture of the fresh mature leaves of Prunus Laurocerasus, L., is used.

General Action.—Essentially the same as that of Hydrocyanic acid. Examine particularly the cough symptoms.

Allies.—Hydrocyanic acid, Kalmia, Hyos.

Generalities.—Tremulousness of whole body. Jerking, < head, back and cervical muscles, then paralysis. Shrieked, threw the head back and was convulsed. Convulsions; with staring eyes, closed jaws and frothing from mouth. Eyes fixed upward, teeth clenched and froth running from mouth. Fell stupidly to the ground. Itching stitches in various parts. Pinching burning pains now in one part, now in another, < limbs. Pain in throat, chest, region of heart and stomach and scapula, only on r. side. Electric shocks at 9 P.M. in bed. Weariness; in morning; towards evening; early in evening, with sleepiness; after eating, with sleepiness; with aversion to all work. Faintness. Heaviness in morning, with disinclination to work. Insensibility. Paralysis. Asphyxiated, paralytic, apparently lifeless condition, pulse scarcely perceptible, barely 30 (compare Kalmia). Healthy feeling when sitting, as after fatigue. Amelioration in open air; though the roughness in throat was worse then; A. after dinner.

Clinical.—Chorea, with spasmodic action of the muscles of the throat and œsophagus; the drink rolls audibly through the œsophagus and intestines. It has been found valuable in conditions of extreme prostration, with sense of suffocation, gasping for breath and slow, irregular pulse. It must, of course, be compared with Hydroc. acid, to which it chiefly, if not wholly, owes its efficacy.

Mind.—Fancy while awake that he saw old men with long beards and distorted faces and sparks of fire. Happy. Lively. Joyous and interested at 2 P.M. Delight in his work. Hasty, impetuous. *Despondent;* and lachrymose, he would rather die than live. Fretful; at 2 P.M., and vexed about everything. Anxiety about trifles in evening in bed, with sleeplessness. Anxious oppression, with inability to work and necessity to go into the open air. Everything is irksome, he goes unwillingly to his business. Indolence and sleepiness. Indifference. Inclination to mental labor. Ideas flow slowly. Memory weak. Stupefaction. Coma, with closed eyes, dilated pupils, hurried respiration, involuntary discharge of urine and fæces, convulsions. Unconsciousness at times, a species of sinking spells, respiration and pulse suspended for several seconds, but before these spells breathing was stertorous, then it stopped and the man appeared dead.

Clinical.—An extremely excitable, nervous condition accompanies nearly all the conditions calling for the drug.

Head.—Hangs over and he cannot raise it. Sticking here and there at 4 P.M.; S. in brain, with crawling. Tearing in evening in bed. Boring. Aching; > open air, < entering house, sometimes < forehead, sometimes < occiput, < over orbits, < hot room, where he felt exhausted; in brain, with constriction; as after intoxication. Anxiety, > open air, with internal and external warmth of forehead. Confusion; at 2 P.M., with pain; when reflecting and writing; in evening, > sleep, with heaviness; with internal heat; with oppression of forehead and small, accelerated pulse; with general confusion as when after violent thirst one drinks several glasses of wine in quick succession; as if stunned; as before violent catarrh; becoming pain, < temporal region and forehead; becoming pain, < forehead and orbits.

Pressure downward; on rising from a seat, with obscuration of vision; > becoming erect. Brain feels as if pressed against upper and forepart of skull, < frontal region, with pressure towards orbits. Feeling as pressed forward. Feeling as if brain pressed to all sides. Heaviness; when walking in the room, with pressure down from vertex; on stooping when walking in open air, with sensation as if something fell from l. side into forehead; < stooping, with dulness and with painful crawling in forehead; extending towards frontal region till 10 P.M.; as before catarrh or after intoxication. Fulness. Intoxication. Apoplexy. Vertigo; on moving in evening, with loss of ideas; on rising from a seat; on rising from prolonged sitting, with dulness of head; after rising from stooping; < open air; < walking; with buzzing in ears, difficult respiration and weakness; then sleepiness; as if head went round and round; as if everything turned around; as if everything turned in a circle in evening.

Forehead.—Sticking in r. eminence; after dinner; in l. eminence at 2 P.M., then in r.; in middle of F. on walking in open air; alternately in sinciput and occiput in afternoon. Tearing deep in; in sinciput at 2 P.M., extending to vertex; in middle, with internal heat. Twinging in sinciput, with sleepiness. Boring above orbits. Pain; in middle; in side; l. eminence; over orbits; in morning in bed; l. side about 2 P.M.; in open air, < in the house, > rest, with heat in face; l. side of sinciput on stooping low, > rising, with sensation as if brain fell forward; with slow pulse; in l., gradually extending over head, making mental operations difficult, returning next morning on waking and lasting till 3 P.M.; alternately in F. and occiput; throbbing; stupefying, anteriorly; stupefying pain in sinciput. Confusion. Periodical pressure beneath bone. Pressure towards orbits and feeling as if water would be pressed out of eyes, then lachrymation. Pressure forward in sinciput, with warmth and sweat on forehead and hands and feeling as if head were enlarged. Pressure outward; on stooping; behind frontal and nasal bones; pain as if bones were pressed outward and raised upward. Pressure inward; not entirely > pressure. Heaviness on going out of the room; H. in sinciput on stooping, not > rising, with stupefying pain; in sinciput, with pressure in orbits as if balls were too large. Drawing in middle. Tension and in l. side of face. Fulness. Feeling above nose as in catarrh. Shock.

Temples.—Sticking in l. Tearing in r.; from l. to vertex, thence to behind l. external canthus and into zygoma, then into a neighboring tooth, where it becomes a jerking; downward in r.; upward in l., not entirely > rubbing. Pain in r. bone; in l. temple at 4 P.M.; in l. on entering a room. Pressure outward beneath r. bone. Throbbing in r. as with a finger.

Vertex.—Sticking, > stooping, < rising. Tearing in l. side. Pain in l. side; intermittent P. in upper part of head. Contraction, with heat. Heaviness; < stooping, > rising. *Feeling as if ice lay on it* (Verat.), then on forehead, then in nape and so on till it occurred in small of back, where it was very agreeable, with disappearance of all head troubles.

Sides.—Sticking in l.; r., < stooping, with beating; in l., with boring in front of l. ear; r., with throbbing; now beneath parietal bone, now beneath temporal bone. Tearing in l. at 2 P.M. Boring in l., then dulness. Pain in l.; in r. parietal bone near vertex, < touch; throbbing, in l., < stooping. Shock in a spot in l., then feeling as if beaten, then dulness in head.

Occiput.—Stitching; in r. Tearing extending towards neck, slightly > friction. Twinging pain, with sleepiness. Painful pressure on l., extending to nape. Pressure outward beneath l. bone, with which his thoughts nearly vanish. Drawing deep internally in r. side. Tension in r. as when a lock of hair is pulled. Sensation as if tendons were too short and head would be drawn backward, like a painful heaviness, with cessation of pain in forehead. Throbbing in l.

Scalp.—Sticking on r. side of occiput. Crawling and itching. Tickling on r. side of occiput, > scratching. Itching here and there; in a spot on r. side; in a spot on l. side, more in upper part; behind sides of forehead at 2 P.M.; now in front, now in back part of r. side, not > scratching.

Clinical.—Neuralgic headache, with feeling of icy coldness of vertex.

Eyes.—Staring. Aching around, < l. Pressure in evening. Painless feeling as if they would be pressed out. Dryness and warmth; in evening by the light. Burning in r. at 4 P.M.; B. in evening by the light. evenings, < r., < inner canthus, with sticking; with dimness and weakness. Biting in r. as from salt at 2 P.M. Itching in l. in afternoon; in l. at 4 P.M. Lachrymation in morning; of l. at 2 P.M. Pupils dilated; < r.; P. immovable. Sensation of a band around ball, with stitches. Tearing in l. superciliary ridge, extending into teeth and r. lower jaw.

Lids.—Agglutination of l.; A. in morning. Tightly closed, pupils dilated. Injected vessels in a spot in l. inner canthus. Burning jerking in r. lower. A stitch from within l. canthus. Lids cause pain in eyes as if they were too dry and he had not slept enough. Scraping in r. inner canthus. Smarting of inside. Drawing in upper margin of upper on exerting eyes. Burning; in l. external canthus. Itching beneath r. upper, > scratching. Itching in r. inner canthus, > rubbing. Itching in l. inner canthus; causing lachrymation, > rubbing; changing to pressure, and vessels filled with blood branching like a tree towards pupil.

Vision.—*Obscured.* Illusion as if everything were very large, > touching the objects (coffee an antidote), with anxiety.

Ears.—Sticking in r.; coming out of l.; in front of l. Tearing extending into r.; coming out of l. and behind it. Pinching; in l. Boring in r. external concha. Pain in r.; burning, in l. Distended feeling in r. Drawing in muscles behind r. Crawling in l.; deep; in r. after dinner as after going to sleep. Itching in r., not > boring into it; in l. at 3 P.M., > boring into it. Whizzing in l.; with roaring.

Nose.—At one time sticking in root, at another pressure inward; S. externally in r. wing at 2.30 P.M. Cramplike pain in r. bone. Pressure asunder in bones. Pressure forward in upper part. Drawing through N. Feeling as before catarrh. Fulness. Stoppage at 5 P.M.; S. in upper part. Tickling in r. nostril. Crawling on l. outer wing, with itching, and when touched on inside pain as if ulcerated. Itching in nostrils; > rubbing; in l., not > rubbing; in upper part of nose. Coldness near wings of nose. Sneezing; at 2 P.M.; 4 P.M.; with yawning; violent, at 5 A.M., then fluent nasal mucus; ineffectual attempts at. Catarrh loosened; stopped C. in morning on stooping. The secretion of mucus is suppressed, without sensation of catarrh. Smells the medicine in the open air.

Face.—Pale. Yellow, earthy; spotted yellow. Liver spots more distinct than ever. Puffy. Sleepy look. Spasmodic distortion. Stitch near l. side of chin in afternoon. Tension in l. zygoma as if pressed with a nail, with itching. Jaws, sticking from r. lower through head and out of r. ear; in l. lower when walking in open air; tearing in angle of l. lower and in lower molars; gnawing on r. side near chin; bruised pain in lower at 7 P.M.; pain in articulation as if it would be dislocated; *inclination to close as in tetanus.* Lips, itching pimples, > scratching; boil in r. corner, smarting on touch; vesicles on margin of upper; clear vesicle in l. corner; itching in middle of upper, > scratching.

Clinical.—It has been used successfully in lockjaw.

Mouth.—Teeth. Sticking; now in lower, now in upper; in r. lower. Tearing in l. upper eye-tooth, > pressure; T. in l. lower, > cold water, and in gum.

Intermittent gnawing in r. lower during supper, with boring. Boring and digging, drawing back and forth, in l. lower molars, during dinner. Pain in l. molars, > biting teeth together. Jerking pain in l. lower in evening. A l. lower molar seems larger and longer than usual.

Tongue.—L. side swollen in evening, stiff and painful as if something were sticking in it. Coated white; C. with dirty white mucus in morning, with flat taste and emptiness in stomach. Sore pain on margin. Burning in tip as from a cut. Feeling after eating as if burnt, causing sensation as if blunted. Back part sticky, with watery saliva in forepart of mouth. Dryness; after eating, with rawness and salivation. Loss of speech.

Dry; in morning, and slimy. Salivation; with dryness of throat; with nausea; with nausea, > eructations; thin; thin, of feverish taste; sourish. Taste insipid; T. feverish; slimy and pasty; offensive, with feeling as if he had an offensive breath; T. and odor of peach brandy in M.

Throat.—A piece of watery mucus comes into throat, which is expectorated without hawking. Hawking; frequent, on account of rawness in throat; of mucus; of mucus in morning; tenacious mucus every morning when fasting; sweetish mucus at 2 P.M. Choking pain in upper part of pharynx, involving chest and causing oppression in it, the pain then extended over neck and face, with sticking in teeth and feeling as if some of them would be pulled out. Gurgling. Sticking, as from a lump, extending to l. side of back. Painful drawing downward, > eating soup. Scraping; before and during cough; and in larynx, with hoarseness and frequent need to cough; on swallowing, with roughness. Rawness; in morning, causing cough; frequent, in afternoon; with hacking; with scraping, provoking cough; making speech difficult. Burning; and pain; and hoarseness; and on palate. Tickling. Able to swallow only after consciousness had somewhat returned.

Stomach.—Appetite great; A. in morning less; lost, afterwards better than formerly. Thirst; at 4 and 8.30 P.M. Eructations; empty; empty after breakfast; incomplete; of the breakfast; tasting of the porridge that had just been eaten; tasting of food at 2 P.M.; sweetish; rancid; bitter during and after breakfast; tasting of bitter almonds. Hiccough. Nausea; in morning, with colic; in morning, with hunger, yet food nauseated him; in morning in bed; after dinner, with stomachache; > eructations of tasteless water; in epigastric region; about heart in afternoon, with anxious warmth, as if he had taken an emetic and could not vomit; with feeling as if stomach were full of water; faintlike, in morning. Heaving. Vomiting.

Distention. Rumbling; then sour eructations. Gurgling. Movings. Sticking in pit; through pit into small of back; cramplike, above pit. Pain; in epigastric region; in epigastric region when urinating; similar to faintness, in morning. Cramplike pulling pain in pit in evening on getting into bed and lying on side, > lying quietly on back, with small, weak, contracted pulse. Contractive feeling at 2 P.M.; C. feeling in epigastric region. Disordered feeling after dinner, > eating bread. Peculiar feeling in epigastric region, not exactly nausea, but similar to the sensation that precedes vomiting. Feeling of weakness. Emptiness. Discomfort as from fasting. Burning; in pit; in morning after beer, with warmth in abdomen; cool, and in abdomen; rising from S. Feeling as if hot vapor arose to shoulders. Agreeable warmth and in abdomen.

Abdomen.—Distended and hard; D. by all food, and he feels stuffed. Retracted, and if he presses it out there is a stitch externally towards r. clavicle. Drawn tightly together, with general comfort. *Rumbling;* from below upward at 2 P.M.; *with coldness.* Movements during supper; M., with burning. Emission of flatus; after stool, after dinner; loud.

Cutting in afternoon when walking; C., then diarrhœa at 2 and 4 P.M.; C. and contractive pain, waking at 2 A.M., > diarrhœa twice. Pinching, < middle, at 2 P.M.; P., < l. side, then soft stool. Pain. *A feeling extending into small of back as if something fell down.* Burning; in evening till 1 A.M., with sleeplessness, without thirst, with necessity to put her hands out of bed, where even she could not bear to have them long. Sensation as if hot vapor arose into shoulders. Warmth, with drops of sweat on nose after dinner; W. extending into shoulders, with sweat on back and in axillæ.

Upper.—Movings, with sticking in stomach. Sticking in middle, then in r. hypochondrium. Cutting, with stitching in l. hypochondrium; C. about middle, coming from sides, at 9 P.M. Pinching, then a stitch in middle of it; P., with contraction, then sticking in l. hypochondrium near back.

Hypochondria.—*Distention in hepatic region, with pain as if suppurating and as if an ulcer would burst.* Sticking in l.; *in liver; in r., with burning and pain on touch; in r., then burning extending backward; in r. extending towards back; in r. extending backward,* then a stitch in nates; in r. at 1 P.M., extending towards axilla at 2 P.M.; in l. at 2 P.M., extending forward; burning, in r. towards back, which after rubbing goes to middle of scapula. Twinging extending to umbilicus, where it is most painful; T. in l. *Pain; indescribable, in r., extending towards small of back. Paralytic bruised pain in liver on inspiration, extending to shoulder* (Chel.). *Beating and bubbling in liver as in a sore finger. Burning in r. at* 3 P.M.

Sides.—Moving about from r. to l., where it becomes a sticking. Rumbling in r. Sticking in l. after morning beer-soup; in l. at 3 P.M.; pinching, in l., that chiefly spreads upward. Cutting, > emission of flatus. Pinching, sticking, flatulent pain in r., > emission of flatus, but returning. Griping extending towards centre, then diarrhœa twice, with tenesmus. Drawing pressure in r. Contraction in abdomen from sides at 2 P.M., with pinching.

Umbilical Region.—Distention; distended feeling below umbilical region. Sticking in r. side coming out at l. groin. Sticking drawing in r. side above umbilicus. Tearing at 6 P.M., extending towards r. groin. Feeling at 2 P.M. as if something had been torn loose. Feeling below umbilicus as if intestines were cut to pieces, then movings in abdomen, > emissions of flatus at 3.30 P.M. Twinging at 3 P.M.; above umbilicus at 10 P.M., with sticking in small of back. Griping, with two pasty stools. Pinching at 2 P.M., with tearing. Pinching about middle of abdomen.

Hypogastrium.—Flatus presses upon bladder. Flatus accumulates towards perineum and causes pressing outward. Fulness > emission of flatus. Stitches in l. groin; r. groin; in r., on ilium, at 1.30 P.M.; in l.

at 2 P.M. if she inclines to left, > becoming erect; in r. after dinner, extending towards thigh; in l. on stooping, > becoming erect; in r., then moving about in stomach; above r. pubis, extending along spermatic cord when lying and on moving about, > sitting up; like a flea-bite in groin during dinner. Twinging from sides towards middle, then stitches in r. hypochondrium. Pinching in sides extending into small of back. Contractive pain on both sides above pubis at 7 P.M. and in bed; in r. groin after dinner; in groins at 4 P.M., extending downward, so that she must bend up. Bubbling pain above l. ilium. Pressure beneath Poupart's ligament, with tension as if the part would press through. Feeling of a swelling in l. side at 2 P.M., with sticking if she presses it with the fingers when stooping, > becoming erect. Weariness in r. flank.

Clinical.—It has been praised as a valuable remedy for chronic indurations and inflammations of the liver, especially for threatening abscess, and for dysmenorrhœa, with coldness of vertex, cold tongue, rumbling in abdomen, etc.

Rectum.—Periodic rumbling and gurgling. Sticking after urging to stool; S. downward during stool, then pasty fæces. Tearings. Constricted feeling. Crawling in evening in bed; in morning, with itching. Urging when walking, with emission of only flatus; U. after dinner, with soft stool; ineffectual U.

Anus.—Cramp extending into rectum. Burning in morning; B. after stool; after diarrhœa.

Stool.—Thin. *Diarrhœa; twice in morning, with tenesmus; in afternoon, with tenesmus; frequent, of thin greenish mucus*, with contraction in groin; in evening. Soft; after dinner, with twinging in upper abdomen, then burning in anus; with pressure; then tenesmus; and frequent. Pasty at 5 A.M., with pain as from a cold. Constipation. Hard; and delayed; and difficult; with urging; with pressure, then burning in anus; at first, then soft, with colic as from taking cold and tenesmus as if more stool would follow. Involuntary S. and micturition. At 6 A.M., with pressure. Frequent; then tenesmus. Delayed. Omitted. Every two or three days, then fulness in abdomen, with feeling as if no stool had occurred and peevish mood.

Clinical.—Diarrhœa of green mucus, with suffocative spells about the heart.

Urinary Organs.—Itching in forepart of urethra. Burning in urethra when urinating; B. and urging after urinating. Painful urging, then necessity to wait for urine to pass; after dinner. Obliged to rise early to urinate, but only a little passes. Frequent micturition; of scanty urine; M. slow and indolent; M. rare, with scanty urine each time; M. impossible.

Urine.—Pale, deposits a cloud. Acrid. After standing an hour looks like clayey water. Frothy. Clear when passed, but deposits a red sediment with white, gelatinous flakes. Golden and a cloud soon forms in the middle. Clear, with a pellicle like a spider's web, large flakes float in the middle and there is a reddish sediment. Increased; in morning; in afternoon, and becomes turbid over night; when walking; and pale. Scanty; and yellow; and yellow, watery; a few drops during stool. None. Deposits a cloud; thin; thickish red sediment.

Sexual Organs.—Voluptuous itching beneath prepuce, with sexual desire. Erections at 7 and 9 P.M., without fantasies; E. in evening and at night. Menstruation too early; and during the first four nights tearing in vertex, the discharge lasted eight days, was profuse, painful and thin; M. profuse and long-lasting; M. profuse, on the second day toothache, on the third day cutting colic from 2 to 4 P.M., > application of warm clothes to abdomen, lasting one day longer than usual.

Respiratory Organs.—Larynx, sticking from without, taking away the breath; scraping, with hoarseness, then increased mucus in larynx and frequent provocation to cough; tickling; itching beneath larynx, causing hacking cough. Hoarseness; and feeling as if breath were impeded in trachea; and ineffectual provocation to cough. Squeaking, afterwards thick voice. Bass voice. Trachea, tenacious mucus, < upper part; pain in forenoon on coughing; rawness; R. and tickling; R. and scraping; R., with painful drawing and hacking cough; R. as from mucus which he could not loosen, with dryness and constant necessity to hawk; sensitiveness low down, < swallowing, with drawing; tickling provoking cough. Crawling in upper part of bronchi as if tickled with a feather.

Cough from tickling in throat; C., with whistling sound and with dry feeling in throat; **C. in paroxysms**; *frequent, short C.; coughing up blood; dry C., with feeling as if mucus were hanging in throat and could not be loosened, an hour afterwards the mucus loosened easily.* Hacking cough at 2 P.M.; H. cough from rawness in trachea; as from tickling in larynx.

Respiration.—Sobbing. Frequent, deep. Short on account of sticking in r. shoulder and liver. Slow and scarcely perceptible. Slow, moaning, rattling. Inspiration impeded in epigastric region.

Clinical.—It is a valuable remedy for the dry harassing cough of phthisis. Spasmodic cough, especially the later stages of whooping cough, when the patient is very much prostrated and has many symptoms of nervous spasm. Cough associated with valvular disease of the heart, the patient coughs almost incessantly, especially on lying down (Hyos., Sang., etc.). Feeling of fluttering in region of heart, and gasping for breath, with cough.

Chest.—Stitches in l.; through l.; in l. female breast; beneath l. mamma; beneath l. arm; in r. near sternum; in middle of sternum; in r. ribs towards back; in last ribs at 10 A.M.; beneath l. mamma at 2 P.M.; in r. side when standing at 6 P.M.; in lower part of sternum, somewhat to r. side at 6 P.M., and on inspiration S. through chest into back; in l. breast on inspiration; in l. female breast on laughing, not on inspiration; in l. female breast, with burning; in sternum, then burning; from both sides to about a hand's breadth from sternum; beneath l. breast, extending to scapula; intermittent, in l. ribs, near ensiform cartilage; creeping or moving, in female breast, with sensitiveness to touch. Pain like knife-thrusts in flesh and bones of l. in evening in bed.

Pinching in outer surface of l. intercostal muscles. Pulling pain in r. pectoral muscles. Bruised pain in ribs when lying on side. Pain; in a spot below l. ribs; in all parts on motion; with oppression; concealed P. in l. Pressure in middle; in middle of sternum; in lower part of sternum; above ensiform cartilage; in upper part of sternum at 2 P.M., not affected by breathing; at 2.30 P.M.; on inspiration; in the room; < sitting; upon sternum, < inspiration; superficial, when walking in open air; with tension and fretful mood; on middle, causing pain on deep inspiration; impeding breathing and causing cutting; P. inward in a spot on sternum at 2 P.M., not < inspiration. Heaviness on sternum on stooping, > rising. Sticking tension in l. side in morning, extending into neck, and there causing tensive sticking on bending towards l. side. Oppression; cramplike, during rest. Tightness; during and after breathing; on stooping, not > becoming erect; on both sides. Anxiety. Burning beneath l. mamma; on r. clavicle, by shoulder; above ensiform cartilage at 2 P.M.; on breathing. Paralysis of lungs.

Heart and Pulse.—Intermittent sticking in region of heart, < inspiration. Pulse 80; rapid and small during headache. Pulse slow; and weak; and small; and small, contracted. P. small.

Neck.—Sticking in r. side; in nape towards l. shoulder at 2 o'clock. Tearing in nape after dinner, then in l. shoulder. Cramplike pain in l. side of vertebræ on turning head towards l. Pain in l. side as from stiffness. Pressure in nape in open air; in nape compelling her to hold head forward at 6.30 P.M., on raising it a painful tension. Tension in r. side on moving head. Spasmodic contractive sensation in anterior muscles when drinking. When running, beating in r. side as with a hammer. Stiffness.

Back.—Sticking; through chest into sternum at 2 o'clock. Painlike stiffness in B. and small of back when writing, > becoming erect. Tension, and between shoulders, extending into neck. Sticking between scapulæ; on taking off corsets; in r. S., towards axilla, when standing at 3.30 P.M.; in tip of l. on inspiration; in lower part of r.; in r. towards axilla; in middle of r.; in middle of r., with burning. Tearing on upper part of l. scapula. Burrowing between S., < rest, with boring. Pain beneath point of r. S. Pressure inward between S. Stitches in r. loin. Pain in small of B. as from weariness, on becoming erect.

Extremities.—Small and remain wherever placed. Feeling as if loosely articulated. Paralytic pain in articular extremities of joints. Paralysis; and insensibility; and coldness, without insensibility; of hands and feet; of hands and feet, without insensibility. Insensibility; with weakness and prickling.

Upper Extremities.—Shoulders.—Sticking; in r. at 2 P.M.; beneath l. towards forepart; in front of r., with S. in axilla; in forepart of l., with tearing; on anterior surface of l. joint on stretching shoulder forward, with tension as if tendons were too short. Piercing pain in r. joint woke him in evening, momentarily > laying arm above head. Tearing; in l. from 6 to 8.30 P.M.; in l., > rubbing. Pain in bones; in r. joint woke him every half hour, and he tossed about; rheumatic, in r. joint, < bending arm backward; bruised, on top of r.; paralytic, in r. Painful pressure in ligaments of l., with tension. The suspender over r. became very annoying. Weariness.

Stitch in r. axilla at 2.30 P.M.; beneath r. axilla, afterwards extending forward into chest. Arms feel as if drawn inward. Upper arm, stitch in r., then bruised pain extending into shoulder; burning S. by r. elbow; tearing in muscles of r.; T. on inner surface; T. in middle of humeri; pinching on anterior surface of r.; gnawing in r., > pressure, afterwards sensitiveness to pressure; pain in tendon of deltoid; pain in head of r. humerus as if swollen and as if it had not room enough in the capsule; tension on inner surface by elbow as if skin were raised by a needle, at 2.30 P.M.

Sticking in l. elbow; in lower surface of r. Tearing through bend of r. E. into tip. Pain in l. E. Forearm, tearing in middle of l.; cramplike pain in l., < lying upon it; tensive pain in tendons of r.; heaviness, with pain on inner condyle of elbow when touched. Wrist, stitch on outer condyle of l.; stitch in r., > rubbing, but returning, then S. in upper arm; tearing on inner surface of l. at 2 P.M.; jerking tearing in a spot on r.; sprained pain in r.; stiffness in r. as if sprained.

Hand.—Trembling. Distention of veins. Cramplike pain in ligaments of l. bones during rest, with stitches. Tearing on back of l. at 2 P.M.; T. on back of r. towards fingers, > rubbing; on margin of l. towards little finger, > rubbing. Swollen feeling in r., a tension on stretching it out and on clenching it.

Fingers.—Sticking anteriorly in ball of l. little; in last joint of r. thumb in morning in bed; on outer surface of l. index about 1 P.M.; behind back of r. thumb after dinner. Tearing in r. little; in r. thumb, then from wrist to middle of forearm, then bruised pain in upper arm; behind nail of l. thumb at 2 P.M., with sticking; in upper end of l. middle, < touch; in l. middle, > rubbing; in r. thumb, > rubbing, with feeling as if tendons would be contracted; extending up l. ring. Twinging in second joint of l. middle as if it would be forced asunder, in evening in bed. Pain in first joint of r. thumb as from dislocation. Paralytic pain in r. thumb and metacarpal bones; in second joint of l. middle, extending upward and downward. Acute periodic drawings in l.; painful D. in l.

Lower Extremities.—Thighs. Jerking (a misprint for itching possibly may have occurred in the original) on outer surface of r. in evening, burning after scratching. Stitching in nates; posteriorly in r. thigh, also at 4 P.M.; in r. natis, rather by anus, at 2.30 P.M.; in l. natis during dinner; deep in r. hip when standing, > moving about; on inner surface of l., < pressure; in r. hip extending forward; in r. hip extending backward. Pain in l. hip-joint as if dislocated, on motion. Jerking pain just above l. knee. Paralytic pain in l. extending below knee. Pain on inner side of middle of l., which on touch pains as if beaten. Bruised pain in middle; middle of l.; in gluteal muscles when sitting or touched; pain in middle on motion as if bruised or as if he had walked several miles.

Knee.—Trembling on walking in open air, > sitting. Unsteadiness on descending steps, as if they would give way. Jerking in bend of r. Sticking in l.; on inner surface of r.; in l. on stretching out leg. Tearing in l., then jerking T. in r. shoulder; T. in r., > rubbing. Tension after rising from a seat, > open air. Weariness after rising from a seat.

Leg.—Visible jerking in r. calf in morning in bed, > stretching out foot. Tearing on outer surface beneath l. knee; in lower part of tibia, with tension and feeling as if skin were pulled; extending down r. tibia; about r. tibia, extending to inner surface of calf; extending from l. calf to inner malleolus, > walking. Pinching outward beneath l. knee. Gnawing on upper part of r. tibia, extending into inner surface of knee. Intermittent beating pain in r. tendo-achillis at 4 A.M. in bed. Tensive pain in l. calf; on outer side. Paralytic pain in l., < motion. Pain as from stiffness in tendons of inner muscles of r. Heaviness when spinning, < r. Falling asleep of r. on motion.

Ankle.—Tearing in a spot beneath r. inner malleolus, > rubbing and walking, with burning. Sprained pain. Painful jerking on r. outer malleolus, then bruised pain on back of foot. Paralytic pain about l. inner malleolus. Weariness on motion, with lameness.

Foot.—Jerking on outer border of r. at 2.30 P.M., then sensation as if a worm moved about on external malleolus. Ulcerative pain in soles of heels on rising from bed, > walking about. Sprained pain in l. os calcis when walking. Contractive pain in r. plantar muscles. Weariness when standing after walking; W. > walking; W., with bruised feeling. Stiffness at 2.30 P.M., after rising from a seat, > walking. Falling asleep of l.; of r. when sitting; of r. on riding the leg over the other.

Toes.—Sticking beneath l. great. Tearing in r. second, > rubbing.

Skin.—Flea-bite on outer surface of l. upper arm. Itching pimples between chin and lip, the I. > scratching; above bend of r. elbow, not > scratching, afterwards an itching pimple higher up; burning P. between chin and lip; P. between chin and lip, painful on touch. Rawness between index, middle and ring-fingers, with cracks, and on putting hand into water burning, which was relieved when dry. Redness between index, middle and ring fingers, with vesicles which could only be felt, itching and after scratching burning. Itching vesicles on l. side near lower lip, not > scratching. Red boil in front of r. ear, with suppurative pain on touch.

Stitch like a flea-bite in nape, in r. great toe at 2.30 P.M. Tickling on l. wing of nose; on l. leg, not > scratching; posteriorly beneath l. heel at 2 P.M., > rubbing; here and there on face as from a hair. Feeling as if a hair were moving on r. cheek. Crawling on r. side of face; on l. sole; on forehead at 7.30 P.M., > rubbing; between l. thumb and index, > rubbing.

Itching on l. side of forehead; on r. frontal eminence; in l. brow; above root of nose; l. wing of nose; nose, < tip; on back near r. scapula; on inner margin of r. foot; in r. side of nose in morning; between shoulders at 3 P.M.; on r. natis after dinner; between shoulders, with crawling. Itching > scratching, on l. frontal eminence; in l. brow; in r. groin; on coccyx; on external surface of l. elbow; on r. leg; on l. calf, but returning. I. not > scratching, in l. lobule; between r. side of chin and lip; behind r. shoulder. I. not > rubbing, on forehead. I., then burning after scratching, on r. frontal region; in bend of l. elbow; on r. forearm. I. and after scratching a pimple, on l. forearm; burning P. on r. upper arm; itching P. on l. lower jaw, with burning after prolonged scratching.

Sleep.—Yawning; without sleepiness, also after dinner; with sleepiness and stretching; with chilliness; with shivering; then shivering and gooseflesh. Sleepiness; at 11 A.M., and after sleeping in an uncomfortable position it was impossible to rise and walk; in evening, with burning in eyes; in evening, it was difficult to rise in morning; early in evening; after dinner; in the house; irresistible, after dinner. Sleep sound and long; with sweat. Sleep from noon till 3 P.M. though he slept well the previous and succeeding nights. Sleep in evening, was awakened for supper at 7 P.M., he sat up and ate, but fell asleep again without speaking, after awhile he started in sleep, then jumped up high, stood up and walked to the middle of the room, with staring eyes and red face, at last he lay down without speaking and slept soundly till morning.

Sleeplessness till 11 P.M.; till 1 A.M., with tossing about; after midnight, with tossing about as if the bed were too hard. Difficult falling asleep. Uneasy S., with frequent waking. S. disturbed by excitement and flushes of heat.

Dreams lively and sad. Frightful, of fire, waking her; F., of fires or dead men. Heavy, anxious. That he was standing upon a high and not very secure ladder or upon a high scaffold, without being anxious. Vivid, but unremembered. Confused.

Fever.—Chilliness; in forenoon, with feverish taste; in afternoon on going into open air; in afternoon, with shivering through skin; at 2 P.M. in open air; at 3 P.M., and nose is icy cold; from 6.30 to 8.30 P.M.; in house at 9 P.M.; after rising about midnight; in the house; in open air; with flat taste; with pains in back; with heat in face, without thirst. Internal; and external from 2 to 4 P.M., with warmth of feet. Shaking C.; at 6 P.M., not > warmth of stove, > application of warm clothes to abdomen; in evening after walking in open air, not > warmth of stove; in the house. Shivering, with gooseflesh; on going into open air. Shivering in face and hands in open air. Agreeable coolness of head after the sweat. Coldness of feet at 7 P.M., with much thirst; C. of l. foot; feet in open air; feet, with warmth of upper part of body; feet, > open air, with heat in head and sweat on forehead.

Heat in afternoon, with burning of palms and thirst; H. from 2.30 to 3 P.M., with sweat; at 6.30 P.M., with sweat on face; at 8 P.M., > sleep, with thirst; in evening, > in bed, with thirst; with hot and dry palms, without thirst; with sweat on forehead and warmth in hands; with feeling as if it spread from shoulders. External H. before midnight. H. in flushes at 2 P.M., with thirst; in F., with anxiety rising from abdomen into head, with redness of face and warmth of forehead. Orgasm and stupefaction of head; O. up to abdomen and back, after breakfast, with heat and anxiety (in head).

Heat of head; with indolence and ill humor; of H. and hands, with sweat on them, then coolness; of H. and hands at 4.30 P.M., with sweat on them; in a sudden flush at 2 P.M.; of forehead, with sweat; on sinciput and hands, with sweat; about forehead at 1 P.M., then general, > open air; in middle of forehead, *then coolness as from a draught of air;* in face and forehead, extending down back, with warmth and redness of forehead and headache.

Heat in face, with redness; internally in r. cheek; H. in coccyx at 4 P.M.; creeping up back; under axillæ; internally in hands at 2 P.M.; suddenly on outer margin of l. hand; jerking burning on back of l. hand at 4 P.M.; burning about nail and ball of l. thumb; in l. thigh near pubis; in r. leg when spinning; in ball of r. great toe, > rubbing.

General sweat from 10 P.M. till morning, with weakness. Sweat and heat of face during dinner and about 1 P.M.; cold on forehead and face; cold and clammy on legs and arms.

Clinical.—Alternations of chills, fever and sweat in phthisis.

Ledum.

A tincture of the fresh herb of Ledum palustre, L., is used.

General Action.—Pains, gouty, in the joints of feet

and hands, shifting from place to place, involving also fibrous tissues in various parts. The smaller joints become swollen and the pains simulate true gout. Veins enlarge and venous engorgments result, with hæmorrhages from lungs, in eyes, etc. Papular eruptions on face and other parts. It has been found useful for stings of insects and penetrating wounds.

Allies.—Arnica, Kalmia, Dulcamara, Rhus, Puls., etc.

Generalities.—Pain in knees, l. wrist, l. side of occiput, after rising in morning; in lower part of l. leg, in r. knee, in lower part of l. upper arm, in first phalanx of r. third finger, in wall beneath r. nipple, < walking; **pains changed their location suddenly** (Puls.); *P. in bones of ankles, in knees, toes, bones of wrist, in evening when sitting, alternately shifting from place to place, alternating with drawing pain in calves, pressure in r. or l. frontal bone, drawing in toes, l. clavicle, muscles of arms, hip-joints, lumbar muscles, sticking in region of spleen and tearing in r. tibia.*

Bruised pain in whole body (Arn.), (with oppression in all limbs). Tearing rheumatic pains, < motion. Pressure and tearing pain, < 5 P.M., < rest, < knees, dorsal muscles, elbows, hands, temples and finger-joints. Drawing pains, < legs, with heaviness in knees and sticking in calf, even when walking; D. pains alternately in l. leg, r. knee, l. hip-bone, l. wall of chest, l. lower jaw and r. wrist. Pressive and drawing pains, < posterior and outer side of l. thigh and in muscles of l. forearm, when sitting. Pressive drawing pains in knees, inner side of upper arm, frontal bone, metatarsal bones, shoulder-joints, < evening and during rest. Drawing in l. tibia, on posterior margin of r. scapula, in r. deltoid at its insertion into humerus, in muscles along dorsal vertebræ, in r. parietal bone, r. toes, in soft parts above l. knee.

(Weakness after nocturnal emissions); W. when sitting, standing and walking, and after prolonged sitting pain in coccyx; with heaviness; sudden W. in evening, then shivering, with cool skin, general trembling of muscles, heat and heaviness of head, small and rapid pulse, the next night wakeful and restless, with confused dreams, frequent micturition, with cutting, pain in limbs, cranium and walls of chest, next morning early waking, weakness all day, shivering, sensitiveness of limbs and cranium to touch, pain and tearing in bones of legs especially, boring in bones of vertex, flushes of heat in sinciput, redness of face, stitches in throat, swollen tonsils, small, rapid pulse, ill humor. Faintness.

Aggravation during the day; *towards evening; of pains from* 5 P.M. *till lying down* (> night, except on waking); when sitting; during rest; cold, wet weather (Dulc., Rhus t.); of pains by wind and cold air; after two glasses of Malaga at dinner; on l. side. Amelioration of pains at night; A. after camphor.

Clinical.—General tendency to rheumatic inflammations, especially of the joints, with soreness of the muscles, without fever. Like Arn., it has marked tendency to ecchymoses and hæmorrhages, especially of bright red, frothy blood. It has been used as a local application for penetrating wounds, and for the stings of insects. As a rule, the pains of Led. are sticking, tearing and shifting; various parts of the body seem bruised. Slight injuries cause ecchymoses.

Mind.—Reason lost after prolonged intoxication. Unmanageable drunkenness. Passionate. *Discontentment with his fellow-creatures all day, at last amounting to misanthropy.* Inclined to anger and peevishness. Fretfulness; with uneasiness and irresolution; he went by himself and almost weeping, wished to die. Fear. Anxiety. Earnest all day.

Head.—Tearing, and in eyes, white of eye and conjunctiva inflamed, the T. in eye < lying, > sitting, lids agglutinated in morning and offensive moisture discharged from between them, with shivering in evening, then heat, nightly thirst, rumbling in abdomen, heat of head, rather internal than external, and sweat on back and in hair. Aching in morning sleep; A., with the intoxication; A. causing dulness; raging; as from a blow; brain painfully shattered by a false step; wandering A. Pain in brain like a weight, next day pressure in a spot in r. temple; like a weight in brain day and night, with slight interruptions. Drawing in bones after meals.

Confusion; < covering it, with pain in upper part of forehead. Stupefaction as in vertigo. Vertigo; when walking and standing; < stooping, on walking it increases to falling forward as in drunkenness, with general heat, < face, without thirst, with pallor of cheeks and forehead; with emptiness and drunkenness; *the head tends to sink back;* as if body swayed to one side when walking, always > standing still. Drunken feeling when walking in open air.

Forehead.—Sticking in brain beneath r. eminence. Tearing in bones; in morning. Boring above beginning of l. brow; in l. bone and l. temple; in l. side; coronal suture; extending through bone; downward to eyes and in balls. Drawing pain in l. side. Stupefying pain externally as after a debauch. Pressure; in bones; in bone above r. eye; with warmth. Drawing in bones; l.; above r. eye; with pressure and boring. Confusion in sinciput; with staggering when walking, < rising from stooping. Heaviness in sinciput; like stupefaction; in F., with heat in it and pressure in r. temple. Vertigo in sinciput.

Boring in l. temple; when reading, and in l. frontal bone. Pressure in temples; r.; < l.; below l.; in l., < evening; in T. and sinciput, with heaviness; P. inward in l. Pain in temples on touch. Boring in coronal suture. Pressure in l. side of vertex. Drawing beneath scalp of vertex and its sides, extending towards forehead.

Tearing in parietal bones; backward above ears; T. above r. ear, extending into cranial bone. Boring in r. parietal bone; in l. eminence; in upper part of l. side, then further forward in forehead. Pressure behind r. ear and in l. side of forehead; on l. side of head, with heaviness of head. Intermittent drawing in r. side. Tearing in l. side of occiput. Crawling itching on scalp and forehead.

Eyes.—Inflammation, with tensive pain. Stitches in l. towards inner canthus. Burning pressure, < evening, with agglutination in morning, with lachrymation during the day. Acrid lachrymation. *Pupils dilated;* contracted. Lids agglutinated; lids full of matter. Stitches in margins of lids towards inner canthi; S. in r. inner canthus. Itching in inner canthi. Pain behind ball as if it would be forced out. Tearing in bone above l. eye. Boring in r. lower orbital margin. Pressure on outer margin of r. orbit, < moving about. Vision flickering; (as in vertigo) on looking steadily at an object. Vision weak. V. of black floating points.

Clinical.—Ecchymoses of the conjunctiva. Intraocular hæmorrhages.

Ears.—Pressure behind r.; in bones and soft parts behind r.; in bone behind l. *Ringing or noise of wind. Roaring as of wind;* interrupted R. Dull hearing in r.; with feeling as if stopped with cotton, and as if he heard from a distance. Deafness, as if something were before drums.

Clinical.—Inflammation of the ear, with deafness, from getting cold, as from having the hair cut.

Nose.—Boring in l. bones. Pain at union of nasal cartilage with bone of l. side, < touch, with much thick mucus in l. nostril, so that it is difficult to get air through it, as from a swelling of mucous membrane. Burning pain internally, with soreness on pressure or blowing nose. Sneezing on account of tickling in l. nostril; frequent S., with increased mucus. Bleeding, bloody mucus in nose.

Face.—Pallor. Tearing in zygoma. Boring in zygoma; l.; in l., in frontal bone and above r. frontal eminence; in r. in evening, and in l. lower jaw; on upper margin of l. Pressure in r. zygoma. Drawing pain in middle, extending across forehead, vertex and occiput to nape. Drawing in l. half, across l. temple to forehead. Pustule on margin of upper lip, with burning itching, < scratching. Boring in l. upper jaw; l. lower; r. lower; r. articulation; r. angle of lower; in r. lower and in zygoma, also in evening; in l. angle of lower when sitting. Pain in jaw on both sides of nose; in r. joint; deep in angle, now r., now l. Pressure inward on l. lower jaw. Drawing in l. side of lower jaw.

Mouth.—Stitches in teeth, then tearing externally on r. side of face, head and neck, which disappears after more stitches in teeth, but returns from time to time, the attack ends with shivering, deep sleep and loss of hunger and thirst. Drawing pain in lower incisors, with coldness. (Pain in a lower and upper incisor.) Stitches through tongue; on forepart; in tip; beneath tip; in tip, with burning; S., with burning. Dryness of mouth on waking; D. of palate, with thirst for water. Salivation; causing nausea. *Sudden running out of water, with colic, waterbrash.* (Breath offensive.) Taste bitter.

Throat.—Swelling of a gland beneath chin, with pain on touch. *Soreness, with sticking.* Sticking when not swallowing, in forenoon, on sneezing there is only pressure in back part of throat. Scraping in evening. Sensation of a plug, obliging him to swallow, with feeling of a foreign body in throat, repeated on going to sleep in evening. Clogging sensation on waking.

Stomach.—Appetite lost; and if she eats feels immediately as if she had eaten too much, it oppresses and nauseates her. Desire to smoke in one unaccustomed to it. Aversion to smoking. Thirst during the day and in evening before sleep chill; (obliged to drink at night); for cold drinks, especially water; lost. Eructations; with loss of appetite and warmth in stomach; of air; of air, with pressure in pit of stomach; (bitter after eating). Hiccough.

Nausea; in morning; when he expectorates; during rest, < sometimes after eating; on walking in open air, with general sweat, < forehead; with musty taste; with salivation, yawning, cold hands and frequent chills over back; with weakness, sweat, that afterwards became cool, with cold hands and feet and creeping chills over back. Retching in morning after rising, with eructations, puffiness and straining in pit of stomach. Pain; in epigastric region, < pressure; in pit, < pressure; in pit, < retracting abdomen. Drawing in pit when eating, with pressure.

Abdomen.—Distention from air, with tasteless eructations. Rumbling. Movings. Emission of flatus. Sticking in muscles, with pressure between pelvis and l. lowest ribs. Cutting every evening; wandering C., < retracting walls of abdomen. Colic (cutting?), with flow of blood from anus. Pain deep in A., < pressure; P. as if intestines were crushed and weakened, a feeling as after a violent purge; P. as in dysentery; drawing P.

After walking in open air, pressure and tension extending from side towards shoulder across chest, a grasping in sternum, vanishing of hearing and vision, necessity to lie down, pallor, anxiety, cold hands and diarrhœa. (Feeling in l. side as if from overloading stomach a pressive swelling had appeared there.) Distention of upper, with pain. Tension in hypochondria on inspiring or holding the breath. Cutting in umbilical region, with retraction of walls of abdomen. Digging below umbilicus, with running of water from mouth like waterbrash. Pain in U. as before diarrhœa, extending to anus, with loss of appetite and cold feet.

Hypogastrium.—Sticking above hip; S. deep between l. ribs and crest of ilium. Boring in l. tuber ischii; in crest of l. ilium, < towards forepart. (Clawing as if in bladder.) Pain posteriorly in crest of l. ilium when walking. Pressure deep in pelvis, towards bladder, with urging to urinate; P. on upper margin of l. pelvis, as far as last ribs, < walking.

Rectum and Stool.—Stitches in rectum. Stool pasty; fæcal diarrhœa, with mucus; hard, scanty, delayed; mixed with blood; retained. Constipation.

Urinary Organs.—Urging; constant; all day, not at night; frequent, with scanty discharge; frequent all day, but no increase of urine. Stitches in meatus; tickling, in meatus. Voluptuous tickling in meatus. (Burning in urethra after urinating.) Micturition frequent; and much urine each time; infrequent and scanty. Urine is frequently retained, after passing it there is sticking. Urine reddish. (Urine yellow, with chalky sediment.) Urine increased; and light yellow. Urine scanty; and no stool during the day.

Sexual Organs.—Swelling of penis and the urethra seems swollen, he must press in order to urinate and the stream is very thin. Tickling of glans. (Itching of glans.) Excessive and constant erections. Emissions at night; without dreams; of bloody or watery semen. Menstruation too early; every fourteen days; increased.

Clinical.—Uterine hæmorrhage, bright red, frothy.

Respiratory Organs.—Stitches in larnyx; and tickling. Scraping in larnyx, with tickling and short dry cough. Pressure on sides of larnyx. Hoarse, raw, scraping feeling in trachea. Crawling in trachea, with rapid, impeded respiration. Cough only at night or in morning, with purulent expectoration. *Violent cough, with expectoration of bright red blood.* Cough without expectoration. Tracheal asthma. Dyspnœa when sitting; D. on ascending steps; D., with rapid breathing as from constriction of chest, with pain in sternum. *Breathing painful, impeded.* Heavy breathing on waking. Inspiration spasmodic, double, with sobbing. Cannot get the breath all day. On coughing loss of breath as if she would suffocate.

Clinical.—Cough, with bright red, frothy hæmorrhage from lungs. Hæmorrhage from the lungs, alternating with attacks of rheumatism.

Chest.—Stitches in walls and in arms; in last r. true rib; in morning; in r. in morning on inspiration; in places in r. wall in afternoon; in l. wall in evening; in walls, < l., in evening, not impeding respiration; between l. lower ribs on inspiration; in r. pectoral muscles on deep inspiration; in lower and anterior part of r. when walking, preventing deep inspiration; in l. lung, not < inspiration; intermittent, in walls, extending to sides of sternum, in morning; tearing, in side above pit of stomach on motion of arm and when sitting.

Spasmodic cramplike pain beneath short ribs and above hips towards evening, taking away his breath and preventing his rising from his chair alone. Paroxysmal pain in sternum like digging, rubbing and scraping. Pain on breathing as if something alive there caused uneasiness. Pain externally as if some one pressed upon a sore spot, < touch. Pain; in sternum; behind sternum; in l. clavicle; in places in l. wall; in places in r. wall; in places in wall, on sides of sternum; in upper part of l. side; in l. wall in afternoon; in pectoral muscles, < inspiration; deep internally at r. margin of sternum, between fourth and sixth costal cartilages on waking, < inspiration and hard pressure; in r. pectoral muscles, extending into upper arm; in upper part, impeding respiration. Drawing and pressive pains in muscles of sides and in lumbar muscles.

Constriction in afternoon, with cutting, as if middle of chest were constricted by a string, which takes away the breath; C. from eating rapidly; *asthmatic C., < moving and walking.* Pressure in and behind sternum; upon C. when walking; on sternum in bed, < moving about; on chest when sitting, with pressure behind seventh and eighth l. costal cartilages; at l. margin of sternum, between third and fifth ribs, extending into chest; P. outward a hand's breadth beneath r. nipple in morning in bed, < expiration. Drawing externally when walking and on inspiration, with stitches; D. in sides, < inspiration, with stitches.

Heart.—Pain deep in region. Palpitation.

Neck.—Pressure in lower vertebræ, < bending head far forward; frequent P. in l. muscles, momentarily > moving head. Drawing extending to r. shoulder. Stiffness of l. side; of r. muscles; of l. muscles, > moving head.

Back.—(Tearing.) *Painful stiffness, and in scapulæ;* in B. and loins after sitting. Stitches in muscles near first dorsal vertebræ; near dorsal vertebræ, < inspiration, with pressure. Tearing in l. scapula. Pressure in dorsal muscles; in lower angle of l. scapula; in r. scapula; in muscles of r. scapula; in muscles to right of dorsal vertebræ; between l. scapula and spine. Drawing pain in dorsal muscles. Drawing and pressive pain in muscles on sides of dorsal and lumbar vertebræ. Bruised pain beneath l. scapula.

Lumbar Region.—Stitches; in l. tuber ischii; intermittent, in muscles. Tearing in sacrum, extending into occiput, l. half of brain and l. jaw, < evening, with hot, red, bloated cheeks and inflamed eyes. Boring in sacrum. Pain; in vertebræ; to left of vertebræ; deep internally, to left of vertebræ; deep internally in sides of vertebræ; *after sitting;* in sacrum on rising from a seat. Drawing pain in sacrum when standing, > pressure. Drawing in sacrum, with stiffness of back.

Extremities.—Painful nodes *and lumps on joints. Trembling of knees (and hands) when sitting and walking.* (Tearing jerking in joints.) Stitches in ball of l. foot, above l. knee, above r. wrist, on dorsal surface. Tearing in r. elbow, lower part of l. calf and in r. knee; in l. ankle and in l. fifth metacarpal bone; in l. tibia, r. wrist, on outer side of l. thigh; sticking T. in joints. Boring below l. elbow and in r. ankle, when sitting.

Pain in various joints; in r. wrist, then in first joint of r. great toe; ankle and r. wrist; flesh of l. upper arm and above l. ankle; knees, wrist, above ankle, in muscles on inner sides of upper arms; external muscles of l. thigh and in muscles of r. upper arm; knees, great toe, joint of r. thumb, in fingers, after rising in morning; *knees and wrists in evening when sitting;* knees, tibiæ, ankles and shoulders, in evening during rest, afterwards in knees when walking; r. thumb-joint in cool air, then in r. great toe; < motion; *in joints, < motion;* in joints, > motion; l. shoulder, > moving arm, but immediately occurring in r. ankle and wrist, changing to heaviness of whole arm, < rest; first joint of l. thumb, and sticking drawing in r. metatarsal bones.

Paralytic pain in all joints on moving body at night in bed. Bruised pain in r. knee and in middle of l. forearm; in l. leg, above r. knee, in r. forearm, r. metatarsal bones and above r. wrist; B. and heavy feeling in knees, r. thigh and l. arm, often changing places. Pain like a pressure, compression and drawing, on inner side of l. upper arm, in l. ankle, anterior surface of l. thigh, in metatarsal bones. Drawing and pressive pains in r. toes and in l. shoulder when sitting; alternately in knees, shoulders, fleshy part of thigh, in legs, when sitting. Drawing pain above l. elbow, in l. tibia and l. metatarsal bones. Drawing in l. upper arm and lower part of l. thigh; l. upper arm and lower part of r. calf; on inner surface of l. upper arm, in l. ankle, on r. tibia; in all long bones of body on motion; *various parts and joints, < wine.*

Compression in muscles of l. upper arm and in ankles; in calves, forearms and lower part of legs; lower part of calves, on sides of tendo-achillis, in l. forearm, in shoulder-joint; in lower part of r. forearm, then in legs. Throbbing in affected joints, impeding motion. Weakness above l. elbow and in l. knee. Heaviness in l. arm, < elbows, < rest, with bruised sensation, afterwards the same in wrists and ankles; H. of r. arm, at times < shoulder or elbow, > moving the joint, then in l. knee and leg, even in bed after 11 P.M. some symptoms in limbs are felt. Heaviness and bruised feeling in l. arm, < elbow, < rest, then the same in wrists and ankles. Painful stiffness in l. wrist, elbow and knee. *Numbness and falling asleep;* N. and heaviness, with pain in bones. Freedom from symptoms when in motion.

Clinical.—Synovitis of knee, with great sensitiveness, trembling and numbness of the extremities on attempting to walk. Rheumatoid pains in the extremities, particularly < warmth of bed, lasting until midnight; the painful part becomes cold. Rheumatism of feet, with swelling and coldness. Great soreness of feet from taking cold, as from getting wet; effects of bruises of soles. The rheumatism of Led. generally affects the smaller joints, which become swollen, the pains < warmth of bed. In general, the rheumatism of Led. begins in the extremities and travels upward; it is rarely useful if the joints are hot and swollen (unlike Bry.).

Upper Extremities.—Desire to stretch legs. Weakness, with pressure in places, a kind of paralysis. Drawing extending from r. axilla into inner surface of upper arm. Pressure outward in l. axilla.

Shoulder.—Stitches below r. joint; in forepart of l. joint; in r. joint, < rest, with pressure in muscles extending over it; *on raising arm. Tearing in r. joint; < motion.* Pressure in joints; in r. joint; forepart of joints; *in joints, < movement;* P. and drawing in joints and in l. forearm; P. on r. joint. Bruised pain in muscles; paralytic B. pain in joints. Drawing in muscles about l. joint. Heaviness in joints on motion.

Arm.—Tearing. Pressure in places in r., with tearing and heaviness, < joints, in which the pain is < movement. Heaviness, < elbows.

Upper Arm.—Stitches on upper and inner side of r. Tearing in muscles of inner side; T. in r. humerus; in upper part, with pressure; intermittent, from lower part through elbow into upper part of forearm; intermittent in l., extending backward, < movement. Pressure in muscles; in muscles of r. and in forearm; above l. elbow; in upper part of l.; above r. elbow and along ulnar margin of l. hand; in middle on motion; in l., with heaviness; outward in r. Bruised pain in upper part of l. Drawing in muscles on inner side of r.; D. on inner surface of r. alternating with pressure in several joints and in upper part of r. wall of chest.

Elbow.—Stitches in bend of l. Sudden boring in bend of l. when arm was quiet and partly flexed. Pressing and twisting pain from l. through deep parts of forearm to wrist. Pressure; at sides of r.; in r., < motion. Bruised pain in l. E. and shoulder joint, then in r. wrist; in r., extending into upper part of forearm; in r., extending into forearm, and in first l. metacarpus. Drawing in l., with heaviness in l. arm, < elbow. Frequent weariness of E. and fingers, > moving joints, with bruised sensation.

Forearm.—Painful jerking in upper part. Tearing on anterior part of l. Pressure in middle of l. radius; in lower part of radius and ulna, extending into wrist and metacarpal bones; in l. forearm in morning, with bruised sensation. Drawing in r.; in lower part of bones of l. Tension in muscles of r. as if sprained. Compression in muscles of r.

Wrist.—Hard swelling on tendon of thumb at wrist, painful on bending thumb. Pressure anteriorly on l.; P. in r. in evening. Compression in r. and above l.

Hand.—*Trembling on taking hold of them and on moving them.* Sticking. Tearing; in first metacarpus. Boring in first r. metacarpus and thumb-joint; in first l. metacarpus in evening. Pressure in bones; r.; l. fifth; between first r. and wrist, < motion. Pressing asunder pain in l. Drawing pain in l. fourth and fifth; extending into toes. Drawing in first l. metacarpus; in l. palm; along surface of l. hand.

Fingers.—Stitches in first joint of r. thumb; beneath r. thumb-nail; in first joint of r. thumb and fourth finger during rest, with pressure. Tearing in first joint of r. index; in proximal joint of thumb, > moving thumb; in l. fingers, < joints, < moving them. *Boring in first joint of thumb; r., with stiffness.* **Pain in periosteum of phalanges on pressure.** Pressure in first joint of l. thumb; in r. finger-joints in evening; feeling in nail of l. third finger as if pressed upward, alternately more and less severe, with prickling in tip of finger. Drawing pain in extensor tendons of three l. fingers. Stiffness of r.; l.

Lower Extremities. — Reeling after rising from stooping.

Thigh.—Stretching. Tearing in l. from trochanter major; from hip-joints to ankles, < motion. Boring in l. trochanter major; and in tuber ischii; above r. patella; jerklike, in l. femur when sitting. Boring pushing pain in and behind l. trochanter. *Sprained pain towards posterior part of l., as if muscles were not in proper position, < walking or touch.* Pain in femora; in l. great trochanter and tuber ischii; in hip-joints and sacrum on rising from a seat; *in r. hip-joint,* < moving it; in muscles of r. thigh when walking, so that the knee gave way; jerklike, above r. knee and ankle; in periosteum when walking, sitting and when touched, as if bruised or as if flesh were torn from bones. Bruised feeling in l. muscles posteriorly when standing and walking, extending into knee. Drawing pain in posterior surface of l.; D. and pressive pains along posterior surface of l. when sitting; pinching D. pain in sockets of hip-joints, extending to posterior part of thigh. Drawing in external soft parts of r.; in l. hip-joint; from l. into knee. Pressure on anterior and outer part of middle of l. Posterior muscles feel paralyzed.

Knee.—*Cracking. Swelling when walking, with tension and sticking.* Sticking in l.; in r., < motion, with pressure. (Tearing); *in and below r., < motion.* Boring in r. to left of patella. Pain; in r. on motion in morning after rising; in l. in afternoon when sitting; in l. at night on waking; near r. side of l. patella, < motion; in l., with drawing; alternately in K. and ankles, suddenly appearing and disappearing; in l., extending into posterior and external soft parts of lower portion of thigh; *as if beaten or sore;* pain in front of patellæ as if beaten, when walking. Pressure in l. and on l. tibia when sitting in evening, with tearing; P. inward from l. patella in evening. Compression in l. Tensive pain in K. and heel when walking after sitting. Intermittent drawing. *Weakness; when walking, with tearing.* Stiffness; when walking; in l. K. and ankle when walking.

Leg.—*Swelling extending above calves, with tensive pain, < evening.* Jerking and weariness on bending them. Tearing deep in r.; in bones of l.; in lower and forepart of l. in afternoon; deep in r. in evening; in bones above l. ankle; below r. knee. Pain in bones of l., < lower part in forenoon when sitting; pressing asunder P. in r. when sitting; P. in outer part of l., especially drawing; drawing P. in outer and upper part of legs and r. thigh. Drawing; through l.; in l. fibula; in lower part of r. fibula; to above knees. Compression in muscles above r. external malleolus; in lower part of l. in evening. Heaviness. *Weakness;* > walking, in l., with pulling in tendon on back of l. foot. *Stiffness in morning.*

Tibia.—Tearing; along r.; on anterior surface of r. and above r. knee; in l. in afternoon, then in lower anterior part of both legs; along r. in evening. Stitches in r.; in l. T. and knee, < evening. Scraping on l. when sitting. Boring; in r. below knee; in l. above inner malleolus; in l. when walking, with drawing pain. Pain in r.; l. T. and calf; in upper part of l. when sitting, extending downward. Drawing in r. Weak feeling below r. knee.

Calf.—Cramp when lying at night, > rising, returning after lying down. Stitches. Pain in morning when awakened by a noise. Grasping pain extending down tibia. Cramplike pain. Drawing pain in l.; in lower part of l. Drawing in lower part of l. and deep in sole; in lower part, even when walking. Tensive pain when walking after sitting. Tension in lower part on walking.

Ankle.—Sticking. Tearing on inner side of l. **Sprained pain.** Boring in r. and at sides of l. tendo-achillis; in l. inner malleolus and metatarsal bones; in r. inner malleolus in evening in bed; in bones beneath r. inner malleolus when walking, and in first and second l. cuneiform bones; in r. and metatarsal bones, extending into toes. Pain; in l. external malleolus; and in tarsal bones; *in bones in morning, and in lower part of l. leg;* in r. external malleolus when sitting; in r. when sitting; in l. bones on standing up, at first < walking, then tearing in l. tibia; *above l. inner malleolus, < motion;* here and there in l., < motion; changing to other joints. Pressure as with a finger under l. Drawing in r.

Foot.—*Swelling; about ankles, with pain in ankles on stepping.* Stitches in l. sole; near inner side of l. sole when walking. Tearing on back of r.; in l. heel; towards outer margin of l. sole; in r. metatarsal bones; in l. metatarsal bones in morning in bed. Boring in l. heel; in r. cuneiform bones in morning. *Bruised pain under heel when walking. Pain in soles when walking as if congested with blood.* Pulling pain in outer margin, extending towards back of foot. Pain in l. metatarsal bones, extending into toes. *Pressure on inner margin of l.;* P. here and there; above r. heel; on back of r.; on inner margin and back of l.; on back of r. in evening; upon back of l. in bed; in sole, < walking; burning P. on forepart of r. sole. Drawing in l. sole; in metatarsal bones; on outer margin of l. sole and in muscles above r. patella when walking, with sticking; in r. metacarpus, extending into toes and into middle of ulna; in l. fourth and fifth metatarsal bones, extending into toes; sticking D. in r. metatarsal bones, extending towards toes. Weariness in l. sole, extending to thigh, with pressure, a kind of paralysis or paralytic pain. Stiffness, with chilliness and confusion of head. Gout reappears.

Toes.—**Ball of great soft, thick and painful on stepping.** *Stitches in great; S. in l.; in r. great; l. second and third; in tip of r. great; in joints of great; in first joints of great; in first joint of l. great and in ball of r. great. Tearing in l.; and in joint of r. great; in l., < under surface.* Cutting in l. at night in sleep. *Boring in first joint of r. great; in first joint of l. great; in r. great in morning. Pain in r.; beneath nail of r. great; in joint of r. great; in first joint of r. great; in joint of l. great when walking in morning,* and next morning on rising; in first joint of each great, at 9 P.M.; in tips of r. when sitting; where three last join metatarsus, < motion. Pressure on anterior part of l.; on proximal joints of l. Drawing; in joint of r. great; on under parts in evening; on flexor surface of r. when sitting. Drawing-asunder pains in r. Feeling as of a rush of blood towards great.

Skin.—Red round spots on inner sides of arms, on abdomen and feet. Bluish spots like petechiæ over whole body. Itching rash on wrist. Itching eruption in hollow of knee. Dry, itching tetter, with anxiety. *Pimples on root of nose;* under middle joint of index; on forehead, with boils; on back of foot, itching in evening; red, on l. temple and cheek; *red, on face,* with sticking on touch; red, itching, on back; *on forehead, hard and with a point; on forehead, as in brandy-drinkers, with biting itching on chest, red spots and miliary rash;* dry, like millet-seeds, on forehead, < in middle; like red millet-seeds, over whole body (except face, neck and hands), with itching during the day and only at times during the night, transiently > scratching. Painful red, moist place above anus, with biting, sore itching when sitting and walking. Boil on scapula. Chickenpox on chest and arms, which desquamates after five days.

Cutting burning pain in a spot above root of nose, suddenly ceasing. Sensitiveness like a burning in fold between wings of nose and cheeks, with redness. Stitches over whole body; over lower border of r. nasal bone; itching S. on several parts, > scratching, but returning worse than ever; itching S. and itching corrosion in several parts, < hips, thighs and upper arms, > scratching, but returning worse than ever. *Itching;* general; on knuckles of toes, on ankles and loins; on sides of abdomen and on arms, with biting and with burning after scratching; *corrosive I. on backs of feet, < scratching and in warmth of bed, > scratching feet sore;* burning I. on thighs at night, which on scratching becomes a burning and then disappears; general sticking I. Sticking-itching corrosion on upper arms, > scratching, but returning more violent than ever.

Clinical.—Papular eruption on face, < forehead, in habitual drunkards. Violent itching of whole body, < warmth of bed (urticaria).

Sleep.—Sleepiness; in morning, with inclination to lie down, anxiety and sickness. Sleeplessness till midnight; *S. and restlessness;* S. and constant starting up, if she closes the eyes she has fantasies while almost wide awake. Frequent waking and inability to sleep for some time. Restless sleep, with confused dreams; R. sleep at night, in morning in bed chill, then long sleep; R. and deep sleep, he lies upon the unusual side and cannot arouse himself in the morning.

Dreams uneasy; and that he is now in one place, now in another, busy now with one, now with another subject. D. of murder and violence in morning sleep. Full of anxiety of conscience, with profuse sweat. Full of shame, with sweat. Vivid, of misfortune; V. and voluptuous, with erections without emissions. Lascivious. Waking her and causing her to start.

Fever.—*Chill;* in morning in bed; in forenoon; on walking in open air, with sudden sweat; *with external coldness of limbs;* with febrile drawing in limbs; external, in morning; as if this or that part had been sprinkled with cold water. Shaking C., with thirst for cold water and heat in hard palate; (S. chill towards evening, with trembling, without thirst); *S. chill over back, with cold hands, hot cheeks and hot forehead.* Shivering, with gooseflesh, without external coldness; S. in back; in lumbar region; in back, < between shoulders, then < lumbar region, with cold limbs; in back at 9.45 A.M. and 2.30 P.M., with cold hands. Coldness in lumbar region; internally in legs, not externally, when sitting.

Heat in bed; on walking, with sweat on forehead; without thirst; in head, < forehead, with heaviness; internally in face, not externally; in back, head and cheeks; in hands, with distended veins; *in hands and feet in evening.*

Sweat and intolerance of bed-covers; S. all night; *general on waking, also with general itching; on hands and feet;* on palms during the day; on knees in morning; general, offensive, even the hair was wet; sourish on forehead when walking.

Leptandra.

A tincture is made from the fresh root of Leptandra (Veronica) Virginica, Nutt.

General Action.—An active cathartic, with feeble action on the liver.

Generalities and Mind.—Jaundice, with clay-colored diarrhœa, headache and the other symptoms usual in such cases. Languor; in morning. Gloomy; and irritable.

Head and Eyes.—Headache; < regions of causality; with frequent pains in bowels; with distress in umbilicus. Dizzy when walking. Frontal pain; on frequent waking at night; < walking; deep in cerebrum; deep in region of causality; < temples; with neuralgic pain in r. temple; with sensation as if hair were pulled; with aching in umbilicus. Eyes smarting; and sore; and aching; with pain in balls. Lids agglutinated in morning. Profuse secretion of tears.

Mouth.—Tongue coated yellow in morning; coated yellow along centre. Taste flat in morning; unpleasant in morning.

Stomach.—Great appetite; on waking at 5 A.M., > breakfast, with pain in epigastric region. Sour eructations of food at 10 A.M. Nausea on rising in the night, with deathly faintness. Aching in cardiac portion; in S. and umbilical region; in epigastric region; constant, in epigastric and umbilical regions, with intermittent cutting; burning A. in region of S. and liver. Aching burning in morning on rising, < 10 A.M., so that I cannot sit or stand still, > 9 P.M. Distress in S. and small intestines, with urging to stool and mushy fetid stool; constant D. in lower part of epigastrium and in umbilicus, with intermittent cutting; D., with burning, and in bowels; burning D. in epigastric and hypochondriac regions.

Abdomen.—Rumbling, with cutting and desire for stool. Aching; in morning, with heat and dryness of skin; preventing sleep after midnight. Distress in small intestines, with desire for stool, stool soft, fetid, black. Cutting near gall-bladder. Aching in lower part of r. hypochondrium; *near gall-bladder, with aching in umbilical region and rumbling in abdomen;* **in liver extending to spine, < region of gall-bladder.**

Umbilicus.—*Distress; with burning distress in back part of liver and in spine.* Aching; in region; in region all the afternoon; frequently at night, with rumbling all day; in region, with intermittent sharp pains; in region of U. and hypogastrium, also constantly with intermittent sharp pains, causing weakness and faintness; in region, then soft yellow stool; in region of U. and hypogastrium, < drinking cold water, *with aching burning in region of gall-bladder, chilliness along spine, urging to stool, > profuse black stool,* of the consistence of cream, containing undigested potatoes, *then hot aching in region of liver extending to spine, with chilliness along spine, then pain in whole abdomen, < umbilicus and hypogastrium, with rumbling and urging to stool, > profuse, black, fetid stool that ran out in a stream and could not be retained a moment.*

Frequent pains in umbilical and hypogastric regions at night, being up all night with a patient, stool running out in a stream at 3 A.M., then cutting in intestines, then distress in stomach and small intestines, then at 8 A.M. urging to stool, which could not be retained a moment, fetid, running out in a stream, containing much mucus, then pain in hypogastrium, distress in stomach and small intestines, with frequent pains in umbilicus causing faintness and weakness, with rumbling, at 10 A.M. stool that could not be retained, of water, much mucus and a little yellow matter, then pain in umbilicus, burning aching in whole abdomen, with rumbling and urging to stool, stool of water and mucus, then pain in hypogastric and umbilical regions, another profuse thin stool, with much mucus, then sleep from 3 to 5 P.M., on waking distress in whole abdomen and urging, stool profuse, watery, mixed with mucus, could not be retained, another stool of water and mucus, with part natural fæces, fetid, and at 6 P.M. another stool with much mucus, then cutting and distress in umbilical region, weakness and faintness, another stool at 9 P.M., profuse, could not be retained, then pain in bowels, the two next days no stool.

Hypogastric Region.—*Rumbling in morning, with distress and with soft, profuse, black, fetid stool, then pain in abdomen.* Aching in r. inguinal region, passing to r. testicle.

Stool.—Profuse, black, fetid, running out in a stream (compare Arsen.). Clay-colored diarrhœa. Mushy; and fetid; then weak feeling in bowels and rectum; second part, the first part natural. *At first hard, black and lumpy, then mushy.* Omitted.

Clinical.—It is occasionally indicated by black, tar-like, pasty stools, generally profuse and fetid. It has been used for pain in region of gall-bladder extending to spine, with chilliness and diarrhœa. Dysenteric diarrhœa has been reported cured.

Urine.—Acid before the proving, afterwards scanty, not affecting blue litmus paper, next day red, afterwards neutral.

Back and Extremities.—Aching in lumbar region; intermittent, sharp, with constant distress. Wrists lame in morning and aching, the pain lasting till noon, < l.

Sleep.—Sleeplessness.

Lilium Tigrinum.

A tincture of the fresh plant of the "Tiger Lily" is used.

General Action.—The provings of this drug have developed pressure, heaviness and symptoms of congestion of the pelvic viscera, especially in women. The ovarian pains are very marked. With the uterine and ovarian symptoms many reflex sensations are found, fluttering of heart, pain in back and extremities, etc.

Allies.—Pod., Aloes, Sulph., Pallad., Apis, Ign., Bell.

Generalities.—Emaciation and debility. Hysterics. Convulsive contractions of almost all muscles. Startings. Tremulousness; in morning on waking, with weakness; nervous, towards evening; trembling of knees, abdomen and lower part of back. Twitching sensations about head and in pectoral muscles. Shootings in various parts, < chest. Pain in all the flesh and bones; P. at night, next morning muscles feel bruised and soles so sore that she cannot walk, hands feel as if they had been pounded, every part sore, intolerant of pressure of the clothing; P. in small spots as from pressure with finger-tips.

Restlessness; at 5 P.M., < evening and after going to bed; at night; on lying down after being called out in the night, with miserable feeling, feeling as if everything were too hot; with desire to do something, but no ambition; restless desire to keep walking. Pulsation in all arteries; P. over body in afternoon, with sensation as if blood would burst through veins of hands and arms. Incapacity for mental or physical exertion. Muscles respond sluggishly to her will. Malaise. Weakness; all day, with vertigo on sudden motion; in forenoon, with irritability; in afternoon, with heat; after diarrhœa; with slowness and forgetfulness; with trembling of bowels. Faintness in afternoon; *F. < in a warm room or after being on the feet a long time;* F., with cold sweat on feet and backs of hands. Numbness in various parts.

Aggravation every evening; at night; from 5 P.M. till 8 A.M., then amelioration till 5 P.M. again; as soon as she gave up active control of herself, that is, tried to sleep; A. of pains after moving. Amelioration from a free loose stool at 8 A.M.; A. in a warm room; in open air, in spite of chilliness; from sitting, standing or walking; when she is busy.

Mind.—Delirium, with startings. Excitement at night, with weeping, and feeling as if she were two persons. Wild feeling after keeping quiet; W. feeling at night, as if she would go crazy and no one would care for her, thoughts of suicide and sleeplessness. Everything seems unreal. Overactive; and feeling as if two individuals, afterwards perceptive and reflective faculties benumbed. **Hurried feeling; as of imperative duties, and inability to perform them, during sexual excitement**; yet cannot do much, feels discouraged; and keeps walking fast as by instinct; aimless hurry and motion, with sleeplessness, desire to have some one talk to her, felt as if she should die and did not care if she did. Inert; yet does not want to sit quiet, restless, yet does not want to walk, is cross.

Depression of spirits; *and inclination to weep, with apprehension of suffering from some terrible internal disease, already seated;* < night, with diarrhœa in morning, feeling of slowness and inability to get at her work; with difficulty in expressing her thoughts, of remembering, of selecting words, with fear of insanity. Apprehension of moral obliquity alternating with sexual excitement. Want to swear one minute and to tell a lewd story the next. Impatient. Irritable; in morning on waking; in evening. Dissatisfied with what she has and envious of others. Do not want to be pleased, do not care to talk or read. Vexed with everybody, disliked to be spoken to. Desired to be alone, did not want the trouble to answer questions. *Aversion to being alone, yet no dread*, tranquil, liked to see others and hear them talk. Dreads speaking lest she should say something wrong, yet wants to talk. Taciturn. Disposed to muse. Undecided, must depend on others. Nervous; and irritable, yet jolly.

Mistakes in speaking, uses wrong words. Inability to apply mind. Stupid feeling. Obtuseness in afternoon, cannot find the right word, forget what I want to say. Forgetful.

Clinical.—A large number of hysterical symptoms have been noted, associated with uterine derangements; for example, dread of insanity, great melancholia, with feeling that she is incurable. Religious melancholia, etc.

Head.—Darting pain in different parts. *Aching;* in morning; at 8 A.M., < fresh air; every evening; towards night, with increased pulse; at night; on waking; < walking in open air, > sunset, with heaviness as if too full of blood, blowing of blood from nose, desire to support head with hands; hot P., > 10 P.M. by frequent sneezing. Pressure outward; as if contents would issue through eyes, ears, etc. Fulness, < over eyes. Crowded feeling, and in face. Heaviness. Dulness in afternoon; D. after reading and writing, < after going to bed, with pain. Muddled, > speaking. Absence of feeling. Intoxicated feeling in afternoon, with staggering forward. Dizziness; at 8 A.M., especially in eyes; < hot, close room, > fresh air, with faintness and blurred vision, but cool air causes chilliness.

Forehead.—Neuralgia; over l. eye, extending to vertex. Burning stinging, with feeling of an elastic band over it; pricking in evening in a warm room, with feeling of a rubber band from temple to temple. Digging in angle between F. and l. temple, extending into orbit, in morning after rising, causing winking and spreading over l. half of brain. Sharp pain over l. eye in forenoon; at 6 P.M., > sleep. Pain; r.; *over eyes;* < over l. eye; morning and evening; at night, < morning; over l. eye, < motion and open air in afternoon, < l. side, < evening, with lachrymation of l. eye; with heat; extending through head, < l. side; over brows, extending to eyes, with heat; in sinciput, moving continually to occiput, l. side, concentrating in l. temple. Blinding pain after 5 P.M., changing to occiput and extending down neck, leaving a muddled feeling in head, weakness and desire to lie down. Hot pain in evening, < over l. eye, returning next day between 5 and 6 P.M., < r. side, afterwards again in evening in a warm room, with lachrymation; H. pain between 6 and 8 P.M., with prostration; in F. and eyes in evening; in sinciput. Painful drawing through F. and eyes. Heavy pain in F. and temples, < noon, passing to occipital protuberances, lasting all night. Outward pressure. Bursting sensation in frontal and temporal regions of brain, > pressure. Fulness in morning on waking, < l. side, with heaviness in it and unrefreshed feeling. Sore feeling in F. and eyes as if beaten.

Temples.—Twitching in l. during the day. Shooting in r. passing over to l., causing heaviness in front of head. Neuralgia in r. Pain < pressure; P. in l. in forenoon, < walking, extending into forehead, with vertigo; alternately in r. and l. in morning, < towards evening; paroxysmal, from l. over ear to occiput, with frontal pain, < over l. eye; heavy, in l., with enlarged feeling in head.

Vertex.—Pressure and a crazy feeling, so that she cannot write her symptoms.

Sides.—Paroxysmal neuralgia in l., next day head weak and confused. Shooting in r. Pain in r.; in l. in afternoon; deep in l., with uneasiness; in l. side, temple, parietal bone and malar-bone, > motion and occupation; pulsating, in l., < motion and noise, > lying; heavy, in l., with malaise; heavy, in l., becoming pulsating after noise or jar. Grumbling in r. and in teeth. Dulness of r. increasing to pressure, inclining head to left. Tenderness in l. side of head, forehead and temple, where heat of sun had caused congestion.

Occiput.—Pain; and over eyes; screwing P. in l. protuberance, with drawing pain on l. side of nucha, the latter increasing in bed to burning as from applied electricity, and lame and tired feeling in whole neck.

Eyes.—Wild look. Dull injection in morning. Pressure in r. Pain extending back into head, < night; burning P. from gaslight. Heaviness, with dim vision. Burning after reading or writing, with weak feeling. Feeling as if full of tears. Lachrymation in afternoon; L. of l. eye. Lids agglutinated. Inflammation of r. outer canthus extending to inner canthus. Raw feeling in r. inner canthus, < cold, damp air. *Vision dim; and confused, with disposition to cover eyes and press upon them;* V. as through a veil at 8 A.M. Blurred vision in afternoon; B., *with heat in eyes and lids.* Muscæ volitantes.

Clinical.—It has been found a valuable remedy for certain forms of asthenopia, especially the asthenopia of astigmatism. (In a prover, who was hyperopic, it removed a symptom of astigmatism, *i. e.*, turning the head sideways to see clearly.)

Ears and Nose.—Neuralgia in r. ear. Rushing sounds in ears after going to bed. Rubbed her nose violently. Nose stopped. R. nostril nearly closed, membrane of both nostrils pale. Nasal discharge of thin, clear mucus; profuse D. of yellow mucus.

Face.—Congestion in forenoon. Flushed; in afternoon, < forehead, with heat and with pricking in skin of forehead; l. cheek red in morning on waking, and externally hot. Pain in r. cheek (malar?) bone, with stoppage of r. nostril and feeling in head as before a cold; P. in l. cheek, extending into ear and temple; in r. jaw, with elongated feeling in teeth.

Mouth.—Darting pain from l. teeth to ear. Neuralgia from l. upper teeth to ear. Grumbling in hollow teeth. Tongue coated yellowish-white in patches. Mouth and throat feel coated on waking in night. Saliva abundant. Bloody taste in afternoon; peculiar T.; foul, > eating.

Throat.—Enlargement of r. tonsil, with exudation. Soreness and dryness. Feeling of a lump, with pulsations when lying.

Stomach.—Appetite great, especially for *meat;* great for dinner and supper; great, as if *in back*, extending to occiput and over vertex. Desire for sour or sweet dainties alternating with disgust for food. Appetite lost; for breakfast. Aversion to coffee; and bread. Thirst; then stupidity and despondency, then the severe symptoms. Eructations. Hiccough. Nausea; from the usual cigar, with waterbrash; with inability to vomit; with pain in back; with fulness in abdomen, < across hips and in region of uterus; with sensation of a lump in centre of chest moved down by empty swallowing, but ascending after the effort was over; constant, with frequent hawking of mucus; coming and going suddenly; sweetish, < eating, with fulness in abdomen. Vomiting of chyme, then of yellow mucus, the same as nasal discharge, at last bloody vomiting.

Distention, with eructations and emissions of flatus; flatulent D. of S. and abdomen in evening, with rumbling. Sensation of a hard body rolling around in it, > night. Fulness after eating, with pressure upward. Heaviness. Discomfort in S. and abdomen after 2 P.M. Empty feeling in S. and abdomen. Faintness at epigastrium, with tasteless eructations.

Abdomen.—*Distention;* in forenoon, and of chest. Distended feeling after morning stool and after eating; feels D., but is not. Flatulency; in morning, with bloated feeling in abdomen after stool. Flatulent movements. Rumbling; at night. Emissions of flatus; violent, at night. Cutting at 8 P.M., > Nux. Griping; after diarrhœa; at 3 P.M., < till evening, then free bilious stool, then acrid feeling and irritation in anus and rectum, next day symptoms > free stool, then acrid smarting in anus, and at 8 A.M. again griping, with heat and pain in and across forehead at 5 P.M., < evening and night, as before > 8 A.M. by a loose stool, then irritation as from a hot acrid spray in anus and rectum, then every morning after rising diarrhœa and the acrid feeling in rectum and anus. Pain all night, < r. side, with rumbling; P. > soft dark stool. Grumbling. Dragging downward, extending to organs of chest. Soreness; in morning on pressure; of muscles just before stool, > during stool. Burning in A. and ovaries in morning. At night sensation as before diarrhœa. Trembling sensation, with coldness; T., with weakness; T. and weakness of A. and anus. Discomfort; < r. side.

Bubbling in r. hypochondrium. Lancinations from l. hypochondrium to crest of ilium. Sharp pain between r. hip and false ribs in forenoon, < deep breathing, ceasing suddenly; in r. H., < motion. Rumbling in l. side. L. side sore to pressure. Heaviness in l. side.

Hypogastrium.—Rumbling, < r. side. Bloated feeling around hips and in region of uterus. Stinging in l. groin or ovarian region, with fulness and voluptuous itching in vagina. Griping as before diarrhœa, with restless, weary feeling, then four loose stools, lasting three days, with languor. Cramplike pain from os pubis through to rectum in morning on waking, > stool. Intermittent sharp pain near bladder. Pain and heat; P. in r. iliac region, > motion; burning P. from groin to groin. Drawing in l. groin; in r. groin after 2 P.M.; painful, about l. groin, extending to pubis. Feeling as if menses were coming on, two weeks too soon. Trembling sensation in pelvis, extending down thighs.

Bearing down pains in hypogastrium, < walking, with weight low down in vagina; bearing down > walking in open air and riding, **with constant desire for stool,** *but with every effort at stool only urine was discharged, sensation as if a hard body pressed backward and downward against rectum and anus, the desire for stool < standing* (see Pod., Sulph., Aloes); in pubes and genitals, < from 3 to 5 P.M., > before 8 P.M., with burning and with pressure on bladder, urine scanty and high-colored, she could urinate every quarter of an hour; in pelvis, < afternoon and till midnight; in pubes after supper. *Pulling downward and backward from anterior superior spinous processes of ilia. Sensation in pelvis as if everything were coming through vagina; this dragging is felt as high as stomach and shoulders, < standing, not > lying, with disposition to press hypogastrium upward, next day < riding, third day when walking sensation as if everything were pressing down in pelvis, so that she inhales forcibly in order to draw up the chest and relieve the pelvis.*

Rectum and Anus.—Pressure on r.; and on bladder; urging, then *pressure downward in abdomen and anus when at stool*, feeling as before diarrhœa, but with every effort only scanty urine could be discharged. Anus stiff and painful, with painful drawing through forehead and eyes. *Pressure in perineum.*

Stool.—Diarrhœa in morning, with acrid smarting, then weakness and trembling; *every morning on rising, with griping in abdomen and rasping in anus and rectum;* in morning on rising, with acrid smarting of whole alimentary canal; after eating, with flatus; dark brown, frequent, the first hurrying her; bilious, copious, sudden and peremptory, every day after dinner, *with burning in rectum and anus*, and tenesmus, then exhaustion. Several S. during the day, alternately solid and loose, with constant urging from a feeling as if something pushed against the anus anteriorly, next day constant tenesmus and every half hour a small lumpy, diarrhœic stool, with wind and with burning in urethra. *Constipation.* Hard and dark, then heat in rectum and anus and pain in abdomen. Dark and offensive; and large; and powerful, in morning on rising, then acrid sore sensation extending into middle of bowels. Yellow, afterwards bloody. Two in one day. Difficult. (Compare symptoms of stool with Pod., Aloes and Sulph.)

Urinary Organs.—Constant desire, *urine scanty, then smarting and tenesmus;* constant D. at night. **Frequent desire through the day, with scanty discharge and irritation and smarting in urethra after every discharge; she could urinate every quarter of an hour,** *in afternoon, urine high-colored and scanty* (Staph., Pallad.); *frequent D.* in latter part of night and early morning, *each discharge scanty, then smarting burning in urethra,* urine milky, on cooling a thick reddish sediment. Burning in urethra; *after micturition, with acrid feeling.* **Frequent micturition; during the day, with smarting in urethra during micturition;** F. at night; F. at night, then acrid smarting about urethra.

Urine.—Milky in morning; and thick, soiled in appearance, scanty, with frequent desire, after micturition soreness and heat in urethra. Clear and white. More like boiling oil than water. Of strong odor. Copious; and dark; and light-colored, with whitish sediment; with red sediment. Scanty and clear. None. Phosphates increased, and odor strong.

Sexual Organs.—Testes swollen and tender to touch; sore in morning, and heavy; intermittent neuralgia inferiorly and posteriorly in l. Desire increased; and prostration from coitus, but irritability from suppression of desires. Emission towards morning.

Female.—Bearing down, with feeling as if all internal parts were pulled outward or downward from breasts and umbilical region through vagina, with irresistible desire to press hands against vulva. Tenderness, with feeling as if internal organs were swollen, with smarting and irritation of labia and heat as if parts were inflamed. Itching of labia, with smarting and with uneasiness of the part, sharp pain extending up vagina. Pressure in vagina, with pain at top of sacrum extending to hips. *Thin acrid leucorrhœa, leaving a brown stain,* < afternoon and till midnight, > morning, afterwards returned and produced rash and swelling.

Uterus.—*Low down, fundus tilted against bladder, the os pressing upon rectum. Anteversion, with neuralgia, < touch, motion or jar, or weight of clothes.* **Weight, with feeling as if all pelvic contents would press out through vagina; if not prevented by pressure with the hand or by sitting down;** *bearing down in region, with distress as from approaching menstruation.* Pain in region. Irritation; when at a lecture, with desire to hit the lecturer, > evening, but then desire to swear, to think and speak of obscene things and to strike persons.

Ovarian Region.—Shooting in l. and bearing down when standing, > sitting down. Stinging darting pain all day. Tearing extending down sides of hypogastrium. Cutting in l. in evening and night, extending across lower part of abdomen, > gentle rubbing with a warm hand. **Sharp pain.** Grasping pain in l. and in l. groin, with pain in r. hip extending down thigh. *Pain in r. and in back;* P. when walking, < l., extending down anterior and inner aspect of l. thigh, as if it would be impossible to step, with constant necessity to extend and flex the limb on account of restlessness, at length she went to sleep on back with knees and thighs flexed; *aching and burning pain < r.* (Apis); P. and feeling like coals, afterwards the pain in r. increased till it seemed as if a knife were inserted into the ovary and ripped down groin and anterior part of thigh, the pain extended over lumbo-sacral region and to r. hypochondrium, > pressure on ovary; oppressive P. in r., < deep inspiration and motion (Pallad.). Drawing pain in l., > 10 A.M. by gentle pressure. *Gnawing dragging in r., < walking* (Pod.), with feeling as if something were shaking loose whenever the r. foot was planted firmly. Weight in l. *Soreness on pressure, < r.* (Pod., Pallad.); l., with at times darting to groin and to pubes in front; l., the pain grasping and extending across lower part of abdomen, the pain > rubbing and moderate pressure. Constant irritation.

Menstruation.—Freer than usual, relieving the headache, after flowing twenty-four hours ceased for twelve, then recurred. Not one-fourth as much as usual, then profuse, acrid, bright yellow leucorrhœa. Delayed, scanty and of short duration. Ceased as soon as she ceased to move. Recurred after two weeks, a slight, dark, thick discharge, smelling like lochia. Discharge of bright blood from vagina (for the first time in two years), with heavy pain and weakness in loins.

Desire increased (in a woman); > during physical effort, increasing until suddenly ended by an orgasm, during these attacks a hurried feeling as of imperative duties and inability to perform them, afterwards mental depression and apprehension of moral obliquity, then sudden return of the sexual excitement, this alternation lasted more than four months; sudden excitement, with disposition to use obscene language, then sluggishness and despondency, then hurried feeling of being impelled to work without herself desiring to work.

Clinical.—Most of the symptoms of this drug seem to be referred to the sexual organs of women; it causes severe uterine neuralgia and feeling of heaviness and pressure in pelvis, especially pressure against the rectum, with ineffectual efforts to evacuate the bowels; these symptoms have repeatedly pointed to its use in retroversion of the uterus. It has proved valuable, at least as a palliative, in some cases of chronic metritis, and curative in many cases of prolapsus and of both anteversion and retroversion, particularly with the pressure against the rectum. With the rectal symptoms it has been prescribed for dysentery, with tenderness over the ovarian region, etc., it is also valuable for troubles in the bladder with the same symptoms. The desire to press upward against the vulva or to hold up the abdominal walls is similar to the symptoms of Sepia, but in Lilium there is generally much more tenderness and more shooting pains. Very free leucorrhœa, often excoriating, with distress on urinating. With the uterine displacements and ovarian pains we very commonly find palpitation and numerous nervous symptoms about the heart, as if the heart were grasped, as if it contained too much blood, tremulous feeling, etc., etc.; sometimes terrible pain running up the back to the vertex, spasmodic contractions of muscles, etc., etc. The ovarian symptoms should be compared with those of Palladium, Pod. and Apis.

Respiratory Organs.—Voice could not be controlled when singing. A single dry cough. Dry hacking cough in evening, > open air. Short breath; after 2 P.M., with oppression; in evening and night, with frequent inclination to sigh; when walking, < ascending stairs. Hard breathing at night, with frequent desire to take a long breath. Desire to take a long breath, with frequent sighing, which seems to come from lower part of abdomen.

Chest.—Sticking in l. mamma, with drawing extending to shoulder and neck. **Sharp and quick pain in l., with fluttering of heart**; S. pain in l. mamma. Sharp twinges in l. in morning, then drawing extending to clavicle. Cutting in mammæ at night, > change of position, extending from l. M. to scapula and to spine; C. in l. mamma at night, extending to scapula, < lying on that side. Crampy pain in l. mamma and shoulder. Sharp pains through r. lung, < open air. Fine pains in r., sometimes gnawing, with lameness and soreness of muscles and desire to stretch the parts, the lameness extending through to r. scapula, next day the gnawing and fine pains increased and extended over to the side. Pain in l.; and at shoulder; in l. mamma in morning; in l. mamma and under l. scapula in evening and night; in mamma at 10 P.M. after lying on l. side, with heaviness in it and grasping sensation extending to l. scapula and down that side to lumbar region; in l. mamma and side, < lying down, with constriction and oppressed breathing; under sternum, towards middle lobe of r. lung, > pressure and sighing; in l. mamma, with drawing in l. axilla and shoulder; in l. mamma, passing under scapula to spine. Sore pain in upper part of breast.

Constriction; a hand's breadth below l. mamma; in l. at 2 A.M., extending to r. side, > change of position, but lasting till after rising in morning, with sharp pain running to throat, clavicle and l. axilla; in l. at 6 P.M., < lying down; in lower third, < towards morning, with oppressed breathing; with feeling as if he would suffocate, but as if it would be relieved if the blood shut up in the heart could be discharged, slightly > deep sighing; under l. floating ribs, extending to neck and l. scapula. Oppression at 8 A.M., with heat, a kind of ebullition, must go into the open air for relief; O. < in evening, with congested feeling; in lower third at night, with oppressed breathing towards morning; > sighing. Tightness; of l. in evening. Weight. Full feeling, and in abdomen. Congestion in afternoon; during the chills, with constriction and feeling as if it might be relieved by letting out blood; feeling of C. if the desire to urinate is not attended to. Hot, congested feeling. Nervous feeling in l.

Heart.—Twitchings around; in forenoon. **Pain**; < exercise; < stooping, leaning forward or bowing, in afternoon, < *lying down at night*, > morning and forenoon; sharp pain; paroxysmal sharp pain, leaving general weakness; sharp pain in apex, > rest, with a hurried, forcing feeling, faintness and fluttering, as if she must sit still, feeling as if she must breathe quickly, yet she does not; quick pain, with labored breathing when walking rapidly or ascending steps. *Pain as if grasped, waking him suddenly* (Cact.); the grasping gradually relaxed, *interrupting pulsations of heart and breathing*, > rubbing and pressure. *Heavy pain.* Heaviness; all afternoon; < night in bed, with palpitation when lying on l. side. Fluttering sensation after walking, this with other symptoms > busying herself.

Fluttering, with sharp and quick pain in l. chest. Weak action in afternoon. Palpitation; from slight exercise; in bed or during siesta, with beating of arteries. Intermittent action, after every intermission a violent throbbing, causing involuntary catching of breath, at the same time rush of blood through carotids to head, causing heat and crowded feeling in head and face.

Pulse.—Rapid. Small and weak. Irregular, increased by slight motion. Circulation weak, P. at wrist imperceptible on slight compression, sphygmographic tracings very low, but regular.

Neck.—Pain in nape, with constriction. Soreness in cervical and occipital muscles, < thirst.

Back.—Pain; in evening, > after midnight; with nausea; between scapulæ; sore, in region of scapula; in lower dorsal vertebræ as if back would break. Soreness of spine, with stiffness; < lumbar region.

Lumbar Region.—Shooting across. Gnawing at night, < bed. Sharp pain at night, extending over r. hip to umbilical region, temporarily > rubbing. *Pain; in sacrum; in lower part of sacrum; in sacrum all day; in morning on rising, > evening; in afternoon and evening, and in sacrum; at night, occasionally transferred to between scapulæ in morning; in sacrum, < standing, with pressure downward in hypogastrium; between hips, not much > lying*, with pressure downward at anus; across lumbo-sacral region, with pressure upon rectum; in spine, spreading to kidneys; as if it would break, on bending forward. Heavy pain and weakness. Drawing pain in sacrum in morning, < moving; D. pain near r. hip on changing position in bed, < rising up. Pulling upward and forward from tip of os coccygis.

Extremities.—Pain in second joints of fingers and in ankle, < jolting of the horse; quick P. in ring fingers and corresponding toes. Out-pressing sensation in hands, arms, feet and legs in early part of night.

Upper Extremities.—Tearing from l. shoulder to hand; paroxysmal, from l. shoulder to elbow. Crampy pain in l. shoulder and mamma. Trembling of l. arm, with weakness. Pain in r. arm and wrist. Tearing in muscles of l. upper arm. Pain in r. wrist, with weakness of the part in morning. Trembling of hands. Pricking in hands and fingers in morning. Hands and arms stiff and hot as if parched; r. hand and arm stiff and painful, > after 8 A.M.

Fingers.—Cramp. Pricking in tips at 5 P.M., with heat of palms; P. extending up arms, with sensation as if blood would press through the veins, which lasted into the night. Pain beginning at tip of index, as from an electric current, with throbbing of the pulse; sensation of an electric current beginning at tip of index, extending to other fingers and up arm, in l. at 5 P.M., then in r., with cold feet during the time. Stiffness; of r. at 5 P.M., with cramp in middle finger and up arm.

Lower Extremities.—Staggering; when walking, with inclination to fall forward. Joints seem to lack synovial fluid, can almost hear the crepitus. Quick pains. Lassitude, < fleshy parts.

Thigh.—Intermittent stitches in r. hip-joint; through the day. Boring in r. hip-joint, with stiff feeling in muscles of thigh. Sharp pain in inside of l. thigh, over femoral artery, two inches below Poupart's ligament. Catching pain through r. hip and down outside of r. thigh, < sitting up. Pain in r. hip and down thigh; in l. thigh when moving, with flatulency and lameness in ankles; intermittent pain in a spot on inner side of middle of l. Drawing pain in r. hip, extending down outside of thigh, > moving limb. Soreness in r. hip-joint, < thirst. Lassitude.

Knee.—Trembling. Sharp pain in a spot on inside, extending towards front, at connection of patella with tendon of rectus muscle. Grasping pain. Pain; all day; when walking, with weakness of them, also < ascending an eminence. Heavy pain after lying down; H. pain extending to ends of toes.

Leg.—Cramp in legs and feet after morning stool. Stinging below r. knee at 5 P.M. Darting pains in evening, disappearing as suddenly as they came. Pain, causing her to twist and turn; P. below knees, suddenly shifting from place to place. Rheumatic lameness and pain in l. when walking. Heavy; and full feeling. Weakness. Heavy tired feeling, with shooting from groins down inner side to knees.

Pain in ankles, < motion; P. in A. extending to toes. Neuralgia in foot; r., and toes. Boring on top of l. foot. Pulsation in feet. Feet tender and ankles swollen. Cramp in l. toes at 5 P.M.

Skin.—Tingling in legs. Formication below knees. Itching of calf; in r. temple in evening; on upper part of chest and arms, with itching rash about forehead and around borders of hair; of hands, as from nettles; burning I. in the swell of deltoids, transiently > scratching. Skin of abdomen at intervals felt stiff and stretched. Numbness on pressure.

Sleep.—Yawning and stretching. Sleepiness; in evening. Sound sleep, but sudden waking three times to urinate. Sleeplessness; after 2 A.M.; after being aroused by anything. Restless sleep; and full of unremembered dreams; with frequent waking as from fright. Frequent waking. Sleep broken by disagreeable dreams, arose earlier than usual unrefreshed. Dreams all night; laborious; frightful and laborious; unpleasant; lascivious, towards morning, with emission; lascivious and exhausting; queer, half-waking, with heat all night, things occurring at short intervals appeared as if at long intervals.

Fever.—Chill; in evening, then diphtheritis; towards evening, causing constriction of heart, extending to beneath scapulæ, heart feels as if squeezed in a vise, all the blood seems to have gone to heart, causing a feeling as if I must bend double, I can hardly walk straight, and the heart shakes with the cold; sudden C., with fulness of head. *C. running downward from face,* with congested and constricted feeling in chest, as if too narrow and as if it might be > letting out blood; over face in forenoon, then fever, congestion to chest and twitching around heart; running over face, with hot congested feeling in chest; congestive, beginning in face and extending downward, in forenoon in open air. Chills in back, < going to bed at night, with hot flushes towards morning; down back; in back at night on going to bed, as if cold water were poured over it; C. creeping down back every night on going to bed; C. creeping down back, then violent beating of heart when lying on either side and throbbing of carotids, preventing sleep. Cold feet; and hands; C. hands from any excitement; outer side of l. leg, also as from a wind.

Heat; in afternoon, with lassitude; internal and external; of head; in back; in hands; hands and feet; hands after 2 P.M.; limbs at night; hands all night, with sweat; arms and legs in early part of night, with pulsation in bloodvessels and sweat of palms; in hands, arms, feet and legs at night, with desire to put them out of bed; in palms and soles at night, extending up limbs, with restlessness; in palms and soles, extending over limbs, < evening and after going to bed, > cool air, with general restlessness; in lower limbs, with restless movements; in hands, arms and lower limbs, with general restlessness and feeling as if blood would burst through veins.

Sweat in axillæ, < r. Cold, clammy, on limbs; on hands and feet.

Lithium.

Pure Carbonate of Lithium is triturated for use.

General Action.—In a general way its action is similar to that of the other alkalies, but it is a more powerful diuretic.

Allies.—The alkaline earths in general (especially Magnesia), Lyc.

Generalities.—*Sticking outward in a small spot, < l. side, ending in burning itching. Feeling as if beaten, stiff and sore in all bones, joints and muscles.* Pains here and there, < a spot in r. temple; (P. < l. side). Lax feeling in whole body, < knees and sacral region. *Paralytic stiffness of whole body.* Aggravation on l. side before menses, on r. after menses.

Clinical.—It is generally indicated in a gouty diathesis, with recurring attacks of acute inflammation of the small joints or of the heart. The skin of the Lith. patient is very rough and dry. The lactate of Lith. has been found very valuable for subacute rheumatism of the shoulder-joint.

Mind.—Disposed to weep over his lonesome condition, so that he sobbed, his nose being full of water. Memory for names less retentive.

Head.—Confusion, with pain in sacrum when standing. Burning sticking outwardly over r. eye. Pain in l. side of forehead, then over eyes, gradually becoming worse in forehead and extending to l. side, with nausea. Heaviness in forehead; in sinciput, < frontal eminences. Pain in temples; and vertex; l.; r. during slow driving, then in r. brow; in l., with earache; in l. before dinner, extending into orbit, with gnawing in stomach, the P. in orbit, > eating, returned after eating and was felt in r. temple, a fulness remained in temples all the afternoon. Pressure inward in temples; with pressure outward in middle of chest towards the sides, in region of fourth rib; a confusion, with pressure outward in l. abdominal ring. Tension in temples towards evening, with heaviness in forehead. Fulness in temples, with pain in r. ear; in afternoon and evening.

Stitching in l. vertex in morning; S. superiorly on r., with sensitiveness to touch. Weight upon vertex and pressing in temple, the whole head seems too large and as if seized, the pain worse in spots, causing nausea, eyes difficult to keep open, they pained as if sore from morning till noon, the headache < looking at anything, could not remain lying, head ached everywhere, > sitting and going out. Sticking burning in l. side, extending upward. Pain in l. parietal bone; superiorly in r. side of head in evening; superiorly in r. side, later on l. side. Confusion in sides. Pain in a spot in occiput.

Eyes.—Pain in l.; P. inwardly above globe, above external canthus; twitching drawing P. around r., < above on external side and deep in orbit; as from sand, < l., then stitches in r.; P. during and after reading as if dry, and lids sore. Heat. Sore pain in margin of r. upper lid, a dry feeling. Cooling sensation as from salt in r. inner canthus. Pain at outer end of r. brow, gradually extending to temples and about ear; intermittent, in r. brow. On entering the house during the second day of menstruation **vanishing of the r. half of whatever she looked at, or if two short words occurred in succession that on the right was invisible** (compare Lyc.), > eating, with pain over eyes and tension in temples as if bound, then pressure in temples, > during sleep at night. *Blinded by sunlight in the street*, on a dull day.

Clinical.—Asthenopia. Retinal anæmia, entire vanishing of r. half of an object, for example, of a word, with pain over the eyes. Retinal anæmia or threatening blindness; in one case this symptom occurred previous to the loss of sight in one eye, subsequently he experienced the same symptom in the other eye and was cured by Lith.

Ears and Nose.—Pain in bone behind l. ear, extending to neck and farther. Obstruction of upper part of nose and of forehead in morning and forenoon. Dropping coryza; in open air, later in the room. Must blow the nose much, more mucus hangs behind (in nares) in evening.

Face.—Sticking burning in r. malar-bone, extending upward.

Mouth and Throat.—Molars, sticking burning extending upward in r.; pain in a l. lower late in evening; intermittent pain in r. Pain in root of a tooth (which had been sawn off), extending into r. side of face towards temple, next day after breakfast the same pain in l. side of face. Pain extending from throat into l. ear. Throat sore posteriorly on r. side, as if sore when swallowing; sensation as if T. would become sore.

Stomach.—*Appetite decreased, satisfied on beginning to eat* (Lyc.), no desire for wine, beer, coffee or sugar, all desire ceases when eating and drinking. Slow eructations before dinner, then pain in l. parietal bone; E. of water after drinking water. Nausea, with pain in forehead; easily nauseated when driving before meals. *Sticking burning extending upward in epigastrium.* Gnawing in forenoon, increased almost to vomiturition, < about dinner-time, yet she ate without repugnance; G. before meals, < before dinner, > eating, with pain in l. temple extending into orbits. Fulness in pit before breakfast, she could not endure the pressure of the clothes upon it, pressure with the hand would have made her vomit. Painless, tensive pressure in a spot towards right of and below and behind epigastrium. Sensation after supper as if a heavy hard body were in it. Restlessness towards evening till sleep, with pain and heaviness over brow.

Abdomen.—Distention from wind at noon, and from 3 to 10 P.M. frequent discharges of offensive flatus. Putrid-smelling flatus. Pain in forenoon; P. waking her, then diarrhœa, which was repeated now and then next day. Pressure in region of liver.

Anus and Stool.—Sudden itching in A. Sticking outward and downward in perineal region when walking. Diarrhœa in morning after chocolate; after fruit; offensive, at night. A second stool after breakfast. Stool omitted, next day hard at first, then soft and bright yellow (had eaten eggs in bread-soup).

Urinary Organs.—*Pain in bladder;* flatulent, on r. side of B. region; horizontally in upper region; fugitive, in lower part of B. region, towards the right, before urinating, after urinating pain extended into spermatic cords, < l. Tenesmus in morning, then copious, clear, frothy urine; T. and before and after miturition Lithium-pains in region of neck of bladder and in other parts of urinary organs, the same pain in region of neck of bladder, on r. side; sudden T., urine dark yellowish, more scanty than usually follows such tenesmus with him, afterwards sensitiveness and pain in middle of urethra. *Urine red. Urine scanty; and dark, acrid, micturition difficult;* the two to three ounces in the forenoon are turbid and form a scanty flocculent deposit. Dark reddish-brown sediment after diarrhœa.

Clinical.—Inflammation of the prostate, with pink sediment in the urine. It has proved curative in some cases of albuminuria, with dysuria at times, very acid dyspepsia, almost constant desire to urinate and great debility, the acidity of the stomach being the most marked indication (Mag. c.).

Sexual Organs.—Twitching stitches passing forward and across pubis hither and thither like lightning, leaving an enduring pain. Twitching to and fro in seminal cords and vesical region. Lithium-pains on r. side and at root of penis at 8 P.M., throbbing stitches when sitting. Menses ceased too soon and suddenly; M. late and less in quantity.

Respiratory Organs.—Paroxysmal and exhausting cough without expectoration when lying, from irritation in a spot posteriorly and low in throat, compelling him to sit up. Expectoration of thick masses of mucus from choanæ and fauces, < morning and forenoon.

Chest.—Pressure in middle in afternoon. Constriction on going out after breakfast, then hawking of much mucus coming from middle of sternum. Shuddering running over anterior surface of body like a drawing together, afterwards S. starting from other regions.

Heart.—Sticking twitching. Sudden jerks. *Pain; in morning on bending forward over bed;* in morning on rising to urinate, > micturition.

Clinical.—It has been found valuable in chronic rheumatic endocarditis, with soreness in region of heart, especially < stooping; this chronic rheumatic inflammation of the heart is generally associated with chronic inflammation of the finger-joints.

Back.—Soreness on r. side near spine at night, changing to pain in sacrum, > rising; S. in a spot on r. side near spine, below loins, from rising in morning till bed-time, with sensitiveness to touch. Sacrum, sticking outward and downward; pain in region; *pressure as with a dull point here and there internally as if near bone*, in evening, < l. side; weakness in afternoon, when writing, standing at a high desk.

Extremities.—Pains externally in l. shin, then in l. hand. **Pain in r. shoulder-joint near insertion of pectoralis major, at margin of muscle.** *Pain in metacarpal bone of l. little finger in evening. Burning sticking in ball of l. thumb. Lithium-pains in l. middle finger (which was chafed) coming from other parts towards this spot. Twitching pain as if in or upon bones of r., then l. fingers,* < l. second and third fingers, internally from the hand towards the extremities, throbbing twitching, < during repose, > pressure and motion. Pain along middle finger towards extremity, then in l. metacarpus in an outward direction, with burning stitches as if it would itch, < ball of thumb, *the burning sticking in jerks outward and ending in itching seems characteristic.*

Lower Extremities.—Itching sticking internally on l. thigh. Burning sticking above r. knee and inwardly towards patella. Pain in r. thigh; in l. hip at night; in a spot in front and towards outside of r. thigh, as if it were the seat of insertion of a muscle; itching burning P. in a spot externally on r. hip, then on thigh, then on outside of little toe. Sticking burning extending upward in l. knee. Pains in knees on descending stairs, < above knees. Knees weak in morning on ascending stairs.

Rheumatic sensations now and then in legs. Pain superiorly in r. calf, extending downward. Pain in ankles when walking, first < r., then < l. Pain in feet in afternoon, with weakness in them; *P. through hollow of l. foot when walking, extending horizontally to outside of foot, thence to a little below knee; rheumatic pain in r. foot on waking at night, > rising; twitching P. in r. heel, extending towards middle foot.* Soreness of corns, which had not troubled her so for a long time, after walking on a warm day.

Skin.—Itching on inner margin of l. sole; of l. middle finger, near nail and around on l. side of finger, in evening; on whole inner side of r. thigh late in evening, and on spots in adjacent parts.

Sleep.—Sleepiness in evening, restless dreams that night and great sleepiness next morning. Little sleep without restlessness. Lustful dreams and frequent waking, with erection, tenesmus vesicæ and lascivious titillation in urethra, on account of the erection he could not pass water, the erection > when he succeeded in doing so, with pain in bladder and scanty urine.

Fever.—General heat. Copious sweat; on backs of hands in evening while the palms were dry.

Lobelia Inflata.

A tincture of the fresh plant is used.

General Action.—This drug produces, in large doses, most violent vomiting, and profound prostration, failure of the heart and respiration, collapse and fatal stupor; it paralyzes the pneumogastric and vasomotor nerves. Its most important action in smaller doses is laryngeal and bronchial spasm, hence it is very useful in various spasmodic diseases of the respiratory apparatus attended with deathly nausea.

Allies.—Ant. tart., Tabac., Coccul.

Generalities.—Convulsions. Trembling. Prickling through whole body, even to fingers and toes. Distress. Internal uneasiness. Malaise; towards evening, caused by colic and diarrhœa. *Weakness;* in evening. Its action is like that of tobacco, but more speedy, diffusive and of shorter duration. Amelioration towards evening.

Mind.—Loss of reason, with convulsions. Raving every evening after an hour's sleep, with palpitation and flushed face. Indisposed to mental exertion.

Head.—Aching; towards evening; all night; < waking; < ascending steps; with drowsiness; in sudden shocks through head. Heaviness. Confusion on moving about, < vertex; C. in evening, increasing to headache, with heat of face. Cerebral torpor. *Vertigo; with nausea* (Coccul.); with headache and trembling agitation of whole body. Confusion in forehead. Temples, stitches; *heavy pain passing from one to other round forehead, in a line above brows;* pain, and in l. molars; outward pressure. Pain in l. parietal protuberance. Occiput, pain; in open air; > removing head-covering; tension in region of lambdoidal suture on paying strict attention to it; confusion; dulness.

Eyes.—Pain in r., with soreness. Burning. Pupils dilated. Pain in balls, < upper parts. Smarting of inside of lids. Itching in angles of lids; l. Vision dim.

Ears, Nose and Face.—Aching in l. ear. Sneezing, with gaping and flatulent eructations. Nosebleed. Face of the color of a corpse. Drawing now in l., now in r. lower jaw.

Mouth.—Pricking in back part. Peculiar drawing from r. side to r. eye. Dryness. *Salivation;* clammy; tenacious; thin. *Taste sharp; and disagreeable, < tip of tongue and back of throat.*

Throat.—*Mucus causing frequent necessity to hawk.* Shooting in a spot to left of larynx and on a line with its lowest cartilage, extending into l. ear. Pricking on swallowing the medicine. Scraping; in pharynx; on r. side of larynx; with sore pain and with consecutive constrictions of œsophagus from below upward; then pain; then efforts to vomit, with pressure and heaving in pharynx; burning S., < anterior arches of palate, extending towards larynx, causing frequent hawking of mucus. Soreness. Sensation of a lump in pit impeding respiration and deglutition. Drawing pain in r. side extending to ear. Burning; changing to dryness and lasting all the forenoon. Dryness; at back; in fauces; after a meal, not > drinking, with scraping. Dysphagia.

Pressure in œsophagus and pit of stomach; in O., as from a foreign substance, worse at certain places, as, for example, just below larynx, whence there was a twisting peristaltic motion to pit of stomach, at last only an intermittent twisting feeling as if a plug in pit reached to spine, the sensation extended to right and left through præcordium, > deep inspiration, at 5 P.M. only a sensation in back, hypochondrium and pit of stomach on turning body as if the tendinous expansion of diaphragm were too tense.

Stomach.—Loss of appetite; for dinner. Aversion to food in afternoon. Eructations; with salivation; empty; painful; fatiguing, with nausea; burning; flatulent, with acidity and heat in stomach; of an acid fluid, with burning. Hiccough; towards evening; frequent and violent. *Nausea; all the morning;* **in morning, > a swallow of water** (Bry.); *with vertigo; with cold sweat on head, < face, and ineffectual retching; with heat, pain, oppression and uneasiness in stomach* (with affection of respiratory organs), with uneasiness and vomiting; with shaking of upper part of body; or sensation of a lump, as if caused by undigested food. Excessive vomiting; violent V.

Pain in pit. Painful twisting in cardiac region. Sensation of an antiperistaltic motion in morning, without nausea. Uneasiness or feeling of a lump. Weight in pit. *Oppression of epigastrium* as if too full, < pressure. Pressure, though little had been eaten; P. in region after dinner, with heaviness. Heartburn, with salivation. *Burning. Weak feeling.*

Clinical.—The most marked and persistent symptoms of this drug are the nausea and vomiting; they generally accompany the respiratory troubles. It has been used for gastralgia and dyspepsia, for the nausea and vomiting of pregnancy, especially if with the nausea there are extreme faintness and sinking at the pit of the stomach.

Abdomen.—Distention, with rapid respiration. Rumbling; with passage downward of flatus. Flatulence. Movings. Griping, with movings, then emission of flatus; G. in morning on waking. Cutting in morning on waking, with drawing. Sensation as before diarrhœa. Pain; in afternoon; almost all night; on waking; < till evening; < eating; and in small of back; in r. hypochondrium; in lower; cramplike, in l. posterior iliac region, < touch and motion.

Rectum and Stool.—Discharge of black blood after stool. Scraping in anus during stool, as from passage of a rough, hard body. Stools liquid, copious, frequent, after the colic. Stools soft; and whitish. Stools pasty. S. easier.

Clinical.—Dr. Cooper has reported in the *Monthly Hom. Review* for Dec., 1888, some remarkable cases of chronic diarrhœa and vaginal discharges, in which the tincture of Lob. had entirely failed, but the extract with acetic acid produced wonderful results; these cannot be accepted as a contribution to Lob., since it may fairly be assumed that acetic acid, which we are beginning to appreciate as a great antipsoric remedy, bore an important part in the cures mentioned.

Urinary Organs.—Pain in urethra. Smarting in urethra during micturition. Frequent micturition; at night. Urine of yellowish wine color. Urine increased; diminished, with less frequent desire to urinate than usual, *rosy red sediment*, with crystals of uric acid.

Sexual Organs.—Heaviness. Smarting of prepuce. Brought on menses; but scantily.

Respiratory Organs.—Constriction of larynx. In larynx a peculiar sensation between tickling and smarting, like irritation to cough, which occurred but seldom, and then with oppression. Hoarse. Cough; irritation to; short, dry. Expectorant. **Breathing difficult**; *from constriction in middle of chest, which impedes respiratory movements.* Inclination to sigh, inspiration deep. Respiration insufficient. Respiration accelerated, with sensation as if it were insufficient, the abdominal muscles acted less than natural in breathing, and it was difficult to hold the breath. Inspiration short, expiration slow.

Clinical.—Bronchitis and asthma, with very great oppression of the chest, as if it were full of blood, which seems to stagnate, > moving about. Spasmodic croup, with nausea, vomiting and threatening suffocation.

Chest.—Pain; under middle of sternum; at l. side of lower part of sternum; in breast; < deep inspiration. Burning pain in a spot below r. breast, extending towards pit of stomach, and on deep inspiration or sneezing sensation as if something were drawn from its position and then returned to its place, towards noon the burning pain extended more towards pit of stomach and l. side, and the pain in the original spot was boring, the pains < dinner, returned at 4 P.M., and extended to the back beneath r. shoulder, the part seemed paralyzed and was intolerant of motion.

Distress. Oppression; impeding respiration; obliging deep respiration. Constriction; of sternal region towards evening, with colic and diarrhœa; < at base, after the eructations had ceased. Tightness, with heat in forehead; T., with short and labored breathing and disposition to breathe with open mouth. Fulness, with short, superficial breathing and failure of abdominal respiration. Burning in breast passing upward. Drawing from l. nipple to axilla. Tickling in region of lower end of sternum on deep inspiration.

Heart and Pulse.—Præcordial anxiety. Deep-seated pain in region of heart. Tumultuous action of H. Pulse rapid; and soft. Pulse slow; and irregular; and small, irregular; and small, intermittent. *Pulse small; and weak.*

Back.—Twitches over l. ribs near spine, then drawing pain between scapulæ. Sticking in region of r. kidney. Pain in loins; in third, fourth and fifth dorsal vertebræ; burning, as if in posterior wall of stomach; rheumatic, between scapulæ. Weakness.

Extremities.—(Rheumatic feeling in r. shoulder-joint.) Pain in a space of a hand's breadth in muscles of r. arm on touch, the pain in shoulder gone. Pressing in flesh above l. elbow, with paralyzed feeling in hand. Paralytic feeling in l. arm. Crawling stitches on inside of r. deltoid. Pain in r. elbow; rheumatic. Walking is difficult. Pressing pain on exterior, middle part of thigh, with constriction of head. Pain and stiffness in knees as from fatigue. Cramp in calves in morning on waking. Cramplike feeling in l. gastrocnemius. Tearing extending up fibulæ to knees. Pain in l. leg when sitting. Weakness of legs. Cramplike feeling in hollow of l. foot.

Sleep.—Yawning; and stretching. Sleepiness. Deep sleep. Heavy sleep interrupted by the slightest noise. Sleep restless and full of dreams. Sleep unrefreshing and disturbed by hallucinations. Dreams heavy; D. anxious; numerous D. and frequent waking.

Fever.—*General chilliness;* C. in l. cheek extending to ear; of l. side of head, with feeling as if hair would rise on end; down back, with heat in stomach. Shivering in upper part of body on account of aversion to the drug. Heat towards evening, < face, with inclination to sweat; H. in evening, with headache posteriorly; in face in evening, with tension in head; in forehead, with tightness in breast. Sweat; towards evening (with colic and diarrhœa); at night; cold.

Lycopodium.

Triturations (as prescribed by the Pharmacopœias) are made of the pollen of Lycopodium clavatum, L.

General Action.—A "tissue" remedy far-reaching in its effects. One of its most prominent effects is the peculiar indigestion (see symptoms of Stomach, Abdomen, Liver, Stool, Kidneys, etc.). The productions of the "uric-acid diathesis" is very clear. Its catarrhal symptoms in nose, throat, and especially in the lungs, are prominent. Consult also the eruptions, tendency to boils, carbuncles, etc. In general it is a drug adapted to atonic and sluggish types of disease, though, like sulphur, it is not infrequently required, as an "intercurrent," during the course of an acute malady.

Allies.—Sulph., Sil., Sep., Zinc.; Puls., Bry., Nux v., Carbo v., Chel., *Cycl.;* Phos., Mag. c., Nat. m., Iod., Iris, Kali bi.

Generalities.—Emaciation. Glands thickened and hardened on getting feet cold. Fell suddenly to the ground without vertigo. Shivering when walking, without chilliness. Trembling in afternoon; in attacks in evening in bed. Tremulous sensation through body after eating. Involuntary extension and contraction of muscles in various parts, in paroxysms every seven days, with complete consciousness. Involuntary turning and twisting of whole body, so that he gasped and the face became red and hot. Twitching, now here, now there; T. below stomach pit and on r. thigh. Epileptic attack, with screams and frothing at the mouth, then he thought that he should die and complained of anxiety at heart; E. attack, l. arm bent backward and fingers clenched, then unconsciousness, beating about with arms and legs, cries and frothing from the mouth, then motionless as if dead, then foolish sounds; E. attack, jerking of muscles of r. leg, extending to pit of stomach, then cries, unconsciousness, beating about with arms and legs, with frothing from mouth, then motionless, after cold water was put into his mouth he rejected it and returned to consciousness.

Sticking over whole body; here and there on body; in various parts; above pit of stomach, in sternum and deltoids; in l. ankle, toes, elbows and nape, in evening in bed; on head and upper arms, now in one place, now in another, with coldness of fingers; now in præcordial region, now in l. elbow, now in abdomen; in chest and umbilical region, taking away the breath; crawling, in lower part of back and in other parts; S. and tearing alternately in r. and l. shoulder, elbows, wrists, fingers, l. knee, r. great toe, r. and l. side of chest, in evening; tearing S. in evening, in second joint of r. thumb, suddenly changing to l. shoulder, then to l. elbow, then to r. thumb, l. knee, l. chest in region of sixth rib, the pain lasted in l. shoulder and elbow and r. hand till 9 P.M.; rheumatic tearing S. at times in r. ear and temple, with drawing in r. shoulder (possibly from sudden change of weather).

Tearing here and there; in head, then in other parts. Pinching here and there. Pains felt in sleep and dreams of them; P. appeared and disappeared suddenly; on touch in all soft parts; raging, in parts formerly injured; here and there in trunk as if single muscles were spasmodically contracted and then extended; rheumatic, in head (jaws, extending towards ears) and in limbs, < l. hand, r. forearm, and l. leg. Bruised pain over whole body in morning; in evening; B. feeling in feet and small of back. Feeling as if there were no marrow in the bones. Feeling as if flesh were loose from bones. Drawing now in scapulæ, now in r. leg, now in chest; every other afternoon in limbs and across face; in gum and whole l. side of body, waking her at night. Throbbing through whole body after eating.

Inclination to take cold. Sick feeling in morning after a sleepless night; S. feeling, with disinclination to think, forgetfulness and absence of mind. Discomfort; in forenoon; in evening; *in every position at night*, which vexed him even to weeping; *after eating*. Everything that she sits or lies upon seems too hard. **Desire to go into open air** (Puls.). Aversion to open air. Excitement of whole body. Necessity to walk about and weep when the pains are most severe. Desire to move about. Walking and persistent sitting at writing were irksome and she easily broke into a profuse sweat. Restlessness in morning on waking, with anxiety; R. in evening; R. when sitting, with oppression of chest and necessity to take a deep breath; in blood in evening, amounting to a trembling sensation; internal; internal, as if she would beat about her with her hands and feet, with faintness and headache. Lying at night was intolerable. Aversion to rising in morning. Inclination to rest without weariness. Feeling in morning as after a night of rioting.

Weakness; all day after coition; in morning; *in morning on rising, with heaviness;* in morning on waking, with inclination to draw up feet; in morning, with heaviness of head, reeling and pain in neck; in morning, with dizziness, shivering, nausea and colic, in forenoon diarrhœa twice, in afternoon chilliness, shivering, < over back, abdomen and thighs, with heat in head and colic over whole abdomen, hernia painful and tense when protruded and when touched, frequent yawning, and when lying pain as if beaten in nape, shoulders and limbs, scarcely able to rise, after going to bed some sleep, after rising again shivering, with heat in head, emission of flatus, and after a glass of wine diarrhœa; W. in forenoon when walking; in forenoon after a vexation, with palpitation and trembling; in afternoon and evening; in afternoon after a glass of wine; in afternoon, with trembling of hands; in evening before sleep; in evening, with sleepiness; in evening, with excitement and late falling asleep; (in evening from business); at 5 P.M., when walking; at 9.30 P.M., with incessant yawning; *after every exertion;* on waking; after stool; after dinner, with sleepiness; after eating, with rapid pulse; during menses; after an emission, with trembling; when walking; when walking, with reeling unless he had a firm hold; on ascending steps, when bones of lower limbs ache; (from studying, with heaviness of head); < rest; < thighs, starting from small of back, on dismounting and walking, with bruised sensation; with nervous irritability; with heaviness and trembling of limbs, < hands; with hanging of lower jaw, slow respiration through mouth, and filmy half-open eyes; (in a child), could not hold his head up, could stand upon his feet only with crying, fear and trembling, and wished to be carried, muscles flabby, ill humor, the slighest worry caused weeping and sobbing, restless night, rapid breathing, foolish talk in his sleep and frequent starting up in sleep, next day sank down if he attempted to sit up, cried if any one touch his thighs and was emaciated; so that she could scarcely speak; in frequent attacks, so that she must let the hands fall; sudden, in afternoon; sudden, when sitting; mental and physical, also in evening.

Little fatigue in evening in bed and early waking in morning. Desire to go to bed in the forenoon. Faintness when standing in church during menses, with internal heat, < head, remains stupid all the evening, and confusion of head lasts next day; F. at a certain hour daily, < evening; sudden; in attacks when lying, without desire to relieve the condition by moving. Feeling as if circulation stopped. R. side of body is asleep in morning after heavy, dreamy sleep. Stiffness of muscles in upper part of body and trunk; S. of limbs and small of back, with cracking in joints on bending them. **Aggravation at 4 P.M., better at 8 P.M., but weak.**

Clinical.—It is frequently useful in dropsies of the pericardium, pleura and abdomen. In general it is a remedy for conditions of malnutrition, and is more frequently useful for persons who are emaciated than for those who are well nourished. It is very valuable for children who look wrinkled and prematurely old. General relief in open air.

Mind.—Delirious at night; D., raging, envious, reproachful, presumptuous and imperious. Irrational talking the day before and the first day of menstruation, with weeping. Excitement in evening, busy mood without perseverance, with difficulty in fixing the thoughts and in accomplishing anything, and when reading fell asleep; E., with mirth; E. after a glass of wine, almost mischievous. Involuntary whistling and humming. Mirth, with vertigo. Liveliness; in afternoon, with busy fancies. Hilarity. Joyous. Necessity to laugh if any one looks at her to say anything serious. Inclined to laugh and cry at the same time. Smiles without being pleased, humorous.

Anger; easily aroused to A. and scorn (Nux v.). *Ill humor* (Nux v.); all day, and weeping at slightest causes; in morning; in morning, with disinclination to everything; in evening; in evening, with ravenous hunger; *just before menstruation, with sadness; with apprehension; with violence; with taciturnity;* with obstinacy; with pallor of face and sleepiness during the day; (in a child), it cried and would not go to sleep in the evening; *causing apprehension in pit of stomach.* Passionate mood without fretfulness. Insolent, obstinate, rebellious, passionate. Quarrelsome, makes unfounded reproaches, and strikes those whom she thus insults; quarrels mentally with absent persons; quarrelsome rage, partly at himself, partly at others. Impatience; on waking. Disobedient. *Anthropophobia.* Flees from her own children. Desire to be alone. Dread of being alone. Ennui. Discontented. *Suspicious* (Puls.). Remembered many unpleasant events, which vexed her, even at night on waking.

Sadness (Nat. m., Ign.); *all day, with weeping and discontent; in evening* (Puls.); *with confusion of head. Despair* (Ign.). *Despondent and weak.* Hypochondriac, complaining. *Apprehension when walking in open air,* with attacks of vertigo. *Anxiety;* in forenoon, with internal chilliness like internal trembling; *in evening* (Puls.), with semi-confusion before eyes; on waking after midnight, so that she could not get her breath; on falling asleep; as if about to die, in morning after deep sleep; then inclination to laugh at trifles, then weeping. *Fear; all day;* of going to bed in the evening; in the evening in the dark, when a door that he wishes to open moves with difficulty; in evening, of fancied images, and lachrymose mood during the day; in evening on entering a room, as if he saw some one, even during the day he believes that he hears some one in the room; frightened easily, starting up. Sensitive, cried about being thanked. *Weeping* with the chill. Cries and howls about past, then about future troubles. *Disinclined to talk;* and inclined to weep. Indecision and loss of confidence. Loss of confidence in his own vigor. Listlessness.

Speaks wrong words and syllables. *Difficulty in expressing himself,* < evening. **Confusion about every-day things** (Sep.), *but rational talking on abstract subjects;* C. of ideas when reading; C. of thought and difficulty in reflecting, causing dulness of head and dimness of vision. *Thoughts stand still, mind helpless, like a confusion, without obscuration of mind.* Inability to read because he does not recognize letters, he can copy them, but has no idea of their significance, he knows that *Z* is the last letter of the alphabet, but has forgotten its name, writes whatever he wishes, but cannot read what he has written. *Distraction;* frequently during earnest conversation after dinner; as in beginning of fever. (Thoughts difficult to fix, < when reading.) *Inability to comprehend or remember what is read. Dull in evening after a cup of milk, and without thought. Stupefaction* (Op., Ph. ac., Sep.); in morning, as if intoxicated, difficulty in keeping erect, tottering, weakness of feet and vertigo; towards evening, with heat in temples and ears, and it seems as if everything would vanish from her; on reading, with heaviness of head, sleepiness, falling asleep. *Memory weak* (Anac.); *forgets words* (Bell., K. brom.). Disinclination for work; for mental work; D. to work or think in afternoon. Inclination for mental work.

Clinical.—A remedy of great value in mental torpor, especially valuable for old people, for forgetfulness of words and syllables, and confusion of ideas generally. Lack of mental steadiness; want of self-confidence. Great mental and nervous weakness, with physical relaxation. Melancholia. Hypochondriasis, often misanthropic and irritable. Very easily frightened and startled.

Head.—Turned involuntarily to the left. Involuntary nodding, now to r., now to l.; I. nodding, slow at first, then constantly more rapid. Involuntary shaking, making him dizzy; *shaking head on stepping hard;* S. and jerking in H. Sticking jerking during cough. Sticking; in forenoon, < occiput; < evening; in brain; < parietal eminences; intermittent, after menstruation; with seething sensation. Tearing; in afternoon, then toothache at night; > appearance of painless swelling of cheek; rheumatic. Every step is felt in H., and a shock in brain on every motion.

Aching; in morning; towards noon; in afternoon; in afternoon, < stooping; in afternoon, < l. frontal sinus and in region of l. malar-bone; at 1 P.M., with heat; from 4 to 8 P.M., with tearing in temples; till 7 P.M., with great appetite and increased sweat; in evening; *during ravenous hunger, > eating;* on waking, with pain in abdomen; on stooping; when reading; when reading while sitting, with pulsation; after stool, with heat in it and weariness of thighs; during cough, with pain in sides of abdomen; < shaking and turning head; < lying; worse during rest than when walking in open air; *with stupefaction;* with heat of face; with heat of face and hands; almost like a tearing, during menstruation; like a clang through head, as from the snapping of a piano-string; jerking, at night, preventing sleep; as if head would be forced asunder and as if brain were swashing to and fro, < walking, ascending steps and rising from stooping; so that he could not work and could scarcely step without having a kind of vertigo; more pressive than constrictive, in morning on rising; **throbbing, after every paroxysm of cough** (Nat. m.); undulating, with burning of face; wandering, at night, making the head heavy, she does not know where to lay it on account of the pain; at night, as from lying in an unnatural position.

Confusion; on waking at 3 A.M.; in morning; in morning, with heaviness and also with heat in it; in morning on waking, with heat in it; in afternoon, with pain in l. frontal region; in evening, < in and above eyes; in evening, with heat of it and weariness of limbs, ill humor and sleepiness; after being much in open air; on waking; on waking, with pressure upon chest, > expectoration of consistent, purulent mucus; > sneezing; with feeling as if a board were before it; with pressure in forehead as from suppressed catarrh, with dryness of mouth and lips, and thirst; with nausea; periodic; as from a disordered stomach; as from intoxication; so that she cannot express her ideas, with internal tension; dizzy, < reading; dizzy, in forenoon, with sensation as if eyes were lying deep, with difficult thought and understanding.

Heaviness; in morning on waking, as if stupid and sleepy; in evening after mental exertion, with weakness. Stupefaction in afternoon; in morning, as if intoxicated. Empty feeling when thinking, with inability to fix his thoughts. **Throbbing in brain during the day on leaning head backward**; T. in brain, with heat in head; in evening after lying down; during cough; like a chopping (with sour eructations). *Rush of blood; in morning on waking. Vertigo; in morning;* **in morning during and after rising** (Bry., Pul.); in morning, with heaviness in eyes; towards evening; towards evening, with anxiety; at night on waking, with nausea; *on drinking;* after breakfast; in a hot room; on rising from a seat; as if everything would turn about with her, in forenoon, with nausea; as if he would fall forward at noon; so that he was in danger of falling forward, at 1 P.M., when standing and talking. As soon as she sees anything turning about she feels as if her body were turning about.

Forehead.—*Sticking;* in region of eye; in l. side; in l. eminence; and in temples and l. ear; (on reading and reflecting); above r. eye, in temple and occiput *at night, with tearing;* constant, on eating, then on moving isolated stitches; in eminences at 6 P.M., alternating with throbbing; outward, by paroxysms, during the day. Tearing at 7 P.M., with thirst and heat; T. in r. eminence and brow at 2 P.M., with heat in these places and in eye; above eyes and extending into them, in morning; *jerking, in r. bone, extending to root of nose and eyebrow;* radiating, in and over l. eminence, extending to l. side. Boring in l. side, extending to root of nose. *Aching;* between eyes; in l. side; in morning; on rising and all the forenoon, with weakness; in forenoon, with heat of head; in afternoon; *in afternoon when riding in a carriage, with pressure in stomach;* at 9 P.M., with heat and redness of face; in evening, < l. side; on waking; *above eyes after breakfast;* on eating; beginning when writing; when riding in a carriage, with vertigo, stupefaction and heat of head, as after a night of debauchery; > open air; with heat; with heat of face; with desire to lie down; in sinciput, with inclination to eructations; frequent, sudden, with nausea and weakness; extending down nose, in morning; externally on touch; sore, < stooping; alternating with sticking, in morning; superficial, in upper part, extending to vertex, bones of cheeks, ear and jaw, > afternoon, returning in evening; as from a nail in middle above hairy part; contractive, in muscles of F. and face; as if head were compressed from both sides; (heavy, in F. and vertex in forenoon after reading and reflecting). Throbbing pain in middle from 3 A.M. till evening; T. pain in forenoon, with heat in face; at noon; at 3 P.M.; in afternoon, with heat and redness of face; in l. sinus and eminence in evening; with heat of face; tearing, in r. eminence and brow in evening. Throbbing in sinciput in evening, which afterwards is tensive and extends across occiput to nape. Pressure outward, with drawing through r. side of face, over shoulder and arm. Pressing asunder in F. and above eyes, extending to vertex, with nausea and trembling in limbs. Painful confusion; in morning. Heaviness in l. half. Swollen feeling. Drawing up of skin, with enlarged opening of lids, then drawing down of skin, with closing of eyes.

Temples.—**Shattering in T. and chest during cough.** Sticking; at 11 A.M.; from 7 to 8 P.M., < behind mastoid processes; in l. T. and in r. side of occiput; in l., extending to l. side of forehead. *Thrust during difficult stool.* Jerking tearing radiating into r. half of head. Aching; at night, with dreams of it; on every step, not during rest; now r., now l.; screwing together, as if forehead would burst, during menstruation; drawing, in l., extending into forehead; paralytic.

Vertex.—Sticking; at night, with pressure; in V. and sides of head when reading; deep inward. Tearing from noon till 7 P.M., extending to l. shoulder; in upper part and sides of head in evening. *Pain* during moderate pressure at stool, with roaring in front of ears; P. extending to l. temple, in afternoon, when riding in a carriage; as in coryza. Throbbing.

Sides.—Tearing through l. into ear; T. in l., with heaviness. Pain in r. side of brain; P. in l. side externally, extending into ear and teeth, < evening, reading, writing and pressure on temples, as, for example, from the spectacles; drawing in r. extending to nape. Attacks of throbbing in r. in afternoon.

Occiput.—Sticking; at night, with throbbing; with slow pulse. Tearing; in a spot near l. side of nape. Pinching behind ear. Aching; and throbbing; in r. half extending towards ear; as if scalp were inflamed, in morning; jerking, extending to vertex, in evening; burning, in eminences. Heaviness; < motion, with confused pain in forehead. Fills with blood after stooping.

Skull.—Pain; jerking.

Scalp.—*Hair became very gray* (compare Arsen.). *Great falling of hair* (Graph., Sep., Sul.); but in other parts of the body it increases. *Eruption, with swelling of cervical glands. Boil on occiput; and scurf over whole scalp, which the child scratches raw at night and which then bleeds.* Suppuration. Twitching in places. Shocks. Tearing stitches. Tearing in upper part of r. side of forehead; T. when walking in open air. Cutting from a little cold air, takes cold easily in head; C. transversely across between forehead and vertex. Spasmodic constriction. Contracted sensation, with feeling as if the hair would be pulled up; feeling in upper part of l. side like a drawing on a single hair. Painful tension, < above forehead, with painful drawing about root of nose. Sensitiveness. *Itching;* and on face as far as beard. Corrosion, necessity to scratch. Formication in forenoon when walking in open air, with feeling as if hair were drawn gently upward.

Clinical.—It has been used in tubercular meningitis, sleep with half-open eyes and moaning. Chronic hydrocephalus, with screaming out in sleep, but without general Apis symptoms.

Eyes.—Surrounded by blue rings. Sunken. Swelling of r., with hard mucus in inner canthus, pain and lachrymation. *Inflammation, with itching in canthi, with redness and swelling of r. lids,* **distressing pain on eyes getting dry, with nightly aggravations** (Sulph.); I. of whites; I., with burning pain and mucus, and with redness and dimness of whites and redness and swelling of lids; with redness of whites, swelling of lids, sticking, photophobia, lachrymation and nightly agglutination; with redness and sticking from 5 till 10 P.M. Redness and pain; in white; R. of white, with biting lachrymation. *Dimness;* in morning; in evening; and weakness. *Mucus; and she must wipe them to see more clearly* (Euphras.); *purulent,* with smarting; dry, with pain, lachrymation and pale face.

Sticking; < morning, without redness; in l. Tearing about E., extending into forehead and cheeks. Scraping in l. as from a foreign body. Smarting when writing on dark paper. Pain; in forenoon, with sleepiness; in l. in evening, with sensation as if a veil were before it; so that she could scarcely open them in evening; in l., < moving it and fixing eyes on an object, especially if of variegated colors, it began to tremble; tensive, in l.; *as if dust were in them*, also in morning, with difficulty in opening them; as if something were in r. Bruised pain; as if they would fall out, so that he cannot look sharply, after 1 P.M., < evening. Constriction. Feeling as if pressed into orbits. Compression, with tense skin over cheek-bones. *Dryness; in morning, with difficulty in opening, and also with smarting* (Sep., Sil.); *beneath lids, as from dust, in morning on waking; with necessity to close them.* Heaviness and weariness, as if sleepy from looking. Biting in r. as from smoke, with drawing together of lids. Itching. Coldness in evening. *Burning* (Zn.); in l.; if she closes them; after dinner, with disinclination to talk and dim vision; *and itching;* and lachrymation.

Lachrymation; of r. in afternoon; in open air; in a raw wind. Pupils dilated a few days before and during menstruation. Ball, tearing in r.; pain in r., causing lachrymation; prickling, now in one, now in the other; burning in l. Throbbing pain about outer part of orbits. Brows, sticking; sudden sticking tearing in r. at noon; tearing drawing pain in l. Canthi, dry mucus in inner in morning; pressure in internal; *itching;* biting in external, at twilight, with lachrymation as from smoke.

Lids.—**Ulceration and redness,** *with smarting lachrymation;* **styes** (Puls.); *towards inner canthus.* Pustules. Inflammation, with pain and nightly agglutination of external canthi. *Swelling of l.; S. and pain, with nightly agglutination of canthi.* Agglutination in morning; of l.; *A., < night,* especially of external canthi. Mucus in lashes. Twitching; of r. upper; of l. lower, towards inner canthus. Trembling of upper in forenoon; spasmodic, of l. upper, with at times sticking in l. eye. Sticking on margin of r. upper. Pain on touch. *Smarting and burning; S. and dryness, they cannot be opened in morning* (Sulph., Zinc.); (S., with burning and biting). Pressure on r. upper. Heaviness; during the day, < bright light; of l. upper in evening, with burning. Agglutinated feeling in morning. Itching of r. upper. Burning in evening on closing them, < l.

Vision.—**Blinded by the evening light, he sees nothing upon the table.** *Sees only l. half of an object* (Lith., r.), *especially with r. eye.* Vanishes on reading or exerting eyes. *Sensitiveness to daylight. Weak;* in evening by the light, with pain on turning eyes; with necessity to press eyes on account of pain. *Flickering* (Cycl., Sulph.); *after afternoon nap, and dim;* on going to sleep; like air in summer heat. Trembling of objects at which he looks intently in evening by the light, especially the light itself. Letters run together when reading. Letters indistinct when writing. Dim, as through a fine lattice; D., he is obliged to hold the print sometimes near, sometimes far off; as from a glutinous moisture in eyes, which he cannot wipe away. (As through a cobweb or fog, in morning.) Far-sighted. *Of black floating spots at a short distance from eyes* (Cycl., Sulph.); of black spots after a meal, < shaking head, with pain < l. Of sparks in the dark; of S., < open air.

Clinical.—Polypus in external canthus. Hordeolum. Catarrhal conjunctivitis. Purulent ophthalmia, with associated inflammation of the cornea in the chronic stage. Many cases of hemeralopia dependent upon chronic degenerative changes in the retina. Cataract has been arrested. Asthenopia.

Ears.—Suppuration and discharge. Discharge from l., which had been dry many years. Sticking; on blowing nose, with difficult speech; behind E., extending into jaws; outward in l. on swallowing; tearing, twinging, forcing-asunder, with feeling as if too narrow and as if it would burst. Tearing on r.; behind l.; *in meatus;* in l. concha. Aching in open air; A. behind ears, obliging him to walk bent over. Sensation as if it had been scraped. Jerking in middle. Pressure on back of r. concha. Feeling as if something were forced into middle. Dragging towards E. Feeling of forcing of hot blood. *Rush of blood.* Throbbing in front of E. in morning and evening; T., with tension, and with spasmodic tension of skin behind ears, extending obliquely into muscles of nape. Bubbling; in front of E. during the day. Biting behind r. and on side of it, with sore feeling. Itching in E.

Hearing.—*Sensitiveness to noise* (Sil.); when walking. Diminished. Hissing. Ringing in r., every noise had a peculiar echo deep in ear. Whistling on blowing nose; W. in front of E. evenings. *Roaring;* and humming; with obstruction and hardness of hearing. Humming in front of r.; in front of E., with roaring; H. in l.; internally in head, with heat. Whirring, with obstruction. Noises. Hears in the evening the music that she heard played during the day.

Clinical.—Numerous cases of chronic deafness, with and without otorrhœa, especially after scarlet fever. Polypus. Eczema of external ear, especially behind ear (compare Graph.).

Nose.—Ulceration of inner surface, covered with a scab, which when removed speedily formed again; painful U. inside. Swelling of tip, with pain on touch; S. at tip, with pain, and red spot as if a pustule would form. Throbbing jerking in r. wing. Cutting soreness high up in r. side of septum in evening in bed. Tearing in r. side extending to canthus. Pain on pressure, as if in mucous membrane, < towards root; corrosive P. in l. nostril on moving nose or putting finger into it; biting, corrosive P. in r. nostril. Pressure in bone close to r. eye. **Stoppage;** *towards morning; in evening* (Puls.); **and the child's breath is often stopped in sleep for fifteen seconds, even when the mouth is open;** with inclination to sneeze; of upper part. *Dryness;* in morning; in morning, *with stoppage; in evening, with stoppage; with stoppage at root* (K. bi.). Drawing in r. side. Tension in r. wing. Muscles feel at first as if stretched, afterwards contracted. Tickling, without ability to sneeze. Itching in nostrils. Heat.

Coryza.—C. < afternoon when walking; C., with heat in head, burning in eyes and cold limbs; in morning on waking, after an hour pain in frontal sinuses, vertigo, fulness in chest, hands and feet cold and sweaty, sensation in tendo-achillis as after a long walk, then tension in tonsils extending into parotids and lower jaws, the secretion of nose ceased and inner margin seemed covered with dry mucus, next night violent coryza, and in morning bloody secretion from nose, then drawing pain in tensor fasciæ latæ (tensor vaginæ femoris) of r. thigh, < crest of ilium, then tension in fifth and sixth dorsal vertebræ, towards noon when walking cramplike pain above l. internal malleolus, in evening prickling in upper lip, next day coryza affected upper lip, bronchi and Eustachian tubes, pain in ears, ear-wax increased, on the seventh afternoon headache, with full, hard pulse, C. > that evening by dancing. **Violent, with swelling of nose** (Phos.); *V., with catarrhal headache.* **Stopped; at night, so that he could not get his breath**; with burning in forehead and confusion in head, so that eyes were drawn together, with thirst and heat at night so that she could sleep but little. Fluent; in morning before rising, after an hour dryness of nose; with sticking in head and pain in eyes; with redness of eyes, lachrymation, flushes of heat in face and yawning; with cough; with pressure on chest; with shivering after dinner and cold hands and feet. Watery; then stoppage of nose. *With acrid discharge.* With offensive discharge from l. nostril, which is internally ulcerated (Sil., Aur., K. bi.). Trickling from nose. Hardened mucus in nose. Blowing out of bloody mucus (Aur., K. bi., etc.). Agglutination of nostrils in morning, afterwards much mucus and coagulated blood.

Sneezing; for half an hour every morning; with catarrh; without catarrh; violent, at 5 A.M., then burning in eyes, dim vision, lachrymation and discharge of hot mucus from nose. Bleeding; at 2 P.M., for three days; then frequent blowing out of blood; blowing out of clotted blood; from a small wound in N. in evening, when walking. *Smell acute;* even the odor of hyacinths causes nausea; lost. Odor of crabs in nose on expectoration.

Clinical.—Influenza, with stoppage of the nose, sometimes excoriating. Stoppage of the nose, when Lyc. symptoms are associated with a feeling of dryness posteriorly or with scanty excoriating discharge anteriorly, it is not only valuable in chronic catarrhs, but is too frequently overlooked in acute coryzas. Stoppage of nose in diphtheria. Polypus of nose. Fanlike motion of wings of nose in pneumonia.

Face.—Yellowish-gray. *Yellow* (Sep., Chel.); pale; *pale, and puffy.* Pale in morning, and sunken; P. < towards evening; *and sickly color;* and emaciated; and pinched. Red in morning; cheeks R. after eating, then pale; after eating, with burning; and puffy, full of dark red spots covered with pustules. Frequent changes of color. Swelling of cheeks; of r., with pain (preceded by ulceration of root of a r. molar). Drawn first in length, then in breadth; lines are D., < after supper. Jerking of muscles of cheeks. Necessity to distort the muscles after the excessive good humor. Tearing; in cheeks; in r. cheek; *in cheek-bone* under l. eye; in r. cheek, extending over vertex to occiput; extending from face through r. side of neck down arm to fingers. Pain in l. side on touch. Drawing, < sneezing.

Jaws.—Hard swelling on angle of lower, with heat in head. Lower pushed now forward, now backward. *Tearing in upper;* r. upper; in l. ramus of lower in forenoon, extending to l. temple; paroxysmal, now in r., now in l. Boring in swollen glands of lower. Jerking pain in lower in evening. Drawing pain in lower, < talking and eating, with heaviness in glands under it as from swelling, and throbbing. Drawing. Pressure backward on r. side of lower.

Lips.—Swelling in morning; S. of r. half of lower; of upper, at last with evening fever, first chill, then heat in face, hands and feet, uneasy sleep and night-sweat; of upper, with swelling of gum above incisors. Inflammation of upper, with a pimple on it. Eruption on margins, with cutting on moving or touching lips. Itching pimples on upper. *Ulcer on red of lower* (Sulph.). White blister on inside of upper, with burning pain when quiet, > eating. Sore spot on lower. Soreness in corner. Pale. L. corner drawn outward, then r. Muscles of lips and cheeks draw together and make mouth pointed, then broad distention of mouth. Drawing in upper in forenoon. Stick together in morning. Stitches in region of r. corner. Ulcerative pain in corners. Dryness in morning. Prickling in upper in evening.

Mouth.—Teeth. *Yellow* (Iod., N. ac.). Looseness; *of some incisors;* of two l. lower incisors, with easy bleeding of gum. Bleeding. Sharp, especially broken ones. Involuntary gnashing and biting. Jerks in r. upper molars. Sticking in a r. upper molar; in upper molar after eating, with burrowing; in hollow T., with bubbling and boring; now in upper, now in lower, with drawing, preventing sleep in evening; in slow succession in hollow, > warmth of bed. Tearing in hollow. Boring in crown; (drawing, in hollow, with bleeding of gum). *Aching;* in l. lower; in sound third r. molar in evening; *only at night, and when it ceases in morning excitement and uneasiness preventing sleep;* on chewing; on touch and when coughing; in l. eye-tooth on going into open air; *with swelling of gum;* with ulcer on root of third r. upper carious molar; with periodic tearing in limbs; so that she must constantly bite teeth together; *as if suppurating* **when chewing and on touch,** *with sensitiveness; in a sound T. when eating, as if too long;* as if too blunt. Cramplike pain; *drawing, > warm drinks.* Pain as if crushed in a hollow T., extending into temple; pain as if C. in a lower molar, < biting. Throbbing pain nights; T. pain after eating; *with swelling of gum;* with pinching. Drawing pain in a r. lower molar; (D. pain < cold and warmth); (sometimes in r., sometimes in l., at first extending to ears, at times to temples, with sensitiveness of scalp above l. ear, < touch, over a fortnight after a dose of 30th dilution, during which time he had drunk coffee and wine); tearing, in l. lower molars. Sensation as if l. upper molars would be forced out. Sensitive sharpness of incisors when chewing bread, as if sore, with cold hands.

Gums.—Blue. Swelling preventing opening of mouth. *Profuse bleeding when cleaning teeth* (Iod., Merc., etc.). Boil. Fistula in space where there was a stump, with swelling. (Ulcer between gum and lip opposite r. eye-tooth.) Tearing in G. and roots of l. lower incisors. Pain and heat; jerking P. in lower in afternoon. Prickling and sticking in l. G. and cheek.

Tongue.—*Coated;* in morning, with bad taste; during menstruation, with acidity in mouth; *white* (Bry., Ant. cr.); white in morning; white in morning, with sensation as if raw and rough. White, with prominent papillæ. Yellow. Swollen; in places, and painful, so that it hinders speech. Pimples. **Vesicles on tip** (Nat., Sul.); which is painful as if sore and burnt. Tip covered with red warts, which burn on touch, and near tip a flat, oval ulcer. Ulcer under T., troublesome on eating and talking. Protrudes involuntarily from mouth and back and forth between lips. Strikes involuntarily now between upper lip and upper teeth, now between lower lip and lower teeth. Involuntary clashing, whereby the tone is changed when pronouncing A and O. Soreness; with pain on chewing dry bread. Burning, and of mucous membrane of mouth; B. as after much smoking (he had not smoked because he had lost all inclination therefor). Stammering of the last words of a sentence, as if tongue were affected by a peculiar cramp.

Mouth in General.—Swellings here and there; S. between upper gum and malar-bone, with swelling of cheek and prickling sticking. Mucus; in morning; in morning after waking, tongue sticks to palate and teeth stick together; coating of bloody M. posteriorly. Crawling tearing posteriorly in upper part of palate. Soreness. Roughness. Sensitiveness as if burnt. Heat; in palate and throat in morning; in M. and tongue at breakfast; and at breakfast dry bread causes sore pain on tongue and palate; of mucous membrane, with sensitiveness, and when chewing bread it is torn and sore in places. *Laxity, with heaviness of tongue.* Numbness of M. and tongue. *Dryness;* in morning; of M. and throat in morning, then hawking of mucus; of M. and throat in morning, then expectoration of tenacious, thick, yellowish mucus; at breakfast; of M. and throat only in evening in bed and at night, without thirst; *without thirst;* with acidity; dry feeling, with salivation; glutinous. *Bad odor;* in morning on waking.

Salivation; in morning; mornings, with nausea; in forenoon when writing; in evening; from sublingual glands; from submaxillary glands; < from submaxillary glands, *with tension in submaxillary region, which was sensitive to touch,* next day pressure upon the glands increased the secretion, with drawing and tension in glands; *salty;* metallic-tasting; watery, acid. Forepart of mouth watery after supper, but back part in fauces dry. *Saliva dries on palate and lips to a tenacious mucus.* Saliva runs from mouth at night in sleep. (Spitting of yellow saliva in morning fasting.)

Taste.—*Bitter* (Pul., Bry., Chel., Sul.); *in morning;* at night; in throat; to all food; and slimy, pasty; after eating, and disgusting; sourish, before and after breakfast. *Sour after eating* (Pul.); after drinking milk; < morning on waking; on back of tongue and on palate; on drinking cocoa; *to all food,* even to sweet things; after all food and drink, with inclination to sour eructations. Coffee tastes like vinegar. Sweet; to water in morning. Pasty in morning and feeling as if tongue were rough; P., earthy at 4 A.M.; sour P.; slimy, P., it seems as if mouth were covered with glutinous paste. Flat; (in morning). Cheesy. Mouldy in forenoon. Metallic; on forepart of tongue. Nauseous. Disgusting in morning on waking, and tongue thick and burning, as after much smoking. Offensive after eating, with confusion of head. Disagreeable T. and odor in morning. Bad soon after eating.

Throat.—*Submaxillary glands sensitive* (Iod., Merc.); and swollen. Swelling of internal and external glands, with sticking in T. and ear on swallowing; *swelling of uvula, with elongation of it. Ulceration of tonsils;* like chancres. Suppuration of glands between arches of palate, with sticking on swallowing. Inflammation, with hoarseness and sticking, preventing swallowing; I. of fauces, with sticking. *Mucus; in pharynx; in fauces;* in morning; in morning, obliging hawking, with rattling; *with inclination to swallow;* (tonsils covered by firm, almost milky-white M. after taking cold). Hawking of mucus; in morning; thick, yellow, offensive, easily expectorated, in forenoon; *bloody,* during the daily horseback ride; *in small greenish-yellow masses; granular, becoming less in quantity and less colored;* yellow, purulent; hard, yellowish-white lumps from fauces in morning after dreamy sleep; hard, yellowish-white lumps. *Choking provoking constant swallowing.* Gurgling in sleep. Throbbing in goitre, with jerking.

Sticking; in region of r. parotid; during cough; preventing sneezing. Tearing in l. side; and in l. side of pharynx; T. extending upward. Cutting in sides when coughing. *Pain, with constriction in region of submaxillary glands;* P. on swallowing as if she swallowed too much. *Soreness and pain;* S. in morning on swallowing, with pain and dryness; *on swallowing and coughing;* like a swelling on empty swallowing; as from a swelling, > speaking and swallowing; on eating it seemed as if the food came to a sore spot, then pressure in the place. Scraping in morning, with hawking till a partly dry yellow lump of mucus was expectorated; S. on swallowing, with roughness; < sneezing; with roughness and bitterness. Rawness when walking in cool, open air, with dryness; R. in top of pharynx, with swollen sensation on swallowing.

Feeling as if a ball rose from below into it (Ign., Nux mos.). Feeling in l. side of a lump moving up and down. **Contracted feeling, nothing goes down; too tight feeling on swallowing, food and drink regurgitate through nose.** *Constricted feeling in pharynx, with difficult swallowing of liquids* (Chel.). Sensation as if a stone pressed inward from the outside and pressed throat together, painful on swallowing, not hindering breathing. Tension in back part of fauces, with pressure. Irritation provoking dry cough. Inclination to hawk, with rawness as if mucus were adherent, with tickling in throat provoking cough. *Dryness;* in morning; in posterior nares; but inability to swallow on account of pain. Burning when hawking; P. in fauces and pharynx; in pharynx; in pharynx on swallowing; in pharynx, with empty eructations; in œsophagus. Inactivity on swallowing, food will not go down. Difficult swallowing in evening; difficult S. of solids, with increased hunger. Inability to swallow soup if it is warm.

Clinical.—Tonsillitis, especially on r. side; tonsillitis assuming a diphtheritic character, beginning on r. side, patients worse about 4 P.M., especially with fanlike motion of wings of nose and stoppage of nostrils. Diphtheria of r. side, with stoppage of nose, albuminuria, œdema of face, hands and feet (following scarlet fever).

Stomach.—Appetite. At 10 A.M.; at night on waking; when walking; **after eating, though stomach and abdomen are full and tense;** desire to eat without real hunger. **Great** (Iod., Chin.); **then distention of abdomen;** and hasty eating; and the more he eats the more the stomach desires, so long as he eats he feels well, but afterwards sourish taste, and saliva seems sour; for smoking. *Ravenous* at noon when eating; in afternoon, with feeling as if heavy morsels were in stomach. *Diminished.* **Sudden satiety** *at noon after a little roast lamb,* **with thirst,** *heaviness in stomach and distention in abdomen.* **Lost; and whatever she eats goes against her, even to vomiting;** *and thirst lost;* but much thirst; and no desire for tobacco; *no desire for morning coffee* (Nux v.). Aversion to food; in morning, and even to coffee; *to coffee and tobacco;* to breakfast; to much supper; to bread (Nat. m.), he prefers warm food (Ferr.); to solid food, especially meat (Petr., Sil., Sul.), with thirst. Disgusted with food before he tastes it, but afterwards he cannot eat enough.

Thirst.—At 3 P.M., with heat of head; at 8 P.M., with heat of head and overpowering sleepiness; after eating; with frothy saliva in mouth; *with dry lips and dry mouth*, yet a little drink nauseates her and she cannot swallow it, therewith she is sick and weak; for small quantities at night; burning, caused by slimy, sour, bitter expectoration, the taste of which lasted all night. *Thirstlessness* (Puls.).

Eructations.—After eating; E. into pharynx, where they cause retching. Alternating with yawning. **Incomplete, burning, rising only into pharynx, where they cause burning** (Puls., Phos., Nat. mur.). Burning. Sour; at night; after dinner, with burning in pharynx; after every meal, with risings of digested food; **S., the taste of which does not remain in mouth, but the acid gnaws in the stomach**; with colic; with burning as far as throat; of a sour fluid. *Empty;* all day; after dinner; with pressure in stomach, retching and pressure in throat. Bilious, in afternoon. Of salt mucus. Tasting of food. Of the milk taken in morning, with scraping-clawing taste in throat. Bitter, in morning; of bitter water in morning. **Waterbrash** (Bry., Sil., Sul., etc.); almost every other day, with griping in pit of stomach, nausea, necessity to open her mouth, from which salt water flows, as if it rose from stomach.

Hiccough (Am. m., Cycl., Ign., Nux v.); after supper; after every meal.

Nausea; in morning; *every morning fasting* (Sil.); in morning, with salivation; in morning, with aversion to everything, with white-coated tongue and raw feeling upon it; *in morning after rising, so that she must sit down, with salivation;* in morning after rising, < walking about the room, as if sweat would break out, with emptiness in stomach; in afternoon, with good appetite; in afternoon, with empty eructations; in afternoon, with sourish eructations; in evening; at night; at night, with anxiety at heart, *then vomiting of food and bile; in throat and stomach, even to vomiting, after a meal, with salivation; during menstruation;* after smoking; on looking at food, with insipid salivation; < reading; > *open air*, and again N. in open air, > in the house; > open air, affecting head, which pains as if compressed and confused as far as nape, with trembling of hands; with hunger; with retching of foam; with empty feeling in stomach; with sensitiveness of pit of stomach; with pain in umbilical and epigastric regions and in head; with heat in abdomen and coldness of face; with yawning and griping in abdomen; with oppression of chest and pit of stomach and weakness of legs, all > empty eructations, then returning with crawling in throat and pit of stomach; with tremulous weakness; sudden, at 2 P.M., with heat of face; in attacks, with trembling of limbs (< smoking), and rapid pulse; like a cramp, with confusion of head; as from great hunger, > coffee; amounting to faintness, during dinner, with sweat on forehead and loss of appetite.

Retching after eating, with waterbrash; R., with rising of mucus. Vomiting of clotted blood and sharp acid; V. of mucus after midday nap (in a child).

Rumbling. **Distention and cramp.** *Cramp;* in morning on waking; at midnight; before eating, renewed by wine, with ineffectual eructations. Sticking at cardiac end, in a spot which is tender to touch; S. externally in l. side of pit; sudden, in pit during vexation, then leaden heaviness of legs. Tearing and drawing pain, with nausea and sticking in intestines. *Griping.* Cutting in epigastric region at night, she is obliged to raise herself. Gnawing, clawing and full feeling. Twisting in pit, with flushes of dry heat in face.

Pain; *in pit;* in S. and abdomen in morning, then two greenish, pasty stools; in S. and abdomen in forenoon, with pain on touch and on breathing; **in afternoon after eating a little, with heaviness** (Puls.); in afternoon when riding in a carriage and at night when lying on back, > lying on side, with difficult respiration and sensitiveness to touch and sore feeling; *in evening in bed*, > rubbing; at cardiac orifice in evening; **in epigastric region caused by cough;** in pit before dinner; *after a light meal; after a moderate meal, with fulness, eructations of food and colic;* after every meal; after eating or taking slight cold, with dead feeling in hands and chilliness; after a dinner, with eructations and yawning; after a dinner of veal, with heaviness of abdomen; in pit and lower part of chest after lifting something heavy; in pit, < afternoon and after lifting, with pain on touch; < *sitting bent over; and in region of duodenum; with difficult breathing;* in pit, with choking in pharynx compelling frequent empty swallowing; and constriction, like that associated with nausea; so that she could not bear anything tight about her; rising through œsophagus to pharynx, where there was retching; in pit, extending to umbilicus, with rumbling in upper abdomen; **as if overdistended in evening after eating a little;** bruised, > eructations.

Sensitiveness to pressure (Bry.); in pit; *S. of epigastric region to touch* (Bry.); S. of epigastric region after dinner. **Digestion slow. Discomfort after eating a little.** Heaviness two hours after breakfast. Sensation as if disordered. *Constriction* extending into chest, all day, *with cramp. Tension in S. and hypochondria*, with fulness; *T. beneath stomach, as if everything were too tight, with soreness on chest;* sticking T. in pit on breathing. *Anxiety in pit* (Ars.); in pit if people come near her; in pit, as in rapid passive motion, for instance, swinging. Throbbing in pit; on straightening upper part of body. Emptiness before dinner, causing yawning. Sensation as after long fasting, after dinner, but without hunger. Burning, and in abdomen; B. in afternoon; at 9 P.M.; extending to pharynx. *Heartburn;* in morning when smoking as usual, with nausea, so that he must lie down; after smoking; after eating, < tobacco-smoke; after every meal, with sour eructations and burning in pit of stomach, which almost takes away the breath and makes him weak; after cold roast mutton, with pressure upon chest as from a stone; rising into chest, then acidity in mouth; causing acidity in mouth.

Clinical.—Canine hunger, but the attempt to eat is followed by flatulent distention and inability to take more food, or sometimes the flatulent distention immediately takes away the appetite; or sometimes a feeling of constant satiety, he feels too full before he has eaten anything, and cannot eat. Acid dyspepsia (Mag. c.), the region of the stomach becomes distended and extremely sensitive to touch. Gastralgia. Chronic dyspepsia, solid food causes excruciating pain and sometimes vomiting. Atonic dyspepsia, with bloating. Chronic gastritis, with burning pain and waterbrash. Scirrhous indurations of pyloric orifice of the stomach, with vomiting of blood, burning and extreme flatulence.

Abdomen.—**Distention** (Carbo v., Graph., Mag. c., Sul.); in afternoon from 4 P.M. on; towards evening, with incarceration of flatus; towards evening, with much movement of flatus, colic in consequence and easy discharge of odorless flatus; **after eating** (Carb. v.), *till evening*, **with tension,** *no desire to walk and he remains sitting;* after eating, with heaviness; *after eating to satiety;* after a light meal, with pressure; after dinner, with tension in head; before menstruation; < evening, with urging to stool; > **emission of flatus** (Mag. c.), *with rumbling;* with hunger; with dragging towards rectum; with rumbling and pain, then diarrhœa; with cold feet. **Flatulent distention; after stool** (Carb. v.); after dinner, with burning pain in stomach and umbilical region, salivation, metallic taste, eructations of food, heartburn and frequent yawning; *with frequent diarrhœa.*

Flatulence; in evening, only a part of which is passed, with pressure in umbilical region; *after eating, with empty eructations;* **here and there, in hypochondria, even in back in region of ribs and chest, causing tension and bubbling, > empty eructations;** *here and there, and most of the pains seemed caused thereby;* with rumbling and tearing; with tension, pinching and dragging towards groins. *Rumbling;* in evening, with gurgling; at night on motion, with movements; *after stool; when walking, with gurgling,* also with eructations; *with gurgling; with movements.* Retention of flatus after sitting two hours; R., then bad feelings. *Emission of flatus.* Offensive flatus; in morning; in morning, with relief; in evening; at night; sulphurous. Sinking in, clothing too loose. Jerks. Cramplike contraction. Cramp; in muscles at night, with hardness and pain.

Sticking in viscera, < r. side; S. extending through l. groin to thigh at noon; about abdomen like a ring, with pain in small of back. Twinging as before diarrhœa. Pinching after eating. *Griping; all day; in morning;* in morning, with desire for stool; from 3 till 10 P.M (after a good stool), with nausea; on frequent waking; after eating; after breakfast; after a glass of wine and two eggs, with diarrhœa and sore pain, and during the night brown diarrhœa twice, with colic and urging, became warm after midnight and slept till 5 A.M., when there was diarrhœa again; > emission of flatus; with frequent diarrhœa, with several greenish stools without tenesmus; then diarrhœa; as in diarrhœa. Cutting about midnight, with vomiting and diarrhœa; C. before stool; before dinner, with pressure; on inspiration and when lying on back; then discharge of flatus; extending into genitals; extending into sides and hips, towards evening; paroxysmal, at night.

Pain; all day; all day, even in bed; in morning; in morning on waking; in morning on waking, with desire for stool, two stools, with griping, nausea, retching and aversion to food; at 4 A.M., with ineffectual urging to stool; after midday meal; in afternoon when walking; after rising; before dinner; from a glass of wine, with disturbance in chest; < *region of transverse colon* (Sep., Petrol.), also during a long walk, and lasting into the night; < 9 A.M. by the usual coffee, with milk; < eating; > a carriage ride from 10 to 12 A.M., but distressing fulness remained, and after a moderate meal griping in abdomen, pain in stomach and anger at every trifle; frequently, > bending together, with offensive flatus, then watery diarrhœa; with diarrhœa; with sensitiveness of walls, extending to inguinal region, as after a long walk; as after taking cold; sore, in afternoon, < cool air, even the hernia is sensitive and not easy to reduce. *Flatulent pain;* > walking, with tension, eructations and scanty emissions of flatus. *Drawing pain;* extending into calves.

Tension; and incarceration of flatus; < evening, with desire for stool. *Sensitiveness of skin; S. to pressure,* < *epigastric region* (Bry.); S. to touch in morning. Pulsation, with anxiety as from cramp. Heaviness. *Rising of heat to head, with burning of cheeks;* H. rising over chest to head, with burning in l. side of face, anxiety, cold sweat on face, necessity to go into open air, with weakness.

Hypochondria.—Gurgling in l. Painless jerking in surface of liver on coughing. Sticking in region of spleen; in hepatic region; in hepatic region in evening; in l. at 8 A.M., also in r. at 3 P.M., lasting till next afternoon; pinching, in r. Pinching in hepatic region. Griping in hepatic region when coughing or turning body. Sharp pressure beneath last r. ribs on deep inspiration and on bending sideways, also pressing on r. side of lower abdomen. Cramplike pain in hepatic region and diaphragm on stooping and from any other slight cause, as if liver were wrenched. **Bruised pain in r., < touch.** Pain; in l. in afternoon. *Pain in hepatic region;* **on touch; on breathing;** with natural stool; *in r. hypochondrium, at times < breathing and becoming sticking;* raw P. in liver. Pressure outward in hepatic region. Constriction taking away the breath. Painful tension in l.; *T. in lower hepatic region, with pressure.* **Unpleasant and distended feeling in hepatic region if she eats to satiety.** Itching within liver.

Rumbling in l. side. Pressure in r. side; in middle of l.; drawing, in l. at night. **Weight in l. when walking, sitting and lying, not affecting breathing.** Cutting in upper abdomen in morning in bed, lasting till afternoon, < walking. Intermittent bubbling, tearing in a spot in middle of upper, extending towards l. side. *Sharp pressure on a spot in middle of upper.* Pain in upper, as from flatulence, < retracting abdomen, > empty eructations.

Umbilical Region.—Burning stitches in r. side; tearing S. below U. region on waking at 2 A.M. Cutting towards 4 P.M. Griping; even in morning in bed, with pinching; waking at 2 A.M. from a restless sleep full of frightful dreams, with ineffectual urging to diarrhœa; in forenoon; with urging to stool; below umbilicus, with urging to stool, > soft stool; outward from r. side, extending towards hips and somewhat lower down. Pain; in morning, with yellowish, watery stool; at 2 P.M.; below umbilicus after midnight, so that he must bend together; < cough and deep inspiration; obliging her to bend double; with emission of offensive flatus; and in hypochondria; extending towards spine, so that she can scarcely bear her clothing, < bending backward, at times rising to pit of stomach, where it is a pressure; pulling pain below umbilicus before, during and after stool, with intolerance of hard pressure. Sensitiveness to pressure, with pain in umbilicus as if a worm rose to pit of stomach.

Hypogastrium.—Glandular swelling in groins; red S. in r. groin, with suppurative pain on motion and touch. Inguinal hernia protrudes after menstruation, with tearing; (hernia easier to reduce than usual, though constantly protruding). Rumbling, in afternoon, with gurgling. Cramp transversely across H. and in uterus after stool, < soft stool. Sticking in r. groin; in groins in evening; in l. iliac region, next day also in r.; in r. groin, with pressure; low down in r. side, extending to pelvis, on every breath and when turning body, < evening and night; extending into pelvic and inguinal regions, with dragging; extending into H. and groins at 2 A.M., with twinging; *tearing, in locality of hernia;* boring, above l. groin. Pulsating tearing outward near r. flank. Cutting at night; C. after dinner, then sticking extending into tip of glans penis; in groins in evening. Intermittent pinching in l. Pain in groin; P. in locality of hernia; near now r., now l. hip; in r. side all day, obliging him to walk bent over and to lie down, with short breath; in groins and back on walking; on touch and on purposely taking short, rapid breaths, which also shake the body; in region of l. groin and hip, in open air, with tension; drawing, in l. groin. Drawing in groins as if menstruation would occur, in one too old; pinching D. low down. Dragging towards groins; towards l. G. after a glass of wine, with swelling as if a hernia would form; as before menstruation, sixteen days after previous menstruation. Pressure outward in r. groin; in l. G., then bubbling in inguinal ring. Sensation as if water were running through r. inguinal ring into scrotum. Pulsation deep in r. groin.

Clinical.—Palliative in cirrhosis of liver. Abdominal flatulence, with much rumbling and gurgling, and pains of various sorts. Chronic inflammation of the liver, with enlargement, heaviness and pain. It has proved palliative in strangulated hernia, with great distention and retching. Gall-stone colic. Abdominal dropsy from chronic hepatic disease. Brown spots, particularly on abdomen.

Rectum.—Contraction, so that it protrudes during hard stool (Nat. m., Nux v.). *Discharge of blood during stool; during soft stool. Sticking;* in morning; in morning after ordinary stool, with tenesmus and dragging; in afternoon; with natural stool; with natural stool, with sore pain. *Cramps like labor-pains, and in small of back.* Tearing, taking away the breath. Pain, with spasmodic pain in abdomen, so that she (being pregnant) thinks that she is near confinement (which follows only after sixteen days). Burning during stool. Itching; burning, after soft stool (Sulph.). Pressure at night. Full feeling even after copious stool. Urging; only in rectum; after normal stool, then pasty fæces mixed with mucus; then spasmodic pain in rectum preventing stool; with emission of flatus and relief of gastric symptoms; as if much would pass, but only a moderate quantity came. Ineffectual urging after stool; I. often in afternoon; almost constantly at night. Inactivity at stool.

Anus.—*Hæmorrhoids swollen; protruding; burning, sticking, protruding during soft stool;* **painful on touch** (Ign., Graph., Iris, Æsc. h.); *painful when sitting.* Itching eruption, painful on touch. **Painfully closed** (Sil., Nux v., Nit. ac.). Sticking; and in neck of bladder; in margin, with twinging. Pinching cutting in A. and perineum in morning. *Burning* (Sil., Sul.); *with frequent stools;* with watery stools. Biting; with thin stool. *Itching;* in evening; and on pubis. Pinching in perineum close to anus. Contractive pain in perineum after a hard, scanty stool.

Clinical.—Hæmorrhoids which become very painful when sitting, with distention of abdomen and mental depression. Hæmorrhoids which frequently bleed, even when the patient is not constipated. Rectal fistula is occasionally cured.

Stool.—Watery; and frequent; and yellow, frequent; and painless, undigested, fetid, with flatus. Diarrhœa; in morning; < about 2 or 3 A.M., with colic; mixed with hard lumps; afterwards hard stool (the first in two days), with tenesmus and burning from anus deep into rectum; offensive. Frequent diarrhœa; with pain in abdomen; with griping; with griping and tenesmus; and green, offensive; and yellowish white, with increase of pain in abdominal walls, so that laughing was painful. Soft, but difficult; and frequent; and painful; S., but painless. Pasty; and yellow; accompanied and followed by tenesmus and dragging in rectum as in dysentery; then urging as to diarrhœa, but a scanty stool firmer than the former.

Hard; and difficult; and difficult, scanty; and difficult, twice, with pain in anus, then none for two days, then hard, difficult, with tearing in rectum, two days afterwards a hard one, with great pressure; indolent; and delayed; with urging, then all night excessive flatulence; with much urging, after two hours pressure in abdomen, renewed urging and soft stool; at first, then liquid. **First part lumpy, second soft.** Crumbly. Of blood and mucus, urgent, frequent, with offensive "earthy" smell. Pale. Of liver color. Green, offensive, twice in morning. Offensive. Small, with urging and burning pain in rectum; S., delayed, hardly to be forced out though the desire is urgent. Scanty, with profuse discharge of thin mucus; S., with feeling as if much remained, then painful accumulation of flatus in abdomen. Difficult from contraction of rectum. Indolent, without desire, not daily.

Clinical.—It is occasionally indicated in diarrhœa, but usually there are obstinate constipation, hard stools and spasmodic constriction of anus; the attempt to evacuate the bowels causes severe pain in anus; anus and rectum seem constricted (Sil.).

Urinary Organs.—Stitches in bladder. Pain in region of bladder and in scrotum. Urging to urinate in evening; almost ineffectual U. in evening. *Frequent desire to urinate;* at night; at night, with scanty discharge; with pains before and after micturition, urine lemon-colored and scanty. Constant desire in evening when lying, urine passed by drops and caused burning; C. desire, with tickling in urethra, urine flowed almost involuntarily, and I was unable to entirely evacuate it, urine orange-yellow and of strong odor.

Urethra.—Discharge of prostatic fluid; with lasciviousness, without erections; D. of blood without pain; thin, yellowish, in evening; of mucus; of purulent mucus for two days, with burning after micturition, next day pain on urinating, which had formerly extended into scrotum, was diminished and the D. was less. Sticking in forepart, piercing glans. Tearing in orifice for some time after micturition. Twinging along as after new beer, in morning. Cutting in forepart; C. from posterior end obliquely into abdomen. Pain as from a foreign body, in morning. Drawing pain in forepart. Jerking drawing in back part. Smarting during micturition. Constriction, extending into bladder after urinating, with dragging and burning. *Burning during micturition;* at 2 A.M., lasting a quarter of an hour; in forepart in evening; in female; with discharge at first clear, then purulent, like odorless mucus, which in afternoon was streaked with blood. Burning after micturition, in forenoon; crawling B. in evening on going to sleep after micturition.

Micturition ceases suddenly, only a few slimy drops pass, with pain in urethra, then pain in groins. Involuntary micturition at night while dreaming that I was standing at the urinal. Micturition painful during last drops. Frequent micturition; at night; at night, with interrupted discharge and subsequent dribbling; and copious; and copious, watery urine; and urine frothy; every moment, urine of ammoniacal odor. *Urine burning.* Urine very yellow. Urine pale, and the clouds in it collect in bands of grayish-white color. Dark, with burning; D. and profuse; D., with sediment; D., with reddish sediment. Dark brown, with sediment of mucus; dark brown, *only a teaspoonful at a time, wants to pass it, but cannot.* Reddish-brown. Of strong odor. Copious. Scanty; and high-colored. *Turbid; as if mingled with brick-dust;* and whitish. Copious sediment; **red sediment**; yellow sediment; **red sand; reddish-yellow sand**; *red sand, urine rather clear.*

Clinical.—Chronic cystitis, with a milky deposit of bad odor. Tendency to formation of calculus in bladder. Dysuria in children, especially with scanty deposit. Hæmaturia, caused by gravel. Retention of urine (**Nux v.**). Renal colic of r. side. Uric acid diathesis, if there are deposits of red sand. Chronic inflammation of the prostate, with more or less inflammation of the bladder. It is frequently indicated in chronic Bright's disease, with œdematous extremities and the gastric derangements characteristic of the drug.

Sexual Organs.—Tickling. Weakness, and of neighboring parts, with pain in perineum when sitting. Penis, *small, cold and without erections;* sticking in P.; cutting sticking transversely through P. close to abdomen, at night after emission of flatus; jerking pain; drawing and cutting; tickling drawing in tip; burning in P. and prepuce in evening after coition. Erections in morning; E., with relaxed scrotum; without inclination to coition, and after coition weakness; frequent, during the day; painful; transient, with loss of desire; infrequent.

Redness and inflammation of prepuce. *Itching on inner surface of prepuce;* of frænum beneath prepuce. Yellow moisture behind corona glandis, with dark red soft elevations and biting itching. Tearing in region of corona glandis. Scrotum, relaxation even during coition, with delayed emission; sticking; sticking tearing in side in evening in bed; itching; itching at night. Jerking in l. testicle. Sticking in testicles, with griping; pinching S. at night. Sticking in seminal ducts at night, with erections without voluptuous sensation. Drawing in seminal ducts. Desire increased; with emissions at night; then emissions at night, then exhaustion. *Desire diminished; power diminished,* even voluptuous thoughts cause no erections though there is no failure of inclination to coition. Emissions at night; with voluptuous dreams and lascivious fancies; exhausting E. Falls asleep during coition, without emission.

Female.—Tearing stitches. Swollen feeling in pudenda during menstruation, with itching. Burning in vagina during and after coition. *Leucorrhœa,* frequent discharge of blood-red, before full moon; *milky L.;* paroxysmal L. Discharge of blood two days after menses. *Menses too early;* and scanty; *delayed;* prolonged.

Clinical.—Impotency in men. Sexual exhaustion and loss of appetite, especially after chronic gonorrhœa or cystitis. Inflamed ovaries. Chronic inflammation of uterus, with discharge of gas from vagina. Palliative in cancer of uterus. Leucorrhœa, especially with burning in vagina. Chronic vaginal catarrh, with dryness and burning. Varicose veins of pudenda. Occasionally indicated in fibroid tumors of the uterus. Occasionally useful in suppression of menses, with great flatulence and other symptoms. Dysmenorrhœa, with bloating, constipation, low spirits, etc.

Respiratory Organs.—Larynx, pain on swallowing; pain in L. and throat, with irritation to cough; *itching tickling, compelling forcible cough;* dryness; burning extending up to it. *Hoarseness;* < afternoon, and when speaking rawness and soreness of chest. Speech nasal. Tone of voice seemed muffled, though as strong as ever. Trachea, rawness, with expectoration of mucus; crawling scratching below larynx, waking from the deepest sleep at 2 A.M.; feeling as if air rose in waves and streamed out of mouth. *Irritation to cough as from sulphur fumes; I. to cough from deep breathing,* stretching out throat, and at times on empty swallowing.

Cough; in morning, with tightness of breath; in morning and evening; from 4 till 8 P.M., with much drinking; at 9 P.M., with fever, then heat of head, cramp in legs, feet and hands, and rapid pulse; on deep inspiration, with pain in chest; < evening and by motion and lying on r. side, with *difficult respiration,* sticking in r. side of chest, chilliness and trembling of limbs, the pain in chest < lying on back; with pain on swallowing; with sticking here and there in chest; **at night, < before sunrise, affecting stomach and diaphragm**; at night, causing pain in head and sides of abdomen; at night, preventing sleep before midnight, with pain in chest. *Violent cough; with tightness of chest* (Phos.); and fatiguing during the day, sometimes with expectoration of white gelatinous mucus. Paroxysmal, from tickling in larynx, ending with sneezing; P. and exhausting, with vomiting; P. and fatiguing, then palpitation, hoarseness and rawness in throat. Tickling, in throat, amount to retching; fatiguing T. during the day, < evening on going to sleep and in morning. Hacking; in evening in bed, with hawking; from tickling in larynx. Dry; with sore pain along trachea; and fatiguing; and whistling, as in brandy-drinkers; with whistling, piping and crackling in throat; and rough, < night; and short in morning, with hoarse sensation in larynx, without real hoarseness; and hacking, with rawness below sternum; *then yellowish purulent expectoration, with rawness and sore pain in chest.*

Cough with Expectoration.—*At night;* at night, with hoarseness and sore pain in spot in chest where the expectoration is loosened; thick E. in morning after waking; granular E. from 3 till 4 A.M., in morning yellowish firm E.; *thick E.;* thick, yellowish-brown E.; yellowish-gray E., and smarting in chest; purulent E., with fever and night-sweat, as in last stages of suppuration of lungs. Cough with mucous E.; at night; day and night, blackish; in white balls; in grayish granules. *Cough with hawking of thick, firm, yellow mucus from throat, pharynx and trachea.* **Tickling cough as from sulphur fumes,** *with gray salt expectoration* (Sep., Calc. c.); *tickling C., with gray E.* **Overpowering C. in evening before sleep, as if larynx were tickled with a feather, with scanty E.** Violent C., with thick, whitish-yellow E.; violent C., with scanty expectoration, then oppression of chest, difficult breathing, palpitation and heat of face. Distressing, hacking C., with E. of thin, then thick, purulent mucus. Coughing up bright blood in afternoon.

Expectoration.—Salt; **gray, salt** (Sep., Calc. c.); of salt mucus morning, evening and night. *Of thick,* *yellowish mucus from bronchi in morning* (Calc. c.). Gray, granular, morning and evening. White, slimy. Tough, thick, yellowish. Of a sourish, watery, at times bloody liquid. Bloody. Cannot bring off the sputa, but must swallow it again.

Respiration.—**Dyspnœa as if chest were constricted by cramp**; D., with short breath and rush of blood to chest. *Difficult;* in morning; when walking, with palpitation; *as from sulphur fumes.* **Short**; in afternoon when walking, also with at times pressure upon chest; in evening when riding in a carriage; in sleep; before the cough; on ascending steps and walking rapidly. Arrested on ascending steps. Catches his breath three or four times in sleep before he can draw it properly, with a noise, when he cannot get his breath he wakes and cries. Impeded on ascending steps. (Oppressed in morning during physical exertion.) Whistling.

Clinical.—Chronic bronchial catarrh, especially in old people, dyspnœa. Chronic bronchial catarrh, cough < after 4 P.M. Cough, with free expectoration. Subacute pneumonia, with great difficulty in breathing, and fanlike motion of wings of nose, patient < when lying on back. Hard, dry cough, day and night, with emaciation. Cough rather worse when going down hill than up. Many cases of phthisis pulmonaris, characterized by the persistent abdominal symptoms.

Chest.—Rattling and râles. At one time involuntary contraction of pectoral muscles forward, at another of scapulæ backward. Exudation of blood and glutinous water from one nipple, < touch. Swelling of one breast, with pain on touch. Hard lump in l. breast and beneath arm, with burning pain.

Sticking; in sides; in nipples; region of fifth ribs; l.; region of l. fifth rib; in l. near sternum. In morning, in sides; l.; l., near sternum; region of l. fourth rib near sternum; now r., now l., near sternum. In forenoon, in l.; in l. near sternum. Afternoon, in r.; in sternum. At 3 P.M., < running, with oppressed respiration. Evening, in l.; in l., < deep inspiration; in sides in bed; on pulsation, < a hand's breadth below l. clavicle, < cough, deep inspiration and motion, could scarcely move in bed, with chilliness, cough, headache, fever, then heat in head, dreamy sleep and sweat after midnight. At night, beneath margin of l. ribs, on turning to l. side, then uneasy partial sleep, with heat and sweat. S. in r. when coughing and moving body; in region of fifth rib, close to sternum, when at rest, then sticking on l. side; here and there on breathing; *in l. when breathing,* also with jerking; in and beneath C. on breathing after supper; in sternum on deep breathing. Aggravation by deep breathing; in l.; in l. in region of fifth rib; in region of l. sixth rib, till night. S. in r. clavicle, with sensitiveness. S. in l. in evening, causing uneasiness; sudden, close to r. border of sternum in evening; intermittent; intermittent tearing, in lower part of sternum during rest, not affecting respiration; pulsating, in l.; burning, on margin of sternum when walking in open air. S. in l. extending to back, so that he could scarcely breathe; on l. margin of sternum, transversely through chest to back, in morning; in region of l. fifth rib, backward to border of scapula; in region of r. third rib, transversely through chest, < deep inspiration; from ensiform cartilage and r. hypochondrium to dorsal vertebræ and especially to scapulæ, impeding respiration on rising.

Darting pain in r. Cutting in r.; through l. C. and hypochondrium, < stretching. Tearing in region of l. clavicle. Ulcerated feeling beneath sternum in morning, with pressure. Pain in l.; beneath sternum; in morning beneath manubrium sterni, with tightness increasing to dyspnœa; in posterior mediastinum and pit of stomach, with general dulness and weakness; so that he could not lie on l. side, then cough in morning, with greenish expectoration; sprained, in l., alternating with jerkings; flatulent, in lower part, and in præcordial region, with distention under false ribs. Sore pain; beneath sternum in morning. Rawness beneath sternum.

Oppression; all day; *in forenoon, < deep breathing;* in evening; *during respiration; with internal rawness;* with tickling in throat obliging coughing; with sticking in throat, provoking scraping cough; *as if too full;* rheumatic, > empty eructations. Constriction in middle, from walking in open air; C. in region of false ribs, almost taking away the breath. Tension; in forepart of l.; beneath sternum in afternoon; from 11 P.M. to 1 A.M., making respiration difficult; at night on waking, with pressure in epigastric region and rumbling in abdomen; on inspiration, < r. side; in r., with pressure; below sternum, with sore sensation on chest; and pressure, taking away the breath in evening, alternating with distention of abdomen; beneath sternum, with pressure obliging deep breathing. Tightness in open air; T. < moving about, with oppressive pain in pit of stomach; < after walking in open air, with loud thumping of heart.

Pressure upon C. in evening; on a spot beneath l. axilla; as from a knob on r. true ribs. Feeling as if anterior surface of lungs were swollen. Fulness in C. and stomach after eating; F. as from oppression at noon. Feeling as if full of mucus; with whistling in air-passages on breathing during the day. Heaviness; in morning; beneath sternum at 11 A.M. when walking, with pressure; in afternoon, obliging deep breathing; on ascending a height; in C. and epigastric region after supper, with empty eructations; < deep breathing; > expectoration of puslike mucus; with frequent sighing; beneath sternum, with pressure; impeding respiration, > cough and expectoration of white, tenacious mucus; as if catarrh would develop.

Anxiety; beneath heart after violent exertion, on stretching body, with pressure and tendency to pass into sadness. Distress, > excessive eructations, with nausea and ability to speak only in a low tone. Pulsation towards evening when lying; P., with sweetish taste in mouth. Burning beneath sternum in forenoon; B. below lower third of sternum when reading.

Heart.—Sticking in præcordial region; taking away the breath. Pulsating tearing in præcordial region. Pressure in præcordial region after eating, with sticking extending to middle of chest and pit of stomach. Pulsation in P. region, or bubbling internally, not associated with beating of heart. Palpitation; from 4 till 5 A.M.; in morning, > a glass of water with salt in it; *in evening in bed;* on ascending steps, with cough; with rapid pulse; tremulous; anxious, at night on turning over; sudden, after exhaustion, with yawning.

Clinical.—Carotid aneurism is reported to have been cured (Bar. c.).

Pulse.—*Rapid;* at 10 A.M., with very cheerful mood; and full; *with coldness of face and hands.*

Neck.—*Swollen glands;* internally and externally; hard on sides. Involuntary stretching now forward, now backward; at one time I. stretching, at another contraction of muscles. Twitching of muscles and constriction, almost taking away the breath; in morning. Sticking in glands on swallowing, extending into ears; jerking S. from N. to r. foot. Tearing extending into r. shoulder, only in evening in bed and at night; extending into shoulder-joint during rest and at night when lying, preventing sleep, > lying on painful side, < during the day if the parts are cold, > motion. Drawing pinching griping up sides.

Pain; in nape; *in a spot in nape;* on outer side towards nape; in nape on bending head backward; jerking, extending up r. muscles. Drawing pain in l. muscles; in outer muscles, extending to shoulders and elbows. Sprained pain in nape; with sensitiveness to touch. Spasmodic constriction in nape after dinner. *Tensive pain in N.* and shoulders on walking in open air, *with stiffness; T. pain in N. and occiput* when writing. *Tension in muscles ;* T. in nape and sides of neck. Nape feels too short on stooping. *Stiffness* (Zn.); of nape; of l. side; with confusion of head. A kind of paralysis of muscles, head sinks forward, with dizziness (Gels.), without inclination to lie down.

Back.—Curvature of spine in a child. Shock extending towards vertex, so that he must hold on to head, when sitting after eating to satiety. Sticking in middle; S. on r. side in afternoon when walking, < deep inspiration; in l. side on breathing; extending to r. scapula; when sitting, extending into small of back; paroxysmal, cramplike, in middle, preventing motion. Tearing near r. side of spine. Pinching; in r. side, with pain. Attacks of clawing and squeezing, then sticking in side, with blackness before eyes and necessity to lie down wherever she was. Pain when standing; P. extending to shoulders and small of back; in morning when sitting writing, sometimes over whole extent, sometimes in one place, as if a fist pressed against lower dorsal vertebræ, when there was a similar pressure on lower end of sternum, so I must hold my breath; sprained, in l. side extending into l. hypochondrium. *Drawing pain;* when sitting. Painful drawing in evening. Tension in B. and hips at noon; sticking, deep in; rheumatic, in B. and r. side of chest, < inspiration. Throbbing. Weariness when writing.

Scapulæ.—Twitching in l. Sticking between S.; beneath; beneath l.; beneath r., extending to small of back and head; posteriorly in region of r., corresponding to the sticking in forepart of chest; near inner margin, taking away the breath. Tearing below, near spine. Pain beneath; beneath r.; P. then burning on r.; rheumatic, in l., so that he could not raise arm to the head; drawing, between. Drawing between; in evening; D. in and near r. in evening. Tension in l. as from a drawing plaster. Bubbling beneath l. Stiffness extending down back.

Lumbar Region.—Sticking; in region of l. kidney; above region of r. kidney; *in kidney region, < pressure; extending into rectum. Tearing in region of r. kidney;* T. transversely across when sitting erect. Cramp at night (in a puerperal woman), extending to epigastric region, then to chest, making breathing difficult and causing anxiety. *Pain; above hips; in region of r. kidney; in region of l. kidney; in morning on rising during menses, so that she could not move;* at night, with sticking in hips and l. chest; when lying upon it, with weakness; in first dorsal and lumbar vertebræ on touch and motion; < stooping and rising again; so that he cannot sit up straight; so that it draws the chest together, with pressure in stomach and constriction in abdomen; extending to hips; extending to feet; as if flesh were loosened; as if it would break, with hard stool and colic as if intestines would burst; bruised, when busy in the garden; drawing; tensive, when walking and standing, and in hips. Tension as from a hard substance. Constriction when sitting. Gurgling to left of, extending across it. Stiffness; after some exertions, as horseback-riding, walking and stooping, and in back.

Clinical.—In lumbago it is especially useful after Bry.

Extremities.—Unsteadiness as in intoxication. Trembling; drawing. Movements almost as in chorea. Spasmodic contraction and extension, almost without pain. Sticking now in r., now in l. elbow, now in r., now in l. wrist and in knees; in last joint of r. index in afternoon, then suddenly in l. malleolus; S. and tearing in morning, now in l., now in r. shoulder, now suddenly into r. knee and r. wrist; sudden S. in l. great toe at 6 P.M., then tearing in l. fingers. Tearing here and there; T. in l. knee and r. wrist; in various joints, < finger-joints; in morning after a restless night full of dreams; sudden, in l. index at 7 P.M., then in r. knee.

Pain in limbs and shoulders in morning; P. on touch; in joints on motion. Drawing pain in wrists, l. fingers and l. knee, in evening; in second joints of l. index and middle fingers, at 7 P.M., then in l. knee. Drawing; in joints, < knees; in l. hand and ankle in morning; with stretching; intermittent cramplike, in knees, forearms, hands and fingers. Drawing tension in wrists and ankles in morning in bed. Weariness; of hands and feet; arms and feet; in morning on waking, > rising; arms and legs when walking; with heaviness, so that he dreaded to ride horseback; sudden, at times, with fretfulness. Heaviness; of arms and feet; at 4 A.M., with bruised sensation. *Stiffness of all joints* (Zinc.). Asleep at night; fingers and toes A.; arms, hands and feet, with crawling. *All affected.*

Clinical.—A valuable remedy in chronic rheumatism, always worse till evening and in warmth, pains < r. side. Chronic gout, with chalky deposits in joints. Chronic rheumatism of hands; hands and fingers swollen and stiff, etc.

Upper Extremities.—*Axillary glands swollen.* Pulsating tearing beneath r. axilla.

Shoulder.—Jerking upward of one or other. Sticking, and in l. forearm; in region of S.; in l. S., elbow and wrist all day, with intermittent tearing; in l. when walking about while dressing; on r., repeated when writing after breakfast; with tearing in arm; sudden, in l. in afternoon when writing, and from l. elbow along inner surface of forearm to fingers. *Tearing;* in l.; in l. and in wrist; in r. in morning, and in l. elbow; in l. in morning, with feeling as of a wind upon it; in joints in evening; during rest, *and in elbows.* Sharp pressure backward in a spot on l. near neck. Pain; sudden, from joint along ulna to wrist in evening, with external sensitiveness of the part. Sprained pain in joint; in r. joint; sudden, in l., then in r. Bruised feeling in r. joint, scapula and upper arm. Paralytic pain in joint, so that he could not raise the arm.

Drawing pain in S. and elbows in forenoon; D. pain from l. to hand, at times like electric shocks. Drawing in l. in evening in bed; D. now in r., now in l., with tearing; painful, in r. Rheumatic tension in r. joint.

Arm.—Flexed at elbow (in a child), it cannot be stretched nor touched on account of pain. Jerking; at night, with weakness of it. Tearing in l. extending to thumb and dorsal surface of metacarpal bone, with sensation of dryness and heat in arm; intermittent T. in r. all day. Muscles sensitive to touch. Drawing pain in l. in forenoon, extending to wrist; D. pain in l. extending to fingers; in bones extending into fingers. Drawing in l., as if in nerves. Weakness, < r.; W. in morning; during work; when at rest, with paralysis of them. Heaviness, with pain along inner surfaces and sensitiveness to touch. Falling asleep of the one whose axillary glands are swollen. Sudden paralysis of r. in evening.

Upper Arm.—Jerking; of l.; cramplike, of extensor muscles of l. Sticking in r. extending to elbow. Tearing; at insertion of deltoids; on l. in evening, and on wrist; in muscles, with coldness of fingers; drawing, on inner surface. Drawing pain; along inner surface in morning; on inner surface in evening in bed; *in inner surface*, in morning, extending along forearms and wrists; beginning in posterior surface of l. and extending to palm, where it became a sticking, in evening. Drawing in l.; increasing to tearing, then also in shoulder and fossa above clavicle. Heaviness.

Elbow.—Sticking at noon; S., < stretching arm, with tearing, also intermittent S. and tearing in l. shoulder-joint in evening. Tearing; in tip of r.; on moving it; in l., extending into wrist. Pain in bends in morning; P. from r. to little finger, with bruised feeling in arm; drawing P.

Forearm.—Cramp in afternoon. Tearing in l., almost in bend of elbow; in ulnar nerve, extending into hand; from washing, extending into hands. Ulcerative pain in r. Drawing pain in l. ulna; along outer side of l. ulna towards morning in bed, then sensitiveness to touch. Rheumatic drawing in r. in morning. Heaviness of r. in forenoon, so that writing was difficult. Feeling as if asleep when lying upon the table while writing.

Wrist.—Sticking in r. in afternoon, with tearing; in r. in evening, extending to finger-tips; sudden, in r. in afternoon, so that he cannot write. Tearing; in l. at 7 P.M. Sprained pain in r.; in r. when writing.

Hand.—Swelling of r. in evening, with heat; red S. of r. as far as finger-joints. Involuntary shaking. Cramp all day; C. in r. when leaning upon a cane while walking, with tensive pain. Sticking on back; jerking, in r. Tearing in r. between thumb and index; in r. palm below middle finger; between r. wrist and knuckle of thumb; in r. H. and in both middle fingers at night and under the feather-covers; extending towards fingers; in outer side of l. and in knuckle of little finger, extending towards wrist; in r. palm, with burning and itching of skin just below fingers. Pain in r. middle metacarpal bone, so that he could scarcely hold a spoon, in evening. Drawing pain on back of l. Spasmodic drawing and tension in r. when writing, and stiffness of l. fingers when holding a book. Weakness in morning. Heaviness in evening; H. when writing. Asleep in morning in bed; at night; after talking a long time.

Fingers.—Middle bent towards side, without pain. At one time involuntarily spread out, at another doubled into a fist. Twitching of r. in evening; T. of l. index. Sticking in r. thumb; in r. thumb in afternoon; sudden, in first phalanx of middle in evening; sudden, in third phalanx of l. index in morning. Tearing; in r. middle; in tip of r. middle; first joints of l.; l. thumb; ball of l. thumb; tip of r. thumb; first joints of l. index, middle and little, at 7 P.M.; with drawing; in joint of thumb, so that he could not bend it; in joint of r. middle, extending towards tip; paroxysmal, in second joint of r. thumb in evening; sudden, in r. as if they would be torn off, in evening in bed; sticking, in tip of l. middle and beneath its nail; drawing, in l. joints in evening; drawing, in third phalanx of l. index. Pain in knuckles on pressure; P. in r. middle, with heat, inflammation about base of nail, which soon healed after discharge of matter. Sore painful spot on r. index. Sprained pain in joint of fourth on bending up hand. Deadness of two in morning, with blue nails; D. of little in morning on waking, with numbness and coldness, still they are movable. Two last asleep in morning on waking; asleep from tips to second joints in morning on waking, with inability to take hold of anything.

Lower Extremities.—(Reeling when walking.) Uneasiness when lying. Feeling as if sweat would break out in morning. Nates sore; rawness from every motion; sore burning on l.; tearing in l.; tearing in upper part beneath r. hip.

Hip.—Tearing beneath r.; in l. joint; drawing, along sciatic nerves to feet in evening in bed. Pain in region of l.; in l. joint on motion; in muscles about joints on pressure, siting or lying; in r., > walking in open air; from r. joint to foot when walking, so that he must limp. Sprained pain in l. on motion; S. pain in morning on rising extending to small of back, making him lame; sudden, when walking, and in knee; sudden, in l. joint on rapid walking down hill, so that he could not stand. Paralytic pain posteriorly in joint on stooping and on rising from a chair. Tension in l., with tearing; rheumatic tension in l.

Thigh.—Involuntary spreading asunder, then pressing together, afterwards with erections. Twitching; in afternoon; posteriorly on r. Cramp in r., extending to knee, so that he could scarcely ascend steps. *Soreness on inner side of l., with biting itching extending to genitals;* S. between, so that she could scarcely walk. Sticking in l. when stepping. *Tearing in middle of r.;* high up in l.; down l., < sitting, especially when knees are bent; along r. vastus externus and internus in afternoon, extending to patella; sticking, and below knee; smarting, in evening, must draw up leg; periodic, on outer side just above l. patella; pulsative, on outer muscles of l. when walking, with paralyzed feeling. Pain on l. as if wounded, then burning. Bruised pain; in l.; in l. in morning; above knee, < touch and motion; and sensation as if flesh were loose. Tensive pain posteriorly on l. in evening when walking. Drawing pain in posterior part; on forepart of l. Drawing in l. in afternoon; D. and burning. Tension in bones of T. and calves, < sitting. Heaviness and weakness of T. and legs.

Knee.—*Swelling.* Flexion of l., the child could not stretch it on account of pain. Jerking evenings; J. in region of r. Sticking in l.; in middle of l. patella; in l. in evening; in region of r. patella in evening;

when walking; sudden, in l. in afternoon when descending a hill; tearing, from l. to hip, causing lameness. Tearing in K. and ankles, with pain on touch; T. through calf into foot before midnight, so that she must sit up in bed; drawing, in l. Pain as if they would break in morning on rising and on motion. Cramplike pain in hollows when sitting with one leg over the other. Sprained pain; in l. when walking. Sore pain on K. and other parts of legs. Smarting on inner side of r. when walking, with pain on touch, < night if the other leg pressed upon it, sleep restless, with many dreams, next day the pain extended down inner side of calf. Drawing pains. Drawing in hollow of l. Tension preventing stepping. Uneasiness at night in bed. Weariness. *Stiffness in hollows in morning on rising.*

Leg.—Swelling as far as above knees, with red-hot spots, with burning pain < about knees and ankles, so that she could not step on account of pain and sticking in them, with shuddering in them in afternoon, and constipation. Jerking and jerklike trembling. Shaking of r., then of l. Cramp; in r.; of back of r., in afternoon, with sensation on walking as if tendon were too short, < walking over an ascent; *in calves at night*, and even during the day when sitting with knees bent; in l. calf when sitting; in calves, < walking and stretching feet, > rest. Cramplike contraction, and weary pain when pressing upon flexors. Tearing, and in toes; below l. calf; in l. tibia; in l. at night; jerking, in l.; sharp jerking, in lower part of tibia in evening in bed. Pain in bones on side of tibia when touched. Jerking pain below knee. Cramplike pain in l. tendo-achillis on rising and walking. Drawing at night; in r. in evening, and at times jerking; in r. when riding in a carriage; in l., with tearing; from above downward, > motion; rheumatic, in l. at night on waking. Feeling as if tightly bound. Uneasiness in evening; before sleep, > bed; U. and heaviness. Weakness; < ascending steps; as if beaten. Heaviness when walking in open air; H. before menstruation; and swollen feeling. Falling asleep during the day when sitting; of l. leg and foot when sitting. Insensibility on walking.

Ankle.—Swelling. Sticking as if sprained when walking; sudden sticking in r. external malleolus at 3 P.M. Tearing in l. at 5 P.M., with drawing. Pain in external malleolus as if dislocated, even during rest. Sprained pain in r. Drawing extending to knees for two hours, at 5 or 6 P.M. Tension. Stiffness of l.

Foot.—Appearance of corns. Sore, painful indurations on heel. *Swelling; of r.;* of backs; during menstruation; on margins, with pain on walking; of l., with sticking in toes on stepping; with sticking in ankles, < walking; ascending till ascites developed, with swelling of genitals, oppressed respiration and infrequent micturition, with pressure. Cramp at night. Sticking in back; S. in heels; in corns also, with sore feeling; S. on walking in open air; in ball on stepping, and on pressure upon it; cutting, in l. side of heel. Tearing near heel; beneath l. heel; in heels and balls. Pain in a corn; in a corn on r.; in ball of r. on beginning to walk; as from a stone under heel on stepping; (in F. which had been diseased) as if it would break out anew; suppurative, in ball of r.; suppurative, in soles on stepping and when sitting, with burning; drawing, in heel in evening in bed. Drawing below ankle, with heat. Burning tension on back near great toe. Smarting of heel. Weakness; in morning; in morning after waking, with disinclination to rise; in afternoon; in afternoon when walking, with heaviness of them; in afternoon, with sleepiness; at 4 P.M., they give way when standing; on ascending steps; with bruised sensation. Heaviness; in afternoon when standing, with tension in soles and heat in r. sole. Falling asleep and crawling; falling asleep of l. heel. Numbness as far as calves at night, with falling asleep of them.

Toes.—Involuntarily stretched, then drawn together. Sticking in great, then in soles; in r. great, in evening; in r. little, which looks red and as if frozen, < morning; sudden tearing, in second joint of r. great in evening when descending stairs. Tearing in first three r.; in second joint of great, in afternoon, then in r. knee; in a corn on little, with drawing and pain on touch; sudden paroxysmal, in l. great, as if it would be torn out, at 11 A.M. on walking in the room. Pain in r. great at 6 A.M.; P., as from inflammation in nail of great; sudden sprained, in r. great, making it difficult to step. Sore pain, < walking; in ball of great, when walking, with feeling of abrasion; *smarting sore pain between toes* (compare Sil.); burning S., with feeling as if sand were about them; burning sticking, sore sensation. Drawing pain in r. at times during rest. Pressure on ball of great. Dead feeling in r., with formication, when walking. Asleep in morning, and insensible.

Skin.—Freckles on face; F. more on l. side of face and across nose. *Itching "liver" spots.* Red spots on legs; like gnat-bites, coming and going on legs; on upper abdomen, about pit of stomach and thumb-joint, with itching and burning; *redness of finger-joints, with swelling;* R. of joints of middle fingers, with swelling and with swelling of hands. *Brown spots* on inner sides of *thighs*, close to scrotum, extending from inguinal canal to perineum, next day spots *inflamed, with burning pain*, so that walking was painful, next day *red, swollen, burning pain*, < touch and walking. Swelling in lumbar muscles, painful on moving body (> Silicea); inflamed S., like erysipelas, below elbow, suppurating like a boil. Inflammation of a scratch on finger; I. of r. middle finger from a hang-nail, with pain. Chilblain on little finger. Warts on hands. Eruption on face; about mouth; fine, on face; fine, about mouth; itching, on upper part of back. Itching tetter on side of nose near eye; on sides of neck and back; on back; tibia; scaly, bleeding, on face and corner of mouth. Urticaria; on legs in evening.

Pimples on face; and thigh and l. corner of mouth; on forehead and behind l. ear; on r. thumb; knee; beneath skin of forehead, without change of color; on leg, with here and there sticking obliging scratching; wartlike, on index; burning, between scapulæ and on nape; red, on r. upper lid, which contract to a scurf; red, itching around neck. *Itching pimples; on hands; about chin;* between fingers; on forehead, temples and chin; P. partly itching, partly burning, on occiput, small of back and about nates.

Red pustules on wrists and l. thigh; biting itching P. on forearms. *Boil on nates;* on hip; above knee; in l. axilla; on l. nates and one on l. forearm, making whole arm stiff; on hands, with sticking on touch; on l. scapula, with inflammation about it, and burning sticking, and alternations of chill and heat in body; on lower jaw, filled with clear lymph, afterwards discharging and drying to a yellowish crust, which left a coppery brown spot. *Skin unhealthy, corrosive vesicles.* Painful ulcer on l. index, preventing sleep; painless U., bleeding on binding up and then sticking pain.

Smarting of thigh after walking, with feeling as if rubbed sore, causing jerking in leg. Sticking in whole skin in forenoon, worse now in one place, now in another, so that he must rub himself with his clothes, with general heat; S. all over l. foot as if asleep at 5 A.M., > rubbing. Sticking sore pain on hypogastrium on touch even of clothes. Prickling on soles on rising from bed. Tickling on l. heel. Itching biting on knees.

Itching of whole skin; I. on head and face and in nose; about eye; behind ears; face, < forehead and cheeks; of nose; about anus; *on chest;* back; loins; groin and scrotum; upper arms; fingers; fingers that had been frozen, also with sticking; hollow of r. knee; about ankle; on head and back in morning; in evening, on forepart of chin; on back in evening; (< thighs, in evening); on legs, back and nates in evening in bed, with hives after scratching; on calves as far as ankles, and ankles pain at night; of face, with pustules on cheek, forehead and < temples; (on lower limbs, < legs), with hives or papules over whole body, with formication and burning; of cheeks, with burning and redness; on backs of legs, with biting; *on head, back and legs, with biting and shivering;* on thighs, and often during the day, after rubbing, sudden red swelling, with burning pain as in a boil; of r. temple, and after rubbing burning-sticking tearing, then pinching headache; on back extending to neck; of limbs and < scrotum, preventing sleep all night, with sweat; peculiar, at times (sometimes with sticking) transversely across chest in region of fourth to seventh ribs; of face as if the beard were tickling it; as from suppuration of a wound, on two last phalanges of r. index, not > scratching, with redness; burning biting, over whole skin; as from flea-bites in various parts and in tetters; sudden prickling, in hollow of l. knee. *Sticking itching, < scrotum;* on r. nates; here and there.

Clinical.—Eczema; herpes; psoriasis; nævus (compare Fl. ac.); lupus; phagedenic ulcers; impetigo. Varicose veins and ulcers, with œdema; carbuncles; intertrigo.

Sleep.—*Yawning;* all day; all day, with shivering; in morning, with stretching; in morning, with lachrymation and heaviness of head; in forenoon; in evening after reading; after breakfast, with empty feeling; after dinner and supper; with sore pain at root of nose; with pressure and tension in temples; incomplete, often obliged to open mouth wide and then cannot yawn enough; child cries because it cannot yawn completely.

Sleepiness; during the day, with weariness; all day on attempting to read, and weakness from every other work, with apathy; in morning; in forenoon, with yawning, pressure upon eyes and internal chilliness; in afternoon; in afternoon in a carriage; 2 P.M., when riding horseback; in evening; after eating; soon after waking. Irresistible sleepiness at noon, then indolence and confusion of head; I., at 1 P.M.; in evening, but late falling asleep; in evening, but night restless, full of dreams; and went to bed at 8.30 and passed the night in anxious dreams; on waking; after eating; after dinner, then exhaustion. Falls asleep when sitting during the day. Sound sleep; in evening. Heavy sleep, with anxious dreams, and dreams of dead people. Stupefying sleep; and restless, with frequent waking; and late waking; and inability to arouse herself in morning, and weakness.

Sleep, with mouth open. Always gets upon his back at night in sleep. *Laughs aloud in sleep. Anxious crying;* weeping; with unintelligible words. Talking; loud. Moaning. *Starting up on falling asleep;* as if coming from feet. Starting up in bed at night; S. up from sleep; wishes to cry out, but cannot. Twitchings, the legs are jerked forward; T. of fingers. Sleeplessness; till midnight; after midnight; first part of night, then uneasy sleep; on account of trembling and feeling as if everything in body were swinging back and forth; because on closing eyes everything that had happened during the day passed vividly before her. Late falling asleep; with restless, heavy dreams. Waking with a scream; W. after midnight, with sensation of coition, without emission; at 2 A.M., with difficult recollection, heat of head and abdomen and coldness of feet; every morning at daybreak and then falling asleep again; wakened by dreams associated with noises that were going on at the same time in the street; anxious. *Frequent waking; from frightful dreams;* with tossing about, sound sleep only in morning; and remaining awake for hours, then sleepiness in morning. *Sleep bad on account of excitement. Sleep unrefreshing;* and confusing.

Restless sleep; after midnight, and interrupted; when lying on l. side; with sobbing; with starting up and jerking in limbs; (in a child), with groans; (in a child), with frequent and violent talking; sound only towards morning; with rapid respiration; with rush of blood to heart; *and light*, and wandering in mind, as if now in one place, now in another; and short; *and frequent waking, wide awake at* 4 A.M.; and waking at 5 A.M. from a dream, with nausea and salivation; *full of dreams; confused dreams*, in which he seemed to be now in one place, now in another, *with frequent waking*, and in morning on rising he is more weary than when he lay down; full of vexatious dreams; with disconnected D.; full of dreams without ability to wake; with dreams, and awake from 12 till 2.30, with sweat, flow of thought, then slumber till 6 A.M.; and dreams of encounters with wild animals or a giant, anxiety as in nightmare, and on waking general heat, with violent beating of pulse.

Dreams.—*Sleep full of D.;* dreamy sleep, on waking dulness of head and irresolution. *Confused.* Nightmare. Of murder. Horrible, that some one wished to kill him. Of hateful images during midday nap. *Frightful;* and even fright after waking. Sad. Heavy. Bad. *Anxious;* in morning after vivid dreams, as if many young dogs in constant succession fastened themselves on various parts of the body; with childish fantasies; in a fight he hid himself away from danger. Exhausting; with sweat on waking. *Vivid;* of business and studies; of the work of the day, whose execution, even after waking, she believed necessary; of business, with moist skin, sleep till 4 A.M. (formerly always awake at 2); and pleasant, then difficult waking in morning, then dreaming again as soon as he closed his eyes. Pleasant, so that she did not wish to wake. Voluptuous; with emission; with erection and emission. Of coition without emission; that she felt the irritation of coition.

Fever.—Chilliness; all day; in morning; in morning on waking, then heat and pain in occiput; from 8 till 8.30 A.M., then slight heat; at 9 A.M., then heat from 11 A.M. till 1 P.M.; in afternoon, and heat; in evening; in evening on falling asleep; every evening in bed till midnight, then heat, in morning sour sweat; in evening, preventing sleep, with nausea; *slight, in evening, then violent and long-lasting heat, weariness and pains in limbs;* every day from 3 P.M. till late in evening; *at* 5 P.M.; 6 P.M., with weakness; every other day at 7 P.M.; at midnight before menstruation, then heat, < face, with restlessness; *the day before menstruation, also with sick feeling;* after stool, with thirst; when writing in a hot room, > moving about, with pain in forehead; with feeling as if everything internal would come to a standstill; with nausea and vomiting, then sweat without heat, sick feeling in all limbs, sticking in head, next day chilliness, then heat in face.

Sensitiveness to cold air; in morning on rising; to C. open air; S. of skin to every change of temperature, especially to cool air, draughts and evening air, and shivering easily runs over whole body. Feverish dread of open air, < after eating. Internal chilliness in morning; I., as if blood gradually ceased to be warm. Creeping C. in morning; at 4 P.M., then weakness; at 1.30 P.M., then weakness, next day at 4 P.M.; every evening; on backs of legs; down thigh during the day. *C. alternating with heat;* during the day; in evening, with pain in whole body and coryza; *and redness and heat of cheeks;* alternating attacks of C., heat and sweat after a fright.

Shaking chill at 6 P.M., beginning in nape and arms, with coldness of ears; S., from 6 till 7 P.M., beginning in chest and extending over body, then bruised sensation; two evenings from 7 till 9 P.M., with drawing in whole body, and on waking from sleep full of dreams, general sweat, then thirst; from within outward at 1.30 P.M., then heat without thirst or sweat; spasmodic, in evening, with throbbing in forehead.

Shivering; at 8 A.M. when walking, with gooseflesh; in evening; in evening, with yawning; in evening, especially starting from back; *in evening (6th day), at* 6 P.M., *starting from back, with feeling as if water were spurted upon back (7th day), at same hour again chilliness over whole body (8th day), at same hour C., with stupefying sleep, then uneasy sleep interrupted by heavy dreams (9th day), at same hour C. for two hours, with stupefaction of head, sleepiness, tearing in limbs, no thirst, no sweat (10th day), at* 7 P.M. *shaking C. beginning in back, with cold hands and feet, cannot get warm in bed for two hours, tearing in limbs is worse, with nausea and constant yawning, then stupid, restless sleep, from which she wakes in morning, with weakness (11th day), similar attacks at* 7 P.M. *for four days;* from 1 till 3 P.M.; *at* 4.30 P.M., *with cold limbs and general gooseflesh, the second day afterwards a similar paroxysm at* 4 P.M., *with yawning, nausea, shivering starting from back and extending over whole body, with coldness of hands and feet, no sweat, no thirst, but heat in face, the chill lasted two hours and a half, ended with weakness and bruised sensation in feet, sleepiness, and drawing in wrists and fingers, slept well and woke well next morning,* attack repeated at 4 P.M., next day and at 3.30 the following day, next day at 3 P.M., with bilious taste, next day at 3 P.M. creeping chill and all other symptoms less severe; S. at 6 P.M.; between 6 and 7 P.M., with thirst; 7 P.M., with weakness and desire to go to bed; 8 P.M. in bed; on going to bed, with burning on urinating; after drinking; after eating, with dulness and sleepiness of head; on coughing, with headache; with hot, heavy head; with uneasiness, pulse rapid, soft and small.

Shivering in back; and shoulders and legs; in back and chest often during the day; over back and loins during the day; at noon, starting from vertex, extending to chest and arms, with sensation as if the hair were drawn gently upward; in lower limbs in evening, from slightest lifting of bed-clothes, with heat of head; starting from head and spreading over whole body; on entering house after riding and afterwards when riding, alternating with heat in face, and head, < forehead; over back and shoulder, with heat of anterior part of body.

Chilliness on l. side of body; C. of body in evening, with heat in forehead. Coldness of head, with pallor, then heat and burning in face, lasting from 9 A.M. till 4 P.M. C. of cheeks and forehead at night; of face, alternating with heat of it. C. in throat and abdomen on going out in wind. C. in back; in small of; on B. and limbs in forenoon and afternoon; at 3 P.M., < evening after lying down, with cold feet; at 5.30 P.M., extending over skin; at 6.30 P.M., extending over whole body; in evening, starting from back; *creeping over back in evening; creeping over back at* 7 P.M. C. in limbs and shoulders. Cold hands; when reading, with hot head and face; externally in fingers, with internal heat in them. Coldness of legs, with heaviness of them. Cold feet; in evening; after supper and a glass of wine; r. in evening in bed, then also l.; before menstruation; r., with heat of l.; and sweat on them; and hands, with shivering in hips; (and hands, l. hand seems dead after eating). Cold toes.

Heat at noon, with redness of face; H. at noon, then headache; in evening after a glass of wine, < head and face; then chilliness, every evening; every evening, drinks frequently but small quantities, frequent ineffectual urging to stool, and at night frequent emission of scanty, brown urine; with weakness, then chilliness; with burning and sticking in eyes; with short breath, little thirst, pallor and starting up in sleep; and everything seems too heavy and hot, often obliged to take a deep breath, oppression, hair bristles and is drawn together in bunches; < palms and soles, then general sweat and exhaustion; > open air, with restlessness; then after fifteen minutes chilliness, with weakness and weariness of feet at 4 P.M. Heat in flushes; with redness of face; with external heat of forehead. Orgasm of blood; in morning on waking; towards evening.

Burning in skin here and there; B. in skin along spine; in skin beneath l. shoulder; periodic, in spots on skin, often in sacral region, < heat. Hot and dry skin. *Heat of head; after eating, with red spot on l. cheek;* with pain in forehead, also at noon, also at night; internal; rush of, with circumscribed redness of cheeks. H. in forehead; about 11 A.M.; (biting), in F., eyes and throat. Heat of face; of cheeks; in forenoon, with redness, then irresistible sleepiness; at noon; at 1 P.M., with circumscribed redness of cheeks; at 2 P.M., and of hands; in evening, with redness; and of ears; with redness; without redness; with hypochondriac mood; with confusion of head; *in flushes;* in flushes in morning after rising. Burning in back; **between scapulæ as from coals** (Phos.); rising along spine; in lower part of forearm. Hot hands; after eating; l., with anxiety; hands and fingers, with redness of fingers, as after freezing; in palms and eyes, also after walking in open air. Burning in feet; in forepart of F. and soles; rising over back to forehead; in soles in evening; in soles at night.

Sweat over whole body; easy S., with increased urine; in daytime in sleep; every morning; every morning in bed; in morning after a restless night; after midnight; towards morning; all night, with quiet sleep; at night, with coldness on forehead and neck; every night after midnight, < chest; after walking in open air, then exhaustion. (Sourish); in morning. Of the odor of blood in morning. Offensive exhalations, as from onions. He is conscious of a strong sweaty odor about himself. Sweat on palms; on swelling of knee; of feet; **of feet** (Calc. c., Carb. v., Iod., Phos., Puls., Sep., Sil., Sul., Thuj.), *till they become sore;* on joints in morning; on trunk at night; between toes (Cycl., Sil.), softening corns so that they can be taken out with finger-nails; sour on body but not on legs. Dry hands.

Clinical.—Chronic malarial fever, paroxysms recurring at 4 P.M., there is general nervous irritability, with thirst, red sand in the urine, enlargement of spleen, sour vomiting, teasing cough, the chill often beginning in the back. Suppurating fever. Occasionally indicated in typhoid fever, with distention of abdomen, red sand in the urine, great mental depression, lower jaw hanging down, etc.

Lycopus.

A tincture of the whole plant of Lycopus Virginicus, L., is used.

Generalities.—Aggravation on alternate days.

Mind.—Wandering from one thing to another.

Head.—Pressure in evening, and in eyes. Pressure in forehead; all day; in morning, < l. side; at 8 A.M.; at 3.15 P.M., and in eyes. Frontal and vertical part of head pressing out at 8 A.M. Pain in forehead and eyes.

Eyes.—Full and heavy during the day; F. in morning, painful and pressing out. Pressing out. Painful pressure in balls at 8 A.M. Pressing pain in supraorbital region; pain in l. in afternoon.

Clinical.—It has been used in morbus Basedowii, with tremulous action of the heart and protruding eyes; it may relieve the protrusion of the eye and the cyanosis from the general relaxation, but it has no effect upon the glandular enlargement of the thyroid, which usually must be treated by Iodine.

Ears, Nose and Throat. — Burning of r. ear. Catarrhal sensation in l. ala nasi. Pain deep in r. parotid gland and at angle of r. maxillary bone.

Stomach and Abdomen.—Circumscribed pain and compression in epigastric region. Flatulence all day. Colic, then profuse and forcible diarrhœa; C., with rumbling. Griping. Tenderness of A. at 8 A.M. Lugging pain in spleen after 9.45 P.M. Tenderness of l. hypochondrium.

Stool and Urine.—Diarrhœa; could have had a stool at any time of day, but had perfect control over sphincter ani. Costiveness. Tenderness of bladder at 8 A.M. Thirty-two ounces of urine during the day. Specific gravity of urine 1012.

Respiration.—Accelerated during exercise in early part of the day, < ascending stairs.

Heart.—Sticking in cardia. Throbbing pain in cardia at 3.15 P.M. Constrictive pain around H., with tenderness. Cardiac viscera pressing outward, but not painful, at 7.30 P.M. Beat more distinct on r. of sternum than on l. First sound displaced by a blowing sound, two days afterwards the first sound lacking, sometimes faint, displaced by a blowing sound of mitral regurgitation, the second sound pointed, short, sharp and emphatic, afterwards sound distinct at apex, the blowing sound heard in clavicular region, < between scapulæ.

Clinical.—It is indicated in diseases associated with tumultuous action of the heart, with more or less pain and tenderness, often in symptoms associated with hypertrophy of the heart. Palpitation from nervous irritation, with oppression about the heart. Rheumatoid pains in various parts of the body, associated with either valvular disease of the heart, cough and hypertrophy, or with simple palpitation and various nervous symptoms. Cardiac disease following rheumatic fever, with hacking cough, palpitation, dyspnœa, small, weak, irritable pulse, which intermits now and then. Hæmoptysis, with palpitation and pain in l. side of chest. Feeble, irritable heart, with cold extremities and general nervousness.

Pulse.—Irregular in force; and weak; and weak, 48. Irregular, sometimes drags and hurries up. 68, and full.

Back and Extremities.—Pain in lumbar region, < l., and bladder feels distended when empty; pain in loins like lumbago. Huskiness of l. patella on motion; with pain in knee, < motion. L. lower extremity feels half an inch shorter than the other and the foot sounds on the sidewalk as if this were the case.

Sleep.—Night restless, full of troubled dreams.

Magnesia Carbonica.

Pure carbonate of Magnesium is triturated for use.

General Effects.—In general it produces gastric and intestinal catarrh, acid eructations, sour-smelling stools and sour perspiration. Great flatulence (which is said not to be caused by calcined magnesia). One of the most interesting effects in connection with the acid dyspepsia is the great tendency to neuralgia, marked in all the Magnesias, especially about the face.

Allies.—Hep., Puls., Alumina, Calcarea c., *Puls.*, Coloc., Pod., etc.

Generalities.—Twitching in vessels of thighs, shoulders and face. Trembling in morning, > rising, with weakness. Burning stitches here and there. Wandering tearing in forenoon; T. during menses, now in both sides of head, now in vertex, now in nape, > night; jerking T. now in vertex, now in occiput, upper arms and thighs all day. Pains here and there in all parts. Jerking pains on rising from bed. Easily sprained, on bending arm backward shoulder pains as if dislocated and on touch feels bruised, and inability to turn head to left without pain. Soreness of whole body. Sensitiveness of skin of head and body, especially to cold, cold creeping through skin and chilliness through and through from every draught. Internal restlessness, with distraction of mind and trembling of hands.

Weakness; all day, with heaviness; *greater in morning after a good night's sleep than in evening on lying down;* in morning in bed; in morning, with discomfort and apathy; in morning on waking, > lying down again, with bruised feeling in hands and feet, and trembling, and on getting out of bed coldness; in afternoon, when sitting and walking, > standing; in evening; when walking; when eating; after eating, with pallor, nausea and vomiting of dark food; after an indigestible dinner, with sleepiness so that he suddenly fell asleep when standing and talking, with confusion of head, which made thought impossible; during menses; during menses, with sweat; after stool; after diarrhœa; after vomiting; with suffering expression and nausea; with heaviness; with discomfort, anxious warmth and sweat; sudden, when walking in open air; of mind and body.

Dizzy faintness at 9 P.M. in bed, with coldness, then nausea, afterwards frequent waking with nausea, < slightest motion, < morning after rising, with taste and eructations almost like bad eggs, pale face and coldness. Stiffness of whole body in morning on rising. Symptoms which occur when sitting are usually > walking (Puls.). Amelioration in open air (Alum., Puls.).

Clinical.—General tendency to neuralgic pains and general aggravation at night, when there is a great deal of fever and restlessness (Sul.).

Mind.—Talkative in afternoon, everything prospers. Ill humor; all day, > evening; in forenoon; afternoon; evening; at 7 P.M.; when walking in evening; so that she does not know what she shall undertake, with constant sweat; yet humming; good humor on first day of menses, the next three days ill humor. Anxiety all day, < moving about, with sweat; A. at night, the bed felt like stones, with constant tossing about; at night causing late falling asleep, frequent necessity to uncover herself, which she could not endure long on account of coldness; at night, and she could not bear to have her hands covered, but if she put them out they immediately became too cold; after rising, with prostration and with stitches in whole body; when eating soup, with warmth, < head; tremulous A. and fright as if she apprehended some misfortune, > evening in bed. Sadness; and apprehension; and unwillingness to talk. Apathy in afternoon, with apprehension and compressive headache. Confusion from mental labor, with stupefaction. Forgetfulness.

Head.—Sticking in morning after rising, with pressure over eyes; S. at 10.30 A.M. when standing, then bruised pain in r. and then in l. side of head, with feeling as if it would be > moving head, which was not the case; from 8 P.M. till sleep, making her ill-humored; here and there; here and there from dinner till 3 P.M. Tearing in evening and night, with sticking as from knives, so that she thought it would take away her senses. Aching in morning in bed, lasting till towards 10 A.M.; in afternoon, < towards evening, with sensitiveness of head to pressure, as from an ulcer; during menses, with heaviness and internal heat; jerking, at 1 P.M. after vexation, < constantly till > evening in bed, with heaviness; drawing; as from stiffness of neck. Pressure across during mental work; P. over whole, in the house with many people. Feeling as if screwed together from sides at 5 P.M., then also in occiput.

Heaviness in morning, with yawning and nausea; H. in morning during menses, with agglutination of inner canthi; in afternoon, with pain; when lying after midday nap, with bloody saliva. Confusion in morning on rising, > washing and moving about, with stupefaction, as from insufficient sleep. Vibration internally on slight motion. *Rush of blood* in forenoon; R. < smoking. Vertigo in morning on rising, > walking, with heaviness of head; V. in evening when sewing, with nausea, afterwards when lying unconsciousness; when kneeling, as if she would fall into a heap; frequent V. like loss of consciousness; as if everything turned around with her and as if she would fall forward; as if everything went round with her, in morning after rising; with nausea and frequent salivation; objects seem to go around at 11 A.M., when standing, with intoxicated feeling and heaviness of head.

Forehead.—Vibrating jerking above l. eye on motion, extending through head. Sticking at 6 P.M.; intermittent S.; outward in r. side, more externally, at 3.30 P.M., preceded by tickling. Cutting as if skin would be cut through from middle towards l. eye. Tearing deep in centre in afternoon, with beating; T. in afternoon and evening, > in bed, with drawing backward in nape; deep in r. side of brain at 4 P.M., then in l., at last in front of l. ear; in F. and top of head after dinner, with heaviness; in brain as if benumbed and heavy, from 1 till 5 P.M. Pain; in sinciput and eyes; from 8 A.M. till noon; on waking, > 4 P.M.; stupefying, in l. at 3 P.M., and at times in eyes. Drawing pain all the forenoon; in morning, with nausea. Painful drawing to occiput all day during menses, with heaviness of brain. Heaviness at 5 P.M., with suppurative pain in l. side of occiput; H. when standing. She felt the beat of an artery.

Temples.—Sticking in l.; in r. after dinner; in l., then above r. ear. Tearing in l. at 5 P.M.; in l. in afternoon, > pressure; in l. in evening on lying down, > pressure, but returning; in r. involving eye; upward in l. in evening, with aching in last molar.

Vertex.—Stitches at 2 P.M.; S. through brain to r. side of occiput at 10.30 A.M.; in r. side, then on moving head towards the left tearing in r. side of occiput. Jerking tearing, then sensitiveness to pressure. Bruised pain during and after menstruation, with sensitiveness to touch towards evening. Pain as if the hair were pulled upward from 5 till 9 P.M.

Sides.—Stitches in l. at 3 P.M. when standing; here and there in l. at 7 P.M.; in anterior angle of r. parietal bone at 7 P.M.; outward in r. at night when lying upon it, > turning upon other side; in r. after dinner, with internal throbbing; in r. when standing, extending forward; in l. parietal bone and in upper and forepart of r., extending towards each other; extending inward at 5 P.M., with internal tearing; inward in r. when sitting after dinner, with tearing; boring, in upper part of r. through to r. side of occiput at 8.30 A.M. Boring in l. in evening. Pain in l., < temple, waking her at night, > raising head.

Occiput.—Sticking, and even over whole head; S. in evening. Pain. Tension as if something drew head backward during and after swallowing, < standing, > sitting.

Scalp.—*Hair falls out profusely.* Itching in morning after rising, < scratching; on r. side in forenoon, > scratching; every evening; on vertex during dinner; on l. side, > scratching; of scurf every morning; of scurf in evening, > scratching; *of scurf in rainy weather.*

Clinical. — Preparations of Magnesia (particularly Mag. phos.) have been found valuable for neuralgias of the forehead, especially supraorbital.

Eyes.—Matter in them in morning on waking, with burning and dim vision. Swollen in morning after waking, and she could not open them for a long time;

seem swollen in morning after waking, with dizziness. Sticking, with burning and with red vessels in whites. Tearing in morning in bed, then lachrymation, > washing. Pain in l. as if it would burst or were forced outward, with lachrymation, at times much water runs from l. nostril, with aggravation of the drawing sticking above l. eye on blowing nose. Burning; all day; in bright daylight. Dryness; in morning; during menses, with burning and dimness. Biting in l., with lachrymation. Itching in l. at 4 P.M., > rubbing, with biting; I. in r. at 10 P.M., with burning; in r. after dinner; voluptuous, of l. at 4.30 P.M., > rubbing.

Lachrymation all day; in morning; of r.; of r., with burning in it and red vessels in inner canthus. Swelling of ball as if "dropsy of eye" would form. *Agglutination of lids* in morning on waking; A., with pressure in eyes. Inflammation and swelling of lower lids, with redness of one canthus. Jerking in l. lids, causing lachrymation. Jerking tearing in lower lids. Burning in r. inner canthus, with inflammation. Itching in canthi in evening, with burning; I. in l. inner, > rubbing; biting, of r. inner, > rubbing. *Tearing on r. upper margin of orbit.* Pressure about eyes towards evening. Photophobia, with burning in eyes. Vision of r. eye vanishes when looking intently. Vision foggy; in afternoon, < r. eye; dim in the inflamed eye as if feathers were before it.

Clinical.—In some cases the development of senile cataract has been arrested. It has cured styes and chronic blepharitis. Warts on lids.

Ears.—Inflammation of r. external meatus, with suppurative pain, then sensitiveness to pressure. Stitches in front of l. at 5.30 P.M., behind r. at 3 P.M., ending with tension, temporarily > pressure. Tearing in r. external concha at 10 A.M.; in l. concha at 7.30 P.M. Boring in r.; in l. in forenoon, with stitches. Sore pain behind lobule of r. on pressure. Burning smarting below lobule of l. during menses. Tickling in r. at 6.30 P.M. Itching in r. external meatus, > scratching.

Sensitiveness to noise. Noise in l. in morning in bed, with pain on touch; loud N. in r. after dinner. Ringing; in l., or noises; in r. after dinner. Roaring in r. at 11 A.M., with fluttering, whizzing and hardness of hearing; R. in r. at 3 P.M.; in l. at 4.30 P.M., with noises like a storm of wind and with diminished hearing; in r., with diminished hearing, with intoxicated feeling, < in the house; in r. as if near rushing water at 7 P.M.; before ears, so that she could not stay in bed; in front of ears, alternating with whistling. Fluttering in r.; in evening.

Clinical.—It has been prescribed for deafness, especially with abscesses and swellings in ears.

Nose.—Redness in evening, with swelling. Scab in nostril. Blisters in nostrils, with dragging pain. Tearing near margin of l. eye at 7 A.M., extending to l. temple. Stoppage of nose, only at times discharge of a few drops; with a feeling of coryza in morning. Stoppage at 8 A.M.; at 5.30 P.M.; alternating with fluent coryza. Dryness every morning on waking; in morning, with stoppage of l. nostril. Tickling at 10.30 A.M., with ineffectual attempts to sneeze; T. in evening, then sneezing; in r. nostril, > scratching, but returning; in l. nostril, irritation to sneeze. Itching in l. nostril; in nostrils after dinner and at 3 P.M., > scratching.

Sneezing in morning during menses; in morning from tickling in nose; in morning, with stoppage of nose; violent, in morning, with tickling in nose. Coryza, < morning and evening; C. on appearance of menses, with stoppage of nose; C., with stoppage of r. nostril. Stopped coryza; with stoppage of nose, waking her at night; with secretion of nasal mucus. Fluent coryza; in morning, dry in afternoon; in morning on rising, then stoppage of nose all day; C., with discharge of thick mucus and feeling as if nose were swollen from frequent blowing. Unnoticed dropping of water without coryza. A clot of blood is blown out with mucus. Bleeding; in morning; waking at 3 and 5 A.M., with violent sneezing and tickling in r. nostril; and from mouth.

Face.—Pale during menses; P., with suffering and earthy look; P. and of bad color, with general discomfort. Redness from 5 till 7 P.M., with heat of it; with heat of whole body. Fretful expression in forenoon. *Tearing in l. side* in afternoon; *in zygoma at night, > sitting up in bed or driving her out of bed, with burrowing and boring as with a red-hot iron, and with anxiety. Pain, so that she must run from room to room all night, hold the painful side and wag the head, < remaining quiet.* Twinging in centre between chin and lip at 6 P.M., with burning. Tension as if the white of an egg had dried upon it. Throbbing in antrum of highmore, with swelling of r. malar-bone (Nat. m.). Suppurative pain in r. lower jaw and in cheek, < pressure, with redness and swelling and with jerking on talking, sneezing and yawning.

Lips.—Hard pimples in corners. Vesicle on lower, near r. corner; clear V. in l. corner of upper, with tensive pain. Pustule on upper; on lower. Tearing in l. lower. Soreness of upper. Dryness in morning, > noon, without thirst. Burning in middle of upper and above it, with tension. Itching in upper in forenoon, with feeling as if eruption would break out.

Clinical.—Neuralgia of the face, with shooting, lightning-like pains, < touch, draught of air or change of temperature, cannot stay in bed, is obliged to walk the floor.

Mouth.—Teeth. Looseness, with swelling of gums. (Lower wisdom come through.) Sticking after eating; S. in roots of three l. upper at 3 P.M., with tearing, and in open air sensitiveness of teeth and tickling in them. Tearing in roots of l. lower, then also in r. lower; T. in r. lower anterior molars at 4 P.M.; in a r. lower molar at 4 P.M., > salt, with drawing; in r. lower molars at 8 P.M., with drawing; in last l. molars without being able to distinguish whether in upper or lower, in evening in bed till sleep and in morning on waking, > rising; T. rather than throbbing pain at night, with elongated feeling; in r. lower hollow, after menstruation, > applying cold water or lying upon that side, but returning till 4 A.M., < warm room, with drawing, gnawing, uneasiness, ill humor and tensive pain over r. cheek; in a r. lower molar at 1 P.M., then in an upper, as if it would be twisted out; in r. lower after dinner, extending into temples.

Toothache in r. in morning, > prolonged moving about; in lower molars, < l., evening and morning; *beginning in evening in bed and at night driving him out of bed, extending to temples;* when riding in a carriage, < cold; < night; < getting into bed, with salivation; with swelling of cheek. Raging pain in a r. hollow. Jerking pain in morning after rising and in night, with jerking in fingers and feet. Burning pain in evening in bed, with pain as if teeth were loose; B. pain, now in one, now in another, > movement of body, < night in bed and during the day by chewing, with throbbing, tearing and elongated feeling. Beating and drawing pain all night; D. pain in all, with swelling and redness of gum. Elongated feeling; in the back tooth, with pain in morning if cold water touches it, as if it would be torn out, and on chewing.

Gums.—Painless swelling, even in sockets of teeth. Burning blisters, and on lips, palate and inside of cheeks. Pain internally to upper lip as if cut to pieces in middle from morning till afternoon, and burning on touch of tongue. Sensitiveness on eating, with burning in it and sensation as if teeth were too long and as if they would fall out, < lower front incisors.

Tongue.—Pimples, and on inside of cheeks, bleeding on touch and burning when eating, < acids. On forepart of l. margin of T. and on lower lip burning, painful blisters, suppurating on third day. Tensive painful blisters on anterior margin of T. and r. corner of mouth.

General Mouth.—Reddish-blue spot on inside of l. cheek, bleeding when rubbed. Blisters on palate, with feeling as if skin were loosened on eating bread, next day feeling as if the spot were denuded and sore, the blisters and raw sensation > appearance of menses. Palate raw posteriorly in morning. Heat all day; burning in palate in morning as if skin were loosened. Dryness; in morning on waking, and in throat; all day without thirst; at night, without thirst. Itching on inside of r. cheek. Numbness in morning and forenoon, < palate and anterior half of tongue. Slimy and mealy in forenoon. *Bloody saliva.* Salivation during menstruation.

Taste.—*Sour;* suddenly in throat, then rawness. *Bitter;* even to morning broth; in morning, and pasty; in morning, with white tongue and white mucus in mouth; in morning, and slimy, and mucus hangs from teeth and tongue. Bitter sweetish, > eating bread, and mouth full of mucus. Flat during menstruation, with little appetite. Not good at dinner. None to food; and tongue coated white and mouth feeling slimy.

Clinical.—Neuralgic toothache, < warmth of the bed, > cold drinks (Coffea, Puls.). The toothache of this drug, like that of Merc., seems to be worse at night, and from the heat of the bed.

Throat.—Thyroid gland seems larger. Pain in r. submaxillary gland on pressure and on motion of jaw. Expectoration of blood-streaked mucus. Mucus which she must swallow, with rawness and dryness; M., which she attempts to hawk up; ineffectual desire to hawk up something in afternoon. Spasmodic retching at 8 P.M. as if distended. Sticking in r. side in evening on empty swallowing; S. low down when talking. Sensation as if stopped so that no air could pass, in morning after rising. Pain in forenoon on swallowing as if a thick substance lay across it. Sensation of a hard substance in it when not swallowing, with burning and choking, rawness and inclination to hawk. Soreness in r. side, with stitches and burning in l. side on talking, sneezing, yawning and < swallowing; prickling S. in r. posterior nares, as in coryza.

Scraping; and rancidity as from old smoked meat. Rawness; in forenoon, > dinner, with hoarseness; > a few paroxysms of cough, with hoarseness; on swallowing, as if a grain of barley were sticking in it; with burning; with burning acidity. Dryness in morning, with sticking in l. side; D. in afternoon on swallowing, with feeling as if it would split; D. on swallowing. Tickling causing short cough. Irritation in region of thyroid gland in forenoon, with frequent cough.

Stomach. — Hunger, but no appetite for bread; ravenous H. in evening before menstruation, then pain in stomach; great for vegetables, but aversion to meat. *Inclined to eat fruit and acid things in general* (Verat.). Little A. Satiated immediately at noon, with distention of abdomen after eating. No A.; at noon, it only comes while eating. Does not relish warm food, has no inclination for bread and butter. Aversion to food; from 6 to 7 P.M., with nausea; with nausea; with shuddering; with pain and coldness in stomach; *to green food*, **relish for meat.**

Thirst for water in forenoon, but in afternoon dryness of mouth, without thirst; for water after 1 P.M.; T. from 11 till 2 o'clock, with appetite for acids; T. in afternoon; *in evening; towards evening*, she drinks much and is obliged to rise at night to urinate; waking her at night, on appearance of menses; on waking from a dream that she was excessively thirsty; after dinner, then chilliness, in evening heat of face with coldness of feet and mental excitement; for cold drinks after diarrhœa; much T., with little appetite.

Eructations; in forenoon, with pain in stomach; at 2.30 P.M.; towards evening, with sneezing; before menstruation, with nausea; after eating plums, with salivation, vertigo and nausea; ineffectual; acid; tasting of morning soup. Empty E.; in morning after soup; with tearing or cutting from l. to r. side above umbilicus; of cold air. Rising of water into mouth without eructations.

Hiccough in morning after rising, then eructations; at 6.30 P.M.; during and after yawning; incomplete, with spasmodic pain in stomach.

Nausea; in morning, with constant spitting; in forenoon, with salivation; in forenoon during menses; at noon when eating soup, with vertigo, then retching, at last vomiting of salt water, then of the soup, then again only water, with anxiety, so that sweat stood on forehead, then white diarrhœa, then cutting and distention in abdomen; in afternoon, with salivation; in afternoon, > dinner, with general discomfort; from 6 to 7 P.M.; all night, with eructations of the odor of bad eggs; in abdomen after supper, with weakness and sleepiness; with shaking, then eructations; with constipation; with feeling as if stomach were full of water and desire to eructate; with pressure, as from a stone in stomach, and after black coffee faint dizziness, with yellow and blue rings around eyes, then two attacks of vomiting of food and bitter and sour mucus, then relief of stomach, but headache and weakness at 7 P.M.; with vomiting and empty eructations; without aversion to food, but with heaviness of head and ill humor; without qualmishness. Efforts to vomit at noon when eating soup, but vomiting of only bitter water, and then bitter mouth for a long time.

Distention > eructations. Rumbling towards noon; at 7 P.M., with yawning, then R. in abdomen. Stitching in pit; to right of pit, extending into r. chest; sudden to right of pit, as with a knife, at 2 P.M. Pain; after dinner, with contractive sensation; in morning, causing nausea, without qualmishness, > soup; extending into chest, > empty eructations; *constrictive;* like soreness on touch, in S. and hypochondria, even at night in bed. Sensitiveness to pressure, > coffee, with internal feeling as if it would fall out, coldness and prostration. Pain like an emptiness, waking her after midnight; in forenoon, > dinner, with qualmishness. Empty feeling in morning, with empty eructations. Disordered feeling after dinner.

Clinical.—Acid dyspepsia, sour eructations. Dyspepsia from drinking milk, which becomes sour in the stomach.

Abdomen.—*Distention* (Lyc., Calc. c., Sul.); in afternoon, in spite of three loose stools; from 3 P.M. till evening, with tension; in evening, somewhat > emission of flatus; *at night, > emission of flatus* (Lyc.); after dinner; after eating, with colic. *Rumbling all day, with gurgling, movements and cutting;* R. at 9 A.M.; in forenoon on motion, with gurgling; at 1 P.M., with movements. Motions before stool, with general heat; M., > emission of flatus, with griping, at last a soft stool. Rolling in evening and morning on inspiration, > eating, with gurgling. Loud emission of flatus; in afternoon and at night. E. when walking before the usual stool. Flatus of penetrating odor.

Pain as if intestines would be torn out, > smelling Hepar sulph. Cutting in evening till sleep; *C. before stool, with griping. Griping;* in morning in bed; at 10 A.M.; at noon, with profuse emission of offensive flatus, the G. < evening and preceded by rumbling; **G., with rumbling, then thin, green diarrhœa, without tenesmus;** intermittent, in forenoon, < afternoon and evening, > emission of flatus, with distention of abdomen; intermittent, with the usual stool, with movings. Pain in morning, < about umbilicus, > warm soup; *P.* in forenoon, *during menstruation;* in forenoon, then leucorrhœa like water; in bed, with dragging towards genitals, next morning menses appeared six days too early, at first scanty. Feeling as if everything were twisting about, with stitches beneath umbilicus. Cramplike constriction at 8 P.M., > diarrhœa. Empty feeling in morning after rising, intestines feel contracted and painful, as if torn out. Heaviness.

Hypochondria.—Sticking in l.; r.; in l. at 2 P.M., when standing; in r. after dinner; in r., as with a knife, at 7.30 P.M. on stooping, > rising. Griping in r. Intermittent pinching towards umbilicus in forenoon, with constriction; P. externally beneath r. lowest ribs, extending into ribs, then burning, taking the same direction. Pinching movings at 5.45 P.M. Paralytic pain in l. at 8.30 P.M., preventing lying on that side. Feeling as if there were something hard in hepatic region, with griping in abdomen.

Tearing in l. side of A., < walking. Cutting in l. Griping in sides. Pinching in forepart of A. in morning. Pinching in middle of A. at 2 P.M., > emission of flatus, then stool, the first part of which was scanty and hard, with great pressure, but the last soft and easy, then burning in anus.

Umbilicus.—Rumbling beneath U. two hours after dinner. Cutting about U. in forenoon during menses, > emission of flatus; C. beneath U., with dragging. Griping in region in morning, with digging; G. in region in morning, with distention of abdomen, then stool, which at first was hard, then soft; in region at 5 P.M., then thin stool, then burning in anus; in region with thin, scanty leucorrhœa. Twinging beneath U. in open air after micturition, extending into small of back and l. hip, with sensation as if flatus would be emitted. Ulcerative pain in spots to left of U.; on pressure. Painful dragging beneath U. during menses, waking her frequently at night.

Hypogastrium.—Fulness at 2.30 P.M., > walking. Cutting from small of back to pubis; C. in groins, waking her at night, with dragging. Pinching in r. groin at 3.30 P.M. when walking, > rubbing. Intermittent griping beneath umbilicus in afternoon, afterwards the pain extended to stomach; constrictive G. in r. groin at 11 A.M. Pain every morning in bed, > eating; P. at 9 A.M., < till 11 A.M., with griping and dragging towards genitals, after 9 A.M. reappearance of menses, which disappeared in afternoon. Dragging all night and in morning during menstruation.

Clinical.—Colic > bending over (Coloc.).

Rectum.—Sticking, with urging to stool, > emission of flatus; *S. waking her at* 4 A.M., somewhat > emission of flatus, which was painful, *S. again next morning after waking,* > emission of flatus. Tearing extending into abdomen, during stool. Pressure when not at stool. Urging, > breakfast; U. for diarrhœa, waking at 11 P.M., and at 3 A.M., and about 4 and 6 P.M. stool of greenish slimy liquid; constant U. though but little passes, and it is only like a fermentation. Frequent ineffectual urging in forenoon; U., but only a little is passed, then ineffectual U., then burning in anus, after five minutes desire again, but emission of only flatus, then desire and burning; U., but emission of only flatus, with cutting and twinging in anus, then a hard stool with pressure, though it seemed as if diarrhœa would occur; U. as before diarrhœa, but only flatus passed.

Anus.—Painful hæmorrhoids. Passage of round worms when not at stool. Pain as if sore and ulcerated between 2 and 3 P.M. when sitting and walking. Burning after stool.

Clinical.—Ascarides.

Stool.—**Of greenish water, with distention of abdomen** (Pod., Puls., *Grat.*), without other symptoms, eight times before 10 A.M.; *frequent green, liquid, also always preceded by griping, < r. side* (Podo.). Livid brown, liquid, then tenesmus and burning. Semiliquid, without trouble. Thin, then burning in anus; almost daily three thin, without trouble. Diarrhœa; in two attacks before midnight; **green, frothy;** of green mucus mixed with white thread-worms, then burning in anus; *of green mucus* (Merc. dulc.) at 5 A.M. *Frequent diarrhœa; with cutting and pressure;* without difficulty; and green. Soft, at the end, with pressure; S. always preceded by twinging in abdomen, > loud emissions of flatus; S. and scanty.

Constipation. Hard; and not till evening, with pressure and pain; after dinner, and difficult; and scanty, with pressure; with pressure; with pain in anus; in first part, the last part thin, then burning in rectum; and crumbling, it troubled her a long time before it passed. Yellow, with urging. Containing round worms. Difficult, but not hard. Normal, twice daily. *Only every second day.*

Clinical.—Sometimes indicated when the stools have a sour odor (Calc., Rheum). Diarrhœa, stools of green water; the stools are frequently bloody, sometimes have a green scum (Grat.), with white lumps like grains of tallow, rarely of bloody mucus, almost always sour, associated with more or less colic, with acid eructations and sour odor of the body (its most similar remedies in this connection seem to be Rheum and Gratiola).

Urinary Organs.—Discharge of prostatic fluid during

emission of flatus. Stitch in urethra in region of glans. Smarting in urethra during micturition. Burning in urethra in afternoon after micturition; B. during micturition, like salt water, even stinging. Frequent micturition; and copious; at night, and copious. Involuntary micturition when walking; on rising from a seat. Urine diminished in evening, then burning. Urine green. U. pale. White sediment.

Sexual Organs.—Erections slow, but coition natural. Emissions at night. Desire diminished. Itching of pudenda. Leucorrhœa; in afternoon when walking and sitting; scanty, after menstruation; like water; biting; of white mucus, preceded by cramp in abdomen.

Menstruation delayed, scanty and lasting but a short time; delayed, preceded by sore throat; delayed, at first scanty, then profuse, with large clots of blood; D. and profuse. M. too early; with pain in small of back, < sitting, > walking; with tearing toothache and distention of abdomen, lasting four weeks (it is usually very scanty); and thick and black; and scanty, lasting only two days; and scanty, but lasting three days longer than usual; and scanty at first, then profuse and dark; after a foot bath, at first scanty, then profuse, dark, and dragging in groins, during these draggings there was no discharge of blood, but always a flow on emission of flatus, most profuse at noon and in afternoon. **Menses more profuse at night than by day,** *with dragging pains, > pressure on abdomen and stooping.* Profuse menses, with cutting colic; P. and lasting a day longer than usual; when walking and standing; and dark; on fourth and fifth days, with headache, < evening. *M. came on in night, scanty at first, more profuse next forenoon, in afternoon it ceased suddenly.* M. that had disappeared for several years in a woman past the menopause returned and flowed profusely for four days. *No discharge of M. during the pains, only after them, and also at night in sleep. M. glutinous, dark, almost like pitch, difficult to wash off* (Crocus).

Clinical.—In pregnancy, nausea and vomiting of sour odor. Irregular menstruation and dysmenorrhœa, menses frequently prolonged, but worse during the night than during the day; the discharge dark, like pitch. Leucorrhœa, white, acrid, preceded by colic, recurring especially after menstruation (Alumina).

Respiratory Organs.—Hoarseness; towards evening. Soft, pea-yellow, offensive nodules, which he is obliged to hawk up, get into larynx, as if he had swallowed the wrong way. Contraction of trachea, with pain in pit of throat. Cough; in afternoon from tickling in throat; at night; from becoming heated; with scraping in throat; hollow, dull; spasmodic, all night; paroxysmal, at 3 A.M., with expectoration of mucus, with difficult, thin, salt expectoration. Expectoration of mucus and clots of blood of sweetish taste at 5 P.M. Short breath when walking.

Clinical.—It has cured bronchial catarrh in children, with stringy expectoration and with the peculiar greenish, sour stools (Kali bi.).

Chest.—Stitches on sternum, above ensiform cartilage, at 1 P.M.; beneath l. shoulder at 3.30 P.M; beneath l. breast at 7 P.M. when sitting; on lower part of sternum at 9 P.M. when walking, with short breath; beneath l. breast at 9 P.M. when sitting, then in sternum; beneath l. breast after dinner, not affecting respiration; deep in, from dinner till towards 5 P.M., with cutting, not affected by inspiration; beneath r. breast on inspiration; in l. lowest ribs, < sitting; beneath r. breast at 10 A.M., extending towards navel; in l. breast at noon, extending to shoulders on breathing; extending beneath r. breast and up through shoulder at 1.30 P.M. when standing; in l. costal region at 5 P.M. when standing, on inspiration, extending upward beneath l. scapula; extending inward to right of ensiform cartilage. Cutting stitches in ribs beneath r. axilla, not affecting breathing; C. stitches beneath l. breast at 1 P.M. when yawning.

Cutting in middle from 6.30 till 7 P.M., with sticking, not affecting respiration; C. during cough, and in morning yellowish purulent expectoration. Bruised pain in pectoral muscles on motion and touch. Sudden painful pressure taking away the breath. Tightness; intermittent, in afternoon, as if screwed in, with short breath. Heaviness in evening. Oppression, with at times deep respiration. Constriction at 3.30 P.M. when sitting and walking, with pinching and with difficult, short breath; C. about middle at 6 P.M., with short breath; at 6 P.M., > eructations, with weariness in shoulders and pain as if dislocated in r. middle finger. Throbbing in l. in evening on falling asleep. Burning internally beneath l. breast at 10 A.M. when sitting, with sweetish taste in throat, then cough and expectoration of tenacious brown mucus.

Heart.—Stitch in præcordial region at 1 P.M. Sudden sore pain after a meal, with creaking and with nausea. Palpitation.

Neck.—Stitching in nape when sneezing. Tearing, with jerking, afterwards extending down back; T. in tendons of r. side at 6.30 P.M., with drawing.

Back.—Stitching extending inward at 2 P.M. Pain at night so that she could not lie, and in small of B. Pain at night as if beaten to pieces, < motion.

Lumbar Region.—Stitches; above r. hip; in r. at 1.30 P.M., then jerking. Sticking-burning and bruised pain extending from above l. hip to beneath shoulder, < stooping to left, > pressure and bending together, with dry cough and stitches in side. Tearing in lower part of spine, causing shuddering, so that she bent backward, then stitches at 5 P.M. Intermittent pain during menses. Bruised pain from morning till 2 P.M.; from 4.30 till lying down at 9 P.M; in afternoon and evening after menses. Drawing pain during menses, > stooping, < stretching. Dragging before menstruation, < sitting, > walking, with cutting and pain as if contracted and beaten, the flow at first scanty, next day profuse and brown, with relief of the pains, the third day scanty, ceased the fourth day, flow more profuse at night. Tightness above hips. Sudden piercing pain in coccyx.

Extremities.—Soreness of all, and she turned from side to side. Weariness. Crawling uneasiness in evening so that she must move the feet constantly. Paralysis of l. leg, with pain in hips and knees, next day it occurred in r. leg and in arms, when walking he had constant pain and was obliged to plant the feet far apart.

Upper Extremities.—Shoulders. Tearing from l. to wrist; in r., extending to r. clavicle and chest; in l. in forenoon, extending to middle of upper arm; in r. in forenoon, extending into wrist, and on turning over the hand the pain occurred in finger-joints; in r. at 8 A.M., gradually extending to lower part of scapula; in l. at 5 P.M., extending to elbow. Pain in r. Pain in

r. as if dislocated in morning and afternoon during menstruation, so that it was difficult to raise the arm; in r. as if D. in afternoon on moving arm and in bed on some motions; in r. in evening, with feeling as if arm should hang down. Paralytic bruised pain in l. on moving arm and trunk and on yawning. Pressure. Painful contraction in morning, with tearing extending down back. Tension extending to angle of lower jaw, so that he could not stoop nor close the jaws.

Arm.—Jerking. Stitches under r., extending to axilla if she holds the arm elevated and still, > moving arm. Tearing above r. elbow, extending into middle of outer part of upper arm. Paroxysmal cramplike grips above elbows, transiently > compression with other hand, with hardness of muscles. Pain in r. as if dislocated on raising it carelessly. Drawing upward in A. Weakness.

Elbow—Stitches in r. at 8 A.M. on moving arm. Tearing in r. at 10 A.M. when knitting; T. in under surface of r. extending to middle of forearm, as if in periosteum, when standing. Gnawing in l. at 7 P.M. Pain on flexing arm. Sharp drawings about r., as if in bone, in evening in bed.

Stitches in tendons on anterior surface of r. forearm above wrist in forenoon. Drawing in r. forearm, extending into hand, with difficulty in raising arm. Wrist above thumb swollen and red, and bones painful to pressure. Stitching in l. palm, then itching, > scratching. Drawing pain in hands. L. hand upon which she had lain at night was asleep in morning.

Fingers.—Inflamed swelling, with sticking in first joint of index. Tearing on dorsal surface of first phalanx of r. little at 9 A.M.; in first joints of r. at 5 P.M.; in l. thumb and index evenings, then paralysis of both fingers; in first joint of r. thumb, extending to nail; in tips, extending to backs of hands, in morning after rising. Boring gnawing in first phalanx of l. thumb, as if in marrow, in forenoon. Pain in first joint of r. middle as if dislocated at 6 P.M. Cramplike sensation in joints. Throbbing pain as from an ulcer in tip of l. thumb after dinner, > pressure. Tension in middle joint of l. middle, mornings.

Lower Extremities.—Sudden jerking in l. in evening after falling asleep, so that she started up in fright and could not sleep again for a long time. Pain in afternoon, < knees. Uneasiness after prolonged sitting. Weakness when sitting and on rising from a seat, > moving about.

Thigh.—Jerking posteriorly in hip, then in r. hypochondrium. Stitches in l. hip-joint; in l. hip at outer surface of bone. Tearing on anterior surface from centre to knee; T. from middle down to middle of leg, > rising from seat, with stitches; in l. hip-joint from 4 P.M. till morning. Twinging in l. hip and sacral region when walking after dinner, then desire for stool preceded and accompanied by cutting in rectum. Pain till evening; P. in hip, < motion. Bruised pain in l. femur from above knee to middle when walking. Weariness at 5.30 P.M., < walking.

Knee.—Hard swelling in hollow, with pain, preventing stretching of leg. Sticking. Tearing in r. when standing; T. in r., < towards outer surface; from l. to above middle of thigh, not in knee itself, after dinner; intermittent T. outward in bend of l., as if in bone, at last it extends into thigh, and when walking tension as if tendons were too short; boring T. in l. at 8 A.M. Intermittent boring in r. Bruised pain when walking during menses. Pain as after a long walk. Weary pain when sitting, < walking. Painful drawing jerking from r. to middle of thigh when standing and bending leg. Drawing pain extending to soles like a burrowing in the marrow. Tension in hollows; hollow of l. at 8 A.M., when walking. Pain in bend of l. as if tendons were too short on entering house. Heaviness in afternoon when walking, with pain.

Leg.—Cramp in calves in evening in bed; in l. calf at night on turning over and rising in bed. Tearing in r. calf in afternoon. Cutting in tibia. Bruised pain in tibiæ. Burning painful spots on tibia. Drawing downward pain in evening. Painful tension in tendo-achillis as far as calves when walking rapidly. Uneasiness in r. at night, he must constantly put it out of bed into a cool place.

Bruised pain from l. ankle to middle of tibia in morning on stepping on it, > long walking. Cramp in heels in morning in bed. Sticking downward deep in r. heel at 9 P.M. in bed. Jerking tearing in l. heel at 10 P.M. in bed. Pain in feet during menses, even in bed. Drawing pain in soles. Weariness of feet; on ascending, with pain. Heaviness of feet from 5 till 8 P.M., < ascending steps, with weariness.

Toes.—Stitching in bone of r. great extending to its dorsal surface at 7 P.M.; burning S. in great. Tearing in r. great from first phalanx to tip; T. in l. little at 3 P.M. when walking, then in fourth toe.

Skin.—Red spots on chest. Tetter below mouth; red, smooth, elevated, on chest and calves, then desquamation. Fine eruption on mouth. Swelling of r. middle finger on the days when he had no stool, with redness, heat and itching pimples. Subcutaneous nodes in axillæ and above elbows, with sticking. Pimples here and there; P. above knee; on r. side of chin, almost daily giving place to fresh ones; on l. arm, disappearing after scratching, but they do not itch; red, above knee; hard, red, deep in skin in front of l. shoulder, stinging on pressure, with one a red areola; hard, above r. ear, painful to touch. Itching pimples beneath ears; on inner surface of l. forearm; between l. fingers; on wrist, exuding clear water on pressure.

Pustules in front of r. ear; on tip of nose; itching, beneath r. nostril, leaving a burning scab. Boil on l. side of forehead and one on r. side of throat; on l. side of chest; posteriorly on lower part of r. thigh, with redness, afterwards roughness of skin. Vesicles on sides of forehead and in r. corner of mouth; on back of nose; near nail of l. index; on first joint of l. index; in the scar of an old burn; clear, on l. side of nape; clear, above r. breast and on r. shoulder; on hands, with stinging; itching, on sides of nose before menstruation; itching, on l. side of throat, waking her at night, after scratching a red spot. Scab on l. side of forehead as if a vesicle had been scratched off.

Itching stitch above r. hip, > scratching; itching burning S. as from fleas, now in r., now in l. hip, l. sacral and r. hypochondriac region. Crawling under first joints of r. toes, then on dorsum of foot; on various parts, < shoulders, with itching, then after scratching clear vesicles. Itching burning above upper lip, towards l. corner of mouth, at 1 P.M. Itching biting in nape and on throat in evening, with burning after scratching.

Itching on whole body; on nose near l. eye; here and there posteriorly on trunk; in l. axilla; inner surface of l. wrist; above hips; between l. fourth and fifth toes; on r. shoulder in afternoon, then burning after scratching; on neck and shoulders in afternoon; between shoulders at 6 P.M., then burning after scratching; on l. palm from 7 P.M. till lying down; of l. hand at 10 P.M.; here and there from evening till 3 A.M.; here and there on scalp in evening, after scratching it appeared in other places; on back in evening on lying down, then burning after scratching; on shoulders, outer side of thigh and on throat in evening before sleep and in morning on dressing, and after scratching itching pimples in several places; in evening when undressing, on nates and inside of forearm, and after scratching itching pimples, the I. < scratching, but > in bed; here and there at night till 5 A.M., always appearing in a new spot after scratching; on forehead during dinner; on chin after dinner; on l. toes after dinner; on r. hip when standing, then after scratching burning on inside of l. forearm when washing with cold water and soap, and after scratching red itching pimples, which soon disappeared after drying. I. not > scratching, on r. temple; on nates.

Itching > scratching, in various places, < forehead, nose, throat and forearms; sides of forehead; beneath r. ear; behind r. ear; in l. palm in morning after rising; in places on face at 10 A.M.; on back at noon and in evening; from first joint of r. thumb up radius at 1.15 P.M.; on r. calf at 4 P.M.; on nape at 6 P.M.; I. in middle of back after dinner, on scratching it appears on l. shoulder, where it is > scratching; on back, but returning; on shoulders, but returning; in r. groin, with internal burning, and with chilliness of body, the B. also > scratching; anteriorly below r. elbow, then a red spot. Itching on r. side of neck, then burning after scratching; I. on l. palm, then after long scratching clear vesicles; I. between r. third and fourth fingers, then after scratching clear vesicles and on the scratched spots long white streaks. Voluptuous I. externally about throat, > scratching, but returning. Biting I. at night on whole body. Burning I. above nates.

Sleep.—Yawning; after rising till 9 A.M.; in forenoon, with sneezing; in forenoon, with sleepiness, indolence and stretching; in afternoon, without sleepiness; at 1.15 P.M., with sleepiness and indolence; after 6 P.M.; after dinner, with sleepiness, indolence and stretching; violent and frequent. Sleepiness; in morning after a good night's sleep; on second day of menses, with weakness.

Sleepless all night; for several nights, and constant tossing about; till midnight; from midnight till 2 A.M., then imperfect sleep till 5 A.M.; from 1 till 5 A.M.; *after* 2 *or* 3 A.M.; till 3 A.M.; on account of anxiety and heaviness. Late falling asleep; on account of uneasiness in blood, then restless sleep. Frequent waking during menses. Restless sleep, with frequent waking. Tossing about at night, or if his body lay quiet his arms and legs jerked all night, even when awake, on waking he knew nothing of the occurrences of the night. Starting up from sleep in afternoon; S. up to about midnight, then sleepless for an hour; S. upon falling asleep, with uneasiness in limbs. Talking in S. after midnight; loud T. in morning, and she beat her head against the wall and woke, but knew nothing of it. Little and unrefreshing sleep, with restlessness; little S. and many dreams.

Dreams.—The symptomatology of dreams is very full, anxious, fatiguing, frightening, vivid and obscure.

Fever.—Chilliness from morning till evening; at 7 P.M. in bed, > 9 P.M.; in evening on undressing, > in bed; in evening in bed, as if dashed with cold water; at 9.30 P.M., > in bed; all night after a long walk, and even in morning; during menses; during menses, always on waking or uncovering herself. Shaking chill at 9 P.M.; in evening and in bed; at 10 P.M. in bed; at 8 P.M., beginning in feet, > in bed, without external coldness, next morning sweat. Shivering down back every day at 9 A.M., with nausea. Chill down back from 4 P.M. till sleep. Cold feet as if wading in cold water.

Heat from 1 till 4 A.M. during sleep, with sweat; in morning after rising till towards noon; in forenoon; from noon till 2 P.M., with sweat on head; general, with redness of face; *internal, at night, so that he could scarcely remain covered, with dread of exposure;* streaming through whole body; dry at night; dry, caused by animal food. Burning in r. ear; in palms at 1 P.M.; of face and hands at noon, with redness and thirst. Heat in head, with sweat on face; in head and hands, with redness of face and external heat; in head in flushes, also at 6 P.M.; internally in head at 1 P.M., but not externally; internal in head and external in face, with redness alternating with pallor.

Sweat during the day on motion; towards morning; in morning; *at night;* (in a child) in evening on falling asleep; offensive, at night; sour-smelling (Bry., Hep.), oily, difficult to wash off, all night. Parched dryness of skin towards morning in bed.

Magnesia Muriatica.

Muriate of Magnesium is triturated for use.

General Action.—Similar to Magnes. carb., but decidedly modified by Mur. ac.

Allies.—Mag. c., Mur. ac.; *Nat. m.*, Nat. c., Sil., Con.

Generalities.—Jerking from heel through whole body as from an electric shock, in morning when awake. Tearing here and there at night; T. in small of back, in r. shoulder and down outer side of back. Cramp-like nervous pain here and there, now a boring, now a constriction, < scapulæ and chest, with nervous headache beginning in forehead, with drawings in ears and at times sticking tearing in head. Bruised pain in whole body; in evening after lying down. Drawing here and there externally in head, also in ears, teeth and half of face, with confusion of head, the pains > sneezing. Burning tension here and there.

Intolerance of fresh air. *Uneasiness in bed as soon as she closes the eyes.* Weakness; in morning, with vertigo; in morning, with bruised sensation, as from insufficient sleep; in forenoon, with fretfulness; in forenoon, even to falling down, with bruised pain in all limbs; after a sea bath of five minutes; on walking, and when at rest pain in hips as if dislocated; even to faintness the first two days of menstruation, with weariness in limbs and late falling asleep. Faintness during dinner, > eructations, with anxiety, nausea, pallor, red and green vision and general trembling. Heaviness in different parts; general sensation as if everything were too heavy. Most symptoms arise when sitting and are usually > motion (see Mag. c.). Amelioration in open air, except of pains in chest.

Mind.—Illusion of fantasy, it seemed as if some one were reading a book after her and she must read faster, with humming and buzzing before her ear, on rising it seemed as if she were looking over great clouds and rocks above her, then anxiety, apprehension and uneasiness, these illusions > farther looking about, but returned twice on beginning to read again, till she was diverted by several persons coming to her (she had had a similar illusion in her early youth, over which she wept violently and could not be quieted). Excitement the day before menstruation.

Lively during the day, but fretful in evening. Fretful; in morning after rising; and restless internally; and taciturn, disinclined to work. Unfriendly mood. Anxiety in morning, with vertigo, then soft stool, with cutting in abdomen; A. in morning, > open air; towards evening, with apprehension and ennui. Apprehension, despondency, homesickness and weeping; A. after dinner, with lachrymose mood. Cheerless, disinclined to mental labor. Joyless in morning and suffering, everything she looks at is repugnant, she does not wish any one to talk to her, lest she should have to answer. It was irksome to talk, he wished to be alone and busy with his own thoughts. Disinclination to work. Irresolute. Apathy and distraction, as from loss of sleep, in morning.

Head.—Stitches here and there. Pressure, also sharp and pinching, < on vertex and in occiput. *Aching, > wrapping up head;* A. after dinner, with sensitiveness of scalp to touch and sore burning in eyes; A. in morning as if he had not slept enough, with weariness of feet; as if whole brain pressed against forehead. Sensitiveness in morning, even from listening to reading, from talking, every step, etc., with little appetite, diminished taste and smell. Fulness in morning. Compression from both sides when pressing upon forehead, with heat and throbbing. Dulness in forenoon, with heaviness; D., with stupefaction and with sensitiveness of l. thigh. Heaviness; in morning; with confusion. Painful orgasm, > open air, but recurring in house, with pressure in occiput. Vertigo; in morning after rising; in morning, > moving about; even to falling forward, in morning on rising; at dinner, > open air, with dulness of head, and after returning to the house heat in head; even when walking in the room and if she hangs the head a little.

Forehead.—Stitches in middle in evening; S. behind r. eminence and out of r. ear; jerking S. deep in F., then also in r. side of occiput. Tearing in evening, with heaviness; T. in forepart in evening on motion, with sticking; at one time T. on stooping when sitting, at another T. and sticking together; T. in l. side, and farther back stitches; T. and sticking in F. and temples, with sensitiveness of vertex as if the hair had been pulled, with feeling of heat, and cold forehead. Pressure; in F. and sinciput all the forenoon, < on waking, with confusion in head; in sinuses, extending into forehead, where there is burrowing, > sweat, which was caused by violent motion; as if brain would fall out, at 6 P.M. on stooping. Heaviness in forepart in afternoon. Numbness.

Griping in temples in evening after lying down, > **pressing head with both hands** (compare Mur. ac.), *with raging in them, feeling as if he would become dizzy and unconscious.* Tearing in l. temple. Stitches in r. side of vertex. Soreness of vertex.

Sides.—Stitches in r.; in l. and in occiput; in upper part of l.; all day, with tearing; in l. parietal bone on bending trunk towards r. side, with boring in front of l. ear; in upper part of r. during menstruation; in l., with ill humor; outward in l.; *in r. extending to eye, with tearing and necessity to press eye together.* Tearing in l.; in r. extending to eye. Boring in l. in evening. Throbbing in l. in evening, with heat and heaviness in forehead.

Occiput.—Stitches in r. protuberance; in r. side, then burning. Tearing extending to vertex; T. at last extending to whole head, > entering house and sitting, with throbbing; jerking tearing in r.; throbbing tearing extending to vertex. Throbbing pain in morning after rising, during menstruation, with heaviness. Throbbing after rising from stooping, soon involving whole head. Pressure. Heaviness.

Scalp.—Pain on touch and stooping. Pimple on l. side of occiput, with pain < touch, with tearing about it. Boils on top of head. Itching.

Clinical.—Neuralgia of the head and around the eyes, as if the skull would burst, < motion and fresh air, > pressure (Mur. ac., Con.), associated with very obstinate constipation, with small gray fæcal masses, and also with soreness in the region of the liver, which is sensitive to pressure. Neuralgic headaches > tight bandages (Sil.).

Eyes.—Inflammation, with pressure, biting, burning, < looking at a bright light, and lachrymation in evening, they are full of purulent mucus by day, lids swollen and red, and nightly agglutination. Pain, and in canthi; P. as from dust, with dim vision; as from sand, < l., > rubbing, but returning. Burning; in evening on looking at the fire, with dryness; < looking at anything bright; so that she must close them, with sensitiveness; and sticking. Itching; in morning after rising, > violent rubbing.

Red vessels in white of l., then of r. Agglutination in morning; with burning on opening them. Twitching of upper lids, which seem swollen, heavy and half closed. Stitches in r. inner canthus, causing lachrymation. Dryness of lids, < morning and after midday nap. Itching of l. upper lid; in r. inner canthus, > rubbing, but recurring in l. eye. Bruised pain in lower margin of l. orbit. Vision dim; and on looking at near objects it vanishes. Vision of a green halo about the light in evening during inflammation of eyes.

Ears.—Stitches; now in one, now in the other; in l. on bending to the right, with tearing. Tearing in r. and externally in front of it; jerking T. in l. Sticking boring. Painful jerking in r. Pain in r., with pulse-like throbbing. Tickling, > boring in with fingers; T. in r., with agreeable warmth. Obstructed feeling all day, with burning, buzzing and diminished hearing; O. feeling during menstruation, transiently > boring in with finger, without impairment of hearing. Fluttering in r. Roaring; in l. upon which he was lying in morning, or as if water were boiling. Deafness, < l., decreasing and returning.

Nose.—*R. wing red, swollen and painful to touch. Ulceration of nostrils. Scab in each nostril, that pains on touch, with loss of smell* (Nat. m.). *Nostrils sore and painful.* Tearing in upper part of nostrils, causing lachrymation. *Feeling as if she would have coryza, with increased mucus in nose.* Tickling, with lachrymation; *T., with sneezing and sensation of coryza. Burning in nostrils as if sore. Stoppage; of l. nostril; in morning; in evening. Sneezing,* *whereby water flows from nose. Coryza, with stoppage of nose and talking through nose; C., with hoarseness and stopped sensation in nose, from which water often flowed. Alternately stopped and fluent coryza, with dulness of head and loss of smell and taste. Fluent coryza; C., with yellow mucus and diminished smell and taste* (Nat. m.), *with inability to lie down or to sleep and necessity to breathe through the mouth. Discharge of offensive purulent mucus.* Blowing out of much mucus without coryza. Mucus specked with blood. Blowing out of blood. *Smell blunted.*

Clinical.—Nasal catarrh, with itching and burning, nose red and painful, and frequent headache (> open air), or constipation; there is general aggravation from lying on r. side. Ozæna, with ulceration of nostrils and fetid discharge.

Face.—Pale; during menstruation, and sad and irritable; and yellow. Yellow, < white of eye and about mouth. Sickly, suffering look. Twitching on chin. Stitch in r. cheek. Tearing from l. zygoma to l. side of head; T. in sides of lower jaw and in roots of teeth, extending to front of ear, where it was a jerking. Paralytic pain in bones. Tension. Tensive pain in r. zygoma. Pain beneath l. lower jaw as if a gland were swollen, which was not the case. Lips cracked; white pimples on inside of upper; *vesicle on margin of lower, itching, then burning; suddenly tense, burning clear vesicles in red of upper* (Nat. m.); inside of upper feels rough to touch of tongue during coryza.

Clinical.—Vesicular eruption on lips, followed by soreness, with soreness in nostrils and formation of scabs.

Mouth.—Teeth. Tearing in sound during dinner; T. in a lower molar, > biting upon it; in r. eye-tooth, extending into zygoma, > pressure; sudden T. in upper incisors. Jerking in r. from 8 till 12 P.M., with feeling as if cheek would swell. Throbbing in a root. Boring in molars transiently > biting upon them; B. in hollow molar all day, > cold and open air, < warmth, with tearing and on touching cheek sticking in the tooth; intermittent B. or digging in next to last molar in morning and after dinner, < cold, touch of food and pressure, > warmth, sometimes tearing. Digging in last molar, > pressure, then tearing in a hollow molar. Pain, causing restless sleep. *Upper incisors seem too long and sensitive.*

Gum.—Bleeding. Painful swelling of lower and of cheek; of upper, < eating, with throbbing in it.

Tongue.—Coated white in morning. Stitches during coryza, then burning. Burnt feeling with the coryza. Burning, with fissures; B. of whole in morning, of tip in afternoon.

Mucus in mouth and on tongue in morning; M. in mouth and on teeth, with slimy taste. Stitches in palate. Dryness, with feeling as if M. and tongue were covered with mucus; D. of M. and throat, night and morning, without thirst. Heat comes from M. Numb and burnt feeling in morning during menstruation. Salivation before and during the dryness; clear S. that she could not sufficiently expectorate in afternoon.

Taste.—Bitter in morning; at first to the breakfast, > continuing to eat; B. on back part of palate. Sourish in throat in afternoon; S. or slimy to various kinds of food. Salt, and salt salivation. Putrid in morning, with coated tongue. Pasty in morning. Watery, with spitting of water.

Throat.—Hawking of acid mucus; mucus mixed with blood in morning; tenacious mucus in morning; thick, tenacious mucus, that draws itself out in long threads, in morning. Stitches in l. side in forenoon, < swallowing; S. in upper part of pharynx in evening and night, on breathing and talking. Sore pain during coryza, < swallowing. Soreness at entrance of fauces, < evening, with rawness, and when coughing and swallowing saliva sticking extending into ear. *Dryness, with rawness and hoarseness;* D., with heat.

Stomach.—Appetite increased; ravenous, then nausea; A. for dainties, he slyly breaks off some cake to eat; A., but knew not for what, did not desire her usual food; soon satisfied at dinner; A. lost all day, only in evening she ate with relish; no A. in evening. Thirst in morning, with dryness of mouth; at 3 A.M., with dryness of mouth and throat; T. in forenoon; in evening; before and after midnight; after dinner and in afternoon, with coryza.

Eructations of water, with nausea; E. of white froth; bitter-acid; of sour water in morning after rising, with nausea; acid, of food, < milk taken in afternoon, after dinner, < walking; tasting of food; of food when walking after dinner; tasting of onions, after a spasm. Empty eructations after dinner; E. in afternoon; E., then stitch above ensiform cartilage. Violent hiccough after dinner; during dinner, making stomach sore. *Nausea in morning after rising;* from morning till noon, with salivation; all the forenoon; after stool, with salivation; > breakfast, with rumbling in abdomen; *with salivation.* Faintlike nausea; in morning, then coldness and weakness of stomach, with eructations of water.

Grumbling in pit, > rubbing and pressure. Movings about epigastric region in forenoon, then in hypogastrium, > emission of flatus. Stitches in l. side; S. transversely across epigastric region. Cutting in r. side, with pain on pressure. Ulcerative pain in afternoon. Pressure in forenoon, > eructations; P., with nausea; P. in epigastric region on stepping and talking, with shuddering in it; intermittent, in forenoon, extending to throat and back; flatulent, extending into chest and throat, transiently > eructations. Bruised pain; on bending forward, on stretching it tension in stomach. Tension in epigastric region, with ulcerative pain, < touch and evening after lying down, then good sleep till 1 A.M., when she awoke with cutting in bowels, on stretching the body the pain extended over the whole abdomen and into groins, with rush of heat in head, at last it rose into throat like a ball and almost took away the breath, with at first tossing about the bed, then about the floor, the paroxysm > eructation and emission of flatus, during the pain necessity to lie bent and intolerance of covering. *Epigastric region sensitive to pressure.* Throbbing in pit, with vertigo. *Acidity after dinner.* Fasting sensation in morning. Heat.

Clinical.—Indigestion, especially in children from taking milk, which passes undigested. It has cured many obstinate cases of gastralgia, that have lasted for months.

Abdomen.—Distention; in afternoon, > emission of flatus; after eating; after dinner; here and there; with hardness and with sticking in l. groin; in afternoon, extending into throat, so that it took away her breath, with anxiety. Hardness, with pain on touch and distressing pressure towards anus. *Rumbling* before eating; R. at every inspiration after soft stool, with gurgling; with griping, then soft stool; with dragging towards small of back. Fermentation. *Incarcerations of flatus. Incessant emission of flatus.*

Cramps evenings, > sleep, with tearing; C., with pressure upon rectum and genitals and with peevish depression of spirits. Tearing in forenoon; from 9.30 P.M. till sleep; with pinching. Cutting; after breakfast, with profuse emission of flatus, then ineffectual desire for stool, then soft stool with cessation of pain. Griping in morning after rising, then diarrhœa accompanied and followed by burning in anus, then repeated diarrhœa mixed with thick blood; G. as in menstruation. Burrowing and feeling as before diarrhœa.

Pain in morning, with desire for stool, which was hard and crumbly, with burning in anus; P. at 4 P.M.; P. after normal stool, with itching in anus; on every motion after stool. *Drawing pain at night*, and during the day on every motion, as if something were loose. Drawing at night on waking, with tearing; spasmodic D. and tearing from 5 till 6 P.M., extending from below as far as r. side of chest, where there was spasmodic constrictive griping, with oppression of breath, < eating cherries, > pressure of hand, next day a similar attack at 5.30 P.M. Weak feeling. Feeling of looseness and upturning, as if intestines had lost their hold. Heat in walls, with burning in anus and sensitiveness in rectum after stool.

Pressure in l. side. Upper A., movings about; cutting in morning, extending to small of back; griping cutting, with feeling as if something hard were lying upon stomach; pinching, > emission of flatus, then urging to stool, but emission of only flatus.

Hypochondria.—Sticking in l.; in afternoon when walking, during menstruation, < inspiration, > sitting; **burning and tensive S. in r., > pressure.** *Cutting in a spot in l. in morning.* **Sharp drawings in hepatic region.**

Umbilicus.—Attacks of cutting below U. in afternoon. Pinching below U. at 1 P.M., with cutting and with shivering over back, then heat in head and desire for stool; P. about U. after dinner, extending towards stomach, > emission of flatus. Griping about U., with dragging towards small of back, then sudden desire for stool, and soft stool with yellow mucus and piece of a tapeworm, then continued urging. Constriction in region.

Hypogastrium.—Movings of flatus low down in abdomen. Stitches in l. groin; in r. groin, then bruised pain, < pressure; in r. ilium, extending towards small of back. Cutting, waking at 2 A.M., then sticking in pit of stomach, then in præcordial region, < inspiration; C. in morning in bed, with desire for stool, but only emission of flatus with cessation of pain; sudden C. so that she must sit bent over. Pain in forepart during menstruation; P. in afternoon, with dragging towards rectum, then soft stool covered with white mucus, repeated after an hour.

Clinical.—Cirrhosis of liver. Numerous cases of enlargement and congestion of the liver, particularly with symptoms of jaundice, yellow color of the face and eyes, gray stools, swelling of feet and legs, high-colored, scanty, albuminous urine, with the peculiar constipation of the drug, general aggravation from lying on r. side, etc. Enlargement of liver, with sour vomiting, offensive breath, yellow color of the face, constipation. Enlargement of the liver, with bloating of abdomen, tongue large, coated yellow, scalloped at the edges, feet swollen, stool dry and crumbling. Chronic hepatic disorder, with dark yellow fæces, distended abdomen, hard, crumbling stools, scanty, infrequent menses, palpitation, small, weak pulse, swelling of feet, etc. In all the hepatic disorders there is tenderness over the region of the liver and pain extending to the spine and pit of the stomach, aggravation immediately after eating, flatulent colic, dyspnœa, weak, small pulse, constipation.

Rectum.—Prolapsus during diarrhœa. Stitches; extending to abdomen; in perineum. Smarting after a soft stool. Burning deep in. Urging after stool; after diarrhœa, but emission of only mucus; U., and though there was great pressure only a little soft, then thin stool in small portions, with shivering and pain in abdomen; U., but emission of only burning flatus; all day, but only flatus was passed; constant, but nothing was passed, it seemed as if the stool constantly went back, with shivering; constant desire for stool, which was thin. Frequent urging, with pain in abdomen; F., with scanty discharge; F., but only a scanty thin and slimy stool.

Anus.—*Hæmorrhoids pain during normal stool. Smarting after hard stool. Burning after usual stool; during and after stool, with smarting.*

Clinical.—Hæmorrhoids, with constipation.

Stool.—Liquid, brown, frequent. Thin, spurting, then tenesmus and burning in anus, then small thin stool again. Frequent diarrhœa, with cutting in abdomen; F. and greenish; F., containing mucus and blood, with tenesmus in anus. Soft, then tenesmus and burning in anus; S. (after the usual one), with general shivering, then burning in anus and sensitiveness in rectum; S., containing a piece of tapeworm; and frequent, with feeling as if flatus would pass; and difficult though she had to hurry, then shivering. **Hard, like sheep-dung; and difficult;** *H. and covered with streaks of blood; and knotty, enveloped in thick mucus; and knotty, then a soft one enveloped in mucus;* **nodular, with pain in rectum;** at first in hard masses and after some time soft or thin; H. in first part, then soft, then burning in anus and sticking externally in hypochondria and constriction in stomach extending to back; H., then three diarrhœa-like ones, with soreness of anus and cutting in abdomen that lasted till the next stool. **Crumbly and as if burnt,** hurrying her, with sticking in rectum, then burning in anus. At first scanty and large, then urging to stool, which was soft, then she felt unwell, with relaxation of abdomen, extending thence over whole body, and frequent necessity to lie down. Retained; then easy, but with sticking in rectum.

Clinical. — Constipation; stools usually like sheep-dung; sometimes the stools are in large masses, but crumble as soon as evacuated.

Urinary Organs.—Urging; during the day; at night, but he repressed it; yet she passed but little, with burning in urethra; frequent, with scanty emission. During micturition he did not feel the urine in urethra. **Micturition only by exertion of abdominal muscles** (Caust.). *Micturition in drops, and some urine always seemed to remain behind* (Merc., Canth., Caust., etc.). Frequent micturition during the day, always in small quantities; F. at night, but scanty; F., with burning in urethra and frequent erections. Rare and scanty M. Involuntary M. when walking, yet on attempting to urinate when standing nothing passed. Urine pale, with burning in urethra after micturition.

Urine almost opaque, as if mixed with yeast, depositing a cloud.

Clinical.—Dysuria, can urinate only by effort of the abdominal muscles, must even press the hands on the abdomen in order to empty the bladder.

Sexual Organs.—Stitches in mons veneris towards evening. Erections in morning in bed, with burning pain in penis. Itching of glans in evening on going to bed; on scrotum and lower part of penis, > rubbing; on genitals and scrotum as far as anus, and in evening and night sweat of scrotum and an emission. Testicles hang down relaxed. After violent erections and neglecting to have coition, testicles, spermatic cord and small of back pained all day after rising and moving or touching testicles. Frequent emissions.

Female.—*Leucorrhœa;* in morning after micturition; < motion; > stool; *with cramp in abdomen;* watery; thick, then discharge of blood fourteen days before the usual time and three days before the full moon. Discharge of blood five days before menstruation. Menses that had been absent seven months (in a woman fifty years old) reappeared, with pain in small of back. Menstruation delayed, at first watery, with dragging in groins and frequent yawning; D., with pain in small of back and lasting a shorter time than usual. M. too early and profuse; and lasting two days longer than usual. M. more profuse and longer than usual, with pain in small of back < walking, and pain in thighs < sitting. M. scanty the first three days, but profuse and continuous fourth and fifth days. *M. passed in black clots, more when sitting than when walking.*

Clinical.—Uterine pains, with soreness of the liver, aggravation from lying on r. side, constipation, palpitation, etc. Fibroid indurations of the uterus; scirrhus, with the abdominal symptoms of the drug; scirrhous induration of the uterus, with pain extending into thighs, leucorrhœa, menstrual blood black, colic, stools crumbling. It is frequently indicated in women who are subject to hysteria, with flatulence and the numerous hepatic symptoms of the drug, sometimes with a sensation of a ball rising into the throat (Ign.); especially with thick, black menses, constipation, etc.

Respiratory Organs.—Rawness in larynx, with dryness. Hoarseness every morning after rising; H., with soreness in throat and chest; sudden H. in bad weather, with dry cough and pressure on chest, on coughing sore pain in chest, but she felt easier after coughing, only after long coughing was some mucus loosened.

Cough in short paroxysms, then pain in chest. Dry C., with pain in pharynx; D., frequently only in evening and night; D. at night, waking her frequently and obliging her to rise. Cough, with expectoration; of mucus, caused by crawling in trachea; of tenacious, fatty-tasting mucus, from crawling in pit of throat; of gray salt mucus, from scratching in throat or itching in chest. Deep racking cough, also at night, amounting to retching, with rough voice, whistling in throat and easy expectoration of salt, sweetish mucus from chest. Expectoration of blood after sea-bathing.

Want of breath on ascending a hill, he is often obliged to stop and take breath. Tight breath, more after dinner than in forenoon.

Chest.—Stitches between r. ribs; externally in l. upper part; in r. lower rib towards evening; deep in l., not affecting respiration; low down in r., not affecting respiration; beneath r. breast, not affecting respiration; internally in l., with sore pain on pressure. Ulcerative pain in evening and night on coughing. Pain; externally on ensiform cartilage; pressing upward, as from a thread, from clavicle into a lower molar, in tip of which it was a crawling.

Constriction, and of scapulæ; C. after supper, with tightness of breath and sticking near r. nipple. Tensive pain, < deep breathing, with tightness of breath. Heaviness suddenly during dinner, taking away the breath, with nausea, salivation, mounting of heat to face, necessity to go into open air, and it seemed as if eructations or vomiting would relieve her, cramplike pressing upward as with fingers beneath tongue, necessity to loosen her clothes, the attack ended with a shaking chill. Burning when coughing; B. here and there, with throbbing. Rush of blood from a sea-bath; feeling of R. on walking in open air. Feels worse in open air, and cough on every inspiration.

Heart.—Sticking taking away the breath. Oppression. Palpitation; when sitting; in afternoon when sitting and on rising from a seat, > moving about; with pulsation in all arteries.

Neck.—Glandular swellings in l. side, tense on motion and painful on pressure. Painful drawing in r. side, as if in tendons.

Back.—Gnawing in spinal cord, extending up to neck, in evening after lying down, preventing sleep and causing constant tossing about. Pain in B. and small of B., disturbing morning sleep, always renewed on falling asleep. Bruised pain during menstruation; B. pain in spine at night. Burning pain and itching; B. pain in morning waking him, after evening coition, < rest, > motion. Burning in spinal cord and still more sticking, then boring sticking between shoulders, > motion.

Scapulæ.—Tearing; between S.; in r., then in hip. Pain in r., extending across shoulder to clavicle, < moving arm or head, > pressure. Bruised feeling between S., with burning; B. pain in dorsal vertebræ in morning on waking on back. Tension between S. and down back.

Lumbar Region.—Stitches in l.; in r. lower ribs close to back. Tearing in afternoon and night, with burning, and in hips; sticking T. in sacral region, > pressure. Cutting in sacral region, with pain. Pain; during the day on suddenly turning body, < sitting and lying. Contractive cramplike pain. Bruised pain; on stretching and stooping; with sensitiveness to touch, and in hips. Drawing pain after stool. Paralytic feeling in evening.

Extremities.—Trembling of hands and feet; after dinner, with weakness of them. Pain in long bones when walking; in r. middle toe when walking in morning, with drawing-inward sensation, then also in r. thumb. Painful falling asleep of hands and feet at night.

Upper Extremities.—Tension beneath r. axilla when standing; T. in r. axilla extending transversely forward to chest.

Shoulder.—Sticking in l. extending to hip, with burning; feeling as if a wedge were sticking in l., > moving it. Tearing; in forepart of r. and down arm to palm; in r. joint extending to scapula, on pressing arm downward; in r. extending to tips of fingers, so that she could not raise the arm, > letting arm hang down. Pressure upon l. Pain in joint, so that she cannot raise arm to face; in l. joint as if dislocated.

Pain in joint so that she could not raise the arm to the face; P. in l. joint almost like a heaviness, > motion of arm, then sensitiveness. Drawing pain in l. Drawing in l. joint, < moving it, with tearing; D. in joints alternating with sticking, < raising arms. Painful throbbing in r.

Arm.—Twitching of biceps. Tearing on outer surface of r. in morning when lying on l. side, > rubbing, with feeling as if falling asleep, extending into fingers; T. in muscles on outer side of r. upper; in marrow of r. humerus, then of l. Bruised pain in l. upper arm in evening after lying down, with a stitch in elbow and feeling as if the arm were out of joint. Falling asleep in morning when lying on l. side; of r. every night, < towards morning, when lying on l side; of r., < fingers, in evening on lying down.

Tearing in r. elbow; on inner surface of forearm extending to thumb; above l. wrist, extending to index; in a streak on outer side of r. forearm near wrist, > pressure, but returning; lightning-like; back and forth in a serpentine course between skin and flesh of l. forearm. Burning pain in forearm, with itching. Falling asleep of r. forearm in morning after rising, then of l.

Hand.—Tearing in r.; in l. fourth metacarpal bone; in ball of l. in evening in bed, with sticking; on articular extremity of metacarpal bone of l. index, > pressure. Drawing pain in r.

Fingers.—Stitches in tips of index and middle; in tips, > rubbing. Tearing in r. middle and ring; from behind forward in r. thumb; jerking T. in l. index and middle, from middle joints to tips. Cramplike pain in l. index. Numbness in tips, > rubbing.

Lower Extremities.—Reeling. Weariness; when walking in open air; during menstruation, even when sitting. Twitching in r. nates. Tearing in nates when walking, > sitting. Bruised pain in nates.

Thigh.—Sticking jerking so that he must draw the leg up. Tearing in r. hip, then in l., < about knee, as if in marrow, in evening in bed; T. in r. hip in evening after lying down, so that she does not know how to lie, but she feels best lying on sound side; in r. hip-joint in evening in bed, on rubbing and pressure the pain extends farther down; in r. hip, < walking in morning, with bruised pain; in r. hip extending to knee; tensive, in flesh above hollow of l. knee; intermittent jerking, posteriorly in hip-joint in evening in bed. Spasmodic pinching in a spot on inner side of r. in morning. Pain in middle in morning in bed before menstruation. Pain in fleshy part as after a horseback ride. Bruised pain in middle in evening in bed, preventing sleep; in l. in evening, as if it would break. Hips sensitive to touch. Throbbing in l. hip. Uneasiness, > moving legs, with tension. Weakness when standing, > walking.

Knee.—Sticking beneath l. Tearing; deep in r.; now r., now l., when sitting. Weakness, or with feeling as if bandaged.

Leg.—Jerking in calves. Cramp of calf when walking; all night, next day pain so that he could not walk. Tearing in lower part of l. during menstruation; in r. calf extending to heel, in evening; in calves extending upward, when standing; in r. calf, with tension. Acute pain in bony union of tibia broken twelve years before, as if it would be broken again. Paralytic bruised pain in calves and on insteps in evening in bed during menstruation. Drawing pain extending to foot. Tension as if muscles were too short, > continuing to walk. Weakness in afternoon; and heaviness. Heaviness of legs and feet in morning in bed. Falling asleep of r. leg and foot, > moving it.

Ankle.—Tearing in l. outer malleolus.

Foot.—Trembling when sitting. Unsteadiness in morning and evening on beginning to walk. Twitching in r. heel. Stitching on outer margin of r.; tearing, in corns; crawling, in soles. Tearing in r. sole; in evening after lying down, then above r. knee, finally in r. hip, lasting nearly all night; transversely across l. instep and toes when walking; on inner side of r. instep, extending into great toe. Cutting in heels. Bruised pain in l. heel. Tension on back of l. when sitting. Uneasiness in evening.

Toes.—Stitch in ball of l. great. Tearing in r. little; in r. great; in r. great in evening in bed; in l. great when walking and afterwards when sitting.

Skin.—Broad wheal between upper lip and nose. Red spot above wrist, with burning. Tetter that had previously existed behind ear itched violently and burned after scratching. Node on r. wrist. Pimple near corner of mouth; deep in skin on chin; on back; painful, on outer side of r. forearm. Itching pimples on back; between shoulders; on forehead, the I. < rubbing; between shoulders and on chest, burning after scratching; on r. nates, with burning after scratching; and red, on forepart of thigh. Yellow pimples covered with a scab on zygoma, with drawing, throbbing, crawling pain. Pustule on r. clavicle; with matter at tip, on l. temple. Boil on nose; itching, on l. false ribs. Vesicles on nose, feeling tense on touch.

Crawling on soles; over whole body at night in bed, with shivering over face, arms, shoulders and as far down as feet; in soles when sitting; in face, > rubbing; on r. side of chest, then a stitch there; on r. toes, with drawing, then heat; burning sticking, in finger-tips.

Itching over whole body; in bend of thigh; here and there over whole body; here and there over whole body in evening before lying down and in morning after rising, always in a new spot; on small of back and hips in evening before lying down, with burning after scratching; on outer side of thigh and after scratching itching pimples; > scratching, on nape and between shoulders, in evening before lying down; > scratching, on r. frontal eminence, behind l. ear, about nose, l. cheek, tip of l. elbow, inner side of r. forearm and knee. on calves, back of r. foot; not > scratching, on r. side of chest, small of back, back and back of l. foot. I. returning after scratching, in r. groin and lower part of l. tibia; on back of thigh, then burning; I. here and there, always in a new spot after scratching, also in evening after lying down. Burning itching on bend of l. thigh. Voluptuous I. on outer side of thigh, > scratching.

Sleep.—Yawning all day, < dinner; in forenoon, with eructations and salivation; with laxity and disinclination for mental work; almost constant; constant during menstruation. *Sleepiness during the day;* in morning so that she could not open the eyes; in forenoon; early in evening, and at first slept well, but after midnight sweat and thirst; after dinner, and on falling asleep jerking in whole body; with indolence. Difficult waking, with yawning. Late waking, with difficulty in pulling open eyes.

Sleepless till 11 P.M. on account of heat and thirst

after midnight sweat; S. after 3 A.M.; from 2 till 3 A.M., necessity to walk about on account of uneasiness, with sour taste; S. and restless on account of heat; and restless on account of pain in small of back. Restless sleep on account of heaviness in abdomen; R. sleep and frequent waking. *Sleep unrefreshing. Late falling asleep.* Difficult falling asleep, with tossing about; and late waking in morning and difficult opening of eyes. Frequent waking on account of heat. Constant tossing about at night. Starting up in sleep before midnight. Snoring. Talking in sleep.

Dreams.—Numerous, vivid, anxious, frightful.

Fever.—Chilliness at 4 P.M.; in evening, > lying down, then heat before midnight, then sweat and thirst till morning; at 8 P.M., with yawning; at 8 P.M., with thirst and dryness of mouth; at 9 P.M. after lying down, then sleeplessness; an hour after dinner, with gooseflesh, frequent yawning, constant desire for stool and cutting in abdomen; alternating with heat. Shaking chill in evening; from 6 till 8 P.M., > in bed. Shivering over whole body in morning, with cold feet; S. in morning on rising, so that she must return to bed several times; in forenoon; over whole body in forenoon, so that the hair stood up; at 7 P.M. on going into open air, but heat on returning to house; in evening before lying down, then sweat from midnight till morning; after dinner, with constant desire for stool; on upper part of body in evening in bed, almost without chilliness or heat.

Heat in afternoon, with thirst; in afternoon and evening during menstruation, with general sweat and orgasm in head; of body at 6 P.M., with sweat on head; in evening after lying down, with uneasiness; in evening after lying down, < every time on waking; before midnight, also with anxiety, after midnight sweat and thirst; after midnight; in bed, with anxiety; during dinner, with sweat; in flushes, with vertigo. Internal at night, with thirst; I. after breakfast of warm milk.

Heat in head; in a spot behind r. frontal eminence; above l. eye, with throbbing pain in head and dim vision; in forehead and palms in evening, with redness of face; after dinner, rising from stomach, > open air; frequent, transient; and in mouth and throat, so that breath came hot from mouth and nose, with coryza; with redness of face, without external warmth, with internal shivering and desire for stool. Internal heat in face in afternoon. Burning from shoulders to scapulæ and down arms to fingers; posteriorly in r. hip; in soles in evening; on back of r. foot as from a drop of hot liquid; of feet before midnight, > putting them out of bed, after midnight sweat and thirst till morning.

Sweat after midnight; with thirst; in morning, with thirst.

Magnesia Phosphorica.

Pure phosphate of Magnesium is triturated for use.

Clinical.—This drug has been used recently by the disciples of Schüssler in place of the well-proved preparations of Magnesia (Mag. carb. and Mag. mur.). Schüssler's indications are mostly found in Hahnemann's symptoms of the preparations above noted.

Magnolia Grandiflora.

A tincture is made of the flowers of the Mexican Magnolia grandiflora, L. (the Yolotxochitl).

General Action.—Apparently it acts upon the heart and peripheral circulation similarly to its very near ally, *Cactus.* Compare also Amyl nit. and the whole "vascular" group.

Generalities.—Contusive pains in all parts; rheumatic P. in different parts, > morning by rising. Prickling in whole body. Soreness > exercise. Heaviness as from want of sleep. *Weakness;* with loss of consciousness as to actions, defective hearing and sensation as if everything were at a great distance. Aversion to motion; to going out. *Stiffness from slightest exposure to draught of damp air; S. > dry weather;* causing sleeplessness, with pain in heart and apprehension. Amelioration of cardiac and rheumatic pains generally in morning, sometimes after rising; of pain in dry weather.

Clinical.—Pains of various kinds in different parts, < joints, constantly changing places. Muscular and articular rheumatism.

Mind.—*Apprehensiveness;* that she will die. Nervous, easily frightened, illusions and hallucinations of sight, with sharp pains in eyes. *Repugnance to all occupation.* Impatience. Ill humor, with burning in hands. Sadness. Despondency. Uneasiness. *Confusion; and dulness. Debility, with loss of appetite,* also with burning in hands and feet. Memory weak; lost.

Head.—*Lancinations; < l. side;* after eating; and in r. ear. Aching, with griping in abdomen; A., with flushes of heat; congestive, throbbing. *Vertigo* in evening, > going to bed, with goneness at stomach; V., with flushing of face; with dislike for physical labor; *beginning with blurring of sight; as from seasickness;* causing loss of appetite. *Pain in temples on bending forward;* P. in l. temple. Migraine. Pain in occiput and upper dorsal region; in O. as from a blow. Weight in occiput.

Eyes.—Pain from sunlight; sharp P., with nervousness and with visions. Lids heavy; sensation in lids as after weeping. *Vision weak; blurred.*

Ears.—Lancinations in l. traveling to shoulder. Pain in r.; in r. in morning; *sharp in l.;* sharp, traveling to throat.

Jaws.—*Lacinations in joints.* Pain in r. side; in joints; in joints, < pressure, also impeding opening of mouth; sharp, going to ear.

Mouth.—Pain > tepid water. Shooting in teeth. Soreness of teeth, impeding mastication.

Throat.—Fauces red. Pain; on turning head; waking him frequently at night. *Constriction; <* r. side; < bending forward. *Burning; and dryness;* with pain in pit of stomach and often extending to abdomen; preventing sleep. Sensation of mucus, with fruitless attempts to remove it. Difficult swallowing; *of saliva.*

Stomach.—Appetite lost after vertigo; lost, with lassitude. Sensation as from hunger, with acidity. *Nausea* in morning on rising, > breakfast; *N. as from tobacco. Pain; with languor;* with griping in intestines; extending to hypochondria; as from a blow; rapid, pulsating, and in l. side of abdomen; burning, extending to chest. *Emptiness; with general lassitude, vertigo and nausea.*

Abdomen.—Flatulence. Griping; with ineffectual desire for stool. Pain; from pressure; with diarrhœa; in hypochondria, with suffocation; *alternately in spleen and heart;* contusive, in liver and spleen, extending to stomach; in hypogastrium; in l. groin. Lancinations in liver. Constriction of liver and spleen.

Sexual Organs.—Congestion of l. ovary, with pain extending to l. thigh. Thick white or yellow leucorrhœa, with straining when urinating, also with constipation. Bloody flow in interval between menses. Menses delayed; M. pale and scanty; of coagulated blood for two days, then intermission for eight days, then normal; painful; preceded by pain in small of back, hypogastrium and thighs, with headache, flushes of heat to face, nausea and chill.

Respiratory Organs.—Hoarse. Dry cough during the day, > night by going to bed. *Suffocation; when walking fast; when lying on l. side;* after a meal, with desire for pandiculations; with uneasiness; *in paroxysms.*

Chest.—*Stitches in sides;* r. side. Lancinations in r. side. Pain anteriorly; *P., with emptiness of stomach and lassitude;* with suffocation and headache; in r. side, with suffocation; *rheumatic, in r. clavicle; rheumatic, in r. side, then in heart, causing fear of death, with general coldness;* contusive, with headache; *erratic, in sides.* Constriction as from a band just beneath axilla. *Tired feeling. Stiffness of sides;* S. as from exposure to a draught, when overheated.

Clinical.—Rheumatic pains in clavicles.

Heart.—*Stitches; waking him frequently.* Pain mornings on rising; in morning on deep breathing; *when lying on l. side; on deep breathing; with fear; with lassitude;* with itching of feet; *extending to back;* acute; alternating with P. in l. shoulder; *rheumatic, and in l. shoulder.* Soreness after disappearance of pain. *Sensation as if it had stopped beating.*

Clinical. — In cardiac affections, faintness in stomach, with mental and physical debility, vertigo, nausea as from tobacco, fear, frequent breathing, palpitation, suffocation, numbness of l. upper limb, restless sleep and frequent waking as if frightened. In valvular disease of the heart, with lassitude, difficult breathing from pain in heart, fear of death, pain in region of heart and cold sensation in whole body. In endocarditis, pain in cardiac region extending to l. shoulder and sometimes to back; in endocarditis, articular rheumatism and crampy pain in heart alternating with lancinations. Pain in heart, with suffocation, constriction of throat, pericarditis, general rheumatism. In cardiac hypertrophy, constriction of throat. In aortic aneurism, crampy pain in heart; dry cough, nausea, with vertigo and angina pectoris.

Pulse.—Weak and frequent.

Neck.—Weight, with tiredness of spine. Stiffness and contusive pain; *S. and tiredness, and in back.*

Back.—Stitches in r. side. Pain, and in l. side of chest; *in dorsal and sacral regions;* burning; tingling burning, as from overexertion of arms; sharp, in sacrum; sharp, in lumbar region. Tiredness impeding motion.

Clinical.—Rheumatic pains in back, also when alternating with similar pains in different parts.

Extremities.—*Sharp, erratic or rheumatic pains.* Lancinations anteriorly in elbows and popliteal spaces. Sprained pain in joints. Alternating pains in joints. Tired. *Stiff.* Pain in l. upper, with weakness; *P. in l. shoulder extending to heart;* from l. shoulder to l. ear. Stinging in arms. *Arms weak.* Rheumatic pains in wrists. Uneasiness in hands, compelling constant rubbing. Sharp pain in metacarpal joint of r. thumb. *Stiffness of lower.* Rheumatic pains in lower; in thighs, with uneasiness in l. leg; in l. knee; in tibia; soles. Pain in hip; in thighs in morning on rising, > noon, with tiredness; in legs, with tiredness. Legs tired as after running.

Clinical. — Shooting in all limbs; shooting from thighs to feet. Muscular rheumatism of l. arm.

Skin.—Itching; of feet; general, sometimes with uneasiness of legs.

Sleep.—Yawning during the day, with sleepiness. Sleepless early in morning. Extravagant dreams.

Fever.—Chill in afternoon, then fever lasting into night; erratic C. Heat; with burning in throat and headache; flushing, with sweat; *of hands;* hands and feet; upper limbs.

Manganum.

Triturations of the acetate or carbonate are used. (The symptoms of both are here combined.)

General Action.—A "blood" remedy to be compared with Ferrum in part. Its power to produce paralysis of the lower half of the body seems undoubted; its action on the skin is also very pronounced and interesting.

Allies.—Arsen., Ferr.

Generalities.—Stitches are mostly dull; pinching S. in several parts, < inside of thighs; drawing, jerking tearing, in various parts. Burrowing in bones nightly. Pain on touch; as if suppurating in all parts on touch, with heat of chest and cheeks. Drawing tensive pains in several parts, as from a tight band. Tension in various parts or cramplike drawing and tearing. Swollen feeling in head, hands and feet at 4 P.M., after walking in open air. Discomfort in whole body, < stomach, with fretfulness. Inclination to stretch all day. Uneasiness of mind and body as if something troubled him. Bubbling in various muscles, with waving sensation.

Weakness; in forenoon; at 4 P.M.; at 8 P.M., he could hardly keep awake. *Paraplegia. Paralysis, first of lower limbs* (Ars.); < *lower limbs, so that he staggers and inclines to run forward if he tries to walk, slight weakness of arms, weakness of voice, vacancy of countenance from paralysis of facial muscles, and from the same cause saliva is apt to escape from mouth,* < *speaking.*

Clinical.—Preparations of this drug have been found very useful in general anæmia, almost taking the place of Iron, especially when there is tendency to early but scanty menstruation or when there is tendency to menstrual discharge between the periods. Chronic rheumatism wandering from place to place. Periostitis.

Mind.— *Weeping mood. Ill humor;* at every trifle in morning, with wrinkled forehead, even the speaking of others excited him; at 4.30 P.M., and sad; afternoon, contemplative, dull, with general discomfort; *about everything she thinks of; so that he was not pleased with the most joyous music, but was almost cheered by the saddest music;* and discontented with himself, solicitous about the future, he talked little, thought he was weak in mind and made mistakes in speaking in every sentence. Embittered, implacable mood. Anxiety, with short breath and profuse sweat. Uneasiness as if he apprehended something sad. Distraction. Memory weak.

Head.—Shattering in brain on shaking head; in brain on motion, with pain in head and upper abdomen. Aching in house; > open air; from above downward over whole brain late in evening and on waking in night; drawing tensive, here and there. Throbbing as if brain would suppurate at 2.30 P.M., > open air, returning in the house. Confusion when sitting, with gloominess of it and general weakness.

Heaviness morning and evening, with sensitiveness of scalp; *in forenoon, so that he could hardly hold it up, with fretfulness; at* 4 P.M., *and feeling larger than usual;* at 3 P.M., > open air, returning in the house, with dulness, pain and internal heat in it. Rush of blood when sitting, standing, walking and lying, with internal heat in face without redness. Vertigo when sitting and standing, obliged to steady himself to prevent falling forward.

Forehead.—*Contractive sticking here and there in forepart of head, < temples, < open air;* drawing S. in sinciput on going into open air, < in the house, with general shaking chilliness; drawing S. in F. extending into ear, ending at tympanum as a sticking outward, < forenoon on walking rapidly, > standing still; intermittent S. in l. side. Shattering like a sticking above r. eye on rapid walking, even in the house. Tearing from l. eminence to temple when talking; T. in l. bone, < moving frontal muscles; drawing T. from above r. eye. Boring inward between l. brow and root of nose. Pain in upper part of bone; stupefying P. becoming internal sticking and boring.

Temples.—Sticking in l. bone. Tearing in l. on walking in open air. Digging extending to eyes and forehead, > stooping, returning on sitting upright and bending backward. Sharp pain above l. on getting up and walking, > sitting down again. Drawing pain in bones.

Sides.—Sticking externally beneath l. parietal bone, extending to all sides of skull; in l. parietal bone extending forward, on stooping. Tearing in r. and < deep in r. ear, on rising from stooping; drawing, in l.; sticking, deep internally from posterior and lower part of l. parietal bone to in front of vertex, when standing at 8 A.M. and at the same hour next day. Pain in one. Itching spot anteriorly on r. parietal bone on stooping, > rising, returning on stooping and scratching, with burning.

Occiput.—Sticking externally on r. bone extending to fifth cervical vertebra, in morning in bed, < turning neck. Tearing externally in afternoon, < touch, with tearing jerking, at other times pain in the spot. Pain; > application of hand, with emptiness, taking away his senses; throbbing, like suppuration, in r. at 1.30 P.M.; drawing, and in orbits and forehead, < stooping, > pressure; burning, and in sides of head, > open air. Constriction, and in vertex. Pressure forward over vertex into forehead, where it seems as if everything would press out, from morning till 5 P.M., < 1 P.M. Dulness and heaviness, then in forehead.

Eyes.—Pain if he looks intently at near objects, < a light held near them; when reading by lamplight, as from reading too much, with overpowering sleepiness. Crawling jerking here and there in r., causing agreeable tickling. Dryness in evening; D. and heat. *Pupils dilated;* < evening; r. more than l.; and light blinds him and causes pain in eyes, when the light is held before the eyes pupils gradually contract, but suddenly dilate on removing it; *contracted.* Sharp pressure on ball on moving eye inward and upward. Lids swollen; jerking sticking in upper lids; *pain on slightest motion and dryness on looking at a bright light, with feeling as on waking;* throbbing in r. upper. Biting pain in external canthus. Sticking inward in r. superciliary ridge. Vision dim for distant objects; short; vanishes at 4.30 P.M. if she looks long at an object; of sparks like rays in evening on closing eyes, and it seems black as soon as he looks at the light.

Ears.—Drawing cramp in muscles of l. mastoid process, so that he must hold head to r. side. *Sticking on speaking;* scraping S. in region of tympanum. Tearing in mastoid process behind r.; jerking, in r. in morning; jerking, in r. concha in evening on lying down, > in bed. Jerking-sticking pinching in l. outer, > rubbing. Digging in bones at night. Cramplike pain behind l. on going into open air, > touch. Intermittent sharp pain in r. on going into open air. Pain in l.; in external on touch; as from suppuration in r. concha in evening. Crawling tickling in region of tympanum, not > boring in with finger. Itching in l. Coldness as from a draught in r. *Deafness as if ears were stopped.* Sounds like the bell of a clock in morning. Sounds in r. like the croaking of frogs, when walking. Roaring after stooping, with diminished hearing for a moment as if ears were closed. Fluttering as of a large bird before l., with warmth extending into ear.

Clinical.—Earache, the ears feel stopped, and on blowing nose cracking, which temporarily relieves deafness, the troubles always < change of weather, associated with naso-pharyngeal catarrh.

Nose.—Tearing in l. nostril, with crawling, as from sudden irritation to sneeze. *Stoppage; alternating with fluent coryza;* with secretion of thick mucus. Coryza; of l. nostril at 1.30 P.M., with inability to inhale air through it and loss of smell. *Stopped coryza; in evening, with red, sore, painful nose and upper lip.* Discharge of bland watery mucus, with frequent sneezing.

Clinical.—Dry catarrh, with obstruction of nostrils, < cold, wet weather. Chronic nasal catarrh, nose very much stuffed and sore to touch.

Face.—**Pale, suffering, sunken,** as after excesses. Intermittent digging in a spot on zygoma at night in bed. Pain in zygoma as if a boil would break out. Jaw, sticking in angle of lower, extending to parotid gland; itching S. from r. side of lower to above temple, on laughing; cramplike sensation after eating; smarting and sore pain in lower; pain as from a blow in l. upper.

Lips.—Pimple in r. corner, with tensive and corrosive sticking on touch and on moving mouth; red, on lower near r. corner of mouth, with tensive pain. Clear vesicles on r. side of lower, and r. side of upper lip swollen and covered with pimples, with tensive pain on pressure; upper lip full of clear itching V., after these dry new ones appear, the itching < evening. Ulcerative pain in corners. Dryness, and of palate; D., with shrivelled epidermis, without thirst.

Mouth.—Teeth. Sticking now in one upper, now in another, on biting teeth together; S. into arm, causing there paralyzed pain. Tearing in several lower; drawing T. in morning in bed. Aching, < forenoon and evening from 10 till 12, > sucking with tongue, which at first caused acute jerking; A. extending suddenly into ear; sudden, in two hollow molars, extending into arm, zygoma, neck or ear, > biting on something elastic or laying head upon table, < sitting upright, with prostration so that he must lie down, internal restlessness and oppression; frequent, in root of a r. lower as if it would be pushed out; as if ulcerated, on touch; smarting, in an upper and lower molar, < cold drink; drawing, in r. molars, often suddenly disappearing, then drawing pain in neighboring parts.

Pimples painful to touch on r. side of tongue; posteriorly on l. side, and painful on swallowing. Burning blisters on l. side of tongue, returning next day. Soreness of palate posteriorly at 8 A.M., when not swallowing, > eating bread, with sensation of a hard substance. Dryness in morning after waking, so that she could scarcely swallow, with white tongue and acid taste. Salivation; bitter, with qualmishness. Clayey odor in morning after rising. Bitter taste in morning on waking, with dry lips, without thirst; to food in morning; and insipid, all day; B. and insipid after food and drink. Sour taste in morning after waking; posteriorly on tongue in morning after waking, > eating. Oily taste.

Throat.—Sticking in sides on empty swallowing; S. low down on empty swallowing. Constriction of parotids. Rawness at 7 P.M.; *R. on hawking, with feeling as if trachea were closed by a film.* Roughness in morning on rising, with hoarse, rough voice. Dryness in morning, without thirst; D. on going into open air, with rough voice, cutting in abdomen and nausea in chest; and scraping, compelling hawking; itching, in morning, provoking hacking cough. Feeling as from hunger.

Stomach.—Aversion to eating at noon. Thirst for beer or sour milk at 6 P.M., with dryness of throat; loss of T. and of all desire to drink. Eructations; in morning, with yawning and ill humor; tasting of breakfast; sickening. Nausea; intermittent. Disgust at food, though it has a good taste. Vomiting.

Fulness, > food. Drawing sticking, extending into l. ear, in region of tympanum, on laughing. Pain; in epigastric region when eating, > pressure of hand; beneath pit when eating, < walking; in pit, < touch, with pressure on chest; as from a stone in r. side. Constriction in morning after rising. Drawing in epigastric region and nausea as if pit of stomach were internally dilated. Distress, > dinner, she thought she would feel better if she could eructate, with attacks of nausea. Burning, extending into chest; in pit, extending up under sternum to palate, with soreness and uneasiness; as after long hunger, rising through pharynx into head, generally causing jerking or tensive sticking in temples or forehead; qualmish, rising into mouth in morning, with sourish-bitter dryness of mouth. Acid burning like heartburn, rising almost to mouth in evening; rising to mouth in morning on rising, with nausea.

Abdomen.—Large. Frequent tympanitic distention, > emission of flatus. Cutting in evening. Griping in A. and sides; > pressure and loose, tenacious stool, with shaking chill; G. in morning, then usual stool, with cutting in rectum; at 4.30 A.M., with movings, then soft stool; with movings, as before stool; then pale, yellow, sandy stool. Pain; < cold food; as if ulcerated, in evening, with pressure in hypochondria; drawing, when eating; flatulent, in morning in bed, not > emission of odorless flatus. Shaking, as if intestines were loose when walking. Discomfort, extending into head, as from smoking tobacco.

Rawness in upper, extending into sternum. Sticking from l. lowest ribs to pit of stomach on rising and stretching body. Bruised pain beneath last ribs. Sore pain beneath last ribs, < touch and motion. *Constriction rising from middle into chest (pharynx), with nausea and warmth.* Painful contraction, now in r., now in l. side, so that she sat bent over. *Umbilical region, cutting,* on deep breathing; drawing pain in morning; tensive pain about and above umbilicus, then flatulent pain and emission of flatus; warmth, gradually extending over whole abdomen. Hypogastrium, sticking, then soft stools; S. in r. groin; tensive pain as if a sinew were swollen, with pain on touch; warmth, as from a hot drink, moving back and forth, at last rising to stomach; burning soreness in bend of r. thigh.

Rectum and Stool.—Rumbling in r. Tearing in R. after dinner. *Constriction of anus when sitting.* Two soft stools in evening. Stool dry, difficult, infrequent. Constipation; for twenty-four hours, then yellow, sandy stool, with tenesmus and constriction in anus. S. omitted.

Urinary Organs.—Cutting in region of bladder in evening when sitting, < standing and walking, but he urinated without trouble. Sticking into urethra when sitting if he quietly emits flatus; S. in meatus urinarius when not urinating. Cutting in middle of urethra when not urinating. Urging; after eating an apple; *frequent urging; during the day;* with profuse discharge; with scanty discharge. Frequent micturition of golden-yellow urine. Urine turbid and deposits an earthy sediment; U. deposits a violet earthy sediment.

Sexual Organs.—*At times burning dragging from vesiculæ seminales to glans.* Drawing pain and weakness in testicles and spermatic cords as if they would be pulled out, with weak feeling in genitals. Sticking in prepuce. Itching within scrotum, not > pinching or working skin; voluptuous I. of corona glandis.

Female.—Pressure. Abortion. Leucorrhœa; intermittent. Menstruation at an unusual time; **too early and scanty** (Nat. m., Ars.), *lasting two days;* woke at 1 A.M., with griping and pinching above pubes, coldness of trunk, head and arms, profuse cold sweat, internal heat, dry sensation of tongue, which was moist, warmth of lower limbs, apprehension, restlessness, tossing from side to side, intolerance of uncovering in spite of heat, after fifteen minutes ineffectual inclination to eructate, then empty eructations and emission of flatus, thirst, eructations of water into throat, nausea, pallor, warm sweat on lower limbs, weakness of feet so that she could not raise them, inclination to stool, hardness and sensitiveness of hypogastrium on rubbing, then after Ipecac. sound sleep, waking at 6 A.M. with heaviness of head and too early appearance of menses of thick, black blood (compare Arsen.).

Respiratory Organs.—Sticking on each side of larynx extending into l. ear, on swallowing food and drink. **Rough voice in morning,** > smoking. *Inclination to cough in morning. Irritation to cough, he tries to cough loose something in larnyx, but it is difficult, and mucus is loosened more by forcible expiration than by real cough.* **Deep cough without expectoration, > lying down,** recurring next day with firm mucous expectoration and shattering pain in pit of stomach and chest, suddenly > noon. Paroxysms of dry cough; *dry C. from reading aloud or talking, with dryness, roughness and constriction in larynx, causing sensitive cough, with which mucus was loosened after long hawking* (Kali c.); dry C. causing shooting into sides of head. Cough in morning, with expectoration. Bloody expectoration. Expectoration of much pale green, yellowish mucus in lumps in morning, almost without cough.

Clinical.—Cough, laryngeal catarrh, with dryness and tickling in larynx, especially with hoarseness or loss of voice, the attempt to clear the larynx causing a sensation of rawness and sometimes stitches; particularly valuable for anæmic persons who are predisposed to catarrhal troubles. A very valuable remedy for boys and girls when the voice is changing and persists in being harsh, especially when associated with catarrh and frequent efforts to clear the voice The cough is apt to become worse in the evening until lying down, not worse through the night; the expectoration is scanty and tough; cough, < talking or breathing, associated with sore bruised feeling in chest. Cough from reading aloud, with dryness and rawness in larynx. Laryngitis, with great accumulation of mucus and rough voice. Palliative in phthisis of the larynx, especially with rawness and great hoarseness.

Chest.—Sticking in upper part of sternum; in l. clavicle and axilla; now in r., now in l. side in morning; in upper, on expiration; beneath l. axilla on motion of trunk; on r. lowest ribs on stooping; inward in r. side near sternum; drawing, extending upward and downward in l.; drawing upward, at times on expiration; constrictive, in forenoon on deep breathing; itching, in r. nipple. Sudden shock downward in l. as far as last true ribs when sitting. Cutting like a digging in sides of sternum, above pit of stomach, in evening. Digging in r. clavicle, with gnawing. Pain on coughing; P. behind sternum; sticking burning, beneath l. second rib, < expiration and motion, > rest and inspiration. Bruised pain; in sternum in morning; in upper, on bending forward, > rising, returning on stooping. Cartilaginous sensation drawing downward in lower part. Oppression in morning, with constriction of breathing. Throbbing in r. as from the beat of the heart there, in evening in bed. Warmth in evening, with stopped catarrh and hot breath, which he feels in fauces on inspiration and expiration, preceded by internal chilliness; burning beneath upper part of sternum, then also in stomach; by l. shoulder, more externally, < pressure and rubbing; internal. Nauseous warmth, with hot breath and burning in trachea; N. warmth, with feverish weakness, coryza and stoppage of nose; with coryza and burning in cheeks, at last external heat.

Heart and Pulse.—Palpitation. *Pulse irregular, scarcely perceptible, now faster, now slower* (Ars.).

Neck.—Digging in vertebræ at night. Cramplike pain in muscles in evening on moving them. Whirling rising from nape over vertex to forehead in afternoon during motion, with stupefaction and confusion of senses when standing. Stiffness of nape; drawing tensive, in nape, alternating with toothache; S. and swelling, with pain in muscles coming from teeth.

Back.—Sticking between scapulæ; in ischia when sitting; in region of l. kidney, then jerking constriction; itching, in middle, > rubbing. Tearing along spine; T. in l. scapula when sitting. Pain in small of, on bending backward. Burning pain in a spot above l. sacral region extending to first lumbar vertebræ.

Extremities.—Weakness of joints, with feeling in them as if stretched, trembling of limbs, tremulous feeling in knee and shoulder-joints, and anxiety.

Upper Extremities.—Sticking beneath l. axilla, with twinging, then sticking in condyles of l. elbow, with twinging. Tearing externally on r. shoulder, then itching. Sprained pain in shoulder-joint; and in elbows, with yawning. Drawing tensive pain in shoulders extending across nape, as if laced by a band. Bubbling in S.-joint, with pain like a boil when touched.

Arm.—*Tensive pain in joints of A. and hand*, here and there. Paroxysmal pain in joints. Drawing through whole A. to shoulder, with tearing. Sick, weary feeling. Weakness. Upper arm, sticking in r., extending towards shoulder; boring sticking outward on inner side of r.; pain on outer side of r.; sudden painful jerking on outer side of r.; drawing in inner side of r., with tearing; sudden weakness so that it must hang down, with drawing in biceps. Humerus, gnawing in lower end at night; boring in marrow of r. often aggravated, when it extended into shoulder, > pressure and motion of arm, but often returning; intermittent digging at night when lying on same side.

Sprained pain in elbow, with much yawning. Bubbling in elbow, with pain like a boil when touched. Drawing sticking on back of r. forearm; tearing S. above r. wrist, extending to forearm. Tearing in lower end of radius. Pain in muscles of forearm close to wrist; tensive P. below elbow as if too short, on stretching arm. Sticking in bones of r. wrist, then pain as if capsule of joint were distended and bones seized and pushed forward. Jerking tearing in marrow behind r. ring finger extending to arm, in afternoon. Tearing-sticking pinching in l. palm, in ball of thumb. Tearing cramplike pain in muscles of r. hand, < thumb and index. Drawing tensive pain in bones and joints of r. hand, almost as if laced, then heat of hand. Tension in hand as if swollen at 4 P.M. if she clenches it or stretches it out.

Fingers.—Sticking in first joints of l. ring and middle, < pressure. Drawing tearing in l. middle. Tearing as if tendons would be torn out on back of l. middle; in margin of l. thumb at 9 A.M., with sticking. Cutting in first phalanx of r. index, with warmth in it. Cramplike pain in first joints of r. middle and ring as if tendons would be contracted, but motion was free. Jerking or drawing pain in index in evening. Paralytic pain as after a blow in first joint of l. index, < rest.

Lower Extremities.—Jerking of all muscles on slightest motion. Cramplike drawing in l. nates extending to anus, on stretching thigh, < standing on that leg and by sitting down, > drawing up foot and while sitting, < rising from a seat, so that he could not walk unless he pressed upon the spot. Burning pain in a spot on l. nates, as if a pustule would form, < sitting. Pinching sticking on outer side of thigh, > sitting, < walking so that he must stand still; *jerking S. above knee* extending to upper part of thigh, in evening. Twinging in muscles of inner side of thigh after walking, causing anxiety and faintness as if he would sink down. Bruised pain in muscles of r. hip, < sitting; B. pain transversely across thigh. Weakness of thighs and legs, with sleepiness; paralytic, in r. hip-joint in morning, with stitches, making him limp.

Trembling of knees in evening when walking. Sticking in bends of knees when walking and sitting; tearing S. in l. calf when sitting. Tearing a hand's breadth above and below knee, on outer surface; on outer surface of l. calf, with itching; internally in r. calf, with external burning; drawing, on r. tibia when sitting. Griping in l. calf, with pinching and with pain from bend of knee to external malleolus. Pressure in muscles of l. leg near ankle. Smarting in r. tibia as if beaten. Drawing in l. tibia when standing, with sore pain as if broken. Tension in r. leg as if stiff when walking in open air. Stiffness of r. leg, < calf, in evening when sitting, > rising, with coldness and smarting. Inflammation of l. malleoli, with swelling and with sticking from external M. up leg. Drawing on back of l. foot, in joint, > motion. Heaviness of feet at 6 P.M. Falling asleep of r. foot at 2 P.M. when standing, with crawling.

Skin.—Red swollen streak on l. side of neck. Tetter on inner surface of l. forearm, returning, and itching < scratching, afterwards roughness. Pimples on upper part of chest; tense, on nates, with suppurative pain on pressure; itching, on inner surface of l. wrist, the I. < scratching, then a red spot; tips covered with scabs, on thighs, with itching burning morning and evening, and after rubbing pain as if sore and ulcerated. Pustules on r. wing of nose; on chin, with tensive pain, leaving a red spot. Suppurating ulcer, with blue margins and sticking, < night, developed from a scratch on first joint of little finger. Painful fissures on bends of joints of thumbs and in bend of middle joint of middle finger.

Tearing between root of nose and r. brow as if seized. Twinging in front of l. axilla as if pulled; T. on anterior surface of l. thigh as if pinched or raised by a needle, in open air, then pain for a long time. Pinching on inner surface of l. forearm, > pressure, but returning. Pain on chin as after shaving with a nicked razor, or as from an ulcer. Corroding acridity just below nose. Itching soreness between r. fourth and fifth toes. Tension on ring finger on separating fingers. Formication over l. mamma. Tickling in hollow of r. sole.

Itching on tibia; in middle of r. scapula; on inner surface of l. forearm in forenoon, and after scratching small pimples; on outer surface of l. forearm at 6 P.M. and on scratching a burning pimple appeared and skin became rosy, but white on pressure; *on knees* in evening; in hollows of knees, preventing rest at night. *Itching > scratching, here and there;* on outer surface of r. elbow; in l. palm; on forepart of l. knee; beneath l. lower jaw; *on outer surface above elbow* at 10 A.M. Itching followed after scratching by pimples, beneath corners of mouth; I. followed after scratching by itching pimples, below l. calf; I. followed after scratching by itching, deeply-seated pimples, on anterior surface of r. upper arm; I. followed after scratching by itching vesicles, not > scratching, then burning, on l. shoulder. Itching of fingers, and after rubbing transparent vesicles. *Voluptuous itching below r. calf, and after scratching deeply-seated pimples, which ceased to itch soon after being scratched bloody, then the place itched a long time;* V. I. on nape at 7 P.M., not > scratching. Tickling itching in palm in evening, < scratching, > licking with tongue. Biting itching over whole body after becoming heated and sweating. Burning itching on under side of l. thigh at 6 P.M., and after scratching sore pain, and on touch bruised feeling; on outer margin of r. thumb, and after scratching a red spot, then a vesicle full of serum, with biting.

Clinical.—Numerous skin symptoms have been palliated by this drug, notably lichen, pityriasis and psoriasis.

Sleep.—Yawning. In his dreams he always lay on his back, instead of on r. side. Sound sleep, with anxious dream of danger to life. Half awake at midnight, no sound sleep till towards morning on account of anxious restlessness and tossing about. Restless sleep, with heavy dreams and weakness on waking. Dreams as soon as he falls asleep. Lively dreams. Peevish dreams. *Vivid, anxious dreams;* and frightful; and confused; V., confused, of constantly varying objects; V., of a reconciliation; V., of something that really happened the next day; V., of objects in rapid alternations, with frequent waking and consciousness of the dream, which in the morning was only vaguely remembered; V. at 3 A.M. that he was with his physician.

Fever.—Chilliness all day on going into open air; in morning after rising, with gooseflesh, also from 7 till 9 P.M., then thirst; every evening. Shaking chill in morning, with cold hands and feet; in evening, with greater coldness of feet than of hands, with sticking in sinciput, the C. > in the house; late in evening, with coldness of feet and of r. leg, without thirst or heat; on walking in open, not cold air, > rapid walking, but hands and feet only became warm in the house. Shivering; sudden, as from a fright, in morning; over back, with sticking in head. Coldness in a spot on vertex, even when head is covered, with bristling of hair; C. of hands and feet, without chilliness; of feet when walking; sudden, in soft parts of tip of l. thumb.

Heat in flushes, < standing, with redness of face. Burning over whole skin in evening on rising in bed, > lying down. Heat in head at 4 P.M.; H. in head, with chilliness in rest of body; *frequently rising into head, with thirst;* burning in bone above r. temple; B. in one spot on r. frontal bone. Sudden heat in back when sitting, with contraction of pupils, then sweat. Peculiar lukewarm sensation in l. leg. Burning externally on r. side of chin; on lower surface of r. upper arm, extending towards shoulder, with yawning. Sweat at night on waking; and compelling scratching; on legs, < feet, at night on waking; on throat on waking.

Marum Verum.

A tincture is made of the fresh plant of Teucrium Marum, L.

Allies.—Lyc., Staph., Sil.

Generalities.—Excited tremulous sensation. Longing for motion in open air, where he is in constant motion without weariness, with joy. *Physical and mental indolence.* Prostration (as after intoxication) about dinner-time, < eating, with sensation of fasting.

Mind.—*Almost irresistible inclination to sing.* Exaltation towards evening, with inclination to talk much and with bodily heat. Fretfulness; during and after dinner, with pressure in forehead.

Head.—Frequent pinching. Dulness; with weariness. Dizziness; and on walking he puts one foot over the other and reels. Frontal pain in r. half; *above eyes;* in a spot above eminence; under the hand on continued pressure; in l. eminence on bending forward, > becoming erect; in r. eminence, with oppression; extending outward from deep in middle and < temples. Burning pain externally in forehead; now in r., now in l. eminence, with tension. Tearing in temples, extending into head. *Painful pressure in r. temple alternating with the same in r. frontal eminence, and* *in l. temple.* Jerking tearing in r. side. Sticking in occiput and even over whole head. Pain in occiput.

Eyes.—Watery look as from weeping, with biting in them. Redness and inflammation, with coryza. Tearing beneath r. Pressure in r. as from sand. Lachrymation of l. in open air. Upper lids red and congested. Biting in internal canthi, with increased redness of conjunctiva.

Clinical.—Tumor of the lower lid (Staph.).

Ears.—Stitches in l. Sticking tearing in l. Pinching. On passing hand through hair and across r. ear a hissing sound down parietal bone and through inner ear, a similar sound afterwards from talking or forcibly drawing air through nose in morning. Ringing in r. on blowing nose, a crackling as if air were forced through mucus, after which the ear seemed closed and then opened with a dull sound.

Clinical.—Otalgia, with lancinating pains.

Nose.—Sticking tearing high up in r. nostril. **R. nostril partly stopped, necessity to blow nose and sneeze, but obstruction not relieved thereby** (Lyc.). *Obstruction on reading aloud, < evening.* Sensation as if he would have coryza. *Crawling in nostrils; in l., with lachrymation of r. eye; with sneezing, without coryza.* Violent sneezing, then fluent coryza. Coryza, with moist stoppage of l. nostril and tearing below l. jaw; fluent C. in open air.

Clinical.—Polypus in the nose, with all the symptoms which would naturally accompany such a tumor, obstruction, catarrh, pain in forehead and nose, etc.; numerous cases have been reported cured.

Face.—Swollen and red. Pale in forenoon, with suffering expression, sunken eyes and sensation as if they lay deep. Tearing in r. cheek-bones, extending to r. teeth.

Mouth.—*Tearing in roots and gums of r. lower incisors.* Drawing pain in last upper molars; short D. pain in anterior molars of both sides. Grumbling in incisors. Incisors and gums are sore when chewing. *Biting as from pepper in l., then on r. side of root of tongue.* Corrosive pain on r. side of tip of tongue as if sore or crushed by teeth, < touch of teeth. Fissures, with elevated edges internally on sides of lower lip, and on l. side a pimple, on touch of tongue these places seem sore, velvety, but painless. Mouldy taste after hawking up adherent mucus. Bitter taste in upper part of throat after dinner, with eructations of bitter food.

Throat.—Hawking of mucus. Sticking impeding swallowing. *Biting posteriorly in fauces, < l. side, with scraping.* Pain in l. side near pharynx. Drawing in pharynx at times, with tearing. Warmth extending down pharynx.

Stomach.—*Appetite increased; so as to prevent sleep.* Eructations tasting of the drug. *Violent hiccough* on eating, with shocks in pit of stomach. Qualmishness in pit, without nausea. Pressure in pit; pressing-in pain in pit. Anxious oppression when standing. Emptiness extending low down in intestines, with rumbling in epigastric region.

Abdomen.—Rumbling; with griping and loud emission of odorless flatus. *Emissions of noiseless but hot flatus, often of a "hepatic" odor.* Flatulent pain after a little brown beer at noon, with emission of offensive flatus, sensation of impending diarrhœa and copious, papescent, offensive stool. Griping in r. side towards small of back; G. in r. hypochondrium almost as from incarcerated flatus, < morning and evening. Paroxysmal tearing drawing in soft part between r. short ribs and ilium, then also in l. Pressure outward in l. upper. Pain in a spot to left of umbilicus, < pressure; P. transversely through umbilical region, with rumbling and emission of flatus.

Hypogastrium.—Griping extending into testicles, as if they had been squeezed. Sudden colic transversely across low down in A. in morning, evening, fasting or after bread, if he drinks water, or nausea as if he could not tolerate water. Pain in groin after eating. Pressure above r. groin; P. outward in r. groin. Painless dragging down in r. towards inguinal ring, in spermatic cord in evening in bed, with compressed feeling in spermatic cord, returning at intervals next morning, when sitting after breakfast and again at 5 P.M., when eating.

Rectum.—*Crawling after stool; C. in anus in evening in bed, with at times sticking.*

Clinical.—Ascarides always < night in warmth of bed.

Urinary and Sexual Organs.—Sore pain in forepart of urethra, > when urinating. Burning in forepart of urethra in morning on first urinating, with long-continued pain. Biting in forepart of urethra when not urinating. *Urine increased and watery.* Drawing pain below l. side of root of penis, extending into l. side of scrotum, so that it became sore to touch. Sexual desire diminished, no tendency to erections.

Clinical.—Polypus of the vagina.

Trachea.—Tickling in upper part, causing short, dry, irritable cough; T. in evening after lying down, as from dust, causing dry, irritable cough, < continuing to cough and preventing sleep. Sensation as if coated, beginning with dryness, compelling constant hawking of mucus.

Chest.—Stitches in ribs a hand's breadth below nipple; S. deep in r. side on inspiration. Tearing on r. short ribs; wavelike T. below r. axilla. Pinching in l. short ribs; P. in lower part on bending backward when sitting, > bending forward, with pain beneath l. ribs close to spine; in lower part, always > walking, and in pit of stomach, extending into chest and abdomen and causing anxious discomfort. Pressure in r. Tightness in forepart.

Neck and Back.—Short drawing pain in r. side of neck, < touch. Rheumatic drawing and tension near l. axilla. Pressure on region of r. kidney.

Extremities.—Twinging in muscles of arms and legs, < region of hips. Falling asleep in morning in bed, and in afternoon when sitting, with crawling.

Upper Extremities.—Suppurative pain in l. axilla. Pain on top of r. shoulder; tensive, in joints near axillæ. Rheumatic drawing in bones of l. shoulder. Paroxysmal anxious, painless jerking transversely across r. arm where heads of biceps unite. Heaviness of l. arm so that it must hang down. Paralytic pain at insertion of r. deltoid into humerus, < raising arm and drawing it backward, > hanging quietly or moving moderately, but if he attempts to bend the arm down when it is raised high it loses all power and sinks down. Rheumatic tension in l. elbow.

Sudden cutting transversely through muscles of r. forearm an inch from wrist. Tearing on surface of r. forearm close to tip of elbow; T. above r. side of r. wrist;

in surface of l. F. close to wrist; in lower surface of of thick part of r. F.; drawing, in ulna and radius. Tensive painful heaviness in muscles of l. forearm. Tearing in r. wrist; < pressure of other hand; T. on back of l. hand; in l. metacarpal bones; in r. external metacarpal bones. Intermittent drawing pain on back of r. metacarpus.

Fingers.—Tearing in lower joints of l. ring and middle; in second phalanx of l. middle; beneath nail of l. middle; in ball of l. thumb; in knuckle of little, extending to wrist; paroxysmal drawing T. in first phalanx of l. index at 9 P.M. On bending r. index, pain in a spot in tip as before a panaritium. Painful bubbling deep in second phalanx of l. index. Rapid beating of the pulse in middle of phalanx of l. index in evening, and with every beat goutlike drawing pain from behind forward in middle of bone. Slow and painful dragging of last phalanx of l. little, as, for example, when rubbing palms together. Sticking burning on inner side of first joint of l. ring and middle. Crawling in last phalanges of l. thumb and index as if they would fall asleep.

Clinical.—Rheumatism in the arms.

Lower Extremities.—Sticking tearing above l. knee; paroxysmal tearing in articular extremity of l. thigh, streaming downward. Pain from middle of thighs to hollows of knees as from pressure upon sciatic nerve, if the thighs rest upon the chair. Pain in front below l. knee. Tension above and in l. tendo-achillis. Tearing heaviness in r. leg, < calf. Paroxysmal tearing in r. ankle when sitting, > walking. Pressing-asunder tearing in lower extremities of l. metatarsal bones close to ankle. Great inflammation to left of r. great toe-nail and above it in morning, > walking and afternoon, *with pain as if the nail had grown into the flesh.* Tearing in last joint of l. great toe; tensive T. in last joints of three smallest r. toes.

Skin.—Red spot in middle of r. cheek, in centre of which was a pointed elevation, becoming pale under pressure. Scaly tetter on lobule of r. ear, then desquamation of white scales, the ear sore and painful to touch. Red pimple beneath l. nostril during coryza, with sore biting on touch. (Rash on forehead and upper part of face, the face feels like a grater, with burning itching < evening and in warmth, sticking in the cold, becoming red on rubbing.) Itching sticking as from fleas here and there in morning in bed; during the day, now in upper part of arm, now in forearm, legs, hips, chest, neck.

Sleep.—Sleepy all day. Inability to wake completely in morning, with weariness on waking and rising. Napping in afternoon, he wishes to sleep, but cannot on account of a throng of confused ideas. Sleeplessness till after midnight, then frequent waking, turning from side to side, dreams, and towards morning heat. *Restlessness at night on account of excitement, with vivid and in part anxious dreams, with starting up till after midnight. Dreams vivid, mostly agreeable.*

Fever.—General shivering, with cold hands, frequent yawning and desire to stretch; S. after eating, with feeling in abdomen as before stool and as if the S. were dependent on it. Chilly trembling in trunk in evening during conversation on a disagreeable subject. *Flushes of heat in face without redness.* Burning on l. scapula; in bend of l. elbow; in tips of three l. middle fingers.

Melilotus.

A tincture is made of the fresh flowers of Melilotus officinalis, Willd. (the *yellow* Melilot).

General Action.—On the peripheral (capillary) circulation, dilating the arterioles and causing intense congestion (see physiol. action of Amyl n.).

Allies.—Amyl n., Glon., Cact., Magnolia, Bell., Ferr.

Generalities.—Sudden, shooting, stinging, burning, rheumatic pains, < knees and elbows, yet metatarsal joint of great toe is most swollen and red. Bruised, sore, tired feeling all over body. Oppression in morning, with heaviness and weariness. Weakness; in forenoon. Wearied easily, as if I could not get air enough to do any good. Stiff on trying to walk; on rising from a seat, with dizziness. Many symptoms appear in forenoon and wear off during the day; return of all symptoms at 3 P.M. *Amelioration in open air; A. from walking and change of position.*

Clinical.—Epilepsy resulting from a blow on the head has been cured. Puerperal convulsions. Convulsions of teething children.

Mind.—Furious, had to lock him in his room for twenty-four hours. *Irascible, impatient, discontented, fault-finding. Indolent,* reluctant to rise in morning, unwilling to set about anything, desire to do something else than the task belonging to the hour. Weeping in three attacks, without melancholy. Nervous and easily annoyed. Desire to be in the open air. *Unable to fix mind, stupid, indifferent. Omit words and letters in writing. Unable to study, memory will not retain anything.* Talk incoherently, know what I want to say, but seem unable to express myself clearly, "words trip each other up."

Clinical.—Religious melancholy. Hypochondriasis.

Head.—*Aching;* > *nosebleed,* with cough and oppression of chest; so that he was almost delirious; *causing purple redness of face and bloodshot eyes,* > *epistaxis; sick,* > *epistaxis or menstrual flow, blood bright red; periodical, nervous, every week or once in four weeks, more frequent in winter;* worse once in three or four days; oppressive; oppressive, at 9 P.M. after a hard day's work, with dizziness, faintness and nausea; *heavy,* > applying vinegar; heavy, in afternoon, becoming towards night heavy throbbing. *Heaviness.* **Fulness;** *and oppression;* **as if all the blood were there;** *as if blood would burst through nose, eyes and ears, with dizzy, sick feeling that is < motion.* **Throbbing** (Glon.); *and sensation as if all the bloodvessels of the brain would give way and cause some lesion of that organ.* **Congestion,** which has left meningeal capillaries enlarged, and this has made me very nervous. *Swaying sensation in brain, with tired pain,* coldness and listlessness. *Vertigo; on moving;* with nausea, with wavelike movement in brain and tension.

Frontal pain in forenoon; every day at 9 or 10 A.M.; in afternoon *preceded by hot, flushed face* and feverish sensation; in l. supraorbital region, < motion or thinking hard, > lying down, on talking it changed to occiput and returned to forehead when I stopped talking, it took about a minute to travel back and forth, I could feel it migrate, especially when returning to forehead, when I walked the whole head was affected, < over eye (I am right-handed and have a weak r. eye); *throbbing, preceded bg prostration; throbbing, in r. eminence, < from 9 till noon.* Sharp pain in r.

temple alternating with sharp pain in r. knee. Headache in r. side waking him at 4 A.M., < motion, < afternoon, with gastric flatulence.

Clinical.—Neuralgic headaches recurring every day at 4 P.M. Violent neuralgic headache, driving him almost crazy, with violent congestion of the head, pulsation, purple redness of the face, extreme nervousness, symptoms associated with nosebleed, which relieved.

Eyes.—Tired and sore, desire to close them tightly for relief. Sensation as if too large for orbits and as if pressed outward. Heavy, hot and as if pressed outward. *Lids heavy.* Sensation in lids as if unable to close them. Vision imperfect; blurred; almost unable to focus objects; floating bodies before eyes when studying.

Ears, Nose and Face.—Sensation of puffing of wind from ears. *Nose dry;* N. stopped, must breathe through mouth. Hard clinkers in nose. *Nosebleed;* with high fever and congestion of head and face; gush of bright red blood; gushing, with loss of consciousness. **Redness of face and head, with throbbing in carotids** (Amyl n., Bell.); *red face all day*, and feverish; *red* in afternoon, and hot; red before hæmorrhages from nose, lungs and uterus; *almost livid* (Bell.). Pallor.

Throat.—Soreness on l. side, swallowing painful, swallowing caused the wind to puff out of ears. Tickling, with cough and spasmodic breathing, causing nervousness. *Fulness.*

Stomach and Abdomen.—Very hungry, but nothing satisfied the taste; ravenous about 10 A.M., with the onset of frontal headache; appetite capricious, < morning; A. lost, especially for breakfast. Eructations burning, acid, smarting, all day; acrid, burning, all the evening. Cramp in stomach. Congestion of stomach. Abdomen full; at night before sleep, with crawling as of worms near rectal muscles. Flatulent distention of A., < during menstruation.

Rectum and Stool.—Internal piles, with oppressive fulness; and heavy throbbing. Shooting, cutting pain in rectum when walking, > sitting. Constipation, with gastric discomfort, fulness, flatulence and other symptoms. No stool for three or five days, then daily stool for three or four days. No desire until there is a large accumulation, then difficult, painful stool, with constriction in rectum and discharge (with the fæces) of stringy, glairy, milky-white mucus, each succeeding stool less painful till normal, then constipation again.

Urinary Organs.—*Frequent micturition; and excessive* (Bell.). *Urine profuse, watery, relieving the dull, congestive headache* (Gels.).

Sexual Organs.—Leucorrhœa excited by walking, with pain and soreness in back and pelvic organs. Stitching or cutting through uterus; *frequent momentary S. in external genitals* (< labia) at close of menstruation, with nausea and dull, heavy pain in pelvis, menses lasted four days (usually only from twenty-four to thirty-six hours), intermittent only during the day. Enlargement of l. ovary. Congestion of ovaries, with heaviness and oppressive pain. Scanty, intermittent menstruation, thin, pale, offensive; scanty, intermittent, with nausea, pain in back and bearing-down pains in pelvis; scanty, intermittent, with headache, vertigo, stiffness in back and limbs, dull, heavy pain in pelvis.

Respiratory Organs.—*Cough from fulness in chest;* C. > nosebleed, blood bright red; hacking C. from tickling; dry, spasmodic, distressing; harsh, dry, spasmodic, causing anxiety, towards night slight expectoration difficult to detach, relieving somewhat, heaviness and oppression so that he could lie on neither side; harassing, as I could not relieve throat or bronchi by getting anything up till near midnight, could expectorate freely next morning on waking. *Hæmoptysis, bright red. Could not get air enough, felt as if smothering.* Breath short, difficult on climbing a hill or from rapid walking; *difficult, from weight on chest* (Ferr.).

Chest.—Pain in r. lung before 10 P.M., with occasional pain in l. hip and with twitching of muscles. Oppression; with smothered feeling and difficult breathing, next day oppressed, spasmodic breathing, with fulness of chest. *Smothering.* Soreness; internally and externally; just under ribs, as if in pleura; internally, on waking from bad sleep, with oppression, through the day *difficult breathing, with fulness of chest and head*, next morning woke with spasmodic cough, same oppression and spasmodic breathing, during the day was nervous and had oppressive, heavy, throbbing headache, was easiest when perfectly quiet, towards night was sure that I had internal hæmorrhage from the congestion, next day distressing cough causing anxiety, easily wearied, with inability to get air enough, towards night slightly > scanty, difficult expectoration, all night had hot cloths applied to the chest to give relief, delirious a part of the night and talked incessantly.

Back.—Broken sensation in lumbo-sacral articulation; in sacro-lumbar region on sitting, > walking or standing, constant change of position to obtain relief, inclination to press or strike the part, this backache alternated with headache.

Extremities.—Rheumatic pains in all joints on approach of a rain-storm or in rainy, changeable weather. Feeling as if I had taken a hard cold, stiff and sore when rising, > careful movements. Uneasiness in large joints. Arms heavy. Soreness about hip-joints, with bruised sensation on pressure. Cutting in knees alternating with frontal, r. orbital and occipital headache. Gnawing, throbbing pain in r. knee, with desire to stretch the leg, but stretching does not relieve. Numbness and aching in r., then l. knee. Rheumatic pain in r. leg, < about knee and hip, > motion.

Sleep.—Sleepiness; in afternoon, with dulness. Sleeplessness; from unpleasant, disconnected, meaningless things coursing through the brain. Sleep poor; > towards morning. Disturbed for weeks, one night sleepless, tossing, dozing, dreaming, the next, probably from exhaustion, sleep without waking, but rise tired. Head seemed too high though I lay without pillow or bolster. Dreams full of contention and bickering.

Fever.—Chilliness; all the forenoon; between 12 and 1 P.M., with sharp pain in cardiac region of stomach and flatulence; with sleepiness, dulness and listlessness; at 10 A.M., beginning in back, lumbar region or occiput and passing in waves to vertex. Cold limbs; hands and feet.

Mentha Piperita.

A tincture is made of the fresh plant of peppermint.

Eager for work and dispatches it quickly. Insensible. Motionless, limbs relaxed, pulse slow and full, breathing stertorous, skin cold, lips livid, pupils immovable, eyes fixed. Headache beginning in morning, tension towards ears, < r. Sharp pain in l. temple when writing. Pain from one temple to other at night on waking; from one ear to other on rising, > returning to bed, but returning on rising again at 7 A.M. Lancinations from one ear to other on stooping or turning head; all day when walking, as if abscesses were forming in them, < l. *Confusion of head.*

Flashes before eyes when writing. Lancinations in l. ear when writing, extending to all of l. teeth. Tip of nose swollen. Tip of nose sore to touch. Aching in lower molars when chewing sugar. Lancinations in parotids, > during breakfast and dinner. Pharynx dry and painful when swallowing, as if a pin were sticking crosswise. Weight in stomach two hours after dinner, extending to ears.

Trachea painful to touch. *Voice husky from reading aloud. Cough; excited by reading aloud, exposure to cold, tobacco-smoke, or any smoke. Dry cough caused by passage of air into larynx* (Hep., Rumex); *D., caused by speaking*, and expectoration every morning of mucus like the core of a boil.

Neck sensitive to touch. Feeling in r. sole, at end of metatarsus, as if the shoe-sole were too thick and made walking painful. Skin liable to inflammation, every scratch becomes a sore. Itching pimple near l. ear, with heat of part. Formication of arm and hand when writing. Itching behind lobe of r. ear. Early waking.

Clinical.—Bilious colic, with great accumulation of gas. Valuable as a topical application for pruritis of the vagina. Irritable cough from supersternal fossa, < cold air (Rumex). It seems to have removed extreme sensitiveness to cold. It has relieved the severe pain of herpes zoster.

Menyanthes.

A tincture is made of the fresh plant, Menyanthes trifoliata, L.

Allies.—Nat. m., Cact., Aranea.

Generalities.—*Twitching of small portions of muscles in various parts* (Nat. m.); *T. in various parts at the same time, not exactly painful, < rest.* Sticking pinching here and there. Increase of vitality, hastiness in all movements. Weakness; when walking, with general chilliness; of whole body, with pain above sacrum when standing; (with heat and headache).

Mind.—Joyous. Keeps aloof from amusements, afterwards inclined to joke. Prefers to be alone, though not ill-humored, because he would rather be quiet than talk. Weeping mood. Despondent, inclined to think of past sad, disagreeable subjects. Apprehensive about heart, as of impending evil and as if he had to endure some calamity. Fretful and gloomy; F., discontented with himself and his circumstances, and anxiety driving him from place to place. Disinclined to work.

Head.—Aching on leaning head to one side; A. < open air; < eating; < ascending or descending steps, when it seemed as if there were a weight upon brain and pressing outward at forehead; > laying head upon one side, with heaviness and intermittent stitches in l. frontal eminence; *stupefying, < forehead;* like a pressure from both sides, with stitches in occiput. **Pressure from above downward, > hard pressure of hand,** *but returning.* Confusion; in the house, thought difficult though he could readily remember. *Heaviness.* Emptiness after eating. (Vertigo on stooping and rising again.)

Forehead.—Stitches extending towards vertex; burning S., less on scalp, with heat in face. *Stitchlike tearing near r. temple.* Pain on r. side, > applying palm. Drawing pain; in r. side; above root of nose; internally along l. bone. Pressure outward; in forepart.

Temples.—Pressure in l., with stitches. Compression, > pressure, but returning. Sore feeling in skin of l. when touched.

Vertex.—*Compression from sides,* **with sensation on ascending steps as if at every step a weight pressed upon brain** (compare Cact.). Tensive pain. Gnawing pain externally. Jerking pain, < stooping.

Stitches in l. side of brain extending towards vertex. Pain in r. side. Drawing in occiput when sitting; pinching D. on side of O. Drawing upward pain in r. half of cerebrum, ending in occiput. Hair stands on end, without chilliness.

Clinical.—Violent neuralgic headache beginning in r. side of nape and extending over whole brain to forehead, > sitting, stooping or pressure (Sil.). Neuralgic headache pressing from above downward, > pressure of hand, < going up and down-stairs, with feeling of a heavy weight on the brain pressing it outward at the forehead.

Eyes.—Pressure on a spot, as if in lens, when sitting, with sensation like vertigo or vanishing of sight or of squinting, but without obscuration of vision. Lachrymation. Pupils dilated; contracted. Stitches in balls. Twitching of lids, > eating, with pressure in balls. Stiffness in one or other lid like a tonic cramp. Tearing stitches in inner canthi, with lachrymation. Sensation internally on l. lower lid as if a not very hard body were lying under it. On holding lids still sensation in them as if swollen or as in a stye. Burning tension above l. upper lid, > touch. Vision dim in open air; V. vanishes on reflecting when reading; V. flickering.

Ears.—Stitches in r., then l.; in l. inner; extending into head, and in muscles below eye of same side. Sticking tearing posteriorly in cartilage and in mastoid process. Pinching. Itching within r. Coldness internally as if water were in it. Ringing in r.; > rubbing ear internally, but returning. Chirping as from crickets in front of ears. Roaring in l. on blowing nose, as if air rushed out through it.

Nose.—Tension in root. Sneezing without coryza. Involuntary running. Fluent coryza, with stopped sensation, though he could draw air through it as usual. Blowing out of blood in morning. Odor like bad eggs, causing nausea.

Face.—*Twitching of muscles, < r., < rest.* Painful cramp in muscles of r. cheek during rest. Stitchlike tearing in l. upper jaw. Tension in jaws. Lips dry and cracked.

Mouth.—Grumbling in upper teeth. Stitches on under surface of tongue, > moving it. Pressure in upper part of palate. Dryness of palate causing sticking when swallowing, without thirst and with ordinary saliva. Paralyzed feeling in l. side of palate on yawning and coughing. Salivation; with nausea. Bitter-sweetish taste. No taste to bread and butter, he has appetite and relish for meat only.

Throat.—Sticking in r. side. Dryness; with roughness of œsophagus, so that swallowing of saliva was difficult; of œsophagus.

Stomach.—Sudden ravenous hunger, > eating a little. Although not hungry, he relishes food as usual and eats more than usual. *Empty eructations.* Hiccough. Nausea; with painful retching and constriction in stomach. Rumbling in epigastric region. Pinching in region slowly descending towards rectum, > emission of flatus, but returning, > stool. *Pressure, then nausea, with coldness extending up œsophagus.* Constriction. Sudden heat, then excessive hunger.

Abdomen.—Distention, then emission of flatus; *D. as if overloaded with food, with undiminished appetite, sensation of incarcerated flatus and ineffectual efforts to emit flatus, in evening the D. < smoking tobacco.* Rumbling after eating. Flatus moves about making him qualmish. Griping, then hard stool. Tension in a part, with pressure. Coldness, < pressure of hand; C. in morning on rising, with creeping coldness over back and sides, like a shivering when listening to a horrible tale.

Parietes sore to touch and to rubbing of clothes, as if covered with pimples. Painful soreness of skin of upper A. when lying and on moving about, < stooping. Sticking beneath short ribs when sitting, transiently > pressure. Cutting in hypochondria. Gurgling in r. side, with heat over whole abdomen and sensation as before diarrhœa. Griping in umbilical region, sinking like a weight towards hypogastrium, > emission of flatus.

Hypogastrium.—Sticking in l. side when walking, then on standing sudden jerklike stitches; sudden jerking S. in l. when sitting, causing shuddering; sudden S. in sides when sitting, > touch, but returning. Griping; with urging to stool. Pressure in glands about rings on bending forward; P. in groin, as if in spermatic cord, with pain on touch.

Rectum and Stool.—Itching in rectum. Twitching in anus. Constipation. Stool hard and delayed. Stool retained; and next day hard, difficult, with drawing griping in hypogastrium.

Urinary Organs.—*Frequent desire, with scanty discharge.*

Sexual Organs.—Retraction of testicles, < r. Painful jerking in r. testicle, < rest. Stitches in l. scrotum; burning S. in scrotum and symphysis pubis. Drawing cutting in r. scrotum or feeling as if one side were squeezed. (Tensive, pressive pain in mons veneris when walking and sitting.) Great desire without sexual phantasy or erections.

Respiratory Organs.—Sticking anteriorly in larynx on swallowing. Frequent crawling tickling in larynx. Spasmodic constriction of larynx, with cough from exertion of drawing in air. Hoarseness. Voice rough; with stoppage of ears. Dyspnœa. Respiration accelerated, even when standing, with increased pulse and redness and heat of face.

Chest.—Stitches in r.; S. on moving; close to l. clavicle on inspiration; *in sides, < inspiration, with pressure on them;* in region of heart and in corresponding spot on r. side, < pressure and making parts tense; in sternum, with pressure; boring, in l., when sitting and on moving about, < inspiration and expiration; itching, in l. false ribs during inspiration and expiration. Grasping from both sides, with stitches. Aching after dinner. Drawing pain in r., extending towards axilla. Soreness as if beaten on sitting bent. Pressure on l. side, as from flatulence; P. upon l., with stitches, alike on inspiration and expiration. Anxious compression when sitting, walking and standing. Throbbing in l. during inspiration and expiration, only when lying.

Heart and Pulse.—Sticking in region of heart, < holding breath. Drawing pain in region after eating. Pulse slow.

Neck.—Tearing in nape. Cramplike pain in r. muscles ending in a stitch, > touch, but returning. Pain in muscles as if sprained, paralyzed and tense, as after long bending backward, on walking in open air. Heaviness of muscles, obliging him to bend neck backward. Stiff, drawing sensation in nape, with dulness in occiput. Stiffness of nape; in evening.

Back.—Shooting cutting from spine out through abdomen. Twitching of r. dorsal muscles. *Boring sticking in l. scapula, extending across spine. Tearing between scapulæ, extending downward, < deep breathing,* > sitting, but returning, then during rest soreness. Pinching between scapulæ near spine. Drawing pain near lower dorsal vertebræ on bending forward when sitting. Heaviness between scapulæ, > bending backward and forward when walking. Twitching in r. lumbar region when sitting.

Sacrum.—Pain on stooping; above S. on stooping; extending upward when sitting. Bruised pain in evening when sitting; B. pain < sitting, > touch; drawing B. pain in S., l. loin, region of kidney and outer side of thigh in evening when sitting. Drawing pain on stooping. Constriction in evening as from pressure of the thumb, and when it became worse a crawling in it.

Extremities.—Weakness. Shooting into axilla on moving arm; in r. axilla, extending towards chest; in deltoid at shoulder-joint. Burning scraping on top of shoulder. Painful visible twitching in l. arm, < rest; *T. in r. upper arm.* Sudden cramplike tearing in upper arm when sitting.

Forearm.—Stitches below elbow and on wrist. *Cramplike pain in muscles of l., almost like paralysis, extending to palm;* C. pressure close to bend of elbow, > touch, but returning. Cramplike drawing in inside of l., then four fingers were involuntarily contracted, the arm spasmodically stiff so that it could not be moved.

Sticking in l. wrist. Paralytic tearing in wrists, < motion. Cramplike pressure in r. wrist and metacarpus. Distention of veins of hands and above them, with coldness of feet. Cramplike drawing on back of hand, in muscles of thumb. Drawing pain in hand on writing and on moving it.

Fingers.—Painful jerking in l. fourth. Stitches in proximal joints, > motion; S. in r. thumb and index, extending outward. Cramplike pressure in ball of r. thumb; in l. index, rather externally, > motion. Sticking pinching in outer side of proximal phalanx of thumb.

Lower Extremities.—*Jerking stitches in upper margin of l. gluteus maximus;* sudden S. in r. gluteals.

Thigh.—*Starting in r. T. and leg only when sitting with them outstretched.* Twitching of muscles of l. Stitches in r. hip-joint when walking and standing; burning S. on anterior surface above l. knee when sitting. Sticking constriction in hip-joint about acetabulum when walking. Intermittent pinching in upper inner part, < sitting, with bubbling as from something alive. Numb, tense, bruised pain when walking and sitting. Tension in T. and leg near knee, with stitches on anterior surface. Cramplike drawing on forepart when sitting. Cramplike drawing, bruised pain in shaft of femur. < sitting, with heat in back and over upper part of body.

Knee.—Stitches outward in patellæ, with heat in knees; itching boring S. on inner side of r. knee. Pain as if dislocated, extending inward. Drawing in hollow of r., extending through calf, when standing and sitting.

Leg.—Jerking in l., < rest. Stitches below knee; in middle of tibia during rest, with jerking clutching, as if he had held the foot in a difficult position; burning, above ankles when walking; pulsating, below middle of tibia during rest. *Cramplike paralytic pain extending upward in muscles of r.* Cramplike drawing upward on outer side of l. when sitting. Sharp pressure on tibia. Sprained pain near inner malleolus, now l., now r. Corroding biting pain in a spot between r. external malleolus and tendo-achillis when sitting and walking. Tremulous sensation in calves, < sitting.

Cutting in external malleoli, > motion. Sprained pain from one l. malleolus to the other when walking in open air. Sticking in r. heel; in soles when walking.

Clinical.—Sciatica of l. side. Sciatica, especially with spasmodic jerking of thighs and legs, the pain generally > motion.

Sleep.—Yawning. Uneasy sleep. Redness and heat of face during sleep, he woke and cried "There, there," pointed with his finger and fell asleep again. *Vivid, unremembered dreams;* and lascivious, without emissions.

Fever.—Chilliness; < fingers; < back, not > warmth of stove; internal in trunk; then internal heat on trunk, < back. Shivering; creeping, external, < legs, without internal chilliness; *over upper part of body, with yawning.* Shivering over back; as from listening to a horrible tale, in morning, also when sitting. Coldness of spine, with shaking. **Cold hands and feet, with warmth of rest of body.** *Cold feet as far as knees, as if in cold water* (Nat. m.); C. feet, with heat of body, without sweat or thirst.

Heat in evening without thirst; after walking in open air, with sweat. Burning in scalp above r. side of forehead. B. above l. brow. Especially in face, then chill without thirst; in cheeks in flushes towards evening. Of ears. Internal, in trunk, < back, at times with coldness, without thirst, heat or redness of face, afterwards red cheeks.

Sweat in evening on lying down; from evening till morning.

Clinical.—In intermittent fever its chief characteristic is the extreme coldness of the tip of nose (Apis), tips of fingers and toes and *icy coldness* of feet and legs to knees; the chill always predominates and forms a pronounced part of the paroxysm (Aranea).

Mephitis.

The liquid obtained from the anal glands of the skunk is diluted with alcohol.

Clinical.—Spasmodic cough, especially whooping cough, with mucous râles through upper part of chest and suffocation, feeling as if he could not exhale, vomiting of food, etc. Asthma.

Mercurius.

Triturations of pure Quicksilver, or of Hahnemann's black oxide (Mercurius solubilis, Hahnemanni), are used. It is probable that there is no essential difference in the effects of the two preparations. Pure Quicksilver is, however, to be preferred as more stable and perfectly pure.

General Action.—Mercury produces in general profound anæmia, with degeneration of the red corpuscles, loss of albumen and febrin and diminished coagulability of the blood; with this there is a marked tendency to destructive action, as seen in the inability of wounds to heal and in ulcerations of mucous surfaces and of the skin. Sore mouth, salivation, destruction of the teeth and gums, with enlarged glands, are among the earliest manifestations. Inflammation of the liver, and especially of the kidneys, is an almost constant effect. A low type of fever and a condition resembling scurvy frequently ensue. Instead of the ulcerations and inflammations nervous phenomena sometimes occur, paralysis agitans, epilepsy, melancholia, neuralgia and a remarkable chorea. The long bones are attacked rather than the flat ones (opposite of syphilis). The iris is never affected.

Allies.—*Iod.*, Nit. ac., *Hep.*, Lyc., Nat. m.; Plat., Aur., Tellur., Phos.

Generalities.—*Foul smell of whole body and breath. Emaciation* (Iod.); then the frame speedily acquired greater bulk than it previously had. Cachectic condition. Child of a woman-worker was badly nourished and when a year old had no teeth. A daughter born during her mercurialismus was very small, only learned to walk when three years old, never was over four feet in height, had kyphoskoliotic curvature of the spine, head was drawn to chest and somewhat to left, and there was imperfect development of muscle and bone. Consumption. Scrofula in children; and rachitis. Chlorosis and amenorrhœa, palpitation, weakness, loss of appetite; C., face and mucous membrane pale, eyes watery, pulse small, rapid, great thirst, palpitation, dyspnœa, pains in head and stomach, œdema of lower limbs, weakness, depressed mood, blowing sounds in carotids.

Periostitis, then necrosis. Caries affects bones and joints that are never or rarely affected by syphilis. Exostosis, < tibia, seldom on upper arm or head, with swelling and sensitiveness of periosteum, < night, warmth of bed, cold, damp weather, thunder-storms, etc. So full of mercury that on putting brass into his mouth or rubbing it in his fingers it immediately became white like silver. She rubs temples and cheeks with both hands and becomes faint. Fell to the ground on attempting to stand. Cramp in several parts on motion. *Hastiness in all motions. Involuntary motions of head and hands.*

Trembling (Arg. nit., Plat.); **of hands and tongue;** of neck and hands; limbs and head; fingers and arms, then knees, limbs and tongue; < limbs, especially thighs, legs and forearms, while dorsal and gluteal muscles and those of pelvis and shoulder were less affected, those of upper arm, anterior chest and face not at all; after long standing or walking, > rest; on attempting to move; on muscular exertion, except of neck and face, then they extended to muscles not in motion, so that the outstretched hand trembled, < stretching fingers, and on repeated pronation and supination of arm the whole body trembled and the protruded tongue trembled; < night; < surprise or fear; < excitement, preventing speech; beginning in hands, < attempting to hold anything, attacking knees and rarely neck; < closing eyes, when it is noticed even in feet, > walking and standing; of muscles of head and spine, > sleep in bed; sudden; alternating with convulsions; usually prevents sleep, or a convulsive shock wakes him as soon as he falls asleep and the T. begins anew; paralytic. *Paroxysmal trembling;* generally worse in morning than in evening; from excitement or physical exertion, at times resembling the shaking of ague; so that he was liable to break whatever he touched, movement of legs so irregular that in descending stairs he must sometimes jump over two or three steps at once, to avoid this he crawled backward and on his hands, if he drank out of a glass it was crushed by the spasmodic clenching of jaws; and regular vibrations of almost the whole locomotive apparatus, apparently caused by alternate muscular relaxation and contraction, more in upper than lower limbs and on l. side, < attempting certain movements, especially if of a tonic character, and these more disordered in proportion as they required precision and voluntary effort. Those who had salivation rarely had tremors.

Jerking (Plumb.); in tendons of fingers, toes and tendo-achillis in evening, with shaking chill that tossed him into the air; of head, arms and fingers, < l., angles of mouth retracted, brows twitching, head constantly thrown back, but the agitation scarcely raised the arms, nostrils spasmodically dilated, short, rapid and painful contractions of sterno-mastoid, trapezius, scaleni, diaphragm and abdominal muscles, hiccough, speech interrupted and indistinct from jerking of tongue, attacks caused by a sudden cold blast, application of cold hand to the skin or abrupt entrance of any person into the ward, when he transmitted volition to any part it was instantly affected, when he tried to raise his foot from the ground it quivered and fell useless, when he attempted to put a vessel to his lips he carried it towards his ear, nose or forehead and spilled the contents on his face or neck. Motions as in chorea before the desired motion is affected, or convulsive motions involving neighboring groups of muscles, better able to hold heavy objects than light ones, hands and arms affected first, then lower limbs, then head in violent cases, the general trembling alternates with stammering, sometimes one half of body affected more than the other, sometimes they can ascend and descend steps with difficulty, as in tabes dorsalis, but cannot eat or drink, while in others these conditions are reversed, some cannot drink without assistance, because the water is spilled before it reaches the mouth, but they can carry food to the mouth by supporting the arm, one has to be held by several persons while he drinks. In its first attack it may be taken for St. Vitus's dance, in its later stages for delirium tremens.

Convulsions; < l. hand; of whole frame if he attempted to move or was asked a question, could not walk, hardly speak; during which he rarely lost consciousness, > tightly binding body and limbs; < evening, with loud screams, consciousness not wholly lost; whole body tossed to and fro, every muscle in activity, head rolled about, jerked backward and forward and from side to side, eyelids opened and closed, eyeballs rolled from side to side, wings of nose and corners of mouth twitched, face distorted, jaw moved backward and forward, limbs jerked as a whole and each muscle by itself, it tossed him to and fro and threw him out of bed; clonic, in r. half of body, affecting one or several groups of muscles and certain fibres.

Sticking in last r. rib and in groin when walking in open air, with tightness of breath on inspiration; in sacrum and lower limbs on touch, with no steadiness or power in sacrum or from knees to soles; *in chest,* knee, zygomatic process and external condyle of elbow, < forenoon and when walking; in various parts, with formication; in several parts, as if in bones. Tearing in various parts; in face, head and neck, sometimes with stomatitis; in hands, back, sides of chest, with internal headache.

Pains returned in evening on going to bed and banished sleep (Iod., Nit. ac., Colch., Plumb.); **pains in bones;** periosteal P. down l. forearm, then down r. forearm, then in r. elbow, then down spine; in affected parts; all over, < night; < *just after falling asleep, and he woke;* wandering; *jerking, in affected parts;* bruised, in whole body, < thighs; drawing, in head and limbs nightly. Drawing, in bones (Colch.). Dragging in whole body before diarrhœa, with anxiety and trembling, after the stool bitter scraping eructations and heartburn. Rheumatic troubles; R. pains, < shoulders and arms. Internal sickness, and he was taciturn and would not leave the bed. Distressed by evening air. Clothes and bed-covers seem too heavy.

Restlessness towards evening, he could not remain sitting and he could not lie on account of jerking in lower limbs, they became heavy, at night he rose constantly, with jerking even of head and throwing about of arms in sleep; R. from 8 P.M. till morning, no rest when lying, then he lay down because walking was intolerable; all night; *and anxiety; so that he could not remain a moment in one posture;* and could neither stand nor lie, was delirious as if he had committed a crime; and noisy.

Weakness; every day about 5 or 6 P.M. (Phyto.); in evening (Nat. m.); after midnight in bed, with tearing-drawing pain in thighs, and on stepping after rising from bed pain from groin to knee as if flesh on anterior part of thigh had been beaten loose; **after stool,** with griping; when washing his feet, with trembling and vertigo; after slight effort, with trembling and heat; on slightest walking; on walking, so that lower limbs ached as if he had walked far, > sitting; less when walking than when standing; < sitting, with feeling as if lead were in veins; *with depression of spirits; with inexpressible sick feeling of body and mind, obliging him to lie down; < sitting, as if all his limbs would fall from him;* of lower limbs, then of arms and hands, then general, then tremor; general, first affecting l., then r. arm, with general tremors, then pains and cramps in r. arm, then paralysis, delirium, aphonia, almost complete blindness and loss of hair, her mind returned slowly, r. arm was emaciated, never strong, and at times trembled; of a child born during the mercurial disease, it had to be fed because the mother had no milk and died after seven weeks, the woman afterwards had eleven confinements, but only five living children; in sudden attacks, with trembling; paroxysmal, of body and mind; approaching palsy.

Had to be assisted in everything like a child. Collapse, with swelling of gum, fetid breath, hiccough, agrypnia, retention of urine. Faintness, once caused by starting at something falling to the floor; F., < lying, without unconsciousness, with gasping and with indolence in all limbs; with distress in r. hypochondrium; with tolerably good pulse. Falling asleep of head, arms and thighs when lying; of all parts on sitting down, less in abdomen, back and chest, everything seemed dead, and on motion crawling in the part moved, as of falling asleep of any part. Torpor. Numbness, < fingers, with fuzziness. *Paralysis. Shaking palsy. Better when walking than when lying or sitting* (Rhus t., Con.). Aggravation in evening; A. on l. side. Young people more affected than the old.

Clinical.—Occasionally useful in hysteria, with restlessness. All the affections of Merc. are < night and accompanied by profuse secretions, especially profuse perspiration. Inflammation of lymphatic glands. Valuable for subacute rheumatism, always < warmth of bed at night, it affects the joints with pale swellings, soreness and sometimes sharp pains. At times useful in true rheumatoid arthritis. Chorea (Merc. vivus produces the most remarkable chorea of all drugs known to medicine; it is of the most violent character and extremely obstinate; but few cases of chorea have, however, been reported cured by this drug; it may be indicated by the general cachexia of the patient rather than by the character of the spasms). Diseases of the bones, especially periostitis of the long bones; rarely indicated for affections of the bones which syphilis attacks; it is almost completely complementary to syphilis, attacking only the bones which syphilis does not attack. General tremulous weakness. Paralysis agitans. Emaciation, with dropsical swellings, etc., etc.

Mind.—Delirium; nightly; *like delirium tremens; muttering* (Hyosc.); speech disconnected, he would not answer questions, increasing to rage, so that he was confined in a strait-jacket, with rolling of eyeballs, clonic spasms, discharge of yellow, frothy liquid from mouth and nose and rattling in trachea, then trismus and tetanus; uncovers herself at night, pulls the straw about, scolds, during the day she jumps up high; talks and scolds to herself, does not recognize her relatives, spits and rubs the saliva on the floor with her feet, then partly licks it up, licks up cow-dung and mud, puts stones in her mouth without swallowing them, and complains that they cut her intestines, stools contain clots of blood, resists any attempt to touch her, obeys no one, eats and drinks irregularly, pale, haggard and weak. Mind wandering occasionally. Knows not where he is. Hallucinations; < night, with desire to escape. *Believes that he is losing his reason in morning, thinks he is dying, and illusions, for example, sees water running where there is none.* Believed that he was enduring infernal torments without being able to explain himself. Foolish, made a fire in the hot summer, laid swords across each other, placed lights in one corner of the room, boots in another, indifferent to cold and warmth, head confused and heavy. Foolish fancy, with inclination to weep, then exhaustion. Inclination to pinch the noses of strangers whom he meets when walking. Excitement. Easily agitated. **Hurried talking** (Hyosc.); senseless talk.

Anxiety; all day, with apprehension, as if he had committed a crime, did not know what to do, with feeling as if he had not control over his senses, without heat (Ign., Verat. a.); all day, thought that he was going to hear bad news; at night, with orgasm of blood and sticking in bloodvessels; as soon as she eats, with sweat on head and forehead, which seem to her cold, sweat > open air, with want of breath and sticking in r. side below ribs; so that she does not know what to do, during menstruation; with apprehension, then sudden pain in pit of stomach, sweat of hands and heat of face; as if it would drive him away, as if he had committed a crime or as if a misfortune impended.

Sadness; with wretchedness and diarrhœa; with restlessness and anxiety, without particular thoughts. Constant weeping; almost involuntary W., then relief. No courage to live. Serious, offended if others laughed at a trifle, yet indifferent to everything that took place about him. Longing for home. Easily startled. Fear in evening, even to starting up; F. from slight cause, general trembling, she seemed paralyzed, heat mounted into r. cheek, which became swollen and bluish-red, bruised feeling in limbs, shaking chills, tottering of knees, so that she must lie down.

Irritable; *all day, and mistrustful, he treated his associates almost insultingly and looked upon everybody as his worst enemy;* all day, and taciturn and serious; all day, thought that all his efforts would miscarry; and vexatious, daring; and intolerant, suspicous. Anger, aggravating the trembling. Quarrelsome; and opinionative. Discontented with himself and his condition; with himself, and fretful, no desire to talk or joke. Averse to everything, even to music; to everything, indifference to even the dearest objects, and wish to die. Indifference; to everything, with no desire to eat, but ate as much as usual and relished it. Desire to take a distant journey.

Slow in answering questions (Lyc., Ph. ac., Op.). Idiocy. *Intellect weak, shows every mark of imbecility,* smiles foolishly, screams constantly, speaks only a few disconnected words, does not understand the simplest questions. Mental condition defective, cannot give a history of his illness, cries at least excitement, cannot remember his age to within ten years, speech thick, words are drawled out and often incomplete, after he has talked awhile articulation is less distinct, apparently from defective control over muscles. Talking was irksome, could not read, head confused, could work at nothing, and fell asleep when sitting. Acuteness of thought affected, vertigo, does not hear what is spoken, does not retain well what he reads, and makes mistakes in talking. Distraction. Thoughts wandering and impulses whimsical. Thoughts difficult to collect, makes wrong answers (that he himself notices). Cannot calculate, cannot put his mind on anything. Thoughts vanish; and he feels as if he had done wrong. No desire for earnest work.

Memory weak (Hyos., Lyc.); *and will power lost; M. lost;* forgot the names of persons and places. *Inclined to sopor, coma.* Stupor. Unconsciousness; and loss of speech, she seems to sleep but is pulseless, with usual warmth, but the look of a corpse, later she tries to speak, but cannot.

Clinical.—Suicidal tendency. Imbecility. Mental alienation, with hurried talking, restlessness and apprehension of impending evil; sometimes the sufferer is morose and mistrustful.

Head.—Swelling. *Constant rotary motion even when lying.* Trembling, almost preventing sleep. Jerking shocks in brain, < motion and stooping. Sticking through head; tearing slow S., with bruised sensation. Tearing externally; T. in skull, < frontal bones. Suppurative sensation beneath scalp on touch of palm.

Aching; every morning on rising; < a glass of beer, with vertigo; with nausea; with heat; with sensation as if he were pulled backward; preventing sleep, with pain in abdomen and back; throbbing, with vertigo; *in brain just beneath scalp, as if heavy and tight;* as if brain would be forced asunder; as if upper part would fall to pieces, and pressure as if everything would press down to nose; uneasy, in evening till sleep, > sitting up and resting head on something, loud talking disturbed him.

Pressure outward. Constriction; *in brain, as from a band* in evening (Iod.). *Pain like a tension encircling head above eyes and ears.* Fulness of brain as if head would burst. Confusion; *in morning on waking;* in morning on rising; in morning after rising, > open air, with feeling as after night-watching; in the house, with heaviness. *Weakness like a dulness and as if there were a vibrating in forehead and turning about in a circle.* Heaviness. Congestion of brain. Apoplexy, one side and tongue being paralyzed; fatal A. Intoxicated feeling after eating, with heat of face and redness and swelling of it.

Vertigo; during the day; at noon and in afternoon for three days, when sitting at the writing-desk, he stood up and reeled about the room, then anxious heat, nausea and headache; in evening; even when sitting; on ascending or descending steps; in the house; on entering the house, with staggering; on turning suddenly, everything turned with him; on rising after sitting bent over; when standing, during which he bent the head forward; on walking in open air, with nausea and sensation as if a worm rose from chest into throat; when walking in open air, with staggering, but in the house only heaviness of head; when lying on back, > lying on side, with nausea; more when sitting than when standing, with blackness before eyes, < towards evening; with cold hands and shivering, then dulness of head; with confusion of head, then clonic spasms of all muscles, spasmodic pains and ravings, consciousness never lost and tongue never bitten; compelling him to lie down; even to falling; in attacks, < evening, with flickering vision, pallor, sudden falling down if he was not lying, sometimes with unconsciousness and sometimes with nausea and vomiting, and once in the morning he became unconscious and fell out of bed; as if waving lengthwise, when lying.

Forehead.—Sticking; when walking in open air; tearing, in l. side when standing; tearing, in l. side when sitting, with general shivering, chilliness, cold hands, hot cheeks and lukewarm forehead, without thirst; intermittent boring, in l. side when sitting. Tearing externally; in l. side; T. in sinciput, extending to crown. Digging on stooping, with heaviness; drawing D. in anterior part of head. Aching; in r. side; above l. temple in morning; in l., < pressure upon the nodal point; passing to occiput, with fulness and vertigo; bursting; tensive, in sinciput, > holding palm upon it. *Pressure outward; with pain in bone beneath brow, even on touch;* P. outward, < lying, > pressure of palm. Head seems screwed in, now in sinciput, now in occiput, now in l. side, with lachrymation. Drawing pain, rather than tearing, sometimes in F., sometimes in occiput. Painful confusion in anterior and upper part of head in evening, with ill humor. Dulness above nose on rising after eating, < warm room, > open air, with whirling and blackness before eyes. Waving in sinciput, with throbbing. Vertigo.

Pain in l. temple. Drawing in r. temple. Pressure outward in parietal bones. Tearing in lower part of occiput; in O., extending to forehead, where it is a pressure. Boring in occiput. Pain in occiput; in upper part of bone. Jerking drawing and pinching in occiput extending to nape, and in r. temple.

Scalp.—*Falling of hair* (Nat. m., Lyc., Kali). Scurf, with itching, and after scratching burning. Dry eruption all over head that pains when grasped. *Moist eruption eating away the hair, with pressure, especially in the sore places.* Elevated, firmly-seated scabs between the hairs *Itching eruption.* **Pain on touch;** burning P. above l. side of forehead, > touch. *Itching; day and night;* and burning, also in forehead. Itching biting, and on nape.

Clinical.—Occasionally useful in headaches, < night, with feeling as if the brain were constricted by a band, or as if the head were in a vise. It has been used occasionally in subacute forms of meningitis. In hydrocephalus; more frequently in diseases of the cranial bones, though Merc. very rarely affects the bones of the skull, being unlike syphilis in this respect.

Eyes.—*Inflammation, with swollen, inverted tarsi and sensitiveness to light;* I. < open air, with burning biting pain. Swollen. Sunken, surrounded by brown rings; S., surrounded by blue rings. Surrounded by bluish-red rings, < beneath them. Staring, with watery obscuration. Bleared and weak. Sticking; in l. **Forcibly drawn together,** *as if long deprived of sleep,* when sitting, standing and walking. *Pressure;* on moving it and on touch; as from sand. *Heat; and biting as from horse-radish; with redness;* with redness of one. *Lachrymation;* of r.; in morning; in open air. *Pupils dilated;* contracted, scarcely reacting to the light. *Chronic conjunctivitis, with fine injection around cornea.* Blennorrhœa. Inflamed swelling in region of lachrymal bone. Constant motion of balls. *Itching of ball.*

Lids.—*Agglutination in morning.* Redness, swelling, constriction and sensitiveness to touch. Upper thick and red, like a stye. Twitching; of lower; when closed; as in chorea. *Sensation as if a cutting substance were beneath l. upper* (compare Sulph.). *Inability to open well, as if agglutinated to balls.* Burning in r.

Vision.—**Dim**; in l.; **if she attempts to look at anything, and eyes are almost involuntarily drawn together, the more she tries to restrain the contraction the less able she is to prevent it, she must lie down and close eyes. Intolerance of firelight or daylight. Blinded by firelight;** B. of l. eye when walking in open air; V. vanishes for five minutes every half hour. Weak; with atheroma of l. arteria centralis retinæ. Impaired in l. eye. *Of floating black insects or flies* (Lyc.). Of black points; moving downward. Play of colors. Of sparks. Of fiery points tending upward towards the clouds, < afternoon. As if a straw were hanging before eyes. Pointed objects seemed to have double points. Everything looked green and black when eating, the room whirled around, she was obliged to lie down. Flickering; when reading; (in evening when reading).

Clinical.—A very valuable remedy for various forms of inflammation of external parts of the eyes, catarrhs and ulcerations of the cornea and lids, and also some forms of inflammation of the lachrymal apparatus, episcleritis, with much aching in eyes, < night (Thuja). Scrofulous ophthalmia < night, and < heat of the fire. It is rarely useful in syphilitic inflammation of the eyes, as it has no power whatever to affect the iris, but it is sometimes useful in inflammation of the retina, especially when caused by working in the glare of a fire (workers in foundries); the pains always < night, and the discharge from the eye mucous and excoriating. Ulceration of the cornea, especially of the serpiginous variety, with turbidity and danger of sloughing of the whole cornea, sometimes with accumulation of pus in the anterior chamber, photophobia, nocturnal aggravation, etc. Catarrhal ophthalmia, with muco-purulent, excoriating discharge, soreness and burning of lids, photophobia.

Ears.—Bloody and offensive matter flows from r., with tearing (Tellur.); oozing of blood from l. in morning; *moisture runs from them; matter flows from* *both, the forepart of r. is a sac of matter, which when touched discharges through ear, with pain in r. half of head and face, so that she cannot lie on that side;* yellow discharge from l. Thin wax runs out. *Internally sore and denuded,* < r. Lobule red, hot and painful, then a pimple.

Sticking on stooping; *S. deep in,* < *l., with burning;* S., and the warmer she became in bed the colder and more moist was the ear, till it seemed as if ice were in it. Tearing deep in l. on appearance of menses. **Feels inflamed internally and externally, with pain partly cramplike, partly sticking, and feeling as if stopped by a swelling.** Pain; as if inflamed, in l., also in meatus; as if something were forcing its way out; burning, in cartilage of l. Pulling behind l., with jerking, preventing sleep, and soreness on touch; P. and pinching. Sudden attacks as if cold water were running out of middle ear, between the attacks itching.

Paraplegia of l. Deafness. *Hearing difficult;* hears scarcely anything, yet every sound re-echoes loudly in ear. H. sensitive, the noise of a horse or carriage made him start so that he would have been run over if he had not kept close to the walls, he was then obliged to stop for fear of falling. *Various kinds of ringing,* < evening; ringing as of high-sounding glasses, < evening. Humming as of wasps in l. Rushing in morning; R. before ears in bed. Whizzing before ears as if he would faint. *Roaring;* before l.; *with stoppage;* in r., with difficult hearing; with difficult hearing; *pulselike, before ears;* as if something had been stuffed into it. Fluttering before l.; in l., with crawling.

Clinical.—Inflammation of the auditory canal, furuncular, herpetic, suppurative and ulcerative, with intolerable pain involving the whole side of the head, < night. The discharge from the ear is offensive, purulent, excoriating. A valuable remedy for acute and chronic catarrh of the tympanum involving the Eustachian tube, with deafness, enlarged glands, etc. Chronic catarrh of the ear and deafness, following measles.

Nose.—Swelling of septum, with cracking; S. of tip, with redness, inflammation and itching; S. on l. wing, as in severe fluent coryza; < l. side, with redness and shining and with itching, < within alæ; inflamed S. on nose. Scaly internally and bleeding on cleaning it. **Offensive odor from nose, as in violent coryza** (Aur.). **Pain in bone when taken hold of** (Aur., Hep., K. iod.). Pinching in r. wing. Pressure downward, as if a weight were bound upon it. Tension transversely across. Distention at root. Congestive fulness in nostrils, < r. Obstruction; of r. nostril at 8 A.M. Irritation of mucous membrane, as from catarrh.

Sneezing; violent; once daily. *Frequent sneezing;* < morning; *without fluent coryza;* for three days, then swelling of l. lower lid, < towards external canthus, with burning pain in it, and lachrymation. **Acrid flow,** *having the odor of old cheese.* Dropping of moisture all day, without coryza. *Coryza;* with thin discharge, hoarseness and frequent loss of smell. *Bleeding;* **during sleep;** *during cough;* clotted, so that it hangs in a string from l. nostril.

Clinical.—Nasal catarrhs of various sorts, especially with thin mucous discharge that excoriates the nostrils, sometimes of green acrid mucus, sometimes < night. Ozæna, with offensive odor in the nose and soreness of the bones.

Face.—Earthy-colored, puffy. *Pale; and bloated; and sickly;* and earthy, sunken, elongated, and eyes dim, obscured; and anxious-looking; with intoxicated look; *with coldness,* heaviness, indolence and sleepiness. *Sallow.* Pale yellow. Cadaverous; and yellow. Dirty greenish. Red spots; red cheeks, with heat of them, then burning griping in upper abdomen. Cachectic. *Swelling;* of cheeks; of l. cheek; with redness and itching, and with swelling on hand; r. side, < beneath eye, with heat. Wrinkled, with a prematurely aged look. Stupid expression. *Masseter muscles contracted so that speech was difficult;* muscles between lower lip and chin visibly C. Twitching. Trembling of muscles on speaking, and T. of masseters when told to open his mouth. Tearing; in r. masseter muscle; in l. cheek and ear. Pressure outward in zygomata.

Jaws.—*Periostitis of lower. Necrosis* (Phos.). *Inflammation of lower progressing to caries, with falling out of teeth. Atrophy of alveolar processes of lower. Exfoliation of alveolar process.* R. lower very thin. Sticking near l. eye. *Tearing in lower towards evening.* Pain in lower; beneath lower; P., with almost complete immobility; mastication painful and even impossible. *Tension in joints on opening mouth. Cannot separate;* and tensive pain in r. side of hyoid bone, bitter taste to all food except milk, tearing and difficult hearing in r. ear, loud emission of offensive flatus and moist eruption on head; *almost unable to move lower or to chew.*

Lips.—Whitish-blue spot on inside. Lower rough and dry, as from cold, raw air. Papules, with biting on touch, beneath red of lower and towards corner of mouth. Herpes oris. *Fissures in corners* (Graph.). White patch, bordered with red, inside upper, near r. corner, and inside of lower covered with gray patches bordered with red. Eruption on upper, < margin, with yellow crusts and biting burning pain. Swelling; *internal, of upper.* Spongy swelling of mucous membrane of lower, with pustules like swollen mucous glands, also spongy appearance of mucous membrane of cheek and upper lip. *Soft, red swelling of upper, separating from gum, where it looks shaggy, and on its inner and outer surface deep suppurating sores, with sticking, at times with itching.* Red swelling of upper lip and lower part of cheek, in which holes an inch deep penetrate, looking as if painted with grayish-yellow matter, with watery, yellow discharge, offensive odor and bleeding of margins on touch. **Ulcers in corners, with painful soreness** (Hep.); painful U. on inside of lower, opposite incisors; dirty white U., easily bleeding, with livid borders; whitish, deep, easily bleeding, with elevated, livid margins. Distorted to one side at 3 A.M. Trembling about corners, < talking. *Pain on touch,* as from nettles; P. in corners as if they had been cut. *Dryness.*

Clinical.—Neuralgia of the face from taking cold, pains tearing, < night, associated with salivation, etc.

Mouth.—Teeth. **Decayed; and became loose in succession,** *and fell out at the slightest shock, especially the molars were gone, those that remained were* **black, laid bare, loose and carious;** and greenish-black; all lower incisors, and chipped, pegged, flat on top, centre brown; *crowns of all except incisors lost, gums very red and soft. Gray;* coating; blackish-gray, black. Covered with tartar. **Loose; and black** (compare Staph.); < *molars,* **and black, denuded of gum, with nightly pains in teeth, jaws and head;** and painful on touch of **tongue;** *and discolored;* and yellow; *and dirty gray;*

< anterior molars; < lower incisors. Falling out. Grating at night in sleep, and biting them together so violently that the pain wakes her. Sticking; in evening; in incisors on drawing air into mouth. Tearing in all roots all day; T. after midnight, and < morning; < eating; *shooting into ears, < night, so that he must sit up all night. Incisors feel as if out of their sockets.* **Jerking pain, < night; pulselike, from lower into ear, and from upper into head,** > *lying down and sleeping,* **with pain of gum from 9 P.M. on.** Neuralgia in a r. dental nerve, radiating upward over side of face. **Aching**; in incisors; in l. lower sound molar; r. lower (decayed) molar at 4.30 P.M.; in l. lower molar, passing to upper molar, both sound, at 6 P.M.; **at night, then general chilliness**; in anterior incisors on drawing cold air into mouth or taking warm or cold drinks; **with swelling of gum and salivary glands**; as from teeth on edge; as if corroding, < eating. Drawing in l. lower (sound) molar; in anterior teeth in morning. Disagreeable sensation. Weak.

Gums.—**Red; bright red margin**; and elevated, with grayish-red margin. *Red and swollen; and livid; and covered with thin, white patches, easily removed from a non-ulcerating surface,* and to left of and behind second molar a red patch which has been covered with a white film; and covered on the free borders with a dirty yellowish-white substance, which extends to the tooth-cavities, on removing this the surface is seen to be spongy and bleeding, without ulcerations; and worn away, covered with white film, free edges coated yellowish-gray. Purple margin. Margin bluish-gray and inflamed. Gingival line. Blue line on lower. White line on margin. *Upper margin jagged, white and ulcerated.* Inflammation. **Swollen**; only in morning; *every night;* **and separates from teeth**; *and sore, bleeding, pain on eating bread and food was bloody when chewed; and painful; and livid red;* and sore, with tearing in various places; with violet margin; S. and copper color of gum and mucous membrane of mouth, then excoriations on inner surface of lips and gums and salivation. *Atrophy, < lower anterior part; < lower, leaving necks of teeth bare;* and coated dirty yellow; and teeth grayish-brown. *Loosened from teeth;* and discolored and white at tip. *Spongy and partly destroyed; S. and covered with a pultaceous exudation; and ulcerated, loose, offensive;* and bleeding, loosened from teeth, with tearing in them and in roots of the denuded teeth almost all day and in morning on rising, > evening by smoking tobacco. **Bleeding; from slightest touch; and spongy;** *and soft.* **Ulcerated. Suppurating**; *between G. and teeth.* Boils close to roots of teeth, then teeth fall out. **Sore. Pain; on touch and on chewing,** < *hard food;* burning throbbing, < afternoon, > lying down and in night; burning, at night on falling asleep, waking him. Itching.

Tongue.—**Black, with red edges. Red, swollen.** *Pale. White, tremulous.* **Coated; and showing impress of teeth on edges** (Ars.). **Coated white**; < morning; **with whitish swollen gums that bleed on touch. Swollen; and showing imprint of teeth in scallops, which looked ulcerated; and its movement difficult**; *and painful, covered with foul ulcers, oozing of blood, the ulcers make swallowing difficult; with painful ulcerated margin;* and hollow internally, suppurating; < l. side, movement difficult, dirty yellowish coat on its upper surface, with gray patches on its edges; < r. side, which was covered with superficial ulcers, the swollen part of T. and mouth hard to touch, T. and palate bright red, painful, and submaxillary and cervical glands swollen and sensitive to touch. Inflammation. Roughness. Cracked, with dirty white coat; fissure lengthwise, with sticking in it. Anterior half so hard that it rattled when struck with the finger-nail, and was dry. *Gray patches on edges, and a dirty yellow coat on upper surface.* Instead of gray patches on edges a granular surface stands out upon the healthy mucous membrane, which bleeds on touch and has the white border of a true cicatrix. Ulcers; on l. margin and on r. cheek; long pale, on edges near tip; as in diphtheritis, upon r. side of mouth and T., with swelling of r. submaxillary glands and fetid salivation; on edges, cicatrized in their anterior third, but a granular surface on posterior two-thirds of l. ulceration, the r. ulceration has a granulated surface rising above the healthy mucous membrane, later a white border around the raised granulated surface, cutting it transversely in several places. *Trembling;* when protruded. Wavy from nervous debility. Vibrating like a pendulum as soon as it is put out, at first in small arcs, which rapidly enlarge if it is kept protruded. *Psellimus* (paresis tremens of organs of speech). Sticking in tip. Pain, with blisters on margins developing into ulcers; burning, as if cracked. Soreness at r. side of hyoid bone, with stiffness. Sensitiveness to open air. Crawling. Insensibility and fuzziness. Motion difficult.

Speech.—**Stammering. Difficult; on account of trembling of mouth and tongue.** *Tremulous. Impeded. Unintelligible.* Could scarcely speak intelligibly from the agitation into which they were thrown as soon as they were addressed or attempted to articulate. Embarrassed, indistinct and hurried. Slow. Lost; on excitement; desired to speak, but could not make a sound, > Hyoscyamus, with sunken face, weeping about her condition, sleeplessness, weakness, with desire for all kinds of food and then for beer.

Mouth in General.—**Salivary glands swollen and painful**; *orifice of excretory duct between last teeth S., white and ulcerated; r. sublingual glands S. and hard.* Trembling of sublingual glands. Swelling of mucous membrane; with pain; *of mucous membrane of palate, with redness;* of inside of cheeks, < r., where there is a red patch that has been covered with a white film, and palate shows some of these films, and on mucous membrane of lower lip white patches bordered with red, these last are replaced by red elevations with a gray coat between them, this granulated surface stands out in bold relief upon the healthy mucous membrane, leaving blood on cloth when touched, contact is painful; S., with redness; and on cheeks, gum and palate white patches that were easily detached from a non-ulcerating surface, and on lower lip, < l. side, yellowish patches that could not be detached, the gray patches on lower lip and inside of cheeks and on edge of tongue were bordered by a red line, later on removing with a cloth the patches that extended from lower lip over inside of cheeks the mucous membrane was seen to be rough, the cloth was stained with blood and pain was caused, the gray patches left red spots, afterwards reddish-gray elevation on inside of r. cheek near corner of mouth, the red spots were true granulations. Partly covered with thin white patches, but in some places thick layers which cannot be wholly removed by the nail, afterwards patches on inside of cheeks bordered with red, changing to grayish-red and granulations. Palate almost covered with a thin, white, false membrane, which can be removed from a non-ulcerating surface. *Pale and eroded.* Roof of palate and uvula copper-colored. Livid. Bluish, < inside of cheeks. Roughness of hard palate, with biting soreness on touch of tongue. Pimples. **Aphthæ. Bluish-red** *in places,* **and spongy,** *next day these spots are whitish, with dissolution of mucous membrane, the whitish-gray substance changes to a fetid ichor, flows off and shows a shaggy, flat ulcer with an almost spongy base and sharply-indented edges,* **the ulcer spreads without penetrating into flesh,** *and pains,* if left to themselves the ulcers appear dirty, foul and become phagedenic and ooze blood, the bottom of the ulcers often present unequal elevations, often with these sores irregular and quick pulse, sleeplessness, restlessness, night-sweats, nervousness and impatience (compare Kali chlor.). **Stomatitis**; sometimes with swelling of cervical and submaxillary glands. *Ulcers;* inside cheek; to left of uvula, with red palate; with fissures and burning biting, < evening; which as soon as cured appeared in another place; in back part, as in syphilis; foul, with copious, offensive sanious discharge; and ribbon-like U. on borders of tongue, in form of a half moon, erosions on free edges of gums, and small cryptiform losses of substance on cheeks; superficial, in angle in front of arch of palate, sometimes l., sometimes r.; deep, on inside of cheeks, with inflammation; deep, inside of lips and cheeks, with elevated, eroded margins, with swelling of tonsils and cervical glands; deep, on inside of r. cheek, descending as far as tonsil, and as mouth healed tremor so that she could not leave her bed nor speak. Pigmented scar on r. side between hard and soft palate, with a mercurial ulcer. *Blisters;* round, elevated, white, on inside of cheeks, from which the skin loosened, with burning pain.

Sticking posteriorly in palate. Drawing from palate into brain, where there is bruised pain, in morning after lying in an uncomfortable position. *Soreness;* and swollen feeling. Burning at night. Dryness; *of palate, as from heat.* **Salivation** (Iod.); *at* 1 A.M., *with nausea that wakes her and obliges her to vomit a bitter substance;* caused by smoking; *offensive* (Iod.); *soapy, often rather slimy and drawn out in strings;* acid. *Saliva bloody* (K. iod.); S. slimy; tenacious, offensive, < certain hours in night and evening. **Bad odor; sweetish** (Puls., Aur., N. ac.); *more noticed by others at a distance than by himself.*

Taste.—**Sweet** (Iod., Puls.); **to bread;** at tip of tongue; *and sensation as if body were made up of sweets. Salt; on lips;* to soup; S. and slimy to all food and drink. *Slimy.* Sour; in morning, > eating; during and between meals; to hop-beer. *Putrid; in throat. As of bad eggs on moving tongue, then involuntary swallowing.* Of matter in throat. Feculent, with salt saliva. *Metallic* (Nux v.); almost causing vomiting. Bitter; in morning; after drinking coffee; before and after eating; on lips and tongue during and between meals; < between meals and when she has eaten and drunk nothing; to rye bread; constantly, with sour eructations from bread. Bad; to butter. Of food as in intermittent fever. Lost to food, with loss of appetite.

Clinical.—A remedy of prime importance for dental periostitis, with great soreness and elongation of the teeth, pain < night in warmth of bed, teeth loose, salivation offensive. Gums unhealthy, bleeding, spongy, pale, receding from teeth, with offensive odor from the mouth. Valuable for patients who habitually suffer from receding gums, followed by decay of the teeth. Ulcers and pustules on the gums and mouth. The Merc. tongue is almost always swollen, flabby, taking the imprint of the teeth, sometimes watery, as if œdematous, sometimes covered with whitish fur. It has proved valuable in interstitial inflammation of the substance of the tongue. Inflammation of the salivary glands, very free secretion, with swelling of the glands, and soreness leading to suppuration. Aphthous stomatitis, with ptyalism, bad odor, etc. Salivation of pregnancy.

Throat.—Parotid gland hard. *Swelling of submaxillarg glands* (Iod.); < l.; r. side of thyroid gland; *lymphatic glands, with hardness;* of parotid, with burning pain, > cold, returning in warmth, if he applies wool to it he is constantly inclined to cough; *of mucous membrane of pharynx in spots; tonsils;* l. tonsil; *uvula, with elongation;* tonsils, with redness; circumscribed, of mucous membrane of pharynx. Redness of tonsils; of fauces, and streaks of mucus; *coppery, of soft palate and < uvula, and on l. side a long superficial ulcer.* **Suppuration of tonsils, with sticking in fauces on swallowing** (Hep.). Ulcers on posterior walls of pharynx; on r. side of soft palate; in fauces, in all workers not salivated. *Tonsillitis; and formation of an abscess* (Hep., Bar. c.). Chronic angina in fauces; and at root of palate, uvula and tonsils; dark red angina in fauces; *coppery red A. in fauces.* Hawking up of mucus that had passed through posterior nares. *Something hot comes into it.* Blood rises into it and comes out of mouth without vomiting or cough.

Sticking in pharynx; *in tonsils on swallowing;* posteriorly on swallowing, extending to ear. *Sensation as if something were sticking in it;* which he must swallow; dependent upon voluntary contraction of muscles of pharynx; *as of an apple-core* (N. ac.). Sensation of a worm rising in it, so that he must swallow constantly. Pain in side on blowing nose, with pain and swollen sensation internally in pharynx; P. like a pressure. *Pain as from dryness;* at back. Soreness in r. side of pharynx. **Dryness; and pain as if tight posteriorly, with pressure in it on swallowing, yet he is obliged to swallow constantly because the mouth is always full of saliva;** *of pharynx, so that he must swallow constantly;* posteriorly, but forepart slimy; in fauces, with constriction.

Inability to swallow a liquid below region of larynx, it returns through the nose. Swallowing was convulsive and often almost caused suffocation. Swallowing painful, with hoarseness; S. or speaking painful; painful, as if he had been burnt low down in throat or had swallowed boiling oil. Swallowing difficult. Paroxysmal pain in œsophagus as if an ulcer would form; pain in O. in region of larynx, < eating, as if she swallowed over raw flesh, with burning pain. Burning extending down œsophagus, later in abdomen.

Clinical.—Useful in various forms of sore throat, catarrhal, follicular, ulcerative, rarely diphtheritic; in all these forms there is free salivation, with swelling of glands, aggravation at night, offensive breath. When there is ulceration of the throat it tends to spread rapidly and superficially. The pains on swallowing are sharp sticking (Nit. ac.). Parotitis (Bar. c.).

Stomach.—Appetite. *Ravenous; she feels that it is not a genuine hunger* (Iod.); excessive A., yet he could eat but little because he had no relish for food and everything was tasteless. Satisfied by a few morsels. The smell of food is more agreeable than eating. Little; during salivation, but ravenous when she had no salivation; but much hunger. No longing for food, but it is relished when it is set before him. *Lost;* < morning; *for wine and brandy, to which he is accustomed;* for dry food; for warm food, A. only for cold **bread and butter**, etc. *Aversion to butter;* to coffee; to sweets; to beef; meat; meat, afterwards vomiting.

Thirst; during the day; *day and night;* for water towards evening; for ice-water; for cold drinks, especially fresh water. Thirst greater than hunger; with constant chilliness. Eructations; after eating and drinking; after dinner, with putrid exhalation from mouth; < eating, also with pressure in stomach; empty; sour; as of freshly-baked bread; bilious, in afternoon; of bitter taste and putrid odor; of bitter water; of acrid liquid while eating; of acrid liquid like brandy into throat. *Hiccough;* < forenoon; after eating; like eructations, during dinner.

Nausea; in morning, with heaviness of lower limbs, weakness and sleepiness; all day, with shivering; *when coughing;* after eating, also with pressure in pit of stomach; when urinating; with sweetness in throat; with eructations and diarrhœa; with vertigo obscuring vision, and flushing heat; with cutting in chest and stitches here and there (towards sides of chest) and cutting in abdomen and pit of stomach; as from something sweet; so that hearing and sight vanished; high up in throat, not in stomach, so that he could not vomit, < eating; in pit of stomach, then eructations, which at times take away the breath; extending almost from pit of stomach to pit of throat, caused by smoking, with oppression and cutting; in epigastric region, afterwards bruised sensation above r. hip, < motion and touch; in chest, with cutting there and with anxiety driving him hither and thither.

Vomiting; frequent, of saliva and bile after eating; violent, of bitter mucus; of bile and food, with constipation, coated tongue and vertigo.

Fulness and constriction; F. in pit, with tension restricting respiration, with diminished appetite. Constrictive tearing in pit, afterwards extending into chest. Griping in pit in evening, then soft stool, then griping and rumbling in abdomen. Ulcerative pain in S. and abdomen. Acute pain, < deep breathing and on touch. Pain; in epigastric region, with tightness; in epigastric region, with constriction; on walking, from l. side of pit to thyroid cartilage, where there is severe pain; as after violent vomiting; in pit like a scarification; *burning, in pit* (Ars.). Drawing down S. if he eats a little, with cramp in it. Contraction in epigastrium, < during a sleepless night, with dyspnœa, hiccough and cough, then vomiting.

Digestion difficult; disturbed; impeded on bending forward; bread lies heavy; food lies like a stone in pit, as if collected into a ball, when sitting; he cannot tolerate the most easily digested food, even a little bread lies in stomach and drags it downward, though he is very hungry, if he eats a little more he is ill-humored. Heartburn; rancid, scraping, after supper. Heat in pit when sitting on a low seat, with blackness before eyes.

Clinical.—Chronic gastritis, with burning pain, etc.

Abdomen.—Parietes tense; muscles tense. **Distention; from gas; and hardness.** Retraction. Rumbling after drinking; R. before stool, with gurgling. Emission of flatus. Flatulence in evening before lying down and on urinating, A. distended, then emission of odorless flatus. Tearing, in muscles. Cutting on urinating; C. before stool; C., with twisting and nausea; at night, or rather tearing, with external coldness of it. *Griping; with constant desire for stool, but little is evacuated* (Nux v.); with twisting, then stool; waking at midnight two nights in succession.

Pain; in muscles; *caused by evening air, with diarrhœa;* if he takes hold of anything cold; indescribable, > lying; *as from a stone;* as from a ball, then stools of dark green mucus; twitching; *in r. side,* as if intestines were twisted out; flatulent, with constipation; rising to larynx, as if a crust were scraping œsophagus and as if eructations and heartburn would occur; tensive, < pressure, > expiration, becoming when walking a cutting, < ascending steps; as if intestines were relaxed when walking; as from taking cold. Sensation as if he had taken cold, when walking in open air. Sensation as if intestines were too loose, and when walking they were shaken as if they had no firmness. *Intestines sore as if pressed, so that he cannot sleep on r. side.* Painful pressure on r. side in morning in bed. Bubbling rhythmical with pulse in A. or abdominal muscles, after eating. Burning. Hot vapor rising into throat after a moderate meal, causing thirst, with pain in throat. Chilliness.

Cutting in upper A. Deeply-seated tensive pain above umbilicus, > eating. Burning about umbilicus. Twitching in muscles of r. hypochondrium. Violent beating of an artery in r. hypochondrium near to and on a line with pit of stomach. Liver, *chronic atrophy, with emaciation and desiccation of body* (Lyc.); (chronic hepatitis in a man who escaped salivation); *sticking in region so that he could not breathe nor eructate* (Bry.); aching in region; pressing-out pain in region.

Inguinal Glands.—**Swelling, with circumscribed redness,** *with pain on pressure and long walking; S., with redness, inflammation and pain on touch and rapid walking; S. surrounded by redness, pain on walking and pressure, then red on its apex and inflamed, pain on walking and standing, obliged to lie down;* with indurated chancre, but no other symptoms of syphilis. *Bubo.* Pain as from swelling; intermittent P. Crawling. (Compare Calc. c. and Clem.).

Hypogastrium.—Painful contraction. Sticking in r. groin; in r. groin, on ilium; in groins (and heels) towards evening; in l. groin, < inspiration; rhythmical, in anterior inferior spine of l. ilium; boring, vertically from middle out through anus; cutting, low down, from r. to l. side, worse when walking than when sitting and standing, with painful ineffectual straining for stool. Cutting in evening, with pain in upper A., compelling him to loosen his clothes there. Griping. *Boring in r. groin* when lying and walking. Pain in groin; drawing, in groins and testicles. Tension in l. groin. Pressure towards pudendum, with pulling pain in thighs as if muscles and tendons were too short.

Clinical.—Chronic inflammation of the liver, with jaundice, great soreness, aggravation from lying on r. side on account of the soreness (Mag. m.). Catarrhal enteritis, with various symptoms, mostly cutting and tearing pains and discharge of mucus. Perityphlitis, with the peculiar symptoms of Merc. Very frequently indicated for inflamed and enlarged liver, with severe pain, < lying on r. side, < night, etc. Subacute colitis, with profuse mucous discharges. Ascites, with indurated liver.

Rectum.—*Evacuation of large round worms.* Ascarides crawl out. Sudden urging. Anxious dragging to stool, preceded and accompanied by nausea and pressure in temples. Frequent urging, then a few large hard fæces with exertion, at long intervals. **Constant ineffectual urging, with tenesmus in rectum** (Sulph.); *ineffectual U., with protruding, painful sore hæmorrhoids;* ineffectual U. in morning (Nux v.).

Anus.—*Prolapsus.* Hæmorrhoid protrudes, with shooting during stool and on touch. Discharge of blood after stool; D. of blood when urinating. Sticking. Pinching as in diarrhœa, with emission of flatus. Soreness. *Burning pain, with soft stools.* Burning; after stool. Itching as from thread-worms. Boring sticking in perineum when walking and sitting.

Stool.—*Diarrhœa; in evening; in night; with cutting and pressure in rectum; with streaks of blood;* with blood for several days, then hard stool with blood; **of green mucus** (Arg. n., Gam., Ip.), **with burning and protrusion of anus; green,** *with cutting and griping;* green, afterwards constipation; yellow, twice daily, without sensation; offensive, at times involuntary; exhausting; burning; alternating with constipation. *Soft, brownish, easy, floating on water;* S., orange-yellow, flatulent. Pasty, with mucus; P., urgent, involuntary if he neglects it.

Constipation; with catarrhal fever, hypochondriac prostration and aversion to all food except beer; with occasional griping, stool on alternate days. Hard; like sheep-dung; H., little, with pressure; H., could not be evacuated for a long time, with pain in anus. *Green, slimy, acrid, excoriating anus.* Dark green, bilious, frothy. *Whitish-gray* (Pod.). Sulphur-yellow. Bright yellow. Red, slimy. *Bloody; with painful acrid sensation in anus;* blood and mucus on fæces. Of sour odor. Tenacious. *Scanty, with much dragging; S., frequent, burning-biting, causing distress in anus; S., of bloody mucus, with cutting in abdomen and tenesmus;* S., with mucus, four or five times. Involuntary. Indolent. Only once every three days. Only at night.

Clinical.—The stools nearly always contain mucus, and there is usually more or less tenesmus; there also may be numerous symptoms of the rectum, pain extending up the colon, sometimes very severe, sometimes violent colic, sometimes the stools are preceded by chilliness and followed by tenesmus and burning; (for children who have catarrhal enteritis, with green mucous stools and very little tenesmus, Merc. dulc. is usually required). Dysentery, with fever, but easy sweat, < night, discharges of blood and mucus, with tenesmus and burning pain, sometimes with prolapsus (Pod.).

Urinary Organs.—Pressure after micturition. **Constant desire, but little is passed;** constant ineffectual D. *Frequent urging* after nocturnal emission; *F. urging, with scanty discharge; so that he must urinate at least every hour day and night, with burning in urethra on beginning to urinate.* Micturition in a weak stream. *Involuntary micturition; if he does not hurry. Frequent micturition; at night; and profuse,* also at night; and urine thin; obliged to urinate every night at 4 A.M.; *with burning-biting pain* (compare Canth.).

Urethra.—**Discharge, greenish, painless, < night.** Discharge of blood. *Swelling of forepart, with suppuration between glans and prepuce, which is red and hot to touch and painful on walking and touch, with raging pain in forehead and rough, itchlike eruption on hands, < region of first joint of thumb, more on upper surface, itching much at night.* Sticking; in forepart when not urinating; towards evening extending towards abdomen; drawing when not urinating. Bubbling like a sticking. Throbbing rather than sticking. Cutting in morning during micturition; C. on beginning to urinate; biting, when urinating, < towards the end, therewith he cannot urinate quickly enough and some passes involuntarily. Biting in female, when urinating. **Burning** *when not urinating; on beginning to urinate; when urinating;* first B. when urinating, then biting; in male, during coition.

Urine.—*Dark. Reddish, causing biting, becoming thick on standing;* brownish-red; fiery red, seldom discharged; dark red, seemed to be mixed with blood. *Acrid.* Of sourish odor. Copious; and red and brown. *Scanty, dark yellow, albuminous; S. and mixed with blood.* Clear at first, but afterwards as if mixed with chalk, then pain, with burning in urethra after even touching penis. *Turbid when passed and depositing a sediment.* Looks as if mixed with meal, with thick sediment. White flocculent cloud. Large white fibres and flakes pass after the urine, without pain. Contained pieces of hard mucus, like pieces of flesh.

Clinical.—Cystitis, dribbling, discharge of mucus with the urine and more or less tenesmus of the bladder, especially burning after urinating. A remedy of very great value for inflammation of the kidney, albuminuria, urine sometimes bloody; indicated by burning and tenesmus, pain in back and nocturnal aggravation. Albuminuria of pregnancy. Gonorrhœa, with swollen inguinal glands, greenish mucous discharge, etc.

Sexual Organs.—Prepuce. *Swelling as if distended with air or water to a blister; S., with inflamed redness of its inner surface, with sensitiveness;* with biting, burning and redness, and on its inner surface chaps and rhagades, but externally fine red eruption. Inflammation, with burning pain. Voluptuous itching; sticking I. on frænum.

Glans.—*At end of penis, under prepuce, red vesicles, becoming ulcers, which discharge offensive yellow-white matter, staining the shirt, then the* **large ulcers bleed,** *and on touch pain affecting the whole body, they are round,* **margins everted like raw meat, caseous coat on bases;** *on forepart and one side vesicles eating deeply and spreading, small white V. which also ooze a fluid.* Tearing sticking from forepart through penis to anus, and at times in groins; itching S. on pressure; itching S. after urinating. Itching; agreeable tickling, on forepart; crawling. Cold and shrivelled. Burning about it in evening, then blisters on inner surface of prepuce, which become ulcers. Falling asleep (deadness) of penis. Painful erections; incomplete E., with tension of pudendum as from flatulence. (The symptoms of ulceration and discharges are taken from Hahnemann and are doubtless clinical, as cases of poisoning do not develop similar effects.)

Sticking in scrotum. Crawling in scrotum and frænum of glans. Paroxysmal drawing in spermatic cord. Testicles, swelling, sensitiveness before emission of flatus, not painful; spasmodic tearing between T., extending into penis and causing itching in ulcers; drawing pain, and in groins; drawing rather than pressure; itching of r.; *coldness every afternoon and evening. Power lost. Emission at night; and mixed with blood;* during midday nap, then burning pain in orifice of urethra when urinating; E. without voluptuous dream.

Female.—Pressure, whereupon she must urinate much. Pimple on labia; on pudenda. Itching of pudenda; before menstruation. Prolapsus of vagina. Inflamed swelling as if raw and sore internally in vagina. *Leucorrhœa, < 8 till 10 P.M., it does not drop,* **is greenish, causes biting in forepart of genitals, so that**

she must scratch much, < evening and night, and burning after scratching; *corrosive L.;* bland; purulent. Discharge of flakes of mucus and pus as large as hazelnuts from vagina. Profuse hæmorrhage; suddenly. Discharge of blood from a woman whose menstruation had ceased eleven years before; D. of blood six days after menstruation. Menorrhagia for three weeks. Profuse metrorrhagia, once there was menstrual flow for ten weeks. *Menstruation too profuse,* with colic; M. irregular, sometimes omitting, sometimes too copious and too late. Menses scanty; and irregular; and pale, lasting only a few hours. Menses suppressed. Abortion. Child born four weeks too early, weak and died within a year and a half. Coition very easy, with certain receptivity and conception.

Clinical.—Frequently valuable for venereal ulcers, with nocturnal aggravation and profuse muco-purulent discharge, swelling of inguinal glands, etc. Herpes of the prepuce. Orchitis. Catarrh of the vagina, with greenish excoriating leucorrhœa, < night. Ulcers of the vagina and os uteri. Subacute ovaritis, sometimes with peritonitis, pains < night, always more or less tenesmus of the rectum or bladder, or of both. Abscess of the vulva. Women who require Merc. are prone to uterine hæmorrhage. Pruritus of vulva.

Respiratory Organs.—Voice tremulous, as during rigor; tone of V. altered. Laryngeal phthisis, with erosions and ulcers on posterior wall of pharynx. Chronic bronchitis in one who escaped salivation.

Cough.—With tightness of chest; with pain in l. side and l. shoulder; with sweat and prostration; (waking him about 2 or 3 A.M.); rough; *violent, nights,* caused by irritation that comes from stomach; racking paroxysms as if chest and head would burst, every other night as he was about to fall asleep, then excessive stretching; *which rings and feels as if everything in chest were dry, with pain in chest and small of back. Dry; and short, fatiguing, from tickling beneath upper part of chest,* which was especially excited by talking; at first, then with white frothy expectoration, with emaciation and weakness. Loose, with such acute pain in chest that leeches were applied, the leech-bites bled upward of twenty-four hours and the blood was thin. With expectoration; of blood; and emaciation.

Expectoration.—*Salt* (Lyc.). Of bitter, tenacious mucus. Bloody, when working; B., when walking in open air; of over a pound of blood in three hours in fornoon when lying.

Respiration.—Asphyxia. *Asthma;* with constant rattling, no cough or expectoration, at last she could not walk or bend over for fear of suffocation. Dyspnœa; after eating; in evening if he lay upon l. side, with necessity to breathe deeply, when, however, there was pain in l. groin. Difficult in morning, as from want of air. *Short; on ascending stairs; with suffocation;* when walking, as if he could not inspire air enough. Rapid; with constriction and cough. Inspiration and expiration in two or three jerks on attempting to breathe deeply. Oppressed, < night; O. from diaphragm upward. It seems as if he would lose his breath when coughing.

Clinical.—Chronic forms of laryngitis and bronchitis, with violent nocturnal cough, sometimes spasmodic, always < lying on r. side.

Chest.—*Swelling of female mammæ, < nipples, which were hard. Emphysema of lungs.* Tuberculosis of lungs; (of r. side of chest). Hæmorrhage from lungs. Diaphragm seemed scarcely moved on deep inspiration. Twitching of r. pectoral muscles. **Sticking** in l.; S. on stooping; **in r. on stooping and coughing**; in r. only on expiration, when lying and stooping; in side beneath l. short ribs on inspiration; **in anterior and upper part, extending through back**, *on sneezing and coughing, not on breathing, it constricts chest;* constricting, in upper and anterior part, extending to back, on breathing. Tearing in muscles near l. shoulder. Jerk-like griping beneath mammæ after eating. Pinching in l. side below ribs, with tension, dyspnœa, and on slightest motion or speaking a word it seems as if the soul would leave the body.

Pain in mammæ; in r. side if he hold his breath and again expires, > inspiration and expiration; in various parts, < deep inspiration; in l. side, < inspiration; in l., preventing deep breathing; in side of sternum, extending through back, in evening, < walking, then bruised pain; periodic suppurative, in mammæ; as from a swelling in l. side beneath last ribs; tensive, in forepart, impeding respiration (when sitting); *sore.* Bruised pain across forepart; in upper part in evening; in l. side on touch. Anxiety, a kind of dyspnœa; A. beneath sternum, he must breathe deeply. Pressure. Tightness; in region of sternum. *Constriction;* in various parts; in lower lobes (diaphragm ?). Oppression; of lungs. Burning extending to throat; B. in l. side at last rib. Rising of something sweet, then faintness passing into sleep.

Clinical.—Useful in some cases of pneumonia accompanied by hepatic disorder, loose nocturnal cough, general aggravation from lying on r. side. Occasionally useful in chronic pleurisy, with sharp sticking pains in chest; aggravation at night and lying on r. side will characterize it. Pneumonia of infants, lobular. It may be prescribed during the course of phthisis for the night-sweats and cough.

Heart.—Pain at apex, extending towards base (pericardial). Oppression. Palpitation; *on slightest exertion;* on walking; irregular; with pulse that could not be counted.

Pulse.—Rapid; at night on going to bed; on slightest excitement; and violent; and full, tremulous; and small; and small, weak. Slow; and small; and weak; and heart's impulse weak. Weak; and sometimes rapid, sometimes slow. Soft; and small, anæmic.

Neck.—*Indurated lymphatics. Cervical glands swollen* (Iod.); r.; r. posterior; and parotid, so that jaws are closed and cannot be moved on account of pain; *and hard,* also parotids. Loud *bruit de souffle* in veins, < l. side. Sticking in glands. Boring in r. side. Rheumatism in nape like a pressure, < bending head backward. Stiffness and heaviness; S. and swelling; stiffness of nape and sticking in it on motion.

Back.—Softening of spine, with curvature (*Merc. c.*). Sticking in muscles when walking. *Bruised pain;* on l. side, as from much stooping, on motion, < open air. Twitching pain. Periosteal aching down spine. Biting pain, < sitting. Hyperæsthesia in upper half, with heat.

Scapulæ.—Twitching in r. Sticking in spine, between S. Tearing. Pinching after midnight on motion in bed. Aching beneath lower angles; beneath r.; under r. at 11 A.M., then between S.; under r. on waking, extending over hepatic region; between S.; between S., where neck joins back, on turning head or if when lying he turns the rest of the body, < raising himself somewhat; in middle of dorsal region, to right of spine. Bruised pain in l. in morning after waking, < turning head, with sticking and tension. Tenderness on pressure over fourth and fifth dorsal vertebræ. Painless throbbing, that ends in trembling.

Lumbar Region.—**Sticking in sacrum on breathing**; S. in r. side of sacrum, near false spinal processes; in S. and thighs, with unsteadiness in S., knees and feet; posteriorly on r. ilium. Tearing in coccyx, > pressure upon abdomen; cutting, above region of l. kidney. Griping in sacrum, < standing, > walking. Pain; in sacrum, > sitting; in sacrum, as from a hard bed. *Bruised pain* in sacrum; < sitting. Throbbing over l. acromion.

Extremities.—Caries once in elbow, once in ankle. Nails eroded and itching. (Cracking of joints.) *Trembling;* **of hands and feet, so that patient could not write**; < upper; < arms, walking so difficult that he often fell on his back, even when striving to keep up by bending forward; after a chill; < being spoken to severely; periodic. *Jerking;* of arms and < hands when in a horizontal position, < attempts to restrain it, and by slight emotional disturbance lower limbs similarly affected, she can scarcely stand, walking is difficult and staggering; rapid (when volition was exerted upon muscles), which moved the limbs in all directions except the desired one, < anxiety or agitation of mind. Constant motion of bends.

Tearing; in r. shoulder-joint, shaft of humerus, in wrists, knee, hip-joints and shafts of femur; < arms; hands and feet, at night; here and there, more in muscle, < pressure; *with drawing;* rheumatic, in arms and legs, < in bed. Pain; in arms and legs; forearms and legs; in joints; in joints, < wrists, elbows, knees and ankles; goutlike, in joints, with swelling; as if dislocated, < sitting; in joints as if dislocated, consisting of compression and crushing, obliging him to turn in every direction; *bruised*, with weakness of thighs; drawing, < night; as from fatigue, in bones of forearms and shafts of tibiæ, < touch.

Painless throbbing in joints. Uneasiness in evening, as if there were a jerking in them. **Weakness**; with hastiness of motion. *Heaviness;* < night, especially feeling sleepy; with fuzziness. Falling asleep of arms and legs, < night. Rigidity so that he could not raise them. Electric irritability good, but limbs contracted tremulously, so that fingers upon the electrode felt a kind of whirring. Paralysis, except of l. arm, afterwards motion returned in arm, but not in lower limbs.

Upper Extremities.—Drawing pain, with formication and fuzzy feeling, then trembling in upper, then also in lower limbs, at last in all voluntary muscles, < excitement and attempt at motion. Loss of control of l. Paresis of r., with trembling.

Shoulder.—L. higher than r., with pain, even waking him, < motion. Jerking in joints rather than throbbing, every quarter of an hour. Sticking in joint in evening. Pain like a pressing down. Burning pain from r. up to nape when sitting. S. and upper arm asleep in morning in bed.

Arm.—Trembling. Jerking of r.; all night. Tearing in l.; on inner surface of r.; jerking, in upper, then soreness to touch. Periosteal aching in outer side of l. in morning, changing to l. wrist and forearm. Crushing pain in humeri. Rheumatic pain; in l.; in upper. Drawing pains, and in hands. Weary pain if it lies long in one place, he must alternately flex and extend it, but it is better when extended. Soreness in muscles. At times disturbance of sensibility in l. Fuzzy feeling in arms and hands. Heaviness of l. on raising it high, with sprained pain. L. cannot be raised, forearm moved with difficulty, hand more easily, r. arm less affected. R. arm and hand asleep, > motion.

Elbow.—Cracking, and in shoulder-joints. Stitches; slow tearing. Tearing.

Forearm.—Cramp in extensor muscles, with paralysis of them. Convulsive movements on radial side, causing flexion of thumb and index. Sticking cramplike pain on inner part of r.; in muscles of outer part of l.; in periosteum of inner side of r. when walking. Aching in flexors of l. Weakness, with pain in elbows.

Wrist.—Permanently flexed at a right angle with forearm, but easily straightened. Swelling of l., with pain when tightly seized and on motion. Aching in l. and in dorsum of hand. Weakness, cracking and sticking; in l., with paralysis. Attacks of painless throbbing. Painful stiffness of r.

Hand.—Swelling of l. *Could neither feed nor dress himself.* **Tremor**; then of limbs, then of whole body; *with weakness. Jerking of H. and fingers, < every exertion.* No power of directing them with decision, thus they caught at a paper with jerks, and when at last the paper was seized it was crumpled in the hand. Cramplike contractions of H. and fingers, they become flexed. Burrowing in ball of r., on outer side below little finger, < rest. Pain in bones of l. on stretching it and grasping, then pressure as if paralyzed and stiff; cramplike, in l., < fingers, on moving hand; drawing, with coldness of fingers. Tension. Weakness at times, generally > ardent spirits. Stiffness; of H. and fingers when at work, with cramplike pain. *Paralytic, so that he could not with both hands carry a glass half full to his mouth without spilling it.* Could not hold a glass without spilling the contents, > when intoxicated.

Fingers.—*Exfoliation of nails.* Nails blue. Painful swelling of proximal joints. Permanent contraction of l. *Flexed, < thumb, so that it is drawn inward as in epilepsy, with difficult opening,* **and with trembling of hands.** L. thumb and index compressed together so that they could not be separated in afternoon when held horizontally while sitting, with sticking in thumb, then thumb moved involuntarily from index. *Trembling* (Nat. m.); gradually increasing in violence and extending over whole body. Cramp of F. and hand, at first they are extended so that she can hardly close them, but after closing them cramp draws them firmly inward; sudden C. after hard work, then trembling of upper limbs, continuing even during sleep, with gnawing pain, after a week lower limbs affected so that the whole body was in constant motion, the trembling of r. arm > latter part of the day, but the limbs remained almost paralyzed. Tearing here and there in joints. Sticking cramplike pain in l. index. Pain in middle joint of middle finger on flexing it. Burning jerking beneath thumb-nail when writing. Asleep in morning, then tickling in them, then tearing extending half way up forearm. Deadness; and coldness.

Lower Extremities.—Œdema. Veins dilated; saphena vein as large as the thumb. Coarse tremor of r. when told to raise leg off the ground while sitting.

Movements slow, those of hip-joint difficult. Inability to stand steadily. Staggering; when eyes are closed, would fall unless prevented. Gait hesitating and difficult; H. and uneven; as in tabes dorsalis. Inability to walk. *Heaviness;* causing unsteady gait.

Thigh.—Shining, transparent swelling of T. and legs. Must lie down in forenoon on account of jerking and heaviness in T. and general sweat. Cramp above hollow of knee. Cramplike pain in tendon on outside near knee when sitting. Sticking in T. and legs on motion; in r. hip-joint when walking. Tearing in hip-joint at night; sticking, in muscles of r. Boring in r. gluteals when sitting. Bruised pain in r., < touch and walking. Tensive pain in r. when sitting; T. pain in l. nates as far as hollow of knee, < along crease between nates and thigh, when dozing at night, > lying on back with something under thigh, < resting thigh on chair when sitting, and worse periodically. Drawing pain on anterior surface of l.; D. pain extending through leg. Dragging downward deeper than muscles. Hamstrings feel too short. Weariness above knees when walking. Paralysis as if asleep.

Knee.—Jerking and feeling as if too large. Sticking when walking in open air; tearing, in r. when sitting and walking. Tearing. Pain at times; P. as if broken when lying; P. in r. as if stiff. Throbbing. *Weakness and giving way;* W. of K. and ankles, as if tendons had lost their power and steadiness, < standing.

Leg.—Swelling. Long, deep depressions in calves. Excessive development of one calf. Varicose veins. Trembling; when walking; when walking, < about knee and in groin. Moved forward involuntarily. Jerking. Cramp; of r. calf. Spasmodic contraction of calf, with knots. Drawn up spasmodically all night. Sticking as if too short on stepping hard; S. in calf when walking in open air. Sticking tearing in muscles of r. when walking in open air. Sticking cramplike pain, almost like a tearing, anteriorly in periosteum of l. tibia when standing. Boring in tibia. Pain in tendo-achillis when walking*; in periosteum of r. tibia,* almost like a cramp, when standing; anteriorly in periosteum of l. tibia in morning. *Drawing pain in tibiæ;* on inner side of l. leg above calf. Bursting sensation in r., then periosteal tingling. *Giving way. Weakness so that he could scarcely stand; W. in evening, with uneasiness.* Heaviness and drawing. Stiffness on walking; S. of l. extending to hollow of knee.

Ankle.—Swelling of r., with sticking in it, < evening and walking. Sticking from external malleolus to hollow of knee. Tearing extending to back of foot, with swelling about it. *Sprained pain in r. tarsal joint.* Painful drawing below external malleolus and in hollow of foot, at first like a sticking and griping. Pressure beneath bones and in flexure, when walking. Weakness.

Foot.—Swelling; *of backs;* of heels, so that she could scarcely step upon toes, with burning and biting in whole foot, even obliging her to rise from bed. Soles turned inward and upward, tendon of tibialis anticus rigid and prominent. Sticking in heels and groin in evening. Sticking, cramplike pain in r. sole near heel when sitting. Tearing in l. heel as from a sprain, when sitting. Tearing-drawing pain from heel to nates, < night, inability to walk because knees give way. Burrowing in r. sole when standing.

Toes.—Swelling; intermittent, of three, with pain at night. Cramplike contraction at night. Itching stitch at root of two last l. during rest. Paroxysmal tearing from great T. to above knee. Boring in tip of third. Burning pain beneath l. great T. during rest. Tingling of l.

Skin.—Fresh wounds heal slowly. *Jaundice, with biting itching on abdomen.* Brownish and dry. Earthy color. Pale and dry; P. and soft. Thin and glistening on back of hands. Scaling of back of hands. Itching redness between fingers, swelling of face, and especially of inner side of elbow, with loathing. Feverish exanthem, resembling roseola, beginning in throat and face and spreading over body. Tetter about mouth and on cheek, with hard and superficial ulcers; T. posteriorly on thigh, and on scratching pain and desquamation; T. burning on touch; on r. forearm, becoming round, with desquamation, causing voluptuous itching; rough, partly red, partly white, on l. zygoma; red, round, scaly, with burning pain, on forearm and wrist; dry, elevated, burning, itching, over whole body, < lower limbs, arms, wrists and hands, even between fingers.

Tetter on forearms and chest, extending over whole body except face and posterior part of limbs, beginning as small scattered red spots, gradually enlarging in a circular form, the spots gradually run together, light red, then scarlet or bluish-red, darker on margin, as spots enlarge the skin in centre becomes healthy, they are elevated, rough, dry, covered with whitish scales, in evening the clothes look as if sprinkled with meal, tetter < axillæ, bends of elbows, groins, hollows of knees, burning and pain, when at its height fever, the affected parts of skin swollen, red, sensitive to touch of clothes, use of arms impeded, sleep wanting or restless, itching from cold air on undressing, burning after contact, rubbing, washing or taking wine, axillary and inguinal glands swollen and painful, and in some places, for example, *groins, superficial ulcers on the tetter, which become covered with yellow scabs and heal,* tearing in joints, < elbows and knees, in evening, and on palms transparent vesicles without sensation.

Eruption appearing suddenly and returning, maculous, papulous or squamous, the latter < old people (on chest, back and scalp). Itching rash on forearms. Nettle-rash becoming a red spot; N. on genitals and thighs and in spots on chest and abdomen. Itching eruption on thighs, < their inner surface. Itchlike eruption on abdomen and thighs. Psoriasis in spots over whole body, *except palms and soles.* Swelling, hard, smooth, painful, of the size of a hen's egg in l. mamma; S. in spots, upon which gray flat scabs develop without previous moisture, then relief of S. and pain. Red elevations, with itching sticking; hot red E. on l. elbow, extending to hand, with burning, tearing and formication; red E., the tips becoming white, scaly and itching, burning after scratching, on l. arm, < elbow; and hard, shiny, on r. tibia, with tensive pain in it; and sore, moist, itching, on lower limbs, genitals, hollows of knees, throat, abdomen, in several places looking like pustular itch.

Swelling, with itching, heat and inflammation, < face and lids, preceded and accompanied by alternate cold and hot fits, languor, loss of appetite, thirst and watchfulness, after this condition had lasted fourteen days, scarlet eruption over whole body, < inside of arms, thighs and legs, with offensive exudation, < from groins and thighs, in a few days the eruption became white and dry, later cuticle peeled off and left cutis tender and itching, and new cutis affected in the same way as the former.

Pimples; on inner side of thigh; on scapulæ and abdomen, with boils; over whole body, with nightly bone-pain; *round, < thighs and legs, becoming round ulcers, at last scurfy;* red, with white tip and sticking, on nates; on lobule of ear, from which it was immovable, at first painful; red, on back of hand, burning at first; itching, on l. leg, then suppurating sores, then desquamation of surrounding skin; itching, changing to ulcers, then desquamation of surrounding skin; burning, corroding, itching, moist, scaly, on lobule of r. ear. Node beneath skin of l. cheek.

Pustule on chin; painful, on nose; itching, on limbs. Pocklike eruption above anus, with pain, < sitting. Boils in l. groin, with burning during micturition; B. on upper part of l. thigh, painful on walking and on touch. *Soreness between thighs and genitals.* Eczema on back of foot. Cracks on hands; on fingers, < inner side; on fingers, the bases of which are sore and bleeding; bleeding and painful between thumb and index; ulcerating, on finger-joints. Eruption below skin, with yellow scab. Eruption on thighs, itching in evening, oozing burning water after scratching (after heat of head and on back of foot), about midnight sweat on abdomen and thigh.

Erysipelas of forearm and legs; of lips, and gangrene, with fever and coated tongue, the gangrene destroyed a part of r. cheek, also gangrenous spot on r. temple, which on opening discharged gas and pus (death after three weeks, with hepatization of upper part of l. lung). Gangrene of feet.

Eruption on thighs, with itching and pain in thighs and groins, then rough elevated erythema over limbs with red eruption, in some places vesicles, eruption over greater part of body, exudation of a serous, yellowish fluid, < inside of thighs, groins and contiguous parts, stiffening the linen, in a few days the erythema was over the whole skin, which was painful, swollen and itching, with desquamation, exudation became general and offensive, swelling, < feet, lips and eyelids swollen, tarsi and eyes inflamed, later desquamation extended to scalp, afterwards swelling in many places where skin had peeled off, the new cuticle cracked, then exudation, later pain in skin < moving, with feeling as if his flesh were cracking, restless night, later flushing of face and increased redness of trunk and limbs, discharge of purulent matter from hand, exudation even from occiput, from which the hair fell, then a tumor on l. breast towards sternum, and one on l. loin, darker than the rest of the skin, containing a fluid, soles so tender that he could not put them to the ground.

Ulcer on foot; on legs, then desquamation from the thickened epidermis in red scales, under them the skin had a dark red pigmented look; *with whitish-gray bases,* **bleeding easily** (Hep., Phos.) *and exuding thin matter;* **bleeding of U. that had previously existed;** *serpiginous; offensive, rapidly decomposing, on thighs, in dropsical patients, instead of the swelling which had rapidly disappeared;* varicose, on limbs; red, on r. side of chin; red, suppurating, on l. side of chin; corrosive itching, externally on r. thigh.

Mercurial sores often have ragged, loose and undermined edges, often bordered by a cuticle like that of new cicatrix, giving them a silvery appearance, bases not hard nor surfaces covered with tenacious lymph, the ulcer may be sloughy in one spot, excavated and ulcerating in another, exuberant granulations at a third, and tendency to heal at a fourth, the ulcer spreads quickly and may attain any size. Mercurial ulceration often attacks the cicatrix of a recently healed chancre and forms a fresh sore.

Vesicles full of water on inner side of wrist; *transparent V. containing water, on various parts before daybreak;* itching, on back. *Erythema, upon which vesicles form and pour out a thinnish, clear liquid, V. quickly broken, the contents desiccate, then redness.* Sudamina on abdomen, chest and upper limbs, appearing at first as round, transparent vesicles, with red areola, filled with clear liquid, except on abdomen, where it was turbid, under lower jaw were shreds of epidermis caused by desquamation of vesicles, on some parts of chest and abdomen desquamation in patches from coalescence of the swellings, afterwards new sudamina.

Drawing pain anteriorly on l. thigh. Formication; from r. knee up front to middle of thigh; at root of nose, with gnawing. Fuzzy feeling in arms and hands. Tickling in palm, compelling scratching. Diminished sense of touch; more in limbs than in trunk, and more in r. lower limb than in l.

Itching on forehead; on r. side of nose; l. elbow; r. scapula and back; on pubes and above penis; thighs; legs; on joints day and night, < evening; on lower limbs in evening; on back in evening in bed; on sacrum when walking; *on all parts, < night,* and face red and hot; between toes, < afternoon and evening; on thigh, waking him at 3 A.M., with sticking. *I. that becomes pleasant on scratching;* on inner side of thigh, then pimples. *Sticking I. here and there in evening;* in sacrum when walking; on abdomen, and in evening burning after scratching; tickling sticking I. on first phalanx of r. thumb. Corroding I. on backs of hands in evening in bed, returning after scratching. Tickling I. on l. side of back. (Burning I. over back, < walking in open air, with heat of back.)

Clinical.—Moist intertrigo. Varicose ulcers, which bleed easily, generally with severe lancinating pains. Moist eczema. Herpes. Herpes zoster. The vesicular eruptions tend to ulcerate. General tendency to suppuration and ulceration. Very valuable in measles, with coryza, cough and nocturnal aggravation.

Sleep.—Yawning; before dinner and supper; with pain in small of back, then rigid extension of limbs, with clenched thumbs, then weakness. Sleepiness; during the day; when sitting, > walking; with anxiety; with weakness, but inability to sleep; then loss of sleep; but sleep interrupted and disturbed by bad dreams; interrupted by starting up in fright; palpitation and attacks of fantasies, for example, as if he dreaded epilepsy; irresistible, when standing. *Sleep too long; and profound.* Much sleep by day, but sleeplessness at night. Sleep from 3 till 5 or 6 P.M., against her will.

Sleeplessness; in evening on account of frightful fancies; before midnight, and early waking, with sweat; till 1 A.M.; till 1 A.M., with tossing about; till 3 A.M., with sweat from 2 till 3 A.M.; till towards morning; < after midnight; *with tossing about, and in morning inability to rise on account of lassitude;* with restlessness, anxiety and bad feeling; with hallucinations, heavy dreams, nightmare. Had no rest at night, stood up, wanted to walk about, saw ghosts, animals which were jumping at her, thought men were on the bed, thought living things were creeping into her mouth and vagina. Almost no sleep, dreaded to fall asleep. Constant dozing, but no real sound sleep. Unsound sleep after midnight and during the night tensive pain in l. leg. Half awake, with heavy dreams. Sleep every moment day and night, and waking every moment so that he had no natural sleep and no natural waking. Distressing sleep, if he woke everything in his head turned around.

Restless sleep; with frequent waking; with frightful dreams; with dreams of highwaymen; with heat, he thought when half awake that he heard thieves breaking in; with open mouth. Starting up in sleep; and throwing up of arms; in fright, on falling asleep, which caused shooting in teeth and through knees, with shivering; in fright soon after falling asleep, and anxiety till he was awake. Delirious talking in sleep. Groaning, whining, talking, rapid respiration and coldness of hands, during sleep. Sleep interrupted by jerkings and disturbed by heavy dreams. Late falling asleep. Waking early; every night from 2 till 4; at 11 P.M., as from fright, and loud cries and tears before she could collect her senses; easy. *Frequent waking;* and stretching; with sleep only like a dazedness and tossing about as if the clothes were a burden; as if he had slept enough, with tossing about; as from fright; as from noise; every quarter of an hour.

Dreams.—Many. Frightful; of shooting; that he fell from a height; in which he started up, thought that he was not in his own house, sat up in bed and talked about a distant village. On falling asleep he fancied that some one called him, started up in fright and became chilly. Anxious, for example, of swallowing a needle; A., from which he could not wake, with palpitation; A., after midnight, of being bitten by a dog, of rebellion. Nightmare and half-waking D. Heavy. Vivid, forgotten; V., agreeable and disagreeable; V., of the business of the day. Historic. Of a flood. Of people standing before the window, then waking, she could not persuade herself that they were not there. Amorous, with erections, without emissions. Unpleasant. Pleasant, after midnight (perhaps curative).

Fever.—Chilliness; in morning on waking; in morning after rising, after nightly emission; in morning, heat towards noon; morning and evening in bed; after midday nap; towards evening, < trying to get warm by the stove; evening in bed; evening in bed till midnight, then heat and thirst; at 9 P.M., and all night, with micturition every hour, and jerking of head, arms and lower limbs when lying and slumbering; in forepart of night, then alternations of chill and heat; *on going into open air;* on walking in open air; when not in bed, but heat in bed, with thirst for milk at night; during griping in abdomen; before stool; before diarrhœa, with dragging and flushes of heat; between diarrhœa-like stools, but during the stools flushing of heat, < face.

Internal chilliness in those suffering from tremor, without diminished temperature, **one wore a heavy overcoat, even in the hot summer**; I. chill in morning in bed; in forenoon; with heat of face; *alternating with internal heat.* Alternating with heat; with heat in head and face; with paroxysms of heat and anxiety, as from compression of chest, with prostration, without thirst. Quotidian ague in one who escaped salivation. C. as if dashed with cold water. Creeping C. during pinching in abdomen, with shivering; C., < hands, with dry heat behind ears.

Shaking chill in evening in bed; and twitching in tendo-achillis and flexor communis digitorum pedis; morning and evening. Shivering; all day, with internal and external coldness, blueness of body and necessity to bend forward; mornings in bed; morning on rising; evening in bed; before stool; from above downward on motion, between the paroxysms of heat; with chattering of teeth; with frequent flushes of heat; (< face, back, chest and arms), with flushes of heat; alternating with heat of face; over the scalp, that makes the hair bristle or that makes the scalp contract and seem to tremble.

Cold hands and feet (Iod., N. ac., etc.); feet in evening in bed; C. sweaty feet towards morning; sensation as if soles were put into cold water, with burning in them; thighs; chill extending from nose and ears to occiput, before midnight, in bed, with tearing externally; over back, with heat in lobules of ears; in limbs, like catarrhal fever, and necessity to lie down; of whole body, with heat of face. Skin cold and dry.

Heat; in cold, raw air; from slight effort, with ebullition of blood; with uneasiness; in attacks, < night. Hectic fever; and phthisis pulmonalis. Erethic fever, or fever of salivation, with quick pulse, hot and dry skin, red gums, swollen tongue, salivation, loss of appetite, restlessness, headache, etc., another kind is the adynamic mercurial fever, with depression of strength, præcordial anxiety, frequent sighing, partial or universal trembling, small, quick pulse, pinched and cadaverous face, coldness, tongue seldom furred, a sudden and violent exertion may prove fatal. (Intermittent fever prevails among workers, but whether due to mercury or local causes is uncertain.)

Burning in head; l. temple; r. superciliary ridge; in r. ear; all over back; between shoulders, extending down back; in elbows; *nates;* (in soles in evening); l. cheek after midnight, with redness of it and sweat on palms, then diarrhœa and aversion to food; cheeks and head, if he sits some time, with redness of face, without thirst; in face, with pallor; intermittent, in head and face; of face, with redness, then general internal heat, < palms, then alternations of internal chilliness, obliging him to lie down, a shaking chill lasting into the night, with heat in palms and coldness in finger-tips; on arms, so that everything falls from his hands, and he must let the arms sink down. Heat of skin; on l. side of forehead; on cheek, in front of chin; with dryness.

Sweat; during the day, with nausea; *in morning;* in morning, with thirst, nausea, vomiting and palpitation; *in evening in bed, and he fell asleep while sweating;* **at night** (Iod., Lyc., N. ac.); at night, and easily chilled; **on motion**; *on walking; on drinking anything warm;* though in a state of collapse; causing burning; **oily at night** (Thuj., Magn.), making linen stiff and yellowish. **Offensive** (Carbo v.); *at night; soaking the bed-clothes.* Sour, making fingers look spongy and wrinkled, like a washerwoman's; S., and if she puts a limb out of bed there is tearing. *Linen stained saffron yellow (that washing will not remove) by imperceptible exhalations from body* (Graph., Lach., Selen., Mag.). Sweat on palms and soles (Am. m.); face and chest; in spots at night, but not on face and head; on legs at night, > uncovering legs; on forehead on walking in open air; on genitals and neighboring parts when walking; *cold on face;* cold, anxious, on face, with discomfort, then diarrhœa. Skin dry, easily desquamating.

Clinical. — General catarrhal fever from suppression of catarrhal discharges, always indicated by the tongue, nocturnal aggravation, etc. Hectic fever. The perspiration of Merc. is sometimes oily. Patients are not relieved by perspiration, but rather get worse thereby. General tendency to free perspiration.

Mercurius Corrosivus.

Corrosive Sublimate is dissolved in alcohol (1 to 99).

General Action.—Similar to Mercury, but much more violent. Its symptoms of ulceration, diarrhœa, dysentery, nephritis, cystitis, *et cetera,* are attended with more pain and fever.

Allies.—Compare the list under Mercurius and add Ars., Canth., Lach.

Generalities.—*Dorsal decubitus.* **Lying on back with knees bent up.** Lies with knees drawn up. Lies with eyes half shut and with a choleraic aspect. Appearance as in the last stage of typhus fever. Collapse. Emaciation. Jactitation and trembling. Trembling of whole l. half of body when leaning heavily on l. arm while standing. Rolling incessantly from side to side. Convulsions; of face, arms and legs; in toes and feet, then in fingers and hands, then extending up legs and arms; with rigors; and face flushed, cheeks and forehead hot, but white around mouth and purple under eyes, pupils dilated, eyes rolled up. Convulsive shudderings in whole body alternating with drawing in arms and tearing in all limbs, and unconsciousness and oppression of heart. Cramps; even of hands and fingers.

Sticking here and there in muscles during the day; S. in parenchyma of organs, as in lungs, liver, and very fine in testicles. Myalgia. Pains; on every motion; over whole body; over whole body, < motion, with stiffness; intermittent, < about scrobiculus cordis and umbilicus; so that she ran about the room out of her senses and screaming. Malaise. Discomfort in periosteum of all bones, like onset of intermittent fever, with heat in head towards evening. Restlessness; obliging him to leave the bed. **Debility**; in morning, with suffering; < joints. Faintness; frequent. Aggravation in morning, especially weakness and vertigo, weakness > work; A. on walking in open air; from acids; from fat food. Amelioration from rest.

Mind.—*Delirium; and stupor;* at night; must be forcibly confined to his bed. Indecent exposure of person. *Ill humor; all day;* in afternoon; alternating with joyfulness. *Low spirits.* Anxiety; at night. Disinclination to talk. *Intellect weak, looks at us with wide-open eyes and does not understand us;* dull, but rational when fairly awake. *Stupor;* with pallor and dry, unsteady eyes. Thoughts disconnected, spoke of three kinds of headache, tried to correct himself, till he was obliged to stop from vexation. *Coma.* Unconscious, pulseless at wrists, tossing about.

Head.—Aching; *like a drawing in periosteum of skull;* as if on fire. Uneasiness. Confusion; < above brows; > emission of flatus. Heaviness. *Congestion of H. and face, with burning in cheeks.* Vertigo; on lifting head from pillow; < 8 P.M. on lying down, with almost loss of hearing and tearing in occiput. Sticking in forehead; above l. eye, mingled with pressure, < stooping. *Frontal pain;* in r. eminence. Dulness in upper part of forehead; in forehead, with waving pain in both hemispheres of brain. Pain in temples; changing to pressure above l. eye. Sticking in l. parietal bone.

Eyes.—Staring. Protruding; and bloodshot; and inflamed. Sparkling; and red; and in constant motion. Dull and expressive of agony. Tearing from l. down into a molar. Pain, with injection of vessels of conjunctiva; burning P. Burning; and dryness; of E. and margins of lids as in beginning of conjunctivitis. Itching of l. *Pupils insensible to light;* and dilated; dilated; contracted. *Pain behind balls as if they would be forced out.* Itching sticking in muscles of r. ball. *Redness of conjunctiva;* of lids. Burning tearing in upper part of l. upper lid. Contraction of corrugator supercilii, with partial strabismus. *Tearing in bone above l., near root of nose and in other parts of bone.* Photophobia when walking in sunlight. Objects seem smaller and more distant, especially letters, < violent yawning.

Clinical. — Ophthalmia, involving external layers of the cornea, with extreme photophobia, so that it is almost impossible to get a view of the eye, with swelling of the submaxillary glands. Numerous cases of pustular ophthalmia and ulceration of the cornea. Severe burning soreness of the eye often indicates it. It has been used with success in some cases of iritis. It has been found valuable for the retinitis of Bright's disease. Retinitis hæmorrhagica. Choroiditis. Inflamed sclera, with burning pains. Kerato-iritis, with adhesions. Hypopyon.

Ears.—Sticking in l.; in afternoon, with digging. *Pulsation, < l.* Stopped sensation. Whirring in l. rhythmical with pulse. (Increase of the usual roaring and humming in r.)

Nose.—**Coryza.** Dryness posteriorly, as if in upper surface of soft palate, < open air. *Frequent nosebleed.*

Clinical.—Fluent coryza, with extremely violent symptoms, burning heat, mucous discharge, not profuse, nostrils very sore. Ozæna, with ulcers in the nose, excoriating discharge, particularly if there is a thick gluey discharge from the nose, always associated with burning pain.

Face.—*Swollen;* < lower part; *and red;* and red and covered with cold sweat; and pale; cheeks, and shining and tense. *Red. Pale;* and anxious; *and anxious, pinched;* and sunken; and drawn and fixed in expression. White streak from angle of mouth to lower edge of jaw, and corrosion of dorsum of tongue and throat. Bluish-white, pinched and anxious. Blue, and lips. Yellow, hippocratic. Livid. Greenish. Collapsed and covered with cold sweat. *Expression of exhaustion.* Aspect as in cholera which has not yet reached perfect collapse. Expression of anxiety; E. of mental exaltation and bodily pain. Distorted. Convulsive motions. Tearing in l. zygoma. *Jaws stiff and sore.* Tearing in antrum highmorianum towards eye, then swelling. Pain in jaws; at l. angle of lower on touch.

Lips.—**Black** (Ars.). **Swollen and tender;** *lower S. and a blister on inside of it;* S. and white; S. and dark red; *S. and incrusted with a dry secretion. Dry and cracked.* Deep color. Blue. Lips and tongue whitish and sunken. Sloughing of lips, gum and tongue. Convulsive motions at corners.

Clinical.—Many cases of facial neuralgia, especially if the pain seems to be in the bones.

Mouth.—Teeth. **Loose**; and blunt. *Sordes.* Tearing sticking in a molar extending to ear. Tearing burning pain from upper to eye. Drawing pain. *Aching at night, disturbing sleep, with anxiety;* A. preventing sleep, with swelling of gum and prostration; *with swelling of gum;* with tearing from infraorbital region to upper jaw (the pain is like that caused by urtica urens touching the mucous membrane).

Gums.—**Bleed easily** (Lach.). **Swollen and spongy;** *swollen and pale;* swollen, red, discharging yellowish pultaceous substance from around necks of teeth; S. and painful, covered with white pellicles; and tender; and S. salivary glands, with ptyalism; about r. molars; about last molars, with burning pain. *Purple. Red and detached from teeth; R. and tender, with swelling of glands beneath jaw. Spongy and ulcerated.* Ulcers, and on inner surface of lips. Burning pain. Tenderness, and of teeth.

Tongue.—*Swollen; and inflamed; so that it could not be protruded, and white;* at base and coated white. Mucous membrane white. *Red, with blackish coat. Covered with grayish-white crust. Coated; and moist, edges red; pale, dirty yellow posteriorly and along edges; white anteriorly, yellow posteriorly;* white. Yellow, moist. Slimy. Frequently thrust out. Sore. Felt numb and large. Dry; and red; with red streak in centre; and hot, with red edges; dry patch at tip, the rest coated white. Cool. *Could not be protruded.* Speech difficult; lost.

Mouth in General.—Swelling so that he could scarcely speak; S. of inner surface of cheeks, tongue, palate and throat; inside of cheeks, < behind last molars, on l. side a sensitive, hardened ganglion; of mucous membrane, with gray sloughs and violet patches; M. and fauces swollen, white and sore. M. and fauces white and raw. *Inflammation; and of gums, with discharge of clear water;* with scars on gums and inside of cheeks, beneath which the flesh was fungoid and bloody, afterwards jaw-bone denuded, and hæmorrhage; of inside of cheeks, with pultaceous deposit like false membrane. *Ulceration.* Cancrum oris (K. chl.). Mucous membrane of M. and pharynx destroyed. From M. and throat pieces of dead skin resembling peelings of roasted potatoes and pieces of gum came away from the place where a tooth had been drawn, and a piece from side of tongue, with tenderness of tongue, gum and throat. Tough lymphatic exudation, loose at edge, on inside of cheek, lower lip and on r. tonsil, and beneath this one or two abrasions. Blood oozed from M. and nose; dribbling of dark B. and brick-dust-colored froth; fluid B. escaped without any effort like vomiting.

Burning pain; to epigastric region. Sore; and difficult to open. *Dry;* in evening, and sweat on skin; *mouth and tongue dry and burning.* Feeling of mucus. Offensive breath; gangrenous. **Salivation;** in evening; *tenacious, difficult to expectorate;* constant flow from mouth of yellowish saliva.

Taste.—**Bitter;** *in morning, and slimy; to food during the day.* **Salt.** Brassy. Metallic; and acid, styptic; and styptic, astringent; and sharp, astringent. Coppery; and nauseous. Astringent, with salivation. Fatty. Disagreeable.

Clinical.—Violent stomatitis, large aphthous patches, with burning pain. Syphilitic patches, with burning pain.

Throat.—*Swelling of submaxillary glands; with tenderness; of submaxillary region;* of external fauces, < r. side, and of r. side of neck. **Swelling; threatening suffocation** (Lach.), *extending to neck, head and tongue, throat so inflamed that speaking and swallowing were difficult, with heat in mouth and throat, afterwards raising of clots of blood and thin blood, ulceration of throat and soft palate, salivation, frequent headache, < temples, afterwards delirium, expectoration of clots of blood and pieces of membrane from ulceration of throat, with prostration and salivation, sloughing extending to cheeks, gum, palate, and even jaw was laid bare, lips black;* **uvula;** *of uvula, with elongation;* of uvula, with ulceration; **of pillars of velum palati, with dark redness, and in tonsillary folds** (Lach.), on edges of pillars are soft gray excrescences; of tonsils; S., with soreness and with grayish ulcers in throat, on inside of cheeks and border of gums, with offensive breath.

Inflammation and pain; I. of fauces. *Dark redness of pharynx, with pain on pressure;* redness of fauces; redness, and tonsils covered with bloody mucus. Bloody mucus from posterior nares. Glairy, sticky mucus. Gray coat between pillars of velum palati. Snapping noise when almost asleep, waking her.

Sticking near larynx on empty swallowing, with hoarseness. Pain; on alternate days, extending through Eustachian tubes to forehead; on swallowing, extending up Eustachian tubes; on pressure; < dry bread; at times in uvula. **Burning pain;** *in fauces;* in pharynx; **and in œsophagus, < external pressure;** and in stomach, < taking anything more than milk-warm; and in upper part of stomach, gradually sinking lower. Soreness; *of fauces;* of pharynx. Scraping caused by beer, with heat and redness of face. Roughness; scraping posteriorly in pharynx, compelling hawking. Rawness; in pharynx, < swallowing a liquid; with catarrh; that makes talking, not swallowing, difficult. *Constriction;* of muscles of pharynx; of pharynx, changing to paroxysmal pain and tickling. Uneasiness. *Dryness of fauces. Swallowing,* **even of fluids,** *painful;* S. and expectoration painful and difficult; *S. difficult;* impossible.

Œsophagus.—*Spasms of O. and stomach on attempting to swallow a drop of liquid, with vomiting of whitish, slimy, tenacious masses, which became mixed with bile if the vomiting continued.* Sticking as if distended by morsels of food which could not descend, < swallowing and eructations of air. Pain. *Burning.* Constriction.

Clinical.—Inflammation of the uvula and arch of palate, with great swelling. Intense inflammation and ulceration of the throat, with burning and suffocation. Occasionally useful in diphtheria.

Stomach.—Appetite great for Cayenne pepper; A. diminished; lost; lost in evening. *Thirst;* in evening; at night; *for cold water; for large quantities of cold water;* for hot or cold drinks; and desire for ice; constant, for cold water, which is very repulsive and soon vomited; but every attempt to take liquids was followed by retching and vomiting.

Eructations, with nausea and ineffectual retching. *Regurgitations of food and drink through nose.* Hiccough; at least movement; with the vomiting; < least quantity of water; with great regularity twenty-six times a minute; in violent fits at night. Nausea; in attacks at night. Retching; and head thrown back and tossed from side to side; on attempting to swallow, with vomiting; violent; *spasmodic and painful.*

Vomiting; at night, with thirst; renewed by cough; < pressure on stomach, with pain; incessant; violent; copious; nothing would remain on stomach; water was rejected immediately. Of food, then of serum; ingesta and tenacious mucus, then of bile and blood; food and dark matter, then yellow bile. *Green;* greenish and bloody, with retching and pain; and bitter, with diarrhœa; **incessant** (Ars.), **green, bilious.** Of bile; in early part of day; and copious, with copious bilious stool. Of blood; or belching of blood, as she lay on her back she raised blood mixed with water by a peculiar action of stomach without exertion; *matter streaked with B.;* of drinks mingled with B.; like water mixed with fresh B.; and of white froth; scanty, thick, yellow, frothy matter tinged with B.; frequent, of yellow matter interspersed with B.; of bloody fluid; and water, in evening, with bloody, watery stools. Of the color of coffee-grounds; and coagulated blood. Spasmodic, of serous substance, without previous nausea; dark, copious, muddy-looking material mixed with half-digested food. V. and purging of dark grumous matter. Of mucus, then of blood; bloody mucus; V. and purging of bloody mucus and membranous flakes; tenacious M.; frequent, of bluish M.; copious and incessant, of viscid, frothy M.; violent, of M. and water, with great retching; violent, of M. and bile; and violent, frequent, thick, metallic-tasting, with constriction of throat. White, frothy, tenacious masses, with frightful retching. Thick, stringy, albuminous-looking substance. Of pieces of membrane. Of pus. Dark frothy substance, frequently with purging. Slate-colored, semi-fluid. Copious, purulent, salt matter.

Swelling, with pain so that she could scarcely speak so to be heard; *S. of epigastric region, with sensitiveness to pressure;* S. of epigastric region, with burning sticking, < pressure; S. of l. side of E. region, with sense of weight and hardness. Sticking; in pit in morning; in epigastric region after soup. Tearing in pit, waking from afternoon nap, < region of stomach and extending thence over whole diaphragm, > bending up, abdomen sunken and painful to pressure in epigastric region. Pinching. Griping, and in abdomen.

Pain; *in pit;* in region; in epigastric region; along alimentary tract; all night, with frequent vomiting and painful retching; < drinks; caused by anything liquid or solid; in pit, < pressure and coughing; and on pressing hand firmly on it felt wind rolling about under it. Sensitiveness to pressure; **in epigastric region**; *in region. Burning* (Ars.); in pit; with griping, tearing and nausea; with constriction extending into intestinal canal, congestion of heart and anxiety, then soft stool; with pain and vomiting of everything she took, always most > when after several efforts she had vomited something that tasted like milk which had stood in a brass pan. Burning pain (Ars.); in epigastric region; in pit. Sensation of a lump in pylorus, with pain. Obstruction and anxiety in epigastric region and præcordia, then palpitation. Uneasiness in epigastrium and abdomen, < pressure. Sweet apples have a good effect, but sour ones distress.

Clinical.—Dyspepsia, with soreness, distention, burning pain, desire for cold food, aversion to hot food.

Abdomen.—*Swelling;* at night; *and pain on touch;* and hardness and pains at regular intervals, like labor-pains. Tympanitic on percussion and painful and tender on touch. Rumbling at night; R., with sharp pain and profuse bilious stools. Emission of flatus. Flatulence after milk. Griping; at times without distention, > emission of flatus, with sudden attacks of weakness and confusion of head. Cutting, with chilliness in open though warm air; C., then thin bilious stools, with straining. Tormina. Pain; in afternoon after potatoes, with desire for stool; at night, with tenesmus and six stools; from slightest cold; after eating various things, fruit, < potatoes, cherries, etc.; > bending double; then several bilious stools, with tenesmus. Smarting pain. **Bruised sensation, < cæcal region and along transverse colon, and bruised sensation in cæcal region and transverse colon on moderate pressure.** Tenderness. Burning.

Pinching sticking in muscles of upper A. Pain in upper. *Sticking in hepatic region;* in middle of liver. Cutting in r. hypochondrium. Pain in hepatic region.

Umbilical Region.—Itching sticking. Cutting below umbilicus after sour apples, when walking in open air, < evening, with desire for stool. Griping at right of umbilicus at noon after sugar. Pain at umbilicus at night; about and above U., after bread and unsalted butter; at U., then in lumbar region; in region, then three thin stools, with tenesmus. Constrictive jerking pain in some fibres in inner side of r. rectus muscle. Pressing down in front below umbilicus after stool. Tenesmus on pressure. Discomfort.

Jerking in r. rectus abdominis. Inflammation of large intestines, with ulceration as in severe dysentery, yet slight dysentery. Pain in l. side in morning. Pain in l. region of cæcum. *Bruised sensation in cæcal and mesocolic regions, < pressure.* Pain in hypogastrium; in a r. inguinal gland as if it would swell, in morning, > rising; tensive P. in l. groin at 5 A.M., with sensation as if a gland were swollen. Sticking drawing in l. groin. Apprehension in hypogastrium.

Clinical.—Inflammation of the colon, especially the transverse and descending, which is very sore, with burning pain.

Rectum.—*Oozing of corrosive ichor.* Discharge of blood; after stool. Sticking; in anus. Pain; *burning. Burning; in anus during stool.* Smarting during stool. **Tenesmus; but nothing passes except mucus tinged with blood** (Canth.); *during stool, with burning.* Constant urging; and in bladder; *frequent ineffectual U., causing pain;* frequent U., with increased emission of flatus. Itching in anus; when walking.

Stool.—Looked like strong saffron water. Liquid, yellow, after a meal; L. green, copious; L., dark, frequent; frequent, with colic; containing much blood; for the most part L., containing blood, mucous membrane and thick scum, frequent, at night, and vomiting of similar matter; L., dark, frequent, containing small lumps of dark green fæces, afterwards almost entirely of dark fluid, some with flakes of mucus, then fluid, bloody, with coagulated albumen, free from fæcal odor, but of fleshy smell. Soft, twice in morning. *Pasty, dark green, blackish, offensive;* P., dark, offensive, with tenesmus; P., brown, frequent, with rumbling in abdomen.

Diarrhœa; **scanty, chiefly of blood and mucus, with constant desire** (Canth.); *bloody; bloody, frequent, offensive, slimy;* involuntary at night, containing little blood; *sero-sanguineous; blackish;* frequent; yellow, painless, with frequent urging, then continued desire; violent, frequent and offensive; violent, of coagulable lymph, clots of blood and fine pellucid membrane. Of coagulable lymph like sheets of boiled maccaroni, stools next day livid, fetid, grumous, third day dirty, grumous, enveloping a lumbrieus. Dysentery and tenesmus.

Bloody; *mixed with blood, with small, hard, frequent pulse;* with cramps; of blood and shreds of membrane, with tenesmus; and small, offensive, frequent; brown, small, viscid stool mixed with blood. **Of blood and mucus, with pain and tenesmus; of B. and M., and frequent, with tenesmus; of scanty, bloody mucus, frequent, day and night, with cutting in abdomen, and almost ineffectual tenesmus;** *frequent, of blood and mucus, each stool preceded by cold pain low down in pelvis, and followed by tenesmus;* fæces mixed with blood and watery mucus; *fæces mixed with mucus and dark clotted blood.*

Bilious, frequent, with tenesmus; B., slimy and frequent; B., slimy, frequent, in morning, with tenesmus, no stool in afternoon, bowels sensitive to touch and flat, next day no stool. Slimy and reddish; S., dark brown, frequent, day and night, afterwards hæmorrhage from bowels, then involuntary discharges. Of thin-formed fæces.

Constipation. Hard; and scanty; and dark brown. *Of tenacious fæces.* Green; dark and frequent. Dark, offensive, frequent. Brown, offensive. Light-colored. Clayey, light yellow, twice a day. Yellowish, frequent. Involuntary S. and micturition. **Frequent;** at night; **with great tenesmus,** *offensive;* and copious. *Omitted.*

Clinical.—The extreme tenesmus, which is greater than that of any other drug, and is associated with tenesmus of the bladder, generally suffices to indicate this drug; the discharges are usually mucous and bloody. It is found useful in dysentery of the worst type and in catarrhal inflammation of the bowels, with extreme pain in the rectum.

Urinary Organs.—Pain in bladder. Apprehension in region of bladder when walking, with discomfort, as before stool. Inflammation and swelling of bladder and urethra.

Urethra. — (*Gonorrhœa thin, then thick, at last with biting pain on urinating and sticking, extending back through urethra.*) Sticking in forepart; in evening after micturition, and in sphincter ani; in evening when walking, and in l. testicle, with desire to urinate; when walking in open air; burning S., with feeling of vigor and lightness after coition. *Burning during micturition;* before micturition; *B. in orifice.* Itching in forepart; in orifice, which was biting when urinating, with sticking through whole urethra. Urging, with scanty emission, then no inclination, with a full bladder, but after the evacuation of bladder fulness remains.

Ischuria. Strangury. *Micturition frequent,* **by drops, and painful** (Canth.); M. infrequent and difficult.

Urine thick, acid, **flakes of albumen precipitated by heat and nitric acid,** *the microscope showed many granular, fatty tubuli and on their surface* **epithelial cells of the tubuli uriniferi,** *also in a state of fatty degeneration.* Pale brown, turbid, *coagulated by heat and nitric acid.* Pale, turbid, with traces of mucous flakes, after standing strongly ammoniacal, with pale gray sediment, covered with whitish coat. Acid. *Bloody. Albuminous;* and blackish. Copious, afterwards suppressed, then scanty. Scanty; with frequent desire; and burning; and red, with brick-dust sediment; with acute pain in region of kidneys, reaction acid, milky, albuminous, squamous epithelium in the deposit, afterwards more copious, albuminous, granular casts in sediment, afterwards involuntary micturition, tenderness to pressure in region of kidneys. Suppressed.

Clinical.—Violent inflammation of the bladder, with extreme tenesmus and burning (Canth.). Inflammation of the kidneys, urine scanty, albuminous, containing more or less mucus, always associated with much inflammation of the neck of the bladder (Canth.). Suppression of urine, with vomiting of coffee-grounds. Occasionally useful in gonorrhœa, with greenish discharge, burning pain and great tenesmus.

Sexual Organs.—*Penis and testes swollen.* Violent erections, with great desire; violent, during sleep and after waking, and during coition delayed and slow emission. Sticking in r. testicle; in middle of l. (When touching os uteri during coition pain, then pressure.) Desire diminished (secondary action), scarcely ever an erection.

Inflammation of vulva. Vulva sloughy (after death). Lower part of vagina swollen, red, hot, with forcing downward as in labor, discharge of watery mucus, then of mucus tinged with blood. Pain in vagina and abdomen, with copious discharge of watery mucus. Pale yellow leucorrhœa, of nauseous sweetish odor. Slight hæmorrhage from vagina. Menses too soon; M. increased.

Clinical.—Occasionally useful in venereal ulcers which spread rapidly, in both male and female genitals.

Respiratory Organs.—*Spasm of glottis on swallowing.* Irritability of larynx. Voice hoarse; and rough. Voice almost lost.

Cough. — Spasmodic; at night; and pharyngeal, from tickling in throat, with pain, then expectoration of bloody mucus, then suffocation and anxiety. Dry; towards evening, from irritation in larynx, with dryness of pharynx; and hollow, fatiguing. Loose, rattling; with almost complete aphonia and raising of gray, salt mucus. *Coughing up mucus tinged with blood.* Spits up pellets of mucus mixed with blood.

Respiration.—*Difficult;* from swelling of mouth and throat; and deep; by aid of intercostal muscles, and irregular. Oppressed, with rattling in throat. Inspirations deep and heavy. Uneven. Quick and catching. Short; and labored. Slow; and interrupted, at times deep and sighing. Groans. Sighs.

Clinical.—Inflammation of the larynx, with hoarseness or aphonia and burning, stinging and other Mercurial symptoms, especially with great pain in larynx and epiglottis on swallowing food, a feeling as if a knife were cutting.

Chest.—**Painful glandular swellings about nipples.** Often violently expanded. Convulsion of r. breast shooting through to back, just under scapula, the breast contracted and its milk speedily dried up. Rattling. Sonorous râles in all parts. **Sticking through it;** *S. in lower part of r.;* through both sides in morning after rising; transversely through at night; internally in upper part of l. on deep breathing; *deep in upper part of r., scarcely < deep inspiration;* in upper part of l., < deep breathing; burning, in r. muscles; itching, in muscles of r. lower costal region. Tearing in lowest cartilages of r. ribs; in middle of sternum after midnight. Pain; burning, beneath sternum. Constriction. Oppression. Congestion of lung.

Heart.—Sounds dull and intermittent. "*Bruit de souffle*" at base. Pain in præcordia. Anxiety in præcordia. Palpitation; at night. Beat tremulous. Beat intermittent; every 15th or 20th beat. Stopped for a few seconds. Beats seemed remote and slow.

Pulse.—*Rapid;* and hard; and full; *and intermittent;* intermittent and corded; *and irregular, intermittent,* small; and small; and small, irregular; and small, tremulous; and small, contracted; and small, corded; and small, hard, with diminished temperature and moist clammy skin; and small, indistinct, next day slow; and feeble; and feeble, irregular; and feeble at heart and carotids, not to be felt at wrist, afterwards rapid and varying in strength at wrist. Feverish at night; after dinner, at 1 P.M.; F. and small. Not to be counted. Full and hard. *Intermittent and uneven; I. and small.* Perceptible at wrist occasionally. Small, contracted, irregular. Feeble; and slow; and unsteady; and small; and laboring in its diastole; and small, tremulous.

Neck and Back.—Tonic cramps, during which respiration stopped. Tearing in upper part of bone of l. scapula. Tension externally near l. scapula.

Clinical.—Potts' disease of the spine, and other diseases of the bones, attended with destruction and formation of abscesses; extremely valuable if characterized by nocturnal aggravations, sweats, etc.

Extremities.—Hands and feet livid, shrunken and cold. Trembling; < stretching them. Twitching. Convulsions of fingers and toes; convulsive motions of r. Cramps. Sticking, < hip-joint and knee; in muscles of back of hand, < abductor and extensor of thumb, and in extensor of foot. Tearing in bones (joints of fingers, hips, etc.). Pain; in arms and legs, < evening, with peculiar numbness; with general weakness; in limbs and arms as after long exercise, < sleep. Drawing in bones. *Weakness, with trembling when standing up and without moving;* W. and shivering; with stiffness and pain on attempting to change position, increasing to paralysis; of deltoid and of muscles of calves and thighs. Loss of control. Paralysis. Paralytic stiffness. Numbness of hands and feet.

Upper Extremities.—Sticking in l. axilla, with sensation as if glands would swell. Tearing in l. shoulder. Rheumatic pain (as in windy weather) in r. deltoid when walking. Cramps of hands. Tearing in l. metacarpal bones. Jerking constriction in r. metacarpus. Sticking in tip of l. thumb in evening when walking. Tearing in joints of l. fingers; in first joints of l. index and ring finger and thumb.

Lower Extremities.—*Drawn up in bed.* Spasms. Sticking in muscles. Rheumatic sticking at night. Myalgia of thighs, with coldness of hands and feet. *Sticking in hip-joints;* in afternoon; > *motion;* outward in l. Tearing posteriorly in r. hip-joint, then more to side and externally. Drawing in femora. Knees drawn up. Cramp in legs; l. Twitching of various muscular fibres of calf, inner side of gastrocnemius. Tearing in l. calf extending inward. Drawing pain in bones of leg. Stiffness of legs. Numbness of legs. Leg seems asleep. Trembling of feet; when walking, < l., < morning on rising and in evening. Pain in feet. Weariness of feet in evening, with sleepiness.

Skin.—Pale. Yellow. Livid, finally dusky. Swelling and mercurial erythema; S. of whole arm, with inflammation in places, and in places vessications filled with lymph. Brown scar on the part that had been powdered, surrounded by bright redness, afterwards the scar black and dry in centre and humid at circumference. Ecchymoses, < lumbar region. Rash around mouth. Itching eruption like rubeola, over whole body. Papulous eruption (lichen). Livid pustules on face and breast. Blisters; (painless, on arms and abdomen in morning, > during the day). Felt dry and harsh to the hand.

Tingling as if asleep. Burning and pricking, with redness and inflammation, afterwards vesicles at many points. Itching burning in many places just under skin, with sticking. Itching of skin, which looks dry and shrivelled; I. between r. great and second toes; in middle of back changing to sticking; in various places changing to sticking and burning.

Sleep.—*Yawning; and stretching;* and stretching, without sleepiness. Sleepiness; in afternoon. Sleeps with eyes half closed. **Sleepiness**; till 3 A.M.; from midnight till 3 A.M., with tossing about the bed; on account of anxiety; *could lie comfortably upon neither side.* Late falling asleep and immediate starting up as from a shock in whole body, then sleeplessness from heat and pressure in chest, with anxiety. *Starting up from sleep;* on falling asleep, also with shuddering in whole body. Frequent waking; and unpleasant dreams. Interrupted towards morning. Soporous, from which she was occasionally awakened by return of pain. Light, with frequent waking and inability to sleep on account of confusion of head. Restless sleep; with mild delirium, she tried to get up; often interrupted by distressing dreams; and dreams of falling from high banks or being let down into deep wells or trying to get away from some one who intended to murder her. Frightful dreams, she was hurried by fancying that a horrid-looking figure at her bedside presented a bottle to her. Dreams of incendiarism and murder. Vivid D.; of remarkable, ludicrous and disagreeable things, journeys, etc. Voluptuous D.

Fever.—Chill; towards evening, with sudden transient heat; in evening, < head; at night; at night in bed; from slightest motion, with cutting colic; in open, warm air, to which she was averse, with cutting colic and tenesmus; < along spine, with formication; creeping, at night; creeping, towards evening, with coldness over small of back as if a lizard were creeping over it; alternating with heat. Shivering; *during and after swallowing;* over whole body in evening in bed, then sleeplessness on account of heat and pressure in chest, with anxiety; < open air, often with chattering of teeth, often > warm sweat.

Cold skin; with small, **intermittent pulse**; *with sweat;* on abdomen; except on abdomen and inside of thighs, with internal heat and burning pain in lumbar region; < limbs. Chilliness in head; in evening before sleep. In l. side, < after midnight. Cold back and feet. *Cold limbs;* with sunken face and rapid, small, contracted pulse. Cold feet; and hands; and feet, with salivation and difficult swallowing, then shaking chill, then dulness in head except in temples, inflammation of skin of l. side of lower jaw.

Heat; febrile excitement in evening; *at night, preventing rest in any place, with anxiety;* on stooping, but coldness on rising again; internal and external, > drinking cold water and sponging body with cold water. *Of skin;* < forehead; on face. Dry, of face.

Sweat; *at night;* at night, frequently on waking. Anxious. *Offensive towards morning.* Of mouldy smell, for the most part partial. *Cold; with pale skin;* on forehead, with dryness of rest of skin. Cold and clammy; and skin blanched; *on limbs.* **S. on forehead,** *temples, chest and hands, with coldness in these parts;* in drops on forehead; in l. axilla, then general, waking at night. Skin dry at night.

Mercurius Cyanatus.

Pure cyanide of Mercury is dissolved in distilled water (1 to 99) for use.

Ally.—Kali chloricum.

Generalities.—Appearance as in first stage of cholera. Lying on r. side, supported on arm. **Weakness; so that he cannot stand up**; from frequent nosebleed; during diarrhœa, and at last he fell to the floor in a swoon. Frequent fainting.

Mind.—Excitement at night; with incessant talking, anger at the attendant and raving.

Head.—Tearing, < forepart of night. Aching; at night. Vertigo; on sitting up in bed, with loud ringing in ears.

Eyes.—Fixed. Sunken. Conjunctiva injected. Pupils dilated.

Ears and Nose.—Ringing in ears. Frequent and profuse epistaxis.

Face.—Pale and wan. Cyanotic. Flushed. Serious expression. Lips, tongue and inside of cheeks covered with grayish-white pulp.

Mouth.—Toothache. Gums swollen and covered with adhesive, whitish coat, above which is a border of bluish-red. Tongue coated grayish. Tongue pale, afterwards with yellow coat at base, next morning edges redder, and a gray, metallic-looking coat at base, third day swollen, red on edges and covered with adhesive gray coat. Blisters on l. margin of tongue and on soft palate, developing into irregular ulcers, these ulcers afterwards appeared on r. margin of tongue. On inside of r. cheek a round ulcer, with grayish base and upright edges, encircled by bright red, the ulcer afterwards covered by a gray leathery coat. Inflammation. Redness. Salivation smelling as from Mercury. Taste metallic. Taste bitter. Taste styptic.

Throat.—*Swelling of salivary glands. White opalescent coat resembling superficial mucous patches of syphilis, on pillars of velum palati and on tonsils. Redness of fauces and difficult swallowing; R. of pharynx; R. at base of pharynx. Roughness. Swallowing difficult.* **Necrotic destruction of soft parts of palate and fauces.**

Clinical.—A valuable remedy for the form of diphtheria characterized by the Mercurial symptoms and aggravations, with extreme prostration; the disease invades the nostrils and there is threatening collapse, with very small, rapid or intermittent pulse. It follows Apis well.

Stomach.—Aversion to food. Thirst; burning; but drinks are speedily vomited; but he cannot bear soups or hot drinks, which seem too salt. Hiccough. Nausea. Violent retching from merely thinking of sugared water. Vomiting; frequent, after drinking; repeated, of bloody matter; bilious, scanty, twice, with much retching; greenish-yellow, scanty, after soup. Epigastrium sensitive to pressure. Burning. Irritation.

Abdomen.—Pain; on pressure; < every evacuation.

Rectum and Anus.—Small hæmorrhoidal tumors around anus, with knobby swellings of mucous membrane. Pain in rectum and around anus when sitting, then sensitive, light red swelling around anus, afterwards no stool, but on straining discharge of clear black blood, next day grayish diphtheritic-looking deposit around anus similar to that on inside of cheeks, and the part is eroded, third day fetid, liquid discharge, of gangrenous odor, leaving black stains, fourth day discharge more purulent-looking, afterwards serous and almost odorless. Frequent tenesmus. Urging, with diarrhœa and vomiting.

Stool.—Diarrhœa; frequent, offensive; frequent, preceded by colic. Liquid, copious, black, offensive, frequent. Slimy at night, and frequent, offensive, green. Thin, bloody. Mixed with blood for five days, then mostly pasty, dark and flocculent, then normal, then constipation. Bloody. Scanty and mixed with blood. Constipation. Hard, then soft the same day, and that night two liquid stools preceded by griping. Yellow, frequent. Frequent and copious.

Urinary and Sexual Organs.—Painful micturition. Urine amber-colored. Urine albuminous. U. suppressed. U. retained. Scrotum and penis dark blue. Semi-erection of penis.

Respiratory Organs.—Cough.

Clinical.—Chronic ulceration of the larynx, with swelling of tonsils, offensive breath, etc.

Heart and Pulse.—Violent and abrupt beating of heart. Palpitation lifting up hand applied to it. Heart's impulse and sound weak. Pulse rapid; and weak. Pulse slow, afterwards rapid; S., full and hard; S., small and contracted. P. small, compressible. P. irregular and intermittent.

Extremities.—Spasms. Pain in l. calf, the veins form two hard cords, which meet above popliteal space, with pain on touch, afterwards with swelling when standing.

Sleep.—Drowsiness, with easy waking. Sleeplessness, with restlessness.

Fever.—Coldness; of limbs; of limbs in evening; of skin; *cold and moist skin.* Fever at night, with sleeplessness and headache.

Mercurius Dulcis.

Triturations of pure Calomel (Mercurous Chloride) are used.

Allies.—The Mercurials in general.

Generalities and Mind.—Convulsion. Prostration. Languor in evening. Uneasiness. Faintness. Agitation. Apprehension.

Head and Eyes.—Headache; in morning. Pain or heaviness across forehead in evening. Conjunctiva red.

Clinical.—Scrofulous ophthalmia, ulceration of the cornea; chronic blepharitis.

Ears. Clinical.—A very valuable remedy in catarrh of the Eustachian tube and middle ear.

Face.—*As pallid as a corpse.* Flushed. Swelling, and of throat; of cheeks. Exfoliation of lower jaw. *Inflammation of lips and tongue.*

Mouth.—Teeth loose; and some came out. Uneasy sensation on gnashing teeth, in evening. Gums spongy. Tongue coated in morning; C. white, creamy; narrow coat in centre. Tongue so tumid that speech was gone. *Filled with ulcers. Inside of M. and tongue black, and constant flow of dark putrid saliva of intolerable fetor,* greater part of mouth and tongue mortified and part of tongue, under lip and part of one side of face sloughed off. Inside of cheeks inflamed and tender, and bloody puriform matter from r. cheek. *Salivation;* returned every October and February, often on the same days of the month as at first, sometimes a few days later. Fetor of breath. Unpleasant taste in morning on waking.

Throat.—*Ulceration. Swallowing difficult.*

Stomach.—Loss of appetite in morning. Thirst. Nausea, with faintness. *Vomiting;* profuse, also profuse diarrhœa; of milk and water that she had drunk, without appearance of calomel. Weight and pain in epigastrium and r. side, > vomiting a thick, ropy stuff consisting of calomel entangled in mucus.

Abdomen.—Griping; and fulness, with burning pain in epigastric and umbilical regions, then frequent copious serous stools, stools gradually becoming less and composed of bloody mucus, with tenesmus and constant desire. Pain. Tenderness; in evening on firm pressure.

Rectum.—Burning pain. Soreness around fundament. *Tenesmus.*

Stool.—*Dysentery. Small,* **of mucus and blood, covered with bile,** in evening, *with constant desire* and feeling as if it would be a relief to discharge whole contents of abdomen, he had had two large bilious stools about 10 A.M. *Watery, green; and small. Dark green, with griping* (Mag. c.). *Tinged with blood at night.* Frequent, and black particles similar to those precipitated from the vomit adhered to the vessel.

Clinical.—Valuable in diarrhœa of infants, with scarcely any tenesmus, stools grass-green, excoriating, liver enlarged, mouth pale, ulcerated, with offensive odor, swollen glands, ptyalism, etc.

Asthma. Pulse rapid and hard; and full; and small; and small, in morning. Trembling of hands and feet.

Skin.—Erythema beginning in pubic region and extending like scarlet redness over whole body, without pain or fever. Redness and swelling of face, extending over neck, shoulders and upper part of back, ending in serous exudation and desquamation. Round deep ulcers in mouth and fauces, on face, genitals and other parts, with white bases and inflamed painful margins, fever, night-sweats, weakness, tearing in limbs and trembling.

Fever.—Temperature low.

Mercurius Iodatus Flavus.

The pure proto-iodide of Mercury is triturated for use.

Allies.—Compare lists under Mercury and Iodine.

Generalities.—Sticking in scapulæ, r. temple, r. chest, l. ear, along outer borders of hands and little fingers. Pains are generally deep in bones. Pains proceed from right to left. The following appeared in rapid succession at night: Pain behind l. ear, then in tips of r. fingers and in r. sole near toes, then in l. toes, then in occiput, then in forehead, then near r. ear, then sharp pain in r. toes, pain about heart, violent pain in r. side of head, pain in r. heel, then above r. temple, then sharp pain in l. side of neck. Weariness after sitting several hours; W., < limbs; W., with sleepiness; at 4 P.M., > lying down, with disposition to sleep, but sleeplessness. Indisposition to do anything, with desire to lie down and rest. Faint feeling when in church; *F., with feeling that it would be > lying down;* F., with loss of muscular power, then spasmodic motion upward and downward of lower jaw.

Aggravation in morning after rising and in forenoon; from time of waking till noon; in evening; at night till 1 A.M., and in morning before and after rising; *many symptoms appear at night in bed;* after dinner till 4 P.M.; *from passive motion* (moving the part when sitting or lying); *during rest on r. side.* Amelioration after rising till noon and from 4 till 6 P.M.; A. in open air; from care, grief, anxiety, etc.; active motion (walking or riding); steady pressure; during the pressure, the relief passes away as soon as the pressure is removed; the pains that he had at night when lying on l. side > lying on r.

Mind.—Imagined that there was a man in the room who intended to perforate his throat with a gimlet. Lively, talkative; L., whistling, singing (soon after great depression). Moodiness. Depression from noon till 4 P.M., then liveliness till 6 P.M., then aggravation of symptoms till morning; D. in a warm room, with dulness. Destructive disposition, he can scarcely resist the temptation to throw his lamp through the window.

Head.—Stitches through H. and face. Aching; *in morning on waking;* in morning on waking, > exercise; in morning when rising; in forenoon; in evening, with soreness of bones of face and nose; at night on waking; after dinner; on waking; in a warm room, with dulness; in church, with faintness; < morning before and after rising; < walking about the house; < pressure; in H. and face, > during pressure, < after pressure is removed; with soreness of bones of face; with wavelike motion of blood; < r. temple, with nausea. Throbbing pain, < forehead. Dizzy pain like a rush of blood, then pain above r. temple. Heavy pain at base of brain and in throat and nostrils. Heaviness and fulness; H., with soreness of bones of face. Dulness at night on waking, with frontal pain; D., with compression and feeling as if pressed down upon the pillow.

Forehead.—Shooting, and in superior arch of r. orbit and in root of nose. Sharp pain above l. temple; suddenly above r. *Pain;* all day, with occasional sticking through head and face; in evening; at night on waking, with pain in orbits and root of nose; *with pain at root of nose* (Iod.); over r. temple; above l. temple, then throbbing pain in r. temple; in r. half, with pain in r. orbit and eyeball; over r. half of frontal and r. parietal bones, also with pain in r. ear, with soreness of r. orbit and r. eyeball. Heavy pain in F. and temples, extending down sides of face.

Temples.—Stitches on descending stairs; occasional S. Pain as if a sword were run through from l. to r.; on waking, with bruised pain in occiput. Sharp pain in r. at night in bed. Pain; in r.; in r., extending over entire side of head to nape.

Vertex.—Sharp pain, then pain in l. hip; S. pain in posterior fontanelle. *Headache is always on vertex or r. side.* Pain; with wavelike motion of blood; proceeding after some time into forehead; dizzy P., with nausea (after slight pain at heart).

Sides.—Sharp pain in r.; over parietal bone, extending to neck and r. eye. Pain; in l. near temple; in r., with stiffness in nape and sensation as if r. ear were closed; in r. parietal bone, < touch and combing hair.

Sharp pain in occiput in morning after rising. Numbness of occiput and nape, with stiffness of neck. Sensation as if skull were cracking; in afternoon. *Itching of scalp;* on vertex at night in bed; on l. side of vertex at night in bed. Numbness and tingling of scalp.

Eyes.—Sharp pain in superior arch of l. orbit; superior arch of r. in morning on rising; in inferior arch of l., and in l. eyeball, also with feeling as if lachrymation would appear; suddenly in superior arch of r., < stooping. Pain in superior arch of l. orbit as from a knife. Pain in l. orbit; r. orbit, with soreness; r.

orbital and l. malar-bones; superior arch of l.; inferior arch of r.; superior arch of l. and in l. malar-bones on touch; superior arch of l., < noise and talking, with headache. Vision of black floating clouds when lying on l. side.

Clinical.—Syphilitic iritis < night, with yellow fur at base of tongue. Ulceration of the cornea, sometimes serpiginous; symptoms associated with agglutination of the lids, yellow coat at base of tongue, nocturnal aggravation, etc. Pustular conjunctivitis. Ciliary blepharitis, with ulceration of margins of lids, etc.

Ears.—Stinging, throbbing pain in l. external. Boring in r. inner meatus; sharp intermittent B. in r. inner meatus; sharp throbbing B. outward deep in l. Sudden sharp pain in r. external meatus. Pain in front of ears; P. in r. inner meatus at night in bed. Touching r. or introducing finger into it causes sore pain and aggravates headache on that side. Sensation as if r. were closed, but hearing was good.

Nose.—Much mucus. R. nostril and r. side of septum sore and swollen. Sore, painful spot on l. side of septum; on l. wing. *Shooting at root.* Sharp pain in septum. *Pain; at root.* Heavy aching in nostrils. Throbbing in r. side, deep in bone.

Clinical.—Catarrh of the frontal sinuses, with offensive discharge from nose and dull boring, pressing pains over eyes, with bursting sensation. Chronic catarrh of the posterior nares and constant efforts to swallow.

Face.—Sharp, throbbing pain in r. cheek and on external surface of r. forearm. Pain in l. malar-bone, with pain on touch. Sharp pain in upper part of malar-bone, with pain on touch; sharp pain in l. cheek, with soreness of l. half of lower jaw-bone. Bruised pain in r. malar-bone radiating into forehead and r. side of head. *Soreness, < bones, with frontal headache;* S. of bones; S. of r. side, < r. lower half of lower jaw. Boring deep in r. ramus of jaw, extending into orbit. Dryness of lips, with burning dryness of lower lip and sensation as if upper teeth were pressed tightly together.

Mouth.—Teeth. Grinding sensation in roots, with occasional pain in abdomen; creeping G. sensation in roots at noon, with pressing together and with soreness deep behind umbilicus; G. sensation in roots, with fulness and drawing, and with desire to press teeth together, he pressed them so hard in sleep that the muscles were lame on waking. Feeling as if too tight in their sockets. Feeling in upper as if pressed tightly together. Pain in two l. molars, < bringing them together, with feeling as if teeth were too long. L. lower molars felt so long that he could not eat. Dry sensation. Gums feel slippery.

Tongue.—Coated, occasionally light brown; *C. at back;* C. yellow; dirty yellow; **dirty yellow at back**, *in morning on rising; bright yellow* (Chel.), *the tips and edges being red;* yellowish white. Papillæ prominent through the coat. Red elevations. Raised blisters on back part.

Fine red eruption on roof. Dryness, and of throat; with frequent empty swallowings. M. and lips dry and sticky; M., gums and teeth dry and sticky. Saliva increased in morning; increased, with congested feeling at root of a tooth.

Throat.—*Posterior wall of pharynx red, inflamed, with patches of mucus,* **and ulcerated spots**; *tonsils, uvula and pharynx red and congested.* Mucus; descended from posterior nares; *difficult to dislodge and causing retching* (Nit. ac.); in throat and on l. tonsil, which he constantly tries to hawk up; mucous patches on tonsils and walls of pharynx, easily detached. *R. tonsil swollen, and painful.* **Pain in r. tonsil, with swollen sensation and pain on swallowing.** *Soreness, with pain on swallowing saliva; S., with difficult swallowing and frequent empty swallowing. Swollen sensation. Sensation of a lump.* Dryness; with sharp pain above epiglottis and in l. tonsil when swallowing, also in l. half of hard palate; in throat and nose, with feeling as if closed by mucus; of roof of mouth and fauces, with moisture of gums and sides of mouth. *Burning;* when swallowing saliva; with dryness and pain on swallowing; prickling B. in r. side of pharynx. Frequent empty swallowing.

Clinical.—Various forms of sore throat, particularly tonsillitis, follicular, occasionally diphtheritic, nearly all cases < r. side or beginning on r. side, associated with yellow fur on tongue and general Mercurial symptoms.

Stomach.—Desire for acids. Appetite at one time excellent, at another wanting, sometimes excellent till sitting down to eat, when, at sight of food, it vanished. Appetite lost at smell of food when cooking; lost, and disgust at sight of food. Thirst; < evening; for sour drinks; for water, of which he drank large quantities. *Nausea;* all day, with cutting in stomach; at dinner; before supper, with disgust at sight of food; with weak, empty feeling at stomach; with dizzy pains over vertex, then pain at heart; with suffocation at heart and dizziness; with pressure high up in rectum and fainting.

Cramps, then pain in r. side of back. Sudden sticking as with a knife. Sharp pain, with hardness of stomach and abdomen, the pain < pressure. Pain in l. side. Bruised, burning pain. Burning, with pain as from a blow. Burning pain in l. side. Constriction.

Clinical.—It has cured vomiting of pregnancy, with the characteristic symptoms.

Abdomen.—Hardness; as from incarcerated flatus. Rumbling; at night in bed, with escape of flatus. Offensive flatus, then immediate inclination to stool, which was small, thin and offensive. Cutting at night, with discharge of flatus, then small, hard, black stool, with stinging and burning at anus; C., with inclination to stool, but emission of only wind; C., then scanty, thin fæces and froth; then copious, thin, light brown stool, with froth and wind; then copious, soft, yellowish-brown stool (the stools always follow immediately after the colic). Pain; in morning on waking, with great discharge of flatus; on waking; with sensation as if escape of flatus would relieve. Feeling as if diarrhœa would come on.

Hypochondria.—Sticking below r. ribs, somewhat > standing with hand pressed against side, he could not speak with gasping. Sharp pain in l.; in hepatic region; under r. floating ribs; in r., then sharp pain through stomach, with sensation as if the pain had turned around. Pain in l.; pain all day, with dizziness; in hepatic region, proceeding from r. to l. side, causing dizziness and nausea.

Umbilicus.—Sticking, < using arm after lying down at night, with dull, tired feeling in small of back, oppression of chest, pain above r. temple and in r. shoulder. Sensation of strings of air-bubbles running transversely across below U., with shooting as of a knotted string down, through and across, above U.

Heaviness below U. daily at 2 A.M., with uneasiness, as if full above and empty below, with pressure towards anus and sensation as if it could not move, then sensation as if a proper acrid loose stool would be discharged, then faintness and sickness in hypogastrium, then frequent emissions of inodorous flatus. Heat, < inspiring.

Frequent darting pains in l. side, with an occasional one in r., from deep in pelvis into region of liver. Pain in r. side proceeding to l., causing nausea and dizziness. Pressure in hypogastrium.

Stool.—Thin, light-colored. Scanty diarrhœa. *Stools of the daytime soft, copious, dark or light yellowish-brown, stools at night scanty, hard and black;* soft, copious, dark brown, with soreness at anus; soft, copious, dark brown, with burning and stinging at anus; copious, light brown, at first tolerably compact, then soft, finally consisting of froth. *Small, almost of the consistency of putty, requiring great straining.* Hard, black, in two small lumps, covered with white and green mucus, at night, after much straining.

Urinary and Sexual Organs.—Constant discharge of mucus from urethra, with sore sensation around glans. Urine copious and dark; C. and in a larger stream. Profuse sweat on genitals. Shooting from end of penis through glans. Erections in morning without desire. Emission towards morning; E. of which he knew nothing till morning.

Respiratory Organs.—Hacking cough when inspiring.

Chest.—Sticking in r.; in l.; in l. caused by pressure on stomach. Pain in l. as from a sword point; suddenly through r. Boring in r. at sixth rib. Sharp pain in l.; in upper part of r.; below l. axilla; in r., then slightly in l.; behind sternum; downward in r.; in r., then under r. arm, with aching in r. side of chest, then soreness of chest as from a cold. Sharp throbbing pain in l. Throbbing pain behind sternum. Pains; in r.; in r. at night in bed; in l., those which appear on r. side always proceed to l. Rheumatic pain in r. Oppression. Tightness and pressure on lungs.

Heart and Pulse.—Sticking. Pain, with yawning; sharp pain; sudden pain taking away the breath. Sudden spasmodic action (she thought it had jumped out of its place). Pulse about 80, weak, irregular and laboring.

Neck.—Sharp pain in l. side; r. side, extending over r. side of head. Soreness of r. side, with stiff sensation (without stiffness), then pain in internal meatus of r. ear, extending into throat and causing dulness in ear and swollen sensation in throat, with disposition to swallow frequently. Stiffness; with pain on turning it, also with soreness; and soreness, with soreness and numbness between scapulæ.

Back.—Sticking. Pains. Sticking in dorsal region; back of r. shoulder. Cutting between scapulæ, then about last dorsal vertebra; intermittent, in l. scapula, > motion. Sharp pain in l. scapula; suddenly. Pain over l. scapula. Throbbing pain between scapulæ; on r. Bruised pain in scapular region. Sharp pain in lumbar region.

Extremities.—Sharp pain in l. wrist, extending (but more severe) into thumb, then sharp intermittent pain on dorsum of l. foot extending into third and fourth toes. Pain in r. arm and r. sole; in r. forearm and l. hip; on dorsum of l. great toe, with sharp pains in r. fingers; on posterior surface of r., then pinching on posterior surface of r. forearm. Weariness; < lying on l. side, > lying on r. side. Heaviness, with laziness and drowsiness.

Upper Extremities.—Sharp pain in r. shoulder; with aching in back; S. pain in r. axilla. Pain in r. shoulder and arm; < *writing*, and in hand. Lameness and stiffness of r. shoulder; L. and soreness of l. shoulder and arm every night when lying on l. side. Lame numbness of l. shoulder and arm.

Arm.—Boring above r. elbow. Pain above l. elbow; P. in r., < bend of elbow, in morning on rising, < passive motion; deep in bones of r., < writing; P. and soreness in l. arm and elbow in evening, night and morning on waking; P. and soreness of r., < pressure, rubbing and passive motion; P. and numbness of r., with lameness of r. elbow. Laming, rheumatic pain in r., < writing. Weariness and lameness of r. after writing; W. and numbness of r., < *writing.* Heaviness of r.

Stabbing in bend of r. elbow. Pinching in r. elbow. Pain in l. elbow; in r.; in bend of r. Pains in forearms; laming, in l. and in hand; aching and drawing, in bones of l.; rheumatic, below l. elbow, proceeding afterwards into l. thumb. Pulsation in a spot at end of radius, with burning. Sharp pain in radial side of r. wrist all day, < using the limb or twisting wrist.

Hand.—Sharp pain in r. palm. Pain on back of r.; in r., then rheumatic pain above l. elbow; in l. palm at night in bed, with numbness of fingers and inability to grasp objects; rheumatic, in r. at night in bed; throbbing, in l. palm, extending up arm into l. chest. Weak, numb feeling in r., with cramplike pain.

Fingers.—Sticking in first joints of third and fourth of both hands, with stiffness of the fingers, the S. < moving or bending fingers; throbbing S. in base of l. index, with lameness and stiffness of whole finger, Sharp pain in l. index; in palmar surface of r. thumb. Throbbing pain at base of l. thumb (palmar surface), with paralyzed feeling. Numbness.

Lower Extremities.—Sharp pain in r., extending into foot. Weariness, with pain and tingling. Tingling through r. even to toes, on passive motion.

Thigh.—Tearing along anterior surface of r. hip to middle third of leg, > pressure and motion, < rest. Boring; in a spot on external surface of l. femur. Sharp pain in r.; above r. knee. Pain in r. hip-joint; P. on shaking limb, with tingling in legs, feet and toes as if they would go to sleep; P. in femur and sacral region, > stretching, motion and turning from side to side; wearying, in anterior and external surfaces of l. (deep in bone), > stretching, motion and turning from side to side, with pain in sacral region. Bruised feeling.

Knee.—Pinching in r. Squeezing pain in l. Throbbing pain on internal surface of r. in evening.

Leg.—Pinching on posterior surface of lower third of r. Sharp pain in l. Pain on anterior surface above r. ankle; on anterior surface of l.; on internal surface above l. ankle; above l. ankle at intervals of fifteen minutes. Throbbing pain in external surface of r., apparently in tibia. Heavy laming pain in calves, with pain in l. knee.

Ankle.—Cutting in r. Squeezing pain in r. Boring on anterior surface of l. Pain on posterior surface in morning on rising. Laming pain on posterior surface in morning on waking.

Foot.—Cramplike pain in l. side of l. sole, with numbness of l. leg. Boring in l. side of l. sole at night in bed. Sharp pain on l. sole. Pain on dorsum of r.; in l. sole; in l. sole, > moving foot; in l. sole extending into great toe and half way across dorsum of foot; in l. sole, causing faintness. Lame sensation.

Toes.—Cutting in l. little. Pain in l. great; with itching on both great toes. Sharp pain in r. great; in r. fourth and fifth.

Skin.—Fine bright red eruption on chest, stomach and abdomen, pitting and disappearing after pressure but returning when it has been removed. Stinging pimple on r. cheek, and one itching more than stinging in same position on l. cheek; itching and burning P. on r. scapula, near lower border, sore and painful at night in bed after scratching; painful P. on second joint of r. thumb; sore and painful, on r. side of septum naris. Stinging in l. cheek; on back of r. hand; on dorsum of l. great toe; in bend of l. knee at night, causing scratching; posteriorly on r. thigh, > rubbing and scratching.

Itching; *in spots over whole body;* on various parts; on l. sole; < chest, abdomen, back and hips; over whole body in daytime. *Itching at night;* over whole body; posteriorly on l. elbow; < bed. Itching at night in bed, behind r. ear; in various parts of r. side of face; on r. side of neck; on r. buttock. I. < scratching. I. not > scratching; in day and evening, but at night in bed > scratching. I. transiently > scratching, on r. side of chest. Pricking I. on various parts; on l. scapula; in r. axilla; on external border of r. foot at night in bed, > scratching, then itching above r. ankle, then stinging I. on r. knee, then on l. foot. Itching spot on r. cheek which he has scratched pulsates and stings.

Sleep.—Sleeplessness till 1 A.M.; on account of fancies which he could not expel; without restlessness. Early waking. Nightmare, she thought that an immense sheet of letter-paper was coming down to smother her. Frightful dreams and nightmare; F., of coffins and drowning. Lewd D., then copious emission. Dream that he was proving the drug, then an emission. D. that he must urinate, then an emission.

Fever.—Chills occasionally; C., with general trembling. Heat in nape and occiput. Burning in r. side of neck.

Mercurius Iodatus Ruber.

Pure deuto-iodide of Mercury (Mercuric iodide) is triturated for use.

Generalities.—Sticking in forehead, throat, l. eye and l. cheek. Tearing gnawing, < night, so that it disturbed sleep. Pain in head, throat and eye. Rheumatic pains, < r. forearm and hand, with weakness; R. pains, now here, now there, generally in limbs, mostly muscular, alternately in arms and hands, legs and feet, and occasionally in l. ear. Restlessness from midnight till morning, with constriction in diaphragm, almost like a cramp. Weakness; with bruised pain in whole body. Symptoms disappeared at noon. Amelioration towards evening.

Mind.—Merry, though the head is worse. Very cheerful in evening after pleasant things had happened. *Ill-humored in morning; on waking, and taste bad;* I. during toothache. *Low-spirited and disposed to cry.*

Head.—*Aching;* all day; in morning, with coryza, which ceases at noon; from morning till 2 P.M. and in evening, < forehead, with nausea; at 4 P.M., < forehead; at 8 P.M.; at night and next morning, later only on r. side congestion as with a cold, in afternoon changing sides, next day more congestive, in evening on r. side only, next morning in bed, > rising; when sitting still after sleep during the day; < afternoon and evening, with drowsy, stolid feeling in head; *with heat;* with sleeplessness; and in ear; *in bones, < occipital.* Heavy pain. Heaviness, with soreness over bowels. Dulness in afternoon; D. on waking; > *walking in open air, with pain in l. side, as during coryza.* Fulness. Vertigo, *everything seemed to reel around her.*

Forehead.—Tearing gnawing pains, < night, disturbing sleep. Sharp pain over eyes at 11 A.M. Pain; in region of comparison; over eyes; over l. eye; in F. and l. side at 9 P.M., drawing and sticking at 10 P.M.; intermittent, < r. side, from 7 till 10 P.M., next day till 9 P.M., with sticking in heart, third day at 3 P.M. Heavy pain through F. up to vertex and in outside of skull. Heaviness, and with it in the evening throbbing in r. side of head from front part to vertex. *Sensation as if bound with a tight cord* (Iod.).

Pain in temples and jaws. Throbbing from r. side of vertex down to nose in afternoon, with heaviness. Sticking above ears at 4 P.M. Pain in l. side of head; in l. side of brain from 6 till 8 P.M.; l. on waking, > evening; in l. half, with sensation in anus as from piles; r. side, > rising; P. goes from r. to l. side, > dinner. Pressure in cerebellum below occipital protuberance. Pustules on scalp; forming crusts.

Eyes.—*Inflammation,* < r., also with irritation from a bright light, so that he keeps it closed; I. in afternoon, with burning; of r., with lachrymation; *with burning.* Pressing or sticking. Pain; in and over l. Weakness and heat. Watery, swollen. *Albuginea inflamed and painful.* Lids affected by the catarrh. Vision dim.

Clinical.—Scrofulous ophthalmia, granulated lids, ulceration of cornea; particularly valuable in old cases of pannus and granulated lids.

Ears.—Wax increased. Pain in r. in morning in bed. *Itching all night;* I. in r.; in r. external auditory passage. Hearing dull; in morning; in morning, returns after going out at 10 A.M., closing only for moments; > evening; > noon and 2 P.M.; r. ear opens at 2 P.M.; H. better with r. ear as long as he takes every morning a shower bath; H. better with r. ear, disposed to put his finger in r. ear to cause pressure of air on drum, at the same time r. nostril runs, < evening when drinking tea; H. returns in evening after painful jerks in teeth; H. returns suddenly in r., then itching in meatus externus. Singing in evening.

Nose.—Dryness in nostrils and throat; and pain. Irritation of mucous membrane causing constant snuffing. Tickling causing sneezing. Stoppage in morning or from 8 till 10 A.M.; S. of r. nostril. *Much mucus in N. and throat. Coryza;* in a warm room, > open air, with cough; > getting warm from walking, with dull hearing; *with hoarseness;* with swelling, heat and inflammation of r. side of nose. Fluent coryza in forenoon; F., > evening; with much sneezing. Discharge of much mucus in morning; D. of bloody mucus on blowing; of much clear mucus without coryza, with lachrymation.

Clinical.—Nasal polypus, involving even the orbit, entirely cured.

Face.—Sticking in cheek. Pain in l. cheek. Heavy aching in upper jaw, then in lower, < sides, worse in r. **Lips slimy and sticky on waking**; *sticking together, with headache.* Sore spot inside lower lip. Sticking in lips.

Mouth.—Teeth. Stinging at times. Rending pain in r. Aching, < l.; in r. molars; in r. hollow T.; in l. at night before sleep; in all during dinner, from chewing; in r. hollow lower, then painful jerks in l.; threatened after meals. Sensitiveness during breakfast. Pressed so much in sleep that the muscles were lame and tired on waking. Gums red. Gums feel sore as if he would be salivated. Gum over second r. upper molar tender to touch as if an abscess were forming.

Blisters on point of tongue. Tongue dry. Tongue and mouth sensitive as if burnt with tea. Scalded feeling in tongue after breakfast. Burnt sensation in mouth in forenoon. Soreness of middle of inside of l. cheek. Sensation as if fibres were in mouth. *Salivation; with pain in lower teeth;* at noon; metallic-tasting. *Taste bitter;* T. flabby; T. metallic in evening; slimy on waking; bad on waking; fresh after salivation; pappy, with good appetite.

Throat.—R. parotid sore to touch and the region painful during eructations. *Mucus. Disposition to hawk; hawking of mucus;* H. through the day and spitting of scanty, white, tough expectoration. Superficial ulcers in patches. *Painful swelling of tonsils and submaxillary glands.* Sticking; and pressing. *Sensation of a lump, with disposition to hawk it out all day, hawked up a hard greenish lump.* Soreness, < empty swallowing; *S. and inflammation, with frequent cough and expectoration, next day* **inflammation and swelling of l. tonsil,** *elongation of velum, which seems to cause the cough, next day inflammation and swelling of both tonsils.* Scalded feeling all day, < empty swallowing. Almost constant desire to make an empty deglutition from salivation and fulness in throat.

Clinical.—In sore throats the inflammation is worse on or confined to l. side, otherwise the symptoms are very similar to the protoiode; it usually has the same yellow-coated tongue (though in some cases the tongue is clean); there are in general more febrile excitement and more tendency to headache than in the protoiode.

Stomach.—Inclination to have the food more salted. Thirst for small quantities. Loud and bitter eructations. Nausea in evening, with uneasiness and laziness all over limbs and sleepiness; during meals; when passing diarrhœa; with uneasiness and laziness all over limbs, at the same time with rheumatic pains; with sinking at stomach or in epigastrium, with general sick feeling; with urging to stool; with headache; with sore throat. Heartburn after dinner. Pain at 10 A.M.; *P. in epigastrium on pressure.*

Abdomen.—Rumbling; or purring; with soreness all over abdomen and heaviness of head. Motion all night after 11 P.M., with ineffectual urging to stool. Griping forcing him to stool, stool large, copious, light brownish, inability to urinate as long as the stool lasted, after the stool the urging continued with itching in rectum, all around sphincter ani, which felt protruded, colic again at 11 o'clock, > loose, light yellowish-brown, watery, bloody stool, coated with mucus, then tenesmus and soreness of bowels, again after dinner, at 2 P.M., colic, with loose stool, then tenesmus, in afternoon and evening only soreness in bowels. Pain all night after 11 P.M., with diarrhœa; P., with frequent desire for stool; P. as before stool, in evening; threatening of P. in evening till fully asleep. Weakness in abdomen, stomach and partly extending into chest, from 6 A.M. till 3 P.M., with eructations and feeling as before stool.

Sudden cutting in liver region. Pain in r. hypochondrium, with full feeling; P. in r. hypochondrium (yesterday in l.), with drawing in anus as if hæmorrhoids were coming on; sprained, in r. hypochondrium near pelvis; intermittent heavy pain in region of liver, pancreas and spleen; drawing, in l. hypochondrium, afterwards lame sensation there in morning. L. waist felt sore on bending. Distention of umbilical region, with pain on pressure. Pain around umbilicus. Sprained pain in r. pelvic region in morning after a good night's rest, > walking.

Stool.—Diarrhœa in morning. Soft. Easier and not so thick as usual. Four firm S. in twenty-four hours, more at night.

Urinary Organs.—Ulcers in bladder. Bearing down on bladder. Frequent desire, she cannot retain the urine a moment. Sensation in urethra as if urine were hot in morning during normal stool. *Urine increased.* Urine red. *U. thick* and dark.

Sexual Organs.—Sensitiveness of r. testicle and spermatic cord. Emissions at night; towards morning. Desire < going to sleep.

Clinical.—It has been found useful by many physicians in true syphilis, which is doubtless due to the Iodine in the combination, though the depressing effects of the Mercury undoubtedly determine a more marked action of the Iodine than would be obtained if the Iodine were uncombined with it. Ulcers and erosions of os uteri; inflammation of cervix and uterus internally; enlarged nabothian glands; especially valuable in cases of venereal origin; leucorrhœa profuse, greenish, corrosive. Extremely valuable in inflammation and enlargement of the uterus.

Respiratory Organs.—Voice covered and rough. Voice hoarse and husky in evening after getting a little wet in a rain. Cough by spells during the day; C. through the day, with scanty, loose, whitish, slimy expectoration and difficult breathing, next day cough, with thick, white expectoration, cough dry in evening. Profuse yellowish expectoration. Breathing difficult.

Chest.—Sticking in muscles of l. ribs in afternoon after walking in thawing weather; S. through r., like rheumatism, going down arm, in afternoon; during a walk, sudden S. in l. muscles, where two years ago acute rheumatism began. Cutting, with sticking in heart. *Catching pain under r. breast,* oppressing respiration. Pain; behind sternum, irritating to cough; occasionally in C. or heart, < l. side. Soreness of breast waking him. *Constriction;* < l. side.

Heart and Pulse.—*Sticking in heart;* all day. Pain at heart. Pulse rapid, stronger.

Neck.—Glandular swellings in scarlatina. Sticking along l. side and in heart till sleep, from 7 till 10.50. Aching in r. splenius capitis, with stiffness; in region of first or second cervical vertebra on waking, with stiffness; in nape at 7 P.M. as if he had been struck; rheumatic, in muscles of neck and nape.

Extremities.—Stiffness, > walking. Rheumatic pain in l. arm, < motion, especially putting on his coat, and at noon, > evening and night, with soreness and stiffness. Rheumatism in joint of l. humerus. Strained pain in middle of humerus as if about to break, with wavering stitches through all the muscles and sensation as if they were sore, with desire to stretch the limbs and body. Aching and drawing pain in bones of l. forearm. Synovial inflammation of l. index. Jerking in l. fingers in evening till sleep. Pain in l. fingers in morning; sore.

Lower Extremities.—Pain in evening, > walking. Sprained pain in l. hip-joint in evening. From hips to ankles pain as after a long walk, < bones. Sudden intermittent throbbing pain through and around head of r. tibia when walking and at the same time pain in r. parotid, afterwards a similar throbbing pain in l. rectus femoris, about a third the distance from knee upward. Rheumatic pain in r. knee and hip in forepart of the day. Weakness of knees. Pain in feet; < soles. Pain in great toe and ball of foot, > walking; sore P. between r. toes; in r. great toe like podagra, towards morning, but without swelling and redness, > rising, returning afterwards.

Skin.—Forehead pale reddish, afterwards dirty gray. then full of fine wrinkles, afterwards peeling of in fine scales, cracks and rhagades in all directions (from external application). Pustules on outer side, below r. knee, itching, sore to touch, with inflamed bases, on the third day they scabbed, but matter continued to accumulate under the scab, afterwards a similar sore to the left of these. Itching on parts of r. forearm; on neck, dorsum of hands, < r. fingers; pricking I. all over r. hand from 3 till 4 P.M., next day on lower part of r. upper arm from 3 till 3.30 P.M., and on upper part of r. upper, < axilla, at 6 P.M.

Sleep.—Deep in afternoon. Sleepless from 5 till 6.30, then sleep till 8 A.M. Restless sleep, with headache. Many dreams. *Frightful D.* Anxious D.; about removing and his relatives. Foolish. Quarrelsome. Lascivious towards 5 A.M., by his will prevented a pollution. Troublesome, such as swimming and wading in water, pushing through low places and under a shed, of detecting robbers in the night attempting to enter dwellings, half-conscious sleep, with fear. D. of gunning and farming; G. and traveling.

Fever.—Chilliness in forenoon, with aching in lower limbs; C. at bed-time; sometimes with creeping over back; with creeping over skin and uneasy sore feeling all over bowels; alternating with warmth; then flushes of heat over face. *Shivering, then feverishness.* Cold hands in afternoon and hot face. Flushes of heat, with tickling over whole body. Flushes in face; with tickling. *Objective heat on vertex* all day; **vertex felt hot** *in evening,* at 11 P.M., *and pulsation in it.* Burning in forehead at 2 P.M., with burning and inflammation of eyes till 10 P.M. Sweat on going out in thawing weather; *copious S. at night;* hot S.

Mercurius Nitrosus.

Pure nitrate of Mercury is triturated for use.

Generalities.—Cachectic condition, with discoloration of mucous surfaces and flabbiness of tissues. Tremor. Subsultus tendinum, so that muscles jumped under skin like a mouse under a cloth. Pain; so that he rolled about the floor and called for a knife to kill himself. Indisposition. Weakness. Faintness.

Mind. — Delirium. Anxiety. Stupor. Memory poor.

Head, Eyes and Ears.—Headache. Dizziness. Eyes sunken. Pupils dilated, to a certain extent obedient to light. Ringing in ears.

Clinical.—A very valuable remedy in pustular conjunctivitis and keratitis, especially with burning pain, lachrymation, photophobia, great sensitiveness to heat or cold, sharp sticking pains. It is useful in various forms of ulceration, with Mercurial conditions and with sharp pain. Staphyloma, with kerato-iritis.

Face.—Pale and livid; P. and anxious. Flushed. Features contracted. Lips bluish-red.

Mouth.—Gums swollen and bleeding. Blackish line on free border of gums, < around insertion of lower incisors and canine teeth. Tongue and lips tumid, parched and painful. Tongue coated. Tongue cannot be protruded well. Mucous membrane red and tumefied; mouth and fauces red and painful. Pain, and in throat. Salivation. Mercurial fetor. Coppery taste.

Throat.—Soreness; of fauces, with redness and dryness.

Clinical.—"Mucous patches," with sticking pains.

Stomach.—Eructations, with frothy discharge from mouth and occasional vomiting, first of a fluid containing a red powder, which sank to the bottom of the vessel, then V. of mucus. Hiccough. Nausea. Vomiting; of glairy and tenacious matter; of bilous matter streaked with blood; frequent, of bilious matter at night; and pain. Pain in epigastric region; in region of S. and abdomen on pressure.

Abdomen and Stool.—Pain in hypogastrium. Tenesmus. Diarrhœa, with colic. Constipation. Frequent stools. Bloody S., with collapse.

Urinary and Sexual Organs.—Micturition painful. Urine high-colored, passed involuntarily. Urine suppressed; and urea was found in blood drawn from arm; but large quantities of water were taken. Sexual power diminished.

Respiratory Organs and Chest.—Voice feeble and almost suppressed. Spasmodic movements of muscles of chest, so that heart-sounds cannot be distinctly heard.

Pulse.—Rapid and small; and weak; and thready. Small and thready.

Extremities.—Tremor causing difficulty in prehensile movements and in walking. Sore feeling where they came in contact with the bed, they looked red and inflamed. Control lost when standing and walking, twitchings in bed, with trembling when standing, and even in bed, spasms < towards evening. Cramp of lower.

Skin.—Brownish-red eschar projecting above healthy parts, on l. chest and one on back (parts rubbed with the solution), skin red, inflamed, ecchymosed, with yellow-brown patches, and a similar tract towards r. haunch, where the liquid had flowed down.

Sleep.—Sleeplessness.

Fever.—Chill. Cold skin; < limbs, and clammy. Cold and ecchymosed limbs. Heat; of skin. Sweat.

Mezereum.

A tincture is made of the fresh bark of Daphne Mezereum, L.

General Action.—It produces violent inflammation of all mucous membranes and of the skin; internally the inflammation is characterized by burning, externally by violent itching. In addition, its neuralgias are very marked, they attack principally the face, but occasionally other parts. The periosteum of the jaw and of the long bones becomes the seat of an inflammatory process which is followed by its legitimate results.

Allies.—Mercury, Rhus t., Ars., Nit. ac., Iod., Phyto., Nux v., Zinc.

Generalities.—Flesh dried and shrivelled. Stretching. Tremulous condition as after too much wine. Stitches over whole body; in various parts; in evening, < l. chest; in various parts, with crawling; *hot, jerking, on various parts.* Tearing in different parts when sitting. Boring in knees, tibiæ, wrists and behind ears, all day when walking and sitting; drawing B. in arms, knees, skull, bones of feet and ankles, < above ankle and wrist. Pain in l. upper arm, r. thumb-joint, l. ankle and r. temple, in morning after waking, with boring; P. in tibiæ and other parts of body, even when walking; shifting P., inclined to return to original spot; rheumatic, in nape, throat and occiput. Drawing pain through whole l. side of body, with sensation of falling asleep, < hand and foot; wandering D. pain in lumbar region, occiput, shoulders, flesh of thighs and in various parts of head. Drawing or jerking, now here, now there, then aching. Cramplike constriction across lower pectoral muscles, lower part of back and upper arms, when walking in open air.

Oppression. *Feeling of great lightness of body. General sick feeling;* amounting to nausea on going into a close room, > open air. Discomfort, > towards noon; D., with yawning, stretching, pain in abdomen and eructations. Swollen feeling in affected parts on touch, without swelling. *Sensitiveness to cold air* (Ars., Kali, Dulc., Mosch., Nux v., Rhus); < head, and sensation when sitting in the house as of a cold wind on head. Sensitiveness to cold water in morning when washing and in teeth when drinking. Desire to walk in open air alternating with dread of open air. When walking inclination to go with upper part of body bent forward, to hurry and to sing, though everything is performed with difficulty. Restlessness (Ars., Rhus t.). Indolence; after deep sleep, with weakness. Weakness; in morning on rising; in afternoon; in afternoon, and sleep for four hours, with agreeable dreams (with faceache, which never quite woke her); in evening without ability to sleep; when walking; > a short nap; with inclination to sleep, at least to lie outstretched; with mental depression bordering on idiocy. Aggravation in l. half of body; of pains, by rest (Rhus t.); (of effects of wine). Pains rarely appeared in bed, did not disturb sleep, but reappeared after waking.

Mind.—Delirium. Feels intoxicated, speaks without reflection, but very lively. Merry after dinner, inclined to sing, dances, jokes and laughs, as if intoxicated by wine; M. mood changing to depression. Cheerfulness and desire to work. **Hypochondriac,** *everything seems dead, nothing makes a vivid impression on his mind. Sad* (Ign., Nat. m.); and every trifle affects him disagreeably, indifferent to the whole world, disinclined to work. *Weeping mood.* Anxiety; at noon before eating, with palpitation and necessity to lie down; in evening, with trembling; in attacks in evening, with weeping, palpitation, coldness over whole body and weakness of limbs.

Anger, with desire to say vexatious things; A. which he soon regrets. Quarrelsome. Inclined to reproach others. Ill humor; after sleep; with sensitiveness; with desire to run away; with restlessness and redness and heat of face and forehead. Discontented with himself and his surroundings. Averse to talking. No rest when alone, desires company. Indifferent. Quiet and contemplative, longing for death. Frightened easily, then palpitation.

Distraction. Dulness. Difficult to make a resolution. Thought difficult, with pressive dulness of head. Thoughts vanish; when talking; as soon as he began to think of anything, inability to repeat anything from memory, confusion, with pressure in sinciput. He looked out of the window for hours without thought and without knowing what he was looking at. *Forgot what he had recently heard, every intercurrent remark of others confused his ideas.* Stupefaction on waking from a sound sleep. Coma, with convulsive movements of eyes and upper extremities, dilatation and insensibility of pupils.

Head. — Tearing. Boring in several parts; < motion. Acute pain as if everything would fall out at forehead. Aching; here and there; in morning on waking; in afternoon; *in afternoon,* **with pain on slightest touch (after a vexation)**; *after moving about and talking much, < temples and sides of vertex;* < towards evening; < open air; < warm room, < forehead and sinciput; > stooping low; with shivering; sudden, with inclination to close eyes, discomfort in stomach and vertigo; just beneath skull, as if brain pressed hard against bones; as if brain were shaken, all the afternoon on suddenly moving head; as if brain hung loose against skull, hit against bone here and there on moving head. Dulness; all day, with pressure in temples; towards evening; > eating; dizzy, with difficult thought; *as if intoxicated, > work; as if intoxicated, and as if he had been up all night* (Nux v.), as after excessive emission. Heaviness; with inclination to support it. Numbness. *Intoxicated sensation.* Vertigo; with flickering before eyes; with contracted pupils; he would fall to the left; faintlike.

Forehead.—Stitches, and in vertex; S. in l. upper part in morning in bed; tearing, in l. eminence. Tearing; in r. side; above eyes; in morning when sitting; in forepart, with jerking stitches. Burrowing superficially in middle. Pinching in F. and temples, with pressure on eyes and jaws, as before violent coryza. Boring; in l.; in various places in bones; in l. bone; above l. eye and in nasal bone; frequently in l. side, extending towards temple, with tearing, afterwards extending to occiput; burning and drawing, in cranial and frontal bones. Boring drawing pain in bones; B. drawing pain in l. side and temple; above eyes, < l. Pain; in r. eminence; above eyes; in upper part; in sinciput in morning on waking, with drawing; in afternoon; in bone on pressure, extending to feet; beneath bones, extending into nasal bones; transversely through forepart of head; in morning as if brain became hard, with inability to collect his thoughts; pressing asunder, in forepart of head. Pressive throbbing. Confusion. Stupefaction in sinciput and occiput in evening.

Temples.—Stitches in l., with tearing. Tearing from one to other through head; (T. in evening when sitting). Boring; < r. Boring drawing pain. Compressive griping, extending into forehead and nose. Pain; and in supraorbital region. *Pressure outward in l.;* inward on l., extending to above orbits, when sitting reading, > motion. Compression from both sides after violent motion, whereby he forgot the word he was about to speak and could hardly collect his thoughts.

Vertex.—Stitches in region; S. extending to forehead, with heat of face.

Sides.—Sticking in l. half of brain. Tearing in l.; in r. side of skull; r. at night when awakened; in l. as if broken, then on vertex and in l. ear. Boring in r. side of skull. Pain beneath l. parietal bone; on l. P. bone, > pressure, < removing pressure; as if a plug were driven in on r. side of vertex, then also in l. side of forehead, then external to and above r. eye; in r. parietal bone as if suppurating, < walking, with sensation as if bone must be painful to pressure, which was not the case; remittent P. in r. parietal region as if brain pressed against bone, < bending head to right; drawing pain in bone above r. ear, returning at night, noticed on every step. Drawing in bone above r. ear.

Occiput.—Tearing; back and forth in bones. Tearing throbbing in spot above nape. *Boring in bones.* Sharp pain in l. side, with tension. Pain on entering house; P. in O. and nape on moving head; sore pain; *stupefying P. through r. hemisphere of brain to forehead.* Drawing pain in r. side. Pressure outward in l. side in evening. Heaviness.

Skull.—Tearing on waking in night and morning, with pressure. Boring; in various places; in shock-like paroxysms, < vertex. Pain; < touch. Drawing.

Scalp.—*Dry scurf;* scurf was *whiter*, more profuse and *drier* than usual. **Covered with thick, leather-like crust, under which thick and white pus collects here and there and hair is glued together** (compare N. ac.). *Elevated white scabs, under which ichor collects and which is offensive and breeds vermin. Scabs look chalky and extend to brows and nape.* Hair hangs soft; H. inclined to bristle; the long hairs were troublesome to him, they seemed rough, the hair became curly and grew rapidly. Pain on touch of hair; *P. on both sides of vertex on touch.* Biting as from lice in evening, > scratching, but always recurring in another place. *Itching on vertex and occiput; near r. side of vertex, > touch; sticking I. > scratching.*

Clinical.—Neuralgic headaches, in one case beginning in the occiput and extending over the whole brain, with tenderness of the scalp, the pain burning and boring, extending to eye and teeth, and even down to the shoulder; in another case it appeared to involve the periosteum of the vertex and occiput, during the pain cold shivering, the parts very sensitive to touch, and the scalp felt thicker over the seat of the pain; in another case the pain involved the supraorbital nerves, was generally one-sided, < warmth; in one case the neuralgia involved the ear, which was sore, as if bruised. A valuable remedy for eruptions on the scalp, particularly when thick crusts form, from under which there oozes a thick purulent matter; in one case the eruption was preceded by violent cough which had lasted for several months and which disappeared as the scurfy eruption appeared, with falling of the hair, and with violent itching, intensely < heat; in another case the eruption was preceded by pain in the cranial bones, < night, the eruption itched and burned. Pityriasis.

Eyes.—*Inflammation, < l., in morning on rising, conjunctiva of ball dirty red, < near external canthus, with pain and* **dryness** (Lyc.). Surrounded by brown rings, < about inner canthus, with yellowish pale color of face and at times circumscribed redness of cheeks. Dull, pupils dilated and sluggish, and eyes turned upward in sleep. Staring; without thought. *Pain; about l.;* in evening when reading, vision not clear; **with dryness,** *as if conjunctiva of lids were inflamed. Pressure and tearing on and in eyes, < orbits. Smarting compelling rubbing.* Biting. Itching of r. Heat, with pain in lids; H., with pressure upon ball. Sleepiness. Symptoms of catarrh in E. and nose, with thirst, heat of skin and rapid pulse.

Lachrymation, with biting in eyes. Pupils dilated; and vision obstructed; contracted. Pain in balls; in r. at noon on closing eyes; < light, and in lids; as if too large, also with frequent necessity to wink. **Jerking of muscle of l. upper lid;** J. in l. external canthus. Agglutination of external canthi, with pressure and itching, with fluent coryza and lachrymation through the day. Canthi feel agglutinated. *Inclination to blink. Inclination to close lids;* lids close when writing. Burning-prickling stitches on margins of lower lids. Biting in margins of lids; in canthi, < inner; *itching P. of margins and near nose.* Itching on margins of lower lids; I. in l. inner canthus; in r. external canthus, with agglutination. Boring in region of brows. Pain in middle of r. brow. Burning in r. brow, with itching. Far-sighted. More short-sighted than usual. Cannot see well till towards 4 P.M., lashes seem too long. Flickering. Vision of sparks. Of white, glistening spots. Of black spots on rising from stooping. Muscæ volitantes in a dreamy way.

Clinical.—Ciliary neuralgia after operations, especially after removal of the eyeball. Ciliary neuralgia, the pains radiate and shoot downward, with cold feeling, especially with soreness of the bone.

Ears.—Painful swelling of r. external meatus, < lower and posterior part. Sticking in l.; deep in in morning and on putting finger into ear the external meatus seems more open than the other; intermittent S. < l.; intermittent, and in teeth; itching S. in r. Tearing deep in l. (Twinging in one); in r.; in l. external meatus in evening, with swollen sensation. Boring behind r. Pain; above r.; in l., with painful drawing; superficially above r. in evening, extending to outer margin of concha, it seemed as if upper ear were painful to pressure, but it was not the case.

Sensation as if air were distending r. external meatus, *and as if roaring in ears would occur, then in l. meatus, with stopped sensation in ear;* ear feels stretched wide open in evening and air seemed to enter cold; feeling of air in r. external meatus in evening, and distended feeling, also < yawning, > boring in with finger; dilated feeling when walking in warm weather, with coldness and desire to bore into ear; sensation of air in r., then l., with twinging, < r. Sensation of a wind in r. Throbbing behind r., with pressure, changing to pressure in head, forehead, nose and teeth, < motion of head. Stopped sensation in l. Tension behind l., with tearing in alternating jerks. Drawing from r. mastoid process into lower teeth. Itching in r., > rubbing.

Hearing difficult. Ringing; in r. in morning on rising; in l. in morning after dressing; with sleepiness; in r., with yawning. Rushing noises. Sudden humming or roaring in r. Sound as of a distant mill when lying on l.

Clinical.—Deafness appearing after the suppression of an eruption on the head, with thickening of the tympanum, entirely cured, with return of the eruption. Chronic inflammation, feeling as if the drum were exposed to cold air, itching behind the ears, etc. Violent pains involving the teeth and pains in the face, with constant chilliness, especially after the abuse of Merc. or when Merc. has failed.

Nose.—*External margin of r. nostril inflamed and painful.* Thicker and shiny. Jerking at root. Tearing near l. side; T. in bones. Boring in bones; and neighboring parts, with drawing pain. *Pressing asunder pain in root in morning extending into forehead, with pain in temples on touch, heat and sweat on head, with coldness of rest of body.* Drawing pain in both sides. Drawing in bones. Rawness internally, with soreness. Biting like mustard; B. in l. nostril, with dryness and crawling in it and stoppage of r., and *vice versa. Dryness, with diminished smell* (Nat. m., Lyc.). Burning; in wings; near wings; near r. side; on back extending towards l. side at 8 P.M., with biting.

Sneezing; in forenoon; *with fluent coryza; with sore pain in chest;* violent and painful; violent, whereby granular mucus flies out of fauces; *ineffectual inclination to sneeze.* Coryza; with sore pain in r. nostril; stopped; stopped, and r. nostril scabby. Fluent coryza; in evening, with stopped C., r. nostril stopped by scabs and painful; *discharge of yellow, at times bloody water, which causes soreness and burning pain; D. of thin mucus, which makes nostrils sore and is sometimes streaked with blood* (Merc.); thin discharge; tenacious bloody mucus. Mucus increased and harder than usual, without coryza, with great noise on blowing nose. Bleeding; brick-red blood from r. nostril in evening before sleep; trickling from r. nostril. Odor like warm offensive exhalations, in evening.

Clinical.—Chronic ozæna, diminished sense of smell, burning pain in bones of nose and face.

Face.—Inflammatory redness, the eruption is "fat" and moist (impetigo); F. and forehead red and hot, with restlessness and peevishness. Pale; and sunken, and expression suffering; and expression ill-humored, prostrated; and collapsed, and limbs collapsed. Gray, earthy. Sunken and ghastly. Shrunken and cold. Cheeks painfully swollen and painful to pressure; r. side swollen, with heat in face and more pain than usual in eyes. *Jerking of r. zygomatic muscles; in middle of r. cheek. Tearing; below l. eye; in morning; in l. side and teeth after morning walk; in side, waking her before midnight, and pain < r. side of head. Boring in l. cheek, with burning. Cramplike pain on r. cheek-bone, with tearing. Sudden pain on waking from sleep. Tearing in lower jaw; drawing T. in l. lower jaw and teeth. Boring in upper jaw; l. side of upper; l. lower; sides of lower.*

Lips.—*Eruption outside of red, with fluent coryza.* Swelling; *of upper;* below l. nostril, with burning pain; lower thick, dry, cracked, scaly and painful. Anterior part of lip, gum and tongue denuded. Outer skin of inner surface of lips as well as anterior gums loose. *Sticking together.* Sticking in upper by r. corner; S. as if a blister would develop. Sore pain in red of lower, with inflammation, burning on touch, > moistening with saliva or drinking, < evening. *Dry; < boundary between internal and external parts, and shiny, painful, in evening sore, burning.* Burning of upper; and below l. eye; B. of lips and forepart of tongue; *of lips and tongue as if sore;* in r. corner as if cracked, in evening; in lower as if it would crack, < evening and on closing mouth. Biting, and on tongue. Itching, and on tongue; I. on l. side of margin of lower.

Clinical.—Infraorbital neuralgia involving the face, so violent that the patient could not wash his face, with profuse lachrymation; another case of facial neuralgia, < heat, the pain leaving numbness. Facial neuralgia, which seems to arise from the teeth, < night, involving the head, after the failure of Merc. Violent neuralgia of the face and head following herpes zoster. Periostitis of the lower jaw, with swelling and burning pain.

Mouth.—Teeth. Offensive mucus. Carious odor of mucus on lower incisors. *Hollow T. decay very rapidly;* upper molar, with drawing, burning and sticking, the pain < evening. Sticking in l. upper molars; in roots of lower incisors. Cutting in hollow, like soreness, in morning, < biting, waking him next night. Boring in one or another, < r., with sticking, sometimes changing to sticking in r. cheek-bone, therewith r. side of head so affected that even to touch the hair was painful, with uneasiness, fretfulness and aversion to everything. Jerking in upper incisors; in last r. molars in afternoon; in l. upper jaw, in which there were broken teeth, with vesicular swelling, bleeding and suppuration of gum, and cheek externally painful to touch; tearing J. from a r. upper hollow molar into temple. Drawing in l. upper; like incipient tearing in r. lower, also in l. teeth. Pain in last l. lower molar as if it should be pulled out. *Aching; in hollow;* in hollow molar; in hollow in morning; in morning on rising, on pressing them together, < upper incisors; *in hollow in evening; on touch of tongue.* **Feel too long and blunt** (Merc.), < l., with boring and sticking in them; l. seem too long; too long in afternoon, with coldness; *on biting on them and from fresh air,* < l. upper and in upper incisors, with drawing pain; in morning on rising, < pressing them together, < incisors. *Blunt,* at night; upper incisors. Hollow teeth seem very sharp.

Gums.—Bleed easily. Swelling like a blister back of upper incisors, then swelling involving forepart of hard palate, wherewith upper incisors were painfully blunted in evening. Drawing in l. upper alveolar processes.

Tongue.—Inflammation, and of mouth. Swelling, redness and white coat; S., < tip, with white, almost loamy coat (almost like that of Mercury), with prominent papillæ, each of which looked red on a white ground, tip very red (denuded), in middle of T. a deep fissure. Coated; white; whitish-yellow. Burning painful blisters, and on gums. Sticking. Biting; posteriorly. Tip painful as if burnt; tongue and hard palate in morning. *Burning, and on forepart of mouth, with salivation; B. extending to stomach; extending over whole mouth,* < hard palate, with dryness of hard palate, < posteriorly and in upper part of pharynx; on forepart, with dry rawness; in tip, with boring; biting burning. Sensation on moving it as if forepart were soft like butter. Speech difficult, at one time as if breath or saliva were wanting, at another as if tongue were too thick.

White ulcers within corner of mouth and on r. cheek. Discharge of reddish mucus. Pain; posteriorly on palate from eating not very warm soup. Prickling posteriorly on palate and at base of tongue, with dryness and heat of tongue posteriorly, after a cup of white coffee the heat involved tip of tongue, inside of lips, cheeks and gums, with sweat, < of face. **Burning** (Ars., Arum t.); *extending to stomach* (Merc. cor.); posteriorly on palate and on uvula till dinner; < pharynx, > inspiration, < expiration; in palate and throat, > eating, except the sensation as if burnt with hot soup, next day rawness, < morning after waking, with roughness and dryness; *in palate and fauces, with scraping;* and biting, with spitting of much watery saliva. Dryness < tongue, in morning on waking. Salivation; salt.

Taste.—Peppery; always after eating. Hard and

rough. Catarrhal. Bitter to beer; B. all day, with nausea. Nauseous posteriorly in fauces as from hollow teeth, and odor similar to it far back in nose. Alkaline salt, with metallic offensive odor from mouth. Sourish-salt. Sweetish-salt, < becoming heated. Flat sourish. Strawlike to tobacco. Diminished, tongue as if burnt. Lost, smoky taste to milk.

Clinical.—Decaying teeth, with burning boring pains involving the bones of the face and head, temporarily > drawing in cold air.

Throat.—Swelling; of glands below l. ear, on margin of ramus of jaw, with pain on pressure in evening. Hawking of mucus; easy, of granular transparent mucus; secretion of mucus posteriorly through choanæ, extending into air-passages, causing hawking, with lachrymation; mucus, making singing difficult, she could not utter a pure tone. Inflammation of pharynx. Sticking in submaxillary glands. *Feeling as if full of mucus, not > expectoration.* Feeling as if a foreign body were sticking in pharynx when swallowing. Pain; posteriorly in pharynx when not swallowing, at times on only one side; in pharynx on swallowing a morsel, with sudden shuddering, starting from pit of stomach, with nausea and shaking of head and chest; as if palate-bones separated on swallowing; as from a plug, on swallowing. Tensive pain in l. side of pharynx on empty swallowing. Soreness of fauces on inhaling open air; S. < when not swallowing; posteriorly, < swallowing, with rawness.

Scraping; **in fauces;** in evening after bread and butter; till 9 P.M., at times provoking cough, < eating; *posteriorly in fauces and pharynx,* < empty swallowing, *with biting,* as in coryza; *posteriorly in upper part of fauces,* > drinking milk and eating bacon, *with burning* (Phyto., Merc. c.); *in fauces,* with tenacious mucus; and on tongue, palate and pharynx, with heat and hot breath; posteriorly in fauces, with salivation and constant inclination to relieve the burning scraping by swallowing saliva. *Roughness. Rawness of fauces; and soreness of F. and palate; of pharynx, < expiration with open mouth, with burning pain. Constriction, and of stomach;* of pharynx, with crawling; of pharynx, with pressure on swallowing food.

Burning, and in pharynx (Phyto.); *in œsophagus;* **in fauces;** in œsophagus if he swallows water; *in pharynx, < inspiration;* in fauces, pharynx and stomach, > swallowing food, with anxiety and sensation of diarrhœa; *with irritation to hacking cough in larynx, like dryness, anxious oppression of breath and loosening of scanty mucus on coughing;* extending from fauces to corners of mouth and lips, where epidermis desquamated, with pain; scraping B.; cool B. on tongue and throat, extending to stomach, as after peppermint; biting B. gradually extending from pharynx over mouth and outer margin of lips, in evening pain in pharynx on swallowing as if swollen or like scraping, then sticking in pharynx on empty swallowing, swallowing painful, especially to uvula and arches of palate. Dryness; *in fauces, and irritation, causing dry fatiguing cough.* Drawing and tickling posteriorly in fauces and pharynx. Pharynx posteriorly affected by talking.

Clinical.—Syphilitic sore throat, with burning and dryness extending down the œsophagus, and inflammation extending into the larynx, with hoarseness, the cold air relieved the burning but caused pain in the gums. Syphilitic ulceration of the larynx and œsophagus, with violent burning and soreness.

Stomach.—*Appetite great; at noon and in evening;* hunger at 6 A.M., with rumbling in abdomen; intermittent hunger; constant desire to eat without real appetite, whereby he has less pain; A. for bacon; desire for wine and coffee; A. disturbed at dinner; A. diminished; does not relish the first morsels; *A. lost;* lost, as from too much mucus in throat. Aversion to meat. Thirst; in forenoon; in evening; during chill; for fresh water; lost, next day great desire to drink, without dryness of mouth or really excessive thirst.

Eructations; from drinking cold water; hiccough-like; in two paroxysms, first a shock, then hiccough-like forcing out of gas; *empty;* empty, with burning and anxious sweat; with clean taste of food and drink; sour and scraping, tasting of meat; sour, rancid, < supper, with pressure in stomach; of acrid fluid; of liquids, which do not reach the mouth; ineffectual efforts to eructate. Violent hiccough.

Nausea; in morning after eating, < fat; in afternoon, > eating; frequently in afternoon; on waking at night; when walking, with heat in forehead; < walking, with intoxicated sensation; < in house; > motion, with retching and eructations of water; *in throat; in throat,* > eating; with general shivering and salivation; shuddering.

Vomiting; *of beer* (**which tastes bitter**); bloody; easy, *of green bitter mucus,* with confusion of head and throbbing pain in r. frontal eminence; violent.

Twitching of muscles of pit and vicinity. Inflammation. Contraction. Sticking after dinner, with pain in chest. *Pain; in pit; epigastric region;* at noon after cooked food; *in pit in evening, worse by paroxysms; at night;* after eating, then sensation of undigested food; in S. and chest after eating; and in intestines, with stinging burning in skin, restlessness, loss of appetite, fever and irregular action of tendons; as if arteries were beating against abdominal muscles as far as præcordial region; tensive and spasmodic, < before eating; pulling tensive P. in pit on inspiration as if a part of diaphragm were adherent.

Burning; in pit (Ars., Merc. c.); *in pit on pressure, with pain; B. pressure extending transversely at intervals, < pressure.* Anxiety in pit, then diarrhœa. Apprehension in pit as if expecting something disagreeable. Feeling as if S. and intestines were empty and swashed about on walking in morning after sufficient breakfast. Sensation of too long fasting, and S. hangs down; S. as after long fasting, in S. and lower part of pharynx, without longing for food, > eating. Fulness, with pressure after eating. Satiety after a light breakfast, with sensation as if undigested food lay in it, with uneasiness in abdomen, depression and indifference. Disordered by eating too much or fat.

Clinical.—Symptoms of gastric ulcer, with burning and great uneasiness in stomach, temporarily > eating, hence constant desire to eat (Iod.). Many cases of ulcers in the stomach, one of which was supposed to be malignant and incurable, have been cured or greatly relieved by this drug, always with extreme burning and distress as if the whole stomach were raw, at times with vomiting of blood, in one case associated with diarrhœa, passing quantities of blood from the bowels.

Abdomen.—Hardness; at night, with tension and pressure, < every position except lying on back, with distress for breath and rapid pulse. Distention; tympanitic, after vomiting and purging; painful, in evening, with short, anxious respiration so that he must loosen the clothes, eructations, rumbling, difficult loud emission of flatus, chilliness, shivering and yawning. Sunken, so that sternum stood out prominently when lying. *Rumbling, with noises;* R. during and after eating. Painful movings as before diarrhœa. Inflammation of intestines. Flatulence. Emissions of flatus; after pain in small intestines; with soft stool; *loud; short and interrupted; short, offensive,* < *before stool;* offensive.

Tearing. Cutting towards evening; C. and twisting. Twisting before copious pasty stool, then colic and pressure in anus as if more would follow. Griping; < about umbilicus, with drawing; spasmodic G., with sticking low down in A., starting from middle of A., at times extending into l. side, with hard tension of A., transiently > emission of flatus, with weakness, < lower limbs, with paroxysms of aggravation.

Pain; from taking cold in night under light covers, at last preceded by chilliness in abdomen, with offensive stool, at first pasty, nodular and brown, then thin, trickling, with dragging in rectum; waking him at night after vivid dreams, with anxiety as if A. would become rigid, hard and adhere to chest, though there is moving about in it as of flatus that frees itself; on walking in open air after eating, then sweat and deathly anxiety, > eructations; > rising and stretching; with anxiety; with drawing in upper part of femur and in nates; in bed, as from cold, wet weather; as if intestines were seized one by one and constricted. Compression and weight in it. Heaviness, with anxiety. Sensation of diarrhœa extending to rectum, then creeping shivering over whole body. *Burning* (Ars., *etc.*).

Stitches in region of l. short ribs. Pain in region of spleen, < deep inspiration, at times more posteriorly in region of false ribs; beneath l. ribs, as from incarcerated flatus, < pressure, > eructations; in r. side of A. as if a piece of intestine were incarcerated, after dinner. Griping flatulence becomes incarcerated in sides.

Griping in upper. Tearing stitches in r. half of upper, then pressure. Pressure over upper, with tension. Sensation as if bubbles formed in upper. Twisting about umbilicus, with nausea and sensation as if water would rise, or like a faintness. Twisting griping in umbilical region, > emission of flatus. Cutting below umbilical region.

Hypogastrium.—Sticking, < just above penis; in r. inguinal region, then tearing; in l. side, < pressure and walking; extending to ilium; outward in r. flank; above crest of l. ilium, more towards back, taking away breath; in r. half, and in upper part of r. thigh, with tearing. Pain extending towards abdominal ring; sudden P. in l. groin like pressure upon a sore spot, < expiration and bending over. Pressing asunder in r. inguinal ring on urinating, > bending up knee, returning on becoming erect. Drawing pain in inguinal glands.

Rectum.—*Stitches.* Drawing pain, and in anus. Urging, then scanty, soft, difficult stool, then soreness in rectum.

Anus.—Constricted around the protruded rectum, which is then incarcerated, sore and painful to touch. Sticking; and drawing extending upward. Pinching in evening, and in l. side near anus, in lower limbs and on scrotum. *Biting sore pain on walking, and burning in rectum.* Pain, and in anterior part of anus. Tenesmus, and in perineum, extending through urethra, with tearing and drawing. Crawling before and after stool. Itching; *in region during day and evening before sleep;* like tenesmus.

Stool.—*Diarrhœa; constant, with pain in abdomen.* Thin, with discharge of thin blood; T. and at times frequent, afterwards hard and infrequent; T., frequent, preceded by pain in umbilical region and straining. Soft, copious, offensive; S., copious, fermented, undigested, brown, passing into yellowish-gray, of sour odor, delayed; S., brown, of sour odor, very early in morning; S., grayish and black, with rumbling in abdomen during and after stool, which was the second one; S. and scanty; S., small and frequent. Pasty, copious, at short intervals, after urging, then tenesmus in anus, as in diarrhœa; P., thick, smeary, preceded by sudden pressure and followed by biting in anus.

Constipation. Hard, slow, with pressure; H., copious, brown, nodular; the second one H., unsatisfactory; H. in morning at short intervals and after long sitting, and after eating other pasty S. at short intervals, and in evening repeated urging, > emission of flatus, at last a small, urgent stool, that was first natural and then pasty. *Brown fæces, containing white, shining grains;* yellowish brown, streaked with blood; dark B., nodular, with pressure, but without much pain, for the first time in three days and a half; dark, nodular, not very hard, with pressure. Clay-colored, scanty. Pituitous, almost uninterrupted, mixed with blood and causing excruciating pain. Fermented, in part dark, in part yellowish, with undigested parts and offensive. Speedy, then great relief. Scanty, tenacious; S., frequent. Unsatisfactory, with bright blood. Discharge of bright blood during and after stool; without pain or straining.

Clinical.—Chronic diarrhœa in a patient who was subject to eruptions on the skin similar to those of Mez., stools watery, with painful tenesmus, which sometimes involved the urethra. Diarrhœa of sour, undigested stools, sometimes with much colic, stools followed by chilliness. Constipation, with dark brown, very hard stools, at times with prolapsus.

Urinary Organs.—Pinching in bladder. Urging; in morning; frequent. Frequent micturition; in forenoon, of much watery urine; even at night, of pale urine. Micturition towards morning; only once or twice a day and urine pale; delayed; indolent in morning, after rising.

Urethra.—*Discharge of a few drops of blood after micturition;* tenacious, transparent liquid in forenoon before micturition; of mucus; watery mucus on moving about. (Blennorrhœa, dark inflammation of inner surface of prepuce, with itching, without swelling and with sore sensation in evening and tearing and drawing in glans.) Sticking in orifice, with frequent desire to urinate. Sticking crawling pain, with emission of fluid. Cutting in orifice; after micturition; C. in forepart after micturition. Drawing; and cutting-drawing pain in forepart and in neck of bladder, when walking in open air. *Sore pain sometimes on touch, sometimes when urinating.* Itching soreness, < pressure. Sticking itching in evening. *Biting burning in forepart at close of micturition* (during stool).

Urine.—Red. Dark. Dark wine-yellow, becoming turbid after an hour, later floating flocculi and reddish sediment. *Bloody. Hot, with reddish sediment. Burning.* Copious, pale. Scanty; in morning; in morning, and dark, hot, of strong odor; in morning, with increased thirst.

Clinical.—Gleet, with watery discharge, soreness and burning in the urethra, particularly in its anterior part, sometimes with hæmaturia.

Sexual Organs.—Penis. Swelling, with warmth. Sticking jerking on back. *Stitches, and in tip.* Tearing and jerking tearing; jerking T. in P., with wavelike pain above, in r. side of abdomen. Acute pain; (pain in forepart). Burning in region when urinating; in region of forepart when urinating. *Itching;* internally on prepuce in evening; on inner surface of prepuce after urinating. Frequent erections during the day; violent E. in evening, with yawning and sleepiness.

Swelling of l. side of scrotum. Stitch on r. side of scrotum. Testicles painful to pressure. Drawing pain in spermatic cords. Excitement after an emission, with crawling over whole body, as from lasciviousness.

Mucous discharge from vagina. Leucorrhœa like white of an egg. Menses too frequent and lasting too long.

Clinical.—Obstinate ulceration of the vagina and cervix, with albuminous leucorrhœa.

Respiratory Organs.—Tightness of larynx and on deep inspiration he hears and feels air pass through larynx. Tickling in larynx as with a feather, causing cough. *Hoarseness; with cough and rawness in chest;* as far down as pit of throat. Voice rough and husky. Voice trembling. Inflammation of trachea, with burning pain between hyoid bone and thyroid cartilage, > eating. Pain in trachea in morning. T. feels closed when breathing.

Cough.—Only between 6 and 7 A.M.; nightly, < after midnight; after walking; interrupting sleep; *after eating, till he vomits* sour or bitter food; from irritation low down in chest, > vomiting and discharge of watery saliva; with retching and scratching, or scraping in pit of throat as if something sweet there could not be coughed up; in afternoon and night, with bloody expectoration, restless sleep and heavy, frightful dreams. *Violent in evening in bed and in morning, from irritation lower in trachea than can be reached by the cough;* V., uninterrupted, causing vomiting. Dry; at night; day and night, with emaciation, tensive pains across chest and weakness; in afternoon and towards evening, with retching and vomiting; with scraping in lower part of sternum and sticking in r. frontal eminence; with soreness beneath sternum and headache, then expectoration of mucus; D. and short day and night from tickling in larynx, one day when the cough was more frequent the symptoms in limbs were less frequent.

Expectoration of mucus; bloody E. in morning.

Respiration.—Whistling in nose during inspiration. Dyspnœa; paroxysmal, as from weight on chest. Tight because chest seems constricted from both sides. Lost on stooping forward when his mouth was full of water; L. in the middle of his speech and he must begin again. Slow; and suffocative. Short, difficult. Full, uneasy. Inclined to take a deep breath.

Chest.—Rattling on breathing, then constant inclination to cough and sore pain on coughing anything loose. Exhalation from lungs offensive like bad cheese. Twitching by r. lower ribs in evening, then on lower part of r. scapula; painful T. like electric shocks in l. side. Contraction at times of diaphragm beneath ribs.

Sticking; in clavicle; beneath l. breast; in lung back of heart; between ribs beneath l. axilla; in r.; deep in, on laughing; on inspiration; in pectoral muscles and beneath l. short ribs, near spine, on inspiration; beneath heart on deep breathing; in r. side, < breathing; in region of last r. ribs, < deep breathing; in intercostal muscles near heart, < coughing and sneezing, and < evening on falling asleep and in morning after waking; beneath l. breast, extending out between shoulders, < inspiration; shooting to r. side after coughing; outward, suddenly in r. mamma; intermittent, < r. side, impeding respiration; rhythmical, below l. clavicle, extending deep into chest, then aching, < every inspiration.

Tearing transversely across forepart; T. in r. clavicle and in neighboring parts of neck. Sharp pain in a spot in anterior wall of chest and region of heart. Cramplike pressure on both sides of sternum when sitting. Pain in r.; l.; in a spot in r., then l.; in region of l. nipple; in lung, in region of l. fourth rib, in evening; in r. pectoral and dorsal muscles in evening; on coughing anything loose; in middle on stooping; in middle extending to throat, on holding head up; in sides on deep inspiration, as if lungs were adherent and could not be freely distended. Soreness. Rawness and scraping in C. and throat on coughing and breathing, it seems as if something would be loosened, but it is not, with constant inclination to cough. Anxiety.

Constriction; transversely across forepart, with and alternating with the same sensation across region of scapulæ; in back part on becoming erect, < deep inspiration and then extending through lower part of chest, the pain > bending forward, but is like rheumatism on moving arms, while bending far backward. Oppression; with palpitation; < about heart, with anxiety and with deep and frequent respiration; as from heart, with long, deep respiration. Tightness; in C. and trachea on inspiration; in region of fourth and fifth ribs on deep inspiration; on stooping and when sitting, necessity to loosen clothes, respiration slow and short; > becoming erect, standing and towards evening, < sitting and after supper. Tension in various parts; T. in pectoral muscles on stretching arms.

Sore burning in a spot on r. side of sternum, near pit of stomach; intermittent burning behind ensiform cartilage; sudden B. pain between mammæ. Weakness in region of l. fourth and fifth ribs, about four inches from sternum, where the bloody expectoration comes from (it only occurs from special cause, drugs, taking cold, etc.).

Clinical.—Intercostal neuralgia, especially after herpes, always < night and heat.

Heart.—Rubbing sound in præcordial region, > moving about, < evening after lying down, lying on l. side and deep breathing, with sensation as if chest were too tight, heaviness and impediment in region of heart. Cramps. Apprehension, with uneasiness. Action accelerated. Irregular beating when sitting and afterwards at night when waking on back.

Pulse.—Rapid in forenoon; towards evening, with heat and excitement; in evening; after eating, with feeling as if heart were beating near stomach on l. side, twitching of eyelids, unusually distinct vision, sensation as if he were looking through concave glasses and swimming before eyes; and full; and irregular, hard; and feeble. Feverish. Slow; and compressible, intermittent. *Hard; and intermittent, full, tense.*

Neck.—Tearing jerkings on l. side. Tearing on l. side extending into ear and near clavicle. Pain extending from nape to forehead. *Stiff pain in nape and external cervical muscles* (Dulc.); *in r. side of N. and throat, < motion.*

Back.—Sticking from l. side through chest, on inspiration; sudden S. near spine extending through chest into l. costal cartilage anteriorly, in evening. Tearing in l. side in morning. Pain in l. side. Tensive constriction extending down to small of back.

Scapulæ.—Sticking < afternoon; S. near r. impeding respiration, < motion; burning, below l., with jerkings; drawing between, extending downward, > moving the part. Tearing on r.; in tip of l. Boring in dorsal vertebræ; when sitting. Acute pain beneath l. shoulder in evening. Pain in r.; beneath angle of l.; in dorsal muscles; in dorsal and lumbar muscles. *Rheumatic pain in l. in morning after rising; R. pain in muscles like tension and as if swollen, making motion difficult;* tensive R. pain on r. Rheumatism of l. scapula and nape, < turning to opposite side. Pulsating pain near middle of spine. Drawing pain beneath l.; D. pain in dorsal muscles. Drawing in l.; D. in dorsal muscles. Pressure on S.

Lumbar Region.—Sticking in outer part of r. side of vertebræ, < motion; S. in kidney and pain as if torn. Tearing in muscles; cutting T. low down on both sides. Pain in r. side; P. < walking; extending to all parts of body; drawing P. near l. side; drawing P. in muscles. Drawing in muscles.

Extremities.—*Trembling.* Joints unsteady, as if they would give way. Tearing on tibia, in fingers and toes; drawing T. outward below r. knee, in metacarpal bone of l. thumb, last phalanx of r. fourth finger, also in r. wrist at articulation of metacarpal bone of index as if it had been injured by grasping something. Boring in wrists, ankles and r. shoulder, < during rest; in knees, toes and forearms, with drawing pains.

Pain in wrists and ankles; *in periosteum of long bones, < tibiæ, < night and in bed, with intolerance of touch.* Pain in all joints as if beaten and weary. Drawing pain in muscles; in various places in soft parts; in places, < bones of feet, hands and fingers; in shoulders and knees; paralytic, on various places of hands and lower limbs. Drawing in flesh of limbs, fingers and toes; in joints, < knees, ankles and wrist, with weariness; in joints, with bruised sensation, often with pressure and boring when sitting; *in long bones, with tearing in them and with chilliness, shivering and sensitiveness to external air;* in all joints as if dislocated. Weakness. Heaviness on motion; H. and dread of motion, cannot make up his mind to anything; H. and bruised sensation, as in suppressed catarrh. Hands and feet fall asleep.

Clinical.—Periosteal inflammation of the long bones, particularly of the tibia, with violent burning pains at night, soreness and swelling of the periosteum. Periostitis of the femur, with great sensitiveness to pressure and burning pain extending into the knee, the parts become erysipelatous and threaten to suppurate.

Upper Extremities.—*Sore sensation in r. axilla.*

Shoulder.—Cracking in l. joint in evening in bed on raising arm, with paralyzed feeling in upper arm and tearing in elbow on bending it. Burning stitches on r. *Tearing; as if it would be torn asunder* in evening, < motion, with throbbing and burrowing. Boring; in joint; in morning in bed; in l. when walking, and in wrist; in l., < rest, > motion; in lower side of r. joint, with pinching. Sprained pain where r. scapula unites with clavicle, on moving arm. Bruised pain, and in upper arms. Pain; on margin of joint; *in r. joint;* in l. at night; in r. joint, < rest; in joint as if head of humerus were too large for capsule; burning, on r. in evening, then on l. behind acromion; as if he had carried a weight, with jerking; paralytic, in r. joint, with pain in bones of shoulder. Painful paralytic pressure on r. acromion in evening when sitting quietly, < letting arm hang down. Drawing. Tension in r., with drawing in l. Burning in r. acromion in afternoon.

Arm.—Tearing jerks in r. A. and fingers. Tearing; as if in bones. Bruised feeling. L. felt out of joint, almost as if paralyzed. Drawing. Weakness when writing. Weary pains, < shoulder-joints.

Upper Arm.—Jerking in l., < touch. Intermittent sticking in l. humerus. Tearing in muscles of l. Pain in lower part. Bruised pain on touch; B. pain, with heaviness and drawing downward in bones. Paralytic pain in l., extending into elbow, < bending arm outward. Drawing.

Elbow.—Tearing; in r.; and in forearm. Boring in l. Pressure in r., < rest, transiently > motion, with drawing. Pressive drawing, extending to fingers. Rheumatic drawing and tension in region of r. Tensive paralytic sensation on raising arm, and sticking on straightening it out.

Forearm.—Tearing in l. ulna; in l. forearm and fingers in morning, with sticking; drawing T. close to wrist. Boring and drawing. Pain in lower part of l.; in periosteum of r. radius, < pressure; in r., with drawing; in ulna by elbow, as from a blow; drawing P. in soft parts. Constriction in muscles during and after a walk in open air.

Wrist.—Tearing in l.; drawing T. in r. Boring. Pain in l.; in r. and finger-joints, with drawing; paralytic, in r. W. and arm, as from dislocation, < muscles, only on motion. Burning pain in bones of l. in morning after rising. Drawing pains; in l. Drawing. Paralytic sensation in r. Weakness.

Hand.—Veins distended in afternoon and evening, skin soft and pliant. Swelling, with crawling, as if asleep; S. of hand and arm, with heat, jerks and prickings; S. of back, with bruised pain in metacarpal bones and little finger. Trembling; towards evening; of r., with weakness of tips of fingers. Jerking stitches on back between metacarpal bones of two fingers; slow, jerking S. in l. Tearing on back of l. and between knuckles; wavelike T. in back of l. Boring in l. palm. Pain causing weakness, with swollen feeling; paralytic and pressive P. in r. bones. Weakness, < *when writing.* Dead on waking from afternoon nap.

Fingers.—Intermittent jerking and grumbling in bones. Stitches in tip of thumb, > taking hold of something. Tearing; in l. index in evening in bed; on inner margin of l. index and middle, with biting burning. Cutting in flesh on anterior surface of last phalanx of r. thumb. Boring; and in joints; tearing, in third phalanx of r. middle. Pain; sore, beneath r. thumb-nail, < pressure; drawing P. Drawing.

Paralytic pains in bones of thumbs, extending forward. *Paralysis of flexors.*

Lower Extremities.—Pain in evening, with coldness and falling asleep. Uneasiness in r. in evening in bed. Weakness; with uneasiness. Tearing in r. nates. Tearing above and on r. hip, with tensive pressure. Boring in hip-joints; r.; in l. trochanter. *Jerking pain in hip-joint,* extending to knee. Sprained pain in region of r. trochanter major when walking.

Thigh.—Movable hardish swelling above l. knee. Cracking in r. in evening when walking after sitting. Jerking in lower part and on l. patella when standing; J. in l. as if bubbles of air were forming. Sticking in flesh, with burning. Tearing, and in tibiæ; T. in thin part of r.; in r., and drawing in middle of l.; above r. knee when walking, then above l.; paralytic, high up on outer part when standing. Boring. Sharp pain externally above l. knee, > pressure, but immediately appearing on inner malleolus. *Pain in bones of T. and legs;* in muscles; in gluteals in morning in bed; in muscles of l. extending into knee. *Sudden sprained pain below r. nates when walking.* Bruised pain on inner side when walking rapidly; B. pain above knees, < ascending steps and walking on a level. Burning sore pain posteriorly on r. as from a fresh bruise. Boring drawing pain in joints of T. and ankles; wave-like drawing pain extending down whole T., then painful weakness. Drawing in muscles and skin. Tension in l. T. and knee as if he had walked too much; rheumatic T. and drawing above knees and in legs.

Knee.—*Jerking in l.* when sitting. Cracking in r. in evening when walking after sitting. Sudden stitch in r., then aching. Tearing; in l.; in r. popliteus extending into thigh. Boring; when sitting. Sudden sharp pain between articular surfaces of l. in morning on getting into a cold bath. Pressure; when sitting; during rest. Sprained pain in l. in evening, < inner side. Bruised pain in outer and anterior part of r.; in hollow of r., every motion is painful, < sitting; sudden B. pain. Drawing pains in K. and legs when sitting, with fatigue; boring D. pains in K. Rheumatic pain in r. on stepping in morning after rising, then sticking in r. foot, back of third and fourth toes, then in l. metatarsus. Weakness; when sitting; of r. (perhaps also of hip) after rising, so that he could not use r. leg in walking. Stiffness of tendons of l. popliteus.

Leg.—Swelling of l. in evening; S. from long standing, < towards evening; of l., which was somewhat varicose; hard S. of calf on walking in open air, with burning pain. Jerking in lower part of calf, with drawing; J. in middle of tibia, with painful drawing; of whole r., towards inner side, a pulling and twisting, at 3 P.M. when sitting and writing; slow, in lower part of l. tibia; sticking, on upper part of l. tibia when sitting with knee bent. Slow jerking stitches in r. tibia. Tearing; in l. tibia; in calves; above malleolus; frequent, in tibiæ; paralytic, in lower part of tibia in evening in bed. Boring in calves; above ankle; in tibiæ, < l.; in l. tibia at night on waking; in tibiæ, < l., even when walking. Pinching in lower part of r. tibia. Pain above ankles; below l. knee in evening when standing and walking; in tibia when walking; *frequently in r. tibia;* in tibia on every step, as if broken in middle. *Pain in tibia as if beaten or as if periosteum would be torn off after midnight, disturbing sleep, with general chill and thirst.* Sprained pain below l. patella in evening when walking. Drawing; in calves; when standing; jerking, in calf; rheumatic, in lower part of r., extending into ankle. **Burning in l. tibia** (see Zinc.). Weakness; when walking. Falling asleep of leg and foot.

Ankle.—Twitching about r. external malleolus. Tearing. Boring; < l.; in bones of l. A. and toes; in malleoli and bones of feet; in A. and bones of feet when walking. Pain in l.; about l. external malleolus, > rest; bruised P. during rest; cramplike and dislocating P. around l. external malleolus. Weakness when running, with pain as if they would break; paralytic W. of outer side when walking in open air.

Foot.—Sticking in r. in afternoon, < toes; (and crawling). Tearing on back of r.; in both heels and r. tendo-achillis; in r. side of l., extending towards sole and heel. Boring in back; in bones; in r. sole. Pain in r.; *P. in bones;* in process of r. os calcis; *in bones of instep, < walking;* in r. metatarsus on stepping after a nap over his work from 10 till 11 P.M., from which he woke senseless, with rapid pulse. Intermittent burning pain on r. Drawing pain in r. sole when stepping on it. Painful stretching beneath l. inner malleolus, extending into sole. Falling asleep.

Toes.—Twitching in knuckle of r. great, like muscular jerking or like bursting of bubbles; painful T. in great in morning in bed. Sticking in tip of l. great; in tips of l. when sitting; rhythmical burning-prickling, in tip of l. great. Tearing; in r.; l. middle; in last phalanx of l. great and in r. side of l. sole; *in ball of l. little,* extending to sole. Boring in l. Pain in bones; P. in r. great like a dislocation; as from pressure of hard boots, even when walking but little. Sprained pain in l. great, when walking, with coldness of feet. Bruised pain in tip of l. middle, sometimes a grumbling. Sore pain between T., epidermis became whitish and shrivelled. Drawing; in l., with pressure; tearing D. through r. great.

Skin.—*Usual liver-spots on chest and arms became very dark, with desquamation.* Roughness, with desquamation here and there. Suggillation on back of r. hand, above index, with itching, < wrist. *Itching rash on nape; and back and thighs, worse and gnawing after scratching, with sticking; red, itching R. on arms, head and over whole body,* partly in spots. Brownish rash on chest and arms. Eruptions like flea-bites on chest, the burning lasts longer than the spots; E. like flea-bites over whole body, becoming scurfy on head. Itching elevations on forearms, becoming hard after scratching. Blotches over whole body. Desquamation; of whole skin.

Inflammation of a fresh wound (on knee), with burning and with intermittent stitches extending into legs; I. of knuckles of l. foot extending over calf and instep and hard tubercles in cellular tissue, which itch on touch, then burning pain. Swelling of face, < nose, eyelids and scalp, with burning pains and with severe and painful sneezing, deliria, pain in forehead, nauseous dryness in throat, irritation to dry cough, face soon took on the expression of erysipelas bullosum, nostrils closed, so that she could breathe only through mouth, febrile pulse, burning urine, afterwards desquamation in large pieces. Pimples on chest; lower limbs, with sticking on touch; red, on forehead, itching at times; smooth red, on r. side of neck, sore to touch, becoming flat under skin; on l.

lower part of chin, became a painful boil, with thin, oily discharge.

Pustules in beard on lower part of l. side of chin; like millet-seeds, on forehead at margin of hair; burning, red, rash-like on thighs; red, on outer part of arms and lower limbs, with tickling burning only on undressing. Boils on face; l. arm. *Ulcers on bony protuberances;* papular ulcerating eruption on finger-joints, itching < evening; **U. covered with thick whitish-yellow scabs, under which thick yellow pus collects**; with red, shining areola; with burning pain in evening in bed; linen or charpie sticks to U., and when it is torn away they bleed; throbbing around U., with red areola and burning pain; drawing pain in U., with sticking on its margin; itching about U., with redness; itching about U., with pain on touch.

Itching and burning vesicles around the ulcers, *the V. dry, leave scabs, the tearing off of which causes great pain and retards the healing; burning V., with red areola, on sides of fingers,* in skin, they dry and leave red spots or epidermis desquamates in round scales; V. full of clear serum on back of nose, inflamed skin beneath the ruptured vesicle, then a brown scab; heat V. on ball of r. hand. *Ichor from scratched face excoriates other parts.* Pale red eruption, itching after scratching, scabs adherent and depressed in middle. Scabs scratched from nose and cheeks, but others formed in their places; *honey-like S. around mouth; white, elevated, over whole body;* on hard bases, surrounded by dark redness, between glutei.

Sticking in l. side of forehead; in l. palm and tips of fingers; in scar on tip of r. middle finger, in which there had been no feeling for two years; in evening, in a previously existing ulcer; here and there, at times itching, < evening in bed; in axilla, < scratching, with biting. Sticking and burning in axilla; on outer aspect of r. shoulder; on inner side of l. upper arm; in r. cheek and on back of nose, where it was associated with boring. Burning stinging in various parts; on l. scapula and shoulder; now in r. arm, now in lower extremity. Stinging burning. Much pain in a slight cut. Gnawing in a bruised wound, with throbbing. Sensation of a cobweb or draught of cold air, in beard on l. side of face. Crawling in foot; in great toes every night, once in fingers as if starting from surface of bones.

Itching over whole body; in brows; in beard of l. side; posteriorly on margin of lower jaw; on backs of hands, < r.; hollow of r. knee; legs; in a wound, even after it is closed; in hollows of knees and vicinity in evening; in evening, < scrotum and in nares; here and there in evening, with heat; of legs, waking at night, with pain after scratching; < towards evening, changing to another place after scratching; now here, now there, > scratching, at times burning I. or tickling on chin, shoulder, clavicle, r. chest, along lower ribs and back, the later the I. began the greater the inclination to scratch; on inner side of calf, not > till it is scratched bloody, then burning, afterwards swelling of calf and a bloody scab, beneath which there was yellowish matter, with bruised pain; *on head and over whole body, recurring in another place after scratching;* on inner side of calves, with smarting after scratching; on small of back, chest, throat and neck, with sore pain and soreness after scratching; as from fleas in spots, < evening, > night. Burning itching on nape and calves; inner side of r. thigh, and on scrotum; posteriorly on lobule of ear, with tension, and on scratching desquamation in scales; of arms and legs, and on scratching sticking. **The child scratches its face continually, it becomes covered with blood, and the bed is covered with blood in morning, face covered with a scab, which the child constantly tears off, and on the spots thus left raw, large ("fat") pustules form.** *Itching behind ears,* after scratching pimples that are scratched sore and painful; I. on scapulæ and r. nates, then elevations, with biting pain on touch, soon opening on rubbing and discharging blood; posterior surfaces of wrists, in region of radius, are scratched sore, then dry, superficial dark brown scabs; I. on wrists, then after scratching superficial dark brown scabs, these at last became white, scaly and conical, the ulcers when healed were brownish and had brownish areola. Skin (compare Rhus t. and Ars.).

Clinical.—The eruptions are herpetic or eczematous, as a rule; they often ulcerate and form thick scabs, from under which purulent matter exudes, this occurs particularly on the head; the itching of the eruptions of Mez. is intolerable, < scratching, associated with burning, < night and heat (Ars., Sulph.). In eczema it is particularly to be compared with Rhus tox., though the tendency of Mez. is to the formation of more purulent matter, that of Rhus more serous; in both drugs the itching is worse at night in the warmth of the bed, and frequently numerous small pimples appear around the main eruptions. Eczema on the backs of the hands and wrists. Eczema impetiginoides on the whole face from one ear to the other, with yellow-brown scabs a quarter of a inch thick, which at times crack open, bleed and ooze offensive matter. In herpes zoster extremely valuable even for the after-pains. Pustules on the chin, forming scabs. Abscess on antrum of Highmore, with intolerable burning pain at night, extending to the bones of face and head. Psoriasis of the palms. Copper-colored spots on thighs and body, syphilitic. On the leg, varicose ulcers surrounded by bluish-red discoloration, the slightest pressure causes the most intense burning pain. A horny growth on the middle of the forehead. Vesicular eruption on the back of the nose, forming a scab and oozing matter. Pruritus of old people, temporarily > wine and coffee; in one case the itching always < night, always involving those parts of the skin which were the most shrivelled, neck, abdomen, arms, legs and face, with sensation as if a thousand insects were crawling over him, and when the itching was most intense he had shuddering in the back and extremities.

Sleep.—*Yawning and stretching;* in forenoon; Y. in morning. Sleepiness; *during the day;* in evening; in evening, with yawning; in evening after three glasses of hock, with dulness of head; early in evening, eyes closed when at work and r. leg jerked; after supper; when sitting and reading; fell asleep in evening when reading. *Irresistible sleepiness;* after dinner, with painful pressure in eyes and inflammation of conjunctiva of lids. Long sleep.

Sleeplessness till 3 A.M. Falls asleep late and wakes before midnight with diminished sensibility in all limbs, even in penis and abdomen. Difficult falling asleep in evening and sleep at night longer than usual; D. falling asleep and frequent waking with pain in bones, < l. wrist and knees. Frequent waking; with erections and sexual excitement; after midnight till towards morning, he then lay upon back, with open mouth, dry tongue, tensive pain and heaviness in occiput; till after midnight on account of flow of ideas and chill. Woke at 2 A.M. and again at 5 A.M., with scanty, thin emission. Woke at 3 A.M., with heaviness in head and limbs, inability to sleep for a long time, then anxious dreams. Frequent starting up in sleep. Restless sleep, disturbed by anxious dreams; R. disturbed by confused dreams; and dreamy, disturbed by formication of fingers; R. and unrefreshing. Arose in morning satisfied with a little sleep.

Dreams.—Frightful. Nightmare after midnight and after waking falling asleep of limbs and weakness of hands. Vivid, with starting up as if falling from a height; V., then sleeplessness after 2 A.M. on account of irritability; and anxious before midnight, after midnight ludicrous; and unremembered. Unremembered. Remembered, towards morning. Varied, uneasy, with confused memory. That his back was covered with warts and excrescences. Voluptuous, and sensation as if he had had an emission.

Fever.—*Chill;* in morning; in forenoon, with cold hands and feet and rapid pulse, skin, at least of hands, dead and shrivelled, as if they had been cold a long time and as if they would desquamate; in evening; out of bed, heat in bed; on motion; > open air, with fretfulness, suffering as before a severe illness, some appetite, but discomfort after slightest food; with sleepiness; with thirst for cold water; with cold hands, dryness of mouth posteriorly and salivation anteriorly, without desire for drinks; with asthmatic constriction and oppression of chest. Internal. *External, with thirst, without longing for warmth nor dread of open air.* As if repeatedly dashed with cold water, < arms, abdomen, hips and feet, with yawning, lachrymation and perfect warmth of face and hands. Creeping, on both sides of upper arms, over back and feet, with yawning.

Shaking chill. Shivering; at 9 A.M., with cold hands; in forenoon; in evening; general, in evening, also in different parts, down l. leg; in sleep, so that he bit his tongue; after stool; before and after stool, with prostration and sensitiveness to open air; with gooseflesh and cold hands and feet. Creeping shivering, with yawning and heat; C. shivering, < back and down lower extremities, in evening, with internal heat. Shivering in back, chest and upper abdomen; over back and arms; over back at 8.30 A.M., with cold hands. Coldness of back; limbs; arms and legs; hands; hands and feet; hands at 4.30 P.M.; hollow of l. knee in afternoon; foot in afternoon, it frequently falls asleep; feet, > in bed; r. hand when writing; over abdomen and arms, with dilated pupils; feet and legs to above knees, with heat of hands and rapid pulse; externally in arms and legs; creeping on both sides of upper arms, over back and feet, with yawning.

Heat; towards evening; in evening in house, with sweat on face; in evening, with sweat. Burning in l. cheek; r. cheek; hand and arm; l. palm; l. calf; r. shoulder, with pulsation; in spots about external condyles of wrists after working in cold water; ball of l. foot, more when standing than walking, with stitches; of scalp, with necessity to scratch it. Burning in skin; in different parts; forehead; r. temple, extending to cheek; cheek; r. cheek and in tip and septum of nose; nose, with burning on dorsum of nose and extending across tip and towards wings; nape; inner-surface of upper arm; nates; various parts of leg; l. calf; r. tibia. Typhoid fever, then weakness and finally death from hectic fever.

Sweat; at night. Cold; on forehead; feet, when sitting in a warm room; on legs, then general heat, < head.

Millefolium.

A tincture is made of the fresh plant of Achillea Millefolium, L. (Yarrow).

Allies.—Erigeron, Arnica, Carbo veg.

Generalities.—Stretching in forenoon, then comfortable feeling. **Hæmorrhage.** *Congestion to head, face, lungs, heart, etc.* Slow stitches or throbbing pains always near bones and not far from joints, < l. side and < hands and feet. Oppression and uneasiness. Aversion to work. Desire to do nothing, without feeling sick. (Amelioration from a glass of wine.)

Clinical.—Hæmorrhages, with profuse flow of bright red blood, which is thin; bleeding piles; hæmorrhage, with chilliness; bright red hæmorrhages from uterus; bright red hæmoptysis, with oppression, palpitation, not much cough, especially during the progress of tuberculosis, raised without cough; the hæmorrhage is only distinguished from that of Aconite by the absence of anxiety. Painful varicose veins during pregnancy.

Mind.—Violent and irritable about everything that happened inopportunely after dinner and in evening, when he wished to rest. Stupefaction, vertigo and intoxication.

Head.—Sticking in brain. Aching all day, < occiput; A. on stooping; intermittent; paroxysmal, < evening; confused, towards noon; confused, towards evening, < occiput and extending towards l. shoulder. Dulness after eating. Confusion, < evening and after wine and coffee, it seems as if he had forgotten something, he does not know what he is doing or wishes to do. Fulness in afternoon after sound sleep. Beating of arteries, with rapid pulse; B. of arteries in H. and face, with rapid, full and strong pulse. Feeling as if all the blood mounted to it. Rush of blood in evening in bed; on stooping, > rising; caused by coffee, with pains here and there in limbs. Vertigo, even to falling to the right and backward, on every slight motion when walking, not on violent motion, with nausea, < stooping, > lying down.

Tearing in l. frontal eminence. Pain in l. side of forehead. Feeling of a band across F. on drawing up skin of forehead. Sticking in upper part of vertex. Pain in vertex. Sticking in side; in l. parietal bone, with a blow on r. side, then S. in same place; tearing S. in whole r. side. Tearing in upper part of r. parietal bone. Pain in r. side as if screwed in. Painful tension in upper part of r. parietal bone. Sticking in side of occiput. Pain in occiput on waking. Drawing in O. after eating. His long hair becomes entangled in spite of cutting it shorter.

Eyes.—Sticking in evening on reading, pressing inward as far as root of nose and sides of forehead. Lids agglutinated in morning. Jerking in l. upper lid, with tension. Crawling in l. inner canthus as from a fine feather. Hair of brows falls out. Vision as of a fog at a distance, not near to.

Ears.—Sticking in l.; inward lengthwise in r. Drawing pain in l., with feeling as if liquid were running from it. Crawling in l., > boring in with finger. Itching in r., not entirely > boring in with finger. Stopped sensation; after dinner and all the afternoon. Painful noise. Ringing in r. Sound of a bat in l., then when laughing sensation as if cold air passed out of ear.

Nose.—**Bleeding.**

Face.—Redness without internal heat. Frequent tearing in l. side extending to temples, in evening. Painful jerking in l. lower jaw. Tearing from r. articulation of jaw to vertex; T. in r. lower jaw, extending now towards ear, now into teeth. Pimple on inside of l. lower lip, with pressing and sore pain in evening, next morning a superficial ulcer still covered with white epithelium, slightly painful. Sticking in upper lip.

Mouth.—Toothache; in l. lower molars. Contractive sensation in forepart of tongue, with burning. Sticking in palate and sensation as if cut to pieces. Dryness.

Throat.—Shooting back and forth anteriorly on r. side of pharynx, extending backward, towards evening. Pain in l. side on swallowing. Soreness every day from 9 till 10 P.M.; S. during and after swallowing. Rawness.

Stomach.—Hunger increased. Thirst. Eructations; empty; empty after eating soup. Hiccough. Cramp extending towards anus, with sensation as if a liquid were in S. Gnawing and griping as from hunger. Pain in morning as from fasting. Pressure as from a plug. Fulness. Sensation as if coated with astringent earth. Burning, and in abdomen; B. extending into chest; B. on bending together, worse towards r. hypochondrium, where it became a drawing and burning pain.

Abdomen.—Flatulent distention in afternoon, with frequent emission of flatus. Rumbling and cutting, then two attacks of diarrhœa, with subsequent tenesmus. Offensive flatus; < afternoon and evening. Flatulent pain; P. as if flatus were incarcerated in a spot to left of umbilicus, then movement downward in abdomen without emission of flatus. Sticking in l. hypochondrium; in l. side when eating; in crest of l. ilium. Pinching in l. hypochondrium, then in both sides as far as heart, > rising from a seat, with anxiety. Indefinite sensation in l. hypochondrium, then in pit of stomach.

Stool.—Soft; then smarting. The whitish, grayish-green, soft S. became yellowish-brown and was repeated in afternoon, the next two days stool in forenoon instead of in afternoon, afterwards small, soft stools in forenoon instead of in afternoon, afterwards hard stool in morning. Frequent. Omitted two days.

Urinary and Sexual Organs.—Constant desire to urinate, urine copious. *Hæmaturia.* Urine dark. Abortion. Leucorrhœa. Menses sometimes too scanty, sometimes too profuse; M. suppressed if used too long for hæmorrhoidal flux.

Respiratory Organs.—Secretion of mucus in larynx.

Chest.—Sticking in r.; l.; r., beneath fourth rib; in lowest r. ribs; beneath l. arm, not affecting respiration; jerking, in l. false rib. Bruised sensation. Fulness.

Pulse.—Rapid; in evening in bed.

Back.—Frequent drawings. Sticking drawing pain beneath l. scapula when sitting. Sticking between scapulæ; in middle of l. S.; in l. S. during inspiration when standing, but after stretching and again bending body together sticking in r.; in small of back; in r. lumbar region near spine.

Upper Extremities.—Sticking in l. shoulder; towards forepart of l., with burning; in upper part of r. upper arm after 9 A.M. Pain in bones of l. arm. Frequent attacks as if l. arm would fall asleep; falling asleep of l. arm in forenoon, with prickling. Sticking externally in r. elbow, with burning; S. on inner surface of r. forearm, then itching, > scratching. Pain above l. wrist. Sticking on margin of r. hand, above little finger. Throbbing pain in metacarpal bones of l. index and thumb in evening. Suppurating pain, as if bruised, beneath r., then l. thumb-nail.

Lower Extremities.—Tearing in l. nates in forenoon, < walking, with tension. Pain in r. nates as if he had fallen upon it, in evening and next morning, < pressure and making tense the gluteal muscles, < insertion of gluteus major into sacrum. Pain above l. knee at 11 P.M. when sitting. Sticking in bend of l. knee. Tearing in r. knee. Sprained pain in tendons of hollow of r. knee. Tearing downward in r. tibia in afternoon when walking. Pain in r. tendo-achillis as after a blow or sprain, increasing and decreasing at intervals, > walking or ascending steps. Drawing in l. tibia; in legs when lying. Pain in r. external malleolus at 3 P.M., > evening. Pain in bones of r. foot. Intermittent throbbing pain in l. foot, in joints of last toes and in metatarsus. Crawling in forepart of r. foot as from falling asleep. Sensation in l. foot as if it would fall asleep, not > by rising. Falling asleep of r. when sitting, not > by rising after dinner.

Skin.—Constricted sensation in forehead. Raw sensation as from a coarse brush, on inner side of l. forearm. Itching on shoulders; on back, and itching pimples.

Sleep.—Yawning and stretching; Y. at noon when riding in open air; Y. < evening, without fatigue; Y. and sleepiness. Sleepiness and prolonged sleep. Sleepless till 3 A.M. Sleep interrupted and dreamy. Paroxysm when asleep at midnight as if a gust of wind raised him in bed (extending from chest to head, with feeling as if a storm howled through the head and out of r. upper part of head like a flame), therewith r. arm seemed paralyzed, then he thought in sleep that he was awake and dreaded another attack, but when it occurred, with redoubled violence and made him cry out, as he supposed, he woke.

Fever.—Heat, < face; in face as if blood rushed to head, even in eyes and nose feeling as if congested with blood. Burning on inner surface of r. little finger, with sensation of a flea-bite.

Morphinum.

Pure Morphine is triturated for use.

General Action.—See Opium.

Generalities.—Emaciation. Cachexia. Perfectly limber. Trembling; with crawling. Fell to the ground as if struck by lightning; suddenly falling back unconscious, can at first be awakened only by most energetic means, face sunken or deathly pale, nose pointed, pulse perceptible only at heart, or face is red, eyes shining, pulse 44 or 40, transient nausea and deathly sensation, then unconsciousness again, when raised up the head sinks forward on chest, this condition is repeated at short intervals in twenty-four hours, during which he is conscious or partly conscious, or he may die with symptoms of paralysis of brain.

Cramps of muscles. Twitching; of whole body; in arms, on head, and < face; muscles of face and limbs; of both sides of mouth, and arms bent and moved backward and forward convulsively; on touching skin, with cramps. Convulsions; of facial muscles, and she fell back as if dead, face blanched, pulse and respiration not to be perceived; tetanic. Partial opisthotonos; without unconsciousness, with convulsions of limbs and face, renewed by tickling or pressure on skin. Eclampsia.

Neuralgia; in various parts, forehead, occiput and stomach. Distinct interval of two or three minutes between paroxysms of pain and convulsions. Sensation as if flesh were trembling on the bones. Sore all over body in morning. Oppression. Drawing in muscles, with stiffness. Discomfort, with restlessness, depression, anxiety and paroxysms of cough. Agreeable sensation. Hyperæsthesia. Paræsthesia. Restlessness. *Weakness;* and apathy; mental and physical; of muscular system; of limbs, small of back, neck and joints; sudden, inability to stand up; pleasant. Could not get up in morning. Sudden collapse. Faintness; in morning, with dilated pupils; on rising suddenly from stool. Heaviness. Immobility. Phrenic and pneumogastric nerves narcotized. Reflex irritability increased; gone.

Mind.—Hallucinations. Delirium; so that three or four persons held her in bed, alternating with convulsions; similar to that from alcohol, but melancholy, that of alcohol is more joyous. Excitement; and partially incoherent talking. Incoherent speech. Lively and wide awake, uneasiness, unsteadiness and haste, and glistening of eyes. Rapid and pleasant flow of ideas. Alternating moods. Cried out in alarm. Tears and sobs. Terror. Starting up in fright if one approached him. Nervous, so that she sprang out of bed at the least movement in the room. Mute despair. Melancholy; so that he desired to commit suicide. Anxiety; and restlessness; and hallucinations and illusions of almost all organs of sense; but after cold coffee fancy roved through scenes of rapture and splendor, and I cannot determine whether I was asleep or not, then sound sleep, then lassitude. Ill humor. Some endure their troubles with resignation, they remain quietly in bed, scarcely speaking, a few are in a sopor, others have no rest, anxiously run about the room, howl and cry.

Activity, without control of the will, jumping rapidly from one subject to another. Dulness. Confusion. Impossible to fix mind. Have to stop in the middle of a sentence to think what word to say next, in morning after rising. Incapable of thought or of recognizing any one in the room. Memory lost. Stupefaction; bordering on faintness; approaching S., with occasional waking and fretting. Coma; from which he could be aroused for a short time by persistent shaking and loud talking. Unconsciousness. Similarity to cerebral paralysis, especially in motor symptoms, but from Morphine there is complete consciousness and memory and ability to concentrate the mind, unless there is mania.

Head.—Drawn backward. Rolling slowly. Shooting to head. Pain; after eating; on waking; on waking, > moving about; < reading and thinking; < r. side; sudden. Tension; as if skull were too small for brain, making reading, writing or thinking difficult. Throbbing as if it would burst. Dulness; < forehead; with difficult thought; with heat; as from a disordered stomach, after a nap, the nausea and headache < a swallow of vinegar, and the heaviness and stupefaction of head < eating. Heaviness; with heat; with pressing asunder at parietal bones, making thinking and writing difficult. Lightness, with sleepiness. Congestion. Apoplectic, unconscious, with stertorous respiration and bluish congestion of face. *Vertigo;* in morning on rising; with nausea; with sleepiness; frequent, with loss of sight.

Frontal pain; above eyes; in morning; in r. side in morning; on waking; < r. side; as if bone would press outward; throbbing P. in sinciput. Dulness in forehead on waking. Heaviness in forehead. Pain in r. side of head; on waking. Violent pulsations in temporal and cervical arteries; r. temporal artery beating full and quick. Pain in occiput.

Clinical.—Brain feels shrunken.

Eyes.—Injected. Sunken; < r.; and half open, staring straight ahead. Glistening. Lustreless, having a look of exhaustion and fear, becoming after a new injection lively, fiery or as in delirium. **Look unsteady.** Staring; and unaffected by light. Pain over and at side of l. all day, with pain in l. ear. Feeling as if too small for sockets, in morning. Heat, > application of ice, with lameness of them.

Injection of conjunctiva; of balls, and < subconjunctivæ tissue, with a rosy circle in anterior ciliary region, as in iritis; of cornea. *Strabismus.* Convulsive motions of balls; upward and outward. Balls rigid, turned upward. Balls protruding. Pupils unequal. Pupils dilated. Pupils contracted; and insensible to light, also in morning; and almost blind; and vision of red and black floating spots. **Paresis of recti interni.** *Ptosis.* Paralysis of upper lids. Lids bluish, drooping. Full feeling in orbits.

Vision.—*Weak. Foggy at times.* Distorted. Increase of far-sightedness. Lost. Could distinguish only one vertical half of objects. Double and indistinct; *D., and accommodation disturbed, often with lachrymation;* D., with diminished range of accommodation, pupils usually contracted, often unequally, seldom dilated; D., with dilatation sometimes of one, sometimes of other pupil.

Ears and Nose.—Ringing in ears. Roaring in ears. Sneezing; in paroxysms; in frequent attacks, with yawning. Coryza.

Face.—Pale; and sunken; and cold; and anxious; with contracted and painful expression; ashy gray. Red; cheeks; circumscribed redness of cheeks; and puffy; and drops of sweat on it; and almost cyanotic; and puffy, and lips livid; and lips pale; then vomiting, then dead faint, struggling for breath, pulse scarcely perceptible. Bluish. Cyanotic. Purple. Dark. Livid. Swollen. Haggard in morning, and eyes watery, as from dissipation. Wild look; after sleep, with confused look. Heavy look. Stupid look. Jaws and eyes wide open. Trismus. Jaws could scarcely be opened. Jaws feel clenched. Lips discolored. Lips pale. Lips livid.

Mouth.—Tongue. Livid. Red; at tip and margins; at tip, palate scarlet, painful; on margin, violet in middle. Pale in morning; P., heavy. Foul, in morning. Coated white and indented. Dry and brown; D. and cracked; D., with dirty mucus on it; D. anteriorly. Muscles so affected that articulation was almost impossible. Speech embarrassed and incoherent; stammering or hesitating; hasty; slow.

Mouth in General.—Strange noise. Mucus. Dry, and throat; D. in morning and after eating; mouth and fauces after sleep; with thirst, nausea, vomiting, aversion to meat, loss of appetite, trembling of tongue on protruding it, stool usually retarded, diarrhœa seldom. Discharge of watery saliva. Saliva churned into froth, which welled up and disappeared at every return and subsidence of respiratory movement. Pasty. Bitter, sticky. Clamminess. Taste perverted.

Throat.—Swelling of jugular veins. Pain posteriorly in morning, with obstruction (?). Dryness and constriction. Irritation. Burning posteriorly in fauces. Peculiar sensation in fauces. Paralysis of pharynx. Muscles of fauces and glottis so affected that swallowing was almost impossible. Inability to swallow.

Stomach.—Appetite diminished; lost. Aversion to food. Thirst; burning. Eructations; violent; of sour mucus, with nausea. Hiccough. Nausea; after eating; in morning on rising, > lying, lasting till 4 P.M.; transiently > vomiting of sour, bright green fluid; waking him; with heat of face; with faintness; with constant retching, faintness and alternate flushes of heat and cold. Retching. Vomiting; in morning after fresh milk; in evening; of coffee; of green matter; of scanty frothy liquid; of bile; with diarrhœa.

Cramp; intermittent, with loud cries, grinding of teeth and violent throwing about of arms, later the pain was worse in umbilicus; in epigastrium, as if clenched by a hand. Pain; in pit; in epigastric region; in evening, and in umbilicus and bladder; after eating, so that he had to go to bed; in epigastric region, then about umbilicus, then about loins; in pit and bladder, waking him; in pit extending to bladder. Constriction. Crawling. Dyspepsia. Digestion irregular.

Abdomen.—Meteorismus. Rumbling. Pain; in morning, > turning on back; waking him; in umbilical region; acute, in A. and along spine, on every inspiration.

Rectum and Stool.—Desire for stool for two hours in morning, then small stool with great straining, and at 2 P.M. loose stool with tenesmus, straining and burning in rectum, almost causing frenzy. *Diarrhœa;* in morning; in evening; watery; watery, in morning; frequent. Constipation; then diarrhœa. Copious stool. Painful S. twice in one day. Delayed and sluggish S.; and scanty, with painful urging. S. and urine almost stopped.

Urinary Organs.—More affected in men than in women. Pain in bladder. Paresis of bladder. Ineffectual desire; constantly. Strangury. Ischuria. Urine copious; and limpid, sp. gr. lowered. Urine scanty; at night, passed with difficulty; and turbid; and high-colored; with great urging; frequently, but at times increased. Urine suppressed. Acid; and pale; and bright yellow. Urine turbid and slimy. Sp. gr. increased, U. alkaline, afterwards acid; U. diabetic, possessing reducing and levogyrating properties. U. contained waxy cylinders and white blood-corpuscles. U. yielded albumen; without structural elements; in severe cases micturition often difficult, often scanty, the U. of nearly all suffering from Morphine intoxication reduces an alkaline solution of Cuprum sulphate without precipitating it as an oxide, at the same time the urine usually turns the polarization ray to the left.

Sexual Organs.—Pain, < r. testicle; and in urinary organs, < r. spermatic cord. Erections incomplete or wanting. Excitement, then impotency. Desire diminished. Impotency. Weakness. Pimple on labia. Bland leucorrhœa. Sterility in women. Abortion. Menstruation too early; and more profuse. Menstruation irregular or suppressed. Amenorrhœa gradually developed from dysmenorrhœa or it occurred suddenly.

Respiratory Organs.—Rattling in trachea. Hoarse. Speech inaudible. Aphonia. Respiration loud and rattling. Respiration stertorous; and at times arrested. Difficult R.; with tightness of chest, she asked to be raised, saying that she felt as if dying. Irregular R., with frequent sighs; l. and short. Rapid R.; with acute pain in chest. Slow R.; and rattling; and stertorous, also irregular; and superficial; and difficult. Indescribable R., thoracic R. apparently suspended. R. suspended.

Chest.—Pain and inability to take a long breath, afterwards pain, < middle of sternum, breathing short and quick and frequent sighing. Indescribable sensation worse than pain, behind lower half of sternum.

Heart.—Violent throbbing, and in carotids. Palpitation. Beat could not be felt, could be indistinctly heard only at times.

Clinical.—Piercing pain in region of heart, with difficulty in breathing.

Pulse.—Rapid; and full; and strong; and soft; and feeble; and weak, fluttering; and small; and small, contracted; and small, weak, intermittent; and intermittent. Strong and full. Hard. Feverish. Tense, suddenly becoming scarcely perceptible, thready, slow and intermittent, which marks the beginning of collapse. Slow; and laboring; and full; and full, intermittent; and weak; and of less power and volume; then rapid. Small; and hard; and at times tense or thready; and contracted, intermittent. Weak. Contracted. Intermittent, almost imperceptible at wrists, fluttering on sides of neck. Irregular; afterwards not to be felt. Imperceptible. Tracing almost a straight line, representing the maximum effect on arterial tension, which thereafter began to increase, forty minutes afterwards marked increase in the swell corresponding to the arterial diastole, but the smaller prominence caused by dicrotism is not yet visible, an hour later tracing normal.

Neck and Back.—Stiffness of neck in morning. Sensation of stiffening and thickening in muscles of nape, soon extending to flexors of all limbs, not the rigidity like that in cramps, but subject to volition. Pain in back; along spine; down spine, with twitching; across kidneys, then diuresis. Loins weak.

Extremities.—Bluish. Trembling; with general oppression. Twitching. Involuntary contraction and extension of fingers, with uneasiness in elbows and knees, after another dose muscles of hands and feet were rigidly contracted, legs drawn upon thighs, and they upon abdomen, arms alternately flexed, extended and then contracted across chest, simulating traumatic tetanus, from 2 till 5.30 P.M. Arms and legs felt as if alive and as if they would jump up. Pain in joints. Abnormal sensations, with salivation. Tingling or prickling. Weakness; of joints. Heaviness; or stiffness. Paralysis.

Heaviness of arms. Stiffness of arms after sleep, with pain. Peculiar, almost painful drawing in wrist. Trembling of hands; when writing; after sleep. Finger-nails dark. Fingers numb and thumbs firmly drawn into palms. Lower limbs deficient in sensibility and lying motionless. Staggering; in morning. Legs swollen so that he could not put on his boots. Twitching of l. leg; T. upward of legs, and feeling as if worms were in them. Tingling in feet.

Skin.—Pale; and cool, bathed in sweat. Livid; < lips and nails, and cold, covered with cold, clammy sweat. Cyanotic about face, neck, chest, arms and hands. Dark bluish spots on back and thighs. Yellow and shrivelled. Lost its elasticity. Loses its turgescence, color and tension, the subcutaneous cellular tissue atrophies (but in some cases, especially in women, it contains fat).

Eruption on face and large part of body; over whole body in morning. Rash like measles on face, spreading over body. Eruption in eighth intercostal space, painless, otherwise resembling herpes zoster. Inflammation of sebaceous glands, zoster, < chin, cheeks, intercostal spaces, sometimes returning. Red pimples; covering arms and legs; itching P., with red areola, a minute and a half after the operation, after twenty minutes it is flattened, its color more like that of the skin, hard, with red areola, with heat. Abscesses infiltrate the skin at the point of injection of morphine.

Pricking. Biting, sometimes with round elevations. Formication; over whole body; general, with tickling and itching. Constant rubbing of face, eyes and nose. Itching; over whole body; on face and back; on nose, neck, loins and inside of thighs; < arm; over whole body in evening; at night, with dryness of skin; over whole body, waking frequently, with sensation of cobwebs on face and sensation of chilblains on soles, I. next day and evening here and there, at intervals.

Sleep.—Yawning. Sleepiness; all day, with heaviness. Sopor. Fell asleep when standing; when talking. Almost constant sleep, in which he dreamed different things, heard everything going on about him and was almost always conscious of his condition. Sound sleep, with muttering. Profound sleep; and calm, with pleasant dreams; at times interrupted by convulsive cramps. Heavy S., with red cheeks. Sleep long and quiet. Did not wake in morning. Difficulty in arousing herself in the morning.

Sleeplessness; all night, with restlessness; till 2 A.M., but as much refreshed in morning as if he had slept all night; then sopor. Restless sleep; with frequent starting up; with fever, headache and itching. Unsound sleep, frequently interrupted by lively imaginings, wakeful early in morning. Light slumber, during which he was conscious of jerking of limbs. Troubled, delirious sleep, from which she woke in a few moments feeling as if she had slept weeks, this sleeping and waking were repeated all day. Half waking, half stupid condition, with ability to think of different things, but he was busy with confused fancies. Frightful dreams.

Fever.— Chilliness; and pallor; and trembling. Temperature falls; afterwards rises. Shudderings. Creeping chills, < from hips to knees and back again to hips. Cold skin; with warm feet. Cool head, face and hands; cold limbs; lower limbs; feet; hands and feet; limbs, with blue nails. Cold and livid limbs and hands.

Heat; at night; with itching; with flushed face and forehead; more in women than in men, with sweat and redness. Temperature rises. Hot skin; and dry; and moist. Hot head; and face; face, with flushing, also forehead. Tertian fever, with delirium during the paroxysms. Intermitting fever, tertian, then quotidian; intermittent, shaking chill, headache, oppression, heat, sweat, > change of locality, brought on again by imprudence (a voyage on the water, errors of diet), sometimes it appears like febris arthritica, at indefinite times attacks with chilliness, heat and sweat, usually the intermittent is tertian or quotidian, if the paroxysms are relieved at the time when the fever usually occurs he feels uncomfortable, especially exhausted, with the febrile paroxysms are associated neuralgia in numerous nerve-centres, supraorbital, intercostal and cardiac pains, temperature rises, spleen is usually enlarged, after the paroxysms sediment in the urine, in the more violent form there is delirium at the height of the fever, so that he cannot be kept in bed, after the fever and during the apyrexia exhaustion.

Sweat; at night; with relaxation; exhausting; clammy; cold; cold on walking; on face; cold, on face, scalp and hands, in beads coalescing about nose and mouth and trickling down; cold, on back; viscid, on upper part of body.

Clinical.—Icy coldness of l. sole, as if it were on oil-cloth.

Moschus.

A tincture is made of the dried preputial secretion of the musk ox, Moschus moschiferus, L.

General Action.—A general stimulant to the nervous system, especially of the sexual organs.

Allies.—Asaf., Nux mos., Ambra, Castor.

Generalities.—*Trembling of whole body;* with general sticky sweat; with bruised sensation and rapid pulse. Convulsions. Equilibrium lost. Circulation accelerated. Hæmorrhage. *Pricking in body and "fidgets," preventing sleep.* Prickling in all muscles. Pain over whole body, with shivering, but he was warm to touch; complained of intense P., and when asked where complained more violently than ever, but did not answer the question; bruised P. over whole body; jerking P. in all parts, < night, waking him. **Nervous.** Discomfort. Weakness; with pain over whole body, < joints. She became busy, but had scarcely begun to put things in order when they fell from her hands from weakness. *Faintness.*

Clinical.—Hysteria, with easy fainting, faints dead away from the least excitement, even from eating (Asaf., Nux mos.). Hysterical spasm ushered in by contraction of throat and suffocation. Globus hystericus. Frequently recurring syncope.

Mind.—Raved, spoke low, as if afraid of disturbing some one, saying "pst, pst, pst," then sighed deeply and played with the buttons of his waistcoat as if he would open and close it. Rage, > striking a vessel near him. Anger and raving till her mouth was dry, lips blue, eyes staring, face pale, when she fell to the ground. Excitement as from wine, with rapid, full, soft pulse. Anxiety; and starting in fright and trembling if any one opened the door; about death, and fell down in a faint. Said nothing but that she must die. Fretful; and weeping mood. Low spirits. Listlessness alternating with restlessness and quarrelsome mood. Sits in thought, talks indistinctly to himself, strikes with his hands and then suddenly cries "ah, ah;" sits in thought and makes various gestures, so that others fear that she will lose her reason.

Stupefaction; with vertigo; and all objects in the room seemed like large black figures, which would spring upon him; half stupefied, > open air. Dulness, and memory diminished. Distraction. Answers confused, as if thinking of something else. Mind lost. Senses lost so that he could not answer questions though he heard everything, and eyes staring, glistening, prominent; senses lost suddenly, he thought that his fingers and toes were cut off, against which he remonstrated with such rapid and confused speech that nothing could be gathered from it. Memory lost; suddenly, with pressure upon vertex. Coma.

Head.—Aching; deep in brain; on violent motion, as, for example, ascending steps; < evening; with coldness as from cold applications to head; with nausea and vomiting; with drawing in r. ear; extending deep into brain; raging, > camphor; as if brain would fall out; as if tightly laced; tensive, with sensation as if something in brain were moving; as if half of skull were cut through, > open air; pressive and boring, at one time in whole head, at another behind ears, at another in forehead, at another in vertex, and then in occiput; stupefying, that made him close his eyes; as a sore, < touch; externally as if scalp were sore, < touch.

Drawing here and there as far as nape, where it is a tension, > open air; spasmodic D. through the whole. Heaviness; amounting to pain, < forehead. Pressure on H. and upper part of forehead; P. < motion. Confusion; with stupefying pressure in brain; with tension in upper part, without pain; as if intoxicated. Stupefying compression of brain, with feeling as if senses would vanish. Stupefaction; like vertigo, with pressure upon vertex. Rush of blood; with staring eyes, cramp in mouth so that he could not speak, afterwards he talked rapidly and confusedly, then deathly pallor and sweat dripping from face and hair.

Vertigo; on stooping, > rising; on moving lids, > open air; with sudden faintness; with nausea and vomiting; with nausea and desire for black coffee; with nausea and throbbing pain posteriorly in head, with drawings as from a thread (extending into spine as far as first lumbar vertebra), sudden, with dim vision; even to unconsciousness; so that he thought he fell from a height; as if she stood very high and would fall; as if whirling violently, so that he even felt the air on his face; as if everything turned in a circle, at first very slowly, then faster and faster, at last it seemed as if she floated in the air, then stupefaction, in which it seemed as if she fell from a great height, and she lost consciousness.

Forehead.—Sticking. Aching; in afternoon, with sleepiness; < moving about; with a red spot upon it; extending into eyes and nose; extending between brows to nose and into bones of cheeks; alternately in F. and occiput; compressive, above root of nose, causing dulness. Sensation above orbits as if a dull instrument were pressed into brain. Stupid feeling. Turning in F. and before eyes, < stooping.

Pain in r. temple; drawing P. in r. Sudden drawing in temple. Pain as from a weight on whole upper part of head, > moving about in open air. Creeping on top of brain. Tearing in r. half of head. Pain in cerebellum. Throbbing pain in occiput. Pain as if something had been driven into occiput, thence the pain extended to forehead. Painful drawing from occiput to ears and from ears into teeth, < r. side. Itching here and there on scalp, > scratching.

Clinical.—Violent neuralgic headache, with feeling of coldness, the pain > open air, < warmth of the room.

Eyes.—Distorted upward. Dim, and pupils dilated; D. and pain in inner canthus. Pressure as from sand. Stiff; and protruding. Biting as from smoke, with lachrymation. Itching. Lachrymation of l.; with pressure. Upper lid swollen and painful. Pinching in external canthus, > rubbing. Stupefying pressure on l. brow. Vision dim; suddenly. Dizzy unsteadiness of V. on least motion of head. V. of black points. V. lost and pupils contracted.

Ears.—Discharge of much wax from l.; from r. at night. Pain in cartilage of l. as if ear had been pressed into head. Sensation of a wind blowing into l. Rushing, as in faintness; as of a violent wind; sudden R., as from the fluttering of a large bird, now in r., now in l. Flapping and sensation as if a flea were in l. Explosive sounds. Sounds like the firing of a cannon; in r., with dropping of blood from ear. Creaking in r., with a disagreeable sensation. Difficult hearing.

Nose.—Tickling in nose, changing to burning. Sneezing, with tickling, then burning; S., with pain in middle of nasal bones; severe S. Stopped by dry catarrh, became suddenly free after a copious clearing out. Fluent coryza, with peculiar burning, alternately in r. and l. nostril. Bleeding; of a few drops always on violent sneezing.

Face.—Pallor; and sweat; earthy. Redness; of r. cheek, without heat, and pallor of l., with sensation of heat in it. Muscles drawn, so that he was not recognized. Tension in muscles as if too short. Frequent pressure on l. zygoma. Motion of jaw as if chewing. Scaling of lips. Upper lip swollen.

Mouth.—Half open, and white mucus running from it. Dryness; with little thirst. Taste bitter in morning on waking; nasty, bitter; bad to everything that he ate except milk; little to food; flat; lost.

Throat.—Dryness; in œsophagus; in œsophagus, without thirst. Burning in pharynx.

Stomach.—Appetite great for dinner; lost for dinner. Aversion to food, with nausea at sight of it and vomiting if it is not taken away. Longing for brandy. Thirst for beer. Eructations; with hot saliva in mouth; leaving a taste of garlic; of air and uprisings of tasteless fluid; violent, of air; violent, with nausea and also with vomiting of food that had just been eaten.

Nausea; all day; in morning; in afternoon, with headache, so that she must lie in bed; in evening; after eating; with inability to vomit; coming from pit of stomach, wherewith navel was retracted, with cramplike sensation; in paroxysms; as in waterbrash, with scraping rising up œsophagus like heartburn. Retching in morning on rising. Vomiting in morning on rising, he vomits everything that he has eaten; V. for several days at 11 A.M., whether he has taken anything or not; V., with constant pressure in stomach and distention of epigastric region; with burning extending upward on sternum; with heaviness upon chest, but respiration free; with tensive pain across chest, < pressing together; violent; of mucus.

Cramplike pain. Pain in epigastric region; in pit; near l. side of pit; in and above pit (in chest), < inspiration, with anxiety in chest; below pit, > stooping; in epigastric region, > eructations; as from something hard in it, < drinking. Pressure in epigastric region towards spine, with nausea. Oppression above

S. Everything seemed too tight about pit after dinner, with biting, burning, sore sensation. Tension in epigastric region as if he had eaten too much. Tension in region, involving whole abdomen, with pain in abdomen. Fulness and pressure; F. in epigastric region, < moderate meal. Throbbing in epigastric region.

Abdomen.—Rumbling, with sticking in it and anxiety through whole body; R., with urging to stool, which was at first hard, then soft, at last natural; with emission of flatus; without flatulent symptoms, > eating. Distention, with ineffectual urging to stool. Flatus of the odor of garlic. Trembling, with general clammy sweat. Griping, > crouching together; G., > pressure, with dragging and pressure upon bladder. Dragging causing ineffectual desire for stool. Pressure as before menstruation. Tensive pain as if everything would burst out. Tightness without pain, with anxiety so that she must run about.

Swollen tension in hypochondria, with jerking. Sticking in liver region, < every inspiration; itching S. beneath r. short ribs, the I. continued after the S.; S. deep in umbilical region, < inspiration. Jerklike clawing above umbilicus, taking away her breath. Pain in U., with burning on chest; P. in r. side below umbilicus. Constriction in umbilical region so that it formed a deep fossa. Forcing downward in l. side, with constipation.

Rectum and Stool.—Sticking in anus; extending to bladder. Crawling in anus, > rubbing. Urging, then emission of flatus, then natural stool. Diarrhœa at night in sleep; < night, with urging and pain in anus; D., with violent colic; profuse, with retraction of stomach; frequent thin stools mixed with fæces. *Constipation;* > drinking coffee. Stool looks as if he had taken Sepia.

Urinary Organs.—Burning in urethra, especially with erections. *Urine as clear as water and copious.* Urine scanty and as thick as yeast. Urine smelled of musk.

Sexual Organs.—Painful emissions without erections. Desire; in both sexes, with tickling; with involuntary emissions; with tensive pain in penis; then great relaxation; and after satisfaction nausea and vomiting. *Dragging towards genitals as if menses would appear.* Menses brought on; too early and profuse; too early, with drawing pain low down in abdomen; with unusual drawing pains; M. irregular.

Clinical.—Suppression of menses, with hysterical spasms, choking in throat, fainting.

Respiratory Organs.—*Sudden sensation in upper part of larynx as if it closed upon the breath,* almost as from sulphur fumes. Feeling in larynx as of sulphur vapor, with constriction in trachea. On inspiration, which was free, sensation as if he had previously inspired S. vapor. Dry cough, < morning, and pain under l. breast on coughing. *Breathing oppressed;* **and she must take a deep breath.** *Difficult respiration, with sticking in chest so that he could take only very short breaths. Short R., > during rest, with sticking in r. side.*

Clinical.—Laryngisimus stridulous, crowing inspiration, attacks excited by eating or laughing. A large proportion of the cases requiring Mosch. are associated with spasmodic constriction of the larynx and chest and sense of impending suffocation. Spasmodic asthma. Attacks of sudden dyspnœa, with violent cough, the chest filled with mucus, with great rattling and with cramplike, suffocative constriction of chest. Threatening **paralysis of the lungs, with great collection of mucus and great difficulty in expectorating it. Angina pectoris, with extreme tightness of the chest and constant desire to take a long breath. Whooping cough, with extreme suffocation and rattling of mucus. Extreme palpitation, with dyspnœa and deathly anxiety.** Dyspnœa.

Chest.—Tenacious mucus without cough, which took away the breath, > drinking. Stitches, with red, puffy face, dilated pupils, dry, bright red tongue and great thirst; S. in r. side extending into hepatic region; almost like fine pinchings, in r. side beneath short ribs, that oblige rubbing; intermittent S. in l. half; intermittent S. in l. side under short ribs. *Cramp in lung, beginning with inclination to cough, gradually increasing and making him desperate. Gnawing, with sensation of suffocation.* Pinching in l. side beneath short ribs on deep inspiration; itching P. in side by short ribs.

Pain, with violent dry cough; P., now in l., now in r., extending into spine; in l. as if the pain would force itself out through nipple. *Tightness so that he must breathe deeper and more frequently than usual. Suffocative constriction; so that he could not lie down and gasped for air.* Pressure frequently stopping his breath. Compression and fulness.

Heart and Pulse.—*Palpitation* as from anxious expectation. Pulse rapid; and large, full; but less full. Pulse slow, full.

Neck.—Sticking now in neck, now in shoulders. Pain in nape; in neck as if muscles were torn from their attachments; in nape so that he could not turn head; drawing, in one muscle in nape; drawing P. from second cervical vertebra to r. shoulder.

Back.—Intermittent sticking in l. side of spine, in middle of trunk. Drawing pain, with tense feeling as before menstruation; D. pain extending from spine into hip-joint. Pains in spine, partly jerking, partly drawing, becoming firmly seated, < upper part of thighs, and so impeding walking. Pressure as from a dull instrument in l. side of sacrum, above coccyx.

Extremities.—Involuntary throwing about of hands and feet, which pain violently. *Aching.* Stiffness, with desire to urinate; S. of hands and feet.

Upper Extremities.—Tearing sticking in l. shoulder, causing heaviness of upper part of arm. Jerking pain from r. shoulder-joint to thumb. Jerking of r. arm, with cramplike pain and falling asleep of fingers. Pain in muscles of arms from shoulder-joints to elbows. Cutting in r. forearm, then burning. Pinching on inferior surface of l. forearm near elbow. Paralytic drawing just above r. wrist. Drawing from l. wrist into elbow in evening in bed, with sticking, preventing sleep, with necessity to put it out of bed and move it up and down.

Swelling of hands and stinging in them. Stitches in l. hand. Cramplike drawing in hands and fingers as before a rigid spasm; in l. thumb. R. hand, in which she held the pestle, became stiff and r. fingers outstretched. Paralytic jerking in l. thumb. Involuntary motions of fingers as if he picked up something or counted with them. Sticking in joints of fingers. Internal pain in last phalanx of l. index, making index tremble. Stiffness of r. fingers.

Lower Extremities. — Uneasiness when sitting, > moving them, with weakness of them. Numb pain in joints. Tingling as if they would fall asleep, if he keeps them still when sitting.

Thigh.—Paralytic jerking in inner side of l. Sticking here and there in T. and legs as if he had been beaten. Pinching in muscles of hips; posteriorly in flesh of r. thigh, < towards outer part; sharp P. above r. knee. Pain as if dislocated, so that she could not get out of bed. Pain in T. and legs somewhat > motion, not at all by walking; P. in hips so that he must lie down; P. from gluteals into groins, with drawing; on outer side, above l. knee, with weakness; in r. as if flesh were beaten to a jelly. Sudden pressure on inner side of l.

Knee.—Pain in r. so that he could not tolerate the bed; P. extending to hip and great toe, only in bones, < lying on painful side. Drawing pain from hollow to calf. Compressive pain in hollows as if tendons were too short. Paralytic weakness on sitting down.

Leg.—Cramplike pain extending downward in tibia, with general sweat. Pain in calves so that he could not touch them hard, with external coldness on outer side. Paralytic pain (painful weakness) down through l. leg, as if it would become rigid, when sitting. Uneasiness in l., a paralytic sensation that obliged him to move the leg at intervals. Tingling in legs and somewhat in thighs as after a long journey, or as if they would fall asleep, if he draws the feet backward when sitting.

Sticking outward in ankles, with dread of walking. Sprained pain in ankles, with sticking in four first l. toes. Drawing pain in all joints of feet, with sensation as if muscles pressed strongly against bones. Pinching in r. little toe, as if it had been stepped upon. Sprained pain in r. great toe, < pressure. Jerking pain in nails of two first toes as if they would suppurate, so that he could only walk barefoot upon the heel. Burning pressure in tips of r. toes. Pain like a burning in toes or as if squeezed by short boots.

Skin.—Blue spots on abdomen and thighs. Red spots like flea-bites above eyebrows. Eruption within cartilage of r. ear, with pinching itching, and after scratching burning. *Pimples, with burning in face;* itching P. in various parts; itching P. on back of r. foot, burning after scratching; red P. tipped with pus on upper lids. (Burning in a venereal tetter, which is usually quiet.) Itching sticking anteriorly on thigh. Itching, twinging S. in various parts. Tingling over whole body. Crawling on tip of nose, not > wiping. Itching posteriorly on ears; between shoulders; between toes; on outer side of l. tibia, towards calf, > rubbing; on l. upper arm, > scratching till the blood came, then burning, then itching pimples here and there, > scratching.

Sleep.—Yawning and sleepiness; when not actively employed; deep and frequent Y. Sleepiness, with inability to sleep, when walking in open air he could scarcely keep his eyes open on account of sleepiness. Feeling as if she had not slept enough. Sound sleep; and when awakened he spoke connectedly, with open eyes, but in the morning he remembered nothing of it.

Sleepless; all night, but there were moments in which she lost consciousness and on recovering from this condition, which was neither waking nor sleep, she was exhausted. Uneasy sleep, with waking every half hour and dry heat. Night full of vivid, slanderous dreams, wherein everything conspired against him, and from which he woke excited. Dreamed incessantly of strife and effort, unable to lie long in one spot because the spot on which he lay felt as if sprained or broken.

Fever.—*Coldness;* on going into open air, not cold air; in paroxysms; sudden, as from a wind, < uncovered parts, chiefly hands; sensation of external C., with sensation of internal burning in the same spot; < spine, with drawing pain. Shivering from slightest contact of air, > in bed; S. > open air, with flushes of heat in the house; alternations of S. and heat all day, with weakness; S. on scalp, extending over whole body. Coldness from soles to knees; suddenly on l. tibia; of thighs and legs, rather external than internal, but not perceptible to fingers. While the hands seemed to him naturally warm, the l. felt hot, the r. cold, to the face they both seemed cold.

Heat; with sweat and increased liveliness; < r. side, at 9 P.M., on getting into bed, with heat, dryness and scraping in mouth and throat and moderate thirst, necessity to lie uncovered, sticking in forehead, dizziness before eyes, general bruised sensation, sleeplessness, restlessness, tossing about, jerklike grasping above umbilicus, dragging towards genitals and ill humor. Hot head, with sweat on it posteriorly. Heat of face, with dim vision; of face without redness. Cooling burning on r. zygoma; in last joint of r. index.

Sweat; every morning; without heat; on forehead. Exhalations of skin smelled of musk.

Murex.

The fresh juice from the color-sac is triturated for use.

Clinical.—Polyuria, < night; one case in which, associated with other troubles, there was frequent need to pass urine, but it was scanty and very fetid, with the odor of Valerian. This drug has been used almost solely for prolapsus of the uterus, with pressure and bearing-down pains and with the particularly characteristic sensation of sharp pain extending upward to the breasts; some cases < lying down, with aching in the sacrum; other cases with much leucorrhœa, green or bloody, with unnatural sexual excitement and enlarged, indurated uterus; other cases with great soreness of the uterus felt on sitting down; sensation of prolapsus so great that the patient wants to keep the legs tightly crossed in order to relieve the tendency to protrusion. Dysmenorrhœa, with uterine displacement. Chronic inflammation of the uterus following miscarriage or labor, with tenderness, also with soreness over r. ovary, which extends up into r. chest. Subinvolution after confinement, heavy pressure upon rectum, swelling of the hæmorrhoids, greenish-yellow leucorrhœa, sometimes bloody, sometimes discharge of blood from the vagina when at stool, great weariness in the loins and pain in the lower extremities, sharp, lancinating pains in uterus, etc. Pulsation in neck of uterus (compare Sepia, Lilium tig., etc.).

Muriaticum Acidum.

A solution of pure Muriatic acid (Hydrogen Chloride) (1 to 2) is called the 1st decimal dilution.

General Action.—It is, in a general way, indicated in atonic conditions, feeble digestion, low fever, unhealthy ulcerations of skin and mucous membranes, cutaneous eruptions, etc. Its allies are Rhus tox., Arum tri., Carbol. ac.

Generalities.—Emaciation. Almost spasms. Pain in periosteum of all bones, as in intermittent fever. Relapse on forty-fourth day, rise of temperature and pulse, bloody vomiting, sticking in back, < below r. twelfth rib, about three inches external to spinous process, abdomen sunken, doughy, l. hypochondrium more distended than r., dulness across upper part of abdomen, pulse weak in relation to impulse of heart, rubbing sound in lower margin of diaphragm, in region of apex of heart, extending to axilla, synchronous with respiration, urine albuminous, pain in lower part of back, death in a week.

Discomfort. Increase of activity. **Weakness**; in morning, < lower limbs; in evening after walking; at night in bed, with difficulty in collecting ideas; after eating, > towards evening; when walking and standing, so that he fell asleep when sitting; when sitting, so that eyes closed, but on rising and moving about she is immediately wide awake; with sleepiness and dim vision, she fell asleep at the table. Indolence in forenoon, with stretching; I. and relaxation, but not wearied by walking. Unwilling to move. Fainted.

Clinical.—In a general way it is adapted to a low typhoid state, the patient slides down in bed and mutters, with sordes on the teeth and offensive odor from the mouth. General muscular debility following typhoid, diphtheria or the use of opium, with restlessness. It is particularly to be compared with Rhus.

Mind.—Easily excited. *Irritable*; in evening; in evening, reluctant and unsuccessful in work; and timid, despondent; and quiet, staring in front of him, abrupt in speech. Discontentment with everything in afternoon in open air, with prostration. Inclined to start up in fright. Sad; during menses, and taciturn, as if she had no life; during menses, absorbed in herself, as if she had no life; and quiet, discontented. Anxiety at 8 P.M., with fulness of abdomen as if it would burst, sweat runs from head, arms fall down and she is weak as if paralyzed; A., with cold sweat on face; and inability to free himself from the slightest trouble. Deep reflection and quiet absorption in himself as if something disagreeable impended, but with desire to work. Thoughts of events that had just happened forced themselves upon him when at work and were very vivid. Disinclination for mental work.

Head.—Forcibly twisted backward without spasms, and sitting up in bed. Sticking; on blowing nose; extending into head after rising from stooping, after dinner. Aching from walking in open air; A. waking her at 5 A.M., then sticking above r. ear; in brain, as if torn and beaten, as in pernicious fever, in morning. Aching as before coryza; pressing towards eyes, > lying, after frequent sneezing. Pressure from middle of brain out to l. side of forehead. Heaviness in morning after rising, < exertion of vision, till vision became confused, with reeling and sleepiness. Brain felt loose when carrying a heavy weight. *Vertigo in open air and unsteadiness when walking*; V. < in house, with dim vision; with stupefaction; with tearing in vertex and sensation as if hair were drawn up; suddenly in open air, objects turned about with her.

Forehead.—Sticking extending to temples, < stooping and pressure; S. in eminences extending towards middle. Tearing; in sudden shocks, extending to r. orbit, with pressure. Pain in F. and occiput, < rising in bed, especially that in F.; P. in forepart of brain, < moving eyes; afterwards involving whole head; from within outward in F. and temples; burning, externally above l. eye; stupefying, > touch. Dulness in front part. Heaviness pressing down upon eyes, > pressure, with dulness. *Feeling of falling asleep* and deadness.

Temples.—Sticking above l. Stitchlike tearing in r. when standing, > touch and yawning. Pain in l.; ulcerative, externally in T. and forehead; tensive, in r. Pulsation in r. artery when lying upon it.

Vertex.—Sticking in V. and forehead from noon till going to sleep. Tearing, with at times sensation as if hair were drawn up. Boring through bones into brain. Pain in V. and l. temple at night, preventing sleep, with restlessness; jerking, in evening.

Sides.—Sticking in r. parietal bone, then tearing in r. lobule and about ear. *Tearing in r. parietal bone*, with at times sticking extending into forehead, at times into margin of orbit, at times with tickling in l. ear and burning in concha. Pressure in l.

Occiput.—Sticking and tearing; S. in evening, with tension. Paroxysmal tearing in sides, extending into forehead. Pain in l. protuberance from walking in raw wind; tensive, in bone, extending through brain to forehead. Painless drawing in protuberance, extending to l. eye, causing twitching of upper lid. *Heaviness*, with drawing stitches on it extending towards nape, swelling of a cervical gland that is painful to touch, and heaviness of head, vertigo and dimness of eyes; H. as if head would sink backward, as from weakness of cervical muscles.

Scalp.—Burning pain above temples. Tension in l. side. Feeling as from bristling of hair after fright. Itching on vertex, not > scratching.

Eyes.—Easily inflamed. Redness, with sticking outward. Burning in morning, with agglutination; B. in morning when washing them; B. and pressure, as after exerting vision in evening. Itching. Pupils dilated; contracted; now dilated, now contracted, at intervals of four or five hours. Cutting in r. ball during rest. Swelling of lids, with redness. Agglutination in morning. Jerking through upper lid towards zygoma, as from a thread drawn through it. Itching stitch in r. external canthus during rest. Corrosive biting in l. external canthus in evening; itching B. in r. internal C., not > rubbing. Tearing in margin of orbit. Sensitiveness to light. Flickering vision, with hemiopia, during which one vertical half of an object seemed cut off from the other.

Ears.—Itching stitch in l., > boring into ear. Tearing in l.; in r. outer; in lobule of l.; drawing, behind ears, extending towards nape and causing stiffness of neck. Cutting posteriorly on mastoid process, and on touch pain as if suppurating. Pinching deep within r., with at times sticking extending behind ear, where it is then painful to touch; jerking, deep within l., with frequent cramplike pain. Gnawing in r. in evening. Ulcerative pain in l., < boring in with finger; U. pain in lobule on touch. Pain in r. like a rhythmical pressure outward, with sensitiveness of external ear to touch. Drawing pressure in antitragus, and on pressure pain extending into ear. Itching in l.

Very sensitive to noise (Sil.). Hears the ticking of a watch better than the sound of the voice. Hearing diminished, and ear-wax dry, a few days afterwards a sudden noise in the ear and he hears better. Singing. Chirping at night. Whistling; and ringing and roaring. Roaring; in r., with whistling.

Nose.—Sticking in nostrils as if they would ulcerate. Stoppage; in upper part, with profuse mucous discharge. Irritation of mucous membrane as in coryza. Sensation of coryza, with dryness. Constant inclination to sneeze, with itching and tickling. *Sneezing*; in afternoon and evening, without coryza; violent, with discharge of water. Discharge of much mucus. Coryza; with acrid water; with thick mucus. *Bleeding* (the Carbons in general).

Face.—Heightened color. Red cheeks when walking in open air. Pale. Cramplike pain near l. articulation of jaw, and on pressure sticking extending into ear. Tearing in jaw just below l. orbit. Drawing in jaws. Tingling in l. lower jaw, extending as a crawling into corresponding teeth.

Lips.—Lower swollen, it feels heavy and burning, < touch. *Margins raw and skin dry and cracked. Mucous lining red, inflamed and painful, stripped of epithelium to a considerable extent and dotted with whitish points.* Pustules in red of lower. Vesicle on l. side of upper; in upper, close to corner, with suppurative pain on touch and tension on moving lips; yellow burning, on l. side of lower. Pain and smarting on lips, mouth and throat. *Burning* (Arum, Carbol. ac.). Burning tension in r. side of upper.

Mouth.—Teeth. Very white. Tearing in r. upper and in zygoma; in a r. upper molar, with sore pain in gums. Boring in roots of l. lower as if they would be pushed out. Jerking, with burning in gums. Aching, > warmth and wrapping up, with pain in cheekbones, ears and temples; pressing asunder, in a lower canine, > pressing jaws together; throbbing, in l. lower mornings, < cold drinks. Cold drink painfully penetrates diseased T. Itching, with desire to bite them tightly together. Gums inflamed. Gums swollen; in morning, lasting till noon; and red, covered in places with thin films of a dead white color.

Tongue.—*Thick, dark and with most of mouth and fauces covered with a grayish-white membrane.* Wastes away. Bluish and sore. White and abraded, also inside of lips and fauces. Coated white in morning, with bitter taste; C. as with coagulated albumen on dorsal surface, while borders were red and raw. *Painful blister, with burning;* red, burning B. on tip. Deep ulcer, with black base and everted edges. Burning and pain, also in pharynx and œsophagus. Heaviness < talking, with feeling as if too long, so that he can scarcely move it, with dryness of mouth and fauces.

Redness of inside of cheeks and of arch of palate. Mouth and fauces white or ash-gray. Adherent mucus posteriorly. Slimy in morning after rising, > breakfast. Painful pimples on sides of palate. *Rawness in a spot on palate, with soreness.* Burning, and in fauces and stomach; in palate in evening and night; in mouth and throat, with pain; sore, on palate in evening and night. Sticky sensation as of tasteless mucus. Dry, in morning, so that she can scarcely talk. Salivation; which seems to come from throat; and taste astringent and as of bad eggs. Taste as of rancid fat in throat. Taste as sweet as honey to beer, causing nausea.

Clinical.—Inflammation and ulceration of the tongue and mouth, sometimes with hard lumps in the tongue, always with easy bleeding, tendency to slough. Epithelioma of the tongue, the edges of a bluish-red color (Carbol. ac.). Aphthous mouth in nursing children. It has been found useful in aphthous sore mouth occurring in the last stages of wasting diseases, sometimes with watery diarrhœa and irritable stomach.

Throat.—*Swelling of uvula; of tonsils; of mucous lining, with redness; of fauces, with white color; of fauces, with inability to swallow, the attempt causing spasm and choking;* behind base of tongue, formed by epiglottis and œdematous arytæus-epiglottic folds. *Deep redness, and of velum palati. Mucus that he must swallow. Grayish-white deposits, then ulcers. Dead white patches over velum and pillars of palate, tonsils and posterior part of pharynx, like the false membrane of diphtheritic angina.*

Pain in lower part of pharynx and in epigastrium and abdomen; in pharynx, with difficult swallowing; burning, and in pit of stomach. Scraping in pharynx. Rawness evening and morning, with scraping, and cough with sore pain in chest; R. in pharynx night and morning, with smarting; with hoarseness and soreness in chest; with burning like heartburn and cough. Sensitiveness of l. side. Dryness, with burning in chest. Swallowing difficult; difficult from sharp pain in œsophagus; painful; impossible. It seemed as if food would not go down properly at noon and oppressed her.

Clinical.—Ulceration of the throat, diphtheritic, the lips are sore, cracked and scabby (Arum tri.), sordes on the teeth, fetid breath, hæmorrhage from the nose, false membrane covering uvula and tonsils. There have been several cures of diphtheria, with more or less œdema, excoriating discharge from the nose, hawking up of tough, fetid phlegm, general typhoid condition, sordes on the teeth, great prostration, not much fever.

Stomach.—Ravenous hunger. *Appetite lost.* Aversion to meat; to eating, because almost everything tastes sweet; to food, with much yawning. Violent thirst. Eructations; after eating; empty, at night, with colic; bad-tasting; bitter; of sour fluid. Hiccough; violent, before and after dinner. Nausea; in epigastric region; in morning, > after rising by emission of flatus, with distention of abdomen; at night on waking, with eructations. Retching; ineffectual. Vomiting; at night; violent; of food; of bloody, frothy liquid; like coffee-grounds, after eating or drinking; of matters with alkaline reaction, and after milk brown V. streaked with blood and containing shreds of mucous membrane; copious, of a stiff, glairy mucus; copious, of a substance that bubbled up on the ground.

Epigastric region hard, tense and sensitive. Inflammation of alimentary canal. Fulness when fasting; F., with ineffectual attempts to eructate. Pain; in epigastric region, also with tenderness; in pit, < vomiting and pressure. Constriction. Painful sensation of retraction in a spot after dinner. Burning; on a spot near l. side of pit, with throbbing. Emptiness at times; *E. in epigastric region, < œsophagus, not > eating,* with rumbling in abdomen.

Abdomen.—Distention all day; in evening, > lying down; after a moderate meal; with pain, and shooting into body on every step; then profuse emission of flatus. Rumbling; during and after eating, with pain; with gurgling; with empty feeling; when sitting, as from emptiness. Profuse emission of offensive flatus. Fermentation, sometimes firmly seated low down, with whistling noises. Cutting when sitting, standing and walking. Griping now here, now there; G. on motion and emission of flatus; then profuse emission of offensive flatus; cutting, when standing and walking, > sitting. Pain; in morning in bed; at night; and contracted sensation; and diarrhœa. Anxiety, > emission of flatus and stool. Painful emptiness in morning after usual stool.

Hypochondria.—Sticking in l. side beneath ribs; in l. on stooping; in r. in evening, then burning, > pressure, but reappearing near the same place. Pinching beneath l. short ribs, not affected by respiration. Pain. Tension in r., extending now upward, now downward, when sitting, with sore pain; burning, in a spot in r. Burning and bruised pain in r.

Jerklike griping externally on a spot of l. side of

abdomen, < inspiration. Griping in muscles in and below umbilical region; G. from U. region to sides, with rumbling; in U. region, with emptiness, extending to pit of stomach, and there causing oppression; beneath umbilicus, then hard stool. Sticking about umbilicus; in abdominal ring; in r. groin in evening. Burning sticking in l. groin; in r. groin in evening. Cutting through middle, beneath umbilicus.

Rectum.—*Prolapsus as if everted, when urinating.* Sticking. Cutting griping, extending to upper abdomen, then desire for stool, stool soft. *Smarting, and in anus, with soft stool.* Itching as from thread-worms. Urging in morning, yet difficult stool. Inactivity, with great pressure he can discharge only a part of the stool.

Anus.—*Swollen hæmorrhoids, with burning sore pain* (Nit. ac.); *swollen, blue H., with pain on pressure.* Cutting during soft stool. Burning sticking. Pressure. *Burning after stool. Itching* and tickling; I., with sore pain and crawling sticking.

Clinical.—Hæmorrhoids < cold water, > warmth, extremely painful, with prolapsus of rectum, accompanied by sticking, biting; especially useful in the hæmorrhoids of pregnancy, bluish-red, hot and very sore. Hæmorrhoids in children, bluish, with violent stitches and great sensitiveness.

Stool.—*Diarrhœa;* in evening and morning, *then burning in anus;* with smarting in rectum. *Watery, passed unnoticed,* when urinating. Soft; with emission of flatus, contractive burning and sticking in rectum and sensation as if stool and flatus went back; with cutting and nausea in abdomen, as from taking cold, he felt better after the stool. Constipation. Hard; and difficult in morning, softer in afternoon; at one time, at another soft; then four times diarrhœa, with tenesmus and rumbling and gurgling in abdomen. In small pieces, with pressure. With blood.

Clinical.—Thin, offensive diarrhœa in typhoid or in old people who are debilitated and sink down in bed, but are restless and inclined to delirium, with dry, burnt tongue, sordes on lips, etc. Dysentery, with low typhoid state.

Urinary Organs.—Bladder weak. Desire to urinate, but he must wait before the urine passes. Constant desire, with scanty but frequent micturition, then tenesmus. *Frequent desire and copious urine;* and scanty urine. Almost ineffectual urging. Frequent and profuse micturition; with urging. Frequent M. at night, but little urine at a time. Involuntary M.; in bed. Slow M., as if bladder had no power to expel the urine. Cutting far back in urethra when urinating during stool. Sticking biting in orifice of urethra after micturition. Copious urine; and watery. Urine diminished, with burning. Urine turbid, like milk, when passed.

Sexual Organs.—Prepuce easily inflamed. Pain on margin of prepuce as if torn or wounded. Burning sticking posteriorly in penis. Erections in morning in bed; weak but frequent E.; no E., weak feeling in genitals, penis flabby. Boring tension from r. testicle to middle of penis. Itching of scrotum, not > scratching; I. about scrotum. Desire increased. Sensation as if an emission would occur woke him in morning, then with slight erection a watery, frothy, odorless emission, then long-lasting erection with tensive pain in penis. Sticking in vagina. Leucorrhœa. Distress in genitals as before menstruation. Menses too early; with colic.

Respiratory Organs.—Epiglottis swollen, white and corroded. Hoarseness. Voice thick and inarticulate. Inclination to cough, with sticking scraping in throat, then mucus that at last collects in masses. Violent cough at 3 A.M., with nausea and vomiting of bile; V. cough, as if it would burst out the sternum, from dinner till towards evening, < talking, laughing and yawning, with sore and bruised pains. Whooping C., then rumbling extending downward in chest. Hacking C. from tickling in throat; H., with burning in throat. Dry C. day and night, with exertion; dry, from tickling in chest. Cough with bloody expectoration; loose C. in evening and morning, with expectoration of mucus. Expiration of white fumes. Sighing; and frequent respiration. Deep respiration and groans. Suffocating sensation. Difficult breathing, with moist râles all over chest; inspiration D. and wheezing.

Chest.—Sticking beneath sternum, just above pit of stomach; in r. nipple; in l. side in evening, with cough; on violent motion and on breathing; between two l. true ribs on expiration; on r. true ribs on expiration when sitting; on l. lowest true ribs, not affecting respiration; beneath r. nipple, gradually increasing and decreasing; upward externally on sides; below præcordial region, extending into l. costal region, with tearing behind l. ear; tensive jerking, from l. false ribs to r. ribs; boring, in r. intercostal muscles when sitting, not affecting breathing; burning, externally beneath l. mamma. Paroxysmal cutting thrusts internally in middle of sternum, with pressure posteriorly in chest, general oppression of chest and tightness of breath.

Pinching, without tightness of breath; P. in r. side, < inspiration. Tensive boring during inspiration and expiration. Sore pain and cutting, with inclination to cough. Pain in sternum above pit of stomach, extending to chest, in evening; in l. side close to spine, on inspiration; on r. side, not affected by breathing; in l. side, with bruised pain; tensive, in sternum, preventing breathing, as if it came from stomach, with pain on touch. Pinching tension beneath short ribs, often obliging deep inspiration, > emission of flatus. Scraping, with cough and expectoration of mucus. Paroxysmal asthmatic pressure. Oppression, < r. side; O. transversely across in evening when walking and sitting. Sensation as if a hard substance rose to throat, where there was tickling, when sitting, with dry cough. Drawing beneath r. nipple, extending towards neck. Burning externally on r. side of chest and on a spot in middle of sternum, with sticking internally, afterwards only sticking in the same place.

Heart and Pulse.—Sticking in præcordial region, so that it was difficult to become erect, > rubbing, with arrested breath; S. deep in præcordial region, extending to axilla and back, in evening when sitting, > rising, with S. in thigh extending to knee. Heart beat so violently at night during fever that he felt it in the face. *Pulse rapid;* **and feeble**; *and small.* Pulse intermits every third beat.

Neck.—Swelling of posterior glands, with tensive pain on turning head.

Back.—Sticking on l. side when sitting; on l. side, > moving. Pressure along spine when walking in open air, > standing and sitting; P. in middle and l. side, as from much stooping; in middle when sitting and standing, as from long stooping. Sprained pain after writing with back bent. Sticking in scapulæ; in r., beneath axilla; on lower margin of r.;

with drawing and heat. Drawing tensive pain alternately between scapulæ and lowest ribs, not affecting respiration. Sticking in small of B. on rising from stooping; burning S. in sacrum. Drawing tearing from middle of sacrum towards lumbar vertebræ.

Extremities.—Jerking. Cramps and contractions of muscles. Tearing in upper arms and calves. Pain in arms and legs. Bruised pain in all joints. Weakness so that he must stand still when walking.

Upper Extremities.—Anxiety in evening, with uneasiness in them, as if in veins, with joyous mood, it was like a heaviness of arms, necessity to move them constantly, with uneasiness of whole body, except of feet, and heat, without thirst.

Shoulder.—Sticking on r., changing to twinging; burning S. in l. in evening. Tearing in r., with pain on touch. Pain in linea axillaris. Sprained pain in l. during rest, with sensation on raising arm as if it would crack in the joint. Weary pain in r. joint, < motion. Pressure. Throbbing in r., with paralytic pain.

Arm.—Tearing just above elbow and wrist, < rest; tearings extending from middle of upper arm and forearm towards each other. Heaviness. Upper arm, pulselike twitching of single muscle fibres in r.; cramp on exerting arm; drawing tearing in r. on writing, > moving about and stretching upper arm; paralytic pain in middle of r., extending to elbow; drawing in l. Elbow, sticking tearing in tip of r.; cutting in bend, < flexion, > extension of arm; *frequent drawing tension.* Forearm, paroxysmal cutting tearing in posterior muscles of r.; drawing tearing in posterior muscles of l., extending into fingers; cutting below r. elbow; bruised pain on inner side of r., < rest; burning pain externally on r.; cramplike pain on flexing arm; cramplike heaviness close to wrist. Cramp of l. palm, > by moving hand. Goutlike tearing on outer side, above knuckle of little finger. Drawing pain in l. hand.

Fingers.—Swelling of tips, with redness and burning pain. Sticking in tip of l. index on touch. Cutting tearing in ball of l. little; drawing T. from middle joint of l. fourth to metacarpal bone when at rest, > bending finger, < stretching it. Cramplike pain in ball of r. thumb when writing, > motion. Stiffness of two last l. at night. Crawling as if asleep in r. Numbness of middle, with coldness and deadness.

Lower Extremities.—Weakness. Cutting griping in r. hip only when sitting.

Thigh.—Twitching of single muscle fibres, now on r., now on l. Cramp in muscles of l. in bed. Sticking in muscles of l. when sitting; drawing, in muscles close to l. groin when sitting; burning, on outer side of r. when walking and sitting. Spasmodic constrictive tearing in anterior muscles of l.; sticking T. in r. femur when walking. Spasmodic drawing pain down l. when sitting. Pain in muscles. *Weakness causing tottering.*

Knee.—Swelling. Twitching near r. patella. Burning sticking externally on r. Tearing when sitting, < r.; T. in hollow and in calf, < at night and more when sitting than when walking; in bend on rising from a seat, extending into hip, with sticking at times in l. knee, < bending it and walking, > stretching it and sitting; sticking, in r. if l. leg lies over it. Tensive pain in l. Bruised pain in r. on walking and ascending steps. Stiffness of l. on rising from a seat.

Leg.—Paroxysmal sticking in tendo-achillis, partly inward, partly transversely through it, even disturbing sleep at night and preventing walking. Sticking cutting in r. calf when sitting. Tearing in tibiæ and l. thigh when sitting; in lower part of r. tibia, when sitting, extending downward; in tibiæ extending into knees, > sitting. Pain in l. calf. *Drawing in tendo-achillis when walking, with tension, so that foot seems paralyzed and walking is impeded.* Painful tension near hollow of knee, in l. calf, when sitting.

Foot.—Burrowing twitching in ball of r. during rest. Sticking on back of l., < rest; on inner margin of r. sole when sitting, > walking and standing; drawing, on back of r. when standing, > walking, recurring when sitting. Tearing in sole of r. heel when spinning and (after several days) when sitting. Cutting cramplike pain in hollow of r. sole. Sprained pain extending from l. sole to thigh on ascending a mountain. Sore pain below l. external malleolus during rest, lasting all night, < touch and lying upon it. Pain in l. as if tightly bound.

Toes.—Swelling of tips, with redness and burning pain. Tearing in r. great when spinning. Throbbing pain in three l. middle, during rest. Sore pain in l. little, with swollen sensation.

Skin.—Spots on face, lips and throat. Sore place on each side of mouth, curving upward, looking as if made by the edge of a drinking glass. Eruption on hands, itching on getting warm in bed. Nodes, itching and burning, on forearms and elbows. Red, tensive pimples on r. side of neck; itching P. behind and below l. tragus, not > rubbing, with smarting; P. that within a day and night ran together into a scab, on forehead, on concha, about lips and on back of hands and fingers. Pustules on forehead and temples. Boil on r. temple; on back, with sticking on touch. Round, raw, itching tetter on inner part of thighs. Vesicle on r. side of lower jaw, painful on touch. Ulcers offensive, but covered with a scab; unhealthy U. on legs, with dropsy and cachexia; painful, < sitting and lying; with more burning about it than in it, and after walking throbbing in it.

Sticking on hypogastrium; S. here and there, at times with burning (on r. scapula). Itching sticking in ball of r. great toe during rest; on back of l. foot, < rest; in r. gluteal muscles, the itching < rubbing. Tickling in ball of l. heel, > rubbing.

Itching of thighs; calves; l. sole; on tip of nose, returning after scratching; over whole body, < evening after lying down, not > scratching, with biting; sticking, here and there in evening, > scratching; tickling sticking, transiently > rubbing; voluptuous, in palms, with sticking tickling; burning, voluptuous, in perineum, close to anus, not immediately > scratching; burning, on knees, malleoli and toes on falling asleep.

Clinical.—Carbuncles, with scorbutic appearance of the gums. Foul-smelling ulcers on the lower extremities, with chilliness and weakness. Papular and vesicular eruptions, with great itching (Rhus t.).

Sleep.—Sleepiness all day; in morning, with yawning; in afternoon; when at work. Sleeplessness before midnight; after midnight; after 4 A.M.; with restlessness, and in morning sleepiness. Difficult falling asleep, light sleep and difficult waking. Wakes always on his back. Slides down in bed and groans and moans in sleep. Starting up after falling asleep on account of uneasiness, < legs. Raving soon after falling asleep. Loud incoherent talking in sleep before midnight, she knows nothing of it in the morning. Snoring, occasionally a stridulous noise, as from an obstruction in larynx; snoring before midnight and tossing about, but easily awakened. Restless sleep before midnight, often talks aloud in a joyous tone, but frequently groans; R. sleep, often interrupted by vivid, anxious dreams, and copious sweat in sleep, except on head. *Frequent waking;* with tossing about; every quarter of an hour, with pain, now here, now there, with restlessness.

Dreams.—*Anxious;* and vivid; and frightful, vivid; or sorrowful or joyful. Unremembered. Happy, of home. Of the death of her mother. That she had lice, which made her much ashamed. Voluptuous. Restless, vivid, full of solicitude and frights, with erections, without emissions.

Fever.—Chilliness; all day, not > walking; in morning and forenoon; from 6 to 7 P.M., with coldness on back; at 8 P.M., with external warmth; *in evening,* with burning in face and *dryness of mouth;* in evening, with thirst, and after lying down sweat, and necessity to drink at night; at night, with tossing about; waking him before midnight, less in parts on which he lies, then heat and sweat; with gooseflesh; with thirst. Shivering; with hot cheeks and cold hands, without thirst; with shaking chill, yawning and stretching, without thirst or subsequent heat; with slight fluent coryza, yawning, cold, dead tips of fingers, blue nails, weak, slow pulse. Cold skin. *Cold limbs;* lower; internally; feet soon after lying down (on account of sleepiness during the day), with heat of head and hands.

Slow fever. Heat at night, with orgasm of blood and sweat, preventing sleep. Burning beneath skin from coccyx up back; in posterior muscles of l. upper arm close to elbow; in head, < forehead, in morning on stooping; in soles when sitting, < putting them to the ground; < palms and soles, without redness of face, sweat or dryness of mouth, with some inclination to uncover himself; in l., then r. ear, as if a vapor would issue from them, then redness and swelling of backs of hands, with wrinkling like a smarting, lachrymation, diminished smell and hearing, then redness and burning of face.

Sweat in morning; in evening on falling asleep; at night; before midnight, with dry cough; before midnight, during dreams full of difficulties, then good sleep till morning without sweat; clammy; on head and back every second or fourth evening; cold, on feet in evening after lying one or two hours.

Clinical. — Malignant scarlet fever, profound prostration, mouth full of ulcers, intermittent pulse, involuntary discharges. Typhoid fever of a low, stupid type, hæmorrhages, dry tongue, sometimes spasms, involuntary discharges, restlessness, or sometimes in typhoid fever, when the patient is very quiet, has involuntary discharges, bed sores, aphthæ in mouth and sinking down in bed. Low types of remittent fever.

Myrica.

A tincture is made of the fresh bark of the root of Myrica cerifera, L.

Generalities.—Pain in whole body, as before ague, at 10 P.M.; shifting P. Muscular lameness, < lower limbs, with soreness. Malaise and feeling of unfitness for duty. Languor; in morning on waking; in morning, with pain in back; with soreness of muscles of thighs, as if he had taken cold. No inclination to move at 9 A.M. Aggravation from warmth of bed at night, disturbing sleep. Amelioration after breakfast; A. in open air.

Mind.—Exhilaration, then depression and pressure about head; E., then excitement preventing sleep, with restlessness. *Despondency.* Irritable; and did not want to speak or to be spoken to; and he looked upon the world as a place not fit to live in, in the morning he considered himself better than the rest, in the afternoon he condemned himself for imaginary faults. Loss of energy. Difficulty in concentrating the mind. Intellect dull. Semi-stupor, with pain through head, < temples, with throbbing in superficial veins.

Head.—Aching; in morning on waking, also in eyes, also in back; in morning, < stooping or moving about; on waking at 6.30 A.M., with pressure in forehead and feeling as if he had not slept enough; at 11 A.M., < over l. eye; at night; > rising and washing with cold water; and in neck; causing confusion of thought and staggering; grinding; heavy, at 7 A.M., < frontis, and through temples. Bruised feeling in morning. Heaviness. Dulness in morning; in morning on waking, with drowsiness; D. and heaviness in head and eyes. Fulness in morning, with bad, indescribable taste. Throbbing in arteries; and in face with fulness; in superficial veins on waking. Empty feeling. Vertigo; in forenoon, with dulness and drowsiness during lectures.

Pain in forehead; in morning on waking, also in temples; over eyes at 8.30 A.M., < motion; in evening, and in eyes; and in temples and muscles of neck; and in vertex, with throbbing synchronous with pulse; sharp, on l. side; oppressive, at juncture of r. parietal and frontal bones in afternoon and evening, with fulness in head; heavy, in sinciput, < l. temple. Dull, heavy feeling over eyes, then stricture across nose. Pain in temples; < r. Numbness in r. temple as from pressure of a hard substance. Drawing in vertex. Sensation in vertex like foam rising in anything fermenting. Pain in sides near temples, which settles into heavy grinding feeling in vertex. Occipital pain; on r. side. Heaviness in occiput. Scalp sore to touch in morning on waking.

Clinical.—Dull headache in morning on rising, associated with pain in nape of neck and small of back, > open air.

Eyes.—Congested and yellow; yellow in morning, and feel swollen. Smarting; in l.; with dryness and feeling of sand in them, making it difficult to close the lids. Sharp pain in l. at 9 A.M. Soreness in morning; of l. in morning, with inflamed look. Heaviness and dulness; in forenoon; H. in morning on waking, with weakness. Burned; and tired easily on reading. Conjunctiva congested and yellow. Smarting in l. conjunctiva, then pain in r. ball. Heaviness in lids in morning, with swelling. Fulness in l. lid, approaching to soreness. Quivering sensation in l. upper lid. Pain in r. brow.

Ears, Nose and Face.—Pain in back of l. ear. Ringing in ears; in l. Pain in nose; in l. side, shifting to l. axilla, where it was sharp and lancinating. Coryza. Face and neck yellow. Pressure in malar-bones. Sharp darting pain in r. articulation of jaw.

Mouth.—Tongue coated; yellow; dirty white or yellowish. Adhesive coating in mouth. M. and fauces dry. Breath offensive. Bad taste; in morning. Sweetish taste about palate.

Throat.—Stringy mucus difficult to detach; T. and nose filled with offensive tenacious mucus. Semi-lancinating pain near r. tonsil in afternoon. Excruciating feeling in posterior nares, as from a fresh cold. Soreness; in pharynx, with dryness, then difficult swallowing. Roughness; with frequent and difficult deglutition; requiring it to be cleared constantly. Constriction; causing constant need to swallow. Swollen feeling inside in morning. Sensation of a foreign substance, requiring it to be cleared constantly. Dryness.

Stomach.—*Appetite increased; with full sensation in stomach and abdomen*, also in morning, with rumbling in bowels; poor; poor in morning; lost. Loathing of food, but desire for acids. Empty eructation. Nausea; in morning; with light-headedness; with vertigo; with gagging, but inability to vomit. Distention; and of upper abdomen, also in forenoon. Fulness of digestive organs, as from slow digestion. Griping, then empty eructations. Pain; in region; in epigastrium when walking, with stinging; temporarily > empty eructations. Distress caused by dinner. Strange sensation, not nausea. Acidity at 8.30 A.M. Burning, with bitter, nauseous sensation in fauces, the B. changing into griping from l. epigastrium in a straight line to left of navel. Heartburn, with increase of saliva, which had to be expectorated frequently. Sinking feeling in epigastrium, with pressure, sometimes approaching nausea, < breakfast, > rapid walking towards evening.

Clinical.—Hunger, with great fulness in stomach and abdomen, > open air.

Abdomen.—Offensive flatus; when walking. Flatulency; in afternoon, with rumbling and urging to stool, but emission of only flatus. Griping at night; intermittent, in afternoon. Pain; occasionally in afternoon and evening; grumbling, in afternoon. Sensation of approaching diarrhœa. Faintish feeling as in diarrhœa. *Pain in hepatic region;* in umbilical region after breakfast; in a spot in umbilical region an hour after dinner, with accumulation of flatus; heavy, in U. region. Rumbling above umbilicus; in umbilical region, with griping.

Clinical.—In jaundice, with thick tenacious mucus from mouth, though the mouth and pharynx are painfully dry, as if they would crack, constant efforts to clear the mucus from the mouth, with feeble pulse, in an old man. In jaundice, with dull, heavy headache in morning, yellow color of the sclerotic and face, tongue yellow, very heavy and drowsy, general soreness and aching in the muscles, slow pulse, dark, turbid urine.

Stool.—Loose; with pain and tenesmus, also after dinner. Mushy; and straw-colored. Soft, with effort. Papescent, copious, with tenesmus and cramplike sensation in umbilical region. Light-colored. Constipation.

Urinary Organs.—Micturition difficult, bladder seemed to lack contractive expelling power. Urine increased; and limpid. Urine dark; and scanty, frothy; and frothy, with pinkish-brown sediment. *Urine looks like strong beer, with much yellowish froth.* Sediment light-colored; light-brownish; pinkish-brown.

Sexual Organs.—Desire lost.

Respiratory Organs and Chest.—Smarting in larynx and trachea. Tickling cough which had troubled him on lying down at night was relieved in morning. Pain in l. chest; in middle lobe of r. lung; in l. lung at 8 P.M. Constriction of chest at night when lying on l. side, with audible beating of heart.

Heart and Pulse.—Stinging, cramplike sensation in l. part of præcordial region and under ribs. Sharp pain in region of heart. Heart's impulse increased, but the number of pulsations diminished. Pulse full; and strong; and soft. Pulse slow; in morning; in morning, and small, feeble, also irregular.

Neck.—Pain in nape at 2 P.M.; in neck at 7 A.M., < nape, with stiffness.

Back.—Pain; in morning, with lassitude; in forenoon; at night. Dragging pain in morning on waking; in evening. Bruised pain, with feeling as if severe illness had seized him. Pain under scapulæ; under l. scapula at 11 P.M.; in l. scapula and arm, extending to end of little finger. Sharp plunging pain in region of l. kidney. Pain in lumbar region; with general chilliness on going out-doors; heavy; dragging, in morning on waking, also till afternoon.

Extremities.—Pain; at 7 A.M.; centering in muscular parts above knees, also soreness and occasional darting pains. Sharp lancinations in l. axilla. Tearing in l. arm, < upper, sometimes extending to forearm, with darting pain in middle and ring fingers. Lame feeling in r. arm, < about wrist, with heaviness. Pain in l. upper arm at 8.45 A.M.; in r. third and little fingers at 9 A.M. Sharp shooting in r. thigh, then in l. thigh, then pain in l. shoulder. Drawing pain in muscles above knee at night. Piercing pain in inner side of l. knee. Pain from knee down, at 12.50 P.M., with coldness of lower limbs; contractive, in middle of leg, a little outside of outer edge of tibia, < motion, occasionally changing to burning pain, with soreness to touch. Pain in calves, with trembling, so that walking is unpleasant, pain < l.; P. in l. tendo-achillis, < touch and motion, with soreness; in hollow of r. foot; bruised, in l. heel.

Skin.—*Yellowish.* Pimples in different parts, a painful one on nose. Itching, < near insertion of deltoid in both arms; of face, then creeping sensation; and stinging like flea-bites, on r. side of face, then on neck, shoulder, forearm, midway between r. knee and ankle.

Sleep.—Yawning. Sleepiness; in forenoon during lectures, with dulness and vertigo; in afternoon, > open air; in evening, > walking in open air, with stupidity. Sound sleep in his chair. Unrefreshing sleep, with exacerbation of all symptoms on waking; U., with frequent wakings and bad dreams. Frequent waking towards morning, with feeling of insufficient sleep; F. waking, inability to sleep after 5 A.M. though sleepy. Restless sleep; towards morning; until 2 A.M.; with unremembered dreams. Amorous dream, with emission. Ugly dreams, at one time that his head was attacked by enormous bugs, which he felt obliged to kill with difficulty.

Fever.—Coldness; at 10 P.M. in open air; when going out of doors, with pain in lumbar region; with quivering sensation in l. calf; alternating with excited, feverish feeling; running over vertex, with tightening of scalp. Feverish feeling, with pulse at 60. Burning in face; at 8 A.M., with redness; and in head, also < after being in open air; in soles at night. Warmth along spine, < between scapulæ, then chill and sweat, < over dorsal vertebræ.

Naja.

The virus of the Cobra (Naja tripudians) is triturated with sugar of milk.

Allies.—It is to be compared with the serpent poisons in general, and especially with Lachesis.

Generalities.—Swelling of body. Local inflammation. Appearance as if intoxicated. Convulsive movement of mouth and limbs. Rolling about as if weak and faint. Moaned, grasped his throat, tossed his head from side to side and moved his arms and legs uneasily. Unnatural quiet, with groans and complaints of slight pains in the bitten arm.

Shooting in upper part of chest, in ankles and lower third of thighs. Occasional crampy pains in thighs, shoulders and nape. Cutting shifting about. Pain descended from body down leg till it ceased at the spot where he was bitten. Malaise; at 8 P.M.; as before a fever, towards evening. Indefinable sensation (*sorte d'enrahissement*), with lightness in head (*entreprise générale*). Sensitiveness to draught of air about head and face. Sensation of wasting away. Restlessness in afternoon. Great desire for and power of walking. Weakness; in morning; with restlessness; with indifference; mental and physical, suddenly at 8.30 P.M. Inclination to lie in bed in morning. Inability to support himself in a sitting posture. Swooning fits. Torpor; and listlessness. Loss of sense of feeling. Stiffness and insensibility. All symptoms > walking in open air.

Clinical.—In a general way it is indicated when organs seem to be drawn together, especially ovary and heart.

Mind.—Insanity, he suddenly split his own head in two with an axe. Excitable and playful. Quick-tempered. Irritable and restless. Displeased with everything. Cried and seemed to suffer much pain. Weeping mood from slight emotion, pleasing or otherwise. *Sadness;* > evening; *with irresolution;* with distress about sexual organs; with headache and inability for any exertion; as if everything were done wrong and could not be rectified, with increased perception of what I ought to do and uncontrollable inclination not to do it, causing restlessness. Brooding over imaginary troubles. Affected easily by wine or alcoholic drinks.

Mental and physical weakness, anxiety to do many things, but not inclined to move about them, disposition to huddle up near the fire and brood over one's business. Absence of mind. Dulness in evening. Stupid and confused feeling. Memory confused. Forgetful. Consciousness almost or quite lost. Insensible; and speechless. Comatose.

Head.—Aching; all day; in morning; in morning on waking; in evening; at 9 P.M., caused by eating a pear, with pain in abdomen; at night; at night, with much sleep; with melancholy, the pain usually began in temples, < r., deep-seated, involving eyes, occasionally shooting, extending as a dull aching over forehead and vertex, < motion, slightly > open air, > smoking and alcoholic liquors; throbbing A. at 3 P.M.; like a scald, < over l. eye, after breakfast; oppressive, at 8.30 A.M. Confusion; in morning. Hollow feeling. Heaviness. Congestion at noon; C., with fluid discharge from nose. Vertigo, then "stounding" pain in r. side of head.

Forehead.—Shooting; at night preventing sleep. Darting across F. Aching; above eyes; above r. eyelid and in r. temple; in l. protuberance; in lower part of brow; all day, with yawning and lassitude; in morning; in upper part in morning, with fulness; at night; < over temples, > going out, < motion or any exertion, > smoking mild tobacco, with weight over upper lids, tightness across vertex, soreness of scalp to touch, next day the same pain > 2 P.M. by pale brandy; A. waking in the night and in morning on waking, with occasional stitches in protuberances and with fluttering of heart; A., with weariness; in upper part, with fulness; with tightness of it and dryness of throat; with dragging and weariness in limbs; intermittent. Throbbing pain in afternoon; T. pain above eyes. Heavy aching; over eyes. Constriction across from one temple to the other; C. at night on going to bed, with heaviness of eyes; C. > breakfast; with anterior headache, not accustomed to this in afternoon; with dryness of mouth and cold feet. Fulness in F. and root of nose towards evening. Sensation as if brain were loose.

Stitches in l. temple; from one T. to the other after breakfast, > open air. Throbbing in temples, with fulness of head when lying. Aching in temples; in morning on waking, with heaviness in eyes; about noon over r. T. and gradually extending to forehead, > afternoon; in evening; in vertex; in vertex, with coldness of feet. Shooting up occiput. Feeling as of a blow from behind on head and nape. Scurf on scalp. Sensitiveness of scalp.

Eyes.—*Staring;* and pupils large and sluggish. Constriction, < breakfast. Heaviness; in evening; with pain and suffusion. Require constant cleansing with lids, frequent prickling, vision confused on looking at small print, have to rub eyes and look at it closely. Pupils dilated. Pain in balls requiring them to be rubbed frequently, with tired feeling on looking at a book. Hot pain at back of balls. Ptosis and paralysis of iris. Eyes wide open and insensible to light. Lids swollen in morning; r. swollen, < upper, and livid, the lividity extending to r. side of nose. Heaviness of lids; in forenoon, and edges of tarsal cartilages livid. Numbness of r. lid at night. Pricking in l. brow. Pain in brow. Vision weak; lost.

Ears.—Whizzing in l., with insipid, almost nauseous taste in mouth. Noise as of a mill, waking him in morning.

Nose.—Soreness of l. wing, with irritation; S. of r. nostril, with ulcerated feeling; S. of wing, with heat and tenderness, worse next day, with swelling and pain, secretion suffused, next day > an eruption on its edge; S., with heat and thin discharge. Stuffed, < evening by walking in a fog, > on returning home, by free discharge of watery mucus, next day nostrils clogged up. Coryza; at night, with headache over eyes, < r.

Clinical.—Hay fever, with asthmatic complications, after the stage of coryza and sneezing has mostly subsided, especially with a feeling of dryness in the larynx, suffocation, especially on lying down, has to be held erect in order to breathe; the suffocative spells occur after sleeping (Lach.).

Face.—Red on rising, > washing, and covered with knots like erysipelas; R. in evening, and burning; cheeks, < cheek-bones, patchy. Greenish-yellow. Livid. Pale and looked ill. Thin and haggard, dark around eyes. Anxious expression. Sticking deep in r. side. Jaws locked. Gnawing in l. upper jaw, waking soon after midnight, sometimes shooting to eye and temple. Bruised pain in l. condyle of jaw, < moving it. Drawing pain in r. jaw. Mouth wide open and tongue cold. Sore on under lip opposite l. canine tooth, and gum swollen and inflamed. Pimple on upper lip. Purple sordes on lips, gum and tongue. Lips feel hot and sore. Lips dry and cracked; and black pores; D., painful, excoriated.

Mouth.—Gnawing and aching in l. teeth and side of jaw. Pain in stumps of decayed teeth towards evening, with feeling in face and limbs as after catching cold, pain in face < night, and gums painful and swollen, next day teeth loose and gums hot, swollen and painful to touch, third day the swelling of gums extended to the other side, afterwards gnawing in l. sound teeth, next day drawing aching in l. teeth, < when stomach is empty.

Ulcer on frænum of tongue. Tongue coated white; coated yellow. Raw feeling on T. where the powder fell, as if it would rise to a blister. Dryness of T. in morning without thirst. Inarticulate speech. *Foaming at mouth.* Pain in a spot about centre of l. palate as if aconite were chewed. Rawness of palate; acid. *Dryness;* in morning on waking; at 8.30 A.M., with frequent expectoration as if from throat; and of throat, with disagreeable taste as if breath were offensive. Clammy in morning. Salivation. Breath hot and offensive, next day the heat and foul taste extended slowly to stomach. Taste sour; in evening, with nausea and roughness of tongue and palate; and raw; T. cuprous, metallic; bitter; "horrible."

Throat.—Pressure on upper part of r. sterno-mastoid muscle, extending over skin to angle of jaw. Hawking of mucus. Redness of l. side in morning, with pain on swallowing. Inflammation of l. tonsil at 8 A.M., with pain. Spasm. Starting about T. Sudden grasping, rousing him in morning when dozing, then sudden jerking of l. masseter. Shooting in l. tonsil. Pricking in l. side of pharynx; after fasting. Pain in morning, with gagging and with sad thoughts; in afternoon; as if she had taken cold; P. in one tonsil. Burning pressure on a point at back of pharynx in afternoon. Soreness of l. side. Tenderness in T. and over sternum.

Scraping at night; towards night, with hoarseness, and more effort required to swallow, next day scraping and at top of throat tenacious mucus inducing frequent inclination to swallow, third day mucus easily detached and always swallowed. Rawness. Roughness from reading aloud a short time. Discomfort like indigestion, low down. Dryness on waking; D. of fauces. Constriction; and dryness; of pharynx; of œsophagus, so that nothing could be forced down. Power of swallowing gone.

Clinical.—In diphtheria it is similar to Lach., the patient grasps at his throat, has a feeling of choking, fauces dark red, breath fetid, hoarse cough, with rawness in larynx and upper part of chest.

Stomach.—Appetite lost. Craving for stimulants, which aggravate the state. Desire for wine. Thirst. Eructations tasting like barley water; E. of hot, foul air. Acidity in S.

Nausea; all day; in morning; in forenoon, with empty eructations; in evening; in evening, with parched mouth and frequent inclination to expectorate adhesive saliva, but constant desire, to drink; in evening, with dulness, the D. > walking in open air, then excitement and mental and physical energy lasting all night, with a lively waking state, giving a sensation in morning of having been awake all night, the excitement lasted till next evening; at night; on going to bed; after breakfast and dinner; after a few walnuts, with pain in stomach; > open air, with pain and beating in stomach and prostration; with disagreeable sensation in mouth; sudden, after breakfast, > acid fruit, with faintness. Frequent faintish sick turns. "Sickish" from a feeling in throat opposite top of sternum, afterwards nausea with discomfort about stomach and headache above eyes till afternoon, belching of water and flatulence.

Vomiting; plentifully. Pricking; after dinner. Griping. Pinching; at night, like incipient gastrodynia. Spasmodic pain at night. Heat when empty, with hot and foul eructations. Uneasiness. Discomfort. Feeling as if loaded at night. Pressure as from stones after each meal. Feeling of indigestion, sensation of a lump in S. and upper part of œsophagus. Sinking.

Abdomen.—Swelling, with feeling of tightness and flatulence; S., with tension and pain, the T. spreading towards heart. Rumbling in afternoon, with cutting; R. in evening after dinner, with aching as before diarrhœa, and often when sitting still a heavy pulsation appeared almost to lift up the bowels; R. after dinner, with aching. Flatulence; during the day; at night, with pain; with pain.

Tearing in morning; at night; intermittent. Cutting; extending to lower part of back. Griping after dinner, > large bilious stool. Sharp pain. Pain; at night; occasional; flatulent, at night before sleep; contractive, in A. and loins at night on going to bed. Empty sensation, > pressing arms over it.

Intermittent sticking backward in hypochondria during the day. Anguish in l. hypochondrium and l. loin after dinner, with flatulence. Frequent griping in umbilical region. Frequent cutting in U. region and small of back in afternoon, then profuse and sudden leucorrhœa. Occasional twisting pain in U. region. Uneasiness in U. region. Griping in l. side. Pain along l. side, > flatulent eructations. Internal cutting shooting upward in lower A. Darting forward from l. ilium into abdominal muscles in evening. Griping in lower A., with desire for stool. Tormina in lower A., with desire to evacuate it.

Rectum.—Feeling of a large stool, which when voided was small. Urging always sudden, whether followed by diarrhœa or not; sudden U., then small bilious stool. Heat in anal region, with itching smarting at anus.

Stool.—Watery, light, forcible, after sudden urging when walking. Diarrhœa in an infant; D., with much flatus, after pain in abdomen; D., with pain in abdomen; profuse; sudden; slimy, white or green (in an infant); bilious, always preceded by sudden urging and griping in abdomen; then stool omitted for two days, then S. partly costive, partly loose, with pain in abdomen. Constipation. Hard, passed with distress and feeling as if more fæces remained. Scanty.

Urinary Organs.—Uneasiness in bladder, with pressure. Urine of deep straw color. Urine loaded with lithates and mucus. Red sediment, mixed with mucus.

Sexual Organs.—Peculiar distress, great desire but

no physical power, with depression of mind. Stinging, somewhat burning pain along r. side of penis, immediately under skin, at night in bed and in morning after rising. Instinct and power excited. Desire on going to bed, with little physical power, with frequent waking, vivid imaginations, painful state of mind, involuntary emissions, then prostration and distress. Crampy pain in region of l. ovary. Thin, whitish leucorrhœa in afternoon.

Clinical.—Neuralgia of l. ovary, with palpitation and pain about heart.

Respiratory Organs.—Larynx. L. and trachea clogged up with thick mucus, which was hawked up with difficulty. Pricking, with desire to cough. Raw feeling > coughing. Tightness after getting into bed at night and next day, with stuffed sensation and cough. Uneasy constriction or irritation, causing desire to cough without the organic inclination. Irritation, < at night by going out in fog, with cough; I. evinced by short frequent cough on going into a cold room or into open air; and in trachea; and in top of trachea, as from an irritating vapor, with warmth and rawness, as after fast running, causing short tickling, hoarse cough, with hoarseness. Tickling at top, with teasing constriction and tenacious mucus; T. in morning on waking, with nausea, sneezing and coughing, the T. continued in afternoon, with scanty, viscid, mucous expectoration.

Hoarseness; in morning; when reading aloud. Speechless. Tenderness over trachea. Feeling in trachea between larynx and top of sternum as if it had been skinned. Tickling in trachea. Feeling as if a hair were in T. Irritating, raw, rough pain in T., causing hard cough, which made me giddy and caused noise in head and pain in chest. Irritation in T., with heaviness at top of chest.

Cough; in morning, with taste of blood; with wheezing; short, tickling, hoarse; in fits when warm in bed, with peculiar sensation about fauces and larynx; dry hacking, towards noon, with tickling at top of throat, then hoarseness, the last < towards night, with scraping in throat. Expectoration of whitish, viscid mucus in morning on waking. Spitting of blood, which had no tendency to coagulate.

Respiration difficult; and stertorous. Gasping for breath; with several deep-drawn inspirations. Respirations 20 per minute and very shallow. Respiration hardly perceptible; could only be recognized by hand on abdomen. R. and pulse imperceptible.

Chest.—Milk decreased, next day returned freely, afterwards scanty. Shooting in r. side; in various places in l. Occasional "stounding" pains in C. and abdomen. Warm pricking in many points over lower half of front, from fifth rib downward, in evening, with heat extending up bronchi into pharynx, with hard cough ending in expectoration of a little thick mucus.

Pain in l. pectoral muscles in forenoon; occasional P. at top of mammæ; P. and oppression as if a hot iron had been run in and a hundred-weight put on top of it, > hartshorn and water. Heavy pain on lower half of r. in bed, with stabbing on deep inspiration, an attempt to breathe deeply caused sudden, short, puffing cough, a real cough impossible on account of the stabbing, cannot lie on l. side, but > lying on r. side, next day at 8 A.M. dulness on percussion as high as r. nipple, third day sticking in front of l. chest at 8 A.M., at noon it extended all over l. side, could not ride, could hardly walk, had to press l. side and bend towards that side, on walking fast it was as if a broken rib tore the lung, on attempting to breathe deeply lancinations in all directions through C., also short, puffing cough, respirations 34 per minute, could not lie on r., > lying on l. side.

Asthmatic constriction in evening, > mucous expectoration. Contractive pains. Hard pressure just above r. nipple in afternoon. Tightness across upper part; with pain to right of sternum, just behind r. rib, passing under sternum, the spot tender to touch. Uneasy aching in evening, < l. side. Uneasiness in upper part; U. about l. after fasting. Tenderness over sternum. Heat in l., < two inches below middle of clavicle, after a moderate walk, with uneasiness and pain.

Heart.—Shooting about præcordial region after breakfast. *Pain near H.;* P. extending to l. scapula after riding, not affected by deep inspiration. Nervous sensation. Peculiar oppression. *Depressed feeling.* Felt a want of something about præcordia, tried to sing, but had no power to throw out the voice. Uneasiness when walking. Heat towards evening, with uneasy aching. Palpitation. Audible beating. Fluttering during headache; sudden F. when writing, with rising in throat. Action only recognized by pushing hand up behind sternum, then felt only a faint thrill resembling the cardiac thrill felt in the same way on a new-born infant.

Clinical.—After diphtheria, threatening paralysis of the heart, the patient becomes blue, gasps for breath on waking, pulse intermittent and feeble. A kind of angina pectoris, acute pain, with loss of breath. After articular rheumatism, severe pain in heart, extending to shoulder, neck and arm, with deathly anxiety, the attacks wake from sleep, palpitation, constriction, dry cough, etc. Persistent palpitation for nearly a year, without organic disease of the heart.

Pulse.—Rapid; and full; 120, some beats tolerably full and strong, afterwards 32, irregular in rhythm and force, some of the beats full and bounding. Weak and thready. Hardly perceptible.

Neck.—Cutting in nape. Aching in nape. Tired feeling in cervical and dorsal vertebræ all day, with the peculiar burning often attendant on exhaustion.

Back.—Shooting from inner and upper angle of l. scapula to front of chest. Uneasy dragging in spine between scapulæ. Pain between scapulæ, < moving arms; in region of spine; in spine between scapulæ, afterwards involving scapulæ; rheumatic, in muscles of scapula, < moving scapulæ. Gnawing in lower part of back, < after going to bed. Pain in loins; in morning; acute, in evening; occasionally during the day, constant at night after going to bed and then with languishing pain in abdomen and flatulence; in r. as on running soon after a meal, somewhat as from pressing on testicle, with occasional shooting, a similar feeling spread over abdomen and to r. groin, > bending forward. Weakness of loins.

Extremities.—Drawing, lacerating in various parts of r., < motion. Aching in ankles, lower part of thighs, wrists and shoulder-joints; in all parts on waking; bruised, on waking. In afternoon occasional rheumatic pains in thighs and arms, < shoulder-joints; shifting R. (drawing-aching) P. in arms, shoulders and legs, < l. *Sudden weakness* when walking in evening.

Upper Extremities.—Rheumatic pains in shoulders; R. drawing in l. shoulder in morning. Aching in shoulder; in arm up to shoulder all day; acute, in bitten part, which soon extended to top of arm. Drawing shooting in l. elbow in afternoon. Burning pain in wrist, and he hung down his arm, from which a few drops of blood fell (from the bite).

Hand.—Swelling of H. and thumb; of H. and arm, with spots; of the bitten H. and of arm and breast of same side, with livid spots. Crampy pain in l. palm and numbness and shifting rheumatic pains, < shoulder-joints, and numbness of hands as if asleep. Numb pain and feeling as if ether had been allowed to evaporate. Pain (in the part bitten) spreading over palm and arm, with swelling, pain in arm, gangrene about the punctures, then spreading over palm and back of hand and part of wrist, laying the tendons bare and forming an ulcer.

Fingers.—Aching in r. fourth and little, then sensation of thumbing (*fouillement*) in middle of l. triceps. Acute pain under l. thumb-nail (where virus had entered), running up arm.

Lower Extremities.—Staggering when walking. Dragging when walking, with weariness. Pain on points, with drawing, and in feet. Pain anteriorly in r. thigh; posteriorly in thighs in afternoon. Shooting down leg and tingling in feet. Drawing pain in lower part of tendo-achillis, < motion, afterwards increased to lameness, > evening. Pain in the bitten toe, ascending to top of thigh, then pain in belly, which was tense and swollen, then the pain descended in the same track in which it had risen.

Skin.—Dark color of the bitten ankle, spreading up the limb. Boil-like swelling on back of middle phalanx of r. little finger. Painful chilblains on feet. Pimple on l. ala nasi; on inflamed base, on tip of nose, and nose sore in consequence; painful, on brow. White, itching blisters on inflamed base, on neck and body in afternoon. Pricking in the wound. Tingling in legs and feet when standing. Itching in scar of an ulcer; creeping I. in various parts.

Sleep.—Yawning. Sleepiness; in evening, and weakness, went to bed at 9 P.M. and fell asleep immediately; < after tea, > hard walking and profuse sweat. Dozing and moaning. Little inclination for sleep, brain irritable. Slept ill the first part of the night and head ached. Restless sleep; and dreamy. S. broken and disturbed. Frequent waking, with dry mouth, dreams vivid, mind active, body not restless, next morning not fatigued as after an ordinary bad night. Many dreams. Long and vivid D., little recollection of the subjects; vivid, of the affairs of the day, with additions and new plans for the morrow. D. of murders, suicides, fires, etc.

Fever.—Chilliness; from 6 to 8 P.M.; at 8 P.M., with partial heat, at 11 P.M. fever with partial chills; and collapse; and starved, miserable feeling, glad to huddle into bed, offended with the least draught of air. Coldness of whole l. side, the skin icy to touch, but no numbness or stiffness of joints, next night shifting to r. side. Cold limbs, < hands; l. arm and back of hand; limbs, and corpselike, up to upper part of thighs and axillæ. Cold feet; all day; in morning; on going to bed; with aching on vertex; and legs, with hot hands; chilly creeping over l. foot and leg.

Heat, but he refused water; H., with prostration; with discomfort, dry lips and tender and hot mouth. Hot skin and pain in an encysted tumor over upper part of l. acromion process, like pain in a finger that has suppurated and is healing. Head hot; and full of blood. Burning of ear. Flushes of heat in face at different times of day; flushes in face, < l. side. Hot palms; hands and sweaty palms. General sweat; cold, clammy.

Naphthaline.

Pure Naphthaline is triturated for use.

Clinical.—It has been found a valuable remedy for hay fever, many inveterate cases seeming to have been entirely arrested; sneezing, eyes inflamed and painful, head hot; also spasmodic bronchitis and asthma, > open air, with soreness in chest and stomach, has to loosen the clothing; also pulmonary emphysema, with great dyspnœa, sighing inspiration, > violent motion, it seems as if she could not get air out of the chest; it is also valuable in whooping cough, with long-continued paroxysms, cannot get an inspiration. Dysmenorrhœa. For gonnorhœa, following the acute stage.

Natrum Arsenicatum.

Pure Sodium arsenate is triturated for use.

Allies.—More related to Nat. m. than to Arsen.

Generalities.—Weight diminished. *Embonpoint*, then emaciation. Venous trunks full when seen on surface. Takes cold easily. Miserable feeling at 8 A.M. on rising. Indisposition, > in the country. Restless; and nervous. Weakness; during the day; in morning on rising, with bruised sensation; on waking; easy, from walking; with sensation as if I should get out of breath if I walked fast; with desire to lie or sit; with listlessness and desire to sit still; with malaise, so that I could not eat dinner. Aggravation after eating. Amelioration of all symptoms on walking in open air, but dulness returned on sitting down in the house.

Mind.—Irritability; and no desire to study; and feeling of taciturnity. Anxiety about everything. Feeling as if something were impending, causing him to move about. Depression; and desire to sit quietly. Listless. Stupid feeling all day. Dull; all day, and languid. Do not wish to read, think or exercise, feel better doing nothing. No disposition to attend to his accustomed business. Forgetful. Inability to concentrate mind; during afternoon headaches, unable to recall names, indisposed to study or speak; when reading; with confusion. Difficult to concentrate mind. Inability to think, and restlessness; I. to think readily, > afternoon. Studying is easy, reconciled to circumstances, feel like working hard, no undertaking too large for me.

Head.—Aching every time he woke; intermittent A. in morning. Sore feeling. Brain jarred by every motion. Throbbing on ascending stairs. Dulness; from 6 till 9 P.M., with heaviness; in evening, with heaviness of it and nausea; < vertex, increasing till I went to bed, < stooping and moving head; > afternoon, with heaviness; with heaviness, then aching, < every motion, taking away the appetite, > 3 P.M., by tying a handkerchief tightly around it; as if he had taken cold. Fulness; in morning; at 8 P.M., with heat in it. Vacant feeling. Heaviness. Wavering, floating sensation on turning head quickly.

Forehead.—Shooting through F.; and r. temple; S. above r. eye. Aching; and in temples, < in and above orbits; over r. eye; during the day; all day till 4 P.M.; in morning on waking; from morning on waking till 1 P.M., and in temples, < from temple to temple; in morning on waking, < during the day, *aching across brow, over orbits and in eyeballs;* in afternoon, with sweat; in F. and temples from between 2 and 3 till 5 P.M., with soreness to touch, listlessness and absent-mindedness; every day from 3 till 9 or 10 P.M., with dulness and indisposition to study or speak; *above orbits*, reaching into temple; heavy, in ethmoid bone. *Dulness in F. and root of nose;* at top, with heaviness, and occasionally sharp pain in side and top of head. Heaviness. Fulness in afternoon, with throbbing in vertex. Numbness in evening.

Temples.—Boring outward, < r. and extending to l., in afternoon, with nausea, internal heat in head, but external coldness of forehead, the pain < heat, pressure and tobacco-smoke. Pain; from one to other over orbits all day; in r. in morning on rising; in T. and supraorbital regions in morning on waking, passing at 4 or 5 P.M. into orbit posterior to and in eyeball, also with photophobia, pain < orbit, compelling him to lie down; in r. at 8 A.M.; through r. during breakfast; in r. at 5 P.M., < evening by stooping, pain shifted to orbital region, two days later > noon by eating, returned on walking in hot sun, > next day at 6 P.M.; through, across and above T. and in superciliary ridge, < forenoon. Drawing pain in r. Throbbing in artery.

Vertex.—Aching; all day, and above eyes; at 9.30 A.M.; in afternoon and evening, and above eyes, < above r. eye; at 8 P.M.; till after dinner, and in sides of head; intermittent.

Occiput.—Pressure on sides of posterior inferior part, as if in a photographer's rest.

Eyes.—Red; in morning on waking; and watery. Swollen; in morning on waking, and sore; eyes and orbital region S. in morning on waking, and agglutination; < l., and inflamed; < rising, and painful. Dim at 8 A.M.; D. on looking long at an object. Pain; in morning; at 8 P.M. when reading and writing; on looking at anything; when reading and writing, and tired feeling all day; < light; < sunlight, with tired feeling; < just after rising, with soreness. Sore all day, < 7 P.M. by reading; at 9.30 A.M., with full feeling; on rising; on pressure; on moving them, with aching; l., < light, with scratching beneath lids on rolling ball; and sticky. Smarting; on reading; in open air, with lachrymation; as from wood-smoke. Swollen feeling; in morning; and inflamed feeling, with pasty matter in canthus and on lashes. Burning; all day, as from wood-smoke. Discomfort in open air; on reading by lamp or gaslight. Heaviness; in morning, < r.; in evening. Feeling as from loss of sleep. Irritable. Symptoms < open air.

Lachrymation; in morning after waking; at 9 A.M.; at 9.30 A.M. when reading; on looking steadily at an object; in open air; in open air, < morning. Pain deep in balls after reading, < opening eyes widely, > closing and resting them. Balls sore on pressure all day; S. at 12 P.M., < pressure; on touch; on closing lids; and smarting. Balls seem too large in morning on waking, when closing lids. *Balls and inside of lids are full, causing feeling on moving ball as of something granular between them.* Balls stiff. Pupils dilated; l.; in morning; l. at 5 and 11 P.M.; l., > 1 P.M. when walking, with misty vision.

Lids.—Agglutinated in morning. Inside of lower granular. Swollen; < lower; lower looked and felt like a bag, livid circles around eyes; lining thick and red, and as eyes are rolled the lining gathers in folds between balls and lids, l. eye worse. Swollen feeling, < r.; < r., and < outer canthus, in morning, r. lower feels S. and itchy, as before a stye. Disposed to close; and unable to open as wide as usual. Stiff. Burning in morning; B. on edges, with itching.

Gum in external canthus; whitish, in external C. in morning. Inner canthus red and sore. Inner canthus itches in morning and feels pasty. Sclerotica congested. Conjunctiva congested; in morning on waking; from slight exposure to cold or wind; and jaundiced; and white of eye yellow. Orbital region swollen; < r.; in morning on waking; supraorbital; infraorbital. Aching across orbits; through O. and brow; in supraorbital region, with dulness; in supraorbital region, extending up forehead, < just above orbits. Aching across brows in morning on waking, with vertigo on moving about, and lightness or largeness of head when sitting. Heavy, full feeling in orbital region, reaching to temples.

Vision.—Blurred. Dim; at noon on rising from a seat; for long distances. Flickering before eyes when they are closed, at 8 A.M. Photophobia. Eyes feel weak, as if lids must be closed to protect balls, conjunctiva dry and painful, vision blurred after looking at an object a short time, eyes sensitive to light, eye symptoms < morning, > towards evening.

Clinical.—Chronic conjunctivitis, membrane very rough, eye dry and painful; granular lids.

Ears.—Shooting over r. in afternoon. Hearing dull.

Nose.—Redness of r. side and bridge, with sore and indurated pimple on r. side. Nostrils indurated and sore; nostrils I. and inflamed. Mucous membrane thick and nostrils obstructed. Pain at root; compressive, at root. Nostrils tender on touch. Dryness. Stoppage; of r. nostril; in morning; in morning on waking; in morning on rising; < night and morning, little discharge during the day, but feeling as if mucous membrane were swollen, hard bluish mucus blown out in morning, then mucous membrane feels sore and raw; of r. nostril, with dryness; of r. nostril, with blowing of thick yellowish mucus from it; but air can be drawn through freely. Sneezing; through the day; in morning on inspiring cool air, with free watery or semi-mucous discharge, S. always renewed on inspiring cool air; paroxysmal, by day.

Fluent coryza; in evening. Discharge less in afternoon; D. whitish and thick; thick, yellowish; of tenacious whitish mucus; of yellowish mucus; tough and yellowish; tough, hard, sometimes when dislodged it causes bleeding, dropping from posterior nares of mucus which collects in a tough and tenacious mass, causing considerable hawking to dislodge it. Watery discharge; from l. nostril in morning on rising, > after 10 A.M.; in afternoon and evening; < l. nostril; or semi-mucous; from l. nostril, more gluey from r., with chafing from frequent use of handkerchief; becoming tough and yellow. Bleeding in evening. Sense of smell defective; lost (Nat. m.).

Clinical.—Nasal catarrh, with supraorbital headache, burning in eyes, watery discharge, dry throat, < morning. Nasal catarrh, with pain at root of nose, the discharge passes into the throat and has to be hawked up. Nasal catarrh, the nose constantly feels stuffed, with more or less affection of the eyes.

Face.—Red; and hot; or purplish. Swollen in morning on waking, < orbital region. Swollen feeling, with heat; S. feeling in malar-bones. Muscles of mastication stiff and motion of jaw painful. Corners of lips, < r., indurated and painful, two days later fissured, < r. R. corner of lips ulcerated, as from a cold.

Mouth.—Teeth and gums tender. Tongue fissured, large and moist; F., large and soft; F. and flabby. Blister on r. side of tongue near base. Tongue coated; on waking, at back, and papillæ large there, but anterior part fissured; and red, cracked, uneven; and deep red, corrugated, next day papillæ stand up on posterior part. Tongue coated white; in morning on rising; along middle from tip to base; except edges and tip; < back part; densest near base, in morning; with rough feeling; with metallic taste after drinking water; grayish-white; grayish-white in morning; yellowish-white. Tongue coated yellow; whitish; whitish, posteriorly, becoming lighter nearer the tip, and tongue corrugated. Tongue feels dry as if burnt, not > liquids. Sore ulcer in mouth. Salivation, with nausea. Taste bitter; at 9.30 A.M.; T. sour at 9.30 A.M.; clammy; pasty; insipid.

Throat.—Pain all afternoon in r. side at bifurcation of common carotid, on moving head or on pressure. Stiffness of upper part of sterno-cleido-mastoideus at 11.45 A.M., with tenderness. Redness after trifling exposure to cold, with puffiness; R. of throat and pharynx, < fauces, less on soft palate, lost on arch, next day throat purplish-red and raw-looking, next day pharynx and pillars of fauces red, thick and angry-looking, no soreness on swallowing; of fauces and pharynx, with glassy look; of tonsils, uvula and soft palate, and thickness and sore look, without special pain on swallowing. Purple, rough, pitted in places and studded with points filled with mucus; tonsils, fauces, pharynx and most of soft palate purplish-red and œdematous and covered in places with a tough, whitish, viscid mucus; tonsils, uvula and pharynx purplish-red, and yellowish or yellowish-gray mucus, color deepest on inner edge of tonsils and uvula. Swelling, with discomfort on swallowing. Rough; and clogged with tenacious, dark slate-colored mucus. Tough yellowish mucus in upper part of pharynx and in posterior nares.

Hawking; all day; in morning; < open air; of tenacious whitish-yellow mucus till 10 or 11 A.M.; tenacious white mucus in afternoon; tenacious starchy-looking mucus; tough and yellow mucus; yellowish, consistent mucus from posterior nares; grayish, viscid, tenacious mucus, with rough feeling in throat; semi-solid whitish mucus from throat and posterior nares, < lying down to sleep; thick white mucus, < inhalation of dust, smoke, etc., with discharge of thick yellow mucus from posterior nares.

Scraping and raw tickling. Smarting in posterior nares in afternoon. Posterior nares feel obstructed, preventing easy and clear articulation. Constriction in afternoon; below larynx in evening and next day; in region of thyroid cartilage, as if pressed between thumb and finger. Heaviness and pain. Dryness; of fauces and pharynx; during the day, and soreness and emptiness; fauces and pharynx all day; fauces and pharynx in morning on waking; fauces and pharynx on waking, with stiffness; of fauces on inspiration and swallowing, < morning and after taking cold; with stiffness; fauces and pharynx, with stiffness; with gagging on trying to dislodge stiff, tenacious mucus in upper part of pharynx. Swallowing painful; empty, but not of food and drink. Constrictive, burning feeling in œsophagus.

Clinical.—In diphtheria, with excessive swelling and great prostration, throat dark purple, uvula excessively swollen, like a sac of water, body cool and sweaty, great oppression of heart, feeble, intermittent pulse.

Stomach.—Appetite great; poor. Appetite lost at breakfast; and dinner; ate no breakfast, and from 11 A.M. till dinner (12.30) had darting sticking in great cul-de-sac; at noon, but took some food and a cup of coffee, which relieved the head for a time, at supper desired pickles, which gave a relish for bread and butter, of which I ate freely, and by 8 P.M. felt much better; except for juicy food or fruits; for tobacco; afterwards very great. Aversion to the accustomed cigar, and aggravation of symptoms after smoking. Thirst; all day; all day, wanted water often, but little at a time; every day till 10 A.M.; at night; on getting out of bed; but feel worse after drinking; absent.

Eructations caused by breakfast becoming sour in stomach; sour E. after eating. Pyrosis below thyroid cartilage in afternoon. Nausea; in night after a supper consisting principally of fruits, then chills on back; on going to bed; after dinner, > soda-water without syrup; after a drink of cold water; passed off with a flash of heat and feeling of moisture on skin, which before was very dry; with pain and urging to stool; alternating with pain in stomach and abdomen. Empty retching. Gagging when the tenacious mucus behind soft palate is brought into pharynx. Vomiting of much sour water; > lying quietly; V. of sour fluid at 5 P.M., at the first bite of food, the odor of which is pleasant to him.

Fulness at 9.45 A.M., with pain; F. after moderate eating, and of abdomen. Cramp in forenoon; at 1.30 A.M., and in chest. Feeling in epigastric region as if some irritating or burning substance were in it. Epigastric region tender; on pressure; on pressure in morning; < below ensiform; on pressure extending to upper part of ensiform; on deep pressure, and in umbilical region. Tightness. Heaviness after a moderate dinner. Discomfort; so that he cannot sleep late. Distress in epigastrium on walking about the room, soon extending through abdomen. Sinking in epigastrium at the same hour that he had had headache, with yawning and dulness in supraorbital and frontal regions. Sickening feeling, not nausea; < eating. Sourness. Indigestion, with sore feeling in stomach, and anything warm or heating causes burning and can be felt on entering stomach.

Abdomen.—Distention at 11.20 A.M., with pain and escape of gas; D. > passage of gas, with pain, but straining pressure on walking caused sharp pain; > 5 P.M. by passage of gas and sour urine, with pain; compelling opening of clothes. Rumbling when pressed; R., with pain; in morning, as before diarrhœa. Emission of flatus; when abdomen is pressed. Cutting waking him at 3 A.M., > emission of flatus. Occasional griping. Pinching and soreness. Pinching-burning pain at 10 A.M. Cramplike pain at 10.30 P.M.

Pain; through A.; on early waking, with headache; in morning, with diarrhœa, the returns of pain farther apart and less severe each time till 1 P.M.; in afternoon, > loose stool, with burning; on pressure;

through A. on sudden pressure, > emission of flatus; before normal stool, > emission of flatus; > emission of flatus; > stool; > diarrhœa; with urging to stool; with urging to stool, stool soft and large, later a small thin, dark, slimy stool, next day stool dark, large and lumpy, an hour later felt weak and nervous, hands trembled, then scanty stool, then burning; waking him, then copious, lumpy, urgent stool, then at 8 and 11 A.M. loose lumpy stools with wind; flatulent, > stool or escape of flatus; occasional, through A.; shifting, through A. in morning on getting out of bed and at times through the day; making him sick. Discomfort. Symptoms < during the day.

Umbilical Region. — Distention and pain, and in hypogastrium. Pain in morning, > free discharge of flatus; P. at 9 P.M. from distention by gas; before stool; and in hypogastrium, with frequent discharges of flatus; occasionally through U. region in morning, with frequent emissions of flatus.

Borborygmus in l. side between costal cartilages and anterior part of crest of ilium, with sharp pain. Shooting over liver in morning; S. in l. hypochondrium before stool; occasionally in spleen. Sharp pain in ilium at 4 P.M. after rising. Frequent crampy pains through small intestines. Pain through small intestines before escape of gas. Flatulent pain in region of transverse colon.

Hypogastrium.—Shooting once from l. groin across umbilicus to costal cartilages. Cutting at 1.30 A.M., then large stool, in ten minutes another stool preceded by cutting, and at 8 A.M. a yellowish, watery stool; periodical C. along both Poupart's ligaments at the same time, after each pain sickening bruised sensation in l. testicle, with sensitiveness of testicle to touch, the pains more frequent by day. Pain in afternoon; P. in l. groin; in groins after going to bed; occasionally in morning.

Rectum and Anus.—Excoriation of A., < at stool. Tearing in A. during stool. Gnawing in lower part of R., as of worms, at 11.45 A.M. Ineffectual urging; all the evening, with burning in region of A. Dragging in perineum and lower part of scrotum.

Stool.—Liquid, large, pungent, at 6 A.M., preceded by pain. Diarrhœa; at 10 A.M. (usually have stool before going to bed at night), with griping and burning at anus; with flatus and tenesmus; painless; forcible, with tenesmus; dark, then burning in anus, three times daily, relieving pain; scanty, three times before 9 A.M.; copious, brownish, painless, with much flatulence; last part laxative and pungent, twice in one day, with desire for stool twice besides, > emission of flatus; alternating with constipation. Soft, dark, then burning in anus, three times in a day; first part of morning stool soft, another in evening thin and lumpy. Mushy; and frequent, with flatus. Pasty and dark; and small, twice a day; P. and copious; P., small, light brown, preceded by pain through abdomen, followed by burning in abdomen, afterwards frequent desire for stool, > passage of gas or urine.

Lumpy. Firm and small, twice a day; F. and large, with much gas and with relief of abdomen, afterwards small, firm stool. Almost black. Light. Yellowish and sticky; Y. and scanty. Small, with much gas, relieving abdomen; S., only about every alternate day. Twice a day. Frequent, muco-purulent, with flatulence and tenesmus. Omitted.

Urinary Organs.—Soreness in region of bladder, > micturition. Urging, waking him. Micturition frequent and copious, watery, without discomfort; M. twice at night, of copious pale urine. Polyuria, had to urinate every two hours day and night, tenesmus vesica if I restrained the desire, urine of the color of Catawba wine, a little over a gill at each discharge. Micturition but twice in twenty-four hours. Burning in urethra when urine begins to flow. Urine copious; with urging; and clear; and light-colored. Urine dark. Urine as clear as water. U. light yellow, cloudy, a deposit after standing two hours, reaction acid, sp. gr. 1029, heat precipitates a dense white granular substance, which dissolves when nitric acid is used, leaving urine clear and reddish-brown, a few epithelial scales, a cast, some fat-globules and phosphates are seen, two days later urine dark straw-colored, of mild odor, reaction acid, sp. gr. 1030, phosphates abundant.

Sexual Organs.—Emission at night in sleep.

Respiratory Organs.—*Oppressed or stuffed sensation* all day from larynx to bottom of sternum. Constriction in lower part of larynx, < r. side, with burning. Dryness in larynx, with inflamed feeling and difficulty in detaching scanty, dark slate-colored mucus. Voice husky. Difficulty in modulating voice.

Cough; on waking; after deep inspirations; < forenoon; < heat of room; < when throat is dry; > night; paroxysmal. Dry cough; all day, < forenoon, causing gagging; during the morning, with irritation in bronchial region; on walking or any exertion requiring increase of volume of respiration; with dryness down trachea and into bronchia; with oppression of chest; with tightness and oppression in middle and upper third of chest; spasmodic, evenings, with roughness of larynx and disposition to hem. Dry, hacking cough; all day; at 4 P.M., < heat of room; after supper; < forenoon. Loose cough when up at night; L., and once or twice per day a little starchy-looking substance is dislodged from a spot under fourth rib to right of sternum, where there is soreness on pressure. Cough, with grayish or bluish-black expectoration; spasmodic C. in morning, with expectoration of lumps of grayish mucus.

Respiration.—Sixteen per minute. Sighing. Oppressed and short, at 9 A.M., often compelled to take a deep breath, with occasional pain in r. side of chest. Sounds not clear; in lower lobe of r. lung; sounds dull in lower half of lungs, but the usual resonance on percussion all over chest; sounds very indistinct, except in upper part of lungs.

Clinical.—In tuberculosis, hectic fever, night-sweats, emaciation, etc., greenish profuse expectoration with racking cough.

Chest.—Sticking under r. mamma; in both sides, in space between fourth and seventh ribs; between sixth and seventh ribs, at about junction of ribs with cartilages, at 9.30 and 10 P.M.; near cartilage of fifth rib, reaching back to scapula; from short ribs down across l. hypochondrium in afternoon. Pleuritic pain over liver in afternoon. Sharp, quick pain anteriorly below seventh rib. Pain below seventh rib, about two inches from sternum, but not in both sides at the same time, later oppression and soreness; P. under ensiform cartilage at 12.05 P.M.; most of the day anteriorly through upper lobe of l. lung, without soreness on pressure; over region of lower ribs, with soreness on pressure; in r. side, with soreness; in r. side, beneath cartilages of fourth and fifth ribs, with irritation and soreness, afterwards uneasiness, which, on physical exertion, causes a teazing, producing a dry, hacking cough and soreness, these symptoms < deep inspiration, dust and close air; between nipples, with hollow feeling there and choking sensation in throat, < inhaling carburetted hydrogen.

Bruised feeling under sternum and to left of it, at junction of upper and middle third of bone, on throwing shoulders upward and backward, at times extending to lower angle of scapula and to shoulder-joint, where there had been for five days weary aching on raising arm. Soreness of lungs; S. all day; in morning; on full inspiration; on inspiration, and on deep inspiration pain, at times cutting short the inspiration; on touch, anteriorly between sixth, seventh and eighth ribs; anteriorly on moderate percussion. Soreness on pressure, under r. mamma; in supra-clavicular region all day; between sixth and seventh ribs in morning.

Oppression; in centre, in afternoon; during motion, with soreness; < inspiration, lasting the rest of the day, with fulness, soreness and with short, dry cough from irritation behind upper half of sternum; > copious micturition; *with fulness;* as from a weight on lungs. Lungs feel clogged. Stuffed sensation all day, < behind sternum and from larynx to epigastrium. Constriction, and at times desire to breathe deeply. Distress, > repeated doses of Pulsatilla. Discomfort behind sternum on full inspiration. Irritation behind lower part of upper third of sternum. Feeling as if smoke had been inhaled, causing cough.

Heart.—Sounds loud and distinct, so as to prevent hearing clearly the respiratory sounds; sounds heard distinctly through nearly all of chest. Beating felt through chest; beating violently on unusual or prolonged exertion.

Pulse.—Rapid; and full; and intermittent; and in early part of day slender and intermittent; and variable in volume; and slender, irregular; and at times slender, at times full and irregular. Full. Slow; and irregular in volume and beat. Irregular.

Neck.—Soreness at lower cervical vertebra, extending to points of and under scapulæ, first felt at night, on getting out of bed and moving arms and shoulders. Stiffness; of l. side, with soreness.

Back.—Soreness; and in abdomen. Sticking between scapulæ on deep inspiration. Pain between scapulæ on inspiration, from 8 till 9 A.M., causing inclination to bend forward, gradually passing around below point of r. scapula to r. side below ninth and across tenth rib.

Lumbar Region.—Pain; across sacrum; in kidneys; in region of r. kidney, < walking; in kidney region, with profuse urine; in evening, extending over back, < between shoulders, and even affecting arms; across sacrum and down thighs, > walking, returning on sitting down. Tenderness in renal region; in sacrum on walking or stooping, first felt in morning on getting out of bed, < pressure on each side of sacrum on a line with acetabulum, < l. side, > walking some time. Weakness in sacral region; from crest of ilium down outer side of thighs to knees, beginning in afternoon.

Extremities.—Aching in all; wandering, < joints and l. side; rheumatic, < lower, running from hips to toes, < rest, > motion, these pains remain a few moments in muscles supplied by sciatic nerve, < flexors of thighs and legs. Joints felt stiff.

Upper Extremities.—Neuralgic pain from axilla along inside of arm to little finger at 9 A.M. Shoulder-joints crack on raising or depressing arm, the pain in shoulder passes down median nerve to finger-tip. Rheumatic aching in r. arm, < shoulder and wrist. Weary aching in l. arm on raising it, < pressure and motion. Aching in flexors of l. forearm, near their insertion at elbow, in morning when riding. Stiffness of flexors of l. forearm on holding anything in hand with arm flexed.

Sticking along palmar surface of fourth metacarpal bones, not in both hands at the same time. Metacarpo-phalangeal bone of r. index sore on pressure, so that it is painful to hold a pencil for any time. Twitching of l. middle and index fingers. Pain in second joints of fingers; from tips of l. fourth and fifth F. to elbow; sharp, in r. little F. at 9.45 A.M.; rheumatic, in r. index; flying, in F., palms and forearms.

Lower Extremities.—Neuralgia in nerves supplying flexors, < l. Pain in flexors; P. in l. iliac region, hip and knee, with occasional twinges in r. knee. Heaviness. Pain in l. hip-joint; and inner aspect of thigh; in l. hip-joint when walking; bruised, in l. hip-joint and along thigh in crural nerve, < beginning to move the part, > continuing to move it.

Thigh.—Sudden sharp pain below l. trochanter on moving, extending to l. spermatic cord, which is sore to touch, returning on crossing thighs, next day occasional aching under trochanter. Rheumatic pain shooting from acetabulum to knee, < moving about. Aching; in anterior and inner part of l. about noon; in anterior muscles on walking, with tenderness on touch; in sciatic nerve, < walking, with soreness; anteriorly, extending to leg and ankle, increasing till it caused restlessness, also at 3 P.M., lasting till he went to bed at 9.30 P.M.; on inner side from groin to inner edge of popliteal space, < l., with soreness. Soreness; of extensors.

Knee.—Cracking at night when flexed. Rheumatic feeling extending from r. to ankle, with cracking of knee when flexed or extended. Cramplike pain in lower part of popliteal space at junction of head of gastrocnemius and running a short distance down muscle, in morning. Pain; in l. in morning in bed; in l. at 9.35 A.M.; in outer part of l. beginning in morning soon after rising, extending all over leg to tarsus, < junction of head of gastrocnemius, with general soreness, < l. leg, next day the same pain in knees and legs began about 3 P.M., < l. hip-joint at 4.50 P.M., third day at 7 P.M., neuralgic pains as before; in l. popliteal space at 7 P.M. when walking, then intermittent cramp in r. sole, between os calcis and metatarsal bones, the rest of the evening (had felt something like it when swimming); in r. on beginning to move, with soreness; on inside of r. popliteal space, with discomfort through posterior muscles of legs, but was > by walking, also began at noon when lying.

Sticking in tibia when walking. Bruised pain in flexors of legs all day on motion. Feet twitched when I lay down, boots felt too tight, limbs jerked. Cramp of r. sole. Corn on bottom of r. little toe, later a painful corn on each phalanx of each little toe. Sprained pain shooting through metatarsal joints of r. fourth and little toes, extending to tips, at 8.40 P.M., causing limping. Bruised sensation externally over metatarsal joint of little toe.

Skin.—Yellowish blotches resembling moth patches, on cheeks and forehead. Reddish irregularly shaped spots on nose, becoming irritable and tender. Eruption on sacrum. Squamous eruption along sternum, the scales thin, whitish, when removed they leave the skin red, if they remain there is itching under them, < warmth from exercise. Miliary eruption on face and neck, with here and there a pustule or reddish pimple; red rash on face and neck, < r. side; red, blotchy, irregular in shape, on forehead and spreading over face.

Heat of body and lower limbs, then itching eruption on inside of thighs and elbows, when scratched red and burning, looking like first stage of scarlet fever, after scratching tumefied and darker, looking like erysipelatous eruption, on touch the parts gave to the hand the sensation of erysipelatous eruption, the eruption appeared first on back, < under suspender, then hands swelled, fingers felt stiff, after washing always worse, soon miliary eruption between fingers.

Diffused irregular patches, with papular elevations, without areola, with pointed apex, on face, < between zygoma and ramus of lower jaw, and on neck, < r. side. Hard, red, not very painful pimples on l. upper jaw. Boil on r. side of chin and one on tuberosity of ischium; on l. outer hamstring. An ulcerating sore near r. mental foramen, existing before taking the drug, becomes painful in morning. Itching on back, stomach and arms at night in bed.

Clinical.—Eruption on the chest, with dark brown spots, scaly, on a red base, without itching.

Sleep.—Yawning; in afternoon, without sleepiness. Sleepiness; in afternoon at work, that night frequent waking; and heaviness. Prolonged sleep. Sleeplessness all night; till after midnight, with tossing about; till after 1 A.M., from restlessness; till 3 A.M., with restlessness; S., with restlessness, and in morning general depression. Had to lie on the face to get to sleep. Difficult falling asleep from nervousness. Jerking before falling asleep. Sleep disturbed; poor, with starting up wide awake and much frightened. Restlessness at night, with alternations of chill and heat. Sound but restless sleep, when aroused he wakes up anxiously as if in fright; S. but restless sleep, when it was attempted to arouse him he rose in bed excitedly, lay down again, and was unconscious of it in the morning. Frequent waking and restlessness; F. waking to find the covers pushed aside and myself in another position from that in which I went to sleep.

Dreams.—Many; with restlessness. Indefinite, troubling sleep. Of quarrelling. Of murder and fighting. Visions of small black animals, arousing him on closing eyes, and while sleeping dreams of black objects.

Fever.—Chilliness; on going to bed; alternating with dry heat from 11 P.M. till 3 or 4 A.M. More impressionable to cold than formerly. Shuddering chills in back in afternoon. Heat; in face and dulness in forehead. Skin hot and dry; with lassitude; with heat in bed and on getting up tired feeling.

Natrum Carbonicum.

Pure Sodium carbonate is triturated for use.

General Action.—A "tissue" remedy of very general action, simulating a general lithæmic condition, with acid indigestion. In catarrh of the nose, throat, eyes, etc., it is similar to *Nat. mur.*, by which it is usually supplanted as a remedy. The salts of Sodium are much less active than those of Potassium, and they do not paralyze the heart as Potassium salts do. The urate of Sodium is deposited in the joints of gouty patients.

Allies.—Nat. m., Nat. sulf., Mag. m., Alumina, Calcarea c.; *Sepia*, *Puls.*, Phos., Lyc.

Generalities.—Puffiness of whole body in morning, > afternoon. Emaciation, pallor, dilatation of pupils and dark urine. Awkward, things that he usually accomplishes easily he cannot do at all. Jerking in whole body, with beating and with sensitive mood; J. in one or another part, in scapulæ, calves, eyelids and arms; *in lower limbs and < parts of lower portion of body.* Sticking in diseased spots; S. here and there in whole body alternately with tearing, during menses. Cramplike tearing in whole body, < limbs. Paroxysm in evening, blackness before eyes, with paralytic tearing in head, eyes and jaws, weak consciousness, confused, distracted thoughts, then crawling pain in lips, r. arm and < r. hand and tips of fingers, < thumb, with timidity.

Pain on every touch. *It hurts to lie on l. side* (Phos., Puls.). Everything hurts on rising from a seat, > walking. Drawing in lower limbs and jaws at night, with tension in them and with drawing in teeth. Painful tension of all nerves, < head, with nausea. Affected by playing on the piano a short time, with anxiety in chest, general trembling and weakness so that she must lie down. Discomfort, she thinks that she is very sick. Takes easily cold and has therefrom colic and diarrhœa or coryza. *Restlessness;* in evening during mental work; and fretfulness.

Heaviness; in morning; on rising, with indolence, when in bed awake she was bright. Dread of motion, which always aggravated symptoms. Indolence, > motion, with feeling as if everything on her were tense and with swelling of face and hands. Inclination to lie down. *Weakness;* during the day, with sleepiness; during the day, and she slept while sitting at work; during the day, with affection of head; in morning; during menses, with nausea; after toothache and fever; with pallor, walking is irksome. Stiffness of neck and l. wrist on holding a glass, he must put it down and move the hand, which is painful. Most symptoms arise when sitting and disappear on motion, pressure or rubbing.

Clinical.—General debility during the summer, especially with headache, worse from heat (Phos.). Glands swollen and indurated.

Mind.—Resolute, persevering, self-possessed, courageous. Lively, sociable; L. all day, with joyous talkativeness. Inclination to sing and singing half aloud. Excited by a slight cause, so that he talked with passionate vehemence till exhausted. Every event makes a strong impression upon her, a wavy trembling in nerves, with faintness. **Melancholy** (Nat. m.); **and apprehensive**; alternating with joy; and trembling, inclination to weep, constant sighing and physical prostration. Lachrymose.

Anxiety daily, with sweat on face several times a day; A. all day, with hasty restlessness, he could not keep limbs still, < arms, obliged to stretch them, it seemed as if they would be drawn asunder; in evening after foot bath, so that she could not fall asleep for an hour and a half; at night before sleep, as if his whole body were very thick and heavy; with restlessness, he thought that he could do nothing properly; with tremulous beating in whole body; about himself. Apprehension all day, with ennui, so that she does not know what to do, and she thinks that she is forsaken; A. from after dinner till evening; and desire to be alone.

Fretful; all day, discontented, he felt as if he could fight, life was lonesome to him, he preferred to have no existence, solicitous about the future and inclined to despair; in evening; after eating, > towards evening; after dinner, < supper; after dinner, > towards evening, uncomfortable everywhere, room seems too small for him, and even in the open air he walks about without anything seeming right; after supper, < copious drinking, with pressure in pit of stomach and in hypochondria; and discontented, almost inconsolable; but desirous to work. Easily provoked to anger; with lively mood; angry in forenoon, inclined to strike, cannot tolerate contradiction. Sensitive in forenoon, as after vexation.

Timidity; and starting at slightest noise. Anthropophobia and fear. Shuns mankind. Disinclination to talk. Dread of taking cold. Aversion to open air. Internal restlessness. *Indifference.* Weary of life in morning on waking. Ennui in morning, absorbed in himself and does not know how he is. Sluggish, phlegmatic. No desire to do anything and inability to keep at anything long. Dislike for business, he goes about it idly, but when once at work it goes on as usual.

Mistakes in writing. Thought weak; with vertigo. Distraction in morning. Power of concentration lost. Sensation of loss of will power in morning on waking. *Dulness of sense,* staring without thought, as if stunned. *Forgetful, he must think long before anything comes to him. Memory lost. Stupefaction in morning on waking.* Almost unconscious of external objects, he reels when walking.

Clinical.—Failure of memory. General mental impairment, inability to perform any mental work, stupid feeling in head. Effects of overstudy. Extreme melancholy and apprehensiveness.

Head.—Sticking through H. during physical exertion. Tearing in afternoon. Acute jerkings in H. Aching externally here and there, in sides, in ear, etc.; A. at noon, < low down in occiput; when walking in open air, with coryza; before menstruation, with tension in nape; after vomiting, with loss of appetite, white-coated tongue and flat, nauseous taste; with confusion, preventing mental work; like a reeling, with painful confusion, then heat in head, > moving about in open air, < rest and sitting; confused and drawing, after dinner; bruised, internally and externally.

Constriction. Apprehension. Dulness as after too long sleep. Heaviness at night on waking, with pain in it and flat taste; H. after dinner, with burning in eyes. Rush of blood; when sitting in the house, < evening, with heat in head; on stooping, as if everything would come out at forehead, if he then lifted and carried anything a beating in head, > rising. Vertigo often during the day, even when lying; at night, < motion or speaking, with slow violent beating of the heart, roaring in ears, heat, anxiety as if he would die, orgasm of blood, then chilliness and trembling; on turning head; when walking, with reeling; after mental labor, with pressure inward in temples; during fatiguing work, especially in sun, with dulness and heaviness of head; *like a faintness, after a spoonful of wine;* threatening to fall to the left; even to falling, when walking about the room, then weakness of hands and feet.

Forehead.—Sticking; behind r. eminence; in r. side, then in r. side of occiput; in evening till an hour after lying down, with internal and external heat in it and sticking in temple. Sticking throbbing in forepart at noon. Tearing from l. eminence to behind ear, with sticking; cramplike T., extending into eyes and tip of nose. Pain in l. side in morning on rising; P. in forenoon, with heat in it; *on suddenly turning head;* and in vertex, with heat in them; as if it would burst, many days from 7 A.M. to 5 P.M., < moving about, with stopped sensation in head; intermittent beating, extending through F., above margin of l. orbit; stupefying; tensive, in r. sinus. Sensation of a tight cord about it, spreading warmth.

Tearing in r. temple and side of forehead during menstruation, transiently > pressure. Pressure outward in r. temple in afternoon. Vertex, pressive shocks in evening on falling asleep; sticking in l. side in forenoon; throbbing pain daily, < morning; painful throbbing in bone in forenoon; throbbing after dinner, with sensitiveness to touch. Sticking in l. side of head; in upper part of l. parietal bone. Tearing in l. side during menstruation, with throbbing.

Occiput.—Sticking in r. side in evening; S. in r. side, then burning. Pain; in r. side; externally low down; in protuberances on touch; extending to vertex; extending to nape, with drawing pain that at last extends to forehead, with vertigo, eructations and dim vision. Tension. Drawing on r. side, with tension as if it would draw head backward. Dulness like a dull pressure, in forenoon. Painful emptiness, with weakness and hoarseness of voice.

Scalp.—Falling of hair. *Boil on occiput,* more towards nape; *almost painless B. on occiput.*

Clinical.—Headache from exposure to the sun or from working under gaslight. Vertigo from exposure to the sun's rays.

Eyes.—Swelling beneath l. in morning on rising, with burning, now in r., now in l. eye. *Sticking after dinner;* S. in r. when sitting; with inflammation. Pain in morning. Burning in forenoon; in evening till after lying down; when at work, < *reading and writing, with dryness, as if he had wept much;* < afternoon, with involuntary winking. *Dryness, with heat* and contracted sensation. Stickiness of r. all day, as if full of mucus. Itching in r. in morning, > rubbing; in r. at 11 A.M., with lachrymation on rubbing; in r., little > rubbing, > moistening with saliva, with biting.

Lachrymation. Balls sensitive to touch, with sensation as if they would be dilated. Pupils contracted. It dissolves the fibrin of the blood, causes excessive fluidity of it, produces a kind of leucoma and finally *ulceration of cornea. Ulcers about cornea, with stinging in eye so that she must shade it. Ulcerative keratitis.* Pain in orbit. Canthus, inflammation of internal, with purulent swelling of lachrymal sac; sticking in l. internal, forcing out tears, at 11 A.M.; sudden burning in r. external, at 2 P.M., then in middle of eye, extending into internal canthus, then sticking in l. eye extending towards external canthus, with feeling as if a hair were in it.

Lids.—Swelling of upper; inflammatory, of r. upper, with pressure in it, feeble-looking face and mucus in canthi. Agglutination in morning and lachrymation all the forenoon; A. in afternoon. Constant closure, then sleepiness, even when walking. *Difficult opening, they closed involuntarily* (Sep.). *Heaviness of upper.* Tearing in r. lower, extending from inner canthus towards outer, at 5 P.M. Itching of lower, < l.

Vision.—*Dim; and he must wipe eyes constantly;* for distant objects, in one usually far-sighted. As if something were drawn before axis. Everything runs together at fine work, yet she can read well. Vanishes on reading. Flickering like rain. *Of blinding lightnings when awake,* of lightnings in evening on falling asleep. *Of black floating spots when writing.* Of sparks.

Clinical.—Ulceration of the cornea, with great photophobia and stinging pains. Lachrymal abscess. Dry catarrh of the conjunctiva (Alumina).

Ears.—*Sticking;* in l. concha; behind lobule of r. at 1 P.M., > pressure, but returning; in r. at 4 P.M.; > opening mouth, returning on closing it; outward in r.; outward in l. at 3 P.M.; itching, in lobule of l. in forenoon, > pressure and rubbing. Tearing and pressure; T. behind r. at 1 P.M., with sticking; intermittent, in r. at 8 A.M. when standing and sitting. Pinching in r. in morning, with dragging. Pain in l.; P. in evening on walking in cool wind, with drawing in r. joint of jaw, extending into inner mouth and r. side of tongue, and pain in tongue on touch of teeth. Throbbing behind lobule of l., as if in bone, > pressure, with ulcerative pain. Tickling in l. external meatus at 8.30 A.M., > scratching, but returning. *Stopped sensation* in r., with diminished hearing.

Ringing on turning head. Rushing. Roaring; with throbbing in l. Music as of a distant bagpipe, as when at times one hears fine tones, when lying on back, > rising, but if he sits upright a short time it returns, > lying down, but it soon returns while lying, together with earache.

Clinical.—Chronic deafness and roaring in ears, pain in the face, etc. Sharp piercing stitches in ears, ears feel closed.

Nose.—*Red, with white pimples upon it. Ulcers high up in nostrils.* Drawing pain in r. outer side, > rubbing. Sensation as if a hard substance were sticking in upper part of l. nostril, not > blowing. Dryness. Tickling in nostrils, not > scratching. *Stoppage;* when talking; *with hard offensive pieces from one nostril.* Frequent sneezing; without coryza; forcible S., with rush of blood into head, so that he saw white stars. **Much nasal mucus passes through mouth.** *Discharge yellow, offensive; D. of thin mucus, with frequent sneezing; thick green mucus. Profuse coryza. Fluent coryza;* in forenoon, > afternoon; with general chilliness, cold hands and cheeks and hoarseness, without thirst; *alternating with stopped C. Intermittent coryza, with burning in eyes. Stopped coryza;* < dinner, with frequent sneezing; and she thought that she would suffocate at night, and was obliged to keep her mouth open. *Bleeding.* Blowing out of blood in morning. Smell more acute (secondary action).

Clinical.—Catarrh, with thick yellow mucus. Acute coryza, with violent sneezing and profuse discharge of thin mucus, < slightest draught on undressing. In general, the catarrhs are < slightest draught, discharge through the day and stoppage at night, > free perspiration, and, as in Nat. mur., there is absence of smell and taste.

Face.—*Swelling; of cheeks, with redness. Pale; and blue rings around eyes and lids swollen;* alternately P. and red at 3 P.M. Red, with warm forehead, without internal heat. Yellow. Earthy, wan. Sticking in upper part of l. cheek at 3 P.M. Tearing in r. zygoma, returning after rubbing; T. in l. zygoma at 4 P.M., extending into head, with sticking in forehead; in r. zygoma as if the bone would be torn out, at 3 P.M., with sensitiveness to touch. Pain in cheek-bones; in bones of face, < walking in open air. Drawing in l. cheek-bone.

Jaws.—Twitching in l. side of lower at 1.30 P.M. Intermittent tearing in l. lower in afternoon. Rheumatic pains. Bruised pain in angle of l. lower after dinner, > pressure. Beating in r. side of lower, extending from middle towards chin, after breakfast.

Lips.—Twitching of upper; of r. upper in afternoon. Tetters. Eruption in r. corner. Pimple on lower; on l. side of upper; on red of lower, with smarting, painful soreness in corners. *Burning crack in lower* (Graph.). Boil on upper. Whitish vesicle on red of upper, with sore burning pain on touch. Burning as if in a vesicle, on upper, in r. corner. Itching as from a feather on upper, at 6 P.M., and on drawing fingers across lip sticking in middle of it as if a hair would be torn out.

Mouth.—Teeth. Looseness; of a l. upper molar. Sticking in hollow, after dinner, > smoking, returning on eating pears, and in evening burrowing when walking, that after supper became pulsative, > falling asleep; sudden S. in sound. Tearing in l. upper molars; in l. lower anterior molars at 10 A.M. on walking in open air; in tips of l. lower, at 11 A.M., then under chin, then again in a lower tooth. In r. lower anterior molars and their gum in forenoon; in last l. upper molars in afternoon; in l. canine in evening, > lying down, with jerking; at night after 9 P.M.; pain (tearing?) all night, then swelling of lip and cessation of pain; in last l. lower molars, as if coming out of teeth, day and night, < after dinner, with jerking. Jerking tearing in r. lower molars in forenoon; in l. lower teeth in evening. Jerking when eating; J. in r. lower in afternoon, with sensitiveness of tips of teeth. Pain as if they would be pulled out, day and night, > warmth, with bleeding of gums on touch, and coldness of body all day, and thirst. Drawing pain in hollow T. after taking cold. Boring in l. lower anterior molars at 10 A.M.; in hollow teeth in afternoon, with pain; drawing, in hollow. Burrowing after breakfast of bread and butter, < touch, especially by pressure on upper jaw, with swelling of r. cheek; B. in hollow, > sleep, with boring; boring, in hollow, waking him at 4 A.M., < touch of tongue, returned after breakfast, when he ate honey, and after sweets at dinner, less from 4 till 7 P.M., when he was out in a cold rain, > during supper. Aching evenings after lying down; A. when half asleep and on waking; with swelling of gum and fever. *Sensitiveness* of lower; S. as if scorbutic and as from bog-water (moorwasser). Cold crawling through r. upper molars at noon. Sensation as if cold air came out of r. upper carious T. after dinner.

Gum.—Looseness. Roughness on inside of anterior lower teeth at 3 P.M. Bleeding. Pain in l. lower as if ulcerated.

Tongue.—Pale. *Pimples on tip;* P. on l. side, with sticking; painful to touch, beneath tongue. Pustule near frænum. Tensive blister on r. margin. *Burning about tip as if full of cracks* (compare Na. sul.) at 2 P.M. Sore pain in tip on touch of tongue. Biting on tip as from salt water. *Not facile, speech difficult.* Speech irksome. Lisping.

Blister on inside of l. cheek, exuding water after pressure. *Superficial ulcers, with burning pain on touch.* Insipid mucus. Painful soreness on inside of cheek when chewing. *Dryness,* and of tongue, calling for drink; *and of lips, which she must constantly lick, as if caused by heat of breath;* every morning after rising, with heat and thirst. Saliva gluey; S. salt, with biting on tip of tongue. Salivation at 1 P.M.; sour, in forenoon; tasteless, watery. Musty odor.

Taste.—*Bitter* in afternoon; *B. to dinner;* B., slimy in morning, < rising and eating; B., slimy, flat, on waking, with white-coated tongue; B., flat mornings; rancid B. to all food, > eating; suddenly, then eructations of bitter water; in throat, like a vapor. *Metallic in afternoon. Sour;* in morning; *and tongue coated.* Sweet. Bloody, on exhaling. Purulent in throat, suddenly, as from an ulcer. Nauseous, waking at 4 A.M., with violent erections. As of an old tobacco-pipe at 4 P.M. after spitting watery saliva, then biting, on tongue. Bad, in morning on waking, > soup, with burnt sensation.

Throat.—External. *Swelling of glands; submaxillary* (Calc.); S. on l. side, painful to touch, with hoarseness, her voice gave out when speaking, throat raw as far as into chest, scraping in throat, < cough, at the same time pressure on vertex so that she could not press upon it. Goitre increases; pressure in G. Sticking in parotid gland, with pain on touch; S. in thyroid gland, anteriorly and externally, in forenoon.

Inflammation morning and night, with swelling of r. tonsil, and sticking and choking on swallowing, as from a swelling, < l. side, where tonsil was not swollen. **Violent hawking of thick mucus, that constantly collects again** (Puls.); easy H. of mucus in morning. Adherent mucus, causing scraping; a piece of M. at night, waking him in morning by tickling and irritation, but he easily raises it, soon a second piece, which is easily raised, with rawness of chest, which is > rising.

Sticking in l. side in morning on swallowing, with redness; S. in afternoon; in r. side in afternoon, in open air; at 6 P.M., on yawning and swallowing; with ecptysis; with rawness and dry cough; as from mucus at 4 P.M. Pain in l. side on yawning. Soreness, and in trachea; pressing S. after stooping, with difficult swallowing, several days afterwards sensation as if something were sticking in T. Rawness; < evening, with scraping; > eating, with scraping; > hawking, with dryness, as if hoarse; felt even in brain, with scraping. Dryness of T. and tongue at night, without thirst; D., he hawks much without raising anything; scraping, in fauces by posterior nares, < open air. Rancidity; at 6 P.M. Sensation as if something arose in it on rapid running. Tickling in afternoon, < swallowing, with sticking; T. causing inclination to cough. On swallowing the morsel descends only by pressing with the mouth. Pressure in œsophagus.

Stomach.—Appetite. *Great;* for breakfast; for breakfast, but he had scarcely satisfied himself when there was pressure in stomach and he became ill-humored; towards noon; in forenoon, little at noon; in afternoon; for a pipe of tobacco after dinner, tobacco had not tasted so good for a long time. Disposed to nibble, as soon as he sees anything eatable he wishes to taste it. Little, though stomach seems empty. Not as good as usual, for dinner, meat not relished, bread tastes best. Lost; at noon and in evening. Aversion to milk; to meat and to fat food.

Thirst great; T. even in morning; in forenoon; towards noon; *in afternoon;* in evening after sleep; after walking; only when eating; for cold water a few hours after dinner.

Eructations; in forenoon; when eating, with vertigo; **sour**; *sour in afternoon; empty;* empty at 2 P.M., then heat in pharynx; tasting of food, after every meal; bilious, penetrating nose, in afternoon; bitter, that he tasted a long time, in forenoon; of sweetish water, only as far as throat, at 3 P.M. *Waterbrash.* Hiccough; every afternoon after eating. Violent hiccough from 6 till 6.30 P.M., so that it caused bitter eructations; and so prolonged in evening that everything became sore; during dinner, making stomach sore.

Nausea nearly all day, with eructations of water; N. in morning, > soup, with sensation of fasting; from morning till noon, with crawling and twisting about stomach, salivation and eructations; in forenoon, with yawning; in forenoon, but without inclination to vomit, > eating; after fruit, with tension in hypochondria; > towards evening by eating, with heat of face, hawking of mucus, retching till vomiting of frothy, tasteless mucus; with fulness in stomach and shuddering; with looseness in stomach, as if he had taken cold, then warmth in pit of stomach. *Ineffectual retching in morning.* Vomiting of offensive sour liquid, like muddy water (when coughing).

Rumbling in forenoon, > eructations, with pressure. Sticking deep in l. side at 3.30 P.M., then burning; in epigastric region, in a broad streak across to r. side in afternoon, with retracted feeling; in epigastric region before dinner, then beneath l. breast on inspiration. Cutting towards small of back in forenoon; in epigastric region at 4 P.M. when walking, then extending towards umbilicus, with feeling as before stool; internally and externally, with drawing. Griping after the morning drink; in epigastric region in morning, > moving about, with pressure; in epigastric region at 2.30 P.M., with beating, as of a worm; when walking, with pressure in it and with tremulousness; extending towards l. side at 1 P.M.

Pain after breakfast and dinner; after milk soup; > 4 P.M. by bread, with sensitiveness, even to pressure, and salivation; then at 1.30 P.M. sticking in region of l. lower ribs; as from a stone at 3 P.M.; about epigastric region like a pressure and retching, > moving about. *Painfulness to touch;* epigastric region in forenoon. Sensation of a lump after dinner. Soreness of pit when talking, and frothy saliva. Painful contraction in evening, afterwards extending to hypochondria, so that she must bend up, > stretching and walking, < stooping and sitting, lasting till morning, with jerking as if a worm were turning about in r. side below stomach.

Fulness in evening; at 4 A.M. in bed, with feeling as if something were rising. *Swollen feeling and sensitiveness.* Tension above pit. Stoppage from below upward after eating, as if digestion could not go on from above downward, then relaxation of hands and feet.

Fasting sensation in forenoon. Disordered feeling, > warm soup, but returning. *Weak and easily disordered.* Burning in l. side near pit at 5 P.M. when walking; sudden, near r. side of pit in afternoon. *Scraping heartburn after fat food.*

Clinical.—Indigestion, mostly acid, with palpitation and distress about the heart.

Abdomen.—*Distention* in afternoon, > towards morning; in afternoon, > emission of flatus; in evening, > lying down, with emission of flatus; < *eating;* slight, > emission of flatus; with frequent urging to stool, partly ineffectual, partly slight discharge of natural stool; here and there as by gas; painful, in morning, during menstruation, > slight diarrhœa after rising. Rumbling; at 6.30 P.M.; with gurgling and with distention in places; griping, > open air. Movements, even in morning in bed, then two thin stools. Flatus of the odor of bad eggs; sour-smelling; offensive, in afternoon. *Incarcerated flatus,* whereupon it mounted into his head, and he had twitching in face.

Cutting in morning; nights, with tensive colic in upper abdomen and diarrhœa; before somewhat hard stool, and in small of back; with movements, then four thin stools in half an hour; in attacks in afternoon, with griping as before diarrhœa. *Griping after eating;* after stool; with movements, then hard, crumbly stool; intermittent; as before diarrhœa, in morning, with nausea. Pinching, then soft, then diarrhœa-like stool, with sore pain in anus.

Colic towards morning, abdomen hard and umbilicus retracted; C. at 11 A.M., > soup; in afternoon, with urging to stool and urine, after long pressure some urine passes, wherewith penis is erect, and this pressure with erection continues after the discharge; at night; on touch and on walking; before soft stool; < 11 A.M., > eating; in a child, > sleep, with nausea, pallor and necessity to lie down; twice daily, > vomiting; with urging to stool, > scanty stool, then feeling as if much remained; waking her at night; waking him, > stool; flatulent, with constant urging to stool; bruised, when riding horseback, with sticking in r. side of chest; sore, > external warmth, with pressure downward, as before menstruation. Jerking contraction, with an affection of small of back. Painful tension, and in testicles. Heaviness.

Hypochondria.—Jerking at times in r. in evening. *Sticking in r. in forenoon, then griping in hypogastrium; in region of spleen* in afternoon when walking; in l., extending into pit of stomach, during the day when sitting, with pain on touch; as with crossed knives in r., with screwing-together sensation and oppressed breathing. Pain in l. on pressure. Stoppage in region of spleen waking him, with oppression across chest and stomach as from flatulence.

Sticking in l. side, with drawing, as from incarcerated flatus. Upper A., distention; griping rumbling in afternoon, > emission of flatus; cutting in middle in morning; inflated sensation. Umbilicus, griping about, in afternoon; intermittent griping in a spot in forenoon; pinching about, then usual stool, with clawing in anus; drawing towards small of back like urging to stool, in morning, with yawning; tensive burning in spot to l. of U. in forenoon.

Hypogastrium.—*Swelling of inguinal glands; (generally painful) and of axillary glands.* Intermittent twitching like a beating in r. flank. Sticking above r. hip, with drawing; S. in r. flank, extending into r. rib near pit of stomach, and then on deep breathing into sternum, above ensiform cartilage, > inspiration, returning during expiration; in r. groin, so that she must bend double, when hawking after rising from a seat. Tearing extending through genitals to urethra. Cutting in sides towards umbilicus, in forenoon when sitting, then in whole abdomen, as after taking cold; intermittent C. low down in afternoon, before menstruation. Paroxysmal griping; rather externally in r. flank after dinner; cutting G. Pain above l. groin on yawning and deep breathing; in U. and sides of abdomen, < walking, with pain on touch; *extending to genitals, as if everything in A. would fall out and menses would come on;* bruised, in a spot on r. ilium, on pressure. Dragging in groins and region of bladder. Biting as from worms in afternoon. Tension below umbilicus, < walking and stooping.

Rectum.—*Incarcerated flatus.* Cramplike pain, and below umbilicus. Pain as from hard lumps during stool and emission of flatus. Distress as from incomplete stool, with sticking. Itching; and pressure, as if hæmorrhoids would occur. *Burning after stool. Urging so that he could scarcely reach the closet, then thin,* **forcibly spurting stool** (Nat. sul.); U. waking at 3 A.M., stool soft, then thin, with burning and tenesmus in anus and evacuation of a piece of tape-worm, later two thin stools; U., stool soft, then rumbling in abdomen, cutting below umbilicus and constant U., but only one slight stool, after half an hour, during which the straining never ceased, great U. and a thin, yellow stool, with burning and tenesmus in anus and pain about umbilicus. Ineffectual urging; with sticking in anus.

Anus.—*Discharge of blood during stool.* Sticking. Twinging. Burning after stool, with biting. *Itching;* biting and burning I. Crawling.

Stool.—**Spotted with blood.** Diarrhœa after milk; profuse D., at first of thick mucus, at last more and more covered with blood, painless, but preceded by pain in stomach; frequent, with burning in anus. Soft; and small, thin-formed, with pressure. Pasty, preceded by discharge of flatus, with burning cheeks.

Constipation or diarrhœa. Hard, with straining; H., with burning in anus; especially at first, and difficult, soon followed by urging again, but stool was insignificant, then tenesmus; and coated with blood, with sticking in rectum, then burning in anus; then soft, followed by burning; then soft, mixed with bloody mucus, then burning in anus. *Like sheep-dung, after great straining* (Mag. mur.), *with burning. With balls of mucus like peas. Difficult, not hard.* Not hard, but causing cutting during evacuation. With pressure, then pain in rectum. With straining after dinner, then burning in eyes and urethra and voluptuous irritation, the burning in eyes returned during approach of a storm, with heat of head and sweat on forehead. Two or three times a day, the last usually with pressure in rectum and tenesmus in urethra and a little crumbly mucous stool, at times only flatus.

Clinical.—Watery, gray diarrhœa, < during the day, after eating, gushing, preceded by cutting in upper abdomen, stools sudden, followed by burning and soreness in anus and great weakness, sinking in hypogastrium (compare Nat. sulf.).

Urinary Organs.—*Frequent desire, with copious urine; with scanty urine;* continues after urinating, though there is always only a spoonful passed; constant D. and during the last drops cutting in bladder and discharge of mucus from urethra; sudden D., with sticking forward in urethra. Dribbling after micturition. *Nocturnal micturition.* Child wets the bed at night. Frequent micturition at night; and copious; and burning in urethra; F., urine watery; F., but scanty; F. and profuse, also with yellowish leucorrhœa.

Prostatic fluid passed with urine; passed with difficult stool. Jerking in urethra. Tearing in urethra during micturition; periodic T. in urethra and testicles. Smarting in urethra during micturition. Burning in urethra in evening, with smarting; B. during micturition, with sticking; during and after micturition; when not urinating. Copious urine; and necessity to urinate after midnight; with burning before and during micturition. Two pounds of lemon-yellow urine every morning. Urine offensive; sour-smelling, bright yellow. Urine turbid soon after passing; becomes T. and deposits a mucous sediment.

Sexual Organs.—Itching; on and about them; stitch-like, on and about them; of prepuce; of glans; of glans in forenoon. Prepuce inflamed; and glans; retracted in morning. Smegma behind corona glandis. *Glans easily become sore*; G. swollen; pain back of G., with erections after coition. Priapismus towards morning, then emission without desire, with tensive pain and cutting in penis. Erections mornings without desire; frequent E. during the day; three times in morning, the last time painful; violent in morning on waking; almost painful in morning in bed; *weak;* ceased.

Sticking beating in scrotum. *Soreness between scrotum and thighs.* Itching of scrotum, not > scratching. Testicles, pain in l.; bruised pain; heavy pressive drawing in T. and spermatic cords, more in morning than in evening; numbness. *Emission* at night, with pain, but sleep so sound that he could not entirely wake, next day fretful, discontented and persistent at nothing; *frequent*, in an old man; *without erection;* without lascivious dreams. *Coition incomplete, transient erection and speedy emission.* Desire in morning after beer, then flat, sweetish taste; in a warm bath and on leaving it burning in palms; even on touching a girl. Desire for emission after dinner and in evening, without real sexual desire, after dinner it returned while legs were crossed, > walking, returned in evening when lying.

Female. — Pressure towards them during stool. Pulsation after coition. Soreness between pudenda and thighs. Tearing in one side of pudenda. Biting, burning itching in region of pudenda. *Leucorrhœa;* thick, after micturition; profuse day and night, always after paroxysms of cutting and twisting about umbilicus. Movement in uterus, as of a fœtus. Menses too late; and scanty, like water from meat; too early; more profuse and longer-lasting.

Clinical.—Induration of cervix uteri, with pressing towards the genitals as if everything would come out (Sep.), metrorrhagia, offensive leucorrhœa, etc.

Respiratory Organs.—Dryness of larynx; in open air, noticed on talking and breathing. Rawness of trachea. *Hoarseness;* with coryza and oppression of chest.

Cough; at night, with scraping in throat and uneasy sleep; with wheezing in trachea; tickling; hacking, with rattling in chest. Scraping cough, at times with hoarseness and heat of hands; S. cough, with sore pain in chest and alternating hoarseness, heat, and burning in hands and soles, with bruised feeling in legs, loss of appetite, nausea, heat, sweat at night. *Dry cough, with stopped catarrh;* D. cough in morning, with tickling in chest; and violent, < afternoon and evening, *especially on coming from cold air into a warm room* (Bry.). Cough, with expectoration of blood in evening; *C., with E. of greenish, purulent mucus and rawness in chest; C., < morning, with partly salt, partly offensive, purulent E.* Slight expectoration, with rattling in chest.

Dyspnœa in forenoon; D., with sexual desire; suffocative, with hoarse, deep voice and scraping in pharynx and trachea, then cough, short during the day, fatiguing at night, rough and hollow, > sitting up, with sore pain at first in chest and trachea, and throbbing rush of blood to vertex, with whizzing and rattling on breathing, afterwards with purulent, bloody expectoration. Easily gets out of breath on walking. Anxious respiration in morning in bed.

Clinical.—Cough on entering a warm room, short and dry. Cough, with greenish expectoration of salty taste. Cough, with burning soreness in r. chest.

Chest.—Painful jerking in region of l. clavicle; sudden J. in one of the middle l. ribs, > deep breathing, with feeling as if it would take away the breath; burning J., as from electric sparks in r. side in forenoon. Sticking in r.; in l. lower ribs; in side of C. and abdomen; here and there externally; beneath l. breast in forenoon, so that she could scarcely breathe, with cough; below r. axilla in evening, < night, by lying on r. side, when there was S. in r. side of chest; below axillæ at night, so that she could only lie on back, and even when walking; here and there on rising; beneath l. false ribs on breathing; in l. side on rising from a seat, < inspiration and expiration, with pinching in l. side of abdomen; after eating pork, with short breath; intermittent, in front of l. axilla in afternoon; upward in r.; outward in side in afternoon. Sticking throbbing in sternum just above ensiform cartilage in evening in bed, then sticking in l. chest, then in r.

Pain in l. side from not breathing. Drawing pain in muscles, < morning and evening (with tightness of chest). Bruised pain in lower end of sternum and on ensiform cartilage in afternoon, with cutting; cutting B. pain in forepart of sternum in forenoon, when sitting, > moving about and inspiration. Sensitiveness of lower part in evening. Rawness all day, < evening, with pressure beneath sternum and oppression and at times palpitation, the R. > eating, but returning, at last dry cough that gradually aggravated the scraping and R., chest > loosening of mucus, with this thirst, chilliness, fluent coryza and frequent, tense, hard pulse; R. after dinner, with ill humor and pressure in pit of stomach, he felt better after midday nap, and while lying the scraping in throat was relieved, but after rising it returned and he was obliged to hawk up with exertion pieces of green tenacious mucus. Oppression after eating. Pressure after eating; P. beneath sternum in morning on deep breathing. Tension on deep breathing. Burning externally in r.; B. in l. in forenoon, with throbbing.

Heart.—Sticking in præcordial region in evening; in forenoon, < inspiration. Pressure. Feeling as if a hard substance extended from præcordial region to pit of stomach after dinner, with constriction in stomach. Painful cracking during the day. *Palpitation on ascending stairs; waking her at night when lying on l. side; so that she could not lie upon the side* (Nat. m.); from slight cause; when sitting if his attention was directed to anything, and in evening when lying; and bellows sound; anxious, on stooping; anxious, when writing, with pain in forehead and confusion in head.

Clinical.—Palpitation and violent beating of the heart, after eating or with general dyspeptic symptoms, especially acidity.

Neck.—*Cracking in vertebræ on moving head.* Sticking in nape; frequently in evening. Tearing in muscles of nape in forenoon; sticking, in r. side in afternoon and next forenoon; sudden drawing, in nape, causing stiffness, < moving head. Drawing pain in nape when reading, causing ill humor and impatience. Spasmodic drawing in nape, making motion of head difficult. Tension in nape when sitting and walking, < moving head. Stiffness; and lameness. On swallowing she feels in nape the movements of pharynx.

Back.—Sticking in l. side; S. at 3 A.M., > rising, with burning, then sensitiveness and sensation as if beaten; preventing sleep all night, and she cannot lie long upon either side. *Aching;* < night, speaking and deep breathing, she could lie only on side; sore. Bruised pain; extending into nape in evening after lying down; waking at midnight, > towards morning, she dared not turn over. Tensive pain at night and after dinner. Tension in afternoon on sitting bent, > stretching; T. and drawing extending into anus in jerks, when sitting and lying, and ending with a stitch.

Scapulæ.—Sticking on r. after dinner; beneath l., with pain and sensitiveness to pressure; below l., extending through l. chest and to r. side, in evening; between S., then in whole back in evening and all next day, < inspiration, and on moving trunk tension over back, > walking. Tearing between S. and in l. shoulder. Boring in tip of l., felt as far as end of r. ensiform cartilage. Gnawing between S. Paralytic pain between S. and in nape in morning. Tension between S., with drawing pain; T. between S. on taking off the coat in open air, with drawing and with sensitiveness to wind.

Lumbar Region.—Sticking in r. in afternoon, when bending towards the left, then griping in upper abdomen; S. when sitting, with pain, lightning-like, above small of back, so that he cannot move, in evening. Cutting, burning and scraping. *Pain after walking;* P. during menses, > night; so that stooping or becoming erect was almost impossible; jerking, starting from it, on lifting anything heavy, then weakness in the vicinity; sudden, like a heaviness, in forenoon when sitting, > moving; bruised, in forenoon and for a still longer time; sore; sore, internally, extending towards abdomen. Drawing in lower part of back as from incarcerated flatus.

Extremities.—Jerking; in joints, or a jerking sensation. Tearing and bruised sensation; T. more than sticking in joints, < evening on lying down and often waking at night. Uneasiness of arms and legs in evening, with stretching. Drawing in joints, and after waking paralyzed feeling. Lameness in morning on waking. Weakness.

Upper Extremities.—Shoulder. Sticking; and itching; in l. joint, then tearing along outer surface into elbow, thence along inner surface to middle of forearm, first <, then > motion, then weak feeling in arm. Tearing; in l.; and in elbows and wrists; intermittent; in l. joint, often extending along outer surface of arm to little finger, first <, then > motion. Pain on l., > pressure, but returning; in joint, so that she could not raise arm; bruised, in joints; drawing, in r. joint.

Arm.—Twitching during the day. Tearing in r., < shoulder; in r., extending into wrist, < rest; in r., extending into finger, at night during sweat, > rising, with weakness. *Heaviness;* of r., so that she could not raise it. Stiffness, she could not raise it.

Upper Arm.—Tearing posteriorly in humerus, above l. elbow; in r. at 3 A.M., and in little fingers, wherewith they fell asleep, whereupon she woke, > rubbing, but returning, > rising; in l. deltoid in forenoon when standing; in r. deltoid, > rubbing. Pinching in flesh, > rubbing. Griping in l. humerus, extending to skin, at noon on taking off coat, without being heated, with burrowing, ending in skin as a burning pain. Pain in r. so that he cannot raise it. Bruised pain in muscles of l. and in pectoral muscles, on touch and motion of arm.

Elbow.—Tearing from tip of l. into bend; from r. into two smaller fingers; from l. to little finger. *Drawing pain* in evening on lying down.

Forearm.—Twitching below bend of l. elbow. Sticking in r. Cramplike pain in outer side of r. Sprained pain in r. Drawing tension in tendons on inner surface of l., extending from wrist to four inches above it.

Wrist.—Jerking in r., or jerking sensation. Boring in r. pisiform bone in morning in bed; < lying or pressing upon it.

Hand.—Swollen in afternoon. Jerking, < taking hold of anything; painful J. on back of r. in morning. Trembling in afternoon, < next morning. Tearing in metacarpal bone of r. index in evening; drawing, in metacarpal bone of r. ring finger in open air. Boring in metacarpal bones at 10 P.M. in bed; in metacarpal bone of r. thumb, then in ulna and radius. Pain in back of r. as if tendons were tight, > pressure; P. between l. ring and middle fingers as if tendons had been torn, on holding a vessel high up. Painful drawing in ball of r., often when writing, first <, then > pressure, but returning, and on moving hand tension extending into forearm and sensitiveness, > stretching hand and arm. Sensitiveness of palms and < tips of fingers, on stroking or rubbing anything, with heat in them. Falling asleep of l. at 4 A.M., though it was not lain upon.

Fingers.—Inflammation of l., then a vesicle. Jerking in l. thumb; on inner surface of r. thumb, > rubbing, with crawling. Sticking above r. thumbnail; in tip of index; in tip of r. index in evening; in r. ring, with twitching; in r. ring, as if a needle were stuck through the skin that was raised up. Tearing anteriorly towards tip of l. little; on backs of all r., and in elbow, > rubbing; from middle of l. ring towards last joint; in little, as if it would be torn out; cramplike, in l. index, with flexion. *Jerking sensation in joints.* Tensive drawing between phalanges of l. in forenoon, extending above wrist, usually > motion. Painful throbbing between middle and last joint of l. ring. Swollen feeling in morning. Crawling in middle joint of r. thumb as if it would go to sleep in afternoon.

Lower Extremities.—*Unsteadiness when walking, stumbling, slipping.* Œdema. Tearing extending up and down, < knees and ankles. Tension when sitting and walking. Uneasiness at night. *Weakness. Heaviness;* when sitting; *and bruised sensation.*

Hip.—Paroxysmal sticking forward through r. on walking, > standing and bending over. Tearing in r. in forenoon during menses, with bruised pain; T. in l. in forenoon on cessation of pain in back, > motion, with sticking; in l. in evening after lying down. Bruised pain in l. in afternoon on rising from a seat, > walking. Drawing in flesh in region of r., with pressure.

Thigh.—Sudden jerking as if a worm were crawling over it; J. in l. natis when sitting. Sticking in l. thigh, tibia and knee from morning on rising till afternoon; through r. in afternoon when walking. Tearing in l. extending into knee in afternoon; in l. natis in evening when standing, > sitting; in middle, along outer surface of middle of leg, in evening when standing; intermittent cramplike, in outer side of r., close to knee. Bruised pain in anterior muscles as if flesh were loose, on walking and touch. Burning pain in fold between nates and thighs, as after a violent horseback ride, when the clothes form a fold and rub against it. Jerking sensation down r. Weary pain; in middle in morning, with general weakness.

Knee.—Boring in r. patella in forenoon. Tearing in r. at night in bed, > wrapping with warm clothes. Sticking drawing in r. in evening. *Pain in hollow on motion;* acute, in r. on stepping; sprained, in r. in forenoon when walking; bruised.

Leg.—Cramp in calf in morning on stretching leg in bed. Twitching in calves in forenoon when sitting. Tearing in lower ends, and in forepart of feet; in r. tibia, extending into great toe, in which there is crawling as if it would fall asleep, in afternoon; in calves in afternoon, then in thighs. Pinching in calf on moving foot after walking, with tension as if too short. Boring in tibia in evening when sitting, > walking. Drawing pain around leg above malleolus. Drawing in r. in evening; in r. from knee to foot, with uneasiness in it; cramplike, down tibia; pressive, in l. calf, < walking. Uneasiness of l. leg and foot at night. Weariness in afternoon.

Malleolus.—Tearing in l. external in afternoon. Sticking below l. external when walking; S. in r. ankle.

Foot.—*Swelling of soles.* Jerking in heels at 11 A.M., with pinching; J. posteriorly in l. heel in afternoon when walking. Cramp in r. at night; on inner margin of sole on bending foot inward. *Sticking in r. sole in afternoon; in a corn.* Tearing in forepart, < moving foot; in r. sole in forenoon, with heat; cramplike, on back of r. near toes. Cramplike pain in r. foot and toes; in l. sole, almost a tearing. Boring in corns. Sore pain in ball, where there are corns, on stepping. Drawing pain in corns. Tensive drawing in r. instep in evening when standing, > rubbing. Sensitive and cold. Uneasy. Heavy. Prickling in soles. *Throbbing* in heels in evening in bed, *with crawling*, as from an ulcer. Crawling in r. as if it would fall asleep at 5 A.M. in bed; in forepart of r. as if it would fall asleep in afternoon when sitting. Falling asleep of l. in forenoon when sitting.

Toes.—Twitching in l. great in afternoon. Swelling of great, with tearing like sore pain, preventing sleep. Tearing in r. great; in forenoon; in outer side of r. great in afternoon; in extensor tendons of r. great in afternoon, > rubbing. Pain as from suppuration in l. great. Smarting between T., with soreness.

Clinical.—Weakness of ankles, with gastric symptoms. Pain in tendo-achillis, with dyspnœa and palpitation. Soreness of the soles, with swelling.

Skin.—White spots on r. cheek and side of neck in morning. Red spots on back of l. hand, one behind little finger, one behind index; as if bruised, on great toe, from which intermittent tearing extends along side of sole; redness of l. leg, with inflammation, swelling, itching, gnawing, and itching and sticking painful ulcers. *Eruption on nose and mouth;* dry, on nates and coccyx, itching in morning on rising. Tetters on l. hand. *Dry, rough and cracked; hands rough and cracked.* Desquamation on back and tip of nose, with sensitiveness to touch. Beginning of warts; W. begin to bleed, grow larger and disappear; W. begin to pain on pressure. Pimple on side of nose; on chin, with burning pain; on face by ear, with sticking when touched; itching, beneath lower lip; itching P. and nodes on scalp, chest and abdomen.

Itching, moist eruption on nose and mouth. *A tetter exudes a purulent liquid*, becomes larger and is aggravated. Pustules about mouth; *black, ulcerating, on heel;* with red areola, on l. wing of nose; red, on forehead, with burning sore pain; on neck, with sore pain on touch; sensitive to touch, on small of back. Boil behind ear; red, above r. side of chin, disappearing after two days without suppurating. Ulcers about mouth. Vesicle near and beneath r. corner of mouth; clear, containing matter, beneath r. corner of mouth; white, with red areola, burning as from nettles, on first joint of l. index; red, itching, filled with water, on chin; red, filled with liquid, in bend of elbow and groin, with sore pain on touch; on back, itching, < evening on undressing; near r. wing of nose, with burning pain on touch; with burning pain as from nettles, in inside of r. index, disappearing after washing with cold water; on tips of fingers and toes, as if scalded, with festering about them as if nails would slough off.

Itching sticking between second and third phalanges of r. ring finger, > scratching. Burning drawrng over outer side of r. tibia. Intermittent sensation of a plaster on upper surface of r. forearm, so that skin was drawn up, from 9 A.M. till 4 P.M. Crawling in r. middle toes in afternoon, > touch; on back, with itching; itching, posteriorly on ball of r. thumb, > rubbing, but returning.

Itching on limbs; on soles, < balls of feet; in beard in evening; general, in evening on lying down, till sleep. I. > scratching, here and there on face; on r. side of neck; outer side of r. thigh; bend of r. knee; r. calf; in a spot on r. index towards thumb, in morning; on back, but returning; on outer side of r. knee, then burning. I. not > scratching, on r. side of abdomen and hip; in hollow of l. knee. I. and after scratching pimples, in bend of l. elbow; burning P. in evening, on nape and outer side of l. leg. I. and after scratching hives, on abdomen, genitals and lower limbs. I., with biting in bend of elbow; on abdomen. *I., as from fleas over whole body;* on back; beard, chin and chest; back of hand. I., with sticking in raphe of perineum; soles and heels. Sticklike I. on hypogastrium and thighs, < afternoon. I. on third joint of r. index, with burning and under the skin a pimple. Burning I. on great toes; on back of l. middle finger in morning; in region of r. lower jaw, > scratching.

Clinical.—The skin on the dorsal aspect of the extremities, hands and feet become dry, rough and chapped.

Sleep.—Yawning in forenoon; in evening; after dinner, > work, with sleepiness and indolence; with lachrymation and sleepiness, then light sleep. *Sleepiness during the day, with yawning;* when sitting and reading; S. in morning and difficult rising; S. in forenoon, and he lay down on the lounge, but after dinner, when he usually had a nap, he was not sleepy, only dozed briefly and lightly; from 1 till 3 P.M., with yawning. Sleep overpowering in afternoon. Heavy, stupid sleep. Sleep very sound first nights, afterwards very restless. Could scarcely wake from a partial slumber in morning.

Late and difficult falling asleep. Sleep vanished in evening if he lay down in bed, yet he soon fell asleep. Sleeplessness after 1 A.M., because she could not find a comfortable position; S. till towards morning, with necessity to urinate much, and restlessness all night; with ability to lie only on l. side; without anxiety and without ability to open eyes. Woke towards 2 or 3 A.M., but soon fell asleep again; W. suddenly about midnight, as if some one had pulled his nose. Frequent waking as from alarm; F. waking and restless dreams; and difficult falling asleep again; and restless sleep. Restless sleep and frightful dreams; R. sleep, with jerking and stretching of limbs. Night restless, uncomfortable. Jerking and starting up in fright; from midday nap; in evening on falling asleep, < l. leg. Jerking now of one finger, now of an arm, now of facial muscles, now of whole body, at night; J., now in hands, now in feet, before and after midnight, always waking her. Throwing about of hands. Talking after midnight.

Dreams.—*Sleep full of D.* Lies in a dreamy condition at night. With chilliness in sleep. *Anxious, confused* on falling asleep, from which he awoke in an hour with distressed abdomen and dry tongue; A. in first sleep. Difficult to remember, of past events, but oftener about things he had heard spoken of in the evening. Vivid; and frightful, of thieves, from which he started with a loud cry, and when awake could scarcely realize that his fears were groundless; of the features of a corpse. That she saw a corpse, at which she woke in fright, when it seemed as if a dead acquaintance stood before her, which made her scream. Of robbers, thieves, etc., all night. Troubled. Of a flood and threatening danger. Of a quarrel, in which he stabbed his antagonist in the chest with a large knife. Of a journey that she could not take because something held her back, a kind of nightmare. Nightmare at the full moon, he could not move on waking. When half asleep in evening she sees figures, visions of soldiers marching in the air, she often rouses herself, but they return immediately and only disappear when she stands up and walks about. At first mostly agreeable and amorous, of marrying two women, of parties, drives, entertainments and excursions on horseback, later they were often anxious, of going astray, of murders, having his ears cut off, also vexatious, he would take a journey but could not get away, and when he reached the first station he was obliged to turn back because he had forgotten something, etc. Voluptuous; and confused, with restless sleep, violent erections and emissions; in which he had an emission without waking, later he was almost aroused by a storm, felt sexual desire that almost induced onanism.

Fever.—Chilliness; all day, and no stool; morning and evening; in morning after rising; at 10 P.M. on lying down, with burning in abdomen, then heat till sleep, at 3 A.M. she woke with sweat and thirst, which lasted till morning, and with which she could not endure to be uncovered; before stool; after eating, with internal heat, and chilliness on going into cold air. Something like a febrile paroxysm, pain in temples and eyes and dulness of head, then nausea and chilliness, < chest and arms, somewhat > in bed, but there were yawning, stretching, stiffness of nape, and chilliness alternating with heat.

Shaking chill all day, with cold hands and warm cheeks, but in evening cold hands, red cheeks and hot forehead, without thirst; S. chill suddenly in forenoon. Shivering all day, with thirst; all day, with hot hands, cold cheeks and lukewarm forehead, without thirst; in morning after rising and often in afternoon; in morning, > rising; in forenoon and afternoon; at 11 A.M.; at 5 P.M., then after lying down heat and thirst; from 5 P.M. till after going to bed, during menses; in evening; in evening before going to bed, then heat, but she could not endure to be uncovered; on back in evening on lying down.

Cold feet; and hands; *and hands, with hot forehead;* < morning and evening on going to sleep, mostly with heat of face, violent beating of heart and apprehension. *Coldness of lower limbs, even during the day.* Cold, dry hands.

Heat, sweat and exhaustion, without thirst; H. in attacks, with weakness; frequent flushes of H., with ill humor, sadness and anxiety, then weakness. Orgasm over whole body at night, making him so fearful of apoplexy that he was obliged to rise often from bed.

Heat in r. side of sinciput, extending to occipital protuberances, at 9 A.M., with sensitiveness to touch in anterior places; H. in head and face on rising from a seat, with sensation as if all the blood mounted into head; in head, < dinner, > evening and in bed, with redness of face and with feeling of heaviness; sudden intermittent, in a spot above l. orbit at 9 A.M.; sudden, mounting into H., with redness of face; dry, of H. in forenoon and afternoon; internal, in H. and eyes, without external H. of face, but with thirst, also at night.

Heat of face from 5 P.M. till lying down, with red cheeks; of face, < r. cheek, at 11 A.M., with redness of face. Heat creeping from nape down over back, with drawing pain. Burning at lower end of r. scapula, > motion, but returning, with pressure; B. in palms; *in feet, < soles, when walking;* in soles; in soles in evening, > in bed; in r. little toe in afternoon on walking.

Sweat.—*In morning;* in morning till breakfast, with thirst; towards morning, with thirst; at night; on motion, even in cool weather; on walking or ordinary exertion, < back; inclination to, after coition; exhausting, < hands; burning, < forehead, where hat rests; on hands; on feet when walking. Dryness of skin; distressing, at night, < after midnight; of. hands, without their usual smoothness.

Clinical.—Coldness between scapulæ.

Natrum Muriaticum.

Pure table salt is triturated for use.

General Action.—In general a scorbutic cachexia, with marked tendency to an unhealthy skin and catarrh of mucous membranes. (Eruptions, ulcerations, altered secretions.) It produces constipation, but increases the secretion of urine. It causes delayed and scanty menstruation and in most cases produces a well-marked depression of spirits amounting even to melancholia. Its power to rid the system of malarial poisoning is abundantly verified, and in numerous cases of malnutrition presenting peculiarities similar to the drug it has restored the tone of the system.

Allies.—Mur. ac., Sep., Nux v., Nit. ac., Puls., China, Ars., Ign.

Generalities.—**Emaciation** (Iod.); *of body, but face was tolerably plump.* Falling of hair of beard and mons veneris. Increase of blood-corpuscles, fibrin, fatty matters, and of extractive and salts, in blood, with decrease of water and albumen. Circulation excited by every motion; impaired C. in arm when lying on table, and often in all parts. Awkward. Shivering when sitting, without chilliness. *Trembling; in evening; caused by tobacco-smoking* (Ars.), with sweat; < hands and feet. Motion of head and limbs greater than he wished. Vibrating motion of muscles of back, r. upper arm and calves. Jerkings here and there; J. in upper part of body when lying awake in afternoon. Sudden shock on whole l. side of body. Attack like epilepsy, it extended from l. shoulder to head, then pressure in temples as if head would burst, sore pain in brain, drawing pain from shoulder to head, nausea, necessity to lie down, with chilliness and heat in face. Sensation of epileptic attack. Attack, it runs from the stiff nape into head, eyes hurt, with nausea, chilliness and loss of senses.

Sticking here and there; < lips and along urethra; < tip of r. thumb, in l. umbilical region and in thighs; S. in shoulder-joint and from r. mastoid process to forepart of neck in morning, < motion; S. outward in teeth, side of head and about ear, all day. Paroxysmal gnawing in evening, now in pit of stomach, now in chest. *Pain as if flesh were loose, < thighs and upper arms, on motion.* Pain at night (for example, in boil on back), taking away the breath, even to suffocation and causing one-sided paralysis, so that arm and leg are powerless. Tickling, weary pain. Bruised pain on r. zygoma and coccyx, < touch, lasting all day in coccyx; B. pain on touch, < about loins. Attack of pressure and burrowing beneath r. ribs, with drawing in back extending to head, preventing sleep at night, and with sticking in head, all > continued talking, physical exertion, rumbling in abdomen and emission of flatus, or after eating. *Sensitiveness to touch* (Arn., Chin., Nux v.). *Takes cold easily* (Kali c., Nux v.). *Dread of open air.* *Pulsation in whole body, even during rest;* P. so that all parts moved frequently; violent, in bloodvessels at night on waking. Uneasiness.

Weakness; *all day* (Ars., China, Ferr., Kali c., Nux v., Sep., Iod.); during the day, with sleepiness; the day after a restless night, with suffering expression and sadness; in morning, with ill humor; in morning on waking; in morning, > rising; all the forenoon; after midday nap, with trembling; in afternoon, also with dulness of head; in evening, also the longer she sits up the weaker she becomes; *when standing, with heaviness of feet and sensitiveness to touch, < about loins;* when sitting; when sitting after dinner; *after walking,* also with nausea; *after eating, with necessity to lie down; during rigors;* < rising from bed; > walking; *with trembling of hands and feet;* with yawning; so that she could not stand; of upper part of body. *Weakness of mind and body;* in evening; with increased appetite. Faint. Stiffness of scapulæ, hip-joints and small of back; of all joints. Riding horseback affected him more and more from time to time. Aggravation when lying, she must sit up in bed at night to get relief.

Clinical.—Marasmus in children, with ravenous appetite (Iod.), especially with emaciation of the neck, thirst, dry mouth, hard stools, fissures at anus, etc. General anæmia, with great depression of spirits, palpitation, coldness about the heart.

Mind.—**Excitement;** in morning after early waking; then falling asleep and deadness of limbs; and scorn; < towards evening, with anxiety, then crawling beginning in finger-tips, hands and arms, arm fell asleep as if dead, crawling mounted into throat, lips and tongue, which became stiff, with boring in a tooth, then weakness of head, with impaired vision, even lower limbs felt asleep and joints seemed dead. Lively; in afternoon, conscious of physical and mental power; towards evening, she wished only to sing and dance. She felt happy and light after coition, but soon was peevish. *Laughed immoderately at something not ludicrous, so that she could not be quieted, and tears came into her eyes, so that she looked as if she had been weeping;* easily made to laugh, though not lively; inclined to laugh in evening.

Hastiness; anxious. Frigidity of manner. **The more he was consoled the more he was affected** (Ign.). **Weeping mood;** *when alone; if one looked at him; because he concluded from the look of every one that he was pitied for his misfortune;* all night after a slight vexation, with cough and ineffectual retching; at thought of a want long past. **Sad** (Ign., Puls.); *all day, apprehensive, disheartened, with palpitation;* during menses; **and preferred to be alone** (Puls.); in afternoon, as if insulted; in sudden attacks. *Despair that deprived him of all power.*

Anxiety in morning before appearance of delayed menses, with nausea, something sweetish came into mouth, then expectoration of blood and saliva; A. in evening, then inclination to sweat; at night, with heat, necessity to uncover, vivid dreams on falling asleep (with profuse flow of menses); at night during a storm, anxious heat forced her to rise; before menses; during menses, with faintness, cold cheeks and internal heat; with heat and sweat; A. and restlessness alternating with indifference; about the future; sudden, forenoons, with palpitation; about herself when alone, with weeping; as if she had done something wrong, with heat and night-sweat; as if he would fall when walking. Looks often into the mirror and imagines that she looks wretched. *Easily startled;* in evening. Fear of dying; of insanity; he seemed paralyzed by F. in evening, afterwards he seemed horrified and apprehensive.

Anger at trifles. Anthropophobia. Hatred of people who had insulted him. Offended by a joke. Quarrelsome (Nux v.). Passionate; towards evening; passion and vehemence alternating with moodiness and silence. Loathing of life. *Ill humor ;* all day ; *in morning* (Nux v.) ; in morning on waking, then quarrelsome mood (Nux v.) ; in forenoon ; in forenoon, with indolence, prefers not to speak ; evenings ; < being spoken to ; about persistent thoughts of affronts he had given and received, and he had no real interest in anything ; I. and exhaustion alternating with cheerfulness and lightness of limbs ; but necessity to sing and hum to herself. Taciturn ; and fretful when questioned. Talked more than usual, but did not like so much to be talked to, when she had nothing to say she became melancholy. Much affected by conversation. *Indifference* (Phos., Puls., Sep.). Lack of circumspection. Lack of independence. Irresolute at his work. Sluggish. *Disinclined to work ;* in afternoon ; but disposed to think acutely. *Disinclined to mental work ;* in evening.

Clinical.—Brain fag, with impaired memory and irritability, inability to fix the attention, sometimes with numbness of the extremities (Pic. ac.). Melancholia, with frequent weeping, pain in occiput, chilliness, restlessness, etc. Melancholia during pregnancy, fear that the child will be marked. Despairing melancholia, hopeless of the future, with dry mouth, constipation, anæmia, palpitation, etc. Melancholia, constant dwelling on past events, weeping if looked at (Puls.). Melancholia at the age of puberty, wakes with headache, patchy tongue, palpitation, etc. Hysterical alternations of laughing and weeping (Ign.).

Easily makes mistakes in talking ; in writing. *Distraction ;* in evening ; *when talking.* Confusion all day, with pain in forehead. Felt almost as if losing his reason. Loss of ideas ; from 3 till 7 P.M., with sleepiness ; after physical exertion, with apathy. Thought suddenly leaves him if he follows an idea. Control over thoughts lost in evening. Inability to perform mental work. Thought difficult. Lost in thought of what would become of him. *Memory weak ;* everything remained in his mind like a dream ; *lost,* and he thinks he has lost his reason ; forgetful all day ; forgetful in evening.

Head.—*Involuntary nodding forward.* Shock in brain like a jerking or pressure, on rapid running. *Sticking ; through H. ;* in brain ; with constriction behind ear ; in various parts, with gnawing as if in bones ; forward through H. on entering house ; through H. into nape and chest. Cutting at 3 P.M., at times somewhat less in r. side, but worse in l. side (< open air), on l. side it extends as a drawing pain above l. eye to zygoma and angle of lower jaw (only on entering house). Anxiety as if he would lose his senses in evening after lying down.

Aching ; all day ; in morning on waking, lasting till towards noon (Nux v.) ; morning after waking ; morning on rising ; mornings, > rising ; morning, after smoking, > dinner and drinking coffee ; at 4 P.M., and on taking hold of forehead sensation as if everything in head were beating ; at 5 P.M. ; at night on waking, with sweat ; externally at night when lying on occiput ; *from sneezing or coughing, > compression ;* from violent motion ; on turning body ; *during rigor* (Chin. s.) ; on touch, in a spot bruised six years previously ; from cold air ; caused by vexation, she feels every step in head, with loss of appetite, sticking in upper part of l. chest, heaviness of feet and weakness ; > walking ; > yawning ; in middle, with compression in skull ; **as if it would burst ;** *stupefying, from morning after waking till noon. Throbbing pain all day* (Ferr.), *< l. frontal region ; T., with heat of head and face, nausea and vomiting. Pain that seemed to press out the eyes, > pressure upon eyes. Sick headache from morning till noon ;* in afternoon, obliged to lie down, and on rising threatened to vomit and faint, the slightest step hurt the head, pain suddenly > 8 P.M., but weakness of head remained ; < from afternoon till sleep, with pressure in forehead.

Dulness ; *in morning ;* in morning, with vertigo, heaviness of head and pressure outward in forehead and temples ; *in morning on waking ; in forenoon, also with vertigo ;* at 10 A.M., with heaviness and on stooping vertigo ; from 5 till 6 P.M., with vertigo ; in afternoon, also with vertigo ; in afternoon, with sudden pain above eyes ; in afternoon, with pain in temporal bone and root of nose ; in afternoon, with throbbing in occiput ; in evening, with vertigo ; at night on rising ; on waking, with heaviness and vertigo ; on waking after a restless night disturbed by vivid dreams, with heaviness of it ; *after thinking ;* after eating ; after a long walk ; after menses, with heaviness as from rush of blood ; < pressure, with pain in temples ; < stooping, with pain < temples ; with pressure above eye and in temple ; with ringing in ears ; as if sleepy ; as before coryza, in morning ; causing peculiar feeling of resolution, even in regard to indifferent things ; soon becoming a pain in one temple, with dry heat in head ; as if stupid and as if not his own.

Feeling as if in a net. Constriction of brain in morning. Fulness after black coffee ; F., which seems to press out eyes. Tension in brain after an affecting farewell. Feels thick and swollen internally. Seems mellow (soft). Brain seems loose, and on shaking head sticking in temples. Feeling in brain in forenoon as if something in it were disturbed, < turning head. *Weakness* as after much turning in a circle. Emptiness, with apprehension. *Heaviness ;* all day ; in morning ; in morning on waking, with dizzy confusion ; in morning after rising ; < talking or thinking ; with compression in brain from all sides ; with drawing pain upward from root of nose ; in attacks so that he must lie down, > sweat after lying down ; repeated H. and congestion, amounting in evening to sticking in r. side of forehead and in eyeball, > towards 9 P.M., then restless night, and on waking heaviness and dulness of head. Stupefaction. Pulsation at night, with heat in body ; P. at base of skull. *Rush of blood ;* at noon, with sweat on forehead.

Vertigo ; all day ; *in morning after rising, > lying down again ;* in morning, < rising, > cold applications ; waking her at 5 A.M., with nausea, the V. > lying with head high, returned on rising, < stooping, > cold applications, < afternoon ; *on walking ;* on stooping ; on stooping and rising again, with obscuration of vision ; on rising from bed and on waking ; on turning around ; before sleep, with nausea and trembling ; < forenoon ; > quiet ; *with dulness of head and flickering before eyes ;* pressing head downward, when sitting ; in attacks, also towards 7 P.M. ; intermittent, < moving head, like a thrust from vertex to forehead, depriving him of his senses ; as if everything in front of her turned in a circle, on walking ; as if the stones were sinking under his feet when crossing a stone bridge ; like a faintness in morning on rising in bed, her senses vanished and often she was obliged to lie down.

Forehead.—Sticking ; in upper part ; above F. ; above brows ; in evening ; at night ; above arch of l. brow after dinner, lasting till evening ; with burning ; in l. side, with loose feeling ; extending to occiput, taking away her appetite; now in r., now in l. half, after dinner; now in r., now in l. side, in open air, < entering house. Cutting from l. half to occiput. Drawing boring in r. half. Burrowing deep beneath l. brow. **Feeling as if it would burst when coughing. Heavy and pressive pain above eyes.** *Pain; above brows; in r. side;* in l. half; all day; at 7 P.M., with vertigo and weariness; *during and after sneezing;* on rapid motion; in open air, and in temples; < wrinkling it, then sore pain in bone on touch; in afternoon extending to temples, > yawning, with dulness and with stoppage of ears; now in l., now in r. half; *and in eyeballs, so that opening lids was painful and difficult and he could read no longer,* < dinner, so that he must lie down, then lachrymation, the same symptoms returned after two hours and followed the same course; *dragging;* as from a swelling above r. eye, < raising brows; sore, in and above F.; in F. and eyes as if head were asleep, when leaning it upon arm. Compression after supper. *Confusion.* Throbbing in morning on rising, with drawing back and forth. Sensation as if brain beat against F., > night, but returning in morning, and on ascending steps towards 11 A.M., with trembling of lower limbs and feeling as if feet were swollen and insensible, returning again about 3 and 5 P.M. Sensation as of some one beating with the finger above brows, if she made an effort to think or talk much.

Temples.—Sticking; anteriorly in r.; in l. from after dinner till evening. Pain; interrupted by sudden pain in l. half of head; sudden, extending from r. T. to half of forehead and r. eye, from 5 till 9 P.M. every second day, < touch and light, with sensitiveness of eyeball, > drinking much water, but not entirely disappearing till after a hearty supper; cramplike, in r., extending into teeth; in T., forehead and ears as if brain were forced out; jerking, in l. bone, extending towards outer canthus and at last to eyeball, towards evening, in open air. Pressure as if in a vise. Compression. Tension in l. as if full, more in evening than in morning. Pulsation in l. extending towards occiput.

Vertex.—Sticking; > resting head on something; with burning; extending through brain into palate. Pain; after dinner; like a soreness of scalp. Pressure on V. and in temples.

Sides.—Sticking in parietal bone; in evening on eating; in l. side of head at night; through l. half of brain, alternating with pressure and heaviness above orbits; cutting S. back and forth in r. side at 3 P.M. Boring, and in occiput. Pain from sides of skull, < r., < working and writing; P. in l. half of brain woke him after midnight; in r. half, extending towards vertex; in l., extending into eyeballs, with sensation as if a nerve were drawn tense and suddenly loosened; drawing P. externally, extending across cheek to eyetooth; bruised P. in parietal bone on touch.

Occiput.—*Sticking;* between r. protuberance and styloid process. Pressure; and in l. side of nape. *Throbbing. Heaviness;* in afternoon, with pulsation and stiffness in nape.

Scalp.—*Falling out of hair;* and of beard. Scurf. Raw on temples. Itching eruption. Smells musty and hairs stick together. Movement from nape towards forehead and back again. Contraction on vertex; on side of vertex. *Sensitiveness. Itching;* **and of nape**; and of beard. Impatient scratching of his head.

Clinical.—Vertigo > lying down, things seem to turn around, she has a tendency to fall forward or to the left. Headache in morning on waking, with constipation, salty taste, aversion to food, tremulousness of the heart, indistinct vision on trying to read, etc. Persistent frontal headache from straining eyes, especially from muscular asthenopia, thus often useful in the headaches of school children. Periodical headache comes on with menstruation. Supraorbital neuralgia, with soreness (Ced.). Neuralgia of r. side of head recurring at 10 A.M. every morning, with vertigo, flickering before eyes, faintness and sinking, relief on perspiring. Sick headaches of the menstrual period, beginning before the menses and continuing throughout, desires to be alone, does not want to be spoken to. Sick headaches in the forehead, with creeping chilliness, vomiting, blinding of eyes, etc. Sick headache, bursting with throbbing, stitches extending to neck and chest, with nausea, vomiting, heat of face, during and after menstruation, disappearing with perspiration. Headache from nervous shock, < lying, involving r. eye. Headache in vertex, like a weight, > pressure. Throbbing headache every morning on waking, < talking or reading. The headaches are usually frontal, but a few occipital headaches have been cured when the other symptoms were extremely prominent. Eruptions on scalp, exanthematous or impetiginous, usually at the border of the hair, especially at the nape and behind the ears, the discharge glutinous, the skin sore and red. The eczematous eruption on scalp exudes a glutinous moisture, which mats the hair.

Eyes.—Redness of white; and lachrymation; *with inflammation and* **feeling as if balls were too large** *and compressed. Inflammation in slight wind, with lachrymation. Dim and weak.* Jerking; frequently during the day, then itching. **Sensation as if sand were in them in morning.** *Sticking in r.;* in l. in morning on waking, with pressure and agglutination; itching, below l. Boring. *Pressure;* in r.; in evening, < r.; at twilight; in r. towards 11 P.M.; **on looking intently at anything;** *as from a foreign body. Smarting. Sensitiveness.* Tension. L. feels smaller than r. On blowing nose in afternoon it seemed to blow into l. eye, and a spot on upper lid by inner canthus seemed distended with air, he thought, especially the first time, that something had come out of the eye, later soreness of the spot, < touch. *Itching.* Dryness in evening, with pressure in inner canthi; *D. as after long weeping, when riding in a carriage. Burning in evening; B. and increased mucus, agglutination and sensitiveness to lamplight;* B. point; (*dry B. in evening when writing*).

Lachrymation; *in open air; biting, in morning;* acrid, making canthi red and sore; burning, and mucus in eyes. Jerking tearing in l. ball in evening. Sticking in r. brow, extending horizontally through brain. Twitching on lower margin of r. orbit. Bruised pain on outer margin of l. orbit. Sticklike itching on margin of l. orbit (towards external canthus) in evening.

Lids.—*Redness of margins and of conjunctiva; of margins, and in morning agglutination, with scabs; of margins, with burning, < evening when reading;* of lower, with ulceration. Pimple on margin of lower, not in Meibomian glands. Soreness of r. lower. *Agglutination in morning.* Trembling. Twitching of r. upper in morning; of l. upper after dinner, with trembling. *Spasmodic closure* in morning on rising, in the twilight and at night, even when she closed the eyes she felt the contraction. Spasmodic drawing in r. and when she wished to go to sleep pain, then trembling of upper lid. **Irritability of margins and of their conjunctiva.** Pain. Heaviness; of upper; of r. upper. Difficult to open at night when awake. Sensation in r. lower as if skin were rough. Biting in upper in afternoon, and they seemed moist to touch. Margins and canthi (< external) burn all day and secrete an acrid fluid, with pain in eyes as if inflamed, and on reading foggy vision.

Canthi.—Stye in r. inner. Jerking in l. external, < evening. Sticking; in l. inner, alternating with the same on crest of r. ilium; as from sand in l. external. Tearing, with darkness before eyes. Burning in r. inner, provoking rubbing. Dryness in evening, provoking rubbing. *Itching in l. inner;* in external; *in inner, with lachrymation;* sticking, in l. inner.

Eyes give out; on writing; on reading, *with pressure in r. eye extending into head and > walking about the room.* **Letters and stitches run together. Objects become confused on looking at them.** *Sudden darkness at 6 P.M. on looking long at anything, > looking at another object, with sleepiness.* Only one-half of an object is visible. *Dim vision; all day;* in morning; from 10 A.M. till 3 P.M.; in afternoon; when walking in open air; as if eyes were covered with mucus; as if through feathers when looking at white objects; as if looking through rain. Intermittent feeling of a mist before eyes when standing. Short-sighted. Far-sighted. *Vision of fiery points;* when walking in open air; fiery zigzags about everything. Many points of light and shade.

Clinical.—A large number of affections of the eye, resulting from muscular asthenopia; it is curative when the symptoms are aggravated by any use of the eye, especially when there is burning or smarting as from salt, when the vision becomes blurred after reading a little, or if the patient wakes in the morning with headache and soreness of the eyes from having read the night before. Blepharitis ciliaris. Ulcers on the cornea. Pustules on the cornea and conjunctiva. Granulations of the lids. Ciliary neuralgia. Insufficiency of the internal recti muscles, even amounting to strabismus. It has been indicated in a number of cases which have been abused by the local application of nitrate of silver, especially in entropium and pannus. It seems to have cured dermoid tumors of the margins of the lids. Stricture of lachrymal ducts and fistula. Styes. Morbus Basedowii.

Ears.—*Discharge;* with swelling of meatus auditorius. Swelling of l. concha, with redness, heat and burning pain; and after some days itching behind ear; S. of l. external meatus, with sensitiveness to touch. Shock in l., then ringing. Sticking in r. meatus; S. in forenoon when sitting still; burrowing, in r.; drawing, in r.; itching, in lobule of r. Aching in and behind l.; behind r. in evening on drinking rapidly; intermittent; in r. as if something were jerked out with a hook at 6 A.M.; drawing, in r. Drawing extending to shoulder-joint, with sticking. Stoppage in afternoon. Crawling in r., with bursting as of bubbles. Itching within r.

Hearing difficult. Singing in l. Ringing all day after 11 A.M., at times alternating with sensation as if bubbles of air were in it; R., < a cup of coffee, with noises, and on rising sensation as if he were falling; sudden, harsh R. in r. *Cracking on chewing* (Nit. ac.); in l. on swallowing; in l., with sensation as if tenacious liquid were flowing from it. Roaring; in morning in bed and when sitting. Humming in morning on waking. Fluttering as of a butterfly in l. during dinner. Ticking as of a watch in l. in evening. Rushing in l. in bed; sudden R. through ears.

Clinical.—Chronic catarrh of the ear, with deafness and various noises, especially cracking when chewing.

Nose.—*Swelling of l. wing* towards evening, *with heat and sore pain,* the last < touch; *swelling of l. half, with inflammation and pain as if nostril were contracted, with soreness on touch and itching.* Tip red, hot and painful, then a group of vesicles filled with transparent lymph, at last confluent and forming a scab. *Internal soreness* (Nit. ac., Sil.); *with swelling inside* and pimples upon nose; of l. nostril, with difficult passage of air. Twitching in l. side of root. Sticking deep in r. nostril at 4 A.M.; S. deep in root, extending towards r. frontal sinus. Boring in bones, root and towards r. cheek. Pain < blowing; P. at root. *Dryness* (Lyc.). *Stoppage* (Lyc., Nux v.). Sensation of coryza every morning. Burning, and in eyes. Crawling in nostrils; in r., with pressure in r. eye as before sneezing. Itching in nostrils all day; I. in r. as if a worm were boring through it. Insensibility in one nostril, with deadness.

Sneezing; at 10 P.M.; ineffectual attempts at. *He easily takes cold in the head, must wrap it up, if it is uncovered during the day he has stoppage of nose at night* (Nux v.). *Coryza and tickling cough, as if he had taken cold; coryza, with loss of smell and taste; violent C. for one day, with sneezing;* stopped. Fluent coryza; with at times stoppage of l. nostril; *and discharge of thick mucus;* after several days affecting eyes, throat, trachea, with dulness of head, prostration, short, dry cough and dryness and soreness in chest, the nasal secretion ceased without becoming yellow or thick; burning; then stopped. Water drops unnoticed. Watery mucus now in r., now in l. nostril, in a carriage on exposing nose to open air. Bleeding; at night; on stooping; *blowing out of clotted blood.*

Clinical.—Coryza, fluent or changing to stopped, with feeling of dryness or with occasional sudden discharge of clear water, also with constant lachrymation from obstruction of nasal duct. Loss of smell and taste. Nasal catarrh, with very profuse, thick, yellow, mucous discharge (Puls.), with complete loss of smell and taste (cured after Puls. had entirely failed), the complete absence of taste seems to be decisive. Coryza, with dry, cracked lips, especially swelling, with eruptions around mouth of vesicles or of hydroa (a good symptom, but not characteristic in intermittent fever). Hay fever, with watery discharge from eyes and nose, loss of taste, etc. Chronic naso-pharyngeal catarrh, especially with morning aggravation, loss of taste, general weakness, elongated uvula. Naso-pharyngeal catarrh, which is generally worse at the seaside (this, however, is true only in persons who are very susceptible to the action of salt). A great variety of chronic nasal and pharyngeal catarrhs which have been abused by local applications, especially of nitrate of silver.

Face.—Red in morning on waking; **L. cheek,** < afternoon; cheeks, in open air, pale in house. Pale; and lips; < morning and after dinner, with sunken look. *Earthy. Yellow,* with pain in hypogastrium. *Shining as if greasy. Beard falls out* and afterwards hair on mons veneris. Confused look. Sickly look. Jerking of muscles. Pain in malar-bones and by ear; in l. side in evening, < region of eye, nose and temple; drawing, in r. cheek-bone. Pressive and broken sensation in l. cheek-bone, extending to l. teeth and thence to all teeth, it seemed as if he could not bring the teeth well together. Bruised pain in r. zygoma; in zygoma, < touch.

Jaws.—Sticking in joints; l. joint at 4 A.M. Tearing in lower, extending into temple and into parotid and submaxillary glands, > binding up cheeks, with intermittent boring and pinching in the indurated glands, < night. Gnawing in J. and l. lower teeth on smoking. Pain in lower on touch; drawing P. in lower. Sensation from r. lower to temple as if flesh were scraped from the bone or were being torn from the bone, from below upward, in afternoon, constantly < from 4 till 7 P.M. Cramplike tension in joint. Compression in l. joint, < opening mouth.

Lips.—Swelling, and of l. side of face; **of lower, with burning, then a vesicle, next day a scab and desquamation**; *of lower, and of tip of tongue, with burning on it, waking him at night; around lips, with vesicles upon it, the red of lip sore and ulcerated and tongue covered with smarting vesicles.* Pale. *Peeling on red margin of upper. Dry; and cracked* (Graph.). *Painful fissure in middle of upper.* Bleeding easily. *Eruption on red of, with smarting;* E. in corners. Pustule in r. corner, with pain, < touch. *Blister on red of upper began to dry towards evening;* B. on red of lower, that burn and smart when moistened; on red of lower, becoming covered with scabs; *about mouth, forming a kind of tetter,* becoming covered with a scab that left a red spot on lower, containing much lymph; ulcerating, painful to touch, in r. corner. Ulcers in corners; U. on inside of lower, with sore burning on touch. Ulcerative pain inside of lower, < touch. Tearing sticking from upper across cheek into ear. Sore feeling in corners on opening them. *Dryness in evening, with desquamation, pain and on sneezing crack in the middle.* Burning; on margin of upper. Numbness, < evening, with crawling.

Clinical.—Neuralgia of face occurring periodically in place of the ague paroxysm (Nux v.).

Mouth.—Teeth. *Looseness;* of incisors, with pain. Bluntness. Rapid decay. Sticking in decayed; S., now in one, now in another every forenoon; in first and second molars, with painful drawing where an upper tooth had been. Pain as if something were sticking in them. Pain in first r. upper molar as if something sharp were thrust in and out, and on pressing finger upon cheek at this point cutting in the root of the tooth. Tearing during menses if cold air enters mouth, with stitches; T. extending to temples; now in r. upper, now in l. lower. Boring. Acute pain on drawing in air. Pain in r. upper; in a hollow; on touch of tongue and on chewing; in l. molars and their gums, waking after midnight two nights; in hollow and neighboring T., > touch and hard pressure; with swelling of cheeks; extending into ears, with stitches. Pain as if pulling and breaking in hollow molar, extending into throat and pharynx, so that she could neither open the mouth, swallow nor speak a loud word, and extending into ear, where there were itching and sticking, < evening and forepart of night. Throbbing pain; in incisor, with sticking; in incisor, with burning boring; after midnight, then drawing outward extending into ear, with heat of face and swelling of gum and elongated feeling in teeth. Drawing; in r.; after eating and at night, then swelling of cheeks; every other day, extending into eye, with stitches. Sore pain. Feel elongated; and as if they did not fit together, and numb on pressure. *Sensitiveness;* to the brush; *to cold; to air,* < r.; to air, < r. lower.

Gums.—Swelling about a hollow tooth; S. in morning, so that she could not chew on that side; with inflammation and with swelling of cheeks; with sore pain; back of upper incisors, with sore pain. Painful swelling; of molars; behind l. upper middle incisor. *Painful ulcer;* on inner side of lower, > eating; on inner side of l. towards tongue, > eating. *Bleeding.* Sticking on touch of tongue. Drawing pain now above, now below, with swelling and pain on touch. *Sensitiveness to touch; S. to cold and warmth.* Affected about l. eye-tooth.

Tongue.—**Blisters** (Nit. ac.); *with burning pain on eating.* Red and shining. Coated white; < about root; C. whitish-yellow; yellow, and flat taste. Swelling under T., with sticking. Trembling sensation in tip. *Dryness; without thirst. D. and stiffness of T. and of hard palate.* Sore sensation. Astringent feeling, papillæ seem blunted. Heaviness. Crawling as if asleep. One half numb and stiff. *Difficult speech like a weakness of organs of speech coming from hypochondria.*

Mouth in General.—*Blisters and soreness. Ulcers, and on gum and tongue, in which food and drink cause biting. Open blister on inside of r. cheek felt during dinner, with burning pain in it from warm food.* Sore spot on inside of r. cheek, with burning pain on touch of warm food. Obstructed by mucus; mucus on inner surface; M., < morning. *Dryness;* of palate; of hard palate. Hard palate felt burnt, and on touch painful. *Breath offensive.* Breath hot. *Salivation;* in evening in bed, on account of which he choked and this caused a fit of coughing; at night, also waking him frequently; with dry sensation in mouth; with nausea; with retching; with frequent ecptysis; with shivering and shuddering, nausea and burning in stomach; then liquid vomiting; sudden. *Constant spitting;* at night. Discharge of saliva from mouth at night. Fine stream of saliva spurted from mouth in evening when chewing. *Saliva salt;* watery; sour-tasting; bloody; bloody, running from mouth at night.

Taste.—**Bitter** (Puls.); *in morning* (Puls.); *to food; to beer;* to tobacco when smoking; and slimy; and slimy, but food has a natural taste. Salt; *on lips;* on lips and palate. *Bad; in morning;* to water. As if she had eaten tallow. Sour in morning; S. till evening; after eating; on lip when touched by tongue; and flat, with salivation. Watery in evening, with loss of thirst and lack of urine; W. and flat to beer in evening; W. and flat, with loss of appetite, but food tastes tolerably well. Pasty; and nauseous; and sticky, but good appetite and good taste to food. Taste of the food for a long time after eating, or she smells it in the nose; after-taste of food, especially acid, for a long time after eating. Bread tastes better than anything else, he can scarcely eat enough of it. **Loss of taste.**

Clinical.—Gums scorbutic, bleeding. General dryness and heat of mouth, with catarrh of the pharynx, fluttering of heart, etc. Mapped tongue. Vesicles on tongue and mouth. Aphthæ of mouth and cheek, with burning; relaxed uvula (compare Alumina).

Throat.—Submaxillary glands swollen, stiff and painful; painful on stooping; painful as if swollen or crushed. Tension in l. sterno-cleido-mastoid, with stiffness; T. in l. sterno-cleido-mastoid after a walk, with roaring in ears. Tonsil, root of palate and uvula red. Uvula swollen and elongated, forming a loop by contact with r. tonsil, with congestion of throat. Ulcers on pharynx, with sore throat, inflammation and dark red swelling of gum. Mucus; green, from fauces in morning. *Hawking of mucus;* in morning; in morning after waking; in morning on going out, from posterior nares; when smoking; (when smoking, with nausea); *of salt mucus;* of watery; bitter, in morning; scanty, gray, lumpy, compact; that is more easily expectorated than usual. *Chokes easily when swallowing;* C. when laughing while drinking, so that the drink regurgitates through the nose and she almost suffocates.

Sticking in uvula; in r. tonsil; S. at night on swallowing; in l. side on swallowing; behind r. tonsil when yawning, extending to ear; and burning like an inflammation, with elongation of uvula and impeded swallowing. Tearing about parotids when drinking. *Sensation of a plug* on swallowing; on touch, in region of thyroid cartilage, and on drinking a jerking there; sensation of a plug, < night, waking him, with sore pain and anxiety as if throat would be closed by a swelling; *with rawness, burning pain and anxiety as if everything would be closed by the swelling.* Pain on coughing, and in chest. Soreness, < morning and evening; S. as from swelling of submaxillary glands, without swelling. Rawness. Scraping; in pharynx; in evening; at night, with salivation, hawking of blood and sleeplessness; sourish, in fauces. Scraping heartburn. Biting in pharynx as from inflammation and tightness, on swallowing.

Drawing in l. tonsil, with cramplike pain and roaring in l. ear. Tightness of pharynx, with difficult swallowing. Constriction in r. side caused by frequent yawning, extending to nape, which thereby becomes stiff. Dryness after eating; posteriorly in pharynx after eating; in posterior nares. Heat in pharynx, so that warm drinks seem cold. Cramp in œsophagus on swallowing, she could not get the morsels up or down, so that it seemed as if she would suffocate.

Clinical.—Follicular catarrh of pharynx.

Stomach.—Appetite. *Great;* waking him in morning, with restlessness; *towards noon, and after eating weariness and sleepiness;* at noon; in evening; with but little taste to food; constantly, but inability to eat more than a few mouthfuls; painful, but satiated immediately on eating; alternating with loss of appetite. For coffee. For cold things in afternoon. For sweets (at the time she usually wanted beer, which to-day she disliked). For beer. For wine only, all day; for wine, all wine seems sour. For fish in evening, but aversion at the first mouthful, the aversion > black coffee, he relished white bread. For bread only, he ate four pieces, with constant drinking and involuntary motion of masticatory muscles, afterwards swelling of abdomen prevented further eating, then sound sleep, woke at 1 A.M. with pasty taste and thirst. Diminished; at noon; but return while eating; for coffee. Returns after drinking wine several times. *Lost;* in afternoon after drinking water, with sensation of hunger in stomach; in evening; in evening, with nausea after eating; caused by a small piece of herring eaten in the evening, with moving and distention in abdomen and restless sleep, often interrupted by drinking; but there is a relish in mouth on eating, also with full feeling; *for smoking, he could not smoke at all;* for meat; for beer. Lost for coffee after rising; for C. in morning, and nausea after drinking it; and after drinking it cutting in region of spleen; but desire for wine and soup. Satiety in afternoon. *Aversion to eating; to meat* (Mur. ac.); *meat and bread;* black bread; *coffee* (Nux v.); salt; wine and beer (later effect); beer and tobacco in evening; smoking.

Thirst (Ars., Chin.); all day; at night; especially for wine; > drinking water; but scarcely any desire to drink; but aversion to wine and beer, beer had a flat, watery taste; **unquenchable;** almost unquenchable, with frequent profuse micturition; lost.

Eructations; *after eating* (Nux v.); after eating and after diarrhœa; after bread; with rancid heartburn; of beer, so that it comes through the nose, though made of hops; *incomplete;* bilious. Sour E. afternoons after eating, with burning rising from stomach; S. of food; of liquids, late in evening; and scraping; of food. Empty E.; in morning; in forenoon, with discomfort in stomach; after drinking much water; after every meal or in open air. Waterbrash; after eating. Hiccough; after eating; alternating with yawning; *violent.*

Nausea; in morning; in morning on waking, with pain in stomach; in morning after rising, with vertigo and empty eructations; in morning after milk, with trembling of limbs, vertigo and blackness before eyes; in pit of S. every day from 7 A.M. till noon; every day at 8 A.M., with burrowing in pit of stomach; all the forenoon; in forenoon, with burrowing in pit of stomach, chilliness as if dashed with cold water, vertigo as if everything turned in a circle with her and as if she would fall forward, and head so heavy that she could scarcely walk; towards noon; towards 4 P.M., after a little coffee, with empty eructations; in evening in bed, with hiccough and yawning; after breakfast; after dinner; after walking in open air after dinner, with yawning, thirst, salivation and mental and physical exhaustion; after eating, without appetite, with cramp in chest; after a pleasant drink, > lying on r. side; when yawning; as soon as she presses the painful spot; < inspiration, with heartburn and pressure in stomach extending to back; > a cup of broth; with salivation; with vertigo; with twisting and turning in stomach; with heaviness and griping in stomach like beginning heartburn; with pressure in stomach as from a stone (there was a remarkable connection between this affection and the tearing in tip of index and thumb); with fulness and tension in hypogastrium; with tendency to diarrhœa; even to faintness; as from an empty stomach; as from ravenous hunger, towards noon. Shuddering nausea at thought of the drug; S., with rumbling in abdomen and frequent yawning. Attacks of N. in morning, with weakness, pallor and necessity to lie down; in evening, with pain in stomach; before supper, with chill during every attack, the chill > going to bed, at night waking twice with acute drawing pain back and forth in forehead and throbbing between the attacks; after eating, with heaviness in head and empty, bitter eructations.

Retching in throat; ineffectual R.; ineffectual, in morning, after a warm, pleasant drink. Vomiting.

Distention; after eating; in epigastric region after eating and drinking; after dinner, with pressure; at præcordium after eating or drinking, with pain; D. and rumbling in epigastric region and abdomen. Sticking; in pit; in pit in morning; at r. side every day at 2 or 3 P.M.; in pit, < motion. *Sensation as if a foreign body were sticking in cardiac orifice and behind sternum.* Cramp from towards evening till next morning; *constrictive,* towards 5 P.M., with coldness in back and stomach. Griping in pit after eating.

Pressure; in epigastric region; in a spot in epigastric region; in forenoon, > eructations and emissions of flatus; in pit in forenoon; till towards noon, with emptiness and yawning; in evening, with tightness of breath and sensation as if diaphragm pressed against lungs and prevented their expansion, with frequent yawning and rumbling in abdomen; after eating; from eating, then waterbrash, then nausea, then vomiting at first of food, at last of bile, with colic; > yawning; *in pit, with sensitiveness to touch;* in pit, extending downward, with sticking; extending towards pharynx; extending into chest, four and six hours after dinner; cramplike, all the evening and next morning, extending across hypochondria to back and shoulders, with frequent yawning; as after taking cold, in morning; impeding respiration; intermittent, impeding respiration, all the forenoon; intermittent, extending to back and causing constriction in pharynx; worse periodically, and in liver and through whole back, < near spine, urine black, as if saturated with burnt coffee, and opaque, no change in color of skin; as from a stone, also with much yawning; as from something hard in pit, often causing deep inspiration; as if something heavy were in it in morning, with trembling of hands and feet; sensation of a hard swelling in pit in afternoon, with tightness transversely across hypochondria.

Sore pain after eating (Nux v.). Bruised pain in l. side near pit, on touch. Scraping; all day, with white, dry tongue, without thirst; as from something indigestible. Constriction; in morning, then cutting and rumbling in abdomen; in evening in bed; with cutting and with pressure before dinner and frequently recurring till evening; spasmodic; spasmodic, in cardiac orifice. Tension, with great appetite. Oppression in pit when standing. Dull, disagreeable sensation, > stooping. Anxiety in pit. Throbbing in pit; in pit while eating; in pit, < after eating.

Sensation as if hanging by a thread, then emptiness till towards noon. Emptiness; in morning; in forenoon, with coldness; as if hungry, but he had no appetite. Faintness in forenoon. Flatulent sensation in region. Digestion disturbed, tongue coated, taste bitter, flat (< morning). Weakness. Trembling. Coldness; in pit at 7 P.M., sticking extending upward and backward into chest; and painless diarrhœa four times. *Burning;* in external parietes in evening; in pit (between S. and parietes of S.) in evening in bed; *paroxysmal, in pit;* peculiar, extending over chest, then towards abdomen, < umbilical region; with shivering over surface of body; in part in pit, in part coldness; cool. *Heartburn;* in evening; all day, < evening.

Clinical.—Thirst is a general accompaniment of Nat. mur. symptoms; there are generally sour eructations, heartburn, especially waterbrash, sometimes vomiting of food. There is very frequently a feeling of great weakness and sinking in stomach (Sep.).

Abdomen.—Distention; in evening; at night, with incarceration of flatus and heaviness; after eating, with heat of face and slumbering, then herby taste, with stupefaction and intoxication in head; after eating, < drinking, with sensation as if everything in it were loose; *after dinner, also with emission of flatus;* after breakfast, > soft stool and emission of strong-smelling flatus; *from water and beer, with swashing in it;* with burning about umbilicus; flatulent.

Rumbling; in morning after coffee; *all the forenoon, with gurgling, then four pasty stools;* in evening, then diarrhœa; during breakfast, with screwing-up cutting; after breakfast, of coffee, < during rest, with gurgling and cutting; when drinking coffee, after drinking the pain ceased, but returned from 9 till 11 A.M., and after dinner; after eating; after eating, with movings, then two watery stools, almost without pinching in abdomen; after thin stool; with movements, gurgling, griping, urging to stool, forcible, copious, almost watery stool, much flatus, an hour later a less prolonged and less violent stool, with burning in anus, repeated after four hours.

Gurgling; and feeling as of the bursting of air-bubbles. Croaking; all the evening, with cracking. *Emission of flatus;* after dinner; copious, with feeling as if liquid escaped; frequent; frequent in forenoon, also with feeling as before a soft stool. Offensive flatus; in morning; forenoon; sour; like bad eggs, also in evening. *Fermentation.* Flatus moves about without being emitted, with heaviness of head, roaring in vertex and ears and stoppage of nose. Flatulence; in forenoon when walking, with feeling as before diarrhœa, at 3 P.M. urging to stool, stool scanty and hard; causing tension and stitches.

Sticking; on waking, < below last r. rib, with general chilliness. *Cutting;* mornings in bed; morning on rising; in morning after rising, < below r. ribs, also after coffee, with ineffectual urging to stool; in morning after coffee, and diarrhœa twice; in morning after coffee, with tenesmus, often returning in forenoon; in morning, > stool and emission of wind; at 4 A.M., with desire as for diarrhœa, but stool in two hard pieces, then tenesmus; every day about 5 A.M.; towards evening; every night; before midnight, with uneasiness and anxious constriction in epigastric region; on rising, then profuse diarrhœa without tenesmus, then C., < about umbilicus and liver; after dinner; < forenoon; < afternoon; intermittent; as with a two-edged knife in morning after coffee; as if everything would be drawn forward towards umbilicus in morning after rising, with anxiety, C. again after breakfast of coffee, after dinner and in evening; griping, after eating and drinking.

Griping; and in small of back; in morning in bed, with soreness, then pressing and sore feeling in back and scapulæ, > rising; in morning after rising; in morning after coffee; every afternoon; with coldness; as from worms in evening; *as in diarrhœa* in morning *after stool,* without result; as before diarrhœa in morning on waking; as before diarrhœa in morning after rising. Pinching, with pasty stools; P. as from worms, in evening.

Pain; waking at 5 A.M., and < stomach, with dryness and burning along œsophagus and throat; at 5 P.M., with ineffectual urging to stool; after coffee; > emission of flatus; as if everything would be torn out. *Flatulent pain,* < motion; F. and tensive, in morning on waking, > sleep, with itching about genitals; at night, moving about abdomen, with griping and with light, interrupted sleep. *Labor-like pain* when riding in a wagon; L. pressure downward during stool that was not hard, or during emission of flatus, necessity to press with her hands. Pain when walking, as if everything were loose, too heavy and would fall out. Loose feeling in morning after waking, half an hour later pasty stool, with flatus. Feeling as before diarrhœa.

Soreness all night. Sensitiveness along linea alba. Constriction towards evening, she must bend up, > walking; C. after dinner, then emission of flatus and hard, scanty stool, with burning in anus, lasting nearly all the evening; with desire for stool, stool hard and painful; and about umbilicus, with stoppage of breath, then sticking from small of back into thighs; jerking, in morning in bed. Tension; all the forenoon, > afternoon by emission of offensive flatus; with incarceration of flatus; flatulent, > eructations. Heaviness during menses. Burning; < pressure.

Upper.—Distention, with sticking in stomach, which on deep breathing extended up under sternum. Rumbling; with diarrhœa; with yawning. Griping. *Pressure.* Heaviness transversely across below pit of stomach, with tightness.

Hypochondria.—Flatulent, colicky distention, > emission of flatus. Sticking below last r. ribs in morning on waking, > dinner, returned in evening on going out, > returning to the house; in region of spleen in forenoon, < walking; below last r. ribs on entering the house, with frequent yawning; in l. on breathing; below last r. ribs on yawning; in l., < rapid walking; in r., with heaviness and fulness; below r. ribs, then desire for stool. Griping in r. Pinching in flesh, first below short ribs, then below umbilicus. Boring in l., then headache. Pain in a spot beneath r. false ribs, with tension; P. below last l. ribs as before diarrhœa, waking her at 5 A.M., with vertigo and nausea; P. in r. extending to back, > emission of flatus, but returning, with tension and with rumbling in abdomen; flatulent, low down in r.; drawing, as from a round, rough substance, extending from deep in r. towards back; burning, towards evening. Tension deep in l., extending to back, with clawing; T. in l. as from incarcerated flatus, in afternoon.

Hepatic Region.—Sticking; daily at 2 or 3 P.M., when sitting; after dinner; with sensitiveness to pressure. Digging deep in. *Pain;* frequently through the day; extending backward through it when walking, > bending forward and towards r. side. Drawing pain; extending downward, then griping below umbilicus. Scraping. Stiffness on bending trunk to l. side.

Sides.—Rumbling in l.; and about umbilicus, with gurgling. *Pinching in r.*, < lying on l. side. Intermittent cramplike pain in l., > emission of flatus. Dragging towards genitals in morning, so that she must lie down gently to avoid prolapsus of uterus. Compression in l. when walking and lying. Painful tension in r.

Umbilical Region.—Umbilicus protruded and sensitive to touch. Painful distention below umbilicus, > emission of flatus. Sticking above umbilicus; to r. of U.; in parietes to r. of U. in forenoon; between 6 and 7 P.M. on entering house; in parietes to l. of U. alternating with sticking in middle of anterior surface of thighs. Sticking twisting during stool, and in hypochondria. Cutting; all day, < pressure; intermittent; intermittent, in evening in bed, with nausea, vertigo and thirst. Griping; with ineffectual desire for stool; drawing, in l., extending to rectum and anus; sticking, above U. Pinching at night. Boring all day, with palpitation. Pain above umbilicus, > pressure; cramplike, in umbilicus, extending into small of back, in morning on rising, ending as sticking in hips and thighs; drawing, extending into thighs. Sensation as if walls were pressed outward by a hard substance. Pressure outward to r. of umbilicus, as if part of a child were pressing there, and whole abdomen tense and distended. Constriction; > emission of flatus; < night, > diarrhœa, which with the pain returned eight times during the night.

Hypogastrium.—Fulness. Protrusion of hernia. Rumbling in l. flank, and emissions of flatus; R. in evening, with flatulence. Cramplike contraction after micturition. Cramp above symphysis pubis, in morning. Sticking in l.; r. side above symphysis pubis, towards groin; alternately on crest of r. ilium and in l. inner canthus; tensive, above symphysis pubis, extending towards r. groin. Cutting; in evening; before stool; with urging to stool, then copious pasty stool, an hour later a watery stool; sticking, in anterior superior spine of r. ilium, extending partly over trochanter towards anterior and outer surface of thigh, partly across back to vicinity of scapula when sitting, shaking the whole body, next morning a similar C. starting from l. hip. Feeling of ulceration in r., and in r. groin. Pain every morning; P. before stool; *in ring when coughing, extending into testicles, as if spermatic cords would be torn to pieces;* towards rectum, as if flatus stopped it, before stool; wind colic; wind colic at night after usual beer; as from indigestion; with griping and sensation of generating flatus, which is passed offensive; sore, before stool or emission of flatus; drawing, in ring extending to testicles; constricting, labor-like, with weakness. Sensitiveness. Labor-like drawing extending into thighs. Intermittent constriction at 4 A.M. Feeling of a tight band on deep breathing. Tension, < r. groin. Anxiety at night caused by constant ineffectual desire to urinate. Heaviness; on walking.

Groins.—Swelling of glands. Sticking in r.; pinching drawing, in l. Cutting on urinating and at dinner, during menses, with burning. Griping in r., worse by paroxysms. Ulcerated feeling in r. when sitting, and on coughing it seemed as if a part of the intestines became incarcerated. Pain on rising from a seat and on rapid walking. Sprained pain, and in upper part of thigh; S. pain in l. Cramplike drawing in bend of r. thigh towards evening. Tension in r.; T. in evening.

Clinical.—General weakness and sinking of the abdominal muscles and viscera, extending down into pelvis; women have to sit down, apparently to prevent prolapsus (Sep.).

Rectum.—*Protrusion*, with burning in anus and discharge of much bloody matter, and inability to sleep at night on account of the pain (Sulph.). Sticking; < afternoon; with soreness, so that he could not sit; through R., with tickling in anus; *itching, in evening in bed.* Griping, with urging, but emission of only flatus and mucus. Pain. Scraping during hard stool. **Contracted sensation during stool, stool difficult, hard, causing tearing in anus, so that it bleeds and pains as if sore,** *then thin stools, constipation every other day. Sensation of a foreign substance or rough hard fæces, with constant looseness of bowels.* Sensation as after taking cold, at night on waking, with involuntary, scanty, slimy stool. Tickling. Itching, > scratching. Burning; at night; when walking. Dragging after stool. Desire for stool after eating. Urging, waking suddenly at night, then thin, pasty stool, then painful flatulent distention above pubis and exhaustion; U., with unsatisfactory stool and flatulence; with feeling as if rectum would be forced out, stool hard, crumbly, then sticking in anus, < walking; all day, as before diarrhœa; colicky; as in violent purging; frequent, with scanty discharge. Ineffectual urging; after stool; *frequent.*

Anus.—Hæmorrhoids, with moisture and stinging; H. swollen, painful to touch; painful, protruding in evening. Redness about. Tetter. Twitching. Sticking; in sphincter; when not at stool, extending up rectum; from ascarides, with biting and itching;

burning, at 10 A.M., < walking, with sore feeling. Burning pain. Spasmodic constriction. Seems swollen and sensation of plug in it, constantly driving him to stool. Soreness; about A. and between nates; biting, after a thin stool. Biting after stool; B. and scratching. Scratching after stool. Itching; in morning when walking; after a bloody stool; sudden, extending to neck of bladder and prostate gland, in morning on waking. Feeling as if bubbles of air passed through it. Burning, and in l. testicle; B., < a vexation; during pasty stool; *after a hard stool;* after soft stool.

Clinical.—Hæmorrhoids, painful, stinging, oozing glutinous moisture. Herpetic eruption about anus.

Stool.—*Watery;* and copious; half liquid, copious, with biting in anus; partly, partly pasty, copious, after urging; partly, partly pasty, an hour later a small thin stool. *Diarrhœa;* in morning; and small, in morning and after dinner; after dinner; at 11 P.M., at 3 A.M. he woke with urging to stool that was yellowish-brown, pasty and offensive, then distention of abdomen with rumbling and ulcerative feeling and on turning around noise like the croaking of frogs, general weakness and uneasiness, tongue and palate stiff and dry, at 7 A.M. wakened again by urging and diarrhœa with flatulence, rumbling and ulcerative feeling in abdomen, repeated at 11 A.M.; slimy; frequent; frequent, with colic, after ineffectual urging; scanty, with tenesmus; *painless;* painless, in evening; profuse, two days, no stool third and fourth days, scanty, delayed fifth day; sometimes D., sometimes no stool; sometimes D., at times soft stool, at other times hard.

Soft; towards morning; after dinner; and scanty, after dinner; with tenesmus, then sticking in rectum; but difficult; and copious, and in an hour and a half a thin, profuse stool with biting in anus; and unsatisfactory, with much pressure, next day none; partly S. and scanty, *difficult from inactivity of rectum.* Pasty; morning and evening; relieving abdominal symptoms; and urgent; and dark brown, offensive after urging; and orange-yellow, after dinner; and yellowish-brown, offensive, mixed with small whitish-gray lumps (looking almost like masses of tubercle).

Constipation; every other day. **Hard;** *during menstruation;* after dinner; after dinner, with tenesmus; **and crumbly,** painless; *and indolent; and unsatisfactory* (Mag. m.); *and unsatisfactory, difficult, with pain as if rectum would burst, then bleeding of hæmorrhoidal vessels and pain in rectum, with frequent micturition;* and difficult; and difficult, every other day; every two or three days, with exertion and often with ineffectual urging; and difficult, scanty; and scanty, less frequent; and delayed; like sheep-dung, *with sticking in rectum;* at first, then soft, with tenesmus, *then burning in anus when walking;* at first, then soft, with feeling as if rectum were protruding, then stupefied sensation and nausea, then vertigo and almost loss of consciousness.

Clotted blood passed with the natural stool (Alumina). Contained blood. Dark brown, profuse, and in half an hour a tumultuous, copious, watery one. Slimy after dinner, with tenesmus and burning in anus; tenacious, slimy, four times in forenoon. Copious. Scanty though it seemed copious; scanty in morning, profuse and pasty at noon, a fluid one towards evening with distention of abdomen. *Unsatisfactory; and irregular; with pressure; with sticking in anus;* and delayed, difficult; and delayed, then bleeding of hæmorrhoids. Difficult; and irregular, with itching and burning in rectum. Only after ineffectual urging for some time. Involuntary discharge of some drops of slimy liquid from anus. Frequent; and small; the last time very tenacious. *Irregular, sometimes two or three a day, then constipation.*

Clinical.—Dry and hard stools, which fissure the anus and cause bleeding. Constipation, with feeling of constriction of the anus, stool is difficult to expel and causes fissure, bleeding and soreness (compare Sil.). Chronic diarrhœa, watery, profuse, with burning in anus during the passage, general emaciation, especially of the neck, and greasy appearance of the skin. Ascarides.

Urinary Organs.—Sticking in bladder on urinating; pinching S. transversely through base of B. when walking. When urinating pressure upon bladder and in hypogastrium. *Urging;* at night; after dinner, with frequent micturition; **with pale, watery urine;** with pressure in rectum; and inability to retain the copious urine; and on retaining urine crawling along ureters, with heaviness and pressure in l. frontal region; constant, urine scanty, acrid, depositing much uric acid; *frequent urging, urine copious, and waking him at night; at night, and much pale urine;* after dinner and till evening, urine clear, pale; and copious, colored urine; and scanty urine; suddenly, with copious, thin urine. Ineffectual urging; at night.

Urethra.—*Discharge of thin liquid after urinating, that causes itching and biting; yellow, purulent D., spotting linen like gonorrhœa, without pain on urinating, only with tension in inguinal glands, which are not swollen;* of a drop of thin, glutinous liquid that sticks to the linen; of prostatic fluid, with lascivious thoughts, without excitement of fantasy or of sexual organs and without erections; milky, after micturition. Constant moisture at orifice, with drawing in spermatic cord. Sticking along; S. in navicular fossa; when not urinating; after micturition, after coition; itching, when not urinating. **Cutting after micturition** (Canth.); *and burning,* with discharge that leaves stiff transparent spots on shirt; C. towards close of micturition, then thin moisture from urethra; (after an emission). Pinching, then whitish, turbid urine. *Sore to pressure.* Periodical sensitiveness, with constriction in it and in rectum, urging to stool and urine, when the urine was passed the urging to stool usually disappeared, but several soft, painless stools a day. Drawing after micturition. Biting on urinating. Itching in orifice; at times like a sticking, with agglutination. *Burning* in morning after an erection; at night on urinating, as after new beer; *when urinating;* in navicular fossa, also when urinating; in orifice in evening when walking, with itching.

Micturition.—**Involuntary** *when walking;* I. and scanty. In a weak stream and only with great pressure. Dribbling after micturition, and pressure in rectum so that he could not sit down. *Frequent; all day and even at night;* all day, urine turbid and yellowish-red, always followed by sore burning in vagina; at night, and ineffectual urging; after eating; < after dinner; with sticking forward along urethra; *and urine pale; and urine turbid and dark;* and urine watery; and urine pale, clear, of strong odor and sweetish taste; and copious, hot urine.

Urine.—*Clear, pale.* Dark. Dark green. Yellow, scanty, causing burning in urethra. Clay-colored, sediment red. *Turbid;* and of strong odor, acrid. Milky in morning, depositing a white sediment. Hot. Scanty; and acrid, corrosive, like brown beer, depositing a red adherent sediment (during menstruation). Copious; during stool; micturition frequent, urine clear, greenish, reaction feebly acid, frothy on shaking, albumen in the morning urine, none in afternoon, no tubular casts, a few epithelial cells, normal or granular, occasionally containing a fat globule and some crystals of lithate of ammonia. Increase of chloride of sodium. *Brick-dust sediment* (Lyc.).

Clinical.—Polyuria. Involuntary micturition on coughing or sneezing. Hæmaturia. Gleet, especially after injections of nitrate of silver, with cutting and burning after micturition, with glutinous moisture from urethra; the whole of the urethra is sore.

Sexual Organs.—Papules on mons veneris. Offensive odor. Weak feeling. *Prepuce retracted from glans,* causing dry sensation that is < by walking whenever the glans touched the clothes; P. retracted and smegma had the odor of Chenopodium vulvaria. Itching of corona glandis, with moisture; I., with crawling; prickling I. Glans, red tip; (red elevations); jerking, also when not urinating; sticking towards glans; rhythmical throbbing sticking in evening, with sticking in orifice of urethra; itching, and in region of frænum; itching on tip; itching on tip, then desire to urinate, urine light-colored. Erections in morning; at night, and dream that he had gonorrhœa; frequent at night, also glutinous discharge; painful at night, disturbing sleep; violent; violent in night and morning, afterwards omitted or infrequent; none, and no emissions.

Sticking in r. spermatic cord in evening, extending into testicles. R. spermatic cord sensitive on motion. Swelling of scrotum, with sensitiveness of it, and with tension, < motion, extending from small of back towards groin during the stools. Scrotum relaxed. *Itching* of scrotum and prepuce; of S. or between S. and thigh; in a red, inflamed spot *on and under S.* and on l. thigh. Pinching in testicles. Pain in r. testicle.

Sudden voluptuous irritation when sitting, > walking. Desire increased; with erections and unusual voluptuous sensation during coition, later corresponding depression; D. is rather physical; weak; slight and emission delayed during coition; lost. Aversion to coition. Coition fiery, with speedy emission; C. weak, emission speedy and rather cold; inefficient, and yet some emission towards morning; much affected by C., to which he had not been accustomed for a long time, then exhausting emission in deep sleep at night. Emissions; with the usual morning stool; *every night;* towards morning; in sleep without erection or voluptuous sensation; *soon after coition* and third night afterwards; with biting on glans; profuse in one impotent, with much desire, then all night almost painful erections; lacking, on abstinence from coition for five weeks.

Female.—Itching on mons veneris. Biting in pudenda when urinating. Leucorrhœa; in morning; in morning, preceded by constricting and pressing colic, pressing downward as before menses; at night; *profuse; greenish,* < *walking;* with smarting; causing itching of pudenda. Impotency after menstruation, with aversion to coition and with dry, painful vagina on coition. Aversion to coition and to men.

Menses.—Too early; and scanty, and on coughing, stooping or sneezing, pain as if head would burst; and rather profuse, painless (usually she had some pain); *M. that was expected shortly appeared instantly and profusely,* the secondary action delays it and makes it scanty; M. that had ceased in morning returned in evening after anger; returned after a suppression of six months, in a woman of fifty years; suppressed for eighty-five days, returned with heaviness in lower limbs; afterwards delayed. *Delayed;* and during this time heaviness of feet and prostration, at last M. came on with pain in pubic region and nausea. Lasted only three days, then dulness of head and rush of blood to it. Period shortened, then lengthened. Scanty; first and second day, next day profuse, with colic-like soreness. Profuse; and dark; and blackish; with less colic, but chilliness all the first day, with yawning, < afternoon.

Clinical.—Pruritus of vulva. In vagina, feeling of dryness and soreness, with great weakness, etc. Sterility, with early and profuse menses, prolapsus, great weakness of abdominal muscles. Delayed menstruation in girls. Dysmenorrhœa from getting feet wet. Profuse acrid, greenish leucorrhœa, with itching, smarting, constipation, etc. Chlorosis in girls, with delayed menstruation and dysmenorrhœa preceded and accompanied by headache, weakness and soreness in abdomen, sometimes with diarrhœa, colic, thirst, dry mouth, etc. Subinvolution. With the uterine troubles of this drug the patient is generally relieved by lying on her back, on a pillow.

Respiratory Organs.—Larynx, sticking extending into ear, with at times pinching; drawing pain in region; scraping, with rough voice; scraping as after rancid heartburn; soreness on coughing, and in trachea; peculiar pressure on posterior wall of larynx and fauces, extending along Eustachian tube and towards tonsils; dryness in morning on waking. Hoarse whistling in bronchi on expiration. Hoarseness; *in morning; in morning, with much mucus in throat* and cough. Voice rough, stopped coryza and sneezing. Voice husky and monotonous, resembling that of a woman addicted to ardent spirits.

Cough.—*Day and night, with loss of breath; in morning; in evening in bed;* at night, with bruised pain in all limbs; at night, with scraping in chest in morning; *from tickling in throat;* from tickling in pit of stomach, with dyspnœa; < night; < from 8 till 11 P.M.; with tickling in chest; *with vomiting of food;* with short breath and tightness of chest and as if a stick of dry wood were down her throat. Violent, almost to vomiting. Hacking, raw, hoarse. **Dry,** from 6 till 7 P.M., from tickling in larynx; D., hacking during the day; hacking, tickling at night; short, at 5 P.M., with tickling in larynx; racking, at 10 P.M.; tickling, scraping, at night; tickling, paroxysmal. Cough, with expectoration, day and night; *with E. of blood;* of offensive taste in morning, and pain in chest as if it would be torn open; purulent, in one attack; of frothy mucus on waking at 2 A.M., with tickling in larynx, the inclination to C. < lying on back, yawning alternating with the C.; *tickling C.,* < *morning, with hawking of mucus;* paroxysms of tickling C. towards evening, ending with E. of salt mucus; paroxysm of tickling in evening, with scraping in throat, ending with expectoration of tenacious mucus; *hacking C.,* with râles in chest and expectoration of mucus; choking C., with expectoration of bloody mucus that seems to come from a dry spot in larynx. *Irritation* *to C.* caused by empty swallowing; I. from talking, with oppression of chest.

Expectoration of blood and blowing of blood from nose.

Respiration.—*Dyspnœa;* during the rigors; on rapid walking, with short breath. Difficult; in afternoon; at night, so that she must rise from bed; *on ascending stairs,* also with palpitation; when walking; < between 5 and 7 P.M., also when she was quiet; with pain in chest; with trembling of hands and feet. Impeded, with palpitation, also after eating. Frequent deep, with pain in abdomen. Rapid on standing, < walking. *Short;* and chest oppressed; paroxysm of, at night, with palpitation. Want of breath in evening on lying down. Tightness, with sticking in sternum, then in hepatic region.

Clinical.—Bronchitis from tickling behind sternum, extending up to pit of throat; the cough causes bursting headache (Bry.), involuntary micturition, lachrymation and palpitation; it may be < night in bed. Cough, with stitches in chest and sides.

Chest.—Bones of r. prominent. Mucus causing tightness, dislodged on walking in open air. Gurgling in r. side; in l. side near stomach, with rumbling. Cracking in sternum on motion. Twitching below l. axilla; T. in l. pectoralis major; beneath r. arm, extending down side.

Sticking in sides; in middle; behind sternum; along sternum; in middle of sternum; beneath nipples; in r. half at 3 P.M.; in region of sternum on every breath; in r. side on walking, > pressure; in r. side, < walking, > bending up; in r. side, with oppression; in r. side, with hoarseness; in l., with tensive pain under arm; beneath sternum, extending along margin; from ensiform cartilage to back in forenoon, < afternoon; at times extending from deep in C. towards back, < deep breathing; through pectoralis major to shoulder-joint; from l. pectoralis major to clavicle in afternoon; backward beneath clavicle at 4 A.M.; outward in l. clavicle along side of chest; upward on r. margin of sternum; in attacks transversely through lungs; tearing from l. upper into shoulder-joint; in l. in evening, taking away the breath, > open air; cutting stitches inward, crossing each other, at 11 P.M., with tightness of breath; as from an electric spark in r. pectoralis major, an hour later in region of r. nipple, then tightness as from a band about lower third of C., with difficult breathing; drawing, beneath upper part of sternum in afternoon.

Cutting in l. on coughing. Pain in l.; above r. nipple; beneath sternum; in middle of sternum and in back below l. shoulder; in sternum at 3 P.M., in open air, < touch, > motion and towards evening, with bruised sensation, returned next forenoon, > evening; in l. half when walking; after standing or talking much; below l. arm on moving arm and on breathing; in middle of sternum, < deep breathing; paroxysmal, in sternum; intermittent, in spots in r. side; sprained, in r. pectoralis major on motion. Bruised pain externally; B. pain in sternum; in a spot in sternum; in a spot in l. side; in l. on bending forward and on breathing; in l. lower ribs, < touch of vest and by pressure. *Sore pain.* Sensitiveness of external in evening; S. of breasts.

Pressure upon C.; on forepart; on sternum in afternoon; towards morning; at night, < towards morning, so that she must sit up to breathe; periodic, < night, with arrest of breath towards morning and need to sit upright. Constriction; with burning in hands; spasmodic, impeding deep breathing. Tightness on lying down in bed and in afternoon. Oppression; in evening; on becoming erect after sitting bent over; on motion, with pressure in middle of sternum; > open air, with weakness. Tension in morning; T. on stretching, and soreness on inspiration. Tensive pain in clavicle extending to cervical muscles, even painful to touch; T. pain in muscles in forenoon, so that he must walk bent forward, with pain on other motions of trunk. Heaviness.

Apprehension. Anxiety, < deep expiration, with pressure in pit of stomach. Scratching in middle. Weak sensation on walking in the sun, obliging him to speak softly. Disagreeable warmth in morning on waking.

Heart.—Sticking; *after reading aloud;* an hour after a moderate dinner; in evening, when walking in street; in apex in afternoon, not affected by respiration. Pain < night; in morning; jerking, in præcordial region. Bruised sensation in morning in bed. *Constriction, with intermittent pulse and oppression in lower part of chest as if lungs had not room enough to expand.* Tension when lying. Pressure below H. as if some one were pressing from abdomen towards heart, till sleep, < lying on l. side, > turning to r., with palpitation, which was less rapid than violent. **Coldness** on mental exertion. **Intermittent beating** during midday rest. **Fluttering** (Lil. tig.). **Palpitation;** *on ascending steps;* when standing; on motion; after dinner, with rapid pulse; > pressure of hand, with pressure downward at heart; *with anxiety;* anxious, without anxious thoughts; waking him, > a glass of cold water.

Clinical.—Palpitation, the pulsations are violent, shaking the body. Particularly valuable in hypertrophy of the heart, attacks < lying down, especially on l. side, the patient is weak, has faintlike sensations, feels the need to lie down frequently, has cold hands and numb extremities.

Pulse.—*Rapid;* all day; after dinner, with anxiety and oppression of breath; when sitting upright, and full; *and intermittent* (Dig.); and full; and full, soft; and small, weak; < drinking, with rapid respiration. **Intermittent**; after dinner.

Neck.—*Swelling of l. glands;* of glands, with tension of nape. *Sticking externally down neck, even through the night; S. in nape at night;* in nape, extending into occiput; rhythmical, in r. muscles. Pain in glands on touch; in muscles on touch and on turning head; in nape, so that she could not turn it; in muscles on coughing; in glands and low down in chest on coughing; bruised or weary, in nape; intermittent paralytic, in nape, extending over shoulder to middle of forearm, till evening; drawing, in nape, so that she could not turn it. Intermittent drawing in nape towards occiput, repeated in evening. Painful rhythmical throbbing in r. muscles. Tension in nape in evening. Stiffness of r. side; S. of nape; of nape and throat; nape and occiput; nape, extending to occiput, with pulsation.

Back.—Tearing downward in spine. Pain in spine at night on lying down, < lying on back; *P. as if broken;* in l. side as from pressure upon an inflamed spot; bruised, in B. and between scapulæ when sitting, < lying, > walking or working with hands. Drawing pain at night, > frequent turning; D. pain extending upward. Jerking sensation in B. and nape extending towards head. Tension obliging him to stretch; T. in l. side. Lameness in B. and small of B. in morning on rising. Paralytic weakness in B. and small of B. in morning on rising, at times extending across abdomen.

Drawing pain in upper part. Burning smarting on uppermost vertebra. Pain near last dorsal vertebra. Sticking beneath l. scapula; in r. S. at night in bed, on deep breathing; beneath l. shoulder, < drawing back inward, > deep inspiration; drawing, below upper part of scapula in afternoon. Pain beneath r. scapula; bruised, in scapulæ and hips. Stiffness between scapulæ, with drawing pain. Pain above small of B.

Lumbar Region.—Sticking on deep breathing; S. deep in region of r. kidney, with pressure; in coccyx, with paralytic drawing; from region of kidneys to uterus in morning, > bending up, pressure upon abdomen or sitting down, < walking; from r. towards uterus in forenoon, intermittent in afternoon; to thighs as the pains about umbilicus cease; transversely through above hips; intermittent; periodical, near spine, corresponding to posterior surface of liver, extending to below r. scapula; rhythmical, deep in region of r. kidney, also rhythmical with pulse. Pain before sleep; P. after stooping; with feeling in legs as if they were stiff or bandaged; causing him to straighten up; near spine, corresponding to posterior part of l. hypochondrium, extending to scapula; *as if broken;* paralytic, < becoming erect. Bruised pain on stooping and rising again; B. pain after stool; on touch; < sitting; in coccyx. Painful throbbing; in evening after lying down. Tension in region of kidneys, even when sitting, with heat, and walking soon fatigues. *Pulsations. Paralyzed feeling in morning on rising. Paralytic weakness nearly all day, > lying, < eating.*

Clinical.—Backache, with general weariness, > lying down; the back feels broken. Backache between the paroxysms of intermittent fever.

Extremities.—Cracking in joints of shoulders and hips on moving them. Trembling after slightest exertion, with rapid pulse; of hands and feet at 11 P.M. on rising from bed, she could hold nothing on account of weakness; of hands and feet after unpleasant news. Jerking; < thighs; in upper arms and lower limbs; of one or another when he wished to write; hot, on backs of hands and in tips of toes in morning on rising, with weakness of feet and less of hands. Sticking in joints; shoulder and knee-joints, with tearing; tensive, on front and middle of r. thigh and beneath l. thumb-nail. Tearing and drawing pains in ankles and wrists, waking him at night. Bruised pain. Rheumatic pains in arms and legs, feet and ankles particularly painful and stiff. Drawing pain in joints. Drawing paralytic pains in almost all joints at times. Frequent drawing in thighs, l. arm and thumb. Tension here and there in joints as if tendons were too short or as if beaten, the tensive pain in groins and in hollows of knees at times almost prevented walking. Cramplike sensation as if asleep. Pulsation in arms and lower limbs. *Weakness;* of hands and feet; thighs, upper arms and shoulder-joints; morning in bed, > rising, with heaviness; of hands at 10 A.M., and < feet; in evening after a short walk, < arms, with nausea and sleepiness; *and heaviness;* paralytic, in hands and r. foot in morning, > rising. Insensibility of little and ring finger and of l. foot.

Upper Extremities.—Swelling of r. axillary glands. Sticking in l. axilla, with tearing.

Shoulder.—Painful cracking of joint on motion. Sticking in r. Tearing on posterior surface of joint and axilla; T. in r. in evening in bed, with drawing, compelling deep breathing; and paralytic pain; in r., with drawing, and then in upper arm; and drawing like rheumatism, then in upper arm; and broken sensation, with stiffness in nape and back. Burrowing about r. joint in morning on waking, so that arm seemed lame. Pain in joint so that she could not move arm; bruised, in joint so that he could not raise arm; sprained or fatigued, in joint. Tension in joint in morning in bed on uncovering, with drawing, like pain after taking cold.

Arm.—Jerked forward. Broken sensation in bones of r. Drawing pain in l. so that he must constantly stretch it. Bruised pain in l., < region of deltoid and in joint, pain in joint on slightest motion. *Weakness;* < shoulder-joint; *with heaviness and sinking down;* speedy, in r. arm and l. wrist when triturating. Asleep sensation in l. arm and hand. Deadness (falling asleep) in l., with insensibility and crawling, with crawling in finger-tips.

Upper Arm.—Spasmodic contraction. Sticking like electric shocks in middle of l. extending from back and in part from chest. Pain at night from lying upon them; P. in deltoids on raising anything; bruised, on motion, < shoulder-joint; rhythmical throbbing, in deltoid near its insertion into arm. Cramplike drawing above point of l. elbow during rest. Painful weakness. Sensitiveness to cold.

Elbow.—Painful cracking on motion. Jerking in l. so that everything fell from his hands; in l. so that hands seemed paralyzed, the pain > stretching arm. Sticking in tip; jerking, in muscles in region of l. elbow, returning in afternoon. Tension in bend of l. as if arm had been exerted too much.

Forearm.—Twitching perceptible to finger. Paralytic tearing on inner side; drawing T. in tendons above l. wrist. Pinching in l. Pain in ulna and radius, < letting hands hang down, > moving arms; bruised, in ulna and radius and in phalanges of fingers, < first r., < touch. Drawing in ulna; cramplike, along inner borders of radii, above wrists; cramplike, through r., towards articulation of radius. Weary pain. Paralytic falling asleep, and if she uses the hand the wrist cracks.

Wrist.—Sticking in r. on taking firm hold of anything. Pinching in l., with drawing pain; drawing P. in l., < touch, > warmth. Sprained pain in r., and in last phalanx of index, with weakness and fallen-asleep sensation in hands, < laying hand upon a hard substance or putting it into the pocket. Bruised pain. Cramplike tension in tendons of dorsal surface of l.

Hand.—Swelling of r. all day. Involuntary movement of r. *Trembling;* on writing. Cramp on taking hold of a cold stone. Sticking in r., < thumb and index, with movements as in chorea and weakness of it; itching S., and on backs of fingers; as if falling asleep. Sudden tearing in metacarpal bone of l. little finger. Weakness; of r.; < closing them. Paralytic heaviness like a falling asleep. Falling asleep when he lies on arm.

Fingers.—Trembling. Sticking; in tip of r. index; in little; on side of middle phalanx of l. ring; in joints of r. middle; (in joint of r. index in evening);

in tips of r. ring, index and thumb after waking, with crawling; in r. index and thumb, with crawling drawing; tip of r. index, with digging; first phalanx of r., with electric shocks through r. arm; tearing, in r. index; itching tearing, in middle joint of index. Tearing in extensor tendons of r. index, extending into forearm; sudden, in second phalanx of r. index, as if it would be torn out; sticking, in tip of r. index. Pinching in l. ring, with clawing and inflammation. Pain on sides of nails of middle and ring, with inflammation; sprained P. in first joints on writing; cramplike P. in first phalanx of l. index when sitting after eating, < laying hand on anything, then in r. thumb; drawing throbbing P. in tip of r. index in evening, as from beginning suppuration; paroxysmal scratching P. extending backward in tip of index and in thumb, paralyzing hand. Tension in r. index. Weakness of r. middle, index and thumb. Joints could hardly be bent. Falling asleep of l. middle, index and thumb in morning.

Thumb.—Sticking in l.; in tip of l.; through tip of r.; in volar surface of r.; on back, near root of nail, rhythmical with pulse; drawing, in metacarpal joint of r.; intermittent drawing, in metacarpal joint of r.; frequent drawing, in volar surface of tip of r. thumb and < index, during rest, and at times beneath nails. Drawing sticking pulsating pain in metacarpal joint of l. Tearing in first joint of l. as if it would be torn out. Pinching in second phalanx of l. Sprained pain in l.; in second phalanx of r.; in first joints. Cramplike pain in r. at 11 P.M.; in metacarpal joint of r. Clawing in tip of r., with crawling, as from a needle. Sensation of a hair upon inner margin of l. towards wrist.

Lower Extremities.—Reeling on walking. *Trembling from weakness on rising from a seat, > continued walking.* Spasmodic contraction of l., < muscles of calf. Lameness in morning; sudden L. after writing, > rapid walking. Drawing pain extending down; spasmodic, in l. and in foot. Strained pain in tendons of l. Uneasiness at 11 P.M., < laying hands on a hard substance; U. at night; when sitting; late in evening, as if joints were bandaged, frequent necessity to stretch. Dread of walking. Weakness of r.; *W. in morning, < knee, > towards noon;* < morning; paralytic, of r. in morning, > rising. Heaviness; in evening. Falling asleep of l. during midday rest. Tearing sticking above nates, extending to groin and hip. Drawing pain in nates.

Hip. — Unsteadiness, with wavering of thighs. Cramp. Cramplike pain in r. joint, < walking. Sticking in r.; *in r. joint,* more when walking than when sitting; from horizontal ramus of pubis through r. hip-joint in evening on walking, afterwards when sitting less severe in a spot on l. side. Electric shock extending downward and inward from r. joint at 7 P.M., when walking. Drawing tearing in region of ischiatic notch of l. Sprained pain in l.; in r., soon extending into small of back, < rising from a seat and by deep breathing, and preventing straightening himself and walking. Sensation as if the head of the bone slipped out of the joint on moving or turning body. Bruised pain in l.; in hip, knee and ankle, so that she could not lie on r. side at night. Tension as if everything were too tight, necessity to loosen the clothes; T. in joints almost as if sprained; painful T. in joint, with soreness on touch. Rheumatism in l., preventing walking. Heaviness, extending along posterior surfaces of thighs to bends of knees, with weariness. Paralyzed feeling.

Thigh.—Painful distention of hamstrings when sitting. Twitches. Sticking in l. at night; in l. when riding in a carriage; in l. near scrotum. Tearing in r. after riding in a wagon. *Drawing pain,* extending to knee, < walking; D. pain in bones to malleolus, < leg, and on ascending steps it seemed as if some one were pulling her back; intermittent, *in r., extending to knee.* Tension on walking, with pain; T. above knee on ascending steps, with feeling as if lower limbs were too short; drawing T. in middle of anterior surface of l., preventing walking.

Knee.—Cracking in evening on walking. *Sticking in l.;* in r.; in hollow of l.; in r. patella; in r., slowly appearing and disappearing on walking; outward in inner side of l. about 1 P.M. Pain in l., impeding walking; sprained; in l. on walking. *Drawing pain when sitting;* sticking, above and below knee when sitting. Compressive pain as from fatigue, and in ankles, then drawing in whole of lower limbs. Tearing drawing in hollows, < walking; paralytic D. in l. knee in evening. *Sensation as if tendons of hollow were too short; in forenoon;* in l. in forenoon, < rising from a seat; in r. in afternoon when walking; on rising from a seat and on walking, increasing from morning through the day; in l., and in three last r. toes. Sensation on ascending steps as if some one were striking hollows, with trembling of knees whenever she stepped up a step. Bubbling as of water beneath skin of l. Weakness in evening. Stiffness of one or other after rising from a seat.

Leg.—*Swelling from middle downward in evening and next morning, with feeling as if feet were filled with lead.* Tremulous unsteadiness of calves when walking, standing and sitting. Cramp at night; C. in l. calf; in calf on turning foot when sitting; periodical, in calves. Sticking now in r., now in l. tendo-achillis; cramplike drawing S. in inner surface of l. leg. Tearing in calves; drawing, below head of l. fibula. Cramplike pain in l. tibia as if tightly bound, in evening; in r. tibia, extending towards malleolus, in afternoon when walking, it seemed as if the drawers were too tight. Pain in r. tibia, with feeling on walking as if it were loose at one point, so that he began to walk with anxiety. Cramplike constriction in calves when walking. Bruised pain in a spot in tibia, > touch. Sensation in l. calf and nates as if he had fallen upon them. Drawing in l. tibia; sticking, in r. tendo-achillis; paralytic, in r. leg, at last extending into thigh, with scarcely any power on standing. *Tension in calves;* as if muscles were too short, *when walking;* as far as knees when walking. Throbbing in l. calf. One leg difficult to put over the other. *Heaviness,* and on ascending steps bruised feeling.

Ankle.—Sticking in r.; r. inner malleolus, then in r. tendo-achillis. Tearing in r. malleolus, increasing from morning till evening, preventing sleep at night, with pain in back; drawing T. in tendons above l. inner malleolus. Sprained pain; in r. Sore pain above and about l. malleolus. Ulcerative pain in malleolus extending into calf on stepping and on touch, but when sitting there is only tensive pain. Throbbing, cramplike pain above l. external malleolus, towards tendo-achillis, during midday nap. *Paralysis, or like an internal falling asleep, when sitting and walking.*

Foot.—Cramp in soles in evening. Cramplike contraction in l., < muscles of calves. Sticking in corns; in corns in morning on waking; in corns all the afternoon; in l. heel in afternoon; in corn all night; in l. foot at 7 P.M. on lifting it when walking, with shuddering pain extending from knee along axis of thigh; *cramplike in l. as if sprained*, on stepping upon the whole sole; as with a glowing needle in forepart of l. in evening; itching, in heel; gnawing itching, in r. heel at 4 A.M.; itching, on back of l., rhythmical with pulse (after a thin stool). Tearing in l. Gnawing in heel in evening; in bone of l. heel. Boring in a corn. Pain on walking; P. in r. extending to middle of tibia; cramplike, in l. Tension; in l. in afternoon, < inner side of thigh. Throbbing. *Uneasiness* from 10 till 11 P.M.; *U. > walking;* > 10 P.M. by walking, with sticking; in F. and legs, > 11 P.M. by walking. Weakness; of r. on waking, especially beginning in knee; on standing, so that she falls; paralytic, of r. in evening. *Heaviness; in evening on walking;* when standing; < evening after beer, with uneasiness (she always has these sensations before menstruation, which was due in a week); next day they felt very light. Falling asleep.

Toes.—Redness of first joint, with coldness and on touch pain like a boil, and when standing and walking tearing and sticking. Cracking in metatarsal joints. Sticking in root of nail of r. great; in flexor surface of r. second at 7.30 P.M.; in l. great in evening; sudden, in r. great when sitting; smarting; burning, on back; itching, in r. great at 4 A.M. Drawing pain in great. Intermittent. Drawing beneath l. great, with tension.

Clinical.—Paralytic condition of the lower extremities after fever, diphtheria or excesses.

Skin.—White spot on l. sole, towards middle toe, painful when stepped upon. Redness of an old scar, with pain; in spots in epigastric region, with sticking on touch, obliging rubbing, becoming itching pustules; dark red mottled spot by nail of l. third finger; red itching spot on chin, that ulcerated after rubbing; R. itching elevations on inner side of r. forearm; red swelling and sore pain on pressure, on l. third and fourth fingers where hang-nails had been cut. Brown spots on back of hand as if bruised. Pale, dry, but elastic.

Hands dry and cracked; < about fingers and nails. Hang-nails. Warts on palms, with pain on pressure. Scurfy. Rash on outer side of calves and over thighs; on forehead, only noticed on touch; *over whole body, with sticking.* Itching gritty eruption behind ear; on chin; on knee. **Itching eruption on margin of hair at nape,** *temples and in brows;* over whole body, as large as millet-seeds on neck and arms, as large as peas on abdomen, nates and thighs, becoming red and hard on scratching, the itching prevented sleep, but was transiently > scratching; E. in groups on legs, with corrosive itching, < touch. Urticaria after violent motion. *Whitish hives on arms and hands, becoming red after rubbing; red H., with itching over whole body and on neck.*

Red tetter in hollows of knees; T. on thigh and leg, with red areola, cutting itching, and on scratching painfully sore; round, itching T. on arms; red, itching, on lower end of inner side of l. forearm, next morning the spot had a raw look; itching, moist, on scrotum and opposite on thigh; T. which she usually had on hands became worse, with biting and burning. Herpetic eruptions on calves. *Herpes circinatus in various parts;* H. C. over whole body. (Ringworm on thighs, abdomen and arms, disappearing here and appearing in other places, < between breasts, and itching < warmth, then ringworm extends over whole body.)

Pimples on face; on forehead and nose; behind l. ear; on abdomen and lower limbs; here and there, with ulcers; white, about nose; hard, in middle of forehead and on nape, with burning pain on touch; painful, below septum of nose; burning, beneath septum of nose, with sensation as if acrid water were running from nose. Soreness of thigh near scrotum; between nates from walking. A sore became more painful and inflamed, suppurated profusely, with swelling and with irritable disposition, so that the sore could not be touched without weeping. A small puncture begins to bleed again several days in succession.

Pustules on hand; on back; itching, on back. Boils; on l. cheek; on neck; knee; above eye, discharging matter; painful, discharging matter and blood, on lobule of l. ear. Ulceration of breasts and pain on touch. Vesicles behind l. ear; on forehead and nose; on hands, then desquamation; **painful, below septum of nose, burning** next day, *and it seemed as if she had a moist nose, afterwards they became confluent and covered with a scab, which left a red spot; filled with bloody serum, on nape near hair;* discharging bloody serum, on l. sole; smarting, on root of nose, becoming covered with scabs; itching, on hands and l. wrist; itching, on little finger; red, itching, here and there on arm; a denuded spot on r. hand became inflamed and formed a V., under which pus collected.

Sticking in various parts; < chest, pit of stomach, wrists and thighs; < lips, chest and under shoulder; S. beneath skin in hepatic region in morning; sudden, here and there, < toes, r. index, lips, glans, prepuce and axilla, all day, with itching; here and there, as if nettle-rash would break out; as from electric sparks here and there, < middle of anterior surface of r. thigh, then coldness; itching, in evening in bed; itching, here and there, with internal creeping heat.

Prickling of fingers, < tips; of hands on putting them into pockets, with asleep sensation in them. Itching gnawing in tip of r. thumb. Smarting in old warts. Sensitiveness. Crawling in tips of fingers; in tip of r. thumb; tip of r. index. Sticking crawling in tips of fingers; tip of r. thumb; third phalanx of r. index in afternoon; tip of r. index alternating with itching in anus; in r. sole.

Itching over whole body; I. here and there, < calves; on lobules of ears; on l. wing of nose; in beard; hypogastrium; chest; back and thighs; lower limbs; on small of back extending to abdominal and hepatic regions and to thighs; internally in hips; r. calf, later on l. inner malleolus, then on r. calf; on back of foot; feet and < inner sides of calves; on toes; all day, < morning, on forehead where she parted the hair and in brows; in morning, about neck and under chin, < sides of neck, not > scratching, with red swelling and burning, during the day the I. extended down breast and arms, then to lower limbs, finally I. and burning in legs and feet, after black tea the I. and burning began again in neck and passed down to soles and he felt as if he had walked on hot coals, he walked the floor barefoot in agony, feet felt swollen but were not, this suffering lasted three-quarters of an hour, in night slight I. of body, repetition of these symptoms for three days, always < after tea; in afternoon, in r. palm; evening, on pubis; in evening in bed, over whole body, also on small of back, also on fingers; at night, on l. leg; on going to bed, on calves; over whole body, < night and preventing sleep; on chest, < open air; on first phalanx of l. third finger, with crawling; < l. side of chest, on head, arms, neck and thigh, and in the latter sensation as if flesh would be loosened from the bone; behind r. ear, then burning; then vesicles after scratching, also on inner margin of wrist; on various parts, < l. knee, after scratching nettle-rash.

Biting itching on lower limbs in evening; (in l. palm); near genitals, with smarting after rubbing; on various parts, and on several parts herpes circinatus, usually disappearing with desquamation in from eight to twelve days, only to give place to another tetter. Itching on calves as if asleep. Sticking itching on margin of lower jaw; in tip of r. index; on back of r. index and on lower margin of r. orbit in evening; between scrotum and l. thigh. Sudden voluptuous irritation when sitting, > walking.

Clinical.—Greasy skin. Eczema of eyebrows; behind ears. Purpura hæmorrhagica. It has cured warts in palms of hands. Herpes circinatus (Sep.). Eczema on hands, < water (Sul.). Urticaria in intermittent fever sometimes indicates this drug. Hang-nails, skin around the nails dry and cracked. Eruption in the bend of the knee, with itching and smarting, skin very sore from the oozing of an acrid fluid, which forms crusts and cracks.

Sleep.—*Yawning;* in morning, > towards noon, with empty eructations; at 6 P.M., when riding in a carriage, then hiccough; with stretching; with lively mood and inclination to joke; spasmodic, after sound sleep; spasmodic, > drinking wine.

Sleepiness; during the day; in afternoon; in evening; in evening, but sleep restless, with many dreams; before eating; after eating; after dinner; after dinner, with inclination to lie down and inability to think; *but inability to sleep.* Sleep in afternoon always on sitting down; after 5 P.M., when sitting; when reading; when unoccupied, but waking every moment. Long sleep; and sound. Sound sleep after dinner; in afternoon, with vivid dreams. Light, after dinner. Deep sleep after midnight, and full of dreams.

Sleeplessness; after midnight; after 2 A.M.; from 3.30 till 4.30 A.M., then anxious dreams; after 5 A.M., she seemed anxious, if she slept she dreamed and woke immediately, with internal heat in head and pain in abdomen as before diarrhœa, from internal restlessness. Late falling asleep; and early waking; and twitching in limbs, and electric shocks through body, once it seemed as if heart and knees were knocked together. Frequent waking; caused by vivid dreams; in anxiety; with uneasiness; every half hour. Early waking. Waking at 2 A.M. in sweat and with anxiety as if shut up in a dark cellar, > seeing a light through the window; at 3 A.M., then sleep, and at 7.30 difficult waking; at 4 A.M., as if he had slept enough, afterwards sleep till 7; at 5 A.M., with thirst; from fright, **thought there were thieves in the house** and dared not go to bed again, with oppression of chest and palpitation.

Talking in sleep; screaming out; sobbing. Twitching in sleep; of lower limbs, waking him from midday nap; in limbs, as from an electric shock, on falling asleep at noon. Shocks through r. half of body on attempting to fall asleep; jerking S. coming from heart in midday nap. Starting up; in evening on falling asleep, when one came into the room, so that it caused palpitation. In the beginning of sleep he arose from bed, woke in the middle of the room, lay down in bed again and fell asleep.

Anxious sleep. Unrefreshing sleep. Restless sleep; after going to bed early she woke at 11 P.M., with vertigo, nausea, weakness, trembling of limbs and giving way of all nerves, at midnight she had to get out of bed, on rising vertigo even to falling and she went back to bed, soon vertigo even to loss of consciousness and three times vomiting of food tasting of red wine, then general chilliness, about 2 A.M. many dreams that she quarrelled and disputed.

Dreams.—About which she was *busy long after waking.* Sad. Heavy. Peevish. Vexatious. Exciting. Troubled, < after midnight, especially of illness, with interrupted sleep. That he had been poisoned. Of conflagrations. That he reproached himself for past mistakes. Confused, of crimes, for which he was held to answer, after eating a little more supper than usual. Lascivious; or of ghosts. That she herself pulled out a fine tooth. On closing eyes for midday nap she saw many persons, large cities and large bodies of water pass before her. Unremembered, in morning sleep. *Vivid;* all night, and confused; on falling asleep, with inclination to compose verses, which on waking seemed ludicrous; < after midnight, disturbing sleep; and connected; and unpleasant; and remembered; and pleasant, remembered; of people near to him; of long journeys; of a dangerous sail in a small boat; of burning thirst that was not quenched by beer, and on waking the tongue was dry. *Anxious; in afternoon; with weeping;* and walking about the room in a somnambulistic state; so that he cried out, with frequent waking; and sleep only after midnight; of battles, on waking she was in an anxious heat and sweat; that she would be beaten, so that she sweat and remained anxious all day. Terrible, which seemed real after waking. Horrible, disgusting. Frightful; of death, fire, etc.; of scenes of murder; of murder and of being taken a prisoner, waking in sweat, and next morning exhaustion. Nightmare, as if abdomen were constricted, with anxiety, she tried to cry out, but could not open the eyes nor move a limb.

Fever.—*Chilliness;* during the day; in morning sleep, then sweat shortly before waking; every day about 3 A.M., with languor, headache and dyspnœa, then heat and thirst, then sweat; **from 8 A.M., till noon, then heat till evening, with sweat or thirst,** *with unconsciousness and headache;* **in forenoon**; in afternoon; afternoon, with thirst. Evening; after drinking; after lying down; on rising from bed; till sleep; *with thirst;* then at night sweat and itching; **fever, with headache** on waking from a nap, first C., then heat in paroxysms, but heat predominated; between 4 and 6 P.M.; between 4 and 7 P.M., with external warmth on face; from 4.30 till 7 P.M., < warm room, > open air; 5 till 7 P.M., with external heat and yawning, alternating with hot twitches; between 6 and 7 P.M., with sleepiness, the latter > rising and walking about the room; at 7 P.M., gradually spreading over whole body, then heat for an hour, with sticking in skin and frequent sneezing, then sour sweat till 2 A.M., when the paroxysm ended suddenly. At night, with languor, headache and dyspnœa, then heat and sweat. Only in a warm room, > at 5 P.M. on going into open air, with frequent yawning; in bed after being much heated, with roaring in head and weakness; after an emission, with weakness of joints. Weakness before dinner so that he must lie down, then chill in bed, then heat, then sweat. C., but sweat on motion; with weakness, with sharp pain in lower incisors; *over whole body, with heat in forehead, pressure in region of root of nose and thirst;* C. at one time, at another heat and sweat.

Internal chilliness in afternoon, with yawning and pallor; I. in afternoon on going out, with rapid pulse, ill humor and disinclination to talk. Creeping C. frequently about 5.30 P.M., then heat and sweat till 7.30; over whole body (except head) at 11 P.M. on lying down, with heat in head and general warmth of skin to touch, then burning of hands, less of feet, tossing about, inability to sleep for an hour, then uneasy sleep, with dreams of strife; during stool, with tenesmus. Cold and hot creepings over body.

Shaking chill; in evening, with aggravation of pains, then heat, < head, and redness of face; with sleepiness, he slept and became warm while sitting and perspired. *Shivering;* in afternoon and burning of hands in evening; in afternoon when sitting, > 5 P.M. on going out, returning in evening when sitting; in evening, also with rapid pulse; in evening in bed, so that hands and feet trembled and teeth chattered; *with yawning;* with yawning and nausea; with sensation of gooseflesh; internal, from 4 till 7 P.M.; sudden, through whole l. side of body; over back towards evening, then thirst; in back, < sitting.

Chilliness in various parts frequently during the day. Cold skin; in evening in bed. *Cold feet; and hands;* hands, in forenoon; arms; vertex, with sensitiveness of scalp and closure of lids; lower limbs, with rush of blood upward to stomach, chest and head. Burning C. on r. patella. Chilliness in back; in evening, with cutting; at night, with restlessness. Creeping coldness over back; at times with cold sweat on forehead, anxiety and shuddering; over small of B. at night.

Heat in morning after thirst and drinking of warm milk, with trembling; H. after midday nap, then shivering till evening; at 11 P.M., and uneasiness of feet, so that he could scarcely stay in the carriage. At night, with uneasiness and much drinking; at N., with anxiety, necessity to uncover herself, profuse flow of menses and vivid dreams; after appearance of menses, with thirst and sleeplessness; preventing sleep, without thirst, with labor-like pain in hypogastrium; of body, then sweat, < head. Heat of blood after a little wine; H., with sweat under arms and on soles; of body alternating with creeping coldness and shivering over back, without thirst; as if dashed with hot water, in afternoon after coffee, then r. ear burning and scarlet. In flushes; and easy sweat. Orgasm of blood at night waking him.

Heat in head; vertex; in afternoon, and in face; in afternoon, on entering house, with redness of face and rush of blood to head; at 6 P.M., with anxiety, then sweat, next day sweat at the same hour; in evening, then sweat; at night in bed; with inclination to cool it with cold water; with roaring in ears; in forehead, with headache; internal, < forehead; in flushes in evening, with anxiety and nausea, even to vanishing of senses, objects seem entirely changed. *Heat in face;* in evening during menses; and on abdomen, arms and lower limbs, *then red spots of the size of the head of a pin over whole body,* with itching and after rubbing redness of whole body. Heat in l. (weak) ear evenings; of ear or of lobule. Burning in feet on walking; in a corn at night; internal and external heat in r. upper arm; in l. scapula as if dashed with hot water; biting, in axilla, with swelling after scratching; itching, as from nettles on l. hand.

Sweat; during the day; mornings; during midday nap; *at night;* before midnight; about midnight, < chest; on slightest exertion; sour, in morning; so saline as to excoriate parts where the skin was thinnest; on head in morning on rising; on head at night on waking; *on hands;* soles; S. on feet that had disappeared was brought back. Dryness of body.

Clinical.—Intermittent fever, chill beginning at 10 A.M., with thirst, pains, fever with thirst, drinking does not relieve; profuse sweat relieving all symptoms; throbbing frontal headache generally accompanies the chill and fever. In malaria there is sometimes profuse watery stool, with great oppression of breath, coldness about the heart, headache, great prostration, irregular pulse. Intermittent fever, the onset of the paroxysms characterized by intense itching over the whole body, during the chill the patient shakes violently. Intermittent fever, sometimes the chill begins in hands and feet, without much shaking, preceded by headache, which grows worse during the chill. Malarial fever characterized by stitches in hepatic region during the apyrexia.

Natrum Phosphoricum.

Triturations of pure Sodium phosphate are used.

Generalities.—Intermittent pains here and there. Sore feeling, < joints. Pulse felt all over body. Nervous in morning on rising; from 11 till 12 o'clock, before breakfast, with sick feeling; after breakfast, went to bed again; when studying, so that he must get up and walk about; < thunderstorm, with goneness at stomach, headache and crick in neck. Weakness; in morning and weak feeling in legs, > forcibly stretching; in afternoon, and falling asleep while sitting; after nocturnal emission; in hot weather; after dinner, with ill humor and desire to lie down.

Clinical.—This drug has been used empirically according to Schüssler for ailments resulting from excessive acidity, diseases of infants, diabetes, etc.

Mind.—Imagines on waking at night that pieces of furniture are persons. Startled by the least noise, < night, then palpitation. Despondency; in evening, with inability to study; in attacks in evening; < emissions; and imagination that he was going to have typhoid fever. Anxiety about home, fear of bad news; A. about his health. Apprehension of some approaching evil. Fear on waking that his child, who had a trifling ailment, was dead. Ill humor; < forenoons. Inclination to study in evening. Study is burdensome, it is difficult to remember what is read. Dulness, forgot what I had just committed to memory. No ambition to do anything.

Head.—Aching at 9 A.M., preceded by gagging and faintness, the A. at first > pressure, suddenly > 8 P.M.; A. at 10 A.M.; every afternoon, after menses; after dinner; > before breakfast; > after breakfast; throbbing; heavy, with dim vision; tensive, with dulness and heaviness and dim vision. Dulness in morning, and at root of nose. Fulness in afternoon, with heaviness and flashes of heat, then sweat; F. towards evening; F. when studying, with heaviness and vertigo; with throbbing pain; with pulsating pain on stepping. Empty feeling. Vertigo; in morning on rising.

Forehead.—Acute pain over l. eye; every forenoon. Aching over l. eye during menses; over r. eye, < before and after, > during menses, with sighing as if room were too close; alternately over each eye every afternoon, after menses; intermittent, in morning when studying, with fulness. Throbbing, < suddenly raising head and when ascending. Fulness, with cutting in r. temples; F. over eyes in morning.

Temples.—Cutting in r.; in l. at 3 P.M. when walking. Pinching in l. descending to l. ear and nostril. Sharp pain in r. Pain nearly all the morning; P. in r.; intermittent, in r.; in r. extending to eye and ear, at noon, > 5 P.M., after eating grapes, and in evening P. over l. temple when riding in a street-car.

Tearing in l. side of H., < temple and front of ear. Cutting in r. side, with intermittent aching over eyes. Rheumatic drawing up l. side of occiput into forehead.

Eyes.—Bloodshot. Sticking, inducing winking and lachrymation. Cutting in r. Feeling as if sand were in them, < l. Sore feeling in evening when reading. Weak feeling at 8 P.M., < gaslight. Feeling as if bathed in hot water. Burning, causing rubbing of eyes and lachrymation. Burning lachrymation. Quivering of r. lid when reading, before sleep and on waking. Lids feel heavy and itch along margins. Soreness of r. inner canthus, desire to rub it, and redness; S. of r. inner C., with shooting. Aching of r. ball. Dryness of l. ball, with bruised pain. Infra-orbital neuralgia on r. side. Pain over eyes; < closing eyes, on retiring; in l. orbit, with pain in abdomen extending into chest, and flatulence; in orbit above ball on using eyes, and lids feel sore, itch and burn; in centre of l. brow. Flickering before l. eye on rising at 5 A.M. Vision misty, halo around gaslight, with sore, weak feeling in eyes.

Clinical.—Ophthalmia, with yellow, creamy discharge. Squinting from worms. Granular lids. Scrofulous ophthalmia.

Ears.—Aching in r. meatus auditorius. Fulness; in evening. When lying, sensation as of water dropping from a height into a long narrow vessel. Tickling from middle into Eustachian tube. Itching in r. meatus auditorius. Imagines that he hears footsteps in the next room.

Nose.—Pricking in nostrils. L. nostril sore, painful, picks it constantly, scabs form. Feels full of mucus, discharge slight. Fulness at root in evening and skin feels tight over it; F. at root in evening, and in ears. Stoppage of l. nostril, < open air. Offensive odor in morning. Bleeding in morning.

Clinical.—Offensive discharge from nose. Naso-pharyngeal catarrh, with thick, yellow mucus.

Face.—Shooting in r. cheek; along cheeks into ears; through l. lower jaw. Soreness in r. angle of lower jaw, with occasional dartings through jaw. Pain about chin.

Mouth.—Teeth in morning and mouth all day covered with brownish mucus. Gumboils, one opposite first l. premolar, another opposite last r. molar. Pain in gum over last l. upper molar. Tongue coated dirty white, with dark brown centre. Blisters on tip of T. Stinging in tip of T. in evening. Sensation of hairs on tip of T., then prickling numbness of whole mouth, next day a pimple. Taste bad in morning on waking. Taste coppery at 5 A.M.

Clinical.—Yellowish, creamy look on soft palate. Thin, moist coat on tongue. Moist, creamy, golden-yellow coat at root of tongue and on palate.

Throat.—Mucus; tough, clear, white, from posterior nares; dropping of thick, clear M. from posterior nares, < night, waking him, he must sit up to clear his throat. Much hawking from posterior nares; H. in afternoon, with tickling and cough. Pricking in r. side, < swallowing liquids, > swallowing solids. Sensation of a lump. Feeling as if something closed it, preventing speech. Soreness of r. side. Throbbing in region of l. tonsil.

Stomach.—Canine hunger. Appetite for strong-tasting things, even alcohol; for beer, it relieves the goneness; for eggs; fried eggs. Little appetite; most for supper; little for dinner. Appetite lost, with a sick, gone feeling. Aversion to bread and butter. Eructations after eating; of food after dinner. Pressure in pit after menses, > eating. Full feeling; after eating a little; < eating. Heaviness after tea, causing restlessness; H. in epigastrium and lower third of sternum during menses, < ascending stairs; in epigastrium, > eating. Goneness; all day, < eating; in morning on rising; from 11 till 12 o'clock, before breakfast; and in abdomen and even in chest; and in abdomen, with weight above ensiform.

Clinical.—Sour eructations and vomiting. Acid dyspepsia, with flatulence.

Abdomen.—Flatulence during the day; F. after eating, with rumbling; F. < dinner. Bloated feeling, < evening, with flatulence, necessity to loosen clothes and urging to stool. Colic in evening when lying, with discharge of flatus; C. after breakfast when walking in the room; after supper when walking; after stool; as from wind pressing on bladder, causing frequent micturition, with urging to stool. Anxiety. Empty feeling in A. and chest after eating; in A. and chest after dinner.

Sensation in descending colon as if a marble dropped, when at stool. Cutting in hypochondria and l. iliac region. Pain through r. groin the day after emissions; in hypogastrium in morning; in hypogastrium, with desire for stool, much flatus before stool, after supper, when walking. Soreness in hypogastrium after micturition, > lying on back, < lying on belly in evening.

Rectum.—Urging; after coitus, U. to stool and urine, S. small and loose. Must bring my will to bear to prevent the escape of fæces. Sudden urging, stool copious, easy, first part fluid, second fæcal; sudden U. at 6.30 P.M. and after supper, during stool, difficulty in retaining fæces, stool mushy, yellow-brown, with flatus before and during, and colic during stool; sudden urging after a light supper, with colic, had to contract sphincter to prevent escape of fæces, stool watery, gushing, painless. Ineffectual urging.

Anus.—Sticking on walking. Burning, contracting pain in A. and lower part of rectum after waking from a troubled dream. Sore feeling. Rawness; on waking, < scratching; sore R., with desire to retract it, which relieves. Itching; and soreness.

Stool.—Watery, yellowish-brown, containing fæcal lumps; W., yellowish-brown, small, and, after four hours and a half, another thin, profuse, yellowish-brown, before each stool weak feeling in rectum and sphincter. Diarrhœa before morning, with colic; D. after rising, with rumbling in abdomen, and after breakfast a small, dry, difficult, dark brown stool, next day dark brown S. requiring straining; frequent D., with flatus and with cramp in stomach and abdomen, afraid to pass flatus lest fæces escape also. Soft and large; and easy, afterwards feeling as if much remained behind; soft and small, difficult, before breakfast, sudden urging while eating, afterwards watery, yellowish-brown, painless stool.

Constipation; next day diarrhœa. Small stools twice a day. Scanty, at 7.30 A.M., with flatus, after breakfast a large soft stool, with much flatus. Difficult, in two small lumps at 9 A.M., normal S. in evening.

Clinical.—Greenish diarrhœa. Diarrhœa from acidity.

Urinary Organs.—Distention of bladder at night. Bladder seems incapable of properly expelling its contents, flow soon stops and requires straining, each effort resulting in a small spurt. Obliged to urinate, but pressure not thereby relieved. Desire to urinate, but had to wait for urine to flow and had to strain at the end of micturition. Constant urging. Burning in urethra during micturition; B. at meatus after coitus, with itching. Frequent micturition; from wind pressing on bladder; but little passed at a time. Urine dark red. U. dark and scanty. Copious U. in morning after rising; C. and pale.

Sexual Organs.—Erections almost every night (in a married man), preceded by pain in testicles, < l. Emissions every other night; at night without dreams; at night, with dreams; at night, with vivid dreams; some hours after coitus, no dream or erection; watery, smelling like stale urine, every night, no lascivious dreams. Itching of prepuce; of scrotum. Pain in l. spermatic cord. Drawing in r. spermatic cord; D. in testicle and cord. Pain in l. testicle; about l. testicle. Excitement. Desire, but no erections, later no desire. Desire diminished.

Female.—Excitement, with sleeplessness till 1 A.M., waking at 5 unrested. Menses too early; and feet cold by day, burning at night in bed, flow pale, with pressure over r. eye and desire to take a long breath as if the room were too close, three days later headache over l. eye, all < from 3 till 4 P.M., on fifth day flow as dark as usual, after menses much worse, trembling about heart, < ascending stairs, pressure in pit of stomach, > eating, headache every afternoon, alternately over each eye, sleep restless, next period too early, with same symptoms as before, but flow stopped two days and returned with headache, chilliness, restless sleep, paralytic aching in r. wrist, feeling in knees as if cords were shortened.

Respiratory Organs.—Cough after drinking water; C. from tickling in throat; constant, with hawking pain in mammary region; dry, tickling, from irritation in throat.

Chest.—Pain in lower third of sternum as if torn in two. Aching; through l. C. and in l. shoulder; through C. after dinner, < l.; diagonally from r. clavicle to stomach, then hoarseness. Bruised feeling in a spot in r.; about cartilages of r. fourth to sixth ribs, < deep breathing, deep pressure, and late in evening inability to breathe deeply, or move arms or bend backward. Intercostal muscles feel sore and as if drawn when sitting erect or moving chest, not in ordinary breathing. Contracted feeling in walls of r. Sudden fulness in upper part. Burning deep in, < r., in evening in bed.

Heart and Pulse.—Uneasiness and pain in H., < about its base, when the pains in limbs and great toe are better. Feeling as if a lump or bubble started from the heart and were forced through the arteries. Heart's beat heard as if it came from under the pillow, when lying at night. Palpitation at every strange noise. Pulse quick, jerking, 11 till 12 o'clock, before breakfast. Pulse felt in different parts of body as if shot were rolling through the artery.

Neck.—Crick in both sides. Shooting extending over r. shoulder.

Back.—Sticking to r. of spine in morning on breathing deeply. Pressure from spine to stomach before breakfast. Weakness; towards evening. Pain in l. scapula in evening. Feeling as if a round stick pressed upward and forward from about last dorsal vertebra into stomach, waking at 2 A.M. Sticking in r. renal region; in l. Cutting in r. sacro-iliac articulation. Pain on l. side of articulation of lumbar vertebræ and sacrum, pressing the spot caused pain down thigh to knee, later the same spot grew more painful and the leg seemed to give way when walking, as if knee were weak. Weakness of small of B. at 11 P.M. in bed, < lying on back, then deep-seated twitching in l. groin.

Extremities.—Drawing in hands, feet, wrists and l. shoulder. Weakness of r. wrist and l. ankle after menses, with pain as if paralyzed.

Upper Extremities.—Synovial crepitation. Rheumatic pain in r. shoulder and nervous feeling. Drawing in l. deltoid in morning. Frequent contractions of extensor muscles on back of arm when writing. Heaviness of r. arm. Weakness of arms; l. Pain deep in r. wrist, going to middle of palm; sudden drawing cramping pain in l. wrist, extending over dorsum of hand to fingers, index very painful. Drawing in r. wrist. Hand trembles when writing. Crampy pain in l. hand, < index. Numbness of r. hand and arm. Sticking in r. middle finger; in l. middle and index. Pain in r. little finger; in an old gouty joint of r. index; rheumatic P. in joints of l. little; darting P. in l., then r. little, < riding. Numbness of r. fingers, with occasional darts, < ring fingers.

Lower Extremities.—Gait unsteady. Synovial crepitation.

Thigh.—Shooting anteriorly in l. Aching in r. Boring in l. T. and knee. Bruised pain inside of T. when ascending stairs. Drawing in inner side of l.; in l. ischiatic nerve, from foramen to middle of thigh; in l. hamstrings when walking. Stiffness of hamstrings on attempting to rise.

Knee.—Trembling on rising after sitting. Twitching in l. Stabbing in l. Cutting in r. Pains about patella; in K. and ankles when walking fast; in l. popliteal space on descending stairs; in muscles of l. as if hamstrings were too short.

Leg.—Sticking in calf when walking. Pain about shins; along shins when walking; P. when walking fast; in calf, < on first rising. Feeling in r. calf as if bandaged. Calves feel as if pulled tight when walking. Heaviness as if paralyzed mornings after rising. *Sudden giving way when walking, as if they would be paralyzed*, and she fears typhoid fever. Weariness when standing.

Cutting in l. foot, through middle of instep to toes. Pain in ball of l. foot; when walking; in hollow of r. after ascending stairs and when riding; alternately in hollow of each, < exercise; in muscles when flexing l.; in big toe; in r. big toe, as this gets better pain in heart. Prickling in big toe as if going to sleep, when rubbed.

Skin.—Pimples, with broad erythematous base, on l. natis; reddish, itching, about tendo-achillis, then on lower limbs, < bends of joints, eruption about joints, <, then > Sepia; itching, near r. ear; itching, burning, on l. leg. Hives on second joint of ring finger. Itching of nose; about mouth and neck; about anus; on joints; arms and coccyx; like insect-bites, on face, < nose, and in spots on body and limbs; < lumbar region and hips, rubbing causes pimples; about joints, elbows, knees and r. external ear, and vesicles form; about mouth and neck, and vesicles and pimple-like nettle-rash form; here and there after going to bed, and hives, the itching > scratching, then burning and sleeplessness, hives > Apis.

Sleep.—Sleepiness all day, < forenoon; at 10 A.M.; in afternoon, must lie down; from 3 P.M. till bed-time, then sleepless from thoughts, finally urging to sleep, dreams of these thoughts; after dinner, with weariness. Sleepless from 12 P.M. till 3 A.M.; waking after 12 P.M., soon afterwards electric shock through body and trembling and palpitation as from fright. Wide awake from least noise. Restless sleep. Sits up in bed, seizes the sheet and folds it precisely along the hem. Dreams troublesome; vexing; of the dead, tired on waking; sexual, thinks she is with her husband, but the act is prevented by the unbidden entrance of a stranger.

Fever.—Chilliness, < chest; C., then hot flashes around body. Cold feet. Heat preventing sleep, and thoughts crowd upon his mind; H. in flashes every afternoon, with headache (woman of 50, who had never had them before); in flashes in evening, with sweat. Burning of face; lobe of r. ear, with itching.

Natrum Sulfuricum.

Pure Sodium sulphate (Glauber's salt) is triturated for use.

General Action.—Like other alkaline sulphates, an active cathartic. In addition, however, it exhibits a marked similarity to the "uric acid diathesis" in general, and is certainly a valuable remedy for combating numerous phases of that polymorphous malady.

Allies.—Nat. m., Puls., Bry., Kali c., etc.

Generalities.—Trembling, < l. side of chest, with fear of misfortune. Sticking in places, with burning. Piercing pain as of knives, in abdomen, small of back and l. hip after a fall, > moving and rubbing. Inclined to mental and physical activity. Weakness; at 9 A.M., with dulness of head; in afternoon, with sleepiness; after vomiting, with burning headache; < 3 P.M., > walking. Many symptoms appearing in morning cease after dinner. Amelioration in open air (Magn., Puls.). *Aggravation from lying on l. side* (Nat. m., Phos., Puls.).

Clinical.—All conditions are < dampness. It corresponds, in a general way, to the "hydrogenoid" constitution. A great remedy for lithæmia. Aggravation from lying on l. side, especially of the hepatic symptoms.

Mind.—Taciturn; < morning. Melancholy from hearing music. Lachrymose. Disheartened, tired of life, despairs of getting well. Dreads a misfortune. Irritable; < morning. Succeeds in nothing that she undertakes and does not know why.

Head.—A sudden jerk in head throwing her to the right in forenoon when sitting. Tearing in various parts; wandering T. Aching; deep-seated; pulsating; wandering; when reading, causing heat and perspiration, the heat and perspiration > walking; burning, after vomiting, with weakness. Confusion; towards 9 A.M., with feebleness; when eating, with darkness before eyes. Stupid feeling. Heaviness. Brain feels loose in forenoon, and when stooping feeling as if it fell towards l. temple. *Vertigo at 6 P.M., then vomiting of sour mucus;* V. when rising, with dulness of head; after dinner with buzzing in head; after dinner, then heat rising from body towards head, increasing till sweat broke out on forehead; with inclination to fall to the right.

Forehead.—Sticking in front of l. protuberance; from l. side to occiput at 10.30 A.M., when sitting. Tearing in r. side; in l. side of bone; in sinciput. Boring in l. side; in bone; in r. side of bone; in bone in evening when sitting; as if it would burst; in l. side, which seemed to forcibly close l. eye. Pain; in r. side; < eating; wandering; periodical, in r. side; grasping, in middle, > cold foot bath, but returning more violently after an hour; breaking, after dinner, then sleepiness; drawing. Drawing; in l. side; frequently in sinciput. Pressure as of a hard substance in forenoon; P. as of two fingers above l. orbit at noon. Heaviness.

Temples.—Tearing on r. towards facial bones; in r. towards vertex from 4 P.M. till next morning, with chill running up back, chattering of teeth and shaking, without external coldness. Boring in l.; l. at 5 P.M.; r., then l. Painful beating when walking and on touch during menstruation, > night in bed, with pain as if top of head would split. Pressure as with a plug in l.; as with a dull instrument in r. in evening.

Sides.—Sensation like an electric shock in l.; on vertex towards r., once during forenoon and afternoon. Sticking in l. on exerting arms. Tearing; in upper part of r. Boring in l. Pain; wandering, in l., < behind ear; in r., so that she held the head with both hands. Pressure inward in r. all night. Drawing in l.

Occiput.—Tearing; then in forehead; in r. side when quiet; r. side, with pain, also in evening. Boring; in l. side. Pain on entering the room after coffee; squeezing P.; wandering. Pressing from both sides at 6 P.M., returned for two hours next morning, and extended over r. side of face, repeated three mornings. Drawing; in l.; with pain, heat and heaviness.

Tearing in cranial bones. Pain in bones. Pimples on side of occiput, sensitive to touch. Scalp sensitive when combing.

Eyes.—Pain transiently > rubbing; *P. in evening when reading by candle-light, with heaviness of lids* (Nat. m.); as if a lentil were in l. Burning in morning and evening when near the fire; in r. in morning, with watering; in r. in afternoon out of doors, with burning lachrymation; in evening, with intolerance of light; < afternoon, with dryness; with redness and dryness (Nat. m.); with tearing and dim vision. Sensation as if a bug were crawling in l., > rubbing. Itching sometimes in l., then in r.; in r. eye and l. ear. *Agglutination in morning, with photophobia* (Nat.

m.); A. of l. Stitches in l. inner canthus. Breaking pain around eye in forenoon. Intermittent tearing at lower edge of l. orbit in forenoon. Photophobia. Vision dim; as if a white leaf were before r. eye, transiently > washing, but always returning till towards evening. V. blurred in morning, with lachrymation. V. of yellow, glittering, pointed bodies after blowing nose hard.

Clinical.—Granular conjunctivitis, with burning lachrymation, with maculæ on the cornea. Granulations of the lids, with general sycotic constitution, tendency to warts (about anus, on scalp, forehead, chest, neck, etc.), stiffness of knees, cracking of joints, etc. (compare Thuja).

Ears.—*Sticking* in r.; into r. at 3 P.M.; suddenly into r. at 8 P.M.; *like lightning out of r.* Tearing above ears; twitching, in l. lobe in evening and night. Boring in bone behind r. Pain behind l.; in r., < towards 9 A.M.; as if tympanum were pressed out; near l., as if skin were pulled. Itching in r. Hissing in l. Ringing in r., with stoppage in both; sound in l. as of distant bells; in r. as if near a belfry; as of a tinkling bell.

Clinical.—Earache, lightning-like stitches, always < damp weather or from wet ground.

Nose.—Tearing on back; in r. side, extending to forehead. Wandering boring in bone at root. Pressure near it at noon. Drawing near r. side. Sneezing. Stopped coryza. Bleeding, light red and fluid, during menstruation.

Clinical.—Nasal catarrh, with thick, yellow discharges, sometimes scabs and blood, and offensive odor, the patient always hawks up salty mucus, also symptoms of oppression of chest.

Face.—Flushed. Pale and wan in morning on waking, with gloomy expression and quarrelsome mood. Sticking in l. zygoma, with sensation as if skin were pulled. Tearing in side; in zygoma; in l. zygoma at 9 P.M.; in l. zygoma, generally in morning, < cold air, afterwards grasping and raging in root of a l. upper tooth; in l. zygoma, > rubbing, but returning; twitching, in evening and night. Pain in l. zygoma; wandering, in zygomata. Pressure on r. zygoma. Drawing in l. cheek, as if skin were pulled. Boring in r. angle of lower jaw, then in r. side of forehead, then extending over forepart of head. Pain in joint in morning, with stiffness. Pressure in l. angle of lower; as with a plug in r. angle of lower in evening. Drawing in l. side of lower jaw. Upper lip dry and peeling. Vesicles on upper lip; with inflamed edges and burning pain on l. side of upper. Lips burn in evening.

Mouth.—Teeth. A r. upper is loose, seems longer, with drawing pain, > cold air and tobacco-smoke. Sticking in last l. molar by day, with tearing. Tearing in decayed l. lower at night, when out of bed. Jerking pain in an upper l. molar. Grasping, raging pain in root of an upper l. Beating pain in l. upper in evening, preventing sleep till morning. Raging, pulsating pain in l. upper molar, waking her at 2 A.M., with heaviness in head, general heat and restlessness, so that she did not know where to lay her head. Drawing in lower; r. upper; lower incisors in evening.

Movable, painless swelling on outside of l. lower gum. Blister on upper gum, suppurating and then drying. Burning in gums, so that she cannot eat bread. *Tongue furred.* Shooting through root of tongue. Biting in tip of T. in evening. *Burning on tongue; on tip*; l. side; on tip, with sticking; on tip and margins, and (towards evening) on lower lip; *on tip, as if covered with blisters*, in afternoon. *Burning pain on tip, with blisters. Blisters on palate, with sensitiveness so that she could hardly eat, > anything cold. Burning as from highly-seasoned food;* B. in palate as if sore or as if raw, during menstruation. Dryness in morning while perspiring, without thirst; D., with thirst and redness of gums. *Salivation* after eating; *thin*, after eating, with nausea and heaving in stomach, but no vomiting. Taste slimy in morning and afternoon, and tongue coated with mucus. Food does not taste well. Taste lost in morning, mouth feels rough and almost insensible.

Clinical.—Toothache > holding cold water in the mouth (Puls., Coff.). Dirty grayish-green coat at root of tongue.

Throat.—*Hawking of mucus in morning; salt mucus in morning* (Calc. c., Lyc.). Intermittent tearing in tendons of r. side when sitting, with tension; I. tearing in veins of r. side, so that the pulsations in the arteries can be seen. Pain on swallowing in evening, with frequent necessity to swallow saliva. Soreness on l. side in morning before and during menstruation. Obstacle on swallowing, tonsils and uvula swollen and inflamed, the inflammation < morning. Intermittent contraction when walking. Dryness; without thirst, it often extends into œsophagus.

Clinical.—Pharyngeal catarrh, profuse, thick, tenacious, white mucus.

Stomach.—Appetite great; then lost; with boring in stomach; hunger, but no A.; while eating disgust; lost, in morning, with yawning and thirst. *Thirst* in forenoon, in afternoon sweat without T.; T. in afternoon; *evening; evening* after violent exercise; at night and in morning before rising; *for something very cold*, with dryness of mouth; wanting. Eructations of disagreeable taste and smell; constant rising of sour water in mouth. Hiccough in afternoon after bread and butter; debilitating, towards evening, in the room. Nausea in morning, with diarrhœa, then boring in stomach; N. in forenoon on descending stairs, *not > vomiting of salty, sour water;* in afternoon when walking, *with waterbrash;* before meals; *with stitches in r. groin;* with almost a beating pain in stomach; with collection of sour water in mouth and with nocturnal headache; with stitches in eyes.

Rolling in S. and abdomen when riding in a carriage, with grumbling. Pain in pit at 3 P.M. when walking; in epigastric region when sitting. Trembling in pit when sitting and walking, with pressure, want of breath and faint feeling. Fasting sensation, with griping. Fulness in evening in bed during menstruation, with difficulty in breathing. Burning in morning, > breakfast, with pinching.

Clinical.—Bilious vomiting. Acid dyspepsia, with heartburn and flatulence.

Abdomen.—*Collection of flatus without evacuation of it, with pain. Flatus rolls about and becomes incarcerated here and there.* Incarceration of flatus towards evening, with salivation, nausea and eructations of disagreeable taste and smell. Fetid flatus in morning; after dinner. Loud, but difficult emission of flatus in afternoon. Painless motion and first hard, then soft stool. *Rolling; and grumbling, with sudden pinches, as after a purgative, then diarrhœa.* Grumbling after meals, with fermenting. Griping, > emission of flatus. Pinching, then diarrhœa; P., then hard stool with blood and scum, then several soft stools; extending into genitals, then diarrhœa; here and there; intermittent, with feeling as if intestines were being stretched. Digging as from flatus towards noon, increasing till 4 P.M., till flatus began to pass, with pinching. *Pain; before breakfast;* > emission of flatus; waking her at 5 A.M., with urging to stool, after which it ceases; as before purging; *flatulent, > difficult emission of flatus;* as if bruised, and in small of back, waking her at 2 A.M., > *lying on (r.) side*, preventing sleep and lasting after rising. Painful contraction extending into chest, so that it oppressed her breath, then diarrhœa. Drawing together, extending into chest, then diarrhœa. Wanderings as from a purgative, with profuse odorless flatus. Wandering burning in evening.

Grumbling in upper part in evening, then fetid flatus. Frequent pinching from sides towards the front. Stitches in r. side in afternoon when walking, with pulsation; S. in l. hypochondrium; in hepatic region in morning when walking, with pulsating pain; in l. hypochondrium and l. side of chest in forenoon when sitting, then in r. side of chest; *in hypochondria when walking in open air, also with tension in r. H.; as if hepatic region would burst open, at* 4 P.M. *on deep breathing while sitting. Hepatic region sensitive when walking, with pain on touch at* 1.30 P.M.

Umbilicus.—*Tearing around,* > breakfast, but returning, with **flatulence.** Pinching around, extending into groin, when sitting, with urging to urinate, the urine was so burning that it was retained, with pain in small of back. Pain around, when sitting; flatulent, above U. in evening, flatus will not pass.

Hypogastrium.—Digging at 9 P.M. during menstruation, > in bed, with chill, then thirst.

Groins.—Stitches in afternoon when walking in open air; S. in l., with pain as if drawn together; deep in, with urging to urinate; in l. extending into axilla, at 5.30 P.M. on motion, > rest; extending into small of back, then diarrhœa. Pain in r. at night, waking him frequently, with sensation of a soft body lying inside there; P. in r. as if distended (which it actually is), extending up into stomach, in evening when sitting and next morning. Full feeling in r., with tension as if it would burst, and with intermittent pinching here and there in abdomen. Burning in evening between menstrual periods, > in bed, in evening when walking, with soreness.

Clinical—Sensitiveness of the region of the liver, < *lying on l. side.* Sometimes used in jaundice, with brown tongue and loose stools. Lead colic. Typhlitis.

Rectum and Anus.—Constant urging to stool. Burning in A. during and after stool. Itching in A.

Stool.—*Diarrhœa;* (after pie); *fluid, yellow, in morning; with full feeling in abdomen and emission of flatus;* later a hard one. Soft from the first doses, hard from later doses; soft, at an unusual time; and frequent, also with flatulency. *Knotty*, with smarting in anus during and after it. Constipation. Hard; and streaked with blood; with much straining; later a soft one. Difficult, but not very hard. Two or three, one semifluid, during menstruation, with tenesmus in anus.

Clinical.—Diarrhœa, thin yellow, liquid, gushing, often involuntary, < *morning, after moving about* (Bry.), preceded by rumbling in abdomen, accompanied by profuse flatulence, often associated with soreness and pain over the region of the liver, which hurts on every jar, sometimes with inflammation and suppuration around the roots of the nails. Diarrhœa, with pain around the shoulders, sometimes blood with the stools Diarrhœa after rising in the morning, with great desire for ice-water; greatly > kneading abdomen, stitches running up into l. side of chest. Chronic diarrhœa; stools sudden, scanty, light red or bloody, forcible, occasionally involuntary when passing gas, aggravation from cold food or drink, eating, or damp weather, in tolerance of tight clothing, of rheumatic habit, especially with discharges from the ear.

Urinary Organs. — Stitches in meatus urinarius. Cutting in forepart of urethra when urinating; in orifice when urinating, also afterwards. *Burning during micturition* (Puls., Hep., Thuja); *with copious urine; with scanty urine;* B. after micturition. Urine increased; *with brick-red sediment* (Lyc.); *and dark and passed more frequently; so that she had to get up several times at night. Urine scanty; and passed more seldom;* afterwards copious. Sediment whitish-yellow in urine of the morning; yellow-red in the urine of the evening.

Clinical.—Uric acid deposits. Enlarged prostate. Chronic gonorrhœa.

Sexual Organs.—Itching on mons veneris; glans; lower part of penis; lower surface of prepuce in forenoon and afternoon, > scratching; scrotum, seldom > scratching; scrotum, and after scratching burning. Sweat on scrotum when sitting towards evening. Desire excited in evening; in morning, with erection. Stitches in pudenda and vagina in afternoon when sitting. Leucorrhœa. Copious menses in afternoon when walking; C. on second day; for a day, before the end of the period, and more fluid; and too late, with pain in abdomen. Scanty menses. Menstruation too late, with pain in abdomen and constipation or hard stool. Menses acrid, making the thighs sore and only flowing much the first two days. Menses every forenoon for five days, lumps of coagulated blood. Passed white, bloody mucus instead of blood on third morning. During menses pinching pain in morning in bed, and when walking in forenoon several times passed coagulated blood.

Respiratory Organs.—Cough at 1 P.M. when moving about, with stitches in l. side of chest and want of breath; *C., with expectoration, if he coughs while standing stitches in l. chest, with shortness of breath;* loose, in morning from tickling in throat. Dry cough; night and morning, with tickling in larynx; < *morning after rising;* < *night, with soreness in chest and rough feeling in throat,* **relief from sitting up and holding her chest with both hands;** with tickling in trachea; with scraping in larynx. Expectoration of mucus after heavy, anxious dreams. *Short breath when walking, gradually > rest,* later want of breath even when sitting.

Clinical.—Bronchial catarrh, cough < 3 or 4 A.M. (Ka. c.), glairy expectoration, vomiting after eating, < damp weather. Asthma, cough at night, sits up and holds his chest, < cold, damp weather. During damp weather dyspnœa and oppression, > open air.

Chest.—*Stitches* anteriorly below l. ribs; above r. nipple at 5.30 P.M. when sitting; towards evening when walking fast; *in l.* after meals; in l. when yawning; in l. when standing; in l. while coughing when standing; in l. on inspiration; in region of l. nipple when sitting, without difficulty in breathing; in side to which she stoops; in region of l. short ribs when walking and sitting; anteriorly below l. ribs when walking, < inspiration and pressure; in r. pectoral muscles, < inspiration; in l. side, with short breath; in l. side extending up into ribs after emission of flatus, while sitting; in l. side, preventing cough.

Cutting anteriorly beneath r. ribs while sitting. Pain in l. pectoral muscles; P. between nipples; between sternum and r. nipple when sitting, < pressure and inspiration; *near l. loin, < motion and pressure;* in pectoral muscles, with drawing; anteriorly beneath l. ribs, with drawing; wandering, in l. wall, < below nipple, not affecting respiration. *Oppression;* in morning on waking. Internal trembling, making her irritable.

Heart.—Pressure in region; in præcordial region when sitting. Anxiety, a sudden short beating, with dim vision, necessity to go into the open air, then relief.

Neck.—Stitches in nape; in l. side. Tearing; in nape; in l. side; and throbbing. Pain in l. side; P. and stiffness; in l. side, with burning, then coldness; frequently in l. side at night; in l. muscles, extending to behind l. ear, with stiffness and pain on moving head; extending to occiput, < moving neck; in l. side, extending into occiput and towards clavicle, with burning and stiffness, then coldness and prickling in skin; indescribable, in r. side, extending into occiput, when sitting, making her scream, > rubbing; bruised, in nape and scapulæ, < stretching and yawning, which he had to do often. Pressure on l. side. Drawing in nape; in l. side. Painful burning in muscles, with stiffness. Stiffness of l. side.

Back.—Tearing down, with feeling in bones as if dogs were gnawing them. Stitches in region of middle dorsal vertebræ. Pain in dorsal muscles. Pressure at sides of dorsal vertebræ. Drawing in dorsal muscles. Stitches between scapulæ in evening when sitting. Tearing in scapula; between S.; on l., extending to nape, < moving head, with burning pain; extending to nape, when walking, and in l. pectoral muscles. Pressure on scapula; in r. in morning in bed; on r., gradually increasing and extending across shoulders. Drawing between scapulæ; below l., then in cervical muscles and l. thumb. Sudden pain below l. scapula. Stitches in middle of sacrum when sitting. Tearing from os coccygis into middle of l. thigh, in the bone, in evening, with piercing. Ulcerative pain in small of B. at night, so that she could lie only on r. side, > rising. Bruised pain in small of B. from morning till evening, > going to bed. Pain in small of B., with burning urine.

Extremities.—Twitching now here, now there, in all; of hands and feet at night, < after midnight in sleep. Stitches in tips of fingers and toes. Tearing in joints. Twitching tearing here and there; at night. Pain in joints; when walking; transiently > motion; > walking; drawing. Drawing in joints; in evening. Pain as if bruised or as after a long walk, in forenoon. Weariness in hands and feet in morning after nocturnal fever.

Upper Extremities.—Axilla. Stitches; in l. when sitting; in soft parts below l., extending backward. Drawing in r.

Shoulder.—Stitches in r.; in l. joint. Tearing; in r.; in joints; at 11 P.M. Boring in r. joint; in forepart of l. Pain; in joints; in r. joint, then in l.; in l. in evening; suddenly in r. Sudden pressure on r., then in l. and in both knees. Drawing pain in l. extending through arm; in r. joint in evening. Drawing; in r. joint. Stiffness in l. Heaviness in r. joint.

Arm.—Tearing in middle of bones of l. Pain; in r., with tension; bruised, in r. Drawing. Heaviness of r., with tearing in middle of upper arm.

Upper Arm.—Tearing in inner side of both; on inner side of l.; in middle of l. humerus in afternoon; in tendons above l. elbow at 3 P.M., with pinching; under shoulder-joint when sitting; intermittent, in r. humerus. Pain above elbow; in muscles; in deltoid. Pressure on inner side of both. Compression above l. elbow; in muscles of l. Drawing on inner sides of both.

Elbow.—Tearing; in r.; in bend of l.; extending to tips of fingers in morning in bed, transiently > rubbing, with asleep sensation. Boring in l. Pain; in and above r.; above and below l.; ulcerative, in r. and in tendon of r. forearm, with pain on touch; bruised, in r.; bruised and weary. Compression; in evening. Drawing in r.; about r.

Forearm.—Tearing; in bone of r., on upper side, in afternoon; about middle of r. in afternoon during rest; on back of l. in evening; in bone below bend of r. elbow in evening. Pain in r.; in flexors of both; in l. in afternoon; above l. wrist, extending to fingers. Drawing in flexor surface of l. Compression in l.

Wrist.—Tearing; in l.; at 11 P.M. Boring in l. Pain; in evening on lying down; in l. in evening; in l. on lying down, < motion; frequent, in evening; frequent about r. when walking; in l., extending into fingers, especially into thumb. Compression. Drawing; in l.

Hand.—Redness of backs of both in afternoon, with burning as from nettles. Trembling on waking; when writing. Stitches in middle of r. palm in afternoon; between metacarpal bones of r. index and second finger in evening. Tearing; between r. middle and third fingers, then backward on back of hand. Pain; deep in palm; sticking-beating, on back of l. in forenoon, transiently > motion; drawing, in r. palm in evening. Pressure on ulnar margin of l. Drawing; in metacarpus; deep in l.; deep in r., extending to fingers and arm, with feeling of lameness, weakness and internal heat. Sensation in r. as if filling with blood, so that the skin feels too tight, in afternoon when knitting, with stiffness of fingers. Weakness of l., and on closing it or grasping anything pain in flexors of hands and fingers, from wrist to above elbow, as if they had been too much extended.

Fingers.—Stitches in tip of r. second in afternoon when writing; behind l. thumb-nail in evening; jerking, through l. thumb; in tips of r. thumb and index, as if veins were being pulled out, at noon while knitting. Sticking, ulcerative pain under nail of r. index. Tearing; in l.; l. thumb; joints of r.; joints of l. little; r. in morning; last phalanx of l. index, towards tip, in afternoon; tip of r. index in afternoon when sitting; r. first and second in afternoon when spinning; along l. thumb towards tip when sitting; cutting in l. little, extending towards margin of hand. Boring in joint of l. third; second joint of l. thumb; joint of l. index in evening. Pain in l. fourth; r. thumb and index and their metacarpal bones; joints; joints of index; joint of l. thumb; joints of l. middle; joint of r. thumb in evening; joints of l. middle on moving it; l., with tension. Drawing; l. thumb; l. little; joints; joint of l. thumb; l., and along margin of hand. Drawing stiffness in r. Pulsation in tip of l. little. Crawling in tips of r. as if going to sleep in evening and next morning.

Clinical.—Panaritium, the pain better out of doors.

Lower Extremities.—Hip. Pain < some movements, always on rising from a seat and moving in bed; in l. joint on walking; deep, in r. joint; excruciating, in r. joint, < *stooping, rising from a seat or moving in bed,* > stretching or walking; in l. joint, as after lying in a bad position, making it difficult to ascend, sit down or get up, waking him at night, can bear any position for only a short time, with intermittent sensitiveness to pressure in one spot.

Thigh.—Sticking in muscles; in l. trochanter in evening, < pressure. Tearing anteriorly in r.; in muscles of r. Pain in trochanter; muscles above r. knee; muscles of r.; anterior muscles of r. when sitting, then in l. knee; in extensors of l. as if they had been stretched too much; bruised, in anterior muscles of r. in afternoon, < walking. Drawing in muscles of r. Prostration in middle, and in lower part of leg. Stitches in l. Tearing; in r.; in r. in evening on lying down, and on back of l. foot; at night on waking, and in toes; in l., extending down leg. Boring in l.; then r.; wandering B. Pain; to side of r. patella; in l. in evening; evening when sitting, < l.; r. when sitting; when walking; intermittent, when walking; bruised, in r. when walking; weary, in r. Compression. Pressure on inner side of l. Drawing; about l.; in hollow of r. when sitting, > motion; in r. extending down leg. Weakness.

Leg.—Stitches in muscles. Tearing in forepart of r.; on outside of l.; in tibia; in r. tibia, with breaking pain; in calves, as if in tendons, < stepping, with drawing; from r. calf into hollow of knee in evening when spinning, > rubbing. Boring in r. tibia when walking. Pain in calf; l. calf when standing; in tibiæ when walking and sitting; weary, above l. ankle when walking, then above l. knee, then in r. knee. Drawing pain in evening when sitting, then in r. knee; in tendo-achillis, then in calves. Drawing in muscles of r.; in calves; tibiæ; when standing and walking; upward in calves and tendons at 10 A.M. when standing; acute, on l. tibia. Compression in l., then stitches in l. toes; C. on lower part of l. calf. Cramplike contraction in muscles of l. calf when walking. Sensation deep in r. on walking as if it were swollen or as from too much blood. Feel weak and bruised.

Ankle.—Tearing; in l.; l. in morning on waking, and in toes. Boring in l. Pain; in l.; in and below l. external malleolus; in r. in evening; in evening on lying down; in r. when sitting; in r. after walking; l. when walking, then above l. knee, with weary pain in both knees; in l., at first < motion or stepping, but continuing during rest; in r., extending to tibia. Sprained sensation in r. in morning on getting up, could not step well on it until after he had walked up and down the room several times. Drawing pain in l., in evening. Drawing; behind l. inner malleolus; when sitting and walking. Compression in l.; on l. inner malleolus.

Foot.—Stitches in l. heel in afternoon when sitting; in l. sole when standing, making her twitch, > rubbing. Tearing in l.; on back of r.; in r. sole and toes; in outer margins; in r. heel in afternoon when standing, > rubbing; in heels at 9 P.M. when spinning, with stitches; on back of r. when sitting; in r. sole when sitting and standing; in r. heel when walking, > rubbing, with stitches. Boring on back and outer side of l. Pain in r.; in joints; ulcerative, in r. heel, so that she could hardly step. Pressure on r. Drawing on back of r. Sensitiveness in morning on waking, with heaviness. Weariness at night, making her often change their position.

Toes.—Stitches in l.; in great; l. great; joints of l. great; tips; tips of great; tip of r. great, then l. great; in l. in evening; beneath nails at night; in l. fourth when sitting; in r. second and third when stepping; in joint of l. great, < pressure; suddenly in r. great. Tearing; when walking; in r.; r. little. Boring in joint of great; alternately in joints of r. and l. great. Pain; in r. great; l. little; joints; joints of great; joint of r. great; in joint of l. great, then r. great; in r. great in evening; in joints at night on waking; joints of r. great at night on waking, with burning under nail; in l., with tension; joints of r. great, impeding walking; jerking, in joints of r. great. Drawing pain; in r. in evening. Drawing; in joint of l. great; in r. and on outer margin of foot. Going to sleep of r. great in morning when sitting.

Clinical.—Useful in affections of the hip-joint, with pain at night, > turning over.

Skin.—Pimples deep in skin on r. side of lower jaw; on chin, with burning tensive pain on touch. Itching pimples inside r. hand; on inner side of r. forearm, burning after scratching, also containing limpid water, during menstruation. Itching vesicles containing water, between l. thumb and index. Stitches like flea-bites on l. chest, and then again on r. side of forehead. Tearing on external surface of upper arm in evening, > rubbing, with sticking. Drawing on r. zygoma; l. leg. Crawling on back of nose; on r. side of back of nose in evening when walking. Itching in forepart of nose; externally on wings of nose; on perineum; alternately on soles and toes; now here, now there, on face; on back in evening on undressing; toes and between them in evening on undressing, < rubbing; top of feet from ankles to toes in evening on undressing, < scratching; between r. fingers, and after scratching burning; toes in evening on going to bed, > scratching; balls of toes, > rubbing, with feeling as if they would be constricted.

Sleep.—Sleepiness; after breakfast, with no inclination to work; in forenoon when writing; after dinner; at 9 P.M., earlier than usual, but he also woke earlier. Fell asleep in forenoon when reading. Starting up when she is hardly asleep, without waking up entirely. Late falling asleep from restlessness. Restless sleep, with frequent waking from headache; R. sleep, with frequent waking, heavy anxious dreams, then expectoration of much mucus.

Dreams.—Unremembered. That she bought beautiful bouquets of flowers in the market. Of gardens, flowers, delightful picnics. Of a wedding procession that passed by her. Of a lottery, he saw the numbers which he had taken. That a gentleman she knew lay sick in her house. That he was hurt and provoked because he had been insulted. That insults had excited him so that he began to fight. Of a mob fight, into which he was inveigled. That her daughter had vexed her. Vexatious, that a gentleman of her acquaintance did not take her to a ball. That wood was floating down the neighboring stream and might cause much damage. That she was sailing on the Danube and was afraid. Of a great expanse of water, in which her daughter went down, and then cried for help; that her daughter had been struck with paralysis, which frightened her so that she woke covered with perspiration. After midnight, that an acquaintance was going to cut off his r. great toe, the fear of it woke him and he felt sticking in this toe. Before midnight, that she was thrown from a carriage. That she was flying in the air and feared to fall to the ground. Anxious, of falling from a height, etc., making her start up; A., for instance, that she poured boiling lard into the fire; A., that priests had discovered that she had committed crimes.

Fever.—Chilliness towards evening; in afternoon during menstruation, without thirst; in evening; in evening, > lying down, without heat or thirst; at 4 P.M. during menstruation, increasing till 8 P.M., with goose-flesh, > in bed, and at 4 A.M. sweat without thirst; at 7 P.M.; all night; at night, with thirst; internal, with yawning and stretching; internal and external, in morning after rising, without thirst. Shaking chill at 1.30 A.M., with chattering of teeth and anxiety; S. chill in morning after walking, on an empty stomach, with internal heat in head and pale face, the C. lasts all day, > lying down; with thirst, the thirst lasting all the forenoon. Chill up back, with chattering of teeth and shaking, without external coldness. Feverish. Febrile paroxysm, with warm forehead and hands. Dry heat afternoons. Heat in flushes towards evening. Burning in tips of fingers; in places above and below elbow; beneath nail of r. great toe; on outside of l. foot near little toe in afternoon; in legs in evening before going to bed and next morning; in l. sole all night. Sweat at night; S. on face when sitting after eating, with oppression of chest and sensation as if r. eye were filled with water.

Nitrum Acidum.

For use, pure Nitric acid, sp. gr. 1.42, is mixed with distilled water (1 to 9), making the 1st decimal dilution.

General Action.—A tissue remedy of wide application, but with a particular affinity for the skin and mucous membranes; general tendency to destructive ulcerations, with sharp pains. In many particulars it resembles Mercury, in others the potashes and Iodine. It presents many points of resemblance to the lesions of syphilis.

Allies.—Merc., Kali, Iod., Lyc., Graph., Hep., *Sil.*, Aur., etc.

Generalities.—Emaciation (Iod.); < upper arms and thighs. Anæmia of mucous membranes. Collapse, with sinking of pulse and delirium. Trembling in morning on waking; T. from weakness. Tossing about. Twitching. *Epileptic attack after midnight, it began like a mouse moving up and down his l. side, then loss of consciousness*, arm jerked, head and mouth drawn back and forth so that he bit his tongue, then stiffness and snoring; E. attack when sitting, first drawing in l. side of chest, then convulsive drawing back and forth in arms, with tolerable consciousness.

Stitches; here and there in all parts (Kali); under skin of whole body; head, face and body; through forehead, temples and malar-bones and in gums and teeth; head, face, lips, gums, and sharp aching in jaws, *these pains partially > binding head tightly with cold compress.* Painful hammering, < head. *Pains in bones;* P. when half awake that he could not distinctly remember when awake; burning. *Drawing pains in almost all parts,* **suddenly appearing and disappearing;** *D. pain in periosteum of all bones, as before intermittent fever.* Drawing in whole body, with tearing.

Tension in head and whole body; T. of nerves, with thirst. *Inclination to take cold* (Ka. c.); and has pain in back in consequence; in weak parts in evening in cold wind, and then drawing pain in the parts. Sensitiveness of whole body to open air. Pulsation in upper part of body. Confusion of body, not of head, as after severe illness. Malaise; after dinner becomes warm, limbs feel prostrated and tremble, she is obliged to lie down; of whole body, with weakness of joints and heat of head. Restlessness; internal, in morning on waking, < arms. Sensation in all muscles as on resting after great fatigue. Disinclination to walk.

Weakness (Ka. c., Phos. ac., Merc., Mur. ac., Sul. ac., etc.); of mind and body; all day, with sleepiness; in morning after rising till 10 A.M.; towards noon; in afternoon; in evening, < lower limbs; in evening, with trembling; on slight movement; after stool; when sitting and walking, with indolence and bruised sensation; after dinner, limbs relaxed, < knees and elbows; from too frequent coition (though with sufficient sexual desire), with renewal of old complaints; with atony; *with trembling and sensitiveness;* **so that he was almost constantly obliged to lie down;** sudden; so that she could not speak during menses, it took away her breath, and she was obliged to lie down; faintlike every other morning, with anxiety.

Faint; all day. Heaviness; on walking in open air; of head and limbs. Spasmodic stiffness of back and whole body. Aggravation towards evening, especially of the drawing pains here and there; A. on lying down. *Most symptoms disappear when riding in a carriage* (Graph.).

Clinical.—Epileptiform convulsions at night on going to bed, during the day frequent vertigo, always felt well when driving in a carriage, a long drive would keep off the paroxysm, promptly cured. In general, indicated for the bad effects of Mercury, to which it is similar. General aggravation from water, on washing (Phos.). Foul odor of all excretions; foul breath, offensive salivation, etc. The pains are almost always splinter-like (Hep.).

Mind.—Delirium at night; D., fancying himself suddenly rich, ugly, raving, later angry at his attendants. Images of all sorts appeared to him in evening in bed, they walked, ran, disappeared, became larger and smaller, with chilliness. Beside himself from slight pains. **Easily excited, much affected by peevishness.** On being questioned he raised his eyelids, whispered briefly and quickly and apparently with increased suffering, for to other questions he answered by a look or nod. *Fancy that she shall die soon, but is not physically ill.*

Changeable mood, at one time lively, at another sad. Violent about trifles all day and then he has to laugh at himself. **Vexed at trifles,** even at himself if he makes a mistake. Rancor, insensibility to apologies. Attacks of rage and despair, with curses. *Ill humor;* in morning on waking; in morning after rising, with discomfort; at himself. Inclined to be angry and to use insulting expressions. *Discontented with himself, > violent weeping;* D., despising life. Quarrelsome. Impatient; in afternoon.

Despondent; not lachrymose; and in deep thought. *Weeping mood. Sad; and peevish, obstinate,* lachrymose;

and absorbed in himself and silent. Homesick. Tired of life. Wishes for death, yet dreads it. *Tendency to start. Fright;* for a moment after waking; thinks that he is going to die. Peculiar anguish, > driving, returning when she was at home, so that she was forced to drive all day. Taciturn. Apathy; interrupted by murmuring.

Anxiety; all day; in evening, before menses; *at night;* after eating; during a storm; after stool, with irritability and general indisposition; if she walks rapidly, with oppression and with sweat on back and chest; with palpitation that takes away the breath; with stitches above heart, fantasy as if she were speaking irrationally, coldness of body and inclination to fall; *as if engaged in a lawsuit or dispute, causing uneasiness;* like palpitation, at night, as if she had committed a crime, so that she could not remain in bed, with nausea, no palpitation was perceptible to hand; paroxysmal, so that he could not sit still in evening. Lost in thought about a long past, anxious event, from which she could not free herself, almost like a waking dream, at times she aroused herself from it as if in fright, but was always buried again in the same thought.

Thoughts vanish; if she exerts herself to reflect upon things important to her. Indisposed to earnest work; no desire to work; I. to scientific work, diminished power of thought. *Memory weak;* diminished as the physical weakness increased. No thoughts and inability to comprehend anything. Stupor; all day, with chilliness in afternoon.

Head.—Sticking, < frontal and temporal regions; in almost all parts; extending into r. eye and l. ear, then inflammation of eye, white of eye very red, in open air he cannot see; sudden, on stooping, as if heavy. Cutting. **Feeling as if in a vise from ear to ear over vertex** after breakfast, then feeling as if she had no head, it felt light on her shoulders, it felt numb or as if made of putty. *Feeling as if forced forward.* Shocks from a slight noise. Sensitive to jar of a carriage and to a hard step.

Aching; in bones; in morning on waking, > *rising;* on waking, involving eyes; in morning in bed, after rising pressure in r. temple, chilliness, qualmishness in umbilical region, at last pain in abdomen as from incarcerated flatus, and eructations, every afternoon, then nausea and anxiety, and at night vomiting, with faintness and diarrhœa; on coughing; on walking in open air; *with heaviness in lower limbs;* with the dysentery; with inability to apply mind; with tension in eyes on moving them; **as if tightly bound** (Merc.); bursting, with soreness of scalp as from ulceration, > *tying up head tightly* (Sil.); waking two or three times at night, and he could not sleep again for an hour or two; paroxysmal, in morning on waking, with nausea and sensation as if all parts of mouth were numb; drawing; as after intoxication, < stooping, with pain in eyes as from smoke; as from rush of blood, so that she could not collect her senses, with dim vision; in H., eyes and upper part of nose, as from fulness of blood, on shaking head and blowing nose.

Tension, and in eyelids. Fulness; as if it would burst at times during the day. Confusion; < after a meal; and weakness; at times, like loss of consciousness, < open air; with spasmodic painful drawing. Sensation as in violent coryza, without special discharge of mucus. Jerking in H. in evening. Jerk-like beating on stooping and lying down again. Heaviness; at night when sleeping and dozing, with oppression; as from coal-gas, waking him in morning. *Rush of blood; with heat.* Crawling, asleep and numb sensation. Vertigo; *in morning on rising,* with obscuration of vision *and necessity to sit down; in morning immediately after rising, with weakness;* in morning, with nausea, then eructations; in evening immediately after lying down; in evening, with pulsation in head and pressure in middle of brain; in evening, she could scarcely hold herself on rising from a seat; at night on rising, so that she did not know where she was; on stooping; on rising from stooping; on rising and walking, with flickering before eyes.

Forehead.—Stitches over l. eye; over eyes every morning; in eminences, with sharp pain; in l. eminence, at times throbbing, at 4 P.M., < evening, and waking him at night, with feeling as if it closed eyes; pain above eyes, more S. than pressing, after eating. *Pressure in forepart of head and upon eyes,* that were then immovable. Pain; every morning; with heaviness and with darting pains in ears and vertigo; drawing, above l. eye; acute drawing upward P. from F. Constriction externally above l. eye. Compression anteriorly in afternoon.

Temples.—*Stitches;* in r.; *in l.* in evening. Pain; *drawing, in r.;* sticking beating, in l. in afternoon; throbbing; throbbing, in r. in morning on waking, with nausea. Drawing in muscles. Heaviness, with frequent chilliness.

Vertex.—Sticking as if it would tear head asunder every day, < afternoon, obliging her to lie down and preventing sleep; boring S. in evening. *Pressure as with the thumbs,* and in temples and eyes.

Sides.—Twitching in l. hemisphere of brain, extending to temples; T. backward in lower part of l. hemisphere of brain. Sticking in r., and in occiput, that even was sore to touch. Throbbing pain in l. in afternoon; in l. towards morning, beginning near vertex, descending to region of l. ear, then gradually over vertex to r. side of head, but still worse on l., she felt as if she could beat the head to pieces, > about breakfast. Bruised pain in r. *Pressive and drawing bone-pains in l., even in teeth and meatus auditorius.* Drawing, at one time above r. orbit, at another in region of l. ear.

Occiput.—Sticking in protuberances, extending to lower jaw; S. in l. side during breakfast, so that head was drawn backward and respiration impeded; sudden, in r. side in evening, then another kind of headache in occiput, both > sleep. Pain, > slight exertion, especially thinking; bruised. Throbbing.

Scalp.—**Falling of hair** (Graph., Sep.). *Offensive scurf. Scabby, moist, itching eruption.* Stitches and drawing. *Sensitiveness; in evening, even the cap oppresses him, and anxiety.* Pain in spots on touch; P. in roots of hair on vertex when touched; suppurative P. on touch. Pain as from subcutaneous ulceration, heat, hot and throbbing pain, so that he could not well bear the weight of a towel. Tension. Crawling about r. ear.

Clinical.—Headache as if in the bones, feeling as if constricted by a band, < night (Merc.). Falling of the hair, with humid eruptions. Moist, burning eruptions on the scalp.

Eyes.—*Yellowness about E., with red cheeks;* Y., sickly look below E. in morning after rising, with a relaxed sensation. Red. Wild, staring. Sunken. Acrid moisture. Puffiness about E. in morning on waking.

Twitching below r. after dinner. *Stitches.* Pinching. Pressure and itching; P. in l., with smarting; drawing; as from sand; as from pressure upon an ulcer; as from looking at the sun, with hard mucus, redness and itching. *Biting.* Smarting. *Burning;* during menses; and in l. temple; with excoriated feeling. Compression in r. Constriction in l. Dryness beneath upper lids. Stickiness as from hardened matter. *Sensation as if full of tears.*

Lachrymation; of r. in open mild air; < reading, with pains in eyes; and itching. Pupils dilated. Redness of white. Dark spots on cornea. Conjunctivitis of r. Stitches externally near l. ball, extending to inner canthus. Lids, swelling; S. of upper, with itching pimple upon it; agglutination of r. over night; twitching; trembling of r.; pressure in evening; periodic pressure on inner surface, < lower, with blinking and sensitiveness of eyes to light; burning in morning; *difficulty in raising in morning.* Canthi, dry mucus; pressure like sand in outer; itching in inner.

Vision.—**Double; of horizontal objects at some distance** (compare Aur., Ka. cy., etc.). **Obscured; when reading;** before r. *Obliged to stop reading in the twilight sooner than usual. Short-sighted.* Eyes weak and hurt as if weary. Sensitive to light. Blinded on looking intently at anything; B. by the daylight as usually in evening by candle-light; suddenly in open air, head confused, his thoughts go hither and thither and he is faint. Wavering. Sensation as if cobwebs were floating before eyes by candle-light, > closing or moving them. The halo around the candle-light increases. Of black spots; of a green spot near every letter when reading; of gray spots at some distance before eyes, preventing distinct vision. Of sparks, then blackness, in four attacks during the day.

Clinical.—Ulcerations of the cornea. Syphilitic iritis, < lying down, feeling as if water were running from both eyes. Opacities of the cornea.

Ears.—*Swelling of glands behind and beneath l. at 6 P.M., > warmth of bed, with sticking and tearing in them extending through ear.* Soreness behind l. Jerking in meatus. Stitches; in r. when pressing on forehead; in r., with roaring. Tearing, now in r. tragus, now in l. Pinching. Pain, then stopped sensation; cramplike P.; as if something in it would burst; in l. as if distended; as if drum were pressed inward. Drawing in r. and in r. cheek; in meatus externus. Dry sensation in the swollen E. Throbbing in drum. Itching in E. Itching heat in E. Sudden closure of r. as if stone-deaf.

Hearing blunted. Cracking when chewing (breakfast). Ringing, with stopped feeling, and for a few minutes after trying to sing, deafness. *Roaring;* in l. Sudden noise in l. like the spitting of a cat. Loud reports. Humming; as if water were in them. Reechoing of her own voice (Caust., Phos.).

Clinical.—Difficult hearing and obstruction of the Eustachian tube. Caries of the mastoid process, syphilitic or mercurial.

Nose.—**Sore,** *nostril ulcerated* (Aur., Graph., Merc.); *S. in nostrils, and scabby* (K. bi.). *Redness of tip* and scabby vesicles on it. **Stitches on touch;** *S. in root, that is distended, < sneezing and coughing. Sore feeling in nostrils; in wings. Itching in nostrils.* Smarting. Constriction, and in malar-bones and about eyes. Burning. Stoppage; of l. nostril; in morning on waking, with trickling of water. *Sneezing; every day, without coryza;* during the day; when coughing; with prickling tingling; with crawling in nose and sensation as if it would bleed; with chilliness, then fluent coryza; violent; violent, in morning and evening, without coryza.

Coryza, < night, with swelling of nose and upper lip and cough; **with soreness within nose and bleeding** (Graph.); *with cough;* with headache; with waterbrash; violent, with pressure downward in head. **Stopped coryza;** at night; **with stoppage of nose,** *the nasal mucus discharged only through choanæ; with dryness of throat and nose, with swollen, inflamed alæ.* **Fluent coryza; and at the same time stopped,** *with difficult breathing, even through mouth, with sticking in throat on swallowing;* with tearing in all limbs; with hoarseness and cough, with stitches in throat on every paroxysm; with roughness of throat on breathing, not on swallowing, and oppression of chest. Discharge of mucus; *offensive yellow matter;* thick, corroding; of acrid water.

Bleeding; in morning; *blowing out of blood in morning; at night;* from weeping; black. Disagreeable odor from N., evening after lying down (Puls., Hep.).

Clinical.—Nasal catarrh, the discharge mostly passing into the pharynx, with a feeling of obstruction. Herpetic eruption on the wings or tip of the nose, the tip is red and covered with vesicles. The nasal discharges are mostly fetid, associated with a feeling of obstruction, or sometimes with dropping of water from the nostrils.

Face.—*Yellow;* greenish. Pale; and bluish, pinched; and veins turgid, with cyanotic lips; with internal heat in it, < eyes, so that he could hardly keep them open. Red. Of leaden hue in morning. Swelling of cheek and upper lip. Sunken. Expression anxious; and worn. Drawn. Twitching of one or another muscle, < masseters; T., with distortion of visage. Sticking; on lying down, > rising. Tearing deep in muscles or in periosteum of malar-bone woke him after midnight; T. in malar-bones as if they would be torn asunder. *Pain in bones;* cramplike, in bones, < cheek-bones. Bruised sensation in bones. Drawing in r. cheek, extending towards nose. Painful pulsation in l. side.

Jaws.—**Cracking of joint when chewing and eating.** Jerking in r. lower, extending forward from region of ear. Sticking in region of joint. Tearing in angles of lower, extending into cheek-bones. Pain in lower in evening, with weakness; cramplike, in r.; as in secondary syphilis; as from Mercury; as from Mercury, and on occiput, the gums being red and enlarged. Could not open readily when requested to protrude his tongue, which he did not do.

Lips.—**Ulcers in corners, with scabs** (Graph.); **U. in corners, with sticking in them** (Hep.) *and soreness of tongue, palate and inside of gum;* U. on lower. Swelling; *of lower;* of upper lip and gum; *with itching;* with burning pain. Itching eruption on upper. Corrosive itching pimples. *Sticking in upper on touch.* Cutting in upper. *Smarting pain in a wart that had been on upper for eight years, it bleeds on washing and is painful on touch.* Feels as if covered and gives a sour taste when touched with tongue. Itching of upper.

Clinical.—Caries of the bones of the face, especially of the malar-bones, which become sore and painful as from splinters.

Mouth.—Teeth. *Yellow* (Iod., Lyc.). *Loose; and painful on chewing* (Merc.). *Feeling as if soft and spongy,* *fear of biting them together lest they fall out, on slightest sucking of teeth blood exuded from gum.* Sticking; at night, with burning in them; *on taking anything cold or warm into mouth;* with swelling of cheek; in upper molars, extending to their crowns. *Tearing;* with swelling of cheek and a red spot in middle of it. *Boring on touch of anything cold or warm.* Jerking, < hollow T. and in evening; constrictive, in hollow, with bubbling sensation. Throbbing, now in one, now in all, < evening in bed, preventing sleep. Pain during menses; P. in a lower molar on chewing; < leaning head on pillow; in upper, with swelling of cheek and tightness in it; in upper incisors and a lower hollow molar, as if loose and blunted, or as if they had been bent forward and were loose, in evening, > warm food. Drawing; at night, with grumbling, and in jaws; about midnight, with sticking in them and swelling of gum; extending to larynx; sharp, in r. and in head. Seem too long. Coldness. Sensation of softness (Weichheit), > eating.

Gums.—*Swelling* during menses; *S., with such looseness of teeth that she could have taken them out* (Merc.); *of upper*, even of sockets of teeth; *and white.* Bleeding. *Feel affected and are red and enlarged between teeth*, next day tender. Cutting in upper. Pain and sore feeling. Itching.

Tongue.—**Blisters, with burning pain on touch** (Nat. m., Lyc.); painful B. on sublingual glands; and dry, brownish, with swollen papillæ. **Painful pimples on sides.** Painful, raised papillæ. Pale, moist. Swollen and of citron appearance; S. and of lemon color. T. and inside of mouth yellow and denuded in places. T. and inside of lips covered with a lemon-yellow membrane. Coated; in morning, and dry; with the febrile symptoms; yellow in two stripes, with red excoriations; whitish, whitish-yellow, with bitter taste. *Bitten when chewing.* Hits against teeth. *Sticking in root when not swallowing*, in evening in bed. *Sore pain in red part. Sensitive, even to soft food, which causes biting.* Dry; and white; and sticking to palate in morning on waking. Stammering. Speech almost impossible in morning.

Ulcers on inside of cheeks, with sticking (compare *Ka. chl.*); *inside of cheeks, uvula, palate, fauces and as far as could be seen covered with U. and yellowish-gray membrane, red, swollen, painful and offensive. M. and throat swollen and bright red, with pain and burning in mouth, throat and stomach. M., fauces and tongue covered with a white membrane that could be torn off easily.* Covered with a whitish-yellow membrane. White. M. and fauces deep yellow, and tongue looking as if covered with Indian meal. *Mucous membrane of cheeks easily gets between teeth so that he bites it when chewing.* Tenacious mucus. Spitting out of blood-stained mucus. *Pain, and in throat and stomach; in M., palate and œsophagus, with burning.* Burning at night. Soreness; and of throat. Constriction. All parts seem stiff and swollen in morning on waking. Sensation as if all parts were asleep.

Dryness; superiorly on palate; in morning; in morning, with scraping as after much smoking; *without thirst, with swollen, hot lips;* with dry lips, tongue feels scalded, tips and edges very red. **Salivation** (Merc.). *Bloody saliva is expectorated in morning;* S. colored with blood, < mental work; spitting out much tenacious; sweetish. **Foul odor** (Iod., Merc.). Taste sweetish in morning; T. of blood caused by cough; salt to water; of the food long after eating. Bitter taste; in forenoon; afternoon. *Sour taste;* in morning; in evening; after eating; caused by black bread, with vomiting; that burns the throat.

Clinical.—Gums become unhealthy and bleed easily; the teeth are loose and the saliva is bloody, and there is a putrid odor from the mouth; with these conditions the drug is frequently indicated in a mercurial cachexia. Ulceration of the mouth, with great fetor, the ulcers spread rapidly, like mercurial ulcers, but when touched they have sharp splinter-like pains; these ulcers extend into the throat and simulate diphtheria. Ulceration of the sides of the tongue, with tough, stringy mucus. Tongue coated yellow as a rule, though sometimes white in the morning.

Throat.—*Submaxillary glands swollen* (Iod., Merc.); with pain on moving and touching neck; swollen sensation. *Pain in submaxillary glands;* r.; and in neck. Itching of the swollen parotids. *Hawking of mucus. Mucus posteriorly.* **A morsel sticks in pharynx when eating, as if P. were constricted. White patches on tonsils, then on back of throat, then inside of mouth and lips,** *the deposit becomes yellowish and tongue coated yellow, with red tip and margins*, swallowing painful, throbbing in tonsils and stiffness in muscles of throat. *Swelling of tonsils; and uvula; and arch of palate, with pain and injected vessels. Redness of fauces, with excoriations and yellow membrane; of fauces and posterior pharynx;* R. and swelling of pharynx, epiglottis and aditus laryngis, with burning and titillation in larynx and pharynx. *Ulcers in fauces, with salivation.* **Hawking of mucus.**

Sticking (Ka. c.); *on long talking; on coughing; with swelling; in tonsils, with burning in fauces behind uvula.* Tearing sore pain in pharynx, chest and stomach after drinking at beginning of meal. *Soreness; with tickling cough. Pain;* and in larynx; region of hyoid bone and of pit; < lateral compression on larynx; behind suprasternal notch, < drinking water; in pit extending to pit of stomach, in morning; posteriorly on swallowing food, extending down inner surface of back; in tonsils, with soreness of uvula; *sore, in pharynx; on swallowing, as if swollen, raw and ulcerated; as if swollen and thick* during day and evening, *with sore pain; on swallowing food, as if it would not go down;* burning, and in epigastrium.

Feeling of a lump on empty swallowing. Rawness, with smarting down œsophagus. *Scraping;* and cough; and inclination to cough on reading aloud; with roughness and dryness; as if something prevented speech and swallowing. Tickling. Bitterness. Acidity; after eating fat. *Dryness and heat; D. low down posteriorly*, with heat at night. Burning after supper. **Swallowing difficult**; possible only for liquids; referred to a line from top of sternum down to l. side; *S. painful; impossible. When eating food is forced into choanæ, with a disagreeable sensation, then it is drawn downward with mucus.* When eating food is forced into choanæ and towards nose, as if pharynx could not grasp the food. Food arrested at a point corresponding to upper edge of sternum.

Œsophagus.—Pain; < swallowing. Feeling of a knot rising in it. Constriction so that he could swallow only by gulps, a part of the fluid regurgitating through nostrils. Heartburn down to pit of stomach.

Clinical.—Sore throat, with pain as from splinters on swallowing, with much salivation. Syphilitic ulceration of the mouth and throat. Enlargement of the parotid glands. Diphtheritic sore throat, with high fever, nausea and vomiting, deposit on tonsils and posterior walls of the pharynx, feeling of a foreign

substance on swallowing, with cutting pain. Diphtheria, with excoriating discharge from nose or corners of mouth; sometimes it seems as if the discharge from the throat affected the stomach, on account of the taste, uneasiness and aversion to food. Rheumatic soreness of palate muscles following severe influenza.

Stomach.—*Hunger great* (*Iod.*, Lyc.), *with weariness of life.* Ravenous H.; dissatisfied with milk and gruels; constant H., but speedy satiety on eating. Desire for fat and herring. Craving for food, but everything was soon rejected. Little appetite, immediate satiety, with eructations after a little food. Cannot eat bread, she can eat only cooked food. Satiety, with dulness in head. *Appetite lost;* < morning; but she eats and soon becomes qualmish. Aversion to food; to sweets; to cooked meat; to animal food. *Thirst great;* for water in morning on waking; at night; obliged to drink while eating.

Eructations the first half of the night, with cramps in stomach; *before and after eating;* after dinner, with flatulence; after eating, with bitter and sour vomiting; after eating, then heartburn from stomach to throat; with heartburn; *sour; empty;* empty, in morning; tasting of the dinner eaten hours previously; offensive; bilious, when eating, < evening; of partly digested food, with insipid taste in mouth. Hiccough; from morning till evening.

Nausea; all day; in morning before breakfast, till she fell asleep again; in evening, with weakness, then excessive yawning; after soft stool; *after eating;* after eating, with diarrhœa; in throat after eating, > moving about; < moving about, with sick feeling like faintness and anxiety as if she would eructate alternating with ravenous hunger, pain in stomach as from emptiness, and waterbrash; > vomiting; > eating and drinking, with heat from pit of stomach to pit of throat; *with heaviness and dulness of head;* with anxiety and trembling; with stitches in side of chest; with unquenchable thirst, but drinking caused increase of pricking in stomach and of nausea; with general sick feeling and movements of body, as after an emetic; with general sick feeling, chilliness after the usual coffee and necessity to lie down; as from heat.

Retching. Vomiting; caused by drink; after dinner, with pain over eyes and in parietal bones as if head would burst; with excruciating pain and anxiety; with pain in mouth, throat and stomach; with burning thirst; with restlessness and delirium; violent; of everything but cold milk; of food and watery fluid after swallowing; bitter and sour; *constant, of tenacious, purulent and bloody mucus;* of a fluid neutral to test-paper; of green mucus about every fifteen minutes, then neuralgia in gums, teeth, jaws and throat lasting about fifteen minutes; of blood; coagulated blood and fluid, next day V. of bloody fluid, with a shred of offensive mucous membrane; black, offensive blood; thin, black blood and of an offensive black, fibrous membrane nearly a foot in diameter, containing bloodvessels; of a ropy, white and yellowish substance streaked with blood; serous brownish fluid mixed with blood and yellow mucus; incessant, of dark, sanguineous and grumous fluid.

Epigastric region distended and sensitive to pressure. Motion near l. side of pit. Sticking anteriorly beneath pit. Cramps, with pain and tenderness; C. as after taking cold. Spasmodic griping; and pinching. Clawing in morning after rising, extending into chest, then attacks of griping in abdomen. Gnawing in morning fasting. Pain; in epigastric region; in morning on waking, and in back; at night; at night, waking her; at night in sleep, > waking; in epigastric region on touch; below S. caused by cough; when fasting; after eating, with coldness of it; in region of cardiac orifice on swallowing food; above S. and pit when walking in open air; < pressure; < before eating, > eating, with empty eructations; in epigastrium, ileo-cæcal region and region of S. Romanum, with sensitiveness to pressure; in pit, with sudden burning as if he would vomit blood; above S. so that he dared not stretch out straight, > eructations; sore, during the day; intermittent; spasmodic, in pit; spasmodic drawing, in pit, extending to navel, with tension, causing short breath.

Tenderness at pylorus. Pressure upon S. and pit when walking in open air. *S. and abdomen tense after a moderate meal, clothes seem too tight* (Lyc.). Uneasiness in epigastric region on pressure. Spasmodic constriction. Pulsation in pit. Orgasm in region of pit. Burning; in epigastrium; and in chest.

Abdomen.—Threw himself on A., writhing in paroxysms of agony, pressing his A., groaning and beseeching to be stabbed. Distention; in the place of a hernia; in morning on waking; in morning, not > soft stool, with colicky uneasiness, movements, pain and rumbling; during menses; with constipation; < l. hypochondrium, extending to umbilical region, dulness on percussion, fluctuations, pressure painful; flatulent, with rumbling from morning till evening. Contraction of muscles. *Rumbling;* after eating; with *uneasiness* and thin stools. Gurgling after eating. *Emission of flatus;* offensive. Movements of flatus, with discomfort.

Sticking, < pressure. *Cutting in morning in bed,* then soft stool; C., with diarrhœa and cold feet; through A., centering at pit of stomach. Cramp; at night; about once an hour, not > black fluid stools, which occurred about every fifteen minutes; and greenish stools, with tenesmus. *Griping;* in morning after a good stool; in morning, with emission of much flatus; *at night,* with restless sleep; before a good stool; when drinking water during a meal; then soft stool. Pain; *before stool,* with drawing; before emission of flatus; during menses, and in small of back; after frequent and in part ineffectual urging to stool; flatulent; flatulent, in morning after rising; as from taking cold; drawing, extending into thighs; twisting drawing, before emission of flatus; in a spot as if something would come out there. Sensation as before diarrhœa. Constriction, with itching; spasmodic C. Tension. Sensitiveness. Uneasiness at night, with frequent waking; U. at night, with anxiety in A. and heat of head and hands. Qualmishness some hours after a meal.

Hypochondria.—*Sticking in hepatic region, < motion;* in region of spleen on motion. Pain on coughing; P. in hepatic region during menstruation; in l., < towards front; *in hepatic region, with tension;* in morning passing up walls of chest, meeting at upper third of sternum, causing a terrible fit of coughing, with bursting headache and pricking in face, temples, etc. Swollen sensation in spleen. Nausea under short ribs frequently during the day, with anxiety, without inclination to vomit.

Side.—Sticking in a hernial spot in l. Pinching in r. during afternoon nap. *Pressure in l.*

Umbilical Region.—Distention. Griping, < moving and bending body, with drawing. Burrowing below umbilicus. Pain; after stool. Constriction. Pressure in middle abdomen as from a lump.

Hypogastrium.—*Swelling of inguinal glands, suppurative, with pain on walking, the whole limb seems paralyzed and muscles tense.* Sticking above pubis when urinating; intermittent S., with pain on touch. Burrowing and griping. Cutting in r. side, with tension. Cramplike pain on appearance of menses; C. pain, as if it would burst during menstruation, with constant eructations and inability to remain quiet in any place. Labor-like pain during menstruation, then dragging into vagina. Pain as if everything would come out of genitals during menstruation, with pain in small of back extending into hips and down legs. Drawing pain, with shivering. Pain in l. groin as if from a rupture, > walking. Constriction of inguinal glands.

Clinical.—Chronic enlargement of the liver.

Rectum.—*Fissures more in R. than in anus after stool* (Graph., Sil.). Painful protrusion. **Stitches** in evening; **during and after stool, with spasmodic constriction in anus** (Sil.); *in R. and anus after stool, with scraping;* when coughing. **Pain during stool, as if something would be torn asunder** (Sul. ac.). *Sticking cutting in R. and anus during stool, with dragging.* Griping. *Pressure.* **Itching**; from thread-worms. **Burning**; *at night on waking, and in morning; with pinching; extending to perineum,* with ineffectual urging. *Inactivity and inability to evacuate fæces.* Dragging towards R., then painful hæmorrhoids. Urging, but a scanty stool. Sensation after stool as if more should be passed. *Ineffectual desire after stool; constant ineffectual desire.*

Clinical.—Ulceration of the rectum, with severe pain after stool. Extensive ulceration of the rectum, following dysentery which had been badly treated by local injections.

Anus.—*Hæmorrhoids* after pressure downward in back, when standing; *swelling; protruding, painless, discharging blood with every stool; with* **prickling in rectum**; *painful; burning.* Fissures in evening. *Discharge of blood with stool; D. of bright red blood; fetid D. Moisture and itching. Soreness; moist, between A. and nates when walking.* Biting acridity with the stool. Pain as if hæmorrhoids would form. *Constriction. Itching* when walking in open air and after stool. *Burning* (Sil.); *all day, < after urinating; with hard stool; after stool* (Iris). Perineum, painful pimples; drawing stitches extending towards anus.

Clinical.—Fissure of the anus, with constant oozing of fetid moisture, frequently burning stools, raw smarting, as if cut with a knife. Stricture of the anus, with accumulation of pus in fistulous ulcers. Hæmorrhoids that have ceased to bleed, but are very painful and pendulous.

Stool.—*Diarrhœa; frequent;* every other day; *twice in morning, with tenesmus;* yellowish-white. Pasty. Soft, twice daily. **Constipation; painless. In hard masses.** *Hard, scanty; H., enveloped in mucus,* at first only every other day, afterwards daily; *with pricking cutting in anus;* like sheep-dung, with pressure and with mucus; alternating with a thin one. *Bloody, with tenesmus* (Merc.); *and painful; and dysenteric, with tenesmus, fever and headache; of much black, offensive blood; of B. and pseudo-membranes, painful and frequent. Dysentery; with fever. Offensive, with offensive flatus.* Containing undigested food. Small, dark. *Frequent, of only mucus, at times with cutting and urging;* F., with shivering and qualmishness under short ribs. Difficult, but not hard; *D., with straining and burning in rectum.*

Clinical.—Dysentery, with exceedingly painful discharges, great tenesmus and frequent unsuccessful efforts at stool. Diarrhœa, with burning, slimy stools and violent colic; the discharges are usually offensive, dark green or watery, with pieces of membrane varying in size, like scrapings of the intestines, sometimes streaked with blood. Diarrhœa, with most violent cutting pain lasting for hours after the stool (during typhoid). Constipation; stools hard, scanty, with painful burning in rectum (*Iris*, Sil., Sul.).

Urinary Organs.—Burning pain in bladder. *Urging;* at night, with cutting colic; *at night with scanty discharge* (Merc.); *frequent, with scanty discharge.* Micturition easy, profuse; frequent M. at night; involuntary (in a child); *in a thin stream, as from stricture of urethra.* Polyuria. Urine suppressed; (bladder empty).

Urethra.—*Orifice swollen and dark red. Discharge of bloody matter; of prostatic fluid after a difficult stool;* drops of thin mucus, not stringy like prostatic fluid, after micturition; tenacious mucus after micturition; drops of mucus when not urinating; yellow matter. **Sticking in orifice.** *Cutting. Smarting when urinating.* Pain on touch; sore P. when urinating. *Burning when urinating; after U.;* in forepart compelling micturition, which aggravates it.

Urine.—Brownish, offensive, biting; B., causing stains like coffee stains. Dark; but soon becomes white and turbid, after micturition increased dryness of throat; a pint, of the consistency of pea-soup. Like brandy, but not strong in odor, afterwards copious and straw-colored, with occasionally a slight hippuric odor. *Cold when passed. Offensive; like horse's urine;* odor like tobacco; ammoniacal odor and whitish sediment. Clear on passing, but on standing it becomes cloudy and thready and deposits a bright red tenacious sediment. Copious, pale. *Scanty; and turbid, offensive. Sediment red.*

Clinical.—Ulceration of the urethra, with smarting and burning when urinating. Albuminuria, with pressing pain in the region of the kidneys, fetid breath, scanty urine. Frequent micturition, the urine has a strong odor. Cystitis, with violent pain in the region of the bladder and passage of almost clear blood, with urging to urinate. Oxaluria. The strong-smelling urine, which the patients requiring Nit. ac. usually have, is to be compared with Benzoic acid.

Sexual Organs.—Falling out of hair. Itching. **Penis, denuded spot becomes ulcerated and will not heal;** itching pimples; *ulcer, with elevated, lead-colored, sensitive edges;* red spots become covered with scabs; moisture; *sore pain in tip when urinating;* throbbing and pressure; *itching; itching, < glans, beneath prepuce;* itching tickling as from gnat-bites. Great inclination to erections; E. in morning in bed, with pain in urethra; E. in evening after lying down; with burning and sticking in urethra; *violent, at night,* even after an emission; violent, at night on waking; spasmodic, disagreeable, after midnight, obliged to toss about uneasily; wanting.

Corona Glandis.—**Superficial ulcers, looking clean, but exuding offensive matter.** *Flesh-colored excrescences, exuding offensive moisture and* **bleeding on touch** (Hepar). Brown, painful spots.

Prepuce.—**Itching vesicles that open and become covered with dry scabs.** *Burning itching pimple on inner surface, and after rubbing a yellow ulcer even with skin, covered with thick matter,* without pain, surrounded by redness. *Superficial, yellow, ulcerating spots like flat chancres,* moist but painless, on inner surface, on both sides of frænum. *Inflammation and swelling, with burning pain, and on inner surface soreness and small ulcers secreting an offensive ichor, that stains the linen like bloody matter.* Swelling of P. and phimosis, without much redness, and on its inner surface and margin and in meatus urinarius chancre-like suppurating ulcers, with flat edges, without inflammation, *with sticking tearing, < towards evening, preventing sleep at night,* still more < violent erections towards morning. Mucus beneath P., behind corona glandis. **Sticking.** *Itching,* with moist spots on its inner surface.

Itching of scrotum; with sore spots. Crawling on scrotum, extending through groin. Swelling of testicles; of r., with pain on touch. Testicles painful to touch, with tearing in spermatic cords; bruised pain in l. T.; twisting pain in l.; burning pain in l.; drawing pain.

Power diminished, at times absent, with slow, unsatisfactory erections, only excited by fondling, that at the next time are all the more satisfactory and complete. Excitement; with discharge of prostatic fluid; and erections without lascivious fancies; *wanting.* Slight voluptuous sensation during coition. Frequent emissions.

Female.—Constriction towards genitals during menstruation. Dry burning. *Itching of pudenda* towards evening; *I. when walking, then soreness;* I., and she rubs the fœtus almost sore at night. Vagina, swelling of one side and of labia minora, with burning itching; *ulcer even with surface, covered with yellow pus, with burning itching pain;* sticking; sticking extending upward when walking in open air; itching and inflammation of V. and labia majora. *Cherry-brown, offensive discharge from vagina.* Leucorrhœa profuse; *L. of bad odor; stringy, mucous, flesh-colored; greenish, mucous, after menstruation.* Menstruation too early; reappeared a few days after close of menstruation and was pale; too late; too late (at the full moon) and rather too profuse, with headache and colic (in a young person); too profuse.

Clinical.—Syphilitic ulcerations and erosions of the penis and prepuce. It is particularly useful for venereal ulcers when the ulcers bleed easily and there are sharp, splinter-like pains. Condylomata on the prepuce, with offensive oozings. Inflammation and swelling of the testicles, with pain in the cords, extending to the abdomen. Herpes of the prepuce. Leucorrhœa yellow and acrid. Inflammation of the cervix uteri, with warty excrescences and excoriating discharge, general tendency to uterine hæmorrhage. Erosions and ulcerations of the cervix, with yellow discharge. Obstinate hæmorrhage from the uterus, with pressure in the hypogastrium, pain in thighs, strong-smelling urine; aching in rectum after stool, general anæmia.

Respiratory Organs.—Rattling in trachea in morning in bed, then retching cough and bloody expectoration, then sick feeling, chilliness, etc. Scraping in trachea. Sticking in region of larynx. *Hoarse;* in morning. Voice rough; feeble.

Cough; on deep breathing; from constriction of throat, < night during sleep; < *night,* and in the day when lying down and falling asleep, *he can sleep only towards morning;* < night, with shattering of whole body, often taking away the breath, as in whooping cough, with stitches in chest, sore throat and fever; with redness of face and body. *C. causing anxiety and vomiting of mucus and food.* Retching, in evening in bed. Violent, after midnight; V., with whistling inspiration, redness and sweat of face and body, the paroxysms of cough so increased by the inhalation of the gas that it caused a taste of blood, nausea and vomiting of mucus and food, longer exposure caused oppressed breathing and anxiety, afterwards rawness, soreness and weariness of chest. Spasmodic, with fits of suffocation; S., ineffectual, ending in gagging; croaking, paroxysmal, from pit of stomach, > night. Hacking, in morning; H. after eating, with irritation and crawling in larynx. Dry; *before midnight,* in sleep; *and rough before midnight;* and barking, < evening. Loose. Cough with expectoration of mucus; of bright blood, then easier breathing; C. and hawking of much black blood and blowing of the same from nose; retching C., causing expectoration of black, clotted blood.

Expectoration.—Yellow, bitter. Of green, frothy mucus.

Respiration.—Threatened with asphyxia. Difficult; in morning; in morning, and painful, stridulous; at night, interrupting sleep; on waking in night and in morning, with anxiety; *from cough;* when walking in open air; as from rush of blood to chest; and rough, the quantity of air taken into lungs appearing to the ear applied to chest to be small, afterwards breathing more labored and a low whistle at each inspiration, later respiration more croupy. Short. *Catching;* at every attempt at a full inspiration. Could be heard in bronchi. Slow and feeble. Lost when walking in open air, and feet heavy.

Clinical.—Cough < forepart of night, with feeling as if the chest were too full, pain as if bound with an iron band, with tendency to tuberculosis. Chronic cough from the larynx, with stinging and smarting as if ulcerated. Phthisis of the larynx, with extensive ulceration. Night cough, fatiguing, paroxysmal, cough caused by laughing or crying, great weakness.

Chest.—*Whistling on inspiration, with râles.* Adherent mucus. Lungs filled with frothy mucus, and death with symptoms as in drowning. Broncho-pneumonia, with violent fever. Signs of commencing tubercle in apex of r. lung. Dulness on percussion over lower part, with dulness of respiratory murmur, raising of frothy mucus and rawness of chest on coughing.

Sticking in r. side and scapula; externally; under sternum and borders of ribs; through lungs in forenoon; in r. breast in evening after lying down; in middle of l. evenings, on nearly every breath when coughing and breathing, < lying down; at night when lying on back he started up and was attacked by S. in r.; S. and pinching at one time below breast, at another in back, at night; in r. side on breathing; in sides on stooping, breathing deeply and reaching high up, with suppurative pain; on sternum, with drawing; in upper part, inside r. ribs, extending to abdomen and back; in l. in morning, making respiration difficult; in and below l. as from incarcerated flatus.

Cramp. Spasmodic pain anteriorly and in back, waking him at night; S. pain in C. and opposite in back after midnight, < inspiration. Twisting pain in r. Pain in r. in morning after many empty eructations; P. caused by cough; externally, < stooping; anteriorly on ribs, even on breathing, with bruised sensation; in l. as if blood would not go through heart. Sore pain when eating; when coughing; on respiration. Soreness; in folds beneath breasts; under sternum, with burning pain; caused by cough, with rawness and weariness; muscular, through intercostal spaces. Spasmodic drawing.

Fulness. Tightness; when sitting and walking, < bending backward. *Oppression;* with short, anxious, difficult respiration; so that she could not get her breath. Constriction; of lower part; in r., < sitting; across lower part, with dyspnœa, incessant cough, with raising of greenish, slimy sputa; about lower, a feeling as if he could not inflate lungs; above heart, taking away the breath; spasmodic, of r. upper muscles, obliging him to bend together.

Throbbing like palpitation, above stomach, < rapid walking, > drinking wine, but returning. Heat; in upper part, recurring at times during the day; if she eats anything salt. *Rush of blood to upper part;* to C. and heart at night. Symptoms of œdema of lungs.

Clinical.—Pneumonia in old people. Useful in some stages of phthisis, with hectic, soreness of the chest, hæmorrhages from the lungs, offensive, bloody and purulent expectoration (Cap.).

Heart.—Stitches at night, with heat and thirst. Anxious constriction, > a violent beat of heart. Rush of blood; with anxiety. Paroxysmal trembling. Palpitation; in evening in bed; *when walking slowly, with sudden loss of breath; on ascending steps, with loss of breath and anxiety;* on exertion, with sweat; on exertion after dinner, with heat; from excitement; during diarrhœa; < motion, with weakness and anxiety as if he would faint; in paroxysms, with anxiety, causing oppression of breath. Violent beating and pulsation below clavicle, waking him after 3 A.M. Action weak; and retarded.

Pulse.—Rapid; in morning, and small; with heat; and hard; and small; and small, hard; and small, contracted; and feeble, intermittent every fourth or fifth beat. Small; and weak. Weak. Irregular and fluttering; I. and weak; and slow; I., after a regular beat two small quick ones, the fourth omitted. Nun's murmur could be distinctly heard on r. vena jugularis.

Neck.—Swelling on r. side similar to a goitre; glandular S. on r. side, with stiffness of neck and tongue. Cracking of vertebræ. Tensive pain in muscles. Drawing in muscles as if a weight were hanging upon them. Weakness of nape. *Stiffness of nape.*

Back.—Sticking in vertebræ when standing. Tearing in B. and chest on motion, < night, with sticking. Pinching in flesh. Pain after taking cold; burning pain; drawing, in evening; drawing, and in loins. Stiffness of spine.

Scapulæ.—Spasmodic jerking in dorsal muscles during manual labor. Stitches between S. at times, always followed by eructations; S. between S. and in forepart of chest, impeding breathing, more when stooping than when sitting quietly; tearing S. when walking in open air, could not lie upon it at night. Pinching between S. *Pain between S.;* in l. S. and region of kidney when walking in open air; drawing, under S. Attacks twice daily, at first a drawing in back like a grasping in dorsal sides below ribs, extending around into stomach, where it turns about and disappears as with an eructation.

Lumbar Region.—Stitching and coughing. Pain; in region of kidneys; on appearance of menses; at night, so that he must lie on abdomen; in bone, almost only on motion, so that he could scarcely walk; *drawing,* towards evening; drawing, after coition, and in spine and thighs; *as if stiff;* burning, in r., that disheartened him and made him unable to think or work. Spasmodic constriction from kidneys to bladder. Tension so that he could not breathe deeply. Pulsation.

Extremities.—Swelling of hands and feet. Trembling during a quarrel. Cracking of joints on motion. Jerking in joints, with tearing. Aching; in bones; in gouty joints, hitherto painless; as if dislocated, after walking. Bruised pain the day before and during menses; B. pain, she could scarcely move arms and lower limbs. Pain like rigidity in l. lower and arm. *Drawing,* > stretching; D., with burning. Tension in lower and arms. Sensitiveness of joints in morning, without distinct pain. Weakness; of joints; of joints, with trembling of them; of joints, with bruised feeling in them; limbs and hands seem weak and paralyzed on pressure or when lying in an uncomfortable position, as if the circulation were arrested by a band. Heaviness as from weariness in morning in bed, and in joints. Paralyzed sensation.

Upper Extremities.—*Axillary glands swollen; and painful, and inflamed;* r. A. gland sensitive all the forenoon. Stitches in l. shoulder on touch, respiration or if she is chilly. Pressure upon r. shoulder. Pain in l. shoulder-joint; bruised, in l. shoulder; P. in shoulders as if she had carried a weight upon them. Tension and constriction in shoulders and arms, drawing arms to body.

Arm.—Jerking and drawing, and in fingers. Tearing, < motion, also disturbing sleep. Pain in r.; bruised, in r.; *drawing;* sprained, in l., she could not move it backward nor forward; weary, and tingling in muscles. Drawing as if sprained, and in hand. Weakness as after fever. Falling asleep of r. at night. Paralysis of r.; seems paralyzed after shaking.

Upper Arm.—Jerking of muscles all day, < deltoid. Trembling of muscles of r. *Bruised pain,* so that she could not raise it, with coldness of hand. Hammering pain in humeri as if they would be shattered. Drawing in humeri.

Elbow.—Tearing extending to wrist, with jerking. Pain on stretching arm.

Forearm.—Trembling, and of hand. Sticking extending to back of hand and finger, with pain. Tearing in l. F. and hand, with pain on touch. Bruised pain externally on motion and touch. Paralytic drawing pain nearly all day. Drawing deep in muscles, extending into bones.

Wrist.—Tearing in region; T. in l. Pinching in r. during afternoon nap. Pain in r.; bruised P. Drawing in r.

Hand.—Trembling. Twitching. Stitches in r.; in l. palm. Cramplike pain when grasping anything. Stiff pain in l. palm on grasping anything. Drawing pain towards evening; paralytic D. pain in H. and first joint of thumb on falling asleep and on waking. *Drawing. Falling asleep* in morning in bed; immediately on resting it on anything, with numbness.

Fingers.—Swelling in morning on waking; painful S. of a joint. Stitches in middle joints, he could not bend them without pain. Tearing in l. little. Pain on moving them, with tension in middle joints; bruised P. in l. little; burning, in l.; frequent drawing, in extensor tendons, extending forward. Falling asleep, with crawling in them. Dead in cold air.

Lower Extremities.—Gait weak and tottering. The child limps and steps only upon toes. Jerking in l.

at night in bed. **Tearing, < night**; *T. in bones. Bruised pain as from fatigue.* Aching in afternoon, as if she had taken cold in them, and she woke in night with deep-seated coldness and *deep-seated feeling as if dogs were gnawing the flesh and bones and as if the sinews were pulled up*, < feet and thighs, kept her awake all night, transiently > hard rubbing (chattering of teeth always on waking with the coldness), disappeared suddenly after breakfast, leaving the parts tender to touch and as if clothes were too heavy. Drawing pain in r. Drawing extending downward in evening. Heat in joints, with lassitude in them. Weakness when lying. Heaviness; < sitting; with bruised pain. Stiffness. Inability to walk.

Thigh.—Sticking in r. at night; S. at head of femur. Prickling. Pain in region of r. gluteals; in nates at night when riding in a carriage; inferiorly and internally above knee, making lower limb weak and stiff. Bruised feeling in l.; B. pain in lower part on moving it forward; as if broken. Paralytic pain in l. thigh and leg at intervals of two hours. Sore pain in nates on touch. Soreness near scrotum. S. between thighs on walking. *Tensive pain in r. hip-joint* on rising from a seat and beginning to walk, as if head of femur would be put out of joint. Drawing pain about hips. Drawing in evening, with itching on skin; D. in muscles as if a weight were hanging on them; D. in nates extending into feet. Spasmodic constriction in middle of T. and below calves often during the day. Throbbing as if internally ulcerated, they do not tolerate the slightest touch, are at one time hot, at another cold. Weakness of l. after a walk, with sensation of stagnation of blood in it.

Knee.—Cracking when walking, so that sometimes he could not move from the spot. *Stitches* in hollow at night; S. when standing; on outer side when walking; when coughing, so that it cracks, with pain in patella on walking. Tearing extending to hip, at night in bed, after much walking; extending up thigh, when walking. Sharp pain extending to tips of toes. Sprained pain, < descending stairs; S. and bruised pain in patella, when walking, < descending steps, > walking on a level, also pain on bending it excessively, with cracking in knee. *Pain in hollow as if stiff*, so that he must limp on beginning to walk. Pain in l. patella so that he could scarcely step. Drawing pain about K., ankles and other joints. Drawing ending with a jerk; D. extending up thigh on sitting down, > sitting, with tearing; to groin, with rheumatic pain, and with soreness of testes. Painful contraction. Tension in hollow in afternoon, with contracted sensation; T. on motion; in hollow, as if tendons were too short. Swollen sensation in hollows on walking in open air. Stiffness of r.

Leg.—Painless lumps in calves in morning. Calves, cramp in at night; towards morning; on drawing up leg; on stretching out foot, for example, on drawing on boot. Cramplike pain in muscles and tendons of lower part, with pain on touch. Drawing extending to knees; paralytic D. in bones; paroxysmal, in middle of calf, sometimes changing to sudden jerks. Paralytic pain in whole, with such heaviness and lassitude that he does not know where to put it. Weakness in lower part after walking a little. Numbness in evening in bed, then cramp in it, < calves, at last sticking and prickling in heels.

Ankle.—*Cracking when walking.* Sprained pain in morning on rising. Stitches in malleoli. Heaviness in malleoli as if compressed, extending through feet, on walking.

Foot.—Swelling after walking in open air. Sticking in r. Tearing; in r. metatarsus; in r. in morning. Pain in periosteum of os calcis; in corns; with intolerance of shoes. Drawing pain when walking; D. pain from ball to heel, with weakness. Drawing extending to knees; D. in upper part of r. metatarsus; extending to back, on motion. Smarting in corns. Weakness; at night.

Toes.—Corn on l. middle, with burning pain. Stitches in r. great and sole, delaying sleep. Pain beneath nail of great; ball of little, when walking. Toes, soles and corns sensitive as if inflamed.

Skin.—*Jaundice, yellowness, with constipation. Face scaly. Dark freckles. Black sweat-pores on face. Redness of great toe and its ball, with heat and sticking in it, as if it had been frozen;* R. of one toe after wetting feet, with inflammation and swelling; behind l. ear, with suppuration and itching. *Chilblains* on great toes. Inflamed swelling (erysipelas) of l. cheek, with stinging, nausea and chilliness, then heat, the shivering always returning on rising in bed. Blue protuberances and spots on hands, itching mostly at night. Warts on neck; on middle of sternum; on upper lid, with a pimple; a congenital growth on abdomen like a wart becomes sensitive, sore and scabby.

Eruption on hands and between fingers, with itching burning, > rubbing; herpetic E. close to mouth, extending to chin; itching, in beard on chin. Itching tetter in beard on cheek; on wings of nose; dry tetter, painful to touch, on outer side of thigh. Pimples on forehead; on forehead below hair; at margin of hair on temple; on face; here and there, with ecchymoses; painful to touch, posteriorly on lobule of ear; on chin, with red, hard areola, at first painful to touch, > as soon as pus forms at tip, then becoming indurated, with red areola; dark red, in clusters on trunk and neck, with soreness and itching.

Pustules; on chin; on tip of thumb; red, itching-burning, here and there. Boil on side of chin; on thigh; below r. hip-joint, with tensive pain; *numerous*, particularly large on scapulæ, nape, nates, thighs and legs; numerous, about head, chin, nape, etc. Itching blisters on fourth finger; spreading B. on toes. Ulceration of an abraded spot; profuse bleeding of U. on dressing it; bloody ichor from U. corrodes the skin wherever it flows, with biting pain.

Sticking in an ulcer; S., though rather a burning, as from nettles, in and about an ulcer; in warts, with picking; in a boil in groin, with sticking itching in indurated part of it; itching, over whole body, with hives after scratching. *Tension on forehead;* on face in morning. Crawling all over body, with sticking; C. frequently from hips to toes.

Clinical.—Dermoid swellings of various sorts. Eczema. Crusts, scabs and soreness of angles of eyes, mouth, etc. (Grap.). Warts on hands. Bleeding warts. Bleeding ulcers, spreading rapidly and oozing offensive pus. Carbuncles. Urticaria. It is said that freckles have been removed by this drug.

Itching over whole body; on back; on nape; below arms; on l. hand; tip of elbows, on patella and back of foot; thighs; between thighs; in hollows of knees and bends of elbows; on feet; in warts; great toe in evening, with crawling in it; on outer part of thigh at night in bed, soon returning after scratching; neck when walking in open air; in spots like freckles, on chest; *on back*, and pain after scratching; of hands, with chilblains and swelling; in spots, bleeding on scratching; burning, on r. lower limb.

Sleep.—Yawning; after a meal. *Sleepiness; during the day;* in morning after rising; in afternoon; dizzy, so that he almost fell asleep when walking and standing, with drawing pain along skin on inner side of thighs. Overpowering sleepiness all day; after a meal; after supper, with stretching and impatience. Sleep heavy, unrefreshing, from which he woke with anxious effort in morning.

Sleeplessness; till 1 A.M.; after 1 A.M., with sweat on l. side of head and neck; *every night after about* 2 A.M; till 3 or 4 A.M.; till 4 A.M., with restlessness, then anxious dreams; after 4 A.M.; with restlessness; with heat. *Only partial sleep;* and in morning it seemed as if he had not slept at all. Visions instead of sleep every night. Little sleep, with yawning, she could not get warm before midnight. *Sleep restless; and unrefreshing;* with late falling asleep, frequent waking and many and frightful dreams.

Sleep anxious, with sobs. Starting up as from fright on falling asleep; S. during midday nap when sitting; S., with jerking in limbs. Jerking of limbs, with stretching, waking him from midday nap. Sprang out of bed several times from the deepest sleep, quite awake, about a fancied frightful event, walked about, and then knew that it was an illusion. Talking and snoring, with hands above her head. Waking at night to drink and urinate; W., with anxiety; with anxiety, obliged to cough and if he had no drink he vomited. *Early waking. Frequent waking; and inability to sleep again for a long time;* and tossing from side to side.

Dreams.—*Anxious;* and violent starting up; and crying out in sleep; so that the pulses beat on waking; and sad, vivid; as if he must die. Frightful. Of crimes that he commits. Vexatious; during the restless morning sleep. Of corpses. Confused, with partial sleep. Joyous, then horrible. Visionary, of carousing and feasting; V. and vivid, of the business of the day, in morning, then weariness. Nightmare soon after falling asleep; N., a wonderful lascivious dream, with sweat; as if some one were lying under him and holding him fast with the arms about his abdomen, as soon as he fell asleep.

Fever.—*Chilliness;* in morning in bed and all day, only in afternoon heat in face; in afternoon, then heat, then sweat, all without thirst; in afternoon in open air, then in bed dry heat, with half-waking fantasies, without sleep, only towards morning sweat and sleep; in evening, with sleepiness; in evening on moving in bed; in evening from going to bed till midnight (in August), then dry heat of lower limbs, head and body; after dinner, with pale look and coated tongue; from taking cold by riding in a wind, then heat, with sweat; < *evening;* and pallor; sensitive to cold wind; of whole body, with warm feet; especially in back, he cannot get warm and yet is internally hot; internal, in evening, with external warmth and headache as if tightly bound.

Shivering; in evening, then flushes of heat, with dryness of throat; < forenoon; as from gooseflesh, with bristling of hair.

Cold skin; and pallor. Cool sensation in head and abdomen. *Cold hands;* with ill humor; in evening, with heat of face; and feet. C. limbs in morning; limbs, with rapid, small pulse, then collapse; r. lower limb; knees; legs externally, with internal heat. *Cold feet* as far as calves during the day; feet and lower limbs towards noon; at night, preventing sleep; soles at night, preventing sleep; after a walk, with heat of head.

Heat; in evening, < feet; at night, < thighs; *at night* waking her frequently, without sweat, with *thirst* caused by dryness low down in throat and with tossing about; after slight exertion; on walking, with headache and vertigo; soon after appearance of menses, with palpitation, anxiety and trembling of all limbs; without thirst; with thirst and with scanty, turbid urine; with hot skin, full, hard, tense pulse; as after alcoholic drinks, with increased inclination to sweat; alternately feverish, cold hands, with heat of head. *Flushes of heat;* during the day, also *with sweat of hands;* towards evening, with transient sweat; in evening before going to bed, with nausea. **Dry heat; at night;** in morning in bed, then chill; internal, with thirst and febrile weakness.

Heat of blood, < hands at night, so that she could sleep but little. Orgasm of blood and weakness of limbs. Hot skin; and dry. Heat in joints; in forearms; l. wrist and palm; feet; above malleoli; beneath nail of l. great toe in evening in bed. *Heat of head; all day;* sensation of burning points or sparks on head. Heat of face in morning on waking, with inclination to sweat; H. of face in afternoon; in evening; in evening, with tremulousness; after eating, with redness of it; with coldness of rest of body; *frequently, and in hands*, with weakness of limbs; internal, in cheeks; in cheeks in flushes, also with thirst, afterwards in evening sleepiness.

Sweat in morning; and at noon *after eating; at night;* **every other night;** at night immediately on covering himself; at night in sleep; at night, during which he woke with pleasant thoughts; on walking in open air, then headache and nausea; *with cold hands and blue nails;* inclined to sweat and take cold. *Offensive*, at night; O., during physical exertion; like horse's urine. Sour, at night. Cold. Sweat on nape; head; forehead; forehead when eating; cold, on forehead. On hands; palms, with heat and redness of face; on chest at night; on parts on which she was lying at night; cold, on hands and feet. **On soles, causing soreness of toes and balls of feet, with sticking as if he walked on pins.** *Feet;* l.; *at night;* cold. *Offensive, in axillæ.*

Clinical.—It has been prescribed occasionally in scarlet fever, with red tongue and foul discharges, also in typhoid fever, with offensive, purulent, bloody stools, great prostration, especially with sore tongue, intermittent pulse, herpetic eruptions between fingers. Foul-smelling perspiration of the feet (Sil.).

Nux Moschata.

A tincture is made of the dried Nutmeg, Myristica moschata, Thun.

General Action.—A soporific or mild narcotic; characterized by marked tendency to attacks of syncope, with cardiac failure, cold extremities and extreme dryness of the skin and mucous membranes (Sec. c.). Twitchings of muscles and even general spasms have been observed. It retards and suppresses menstruation, rendering the flow thick and dark.

Allies.—Hyosc., Cannab. ind., Mosc., Nux v., Sepia, Lyc., Op., Dig.

Generalities.—Blood seemed dried up, ears and lips were white. Trembles, cannot hold still, begs to be held, legs and body jerk violently, knees up and body forward. Erethism, < limbs, simulating chorea. Convulsions. Opisthotonos.

The effect of some brandy was as if I had been electrified from mouth downward in a straight line and dying off towards feet, then it diffused itself over whole body, feeling generally as if I had hold of galvanic wires working in antagonistic directions, out of time and keeping. *Strange feeling over whole system,* **with almost irresistible sleepiness,** *jactitation of muscles* (Hyosc., Nux v.), pain and vertigo in forehead and confusion of ideas. *Intermittent wandering digging in small spots.* Wandering pinching that increased and decreased in waves, in spots in bones. Pains generally; in parts on which he lies, if he lies on a moderately hard substance; wandering, always in a small spot.

Soreness and bruised sensation. Condition as if he had cooled off after sweating violently, nape and all bones hurt, with pressure forward towards forehead. Throbbing in every part. Restless, jumping and starting. (Anxiety over whole body, with inclination to tremble.)

Weakness; on waking, with drowsiness, felt unwieldy, like a mass of metal; *and sleepiness; knees affected as if he had walked far, and sleepiness,* even talking fretted him; and lazy feeling; *so that he must lie down after accomplishing a trifle.* **Faint** (Mosch., Sep., Dig.); all day, she was forced to gasp for breath; at 5.30 P.M., with lightness, giddiness and emptiness in head; *and sickly sensation.* Sinking sensation as soon as she lay down, as if going to die, but at ease in mind and free from pain, happy and unconcerned, sensation not complete, knew all that transpired about her, but could not express herself clearly (ideas muddled, tongue thick, and coldness beginning in lower limbs).

Immobility. General numbness; except in head, only when she moved, even to eyelids, something like an electric shock would run all over her, starting from small of back, > if any one touched her, although she felt that she could not move, if by great effort she did so she was surprised at the power she had. Symptoms, especially of head, occur after eating, < after breakfast of bread and milk. Amelioration from an hour's sleep towards evening; A. in open air; dose of Nux vom.

Clinical.—Hysteria during pregnancy, with attacks of faintness. Hysteria, with enormous bloating of the abdomen, dryness of the mouth, etc. General tendency to syncope from slight causes.

Mind.—*Delirium;* with vertigo, he made remarkable gestures, used improper language in a loud tone, could not be quieted or made to sleep until he had taken tea and been bled, then profuse sweat and deep sleep, from which he woke well; delirious sleep in afternoon, with pleasant, peaceful dreams, afterwards he went to the theatre, but the way seemed to have no end (Cannab. ind.), he had control over his limbs, but was obliged to tear himself away from fanciful images in order to continue on his way, at times he was unconscious, he went straight on without recognizing the streets that he crossed, he was most concerned about the time, but he arrived earlier than he thought, and during the play fancy and reality battled with each other.

Lively, laughing and bright in forenoon. *Laughing at everything,* < going into open air, he stood still upon the street, made foolish gestures, between the attacks absence of mind and on collecting himself *everything about him seemed ludicrous,* during this he looked like an idiot, > being brought into the house (Cannab. ind.). Elated, light-headed and bewildered. Joyous fancies and he saw something ludicrous in everything. Foolish. Foolishly happy in evening, but not desirous to talk. Ridiculous or extravagant acts or expressions, like idiocy, the next moment chagrin at her conduct, said she could not control her actions, *disposed to laugh and jest at everything, stupid look for a moment,* **changeable, one moment laughing, the next crying** (Ign.). Earnest at one time, at another inclined to laugh. *Variable mood,* at one time wishes to do something, but when he is about to accomplish it changes his mind.

Alarmed, puts out hands to ward off danger, laughs heartily, then cries, sighs frequently, then starts and asks, "Where am I?" "Such blackness, the whole world seems black to me," forgets her sensations as soon as passed and her words as soon as uttered, but suddenly remembers, cries out in sleep, then suddenly asks if she has cried out, "I am crazy," "Don't let them make fun of me," can answer questions if asked very emphatically, says she has some pain, but forgets when and where, notices her own mistakes, but instantly forgets again, impatient of any delay, appeals to others to know if they do not see, hear and feel her various symptoms, sounds as if chains were in her head, pains mostly at back of head, if touched there says it touches her brain, "Oh, don't you hear my brains crack? head so queer," says her brains hit together, jumps up with an outcry of pain and says, "Oh, can't you hear them?" (the brain), cries easily, it hurts her to laugh or cry, afraid to lie down.

Fear of death at 5.30 P.M. Startled by trifles, for instance, if spoken to quickly or called by name, palpitation, with difficult breathing. Anxiety; and reeling. *Weeping mood, with burning in eyes and lachrymation* (Puls.). Ill-humored; and nervous. Annoyed by touch of any part of her body; A. by the running to and fro of the family. Indifferent. Careless in evening, nothing could have offended me.

Absence of mind, inability to think, *indifference to everything, scalp much stretched; A., he never accomplishes what he undertakes, but remains standing in one place; with senselessness and intoxicated condition; when reading, which passes into sleep. Staggering when walking, and when reflecting his mind ran upon one idea till all at once he woke from abstraction and was obliged to collect his thoughts before he knew where he was. Thoughts vanished when writing. Slowness of ideas, so that he must wait before he can answer a question* (Ph. ac., Op., Sep.).

Confusion; with strange feeling in whole system; with pain in upper half of skull and brain as if pressed together from above and the side and spasmodically seized or constricted, with sleepiness. *Talks very little, confused images before his mind, obliged to collect his thoughts before he can say anything. Omitted letters when writing, wrote in different alphabets against his will and changed from one subject to another. Incoherency on attempting to express her ideas.* Used words the opposite of what he should to express his sensations. Inability to use words properly, frequent necessity to stop in the middle of a sentence and change it entirely because she could not think of the appropriate words.

Memory lost (Hyosc., Verat., etc.); forgot what she was saying in the middle of a sentence; and inability to connect any train of thought, it seemed too much trouble to think, voices of persons in the room seemed far distant, and words spoken to her seemed spoken long before, objects in the room appeared multiplied in different sizes, she saw several bureaus, one above the other, each larger than the one below, head felt as if many times its natural size, with drawing in nape, drawing the head backward, dared not move lest she should become unconscious, dared not yield to a strong impulse to sleep lest she should die (Cannab. ind.).

Stupor; and loss of motion and sensation. Comprehends not what he reads. Dulness of senses in evening, with loss of control, she could have been led anywhere without resistance, loss of power. Uncontrolable thoughts at 2 P.M. State similar to that of an opium eater, not apprehensive though aware of some danger. Unfitted for work. *Unconsciousness; momentary, but seeming to her of half an hour's duration;* semi-conscious, unable to answer questions although her eyes were open and she apparently understood everything transpiring around her. Coma.

Clinical.—Coma, with almost complete insensibility, with great slowness of comprehension. General inclination to become unconscious during acute attacks. Bewildered senses, increasing to faintness and unconsciousness.

Head.—*Dropped forward when sitting; D., chin resting on breast, it could be raised only with much effort, and it again dropped forward. Seemed bulky and rolled about, obliged to support it with one or both hands, when sitting at a table.* Aching; in afternoon and evening; so that everything turned dark, by strong effort could see at times, but only one object at a time; < *temples, and on nodding a loose feeling as if brain beat against skull,* temples would not tolerate touch, with heat in head.

Dulness. Seemed compressed from forehead and occiput on waking from midday nap. Heaviness and pressive dulness, with swollen sensation in l. half of face and head and prickling as from an electric current. *Felt full and expanded; in evening, but painless.* Swollen sensation, and in face. Tingling. *Throbbing.* Apoplexy. Shocks. Intoxication; and indolence; all day, heaviness of head, aching between l. temple and forehead, afterwards extending towards occiput.

Rush of blood obscuring the sight; rush of blood on rising from dinner, but feeling as if an electric current passed from vertex downward, I made an effort and got mechanically down stairs, and then twice I felt as I suppose one does who is nearly insensible from cold, and that if I yielded to it I could sleep out of existence without pain, then a cold shiver, then every variety of heat and cold, every time the blood went from and returned to my head the sensation changed, sometimes feeling very hot, next very cold, once it appeared as if all the blood in the body had rushed to the head, and I thought I could hear it gushing in my ears.

Vertigo; on standing; with vanishing of thought; with lightness of head; with pressure towards forehead and feeling as if head were twice as thick as natural; with uneasiness of muscular system; with derangement of intellect, loss of memory, but conscious of all that I said and did, became loquacious, seemed to be neither in this world nor the other, felt happy and free from pain, and as I suppose one might feel who had been magnetized; as if intoxicated and sleepy.

Forehead.—**Pain; in a spot** *above l. eminence;* in l. side of sinciput; in morning; in a spot in r. upper part in morning; in l. organ of wit, afterwards it extended over l. eye, a gnawing in the organ of locality and smell; with vertigo and strange feeling in whole system; with tension and pain in scalp; (with stupefaction, at times it closed the lids and he yawned); above l. eye, pressing forward, in morning; in sinciput, extending towards l. eye, with stupefying sensation; throbbing, above l. eye in morning. Confusion and dulness; C. in forehead and temples, with fatigue.

Sticking in l. temple, with pain; intermittent S. in r.; paroxysmal S. outward in T. Pain between vertex and occiput; in a spot in V.; on V. in forenoon; drawing, in V. extending into eyes in morning. Constriction in vertex, with pressure inward and rising of warmth towards it. Pressure in V. towards forehead on stooping.

Pain in r. side in afternoon; in l. on falling asleep at noon; in various parts of l. side above forehead. Hot pressure outward in side, < temples. Pressure inward upon bone, in part above r. ear, in part at r. angle of occiput. Pain in occiput; in l. side towards nape.

Clinical.—Feeling of looseness of the brain on moving the head or on walking, < hot weather. Congestive headache, the pain seeming to be just under the bone. Neuralgia over l. eye, constrictive, burning, stinging pain, with redness of the face, difficulty in speaking, unconsciousness when the attacks are violent. Headache from overloading the stomach.

Eyes.—*Surrounded by blue rings;* at 5.30 P.M. Injected; and swollen. Enlargement, with intolerance of light, while objects seemed to float. Dull; and heavy look. Sunken. Staring into vacancy. **Dryness;** *in evening, reading by artificial light was difficult, eyes would close from sleepiness, head and forehead were dull; and roughness, so that it was not easy to open and close them* (Sep.); *with agglutination,* and with inclination of head to the left from sleepiness. Burning, with lachrymation. Felt as if starting from head. Tension about r., < lower lid, as if she could not open it, with pressure in eyes, she was obliged to draw the eye together, whereby it seemed as if she could open it wider. Swollen feeling in evening, and in lids.

Pupils dilated; and insensible; contracted, and eyes felt full. Lids spasmodically closed under influence of the spasm; unable to open, they felt heavy and stiff; upper swollen and red around the border in evening, and drooping, looking as after weeping; pressure as from sleepiness; tension and dryness. Puffiness of r. infraorbital region. **Everything looked too large** (Hyosc.) **in evening,** *my hand looked double its natural size; her hand looked too large to her* and as if spotted red. Vision misty; in evening and everything looked red. Vision vanished for an instant at 2 P.M.; momentary paroxysms of blindness, when she grasped her head and said, "How strange my head feels." By strong effort she can see, at times, but only one person or object at a time.

Clinical.—Ptosis.

Ears.—Stitches; in r. in forenoon. Pain; between

a pressing and sticking, in r. in morning; sharp, in l., < motion of jaw; as if a not very dull instrument were pressed back and forth in it. Painful heat extending towards posterior wall of pharynx (tuba Eustachii), almost as if a rough body had to be forced out, towards evening when riding in a wagon before a storm of wind and rain, the sensation began in posterior wall of pharynx, then in ear, at last extended to buccal cavity. No answer to loud summons. Buzzing. Voices sound as if far away.

Nose.—Irritation and stinging. *Dryness* (Lyc.). *Stoppage* of l. nostril; < l. nostril, with crawling as from coryza and sneezing, the stoppage > moving about and rising. Sneezing; in morning; with feeling of catarrh in nose. Catarrh of l. nostril, it is neither dry nor stopped, but it seems to him as if he could get no air through it.

Face.—*Pale;* ashy. Hippocratic at 5.30 P.M. Suffused, and eyes. Muscles drawn, denoting suffering, during spasms. Expression singular; distressed; bewildered; sick; silly, occasionally a diabolical grin. Hot stitches in l. side of chin. Pain in r. cheek-bone at night; in r. cheek extending to ear and joint of jaw, in morning. Tingling and itching. Jaws firmly closed; spasmodic constriction extending forward from joints; drawing pain in flesh on r. margin of lower. Lips swollen and stuck together; *lips, mouth and throat dry without thirst* (Stram.); *lips, palate and velum palati dry* and burning, as in catarrh; lips, mouth and throat burning.

Mouth.—Teeth. Gritting, margins of tongue torn, and bloody froth escaped from mouth. Stitch into incisors in evening; S. in teeth and l. eye, a taste in teeth like calomel, salivation, burning in eye, he is afraid to go to sleep. Boring in root. Pain in l. upper; in l. molars in evening; *when eating* dry bread; *in incisors and anterior molars on drawing air into mouth,* < *cold or damp air,* at first warm drinks caused a similar pain; in l. anterior lower molars in morning on looking out of the window, extending into a r. molar, where it was a pressure outward, it returned after washing and taking cold in evening; as if a loose tooth were grasped for extraction, with sensation as if a jar had caused it, which was sometimes the case (ascending stairs, etc.). Jerklike drawing in l. upper molars on loud and continued talking and on inhalation of cold air. Grumbling. Painless jerking in molars after drinking cold water, with redness of cheek. Felt every nerve, but no pain. Felt as if covered with chalk. Felt too large laterally and soft. (Seemed blunted and soft.) (Increased inclination of gums to bleed.)

Tongue.—White mucous coat, mouth slimy, *throat dry,* and thirst. Red, shining, sore elevations (mucous glands) anteriorly where frænum passes into mucous membrane of mouth, < l. side. Disagreeable sensation, almost an aching, at sides, at orifice of salivary ducts. **Dryness of T. and mouth** in evening, **as if it would stick to palate, without thirst,** *and without actual dryness of T.,* it seems as if she had eaten herring; *T. and mouth dry and pasty,* with a velvety and spongy feeling; T. and palate dry at night, without thirst, T. feels to the finger like leather, nose stopped by thick mucus; constantly pressed against palate on account of dryness in mouth and a taste somewhat like the after-taste of very salt things. Stiff, and articulation indistinct. Stammering. *Speech difficult, indistinct,* T. rolled in mouth like one intoxicated, and felt numb.

Dry mouth without thirst (Cannab. ind., Verat., etc.); **in evening, so that tongue sticks to palate,** *also back of mouth and throat in morning on waking; D. at night, with slimy feeling,* thirst, sensation of flour on palate and dryness of nose; *D., and the saliva seems like cotton. Saliva and mucus so thick that mouth was dry and he was inclined to drink, but had no real thirst,* with sensation posteriorly on tongue as after eating much salt. Saliva thick and pasty. *Taste chalky; in morning fasting;* T. foul; in morning as after intoxication; (sour).

Clinical.—Toothache in pregnant women. Excessive dryness of the mouth and tongue in sleep, always wakes with dry mouth and tongue.

Throat.—Fauces and velum palati red, bloodvessels injected, but mucous membrane between them white, with raw sensation. Stitches provoking hawking, not > thereby. Pain in l. tonsil and in region of arch of palate as if he had swallowed a hard substance, with slight redness. Scraping < swallowing. *Dryness so that he could not swallow a bite of an apple; D. posteriorly, with stiff feeling, without thirst;* D. of fauces and choanæ, extending forward, with inclination to swallow, but without thirst; *scraping.* Paralysis of organs of deglutition, making it difficult to swallow saliva. Chokes when she tries to swallow. Food stopped in œsophagus or went down very slowly. Intermittent burning in œsophagus in afternoon on going into street.

Stomach.—*Appetite great; at noon, he ate with haste and though it oppressed the stomach he could have eaten more;* in evening; afterwards diminished; lost; lost, dinner tasted like sawdust; little. Aversion to tobacco-smoke all day. *Thirst.* Drinks much.

Eructations as of pine oil; scraping E. after eating. Nausea; in morning, with salivation and sleepiness; in forenoon, at times alternating with increased appetite; at 2 P.M.; with shuddering aversion to food; but inability to vomit; *deathly, if her head was raised from the pillow.* Retching at night. Vomiting.

Distention. Feels sour. Pain; in pit; as if laced, as if she had to vomit (drawn up as if it would break). Intolerance of touch, slightest touch causes nausea. Oppression in pit; O. on ascending stairs, with weight; in pit, extending to chest. Heaviness and weakened digestion; and impaired appetite and tendency to inflammation of mucous membrane of stomach; H. over epigastric region after eating, then eructations of wind, prior to which feeling of a lump in throat (globus hystericus), which is in part > eructations. Emptiness, but when food was brought she could not eat. Burning; extending upward; in pit, waking her at night, with præcordial anxiety; like a sensation of fasting.

Clinical.—Nausea and vomiting of pregnancy. Dyspepsia < any mental effort, stomach and abdomen became excessively bloated from any unpleasant emotion. Dyspepsia, distress appearing while the patient is eating, feeling as if the food formed hard lumps, with soreness in stomach.

Abdomen.—Distention towards evening, with nausea, a twisting about umbilicus that extended now to heart, now downward, and discharge of thread-worms with the stool; D., with qualmishness in it and pain in small of back; as from flatus. Hardness, with constipation. *Rumbling; and gurgling. Movements as if he would have colic.* Offensive flatus. Flatulent trouble, pressing outward in l. groin. Muscles drawn up as in chorea, during spasms. Jerking now and then.

Cutting, < across bladder, with pressure, as before diarrhœa, in evening, next day difficult stool. Griping in evening, > emission of flatus. Pain, with inclination to flatulence and sensation as before diarrhœa, yet a difficult stool of normal consistence, bright yellow, with pieces of undigested food; P. as if full of knots, with chilliness, little appetite, feeling of fulness, next day more cutting in abdomen, necessity to sit down, she could scarcely walk on account of weakness, some diarrhœa; crampy forcing-down P. in A. and rectum at 2 A.M.; (and troubles as before a hæmorrhoidal flow). Discomfort as if he had eaten too much and A. were distended.

Upper A. distended, and attacks of colic. Griping below stomach and feeling as if it would change to real colic. (Pressure from sides towards pit like that he usually felt before a hæmorrhoidal flow, at night.)

Hepatic Region.—Jerking in side below liver. *Tearing as if stones would cut their way out, with diarrhœa, always preceded by an agreeable sensation in stomach,* the relief was such that it seemed as if the evacuations came down from liver (in a woman suffering from enlargement of liver). Plucking in liver and upper abdomen in afternoon, as if the parts would be lengthened, a heaving motion, a feeling as if the liver were pulled down or twisted around. Constriction like a forcing outward when walking. Scorching, next day blood with the stool, without pain, but at the same time constipation and nausea around region of pit of stomach.

Umbilicus.—Sticking from r. to l. side of abdomen, at about level of U.; splenetic, to r. of U., doubling him up. Cutting extending in two rays to both sides, downward and backward, at night; C. in middle of abdomen in evening, with inclination to flatulence and diarrhœa and with aching in temples. Griping in evening in bed after the chill; in region at night in bed; (in a spot to r. side of U). Colic in region, > pressure.

Hypogastrium.—Griping mornings after breakfast (of cocoa), > keeping quiet. Colic in l. side extending towards r. and downward.

Rectum.—Protrusion in evening. Sensation in evening as before diarrhœa, it seemed as if a part of R. were dragged downward, next morning scanty diarrhœa, with tenesmus. Urging at 2 A.M., with sensation as if everything had fallen against it; ineffectual U., with swollen sensation in anus.

Stool.—Dysentery in a pregnant woman, that continued after labor, which was premature on account of it. Diarrhœa; towards midnight; painless, all day; slimy, as in worms; frequent, with pressure towards pelvis and sensation of an acrid liquid in rectum, after the stool sensation as if more should follow; twice a day. **Soft, but difficult,** with distention of abdomen; *soft, but difficult, indolent, also with sensation as if a part remained.* Pasty, easy, frequent. Hard and difficult, no real desire at usual time; H., with the greatest effort of rectum, with sticking in it, with constriction of rectum and anus during stool and worse afterwards; H. and black, afterwards watery, then mushy. Indolent; next day diarrhœa in morning after milk. Copious, afterwards constipation, stools preceded by cramps in abdomen, stools small, narrow, with lack of expulsive power. Omitted, next day hard and difficult, third day a watery one instead of flatus.

Clinical.—Diarrhœa like beaten eggs, undigested, profuse, putrid stools, followed by drowsiness and even by faintness, with flatulent distention of the abdomen.

Urinary Organs.—Irritability of bladder during menstruation, with frequent desire to urinate, bearing-down pains and a sort of strangury with the last drops of urine. Frequent urging at night, but scanty urine; constant desire in evening, with frequent scanty passages of urine like well-water. Micturition involuntary, scanty at night, during the spasms. Strangury. Burning in urethra when urinating. Urine violet-colored. Urine increased; and smelling strongly of nutmeg; and frequent micturition. Scanty; and concentrated, also clear.

Sexual Organs.—Spasmodic pains in penis, extending upward. *Erections weak and of short duration though there was some inclination to coition;* want of E., even with voluptuous thoughts. (Pressure in spermatic cord on same side where testicle had been bruised some years before, with drawing downward.) Desire, with relaxation of genitals; lack of D.

Female.—Pains similar to labor-pains, at 2 A.M. Irritability about pelvic viscera, < during menstruation, when ovaries and womb were swollen and sensitive to pressure. Cutting in ovarian region. Leucorrhœa greenish, acrid. Dysmenorrhœa, with clonic spasms, delirium, stupor and loss of use of lower limbs. Menstruation ceased immediately; and womb and ovaries were swollen, with tenderness over ovaries, < l; M. too early, with dragging downward from umbilicus and drawing in limbs; too late, dark, thick and when dry more glutinous than usual, preceded by pain in small of back as if a piece of wood were lying across it and pressing outward, concealed aching on vertex, weakness, pressure in stomach, running of water from mouth and pain in liver, but at the time when menses should have appeared there was discharge of only mucus.

Clinical.—Suppression of menses, with persistent fainting attacks. Suppression of menses, with mental confusion, cold extremities, drowsiness. Obstinate uterine hæmorrhages, with repeated fainting, dryness of mouth and throat, etc. Uterine hæmorrhages of thick, dark blood. Vaginal flatulence. Disorders of pregnant women, mental bewilderment, repeated syncope. During pregnancy extreme flatulent distention of abdomen.

Respiratory Organs.—*Hoarse. Voice lost and unsteady;* suppressed after waking; like that of a sheep, and in larynx dry sensation, without actual dryness. (Soreness in trachea, with inclination to cough.) Coughs up blood partly mixed with mucus, with stitches in chest. The dry cough becomes moist and he expectorates much mucus.

Respiration oppressed; and shallow; unless clothes are loose. Long gasps. Sighs; and rapid breathing; desire to sigh or take a long breath, which she cannot accomplish satisfactorily. Breathing slow during the spasmodic condition; S. and heavy. Want of breath after eating; W., with oppression of chest, to relieve which he would straighten up, when other distressing effects ensued, rush of blood to head, obscuring vision, quivering of heart, palpitation, intermittent pulse, hands placed on sides on account of the constriction about waist and abdomen.

Clinical.—Nervous aphonia. Aphonia, with apparent constriction of the vocal organs. General loss of voice from walking against the wind.

Chest.—Jerking stitches in forepart extending obliquely upward and arresting breath. Pain anteriorly in evening, making respiration difficult, at times with pressive pain anteriorly in r. side; sudden P. round about region of diaphragm in forenoon on inspiration; as if raw when coughing. Bruised pain in forepart in evening, < inspiration and during flatulent colic; B. pain in region of pectoral muscles on moving arm, < touch and pressure.

Pressure inward in r. lower part, ascending to throat and mouth, with collection of bitter water in mouth and dry cough. Spasmodic pressure outward and inward in region of insertion of diaphragm, extending from pit of stomach to scapulæ, with difficult respiration, necessity for deep breathing and expanding chest, with dry cough, that was somewhat loose in morning and came from the back, this attack was associated with sleepiness and dryness of nose, on third day pain between scapulæ, seeming to be in lungs.

Oppression; with rush of blood to heart; with tightness of throat as if they would choke; (as if it were fatty, or as if there were a piece of perforated bacon in trachea, which did not allow enough air to pass, towards evening when walking in cool air, fear of suffocation). Constriction in C. and abdomen as if everything were drawing into a knot; C. of muscles, with tightness of chest, obliging deep respiration on moving about, forcing him to sit down.

Weight in evening making respiration difficult, also in forepart; W. anteriorly all day, < beneath sternum, < falling asleep in evening and waking from noonday nap, sometimes compelling a deep inspiration, respiration was difficult and caused distress in chest. Fulness in upper and anterior part, preventing deep inspiration, but on deep breathing jerking pain under sternum. Crawling in r. upper part in morning, with tickling, provoking cough.

Heart.—Sudden spasmodic stitches in morning after waking, with colic. Sensation as if grasped about 5 P.M., with cutting in cardiac region. Præcordial anxiety. "Awful feeling." *Feeling as if blood rushed to it, thence to head, then over whole body,* again to heart, and repeat (the coldness and other symptoms still present), the alternate paleness and redness of skin indicating this action were visible about 4 P.M. Circulation increased. Palpitation.

Clinical.—Fluttering of the heart as from fright, with faintness.

Pulse.—Rapid; and full; and small and feeble, during the spasmodic condition, with slow respiration; and small, but during unconsciousness irregular, fuller and weak. Varied from 70 to over 100 during the sexual paroxysms. *Slow and small.* Almost imperceptible at 5.30 P.M.

Neck and Back.—Drawing pain in muscles of nape from a draught of damp air. Constriction of nape. Backache on riding in a carriage. Scraping between scapulæ. Pain in lumbar region; with weakness of lower limbs, as from a blow upon small of back and calves; *as if broken,* in evening, < rest. *Bruised pain at side of lumbar vertebræ;* in muscles at side of lumbar vertebræ; in lumbar region and lower limbs, with weakness.

Clinical.—Neuralgia of the sacrum and coccyx, especially when driving in a carriage.

Extremities.—Twitching, then burning at umbilicus, with restlessness and lassitude, she had to lie down and fell asleep, on waking burning in chest, vexation and irritability. (Drawing pain in muscular parts as after taking cold, < during rest.) Drawing in calves < standing, > lying, then trembling and weakness of hands and lower limbs. Arms and legs felt sorish, large and heavy. Weakness, < lower, and numbness on ascending stairs, with sensation as if floating through the air. (Relaxation, < arms, with pressure here and there.) Rigid and hands clenched above breast, so that on attempting to separate them a convulsive effort was made by the patient, then clonic spasms. *Numbness.* General affection, < legs, < towards lower part and on r. side.

Upper Extremities.—Paroxysmal sticking in bloodvessels on flexor side of shoulder, upper arm and elbow. Pain in l. shoulder as if it contained lead; pressing P. in shoulders and sensation as if a six-pound ball pressed from abdomen into pit of stomach. Arms feel in evening as if a string were tied around them and all the blood rushed into hands; jerklike drawing in arms, sometimes with boring outward in elbows. Upper arm, pain in l.; as if grasped below middle of l.; sensation of fomentation in muscles. Tearing in extensor muscles of l. elbow, impeding motion. Gnawing externally on l. forearm near elbow. Hands lost all power; H. numb and full in evening. Inability to grasp firmly. Pain in bone of r. middle finger; sprained, in some joints of l. little in morning, on grasping anything; drawing from F. to shoulder from holding a nutmeg in hand, there remains a tearing rheumatic pain in shoulder.

Lower Extremities.—Reeling in evening when walking, with stumbling; R. to the left in evening when walking in open air; R. that increased to relaxation and insensibility, he fell from his chair, being laid in bed he fell asleep, but woke at times in delirium, also headache. Trembling, < walking or going up or down stairs, with weakness of them. Painful weakness, with bruised pain in back of feet, the farther above the ankles the less the pain, though stepping aggravates the pain yet he must move the leg back and forth constantly on account of uneasiness (trampling).

Thigh.—Bruised pain on upper and inner part, < touch; in posterior muscles of r. in morning on walking and on touch. Painful drawing here and there. Numbness of r. when riding one leg over the other, then sensation as if l. leg would fall asleep, with rush of blood in it, prickling, etc.

Knees.—Knocked together. Sprained pain in r. on moving it, < ascending stairs. Sensation as if grasped anteriorly in r.

Leg.—Cramps; (in r. calf on sudden motion of lower limb while lying, > pressing foot against something). Pain on anterior surface of l. in morning when standing; drawing P. in periosteum of r. tibia; P. in shins as if bone were smashed, < afternoon, so that he could hardly walk through the room. (Throbbing in l. calf as if a bloodvessel had burst.) Numbness, and of feet. Falling asleep of r. when standing.

Burrowing in middle of soles in morning. Throbbing on inner margin of r. foot at noon when lying, with warmth in it. Boring in r. great toe after lying down. *Tingling in toes as after freezing, < metatarsal joints, it extends over sole and heel, which also pain as if bruised.*

Skin.—Blue spots. Mottled. Red spot, burning, with pain on touch. Alternately pale and red at 4

P.M. Pustules on border of l. jaw. (Boils, with broad, red areola, on chin.) Pain all day below chin, as if pimples would form.

Sleep.—Sleepiness ; eyes closed constantly ; all the time or faint feeling, drops off almost asleep, with eyes open ; but inability to sleep. **Falls asleep on sitting down.** Irresistible sleep, disturbed by vivid dreams. Profound, was called to breakfast several times ; P. and long at noon. Not very sound after dinner. *Starting in sleep, but does not always wake*, sometimes with unpleasant dreams, even nightmare. Sitting up in bed at 5.30 P.M., tossing from side to side. Restless sleep ; with difficult waking. Very wide awake on going out after sleep. Little sleep. Voluptuous dreams disturbing sleep ; and awoke weak, with swollen sensation in ovaries. Dreams of falling from high places, again of being pursued by persons seeking to harm her.

Fever.—Chilliness ; in evening in bed ; in evening on going into cold, damp air, with pallor ; towards evening in open air and from external cold, increasing to shaking, > warm room, with pain in small of back, dulness of head, < forehead, diminished appetite, slimy tongue, disposition to make fun ; sensitive to cold air. Shaking C. in evening and morning, then heat ; at 9 P.M., with coldness beginning in lower limbs, then chills at intervals, *sleepiness between them if left alone ;* extending from loins, < uncovering himself or going to stool, > warm room. Shivering on going into cold air ; S. in evening, with colic, pain in small of back, little appetite, white-coated tongue, pain in soft palate, difficult respiration on account of pain in chest and sleepiness. *Cold skin ;* at 5.30 P.M., and blue ; C. limbs ; feet ; feet, with hot head ; hands, and numb ; hands, and on entering house humming and tingling under nails, obliged to throw his hands about as if they had been frozen.

Temperature increased. Dry heat all night, with uneasiness, sleeplessness, dry, sticky lips and tongue, without thirst, throbbing in all vessels, throbbing pain, < head, in small spots, < l. superciliary ridges. Heat in skin. Heat in face and hands forenoons, with prostration and hypochondriac mood ; of cheeks, with redness ; of hands ; externally on l. side of l. elbow. Skin dry.

Clinical.—In general, the skin is cold and dry, never perspires, with general coldness ; this dryness often extends to the mucous membrane ; with sensitiveness to cold, moist air.

Nux Vomica.

A tincture of the seeds of Strychnos Nux vomica, L., is used.

General Action.—Its most pronounced characteristic is spasm of all muscle fibre, both voluntary and involuntary, characterized by extreme hyperæsthesia of the general nervous system ; these spasms are tetanic and seem to arise from the action of the poison on the motor tract of the spinal cord ; consciousness is rarely affected. Careful experiments have developed very prominent effects on the gastro-intestinal canal as well as on the vaso-motor nerves ; well marked gastro-intestinal catarrh accompanies an irregular action of the peristaltic muscles of the stomach and bowels ; well defined paroxysms of chill, fever and sweat are associated with the disturbances of the circulation. Very few tissue changes have been observed (mostly resulting from malnutrition).

Allies.—Ign., Sulph., Puls., Lyc., Sec. c., Cic. v., Coccul., Cedr., Coff.

Generalities.—*Emaciation.* Loud involuntary cries. Knits his brows and folds his arms. Lying on her back. Extended rigidly along the floor. Stretching in morning in bed, seeming to start from abdomen, arms stretched upward. Awkward. Trembling ; as from an electric shock, constant necessity to rise and walk about ; *tremulous sensation in morning.*

Twitchings. *Convulsions ;* **on slightest touch** (compare Stram.) ; < limbs, with pain in all parts affected ; with red face and closed eyes ; with rigid muscles, jaws clenched, restless, and short cries ; woke in C., uttering loud cries, on cessation of the spasm faintness, on coming to himself the first drop of water on his tongue caused spasm, with shrieks and opisthotonos, spasms > forcible extension of body, in intervals constant twitches of limbs ; like electric shocks, on rising from a chair vertigo, then spasms of limbs, > rest, renewed by movement, speech hurried, when talking C. of facial muscles, trismus, pale face, weak pulse, sweat on head ; whole body straight and stiff, legs wide apart, pulse and respiration imperceptible, face and hands livid, face and lips agitated, moaning, chattering, afterwards asphyxia ; head drawn back, teeth clenched, heels fixed to the ground, eyes protruding, unable to move, but crying "Hold me."

Tetanic spasms, < wiping sweat from face ; T. spasm when arm was touched to feel the pulse, eyes wide open, protruding, rigid, jaws clenched, lips wide open, face distorted, limbs rigidly outstretched, spine bent backward, jerks along lower part of spine, which raised the body, breathing intermittent, face blue, during a pause the child breathed with exertion and in a catching manner and desired coffee, spasms returned if lips touched the cup, if any one touched his person, at noise and without apparent cause, after the spasms eyes were usually closed, face and forehead covered with sweat, lips blue, groans, pulse 102, spasmodic and irregular, afterwards irregular and soft. Tetanic spasms, head drawn backward, arms extended, fingers flexed to palms, jaws contracted, face livid, eyes open, fixed, protruding, trunk stiff, legs extended, feet turned outward, toes flexed to sole, skin dry and warm, breathing loud, perfect sensibility between the spasms, at last the slightest movement or an attempt to speak or drink caused the paroxysms, she begged to be let alone on account of the pains during the paroxysms.

Tetanic spasms, limbs stretched out, hands grasping sides of bed, legs apart, feet everted, afterwards opisthotonos, with difficult breathing, prostration between the spasms, then jerking of whole body on touch or movement of bed or sudden noise. Tetanus, jaws locked and limbs rigidly extended. Tetanus and trismus, jaw moved spasmodically from side to side, arms cramped towards chest, thighs drawn up against abdomen, fingers and toes flexed, whining and groaning, loss of voice, anæsthesia of skin, no pain. *Spasms, with tetanic rigidity of nearly all muscles, with interruptions of a few minutes during which muscles were relaxed* (compare Sec. c.), pulse became soft, with consciousness and speech, spasm renewed by slightest touch, but at times > grasping the patient or straightening the elbow.

Opisthotonos (Cic. v.) ; beginning with a sense of impending death, brought on by touch, > applications of ice to spine ; and all muscles rigid and respiration suspended; alternating with trismus, tongue protruded and injured by sudden closure of jaws; and impulse of heart marked, pulse slow, scarcely perceptible, biting at everything brought near the mouth. Convulsive tossing about of arms, bending backward of head, biting teeth together, hands clenched. Stretched out her arms, clenched her fists, threw her head back, jaws firmly closed, face distorted and expressive of agony. Spasmodic flexion of arms on elbows, fingers clenched and pressed against pit of stomach, abdominal muscles spasmodically contracted. First nervous excitement, then spasmodic contraction of jaws, with grinding of teeth, bending backward of head, rigidity of trunk, forcible extension and inversion of feet and subsultus of calves. Spasmodic drawing sideways of body, ineffectual efforts to hold himself erect with the hands, then vomiting, then involuntary quick discharge of stool and urine, with consciousness.

Stiffness, < neck; tetanic S., with shuddering of trunk and limbs; as in catalepsy (one fell suddenly to the ground while conscious), jaws clenched; stiff and lifeless suddenly, feet and toes turned outward, eyes staring, jaws clenched.

Frightful tortures. Stitches at times in affected parts; S. here and there, with sore pain; *like jerkings in various parts, causing shuddering;* burning here and there; burning, or stitches here and there that end in burning. **Contractive pain through whole body.** Pain in all parts on which he was lying during morning sweat; P. in voluntary muscles, < neck and limbs, < motion; sore, renewed in old wounds that had healed; (intolerable, from 8 till 9 P.M.). Bruised sensation.

Drawing, crampy pains in nape, with paroxysms of internal rigidity from nape downward, sometimes muscles of chest and throat were affected as well as those of neck, causing difficult breathing and choking, < attempting to swallow anything, also muscles of head, < forehead, causing contraction of brows, sometimes all muscles of back and legs were affected and the whole body became rigid and bent backward, at times he could not keep his seat, and when he attempted to get on his feet he could scarcely stand or move his legs, he always attempted to move about when the attacks came on and to rest the affected parts.

Sensation in muscles of limbs, back, scapulæ, etc., as if something in them were drawn back and forth, more spasmodic than painful. **Everything makes too strong an impression** (Coff.). Whole body feels electrified. Attack in evening, it arose to the heart, he became sick, apprehensive, trembled, obliged to bend head forward and rest it on the table. Attack after midnight, crawling in hands and feet, rising (with heat of face) to pit of stomach, then to throat, then nausea and apprehension, thence it rose into head, with dulness of head and ringing in ears.

Takes cold from the slightest draught (Sul., Kali c., etc.), (discomfort in skin, colic, etc.). Oppression; of whole body, with pain in legs as after a long walk. Uneasiness at night; in evening after lying down, with anxiety so that he was constantly obliged to stretch the limbs; with easily dilated pupils. Inclination to sit. Inability to sit up.

Weakness; in morning after rising greater than in evening on going to bed; in morning, > rising; in morning on rising, with soreness of lower limbs and arms; morning on walking in open air; in afternoon, with loss of appetite; about 2 P.M., during menstruation, with headache as if eyes would fall out, inability to hold head up, chilliness and shivering, then internal heat, with dry lips; in evening; in evening after walking in open air; when walking in open air; after walking in open air; after being in open air, with stiffness of l. foot; after stool during menses; on waking, > open air, with headache; with frequent sighs and irregular respirations; sudden; drops things involuntarily.

Faintness; in morning after rising, during menstruation, preceded by spasmodic motion in abdomen, then weakness and chilliness on rising; in morning in open air, with staring eyes; about 8 or 9 P.M. when sitting. Stiffness, < neck. Aggravation from slightest touch. Amelioration from frequent stretching; A. after dinner; of all pains by cold sweat.

Clinical.—Chorea. Convulsions from indigestion. Tetaniform convulsions without loss of consciousness. Palliative in epileptiform convulsions, especially when brought on by indigestion. There is disposition to lie down and rest, with easy mental and physical fatigue. Paralysis resulting from apoplexy, in high livers. Various paralyses. Partial paralysis, with vertigo and nausea, especially in drunkards. There is aggravation of all symptoms early in the morning. Aggravation from any mental effort, sometimes worse in open air and from motion, sometimes relief in the house or when at rest, or *vice versa.* There is general relief from unbroken sleep, but aggravation when the sleep is disturbed; the patient is usually very drowsy early in the evening and wakes very early in the morning, but after falling asleep a second time he wakes finally with all the Nux aggravations.

Mind.—Delirium, a kind of coma vigil. Rushed into the room, exclaiming that her mother was murdered. (Anxious, delirious fantasies about 9 P.M., as if some one would get into his bed and there was no room in it, as if some one had sold his bed, etc.). **Quarrelsome** (Anac., Lyc.); **even to violence**; *and reproachful, scoldings,* **insults from jealousy,** *with unchaste expressions, then he howls and weeps aloud.* Hasty, he looked angrily at any one who asked him a question, without answering, as if obliged to restrain himself to avoid being insulting, he was so irritable that it seemed as if he would like to strike any one in the face who spoke to him.

Ill-humored after eating, and sad. **Intolerance of noise or talking, music and singing affect him** (Coff., Bell.). **Sensitive to impressions on the senses** (Ign., Plumb.), **intolerance of strong odors or bright light.** Impatient of lightest step or jar of floor. *Beside herself at the slightest contradiction or reasonable representations to do differently.* Resists obstinately what is desired by others. *She cannot get over the slightest trouble.* Moans and groans piteously without stating the cause. Pain seems intolerable, she would rather take her life (Cham.).

Hypochondriac; after eating, and affected by the slightest thing; after dinner, < after supper. Silent grief and sadness. (Sad, but unable to weep.) *Ennui.* Weeping; at the least thing done contrary to his wishes; and sobs; loud, solicitous, inconsolable, with complaints and reproaches that at times change to groans, with red, hot cheeks; alternating with laughter (Ign.).

Anxiety; in morning on waking, and at 5 P.M.; *in morning on waking, > rising, with orgasm of blood and ill humor;* in evening after lying down, then sweat after midnight; from suspicious and apprehensive solicitude, < after midnight; with impulse to commit suicide; with inability to remain in any place; fretful; causing internal heat, then sweat on forehead; as if he had committed a crime. Apprehension in evening when walking, with oppression and intoxicated feeling. Easily startled. Alarm; kept hold of her husband. Dread of death. Believes that she is near death. Agitation, and on moving he grasped the nearest objects for fear of falling.

Taciturn as if averse to everything; T., slow flow of ideas. Dreads to go into open air. *No patience for work.* Aversion to work, but not to moving about. Irresolution; and dawdling. Wishes to accomplish much, but thinks that it will not succeed. Everything miscarries. Tender, gentle mood, music affects him to tears.

Dread of literary work at which one must think, in morning, but no aversion to reading or committing to memory. *Disinclination for mental work,* blood mounts to the head till evening. Hindered in scientific work. Mistakes in talking and writing, omits syllables and words. *Inability to think properly;* and mistakes in talking, trouble to find the words, uses unsuitable expressions, makes mistakes in weights and measures. Flow of ideas in morning after rising, so that he is scarcely conscious. Remembers scarcely anything from the time of her fall to being brought home. Stupefaction. Unconsciousness.

Clinical.—Very useful in effects of mental strain at night, especially when it results in a condition of irritability and great nervous sensitiveness. The disposition is generally passionate and jealous, becomes angry easily. Indescribable anxiety, gets no rest, with coated tongue, nausea, vomiting and trembling. Hypochondriasis in persons of sedentary habits, or those who sit up late at night, with alternations of constipation and diarrhœa. Generally a fiery and excitable temperament.

Head.—Sticking. *Tearing after eating, with heat in cheeks and chilliness over body, at least in hands;* T., extending to root of nose and jaw, < walking; *drawing, in morning, with burning pain. Pinching. Sticking throbbing pain, < stooping, when it seems as if a piece of the forehead would fall out.* **Aching in morning in bed, as if beaten with an axe,** > *rising. Bruised sensation.*

Aching; in morning after yawning; *in middle of brain* **in morning on waking, even before opening eyes;** in night on waking; before dinner; *before dinner,* < **eating,** *then sticking in l. temple,* **with nausea and sour vomiting, symptoms > evening after lying down; in morning, as if he had not slept at night; stupefying, in morning on waking, > rising; composed of heaviness and pressure after dinner, < moving eyes;** *on stooping, as if a weight fell forward in it; as if brain would be pressed asunder, when lying after slightest thought; over surface of brain as if skull would burst, in morning in bed;* (burrowing?) *in morning, > rising;* as if brain were split in two; *drawing jerking, in morning; tearing drawing;* drawing; drawing, externally; tensive, at night; as from emptiness; as if sore externally, though the spot is not sore to touch, in a raw wind; in middle of brain on closing eyes, as after vomiting.

Heaviness in morning; H. on stooping; **dizzy H. in morning. Intoxicating confusion;** *C. after dinner.* **Dulness;** and on moving it blood rushes into it, with sluggishness of rest of body. *Fulness, partial pain,* inability to study, buzzing in head, > evening. Painless drawing here and there. Jerks; or beats. *Stupid feeling; if he holds it erect, if he bends it down sensation in forehead as if a weight fell into it;* in open air and in sunlight; (with black points floating before eyes). Tingling in brain when walking and running, with quaking. Apoplexy. Mounting to H. on walking rapidly in open air, thought vanished, obliged to stand still, blood rushed to heart, constriction of upper part of trachea, sparks before eyes, could not see where she was. Swashing in brain when walking, with bubbling. *Intoxication.*

Vertigo; **after dinner;** when eating; on moving; on moving, with burning pain in temple; when walking after eating; > standing still; during eructations; when lying on back, so that it was impossible to raise head, with obscuration of vision; here and there in brain; with obscuration of vision; with shooting through head; with congestion of brain, roaring in ears and blackness before eyes; *in paroxysms, as if brain were turning in a circle, with momentary unconsciousness; as if he would fall to one side; as if he would fall to one side or backward when walking;* as if the bed were whirling around with her evenings; sudden, on going out; faintlike; as on going from cold air into a warm room, when eating, with obscuration of vision; as if one neither saw nor heard and would fall, when sneezing, coughing, or rising after stooping low down.

Forehead.—**Tensive pain. Pain as if he had not slept enough.** *Bruised pain over l. eye and in bones, with inability to open eyes.* Pain > laying head upon a table (Ign.), < open air, with weariness of feet on ascending; P. above r. orbit in morning if he lies on r. side. Drawings back and forth, extending to root of nose. Buzzing in afternoon and evening. Obscuration in evening in open air, as if consciousness would vanish.

Temples.—Pain from exerting head; P. in r.; *drawing, then in forehead, then in occiput.*

Vertex.—Tearing, and in forehead and eyes, with nausea in region of chest and weakness of vocal organs. *Throbbing pain from fixed attention.* Deep-seated, pressing-downward drawing pain.

Side.—Tearing in r. hemisphere of brain in morning when lying on l. side, > lying on r. side; T. downward at ear. *Intermittent pain in one half as if a nail were forced downward deeper and deeper into parietal bone* (Ign.). One-sided pain from 4 P.M. till night, with weakness. Drawing-upward pain in r. side of brain near ear.

Occiput.—Pain; in medulla oblongata; *in morning after rising;* as from an ulcer in brain, during menstruation, < lying; as if brain were thrust forward; as if skull were forced asunder, momentarily > pressure of hands, with heat in brain. Obscuration.

Scalp.—*Pain, < touch;* P. on occiput. Bruised pain on vertex on touch; B. pain, and the hair stood up in this place and was painful to touch. Crawling on skull.

Clinical.—Vertigo before breakfast, recurring after dinner. Vertigo in the morning, resulting from alcoholic excesses on the previous day. Congestive headache, with bloated face, < morning. Frontal headache, with nausea and vomiting, desire to press the head against something. Persistent headache recurring after sleep, even in the daytime. Headache from the abuse of coffee. Supraorbital neuralgia, recurring early every morning (compare Ced., Sang., Iris). Congestive headache, associated with hæmorrhoids or with other abdominal troubles, bruised feeling in the head, < walking or drinking coffee.

Eyes.—*Inflammation. Injection of whites. Swelling, with red streaks in whites and tensive pain.* Glistening, staring. Staring, often turned upward so that pupils could not be seen. Wild. Sunken and moved rapidly. Oozing of blood. (Stitches.) Bruised pain in l., with purulent mucus in external canthus. *Itching*, > *rubbing. Biting*, < *external canthus, with lachrymation.* Burning; crawling. Dryness of r. *Movement difficult on account of stiffness of muscles* (Kalm.). *Lachrymation; in morning when yawning.*

Itching of ball. Pupils contracted; and insensible; dilated. Lids, *blinking;* twitching; wide open; contraction as from heaviness of upper lids, with a gush of tears; drawing tearing; *pressure in upper*, < *morning; pain in margins as if rubbed sore*, < **morning**, *and on touch;* burning itching pain; itching towards inner canthus in evening; itching of forepart. *Canthi purulent;* external agglutinated in morning; l. external red in morning; **smarting dryness in inner in morning in bed**; *pain as if sore and rubbed, also inner;* biting in inner in evening in bed. Sticking above lids, with pressure; *jerking S. extending from l. orbit through l. hemisphere of brain towards parietal bone and occiput after eating.* Pain in r. brow on touch. **Photophobia; in morning,** *with obscured vision.* Presbyopia. *Vision sensitive; cloudy;* distorted; lost. Glistening flickering outside the field of vision, < l. side, in forenoon.

Clinical.—Infraorbital neuralgia, involving the face, with watering of eyes and running from the nose, numbness, caused by the abuse of coffee or liquor. Ciliary neuralgia. Catarrhal conjunctivitis, with great photophobia in the morning. Keratitis, even scrofulous, with excessive photophobia in the morning, so that the child buries its eyes in the pillow, the photophobia disappears later in the day. Extreme hyperæsthesia of the retina in the morning, the attempt to open the eyes is resisted and attended with gushes of tears. Amaurosis from alcohol or tobacco, with restricted field of vision. Asthenopia on account of retinal hyperæsthesia. Spasms of the lids. Atrophy of the optic nerve.

Ears.—Sticking in morning in bed; S. externally in meatus; tearing sticking inward towards evening. Pinching and pain. Sharp thrusts. *Itching within, through Eustachian tube, which compels frequent swallowing and disturbs the rest at night;* I. within, with creeping, crawling. (Hollow feeling in morning, so that his words re-echo in his ears, > dinner.) Hearing sensitive. *Ringing. Ringing hissing.* Chirping as of locusts at night. Rushing as of a fulling machine, at night. *Roaring in morning after rising;* (R. and humming as of bees).

Clinical.—Otalgia, intermittent pains, < going into a warm room or in bed. Deafness, with roaring, etc., auditory canal dry and sensitive, with coryza, itching in the Eustachian tube, headache, nausea, creeping chills, etc.

Nose.—Nostrils wide open. *Pain in anterior angles of nostrils as if ulcerated and as if cutting into a wound. Margins of nostrils sore as if ulcerated on moving nose*, < *evening. Nostril sensitive internally. Heat, with frequent premonitions of coryza. Obstruction and itching; O. in morning, with tensive pain in limbs.* (Air passes through nose, but it is dry.) **Sneezing; in morning in bed, but after rising sudden fluent coryza.**

Coryza in morning and after dinner; C., with scraping in throat, crawling and scratching in nose and sneezing; with headache, heat in face, chilliness *and much mucus in throat;* dry in morning, with dryness of mouth. **Fluent coryza in morning; during the day, stopped at night. Discharge of mucus from nostrils that seem obstructed by dry catarrh, also from one nostril.** *Discharge of mucus without coryza; D. of bloody mucus; of acrid fluid.* Bleeding; clotted blood in morning. Smell acute; S. as of bad cheese; as of a smoking candle-wick; sulphurous; offensive breath through nose. Disgusting odor to food and drink.

Clinical.—Coryza caused by dry, cold weather, with sneezing and stuffiness in the nose, which seems dry, or there is sometimes a little watery discharge, < in the house, > open air. Often a valuable remedy in the beginning of a severe coryza, which is sometimes fluent during the day and stopped at night, or the stoppage may alternate between the nostrils, with somewhat acrid discharge. Coryza in nursing infants, preventing nursing.

Face.—*Pale;* and earthy, yellowish, suffering. Dusky. Red; cheeks and eyeballs; cheeks, in morning after waking; and swollen; cheeks, with heat and crawling here and there in them; r. side, upon which she was lying, and swollen, hanging down; livid. Expression anxious; suffering; excited. Distorted. *Twitching;* in evening after lying down; of r. side, as if drawn by a thread, in evening. Drawing on stooping. Tension about mouth, eyes and nose, with distention of these places. *Drawing in masseter muscles, with stiffness.* Masseter muscles sensitive.

Jaws, contraction like lockjaw; *drawing tearing in J.; drawing pain in muscles;* sensation in J. and masseters as before tetanus, or as if J. would be drawn together; *tetanic rigidity.* Lips wide open; ulcers in corners; *ulcer painful to touch, on inside of lower* (Ign.); ulcer on red, with scab and burning pain; ulcerative scurf on margins, that when appearing causes sticking; crack in middle of lower; itching pimples above margin of upper; *painful desquamation;* stitches in morning; sticking on touching a hair in beard; *sore sensation inside lower.*

Clinical.—Facial neuralgia recurring periodically in the morning.

Mouth.—Teeth. Falling out of sound, that had never been loose. *Looseness;* with pain caused by chewing, late in evening and in morning before rising; of a sound T., with pain when knocked against. *Stitches; in an indefinite T., with drawing;* in an upper incisor; burning, or pain like fire, on exposure to open air, with taking cold; after dinner, or beating pain, then tingling like painful buzzing, that extends to eyes and is < walking in open air, that also at times lasts into the night, when it is > wrapping cheeks warmly, when it reappears it always begins with sticking. Paroxysmal tearing in a hollow T., then in all upper T., then in all lower, then through bones of face into head and temple of same side, > sleep, renewed by cold water or food getting into a hollow tooth. Jerking in morning on waking and in evening, with jerking and twisting screwing in ear; J. in various, always ending with a stitch, in open air; as if caused by swelling of gum; rhythmical with pulse, with swelling of gum. *Burrowing on exerting mind and reflecting,* towards evening, then pain in a gland below angle of lower jaw. Boring gnawing, > drawing in cold air, < warm room. Drawing pain from warm drinks and soup; in a hollow T. if sucked with the tongue; < *drawing in air with open mouth* (Calc. c.), *with stitches in one row of teeth; now in an upper, now in a lower molar, then in other T. towards the front*, < *eating, at noon and evening, with red, hot spots on cheeks and throat, with complaining mood, full of reproaches and despondency. Sore pain*, < *exerting mind and reflecting;* when walking in open air, < opening mouth. *Pain in hollow T., extending into head, if air enters mouth.* Pain as if air entered a hollow tooth, on breathing deeply in open air. Pain as if a T. were out of place and loose, on drawing in air with open mouth, with stitches. Pain in morning as from soreness of gum.

Gum.—*Swelling;* before dinner, with toothache; with drawing pain; with toothache; with bubbling pain as if an ulcer would break; with bubbling pain as in an abscess, so that she could not eat; painful, with painful pimples on inside of lips and on tongue. *G., mouth, tongue and palate slimy, with raw and sore feeling as from something acrid.* Red. Ulcer over incisors, with drawing burning pain.

Tongue.—*White.* Coated white, difficult to protrude. *Painful blisters.* Inflamed and contracted. Stitches in tip at noon on going to sleep. Dry. Itching on l. side of root. *Heavy when talking. Speech difficult; and lisping. Unable to articulate any sound.* Speech interrupted by sighs, weak, monosyllabic, often unintelligible; interrupted by spasms of limbs and spine (opisthotonos.)

Mouth and fauces covered with mucus in morning, with yellow, hard mucus in canthi. Swelling of palate, with pain in it and biting posteriorly; S. of roof of palate and uvula, as from adherent mucus, noticed especially on swallowing. Painful pimples on palate behind incisors. Sticking drawing pain in mouth, almost like a cramp, extending to inner ear, on chewing and compressing jaws. *Dryness in morning, without thirst, as after alcoholic stimulants the previous evening; D. after midnight, as if tongue stuck to palate, without thirst,* **with much saliva in fauces**; in forepart, < tip of tongue. *Salivation;* watery, after waterbrash. Profuse discharge on stooping. Saliva discharged in sleep; discharged by jerks; bloody. Spitting of blackish, almost clotted blood at 2 A.M., and at 2 P.M. with peculiar taste, odor of blood in nose, and blowing of blood from nose. *Breath offensive* (Nit. ac.); *in morning* (Puls.); *after dinner; sour.*

Taste.—**Bad; in morning, though food and drink have a natural taste**; *in morning, > eating; low down in throat on hawkimg;* as from hollow teeth, in morning. **Sour** (Ign.); *< morning; after swallowing food that had a natural taste;* after food and drink; after drinking milk; to bread and rolls. *Bitter* (Puls., Sul.); *in morning* (Puls.), *though food and drink have a natural taste;* on spitting out saliva; low down in throat on expectorating mucus from chest. *Spoiled to milk in morning.* Coppery. T. and odor in mouth and nose almost sulphurous. As from a disordered stomach. Herby, to beer; nauseous, H., in throat, almost like that of carrots. Slimy, composed of herby and metallic T. in morning, with ill humor and laxity. Smoky to bread. (Salt in morning.) (T. and odor about himself, sweetish, offensive.) Lost to food; to meat; to coffee; to milk, in morning.

Clinical.—Tearing toothache, extending to head, > warmth. Neuralgic toothache from taking cold, involving even healthy teeth, feeling as if they would be wrenched out, usually < cold air, especially worse immediately after eating. Ulceration of mouth and gums, with fetid odor and other symptoms.

Throat.—Hawking of salt mucus from fauces. Stitches in upper part in afternoon; in uvula and submaxillary gland when swallowing, with shivering during the day, sweat at night and headache; in sides when not swallowing, < stooping and ascending stairs; itching, extending to ears, on swallowing or moving jaws; as from a plug, < not swallowing. **Rough from catarrh. Rawness that provokes cough; pain at palate as if raw and sore**; *R. on swallowing;* **R. in fauces** *on drawing in cold air and on swallowing.* **Scraping as after heartburn**; *and at orifice of larynx; S., not on swallowing. Sharpness on coughing, causing pain in pit of throat. Spasmodic pain from pharynx to pit of stomach in morning.*

Swollen sensation; in pharynx, < swallowing; on palate, not when drinking. Pressure on swallowing saliva. *Constriction of pharynx.* Dryness posteriorly after dinner; in fauces in morning on waking, and after rising bad breath. A rising up, bubbling and burning extending into throat. Burning; in pharynx; at night, < lying; and in chest, with suffocating sensation; in œsophagus, extending to mouth; in fauces like heartburn. Crawling upward in pharynx in evening after lying down, during menstruation. *Swallowing impeded.*

Clinical.—Sore throat, catarrh, with smarting burning, usually associated with coryza. Tickling in end of l. Eustachian tube.

Stomach.—*Appetite great;* in morning; but soon satisfied; *but aversion to food;* but lost next day at lunch time, sleep instead; periodically in afternoon, < after weiss beer, if the hunger passes off without eating he feels quite full. Longing for tobacco. Appetite diminished; *lost;* lost after walking. **Aversion to food; to the usual food, drinking, tobacco and coffee;** *to the food just eaten, < if she does not lie down; to the odor of food* (Colch.); to bread; to rye bread, it causes salivation; to sour (black) bread; to fluids, which were swallowed with difficulty or not at all.

Thirst; in afternoon and evening; in evening, *but nausea soon after drinking; for milk;* yet aversion to water and beer; yet drink distresses stomach; *for beer during chill; for small beer, with shivering; for small beer after morning sweat.*

Eructations; after eating and drinking; **of bitter and sour liquid,** *also at night; bitter when fasting; sour, all day; sour, as far as tongue,* after walking in morning; sour after eating, with yawning; *of water after eating;* of food; painful. *Hiccough;* before dinner.

Nausea; in morning (Lob.); **in morning during menstruation, with chilliness and faintness; in morning in bed,** *with bruised pain in intestines and loins; during morning sweat; in morning, with qualmishness about heart and salivation, in afternoon shivering;* about 5 P.M.; in pit of stomach in afternoon; in pit of stomach towards evening; **from smoking; after eating** (Ferr.); before dinner; *during dinner, > lying down, with faintness and flashes of heat;* **after dinner**; after dinner and drinking, then thirst, and after drinking distention of abdomen; whenever she wishes to drink; after palpitation; *after anxiety,* with rapid respiration, then dry cough caused by the nausea, with vomiting; **from colic, more cutting than griping; with cutting colic; < pit of stomach,** *with cramp in l. side of abdomen; rising from pit of stomach,* **after eating, as from a purge, with anxiety;** *extending through body here and there, as if everything were fermenting,* **in morning**; *sudden, after dinner, then vertigo and attacks of faintness, then eructations;* sudden, rising from pit of stomach after dinner, with general anxiety, trembling, beating and weakness.

Retching; on hawking mucus from fauces. *Vomiting; violent;* **of sour mucus in forenoon; of sour-smelling and sour-tasting mucus** *towards evening, with headache like a tearing (?) around lower part of skull; hæmatemesis;* copious, after much milk.

Distention, with pain on touch, also in pit; D. in pit and abdomen after eating, with pressure. (Stitches in pit in evening and after lying down.) Tearing. *Constrictive pinching.* **Scraped sensation in pit.** *Pain; in pit; epigastric region; and in chest;* **in pit in morning, then cutting in abdomen and nausea; in morning after eating a little; after eating, with return of a metallic and herby taste;** below pit, < walking in open air; *with weight and heat in it;* **as from a stone; in epigastrium, as from a stone in morning, < walking, > sitting; in epigastric region, as from overloading stomach, after eating;** *in pit after drinking, causing tightness of breath, with distention of abdomen;* as if beaten, before eating, > eating. *Clawing towards morning, as from a purge, changing to burning in pit of stomach. Epigastric region sensitive to pressure, nausea if hand lay on S.*

Tension; **above S.**; transversely across epigastric region, above S., about 3 P.M., then pain as if everything were raw and sore. *Sensation as if something in epigastric region turned over.* Throbbing in epigastric region; after supper, most noticed on laying hand on it. **Heartburn;** *as after overloading S. with rancid fat* (Puls.). Burning; in orifice; in pit, extending upward; cool, in pit, rising to pharynx, < night. Burning pain in pit and farther down after supper, with anxiety. *It often seems as if she would eructate, but she does not, it then seems as if œsophagus were constricted by a spasm. Discomfort in pit, ascending to throat, choking him and stopping his breath.* Heaviness from a light dinner, afterwards distention and flatulence in bowels. *Fluttering,* sinking feeling in *epigastrium,* with palpitation. Acidity caused by milk.

Clinical.—General desire for stimulants. Indigestion characterized by extreme distress in the stomach immediately after eating, feeling as if the stomach knotted up, at times with bitter eructations or with sour or putrid taste in the mouth, nearly always associated with nausea and efforts to vomit. Persistent efforts to vomit food. Vomiting of pregnancy. Nausea and vomiting every morning. Chronic vomiting. Nausea and vomiting are a very frequent accompaniment of the state requiring **Nux v.**; the efforts to vomit are usually spasmodic and associated with great distress in the stomach, < eating. Severe gastralgia or cardialgia, < least nourishment, the stomach seems very irritable and contracts painfully upon its contents. Atonic dyspepsia, with slow and imperfect digestion, fulness in the stomach, belchings, pain extending all around the chest and up to the shoulders. Various forms of inflammation of the stomach, caused by the habitual use of powerful drugs or of alcohol. Dyspepsia from drinking strong coffee. Gastro-duodenal catarrh, with headache, vertigo, bitter taste, nausea and vomiting, soreness of the stomach and abdomen, uneasiness in the bowels. Gastralgia, < light, > hard pressure, transiently > vomiting.

Abdomen.—*Twitching of muscles. Distention;* **flatulent after eating** (Lyc.); *flatulent, after drinking.* Rumbling; *in morning, with gurgling, also in bed, with spasmodic and griping flatulent colic and heat in palms and soles;* in afternoon; with motions as if stool would follow, with weakness and necessity to lie down. Croaking as of frogs. Movements in morning. Agitation from below upward. *Flatulence rising and becoming incarcerated under short ribs;* rising into chest, tightening it and causing sticking here and there; caused by all food, rising up and causing anxiety; here and there, causing pressure and anxiety.

Stitches. Cramp. Tearing after 4 P.M.; *griping T. extending to chest; drawing;* drawing, that comes from both sides above ossa innominata. *Griping; in A. and uterus, with clawing, with profuse discharge of clotted blood;* with bubbling and digging; as of worms, after coffee, > bending backward, returning on stooping. Burning cutting, < upper, and < moving about.

Pain; on touch; in a spot on touch or on pressure of clothes, after walking violently, with sticking; with dryness of lips and heat in face; with desire for stool, but emission of only flatus; *then discharge of dark mucus, causing biting burning in anus;* **as before diarrhœa from taking cold** (Sulph.); *in open air, as from taking cold; as from taking cold, in morning on slightest uncovering during sweat; as if everything were sore, on every step; as from incarcerated flatus; flatulent, after stool, as if intestines here and there were pressed by stones;* drawing-tensive; drawing, extending through thighs. *Bruised pain in muscles on motion; and on touch.*

Constriction. Weight. Sensation as if everything would fall down, obliging him to walk carefully. Sensation as if intestines swashed about on walking. Warmth in morning; not disagreeable W., with sensation as if something unfolded itself and were in motion.

Upper.—*Griping when she wishes to go to stool.* Grasping and clawing alternately. *Flatulent colic in evening after lying down.* Pain as if clothes were too tight. Pressure below pit of stomach causing eructations. *Fulness on beginning to eat.*

Sides.—Stitches on moving; in l. on deep breathing; in r., taking away the breath in forenoon, > pressure. *Pinching. Pressure outward during menstruation.* Bruised pain on touch, and in loins. Drawing pain from l. over umbilicus. Bubbling, with anxiety. Creeping in r. muscles, the place felt dead and seemed swollen.

Hypochondria.—*Sticking in hepatic region. Constriction. Throbbing in and below hepatic region as if an ulcer would form.* Sensation of internal swelling.

Umbilicus.—Sticking in region. *Griping about U. on eating, with pinching. Pain below U. as from a stone, taking away the breath, after dinner.* Kneading in region as if something drawn from the limbs were collected into a ball.

Hypogastrium.—**Development of a tendency to inguinal hernia** (compare Coccul.). (Glandular swelling on bend of groin.) *The band of clothes above hips is tight. Cutting mornings, with nausea, sweetish disgusting taste, weakness and sleepiness; C. rising to upper A., where it amounted to griping. Pinching* **in morning,** *with fermenting rumbling, then watery diarrhœa.* **Pain in ring in morning in bed as if a hernia would become incarcerated.** *Pain in pubic region. Pain especially extending towards anus. Colic as if flatulence, with cutting, were forcing out bladder, neck of bladder, beginning of urethra, perineum, rectum and anus, < every step, obliging him to walk bent,* > **rest when sitting and lying** (Sul.). Pressure like a distention, on inspiration, talking or touch. **Forcing down towards genitals.** *Griping drawing in ring, extending upward in side of abdomen. Constriction when walking in open air, with forcing downward towards genitals. Soreness on bend of groin.* **Weakness in ring as if a hernia would form.**

Clinical.—Engorgement of the liver, with stitches and soreness and yellow face (symptoms of gall-stone). Colic from indigestion, with pressure upward causing shortness of breath, and downward causing desire for stool, with general soreness. Colic, with constipation and frequent desire for stool. Jaundice resulting from fits of anger. Affections of the liver in persons who habitually use alcoholic liquors, especially if constipated and subject to hæmorrhoids. Incarcerated hernia; numerous cases of apparently irreducible hernia have been reported as cured by this drug, which seems to relax the unnatural condition of the irritated

muscles; in more recent hernias a complete cure is made by Nux v., by restoring tone to the relaxed muscles which have permitted the hernia to protrude; this is especially true in infants who have hernia from extreme constipation or from crying, with colic and indigestion, especially if they are very cross.

Rectum.—Sticking during stool. **Sharp pain after stool and after eating, < exerting mind or studying**; *in morning before stool.* Pain in evening, and in anus; deep in, taking away the breath about midnight; as from constipation, in evening after eating, > emissions of flatus. Contraction in morning after rising, and in anus; *C. at times, as if he must go to stool.* **Constriction during stool, with discharge of bright blood; C. after stool, with sensation as if some could not be evacuated; in R. and anus after eating, exerting mind and reflecting, with tearing sticking**; *preventing stool. Raw, sore feeling.* Itching; voluptuous; tickling in R. and anus, with crawling. **Sensation as if stool were incomplete,** *with colic.* Urging, with pain in hepatic region and other parts of abdomen; **anxious U.; ineffectual; frequent, ineffectual, after the usual stool; frequent, ineffectual, with griping, and stool when passed was soft;** ineffectual, after eating. *Pressure before stool.*

Anus.—**Blind hæmorrhoids**; *H., with burning and sticking in rectum.* Hæmorrhoidal excitement. *Hæmorrhage. Discharge of blood with the stool;* D. of thread-worms. *Jerking when not at stool. Burning smarting some hours after stool, with cutting as in a sore. Biting in evening after stool, with sore pain.* Burning pain externally after stool. *Itching,* when walking in evening, *with sore pain as from hæmorrhoids; I. on margin becoming a smarting and sore pain as from blind piles;* and hot stool. Crawling at night as from thread-worms. Pain in perineum after dinner.

Clinical.—Hæmorrhoids, with itching and frequent urging to stool. Blind hæmorrhoids, which are extremely painful.

Stool.—Watery and copious; W., yellow, frequent; W., involuntary, during emission of flatus, then hard fæces. *Diarrhœa; in morning after rising* (and drinking), then weakness, yawning, sleepiness, chilliness and dulness of head, then refreshing sleep; **dark, < morning and after dinner**; *scanty and corrosive in morning;* green, slimy; offensive; and copious, two hours later watery and urgent, with colic; afterwards hard. *Soft, with griping.*

Constipation; with rush of blood to head; **as from constriction of intestines**; *as from inactivity of rectum. Hard, then sticking as from hæmorrhoids;* H. and large; H. in morning and after eating (and drinking), mixed with soft fæces and flatus. *Whitish, mixed with tenacious mucus and streaks of blood.* Coated with white mucus; with blood and mucus. Two, in forenoon, with straining. Small, frequent. Difficult, with burning. Delayed, with urging, after five hours and a half urging again, stool loose and scanty, with straining.

Clinical.—It is generally indicated in constipation when there is now, or has been, repeated ineffectual urging to stool throughout the whole abdomen, in this respect differing from Sul., which is indicated when the uneasiness is in the rectum; the constipation of Nux v. usually results from inharmonious action of the persistaltic muscles of the bowels, while that of Sul. is from dryness, irritability and relaxation of the rectum, particularly caused by injections of water. Diarrhœa consisting of frequent small evacuations, with backache and constant feeling as if there were more to be evacuated. Dysentery, with backache, violent tenesmus, nausea and vomiting. Dysentery, especially after the administration of allopathic remedies, with disordered stomach, morning aggravation, discharge of bloody mucus.

Urinary Organs.—Bladder, *discharge of tenacious mucus during micturition;* (sticking after dinner, > emission of flatus); *pain in neck before micturition; pressure in neck after micturition;* **burning in neck during micturition, with tearing**; *itching burning in region of neck in morning in bed,* seeming like sexual desire. **Urging**; in afternoon; **frequent; ineffectual**; and urine scanty. **Micturition difficult**; *M. in a strong stream;* painful, of thick urine; delayed. Slight incontinence of urine.

Urethra.—Discharge of mucus. Sticking or jerking before urinating; itching stitch in forepart, extending backward. Pain in meatus, with shivering; P. in meatus as if sore before and after micturition. *Constriction in forepart, extending backward, in morning and when reflecting. Itching when urinating. Burning in urethra when urinating;* and at other times tearing; *before micturition after dinner, with sticking. Burning pain in forepart when urinating.*

Urine.—*Turbid, with dirty yellow sediment.* Reddish and thick. Watery. Pale, then discharge of a thick, whitish substance like matter, with burning pain.

Clinical.—Extremely irritable bladder, with strangury, frequent and painful efforts to urinate, with discharge of only a few drops of burning urine. Paralysis of the bladder, with dribbling of urine. Retention of urine, and spasmodic closure of the neck of the bladder. Hæmaturia, with suppression of the hæmorrhoidal flow or of the menses. Renal colic of r. side, extending to the genitals, with frequent ineffectual efforts to urinate, but the urine only dribbles.

Sexual Organs.—Pressure outward in morning in bed. Irritation in morning after rising, with desire for an emission. Sore pain in tip of glans after micturition. Biting in glans. Itching of glans; in morning; biting; burning, posteriorly; corrosive, evening and morning. *Erections mornings; after midday nap;* persistent. Prepuce retracted above glans; *P. sore on margin,* < towards evening; *biting itching on inner surface,* < towards evening. Profuse smegma behind corona glandis. Pinching on r. side of scrotum. *Itching of scrotum. Testicles, stitches;* constriction; aching in r. T. and spermatic cord, > camphor or brandy, with heaviness; heat. *Desire on slight provocation;* < *morning in bed;* D., but during an emission he became impotent. *Emission at night, with lascivious dream;* E. at night without erection, then relaxation of lower part of body; at night, then coldness of feet.

Female.—Discharge of yellow mucus; offensive mucus. *Internal swelling of vagina like prolapsus, with burning pain,* < *touch.* Corrosive itching eruption on pudenda. *Burning in pudenda,* with great sexual desire. Pressure in uterus at stool, as if the child would pass. **Menses too early; with cramps**; and scanty; and scanty, and shorter than usual; delayed till full moon; at full moon; M. that had ceased the day before returned for a few hours.

Clinical.—Sometimes indicated in venereal ulcers, with the general irritability characteristic of the drug. General effects of sexual excesses. Prolapsus of the uterus, recent, resulting from sudden strains, associated with the bladder and bowel troubles characteristic of the drug. During pregnancy useful for morning sickness, possibly with jaundice, constipation, etc. Valuable during labor, when the pains in the back go down the thighs, or when the os is rigid, with constant desire to evacuate the bowels and bladder. Too early and profuse menstruation, with morning nausea, chilliness, and pressure in genitals. Intense, agonizing dysmenorrhœa, with constant desire to evacuate the bowels and bladder. Dysmenorrhœa, with cross disposition, pain in sacrum as if it would break, bearing down in uterus, constant desire for stool. Dysmenorrhœa, with nausea, red face, etc. Generally in the irregular menstruation characteristic of Nux v. new symptoms appear and some of the old ones become worse.

Respiratory Organs.—Larynx. **Roughness and scraped feeling, provoking cough.** *Dry, painful catarrh in evening before sleep; in morning, with heat of hands and feet, then general sweat, relieving the catarrh. Itching, provoking cough.* Inability to speak aloud.

Trachea.—Hawking of mucus, without cough. *Adherent mucus high up, provoking cough; A. mucus in upper part in morning on rising, chest seems stuffed up. Upper part constricted by mucus, which he must forcibly expectorate by short coughs. Tickling itching in middle of sternum, provoking cough.* Tickling on expiration, provoking cough.

Cough; at night; *at night, preventing sleep* (Puls.); at night, with oppression of chest; *on physical exertion; after eating;* from reading or reflecting; disturbing sleep till midnight; violent, every other day; *causing sore sticking; causing headache as if skull would burst; causing bruised pain in upper abdomen;* causing heat; (causing cracking in ear); *scraping.* **Dry cough from midnight till daybreak;** D., from tickling in region of palate; *in violent paroxysms in evening after lying down and* **in morning;** *and fatiguing, about midnight if she lies upon back, > lying on side.* C., with sweetish expectoration; C. < walking in open air, with expectoration, then weakness; **violent C. in morning before rising, with expectoration of clotted blood and aching in chest.**

Respiration.—*Tight, and thereupon hacking cough. Dyspnœa; morning and evening;* in morning when lying on back, but headache after turning on r. side; *at night on waking from frightful dreams,* with roaring in ears, rapid pulse and sweat; after dinner, obliged to breathe deeply and slowly, but after some hours short, rapid respiration; > lying; with anxiety and intermittent sweat. Irregular, superficial, suffocative. Short, she could not inspire sufficient air, with rapid pulse. Rapid and labored; R., sighing, constantly interrupted; R., with great heaving of chest; R., difficult, with pain in præcordial region. Slow, with dilated pupils. Suspended. Unable to breathe when walking if the clothes are tight under the ribs, > loosening them somewhat, but respiration again difficult if the clothes are removed.

Clinical.—Irritable cough coming on in the morning, > warm drinks, sometimes with involuntary micturition. Reflex cough < mental work, or cough associated with indigestion, always after eating, with soreness over the stomach. Asthma recurring towards morning and < eating heartily. Occasionally useful in whooping cough, < towards morning, cold air, eating or drinking.

Chest.—Catarrhal accumulation in morning, so that he cannot loosen it by coughing without pain in trachea. Catarrh (like felt) in morning, > rising, with hoarseness and roughness in chest and a sore spot in trachea, from which mucus is loosened by coughing.

Sticking in sternum in afternoon; in pectoral muscles, not caused by breathing; in middle, < moving about; in pectoral muscles, with internal and external warmth in chest; itchlike, below nipple; (jerking). **Scraping causing cough.** Pain after eating, with cutting; P. in l. if she sits awhile, > eructations; beneath axilla on touch; in r. nipple on touch; anterior to r. scapula, with cough; extending transversely across, with shortness of breath; transversely across, impeding respiration; in nipples, as from milk rushing into breasts after childbirth; as if sternum were pressed inward; in region of sternum as if too short, during the day on breathing. Bruised pain in sternum on touch; below shoulder, < motion and touch; in sternum, extending to scapulæ, during the day, with stitches and shortness of breath. Drawing pain; in ribs; pinching, near sternum. Drawing in l. side in morning, with burning tearing; D. beneath l. breast, with anxiety, a kind of oppression of heart, which makes respiration difficult.

Asthmatic constriction transversely through C. on walking or ascending a height. Oppression; in evening; as from tight clothes, on ascending steps, > sitting down. *Compression; at night in bed. Weight in open air;* W. externally at night, with paralyzed sensation in sides. Feeling as if something would fall down. Anxiety. Stuffed feeling, he cannot loosen it by coughing. Nipples sensitive. Throbbing; in side in morning. *Heat; rising into mouth, causing uneasiness, anxiety and sleeplessness.* Warm orgasm that causes anxiety. Warm tension. Painful weariness, > bending backward.

Heart.—Stiches; in præcordial region in morning after rising. Painful thrust towards H., rhythmical with pulse. Pressure on H. in region of pit of stomach. Action rapid and fluttering; slow and feeble. *Palpitation;* in morning, with orgasm of blood; after midnight, with anxiety that impels him to suicide; *on lying down after dinner.*

Clinical.—Angina pectoris from suppression of hæmorrhoids, constricting, agonizing pain, with vomiting, opisthotonos, etc. "Cardiac complaints, with portal obstruction," with distress in the region of the heart, dyspnœa, etc.

Pulse.—Rapid; and irregular; and irregular, during spasms; and small, irregular; and hard, small; and faint; and faint between spasms. Throbbing in carotids. Hard and excited. Irregular; during the spasms, almost lost. Weak. Slow and indistinct.

Neck.—Swelling of l. muscles, with pain on moving head as if tendons were too short. Crackling in vertebræ on moving head. *Paroxysmal tearing in nape in evening.* Pain in joints of vertebræ; in nape and between scapulæ on moving head; bruised, in nape on motion and touch; as if flesh were beaten loose from last vertebra, he could scarcely tolerate the shirt against it; paralytic, in nape, then extending into wrist, on walking in open air, > evening on going to bed, with inability to grasp anything firmly. *Drawing pain in muscles;* in nape; in nape in morning, with feeling of a load on it. Drawing in nape extending down back in afternoon when sitting, with pain in pit of stomach like a crawling, so that she must sit bent over. Stiffness in muscles, with drawing; stiff and drawn to r. side; S. of r. side at night, as if head had been lying in an uncomfortable position.

Clinical.—Wry neck from cold or from nervous shock.

Back.—Tearing and pulling pain; *burning T.;* drawing T. *Pain;* in vertebræ; indescribable, then tetanic spasms; *bruised;* drawing; as if congested, on touch and pressure. Constriction. Stiffness. Stitches between scapulæ; on motion and breathing; burning. Sprained pain in scapulæ. Bruised pain in dorsal muscles on touch; D. pain between S., < stooping, with drawing. Constriction between S.

Lumbar Region.—Sticking taking away the breath, on turning upper part of body sideways; (during afternoon chill, then extending into sides and impeding respiration); burning, extending through thigh on stepping and walking; jerking, and in ischii, so that she could not turn in bed, also pain in lumbar region during rest, inability to lie still, cough or sneeze on account of the painful jerking. Tearing; when walking and sitting, > lying, with pulling. **Pain in morning,** *with pain as from incarcerated flatus low down in hypogastrium; P. passing to hips;* at night, preventing turning over in bed; extending towards spine, in morning after drinking, then it presses towards hypochondria, as from incarceration of flatus; extending up spine, causing anxiety, after supper; as if dislocated, in pelvic region, on motion; as if it would break, caused by a draught of air, was obliged to walk bent over; heavy; throbbing, during shaking chill, with eructations; drawing, extending up back, with paralytic stiffness. *Bruised pain in L. region and in knees* in morning in bed, with drawing pain; *B. pain* on bending far backward, < bending far forward; < motion. Pain as if beaten or weak, as after childbirth, during the day. Constriction extending into side. Tense and sore on touch.

Clinical.—Lumbago, the back feels bruised and lame. General rheumatism of the large muscles of the back and trunk, with extreme sensitiveness to pain and to cold, with gastric symptoms. Lumbago < night in bed, inability to turn over, the longer he lies the worse it gets. Spinal irritation, with loss of power in the extremities, which go to sleep easily, numbness. Formication along the spine. Occasionally useful as an intercurrent in locomotor ataxia. Multiple sclerosis.

Extremities.—Lower outstretched, stiff and cold, upper cold and affected by cramps. *Trembling, with jerking of heart.* Jerking in evening in bed; J. under skin. Tearing in l. arm and r. thigh after midday nap during menstruation. Pain in l. wrist and tibia; in joints after midnight, < motion; *spasmodic, after yawning and stretching, with chilliness and internal beating;* crampy, on motion of them. *Bruised pain; in morning, < joints, worse the longer he lies, > rising; in joints and shafts of long bones in morning,* > rising, with incarceration of flatus low down in abdomen; in joints on which she was lying in morning in bed, compelling turning over, > rising; in joints on motion; in joints on which he was not lying, compelling frequent turning, with tearing. Drawing on backs and soles of feet and toes and in arms and hands, with sticking.

Weakness; of arms and feet in afternoon, with heaviness; *after taking the open air;* < ascending steps; with rending; with painful, contractive sensation through whole body; *sudden, of arms and lower extremities in morning;* sudden paralytic, < motion. Heaviness of arms and lower limbs. Stiffness; of joints; with jerking; of joints, with soreness; with tension.

Upper Extremities.—Shoulder. Indescribable pain in joint on which he was lying about 3 A.M., > turning over, with general sweat; P. in l. joint, as if ligaments were torn, in evening when lying on r. side, > lying on l. side; rheumatic, in r. and deltoid; drawing, in top; paralytic, in joint when sitting and walking, with heaviness and weariness of whole arm, after some motion he could not hold up the arm. Bruised pain in joint and scapula on bending head to opposite side; B. pain in joint so that he cannot raise arm; B. or wearied pain in joint if arm hangs down on walking in open air.

Arm.—Pain impeding motion. Drawing pain; extending upward in arm, with paralytic stiffness. Burning, painful spot in deltoid, with external heat. Uneasiness at night, at one time he wishes to cover them, at another to uncover them. Indolence. Falling asleep at night. Sensation as if falling asleep, without prickling, then contracted sensation.

Elbow.—Boring about 2 A.M. when lying on opposite side. Contractive pain.

Forearm.—Always partially flexed. Swelling of muscles on inner side of l., and pain as if burnt. Drawing pain, with a stitch in fingers. Paralytic pain in middle of r., extending outward. Numb pain down l. ulnar nerve to fingers. Weakness; after midday nap, and of hands. Falling asleep every or every other morning after rising, it seems dead, with coldness, but with distention of veins.

Wrist.—Drawing sticking in r. external condyle in evening before sleep. Pain in r. as if dislocated on moving hand. Lameness and stiffness of r. W. and hand.

Hand.—Pale swelling, and of fingers. (Often dark red, full of distended veins.) Cramplike contraction of palm so that it cannot be spread out without pain. Twitching, and of fingers. Sharp pain in r. palm. Drawing pain extending upward, then in elbow. No power to write. *Falling asleep.*

Fingers.—Dislocation of thumb on motion. Spasmodic contraction when yawning. Cramp after midnight in bed. Jerking sticking extending backward along bone of thumb. Cramplike sensation shooting into F. on stretching out arms, with sticking. Sharp pain in r. third. Drawing pain up and down. Pain in joints as after hard work and as if tendons were too short. Falling asleep during night-sweat.

Lower Extremities.—*Unsteadiness;* with dread of falling. The child often falls when walking. Separated, straight and stiff. Shock on looking at a vexatious body, then whole body is affected and she almost loses consciousness. Tearing above and below knee in evening, with sticking. Inability to flex on account of pain. Bruised feeling. Sudden sensation of holding back when walking, so that she must often stand still, with electric shocks in them. Uneasiness before midnight, with an almost voluptuous, agreeable, but intolerable sensation, preventing sleep, forcing him to alternately draw up and stretch out legs. Weakness; of r. on walking in open air; with heaviness; and falling down. Heaviness, obliging him to sit down, Sensibility blunted. Stiff, immovable, muscles hard, tetanically contracted. Falling asleep when sitting during dinner. Paralysis before tetanus.

Thigh.—Jerking in flesh; in hip-joint before dinner; in side of r., as if a thread were pulled. Sticking in r. hip as if sprained. Drawing tearing extending to knee, from fatigue. *Bruised feeling;* in flesh; in r. natis; in muscles of middle on walking; *in muscles of T. and knees, < motion and touch;* in posterior muscles, < rising from a seat. Paralytic pain in head of femur, extending below knee, when walking. Drawing-downward sensation. *Paralytic drawing in muscles of T. and calf, painful on walking.* Gnawing, biting-itching pain in T. and over knee in evening in bed. Painful tension as if too short. Heaviness of r. Burning in r. hip-joint.

Knee.—*Painful swelling. Tottering.* Trembling, and of one foot; evening when standing, with an excited, even agreeable tension of mind. Jerking in hollows when standing after walking in open air. Bruised pain during the day. Feeling as if it would crack when walking. *Sensation in hollows as if too short on rising from a seat.* Tensive pain in patellæ as if weary, on ascending steps, < morning. Weakness. *Stiffness in hollows, < standing, with tension.*

Leg.—Cramp on getting into a warm bed. Cramp in calves; in morning in bed on flexing leg; in evening in bed on stretching out leg; after midnight in bed, if thigh and leg are flexed on body; caused by washing feet. Cramplike pain in calves. Sticking in calf on exposure to cold air, as if leg had been asleep. Sticking burning pain in a spot in tibia. Tearing in l., extending to toes, in afternoon. Pressure on side of calf; on outer side of calf, as before cramp, mornings on rising. *Tensive pain in calves.* Spasmodic drawing. Heaviness. Stiffness; and numbness. Falling asleep after sitting, when walking and standing; in calves and feet in morning; when sitting and standing; and sticking in it if it rests against the other leg; sensation of, without prickling, then contracted sensation.

Ankle.—Easy dislocation when walking, with giving way. Tearing in malleolus after midday nap. Sprained pain in morning when walking, on stepping shooting up into leg. Pain as if fatigued, on walking, with pain in tendons as if too short. Drawing in r. external malleolus in evening before going to bed, with sticking. Weakness of l., with pain on walking.

Foot.—Swelling of back; S. of sole in morning (that leg has an ulcer); S. and dampness. Sticking jerking from feet to hips in morning in bed, > lying on painless side. Spasmodic contraction of r. sole; of soles when thighs are bent. Cramp in soles often during the day on rising from a seat, > stretching out feet and running, and at night cramp on drawing up feet or bending thighs, preventing sleep. Stitches in heels; in soles. Tearing in sole in afternoon when lying (preceded by burning in ball of thumb). Pain as if shoes were too tight and as if soles were sore from walking. Pain like a burning on side of F. and toes and on top of toes, and as if shoe pressed foot, in evening. Burning pain in soles. (Pain as if heels were sore from walking, when stepping upon them, < stepping upon a stone.) Beating pain in a chilblain as from cold, in summer. Feeling in r. when walking as if it would trip, > getting warm from a sharp walk. Peculiar drawing in backs and soles. *Falling asleep of soles (deadness).* Numbness of heels as after jumping from a height.

Toes.—Spasmodic contraction on yawning. Cramp after midnight in bed. Cramplike pain in r. great during rest. Ulcerative pain in roots of nails on touch. Sore pain in corns. Falling asleep of great.

Clinical.—Partial paralysis of the lower extremities from overexertion or from being soaked, sensation impaired, legs cold, bluish.

Skin.—Painful swellings on forehead; hot S., painful to touch, on thumb, that by the joint develops into an abscess. *Jaundice, with aversion to food and attacks of faintness, then sickness and weakness.* Congestion on face, neck and chest. Red spots on fingers, which seem frozen, with burning itching, < in bed or on entering a warm room. Inflamed redness about a previous ulcer on leg, on motion.

Eruption on inner side of r. forearm; itching E.; itching burning E. Tetter on lower part of chin. Itching rash on arms, with smarting after rubbing. Burning itching rash on knee; on thighs during menstruation. *Itching pimples on chin, the larger surrounded by redness;* P. painful on touch in skin of lower jaw; itching biting, on nates. Pustules on cheeks; about lips; red, painful, on scalp and face. Boil anteriorly on thigh; posteriorly on thighs; on thigh, with sticking; on knee, making whole foot stiff.

Tearing in an ulcer on leg if exposed to open air. Pain above l. eye as if it had been burnt. (Sensitiveness of whole body as if sore, and on touch it seems as if different places were asleep.) Burning itching stitches in various parts; in evening after lying down. Crawling on face; forehead and vertex; from feet upward; in calves after walking in open air. Insensibility.

Itching on finger-joints; on leg at some distance from an ulcer; in hollows of knees in morning; on perineum after midday nap; thighs when walking; (scalp and nape, < forenoon, with gnawing, as if an ulcer were healing); l. thigh and foot, < evening on getting into bed; on face, > scratching, but returning, with crawling; on toes, as after freezing; biting, here and there, < outer parts of body, on limbs and joints, in evening after lying down. Burning itching over whole body; in evening in bed; on upper arms, thighs, abdomen and back in morning when dressing and in evening on undressing, and even in night.

Clinical.—Acne of the face, the skin is red and blotchy. (K. bi.).

Sleep.—*Yawning during the day, with sleepiness; in morning after rising;* in morning, with stretching, then spasmodic pain, < knees; in afternoon, with stretching; then weakness; that causes cough. Sleepiness; during the day, as from stupefaction of head; *late in morning;* at 11 A.M., before dinner; **in evening, with yawning, in bed immediately falling asleep, sleepless for a long time after midnight, then sleep late in morning, with vivid dreams of the events of the previous day, in morning he did not wish to rise;** *after eating;* when walking in open air, then palpitation and anxiety, with swelling of veins of hands. *Aversion to rising in morning. Inclination to lie down again in morning; in forenoon. Difficult waking in morning. Lies mostly on back, with one or both arms under head; on back, with one or both arms stretched above head, talks in sleep, and* **wakes between 2 and 3 A.M.;** *on back, with head bent backward, arms above head,* so that hands lie on nape; *on back, with head low.* Stupid slumber (coma), with dreams of strife and excitement, and the night seemed too long and wearisome.

Sleepless till midnight, with heat without thirst; except from 11 till 1, and necessity to rise at 3 A.M.; S. or frightful dreams. *Sleepiness only after daybreak.* Late falling asleep; on account of many conflicting ideas. Sleep restless and full of care; R., with convulsive movements at times; and little; and broken by flatulent colic, sour eructations and sexual excitement, next night heavy S. *Snoring before midnight; before midnight as if posterior nares and palate were constricted;* with whistling expiration through nose. Groaning moaning. Ravings at night. Anxiety, he threw off the covering. Unintelligible morose prattling before midnight; anxious whining prattling about 4 A.M., then emission of flatus. Jerking in afternoon nap, with fright; J. of limbs, on falling asleep, causing palpitation. Starting from sleep; *on falling asleep;* starting from sleep at night and during the day when awake. (Sprang from bed delirious during evening nap.) Waking in fright at slightest noise. Waking early at night, with apprehension. Frequent waking, with difficult falling asleep again, then vivid dreams.

Dreams.—In midday nap, and talking aloud. *Frightful;* as, for example, of wild beasts; waking him. Anxious, with weeping. Disagreeable, of things that happened or were talked about the previous day. Of lice and vermin. That the teeth fell out. Of sick or mutilated people. Of indifference at horrible mutilations and lacerations. That he is engaged in an absorbing occupation. Delightful. Half-waking, with fatiguing thought; H., sad, as, for example, of the heads of deceased acquaintances without bodies.

Fever.—Chilliness; mornings after rising; at 3 A.M., *preceded by drawing pain through thighs and legs obliging him to draw them up and stretch them out;* **in afternoon, with blue nails, then general heat, with burning of hands, with thirst for water, then for beer,** *without sweat;* towards 6 A.M., with at times general heat and drops of sweat on forehead and again chilliness towards 6 P.M.; towards 6 P.M., with intercurrent attacks of heat, recurring at same hour next day; in evening before sleep, and if she wakes; *in evening before lying down, in bed heat of head and face; in evening after lying down, sleep for an hour, then heat,* with headache, roaring in ears and nausea; in evening after lying down, with trembling, then heat of face; at night in bed; at night, with tossing about; in bed, but towards morning sweat preceded by crawling; after dinner; after supper; on slightest motion; from slightest contact of open air, with shivering and pain in back; < afternoon, with weakness, heat and necessity to lie down or to be warmly covered; **with blue hands;** *with blue skin;* with chattering of teeth; with yawning; without thirst.

Shaking chill; then heat and moist skin; in morning in bed, without external coldness, then cramplike contraction of toes and soles. Shivering in morning, with horripilation; S. in evening, with coldness of limbs, redness of face and thirst for beer; *after drinking;* when lying down after dinner, with drawing pain in limbs, as if caused by pain in small of back; on slightest motion; with yawning; then anxious heat, then thirst for beer; then sleep, then shivering again, with coldness of toes. Rigors, then warm sweat.

Internal chilliness, with hot cheeks; I. at night, with internal heat, dryness of mouth, but dread of drinking; I., and it seemed as if she steamed from the throat, and much drinking. Chill alternating with heat at 8.45 A.M., especially heat in head.

Cold skin. Chilliness of face and head; intermittent, about head; externally on head, with internal heat in it. **C. of back and limbs in morning, with pain of skin as from freezing cold, and falling asleep of limbs;** *in back and arms in evening after lying down;* in back after a vexation, with heaviness of lower limbs; creeping, in back, with restlessness and occasional griping in bowels. C. in arms after eating, with gooseflesh, photophobia, heat of cheeks and easy dilatation of pupils; sudden C. of either arms and hands, or of legs and feet in afternoon. Cold hands; and moist, with cold tip of nose; hands, soles and scalp, with external heat of rest of body, redness of cheeks and recurring chilliness, without thirst. Of lower part of body, with heat of face. Cold feet; in morning; in evening, with red cheeks, hot hands and recurring shivering; and damp; and stiff, then cold and stiff toes; as if dashed with cold water, with trembling; then dry heat of face. Cold thighs at night. Creeping coldness over face; in hepatic region; over chest, with tensive pain. Shivering across breasts.

Heat; at 2 A.M., with thirst and drawing pain through thighs and legs; in morning, with thirst for water; in morning on walking in open air, also with full pulse, without thirst, then sleeplessness; in morning in bed, < cheeks, hands and feet, particularly in palms and soles, but cool on uncovering, cool places in bed caused general distress, partly griping or cutting colic; in afternoon or evening, then chilliness; at night, with thirst and almost without sweat; after dinner, < face, that rises from abdomen, with sweat, < back; in bed, with sweat, but shivering on slightest uncovering, after the sweat chilliness, then again sweat; with full, rapid pulse, desire for the bed and thirst.

Dry heat about midnight in bed, without thirst; *D., that does not tolerate uncovering,* after coition, with dryness of mouth, without thirst. Flushing H. on moving about; F., with irritability and rheumatic pains in shoulders and hips. Anxious H., with red cheeks, lips dry, though mouth is full of saliva, desire to drink, but does not relish it, sleeplessness, lying with arms under head, after the heat thirst for beer; paroxysm of heat, with sweat on forehead and anxiety, without redness of cheeks. *Internal H.;* with full pulse, without thirst, then sleeplessness; and it seemed as if she steamed from the throat, during which she drank much. Heat running through all veins, > vomiting.

Heat of skin; with clammy sweat. Heat of head in evening; during dinner; in brain beneath frontal bone; with redness of cheeks and chilliness over rest of body; as in coryza, with one red cheek and discharge of mucus from nose. Heat of face in morning after rising, with constipation and flatulent rumbling in abdomen; face in evening in bed, and restless sleep before midnight; in evening after lying down, and in soles and inside of hands; cheeks after eating, with redness of them and dulness of head; without redness; with shivering over rest of body; internal; internal in F. and head in morning on waking, with general sweat, without thirst; *flushing, in cheeks on slightest exertion;* flushing, towards evening; flushing, when walking. Heat here and there on top of shoulder and arm. Burning on back of hand; in hands in morning, but need to cover them because coolness causes pain. Burning in ball of thumb on lying down after dinner; heat in soles in morning, he tries to cover them because cold causes pain.

Sweat; in morning; in morning, < upper parts, then drawing pain in l. side; after 2 A.M., in sleep; at 3 A.M., < below nose, on forehead (scalp), nape, throat, pit of stomach and between thighs, with anxious heat and dryness of tip of tongue, anterior part of palate and lips, without desire to drink; every day about 5 A.M. after waking; *after midnight;* on moving about the room; during and after anxiety; between the spasms; (in bed and on rapid walking); (> open air); in attacks, followed by dry heat; offensive; offensive, all night; sour, at night; cold; warm, except on lower limbs, which were moist, cold and rigid; of the odor of musty straw (except on face), at night and in morning. Sweat except on head and face, in morning after waking. On one side of head and face; on forehead and scalp when eating; clammy, on forehead when walking in open air. On face; and hands; diseased side of face, with one-sided headache. On inside of hands; on walking in open air; cool. On thighs and calves after midnight. Offensive, on side.

Clinical.—Frequently indicated in intermittent fever, the paroxysms anticipating in the morning, the chill accompanied by blueness of the finger-nails, yawning, aching in the back and limbs, after the chill thirst occurs and is followed by fever, which lasts a long time and is followed by rather light perspiration, during the intervals there are numerous symptoms indicating the drug, especially in the abdominal organs; sometimes there is a feeling of paralysis in the limbs during the fever; as in Ign., the patient is inclined to cover himself during the fever in order to avoid feeling chilly.

Ocimum.

A tincture is made of the fresh leaves of Ocimum canum, D. C.

Clinical.—This drug has been found useful in renal colic, especially of r. side, associated with violent vomiting. The late Dr. Dunham used it very frequently for uric acid diathesis, with large deposits of red sand, particularly if the patient was subject to a pain in the ureters.

Œnanthe.

A tincture is made of the fresh root of Œnanthe crocata, L.

Ally.—Cicuta.

Clinical.—Epileptiform convulsions, in one case coming on in the seventh month of pregnancy, almost immediately cured by the 3rd dil.; in another case, convulsions in a child, apparently preceding the outbreak of an exanthema; another case of epilepsy, worse during menstruation. It is reported to have cured tickling cough, with rattling in the lower part of the chest and thick, frothy expectoration.

Œnothera.

A tincture is made of the fresh plant of Œnothera biennis, L.

Clinical.—Chronic diarrhœa, exhausting, watery, almost involuntary.

Oleander.

A tincture is made of the fresh leaves of Nerium oleander, L.

General Action.—A narcotic poison, with tendency to convulsions. General paralytic symptoms supervene, with a weak, irregular pulse. It exerts a marked effect on the skin, especially on the scalp (compare Anacard. and Silicea).

Generalities.—Fell senseless. Lay as if in slumber, but conscious and able to move (Gels.). Stretching of upper part of body and of arms. Outstretched, stiff, pale, limbs cool. Arms drawn up against chest, lower limbs to abdomen and chin against chest. Spasm, with cold, clammy skin and barely perceptible pulse. Spasmodic contractions of all muscles, more in upper than in lower limbs, on attempting to rouse him, > towards evening, between the spasms he lay on his back, but the superior contractions of l. side threw him over on the right.

Tearing in l. side of neck and l. scapula, alternating with T. in temple and second l. molar, towards evening and in night. Pinching in several parts of body and of limbs, fingers and toes, as if bones were crushed. Pressure inward in several parts. Bad feeling, with weakness in abdomen and chest. General sick feeling, with weakness of limbs. Restlessness. Weakness; < rising. Faint; and down-hearted, general giving way. Stiffness of limbs, < l. fingers, and S. of back, so that rising in bed was difficult. (Symptoms more severe on second than on first day.)

Clinical.—Hemiplegia preceded by vertigo.

Mind.—Lively in afternoon and jumping about. Screaming. *Fretful;* and reserved. Passionate, but he immediately repented of it. Intolerant of contradiction. Anxiety. Loss of self-confidence, causing sadness. Disinclination to work; or to undertake any other agreeable occupation. *Confusion when reading, if he makes a great effort to understand the book. Difficulty in grasping the connection when reading a long sentence. Disturbed by other ideas of his own when reading.* Busy with beautiful images concerning the future when studying. *Loss of memory* (Anac.); of the names of his acquaintances. Stupidity. Insensibility. Coma, from which she could be aroused by loud talking, speech connected but difficult, as soon as she stopped talking she sank back into coma, with distortion of eyes.

Clinical.—Said to be valuable in the mental condition of slow perception.

Head.—Boring in brain. *Pain in brain;* P. as if head were pressed forward. Tightness, more stupefying than painful. *Heaviness;* > lying, with dulness of it, nausea and other disagreeable sensations. Dulness. Vertigo; on rising from lying; on walking in open air, swimming of objects, darkness before eyes, with flashes of lightning; if he looked towards the ground when standing erect, with double vision (Gels.); as if hearing and vision would vanish, especially as if it would become black before r. eye, during dinner, which he swallowed in haste.

Forehead.—*Pain as if it would burst.* Hammering in a spot in forepart. Pulsating pain. Sudden, stupefying pain in forepart, as from a blow. Pressure on r. eminence. *Pressure outward; above F.;* in l. eminence, > pressure of hand. Compression. Uneasiness. Whirling vertigo, with tottering of lower limbs.

Temple.—Pinching in r. Pain, now higher up, now lower down, when chewing; P. like a shock in l.; in l., drawing upward and downward, > open air. Drawing in l. Sensation in l. T. and meatus auditorius like that caused by yawning.

Vertex.—Deeply-piercing stitches in r. side. Boring in upper part of brain. Pressure in upper cranial bones as if sore. Contractive burning pain externally on l. side.

Side.—Pressure inward in r.; stupefying. Pain over mastoid process as if a nail were driven into it, with stupefaction.

Occiput.—Tensive stitch in bone. Sharp pain externally on l. side. Pressure in a spot.

Scalp.—**Desquamation.** Itching pimples. **Gnawing itching; biting itching at night, as from lice. (Itching) eroding as from lice, after scratching smarting as if scratched raw.**

Clinical.—Vertigo on looking fixedly or on rising in bed or on looking down. Headache, > forcible squinting (Farrington). Crusta lactea; the eruption is moist and scaly, occurs especially on the occiput and behind the ears; after scratching there are burning and soreness, with occasional biting-itching.

Eyes.—Fixed; and lustreless. Turned upward.

Distorted. Sunken. Aching as from overexertion. Pressure as from a hard substance. Pressure downward in l. eye and malar-bone. Biting in l. Lachrymation on reading. Itching of r. ball. Pupils dilated; contracted. Lids involuntarily drawn together, as if sleepy; sticking in l. upper, with itching; tension in l. on reading; burning tension in r.; burning in r. upper; burning in lower, with itching about it. Tensive pain in one canthus as if eye were turned upward excessively, in evening, it was difficult to turn eye the opposite way. Sore pain on touch, in r. brow towards temple. Intermittent pressure on upper margin of orbit. It seems as if it would become black before eyes. Blackness before eyes on rising up; B. on looking sideways without turning head.

Ear.—Sharp pain within. Cramplike drawing on outer, and below it, as if it were drawn outward. Burning in entrance of l. Shrill, stupefying ringing in l. Singing in l. Howling in l.

Nose.—Numbness on back, like a painless pressure. Violent sneezing.

Face.—Redness of cheeks without heat; R. of face and eyes, face pale towards evening. Pale; in morning after rising, and disturbed look, eyes surrounded by blue rings, and cheeks sunken; with brown lips, < lower. Twitching, < about mouth. Benumbing pinching in malar-bones. Pain in bones of r. side. Pressure on r. cheek near angle of lower jaw; numb, painless, on l. zygoma close to ear; stupefying, between root of nose and l. orbit; tensive, more stupefying than painful, on malar-bone, extending deeply into head and root of nose. Pain in r. upper jaw, below malar-bone. Stiffness of muscles of jaw. Lips, twitching outward of l. corner; sudden swelling about l. corner; swollen (numb) sensation in upper; burning pain in r. side of lower during and after motion; burning sticking over l. corner.

Mouth.—Teeth. Cutting when chewing. Drawing in r. lower molars; in second l. molar; tearing, in first l. molar, and at times in the next hollow tooth, at night, > rising, returning in bed, with anxiety as if he were to die, frequent micturition, nausea and heat of l. cheek. Molars sensitive on chewing, as if they were hollow. Loose sensation, with bluish-white gum.

Tongue coated white, with dry mouth and lips; T. dirty white and papillæ elevated; stitches; burning stitches in l. side. Speech unintelligible; lost. Foaming at mouth. Taste bitter; *T. flat and nauseous to food in evening;* insipid, as from a disordered stomach.

Throat.—Sticking in thyroid cartilage. Sharp pain in l. side, near Adam's apple. Pushing in anterior cervical muscles, so that he must loosen the neckband, a suffocating, choking sensation. Pain as if a dull point were pressing upon r. side of œsophagus, with pain in cervical muscles on external pressure. Burning in pharynx extending to stomach. Irritation of pharynx.

Stomach.—**Ravenous hunger** (Cannab. ind., Lyc.); *after the nausea;* after rapid walking, *with trembling of hands when eating and general weakness;* yet no appetite, but he greedily swallowed large amounts. Longing for the food before him caused his hands to tremble. Speedily satiated though he relished the food. Appetite lost; for food and smoking; and everything nauseates him, as if afterwards he would vomit or have diarrhœa. Aversion to cheese. Thirst; for cold drinks, especially cold water.

Eructations; of bad odor; empty, violent; empty, violent, when eating at noon.

Nausea; in mouth; in mouth, and with every act of retching running of water from mouth, cervical muscles spasmodically and painfully contracted, as if it would strangle him, abdominal muscles similarly affected, and at first with much retching he raises only mucus from fauces, then sour liquid portions of the food; in pit of stomach, in bed after sleep, with difficult breathing, > rising; < rising; < stooping, momentarily > eructations; with general sick feeling; with collection of water in mouth; with collection of water, if he swallows it the N. disappears for a moment, with flat taste; forcing him to stop eating though he relishes the dinner.

Vomiting; and retching; copious, painful; frightful, then thirst; violent, of a green, bloody liquid; repeated, of mucus and bile; of bitter, yellow-green water; of the bread just eaten, with water.

Pain; in epigastric region; in a spot in gastric region beneath l. short ribs on every expiration, > inspiration, < external pressure. Oppression in pit when lying, with vomiting of mucus, water and bread. Heat and constriction. Intermittent throbbing in l. side of pit. Sensation in pit as if he felt every beat of heart through whole chest, as after great heat, though the heart did not beat violently. Emptiness in pit, with full feeling in abdomen.

Clinical.—Extremely weak digestion, with ravenous hunger; vomiting of food and greenish water, followed by renewed hunger. Pulsation in the pit of the stomach, as of the beating of the heart.

Abdomen.—*Rumbling;* and gurgling, then thin, yellow stool. Emission of flatus; *of the odor of bad eggs.* Cramps. Pinching-sticking when walking. Griping; intermittent, with indications of diarrhœa. Colic; then thin stools. Weakness, with feeling as before diarrhœa. Itching stitches beneath l. short ribs. Stitches posteriorly in ilium, with pain on pressure. Jerking pain above l. hip-bone. Emptiness in upper A. Coldness in r. side. Jerking thrusts above root of penis.

Umbilical Region.—Rumbling and gurgling, with emptiness in abdomen, then emission of flatus. Stitches below umbilicus; S. or blows in l. side below umbilicus; long-drawn S. as if winding out of abdomen, near r. side of U. Gnawing in l. side above U.; G. internally below U. Sensitiveness, with discomfort in hypogastrium and uneasiness about U. that at times becomes a pressure, at times a gnawing.

Rectum and Anus.—*Burning in anus when not at stool and before and after stool* (Sil., Sul.). Ineffectual urging.

Stool.—Watery and scanty. Diarrhœa; the first part, the last harder, so that he must strain. Soft. Hard and difficult. **Food eaten the previous evening passed rather undigested,** when he thought he emitted only flatus (compare China). *Involuntary.* Bloody. Only after twenty-four hours, first part hard and crumbly, the rest thin. Omitted.

Clinical.—Diarrhœa, containing undigested food which had been eaten the day before. Involuntary evacuations on emitting flatus, in children. Diarrhœa of phthisis.

Urinary Organs.—Frequent urging, with scanty discharge. Frequent and copious micturition. Involuntary micturition.

Respiratory Organs.—Tickling in larynx on inspiration, causing short cough that shakes the whole body.

Tenacious mucus in trachea, with hacking cough in morning on rising. Stertorous breathing.

Chest.—Jerking in r. muscles. *Sticking in sternum;* in l. side; *in l. during inspiration and expiration;* in r. during inspiration and expiration; in l. when walking; when walking, < expiration; in diaphragm during respiration when lying; in a false rib, near r. side of sternum, with pain on pressure; crawling, in sternum; pinching, in l., coming out at false ribs; tensive, in middle; tensive, in sternum, < stooping.

Burrowing in r. costal cartilages, < pressure, with intermittent pressure upon a spot. Intermittent gnawing on one rib of l. side, opposite pit of stomach. Intermittent thrusts in ribs of l. side. Beating like dull thrusts below r. shoulder. Pain in sternum. Pressure on upper part of sternum. External soreness of r. as if pressed hard. Compression when walking, standing and lying, causing deep, anxious respiration. Tightness when lying, with necessity to take long and deep breaths. Emptiness.

Heart.—Anxiety, without anxious thought, with general trembling; A., with distress. *Drawing pain, < stooping and at last during expiration.* Palpitation; with enlarged sensation in chest, he then breathes with great heaving of chest, without anxiety.

Pulse.—Rapid and full in evening; R., later it sank to a thread. Slow in morning after rising; slow, weak; S., violent and full in carotid. Intermittent. Small, irregular, periodically intermittent. Irregular, at one time slow, at another rapid, at one time full, at another soft, small and weak. Weak, thready, afterwards scarcely perceptible.

Neck and Back.—Numbness externally in neck, ascending to head. Tensive stitches in spine when walking and standing; sudden stitches deep internally in r. half of back; burning S. below l. scapula when sitting. Pain in r. side of back as if the hand pressed it, or as from a sprain.

Extremities.—Stretching, with general comfort. Convulsions. Cramps. Pain in joints. Cramplike drawing in several parts. Weakness.

Upper Extremities.—Sticking in l. axilla, > rubbing. Pain in shoulder-joints as if dislocated if he raises arms high or puts them under head when in bed. Pressure on top of r. shoulder. Twitching of muscles of l. arm. Upper arm, itching stitch in l.; jerking sensation in r.; pinching externally in upper part of l. Rhythmical cramplike drawing in shaft of l. humerus, by elbow.

Forearm.—Stitches or thrusts in l. near wrist; burning S. in l. Pressure below elbow; P. as from a blow; intermittent P. in a spot on outer side of l. Pulsating pain on inside of r. by wrist. Drawing in r. above wrist.

Trembling of wrists; of hands when writing (before eating). Swelling of veins of hands. Cramp in l. hand. Intermittent pressure in palm.

Fingers.—Sudden swelling of ring, with burning pain and inability to bend it. Twitching. Burning stitches in tip of l. index; in distal phalanx of r. index, making the finger tremble. Cramplike jerking tearing in proximal phalanx of l. middle. Pain in last phalanx of thumb, with sensation of a blow upon it, so that thumb trembled. Cramplike drawing pain. Drawing in metacarpal joints. Rigid, and thumbs turned into palms.

Lower Extremities.—Quivering extending downward.

Thigh.—Jerking on under surface of l. Sticking on r.; in muscles on inner side of l.; in a spot above r. knee, with burning; drawing, in r., > walking or ascending a hill. Bruised pain in forepart on walking rapidly. Constriction in gluteals when walking, as if sprained. Pressure above knee; intermittent, on upper part of r., < pressure on it; benumbing, on outer side of l., as if tightly bound, so that circulation was impeded. (Burning tension in r.) Bubbling sensation in r. *Weakness of T. and legs when walking, with an asleep sensation in forepart of feet, < soles.*

Knee.—Pulsating pain in hollow when the leg was drawn up. Cramplike drawing in r. knee, that was drawn up. Weakness.

Leg.—Cramp in r. calf when sitting. Twitching sensation in r. calf. Tearing in l. calf when walking. Aching when sitting, obliging him now to stretch them out, now to draw them up. Intermittent painful pressure above r. ankle when standing. Surging sensation when sitting, as after a walk. Wavelike drawing in shafts of bones. Painful weakness, as after a long walk; paralytic W. when walking after sitting with them drawn up.

Foot.—Intermittent bruised pain in a spot in r. sole. Pain in soles after a short walk, with weariness. Pressure on back. Painful throbbing above ball of l. great toe.

Toes.—Stitches in l. fifth; tensive, in tip of l. great. Pain as after hard pressure in T. and its ball.

Skin.—Swelling; red, below eye. Pustules on sides of chin. Itching vesicles on nates. Soreness from slight rubbing of clothes, with rawness and pain. (Itching?) biting on r. cheek.

Itching; *here and there;* on r. scapula; on tip of r. elbow; above bend of elbow; on nates; about nose all the afternoon; on outer and anterior part of r. thigh, temporarily > scratching; on r. thumb, at first > scratching, then changing to gnawing; burning, on forehead, l. cheek and tip of chin, then pimples with hard, elevated margins. *Biting itching on undressing;* B. itching on root of nose, towards l. eye, as if there were smoke in the room. Sticking itching on root of nose and l. malar-bone near eye; on proximal phalanx of middle finger; on l. heel. Itching stitches towards forepart of r. ankle; in r. sole during rest; in posterior muscles of thigh, with burning after scratching; on r. inner malleolus, > scratching.

Sleep.—Yawning, always with shivering running over whole body, causing muscles to shake and then to tremble. Sleepiness. Sleep with open eyes, pallor, pupils small, coldness and insensibility, pulse and respiration small and irregular, he could not be roused, after emetics the child vomited, but whenever aroused he soon sank back into deep sleep. Sleeplessness; and no rest. *Voluptuous dreams, with emissions.* Uneasy dreams.

Fever.—Coldness, with cold sweat; chilliness, with internal and external heat, without thirst; shaking, with cold hands and warm cheeks, without thirst. *Shivering, without thirst;* S. when yawning; S. as from chill or sudden fright. Skin cold and clammy. Cold limbs. Sudden C. on l. chest. Sensation of a cold wind on l. side of neck; on r. side of hypogastrium; on l. cheek, > pressure of hand, when it feels hot to hand.

Heat forces itself out of the body when reading. Flushing heat, < doing anything eagerly, also if he walked rapidly, the heat causing prickling in face. Hot skin. Hot head, with sweat on it. H. beginning at one time in r., at another in l. lobe of ear and extending over side of head and thence over whole face; H. in cheeks, without redness and with dryness of palate and throat; in tip of r. great toe when sitting; tensive, on tip of l. thumb; internal, in side of thigh, then internal coldness low down.

Cold sweat.

Onosmodium Virginianum.

A tincture is made from the fresh plant.

Generalities.—Tremulousness from least exertion. Nervous, trembling feeling, as from hunger. Nervous and shaky feeling that physically and mentally unfits her for any duty. Muscles feel unsteady and treacherous. Inability to lie on l. side. General aching, as if I would have a chill. Every day about 12 or 1 o'clock feeling as if I would have a chill. General distress and full feeling. Light feeling, somewhat like that caused by chloroform. Weakness; in morning, with stiffness; in morning, with soreness; in morning when walking, with sore and lame feeling; with aching, stretching, gaping and disagreeable feeling. Aggravation from pressure or tightness of clothing; from motion or jar; on l. side. Amelioration in open air; from quiet, lying on back, sleep, undressing, cold drinks and eating; temporary A. of all symptoms, except tired feeling in limbs, by eating.

Mind.—Talkative, but in a disconnected way. Irritable. Irresolute. Desire to change the position constantly, followed by desire to lie down and be quiet, with sleepiness. Impatient, my team travels too slowly. Minutes seem like hours. Feeling as if something terrible were going to happen and that she was powerless to help it. Fear to look down lest she might fall in going down stairs; that he might fall into a fire when walking by it, and in spite of all his will power he did stagger into the fire. Wants to think and not move, and thinks until she forgets everything and where she is. I write very fast, but cannot keep pace with my thoughts, before one sentence is completed I begin on another, I omit words and letters, when writing and talking I cannot concentrate my thoughts on the subject. Wish not to talk or make any effort. Listless; and apathetic, as if it were impossible to think. Drowsiness and confusion. Confusion of ideas, forgets the subject of conversation, will begin a subject and before it is complete changes to another. Dull. Forgetful; that he is reading, and he drops the book in vague and listless thought.

Head.—Fulness, > eating and sleep. Heaviness. Cannot bear to move. Lightness. *Frontal pain over eyes; < over l. eye; over bridge of nose; in l. eminence; in r. eminence, changing to l., where it remained; running back into neck; heavy, and the same pain in temples and mastoid region. Pain in l. temple; sharp, darting, in l. temple; darting, throbbing, in l. temple. Pain in mastoid. Dull, heavy pains in l. side and over l. eye, extending around to back of head and neck, < movement and jar, forcing her to go to bed, when they were > sleep, but returned soon after waking.* **Occipito-frontal pain in morning on waking. Dull, heavy pain pressing upward in occiput, with dizziness** (Gels., Cimicif.).

Clinical.—Dull headache, < occipital region, usually extending down nape or over one side of head, generally l.; with the headache usually dizziness and sometimes nausea, and either preceding or following the headache pain in or over the corresponding eye, with stiff, strained sensation in the eye, < reading or near vision; in another case deafness, with roaring, hissing in ears, dull, pressing pain in occiput, < evening, with pain in ear and shooting in front of auricle, vertigo, results of chronic catarrhal inflammation of middle ears, Onos. relieved the headache and pain in ears, but did not affect the hearing or tinnitus. A case of myopia, with dull, stupid aching in r. side of occiput and r. eye, < fatigue, coughing or sudden motion, with vertigo and strained feeling in r. eye. Vertigo, with ringing in ears, inability to lie on l. side or raise her hands above her head.

Eyes.—*Pain in and over l.* Feeling as if she had lost much sleep. Heaviness and dulness. *Feeling of tension, as when straining them to read small print.* Desire to keep them wide open. Feel tired and as if stretching them open. Feeling as if they were very wide open, and he feels as if he wanted to look at objects far away, distant objects look large, it is disagreeable to look at near objects, tense, drawing and tired feeling in ocular muscles. *Optic disc hyperæmic. Retinal vessels engorged,* < l. Aching in upper part of balls. *Dull, heavy pains in balls, with soreness. Lids heavy.* Pain in upper part of l. orbit, with feeling of expansion. Vision impaired; blurred.

Ears and Nose.—Fulness in E. Feeling in E. as in catarrh. Hearing impaired. Singing as from Quinine. Dryness of nose; with feeling as from taking cold. Pain in nasal bones. Sneezing much in morning; and l. side of nose and l. eye seem affected; on first getting up.

Face.—Flushed; < least motion or excitement; with relief of headache; with full feeling. Pain in r. malar-bone where it articulates with frontal bone; darting, through r. malar-bone, with numbness.

Mouth.—Dryness; and of lips, without thirst; > cold water, with scanty saliva. Clammy, sticky, feeling. Bitter, clammy taste.

Throat.—Whitish sticky discharge from posterior nares, causing constant hawking. Raw scraping. Soreness lasting longer on l. side; it hurts to swallow or speak; S. momentarily > drinking, with scraping. Constriction of pharynx when swallowing. Stuffed feeling in posterior nares. Dryness; in pharynx and posterior nares; with stiffness; in pharynx, with soreness. All symptoms > cold drinks and eating.

Stomach.—Appetite increased. Hunger after siesta; nervous, all day. Appetite and thirst diminished. Thirst for cold drinks, wants to drink often. Distaste for water. Eructations after eating; nauseous E. Nausea, with bitter, clammy taste; N. in morning, as in pregnancy.

Abdomen.—Distended feeling; > removing clothing; with griping and rumbling. Colic, > bending backward; C. below navel; in lower part, > undressing or lying on back; in lower part as from ice-water; uneasy, in hypogastrium, as if diarrhœa would come on. Soreness in hypogastrium.

Stool.—Shining, bloody and stringy, with tenesmus. Mushy, greenish-yellow and stringy, with tenesmus. Yellow, mushy. Hurrying him out of bed in morning.

Urinary Organs.—Burning in male urethra, with itching. Pain in prostatic urethra before and after micturition. Seldom any desire to urinate. Micturition frequent, scanty. Urine scanty, high-colored, dark straw and brown, very acid, sp. gr. high, also of balsamic odor and heavily loaded with urea.

Sexual Organs.—Cold feeling in glans. Desire diminished; destroyed (in a woman). Itching of vulva, < scratching and contact of leucorrhœa. Constant feeling as if menses would appear. Pain in ovaries, < pressure; cutting and throbbing P.; heavy aching and slowly pulsating pains beginning in one ovary and passing over to the other, leaving a soreness that lasts until the pains return. Uterine and ovarian pains that had not been felt for years were re-excited. Uterine cramps as from taking cold during menstruation. Uterine pains; > undressing and lying on back; bearing down. Soreness in uterine region, < clothing and pressure. Leucorrhœa light-yellowish, offensive, excoriating and profuse, running down the legs. Menstruation too early and prolonged, the two next periods anticipating and profuse.

Respiratory Organs and Chest.—Voice husky. Hacking cough, with tough, sticky, white expectoration. Laryngeal cough, > drinking cold water, with expectoration of whitish, sticky phlegm. Aching in breasts, < l.; from l. nipple through breast; sharp, under l. breast. Soreness of chest. Bruised feeling in l. breast, with pain on pressure. Breasts feel swollen and engorged; feel swollen and sore, with itching about nipples.

Heart.—Pain causing apprehension of death; P. in region of apex. Oppression. Depressed feeling as if it would stop beating. Action rapid, pulse full and strong.

Pulse.—Rapid; and irregular. Irregular and weak; and slow. Weak, and occasionally the diastole seems prolonged. With every third or fourth beat the diastole is prolonged almost to intermittence.

Neck and Back.—Pain in neck; in a spot in l. scapular region; in lumbar region; over crest of l. ilium; in lumbar region in morning on waking, > about noon; low down when walking; across lumbar region, with stiffness; bearing down, in lumbar region. Sore, lame feeling in lumbar region. Tired feeling in lower part of back.

Clinical. — Pain in dorsal and lumbar regions, constant sexual excitement, severe erections, numbness and tingling in feet and legs.

Extremities.—Weariness; of legs, knees and hands, with numbness; of arms and hands. Trembling of arms and hands. Aching in biceps, elbows and wrists. Sore feeling in biceps and muscles of forearm. Tired feeling in forearms and flexures of elbows. Numbness of l. forearm and < leg. She cannot write nor use the hands well in eating, because she cannot properly co-ordinate the movements. Shooting in joints of l. fingers. Pain in joints of fingers.

Lower Extremities. — Staggering. Disturbance of gait, with sensation of insecurity in the step. The sidewalk seems too high, which causes him to step very high, this jars him and makes his headache worse. Numbness mostly below knees. Pain in l. hip; in knees; in knees and tendons about them. Weariness and numb feeling in knees and legs; in popliteal spaces, < l.; deep-seated in legs and popliteal spaces. Tremulousness of legs. Aching in l. calf when walking. Tingling in calves and feet, < l. Weariness of legs; in evening when walking, with unsteadiness. Œdematous swelling of ankles. Heavy pain in l. instep. Numb tingling pain in outer side of both little toes.

Skin, Etc. — Formication in calves. Sleepiness. Sleep uneasy and interrupted; restless, and waking early. Dreams many, varied, neither pleasant nor very unpleasant. Sensation as if chill would come on. Flushed feeling over whole body. No perspiration in very warm weather.

Opium.

A tincture is made of the inspissated juice of the white Poppy, Papaver somniferum, L.

General Action.—It produces stupor and profound coma, with stertorous respiration, contracted pupils, slow, feeble respiration and pulse, cool, moist skin, and finally death from failure of respiration. Rarely, instead, it produces delirium or convulsions.

Obstinate constipation, with diminished secretion and atony, usually follows. Retention of urine is common. Its power to diminish reflex irritability and destroy the consciousness of suffering pain is well known.

Allies.—Cannab. ind., Gelsem., Hyos., Sec. c., Bell., Nux v., Carbo v.

Generalities.—*Emaciation.* Muscles flaccid. Intoxicated appearance. Lying on back. Lying with knees drawn up. *Sinks down in a heap, with short, anxious respiration.* Raises himself at times and violently scratches his face or chest. Whimsical gesticulations. Wry neck, head contorted to one side, one shoulder higher than the other, or head is almost buried beneath shoulders. Relaxation of muscles; so that tongue hung out of mouth, in certain positions folding back into fauces and obstructing respiration. Stooping, and peculiar shuffling gait. Tottering of body when erect. *Trembling;* of whole body, with twitching of flexors of limbs and external coldness of body; < lower limbs and about lumbar region. Excitement of whole system. Hysteria. *Twitching;* of tendons (Hyosc., etc.); < limbs, with pain in muscles.

Convulsions; alternating with subsultus; of face and limbs; with comatose intervals; with images before eye; with terrible pains; with bloody liquid exuding from nose and mouth; and face, neck and limbs turgid, livid and cold; and she groans and tears everything within her reach, bites her hands and arms; with screams, bending of head backward, at times opisthotonos; with deep, difficult, interrupted respiration; with clenched hands and teeth and loud breathing, stertor after the C.; eyes shut, pupils contracted, breathing stertorous, between the spasms he was limp, had no control over his limbs, and head fell forward or backward; started up in a fit, threw his arms about, vomited and then sank as if exhausted; convulsive throwing about of r. arm and leg, with loud cries, difficult respiration, coldness of face and hands, that were covered with drops of sweat; spasmodic contractions of limbs alternating with relaxation, at times with bending backward of head and trunk.

Convulsions at regular intervals, with staring eyes and twitching and contraction of muscles of limbs; C. making stiff, afterwards warm sweat. Tonic spasm. Clonic spasms, with screams and tears; C. spasms, < lower limbs, with unconsciousness. Epilepsy; with violent delirium. Opisthotonos; with blue color of skin, < genitals; with distortion of eyes, contractions of fingers and screams alternating with stertorous respiration; ending with trembling, then profound quiet with relaxation of limbs.

Rickets. Dropsical tendency. Strumous affections.

and the constitution is prone to succumb without resistance under all violent diseases. Those seldom attain the age of forty who begin to use Opium early.

Gnawing in bones in morning. Pains; in limbs and loins in morning on waking, and bathed in sweat; piercing through the marrow of bones; nervous or neuralgic; burning, with irritation. Bruised sensation in r. half of body, with flushes of heat and burning pain. Inability to lie on l. side, and pain in it even on attempting to turn in bed. Intolerance of open air, with sensation as if he would take cold. Restlessness; with oppression, confused ideas, sparks before eyes and heat of head extending over body; anxious. Sensation of strength.

Inclination to lie down. Inclination to lean against something, to stretch out feet and support the head upon the hand. Feeling as after a night of debauch. *Weakness;* of mind and body on waking; on waking from restless dreams; and stunted, decrepit; and voice not firm; of knees, elbows and masseter muscles; with bruised sensation so that it was difficult to move limbs, yet internal restlessness constantly impelling him to change his position; extending through all nerves, < sciatic nerve; pleasant.

Faintness; sudden. *Collapse, with cold face and limbs,* pupils contracted but before death dilated, pulse rapid, small, weak (Sec. c.), smaller in r. arm than in l., violent beating of carotids, distention of jugular veins, respiration sometimes superficial, sometimes deep and noisy, as in agony, with distention of anterior and upper part of neck, abdomen retracted, hard and tense, running of mucus from mouth, child became rigid, opened its eyes and mouth, face at last violet, puffy and drawn, then death.

Heaviness. Numbness. **Insensibility to pulling of the hair, pinching and sudden affusion of cold water.** *Sensation diminished; afterwards reflex irritability.* Loss of the senses of taste, smell and touch in relation to external objects, though he feels his cheeks cold when he touches them. Activity of voluntary muscles destroyed, sensation diminished, and hence sleep. Paralysis. Stiffness; of whole body, limbs cold, eyes convulsively distorted and half open. Cold, rest and especially sleep retard the appearance of effects and prolong them. Refreshed for a moment by cool air. Amelioration from vomiting; from black coffee (Cham.); from coffee, of all symptoms except trembling, but they soon return.

Clinical.—There is a general tendency to twitching of muscles or tremulousness of the head, arms and hands, with occasional jerks, especially of flexors. Puerperal spasms, with the characteristic coma between the spasms. Sometimes indicated in spasms resulting from fright, especially in infants, the spasms ushered in with a loud cry, with purple face, hot sweat, etc.

Mind.—Delirium; at night, with jactitation and frightful dreams; and great attempts to resist treatment, then unconsciousness; *talking about all sorts of things, with open eyes,* afterwards remembered them only as in a dream; *saw frightful animals and other objects; said many disconnected things, pointed at imaginary masked persons approaching him,* now loud laughter, now staring in fright at fancied swordsmen who threatened to stab him, angry with any one who talked to him or thought him delirious, but blamed himself for his folly; and rolling about the floor, anger, threatenings, does not recognize his friends, head and face swollen, lips reddish-blue and swollen, eyes protruding, inflamed; *distressed by ghosts and chimeras that collected about her bed;* talked of his business, cast up columns of figures and started at any noise; violent, with red face, glistening eyes and great activity; raging, with distortion of eyes; in paroxysms, during which she leaped from bed and escaped from the doors, but she soon became faint, fell and begged to be carried to bed, after which she was composed till another paroxysm; he seemed to be flying or floating through the air and to whirl with everything about him. Sensation as if in heaven; driving away slumber. Amiable, and employed himself in drawing maps of apartments in heaven, which he said he visited every night. Wild expression of face, delight, gesticulations, talking, some compose verses and address bystanders in excellent language, in an elysium, then miserable reaction. Agreeable reverie, in which they throw themselves into a thousand postures, extravagant and merry, absurd talking, they imagine themselves possessed of whatever they wish. *Visions.* Hallucinations. Conscious of being possessed of another self beside his real self, and is not always sure which will conquer the other.

Excitement; with risus sardonicus; pleasant, they carouse, sing amorous songs, laugh, play pranks, then anger and raving, then sadness and weeping, then sleep, then their ordinary condition of sadness and stupidity; threaten alternately self-destruction and injury to others. Agitated, often rising from bed and walking hastily across the room. Joy; increasing to delirium. Exhilaration, but all is order, harmony, vigor and tranquillity. Liveliness, with great strength. Laughter. Cheerfulness alternating with sullen grief.

Quiet enjoyment, lightness of head, tingling in limbs, eyes seem enlarged, hearing acute, elasticity and inclination to mount on high, pain and weariness gone, loathing of food is changed to a relish for what is piquant and often great desire for some particular food, tongue loosened, calmness, smiles, then broken sleep, from which he wakes to a conception of his miseries. Hardly sensible that my feet touched the ground, it seemed as if I slid along the ground impelled by an invisible agent, and that my blood was composed of an etherial fluid which made my body lighter than air, and visions of delight filled my brain all night. Alert and sprightly. Courage; and endurance; with mirth and lustiness, then dulness of head, etc. Undaunted in danger. Fear of death lost (compare Cannab. ind.).

Loquacious, then conversation droops, frequent loud laughter, then vacancy of countenance, with pallor and shrinking of features, then silence, then sleep with slow, soft and small pulse (in the Chinese), but the Malays, before they sleep, often become violent and quarrelsome, and lives are occasionally lost. Whimsical gesticulations. Screams. Lamentations and howls. Moans. Groans. *Starting at least noise, and a fly on any part of the body was a burden to him. Sullen.* Weeping mood; at night; from vexation about a pain. Feeble wails or cries.

Fear; **of impending death** (Acon., Cann. ind.); of the people around him, and jealousy. *Anxiety*; in attacks, with short, oppressed respiration and trembling of arms and hands; with heat and intoxication, talked of all sorts of things, took her words back at one time, started up in fright, at another angrily seized the hands of those about her. Sadness; in afternoon. Despondency; then a condition somewhat similar to a low state of delirium tremens with prostration, exhausting diarrhœa and vomiting, pre-existing diseases are aggravated, often dropsy, death may result, generally from effusion into the great cavities and general anasarca.

Fretful. Mistrustful. Pleasurable feelings only when his eyes were open, as if external objects only were acted upon by the imagination. Anger. Rage. Ferocity. Inconstant, they often promise what they soon refuse to abide by. Hastiness at work. Inclined to work. Indolence; *and intoxication;* in morning on rising; and theft often supplies the means for persevering in the fatal pleasure. Indifference; after the delirium. Taciturnity.

Mind active; and filled with gigantic schemes and theories, faculties keen and expressions terse and convincing, but after sleep suicidal depression as if haunted by evil spirits. Intellect brilliant, language eloquent and his talent for writing easy, with kindness and benevolence. Sublime contemplation all night, without sleep. Imagination and memory increased, so that he passes the night in profound meditation, he slumbers a few hours at daybreak, unable to remember what he thought about at night.

Imbecility. Confusion. Dulness, with short, anxious respiration, heaving of chest, eyes look dead and are full of water. Mind weak; and obscured, illusion as if eyes were four times larger than usual. Loss of ideas. Answered questions with difficulty; answered only after a pause and not always correctly. Comprehension wavering. Inability and disinclination for work in afternoon. Ideas difficult to collect. Memory weak; lost. Will power weak; over muscles, with heaviness of head and weakness. Voluntary powers suspended.

Insensibility; **with apoplectic respiration**; with loud snoring; *with immobility;* to shame and the more refined sensibilities. Unconsciousness; sudden, with blue face and contraction of upper limbs. Lethargy. Stupefaction; soporous; as if a board were before head, with vertigo, obliging him to lie down, then trembling of body. *Coma;* lying on her back and resting as if inert; with head drawn backward and partial consciousness; with snoring; with insensibility to pinching, arms rigid, fingers clenched.

Clinical.—Valuable for the after effects of fright, with delirium, flushed face, sleeplessness and cold extremities. Violent mania in low types of fever, with frightful fancies, fear that they were going to be executed for crimes and attempts to escape; there are generally staring, twitching of facial muscles and trismus. Delirium tremens, < least amount of alcohol, expression of fear (Stram.). Complete stupor in low types of fever, with open eyes and mouth, speechless, muscles rigid; this condition may alternate with delirium, attempts to escape, head and face flushed and dark, respiration slow and sighing, stools involuntary.

Head.—Swaying back and forth. Lateral motion. Drooping. Fell backward or sideways when sitting. Sticking; extending outward. *Sensation like that following sleep after a debauch.* Tearing as if everything were torn to pieces, with sensation as if everything in body were turned about, and general discomfort, making him indignant. *Aching;* in morning; in morning on waking; in morning, < rising, > open air in forenoon; on waking, with stupefaction; after a nap; < at 10 A.M., with throbbing in brain; < sitting quietly, with confusion of head; > leaning against a cold wall; > vomiting, with drowsiness and nausea; with feeling as if there were bees in a hollow in it; extending along median line, in afternoon, at times throbbing; becoming vertigo, making thought difficult; as if splitting.

Confusion; in morning; in afternoon, and next day from 8 A.M. till noon; after sleep; *with no mental grasp;* with weakness; with rapid pulse; with full, hard pulse; with pressure in eyes; with congestion, and with glowing heat of face and sweat on head; with dry heat in eyes and inclination to close lids without sleepiness, with sensation as if he had watched the previous night; as after intoxicating drinks; as if smoke rose into brain; becoming vertigo and making thought and speech difficult; becoming a pain extending over orbit and to nape; becoming a pain, < forehead, extending towards eyes and to nose.

Sensation as if in a vise, > motion. Tension. *Heaviness;* and on raising it sensation as if a weight moved to and fro; with feeling as if it had been hanging down for a long time; *making thought and writing difficult.* Fulness. *Rush of blood;* heard the R., with a dull but loud noise at every beat of heart; painful, < forehead. Pulsation of arteries; with heat. *Apoplexy;* threatening of A., with all the symptoms except stupor, then insensibility and death; apoplectic condition, with stertorous, rattling respiration, open mouth, pale face covered with cold sweat, l. eye closed, r. partly open, pupils dilated, eyeball paralyzed, nails blue, pulse full, insensible and motionless. *Intoxication;* on waking from a nap.

Vertigo; after waking; on attempting to get up; on looking to r. or l.; on stooping; on rising in bed; < trying to walk; > vomiting; with sickness; with difficulty in holding up head; with stupefaction of head; with vanishing of thought; with blackness before eyes; with swaying back and forth of body; with numbness of limbs; as if everything turned about with him in a circle (compare Gelsem.).

Forehead.—Stitches; in l. side, extending deep into brain; to occiput, < r. half of head, with sleepiness; alternating with drawing pains within ears. Tearing and beating, with sour eructations and necessity to lie down, when she perspired. Intermittent boring, at times extending to vertex. Aching; in r. half; in r. eminence; in r. eminence and above eye; in supraorbital region; in region of glabella; all day; over eyes in morning; l. side of F. and vertex in evening; *above r. eminence when reading, with heat, then pinching in r. temple as if something pressed upon it and then relaxed;* with warmth in it; with external warmth in it; in upper part, with digging, and with heaviness of lids, < l. eye; and over eyes, with sensation as if eyes would be pressed together, with tremulous drawing in scalp of forehead and vertex, the pain changing to dulness, sleepiness and feeling in head as if he had not slept enough; extending to eyes and nose; extending to root and tip of nose, and changing to pinching; in periosteum of eminences, extending to nose, then pain in forehead, < above eyes, with dulness of head; intermittent, in l. eminence; sticking throbbing; stupefying, in r. side. Pressure outward; in one side, > pressure; in r. eminence, preventing writing, then in occiput, > rubbing and pressure; paroxysmal, in l. side, extending over r. side from head to tips of toes. Straining sensation reaching to eyes and nose. Dulness; in sinciput; in r. side, with heat in it; sometimes interrupted by sticking above brows that afterwards extended over head, > towards noon, in afternoon dulness, with at times sticking in head, with warmth and flushes of heat in face. Heaviness in sinciput; over eyes. Stupefied sensation above eyes.

Temples.—Twitching. *Pain;* in r., and in external canthus; as if pressed together; as if pressed asunder, and especially in forehead.

Vertex.—Pain, with dulness; P. on r. side, under forehead; extending outward and from V. to r. orbit in afternoon and evening; P. between sticking and boring in coronal suture, and in sagittal suture as far as middle of vertex.

Side.—Dulness in l. extending to r. temple.

Occiput.—Drawing tearing from scalp to ears, in region of fontanelle, in afternoon, suddenly disappearing, but returning and extending down spine. Pain; in evening; tensive, at insertion of trapezius muscle, extending across neck to upper margin of acromion process and inner margins of scapulæ to tips, in general corresponding to course of muscular fibres, < motion, > rest, < region of fourth cervical vertebra, whence it extended to last dorsal vertebra. Feeling like lead, so that head constantly fell backward.

Scalp.—Hair gray. Bruised pain, and in nose.

Clinical.—Of extreme value in apoplexy when there is stupor with cold extremities; it has frequently produced the most rapid and beneficial results in temporary paralysis, apparently resulting from serous effusion in the brain, and it is certainly of great value as a palliative in cerebral hæmorrhage. In threatening apoplexy of drunkards, the occiput feels as heavy as lead and there is a tendency to stertorous respiration, with free perspiration, which does not relieve, with spasmodic jerkings of limbs, numbness and variable pulse.

Eyes.—Red. Staring; and wild. Prominent and motionless. Sunken. Glazed, half open, pupils moderately dilated and immovable. Glassy and sunken; G. and dark; G., and conjunctiva straw-colored. Sparkling; and full. Lustreless. Dimness alternating with moisture. Expressionless. Heavy look. Distorted. Turned upward; and outward; and open. Pressure upon r. as from long reading; P. causing sensation as if he could not hold lids open. Sensation as if too large for orbits. Dryness of r.; *D.* in evening, > night, *with weakness, burning and sensation as if dust were in them;* with stiffness and sometimes with water in them; with frequent pressure on them, frequent necessity to forcibly open and close them and redness of conjunctiva. Seem moist in open air. *Burning.* Heaviness; on waking, with dulness; with uneasiness. Stiffness.

Lachrymation. Balls turned upward; pressing-together sensation in B. **Pupils contracted;** and turned upward and outward; with divergent squint; and insensible; *dilated;* insensible; oscillating. Lids, swelling of lower; swollen, dark, half closed; livid, and lips and wings of nose, also lips and nails; drooping; closed; spasmodically closed; open; half open, and eyes fixed; tremulous and half open; sealed up or dropping rheum; immovable, and balls; upper heavy as if swollen. Canthus, sticking in l. external; cramp-like sensation in r. external. Conjunctiva red; red, with swelling of caruncula lachrymalis; insensible, also cornea. Dim vision; in forenoon when reading; intermittent. Objects looked larger; smaller. Letters swim when writing. Vision double; flickering. He thought that flashes of fire came out of his eyes. Blindness.

Ears.—Livid, and nape; tips. Jerking within l., then r. Pressure towards external meatus. Throbbing. Hearing acute; during the torpor; indistinct; difficult in l. Could hardly detect the voice of any one who spoke, but her own sounded disagreeably loud to her. Ringing. Singing. Humming; when talking or whistling; as of bees, with stopped sensation and diminished hearing. *Roaring;* in evening when sitting still; after eating.

Nose.—Pinched, and could not inspire through it. Stoppage in a warm room after walking in open air. Dryness; in afternoon and evening. Much mucus; frothy mucus; frothy fluid tinged with blood. Sneezing. Loss of smell.

Face.—Flushed; during sleep; *and bloated;* and neck; and head hot; alternately F. and pale. *Livid.* Dusky. Black in morning. Cyanotic; and earthy. Purple. Cherry-brown. Lead-colored, with blue lines; F. and lips lead-colored. Yellow; and withered. **Pale;** and sunken; and bathed in cold sweat; cheeks, with red spots; cheeks, and furrowed. Earthy. Swollen; and dark; and expression unmeaning, ghastly. Blotched. Veins distended. *Distorted;* and purple. Full, smooth and glassy. A new air of life and brightness. Horrid look. Wild and fierce-looking. Alarmed and bewildered expression, apparently recognizing no one. Sickly. Cadaverous; and livid, cheeks and nose cold, eyes sunken, surrounded by dark circles. Ghastly. Haggard. Look as if he had not slept enough, with sunken, blinking eyes. Expression of premature old age. Vacant look. Languid and stupid expression on waking. Muscles relaxed, giving a stupid expression, lower lip inclined to hang down, nostrils wide open, upper lid difficult to raise. Spasms. Convulsive trembling, and of lips and tongue. Confused feeling in l. side of chin.

Lips.—*Purple. Livid.* Pallid. Cracked. Swollen; < lower, and blue; lower, towards r. corner, and hard, with excoriation (possibly from biting lip). Distorted. Pain in lower on touch.

Jaws.—*Falling;* and fixed; spasmodic. Lower protruded and tremulous. Sudden trembling. Clenched. Stitches, < region of condyles. Pain; in joints and in cheek-bones, with heat in them and in lobules of ears.

Mouth.—Teeth, gnawing in nerves; aching; looseness. Gums eaten away, so that teeth stood bare to the roots.

Tongue.—*Black. White.* Coated; brown; yellow; and taste sticky, pasty. *Purple.* Ulceration, and of palate; and of mouth. Projected, tumefied and blue. Thrust backward and up against palate; thrust between lips, swollen and trembling. In constant motion. Rapid trembling. Thick, and speech difficult. Dry; and brown; and edges dark; and edges red, centre coated white; and palate; anteriorly in morning, without thirst; T. and mouth dry, widely extended, with rasping sensation on touch; and palate and fauces, without inclination to drink. Cold. Burning, and in mouth, with inflammation of larynx; biting B. Difficult to move after waking, with dry mouth. Paralytic. Speech difficult; and slow; stammering; impossible.

Foaming at mouth; at times. Discharge of yellow, tenacious, mouldy-smelling mucus from M. and nose, without cough or inclination to sneeze. Pale and tumid. Occasionally puckered, not drawn. Dryness; and in œsophagus; M. and fauces dry and covered with tough, viscous saliva; with little thirst; with chilliness over abdomen, without desire to drink. Salivation; constantly flowing from mouth. It thickens saliva and mucus of nose and trachea. Frothy sputa. Taste impaired; bad, with salt taste to saliva; sweetish; sour; bitter; bitter in morning; bitter burning; pasty; flat, insipid; lost.

Clinical.—Paralysis of the tongue and pharynx, with difficulty in articulation and inability to swallow.

Throat.—Vessels distended and pulsating violently. Fauces red. Râles. Rattling, then deep breathing. Choking, then eructations. Spasms. Scraping rawness in fauces. Sensation of a band, with stupid feeling in head. *Constriction; in pharynx* (Nux v.); anxious; in fauces, with scraping. Dryness; posteriorly; in fauces; fauces and larynx; with inability to swallow; or burning. Cramp in œsophagus on swallowing; and afterwards. *Asphagia, as from paralysis of muscles* (Gelsem.). Swallowing painful; impossible.

Stomach.—Appetite. Increased; for supper; with weakness. Ravenous; in paroxysms, at times with flat taste; with dread of food. Gluttony. Changing on eating to emptiness and pressure in stomach. Diminished; for dinner; for supper. Capricious. He wishes to eat, but has taken scarcely a bite when he has no desire for the rest. *Lost;* at noon; for food and drink; except for bread; or depraved, sweetmeats and sugar being most relished. Aversion to food; to meat, with unclean tongue; to tobacco; to tobacco-smoke.

Thirst; all night; during the chill; especially for thin beer; *unquenchable.*

Eructations; empty; bitter; tasting like chamomile tea. *Hiccough.* Nausea; in epigastric region; at 10.30 A.M., on attempting to smoke a cigar as usual, momentarily > a glass of water, with vertigo, trembling of limbs and cold sweat; at night on rising, with vertigo; on waking; after waking; on moving about; when walking in the street, with exhaustion that lasted all day; > eructations; > white sugar, with salivation; > vinegar, with headache; with salivation; with emptiness in stomach and general discomfort; then eructations; as after fasting; faintlike, with vomiting and prostration. Ineffectual retching.

Vomiting; before a convulsion; on waking; after eating; then bitter taste; violent, with purging; *green;* of food and drink; of everything that she swallowed; of blood; almost incessant, of brown, sour-smelling fluid; of dark fluid smelling of laudanum; of coffee, with much mucus; grayish mucus and unripe poppy-seeds; of phlegm, then copious discharge of bile, every kind of drink was thrown up as soon as taken, at last vomiting of a dark greenish liquid, which deposited a sediment of the same color.

Distention; with pain on touch; meteoric; flatulent, at night; painful, in pit. *Accumulation of flatus, and in abdomen.* Rumbling, and in abdomen. *Cutting in epigastric and umbilical regions.* Griping in epigastric region. Gnawing. *Pain; in epigastric region, also in umbilical region;* in region; on pressure, with heat; in epigastrium on pressure; when turning in bed or taking food, which "seems to lodge;" in epigastric region after eating, > walking; in epigastric region on inspiration, with tenderness; *< pressure; in epigastrium, with tightness; in region and lower down, with cutting, and with dulness of head, changing to pain, < forehead and temples,* with slow and weak pulse; in pit, with anxiety; sudden, with compression of diaphragm; as if a stone were in it; above S. after dinner, as if he had eaten too much or too hard food, > moving about in open air.

Constriction; with constipation. Acute throbbing when lying after dinner, < lying on back, > rising and walking, with visible rising and sinking rhythmical with pulse. Discomfort; somewhat as after a purge, extending into ilium. Heartburn. Heat extending over body, with moist skin; H. in epigastric region, streaming over body. Coldness. Emptiness; with frequent empty eructations; > breakfast, but it returned and lasted, with slight interruptions, all day, though I ate often. Heaviness, with compression and with distress in pit. Digestion impaired; after an early dinner, at 1.30 P.M.; slow. Weakness. Insensibility to emetics.

Abdomen.—Distention; but no power to expel its contents (Carbo v.), > **catheter;** > moving about, with pressure, the latter returning on sitting; increasing from noon till evening, and late in evening a scanty, difficult, not hard stool; *tympanitic; hard and sensitive to touch. Rumbling;* and gurgling and griping; and moving about. Emission of flatus; after eating; difficult; offensive, at night.

Cutting. Griping; all the afternoon; > a tumbler of milk drunk as soon as it came from the cow; **with constipation**; with contraction; with pinching, then emissions of much odorless flatus through the night and eructations of gas; *with flatulence, then hard stool.* **Colic**; before and after stool; *with spasmodic closure of anus and difficult emission of flatus;* with desire for stool, > soft stool, then weariness, with yawning; then diarrhœa; then diarrhœa in morning; *tensive;* as from taking cold; as after a purge; drawing; as from a stone. Bruised pain. *Tension. Grumbling;* and contraction; G. motions. Throbbing. Heaviness; in morning. *Intestines sluggish, so that the strongest purgatives lose their power.* Intestines seem paralyzed.

Fulness of upper A., with tension. *Griping in upper A.* Pain in hypochondrium; in region of spleen and back. Umbilical region, distention; cutting, then a stool not hard; griping, then pasty, yellowish-brown stool of mouldy odor; pain; pain on pressure; pain, a few hours later diarrhœa; weight and anxiety, with flushes of internal heat and stupefaction of head. Stitches in l. side; in l. flank. Rumbling in transverse colon at midnight, with twisting, then urging to stool, which was copious, watery, with sudden loud flatus, then burning in rectum. *Tension in hypogastrium, with pain on touch.*

Clinical.—Colic, with great tympanitis, especially in obstinate constipation. Valuable in intestinal obstruction, with fæcal vomiting and violent colic.

Rectum.—Distending pain. Pain as from hæmorrhoidal congestion, < touching anus. Sensation as if closed on making exertion at stool. Indolent, it seemed as if it could not evacuate the stool, in the evening a not hard stool. Ineffectual efforts at stool.

Anus.—Spasmodic closure. Spasmodic constriction, with burning pain on touch. Tickling ending with itching.

Stool.—Dysentery. Watery; at 9 and 12 P.M., with griping; about midnight; frequent, afterwards constipation. Diarrhœa; *whitish, frequent, also causing burning in anus;* frothy, profuse, then great relief; frothy, with itching burning in anus, and tenesmus;

frequent; frequent, with dragging and burning in rectum and anus; bilious, with pain extending from r. hypochondrium to umbilicus. Soft. *Pasty;* and copious, dark, almost odorless, waking him about 5 A.M. Loamy, tenacious, dark brown, difficult, of mouldy smell, delayed.

Constipation. **Hard; and dark brown; in small pieces, only after clysters, with loss of appetite;** *not till* 10 P.M.; *and gray; and crumbly; and unsatisfactory, also delayed;* and difficult, also scanty; in hard nodules, with labor-like pains; first part H. and difficult, the last diarrhœa-like. *Offensive.* Contained a blackish substance. Tenacious, gluey, yellowish-brown, of mouldy odor. Profuse. Indolent; and scanty. Difficult. *Involuntary; and micturition.* Infrequent. *Delayed;* preceded by ineffectual urging. Retained two days, then sudden desire for soft stool, next day, pasty, unsatisfactory.

Clinical.—Constipation from inertia of the bowels, especially of the rectum, with no inclination for stool; in these cases gas accumulates in the upper part of the bowels and causes great pain. Particularly useful in constipation resulting from unwise use of enemas of water and soap. It has cured chronic catarrh and ulceration of the ilio-cæcal region, with persistent discharge of enormous quantities of flakes of mucus, constipation, fæcal stools completely enveloped in mucus, the indication being complete atony of the lower bowel and the accumulation of hard balls of fæces. Occasionally useful in cholera infantum, with involuntary offensive stools, great weakness, dark red face, collapse and sleepiness. Useful in cholera infantum when the discharges have been suppressed and the child has become unconscious, with insensible pupils and flushed face. Diarrhœa during typhoid, with bloated abdomen, etc.

Urinary Organs.—Bright's disease. **Urine retained** (Nux v.). **Expulsive power of bladder weak** (Caust., Gels., etc.). *Pain in bladder as from need to urinate without being able to accomplish it.* Tenesmus, on beginning to urinate, necessity to wait on account of twitching of sphincter vesicæ. Micturition violent. Stream interrupted; *after long waiting on account of cramp of sphincter. Micturition only after long exertion. M. difficult;* on waking from a nap; *with full bladder, on account of cramp in sphincter vesicæ, even after much urine began to pass the full stream was interrupted, this lasted all day.* Dysuria, with frequent interruptions in the stream of urine; D. as if passages were closed. Strangury, with frequent ineffectual desire, burning and cutting at neck of bladder, cutting along ureters and urethra and tenesmus. *Ineffectual attempts to urinate;* later high-colored urine. M. painful and scanty. Involuntary M. Frequent, scanty M.; E., of turbid, mucous urine, sometimes from vesical, sometimes from renal disease.

Urethra.—Burning during micturition. Spasmodic constriction, > urinating. Feels closed during micturition.

Urine.—*Red, scanty, with clouds;* dark red, scanty, passed with cutting; dark red, turbid, frothy, depositing a yellowish-red, slimy sediment. Lemon-yellow, with much sediment; lemon-yellow, turbid, scanty. Brown, with iridescent film. Dark; and turbid; and depositing a sediment. Bloody. Of remarkable odor; and wheylike. Of intolerable odor. Copious; in afternoon; in evening, and pale yellow; at night; after midnight, and on waking next morning; at times, at other times suppressed. Brick-dust sediment.

Clinical. — Retention of urine, especially resulting from fright or following parturition (Nux v.). Renal colic, with cold sweat.

Sexual Organs.—Cutting in male during micturition. Erections in sleep, and after waking impotency; frequent E. at night in sleep; excessive E. Masturbation. Desire, with erections, emissions and lascivious dreams; D. at first, then organs gradually lose their tone; increased in some, diminished in others. Impotency. Emissions at night; involuntary, even when wide awake. Procreative power in both sexes lessened, and in those women who do bear children the secretion of milk is defective. Painful movements of child in uterus. Uterus so soft that the movements of the child can be felt externally, with a general paralyzed state. Labor-like pain in uterus, obliging her to bend together, with anxious, almost ineffectual desire for stool. Mucous discharge from vagina. Menstruation increased; irregular; did not appear.

Clinical.—Amenorrhœa from fright. Occasionally useful in uterine hæmorrhage.

Respiratory Organs.—Spasms of respiratory muscles. Larynx dry. *Tickling in larynx, > a glass of water, with dry, racking cough causing lachrymation,* afterwards paroxysms of cough waking him at 3 A.M., repeated at 3.15 P.M. *and second night at* 2 A.M., fourth night at 3 A.M. awakened by dry cough, with tickling and scraping in larynx. Voice harsh and deep; H. and hollow; gruff; hoarse; quivering.

Cough on swallowing; on swallowing liquid; < eating; dry, hollow; violent, dry, in paroxysms, then yawning and a sudden loud cry; *with scanty, tenacious expectoration and rattling in chest.* Expectoration, with bronchial irritation. Expectoration of blood. Expectoration of mucus and pus; frothy mucus; thick, bloody mucus.

Respiration. — Asthma. Suffocative attacks; in sleep; and suddenly became blue in face and tried to cough, but had no breath, then deep sleep, with cold sweat. Choking sensation. Dyspnœa; as if threatened with pleurisy, and tension in scapulæ. *Difficult; at night* on waking; *and loud, rattling;* and rattling; and deep; and rapid; and rapid, anxious; and slow; and slow, rattling; and slow, with loud mucous ronchus; and anxious, with open mouth; *at long intervals;* and long intervals between inspirations and expirations, with rattling; and each inspiration giving a long struggling sound, it would draw four inspirations at the rate of 16 per minute, then cease to inhale about thirty seconds, then the four inspirations, and at the fourth a general spasm of muscles, after remedies breathing difficult, at the rate of 30, afterwards three inspirations at the rate of 12, when spasms would occur and the suspensions of breathing became longer, afterwards two inspirations together, about twelve seconds apart, then suspended for nearly a minute; as if pectoral muscles were tense; as from nitrogen, the air seeming to leave the lungs without having performed its function, with dryness in fauces and larynx; gradually increasing to suffocative, generally dependent on œdema of lungs or effusion into pleural sac.

Respiration. Short; and rattling, at times stopping for half a minute. *Rattling.* Grunting. Sobbing, interrupted. **Long and sighing; deep and frequent sighing. Frequent, deep;** with convulsive motions of jaws; D. and anxious; D. and sonorous; and heavy, with slow, large pulse; single D. at times, suspended at times. Loud. Weak. Shallow. Interrupted; inspiration. Irregular; and feeble; and not full;

often only 5 per minute; occasionally full and deep, then ceasing for a time. Convulsive, 10 per minute, then did not breathe for a minute. Rapid; and anxious. Suspended; for a minute at a time, then begins with a sigh; then short, sudden gasps as if he would suffocate.

Slow respiration; and groaning; and sighing; and now and then moaning; and stertorous; and stertorous, irregular; and stertorous, deep, puffing; and stertorous, jerking; and stertorous, interrupted, gasping; and sonorous; and loud; and rattling, irregular; and irregular in time; with at times deep inspiration; and deep; and heavy; and feeble; almost imperceptible, intermittent; obstructed by mucus; and stertorous, labored, irregular, sometimes more than a minute between the respirations, then sudden snoring inspiration; with rapid, thready pulse.

Stertorous respiration; *and deep;* and deep, moaning; and rapid; and rapid, with stridulous inspiration; with rattling in throat; and loud at one time, at another heavy and weak; and irregular, sometimes interrupted; with occasionally such an impediment that the face became livid and the child apparently dead; with hiccough; with large, slow pulse; at times S., at times stridulous. Apoplectic breathing.

Clinical.—Aphonia from fright. Cough at night, dry and spasmodic, from tickling in the larynx. Threatening paralysis of the lungs, with superficial respiration and occasional deep breaths. Bronchial catarrh, with dyspnœa, suffocative attacks during sleep, deep snoring respiration, great difficulty in lying down. Bronchial catarrh, wakes with suffocation, great dyspnœa and blueness of the face. Pneumonia, with complaints of the heat of the bed, profuse hot sweat and tendency to stupor.

Chest.—Stitches extending outward, < towards r. scapula. Drawing tearing in side. Pinching in sternum and back on motion. Pain; in r. side, even when not breathing, with stitches during inspiration; P., with cough; P. all the afternoon, making respiration difficult; frequent, causing hacking cough, which relieved it for a time; tensive, beneath short ribs, along attachment of diaphragm, when breathing. Contraction, tightness and anxiety. Constriction as if stiff, with difficult respiration. Oppression; of lungs; waking him about midnight. Heaviness, with frequent need to breathe deeply, with at times gasping, the clothes were too tight, *beat of heart could not be felt.* Heat.

Heart.—Sound weak. Stitches. Pain, with irregular and feeble pulse. Anxiety; with restlessness. Heaviness and oppression. Burning. Faintness as often as he dropped to sleep. Circulation rapid, with heat. Beats rapid; violent; imperfect and irregular, more when reclining than when sitting; feeble; suspended.

Pulse.—*Rapid;* at night; and full; and full, strong; and full, soft; and full, sometimes slow afterwards; and hard; and hard, full; and hard, contracted; and hard, large; and hard, violent, with impeded respiration; and large, soft; and irregular in volume and rhythm; and irregular, full; *and irregular, feeble;* and irregular, small; and irregular, small, intermittent; and intermittent; and intermittent, feeble; and small; *and small, weak;* and small, soft; and weak; and weak, sometimes fluttering; afterwards slow; afterwards slow, full, without much tension.

Slow; with slow, stertorous respiration, red, distended face and sweat, with convulsions; with chilliness, shivering, diminished activity, weakness, but increased hunger; and strong; and laboring; and large; and full; *and full, with deep stertorous respiration;* and full, soft; and full, irregular; and irregular; and irregular, feeble; *and soft;* and undulating, soft; and small; and small, faltering; and small, weak; and weak; afterwards rapid; but rapid and weak during the spasm and suspension of breath, ceasing at wrist about six seconds before the breathing was resumed.

Strong in carotids. Sharp. Violent in carotids. Laboring. Hard; and contracted. Full; and hard; and strong; and soft. Intermittent; and irregular. Irregular in carotids, about 50. Small. Thready. *Weak; and irregular;* and irregular, small; and irregular, tremulous; in morning, and tremulous; and small; and threadlike; and fluttering. Imperceptible; at wrists and temples; at wrist, slight in carotids; and heart's action feebly dicrotic, irregular, slow.

Neck.—Swelling of veins, with violent pulsation in them. Tonic spasm, so that head was bent backward. Weakness of muscles that support head.

Back.—*Arched, from trembling of limbs,* that irritates all limbs. Bent, often in a circular form. Tonic spasms. Pressure inward in B. and chest up to nape, and muscles and vessels seem contracted. Pain; in dorsal muscles, at times extending into chest; between tip of r. scapula and posterior wall of chest; in lumbar region. Heat along spine alternating with coldness.

Extremities.—Flaccid; and unable to walk; and hanging down. Lie, immovable wherever placed. Drawn up. Nails purple. Cramps. *Trembling;* of hands and feet; spasmodic. Spasms; clonic. Involuntary motions of arms, fingers and toes. Pain on walking far. Distress about joints. Uneasiness. Weakness; of legs and forearms. Heaviness; of arms and feet; and asleep; and stiffness in them on rising. Rigidity of muscles of arms and legs. Power of motion diminished, with pain in recti and vasti muscles of thigh, also pain in arms and legs on motion. Insensibility.

Upper Extremities.—Violent shaking. Numbness from l. shoulder to tips of fingers, < palmar surface of hand, thumb and little finger. Arm, trembling of l.; automatic motions; twitching; convulsive motion back and forth of one or another; hung motionless; heaviness of l.; paralysis of l. Drawing and tearing now in r., now in l. forearm, in evening. Hands purple; livid; *trembling;* twitching; *numbness and swollen sensation, and in forearms.* Fingers blue; congested, and nails; thumbs rigidly extended at r. angles; jerking, and of wrists; sudden drawing tearing in second joint of r. ring, < motion, > rest, afterwards extending above wrist to head of radius; crawling as if asleep, < grasping anything; touch so affected that she could do no needlework; numbness from second joints to tips of l. little and ring, as if they had been constricted, in evening, > rubbing.

Lower Extremities.—Gait stumbling; and slow; lame gait. Flexed and cold. Trembling. Weakness. Crawling. Numbness of l. after short sitting, not > walking, with prickling. Thigh, trembling; rheumatic pain; tensive pain in flexor muscles, extending to hollows of knees, in forenoon; drawing on outer side of r.; sensation as if a liquid were moving up and down in l.; heaviness. Knee bent; lightning-like tearing along outer side of r., extending down outer surface to malleolus, disappearing as suddenly as it came; pain in hollow; pain in K. and hip-joints so that I could neither sit nor lie; weariness; weariness in l.; paralyzed feeling, also with trembling, also with pain; stiffness. Legs drawn up; *jerking in calves;* weak; weariness on rising from a seat, lasting till towards 6 P.M., with heaviness; crawling; heaviness; almost insensible; stiff. Feet, swelling; tossed up and down as in convulsions, with a sudden, loud cry; heavy after eating; stiff and sensitive; numb.

Skin.—Pale; and contracted; and covered with sweat; and bluish. Blue; in spots; on limbs and face; lips and tips of fingers and toes. Violet, with swelling. Purple face, hands and feet. Livid; < limbs. Almost black. Brown. Red; on neck and chest; and itching; and all veins distended. Leathery. Swollen, < face and hands. Dry, rough and of a dirty color; D., of sunburnt color; D., shrivelly and tawny. Eruption, with at times itching; E., with biting itching of skin after the sweat. Red, itching tetter here and there. Itching blotches on extensor surface of forearms near wrists, > night. Hives on middle of extensor surface of l. thigh. Erysipelas in face extending to head. Pimples sensitive to touch on side of neck. Boils. Carbuncles. Foul, indolent ulcers. Blisters.

Burning sticking about r. wrist, with pimples surrounded by red areola on back and in palm of hand, which arose to blisters, similar to pimples on r. cheek, sensitive to pressure. Tension on forehead, > stroking. Biting, < face, with burning in it. Crawling on l. leg; on hands and feet, changing to rolling. Itching; of nose; arms and shoulders; about anus; on legs in evening; < upper part of body, extending from chest over face, < nose; of skin, which was warm and dry; face, with heat in it; with removal of hair; and after scratching red, itching pimples; sticking, here and there; burning, with pustules. Insensibility.

Sleep.—Yawning; with stretching; with pain in joints of jaws as if they would break. **Sleepiness;** all day; at 8 A.M.; after eating; when writing at a table; *with the headache;* **with inability to sleep, also with slow pulse; but during the night restless sleep, with much sweat;** with desire to be let alone. Sleep; sudden; instantly on lying down; when sitting, with startings and a strange chaos of happy and disagreeable visions; irresistible; from which it could not be aroused; could not arouse himself in morning; *deep, sound, with rattling respiration, as after apoplexy;* deep, with frequent sighs and at times jerkings; ending in coma or apoplectic death, with convulsions; constant, with half-open eyes, carpholgia and picking all about; quiet, from which he was constantly awakened by jerking of limbs; intoxicated, with unintelligible prattling. *Stupid sleep; with half-open eyes;* with half-open eyes, eyeballs turned upward, mouth open, with stertorous inspiration; with rattling in chest.

Sleeplessness; at night, in the daytime only a little confused sleep, easily ended; from heat and headache; *with unwelcome fancies that were distinct from surrounding objects, as in delirium;* with restlessness; with restlessness and delirious talking. **Snoring;** on expiration. *Whining in sleep;* moaning cries; sudden jerking over whole body, waking him. Starting in S.; with incoherency in language and action; and after waking he seemed intoxicated and half delirious. *Sleep unsound.* He heard everything in sleep, but could not rouse himself. Unrefreshing sleep; with sweat. *Restless sleep;* forepart of the night, sound and refreshing the latter part; often interrupted and only partial, conscious of every noise, dreams varied, unable to rise as early as usual, weaker than on going to bed, head heavy and dull, after a glass of water became fully awake; from which he woke stupid; night restless, slumber alternating with waking, with irrational talking, hot skin, stupefaction, during which he lies coiled in a heap. Frequent waking and inability to sleep again for a long time, one night arose at 3 A.M. Sopor at night, alternating with delirium; waking sopor.

Dreams; with grimaces; joyous; agreeable; delicious, on waking prostration of mind and body; restless; lascivious, with emission; sad; anxious; busy, with numerous fancies all night; vivid, wonderful, during which he spoke aloud; vivid, fretful, he always fails; wild; wild, with waking once after midnight; frightful; she had scarcely closed her eyes when she was aroused by frightful images, she spoke disconnectedly and did not recognize bystanders; sleep full of horrors, whenever he closed his eyes it seemed as if he had lost his reason; of falling from heights; of humming-birds, continued after repeated waking; (in a condition between waking and sleep) of dragons, skeletons, frightful ghosts and grinning spectres.

Fever.—Coldness; in evening in bed, but on falling asleep sweat, < about head; > supper, with discomfort; with insensibility of limbs; with weakness; with discomfort; with stupefaction; with pulselessness; with lifelessness; with sleep, without thirst, during the heat thirst and sweat; then heat of face (with white tongue and sweat before midnight), alternating with moderate warmth; sensation at one time as if in ice-water, at another as if flashes of fire were running through veins; shivering; shaking, then heat with sleep and sweat; (trembling, with thirst, then heat, inclination to uncover, strong, full pulse, dryness of fauces, without thirst, with vivid ideas and vivid memory).

Cold skin; and pale; and bluish; and purplish; and livid; and dry. *Cold body; and head somewhat warmer.* Face cold and exsanguine; C. and livid; and livid, afterwards flushed. Chilliness in back; with scarcely perceptible pulse. **Cold limbs;** and clammy; with tetanus; and livid, and rigid, with cold nose; externally; with sweat on the moderately warm face; lower; feet; arms, hands and feet. Shivering anteriorly on r. thigh, down to knee, at 6.30 P.M., afterwards extending from nape down to small of back.

Heat; with sweat; with thirst; with anxiety; with redness of cheeks, with rapid, full, hard pulse; with fantasies, which come after a short sleep and last twelve hours, then weakness, nausea and weak pulse, three hours afterwards again fantasies that last forty-eight hours, with full, hard pulse, then sleep for eight hours; when applied as a plaster, with pain, blisters, irritation and mortification; < head, then sudden sweat; sudden, then sweat and increased vigor.

Heat of head; extending to r. forearm. *Heat of face, with drops of sweat; of cheeks, with redness;* with flushes in it; and scalp, with headache; evenings, < about eyes, without thirst. Hot body, with sweat, thirst, full, hard pulse, bright eyes and mental activity. Heat in r. half of body. Hot skin; on face; with clammy sweat; with roughness and dryness; with dryness and injection of bloodvessels. Heat creeping through limbs, < palms, then exhaustion.

Sweat; *in morning during sleep, with inclination to uncover;* in afternoon; about midnight, an hour after falling asleep; at night; at night, and towards morning chills; in sleep; on physical exertion; on rapid walking; with red rash and itching; when S. is more profuse then there is more itching, with eruption, while all senses vanish; < upper parts, while lower are hot and dry; colloquative. On forehead. *Cold sweat; except on feet, < head;* **on forehead**; on limbs. Cold, clammy; on forehead; on body and hands. Strong sweat. Thick sweat on head, then over whole body like drops of dew, and sleep. Dry skin.

Clinical.—General low temperature, with inclination to stupefaction. Occasionally called for in puerperal fever, with approaching stupor. A valuable remedy in intermittent fever, too often overlooked; the cold stage predominates; the chill is very violent, with weak pulse, which may be followed by diarrhœa and stupefaction; as a rule the patient sleeps through the fever and even through the sweat; hot sweat over the whole body, which does not relieve the stupor. Congestive chills; great heat of the head, with stupor, stertorous respiration, then profuse hot perspiration over the whole body. Congestive chill, with stupor throughout the paroxysm, snoring, with wipe-open mouth, twitchings of the limbs, followed by profuse hot sweat, with no relief of the stupor. Intermittent fever, chill the latter part of the night, with thirst, heat of the head and sleepiness; during the fever sleepiness, vomiting; after the fever sweat, mostly on the lower extremities.

Osmium.

The pure metal is triturated for use.

General Action.—It produces most violent irritation and catarrh of the whole respiratory tract, with a secretion of tough mucus, difficult to expectorate. The kidneys also become inflamed. Its eye symptoms are valuable and extremely interesting, since it has actually cured glaucoma!

Generalities.—Tearing to and fro deep in r. upper side of forehead and in bones of limbs, in evening. General sick feeling. Restless. Weakness; all day, with muddled head and aching limbs and body; on rising; on rising after a restless night.

Mind.—Morose. Angry. Indolent. Misplaces words in the same phrase. Thoughts of accidents having happened to others, these thoughts grow upon him, as if he were to do the same injuries to others. Weakness in evening when riding.

Head.—Aching in base of brain and in jaws at night; extending from base of brain into jaws; < temples, with pain in larynx and hoarseness; nearly preventing sleep; like a band around head above ears. Muddled. Dulness and heat; D. and fulness; D. < l. frontal eminence, with pressure and heaviness. Heaviness. Peculiar feeling. Headache above and under eyes, on one side, tearing towards ear, < under brows, eye waters and is weak. Compressive pain in forehead and temples. Pain in organs of ideality; in r. upper side of forehead; forehead at 9 P.M.; in l. petrous bone above and behind ear; in occiput; vertex and occiput all the afternoon, < throwing head backward, with fulness. The falling of hair is increased.

Eyes.—Veins of fundus large and tortuous. Pain; sharp, lids spasmodically closed, light distressing, pain in globe, conjunctiva and sclera injected, lachrymation, dim vision; burning. Burning, with lachrymation. Smarting, > open air, but leaving them weak, so as to prevent reading, all objects surrounded by a colored halo, eyes red and swollen. Irritable and suffused, and sight weak. Sensation as if axis of vision were moved back and forth, without moving eyes, in evening, with closed eyes. Lachrymation, < fixing eyes upon any object. Twitching of levator of r. upper lid in morning, > rubbing, but returning. Itching in l. inner canthus. Pain in balls; externally on l. orbit. Burning in conjunctiva.

Vision dim; < r. eye. Letters run together when reading. Flame of a lamp seems confused and larger than natural. *Candle-light surrounded by a yellow circle; by a rainbow-hued circle; by a green circle with red margin, larger or smaller according to distance; by a bluish-green circle with ashy gray margin, becoming larger as the light was removed; by bluish-green circle, the outer margin of which is bright red, if the light is ten or fifteen paces from eyes the flame seems enveloped by dust or smoke.*

Clinical.—Violent supraorbital and infraorbital neuralgia, with lachrymation. Glaucoma, with iridescent vision and severe pain around the eyes.

Ears.—Pain in r., then l. in evening. *Ringing in r.;* with pain.

Nose.—Sensation as if blood rushed into it from head. Burning irritation; as from hot water, and in throat, œsophagus and trachea. Full sensation, as if coryza would come on. Prickling, with increased mucus. *Sensitiveness to inspiration; to cold air, and in larynx. Irritation of Schneiderian membrane as from snuff. Ineffectual efforts to sneeze. Sneezing. Coryza. Constant discharge. Constant running, with sensation as if it were full.* Smell similar to chlorine; the stinking odor of the drug remained long in nose, afterwards changed to a sensation as from a blow on nose (odor of blood). Smell diminished.

Clinical.—Violent fluent coryza, with tickling in the larynx and dyspnœa.

Face.—Pain in muscles on chewing after eating wheat bread. Cold jerks in l. upper jaw and front teeth.

Mouth.—Teeth creak more than usual when rubbed with the finger. Jerking pain in a r. upper hollow molar, often preventing speech, afterwards the pain returned but was drawing, > sucking it with tongue. Sudden swelling of gum above root of an upper l. incisor after eating pears, > Silicea, with pain and numbness. Tongue coated and sensitive to hot and cold drinks; coated, and bad taste to coffee; fissured and one spot denuded; red stripe on middle, paining as if sore, edges of T. rough and covered with pimples, T. sensitive to touch when eating and drinking. Mouth sticky and pasty. Salivation; with constant expectoration of mucus, causing nausea; watery, with eructations of the odor and taste of drug and nausea. Taste of blood; T. metallic; unusual to tobacco, it causes scraping in throat, cigars cannot be smoked because they provoke cough and aggravate the rawness in larynx; blunted.

Throat.—Lumps of mucus easily loosened from posterior nares. Hawking of mucus, often with nausea. Burning irritation in pharynx. Warmth along œsophagus, in chest.

Stomach.—Appetite diminished; lost; lost for dinner. Aversion to coffee and tobacco, disgust at their odor. Eructations of the odor of radishes. Nausea;

in morning, with discomfort in pit of stomach; on coughing; after eating, with pain and heaviness in pit of stomach and discomfort; in pit of stomach when riding in open air; > empty eructations; with accumulation of water in mouth, obliging frequent spitting; with discomfort below navel and weakness. Vomiting of watery mucus of the odor and taste of the acid, with blackish-gray flakes of mucus; paroxysmal V. of water, afterwards of yellowish and tenacious substances.

Distention of stomach and abdomen in evening, with difficult passage of flatus; D. of stomach and abdomen all the evening after a dinner of roasted mutton and potatoes. Constriction in forenoon; in epigastrium before dinner (which I take at 12.30), with weight, and often a feeling in stomach as if I had swallowed stones. Uneasiness increasing to anxiety and contraction, < food and stimulants. Weakness at 6 P.M., almost amounting to nausea, after meat pudding, > 10.30 by a glass of brandy and water, with aversion to cocoa. Indigestion.

Abdomen.—Distention in afternoon; and evening; in afternoon, with sensitiveness. Rumbling and movements; R. and gurgling, and one could feel bubbles of air passing through intestines, but no pain. Griping at night. Pain; in groins, that on coughing extended into testicles. Pressure on inguinal rings. Weakness in groins towards spermatic cords.

Rectum and Anus.—Tendency to piles. Urging, but passage of only flatus; U., then stool, first part hard, then soft, with burning in anus preventing sleep, with desire for stool, but evacuation of only a little yellow mucus.

Stool.—Diarrhœa nine or ten times daily, preceded or followed by colic, nearly always with black blood (no hæmorrhoids); (D. after coffee). Mushy, frequent. Soft at 9 P.M. after a normal one at 10 A.M. Bilious, partly fluid, delayed, hasty, with burning at anus. Constipated; and small, delayed. Hard, then soft, orange-colored. Dry, full of air, delayed, next day scanty and small. Only a small lump like a marble, difficult.

Urinary Organs.—Nephritis, urine at first scanty and of the color of porter. Urine high-colored, smelling of violets, apparently full of bile. Urine scanty and brown, next morning scanty and strongly scented, third day scanty and dark. Urine albuminous. Bright red sediment on bottom and sides of vessel.

Sexual Organs.—Glans red on l. side, during coition a long-lasting emission of semen; throbbing, stinging, *pinching* on l. side of G.; *undefined pain in tip and in foreskin.* Hard erections; often after midnight, always on waking in morning, later they last longer, even after rising, desire moderate; E. every morning, earlier and harder. Pain in r. testicle; in testicles, preventing sleep all night; in spermatic cords, < l.; in spermatic cords, extending into testicles, with inflammatory swelling of r. inguinal glands. Appetite suppressed, the conjugal act done by act of volition, and the usual thrill in ejaculation absent.

Respiratory Organs.—*Mucus; in trachea, with constant inclination to cough. Bronchitis. Larynx, lumps of mucus easily loosened; mucus hangs like a thread, irritates to hawking and cough and causes vomiting, after sneezing it is easily loosened; pain, with cough and coryza and pain on talking; sore pain; rawness; scraped, raw sensation and prickling; scraped, raw sensation in epiglottis; tickling, also in trachea; irritation, with hacking cough; irritation, and in trachea; burning irritation, and in trachea; sensation causing hawking. Hoarseness; with pain in larynx, the H. < singing and worse entering house.*

Cough only in morning; *C. from scraping in larynx; with pain in larynx; with constriction of trachea; convulsive; in short bursts on rising, without expectoration;* in short bursts (after coryza) returned during the day, disturbing sleep till midnight, *from tickling in larynx, after sneezing a lump is loosened, which he must swallow; dry, spasmodic; dry, rattling, difficult to loosen; short, dry, paroxysmal, as if mucous membrane would be torn off, with and followed by raw, sore pain in larynx and trachea, extending to middle of sternum. Hacking cough;* > deep inspiration; < motion in open air, with irritation in larynx. Cough, with secretion of colorless mucus. Expectoration of mucus causing nausea.

Dyspnœa; one day better, the other day worse; almost asphyxia, with dry skin and temperature 40.6 C. Respiration difficult, whistling.

Clinical.—Acute laryngitis, with cough, efforts to vomit and increased secretion of stringy mucus. Spasmodic cough, with great efforts to expectorate, but he has to swallow the mucus.

Chest.—Moist râles on breathing, and in larynx. Wandering, pneumonia. Sticking near l. lower rib. Pain beneath sternum on coughing, extending to sides of chest, with burning soreness, after coughing long lumps of yellow, tenacious mucus were loosened. Rawness provoking hawking and hacking cough. Oppression; > deep inspiration, with difficult respiration as if lungs were collapsed and could not get air enough. Tightness, dread of breathing, sore pain when air enters lungs. Dryness.

Pulse.—Rapid.

Back.—Pain in lumbar region; in sacral region; peculiar, extending from scapula to sacral region, < motion and cough.

Extremities.—Heaviness and weariness, < knees. Pulsating stinging on inner side of r. shoulder-joint. Pinching above l. elbow, inwardly and on inner posterior side. Pain in middle of l. humerus, then in l. fingers; in bone of l. elbow; paralytic, deep in radius, < lifting anything or allowing hand to hang down. Pinching in bones of r. forearm. Burning pressure on outer side of r. forearm. Drawing on inside of r. forearm. Pain in bones of l. wrist in morning after stool; P. in r. index, < phalanx, stinging and twitching towards tip, in forenoon. Stabbing in tips of l. fingers and thumb; in attacks, in finger-tips, < l. Burning pain in l. ring finger.

Lower Extremities.—Sudden pain in hip-joint as if it would be dislocated, preventing walking. Ulcerative pain in l. leg and gluteal muscles. Fulness in legs and feet; in legs at 9 P.M., with restlessness in them so that he has to lie down. Legs almost insensible. Pinching in ankles. Pain in r. ankle. Flying cutting in bones and joints of r. foot. Pinching in bones of l. heel, then r.

Skin.—Fold remains attached to growing nail, < r. side and mostly middle finger. Red spots on back of hands. Face red, tender, covered with pimples with watery heads, then pimples on knuckles, gradually spreading over hands and arms, later hands and forearms covered with red, slightly raised circular or elliptical patches, covered with concentric scabs, resembling later stage of herpes iris, most of patches deeply fissured, patches irritable, < morning on rising and at night on undressing, papules on neck.

Redness of hands and arms, with swelling and itching pimples, gradually becoming vesicular, on face, neck and forearms patches of vesicles on an elevated base, the latter hard, brawny and pitting on pressure, towards the edges the patches consist of one or two vesicles on the summit of a large pimple, contents of vesicles watery, occasional cracking of affected skin and constant oozing, the itching makes him irritable.

Eruption on forearms, head and side of face. Exanthema on forearms, hands and cheeks. Eczematous rash on face and upper limbs. Prickly heat disappears on upper half of body and increases on lower, first on thigh, then on leg, then on ankle. Red-brown papules on forearm and hand, with desquamation. Itching, pointed vesicles, with red areola, on back of l. hand, between thumb and index (where six years before scabies had broken out) and on ulnar margin of l. hand, from metacarpal joint to phalanges of little finger, and on outer surface of wrist, on r. hand itching, but no vesicles.

Burning stitches in many places, < r. upper lid and at inner border of nail of l. fourth finger. Itching on legs and ankles; in spots near l. hip, 3 till 4 A.M., when erections return; above crest of l. ilium, with redness and pointed spots as if tetter would appear; as from crawling insects, on shoulders and back in evening on going to bed, it scarcely permits sleep.

Sleep.—Sleepiness; overpowering. Sleepless. Restless sleep; with painful dreams. Sleep heavy, interrupted by nightmare. Dreams of fire, confused, but not frightful. Unremembered dreams of activity and of serious and important events.

Fever.—Shivering, < back. Fever, with difficult respiration; F., with hot and dry skin. Sweat in axilla, smelling of garlic, < evening and night.

Oxalicum Acidum.

Pure oxalic acid is triturated for use.

General Action.—It causes violent gastro-intestinal inflammation, with irregular pulse, stupor and collapse or convulsions. It paralyzes the motor centres in the spinal cord, and also causes apparent inflammation of that substance and its sheath.

Allies.—Pic. ac., Ph. ac., Colch.

Generalities.—Lies supine, on his back, with knees drawn up. Emaciation. Convulsions; with two or three deep inspirations. Mimic spasms and feeling as if they should never laugh again; mimic spasms or pulling of face, as from acid fruit and vegetables. Spastic contractions of muscles of jaws and limbs. Twitching; sudden, in metacarpal bone of l. index; then externally in ulnar side of hand, then in r. side of head, etc., and intermittent jerking pains like stitches, in spots. Tremors.

Pains occupy a small space, one-half to one inch in length and of the thickness of a quill, at times they move through this space, often they occupy the whole of it; pain in l. side; *P. < movement;* excruciating P. Bruised feeling in morning after sound sleep, with stiffness. Distress, < ascending stairs. General sick feeling, sensation as if hands and feet were trembling. Feeling as after a debauch, > walking in cool, open air, headache, with gnawing pain and soreness in eyes and superciliary regions, lassitude, disinclination to occupation, inclination to stretch and yawn. Sensation in upper part of body, < head, like a rippling and surging three times to every beat of the pulse in forenoon, when lying, < directing attention to it, it seems as if the blood streamed in this manner through the capillaries, he distinctly feels it streaming upward and outward in head. Restless; at night.

Indolence in morning, he lay down and felt well while lying. Inclination to lie down in morning and close the eyes, without sleepiness. Weakness; in morning; in forenoon during diarrhœa; on ascending steps and afterwards; < lower limbs; with sweat; with trembling; with feeling as if spine were too weak to support the body; crawling, at noon after eating and in evening, obliging him to lie down, with general fulness (Pic. ac., Phos. ac.). Faintness; and rattling respiration. Collapse. Numbness; approaching palsy. Symptoms reappear as soon as he thinks of them. Symptoms usually intermit and then return in a diminished degree.

Clinical.—Pains occurring in small circumscribed areas, lasting a short time, but very violent. Pains of rheumatic gout, especially worse from sweets.

Mind.—Delirium; in evening; at times; with paroxysms of violent struggling; and he got out of bed. Hallucination at night. Excitement in evening; E., with dry coldness of skin and imperceptible pulse. Hilarity; with frequent and tense pulse. Exhilaration. Cheerfulness; with quickness of thought and action. Animation through the day, with playfulness and mirth. Vivacity in forenoon, < afternoon, with unusual power of understanding. Manner quick; and nervous; M. agitated; heavy. Starting, external rather than internal, when the door slams. Fear; of death. Anxiety and distress; A., with apprehension, vertigo and headache. (Ill humor in afternoon and evening.) Greater love for his children. Aversion to talking; with full feeling in face and excitement.

Unusual power of concentration; after the opposite effect. Presence of mind greater, the relations of the world seem clearer to him. Power of meditation difficult and slow in morning, hardly able to answer questions. Power of understanding lost when reading, necessity to read a sentence three or four times before he can comprehend it. Stupor; with depression and vomiting of blood; fell to the floor and appeared stupid. Unconsciousness. Disinclination to mental work.

Head.—Aching; after exerting mind, < forehead, with dulness; in spots, with sensitiveness to touch; pulsating, in evening after wine. Dulness before and during stool, with screwing-together pressure above and behind ears. Lightness like a flying forward, when walking, though dependent on weakness. Faintness as if all the blood had left the brain, with anxiety. Apoplexy. Vertigo; all day; in morning; in morning, with anxiety and headache; in morning, with thirst and weariness; in evening on looking out of the window; like a swimming towards the left on lying down; in upper and internal part of head, like a vanishing of sense, on rising from a seat, without whirling.

Forehead.—Cutting in r. side, extending behind ear to insertion of sterno-cleido-mastoid. Sharp pain, and in vertex, < over l. eye and in l. temple, with light feeling in head. Pain; in sinciput; in l. side in morning on waking; in morning on waking, > 11 A.M. by a copious stool; in forenoon on rising; in eminence, extending laterally towards temple, then closing of eyes so that she wished to sleep; dull, with occasional sharp pains; throbbing P.; P. in F. and eyes, as in beginning of coryza. Heaviness in F. and vertex in morning. Fulness above eyes.

Pain in temples; in l., extending to lower jaw; jerking, in l.; jerking sliding, in a spot in r. Pain in vertex; intermittent, along base of occiput. Pressure inward in a spot between vertex and occiput, on middle line.

Eyes.—Glassy. Sunken. Pain in a short streak in l.; P. in upper part when walking. Gnawing and soreness in E. and orbital regions, with headache. Sensation of sand in l. in evening. Pupils contracted; and insensible. Balls prominent. Pain in balls, < l. Conjunctivæ dusky, with distinct arcus senilis at upper part of eyes. Dry mucus in margins of lids in morning, which could be removed only in granules. Lids pressed together. Biting in l. inner canthus. Brows corrugated. Eyes weak, with a general sick feeling. Small objects at a short distance seemed large, at the first look he thought they were at a greater distance than they were (in a myope). Loss of vision.

Ears.—Sticking in l. in evening. Pressure behind ears before and during stool. Occasional pain in Eustachian tube near throat, < r., in afternoon. Blowing noise in l.

Nose.—Alæ dilated. Vesicle in r. nostril in morning on rising, with stitches and burning on touch, and every two or three days for two weeks the wings are swollen, < r. at times, < l. at other times. Sticking through r. nostril on inspiring through nose. Sticking burning pain extending from tip towards r. side, with swelling and shiny redness. Pain. Stoppage. Sneezing in evening after tea, with shivering; S., with watery discharge, also with expectoration of hard lumps of mucus.

Clinical.—Pimple in r. nostril, with red, shiny swelling of the tip of the nose.

Face.—*Pale; and livid;* and haggard; at noon, and appetite lost; and lips blue; and yellow, and eyes sunken. Blue, and lips. Hippocratic. Red. Dark. Sunken. Livid; and swollen, also lips, throat and tongue. Expression anxious; desponding; stupid; dull and heavy. Twitching of muscles. Full sensation. Lips puffed; shrivelled and sore; upper trembling, lower relaxed. Jaws spasmodically closed; and angles of mouth drawn down. Drawing pain near angle of lower jaw, l., then r., but longer in l., with rigidity.

Mouth.—Teeth. Covered with sordes, as in low fever. Cutting in hollow molars at noon. Cold jerking in a l. upper incisor. Pain in first r. upper molar; nearly all day in molars, < r. upper, > towards evening; in a hollow M. in evening; in a hollow tooth in evening. On edge. Roughness when ground together, with pain when air rushed through the open mouth, as during yawning, and such tenderness of teeth on voluntary deep inspiration that it causes gooseskin. Bleeding of gums during friction (had had it before, but it is increased now). Pain as from blisters, in places on gum. Burning pain in gum of a l. lower incisor and a pustule surrounded by red areola and swelling.

Tongue.—White; and dry; and fauces as if they had been boiled. Pale, and lips. Pale gray. Occasional inflammation, and of mouth. Brown and dry; reddish B. and dry. Red, and fauces; R., swollen, firm and tender on pressure; T. and throat red and sore, afterwards a yellow coat on tongue; T. and throat red, afterwards dingy white, hot and dry to touch; T. and pharynx covered with red and white spots, swollen and painful, swallowing difficult. Swollen and coated white; S. and a wooly coat, next day red at sides and aphthous; S. so that it was difficult to project beyond the teeth, and livid. Rough. Coated; yellow; brown, with a red, dry tip; white, with red interspaces; like the dry coating of sugar on sweetmeats, interspersed with red patches. Dry; < towards tip, and sore and painful. Burning on l. half. Cold. Speech labored.

Mouth inflamed. Mucus. Palate vesicated. Soreness; and of tongue; and of posterior nares. Burning pain, and in fauces, so that swallowing was difficult. Burning, and in throat and œsophagus; acrid, in M., gullet and stomach. Scraping posteriorly on palate and fauces, obliging hawking. Discomfort in soft palate and uvula after gruel. Dryness; with ulcers in it. *Salivation;* after yawning, or the mouth feels empty. *Sour taste;* in morning; in forenoon, during a nap; on rinsing mouth; and astringent. Sweet taste to water. Dry and burning taste in M. and fauces. Taste of the drug in the evening. Taste of food lost, with nausea and coated tongue.

Throat.—Mucus; pulling out of string of M.; expectoration of thick, yellowish; hawking up of lumpy, tenacious; hawking up of thick, yellowish-white M., with a black lump in the centre; natural secretion of M. is diminished. Inflammation of pharynx. Soreness resembling cancrum oris, with ptyalism, but no fetor. Pain; in fauces in morning on swallowing; in morning on swallowing after rising, > noon; in evening on swallowing; burning P. Scraping in upper part; S. in morning on rising, with soreness; on rising, with roughness, speech difficult; with difficult swallowing, tonsils and velum palati red and covered with adherent mucus that can be expectorated only after long hawking; in tonsils, with biting, as if uvula were swollen; in fauces, as from mucus. Sensation in fauces as from acidity of stomach. Constriction; and uneasiness; of œsophagus. Irritation in fauces. Dryness, with pain on swallowing; D. of pharynx in forenoon after diarrhœa. Burning; in evening; with pain on pressure; and in fauces; in pharynx and œsophagus. Swallowing difficult.

Stomach.—Appetite increased; A. little at noon, with thirst. Appetite lost; at noon; in evening. Aversion to tobacco-smoking in morning, but longing for it in the evening. (Coffee is not relished at noon.) Thirst; at 3 P.M. Repugnance to water.

Eructations; acrid; painful; sour; sour after coffee at breakfast. Empty eructations; at noon, with emission of flatus and rumbling and gurgling in abdomen; in afternoon; *tasteless, after eating;* tasting of the food. Hiccough; during the day, with painful hawking; at 11 A.M., returning as soon as he thinks of it. *Nausea;* in morning, with cutting in abdomen; at 10 A.M. after diarrhœa; during dinner; after eating; at pit of stomach; with emptiness in stomach; with emptiness in stomach and discomfort in whole body. Retching.

Vomiting; *frequent;* with purging. Violent; after

the accession of pain; with frequent desire for stool; like beer, only redder. Of food. Of blood; mixed with mucus every half hour; at first tinged with blood, afterwards of arterial blood, then coagulated blood; bloody fluid, with white membranous patches; bloody matters and a white fluid; fluid of a dark bloody color; dark, grumous, bloody matter; bile and clots of dark blood. Of mucus tinged with blood; bloody, frothy mucus; thick mucus. Of a brown matter like chocolate. Of thick, black fluid. Of a dark liquid. Of frothy, watery fluid, after standing a brownish precipitate fell leaving a transparent brownish fluid. Of greenish-black matter. Grass-green, with grumous sediment; grass-green fluid, with mucous sediment and white flocculi; of yellow-green, jelly-like fluid mixed with white flocculi, with jactitation and distress. Of a yellow fluid; thick, at night. Of matter like milk.

Griping and twisting pain; G. in pit. Grasping. Excruciating pain in epigastrium. Pain; in region; in epigastrium; at night; after eating; in epigastrium, < pressure; with oppression and continual efforts to vomit; in pit, with heat and soreness; in epigastric region, with heat and oppression; in S. and abdomen, obliging him to sit bent over, < sugar in tea and coffee. "Gathering." Gnawing in region; G. like hunger, it was scarcely possible to eat a morsel at dinner, the first spoonfuls of soup caused urging to stool, which was diarrhœa-like, yellow, slimy, serous, with tenesmus.

Pyrosis in evening; after tea, with emission of flatus and pressing downward. Burning pain; in epigastrium; in epigastrium, extending to œsophagus and pharynx, so that he rolled about the floor, with ineffectual retching; in epigastrium and in r. hypochondriac and iliac regions, with tenderness on pressure, < over cardiac end of stomach, abdomen generally hot to touch. Burning; *in pit;* gnawing. Tenderness on pressure; at cardiac extremity and epigastrium; in epigastrium, with burning; in epigastrium, with resonance on percussion; and in abdomen. Intermittent weight in pit at night waking him, > eructation. Emptiness similar to hunger, > eating; E. so that he must eat between meals. Irritation.

Clinical.—Gastralgia, with feeling of coldness between the stomach and navel (Colch.).

Abdomen.—Distended; by flatus. Movements day and night. Rumbling; in afternoon, with gurgling; in evening, with rolling as from water; all the evening, with pressing downward; after coffee at breakfast, < l. side, with gurgling, then diarrhœa, then nausea; after dinner; with colic, then pasty stool. Emissions of flatus; *difficult;* difficult, in evening and next morning; offensive. Flatulency all day and at times during the night, with emissions of flatus, swelling of abdomen, with intermittent pain in and around umbilicus, worse in r. iliac region, and itching and crawling in anus, > rubbing.

Sticking extending to region of spleen, > deep breathing. Cutting in forenoon after a thin stool in the morning; C. waking her at 5 A.M., returning periodically all day, also chilliness alternating with heat, the same C. next morning. Griping; which drew her up double. *Pain;* in morning after rising, then copious diarrhœa, which was repeated; in evening, with urging to stool and sickness, so that he drank a glass of wine, then painful dulness of head; < pressure; *with burning;* with frequent inclination to stool; with diarrhœa; intermittent; flatulent, with distress and weakness of it. Pain as before diarrhœa; at night; after coffee. Tenderness.

Sudden distress at 6 A.M., then twisting in and around umbilicus, then scanty, hard, dark brown stool, in half an hour again pain and bearing down, then loose, muddy, brown stool, with colic in umbilicus, bearing down below umbilicus and griping in anus, the latter causing nervous pains through head, with heat in head, after going to bed return of the same pains, then copious, consistent, dark, muddy, brown stool, the pains always returned on going to bed, obliged to sit or stand, > motion (pain > Merc. sol.).

Sticking in l. hypochondrium. Pain in l. hypochondrium after retiring; bruised. Pain in a spot in r. side of A. in forenoon.

Umbilical Region.—Sticking in evening. Cramp-like pain to l. of umbilicus at 5 P.M., then colic in r. iliac region and eructations of tasteless wind. *Pain;* at night, with emission of flatus; before stool; during stool, and below umbilicus and through ilium and jejunum; always after symptoms in head; with pressing towards anus and flatulent troubles; flatulent, between umbilicus and l. hypochondrium; periodical flatulent, below umbilicus, as from unripe fruit, at night on waking, < movement after rising, > rest, returning in morning on walking after breakfast, > at noon; paroxysmal, and in r. iliac region. Scraping at night, often waking him, with sensation as if stool would occur, which did not. Soreness on touch.

Hypogastrium.—Rumbling in r. groin, in cæcum, and noises of flatus after stool. Sharp pain in l. iliac region. Pain in a spot deep above r. ilium, towards the side, when yawning, breathing and in different postures; P. in descending colon in evening, then mushy stool. Constriction in descending colon in evening after supper, with cutting in abdomen and constant desire for stool. In a spot in l. iliac region, urging to discharge flatus on sitting down after a walk, a sensation as if the part would burst.

Rectum and Anus.—Discharge of mucus after stool. Cutting downward in a narrow streak in r. side of rectum in morning on rising, repeated on sitting down to stool, afterwards C. in r. side of rectum and after stool an undefined sensation in anus. Burning in rectum at night. Frequent stitches in anus, with pinching near anus, as from flatus. Frequent pain in anus at night, disturbing sleep. Pressure towards anus. Constant tenesmus, ineffectual efforts for stool. Ineffectual desire. Desire for stool and to urinate in morning on lying down (an hour after taking milk).

Stool. — Watery, frequent; constant involuntary, watery, *occasionally mixed with blood;* thick, black, offensive, containing bloody shreds. *Diarrhœa; frequent.* Violent diarrhœa; in morning, then eyes sunken in forenoon and surrounded by blue rings; at 3 and 7 P.M.; with blood. Copious diarrhœa in morning after rising, preceded by colic, at 9 A.M. watery stool with prostration, then nausea and tension in calves, in afternoon again diarrhœa. Pasty, copious at 7 A.M., preceded by colic, followed by more violent colic, then general sick feeling, desire for stool and recurrence of diarrhœa in forenoon, in afternoon constant desire and diarrhœa containing the undigested dinner. Pasty, tenacious and difficult; with general weakness. Pasty and scanty at 8 A.M., and a copious one, with urging at noon. Pappy, light brown, with scanty, light urine, again in afternoon a pappy, thick, short stool, with cutting in fleshy part of l. thumb, then heavy rumbling in r. side of abdomen (cæcum) and noise of flatus.

Constipation. Hard and frequent; H. and difficult; H., with mucus and blood; H. and copious, covered with mucus. Serous, with streaks of blood and with tenesmus. Mixed with blood; with bloody mucus and tenesmus. Containing filaments of whitish matter, similar to the crust on tongue. Green, slimy. Irregular. Indolent; and micturition frequent, but scanty. Frequent; at night. Omitted; next day thin, loamy.

Clinical.—Diarrhœa < coffee, stools profuse, watery, with frequent ineffectual urging. Dysentery, stools of blood and mucus, preceded by colic, followed by nausea and pain in the calves.

Urinary Organs.—Bladder distended by urine, but inability to pass it. (Full feeling in bladder.) Urging, with copious, light-colored urine. Frequent desire, urine light-colored; F. desire and copious urine each time, with burning during micturition, urine clear and straw-colored. Diminished desire. Frequent micturition in small quantities; F. micturition, in evening of copious light-colored urine. Involuntary micturition. Micturition by drops at night, with burning.

Burning pain through urethra to orifice, as if a drop of acrid urine would pass, in the evening. Burning in urethra at noon during micturition, with voluptuous sensation. Urine passed in morning and evening very acid, deposit of numerous crystals of uric acid, indications of oxalates of lime in the milky-white sediment. Urine loaded with enormous crystals of oxalate of lime, and it contained some blood-discs. Urine profuse at 5 A.M. Urine scanty in morning. No urine during the ten hours.

Clinical.—Oxaluria, with general gouty symptoms and exhaustion.

Sexual Organs.—Red points on glans. Thrusts in glans on urinating. Erections in forenoon after sleep, with dulness in occiput; E. in forenoon on lying down, then pain in testicles on going out, after going out pain in testicles and spermatic cords, < latter and < r.; *E. at night, with lascivious dreams* (Pic. ac.). Heaviness in testicles in evening when walking, < r., with pain and with shooting along spermatic cords. Itching of testicles and spermatic cords. Emission at night; interrupted by waking. Desire increased; during the night and morning, with voluptuous dreams at night. Burning in female genitals.

Clinical. — Neuralgia of the spermatic cord, < slightest motion. Amenorrhœa, with great asthenia. Amenorrhœa from taking cold.

Respiratory Organs.—Irritation of glottis. Tickling in larynx on walking in open air, with sticking, swollen feeling and cough. Hoarseness; and frequent hawking. Voice rough; before going to bed. Voice altered from a deep bass to a low key, like a person talking in an undertone, afterwards like an old man's voice. Cough; in evening, with tickling in throat; from tickling in larynx and trachea, with soreness in larynx; with soreness of chest; *dry, on violent exertion;* dry, violent, in morning from tickling in throat, with pains in chest; with expectoration of greenish mucus; desire to cough, but cannot for pain in chest. *Spasmodic breathing. Difficult breathing; with constriction in larynx, wheezing and oppression of r. side of chest;* in forenoon. Dyspnœa, with tracheal râles. Felt as if his breath were going, almost strangled. Respiration tight in evening on violent motion. Respiration rapid; and labored. Respiration slow. Moaning.

Chest.—Sticking in l. lung in afternoon; S. in l. breast, < walking; *in l. lung and heart, extending to epigastrium;* sudden in l. lung, depriving him of breath; sore, at 2 P.M., afterwards extending to between scapulæ. Pain when coughing; P. in middle, extending to scapula. Pressure upon C. as if ulcerated, at noon. Constriction, with short breath. Tightness, with inclination to breathe deeply.

Clinical. — Congestion and inflammation at the base of l. lung.

Heart.—Sounds imperceptible, and pulse could be felt only at long intervals. Sticking extending towards abdomen; S. in præcordial region. Pain in posterior and lower part extending forward, in forenoon when lying and afterwards when walking in the street, and electric-like beats extending outward below nipple to sternum. Ulcerated sensation in præcordial region in evening, with heaviness of chest as in asthma or dropsy. Oppression of præcordia, with sighing. *Fluttering palpitation; P. at night on lying down.* Beats attracted attention at night after going to bed. Action irregular and sounds distant. Action feeble and sound barely audible. Impulse diminished. No capillary circulation and no pulsation in radial artery, and very feeble in brachial.

Clinical.—Palpitation coming on after lying down at night. Angina pectoris, with peculiar numbness, pains < least motion, like short stitches, confined to a small spot, lasting a few seconds; sharp darting pain in l. lung and in the heart, with forced expiration.

Pulse.—Rapid; with heat; and sharp; and full; and hard; and full, hard; and full, hard, intermittent; and wiry; and small; and small, wiry; and small, threadlike; and small, irritable, intermittent; and tremulous; and weak; and weak, and so irregular that it could not be counted. Slow. Hard and contracted. Irregular. Small; and irregular; and weak; and tremulous, intermittent. Weak. *Scarcely perceptible;* at wrist and temples, later rapid and firm. Imperceptible; with deadly coldness, clammy sweats, sometimes lividity of nails and fingers.

Back. — *Acute pain gradually extending to thighs. Bruised sensation from shoulders to loins in morning instead of the habitual pain in small of B.; bruised feeling in morning, < beneath tip of l. scapula, with stiffness. Numbness and weakness, and in limbs; N. and W., and in lower limbs, so that it was difficult to ascend stairs; N. and tingling or pricking, and in thighs.* Sticking beneath point of r. scapula when sitting. Burning pain deep between scapulæ in evening.

Small of Back.—Sticking above hips during hiccough; above r. hip during hiccough; above r. hip, taking away the breath, on yawning; from loins down to limbs, the patient seeks relief in a constant change of position. Excruciating agony in lower part of back, extending down thighs. Pain; all day, somewhat > hard stool; in region of kidneys; in region of r. kidney in evening; in region of l. kidney, waking him towards morning; in r. loin after rising from lying; between last rib and hip extending towards r. side after rising from a bent position. *Weakness in loins and hips extending to lower limbs. Numbness* (compare Ph. ac. and Pic. ac.).

Clinical.—Neuralgia of the spine starting between the shoulders, with tenderness over the spine and pain in the occiput. Spinal symptoms, with numbness and weakness in the back and limbs; peculiar numbness of the whole body, with coldness and loss of motion in the limbs, the pain darting and lancinating, especially in l. lung and about the heart, with jerking inspiration and forced expiration, apparently trying to relieve the intense pain by emptying the lung; dyspnœa, great aggravation from motion; the attacks recur with periodical remissions. Posterior spinal sclerosis, with violent shooting pains down the extremities, dyspnœa and numbness; also with pains confined to small spots, lasting only a few seconds.

Extremities.—Livid; hands, arms, legs and feet livid and cold, and legs difficult to move. Trembling. Contractions of arms and legs. Uneasiness, < feet. Weakness; extending over whole body; and heaviness. *Numbness;* and tingling, and legs drawn up on abdomen. Joints of ankle, knee, hip, wrist and shoulder affected.

Upper Extremities.—Sudden shooting in r. shoulder-joint. *Numbness from shoulders to tips of fingers;* towards noon. Pinching stitch in l., then r. deltoid after lying down in bed. Pain in middle of humerus in evening, often a jerking, so that he must stretch or move arm. Pain in muscles of upper arm as if beaten. Numbness of arm. Hands clenched. Sensation in hand as if dead. Heaviness of l. hand, motion of fingers slow and difficult.

Fingers.—Livid. Nails dark; and fingers contracted. L. drawn inward, < index. Semi-flexed, rigid, and thumbs bent into palm. Sticking in ball of r. thumb in evening when writing; burning S. similar to gouty pains, deep in r. fingers, < last phalanx of middle. Tensive pain in fleshy part of l. thumb, with heat, numbness and swollen sensation. Tingling.

Lower Extremities.—Gait slow and unsteady. *Blueness, coldness and almost complete immobility. Lameness and stiffness.* Sticking in r. hip-joint. *Contracting pain in external tendon of l. patella.* Jerking-sliding pain in hollow of l. knee. Weakness of knees on ascending stairs; W. of legs extending over whole body, with sweat, < axillæ. Cramp of legs and feet, > pressure. Legs fell asleep. Sharp pain in r. ankle; pain in r. ankle, with swollen feeling in it and in r. foot. Shooting in r. instep; intermittent. R. toes spasmodically flexed in morning on rising and at noon after sitting.

Skin.—General redness; red spots or petechiæ, as if spattered with blood, on face, head, chest and nates. Arms, chest and face mottled. Eruption not unlike the roundish red marks on arms of healthy children, but of a deeper tint. Eruption like roseola, then dark skin, then desquamation. Eruption over whole body like maculæ of typhus. Efflorescence on greater part of body. Fold around nails of third, fourth and fifth fingers cracked and inflamed. Itching papules over whole body. Painful pustule on r. index, where a cut from a penknife had healed. Smarting soreness around neck as if chafed by the collar. Sensitiveness when shaving. Itching on nape; in spots on r. side of nape, r. side of scalp and l. side of abdomen, in evening, when sitting after walking.

Sleep.—Violent yawning; constant Y. in evening, then salivation; inclination to Y. and stretching. Sleepiness by day; S. in morning. Tendency to sopor alternated with restlessness. Conscious when aroused, but immediately lapses into a sleepy state. Profound sleep when sitting after dinner; P. and long, and on rising he feels stupid, lies down again and sleeps an hour longer. Long and undisturbed sleep (unusual), with sweat, the wet shirt feels very cold on waking.

Sleepless after being awakened by a noise. Restless sleep; without dreams. Little sleep; with constant unpleasant dreams, starting and waking in fright. Frequent waking on account of pain in stomach and urging to urinate. Frequent starting in sleep. Raised himself in alarm, looked around the room, but remembering where he was lay down again, repeated the action in an hour. Dreams unremembered; D. vivid, agreeable and lascivious; constant, vivid, frightful, with frequent waking; of rapidly sliding walking, also that water is poured upon him.

Fever.—Chilliness all day, with heat on slight exertion; C. all day alternating with heat; shaking, in evening, with small contracted pulse, red face, internal heat of head and cold hands as if dead; creeping, < upward from lower part of spine. Rigors. Cold skin; and clammy. Cold and livid face and hands; C. and pale face and limbs; C. and sweaty face, hands and feet. *Cold limbs; and livid nails;* and trunk; *feet and legs;* feet, in evening.

Exhausting fever, with dyspepsia and singultus. Heat; *internal, < face,* in forenoon; *in flashes, with sweat;* in flushes in morning, with sweat and with sharp pains in forehead and vertex. Hot skin. Heat in face and hands; in face, then in l. thigh. Sweat, < axillæ; on forehead; cold, < about forehead; cold, partially bedewing skin; clammy; cold, clammy. Skin dry.

Oxytropis Lamberti.

A tincture is made of the entire plant. This is one of the family of "Loco" weeds of the western plains, which have proved so poisonous to horses; there seems no doubt that, like its ally, the Lathyrus (chick-pea), of Europe, it produces congestion of the spine and paralysis, possibly also convulsions.

Allies.—Physostig., Lathyrus.

Generalities.—Pains come and go quickly, but muscles stay sore and stiff after the pain is gone; P. in helix of l. ear for two or three minutes, then between eyes, went up over head and down to base of brain, heavy aching in lumbar region for a short time, pain across base of brain, gone in a minute, next down inside of l. leg from groin to knee; frequent fine P. all over body, > 3 P.M.

Sick, exhausted feeling at 10.30 A.M. Languid all the forenoon. *No life.* Feeling as if I would lose consciousness, or as if I would fall when standing. Inability to move around on account of uncertain feeling of numbness, with prickling in l. arm and hand. *Aggravation of any symptom from thinking of it;* A. on alternate days; from eating. Amelioration after sleep; *after stool;* from motion and going into cool, open air.

Mind.—*Disinclination to talk, study,* or work, *desire to be alone. Sadness;* all day; on rising, with weariness. Weak, cannot study with the usual vigor, forgetful. Forgetful of words and names. Less able to concentrate thoughts.

Head.—Aching; from 2 till 4 P.M.; from 2 till 5 P.M. Pressure, > sleep; < moving legs, with strange sensation in it; with heavy pain and with pain in eyeball. Full, uncomfortable feeling; F., with heat of head, coldness of feet and instability when standing or sitting. Vertigo, with uncertainty of gait. Pain over r. eye. Dulness in frontal region obliging me to lie down. Weight in forehead on waking, gradually increasing till 2 P.M., then gradually decreasing. Pain in vertex and occiput in forenoon, over eyeballs about 12 P.M. Sensitiveness of the side on which I lie. Pain as if a weight were attached to lower edge of occiput.

Eyes.—Dull feeling. Pupils dilated. Vision blurred. When reading it seems as if a light were reflected from a bright copper plate seen at the left side, as if the light were at the end of the room.

Nose.—Pressure over bridge. Feels as if sunburnt, red and shiny, < alæ. Dryness and scabs. Fluent coryza in evening, with sneezing; bloody, fluent C.

Ears and Face.—Roaring in ears. Pain in l. lower jaw.

Mouth and Throat.—Tenderness of molars. Gumboil on l. lower gum. Dryness of mouth, < morning. Salivation. Taste metallic; in morning on waking; T. greasy. *Throat sore;* and dry. Inflammation of pharynx, "husky" feeling.

Stomach and Abdomen.—Appetite increased; lost. Eructations as if I had taken soda-water; empty E. Nausea in forenoon on lying down, > rising, returning on lying down again; intermittent N. all day. Soreness of stomach. Epigastric region tender at 10 P.M. Lancinations through abdomen in evening. Sharp pain running across A. from r. to l. Colic, with looseness of bowels (constipation was marked when I began). Griping in umbilical region working down, at 8 P.M., then discharge of flatus at 10 P.M.

Rectum and Stool.—Sore feeling in rectum. Crawling in rectum. Urging, > emission of flatus. *Stools slipping from anus like lumps of jelly;* and mushy, of carrion smell; *and sphincters seemed relaxed.* Stool hard and unsatisfactory; hard at first, then diarrhœic. Stool dark brown. S. frequent; omitted.

Urinary Organs.— *Urging always on thinking of it,* urine profuse, light-colored, of strong odor. Urine profuse; and clear like water; and dark. Urine scanty and looking like that of a child troubled with worms, light red, stain on bottom of vessel; scanty, with irritation, muscles of bladder seem to contract.

Sexual Organs.—Intermittent pain in glans. Bruised pain in testicles extending along spermatic cord and thigh; B. feeling after going to bed, beginning in r. testicle and extending to l. *Desire diminished;* lost, almost impotent.

Respiratory Organs and Chest.—Mucus in larynx, hard to cough up. Dry cough from any exercise. Breathing short and quick on account of full feeling in abdomen, after lying down. Pain in upper part of r. lung. Oppression of lungs at 9 P.M. Tightness across chest in morning, with hacking cough. Warm tingling under skin of l. side of chest.

Heart and Pulse.—Pain over heart like a wave. Palpitation after lying down at night. Pulse 84, intermittent, at 2 P.M.

Neck and Back.—Pain in nape and stiffness in muscles. Sore feeling in r. muscles of neck. Back weak. Pain in kidneys, < r., with tenderness; heavy P. in kidneys on waking.

Extremities.—Stitches in r. leg and knee and r. wrist in forenoon, leaving tired feeling in joints, flesh on under side of these limbs felt sore all the afternoon. Cutting running from point of shoulder down front of chest to point of hip-bone. Sharp pain in l. shoulder extending down arm, < around shoulder-joint, lasting till after sleep; in l., extending down arm, with coldness. Rheumatic pain in shoulder and arm; intermittent, at lower end of l. radius. Pain streaking along ulnar nerve from tip of fourth finger. Flesh of arms and hands feel as if I had taken a heavy cold. Gait uncertain. Weakness of knees; of l., with rheumatic pain. Pain in l. great toe-joint.

Sleep.—Twitching of all muscles just as I would go to sleep. Frequent waking. Did not sleep well, dreamed, woke at 4 A.M. feeling stupid and weary. Dream of spiders, bugs, etc.; D. pleasant; lascivious.

Fever.—Chilliness all day, with sweat of feet and axillæ, sensitiveness to cold air; C. between shoulders going down to feet at 11.40 A.M., stomach feels cold, repetition of all pains, also peculiar crawling in bowels like a contraction of muscles, < around navel, as chill goes off smarting in throat and feeling as if lungs and bronchi would shut, breathing hard, C. passed off about 1 P.M. with sweat of palms and soles, changeable pains until 3 P.M., no thirst, at 1.30 grasping pain in l. ovary for an hour, pain in abdomen as before stool, stool thin, yellow, felt bad at the same time for three days, then for four weeks on every seventh day had a chill with all the symptoms recorded, after the first chill cold feeling in spine for eight weeks.

Pæonia.

A tincture is made of the fresh root of the Pæonia officinalis, L.

Compare Silicea, (Sulphur, Ratan.)

Generalities.—Weakness; when walking, with heaviness of chest and limbs, so that often she must stand still; > eating, with heaviness of limbs. Aggravation after sleep at night, at noon and in rainy weather.

Mind.—Delirium. Excitement. Apprehension; in evening, with anxiety. Ill humor. Depression; after 5 P.M., with irritability.

Head.—Pain and confusion; P., with dulness of it, roaring in ears and flickering before eyes; gnawing P. Fulness. Rush of blood; after 5 P.M., with pain below forehead; and to face, with sweat. Vertigo; on motion; in a warm room, with confusion and heaviness of head; on walking, with staggering of limbs; < walking about the room; > a glass of water, with nausea; with heaviness, dulness and heat of head. Pain in forehead; in morning and evening, and in orbits; above l. brow, with sticking. Jerking tearing in r. temple, extending into head. Boring outward in r. temple. Pain in l. side of head after dinner. Pain in occiput; in morning; and in nape. Heaviness in occiput.

Eyes.—Red and watery. Pain in l.; becoming a tearing, with inflammation, injection of conjunctiva, difficult opening of eye on account of pain and photophobia, with lachrymation. Dry, smarting, not easy to open. Burning, itching and dryness; burning of eyes and lids. Conjunctivitis of ball and lid, with lachrymation and contracted pupils. Inflammation of l. ball, with pain as if a grain of sand were under upper lid. Sticking in r. upper lid, towards inner canthus. Itching in r. upper lid at short intervals.

Ears, Nose and Face.—Sticking outward in r. ear. Pinching behind r. ear. Ringing in ears; in l. Stoppage of nose in evening; in morning in bed, with dryness. Face red and puffy. Pain extending from articular fossa of lower jaw through inner ear, > keeping jaws open for a long time, as, for example, when drinking, < pressing them together. Crawling in upper lip.

Mouth and Throat.—Tongue red. Biting posteriorly in palate in evening. Hawking caused by tenacious mucus in throat, with scanty expectoration. Scraping in throat, necessity to cough and hawk to loosen it, and feeling in posterior nares as if full of mucus. Sensation as if an acrid, burning vapor ascended throat. Heat in fauces extending to pharynx; in throat and œsophagus, < hawking. Swallowing difficult.

Stomach.—Appetite lost. Thirst. Nausea; (on entering a warm room after a moderate walk, with seething in head, vanishing or obscuration of senses and attacks of faintness). Vomiting and painful diarrhœa. Periodical sticking upward from middle of epigastric region. Cutting in region of stomach and transverse colon, then soft stool. Burning in epigastric region at night.

Abdomen.—Rumbling. Griping in forenoon, preceded and especially followed by anxiety, trembling of limbs and arms, as if frightened, and apprehension when any one spoke to him, unpleasant news affected him exceedingly. Cutting; in umbilical region. Colic; with diarrhœa; transversely across upper A. Sensitiveness, < along transverse colon and epigastric region, that were hard and retracted. Crawling in A.

Anus and Stool.—*Biting itching in anus* in afternoon, **the orifice seems swollen.** Diarrhœa five times; *sudden pasty D., with faintness in abdomen and burning in anus after stool*, returning after six hours, *then internal chilliness*, generally a few hours after he felt the worst. *Stools thin, frequent.*

Clinical.—Pasty diarrhœa, followed by burning in anus and internal chilliness. Hæmorrhoids, with ulceration; the anus and surrounding parts are purple and covered with crusts, ulcers within the anus, exquisitely painful, the whole mucous membrane studded with ulcers and cracks. Fissures of the anus; stools followed by burning and biting, lasting several hours, has to walk the floor on account of the pain, with exudation of offensive moisture (Sulph. in part, Ratan.).

Urinary and Sexual Organs.—Constriction in region of neck of bladder, so that urine passed only in driblets. Frequent and copious micturition, disturbing sleep at night. Micturition burning and urine scanty. External genitals swollen and painful.

Chest.—Sticking in l.; in l., parallel with axis of body, on every inspiration from 3.30 to 5 and at 9 P.M.; in r. side near sternum, on a level with nipples, at 4 P.M.; near r. nipple, < walking; to right of ensiform process, with pressure; downward in l.; backward, as if through heart; through whole l. half, beginning beneath clavicle and extending to diaphragm, < region of heart at the moment of expiration and < walking. Cutting in l. side when sitting bent over. Sharp pain in ribs above hepatic region, in morning. Pain; near middle of sternum; beneath manubrium in morning; near both sides of lower part of sternum when eating; in middle of sternum, > night, < next morning and recurring all the forenoon; beneath heart, as from anxiety. Throbbing extending through r. side and from posterior part to nape, where it ended in intermitting pinching. Rush of blood. Heat.

Pulse.—Contracted.

Neck and Back.—Periodical sticking in last cervical vertebra; S. in scapulæ; in places in back, > scratching. Pinching now in dorsal, now in abdominal muscles. Griping now in dorsal, now in abdominal muscles. Boring in l. scapula, > motion.

Extremities.—Jerking and tearing. Paroxysmal tearing, then numbness. Weakness in evening. Aching in r. upper arm, extending to region of elbow, > motion. Tense feeling in muscles across elbow on flexing arms. Cramp in ulna at wrist. Sticking griping in l. wrist, behind thumb. Pain, almost a tearing, in l. finger-tips. Dead feeling in one finger. R. ring finger, which received four weeks previously a blow from a blunt rapier, seems as far as the first and second phalanges dead, cold, devoid of blood, shrivelled, yellow, and without sensation, in afternoon.

Lower Extremities.—Cramp in r. knee when sitting. Sudden thrusts outward on inner side of l. knee. Sensation in lower part of calf as if aponeurosis of muscles and tendons were tense or bruised, making walking difficult, towards evening. Weary pain in ankles when sitting. Pain in corns. Swelling of toes, with contraction, intermittent sticking through them and burning itching. Sticking in skin of r. great toe, as if pressed by shoe, in evening. Pain in l. little toe as from pressure.

Skin.—Painful ulcer, oozing offensive moisture, on perineum, near anus. Crawling in tip of nose; in a spot on l. forearm, with a bristling sensation; sticking, in the fingers, in the sides; drawing, beneath umbilicus, > scratching. Itching in concha; on calves, > rubbing; on head, chest and limbs, with burning biting as from nettles; prickling in open air, with sticking; prickling, on chest, then in axillæ and arms down to sides of chest.

Clinical.—Abscess below the coccyx. Obstinate ulcer on the jaw. Ulcer on r. instep from blistering the foot. Large ulcer on lower part of leg. Ulcer on the breast of an old lady, from an abscess which had never healed.

Sleep.—Sleepiness all the afternoon. Starting on falling asleep, even during the day. Sleep restless and dreams unremembered; restless, disturbed the first night by burning in epigastric region, afterwards by voluptuous dreams with emissions, or by anxious, sad and vivid dreams of death, etc. Sleep unrefreshing, disturbed by many and unrefreshing dreams. Dreams unremembered; frightful, of the death of relatives, etc.; quarrelsome; anxious; vivid, wonderful and amorous; amorous, with emission; amorous after midnight, disturbing sleep; of a ghost sitting upon his chest and oppressing his breath, so that he often woke groaning; of a figure sitting upon his chest, making respiration anxious.

Fever.—Shivering. Coldness of one ear at 5 P.M., with heat of the other. Coldness of limbs, with heat in face, back and chest. Heat at night disturbing sleep; general, waking after midnight, with heat in region of stomach. Hot skin. Heat in head; in face; as from nettles, on chest, neck, back and shoulders.

Palladium.

The pure metal is triturated for use.

Compare Plat., Pod.

Generalities.—Pain in abdomen in morning before rising, then in r. temple, at 7.30 when walking rheumatic pain in r. hip, at 9.15 pain in r. thumb, then in forefinger, then in r. temple, then in l. temple, r. shoulder and arm, then again in r. temple, in small of back extending over r. thigh, then in r. wrist, l. hip, r. hand, r. lower jaw, after a walk at noon pain in r. temple and r. arm, the pains change place so quickly and at times are so transient that they are hard to describe, they appear oftenest and longest in temple. Pain in head and hips in forenoon, > 2 P.M. by sleep, from which she wakes with a start, headache cured by half an hour's sleep before dusk. Peculiar pain somewhere in l. side (forgotten because it disappeared on turning) towards morning. Throbbing throughout body at 2.30 P.M., delaying sleep. On walking, feeling as if he had grown taller. Heaviness in morning, with tired feeling in limbs, inertia and indecision. Tired in evening; on walking, he reels on entering the room. Aversion to exertion. Aggravation in afternoon; towards evening; from motion.

Mind.—Irritable; in evening. Impatient. Inclined to use forcible language and violent expressions. Time seems long. Tired in evening.

Head.—Aching; in morning; internally in places, or crocked stitches; making her irritable and impatient, with inclination to be pert and to make faces; dreamy, < vertex and occiput. Dulness, with sticking to and fro in l. side of head.

Forehead.—Aching in F. and over eyes in forenoon, with heaviness, next morning heaviness. Fluttering pain, between stinging and pressing, in "cautiousness," r. side, > touch or fixing attention upon it. Cooling or slightly burning pressure in a spot on r. side, in boundary line of hair. Dulness as from a load, < central part of brain, and on each expiration feeling as if this load were pushed from occiput to forehead. Fulness and sensation as if brain were shaken.

Pain in temples and vertex; l. temple; temple and orbit on walking in open air. Tension in temples. Pain in l. vertex; *P. in vertex* at dinner, causing numbness, as from great heat or cold, < between 2 and 3 P.M., necessity to lie down, *head felt as if swung backward and forward*, the pain > an hour's sleep. Sharp pain, neuralgia, in l. side of head in evening. Constriction in r. side at 12 o'clock, through l. side at 1 o'clock. Dulness in occiput all the evening. Pimples on scalp behind l. ear.

Clinical.—Headache across the top of the head, from one ear to the other, with sensation as if the head were swinging from behind forward and the brain were shaken.

Eyes.—Pain around l. when walking, extending beyond r. brow. Heavy pain in l. and in back part of orbit from 6 till 7 P.M. after walking, spreading over forehead and vertex, and next day towards 8 o'clock, after a walk, pain in r. eye, temple and around ear, during dinner pain in r. temple near eye and unpleasant sensation around l. eye. Dryness in evening, with itching, not > rubbing; D. of edges of lids. Vesicles as clear as water on edge of lower lids. Lids felt heavy in afternoon.

Nose and Face.—Burning in nose, as from horseradish, in evening, then watery discharge. Coryza. Diminished growth of beard. Vesicle on inside of lower lip, near l. corner. Pain in r. corner of lips as if sore.

Mouth and Throat.—Sensitiveness of second l. upper incisor, and feeling as if it were a dead foreign body. Hawking up of small solid lumps of mucus that he must swallow again. Fauces and tongue dry, tongue red in middle.

Stomach.—Aversion to beer. Eructations, the last leaving a sourish taste. Digging to right of epigastrium, where eighth and ninth ribs ascend to sternum, then pressing pain under l. ribs.

Abdomen.—Frequent, small and short emissions of flatus; frequent, small and odorless. Pain, < region of spleen; P. before rising; in liver, with soreness; in l. groin at every step. Cutting in hypogastrium soon after rising, between 6 and 7, > stool, two slight attacks after breakfast, with inclination to stool, but emission of only wind.

Rectum and Stool.—Sticking in l. side of rectum or aching twitches, at approach of stool, the sticking returned in evening. Pain in rectum, with a retained stool, no urging, the pain < till 1 P.M., just before dinner, then > soft stool. Inclination as to diarrhœa when walking in the street. Fulness in anus in evening after stool, with much pressing. Thin stool, with urging as if diarrhœa would set in. A hard stool, then a mushy, thin stool, with protrusion of anus (Pod.). Frequent stools, then colic; F. and soft. Stool every other day. Stool usually in afternoon or evening.

Urinary Organs.—Sticking through bladder and painful weakness. Urging in evening, he passes more, but not often. Frequent micturition, bladder feels full, yet little passes.

Sexual Organs.—Erections every morning, none in evening or night, even from excitation. Pain in uterus or region of bladder. Menses too soon; reappeared after rapid walking, as they had often done, but were more like clear blood than usual, it was the seventh day since they began and for thirty-six hours nothing had been visible, they still continued two days afterwards, but were less copious and watery.

Clinical.—Swelling and induration of r. ovary, with soreness and shooting pain from navel to breasts, where there is heaviness. Neuralgia of r. ovary, drawing downward during and after menstruation, < standing and moving, > rubbing and lying down, associated with feeling as if the uterus were prolapsed, accompanied by headache and nausea, glairy mucus in the throat and glairy leucorrhœa, also with soreness over r. side of abdomen, pains shooting down r. thigh; pain in region of liver and spleen, flatulence and constipation, frequent micturition, with sticking in urethra; pains in different parts, changing about, with great lassitude, cold hands and feet (this condition occurred in a nursing woman who menstruated every month, at one time after three weeks, at another after five weeks, alternating regularly, with profuse hæmorrhage after the five weeks' interval). Jelly-like leucorrhœa before and after menstruation, with heaviness and weight. Uterine displacement, with constant pains in back and hips and cold extremities (r. ovary compare Plat. and Pod.).

Chest and Heart.—Sticking on inner side of collarbone on entering room from a walk in open air; S. in region of r. nipple, running deep in, < deep breathing, > walking in open air; flying S. from middle of C. in direction of shoulders, on bending forward while sitting. Congestion in r. side of C. after sitting awhile. Aching along edge of ribs and diaphragm; A. in cardiac region at 2 A.M. Intermittent painful pressure in cardiac region and low down in l. chest.

Neck and Back.—Painful contraction of several muscles on r. side of neck. Painful drawing in neck and shoulders and down l. arm. Pain in l. trapezius as from lying on it too long, < turning head to left. Backache in afternoon as from sitting up stiffly too long; B. across hips at night, perhaps because her child was restless and she was anxious about it; B. in region of l. kidney as if urine had been retained too long, < sitting, > pressure, but worse afterwards, < towards evening, frequent urging to urinate and aching in bladder, next day pain in l. kidney when sitting. Back weak in morning.

Extremities.—Bruised pain in afternoon, > evening, with feeling as if menses would appear; B. pain in muscles of shoulders and upper arms. Lightning-like sticking in r. shoulder. Rheumatic pain in r. shoulder in evening. Painful drawing in r. shoulder on entering room after walking in open air. Sensation in l. arm as if it were going to sleep. Numbness of arm, > evening; N. of r. arm and hand in night; N. of r. forearm, extending to fingers. Drawing pain in l. forearm as if lame, < radial side, > open air. Pain in r. wrist extending into forearm. Sudden twitching in r. wrist and metacarpal bones. Stinging in l. metacarpal bones and thumb; suddenly in l. middle metacarpal bone at noon. Burning pain and boring as if shattered, deep in l. hand at night, waking him. Twitching of fingers, < index, which crooks the fingers, when sitting, till 12 o'clock.

Lower Extremities.—Gnawing in l. hip. Pain above l. knee, extending thence into chest, in morning; twitching P. in l. hip-joint during the morning. Feeling in femora, < l., as if they expanded or were pressed out of their sockets on pressing down as if for stool.

Skin.—Pimple on back part of r. zygoma, next day one in the same place on l.; red, deep-seated on r. cheek, near wing of nose; painfully sore, < back of l. ear; itching, in l. side of whiskers in evening; itching and burning, on r. side of neck; burning and biting on touch, beneath r. brow, near canthus. Something similar to flea-bites above r. side of lip, on l. nostril and various parts of body and head, between 2 and 3 P.M. Elevations like nettle-rash here and there, red on a base whiter than the skin. Pustule above tip of nose, bleeding a long time after the pus was squeezed out.

Tickling in r. shoulder. Itching on inner side of l. ankle, inner side of r. thigh, on r. elbow, l. brow, l. arm, < nape; at 1 A.M., above l. zygoma, above eye and nostril, later in r. side of face, near eye, and on side of head; in a spot on r. side of face in morning, with burning in it; general, in evening on undressing; in a spot in l. groin in evening, with burning; over back and thighs, > scratching, but soon appearing in a neighboring place, with crawling; in spots on r. thigh and leg and below point of r. scapula, with burning; on various parts, back, arms, abdomen, thighs and ankles, with crawling; on forehead, with roughness.

Sleep.—Sleepiness in evening, later every day, with fatigue, he lies down and sleeps if he can; overpowering S. from 3 till 4 P.M.; S. in evening when riding in a carriage and seeing patients. Dream of the same kind every night for a week, of a house, buildings, in which he was or beside which he stood, often as if he stood at a window, walked up and down stairs, through various apartments, etc.

Papaya Vulgaris.

A tincture is made of the milky juice of the green fruit of the "Pawpaw." (It contains a digesting ferment.)

Generalities.—Loses flesh. Takes cold easily when riding; takes C. easily during menses. Nervous before and during menses. Pains < towards evening; P. > rubbing. Dull feeling in morning on rising. Muscular debility. Languor; and drowsiness. Papaya has evidently waked up an old psoric taint caused by suppression of itch forty years ago.

Mind.—Impatient. Wants to be alone. Dislikes to be talked to or to answer. Listless, lacking in ambition. Unusually active, can study longer without weariness, likes to read. Unable to think quickly. Stupid, confused feeling. Easily confused. Could hardly trust herself to do anything during menses for fear of making mistakes. Forgetful.

Head.—Aching after eating pop-corn and candy, < towards evening; A. < bright light, warm air and motion, > cold air and sleep; > rubbing; involving eyeball; increased for twenty-four hours, passing backward to occiput and nape, drawing head backward. Dulness. Fulness in evening. Vertigo and throbbing frontal pain, with nausea. Frontal pain. Piercing pain traveling like lightning from r. side of H. to r. side of foot. Bruised feeling in l. side. Soreness of parietal region, with throbbing. Itching greater, but dandruff less than usual.

Eyes, Nose and Face.—Prickling in eyes. Pain in eyeballs. Dry feeling in eyeballs. Inflammation of r. lid, feeling as if a foreign substance were in it, preventing much reading by artificial light. Vision not as good as usual. Nose stopped, < l. side. Thick discharge from N. Watery, colorless, bland coryza. Neuralgia on l. side of face.

Mouth.—Toothache < cold water; T. in l. lower molars; in r. lower molars, with soreness. Tongue dry at night. Taste bad; flat to food.

Stomach and Abdomen.—Appetite diminished in morning. Thirst, but inability to drink cold water on account of toothache. Drinks much water. Tasteless eructations. Nausea after dinner. Faint for want of food, but food distresses stomach. Pain around waist.

Stool.—Soft. Constipation. First part large and hard, breaking into balls, latter part mushy, with wind. Irregular.

Urinary Organs.—Tearing in bladder, with desire to urinate. Straining with the first urinary effort in morning, with burning as if an obstruction were being overcome, which being removed the urine passes easily. Frequent desire; irresistible desire at sound of running water, even in a horse's throat when drinking. Burning in urethra during and after micturition, with continuous desire. Urine increased; scanty. Less sediment than formerly.

Sexual Organs.—Flaccid and lifeless. Pain running from perineum to middle of penis as if a rough, jagged body forced its way out. Erections towards morning; E., but no emissions; not long-lasting and not due to sexual thoughts. Pain in l. testicle, waking him at night. Instinct abnormally aroused. Functions depressed. Emissions without lascivious dreams.

Respiratory Organs and Chest.—Pain in larynx. Hoarse in evening. Cough keeping him awake at night; violent, sudden, spasmodic C.; with easy expectoration and soreness of l. lung. Shooting in lungs and around heart. Pain in l. lung; deep in upper lobe of l. lung; from l. chest to l. thigh and knee; heavy, in l. lung, extending through to back and becoming stabbing. Lungs feel tired and hot.

Heart and Pulse.—Shooting in heart. Pulse 100, temperature 102. Pulse slow; and weak.

Back.—Bruised pain in l. side. Sore pain in point under l. scapula. Pain in region of kidneys; region of l. kidney, running around ilium.

Extremities.—Go to sleep easily. Numbness, > walking; N., pricking and sleepiness. Rheumatic pain in l. shoulder. L. arm helpless. Numbness of r. hand and fingers while asleep, < little finger; N. of r. ring finger, < outer side. Trembling of lower, with weakness of them. Prickling in lower, but not in foot, with tingling. R. leg went to sleep when writing. Pain on ball of r. foot under little toe, with swelling and with heat extending to toes.

Skin.—Eruption in groins, bends of knees and r. elbow, extending along flexor surface, and on r. forearm and abdomen. Pimples on face and body. Red, sore, elevated points like acne, on thighs; red, itching elevations, < evening and warmth of bed, > scratching. Itching eruption over r. eye. Eruption like nettle-rash after scratching. Pinkish erysipelatous swelling on dorsum of l. great toe, with itching, > scratching or rubbing. Itching all over body; behind l. ear; on mons veneris; on r. ankle on going to bed; forearms and anterior part of thighs, with diffused redness, < forearms; < warmth of bed.

Sleep.—Yawning and stretching. Drowsy, but cannot sleep. Heavy. Disturbed. Frequent waking. Dreams horrible, vivid, of shipwreck, fire, being drowned, shot, etc.

Fever.—Chilliness; at night; in open air. Cold hands and feet; forefingers, with deadness, stoppage of circulation.

Pareira Brava.

A tincture is made of the dried root.

Stool hard and urine dark.

Clinical.—Cystitis, constant urging to urinate, with violent pain and straining, < from midnight till morning. Cystitis, with strangury, ability to urinate only when on the knees and pressing the head against the floor, the urine scalds the whole length of the urethra. Cystitis, the urine very strongly ammoniacal, containing large quantities of thick, white mucus, < early morning hours. With the cystitis severe pain in the thigh (Berb. in the hip). Feeling as if the bladder were distended, with pain < after micturition, and neuralgic pains in anterior crural region going downward, urine always clear, of high specific gravity, rather strongly urinous in odor, without a trace of pus, at times increase of mucus.

Paris Quadrifolia.

A tincture is made of the entire fresh plant.

Generalities.—Subcutaneous sticking on upper lip, nape, hands and feet. Feeling as after intoxication. Discomfort so that he must lie down. Weakness; as after a journey on foot.

Mind.—Lively, talkative. Foolish, talks about every subject, changes from one subject to another, would talk if alone, is delighted with his own frivolity and ridiculous talk. Inclined to be vexed and to relieve himself in a few contemptuous words. Disinclined to mental work.

Head.—*Sticking in middle and in temples, then weight upon forehead, < stooping.* Pain, < temples; P. on smoking the customary tobacco; < thought; feeling as if P. would occur, < towards evening in open air; internal, like a bubbling, at night on waking, and inability to sleep again on account of internal restlessness. Pressure outward. Sensation as if puffed up, especially as if temples and eyes were forced outward. Sensation as if dura mater were drawn tight over brain, < occiput. Tension in meninges and brain, with tension in occiput as if the skin were thick and could not be wrinkled. Heaviness and sinking forward. Dulness; like vertigo, > walking in open air. Vertigo after reading aloud, so that talking and looking intently were difficult, with feeling as if headache would come on and pressure outward in head, all < towards evening in open air, also < walking; sudden V., < sitting; everything whirls around with her.

Forehead.—Sticking in l. side, with gnawing, then gnawing in l. lower jaw; benumbing S. in l. side; sensation as if a sharp point were pressed against r. eminence (superficial sticking pressure). *Aggravation in evening, the pain in F. involved the whole sinciput, it seemed as if the scalp were contracted and skin scraped sore, margins of lids red and hot,* **with pain as if a thread were drawn tightly through eye to middle of head.** Pain deep in r. eminence; P. above l. orbit, that seemed to press down upper lid; stupefying throbbing, in l. side; waving and throbbing, in l. side on ascending stairs. Constriction.

Sticking in l. temple. Pain in l. temple; *in r., > pressure of hand.* Sticking in r. side; to l. of vertex. *Bruised pain in l. parietal bone on touch,* at night. Pain in occiput; intermittent drawing, in muscles of r. side. Hair falls out and is painful on vertex. Scurf. Tension as if scalp of forehead and occiput were adherent to bone and almost immovable. Pain in scalp on touch, as if hair were painful. Itching, with burning after scratching.

Clinical.—Neuralgic headache, with the characteristic feeling as if a thread were drawing through the eye backward to the middle of the brain. Occipital headache, with a feeling of weight.

Eyes.—Mucus in morning. Discharge from E. and nose of thin mucus, that causes wheezing. *Sticking through middle,* with cloudy vision. Burning and lachrymation; B. and biting. Swollen feeling as if orbits were too small (so that he could not move eyes easily), with inability to fix vision, as if objects moved. Painful tension beneath l. Coolness in r. Lachrymation in morning after rising. Pupils dilated. *Balls seem too large.* Tearing on upper surface of r. ball. Painful pressure in upper margin of orbit. *Twitching of r. upper lid.* Crawling on margin of r. upper lid. Hard matter in inner canthi during the day, with burning pain, < touch. Burning in inner canthi. Swimming before eyes. Vision unsteady, as after weeping.

Ears.—Tearing in l.; in r. as if it would be torn from head. Sudden pain as if a wedge were driven into meatus in evening when walking in open air, at last < r., transiently > boring in with finger. Sensation as if heat came out of them. Sensation of a mist before them, so that he could not hear well. *Ringing in l.;* ringing and twinging.

Nose.—Fulness in upper part, with blowing out of blood-streaked mucus. Stoppage in morning after rising, difficult blowing out of bloody mucus. *Stopped coryza; alternating with fluent. Blowing out of red and greenish mucus.* Sneezing; violent. Bleeding. Smell altered, milk and bread smell like bad meat.

Face.—Pallor. Hot stitches in bone of l. cheek, with pain on touch. Scratching beneath malar-bone. Tension in l. cheek, with pressure. Upper lip thick and cracked, with tetter about mouth. Blister within lower lip.

Clinical.—Facial neuralgia, hot stitches in l. malar-bone, which is very sore.

Mouth.—Toothache almost like a tickling, < afternoon and night, and by cold and warmth. Drawing and throbbing in teeth. Drawing pain in a hollow tooth; hollow molar, < forenoon, > walking, and cold causes jerking pain. Pain in teeth as if hollow and as if open air penetrated them and caused coldness, with wrinkled sensation in gum and pain as if burnt. Cutting in gum every morning. Loose sensation in gum. Tongue rough and dry; rough and coated white, as if covered with millet-seeds; T. brown at root in morning after rising; seemed too large and broad.

Tense, almost painless swelling on hard palate, near last molar. Pain in skin of palate, next day desquamation. Denuded sensation on palate. *Dryness in morning on waking; and in trachea, with hoarseness;* D. on hard palate, with tickling burning; at times sudden D. far back on palate, with scraping there and with much tasteless water in mouth, as in hunger. Salivation after breakfast; astringent S. Frequent spitting of watery saliva. White, slimy froth in corners of mouth in morning. Taste flat, slimy; T. bitter, with dryness and roughness of tongue; T. and odor of cresses and onions in mouth.

Throat.—*Hawking caused by mucus in fauces.* Sticking in pharynx. Sticking scratching, < evening. Burning, then scratching. Scraping posteriorly. Pressure as from a ball; that continued to grow larger and would burst the throat open, on stooping, < evening. Pressure in r. tonsil. Dryness of pharynx.

Stomach.—Appetite great. Smoking tobacco is not relished. Eructations; empty, in forenoon, with pressure extending up into chest; nauseous; of clear, tasteless water in morning. *Hiccough;* after eating. Nausea; and acid taste. Fulness; flatulent, in epigastric region, with sensitiveness to touch. Rumbling extending to throat. Griping in afternoon, > eructations. Pressure, > eructations. Sensation of a stone in it in morning. Warmth in epigastric region. Burning extending into abdomen. Digestion not as good as usual.

Abdomen.—Fulness after eating, with discomfort. Movements and emission of flatus. Cramplike tearing in muscles, extending to pit of stomach, worse when sitting bent over than when walking. Cutting after dinner, with ineffectual desire for stool; C. and rolling, with two stools. Griping in afternoon when sitting, < about umbilicus, > walking. Pain. Tension. Burning, like heartburn and nausea, rising into chest, after breakfast. Uneasiness.

Rumbling below stomach, as from emptiness. Sticking in r. hypochondrium. Pressure in a spot in l. side; in a spot in l. side above umbilicus, as from something hard. Rumbling and gurgling in hypogastrium. Cutting in l. groin when walking.

Stool.—Ineffectual desire. Frequent urging, stool always unsatisfactory and pasty. Diarrhœa; twice in one day; thin, slimy. Hard, difficult. Offensive, like bad meat. Frequent; two normal stools in quick succession.

Urinary Organs.—Tenesmus in morning after urinating. Urging, but necessity to wait a few minutes before any passed. Desire every ten or fifteen minutes, with burning micturition. *Sticking in forepart of urethra. Burning in orifice of urethra when sitting;* in urethra above glans during micturition. Drawing in anterior part of urethra. Urine dark yellow; pale yellow; acrid; *turbid on standing and covered with a fatty film;* fiery, and after standing a flocculent film in middle, later a reddish sediment and *iridescent film on surface;* copious.

Sexual Organs.—Nightly emission. Desire increased and hard erection; D. increased, and increased voluptuousness during coition. Menses too early.

Respiratory Organs.—*Hawking and expectoration of greenish, tenacious mucus from larynx;* H. of white, tenacious mucus from upper part of larynx. Constantly obliged to loosen mucus from larynx and trachea. Burning in larynx; and posteriorly in throat; then scraping. Hoarseness; periodical, so that he could not speak a loud word. Rawness in trachea, causing bass voice. Frequent inclination in larynx to hack, as from sulphur fumes, with scanty expectoration of mucus. *Hacking, he tries to loosen tenacious mucus from back part of larynx;* H. in morning after rising, without expectoration, after half an hour expectoration of greenish, tenacious mucus. Cough as soon as he lies on l. side; C. on lying down, without expectoration, with such violent hacking that he sees sparks. Expectoration of lumps of mucus from upper part of trachea, without much hawking. Frequent deep inspiration. Oppressed respiration.

Clinical.—Catarrh of larynx, with green, tenacious expectoration. Catarrhal bronchitis, with expectoration of viscid mucus, in morning and evening. Hoarseness, with constant hawking of mucus and with burning in larynx.

Chest.—Mucus without inclination to expectorate it. Sticking in l.; in l. nipple during inspiration; frequent, through lungs; in r. extending into r. clavicle and into a r. molar and lastly into r. calf. Cutting in r. side near ensiform cartilage, midway between back and sternum, alternating with sticking. Drawing cutting in l. side above diaphragm in evening when lying on l. side, extending into abdomen, then cutting through small intestines to entrance of true pelvis, where it disappeared, but at the same time appeared again in chest, gradually > lying on back, with difficult, superficial respiration. Biting gnawing on sternum. Pain in r. side; pulsating P. in a spot beneath l. nipple, with sticking on touch.

Clinical.—Neuralgia beginning in l. intercostal region and extending into l. arm, which becomes stiff, with clenching of the fingers and with weight in the nape.

Heart and Pulse.—Pinching in heart and lungs, and when stooping it seemed as if a stone were upon the back. *Palpitation* in evening. Pulse slower than usual.

Neck.—Cramp in l. sterno-cleido-mastoid muscle. Tearing in muscles of N. and nape. Paralytic pain in l. side of nape on turning head to that side. *Stiff and swollen feeling if turned around.* **Weight upon nape.** Tension in muscles of N. and nape, so that the head was almost involuntarily drawn forward.

Back.—Stitches through and through both sides of B. and nape; extending into B. when sitting; close to spine, between four last r. ribs, < inspiration; beneath l. scapula; between scapulæ, as if in bones; pulselike, in coccyx. Tearing in coccyx when sitting.

Clinical.—Neuralgia of the spine, pain located about the sixth cervical vertebra, extending upward, and downward to the shoulders, with weight, numbness and heat, with soreness of the top of the head so that he could not brush his hair, heaviness of eyelids, etc. Neuralgia of the coccyx, a pulsating sticking when sitting, with pain between the scapulæ.

Extremities.—Sticking, < evening. Cramplike twinging in joints. Tearing in r. elbow and malleolus. Sensation in joints on motion as if broken, and on stretching them out as if they had been pressed in, on turning about sensation as if swollen and sprained. Several tendons are sore to touch. Heaviness in evening, with internal coldness.

Upper Extremities.—Tearing in l. shoulder; in shoulders extending into fingers. Burning in l. shoulder as if in bone. Heaviness of arms; of r. Drawing in upper arm. Tearing in r. forearm. Pain in forearm as if he had been writing a long time, < hanging arm down. Cramplike pain above l. wrist. Trembling of hands. Sticking in l. palm. Tearing in r. palm. Drawing in metacarpal bones. Sticking on back of index; bubbling S. in bone of index. Tearing in thumb; in l. index; in first joint of r. middle finger. Pain like suppuration or like congestion of blood in tip of middle finger. Drawing pain in thumb and index. Drawing deep in middle finger. Paralytic sensation in finger-joints, then in arm and in other joints. *Fingers often feel asleep.*

Lower Extremities.—Drawing; paralytic, in r. Sticking in l. nates; paroxysmal, in r. hip. Tearing in hip-joints; suddenly in r. hip when sitting; on outer side of r. thigh extending to heel, when sitting. Gnawing in posterior surface of thigh. Pain in r. hip-joint when walking, and if when walking he puts the l. foot to the ground while the r. is extended backward to its farthest point, just before bringing it forward there is drawing in r. hip-joint as if the foot were pulled backward. Drawing on inner side of l. thigh.

Tearing in l. knee. Cramplike pain about r. patella, not > motion. Pain along tendons of r. popliteus when standing. Painful tension in r. knee only when resting part of his weight upon it while bent. Tearing in calves. Drawing in lower end of tibia in bed. Sticking in l. inner malleolus when sitting; rhythmical S. in ankles. Tearing in r. external malleolus. Paralytic pain in l. ankle as if ligaments were relaxed. Numb pain in inner malleolus. Drawing in external malleolus.

Sticking on back of r. foot; in sole, transversely across balls of toes. Tearing in sole; in r. heel and thence along outer margin of foot to little toe. Pinching on back of foot. Paralytic pain in l. sole on stepping upon it. Drawing in os calcis. Weariness of feet when walking, with trembling. Jerking in r. great toe in evening when sitting. Sticking in fore-part of r. great toe. Tearing in r. great toe when sitting. Drawing burning beneath toes, < evening.

Skin.—Red curved stripe above navel, along anterior line of ribs, with pain, < middle. Red, itching tetter like millet-seeds, on cheek and on ramus of jaw, painful on rubbing and scratching. Itching pimples, painful after scratching, on r. side of chin; on metacarpal bones of r. index and middle fingers; dry pimples above l. brow, with itching biting, the biting < scratching, and then sticking; pimples on forehead, painful on touch. Pustules, with red areola, outside of red of upper lip; beneath nose.

Soreness on touch. Crawling in places; C. on heel; on inner surface of hand, almost as if asleep. Itching biting on l. side of lower jaw and beneath its l. margin in evening before sleep, with burning, and in morning bloody pimples like millet-seeds, that had been scratched open. Itching here and there; I. on coccyx.

Sleep.—Yawning; in afternoon, with sleepiness; with sleepiness. Sleepiness during the day; in evening; after dinner, and sleep with restless dreams. Partial sleep all night. Tossing about, only half asleep. Restless sleep. Short, broken sleep. At night on waking he thought to find himself in a strange and solitary place. Sleep full of dreams. Anxious dreams all night. Voluptuous dreams in afternoon, with profuse emission and hard erection.

Fever.—Coldness in evening on lying down; in evening and forenoon, as if he trembled internally; as if all internal parts were drawn together by the cold and they trembled back and forth. Creeping shiverings. *Shivering in chest, abdomen and lower limbs, with gooseflesh, yawning and cold feet;* S. in lower limbs, with contracted sensation in skin, while abdomen, upper limbs and feet are warm. Cold skin in spots. Coldness of whole r. half of body; of feet, < night; of fingers as if dead at one time, with color as if dead, at another time heat of them.

Heat; with sweat; with anxiety; flushing, after a light dinner, with sweat on back and forehead, then shivering in back, with redness of face and dry burning; of upper part of body, with sweat of it and with increased full pulse; in face; H. and sweat on head after breakfast, with nausea; intermittent, in nape extending down back in evening. Sweat; on waking about 3 A.M.; *biting itching in morning on waking.*

Petroleum.

A tincture is made by dissolving one part of the crude rock-oil in 99 parts of alcohol.

General Action.—Very complex and not clearly defined. Its nausea and occipital headache are marked; examine also its skin symptoms; it is generally allied to all the Carbons and the tissue remedies.

Allies.—Sulph., *Graph.;* Tab., Colch., Puls.

Generalities. — Emaciation; with good appetite. Swelling began in feet, spread over abdomen and chest, disappeared, but returned, at the necropsy the body was extremely œdematous and the epidermis in places was raised in little blebs, dissection showed dropsy of the cavities and œdema of lungs, but no lesion to account for the dropsy, there were traces of fatty degeneration of the epithelium. Trembling in morning on rising. Convulsions; tetanic, frightful pains, at times followed by general rigidity, with incessant cries, after ten minutes' quiet the paroxysms returned with renewed violence, no liquid could be taken and six men could not hold the patient. Jerking together of body in evening in bed, when awake.

Stitches here and there. Pain > lying; sprained P. in arms, chest and back in forenoon; sharp jerking, in one or another part; weary, in shoulders, spine and loins; drawing, here and there in bones; drawing, in r. arm, then in head. Frequent drawing in trunk. Indescribable feeling of sickness, with anxiety. Tremulous tension through whole body, with apprehension, ill humor and cracking in joints. Affected by a slight vexation, taste bitter, appetite lost, a short walk then affects her, she has frequent diarrhœa, orgasm of blood on falling asleep, eructation, nausea, restless sleep, next morning trembling and waving through whole body, diarrhœa and internal misery, so that tears stood in her eyes. *Takes cold easily*, which causes faintness. Aversion to open air when walking. Everything seems too hard when sitting and lying. Restless; at night.

Heaviness of feet and of whole body. Indolence; with heaviness of limbs. *Weakness;* in morning; *in morning in bed*, with bruised feeling in limbs; in morning on rising; after a walk; during menses; after stool, with vertigo, vanishing of vision and necessity to close eyes in order to recover himself; < evening on lying down, with bruised feeling in limbs; > eating; with trembling and intolerable sensation as before severe illness; of body, with heaviness of lower limbs; so that limbs were painful; so that she fell asleep when sitting; nervous, after a short walk. Faintness in morning on entering the house, he felt sick, heat mounted to face, a veil seemed to come before the eyes, compression in temples. Amelioration at noon.

Clinical.—General relief from warm air.

Mind.—Excitement. Extravagant and exaggerated condition, with internal trembling, then despondency. **Imagined that some one was lying near him.** Arose up and got out of bed. *Violent, offended at trifles. Irritable;* and indolent. *Quarrelsome;* in morning on waking; and lachrymose. The child became fierce and uncontrollable. Inclined to be angry every morning. Discontented with everything. Constant complaints. Irresolute. Little ambition. Ennui. *Fear,* violent shock from fright at a trifle; F. and weeping at trifles; F. of death. Anxiety at the noise of a crowd. Dejected; in morning, and quiet, with dim vision; when walking in open air, and inattentive to intellectual conversation or other diversions; with feverish condition; with sick feeling of weakness of heart.

Clinical.—A peculiar fancy that another person is sick in the same bed has been verified in many cases of low fever, for instance, in puerperal fever there was a delusion that there were two sick babies and she could not take care of both (compare Bap.).

Forgetful; and disinclined to think. Impairment of powers. Loss of power of thought; of will power. Cannot easily free himself from the subject on which he is talking. Stupidity caused by a little wine at dinner. *Unconscious;* partly, all day. Comatose.

Head.—Sticking jerking on stooping and walking, obliging her to stand still every few minutes. Sticking; and heat. Tearing in evening. *Pinching.* Boring. Aching; *every morning;* every morning on rising; in morning, > breakfast; from morning till evening, with drawing towards forehead, together with chill till noon; in evening after walking in open air; at night, < above eyes; on stooping; from taking cold, with lachrymation, inflammation of throat, cough and coryza; with pain in teeth and antrums of upper jaw; with nausea. Distress as if everything were alive and twisting about, with dread of work. Screwing-together sensation. Compression of brain. Constriction; on coughing, with sticking in chest. Tension; of dura mater, with pulling; of dura mater, with dulness.

Dulness as if enveloped in a fog. Confusion after eating a little, with vertigo; C. from the customary smoking; C., with general discomfort. *Heaviness in morning,* < stooping and sewing, with fulness and heat; H. in morning, with dulness, thick feeling and heat. Beating. Trembling, waving and roaring in H. and ears, as from rush of blood. Rush of blood after dinner; feeling of rush of blood on rapid motion, that causes a stitch through brain. *Vertigo;* in evening, with roaring in ears; in evening in bed, < lying with head low, with nausea; *on stooping* and on rising from a seat; on stooping, with nausea; after dinner; on rising from lying down, while lying heat in face; often when walking; obliging him to stoop forward, < standing, > lying, with pallor, nausea, slow pulse, eructations, yawning, loss of appetite and pressure in abdomen.

Forehead.—Sticking in morning on waking, soon extending over occiput; throbbing S. above one eye. *Pain,* with sticking over eyes; P. the last part of the day and night; worse during nausea, > nosebleed; drawing, with sticking above eyes. Pulsating waving < forehead, as if head would burst, > motion.

Cramplike pain in l. temple. Drawing in r. temple, even during a nap; cramplike, in temples, also in l., with pressure; pinching, extending up to l. temple. Jerking stitches on vertex extending into head, in evening, then persistent pressure in it. Bruised pain as if vertex were soft. Pressure on vertex, with vertigo. Suppurative pain in l. side; in sides on touch. Headache on r. side, inability to open eyes or hold head upright, necessity to lie down.

Sticking in l. side of occiput in afternoon. *Pinching in occiput.* **Pressure in occiput;** *in morning, with sticking.* **Leaden heaviness in O.** (Chel.). Throbbing in O. all day; *when lying upon it.* Vertigo in O. as if she would fall forward, < raising eyes. *Falling of hair.* Soft swellings, painful on touch. Papules. Bruised pain in scalp. Scalp numb, like wood. *Itching; and after scratching sore pain.*

Clinical.—Neuralgic headache beginning in occiput and extending forward. Occipital headache extending to vertex, with vertigo, stiffness of neck, swelling of muscles; rapid motion of the hands seems to relieve the pain. Vertigo in the occiput, with general feeling of numbness, stiffness and nausea. Occipital headache, with nausea, especially in seasickness.

Eyes.—*Dim.* Sunken. Glistening. Staring and glassy; S. wildly about. Rolled up occasionally. Twitching. *Stitches; and itching;* with lachrymation, itching S. and burning. Cutting on exerting them by reading. *Pressure,* < evening by the light; P. as from sand; throbbing P. in r. Painful drawing in r. extending into ear, with loss of hearing in r. ear. Biting; as from smoke. *Burning; and pressure, and on exerting them dimness.* Feeling as if they would be distorted. Weakness. Lachrymation; in open, not cold air. Much water presses out of both canthi.

Pupils contracted; and insensible to light; dilated, with l. eye he cannot distinguish letters at a short distance, at a greater distance they are distinct, but small. *Conjunctivitis and blepharadenitis. Inflamed swelling in inner canthus, like an incipient lachrymal fistula, with dryness of r. side of nose.* Papules on lids. Trembling and twitching on lids; twitching of r. Blinking and winking. Sticking from outer canthus towards inner. Biting in lids. *Itching of lids;* of lower, with dryness. Lids cannot be opened in morning, vision misty. Burning in inner canthus, with pressure. Sticking in brows, with beating. Far-sighted. Photophobia. Vision disturbed; V. *weak* and misty; double; of sparks; of blacks spots that prevent reading; flickering; twitching before eyes in evening; floating and twitching of objects, > fixing eyes upon them; of flickering and black figures.

Clinical.—Inflammation of the margins of the lids. Inflammation of the lachrymal canal. Lachrymal fistula.

Ears.—Thin, yellowish discharge, more copious from l. *Swelling of meatus; inflamed and painful.* Sticking; and tickling, then stiffness in articulation of jaw as if it would crack. Tearing in r. Cutting in l. Pain, with heat; *P. externally;* cramplike, in r.; jerking, in l.; painful drawing and jerking in r. Cramplike drawing in r. Bubbling. Itching within l., with bloody discharge. Something seemed to come before it on eructating, so that he could not hear. *Diminished hearing; with roaring as of wind. Ringing. Cracking at times.* Singing; during menses, with roaring. Roaring and pain; *R. in l.* evenings, like the rushing of water, with at times cracking in it. Noises, at one time as of a clock, at another as of a waterfall.

Clinical.—Deafness, with frequent occipital headache, tearing pains in the ears, as if water were in them. Pain in the Eustachian tubes, with noises in the ears and deafness.

Nose.—*Ulcerated nostrils; and stopped catarrh.* Pustules, with red areola, internally on lower part of septum. Pimple inside. Tensive pain in root, extending from one brow to the other, with ulcerative pain on touch. Burning on and near it. Sneezing; towards evening, with sleepiness; with catarrh in throat that provokes cough. Coryza. Blowing out of bloody mucus in morning. Stoppage of mucus, necessity to blow out small masses at night. *Bleeding.*

Clinical.—Nasal catarrh, with obstruction of the posterior nares. Ozæna, with formation of scabs, discharge of purulent mucus, and cracks in nostrils.

Face.—*Pale.* Distorted. Bluish-red; lips. Eruption on lips. *Papules in corners of lips,* with sticking. Boil on upper lip. Lips cracked. Swelling of lower jaw, painful on stooping and on pressure. R. articulation of jaw easily dislocated in morning in bed, with pain. Drawing and tension in jaw beneath ear.

Mouth.—Teeth. Constantly unclean. Sticking, < night, so that she could not remain in bed; S. in hollow incisor. Tearing in hollow, from evening till midnight, with sore, painful gum. Cutting and constriction. Stitchlike jerking every evening till 11.30 P.M. Boring. Aching after breakfast; if open air enters them; in r. molars; with swollen cheek, preventing lying on it at night; ulcerative, with throbbing pressure in r. lower jaw extending to ear and posterior cervical muscles. Drawing pain; in upper incisors, with coldness. Canine T. seem too long in morning; all of lower and some of upper seem too long, and pain as if ulcerating. Numbness and pain on biting on them.

Gum.—*Swelling,* with sticking on touch. Inflammation between lower incisors, with sticking and burning pain. Blister; black, hollow, sensitive to water and cold air, by a lower molar, the tooth pains even on opening mouth. *Pustule above a hollow tooth like a dental fistula. Painful soreness on chewing.*

Clinical.—Abscess at the root of a tooth, with external swelling, dental fistula.

Tongue white. Yellow spots on T. Tongue coated; white in centre, with dark streak along edges. Tongue and r. side of palate towards cervical muscles raw and sensitive, so that he dares not eat or move anything hard in mouth, and acid and salt things cause smarting. *Much mucus in mouth and nose.* Ulcers on inside of cheeks. Mouth pasty. Slimy, with no desire for food or drink. Dryness in morning; and of throat, so that it took away her breath; D., with swelling of throat. Burning, and in throat and stomach. Salivation after eating. *Bad odor;* and even the saliva has an offensive odor; at times, like garlic at other times. *Taste sour; T. slimy,* with white tongue; acid, slimy; *bitter* after breakfast, with scraping in throat and eructations; bitter sour in morning; as of spoiled meat; rancid in throat; as of a disordered stomach, with heaviness of head; bad; insipid, with saliva, as from disordered stomach; insipid after eating, with uneasiness.

Throat.—*Swelling of submaxillary glands;* painful. Hawking of mucus in morning, with headache; H. of thick mucus, < morning. Covered with mucus. Inflammation. On swallowing a part is forced into choanæ. Sticking on swallowing; as if it were prevented by a fish-bone. Sore pain and feeling as if ulcerating. Scraping; with cough. *Rawness in pharynx on swallowing;* R. in pharynx, extending to stomach. Constriction of pharynx. Seems swollen internally. Stopped sensation in posterior nares. *Dryness;* with eructations and loss of power. *Burning; in pharynx;* and in stomach and r. side of abdomen; in fauces, œsophagus and upper part of chest. *Tickling on swallowing, extending to ear.* Crawling in pharynx and nose, as from snuff.

Clinical.—Pharyngeal catarrh, with feeling of dryness, but with accumulation of much mucus, with stinging and burning, the pains extending along the Eustachian tubes into the ears (Gels.).

Stomach.—*Ravenous hunger, but speedy satiety after stool; R. often, making her sick* and waking her at night; insatiable hunger at dinner. Nibbling appetite. Appetite variable, at times lost, at times relished a hearty meal. Loss of A. and thirst. Thirst; all day; *for beer.*

Eructations; all the afternoon, after eating; empty; tasteless all day; with pressure in abdomen; *tasting like bad eggs,* in morning; *sour,* that set the teeth on edge; *hot, sharp and sour;* sharp, sour during dinner; sour, with weak vision; of sour water after breakfast; scraping, even after a light meal; unpleasant. Hiccough in evening, then sneezing; violent H.

Nausea; all day; all day, with loss of appetite, sour taste and dry, white tongue; **in morning, with accumulation of water in mouth;** *in morning on waking,* till breakfast; *every morning immediately after waking, she could not eat breakfast;* in morning or evening, with retching; in morning fasting, with pressure in pit of stomach; waking him at 4 A.M., *with cutting in upper abdomen and diarrhœa;* on coughing; after a normal (second) stool, with weakness; with sticking in r. side of abdomen and also *with cold sweat;* **incessant;** *so that it takes away the breath, all day, without vomiting; sudden, on walking, with salivation, sudden heat of face and vertigo;* sudden, after riding and then walking in open air, with weakness so that she sank down, inclination to stool, cold sweat on head, throat and chest, pallor of face and blue rings around eyes, after stool chill, then in evening heat; in attacks during the day, extending into throat, > lying down, with constriction about larynx.

Violent vomiting. Distention in afternoon; of pit after a moderate meal, with pressure; of epigastric region, so that he must press the hands tightly upon it in spite of sensitiveness. Sticking in pit in afternoon. Tearing in pit as if something would be torn away. Cutting in region, with desire for stool. Pinching in pit. Clawing as from taking cold, waking her in morning; C. as from taking cold, in evening, with anxiety. Pain in morning; when fasting, > eating; frequent, in S. and abdomen, at one time constriction, at another distention. Constriction in pit and about umbilicus; of diaphragm. Burning; in pit at night. Heartburn in morning; *towards evening,* with eructations; rancid. Heaviness, > violent exercise on foot. Relaxed feeling. *Emptiness;* with stupefaction in head. Discomfort after supper; intermittent D. in S. and abdomen. Disordered by a little food; < sauerkraut, "braunkraut," etc., < stormy weather, so that he has diarrhœa day and night. Paralysis, and of œsophagus, so that emetics had no effect and vomiting was induced only after friction of epigastric region.

Clinical.—Dyspepsia temporarily > eating (Puls.). Dyspepsia, with violent pain extending into the chest, with nausea temporarily > eating (Puls.). Nausea and vomiting of pregnancy. Seasickness, with the special indication of the occipital headache. Gastralgia, with feeling of coldness and faintness in the abdomen (Colch., Tab.).

Abdomen.—*Distention;* in afternoon, with tension and with indolence; in evening on going to sleep; after a little drink; < eating, with pressure below pit of stomach; flatulent; flatulent, after stool. *Rumbling* at 5 A.M.; in evening; in evening, with griping. Movements. Offensive flatus; before a thin stool.

Cutting; in morning, then diarrhœa of offensive camphorated odor, then ineffectual urging; *with diarrhœa;* and stools at first fæcal, afterwards of bloody mucus with little fæces; with clawing, then eructations, vomiting of clear water, diarrhœa and headache; *as from taking cold, then diarrhœa, with pressure;* drawing, with eructations and emission of flatus. Griping evenings; all day, with diarrhœa; every ten minutes, she was obliged to bend together; as after taking cold, waking him about midnight. Colic; < along transverse and descending colon; in afternoon, then pressure in stomach and diarrhœa; *in evening,* she was obliged to bend up; *with retching;* with watery stools; as from taking cold. Feeling of diarrhœa in evening without stool. Tension and cramps; paroxysmal T., with pain in l. hypogastrium as if something would break through or as from an internal sore. Itching internally, not > external rubbing. Crawling falling asleep in muscles, extending to thighs, when sitting.

Sticking in hypochondria; in hepatic region on physical exertion. Pressure in hepatic region; in l. hypochondrium. Clawing in umbilical region at night; paroxysmal C. and pinching about umbilicus; C. upward in sides of abdomen, with heaviness in lower limbs and sleepiness. Pain below umbilicus waking at 5 A.M., on movement it became cutting and increased the desire for stool, at 6 A.M. thin, lightish brown diarrhœa, at 7 A.M. urging, but I did not go out and it passed off, soon ineffectual desire, at 6 P.M. natural stool, next day awakened at 3, 5 and 6 A.M. by urging, stool free, watery, gushing, a little pain just before and after it, and at 8 A.M. ineffectual desire. Sticking in r. groin after a nocturnal emission. Pain in transverse colon and in l. loin; in r. inguinal ring; cramplike, in groins when walking and lying, < sitting; in groin, as if a hernia would protrude, on every paroxysm of cough.

Clinical.—Colic > bending double (Coloc., Colch.).

Rectum and Anus.—Rectal fistula. Scabs on margin of anus, with tickling smarting. Sticking and burning. Pain in rectum two days before menses, obliging her to bend forward, and on becoming erect sticking, < walking. *Burning pain in region of anus. Itching of anus;* on going to sleep. *Pressure in anus. Weakness of rectum.* Frequent urging; always with scanty diarrhœa, with pressure as if more were to pass; ineffectual U. as if rectum were too weak.

Clinical.—Hæmorrhoids and fissures in the anus.

Stool.—*Diarrhœa;* twice, then exhaustion; *profuse, mucous; of much bloody mucus; violent, involuntary.* Thin, copious. Pasty, copious, brownish-yellow. Soft, but with tenesmus; S., difficult, as from inactivity of intestines. *Of bloody mucus, frequent, with weakness.* Constipation. Hard (secondary action). Difficult, with blood (in a child); D., with sore pain in anus; D., as if rectum had not power to expel it. Omitted one day, next day two thin ones. Evacuation of ascarides.

Clinical.—Diarrhœa from indigestion, stools offensive, flatulent, consisting of green mucus, sometimes dark, with blood, often with soreness along the colon. Diarrhœa < during the day, not at night.

Urinary Organs.—Catarrh of bladder, kidney and pelvis. Cutting in neck of bladder, at beginning and close of micturition. Constriction at neck of bladder, at both sides of mons veneris, < during micturition, during which the urine often stopped. Burning in neck of bladder during micturition. Pressure upon bladder, necessity to urinate ten times in afternoon, but he always waits long before the urine passes. Frequent desire, but only a little is passed; frequent D., micturition in a divided stream, with burning pain and with tearing in glans. *Dribbling after micturition. Involuntary micturition. Frequent M.;* and copious, also at night; *but always scanty.*

Discharge of mucus with the urine. Jerking in urethra as in ejaculation of semen. *Burning pain in urethra* towards evening; at night during micturition. Itching in female urethra on urinating, preceded by urging. Urine dark yellow, with much red sediment; *U. bloody and turbid;* contained brown clouds after standing; brown, of offensive and sourish odor; odor very ammoniacal; *offensive, it deposits a red, slimy sand that adheres tightly to the vessel* (Sep.); burning; copious at night; suppressed, next day scanty, with brick-colored sediment and of carbon-oil smell; contained albumen and sugar; *contained albumen, hyalin and granular casts; covered with a glistening film and with red sediment;* white sediment.

Clinical.—Nocturnal enuresis. Dribbling of urine after micturition, a condition of atony of the bladder. Hæmorrhages from the kidneys, with constant pain in the back, frequent micturition, chilliness, œdema of the feet. Chronic Bright's disease, with the headache, gastric symptoms, dropsy, etc.

Sexual Organs.—*Reddish eruption on glans, with itching;* smooth red spot on glans. Sticking in penis on urinating. Tearing in glans. Itching in glans, becomes itching. Erections every morning on waking; E. at night, without amorous thoughts; frequent E., without amorous thoughts. Retraction of scrotum, with cramplike pain in l. testicle (spermatic cord). *Red and moist soreness on side of scrotum. Itching of scrotum, with moisture;* pulling I. in r. side of scrotum. Emission in morning, then anxious heat; E. twice at night; during caresses; delayed on coition. Violent desire within genitals for an emission in morning after waking. Desire less.

Soreness near pudenda. Leucorrhœa like the white of an egg; profuse L. Burning, with discharge of blood. Itching caused by menstrual blood. Reappearance of the long-absent menses. Menses too early; and scanty; M. delayed till the full moon. Aversion to coition (in a woman).

Clinical.—It has been found valuable in the eruption of secondary syphilis. Herpes of the scrotum, which was fiery red and almost entirely raw, with occasional burning and oozing of thick, glutinous fluid, with raised vesicles.

Respiratory Organs.—Rattling in trachea in evening in bed, on breathing; R. in trachea in evening before sleep, with dry cough. Bronchial catarrh, with frothy, wine-yellow sputum of oleaginous appearance and consistence. *Hoarse;* in afternoon. Voice weak. *Cough at night;* towards evening from irritation low down in trachea, affecting chest; on smoking; from low down in chest; from dryness of throat; from scraping in throat; with retching; short; spasmodic; dry, vexatious, taking away the breath, she cannot cough it up; violent, at night after falling asleep; violent, with much expectoration. Expectoration of much grayish-white mucus from pharynx.

Asphyxia. Dyspnœa in evening; D. and suffocation, as from constriction of trachea, with tickling, provoking, dry cough. Difficult respiration, < ascending steps, on beginning to walk and on loud talking. Respiration lost if the child fell down or hit anything. Respiration short; and rapid.

Chest.—Pneumonia on r. side (possibly caused by dashing with cold water). Cramplike spasm taking away the breath, in morning and at noon after eating, > stooping, but return of difficult breathing on rising again. Sticking; in side; under r., then under l. arm. Sticking cutting in forepart, from r. to l., if he bends to the l. (during a meal). Pain more tearing than sticking below arm all night after going to bed. Acute drawing pain on l. short ribs, on l. chest and in r. hypochondrium. Pressure and digging; P. in afternoon, with tightness. Pressure upon sternum in morning; upon upper part of sternum at night, > eructations; griping P. from forepart. *Oppression* at night, and restless sleep; O. after exposure to cold air; more O. when sitting than when walking, with difficult breathing.

Heart and Pulse.—Sticking at heart, taking away the breath. Præcordial anxiety. *Coldness in præcordial region.* Palpitation at times, for a moment; P. extending to umbilicus in evening when sitting still. Pulse rapid; slow, hard, excited, not compressible; excited; violent when walking, with pallor and difficult speech; violent, < walking and ascending stairs; violent circulation of blood on slight motion; contracted; radial P. small, empty and of low tension; P. and respiration imperceptible.

Clinical.—Feeling of coldness about the heart.

Neck.—*Pain in nape;* < motion. *Painful drawing extending from nape to occiput;* as from a sprain, extending from muscles of mastoid process to clavicle, and a jerk every five minutes on both sides of neck. *Heaviness of nape.* Stiffness of r. side.

Back.—Opisthotonos. Painful jerking always on swallowing, also with incomplete eructations, at times without swallowing, during rest, always followed by oppressed respiration. Cramp, and in ribs, with drops of sweat on face and arms, then profuse mucous diarrhœa. Pain in morning, with heaviness and weariness in it; P. so that he could not move; in spine from comfortable riding in a carriage, as from a shock; sprained, in back and scapulæ extending into chest, impeding respiration. Drawing, > bending backward. Heaviness. Stiffness; and drawing. Weariness at night, with heaviness of limbs.

Tearing between scapulæ so that she could not move. Pain between scapulæ as from a sprain and pressure, extending forward into chest. Painful jerking in small of back on various motions. Cutting in small of B. in morning after rising and in evening before sleep, only on moving about and stooping, > standing upright. Pain in small of B. on rising from a seat; sprained pain in morning in bed and when sitting; *pain in coccyx when sitting.* Weakness in small of B. after walking; W. and stiffness in small of back and coccyx in evening.

Extremities.—Twitches during the day. Bruised sensation at night, he does not know where to put them. Cramplike drawing and pressure; paralytic D. along extensor surfaces of l. tibia and forearm. Uneasiness. Stiffness in morning after rising. Easy falling asleep. Weakness of joints.

Upper Extremities.—Shoulder. Frequent jerking in r. Pain in joint on raising arm; sprained, in joint on raising arm; drawing, in l. extending to elbow. Pressure upon S. and in back. Tension and drawing.

Arm.—Stretching in morning in bed. Twitches. Internal trembling. Sticking up and down r., extending above elbow, < bending arm. Sudden cramplike pressure here and there. Drawing pain in r., then in head. *Weakness.* Falling asleep of l.; of arms and hands at night if he lies upon them. Cramp of upper when holding a trifle in the hand, renewed by the slightest motion, deltoid hard, next day bruised pain in the spot. Tearing in r. upper. Sharp pressure on r. upper, beginning like a jerking.

Pain in r. elbow, with swelling, the latter so great that it obliterated the fold of the elbow and olecranon, an abscess rapidly formed and rapidly disappeared. Rheumatic drawing in elbows and fingers, pronation of arm caused pain, flexion caused pain, not in the joint, but in axillary fossa, supination was painless. Paralysis about elbow. Sprained pain in wrist. Sticking in r. hand extending into fingers, in morning in bed. Drawing pain in r. hand and index.

Fingers.—Sticking in ball of r. thumb; in bone of last joint of index, with external itching. Sprained pain in first joint of thumb. Scratching pain on first joint of r. thumb. *Bruised pain in nails on touch. Drawing;* in tips. Stiffness of only one in evening, then of others, extending through arm, with faintness, all > walking rapidly in open air, except palpitation and heaviness of arm.

Lower Extremities.—Pain and stiffness; drawing P.

in l. Uneasiness. Paralytic, stitchlike, asleep sensation from above knee to foot when walking and sitting. Heaviness; and tottering on walking.

Thigh.—Cramp all day. Tearing during menses. Pain in l. on motion, so that she could not rise from a seat; P. in hips when sitting; jerking, in l.; sprained, in hips near sacrum on motion; gouty, in hip, knee and ankle at night; tensive, above hollow of knee; drawing, in l. hip-joint. *Stiffness on walking, with heaviness.*

Knee.—Cracking as if a cartilage slipped, with pain on moving it. Cramp in l. when walking. *Sticking;* in r. as if sprained in evening when walking and lying. Tearing in l. in evening, she could not stretch it out. Cramplike pain. Bruised pain in patella; in knees and tibiæ. Pulling pain, with tickling. Tension on the first step after sitting; T. in hollow, with burning. *Stiffness, and in legs; in knees and ankles;* in hollows and in legs. Weakness of r. when walking, > continuing to walk; painful W. in morning immediately after rising.

Leg.—Jerking from r. knee down, painful only when walking. Cramp; *in calves, thighs and feet all day;* in calves at night; in tendo-achillis at night. Tearing in a spot formerly ulcerated, with sticking and pressure. Pain in places on touch during menses; P. in tibiæ on walking. Cramplike drawing in r. tibia. Feeling as if surrounded by an iron band, < ankle.

Cracking in ankle on moving foot. Swelling of feet; of sole anteriorly evenings, with heat in it. *Cramp in soles at night;* C. in feet, with tension of tendons of dorsal surface. *Sticking in corns; in heels.* Tearing in heels in morning on waking. Pain in r. heel; P. in foot, with weakness below external malleolus; *burning P. in corns.* Drawing in feet, with jerking; D. in feet when walking. Tension in feet on walking. Throbbing in soles, < rest. Swollen sensation in feet. Stiffness of foot and on moving it cramp in sole.

Toes.—Drawn inward by cramp in evening. Stitches cross each other in different directions through toes. Sprained pain in first joints on stepping. Pressure in ball of great, as if it had been frozen or as if an iron band were about it. Tearing drawing in ball of r. great.

Skin.—Yellow spots on r. arm. Redness of parts on which he was lying; red spot on l. knee, afterwards with pain; itching R. spot on upper and inner side of thigh; *R. behind ears, with rawness, soreness and moisture;* R. of upper and inner part of lower limbs, with moist soreness. Inflammation in spots, small-celled growths along veins and lymphatics, and in all layers of the cutis there was a widely distributed nuclear proliferation; erysipelatous I. of arm, with burning pain. *Eruption on outer ear; between toes.* **Finger-tips rough, cracked, and sticking cutting in them** (Graph.). *Hands cracked; and rough.*

Nodules (in paraffine-workers), in the acute form, on hands, wrists, arms, feet and legs, < wrists or wherever the dress is tight (palms and soles being free), less on face, neck and other parts to which oily matters find access, the nodules bright red, tender on pressure, consisting each of a hair-follicle, with the parts around it, which are hard, inflamed and red, the hair emerges from the summit of the nodule, orifice of follicle enlarged and containing dry and friable epithelial scales, which cannot be squeezed out, the follicle remains enlarged after the redness and induration have disappeared, successive crops of these nodules are seen at the same time in all stages, while the skin between them is studded with the black mouths of the follicles, men with dark complexion and strong hair especially have their hands and faces dotted with black, but in the chronic form on the backs of feet, toes and hands, and backs of fingers, except over joints, the skin appears honeycombed, elevated, thick and inelastic, so that flexion of fingers and hands is painful, the honeycombed patches are groups of hair-follicles packed with dry epithelial scales, with indurated cutis between them, the hairs have disappeared, the indurated parts are cracked and bleeding, in some instances a follicular abscess, with pale face, foul tongue, emaciation and sleeplessness caused by irritation and pain of skin of the affected parts.

Pimples about eyes; on face; on r. ear, bursting in the evening; inflamed, above knee; burning on touch, on abdomen; itching, on calves; itching, on angle between scrotum and thigh; scabby, above upper lip, with sticking in it; on the exposed skin, with nodules. Scab in fold of l. wing of nose.

Skin unhealthy, slight wounds suppurate and spread. Pustules on face; with white tips; *on nose;* on r. wing of nose, painful to touch; painful to touch, on chin. *Blisters on heel;* on front of thighs and legs and backs of forearms, aggregated in places, isolated at margins, some of them inclined to be pustular at their summits, with a hair in each, and on thighs thickened patches of cuticle and sordes cover part of the eruption, no itching, but some irritation (in paraffine-workers).

Boil on thigh; on anus, disappearing without opening; *painful, on nape, preventing bending or turning head, with moist eruption on margin of hair of occiput, like ezcema, one boil after another discharged and the vertigo and other head symptoms disappeared;* with sticking on touch, on forearm; in axilla, with pain more tearing than sticking, threatening to suppurate.

Sticking in an ulcer; in a painless soft boil that had existed for years on upper and inner part of r. thigh; general itching, at 7 P.M., with anxiety. *Sensitiveness, all clothing is painful.* Pain on l. side of back as if abraded. Burning pain in a wart on finger in evening in bed, as if it would suppurate. Picking in a wart on finger in evening in bed, with soreness on touch. *Itching of tip of nose;* here and there on face; in bend of elbow; in palms; on finger-joints; general, in morning when half awake; *of nipples, with a mealy coat;* with shaking chill; burning, on external malleolus.

Clinical.—Eruption, with thick crusts and deep cracks, on the hands. Herpes zoster. Herpes of the perineum, with great itching and burning. Bleeding fissures on the tips of the fingers, which crack and become very sore, < cold weather. Eczema which had lasted nine years, extending from l. elbow to wrist, raw and moist, though sometimes covered with thick crusts. Eczema on the backs of the hands, which were completely raw from the wrists to the fingers, with burning, smarting and watery oozing. Eczema of the ears, with fetid discharge, greatly increased cerumen, deafness, roaring, etc. Ulcer on the leg, sloughing and spreading. Intertrigo. Psoriasis of the hands.

Sleep.—Sleepiness; during the day; evenings when sitting still; with weariness in all limbs. Constant slumber. Sleepless; and only fantasies about the same disagreeable subject, with night-sweat. Snoring in the morning. Starting up from frightful dreams; S. up in evening in sleep, so that limbs trembled; S. up in sleep, had palpitation, trembling, vomiting and profuse diarrhœa. Twitching in sleep at noon and at night. Tossing about, sleeps only a quarter of an hour at a time. Late falling asleep and tossing about all night. Restless S. and anxious dreams. Sleep interrupted by emissions and desire to urinate.

Dreams; *frightful*, of robbers every night; frightful every night, each dream lasts all night and in the morning she is weak; anxious; vexatious; vivid, horrible; vivid, unremembered; confused, with frequent waking; of lewdness and murder, with anxiety, repeated in midday nap, as if he were murdering the same person.

Fever.—Temperature depressed. Chilliness towards morning, with general trembling, face cool, cheeks, fingers and nails blue, pulse 66, hard, temperature 36.6° C.; C. from morning till noon, with headache and drawing towards forehead all day; from 10 till 10.30 A.M., with cold hands and face, in afternoon heat of face, < eyes, with thirst; every day at 3 or 4 P.M., lasting two hours, with cold hands and dry mouth; at 6 P.M., with blue nails; in evening when walking; in evening, then flushes of heat in face; in evening in bed, then night-sweat; obliging him to lie down; with fever, exhaustion and general pain; then heat, with thirst. Shaking chill; every evening; every day at 10 P.M.; from 7 till 8 P.M., then general sweat except on lower limbs, which were cold; almost shaking at 10 P.M., with heat and weeping mood. Cold and dry skin (gooseflesh). Feeling as if a cold wind blew across head. Coldness of hands; of lower limbs; of feet every evening; of feet at night, preventing sleep; of r. lower limb at night; of a spot on knee, from which a cold stream extended through the whole limb; cold, moist hands, with heat in head.

Heat; in morning on waking; every day from 5 till 6 P.M.; before midnight, with burning pain in mouth, after midnight chilliness; at night in bed; on walking; after eating, with sweat, < head; with full pulse and burning in skin; internal, with heat and dryness in trachea, discomfort, irritability and exhaustion; anxious, at night, with itching; in flushes, also with sweat. Orgasm of blood in evening, with bitter taste. Heat rising into l. side of head after eating, with redness of cheeks. *Heat of face; and head;* with redness of cheeks; all day, < after dinner; and eyes; heat and itching in F. and forehead; in flushes every day from 5 till 6 P.M., with hot hands, dry tongue and accelerated respiration. Heat in palms; in hands, then sweat in palms; in hands in morning on waking; in hands and soles during menses.

Sweat, easy; S. at night; S. in axilla; on hands; *on feet;* on legs and forearms, < wrists; on soles; chest and back during the day when at rest; on head in evening after lying down; on back at night, waking him about 4 A.M., then internal dry heat, with discomfort, preventing sleep.

Clinical.—Fetid perspiration of the feet, with tenderness. It has cured intermittent fever, with the characteristic occipital headache. It is occasionally useful during typhoid fever, when the symptoms correspond.

Petroselinum.

A tincture is made of the fresh plant of the Parsley, Petroselinum sativum, Hoff.

Frequent desire to urinate caused by a crawling stitch behind navicular fossa. Orifice of urethra agglutinated with mucus. Discharge from urethra milky; (yellow); (albuminous). *Drawing and sticking in navicular fossa,* **that changed after urinating to cutting biting;** D. *in navicular fossa*, then itching; D. behind *navicular fossa*, with pressure. *Burning in navicular fossa when urinating.* (Crawling rather than burning, extending from perineum through urethra when urinating.) Creeping crawling in isthmus of urethra in morning in bed; in urethra, in region of Cowper's glands, in morning in bed, then pressure, > standing and sitting. *Voluptuous tickling in navicular fossa. Priapismus, without curvature of penis.* Profuse emission towards morning.

Clinical.—Acute inflammation of the urethra and bladder, sudden attacks of urging to urinate, which, if not immediately attended to, will cause severe pain. Gonorrhœa, with strangury, constant irresistible desire to urinate. (Notice the marked localization of sensations in the navicular fossa; this is quite characteristic.)

Phellandrium.

A tincture is made of the dried seeds of Phellandrium aquaticum, L.

Ally.—Con.

Generalities.—Sticking here and there, in back, groins, etc., if she moves the trunk while sitting. Sensation as if all the vessels were in a tremulous motion when sitting and standing an hour after dinner. Weariness and sleepiness; W. in forenoon, so that she could scarcely move her feet; an hour after dinner, < knees; of feet, then of whole body. Amelioration on motion and in open air.

Mind.—Excited in evening, and joyous. Lively mood, with facile movements of body and agreeable warmth. Sadness; all the forenoon; all day, with fear as of impending misfortune and weeping. Apprehension; an hour and a half after dinner, with tightness about chest. Fretted; by everything, and she had a morose expression. Absorbed in herself and in thought.

Head. — Falling back and forth when walking. Sound in brain as if some one were beating on a metal that was swinging freely, waking him at 5 A.M., then gradually dying away. Aching, < sinciput; A. in forenoon, with dulness; after dinner, with sweat on top of head as far as forehead, then coldness of head; with compression in sides of head. Dulness. Heaviness; with fulness; as if it would be drawn backward to nape. Intoxication; in open air. Vertigo; at 1 P.M., with confusion of head; when sitting and moving about; < open air, > lying down; < walking, it seems as if something projected from forehead so that she could not see over it; so that she could scarcely open her eyes; even to falling backward; with heaviness of head, it falls to the side to which she turns it. Amelioration in open air; A. of headache and most of the head troubles during dinner.

Forehead.—Sticking in r. side. Tearing; extending to r. side when standing after dinner. Intermittent burrowing in l. side. Movement back and forth in it. Pain in l. side, with warmth in it; dizzy P. in l. side, with heat in head and hands.

Sticking in front of l. temple. Sticking burning in l. temple at 9 P.M. Pressure in r. temple. Tearing in upper part of r. side of head on shaking head; T. extending downward in r. side. Sticking in vertex at 3 P.M., with painful throbbing; S. in l. side of V. after dinner, with hot orgasm from occiput to vertex; in r.

side after eating, with tearings; sudden, so that it drew the head backward. Burrowing in vertex, < l. side. *Heaviness as if a hard body were upon V.* Constriction in V. extending to sinciput; almost burning C. on V., < towards forepart and l. side.

Sticking in r. side of occiput. Tearing in O. Intermittent pain in O. Burrowing in l. occipital protuberance. Almost burning constriction in O. Dulness of O. Stitching like flea-bites on r. side of O., then smarting. Biting like flea-bites in a spot on r. upper part of head, > rubbing. Itching, > scratching; on r. side of head; on r. side of occiput; on l. temple at 2.30 P.M.; above r. side of forehead at 9.30 P.M.

Clinical.—Neuralgic headache, a feeling of crushing on the vertex.

Eyes.—Dryness and sticking; D. and burning. Frequent biting in l. Itching, > rubbing, in r. at 8 P.M.; in l. after dinner; sticking. *Lachrymation;* in morning; with biting. Intermittent pressure about them. Frequent tearing in upper margin of r. orbit. *Lids close from heaviness and sleepiness;* twitching of l. lids; tearing in r. lower, near outer canthus, after dinner; tension in a spot on l. lower, with burning; burning in morning; biting burning in l. upper at 9.30 P.M.; biting on l.; itching on l. lower, > rubbing; biting itching on l. at 3 P.M. Itching in r. inner canthus, > rubbing. Itching-sticking biting in inner canthus. Vision dim when sewing.

Clinical.—Inflammation of the eyes and headache, eyes only half open, looks as if she had been crying for a week, photophobia, lachrymation, inner surface of the lids as red as scarlet, with weight on the vertex and burning shooting in the temples.

Ears.—Tearing in r. external meatus; behind l. at 3 P.M.; frequent, in r. after dinner; frequent itching behind l. Boring within l.; deep within l. extending to lower jaw. Itching biting in r., that extended deeper on boring in with finger. Crawling itching externally and internally in r., > boring in with finger and rubbing. Singing in r. at 8 A.M., with ringing.

Nose.—Itching vesicles in r. nostril, becoming confluent and smarting when scratched off. Stoppage, with rough voice; S. in evening, necessity to sit up at night to get air, next morning fluent coryza. Coryza, with hoarseness, redness, burning and swelling of nostrils and swelling of upper lip; fluent C., with hoarseness. Sneezing. Smell lost.

Face.—Pallor. Sticking like a flea-bite on r. side between chin and lower lip after eating. Tearing in a spot on l. lower jaw. Pinching on l. cheek in open air, with tearing to and fro, a kind of twitching. Tension in skin of l. side, with heat; T. in a spot on l. cheek, > rubbing. A pimple that had previously existed on upper lip began to burn.

Clinical.—In a very nervous coffee-drinker, it cured attacks of intense livid redness of the face.

Mouth.—Tearing in the cavity of a r. upper tooth; in last l. upper molar at 1.30 P.M., < touch of tongue, with sticking; in last r. lower molar in evening in cool air, > in the house; in cavity of l. lower molars at 8.30 P.M.; itching T. in the roots of a r. upper and opposite lower molar during dinner. Redness posteriorly of gum of l. lower incisors, with swelling and ulcerative pain on pressure. Tearing in gum of r. upper back tooth. Biting, almost like a burning, on inner surface of gum of anterior lower incisors.

Red, burning vesicles on r. margin of tongue towards tip. Biting burning, as from blisters on tip of tongue. Burning prickling on tip of tongue. Mouth and throat dry at night, so that swallowing is difficult. Salivation. Frothy saliva, which she must spit out often after dinner. Taste slimy; T. like cheese; bitter to beer; sweet after drinking water half an hour after dinner.

Throat.—Mucus provoking hawking; and cough. Hawking of mucus in evening on account of rawness in throat. Chokes easily when drinking in evening. Sticking at 4 P.M., > eating bread, but returning; S. from 4 till 7 P.M., > eating, with pressure; from 4 till 6 P.M. on empty swallowing and swallowing of saliva, with pressure, compelling hawking, then swallowing is painless; S. < swallowing. Rawness, with hoarseness; R., with short breath; intermittent R. Dryness in morning, > breakfast, with thirst, returning that night; at night, and thirst for beer in morning, especially for fresh milk. Burning in œsophagus, extending downward.

Stomach.—Appetite increased; lost, stomach seems full constantly. Eats only soup at noon without appetite. Thirst in morning; *with desire for acids;* for milk in morning, temporarily > soup, with aversion to water; in forenoon and after eating, with aversion to and dread of water, though liquid food agrees with her; at 5 P.M.; for milk and beer, with aversion to water.

Empty eructations at 8 P.M.; E. tasting of the dinner eaten an hour previously; with odor almost like bed-bugs; ineffectual, with pressure in stomach. Nausea; with desire to eructate; with emptiness in stomach and movements about intestines; then pressure in stomach, > empty eructations; so that she was often obliged to spit. Loathing of the veal that had been eaten in the evening.

Stitches above pit. Pinching in epigastric region, with cutting. Sensation as if an acrid, pungent exhalation arose from it, with ineffectual effort to eructate. Sensation as if full of water that would rise up, then sensation of a large, round body twisting about in stomach, that afterwards fell downward, then rumbling in stomach. Oppression, > rising. Burning. Emptiness. Discomfort.

Abdomen.—Distention. Rumbling and gurgling. Movements; causing coldness. Emissions of flatus at 1.30 P.M.; frequent E., with nausea in abdomen and thin stool, without tenesmus. Cutting at 7 P.M., > soft stool. Griping before and during stool, with flatulence, then tenesmus in anus. Pinching, < about umbilicus, with soft stool; P. at 3 A.M., with cutting, as before diarrhœa, > hard stool, afterwards return of the pains with tenesmus, > liquid stool. Pain caused by flatus that is not passed, in morning. Anxiety rising into stomach waking her after midnight (she had eaten potatoes and vinegar in the evening), with nausea, then diarrhœa twice, with pressure and tenesmus, then sore pain in anus. Coldness after stool; as after spirituous drinks. Burning extending into stomach.

Incarceration of flatus by ribs and in sacral region in morning. Constriction in r. hypochondrium when eating, extending in a straight line to l., where it became a sticking, > rising from the seat and walking. Biting internally in r. hypochondrium. Sudden burning in r. hypochondrium. Short movings back and forth in upper A., causing coldness. Pinching in upper A. an hour after dinner, with desire for stool, but emission of only flatus. Pain in upper A. and about umbilicus at 2 P.M.; intermittent, in upper A. at 2 P.M.

Pinching in umbilical region, with constriction; sudden P. Biting in a spot to r. of umbilicus. Twinging in r. side of A. Sticking in r. flank during inspiration after dinner, and on bending to r. sticking in r. groin. Cutting in middle of hypogastrium, extending on r. side to epigastric region. Intermittent pinching in hypogastrium.

Rectum and Stool.—Ineffectual urging; then burning in anus. Itching in anus that becomes burning after rubbing. Stool, with glistening of upper surface, then burning in anus. Thin stool, then tenesmus and sore pain in anus (> Rheum). Soft S. in evening, he usually had a hard one in forenoon. Hard S., with pressure; H., with pain in anus; H., copious, with clawing. S. three times a day, with much flatus.

Urinary Organs.—Desire, but little is passed, with burning; frequent D. Frequent micturition, urine pale. Urine pale, almost greenish. Urine increased; scanty.

Sexual Organs.—Itching of prepuce, > scratching. Menses too early, with weakness, > walking; too early, lasting only a day and a half, and scanty. Menses that had just begun ceased. On appearance of menses, weakness, yawning, bruised pain in inner surfaces of thighs, so that she could neither sit, stand, walk nor lie on account of pain, > bending body towards the l. and in afternoon, menses lasted four days, **flowed only in morning and evening** *and rather profusely.*

Respiratory Organs.—Dry cough in afternoon; in evening, with sticking and short breath. Paroxysmal cough at 1.30 P.M.; at 3 P.M. Easy expectoration of mucus in morning. Short breath when walking.

Clinical.—Bronchitis and emphysema, with rapid respiration, cough compels him to sit up day and night, with sleeplessness, and ulcers on the legs, with tearing, sticking pain. Valuable for the extremely offensive expectoration in the last stage of phthisis.

Chest.—Sticking deep in l.; in r. lowest ribs; in l. lower ribs at 2 P.M.; in costal cartilages to l. of pit of stomach at 7 P.M. on various motions of trunk; in middle on breathing after dinner; on inspiration and yawning an hour and a half after dinner; in upper part of sternum, somewhat to r. side, not affected by respiration; frequently in r. mamma; **through r. mamma near sternum, extending to back between shoulders,** after dinner, *then into r. side of sacrum, < breathing; inward beneath l. mamma, not affected by breathing;* below l. shoulder, extending into l. chest; in last true ribs, extending towards ensiform cartilage, after dinner, not affected by breathing, with screwing-together pain in stomach; *tearing, through l. mamma* at 3 P.M.; biting, in r. nipple in evening before lying down. (Compare above with Con.).

Pressure in l. side in morning in bed, > lying on l. side; when standing, provoking deep breathing; upon chest, with tightness of breath. Oppression, with shortness of breath; O. in a spot on r. side when breathing. Lower part of sternum and pit of stomach sensitive to pressure. Burning in upper part of sternum and in middle of l. scapula, when standing.

Clinical.—Pain in the milk tubes, which is intolerable when nursing.

Heart and Pulse.—Sticking in præcordial region, not < motion or breathing, with drawing. The thumping of heart felt in forepart of chest. Pulse rapid, with warmth; 80, an hour after dinner; slow; full and hard.

Neck and Back.—Twitching in cervical vertebræ and between shoulders. Tearing beneath l. lower jaw, then in l. side of head, extending behind ear and into lower jaw, where it becomes a gnawing. Bruised pain in back when sitting an hour and a half after dinner, > walking. Twinging in lower end of l. scapula, or constriction. Sticking in r. lower false ribs, by back; between scapulæ after dinner; in lower end of l. scapula when eating; in sacrum at 5 P.M.; in lumbar region on deep breathing. Sudden biting in r. side of sacrum.

Upper Extremities.—Tearing in r. shoulder; towards forepart of l. Twitching in middle of inner surface of r. upper arm, or itching. Tearing on inner surface of r. upper arm extending into shoulder, when eating; in r. elbow; in r. radius, from elbow to middle of forearm; on under surface of l. forearm at 8 P.M.; in l. ulna above wrist after eating; in r. thumb towards tip; between second and third joints of l. middle finger, towards back of hand; in first joint of thumb towards the front at 2 P.M.; intermittent jerking, in first phalanx of r. thumb after dinner.

Lower Extremities.—Sticking in r. hip by sacrum. Tearing down anterior surface of r. thigh, just above knee; from l. knee down tibia at 9 P.M. Drawing pain downward in bend of l. knee. Sensation as if blood were accumulating in knees, almost like a burning, at 1 P.M., when sitting and standing. Grumbling in l. calf as after a long walk, at 1.30 P.M. Tearing downward in r. calf; T. posteriorly in l. heel; on margin of r. foot near little toe; in r. sole in morning; lightning-like, in l. sole towards toes at 9 P.M.

Skin.—Blue spots like petechiæ between breasts and neck. Wartlike pimple on r. side of neck. Burning, biting and corrosive itching sticking, like electric sparks here and there, in head, trunk, nose, ears, cheeks, chest, arms, etc., from 8 till 10 P.M. Almost burning or prickling on r. surfaces of calves at 1 P.M. when sitting, walking and standing, in r. calf it extended to heel, almost as if after fatigue. Sensation of a fly above r. eyebrow. Biting in bend of r. knee. Itching on l. scapula near axilla at 8 P.M.; on back of r. hand, by first finger-joints, after dinner. Itching, > rubbing; about l. ear; on l., then on r. ear in evening before lying down. Itching, > scratching; in various places; in r. brow; on nape; on lower surface of l. wrist; on r. side of nose at 2.30 P.M.; in front of r. nostril at 3 P.M.; on r. breast at 9.30 P.M.; on l. cheek after dinner; on r. side of sacrum after dinner. Itching not > scratching, on r. thigh after dinner, with biting. Burning itching on upper margin of l. scapula; on l. concha at 9 P.M., > scratching.

Sleep.—Yawning; after dinner, without sleepiness; with sleepiness; with stretching. Falls asleep when standing at work. Long sleep in morning, during which she hears everything. Sleepless till 2 A.M. Waking early; at times before midnight, then long sleep in morning; after midnight, but soon fell asleep again; frequent; twice towards morning, with feeling as if limbs would fall asleep. Dreams various, unremembered; frightful D., that lightning struck close by him; of fighting, in which he got a good beating; pleasant, of gardens, parties, pleasures, etc.

Fever.—Chilliness; from 6 till 10 P.M., with general shivering, gooseflesh on arms and cutting in epigastric region; from 7 till 9 P.M., > in bed, with shivering; at 9 P.M.; after dinner; internal, from 8 P.M. till midnight, with frequent shaking. Shivering from 4 till 10 P.M.; > sleep; from 4 P.M. till night, with thirst; as if she had been dashed with cold water. Coldness of forehead, > open air, with heat of head.

Rising of heat when standing after breakfast, with sweat about forehead. Heat in head after dinner, with thirst for milk; in head, with dulness; < l. side, with redness of face and heat of hands; internally in head, nape and hands, with sweat on head and nape; in temples, < l., then in rest of head, with sweat on head and hands, with moderate warmth of skin; sensation of heat and sweat on scalp, with feeling of warmth in hands, the H. starts from l. side of occiput, where it continues a burning or distress a long time, as in calves, at 1.30 P.M.; of face, > open air, with redness; internal, in cheeks, with redness of face; in neck beneath l. lower jaw, as if approached by a glowing hot iron.

Clinical.—It has been prescribed in intermittent fever, with pain in the arms.

Phosphoricum Acidum.

One part of pure glacial phosphoric acid is dissolved in 90 parts of distilled water and 10 parts of alcohol are added (making the 1st centesimal dilution).

General Action.—It produces general weakness, with a quiet apathetic state (profound nervous prostration, without excitement). Its collateral symptoms of diabetes mellitus are pronounced, and its curative power in that disease is undoubted. The discharges are usually free and unaltered in character (sweat, urine, fæces and bronchial mucus).

Allies.—Phos., Puls., Sep., Lyc., Sulph.; *Pic. ac., Fl. ac., Sil., Mur. ac.*

Generalities.—Emaciation, with suffering expression and sunken eyes. Twitching here and there, < lower limbs. Epilepsy. Intermittent stitches in umbilical region and in many other parts. Pains at night, > pressure; P. > motion; sore, in every injured spot. *Bruised sensation in all joints in morning, in arms and lower limbs* and in nape; *in hips, arms, thighs and nape, as from growing pains,* < ascending steps and on beginning to walk, with tearing sticking in these parts. **Scraping in periosteum of all bones.** Smarting in wounds, even in wounds of bones.

Discomfort after eating, with anxiety. Dulness of head and limbs as after intoxication or loss of sleep. Invigorated by fresh air, strong in mind and body as from stimulants. Buoyancy and lightness of feeling. Raging in blood. Uneasiness in evening, with itching in canthi, nostrils, face and scalp; U., with forcing and surging of blood, he seems beside himself; and anxiety as if she would be sick. **Weakness; in morning, with apathy;** *in morning after rising,* > lying down, with pallor; *after eating* (breakfast); after ascending steps, with pain in pit of stomach; on walking, with dejection, and on entering house chilliness; *with disinclination for business;* but inability to sleep from itching and sexual excitement, erections weak, with salivation and palpitation; *physical, with mental dejection. Physical heaviness, with mental inactivity* (Pic. ac.). Aggravation from coffee (Nux v., Caust.).

Clinical.—Chorea. Hysteria, with extreme nervousness and debility. A very characteristic sensation, especially in scrofulous diseases, is a feeling as if a bone were scraped with a knife, < night. Growing pains (Guaiac.). General nervous debility, with or without burning in the spine, with general apathy. General relief of pains by motion, sometimes by pressure.

Mind.—Dancing wildly, without consciousness. Lively. **Quiet, indifferent** (Phos., Puls., Sep.), and much boring in the nose. **Speaks unwillingly.** Hasty in speech, he cannot obtain anything rapidly enough. Lachrymose, as if homesick. Sad. Anxious and restless; A., and necessity to lie down in afternoon. Apprehensive as if chest were too tight, with internal heat. Discouraged when walking in open air, worse the farther he walks. Solicitous about the future; S. as if she would be sick. Brooding constantly over his illness. Reproachful of himself. Ill humor; in morning on rising, with weakness and sleepiness. Easily vexed. Beside himself and hot from slightest vexation. Obstinate. *Disinclined to work.* Uneasiness hindering him at work.

He cannot collect his thoughts in proper order (Op.). **Ideas lost and mind weak,** *on thinking he becomes dizzy. Inability to find the right word when talking.* When reading a thousand different thoughts come to his mind, *he understands nothing and remembers with difficulty what he has long known.* He cannot get rid of an idea, and thoughts connected with it do not come to him. *Mind indolent; and unbalanced, without fancy. Memory of the occurrences of the day almost lost* (Anac.). Unconscious in morning if alone.

Clinical.—Delirium, with great stupefaction. Dulness of comprehension, especially in low types of fever; it is difficult to arouse the patient, who seems to require time to collect his thoughts and answer. Valuable in exhaustion of the nervous system from excessive fatigue; any attempt to use the mind brings on headache. Effects of grief and of mental shock, particularly the effects of disappointed love, following Ign. well. Homesickness. In low fever complete apathy and indifference, answers reluctantly; often associated with nosebleed, tympanitis, involuntary stools, great weakness, decubitus, dry mouth, etc.

Head.—Jerking in H.; rhythmical J. forward through H. Burning stitch on H. Pinching here and there in brain, with tearing. Hammering. Hacking as with a hatchet (cured by Staphis.). Painful shattering when walking. Boring as if a hole would be bored through skull, < vertex.

Aching; in morning, with bitter taste; in morning, > rising; in afternoon; from reading a short time, with weakness, heaviness and nausea; < a jar or noise; < ascending steps; *with tingling in head,* and on coughing pain in H. as if it would burst; as if on surface of brain and in periosteum of that part of skull on which he was lying, on waking after midnight, > lying on another place, but it began there; obliging him to lie down, with stiffness of nape; intermittent, with sticking; as if brain were pressed upward, with painful throbbing in it; prickling, from rising in morning till noon; confused, in evening on entering a warm room; as if brain were compressed. *Pressure downward as from a weight, or as if vertex had been beaten. Dulness;* during and after eating; *with inability to think; as after excessive coition;* as from loss of sleep, in forenoon. Heaviness; extending to l. frontal eminence, with pressure; as after lifting. Weakness in morning after rising, as if he would reel.

Vertigo all day; *in morning* when standing; mornings on rising; in morning in bed, on closing eyes it seemed as if the feet arose and as if he were standing on his head; *towards evening when standing and walking*, with staggering; after reading; on stooping; when sitting; on rising after sitting a long time; when walking, with reeling; caused by heat of head, he often nodded involuntarily when writing, things seemed to whirl around, the table to fall down, and when walking and standing he was in danger of falling forward and was obliged to take a step in advance to steady himself; *and head sinks backward and forward.*

Forehead.—Sticking outward in middle; S. above l. eye, extending up into head. Pain; in l. side; in F. and temples; between eyes on waking, with irritability of sexual organs, mental depression and languor; above orbits in afternoon, with stitches behind ears; on suddenly turning head and on stepping hard; at root of nose, with gnawing; extending towards nose; *so that she was stupid, could not open eyes, in morning*, and could scarcely talk, < motion; above eyes, so that she could not open eyes; as after intoxication; bruised, in F. and temples, as if on surface of brain, on reflecting, < evening; crawling, in sinciput, with sweat on forehead. Pressure outward in r. eminence. Dulness in sinciput, < orbits.

Temples.—Sticking in r.; in r. extending deep into brain; in r. extending into eye. Sharp thrusts in r. Tearing in l. extending to forehead, < motion. Pinching in r.; in and on r., < motion; rhythmical, in l.; as if both bones were pinched together. Pain as if both were squeezed to a single piece in evening in bed. Pain on r.; in l., with boring; above l., extending to occiput, with dread of motion. Pressure outward in r. Drawing in l. and in anterior cartilage of ear, becoming a pressure on motion.

Vertex.—Sticking, > pressure, with drawing; S. externally, < touch; intermittent, deep in l. side. Tearing, and in occiput. Burning pain in upper part of brain. Drawing pressure in r. side of V. and occipital bone, < motion. Pressure outward.

Parietal Bones.—Pinching, < motion.

Occiput.—Pinching tearing, < noise and motion. Digging boring in r. side. Pain; in brain behind l. ear; obliging him to lie down; extending outward in r. side; all day in r. side, in part extending forward, < pressure and turning head; as from a hard body, > rubbing; as if he were lying on something hard; bruised, at insertion of cervical muscles; drawing, in bones every day. Heaviness on bending head forward, > bending it backward, with pressing forward.

Scalp.—Falling of hair. Pain. Pain on touch as if sore or as from pulling the hair; with painful elevations. Burning pain on r. side. *Itching.*

Clinical.—Pain in vertex, with loss of appetite. Crushing headache in vertex. The hair becomes gray early and falls out, the effects of mental strain.

Eyes.—Surrounded by blue rings. Inflammation, with a stye on upper lid. Glassy, weak; G., with almost involuntary motion of ball, < staring straight ahead. Lustreless. Sunken, weak. Staring. Pain; in morning on opening them; extending backward; suddenly in l., as from sand or as from a pimple; as after looking too long at an object, obliging him to close the lids; as if being pressed outward, causing blinking; as if too large, with immobility, as if he had not slept enough, with dulness in head. Itching. Burning in evening, with pressure, she cannot look at the light; B., with burning lachrymation; suddenly in l.; biting, < evening by the light.

Lachrymation; biting. *Pupils dilated;* r., < exerting vision; then contracted; contracted. Yellow spot in white, towards inner canthus, with dim vision, > holding hand before eye. Pain as if balls would be forced together and into head. Pain in r. ball at external canthus, at one time sticking, at another burning piercing, then sensation of a broad surface of snow before eyes on which fiery points were falling, then as if glistening white points were falling on a fiery surface. Sticking in thin wall of orbit, towards root of nose. Pinching in upper margin of l. orbit.

Lids.—Swelling of lower, with redness; S. of lower integuments of eyes and beneath lids. *Dry matter in morning, with smarting on cleaning. Agglutination.* Twitching of lower, towards inner canthus. Electric stitches beneath r., so that he must press eyes together; drawing S. from one canthus to the other, with stitches in canthi and around orbits. Pressure in l. lower; beneath l. lower, < pressure, then >; in r., with heaviness. Heaviness. Coldness of inner margin on closing eyes. Burning beneath upper; B. in integuments all day, with burning itching in inner canthus; in inner canthus, as from too much air and light, < afternoon, > pressing lids together.

Vision.—Foggy, of objects farther than six paces. Hazy, > rubbing eyes. Dim for near objects, momentarily > looking away from her work; D. if she looks long at one object, with flickering and pressure in inner canthus, after rubbing lachrymation and disappearance of dimness. Increase of short-sightedness. Weak, more in forenoon than in afternoon, distant objects seem enveloped in mist and are distinct only on exerting vision, every near somewhat bright object blinds him and causes pressure in eyes, the same happens if he goes suddenly into the dark. Flickering when reading by the light. Of ciphers in evening when sitting, and head feels dull and at last hot. Of black stripes, it seems as if he must look out under forehead with head bent over.

Clinical.—Inflammation of the margins of the lids and falling out of the lashes. Styes on upper lid.

Ears.—Swelling in E., with heat and itching. Jerking in r. lobule; in cartilage of l., at times only a tearing. Sticking deep in r.; S. on every musical sound or stroke of a bell and during her own singing; in l., > putting finger into ear; with drawing pain in l. cheek; with drawing pain in jaws and teeth; burning; itching, within r. on moving jaw. Tearing in middle and external. *Spasmodic drawing pain;* in r. Drawing in r. external and middle. Sticking itching in r. lobule.

The watch that he usually hears at twentg paces can only be heard at ten. Cannot hear a watch at a moderate distance, three paces from the ear it is distinct, but close to the ear it is only a hissing. Intolerance of musical sounds. Loud re-echoing of every sound. **Roaring; with difficult hearing;** < r.; in evening, > in bed, returning in morning. Ringing; in l. at night; or sound as if things moved that were lying high up near him out of sight. Screaming on blowing nose. Singing, < lying. Sound at night as if a bird or bat were flapping about the room.

Clinical.—Deafness and roaring in the ears.

Nose.—Swelling in choanæ, with sore sensation.

Crawling and burning. Dryness. Sneezing. Mucus. Discharge of matter. Coryza, with red margins of nostrils. Fluent coryza, with burning in chest and throat extending into mouth, and cough. *Bleeding* and frequent blowing out of blood. Smell acute.

Face.—*Pale;* in morning after rising, with inclination to stare. Often dark red for a moment, and flushes of heat in it. Morose expression. Burning pain in a spot on l. cheek. Drawing through l. cheek into ear. Tension in skin as if albumen had dried upon it, with external heat. Pain in lower jaw in front of ear, as if it would be torn from the articulation, < chewing. Drawing pain in r. angle of lower jaw.

Lips.—Crack in middle of lower; in r. side of upper, with sore pain, < moving lip. Eruption on margin of lower, near corner. Burning, painful pimples on red of lip. Yellowish-brown, scabby pustules on lower, towards corner. Suppurating, excoriating blisters on red of lips, with tensive biting, they became covered with dark skin, which was easily rubbed off on washing, then they bled and were sore to touch, with biting pain. Sticking in a point on red of lip, with crawling. Burning pain in lower; in l. side of lower.

Clinical.—Lips dry, covered with brownish crusts in fever.

Mouth.—Teeth. Bleeding of hollow. Boring sticking, ending with swelling of cheek. Jerking-like tearing in r. upper molars; T. extending into head, as if teeth would be pressed apart and out, < warmth of bed and anything hot or cold. Pain in wisdom T.; in a hollow T. on getting food into it, > picking it out; burning, in incisors at night. Tingling burning in hollow T. Coldness of roots, < molars, when chewing. On edge, as from a corrosive acid.

Bleeding of gums on touch; on rubbing, with sore pain on touch. Gum swollen internally and painful on eating and on touch. Tongue swollen and painful on talking; sticking in r. side; sticking in tip; itching stitches in tip; *dry sensation in T.* and palate, without thirst; dryness; burning; burning in spots; pasty; itching. Bitter mucus often passes from choanæ into mouth and fauces. Mouth slimy and oily in morning, with thirst. Pain as if mouth were sore and raw when not swallowing. Soreness of arch of palate, < expiration, with rawness of throat. Sore burning posteriorly on arch of palate. *Dryness of palate*, without thirst; D. in afternoon, with frequent spitting of tasteless, glutinous, soapy mucus. Much acid saliva. Slimy saliva in forenoon. Much frothy saliva, of sharp taste. Taste foul, musty; foul, insipid; sour; herby in morning and at breakfast; bitter to bread; long after-taste to food, < bread, in morning; long after-taste of bread, with scraping in throat; little to food.

Clinical.—Teeth become yellow. Degeneration of the gums, which bleed easily. Speech difficult, tongue swollen.

Throat.—Inflammation, with a blister and biting pain. *Sticking* on swallowing food; as soon as he swallows saliva. Smarting when not swallowing. Scraping on swallowing bread. Rawness, with pain on talking and swallowing, and necessity to hack; R. that prevents talking. Soreness internally, with sticking in glands beneath l. corner of lower jaw on touch; S. on swallowing; in region of thyroid cartilage on swallowing; on l. side like an ulcer, throbbing, tensive and feeling dry when not swallowing, speech is difficult and swallowing causes scraping sore pain extending into ears, where there is a scratching sticking. Pressure on l. side as if it would become sore internally. Constriction in pit, < bending neck. Tickling in pit causing inclination to cough. Swallowing not easy, as if something were lying behind palate.

Stomach.—Ravenous hunger at night, waking him. Longing constantly for food, without eating much (in a child). *Appetite lost. Thirst;* for beer all day after the colic; for cold milk. *Sourish eructations after eating;* burning, sour, inaudible, not rising to mouth; empty E. Nausea; as if in palate; in epigastric region; in evening obliging him to lie down; at the sight of black bread, especially on account of its sourish odor, and when eating it almost causes vomiting; with tension in abdomen; with accumulation of water in mouth. Vomiting of food, then vomiting nearly every hour, day and night, until morning; *sour V.* (Puls.).

Rumbling after eating, then empty eructations; R. in epigastric region, with gurgling. Stitches in pit, extending to small of back, with drawing; S. in pit as if something would be pulled away. Twisting after eating, then nausea so that she must lie down. *Pain in pit on touch,* he cannot button the clothes tightly. *Pressure* before and *after* eating, < motion. *Weight after a meal;* with sleepiness. Feeling of a lump. *Acidity.* Coldness. Burning beneath pit, afterwards extending to l. side.

Clinical.—Acid dyspepsia, rising of food half an hour after eating, with cramps in stomach (Puls.).

Abdomen.—Distention, > *emission of flatus* (Lyc.); D. after a meal. Rumbling; in l. side; when lying, < upper A. Gurgling as from swashing of water if he bends forward or backward and on touch. Flatulence after eating heartily. Incarceration of flatus. Emission of flatus; smelling like garlic; smelling like garlic, in evening in bed. Sticking in l. muscles; intermittent S. extending to pit of stomach, < becoming erect while sitting; tensive, in r. side of A. and chest, almost taking away the breath. Cutting at night, with drawing in pelvis; C. when walking; with sticking in coccyx; paroxysmal, transversely through A. *Griping* in evening on walking; flatulent, on walking in open air; cutting, as in diarrhœa, in evening before sleep. Pain before coughing. Contraction in morning during stool, then biting in rectum. Shivering, < slightest entrance of open air, with cold finger-tips. Coldness. Tension, with full sensation, without flatulence. Tensive pain in upper, almost taking away the breath.

Hypochondria.—Sticking in hepatic and splenic regions; beneath last l. rib, < inspiration. Griping, extending towards l. side. Pinching just above hepatic region, extending to umbilical region in morning after walking. Pressure, < sitting, with anxiety. Burning pain in a spot in hepatic region. Heaviness in liver.

Umbilical Region.—Griping; when sitting, with pinching; periodic, in umbilicus. Griping constriction in intestines, from both sides of umbilical region. Sickening pain after stool. Burning when walking in open air, with smarting.

Hypogastrium.—Swelling of inguinal glands; with pain, can scarcely stretch the feet. Bubbling-like jerkings in r. groin. Sticking just above pubis on changing position, as when he begins to walk or sits down. Cutting in l. groin. *Pressure in places;* P. towards genitals at end of micturition; outward in r.

groin as if a hernia would protrude, when walking, < pressure.

Clinical.—General tympanitis, with enlarged spleen. Sensitiveness in the lower cæcal region (Sulph.).

Rectum and Anus.—Hæmorrhoids protrude during stool. Tearing in rectum and indications of diarrhœa without stool. Frequent desire; ineffectual D. for twenty-four hours, then difficult stool, next day none. Tearing in anus and penis in evening and morning. Biting itching in anus. Biting in anus after a difficult stool.

Stool.—**Thin, whitish-gray** (Phos.). Watery, with much flatus. *Pasty,* **involuntary** (Hyos., Aloe), *bright-yellow, with sensation as if he would emit flatus* (Pic. ac.). *Diarrhœa, not prostrating;* frequent D., with colic. Soft and frequent. Stool after eating, then sinking at epigastrium. Constipation, with frequent ineffectual desire. Hard; and crumbly; and difficult; at first, then pasty, delayed; first part, then pasty, then tenesmus. Difficult, but not hard. *Omitted;* and abdomen distended; and flatulent pain in abdomen.

Clinical.—Chronic diarrhœa, thin, gray or watery and yellow, painless, preceded by rumbling; as a rule, the diarrhœa does not seem to exhaust the patient, though it may contain undigested food. Diarrhœa after eating. Very valuable for painless diarrhœa, which is very prevalent during an epidemic of cholera and is sometimes premonitory of genuine cholera.

Urinary Organs.—Spasmodic constriction of bladder, without desire to urinate. Urging, with burning; U., with scanty discharge; frequent U. *Frequent micturition; and profuse; of watery urine that often could scarcely be retained.* Retention of urine, then frequent but scanty micturition, with burning in neck of bladder.

Urethra.—Swelling about orifice. Stitches when not urinating; S. in end; intermittent, with frequent rawness. Dragging in U. and rectum as with cutting water. Drawing extending to anus. Crawling when not urinating. Burning when urinating, then increased gonorrhœa; B. when urinating, and before the water flows a cutting, with ineffectual straining; that stops the flow, then desire to urinate; cutting, during micturition, with cramplike pain in small of back.

Urine.—Dark, profuse, forming a cloud. *Pale, copious, flowing freely, as if urethra were very large;* P., in which a thick, whitish cloud speedily formed. Clear, watery; *and depositing a sediment.* Copious; and clear, afterwards dark and turbid. Scanty and irritating; S., and micturition slow.

Clinical.—Milky urine. Urine has a white sediment, jelly-like, consisting of phosphates, with aching in small of back. Incontinence of urine. Diabetes.

Sexual Organs.—Falling of hair. Heat in condylomata; sore pain in C. when walking and sitting. Frænum preputii, itching crawling; crawling, then moist, itching vesicles; vesicles, itching on pressure. Penis, swelling without cause; stitches in tip; itching stitches; burning cutting, with pressing-out pain in groins; heaviness, < when urinating; crawling itching posteriorly. *Erections in morning in bed; in morning when standing;* at night, which formerly had ceased; excessive, without desire (Pic. ac.).

Hardness of spermatic cord, with tension. Swelling of spermatic cord, with dulness of head. Scrotum, inflamed swelling; red, burning pimples, and on posterior part of penis; sore pain; itching sticking; itching; crawling, changing after scratching to burning and sore pain. *Testicles, swelling* of l.; burning tearing in l., with burning in prostate and frequent erections; drawing smarting as from soreness; pressure, < walking and touch. *Emission at night without erection; E. when pressing at stool;* **profuse.** Desire lost; normal, with ability for coition, but the penis finally became relaxed, with satisfaction, without emission.

Leucorrhœa after menstruation; yellowish, after menstruation, with itching.

Clinical.—Involuntary seminal emissions; the seminal fluid escapes readily after urinating or during sleep. Valuable for the general effects of seminal emissions, vertigo, brain fag, deficient sexual power, weakness of the back and burning in spine (compare China). It has been prescribed for swollen testicles, which are very tender to touch. Chlorosis in women, with leucorrhœa and early and profuse menstruation, evacuation of large quantities of urine, debility; meteoric distention of uterus.

Respiratory Organs.—*Capillary bronchitis, < evening, with fever, dyspnœa, pain under sternum, then violent sneezing, thirst and coryza, the profuse secretions purulent rather than slimy. Hoarseness.*

Cough from tickling as with a feather, from middle of chest to larynx; from burning in chest; with nausea; with vomiting of food; *constant irritable;* violent, provoking vomiting; causing headache as if skull would burst; **dry from tickling in chest, just above pit of stomach,** *< evening after lying down. Cough, with expectoration of herby taste and odor; C. in morning, with yellow E.; violent C., with copious E.,* causing pain in abdomen; *mucus thinner than usual.* Inclination to cough, causing sticking in palate, but no cough. *Salty expectoration in morning.*

Respiration difficult; with stitches between short ribs, < l. Want of breath after a nap in forenoon, with uneasiness and sweat. Breath taken away by odors. Sighing.

Clinical.—Inflammation of the larynx and trachea, with hoarseness and loose cough, which seems to come from the pit of the stomach, though the cough is often dry in the evening. Spasmodic cough from a feeling of dust in the air-passages, apparently down as far as the pit of the stomach. Cough < morning and evening, after sleep, from cold air. Capillary bronchitis, with expectoration of mucus in small balls (Stan.).

Chest.—Sticking in region of r. lower ribs; in middle of sternum; in lower part of r. on inspiration while sitting, > walking; in l. side between last ribs and pelvis, extending through whole abdomen, < inspiration; beneath r. arm, taking away the breath; pinching; boring, in l., < inspiration. Sudden cramp in C. or diaphragm, in region of last r. ribs, obliging her to sit bent over, with sticking on breathing. Cutting in l. on deep breathing; burning, on l. when sitting, < touch. Pinching in region of l. nipple; beneath r. axilla, opposite nipple; in region of r. seventh rib; near sternum, beneath last r. rib; intermittent, near sternum, about seventh rib; periodic, beneath short ribs; boring, in l. when breathing.

Pain; on last r. rib on pressure; in l. side, < breathing; **as from weakness** or after sitting a long time, > walking; crawling, during rest, and on touch and motion soreness on sternum; burning sore, internally by last rib; burning itching, in middle of C. and in upper abdomen, with frequent hawking of mucus. Anxiety. Sensation in side as if ribs were beaten in. Pressure at night, causing difficult breathing; at night waking him, extending to abdomen, > emission of flatus; sharp, on l. mammary gland; outward in sternum, < expiration, pressure on sternum, stooping and coughing. Constriction; in afternoon, with stitches. Oppression on beginning to walk; O. behind sternum, with pressure, making respiration difficult; extending to stomach. Fulness on waking, then cough, with expectoration. Burning in middle after a vexation.

Heart and Pulse.—Intermittent pinching in region of H., extending towards sternum, in evening when walking. Palpitation always after starting up in sleep. *Pulse irregular, intermittent;* P. strong; full, with distention of temporal arteries and veins of hands; rapid; rapid and weak.

Clinical.—Nervous palpitations, resulting especially from self-abuse.

Neck.—Jerking in nape during rest, < raising head. Drawing sticking in nape, extending towards occiput. Pinching in a spot. Burning sore pain on side. Pressure in forepart and sides. Spasmodic drawing in r. muscles extending to eye, on turning head. Soreness of r. muscles. Stiffness of nape, > motion; S. of l. muscles, with tension.

Back.—Jerking stitches in middle of spine. Pinching in middle of spine. Tearing at night; T. on l. scapula when sitting bent forward. Gnawing in bones beneath tip of scapula. Aching; from slight exercise. *Boring between scapulæ,* with drawing pain, then restless sleep, next day the pain extended to nerves of l. shoulder-joint, < axillary and radial nerves, it was boring digging and gnawing, increased daily, prevented sleep after 2 or 3 A.M., > 8 A.M., < again from 2 till 4 P.M., and from 7 or 8 till 11 P.M., < beer and wine, lying on l. side, rest, every movement that impeded circulation of blood, > every movement that hastened circulation and motion in open air, afterwards numbness over region of radial nerve of l. hand. Drawing in dorsal vertebræ as if beaten, < sitting.

Lumbar Region.—Sticking in kidney region; on coccyx and sternum; on rising after squatting; on lifting, continuing when sitting, > moving about. Intermittent tearing on rising from stooping, and on standing still jerklike drawing. *Burning pain in a spot above small of back.* Intermittent sudden drawing pain, < standing, > walking, pressure, sitting and stooping. Pain; as from something alive, like a drawing and pressure, at times tearing, only distinctly felt when standing.

Clinical.—Spinal anæmia, resulting from sexual excesses, with palpitation, impotency and pain in vertex. Weakness of the small of the back and heaviness in the lower extremities, resulting from sexual excesses. It has proved a palliative in caries of the lumbar vertebræ.

Extremities.—Jerking tearing. Contracted feeling. Bruised feeling in hands and feet as if paralyzed. Cramplike drawing in hands and feet as if asleep, in evening and morning. Crawling as if asleep, with weakness. Falling asleep of arms and lower limbs at night, so that they must be moved by others.

Upper Extremities.—Swelling of axillary glands. Shoulder, pinching on top of r.; rheumatic paralytic pain in r. joint; drawing extending into arms; drawing in joint, with throbbing. *Arms weak* in afternoon, so that he trembled. Arm that had been injured stiff and painful on motion, hand heavy, picking and sticking in an ulcer, tearing and sticking in ball of thumb and in fingers, internal burning in hand and on allowing arm to hang down blood shot into hand. Jerking of upper arm, > motion. Paralytic pinching in upper arm, < touch. Drawing cutting in elbows, wrists and first finger-joints. Pain in elbow on touch. Drawing extending from elbow to shoulder.

Forearm, sticking boring near bend of l. elbow, < rest; pinching above r. wrist; pinching extending inward and outward; pinching heaviness in r.; bruised pain when lying on the table; paralytic pain externally below elbow. Wrist, tearing transversely across r.; spasmodic tearing in l. (possibly from taking cold in hands when out of bed); stiffness, < motion, with pinching. Hands, trembling when writing, with crawling and itching in them; cramp in r.; drawing stitches in palms; tearing in l. H. and shoulder; tearing rolling up and down in bones of H., fingers and forearms, at times with stitches; griping pinching between r. metacarpal bones; drawing in r.; swollen feeling.

Fingers.—Stitches in joints; through back of r. thumb, extending under nail; intermittent, in ball of thumb. Tearing, < joints, with tension on motion as if tendons were too short; sticking T. on first phalanx of r. middle. Cramplike pain in l. Painful drawing in little, < joint, > bending finger into hand. Falling asleep, coldness, yellowness and wrinkling, with slow, scarcely perceptible pulse. Numbness of tips. Circumscribed deadness on one side of l. index during the chill.

Lower Extremities.—Staggering sensation when walking. Heaviness of joints. Falling asleep when sitting.

Hip-joint.—Cramp tearing through whole leg, < eating and sitting. Pain on rising from a seat; as if broken when walking and on touch; tensive and bruised, in r., < motion. Heaviness on beginning to walk after sitting, > motion, with lameness.

Thigh.—Painful pulsating jerking from middle to knee; itching J. in gluteals. Stitches on motion, < sitting and rising from a seat; boring, in l. near abdominal ring during rest. Tearing extending to great toe. Pinching in r.; P. externally above knee. Pressure; a hand's breadth above knees; sharp, on muscles of r., extending to knees. Bruised pain in femoral muscles; in T. and legs when walking; transversely across middle when walking, so that he staggered. Cramplike drawing in l. nates when walking. Weariness, < after sleep; W. when sitting, with anxious restlessness, so that he must constantly move the feet.

Knee.—Sticking in r. patella, < motion. Tearing from hollow to upper part of thigh. Periodic pinching beneath l. Tensive pain in tendons under K., < motion and touch. Painful drawing deep in l. extending to tibia, when in walking the body is supported by l. leg.

Leg.—Cramp in l. calf. Sticking in lower part of tibia; cutting, in calf extending downward. Tearing in tibia and in outer surface of upper part of thigh; burning, in tibia at night, extending downward. Spasmodic pinching in l. calf, > rubbing. Pain below knees; P. in r. tibia, > walking. Spasmodic drawing, obliging her to rise and walk about during the day, and to move the leg back and forth at night. Pulsation during rest. Crawling in r. Weakness on walking. Rheumatic paralysis of l.

Ankle.—Tensive sticking in r. internal malleolus, extending to tibia. Sprained pain, even in morning in bed. Paralytic pain at rest, with cracking on motion.

Foot.—Swelling, with burning of soles; S., with soreness. Sticking in soles and heels, and during rest heaviness; S. in corns, with burning; burning, in soles, < evening; jerklike, in r. sole. Tearing along r. external plantar nerve, with painful drawing. Pinching in soles. Cramplike pain caused by motion. Intermittent pressure in l. sole, extending towards great toe. Sore pain in soles and balls of toes on stepping. Smarting on outer side of r. in morning. Spasmodic drawing, < r. sole and balls of r. toes, preventing sleep till after midnight, > 1 A.M. Tension in anterior part of F. and in toes when walking, with sensation as if asleep. Numbness of l. on walking.

Toes.—Nail grows into flesh, causing inflammation and pain. Swelling of joint of great, with burning and throbbing, and on touch sticking causing jerking in toes, even hiccough or dread of being approached caused the pain. Tearing stitches on ball of l. great; boring S. in l. little. Pinching in two last r. Sore as if ulcerated.

Clinical.—It has been found valuable in hip-joint disease, with great fever and sleeplessness.

Skin.—Red, burning spots on thighs and legs. Redness of whole body, with red spots on shoulders and red stripes above patellæ, and from hips to umbilicus, with sensitiveness to air, the warmth of the bed feels good. Hands dry, rough and wrinkled. Rash over whole body, burning more than itching. Eruption on dorsa of hands, with a depressed centre like a grain of wheat, hands look as if covered with white of egg, skin dry. Eruption painful on touch, on scapulæ.

Swelling on back of nose, with red spots on sides that now appear and now disappear, with tense sensation. Nodes on forehead. *Pimples on face;* red, on and between fingers, finally with white elevations in the centre; with throbbing in it and painful on touch, in tip of nose; sore on touch, on forehead; sore, < touch, behind lobule of r. ear; red, on back of hands; red, < evening, sensitive to rubbing and touch of clothes, on back, chest and neck; red, smooth, with red areola, sore on touch, on forearm and throat; itching, < evening in bed, on knee and calf, with burning after scratching, then they become confluent, spread and change to ulcers that bleed easily.

Itching scab beneath septum of nose. Red, itching pustules, < touch, on cheek and nose. Boils on l. chest and l. side of back; on r. shoulder; on nates. Inflammation beneath finger-nail, with suppuration. Vesicles on balls of toes; and toes and nates; deep-seated, hard, itching, on ball of thumb.

A bursa between metacarpal bones becomes painful, < night, < touch. Burning pain on l. side of forehead; on r. cheek near corner of mouth; in ulcers. Sore, even shaving is painful; S. spots on toes, groins and pubis. Crawling; *over whole body,* with stitches; now here, now there; itching, on body and hands in evening after lying down. Boring sticking on upper abdomen. Itching sticking on coccyx; around anus; on upper arm, not > scratching; between breasts, waking her about midnight and forcing her to walk about. Itching biting on forehead; on r. false ribs; on trunk and thighs; on coccyx above rectum; on l. leg, < scratching.

Itching of face; ear; of tip of nose; on tibia; r. hip; malleolus; heels; backs of hands, < scratching; on back, with sweat on it; suddenly here and there, transiently > scratching; biting, on l. middle finger, recurring after scratching; sticking burning, < scratching, with redness.

Clinical.—Atonic ulcers on the legs, with stinging, burning pains. Acne, resulting from onanism. Blood-boils. Chilblains. Wartlike excrescences.

Sleep.—Yawning; in forenoon and evening; from 9 till 10 and from 4 till 6, with shivering, and with cold feet in evening; with stretching of upper limbs and sleepiness; that brings water into eyes. Sleepiness; all day, < evening, with yawning; during the day, > walking, with weariness, at night sleeplessness, and from evening till midnight heat and sweat; *early in evening* and in morning. Falls asleep after dinner, when talking. *Could not arouse himself in morning.* Sleep early and sound; fell into sound S. when writing; sound during the day, interrupted at night.

Sleepless from 2 till 4 A.M. from flow of ideas. Late falling asleep; and for several hours nothing but large ciphers before eye, > rising in bed. Waking at 1 A.M., with sad, solicitous thoughts; anxious W.; early W., and difficult falling asleep again. Restless in morning in bed; restless sleep, with dry heat. Laughing expression at one time, at another weeping, with distortion of the half-open eyes. Singing. Moaning; with half-open eyes, talking and jerking of hands. Biting of tongue. Starting up in fright as if he were falling into water or from a height.

Dreams.—**Lascivious, with emissions.** *Sleep full of D., with erections. Causing uneasiness.* Full of strife, *night restless.* Fatiguing, working all night. Anxious, of dead people, with fear on waking. In part vexatious, in part indifferent, towards morning he places arms under head, then they fall asleep. Pleasant before midnight, fearful but little remembered after midnight. Vivid, shocking, unremembered; vivid, of feasting. Wonderful. Every night, of the last thing that happened in the evening.

Fever.—*Chilliness;* towards evening; in evening on lying down, and heat on first waking, without thirst; in open air; waking her every night after an hour's sleep, with drawing in limbs; sensitive to cold air; with cold creeping and palpitation; alternating with heat in evening, dry heat in face without redness, with chilliness, after the heat still more violent chill, cold creeping over whole body, sweat in sleep towards morning, if after waking he falls asleep again; trembling, in evening, next morning heat of face, dryness of mouth and sticking sore throat on swallowing.

Shaking chill in forenoon, with blue nails, tearing in wrists and paralytic weakness of arms; S. chill from afternoon till 10 P.M., then dry heat; an hour after eating, with cold fingers, after four hours heat, without thirst. Shivering in attacks in evening, then exhausting sweat at night; paroxysmal S. in forenoon, with blue, cold hands and dry palate, without special thirst; *more internal S. than external coldness;* alternating with heat, in evening; creeping S., then heat alternating with S.

Coldness on scalp; nose; r. upper arm; from malleoli to calves; feet in evening after lying down, with heat of head; hands on talking much, with heat of head; often internally in r. cheek, with internal warmth in l.; as from a cold wind on face, temples and forehead, with coldness of finger-tips.

Heat from 11 A.M. till 5 P.M., without thirst; *general H. in evening*, then a restless night; with sweat and thirst for water; internal, without thirst or redness of cheeks, with deep respiration and apprehension; dry, on going to sleep. Intolerance of heat. Catarrhal fever, with soreness of limbs and loss of taste.

Heat on side of frontal bone; on chest; here and there in arm and on shoulder; in tips of elbows; palms; feet and soles; soles and head; soles in morning; face in afternoon, without redness, but with thirst; cheeks and ears in evening before sleep; cheeks in evening on walking in open air, with flushes of heat in back; face at night; side of face on which he was not lying; posterior femoral muscles, when standing, > walking; soles, with soreness between toes.

Sweat in morning; and heavy dreams of dead people and of being pursued; all night, with hot feet and forehead; about midnight and on waking, beginning on head, most profuse on chest; on exertion; on walking; on walking in open air, < genitals; in attacks when walking; on nape, < during sleep in the daytime; on forehead; cold.

Clinical.—Typhoid fever, with debility, stupor, diarrhœa, rattling mucus in the chest, deafness, etc. Typhoid fever, with quiet delirium, disconnected talking, inability to protrude the tongue or to articulate distinctly, tongue and lips dry, extremities cold, discharges involuntary. Typhoid fever, with panting respiration, dark blue circles around eyes and mouth, nosebleed, tympanitis, involuntary, undigested stools, red streak in the centre of the tongue, albuminuria, urine milky, temperature low.

Phosphorus.

A saturated solution of Phosphorus in alcohol corresponds to the 3d decimal dilution.

General Action.—A tissue drug of first rank as well as a most virulent poison. It inflames and causes degeneration of the mucous membrane of the entire alimentary canal, causing gastritis, entero-colitis and dysentery, all characterized by destructive processes and hæmorrhage. It inflames the kidneys. It causes acute yellow atrophy of the liver as well as a subacute hepatitis. It causes inflammation of the whole respiratory tract and pleuro-pneumonia. It produces an inveterate myelitis of the spinal cord and other nerves, with consequent paralyses. It destroys bone, particularly attacking the jaw and tibiæ. It disorganizes the blood and produces hæmatogenous jaundice. It causes fatty degeneration of every tissue and organ in the body, predisposing to hæmorrhages.

Allies.—Arsen., Pic. ac., Crotal., Apis; Puls., Lyc., Nat. sulf., Ferr.; Pod., Merc.; Sec. c., Ham.; Nux v.

Generalities.—Mucous membranes pale. Muscular system lax. Lay always on r. side at night (Puls., Nat. sulf.); **always on r. side**, throwing about upper part of body, < head; *on back;* on back at night, with l. hand under occiput; on l. side, with feet drawn up. **Emaciation** (Iod.). *Ataxia and adynamia.* Anæmia. Consumption, with hectic fever, bad digestion, cardialgia and constipation. Appearance as in typhoid fever, depression and prostration, difficulty in raising herself in bed. Swelling of body; < lids and face, so that the depression from pressure of finger was but slowly obliterated, on other parts the relaxed tissues, when pinched, but slowly regained their smoothness (Ars., Apis). Soft parts detach themselves from the bone and leave a bony, gray, rough, but solid surface, and a gray, fetid suppuration exhales, after an uncertain period this separates without any new bone being formed.

Much bleeding of small wounds. *Hæmorrhages from free surface and from tissues* (compare Crotal.). *Blood when drawn was pale and had only about twice as many red as white corpuscles. Regurgitation, without effort of nearly pure blood, with epistaxis and oozing of blood from ears,* **the blood of these hæmorrhages very fluid and difficult to coagulate,** *next day a little blood from throat, with these hæmorrhages return of nervous symptoms, pain and numbness of l. arm, then of other limbs, pain in region of throat, stricture of throat,* **suffocative sensation,** *as the hæmorrhages diminished the skin was more deeply jaundiced,* after a month the H. returned, *with pure blood in stools, epistaxis, hæmaturia,* then prostration, **almost complete loss of voice,** *feeble pulse, cold limbs, bruit de souffle with first sound of heart,* later the H. with pain in r. iliac fossa and r. thigh and weakness of limbs, afterwards *profuse uterine H.*, but miscarriage was prevented, she was delivered without accident, *afterwards diarrhœa, not bloody, which could not be stopped and which ended her life eight months after the poisoning.*

Stretching of limbs and chest in morning in bed. *Motions involuntarg and uncertain, as in palsy. Trembling;* in morning, with jerking of limbs; in morning on waking, with feeling as if teeth were chattering; of chest and hands, as if he had drunk too much coffee. Tremulous sensation in lower part of spine, in jaws and fingers; in whole body, like a pulsation. Twitching of all muscles, < limbs, during rest and on contact. Convulsions; and hands clenched, eyeballs fixed; clonic; hysterical; tonic (the post-mortem showed spinal arachnitis and partial softening of spinal cord).

Sticking; here and there; at times in joints or bones, or pain; in chest, back and r. arm on motion, < night in bed. Tearing over whole body. Pain; *while eating,* at noon and in evening; on slightest motion; before change of weather; in muscles, < calves; in r. side, with occasional stitches; fugitive, during the night; assuming the form of cramps as soon as the bowels begin to move; burning and boring, < bones of skull, palate, nasal bones and teeth, < night; drawing, in bones of l. arm and in lower jaw, and rheumatic P. in other parts; numb and drawing, here and there, < r. side. Rheumatic feeling in knees and small of back. Bruised feeling. Soreness of whole body. Pressure on scalp, in face and on throat. Tensive drawing in glands, even on neck.

Hyperæsthesia of all senses, < hearing and smell. Discomfort, < stomach. General sick feeling, with weakness in joints, < knees; S. feeling, preventing sleep till 2 A.M. Inability to assume an upright position when walking. *Takes cold easily in open air,* which causes griping in abdomen, pain in nape, stiffness of arms, toothache, lachrymation, hiccough, cutting and sticking in and above pit of stomach, dulness of head, or at last coldness and moist coldness of feet and hands, with a hot cheek, etc.; takes cold on rising after slight night-sweat, with toothache and jerking in teeth; feeling of taking cold in whole body, with chilliness and sleepiness (Nux v.).

Sensation as if a fluid ran from trunk into limbs, < into knees, elbows and wrists. Rush of blood into hands and head, as if from stomach, with injected veins on back of hands. Restlessness; at night, from pressure in stomach and nausea; during a storm; in bed; with anxiety; with rolling about of head and moaning; in blood after eating a little, with anxiety. Nervous, < symptoms in afternoon and evening. Nervous sensitiveness, with weakness, < region of last vertebra and in sacrum, every exertion fatigued and the carrying of a small basket caused pain in whole back. Increase of muscular power; of muscular activity; of vigor; of feeling of vigor, next day exhaustion.

Weakness; all day, with oppression; all day, then at night sweat and turbid urine; *of mind and body in morning; in morning, with feeling as if he had not slept enough* (Nux v.); in morning on rising; *in morning after micturition, so that he had to lie down;* in morning on rising, and during the day general sick feeling and heartburn, and after rapid motion ravenous hunger and trembling of limbs; in morning, > rising; towards noon, with sickness; towards noon, > afternoon; in afternoon after a little wine, so that he must sleep a few hours, then a sleepless night; during evening fever; after eating, < affected parts; **from walking**; *from a short walk*, with headache; during menses, < evening, with pain in back as if beaten and torn, drawing in whole body, palpitation, anxiety, griping above stomach, with constrictive pain and inability to keep up on account of nausea; at times > walking, < lower limbs and knees, with loose feeling in knees; **with depression and no desire to attend to ordinary business;** *with ability to lie only on his back; and on ascending stairs muscles of lower limbs refused to act, so that she was in danger of falling; and almost speechlessness;* with evening fever; sudden; sudden, with heat of face; similar to that of typhus; hysterical, so that she could scarcely move the leg, with constant yawning, uprisings, and distress and pressure on chest. **Nervous exhaustion, with general heaviness, desire to keep the bed and dread of motion.**

Faintness; incomplete, towards evening, when drinking a glass of cider. Collapse. **Heaviness of whole body;** *with fulness; of upper part of body* all day, **with sensation as if everything about chest were too tight;** *of limbs and back in morning on waking; of head, spine and limbs towards evening, increased in paroxysms, with ill humor. Paralyzed feeling;* mental and physical, all day; in morning after rising, with bruised feeling; with tremulous sensation; in whole r. side, with nausea. Symptoms of paresis of r. side of face and r. arm, then paralysis of facial and hypoglossal nerves. *Numbness of whole body* (Pic. ac., Plat.); *with pricking* as if encompassed by needles that just touched and on slightest motion entered the body; *of lower limbs and up as far as chest.* Hands, feet and nose seem stiffened.

Symptoms manifest themselves first upon ailmentary tract, then upon respiratory organs, then upon skin. Aggravation in morning after sleep; *of pains from 5 or 6 P.M. till towards morning; in afternoon;* in a warm room; from onanism and emissions. Amelioration in afternoon after eating; after dinner; after supper; after supper and a glass of beer; from rest; after sleeping half an hour; in open air; *in cold, open air.*

Clinical.—General tendency to fatty degeneration of organs. General tubercular diathesis. Hæmorrhagic diathesis. Exostoses, especially of the skull. Cancerous ulcerations with profuse bleeding, burning, etc. Vascular growths. Rickets. Chorea. Marasmus. Chlorosis. Paralysis, face and extremities generally hemiplegic. Post-diphtheritic paralysis, with numbness of the extremities. Pseudo-hypertropic paralysis; with nosebleed, diarrhœa, numbness, inability to grasp objects, etc. General aggravation from sweets; *from wetting hands* and feet; in cool, damp weather; in hot weather.

Mind.—*Delirium;* with cries, striking and biting about him; with fear of death, carphologia, shrill cries, and at times stiff bending backward; with attempts to escape; in which he got out of bed, tossed about the floor and screamed; at times; *loquacious* (Hyosc.); violent; *violent*, with icteric color, *he forgot to urinate*, **respiration difficult**, *pulse small, skin dry, tongue brown; violent, erotic, at first alternating with consciousness, afterwards interrupted, then stertorous respiration and death;* sudden, then coma interrupted by screams; when slumbering and waking, as if she were on a distant island, had much business, were a noble lady, etc.; saw faces everywhere, they swarmed by him in a long procession, leered at him over the footboard of the bed, squinted at him through the windows and trooped in when the doors were left ajar, so that he could not sleep, afterwards he fancied that he was some one else, *or that he was in several pieces and could not adjust the fragments* (Bap., Petrol.). Dread, but inability to resist or move, sometimes it seemed as if I began to bloat and a multitude of voices said, "Fill him up a little more and he will burst," then I heard demoniacal laughter, which made chills run over me, I imagined myself an aurora borealis and could hear shouts of "Beautiful! Oh, was not that splendid!" as the pains became more severe, but the agony soon became so great as to throw off the stupor. Foolish, disconnected talking, then quiet delirium, with lucid intervals. *Shamelessness, she uncovers herself and wishes to go naked, as if insane* (Hyosc.). Imagines that he has hydrothorax. Wild, troubled thoughts, half dreaming, half waking. Vivid fantasies, < evening, causing shuddering; V. fancies caused by reading a foolish story, so that I must make earnest exertion to do my work.

Excitement; with heat and thirst; with singing and laughter, afterwards sleep, next morning anxiety on waking; then delirium, then somnolency, then delirium again; alternating with sopor. Exhilaration. *Spasmodic laughter and weeping.* Liveliness, < afternoon; L., with singing and humming to herself. Cried loudly in bursts. Screams, with clinching of hands; S., with biting and tearing the pillow with the teeth. *Said that he could not recover and gave disjointed directions about his business. Nervous, as if going to die.* Discouraged about his health. **Disinclination to mental or physical exertion; to study; to converse.** Increased activity.

Anxious oppression. Anxiety; every morning on waking; in evening; in evening in bed, with restlessness; *at times in evening, as if he would die;* **at night if he lies on l. side;** all night as if he had murdered some one, with tossing about; *when alone, with irritability; with restlessness, sweat on forehead and heat of head; with heat* (Ars.); *about the termination of her illness. Fear; in evening;* during a thunder-storm; > weeping, then indifference; *as if a horrible face looked out of every corner, in evening; of death at night*, with desire to commit suicide; as if about to be run over by a locomotive. Sense of impending trouble. *Worried about imaginary troubles.* Apprehension on thinking of anything disagreeable. Starting when the door was opened, noise was very troublesome. *Melancholy;* towards morning, on waking from a dream, with violent weeping; *in the twilight; and silent, reflective;* about the future; but obliged to laugh against her will. *Tender mood.* Inconsolable grief in morning, with weeping and crying. *Weary of life.*

Ill humor; in forenoon; on waking after midnight; at the crying of a child; before dinner, then heat and then pressure in stomach, then nausea with heat in face and loss of appetite; and affected by everything, especially people and noises; and profanity. Anger. Vexation from slight cause, with cold hands, hot face and palpitation. Discontented; and irresolute. Capricious, sensitive. Wants numerous and varied. Anthropophobia. Obstinate. Uneasy, hurried feeling. Impelled to walk far in the open air. Dislike to being alone. **Apathy**; in evening, with weakness and heaviness of head; **and almost unwilling to talk; and slow answers and movements** (Phos., Sep.); *at times tossing about the bed and moaning;* but loud screams now and then, at other times she is unconscious and does not answer.

Mind very clear, very distinct remembrance of my past life. Rush of ideas which were difficult to put in order. **Slow flow of ideas,** *absence of ideas.* **Inability to think** (Op., Lyc.); **could not keep mind long on any subject**; on work, in evening. *Thought confused;* and singing, loud cries, involuntary stool and micturition. Distracted in morning, though inclined to work. Forgetful. Took no notice of what was passing around him, but his responses were always correct. Loss of senses, as if he could not grasp a thought, with headache. Loss of intelligence. *Coma.* Sopor, with restlessness, then coma and death. **Stupor**; at night on waking, also with vertigo; **from which he could be aroused for a moment, only to lapse back into muttering lethargy** (Ph. ac.); **and forgetfulness,** so that he did something different from what he wished; with tossing about the bed, often rising up and calling the names of people; and at times screams.

Unconsciousness; with convulsions and black vomiting; and quiet, except during tetanic spasms, with opisthotonos; and quiet alternating with restlessness; and frequent change of position, often drew her legs up against abdomen, *apathy*, pupils insensible, pulse small, thready, inspiration short, expiration long and stertorous, heart gradually became weak, death; sudden, with screams, attempts to escape, biting and sobbing by paroxysms, then quiet for some time.

Clinical.—General mental and physical exhaustion, with trembling of the limbs and vertigo. Generally indicated in brain fag. Softening of the brain, especially with vertigo, stupidity, slow answering, constant tired feeling. Brain fag and feeling of coldness in the cerebellum. Insanity, especially of the form in which there is an exaggerated idea of one's own importance, of his grandeur or of his riches. Delirium, as above, especially with fever of a low type.

Head.—Turned alternately to r. and l., and eyes fixed. Stitches in evening; S. in different parts, or throbbing pain; in various parts, < evening; back and forth in brain; tearing, in various parts. Tearing, < above r. eye. Pinching. Intermittent digging, > cool air, with burrowing and with dulness extending more towards r. side and towards root of nose.

Aching; all day, with vertigo; in morning, with heat of head; in morning, with bad humor; every morning on waking, < motion, or a confusion, with jerking or tearing in head; in morning on beginning to walk, renewed by any motion; in morning when sitting still, with pressure in eyes and sleepiness; from morning till noon; in afternoon, also with the fever; in evening when reflecting; in evening as soon as he lay down; in evening, with stitches in temples; in evening, < quiet; at night, with weight in abdomen, nervousness and erections; before rising; before rising, > rising and eating; on rising from lying, with vertigo; when lying, with nausea, then vertigo; after dinner; after sailing; on riding; after writing; when reflecting; from mental application; from vexation; in open air, from stooping; when jarred, with soreness; < towards evening and by motion; < slightest motion, > quiet and gentle pressure; > lying quietly and partly sleeping, returning after rising and moving about, with dizziness, disinclination and inability to work, especially mentally, sleepiness, feeling as if there were no firmness in head and sore pain in places on touch; > walking in open air after dinner (except confusion and stoppage of ears), returned in a warm room; with heat of head; with the fever; with feeling as if he had not slept enough (Nux v.); with nausea, eructations and accumulation of water in mouth; with vertigo so that he could not hold head up well and could not see well, < turning head, when it extended into face, > leaning it forward, with accumulation of water in mouth, general prostration and sickly look, the symptoms only somewhat > sleep, then an irregular circle in middle of forehead, with a warm, red, swollen border, the redness > pressure but returning (eczema erythematosum), cold water and cold air caused smarting in the diseased part of skin; extending to occiput, with loose sensation in brain on stooping and rising again; as from too much study, > thinking, with vertigo; as after a night of revelling; in various places, as from pimples under skin; here and there, changing to pain as if surface of brain were bruised; bruised, in brain in afternoon, > sleep at night; as if it would burst from 6 A.M. till after lying down in evening; drawing, in morning, changing towards noon to vertigo, with flickering before eyes, > eating, returning about 2 P.M., with excited circulation, liveliness and excitement, in the evening exhaustion; burning, externally, with external heat in it, loss of appetite and lying down.

Anxiety, > standing, with heat in it and with red, hot hands. Constriction every other day. Fulness; with stoppage of ears, and on swallowing diminished hearing; in brain, not as if filled with blood. **Dulness**; in morning after rising; in morning, with heaviness and weakness of it; in forenoon, < frontal sinuses, after dinner stupefaction and vertigo so that she must lie down, with general feebleness and cramps in hollows of knees; after eating; after dinner; during menses, with general exhaustion so that she fell asleep when reading; < at noon, > repeated washing of face with cold water; > open air; > washing with cold water, cold air or motion, < sitting and stooping, with symptoms of coryza; with heaviness and sensation as if she would have apoplexy; *heavy, after eating;* as from insufficient sleep; as in impending coryza.

Throbbing; in morning on waking; when lying; after ascending stairs; from laughing, stepping hard or stretching limbs, < after long sitting. Vibration on talking loudly. Movements as from a foreign substance, with heat in it. Jerking internally, < during a difficult stool. Tingling; almost all day, with humming. Tickling. Uneasiness in forenoon. *Weakness, so that she could not endure the sound of a piano.*

Heaviness; > open air, with vertigo; < r. side, with dulness of head and tension of cheeks as from too much blood; and he saw as through a veil; extending to eyeballs, as if head were drawn forward by a weight, transiently > smelling spirits of wine and by shaking head, < mental work, with fulness and heaviness of face as if too full of blood, as after too intense study, and with drawing in l. side of occiput when the headache was at the worst. *Stupid feeling;* painful, in morning on waking. Numbness when sitting, vertigo on least change of position. Sensation as if brain stiffened on remaining in open air. Lightness. *Rush of blood;* towards evening; when sitting, with burning and redness of face. Discomfort in a warm room as from too much blood. Feels freer in open air. Symptoms > moving about.

Vertigo; *every morning; in morning on rising,* **with heaviness and pain in head as if he had been lying with the head too low,** with inability to collect his senses; in morning after rising; in morning after waking; after breakfast; in morning and after dinner, followed by nausea, pressure downward in middle of brain, stupefaction and sensation as if he would fall, in afternoon nausea, with heartburn, red face, sensation as if something were seated in throat, sadness and weeping, in evening misty vision and itching of eyelids; in forenoon *when walking everything turned around with her* and she staggered; in forenoon, if she turned herself once she did not know where she was, the same after stooping; at noon; in evening; in evening when walking; in evening after supper and after a short walk, < quiet, > violent exercise; in evening after eating, objects seem partly invisible, with flickering zigzags and rings before eyes, head seems turned around, he does not know whether he is really sitting in the chair; in evening in bed; in evening in bed, obliging her to rise, then diarrhœa four times, with shaking chill, then heat and sweat; on waking at 10 P.M., with nausea; **on rising from lying** (Pic. ac.); *on rising, with roaring in ears; on rising from a seat;* on moving; after eating; *threatened when eating;* after dinner; after dinner, < lying; when lying on face; on suddenly turning and raising head; on stooping, with chilliness and nausea; after a second stool, with faint feeling; on closing eyes; on entering a warm room from the open air, with stupefaction of head; when pressing forehead or when lying, > sitting up; < *looking up and turning around quickly;* with trembling; with exhaustion; with blackness before eyes; with pain in r. mastoid region; with headache and salivation; with headache, shivering, chill, without thirst, alternating heat in head, shivering and general discomfort; with nausea, then sour, bilious vomiting towards evening, with coldness and numbness of hands, afterwards of feet, with cold sweat on forehead, after repeated vomiting two natural stools within two hours, the nausea and coldness > lying; then lightness of head, < afternoon; **like a pressing downward of forepart of head,** *in morning constantly increasing,* lasting till evening, > open air, with faintish nausea, and on stooping blackness before eyes, with sneezing; *several times a day,* so that she staggered against people when walking; *as if all the blood rushed to the head,* in evening on turning over in bed; as if his chair were higher than usual and he were looking downward, in afternoon, then hypochondriac mood till 9 P.M. with sleepiness and weakness; as if it turned him around, he found himself standing with outstretched arms, as if he had attempted to take hold of something.

Forehead.—Sticking through F. and temples, with distracting pain; S. during menses, the eyes close and she desires to lie down; extending to vertex, with hammering; intermittent; in F., vertex and side of head, at times burning, extending into l. side of occiput and into temples, after dinner or in morning, < sitting, > rubbing, with sensation as if hair were pulled or as if head would burst. Tearing; as from a blow, in the flesh of outer and upper part of r. side, with soreness when grasped. Sudden cutting over l. eye. Sharp pain; over eyes; over l. eye; in a shock, in eminence. Shock of pain in r. eminence. Pain; above eyes; over and around r. eye; in l. eminence; *above eyes* from morning till night, with burrowing in vertex; in evening; deep in r. side of F. and parietal bone in evening, with ill humor; above eyes at night; *on waking, with heat in head and disinclination to rise or move about;* over l. eye during breakfast; after breakfast and after walking in open air, < r. side, < till 10 A.M.; in eminences after mental exertion, with heat in face and head; between eyes, > after dinner but returning and lasting till evening, with stupefaction; < walking; < bending forward; < r. side, > eating; > *cold air;* with heat; with fulness in ears; above l. eye, with floating spots before vision; above eyes, waking her every morning, > rising; *extending to root of nose and upper lids, < turning head or any violent motion, with vertigo; in sinciput, extending towards root of nose;* extending from r. side of sinciput to above eye; *extending into eyes as if they would be pressed out; burning P.;* burning at times, with nausea; periodic, in sinciput, < l. side, < afternoon and evening, with stitches; crawling; drawing, in bone of l. side, with heat in it; throbbing, over eyes; periodic jerking-throbbing, in root of nose every day about 9 A.M., also extending into nose and eyes, < about noon, when she vomited. Jerks as if pieces of lead shook about in brain. Pressure outward, rather external, above eyes. Tension, and in face. Fulness after coitus, with throbbing. Dulness; > open air and wrinkling forehead, returning in the house, < stooping, with heaviness, the head falls forward. Numbness, and of vertex.

Temples.—Swelling of r. bone and upper jaw. Jerking in upper part of l. after dinner, then drawing to side of forehead. Sticking in r. in evening; S., with cramplike drawing beneath vertex. Tearing transiently > then < pressure; T., with vertigo in sinciput and throbbing and stitches on vertex. Neuralgia from l. to occiput at 10 A.M. Shock of pain in r. on coming into bright light from a dark room; sharp S. in l. when bending over writing. Pain; in r. in morning on waking, < motion, especially stooping, > open air; towards evening, > during the night; with fulness; intermittent, in r.; alternately in T. and vertex, with fulness in brain, but not like orgasm of blood; *throbbing;* drawing. Numbness, and in vertex.

Vertex.—Stitches. Tearing extending to zygoma in afternoon when sitting. Pain here and there on surface of brain; *stupefying P.;* as if congested; spasmodic contractive, in afternoon and evening; throbbing, < chewing, with pain on touch. Throbbing, and on l. side of head, < occiput. Tension in upper part of head.

Sensitiveness externally, with jerking as if the hair were pulled. Dulness; then nausea and empty belching. Numbness in upper half of head.

Sides.—Stitches; extending towards root of nose and to ball of r. hand; in r. half of brain, extending outward towards r. parietal eminence. Tearing in r., extending upward in evening, when sitting; T. in upper part of r. as if pulled by the hair, when sitting. Pain; in r. from mental application; > walking in open air; cold, cramplike, in l.; as from pressure in front of ears. Drawing pain in r. side, deep in cheek-bone, frontal, temporal and parietal bones; in a spot in r. in evening; now r., now l., with dulness; tearing, in evening, < night, with pain of hair on touch. Pulsating pain deep in r. side of brain in evening. Throbbing in r. parietal bone in evening, with gnawing. Soreness of r.

Occiput.—Stiches; in side; then pressure in it, then throbbing in forehead. Pain; in bone of side; in protuberance; in O. and l. side of head from 3 till 6 P.M.; with fever and flushed face; in O. and nape, with stiffness; in shocks in O. and cervical muscles after working with the microscope. Pulsation; on rising. Heaviness; and in nape.

Scalp.—*Hair falls out* (Sep.); *and the roots seem dry. Bald spot above ear. Much dandruff* (Lyc.). *Itching pimples*, painful on touch. Itching scabs. The eruption smarts and bites, itches but little. Boring in r. side when sitting, with throbbing. Bruised pain, < vertex, < pressure. Soreness on vertex, < pressure. *Itching.*

Clinical.—The brain always feels tired, as if he could not get it rested. Neuralgia of the brain, feeling of a rush of blood to the head, general aggravation after washing. Shocks in the head, following a mental strain. Falling of the hair in circumscribed spots. Sensation of heavy pressure on the top of the head. Brain fag and feeling of coldness in the cerebellum. Stiffness in the brain, sensation of impending paralysis in the brain. Exostosis of the skull, with violent tearing pains at night, swollen glands, faintness, emaciation, etc.

Eyes.—*Sunken. Swelling. Surrounded by blue rings;* with weakness of them; with general sickly look. *Inflammation;* with stitches; of r., with weakness of l.; of r., with redness, swelling, agglutination and burning pain; of r., with heat and with itching at inner canthus, aching around and in the eye. Redness of white, with itching, and smarting, and burning smarting lachrymation. Yellow color of the white. Dull and expressionless. Heavy look.

Sticking behind E.; sticking and dryness; with pressure, dimness and weakness; in l., with a stye on lower lid. Burrowing. Pain; when reading; after writing; of r. after reading and working with the microscope, with heat in it; < light; deep-seated; in a shock in l.; as from sand; as from sand under upper lids; burning, in and about it. Intermittent burning during the day. Tension. R. feels too large. Dryness; in morning on waking. Rush of blood, he is sensible of the ball. Heaviness like sleepiness. Stiffness, with lachrymation. Biting in l.; B. when reading, with dryness. Itching; of l., > rubbing. Burning; in l., with dryness; in r. after being in open air, with dryness, pupil slightly contracted, l. pupil dilated about twice the size of r.

Lachrymation; in morning when at work, with dimness of eyes; of r. in evening, with biting mucus in it; in a warm room; when reading, with dimness of eyes; *in open air;* of r. eye when walking in sunlight, had to keep it shut. Balls, yellow; lower half yellow; redness of inner side, < near corneal margin, < r. eye; sticking extending into r. in afternoon when sitting, with tearing; darting pain; pain as if pressed, < looking; burning; heat in l., with throbbing aching in it and aching over eye. *Pupils dilated;* and sluggish; and insensible; and he did not perceive near objects; *contracted;* sluggish.

Lids.—Closed, and pupils dilated and insensible. *Swelling; and about eyes;* of l., with pain in orbit on touch; of r. upper, with itching and pressure; gaseous, of r. upper. Agglutination in morning on waking; in morning, with burning and sticking in eyes and dim vision; in morning, with suppuration and lachrymation during the day; of inner canthi in morning; on waking; from lachrymation. *Twitching of l. lids and external canthus;* of muscles beneath r. eye. Sticking in inner canthi, < open air in morning. Pain in upper; P. in margins. Feeling as if a stye were coming on l. lower. Pressure. Feeling in r. as if the edge had been grazed. *Frequent itching* during the day. Biting in r. external canthus. Burning of upper.

Conjunctiva yellow; dirty yellow; red, and feeling as if something were in the eye. Orbit, tearing in lower margin as if the flesh would be torn loose; pain; flashes of pain in upper part; pressure inward above margin of l. eye after dinner; tickling in periosteum.

Vision.—*Dim; for distant objects,* **sees better by shading the eyes with the hand;** *sees more distinctly in morning, in the twilight, than during the day;* and dreamy, as if objects passed to and fro before eyes. **Of a green halo about candle-light in evening. Of black floating points;** of black floating spots after eating. *As if a black veil were before r. eye.* Of dark objects and spots. *Flickering, with roaring in head.* Trembling of objects in morning on waking. *Of sparks in the dark.* Dazzling, inability to thread a needle. Dread of sunlight; of candle-light in evening. Short. Weak; in morning on waking, > rising; and unsteady. Inclination to look with only one eye. *Eyes give out when reading.* Blinded by daylight. Lost; in evening; at times; when he sat up, but when lying he sees a feeble ray of light; suddenly, and sensation of a gray covering before eyes.

Clinical.—Paroxysms of night-blindness, a sensation as if everything were covered with a gray mist or veil, especially after sexual excesses. Cataract; a great many cases have been arrested; sometimes it seems to be indicated by a disturbance of vision in which the letters look red when reading, the general condition of the patient sufficing to indicate the remedy. Numerous lesions of the retina and optic nerve, photopsies, chromotopsies, halo around the light, red appearance of objects, flashes of light before the eyes, etc. Muscular asthenopia, dull pain deep in the eyes after reading. Retinitis albuminurica. Glaucoma and detachment of the retina. Myopia. Retinal apoplexy. Lachrymal fistula.

Ears.—Swelling of concha. R. red and hot, l. pale and cool. Moisture within. Discharge of pure blood. Sticking; in r.; in r. lobule; r. external meatus; through E. and teeth at night; with pimples; in E. and in head around it, with tearing; sudden, in l., then roaring, and difficult hearing, then yellowish discharge, hearing momentarily > pressure; jerking, from l. into lobule when sitting. Tearing in r.; beneath r.; in r. in forenoon when sitting; beneath r. when sitting, > rubbing. *Aching;* in a warm room; in r. mastoid process; in outer at night, waking him; in a shock back of l.; in lobule of r. as from pressure with the hand, > evening, with sensitiveness so that she could not tolerate a cloth upon it; drawing, in lobules; acute drawing; burning sore. Pulsation in r. after rapid walking; sticking P. behind, in lobule. Jerking in l. Dry sensation. *Tickling*, as if a veil were over them. *Itching within.* Sensation in r. as if air had been blown up Eustachian tube. L. Eustachian tube occluded. *Feeling as if something were in front of them; in front of r. at times.* R. stuffed up internally.

Hearing difficult; when walking in wind; with feeling of a foreign body in ear. Hearing lost. *Re-echoing of his own and others' words; of every tone that is spoken distinctly in the same pitch; loud, in morning. Ringing;* in l., with noises; with roaring and buzzing, impairing hearing; that at times reminded her of lovely melodies. Singing, < lying. Whizzing. *Roaring;* in r.; < sitting. Rumbling. Noises.

Clinical.—Deafness, with re-echoing of one's own voice. Nervous deafness.

Nose.—**Swelling, painful to touch** (Rhus t.); *S. of bones; S., with coryza. Chronic inflammation of mucous membrane*, **nose swollen and dry, cannot draw air through it**; *internal inflammation, with dry sensation* **and slow bleeding**. *Polypus. Ulceration of nostrils.* Vesicles in r. nostril, burning on touch. Dark redness of one wing, with smarting on touch. Boring into nostrils till blood comes.

Pain in forenoon; P. in bridge; as in coryza; *sore, in nostril, even on touch. Soreness of Schneiderian and mucous membranes, with bloody scabs on margins of nostrils.* Raw sensation, < breathing through it. Sensation as before coryza, > sneezing; sensation of coryza, < upper part of l. side, with fulness, with loose mucus. Sensation as if water dropped from it. Frequent desire to blow it. Crawling, changing to scraping when speaking. Itching; in l. nostril in morning; and pimples; and bleeding after rubbing. Itching, tickling in and on N.; after dinner. Burning in r. nostril extending above and around r. eye during dinner. *Dryness;* at night, with heat; *with sensation as if it would be stuck together. Fulness. Stoppage;* now of r., now of l. nostril; every morning; in evening in the house, with sneezing; at night, with difficult breathing, waking him; *with dulness of head as before coryza;* with pain extending to middle of forehead; of r. nostril, with passage of mucus through posterior nares; of r. nostril, with seeming dryness, but suddenly clear, watery mucus runs down to point of nose.

Sneezing; in morning, with dread of it on account of pain in throat as if something would be torn out; evenings, without coryza; after dinner; with irritation of r. nostril; with watering of nose; with rumbling in l. flank; then stoppage; violent, towards evening, with dulness of head and heaviness of limbs; spasmodic, with headache, distortion of limbs and constriction of chest; ineffectual efforts to sneeze and to eructate.

Takes cold in head easily. *Coryza;* during the morning; in evening; after a walk; < open air and entering a warm room from a cool one; *with inflammation of throat and dulness of head;* with hoarseness; with sneezing and pain in sides of head; with heat in head; with bronchial catarrh; serous; sudden, disappearing suddenly; *stopped; alternately fluent and stopped.* Fluent coryza; with chilliness; with dulness of head, loss of appetite and general sick feeling; with stoppage of nose; from one nostril, stopped in the other; from r. nostril soon after getting up, l. stopped; from r. nostril. Discharge of mucus without coryza; *D. of bloody mucus; purulent mucus and blood on blowing; yellow mucus and blood in morning on blowing; greenish yellow;* two greenish clinkers from r. nostril; membranous clots; thick, yellow, from l. nostril; thick, yellow, from r., with thin from l.; of water in open air.

Blowing out of blood. *Bleeding* (Ham., Sec. c.); in evening; *with sweat;* < during stool. *Smell acute, with the headache;* acute, especially for offensive odors; smell of the drug was constantly with him; lost.

Clinical.—Nasal polypus, bleeding profusely. Chronic nasal catarrh, with green, bloody mucus. Caries of the nasal bones and of the jaw. Fanlike motion of wings of nose (Lyc.).

Face.—*Redness;* of cheek; in morning, < afternoon and next day, in afternoon bluish-red, except in middle, a colorless band from highest point of forehead to chin, next day the bluish-red color had changed to a cyanotic hue, the median line remaining colorless; almost bluish, in cheeks at 8 A.M., without heat; frequent, livid, in l. cheek; alternating with pallor; greenish. *Pale; in evening and sickly; and yellow; and puffy; and sunken;* and sickly; and cool; suddenly, with chilliness, colic and headache. *Yellow.* Of the color of old parchment. Lead-colored.

Swelling; of cheek and gum; on the side on which he was lying; of r. cheek, corresponding to three carious upper teeth; of cheek, next day harder, painful and extending over l. side of throat. *Sunken; and earthy.* Pinched; and stupid. *Expression of weakness;* of pain; of anxiety; peritonitic; bewildered; sleepy. Twitching of cheeks; in l. malar-bone, > rubbing. Features fixed, anxious; fixed, with expression of sadness, languor and wandering of mind.

Sticking in l. cheek. *Tearing;* in malar-bone; in bones of F. and temples, < till 8 P.M. Pain in front of l. ear; P. in bones; in malar and maxillary bones and in teeth, < chewing, swallowing food and on going from a cold into a warm room. Burning smarting, as after being in cold, sharp air. Tension in skin; in malar-bones as if they would be forced towards each other, > rubbing. Rush of blood in open air, with distended feeling.

Jaws.—Lower denuded of soft parts, grayish, rough, rugous and covered with fetid suppuration. Glandular swelling of articulation. Swelling on r. side of lower, with toothache, the pain > extracting teeth, but the swelling increased till an opening formed on under side of jaw, with discharge of pus, lower jaw necrosed on r. side and partly on l., jaw painful and side of face swollen, the discharge was partly through mouth, mastication difficult and painful. Swelling where a tooth had been extracted, extending over whole bone, with pain in it, sleeplessness, emaciation, sick look, mouth pursed up into a round aperture from protrusion of the enlarged jaw, fistulous openings, jaw dead, condyles imbedded in soft tissue, fetid discharge around bone, < near condyles, outside of cheeks about masseteric regions thick, teeth all gone and jaw appeared like an edentulated cranium. Red swelling on under part of chin, quickly extending to eyes, pale and doughy except on chin, on the original swelling on chin a group of vesicles, with a thin, turbid discharge, then forming an ulcer, the parts beneath disorganized into a thin, discolored, offensive, purulent mass, with disagreeable odor from mouth, gums and teeth, < incisors, loose from salivation, with toothache and headache, the ulcer destroyed the soft parts to the bone and pieces of bone detached themselves. Inflammatory swelling of gum and soft parts of mouth, extending over face and neck, with masses of osteophyte of varying extent and thickness about jaw, in the second stage teeth black, gum recedes, the osteophytes suppurate, jaw denuded, rough and blackish or grayish-green, teeth fall out, pain in face and head, disturbance of digestion, sleeplessness, fever, salivation, fistulous burrowing of matter in muscles and integuments of face, which becomes erysipelatous, then exfoliation of bone, sometimes extension of necrosis to all bones of skull, and death with hectic fever. Abscess in upper jaw, which left it carious. *Necrosis of lower;* of r. upper; with erysipelas; with swelling of face and neck; with soundness of all teeth; of l. upper, with hectic fever, sleeplessness and loss of appetite; after extraction of a r. lower carious molar, with indurated swelling of face, < r. side and about chin, on r. side of neck three fistulous openings surrounded by flabby granulations and exuding fetid pus, offensive odor from mouth, constant dribbling of saliva and pus, gums spongy on margins, indurated at sides, jaws could not be parted enough to introduce finger easily, examination painful. *Lower jaw affected in nine cases out of ten,* first tensive pain in teeth, then looseness of teeth and discharge of matter between gum and teeth, if now the teeth be drawn the swelling and pain increase and involve the whole half of jaw, usually the disease progresses slowly and irregularly, with transient periods of improvement, soft parts covering jaws, cheeks and sides of mouth swollen and painful, one tooth after another becomes loose, pus discharged on pressure upon gum, pus often discharges externally through cheek, skin of margin of lower jaw red, soft, loose, at last infiltrated, from this infiltration discharge of matter that seems to come from alveolar process, when the opening is probed denuded bone is found, the periosteum that has been loosened from the bone has a new deposit of bone on its inner surface, so that the sound passes between two surfaces of bone, the old bone and the new growth, the denuded bone decays and is discharged with the matter, also fever, emaciation, swallowing difficult, digestion suffers from the mixture of offensive matter with the food, sleep only by means of Morphia, and the patient gradually sinks with hectic and exhaustion, **often tuberculosis develops during the prostration, at times also lobular pneumonia, ending in gangrene of the lung and pyæmia.** Sticking in middle of l. lower, extending through cheek and eye to forehead. Tearing in evening when lying, > eating and moving jaw; T. in r. lower, extending backward from mental foramen; in lower, extending towards chin, with pressure and drawing. Sharp pain in middle of l., with difficulty in chewing. Pain in lower, then necrosis; P. in antrum of r. upper; in r. upper, then swelling and abscess of gums, teeth decayed rapidly and were removed, but the swelling increased again and extended to cheek and part of neck, then necrosis of upper jaw; in l. upper, with swelling of upper lip, abscesses in mouth, discharge of matter between teeth, pain temporarily > removing molars, then it increased, gum was swollen so that mouth could scarcely be opened, and bone denuded. Jerking in lower, almost like toothache. Drawing in lower. Sore spot at l. articulation with malar-bone. Difficulty in opening. Trismus.

Lips.—Dark. Blue. Livid. Pale. *Swelling;* of upper every morning. Eruption on red, at times with stitches. Tetter in l. corner, with cutting and sticking. *Crack in middle of lower.* Denuded and hot. Papules in r. corner. Pustules in corners. Ulcers in corners; painful, on inner surface of lower. Painful blister filled with lymph on inner surface of lower. Burning stitches on margin of upper when sitting. Heat. Burning pain on red of lower, with white blisters inside. *Dryness;* all day; and of palate, without thirst. Itching of upper, with pain after rubbing. Numbness of r. side of upper, and of tip of tongue.

Clinical.—Necrosis of the lower jaw; with destruction of the gums, red, dry stripe through the centre of the tongue.

Mouth.—Teeth. Gray. Sordes. Sudden bleeding of upper molars. Discharge from all sockets; purulent D. from sockets. Looseness; of lower; of lower incisors; of last r. upper molar, with sensitiveness and elongated sensation. Blunt. Feel smooth when biting, as if they had been rubbed with soap or fat. Gnashing as from spasm. Carious; and painful, swelling about l. lower jaw, with pain in the bone extending to different parts of head and face, the remaining incisors loose, l. gum swollen and spongy, on pressure fetid pus escapes from the previous site of an extracted tooth, a probe passed into these openings strikes on the bare bone, pulse quick and feeble, general weakness, face puffy and pallid, sleep disturbed by pain in jaws and joints, r. half of face soon affected like l., jaw soon denuded, and fetid suppuration. Second l. upper molar carious and painful, after it was removed the wound always remained open, afterwards swelling of l. upper gum, extending partly over roof of mouth, discharge of pus from alveolus and from l. nostril, other teeth loose and painful, and were extracted, l. cheek swollen, pieces of dead bone were removed from jaw, antrum open, discharge semi-purulent, offensive. Sticking in upper incisors, with swelling of upper lip. Tearing in r. upper molars; T. every day, evening or morning, < open air or after entering house; in a l. lower cavity, > pressure; in a l. molar, with boring; in molars, extending to zygomatic arch when sitting, > rubbing; in r. upper molars, at times shooting, often returning, always > pressure; sticking, in roots of several r. upper in evening, > pressure; jerking, in roots of r. upper. Boring in a r. molar. Boring burning, < cold or warmth or chewing, at times the pain becomes dull, like a numbness, at times teeth are loose. Twitching in decayed T.; in hollow T. on opening mouth and if food gets into them, with sensitiveness to touch of tongue; throbbing, in open air, with sticking in them. Gnawing in a l. lower molar; G. in morning and evening in bed, with boring. *Aching;* in l. lower; l. upper molars; in two lower molars in morning, > rising; in evening in bed; at night in bed, > rising; on walking in open air; on becoming heated; when pressed; on eating candy; during menses, beginning when eating; in l. molars on violently blowing nose, ending with chattering of teeth, then heat in cheeks; in a hollow T., < warmth of bed; in l., then painful swelling of throat and white blisters in mouth; in r. lower, afterwards extending over cheek to temple and neck, with rigors, swelling of gums and cheeks, erysipelatous redness of cheeks, r. cheek tense towards eye, mouth, chin and neck, the tenderness greatest near lower jaw, throbbing, piercing pain deep-seated, at angle of jaw, radiating thence over adjacent soft parts, the diseased gum and inside of cheek swollen, tense, dark and tender, between angle of jaw and first molar fetid, phlegmonous pus oozed on pressure, some teeth carious, the swelling extended to soft palate, dysphagia, salivation, jaw almost immovable, teeth loose, suppuration ichorous and rusty, gums soft and livid, sinuses through which the probe reached the bone, which appeared in part rough, finally the bone appeared almost detached in soft parts and floating in a sanious fluid. Aching, with swelling of r. side of face, teeth drop out, general weakness, swelling below r. orbit, discharging white pus, later r. cheek swollen, at r. angle of lower jaw an opening discharging pus, through which a probe can be passed along the bare bone, anterior to this another aperture leading to dead bone, on opening mouth the lower jaw is dead, denuded and leaden grayish. Pain (tearing?) caused by inspiring cool air, by warm food and by touch. Sore pain. Throbbing pain in two r. upper molars; in l. hollow canine, from cold air in it. Drawing in a lower molar; in anterior incisors; in a lower molar in morning, then sticking in r. upper jaw, extending into ear; with burrowing; with cold hands and feet. Pressure forward upon l.

Gums.—*Inflammation. Bleeding; easily and separated from teeth;* and painful. Violet. Red, ulcerated line at junction with teeth. Swollen; above a bad tooth; of G. and cheeks before and after menstruation; with pain; with itching; and soft, with pain in upper teeth, swelling extending over cheek, teeth decayed, fell out, fetid suppuration from sockets, bone diseased. Loose, with a dirty brown coat, bleeding on touch; G. and teeth, < incisors, loose from salivation; loose over incisors, bleeding easily and feeling full, and every morning on rising incisors covered anteriorly with mucus and blood, gums of incisors and eye-teeth swollen, very red, margin grayish-yellow, looked as if suppurating, bled on pressure (posterior surface of gum normal). G. and tongue covered with tenacious, dirty yellow or blackish mucus. *Ulcers* after toothache; *with sensitiveness so that he could not eat;* with swelling of upper lip; bleeding, by a hollow molar. Sore pain; on inner side of upper incisors, with burning. Sensitiveness. Itching and throbbing.

Tongue.—*Chalky white;* pale and moist; tip white, with red papillæ. Red, denuded, papillæ prominent; *red in middle* and shining. Brownish-black. Yellowish posteriorly, with a red stripe anteriorly. *Coated;* in morning; with dark centre and red edges; *yellow;* yellow in middle third; dirty yellow, afterwards dry, fissured and coated dirty brown; white; white at night, with burning; dirty white, and mouth; white, with much slime; gray; black; blackish, and swallowing difficult and painful; two slimy streaks along it. *Swelling* about root; l. margin; *dryness and blackish along median line* (Verat. v.); and moist; and red; < l. side, with redness and vesicular swelling of papillæ. Ecchymoses, and on lips. Cracked; in centre from tip to base. Blisters an hour after eating; clear, burning on touch, on tip. Sticking, and in œsophagus; in tip. Prickling on frænum. Pain in frænum and in palate, preventing eating and talking. Soreness in r. side. Tip feels burnt; and raw. Burning; posteriorly on r. side; on tip; in tip, with sensation of eruption; in points anteriorly, with redness and bleeding; extending to soft palate; extending to larynx, where it provoked cough, afterwards extending into choanæ, causing an unnatural smell. *Dry;* on waking; *in middle,* and gray; *in middle, and brown; and white; and red; and black;* and red, rugose; and brownish-yellow; and coated brownish; with thirst; without thirst. Swollen sensation. Stuttering. *Speech difficult; and weak; and slow;* and slow, answers unsatisfactory and disconnected.

Mouth in General.—*Bloody erosions on inside of cheek.* Discharge of blood; of bloody fluid constantly from l. corner. Painful pimple on inside of cheek. Blisters that suppurate and burst on palate; painful B., with sore throat on swallowing, and thirst. Redness of inside of cheeks, with soreness. Slimy. Mucous membrane pale; M. membrane separated from palate and jaws; destroyed in patches. A stitch superiorly in palate after dinner. Rawness, with sore feeling in places. Scraping in palate and fauces during breakfast; S., with weariness after eating, walking affects him much, chilliness and bad humor. Aching from roof and pharynx to eyes and root of nose; in a spot on palate; burning; sore burning, in all soft parts of M. and face, extending through Eustachian tubes, with redness, swelling and feeling as if all the parts were covered with ulcers. Sensation as if palate would be denuded, it became wrinkled and painful. Burning and irritated by the air breathed; B. on palate; superiorly on palate. Burning and biting on palate. Itching on palate; prickling, posteriorly on palate as in catarrh. Tickling about palate. Soreness of roof, < l. side. Sensation of blood. *Dryness;* on palate in morning, with rawness; *on waking and in nose;* at night, with heat; with burning on tongue, compelling him to drink at night; *and in throat;* with tenderness; with glutinous sensation and thirst; with cold feet; alternating with moisture.

Salivation; with bitterness in throat; with sensation as if he could only swallow it; **watery;** sour, with nausea. *Saliva runs from mouth in sleep,* even when sitting; bitter, sour S.; S. like thick soap-suds, without bad taste; S. that tastes like foul water expectorated in evening. Breath phosphorescent; and what he vomited; offensive; cadaverous; garlicky; smelling of phosphorus; cool.

Taste.—*Bitter;* all day; in morning; in mouth and throat in evening, > lying down, with dryness, thirst and copious drinking of water; to breakfast; < after eating bread; with rawness in throat. *Sour; after milk;* < morning; with constant desire to swallow; with necessity to spit much; S. and insipid, in morning, > bread; metallic; salt, sweetish, with sensation as if saliva were collecting in mouth. Slimy; on rising; sweetish. Glutinous in morning on rising. Metallic in morning. Inky. Burnt to milk. Of the food after eating. Doughy to bread. Unnatural to bread, < morning. Right to nothing. Flat. Bad; on waking, with irritation in fauces. T. of the drug always with him.

Clinical.—Persistent hæmorrhage after drawing a tooth.

Toothache in washerwomen (the aggravation from having the hands in water is a marked indication for Phos. in many diseases). Dental fistula. Retarded development of speech in children. (Compare teeth with Mercury.)

Throat.—Parotid gland tense, < stooping, with pain on touch. Intermittent burning in parotid. Uvula and palate dark red. *Tonsils swollen;* and red; T., pharynx and uvula S. and red; l., and sore on pressure; l., impeding swallowing and motion of head. Mucus on waking, difficult to expectorate; M. in pharynx; from posterior nares, pharynx streaked with gray mucus and soft palate streaked with a dark brown coat; a lump of greenish-yellow M. from posterior nares; glairy discharge from posterior nares. Hawking constantly, < singing, with clearing of throat; from sensation of something dry in upper part of pharynx; ineffectual. Hawking of mucus in morning; *of cool, in morning;* gray, salt; tenacious; tenacious, white; sour; sour, transparent; yellowish-green clinkers; greenish, yellow, thick and viscid, from nose; grayish, blood-streaked, from posterior nares.

Sticking in pit; S. on swallowing; burning, in upper part of pharynx. Pain; in morning; on sneezing and yawning; in r. side at breakfast, > swallowing a few times; with swelling of tonsils, touch of which causes hacking cough; in pit, with nausea, sensation as if he could not vomit on account of this pain, with salivation; in pharynx, extending to r. ear; paroxysmal; burning, and in stomach; sore; sore, on coughing. Soreness; on side; during the day; all day, with hoarseness in morning; on r. side after breakfast till 11 A.M.; on swallowing, extending into posterior nares; posteriorly, with rawness and dark redness; with sensation as if grown together, and with pain in larynx on pressure; as from a cold; as from swelling of uvula.

Roughness. Rawness; after cough; on swallowing saliva after hawking; in damp weather; from sensation as if he had eaten something rancid; in pharynx, with sharp bitterness; provoking cough in morning. *Scraping;* in afternoon and evening; in afternoon, in open air, provoking cough; from heartburn. Sensation when coughing as if a piece of flesh would be raised. Sticking irritation to cough. Crawling which afterwards when talking changed to scratching. L. tonsil feels swollen and as if it would drop into throat. Oppression in pit. Constriction. Tightness. Fulness up into throat, taking away her appetite; in upper part of pharynx, as if the food stood high up and must be vomited, without nausea.

Dryness; in pharynx and fauces; in posterior nares; in morning, so that he could scarcely swallow, > eating; with sensation as if a flame of fire passed through me. Burning; in pharynx; after vomiting; and in nose. Irritation. Rancidity. Acidity, with scraping in pharynx. Sweet taste causing salivation. Swallowing difficult; towards noon, with pain; painful. Constant desire to swallow; with feeling as if something must go down from posterior nares.

Œsophagus.—Pain; and in pharynx; acute. Twinging in upper part. Heat. Sensation as if little lumps rolled up to throat, > swallowing, returning with nausea.

Stomach.—Appetite. *Ravenous; at night,* then weakness with heat and sweat, then coldness with chattering of teeth; > eructations, which only occurred after pressure; but eating caused nausea; but as soon as the least food entered the stomach vomiting, stool and micturition, afterwards a few mouthfuls satisfied the ravenous appetite, later could eat nothing but the most easily digested food, spices and pastry caused diarrhœa. *Longing for acids and spicy things.* Impaired and irregular. Diminished; for breakfast. Satisfied with a little in evening, immediately discomfort in pit of stomach, sleep restless, and no appetite next morning. Easily satisfied with tobacco. When eating I do not know whether I am satisfied or not, hence eat less than usual. *Lost;* in morning; in morning, with white tongue and fulness in pit of stomach; and after breakfast overloaded feeling; for dinner; for supper; and nausea after eating; and almost everything tastes alike, alcoholic drinks taste watery, and not the usual desire to smoke. Aversion to food; to cooked milk; to meat, especially fat; to the cigar, it causes emptiness in stomach and abdomen, > sleep.

Thirst; in morning after rising; at noon before eating; at night; during supper; after eating; < drinking water; but no relish for food; *unquenchable;* drink did not quench it, but caused drops of cold, clammy sweat as soon as it entered the stomach; and large quantities of water were taken at a draught; for small quantities, also frequently; burning; burning in afternoon; none.

Eructations.—After a meal, with waterbrash, nausea and running of water from mouth; with salivation and constriction in mouth, increasing to retching, with mucous expectoration, then eructations and yawning. **Of food,** without bad taste; of food after supper; *tasting of the food. Empty;* when eating; after eating, then of food, as if there had been no digestion; < eating; < drinking cold water, with nausea; with scalding in throat; of alliaceous odor and painful. Sour; in evening; after eating; after milk; of food; of S., bitter water. Bitter; of B. water; B., rancid water. Of water into throat, as after saltpetre; tasteless water. Waterbrash. Of fluid after breakfast, once of a sour taste. Of bile on stooping low. Of white, tasteless mucus. Loud. Foul; towards evening. Tasting like bad eggs; at night; with feeling as if diarrhœa would occur. Tasting of urine. Tasting like oranges. Of a scraping taste. Burning, into chest, when sitting, with anxiety and sweat on forehead and chest. Of the odor and taste of the drug, blue exhalation from mouth. Of the odor of olive oil and a rising up through nose, from which a white vapor issued. *Ineffectual; with pressure in chest;* with griping in abdomen; with feeling as if everything about hypochondria were filled with air that could not be sufficiently expelled; with ineffectual efforts to yawn; with nausea in pit of stomach.

Hiccough; during the day, even before eating; after eating; after dinner, causing sore pain in pit of stomach.

Nausea; all day and vomiting in the evening; in morning; in morning till breakfast; in forenoon when sitting; towards noon and in afternoon, > *drinking;* in afternoon, with salivation and frequent spitting; from 1 P.M. till going to bed at 11 P.M.; from 1 till 5 P.M., then pain in occiput, then fever till 9 P.M., with flushed face and thirst and loud emissions of flatus; in evening; in evening in bed, making her voice weak; in evening, then headache at night; at night; *at night, with eructations of food;* after breakfast; after eating a few spoonfuls; after eating, with uneasiness in stomach like efforts to vomit; after eating a few pears, with empty eructations; when smoking; on rising in bed, on appearance of menses, with sour vomiting, oppression of chest, cold sweat on forehead and vertigo when walking; < every odor; > *drinking water* (compare Bry.); > supper, with empty eructations that made the chest sore; > eructations, with pressure and fulness in stomach; with shivering; with flatulence; with constant inclination to eructate; with mucous expectoration without cough; with vertigo, oppression in pit of stomach and eructations tasting of phosphorus; with attacks of faintness and with pressure in pit of stomach so that she could tolerate no clothing; in pit of stomach, then shivering. Faintlike nausea from 8 till 9 A.M.; in forenoon and evening; late in evening, with vomiting; a few hours after dinner.

Retching; of watery fluid; ineffectual; ineffectual, > drinking cold water, with pain.

Vomiting.—In morning; at night; after eating; after milk; during the cough, < eating; when riding in a carriage; with diarrhœa; with pallor, collapse, scarcely perceptible pulse and falling of temperature; with internal spasms, unconsciousness, paralysis of arm (then death); with pain; with pain in epigastric region extending to hypochondria and afterwards to lumbar region; with pain, and death in about forty-eight hours, having been previously delivered of a stillborn child; with weakness, small, rapid pulse and pain in abdomen. **Vomiting of food** (Ferr., Lyc., Puls., Verat.); in evening; *violent*, colored grayish-yellow, during the first and second chills, and usually after the succeeding chills. **Of blood**; *nearly pure B.* towards evening; *mixed with dark acid matter; mixed with bile and mucus;* and reddish-brown; decomposed, black. Of bloody mucus. *Black; acid liquid*, a mixture of fatty substance and blood-corpuscles, mostly misshapen or reduced to amorphous molecules. *Like coffee-grounds* (Ars.). Brownish-black, metallic-tasting. Dark; grumous fluid, morning and evening. Dark brown liquid. Dark reddish-brown and thick. Greenish; blackish, at first tenacious, afterwards watery; yellowish-green fluid. Bilious; all night; violent; violent, in evening. Yellow masses; mucous, afterwards dark brown substances; afterwards blackish-brown, with pain in stomach. Dirty gray and mixed with mucous flakes, alternating with hiccough. Sour, mornings after stool, or retching; S. on coughing; brown liquid. *Offensive.* Violent; smelling of garlic, with similar eructations. Painful towards evening. Of mucus tasting of olive oil at night. Water, mucus, epithelium and portions of mucous membrane, later scanty, with clots of blood. Liquids ingested.

Distention; epigastric region; with movements; and abdomen retracted; flatulent, also with hunger. Inflammation; and of intestines, with gangrene, burning and cutting. Gastro-enteritis, lips red, tongue white, epigastric region painful to pressure and hard, abdomen tympanitic but painless, great thirst, respiration 40. Gastro-enteritis, cold, pale, as if dying, unconscious, sunk down in bed, cold, clammy sweat, here and there a waxy color, face almost leaden gray, with dark rings around mouth, mouth closed, lips blue, respiration retarded, short, difficult, heart's impulse weak, intermittent, radial pulse small, slow, irregular, now and then intermittent, epigastric region and abdomen distended, sensitive to touch, could scarcely bear the weight of her nightdress, so that she made constant automatic efforts to free herself from all clothing.

Sticking in epigastrium; in pit every day at 10 P.M., so that she could not get a breath, > eructations; in pit when coughing, so that she must press upon it, with raw pain in throat; above S., through abdomen, which then became large. Tearing in cardiac orifice during eructations. Cutting in epigastric region; lightning-like C. to umbilicus. Cramps; in evening on lying down. Spasmodic sensation before and after supper, it then extends into chest from both sides; S. sensation in pit and chest, with chilly trembling in them. Painful jerks up into throat, as from mucus, when sitting. *Cardialgia.* Griping at night, with twisting; constrictive G.; intermittent, in epigastric region; in epigastric region, extending to transverse colon, afterwards farther down on both sides of abdomen, with warmth, as from incarceration of flatus. *Sharp pressure; in pit with every cough.*

Pain; in epigastrium; in pit; in a spot, and in r. temple; *in morning on touch* and on walking; in morning in bed; *at noon a few hours after eating, with nausea and dulness of head; in evening; towards evening, and in abdomen, with painful vomiting and diarrhœa;* on coughing; after eating; an hour after dinner; after dinner, with tension in it and distention of abdomen; *at cardiac orifice, < swallowing bread, which seems to remain there;* in pit, < sitting; in epigastric region, with tension; with rapid pulse, restlessness and cool skin; then distention from 9 P.M. till midnight, with nausea, retching and eructations of gas; *gradually extending over abdomen, with vomiting, first of green, then of blackish substances;* encircling base of thorax like a girdle. Distended pain in morning; in evening, lasting till sleep. Bruised pain in epigastric region.

Sensitiveness to pressure; **in region of pylorus;** with tympanitic percussion-sound. *Epigastric region sensitive; in morning, < towards evening; to pressure; to pressure, with enlargement of liver; to pressure, with tension; to touch.* **Pressure as from a hard substance above pit,** *with coldness;* P. in and above pit, then also in sternum and on ribs, taking away the breath. *Heaviness; after eating; < pressure. Oppression in epigastrium;* in pit. Tightness in pit. Compression from both sides when sitting; C. in morning in bed, preceded by sweat. Constriction in pit and chest; C., with gnawing; tensive, with sourish eructations; griping, in epigastric region, with sensitiveness to pressure, afterwards the pain extended upward and downward, so that he was often obliged to bend forward, which caused pain in forehead, these pains > eating.

Drawing pain in pit, extending into chest. Drawing in pit; D. when riding in a carriage, with tension. Anxiety in epigastric and præcordial regions. Emptiness; in morning after rising, with uprising nausea; at pit, with weakness; without appetite. Pulsation beneath pit after eating. Stopped sensation in pit. Discomfort in epigastric region. Uneasiness. Sensation as if he had drunk much water. Digestion difficult. Disordered feeling at night; all day, and in evening sensation as if pressed together, < pressure. Acidity after eating; with pulsating pain in forehead. Coldness, at times alternating with warmth.

Burning; in pit; in epigastric region; in epigastric region, < deep pressure; with cold hands; with prickling and with eructations of whitish vapors through mouth and nose; with thirst, anxiety, facial convulsions, shivering, cold limbs, bright, watery eyes, pale lips, weak pulse, weakness (then death); in epigastric region and abdomen, extending into fauces. Heartburn; in morning and afternoon; after moderate eating of fat; after a glass of beer with a cigar; extending into throat.

Clinical.—Gastric ulcers. Vomiting of pregnancy. Hæmorrhage from stomach, temporarily > drinking cold water. A general gastric indication for Phos. is vomiting of the contents of the stomach, temporarily > cold drinks, but as soon as these become warm the vomiting is renewed. Burning fermentation in the stomach. Atonic dyspepsia. Chronic gastritis. Excruciating gastralgia, pains as from knives, or burning, or constricting, or associated with great external weight. Inflammation of the stomach, with swelling of the liver, vomiting of blood and mucus, yellow tongue, etc. Burning heat in stomach, extending to back, with faint, empty feeling in stomach and bowels. Although there is sometimes excessive thirst with the symptoms of inflammation of the stomach, yet generally the Phos. patient is not thirsty. Gastric troubles always < hot weather.

Abdomen.—*Distention;* at night, < after midnight, and pressed towards stomach; after eating; after eating, with anxious pressure; caused by moving flatus, with evacuation of a thin stool instead of flatus, next day bruised pain and moving of flatus, third day incarceration of flatus in r. side, with pain; fourth day incarceration of flatus in r. side, with griping; > coffee; with oppression of breath; with sensation as if food were not digested, sour belching, taste of coffee, etc.; hard; *tympanitic;* at times pressive, > motion, at times with difficult, deep respiration, or with bruised pain in small of back and abdomen on touch.

Retraction. *Tense;* and covered with cold, clammy sweat, and sensitive. Hardness on eating a little, with tension and with little appetite. *Rumbling;* in small intestines in morning after rising; at noon and in evening after eating, with twisting; after eating; < before and after supper, with emissions of flatus; and gurgling or sensation as if bubbles of air would burst, with inclination to eructate; but slow stool; painful; as before diarrhœa; at times extending towards sacral region, with moving about, dragging and gurgling. Movements; with griping about umbilicus, then stool at first consistent, then semi-liquid, accompanied and succeeded by burning in anus. Rising up to throat like flatulence, then eructations, when it went down.

Emission of flatus; during the day; after breakfast; easy, in evening, with desire for stool; odorless; loud; unsatisfactory, in evening after lying down; ineffectual efforts. Offensive flatus on rising; in afternoon and evening; with several loose stools; then hard, dark brown stool. Incarceration of flatus, with coldness of body and heat of face. Paralysis of intestines.

Sticking at noon, with pallor, chilliness and headache; S., > lying on abdomen, with sore pain; transversely through A.; extending into A. when sitting. Cutting; in evening before sleep; before stool; before diarrhœa; < evening; > stool; with urging to stool; waking at 1 A.M.; waking her at 3 A.M., > thin, forcible stool; starting from one point and flashing over whole abdomen, each C. having a separate starting point.

Griping; in morning, then sour-smelling diarrhœa, then tenesmus and burning, with erection; at 2 A.M., then thin stool, then burning in anus, all repeated at 5 A.M.; after dinner; > brown liquid stool, with movements in abdomen, then burning; with tenesmus; *then stool, with constriction in rectum,* two hours afterwards emission of much flatus, then another stool, then renewed constriction of anus; as before diarrhœa. Sharp pain; burning.

Pain; in morning before a hard stool; in morning after moving about, then diarrhœa; in evening; at night; on pressure; on touch; on change of position; in cold weather; during menses; before watery stool; < morning; > stool; > thin stool; > bending up and lying on r. side; with frequent ineffectual desire for stool; with diarrhœa; with emission of flatus, then thin, brownish stool; with shaking chill and moaning respiration; waking her at 4 A.M., with diarrhœa; jerking; burning; fugitive, and in chest; as if something burst; as before diarrhœa, intermittent, then on pressure inward above ilium sore pain; flatulent, < sides, as from incarceration of flatus here and there, with difficult, short, interrupted emissions of flatus.

Sore, but not tender to touch. Sensation as before diarrhœa. Constriction, with chilliness; intermittent C. Pressure upon small of back as from flatus, which is scantily emitted, with some relief. Weight at night, with flatulence. Uneasiness. **Emptiness and weak feeling** (Sep.); E. after emission of much flatus. *Weakness, and in back; so that she must lie down;* W. after a soft stool. **Coldness** (*Colch.*). Burning; when eating, and after an hour a soft stool.

Upper A.—Griping when walking, with cutting as from a purge. Pain; drawing, with soreness. Tension, even caused by every motion of trunk. Agreeable warmth. Coldness internally above umbilical region.

Hypochondria.—*Enlargement of spleen; with pain. Enlargement of liver;* with doughy and smooth feeling, lower margin obtuse; surface smooth, margins blunted; with pain; with pain on pressure; with distention and hardness of r. hypochondrium; towards the left, with pain in the region; with icterus; with icterus and disappearance of sweat; with dulness over it extending to above fifth ribs, the pain on pressure < during and after the chills, afterwards the dulness over liver was unnaturally small, and spleen enlarged. Liver became small, with meteorism, thin, colorless stools, next day furious delirium, with jaundice, albuminous urine, then sopor, frothing from mouth, rapid pulse, contracted pupils and death. Inflammation of mucous membrane of duodenum, which seemed to close bile-ducts and caused accumulation of bile in gall-bladder. *Incarceration of flatus, with oppression of chest.* Sticking in l.; hepatic region; even when sitting, then at times sensitiveness; in hepatic region on deep inspiration; in r. after dinner, then diarrhœa; in r. at times, with burning in skin, > rubbing, or sensation as if it were tightly adherent. Griping in a spot, < r., > rubbing; in l., extending towards epigastric region, when standing and sitting, then sensation of something living there. Pain; in l.; r.; liver; r. lobe of liver; at night; r. when walking; on pressure; *hepatic region on pressure,* also with diminished area of hepatic dulness; region of spleen on pressure; hepatic region on touch; r. on touch; in spleen and groins, < thirst; in l., with inability to stoop or lie on r. side. *Sensitiveness in hepatic region, < lying on r. side, with pain on touch. Painful pulsation in r.* (Compare above with Sulph. and Pod.).

Sides.—Distention of r. Colicky flatulence in r. Sticking in r.; in r. when sitting, with tearing in head. Cramp colic in r., afterwards extending towards back (also in r. testicle), extending upward in epigastric region, with sweat, groans and distortion of facial muscles. Griping in l., then in epigastric region. Constriction in l.

Umbilicus.—Fulness above U., with general discomfort. Tympanitic above U. Griping; below U., with movements and dragging, then urging as to diarrhœa, but a consistent stool was passed. Pain in region; below U. on touch; labor-like, in region and in back, so that the patient lay as in opisthotonos; paroxysmal, in region extending inward, with nausea, salivation and sensitiveness of pit of stomach to pressure.

Hypogastrium.—Swelling of inguinal glands. Hernia protrudes during a soft stool and is painful as if incarcerated on stooping, touching it or walking, even when lying on the side he dares not reduce it with the hand. Rumbling in place of a hernia, with gurgling. Incarceration of flatus when sitting and lying, it seems as if the abdomen were drawn inward, with discomfort. Jerking above genitals in morning in bed, with sticking; griping J. in afternoon, then emission of flatus; with drawing, as before menses. Sticking extending to perineum. Cutting in l. side extending across umbilicus, on inspiration when walking after dinner, with pain as from a tense swelling on pressure. Sharp pain above r. hip; in l. groin; in region of Poupart's ligament and in region of bladder. Pain; in l. groin; in morning before rising and before stool (after sweet cider), > diarrhœa, which was accompanied by rumbling; *in forenoon* and in evening after eating; at 10 P.M. on going to stool, with rumbling and urging, later light clay-colored stool, with flatus, pains lasted some time after stool; on touch; in place of a hernia during menses; extending from an inguinal hernia to stomach; in r. iliac region, as in diarrhœa; as from a swelling and injury above r. hip, but on touch bruised pain; as from soreness or inflammation, extending to pudenda, < touch, with weakness. Sore feeling. Sensitive spot in r. iliac region. Pressure, almost as if on bladder every morning on waking; waking him at night; cramplike P. low down, in genitals, in morning in bed. Dragging towards inguinal rings, with flatulent colic as if a hernia would occur. Burning constriction at night, as before menses (that had already stopped for several days). Tension above bladder. Uneasiness. Burning in colon.

Clinical.—Chronic enteritis, stools pasty and yellow. Chronic inflammation of the pancreas, with greasy stools, or stools like cooked sago. Diffuse hepatitis, with jaundice. Malignant jaundice, with sleepiness. Cirrhosis of the liver. Threatening suppuration of the liver, with hectic fever and night-sweats. It is generally found useful in the course of fatty degeneration of the liver and heart.

Rectum.—Spasm in morning in bed. *Sticking* when not at stool; before stool, with constriction. Tearing; and in genitals, even to sinking down. Cutting, < evening, and in anus. Pain above anus after slight exertion at stool. *Smarting during a stool that was not hard. Burning; in R. and anus after soft stool, with exhaustion.* Sensation in evening as if there were something in it that prevented stool, with a not hard stool. Seemed contracted and during and after a soft stool a sharp biting, sore pain extended into abdomen. Crawling during a soft stool, with itching. Cramplike dragging. *Urging; on rising;* in morning on rising; at night, partially waking him; after eating; *before a stool, which shot out as from a gun;* before a difficult soft stool; before a pasty stool; after stool; moving about, with pain; with thrill all over; frequent, ineffectual; but only forcible emission of flatus. Pressure, with the not hard stool; after stool. Insensibility, with paralysis of sphincter, and after each stool prolapsus ani.

Clinical.—Desire for stool whenever she lies on l. side.

Anus.—Hæmorrhoids protruding; protruding during stool, with burning pain on touch, sitting and walking; painful after stool; sore pain when sitting and lying, with sticking and pressure in them on rising; sticking itching during menses. *Hæmorrhage from abdomen.* Blood from A.; during emission of flatus; *pure B. during stool.* White, corrosive mucus from A. awhile after stool. *Stitches;* in l. side after dinner, with clawing; crawling, when walking. Pain as if body would be torn asunder, with cutting and movements in abdomen, constant, ineffectual desire for stool, heat in hands and anxiety, the pain > warm cloths. Soreness after stool; before and during a hard stool. Burning pain. Burning; after stool, with scratching in it and burning desire to urinate, and scanty urine. *Itching;* in evening, with tickling; in evening and after walking; when walking, > in the house; after walking in open air, with crawling; *and biting.*

Clinical.—Bleeding hæmorrhoids, a small stream of blood with every stool. Paralysis of the sphincter ani, the anus is always open (Sec. c., Apis).

Stool.—Watery; four times from 4 till 6 A.M.; waking him at 5 A.M., with empty eructations like rotten eggs, no pain and no control of sphincter, no appetite for breakfast; with urging and sick feeling; and dark, bloody; and dark, offensive, frequent, < afternoon, with pain before and after stool and between times. *Semi-fluid,* scanty, forcible; S., three times in morning.

Diarrhœa; at 4 A.M., with colic; twice at 6 A.M.; every morning on rising, with pain in abdomen and with heaviness and weakness in limbs; towards evening, then no stool for six days, then involuntary stool; in night; < morning and afternoon; > drinking coffee, with tenesmus in anus and rumbling in abdomen; with discharge of thread-worms; with colic and emission of flatus; *profuse;* dark, with pain before and after it; *bloody; containing mucous membrane and clots of blood;* bloody, fetid; dark, grumous; unsatisfactory, with burning in anus; frequent; infrequent; alternating with constipation.

Soft; with pressure and cutting in colon; **with lumps of white mucus;** and colorless; and green; and light-colored; *and clay-colored, offensive;* and large, yellowish-gray, streaked with blood (from piles), then scalding in anus; and small; and frequent, with colic; the last part with much florid blood. *Pasty; at an unusual time; and lumpy, light clay-colored, with urging and inactivity of rectum.*

Like scrapings of intestines, almost constant, with tenesmus, *involuntary on least motion,* after eight hours they changed to *mucus and mucus mixed with blood and slime, still involuntary,* afterwards periodical, **involuntary the moment that anything entered rectum,** later on going from a warm room into open air, always of a slight mouldy smell, for more than two months spices and pastry caused loose stools.

Constipation; with sensitiveness about l. Poupart's ligament and hardness low down in l. iliac region, afterwards almost dysentery of watery stools **mixed with whitish-yellow and cheesy masses**, *and tenesmus;* for three days, then stool of blackish masses, seemingly of only inspissated blood; then bloody diarrhœa. Hard; only every second day; with cutting in anus; (secondary action); and covered with mucus, with some blood; in small lumps; and crumbly, like clay; and knotty, light yellowish-brown; and large; and large, dark brown and crumbling, then scalding in anus; **and small, dark;** *and small,* with urging and sharp pain in bowels; and sluggish; **and difficult,** *apparently from inactivity of rectum.* In little balls after urging. Crumbly (after emission of flatus), with stitches in rectum, then sensitiveness; C., at first, then consistent, then soft, with pressure. Claylike, only by injection; C. large, then darker, fluid.

Gray. Whitish-gray (Pod.). *Green.* Grayish-red. Greenish-blue. Black. Light brown. Dark brown; and small, slimy; and lumpy. Clay-colored, difficult. White, offensive. Almost colorless. Luminous. *Bloody;* and profuse; and frequent, with tenesmus; frequent, of bloody mucus or of fæcal masses mixed with blood, with desire for stool, then spasmodic tenesmus and burning pain in anus. Of offensive mucus. Feeling hot when passed. In small pieces, with pressure. **Involuntary**; and colorless; and dark, apparently containing coagulated blood. Urgent, then two teaspoonfuls of florid blood. Frequent. Twice daily. Irregular. Scanty, but frequent; S., then blood from anus. *Difficult. Sluggish.* Delayed.

Clinical.—Chronic diarrhœa, painless, worse in hot weather, stools fetid or containing particles like grains of tallow. Involuntary, undigested stools.

Urinary Organs.—Bladder. *Discharge of pure blood.* Empty in spite of copious drinks. Sticking from neck into penis in evening on falling asleep. Pain, and in kidneys. Spasmodic sensation in neck. (Severe pressure during menses, usually it occurred only the first day and was slight, with cutting and burning during micturition.) Urging; during the day; more when sitting than when walking; in neck of B., > evacuation of the first drops, later this pressure extended to meatus; afterwards incontinence of urine, < walking; constant, when standing, but only a few drops passed; sudden, in morning. Frequent desire; with scanty discharge; sudden. Ineffectual desire; with emptiness of bladder and sensitiveness over region of r. kidney; constant, later frequent passage of copious, scalding, high-colored urine of strong ammoniacal odor. Loss of desire, even when bladder is full, but micturition without trouble.

Micturition.—Dribbling and burning; D. after urinating. Stops for a moment, with flatulent distention. Strangury, with ineffectual urging, the moment that micturition was accomplished the trouble began anew. Dysuria, with burning urine. Painful. Difficult; and burning; as from an impediment; on account of pain in hypogastrium, in morning in bed, preventing him from passing the last drops, soon urging again, then scanty micturition by drops. Frequent; in morning; in morning, though I had four watery stools after midnight; at night; *at night* of only a few drops of clayey urine; after drinking coffee; and increased; but little at a time. Involuntary; of a few drops when coughing; of reddish urine, if he does not obey the first call.

Urethra.—Moisture at orifice, as from prostatic fluid. Discharge of prostatic fluid during hard stool. Sensation as if prostatic fluid were at orifice, causing moisture when walking. Moisture in orifice, that afterwards became yellow and caused a yellow stain. Dribbling of fluid (not urine) during stool, after micturition, from friction of his clothes and when talking to a woman. Oozing of mucus while genitals were relaxed. Glairy mucus in orifice. Discharge of mucus on urinating the first time after a stool, with pain in perineum. Sticking; and in anus. Cutting on micturition, with bloody urine. Pain, < when urinating, and in penis; cramplike, and in upper part of scrotum. Drawing extending to meatus; D. and in penis, with occasional burning; sticking, in middle; sudden D. back and forth, extending to bladder, with constriction. Burning pain anteriorly during micturition; extending forward from scrotum, often when not urinating; sticking, provoking to micturition. *Burning; in evening, with desire to urinate;* when urinating; when urinating, with cutting. Discomfort in forepart. Biting near orifice, with smarting and with pale red swelling on r. side of apex of glans, beginning at upper surface and extending to within orifice of urethra, after micturition a drawing from meatus to membranous part of urethra. Itching in meatus; just back of meatus.

Urine.—*Copious;* before daybreak; when riding in a carriage; during the attacks of pain, and *watery, colorless;* and pale; and dark brown, smelling of garlic and sulphur; with copious sediment; with much urea, the etherial extract contained hippuric acid, parts insoluble in alcohol contained many urates, on ninth day contained creatin. Scanty; and dark; and dark, containing bile pigment; and red; and orange-colored, thick; and high-colored, odorous; and deep yellow, smelling like garlic; at times mixed with blood. Retained. Suppressed; with sensitiveness over region of r. kidney; and on attempting to pass catheter, burning and pain in region of bladder; afterwards almost black, turbid. **Hæmaturia** (Ter.); *with acute pain in region of kidneys and liver, and jaundice,* later H. returned after excitement, with profuse bloody vomiting. *Brown, with red, sandy sediment. Dark; and turbid;* at one time, at another light, often turbid, often a mucous sediment that disappeared on heating, at times acid, at others neutral. Dark yellow, with a gray pellicle; D. yellow, clear, frothy, nitric acid caused a sediment that formed slowly. Golden yellow, soon a whitish sediment. Red and turbid; R., depositing a sediment; R., smelling of sulphur, depositing a thick, copious, white, slimy sediment. Dark red, depositing a bright red sediment; D., with greenish-yellow foam; D., contained many free phosphates, with yellowish-green froth when shaken. Pale; and of strong odor; soon showing a cloud; forming a white line around side of vessel. As clear as water. Turbid; on standing; depositing a brick-red sediment; of strong ammoniacal odor, depositing a whitish-yellow sediment. Offensive; and acrid, smelling of violet root. Of the odor of violets. *Covered with iridescent fatty membrane.* Contained bile; bile pigment, exudative casts and epithelial cells. Much creatin. Sp. gr. high. *Sediment copious; white-wheyey S.; whitish; like white sand; white, flocculent;* yellow; dark.

Albuminous urine; and bloody; with acute, fatty degeneration of all viscera; and copious, acid, with bile; copious, sp. gr. diminished, with bile pigment, *many casts of fat drops*, triple phosphates at first were abundant, but gave place to abundant sediment of urates, urine dark and contained much bile pigment, hyaline cylinders, with here and there fat or fatty cells of kidney epithelium; copious, greenish yellow, with bile pigment, sp. gr. 1009; scanty, sp. gr. diminished; scanty, with epithelium, casts of tubes and a few blood-corpuscles; scanty, contained bile, loaded with salts; high-colored, frothy, sp. gr. increased, exudation cells, increase of coloring matter, sulphates and phosphates and decrease of chlorides; brown, with bile; dark brown, with bile, coloring matters, casts, fatty degenerated epithelium from kidneys and large cells from bladder; reddish-brown, with bile, and turbid; brownish-black, with pus-cells and blood-corpuscles, as brown as beer, with bile pigments, many urates, increase of uroxanthin, uric acid, phosphates and sulphates, diminution of urophan and urea, no chlorides, acid, with copious sediment; dark brown, with bile pigment, granulated casts, with fatty epithelium, acid, flocculent sediment; and contained biliphæin; evacuated by catheter, with bile, acid, turbid, light flocculent sediment; with hæmatin, constituents of bile, blood-corpuscles, cellular elements, epithelium, fibrous cylinders, leucin and tyrosin; with bile pigment, increase of extractive matters, small amount of urea and much lactic acid; with bile pigment, granular, fibrous casts, urea gradually disappeared, lactic acid copious; with numerous small polygonal and oval epithelial cells presenting the highest degree of fatty degeneration, no trace of nucleus or protoplasm, but closely compressed, generally large drops of fat partly concealing the borders of the cells, and abundant small drops of fat floating free.

Clinical. — Urine milky white. Diabetes, with phthisis. Bright's disease, especially when the urine contains fatty casts.

Sexual Organs.—Tearing as from a sore during or after a walk. *Irritation.* Relaxation, erections weak. Sensation in mons veneris as if a testicle had slipped up there. Glans, sticking; in region of frænum; in forepart after micturition; pain in tip; biting pain at close of micturition and afterwards; pruritus in evening. *Erections; day and night;* in evening, without desire; violent, in morning; *frequent and painful*, waking him; painful at night during coition; *ineffectual during coition; none.* Ulcer on prepuce. Pain in prepuce when urinating. Spermatic cord swollen, with pain in it and in testicle (during stool); drawing-tensive pain in S. cord; drawing in r. Pain in scrotum; in testicles; sharp, in r. testicle. Sensation as if one testicle were pushed upward and compressed. Drawing in testicles. Impotency. **Desire extreme**; *with feeble erections; afterwards disappeared and erectile power left him;* D. in forenoon; in evening; diminished; diminished, with too sudden ejaculations of semen during coition; gone. Aversion to coition (in a man). *Emissions; at night;* at night, with dream; about midnight during restless sleep, then better sleep; *soon after coition;* with confused dreams; without dreams; without erections; without excitement of fancy.

Female.—*Hyperæmia, the parietes of the vessels are lowered in their power of resistance by the fatty metamorphosis, and the hæmorrhages become more severe, often causing general anæmia.* Painful heat after emission of dark, turbid urine. Œdema of l. labia, then of both, then gangrenous slough and hæmorrhages. Pimples on margin of labiæ, with burning sticking. *Hæmorrhage. Discharge of blood between the menses;* scanty, the menses had been suppressed for five weeks; reddish D. in an old woman; fetid, bloody (after death the patient was found to be pregnant and the fœtus had become putrid). Whitish discharge in evening, with fever. *Leucorrhœa; acrid, causing soreness*, also after menstruation; milky; slimy in morning when walking; tenacious, instead of menses. Dragging towards pudenda and rectum as before menses, with ineffectual desire for stool. Spasmodic griping in uterus in evening, during and after stooping, with constriction. Pain in uterus and vagina, afterwards resembling labor-pains, and in back, < hypogastrium. Bearing down in uterus and bladder when walking, with pain and smarting. Constant sensation as if menses would occur. *Aversion to coition.*

Menstruation.—**Too early; and scanty**; and scanty, dark; and profuse; formerly very thick, now *bright red; too early, sudden, short, ceased on third morning, returned slightly in afternoon and lasted till next day;* M. that ceased a few days previously returned. *Delayed;* and profuse and long-lasting; and short, slight, ushered in by pain in abdomen and small of back. *Pale, with colic, nausea and diarrhœa.* Copious, black, viscous, coagulated, painful, at an unusual time. Scanty, with spasmodic pains in uterus and ovaries. Less profuse, came on with less pain, lasted only five days, in a subsequent proving came on almost unnoticed, *but lasted only two days.* Came on violently, lasted five days, offensive (in a woman 51 years of age, who not had menstruated for a year and a half). Came on with colic, pain in small of back, drawing in lower limbs, bruised feeling in all limbs, making her very sick and taking away all desire to eat or work.

Clinical.—Sexual excitement, with weakness, seminal emissions accompanying erotic dreams. Nymphomania; with sterility. Metrorrhagia, especially in nursing women. Menorrhagia followed by great weakness. Chronic inflammation of the uterus. Membranous dysmenorrhœa. Suppressed menstruation. Vicarious menstruation. Post-partum hæmorrhage. Anteversion, with ulceration of the cervix, profuse, acrid leucorrhœa, vagina filled with condylomata, cured.

Respiratory Organs.—**Rawness in larynx and trachea, with hacking cough and hawking** (Brom.). *Suffocative contraction in larynx and trachea at night after waking.* Irritation in larynx. **Hoarseness; in morning; and larynx seems coated; inability to speak aloud; so that he could not speak above a whisper. Voice husky; rough**; *almost lost, with prostration, it was difficult to answer questions* though the intellect was not impaired; broken on attempting to sing high. Frequent bronchitis, with exhausting purulent expectoration depending on bronchial blennorrhœa, with emphysema of lungs. Mucus in trachea. *Irritability in lower part of trachea,* **with suffocative pressure in upper part of chest.** Tickling in trachea waking her about midnight and causing dry cough.

Cough; in afternoon, *from irritation in trachea;* **from tickling in throat**; *from scratching in throat;* after dinner; after dinner, with soreness of throat; caused by cold air, which affects the chest much; < *drinking;* < *exercise and entering the house;* < warmth; < warmth, but he is sensitive to the cold; **with difficult respiration** *and* *bronchitis, at first without fever, with soft pulse, prostration and emaciation; with faintness;* with chilliness; with burning in throat; with sticking beneath hypochondria; with sticking below pit of stomach, so that she must hold the chest; with sensation as if something were tearing loose in chest; with dragging in lower part of chest; *causing pain in abdomen, so that she must hold abdomen;* in open air, causing pain in chest and abdomen; causing pain in base of sternum; in two shocks after dinner; two or three single coughs come together. *Loose rattling C. as in old people, when eating; L., without expectoration, with pain and soreness in chest, so that she dreaded to cough;* a paroxysm of L., without expectoration about midnight, > sitting up, after which she fell asleep with the cough, in morning soreness of throat. *Hacking C.;* and tickling; waking him in morning. *Hollow C., < morning in bed and at night, preventing sleep; H., mostly dry, with pressure in pit of stomach, so that he could not sleep at night.* **Dry C.**; *with pain in head as if it would burst,* and coryza; with itching in trachea and beneath pit of throat; *with bronchial catarrh, afterwards with slimy, purulent expectoration, rapid respiration,* **oppression of chest,** *necessity to sit up when coughing, pain and constriction beneath stomach, remarkable sonority in upper third of r. chest, moist sibilant râles in lower part, ribs almost immovable, chest arched;* **with scanty expectoration,** *catarrhal symptoms in posterior and lower part of lungs, < r.,* (chill), **percussion showed slight dulness in r. lower part posteriorly, with diminished respiratory murmurs and fine vesicular rales,** *change of posture caused a change in area of dulness, vocal fremitus diminished beneath line of dulness on r. posterior part of ninth dorsal vertebra, next day (second chill) the dulness extended upward half an inch and bronchial breathing was distinct over area of dulness, afterwards the cough was paroxysmal, < after a chill,* **with expectoration of tenacious, purulent mucus;** with frequent excitement to cough, shootings under sternum and towards r. side of chest, copious muco-purulent expectoration, with tickling and scratching at bifurcation of trachea; **causing soreness in forepart of chest,** *waking her every night;* **violent, on reading aloud** *in evening;* violent, all day, with headache; when sitting and lying; *hacking, all day,* < evening, *from tickling in throat; hacking,* preventing sleep; *irritating,* next day with mucous expectoration, < lying on r. side or on back, later racking and deep, for two months deep harrassing, but dry chest cough, when the spells came on fluttering sensation in lungs, which caused tickling, often nausea and vomiting with the cough, < after eating. **Cough, with oppression of chest, to expectorate she must sit up in bed, when there is great pain, with constriction under sternum,** *mucous rattling, rhonchus sibilans in the two inferior thirds of r. lung, in upper third of r. lung anteriorly and in lower half posteriorly, on percussion uncommonly clear tone, almost immobility of ribs at these parts, pectoral walls arched; C., with expectoration, even at night;* **with expectoration of blood and mucus,** *also with short, slight cough;* **with E. of transparent mucus in morning after rising,** *and sensation in middle of sternum as if something were torn loose; spasmodic C., with expectoration of mucus,* **with oppression of chest;** *hacking, fatiguing C.* the day before and first day of menstruation, *with expectoration of blood; C., with difficult expectoration; white E. difficult to loosen;* with mucous E. day and night, after some days with stitches in chest; with mucous E. and with tensive pain in chest; *with great exertion till E. of tenacious mucus; with much grayish mucus, as if mixed with dust,* after rising; with thick, white, mucous E.; with slight mucous E., next day E. more copious, phosphorescent, and when dry burned readily from application of a lighted match, later puslike and profuse E.; violent C. waking her about 2 A.M., with mucous E.

Hæmoptysis. **Bloody expectoration from lungs; bloody E., with mucus;** *blood-streaked mucus from chest;* E. of tenacious mucus; of flakes of mucus, with smarting burning behind sternum; scanty mucus in thick, light-colored lumps.

Respiration.—*Suffocative feeling.* Choking. **Dyspnœa;** on taking a deep breath; after sitting long, with at times pain or sticking above heart; *with prostration;* with nausea. **Oppressed;** with chilliness and headache, so that he could scarcely collect his senses. **Impeded by rapid walking;** I. in forenoon by fulness of abdomen. **Difficult;** in evening in bed; inspiration, on account of tension in pit of stomach; and deep; and irregular; and quick. **Anxious, panting;** *A., frequent; and short, hurried, with elevation of whole chest, < l. side;* when reflecting. *Tight after slightest food.* **Short; after coughing;** *with pain in upper part of sternum. Complained of want of breath though she often took a deep breath.* Deep; *inclination to take a deep inspiration,* also with discomfort on doing so. Moaning and groaning. Gasping on ascending a hill. Rapid; *and superficial;* interrupted by attacks of dyspnœa; and deep, with contraction of sterno-cleido-mastoid, at times stertorous. Slow; and rattling before death. Like suppurating bronchitis. *Loud and rattling.* Stertorous before death. Weak vesicular, with moist râles. Vesicular respiratory murmurs, with sonorous, almost tympanitic percussion.

Clinical.—Laryngitis, with great sensitiveness of the larynx, amounting even to aphonia, inability to speak on account of the pain in the larynx. Inflammation of the respiratory tract in general, occasionally capillary bronchitis. Bronchitis, with night-cough, frothy expectoration, oppression of the chest, etc. Bronchitis, with violent cough and involuntary micturition. Cough < lying on l. side. Hacking night-cough, < lying on back or l. side. Chronic cough seeming to start from the pit of the stomach, cough easily caused by any excitement.

Chest.—**Tubercles in lungs, with hectic fever.** *Rapid suppuration of lungs, with formation of cavities and purulent exudation into cavity of chest, infiltration of messenteric glands, tubercular ulcers in intestines, etc. Mucous râles in different parts of lungs, <* **lower lobes.** Catarrh of lungs. Catarrhal coating in morning. *Percussion dull on r. lower part, with indistinct bronchial respiration and râles, partly dry, on l. side vesicular murmurs and moist râles.* Clear tone in middle of r. side on percussion, auscultation revealed diffused mucous râles, with pectoriloquy. Constant rubbing of breast and region of stomach during unconsciousness.

Sticking in l. side beneath ribs; in sides; r. side; r. clavicle, at shoulder; at origin of neck; half an inch below nipple; in lungs; in mammæ; *in l. side on breathing;* in r. side on breathing; r. side under false ribs when riding horseback; deep internally beneath l. breast on rising from a seat; *through lungs, < deep inspiration; in various parts,* < sitting, at times with burning; in l. side, > deep inspiration; beneath l. breast, with anxiety; externally, not affecting respiration; extending backward in r. upper part; in middle of sternum, extending to r. scapula, from morning till evening, > during breakfast, so violent that it took away the breath, < inspiration, > motion; in sternum, extending through chest to l. scapula, < working, worse in evening when spinning, in the evening the S. was usually accompanied by shivering, then sweat, during the paroxysm necessity to keep quiet, else there were apprehension and palpitation, *the corresponding part of back sensitive to pressure.*

Darting pain. Cramp in evening; towards evening after riding in a carriage; *at night, he thinks that he shall suffocate;* in attacks high up under sternum during the day, > flatulent eructations. Cutting to r. of sternum; drawing C. beneath short ribs when walking. Acute pain behind sternum; A. pain in l. side on inspiration, < full respiration. Pleuritic pain through C. extending into throat and down r. arm.

Pain; in pectoralis major; in lower ribs; beneath r. short ribs; after violent eructations; in lower part when drawing a long breath; < inspiration; posteriorly in l. lung, sometimes < inspiration; below middle and to r. of sternum, > eructations, with oppression of chest; in l. side, with distinct pleuritic friction; behind sternum, extending into stomach; from l. nipple to r., then to r. shoulder, thence to little finger, at 3.30 P.M.; in r. upper part, changing to a deeply-seated pain corresponding to sixth and seventh ribs, at times preventing deep respiration, with this burning pain a constant desire to cough, which was with difficulty suppressed on account of the pain; fugitive, and in abdomen; burning, in lower part (œsophagus), stomach and abdomen; drawing, in l. side of C. and abdomen towards morning, disturbing sleep, > rubbing, eructations of wind and emission of flatus; drawing downward, in upper part, then empty eructations; above heart, as from incarcerated flatus, extending to region of thyroid gland, with nausea and frequent need to take a deep breath; as if skin were raised by a needle, in r. side; rheumatic, in l.; bruised, beneath r. axilla on pressure; bruised, in upper part on motion, stooping and touch; sore, in clavicles; sore, under short ribs on pressure.

Anxiety and pressure amounting to suffocation, so that deep inspiration was difficult, *with burning and sticking behind sternum; A. in evening; with want of breath;* with throbbing in its r. lower part; *below l. breast causing general trembling,* at times with bitter eructations and *palpitation.* **Soreness of lungs, with difficulty in taking a full breath.** Irritation of lungs. Rawness; *of lungs,* < l.

Heaviness; on inspiration, when walking after dinner. *Clogged feeling in lungs, with dyspnœa. Stuffed sensation, < sneezing, with discomfort in it.* Fulness at 5 P.M. *Oppression; in morning in bed;* in morning, with palpitation and nausea; *of lower part* in evening, *with short breath;* above ensiform cartilage in evening on stooping, > becoming erect, with tightness of breath; *at night after walking in open air, so that she could not yawn perfectly; after dinner, with anxiety;* < sitting, > eructations; anxious; as if hot blood surged up into throat in morning. *Constriction;* in morning, *with painful, difficult breathing. Pinching high up.* Contraction in l. upper part; of whole lung; with pressure or pinching in upper abdomen; spasmodic. Pressure upon lower part; P. after eating, then short breath; upon r. ribs, with dulness of head, < parietal parts; in glands of fleshy part of r. breast; *so that he could not breathe easily.* **Tightness; of upper part;** < **lying on l. side;** *as if air were forcibly kept out; as from rush of blood,* < morning on waking. *Tension;* behind C.; *without dyspnœa; as from a band about it. Inability to fill lungs as usual.*

Distress. *Dryness.* Beating as with a finger on r. side when sitting. Feeling as if everything in C. and abdomen would sink together. *Weakness; of lungs;* from towards 6 P.M. till after going to bed, with pain in different parts of chest and cough; with feeling as if she would discover pain in it. *Rush of blood; and to head;* on every emotion, with cramplike constriction between scapulæ. *Heat; in lungs; behind sternum;* externally beneath r. breast, with pinching and mounting of heat to head; extending to head and abdomen, after soup, with sensation as if sweat would break out; on lower end of sternum, extending towards l. clavicle, after dinner; above r. side of heart and beneath l. clavicle, afterwards extending to tip of l. scapula and to acromion process, while at the heart it disappeared. Itching internally. **Aggravation on l. side.**

Clinical.—Phos. is indicated in a great variety of diseases of the bronchi and lungs; there is a general tendency to easy hæmorrhage from the lungs (from violent fits of cough or from emotional excitement); there is generally absence of fever, so that Phos. is rarely indicated in the beginning of acute diseases; there is generally exhaustion; in pneumonia Phos. is indicated after the febrile symptoms have mostly subsided, when there is great oppression of the chest, as from a weight, especially if the patient is worse when lying on l. side. In phthisis the patients are generally thin and tall, have a sensation of a weight on the chest, a tormenting cough, with sweet or salty expectoration, general tendency to hoarseness, palpitation, expectoration of bright blood, inability to lie on l. side or even on the back, tendency to painless diarrhœa, mental and physical indolence, etc. Typhoid pneumonia. Broncho-pneumonia. Pleuro-pneumonia. (Compare chest symptoms with Ferrum.)

Heart. — *Bruit de souffle with first sound. Systolic murmurs at base. Marked bellows murmur with first sound. Impulse whirring, first sound at apex is blowing, second clear, at orifice a systolic murmur. Blowing sound; peculiar, synchronous with systole of heart, over arch of aorta;* peculiar, with second sound, < at base, action weak, pulse 20; sounds dull, *systole always accompanied by blowing sounds; always with the first sound,* sound weak, whirring. Sound feeble; with systolic murmur; second; first, and no pulse at wrist. Second sound of heart and great vessels inaudible.

Pain; in præcordial region, not > eructations; in præcordial region on every paroxysm of cough; sharp, in præcordial region. *Anxiety after* 10 P.M., *with nausea and* **peculiar hunger, somewhat > eating, distressing her even in bed.** Heaviness in præcordial region.

Palpitation; in afternoon after excitement, so that he could not remain lying, another attack on going to sleep; *in evening and morning on waking, with anxiety;* in evening in bed, with ringing in ears, uneasiness in blood, tossing about and numerous unpleasant fancies, preventing sleep; at night; when walking and sitting after a meal, *and at night when lying on l. side;* after breakfast; < eating, with rush of blood to heart; with weeping mood and unhappiness. Violent beating in morning on waking and in evening on lying down; *on slight motion,* < l. arm. Thumping after dinner, often provoking cough, with redness mounting to face. Deep beats. Impulse noticed over an increased area, at times intermittent. Weak; and pulse small, often imperceptible.

Clinical.—Fatty degeneration of the heart.

Pulse.—*Rapid;* in morning, rapid, small and weak.

in afternoon; and full; and full, hardish; and hard; and hard, small; and tense; and wiry; *and soft; and weak;* and weak, irregular; and short; and very compressible; and thready, easily compressed; and small; and small in evening; *and small, compressible;* and small, soft; and small, weak; and small, thready; and small, irregular. Slow; and at times full and hard; and weak; and contracted, scarcely perceptible; and small, soft. Labored. Hard, towards next evening it disappeared at wrist. Throbbing in carotids. *Small; and soft;* and weak; and thready; and thready, compressible. Intermittent; after every three to six beats; and thready, varying from 53 to 135. *Weak;* and thready; and irregular in morning, afterwards rapid and weak. Pulseless.

Neck.—Swollen glands. Twitching of muscles. "Crick" in nape. Sticking in l. side; S. anteriorly extending towards r. ear, and tearing extending thence to vertex. Tearing in nape; in l. side, with coldness; in bloodvessels of r. side, extending to shoulder. Pain in nape; in r. side; anteriorly in muscles on touch and motion. Soreness of muscles of nape; of nape beginning at 9 A.M., < twisting head to left, < in r. side by pressure. Weight on nape. Stiffness; *of nape.*

Back.—Sticking in spine all day. Pain; after walking; on sitting a long time; < pressure, and in r. hypochondrium; so that he could scarcely rise from a seat; periodical, preventing walking. Bruised pain during menses; B. pain obliging her to turn constantly in bed. Tension of muscles. Dulness in spine, as from fulness of blood, with at times paralytic sensation in os sacrum. *Weakness as if crushed, then weakness in limbs and trembling on least exertion.* Heaviness; on lying down, with weariness. Paralyzed feeling after midday nap, and in arms. Feeling as if asleep or sprained after midday nap.

Scapulæ.—Sticking; *in r.;* beneath S. Tearing in r.; in l., > rubbing; in bones of r., with throbbing, soon recurring after rubbing. **Spinous processes of dorsal vertebræ sensitive to pressure** (see Chin. sulf.), *also muscles between spinous processes and l. scapula, < l. side,* with sticking near l. scapula, extending forward through chest, or from before backward, at times extending to upper arm, > firm pressure upon back, rest and warmth, < lifting, working, during menses and *unpleasant excitement and vexation. Pain between S.;* under r.; under S.; in dorsal region; **burning, between S.** (Lyc.); *throbbing, in a spot between S.;* as from a plug in l.; jerking, in l., extending into shoulder, when sitting. Sensation as if grasped on lifting or carrying anything with both hands. Heaviness in upper part of back.

Lumbar Region.—Sticking; in vertebræ; and in splenic region; through female pelvis; in muscles above l. hip; behind l. sacro-iliac region; deep in region of kidneys, with sensitiveness to great pressure. Darting towards splenic region. Acute pain in region of kidneys; during micturition. *Pain;* in lower part; at base of spine; in region of insertion of last ribs; in kidneys; in kidneys, < r.; in kidneys in morning; region of kidneys on pressure; after sitting a long time; in last vertebra, near r. side of spine, when sitting, and at times when standing; on rising from stooping and on standing, > walking; in kidneys, < open air; above sacrum and in neighboring parts of ilium, < sitting bent and after dinner, with weakness; in coccyx, impeding every motion, she can find no comfortable position, then painful stiffness of nape; in coccyx, extending through spine to vertex, during stool, drawing head backward; ulcerative, in coccyx on touch; rheumatic; heavy, in region of kidneys; as after exertion in lifting, extending down posterior surface of thigh to knee, < rest, > moving about; as from lifting too heavy a weight, at union of sacrum with last vertebra when standing and walking, < standing with sacrum bent backward, coughing, < standing on one foot with the other turned inward and outward, and bending towards one side, > towards evening, with numbness and rigidity in feet when pressing on spinal processes of two last vertebræ and neighboring parts. Gnawing, > rubbing, and in sacrum. Weakness; and lameness; nervous, after an emission; as if asleep when sitting and on rising from a seat. Paralyzed sensation in upper part of os sacrum and in lower vertebræ.

Clinical.—Spinal irritation, with burning pain between the scapulæ (Lyc.). Locomotor ataxia, with burning in the spine, formication, exhaustion, etc. Paralysis following exposure to a drenching rain, sensation as if quicksilver moved up and down the spine, etc. Caries of the vertebræ, with intolerance of heat near the back and feeling of a tight band around the body. General neuritis, subacute, with numbness, feeling of constriction in the extremities, etc.

Extremities.—Blue. Toes and elbows bluish-red. Nails hard and dry. Crackling noise in joints on motion. Trembling. Jerking alternating with quietness as from sleepiness. Convulsions; tonic, of lower limbs and feet, which were outstretched, then spasms of upper limbs, then trismus. Cramps; at night, with lancinations and contractions. Sticking on pressure of finger; S. in elbows after a fright, then in an abraded spot on foot; in one or another joint, with pain. Tearing in r. forearm and knee as soon as she becomes cold; in l. shoulder, in joints and l. knee, < after dinner; as from a blow in flesh of outer upper part of r. forearm, with pain on grasping it, tearing in leg and general weakness. Feeling as if dislocated on rapid motion. Pain; in bones; in joints; in knees, then at 3 P.M. above l. elbow; on touch; on walking, with general weariness; in joints, < motion; spasmodic; cramplike, at night, with occasional exacerbations, during which the muscles are stiffly contracted; tensive, in inner condyles of r. wrist and l. knee. *Bruised pain;* on ascending stairs; in l. knee and elbow, with heaviness. Drawing pain; in joints in morning after rising; in one or another joint during rest. Drawing in r. arm and leg at night; in arms and lower limbs, with weeping mood.

Weakness; in joints; hands and feet; arm and knee-joints; muscles of legs and arms; in morning after rising, < thigh; in evening; after getting feet a little wet and cold, with burning in hands, headache and lying down, next day coryza; *< joints, with paralyzed feeling;* < forenoon; < knees, < morning after rising and by rest, > walking, with sticking and burning in them. *Heaviness; of hands and feet;* in joints of arms and knees; in morning before rising; during a storm; *and at last paralysis, with pain in muscles.* Could not be extended, but he lay with them drawn up. Falling asleep; of hands and feet; of arms and legs; alternately of arms and feet at night, waking her. Numbness; when sitting. Hands and feet feel dead. Paralysis in morning, > rising; feeling of P. in hands and feet in morning after rising.

Upper Extremities.—Axilla. Glandular swelling; two hard, red, painful, < afternoon, evening and forepart of night and < hard pressure, in l., with lumps down inner surface of arm, < pressure or rubbing quickly; hard, in r., with sticking in afternoon, during night, less towards morning, later discharge of offensive, thin, bloody pus; with burning pain in skin of arm; in l., with suppuration and discharge. Stitches extending through shoulders; under A., extending broadly from each other.

Shoulder.—Cracking of joint. Sticking in r.; in l. after dinner, > motion, then sensitiveness. *Tearing in l., < night in bed;* in l., with headache. Boring in r. after dinner, < motion, > rest. Pain in r.; in region of r.; in r. and in arm; on motion and on touch; in joints after walking in open air; with drawing; extending from l. bone to muscles of arm above and below elbow, with coldness at back of hand, ending with pricking at finger-tips; sprained, in r., < raising arm; burning, in r. joint, < raising arm when washing. Rheumatic pain in r. in morning after waking; in r., extending to upper ribs. Tension in muscles of r. and r. side of nape, with pressure; T. in r., when brushing teeth, with stiffness and heaviness, so that arm must hang down, also on combing hair and washing; in muscles, extending half way down forearms. Tensive pain in deltoid and upper dorsal muscles, extending to nape. Heaviness, and of arms. *Stiffness in morning on washing, with pressure in it and heaviness of arm;* S. of r., a kind of tension, extending to occiput.

Arm.—Shooting down r. into little finger. Tearing in r.; in l. A. and hand; in bones of r. A. and hand; with drawing. Pain; < about elbow in evening in bed, > moving it, but recurring, also numbness and weakness; sprained, in r.; drawing, < evening; paralytic sore, if she holds anything in hands, with trembling. Heaviness of r.; of r. in morning when writing; when writing; of r. during and after washing; in r., with pressure; in r., and when it hung down sensation as if it were drawn downward; of r., so that he could not raise it easily, as if shoulder-joint were stiff. *Weakness;* of r. A. and wrist; of joints, with distended veins of hands. *Falling asleep;* of r. in morning; of r. in evening; *of the one on which head was resting;* of l., < morning, with numbness of fingers and contraction of them, then weakness of arm; in r., with crawling. *Numbness when working.* Paralysis of l.

Upper Arm.—Tearing; in outer surface of r. after rubbing forearm, with twitching. Pain in periosteum of humerus and radius; in biceps when writing; rheumatic, in r. Bruised pain in r. when sitting; in l. humerus, extending up and down, from elbow to shoulder, when sitting. *Weakness.*

Elbow.—Tearing in r., with drawing; in r., with sticking; extending towards shoulder, with boring; extending along inner side of forearm towards thumb-joint, as if the bone would be torn out, > rubbing. Gnawing in r. extending towards shoulder when sitting. Pain as if broken. Drawing pain from r. to knuckles, with nausea and ravenous hunger. A blow in condyles when sitting, with jerking.

Forearm.—Tearing, < about wrists; T. on inner side of l. as if skin would be rubbed off in morning; paralytic, in bones of r., on dorsal surface of metacarpus, towards evening, once extending into humerus, with numbness of dorsal surface of r. hand. Pain in l.; in muscles on ulnar side of r. in morning on washing, then heaviness of arm; drawing, neuralgic, in l.; bruised, in r. radius. Weakness. Stiff, sore sensation in r. Numbness towards evening, and of hands, with shaking of hands.

Wrist.—Swelling after taking cold (?), with throbbing in it as in an ulcer and with tearing extending into fingers, < moving wrist, which was stiff. Sticking during rest. Tearing in evening, with paralytic weakness. Pain in r., with paralytic weakness; P. in r., with stiffness; sprained P.

Hand.—Red from rush of blood. Emaciation, so that veins were very prominent. Rapid swelling, and of fingers; soft swelling of r., index thickened, grayish-black, gangrenous, whole bone mumified, as in gangrenous senilis, amputation of first phalanx necessary. *Trembling;* in morning; *when writing;* when hanging down, with heaviness, redness and distended veins and feeling as if blood were forced into them. Contractions, r. pronated, thumb adducted towards middle finger, index and middle finger extended, fourth and fifth fingers partially flexed, l. hand in similar condition, only the three last fingers were strongly flexed, with drawing and pain in hands and arms and fibrillar twitchings of muscles of thumb and little finger; paroxysmal contractions, with tearing in limbs (appearing like hysterical attacks). Sticking in a spot on inner margin of r., with burning. Tearing in bones; in H. and wrists, with cracking; < knuckles, < night in bed. Pain in bones of r.; in bones of l. H. and fingers. Drawing in r.; in H. and fingers after wetting hands with warm water. Restlessness, and of arms. Weakness. Numbness on flexor surface of r. *Falling asleep in morning on waking,* **with numbness**; F. asleep of r. in morning in bed. Stiffness, < r. middle finger. Paralysis; of one; and of fingers.

Fingers.—Tips cyanotic. Swelling of one, with pain, < pressure; S. of first joint of thumb, with pain on touch and tensive, sprained pain on motion. *Drawn, bent at times, as from cramp.* Contraction of adductors of thumb and flexors of index. Jerking of certain ones; in l. little; of one all day, with weakness; paralytic, of r. thumb when writing. **Were all thumbs.** Sticking in bone of ball of r. little; burning, in tips of r. in evening. Tearing in r. little; in thumb and knuckles; cramplike drawing and T. in little. Gnawing in second phalanx of r. middle. Sprained pain in joints; in thumb on grasping anything; in first joint of thumb on motion. Pain in r. middle and in elbow; in adductors of thumb; in extensor digiti medii, extending into middle of forearm, often the same in second and fourth finger. Tension of l.; sprained, in fourth and fifth. *Heaviness of tips.* Sensation of stiffness and swelling in r. joints. Numbness in tips of r. little and of thumb; *of F. of one hand, with falling asleep of the others,* r. middle numb, bloodless and cold, in moderately cold air. *Paralysis,* she had the power to feel but could scarcely move them.

Lower Extremities.—Gait unsteady. Walking as if paralyzed without noticing it himself. Anasarca. Cramplike contraction, with jerking, and of feet; spasmodic C., so that she could not stretch them out during menses. Cramps, and in calves and feet. Tearing. Pain; on touch; in muscles on pressure, < thighs; < motion; in morning on rising, as after a long walk; bruised, as from weariness at night. Tension, with stiff pain in l. Tightness in r. Seemed swollen and glued to the floor on attempting to walk.

Uneasiness, < evening, with cold hands. *Weakness;* in morning; < *ascending steps, with heaviness. Heaviness.* Falling asleep of l. in morning. Sensation as if she had been deprived of them, though their sensibility and motility were intact. Paralyzed sensation in r. at night.

Thigh.—Twitching of nates; visible, painful, of T. and natis; tearing, on posterior part superiorly, extending to knee, every four minutes during and after walking in open air, with sore pain on touch. Sticking in l. hip after dinner, > rubbing; in r. hip, extending to chest; intermittent, above r. knee when sitting, > rubbing, with burning. Rhythmical tearing posteriorly in evening after lying down. Pain; *in r. hip-joint;* in hips; region of r. hip; r. hip and leg; l. ischium on sitting long; in bones of l. T. and leg, with boring; *suppurative, in nates* on sitting long; sprained, in hips; in hip-joints at night as if bed were hard, obliged to change his position constantly; bruised, in muscles; bruised, in middle, with pain on touch and inability to walk; drawing, in tendons of semi-membranosus and semi-tendinosus; drawing, > walking, which he was obliged to do. Drawing back and forth during midday rest. Soreness on inner part. Pulsation in nates. Feeling in r. hip as if held tightly when sitting. Weariness. Painful, paralyzed sensation in l. hip in evening, > sitting and lying.

Knee.—Drawn up. Sprung forward when walking, as if weak. Trembling. Sticking in r.; in r. patella on stepping; on inner surface of r. on every step, but on raising limb while sitting a bruised pain above knee, > rising from seat; paroxysmal, at night. Tearing evenings in open air; in hollow of r. at night; in l. extending up thigh; to back of foot, > rubbing, with falling asleep of anterior part of l. foot; to inner side of calf, as if flesh would be torn from bone, > rubbing, after dinner; intermittent, in K. and patellæ, as if in bones, sometimes > rubbing, also after dinner. Pain; on inner side of l.; when walking; sprained, in l.; *drawing, to feet;* drawing, extending to tips of toes, < putting one leg over the other; rheumatic, in morning. Rheumatic symptoms in l., < ascending stairs, tightness of tendons on suddenly bending knee, and internal condyle of thigh sensitive to pressure (she had this symptom the previous year, at this time there was no apparent cause for it). Goutlike tension as if sprained, they are hot to touch; cramplike T. in hollows all day. Tightness of tendons under K. as if too short, when walking. Drawing from l. to foot; to foot in evening, then painful jerking; spasmodic, in hollows; spasmodic, when walking. Sensation in K. and ankles as if a soft, foreign substance were lying between articular surfaces, necessity to be very careful when walking to prevent falling, with swelling of soft parts about the joints and rigidity on flexion. *Heaviness in hollows.* Paralyzed feeling in l.

Leg.—Two wounds below knee, after the necrotic parts had been thrown off and granulation was beginning they were attacked by nosocomial gangrene, after this had been subdued by strong caustic remedies **gangrenous periostitis of tibia, with fever, the periosteum peeled off as far as knee, the bone was rough,** with sleeplessness, during amputation of femur above condyles it was seen that the periosteum adhered loosely to the bone and could be turned back easily as far as condyles, as soon as the sutures were removed (on account of pressure of shaft of bone on the soft parts) the periosteum of the whole shaft peeled off up to the trochanter minor and fell back with the soft parts in the form of a flabby, funnel-shaped sac, so that the superficially necrosed shaft stood out free half a foot, with high fever, irregular rigors, collapse and death. Trembling; like a shuddering. Cramp; *in calves;* at night, and in feet; in calves, then jerking in legs on stretching them when walking. Tearing stitches extending down tibia; intermittent burning S. about middle of r. tibialis anticus and at origin of communis dig. ped. when sitting and on crossing legs and when standing, > motion. Rhythmical tearing in l. tibia, in forepart above foot, in morning on waking. Pain; in l.; in calves; in l., waking at night, with erections; in tibiæ on walking; in muscles of calves on pressure. Bruised pain on ascending stairs; B. pain in tibiæ; *in periosteum of tibiæ, with soreness on touch.* Soreness; resembling "bone-pain," < motion. Tension in r. calf when walking. *Weariness; and heaviness.* Hyperæsthesia; of muscles of calves. Numbness; after sitting a long time, > walking; of l. when lying on l. side, > lying on back or r. side; of l. to toes, with sensation as if hot blood circulated through it. Falling asleep when riding one over the other; F. asleep from calves to feet, as if circulation were arrested by a band below knee.

Ankle.—Swelling of a tendon by r. malleolus. Sticking in l.; in malleolus, > motion; in r. malleolus, preventing stepping, with swelling. Tearing in l. malleolus at night, preventing sleep. Pain in l. extending to calf; paralytic drawing, in malleoli, extending to knee; *sprained, on walking,* tension on stepping upon it; sprained, in r., < motion. Easily sprained when stepping. Tired.

Foot.—Swelling; of one; in morning; *in evening; on walking;* with pain in their bones and soreness, later pain in the joints, afterwards the swelling of feet and toes and the gouty pain in great toes made it painful to walk and stand. L. dark bluish and cold. Redness of soles, with pain on walking. Jerking; with crawling cramp in soles. Cramp in soles. Sticking; in corns when walking; in corns, which afterwards disappear; in corns, with boring; in soles, with tearing, so that he could not step upon them; tearing, in soles. Tearing; at night, with sticking, preventing sleep; in l. heel, extending along inner margin of sole, when sitting. Pain; in l. instep; in corns on heels from slightest pressure; in heels and toes (formerly frozen), < shoes when walking; in soles, as if she had walked too far; in corns, piercing through the bone and marrow; beating, in heels at night, > rubbing them till warm. Drawing in r. metatarsal bones. Tension in heels in morning in bed. Tingling in soles. *Weakness;* with sensation of falling asleep and uneasiness. *Heaviness;* with stumbling over an uneven path; as if swollen. Feeling in l. sole as if on velvet. Numbness; < crossing them while sitting. Crawling at night as if asleep. Falling asleep of r.; of l. when riding it over the other leg. *Paralyzed feeling.*

Toes.—Jerking in l. great when sitting. Inclination to cramp. Sticking in r. great; in r. great, < walking; in l. great, < motion and in evening; in ball of great, with inflammation. Tearing when sitting, >

rubbing. Acute pain in joint of l. great. Pain in l. great; on inner side of metatarsal joint of r. great when walking; in those that had been frozen, on walking, with burning; in old corns on little, with swelling of toe; around joint of l. great, with swelling and inflamed appearance; in great, as if frozen.

Skin.—*Jaundice;* towards evening; of eyes, chest and limbs; < chest and abdomen; except of face, which was congested; of whole body and of conjunctiva, but spots of a deeper and redder color on face, as from circumscribed erythema or subcutaneous effusion; with confusion of mind, later with delirium; with delirium and rapid pulse; with fever, delirium, irregular pulse, then prostration and death; with pain in epigastric region and vomiting of black, thready substances consisting of blood; with enlargement of liver, which was painful to pressure; with enlargement of liver and spleen, and bile in urine; with enlargement of liver and weakness of heart's action; with distention and sensitiveness of epigastric and r. hypochondriac region, constant moaning, semi-consciousness, half-open eyes and mouth, pulse 150, respiration difficult, twitching of face and arms, then distention of abdomen, swelling of liver, which was sensitive to touch; beginning in eye; beginning in face and extending over body; afterwards paleness of skin and of mucous membrane; yellowish-brown; dark; dark, with livid lips, nose, forehead and limbs.

Yellow spot at side of umbilicus. Dirty yellow in face, other parts gray, with dryness. *Pale, and mucous membrane;* peculiarly; as in leuchæmia; at times dirty yellow, puffy, < face. Dark. Livid. Bluish. Freckles on lower part of tibia; on nose in morning after being heated by exercise at night. Transparent coppery spots. Brownish, dark spots, at times elevated, in hollows of knees, on chest, forehead and below corner of mouth. Red spots on arms, > pressure; corrosive-itching red spots in bend of r. elbow. Bluish-red spots, < legs, bleeding from leech-bites difficult to stop; almost like petechiæ, on legs. *Petechiæ;* dull livid, over epigastrium. *Ecchymoses;* over abdomen; on chest and face. *Spots similar to purpura hæmorrhagica* at base of neck, on shoulders and backs of hands. Purpura on chest; P., with weakness, next day the oldest spots were brownish-red, the newest bright red. Covered with peach-colored spots, with red spots of purpura in centre.

Inelastic. Soft, relaxed feeling. Wrinkled and dry. Roughness; of hands, with dryness; on anterior and posterior borders of r., then l. axilla, with scales. Desquamation; on face. Cracks on finger-joints as from cold. Warts on hands. Eruption on thighs and legs; on anterior surface of ulnar side of r. hand, and over metacarpal bone of l. thumb; gritty, on forehead and chin. Itching eruption; anteriorly on arms; anteriorly from bends of elbows nearly to wrists; and scabby, cracked, scaly, < arms and hands. Tetter above upper lip; above knees and below patellæ; *in round spots over whole body.*

Indurations on nates; painful to touch, beneath chin. Itching enlargement as from an insect-bite, on back of lower third of l. thigh. Shiny swelling on forehead, with headache above eyes. Raw, red, mottled elevations on face. Sudden red, inflamed swelling between calf and hollow of knee, with smarting. Exanthematous spots over anterior part of abdomen, > pressure; purple-like exanthema over whole body, < lower limbs. Dry eczematous spots on l. cheek, < waking, extending over nose and r. cheek. Chilblains on feet. Inflammation of l. nipple and breast, with swelling, pain and suppuration; erysipelatous I. of one breast (covered with eruption), with swelling, redness, burning, sticking, and at last suppuration.

Urticaria, with large hives; U., with large blisters; U. in one resembling measles, in the other more raised, crimson and less crescentic. Pimples on face; and wings of nose; on cheeks; behind and below angles of jaws; with indurated spots, and brownish and reddish-blue spots have an increased color; red, on face; bright red, itching, transiently > scratching in afternoon; hard, below angles of jaws; painful, on r. wing of nose; painful to touch posteriorly on thighs; itching, in axilla, burning after scratching.

Pustules on chin; on face, after slightest injury to skin, with scabs; on forehead, afterwards on face, with red areola, in the centre was the opening of a hair-follicle, at the same time ecthymatous pustules on nates, about anus, afterwards a boil that discharged greenish, bloody matter on l. natis; like ecthyma on hands and arms, with purpura of whole body. Hard swelling, oozing a sticky, watery fluid, on chin, after a little irritation throbbing and twitching in it, with pain in chin.

Ulcers bleed on appearance of menses; *U. that would not heal, about the nail.* Boil on margin of orbit; on abdomen; nape, chest and thighs; forehead; with red areola, with dark color in centre, on thigh; with burning pain, in groin. Gangrene and inflammation. Vesicles behind ears; in and about nose; V. and ulcers on feet increased; on chin, with inflammation; in concha, with burning pain; on heel, breaking, becoming moist and is painful on walking; with thin, transparent fluid, afterwards milky; in groups, without areola, about joints, then desquamation in thin scales; painful, hard, here and there; crusty and cracked, more on r. than on l. hand, also between fingers of both hands; like gangrene, bursting and exuding water; heat, on backs of hands, with itching, < night; itch; itching, between fingers and in hollow of knees.

Sore, abraded spots in various parts, with redness and smarting or sticking. Raw bleeding surface under scabs. Exudation of black blood from scar of an old blister. Hæmorrhage from subcutaneous cellular tissue of chest and < lower limbs (after death, also found in anterior and posterior mediastinum, endocardium, pleura, parenchyma of r. lung and mesentery).

Sticking on abdomen; in a boil on throat; like flea-bites. Prickling on scalp, chest and r. arm during sweat. Sticking pinching on neck when walking in open air. Pinching, contractive pain in an old scar. Bruised pain, < vertex, < pressure. *Sensation on forehead as if too tight,* with anxiety. Hyperæsthesia. *Anæsthesia;* on limbs, so that she could not pick up a pin. *Formication;* on limbs; l. arm; l. thumb; r. fingers; tips of fingers; r. fourth and fifth fingers; second knuckle of l. third finger; heels; feet and toes; beneath toes; thighs at night; hands in open air, when yawning; upper part of body, < nape, chest and occiput, on entering house; with twitching sensation; r. fingers, l. index, l. thumb, r. outer toes, red of upper lip, with at times warmth in r. thumb; *numb, in tips of r. fingers,* in l. thumb and in r. little toe; numb, in ungual phalanges of r. little finger and thumb; *itching, in paralyzed parts.*

Itching of whole body; face; wart on forehead; about eyes; in a spot on l. side of lower jaw; at point of sternum; on back and in hollows of knees; arms; hands; back of r. hand; *legs;* hips; thigh and patella; calves and tibiæ; soles and beneath toes; soles and toes in evening; hands in evening in bed; over whole body at night, with heat and dryness of mouth; at night on arms, lower limbs, back and abdomen; inner side of thighs when walking, with sensation as if a hair were pulled on inner side just above l. knee; < scratching and by thinking of it; not > rubbing, on navel; I. (or biting like formication) here and there, > rubbing; between scapulæ, > scratching; on r. side of chest and abdomen, > scratching; temporarily > scratching, continued scratching caused a raw, smarting, burning, sore feeling; *in r. axilla,* with glandular swelling; on l. buttock, with prickling; in a spot on thigh, with smarting after scratching; about abdomen, with biting, and on arms and thighs, red streaks, caused by scratching; under chin, extending to neck; sticking, over whole body during menses; sticking, on backs of hands, preventing sleep at night, not > scratching; burning, over whole body.

Clinical.—Psoriasis of palms and soles. Fungous hæmotodes. Fungous excrescences.

Sleep.—*Yawning;* in evening, with chilliness; after dinner, with stretching and sleepiness; during the attacks of pain, with watery urine; ineffectual desire for. **Sleepiness; during the day, even before dinner;** during the day, after walking in open air; all day, poor sleep at night on account of amusing dreams; one day, next day restlessness; till 11 A.M.; early in evening; *early in evening, then restless sleep;* in evening when walking; *when eating; after eating;* after dinner; when walking; on attempting to read; *but long in getting to sleep;* with beginning of enlargement of liver; with inability to sleep or to find a comfortable position; with inability to sleep; as if dizzy, with inability to sleep. Overpowering sleepiness after dinner; (in evening); and on falling asleep sudden starting up, with irrational talking, or during sleep erotic ecstasies or lascivious dreams, also with automatic movements as in sexual intercourse. Slept nearly all the afternoon while trying to study. Fell asleep when writing. Inclination to sit sleeping with head bent forward. Stupid sleep during the day; stupid and long; S. and sound, and in morning on waking she had no desire to rise. Long in morning. Sleep for twenty hours, with scarcely an interruption. Somnolence, when aroused he was in a raging delirium and beat about him.

Sleeplessness; *in evening in bed, with restlessness;* in evening in bed, then light sleep, so that every noise woke him; **before midnight,** *necessity to get out of bed and only after lying down can he get to sleep; for a long time after waking in evening and night; till* 1 A.M. *on account of restlessness, also he cannot get his feet warm;* from 1 till 4 A.M.; on account of a feeling as if eyes would not close but had to be kept closed with the hands and turned about in head; from restlessness; with restlessness and delirium; with inclination to study later than usual. *Late falling asleep;* on account of numerous fancies, then partial sleep with confused fancies; preceded by restlessness, then she woke with oppression as from weight on chest and difficult respiration. Sleep unrefreshing; and heavy. Frequent waking; *on account of dry heat;* with chilliness; with boring in teeth.

Restless sleep; with constant dreams; with dreams, and when awake anxiety in whole body; full of dreams, then headache in morning on waking; then sleeplessness after 4 A.M. Fitful sleep filled with dreams of fighting or of violent physical exertion, with a running comment of incoherent talk. Starting up on falling asleep; starting up towards morning. Crying out and talking. Sopor interrupted by screams. Anxiety during unconscious sleep, wringing hands as in despair, sobbing, lamenting, tossing about, short breath, in fear she grasps at bystanders or deliriously grasps after them.

Dream just before waking; *D. of fire,* with crying out and beating about her; nightmare, so that he cried out; of danger just before waking, of falling from a height out of a hammock; hideous; sad; fretful; of robbers; distressing, of vermin; of dead people, fights, etc.; interrupted, exhausting; confused; unremembered; of money matters; of the business of the day; that she was pinched on back and breast and tickled on soles; ludicrous; of a hæmorrhage; historical, every night; of scientific and philosophical subjects. Unpleasant in morning; with restlessness; indefinite, troubled. Vivid; and constant; *of restless work and business which he could not finish;* and partly remembered; and fearful, of being bitten by a ferocious black horse. Anxious; immediately on falling asleep, waking him; towards morning; and frightful; with tossing about and whining; *of biting animals, she cried out and woke in anxiety;* on falling asleep, as if a man grasped him by the throat and tried to choke him; as if an insect were stinging behind his ear; of necessary business, for attention to which she often rose and made preparations. *Lascivious, with emissions;* L., with erections; with emissions, whereupon he was very wide awake, then little sleep, only confused sleep in morning before 6.

Fever.—Typhus, often with pneumonia and bronchitis, that developed into consumption. Chilliness; in morning; in morning, with yawning; every day from 1 till 5 P.M.; every afternoon, and weakness for several days; in afternoon during menses, then heat and headache, without thirst, next day chilliness at noon, then spasmodic shaking of whole body with chattering of teeth, then heat, < head, and headache; *towards evening; in evening, with anxiety; in evening on going to bed;* in evening in bed; *at* 5 P.M., *then heat, with thirst and internal chilliness, then heat and sweat all night;* towards 6 P.M. and falling asleep from weakness, towards midnight waking from heavy dreams, with sweat; at 7 P.M. when walking in open air, with cold hands, pallor, nausea and empty eructations; at night; at night, with fever; at night (preceded by restlessness for two days), then sweat; at night on waking from an anxious dream, with trembling, < abdomen, then orgasm of blood and oppression of chest, so that he could not breathe and could scarcely rise; at night, then thirst, after the fever delirium; when sitting; on rising; before stool; during menses, with cold hands and feet; when eating (after sitting in a cold room), < limbs, with blue nails; sensitive to cold; with symptoms of fever; with increased temperature and pulse; with ringing in ears, < r.; *then fever, with* **flushed cheeks,** < l., *next day fever with headache, fifth day fever in evening with whitish discharge from vagina, next afternoon fever with headache.*

Chilliness alternating with heat; waking at night, with

pain in head, abdomen and lower limbs, then in forenoon vomiting, lasting more than twenty-four hours, with loss of appetite and sleep; alternating with heat of skin at night, then sweat in sleep; *C. alternating with sweat on head and hands.* **Shivering; every evening, without thirst**, but with dryness of throat; at 7 P.M.; *more than warmth, the S. not > warmth of stove;* with yawning, and at times with gooseflesh on arms; with loss of appetite; with pain in head and stomach; without chilliness; alternating with heat of head and hands. Shaking chills; *at night, with diarrhœa four times, then heat and sweat, later every night sweat before midnight;* with cold creeping over back, necessity to lie down, on putting hands out of bed renewed shivering, with stiffness of hands from cold and painful dulness of head; then heat in forenoon, with thirst for beer, then chilliness, all this in a dreamy slumber, with much motion of hands. *Internal C. afternoons,* with at times sensation of hot water in pit of stomach and in back.

Chilliness except in forehead. Cold skin; and dry; *cold limbs;* C. and bluish limbs; *hands;* hands, though they were warm, red and veins distended; face and hands; *feet;* lower limbs; insteps, hands and feet all day; face in forenoon, with sweat on it and nausea; **knees at night in bed**; of head, with sweat of body; l. side of head, with pain deep in ear; head and body often alternating with heat; over whole trunk, as if it were in cold water, not > an overcoat and a glass of beer; creeping up back during the day; as from a draught, in muscles of r. scapula and posteriorly along r. upper arm to elbow, or sensation as if a raw wind were blowing upon a moist surface, changing at elbow into a numbness that extended to fingers. Shivering over back; and arms, then chilliness in head.

Heat; from 1 till 4 A.M., with short breath, without thirst, with sweat, dry lips and dry tip of tongue and moisture posteriorly in mouth; from 7 till 12 A.M., with sweat, without thirst; *every afternoon,* with or without previous chill; from 2 till 3 and from 6 till 7 P.M., < face; towards 8 P.M., with loss of thirst; in evening, < face, with vertigo; *moderate but regular rise of temperature every evening the first five days,* in morning it was normal or even lower, with frequent pulse, sixth day remittent fever, *which reached the highest point in eighth evening, when pulse was small and soft,* after eighth day temperature fell, on thirteenth day began a more regular intermittent fever, with shaking chill (generally in morning), high temperature and rapid pulse, then sweat; **at night, without thirst** *and sweat, with frequent waking;* **at night, with sweat and hunger that could not be appeased,** *then chilliness, chattering of teeth and external coldness, then internal heat, < hands, with external coldness;* at night, with vomiting; after dinner, < shoulder, with sweat except on feet; before stool; during all pains; at times when sitting, > open air or after dinner, at times with anxiety as if sweat would break out; > cool, open air, with heat in head, < forehead and face (in hands), at times with throbbing in head, at times mounting from back; with tossing about the bed; with red, hot face; with quick pulse; with coated tongue; with sweat and thirst; with itching internally, also with rush of blood to head; < head and hands, with bitter taste and nausea; then sinking of temperature.

Internal and external heat; I., with dulness of head. Anxious H.; after breakfast. Sudden, with restlessness, pain in epigastric region and retention of stool and urine. Inflammatory. Dry, at night, without thirst, with pain in parts on which she lies, as from a hard bed. As if dashed with hot water, on thinking intently. Flushing, < evening, with febrile restlessness and burning in palms; oppressive F. In paroxysms, < face, with dryness of mouth without thirst; anxious P. Sensation as if a flame of fire passed through me. Orgasm of blood; in evening, with warmth; at night, he hears a rush through the body; at night, with chilliness and trembling, with uneasiness in intestines; from the ordinary smoke.

Burning in whole r. side. Heat in paralyzed parts. Hot skin; and dry. Burning in a wart, as in a suppurating wound, in evening after lying down. Heat of head; forehead; on excited talking, and in chest; an hour after dinner, then in whole body, then in feet, as if sweat would break out; > moving about, with dulness; and of hands, with sweat of them; and of hands and feet, with sweat, but only moderate external warmth; dry, and in face and feet, so that the warmth of the room seemed intolerable. *Heat of cheeks;* face and abdomen in morning; *one or other cheek* every evening, without thirst; face towards evening; after eating; with redness of it, sweat on forehead and dulness of head; with red spots after washing; creeping over upper part, with redness and with dim vision; about nose and upper lip, as from something acrid. Heat of ear, with redness. Externally on chest. H. frequently rising from back into head in afternoon when sitting, with redness of face; H. in small of back, < during delayed menses. Flashes of H. and cold across shoulders. Burning in arms and thighs; skin of upper arms. Burning in palms; hands and lower limbs; internally in hands; hands and feet at night; hands, then in head, then in nape, with feeling as if sweat would break out. Burning, moving back and forth along bone of second phalanx of r. index. Burning in thigh, < touch.

Sweat; over whole body in morning; **in morning in bed,** about feet and hands; *in morning after waking; at night; from midnight till morning, in sleep;* **towards morning, with anxiety; on slight exertion;** during dinner; with increased urine; **exhausting, every morning;** exhausting, *then painful heaviness, now in chest, now in head, now in thighs and legs, now general, making him inactive and fretful; anxious; cold;* cold towards evening; clammy; *cold, clammy;* in flushes in forenoon; of garlicky odor; of sulphurous odor; of phosphoric odor, < evening. Sweat on head; forehead; on head, afterwards in the house, after moving about in open air; head and palms after soup; luminous, on forehead; chest; palms; feet; anterior half of body, < abdomen, then on chest, then under shoulders and on back, > after dinner. Dry skin; distressing dryness in soles.

Clinical.—During typhoid fever when the liver and spleen are swollen and there is painless diarrhœa.

Physostigma.

A tincture is made of the "Calabar bean," Physostigma venenosum, Balfour.

General Action.—This ordeal poison produces muscular tremors and tetaniform spasms of voluntary and involuntary muscles, as well as vasomotor spasms, followed by diminished reflex and paralysis. It also produces violent vomiting and purging. Death occurs usually from failure of the respiration. One of its most marked effects is the contraction of the pupil, which is supposed to be due to a paralysis of the sympathetic fibres. Its most marked ally is Muscarine.

Allies.—Agaricus mus., (Opium), Nux vom., Tabac.

Generalities.—Tremblings in front of body, with wavelike motions up and down in it, but in back of body paralysis, numbness and pain as when the nerve of a tooth is being killed; T. in paroxysms, first in legs, sometimes general, at the least thing that startles, once in hands, then soreness in pit of stomach; T. and shuddering, beginning in head, running down through pit of stomach, womb and whole body, the chief sensation in the head was the one in the middle of forehead, and in l. eye a pain with muscæ volitantes. Nervous motions down through body and through arms at 3 P.M., with palpitation, next day with weakness at pit of stomach. Convulsions and twitchings (< back). Twitching of mouth, eyebrows and between brows at 8 P.M., with throbbing between brows and numbness from between eyes down through nose. Hinders voluntary motions as well as causes involuntary motions.

Lancinations in l. hypochondrium, l. thigh, l. index, at 9.50 A.M., then sharp pain in region of liver, passing towards sternum. Darting pains wandering from one place to another. Occasional sharp pains in different parts. Twinging pain in various parts. Strange indescribable sensation through system. Feeling as if he had taken cold; and soreness and stiffness, all over body. Discomfort in morning. Floating sensation on raising my foot when walking, and when the foot touched the ground an unpleasant sensation that caused shuddering. Pulsation through whole body when sitting still, < chest, each beat of heart was distinctly perceptible in chest and temples. Soreness around waist at 6 P.M. Sudden access of vigor at 6.30 P.M., and the symptoms that followed came like a reaction. Restless; at 10 P.M., in bed. Constant desire to change from side to side. Disinclination to move. Aversion to the usual cold bath; to the usual bath, and discomfort after bathing.

Weakness; of r. side; in forepart of day (which was sultry), with uncommon mental activity; in forenoon; at 8 A.M.; 9 A.M; at 9 A.M., < groins; at noon, > 10 P.M., with headache; at 1 P.M.; in afternoon, with fulness on forehead and tendency to ache, < r. side; at 4 P.M., with leucorrhœa; at 8 P.M.; 9 P.M.; 10 P.M.; after stool; on ascending stairs; on walking; when walking in the street, with stupidity and vertigo; and whole frame seemed loosened; with stupidity and feeling as after carousing; with torpor; with necessity to lie down and desire to have the doors shut; at 6.30 P.M., as if every nerve were unstrung, even to eyes, which felt as if all power to see were going from them; extending from head through back and legs, with thrilling in legs, slight exertion caused lameness and weakness in small of back; muscular, with fibrillar twitchings; nervous, tremulous, at 7 P.M., < l. arm.

Faintness. Collapse after the vomiting. Shock of nervous system, amounting to collapse in the worst cases. Paralyzed feeling in whole l. side. State like the effects of an overdose of Aconite. (Old ailments return with renewed force.) Aggravation from motion; from mental activity and exercise; on l. side. Amelioration in open air; and from walking; of pain, by walking, but I had not the strength to walk far; from closing eyes and quiet; in warm room, from not moving; from odor of camphor; from Arnica (selected because the pain was caused by hard pressure on lower end of sternum).

Clinical.—Traumatic tetanus. Chorea. General emaciation. Numerous cases of tetanus in horses. Paralysis agitans. Congestion of the spinal cord, with tetanic spasms.

Mind.—Foolish actions, said it made him crazy. Exhilarated in morning, gloomy towards noon. Nothing was right, too many things in the room, continually counting them. Irritable. Nervous, cannot endure pain, sensitive during the filling of a tooth. Anxiety about friends at home. Not the usual flow of spirits, and it was an extra effort to speak. Disinclined to speak to some of his friends. Dull and sluggish all day; at 8 A.M., and confused feeling, stupid. Felt no alarm where some of my friends saw some reason for it. *Uncommon activity.* Exhaustion, cannot remember anything. Difficult to concentrate thought; D. to work.

Head.—Drooping listlessly. Darting pain; in various parts, < motion. Aching; in morning, with epistaxis, l. side; in morning, < over l. eye, < afternoon and till 10 P.M., with warm sweat on head; at noon, could not put my mind on anything nor remember anything, a mental exhaustion; in afternoon, < towards evening, > 10 P.M., with a strange and confused feeling; in evening and next morning; at 8 P.M.; in brain on waking, < l. side; after drinking new milk; < motion, with confusion of head; < walking; > mental application, < walking in open air; preventing study; congestive, all the forenoon; tensive, and brain and scalp feel tight; burning, at 7 P.M.; bruised, in brain all day, < a heavy step or misstep; heavy, bruised, in brain all day till evening, < l. temple, with general fatigue and sensitiveness to cold or change of temperature.

Pressure encircling it, with sleepiness. Constriction as from a bandage about it; C. as if a tight cap were pressed down as far as temples, with pressure along sagittal suture as from fulness in longitudinal sinus, and aching in temples. Fulness at times, almost to faintness. Heaviness at 8 A.M.; at 2 P.M., with pain in eyes and heat in head and face; < motion, with darting through temples; with dulness and fulness; with confused, feverish feeling alternately in forehead and vertex. Brain confused on waking from midday nap. Stupid feeling; at 7 P.M. Solid feeling; brain feels tired. Constant desire to move it from side to side. Sensation as if brain rolled about in skull. He felt as if he had drunk a glass of liquor, confusion of head, vertigo, legs weak, staggering, at night frequent waking, with terrible thoughts, fear that he was becoming crazy, that he might get up and do some mischief. Vertigo; at 3 A.M.; at 1 P.M. on moving, with faintness and muscæ volitantes; at 4.30 P.M., with nausea; in evening, if people stepped in front of her in the doorway; at night; when reading; on getting up after dinner; when walking; on descending stairs, with dim vision and unsteady gait; with weakness and faintness; with wavering sensation in brain when walking; with feeling as if head fell forward, and stumbling on going up and down stairs; with the peculiar torpidity of Opium and Indian hemp.

Forehead.—Darting pain, < motion, and in temples.

Sharp pain in supraorbital region, running off towards nose. Pain; over r. eye; in morning on waking, by noon pain in whole cerebrum, fulness of bloodvessels of brain and contracted feeling in skin of forehead, which extended to eyelids, causing an effort to open or close them; in l. side at 10 A.M., with heat in abdomen and nausea, the pain is heavy at 11, pain over whole head from 4 till 10 P.M. with nausea and general sweat, headache next day with lame, bruised feeling in region of kidneys; at 2 P.M.; in evening; over r. eye all the evening; at 8 P.M. with chills and fever, next day at 10 A.M. hot and dry skin, at times in afternoon extending to vertex; across top at 5 o'clock, < till going to bed and sleep; on waking; in sinciput and over l. eye, waking me at 3 A.M.; deep-seated, with desire to rub it; sudden, over r. eye at 2 P.M., with pulsation in occiput; as if something hard were tightly bound on it, all the forenoon, with dizziness when walking; weary, over r. eye; stupefying, < over l. eye. Burning pain from 9 A.M. till going to bed at night; at 1 P.M., and pain at 4 P.M. on eating, exercise or mental exertion. *Heavy pain over eyes* in morning on waking, > rising; H. pain before rising; in l. side on waking, afterwards extending over head, < l. side of forehead at 1 P.M., next day headache preventing study, > 10 P.M., third day H. pain in l. frontal eminence, extending deep into brain, preventing study; over eyes at 5 P.M.; over eyes at 8 P.M.; < motion; *H. oppressive pain at* 10 A.M., with inability to express my thoughts clearly. Constriction around F. and temples, changing to oppressive pain over l. orbit and extending to forehead and temples, < reading. Fulness, with tendency to ache and with fatigue, afterwards heavy aching, < r. side. Sensation of rush of blood in F. and temples.

Temples.—Shooting from r. to second bicuspid. Darting pains, < motion. Pain; > supper; in T. and forehead at 11 A.M., in church, with intermittent tension in skin of forehead and nose, making it difficult to close eyes, in evening the sound of the organ caused headache, < forehead and temples, same headache on following days, sometimes < warm room, especially after being in open air, with such sleepiness that efforts to keep awake caused nausea; with pressure outward in forehead; through T., as from rush of blood to head, at 4 P.M., with throbbing of arteries on side of neck; heavy, in r., becoming pulsative and occasionally darting and quivering. Throbbing in arteries and in carotids. Numbness at 4 P.M., with crawling over head.

Vertex.—*Pain extending to occiput, with pain in temples, obliging him to lie down, with pain over orbits, cannot bear to raise eyelids,* feeling as if something heavy were pressing out the brain; pain in V. and forehead, obliging him to lie down, > sitting up in bed and by strong pressure; stupid, extending down through head, in evening. Bearing down on V.; < l. lobe of brain. Expansive sensation. Pressure outward, and in temples.

Sides.—Shooting through r., extending into nape, at 11 A.M., < rising or walking; paroxysmal, in r. eminence, leaving a bruised feeling, the pain > evening by close attention to a sermon, renewed by going into open air. Sharp pain in r.; in l., then r. Lateral headache, deep in brain; lateral, in morning, with fear of opening his eyes lest it should increase the pain; beginning when riding in a carriage; caused by the crying of a child; deep in brain, > eating. Pain in r. side; indefinable, in r., all day, with feeling as if it would increase, but it did not.

Occiput.—Pain in l. Stimulus in O. and neck, extending through head to eyes, in afternoon and evening. Weak feeling as if paralyzed, passing through back to lower limbs, the feeling in legs was as if asleep. Creeping numbness in O. and down spine, between 8 and 9 P.M., < between hips.

Eyes.—Bloodshot all the forenoon, with burning in them. L. red and swollen. Inflammation of r., then l., sclerotic red, dry and swollen, eyes feel best when closed. Sleepy-like. "Were working." *Shooting in r.* at 1 P.M., *with drawing in it. Drawing, twisting sensation; at* 3 P.M.; from 11 A.M. till 8 P.M. *Drawing at* 6 P.M. *Smarting, with sore feeling in lids.* Pain in l.; in l., with muscæ volitantes; P. on attempting to use binocular vision, as in reading, with burning and straining, so that one eye must be closed, > a weak concave glass. Pressure, with muscæ volitantes, dark and light long worms or snakes, also tremulous vision. Heaviness; at 2 P.M., with dulness. Sensitive. *Weak feeling.*

Lachrymation. Pupils contracted; in morning; by small and rapid jerks, with sensitiveness to light; then mydriasis, < morning, seeming to depend on fatigue of sphincter, which was relieved during the day by the reflex stimulus of light; dilated.

Ball.—Intermittent darting outward in r., > pressure on eyes, lasting from 6.30 till 10 P.M., then shifting to supraorbital ridge and lasting till 12, next day on rising at 7 A.M., darting outward in eyes, > breakfast, on sitting down to study at 7 P.M. same pain in l. eye and superciliary ridge, > pressure and moving about. Drawn, twisted sensation at 8 P.M., < r., next day at 7 P.M. *Pain;* in r. ball and frontal bone in evening, with stitches and with pain running obliquely into temporal bone, next day *pain deep in over top of ball, ran up from inner canthus to r. frontal eminence, then down obliquely outward into temple, the same returned in eye and forehead but was more general in forehead,* > motion out of doors; nervous, extending along supraorbital nerves and over half of head. Painful tension, partly in equator of ball, partly in ciliary region. Burning all the morning.

Twitching of lids; upper; upper, < l.; upper at 4 P.M. Contracted sensation in lids, with difficulty in opening them and lachrymation when wide open, difficulty in keeping l. open. Lids heavy. Lids immovable. Tight feeling in ciliary region, as if something were creeping about in it, with sharp pain, < reading, vision confused, spasm of accommodation in l. and diminished power in r. eye, type looked smaller with r. than with l. eye, afterwards type now clear, now indistinct, coinciding with sensation as if ciliary muscle were irregulary contracted, with sudden contraction of l. pupil and sudden gloom, as of an eclipse of the sun, < when l. eye only was open, astigmatism. Pain in posterior part of orbit, extending back into brain, preventing reading and causing nausea.

Vision.—*Blurred, then dull pain over and between eyes.* Dim; when walking; for objects more than a foot distant, all objects seem nearer and larger, afterwards with contracted pupils and on reading heaviness and fatigue of eyes. Double. *Accommodation recovers before the pupil;* recovers before the myosis, the approximation of the near point lasts longer than that of the far point. Jerklike approximation of far point, then of near point. Letters seem in constant motion, and can only be seen at a large visual angle. Muscæ volitantes; black and white; bright marks when looking at an object, and when reading dark, yellowish spots covering one or two letters.

Clinical.—Physiologically this drug has been used to tear adhesions of the iris, especially when complicated with ulceration of the cornea at the margin, on account of its extraordinary power to contract the pupil. Curatively it has been used in myopia for spasm of the ciliary muscle, especially with symptoms of irritability, pain after using the eyes, flashes of light, black specks, etc. Torpor of the retina. Nearsightedness from a blow, a rigidity of the muscles of accommodation so that the patient can only see very near objects. Increasing myopia.

Ears.—Shooting in l. at 3 P.M.; in r. at 6.45 P.M. Sharp pain in r., with stiffness of neck, next day a little soreness. Pain in r. when writing. Hammering in r. in evening, with feeling in external ear as from a hot wind. Painful pressure on tympani. Discomfort in r., with inclination to bore in with finger, and after removal of wax and with eructation, a sudden pain from throat along Eustachain tube to middle ear, leaving stabbing pain in middle ear, the desire to bore in occurred repeatedly every evening. Crawling in l. Fulness. Stopped feeling. Partial deafness of r. Sensitive to every sound. Singing or tuning like escaping steam, at night after lying down. Buzzing in r. at 7 P.M., with ringing.

Nose.—Twitching, with involuntary expansion of nostrils. Fever-blisters in and around l. nostril. Boil inside of r. nostril, with pain extending to eye and r. side of head, scanty discharge after breaking. Feeling as if a cold were coming on, smarting, tingling and sneezing. Contracted feeling in wings and in upper lip, > rubbing. Itching in l. nostril in morning, with tingling and *moisture*, return of the itching in afternoon with *dryness*, again in evening with *moisture*. Stuffed and hot. Sensation as if it would bleed at 4 P.M., with heat in it; sensation as if it would bleed at 2 and 8 P.M., and the peculiar taste that goes with it. Sneezing. Fluent coryza. Bleeding from r. side in evening, next day from l. side in morning and at supper, with headache.

Face.—Red; on rising from a seat, with pain. Pale. Tired look in morning. Occasional darting pain in r. malar-bone and ramus of jaw. Neuralgia in r. side. *Contracted sensation in l. side*, with numbness. Feeling as in spasms, > opening mouth, at times extending into neck, when it was the worst the l. hand became numb and it bothered me to hold on to anything, noticed most when looking at my watch. Pain in mastoid processes; in r. lower jaw; in side of jaw where there were teeth; like toothache in r. upper jaw (from which all the teeth had been extracted).

Mouth.—Teeth feel rough in morning, not > brushing. Quivering sensation in teeth, as if resting on the sounding-board of a piano. Tongue rough to touch; T. coated, < towards root; coated white, with oily feeling in it and bad taste; scalded feeling, next day only on l. side, two days afterwards on r. side; raw feeling, < swallowing; *felt sore on tip* at 4 P.M., and rough; sore, rough and dry; sore on l. side, with difficult motion of it as if stiff; *smarting at end;* dryness in tip and in lips, with smarting; numbness and tingling smarting in T. and lips, with constant desire to moisten them. Felt a sluggishness of articulation, and to avoid any show of this made a strong effort to speak slowly and firmly.

Roof of yellowish copper color at 9 P.M., with feeling as if covered with patches of loose skin. Running out of mucus. Thick, lathery saliva. Salivation. Taste bad all day; bad in morning on rising, as if I had been in a close room all night; bad, with salivation; brassy, with salivation; metallic at 9 P.M.; like creosote in morning on waking.

Throat.—Submaxillary gland tender and tumefied. Clear mucus at 6 P.M. *Feeling as if a ball ascended.* Pain extending to l. ear at 3 P.M. on swallowing. Soreness at 2 P.M., with constricted feeling on swallowing, S. next day at 5 P.M.; S. at 8 P.M., < swallowing; in back part in evening; in evening, tonsils and soft palate inflamed, dark red, with stinging; at 9 P.M., with feeling of a fish-bone in it, swallowing of saliva painful; in a spot on r. side, < swallowing; on swallowing. Raw, scrapy burning at 9 P.M., on swallowing. Burning scraping rawness, with constriction on swallowing. Smarting of l. tonsil. Fulness.

Constriction in evening when swallowing; at 7 P.M., with soreness posteriorly in pharynx and painful swallowing of saliva, throat dry at 10 P.M., next day the pain and constriction of pharynx continued, with ulcers with yellow centres on r. side of pharynx, behind tonsil, and redness of posterior nares, afterwards swallowing difficult, ulcers < r. side, pain < r. side, afterwards with elongation of uvula; C. in upper part, with difficulty in eating, > before breakfast is eaten, injection of posterior superior part of mouth; C., with difficult swallowing, tonsils enlarged, uvula elongated, speaking painful, posterior part of tongue painful to touch. Gone feeling in œsophagus. Inability to swallow.

Stomach.—Appetite increased; morbid; diminished; lost; lost for breakfast; hunger, but can find nothing to satisfy it, disposed to try one thing after another, food has a flat taste. Disgust for food. Thirst; in afternoon; for cold water in evening, < drinking; lacking. Eructations; at 4 P.M.; tasteless; empty; empty at 7 P.M.; of warm air. Hiccough; from 9 till 11 P.M., > going to bed; violent, from 5 till 8 P.M.; violent, at 8.30 P.M., > sleep, with distress for breath, violent H. on waking at 2 A.M.

Nausea; in morning and at noon, so that he could not eat much dinner at 1 P.M., > lying down, then he could eat a little more, after resting again all symptoms passed off; in morning on waking; at 10 A.M.; 2 P.M., with chilly creeping up back; 3 P.M.; 4.30 P.M., with vertigo; 7 P.M.; 10 P.M.; on lying down; caused by breakfast; caused by sound of the organ; caused by pain in orbit; with the headache; with sinking feeling in stomach; in attacks. Vomiting; of acrid fluid; with great retching, then collapse and cold sweat in drops over whole body; in attacks, with diarrhœa; copious, with such weakness that he could not completely eject the vomited water; later I could not vomit, the abdominal muscles acted too feebly.

Trembling of nerves at pit, with nausea and faintness. Pricking in S. and abdomen, then rumbling and pain in region of transverse colon, next day P. in stomach and abdomen at 9.30 A.M. Sharp pain shooting upward at 9.30 A.M. Darting pain in epigastric region, except during sleep. Griping and oppression; G. in pit; in pit, with soreness on pressure. Crampy pain, with desire for stool. Pain; in epigastric region;

on going out of doors after dinner, causing nausea, then crampy feeling in fundus of bladder; in epigastrium, just under ensiform cartilage, extending into chest and down arms, waking at 2 A.M., pain in epigastrium produced by hard pressure on lower end of sternum, extended along lower edge of ribs, at attachment of diaphragm, and through to about third dorsal vertebra, sensation as if the pain were squeezed out into arms, the pain alternated between an ache and an acute quick pain, but was occasionally pulsative.

Sensitiveness to pressure in region; in epigastric region; in pit at 10.30 P.M. Nervousness, < *front of body.* Oppression in epigastric region. Contraction in region, afterwards with dull pain in l. side and forepart of head. Feeling as if mucous coat (?) swelled. Burning, with hot eructations. Peculiar sensation in epigastrium, afterwards increased to an intermittent sensation as from suddenly swallowing large pieces of food, first near upper part of sternum, becoming more intense till it reaches the epigastrium, when it is almost painful and eructations usually occur, escape of gas, then reversal of pain from lower sternum to throat. Sensation in pit as if undigested food oppressed it; at intervals, and intermittent breathless sensation and disposition to inspire deeply. Digestion slow. Unsettled. Weakness in pit, with the nervous symptoms. Food lay hard all day. Heaviness; as from undigested food. Emptiness at 3 P.M., with weakness of it, without hunger; E. in stomach and abdomen.

Abdomen.—Bloated feeling; in morning, with soreness; B. by gas, with pain, compelling me to lie down, < standing erect. Rumbling at 10 P.M.; at 8.40 P.M., with gurgling, heat and colic, all but the colic lasting till 11 P.M.; with full feeling and heat. Emission of flatus; noisy; odorless; foul-smelling; smelling like carrion. Pinching crampy pain at 3 P.M. Clutching pain at 4.30 P.M.; at 7.30 A.M., before stool. Pain; during stool; with feeling of looseness; waking at 3 A.M., > 11 A.M. by stool. Heat with the headache. Uneasiness as if bowels would move soon.

Stitches in l. side. Sore spot in l. side, with pain on pressure and moving about, < riding. Pain in l. side; in transverse colon; in transverse and descending colon, with full sensation; in transverse and descending colon during diarrhœa, with tenesmus; in region of arch of colon, < r. side, < night, often waking me, with stitches through to back.

Darting pain in r. hypochondrium. Griping in r. hypochondrium. Pain in hepatic region at 10.20 A.M.; stiff pain posteriorly in hepatic region in morning on waking, with tenderness on pressure and first moving, > moving. Sore pain in spleen; descending to groin, < motion, so severe in evening as to cause me to extend my legs. Pain in umbilical region; drawing; sharp. Soreness of umbilicus, with sensation as if corset had pinched it, with blood red color.

Hypogastrium.—Shooting in l. iliac region; occasionally in groin, extending into r. testicle. Cutting, more in muscles than in organs. Pain in groin; in groin at 7 P.M.; in groin at 8 P.M., with swelling; alternately in r. and l. groin at 6 P.M.; low down in abdomen, then copious, loose stool; return of a pain in r. that had been absent two years; drawing, in r. iliac region, > lying on r. side, pressure, walking in open air and eating, < lying on back and l. side. Soreness, hurting me to stand, and in l. side.

Rectum and Anus.—Return of piles which had not troubled him for years. Anus sore, inclined to protrude (as from relaxed sphincter). Tenesmus before and after stool; after stool; with diarrhœa; as if he had been to stool, then a thin stool. Feeling for half an hour before stool as if I had been to stool. Frequent ineffectual desire. Desire, stool hard, scanty, three hours later watery stool, with flatus, on following days loose stools.

Stool.—Diarrhœa; and vomiting; weakening; copious, with burning at anus. Loose and irregular. Soft and light-colored, next morning thin and light-colored, then tenesmus, thin stool at noon, soft at 9 P.M. with tenesmus. Soft, brownish, fetid, frequent, with tenesmus and pain in transverse and descending colon, and tenesmus on bladder, next day two mushy stools after breakfast with same kind of pain, same kind of stool and pain after dinner and supper, with tenesmus, afterwards constipation on the days when I did not take the drug, and when I recommenced had four stools in one day, but not loose. Soft, large, brown, at 7 A.M., small, thin, yellow, sour-smelling at 2 P.M., small, watery, mixed with undigested food, sour-smelling at 7 P.M., small, watery at 10 P.M., next day (third day) watery, then tenesmus, fourth day no stool, fifth day a large stool, a part black like tar, sixth day natural-looking stool mixed with black lumps, then slight discharge of mucus, seventh day thin, small, lumpy, tenesmus before and after it, ninth day small, hard stools covered with jelly-like slime at 7 and 7.30 A.M.

Constipation. Hard and in balls, but easy. Lumpy, mingled with a watery discharge, at night, next day constipated. Yellow, at 5.10 A.M., with pain below umbilical region. Twice in one day, once with much straining to pass a small amount. Natural looking at 3.45 A.M., a small, sour-smelling one at 8 A.M., then none for sixty-nine hours. Copious at 11 A.M., a soft, yellowish one at 3.30 P.M., an offensive one at 6.30, another stool at 10.30 P.M. and at 6.30 A.M. next day, afterwards two or three stools a day, at irregular times, not large, yellowish. Omitted second day, third day ineffectual desire several times, fourth day small, hard stool, fifth day copious, light-colored, twice, with crampy pain in hypogastrium, seventh day stool almost impossible on account of contraction of sphincter, eighth day desire in morning in bed, with cramp in stomach, but the desire left me after rising, ninth day constipation, tenth day hard, dark at 9 A.M., with urging and pain in abdomen, urging at 9.05 A.M., with light stool, copious, yellow diarrhœa at 9.15 A.M., with burning smarting, eleventh day constipation.

Urinary Organs.—Full feeling in bladder, as from retention of urine. Frequent ineffectual desire. Frequent micturition. Pain in urethra after micturition. Urine muddy. Urine high-colored and smelling strong. Urine scanty. Urine copious; in morning; in morning on rising, and clear, slightly yellow; in forenoon, with difficult retention of it; at night, and frequent micturition; and colorless; during the pain, and pale, odorless, and frequent micturition; containing mucus; and clear, urates diminished, phosphates increased.

Sexual Organs. — Strong-smelling sweat, prepuce tender and swollen, with eruption on glans, which was easily excited, with burning itching. Frequent erections in forenoon, with slight desire. Emissions without dreams or excitement. Pain in womb as if menses were coming on. Leucorrhœa; at 4 P.M., with weakness. Condition like that induced by profuse flooding after delivery.

Clinical.—Irregular menstruation, with palpitation, congestion of the eyes, with occasional tonic spasms, rigidity of every muscle, but without loss of consciousness, sighing respiration.

Respiratory Organs.—Cough from tickling in throat; in evening; C. till expectoration of a plug of white mucus, with irritation of r. bronchus; constant inclination to C. from filling lungs. Dyspnœa; at 10 P.M. *Sighing; and yawning.*

Chest.—Twitches across pectoral muscles. Sticking near apex of r. lung at 5 P.M., in l. breast all day, preventing a long breath. Pain in lungs, < l.; P. in r. side, in region of sixth and seventh ribs, at 7 P.M.; muscular, beneath clavicles, extending down inside of arms, at 3.45 P.M. L. lung cannot be filled, as the attempt causes pain in upper part, > pressure.

Heart.—Pain in region. *Palpitation*, with the nervous motions. Action regular after strong coffee; tumultuous when lying on l. side, > lying on back; heart and pulse feeble and tumultuously irregular.

Clinical.—Spasmodic action of the heart, with feeling of pulsation through the whole body, especially in the chest, the beats of the heart distinctly perceptible in the chest and head.

Pulse.—Rapid; and full, strong; and small; then slow, feeble and thready; then slow, small and wiry, then slow, thready and difficult to count, then slow, thready, intermittent. Slow; and feeble; and feeble, afterwards could not be counted; and soft, compressible, with occasional intermissions. Full. R. side nearly double in strength to that of l. Could count it in carotid and hear two sounds of heart as my head lay upon the pillow. Variable; and full, strong. Feeble.

Neck.—Pain across nape at base of brain as if it were cutting the body off from the head, extending to back of throat, which was stiff and sore, in afternoon, with loss of power and sensation in occiput as if head would fall forward, then pain down nape, < the most prominent bone there and on each side of it, *drawing* whenever the head was turned. Pain in nape reaching to first dorsal vertebra; rheumatic, in l. side and l. shoulder; rheumatic, in l. side, with soreness. Inclination to "run the head out" from uneasiness in nape. Stiffness of l. side; of r. side, inability to move head, with drawing and tension; sudden, in r. side when taking the usual cold morning bath, extending during the day to r. shoulder and also to clavicle, which felt sore and was swollen over sterno-mastoid, > leaning head towards r. side, extending towards evening through r. lung, the pain in neck and shoulder at times caused nausea, sharp pain in r. ear, afterwards soreness of neck.

Back.—Cramplike stitches up and down spine. Pain at 2 P.M.; down spine at 1 P.M., with stiffness and inclination to bend forward; with downward pressure and appearance of menses; with almost constant desire to urinate and copious reddish urine. Weakness, inability to stand erect. Sticking under inferior angles of scapulæ during expiration. Pain in region of r. scapula and below it; deep under r. in afternoon when sitting; heavy, under l. after dinner.

Lumbar Region.—Pain; in l. side of sacrum in afternoon and next morning; between hips at 6.30 P.M., with numbness in region of womb; in kidney region, causing restlessness all night; dragging, over l. hip in sleep the rest of the night after 3 A.M.; drawing, low down in back and in abdomen, with bearing down as if menses would appear, a week later the menses came on at the right time without the usual unpleasant premonitory symptoms; heavy, over l. hip, extending to back, in afternoon and evening, with bearing down as before menses. Bruised feeling in kidney region. Soreness; with heavy pains.

Extremities.—Neuralgic stitches in muscles of knees and arms. Darting pains in joints, more in legs than in arms, extending up into body, pains in knees, < flexion. Pain; in joints of wrists, hands and knees. Bruised feeling in joints. Weariness, with constant desire to move them; W., with heaviness; W., or numbness. Pleasant numbness, as before the sleep of Opium or Morphia, at night when awake. Stiffness of joints at 9 P.M.

Upper Extremities.—Shooting in l. shoulder at 7 A.M. Rheumatic pain in l. shoulder at 8 P.M.; drawing, through l. Arm, uneasy pain in r.; uneasy pain in r. deltoid, preventing sleep the forepart of the night, > violent motion; sharp pain in l., then in r., involving shoulders; pains extending downward, with weakness of them; burning throbbing in l. arm and hand as if it had been out in the cold, at 11 A.M., with the sensation felt on coming to the fire, also a nervous, tremulous, weak feeling in arm; sudden constriction around l., above elbow; weakness; tired feeling and difficulty in lifting them; numbness of l., also at 7 P.M. and down ring finger.

Elbow.—Darting pain in r., extending down outside of arm to the two middle fingers. Acute pain in l. and darts of pain thence to fourth and fifth fingers (these pains began in l. side of neck and elbow, extended thence to l. leg, locating in l. knee). Tingling pain (as from hitting the nerve) in r., extending down ulnar surface of forearm and into third finger.

Numbness of l. forearm at 5 P.M., with sticking down arm. Pain in wrists, with weakness; P. deep in muscles of r. forearm and wrist at 8 P.M., next day pain moving, gnawing deep in inner aspect of wrist, thence it ran up ulnar side of forearm to elbow, with desire to move the arm, which did not relieve; sharp, in l. wrist at 11 A.M., recurring frequently at 8 P.M.; in bone of r. wrist, as if squeezed and gradually let go, in afternoon. Stinging in r. knuckle from 2 till 4 P.M. Hands, trembling sensation; pain in dorsum of r.; weakness; numbness of l.; numbness at 11.30 A.M., < feeling pulse. Twinging in l. fingers. Darts of pain through r. thumb, at root of nail, at 3 A.M., less severe through r. finger-joints. Sharp pain in l. index.

Lower Extremities.—Staggering. Walking difficult. Could neither stand nor walk. Pain at 9 A.M.; twinging pain. Weakness at 6.30 P.M., coming from a spot in back between hips.

Thigh.—Twitchings in lower third of vastus externus every time I sat down. Intermittent shooting in or near l. popliteal space. Thrusts in l., with aching down it. Cramplike pain in l. popliteal space, < walking, > rest, returned on motion, > continued motion. Aching in r. gluteals; in l. thigh and both knees about noon, after a few steps; in l. hip extending into groin, at 2 P.M. Stiffness in rectifemoris muscles in afternoon when walking; S. in hip and knee-joints; in l. hip at 2 P.M., next day at 9 A.M.; l. hip and r. knee at 6 and 9 P.M.; l. hip at 7 P.M.

Knee.—Pain on outside; in patellæ on descending stairs; numb, in knees and ankles when sitting, with desire to move frequently. Drawing in posterior cords of leg and knee at 6.30 P.M., < walking, especially up stairs. Weakness of r. at 9 A.M. Unsteady feeling from knees downward when walking, < *shutting eyes*, > exertion of the will, with weakness about ankles. (Better in morning.)

Cramp in l. calf at night in bed. Gnawing in l. tibia. Intermittent constriction around l. leg above ankle. Weight in legs. Twinges of pain in ankle; in r. instep. Cramp in l. foot in evening in a warm bath. Numbness of l. foot. Pain around r. great toe.

Skin.—Eruption about the size of flea-bites on back and arms. Itching of l. palm. Numbness (from local application), with pricking.

Sleep.—Yawning. Sleepiness; all day, with yawning; mornings when riding, such sudden falling asleep after dinner that he was surprised on waking to find that he had slept, the sleepiness > a few hours of hard exercise, he slept at night as well as if he had not slept in afternoon; at 8 A.M. when driving, with pressure encircling head; at 3 P.M., > sleep; < from morning till 2 P.M.; and sleep for two hours, but the mind was so active that I was not conscious of having been asleep. Sleep early in evening and prolonged next morning. Difficulty in arousing myself in morning. Heavy sleep, with tired feeling before rising. Frequent falling asleep and sudden waking, next night eyes scarcely closed in sleep, thoughts active, an idea started kept on with unusual persistence.

Sleepless before midnight, then disturbed sleep. Awake for some time in a dreamy state. (Wakeful in evening, instead of drowsy as usual.) Restlessness at night; restless sleep towards morning. Sleep disturbed, awake from 2 till 5 A.M., then deep sleep for an hour, on waking discomfort as if I had slept too sound, with pain on r. side of head and neck and stiff neck, cannot bear my pillow high. Dreams vivid, pleasant; horrid all night; that he was a lion; in afternoon, that my head was full and as if brain were revolving upward from frontal sinus to occiput and that I was almost blind, next day sleepiness at 9 A.M.

Fever.—Chilliness; at 8 P.M., with fever and frontal headache, next day at 10 A.M. hot and dry skin, < noon; in paroxysms; in back, with yawning and bruised feeling in joints, every draught of air caused shuddering, and the same bad feeling every time I moved; on r. side of back at noon. Chills creeping up back at 7 P.M.; at 2 P.M., with nausea; with feverishness. Chilliness in limbs, with vague discomfort; C. of hands, then heat and redness of them; of lower limbs in evening, with heat in face and down back, as when the sun shines directly upon you on a cold day. Cold and clammy skin.

Heat; at 2 P.M.; dry, over whole body, with uneasiness and distress about heart. Hot head at 2 P.M., with throbbing in temples; head and face at 2 P.M., with heavy headache and pain in eyes; forehead at 2 P.M.; in a spot in the centre of forehead; cheeks; face in afternoon, with redness of it and feeling as if a lower temperature would cause chill; lower limbs; palms by paroxysms.

Sweat; in morning on waking and caused by any excitement during the day; at 8 P.M.; on least exertion; on forehead, from suffering; cold, in drops, after vomiting.

Phytolacca.

A tincture is made of the fresh root of Phytolacca decandra, L.

General Action.—It produces sore throat, even diphtheritic; inflammation of the kidneys, with numerous symptoms of general lithæmia, pains in tendinous parts (periosteum and tendons), heart symptoms, etc. Its action on the mammary glands is pronounced and important.

Allies.—Petrol., Merc., Rhus t., Colch., Wyeth., Lyc.

Generalities.—Increased secretion of tears, saliva, bile, urine and menses. *Convulsions.* Opisthotonos, general rigidity, hands clenched, feet extended and toes flexed, eyes bleared and dancing, pupils contracted, lower lids drawn down, teeth clenched, lips everted and firm, pulse 85 and soft, respiration difficult, mucous râles, later general rigidity with convulsions of face and neck (chin close to sternum), then partial relaxation, then return of symptoms, afterwards twitching of muscles, < lower limbs.

Pains are sometimes followed by itching and burning. Pains transitory; P. in joints, and bones of face and head, preventing sleep and proceeding from the "nodes," < frontal bone, and resembling those of periostitis; P. always came with its full force at once and so continued till it ceased, then drowsiness and stupor or even sleep; all neuralgic, < motion and pressure, they are pressing and shooting, sometimes sore, drawing and aching; shooting inward and upward. *General soreness* at 7 A.M.; *S. in muscles* (Rhus t.); of throat, lungs and stomach; *with stiffness* (Petr., Rhus). Throbbing through whole system.

Weakness; in afternoon and evening; at night, with the headache; on rising and walking, with intoxicated feeling; and could speak only in a whisper; with indisposition to move; with trembling on motion; with discomfort; with the vomiting and purging; as between chills and fever of ague. Faintness.

Aggravation *general at night and in wet weather;* in morning, of symptoms in stomach, throat and mouth; at 11 A.M., of all symptoms except pains in bowels, most symptoms begin to subside at 10 P.M.; on motion and in open air, except headache, which was > open air; in r. side of head and neck, r. limbs, r. side of chest; on r. side, in several instances symptoms first on l. side and either pass over to r. or the next symptom was on r. side. Amelioration when eating, especially of throat symptoms (Ign.); *of pain in open air;* after breakfast, of many symptoms, especially about head and throat, while heat and many abdominal symptoms are < afternoon; when lying, of all symptoms except scraping and excoriation of throat and expectoration of tenacious saliva.

Clinical.—Subacute rheumatism. Convulsions (uræmic).

Mind.—Cheerfulness increased. *Loss of personal delicacy, disregard of surrounding objects and no disposition to adjust their persons under any circumstances. Indifference to life* in morning on waking, with disgust for the business of the day. Gloomy. Irritable. Dread of movement. Desire to bathe in cold water, could hardly keep him from dashing water over himself. Half stupor all the time and sleep as soon as the paroxysm of cramping had passed.

Head.—Thrown backward. *Aching;* all day; after breakfast, through the forenoon, < walking or riding; sometimes in whole head, sometimes in temples, with vertigo, sometimes in occiput; from walking, with nausea; < looking down and stooping; < after dinner, especially in forehead; *with nausea;* moving about, generally in one side at a time, < r. side; as if it would burst, at 3 P.M. *Soreness internally; sore pain over H.* as if sick-headache were approaching, < *r. side* and in damp weather. Dulness; with disturbed feeling in stomach. Heaviness; with burnt feeling in back of tongue; at 11 A.M., extending through shoulders and chest, later in the day through legs, with vertigo. *Vertigo;* with dim vision; with nausea; with heavy headache and indisposition to mental exertion.

Forehead.—*Aching;* over eyes; in tuberosities; in r. side, in region of time and mirthfulness; at 7 A.M., and in temples; in F. and temples at night, with lassitude; after dinner, < glabella; *above one brow, with nausea; with nausea, cool sweat on forehead and weakness,* the nausea and headache > supper, but returned; with acute hearing; with gaping; *extending backward from F.;* heavy, after dinner. Painful pressure on F. and upper part of eyes. Constriction. Fulness, with constant gaping. Heaviness; and dulness. Drawing above root of nose.

Temples.—Shooting in r. Pain; in l., then burning in skin, in l. region of time; with pressure outward; through T. when leucorrhœa began; drawing, in r. Pressure, with constriction in præcordia, as before seasickness. Heaviness.

Vertex.—*Pain, with dryness;* P. beginning at 5 P.M., when riding, < motion, which caused vertigo, P. > night by sleep; P. on stepping from a high step to the ground, with bruised sensation in brain. Heaviness.

Throbbing pain in r. side. Pain in occiput; in l. region of combativeness; bruised.

Clinical.—Headache, syphilitic. Dull frontal pain, with sensation of soreness in the brain or a feeling as if the brain were bruised on stepping down. Headache < wet weather.

Eyes.—Sunken; and surrounded by livid circles. Inflammation and lachrymation. Shooting from l. to vertex; at intervals. *Sandy feeling.* Pain; and subjective soreness. *Smarting;* of l. Sensation as from horse-radish. Burning in l., with smarting and lachrymation. Twitching sensation about E. Aggravation in l.; A. in eyes and lids in morning, but vision is worse in evening. Lachrymation, > open air; L., with running of water from nose. Pupils dilated.

Smarting in internal canthus in evening, < l., < gaslight. Itching of internal canthus, with pain in ball on slightest pressure. Lids agglutinated at night; A. in morning, and œdematous; reddish-blue swelling, < l., < morning, cannot close eyes without pain in forenoon, > afternoon; *feel granulated, and edges have a scalded feeling as if raw, the same next day, with sandy sensation in lids;* feeling as if sand were under l., causing lachrymation from that eye; soreness on closing; feeling as if coals of fire were on them. Pain along lower half of r. orbit. Pressure around eyes in afternoon as if eyes were too large. Photophobia; in morning. Long-sighted. Vision dim. Diplopia on suddenly raising eyes to look at a higher object; D., with twitching; not only two but four and five reduplications, always in the same horizontal plane, < the next evening.

Clinical.—Blepharitis, with styes and tumors, the lids thickened, indurated, dark red and tender; ulcerated, with formation of crusts (similar to Graph.). Granular lids. Suppurative choroiditis, with inflamed hard swelling of the lids, hypopyon. Threatening suppuration of the cornea.

Ears.—Shooting in r. Pain, < r. Irritation in one Eustachian tube. Obstruction in l. Eustachian tube, with rushing sound in l. ear, and feeling as if hearing were dull, but it is sensitive to the most minute sounds. Hearing increased, < r. ear.

Clinical.—Neuralgia of the ear, especially right side, shooting pains when swallowing.

Nose.—Pustule in nostril. *Drawing about root. Feeling in N. and eyes as if a cold were coming on.* Smarting in nostril at 9 A.M., after riding three hours in an open carriage, with stinging. Burning, then dryness in throat, which soon caused soreness, then watery discharge from nose, which increased until nose became stuffed. Tickling in r. nostril. Stoppage of r. nostril; of one nostril at night; S. when riding, so that he must breathe through mouth. Sneezing. Coryza; fluent. Discharge of mucus sometimes from one nostril, sometimes from the other; from one while the other is stopped.

Clinical.—Nasal catarrh, with pain at the root of the nose and stoppage of one nostril.

Face.—*Pallor;* alternating with almost purple redness; with blue, sunken and suffering look; and hippocratic appearance. Red. Sickly-looking, sclerotica and face dark yellow. Expression as if suffering from cholera. Eruption on l. side of upper lip. Pain in upper jaw; at 11 A.M., and in teeth; in jaws, as if he could not move them.

Mouth.—Shooting in r. molars. Pain in teeth, with soreness and elongated sensation. Irresistible inclination to bite teeth together. *Tongue feels rough, with blisters on sides,* **red tip** (Rhus t.), **pain in root on swallowing**; T. coated white; coated yellow and dry; T. and lips dry; T. and roof of mouth tender and hot; T. yellow and swollen; *pain in root of T. and in fauces;* smarting towards tip, with coldness. Swelling of soft palate; and tonsils, with congestion, r. tonsil half as large again as l. Ulcers on inside of r. cheek, as from Mercury. Constant flow of thick, ropy, tenacious secretion from M., throat and salivary glands. Saliva yellowish, metallic-tasting; S. cold, sticky, stringy; no S. *Salivation* (Merc.); in morning. Palate dry in morning. Taste like nuts; metallic; bitter, leaving smarting and coldness towards tip of tongue.

Clinical.—Difficult dentition. Ulceration of the inner surface of the cheek. Ulceration of the margins of the tongue, with thick tenacious secretions in the mouth (Merc.).

Throat.—Peculiar pressure in parotids, with tension in them. *Tonsils and palate dark purple. Tonsils swollen and red; S.* in morning, *and sore.* Eruption in fauces and œsophagus. *Pain in r. side;* in T., fauces and lungs, with suffocation. *Smarting in fauces. Rawness; and scraping, and in tonsils,* as if something had lodged at root of tongue. *Roughness;* in pharynx. Burnt feeling. **Soreness and dryness** (Wyeth.), **fauces congested and dark, tonsils swollen;** *soreness in morning, with swelling of soft palate and with thick white and yellow mucus about fauces,* after removal of which the throat feels better, and still better after breakfast; S. in afternoon, < swallowing, *with dryness; with redness, dryness and roughness; with feeling of a lump on swallowing saliva and on turning head to l.; of posterior fauces extending into one Eustachian tube;* extending downward.

Sensation of a lump. Sensation of a plug in forenoon when riding, not > hawking, *then increased discharge from posterior nares of mucus, which was detached with difficulty and which continually excited attempts to expel it.* On swallowing, sensation as if a ball of red-hot iron had lodged in fauces and œsophagus, so that I could eat nothing but fluids, with constant choking sensation. Sensation as if an apple-core had lodged, causing constant inclination to swallow. Sensation in pharynx as after eating choke-pears. *Fulness so that it felt choked, hawking to rid throat and posterior nares of mucus,* and sensation as if something had lodged on l. side of throat after bending head forward in writing, < turning head to l.; F. in fauces, and next day in upper part of larynx, with sensation of a lid there till afternoon, next day the same F., with ineffectual desire to hawk up mucus from throat.

Dryness; in a spot in l. side of fauces in morning, till after breakfast; on going to bed; < morning; in fauces, < morning; *causing soreness; uneasy, in fauces, provoking hacking and dry cough;* in pharynx towards morning causing cough; *with roughness, preventing swallowing; in upper part of pharynx, and disposition to hawk, without relief,* next day the D. and hawking continued, raised small pieces of tough, sticky mucus at 9 A.M., throat > 1 P.M. after riding three hours in an open carriage, symptoms returned at 5 P.M. after being two hours in a warm room. *Swallowing impossible,* **shooting through ears on attempting it.**

Clinical.—Enlarged tonsils, especially when their color is bluish; feeling in the pharynx of scraping and rawness, with at times dryness. Sore throat in general, with or without ulceration; the general indications for this drug in sore throat are the rawness or roughness internally, with stiffness of the muscles externally, associated with backache, headache, vertigo, etc.; the right side is more apt to be affected. It has even been found useful in some cases of diphtheria, involving both sides of the throat, with a heavily-furred thickened tongue, which may be fiery at the tip, great prostration, aching in the limbs; the throat internally is generally purple, and there is aggravation from hot drinks. Diphtheria, with albuminuria, soreness across the kidneys, scanty, dark red urine. Diphtheria, with pains about the knees, aching in back and limbs.

Stomach.—Hunger soon after eating; canine H.; diminished; lost. Thirst; at night; towards morning, with feverishness. Eructations, with spitting of water; empty E.; empty E. when vomiting; of sour fluid; of food in evening and till sleep. Hiccough, with inclination to vomit, but no nausea.

Nausea; at night on being awakened; > eating, with pain in forehead, returning with increased violence, frequent vomiting of ingesta, relieving the nausea but aggravating the frontal pain, afterwards acrid vomiting, then empty retching, then vomiting after warm water, also after a cup of strong coffee; with the usual appetite; with faintness; with pain in umbilical region; with heat in head; with the headache; with the vertigo, then violent retching and vomiting of ingesta, later frequent vomiting of yellowish transparent mucus; intermittent, on waking from after-dinner nap.

Vomiting; and purging; almost incessant, from 9.30 P.M. till 5 A.M., first of contents of stomach, then of a bitter watery mess; dark brownish, afterwards light yellow; profuse, without much pain, but much distress in stomach; sudden, with cramps so that they had no time to get into bed, but lay on the floor, unable to call for assistance. Easy vomiting, with colic and purging; E. and bitter; and frequent, first of the aliment, then of a dark bilious substance, lasting all the afternoon, with purging, V. > black coffee; but it is slower in its effects than is usual with emetics. Violent vomiting; *of clotted blood and slime, with retching, pain and desire for death to relieve;* of dark red ingesta; and difficult, first of food, then of greenish, finally of black matter mixed with clear blood, diarrhœa began with the vomiting, and tenesmus, could not leave the stool, stool at first yellow, then greenish, finally dark bloody matter, the V. and diarrhœa lasted all night, somewhat > morning, ceased at 2 P.M.

Swelling of stomach and bowels, with burning pain and soreness. Cutting in pit and abdomen. Cutting-tearing straining pain, then soreness on pressure. Pinching. Pain; in pit; in region of pylorus; in morning on waking, > rising, with salivation; on pressure; in pit on pressure; in epigastrium after being aroused from their narcotism, with thirst and chilliness; in cardiac portion, < full inspiration and by walking; in region of pylorus, gradually working up into chest on same side; bruised, in pit; burning, in epigastric region. Tenderness of epigastrium. Distress, and in abdomen. Disturbed feeling, > going into open air, with dulness of head, return of symptoms on sitting down to tea, could eat nothing. Oppression in epigastric region, with weight. Heat; with tenderness of abdomen and peculiar heat in rectum, then tenesmus and mucous and bloody discharges. Weak feeling, causing frequent yawning, that was attended by stitching through the part.

Abdomen.—Rumbling; with pain in umbilical region; with desire for stool. Emission of flatus; fetid. Cutting. Griping; all day, > night, then offensive flatus; in afternoon, with cramp and purging; as before diarrhœa. Pain in evening, finally locating itself in splenic region; P. on pressure and when walking; > emission of flatus. Sensation as before diarrhœa. Weakness. Amelioration of some symptoms at night.

Digging in upper and outer part of liver, preventing motion, first at 2 P.M., then every morning before daylight, and soreness through afternoon and evening. Pain in l. hypochondrium when walking; in l. in evening, so that he cannot sit up, gone in morning, after lying all night on l. side; penetrating, in r., after midnight, preventing lying on r. side; heavy, in hypochondrium, > when leucorrhœa began. Umbilical region, cramp, then copious stool; boring to l. and a little above U.; burning griping; pain; pain, < motion; pain, with desire for stool; distress, and in hypogastrium; burning distress. Pain in region of transverse colon at 7 A.M.; deep-seated, in l. iliac region; neuralgic, in l. groin.

Rectum and Anus.—Hæmorrhoids. *In middle of night, neuralgic pain in anus and lower part of rectum, shooting along perineum to middle of penis,* then neuralgic pain in r. great toe. Inclination for stool, with much straining; continual I.

Stool.—Dysentery. Copious discharge of bile. Diarrhœa; all the afternoon, with griping and cramps in abdomen, in the night stools painless; from increased action of liver, with but little tormina or tenesmus; with sickly feeling in abdomen, but no tormina or tenesmus; violent; light yellow and loud; dark, after vomiting; copious, *of blood, mucus and what looked like scrapings of inner surface of intestines,* with sickly feeling in abdomen, stools involuntary, from straining, which continued even in sleep; copious, at 1 or 2 A.M., till after breakfast, at last watery. Mushy; with undigested food in it, sometimes with straining. Papescent, dark, with undigested food in them; P., then faint feeling. Of mucus, with straining. Hard. Dark, lumpy. Three in one day; the first hard and preceded by griping, the others by pains moving about in abdomen.

Clinical.—Constipation of old people, with great weakness and intermittent pulse. Constipation, pain shoots from the anus along the perineum into the penis.

Urinary Organs.—Uneasiness down ureters. Straining to pass water. Urine retained for ten hours. *Slight suppression of urine, with pain in loins.* Urine copious at night; C. and as clear as water; diminished, then increased, acid, albuminous, sp. gr. increased. Chalklike sediment.

Clinical.—Nephritis, with pain and soreness over the kidneys, especially on the right side; urine dark red, even mahogany-colored, often with painful micturition. It has proved curative in chronic Bright's disease, even after convulsions have appeared.

Sexual Organs.—Frequent gurgling in prostate gland in afternoon. Spermatic cords, grinding pain shooting up, in morning; sharp pain running up each; paroxysmal pains, afterwards soreness. Sensation all the time as if menses would appear. Ropy leucorrhœa towards morning. Almost miscarriage in the seventh month, labor-like pains, involuntary straining, hæmorrhage from vagina, could feel uterus contract under my hand.

Respiratory Organs.—Feeling as if breathing through an open sponge. *Larynx dry.* Tickling in l. side of larynx, with hacking cough, aching in r. chest and dryness of throat. *Hoarseness.* Trachea, sensation as if grasped, < evening; dryness in morning; dryness in lower part and in large bronchi; roughness and heat in T. and bronchi, with dry bronchial cough. Roughness of bronchi.

Cough; towards morning, from dryness in pharynx; dry; dry, irritative, with pain in different parts of head and increase of bile; hacking; with scanty expectoration. Expectoration of tough mucus; with cough.

Respiration.—Suffocation. Difficult, impossible through nose. Moaning and gasping. Sighing, slow. Short; inspiration, and sighing. Shallow.

Clinical.—Laryngismus stridulus. Laryngitis, dry, croupy cough, with burning in the larynx and trachea, < night. Catarrhal laryngitis < night, especially with enlarged tonsils; useful in cold, damp weather.

Chest.—Sharp pain through upper part, preventing a long breath. Pain in r.; in lung; in lungs at 7 A.M.; at night, with restlessness; in r., so bad after midnight as to prevent sleep, < lying on r. side, > morning after rising; from front to back; in region of r. nipple, passing through to back, on taking a long breath and on bending shoulders backward, > afternoon. Tenderness of muscles, as if bruised. Lameness in l. side and shoulder; near cardiac region at night, waking me, with restlessness, sleeplessness for a long time, lameness on moving, < during expiration, these pains returned occasionally for months. Symptoms < after midnight, > afternoon, most of them on r. side.

Clinical.—One of our most valuable remedies for inflammation of the mammary glands, especially after the acute symptoms have subsided; there is violent pain whenever the milk flows into the breast, especially when nursing; pains start from the nipple and radiate over the whole body, particularly up and down the backbone. Nipples sore and cracked, with intense suffering. Inflamed mammæ, even during pregnancy. Tumors of the breast, with enlarged axillary glands; the breast has a purplish hue and the pains radiate over the whole body.

Heart.—*Shocks of pain in region, then in r. arm. Pain in præcordial region,* < *walking. Beat felt distinctly.*

Clinical.—Chronic endocarditis, pain shoots into the arm, especially right arm. Frequently useful in fatty degeneration of the heart. Gouty heart.

Pulse.—Rapid; and tense, strong, full, after he had ceased to purge; and full, but soft; and feeble. Slow and feeble. Hard and full at 7 A.M. Low towards evening. Small and depressed; S., threadlike, irregular, with agitation in chest, < about region of heart.

Neck.—Hard gland on r. side. Pain in nape at 11 A.M., running down spine. *Stiffness in morning on waking; at night; r. side,* < in bed after midnight.

Back.—Pain, with inability to walk. *Stiffness in morning.* Pain in scapulæ; with occasional sensation as if a small piece of cold iron pressed upon it; behind S. when walking; bruised, in l. Weight upon scapulæ. Laming pain below l. scapula towards evening when riding, at 9.30 the pain had reached region of spine and was sticking. *Shooting in sacrum, extending down outside of hips to feet.* Griping in lumbar region. Pain in l. loin, then itching; *heavy P. in lumbar and sacral regions,* < motion. Weakness, pain and soreness in region of kidneys; < r. side, with heat.

Extremities.—Jerkings of arms and legs; hands and legs. Sudden cramps, hard knots in muscles, then in a moment they would be flaccid and sore. *Sticking in various parts, always from without inward and near surface. The pains are always in outer parts.* Sudden translation of internal pains to limbs. *Rheumatic pains in hands and feet, sometimes in arms and legs; below knees and in arms.* Rheumatic drawing along l. ulna and in r. leg. Rheumatic symptoms in joints at 3 P.M.

Clinical.—Subacute rheumatism, pains affecting especially the long bones or the tendinous attachment of muscles; the pains sometimes seem to be in the periosteum, they are generally burning, shooting, always worse at night and in damp weather (Rhus, Merc.). Rheumatism of the heels of very obstinate form, only relieved by keeping the heels higher than the body. Rheumatism affecting the dorsal muscles. Pains fly from one part to another, the patient is pale and puffy (Colch.). General stiffness of the extremities, with tearing pains. Syphilitic pains, shifting. Syphilitic or gonorrhœal rheumatism, joints swollen, red, glands swollen, < damp weather.

Upper Extremities.—Pain in l. shoulder about noon; in l. joint on sudden motion; in muscles of l.; along top of r., along superior edge of trapezius, < pressure and contracting the muscle. Rheumatism of l. shoulder. Arms painful; almost paralyzed, no strength in them. Twitching in muscles of r. upper arm when resting it on the table, with fluttering in them. Pain at humeral insertion of l. deltoid; P. in r. humerus, < motion and extension, with weakness of it; drawing, in r. upper arm. Bruised sensation in muscles of outside of r. upper arm, < two inches above elbow, < pressure, touch and extending arm. Tenderness on outside of l. arm, just above elbow, on pressure and on extending arm.

Pain in bones of forearm after going to bed. Rheumatic drawing in r. forearm. Rheumatic pain in l.

hand, then in r. Drawing pain in r. hand, now and then, by shocks to elbow. Neuralgic pain in r. palm. Sticking in end of l. thumb; in fleshy part of l. thumb; in r. little and ring fingers; in finger-joints, sometimes in one hand, sometimes in the other; suddenly in finger-tips, as from electric sparks. Aching in finger-ends, with throbbing, as if going to suppurate. Rheumatic feeling in r. little finger, < writing.

Lower Extremities.—Cramps. Weakness. Heaviness in afternoon as if asleep. Symptoms < afternoon. *Sciatica. Neuralgic pain on outer side of thigh. Rheumatic pain in r. knee in afternoon, < open air and in damp weather;* R. feeling in l. knee when walking, with sensation of shortening of tendons behind it. Knees heavy, tired from a short walk. Pain in legs, < walking, with stiffness about knees. Pain through ankles and feet. Stinging in l. instep, > pressure. Pain on dorsum of r. foot at 4 A.M.; P. in a spot on ball of r. foot, which had been frostbitten years before, and in a corn never painful before; striking P. in ball of l. foot; neuralgic, in r. great toe, in middle of night.

Clinical.—Sciatica. Violent tearing pain down to the foot.

Skin.—Shrunken and lead-colored. Itching elevations on chest. Eruption beginning on scalp and spreading to toe-nails, pink erythematous blotches of irregular shape, slightly elevated, sore, painful, itching only on desquamation, too sore to allow scratching, ending in a dark red or purple spot, taking about a month to pass through its various stages of eruption and desquamation and about as long to advance from head to feet, so that it could be seen at one time in all its stages, eruption < after Merc. sol. 3d x trit. (which relieved the sleeplessness and pains), and invaded conjunctiva and mucous membrane of nose and mouth, later in fauces and œsophagus. Pustule behind r. ear. Boil behind r. ear; painful, on l. side of neck. Suppuration of painless tumors; S. of a tumor behind r. ear, with discharge of matter and blood.

Drawing in cicatrices. Itching on l. calf, then on r. leg, at last with lichen-looking eruption, the I. always < first part of night, often preventing sleep till midnight. Itching on hands and feet, then spreading over body, then rash following the same course, the I. < scratching and warmth of bed, skin hot and dry, great desire to pour cold water on himself, which relieved for a few moments, but was always worse afterwards, skin red, and if he exercised so as to feel the least warm vesicles could be discerned under cuticle.

Clinical.—General tendency to boils or carbuncles, with swollen glands, burning pains, < night. Chronic ulcers surrounded by small boils.

Sleep.—Yawning; in daytime. Sleepiness. Sleeplessness. Restless night; with pains in knees, arms and chest; with late falling asleep, next night restless, after waking could not get to sleep again for a long time. Restless sleep, he lies on his stomach. Sleep disturbed first part of night by scraping and tickling in throat, which cause disposition to cough.

Clinical. — Occasionally indicated in scarlet fever, with scanty, mahogany-colored urine, skin dry and rough, tongue dry and sore, tonsils purplish, < night.

Fever.—Chilliness; when vomiting; when vomiting and purging, with sweat; with shivering; then fever and thirst; external, at night, with sweat, shivering on putting a hand outside of clothes, coldness and internal shivering in stomach and abdomen during the pains, with external heat of these parts. Skin cold and somewhat bluish. Coldness in head; hands and feet; hands and feet alternating with heat; limbs towards evening; limbs, with withered appearance of them; feet, with increase of capillary circulation about face and head.

Heat, with many symptoms; H. at night; towards morning, < soles, which were bloated, though they were not hot externally, with thirst; with redness of face, fulness about head and coldness of feet; in head; head and face; head, with vertigo and nausea; on l. side of face in afternoon; in face after dinner. Sweat of feet, < under toes; cool, < forehead and hands.

Picricum Acidum.

Pure picric acid is dissolved in distilled water for the 1st centesimal dilution.

General Action.—It causes a profound alteration of the blood, even disintegration of corpuscles; degeneration of the spinal cord, with paralysis, inflammation of the kidneys, etc.

Allies.—Phos. ac., Petrol. (Gelsem.).

Generalities.—Veins sunken, < l. side. Bright yellow color of sclerotic, skin and urine. Trembling of all muscles. Rheumatic stitches in different parts, with muscular debility. Darting pains in various parts, extending into bones, every hour in the day. All pains lasted till 8 P.M.; P. in r. side; P. < l. side. Soreness and lameness, < l. side, in morning when rising, with heavy throbbing pain extending from behind ears to supraorbital notch and thence into eye, with burning-throbbing pains and dilated pupils, conjunctivitis and lachrymation.

Tired feeling (Ph. ac.); in morning on waking; in morning on waking, with heaviness; in afternoon on walking; at 7 P.M. when walking, legs heavy, feet tired all the evening; *on least exertion;* on walking; on ascending stairs; on rising from bed, with lame sensation; > open air; *with lame sensation over whole body; with no desire to talk or do anything, indifferent to everything around me,* sleepiness and desire to lie down. *Numbness,* with pains, as when taking cold. Aggravation between 10 A.M. and 2 P.M.; between 11 A.M. and 2 P.M.; till after 2 P.M. of symptoms of head, eyes, legs and of fever; from least motion. Amelioration in afternoon and from motion, aggravation again in evening; at 7 P.M.; 11 P.M.; in open air; open air and motion; cold water and walking in open air; at rest.

Clinical.—Hysteria. Neurasthenia. Extreme exhaustion at the menstrual period.

Mind.—Nervous feeling, which I never have except when fever is leaving me, feeling as if about to be crushed by the bed-clothes, arms, face, tongue and forepart of brain seemed to reach to the clouds when I was going to sleep. Although enjoying the society of gentlemen the idea of marriage was unendurable. Desire to be alone. Irritable. Low spirits. *Indifference, lack of will power to undertake anything* (Phos.). *Disinclination for mental or physical work, aversion to talking or movement, with the headache. Mental prostration after reading a little; after writing a little. Inability to collect thoughts or to study* (Phos.).

Head.—Aching; all day, < rising, > open air; in morning, probably from oversleeping; in forenoon, < afternoon; in afternoon and evening, with trembling; in evening; in evening, with thirst and heat, chiefly in temples, and burning in external ears; < afternoon; > pressure; > bandaging head; with heat of head; with sleeplessness till 2 A.M., after going to bed at 9; so that I did not feel able to study; peculiar, < motion, turning head and stooping, > lateral pressure; changeable, alternating between r. and l. temple, sometimes in centre of forehead; heavy, blind, dizzy, < vertex and forehead, at 9 A.M., increasing till I go to bed, with fulness, feeling as if it would burst, < stooping, which causes vertigo, head feels too small, scalp sore to touch, sore aching in infraorbital region.

Pressure outward as if it would fly apart, at 8 P.M., < motion and study. Fulness; at noon, with heaviness of it and disinclination for mental or physical work, F. and heaviness increased till 2 P.M., when it developed into throbbing headache, < l. side, chiefly in l. eye and occipital region, < ascending stairs, which causes throbbing pain in eyeball, headache > at 4 P.M.; with heaviness of it, with disinclination to do anything, the headache increased and developed into throbbing pain in l. side of head, < eyeball and forehead, and extending backward to occiput, > quiet, < motion, especially ascending stairs. Heaviness; and dulness; alternating with emptiness. Feeling as if falling forward. Affected in evening; and study prevented. Discomfort at 5 P.M., < supraorbital region, with soreness. Vertigo at noon, < rising from a seat; at 6 P.M. on least motion, with nausea, both repeated at 9 P.M., with pain in forehead and vertex and inability to sit up; on stooping or bending head or lying down; < evening.

Forehead.—Shooting from outside to centre in evening. Intermittent, sharp and vibrating pain in r. supraorbital region. Aching in supraorbital region; and in nape; in F. and temples, < r. side; in upper part of anterior lobes of brain; more or less all day, and in supraorbital region; all day in upper part of anterior and middle lobes of brain, and above eyes, with occasional shooting; in evening, and in vertex; in l. supraorbital notch at 6 P.M.; at 7 P.M. (with vertigo when rising and walking); in F. and vertex at 9 P.M., with vertigo and nausea; over eyes, < study and motion, > sitting still; in F. and r. side of head, with heat in head and upper part of body; in back part of anterior and top of middle lobes of brain, with occasional throbbing pain; in F. and temples, extending to nape; sleepy, at 3 P.M., with sour eructations. Heavy pain in supraorbital region; H. pain extending to vertex, at 10 A.M., < motion, < 1 P.M. by motion or rolling eyes; with heaviness and weakness in small of back and limbs; H. tingling pain extending to vertex, in evening. Throbbing over r. eye.

Temples.—Shooting through, from r. to l., with headache, < r. side. Cutting in l., over a transverse branch of the artery. Neuralgic pain alternately in l. and r. Sharp pain in r., running to occiput, then in l. temple extending to suboccipital region; intermittent, in l. Pain between temples; over r., passing around occiput; in r., extending over brow to inner angle of r. eye; sleepy, over l.; throbbing, in r. Beating of arteries. Formication over r., running up over parietal bone.

Vertex.—Pain; at 11 A.M., with fever; in V. and occiput in night on waking and several times next day; < study and bending head forward; in twinges at 9 P.M.; throbbing, < turning to lie on back, with nausea; full, heavy, < stooping and moving eyes. Fulness; at 8 A.M., with heaviness.

Sides.—Darting pain in r. in middle of afternoon. Pain in r., running behind ear; heavy, in r., spreading to l., lasting all day; heavy throbbing, extending from behind ears to supraorbital notch, thence into eye, with soreness and lameness, < l. side. Pressure outward at 9 P.M., < turning head, moving eyes or least motion, with sensation as if frontal bones would split open. Contracted sensation in l. hemisphere of brain at 6.30 P.M., on going into open air.

Occiput.—*Pain, and in nape;* P. in r. lower part; in r. and lower side in afternoon; in r. and lower part at 4 P.M., finally extending over towards r. supraorbital region, lasting about three hours; in r. lower part from 8 till 9 P.M., with sensation of a band along r. parietal eminence; in r. and lower side in evening; extending to supraorbital region, also < movement or stooping; in O. and neck, extending to supraorbital notch and then into eyes; intermittent, in r. lower part; in r. lower part, as if r. side of cerebellum were loose, 6 till 7 P.M., < walking, > quiet, with throbbing; *heavy, extending down neck and spine;* heavy throbbing and burning pains, extending to supraorbital foramen and thence into eyes, which throb and feel sore to touch. *Confusion in base.*

Clinical.—Violent occipital headaches, always < mental effort, with general fatigue. Brain fag, the slightest mental exertion brings on headache at the base of the brain; the pain is generally intense and throbbing. Any attempt at mental labor causes great general prostration.

Eyes.—Yellow. Stinging at 7 A.M., on waking; S., with lachrymation. Shooting in centre, extending along optic nerve to occiput, with soreness of balls on touch, and photophobia. Sensation of sand in them, with smarting pain and acrid tears. Feeling as if sticks were in them on waking, with inflammation, afterwards feeling as if sticks were in them in evening. Sore feeling. Dryness and feeling as if full of sand; D., with roughness of inner surface of lids; < constant use and lamplight, with tingling or smarting, next morning thick acrid matter in canthi. Gaslight hurts them. Feel worse on moving them. Lachrymation.

Pupils dilated. Conjunctiva injected. *Conjunctivitis; < r. eye, > washing with cold water and by cold air, < warm room, with difficulty in keeping eyes open, and sticky feeling on reading.* Ball, shooting from r. to l. side of occiput; pain, < moving eyes, > closing them and quiet, with soreness; heavy, smarting and burning pains, > pressure; sore pains, < strong light and by turning eyes. Lids swollen and sore; swollen, and styes and soreness; agglutinated in morning on waking; margins red on waking; heat in upper, with lachrymation; heaviness; heaviness in evening, with burning in eyes; heaviness and inability to keep them open; inability to keep them open when studying. Air looks smoky. Vision dim and confused; dim, can read clearly at only one point, about five inches from eyes; blurred; blurred when reading, seemingly from winking mucus over pupils; whirling of objects. Vision of sparks.

Clinical.—Ophthalmia > cold water.

Ears.—Puffy and burning, with sensation as if worms were crawling in them. Pain behind r., running down side of neck. *Buzzing and hissing.*

Clinical.—Noises in the ears, with vertigo and headache at the base of the brain. Chronic deafness, apparently caused by excessive headache, with noises in the ears when tired, membrane pale.

Nose.—Boil in l. nostril. Stinging in r. side. Weight on bridge. Full of mucus, can breathe only through mouth, > open air. Bleeding from r. nostril; with heat and congestion of head.

Face and Mouth.—Irregular pain in lower jaw, with beating in molars. Tingling in lips. White, frothy saliva hangs in strings to floor. Taste bitter; with thirst; sour, bitter; T. sour; bad; bad, of gas.

Throat.—Redness, with raw, scraped, stiff and hot feeling, as if burnt, and with thick white mucus on tonsils, difficulty in swallowing, with sensation as if throat would split open. Rawness in l. side, extending forward to submaxillary gland, < swallowing; R., with roughness and scraping. Soreness back of and above soft palate, with debility, < lower limbs; S. on swallowing, < l. side, > eating, < after sleep, with roughness and scraping, also on empty swallowing. Dry and husky. Feeling of a plug on swallowing saliva and afterwards. Sensation of something in lower part of œsophagus.

Stomach.—Appetite great in evening; increased, then lost; lost; lost for breakfast. Aversion to food; at noon. Thirst; unquenchable, for cold water. Eructations; empty; sour, of gas and ingesta; bitter after breakfast. Waterbrash. Nausea; on retiring; after retiring, with headache; till night, with intermittent griping in epigastric region; as from a weight, with frontal headache; deathlike, in stomach and abdomen on waking at 5 A.M., < rising and moving about, returned on waking a second time, repeated next morning on waking. Vomiting. Sharp pain in epigastric region. Pain in cardiac region when eating breakfast. Oppression of epigastric region. Weight in pit, with ineffectual desire to eructate. Faint feeling in epigastrium all the morning; nauseated faint feeling in epigastrium most of the day, occasionally the next day.

Abdomen.—Fulness. Rumbling; in small intestines; at 7 A.M. on waking, with colic; with crampy pain and flatus. Emission of flatus; during the day; in evening. Crawling stinging. Pain all the forenoon, with slight headache; P. on waking, with strong erections, and on moving emission of much flatus; and in neck of bladder; rumbling.

Sticking through hepatic region, < muscles; S. backward through l. umbilical region. Pain in umbilical region in evening; sharp, on l. side of umbilicus. Shooting, wandering pain in region of coccyx, bladder, rectum and umbilicus, caused by wind. Sharp pain in r. iliac region, above ovary, at 11 P.M., with soreness on pressure. Pain in lower part of large intestines; in l. groin on walking, < ascending stairs. Occasional sensation of giving way in hypogastrium all day. Vacant and sore feeling in hypogastric region.

Anus.—Stinging during and after stool, with itching. Shooting around A. at 9 P.M.

Stool.—Like gruel, yellow or yellowish-gray, twice before 9 A.M. Diarrhœa, with burning and smarting at anus; frequent D., with prostration; light-colored, with cutting and smarting at anus during and after stool. Soft, with tenesmus; S., light-colored, with straining; and small, ineffectual, with tenesmus, then drawing up of anus; and scanty, with burning at anus; in plugs, easy, shooting away, then much flatus. Light-colored, with burning and smarting in anus. Yellowish, copious, oily, frequent. Quick, as if greased, of sweetish smell, as of boiling sap, at night and morning, then much wind. Difficult, next day ineffectual desire for stool.

Urinary Organs.—Pain in region of bladder; sharp, in evening, < r. side. Frequent micturition in morning. Dribbling micturition. Urethra, jerking drawing; pain after micturition; burning pain during micturition; burning during and after micturition.

Urine.—Yellow. Of a milky olive hue. Dark; indications of sugar. Dark yellow, with strong odor; dark yellow, scanty, afterwards profuse and yellow. Red; dark, in evening. Copious; and pale; and light-colored, sp. gr. increased; and hot when passed, with burning pain in urethra; afterwards scanty; afterwards diminished. *Scanty.* Urates abundant. *Contained much indican, numerous granular cylinders and fatty degenerated epithelium.*

Clinical.—Valuable for subacute and chronic inflammation of kidneys, with scanty urine, dropsy, profound weakness, very dark, bloody urine.

Sexual Organs.—Erections in morning on waking; E. at 11 A.M., with bruised pain in l. testicle, extending up cords to external abdominal rings; firm in morning, with pain in abdomen, next morning woke with emission and firm erection, which lasted about ten minutes after the emission; *terrible, at night, with restless sleep;* violent, all night; violent, all night, then profuse emissions. *Desire at night, with emissions; at night,* with hard erections, lewd dreams and emission, *emissions every other night;* D., with almost constant priapism night and day. Occasional aching in l. ovarian region; twinges of pain in l. ovarian region in in evening. Menses delayed, during the period yellowish-brown leucorrhœa, the night before menstruation, in bed, voluptuous pruritus (usually pruritus slight after menses, never before), exasperating memenses painful, bruised pain in abdomen, with sicken, ing sensation.

Clinical.—It has proved valuable for seminal emissions followed by extreme exhaustion, occipital headache, etc. Loss of sexual power, with tendency to boils and carbuncles. Loss of power, with threatening paralysis of the legs.

Respiratory Organs.—Dry cough, as from dust in throat, then nausea. Can get the breath only half way down.

Chest.—Twitching in l. side over eighth and ninth ribs; in l. side over tenth and eleventh ribs from 6 till 11 P.M., with throbbing in muscles. Pain in r. side, extending across l.; P. in l. lung in evening; sharp, under r. clavicle; heavy throbbing in l., under tenth and eleventh ribs at 11 A.M., changing at noon to region of kidneys, extending at 2 P.M. into legs, < l.; stunning, at 9.30 A.M., with twitching in throat. Tightness, as if encircled by a band. Numbness in lower part of sternum.

Heart and Pulse.—Pain in apex of H. in evening. Intermittent fluttering at base of H. all day, it seemed to move. Palpitation. Pulse frequent; slow, feeble, afterwards rapid; slow, small and feeble; irregular.

Neck.—Muscles on r. side felt as if they would give way in afternoon when lying; at night when lying on r. side, with feeling as if neck would be dislocated.

Back.—Pain; < sitting; in B. and lower limbs. with heaviness and weakness; in dorsal region; extending from r. scapula to r. loin when bending forward. Sticking under r. scapula; in upper part of l. loin; in r. loin in evening; in lumbar region on bending forward when sitting. Sharp pain in region of coccyx. Pain in lumbar region; and anteriorly in thighs, in muscles, < motion, with weakness in the same, < legs; extending down legs, < motion, legs and lumbar region sensitive to pressure; heavy, at 6 P.M. Dragging pains in region of kidneys and nape, extending upward and downward till they meet between scapulæ, at 2 P.M.; between hips, descending slowly to l. leg, with throbbing and jerking in muscles in different parts of body, and chills. Weakness in sacral and lumbar regions. Lumbar region and limbs tired at 12 P.M. on waking; at 6 A.M., with heaviness, the same next day at 4 P.M., with heavy frontal headache.

Extremities.—Rheumatic pains in joints. Weakness; from a short walk, with heaviness. *Heaviness, < l.; of arms and legs on exertion, < legs*, legs weak and heavy all the time. Lame sensation in shoulders. Shoulders tired and sore; r. Twitching of lower part of l. biceps; in forenoon. Shooting in l. elbow, extending down arm. Pain in r. elbow, between ulna and radius. Shooting in hands. L. hand goes to sleep.

Lower Extremities.—*Weakness;* on ascending stairs; *and heaviness.* Numbness. Twitching on back of l. hip at 9 P.M. Pain anteriorly in l. thigh, can hardly flex and extend legs. Hips and legs heavy all day. Knees weak.

Legs.—Twitching of flesh of r. Sticking, and in feet. Pain anteriorly on touch; below knees on touch; in calves all night; in back part of l., extending to sole, > motion and open air, with sensation as if foot would go to sleep; intermittent, in a spot in r. calf, with soreness on hard pressure; deep-seated sore, in upper part of l. Scarpa's triangle, < night, > sleep, returning on waking; numb, sleepy, extending to soles, > cold water and in open air. Calves lame and sore. *Weakness;* < l., which trembles; with soreness; *legs and region of hips, with heaviness. Heaviness,* < l.; H. at 9 P.M. Numbness of anterior muscles.

Crawling pain in l. sole and under patella. Feet feel as if frostbitten. Numbness of l. foot. Soreness in ball of l. big toe in afternoon and evening, > continued walking.

Skin.—Yellow. Pimples on face and neck that he had for years were now increased in number and size. Reddish, painful boils about mouth and face, when opened they exude a thin, clear serum, which dries into a transparent scab, then become painful and contain pus like condensed milk; reddish boils on face, becoming pustular, with burning stinging on touch. Tight feeling over epigastrium. Itching; at night.

Clinical.—Very frequently called for in the disposition to boils, either on the back of the neck or within the ears.

Sleep.—Frequent gaping in church. Sleepiness, slept an hour in afternoon, then I felt better; S. in evening, > walking in open air; at 9 P.M.; at 9 P.M., and tired. Sleep sound, but unrefreshing. Sleepless all night. Late falling asleep from a crowd of ideas. Sleep restless till 11 P.M.; till 12; till 12, then heavy, restless, woke unrefreshed. Woke earlier than usual and dozed till time to rise; woke at 3 A.M., then difficulty in going to sleep. Constant dreams, dream that she was pregnant.

Fever.—Chilliness, with cold, clammy sweat. *Cold limbs; feet;* hands and feet. Fever; and chilliness, then cold, clammy sweat, C. predominates. Heat in head; r. side; in forehead. Burning along coronal suture; along spine, < trying to study, > motion. Heat in lower dorsal and lumbar regions. Sweat. Cold, clammy sweat in evening; on hands; on hands and feet in daytime; on hands in forenoon; on feet in evening, next day feet cold and sweaty all day.

Piper Methysticum.

A tincture is made of the fresh root of the Kava-Kava, Piper methysticum, Forster.

Generalities.—Emaciation; and decrepitude. Trembling. *Pains,* < head, *temporarily > turning mind to another topic.* Feeling as if drug descended and impressed lower part of system, causing trembling of abdomen and lower limbs and bloodvessels connected therewith, but on descending stairs the drug seemed to come upward through the circulation, reaching the brain, causing exhilarating dizziness and disposition to swing and stagger, as if under the influence of liquor, felt talkative and happy, after the dizziness felt a "toned-up" condition of brain and nervous system, dizziness returned on beginning to move. Stimulating and sedative effects, then sweat. Vigor; all day, with exhilaration, next day feelings varying and generally depressed. Uneasiness during the day. Weakness during the day, with timidity and apprehension; W. in morning, > rising and moving around; at 8.30 P.M. Want of tone and life in all functions towards night. Amelioration in open air and on motion.

Mind.—Hilarious from 10 A.M. till 1 P.M. Lively after an emission; L. and inclined to work, can dance with more ease than usual. Cheerfulness and ease in his work. Agreeable excitement and support against great fatigue, from increased doses intoxication of a sorrowful, silent and sleepy character, different from that produced by alcoholic drinks. Faculties sharpened. (Capable of working more without fatigue or brain fag.) Lazy and drowsy. Torpor and irritation from least noise.

Clinical.—The symptom of getting worse from thinking of his symptoms is said to be one of the indications for this drug.

Head.—Aching, with pressure in upper part of orbits; A., with sleepiness. Brain fag; in morning, > getting on feet. Tired feeling at night. Fulness, sometimes in one part, sometimes in another, < forehead. Uneasiness. Heaviness. Intoxication, with fantastic ideas and desire to skip about, although he cannot for a moment hold himself on his legs. Vertigo from 5 till 9 P.M.; in morning in bed, with frontal pressure.

Forehead.—Intermittent shooting in l. supraorbital nerve after 3 P.M. Aching; in l. supraorbital nerve; back of eyes; all day, at 8 P.M., < over eyes and deep-seated; at 9 A.M., < 3 P.M.; in afternoon and evening, with drowsy and stupid feeling; above eyes at 5 P.M.; at 7 P.M.; in l. side at 7.30 P.M; < l. side and deep in upper part of orbits, with pain on moving eyes; intermittent, in r. eminence, > open air and motion; above r. eye, radiating over eyes, at 10 A.M.; heavy, in F. and temples, < thinking and reading. Heaviness. Dulness, with fulness and pressure, and on raising head or moving it to either side vertigo, after the noon meal the pressure shifted to lateral and occipital regions, < lying down, but not to real pain, pressure, < remaining in one position, > moving, apprehension of pain by rapid movement, but temporary relief from it.

Shooting in l. temple; in l. side of brain, from front to back, after 3 P.M. Uneasiness as from weight over each ear.

Eyes.—Conjunctivæ red. Pain along r. optic nerve when reading after 3 P.M.; deep in l., as if ball would be pressed out, in the street at 5.30 P.M. Vision obscured. Dizzy blindness when dressing, vertigo, > closing eyes, directing attention to head and exerting the will, at the same time vertigo then rush of blood and fulness in forehead, then similar sensation in occipital and basilar regions.

Ears and Face.—Singular pressure in lobules of pinna of l. ear. Pressure outward in face at 7 P.M.

Mouth—Teeth deep yellow. Teeth sensitive to cold water, cold air, brushing, etc. Tongue feels as if covered with velvet or fur at night; T., mouth, stomach, etc., feel as if mucous membrane were furred and their sensitive power lost, tongue not coated. Burning on tongue. Dryness on waking from afternoon nap, with sweat (in a hot day). Salivation. Taste nauseous; T. sweet, then piquant and sharp; pappy; everything is tasteless at every meal; lost to food, but *ravenous haste* in eating; T. and relish to food not as usual, at noon, but appetite unusually good.

Clinical.—Toothache, with enlarged tonsils, pain involves the whole side of the face, from taking cold. Toothache, with earache and restlessness, forgets all about her pains when amused.

Stomach.—Appetite formidable at 8 P.M.; slight; hungry at noon, but not able to eat much, able to eat but little supper. Sour eructations, < an hour before meals and at night, at times rolling up and rumbling from stomach to mouth, but generally breaking at throat-pit, and in throat-pit sensation of something that cannot be swallowed, the latter temporarily > eructations. Bloating at 11 P.M. Crampy pain, > pressure against edge of table. Warmth.

Abdomen.—Pain every day about 9 A.M.; in forenoon after first stool, with distressing full sensation; > motion; then a large stool, the latter part soft; above umbilicus; in r. groin when walking.

Clinical.—Colic, purely neuralgic, with great restlessness and agony.

Rectum.—Burning. *Urging all day;* **every evening.**

Stool.—Diarrhœa threatened. Loose in morning, more difficult in evening. Soft, difficult. Constipation. Hard; and the same day a small one; and large two days, next day H. and small; and light-colored, small, oblong, afterwards a darker and larger one, then continuous desire, next day forced a large stool, which caused prolapsus ani. Large, next day none; L. and soft; and light-colored; frequent, one soft. Small, a second one softer. Light-colored. Difficult.

Urinary and Sexual Organs.—Micturition at 4.45 A.M. Burning in urethra during micturition; in morning, urine nearly neutral at 10 A.M., hot and over-acid next day at night. Urine increased. Urine scanty in morning. Shooting in penis. Erection in afternoon; at night; at 4 A.M. after an emission. Pain in r. testicle. Emission early in morning, without dreams; E. about 4 A.M., then wakefulness; at night; in forepart of night. Amorousness.

Clinical.—Renal colic, passage of uric acid.

Chest.—Heaviness behind upper part of sternum, as from wind that cannot be eructated.

Pulse.—Steadied.

Back.—Pain on pressure at 11.45 P.M. Soreness about second dorsal vertebra at 5 P.M.

Extremities.—Pain in r. foot and wrist and l. toe, at 10 P.M.; r. elbow and l. knee, with stiffness; r. foot and back of l. hand at 11.30 P.M., with heat of them; P. in r. arm as if marrow would be affected, changing its location in the whole length from shoulder to finger-ends, with paroxysmal paralyzed feeling in hands, pain in r. great toe, pain at 6 P.M. around r. fibula, > toe at 9 P.M., but appearing in r. hand, < metacarpal part, next to little finger.

Upper Extremities.—Pain in l. shoulder; in l. arm in the street, with flushing heat in l. hand, then pain in middle and third fingers, later in second joint of l. thumb; above elbow, at insertion of triceps, at noon; in r. arm, running in all directions, with heaviness, soreness and tired sensation; dragging, in l. arm at 8 P.M., > 10 P.M. Tingling as from an electric current from l. elbow to fingers. Numbness of r. elbow. Pain in r. wrist, < writing, the P. lasted all the next day and evening, began third day at 10.30 A.M., with sore pain and with prickling running up to elbow, afterwards soreness of wrist. Weakness of l. hand. *Pain in joint of l. thumb, < pressure.*

Lower Extremities.—Drunk in his walk, but intellect unclouded, aware of his inability to control the movements of his legs. Numbness. Weakness; all day; in afternoon; in thighs as if unable to stand. Sticking in l. knee at 4 P.M. when walking. Pain in l. knee; making me limp; arthritic, in l. when walking; sharp intermittent, under patella, making me limp. Pain in r. calf; in lower part of r. calf in morning; in calves after bathing. Soreness of r. leg moved down to tendo-achillis at 8 A.M., removed to l. sole at 4 P.M., hardly felt at 7 P.M. Weariness of legs. Heaviness of legs when walking. Pain in feet; l. foot and toe; r. sole; at outer and under border of l. foot and in r. great toe, with coldness of l. foot; r. instep, < sitting, > motion, with tingling; in toe; great toe; r. great toe at noon; arthritic, in first phalanges of r. toes at noon, also in l. when walking at 6 P.M. Sticking in end of l. toe on waking at 4.45 A.M.; in great toe when moving and walking.

Skin.—*Covered as in leprosy with large scales, which fall off and leave white spots, and these often become ulcers.* Dryness, especially where it is thick, as on hands and feet, with scales, cracks and ulcers. Peculiar disease called arevareva. Painful hard swelling in lower corner of l. ear; red, painful lump, threatening to become an abscess, on forehead above r. minor canthus, and on back.

Sleep.—Sleepiness; at 9 A.M.; in afternoon and evening, with stupidity and frontal headache; at 10 P.M., soon afterwards liveliness and wakefulness; irresistible. Sleep in afternoon, laziness on waking, and sleepiness in evening. Hard sleep several times a day. Stupid S. Sound S. in afternoon. Heavy S., with disturbing but unremembered dreams. Sleepless; from 12 till 2.30 A.M.; at 4 A.M., after an emission, then sound sleep, next night wakeful after an emission till I got up for breakfast; latter part of night, mind working on business problems, next morning tired feeling before and after rising; between 1 and 2 P.M., when he is usually sleepy. Difficult falling asleep. Restless sleep last part of night. Fragmentary sleep from 12.30 till 4.20 A.M., with varied and exciting dreams, then sleeplessness so that I had to get up at 4.30 A.M., did excitedly all kinds of unusual office work.

Dreams.—Curious, nonsensical, wild. Amorous. Of traveling by rail. Active, vivid, last part of night, alternating with half-conscious waking, D. unremembered, except that I was proving a remedy which caused frontal pain, sore throat, < r. side, inability to swallow, saliva acid and smarting, and was looking over the system for symptoms to record. Of fighting (orally) for liberty and of giving a surprise party to a friend in his own house, took dinner with him and enjoyed a roast greatly. In afternoon, of fighting unknown men, left them to follow an unknown woman, and when she left me found that she had conducted me to a prayer-meeting, which must have changed to a restaurant, for I ordered a Hamburg beefsteak, but woke before it was served. Of a fire, heard the engines and firemen, the order to come down as the roof was going to fall, saw them coming down, heard and saw the crash, dream that I was awakened, when to my consternation I found it to be the hotel in which I lived that was on fire, my room was only a few feet outside the part that had been burned, made hasty arrangements to move all my things, went out to find an office, was stopped by an unknown man in an open carriage who wanted me to go a little way up the country, where he said it would pay well, but I turned away to find another place, woke from the dream at 5.30 A.M.

Fever.—Chilliness for the last few hours, at 8 P.M. Heat at 9 A.M.; flush of general H. Heat in face and hands, < l. hand; flushing, in cheeks; H. in l. ear flap and l. hand; l. hand, fingers and ear at 10 A.M.; over upper part of body in evening.

Plantago.

A tincture is made of the fresh plant of Plantago major, L.

Generalities.—Sudden boring rheumatic pains in l. wrist, extending over dorsum of hand, in evening on lying down, then shifting to r. ankle, then to l. and extending over dorsum of foot to big toe, continuing this course rapidly for two hours, and sometimes along muscles of l. forearm to elbow, then to shoulder, with tenderness on pressure, *all pains < l. side*, at the same time or alternating with these boring in a spot in l. temple, then shifting to r. Sharp pain in l. side at 5 P.M., sometimes extending to r. shoulder, then to r. side, then spreading over upper part of back. Sharp darting pain in l. side several times during the day, then in r., at one time peculiar sharp darting up r. side.

Pains at first came on at night, were on l. side, extended backward to body and head, but after some days they lasted all day, affected both sides and often extended across from one side to the other, as in head, from one temple to the other. Fugitive pains through l. side. Pain now in head, now in dorsum of big toe. Shifting pain on r. side, beginning at wrist, then in shoulder, hypochondrium, knee and along tibia to ankle, > motion. Bruised feeling in front half of head, face, jaws and gums.

Dulness and sleepiness; D. at 4 P.M., > walking in open air, with stupidity, inclination to stretch and yawn, oppression of chest and aversion to mental or physical exercise. Restlessness; < lower limbs, which became numb, tremulous and painful when quiet. Unwilling to rise in morning. Weakness; < loins; after stool, with faintness; with desire to lie down; painful, - loins and lower limbs. Faintness after eating; F. < least exercise, with tremulous feeling. Symptoms return every four weeks and last about six days. Aggravation when sitting, amelioration when moving. Amelioration in afternoon after sleep; in afternoon after peppermint candy.

Mind.—Excitability; with trembling and pulse at 120. *Irritability;* < evening; cannot bear to be spoken to; with inability for mental exercise; with headache; with pain in r. temple; with trembling of r. arm; feeling of suppressed. Impatient and restless mood, with stupid feeling in brain; I. to finish anything. Desire to do several things at once, but no inclination to move and do one. Restless disposition, with dull feeling over sinciput. Desire to be at home when abroad. Despondency. Low spirits, irritability and disinclination to work; low spirits, with inclination to work, but tired and irritated as soon as I begin.

Aversion to study or thought. Inactivity all day, < afternoon and evening, with shifting pains in various parts. Meditative and unable to associate my mind with any external object. Confusion; with prostration and inability to think, on attempting to think rapid respiration, anxiety and increase of the depression. Memory bad. Nervous and cerebral symptoms < evening and gradually increasing till morning, with some exceptions.

Head.—Aching; during the day; in morning on waking, and in l. side more or less during the day; in morning, lasting till after tea in afternoon, < occiput; at 10 A.M., often centering in ears, < l.; after dinner, with stupid feeling in head and fever; > breakfast; momentarily > pressure or contact of anything cold; with chilliness; intermittent, in evening; in twinges in different parts, now in r. temple extending backward, then through occiput from ear to ear, then in other parts of head; as if brain were stretched, on turning around; stupefying, > motion, < study; stupid.

Bruised, maddening feeling in brain, cannot bear the slightest contradiction. Irritable feeling at 9 A.M., with soreness of eyes; I. in different parts, with stitches. Oppression deep in at night, with sensation of something lying in head, through from one ear to the other. Swollen feeling. Fulness, with sore feeling in temples. Heaviness; with inclination to drowse; in evening, > holding it backward, with weariness of it and stiffness of neck. Dulness. Confusion all day, < evening, with inability to think. Vertigo.

Forehead.—Boring in eminence. Sharp pain over r. eye, extending to temple, after going to bed. Pain over r. eye at 7 A.M.; over r. eye in evening; and over r. eye and temple, < movement, with pressure over eye; over eyes, > exercise; over l. eye, > eating; over eyes, with tenderness on pressure; over l. eye and side of head, with irritability, cannot bear to be spoken to; extending over eyes; paroxysmal, in l. side extending deep into brain; intermittent, in l. protuberance, with tenderness on pressure; stupefying, in sinciput, extending to sides of occiput. Bruised sensation, and in temples; in a spot over eye; over l. brow and deep in scalp at 9 A.M., > shutting eyes; with dimness of eyes. Irritable feeling. Dulness of sinciput, with restless disposition. Heaviness.

Temples.—Distention of arteries and of superficial vessels of forehead. Boring in evening, < warm room; B. in a spot in l. Sharp pain in l. when sitting by the furnace and after being out. Pain in l.; with flushed face; and in l. side of face, > pressure; cloudy; P. in r., with irritability; fleeting P. in T. passing upward. Bruised feeling; with fulness.

Sides.—Sharp pain in l., from over eye back towards occiput, at 6 P.M. when walking and driving in cool air. Pain in r., rather on parietal and frontal eminences. Pain in l. at 10 A.M.; intermittent, in l.; occasional, in l. side of brain at 10 P.M.; fleeting, in l.; in l., as if brain turned over, on turning head suddenly. Bruised pain in l. half, < temple, in morning on waking, at noon all over head, with pain extending to top of nose. Irritability in l. half, with coldness of body and shivering; bruised I. in l. side, > lying on it and pressure.

Intermittent pulsating pain in a spot beneath scalp of vertex. Boring in occiput. Pain in occiput, > changing its position, with thirst. Bruised pain over scalp and occiput in morning on waking, inability to rest long in one place on the pillow, > for a time by resting on the painful part. Scalp and skin of face rigid. Itching of scalp; in morning; on l. side from 10 till 11 P.M.; with eruption on forehead.

Eyes.—Redness and inflammation. Bruised pain in l., < pressure. Œdema of lids on rising; after rising, with redness. Soreness of lids. Dryness of lids. Itching of lids at 10 A.M., with stiffness; I. of r. Sticking in l. ball, then in r., < inner canthus. Pain in orbits, < pressure; darting pain in superior and outer side of r. at noon; bruised pain in r., < pressure. Bruised feeling in l. brow in evening, with pricking.

Ears.—*Shooting in l. Sticking before and above, with stiffness and feeling as if bone were swollen. Pulsating pain in l.* Irritation from a pin or anything behind it. *The least noise goes through one. Hearing acute, noise painful, with trembling sound. Ringing.*

Clinical.—Earache, with toothache, the pains are darting, stabbing or twinging. One of the most valuable remedies for pure neuralgic pains in the ear.

Nose.—Excoriation of r. nostril, with ulceration. Sensation across bridge as if bones were pressed together or inward, at 4 P.M. Drawing over bridge. Soreness of l. nostril on touch. Dryness. Tingling about root. Fulness and stoppage; F. about root. Stuffed up, with pain or fulness over eyes and soreness of lids. (Frequent sneezing at 6 P.M., with discharge of sanious mucus from l. nostril.) Discharge, with stoppage; **sudden D.** of yellowish *water* from r. nostril; **sudden,** of clear water from l. nostril; *like saffron-water;* of sanious mucus from l. nostril, next day from r.; thick D.

Face.—Flushed every evening. Swelling of l. cheek, with inflammation of gums. Neuralgia in r. side. Sudden drawing and shooting pain. Sharp pain in r. cheek, waking at night, with heat and thirst. Pain in l. side at night, preventing sleep, < getting warm in bed, afterwards bruised pain in r. side, < getting warm from walking; P. in r. side, with swelling and stiffness as if a boil would form and soreness on touch; indescribable P. in both sides, > Platina, and head seems swollen. Bruised sensation as if ulcerated in l. side and temple on going to bed. Tingling in nerves of front and upper jaw at night before sleep. Lips livid, dark, sickly and rough; dry, scaly eruption, < lower, with burning and tension; pimple on upper; watery bladder as from a cold, on upper; slimy feeling.

Mouth.—Teeth. Sordes as if mixed with blood, next day S. like white mucus. Decay rapidly, gums bleed easily, teeth feel elongated in morning, *then stabbing pain in them every day from* 2.30 *till* 4 P.M., *and contact along superior branch of trifacial nerve causes pain, he cannot lie on that side at night. Grinding in sleep; with restlessness. Shooting. Boring in a l. lower molar. Drawing pain in l. upper molars at night, feeling as if they would throb. Pain in l.; in exposed nerve of an incisor;* in l. before and after breakfast, after dinner and all the next morning, in l. upper bicuspid and molars *extending to face after rising and washing* the third and fourth days, next day toothache and faceache in morning till after 2 P.M.; *in decayed l. lower after dinner; in decayed second l. upper molar, with swelling of cheek, constant discharge of saliva from mouth, elongation and soreness of sound teeth on each side of the decayed tooth when eating, the pain > night;* intermittent, in l. in forenoon; inclination to P. in a l. lower decayed molar. Grumbling in l. before breakfast, *pain after eating. Soreness; at night before sleep; of sound T. when eating breakfast; of front incisors, as if chilled by cold air, with loose sensation; of l., with elongated feeling and with boring digging in sound l. molars, < walking in cold air, contact and great heat, partially > lying down in a cool room, could not endure the pain, >* Merc., *with salivation.*

Gums.—Inflammation, with swelling of l. cheek. Dark redness. Bleeding; in afternoon and evening; at 10 P.M. on going to bed. Mattery ulcers. Painful gumboil of l. upper, discharging matter from two heads, with swelling of face. Feeling of stiffness and fulness in G. and face.

Tongue coated white; in morning. Spitting of bright blood. Dirty feeling in mouth all day. Dryness in morning. Breath putrid. Taste putrid; in morning on waking. Taste dirty in morning, with hoarseness; D. at night, with thirst; on waking. Taste clammy in morning. No taste to food.

Clinical.—Neuralgic toothache, pains shoot through the side of the face. Violent toothache in decayed teeth.

Throat.—Submaxillary glands swollen and sore. Hawking of mucus. *Scraping;* in morning on swallowing; in evening, with uneasiness. Rawness at 10 P.M., with roughness; rawness in pharynx at night on waking and next day, with soreness in it and dryness and tickling in throat inducing dry, hacking cough; on waking, with relaxation and sensation as if I had taken cold; on waking, with huskiness, soreness and difficulty in clearing it; with soreness, relaxed sensation and acrid expectoration, throat worse next day, with hoarseness, constant desire to clear it of tenacious, white, sweetish mucus, taste burning, acrid, cough scraping. Burning smarting in l. side, afterwards in r.

Soreness; in morning, with hoarseness and sweetish taste; and pain. Constriction in pharynx in morning on waking. Swollen feeling deep down on r. side. Sensation of a foreign body. Dryness all day; in morning on rising; in morning on rising, with huskiness; in morning on rising, > afternoon; in evening, and a draught of air irritates and causes cough; of fauces and pharynx, with continual desire to swallow, but not much thirst; D. and soreness of throat, mouth and mucous membrane of nose. Itching inside.

Stomach.—Appetite little; lost. Thirst; at night, with the headache. Eructations all day, tasting of sulphur in morning on rising and in forenoon, tasting of carbonic acid gas in afternoon, after supper this gas passed down to bowels, caused boring and passed off with the odor of sulphuretted hydrogen, the E. continuing on lying down, and rumbling and inflation of abdomen; empty E.

Nausea; at 9 A.M.; at breakfast; in evening, with griping in abdomen, also rumbling; with griping in abdomen; with inclination to diarrhœa; with faint and tremulous feeling; with drowsiness. Retching. Intermittent pain in evening. Coolish pain as if distended in region of cardiac orifice, < hearty meal. Heaviness after a light supper of biscuit and tea, till late at night; H., with pain and tenderness. Sinking feeling; with pain as if diarrhœa would come on and sickness. Uneasiness in epigastrium; when walking and reading, with nausea.

Abdomen.—Distention in morning on waking, then copious and loud flatulency; D. in afternoon when walking in open air, with heat in præcordia. Rumbling in morning, then griping; R. after eating; with uneasiness and coldness in it; with griping and copious flatulency; then flatulence. Flatulence; in open air; offensive, like cabbage-water; frequent discharge of offensive flatus at 11 A.M., with uneasiness in bowels, then loose stool; with pain. Griping causing sweat, with the brown, fermented, frothy diarrhœa, with urging. Pain; during the day, with inclination to diarrhœa; in evening, < stooping, lasted nearly all the next day, with distention; at night; on eating. Feeling as before diarrhœa; at 9 A.M., with cutting under umbilicus at 1 P.M., diarrhœa with discharge of bright blood and painful urging (dysentery), as if the gut would protrude. Uneasiness and discomfort; U. at breakfast, with qualmishness, then rumbling; U. as before stool, at 7 A.M.; as before diarrhœa, at 10 A.M.; as before diarrhœa, after breakfast. Qualmishness. Gone sensation.

Griping in region of upper A., with pain in forehead. Darting sticking in r. hypochondrium, < laughing or movement. Pain in l. hypochondrium; waking at 6 A.M.; at noon; at 6 P.M.; P. deep beneath l. floating ribs at 4 P.M., lasting all night, < deep inspiration and lying on l. side, returned at times next day. Cutting over umbilicus; above U. as before diarrhœa. Sudden griping drawing pain in l. side of U. Sore pain under U.; in a spot on touch in evening, when going to bed; S. on U. as if ulcerated. Rumbling in hypogastrium. Cutting in hypogastrium, with inclination to diarrhœa. Pain about Poupart's ligaments; in r. inguinal canal as if a stone were in it, at 5 P.M.; intermittent, in the hollow of iliac region, as if struck in the testicles.

Rectum and Anus.—Discharge of blood during stool; painless, bright; painless D. of blood in morning after getting up. Violent purgings of anus caused by old piles. Partial prolapse of rectum during stool. Bearing down in old piles all the afternoon, with burning in them and diarrhœa pains. Pain in rectum and lumbar region.

Stool.—Watery, brown, with excoriation of anus; *W., with little pain or desire,* at 10 P.M., 1 A.M. and about daylight, they were watery at first, then thicker, then watery again, and so on, also passed much wind, similar stools the two next days. Loose; every day, sometimes twice a day, with pain in rectum and colic before stool; but difficult. Free. Frequent. Bowels confined for three days. Omitted, next day loose after uneasiness in abdomen, third day no stool, next morning loose and urgent.

Clinical.—Diarrhœa < morning, stools brown, watery, fermented, especially with very profuse urine, and colic > eating.

Urinary Organs.—Urging in morning on rising, with slight tenesmus of bladder, but scanty urine. *Frequent micturition of clear urine; F., of colorless urine;* micturition twice at night, each time a pint or more of light-colored urine. Urethra, sudden darting stinging up, when sitting; sudden darting up when sitting; cutting outward at 7 P.M.; sudden tingling in orifice in morning, with itching; itching in lips of meatus after micturition, or prickling; sudden itching in orifice in evening.

Urine copious; in forenoon, and light-colored; at night; and white; and light-colored; and light-colored, depositing a white sediment; and limpid; and of deep orange color; and *dark red,* and offensive, in morning on rising, gradually diminishing in quantity and color the same day, while I felt in every respect better.

Clinical.—Nocturnal enuresis, urine very profuse.

Sexual Organs.—Itching and discomfort. Unconscious emission at night in sleep. Desire or power diminished.

Respiratory Organs.—Scraping tickling low down in bronchia at 10 A.M. Itching at top of windpipe. Hoarseness in morning; on rising, as from dryness in larynx, > breakfast, next day it lasted till evening. Cough; in morning, almost making me sick, retching slightly. Dry cough; with irritation at top of windpipe. Troublesome cough; on first moving about, > expectoration; with difficult expectoration of light-colored mucus, causing soreness and roughness of throat. Cough, with expectoration; on going into cold air; of tough mucus, mornings and on going into cold air. Expectoration of mucus; saltish E. Panting on the least exercise, < ascending steps, with palpitation and rapid pulse. Frequent, deep breathing, approaching yawning; often inclined to breathe deeply to relieve the chest.

Chest.—Sticking or catching pain in l. lower lobe of lung at night in bed, on drawing a long breath. Pleuritic pain in l. side when sitting; under l. side of sternum when sitting, > exercise. Darting outward in r. side. Pains through chest, < l. side and posteriorly; frequent, through sides; subcutaneous, near l. side of sternum, below centre, < pressure and sitting, > moving; muscular drawing, under r. breast at 9 A.M. Oppression at 4 P.M.; in evening, with hurried respiration and prostration, and necessity to stop several times to get breath when talking or reading aloud; with rapid and difficult respiration, as if there were no air in the room; with weakness of it and shortness of breath, then nausea. Orgasm; with heat.

Clinical.—Neuralgia of the nipples.

Heart and Pulse.—Sticking in heart after dinner. Violent beating of H. at 4 P.M. on ascending steps. Throbbing in arteries at night. Pulse rapid; in evening, and full and strong; and strong and bounding; and almost imperceptible. Pulse intermittent and irregular.

Neck.—Full feeling in gland of l. side, extending to side of face. Stiffness; in morning on waking; at 2 P.M. on moving head, with soreness; along l. sterno-cleido-mastoid, with soreness; of r. sterno-cleido-mastoid, < moving head to r., > moving it to l., with soreness.

Back.—Spine tender on pressure. Bruised pain at top of spine. Pulsative pain between scapulæ, passing from one to the other, thence to dorsum of r. arm in extensor muscles, darting towards elbow. Pain in sacrum; a little below its union with vertebra, < motion or standing; in loins in morning on waking, < motion; over r. kidney on waking, < moving. Tenderness of kidney region on pressure. Weakness of loins after exercise; W. and pain of loins and lower limbs, also at 10 P.M.; painful, of loins, also at 10 P.M., < standing; of small of back, extending around body, as if the body were broken.

Extremities.—Twitching of muscles of arms and legs. Sudden boring rheumatic pains in l. carpal bones in evening on lying down, then shifting to r., then down to r. tarsal, then to l., these pains shifted rapidly for several hours, all > getting up and walking. Pain alternately in r. shoulder and r. hip, passing down limbs. Heaviness of arms and legs at 3 P.M. Stiffness on getting up.

Upper Extremities.—Shifting pains here and there. Weight. Pain in l. shoulder; intermittent. Trembling of arms and hands in evening. Bruised pain in muscles of l. upper arm on moving it or lifting, and on resting it stiffness as from a blow or wound, afterwards the same in r. Pain in extensor muscles of r. forearm. Swelling of veins of hands. Rheumatic pain in r. index and first joint of the phalanges; suddenly in knuckle of l., then of r. ring finger. Feeling as if the least pressure with fingers would sprain them.

Lower Extremities.—Shooting from r. trochanter into hip-joint. Bruised pain in tops of thighs as from overwalking, when walking, > walking fast. Drawing pain in posterior muscles of r. thigh, with tenderness on pressure. Sharp darting pain at inner upper angle of r. patella at 3 P.M. Pain at superior angle of l. patella, extending beneath it. Boring in r. knee. Sprained pain in l. knee (which was sprained and lame for several weeks five years ago, but has not troubled him since) on stooping, with stiffness, afterwards the pain on moving, the stiffness in centre of hollow is like the stretching of a cord, no strength to get up with it when stooping, leg < evening, > sleep and rest, after walking two miles one day it was intensely painful on rising from a seat, > moving about, leg continued weak and painful, inability to walk fast or run, pain under l. ham on stretching leg.

Soreness of l. leg below knee, as if it had been strained. Contractive pain in l. tendo-achillis, > motion. Tearing in r. ankle when walking. Pain in l. ankle, > motion. Pain in an old bunion. Sharp darting pain at end of l. big toe. Rheumatic pain in dorsum of l. big toe, shifting to l. ankle.

Skin.—Red blotches that burn on rubbing. Reddish, rough, scaly, erythematous patches (resembling barber's itch) on l. side of face and near corner of lips, with tension and tenderness of skin of face. Pimples on chin. Sore pimples, pricking on touch, on face, loins and seat. Hard, white, flat papules, some with a red point in the centre, about lips, thighs, on wrist and between fingers, < inside of thigh, with itching, < scratching, then burning and diffused redness, in several hours they become more elevated or acuminated and finally disappear without suppuration or desquamation and others spring up, afterwards pimples on prepuce, the itching < afternoon and evening, not after going to bed, the prepuce itches, < morning on rising, itching < warm room and evening and morning. Red papules, smarting on touch, around nose, next day yellowish exudation from them, which soon forms a crust. Painful boil on r. shoulder.

Sensitiveness, and when scratching burning. Bruised soreness on face, < forehead, above l. eye and around it, in morning on rising, with tension and when pressed or rubbed sensitiveness. Itching; in differents parts; under skin; on lower limbs and other parts at 10 P.M., not > rubbing, burning as soon as the rubbing ceased; in commissure of l. fingers, < evening and night; in different parts, as from small pimples; tingling, in various parts, hands, face, uncovered parts; stinging, all round neck; stinging, at top of thorax, < rubbing, with redness.

Sleep.—*Excessive yawning* after lying down. Slept with mouth open. Sleepiness; in the daytime and sleeplessness at night; with nausea, but inability to sleep more than a few minutes. Heavy sleep and lascivious dreams. Sleeplessness; after the first nap till daylight, with restlessness; till 1 A.M., then frequent waking; about 3 or 4 A.M., with restlessness; after 4 A.M.; till towards morning, with restlessness. Frequent waking; towards morning; from vivid, frightful dreams. Restless sleep; with anxious, incongruous dreams; and disturbed, < after 4 A.M., with a variety of unimaginable and incoherent dreams; with frequent waking, inability to lie still, fever, sweat, pain in small of back and burning of feet; and unrefreshing, tossing about before sleep, frequent waking, difficult falling asleep again. Tossing about two hours before sleep. Restless till 12 or 1; after 4 A.M.; *at night,* and unable to think.

Dreams; *gloomy, rousing from sleep,* < about midnight; horrid; troubled; disagreeable; anxious, unremembered; constant, of the ordinary occurrences of the day, sometimes mixed with the fantastic; unimaginable and incoherent; vivid, congruous, coherent, also incoherent and disgusting, all in rapid succession; of every variety; of death; of death in the family; of the announcement of the death of a brother, and on waking found myself shedding tears, which continued for hours to affect me as if real.

Fever.—Chilliness through the day; at 1 P.M. on rising after sitting three hours, lasting till 3 P.M., with heat in chest, erratic pains in limbs, chest and head, disposition to stretch, chilliness on moving about and cold hands; in evening, with cold feet; with shivering, also with irritable feeling in head; with cold hands and feet and headache; with flushed face; frequent; running over me at 2 P.M., with gooseflesh and cold fingers. Cold feet; when walking out-doors, and cold legs.

Fever till 1 A.M., with bounding pulse, 120, thirst, oppression of chest, rapid respiration, difficult breathing as if there were no air in the room, pacing the room in anxiety, then throwing myself on the bed and rolling from side to side in mental agony, without knowing why, afterwards frequent waking from vivid, frightful dreams. Heat of the room was unbearable and caused sweat. Heat of head, hands and feet; of head, with stupidity of it; of face, flushed after tea, with pain in l. temple. Hands feel hot and clammy to me, but not to any one else. Cold sweat at bottom of back.

Platinum.

Pure precipitated Platinum is triturated with sugar of milk.

Allies.—Rhus t., Lyc., Aur., Puls., Sep., Bell., Verat., Hyosc.

Generalities.—*Lies in morning on waking with legs spread out*, r. hand under head, l. on pit of stomach, that is uncovered, or with legs drawn up and knees far apart, or with hands above head, *also with erections, always on back, with inclination to uncover legs and body, though without heat* (Hyosc.). *Painful tremulousness of whole body, with throbbing in veins; tremulous sensation at times through whole body* (Arg. nit., Gels.); T. sensation in hands and feet, then chilliness and trembling of whole body and chattering of teeth, with warm face and cold hands. Sticking through whole body. **Bruised pain on pressure in the parts affected by cramplike pain**; B. pain here and there, suddenly disappearing. Drawing in various parts in succession; *cramplike, here and there*, as from taking cold; jerklike, on r. side of neck, then in a hollow tooth, at last in ear, where it was a jerklike sticking.

Necessity to stretch in afternoon, which made her feel better. *Weakness;* in morning in bed, with sexual desire, so that she covered her face and wept hard; in evening, with sleepiness; after dinner, with sleepiness; in open air, even to sleeping; < *sitting, with tremulous restlessness, feet tired out* (Rhus t.); with sensation as if cold sweat would break out on face; even to falling down; as if she had slept but little. **Numbness; painful, as from a blow**, *in spots, < head. If the mind is joyous the body is suffering, and vice versa.* Symptoms all l.-sided. Aggravation in evening before sleep.

Clinical.—Hysterical spasms resulting from nervous excitement, especially with constriction of the œsophagus, globus hystericus. Spasms during labor. Alternations of anæsthesia and hyperæsthesia. General aggravation from rest, relief from motion. Pains generally increase and decrease gradually (Stann.)

Mind.—Arrogant, proud. Contemptuous, pitiful looking down upon people usually venerated, with a kind of casting them off, *in paroxysms, against her will* (Verat.). *Illusion on entering the house after a walk,* **as if everything were too small, all persons physically and mentally inferior, but she herself physically large and superior,** *the room seemed gloomy, with apprehensive, sad and fretful mood*, whirling vertigo and discontent with the surroundings, all > open air and sunshine.

Lively, so that she could have danced, half an hour after weeping; lively for two days, everything seems joyous, could laugh at the saddest thing, then the third morning and evening sadness, with weeping even at joyous and laughable things and if she is spoken to (Ign.). Inclination to whistle and sing. *Weeping mood after mild reproaches; W., < evening; > open air; and out of sorts with the whole world, everything seems too narrow* (Puls.); with sticky tears; with aversion to eating; and laughing, yawning, again weeping, aversion to everything; so that she was vexed with herself, *with silence. Feeling that he shall die soon; with shuddering at the thought. Thinks that she stands alone in the world. It seems as if she does not belong to her own family, everything seems changed after a short absence.*

Anxiety; on attempting to talk in company, with palpitation; < walking, with palpitation; *with trembling of hands and flushes of heat over whole body; deathly, as if her senses would vanish, with trembling of limbs, oppression of breath and palpitation;* frequent, sudden, through whole body. Sad in morning, and fretful, next morning happy, especially in open air; *S. and restless, she thought that she was not fit for the world, was weary of life, but had* **great dread of death, which she believed to be near;** *and morose, she sits alone, does not talk*, cannot keep awake, *then inconsolable weeping, < being spoken to;* and quiet; suddenly.

Sensitive mood. Morose and discontented; M. all day, and anxious about heart; in morning, and indolent; *and easily excited, he could have beaten any one without provocation;* > frequent weeping. Quarrelsome; and spoke only when obliged to, abrupt. Earnest and taciturn, next day she made jokes and laughed at everything. Disgust for everything, no desire for anything. Indifference, does not care whether his absent wife dies or not. Vacillating mood. Disposition affected, < afternoon and evening.

Mental quiet, increased vigor, and inclination to think. *Absent-minded; and forgetful;* in the company of friends in the open air, and reserved, cold. Disinclination for mental work. Memory deficient.

Clinical.—Melancholia; a form characterized by great pride, extreme self-esteem. Mania, especially puerperal, with unchaste talk, at times very violent in her actions. Mental troubles associated with suppressed menses. Religious melancholia; great dread of death, palpitation, weeping; hysterical alternations of laughing and weeping.

Head.—Aching; as if *tense;* as if torn, after the vertigo; as if water were in it, waking her about midnight, with dryness and scraping in throat, ill humor and sweat, < face. **Intermittent cramplike drawing constriction,** *< about forehead, beginning slight, increasing till violent, ending slight.* Painful drawing in various parts. Confusion; tensive, like a board in front of head. *Vertigo, < sitting down or descending stairs;* V. so that she dared not move the eyes, < day, mostly with palpitation; in quick paroxysms, as if he would lose consciousness, in evening when standing.

Forehead.—Sticking in sinciput. Boring in middle. Burrowing in l. side after dinner, while walking in open air and afterwards. Pain above l. brow; beneath r. eminence, increasing and decreasing at intervals; *cramplike, as if screwed in; wavelike benumbing, above r. orbit;* bruised, in r. eminence. Intermittent compression. Sudden pressure inward in l. side. Pressure as if everything would come out, < motion of head, with weight upon head that presses eyes together and forces out tears, before the attack anxiety about heart, followed by stupidity so that she could not talk, headache < till 10 P.M. (it returned at the same hour several days), with anxiety, heat, redness of face and thirst.

Drawing from l. side into temple, where it is a pressure. **Numbness in sinciput as if constricted,** *in a warm room full of people, increasing to burrowing compression, with fretful impatience and heat in upper part of body, < head, as if anxious sweat would break out,* and in evening in cool air heat, and on beginning to walk shattering in brain as if a ball were beating against the skull, later in bed addition of whizzing in ears; *tensive N. in sinciput as after a blow, extending to nasal bone.* Dulness.

Temples.—Burning sticking in l., > scratching. *Cramplike pain in r. in afternoon; in l. beginning gently, increasing and decreasing. Cramplike tension as if screwed in. Cramplike pressure inward;* wavelike P. inward in l. Sudden spasmodic, contractive shocks through head from r. temple to l., then **numbness as if bound,** *with tremulousness of sides of head.* **Crawling on r., afterwards extending down along lower jaw, with coldness in it.**

Numb pain on top of head as if scalp would be contracted and as if a weight were on it. Pressure inward on middle of vertex. Sticking in l. side in evening in bed; intermittent corroding, in a spot on l. parietal bone. Sudden bruised pain in a spot on l. parietal bone. Pain in parietes at night as if lying upon a stone, obliged to sit up; P. as from a blow in r. side and forepart of head; in r. parietal bone, as if a plug were sticking in it. Jerklike drawing in sides. Cramplike drawing extending from l. side of occipital bone through head to lower jaw.

Clinical.—Periodic headache, which increases and decreases gradually, generally < stooping and > exercise in the open air. The sensation of numbness or a contraction of the brain accompanies nearly all the headaches of this drug, indeed numbness is one of the most frequent accompaniments of all the affections requiring Platinum.

Eyes.—Feeling of sand in r., with necessity to wink. Pain in the evening by the light and on exerting vision, at first an itching, so that she was obliged to rub them, then suppuration and pain, with trembling before vision so that she could see nothing and was obliged to close lids, then sleep. Smarting of r., with coldness in it. Sleepy pressure in forenoon, without inclination to sleep. Painless drawing about l., with dim vision and feeling as if eye were agglutinated. Heat, < in house, with sleepiness as if they would close, less pain on closing them, and on looking sharply at anything sensation as if they would water. Cornea red and inflamed. *Lids twitch.* Crawling in r. canthus. Margin of orbit, *intermittent cramplike pain near r. outer;* tensive pain as if pressed together in upper, and in eyeballs; sore biting on upper, as if denuded. Pain as from a blow on arch of r. brow.

Ears.—*Sticking jerking in r. outer, with numbness and coldness extending through cheeks to lips.* Intermittent sticking in r. meatus. Digging in r., with jerklike drawing in l. Cramplike pain. Tearing drawing in r., with sticking. Biting crawling in r. meatus. *Ringing;* in r., with crawling; then tearing. *Whizzing* every morning and afterwards, also every evening after lying down, with *roaring. Roaring,* with sticking in head; R. in r.; in r., with cramplike dulness in head; in r., as from the fluttering of a large bird. Sound of a wind, as if stopped, < slightest noise, so that it was difficult to understand what was said. Thundering jerks in r., like distant cannonading.

Clinical.—Nervous deafness. Otalgia, with sensation of coldness or numbness extending to cheeks and lips.

Nose.—Rhythmical cramplike jerking in l. wing. Cramplike pain in r. side of nasal bone, with numbness. Pulling above l. wing, as if pulled by a hair, then numbness as if a hair had been pulled out. *Acrid biting.* Crawling, with lachrymation and ineffectual attempts to sneeze. Increase of mucus. Stopped catarrh in one nostril, later on walking in open air fluent catarrh, then stoppage of other nostril, then again fluent coryza.

Face.—*Pale, sunken;* P., suffering expression. Bluish veins like varicose veins, on chin. Jerkings in chin, as if it had been knocked up. Burning sticking in l. cheek, necessity to scratch. *Neuralgic pain in l. malar-bone.* Bruised pain in l. mastoid process on pressure. Stupefying pressure in r. malar-bone and in whole half of nose. **Painful cramplike numbness in l. malar-bone. Tense numb sensation in zygomata and mastoid processes, as if head were screwed together;** tense numb sensation in chin, as if screwed in. Slow intermittent shocks beneath chin. Cramplike pain in l. side of lower jaw; on lower margin of lower jaw.

Lips.—Desquamation, bleeding, pain and in open air smarting. Vesicle on inner margin of upper, with sticking on touch; vesicles about outer margin of lower, with biting pain. Intermittent cramplike jerkings in upper in morning in bed. Smarting of inner surface of lower, and in gums; of inner surface, with painful feeling of looseness of upper; just below red of lower, as if denuded. Dryness and roughness; upper dry as if burnt.

Clinical.—Facial neuralgia, a feeling of numbness especially in the malar-bones or a feeling as if the parts were between screws (Verbascum).

Mouth.—Teeth, *numb pain in l. lower in morning after rising;* drawing and throbbing in upper molar, then in lower; cramplike drawing; burrowing drawing in a hollow incisor and in a sound one. Tongue, *burnt feeling,* < rubbing it against teeth; burning beneath and on r. side; *crawling.* Glutinous and slimy all day, < eating, also in morning, with ill humor. Smarting as if raw on r. half of palate, with crawling in l. nostril. Salivation. Sweet taste on tip of tongue.

Throat.—Painful swelling of r. tonsil. Pain extending suddenly through head as a drawing, heavy sensation; P. in the goitre, < touch, with tickling in it. Scraping in evening after lying down and next day, at times provoking short cough; S., with mucus and necessity to hawk; as from catarrh or as from biting food, with frequent necessity to hawk, which caused sticking. Rawness as if a piece of skin were hanging down. Constriction. Cramplike drawing about hyoid bone as if everything were constricted. Uvula feels elongated.

Stomach.—Almost always hungry. *Sudden ravenous hunger during the contemptuous mood, with* **greedy, hasty eating** (Aur., Lyc.), then at mealtime she eats without desire. Though longing for tobacco he does not relish it, is soon averse to it. First morsels are relished, then speedy satiety; satiety immediately in evening on account of sadness, afterwards she eats. Appetite lost. Thirst after supper; T. for water; no T.

Eructations.—*Empty; in morning fasting;* in morning fasting, with fulness in stomach and abdomen as if overloaded; *loud, when fasting and after eating;* with hunger. Sudden, of a bitter-sweet liquid, during which he choked, so that he was obliged to cough, then scraping in throat. Like hiccough, after eating, with emission of flatus.

Nausea in forenoon, with weakness, anxiety and tremulous sensation through whole body; N. in epigastric region; in epigastric region in morning; with appetite; with weariness of limbs; in pit of stomach as from fasting, then griping tension extending into abdomen; in attacks when walking in open air, < walking against the wind, > in the house by laying head on table, < rising again, then with whirling vertigo, < looking up, with smoky vision, and on laying head down a condition midway between sleep and waking, with vivid dreams, all > rising.

Fermentation in epigastric region (Lyc.). Distention of pit and epigastrium, with scraping and tearing in stomach. Visible twitching in epigastric region. Sticking near r. side of pit. Thrusts in pit; intermittent sticking, in pit. Griping in region of pit, then *flatulent pressure towards hypogastrium,* > after collection of flatus, which afterwards was passed with difficulty, the sensation in hypogastrium returned constantly with tension of abdomen. Gnawing in morning, with twisting, ravenous hunger and collection of water in mouth, not > eating. Drawing pain beneath pit, as from a strain; D. pain transversely above pit, increasing and decreasing at intervals, with shooting into middle of upper arm as if pinched, with numb and paralyzed sensation, the pain in side < laughing, inspiration, pressure, and every step caused shattering.

Pressure in pit, even on touch; P. in pit after eating (bread and butter), as from undigested food. Oppression in pit. Constriction in pit, with inclination to eat, as if thereby it would be relieved; C. in pit as if she could not get her breath. Feeling in pit as if he had swallowed too much air, > empty hiccough, with uprisings to pit of throat and ineffectual efforts to eructate. Crawling about pit extending to throat, as if she had swallowed feathers, with necessity to hack.

Clinical.—Gastralgia, hysterical.

Abdomen.— Distention in evening; cramplike, in places, in other places spasmodic retraction. Tense after dinner. Movements. Gurgling in morning fasting, with griping uneasiness. Emission of flatus during the day; E., with sensation as before diarrhœa; *odorless;* difficult, with desire for stool; short, abrupt, not easy without exertion of abdominal muscles. Jerking like thrusts in a spot externally. Sticking in morning; cutting S. suddenly through abdomen, then weariness of knees. Griping on second day of menses, then pressure downward in groins alternately with pressure in genitals, with increased flow; paroxysmal G. here and there. Colic towards morning, < rising in bed. *Constriction.* Anxiety, then pain in it as after a fright, with urging as in diarrhœa, but a small, normal stool. Uneasiness at night as from taking cold.

Rumbling in upper A. in morning. Constrictive griping beneath l. short ribs. Intermittent thrusts below short ribs. Sticking in r. side, when lying it extends forward into umbilical region and into l. side, < lying on l. side. Jerklike griping in sides, > emission of flatus. Jerklike drawing in r., with arrest of breathing. Intermittent burning in a spot in l.; sudden burning shooting downward in r.

Umbilicus.—Sticking; deep above U. on rising suddenly after stooping. Twisting about U., with oppression of breathing and general tremulous sensation. Griping in region, as in diarrhœa; after eating; flatulent G. in region, extending downward, with cutting and with desire to pass stool and flatus. Griping constriction in region, extending to back. Pain as from a thrust below U. Burning in region.

Hypogastrium.—Cutting as in menstruation, with drawing headache. **Pressure** *during profuse menstruation, with ill humor;* P., with nausea, as before menstruation; P. **downward towards genitals, as during menstruation** (Bell.), at times with desire for stool, extending through groins, above hips, towards small of back, where it pained a long time. Drawing from middle of groins towards both thighs, < touch and inspiration, with tearing; *painful D. in groins, as before menstruation.*

Clinical.—Lead colic, pains extend to back.

Rectum and Anus. — Discharge of much blood. Sticking in forepart of R. Sensation as in diarrhœa, extending up rectum, > emission of flatus. With the stool that was not hard great pressure, then sticking in anus, then spasmodic constriction of nates extending towards small of back, she must stop pressing on account of the pain. *Urging, with scanty stool passed in pieces after pressure, with* **painful weakness** *and tight sensation in abdominal muscles;* constant U.; ineffectual. Tenesmus in anus before and after a thin stool; *crawling T. in anus as in diarrhœa every evening before sleep.* Burning in rectum during stool, then itching. Crawling in anus every evening, with itching.

Stool.—Thin, sudden, forcible. Pasty, with thread-worms; P., partly digested, somewhat bloody, then increased tension in l. hypochondrium and small of back. *Indurated, as if burnt, preceded and followed by pressure.* Forcible, noisy, after dinner, at first thin, then hard, with increased urging, in pieces, each of which he must press out, then shivering, < upper part of body, and after rising from stool pain and weakness about umbilicus. *Constipation.* Scanty, tenacious, glutinous, connected, with long pressure and exertion of abdominal muscles. Difficult, with cutting, burning and protrusion of hæmorrhoids. Every two days, with pressure and at times blood. A piece of tape-worm is passed, with desire for stool.

Clinical.—Constipation, from lead-poisoning or from traveling; frequent desire, but small evacuations with great effort. Obstinate constipation, with feeling of a load in rectum which cannot be evacuated.

Urinary Organs.—Micturition slow, but frequent. *Urine red,* with white clouds; pale yellow in morning, as clear as water in afternoon; became turbid and caused red color on sides of vessel.

Sexual Organs.—**Sensitiveness and pressure, and in mons veneris,** *with internal shaking chill and external coldness* (except in face). **Voluptuous crawling, and in abdomen,** *with anxious oppression and palpitation, then painless pressure downward in genitals, with sticking in sinciput and exhaustion.* Sore biting as if denuded on scrotum, so that he must often change its position, even in bed. Erections towards morning; *in sleep, with amorous dreams;* constant, at night, without emissions or lascivious dreams. Coition short, and with little satisfaction.

Female.—*Sticking in r. ovarian region;* in the indurated uterus, with cramp. *Leucorrhœa like the white of egg*, only during the day, after micturition and after rising from a seat. **Menses too early and profuse** (Rhus); **too early,** *lasting eight days, with drawing pain in abdomen the first day;* too early, with diarrhœa. **Much clotted blood the first day of menstruation.** Painful urging to menses, > evening in bed, returns in morning on rising.

Clinical.—Satyriasis. Nymphomania, especially puerperal; in this morbid condition Plat. is indicated generally by the extreme sensitiveness or numbness of the external organs, sometimes even these sensations may alternate. Sexual melancholia in both sexes. Pruritus of the vagina. Fibroid tumors of the uterus, with constant pressure as before menses, menstruation always very profuse, great sensitiveness of the parts, internal chilliness and external coldness and numbness. Prolapsus, with constant pressure in the back and groins, especially with extreme sensitiveness to touch. Chronic inflammation of the ovaries, especially right. Ovaritis has been relieved, even after suppuration has taken place. Dysmenorrhœa, with extreme pressure, external sensitiveness, the pains increase to spasms and screaming, followed by excessive hæmorrhage. Sterility, with chronic ovaritis, internal soreness, etc. Menorrhagia, characterized by dark clots and extreme pressing pain. Very irregular menses, with the peculiar disposition, discharge of dark clots, bearing down. Women requiring this drug habitually have too early and too long-lasting menses, discharge dark and thick, increased sensitiveness and pressure, abnormal sexual appetite and melancholia. Albuminous leucorrhœa. Associated with uterine and ovarian troubles there is usually a large number of reflex disturbances, such as aphonia, cough, palpitation, numbness, spasms, sleeplessness, etc.

Respiratory Organs.—Constriction at bronchial bifurcation. Dyspnœa as if tightly laced, with heavy, slow respiration. Want of breath if she walks a little. Oppressed breath, with warm uprisings from pit of stomach to pit of throat, necessity to breathe deeply and hoarseness. Frequent deep breathing, without apprehension or oppression of chest. Sudden arrest of breath in throat, as on walking against a strong wind.

Clinical.—Nervous dry cough, with palpitation and dyspnœa.

Chest.—Cutting sticking in r. side, < inspiration; sudden S. beneath l. shoulder. Pain in a spot in upper part; neuralgic, in clavicular region; *cramplike in l. side;* intermitting cramplike, beneath r. clavicle; *in shocks in l. half,* partly beneath axilla, partly in middle of chest, not affecting respiration; strained. Thrusts in a costal cartilage, in l. lower part, near sternum; cutting T. upward in r. half. Beating like thrusts on a lower true rib. Hammering in a costal cartilage near pit of stomach, with throbbing. *Cramplike constriction close to shoulder. Weight, causing deep breathing.* Pressure on a l. short rib, and after pressure upon it bruised pain. Oppression, with anxiety and warm uprisings from pit of stomach to pit of throat. Drawing extending to groins, then constriction in genitals. Rhythmical burning between two l. ribs. Sensation of fasting, as after rising too early, lasting long after rising, gradually increasing, > towards noon, with nausea. *Weakness as if respiration failed, she breathed deeply, but could not breathe deeply enough.*

Heart.—Sticking and burning. Pressure in region of apex.

Neck.—Cramp in muscles, as from a hard bed, < motion. Cramplike pain in side on turning it towards shoulder. *Tense numbness in nape close to occiput, as if bound. Nape weak, head sinks forward.*

Back.—Smarting sticking in r. half. *Pain as if broken,* after walking an hour. Pain in middle and l. side, with intermittent thrusts; P. as from a plug in r. side, near middle of spine, and on pressure pain as in a wound. Sore, denuded sensation in l. side when sitting, with burning intermittent sticking. Intermittent sore sensation on outer margin of r. scapula. Jerklike drawing in r. scapula, extending to hand. Pressure on lower end of l. scapula, with cool sensation. Bruised, cramplike pain in sacrum on pressure. Pain in small of back as if broken, < bending backward. **Numbness of coccyx when sitting,** *as after a blow.*

Extremities.—Cramplike throbbing jerks here and there. Wavelike beating pain in spots on forearm and leg.

Upper Extremities.—Shoulder. Sticking, so that it jerked the arm and almost made it sink down. Pain as from a blow on top of l.; P. on top of r. as if he had carried a weight on it. Weakness.

Arm.—Bruised pain; in upper, < moving it; above elbow, increasing and decreasing in waves. Pain in l. as if flesh were torn off. Weakness of l., with drawing in it; W. as if she had carried a weight, > moving it back and forth, returned during rest, with drawing as by a thread from shoulder to hand. Heaviness. *Paralyzed sensation in l.,* so that she must let it hang down, < leaning arm on a chair when sitting and when leaning against shoulder; sudden paralysis as from a blow, in a spot, now in r., now in l.

Pain in periosteum of r. elbow. Forearm, pain in r., with drawing inward of fingers on straightening out arm; cramplike pain on resting upon elbow; intermittent jerking pain in l. ulna, in tendons close to wrist; cramplike intermittent pressure on flexor surface of l.; cramplike rigid sensation in l., and in hand; paralyzed sensation in r., extending downward.

Hand.—Trembling of H. and fingers on holding them free. Cramp on exerting it. Cramplike rhythmical jerking below external condyle of wrist. Cramplike pain above two first fingers; on ball of l.; in r. metacarpal bones; in H. and fingers on grasping anything firmly, < joints.

Fingers.—*Trembling of r. thumb* in morning, *with numbness* as if bruised. Flexion on flexing arm, with painful drawing extending up arm. Jerklike cramp in thumb-joint and metacarpal bone, < violent motion. Burning sticking in metacarpal joint of index, recurring after scratching, which it compelled. Pain in first phalanx of index as if an ulcer would break. Jerking cramplike drawing in r. index and hand. *Numbness* of little.

Lower Extremities.—Staggering when standing. Muscular twitches after walking, < legs. Inclined to uncover at night, though they were not warm. Weakness as if beaten when sitting and standing, with tremulous uneasiness in them. Crawling as if asleep when riding one over the other.

Thigh.—Bruised pain; above l. knee; in upper part of l. when sitting; in middle, more when sitting than when walking. Cramplike pain on inner side of r.; posteriorly when sitting; pulsating, in middle when sitting. Pain as if broken when sitting with legs stretched out, with undulating cramplike shooting through limbs on drawing them up. Pinching tensive pain as from a blow just above hip-joint, increasing and decreasing at intervals. Drawing in upper part of l., so that upon stepping upon it she sank down; jerklike, above knees. **Tightness, as if tightly wrapped** when sitting, *with weakness in them.* Cramplike numb sensation as after a blow on anterior surface.

of r. Weakness when sitting, < towards knees, with tremulous uneasiness.

Knee.—*Pain as from a blow in l.* Burning prickling in r. Pressure on inner side of hollow of l. when sitting with leg drawn up. Drawing, then burning, and on stepping upon it pain as if dislocated. Tension in hollow of l. after rapid walking in open air. *Weakness* when walking, and in thighs when sitting; more when standing than when walking, < ascending steps; *in and about them, more when standing than when sitting,* with tottering; on inner side of hollow of l. when sitting, with numbness and pressure. *Tremulous numbness as if tightly bound, entending to feet.*

Leg.—Cramplike jerks extending down legs when sitting, < evening, *with sense of rigidity,* even in feet. Acute shocks on tibiæ, extending downward. Cramplike drawing through r. calf on sitting down after walking a little. Tension in r. calf when sitting, with beating, so that foot trembled. Smarting pulsation in middle of anterior surface of r. *Tremulous crawling uneasiness when sitting,* **a numbness and rigidity,** < *evening* and in bed. Weakness below knees when walking; below knees when sitting; after a short walk, with oppressed respiration, more when beginning to walk than afterwards, at last nausea.

Ankle.—Sprained pain. Sharp jerking pain at l. external malleolus, extending to hip and ilium.

Foot.—Cramp in soles at night on rising, with flexion of them. Painful twitching in r. sole when standing, and crawling pressure beneath it when sitting. Sticking in balls in evening after lying down till midnight. Tearing on back of l., with cutting transversely across it. Tensive pain in instep when standing, < inclining it forward. Tremulous pain as from external pressure in a spot on back. Hard pressure in r. sole near toes. Cramplike drawing in r. heel. *Weariness when sitting, with numbness;* W. in evening, with swollen sensation about malleolus, when sitting the W., with tension, extended into calves.

Toes.—Swelling of balls, with nightly tearing. Burning-crawling sticking beneath great. Tearing in r., < great, with throbbing, as in an ulcer. *Pain in great as if tightly bound.* Burning pain at night. Sore pain in ball of T. (that had been frozen formerly), < walking. Cramplike drawing, < great. Cramplike burning tension in l. great. Painful throbbing beneath little; intermittent cramplike throbbing in l. great.

Skin.—Blue spot on l. upper arm, becoming smaller and dark red. Sticking above ankle, not > scratching; jerking, on r. chest, recurring after scratching. Itching sticking over whole body, not > scratching; on back of hands, > scratching; on cheek, > rubbing. Burning pricking; here and there. Smarting above ankle. Biting on cheek, > scratching, but returning; sticking, in a spot on sole, he must scratch it; corroding, in lobule of l. ear; itching, < arms, hands and scrotum, < evening on getting into bed, with sticking and burning tickling. *Sore biting* on chin, obliged to rub it; about malleoli, with *smarting,* pain as if raw on touch of clothes; about mouth, provoking scratching, as after shaving with a dull razor. Crawling on inner side of r. thumb; in l. finger-tips, with tickling; itching, on r. great toe; on hand, or a sensation of a cool wind. Itching over whole body at night; I. in epigastric region, > rubbing; on r. wrist, with biting, so that he could not scratch it enough; sticking, beneath great toe; tingling, on l. index.

Sleep.—Yawning; in morning on rising, though sleep had been long and refreshing; in afternoon, without sleepiness; in afternoon, causing lachrymation; violent, after eating, that makes cervical muscles painful; *inclination to almost spasmodic.* Sleepiness in morning after long and sound sleep; in evening, dreams of distant strange things on closing eyes, but immediate waking; so that she cannot follow her own thoughts. Fell asleep in evening when talking; in evening when reading, with frequent waking, afterwards sound sleep at night. Sleep late in morning.

Sleepless before midnight, then short sleep, with constant dreaming; S. till after midnight, with tearing in balls of toes; from midnight till morning, with fixed ideas to which he anxiously clung; after 3 A.M., comfort in no position. Starting up in evening on falling asleep when sitting. Waking about midnight and tossing about; *W. about midnight,* with despondency and thirst, but sleep after an hour; at 3 A.M., every morning, and sleeping again; *every night very stupid and could not collect himself for a long time;* in morning anxious and fretful, as if in sleep he had received an injury, and much crying.

Dreams.—Pleasant, remembered. Unremembered. Disconnected, in evening nap. Confused, of ordinary events, with inability to remember it exactly; anxious, of war and bloodshed. Anxious, and on sudden waking gloomy thoughts. Fires, she could not get ready to go to them. Of the death of a distant sister and wondered that he had had no intimation of it.

Clinical.—Sleeplessness, with extreme nervous excitability.

Fever.—Chilliness in forenoon, with sleepiness; C. in evening on undressing, with chattering of teeth; in evening before going to bed, with uneasy sleep and frequent waking, with anxiety, a tremulous sensation through whole body, nausea and headache; in open air, with shivering, flushes of heat, fretfulness and taciturnity; constant sensation as if he would be chilly, with frequent shivering down lower limbs, < warm, open air; frequent, extending downward over whole body, as if he would have gooseflesh; trembling, in evening; shuddering; shuddering, after stool and micturition, with shivering over head, chest and arms; shaking, over whole body, extending down to feet; shaking, creeping over her on going into open air. Shivering, < through lower limbs; creeping through whole body, after yawning.

Coldness on chin, beneath corner of mouth; **on r. side of face, with crawling and numbness;** feeling as if cold air entered r. ear; creeping over back; creeping in occiput, extending down to cheeks, where it was a burning pain, afterwards drawing in a hollow tooth. Sudden shivering in forehead, chest and arms after entering a warm room.

Burning at one time, at another prickling itching here and there. *Sudden heat, she thought that she was very red, but her color was the same as usual. Heat in face,* with burning and itching in eyes; *in face* every day from 5 till 9, *with redness,* thirst, dryness in mouth, headache and vibrations before eyes, causing vertigo, lachrymation; in face and head, a sultry sensation and a pain in forehead, she does not know what to do. Burning on head; in ears, with redness; in limbs, now here, now there; extending from r. shoulder to wrist; sore, on elbow, as if scraped or rubbed by woolen. Sweat in sleep.

Platinum Muriaticum.

This salt is dissolved in water for use.

Clinical.—This preparation of Platinum has been found valuable in caries of the bones, particularly of the nasal bones and of the tarsus. It has been used in syphilis after Mercury and Aurum.

Plumbum.

Pure precipitated lead is triturated with sugar of milk.

General Action.—It produces general interstitial inflammation characterized by proliferation of connective tissue (nerve, muscle and parenchyma of organs). The most striking effects of lead appear to originate from its action on the spinal cord and the nerves proceeding from it, namely, colic with violent contraction of the intestines and abdominal parietes; obstinate constipation. Paralysis, attacking chiefly the flexors of the extremities and finally becoming general; terrific pains in the extremities. The brain degenerates, epilepsy, various disturbances of the mental powers, even imbecility, result. Various organs undergo degeneration (sclerosis), kidney, heart, liver, etc.

Allies.—Thall., Cupr., Zinc., Ferr., *Phos., Ars.; Lyc.*, Op., Con., Colch., Led., etc.

Generalities.—Emaciation; looking ten years older than he was; and if placed upright he fell over, no control over flexors and extensors of limbs, < upper; of the paralyzed parts, their shrivelled, dingy yellow skin seems loosened from the flabby muscles, hands blue and infiltrated. **Anæmia**; and condition analogous to paralysis agitans. *Jaundice.* Consumption. Great mortality among children. Ganglion. Secretions diminished. Anasarca.

Lies upon his back; with limbs relaxed and powerless; on side doubled up; on r. side, with legs flexed upon thighs and these upon abdomen; on side when quiet, generally on l., with thighs pressing against abdomen. Constant change of position; doubles himself up, but avoids lying on abdomen, pressure on latter aggravates. Sometimes with his head almost on the floor, feet tangled in bed-clothes, he keeps up a rocking movement. Fell back without consciousness. *Blood-corpuscles diminished in number; but increased in size; abnormal number of white globules in blood.* Serum of blood shows a yellow reflection. Muscles flabby and soft; F. and pale. Mucous membranes pale; of waxen hue.

Trembling; of limbs and face; < evening, when he is fatigued; < fatigue or excitement, and in the latter case it extended to lower limbs; < excessive drinking; sudden, < arms. Cramps; in various parts, < hands and feet when those parts were first moved after rest; < behind knee, when walking or even standing still, > pressure, increased motion and cold compresses, with lancinations and sleeplessness; painful, in paralyzed muscles.

Often puts hands to head, with convulsive movements of eyes, hands and feet. Spasmodic shocks shoot like lightning over face and limbs. Twitchings; of limbs and body; epileptiform, in all parts, then paralysis. Spasmodic flexion of arm and r. leg, with automatic movements of eyes, hands and feet. Spasmodic contractions of flexors and adductors, legs forcibly flexed on thighs and thighs on abdomen, sometimes one leg is drawn over the other, impossible to raise arms from chest, forearms and wrists forcibly flexed, head drawn down to chest and to one side, head occasionally jerked from side to side, with consciousness, but inability to articulate, involuntary groans, pain, rectus abdominis hard and prominent, muscles attached to ribs contract so forcibly as to draw them in and he often cries out that they are breaking, afterwards prostration.

Convulsions; of particular muscles; with unconsciousness; with cold, clammy sweat; then coma; of limbs, then general stiffness, he fell to the ground, with consciousness, but inability to answer, afterwards weakness; *clonic and tonic;* clonic, with involuntary micturition, preceded by a cry, pallor, then redness, sweat after the spasms; tonic, in arms, fingers, legs, abdomen and chest; sudden, tonic, < face, neck, trunk and limbs, at the same time head was drawn towards l. side, shoulder drawn up, l. arm and l. foot stretched out so violently that the joints creaked, lips closed and l. corner of mouth drawn downward, l. cartilage of nose drawn to l. side, the attack generally lasted two minutes and ceased suddenly, the clonic C. affected only face and usually occurred after the atonic C.; tetanic; tetanic, then prickings in hands, forearm, lower limb, then stiffness of limbs and convulsive clenching of jaws; sudden, with heavy breathing, eyeballs distorted, body and arms flexed spasmodically, scanty ejection of saliva ended many attacks; sudden, limbs alternately flexed and extended, body shaken, head bent backward, sensation lost, face injected, coma between convulsions; head suddenly inclines forcibly to r., limbs stretched out stiff and convulsed, also face, which turns blue, eyes wide open and rolled upward, pupils dilated, shocks over whole body, bloody froth from mouth, beats of heart and pulse tumultuous and strong, afterwards threatened with suffocation, inspirations deep and difficult, the dark red face becomes pale, only whites of the half-open eyes are visible, body cold, motionless, sleeps a little, pulse 140 and small, wakes, eyes fixed, countenance dull, ill-humored, will hardly answer, turns on l. side and sleeps; formication from r. thumb and index to shoulder, with pricking, at the same time fingers flexed into palm and covering thumbs, forearm flexed and held in forced pronation, wrists flexed, clonic spasm of whole limb, r. hand and arm red from stagnation of blood, with his l. hand he supported his r. forearm, which tended to approach trunk, head shook and was inclined to l., spasms of eyes, circular movement of lower jaw, mind not affected, but unable to speak, afterwards numbness of r. hand.

Epilepsy; face pale, then E. without a cry, clonic convulsions of diaphragm and larynx; in bed, one quick, loud cry, tetanic rigidity of neck and limbs, pallor, unconsciousness, respiration ceases for a moment, face blue, congested spots on forehead and face, facial spasms, clonic convulsions (movements concentric), bloody, whitish foam at mouth, then paralysis of limbs, coma, with stertorous breathing, roused to half-consciousness, drowsiness; fell down with a cry, pallor, stiffness, then contractions, involuntary micturition, afterwards prostration; tongue swollen, protruded and bitten; with biting of tongue, then frequent coma, delirium more generally after than before the epilepsy, pupils dilated; with unconsciousness, convulsions of limbs, tetanic stiffness of head and body, face livid, distorted, stertor, foam at mouth, spasms of eyeballs, then coma, he lay motionless, with half-closed eyes and open mouth, grunting and automatic movements of limbs; muscular contractions began in abdomen, extended to throat, jaws closed so violently that a tooth was dislodged, eyes rolled upward, lastly limbs affected, motionless for an hour after the convulsions, then restless and talked incoherently, three more convulsions, each lasting about a minute, all preceded by dark vomiting and followed by symptoms similar to those after the first fit; sudden, with unconsciousness, pallor, stertor, prolonged inspiration, pulse 112, arms and hands forcibly extended, pronated and convulsed. Epileptiform spasms; one-sided, with twitchings of face, then general epilepsy, with stertor and unconsciousness. (Compare Calcarea c.)

Opisthotonos; with uræmic convulsions, distortions of eyes, unconsciousness, puffy face, then slow respiration, pulse 36; and sometimes emprosthotonos and pleurothotonos.

Hysteria; with loud groans, sighs and weeping; symptoms resembling H., irritability, restlessness, after useless efforts to find an easy position they fell back in bed exhausted, with pain, respiration hurried, heart's action painful and violent, with tears, groans and sighs, often coincident with abatement of the suffering.

Shooting through body; superficial, in several parts; in knees, popliteal spaces, calves, soles, bends of elbows, metacarpi and temples, worse by paroxysms, > pressure, with great sensibility, < popliteal spaces and calves. Tearing; in r. jaw near chin, after rubbing it extends into r. lower ribs, then in the former place and corresponding teeth, later deep breathing causes sticking below r. scapula, then sticking in upper part of r. scapula; through limbs, back and walls of chest (during colic), worse in lower limbs, especially knees, forepart of thighs and in soles, worse at intervals, > pressure, < movement, but he assumes all sorts of positions. Boring; in r. upper arm, with tearing in r. lower teeth, later with sticking in scapula. Feeling as if bones were gnawed. Myalgia.

Pain in whole body; **in trunk and limbs**; in bones; cranial and other flat bones; l. side; lower part of body; muscles and joints, < r. side; neck, walls of chest, back and loins; limbs, shoulders, neck, face and head; knees, ankles, arms and in tendon of pectoralis muscle; at night, with convulsions, delirium and copious stool; everywhere on motion; in joints and muscles on movement; < night; < motion, but he constantly seeks relief by change of position; in joints, < of lumbar vertebræ and of shoulders, < movement and pressure and especially pressing together the bones which belong to a joint, > rest, joints of fingers, toes and jaws almost painless; < cold, forced movement and pressure; except when still in bed; > pressure.

Wandering pains. Pains rapidly changing in character. Neuralgic pains in all parts; < loins. Pain in paralyzed parts, sometimes lancinating, sometimes contusive, < motion and pressure; crawling paroxysmal P. in bones, < above l. knee and in l. forearm; paroxysmal; benumbing; bruised, in affected parts, and sometimes gnawing; bruised, in paralyzed parts, or at times pricking and formication, then numbness, with sensitiveness to cold, which increases the pain.

Arthralgia; rheumatic pains (muscular); arthralgic and neuralgic pains about trunk and limbs; deep arthralgic pains, as if in bones, < flexors, then trembling of fingers passing into paralysis, paralysis of extensors of upper limbs, slightly of lower, arms when left to themselves hung dangling as if turning on a pivot, inability to raise hands or fingers, back of hands arched, fingers bent, rotatory motion of arms lost, all use of muscles attended with injury, they had lost their contractile power, abdominal muscles less affected, the A. pain greatest in parts not paralyzed, pain worse in inside of knees, l. intercostal muscles affected, preventing sneezing, thirst < afternoon and when fatigued, at one time highly nervous pulse, soreness in all the flesh except a spot in inner part of l. thigh, which was insensible, at times burning in soles, > pressing them against the bare footboard, at times pain between scapulæ, nearer r. than l. shoulder, > lying on back and pressing on the part.

Hyperæsthesia of cutaneous nerves; intermittent, sometimes of one part, sometimes of another, < over bony processes, for example, spinous processes of dorsal vertebræ, but deep pressure relieved the pain; H. of muscles. Soreness of muscles. Compressions between the paroxysms, with burning. Tingling. **Restlessness** (Ars.); between the paroxysms. Pulsation in hands and feet after dinner, < head.

Weakness; in morning on rising, with lack of courage; at twilight, he lay down, felt the beating of pulse, burning spots in face, trembling of head and vertigo as if the couch moved, renewed by thinking of it, sensitiveness to noise, at last sleep for three hours, on waking prostration, > moving about, but there remained dulness in head and bruised feeling in small of back; on walking; after motion; < r. side; he lies down, feels beating in neck and abdomen and can sleep but little; r. side becomes weaker and weaker, mobility diminished, atrophy of posterior part of upper arm, limited extension of hand, anæsthesia of r. limbs, r. side of face and trunk, diminished sensibility of r. side of tongue, reflex movements in throat almost abolished, voice nasal and speech indistinct.

Nervous prostration. **Faintness**; in morning; on ascending stairs or on any undue exertion; always on rising from a seat; in a room full of people, with frequent dimness of vision; > food; with præcordial uneasiness. Malaise. Collapse.

Immobility; of large dorsal and pectoral muscles, of shoulders, arms and hands, only difficult raising of shoulders by action of trapezius. Rigidity of limbs, spasmodic closure of jaws, inability to stand, afterwards chilliness; painful R. on movement. Movements difficult; in bed, so that he lies on back; and slow, painful. Movements slow and feeble. Want of co-ordination, so that she fell from her chair.

Anæsthesia; of affected parts; of scattered parts; of r. side of body; r. limbs, r. side of chest, abdomen and back, bounded exactly by median line; r. arm, extending over r. side of face and r. lower limb; of skin; of skin, with pain deep in limbs, thus paralysis may be accompanied by both anæsthesia and hyperæsthesia; of skin in hypogastric and iliac regions, penis, scrotum and upper two-thirds of thighs, pressure on hypogastrium causes pain, but not on other parts, pain is felt when a pin is thrust in deeply or muscles are pinched; to burning of whole r. side, but a blister in the middle of forepart of the insensible r. thigh caused pain; to pricking in r. upper limb (except shoulder), of r. foot, r. leg and lower third of r. thigh, diminished sensibility of r. side of face, r. shoulder and upper two-thirds of r. thigh, the line between partial and entire sensibility on thigh corresponding with the border of the shirt.

Diminished sensibility of r. side of body; r. side of trunk and on front of chest, corresponding to the part of the shirt worn during the work; to pricking; tactile in upper limbs, < r., of r. side of face and of r. lower limb, more on dorsal than palmar surface of forearms; electrical, on r. side; under electricity, difficult contraction of deltoid, pectoralis major, flexors and outer layer of muscles of forearm and posterior rhomboid, trapezius and longissimus dorsi. Analgesia of whole surface, sensitiveness to tickling diminished in palms, < l.; A. of r. half of body, < forearm and hand, l. cornea has little sensibility. Sensibility to temperature diminished; in r. side; in r. side, < upper limb; on r. forearm and l. side of face, which is the one most affected with anæsthesia. Sensibility perverted, pricking caused a sensation as if rubbed, and pinching a sensation as if touched.

Paralytic sensation extending from back towards hands and feet, < l. side of body, which felt asleep, inability to move, this paralytic condition disappeared with a shock, then spasmodic stretching of l. limbs, which seemed dead, l. fingers spasmodically closed, pronation of wrist and gradual extension of arm at elbow, extension of l. leg, this cramp returned at intervals, loud cries from pain, partial consciousness, short, indistinct answers, later these spasms in other muscles, head jerked to l. side, so that the chin rested on l. clavicle, next day frequent spasms and the pallor of the face of the first day changed to redness, on third day similar spasms in r. side with opisthotonos, then rattling in trachea and oozing of tenacious, frothy mucus from mouth, between the spasms jerking of facial muscles.

Paralysis; one-sided; l.-sided hemiplegia, with contractions of l. hand and distortion of face towards the right; dextral hemiplegia, < upper part of body; of r. side, with curvature of spine; (of r. upper limb and r. half of face including tongue); of extensors of forearms and on lower limbs, and symptoms of general P. of the insane, he could not lift the feet from the ground, then bilateral facial spasms, trismus, jerkings of upper limbs, the flexors of which were rigid, while lower limbs were rigidly extended; of all parts, with insensibility; in parts, with sensitiveness to cold; incomplete, < upper limbs, external muscles wasted and soft; motor and sensory, < r. side of body; beginning with numbness of the parts and trembling, ending in loss of motion and atrophy, also ending with loss of motion, and when the trembling parts are moved their muscles oscillate in their contractions, and the trembling parts are weak.

Two or three crises during the day, with prickings in skin, contractions of jaws and limbs, supraorbital pain, twitching and constriction in temples, that night spasmodic cries more frequent but less violent, tingling in limbs. *Aggravation at night; and lying in bed,* they caused such agitation and anxiety that he was often obliged to rise and walk about the house all night aided by some one, bent position when walking as well as when in repose, in the morning he was worn out by fatigue and suffering; A. from drinking; paroxysms renewed by drinking, thence though thirsty he dared not drink often.

Amelioration at night; A. from drinking; *from friction* and strong pressure; from pressure during the paroxysms, but between them aggravation.

Clinical.—General anæmia, mucous membranes very pale, persistent vomiting of food. Chlorosis, with palpitation and œdema of the feet. Inveterate chlorosis, with extreme constipation. (It is said to follow iron well.) Epilepsy; one case always appearing with menstruation, associated with colic, obstinate constipation and sallow complexion.

Mind.—*Delirium;* with violent convulsions; with trembling of tongue and hands; when his attention was strongly attracted to anything what he said at first was rational; his facial expression does not correspond with the conversation he is engaged in or other external influences; nightly, alternating with sopor; tranquil during the day, furious at night; restless; violent, at night; violent, followed by morbid ideas; violent, with screaming and running about, after the epileptiform spasm; resembling delirium tremens; raging, with hallucinations of vision; raging, in paroxysms alternating with quiet; difficulty in putting him to bed, he tore the clothes and spoke incoherently; bites his garments and bed-clothes; impelling them to tear themselves and bite their own fingers; often getting out of bed and desiring to go home, sometimes not recognizing his family, thought they were conspiring to kill him; imagined that he was constantly followed, that he heard voices from the chimney, later was convinced that fiends in the building pursued him and sought his life; did not close his eyes all night, sometimes was silent and quiet, sometimes hurried out of bed, wanted to dress himself, talked incoherently, was abusive, when put into a strait-jacket he resisted, screamed and bit an assistant, later he was quiet and had an astonished look; sudden furious, with shouts and abuse against all who approached him, *thought that he was in danger of assassination or poisoning and that every one about him was a murderer,* he walked about briskly, knocking against every obstacle, face flushed, eyes sparkling and fierce, heat and strength increased, then coma, during which he lay stretched out, motionless, with closed eyes and pale face, then sudden return of delirium, thus alternations of D. and coma; sudden restless, in evening, hears everywhere threatening voices, officers come to arrest him, to seize the furniture and to expel him from his lodgings, voices come from the pillow, the mattress, they enter by the window, where he sees people, and they consult about him with closed doors, he gets up, looks for his clothing, wants to run away, next morning he sits at the edge of the bed, with eyes fixed on the window or looking about restlessly, recognizes every one, replies correctly, but cannot remember what he ate yesterday, etc., insists, but as if afraid to acknowledge it, on the reality of his hallucinations; talked incoherently at night, left his bed and wanted to lie in another bed, eyes projecting and fixed, face expressed astonishment, next day he was listless, at 5 P.M. he began to rave, chattering alternating with silence, face had a wild expression, worse at night, took part in all conversation he heard or fancied he heard; in sudden attacks in evening and night alternating with deep sleep, with the D. restlessness, railing and threats, next day face flushed and covered with sweat, eyes fixed and expressionless, bloodshot, lids swollen, pupils, < r., dilated, expression of face dull, frequent movements so that he had to be put into a strait-waistcoat; with sudden epilepsy, then slight coma, then return of D., eyes sometimes fixed, sometimes rolling, with unnatural expression of face, sometimes unexpected bursts of laughter, slight spasms of limbs and face, sometimes said that he was insane, at night incongruous disconnected talking, tried to get into the neighboring bed, wanted to strike the nurse, urinated in the middle of the floor, pronunciation rapid and incomplete; walked like one groping in the dark, sometimes incoherent, hurried talking in a trembling voice, more often was silent, got into bed and fell into a deep sleep, then began to behave in the same way again, made incongruous demands upon those about him, sometimes cried like a child, sleepless, the D. and restlessness < night; sometimes talks unintelligibly to himself, more frequently is silent, when his attention is strongly attracted he answers rationally at first, then utters some word without meaning or connection, then takes up again the thread of logical thought, he generally waits some time before answering, as if it required great mental exertion to understand what is said; talks like a child who has not learned to speak plainly, sometimes cannot get hold of the right words, especially substantives, then frets and sometimes becomes desperate, less trouble with adjectives; saw palaces and castles; fancied at times that he heard delightful music, which soothed his sorrows, he was never sleepy.

Delusions at night. Hallucination, saw her dead husband and child in a tree out of the window; erroneous ideas as to the identity of herself and those around her and her situation, a mild delirium arose and alternated with a different state, difficulty in finding language and before she could convey the meaning the idea fled, then a jumble of disconnected words, later apathy, with occasionally symptoms approaching catalepsy and ecstasy, on placing arms, for example, in any position they were fixed for some minutes, then slowly relaxed and sank down, at other times unconsciousness with fixed eyes; saw many colored figures in constant motion as soon as he closed his eyes.

Mind affected between the paroxysms, would leave home without knowing where he was going, became enraged with persons he met, generally remembered nothing, when brought home he would shut himself up till he got right again. On recovering consciousness the people in the ward seemed as small as dolls and the opposite side of the room seemed forty feet below his own level.

Wandering in speech now and then; and when he began to rave the facial muscles twitched, giving him a hideous appearance. Speech wandering, lay quiet with closed eyes, insensible to pinching, when limbs were placed in any position and left unsupported they remained there a few seconds, then oscillated and fell back on the bed, body rigid, so that he could not be made to sit upright, and his attention could not be aroused, suddenly a great variety of expressive gestures, tried to speak but was prevented by the liquid in his mouth, very sensitive to pinching, upper limbs too stiff to be moved, then quietude, thus alternations of repose and movement, then he indicated by a gesture that he wished to eat and drink, then he suddenly spouted the ptisan which he held in his mouth over the surgeon, then quietness and unconsciousness, during which the limbs remained in any position they were made to assume, then gestures of varying significance, with his eyes shut and without speaking, at last he suddenly opened his eyes and called for drink, seemed to fall asleep while swallowing his ptisan, but was easily aroused by being spoken to, rambled volubly from one incoherent idea to another, but answered questions rationally, at one time tried to get up, tried to strike and bite the nurses, remembered well what happened a month ago, but could not recollect what occurred a few days ago.

Talked all day, attempted to get out of his strait-waistcoat; T. all night, mostly about how he should destroy his fastening; babbled all night, now and then jumped out of bed, swore and blustered; T. to himself when alone, but was generally silent and quiet; T. at random all night. Answers at random; and in monosyllables. Language extravagant. Utters a few broken, disconnected words. When spoken to he looks everywhere but at the questioner. Quiet in bed, with constant, unintelligible words; Q. when left to himself, and silent. Silent generally, when he speaks his words are disconnected and voice broken, when interested he answers rationally, sometimes sits facing his questioner in silence without looking at him, at times he answers a simple question wide of the mark. Self-absorbed, answers rationally but briefly, pays no attention to his wife and children when they come to see him, when in bed keeps moving his hands, folds and unfolds the coverings, sometimes wanders about the room, now singing, now gradually quickening his steps, now stopping and turning about abruptly, gait uncertain. Searching about on the floor. Screams; frightful, with general convulsions; during the aggravations draws himself together under the bed-clothes, suddenly gets out of bed and gets in again and doubles himself up, etc.

Liveliness; in afternoon; and hallucination alternating with morose mood, disinclination to talk and attempts to escape. Active in afternoon, absorbed in knitting and thoughtful. Disinclination to work; and inability; D. to talk after dinner. Anguish. Grumbling during the intervals of quietude, closed his eyes and shrank under the bed-clothes. Weeping from slight causes. Manner frightened and nervous. Fear; of death if left alone; easily frightened. Avoids society. Melancholy; at the fear of death; and silent; and if a neighbor called to see him he burst into tears and was unable to speak for some time; has no desire to live, threatens to destroy himself, fault-finding with friends; and stupefaction, dulness of senses, drowsiness; religious. Despondency. Ennui; in afternoon, with quiet reserve. Discouragement. Discontented in morning on waking.

Anxiety; and sighing; with inability to breathe deep enough and increased palpitation; with difficult respiration so that he seemed almost suffocated from fright, could get his breath only when sitting. Apprehension. Distrust. Longing for a distant friend in evening before sleep. Irritable; in afternoon, all work frets her; whenever approached it cried, whined and would not play. Hasty temper. *Apathy;* and sopor alternating with difficulty of breathing and headache. Indecision. Nervous; and unwilling to be touched or have anything done for her.

Slow of perception, memory lost (Lyc., Phos. ac.); **so that when talking he was often unable to find the proper word.** Scarcely knew old acquaintances. Imbecility. Stupidity. Answers slow and stammering; slow and short; vague; says and does everything very slowly. Inability to fix thoughts. Reading is tiresome, he mistakes one word for another and skips lines. Intelligence and power of utterance vary curiously at different times.

Coma; with at times automatic movements of hands to occiput; alternating with loquacity; alternating with delirium. Lethargy. Unconsciousness; with falling on attempting to walk; with sudden falling backward; with falling twice, then coma alternating with loquacity, next morning he roused up suddenly, half opened his eyes, uttered many disconnected words, tossed about in bed, urinated on his pillows, put his head down, lifted his buttocks in the air, then relapsed into coma; occasionally, then epileptiform spasms, with bloody froth from mouth, then left-sided paralysis of motion and sensation.

Head.—Trembling. Turned to right, its rotation to l. being prevented by paralysis of sterno-cleido-mastoid. Shooting; here and there, < r. ear, < afternoon and evening. **Aching**; always immediately after colic, < frontal and parietal regions; < morning on waking; with vomiting; with heaviness of it and confusion of mind; with anxiety extending to forehead, dim vision and contracted pupil; with obscuration of vision and sleepiness; so that head could not be held up; contractive, and in cheek. Pressure beneath skull as from rush of blood. Dulness; with dimness of mind, so that he rubbed his forehead. *Heaviness;* when standing, with dulness; < occiput, with sticking in sinciput; it falls forward. Apoplexy; with paralysis of l. arm. *Vertigo;* on stooping or on looking up; > open air. Symptoms > hot-air baths.

Forehead.—Sticking in brain; in eminence; in sinciput at 9 P.M.; across. Tearing in afternoon, with internal heat in head and redness; T. and sensation of contraction; intermittent, in middle; back and forth. *Pain;* supraorbital; rather externally in evening; above eyes on moving them; and in temples; and in temples, < l. side; worse by paroxysms, with feeling of dislocation; with tearing in nape; heavy, in forepart of head. Heaviness after morning soup; H. above orbits.

Temples.—Twitching in r.; T. and constriction. Sticking in r., with external soreness; S., with compression as if in a vise; tearing, in l. Tearing in r.; and then in r. ear. Clucking in l. extending to ear. Throbbing.

Vertex.—Intermittent, lacerating pain worse by paroxysms, > pressure, and in face.

Sides.—Cracking in r. when sneezing, then formication and numbness in whole r. side of body, with weakness of these parts. Sticking in r. in forenoon when walking and standing, with beating; S. in upper part of r. parietal bone, with tearing; inward in upper part of r. parietal bone. Pain in l.; anteriorly in l. parietal bone; in l. extending to l. side of face, < night.

Occiput.—Pain; at times extending to forehead; extending to ears and temples, beginning when asleep, so that he often rose, walked about the room holding his head with both hands, then somewhat relieved he lay down again for a short nap. Pressure towards forehead, > standing, with feeling as if eyes would close from heaviness. Heaviness as if its weight were increased.

Clinical.—Has been used for a form of headache with sensation of a ball rising from the throat into the head. This drug has occasionally been found useful in the form of cerebral paralysis, with blunted consciousness, deficient memory, impaired speech, more or less paralysis of the muscles of the face, throat, eyes and extremities; the patient is either unable to remember words or simply omits syllables and words.

Eyes.—*Yellow.* Surrounded by blue rings; and the rest of face dingy yellow. Large and red. Inflammation. Swollen, painful. Rush of blood. Livid, < inner canthus. Protruding; and glistening. Staring. Wild; and rolling; and shining. Sunken; and dim. Squinting. Strabismus, one turned towards nose and he could not turn it out, paralysis of external muscle, vision double when he looked with both eyes. Twitching. Distortions. White, watery discharge in morning, without other complaints in eyes, soon becoming thicker and agglutinating lids. *Neuritis, papilla swollen, post mortem showed interstitial hyperplasia of connective tissue, sheaths of optic nerve distended by fluid, cerebrospinal fluid increased, brain substance anæmic and the gray part yellowish;* N., with normal field, dim vision, central scotoma and flickering. Sticking; in l. Contraction, < lids. Heaviness on moving them, with pain in internal muscle extending backward. Burning in r. as if tobacco were in it. Fatigue.

Lachrymation; acrid, contracting skin. *Hypopyon. Disc prominent, opaque, bluish-white, its outline hazy,* sclerotic ring invisible, vessels diminished in calibre. *Sclerotics yellow.* Sclerotics lead-colored. Sclera dirty bluish-gray. Fundus black. Varicose bloodvessels in cornea extending like a thick network to centre and obscuring it. Spasms of r. ball. Shooting through balls on closing lids firmly; S. beneath l. ball at 2 P.M., with burning. Jerking tearing in l. ball in forenoon. *Pupils dilated;* but in different degrees, also unequally in their respective circumferences. Pupils uneven, < l. Pupils spasmodically contracted, later dilated and insensible. Pupils insensible; and dilated; and contracted.

Lids.—Red. Swollen and sensitive. Dropping of upper. Violent closure. Agglutination in morning and evening, with a cloud before l.; A., with thick yellow mucus. Twitching of r. upper. Ciliary neuralgia of r., then dull vision. Tearing in morning after soup, with sleepiness. Sensation as if something were under them and as if balls were too large. Heaviness. Paralysis and insensibility. Itching of l. upper, > scratching; I. of l. canthus and pain on rubbing it.

Conjunctiva yellow; and livid; dingy yellow; dingy yellow, with a shade of blue; C. suffused with blood; pale; œdematous; dry. Much hair falls from brows. Fulness in orbits, with weight and excruciating pain.

Vision.—*Dim;* < r. eye; and confused; with frequent necessity to wipe eyes; several times a day, beginning with weakness in all limbs, with roaring in ears and vision of falling snow or showers of fire, he almost loses consciousness and has to lean against something. Weak. Diminished, the ophthalmoscope showed congestion, with sinuosities of vessels. Increase of nearsightedness; nearsighted in r. eye, perception of color feeble, field limited, vision of l. normal, dilated veins in fundus of l. V. and hearing better on r. side. *Diplopia;* except when close to objects; of r. eye, which is affected by strabismus. As if everything trembled and turned in a circle. Yellow; spots before l. eye, covering what is looked at, and at a certain distance things seem to jump. Dazzling. Eclampsia consequent upon uræmic poisoning with albuminous urine. *Lost;* suddenly; suddenly after an attack of headache and colic; suddenly, then sudden paralytic spasm, with unconsciousness; almost, in l. eye, which looks sound. Sees only one-half of an object.

Clinical.—Paralysis of the optic nerve, with greater or less cloudiness of vision. Hypopyon, with nightly pain.

Ears.—Sticking in lobule of r.; in r. in forenoon when standing. Tearing in region of r. after dinner; deep in; sticking, in r. extending to concha. Boring in r. after dinner. Pain in l. ear and meatus. Tension in region of r. and in r. cervical muscles. Scratching in r. as from a spear of grain. Ringing. Whizzing and humming. Roaring; every evening, causing deafness. Sensitive to slight noise. Hearing difficult; frequently in evening; after exposure to cold; with numbness; H. lost.

Nose.—Erysipelatous inflammation. Tearing in r. side of septum. Pain in tip; sharp drawing, in r. wing and in upper lip. Mucous membrane dry. Stoppage. Itching in l. nostril in afternoon, > scratching. Irritation and ineffectual sneezing. Sneezing. Fluent coryza; in afternoon; with watery mucus. Running out of water during dinner. Tenacious mucus which he must draw through posterior nares, where most of it accumulates. Bleeding; during convulsions; with the second attack of spitting of blood. Horrible smell; < l. nostril. Smell diminished, < r. nostril. Smell lost.

Face.—**Sallow. Pale**; and covered with sweat; and anæmic; puffy, and dark under eyes; and cachectic, lips dry, with sordes, mucous membranes pale; dirty, and peculiarly marked. Looks like a corpse. Yellow < night; Y. in spots; and haggard; grayish; dirty; livid; like wax. Lemon color. Dirty gray. Yellowish-gray and puffy. Livid. Red; with a shade of yellow; and warm, moist; cheeks, which were covered with sweat. Dusky. Swollen; < about eyes and lids; r. half, with earache, < swallowing saliva; and purple; with violent pulsation in carotid (apparently the result of retching); but anæmic. Œdematous. Cachectic. Emaciated. Sunken; cheeks. Long, shrivelled. Sharp, pinched. Wrinkled. Shining as if oily, and feeling oily. Skin changed in texture and appearance. Pasty, lustreless.

Expression anxious; and suffering; E. sad; as if silently imploring pity; fatigued; wild; of pain; as if the child suffered from pressure on brain; sardonic smiling; stupid; astonished; astonished, with thoughtful appearance, which was not borne out by his answers; indescribable; altered. Drawn; to l. side. Trembling; of r. side, then of l., and mouth drawn to r. Spasmodic contraction before the paroxysms of colic. Convulsions. Choreic. Almost immovable; except during paroxysms of colic, then expression of acute suffering. L. side fixed and devoid of expression.

Sticking in r. malar-bone; < cheeks, extending into ears, < movement. Pain. Hypalgesia of r. side. Diminished sensibility; r. side. Anæsthesia of side; l. cheek. Paralysis of r. side. Paresis of nerves, when talking all facial muscles twitch.

Jaws.—Loud movement, with grating of teeth. Contractions. Trismus. Tearing in r. upper; in lower and in lower teeth; near chin and in corresponding tooth; in r. side of lower, with sticking; in l. lower, extending towards l. ear, > rubbing, when rubbing a beating in l. side of occiput. Boring in r. angle of lower; in l. lower and in three corresponding teeth.

Lips.—Bluish. Pale; mucous membrane of lips and throat. Desquamation. Covered with thick fissured scabs, and teeth and tongue. Covered with brown scabs. Dry and fissured. Moved as if smoking a pipe. Hair falls from moustache. Sharp drawing beneath r. wing of nose.

Mouth.—Teeth. Black; at their necks; < incisors and canines; yellowish. Brown; at base, yellow at tip; dark; greenish, < at their necks. Dirty gray. Bluish-gray, and gums. Yellowish. Covered with yellowish mucus; yellowish coat at root and a slate-colored border around several. Tartar. Sordes. Covered with dark incrustation. Covered with sulphate of lead, and gums. Decayed; and loose, edges of gums red and ragged, often bleeding, and a blue line; has an offensive odor and breaks off. Loose. Fell out. Chattering. Grinding; at night, with frequent waking. Tearing in two r. lower molars. Jerking pain in r. lower molars in morning, < cold. Aching in sound ones as after eating sour fruit.

Gums.—**Blue; along margins**; between teeth; a line along incisors; margins of upper incisors; line near a lower canine tooth; line opposite bicuspids; crescent over upper molars, towards roof of mouth; and bloodless; bordering on teeth, the rest light bluish-red; reddish, beneath l. lower canine, then beneath all lower incisors and canine; grayish, on border. *Slate-colored; on border;* and bleeding on slightest touch. Bluish-gray. Ashy-gray margins. Black. Dirty brownish-gray. Violet-red, then slate-colored. Pale. White and tense. Discolored and either thin or dwindled in extent, in the latter case the interdental partitions gradually disappear and the concavity of the gums is increased in consequence of molecular absorption, and teeth are laid bare, the gums thus form a projecting pad, sometimes marked by vertical incisions, the discoloration often disappears in proportion to the shrinking, gums more affected anteriorly, and lower more than upper, sometimes gum of only two or three teeth affected. Inflammation. Abscesses on r. Ulceration of superior alveolar border of both jaws, with discoloration of most of buccal membrane. A painful and hard pimple. Congestion, with bleeding on touch. Swollen; at roots of teeth. Soft. Spongy; and tender, and between teeth lead-colored elevations. Retracted; and covered with tenacious mucus. Tender.

Tongue.—*Red; on margins; on margin, brown coat down centre;* and coated white; and rather white on edge; on sides, whitish in middle; and dry, rather pale and moist at edges; and pointed. Bluish line on margin. T. and mouth slate-colored except a few scattered red points. Brownish. End covered with bluish-black spots, upper surface covered with ulcers as from Mercury, with pain in T. and lips and offensive salivation. Pale. *White; and dry;* yellowish, but moist. Inflammation. Flat and broad. Swollen; with saburral coat; with saburral coat in middle; and yellow; and whitish, moist. Flabby. *Coated;* brown; brownish down centre, edges red, indented, speckled, with enlarged red papillæ; brown in centre; whitish brown, clearing off towards edges, and moist; with black crust; covered with frothy saliva. Coated white; and moist; and swollen, margins and tip red; brownish. Coated yellowish-white in middle; about base, with partial paralysis on r. side; saburral, partly dry, edges of T. red and rough, with projecting papillæ. Yellow coat; in centre; posteriorly; on l. edge in morning, and mouth slimy; and greenish; brownish; dirty; dirty, and flabby, indented. Light yellow crust. Clammy. Blisters on frænum. Suddenly burning pimples on tip, painful, < talking, from 6 till 10 P.M. *Dry;* with dark streak in centre; and brown, cracked. *Trembling;* and lower lip; but no hesitancy in speech. Drawn forcibly to l. side and folded in the same direction. Burning in morning, and mouth; in tip as if he had bitten it, about 2 P.M. Heaviness. *Partial paralysis, and of other parts. Cannot be put out.* Insensibility of r. side. *Articulation imperfect, sometimes only confused sounds.* Speech slow; difficult; panting and puffing, as in diaphragmatic pleurisy; stammering; stammering, broken, shaking; hurried and abrupt; suddenly lost, with short, rapid respiration. Inability to talk.

Mouth drawn aside. Bluish spots; blue blotches or lines; various shades of blue. Slate-colored spots. Paleness. Redness of M. and fauces, with tenderness and soreness, all food except the mildest caused pain, heat and smarting. Froth. Mucus; tenacious, in morning on waking. Swelling of glands in M. and beneath chin. Aphthæ, and in throat. Ulcers, with an offensive odor, < sides, later they are yellow; perforating U. on inside of cheeks and under side of tongue so that he cannot eat or drink, he swallows hot drinks best, healed by direct application of alum. Constriction, < lips, often prompted to extend lips. Burning pain, and in throat and stomach. *Dryness;* and in nostrils; and on lips; drier in morning than in evening, but thirst less. Sputa bloody; and lumpy. Saliva bluish, sweet; tenacious; alkaline. Salivation; dropping from mouth, > Merc. sol.; sweetish, slimy-tasting in forepart of M., with dryness at root of palate posteriorly and in fauces, > swallowing saliva. **Breath fetid**; and metallic.

Taste.—**Sweetish**; S. sour. *Bitter;* every morning; < night. *Metallic.* Coppery in morning on waking. Sulphurous and sour low down in throat. Styptic. Acrid. Nauseous. Clammy. Flat. Pasty. Diminished; < r. half of tongue. Perverted; so that he did not recognize ordinary food.

Clinical.—Paralysis of the tongue, with indistinct speech.

Throat.—*Swelling of tonsils;* of submaxillary glands, with pain; parotids, l. painful, red and hot. Inflammation of uvula; *of tonsils, with induration.* Hawking of sourish mucus; easy, of frothy, transparent, lumpy, yellowish-green, tenacious mucus. Choking on swallowing.

Pain. **Constriction**; in pharynx; in pharynx extending to stomach before and after eating, with cutting; spasmodic. Drawing in pharynx when eating, as if œsophagus would be torn open. Rawness. Roughness in morning, with hoarseness. Globus hystericus. Sensation of a foreign body in r. side, with sulphurous odor, afterwards the sensation extended towards ear; sensation of a foreign body all the forenoon, provoking sneezing, on swallowing it extended far down, but immediately returned; as if a foreign body slipped downward, then tearing in r. scapula; when smoking, as if something moved suddenly to base of skull and thence to l. orbital region, where it became a sticking. Swollen sensation on swallowing, with choking; S. sensation that obliges frequent swallowing and does not disappear. Dryness; in fauces; in morning. Heat; in fauces, with tickling. Paralysis of pharyngeal muscles.

Œsophagus.—Crawling. Heat. Feels food descending and reaching stomach. *Swallowing difficult.*

Clinical.—Has occasionally been used for granular sore throat, especially with symptoms of paralysis of pharyngeal muscles, difficulty in swallowing liquids.

Stomach.—Great hunger; in evening; in evening before sleep, with nausea; in throat extending to stomach, returning after eating; for bread and cake all the time. Great relish for tobacco. **Appetite lost**; *diminished. Aversion to food. Thirst;* in morning; after dinner; < evening; but liquid was returned with straining as soon as taken; for cold water; for cold drinks; *unquenchable;* absent. Dread of all drinks.

Eructations; worse at end of paroxysms of colic, with nausea and vomiting; with sensation in mouth as after eating sugar; *sour;* distressing; paroxysmal; nauseating; of strange taste; offensive; of offensive taste; tasting of the food; of tasteless water. Sweetish eructations; relieving temporarily; of water from an empty stomach; as if about to vomit. Empty eructations; after breakfast; in evening before sleep, with nausea; of bitter, fetid smell and taste. Ineffectual attempts to eructate, then yawning. **Hiccough** (Lyc.). **Nausea**; after every meal, with uneasiness; before the colic; with uprising as far as chest; with load at pit of stomach; anxious; fatiguing. *Retching;* with eructations of thin white mucus or greenish bitter fluid; almost convulsive.

Vomiting; in morning; soon after eating during the colicky spasms; with colic; **constant** (Cupr., Phos.); constant, with constipation; **of food** (Lyc., Phos., Ferr.); *of everything taken into stomach; fæcal; fæcal, with colic and constipation;* of lead-colored fæces; *blackish; of a brownish liquid streaked with blood;* bloody; violent; difficult, also with anxiety; difficult, of mucus and bile; causing hard lumps in region of stomach, which were > friction; of a substance like corroded copper; like the white of egg; stringy; of clear, acid fluid or else bile; bilious; of matter tasting like liquorice; yellow mucus and bilious matter; yellowish, offensive, with colic; of bilious yellow substances like green vitriol; blackish-yellow. Greenish vomiting; < *night and early morning,* and watery; and watery, also with momentary relief; and bitter; and bitter, thick; and bitter, bilious; bitter, difficult (with the colic); of bilious fluid; and scanty, thick; dark, and difficult, bitter, depositing a copious, thick, slimy sediment; yellowish; grass; porraceous, æruginous.

Epigastrium tense and hard. Epigastrium depressed. Sticking; in pit extending to back; across S. and hypogastrium. Pricking in pit, gradually amounting to pain, worse at intervals, drawing him double. Tearing in epigastrium and umbilicus, worse by paroxysms, during which he is restless, lies on his belly, complains and screams, abdomen contracted and hard; T. in epigastrium, less at umbilicus and hypogastrium, worse at times, when with a shrunken, wild-looking countenance she threw herself into strange attitudes, uttered sharp cries and begged those about her to press upon her abdomen. Cramp. Enteralgia, with exhausting fever. Cardialgia. Griping in pyloric region.

Sharp pain at epigastrium, worse at intervals, when there is laceration. Intermittent boring in pit extending into r. side; B. in epigastrium, worse by paroxysms, slight at hypogastrium, scarcely felt in umbilicus, acute in r. testicle, the pain > gradual pressure with the flat hand, < sudden and forcible bearing down on abdomen, pressure did no good unless limbs were previously flexed upon pelvis, pressure caused the pain to shift its place.

Pain; in pit; cardiac extremity; epigastrium; after eating; in epigastrium after eating, with fulness; at insertions of diaphragm during inspiration; < hot or cold drinks; in S., abdomen and loins, with internal heat; *extending to loins and down limbs, < l.;* extending over abdomen; in epigastrium gradually extending over abdomen; in pit gradually extending over abdomen; in pit extending to umbilicus; in pit extending to middle of chest; changing to ileus; irregular, about epigastrium; in epigastrium, worse at intervals; as from fasting, in morning, > rising; as from much undigested food, after a moderate dinner till late in evening, with heaviness in occiput, < moving head; heavy, in epigastrium, causing sensation as if abdomen were drawn towards spine; anxious, in pit.

Paroxysmal pain in epigastrium extending to chest, thence along external surface of upper limbs, he sits up in bed, with uneasiness, anxiety, palpitation, suffocation almost amounting to syncope, respiration 35 to 40, then prostration; P. pain in epigastrium radiating to all parts of abdomen, < night and eating, > pressure, later increasing to griping and twisting, afterwards weight in abdomen, tenesmus and throbbing in epigastrium, sleeplessness, restlessness, though the pain prevented walking.

Twisting pain in epigastrium, worse at umbilicus, < pressure, > friction; paroxysmal, in epigastrium, > pressure, also at umbilicus, he lies on his belly, bends double, keeps changing position and face is pinched; paroxysmal, in epigastrium and umbilicus, with distortion of face, grievous cries, lies on belly, doubles herself up, ties handkerchiefs tightly around her, walks the room, etc., but no position relieves; worse by paroxysms, in epigastrium and umbilicus, with tearing in r. hypochondrium.

Sensitiveness to pressure; in epigastric region. Burning pain; at pit; in epigastric region; extending through abdomen, with cutting; worse at epigastrium than at umbilicus or hypogastrium, worse by paroxysms, > gradual pressure; constrictive, later in umbilical region at intervals. Heat; in epigastric region, also with pain that extended to region of heart. Sensation as of boiling water when cold drink reached it, then profuse vomiting of the color and consistence of coffee.

Constriction; in epigastric region; in epigastric region extending to pharynx when the colic is coming on, preventing drinking. *Tightness;* in epigastrium; in pit. Fulness; after eating. *Feeling in epigastrium as if a ball ascended to throat, where it caused suffocation, preventing speaking and swallowing, with anxiety.* Weight; in epigastrium; in epigastrium, with smarting pain and pain on touch. Sensation as if S. and abdomen were drawn upward and backward. Sensation as if it turned after swallowing liquids, aggravating the abdominal pains. Discomfort. Uneasiness after eating, with weight, digestion slow. Depressed sensation in pit, with distress. Emptiness.

Dyspepsia; with constipation and irregularly occurring pain or cramp in abdomen; with loss of appetite, usually clean tongue, sweetish taste, salivation, frequent nausea, pressure and heaviness in pit of stomach, sometimes with pain and confusion in head, malaise and prostration.

Clinical.—Gastralgia, pains sudden, violent, compelling hard pressure on the abdomen, > eructations. Periodic vomiting of brown or black liquid, with violent cramps. Periodic attacks of vomiting food (Ferr., Verat.).

Abdomen.—*Retraction; with hardness and pain at umbilicus radiating to lumbar region and iliac fossæ* so that he rolled on the ground and pressed the abdomen; *with hard knots over its surface;* < over median line, with tension of muscles; < along recti muscles, causing a sort of canal from ensiform cartilage to pubis; in spots, distention in other places, muscles distinctly seen through the skin; anterior wall on same plane with ensiform cartilage and pubis; tense; tense, < hypogastrium; feeling to hand on palpitation as if muscles were affected by cramps; with retention of stool and urine and cramps. Parietes seemed glued to spine, I could grasp the curvature of the spine and take hold of the descending aorta.

Distention; of A. and loins, with pain on touch; flatulent. Ascites, with at times violent diarrhœa. Muscles rigid. *Hard;* and flat; and uneven, sunken along the median line while the sides are elevated; and at times distended by flatulence, often spasmodically contracted. Hard lumps. Uneven swellings on various parts, < during height of paroxysms; movable flatulent S., in various parts. Doughy to feel. *Rumbling;* in morning after rising, with gurgling, later a stool at first formed, then violent purging; in evening, with movements. Gurgling; < pressure. Dull sound anteriorly on percussion.

Movement in afternoon, with desire for stool, but only flatus was passed. Flatulence; and movements, then soft stools; everything that he takes seems to turn to wind. Emission of flatus; offensive; offensive, after eating fish; hot. Ineffectual efforts to pass flatus in afternoon, which afterwards is accomplished by pressure. Spasms of intestines. Spasmodic contractions, < during hiccough, with tearing, > lying on A., sometimes body and limbs are jerked about, with chattering of teeth; S. contractions, with pain and sensitiveness so that he could not bear the pressure of the bed-clothes. Ulceration. Inflammation, with pain on touch, anxiety and burning in intestines and general twitching, then death; I. of intestines, mesentery and peritoneum, with ulceration and gangrene; of viscera and mesentery, with creeping fever, turbid, red and thick urine.

Lancinations; in evening; worse in epigastrium and umbilicus, < pressure; in walls, worse by paroxysms, renewed by bending head on chest when stretched out in bed; extending into back and loins. *Paroxysmal tearing, worse at umbilicus,* > pressure. Cutting; in morning, then emission of flatus; during soft stool, with cutting in anus; transiently > stool; flatulent, in morning in bed. Pinching. Griping; in evening; in forepart rising paroxysmally towards stomach, which is sore, like a faintness, with rumbling after stool. Enteritis. Ileus. Leucophlegmasia. Typhus abdominalis, with nephritis, nosebleed, enlargement of spleen and liver, without marked eruption, often with hypostatic pleuro-pneumonia. Intermittent boring, usually beginning in umbilical region, *often extending to chest, threatening suffocation, to small of back, kidney, blad-*

der, lower limbs, always with constipation, abdomen usually retracted, pulse slow. Acute pain, then profuse diarrhœa.

Colic; after eating, with flatulent distention; then stool, with febrile movement, debility and drowsiness, later attacks of C. with constipation; < morning and evening; < night; < eating; < cold; < touch; < pressure; < slight pressure, > firm pressure (Cóloc.); in front wall, < light pressure, > strong pressure; < sudden pressure, > gradual pressure; < pressure of hand, > lying on abdomen; > warmth; > during pregnancy; > emission of flatus, with painful flatulent distention below navel; most acute in hypogastrium, then in umbilicus and epigastrium; *with pain in kidneys and lower limbs;* with inflammatory symptoms; with tension, then bilious vomiting; worse in umbilical region, with tension and with hectic fever; with closure of jaws, convulsive movements of eyes and limbs, uneasiness and impeded micturition; with anxiety, retching and retracted testicles; with restlessness, delirium and paralysis of upper limbs; with bruised pain in forepart of thigh, in knees, calves, soles and loins, with loss of animal contractility in upper limbs; with nausea, vomiting and constipation; with tenesmus and diarrhœa; with diarrhœa; with diarrhœa, then constipation; with offensive stools; with paralysis; with paralysis of thighs; with paralysis of r. extensor communis digitorum; **radiating to all parts of body**; extending to testicles, > lying on abdomen; extending to lower limbs, < feet; so that she doubled up like a worm; alternating with pain in head and joints; causing uneasiness, confusion of mind and faintness; wandering; arthralgic; periodical. Paroxysmal colic; during micturition, micturition suddenly stops and the painful penis is retracted, when the fit is over the urine flows freely again, during and after micturition smarting along urethra; > pressure, but sensitiveness between the paroxysms; worse at umbilicus, > pressure; > stools, then uneasiness in A. causing him to press it, constipation and attacks of pain; worse at umbilicus, with burning which often changed to insensibility of abdominal walls; with restlessness; with watery stools containing much mucus; doubling him up.

Twisting pain. Paroxysmal twisting pain, worse at umbilicus, > pressure; worse at umbilicus, scarcely felt in hypogastrium, between the paroxysms compression, abdomen tense; worse at epigastrium, or compression, < pressure; worse at epigastrium, compressive pain between the paroxysms, the attacks > inflating abdomen and by pressure, he kept moving, screamed, rose from bed, struck his abdomen, face shrunken, eyes hollow and dim, between the paroxysms abdomen sunken and hard.

Sensitiveness to touch; < food; < below ensiform cartilage; < at stomach and r. side, with pain ascending œsophagus to throat; pain on pressure of two fingers, pressure with palm not much felt. Constrictive pain. Burning pain, < epigastrium, worse by paroxysms, with distended feeling. Tension. Sensation in afternoon as if full and stopped. Confused feeling. Uneasiness; with ineffectual urging to stool, but no excessive constipation, this U. or pain gradually crept around to lumbar region, where it became fixed, but by degrees spread over the system, < lower limbs, with general debility and indisposition to motion, later inactivity of bowels, gnawing, < lumbar region and abdomen, tired feeling in limbs, restlessness, relief from effectual stirring of bowels. Heat; rising into head; internally, with twisting about umbilicus, sticking in back and sensation as if something were lying on it, and pain in pit of stomach. Paralysis of intestines and bladder; intestines gradually lose the ability to expel their contents.

Upper A.—Griping. Pain; acute, between epigastrium and hypogastrium, a less severe P. extending around hypogastrium; contractive, > eating, with increased appetite. Painless sensation as if something were torn off and fell down, then movements in abdomen.

Hypochondria.—Distended and tympanitic, with gurgling in various parts of abdomen on pressure, pain in umbilical region on pressure, retention of stool and suppression of urine. Lacerations as with arrows in different directions in H. and iliac region. Pain < touch; bruised, transversely across muscles below ribs and about navel on pressure, coughing and the like, < rising from lying.

Liver.—Enlarged. Contracted. Cirrhosis. Sticking in region; in region, anteriorly, then posteriorly. Pain; in region on pressure. Heat, and in spine.

Spleen.—Large. Diseased. Sticking in region, > rubbing; S. in region extending backward; inward in region, > rubbing, returning worse than ever. Tearing in region posteriorly towards back, where it becomes sticking, in afternoon. Pain in region. Sensitiveness in region; and in kidneys.

Sides.—Induration of muscles from l. false ribs to crista ilii and from dorsal vertebræ to l. rectus muscle. Sticking in l. Tearing in flanks down to bladder, with regular exacerbations. Pain. Drawing towards back as from distention. Sensation as if something had fallen down in l. Creeping as of a mouse in l.

Umbilical Region.—**Seems to adhere to spine**; with pain involving chest; approximates spine, also anus drawn towards abdomen. Swelling in U. and hypogastrium, evidently from aggregation of intestinal folds, during acute attacks. Movements; back and forth below umbilicus, like a rough substance. Intermittent bubbling. Tense. **Shooting to other parts of A., > pressure,** *so violent at times that he was almost wild, tossed about, pressed his fists into his abdomen, said he must go to stool*, abdominal walls retracted, vomiting of greenish bile, breath offensive; S. extending to r. and l.; S. deep internally below umbilicus; and in pubic region. Intermittent tearing, > pressure. Cramp. Cutting during stool. Griping in afternoon, > emission of flatus; G., then burning; then ineffectual desire for stool, > emission of flatus. Boring and constriction, and above it. Pain; above navel; and in back; on vomiting; > pressure; > gradual pressure, sometimes he can allow two or three persons to lie on his abdomen, at other times aggravation from slightest touch; then constipation; obliging him to draw up legs; extending to r. hypogastric region; extending towards hypogastrium; extending to hypogastrium, with nausea, vomiting and strangury; radiating over abdomen, < direction of recti muscles, with general uneasiness, the pain became lacerating, caused restlessness and moaning, with attacks of bitter, bilious, green vomiting, metallic taste, anorexia, lack of thirst, chilliness, cramp in lower limbs, sleeplessness and anxiety; periodically. Paroxysmal pain; > pressure; and in a circle all around abdomen and corresponding part of trunk, > hard pressure, < gentle pressure; as if bowels were torn out, extending to hypogastrium and testicles. Twitching pains, and in hypogastrium, pressure made them rise up to breasts. Twisting pain; shooting through to back and down limbs. Paroxysmal twisting pain, > pressure, also in hypogastrium and renal regions; > pressure, also in hypogastrium, epigastrium and base of chest, between the pains constriction, < pressure, with hardness of abdomen; and in hypogastrium, with rolling about, etc., face shrunken and expressive of anguish, abdomen, < about umbilicus, retracted and hard, pains < pressure, between the paroxysms constriction; < below navel, less in hypogastrium, with restlessness and rubbing of abdomen. Tenderness. Contraction transversely about middle of abdomen when sitting bent over. Constriction as from a cord around body. Feeling of a bar across under umbilicus, then pain rising towards stomach, sometimes extending into back and loins, > pressure on abdomen, < night, generally with yellow sclerotica, stool once in several days, or two or three stools in one day. Internal burning.

Hypogastrium.—Congestion of inguinal glands. Rumbling in r. iliac fossa. Movements in forenoon, with cutting. Sticking in transverse colon; in small intestines; in r. side in afternoon; in l. groin on stooping after dinner, and on rising S. in umbilical region, > stooping. Griping; in transverse colon; > pressure. Crampy paroxysms every quarter of an hour, with pain and coldness, passing like lightning from groin to leg, without involving posterior part of thigh, if when the attacks come on he is leaning on a cane he falls to the ground, the pain feels as if in the bones, but is > strong pressure, between the paroxysms constriction in limb. Pain; in iliac region; and in renal region; along colon; in region of transverse colon, < pressure; > pressure; in a spot between tip of ilium and symphysis, with distention; myalgic, from fatigue of muscles after retching; twisting, and in testicles, at times excruciating; drawing, from pubic region to middle of spine. Sensitiveness to pressure in r. iliac region; to hard pressure in r. iliac fossa. Sounded well on percussion, but attempting to introduce the catheter aggravated the pains, entrance only affected during the remission and a few drops of red urine were drawn off. Paroxysmal constriction, with anxiety, nausea, eructations, small, rapid pulse, cold skin, later sensation as if two arrows were drawn through abdomen in opposite directions. Compression, < pressure, worse at intervals, with coolness there. Oppression. Sensation of incarcerated flatus. Dragging in colon, with ineffectual efforts to pass stool and flatus. In H. and low down in rectum, painful, ineffectual desire to pass flatus.

Clinical.—Colic, walls of the abdomen tense and hard; about the navel, with terrible tearing pain; with extreme distention of the transverse colon; with tympanitic distention of the abdomen in circumscribed swellings as large as the fist; with complete obstruction of the bowels and frequent vomiting. Jaundice, with nausea and vomiting. Many cases of incarcerated hernia. Chronic inflammation of the liver, with constipation, vomiting of green mucus, pain from the liver to left side and to the back, or a feeling of a string pulling the liver backward.

Rectum.—Closed forcibly upon finger introduced into it during paroxysms. Injections cannot be retained more than five minutes, they are rejected hurriedly. Crawling and sticking. Weight. Tenesmus; and of bladder. Feeling as if he would pass a thin stool, but he does not. Urging to a stool that was scanty and consistent, with pressure. Sluggish desire at times, stool sluggish and tenacious; ineffectual D.

Clinical.—Neuralgia of the rectum.

Anus.—Hæmorrhoids caused by violent efforts to evacuate. *Drawn up; with constriction;* with itching hæmorrhoids. Prolapsus. Formication. Burning during stool. Tenesmus; with pressing boring.

Stool.—Watery; and frequent; at first, afterwards in small pieces, of penetrating odor. *Diarrhœa;* before colic; only during lead colic; with burning in rectum, preceded by tenesmus; with tenesmus; then constipation; *alternating with constipation* during pregnancy, black, small; yellow; yellow and copious; yellow, with pain; frequent, offensive; painless, with rumbling in abdomen. Sometimes thin, sometimes globular, sometimes triangular, nearly always dark, afterwards constipation. Dysentery; bloody, with fever, cutting in stomach and abdomen and eructations so that everything seemed turned to gas.

Constipation; with nausea and vomiting; with heat in abdomen; with pain in epigastric region and back; then diarrhœa, often involuntary; causing fissure of anus, although there was a stool nearly every day. *Like sheep-dung, scanty;* and only two in three days; like S., ashy gray; like S., white, with effort; yellowish, rounded, as the disease progresses they become softer, at last often watery. Hard in morning, with pressure and sticking, three soft ones in afternoon; H. and scratching; and difficult; and light gray, tenacious, difficult.

Blackish, scanty (Op.), *painful, only once in eight or ten days;* B., fetid; every other day, and thick; *or green, in balls, often hard.* Dark; and smooth. Lead-colored. Fawn-colored. Yellow, consistent, passed unconsciously. Pale. *Indolent;* and tough, at last streaked with blood. Bloody; and small; with tenesmus. Scybalous. Copious. Involuntary. Painful. Difficult; before colic; and indolent. Irregular. Twice since 5 A.M. Every other day. Once in two or three days.

Clinical.—Diarrhœa, particularly with a sensation of something pulling the navel backward, with actual retraction; one case of diarrhœa, following typhoid fever; colic, alternating with delirium. Constipation, with spasm of the sphincter ani, especially with the sensation of a string pulling the anus into the rectum; with terrible spasms of the anus, pains in the muscles of the thighs, etc.; with violent pain in the cæcal region, where there is a hard, sore swelling, with retraction of the navel; with most violent colic and retraction of the navel.

Urinary Organs.—Prostate indurated. Nephritis; with fever; parenchymatous. Bladder distended; pain in region; itching and burning pain in neck and in perineum; constriction towards neck, difficulty in introducing sound; sphincter did not permit urine to pass for more than thirty-six hours, so that bladder extended up to umbilicus, at times testes retracted into inguinal canal causing pain in back, loins, scrotum and perineum; inactivity, micturition difficult; paralysis of sphincter, which allowed urine to pass guttatin. *Tenesmus; ineffectual, sometimes after an effort, which increases the pains, urine passes guttatin;* frequent ineffectual. Desire in forenoon, with inability to urinate immediately; frequent D., urine always scanty; frequent D., micturition painful, urine often high-colored, depositing a lateritious sediment.

Strangury. Dysuria. **Micturition difficult**; *and by drops; and a little at a time;* and frequent, scanty; and painful; only affected by forcible contraction of abdominal muscles, which increases the pains; possible only during remission of abdominal pains. Micturition painful. M. rare; and scanty. Frequent M. of usual amount in afternoon. M. impossible at times. Involuntary M.; during epileptic spasms; between epileptic seizures. Ischuria; with inflammatory fever. Urine retained; suppressed; *suppressed,* only a few drops of bloody mucus in bladder. Urethra retracted; painful where it leaves bladder; smarting along U. at beginning of micturition; scalding on micturition, also still more so afterwards.

Urine.—Copious; at 4 A.M., then pain in abdomen as after taking cold, > emission of flatus, then sticking in abdomen; and pale; and watery, with a pellicle looking like spermaceti and leaving a greasy mark, reaction acid, depositing a flaky sediment, which showed a few mucous granules and one cell of renal epithelium, containing several fatty globules. **Scanty; and dark, evacuated by drops;** S. and deep red; and red, easily discharged; and limpid; passed only once in twenty-four hours; and high-colored, with decrease of extractive matters, urea, phosphoric acid, uric acid and chlorides, later with anæmia and double the quantity of normal excrementitious matter in the blood, lastly albuminuria, the amount of urine variable, sometimes almost normal but the density low, extractives diminished, and whether there is albuminuria or not there is no increase of uric acid in blood and no uric acid in serum of a blister. Dark; and turbid; and depositing many lithates on cooling. Red; brownish; and acid; soon decomposing and becoming thick with flaky clouds. Brown-yellow. Orange-colored. Dull yellow. Pale; pale lemon-colored, clear, alkaline, without sediment. Hæmaturia. Contained a little sugar and mucus. Alkaline, but not limpid. Acid. Dark brown sediment.

Albuminous urine; *without œdema; without urea,* sp. gr. 1002; urine scanty; *brownish-red, turbid, acid, sediment flocculent, consisting of red blood-corpuscles and many short, thick, turbid cylinders beset with red blood-corpuscles, all the symptoms of acute, diffuse nephritis;* sp. gr. 1030, yellowish-brown, acid, clear, with many granular cylinders; containing cells from kidneys; containing epithelial casts and traces of lead; color reddish amber, with much uric acid; and alkaline, with traces of lead; *with amaurosis and cerebral* (usually epileptic) *symptoms;* with clonic spasms of face and limbs, unconsciousness, frothing from mouth and puffiness of face; with many casts, it had to be drawn with a catheter, two days afterwards anuria, trismus, opisthotonos, convulsions, during which the tongue was bitten, pupils contracted and indolent, then loss of mind, on following days the amount of urine (in spite of infusion of squills) was 600 and 700 c. cm., seventeen grammes of urea in twenty-four hours, *pains in limbs,* later urine and urea increased, albumen diminished, pus disappeared, mind became free, but death from erysipelas; yellowish-brown, scanty, turbid, sediment of many tubular crystals of uric acid, hyaline cylinders, to some of which adhered cells similar

in the ureters. Acute nephritis, with bloody urine, mental depression, etc. Paralysis of the bladder, with difficult micturition, or even with retention of urine.

Sexual Organs.—Weakness. Impotency. Penis flaccid; P. painful; sensation as if tied at its root or along its course. Erections in morning; frequent E., with spasmodic retraction of testicles and even with emissions during colic. Inflammatory swelling of scrotum and penis, with inflammatory dysuria, constipation, delirium, gangrene of all these parts. Constriction of scrotum; so that at times testicles were drawn up into inguinal canal, with pain in small of back, scrotum and intestines. Skin of scrotum and thigh sore to touch after the sweat.

Testicles.—Swelling; retraction at times. R. rose towards inguinal canal during the paroxysms. Shooting through them, almost causing faintness. Pain in l.; P. > suspending them with the hands; > compression; in T. and spermatic cord, with painful drawing in them and with contraction of scrotum; choking, in l., at times extending into spermatic cord. Constriction. Tension.

Jerking in spermatic cord in morning, in afternoon stitches where it leaves abdomen. Paroxysmal pain along spermatic cord into l. testicle, which is then retracted. Desire increased; diminished; *lost;* seminal weakness. Emissions; in morning sleep, with voluptuous dreams; with biting on frænum preputii; involuntary, causing debility; unconscious, in sleep after wine, with relaxed penis, next morning violent E. on slight provocation; scanty, during coition.

Female.—**Vaginismus.** Leucorrhœa. Inertia of uterus at delivery and post-partum hæmorrhage, the child was very slight. Stillborn infants. Premature births. Abortion; with abundant menorrhagia and colicky pains; then peritonitis; tired, heavy pain in lower limbs, < knees and about umbilicus and in groins, as if a cord were pulling down and extending to the very lower part of abdomen, same pain in upper limbs, feet, toes and back, < over tops of feet and hands, with the nausea of pregnancy, afterwards vomiting, with increase of these symptoms, ending in A. Menorrhagia. Menses absent; for fourteen months, then returned scantily; M. that had ceased for two days returned; disturbed.

Clinical.—Dysmenorrhœa, with the characteristic sensation of a string pulling the abdominal walls towards the spine. Vaginismus, associated with excruciating colic, etc. Threatening abortion (from lack of development of the uterus).

Respiratory Organs.—Spasms. Constriction of larynx. Voice loud; V. nasal; hoarse; hoarse, rough; hoarse, almost toneless; tone impaired; hollow; weak; lost its resonance, weak, like a woman's, articulation impeded, sometimes incomplete; weaker with each return of menses till it was a faint whisper, no approximation of vocal cords on attempting to speak and glottis was wide open, hence fatigue of muscles of chest; panting, stifled; lost. Dry mucus in upper part of trachea, with pain in chest on loosening it, with whistling in upper part of chest on inspiration. Bronchitis.

Cough; in morning from dry mucus in upper part of chest; convulsive; hacking. *Dry cough;* on deep inwithout cough. Hæmoptysis; changing to suppuration of lungs (in a young man who had suppressed erysipelas with white lead).

Respiration.—Asthma. Suffocation; on drinking. Suffocative oppression during the colicky paroxysms. Asphyxia. Dyspnœa. Craving for air, < night. Anxious. Impeded. Difficult; compelling him to jump out of bed at night and open the window. Short; on walking, < ascending a height, with hoarseness and oppression in region of heart, < pressure. Wheezing. Heavy. Sighing; and slow. Intermittent. Slow, expiration stertorous on account of weakness of buccinators. Rapid; during the paroxysms, and short; during the paroxysms, sometimes interrupted and choking during attack of colic; inspiration R., incomplete and noisy during the paroxysms, as if checked by the pain; < during paroxysms of colic and arthralgia, with noise at entrance of nose and mouth; < during colicky paroxysms, and difficult, superficial; < during the paroxysms, and anxious, difficult, irregular; and embarrassed; and painful; and anxious; and irregular; and interrupted, panting; in short jerks; and incomplete, short, suffocating and a kind of jactitation; and feeble. Painful. Suddenly cut short. Arrested in afternoon when standing, sitting or moving r. arm towards the left, with sticking in sternum.

Chest.—*Milk scanty. Suppuration of lungs.* Gangrene of lungs. Tubercles in lungs. Consolidation in apices of lungs, with little cough, scarcely any rising of l. upper chest on inspiration, respiration harsh, almost bronchial. Mucus. Applied perpendicularly over sternum the instrument showed .75 mm. Labored movement of C. and diaphragm. Weak action, < l., dulness in l. apex, then in r. Râles at apices of lungs on auscultation. Vesicular murmur loud, with mucous râles, lungs congested. Friction of muscles, with other symptoms, so that it was difficult to satisfy myself that she had not pleurisy. Bronchial respiration was heard at apex of lungs.

Stitches in l.; in middle of sternum; in pectoralis major; in female breast; beneath mammæ; below r. breast; deep in r. mamma; in l. mamma; in l. mamma, then in r.; in various parts of C. and shoulders; in and beneath mammæ in morning, > rising; in l. in afternoon; beneath l. mamma near sternum in afternoon; now r., now l. side in afternoon and evening; in l. mamma in afternoon on inspiration; in upper part of sternum in afternoon during inspiration; in region of r. lower ribs in afternoon on turning body to right, < turning it backward, > rubbing; in l. upper part in afternoon, on rubbing it extended into mamma and then backward and upward under shoulder; in r. costal region after sitting down, > walking; beneath r. arm when standing, taking away her breath; in l., < inspiration, then tearing; in l. side near sternum, > rubbing; in breasts, with itching, and with suppuration about l. nipple and discharge of serous water, induration of r. breast, adherent towards outer part, livid, with red streaks, pain extending into arm and affecting its use, thin corrosive discharge (after lead ointment on rash of hands); in l. side in afternoon, extending through scapula; below r. breast, extending into r. scapula; in front and sides, worse at intervals; intermittent, in l., not affected by respiration; paroxysmal, in external subclavicular region, near brachial plexus, > pressure; in r. side, becoming twinging.

Pleurisy. Tearing beneath r. arm. Cutting in C. and throat as if scraped by a shell, later the sensation was felt in throat only at times and exhausted him. Sudden boring in l. mammary region extending into back, < pressure, with fever and dyspnœa obliging her to sit up in bed, *beats of heart tumultuous, rapid and resonant.* Oppressive cramp in lower part after physical exertion, with fatigue. Pain; behind sternum; in l. lower intercostal muscles; in anterior parietes, < above costal cartilages, < touch and respiration; dared not dilate C. lest he should increase the pains; intermittent, in r. pectoralis; intermittent, in l. side anteriorly and posteriorly; dragging, as if a string were stretched from it to groin. Sensitiveness of anterior walls and of costal cartilages.

Pressure; upon lower part of sternum; < behind sternum, causing anxiety and making respiration difficult, the anxiety < movement or pressure of hand upon l. chest; upon l. independent of respiration; as from a block of wood against l. anterior lower part, as if on surface of lung, from morning after rising till after dinner, < inspiration, laughing and after dinner when lying on the sofa, with drawing sticking in l. upper arm and at times sticking between scapulæ, with pain in chest. Constriction; at base and all around. Oppression; in morning; intermittent. Tightness. Anxiety. Rush of blood when walking rapidly. Sensibility to temperature diminished in sternal region.

Clinical.—**It has been prescribed in tuberculosis, hæmorrhage from the lungs, cough, purulent expectoration, etc.**

Heart.—*Change in muscular structure, without coincident disease of valves, with or without atheromatous degeneration of vessels, usually hypertrophy and dilatation of l. ventricle, sometimes with parenchymatous nephritis.* Dilated, four beats heard instead of two, pulse vibrating as in insufficiency of aorta. Enlargement; and beats noticed over whole surface and in epigastric region, violent pulsation in the distended jugular veins, pulse small, rapid, with oppression and œdema of limbs, heart's sounds of indefinite double friction murmurs; so that it was impossible to lie on l. side, with pressure upon H., but it maintained its rhythm through the respiratory intermission, slower at the beginning of the period and falling to 100 or 105 per minute, holding that for a time, then increasing rapidly till he breathed, when every available muscle was exercised to give him air.

Sound.—First at apex sharp and metallic; first remarkably ringing, second dull, impulse strong, whirring, with pain under sternum. First short, defective, second unusually distinct, the impulse received in two intercostal spaces is jerky but not forcible, no murmur. *Bruit de souffle* at apex; in cervical vessels; humeral; during first action, more at apex than at base; anæmic, at base and along large vessels. Anæmic blowing in vessels of neck. Sonorous *bruit* at apex transmitted along carotids, the second beat of H. is heard under sternum. Cat's fremitus at apex. Double friction sound without enlargement; D. murmur in crural artery; D. *souffle* in subclavicular region but none in crural artery; D. rough blowing, transmitted along carotids, with swelling of limbs and albuminuria. Sounds over a large surface, instead of the valvular sound a double *bruit*, rasping, which is transmitted along carotids. Redoubled, second rude and like a pericardiac sound. Sound accompanied by metallic tinkling. Chlorotic. At one point a murmur in second sound. Soft systolic *souffle* at base. Dull on percussion, with prominence of præcordial region. Tremor in jugular veins on auscultation.

Palpitation; < ascending stairs or running too long; with dyspnœa, he felt the heart beating along neck and as far as vertex, with full, hard, regular pulse, heart's sound heard nearly all over anterior part of chest. Impulse violent, but pulse rhythmical. Action strong; and irregular. Action irregular; and hurried, shaking præcordial region, the beats seem stifled on auscultation. Action feeble; and slow; and second sound indistinct.

Jerking in præcordial region. Symptoms resembling angina pectoris. Sticking in præcordial region on inspiration, then anxiety with mounting of heat and redness into face. Sudden pain; P., with palpitation. Pressure in præcordial region. Oppression. Anxiety; with anxious respiration; with cold sweat.

Pulse.—*Rapid;* and jerking; and strong, also cordy; and full; and hard, also full; and hard, small; and tense, intermittent; and small, also weak and intermittent; and small, irregular; and irregular, also slender; and soft; and weak; and scarcely perceptible one minute, the next slow and large; by turns R. and slow, large and small; sometimes R., sometimes slow, soft. Slow; and full; and strong; and hard; and hard, vibrating, also large; and hard, tense; and large, tense; large and soft; and contracted; and soft; and small; and small, weak; and small, contracted, hardish, intermittent; and weak; and weak, irregular; and weak, soft, also easily depressed; and indistinct, intermittent and of irregular strength; irregular as to force, sometimes weak, sometimes vibrating; when recumbent, quickened by trifling exertion, weak. Forcible beating in aorta shaking abdomen. Throbbing in carotids and crural arteries. Full and turgid. Hard; in temporal arteries; and tense; and full; and full, tense, vibrating. Intermittent. Tremulous. Vibrating. Irregular; in frequency and force; in frequency, and soft; and deep and easily compressed. Dicrotic. Small; and soft; and feeble; and slender, soft, easily compressible. Weak; and thready, sometimes imperceptible.

Neck.—Tearing in nape, > standing and rubbing, then it appeared in l. shoulder; T. from r. side into shoulder. Pain in region of last cervical and first dorsal vertebræ on pressure. Acute drawing in nape. Tension in nape, < r. side, extending into ear, on turning head sideways. Sensibility diminished. Stiffness. Paralysis of muscles.

Back.—Neuralgic pain. Pain in muscles; in spine extending into occiput; with lameness and weakness; with sensitiveness of spine to pressure; and in hips and down spine, occasionally extending up neck to occiput. Spinal irritation. Rheumatism of B., hips and lower limbs. Weakness; and of lower limbs. Locomotor ataxia, < shutting eyes, strength undiminished, leg cannot be bent upon thigh. Sticking in middle of spine; in middle of back in forenoon when standing.

Scapulæ.—Sticking; between S.; in r., with burning. Tearing in r.; in lower part of r.; in r., with feeling as if something rose up in it, then burning in abdomen, then sticking in r. scapula. Pain between S.; sprained, in r. Dorsal region of spine tender to pressure.

Lumbar Region.—Sticking in l. in afternoon on laughing; in r. in afternoon, > pressure; S. in afternoon, > rubbing, with sensitiveness on leaning it against a chair; in l. and in r. hypochondrium in afternoon on bending towards l., > rising and sitting erect; worse by paroxysms, > pressure, < movement, with cramps there. Tearing in l. in afternoon when standing; T. in renal region worse at the same time as the abdominal sufferings, and like them > friction and pressure. Pain; in sacro-iliac synchondrosis; < stooping; with warmth in it; *usually lancinating, and in nates, posterior part of thigh, knee, sole and toes, equally severe on both sides, felt somewhat on inner surface of lower limb, with attacks of cramps;* rheumatic, and in limbs, extending into knees; drawing. Dragging pain; and in epigastrium.

Clinical.—Spinal paralysis, rheumatic. Infantile paralysis. Symptoms of multiple sclerosis, posterior spinal sclerosis; if this drug has not actually cured this disease it has been found valuable for many of its distressing symptoms, especially for the violent sciatic pains, the colic, constipation, dysuria, etc.; (its ally Thallium, which is even more poisonous than Plumb., has been found to act well in the terrible neuralgias of this disease after Plumbum seems to have lost its effect).

Extremities.—Œdema. Emaciation; with sensitiveness to cold; of r. leg and l. arm, with increased sensibility. Bluish. (Dilated veins on legs and feet, and on upper third of outer surface of r. arm a serpentine varicose vein, and on patella a patch of varicose veins.). *Gout;* in hands and feet; without redness or tumefaction, a tumor on dorsal surface of wrist, in some cases coincident with paralysis of extensors, extends along tendons, is not changed in color, consistence or mobility, it is caused by hypertrophy of tendinous expansions, never begins in joints. He always lies with them drawn up. Legs flexed upon thighs and forearms on arms, and body doubled together. R. fall back more easily than l.

Trembling; of legs and hands, < r.; after colic; > resting them against something; of l. lower, then l. upper, with pain and difficulty in moving them; of hands when stretched out, < r., r. ring finger semi-flexed, paralysis of extensors, < last phalanx, on l. hand only ring finger is paralyzed, grasp weak, < r. hand, lower limbs weak, cramps in last three r. fingers and in calves. Constantly thrust out of bed and then covered up again. *Jerking.* Contractions; of joints; spasmodic, < night, with pain. Spasmodic flexion of arms and legs, so that backs of hands rested on chest, then gradual relaxation till arms hung by the side. Convulsions; and of hands, with tightness. Cramps; in joints and surrounding muscles, with pain; hands and feet; hands and r. leg from lying in bed, < extending them; knees and arms, with pains; l. middle finger and successively in knees, popliteal spaces, calves, soles, etc., sometimes with pain.

Sudden shock so that he fell to the ground, with spasmodic flexion of legs, so that heels touched nates, on trying to extend legs cramp in thighs and calves, abdomen retracted and sensitive to touch, even of his shirt, with constipation, a week later a similar shock in arms with spasmodic pains, hands flexed and fingers spread apart, the pains lasted several weeks and during this time he could sleep only on his back with r. arm clamped between legs, afterwards use of r. arm impaired and fingers hanging down, next year l. hand similarly affected, skin of arms rough, dry and cracked.

Lancinations in arms, forearms and lower limbs;

legs, arms and fingers; in elbows and knees; *along inner surfaces, sometimes with cramps.* Tearing; knees, calves, soles and palmar surfaces of forearms, < movement, > pressure, worse by paroxysms, during which there are cramps. **Neuralgic pains.**

Pains; arm and legs; hands and feet; joints; lower joints of r.; large joints, < knees; joints and muscles of elbow, wrist, fingers and their tendinous sheaths, knees, popliteal spaces and insteps, spontaneous or excited by movement or pressure; during movement and pressure; on forced movement; in flexor muscles on motion; < **muscular parts of thighs,** *then in muscles of arm;* < knees, with weakness and lameness; < legs and l. arm, with swelling of l. knee, then weakness of l. knee; on inside, < about inner angle of elbow and knee; < **night**; < **evening and night,** so that he rubbed one foot against the other; in wrists and ankles, < morning on going to work, with stiffness, lameness and weakness of them; large joints, < heat of bed; in joints, with cracking on motion; hands and feet, with numbness of them; *beginning in fingers and extending through elbows and upper arms, then beginning in feet and finally affecting whole body;* across arms and legs; in joints extending through limbs; sudden; **paroxysmal, so that he cries out,** *also > pressure, < movement; vague wandering;* now in arms, now in feet, with drawing, removing their activity; as if broken.

Bruised pain; < lower; suddenly in lower, with pricking and formication on soles, walking aggravated the latter so that it was painful, < night, > daytime after getting heated at work, next weakness of upper limbs, at last upper limbs immovable and painful, arms hung down and seemed fastened to sides, when raised they fell like dead weights, shoulder depressed, elbow, wrist and fingers flexed, forearm and hand half way between pronation and supination, bruised pain, < movement and at night, in parts around shoulder, subclavian space, axilla and upper limb, when the arm was squeezed he cried out that the marrow was bitten. Drawing pains; tearing. Drawings in arms and legs. Tingling. Heaviness.

Weakness; of joints; wrists, ankles and knees; lower and hands in morning on rising; hands and feet, < calves, on waking at 4 A.M., > walking; < r.; calves and arms, < biceps; < l. upper, with emaciation and arcus senilis; hands and forearms, later sudden pain in thighs when walking, lost use of limbs. Stiffness; of fingers, toes and insteps; with general cold sweat, the patient answered by nodding, later respiration stopped, rigidity extended over body, but heart continued to beat. Diminished sensibility of r. hand and foot; of forearm and thigh, < anterior surface. Numbness; *of arms and legs;* arms and legs < movement; in r., more in leg and foot than in arm; with torpor; arms and feet, with immobility of them; r. hand, r. leg and foot, with impaired power of motion of them; sometimes extending through whole system; in sudden attacks in arms and thighs, with heaviness and pain; gradually becoming paralysis. Insensibility to tickling in r. hand and r. sole.

Paralysis; of l.; arms and feet; hands and legs; hands and feet; both lower and r. arm; extensors; extensors, of upper and of one lower; a group of muscles, one muscle or a single muscular fasciculus; posterior muscles of upper limbs and anterior muscles of lower; with feeling as if weights were suspended from joints; with pain, < pressure and movement; with emaciation, their skin dingy yellow, flabby and as if fastened to bones; with emaciation, tissues soft and flabby and skin yellow and too loose; wrists and ankles, < extensors, with emaciation of ball of thumb; extensors of forearms, emaciation of lower part of forearm, < r., of hypothenar, deltoids and muscles of upper arms, < r., analgesia and anæsthesia of arms, < r., the same symptoms in lower limbs, extensors of feet very little paralyzed; upper, and partial P. of lower, the hands, with palms turned inward, hung by his side and rather forward, powerless, swollen and livid, he could not move forearm nor rise from a chair, nor walk without assistance and then gait was tottering; incomplete, in upper, < extensors of fingers, the supinators, extensors, abductors and adductors of thumbs, with incomplete P. of feet, < extensors of legs, sensation of warmth not entirely lost.

Upper Extremities.—Emaciation; of flexors; extensors completely atrophied, space between radius and ulna sunken, skin dry, gray and rough, hands flexed at wrists, basal phalanges at r. angles with metacarpus, other phalanges flexed into palm, terminal phalanx of thumb at r. angle with basal phalanx, extension and separation of fingers impossible, pronation and supination almost lost, scarcely any power to flex or extend elbow, motion at shoulder free. Trembling; < morning, relieved for the rest of the day if he drank two or three glasses of brandy; rapid and uniform. Cramps; < deltoids, with pains.

Pain; in muscles and joints; neuralgic; lacerating; myosalgic, < where radial nerve leaves the spiral grove of humerus. Pressure, < elbows and fingers, sensitive. Weakness of flexors; r. extensors; < evening. Hypalgesia of l., < upper two-thirds of palmar surface of forearm. Sensibility diminished; to temperature in r. Insensibility; with formication and weakness, then paralysis; in r., and in l. hand, diminished sensibility of rest of l. upper limb.

On attempting to move them contraction only in fibres of deltoid. Extensors do not contract under electricity. Motor power of r. diminished, and posterior muscles of forearm wasted. Inco-ordinate movements, with analgesia. Want of power of motory coordination, < l., when his eyes are shut he cannot touch any particular spot on his face without feeling for it, analgesia to pricking and pinching in arms, < l. Paralysis; of extensors; P. and atrophy of extensor digitorum communis indicator, extensores digiti quinti et pollicis, extensores carpi (except l. extensor carpi ulnaris), abductor pollicis longus and brevis, interosseous muscle, deltoids, biceps, brachiales interni and supinators.

Shoulder.—Depressed. Emaciation; of r. S. and arm, fingers flexed, tremors after attempting to use them, no power to raise arms, which hung useless by his sides, tenderness when they were moved. Sticking; inward in r.; beneath r., extending outward at S.; burning, on r. Acute pain, < l. and along extensor surface of forearm, on moving upper limb, pain on pressure on deltoid, < l., tremor on stretching arm. Pain; in region; in r.; r. on movement; < deltoids, which were paralyzed; extending to elbows, < over deltoids; in joints and flexors of upper arm so that he could not raise arm. Weight, and in finger-tips; W., more in elbows and most of all in hands; more in elbows and most of all in wrist, the pain < exposure of the parts to cold, with internal and external coldness of the limb, < dorsum of hand. Raising difficult; impossible. Numbness. Paralysis of joint and elbow, temperature in morning 39.4° C., in evening 41° C., pulse 126, respiration 28.

Arm.—Emaciation; < l., and < hypothenar eminences. *Moniliform dilatation of veins, and on back of hand, chiefly corresponding to union of veins*, < muscular exertion, and dilated veins on calves; veins only slightly filled, but on compressing deep veins of upper arm they were swollen and had olive-shaped dilatations. Fixed in pronation. Always semi-flexed at elbow; A. and hand held midway between pronation and supination. Hanging down by his side, unable to raise them; hanging down as if fastened to his sides, when raised and let go they fall like inert bodies. L. laid against chest, it cannot be raised by action of deltoid, other movements natural; r. applied to chest, unable to raise it, its other movements natural, with pain in r. side of neck, r. shoulder, inner part of r. arm, bend of r. elbow, palmar surface of r. forearm and wrist, < movement, worse by paroxysms, during which they burn and between which they are contusive, skin of these parts insensible. *Trembling;* of r.; of r. *during voluntary motion;* < r., with a regular to-and-fro motion; < towards evening, < hands and forearms, but extending to upper arms on strong exertion. Convulsive movements. Clonic convulsions on attempting to use them, > walking for some time, r. arm fixed to his side every day up to 10 or 11 A.M., grasping power lessened. Tearing in r.; deeply-seated T., sharp one moment, dull the next, with trembling and occasional cramps. Pain; in joints of A. and hand; in r., with formication; r., with sensitiveness to pressure, and with lancinations from shoulder to bend of elbow. Weakness; of extensors and flexors of A. and hands, < r.; < towards evening, with numbness, then trembling; < r., with numbness and alternately increasing and decreasing trembling, the latter < fatiguing work; with weight at posterior surface of middle part of A. and forearm. Numbness; from middle third down to finger-tips; < r., with analgesia. Sometimes held against the hottest parts of the stove, sometimes he wants them sprinkled with cold water. Paralysis; of extensors; painful; of l., he could flex and extend it but slightly, still the grasp was unaffected; of extensors, when he pronates the hand the wrist drops at right angles to arm and he cannot straighten it; beginning in extensors, gradually extending to flexors, < deltoid, hand remained midway between pronation and supination, with tearing in arm, < pressure and at night, heaviness in wrists and fingers, finally cold feeling in limbs.

Upper Arm.—Atrophy of deltoids. Veins large and knotted, varicose at points of union, but veins on extensor surface of forearm scarcely visible after compression of venous trunk. Twitching above l. elbow. Tearing beneath r. shoulder; in middle of r.; in lower part in morning; on inner surface of l. in forenoon; posterior surface of l., which on rubbing went into elbow. Sudden pain in A. and hands, then inability to use hands. Bruised pain in deltoid. Acute drawing in r. humerus; and in bones of hands and fingers. Diminished sensibility in r. Insensibility of external and anterior surface of region of l. deltoid. Deltoids did not contract under electricity. Unable to extend it laterally or raise it. Unable to raise elbow to the level of his shoulder. Immobility of deltoid while the surrounding fleshy parts are moving in different directions, all other movements of upper limbs slow, feeble and difficult.

Elbow.—Flexed. Boring, < at bend, extending to shoulder, hand flexed and cannot be straightened nor lifted, arm cannot be raised, uses both hands in carrying a glass to his lips, on trying to straighten the arm the supinator longus resists forcibly. Pain; in bends; in r., and in wrists and muscles of r. arm; twisting, in bends and in palmar surfaces of forearms, worse by paroxysms, > pressure. Weight; < l.

Forearm.—*Dilatations of cutaneous veins like strings of pearls*, < exertion and compression of venæ profundæ brachii, *on F. and under surface of lower third of upper arm;* on F. and hands. Arteries rigid and tortuous. Emaciated; extensors; < r. and thumbs; posterior surface, and flabby, also the skin there dried, a bony projection at carpo-metacarpal region. The superior part of outside is not on the same plane with the interior part, which is twisted inward. Muscles, < extensors, flabby, weak and tremulous. Palmar surface hard and tense during the worst paroxysms and affected by cramps, which are removed by movement. Fixed in pronation, with much effort they can be brought midway between pronation and supination. Semi-flexed and incapable of extension and supination; l. semi-flexed, incapable of extension. Trembling of F. and hands, < l. Cramps; of r. flexors. Lancinations from elbows to finger-ends. Boring from middle of r. to near shoulder-joint after breakfast; paroxysmal, in palmar surface, in bend of elbow and in axilla, > gentle pressure, < firm pressure. Pains; sudden, in radial nerves in the daytime, with pain on stretching out hand, only ring fingers and r. little finger could be extended, with uneasiness in elbow like fatigue, also felt in leg behind ankle. Weakness. Diminished sensibility; on extensor surface of F. and fingers. Electro-muscular contractility diminished. Anæsthesia; on back; < extensor surface, with analgesia; F. and hands insensible to pricking and burning, but pain on anterior surface of forearm. Supination impossible. Paralysis; of extensors; < r; extensors, < r., coming on gradually during colic, with withering of the affected muscles.

Wrist.—Emaciation of r. Swelling, with paralysis of extensors of hands. Bony elevation on back from projecting heads of second and third metacarpal bones. Flexed; and fingers form a right angle with metacarpus; r. permanently flexed at a right angle with forearm; r. permanently flexed with W. and hand twisted outward; permanently flexed at a right angle with forearm, turned inward, so that radius projects. R. twisted inward, incapable of abduction, upon attempting to turn it back upon forearm the whole hand is thrown into adduction. Trembling of W. and hands from any emotion. Tearing on lower surface of r. extending to back of hand and fingers, in afternoon. Attacks of pain extending up arms. Weight. Weakness of W. and fingers after the colic; W., with burning pain in them and in forearms, < night, later paralysis of extensors of W., complete on l. side, partial on r. Insensibility; of l. Extension of l. W. and fingers slow and feeble. **Wrist-drop**; < on r. side; with numbness of fingers and muscles of back of arm, he could not pick up a pin though sensation was unaltered; with helplessness of W., but a comparatively good grip with his hands. Paralysis of r. extensors; of extensor carpi ulnaris; of W. and fingers, with tremor on trying to move them. Flexors of W. and fingers cease to act during supination of forearm and hand, so that they are extended by their own weight. L. cannot be extended; cannot be extended unless the hand is placed edgeways, it is with difficulty abducted or adducted at the same time that it is extended or flexed; W. and fingers can be abducted and adducted only by flexing them. W. is brought into abduction (never into adduction) when straightened out, during extension the action of the radial muscles is visible, but scarcely any in extensor carpi ulnaris. L. easily moved when the hand is closed.

Hand.—Back blue, clammy and infiltrated. Emaciation; of r.; with contractions of flexors and stiffness of finger-joints. Palm does not lie upon the bed, but looks the other way. Back convex, projections formed by heads of second and third metacarpal bones and by trapezium and trapezoid. Hard swelling of extensor tendons extending from wrist to middle or two-thirds of metacarpus, painful on pressure, and on back of hand a series of round digitations, with paralysis of muscles. *Trembling;* when he is fatigued; worse when anything goes wrong with him; worse in evening than in morning, and when he is intoxicated, spreading when he is vexed or fatigued over upper limbs; suddenly in r., later T. and paralysis of l. upper limb; then weakness of third and fourth fingers, so that they could not be fully extended, then second and fifth fingers were affected, then wrist, finally shoulders, arms hung down relaxed, balls of thumb, shoulders and arms, < deltoids, emaciated, T. of muscles on passive motion of hands and fingers, at other times fibrillar twitching, on attempting to raise arm the trapezius and sterno-cleido-mastoid contracted and raised shoulder three inches, then pectoral muscles drew arm forward, contraction of all muscles weak. Twitching; in back of l. Cramp of r. Sticking inward in back of r. Tearing in r. at place where the pulse is felt. Pain in l., with loss of motion. Weakness; < r.; r., < inner border, ring and middle fingers semi-flexed and paralyzed, with insensibility of these fingers and inner half of hand. Stiffness of r. and of l. fingers. Difficulty in closing l. Diminished sensibility; in r. palm; < r.; in r., < dorsal surface; of r. and lower part of forearm; of r. and wrist and lower third of back of forearm. Insensibility; of r.; r. palm; skin of l. palm; in night on waking and in morning sudden loss of power; of r. H. and wrist extending to lower half of dorsal surface of forearm, but only three or four centimetres above inside of wrist; extensor communis digitorum almost insensible to electricity. Paralysis; < r.; extensors; r. extensors, also fingers always semi-flexed; with relaxation, dryness, paleness, coldness, the backs raised by scabs, under which cavities are formed; incipient motor, of r., < index and middle fingers.

Fingers.—Nails bluish-gray. Atrophy of balls of thumbs; with pain up arms to nape and occiput; A. of thenal and hypothetical eminences. Flexed; r.; curled up into palm; < middle ones; upon one another without muscular contractions; index and little F. flexed by weight of middle fingers and by action of flexores communi digitorum; and when forcibly extended pain up to shoulder; l., with imperfect extension, abduction and adduction; l. little, it cannot be extended, separated, adducted or brought into opposition; thumb firmly F. and turned inward, it cannot be abducted, extended or brought into opposition; third finger and last phalanx of thumb spasmodically F.; two l. middle firmly semi-flexed. Jerking in l. thumb. Spasms. Cramps; on trying to grasp anything. Tearing in l. thumb; on side of l. index, between second and third joints in afternoon; in r. ring and middle towards tips, > rubbing, but returning. Pain. Painless sensation of tension in l. thumb. Weight; in tips; with swollen feeling. Weakness; of r.; extensors, < r.; r., < middle and ring; r. middle and ring, then index and little; extensors of fourth, then trembling of arm on exertion, then paralysis of arm; extensors of third and fourth when writing, then of fifth and second, then thumb, at last extensor carpi ulnaris, then W. and trembling of hands, later paralysis of arm (the patient was left-handed and the paralysis was < l. side); sudden, in r. fourth and fifth. Sense of touch weak; < r. Analgesia of r., < tips. Numbness; of r.; tips of r., with formication; tip of l. fourth, with fuzziness; < r., with formication, then pricking; of little and ring F., extending to styloid process of ulna and on inner surface of middle F. and third metacarpus, the F. move less nimbly than usual. Difficult to move. Inability to extend them; r. F. and l. middle and ring. Thumb and little F. cannot be placed in opposition. Adduction of r. thumb impossible. Fingers do not fall beyond thenar and hypothenar region, last phalanges flexed; middle F. do not fall beyond thenar and hypothenar region. Difficult to separate; when flexed; when hand hangs down; l. middle, and to approximate. Abduction impossible, in l. index; in F. except by flexing them; in thumb, abductor pollicis longus motionless; A. and opposition of thumb impossible; A. and opposition of thumb impossible when fully adducted; A. and extension of two r. middle F. impossible, with weakness of them; r. ring F. does not go as far down as the others when they are closed and it cannot be fully abducted nor adducted. Paralysis; of extensors of r.; of two last r., with numbness of them; partial, of extensors. Falling asleep of r. thumb.

Lower Extremities.—Œdema. Redness. Gait unsteady; and knees converged, and walking painful, long standing impossible, he drags his feet and can hardly go up and down stairs; G. awkward, he often fell in crossing the floor, it hurt him to walk, pain in feet, < soles. Trembling; when sitting, lying or lifting legs, < r. *Cramp;* **with acute and paroxysmal pains. Neuralgic pains. Lightning-like pains** (Thall.). Tearing; < popliteal spaces, calves and soles. *Pain;* < movement and pressure, with redness and inflammation; < *anterior part of thighs and in calves,* so that it was difficult to rise in bed; encircling them; *paroxysmal,* also < movement, > gentle pressure. Bruised pain, < soles and knees, worse by paroxysms, with at times cramp. Rheumatic pain on pressure; R. pain in knees and feet and in muscular part of thighs and calves, the muscular pains excited by movement and accompanied by cramps. Intense reflex excitability from pressure on the painful parts, < l. Weakness; in afternoon; when walking; with stiffness; (walking difficult, < in the dark, at times with lancinations.) Paralytic sensation. Insensibility; and stiffness. Difficulty in walking; r. leg dragged; D. in moving r.; sudden D. in ascending stairs. Standing and walking impossible, when he tries to stand the thigh is flexed upon leg and leg upon foot, so that the balls and sole form a hollow. Paralysis; of r.; of peroneal muscles and extensors of toes.

Thigh.—Flexed upon pelvis from semi-flexion of leg upon thigh, caused by paralysis of triceps and anterior crural and contraction of their antagonizing muscles. Wasted in anterior part; gluteals and large extensor in front, while biceps and flexors from trochanter to tibia were very strong and contracted; W., with inability to stand upon leg, extend it or flex thigh upon abdomen, loss of motion in all muscles supplied by anterior crural nerve, on trying to raise leg it turned outward by action of biceps and in crossing leg over the other it must be lifted with the hands. Jerking in l. Spasmodic shaking above r. knee. Cramp. Crampy feeling after an hour's drive. Sticking; in anterior part; in posterior and inner parts; in region of r. hip in afternoon, then in r. hypochondrium, > walking; in r. hip in afternoon on moving r. arm towards l.; in r. when walking, then also in l.; *from hips extending to knees;* in forepart and in popliteal spaces and in tibial and peroneal surface of legs, < movement, > pressure, alternating with cramps in thighs; jerking, in inner and upper part of l. in afternoon. Tearing in middle of inner surface of l.; in forepart and in popliteal spaces; *in forepart of T. and knees, worse at intervals, < movement;* above l. knee in afternoon when standing, > rubbing, then sticking in r. hypochondrium after sitting. *Pain;* along r. sciatic nerve; in l. hip and r. knee; adductors of both and extensors of l., with pain on pressure; *paroxysmal;* (in hip-joints, < walking, it extended to malleoli, finally œdema, with pain on pressure and movement, afterwards mostly transferred to knees); paralytic, on ascending steps, and in knee and ankle; burning, in spots; bruised; in a spot in middle of l., a hand's breadth below groin, as if a tendon would snap, always at the beginning of a step. Drawing in r. hip-joint when lying. Weakness of r. T. and leg; W. in extensor and adductor muscles. Numbness over l. T. and buttock.

Knee.—Laxity of K. and ankle, so that gait was tottering. Jerking. Cramps; in popliteal spaces, calves, backs and soles of feet, temporarily > pressure and walking, legs and feet flexed, afterwards tearing. Lancinations; in r. in evening when standing, > moving it back and forth; through and through r.; extending to soles and intermittent heat in soles; intermittent, in K., calves and soles, > warmth of bed and pressure, between the paroxysms constriction; burning, in inner side of l. when sitting. Tearing in K. and soles, < movement, warmth of bed and firm pressure, > light friction, worse by paroxysms, during which there are cramps in feet; T. in popliteal space, calf and soles, < motion, > pressure, worse by paroxysms, during which there are cramps in feet; passing to soles, where they are the worst, also in backs of feet, toes and calves and popliteal spaces, varying in degree according to the order in which they are named, worse by paroxysms, < night and by walking, movement and heat, > rest, with burning, sometimes the cramps are felt in calves and soles, where there are pricking and formication, sometimes jerks through the whole body, < lower limbs. Pain; in bone in bend; popliteal spaces; deep in r. in morning on ascending steps; < inner part; in l., with effusion; *paroxysmal;* and under soles and between lower limbs, even in feet, making walking difficult; in zones in l. K. and ankle, with anæsthesia of legs, < l.; tearing jerking, preventing walking. Bruised pain; in popliteal spaces. Weight; when walking. Weakness; when he is fatigued; on ascending steps. Sudden bending when standing and walking, so that I fell. Stiffness. Inability to extend it.

Leg.—*Enlarged veins on calves, with varicose dilatations;* many reddish and bluish veins on calves. Swollen. R. flexed upon abdomen. Semi-flexed upon thigh, difficult to extend; r. S. upon thigh, extension impossible, thigh flexed upon abdomen, inability to stand upon r. limb alone; r. S. when left to itself while sitting or standing, when lying it is extended by mere mechanical movement; l. almost S., flexion and extension difficult. Trembling. Spasmodic contraction. Jerking in r. tibia. Cramp; *in calves;* r. calf; calves, < night; l. at night, ascending the whole body and affecting throat so that he could not speak. Sticking in calves. Tearing in l. towards instep in afternoon, on rubbing it extends into hollow of knee, then sticking in former place, > rubbing. Sharp pains in calves before the colic. Pain in l. in lower part; calves; r. calf; muscles of calves; at night, waking him often, > sudden jumping and hard rubbing; in tibia when walking; < *night;* in upper part of one, with swelling of principal cutaneous vein at back of r.; bruised, in morning after rising, > walking. Hyperæsthesia in muscles of calf. Throbbing in a spot on outside of r. calf when lying. Weakness; of r.; with flabbiness of muscles. Insensibility of posterior part of r. from two inches below knee to ankle, with a numb sensation. Falling asleep of l. Want of motor co-ordination, he strikes the ground with his heel when he puts his leg out, staggering if he walks with his eyes shut. Paralysis of r., with atrophy of r. thigh; P. of tibialis anticus and peronæus tertius.

Ankle.—Bony projection. Swelling of l., with pain in it; extending half way up legs. Œdema; and legs covered posteriorly with livid spots and superficial ulcerations. Pain; in malleoli; in l. extending to knee. Sprained sensation on outer side of r. in morning.

Foot.—Swollen. Œdema. Shortening, with paralysis and atrophy. Dorsum arched and sole hollowed. Twisted inward, abductors paralyzed, tibial region atrophied. Pointed downward, plantar surface hollowed, so that he can hardly stand, much less walk; l. pointed downward, toes firmly flexed, instep on the stretch, so that the heel is lifted high. Extended, it cannot be flexed, abducted or adducted; r., and it points downward, while the heel is drawn high up. When walking they are lifted like dead weights and when extended they strike hard upon the ground, by pressure against which they are flexed, he seems to move by skips and jumps; dragged along stiff when walking, inability to plant entire sole upon ground. One began to drag, and soon he could only creep, hand of that side soon affected. Cramplike contraction of muscles of l. sole during rest. Spasmodic working from side to side, and they often drew back out of the shoes, inability to draw on a boot, when sitting still the legs insensibly drew back till the feet got entangled under the chair, this drawing back of the leg made it difficult to ascend stairs, a man held the foot on the first step while a person behind assisted me to rise so as to place the other foot on the next stair, and the man held that foot in place, when descending stairs I straightened the whole limb before planting the foot upon the next stair. Cramp; in soles before the colic, with lancinations. Gout of l. Shooting from soles to hips when walking and standing. Pricking in soles; with formication. Tearing in soles; extending upward in r. heel. Pain; in soles; after a mustard foot bath, which removed the headache; remittent; heavy, gradually extending to legs and bowels; bruised, in soles. Soreness in soles in morning, > exercise and warmth; S. of soles so that he dreaded to touch the floor, with shooting extending to loins. Soft sensation in sole on touching ground. Heaviness. Weariness; in soles, < sitting, with heaviness. Diminished sensibility of back of r. Numbness. Falling asleep. Difficulty in putting it to the ground, soles seemed dead, and when stepping felt as if round sausages were under them. Lateral movement impossible. Paralysis of F. and toes, with tenderness of F.

Toes.—Swelling of great, with redness and pain; S. now of one, now of another joint, with pains and sleeplessness, finally extending to ankles, heels, etc.; articular, in great, at the same time as the tendinous tumefaction, with redness, heat and pain. Great joints enlarged by tophacæous deposits. Strongly flexed upon soles, can be slightly separated in way of flexion, extension impossible; bent upon soles, can neither be separated nor approximated; r. great strongly flexed upon sole; r. strongly bent upon metatarsus, they cannot be flexed upon foot nor separated in this way, foot strongly bent upon leg, incapable of flexion, can be abducted and adducted by extending it and causing the leg to move the whole foot at once. Painful drawing inward of two larger r. when standing and sitting, then drawing in hollow of r. knee, then also in hollow of l. knee, where there was sticking, afterwards numbness of toes, > afternoon when sitting. Cramp. Gout in four attacks, first in metatarso-phalangeal joint of l. great, afterwards in corresponding joint of r. great toe, then in l. knee, then in r. knee. Tearing in two first l., > walking. *Pain in great at night;* P. in tips. Drawing by nail of l. great, on walking this extended into ball of foot, > continued walking. Falling asleep of l. extending into instep, with crawling. Cannot extend T. nor flex foot upon leg. Extensors paralyzed, abduction and adduction prevented by want of power in interosseous muscles.

Skin.—**Yellow;** with thick ecthymatous pustules over whole body; livid, < face. Dirty yellow, and eye; and albuginea oculi; and flabby, with desquamation; < face, or earthy color. Sallow, dingy; S., clammy; dry, traversed by larger veins. *Pale.* Cachectic color. Peculiar dead, waxy hue. Light ashen color. Lead color; dingy. Bluish; dusky. Pale gray in folds, and dry. Livid, and lips and gums. Dark brown spots over whole body. Discolored. Face and most of limbs and body covered with white-lead deposit. Flabby.

Red, swollen spots on fingers. Hard, movable elevations where external radial muscle attaches to metacarpal bone. Phlegmonous swelling of back of hand and forearm, then abscess. Eruptions; disgusting. Scorbutic symptoms, with ulcer in lungs. Serous infiltration. Erythematous rash over whole breast. Inflammation, swelling, with itching vesicles that contain a yellow liquid, scabs, beneath which an offensive ichor exudes, and gangrene, with delirium and constipation; rapid I. from a small prick, rapid suppuration and rapid healing. Erysipelas in a wound on face (received in falling in epilepsy) spread rapidly over face and head, with nausea, vomiting, delirium, pulse 52, tongue coated white, headache, stitches. Petechiæ. Eczema in patches about face, neck and under arms. Red pimples on chest; that desquamate after twenty-four hours; itching P. containing clear water, on back of index and one on external condyle of l. wrist, with pain after scratching. Boil on outer side of r. thigh; sores somewhat like B. on back of thigh and somewhat above it. Suppuration comes to a stop and disappears. Pustules, with thick pus in angles of nose, that is red. Vesicles on legs, arms and face; forehead and nose. Gangrene. Bed-sores on sacrum and thighs.

Sticking; here and there on face; on soles. Burning in ulcers. Formication, on forearms and fingers; lower limbs; feet; r. great toe; soles; limbs at night; soles and instep, < r., when standing; soles, it feels as if he were walking on nutshells. Sensitiveness; to air; to touch, < arms and lids. Itching; over whole body; on face; between r. thumb and index; on thighs; of a dry tetter on r. tibia that usually had no sensation; in evening; < night; in a spot on inner side of r. wrist, with burning, < scratching, and after long scratching numbness; between l. thumb and index, > scratching; on coccyx above anus, > scratching; sticking, between l. middle and ring fingers. Insensibility of skin of r. lower limb, but not of subcutaneous tissues.

Sleep.—Yawning; an hour after dinner, with sleepiness; and stretching; constant short. *Sleepiness;* early in evening, and sound sleep; > open air; with heat over abdomen and redness of face. Easy falling asleep when talking and knitting. Sopor. **Sleeplessness;** from acute pain; from nightly aggravation of spasmodic pains in abdomen. *Sleep restless.* Talking in sleep. Starting up on falling asleep. Waking with a start and wakened whenever he stirs by the acuteness of the pain. Nightmare. Dreams; in evening, with talking; distressing; confused, anxious; frightful, of falling; pleasant; lovely, after midnight, of a distant beloved person; of stealing fruit in a garden; voluptuous, afternoons, with erections, without emissions.

Fever.—Chilliness; from morning till afternoon; towards evening, then fever; in open air; before the colic; during the colic, with fever; at the end of the crisis; when walking in the house; < towards evening, head dull, dizzy, with thirst, redness of face, soft, rapid pulse, but in bed external heat, with internal chilliness, at last skin hot, dry, pulse frequent, without thirst, after midnight sweat on chest, abdomen and head, after 2 A.M. sleep with confused dreams, next morning tongue coated, head dull, face pale, and on stepping sticking upward through head; as if liquid ice ran through his veins. Shivering; in limbs. Cold limbs; and face; nose; arms; *hands and feet;* hands, which are cyanotic; hands and forearms, with an asleep sensation; fingers; lower limbs; skin; as far as abdomen, as if seated in cold water, alternating with heat in abdomen; internal and external in paralyzed parts, < ends of affected limbs, < least draught of air.

Heat; after breakfast, with weakness of upper part of body, then weakness of hands and feet; in evening, with hot skin, rapid pulse and red face; with unquenchable thirst; with copious sweat; then sweat on knees; dry; internal, towards evening and at night. Flushes of heat; in afternoon, with redness of face and sweat on upper part on body; anxious, in afternoon, with sweat. Hectic fever. Inflammatory fever, with jaundice. Typhoid fever, with bilious vomiting, delirium and restlessness, afterwards epileptiform convulsion, then coma and death. Hot skin. Hot head, with coolness of rest of body, < hands; heat mounting to head, also with redness of face. Flashes of heat and sweat mounting to face; sudden heat in face and scalp, with redness of them while rest of body was cold and covered with cold sweat. Burning in tip of l. scapula; in limbs; in region of kidneys, diffused engorgement in l. loin, apparently perinephritis from calculus, with urinary fistula, but urine scanty and high-colored.

Sweat; during the colicky paroxysms; easy on exertion and at night, but afterwards dry skin; on face; contained urea; sticky; viscous, on paralyzed parts in morning; offensive, on soles; cold; cold, on forehead, hands and feet. **Dry skin.**

Podophyllum.

A tincture is made of the fresh root of the Podophyllum peltatum, L.

General Action.—An active cathartic, causing inflammation (and ulceration) of the whole intestinal canal, affecting chiefly the duodenum and rectum. It congests the liver and promotes the secretion of bile. It produces symptoms of dysentery and prolapsus of the rectum. Study also the symptoms referred to the uterus and right ovary.

Allies.—Chel., Iris, Sul. ac., Merc.

Generalities.—Sudden shocks of jerking pain. Nervous and crampy. Distress in evening after first sleep. *Weakness; during the pain in stomach;* with relaxed muscles and feeling as if body were bathed in sweat, which it was not. **Faintness, with sensation of emptiness in abdomen after stool** (Sul. ac.). Bordering on collapse, features pinched, limbs cold, pulse feeble. Stiffness on beginning to move. *Aggravation from 2 till 4 A.M. of all symptoms except weakness in epigastric region;* in morning, especially of abdominal symptoms, and amelioration in evening.

Head.—*Aching* in morning, with dulness and sleepiness; A. in morning, with heat in vertex; and fever; *alternating with diarrhœa.* Vertigo when standing in open air; V., with inclination to fall forward; with fulness over eyes. Frontal pain at 10 A.M., after stool, with feverishness and with dryness in forehead and eyes, transiently > bathing the parts with cold water; in l. protuberance, < afternoon; suddenly in evening, with sore throat; darting, obliging him to close eyes, with vertigo; heavy, with soreness. Pain in temples in forenoon, with drawing in eyes as if strabismus would follow; P. in temples and eyeballs, with heat and throbbing in temporal arteries; stunning, through T., > pressure. Pain in vertex in morning on rising. Pain in occiput as if head were being split open for two minutes, then a throbbing ache and heaviness so that head could not be raised from pillow.

Clinical.—Headache preceded by a blurring of vision, then gradually increasing pain, especially in the occiput, with nausea and vomiting (Iris).

Eyes.—Glazed in morning, and motionless. Sunken. Inflammation; in morning; with heavy pain and turgescence of vessels of conjunctiva; of lids. Smarting. Soreness of l., < inner canthus, with discomfort there, conjunctiva of l. ball red, < inner canthus. Heaviness, with occasional pains on vertex. Superficial ulceration of each cornea, its base white in r. eye and looking as if lead had been used, with general conjunctival congestion.

Nose and Face.—Nose pinched. *Soreness and pustules in nose.* Face pale. Face and eyes red in morning and skin about them discolored, the discoloration extended over face, forehead and front of neck during the day, next night pain in eyes prevented sleep, next day the parts were yellowish-red, pupils small, eyes painful and sensitive to light (local effects). Jaw fallen.

Mouth.—Teeth covered with dried mucus in morning. *Tongue white; coated white in morning, with much viscid mucus in mouth;* coated white, except centre; T. and neighboring glands swollen; T. and mouth dry in morning on waking. Salivation. Taste bad; sour; sweet to everything; as of fried liver, at night; lost.

Clinical.—Difficult dentition, with grinding of teeth, rolling the head, disagreeable breath, diarrhœa, etc.

Throat.—*Soreness extending to ears;* S. on l. side, < morning and on swallowing liquids. *Dryness.* Burning.

Stomach.—*Desire for something sour. Indifferent to food. Appetite lost;* impaired in morning, with unusual thirst for cold water. *Thirst;* towards evening; after eating. *Nausea;* in morning after rising; in afternoon, with *acidity;* > in bed; with diminution of pulse; *and retching. Vomiting of hot, frothy mucus; of contents of stomach, then of bile; of thick, dark green bile mixed with dark coagulated blood about every hour;* of contents of stomach, then of bitter, dark green fluid, from half a pint to a pint at each attack, and exhaustion so that she felt as if dying, could not raise her head, with each attack a painless stool, first constipated, then watery.

Such rapid and hard contractions in efforts to vomit that the wrenching pain caused sharp screams. Epigastrium and abdomen tympanitic and tender. Griping sticking in S. and abdomen at 3 A.M., transiently > pressure on abdomen, **about 4 A.M. offensive, yellow, undigested stool mixed with mucus,** *about* 10 A.M. *burning, acrid stool, with tenesmus and bearing down during and after it.* Pain at night, with thirst, burning and prostration; P. extending into abdomen after eating toast. Tenderness; and in abdomen, could scarcely bear the bed-clothes; and in abdomen, < motion. Throbbing in epigastrium, then diarrhœa. Oppression from cold water, with uneasiness, small quantities of the water were ejected, tasted bitter and burned œsophagus. Heat; as from hot steam, after breakfast and dinner. **Hollow sensation in epigastrium.** *Empty feeling* before supper, without hunger. *Weakness in epigastric region* from 2 A.M. till next morning.

Clinical.—Indigestion; food becomes acid. Hot eructations, violent efforts to vomit. Numerous gastric complications of uterine complaints.

Abdomen.—Distention in morning. *Flatulence;* in morning; in evening. Griping; during stool. *Pain;* at daylight, > external warmth and bending forward while lying on side, < lying on back; *with coldness, then heat and warm sweat;* then frequent liquid stools; occasionally; wandering, at 5 P.M. *Heat, with inclination to stool.* Colon, rumbling in ascending; pain in ascending; *pain in transverse at 3 A.M., then diarrhœa.* Hypochondrium, fulness in r., with flatulence; sticking in r., < eating; twisting pain in r., with heat in it; sensation of flatulence in l.; dragging close under l. ribs. Cutting on sides of A., with desire for stool. Hypogastrium, bloating and tenderness; sticking above pubes and along spermatic cords; pain in H. and r. ovary in afternoon.

Clinical.—Chronic inflammation of the liver, with fulness and pain; the pains involve the whole right side, associated with jaundice. Gall-stone colic, with jaundice and twisting pain. Duodenitis, with jaundice. Catarrhal inflammation of the bowels, with hot, watery stools. Ulceration of the duodenum.

Rectum and Anus.—*Aggravation of internal piles, protrusion of rectum after stool* (Ign.), *sudden motion, such as sneezing and mental excitement, sometimes prolapsed for days, owing to the swelling and congestion.* Discharge of mucus. Too much bearing down at stool, as from inactivity of rectum. Ineffectual desire. Intermittent desire from after supper till going to bed, woke at 2 A.M. with the desire and sticking in abdomen, stool about 2.30 A.M., did not sleep well the rest of the night on account of sticking in abdomen, the pain > flexing thighs on abdomen.

Clinical.—Hæmorrhoids, frequently with prolapsus ani following confinement; associated with prolapsus uteri. Prolapsus of the rectum.

Stool.—**In morning, with heat and pain in anus,** *and urging.* With pain and nausea. **Liquid, yellow,** *every hour; L., green, frequent,* also with pain and griping; *L., with colic.* **Diarrhœa; in morning and through forenoon, then natural stool in evening;** *immediately after eating and drinking; alternating with constipation;* frequent. Solid and small at 9 P.M., copious, loose one at 12 P.M., next morning two thin ones, with griping and chilliness. **Green in morning.** Muco-gelatinous, small, infrequent, with flatulence and pain in *region of sacrum.* Frequent.

Clinical.—Diarrhœa; stools profuse, gushing, usually yellowish in color and very offensive; generally worse in the morning, either painless or preceded by violent colic; associated with prolapsus ani and sometimes with pains in the sacrum; in cholera morbus we may find this drug indicated even when there are cramps of the calves and of other muscles. Diarrhœa in hot weather; dentition. Diarrhœa worse from 3 to 9 A.M., then a natural stool towards evening. Constipation, with prolapsus ani and sinking sensation in the abdomen as if the intestines would drop through the pelvis. Dysentery; it has not infrequently been found to be an epidemic remedy, especially in the South, usually characterized by prolapsus ani, sinking feeling in the abdomen, nausea and efforts to vomit. Chronic dysentery, discharges like meat-washings, severe tenesmus, burning pain deep in rectum, extremely weak digestion. Diarrhœa, stools profuse, containing undigested food, extremely fetid.

Urinary and Sexual Organs.—Micturition frequent and scanty; M. painful. Urine red. Inflammation of scrotum or eyes, seldom of both; of scrotum, with pustules. *Sensation in female genitals as if they would fall out when at stool.* After-pains, with strong bearing down. *Symptoms of prolapsus of uterus, with pain in sacrum, flatulence, infrequent, muco-gelatinous stools.* **Pain in uterus and r. ovary** (Apis).

Clinical.—Nocturnal enuresis. Suppressed menses of girls, with great pressure, hæmorrhoids, etc. Prolapsus uteri, especially following parturition, with more or less prolapsus ani. A great weakness of the abdominal walls during pregnancy, generally > lying on the stomach. Ovarian tumor of the right side, pains extend to the shoulder or down the thigh. Endometritis; thick, transparent leucorrhœa. Prolapsus of the uterus and vagina after parturition, with ovarian pain, backache, etc. Numerous cases of acute and chronic ovaritis, right side.

Respiratory Organs and Chest.—Suffocating sensation at night on lying down. Short breath. Inclination to breathe deeply, sighing. Snapping in r. lung like the breaking of a thread, on deep inspiration. Pain in chest, < deep inspiration. Oppression of chest in morning, with inclination to inspire deeply, but prevented from doing so by constriction of chest.

Heart and Pulse.—Sticking in heart. Sensation as if H. ascended to throat. Palpitation in morning, with rapid, small pulse; P. from exertion or emotion; from physical exertion in persons subject to rumbling in ascending colon, with heavy sleep, and fatigue in morning on waking, then drowsiness in forenoon. Pulse rapid. Pulse slow; and weak and small, also with nausea. Pulse weak.

Neck and Back.—Pain in nape, < motion, with soreness. Stiffness of nape, with soreness of muscles of neck and shoulder. *Pain under r. scapula* (Chel.); between scapulæ in morning; between S., < night and morning and by motion, with soreness; in loins when walking and standing, with sensation as if back bent inward; in loins, < night and motion, with coldness; in loins, < a misstep and walking over uneven ground.

Extremities.—Aching, < night. Tingling. Weakness of joints, < knees; wrists, with soreness on touch. Spasmodic sensation in r. thigh and leg. Pain in thighs, legs and knees, < standing; P. in l. hip like rheumatism from cold, < ascending stairs, with weakness of it. Cracking in knees on motion. Pain in l. knee, leg and foot. Heaviness of knees and stiffness as after a long walk. Pain in r. leg in afternoon, with *cramp.* Sharp pain in outer and upper part of l. foot.

Skin.—Rubefacient and vesicant effects. Scabs on arms and legs. Minute vesicles filled with serous fluid, which soon changes to whitish or yellowish pus, with superficial inflammation, the pustules usually slow in healing. Itching on body and arms, and on scratching blotches like hives.

Sleep.—**Sleepiness; in daytime, < forenoon,** *with rumbling in abdomen;* early in evening. Sleep too heavy. Difficult waking in morning. *Unrefreshed in morning on waking. Restless in forepart of night. Moaning, with half-closed eyes.* Rising up in bed without waking.

Fever.—Chilliness; in afternoon, then fever and headache, next day fever and headache. Shivering and prostration. Cold feet. Intermittent, quotidian, tertian and quartan fever. Heat; in afternoon, with occasional coldness, not > heat of stove, but > warm covering in bed; in flashes up back after stool; passing over face and head. Sweat, so that it dropped off finger-tips; S. of feet in evening; cold S.

Clinical.—It has been found useful in some cases of remittent fever, with numerous "bilious" symptoms.

Polyporus Officinalis.

A tincture is made of the fresh fungus.

Generalities.—Shuddering, nervous rather than from chilliness. Tonic effects, afterwards enervating. *Aching in all joints of body and limbs;* rheumatic and neuralgic pains; sudden, sharp, momentary pain in r. wrist, where the pulse is felt, extending two inches up the artery, when riding, soon in r. shoulder-joint, thence outward to deltoid, at 2 P.M., when writing, the same pain above elbow and external to tendon of biceps, then on internal side of l. knee, at 9 P.M. in inner border of r. foot, then in r. arm, and then in l. side of neck. Malaise. *Weakness; with depression and disinclination to physical or mental exertion; with aching in all large joints; with uneasiness.* Amelioration after 2 P.M.

Mind.—*Despondent; and morose.* Dulness.

Head.—*Aching;* in morning on waking, lasting all day, < stooping or shaking head, with soreness in brain; all night; < motion; > *eructations, with nausea;* and in jaws and teeth; semi-lateral. Dulness. Fulness. Light; in morning, with hollow feeling and deep frontal pain; *light dizzy feeling.* Twinge over l. brow. *Pain in forehead;* deep; all day; at 8 A.M., < walking; in evening; < walking; < motion; oppressive, in F. and temples all day; deep drawing, with frequent nausea and cutting in epigastrium; heavy, at night, < motion; heavy, through F. and temples. Heaviness in forehead. Dulness in forehead. Tightness across forehead, with headache; in evening. Frequent cutting in temples. Pain in temples; lacerating, in r. at 9.40 P.M.; sharp; neuralgic; neuralgic in l.; neuralgic, in temples, face and teeth. Aching soreness through temples.

Eyes and Face.—Pain in eyeballs; deep drawing. Face bluish.

Mouth.—Teeth felt as if being forced out. Soreness of gums; and of teeth. *Tongue coated white; coated yellow;* coated light brown; red at tip, coated yellow at base; *yellow;* prickling in end. *Taste bitter;* and sweet; and flat; and coppery; T. coppery; flat, metallic or coppery; sweetish, nauseous.

Throat.—Rawness all the afternoon and evening, with scraping. Feeling in fauces as if I should vomit, but no nausea.

Stomach.—Appetite invigorated. Desire for sour things, which always relieved the symptoms. Little appetite; for breakfast; for dinner; *lost;* lost for supper. *Thirst.* Acid eructations, with heartburn. *Nausea;* < throat and fauces; frequent, but momentary; with loose stool. Vomiting of a bitter, sour, watery fluid.

Cutting, and in abdomen; in epigastrium, waking at midnight, next night waking at 5 A.M., with distress in umbilicus and urging to stool. Cutting lancinating pain. Sharp pain during the day, with almost constant borborygmus; S. pain in epigastrium; all day, < walking, with deep distress in it and dull pain in r. hypochondrium. Pain; in epigastrium; in l. epigastric region and in region of spleen. Burning pain, with dragging pain in hypochondrium. Burning distress in epigastrium and r. hypochondrium; in region of S. and liver, extending to umbilicus, < 10 A.M., with urging to stool, continues after stool. Burning in epigastrium. Coldness, then burning. Feeling of a lump in it in evening.

Abdomen.—Rumbling. Emission of flatus; fetid in evening. Much flatus in A., with feeling as before diarrhœa. Cutting before stools. Lacerating pains here and there at 3 P.M., then located for an hour in hypogastrium, with inclination to stool, at 9.40 P.M. (after stool) in hypogastrium extending to r. hypochondrium. Pain; all night; on touch. Uneasiness; at night; from increased vermicular action; with diarrhœa; as before stool. Sensation as before diarrhœa.

Hypochondria.—Stabbing pain in r. lobe of liver and in lower dorsal region on full inspiration. Sharp pain in region of spleen; and liver and abdomen. Pain in liver; r. lobe of liver, lower part of epigastrium and upper part of umbilicus; r. lobe of liver and in umbilicus, with urging to stool. Dragging in r.; in region of r. lobe of liver; in r. lobe of liver at night. Heavy drawing pain in region of r. lobe of liver, extending through to dorsal region. Heavy pain in region of r. lobe of liver after morning stool. Distress in r. and in umbilicus. Burning distress all the afternoon in region of gall-bladder, with heavy aching in it and cutting in epigastrium and hypochondrium.

Umbilical Region.—Cutting in umbilicus. Sharp pain before stool; S. pain in U. and hypogastric regions. Pain; all day, and in region of transverse and descending colon. Distress; and in hypogastric region, with desire for stool; between stomach and umbilicus all day, with faintness and fever. Uneasiness in subumbilical region, with inclination to stool (an hour after the usual morning stool), during the stool shooting on each side of umbilicus, towards iliac, then to floor of pelvis, in a ring around rectum.

Hypogastrium.—Pain; in morning; in region of transverse and descending colon; burning, in region of transverse colon. Sudden distress, then light-colored papescent stools. Uneasiness all day, as before diarrhœa.

Rectum and Anus.—Pain in anus. Discomfort about anus, < 1 P.M. Desire for stool; with pain in anus; with much flatulence. Disposition to strain when at stool.

Stool.—Watery, copious, with pains; W., copious, forcible, frequent. Mixed with water and contained undigested food. Loose, painful; L., with nausea; *L.*, at 6 A.M., mushy and mixed with mucus at 6 P.M., next (third) day mushy at 5 A.M., then heavy aching in region of r. lobe of liver, after 8 P.M. dark stool mixed with bile and mucus, then aching in dorsal region extending to shoulders, fourth day at 6 A.M. black, mixed with bile and mucus, before it voided a drachm of white mucus, after 8 A.M. a stream of bile, mucus and black fæcal matter, then burning distress in region of stomach and liver extending to umbilicus, at 10 A.M. copious stool of water and black fæcal matter, then desire to strain, then the same symptoms as before, fifth morning hard, black, lumpy stool mixed with bile and mucus, at 1 P.M. soft, black, fetid, then distress between stomach and navel, sixth morning, dark, papescent, at 9 A.M. mushy, with distress in region of liver and small intestines, at 6 P.M. papescent, then a teaspoonful of blood with tenesmus. Mushy, copious, then uneasiness in umbilical region, next day scanty stool.

Constipation. Dry stool; and lumpy the first part of the day, but in evening watery, yellow and frequent; and lumpy, dark, then stools mixed with bile and mucus, stools mixed with blood, stools thin and yellow. Contained something like drops of oil, clear and white. Dark, once to three times a day. Two in morning. Copious. Scanty.

Urinary and Sexual Organs.—Frequent desire to urinate. Frequent micturition; at night; and profuse, pale; of high-colored urine, with pain in region of kidneys. Urine increased; and light-colored. *Urine scanty and high-colored.* Sharp pain in glans penis at 10 P.M. after getting into bed.

Chest and Pulse.—Darting pain in l. lung, with suffocating feeling, causing me to rise in bed. Pain in l. lung; extending through l. scapula; P. in ribs, < motion. Piercing pain in region of heart, < motion. Pulse rapid; at night; and full, wiry; and full, soft.

Neck and Back.—Drawing pain in l. side of neck at 10 P.M. after getting into bed. *Pain in back;* at 5 P.M., with stiffness; with stiffness; *and in hips;* and in limbs; drawing P. through back and legs; rheumatic P. in spine and limbs. Shooting between scapulæ, extending up nape, then soreness of occipital region, with disposition to throw head back. Aching in lumbar region; all day; at night; with weakness of it; and in dorsal region.

Extremities.—Pain in all joints; in afternoon; *P. in arms and legs;* in arms and hands. Rheumatic pain in all joints; and limbs. Weakness of arms and legs. Drawing in r. upper arm at 10 P.M. after getting into bed. Lancinations in hip-joint. Pain in thighs and bends of knees; in feet and ankles; *in knees and ankles,* < motion. Rheumatic pains in shin-bones, < walking. *Weakness of knees.*

Skin.—Itching over whole body, < between scapulæ and on forearms.

Sleep.—*Disposition to yawn and stretch; with chilliness. Restless; and disturbed by dreams.* Much dreaming. Frightful dreams of water.

Fever.—*Chilliness;* all night, and fever; *in open air, with coldness of nose;* then fever and sweat; then pain in hypogastrium, then in hypochondria. Coldness of nose; between shoulders; along spine, with hot flashes and disposition to yawn and stretch; *creeping along spine, intermingled with hot flashes;* creeping up back to nape, < between scapulæ; cold hands and feet. Heat all day and night; H. on waking at 1 A.M. Face hot and flushed. *Skin hot and dry.* Heat and dryness of hands; and feet, also at night; of palms. Sweat all night; at midnight on waking.

Clinical.—This remedy has been used for chills and fever, characterized by rush of blood to the head, vertigo, prickly sensation in the face which is hot and flushed; chill, with darting pain in the back and limbs, heat with headache and flushed face, perspiration not profuse; rarely any thirst; during the apyrexia, disordered liver, jaundice, headache, constipation, etc.; especially adapted to chronic cases.

Populus Candicans.

A tincture is made of the fresh buds, which in spring are covered with a resinous gum.

Generalities.—Emaciation. Rheumatic and gouty pains in muscles to ends of fingers and toes. Bruised, sore, swollen, inflamed, with burning pain; B. feeling the next day after a fitful, restless, dreamy sleep. Whole body feels swollen, bruised, lame, sore and painful, exhausted as in dry, sultry weather, movements heavy, labored, clumsy, stinging, restless irritation *as if an eruptive fever would come to the surface,* feeling as if sweat would break out. Burning irritation of eyes, nose, skin, mucous membrane of mouth, throat and air-passages and oppression of respiration and circulation. Catarrhal feverish state of mucous surfaces. Pulmonic, cardiac and capillary circulation oppressed, feels as if death must result, as if there must be fatal organic lesions. Weakness. Stiffness of muscles, tendons, ligaments, with lameness and with dry feeling in cartilages, as if lame. *Insensibility of surface, < back and abdomen, so that rubbing and pounding were borne without pain and insisted upon for the sake of warmth.* Aggravation morning; *A. before menses.*

Mind.—Hopeless foreboding, < sleep. Fear and anguish. Feels unable to do anything, but as though something must be done, as if the will were paralyzed as to power, with the sense of suffering increased, no rest anywhere, mind anxious, restless, oppressed and all functions seem spellbound, as if they must act and cannot, cannot bear to see or be with any one, but restless, unhappy, fearful and foreboding when alone, as if mind and body must be in action and yet withheld from action by oppression and obstruction.

Head and Eyes.—Confusion in head, with expansive fulness, all parts feel lame, swollen, inflamed, thickened, painful, burning, throbbing in head and brain, < cerebellum and cerebro-spinal axis, dulness of the senses as from congestion. Boring through l. temple. Weight on vertex. Sensation as if l. eye were twisted during the headache.

Face and Mouth.—Face yellow. Tongue white, dry; T. feels thick and numb; T. and mouth feel burnt and dry, but are moist, wants drink, but can take only a little and feels worse after food and drink, as if mouth and stomach were burnt, cold, warm, hot, sour, bitter and sweet things are repulsive, nothing is relished. Speech thick. Taste bitter; T. sweet in morning.

Stomach and Abdomen.—Appetite lost, loathes meat. Nausea, with sinking in epigastrium. Vomits bile. Wears her clothes loose. Flatulent colic doubling the body forward. Pain in r. hypochondrium, with enlargement.

Stool, Urine and Sexual Organs.—Stools watery, green, alternating with constipation. Constipation, bowels feel hot and dry. Urine strong, high-colored, hot, scanty; U. increased, variously colored, red, dark, light, phosphates abundant. Menses scanty, usually delaying, afterwards absent, then abundant, early, with dysmenorrhœa, > hot clothes.

Respiratory Organs, Heart and Pulse.—Dry cough when tired. Suffocation. Breathing dry, asthmatic, with dyspnœa, sits bent forward, < *lifting arms.* 'Pain in heart, stitches. Heart's sounds irregular, usually muffled, with a systolic murmur, < *before menses.* Palpitation when rising or lying on l. side, with vertigo. Pulse rarely exceeded 60.

Back and Extremities.—Numbness in back radiating from spine. Burning weariness in small of back. *Finger-ends thickened, horny, insensible to pinching and pricking.*

Skin.—Harsh, generally dry and cold, with *burning stinging below the surface,* as if eruption would appear, rarely blotches and fine papules. Burning prickling on face, chest and hands, the parts became dark red and swollen, and there were blisters as large as walnuts, hanging down like bags of water, with watery, acrid, sticky oozing, external heat like coals of fire on skin, *at times internal heat, with cool skin, > hot applications,* the eruption returned each year with *fear* and expectation of death, *loquacity*, discussing repeatedly her symptoms, vertigo from lifting head.

Sleep.—Sleepless after midnight, with restlessness, < from early morning till noon. Dreams frightful, vivid; D. fearful, after fitful sleep.

Fever.—Sudden coldness of extremities, with numbness of them and heat of head. Fever and unrest; F., with congestion of brain, fulness, heaviness, dulness, soreness, with expansive pressure, as if swollen, deadening heat in head as if scorched by the sun, vertigo, oppression of vital forces and circulation as if overheated, fatigue, faintness and burning, throbbing oppression. Dry heat. Heat of cerebellum and neck, with feeling as if the capillary circulation were congested and oppressed. Sweat on head and neck.

Populus Tremuloides.

A tincture is made of the fresh inner bark of the "aspen" poplar.

Nervous excitement. Fulness about head. Nausea, vomiting and slight bilious purging, with burning in stomach. Warm, pungent sensation in stomach, then glow of heat on whole surface. Urine copious; *with irritation of bladder and urethra.*

Clinical.—Catarrh of the bladder; urine contains large quantities of mucus and pus, severe tenesmus, especially in old people. Inflammation of the bladder, with pressure and aching in the pelvis. Urethritis, micturition painful, scalding, especially during pregnancy. Valuable for tenesmus of the bladder following laparotomy or ovariotomy.

Prunus Spinosa.

A tincture is made of the fresh flower-buds.

Generalities.—Trembling of whole body. Stitches in various muscular parts. Restlessness, with constant running about, shortness of breath and oppression of chest. Weariness in morning and seemed to have had no sleep, with aching in all bones, especially bruised feeling in thighs.

Mind.—Morose. Joyless, satisfied with nothing.

Head.—*Pressing-asunder pain, so that he almost lost his thoughts; pain beneath skull as if skull would be pressed outward by a plug.* Pain as from heat of sun. Painless compression in brain from all sides. Heaviness; and dizziness. Vertigo and obscuration in forehead. **Shooting from r. frontal bone through brain and out at occiput.** *Painful jerks in forehead shooting backward.* Pain in r. frontal bone, extending through brain into occiput. Pressure outward in forehead; in r. eminence; beneath l. bone; in sinciput; in r. side of sinciput after dinner; in F., taking away his senses. Sore pain in forepart of head, > thinking intently about it. *Twinging in r. temporal bone, extending outward; in r. T. bone, extending into ear. Acute nervous pain in upper part of r. temporal bone, < pressure. Pressure outward beneath upper part of r. T. bone; P. outward extending from beneath r. temporal bone to frontal bone, < pressure. Pain in r. side of vertex as if a sharp corner pressed against it. Jerking sticking posteriorly in l. parietal bone. Jerking thrust through r. hemisphere of brain on motion.* Nervous pain in l. side of occiput, that took away his thoughts. Pain extending outward in occiput; in l. side of bone. Pain in O. on stooping, so that his thoughts vanished; sore P. in l. side of O., extending forward and into some l. teeth. Pressure outward in l. side of occipital bone. Sticking in scalp on occiput.

Eyes.—**Pain in r. ball as if inner part of eye would be torn out.** Lids closed though she was not weary. Itching in l. inner canthus; in r. outer, < margins of lids.

Clinical.—Ciliary neuralgia, severe pain in the right eyeball, as if the eye would burst, shooting like lightning through the brain, to the occiput, sometimes involving all the parts around the eye. Chorio-retinitis in myopia. Irido-choroiditis. Irido-cyclitis. Opacities of the vitreous.

Ears, Nose and Face.—Pain in l. ear; *pressing asunder in r.* Pressing-asunder pains above nasal bones. Tickling in middle of r. nostril as if he would sneeze. Irritation to sneeze and sneezing. Itching sticking on upper part of malar-bone.

Mouth.—Teeth. *Sticking in various;* in l. lower incisors. *Piercing nervous pain in last upper molar. Nervous pain in last l. lower molar as if it would be taken out. Pain as if teeth would be taken out; the pain also shoots from one to another. Wrenching pain in last lower molar; in several molars when anything warm is taken into mouth.* Bubbling pain in last r. upper molar as if it were taken out. Pain in second l. upper anterior molar. Pain as from cold water in mouth; P. in l. lower incisor and canine as from a cold drink immediately after a warm one. Indescribable sensation in several, compelling him to bite them together, which relieved.

Tongue covered with white mucus posteriorly, clean in middle. Sticking in r. side of tip of T. *Burning in tongue as if it had been burnt,* > when eating, but returning. Itching crawling in tip of tongue and in anterior teeth. Taste slimy. Taste bitter in morning. T. pasty after dinner.

Throat.—Pinching in r. submaxillary gland. Scraping, causing hacking cough; S. in evening on going to sleep, with rawness, provoking cough. Crawling, causing hacking cough; C. upward in pharynx, provoking cough.

Stomach.—Seized with hunger at times, but satiated after a few morsels. Satiated constantly. Nausea, with loathing of food and drink, so that he must lie down, then frequent diarrhœa. *Distention of pit;* after a few spoonfuls of soup; *with shortness of breath,* so that she must rest three or four times on a flight of stairs. Pressure in pit so that she could scarcely breathe.

Abdomen.—*Ascites, with loss of appetite, scanty micturition, hard, nodular stool discharged with pain in rectum.* Cutting transversely through, as before diarrhœa, preventing sleep. Cramps from incarceration of flatus; C. > bending forward, with pain on breathing; *obliging careful walking so that A. should not be shaken, otherwise aggravation of urinary troubles.* Colic, then profuse diarrhœa; C., with desire for stool, as after taking cold; as if he had eaten much fruit and then drunk water; as after cold, wet weather; as before diarrhœa; twisting, with incomplete emission of flatus, as before diarrhœa. Constriction so that she could not lie on back or sides. Itching crawling beneath skin.

Sticking in r. posterior and lower lobe of liver, which in walking takes away his breath. Pain in hepatic region; < standing; beneath r. lobe of liver. Pain in upper A. Pinching in spots in r. side. Pain in r. side at night, so that she could not lie upon it; as if something were forcing through r. side opposite navel; in r. side below umbilicus. Swashing like a bladder filled with liquid in r. side of hypogastrium. Sticking in r. groin, > pressure. *Cramp in bladder from pressure of flatus, so that he must bend double.* Pressure outward in region of r. inguinal ring, as if a hernia would force through.

Rectum and Anus.—Bleeding after hard stool. Involuntary discharge of offensive water at night in a case of ascites, then the swelling in r. side of abdomen constantly diminished and the heaviness caused by the swelling disappeared from the side. *Cramplike pain as if an angular body pressed inward in r. side of R. an inch above anus.* Cramplike bubbling in R. when sitting. *Burning in A. as from salt in a wound, after slimy diarrhœa.* Itching in A. Ineffectual desire for stool.

Stool.—Thin, but sluggish. Hard and not daily. Like that of a dog, in small, broken pieces, with sticking in rectum.

Urinary Organs.—**Tenesmus of bladder** *every quarter of an hour. Burning pain in sphincter. Burning biting in bladder and urethra, with efforts to urinate.* Cramp in bladder preventing sleep at night. *Ulcerative pain in urethra so that he dared not take hold of it. Burning biting in urethra.* **Burning pains** *on ineffectual efforts to urinate, so that he must bend up. Momentary relief as the urine passes, but there remains sticking in glans, which causes spasm of urethra, with tenesmus recti. He is hurriedly impelled to urinate,* **but the urine seems to pass into glans and then to return and cause pain in urethra.** *Strangury.* Obliged to make great pressure to urinate. Micturition six or seven times at night, of half a pint each time, preceded by the opposite condition. Micturition in a thready form, with pressure to stool. (Micturition in two streams, as if urethra had two openings.) Urine biting and hot. Urine scanty and brown. U. clear, light wine-yellow, depositing a sediment varying from white to sky-blue.

Clinical.—Numerous cases of dysuria, usually neuralgic in origin.

Sexual Organs.—Prepuce retracted from glans and penis small. Pinching on l. side of scrotum. Agreeable itching in lower part of scrotum, > scratching. Painful throbbing in female. Leucorrhœa making her weak; L. excoriating and staining yellow. Discharge of blood from vagina daily for eight or ten weeks, more watery the longer it lasted. Menses watery. Menses recurred profusely every fourteen days, with pain in small of back. Itching tickling in region of ovaries, not > scratching.

Respiratory Organs.—Voice rough and hoarse. Tickling in trachea on inspiration, provoking cough. Crawling in upper part of trachea, causing cough. Cough from tickling beneath larynx, renewed by holding breath. Whistling cough. **Respiration anxious, short**; *R. short and wheezing when walking. R. difficult, with anxiety about heart.* Breath seems to remain sticking in pit of stomach.

Clinical.—Like its relative Laurocerasus, it has been found useful in respiratory and cardiac complaints, dyspnœa, with palpitation, sense of suffocation, etc. Cardiac dropsy. Enlargement of the heart, with œdema of the feet.

Chest.—Sticking in middle of l. side, not affected by inspiration; S. in r. lower posterior sides of ribs on pressure, and pain as from internal suppuration; in fleshy part of l. mamma on deep inspiration when walking and sitting, extending to every side and above l. shoulder; intermittent, in middle of r. side, preventing inspiration. Pain from talking, with sensation as if she would become hoarse and lose the power to talk; P. beneath sternum and oppression of chest from fulness of pit of stomach and abdomen; pulling tensive, in l. side, < inspiration; externally on l. lower part as if a sharp corner pressed against it. Bruised pain in large pectoral muscles on touch. Seemed pressed inward, pain internally on breathing. *Tightness in upper part of l. Heaviness and oppression; H. in l., obliging deep breathing; in lower part, with anxiety there, often compelling deep breathing.*

Neck and Back.—Pain in nape involving occiput on stooping. *Stiffness of back as from an injury.* Sticking between scapulæ on deep breathing, extending to lumbar vertebræ and taking away his breath. Pain near spine as if a plug were forced inward two inches below l. scapula on stooping. Sticking from r. loin towards umbilicus, taking away his breath; piercing deep inward beneath crest of ilium, taking away his breath, < lying backward. Sensation as from suppuration in lumbar vertebræ, < lying, > gentle motion, when it extended to hip-joint and caused a sensation as if ligaments were too short, then he cannot lie on either side on account of pain in hip. Pain in small of back; *when sitting.*

Upper Extremities.—Suppurative pain in l. axillary glands. Swollen sensation in l. axillary gland. Pain on top of r. shoulder, ending in deltoid, preventing him from raising arm. Paralytic pain in l. shoulder-joint, extending across chest; in l. elbow, extending to wrist. Pinching in r. elbow, with pain on motion. Forearm, jerking pain in l.; P. as from a blow on l.; P. as if burnt on outer side of r.; tensive P. in muscles of l. impeding motion; P. as from stiffness in r. when writing, so that he could scarcely hold the pen; cramplike pressure on outer side of r., < grasping. Wrenching pain in r. wrist during rest. Pain in r. wrist as if a bursa would form. Cramplike constriction in r. hand, extending to tips of fingers.

Fingers.—Pinching shooting in r. thumb, then in l. Constriction in two r. middle. Pain between l. thumb and index; wrenching, in r. thumb when writing, so that he nearly dropped the pen; spasmodic, in l. thumb; *as from stiffness in r. thumb;* as if burned on outer side of r. little; pulling P. extending from l. through arm into l. pectoral muscles. Painful pulling forward in l. thumb. Painful drawing in r. fourth. Bruised pain in ball of little; in metacarpal joint of l. thumb. Paralytic pain in r. thumb.

Lower Extremities.—Staggering. Uneasiness. Needle-like sticking here and there in thighs and nates, so that he scratches, which causes a sensation of hot needles. Tearing externally in middle of r. thigh. Pinching high up on inner side of r. thigh. Pain in middle of r. thigh; P. in hip, < forenoon, scarcely felt in afternoon; tensive, on inner surface of l. T. Weariness in hip-joints. Pinching in hollow of r. knee. Pain in margins of bones of l. knee; twitching, in l. knee; wrenching, in r. during rest; sprained, in r.; as from stiffness on inner side of l. when walking. Sensation about r. knee as from steam. Weakness of knees; when standing. Pain in tendo-achillis as if it would be torn off; P. in tendo-achillis that often is pulsating; as if a plug were pressed against inner side of l. calf; bruised, in middle of l. fibula; paralytic, extending upward in r. leg. *Sprained pain* *in l. ankle; below l. outer malleolus.* Suppurating pain in r. sole. Sticking in ball of l. great toe. Pain in great toe, extending forward, as if last phalanges would be pulled off. Tense pain in l. toes.

Skin.—Seems tense on thighs and calves on ascending stairs, with swollen sensation in the parts. Itching sticking in various parts at night, waking him, > scratching. Itching in middle of r. thigh externally, pimples after scratching; I. in tips of various fingers, as if frozen; sticking, on inner side of thigh and on back, that at last, if he stopped scratching, changed to twitching or pulsation.

Sleep.—Fell asleep when reading after dinner. Slept quietly for some hours on becoming warm in bed, but no more all night. Sleep light. Sleep restless, she was wakeful almost all night. When she woke after a few hours' sleep she was as wide awake as if she had slept all night. Early waking. Late falling asleep and early waking, but seemed to have slept enough. Sleep mingled with dreams and fantasies. Dream of having boils. Dream that he was writing on a table covered with dirt and as he moved the clean paper it became smeared with butter and fat.

Fever.—Chilly and stretchy; C. towards evening. Burning on legs, so that he must pull off his boots. General dry heat, with redness of prepuce and redness and painfulness of glans; dry heat except on arms, < genitals, partly > sweat, > in bed. Sweat on face during sleep.

Psorinum.

A tincture was made of the pus from mature pustules on the hands of a healthy negro who was probably afflicted with the "itch" (C. Hering).

Generalities.—*Looks pale, exhausted and thin, his clothing is too large for him.* Hot trembling over whole body in morning during rush of business, with hoarseness, good humor and love for his business. Soreness. Gouty pains in l. toe, both knees and back. (Old rheumatic pains in neck, head, shoulders, back, stomach, etc., after putting on too light clothing in spring, with eructations, irregular stools and twitching in l. eye.) *Stormy weather affects him,* he feels restlessness in his blood a few days beforehand; S. weather makes him sick and causes hæmorrhoidal troubles. *Weakness;* towards evening, > going to bed; *after riding in a wagon; from a little labor.* Sensation when the sun shines upon her as if it pushed her down, she had to rest in the shade in order to walk on. Heaviness of whole body as before intermittent fever. Amelioration in morning; A. in fresh air; when lying.

Clinical.—Frequently indicated for persistent weakness after debilitating diseases, depressed in mind and body. General anæmia, aversion to food, with foul taste.

Mind.—Good humor in morning, he works with pleasure. Great humor, full of fun. Lively, enjoys everything. Pictures the future in the brightest colors. Excitable before sleep; E., vexed with everything. **Fear. Anxiety**; when riding in a carriage; with trembling of hands and restlessness. **Melancholy;** *so that she could commit suicide, then is full of phantasms,* peevishness and lachrymation; alternating suddenly with liveliness; alternating with frolicsomeness. *Despair, fear of failing in business; D.,* he wishes to die in spite of the best hopes. *Ill humor;* in morning; *and constant thoughts of dying;* if spoken to frequently; could weep about everything. Quarrelsome; in morning; in evening. Affected by every moral impression so that she trembles over the whole body. Disinclination to work; to ride in a carriage, then desire to ride all the time, even in bad weather. Sentimental.

Inability to rid himself of ideas which first appeared to him in a dream. Thinking that he understood what he had read he tried to explain it and found that he did not understand it. Memory lost; so that she does not recognize the room after looking out of the window.

Clinical.—Hypochondriac, thinks he will never recover. Cannot apply his mind to work. Melancholia, religious.

Head.—Sticking, with weakness, she had to lie down towards 7 P.M., and soon fell asleep, copious sweat at night, which relieved her. Thrusts. Tearing; (which he formerly had) this time with fever and general arthritic pains. *Aching* in evening; A., with eructations; with thirst, coldness and with dryness of mouth and lips; intermittent; spasmodically contracting; *as if a hammer were beating in head; especially unilateral* (in a herpetic patient); as if everything would protrude through forehead towards evening. *Fulness during mental labor. Dulness, so that he fears inflammation of brain, > nosebleed.* Cloudy feeling in night on waking, as if he had been intoxicated in evening, with stupor and tumbling about. Heaviness in morning. Weakness. Pulsation of blood during mental labor. *Vertigo;* in morning; everything turns around with him.

Forehead.—Sticking on l. side; in r., extending into eye; drawing, extending to nose. Pinching in upper part, beginning in morning in bed, < morning and evening, with heaviness, sometimes whole sinciput aches and then temples feel pressed in, afterwards it alternates suddenly with pain in molars, < walking in fresh air. *Pain;* in centre; *with weakness of it;* in sinciput, < temples, < steady mental exertion, > motion, especially in open air, < morning and evening, with heaviness in sinciput, often it suddenly passes off and attacks l. molars; *as if brain had not space enough in morning on rising, > washing and breakfast;* contracting. Drawing in sinuses as in coryza. Stupefied feeling in l. half in morning.

Shooting from l. temple into head; boring, in l. temple. Pain in temples; after mental exertion; hammering; crampy, in skin of r. at 7.30 P.M. Intermittent pain in a spot in vertex. Strained pain in r. side of occiput at noon. *Pain in occiput as if a piece of wood lay across from r. to l.* Feeling as of a cord around skin, < about occiput, which feels as if pressed outward.

Clinical.—Chronic headache, associated with inordinate appetite, sensation in the occiput as of a piece of wood lying on the head. Humid eruptions on the scalp, the hair becomes matted and of foul odor. Head sensitive to the air, even in hot weather.

Eyes.—*Gummy.* Surrounded by blue rings. Glassy, with pain in them and agglutination in morning. Swelling, and of face. Inflammation of r. Ophthalmia, with pain as from sand in eyes, and lachrymation at night. Sticking; in l. Pain; in r., < touch; with burning and constant necessity to close them; burning, in the evening when looking sharply at something, and by candle-light; as from sand; as from a foreign body in r. in evening when closed. Biting. Tired in evening as from much reading by candle-light.

Lachrymation; towards evening; on looking long at an object. Pimples like hordeola on upper lid; red, like fresh hordeola on margin of upper lids and sensation as if one were playing with his fingers before his eyes. Itching of r. lid; l. lower lid, from one side to other; of canthi; inner canthi, with heat. *Vision of sparks.* All objects in the room appear to tremble. Dazzling in evening when walking in the street. Vision blurred suddenly.

Clinical.—Scrofulous ophthalmia. Recurring pustular ophthalmia. Serous choroiditis.

Ears.—Discharge of fetid pus; *from l. Otorrhœa, with headache.* Discharge of reddish cerumen from l. Sticking; towards noon; in l. lobe in evening; in l. after the buzzing; in meatus internus, transiently > boring in with the finger, frequently returning, < evening during rest. Intermittent tearing through external meatus, as from temporal muscle to styloid process. Pain in r. in morning; ulcerative, in l., and at the same time on r. ear a pimple appearing like healthy skin, but split into four parts by a cross, like a wart, in the centre a deep indentation. Sensation as if something burst suddenly when eating or swallowing saliva. Sensation in l. as if breath came from it instead of from respiratory organs. Feeling as if stuffed with cotton forenoons. Biting in l. Itching in r. Coldness in r., then sticking.

Ringing in l. in evening; in r. or l., with buzzing in head so that she hears hardly anything, and behind ears, in region of sterno-cleido-mastoideus, a sore pain, sometimes heat extending to vertex, < towards evening, when she feels as if pulled by the hair; increase of former ringing, so that he feels stupefied. Buzzing. Feeling in r. as if he heard with the ears of another person, in evening.

Nose.—Inflammation of septum, with white pustules. Sticking in l. nostril when boring in with finger; boring, in r., then sneezing. Boring in r., then sneezing. Drawing extending up to frontal sinuses, with pain in eyes as if coryza would set in, then discharge of fluid from nose. Dry; nostrils nearly dry, and sensitive when breathing through them. Scratching crawling towards root as if coryza would set in. Stoppage. Sneezing; without coryza. Coryza; with cough and expectoration of yellowish-green mucus; dry; *dry, with obstruction of nose;* fluent; fluent, from l. nostril. *Tough mucus,* he can hardly do a minute without his handkerchief, without coryza, with feeling of a plug high up in nose, which nauseates him, > stooping. Clear watery fluid pours out, < l. nostril, < stooping.

Face.—*Pale.* Sickly looking. Yellow. Pain in zygoma on touch as if bone were suppurating, in evening. Sticking in lower jaw.

Lips.—**Swelling of upper.** *Dryness; and brown and black color. Burning. Painful and seem swollen.* Pimple on upper. Vesicles around corner, and outwardly above them larger sore spots, exuding a fluid, which seemed to originate from scratching the V. and cause continual scratching; yellow, on red edge of lower, sore on touch; clear, on inner surface of lower; burning and painful, on inner surface of lower. Painful itching in r. half of upper as if swollen.

Mouth.—Teeth. *Looseness, < incisors, so that he fears they will fall out,* the pain < touch, > open air, with much mucus of an offensive odor in mouth. Blood suddenly escapes from a hollow molar. Sticking from one side to the other, extending to head, then burning pain in r. cheek, which is swollen; S., on touching them in order to remove something lodged between them; in a carious r. upper, as if it would be pulled, at dinner, then grumbling and hammering pain in all r. teeth, only in daytime, > fresh air. Tearing; jerk-like in l. molars, sometimes only slight pain alternating with headache. Seem on edge in afternoon when smoking.

Ulceration of r. gum after toothache. Inflammation of gum of a posterior r. hollow lower molar, with swelling and crawling pain, < touch. Tongue coated; *white; yellowish-white; ulceration of T. and gums, with sore throat;* **dry**; *dry at tip, as if burnt, painful;* burnt feeling from tip to middle, so that he has hardly any taste.

Thick mucus from choanæ; nauseous tasting M.; tough, of nauseating taste, and teeth stick together. *Adhesion of tough mucus to posterior wall of soft palate, necessitating hawking;* A. to soft palate of tough mucus, tasting like old cheese, coming from choanæ, also on posterior wall of soft palate. Scratching in back part, and when leaning backward asthmatic feeling. Swollen sensation in palate. *Dryness.*

Taste.—*Bitter* mornings before eating, > eating; *when not eating;* > eating and drinking. Bad, finally coppery, like cat's urine, to bread and butter in morning. Oily to the dinner; flat, insipid. Foul, she drinks to get rid of it. Increase of the nauseous T. after eating or smoking tobacco. Sticky.

Throat.—Submaxillary glands swollen and painful to touch, also a painful pustule below l. lower jaw. *Angina, on r. side an ulcer, with sore pain deep in throat and burning in palate.* Painful pimple on fauces. Sticking in l. tonsil; in l. sinews on turning head. Pain in l. tonsil, with swollen feeling; P. on swallowing saliva; intermittent P. and difficult swallowing. Soreness, with difficulty in swallowing; S., with inability to swallow; can take without difficulty only cold food. Scraping as if she would become hoarse (in a herpetic patient); S., with suffocation, causing dry cough. Burning; extending farther downward. *Dryness; in morning, with scraping;* of fauces, with moisture in mouth. Swollen feeling in fauces. Tickling mornings; causing cough; then empty eructations.

Stomach.—Hunger great; in afternoon, with thirst for beer; in evening after a walk; in evening; desire for breakfast; *H. without appetite; appetite diminished;* easily satiated though he has a good appetite; loss of appetite, but constant thirst. Disgust for pork. Desire to smoke in evening, but when not smoking the desire for it ceased. Aversion to smoking after breakfast, but when he begins smoking is relished. Thirst; during dinner; after the chill, then heat in mouth; with dryness and burning in mouth; for beer.

Eructations tasting like rotten eggs; sour E.; rancid E. in evening. Pyrosis; after drinking water; when lying down, colic > eating. Hiccough; after eating; when smoking a pipe after eating. *Nausea; during the day,* a kind of vomiting of *sweet mucus* every day at 10 A.M. and in evening; in morning; in pit of stomach in morning; after all food; after supper, > eating something roasted. *Vomiting sour;* of sour mucus, so that teeth are on edge, in morning before eating; of food, then of a sour, slimy fluid. Bloating. Sticking in pit. Cramp in epigastric region. Cutting in epigastric region. Oppression. Contracting pain in epigastric region. Weakness and pressure.

Abdomen.—*Bloated;* after eating; after eating frozen things. Rumbling in morning. Gurgling and roaring. Foul-smelling flatus. Cutting; in evening, > passage of offensive flatus; as from a purge. Cramps in morning in bed. Griping when driving; G. in women, < pubic region. Pinching in morning, so that he has to run for the closet, > stool. Pain; towards evening, > eating; *after eating, > emission of flatus, with nausea;* and in lumbar vertebræ, with flatulent troubles, pain in spermatic cords and testicles as if filled with blood, a soft, difficult stool; as from canine hunger, < epigastric region, an hour after supper, with accumulation of flatus.

Sticking in sides; r.; *region of spleen;* under last l. rib; in hepatic region; *region of spleen,* > standing still, renewed by walking, later felt even during rest. Swollen sensation horizontally across below short ribs when sitting. Frequent sticking to l. of umbilicus during rest. Cutting in umbilical region. Gurgling in small intestines. Twitching in r. groin after driving. Sticking in inguinal glands. Pain in r. inguinal ring. Bearing down towards pubes, with tenesmus and painful burning micturition.

Clinical.—Chronic hepatitis. Sharp stinging pains in the liver, general aggravation from lying on the right side.

Rectum and Anus.—Spasmodic pain in rectum. *Burning* high up in rectum. Chafed sensation in rectum during a drive. Ineffectual urging. Burning nodes in anus. Itching in anus.

Stool.—**Fluid, dark brown, foul-smelling**. *Diarrhœa preceded by colic; green, bilious D. mixed with mucus;* four times in a day, without pain. *Soft, difficult;* S. and copious. *Constipation.* Either costive or mushy. Of normal consistency, in small balls, almost involuntary, at night, with violent emission of flatus. Two in forenoon. Four or five a day, preceded by colic. Sometimes shooting away as from a syringe, at another time it is mushy, sometimes of normal consistency. Stopped.

Clinical.—Diarrhœa; evacuations dark, liquid and extremely fetid; during teething; after enervating diseases; sometimes with ravenous hunger, debility, profuse perspiration, with a foul odor from the skin, which is greasy.

Urinary Organs.—Discharge of prostatic fluid before micturition. Tenesmus urinæ, and discharge of a few drops when he thinks he has done. Some drops of urine after micturition although he tries to hold it back. Frequent micturition at night. Sticking inwardly from orifice of urethra. Burning during micturition, with cutting. *Urine has a red sediment and a pellicle of fat.*

Sexual Organs.—Relaxation; with indifference to sexual affairs. *Glans inflamed, with an ulcer on it, testes swollen and heavy.* Burning pain at tip of penis on beginning to urinate. Frequent tightness of penis, with drawing. *Absence of erections;* even with lascivious thoughts, afterwards morning erections and pollutions, with satyriasis. Drawing in testicles, but more steady in small of back. Painful suppurating vesicle on scrotum. *Aversion to coitus. Impotency.* No discharge of semen during coition. Menses too late; and scanty.

Respiratory Organs.—*Hoarseness.* Tickling in trachea, with cough. Inclination to cough, with sensation of coldness. *Cough in evening, > keeping quiet, with pain in chest and throat, talking causes cough; C., with weakness of chest;* so that he could not remain in bed at night, with weakness and vertigo. *Dry cough* all day, with nausea and retching and tickling in throat; *from tickling in trachea; with soreness under sternum; with heaviness on chest.* **Cough,** *< morning on waking, and in evening on lying down,* **with expectoration of green mucus, nearly like matter,** *with nausea, chest is affected and expectoration is difficult;* C. in morning, with copious expectoration; sometimes with expectoration of mucus streaked with blood; with expectoration from chest, salivation and vomiting of acid mucus.

Suffocation in larynx when sitting bent backward, *with crawling, causing paroxysmal, dry, hacking cough,* and at the same time contraction and heaviness in chest and pain in upper part of sternum. Dyspnœa in evening. *Short breath; in fresh air,* > riding and lying down. *Want of breath on walking in fresh air;* W. of breath, < sitting, > lying, with pain in chest. Whistling respiration on waking, with constriction, again in evening whistling in chest. Breathes easily when doing some light work, as trimming trees.

Clinical.—Chronic cough from tickling in the larynx. Extremely offensive expectoration, night-sweats. Hæmoptysis.

Chest.—Twitching through l. anterior side. Sticking in l.; l. mamma; under l. false ribs; in r. side on coughing; *in r. when breathing;* even when not breathing; in sternum on deep breathing, and on touch a pressing and bruised pain. *Feeling as if everything in it were torn* when lifting. Pain as if a lung had been torn loose and something were pressing it down. Cutting in evening, with burnt feeling in throat, eructations, then emission of flatus. Boring in r., with oppressed breathing. Pain under sternum when coughing as if something would be torn away, extending to throat. *Pain* on spots; *ulcerative P. under sternum;* P. as from a load, < bending head forward, with want of breath. *Oppression. Pressure.* Contracted feeling. Dull feeling, with pain in back. When in bed he has to remove the arms as far as possible from chest, otherwise they increase the pain.

Heart.—Palpitation; with anxious oppression.

Clinical.—Pericarditis, with effusion.

Neck.—*Glands swollen, and on touch bruised pain extending to head.* Sticking, with pustules. Tearing in nape. Boring in nape, with stiffness. Pain in nape in afternoon, only in the house, when supporting the head with the hands it feels as if it had no body, as if he could pass through it with the hands; P. in muscles of r. side, in their upper sinewy part, as from sudden tension, on turning head to r., backward or sideways, > pressure; tensive, in nape after waking, as if he had lain in an uncomfortable position; drawing, extending to shoulder, after waking.

Back.—Sticking; *extending towards chest on coughing.* Boring in vertebræ in morning, with colic, as from rheumatism. *Aching;* bruised feeling in evening, he cannot straighten it. Scapulæ, sticking between in morning; tearing; rheumatic sticking tearing in and between, down sides. Dorsal vertebræ, boring; pain between second and third in afternoon.

Lumbar Region.—Sticking extending to knee in morning; in os pubis during bodily exertion. Cutting so that she could not walk alone. *Pain;* and itching; like molimina hæmorrhoidalia, < motion, so that he could not walk straight comfortably; as if third vertebra from below were wanting or broken. Drawing, and sometimes in testicles. Tightness in ischii when walking, extending to knees. *Weakness.*

Extremities.—*Trembling of hands and feet.* Stretching. Tearing in l. knee and shoulder; intermittent, in joints of fingers, in humerus, knee and toes, > motion; wandering, < tibiæ and soles, also in finger-joints, at times in r. patella, > motion. **Weakness of joints as if they would not hold together.** Tearing in l. shoulder in afternoon and evening when resting. Arm, tearing; intermittent sticking in l.; spasmodic pain in bones of l. in evening at rest; asleep sensation in l. in morning in bed, with crawling in fingers; asleep sensation in l. in morning, with numbness of three first fingers and of half of hand. Tearing in elbow; r. in evening. Sticking in l. index.

Lower Extremities.—*Legs, < tibiæ and soles, pain as from too much walking,* mornings in bed, > *rising, with restlessness of legs.* Leg on which he lies in bed too weak to endure the pressure of the other, he has to change his position continually. Sensation in r. leg as if it would go to sleep. Tibiæ and soles feel bruised, as after a tiresome walk, mornings in bed. Sticking in r. ankle in morning on every step, with strained sensation. Feet, trembling; inclination to turn l. inward when walking, with sensation as if he really had turned it the wrong way; pain < during rest, with itching; gouty pain in l. Cramp or spasm in toes, < l. great, when stretching them or taking off boots.

Skin.—Roughness from knuckles to middle joints. Smooth warts on l. fingers. L. concha inwardly inflamed, with suppurating pimples. Rash above l. brow and on l. cheek; red, on external throat, beginning with sticking. Nodules on face, neck and legs. Pimples on forehead; on neck and mammæ; with black point in centre, painful when scratched, on external throat; burning like heat-rash, below eyes; causing itching smarting pain, burning after scratching, and feeling sore (in a herpetic patient); and ulcers, from which watery fluid oozed for hours after being opened, < hands, wrists and palms. It aggravates herpes and causes smarting and itching.

A scab on nose which commonly fell off when coughing is now adherent and hard. Pustules on nape, with sticking. Boils on chest and loins; on buttocks, with burning itching, soon disappearing, leaving crusts. *Itchlike eruption on face, hand, back and leg, and agglutination of eyes.* Vesicles on face; *quickly filling with yellow lymph, sore to touch on forehead, face and behind r. ear; filled with lymph, painful to touch on various parts,* some forming itching papules. An old rhagade near r. styloid process suppurated, itched and was surrounded by blisters filled with clear water, these soon changed to pustules, which healed under a crust.

Crawling on all limbs, with falling asleep of them. Itching on forehead; tip of nose; l. arm; biceps of r. arm; r. elbow; soles in evening after a glass of Muscat wine, with tickling and heat; face, neck and hands on touch; *over whole body, after rubbing papules and vesicles; between fingers,* and vesicles filled with lymph; on r. carpus, with red spots like flea-bites; voluptuous, where a flea had bitten, with white, hard blisters on a red base; aggravation of the *I.*, which he had had for years *on knees,* < l. and the herpetic eruption begins to become pustular.

Clinical.—The skin is generally yellow, dirty and greasy, with unhealthy eruptions, especially on the forehead and chest, with constant fretting and worrying. Irritation of the skin in various parts of the body; some distressing cases have been known of whole families tormented with constantly recurring body lice, in spite of all precautions of cleanliness, cured only by this drug. The secretions are always offensive; there is easy perspiration, especially on the extremities; there is always great debility, even with an extreme appetite. Various forms of eczema, worse in the warmth of the bed, always with a disagreeable odor. General tendency to glandular enlargements.

Sleep.—Yawning at noon; and shivering, pale blue rings, with tearing and spasmodic pains in umbilical region, in evening; in evening, with early sleepiness. Sleepy all the time; *in daytime;* early. Sleeps when she sits down. Sleep unusually sound. Cannot fall asleep in evening. Cannot sleep on the habitual r. side, but sleeps on l. Gnashing of teeth at night, so that he wakes. Restless sleep; and unrefreshing; but refreshing; on account of disquiet dreams. *Dreams anxious* in morning, of robbers, travels and danger; uneasy, earnest; that he is on the closet, and thus nearly soils his bed; of his business and of his plans.

Fever.—Coldness frequently during the day; C. < evening, with hot flashes, debility and sleepiness; with heat, thirst and sweat; internal, towards noon, with shivering and horripilation; creeping; creeping, in afternoon, with internal shivering. Horripilations. Feet cold all night.

Heat in afternoon; in evening when riding in a carriage, with sweat; *of whole body suddenly,* at meals and in evening, *with trickling sweat all over face,* frequent thirst, dryness and burning in mouth; in evening, as if she would lose her senses, at night delirium, thirst and sweat, then she feels well. Burning in head; in forehead; in nose, transiently > discharge of mucus; in nose, then fluent coryza; in face, then vesicles; in r. ear, with itching.

Sweat on walking; in morning when out of doors; **with consequent debility,** *and taking cold easily; S. on palms;* on face; palms at night; perineum on moving about.

Pulsatilla.

A tincture is made of the fresh plant of Anemone pratensis, L. (Pulsatilla nigricans).

General Action.—Most extensive action on mucous membranes, eyes, ears, nose and respiratory tract, mouth and digestive tract, vagina and urinary apparatus. It affects the testicles and spermatic cord, the female sexual organs, the veins of the lower extremities and the joints. Its action on the disposition is very marked and important. Its fever is unpronounced, is symptomatic (catarrhal as a rule) and is not attended with thirst or nervous excitement.

Allies.—*Lyc.*, Phos., Ferr., *Cycl.;* Kali bi., Euphras.

Generalities.—*Lies upon back with hands above head when sleeping;* upon back in sleep, with hands crossed upon abdomen and feet drawn up; *most comfortably* *upon back with feet drawn up,* if he lies upon either side spasmodic symptoms occur, for example, hæmorrhoidal pains in anus, headache as if skull would burst, pain in joints, tightness in chest, anxiety. Child grunts and groans if it is carried and during urging to stool. *Trembling; with cold sweat; anxious, with drawing pain in limbs and over whole body.*

Sticking in a fresh wound in evening. Drawing tearing here and there in frequent attacks. Pain in sacrum and knees as if beaten, in bed. Jerking drawing pains in muscles, as if they were stretched on one side. *Pressure in l. hip* and in head, in forenoon, > motion. Smarting as from an internal wound in lumbar region and in wrist. **Discomfort in morning after rising, > moving about.** Distress in whole body, causing despair, he cannot sleep nor become quiet. Distressing throbbing in all arteries, < motion. *Everything about body seems too tight, she wishes to throw off her clothes* (Lyc.). *Tension of face and fingers* (< taking hold of anything), *as if the parts would swell. Sensation in whole body as if he had been awake all night, with emptiness of head as after intoxication. Inclination to stretch.*

Weakness; **weaker the longer he lies in morning, and the more he wishes to lie, he desires to sleep again;** at noon after walking, the more he tries to keep awake the sleepier he becomes; *from a short walk; and necessity to lie down; tremulous;* so that he could scarcely walk a few minutes, then necessity to sleep for hours, and so alternately all day. Faintness all the morning. *Heaviness; with chilliness in arms and legs.* Impairment of motor power. Numbness of integuments, then general anæsthesia. Painful paralytic sensation about ligaments of joints, < evening, with pain in all joints of limbs as in beginning of a paroxysm of intermittent fever, with chilliness. Stiffness; in a child, from fretfulness. Troubles in open air, he dreads it. **Symptoms occur mostly in evening, next in succeeding hours till midnight** (Lyc., Cycl., Euphras., Valer., Phos.), *rarely about* 4 A.M. *and still more rarely in morning, etc. Aggravation every other evening.* **Amelioration in open air; A. of pains when lying on back** (Sang., Bry., Calc. c., Lyc.), *aggravation from lying on side.*

Clinical.—Rheumatism, rarely highly inflammatory, joints may be swollen, with sharp stinging pains, these pains are usually erratic, they constantly change from place to place, mostly tearing, > pressure and by moving about slowly, > cold, < warmth and in the evening. Useful for gouty symptoms caused by indigestion (Lyc.). Gonorrhœal rheumatism (Thuja). Paralytic symptoms, especially with disordered menstruation, with numbness of the extremities. Occasionally indicated in chorea and in epilepsy. Neuralgia of various parts, pains wandering, with the characteristic aggravations and ameliorations. Chlorosis, with chilliness, burning heat at night without thirst, palpitation, longing for fresh air, etc. Various forms of hysteria. In general, aggravation in the evening, on beginning to move, from lying on the left side (Phos.), lying on the painless side. Amelioration from slow motion, cold place, lying on painful side (Bry.), from cold drink.

Mind.—Excitement. Quiet. It seems so quiet in her head and everything feels so empty that she seems alone in the house and in the world, she wants to speak to no one, just as if her surroundings did not exist and she belonged to no one. Careless ease, such as is often produced by a small dose of hasheesh. *Indolence and constant desire to sit or lie.* **Longs for fresh air,** *though colic and nausea are < open air.* **Hypochondriac moroseness.** *Ill humor; in morning when thinking of his business; all day, with discontentment;* about 4 P.M., **weeping** *when interrupted in his business;* in evening, will not answer and takes everything in bad part; *at everything said to him;* after walking about the room, *with loss of appetite; even with himself, and capricious mood; with dread of work; with confusion and chilliness. Disgust with everything. Satisfied with nothing, yet not vexed.* Disconnected in morning after waking, and weeping. Envious, avaricious, dissatisfied, greedy. Hasty.

Restless mood, as if he had not done his duty satisfactorily. Irresolute; and shuns business, sighs and loses composure. Longing now for this, now for that, even with good humor (in a child). Wishes now for this, now for that employment, but when it is given to him he will have nothing to do with it. *Melancholy; from disagreeable news; with much crying. Anxiety;* during the day, with trembling and flushing heat over whole body though hands and face are cold and pale, *and when evening comes dread of ghosts;* in afternoon, with trembling of hands, that are spotted red; *in evening after going to sleep, with rush of ideas and determination of blood to head, forcing him to rise;* **and lachrymose mood; at night as from heat;** *as if in a hot atmosphere; tremulous, as if death were imminent; tremulous, < rest, > motion; thinks that he shall be ruined;* as if he had committed a crime, at night on waking; about his household matters, in morning; about his health; as if he should have apoplexy, in evening after lying down, with chilliness, sounds in ears like music and twitching of r. fingers.

Hesitates when talking, it frets him to answer. Difficulty in expressing himself correctly when talking. Omits letters when writing. *Many wandering thoughts.* He cannot get rid of a thought that he has once grasped. Inattentive, does things hurriedly, does something different from what he intended to do; I., but not indifferent to his surroundings. Disinclination to mental labor, < evening. Mental labor affects him most of all.

Clinical.—This drug is generally indicated for persons who have a mild, yielding disposition, inclined to weep, or for those who are inclined to be very gloomy and too full of care. This sad weeping mood is an almost constant accompaniment of every form of disease requiring Puls. Religious melancholia. (Compare mental symptoms with Ign. and Lyc.)

Head.—*Sticking; through brain from after dinner till bedtime, with shivering and attacks of faintness;* with boring outward; and tearing, < temples. Cutting. *Aching on stooping;* A. on entering a warm room, with obscuration; in various parts of bones; **extending into eyes in evening;** extending into r. eye, it presses in it and tears come out of it; intermittent, < walking in open air; **as from eating too much or as from too much fat** (Cycl., Ferr.); *as in stopped catarrh* **in evening,** *then dry heat in bed, and sopor,* with delirious fantasies and almost waking dreams; *as if in a hot wind;* intermittent, as from a sharp wind through brain; as from intoxication and night-watching; on waking and for some time afterwards, as if brain were confused and torn to pieces, as in putrid fever or after intoxication by brandy; sick; so that he must incline head to one side; *tensive, over brain;* drawing, with lachrymation of one eye; drawing, with heaviness and crawling in brain and vanishing of vision and hearing, then chill. **Throbbing pain; > pressure;** about midnight.

Constriction in brain, with boring in crown. Crackling in brain synchronous with pulse, on walking. *Bubbling at night, he heard the beating of the pulse in it*

Roaring, and more in ears, so that he must lie down earlier than usual. **Dulness**; in evening, and on moving eyes pain deep in orbits as if forehead would fall out and as if frontal bone were too thin; caused by motion, with vertigo; when sitting, with whirring in it and sleepiness; **with bruised sensation in forehead**; *with pain in forehead as if it would be torn to pieces; with feeling as if hollow* and as if intoxicated; with vanishing of thought; *so that eyes ache; as if his memory failed. Heaviness; on stooping, it seems as if he could not raise it again;* with intolerance of the glare of the lamp. *On stooping sensation as if it would fall forward.* Cannot hold it upright, cannot raise it; cannot hold it upright, must lie down, yet cannot remain in bed.

Vertigo; in morning on rising, forcing him to lie down again (Bry., Lyc.); at 2 P.M., when walking; after eating; when walking over a high bridge; when walking in open air, > sitting; *on stooping so that she could scarcely rise again;* > **sitting**; *with nausea;* and he thought that he was unable to comprehend a subject; in paroxysms, with heat; **as from intoxication**; *as from drinking brandy; as from heaviness of head, on walking and stooping, with some whirling even when lying; as if he would fall, on stooping, then inclination to* **vomit**; *as if he would fall or as if he were dancing, on looking upward;* as if falling to right or left in morning on walking in open air; as if blood mounted to head, it surged therein.

Forehead.—*Boring in r. side.* Stitches extending outward in evening. *Tearing in l. side of bone in evening.* Sharp pain. *Pain;* **above orbits**, *involving whole head;* in afternoon, with prostration, desire to yawn and fever; when walking; and in vertex; *tensive drawing, above orbits,* < raising eyes; crawling; throbbing, in evening on stooping and mental exertion, > walking. *Constriction above eyes,* < *looking intently.*

Temples.—*Sticking.* Jerking tearing, as if they would be torn asunder. Pain; *in l. Constriction.*

Sides.—*Tearing in r.;* in l. parietal bone; in side on which he is not lying. Stitches. Sharp thrusts or jerks in r. half of brain. *Pain in one side as if brain would burst and eye fall out;* pain in half of brain on which he was not lying, before midday nap.

Occiput.—Sticking, < lying, > rising; S., extending through ears. Tearing in l. side; in morning. Pain, with frequent heat of body and constant sweat. Drawing pain above nape in morning. Rhythmical throbbing pain.

Scalp.—Swellings, with pain as from suppuration. Pustule in region of occiput, with tearing. Drawing pain on brushing hair. Pulsation on l. side of occiput. *Biting itching.*

Clinical.—Vertigo is a very frequent accompaniment of Puls. symptoms. It is especially noticed on looking up, < while sitting and lying, usually associated with nausea and gastric disturbance or with suppressed menses. Headache, generally one-sided and usually involving the forepart of the head; supra-orbital neuralgia of r. side (Cedron). Headaches, like all other symptoms, < the evening, by mental effort or by warmth. Menstrual headache > open air.

Eyes.—Puffy, and sensation as if squinting. Sticking in l. on shaking head, with lachrymation; S. in one or other, almost without inflammation of the white, with intolerance of candle-light, he can open lids but little; *itching.* (Tearing-boring cutting, in a case of chronic amaurosis, with improved vision.) *Pain in l.; P. as from sand, when reading;* (as if scraped with a knife, in a case of syphilitic ophthalmia). **Burning and itching** (Lyc.). *Burning pain,* < morning and evening; *B. pain as if a hair were in it. Dryness, and in morning sensation of a foreign body; D. of r. in evening, with sensation as if mucus were hanging before it* (Euphras.).

Lachrymation; in wind; in open air; in cold, open air; with deeply sunken eyes. Pupils contracted at first; *dilated. Red (inflamed) spot on white, near cornea.* Itching in ball, in external canthus in evening. Lids, **stye, with inflammation of white of eye,** *now in one, now in other canthus, with drawing tensive pains in eyes on moving facial muscles and with ulcerated nostrils;* **inflammation of margin of lower in morning, with swelling and lachrymation; agglutination in morning**; swelling and redness; twitching; *sticking in evening, and in canthi;* **itching (biting) in evening, with burning**; dryness; dryness < sleepiness. Canthi, **inner seems agglutinated in morning**; sticking in r.; *pain in inner; itching like the healing of an ulcer in inner, after sunset, and after rubbing there is sticking; biting in inner, with sore sensation.*

Vision.—**Dimness**; *in morning on rising; on rising from a seat and walking;* several times during the day, with flashing of fire, as from a slap in the face; **transient**; *dizzy, after sitting, on rising and beginning to walk;* **blackness during menses, and she felt worse on entering a warm room.** Photophobia and asthenopia. Double. (Flickering.) Starry halo around candle-light. Fiery circles, becoming larger towards noon, > towards evening.

Clinical.—Conjunctivitis, with thick, yellow, bland discharge; after measles; from taking cold, etc. The thick discharge tends to collect over the cornea and may be removed by wiping (Euphrasia). Catarrh of the eyes and nose, discharges always profuse, thick and bland. Ophthalmia of infants, following well after Arg. nitr. Granular lids. This drug affects rather the lower lid than the upper. General tendency to styes. Asthenopia. Ulceration of the cornea. Inflammation of the lachrymal apparatus, with profuse muco-purulent discharge and fistula lachrymalis. Various forms of blepharitis and blepharadenitis always > the cool, open air. Tumors of the lid (Staphys.). Pustular conjunctivitis. Episcleritis. Iritis (occasionally). Hyperæmia of the choroid. Retinitis. Progressive cataract.

Ears.—*Redness of outer, with swelling and heat. Discharge of matter from l.* Sticking; *in r.; deep in l.; itching, in middle.* **Pain as from something forcing outward.** *Pressure in bone above r. Jerking; in outer, then heat in it; tearing, through ears. Itching deep in;* in r. in afternoon and in evening. Air penetrates on blowing nose, as if ear were distended thereby, with sticking extending to eye. Rush of blood. **Stopped sensation, with distant roaring**; *frequent stoppage of r.*

Hearing difficult, as if ears were stopped; *every other hour, with trembling and sweat on back.* Words seem too loud on waking, they vibrate shrilly. *Ringing;* in r, then in l., with agreeable tickling in region of drum; tremulous tingling, as from the beating of an iron bar. *Cracking on moving head or body.* Whistling in r., with diminished hearing as if air were forced outward. Twittering as from a cricket in morning in bed. *Humming.* Buzzing. *Sound of wind or rushing of water after* 4 P.M. Noise like a bursting. *Roaring* disappearing by an electric shock that extended from head down across chest, with sensation before eyes as of the bursting of a soap-bubble. Murmuring rhythmical with pulse.

Clinical.—Inflammation and swelling of the external ear,

the concha is swollen and red, frequently with profuse discharge of thick pus, with pains worse at night. Earache relieved by cold applications, pain darting and tearing, involving sometimes the face and teeth and even extending to the throat and preventing swallowing. Otorrhœa; the discharge is purulent, sometimes bloody, generally not excoriating. Deafness following scarlet fever. Deafness, with feeling as though the ears were stopped, or sometimes with pulsation in the ear as from a pulse. Catarrhal inflammation in the ear from a suppressed cold in the nose.

Nose.—*Pain in root; P. in bones as if they would be forced asunder;* jerking; (as from an ulcer in root on stooping). Sensation of an ulcer in l. nostril. *Tickling.* **Stoppage in evening on going to bed, and blowing out of thick, yellow, opaque mucus in morning** (Kali bi.). **Sneezing;** *in morning in bed; in evening in sleep.* **Offensive mucus, as in old catarrh.** *Green, offensive discharge. Purulent discharge from r. nostril. Coryza; with loss of smell and taste* (Nat. m.); occasional. Stopped; stopped, with ulcerated nostrils. *Bleeding; with stopped catarrh; blowing out of blood in morning.* **Smell as in old catarrh;** *in morning.* He smells tobacco and coffee, even in open air.

Clinical.—Nasal catarrh; it is one of our most frequent remedies for an ordinary cold in the nose. There is usually more or less soreness of the nose, which is sometimes swollen; the discharge is profuse, *and does not excoriate the nostrils,* it is generally thick but sometimes thin, usually with loss of smell, rarely loss of taste; occasionally indicated when the discharge alternates with a dry stoppage of the nose, especially when it is stopped in the evening. A form of ozæna, with offensive discharges. Catarrh of the antrum, with orange-colored discharge, especially from the r. nostril discharge of a urinous odor. Occasionally called for in chronic catarrh, with yellow discharge, especially worse evenings. Catarrh, with loss of smell and taste, occasionally indicates this drug, but if the aggravation be in the forenoon, Nat. mur. is indicated.

Face.—A painful gland between tragus and joint of jaw. *Pale.* Redness; every evening, with heat; and heat, then immediately pallor; sudden, with shivering on feet and anxious trembling. Twitching of cheeks. Sticking in parotid gland. *Boring in l. malar-bone.* Aching; in bones of r. side. Feeling as if mumps were coming on, with sense of threatening deafness. Tearing (drawing) pain in lower jaw. Constrictive pain in jaws as from an acid, with shivering and cold sweat on face. Lips fissured; *swelling of lower, which is cracked in the middle, with tensive pain;* peeling down to the raw flesh, on outer margin; twitching of lower.

Clinical.—Neuralgia of the face involving the whole left side, worse in warm room and bed. Pain usually associated with chilliness. Erysipelas of the face (occasionally). Infraorbital neuralgia of the left side, with profuse secretion from the left nostril.

Mouth.—Teeth. Loose in morning. Sticking, > vinegar; S. in last molar from 2 till 6 P.M., < opening mouth. Sticking digging in lower, then in upper, beginning at 2 A.M., changing from root of one T. to another, so that he could not lay his head in a cool place in bed, returning at noon when eating. (Sticking throbbing about 4 or 5 P.M., < cold water.) *Tearing.* **Aching as soon as anything warm is taken into mouth** (Graph.); *A. on chewing and biting;* < wind; *as if they would be forced out.* **Jerking pain** *from picking them,* **< morning, > when cold water taken into mouth becomes warm;** J. from 6 till 11 P.M., preceded by heat in head and followed by sweat; in molars, with swelling on gums; drawing, < cold drinks.

Gums.—*Sticking gnawing,* **< towards evening and by warmth of bed, > uncovering, a draught of cold, open air,** > *evening nap. Pain as if sore;* as if inside were eroded. Throbbing rhythmical with pulse, < warmth of stove. Feels swollen posteriorly, but it is not, and on taking anything cold or warm into mouth there is burning.

Tongue.—**Covered with a tenacious mucus as with a membrane.** *Painful blister on side of tip.* Sticking. Tearing, then heat. *Sensation in middle as if it had been burnt and were insensible at night and in morning.* Edge feels sore as if scalded. *Biting in tip. Dryness in morning; on waking, and in palate and lips,* **then much tenacious mucus.** Sense of "gathering" under it. Seems broader than natural.

Mouth and pharynx dry in morning and covered with insipid mucus, with offensive breath that is not perceptible to himself. *Much mucus; covered with offensive mucus in morning on waking. Sensation as if roof of palate were covered with tenacious mucus and were swollen.* Pain in side of palate in morning when touched on talking, as from a blister or pimple, with dilated pupils. Acrid sensation in palate as if raw on swallowing. *Salivation;* **sweet;** with scraping extending low down in throat and into œsophagus, and heat in stomach; *tenacious; discharge of watery saliva, also like waterbrash. Offensive odor in morning; in evening after lying down; at night.*

Taste.—**Bitter bilious, after eating and smoking. Bitter;** *in morning,* > eating; *in morning fasting, continuing even when smoking;* **at 6 P.M.;** *in evening after beer; after eating, and good appetite;* after vomiting; after coffee, < morning; < *morning* **and after eating and drinking, though food has a natural taste;** *with desire for citric acid;* **to food; to food, then chilliness and cold sweat;** *to bread, rolls and meat; to bread, with aversion to bread;* to black bread, which disgusts him; *to beer in morning, afterwards a sour taste;* to wine; (and slimy, salt, in morning, not without appetite). **Slimy; in morning, with nausea;** and sweetish. **Foul, clammy, insipid. As of bad meat, with nausea;** *as of bad meat on hawking, < morning.* **Disgusting in morning, with white tongue;** *D. sweetish to bitter beer. Nauseous from smoking tobacco; N., as of fasting, as if one had risen too early, in morning. Filthy, and tongue coated, appetite lost. Burnt* (empyreumatic). Bad to fresh meat. Purulent at times, < morning. Sour after eating; to bread, and it seems too dry. Herby posteriorly in throat. Flat, as if he had eaten earthy things. Too salt to all food (except black bread) and after eating a scraping salt taste constantly rises into throat. *Diminished to all food.* Little or none to bread, butter and beer (only plum marmalade has a perfectly good taste), with some appetite. Lost to meat; to milk in morning; when smoking tobacco in morning.

Clinical.—Neuralgic toothache, ceasing entirely in the open air, < in a warm room, always relieved when walking about. Toothache in pregnancy, temporary > holding cold water in the mouth, always < the evening until midnight.

Throat.—Submaxillary glands, boring; pain; drawing tensive pains. *Covered with tenacious mucus in morning.* Sticking; posteriorly, > swallowing. Cutting. *Pain as if raw posteriorly with drawing pain in cervical muscles. Rawness and scraping, with dryness of mouth.* Pain on swallowing as if submaxillary glands projected into throat and as if they were sore and raw. *Pressure on swallowing, with tension. Constriction.* Fulness. *Sensation as from sulphur fumes when coughing.* Soreness, with dysphagia, feeling as if she would be choked. *Dryness in morning;* in morning, with rawness and soreness when not swallowing; after midnight; > swallowing, with clawing, scraping and rawness, as after violent vomiting; *with scraping, causing paroxysms of cough; extending as far as tip of tongue (without visible dryness), with thirst, he can drink but little, because it distresses him and causes nausea.*

Swollen sensation on swallowing, with rawness in trachea; S. sensation posteriorly on swallowing, with constriction; in uvula on swallowing. Swallowing difficult, as from paralysis of pharyngeal muscles. *Œsophagus, sensation of a worm creeping up; attacks of constrictive or retching pain, as if one had swallowed too large a morsel of fresh bread;* burning after swallowing; swollen sensation, at times in upper, at times in lower part.

Clinical.—Pharyngeal catarrh, with varicose condition of the mucous membrane, sometimes with stinging in the throat.

Stomach.—Appetite at an unusual time; increased in evening; ravenous; *but he knows not for what, also he relishes nothing;* (desires no warm food, only bread, butter and fruit); lost; lost on account of tastelessness of food and fulness in stomach. *Aversion to smoking; to meat* and stale bread; *to butter*, it tastes bitter; to milk in morning, though he immediately relished it.

Thirst in evening as soon as he lies down in bed, sweat between 2 and 5 A.M., with thirst, drinking always increases the sweat; for water in evening; (at midnight); *during the heat; < morning, especially for beer; for alcoholic drinks;* for something invigorating; for beer, which however has an unpleasant taste; **lost.**

Eructations tasting of food (Lyc., Phos.); **then nausea; of gas; bilious, in evening; bitter, at night; of a bitter fluid; tasting of rancid tallow after eating cakes; as of bad meat after dinner, the taste remains, with nausea;** *loud; sour in morning; of sour liquid after coffee; ineffectual. Hiccough when smoking;* at night in sleep; inclination to, after drinking.

Nausea; in morning after milk; *in morning, with slimy mouth, changing to an acid taste;* in morning, with pressure in pit of stomach; towards evening after walking in open air, with salt or sour vomiting; *at night during menses, with retching and waterbrash; during suppression of menses, with good appetite; when he wishes to eat; when eating, so that food was repulsive;* from solid food, bread, meat; from the accustomed smoking; when sleeping, with persistent appetite, even for black bread; **in epigastric region, < eating and drinking**; only in throat, > swallowing; **with waterbrash and disagreeable risings;** *with heartburn; with rumbling and gurgling in hypochondria; with chilliness; with obscuration of vision and pallor;* with peculiar aching in stomach; with salivation; with fear to eat lest she should vomit; *rising into throat; rising into mouth;* as from drinking oil; as from heat of body.

Vomiting at night, with sticking drawing pain in back extending towards scapulæ; (a little before midnight, almost without nausea); **of food that had been eaten long before** (Ferr.); *of food in evening, then bitter taste and teeth on edge; short bilious;* violent, of green, slimy, watery substance, of sour odor, burning the œsophagus, evenings after eating, when lying down to sleep.

Distention (Lyc.); hard, with flatulence. Jerking extending to larynx, > eating, with tensive pain in throat, anxiety and internal heat. Sticking in pit on a false step. Sensation in pit as if something were torn loose, then pressure, with rising of a liquid into mouth. Cutting at 5 P.M. *Griping in pit; in epigastrium.* **Pain; an hour after eating;** in pit on inspiration; sudden; extending to umbilical region and pelvis, then jumping to l. side beneath ribs, pains < retracting walls of abdomen; in pit, at first pressive, then jerking; *drawing, in pit in morning,* changing into sticking in side of chest, at last into tearing in back. *Pinching or choking pain in pit, impeding respiration in afternoon. Constriction and pinching in epigastric and hypochondriac regions, < eating, then changing into chest and impeding breathing.*

Scraping like heartburn, and in œsophagus. *Cardialgia during menses.* **Gnawing like ravenous hunger.** *Clawing in morning on rising, as from long fasting, > eating. Tension in region in forenoon, > moving about;* in region of S. and pit, extending into breasts. Anxiety in epigastric region. *Pulsation in pit; P., perceptible on laying hand on it.* **Sensation as if one had eaten too much, food rises into mouth as if one would vomit.** *Seemed to turn over on coughing and as if he would vomit, the cough presses tears from eyes. Heaviness as from a stone in morning on waking.* **Symptoms as if disordered.**

Clinical.—Very frequently called for in disorders of digestion; with pain between the shoulders and heavily furred tongue. Great distention of the abdomen, not relieved by warmth; dyspepsia characterized by regurgitation of food, more or less nausea and vomiting. With the dyspepsia there are usually loss of appetite and thirst, bitter taste, vertigo on rising up, chilliness, and, above all, constant aggravations from eating fat substances (Cycl.). Gastric catarrh, with thickly white coated tongue, dry mouth, nausea, especially when the distress or regurgitation of food takes place a long time after a meal; distress in the œsophagus, as if food were lying there (Abies, China, Bry.); dyspepsia from ice-cream or from too much ice-water; indigestion from buckwheat cakes. Atonic dyspepsia, digestion very slow, the food is tasted or regurgitated a long time after eating. In a general way the distress of this drug comes on only an hour or more after a meal. Gastralgia, with profuse sweat of the face, nausea and vomiting. Vomiting of pregnancy, especially vomiting of food in the evening or at night. General craving for acids and aversion to meat, and fat or rich food.

Abdomen.—*Distention; after eating, with intermittent colic and rumbling; flatulent, after eating* (Lyc.); hard, with tense pain and sensation as if abdomen would burst (with swelling of backs of feet). **Rumbling; and gurgling; in evening, or colic; < evening in bed, with gurgling, griping and moving of flatus from one part of intestines to another;** *with griping pinching and frequent diarrhœa; with working and pinching, then uprisings into throat.* Offensive flatus after eating.

Shooting into penis. *Cutting in morning, with emission of flatus;* when she moves; every other day, < evening; *as from flatulence in evening before eating.* Griping; with shooting into penis, frequent thin stools and thirst for "braunbier"; with sensation of fasting and bubbling, as from fermentation. (Pinching in morning, with chills and heat.) **Drawing tensive pains like labor-pains.** Tormina, > loose stool.

Pain; in evening after drinking; after drinking; after stool; on touch; on touch after purging, with thirst; when walking; in muscles when sitting and on coughing; *with diarrhœa;* in A. and lower chest, forcing her to bend forward; sharp, > loose stool; *as if diarrhœa would ensue, but stool normal;* (spasmodic and almost burning, during menses). *Flatulent pain in morning after waking, flatus rumbled and moved about painfully, < upper A.; F. pain in evening after a meal; here and there after midnight, not > emission of flatus, with general heat, without thirst; after supper, with painful rumbling,*

< *upper A.;* after supper, with pressure in stomach, then nausea; after stool; **moving about,** *in evening in bed.*

Heaviness like a stone just before menses; during menses, and in sacrum, with inclination of lower limbs to fall asleep when sitting, *and with ineffectual desire for stool.* **Chilliness extending around to lower part of back.** Tension as if everything were too full, hard and immovable, as if he could pass neither stool nor flatus, though a slow, not hard stool passed and flatus continued to pass with difficulty in small quantities. Feeling of diarrhœa. Constant desire (in remote intestines) for stool, without straining in rectum or anus, without sufficient stool. Sensation as if eviscerated.

Drawing and drawing tensive pains in upper A., extending through spermatic cords into testicles, which hang low down. Griping sticking in upper A. in morning, with flatulent colic. *Pain in upper, with sensation of tense distention.* Jerking in hypochondrium, extending into sacrum, with sticking as from an ulcer. Drawing tensive pain in hypochondria. Sticking in side as from incarcerated flatus. *Cutting above umbilicus as before diarrhœa.* Tense, prominent, painful ring about umbilicus when walking.

Hypogastrium.—Painful lumps in groins; (swelling of inguinal glands and of a bubo on disappearance of a venereal ulcer). **Cutting low down in abdomen, penetrating into pelvis** (Cham.), < *retracting walls of abdomen, with urging to stool;* C., extending round to loins, with dragging making her faint; low down in A., as if one would vomit, towards 5 P.M., after supper, > stooping, disappeared about 9 P.M., when lying curled up. Colic more cutting than griping, with soft stool. Griping low down in l. side of A., necessity to bind up A. Bruised pain in parietes when yawning. **Constriction as from a stone extending to bladder.**

Clinical.—Intestinal catarrh; in children colic and diarrhœa; colic about the navel, with chilliness, nausea and vomiting, worse in the evening; colic from taking cold, with diarrhœa, or from fruit, ice-cream, pastry, etc.; flatulent colic in the evening or at night; colic during pregnancy or from suppressed menstruation. Intestinal catarrh, with much burning in the bowels, stools covered with mucus. Menstrual colic.

Rectum.—*Sticking as from incarcerated flatus.* Burning during stool. Feeling as of piles. *Desire as if diarrhœa would occur. Pressure after stool.*

Anus.—*Hæmorrhoids, with itching stitches.* **Blind hæmorrhoids; with itching; in evening, with itching;** *in morning, preceded by pain in small of back; in evening till 9 P.M., with sore pain in anus, < motion; with sore pain;* **and painful, protruding.** *Bleeding; during stool;* hæmorrhoidal (with relief of chronic sacral pain). **Frequent evacuations of only mucus, with colic,** before every stool, also after forty-eight hours. Acrid discharges with the stools. *Sore pain after stool.* (Tearing extending into anus when sitting.)

Clinical.—Hæmorrhoids; they usually bleed easily, especially after the stools; frequently associated with gastric derangements.

Stool.—As soon as she drinks. **Watery at night. Diarrhœa** (in morning); **D. of green mucus** (Merc. dulc.); **as green as bile, once or twice at night, with movements in intestines before every stool;** *at first green, then slimy; not exhausting; without colic;* slimy, every morning immediately after rising; involuntary, at night in sleep, and D. three or four times during the day; bloody, frequent, and on least movement, with pinching in abdomen, and with nausea and faintness before and at each stool, and with necessity to keep her bed. **Soft, mixed with mucus, frequent;** soft, acrid biting, in morning. Acrid, slimy, during watery micturition, with weakness in loins. (Thin in form and seem pressed out flat.)

Constipation. Hard (with pain in hæmorrhoids). *White. Of only yellow-white mucus mixed with blood.* Like chopped eggs, preceded and followed by cutting, < morning. Bloody. *Difficult, with pain in back;* D. in morning, then two soft ones during the day. Frequent, with grayish pale face (sickly expression) and faintness.

Clinical.—Diarrhœa from fright; from pastry or ice-cream; the evacuations greenish, mucous, generally worse from being in a warm room, preceded by colic and pain in the small of the back. Occasionally called for in dysentery, with pain in small of back, constant desire for fresh air, stools mucous and bloody. Dysentery, stools bloody and mucous at night, with burning like fire in the anus. Alternate constipation and diarrhœa.

Urinary Organs.—Bladder. Sticking in neck, as from incarcerated flatus. *Pain in region on touch. Sharp (almost cutting) pressure upon neck, as from flatulence, when walking in open air, without desire to urinate.* Pressure before urinating; constant P. in evening and night, without compelling micturition; only when lying on back, and he is soon obliged to urinate; as from incarcerated flatus, towards morning. *Tenesmus.* **Frequent desire;** *and almost ineffectual, with acrid urine and cutting when urinating.* Burning in neck, as if it would compel micturition in evening before lying down.

Micturition involuntary at night in bed (Ferr.); *I. when coughing or emitting flatus; dribbling when sitting or walking. Frequent M.* (Strangury.) Gonorrhœa of the color and consistency of semen, < after urinating, with burning. (Dropping of blood in gonorrhœa, from which he had already suffered.) (Discharge of offensive liquid, gonorrhœa?) Urethra, sharp pressure as with a finger-nail, after urinating; crawling pain in orifice after urinating; drawing pain when not urinating; *burning in orifice during and after micturition,* brick-colored sediment in urine; burning anteriorly after passing brown urine; contraction, micturition in a thin stream. **Urine profuse.** *Hæmaturia. Urine brown;* brownish-red; red; dark red; colorless; with red sediment; with brick-colored sediment (Lyc.); with violet-red sediment; (gelatinous sediment); with violet ring of froth above the sandy sediment.

Clinical.—Incontinence of urine, at night; also during the day when coughing or when walking. Catarrh of the bladder, with spasmodic pains extending to the hips and thighs. Catarrh of the bladder, with incontinence of urine, profuse sediment, etc. Vesical catarrh after exposure to cold, urine very turbid. Vesical catarrh, particularly during pregnancy. Frequently called for in acute symptoms of the bladder and urethra, with enlarged prostate, the fæces are flattened. Hæmaturia. Sometimes called for when the urine is loaded with urate of ammonia, especially in young children. Suppressed gonorrhœa, with vesical catarrh. Gonorrhœa, with profuse, slimy discharge.

Sexual Organs.—(Sticking near.) Glans, constrictive pain behind; pressure after urinating, with crawling; agreeable tickling, then discharge like prostatic fluid. Erections day and night; *in morning for a long time after waking,* not without desire; frequent, with discharge of prostatic fluid. Prepuce, *itching biting on inner and upper part;* sticking itching in evening when sitting and lying; sticking itching beneath P.; biting itching under P. **Drawing pain in spermatic cords. R. side of scrotum swollen.** Itching of scrotum morning and evening.

Testicles swollen; *T. hang low down; l. hangs low down, while r. is drawn up and swollen, and spermatic cord swollen, with tensive pain;* **tearing;** *soreness, so that trousers seem too tight, unpleasant when sitting.* Itching in region of seminal vesicles in morning in bed, causing inclination for an emission, almost without erections and without amorous thoughts. *Desire in morning on waking. Emission at night, without dreams;* at night, with amorous dreams; *twice in one night,* next day lassitude and heaviness of limbs.

Female.—Burning (sticking?) in vagina and labiæ. *Cutting in orifice of uterus.* **Drawing pain extending towards uterus towards morning, with nausea. Contractive pain in l. side of uterus like labor-pains, forcing her to bend double. Leucorrhœa, with burning pain; painless, thickish, of the color of milk, < lying down; milky, with swelling of pudenda; thin, acrid;** *milky, painless; like cream, painless.*

Menses suppressed; delayed, with coldness of body and chilliness and trembling of feet; *only during the day when she walks, very little or none at night; thick, black, discharged paroxysmally, only two or three times a day;* too early; appearance of the delayed; (increased, profuse, in a case of chronic ophthalmia, with formation of matter in eyes); flow like M. in a girl of four years, with pain in back and thighs.

Clinical.—Orchitis. An extremely valuable and frequently indicated remedy for epididymitis; the inflammation and swelling extend from the testicle upward, pains not > warm applications, generally associated with pains in the small of the back, chilliness, nausea, etc. Neuralgia of the testicles. Hydrocele. A remedy very frequently indicated in disorders of women. Dysmenorrhœa, menses too late and scanty and too short, with colic. Dysmenorrhœa from getting the feet wet. Amenorrhœa at puberty, with numerous concomitant symptoms, especially with nosebleed (Bry.), headache, colic, backache, gastric catarrh, tearful melancholia, general chilliness, vomiting of food. Leucorrhœa, from delayed menses, discharge thick, bland, with swollen pudenda, rarely thin and acrid, when concomitant symptoms demand Puls. Prolapsus of the uterus, < lying down and heat, > walking in open air, with weeping mood. Irregular labor-pains; it not infrequently restores a harmonious contraction of the uterus and determines a natural presentation of the child, testimony on this point is so strong that its power to rectify abnormal presentations seems undoubted. Uterine inertia, especially with palpitation, suffocation, must have fresh air (compare Causticum). Phantom tumor, even the breasts contained milk. Disorders of pregnancy, of various sorts, nearly always with desire for fresh air, aversion to meat and fats, nausea, etc.

Respiratory Organs. — Tickling and scraping in larynx, causing lachrymation and dry cough. *Scraping in epiglottis, as in hoarseness. Tickling in region of thyroid cartilage, causing short cough. Hoarseness, inability to speak a loud word.* Constriction of trachea in evening, when standing, so that he could not get his breath.

Cough; *from dryness in trachea; caused by itching from pit of stomach to epiglottis; from scraping in trachea; from constriction in larynx, < after eating,* with vomiting and nosebleed; (after eating a morsel); *with oppression of chest, without expectoration;* with pain in chest; (in a child), then much hacking; *efforts to C. caused by inspiration.* **Constant, in evening after lying down. At night, causing dryness of throat; at night, preventing sleep** *and causing exhaustion;* at night, causing stitches in side; at night, causing stitches in shoulder. **Hard, towards evening.** Shaking the child very much. **Dry, at night, > sitting up, returning on lying down; D., with difficult expectoration;** *with scraping and rawness in larynx;* at first, later C. with easy expectoration of much mucus from anterior part of trachea. **Cough, with expectoration; of yellow mucus;** *in morning after rising, with oppression of chest; bitter E.;* bitter, bilious-tasting mucus; mucus of a biting, burnt taste, almost like the taste of crab's broth, or the juice of an old pipe; black clotted blood till evening; (salt, nauseous, in morning); *violent C., with difficult, scanty E. of tenacious mucus. Expectoration of blood.*

Respiration.—Dyspnœa; *in lower part of chest in morning; in evening;* then slumber, then waking with a paroxysm of suffocation, hacking cough, tearing in forehead extending through eyes, crawling on tongue, cold feet, cold sweat on face and eructations; when lying outstretched on back, with vertigo and weakness of head. Difficult in morning from anxiety in chest. (Asthma on smoking as usual). *Short after dinner. Want of, on attempting to breathe through nose.* Spasmodic inspiration and expiration, changing to suffocation.

Clinical.—Aphonia, reflex, rarely catarrhal. Bronchitis, > open air, < warmth of bed and drinking cold water, the cough is frequently dry, > sitting up in bed, or there may be thick yellow expectoration, sometimes streaked with blood. Night-cough, with feeling as though something were torn loose in the chest. Asthma, especially of children, with a shattering spasmodic cough. Cough dry at night, loose during the day (Calc. c.). Catarrhal pneumonia. Whooping cough, occasionally indicated by itching in the chest and attacks of suffocation, with intense desire for fresh air. Threatening tuberculosis, with soreness under the clavicles, especially < lying on the painful side, involving also the muscles about the shoulders. Hæmorrhages from the lungs, suffocation in the chest, hacking cough, with soreness of the lungs, > morning in open air.

Chest.—Swelling of breasts, with tensive pain as if milk rushed into them and caused pressure, while nursing. (Lungs ulcerated, eroded, with hectic fever and bloody and purulent expectoration, when given in fever with cough, rawness in throat, acrid catarrh and stitches in side.) Sticking beneath ribs; in sternum and l. wall; in l. side in evening after lying down; in middle pectoral muscles from towards evening till morning, on raising arm; on moving body; in side on lying down; on breathing during menses; before and during menses, on moving arm, breathing and talking loud, so that arm felt paralyzed; in side, with tearing; sudden, through C.; sudden, in l. wall when sitting; beneath l. margin of ribs, extending to l. wall of chest.

Cutting here and there; compressive C., almost like a stitch, in a lower rib when lying on r. side, > stretching or lying on painful side. *Cramplike sensation through C.;* C. pain in r., then l. side, then in C. Spasmodic pain across. Pain in side when coughing and on rising; in side during menses, > sweat; in l. wall, preventing respiration; *in a spot in region of sternum as if the breath pressed against it; in sternum, as from an internal ulcer, before midnight, with pain in forehead;* jerking, in l. side; weary, in region of short ribs, as from a long-continued cough, from slight cough Drawing, tensive pain in sternum; in one or other side, < breathing. *Spasmodic tension in lower part.* (Drawing in region of sternum, extending to region of stomach, with burning and clawing.)

Constriction; spasmodic, in r., with orgasm of blood and internal warmth; cramplike, at times, preventing breathing. *Pressure and soreness;* P. on middle; above and upon clavicle. Soreness under clavicles; (S. of ribs when grasped). Anxiety, with rapid pulse. Jerking sensation in pectoral muscles, < morning after waking. Rush of blood to C. and heart at night, with anxious dreams (for example, of being immured), starting up and anxious cries. Painful stiffness of pectoral muscles in morning on deep breathing and on moving chest, after rising.

Heart.—*Sticking in præcordial region, > walking, with pressure and anxiety impeding respiration.* Catching pain, *temporarily > pressure. Anxiety in evening, with impulse to commit suicide and with nausea in pit of stomach.* **Palpitation;** *from talking; after dinner;* **rapid, if she lies on l. side, with anxiety and want of breath;** *and anxiety, forcing him to throw off his clothes.* Action feeble and irregular.

Clinical.—General sluggish circulation, with chilliness, soft pulse, palpitation, suffocative attacks and a tearful disposition. Phlebitis; in disease of the veins, especially of the lower extremity, the characteristic is coldness of the part, with chilliness, with the other symptoms of the drug; it is very frequently useful in varicose veins. Varicose ulcers, with smarting, stinging pain, < warmth, the leg sweats constantly.

Neck.—Swelling of glands; of nape as far as carotids and on touch pain as from an internal ulcer; on r. side, with sensation on moving and touching it as if torn and tense or as from an internal ulcer. Painless cracking in first vertebra on moving head. *Sticking in nape; drawing, in nape, between scapulæ and in back. Pain in l. muscles, with stiffness; P. in nape at night, as if he had lain in an uncomfortable position; rheumatic, in nape, with weariness of feet; drawing tensive, in nape. Drawing-like rheumatism in nape in afternoon, he could only move it with difficulty.*

Back.—*Sticking; and across chest;* when coughing. Tearing. Sensation as if spine would come out. Pain extending up B. Drawing during stool, rarely at other times. Throbbing tickling. *Painfully stiff.*

Scapulæ.—Cracking in morning on motion. Sticking at night; between S.; between S. on motion, impeding respiration. Pinching in r. when sitting. Pain between S.; < inspiration; as from heaviness; as on rising after long stooping, > walking.

Sacrum.—Sticking in S. and abdomen, with cutting colic, impeding respiration; S. in loins in morning in bed, on bending forward; afterwards extending to abdomen, where it became a cutting and sticking and took away the breath, later a crawling in head, heaviness and drawing, with vanishing of sight and hearing, then chilliness as if dashed with cold water. **Sprained pain on motion. Labor-like pain,** *as if a band passed through S. and everything were constricted, taking away her breath, < morning. Pain as if suppurating or as from a band, when lying, with stiffness. Pain after sitting, can scarcely rise; after sitting,* can scarcely stoop; in fourth lumbar vertebra, < walking; on stooping, > rising or bending backward; on rising and on bending backward, > bending forward; *as from fatigue in evening; pressing out, in evening; drawing tensive, in loins;* drawing, in loins on inspiration, extending to pit of stomach, where it became a sticking; as from long stooping in evening, < standing and sitting, > bending backward and walking, with weariness in feet forcing him to sit down.

Clinical.—The backache of Puls. generally involves the sacrum and hips, and extends towards the small of back, < lying on back, > lying on sides, but is usually > change of position, this occurs during many affections calling for the drug, and especially is a symptom during pregnancy. Spinal irritation, stiffness, small of the back feels bandaged.

Extremities.—Trembling and tearing; of l. arm and foot; (trembling of hands and feet on moving about); *anxious tremulous sensation. Drawing sticking, < joints, which are painful to touch as if beaten. Drawing tearing in one or another, with chilliness.* **Pain in morning in bed, < joints, forcing him to stretch, with general heat.** *Feeling as if beaten.* Bursting pain in muscles of thigh and upper arm. *Heaviness and drawing in legs,* less in arms. *Weakness; in morning after rising, with relaxation, without feeling weary.* Stiffness of knee and second joint of thumb as if they had been sprained and as if cracking would ensue. *Falling asleep of those upon which he lies in sleep, with crawling on waking;* crawling falling asleep of forearms, hands and legs when lying, > motion.

Upper Extremities.—Hard glandular swelling in r. axilla, painful and throbbing. Stitches in r. deltoid; (in axilla when sitting).

Shoulder.—Sticking caused by cough; S. in joint on rapid motion of arm. Sticking rheumatic pain in joint in morning on moving arm or bending head sideways. *Tearing in joint obliging him to bend arm,* in morning on waking and half an hour later, then disappearing of itself or on lying on painful arm. Pinching in joint, with heaviness. Sprained feeling from r. joint to wrist, except in elbow; in joint on bending arm backward. Pain in r. joint; in joints in evening; on attempting to raise arm; in joints so that she could not hold a cup; drawing, extending into fingers all night, with falling asleep of fingers; *intermittent drawing, to wrist;* jerking, in joint. Jerking sensation in joint. Bubbling, a kind of trembling sensation on r. in afternoon. Weight in joint on attempting to raise arm, with paralyzed sensation.

Arm.—(Cramps of muscles on A. and hands during night-sweat.) (Sticking here and there in a case of rheumatic paralysis of l.) Jerking tearing. Feels broken and dislocated, < pressure and movement. When she raises the arm she cannot get it down in the same way, it is a sickening pain. Tearing drawing at night, < fingers. Drawing tensive pain in inner part, extending to wrists. Burning pain in evening, with dry sensation in fingers. Heaviness during the day, with tearing in elbow on bending it; *H. on raising it while holding anything with it or working with it, with numbness.* (Feeling as if it would fall asleep on holding anything in hand.)

Pain as if beaten in middle of humerus, extending into thumb, so that she could not use it. Upper arm, sticking; tearing in muscles; pain on touch. Elbow, pain on moving it; on stretching it; *tensive, in tendons of bend on moving arm;* bruised, in morning on motion, with dilated pupils. Shooting low down in r. arm when coughing. Forearm, swollen veins; attacks of drawing tearing in bones during the day and evening; pressure in l.; jerking sensation extending to wrist, < morning after waking. Wrist, sprained pain in bones in evening, < motion, then in arm; on motion pain like stiffness, with sprained feeling in hand; stiffness of r., even if hand is not moved.

Fingers.—Sticking in tips of r. Sprained pain in second joint of thumb on motion. Tearing in extensor tendons. Pressure between l. Pain in first joint of l. index at 5 P.M., > moving fingers; in index, as if a panaritium would form on side of nail; drawing, in thumb on moving it, with stiffness. Tension in last joints in morning. Falling asleep in morning in bed; at night.

Lower Extremities.—Reeling in evening when walking, as if head were dizzy, without dizziness; dizzy, < evening, with internal heat in head and pallor; as from the side. Trembling in morning. He must lie with l. bent or else he has no rest. Bruised feeling. *Drawing as far as knees in evening, with more chilliness than during the day.* Stiffness when walking in open air.

Thigh.—Twitching of some muscle-fibres in evening in bed. Sticking anteriorly in l. extending to knee and from r. calf to heel, when lying. **Pain in hip-joint as if dislocated. Drawing pain in muscles at night, forcing him to move, with sleeplessness, tossing about, even when there is no pain, and general coldness.** *Pain in hip at noon on bending back.* Bruised sensation in bones and muscles; *in femora when pressing upon thighs, inability to bend knee, it seemed as if bone would break; in gluteals, or pain as from internal suppuration, after sitting. Jerking, almost sore pain extending from hip-joints to knees in morning in bed, > walking.* **Drawing in T. and legs in evening, with tension.** (Tension when walking and stooping.) Soreness externally on nates where the fissure begins, with smarting. Sudden paralytic weakness on beginning to walk after long sitting. *Stiffness in r., but on grasping it soreness like a sticking.*

Knee.—**Painless swelling;** *swelling, with tearing. Cracking. Trembling, with weakness of legs.* Tremulous sensation in K. and legs in evening after lying down. *Tearing pain-like jerks.* **Tearing and drawing pain;** T. extending to hip when sitting. Bruised pain in a spot on one side; *in and below K. at night if she moved the affected thigh and leg. Tension in hollow.* Paralytic pain in K. and heel on beginning to walk after sitting. Pressure on inner side of r. *Weariness* on rising from a seat. Give way when walking. *Stiffness of r. when walking, whenever thigh is stretched out straight.*

Leg.—Swelling, and of feet; of calves, with pain. *Bleeding of varicose veins. Cramp in evening after lying down, with chilliness.* Jerking in one part of r. calf in morning in bed, not without an agreeable sensation. Stitches upward in shaft of tibia, with external burning pain and erysipelatous redness. Tearing in forepart of r. Pain; in bones; in l. tibia; in tibia on touch; if he allows it to hang down; *in bones, like pressure upon a suppurating spot, on long walking, < afternoon, > pressure and sitting, but most by resting at night;* in flesh, as if suppurating, < evening after lying down, > pressure; in calves, like a cramp, when walking; paralytic, on rising from a seat, > walking. Bruised pain in tibia; in T. in afternoon; in T., < lifting foot. *Tensive pain in calves;* drawing, in calves. *Drawing pain in evening.* Drawing in l. calf; on inner side of calves on sitting down in the house after a long walk. *Heaviness during the day;* H. < forenoon. Weariness on rising from a seat. *Seem asleep on rising from a seat.*

Ankle.—Sticking in r. internal malleolus all day when walking, with drawing pain. Tearing in morning on moving foot, with dilated pupils; in internal malleolus, < walking. Boring above r. internal malleolus. Sudden sprained pain when walking. Intermittent pain in r. external malleolus when sitting.

Foot.—*Swelling; of back;* above malleoli, not below; of one in evening; **and varicose veins swell up;** *of back, with tensive pain; hot, as far as calves; red, hot, with tensive burning pain, which on standing changes to sticking;* red, hot, with itching crawling as if frozen. Red, inflamed, painful. *Tearing across back to heel* in morning and evening. *Burning pain on back.* Bruised feeling, as after a long walk. Sensitiveness in morning on first stepping on it, with crawling, as from accumulation of blood. Drawing pain to knees as after a long walk, > morning. Drawing downward into F. in evening in bed. Tension after slight overloading of stomach at breakfast. *Tingling when standing, > walking, with grumbling. Inclination to stretch during the day when sitting. Weakness.* Seem insensible towards evening, yet heavy, they tremble when walking.

Heel.—Sticking in morning, > rising; *burning, in ball, with itching, as if frozen; boring.* **Boring towards evening.** Cutting in evening in warmth of bed. Pain.

Sole.—Sticking during rest, and in tips of toes; crawling, as if asleep, when standing. Tearing, and above knee; extending above knees and into back. *Pain as if beaten; burning P.;* in hollow, as from swelling or internal suppuration, on stepping, with stitches extending into calves; as if congested or ulcerated, on stepping; numb, in S. and balls of great toes, as after a great jump and as if deadened, on standing after long sitting, > walking, a pain in periosteum on pressure, with insensibility of skin and muscles.

Toes.—Tearing jerks in great. Sticking in r.; S., < great; in tips of r. in evening; burning, in balls of second and fifth in evening on becoming warm in bed, with itching, as if frozen. Cutting; in r. Pain in great, < evening, > lying down to sleep; P. as if pinched by a shoe; numb, in ball of great; (burning, extending to groins, in a paralyzed leg, coincident with improvement in power).

Skin.—Reddish spots on different parts; the redness about an ulcer becomes hard and glistening. Swellings painful to touch beneath skin above elbow; hard red S. in front of r. ear, with burning constriction; red, painful S. on back of foot, with prickling sticking as if an ulcer would form. Scurfy eruption on tragus, with burning biting pain, watery exudation and glandular swelling farther down neck, which is painful to touch. Pimples on forehead, face, shoulders, chest, and lastly on back; (in hollow of knee); painful to touch, below chin; red, in region of zygoma; (red, as from burning nettles, with itching biting pain); itching, < evening on undressing, on scapulæ and as far as middle of back; itching, on side of neck, the I. not > scratching; containing water, between fingers, with sticking when touched or moved; oozing moisture, on legs, with burning pain.

Pustules in groins, with burning sticking. *Abscess at root of nose, near inner canthus, as if a lachrymal fistula would form. Ulceration externally of wings of nose, and oozing of watery moisture;* ulcer that had existed is inclined to bleed. Boils here and there. (Blisters on paralyzed arm that filled with matter and desquamated.)

Sticking upward in an ulcer on one foot, and burning in an ulcer on other foot; S. in an ulcer, that causes shuddering through whole body, with sticking that often changes to burning about ulcer. *Itching sticking;* in feet and toes, that seem inflamed, < close to nails, as if limbs had been frozen, penetrating whole body, before midnight. Pain in an ulcer is aggravated when about to eat; P. on touch on face and lips; on touch in a place that had been burned but was now healed. *Biting in an ulcer on foot* morning and evening just before dressing it; sticking, in an ulcer, with itching about it; burning, in region of a scab of an ulcer in morning in bed (with dry cough). Itching crawling in toes as if frozen, in evening.

Itching in evening in bed; *on back and across loins; on forearm, < back of hand and between fingers; on backs of feet and between breasts in morning in bed;* (in the paralyzed arm at night); in region of chin, < evening; of r. nipple, not > scratching; *on neck and cheeks, on scratching pimples appear;* **burning, over whole body before midnight, on becoming warm in bed, < scratching, preventing sleep, less during the day and only after becoming heated from walking or after rubbing;** about an ulcer, as if it would heal; crawling, in and above umbilicus, painful after scratching; tickling, under an ulcer on foot. **Biting itching here and there;** on tip of elbow; on upper part of sternum in evening, not > scratching; on side of neck after shaving off beard, not > scratching, but it pains.

Clinical.—Measles, dry cough at night, must sit up in bed, with earache, usually indicated after the fever has subsided. Occasionally indicated in erysipelas, which changes its location.

Sleep.—*Yawning.* Sleepiness; *late in morning or early in evening;* **can scarcely keep awake in evening, but not weary;** *during dinner;* constant, dreamy. **Irresistible sleep in afternoon;** at noon, in the middle of a meal. Sleep too long, at first it is only a nap full of dreams. Stupefied slumber full of visions and thirst for beer and sweat all night.

Late falling asleep in evening and early waking in morning. **Sleeplessness in evening; on account of anxious heat; before midnight, from a fixed idea,** *for example, a melody constantly recurred, but sleepiness prevented activity of memory and fantasies;* before midnight, then sleep only when sitting with head bent forward or to one side; *till* 2 A.M.; all night, except the first hour and a half, obliged to turn over constantly; *with restlessness;* with rush of ideas; *as from orgasm of blood.* **Restless sleep, necessity to throw off covers on account of heat, with internal warmth of hands, without sweat;** *R. and stupid sleep.* Light sleep. *Waking before midnight and dreaming much, quiet sleep only after* 2 A.M., *next forenoon weariness; W. at night as if frightened and dazed, did not know where he was and was unconscious; frequent, on account of vivid dreams, for example, that he was falling; frequent, at night, and sleepiness during the day;* wide awake every three hours during the night; easy W. before midnight.

Jerking of limbs or whole body in sleep; of arms and starting up in fright; of one or another limb on touch when falling asleep; in head and whole body on falling asleep in afternoon. The child drew its mouth back and forth, opened its eyes, distorted them and closed them again and twitched fingers. *Fright and starting.* Screams and starts up, frightened by a black dog, a cat, and tries to drive away bees. She frequently sprang out of bed because she felt better out of bed. She sat upright in sleep, with staring eyes, and said "Drive that man away." *Talking;* about trifles that seemed to float before him after midnight when half awake. Snoring in afternoon nap while sitting.

Dreams.—**Confused.** *Of disconnected subjects,* to each of which the dreamer attaches words in thought, though the names do not correspond to the subjects of the dream, hence disconnected loud talking. *Vivid, of what had happened or been spoken of the previous day; V. after midnight,* causing weariness, almost constant recurrence of same subject till he woke; V. after midnight, with stupefied slumber and sweat. *Frightful, with starting up; F. and disgusting;* for example, that he would be beaten and was unlucky, he sobbed and wept aloud and on waking the dream was so vivid that he was forced to sigh; and he was forced to get up. Anxious in morning, the anxiety continued after waking. Of quarrels. All about men, *dread of men,* she fancies that a naked man is wrapped in her bedclothes and rolled up under her bed, while she has only a sheet to cover her. Amorous, with emission; A. in evening and morning, almost without sexual excitement.

Fever.—Chilliness; all day, and three times flushes of heat in face; in morning on rising; morning and evening; at noon, after dinner; every day about 1 P.M., with hot ears and hands; **thirst about 2 P.M., at 4 P.M. chill without thirst, with coldness of face and hands, with anxiety and oppression of chest, later lying down, drawing pains in back, extending to occiput, thence into temples and vertex, three hours later heat of body without thirst, skin burning, sweat only on face, trickling down in great drops, sleepiness without sleep, restlessness, next morning sweat over whole body;** *in afternoon; in afternoon, then heaviness and heat of head;* towards evening; towards evening, *without sensation of being cold,* mingled with heat. **C. in evening; all the E. before bedtime, even when walking;** *in E., with pain; with external coldness, without thirst, in morning heat as if sweat would break out (which does not), without thirst and without external heat, though with hot hands and with aversion to uncovering; after lying down,* after lying heat; in evening, after a few hours heat rather external, with weakness, the heat during the night was internal, without sweat till 5 A.M., then confusion of head, in a few hours bloody expectoration, later it was of the color of liver. **C. before menses, with yawning and stretching;** *on going into cold air; on taking off her clothes, but she was too warm with them on;* after stool, < *sacrum (with pressure in region of stomach);* during most of the pains; *with trembling, returning after a few minutes, then heat without sweat;* with pallor and general sweat; mingled with warmth, then heat in face and rest of body; *without thirst, thirst during the heat;* then heat in head and hands, with full, slow pulse; then internal heat with shivering, then heat with rapid pulse, rapid respiration and deathly anxiety.

Shaking chill, then general heat and sweat, with drawing jerking pains in shafts of bones of limbs. *Shivering; in afternoon, in evening heat, thirst, starting up preventing sleep, labor-like pains, pain in whole body so that she could not turn over in bed, and watery diarrhœa;* < open air, with redness and burning of r. cheek, heat of r. hand, confusion of head like intoxication and fretfulness; almost without chilliness, so that hair bristles, with anxiety and oppression; as if sweat would break out.

Shivering on one side of face. *Chilliness over upper abdomen and upper arms after dinner. Chilliness along back; with cold hands; shivering up B. all day, without thirst; shivering on B., extending into hypochondria and especially into anterior part of arms and thighs, about* 4 P.M., *with coldness of limbs and feeling as if they would fall asleep;* sensation as if cold water were poured down B. Coldness in arms as if they would fall asleep. *Shivering creeping over arms, with heat of cheeks, the room seems too warm. Coldness of hands and feet, they seem dead;* C. of one hand, with heat of other; of hand and foot of one side in evening and night, with redness, the other side hot; (of hands and feet during rest, when sitting). Internal C. of lower part of body in afternoon, without external coldness, with warmth of upper part of body. Chilliness on thighs towards evening, with external coldness of them; on thighs and legs at 6 P.M., without thirst, with heat on chest and between scapulæ; (of knee at night in bed); internal, in leg.

Heat; in morning in bed, with sensation as if sweat would break out; for an hour in afternoon; at 7 P.M., with inclination to wrap up and thirst for beer; every evening, with red face; **at night, without thirst; at night in bed, with uneasiness**; at night, and on turning over in bed shivering; **with desire to be covered, he licks his lips and does not drink, moans and groans; intolerance of external warmth, enlargement of veins**; with thirst; *then shivering;* then chilliness; waking him; *in flushes;* sudden, with sweat of face, trembling of limbs and faintlike obscuration of vision. **Dry heat of body in evening, with distended veins and burning hands, that seek cool places**; *D. at night in bed;* night and morning. **Anxious H.**, *as if dashed with hot water, with cold forehead;* A. over whole body, hands mostly burning, with tearing in occiput. *Internal H. without thirst;* I. in afternoon, *with thirst.*

Heat of whole body except hands, which are cool, with headache above orbits and anxious lamentations. Heat in sinciput; in outer ear, with sweat on it; in face; in face in evening; sudden, in cheeks, < evening, with redness of them and warm sweat on forehead, during and after the heat of face shivering in back and over arms, boring outward headache, with stitches and with attacks of anxiety; running from shoulder down through arm at night; *of hands and feet;* feet; feet during rest, < walking; soles; *near or above an ulcer on foot, in morning.*

Sweat; inclination to during the day; *in morning; in morning in sleep;* at night; offensive, at night (in a case of chronic syphilitic ulceration and bone-pain); *on r. side of body; on l. side of body; r. side of face; face and scalp;* pouring down back all day; on hands in morning after rising; on feet every morning in bed (curative?), after cure of swelling of feet.

Clinical.—Occasionally useful in intermittent fever, chill without thirst, with distressing desire for fresh air, followed by fever and sweat; during the fever there are frequently heat of one part and coldness of another, perspiration usually profuse during the night. It is also said to be useful in ague without sweat. Usually in febrile disorders it is indicated by predominating chilliness.

Ranunculus Bulbosus.

A tincture is made of the entire fresh plant.

General Action.—The "butter-cups" seem to typify the acrid properties of the Ranunculaceæ in general; their pathogeneses are remarkably free from the mental symptoms found in most of their botanical allies. Vesicular eruptions which are very painful, and violent neuralgic pains without these eruptions characterize these plants.

Allies.—Aconite, Cimicif., Clem.

Generalities.—Twitchings; in abdomen and arms. Epilepsy. Pain in posterior part of thigh, in wrist, thumb and scapula. *Bruised feeling,* < hypochondriac region. Rheumatic pains; here and there. *Smarting of eyes,* nose and fauces, running from eyes, inability to see, whites inflamed, mucus running in torrents from nose, fauces painful during inspiration, less during deglutition. Uneasiness. *Weakness; all day,* with sleepiness; all day, head feels as if he had not slept enough, but he performs his occupation with ease if he chooses; during afternoon walk, with trembling of limbs; *with heaviness;* with trembling; sudden, in morning when writing and standing; in sudden attacks in afternoon when sitting, arising from head, with feeling as if his senses would vanish. Many symptoms caused by change of temperature, for example, going from a warm room into cold air, or the reverse. Aggravation *morning* and evening.

Clinical.—Rheumatic neuralgia, < damp weather or change of temperature.

Mind.—Ill humor; in afternoon, when with a patient. Vexed, quarrels and scolds. Quarrelsome and disposed to scold in forenoon, in evening desponding, apprehensive, sensitive, discontented, next day inclined to be provoked by innocent jests of his friends, etc. Gloominess. Anxiety, with headache and faintness. Fear in evening, she does not wish to remain alone, she is afraid of ghosts. (Dread of labor.) (The objects of his feelings, for instance, chagrin, occupy his mind long in forenoon, one sees that he is thinking of those things, he talks to himself, gesticulates in his anger.) Absentminded and talking to himself. Knows not where he is. Obtuseness of senses during the herpes, even the painful herpes did not affect him as vividly as it ought to have done. *Thought vanishes* when reflecting, he stares at one point.

Clinical.—Delirium tremens. Effects of intoxicating drinks in general.

Head.—Aching in morning; A. when eating, with anxiety and weakness. Confusion; in forenoon, with weakness of it and of body. Heaviness. *Distended feeling.* Congestion when walking in open air, < vertex. Rush of blood. *Vertigo;* when walking; on going into open air (Clem.); deep in brain when walking in open air, with stiffness in r. tarsal joint and whole r. leg; *making it difficult to think.*

Forehead.—*Pain, and in eyes; above r. eye;* in eminences in morning on entering house; in morning after a glass of wine, with nausea, pressure in upper part of chest and stitches in l. side of chest; in F. and eyeballs in morning, > rising, whereas pain in chest increased; *over r. eye in evening,* with disposition to weep and mental oppression, which seemed to emanate from chest; in F. and parietal bone from a slight blow upon nape; *over r. eye, < lying down, > walking and standing,* with heat in face and cold hands; in sinciput in afternoon, as if filled with blood; sore, in hairy part in afternoon, *per se,* not when touched; drawing, in front of F. and upper part of frontal bone after supper, with sensation as if hair of sinciput stood on end. *Pressure outward* in afternoon. Vertigo, then pressure.

Temples.—Superficial stitches in l., then stitches in l. ear and tearing in l. side of occiput. Tearing. Pain in region where r. malar and temporal bones unite, about noon; where l. temporal and frontal bones unite, before dinner; in evening when walking, with drawing, pressure and with feverish restlessness and difficulty in breathing; sudden, in T. and nape in evening on entering house, with vertigo deep in brain.

Tearing in vertex; in morning when writing while standing. Pain in vertex as if pressed asunder in evening on entering house, with pressure in eyeball at outer canthus. Migraine; on r. side. Occiput, drawing, sticking; tearing in l. side as far as nape, in evening, later along l. lower jaw, from behind forward; pain in morning after slight chagrin; pain (beating?) in r. side when sitting, with general debility; beating; beats, not like pulsations, but at longer intervals, in l. side; sudden vertigo when walking, then tearing in r. temple. Scalp, burning prickings in outer and r. side, with sensation as if blood rushed into brain and vanishing of thought; crawling in evening in bed; crawling and stitches, with stupefaction of senses.

Clinical.—Neuralgic headache in forehead and vertex as if forced asunder, < evening or coming into warm room. Headache, < change of temperature. *Herpes frontalis*, with violent pain.

Eyes.—*Inflammation. Pain;* sore; as from a hair, > rubbing. *Smarting in r.; S. as from smoke* in evening. Itching in afternoon in the house, with stretching and yawning, later eructations. *Pupils insensible. Pain in balls; r.;* < l.; *now in one, now in other*, in morning; *pressing out*, with vertigo in forehead. *Pressure downward as with a dull point in r. ball. Balls sore on moving them. Burning soreness in r. lower lid* in morning. Swelling of l. outer canthus, with redness and painful soreness. *Smarting in r. outer canthus, with sore feeling.* Pain in region of r. brow in evening during moderate mental effort. *Vision misty.*

Clinical.—Herpes of the forehead, involving the eyeball, with intense ciliary pains, iritis, etc.

Ears.—Stitches; *in region of r. tympanum;* in l. in evening; through r. into parietal bone in evening. Cramplike feeling in l. middle and outer in evening.

Nose.—External redness and swelling, with internal tensive pain and dryness and with scurf in r. nostril. Pain in region of root when seating himself. *Tingling internally pressing upward from tip to root and from r. brow to temple.* Crawling internally; pushing upward in region of lower turbinated bone, another paroxysm of painful crawling in lower part of nostril, with a sort of pressure, *frequent necessity to blow her nose, during which she discharged blood*, the C. and pressure > blowing, then stoppage of r. nostril, > open air, returning in the house. *Stoppage; in evening, with painful soreness extending deep into nose. Profuse tenacious mucus.*

Clinical.—Hay fever. Smarting and burning in the eyes, nose stuffed, < towards evening, pressure at root of nose, especially tingling and crawling in the nostril, patient tries in every way to reach this sensation by hawking and blowing the nose.

Face.—Stitches near r. corner of mouth. Pain; in r. zygoma. Spasmodic paralytic sensation in jaws in evening after lying down. Spasms of lips.

Mouth.—Sensation in r. sound and lower molars as if a foreign body were between them and forced them asunder. Teeth sensitive. (Toothache in morning on waking.) Burning scraping in palate. Scraping burning in velum palati. Salivation; white, tasting like copper; with sweetish taste on tip of tongue. Taste burnt; T. bitterish, pungent, in morning during and after dry food, which tastes natural; bitter-sour before dinner; flat in morning, with white-coated tongue; (too sweet to butter).

Throat.—Mucus; in afternoon, with frequent hawking. Tenacious mucus; evenings; with roughness. Scraping burning, < during inspiration and by smoke of tobacco. Spasmodic feeling ascending pharynx and œsophagus.

Stomach.—Hunger in morning, with grumbling in stomach. *Thirst in afternoon. Eructations;* in evening; before dinner, with great hunger, still he eats less than usual; empty; hiccoughing, after dinner. Hiccough. *Nausea;* towards noon, with eructations; *in afternoon, sometimes with headache;* in evening, with pressure upon sternum, breathing labored, frequent and deep; in evening, < smoking tobacco as usual, > eating; with drowsiness. *Pain in pit;* and transversely across lower part of chest. Soreness in pit in morning on touch; burning S. in pit. Burning in pit; *in region of cardiac orifice*, with anxiety about heart.

Abdomen.—*Rumbling;* in evening when lying down, with movements; in evening after lying down, with colic; *and movements.* Fetid flatus. Cutting in evening. *Pinching all day, sometimes alternating with pain in chest;* P. in walls after dinner, with pain in them on touch and with shivering; with pain on touch in groins and pit of stomach. Pain, and in back; P. during digestion, with faint sensation; before stool; *subdued, in all intestines when walking, with pain on pressure;* as from subcutaneous ulceration, when pressing it against sharp edge of table, then pinching below umbilicus; now concealed, now sharp, with pinching and with burning sore feeling below umbilicus, sometimes with stitches in side of abdomen, and on pressure pain in intestines as from subcutaneous ulceration. Sensitiveness when walking, with pain. Cramplike paralytic sensation in A. and upper A. in evening after lying down.

Hypochondria.—**Sticking in region of last r. true rib** *in morning when walking after sitting*, **with pressure arresting breath and with stitches and pressure on top of r. shoulder. Pain, with pain in region on touch;** P. in hepatic region; deep in hepatic region when standing, < pressure; external P. **Bruised pain; in evening, and in lowest ribs;** < motion, and in back. Periodical pulsation in l. (Compare this section with Aconite.)

Sticking in r. side; *in l. side in forenoon when walking; in l. side after supper, with sore pain.* Pain in l. side in morning. Pinching in umbilical region at noon when walking; *below umbilicus after dinner*, with sensation as if bowels would fall out, the P. spreads to sides as a drawing aching and then rises to pit of stomach. Colic around U., with coldness creeping up back and arms. Drawing below and around U. in evening when going to bed and moving about, with pinching. Sticking in groin, near anterior superior spinous process of ilium, when walking. Pinching in hypogastrium; after a meal; deep in two hours after supper; then emission of flatus. Pain deep in hypogastrium; from spinous process of r. ilium to flank on stretching body.

Rectum and Stool.—(Profusely flowing hæmorrhoids.) Sticking in anus. Pinching and pain internally in rectum, periodically all day when touched and alternating with each other. *Stools frequent and easy.* Stools twice daily. *Hard stool every morning* *after several urgings, a natural one in afternoon;* H. and scanty, dark brown; and delayed; and painless, though apparently larger than anus.

Clinical.—Dysentery, with violent inframammary pains.

Sexual Organs.—Frequent erections towards morning, with vertigo. Emissions towards morning; at night, with slight erections. Leucorrhœa increased and changed from mild to acrid.

Chest.—Jerking in region of l. short ribs. **Sticking;** *in r.;* in l., and in spleen; *all day, < r. side, in evening pressure on middle of sternum; in r. almost all day, with pressure in middle of C., and with painful inspiration;* **above l. nipple** *in morning on waking,* **< touch and motion,** *with bruised pain in chest; above l. nipple, near axilla, in morning when rising, he dares not move arm or raise trunk, he has to stand with head and chest forward to l. side; in region of l. fifth and sixth ribs in morning when walking,* **with sensitiveness of that spot to touch and debility;** *in r. side in morning on walking in open air;* **in region of r. fifth to seventh ribs,** *in morning when walking after sitting,* **arresting breath, with stitches and pressure on top of r. shoulder; in region of r. fifth and sixth ribs** *in forenoon;* **anteriorly in middle of l., in forenoon during inspiration;** *in region of last l. true rib in forenoon when walking and standing, with pain as if bruised or as from subcutaneous ulceration;* in l. in forenoon when talking; *in l.* in afternoon and evening, < *motion, with sensation of subcutaneous ulceration,* and in evening pain in r. scapula; **in l. side** *in evening,* **with burning** *and with short heavy breathing and frequent necessity to breathe deeply; in upper and l. side in evening, with pressure upon chest,* **breathing and contact painful; now in r., now in l., first in outer part, then extending deep in,** *in evening when walking and standing,* **< moving, stooping or inspiration, with pressure and tightness across lower part;** in l. side of sternum on ascending a hill, with bruised sensation; *in l., with sensation of subcutaneous ulceration;* in interior, in region of l. nipple, then pain below r. true rib (splenetic stitch?); *extending from r. into l., being felt in both sides at the same time,* in forenoon, but ability to breathe deeply when bending forward. (Compare above with Aconite and Bry.)

Pinching, rather external, impeding breathing only when walking. Sharp pain in upper part of l. Pain; *in outer parts;* in sternum; in l. side; in l. all day, < evening, with tenacious mucus in throat; in l. in morning; in l. in morning on rising; on both sides of xiphoid cartilage in morning when walking; *near l. axilla, in region of pectoralis major, in morning, < motion; in forenoon; in afternoon, < l. side, and partly in pectoralis major, where there is rheumatic pain on turning body and pain as from subcutaneous ulceration, at first the pain is external, then in posterior surface of sternum and in pit of stomach,* the pain often gives place to a pain as from subcutaneous ulceration below liver, the pain is often preceded by a bitter burnt taste and forcible hawking; *in evening in bed, < l. side, with anxiety, tightness of breath, rapid pulse and inability to lie on either side on account of pain in outer part of chest;* in upper half of sternum in evening when writing; in middle and in l. side in evening, with increase of mucus in throat; in evening and all night, not < deep breathing; in l. chest, hypochondrium and back on motion and touch; *with restless night;* with cough; with cough and eructations; with shortness of breath when walking on level ground, but no oppression of breath on ascending a hill; alternating with concealed pain in abdomen.

Bruised pain in region of short ribs, with pain in back, lassitude and ill humor; *B. pain in l. half in morning after rising, spreading over whole chest, with pressure and shortness of breath so that he cannot speak long sentences, movement of shoulder causes pain; in region of last l. true rib in morning, or sensation as if he had lain in a wrong position. Rheumatic pain in morning on rising, and on motion of trunk pain as from subcutaneous ulceration. Burning pain. Soreness under l. short ribs, < moving trunk.*

Pushing in lowest part of r. side, towards liver in forenoon. Oppression; in evening, with weeping and sore pain in eyes, < r.; when walking and ascending a hill; *as after an insult,* in evening, *with frequent necessity to breathe deeply.* Pressure on l.; on xiphoid cartilages in morning, < r.; transversely across C. and pit of stomach; on lower half of sternum, in region of xiphoid cartilage on stooping, and on rising a beating there, then pain on touch, later the P. on lower part of sternum spreads towards r. side of chest and pit of stomach, pit and sternum are painful to touch and when stooping, outer chest so painful that even buttoning the coat causes pain. Beating in sternum; B. after dinner, with movements in abdomen during digestion; as from congestion of blood, after dinner, with inclination to lie down. Chilliness in outer parts when walking in open air.

Clinical.—Inflammation of the diaphragm, sharp shooting pains around the hypochondria and back. Pleurodynia, especially < in changes of weather. Pneumonia, with pleurisy, with the characteristic pains about the chest, as from subcutaneous ulceration. Muscular rheumatism, especially about the chest. Intercostal rheumatism, always with great soreness to touch, as if the muscles had been pounded. Inflammation of the pleura or peritoneum.

Pulse.—Rapid towards evening, and hard. Small, hard. Full and strong.

Neck.—Pain in nape; rheumatic, in nape in evening, in l. shoulder next morning.

Back.—*Pain in morning* on rising; P. in r. scapula; rheumatic, between scapulæ *in morning on waking.* Sticking between scapulæ, in region of third and fourth dorsal vertebræ, in morning; in r. scapula in morning when walking; *in r. loin* in morning *when walking, with burning; from l. loin transversely through abdomen after dinner, < below umbilicus and towards r. groin.* Pain in lumbar region in morning (after a restless night disturbed by dreams and emissions), with general indolence.

Extremities.—Trembling from the least chagrin. Pressure on top of r. shoulder, with stitches. Jerking of arms. Rheumatic pain in arms. *Jerking pain in r. upper arm.* Rheumatic pain in elbows and shoulder-joints in morning. Stitches through forearm, then also in l. thumb. *Sudden tearings* (stitches, jerkings?) *in r. forearm and between thumb and index* when writing. Spasmodic contraction of skin and muscles in region of styloid process of l. ulna. Tearing in l. wrist, extending along dorsum of hand, in forenoon. Hands tremble when threading a needle. Jerking of some muscular parts of hands; J. of l. hand when it is lying quiet. Tearing in ball of l. thumb in afternoon, later sensitiveness to touch. Pain at nail of index; under nail of r. index, as if a splinter had caused suppuration, in afternoon.

Lower Extremities.— *Weakness in forenoon when walk-*

ing. Cramplike tearing in outer side of r. thigh in evening when walking, from centre downward, skipping bends of knees and beginning in calves. Tearing boring in middle of l. thigh in morning in bed and later when standing. Drawing pain in r. hip in evening when walking. Painful drawing in posterior and inner sides of thighs extending into half of calves, in afternoon when sitting, < region of inner hamstring. Cracking in knees; in patella in morning on ascending a hill. Tearing in inner side of knees when walking. Weakness in bends of knees in morning, they give way. Pain in tendo-achillis. Tension in r. tendo-achillis when walking. Tearing in l. tarsal joint in evening when sitting. Pain in ankle; in evening on rising from a seat; extending half way up tibia, as if tendons were too short, when walking. Ankles stiff. Sudden cramp as if sprained, in dorsum of foot and in toe-joints when walking. Sticking in dorsum of l. foot in morning when sitting; *pulsative, in l. heel in afternoon when standing.* Pain in dorsum of foot; in heels; in heels in evening, as if pinched by boots (which he had taken off); drawing, in dorsum of r. foot. Sticking in toes in morning when walking; in dorsa of T. in evening; in tips in evening, with sore pain; in l. fourth on entering the house; between T., with soreness. Pain in toes.

Skin.—Inflammation from finger to shoulder; about arm, with fever and delirium, then gangrene of arm. Ulcers on fingers, penetrating to flexor tendons. *Vesicles on fingers,* < r., after being opened they emitted a yellowish lymph, with burning pain, the red skin shining through the blister, after healing **deep transparent, dark blue elevated blisters of the size of a pin's head formed,** crowded together in oval groups, *with burning itching,* when opened they emitted dark yellow lymph, later were covered with an *itching, herpetic, horny scurf* and emitted a clear fluid, after the scurf had crumbled away new blue vesicles appeared, with burning itching, scratching brought on *a shining red, loose swelling of fingers* (they felt like sheepskin), *with inflammation* and burning stinging itching, after applying hart's grease instead of the *horny scurf there were groups of holes (as if they were pores) emitting yellow lymph in the shape of drops of sweat and changing to flat, spreading ulcers, with eroded sharp borders and burning stinging itching, day and night, depriving him of rest.*

Pricking ending in itching, in various parts. Burning, then redness, then a blister emitting a thin yellowish, burning fluid. *Crawling on fingers; single parts of fingers;* in face and hands; face, < about chin and nose. Itching of upper arm; hand; *hollow of hand;* inner side of knee and in tarsal joint, in evening; several parts of hands, with redness; then a blister; stinging, in r. palm; burning, in l. palm in evening.

Clinical.—One of our most valuable remedies for herpes zoster; the vesicles are filled with bluish-black serum. This eruption may follow the course of the supraorbital, intercostal or other nerves, and is always accompanied by the peculiar pains of this drug. It has also been used for vesicular eruptions, with burning itching.

Sleep.—Irresistible sleep in afternoon. Sleeps three hours in afternoon after dinner; in evening over his work, but unable to sleep for several hours after going to bed. Sleepless; from midnight till 5 A.M., then sleep full of dreams. Jerking through whole body in evening when lying down to sleep. *Late falling asleep; and frequent waking;* and inability to lie on r. side, and early waking; from itching of thighs and internal uneasiness, with great fatigue, moisture of skin, and micturition four times. *Sleep disturbed.* Restless sleep, with increase of pain in chest and back; R. sleep, with aching in chest and oppression; and unfreshing, with flushes of heat. Frequent waking and awake a long time from sleeplessness and anxiety in chest. Waking early and wider awake than usual; W. early, with sweat. Dreams vivid, that he was swimming, etc. Anxious D., that he is near drowning, with erections. Voluptuous D., without emission.

Fever.—Chill in evening; in evening, with external coldness; after dinner; after dinner, with fever; during digestion; internal in evening, with heat in face and redness; creeping, *an hour after dinner,* hair stands on end, shuddering across scapulæ, hands and thighs, then pinching in hypogastrium, with stitches like pushes, which dart towards hypochondrium; shaking, in open air (less in house), with chattering of teeth, heat in face, dryness and mucus in mouth. Shivering in evening; after eating, with cold hands and hot face; after eating, with cold tips of fingers and hot face; after dinner, with gooseflesh on calf and forearms; over shoulders, upper arms and thighs after supper. Cold hands; all day; in evening, with heat in face, < r. side, quick pulse and eructations; in evening, with heat in face and ears, < r. side, and general discomfort; with heat in face. Cold feet at 8 P.M., with dry heat in face, redness of cheeks, mouth dry, viscid, so that she could scarcely speak. Cold feeling in great toe in evening, as from a current of air through it.

Heat in evening; after dinner; about forehead in evening when writing, with sensation as if sweat would break out in that region.

Ranunculus Sceleratus.

A tincture is made of the entire fresh plant.

Generalities. — Twitching of facial muscles and limbs, risus sardonicus. Convulsion in face, outer parts of abdomen and limbs. Irritation of pharynx, eyes and nose, with flow of mucus and tears. Prostration with the sweat. Faintness.

Mind.—Delirium. A species of hydrophobia. Anxiety and oppression. Sad mood, grief, in evening. Disinclination for mental labor in morning; for work, with ill humor, absentmindedness, he tears a paper on which he has made notes, looks at it, discovers from the pieces that he has torn it, and toys with it. Forgetful.

Head.—Inflammation of brain. Feels distended and thick. Heaviness and fulness. Feels as if in a vise. Dulness, < morning after the characteristic uneasiness in afternoon; D., with pressure of temples towards each other. Vertigo when sitting; V. and vanishing of thought.

Fulness in forehead. Temples, sticking in l.; sticking from r. to r. superciliary ridge; gnawing in r., with pressure; pressure outward; pressure inward above T. Vertex, *gnawing in one spot in l.; gnawing suddenly coming and going in a spot;* drawing-clawing pressure across; pressure as with a dull instrument; burning pain; jerking. Occiput, pain, with aching in whole head externally; pain in both tuberculis infer. ossis occipitis, > pressure, but returning. Scalp, contraction; (hard blotches above temples); sticking on vertex, with drawing; biting; itching.

Eyes. — Contortion. Smarting. (Inflammation.) Lachrymation; at night. Conjunctiva injected. *Balls painful* all day; P. *on moving them quickly; periodically. Canthi, periodical smarting;* stinging smarting in r. outer. Lids agglutinated, white of eyes light yellow, finer vessels visible; burning in margins. Itching under r. lower lid, > cold.

Ears.—Sticking in r.; in r. meatus externus; in front of r. in evening. Aching; *in r., with headache and drawing in all teeth.* Boring behind r. in evening; in l. outer meatus in evening, with drawing. Drawing along r. outer meatus.

Nose.—Pricking in outer parts of tip. Crawling inside, with smarting. Sneezing. Watery mucus.

Clinical.—Occasionally useful in fluent coryza, with sneezing, burning micturition, etc.

Face.—*Drawing from above r. brow to corners of mouth* in evening, *with coldness.* Feeling as if covered with a cobweb in evening. *Tremulous sensation around lower lip and corners of mouth before vomiting, without nausea.*

Mouth.—Teeth. Tearing in incisors; in r. lower canine in morning, Stinging gnawing in incisors in evening. Burrowing under roots of l. lower molars as if pushed upward, in afternoon. Drawing in upper molars; *in all* in morning, *with jerking;* in canine, in afternoon and evening; *stinging, in all.* Sensitive all day. On edge, later stinging in them.

Pain in gums, with swelling, redness and bleeding. Tongue coated white; in morning, with sweetish taste; *T. peeling and cracked;* shooting in tip; pain, with burning, redness, inflammation; smarting of tip; burning in tip. Much frothy mucus in mouth. Stinging in parts of soft palate. Smarting in region of palate and fauces. Smarting drawing pain in region of palate. Dry at night; and skin, without thirst. Ptyalism. Spoiled taste.

Clinical.—Superficial ulceration of the tongue, with rawness and soreness. Sore mouth characterized by raw patches on the tongue, the rest of the tongue being coated, sometimes indicates this drug in diphtheria or typhoid fever.

Throat.—*Swelling of tonsils* in evening, *with sticking.* Thick mucus that is difficult to hawk up. Choking at night. *Sticking in tonsils.* Scratching; with soreness; with dry cough that increases the sore pain; becoming somewhat burning. Contractive sensation before breakfast, < eating bread. Burning in pharynx; and œsophagus, sometimes with convulsive arthritic pains. Dry in morning. Impelled to swallow several times. Inflammation of œsophagus.

Stomach.—Hunger after eating, with eructations; H. strong, without real appetite. Little appetite at dinner, then nausea; A. wanting in evening. Thirst on waking after midnight, with heat. Eructations after bread and butter; empty E. before breakfast; *tasting of the ingesta after a meal;* rancid, sour, in evening. Hiccough. Nausea; < after midnight; periodical, in morning. Inactivity. Fulness. Sticking in pit. Pain; *in pit, < morning and pressure, with fulness;* and fits of anxiety. Tension in pit. Constriction. Heartburn.

Abdomen.—Passage of flatus after a frugal meal. Gurgling and pinching. Pinching as after taking cold, < region of navel. Cutting at night. Pains in walls; peculiar P.; convulsive, in various parts, with fainting turns. Torpor of intestinal canal. *Sticking in hepatic region;* in region of gall-bladder; *in region of spleen, < deep inspiration. Screwing pressure behind umbilicus* at night. *Sensation of a plug lodged behind umbilicus,* < morning. Pain in groins.

Clinical.—Pain and soreness over the region of the liver, with frequent sensations as though diarrhœa would set in.

Rectum and Anus.—Moisture in anus. Hæmorrhoidal symptoms, especially itching of anus. Sticking in anus. Tickling burning near anus. Itching in rectum in evening, with forcing; I. in anus, < walking, with forcing out sensation, as if premonitory of hæmorrhoids. Urging after the usual breakfast; after dinner, with passage of flatus and after great straining some soft stool; *frequent, and loose stools;* ineffectual, with emission of flatus.

Stool.—Liquid, fetid; L. and frequent. Loose, frequent. Soft, frequent, with the last one pressure in rectum. *Frequent sensation as if diarrhœa would set in,* but stool is natural. Frequent, alternating with ineffectual urging. Delayed.

Urinary and Sexual Organs.—Dribbling after micturition. Frequent micturition of scanty light yellow urine. Burning in forepart of urethra soon after urinating. Tickling crawling in orifice of urethra. Sudden stitches in forepart of glans. Drawing pains in penis. Smarting about scrotum. Emissions after midnight, without lascivious dreams.

Respiratory Organs. — Hacking cough. Sighs. Breath tight and deep.

Chest.—Sticking in r.; in l. and below false ribs; in pectoral muscles; *behind xiphoid cartilage* in morning; *in r., not < inspiration. Gnawing behind lowest part of sternum, arresting breathing* in evening. Pinching around l. nipple; *behind r. nipple* evenings. *Pressure as with a dull instrument behind r. false ribs, < deep inspiration. Sensitiveness of integuments. Bruised feeling* in evening; *with weakness in it.* Pain externally in sternum, pressure on it causes stitches through chest. *Sore burning behind xiphoid cartilage.* Painful drawing in pectoral muscles. Oppression; as if something lay on sternum. Weakness.

Clinical.—Bruised pain and weakness in the chest every evening, with painful sensitiveness externally.

Heart and Pulse.—*Sticking in region of H.* Sticking pinching in region of H. at night, causing tight breath. Pressure as from a blunt piece of wood in region of H. Sometimes rapid, sometimes slow beating of H. Pulse somewhat accelerated, while radial artery feels somewhat thinner.

Back.—Pain between scapulæ. Compressive drawing in region of scapulæ. *Lumbar region, jerks arresting breathing when walking in open air;* bruised pain; paralytic pain; pressure in r. side.

Upper Extremities.—Soreness in r. axilla. Shoulder, stitches in l.; drawing on r.; sensation extending downward from r. as if muscles for sitting erect had been overtaxed and as if they were now relaxed. Elbow, sticking; gnawing in r. Forearm, sticking; *boring sticking along l. to tip of index, where it is most violent;* paralytic drawing. Hand, sticking in dorsum; drawing sticking in ball of r. *Gnawing in l. palm* in evening. Boring in metacarpal bones of thumbs. Drawing in r. metacarpal bones, with pressure. Fingers, swelling in morning; sticking between l. middle and index in evening; sticking in tips of ring and index, with gnawing in bones of same; sticking boring in last phlanges of index; sticking jerking in bones of l. index; gnawing in last phalanx of l. ring; gnawing in bones of r., with boring; pain in r. middle.

Lower Extremities.—Drawing gnawing in r. thigh. Gnawing in r. knee, with boring. Biting in bends of knees. Jactitation in muscles of r. calf. Painful drawing along leg, with pressure. Gnawing in region of r. outer malleolus. Foot, pricking on dorsum of r., with griping; gnawing in region of ball of l.; gnawing in l. heel; stinging boring in ball of r.; sticking boring along r. sole; pain in a corn in ball of r., with sticking and burning; weakness. Toes, *sudden sticking in r. great, passing into burning; sudden intermittent sticking in forepart of r. great;* itching stitches in l.; *boring in r. great, with gnawing;* gnawing in ball of r. great; tingling in l. great, with jerking.

Clinical.—Corns on the toes, with burning and soreness, especially painful on letting the feet hang down.

Skin.—Red spot beside r. nostril, which turns white when pressed and then causes sore pain, next day a vesicle there, with sore pain. Hard pimple below l. brow. Gangrene. Ulcers. Blister, which spreads over arm. Vesicles, with a thin, acrid, yellowish ichor, they do not heal till the ichor becomes thick and purulent.

Sticking on pit of throat; on pit of stomach. Itching stinging below r. nipple; on dorsum of l. foot. Itching prickling in r. heel. Tickling between fingers. Formication on chest and back, with prickling. Itching between r. fingers in evening; in lower half of thighs in evening, not > scratching; *now here, now there, < towards evening, with boring, biting, crawling and gnawing;* with pain, burning and redness of skin; on feet, with prickling; on soles, with pinching; stinging, on some parts of upper arms.

Sleep.—Yawning afternoons. Sleepy; in evening, and peevish, disinclined to any occupation. *Half slumber after midnight, constant tossing about, frightful, anxious dreams about corpses, serpents, battles, etc.* Half sleep all night, he was not sleepy in morning. Sleeplessness after 3 A.M., with anxiety, debility, gloomy, thoughtless brooding of mind and bruised feeling in limbs, in morning the mind feels worn out, he cannot fix his thoughts. *Wide awake for a long time after midnight.* Wide awake suddenly half an hour after going to sleep, but soon fell asleep again. Restless sleep every night after midnight.

Fever.—Coldness in morning after rising, < nape, extending down back; C. evenings, with thirst and pressure inward in forehead; *when eating.* Cold feeling in face. Heat; in evening, < face, with sweat; *waking him every night after midnight, with thirst, full, soft, rapid pulse, later sweat, < on forehead;* then sweat and prostration; in head and face in evening on entering house; in skin of fingers from touch of juice; flushing, in face. Stinging burning in a spot on forearm; in a spot on r. calf. Cold sweat.

Raphanus.

A tincture is made of the fresh solid roots of the black garden radish.

Generalities.—Emaciation. *Hysterical attack,* pain as if a foreign body passed through spine from top to bottom and were stopped at certain points by an obstacle, the pain extends to adjacent parts and causes weakness, it seems to her that she is about to die, inability to speak or stir, pain like a hot ball starting from uterus and stopping at beginning of throat, then drawing pain in occiput, lancinations in ears, pain in jaws, gums, nose, eyes, which burn, drawing pain in temples, swollen feeling in every part, even in bones, abdomen swollen and painful to touch, feeling as if several balls ascended from abdomen to throat, eyes filled with blood, sight lost, ability to lie only on back, loss of power of moving, this hysterical attack repeated at midnight, with sharp, nervous pain in shoulder, next day (first day of menses) less severe attacks, preceded by cramps extending from uterus to chest.

Lancinations in different parts; in whole body, with drawing pain; in fleshy parts, with drawing in all muscles, itching around waist, preceded and followed by sensation as from too tight a girdle. Pain in all joints, painful weariness, all bones crack, < nape; P. in nasal bones, from tobacco, at root, and in ear, with weeping; in l. orbital, nasal and maxillary bones on touch, with numbness in parts near them; in sides when she presses on stomach, pain in dorsal vertebræ, which, when she touches, is felt in middle of chest. Drawing pain all day, < evening. Rheumatic pain in loins, knees, groins, abdomen and thighs, can scarcely stand upright, cannot bend knees. Paralytic pains increase till evening; P. pain, < sometimes on one side, sometimes on other, with difficulty in writing. Pain under skin, like painful weariness of whole body.

Sensation in head, throat and chest as in beginning of a bad cold. Swollen sensation in arms, hands and eyes, but feet appear smaller, and wrist feels as if lashed with a whip. Throbbing in l. lowest rib, neck, temples, back, stomach, < when she wishes to express an idea, later the throbbings became lancinations, two or three near together. Veins feel as if full of quicksilver. Sensitive to the electricity of the atmosphere, it causes pain and low spirits.

Weakness; with bruised feeling; with want of spirit, it seems to her as if she were dead. Difficulty in rising from bed, she lay without thinking or moving, but a multitude of pictures passed before her eyes, inactivity, it seemed as if she were carried somewhere else and conversed with another person, calm and indifferent, it was also like a picture. Numbness and heaviness. Stiffness of muscles. Aggravation from wine and vinegar; symptoms severe in morning, > course of the day, < evening. Amelioration from walking and open air. Feels better when lying than when sitting.

Mind.—She is averse to all women, but she is attracted towards all men, these symptoms increase to furious delirium. Nervous in morning, averse to children, < little girls. Nervous distention and sometimes nervous attacks, great activity of head, sleeplessness every night, strange ideas, forgets what she has to do, dangerous fancies assail her, but she restrains herself from executing them. Agitation till 1.30, then heavy sleep. Return of memory, liveliness, quick intelligence, everything disturbs her. Rage, then depression. Excitement, with sleeplessness all night.

Anxiety, she thought that she should die. Melancholy and numbness; M. on waking, with impulse to weep, then apathy; with irrepressible tears, voice sounds melancholy and eyes have a sad expression; with drawing and throbbing pains running over head, body and limbs, when these pains are felt in abdomen or chest they make her weep. Believes that she has a disease that is not recognized. Capricious mood, stupefaction, sadness and tears alternating with hopefulness, she fears that she will become a burden to every one. Indolence and indifference. Dulness and inclination to weep at the least word.

Inactivity of mind; physical and moral I., loss of memory, which she tries to recover, and this fatigues her, she goes out and at every step forgets what she was going to do. Fatigue of mind and body, loss of memory, indifference, horror of noise. Stupefaction when she wishes to pursue a train of thought, she looks at things without seeing them. Memory lost.

Head.—When writing shock in brain as when sitting down suddenly and sensation in ears as when diving. Aching on waking between 3 and 4 A.M., and drinking of much water; in morning, with confusion in vertex and forehead, then flushes of heat ending in general external coolness; in morning, < occiput, when she presses her hand on occiput the aching becomes general, when placing a finger on middle of occiput tickling, or rather shuddering in back, chest and arms, with loss of thought, appearance of a sheet of water before her eyes; at 12.30 P.M.; in evening, < occiput, head fatigued; on waking; after dinner; in open air, < skin of frontal eminence, especially l. side; with stupefaction of head.

Pressure inward upon eyes, extending to behind ears. Brain feels sore from least jar when walking. Confusion, with pressure in forehead. Rush of blood to head and chest at 11 A.M., causing vertigo and cough, preceded by burning. Intoxicated feeling in morning on waking; after dinner, at which she drank only water. Vertigo, with dim vision; in morning; V. in evening, with feeling as if head were bandaged.

Forehead.—Pain; in eminence, with sticking; over eyes; in morning, and in occiput; in forepart of head at night on waking; < root of nose; < over eyes, almost preventing vision; in l. side like a pressure.

Pain in morning in temples, eyes and root of nose, with fatigue as if bruised. Sticking on vertex. Gnawing in occiput, then numbness. Pain in occiput, > throwing head back, when leaning head to l. side sensation of a sharp substance inside which pricks into temple near ear, > lifting head; pain in O., a kind of uneasiness, of fatigue, with drawing in it and in neck. Scalp of vertex tight.

Eyes.—Red. Sunken. Pricking, heat when shutting them, coldness when opening them, it seems to her that she sees double, that she squints. Smarting and a little lachrymation; S. and burning, with myopia; and redness and agglutination in morning, after shutting them she can scarcely open them on account of her nervous condition, she winks when looking at anything. Itching in l., with deep stitches. Coldness and pressure upon them; C. in l. Pupils dilated. Lower lids œdematous. Fatigue. Vision weak, lost in r. eye, when she turns her eye in direction of ear she feels a pain in temple, ear and parietal bone; V. very acute. Far-sighted. Short-sighted. Vision and hearing lost, then vomiting with great effort.

Clinical.—Distressing twitching of the eyelids, almost prevents vision, with rotary motion of the ball.

Ears.—*Sticking in r.* Sticking tearing in bones of l. Swollen sensation in posterior part on bending head to l., and when pressing on this spot pain in eye as if it were pulled inward, with drawing in ear corresponding to part pressed on. Stoppage, with fulness as from rush of blood.

Nose.—Pointed. Pain in root extending to occiput. *Stoppage.* Weight on back. Sneezing. Pure blood from it every time she blows it, which clears her head, but it seems as if she did not blow it all out and as if there were a deposit deep in nose. Odor of the radish; as of spoiled eau de cologne, or a suppurating spot, or bad oil burning, which seems to come from interior of head or root of nose, with gnawing there, and the breath feels burning.

Face.—*Pale*, with expression of anguish; P., with blue circles around eyes. Red and tumid. Yellowish in morning on rising; cheeks Y. Sunken; and livid. Tearing in r. malar-bone; in r. zygoma.

Mouth.—Teeth. Lower loose, gum inflamed and ulcerated. Two lower incisors loose and gum ulcerated; and gums violet-colored. Lancinations in l. molars. Pricking and burning. Tearing in molars. Pain in hollow, causing salivation; P., with abscess on gums and another in a hollow tooth, decayed teeth loose and lower incisors shake, lower gums black. Excoriating and gnawing pains in T. and gums, T. feel as if made of papier mâché. Feeling as if two lower middle incisors were enlarged and starting from gums. Gum black in front of lower incisors, pale behind, with vesicles. Pain in gums and feeling as if they separated from teeth.

Tongue white; coated white; pale reddish-blue, with fissure in centre, pale red points on margins; burning in forepart; heat in root. *Taste bitter; pasty*; of pepper; bad.

Clinical.—Neuralgic toothache, shooting pulsating pain in the evening < lying, > walking about. Toothache during the early part of pregnancy.

Throat. — R. submaxillary gland hard, swollen. Swelling of tonsils, with redness and constriction. Mucus, with cough. Pain in l. tonsil; in throat, swollen sensation in top of œsophagus, sensation as if a particle of tobacco stuck in œsophagus, owing to a small pimple behind posterior nares; as if alive every evening when air reaches it, sharp pains as if alive in tonsils, uvula, behind nasal fossæ and along œsophagus, cramps in neck, nerves of neck behind ear painful, feeling of viscid mucus at bottom of throat, which cough makes more adherent, and which breathing appears to loosen.

Scraping, not > clearing it, and at night in bed expectoration of white mucus as in catarrhal fever. Soreness every day on waking, with cough and greenish, salt expectoration. Sensation in pharynx, in region of tonsils, forcing him to clear the throat to relieve it of viscid mucus, which is adherent or detached in so small quantity that it cannot be expectorated, the hawking causes irritation, which excites a dry cough, producing a painful shock in head and sides of chest.

Contraction. Stricture at 5 A.M., with expectoration of tenacious white mucus from pharynx and œsophagus. Dry; feeling as if everything swallowed were dry. Burning; in pharynx; below larynx; in pharynx and tonsils, with stitches. Uneasiness high up in œsophagus, the air when inspired feels cold in mouth, when expired burning.

Clinical.—Spasmodic painful contraction of the throat, cannot speak a loud word.

Stomach.—Voracious appetite, and when she has eaten she finds herself smaller and less tight than before, also empty sensation after dinner; A. at 4 A.M. in bed, without hunger; constant A., with aversion to food, thirst; *A. lost.* Aversion to food and tobacco. Repletion in evening from sugar, with vomituritition, bitter risings or rather acrid vapor ascends into œsophagus, she swallows everything with disgust. *Violent thirst.* Drank more than he urinated, though he urinated considerable.

Eructations of liquids, with retching; E. of water and mucus, sometimes mixed with blood; almost putrid; bilious, leaving a bitter taste; of the odor of radishes, < drinking. Wind from eau sucree. *Nausea;* in evening and after breakfasting on chocolate; when riding in a carriage, with headache; *with retching;* so that she must sit up, in spite of great weakness; in faintlike attacks. Retching in afternoon; in evening when walking; at night; when coughing, with pressure mounting into chest and eructations of acrid, colorless liquid. Vomiting; at 7 A.M., of undigested radishes and white mucus; twice at 1.30 P.M., of greenish, bitter liquid, then clear water; of the radish, with mucus and bread; dark, slimy matter.

Sticking, and in region of liver; in epigastric region; in pit; in pit, < deep breathing. Cutting in pit. *Pressure in pit;* intermittent, extending from pit to pit of throat and sometimes to back, < eating and coughing, > drinking, with sticking. Swollen sensation, with throbbing in epigastrium, she can scarcely sit still.

Abdomen.—*Distention* after eating a little; *D. beginning at stomach, A. hard, as if filled with air, without pain, she cannot bear pressure on stomach;* < *hypogastrium, and hardness and pain on pressure,* it seems as if she would choke with the swelling; *then griping,* as before stool; *tympanitic,* with twisting pain in region of ascending and transverse colon and in l. groin, < pressure. Rumbling; at night. *Flatulence.* **No flatus emitted upward or downward.** Flatus smelling of radishes. Trembling. Lancinations in l. side. Griping. *Pain,* then hard stool; before stool, accompanied and followed by heat and pains of swelling in intestines. Heat, < about umbilicus.

Liver, sticking in region; pressure in region as from an internal abscess; pain in r. lobe like tightness or lancinations. Umbilicus, *griping about;* sticking to l. of; pinching to l. of as before soft stool; sharp pains at side of, with pressure; colic about, after breakfast; burning above.

Hypogastrium.—Gland in r. groin swollen and painful to touch. Cramping sore pain in morning on waking, < motion, with distention and tenderness on pressure, could hardly bear touch of her clothes, next day the same, with tenderness from least jar when walking. Loins are relieved when she leans on her side, but at the same time pain in hypogastrium and sensation of a round body suddenly impelled upward and stopping in throat, where it feels like a morsel too large to be swallowed, thence the substance seems to descend into stomach, where it causes a sensation of something hard to digest and leaves emptiness, with hunger and lancinations in hypogastrium, each lancination causes flushing as if blood rushed to eyes, eyes burn, dizziness, ebullitions of blood throughout body, cold feet, with prickings, sensation as if she had put her cold feet into hot water, then heat. Pain in H. and kidneys as before menstruation, lassitude in groins and top of thighs, pain, with heat in sides almost every time she breathes. Pain on pressure. Feeling as if a hernia would protrude. Heat, < side.

Rectum.—Frequent desire for stool, < about noon.

Stool.—*Liquid; and brownish, frothy, profuse, forcible, three times in one day; and yellowish, brown, rather copious, nine times in one day, mostly in morning; and copious, forcible,* painless; and of the color of coffee with cream, every time she eats. *Diarrhœa, dark brown;* scanty, yellow, like fresh butter, twice, with urging, without colic. Soft; and yellowish; and colored like café au lait; and profuse, in morning and at noon. Hard. Dark, profuse. Preceded by colic, twice in one day. Frequent. Omitted.

Clinical.—Diarrhœa, thin, brown, yellowish, frothy, forcibly expelled, with colic and prominence of intestines like pads here and there all over the abdomen during the pains, and especially with the characteristic absence of emission of gas either upward or downward for a long time. Chronic diarrhœa, green liquid stools always mucous and bloody, anxiety, pale, suffering face, small pulse, *no emission of flatus for six days,* chills from the back along the arms and limbs, followed by heat, frequent efforts to vomit, great thirst, great weakness. Chronic diarrhœa, with dropsy, great thirst, weakness in the pit of the stomach, and pain especially on breathing, profuse urine, *no gas.*

Urinary Organs.—Burning in forepart of urethra during micturition. Desire to urinate, with pain in mons veneris like a pressure in fundus of bladder; frequent D. at night. Urging returns as soon as she has urinated, with pain in sides and loins. Did not urinate all day. *Urine yellow, turbid,* depositing a copious whitish-yellow sediment like yeast; *dirty yellow, with sediment like yeast,* equal in amount to urine; whitish-yellow, turbid; pale; pale, copious and passed frequently; very clear, afterwards thick; *copious;* scanty.

Sexual Organs.—Female. Titillation increasing till 1.30 A.M., when it abates, with abundant flow of mucus. Uterus and groins pain, with heat and constant ineffectual urging to urinate; U. and abdomen, pain, and in groins on touch, with inflammation, pain in bones, cracking of joints, weakness of spine; burning pain extending from U. to pit of stomach, where it changes into nervous contraction, giving a sensation as if she would have convulsions; sensation of a round body rising from fundus of U. and stopping at entrance of throat.

Nervous irritation of clitoris, impelling her to onanism. Vagina, great flow of mucus; flow of a little blood, like rose-colored mucus, every day between 3 and 5 o'clock. Menstruation profuse, in clots and long-lasting; M. profuse, with flushes of heat from uterus to head, then into loins and through body, causing sensation as if about to perspire, prickings in legs and under soles, loss of thought, faintness, difficulty in speaking. Desire. Nymphomania in morning, increasing till 11 P.M.

Clinical.—Abnormal sexual desire, with sleeplessness.

Respiratory Organs.—Tickling in larynx; in epiglottis. Hoarseness; in evening.

Cough beginning by tickling at bottom of œsophagus and resonant in chest; C., it seems as if something came fron larynx, also when she laughs, with tickling at bottom of larynx which seems to start from epigastrium, after cough acid risings, as of bitter water; with horseness, and in evening feeling as if chest were in a vise, with difficulty in breathing and speaking; drier, she tries to raise something from throat, but the cough does not bring it up, but creates more of it. Expectoration easy, of round masses of mucus; easy, of round masses of thick mucus; clear and sticky, like gum-water.

Respiration.—Strangulation when she begins to eat and drink. Difficult and short. Possible only with mouth open, till 3 A.M., the air which enters mouth causes pain and burns as if everything were alive, uvula is swollen and red, tongue rather white and red on edge. Uneasy, with general distress, she cannot remain sitting, standing or lying; U., with oppression of chest, difficulty in swallowing, it seems as if water would return through nose, burning in œsophagus and chest, she is better at midday than in morning and worse in evening, better from walking in open air, everything she swallows and even breathing cause pain in back; during expiration pain between shoulders and in sides of chest, during inspiration only tightness of chest, drawing pain as from a prick or bruise, which returns when drawing breath, drawing pains in whole chest as far as back during expiration, it feels as if stretched fibres returned to their place, which causes pain between shoulders and in sides of chest.

Chest.—Sticking in l.; in middle of sternum; externally in a spot in large pectoral muscles, near axilla; in spots in bones, < sternum; when coughing and breathing; < deep inspiration; in sides, like an iron band around waist. Cramp in clavicular part of sterno-cleido-mastoid muscle. Pain in middle; under breasts and in back when she breathes; gradually extending to spine. Drawing pain in sternum, extending to umbilicus and back. Spasmodic tension in l. sterno-cleido-mastoid. Heavy lump in centre between mammæ, with coldness, preventing sleep. Rattling sensation almost under arms, as if something would be loosened, during respiration. Painful weariness, and under ribs. Burning externally in r. side.

Heart and Pulse.—Palpitation. Rapid and violent beating of heart. Pulse rapid; and full; with feverish sensation in limbs, like beginning of a bad cold; *small*, jumping; slow.

Neck. — Pain in muscles, with painful lassitude through body, < occiput, neck and loins. Numbness of muscles near l. ear.

Back.—Pain. Weakness, she must wear stays as a support, feeling as if she would be humpbacked, feeling as if middle of back were crooked, waist hollow and shoulders uneven, she could not keep her balance. Tearing along crest of r. scapula, with tension; T. in region of kidneys, < stooping. Pain in loins, hypogastrium and groins; sharp, in coccyx, as if an abscess were forming. Weakness in dorsal part of spine, with intermittent prickings; painful W. in loins as after running too fast.

Extremities.—Trembling. Pain. Sensation in arms and legs as if her garters were too tight. Weakness; in joints; after a short walk, with bruised sensation; with feverish sensation; as if they had been broken.

Upper Extremities.—Gland in r. axilla swollen and painful to touch. Sticking in l. shoulder. Tearing on top of l. shoulder; in r. biceps, with tension; in l. arm and joint, with pulling, and with weakness in elbow, as if carrying a weight. Sticking in bone of l. elbow; in l. olecranon process; burning, in r. elbow, as if in tendon of biceps; in r. forearm, near wrist, with tearing and weakness. Numbness of hands; and in a slight degree all over, sometimes in one place, sometimes in another. Pain in fingers and pain under nails, < l., as from a burn or thrusts with pins.

Lower Extremities.—Numbness of buttocks and soles; of B., < r., as if asleep. Lancinations in l. hip-joint, back of trochanter. Tearing at top of l. thigh; intermittent, in l. calf, in hamstring. Painful cramps in calves, more a spasmodic pain than a cramp. Legs feel as if bent outward when getting up, tibia painful to touch, burning as if a hot coal were held at centre of tibia. Legs heavy as if almost paralyzed, knees crack as if they would be dislocated. Lancinations in l. malleolus; in soles when beginning to get warm after being very cold; itching, on r. sole and near fleshy part. Redness of r. heel, with swelling and pinching, later a blister, after the opening of which there was no more pain. Pain in a hitherto painless corn; P. in heel when walking, > rest and when boot is off, though the pain is not caused by pressure of boot.

Skin.—Greasy. A black mark on arm near shoulder and reddish spots on chest. Eruption, itching and heat of skin, with fever, pimples are seen beneath skin, but do not come out, a plaster on her leg draws out a kind of tetter. Blisters full of water on breasts, with itching. Tearing on l. thigh. Susceptibility. Itching, < outer canthus, r. wrist, r. thigh, scrotum, anus, back and scalp; in l. ear, with deep stitches; of l. concha, with pain on touch; at night, delaying sleep; over whole body, a crisis every four hours, nervous yawning; over whole body, scratching causes burning; burning, on back.

Sleep.—Yawning; and stretching, desire to go to bed. Sleepiness; in afternoon. Sleeplessness; every night, tension of nerves, melancholy, jealousy, a nervous attack on fifth day of menses. *Restless sleep;* and disturbed from 11 till 2 by confusion of head; *with distressing dreams;* with sweat; with talking; and waking every fifteen minutes with headache and retching. Waked by talking in his sleep. Murmuring in S. at night, as if playing with his companions, he slumbered all next day, but talked as if quarrelling with his companions. Sleep light, disturbed by painful dreams of death, etc., sleep better towards morning, but often interrupted. Dream that he was intoxicated, of difficulties, without sadness or discouragement; lascivious; vivid about 3 A.M.

Fever.—Chilliness; every evening after dinner, with nervousness, pain in throat as if there were something to bring up, and on hawking a smarting, then sweet taste, and once after great effort scanty sputum specked with blood, difficult breathing; in evening in bed, with trembling, then heat; at midnight; after going to bed, with weakness of joints, < elbows; in attacks at night, with the last attack towards morning, nausea and soft stool; with hot, moist skin; with hot skin, at other times after shivering internal heat; alternating with heat and sweat; creeping, often during the day, alternating with heat and sweat. Shivering, then heat; alternating with heat; with heat of head and skin; over back and arms; over back and arms, waking at 3 A.M.; down back at night in bed.

Chilliness in back and posterior surface of arms; < after

drinking water; in back and posteriorly on arms and legs. Coldness of feet and legs; of r. foot at night in bed; of knees and feet at night, also preventing sleep; of feet, with heat of hands; of hands and feet, with burning in abdomen, stomach, chest and loins.

Heat; in evening; in bed, pulse nervous, short and strong; with headache, uneasiness, numb pain, inclination to lie down and chills. Burning here and there, < gland of r. axilla; in a spot on vertex; in a spot on upper and external part of thigh; cheeks, with redness; ears, < l., with redness.

Sweat; in morning; at night; S., breath and whole body had a strong odor of radish.

Ratanhia.

A tincture is made of the dried root of Krameria triandra, R. and P.

Ally.—Iris v.

Generalities.—Jerking here and there. Sticking now in l. ribs, now in small of back, in region of hips, etc. Sore pain now in chest, now in shoulders and in other parts, often with sticking. Malaise, frequent yawning, labored attempts to draw a long breath and constriction across chest. Weakness, with anxiety and sweat. Amelioration from motion in open air and aggravation from mental distress.

Mind.—Restlessness, causing exacerbations. Quarrelsome. Ill humor. Changeable mood. Apprehensive depression when alone, > conversation and giving place to gayety.

Head.—Sticking here and there in evening. Tearing, < l. side; T. or stitching on moving and on deep breathing. Pain as if screwed together; P. as if it would burst, also after the usual stool; bruised, here and there. Jerking deep in brain. Dulness; as if intoxicated.

Forehead.—Sticking in r. side; S. in middle on stooping. Tearing. Pain as if it would burst in evening when sitting bent over; in middle as if whole brain would force out when straining at stool. Drawing behind r. side when walking. Dulness, > open air.

Tearing in l. temple; in spots in r. Jerking in a spot externally in r. temple. Sticking in vertex. Tearing in vertex, then intermittent sticking; T. during menses, > open air, with burning. Sticking in l. side on sitting down; S. in upper part of r., then pain as if beaten. Burrowing in r. side of brain, > open air. Frequent bruised pain in l. parietal bone. Tearing extending from occiput to vertex. Itching not > scratching; I. on r. temple; on l. side of occiput, and glandular swellings.

Eyes.—*Inflammation of white, a membrane seemed to extend to centre of eye, that burned.* Twitching of r. Sticking above r. external canthus. Sensation in r. as if screwed in or as if it could not be moved, still she could move it easily. Biting in r. in morning. Burning in morning on waking; in evening, with constriction; in evening, agglutination at night.

Lachrymation in morning after waking. Lids, agglutination in morning; twitching of r. upper; twitching of r. lower, with weak vision; sticking in l. upper in evening; itching in r. lower; stiffness of upper, with soreness of edges. Canthus, twitching in r. inner, then sensation as if lid were pressed upward, preventing vision; tearing in r. inner in evening. Vision dim; for distant objects. A white spot before eyes in evening, by the light, preventing vision.

Ears.—Sticking in r. Tearing in r.; in middle and outer; in bone behind l., extending upward; piercing in front of r. Crawling in r. Itching in r. Chirping in r. Ringing on waking about midnight.

Nose.—Pimples in r. nostril, becoming scabs. L. nostril inflamed and scabby. Swollen feeling across bridge; in r. nostril. Dryness, < l. nostril. Burning in nostrils. Tickling or itching about nostrils. Itching in nostrils. Stoppage and fulness. Stopped catarrh. Violent sneezing. Bleeding three times a day.

Face.—Tearing in l. malar-bone in evening; in l. side of lower jaw and corresponding teeth. Sensation of cobwebs about r. side of mouth. Lip, pimple on inner surface of r. side of lower; vesicles beneath margin of lower; blisters in red of upper, burning on touch; tearing in a spot in inner surface.

Mouth.—Shooting or jerking in molars in evening and morning, with coldness starting from them; S. in incisor, < eating, with heat, preventing sleep. Tearing in molars in evening, now in r. lower, now in r. upper, now also deep in bone in front of r. ear. Digging in some lower molars in evening. Throbbing in root of an upper tooth; in a l. upper incisor, with bleeding of teeth. A l. upper incisor feels too long and is painful to touch; molars seems too long and coldness seems to come out of them. Gums swollen; fungoid softening; acid blood from, when sucking; painful spot as if abraded. Tongue, tension as if swollen; burning on tip; burning itching on tip. Mouth dry all night. Offensive breath. *Collection of tasteless water.* Insipid taste in morning in bed.

Throat.—Painful spasmodic contraction, during which she could not speak a loud word. Intermittent sticking. Roughness and scraping. Soreness, worse on empty swallowing than on swallowing large pieces.

Stomach.—Hunger increased. She has no relish, food has no taste. Disgusted in morning with everything that he even looks at, he will not hear of eating. Thirst; in evening. Eructations, with salivation; E. tasting of the dinner; empty, after dinner. Hiccough after dinner; **violent H., so that stomach is painful.** Nausea; waking him at 1 A.M., with retching, then vomiting of food eaten the previous evening, relieving the nausea, then sleep till 3 A.M., then awakened by nausea, with rolling and constriction in stomach, > open air. Vomiting of only water; of mucus streaked with blood.

Distention; in morning; before dinner, > emission of flatus. Rumbling when walking, it seems empty; R. after dinner, with movements; in epigastrium in afternoon. Sticking to l. of pit. Pain as if cut to pieces, < deep breathing. Sudden twisting in pit in afternoon. Griping in morning. Ulcerative pain in r. side above pit; in epigastric region in evening. Constriction in evening, > eructations, with cutting in abdomen. Weight in region and sometimes pinching. Heat; in epigastrium. Digestion difficult.

Abdomen.—Flatulent distention in afternoon, with constant desire for stool and frequent emission of flatus. Rumbling and gurgling, then painless diarrhœa twice, some drops of bright blood with the last; R., with dragging in groins and diarrhœa, with blood three times. Movements as after a purge, in morning. Griping, then soft stool. Pinching; in morning, with burning. Colic, with frequent diarrhœa; then five thin stools.

Movements as of something living in r., then in l. side. Pinching in sides. Sticking in l. hypochondrium; in r. H. in evening. Frequent pinching about umbilicus in afternoon. Drawing in U. region, with coldness. Rumbling in hypogastrium, with cutting, then scanty diarrhœa three times in the day. Frequent griping in hypogastrium in morning, with external itching. Groins, sticking in afternoon when sitting; pinching or constriction in r. in evening; pinching in morning on waking, > emission of flatus; dragging downward as before menstruation, with discharge of mucus from vagina; constriction in a spot.

Rectum and Anus.—Painful hæmorrhoids. *Anus, oozing; burning before and after diarrhœa; dry heat and cutting. Straining, then hard stool and protrusion of hæmorrhoids*, **then burning in anus** (Canth., Iris, Sul.). Urging for a normal stool; ineffectual U.

Clinical.—Fissure of the anus, with great constriction, terrible pain following the stool, especially burning like fire, only temporarily relieved by cold water. Hæmorrhoids, with extreme burning like fire.

Stool.—Liquid in morning after rising. Yellow diarrhœa, with burning in anus. Constipation. Hard, with pressure; H., scanty, difficult; H., then diarrhœa.

Clinical.—Bloody stools. Thin fetid diarrhœa, with burning like fire in the anus.

Urinary Organs.—Frequent urging, always only a few drops. Micturition frequent and profuse; at night; frequent, only a little at a time, with burning in urethra. Urine pale. Urine copious. Urine scanty; and soon depositing a cloud, afterwards becoming turbid like muddy water.

Genital Organs.—Burning at root of penis when urinating. Itching of scrotum, not > scratching. (Chronic gonorrhœa becomes worse.) Leucorrhœa. Discharge of blood, the menses had ceased four days before. Menses too early; and scanty; with pain in abdomen; delayed; ceased on fourth day and returned on fifth day; suppressed, with swelling of abdomen and breasts, simulating a pregnancy of several months, with leucorrhœa and pain in kidneys.

Respiratory Organs.—Cough from tickling in larynx; dry C., mucus is loosened with difficulty.

Chest.—Sticking in sternum, above ensiform cartilage; behind r. ribs in afternoon; above l. clavicle in evening, with drawing as if skin were drawn inward; on l. ribs during dinner; in r. side after dinner; in sternum at every step when descending stairs, taking away the breath; on ribs, beneath l. breast, extending downward; burning, in last ribs, near back, on stepping. Sticking burning beneath l., along one rib, in evening, with cutting. Intermittent cutting in a spot in upper part of sternum; throbbing-burning C. beneath l. breast, near pit of stomach, > pressure and motion with ulcerative pain. Ulcerative pain during and after cough. Constriction in sides. Pressure as from a stone, with short breath on slight exertion. Rush of blood and heat, with difficult breathing.

Heart and Pulse.—Sticking in præcordial region, rather external. Pulse often as full as in gastritis.

Neck.—Tearing sticking in l. side, with constriction. Tearing in l. side; in nape extending into forehead, when walking, with heaviness of head. Tearing jerking in nape extending into vertex, when walking. Drawing or tensive pain from nape down spinal marrow after dinner. Drawing in l. side in evening when standing, with tension. Stiffness in nape on turning head, > violent motion.

Back.—Sticking through spine to pit of stomach. Bruised pain in spine; B. pain towards morning, > rising; in region of hips in morning on rising, > motion. Intermittent sticking on inner margin of r. scapula. Lumbar region, pain during menses; forcing as if to stool; jerking, and in region of hips.

Upper Extremities.—Sticking from l. axilla into chest in afternoon, < expiration, > inspiration. Tearing in shoulders; to elbows; from r. almost to wrist. Tearing above and below l. elbow in evening, > allowing arm to hang down, < bending. Constriction as with a cord two inches above and two inches below r. elbow, > stretching arm. Elbow, burning stitch in bend of r., then sudden shaking chill; pinching constriction in bend of r. when arm was bent, > stretching it. Forearm, burning stitch in flesh of l., then tension; tearing in flesh on outer surface of l., extending to wrist; tearing from l. into first joint of ring finger, as if in bone.

Tearing in r. wrist; in r. wrist behind ball of thumb, with sticking; between l. thumb and index; jerking, on back of r. hand. Sticking in middle of thumb, extending into tip. Jerking tearing alternately in each thumb. Constriction in r. middle and ring fingers, > rubbing, but returning frequently; in r. middle and ring fingers in evening, with an asleep sensation, so that she could not stretch them.

Lower Extremities.—Thigh. Jerking in middle of r. in morning. Trembling in r. in evening, or waving sensation. Sticking in a spot in forepart of r., with tearing in l. side of head. Tearing in hips; from hips to knees; T. posteriorly when riding one over the other; in middle of r., when sitting, extending to knee. Tension in flesh above r. knee when standing. Weariness on inner side, with heaviness; W. in r. when sitting, with heaviness.

Sticking in bend of r. knee on rising from a seat. Tearing in r. knee when sitting; in r. tibia; calves; lower part of r. leg; tendons of r. calf in evening and morning when sitting; tendo-achillis, extending upward, then sticking deep in r. knee when standing. Jerking in calves. Drawing in legs; in calves in evening. Weakness of legs in morning after rising and in afternoon. Intermittent contractions in tendons above heels in evening. Tearing in tendons behind r. external malleolus when standing; on back of r. foot; in tendons of r. foot. Jerking in forepart of r. foot. Toes, sticking in l. great, with burning tearing; tearing in three first, extending towards tips; sprained pain in last joint of r. great, when sitting.

Skin.—Pimples in skin of r. temple; on chin; < shoulders and lumbar region; like a boil, itching, on l. hip. Boil on r. sole.

Twitching beneath r. axilla. Stinging in various parts of body, neck and arms, < legs, when walking, > rubbing, leaving soreness and itching, a vesicle on the spot. Burning sticking on inner margin of l. sole; now above r. knee, now in r. upper arm, or in small of back. Stretched feeling once from above root of nose to top of forehead and once from centre of forehead to r. frontal protuberance. Feeling as if drawn together in centre of forehead. Stiff feeling on lower forehead, < knitting brows. Crawling beneath skin of r. knee, alternating with sticking and tearing; C. on back, with itching eruption. Tickling on heels and soles; in ball of r. thumb.

Itching on nape and between scapulæ; on tip of nose, > rubbing; in evening, > scratching, on back, also anteriorly on thigh; here and there over whole body, > scratching; on outer part of l. forearm, not > scratching; on nose and upper lip, returning after scratching; in epigastric region, with red spots; on forearm, and on scratching itching pimples; between shoulders, with pimples, burning after scratching; in hollows of knees in evening, burning after scratching; tickling, voluptuous I. in l. sole.

Sleep.—Yawning; in evening, without sleepiness. Sleepiness in morning and after dinner, with indolence and yawning; S. when sitting; during dinner. Late falling asleep and waking about midnight. Snoring. Starting up soon after falling asleep. Sleep restless, she woke often and could not fall asleep for a long time. Waking at 2 A.M., with trembling, apprehension and fear, so that she started up. Dreams full of quarrels, anger and vexation; of funerals, death of friends, etc.; anxious, of snakes and sick people, from which she woke in sweat and thirsty; frightful, of earthquakes and the like.

Fever.—Chilliness in afternoon and night; from 8 till 9 P.M., > in bed, then sweat till midnight; general, at 9 P.M., with burning in hands and feet and external heat, afterwards in bed sweat till midnight. Shaking chill in morning; in evening and in bed. Shivering in evening. Cold fingers in morning. Heat on l. external malleolus; in head, with heaviness of head and external heat in forehead; in rushes to face; tensive, in thighs and legs in evening on rising from a seat. Sweat at night; at 1 A.M., on waking, with thirst and dryness of mouth.

Rheum.

A tincture is made of the dried root of Rheum officinale, Baillon.

General Action.—An active cathartic not inflaming the mucous membrane, but stimulating peristalsis. Constipation follows its catharsis.

Alies.—Coloc., Mag. c., Sulph.

Generalities.—Twitching in morning. Discomfort. Weakness; when walking. *Heaviness of whole body* after sleep; *as after deep sleep;* as from too little sleep.

Clinical.—In general, there is an acid condition of the system, the whole body smells sour, the discharges are sour and fermented.

Mind.—Excitement. Talking nonsense. Moaning, anxiety, ill humor. Silence, nothing makes an impression on him; S. and sulky. *Child impatiently desires many things and cries.* Gloomy, he cannot continue long at one occupation. Indolent and laconic; I. in morning after sleep, and pinching and tensive pain transversely across forepart of head. State as if half asleep. Inability to collect her senses for a long time.

Head.—Aching; then tearing extending into occiput; beating; tense, dizzy, spreading over brain, < vertex and in temples; as if stupefied and distorted, < motion and stooping, with anxiety as if he had committed a crime. Confusion; with puffy eyes, then pain above one orbit, with dilated pupils; as after intoxication. Heaviness when walking, with intermittent tearing in it; H., with sultry heat rising into it. On stooping sensation as if brain moved. Vertigo; as if one would fall to the side, when standing.

Forehead.—Pain over forepart of skull; drawing, deep, behind eminences; beating, in forepart of head, < standing. Obscuration in forepart of head, a drawing about in it. Inclination to wrinkle it.

Sticking above temples. Pulsative pinching now in l., now in r. temporal bone and over crown. Pain in r. side, < vertex and temple. Pressure as with a finger at point where head unites with neck. Crawling in temporal region.

Eyes.—Beating pain. Biting in l. as from a foreign substance before sleep, with lachrymation. Seem dull and on looking long at anything aching as if they were weak. Lachrymation in open air. Contraction of pupils, with internal uneasiness; at one time greater, at another less contraction. Agglutination after sleep. Gland on margin of upper lid, causing pressive and burning pain. Pressure on lids, even when closed. Drawing in lids.

Ears.—Crackling and bubbling, preceptible even to hand, and in muscles in side of neck. Squeezing in l., with itching. Pressure as from a finger in meatus. Throbbing at times when writing, < stooping. Roaring in r., transiently > violent swallowing, with dull hearing and sensation as if drum were relaxed.

Nose and Face.—Drawing, stupefied pain along root, causing crawling in tip. One cheek pale, the other red, or both pale. Tensive sensation in skin of face. Drawing gushing sensation in r. lower jaw, extending into r. temple.

Mouth.—Teeth blunt; burrowing in hollow T., with elongation and looseness; pain in l. upper incisors, with coldness; pain in l. molars, with coldness, causing salivation. Mouth covered with offensive mucus after sleep. Dryness, without desire to drink. Offensive breath after sleep. Taste sour; insipid; bitter to food; bad after sleep; lost, and tongue insensible.

Throat.—Hawking and spitting. Contraction of pharynx.

Stomach.—Appetite great, yet the food that was relished soon became repulsive; hunger without real A.; A. diminished; lost. **Food soon becomes repulsive,** *though there is a tolerably good appetite. Aversion for certain things (for example, fat, insipid food),* **yet desire for various things, but he cannot eat much because they become repulsive.** Coffee is repulsive unless very sweet. Thirst. Eructations. *Nausea;* in epigastric region; *with colic;* with contractive sensation in stomach; with retching.

Sticking in pit; in l. side near pit. *Fulness as if he had eaten to satiety,* sometimes followed by sleepiness. Pressure as if filled with food; P. in pit after sleep, that on inspiration extended over sternum and changed to bruised pain. Throbbing in pit, with rhythmical gurgling.

Abdomen.—Distention; after eating. Rumbling; and gurgling. Twitching of muscles. Flatulence; rising to chest and there causing tension and pressure. Emission of flatus; offensive, with relief. *Nausea.* Cutting; in morning in bed, on uncovering, with emission of flatus; *after dinner, > bending over, < standing;* twinging, transversely acrosss. *Griping; with ineffectual urging to stool* from inactivity of rectum; then emission of flatus. *Pain; before and during stool, > stool; < plums;* as if full of liquid, on inspiration.

Hammering mounting into head. *Tension.* Gushing-gurgling sensation, which seemed as if it could be heard. Warmth, with pain on pressure.

Pressure in region of spleen. Umbilical region, *cutting;* griping; pressure; intestines seem to press outward. Itching stitches in the last inguinal gland. Pain in ring as if a hernia would protrude, when walking. Pressure as with tip of thumb in pubic region. Tension in l. side above pubis after a meal.

Rectum and Anus.—*Desire for stool after a meal* (Cham.); *D. < moving about; then thin offensive stool, with colic, then ineffectual tenesmus, later another stool, after rising from stool the urging, which had gradually subsided, returned more violent than ever, and the pain in abdomen which accompanied the stool became worse;* partly ineffectual, partly with soft stool. Tenesmus. Urging. Pain in region of anus as after continued diarrhœa.

Stool.—*Semi-liquid, forcible, frequent, followed by tenesmus and burning in anus; S., brown, frequent, followed by tenesmus, pain in back and burning in rectum. Diarrhœa, with mucus.* **Pasty, sour-smelling** (Dulc.), **then shivering** (Puls.), **then urging, with constriction in intestines.** First part soft, then hard, preceded and accompanied by cutting. First part hard, last liquid. Constipation. Mingled with mucus. Of grayish mucus.

Clinical.—Diarrhœa, sour-smelling, brown and frothy, sometimes excoriating, especially during teething, preceded by colic and followed by tenesmus, with desire for all sorts of food of which one can eat but little. Diarrhœa, with colic, tenesmus, alternate chill, heat and thirst, sweat, weakness; stools like chopped eggs, with sour odor, color green.

Urinary Organs.—Burning in bladder and kidneys. Bladder weak, must press when urinating, else the urine cannot be completely evacuated. Urging. Desire to urinate every half hour. Tenesmus during micturition, tickling in urethra and dragging towards bladder. Micturition frequent and profuse. Micturition burning. Prickling in urethra during micturition. Urine bright yellow, tinged with green; reddish-yellow, as in jaundice and in high fever; dark, of an agreeable benzoic odor; dark red, almost brown, thickish, warm and of an agreeable odor; increased; increased and light-colored.

Sexual Organs.—Emissions.

Respiratory Organs.—Cough, with expectoration of mucus; dry C. in evening. Dyspnœa, on taking a deep breath the chest cannot expand sufficiently, as from a weight below throat.

Chest.—Yellow, bitter milk in a nursing woman. Sticking; in r. side; in nipples; sudden, below last ribs during inspiration and expiration. Aching in nipples, caused by flatulence in abdomen; tightening, across sternum, with at times stitches; burning, in l. side of sternum. Contraction. Audible crackling bubbling, as of vesicles, in l., then in r. pectoral muscles. (Oppression.)

Pulse.—Rapid.

Back.—Tension. *Cutting in lumbar vertebræ, < stool;* C. in l. lumbar region. *Cutting drawing in lumbar region, beneath l. short ribs, and in l. side of hypogastrium above pubis, a digging in intestines.* Stiffness in sacrum and hips, with inability to walk straight.

Extremities. — *Pain in all joints during motion.* (Fatigue.) *Falling asleep of those upon which he lies.*

Upper Extremities.—Sticking in arms. Tearing in upper arms and finger-joints. Elbow, twitching sensation in r.; gushing gurgling sensation. Forearms, muscles seem contracted, with tremulous motion of hands; tearing; sensation in lower side as if about to fall asleep. Hands, swollen veins; involuntarily stretched above head before falling asleep; tearing across from thumb to little finger. Sticking tearing in thumb.

Lower Extremities. — Thigh, twitching of various fibres on posterior part when muscles were extended while sitting and on drawing up knees while lying; *weariness.* Knee, sticking in l. when walking; drawing-down weary pain in hollow of l. when standing; *tensive pain in hollow of l., extending to heel;* painless gurgling in hollows, extending to heels; gushing gurgling sensation in hollows; weary tension in hollow of r.; stiffness, with pain on motion.

Intermittent burning pain between inner malleolus and tendo-achillis. Gurgling extending down leg, with stitches. Legs go to sleep when riding one over the other. (Sprained sensation in l. ankle in morning on stepping upon it.) Tearing transversely across instep, with sticking. Sticking in l. sole above little toe. Gushing crackling sensation in ball of l. great toe.

Skin.—Itching rash on forehead and arm. Sticking itching in hollow of sole; in root of little toe, almost as after being frozen.

Sleep. — Yawning. Sleepiness. Raving in sleep, afterwards he walked about in an unconscious state, half dreaming, half waking; R. in evening, tossing about and heat. *Snoring.* Hands stretched above head. *Restless;* with moans and bending backward of head; in a child, it often begins to cry out and says tremblingly "There are men." Child seems to be quarrelling, with convulsive drawing of fingers, facial muscles and of eyelids and pallor. *Dream vivid, sad, anxious;* anxious, of dead relatives; vexatious, offensive.

Fever. — Chilliness; (in morning); C. and heat alternately, with weariness, anxiety and aversion to everything. Shivering without external coldness. Coolness of face, with heat of hands and feet. Heat; and uneasiness; without thirst; about nose; in cheeks; in palms. *Sweat on forehead and scalp after slight effort;* in palms when hands are closed; *cold, on face, < about mouth and nose;* cold in palms while rest of body was warm; yellow, smelling of rhubarb.

Rhododendron.

A tincture is made of the dried leaves of Rhododendron Chrysanthemum, L.

Allies.—Its botanical relatives Led. and Kalmia; *Rhus t.*, Clem., Lyc., Aur.

Generalities.—Lies on back, with feet crossed. Twitchings. Tearing in different parts, < l. elbow and in affected limb. Sprained sensation. *Bruised feeling;* in whole body in morning, disturbing sleep, with digging, drawing pain in back, shoulders and arms. Drawing now here, now there, < joints, with jerking sensation; *D. as if in marrow, < bad weather.* Tingling in gouty parts and abatement of pains. Discomfort in affected parts, with sensation as if a worm were creeping through them. **Sensitiveness in windy and cold weather.** Weakness; from a short walk, with bruised feeling in limbs. Insensibility of affected parts. **Almost all symptoms reappear with rough weather**

(Rhus t.). Most comfortable in bed with limbs drawn up.

Clinical.—Rheumatic pains, especially in the periosteum of the bones, < cold weather, > moving (Rhus t.); these pains may affect nearly every part of the body, and are frequently associated with coldness of the extremities, especially of the feet, but the general indication is *aggravation before a storm.* Chronic rheumatism of small joints (Led.). Rheumatoid arthritis.

Mind.—Delirium; and he tosses his head about and reels, then falls asleep upon his knees, tries in vain to rise but is overcome by sleep, during which he starts continually and appears terrified, but awakes cheerful. Frightful visions. Fits of anxiety. Peevish. Gloomy, indifferent. Phlegmatic. Averse to everything, especially earnest occupation. Stupefaction. Loss of sense. *Forgetfulness of what he is talking about;* F. and sudden disappearance of thoughts, he omits words in writing.

Head.—Sticking, < forehead; burning, through H. Racking sensation when walking as if brain were shaken from all sides, especially from above. Aching; towards evening; in evening; with sensation in head as if everything would fall out of forehead; *almost depriving him of senses in morning* (the day after a glass of wine), > *rising;* beating; as if brain pressed against skull; as if catarrh would set in. (Oppression of brain as from lead, in morning after a glass of wine.) *Confusion;* in morning on waking, with obstruction of nose and humming in ears; after rising; < open air, with drawing towards eyes; < frontal region, > laying head on table and by exercise in open air, with pain in l. temple; with heaviness; with want of attention; with drowsiness. Affection as from brandy. Feeling as if he had been revelling all night. Intoxication. Vertigo; at night; when sitting; in bed; when writing, > motion in open air; with dulness in forehead; as from strong tobacco; as if head would fall backward, when in bed, with anguish.

Forehead.—Drawing tearing in direction of temples and eyes, < moving about in the house; close to bone, like a forcing, < wine. Aching; in l. side; *in l. half, spreading towards l. temple, < wine;* (drawing, over l. eye the day after a glass of wine); beating, > rest, with pressure in head as if everything in head would come out there. Pressure in l. bone as with a thumb; P. outward in region of r. bone. Drawing in l. bone, then shuddering across face. Tension in l. bone; T. in front part, with pressure. Beating in l. region. Dulness in sinciput after rising, with heaviness; D. in sinciput, and on moving head pain in forehead.

Temples.—Sticking in l. *Tearing boring in l.* Drawing pain under l. bone; under r. bone, pressing outward. Pain in l. Pressure in bones; painful, in l. bone; inward in l.; outward under l. bone. Cold crawling above temple.

Vertex.—Pain; suppurative, on touch.

Half.—Shooting in l. Tearing in r. Beating pain in r. Sore pain in l. hemisphere of brain when lying; in r. hemisphere of brain and cerebellum when sitting.

Occiput.—Pain in morning; deep in evening; deep in r. side, with paroxysmal drawing upward; in r. half as if a foreign body had been forced into it; contusive, in a spot externally in r. side, alternating with drawing in direction of ear.

Scalp.—Pain on touch. Biting in various parts. Itching; evenings; evenings, changing on scratching to burning.

Clinical.—Rheumatic headache, < wet, cold weather, involving the forehead and temples. Headache like a tearing of the bones of the skull, < wet, cold weather, > warm wraps and from moving about, also < wine (Lyc.).

Eyes.—Shooting from centre of r. to inner corner. Periodical smarting in r. *Burning pain, and on reading or writing heat in eyes;* B. pain in evening when reading, with dim vision. Burning all day; when looking at daylight before rising from bed; when looking intently; < evening, with dryness; and pressure; dry; periodical, in morning. Weak feeling when reading and writing. Itching. Lachrymation; (in raw air). Contraction of pupil; of l., with dilatation of r., with pressure in l. ball; r. smaller than l. Hot sticking outward in r. ball. Lids swollen and red; twitching of upper; agglutination, with moisture of eyes; suppuration at night. Canthus, pressure in r. inner as from sand; burning in inner in morning, with pressure and increased mucus. Pressure around margin of l. orbit, with sticking and with spasmodic contraction of l. lids. Sensation of a gauze before eyes.

Clinical.—Threatening glaucoma, always < the approach of a storm, > after the storm broke, patient strongly rheumatic. Muscular asthenopia, with darting pains through the eye, < before a storm. Ciliary neuralgia.

Ears.—Sticking in l.; pinching S. outward in r. Darting pain in l. ear and temple. *Tearing in and about r.* Periodical boring or drawing pain in or around ears. *Pain in r. outer nearly all day.* Pain in r. as if pressed asunder. Sensation as if a worm were creeping in l. Beating in l. Tickling in l. external meatus, changing to pain on boring in with finger. *Humming before ears, with ringing;* H. before ears in evening in bed, with ringing. Buzzing in l. in forenoon, < whistling; *B. and sensation as if water were rushing into them, loud sounds re-echo long.* Whizzing in l., < whistling.

Clinical.—Otalgia, tearing pain, with roaring and buzzing.

Nose.—Stoppage in morning; *S. of l. nostril;* of l. mornings; *of l. near root, in open air, with sore pain in r. and sensation of mucus; of l. near root, < morning before rising, alternating during the day with stoppage of r., > open air.* Dryness. Itching in nostrils, with creeping. Sneezing in morning on rising, with heat of face; S. in forenoon, with increased discharge of thin mucus. Increased mucus; in open air; with stoppage of one or other nostril near root. Fluent coryza, with headache and roughness of throat; F., with diminution of smell and taste; alternating with obstruction of one nostril. Dry coryza, with sneezing. Bleeding from l. nostril. All things smell and taste alike.

Face.—Sudden (prickling) biting in cheek. Drawing from l. half into l. ear, leaving behind a pressure in eye. Pain in l. lower jaw and teeth all night, now >, now < pressure, with otalgia, r. side of head less affected. Vesicles on inside of lower lip and lower side of tongue, causing biting when eating. Lips dry; and burning.

Mouth.—Teeth. Sticking in a l. upper hollow. Prickling in incisors, with biting. *Tearing* in hollow; in upper molars towards evening, < warm food and staying in a warm room; *occasionally in first anterior molars, now upper, now lower, now r., now l., with grumbling.* Pain, < damp weather and **before a storm. Drawing pain before a thunder-storm or cloudy, windy**

weather, with cutting, connected with a pain in ear; D. in l. molars; in r. lower T., > eating; in a l. molar, with pricking and intolerance of touch. Pain as if swollen and sore between r. lower gums and cheeks. Itching of gums.

Tongue, greenish coat, with bitter taste; painful, swollen spot on one side of root of T. and gums; prickling; burning during inspiration. Contractive sensation along l. Stenonian duct. Burning posteriorly in mouth, as if catarrh would set in. Dryness. Salivation; sourish, in morning. Taste sourish; T. flat, bitter; putrid bitter posteriorly on tongue; putrid in morning; sourish salt in morning, and nausea on swallowing saliva; of straw all day; all things taste alike.

Clinical.—Facial neuralgia, involving both dental nerves, pains drawing, tearing and jerking, < change of weather, > warmth and eating. Neuralgic toothache, > while eating, caused by cold.

Throat.—Hawking up of white and tenacious mucus. Stitches in uvula; drawing S. from l. submaxillary gland towards cheeks. Pain in posterior surface in evening on swallowing bread. Scraping when walking, with sensation of mucus in trachea, which he cannot cough up; *S. in fauces and sensation as if lined with mucus.* Roughness in morning. Contraction, with burning taste; C. in fauces, with burning. Burning in T. and palate in forenoon after bread.

Stomach.—Appetite unusual, before a meal; good, but speedily satisfied; lost. Satiety, then weakness. Thirst. Eructations; *empty;* of oppressive wind after dinner, causing burning through chest extending to dorsal vertebræ; of bitter liquid; (of rancid fluid, causing scratching in throat). Nausea; when stooping, > eructations; with salivation; with pressure in stomach; with indication for stool; with paroxysmal drawing pain in upper abdomen. Vomiting; after fluid, < cold water; of a green bitter substance.

Superficial sticking here and there in pit and region of short ribs, < l. side, with pressure. Pinching in pit. Clawing pain in pit, sometimes spreading into hypochondria and impeding respiration. Sharp pressure in pit an hour after dinner. Pain; in pit and epigastric region; in pit at night in bed; after drinking cold water; in pit before, during and after dinner; in epigastrium after dinner; deep in pit an hour after dinner, with cramplike drawing; in pit when stooping and when pressing inward; deep in, < afternoon when standing, with alternate drawing and sticking along union of short ribs, often increasing to oppression of breathing, anxiety and heat in face. *Contractive pressure in pit evenings when walking, with tight breath.* Creeping in region.

Abdomen.—Painful distention. Rumbling; and gurgling; after eating and drinking, then painless diarrhœa; < morning in bed and in evening, with heaviness, distention, full feeling, empty eructations and fetid flatus. Incarceration of flatus in morning fasting. Tense, as if distended by flatus, > emission of flatus. Stitches. Pinching; then loose stool; as of flatus. Bruised pain in integuments. Pain now in one part, now in another, > emission of fetid flatus. Digging, with full feeling. Full feeling without actual distention, > eructations and emissions of flatus; fulness caused by breakfast, > eructations. Weight and lassitude, not as from food. Discomfort after a meal. Grumbling. Empty feeling after stool, then pinching. Occasional feeling of looseness as if diarrhœa would set in.

Sticking in r. hypochondrium in evening; in region of spleen in evening during rest, arresting breathing. Pain in hypochondria as from incarcerated flatus; and in small of back. Pain in l. hypochondrium on stooping, with tension. Cutting in upper A. after a meal, then pain. Pinching transversely across upper after supper. Pinching in r. side; P. in umbilical region after a meal. Intermittent sticking outward above crest of l. ilium. Drawing pain in rings when walking, < r., with tension. Drawing from l. groin into l. thigh.

Clinical.—Neuralgic colic in various parts of the abdomen, <l. hypochondrium. Chronic pain in the left side under the short ribs, > eating.

Rectum and Anus.—Sticking in R. extending under ribs. Spasmodic pain in R. as from incarcerated flatus. Drawing from R. to genitals. Tenesmus, with papescent stool. Urging, with hard and difficult stool; U. as for diarrhœa, but a natural stool, with much pressing; frequent, then natural stool, with much pressing, it occurs in evening instead of in morning; sudden, but only flatus is emitted after pressing. Frequent ineffectual desire; then papescent stool. Anus, beating pain; biting, with oozing of liquid; crawling as of ascarides. Creeping from perineum to penis, then erections.

Stool.—Fluid, spurting. *Diarrhœa;* in morning on rising; after a meal; *in damp weather;* from food or drink, without colic; *from fruit*, with weak feeling in stomach, with nausea when walking; which does not cause weakness; *food passed undigested. Loose, but sluggish;* L. and difficult, also twice a day; and yellowish, sluggish, insufficient. Papescent, brown; P., delayed; and frequent; at regular periods, the latter part loose and leaving smarting in rectum. Constipation. Copious, black, fetid. Fermented. Difficult, not very hard, with sensation as if contractive power of anus were diminished. Delayed.

Clinical.—Diarrhœa in wet, cold weather; after fruit, with general rheumatic pains.

Urinary Organs.—Drawing in region of bladder and groins in forenoon, with desire to urinate. Frequent desire. (Dribbling after micturition, causing burning pain in urethra and shuddering through body.) Urethra, twitching in orifice when not urinating; sticking after micturition; sudden pricking in orifice in evening; pain as if suppurated and engorged with blood, at night; pain in orifice when not urinating; burning before and during micturition. *Urine somewhat increased, pale, of offensive acrid odor;* U. bloody; brown-red, offensive; clear, with greenish tinge; cloudy; hot; copious; U. and stool copious; scanty.

Clinical.—Catarrh of the bladder, with frequent urging to urinate and drawing pains, urine offensive.

Sexual Organs.—Burning sore pain between genitals and thighs, < walking. Itching crawling behind prepuce. Pinching jerking pain in glans. Beating pain in glans in evening. Want of the usual morning erections.

Testicles.—*The swelling, which had been painless heretofore, enlarged to the size of a hen's egg, < l., with sticking and tearing in both. Drawn up,* **swollen and painful;** *D. up and when walking contusive pain.* **Painful draw-**

ing in the swollen, hard T. (Clem.), **extending as far as abdomen and thigh,** < **r. side** (Aur.). *Sticking in r.; in r. in evening when sitting; drawing, in r. and in spermatic cord,* > *motion, sometimes a pricking beginning in r. T. and spreading in a zigzag manner along perineum toward sanus and arresting breathing.* **Pain on touch,** < **epididymis. Contusive pain, with alternate drawing,** < *one, now other T.* Crawling pain.

Scrotum shrinks easily, < walking or standing; when air becomes cool; *itching and increase of heat about S.* Emission at night in sound sleep, then long-continued erections. Desire increased, erections easy (later action). Aversion to coition and want of erection.

Menses too early; M. that had ceased two days before reappeared; that had been suppressed six months reappeared for two days, with intermissions; that had been suppressed six months returned with febrile excitement and headache.

Clinical.—Hydrocele, several cases. Orchitis, testicle indurated with a feeling as though it were being crushed.

Respiratory Organs.—Trachea dry in morning. Cough from tickling in throat; scraping C., disturbing sleep, with expectoration of mucus. Dry cough in morning; in morning, from roughness in throat; *in attacks* from tickling in trachea; fatiguing, morning and night; scraping, in evening. Breath suppressed, suffocative sensation. Breathing accelerated by anxious, undulating sensation arising from abdomen.

Chest.—Sticking in middle of l. as far as under scapula, < motion; below l. ribs, extending towards dorsal vertebræ during rest. Tearing in region of lower end of sternum. Cutting in middle of l., < turning upper part of body from l. to r. Feeling as if a knife were plunged through l. and out at back when bending to r. side and backward. Pinching transversely through C.; P. under short ribs in morning, with dragging and with full feeling in pit of stomach and oppression of breathing; periodical, in outer part during motion, < in house. *Pain almost like splenetic stitches extending to l. hypochondrium, when walking fast.* Pain in muscles, < touch; P., with tightness of breath; deep in, in afternoon, arresting breathing; periodical clawing, under short ribs; sprained and bruised; beating paralytic, along l. clavicle; oppressive burning, below ribs, with anxiety, not impeding respiration.

Shocks in the side, across lower part of spine, or rather pressure as with a dull point. Scraping, rough feeling, with heaviness, forcing him to hawk. Constriction; more externally. Oppression; in evening, from tensive feeling in pectoral muscles; in sleep, a sort of nightmare; and pain when stooping or sitting bent; as if sternum were pressed upon. Congestion. (Undulating sensation.)

Heart and Pulse.—Warm undulations at H. Strong beating of H. Pulse slow; and feeble, small.

Neck.—Pain in muscles; P. as if outer part were swollen; drawing, in r. side towards shoulder; tensive, in l. muscles; (tensive, in outer muscles, at noon); tensive, rheumatic, in r. outer side, with drawing extending to behind ear; as if nape were stiff. *Stiffness of nape in morning in bed; of nape in morning after rising, with rheumatic pain.*

Back.—Pain; drawing, in r. side, < scapula, waking him in morning, > turning on other side. Scapula, pain in l. as from taking cold after a sprain, in morning on turning over in bed; rheumatic pain between S., hindering motion; rheumatic drawing pain in l. *Lumbar region, drawing tearing on bone; bruised pain,* < **rest** *and in rainy weather* (Rhus t.); *sprained pain; pain when sitting as if back had been bent too long, and as if one had been lying upon it too long.* Pain in lumbar region; in l.; in l. side of vertebræ during rest; when sitting; *when sitting,* > *motion, with anxiety;* < *stooping.*

Extremities.—Trembling at night. Joints affected by gout become red, swollen and painful. Erratic tearing. *Pain; in bones or periosteum, mostly in spots,* **on change of weather**; joints of l., < motion; drawing, in l. wrist and in r. leg. *Cramplike drawing,* < *forearm and leg down to fingers and toes.* Pressure downward in lower limbs and fingers. Creeping causing uneasiness, < rough weather, and < arms during rest. Sticking crawling in r. foot and hand when walking, as if asleep. Go to sleep easily. Insensibility; and paralysis. Affected in morning in bed, stretching all the time and throwing himself about.

Upper Extremities.—Drawing digging in joints, < l., during rest.

Shoulder.—Tearing in morning in bed; in r. evenings in bed and disturbing night's rest. *Tearing boring in l. joint,* with falling asleep of arm and pricking in tips of fingers. Pain in l. joint all day; *paralytic rheumatic, in r. in morning when resting upon it, sometimes extending below elbow;* boring beating, in r. joint; beating and drawing, in r.

Arm.—Sticking. Tearing in periosteum of r. A. and elbow during rest. Pain in r. as if dislocated all day, so that it is difficult to hold anything in hand. Spasmodic contractive pain in l., with paralytic feeling, so that it is difficult to lift it. Drawing pain in r. in rough weather, < rest. Drawing in r. A. and l. hand, with jerking. Weakness of l., with drawing in muscles of l. upper; W. of r., with prickling in tips of fingers. Heaviness of l., < rest, with feeling as if blood ceased to circulate and weakness; H. of r., > motion, with weakness; of r., > motion, with tremulous paralytic weakness.

Upper Arm.—Sticking coming deep out of l. Pain in periosteum on inner side of l.; in muscles as after great exertion; drawing, along. Drawing. Pulsation.

Elbow.—Tearing close to bone of r., extending upward and downward on posterior surface of arm. Pinching in tip. Drawing pain in l. Drawing in r.

Forearm.—*Tearing in r.; T. in l. at night* in bed. Darting pain in l. Sensation as if circulation ceased, < rest, with distention of veins of hands, pleasant warmth spreading through hands and prickings in single fingers as if asleep. Weakness of l., with paralytic feeling.

Wrist.—Sticking in r. in evening. Tearing in l. when walking in open air. *Digging in l. in evening during rest, with painful drawing;* digging, < rest and rough weather, with drawing. Digging drawing pain, with increased warmth of hands. Sprained pain in l.; S. pain during and after motion; during motion, in r., then l.; with heat; *in r., impeding motion, in rough weather,* < *rest.* Clawing pain in r. as if sprained. Pain in l. moving towards hand, with difficulty of motion. Drawing pain in single carpal and phalangeal bones. Weariness in l. during rest.

Hand.—Puffiness. Trembling. Burning stitch in r. Tearing in r., < thumb and index, in evening;

paroxysmal in r. in evening; paroxysmal, in direction of little finger in evening, with twitching. Pain in metacarpus of l. index; in a spot in metacarpus as if a bursa would form. Weakness and heaviness, with drawing in spots in bones.

Fingers.—Jerking in l. index in evening. Sticking in l. index in evening in bed. Darting pain in l., < little; in l. phalanges. Digging in second joint of r. index in afternoon in rough weather, with tension in joint on moving it. Sprained pain in joints of l. thumb. Pain in joints of l. thumb, < motion; in middle joint of l. little finger impeding its motion; bruised, under nail of r. index all day; paralytic, in l. thumb; drawing paralytic, now in one, now in another, now in metacarpus, now in forearm. Numbness in r. little, then formication.

Lower Extremities. — Tottering. Occasional contusive pain in some muscles in evening when sitting. Weakness of r., with heaviness.

Thigh.—Sticking in region of neck of femur; tearing, in outer side of l. during rest. Digging in r. hip in evening when lying upon it. Sprained pain in r. hip; when walking. Tensive pain in inner surface of r. Acute drawing in r. Sore feeling near genitals. Burning soreness between T. and perineum. Weariness of T. and legs, < l., in morning; of muscles of r. on walking. (Heaviness); on beginning to walk, > continued walking.

Knee.—Tearing close to bone; T. in r., > motion. Tensive, sprained pain in r. when bending it during rough weather. Bruised pain on inner surface of r. patella. Drawing in r. at night in bed, then tearing; D. in hollows when walking; in r. when at rest. Jerking sensation in r. Threatening to give way after the siesta, with indifference and low spirits.

Leg.—Swelling of legs and feet, < r., < unusual exertion. Tearing in r. tibia; in periosteum of l. tibia, beginning in knee. Tearing drawing in r. Boring beating pain in r. fibula. Pain in tendo-achillis when stepping. Drawing along anterior surface. Uneasiness of l. in evening, as if tired from walking. Give way on descending stairs. Weakness of tibiæ. Rigid feeling in l., with crawling.

Ankle.—Acute drawing pain deep in externus malleolus, extending along leg, in rough weather, < rest. Sharp clawing pain in tarsal joints.

Foot.—Stitches through corns; in corn at night in bed; sudden, through l. heel. Tearing in r., < outer malleolus. Pain in r. heel; in r. sole as from a corn. Uneasiness, forcing him to turn from side to side all night. Tingling, < balls and heels; in l. as if asleep.

Toes.—Pain in outer border of r. great during rest; in joints of l. great; as from chilblains, and in balls and hollow of foot.

Skin.—Red blotches on inner surface of thighs; red spot on nose sensitive to touch; dark red spots on inner side of r. thigh causing sore pain when walking. Eruptions. Pimples around l. corner of mouth; painful to touch over outer part of l. brow and under r. corner of mouth. Pustules on forehead; on back and shoulders; on r. forearm; painful, on forehead.

Pinching above r. brow; on dorsum of nose; itching, on r. brow. Prickling here and there. Formication on r. thumb; l. leg; affected parts; (in those limbs which had been affected by gout); sudden, in single fingers or other places of hands and feet; burning F., pricking in limbs. Itching; and pains of all sorts; of nose; on inside of thighs; in different parts evenings on going to sleep, with gnawing; *of r. middle and ring fingers, with erysipelatous redness;* behind l. ear, extending down nape; between l. index and middle finger, waking him at night during rough weather; of l. fingers, then burning, > washing with cold water.

Sleep.—Yawning. Sleepiness; in daytime; during day and deep sleep at night, later the reverse (in a woman who had rheumatic pains); in afternoon; in afternoon, with burning in eyes. Deep sleep in evening immediately on lying down. Restless sleep; disturbed by indifferent dreams. Waking frequently towards morning and tossing about; W. early, then restless sleep; early every morning at a certain time, as if called, and afterwards inability to fall asleep. Sleep full of dreams, greater weariness on rising than on lying down. Dreams about fire, with indifference; anxious, about fire. Lascivious dreams, with copious emission; L. after coition, with emission and long-continued erections; vivid, towards morning.

Fever.—Chilliness all day, the least current of air makes him chilly; C. < morning in bed; alternating with heat (on appearance of menses which had been suppressed six months), with headache, drawing in limbs. Shuddering in lumbar region when sitting. Coldness of three r. middle fingers; in parts of lower limbs, with gooseskin; in l. knee extending along thigh in forenoon; in thighs in evening on rising from bed, with rigidity. Cold undulating sensation above knee, extending to top of knee. Cold feet; < evening, disturbing sleep; at 6 P.M., with heat of head, without thirst, with pressure outward in head, burning in eyes, dryness in nose, burning in nose on inspiration, debility and bruised pain in limbs and weariness of mind, restless, almost sleepless night, dry heat of body, slumber towards morning, during slumber sweat, which alleviated sufferings.

Heat; with thirst; *of hands;* in face and on body down to thighs; of hands, < tips of fingers, with sweat; in upper part of body on entering house, with anxiety there; in r. cheek under eye, with prickling; paroxysmal, in face in evening. Sweat; at night; easy, on walking in open air, with tired feeling; on lower limbs in morning in bed; fetid; fetid in axillæ; often smelling of spice, with itching and formication.

Rhus Aromatica.

A tincture is made of the fresh bark of the root.

Clinical.—Diabetes. Incontinence of urine; both diurnal and nocturnal. Hæmaturia, with general debility. Catarrh of the bladder, with excruciating pain on urinating. Sometimes useful in enlarged prostate. It has been found useful in the summer diarrhœa of children, with weakness, pale tongue, general moisture, etc.

Rhus Toxicodendron.

A tincture is made of the fresh leaves of the "poison ivy."

General Action.—The contact of this poisonous plant produces in sensitive persons the most violent dermatitis, with (1) vesicular eruptions (eczematous), (2) erysipelatous inflammation of the deeper layers, with bullæ or boils, or with an extensive phlegmonous infiltration leading on to formation of abscesses and even septic infection; with these there may be diarrhœa, with or without ulceration of the bowel, dysentery, nephritis and cystitis. Some of the phases of this dermoid inflammation simulate closely forms of scarlatina and typhoid fever. The rheumatoid pains it produces are like multiple neuritis and inflammation of the fibrous sheaths of muscles; its numbness like the effects of neuritis. A low type of fever accompanies the development of its symptoms.

Allies.—(Anac., Ailanth.), Puls., Lyc., Caps., Euphorb., Ferr., Con., Dulc., Viola tr.

Generalities.—Fell down unconscious, no pulse, feeble but ineffectual efforts to vomit, offensive odor from body, pain in epigastric region, frothing from mouth, inflammation of lips (after suppression of erysipelatous inflammation by vinegar and water), later pustules returned and developed into furuncles, then patient recovered. Trembles and reaches out hastily. *Twitching;* in various parts, except joints; across abdomen and of limbs, and when the nervous influx passed to limbs it caused pain in brain so that he exclaimed violently, when asked where his pain was he could not mention any place, but that his limbs were as if forcibly stretched, < after sleep. Convulsions of different parts, with delirium. Extreme mobility in afternoon, with physical activity.

Pain in affected parts causing moans, when sitting; in back at noon in cold weather, then in l. eyeball, then on dorsal side of fourth r. metacarpal bone, extending subsequently to wrist, with lassitude and disposition to stretch, pain at ulnar edge of l. metacarpus, then in radial edge of r. forearm and ulnar edge of r. metacarpus, then < ulnar edge of l. metacarpus, then in l. ring finger, near nail; tearing-drawing, at 8 P.M. when sitting; tingling, in r. hip and rectum; tingling, in l. hip and rectum when lying on l. side; burning, semilateral, above zygoma and in same side of occiput at 3 A.M.; (biting, as from salt in an ulcer, when walking in open air and waking her at night); (crawling, in face, spine and sternum).

Rheumatism after too hot a bath, < legs, a stiffness of all joints on first moving them, with pain in joints and lame feeling in legs. (Twinging on backs of fingers and outer part of arms and on occiput, with pinching.) **Soreness in every muscle, > exercise.** *Can lie only on back at night.* **Restlessness; at night.** *It seemed as if something forced him out of bed at night.*

Weakness; *on waking;* before stool; (after eating); after eating, with dizziness; < **walking in open air;** < **sitting** (Caps., Con., Dulc., Lyc., Puls., Viola tr.), > **walking, with stiffness on rising from a seat** (Puls., Lyc.); *with difficulty in thinking and aversion to talking; as if deprived of sleep; as if bones ached, with constant desire to sit or lie. In morning he did not wish to rise and dress. Desire to lie down;* in church. Faintness; with dizziness; sudden, at 9 P.M., with perfect consciousness, could feel the beat of the heart, coldness, quiet mood, but could scarcely walk.

Stiffness, < knees and feet; S. on rising from a seat; *on descending a hill,* > **walking on a level.** *Paralysis of whole body, in all joints,* < **attempting to rise after sitting and towards evening** (Lyc., Puls.). Aggravation at 2 A.M., then gradual improvement till about 10 A.M., and aggravation towards evening; A. about 6 P.M.; *after drinking cold water; in cold weather and during northeasterly winds; cold air or taking cold* (Dulc.); on going from cold air into warm room, < pit of stomach; from slight vexation, for instance, discharge of coagulæ after menses had ceased, etc. Symptoms of poisoning which had lasted eight years, > after a typhoid fever, which continued thirteen weeks.

Clinical.—Valuable for effects of strains on muscles, especially from lifting or from working in water. Muscular and neuralgic pains, > *moving about.* In muscular rheumatism, generally useful when there is not much inflammation or fever, every part seems sore, general aggravation from cool air; especially valuable for ailments resulting from checked perspiration. Neuritis of almost every nerve in the body, characterized by the peculiar symptoms of the drug, especially numbness and paralytic stiffness. Rheumatic paralysis from getting wet or lying on damp ground. Generally indicated in low types of diseases or when acute diseases assume a typhoid type. Generally indicated in cellular inflammations, which assume a purulent character. Hemiplegia of the r. side after apoplexy. Chorea. General aggravation during wet weather, at rest, on rising from a seat and cold; amelioration from motion, warmth.

Mind.—Delirium. Thought that an enemy wished to poison him. **Sadness; and weeping without knowing why** (Lyc., Puls.); *with anxiety as if a misfortune would happen or as if all about her were dead, or as if she had bid farewell to a near friend,* < **in the house,** > **walking in open air** (Puls.); with dislike to being spoken to, nervousness, starting at every noise; with love of being alone. Grief and inclination to weep.

Apprehension at night, cannot remain in bed. *Fear on account of sad thoughts, which she could not get rid of;* F. from a trifle on falling asleep, as if he had dreaded misfortune. *Anxiety at night, he would flee from bed and seek help on account of indescribable distress;* < after midnight, *with weakness as if he should die; when sitting, she was obliged to take hold of something because she did not think she could keep up on account of the bruised and drawing pains in limbs; with trembling; with pressure at heart and tearing in sacrum;* with hot skin; with mental uneasiness and dryness in throat; *as if he wished to take his own life* towards evening. *Discouragement; in evening, and dissatisfaction with the world;* and apprehension, then short cough from tickling and irritation behind upper half of sternum, after a siesta, from noon till 3 P.M.

Restless mood, *with anxiety* that clawed at pit of stomach and with difficult breathing. *Impatience and vexation at every trifle, intolerance of being talked to. Satiety of life, with desire to die, without sadness. Ill humor;* in open air, he could fall asleep when walking. Disposed to criticise and find fault from 7 till 9 P.M. Cannot be satisfied, indifferent to society. Averse to labor.

Forgetful (Anac.). Confusion, he thought that he should die. Mathematical and mechanical calculations. If disagreeable thoughts came into her mind she could not free herself from them. Ideas slow. Inaptitude for mental labor from 9 till 10 P.M., then itching from middle of l. leg to ankle. Exhaustion. Loss of thought; when walking after a meal; with dizziness; though he seems to be thinking; like a swimming before eyes, often like a vanishing of objects. Coma.

Clinical.—During low fever there is frequently delirium, rather mild, especially with fear of being poisoned. Usually there is extreme nervous restlessness, both mental and physical; it is sometimes difficult to say whether the mental anguish or the physical suffering causes the restlessness.

Head.—Swelling. Twitching in spots of part on which he was lying at night. Sticking outward. Sticking digging. Tearing; throbbing. Aching; mornings after rising; in forenoon; in forenoon, with sleepiness; after eating; after beer; with constipation; reeling, and when writing vanishing of thought and memory; bursting, < motion; throbbing, with burning; intermittent throbbing; as if stupefied, with tingling in head; like a crawling, after walking in open air; (as from a disordered stomach). Throbbing in brain, with compression.

Dulness; in morning, with intoxicated feeling; on turning eyes, with heaviness of it, even the eyeballs hurt; with disinclination for literary work; with weight in r. temple and above and behind r. orbit; *as if intoxicated, when sitting,* **on rising vertigo even to falling forward and backward** (Bry.). *Heaviness so that she must hold it upright to relieve the pressure forward into forehead;* H., and on stooping sensation as if a weight fell forward into forehead and dragged head downward, whereby face became hot; H. and fulness, with sensation on stooping as if brain fell forward; and fulness, with ringing in ears, with at times sticking outward in l. temple.

Weakness, on turning it unconsciousness, and on stooping it seems as if she could not rise again; W., with stupid feeling; sudden, when standing after dinner, with vertigo, so that he thought he should fall forward. Affected so that she could not hold herself up. Unsteady feeling. *On shaking head sensation as if brain were loose and hit against skull.* Swashing in brain at times. Rushing sensation on ascending, she felt every step in it. Sensation as if something in it turned around when walking in open air, without vertigo. *She seemed intoxicated* **on rising** *and thought that she would fall forward.* Swaying sensation in brain when walking. *Vertigo;* in morning; in morning on rising; in morning on waking, > rising; after eating; on walking or stooping; when walking, so that he did not see men in front of him; on lying down, with fear that he should die; when sitting, as if he were elevated; as if everything whirled around with her, > lying; as if she would fall forward when walking.

Forehead.—Shooting inward in l. side, with throbbing; S. outward above eye when eating, then nausea and fulness and warmth rising internally. Sudden pain behind eyes as if brain were torn to pieces, as after intoxication by brandy, on opening eyes after sleep, < moving eyes, then bruised pain in cerebellum, with pressure outward in temples. *Tearing in region of brows and in malar-bones, with drawing.* Pain; in l. side; at l. angle and in l. temple; in r. superciliary ridge; over l. brow; over r. brow and in region of r. hemisphere of cerebellum; at junction with r. temple in morning; at 6.30 and 7 A.M., and in temples and occiput; over r. eye in forenoon after mental labor; at 11 A.M., < region of causality, with fulness and impatient desire to accomplish several kinds of business, chiefly intellectual; over l. brow at 1 P.M., with depression of spirits, yawning and lachrymation; intermittent, above brows, in latter part of forenoon, > afternoon, returning in evening, also depression of spirits, disinclination to conversation and weakness of legs; burning, above l. brow after washing hands and rinsing mouth with cold water; as with a dull point, on violent motion of arms; as if eyes would be pressed out, with yawning and chilliness; pressing forward behind l. eye. Pressure upon bone, constantly increasing and suddenly ceasing. Tension in sinciput after eating; painful, in cerebrum at 6 A.M., on waking, with languor and coldness. Drawing on l. side, extending through cheek and down lower jaw through muscles and teeth, as if toothache would develop.

Temples.—Sticking inward in r.; in l., with throbbing; S. from temples and nape to vertex, and head feeling too large. Sticking jerking extending into jaws and teeth at 7 P.M., with general weakness and with bruised pain in l. temple, he yawned, but could not fall asleep immediately for fear the pain would return. Tearing in r. Pain; in r., with remittent burning bone-pain through middle phalanx of r. little finger, waking him at 5.30 A.M.; radiating upward into r. in evening in bed, < rest, forcing him at one time to sit up and at another to rise; burning, in r. bone. Compression in brain. Heaviness.

Upper Part.—Tearing after eating, with external soreness and at times drawing pain through whole head. Heaviness after walking.

Side.—Tearing from side to side from 5 P.M. till going to bed, < stooping. (Pain in l. side and in occiput as if sore, extending into teeth.) Beating in r.

Occiput.—Stitches on stooping. Pain in l. side; in r. hemisphere of cerebellum and over r. brow; in morning on waking; in r. hemisphere of cerebellum at 11.30 A.M. after intellectual labor; in r. side, with constipation; > *bending head backward;* jerking, in afternoon; burning, at times, in forehead at times; drawing, in O. and temples at 4.30 A.M., with pressure in eyes, driving him from bed.

Scalp.—Scabby pimple above l. parietal protuberance. Tearing transversely across. *Pain on touch;* and on stroking hair backward; P. in l. side, with drawing, both extending upward; as if contracted or as if she were pulled by the hair. Pressive drawing in l. side. Crawling; in a spot on occiput as if it would suppurate, in afternoon. *Itching;* anteriorly at 10 P.M. on walking in open air with head uncovered.

Clinical.—Headache < in wet weather. Headache < morning from lying and from cold, > heat and motion. Neuralgic headache only > walking rapidly. Occipital headache, with rheumatic stiffness in nape of neck (Dulc.). Meningitis, with stiff neck, generally > lying upon something hard, restlessness, etc. Moist eruptions on the head, formed in crusts, offensive, itching < night. Eruptions, with great sensitiveness of the scalp, < warmth of bed. Erysipelas of the head, with vesicles.

Eyes.—Inflammation. Redness in morning, with agglutination; *redness of white in morning, with burning pressure in it,* eyes seem to protrude. **Soreness around** r. Dull. Sticking below eyes; S. alternating with itching and redness. Periodical cutting, with difficulty in opening lids in morning. *Sharp pains running into head. Aching; on exerting vision; as from dust;* as from inflammation in l. in evening, with redness in inner canthus and agglutination; pressive and contractive, in evening; burning, in l.; burning, from evening till morning, > rising. *Swollen feeling in l.;* and bruised sensation, upper lid swollen and itching. *Biting in r.; B., and in morning agglutination. Lachrymation; in evening, with burning pain;* in cold wind. Pupils dilated. Pain in l. ball; *in ball on turning eye and on pressure.* Itching in ball.

Lids.—**Inflammation. Agglutination, with purulent mucus in morning. Swelling;** of r. upper, > open air, with pressure; *with relaxation of them and with hot, flushed face;* closing l., with feeling as if glass or sand were in eye; *hard, red, like a stye on lower towards inner canthus, with pain.* **Closed**; l.; nearly; in evening, as from sleepiness, with dryness. Twitching, with dryness and with febrile chill; T. sensation in l. upper; sensation consisting of T. and contraction in r. lower. **Heaviness,** about 8 P.M., **with stiffness, like paralysis** (Kalm.). Dryness, < inner canthus. Soreness in cold air, as from salt biting tears. Biting on inside of lower. Itching, with drowsiness; biting I. on r. upper, > rubbing.

Jerking near r. inner canthus. Pain in l. inner canthus and in side of root of nose at 9.30 A.M.; P. in r. outer C. on pressure and on closing lids. Swollen sensation in r. inner C. Burning in l. inner C. at 6.30 P.M., with stinging; *in r. inner* before 8 P.M. Itching of r. outer C. Pain in l. brow. Sharp pain from l. orbital region through head to nape, > pressure. Bruised pain on inner side of orbit towards nose.

Vision dim; and objects look pale. Confused from 8.30 till 9.30 A.M., with (< r. half of field) irregular wavering lines and with tendency to hemiopia (and presbyopia?). Double, and sometimes only one-half of an object could be seen, and objects appeared to be at half the real distance. Objects do not appear of the right color.

Clinical.—This drug is valuable for numerous affections of the eye, in a general way characterized by great external swelling of the lids and sub-mucous cellular tissue. Paralysis of the upper lid from cold. Erysipelas of the lids. Pustular conjunctivitis. Scrofulous ophthalmia in general, intense photophobia, yellow, purulent discharge, pains < at night. Affections from getting wet. Conjunctivitis and iritis. Granulated lids, with saclike swelling of the conjunctiva and heavy feeling of the lids. Panophthalmitis, suppurative, with much swelling externally. Orbital cellulitis; one case of most rapid progress had destroyed one eye in forty-eight hours and attacked the other, was making rapid progress, immediately checked by Rhus t. Occasionally useful in glaucoma.

Ears.—*Swelling on lobule.* Shooting inward behind l., with throbbing. Tearing behind l. Aching; sudden, as if a thread were drawn through them. Painful throbbing at night. Sensation as if something were blowing into r. or stopped it up. (Itching crawling as from something alive in them.) Ringing in r. when walking. Singing like a locust, < cold air, > afternoon. Squeaking like young mice. Cracking in l. as if drum burst, on going to sleep at noon, so that he started up and trembled. Sound in l. like a cascade or like heavy rain striking the ground. (Roaring.)

Clinical.—Inflammation of the middle ear; inflammation of the external ear, with thick, yellow discharge. Erysipelas of the auricle.

Nose.—*Tip red and painful to touch, as if it would suppurate.* Median edge of r. nostril inflamed, then a tough and irritable pimple at upper part. Pointed. Sharp pain extending into cheek-bone. *Sore sensation in nostrils;* in l. Feels abraded. Tension beneath r. nostril. Sensation of hardness and swelling below N., > touch. Dryness. (Obstruction, > open air.) Sneezing; during the siesta, with fluent coryza; *violent. Involuntary discharge of mucus in morning after rising, without coryza. Bleeding; in morning; at night; almost only on stooping;* on hawking and clearing throat.

Clinical.—Nasal catarrh, with severe aching in all the bones, caused by dampness. Catarrh, with green discharge, offensive. Frightful attacks of sneezing all night.

Face.—**Swelling;** *and tension. Sunken, with sickly expression and with blue rings around eyes;* S. and drawn, l. side feels drawn up shorter, r. side feels elongated. Redness and sweat; erysipelatous R. of l. side, beginning during stool. Yellow and brown. Sallow. Pale. Stitches in zygoma, with pressure; sudden S. in r. cheek. Cutting at a point in cheek, then itching and sticking, > scratching. Cutting contraction in r. cheek; burning contraction in r. cheek, with pain in crowns of upper molars. Burning cramp in r. cheek in afternoon, as if everything would suppurate, skin of cheek hot and rough, necessity to rise from bed, and thirst. *Pain in a gland under angle of jaw, with digging.*

Cracking in joint of jaw on moving it, even when drinking; on moving it back and forth in morning. *Cramplike pain in joint of jaw; close to ear, > hard pressure and by warm food. Pain in joint as if it would be dislocated in evening during spasmodic yawning. Pain in joint as if bruised or as if it would break on moving it. Lips dry, cracked and covered with a red crust* (Ailanth.). *Clusters of vesicles filled at first with watery substance, on lower lip, near corners, with salty biting and soreness to touch.* Soreness in corners. Pinching point in r. side of lower lip in morning on rising, with sensation as if bleeding.

Clinical.—Facial neuralgia, with chilliness, < evening. Rheumatism of the jaws, feeling as though they would break or crack always on chewing; the jaw dislocates easily. Facial erysipelas.

Mouth.—Teeth. Looseness, with intermittent painful crawling in them, as in a limb asleep; *L. of lower incisors, she cannot bite upon them;* of lower incisors, the gum recedes, it can be pushed off and touched without pain except while the teeth are painful; of incisors, with pain from cold and warm drinks; of lower incisors, two first molars and canines, with crawling pain in gums. *Tearing, > hot applications.* Sticking digging. Cutting and sore pain. Sharp pressure in lower molars, with dull pain in them and with sensation of a mouldy smell in mouth. Pain in lower molars; in incisors on touch of tongue; *in evening in a hollow tooth, which became elongated and loose, then also in other teeth pain partly sticking and partly crawling;* as if too long and loose on biting and chewing; drawing, after dinner; in r. upper as if they were drawn into their sockets by the roots. Jerking pain in hollow; J. pain in canine in evening, with sticking; *at night* (about 10 P.M.), extending into head, > cold hand; upward in a nerve, transiently > a cold hand. Sensation of a tenacious substance between r. Numb sensation in upper molars.

Gum.—Pinching on both sides of lower, with musty taste. Sore pain at 2.30 A.M., with burning extending into roots of molars, forcing him to sit up in bed, with heat in body, < head, with sweat on forehead. Pressure on outer part, over lower molars; P. moving here and there on inner side of incisors, and in periosteum of teeth.

Tongue.—**Soreness, with redness at apex** (Phyto.). *Blisters. Yellowish-white at root. Coated;* reddish-brown, except near edges, in morning on rising. *Brown mucus,* except on edges, in morning on rising. Dark brown mucus on it one morning, coated yellow another. Salt mucus in morning. Burning and smarting, with increase of saliva. **Dryness** on waking at 8 A.M.; *D., provoking drinking; dry sensation at tip* without visible dryness.

Mouth in General.—Inflammation and vesicles. Mucus; grayish, in morning. Cutting throbbing pain as from an ulcer posteriorly on palate where teeth end, and on touch sticking as in an ulcer. Soreness of upper and back part of palate. *Dryness and thirst.*

Coldness as from a wind, when closed, with roaring in l. ear. Sudden heat, and in gullet. Inclination to spit, as from salivation. *Salivation;* in morning, with nausea and hunger; during afternoon nap; *running from mouth during afternoon nap when sitting;* after the customary smoke; with burning pricking in tongue and sore feeling at tip of tongue; salt, in morning in bed. Spitting of saliva and mucus all day, with sour eructations; spitting of tenacious mucus. *Breath fetid.*

Taste.—Bitter (all day, even to food); in morning, > eating; *waking her at night, with dryness in mouth;* (to acids); (to bread); and rough to bread; and acrid, sour. Bloody when coughing; B. in nose and mouth, then bilious, bitter taste. As of bad meat in forenoon, > eating. Sour; after milk. Coppery, with scraping extending into throat. Slimy, mouth seems coated with mucus; S., forcing her to spit much. Fatty, but natural to food. Flat. Bad, in morning after waking and after eating.

Clinical.—Toothache, < cold, > warmth; (occasionally relieves a jumping toothache, momentarily > a cold hand). Sometimes useful for inflammation at root of a tooth, with pain, < night from cold. The tongue is dry, red and cracked, in fever.

Throat.—**Hard swelling of submaxillary and parotid glands. Swelling of submaxillary glands,** *with sticking on swallowing.* Mucus, and in posterior nares; M., < rinsing mouth; hawking of M. in morning; tenacious, > hawking, but leaving roughness. Sticking on swallowing and yawning; on swallowing if throat is dry, but when moist pressure in it on swallowing; near epiglottis, beginning dull and ending sharp, > swallowing.

Pressure on swallowing, < empty swallowing. Throbbing pain posteriorly. Soreness, with burning extending to stomach; S. and apparent smallness, causing difficulty in swallowing. Swollen sensation, with bruised pain, and on swallowing swollen pain and sticking. Sensation in pit as if stopped and constricted in trachea, transiently > eating and drinking. Rawness in l. tonsil on swallowing, with soreness. Roughness provoking hacking cough; R. in throat and trachea as if chest were raw and sore. **Dryness;** after getting into bed. Coldness on expiration, as if a cold breath were exhaled. Burning; about noon, and in chest near œsophagus, with burning pain in back. *Inability to swallow drink, on every swallow the drink chokes her as if epiglottis were paralyzed, with dryness posteriorly in throat.* Pricking low down in œsophagus behind sternum. Burning in œsophagus in forenoon.

Clinical.—Sometimes used for sore throat, with œdema of the fauces, great restlessness, swelling of the parotid glands. Occasionally useful in diphtheria, with bloody saliva, swollen parotids, restlessness, etc. Mumps.

Stomach.—Appetite, in morning, but on going to the table indifference to food. Great. *Ravenous, > sitting, with emptiness in stomach, with loss of appetite in palate and throat;* ravenous, yet mouth seemed soapy, everything tasted like straw and was eructated, appetite disappeared after slightest food and he felt full. Frequent, sudden, for dainties. **Desire for cold milk,** he swallowed it hastily; D. for raw oysters; for cheese, sometimes for hearty food. Food is relished in evening, except bread, that seems rough, dry and scrapy; F. was relished though he ate without desire; ate with relish at noon, though he was indifferent to food; food is relished tolerably, but she has no real desire for it and her stomach seems constantly full (Lyc.). Little appetite, yet a hunger, with a sensation as if hunger affected chest. Satiety if he eats a little, yet hunger (*Lyc.*); S. after a glass of wine, aversion to wine, with heaviness of head. *Lost;* at noon; with flat, slimy salivation; with constipation; and after swallowing a morsel a putrid taste; for tobacco; *beer is not relished;* and neither food, drink nor tobacco tastes good. Aversion to meat and broth; to bread and to eating generally; to coffee.

Thirst; in morning; from 2 till 5 A.M., then sweat; in afternoon and after midnight, *from dryness in mouth;* at night, without desire to drink, with slimy mouth; *for water or beer.*

Eructations.—At 1 P.M., with shooting in r. side of epigastrium and in r. axilla; whenever urinating. Empty, in evening, then hiccough; E. towards evening, with bloating of abdomen; after eating and drinking; tasting of food. Burning; rising from pit of stomach into pit of throat, almost taking away her breath, in evening; *remaining in r. side of chest.*

Nausea; in throat; in chest in morning after rising; in morning after rising, > open air, with anxiety; in morning after rising, with warmth, N. > lying down; in evening on lying down, with tossing about; in chest and stomach in evening in bed, > sleep; *after eating and drinking;* after eating and after coffee, with salivation; when sitting; < stooping; in chest, > eating, with ravenous hunger; > eating, returned with hunger, without appetite; *with pain at l. quadratus lumborum;* with burning pain in stomach, dizziness, feeling as if stomach were too large and hanging down, then chills running from feet to head, then flashes of heat, chill from 2 till 3 A.M. every day during the inflammatory stage, pulse full, rapid; beneath short ribs, impeding respiration; causing shivering.

Vomiting; of the partially digested fruit, later of a tenacious wine-colored fluid.

Sticking in r. side towards stomach; in pit; in pit near r. hypochondrium; in region, impeding deep breathing. Rending pain in diaphragm, < lying. Cramp in pit like a fulness. Griping above stomach, below diaphragm, later lower down in stomach; in pit and thence suddenly in a spot in hypogastrium. Pain; in epigastrium; in pit; at 7.15 P.M., and in abdomen, lasting in abdomen through the evening and remaining next morning; on coughing; in pit on moving about; when about to fall asleep; *then loose dark brown stool,* before the stool pain at symphysis pubis, and during it burning in anus and procidentia ani; in pit and diaphragm so that he could not lie in bed; (in pit during dinner, delaying sleep); in pit as if everything were swollen, making breathing difficult; *after eating* as from undigested food; in pit, as from swallowing too large a morsel; pressive and burning, on swallowing cold water; as if closed and being split open with a knife, preventing lying. Contractive pain in r. side, extending towards stomach.

Fulness in morning so that food will not go down; after a moderate meal, with eructations; after a glass of wine, aversion to wine, with heaviness of head; *as if overloaded* after a moderate meal, with great appetite. Sensation of a lump after a meal, < standing. Oppression towards evening, as if everything in region of pit were contracted. Throbbing in epigastric region; below pit. Crawling, > lying, with eructations, both renewed by rising.

Abdomen.—*Distention; all day,* and sensation of fermentation in it; *after eating;* > eating, with fermentation and hunger; on rising from stooping, with warmth in chest; flatulent, < eating, with apprehension; painful, after a meal, with colic as from incarcerated flatus. Rumbling and griping; R. and gurgling, with thrusts towards mons veneris. *Fermentation.* Flatulence in evening; before 8 A.M., with pain in region of ascending colon, < gradual pressure and more by sudden pressure and percussion, often worse at a distance from the part pressed or struck than at the part itself. Offensive flatus; easy emission of flatus that appears only in rectum. Jerking caused by flatulence. Internal shaking on every step.

Shooting at noon. Cutting, < motion, with tearing and griping; C., then sticking in r. side of abdomen. *Griping* in forenoon when walking in open air, with incarceration of flatus; G. during normal stool; when sitting, with oppression mounting upward; *and jerking;* almost jerking, in various parts. Digging and twisting pain as if a worm were moving in it. *Pain* at night; *P.* > *stool,* but returning and causing other stools; *with contraction so that she must walk bent over;* as if ulcerated in morning on stretching after rising, and skin of abdomen seemed too tight; as in diarrhœa; as from pressure, when sitting, > lying; like a heavy lump; in a spot, as from incarceration of flatus, on violently turning body. Sensation of water bubbling under walls. Crowding as if intestines were pushed towards heart, when sitting. Heaviness when sitting, with emptiness and hunger. Burning, with thirst.

Hypochondria.—Shooting from hepatic region to r. shoulder. Griping below r. ribs when sitting, as from worms, soon extending to umbilical region. Pushing below l. ribs. Crowding forward when sitting bent over, with anxiety as if death were imminent. *Pressive drawing forward in l., with anxiety and nausea in chest.*

Griping in upper A. after eating and drinking. Cramplike pain in r. side in morning from slight cold, with moaning, timorous and disconsolate mood. Cutting in r. side of A., then sticking. Digging in r. side. Drawing pain in l. side during respiration. *Cutting in middle in forenoon, with frequent* but natural *stools,* > bending body, < walking. Contraction transversely across above navel, so that abdomen above and below the line was distended, hard and tense.

Umbilical Region.—Flatulent distention and griping. Sticking at 3.30 P.M.; S. above umbilicus; to l. of U.; extending to præcordial region with every pulse; to anus, first from below and to right of U., then from below and to left of it, towards evening. Cutting in l. during expiration while sitting. Griping in r., with creeping chilliness over upper arms. Drawing pain extending towards pubes. Cramplike drawing. Bruised pain below umbilicus.

Hypogastrium.—*Swelling of inguinal glands.* Griping burrowing waking him about midnight, with exhaustion and emptiness in pit of stomach and nausea. *Pain in region of ascending colon,* and in r. wrist and middle of l. radius; in pubic region; *in region of ascending colon* at 10.45 A.M., *on rising after stool;* at 2 P.M., with flatulence, then pain in r. chest; *in region of r. quadratus lumborum muscles at* 2.30 P.M. *on rising from lying;* in inguinal glands at night on moving; labor-like, as if menses would appear; rheumatic burning, between spine of ilium and ribs in evening; in ring, as if a hernia would protrude; contractive, in l. groin; drawing, in r. side when sitting, with sensation as if abdomen were covered with a cobweb. Drawing transversely across above ring when sitting. Pressure outward in r. groin, with ravenous hunger and gurgling in abdomen. Sensation in l. flank as if a hernia protruded. Stretching in r. flank as if a hernia would protude. Tension in l. flank, with sticking; T. in l. groin by hip as if skin were too tight. Heaviness as if a boil were hanging on l. flank, when walking.

Clinical.—Peritonitis and enteritis, with restlessness, dry, red tongue, putrid, slimy diarrhœa, sometimes involuntary. Typhlitis, painful swelling of the whole r. side of the abdomen, < lying on l. side, > lying on the back and by gentle pressure from below upward. Colic, > bending double and moving. Numerous inflammatory symptoms of the r. side of the abdomen, with feeling of heavy weight pressing in the groin, could not stand.

Rectum.—Procidentia. Pain; at 3 P.M. when urinating. Burning before stool. Crawling as of threadworms. Deep-seated itching. Frequent desire, yet he accomplished but little. Constant urging and straining at stool; constant U., with nausea and tearing in intestines, the U. often ineffectual, sometimes scanty, watery discharge.

Anus.—Painful, sore, protruding, blind hæmorrhoids after soft stool. Sore pain when not at stool. Smarting during and after stool, with burning. Burning at 10.30 A.M., soon with burning at end of penis. Itching pain as from hæmorrhoids. Pricking itching between 3 and 6 P.M. when walking.

Clinical.—Hæmorrhoids, blind, protruding after every stool, with backache and pressure outward in the rectum. Fissure of the anus, with sore protruding piles. Inflammation of the cellular tissue around anus, especially traumatic.

Stool.—*Liquid, with mucus, red and yellow, gelatinous;* L., brown, occasionally with pain before getting up from stool; almost L., frequent, with flatulence. *Diarrhœa;* in morning, with colic and cutting in abdomen; with griping before each stool; as if chopped; *tinged with blood, preceded by lassitude;* dark brown, with procidentia ani; dark greenish-brown, with eysipelatous redness of l. side of face lasting an hour; frequent, gelatinous, yellow and white streaked, without colic; sudden yellow, frothy, scarcely at all offensive, without previous colic, the first drops involuntary; frequent; (frequent, then ineffectual tenesmus). Soft, whitish-yellow.

Constipation; with pain in r. side of occiput; with headache and loss of appetite; with continual urging, ineffectual stool, with flatulence and rumbling in abdomen, ineffectual desire after eating; then dark brown stool. *Stools mixed with blood.* (White.) *With gelatinous substance;* frequent; and sudden, offensive, at first thick, afterwards watery, mixed with flatus, with griping and digging in hypogastrium. Child cries before every stool, afterwards it is quiet.

Clinical.—Diarrhœa of thin, red mucus, or of bloody water like meat-washings, sometimes a jelly-like mucus, with lumps of transparent mucus, sometimes involuntary; it may be without odor or very offensive, frequently associated with tenesmus and tearing pains down the thighs; this may occur during typhoid fever or may result from getting wet. Dysentery, with many of the above symptoms; craving for cold milk said to be very marked.

Urinary Organs.—Stitches from both sides upon bladder while urging to urinate. *Obliged to urinate three times at night;* every minute during the day. Micturition frequent, urine scanty, red. (Micturition in a double stream.)

Urethra.—Cutting when urinating; anteriorly when urinating, with burning and smarting, and after micturition burning and smarting, with irritation and heat in rectum; anteriorly during and after micturition, with burning pain, the last part of urine milky, after micturition heat in rectum. Burning during micturition; with scanty, high-colored urine; posteriorly at root during micturition. Biting in forepart during and after micturition, < rest.

Urine.—*Dark; and scanty, irritating; and soon becoming turbid. Hot. Turbid when passed.* Whitish, becoming more turbid the longer he urinates, the last drops like flakes. Like water, with snow-white sediment. Yellow, occasionally frequent desire, at other times seldom, but copious, sometimes transparent, sometimes smelling saltish, at others sulphurous. Profuse.

Clinical.—Pain and soreness over the region of the kidneys, with symptoms of inflammation, œdema, etc. Paralysis of the bladder. Inflammation of the bladder, with tenesmus. Oxaluria.

Sexual Organs.—Swelling and tightness; tympanitic S., < scrotum, with itching. Frightful eruption, with closure of urethra by swelling. Mons veneris, red, sore spots caused by ruptured vesicles; swelling; distended sensation when walking in open air; pressure.

Glans.—Swelling in morning after rising, with pain on touch and with biting in urethra during and after micturition; S. of glans and prepuce, and around root and in prepuce itching, burning, prickling and cutting, with transparent swelling from prepuce to scrotum, < l. side, with vesicles discharging a transparent fluid, prepuce looks and feels as if scalded. Vesicle beneath prepuce; V. oozing moisture at top of G. *Pain on account of swollen prepuce, causing paraphimosis.* Erections after waking at 1 A.M., without desire; E. at 2 A.M. in sleep without amorous dreams, then mathematical and mechanical calculations; towards morning, with frequent desire to urinate; frequent, at night, with frequent micturition.

Swelling of prepuce; close to its union with glans. Prepuce dark; red spots on inner surface of P., near frænum; *sticking itching on inner surface of P. Scrotum felt like thick hog's hide; thick and hard, with itching, extending especially towards perineum. Scrotum and penis red at* 2 P.M., *scrotum flaccid and hanging half way down to knee.* Moist eruption on scrotum, with swelling of prepuce and glans; M. eruption where scrotum touched thigh and in perineum. Cutting drawing in l. testicle. Emissions at night; irresistible inclination to E. after 3 A.M.

Female.—Sticking in vagina. *Sore pain in vagina* in evening; in evening after touch. Labor-like drawing extending down to uterus when standing. Bleeding from uterus at new moon, without pain, in a pregnant woman. *Menses caused biting pain in genitals.* Menses profuse, they had been long absent.

Clinical.—Erysipelatous inflammation of the penis. Persistent painful erections, > lying on the back, with tenderness in the spine, apparently the result of a strain. Erysipelas of the external genitals, moist eruptions. Eczema of the pudenda, with great swelling, intense itching, < night on undressing, followed by soreness and smarting. Prolapsus uteri. Ovarian cyst. Leucorrhœa. Retroversion. Erosions of the cervix, resulting from distended follicles. Membranous dysmenorrhœa, always < dampness. Puerperal fever of a typhoid character.

Respiratory Organs.—*Burning rawness in larynx* at 6 A.M. on waking. *Hoarseness from scraping rawness in larynx;* H. low down in trachea. *Tickling irritability in air-passages, as if it would provoke cough,* that makes breath short, > moderate exertion.

Cough night and morning; about 3 A.M., < after waking; *at night, preventing sleep;* (after eating); (in open air); < after waking; with tension in chest; in evening, causing vomiting of food; **short, from tickling and irritation behind upper half of sternum, then discouragement and apprehension;** *short, anxious, painful, waking him often before midnight, with short breath; hacking, in evening after lying down, with bitter taste in throat till he falls asleep, and in morning similar cough and taste till rising; tickling, causing dryness in throat, < evening; short, dry, at* 11 A.M., *from tickling behind upper half of sternum when sitting bent forward, with aching in mammary region;* dry, hoarse; dry, before midnight, causing sticking in one loin; *spasmodic, shattering head;* shattering chest, as if everything in it were loose; with expectoration and coryza; (< morning, with black, glutinous expectoration); fatiguing, day and night, with white mucous expectoration.

Respiration.—Choking sensation at times. *Oppressed and anxious.* Difficult after walking a little. Obliged to breathe deeply, as if she would suffocate, < eating, and inability to sit up. *Short at night;* S., < going to stool. *Hurried.*

Clinical.—Paralysis of the muscles of the larynx. Cough racking, < before midnight in wet weather, with pains in the back and limbs, restlessness. Typhoid pneumonia. Hæmoptysis.

Chest.—*Milk disappears from breasts.* Hot vapor from lungs. *Sticking in side;* r.; below r. nipple in morning in bed, with itching in front of chest; near middle of r. side after 1 P.M., when lying on that side; below l. ribs in evening, lasting till midnight; in l. when coughing; in l. when talking and on deep breathing; in side when walking in open air; deep on sides of sternum when sitting bent over; at third rib, about three inches to l. of sternum, on inspiration when sitting at close of supper, at which the principal drink was ice-water; tearing, from r. side of C. to l. side of abdomen in evening; pulsating, above præcordial region in evening when sitting; boring, in one of last ribs when standing. Boring in l. side in evening in bed.

Pain in r.; l.; near middle of sternum, on l. side; two inches to l. of nipple and at lower angle of l. scapula, then at l. scapula and l. shoulder-joint; at insertion of a muscle near middle of sternum in morning, then sensitiveness on pressure; two inches to r. of middle of sternum at 1.30 P.M.; in r. at 2 P.M., with flatulence and pain in hypogastrium; in l. side midway between sternum and angle of ribs at 7 P.M. when walking; at l. clavicle on waking from nightmare; in l., midway between sternum and angle of ribs, soon extending to shoulder, arm and forearm. Burning and pressive pain at middle of lower side of l. clavicle on swallowing cold water; B. and pressive pain behind upper half of sternum at 11 P.M., with excoriation and with short cough excited by tickling in same part. Scraping and burning.

Oppression; at night, with sticking, < breathing; sticking, in sternum, making respiration difficult, with short cough, without expectoration; as after violent weeping. *Weight on lower part, with anxiety, so that she* *breathed with difficulty and sometimes deeply*, when it was easier, pulse at one time slow, at another rapid. Pressure inward on sternum in morning, > rising. Constriction; with nausea; in sternum, with sticking jerking in it. Pushing in l. side not far from pit of stomach when sitting bent. *Tension in evening, with short breath and weakness in limbs.* Drawing down l. side when breathing. Fulness, with hunger, without appetite; F. below sternum, with sensation as if appetite had vanished forever. Weakness, so that talking was difficult, after walking in open air. Heat when walking in open air. Numbness.

Heart.—Anxiety more in afternoon than in forenoon, sleeplessness half the night on account of anguish, and anxiety so that she perspired. *Weak sensation, with trembling of it. Palpitation when sitting still, so that the body moved with every pulse..*

Clinical. — Palpitation from over-exertion. Hypertrophy of the heart in a rheumatic diathesis. Rheumatism of the heart from getting wet, violent palpitation, pains extend into the left arm.

Pulse.—*Rapid.* Slow, at times irregular; S., full and strong, afterwards rapid, small and compressible. Felt in occiput.

Neck.—Stinging in upper and lower part of neck and in upper part of back at 4.40 P.M., after drinking cold water. *Pain in muscles of nape as if asleep or as after lying in an uncomfortable position towards evening. Pressure in muscles on bending head forward;* P. in upper part of nape, with numbness. Drawing over one side of nape when stooping. Weight on nape so that he could not rise again, with rush of blood into brain. *Stiffness; of nape; of nape, with tension on motion; rheumatic, of nape* (Dulc.).

Back.—*Sticking in evening when stooping; worse when walking than when sitting, also on stooping, but < rising again.* Burning pain about noon, with burning in throat and region of œsophagus. Drawing pain when sitting, > walking; D. pain in evening, forcing him to sit upright. Drawing downward, with tension and pressure in rectum, as if everything would press out.

Scapulæ.—Twitching in l. side by S. when sitting; rumbling T. in some parts of S. and above r. knee, with contractive sensation. Tearing between S. and at the same time they were drawn together. Tensive cutting across. Pain in l. and in shoulder-joint; under r.; below l., with drawing upward; *rheumatic, between S., > warmth, < cold;* as from pressure of a finger upon l. Pressure upon r. Drawing beneath r., with pressure, impeding respiration. *Constriction of dorsal muscles when sitting, > bending back, < bending forward.*

Lumbar Region.—Sticking jerking in sacrum when walking. Drawing jerking stitches in coccyx. *Cutting in sacrum when standing and bending backward.* Pain in region of l. kidney, < lying down at midnight; P. behind r. sacro-iliac symphysis and in l. shoulder; above l. sacro-iliac symphysis; **in sacrum when sitting, as after long stooping. Bruised feeling in sacrum; when sitting, with heaviness; in S., > moving**; *in flesh on grasping sacrum; and in r. side of lumbar vertebræ.* **Stiffness of sacrum; with pain on motion.**

Clinical.—Muscular rheumatism in the back, especially umbago, great pain on attempting to rise, > warmth, < cold, > bending backward. Muscular pains in the back from strain. It seems to have cured locomotor ataxia.

Extremities.—*Swelling of hands and feet. Readily sprained. Contraction of l. arm and leg, with stiff feeling.* Twitching. *Unsteadiness during a chill.* **Trembling after exerting them. Sensation similar to trembling in arms and legs, even at rest.** Sticking; in a spot, < lying; in joints when the limb is lying at rest, not when stretching it out, not on touch and not when lying down at night. Aching on ulnar side of upper phalanx of l. middle finger in morning in bed, then in posterior phalanx of l. fourth toe on beginning to walk and on pressure, between 6 and 7 P.M.; *A. in joints, < open air. Bruised pain in limbs and joints on which he does not lie in morning;* B. pain in flesh, < touch. **Drawing when lying.**

Weakness. **Stiffness** (Caust., Lyc.); **on first moving it after rest; during and after walking, with paralyzed feeling in them and with weight upon nape;** rheumatic, in joints, with pain shooting through knees from side to side, wandering pains, sometimes on one side and then suddenly on the other, pricking in feet and fingers, flesh feels as if it would drop from limbs, the pain is deep-seated, < gentle friction, > *hard rubbing*, **desire to move limbs frequently, which relieves the rheumatic pains. Falling asleep of those upon which he lies, < arm.**

Upper Extremities.—*Painful swelling of axillary glands. Stitches in shoulder when lying, > moving; drawing stitches from shoulders down through arms; S. inward in l. shoulder, with throbbing. Tearing in shoulder-joint and on top of scapula.* Pain in r. shoulder; *at top of l.; in l. in forenoon when riding;* in r. at 6 P.M. when walking; *when lying, > moving; rheumatic, in l. S. and arm in region of deltoid;* burning, in l. at 1 P.M. when walking. *Weight on shoulders; upon l. by clavicle. L. shoulder seems paralyzed.*

Arm.—*Swelling and pain.* **Trembling after moderate exertion of it.** Jerking sensation in l. *Shooting through them;* **extending downward in l. and out at finger-tips, with drawing. Tearing, < lying still. Drawing in l. at night, with paralyzed sensation.** Sensation as if something were rolling down in it from shoulder to hand. *Falling asleep of the one upon which he rests his head in sleep.*

Upper Arm.—Sticking in l.; *inward, on r.; burning, beneath l. axilla;* boring, when standing. *Tearing, < work, forcing one to let arms hang down, with pain when in bed, and on taking hold of them pain in bone.* **Sprained pain in l. at 2 and 3 P.M. when arm is carried far upward and backward.** *Pain in l.;* in l. deltoid at 6.30 A.M. on exerting it; about middle of l. at 7 A.M., with itching on back and chest; *on r. side of l. about noon after lying down. Tension in l. in open air. Drawing from below l. axilla to middle of upper arm, on raising arm.*

Elbow.—**Jerking tearing in E. and wrist, >motion.** Pain in l. between 2 and 3 P.M. after drinking ice-water, then in r. scapulary joint, < lower angle of scapula, beginning when pulling; burning itching P. in l., > scratching. *Drawing extending into wrist, with tearing; cramplike, in l. on moving it. Tension on stretching arm, with difficulty in raising arm.* Throbbing in l.

Forearm.—*Pain in middle of l. radius; in region of l. biceps;* region of r. biceps flexor, then in ulnar edge of r. metacarpus; *l. biceps and phalanges of l. fingers about* 6 A.M.; middle of l. ulnar at 1 P.M.; in r. biceps when at rest; *bruised, in l.;* burning, in biceps in bed,

< l. **Weakness in upper part of r. on motion and sprained pain in wrist on grasping anything. Stiffness and weakness of F. and fingers**; *S. of l., with digging in bones on motion and jerking in r. wrist.*

Wrist.—Tearing sticking in l. **Sprained sensation on upper surface of l. on bending it.** *Pain in r.;* l.

Hand.—*Swelling.* (Twitching between r. thumb and index.) Pain at ulnar edge of r.; before midnight, > movement; *rheumatic P.; drawing, in r. palm;* throbbing, in l., extending to elbow; intermittent throbbing, in l.

Fingers.—Twitching inward of thumbs on laying hands down; (T. inward of fingers). *Sticking;* in tendons on back of index. *Tearing in joints.* Pain in middle joint of l. index; in middle joint of r. ring; in middle phalanx of r. little; in metacarpal joint of l. index and in middle of r. upper arm; midway between joints in evening; *on motion, on account of swelling.* **Crawling in tips as if asleep** (Sec. c.). *Falling asleep sensation in l. index. Index and middle numb and asleep in morning.*

Lower Extremities.—*Staggering in morning on rising, with inability to stand upright;* S. to the right when walking; S. without vertigo. Limping in afternoon. *Pain, and in knees; burning, and in knees.* **Weakness, < rest;** W. of joints; *so that they feel bruised. Paralysis; and walking difficult, slow and shuffling.* Cramplike contraction in r. nates. Pain in tuber ischii after rising from a seat; *drawing P. in r. nates, just below sacrum, > pressure;* cramplike, in l. nates when standing.

Hip.—Lameness of l. during first part of a walk. *Tearing extending to knee when walking and standing, with drawing. Pain, and in knees; in l. at 5 P.M. on bending trunk to r.;* **when lying on side, and in sacrum when lying on back** (Nux v.); **in joints on every step, and paralyzed sensation in anterior muscles of thighs;** *in r., consisting of tension and drawing.* **Tension in l. joint when sitting;** *in l. joint, extending down thigh.*

Thigh.—Twitching, with trembling of knee. Cramp in l. T. and nates. Sticking extending outward; boring S. when standing. *Tearing in middle of outer part when sitting, > motion; jerking T. above r. knee. Tearing dragging in muscles of l.* Cramplike pain below r. groin when sitting. Sensation near r. groin like that felt when fingers are spread apart when wrist has been sprained. *Pain in l.; along l. rectus femoris from 4 till* 8.30 P.M., *< beginning to walk, transiently > continued walking; in anterior muscles on touch, < l., the posterior part of which was painful on walking the preceding day;* in tendon above patella on walking; *bruised, in r. rectus cruris on pressure; drawing, on rising from a seat and when standing, forcing her to bend up;* bruised and drawing, in r. *Tension on posterior surface when riding one leg over the other. Heaviness from above knees to ankles, so that she could not stand, > walking and sitting. Inclination to stretch T. and leg in morning in bed.*

Knee.—Sticking on inner surface of l., then r., when walking; *in hamstring just above calf on violent motion, on rising from a seat and on touch; across, on standing up after sitting; outward in side when walking.* **Tearing in K. and ankle, < rest;** *T. to ankle, with drawing. Pain; under knee-pan;* in upper part of l.; in l. in morning on beginning to descend stairs after sitting; *on l. side of upper end of r. patella at noon on rising from a chair;* at outer edge of l. patella in evening on descending stairs after sitting some time; *rheumatic, extending to ankles;* hot, running to groins; intermittent sore, and in legs; *drawing. Drawing in hollow of r. on bending knee.* **Tension in l. on rising from a seat; T. as if too short;** T. in tendons on inner side of r., with pulling, **causing uneasiness in foot;** in *tendons on inner side of r., with crawling.* Tingling in K. and hollows on sitting down after walking, with buzzing. *Heaviness in hollows and in calves, so that he could not move legs.*

Leg.—Cramp in one or other in forenoon in bed, > pressure against sole. *Sticking below r. knee;* at head of l. fibula after drinking ice-water, then pain there on stepping; in lower part of tendo-achillis, < touch and after lying down. **Aching, with inability to rest in any position;** A. above l. tendo-achillis at 2.15 P.M., on ascending stairs; alternating with cold feet; (sudden throbbing and crawling P. at 6.30 P.M., < motion and touch, with cramplike pain, both disappearing suddenly). Throbbing. **Weakness;** *in forenoon; at noon, with desire to lie down;* **in afternoon when walking in open air, with heaviness and bruised sensation;** between 5 and 6 P.M., with pain at anterior tuberosity of l. tibia on first walking, then behind l. outer malleolus, then superficial pain at inferior occipital ridge, < exerting muscles whose tendons are inserted there; **when sitting, > walking;** *in legs and ankles, with pain; with pain above superciliary ridges.* **Heaviness; when sitting, with tension, but only weariness when walking.** *Stiffness* in forenoon, with staggering to r.

Tibia.—*Tearing sticking and weariness.* Stinging below inner side of head of l. after drinking cool milk. **Tingling pain in shafts at night when feet are crossed, with constant necessity to move legs, which prevents sleep.** *Sudden sprained pain at insertion of ligamentum patellæ into T. on rising from a chair, with pain on pressure.* Pain at inside of head of l. at 9.30 P.M. on sitting after walking; cramplike, in l. on bending knee, then burning. Pressure on r., then burning.

Calf.—Jerking. *Cramp after midnight in bed and when sitting after walking, > bending knee;* C. when sitting. Pain in l. at 7 A.M. on descending stairs; in l. at 2.30 P.M. at each step; *in inner, lower and posterior part when heel was raised by action of calf on beginning to walk, > continued walking; in l., > movement;* tensive, in r., with burning. *Tension when walking, with sensation as if hamstrings were too short; T. in skin, with sticking in it when sitting. Drawing internally in r., causing uneasiness in feet;* cramplike drawing upward in l. to hollow of knee. (Throbbing on outer side.)

Ankle.—Sticking in l.; in r. inner malleolus on rising from a seat; cramplike. Deep-seated pain in outer at 8.30 A.M. on pressure. Drawing in r.

Foot.—*Swelling in evening. Spasmodic contraction in inner side of sole, > stretching it out and bending sole. Sticking in heels in morning on first standing; in soles in evening; in heel when stepping upon it; in l. heel after walking in open air;* burning, on back of r., with warmth. *Intermittent pains in heels like running nails under skin.* **Sprained pain in morning on rising.** *Pain in hollow; P. after walking in open air, they seem immovable, > sitting;* in soles, with tension; in r. sole near ball, as from pressure upon a painful spot; burning sore, in a corn, from pressure of shoe; (in heels as if benumbed, when stepping upon them). **Drawing like a paralysis when sitting;** D. extending outward in l. heel, with burning. Throbbing on back. *Weakness as if she had walked too rapidly, so that she cannot easily ascend stairs;* as if blood settled in them, when sitting. *Deadness of r., with numbness.*

Toes.—Spasmodic contractions. Sticking in l. fourth; in l. great; in ball of l. great; from great to middle of l. chest when standing; burning, between fourth and fifth in evening when walking and at night in bed; jerklike, as if a boil were about to break, in affected ball of great, in the evening throbbing in it. Pain in several at some distance from joints, then about hips and small of back, then in l. gluteals, then at connection of l. tendo-achillis with calf, the last three early in a walk; drawing, in r. great, with warmth.

Clinical.—Loss of co-ordination in lower extremities. Various forms of rheumatism and rheumatoid pains.

Skin.—Hard and like leather; then desquamation; *H. on back of hand, and stiff, cracked and hot.* Hands seem coated with nitrate of silver. A black welt, which becomes sore, cuticle sloughs off and leaves a circular cicatrix. Yellow and sunken between knuckles. Blue color of scars when exposed to cold air. *Inflammation at inner side of l. nates, with excoriated feeling;* a wound becomes inflamed and surrounded by vesicles.

Redness of whole body at 2 P.M.; R. as far as four fingers' breadth above umbilicus; extending downward from scrotum, becoming striped at middle of thigh; in a hot spot on r. hip, with burning pain; in round spots on upper part of arm; (in round spots in ball of foot); *erysipelatous, of l. side of face, with burning and smarting.*

Swelling of nose, ears and neck; head, neck and chest as far as umbilicus; every year, with itching, burning and vesicles; of whole body, eyes closed and penis so swollen that he could not urinate; **of lips and nose, and then pale S. of face, later with burning pain in face, lids closed by swelling, lachrymation, face covered with vesicles full of yellow water, S. lasts longest below chin and then fine desquamation there; of face, lids and lobes of ears, with itching; of face, with redness, then scarlet exanthema over whole body, with itching biting, later backs of hands and legs covered with blisters that burst and slowly desquamated;** *of face, with itching and burning on forehead and about eyes, difficulty in opening lids, vesicles filled with watery fluid; r. side of face, with inflammation, itching and burning; of face till eyes are shut, with inflamed vesicles covering neck, hands and arms, inflammation of skin and symptoms resembling those of "milk sickness;"* of face, with heat, itching and stinging; of face, which was blistered and mottled, lids swollen so that she could not see, burning smarting over face and head and fever; **erysipelatous, of face and neck;** *erysipelatous, of face and lids, and finally phlyctenæ over whole body; of face, neck and throat, with rash resembling measles;* of face, ears and neck, with erysipelatous redness of them, hands swollen and blistered; sudden, of l. cheek, upper lip and lids, next night S. of forearm, skin leathery, with itching and heat, after four days pustules on hands and forearms, bursting and discharging clear liquid; hot, of face and hands in evening; red, in a fan shape from root of nose towards scalp, becoming hot, next day face swollen, eyes closed, on r. temple a red, itching and burning circular elevation, in afternoon the circular blotch was covered with minute vesicles and vesication had begun on other parts, later the vesicles appeared milky whitish, on back of r. hand and back of several fingers vesicles limpid at their apices, the fluid was transparent, changed blue litmus to deep blue, which faded after drying and left no discoloration; red, of face, hands and fingers, with itching, then heat, pain, vesication and fever, the vesicles on inside of fingers were large and added to the pain by pressing against each other; lurid red, of face and ears, and vesicles dripping with fluid, neck, chest and abdomen red, with patches of flattened papules and vesicles and moist excoriations, genitals swollen and scrotum running with serum, swelling of arms and legs, with vesicles, itching and irritability so that no clothes could be worn, sleep impossible without powerful anodynes. *Hard swelling under l. ramus of jaw, causing chin to rest on r. shoulder.* Swelling of head, limbs, eyelids and cervical glands, the last sore to touch, with smooth red eruption over whole body, and burning, then vesicles, which ran together in places, later desquamation and itching. *Swelling of lids* and lobules of ears, *with burning, itching and prickling. Dark red swelling of l. eyelid, exuding yellowish-white pus from tarsal margins, anterior part of r. forearm covered with minute vesicles, burning and stinging, next day r. eye involved, later blisters on fingers, which discharged a yellowish-white serum, yellowish-brown scab on arm, then peeling of cuticle of r. arm and fingers.* Swelling of l. ear, with itching and bursting of skin of lobule of r. ear. Swelling of l. side of trunk from axilla to below ribs, with pain. Swelling extending to groin and inside thigh, pubes and abdomen, as far as navel, with itching. *Swelling on arms and hands, with erysipelas, pustules, burning and itching; of arm, with vesicles containing yellowish fluid, then on other parts;* tense, of l. arm and both legs, with strong resemblance to a denuded blister in a suppurating state; *of forearm, with sudden roughness, itching and heat;* of forearms, with redness and small transparent vesicles like eczema, arms stiff, face swollen and erythematous, penis and scrotum red, swollen and painful, with inflamed elevations on inner side of thighs, the inflamed parts painful, sometimes numb, sometimes stinging, the pain < night owing to heat, and < forearms, later the red patches extended up arms and down legs, afterwards at margins of the large patches were reddish spots as at the outset of measles, the large patches resembling the redness of scarlet fever, later the redness extended to back and clavicle, except region of sternum, while the eruption was spreading on lower half of body the upper half was recovering; S. of l. hand, increasing to bursting of skin, with itching; hands, wrists, penis, scrotum, hypogastrium and part of thighs, prepuce swollen and distended by fluid, almost transparent, phimosis, hiding the glans; hands and wrists, with itching and pimples, then vesicles, which became filled with yellowish serum, swelling of head and eyelids so that he could not see, the itching spreading over body, < scalp and privates, desquamation of wrists, which had exuded much serum, and he was cured of a dartre which he had had on wrists for more than six years; S. on little finger, later another on thumb, increasing till it covered lower joints of thumb and finger, changing to a callus, which fell off as a scab; on tibia and loins, with induration.

Erysipelas, with high fever; E. appearing below l. eye at 1 P.M.; **that burst and secreted a slimy liquid; on face, the inflammation spread over forehead and into scalp, eyes closed, ears, cheeks and lips swollen and pitting on pressure, features not recognizable;** *on limbs and face, sometimes on whole body, with pruritus, tingling, smarting,* *with stinging and burning vesicles and blebs crowded together upon a red and swollen base, when these broke and dried, then eczematous crusts, sufficient irritation caused ulceration;* of face, with sweat of face; **a sort of phlegmonous E. of face and head; vesicular, on face and hands, with fever.**

Eruption about mouth and chin; near l. corner of mouth; *scurfy, over body; scurf on face;* crusty, near l. wing of nose and below nose; *burning itching, on hands;* painful, burning, itching, < scrotum, prepuce, eyelids and eyes, with swelling of these parts and yellowish blisters that here and there become confluent and discharge, also vesicles on arms and loins, many of these large pustules or ulcers slowly suppurate, are surrounded by red areola, become extended and heal slowly, the small confluent pustules rapidly dry and desquamate after a few days. *Tetter around mouth and nose, at times with jerking and itching, burning pain.* Red phlegmonous patch over l. hip. *Pemphigous eruption* followed the eschar, such as might be caused by nitrate of silver. *Eruption similar to urticaria. Desquamation of face; from cheeks, then heat and roughness; from affected parts, with itching of l. hand.*

Pimples below lower lip; on r. side of chest and half of back, with pain as if sore and raw and sticking extending outward; *hard, on hands, with burning-biting itching; inflamed, above middle joint of ring finger, with itching burning pain, that sometimes changes into a slow stitch, not > rubbing and scratching; like the itch, on inner surface of wrist and lower part of cheek, with burning itching and smarting after scratching; coalescing into blisters filled with yellow watery fluid, with itching, < after midnight, only > rubbing with something rough till blisters are opened;* miliary, *on scalp, forehead, face and mouth, with biting itching;* red and warm, on hand, itching next morning, then vesicles, a cluster of vesicles on cheek, scratching aggravated the inflammation and caused watery discharge; itching red, behind ears and on neck, next day eyelids and face red and swollen, cervical glands tumid and tender, syncope, later the rash extended over face and hands and between toes and thighs, with burning itching, later the papules became vesicles, which coalesced on face and burst, emitting an acrid serum, which formed a crust so dense that movement of facial and buccal muscles was painful, nose, lids and lips swollen, afterwards unusual irritability (to flannel, etc.) of skin and hypersensitiveness to cold air. Tough pimple at bend of r. elbow; above l. nipple; and deep-seated and irritable to touch, above l. nipple, scratching caused redness, burning and smarting. Deep-seated and irritable to touch on upper lip, opposite l. posterior bicuspid; on median side of nates; *on nates, < median line, near os coccygis;* on dorsum of l. hand, over smallest metacarpal bone, preceded by stinging.

Vesicles below lower end of r. ulna; on fingers, wrists, bare arms and back of hand; in centre of red spots; *between fingers, then over whole hand, with swelling;* **on cheeks, with itching burning;** on hands and wrists and about eyes, with itching burning of skin, < morning, with smarting and redness of eyes, photophobia, obscured vision, headache through eyes and temples, dulness, sleepiness, urine copious and pale, next day tongue furred, appetite not good, and after midnight colic, rumbling and griping during repose, with sulphuretted eructations and discharge of flatus, rheumatic pain in lumbar region and through hips, nausea, loathing of food in morning on rising, amelioration after moving about during the day, later new spots of eruption while the rest was drying up; *on different parts, then desquamation;* on inner sides of knees, with red burning spots and stripes; *some containing milky, others clear fluid, becoming confluent, then desquamation; containing yellowish serous fluid, on r. cheek, with swelling, inflammation, itching and burning, repeated next spring;* yellowish, on palm, with itching, then soreness to touch; *watery, below border of lower lip, with smarting and prickling around mouth;* watery, on l. hand, with swelling; as in chicken-pox, after too hot a bath; filled with opaque matter, on r. hand; dark, with thick cover, on back of a finger, next day one on l. wrist, later burning and itching, afterwards one of irregular shape on back of last phalanx of r. thumb, with so thick a roof as to be almost transparent, as if the effusion had taken place in lowest layer of rete mucosum, later vesicles on other parts of hands and fingers, all itching and burning, in flat, dark brown patches; exuding a turbid serum, beginning at r. mastoid process, spreading over face, neck and upper part of chest, then on hands and fingers, with burning and itching, < scratching, and with swelling, not pitting on pressure; in a thick mass, on a pale red base, on r. wrist, some brownish, glistening from the dried exudations that were pressed out as limpid water; discharging a clear lymph that dried to a yellow glistening pellicle, in a band around arm, the V. more isolated towards hand, some on outer margin of hand were clear and without areola; V. and papules in a red stripe above and below knee, a group of papules on chin, a few of which had reached the vesicular stage, skin beneath one eye puffed and red; *burning, about mouth and nostrils; burning, filled with water, with redness of whole body, except scalp, palms and soles;* itching, on chest; itching, on an elevation in l. palm, discharging serum.

Pustule in l. mammary region; *on side of chin, and when touched burning and pain;* between fingers and on parts of hands touched by the stems, with itching, extending over whole body, with inflammation and itching; (in fold of cheek, with sticking on touch); abortive, on r. fingers and at root of thumb-nail, with itching. Boil on edge of l. upper eyelid, then in groins, legs and abdomen; on hypogastrium, groins and inner part of thighs; on pubes; on abdomen, thighs and groins, with soreness and redness on pubes and abdomen, with smarting, throbbing and burning pain.

Sticking externally on leg; in outer anterior part of leg; in region of a scab in morning on waking; at lower part of cervical and upper part of dorsal spine and at two corresponding points of neck, at clavicular parts of sterno-mastoid, at 5.45 P.M. when walking in house after drinking cool water; in different parts of neck at 6 P.M. on walking in open air after drinking cold water, oftener over sterno-mastoid opposite lower part of larynx, next day at lower part of neck about 6 P.M. when walking after drinking cool water; itching, in nape.

Contraction on l. scapula. (Pain in an ulcer as if beaten.) Crawling; in an ulcer; on last knuckles of l. second and third fingers; *on feet in morning;* across forehead and nose when sitting upright, > stooping; burning, in forehead. Burning biting in an ulcer, with weeping and moaning.

Itching; in various parts, with burning; **with burning, later < touching or moving the affected parts, as if pierced by hot needles, swelling and white transparent vesicles on the inflamed skin**; with stinging; sometimes with dryness and cracking of the skin; it occurs in different places and at different times, is generally < heat and > cold, and is always violent and almost intolerable. (The skin symptoms of Rhus t. may be compared with Anacard., Ailanthus and other poisonous Anacardiaceæ.)

Clinical.—Acne rosacea. Indicated in numerous vesicular and pustular affections of the skin, with symptoms characteristic of the drug. Facial erysipelas, with formation of vesicles, burning, tearing pain, great restlessness. Urticaria. Erythema. Valuable when glandular inflammations threaten to suppurate. It is indicated in skin eruptions of a vesicular type, especially when the vesicles tend to form scabs, intense itching, < warmth. Eczema, which tends to assume an erysipelatous condition. Boils, carbuncles, abscesses, in short, all sorts and conditions of skin diseases which threaten to suppurate or which are characterized by the general restless fever and prostration of the drug. Particularly valuable in the typhoid forms of scarlatina, with enlarged glands, mild delirium, restlessness, etc.; the eruption calling for Rhus is usually not uniform, and causes great irritability. Smallpox, the pustules are blackish or bloody, with diarrhœa. Purpura hæmorrhagica, with dry tongue, tremulous pulse, numbness of the extremities, restlessness.

Sleep.—Yawning; in morning on rising; morning and evening; with lachrymation; *spasmodic, threatening to dislocate jaws. Sleepiness; by day, with sleeplessness and restlessness at night;* during the day, with constant desire to lie down, anxiety, sadness and dryness of lips; during day and evening; in morning in bed; in forenoon, with headache; at 11 A.M., with yawning and indisposition to labor; in afternoon, with languor; when sitting after walking; *after eating*, he could not keep awake; with stupidity; sudden, at 6 P.M., with paralyzed feeling in limbs.

Sleeplessness; in evening on account of mental activity, heat without thirst, but chilliness on uncovering, orgasm of blood, throbbing in vessels and dark clouds moving before his vision, after midnight he became quiet and slept well; *half the night, with anguish at heart and apprehension; before midnight*, with or without sweat; *after* 3 A.M., *then vivid dreams, and on waking it seemed as if he had not slept at all; after* 3 A.M., *she rose anxious, restless, weak and trembling, < knees* (with sweat on back); **with inability to remain in bed**; with restlessness.

Late falling asleep and tossing about. **Restless sleep after midnight, filled with fretful, disagreeable thoughts; R. after midnight on account of burning in whole body, without thirst, with dreams full of anxious agitation**; R. during the day, he moves his hands back and forth and plays with his fingers and hands; *on account of burning in the eruption;* **with raising and throwing off of the covers; and interrupted, with much turning over.** *Slept with open mouth.* Expiration light and blowing, inspiration inaudible. She often rises at night in sleep and heaves as if she would vomit, but nothing comes of it. Starting up every quarter of an hour in sleep in forenoon; S. up in fright on falling asleep, as if he had let something important fall. Loud weeping. Talking aloud in morning; talking about his business, wishes to throw everything away, and desires this and that; talking half aloud of the business of the day, when asleep in evening. Woke early, with fretful mood. Waked at 6 A.M. by an allusion to sleep in a gentle voice.

Dreams.—**Anxious, of his business as soon as he fell asleep.** Of subjects that had been listened to or talked about the previous evening. *Of accomplishing the plans projected the previous day, associated with the subjects whence they were derived.* Light, of what had been considered or accomplished the previous day. *Fearful, for example, that the world was on fire, with palpitation on waking.* Of fire. Interrupted, full of difficulties. That her head was hanging out of bed and she could hear the blood flowing into it, and that she was obliged to accompany a horrible image, in morning after falling asleep a second time. Incubus at 1 A.M. after waking, with pain in occiput. Incubus, with inability to move, pressure on r. upper part of chest, superstitious fear connected with the supposed presence and agency of some invisible, sly and malicious being.

Fever.—Chilliness; on waking, < rising and till afternoon; in afternoon, alternating with heat, with malaise; towards evening; *in evening, with heat, face seemed hot, though cheeks were cold to touch and pale, breath hot;* at 7 P.M., with inability to drink anything cold without suffering, as soon as he lies down external heat, which does not permit him to uncover, without thirst, with watery mouth and dry lips, about midnight sweat during a half slumber, after midnight sweat on face, then on scalp and neck to chest; at 8 P.M., then in bed dry heat, with thirst, cutting in abdomen and diarrhœa, in morning again diarrhœa, at 6 P.M. chill in limbs, then dry heat, then heat with sweat for three hours and thirst, diarrhœa of only mucus, with colic, followed by tenesmus and accompanied by headache, a pressure from temples towards middle and rush of blood and heat in head; in open air; *sensitive to cold, open air, sometimes it causes pain in skin, also without aversion to open air;* with dry lips and less thirst than hunger.

Creeping chilliness in house towards evening. Sensation as if dashed with cold water. External chilliness all day, with internal heat, yet natural warmth to touch, the internal heat < coffee. Shaking chill at 5 P.M., < open air, with throbbing toothache and salivation without thirst, the shaking chill continued by a hot stove, with thirst and cessation of salivation, the chill > in bed, but thirst continued, then stupid sleep, like dulness of head, next morning thirst and dulness of head, > rising. Shaking chill in evening in bed, then slight warmth, without thirst; S. chill on going from open air into warm room; on walking in open air, with thirst and mucus sticking lips together.

Shivering in morning on rising; *about* 5 P.M., *with stretching of limbs, thirst, cold hands, heat and redness of face, again in evening shivering, in morning general sweat, with pressure in temples;* **over body about 6 P.M., with warmth of body, internal and external heat of head, without thirst, with stretching, drawing, weakness in limbs, dulness and compression in side of occiput, violent cough, short breath and pain as if tonsils were swollen, towards morning slight general sweat**; at night in bed, at times in the middle of the sweat, and during the shivering cramps in abdomen; as soon as she goes away from the stove; after walking in open air, with heat, with warm sweat, < palms, without thirst; < eating.

Coldness of r. side of body without chilliness, with heat on l. side. Chilliness, except in head and hands, with heat of them and nausea, then general C., with nausea; in back at noon; *in back and head, with heat on anterior part of body;* about joints, with cold sweat, and on back cold spots as from ice; *internal, in limbs;* in limbs towards noon, with headache and vertigo (> walking), towards evening chill again and necessity to lie down, at night sleeplessness, vertigo and sweat; forearms; l. forearm, with sensation as if rubbed with a woolen cloth or scraped with a knife; internally in wrist, as from a wind; *hands and feet all day;* backs of hands in a warm room, with sensation as if finger-tips were engorged with blood; *on l. tibia;* feet and legs; feet in evening in bed; feet, < hollows of feet, alternating with pains in legs; feet and between scapulæ, then heat of l. side and l. arm; *pinching, in feet and between shoulders, then external heat, with burning pain in l. arm and on l. upper part of body and redness of cheeks.* Shivering in back; in scapulæ, with warmth of face and fingers, without thirst.

Heat; weary with sleep in forenoon, yawning, sleepiness when walking, with anxiety, then stool with cutting, then heat (about 10 A.M.), without thirst, it seemed as if he were dashed with warm water (with shivering) or as if blood circulated hot through the vessels and too violently through head, and as if head were pressed down to stooping, with throbbing headache, about 7 P.M. a chill as if dashed with cold water or as if blood ran cold through vessels, heat as soon as he lay down and covered up; through the night drawing in spine, between shoulders and in limbs, as if he constantly wanted to stretch them, in morning sweat; heat at 2 P.M., with languor compelling me to go to bed; in evening, < hands, with headache; at night without thirst; when walking in cold, open air, with cold sweat; on entering house after walking, with sweat; (when sitting); *with thirst;* with twitching; with distended veins, weakness so that she must lean back when sitting, thirst, also frequent thirst at night, next day shivering in upper part of body, < arms.

Remittent fever, sometimes with brain symptoms. Double tertian, with jaundice. Pernicious intermittent fever.

Burning in skin at night, with twitching in it and sweat, **cough whenever he puts his hands out of bed.** Hot skin; with anxiety; with full, hard pulse. (Burning in affected parts.) Heat of head; in evening, especially internally; mounting into head on drinking beer; extending into throat, without redness of face; external; internal, with dry lips and thirst, then pressing asunder in forehead, with heaviness in it, < entering house or waking from midday nap, headache > evening as soon as she lay down in bed. Heat in l. eyebrow, then pain; H. at inner end of l. superciliary ridge; *in the swollen face, lids and lobes of ears; beneath l. nostril, so that the breath seemed to come out of it hot, > open air;* in face in evening; internal in face, with redness of it, but moderate warmth to touch; *in loins;* in a point at bottom of sacrum, extending to r. side; as if hot water were running through arm; biting, in forearm; in flesh between l. thumb and index; in a point on r. thigh by scrotum; feet.

Sweat; during the day, with desire to be covered; about 3 or 4 A.M. in sleep; *in morning;* in morning in bed, except on head; in afternoon, except on face, which, however, was hot; before midnight; all night; at night, < about neck; at night as soon as he lay down, without thirst, hence he had no rest; *from warm drinks;* when coughing; sour-smelling, in morning, with cold, sweaty cheeks; on thighs in morning; (on feet). Exhalation of a strong odor at night without being wet.

Clinical.—Intermittent fever, chill begins in one leg, with dry, teasing cough, external chill, with internal heat. Malarial fever; paroxysm preceded by stretching and yawning, sometimes by cough; during the fever there is frequently urticaria. Very frequently indicated in typhoid fever.

Robinia.

A tincture is made of the fresh bark of the young twigs of the yellow locust, Robinia pseud-acacia, L.

Features and limbs shrunken. Convulsions. There appeared to be muscular pains, as the child cried when its arms were taken hold of. Weak; in morning. Faint; tendency to when moved from a horizontal position. Relief after flatulent stools. *Low-spirited.* No ambition. Headache; in r. temple; with sharp stitches in temples; *throbbing, in forehead; heavy, in forehead, < motion and reading;* neuralgic, in l. temple, preventing sleep from midnight till daylight. Dulness of head. Inability to support head upright. Eyes sunken. Eyes sore; felt sore and watery. Pupils contracted. Running from nose; continual discharge, with headache and frequent sneezing. Tongue coated white, with red tip; coated whitish-brown, smooth and slimy. Mucous membrane of mouth pale. Throat rough. Dry, scratching sensation in throat.

Called for water. *Eructations; of sour fluid.* Retching. *Nausea* on sitting up, with efforts to vomit; *N., then profuse* **vomiting of sour fluid;** intermittent, in afternoon. *Vomiting; violent;* in sudden attacks, with purging. *Sourness of stomach. Pain in epigastrium; sharp, in stomach day and night.* Distress in epigastric region, with cutting in stomach and bowels, and much rumbling; *heavy aching D. in stomach; burning, in stomach and region of gall-bladder.*

Clinical. — Acid dyspepsia, with constant weight in the stomach, eructations of sour liquid, sometimes with vomiting. Indigestion, with severe lancinating pains extending from side of the chest to top of shoulder-blade. Intensely acid vomiting; this symptom has been relieved, even when associated with cancer of the stomach; and numerous cases of acid eructations and vomiting have been cured. Burning in stomach and between the shoulder-blades. Indigestion, constant squeezing pain in the stomach after eating, can only eat once a day on account of the distress, backache, weakness, etc.

Distention of abdomen; with flatulence; with pain. Rumbling in abdomen. Abdomen sore on motion and pressure. Stool, with slimy look and bilious tinge. Purging an hour after supper, continuing every few minutes for about an hour, when it changed to urging, but with little success, in another hour stool of a little dark liquid, with tenesmus and pain. Constipation; with frequent ineffectual desire. Voice reduced to a whisper, and the effort to cry very feeble, suddenly ceasing with a sigh, as if from exhaustion. Respiration feeble. Heart's action feeble; action more embarrassed when moved from a horizontal position. Pulse 55; P. almost imperceptible at wrist. Inability to move fingers, hands, arms or legs. Body and limbs pale. Urticaria over whole body. Tickling the soles seemed to cause much distress. Lethargy. Sleepiness, with dulness in limbs and head, changing from r. to l. side, also with stinging in temples. Restless sleep on account of frequent sneezing. Cold hands and feet.

Rumex Crispus.

A tincture is made of the fresh root of the yellow Dock.

Allies.—The cough as well as the skin symptoms may be compared with the Kalis, especially with Caust.

Generalities.—Pains intermittent; and wandering; neuralgic P. **Sensitiveness to open air.** Pulsations through whole body; over body in evening, with flushing of face, pulse 80. *Restlessness in evening. Weakness;* in a warm day; on going to bed; with heaviness and with fulness in head and chest; with somnolency, constant change of position and tired feeling in legs.

Mind.—Irritable; and restless. Depressed and indisposed to exertion; D. as if evil impended. Indifferent to surrounding persons and things. Stagnation of ideas in evening, with lassitude and uneasiness.

Head.—*Aching;* nearly all day, *with bruised feeling in forehead;* in forenoon; after retiring late at night; till going to sleep towards midnight, returned on waking and lasted till noon; before breakfast; < motion; with coryza. Bruised sensation in brain in morning on waking, < moving, stooping or sudden movement of head, suddenly > after dinner at noon. Heavy aching during the day; during the day, < forenoon, with deep-seated soreness of eyes; during the day, > afternoon; in forenoon; from 10 A.M. till night, > after 2 P.M. Heaviness in evening. Oppression in morning on rising. Fulness, with deficiency of hilarity, giving a serious expression to face. Vertigo; with nausea.

Forehead.—Shooting over l. brow. Sharp pain in open air. Aching; over brow; in region of causality; at r. organ of causality; in morning on waking; at 11 A.M.; in evening after singing, with heat and redness of face; at 7.30 P.M., with shooting; at 9 P.M.; < motion; with indisposition to think; with pungent tingling in organ of philoprogenitiveness; over l. eye, with soreness to touch; over r. brow, with stopped sensation in l. ear; in F. and temples, with fulness; burning, in l. superciliary ridge, then in r. Bruised feeling, < r. side, < moving head, when brain felt loose, < next morning; B. sensation, > after breakfast next morning, and on moving head sensation as if brain were loose.

Pain in temple; r., then l.; region of r. and hemisphere of cerebellum; r. in morning; l. in afternoon. Pain in vertex. Sharp, piercing pain in l. side of head. Darting pain in l. side at 11 A.M. and 8 P.M. Pain in occiput; low down in O.; intermittent, in O. in afternoon.

Eyes.—Shooting in l. running to r. jaw and arm. Pain; < r.; in forenoon; in or over either or both; in both and over l., with soreness to touch over l.; deep-seated in r.; heavy. Lids feel inflamed and dry in evening. Lachrymation. Shooting in r. ball.

Ears.—Boring behind base of l. Pain; in r. in morning; in l. in afternoon; in r. after rising from bed; when walking; in l. and running to shoulder. Throbbing synchronous with beats of heart. Itching deep in l., then r.; in r. meatus. Obstructed sensation, his own voice (as well as the voices of others) has a ringing, confusing sound, and causes a kind of titillation in ear, yet hearing is as acute as ever. Ringing. Roaring in l., with feeling of a tight thread around neck just below ears.

Nose.—Inflammation at lower edge of r. side of septum, then a vesicle there. Pain; pungent drawing, in l. nostril and side of occiput, with feeling as if coryza would ensue. Sudden, sharp tingling in Schneiderian membrane, then violent and rapid sneezing, *with watery discharge.* Dryness. *Desire to pick.* Obstruction of r. nostril at night. *Sneezing. Coryza; with headache;* with yellow expectoration from posterior nares; with obstruction of voice. Bleeding; from slightest picking of nose.

Face.—Pallor when standing. Pain in l. side; in side, r. temple and ear, and in l. side of upper lip; in r. jaw and molars; in r. jaw in morning. Lip, eruption on vermilion border of lower; vesicle on inside of lower, near l. angle; sudden itching of r. side of upper; sudden itching of upper, near l. side of nose.

Mouth.—Teeth. Lancinations at root of l. lower canine after retiring late at night. Grumbling stinging in r. upper molars when riding in a cold wind, with aching in forehead. Aching; in l. lower; in morning; of both sides in morning, in incisors in afternoon; and pain in lower jaw, in incisors, also on l. side; in r. molars, > dinner; in r. molars, > rinsing mouth with cold water; sharp; running; running, in upper.

Tongue coated; yellow; reddish-brown and dry, with bitterish taste. Stinging at side of tongue, near root. Soreness of r. edge of tongue; S. on touch of teeth, with excoriated feeling at edges and scalded feeling anteriorly. Tongue anteriorly felt dry and hot; T. and mouth dry at night. Flow of saliva. Taste nasty; bitter in morning on waking; bad in morning on rising; flat in morning on rising; like zinc on upper surface of tongue and on roof of mouth.

Throat.—Mucus in fauces and upper part of larynx; M. from posterior nares at night; from posterior nares at 7 A.M., soon after rising, fluent coryza began after breakfast, < r. nostril, < evening, with sneezing, and in evening pain in r. nostril; thick, yellow, from posterior nares; tough, in fauces, difficult to eject; tough, in fauces in evening, with aching in pharynx and inclination to cough. *Scraping* in evening, with symptoms of slight cold. Excoriated feeling in velum palati. Rawness in upper part all the morning, with secretion of phlegm. Burning smarting in fauces and upper part of larynx. Sensation as if a lump were sticking in it. Soreness on l. side on swallowing; on l. side during empty swallowing; S., with feeling of lumps in it on swallowing. Tickling, then soreness; T. in pit and behind upper part of sternum. Dryness; in posterior nares; and deglutition difficult.

Clinical.—Catarrh of the pharynx.

Stomach.—Appetite increased; decreased; lost; lost, with feeling of emptiness. Thirst in evening; at 7.30 P.M. Eructation. Empty eructations; after dinner; with distention of pit of stomach; sour, in morning on waking; forcible, in evening. Hiccough. Nausea; in morning on waking, with movements in abdomen as from a cathartic; in morning when dressing, with vertigo; in evening, > eructations, with fulness in abdomen as if diarrhœa were forming; on going to bed, with fulness of stomach and eructations tasting of the food; with pain in epigastrium, stomach and abdomen.

Distended sensation, > motion of wind in abdomen. Cutting in pit when riding in open air. Acute pain in pit. Pain; in gastric region; on waking; in digestive organs in morning on waking, and frequently; heavy, towards cardiac orifice. Burning pain during the day, and in abdomen; in pit. Pyrosis after dinner. *Feeling of repletion* and as if one had eaten spice, with dry feeling in anterior part of tongue. Weight in epigastrium; *in pit; in epigastrium after eating.* Feeling two hours after breakfast as if food had not digested; sensation of undigested food, > night; *with upward pressure to throat-pit, every empty swallowing carried it downward, but it immediately returned.*

Clinical.—Gastric disorder, shooting from pit of the stomach into chest and throat, with flatulence. Affections from excessive tea-drinking. Gastralgia, aching extending through to the back, obliged to take a long breath. Gastralgia, pains extend to the chest, < motion, > quiet rest.

Abdomen.—Distention and hardness; D. on going to bed. Movements as if stool would occur. Rumbling; in evening, with sharp pain, then dull headache; with yawning; with relaxed sensation; with colic above hypogastrium, nausea, loss of appetite, copious diarrhœa four or five times, in a stream, each discharge suddenly arrested, urging renewed on rising and on returning to the cabinet a new stream poured forth. Flatulence; in morning on waking, with emission of flatus and burnt sensation in tongue and mouth; after meals; moving about at night. Fetid flatus at night.

Cutting in evening, then diarrhœa. Sharp pain in morning after the fever, < deep inspiration, > rising. *Pain* in morning on waking, > emission of flatus; *in morning, then brown diarrhœa;* in morning, then diarrhœa; in evening; at night; wandering. Sensation as before diarrhœa, with pain in rectum; sensation as before D., and in rectum.

Pain in l. hypochondrium when lying on l. side; l. H. when walking rapidly after dinner; r. H. during eructation; r. side about seventh rib, about 5 P.M., with weakness on each side of umbilicus; r. side, in region of ascending colon when walking.

Umbilical Region.—Griping below umbilicus after breakfast, partially > emission of offensive flatus. Pain; above U.; in r. side towards evening; flatulent, in r. side (ascending colon); flatulent, in transverse colon, beginning during dinner, > emission of flatus; sudden, in bed before midnight, beginning on yawning or deep inspiration.

Hypogastrium.—Sharp pain in morning before rising, then diarrhœa twice and pain in abdomen. Aching at dorsum of l. ilium; in l. side midway between umbilicus and crest of ilium when riding, with full sensation as from flatus.

Rectum.—Hæmorrhoids, with heat and irritation about anus and sensation of a foreign body there. Movement of flatus, then pain in pubes. Shooting to l. groin like an electric shock. Pressure as from one side of a stick in afternoon. Feeling as if a rough stick were forced up in evening, painful on walking. Itching in anus.

Stool.—**Watery, brown in morning** (Sulph.); W. at 4 A.M., *the urging waking him.* Diarrhœa. *Constipation.* Hard; and small; and brown, tenacious, accumulating in rectum. Black. Scanty.

Clinical.—Early morning diarrhœa, hurrying the patient out of bed, characterized by a dry cough from tickling in the throat, < night. Chronic diarrhœa, of brown water from 5 till 9 A.M.

Urinary Organs.—Constant inclination to urinate. Urging; at neck of bladder; frequent; sudden, with sensation as if urine had entered urethra, urine pale. Urine copious, colorless; scanty, red, turbid, with flocculent deposit and oily surface, next day brick-dust sediment.

Sexual Organs.—Tendency to phimosis. Redness at end of prepuce, with sore and excoriated feeling; redness of prepuce, < evening and morning, with soreness. Itching of prepuce. Desire diminished; lost.

Respiratory Organs. — *Larynx, mucus removed by hawking; tough mucus, < night, with constant desire to raise it; irritation to cough when eating; pain; pain in top; pain, < l. side;* burning smarting, also on expiration. Burning smarting in l. bronchus, with expectoration. *Hoarseness;* in morning; in evening. Voice nasal at 11 A.M.; V. suddenly rose in pitch at 2 P.M., at 4 P.M. it sounded as in coryza. *Breathless sensation as if air did not penetrate chest, or like what is felt when passing rapidly through the air.*

Cough before breakfast, from tickling in chest; at noon **on breathing cold air,** with piercing in l. lung; **C. in evening on lying down in bed; from 10 till 12 P.M., < lying; at night on lying down; at night in bed, from tickling behind upper half of sternum; on lying down after dinner;** in bed on turning on to l. side after lying on back; when lying, **from tickling behind sternum; from tickling in pit of throat;** *then behind sternum and in stomach;* when riding, from tickling in l. anterior side of chest; *when riding in open air, from tickling in middle of sternum, then easy hawking of mucus;* **dry, spasmodic, like early stage of whooping cough, preceded by tickling in pit of throat,** *during the cough congestion and pain in head and wrenching pain in r. side of chest,* **C. < a few minutes after lying down at night,** *then sleep all night, after two weeks C. with difficult expectoration of scanty, adhesive mucus; hacking; hacking, from irritation behind sternum; C. from 11 till 12* P.M., *at first from tickling in pit of throat, then from tickling and irritation in chest as if a feather in bronchus oscillated on respiration, and with expectoration, which felt as if it came from near centre of chest, the C. causes a sharp pain to extend downward several inches in a vertical line from that spot;* causing shocks in stomach and pain over l. brow and in stomach, from tickling in trachea, bronchi and stomach, with expectoration from bronchi; *causing painful shocks in muscles in region of stomach and in place of muscular attachment on l. of stomach, where there is a spot sensitive to touch,* **in evening on lying down, from tickling in pit of throat.**

Clinical.—Aphonia. Incessant dry cough, with soreness in the chest, < cold air, cough seems to come from the pit of the throat, > warm air. Paroxysmal cough from taking a deep breath, < evening after lying, must keep his mouth covered on account of aggravation from cold air. Night-cough in phthisis. Sympathetic gastric cough. Cough causes pain behind the sternum. Asthma, with violent spasms of coughing, sense of suffocation, especially < 2 A.M.

Chest.—*Sticking to l. of sternum and under breast;* in l. side, just below middle, at angle of a rib; *in l. in morning before rising, then pain in lungs;* around waist at 7 A.M. on deep inspiration; *along l. margin of sternum in afternoon on deep inspiration when riding;* in l. anterior part on lying down at 3 P.M.; at xiphoid or ensiform cartilage and adjacent parts of epigastrium and chest about 3 P.M., < movement; **in substance of l. lung** *at 3.30 P.M., when writing at a desk;* in various parts in evening; l. side near lower edge of ribs during dinner; to l. of epigastrium when lying on r. side after dinner; *raw, to left of longitudinal centre of sternum at night, obstructing deep inspiration; burning, near heart, after lying down, gradually moved into pectoralis major, about two inches above and to left of nipple, < deep inspiration and by lying on back or r. side, > lying on l. side; sudden burning in l. at night on deep inspiration when lying down; almost itching pain below l. nipple, followed and accompanied by stinging-burning pain in back,* with throbbing in ears synchronous with beats of heart.

Cutting in l. breast at noon. Sharp pain; in r.; near anterior border of r. axilla; running to r. and l.; intermittent, at 11 P.M. in bed. *Pain; l.; sides and in lungs;* sternal region; lower border of l. axilla; below and anterior to nipple, < r.; *anterior part of lungs day and night, with headache, pain in stomach and belching of wind;* region of heart at 2.15 A.M., on waking from a dream of an accident; l. side near back, above last true rib, at night after lying down; r. side when lying, *l. side with sense of depression in chest;* above middle of l. clavicle when riding in open air, with burning and sticking pain; upper part of breast, with sense of depression; intermittent, in anterior part of lungs in afternoon.

Burning pain below l. nipple, < deep inspiration. Burning-tingling pain (similar to itching) below and to right of l. nipple. Raw pain under each clavicle when hawking mucus out of throat. *Soreness in l. after turning to that side.* Bruised sensation in r., about a lower rib. Pressure as with a finger between clavicle and axilla at 11 P.M., alternately in l. and r. sides, then aching under middle of l. clavicle. Dry heat in middle, with stinging burning pain in back.

Clinical.—It has been indicated in rheumatism of the muscles of l. side of the chest, < lying in bed at night.

Heart.—Stinging in region in afternoon, extending to apex of l. scapula, with frequent desire to inspire deeply, which increases the pain. Pain; in region, with pain and heaviness in l. upper arm and < elbow; sharp and deep, in l. side; heavy, in region on deep inspiration; burning, in region at times. Sensation as if it suddenly ceased to beat, then throbbing through chest. Action increased by ascending stairs. Palpitation after supper and after conversation.

Pulse.—Rapid.

Neck.—Pain in nape; cramplike, in l. side of nape.

Back.—Pain; in afternoon and evening; running down; in middle; in scapula; under scapula; under and below apex of l. S.; near inferior angle of r. S.; between S. when standing; near dorsal spine; in l. side of dorsal spine, extending half way to spine; sharp, at l. scapula. Shooting from dorsal spine half way to l. side; midway between dorsal spine and l. side on beginning to walk in the room, then in a spot immediately below it, in loin. Pain in loins; at dorsum of l. ilium; with fatigue; burning, in a spot near top of r. sacro-iliac symphysis; sore, at junction of sacrum with l. ilium, < stooping and rising, later pain in loins and lameness as if strained, < sudden motion of body, the lameness > 2 P.M., then pulsation in muscles of nates.

Extremities.—Twitching of r. arm and leg. Pain in r. arm, thumb and knee; r. arm and legs; r. arm, thumb and leg, and in l. foot and ankle; l. arm, thumb and leg; l. arm and foot; elbows, arms and l. knee; r. arm, hand and knee in afternoon; rending, anteriorly in ligaments of ankles, running down insteps, alternating with gnawing in internal condyle of l. humerus, then when riding aching, heaviness and crawling through lower limbs.

Upper Extremities.—Pain in shoulders and scapulæ; in r. shoulder on waking, > rest; in l. shoulder and along arm to elbow. Arm, pain at inner side; in l., and in hand and thumb; in l., and in l. fingers; remittent, near insertion of r. deltoid; bruised feeling in l.; feeling in r. as if muscles were glued together and sore to touch; numbness in l. after lying down in bed, with crawling. Upper arm, stinging on inner side of r.; aching in l.; pain at inner side just above r. elbow; strained sensation in l.

Aching in elbows; in l. wrist; in ulnar half of r. wrist; rheumatic, above back of wrist late in evening. Pain in l. hand; at ulnar side of dorsum of hand; in l. fingers. Numbness of r. hand.

Lower Extremities.—Weariness in afternoon, with aching in bones; W. < moving, > lying, with aching in calves as after long walking or standing. Crawling-tingling. Aching in r. hip-joint when walking, causing lameness. Sticking at inner part of r. knee on stepping. Rending pain in flexure of l. knee when standing. Sharp pain in knees, running down l. leg, on rising from a seat.

Legs.—Pain in r. and in toes; at inner side of l. at each step, then sharp pain at inner side of r. knee at every step; muscular, < pressure and in thighs; drawing, almost a cramp, in r. calf. Rheumatic pains all day, with aching in them; R. pains in afternoon, < r; anteriorly in tibia; in anterior surface of tibiæ in evening. Weakness through the day, < ascending and descending stairs; in evening on ascending and descending stairs. Heaviness in r. calf as if flesh would fall from bones.

Pain in l. foot, with insensibility of leg; P. in l. instep, at upper anterior part of tarsus, at night. Tenderness of feet; with sensitiveness and shooting in corns. Pain in r. little toe, < corn on outside of it.

Skin.—Vesicles on neck near jaw; on r. side of neck, near jaw.

Itching; in face and r. ear; in whiskers on l. side of face; l. upper eyelid, groins and various parts of trunk, limbs, face and neck; abdomen, near l. side; between scapulæ; between spine and l. scapula; anteriorly on l. shoulder and anteriorly on l. loin; at right of middle of sternum, then at l. scapula, then on r. side of face; bends of elbows and to left of sternum, over fifth rib; posteriorly below elbows; backs of hands; legs in evening; lower limbs in evening, on undressing and afterwards; calves at night and in morning; at night when awake, > scratching, which produced burning; buttocks before and after getting into bed; limbs, < night on retiring and in morning after rising; about knees, and < on calves, *at night on undressing,* after scratching minute red pimples, later pustules, afterwards almost the whole surface from thighs to feet covered with this nettle-rash; *of legs when exposed to air on undressing and on rising in morning, > warmth of bed,* after scratching redness and little sores which heal rapidly, on calves and about knees, < posteriorly; in a spot, suddenly changing to another locality; stinging; stinging, in various parts; prickling, on buttocks when exposed to the air during stool.

Clinical.—Prurigo, < cold, > warmth; excessive itching on undressing. Chronic urticaria. (Compare Rhus tox., Caust.)

Sleep.—Yawning. Sleepiness at 11 A.M.; in afternoon and evening after eating heartily; with desire to lie down. *Sleep restless, disturbed, with short naps and unpleasant fancies even when awake;* R., with many kinds of absurd dreams, constant magnifying of trifles disturbed him; R., broken and unrefreshing or disturbed by vivid dreams, he jumps and tumbles in bed, walks about the room and talks in sleep. Restlessness latter part of night; in bed at night, with discomfort. Woke about 2 A.M.

Dreams.—Of being made angry. Of vexatious conduct of a strange servant. Disagreeable; about 6 A.M.; of burglars after 4 A.M.; and sleep unrefreshing. Solicitous, in morning. Of danger from floods; of D. and of disagreeable and wicked persons. Of fear and of hostile conduct of strangers towards each other. Horrid, of dead persons returning to life. Terrific, of autopsies, murdered men running about naked, falling, being drowned, etc., afterwards pleasant. Of murders at 5.30, just before waking. Of killing a small rabid dog and of being in trouble and perplexity. Of stealing a horse, of crime and trouble. Indistinctly remembered in latter part of night; indistinctly remembered, of being in a beautiful country, of being disappointed. Of seeing Queen Victoria. Of seeing friends. Of loving. Of hope and of friendly conduct of acquaintances towards him.

Fever.—*Sensitive to cold during the day.* Chilliness; down back on motion; running up and down back and down calves in afternoon on motion; of lower limbs in forenoon; feet during the day, while face felt hot and pulsated.

Heat; towards morning; in morning on waking, with frontal headache, heat of skin, full and rapid pulse, tongue coated white, then coldness; in cheeks; l. cheek; r. side of nose and adjacent part of cheek; in palms; palms in evening; back and face, with smarting in face, then chilliness, < back, with pain in abdomen, nausea and shooting near middle of chest anteriorly.

Sweat in morning on waking; on lower limbs in latter part of night; cold, clammy, on legs at night, then symptoms of severe cold, as scraping in throat, with tenacious mucus, cough, headache and obstruction of nose.

Ruta.

A tincture is made of the fresh plant of Ruta graveolens, L.

Allies.—Its rheumatic and skin symptoms are closely like those of *Rhus tox.;* compare also *Arn.* and *Puls.*

Generalities.—Looked intoxicated, eyes and face red. **Bruised pain in all parts on which he lies** (*Arn., Cic., Dros.*); *on touch of painful parts, < hips and bones of legs.* Nervousness. *Restlessness;* evenings, with headache and heat; in whole body after dinner, with pressure upon brain and great activity of nervous system; *so that he does not know where to lay his legs, with heaviness* (Rhus t.). Sensation as if he had not slept enough. *Weakness;* in morning; in afternoon, > walking, with sleepiness; in evening after playing with children; on sitting down after a *short walk,* > rising and walking (Rhus t.), with **bruised feeling in limbs** *and pain in sacrum and loins;* after a meal, > open air, with heaviness and sleepiness; when sitting, with indolence; with heaviness. Faintness.

Clinical.—General feeling of soreness as from a bruise. General lameness after sprains, especially of wrists and ankles. Periostitis, the result of bruises. Neuralgias; sciatic and other forms. Pains, especially in the wrist, in cold, wet weather, > motion (Rhus t.).

Mind.—*Fretful;* in afternoon and evening, melancholy, dissatisfied with life; and mistrustful; and irresolute. Dissatisfied, especially with what he did himself, and inclined to weep. Inclined to contradict. Quarrelsome, inclined to anger and vexation. Anxiety, despondency and fear; A. all day as if he had done something wrong, if only the door opened he feared that some one had come to arrest him. Indifference; with discomfort and disinclination to work. Stupefaction. Confusion of ideas. Thought and memory slow. Frequent loss of thought, he did mechanically and at the wrong time things that had become easy from frequent repetition.

Head.—Pain in brain in morning after rising; P. from reading a little; tensive, in brain; stupefying burning compressing, externally; confused. Oppression. Dulness; with heaviness and with tension in forehead; a kind of loss of memory. Heaviness. Uneasiness. Vertigo as if he would fall forward in morning on rising; as if he would fall to the right when walking in open air; sudden, when sitting, then heat of cheeks.

Forehead.—Sticking in l. eminence; *in l. bone when reading;* < coughing; above l. brow, with pressure; intermittent boring, in r. when sitting. Gnawing. Pain above root of nose; drawing, in r. side; *sticking drawing, extending from frontal to temporal bone; rhythmical, in sinciput;* stupefying, in sides, with cramplike tearing on malar-bone. Dulness in brain in evening before sleep, < morning on waking from sleep that was too sound, with throbbing pain. Heaviness.

Tearing in temporal bones. *Pain as from a fall in periosteum of temporal bones, extending to occiput.* Sticking drawing externally on vertex. Tensive drawing pain as from a blow or thrust, externally on sides. (Tearing on r. parietal bone, > evening, next morning a boil painful to touch as if suppurating.) Pain in occiput; with heaviness and tension; beating in side.

Biting-itching ulcer on l. side, and one towards nape. (Sticking in scalp, with tearing, then a pimple, at first painful to touch.) Itching behind l. ear, > scratching, with soreness; biting I., < l. side and occiput, > scratching, but returning.

Eyes.—Staring, with contracted pupils. *Pain in r. like a pressure, with obscuration of vision as if one had looked too long and intently. Pressure on inner surface of l.* in open air, *with lachrymation.* **Weary pain when reading. Fatigue as after reading too long. Heat in evening by the light, with aching while reading.** *Lachrymation* (Senega).

Pupils contracted. *Cramp in lower lid, then lachrymation. Itching in lower lid and inner canthi, that after rubbing become biting;* (I. in lids in evening, with biting). Mucus in canthi in morning. Sticking in canthi in morning, with biting as from dust. Burning in outer canthi, with smarting. Pressure on balls, with spasm of lower lid, which was sometimes drawn upward and sometimes towards inner canthus. *Bruised pain in orbicular cartilages.* Twitching of brows; of lower part. *Pressure deep in orbits;* on upper margin, with tearing in ball. **Vision weak as if eyes were strained** *mornings; dim;* (V. of flitting points).

Clinical.—Valuable in weakness of accommodation, especially in near-sighted people when there are heat and aching in and over the eyes, eyes feeling like balls of fire. Asthenopia from sewing and reading.

Ears.—Itching sticking within r. *Scraping pressure as with a blunt piece of wood.* Pain as from pressure. Tickling, hot pressure, < inserting finger. Sensation as if something in it rolled back and forth on shaking head.

Nose.—Pain in upper part as if a plug were forced transversely through it, with scraping and pressure. Sharp pressure on root. Sneezing; with yawning and shivering. (Bleeding); (blowing out of blood).

Face.—Pinching in l. cheek. Biting, goutlike pain in cheeks. *Pain as from a blow below mastoid process.* Numb pain as after a blow, in bones, extending into teeth and lower jaw. Papules on lips. Itching in corners of lips.

Mouth.—Digging in lower teeth. Bleeding of gums on brushing or picking teeth. Pain on inner surface of r. upper gum as if sore and swollen, < touch, with drawing sticking. Tongue red and swollen; red on margin. Pain in hard palate, < when not swallowing. Soreness of velum palati when swallowing, with pressure. Dry; and glutinous at times. Salivation. Taste wooden to food.

Throat.—Cutting extending to chest when walking, < clavicle and axilla, < walking rapidly. Pain.

Stomach.—Little appetite; for dinner. Aversion to meat and vegetables. Thirst for cold water in afternoon; unquenchable, for cold water in afternoon, he drinks much and frequently without being distressed thereby. *Eructations; odorless;* empty; tasting of food after eating and drinking. Hiccough during the customary smoke; with nausea. Nausea on stooping; on beginning to eat; *in pit of stomach,* with desire for stool, momentarily > emission of flatus; with scraping and gnawing in umbilical region; with stupefying headache, < r. side of forehead, and heat in face. Violent vomiting, with vomiting of blood; violent, painful V., with spasmodic distortion of head, trunk and limbs.

(Stitches in pit.) Sticking tearing in pit. Griping in r. side of epigastric region after bread and butter. Pain. *Tension,* > **drinking milk** (Rhus t.). Gnawing and emptiness; G. in pit at night and in morning; *burning G. Epigastric region sensitive.* Uneasiness. Warmth.

Clinical.—Dyspepsia resulting from straining the muscles across the stomach. Dyspepsia, every attempt to eat meat is followed by distress and eruption like nettle-rash (Puls.).

Abdomen.—Distention in evening. Rumbling and gurgling. Emission of flatus, with sensation as if stool would follow; easy emission; offensive. Sticking extending upward on sitting down. Griping in morning on rising, with eructations. Pressure, then emptiness. Sick sensation, then two stools, soft, but difficult on account of relaxation and inactivity of rectum. Heaviness. Agreeable coolness, and in chest. Burning.

Tense oppression in upper A. and chest as if satiated, as soon as he eats anything. *Gnawing in hepatic region.* Pressure anteriorly in hepatic region near pit of stomach, causing restlessness. Pushing cutting griping as from flatus, in sides. Corrosive burning in l. side. Sticking jerks from below umbilicus to mons veneris on expiration, taking away the breath, > hard pressure. Sticking in muscles of umbilical fossa, obliging him to retract abdomen. Tensive pressure extending from umbilicus through hypogastrium as if menses would come on, at night, < pressure. Coldness internally in umbilical region, with sensation as if something were becoming loose. Rumbling in hypogastrium. Pinching in hypogastrium, with aching and discomfort, as from taking cold. Sharp burning pressure in r. groin.

Rectum.—Evacuation of blood during stool. *Tearing stitches when sitting. Tearing when not urinating, and in urethra. Frequent urging, with prolapsus and emission of flatus, stooping and still more crouching down caused protrusion,* later constant protrusion. Constant desire for stool, which is soft, then dragging and urging.

Clinical.—Prolapsus of the rectum. Pruritus of the rectum.

Stool.—Soft. Large and difficult, as from loss of peristaltic action of rectum. A few hard fæces, almost like sheep-dung. Delayed.

Urinary Organs.—*Pressure in region of neck of bladder like a painful closure of it, after micturition. Full sensation in bladder on every step after urinating, with feeling as if it moved up and down. Urging,* with pain over kidneys; *U., but scanty micturition, then dragging as if more should pass, but it does not;* U. even if there were only a drop, during and after micturition burning in genitals and long-continued pressure; U. only before daylight. Frequent and copious micturition. Urine deep yellow. Urine scanty, after micturition dragging in bladder.

Clinical.—Irritable bladder, constant urging to urinate, forcible retention seems to paralyze the bladder. Incontinence at night (Puls.).

Sexual Organs.—Emissions at night, without amorous dreams. Desire increased. Violent pain in evening, then discharge of blood from vagina and miscarriage. Bearing-down pains in womb. Miscarriage, then slow recovery; M. of dead children at about seven months, uterus well contracted, after two days fever, delirium and spasms, then exhaustion and vomiting of bile, for five days partial intoxication, with contracted pupils, swollen coated tongue, slow pulse, delirium, spasms of arms, vomiting, painful tension in epigastric region, abdomen soft and painless, uterus contracted though lochiæ soon ceased, later lochiæ returned, long-continued slowness of pulse and weakness. (Compare Tanacetum.)

Respiratory Organs. — Bruised pain in larynx. *Hacking cough waking him about midnight,* with scraping in upper part of chest and with slight, infrequent expectoration. Forcible cough in evening after lying down, with expectoration of stringy mucus, C. several times in night, when most violent it seemed as if stomach turned over and as if he would vomit. Respiration impeded, with sensation as if whole body were pressed full. Dyspnœa and shortness of breath; from fulness of chest.

Chest. — Tremulous twitching in last r. true rib. Stitches in sternum on motion; S. on ascending steps, with arrest of breath, causing anxiety; between l. nipple and axilla, < inspiration; internally in l. nipple, < inspiration; oppressive, in sternum, on inspiration and expiration when sitting; burning, like pains in an ulcer, in morning, < beneath sternum. Dull thrust in l. side. Pain beneath l. short ribs at night on waking, < pressure and arresting breathing; P. as from a burning-biting ulcer under r. axilla. *Gnawing in l. side; in r. side, with biting and burning;* intermittent G. or picking on one of the costal cartilages, above ensiform cartilage, at night. *Pressure on sternum internally and externally;* on sixth true rib, < expiration and touch; on last ribs at night, dream that some one was encircling him tightly, which woke him. Painful throbbing or picking beneath l. short ribs. Corrosive biting drawing in l. side. Internal heat.

Pulse.—Rapid. Slow and small.

Neck.—*Tension and pressure in nape and shoulders.* Drawing in nape. Stiffness in morning.

Back.—Stitches in spine when sitting, with sudden anxiety. Tearing pulling-sticking. *Pain;* in evening, > exertion, with heaviness in limbs (Rhus t.). **Pain in spine as if beaten and like lumbago** (Arn.). *Bruised pain extending along back* when sitting, < l. side; in l. side when sitting, > standing and walking; *in spine when sitting and walking, arresting breath; drawing, in spine, often arresting breath.*

Scapulæ.—Sticking at angle, extending to back, with pressure; drawing S. on tip on moving it, so that he must let arm hang down. Pain; between S. in afternoon; *in dorsal vertebræ, as from a fall;* drawing, arresting breath. Pressure internally on r.; on r., with shivering.

Lumbar Region.—Painful jerking in spine opposite pit of stomach, < pressure, when there was aching beneath last short ribs extending into abdomen and impeding respiration. Tearing waking him at 4 A.M., > 9 A.M. *Digging as if bruised just above sacrum when sitting after a long walk, > continued walking, returning when standing still and sitting* (Rhus t.). *Bruised pain in vertebræ; in coccyx, extending to sacrum;* when sitting, with tension across hypogastrium. Pain in posterior process of ilium like a forcing forward, > pressure, with sensation as if something were pressed outward. Drawing pain opposite liver, < inspiration; in region of kidneys extending along loins, when sitting. Pressure on l. lower part of sacrum; on l. side of os innominatum, near spine. Beating on posterior margin of l. ilium, extending over hip to inner surface of thigh and almost to knee, after a long walk, > pressure upon ilium; intermittent, in anterior spine of l. ilium; intermittent painful, above l. ilium, > pressure, but returning.

Clinical.—Rheumatism of the dorsal muscles.

Extremities.—Constant, not convulsive motions. Cramplike tearing, now in upper, now in lower. *Bruised pain in joints and hip-bones so that he cannot bend.* Weakness when sitting, when hands lie upon lap they are so comfortable that he does not wish to raise them; W., with heaviness and aversion to work; of hands and feet, she could hold nothing firmly and when walking could not stand firmly; of lower, with heaviness of them, and with painful jerks, beginning in middle of upper arms, when the pain reaches the elbow it extends down fingers and seems to be in shafts of bones. Heaviness.

Clinical.—Rheumatism of the wrists and ankles, with puffy swellings. Dislocation of the bones of the wrist and of the tarsus. Synovitis from strains. Ganglion on flexor tendons. Bursa of the wrist. Glanglia on wrist (Benz. ac.).

Upper Extremities.—Sticking in shoulders. Sprained pain in r. shoulder; in shoulder-joints, > drawing and turning arm upward, returning on letting arm hang down or lie upon anything. Tearing in bones of arms. Tearing in r. elbow and neighboring parts, extending to lower end of humerus, on stretching out arm it is a rather pressive pain. Pain in elbow, < stretching arm; in l. as from a blow, with weakness of arm. Cramplike drawing in biceps. Shaft of ulna seems bruised. Forearm, cramplike tearing in l.; paralytic pressure on outer part of r.; painful drawing in middle of anterior surface of r.

Wrist, tearing in r., < violent motion; pain in l. as if broken; bruised pain in bones of wrist and backs of hands. Veins of hands swollen after eating. Cramplike pain transversely across hands. Fingers, tearing in l. middle, < middle joint and middle phalanx; sore and ulcerative pain in l. ring; bruised pain during rest; pressive drawing in middle joints of three r. middle; painful drawing in last joints of two last, at night.

Lower Extremities.—Gait unsteady. *Falling from side to side when walking, legs will not support him, no power or steadiness in thighs. He cannot walk at first on rising from a seat, he falls back again,* bones seem broken, thighs refuse their service on account of weakness and pain. Weakness, walking difficult, and weight in legs (Rhus t.).

Thigh.—Sticking as if ulcerated, above r. knee when walking and standing. *Bruised pain on stretching lower limbs; posteriorly above knee* on motion; *in bones about hips* on motion; in middle of femora on motion; *on anterior surface, with pain on touch;* so that he could hardly walk. Cramplike throbbing pain in middle of r., then in both, then on outer side below l. knee. Burning pain on upper and inner surface when sitting, worse on waking in bed. Pain at night as if grasped. Pressure in middle of outer part of r. (Contractive and spasmodically drawing pain extending from middle to hip-joint and thence to sacrum.)

Knee.—Trembling, with weakness of feet. Spasmodic contractions in hollows on rising from a seat. Weariness of l. after walking a little; sinking down on rising from a seat and on beginning to walk. Paralytic heaviness, > walking, with necessity to move feet.

Tremulous heaviness of legs. Pressure in middle of outer part of l.; on upper and inner surface of l. *Legs give out on ascending and descending stairs. Pain consisting of throbbing and hacking, as in an ulcer, anteriorly on l. ankle.* Cramp in l. sole. Slow stitches from back of foot up tibia; stitches in l., then r. heel when sitting. Pain in l. sole when sitting; *in bones of feet so that he cannot step heavily, with heat; burning and biting, in bones of feet during rest.* Toes, cramplike sticking in r. little when sitting, < moving toes; burning tearing in l. great, < pressure; burning pain as after a bruise, where a foreign body had been forced in; painful drawing.

Skin.—Inflammation, with swelling of hands. Red swollen stripes from root of nose to frontal eminences. Redness of hands, with warmth and sensation as if scalded, later covered with water blisters, < finger-tips, later between the vesicles dark redness with bluish tinge, afterwards the swelling spread posteriorly over arm to elbow, afterwards epidermis of hands peeled off, even where there had been no blisters (Rhus t.). Erysipelas of hands and forehead. Corroded and blistered.

Stitches in arms changing to biting itching, with heat and redness. Formication on thigh upon which he was not lying. Hot tickling prickling in sole. Sticking-itching tickling in l. palm.

Itching over whole body, in morning on rising, > *scratching;* I. on one side of face; l. upper arm; sticking, between scapulæ, not > rubbing; I. on hands, with redness, then vesicles with red areola and filled with transparent liquid, most V. between fingers, somewhat like itch-pustules, the itching < night, vesicles became confluent, large phlyctenules formed, then desquamation, then vesicles in palms, itching on great toes and vesicles like those on hands, next year the effects of contact again with the leaves were more intense, hands looked as if they had been boiled and were completely excoriated, with fever (Rhus t.).

Sleep.—*Yawning*, < noon, even after dinner; *with stretching*, then sleepiness; with stretching of legs and < arms; with fever; incomplete and not satisfying. Sleepiness in forenoon; after dinner; overpowering, with heaviness, and head seemed befogged. Sound sleep immediately on lying down, so that it was difficult to arouse her.

But little sleep, with restlessness. Sleep, with partial consciousness when reading after eating, he woke with a cry of fright on slightest touch. Starting up in fright during afternoon nap, with jerking of feet. Restless sleep, with fretful dreams; R. sleep, with copious micturition three times; with waking every hour and difficult falling asleep again. *Frequent waking as if it were time to rise;* F. waking, with restlessness, nausea, painful twisting about umbilicus, at times it seemed as if something arose to pit of throat and as if water would accumulate in mouth. Awake a long time in night from confusion in head. Unrefreshing sleep from 3 till 4 A.M., then sleeplessness, with heaviness of head. *Dreams vivid; and confused;* constant fatiguing D.

Fever.—Chilliness; creeping, < up back; internal, which she always had just before menstruation; shaking, with gooseflesh, yawning and stretching. Shivering frequently during the day; S. of whole body, with coldness of hands and feet, internal and external warmth of face, dulness of head, as in catarrhal fever, with thirst which was > drinking once; over back and chest. *Coldness from spine downward;* running up and down back; creeping over half of head and face; of limbs; hands and feet; internally in arms; (internally, almost like a falling asleep, on inner side of legs).

Heat; in afternoon, < face, with feverish restlessness, anxiety as if he would die, that took away his breath, white coated tongue, that seemed rough and dry, without thirst; with yawning; in flushes. Heat in head; about 11 P.M., with feverish restlessness of whole body and anxiety; *beneath l. eye;* below l. ear about 10 A.M.; in face, with redness; in feet; beneath external malleolus when standing.

Sweat in afternoon when walking in open air; general after walking; on vertex; on back of nose, with heat of nose and cheeks and redness of face, without thirst; (cold, on face in morning in bed, with redness of cheeks).

Sabadilla.

A tincture is made of the seeds of (Veratrum Sabadilla, Schl.), Schœnocaulon officinale, A. Gr. (Cevadilla seeds).

Allies.—Like its near relative, Veratrum album, it is an acrid emetic and cathartic, with a very decided action on the nose; it seems to lack the violent thirst of Verat. and in some respects more resembles *Puls.* (Relief in the open air is a strongly marked character throughout the symptomatology.)

Generalities.—Convulsions. Jerking of upper lip, then of hands, fingers or thighs, < l. side, and always from r. to l. Starting at the least noise. Trembling. Sticking, now here, now there; S. under skin, < about fingers and toes; burning crawling, here and there; beating, in several parts, almost like pressure, sometimes pinching, returning after four or seven beats of pulse. *Pain in all bones, < joints, as if scraped and cut, all day* (see Ph. ac.), < r. arm, < cold, transiently > moving arm rapidly and in warmth and at night. Boring behind l. ear in parotid, lower jaw and submaxillary glands. *Bruised pain in various parts;* B. feeling, she would like to lie all the time, walking and standing are very distressing. Many pains are felt in r., then l. side, or extend from r. to l., for instance, headache, pain in side, pain in limbs.

Indisposition without pain. Discomfort towards evening and falling asleep, worried in sleep by all sorts of strange thoughts, no images in his dreams. Pulsation in all vessels in evening before sleep. Anxious restlessness. *Weakness;* in morning on waking, with pain as if she had lain on blocks of wood; in forenoon while sitting, till he falls asleep, when disturbed he starts up in fright, then heaviness of head; > lying down, with heaviness; with desire to lie and sleep all the time; sudden, with closure of eyes; sudden, in the street after a short walk, with dulness of head as if he had taken liquor, and closure of eyes. Aggravation in last hours of forenoon, especially pains in joints, weakness and drowsiness; of pain by cold, with discomfort. Amelioration when lying.

Clinical.—Convulsive symptoms, especially in children with worms. General aggravation at the same hour each day. General sensitiveness to cold, which aggravates.

Mind.—She lay almost speechless and unconscious or else sprang up with anxious restlessness and ran about the room, pulling at the pit of stomach and at neck, face sunken, pale and anxious. He imagined strange things about his own body, that it had shrunk like that of a dead person, that his stomach was corroded, that the scrotum was swollen, etc., but he knew that it was all fanciful. Mind excited, but disposition cold, afterwards understanding depressed, he comprehends with difficulty, but disposition is more easily excited. Rage. Vexed; and inclined to be vehement. Gloomy, as if he were the greatest criminal. Absorbed in reverie all day. Indisposed to work. Cheerful. Thought difficult and caused headache, otherwise inclined to laugh at everything, afterwards indifferent.

Clinical.—It has been found useful for imaginary diseases, that is to say, a mental condition in which the patient imagines he has various troubles.

Head.—Sticking, < forehead. *Pain from fixed attention; P. < walking*, on returning to the house screwing pain beginning in r. side of head and extending over whole head after going to bed; with heaviness so that he could scarcely raise it; itching, < forehead; in different parts of brain as if pressed against sharp corners, in evening when reading; pressing asunder;

P. inward from all sides. *Dull and heavy*, as if he must hold it all the time. Confusion. Stupefaction. Vertigo; in morning after rising, greater when sitting than when walking; in afternoon till after dinner, > resting head on table, with nausea; on going to bed; < *rising from a seat;* greater when sitting than when standing; as if he would faint, with obscuration of vision.

Forehead.—Sticking in l. eminence; tearing, externally on l. side. Pain; above l. eye, then also in temple; in sinciput, > pressure of palm on forehead, heat in F., then coldness in hairy scalp, even the hair felt cold to hand, as if cold water had been poured over head; in sinciput and temples, with dizziness and occasional stitches in back, then drawing; in skin, ascending to vertex, with vertigo in F.; *tensive, with pressure;* above eyes, as if brain would fall forward; as if a thread had been drawn from middle of F. to occiput above temple, leaving burning; beating, in r., then l. side; beating, in r., afterwards more in upper part, then headache all day; like heaviness, next day in whole head, > staring or reflecting. *Heaviness in forepart of r. side, extending towards l. side* and finally over whole head, < motion, when it is a sort of vertigo. *Stupefying oppression, causing a reeling sensation* and making him stagger. Dull sensation as from a blow, not exactly a pain, with heaviness of limbs.

Temples.—Sticking; in r.; externally in l.; and in scalp. Pain; in l.; *pressure towards r. bone; P. outward in r.;* downward in l.; P. extending towards vertex and thence to lowest part of occiput. Painful beating in l.

Pain in r. side of vertex. Pain in r. hemisphere, extending to l. lower molars. Sticking in r. side of occiput, in region of lamboidal suture, when walking in open air. Pain as if something were thrust from upper part of occiput through brain to forehead. Pressure forward in O., with vertigo. Pain in l. side of O. as if a wound were pressed. Burning pain in scalp. Tension of scalp, < during fever. Itching of scalp; on vertex; when perspiring during a walk, with crawling; crawling, > scratching, with burning.

Clinical.—Sudden vertigo on waking at night, sometimes when rising from stooping. Headaches > eating.

Eyes.—Surrounded by blue rings. Painful drawing upward in r. E. and temple. Intermittent corrosive burning in l., returning after a few pulsations. *Lachrymation as soon as pain is felt in any part of body;* L. when walking in open air, when looking at a bright light, coughing or yawning. Pressure upon balls, < looking upward, > looking down. Hard mucus in external canthi about noon. Margins of lids red and sensation in eyes as if inflammation would arise.

Ears.—Sticking in l.; in lobule of r.; burning-crawling, behind E. Pain internally. Burning itching in interior of lobules. Obstructed sensation. Crackling; and otalgia. Humming before dinner, on forcing air into it; H. and buzzing, with sometimes a sensation as if something heavy had fallen upon the floor and burst, then ringing.

Nose.—Contractive biting as from mustard. *Itching tingling. Sensitive dryness of upper part.* Obstruction of one nostril, with whistling in the other during inspiration; O. of one or other nostril, the air has to be forced out with a snuffing noise and is drawn in with great effort, with snoring. *Sneezing shaking the abdomen, then lachrymation; S., with sticking contractive headache over eyes and red margins of lids. Copious, thin, thickish, whitish, transparent mucus, sometimes in large lumps, on blowing slightly, without catarrh, later frequent blowing of nose because it is full of viscid, yellowish-grayish mucus. Bleeding.*

Clinical.—Influenza, with violent spasmodic sneezing and lachrymation on being in the open air, with symptoms of tonsillitis beginning on l. side and extending to r., pains < empty swallowing. Rose-cold or hay-fever, with burning and stinging and complete obstruction, watery discharge, itching and tingling in nose, nose swollen, eyes watery (Verat. alb.).

Face.—Jaws, rattling in joints as if loose, in morning on opening mouth, < r.; pain in lower on touch, as from swollen glands; drawing, and in teeth; *beating in muscles of l. upper, with itching.* Stinging in lips, gums and tip of tongue, with bitterness and repulsive sweetness. Sore tensive pain in median line of upper lip in morning after waking, as from a crack, or as if it were drawn together and upward with a string, the tension > pressing lip with incisors, then only soreness, afterwards it is seen that the epidermis is torn and retracted. Burning of lips; with itching, tingling and prickling.

Mouth.—A carious molar becomes more carious and breaks, without pain. Sticking downward in r. upper teeth; S. in an anterior l. lower molar, extending towards ear; in a r. lower molar, extending into submaxillary glands. Intermittent beating in teeth, < walking, with drawing. Paroxysmal painful jerking in gums.

Tongue.—*Coated mostly whitish-yellowish, < middle and posteriorly;* C. white, tip and gums are bluish. Intermittent pinching stitches in tip, < r. ride. *Feels sore and as if full of blisters.* Burning pain through r. side of tip, then spitting and taste as of unripe fruit. *Burning on tip;* with soreness of throat, < swallowing saliva, leaving burning when drinking.

Burning, crawling, stinging in palate. Intermittent pain inside l. cheek, where teeth touch. *Mouth and tip of tongue felt sore and scalded.* Salivation; with nausea and retching; sweetish; (astringent, metallic). Hot breath. Taste flat, bitter; *bitter*, rising from throat to nose, > a meal; flat, bitter; sweet as after liquorice; repulsive, burning, sweetish, < the customary smoking, > eating; T. and appetite lost.

Clinical.—Neuralgic toothache.

Throat.—Swelling of uvula. Mucus before breakfast. Hawking of bright blood from posterior nares. Tensive clawing in parotid gland, with salivation on same side. Scraping and pain; S., with accumulation of water in mouth; with roughness and sensation as if a morsel were lodged there, provoking cough; with roughness and constant hawking; and when swallowing feeling as if uvula rested on tongue, the insipidity in throat obliged him to hawk a sweet, flat-tasting mucus; with tightness, causing sticking, he has to hawk in order to breathe freely; as from something acrid, with dryness where nose opens into throat. *Constant necessity to swallow*, with pain in mouth and behind larynx as if something lodged there, with scratching roughness, he hawks constantly, < morning, afterwards all day, also when eating, < after eating.

Sensation of a lump, which it was necessary to swallow. Sensation of a soft body lodged there, < deglutition. Sore on swallowing. Swollen feeling. Constriction as from a string; *in fauces as after an astringent drink. Dryness; when swallowing.* Burning, with pressure as from internal swelling; B. and during empty deglutition pressure as from a plug; in fauces and about uvula, with pungent taste, he had to spit much. Sensation of a vapor rising in it, with bitterness, almost like heartburn.

Clinical.—Tonsillitis beginning in l. side, > warm drinks.

Stomach.—He eats more breakfast than usual, and with haste. Appetite lost all day, then canine in evening; lost for dinner; lost, the first mouthful of food tastes of the drug. Aversion to food; and coffee; *to meat;* with appetite. Thirst; after the chilliness; for cold water in morning; for cold water, < towards evening. Eructations; rancid; sour; bitter, pungent; empty, with shuddering; painful, often ascending only to middle of chest. Hiccough.

Nausea; when eating; as soon as she sees cooked food; after eating, with anxiety; > dinner; > bitter eructations; > tasteless eructations; *with constant spitting of insipid water;* with bitter taste; with discomfort and coldness in stomach; with pain, weakness and feeling as if she would sink down; with retching, then vertigo unto falling, then headache; with retching, the R. < coughing; with gulping up of bitter mucus, leaving behind a greasy substance, as if he had eaten tallow; causing shuddering.

Vomiting of a clear, slimy liquid. Sticking in l. side of pit. Digging on l. side above pit, with pain on touch. Intermittent pinching in middle of epigastrium, between pit of S. and vertebræ. Pain, with bloated sensation; *P. as if a sore spot were pressed, below pit, on pressure and inspiration.* Sensitiveness of epigastric region to touch, with pressure as from a stone. Pain in S. and abdomen as from a stone, with digging in abdomen. Tightness in pit and chest, < inspiration. Sensation just below pit as if S. were turning inside out. Indications of heartburn. Burning pain; *corrosive, when walking.* Burning; in region of S. and liver; after waking, with suffocative breathing, she thought she was relieved by pressing chest with hands, but she was not; *extending to pit of throat.* Emptiness.

Clinical.—Cardialgia, with distention. The gastric symptoms are generally characterized by absence of thirst and longing for sweats, general relief after eating. Cutting colic, especially from worms. Vomiting of round worms, feeling of worm in pharynx.

Abdomen.—Rumbling; with movements; with emission of flatus, then urging and stool, in half an hour another stool; with urging, then scanty, difficult stool, after half an hour a copious, painless stool; with burning in it and tip of tongue and throat, then stool mixed with blood and burning in anus, then weakness and slumber for quarter of an hour, upon waking he felt extremely well; with pinching and stitches in region of bladder; then loose stool, after ten minutes again R., then copious loose stool; *as if empty;* intermittent R. and grunting. Pinching, then urging, but only flatus passes. Pain, and in anus. Burning; after stool, and in rectum; with ineffectual desire for stool; extending to mouth, with ptyalism, the saliva appearing to be as hot as the heat in A., but it is not. Shuddering.

Hypochondria.—Sticking in r., < deep inspiration; sudden, in r. in afternoon when sitting, with lachrymation, he rises and twists in every direction, when the pain suddenly attacks l. side and the pains meet in the middle of the abdomen, > sitting down, stretching, bending the back forward and pressing hands into sides. Digging in r. lobe of liver, extending to l., with paroxysms of painful drawing transversely, and when pressing upon it pain as in an old sore, at the same time digging in forehead, > pressure. Scraping in hepatic region. Warmth in r. not far from pit of stomach.

Spasmodic contractions of l. side, with burning pain, he bent towards l. side. Sticking in l. side when sitting; S. in r. side, < hepatic region; in l. side as from a sore. Pinching around umbilicus, then sudden copious stool, which was soon followed by another, later fetid flatus. Burning around umbilicus. Intermittent sticking in l. groin in evening. Boring in hypogastrium, < one place in r. hip.

Rectum.—Pinching tearing. Crawling as from ascarides. Urging, then scanty difficult stool, then headache; U., with jerking drawing in pubic region, as if coming from spermatic cords and extending to hollow between thigh and scrotum, later noiseless emission of flatus, then shuddering across back; with croaking like frogs, after sitting a long time emission of much flatus, then enormous stool, then a second mixed with blood, then burning pain in abdomen for eight days, then itching which on rubbing changed into burning; sudden ineffectual.

Clinical.—Thread-worms. Numerous symptoms of worms, especially in children, with irritation of the external genitals.

Anus.—Burning pain before stool. Itching, then burning after scratching.

Stool.—*Fermented and brown diarrhœa.* Frequent, after a large dose, none for four days after a small dose. Difficult. Delayed. Omitted for several days, then first part hard, difficult at first, afterwards scanty.

Urinary Organs.—Urethra, dragging as far as tip when urinating; scalding when urinating; burning between micturitions, with urging. Constant desire to urinate, with burning in urethra, the urging < emission of a few drops, with drawing backward in urethra, this symptom > Pulsatilla. *Urine like muddy water.* Urine increased, mixed with blood. U. scanty.

Sexual Organs.—Drawing, beating, sticking, intermittent pain towards tip of penis. Painful erections in morning, without desire. Slow undulating motion in testicles all day, sometimes tingling from thighs to testicles, after which the undulation begins again and is more violent. Intermittent bruised pain in l. testicle towards evening. Insensible to excitement, he is nauseated by amorous caresses. Desire lost, later he can scarcely rid himself of voluptuous thoughts though the penis is relaxed.

Menses one day late, profuse and lasting one day longer than usual, three or four days before they appeared bearing down as if they would come on; M. which had just begun decreased, they reappear irregularly and more or less profusely.

Clinical.—Ovaritis, with cutting pain (Coloc.).

Respiratory Organs.—Hoarseness. Wheezing in trachea during inspiration when lying. *Cough dry, at night,* leaving him no rest, with heat and sweat; *short, dry, from scraping in throat;* short, in paroxysms, with lachrymation; violent. Breathing rapid; *sud-*

denly oppressed in pit of stomach, with anxiety; short, all day; short, difficult, < afternoon.

Clinical.—Has been used for cough, < lying down. Cough, associated with coryza and lachrymation. Reflex cough from worms.

Chest.—Sticking in l. side; in r. side between third and fourth ribs; above ensiform cartilage; externally in r. side during expiration; in l. side, at first more in upper part, then in lower, < cough and deep inspiration; in forepart of middle of r. side during inspiration and cough, waking him at night, necessity to lie on back, cough with expectoration; pinching, behind heart, towards l. side, < inspiration. Pricking borings outward in r. side during expiration when sitting. Oppression; when sitting or lying; with anguish about heart. Painful pressure in middle. Burning pain in l. side. Burning, with bitterish-sourish taste rising from œsophagus into posterior part of mouth; B. in r. side as if he had swallowed hot water.

Heart and Pulse.—Præcordial anxiety, with tossing about and groaning. Præcordial warmth. Palpitation and sensation as if all arteries of body were beating. Pulse rapid and irregular; P. small, spasmodic, with coldness of limbs.

Neck.—Pain in nape on moving it.

Back.—Sticking in r. side. Bruised pain in spine when sitting. Intermittent pain as from weariness in forenoon and afternoon, beginning when walking, > sitting, making his back hollow and leaning firmly against anything. Burning-tingling stinging between scapulæ. Pain in region of l. sacro-iliac symphysis when walking; P. in lumbar region, with chilliness; in upper border of os ilium, not far from superior spinous process, > walking and pressure, < sitting.

Extremities.—Trembling. Cracking in joints on motion. Bruised feeling, < knees, also when sitting. Pain in fingers and toes waking him and obliging scratching, which caused burning. Drawing through all, with sensation as if one were paralyzed; painful D., with heaviness of feet so that walking was difficult; painful, in middle of bones, < lower, causing stretching, > rest, and heaviness and stiffness on motion, < joints. Crawling in all. *Weakness,* he sweats on exertion and at night in bed; paralytic W. late in evening. *Heaviness all day, < latter hours of forenoon and towards evening, obliging one to lie down;* H. < joints, with weariness; < feet, with weariness, she often lets arms hang down, as if they had no strength.

Upper Extremities.—Pain from r. shoulder into chest, as if circulation were stopped by a bandage, all day, < cold and in open air, sometimes the pain is in l. shoulder. Arms, convulsions; r. suddenly and painfully jerked upward; stretching; trembling, and of hands. Upper arm, sticking in muscles of l. during rest; intermittent pinching in flesh in middle of inner side of r.; aching in muscles on moving arm. Elbow, jerking; painful drawing in r. Forearm, sticking outward in muscles of l., > motion; aching below elbow on bending arm; aching in muscles near r. wrist during motion; jerking pain on inner side, < towards hands. Pain in r. wrist, < motion.

Hand.—Trembling of r. when writing; of l. as after apoplexy, when lifting or holding anything. Cramp of r., < fingers, so that hand is stiff, fingers crooked and nothing can be held; sudden C. in r., he cannot grasp anything. Sticking in r. Beating tearing internally in l., on side of little fingers. Dryness.

Fingers.—Cramplike contraction of l. little and ring during rest. Sticking in r. index; burning, in tips of l., then heat, the rest of the hand being cold; tingling, in r. thumb towards index when writing. Jerking darting in r. thumb, < grasping it. Tearing in l. middle; itching, in l. ring. Pain in l. index, > motion; beating P. in bone of r. middle. Paralytic drawing, painful rigidity of l. thumb and index.

Lower Extremities.—Staggering, afterwards movements more graceful than ever.

Thigh.—*Stinging in both;* intermittent, in muscles of r. when sitting; drawing; intermittent jerking, in surface of r. near genitals. Pain in l. hip when sitting; bruised, in anterior muscles of T. when walking, < touch; as if they had been compressed, > stretching limbs, < motion, > continuing to move; drawing, in r. T. and leg. Painful pressure in r. hip-joint, < lying upon it.

Knee.—Sticking in r.; in outer part of l. when sitting. Tearing in r. on every step. Drawing in outer side of l., with pressure. Weakness.

Pinching along r. fibula when walking, with pressure. Tearing-tensive pain in calves after midnight, > morning after rising. Tension in r. calf when walking. Weariness of legs. Swelling of feet, < morning; S. of feet, with pain on walking. Painful pressure in l. sole when standing. Tension of feet. *Heaviness of F.* Pricklings in toes as if asleep.

Skin.—Yellow spots on fingers. Redness of face and hands; of one hand, with red spots upon it; in an elevated streak transversely across l. forearm; in spots on hands, < l.; in spots on l. arm, causing heat; in spots and streaks, < cold; in points on abdomen, hands and chest, < open air. Erysipelatous inflammation on r. tibia, with burning pain. Dryness of hands in forenoon, > afternoon, with roughness. Desquamation on sides of finger-nails. Pimples behind r. ear; burning itching, on forearms. White blister with red areola and burning pain, on forepart of l. knee.

Prickling on forehead when becoming warm and ascending stairs rapidly. Burning crawling over brows. Itching waking him after midnight; at night in bed, scratching causes burning; of hands and feet; between r. fingers at night in bed; on l. cheek, with specks like herpes on face.

Clinical.—Measles, with violent sneezing, headache, sticking in the chest.

Sleep.—Constant necessity to stretch, with cracking in shoulders and back. Weak yawning, with lachrymation. *Sleepiness; all day,* eyes constantly closed. Sleep as soon as she sits down; S. in afternoon, and peevishness on being disturbed from his sleep. Very sound, without dreams.

Sleeplessness in evening from a crowd of ideas. Restless night, with pain in r. thigh and r. upper arm; R. sleep and much dreaming; R., unrefreshing sleep. Starting up in fright from sleep in morning. In evening in bed when half dreaming, strange thoughts as if they were separate from him and more important than he and he could not drive them away. *Dreams confused; and unremembered, disturbing sleep;* vivid D. about helping people and making them glad; lascivious, in morning, with scanty emission and relaxed penis, he is conscious of dreaming and of an emission, then painful erection and lassitude, feels easier in open air.

Fever.—Chilliness; all day; at 5 P.M., coldness over back as if dashed with cold water, chattering of teeth, the chill > only warm stove, then general warmth and sweat, < forehead, lower limbs simply warm, in night sticking in chest and cough; at 9.30 P.M., so that he went to bed, then shaking chill, later alternate heat and coldness, then oppression with sweat and chilliness; sensitive to cold; with gooseskin and moderate thirst; then warmth and sensation as if creeping would set in, < thighs; *internal, with internal heat of head;* general, with shuddering over back; alternating with flashes of heat all day, < forenoon; shaking, waking him at 1 P.M., he feels warm, with prickling in forehead. Shuddering; *intermittent, afterwards sudden heat, < face, feeling as if a hot breath came out of mouth and nose and heated neighboring parts,* **without thirst,** *with clearness in head and general comfort, the paroxysms of heat less frequent but longer than the shuddering.* Chilliness over body, < limbs, with burning in face. *Cold limbs;* feet; forehead, with sudden heat in cheeks, without thirst.

Heat, with redness of face and heat in forehead, without thirst; H., especially internally, at night and in morning on rising, only hands, forehead, lips and cheeks felt hot, hands dry and rough, mouth dry and sticky in morning, moderate thirst, desire for juicy food; in flushes, with redness of face; *febrile condition, sick feeling, restless anxiety, easy startings, short, hot breath, trembling, orgasm of blood, eyes weak and unsteady, irresistible sleepiness, yawning, shivering, nausea.* Heat in various parts of skin, < face, < stooping, > washing with cold water, with pain, later tension, < l. side of face. Burning in l. temple and r. ear, without redness; *corrosive burning point on vertex; internal heat in head and face as from wine;* in face after warm drinks; external, in face, with redness; in face in flushes, with redness of cheeks; here and there in face towards evening, with stinging itching; burning in knees.

Sweat after midnight; S. on soles; on head and face, which were hot to touch, while rest of body was cold; on chest and in axilla towards evening after walking, with itching about nipple; cold, on forehead.

Clinical.—It has been used for intermittent fever, which recurs at the same hour; chills in evening, commencing in extremities, running up the body; heat in head and face, interrupted by chills; sweat commencing during the fever; hot sweat on the face.

Sabina.

A tincture is made of the fresh tips of the branches of Juniperus Sabina, L.

Allies.—Bell., Ipec., Millefol., Calc. c.

Generalities.—Jerklike sticking in anus and in forepart of thighs when walking. Burning pain in the swollen periosteum. Rheumatic pains. General sick feeling, as if he had danced and revelled several nights, with whimsical mood. Discomfort without ability to state what or where he suffers. Prefers to lie on l. side at night. Blood agitated in evening in bed, obliged to change his position constantly and cannot fall asleep. Restlessness in evening in bed, with anxiety, chill and gooseflesh, preventing sleep. Pulsation in all vessels, almost like a jerking. Weakness from a short walk; W., with trembling, drowsiness, yawning and giving way of feet; with sleeplessness after midnight, necessity to stretch and move feet. *Heaviness and indolence of body, forcing him to lie down.* Symptoms cease on going into open air, they return on entering house.

Mind.—*Anxiety.* Irritable nerves, > exercise in open air, music was intolerable, it penetrated marrow and bone, with pain in occiput, weakness and inclination to sweat, < on back. Vexed and weeping aloud. *Ill-humored and hypochondriac;* I., and sensation as if he had taken cold; and indifferent to a jest; and indisposed to speak, timorous, joyless, and all limbs weak. Indisposed to talk in morning when walking. Indifferent. Confusion of ideas. Memory weak. Insensible.

Head.—Sticking through brain, with pressure. Digging boring. *Aching;* through the day; *< forehead, with dulness,* as after intoxication; with congestion of conjunctivæ; drawing; beating, with heaviness and stupefaction. Pressure outward like a wind which rushes in suddenly and disappears slowly. Dulness; after dinner; < forehead, extending towards nose, in which it became a sort of drawing, causing sensation as if l. nostril would bleed. Heaviness till she goes to bed; H. as if she had taken much spirits, in forenoon. Semi-intoxication. *Vertigo* on rising, she was obliged to lie down again; V., with *obscuration of vision;* with stupefaction; *with orgasm and heat in head;* with weakness as if he would fall over and as if his eyes would close; *as if he would fall;* as if he would fall foward, *when standing.*

Forehead.—Smarting stabbing in r. eminence, deep into brain. Boring behind r. eminence, in coronal suture. Pain in l. side; above r. temple; in r. side of sinciput; in r. eminence, with tearing; raging; stupefying; as if skin were fast to skull, on motion, she could scarcely wrinkle it; drawing, then in occiput; drawing, in F. and temples, only in the daytime. *Sudden pressing asunder in r. eminence and temple, disappearing gradually, recurring frequently.* Painful pressure in l. eminence, affecting eyeball, which feels compressed. Sudden pressure inward in l. eminence.

Temples.—Pain; *circumscribed;* extending outward in l. *Painful stricture.* Pressure inward in r., with sticking in l. frontal eminence, coming and going suddenly. Pressure outward in r. Drawing from r. to forehead; painful, in l. on closing eyes, with painful pressure on l. upper eyelid.

Pressure under vertex at dinner. Vertex sensitive to touch and when touched pain in head. Sticking darting into l. hemisphere. Tearing in r. hemisphere from occiput to forehead. Pain in morning as if mastoid processes were pressed towards each other. Pressure in l. side, with heaviness, sometimes sticking darting through l. hemisphere.

Occiput.—Tearing externally in l. bone extending to l. side of frontal bone, in a curve across l. temporal bone, < touch. Pain in r. side. Pressure on sides. Sensation as if a sharp wind penetrated l. side, then boring. Heaviness, > strong pressure upon a hard cushion; H., and in nape descending to small of back.

Clinical.—General rush of blood to the head, with alternating flushes to head and face.

Eyes.—Surrounded by blue rings. Pain and smarting lachrymation. Tensive pain, sensation on looking up as if internal and inferior muscles were too short. Heat. Sensation as if clouds were rising before them, > open air, with tremulousness. Pupils contracted; slightly dilated. Conjunctivæ congested.

Twitching in upper lid. Lids shut. Pricking below cartilage of lower lid. Tearing in l. brow.

Ears.—Sticking behind E. Tearing in l. Deep-seated pinching. Pressure externally above r. (Trembling in front of them when hearing music or sad news, with threadlike drawing extending to brain.) Hearing hard.

Nose.—*Dry coryza;* in r. nostril. Sneezing.

Face.—Turgid. Flushed. Pale, and eyes lustreless. Aching in l. malar-bone, < touch; paralytic A., in r. zygoma. Lower lip dry. Jaw, jerks through l. lower into a hollow tooth when walking in open air after a meal; sticking in l. lower; sticking from lower into malar-bone; pain behind l. angle when touched and pressed upward; *drawing pain in r. angle, in masseter muscles, < touch.*

Clinical.—Facial neuralgia, > open air.

Mouth.—Teeth. *Tearing in roots of molars, <* gums. Aching, beginning in a hollow tooth, almost only on chewing; A. in lower as if gum were swollen and as if teeth were elongated and loose, when chewing, worse afterwards; pressing outward, in evening and night, waking him, > rising, < drinking and smoking, intolerance of the warmth of bed. Drawing pain in all; in root of a hollow T. on eating or drinking cold or warm things, and when breathing through open mouth. Incisors on edge.

Gum.—Ulcer painful to touch over an incisor. Swollen around a hollow tooth, whitish, painful to touch, in morning on waking, with heaviness in tooth and jaw. Pain around a hollow tooth on touch.

Tongue coated yellow in morning, < posteriorly; C. white and brownish, with flat taste. Pricking in tip of tongue. Foaming at mouth. Scraping in palate and uvula, < swallowing saliva. *Mouth and throat dry.* Saliva white, and becomes frothy when talking. Salivation; with frequent yawning. Offensive breath. Taste bitter; after milk; to food, milk and coffee; T. bloody, greasy, and saliva reddish; T. disgusting, like old catarrhal mucus, < hawking.

Throat.—Drawing pain externally. Hawking in morning, the mucus is loose but does not come up. Stitches during rest. *Sensation as if he had to swallow over a foreign body.* Sore pain in afternoon on swallowing. Contractive and pricking pain extending backward, when not swallowing. Pressure on swallowing saliva. Choking in l. side when not swallowing. *Dryness, with drawing pain.* Crawling.

Stomach.—*Desire for acids, especially for lemonade;* for milk. *Appetite poor;* lost. Eructations; after every meal, with acidity in stomach, then heartburn; empty. Nausea in morning, > rising; after breakfast; after eating; after miscarriage, with vomiting; with salivation; with cough; with painful fulness; with pain in abdomen; with pain in umbilical region; in attacks; as when fasting. Retching. Vomiting (the gall-bladder had burst); V. of bile; of green matter looking like bile; of food eaten the day before, the milk thrown up is curdled and sour; violent.

Distention of epigastric region. Sticking from pit through to back. Sticking tearing in epigastric region. Pain; in region of S. and liver; in epigastric region, and on pressure pain internally as if beaten; in a spot near r. side of pit, with pinching; in region of pylorus, < before a meal, with anxiety, oppression and sensitiveness to hard pressure; in pit, then stitches; in region as if distended by air, when sitting bent, sometimes > eructations of gas, < remaining in that position, when it descends into l. side of abdomen, > sitting erect. Sensation as if she had eaten too much, with rumbling in abdomen. Oppression of pit. *Heartburn.* Heat; in cardiac region, > eructations; and weight.

Abdomen.—Rumbling; with cutting; in a fine, high tone in evening. Parietes tense. Distention; and pain; and drawing pain. Flatulence. Inflammation. Griping in morning in bed, < l. side. Pain; in track of colon, with free stool; intermittent, as from taking cold; as if he had taken cold and would have diarrhœa, > emission of flatus. Bruised feeling in muscles in evening in bed. Constriction.

Anxious bubbling in angle beneath pit of stomach on bending forward, as if cartilages were bent outward and as if cartilages and muscles were raised. *Intermittent writhing in umbilical region, with pinching and with sensation as if vomiting would come on, without nausea.* Griping above umbilicus; twisting, about U. Pain above umbilicus.

Hypogastrium.—Sticking inward in evening in bed. Compressive pain in l. side. Painful drawing in r. side, towards genitals. Drawing pressure towards genitals as if menses would appear. Heaviness, < pressure, to which she was accustomed on first day of menses.

Rectum and Anus. — *Discharge of bloody mucus.* Hæmorrhoids, painful, < morning. Biting sore stinging in anus at stool. Pain in rectum during stool. Pressive, almost paralytic pain in sphincter, a kind of ineffectual urging, almost all day, only after a long time he is obliged to go to stool, the first part quick and liquid, the second slow and hard. Creeping in anus.

Stool. — Liquid, slimy, frequent. *Diarrhœa* and much flatus; D. after miscarriage; painless D., with rumbling. Soft at first, then hard. *Hard and painful, then discharge of blood from anus, which is painful to pressure;* (H., with tenesmus). Too early. *Frequent and bloody.* None during the day; next day slight urging several times, then towards evening a scanty, thick, pasty stool.

Urinary Organs. — *Burning pain in vesical region.* Inflammation of urethra, with pain and purulent gonorrhœa. Smarting in urethra during micturition. Urging; but scanty urine, then feeling as if she would pass more. Frequent micturition; even at night he wakes to urinate, urine often turbid when passed; twice in an hour, slight increase in amount. Retention of urine, with burning and dribbling discharge. Urine increased, dark yellow; scanty, but often high-colored.

Sexual Organs.—Glans, dark redness; hard swelling on dorsum of penis not far from glans, the skin over which is movable, the S. feels like cartilage, is flat towards the median line, with a swollen border, is harder and more manifest during erection, with dull, tensive sensation; *burning sore pain in G. and figwarts,* < touch; pressure backward through whole penis, with sticking; stinging itching in morning. Violent and frequent erections day and night. Frænum swollen and tense. Paroxysmal pain in frænum. Pain in foreskin, he cannot draw it back. Intermittent drawing pain in r. spermatic cord. Contused pain in r. testicle. Intermittent tensive sensation in l. testicle, with pressure. Figwarts sensitive. Desire increased;

and slight excitement causes violent and continuous erections, with aversion to coition.

Female.—*Os tincæ is open*, **discharge red, profuse and paroxysmal, < motion.** Sticking extending backward deep in vagina. Leucorrhœa, with itching of pudenda; milky L. causing itching. **Hæmorrhage from uterus;** *at the period of the menses. Contractive pain in region of uterus.* **Menses profuse for nine days;** *P., she passes clots of blood after rising;* violent M. returned three days after menses had ceased, with colic and labor-pains, the blood partly clotted, there was less discharge of red urine, with strangury, and discharge of a slimy fluid from vagina; *miscarriage, metrorrhagia; miscarriage* at three months and a half, preceded by thin, black blood. Desire increased and consequent gratification.

Clinical.—Uterine pains, pressure towards the groins, extending into the thighs. Dysmenorrhœa, pains shooting down the thighs; pain in the small of the back, extending around the pelvis, drawing, aching pains extending through from sacrum to pubis. Uterine hæmorrhage, bright red flow, < every motion, pain extending from sacrum through to pubis. Uterine hæmorrhage in plethoric women; the hæmorrhage sometimes ceases on walking about, especially with the characteristic pains from the small of the back to genitals and down the thighs; adapted to gouty temperaments. Occasionally called for in dark hæmorrhage, with the characteristic pain. Irregular menstruation, becoming almost incessant. Threatening miscarriage, with pains from back to pubis. Amenorrhœa, especially with pain in extremities, etc. After-pains, with tendency to hæmorrhage. Acrid leucorrhœa, with much biting and itching, during pregnancy. Offensive leucorrhœa after profuse menstruation.

Respiratory Organs.—*Crawling and tickling in larynx, exciting cough and slimy expectoration;* C. as if something were crawling out of larynx. *Dry, hacking cough*, with tickling in trachea, next day expectoration streaked with blood. Asthma increasing to arrest of breath. Breathing labored and stertorous. Breathing short.

Chest.—*Hæmoptysis.* Swelling of breasts. Trembling in substance of lung behind r. border of sternum, often during the day, sounding like rattling or snapping, as of electric sparks, somewhat like the creaking of new ice when walking over it. *Sticking in l. nipple;* in l. side; on l. side, below manubrium of sternum; posteriorly in l. side, in region of two last ribs; in region of r. last true ribs, towards sternum, on inspiration; below sternum, < inspiration, sensation as if breathing were difficult from tightness of chest; *intermittent, in clavicle;* inward in l. nipple; burning, in l.; sore, in xiphoid cartilage, < deep inspiration and touch, > rest. Tearing above l. nipple, < touch, and in l. axilla. Cutting above pit of stomach.

Pain near l. nipple; in sternum on touch; *tensive, in middle of sternum, with pressure;* in sternum, as if it encroached upon chest and curved inward, < inspiration; spasmodic, in front above pit of stomach, extending across chest like a band, after a quick walk, < inspiration. Pressure rushing into it like a wind, chest feels dilated and yet oppressed. Oppression, with desire to inspire deeply, which relieves the O., later inspirations are difficult, they cause sticking on l. side behind union of cartilages of short ribs. Fulness, with cough. Burning in r. lower false ribs, with pressure. Crawling in nipples, with pleasureable sensation.

Heart.—Beats stronger, sometimes more rapid, fuller and felt over a larger space, afterwards weaker after the siesta. Beating increased and more violent in afternoon, alternating with pulsations through abdomen, accompanied by drowsiness, but inability to sleep.

Pulse.—Strong; and full. Tense, at times rapid, at times slow. Feeble.

Neck.—Tearing in muscles; T. between l. mastoid process and angle of jaw, with pressure. Pain in l. muscles; intermittent, in a spot in r. side when walking in open air, < pressure; bruised, in muscles and vertebræ. Frequent rheumatic drawing in l. muscles.

Back.—Labor-like pain, extending along Poupart's ligaments down thighs, then bloody, slimy discharge from vagina. Sticking in dorsal vertebræ; in region of dorsal vertebræ, < inspiration. Pain in a spot below l. scapula, > moving arm; in soft parts above border of l. scapula during rest, > evening during motion; paralytic, in muscles of l. S., with burning, gradually extending over l. side of thorax.

Lumbar Region.—Sticking darting into it when stooping, then tension as if parts were torn, obliging him to remain bent for some time, later in bed chill without thirst. Tearing in lumbar muscles, lowest dorsal vertebræ and in adjacent parts of ribs, < bending body, with pressure. **Drawing pain extending into pubic region. Uneasiness and dragging forward like weak labor-pains.** *Pain obliging him to bend inward*, when there is voluptuous pain in the same; intermittent pain in r. renal region; *paralytic pain*, > bending backward, with desire to stretch; paralytic, < l. side. Painful drawing, < bending backward, such as she is accustomed to feel before menses.

Extremities. — Convulsions. Cracking of joints. Tearing sticking in joints, with swollen sensation and with drawing sticking through long bones. Arthritic pain in r. great toe, which was red, shining, swollen, with boring sticking, inability to move foot or toe or bear least pressure upon it, later this pain appeared in r. wrist and hand, hand was stiff, unable to grasp anything, afterwards it changed to l. hand. Drawing pain in bones, < walking, < tibiæ, extending to feet; in bones, beginning in middle and spreading to joints, where the pain was worse, > open air. Paralytic pain in joints, < exertion; intermittent, internally above l. knee, drawing upward, once also above r. wrist. *Weakness, with despondency.*

Clinical.—Chronic arthritis and gout, > open air, < warmth, with general depression; the pains involve the shoulders, elbows, hips and knees; often accompanied by pulsation in different bloodvessels. Arthritic nodes.

Upper Extremities. — Shoulder, sticking like electricity, extending to tip of elbow, and at the same time from wrist to elbow; *sprained pain in r. joint;* pain in l., with drawing; rheumatic pain in l. joint; pressure in joints. Tearing in r. arm when lying, so that he stretched it out. Weakness of l. arm. Upper arm, *paralytic tearing along r. to hand; stinging extending inward near elbows; pain extending inward near elbows, < motion and touch;* pain extending inward in muscles, < touch. Drawing paralytic pain from head of l. humerus to elbow. Paralytic drawing in head of l. humerus during motion, with weakness.

Sticking in outer condyles of elbows; in outer side of l. E., > motion. Paralytic pain in and around l. elbow, < leaning arm on anything. *Pain in r. radius, < motion or touch.* Forearm, sudden prickings when sitting; tingling weakness in l.; heaviness on flexion after coition, with bruised feeling and anxiety, obliging him to move arms often.

Wrist.—Sprained pain in l., increasing till he could not move hand. Paralytic drawings in l. Stiffness of l., with luxation pain, later the pain changed to tearing sticking and distention, with weeping and being beside herself, she had to move the painful hand from side to side with the sound one or keep it straight, hand could not hang down, the pain > Aconitum.

Hand.—Tearing in r. carpal bones; drawing, from middle of r. carpal bones to wrist, with pressure; burning, in third l. metacarpal bone. Drawing pain in l. metacarpal bones; D. pain in palm, extending through fingers. Spasmodic contractive pain in l. palm, worse on stretching hand than on flexing it, upon stretching it out it flexes involuntarily. Sensation as if palm would be spasmodically constricted. Weakness when writing, inability to hold the pen, with chilliness.

Fingers.—Sticking in tip of l. thumb; burning-tearing, in muscles of first joint of r. fourth. Tearing lancinations in muscles of l. index and middle. Tearing in joints; in kunckle of l. little; in second and third joints of r. little, and in third joint of r. fourth; drawing, in r. fourth; paralytic, in l. index. Painful drawing in middle phalanx of r. index. Ring F. goes to sleep.

Lower Extremities.—Thigh. Sticking in region of l. hip on inspiration; sudden, down r. thigh to knee, where it is most violent, when sitting; intermittent, in inner surface. Tearing in soft parts above l. knee; tensive, in anterior surface of l. when walking, obliging him to limp. **Bruised pain in middle of anterior surfaces** when walking on level ground and when descending, but when sitting and drawing up legs tension and pain in T. on touch. Smarting as of a wound in and around r. hip-joint, < moving thigh, > sitting and lying. Pain in region of r. hip; in r. hip-joint in morning on rising, at first she could hardly step, the pain > walking; rheumatic, in l. T. during rest, then down l. tibia, and thence into l. forearm; burning, extending downward and inward; tensive, in tensor muscles as if too short, so that he cannot sit or crouch down. Tension in inner muscles of l. Pressure inward in middle. Pushing and drawing in T. and knees.

Drawing pain in l. knee. Sticking from lower part of tibia to toes in evening in bed; in lower part of calves, as after dancing, < morning. Sticking tearing in tibia below knee. Tingling-drawing tearing in lowest part of tendo-achillis during rest, with occasional darting sticking. Clawing pain in r. tendo-achillis, becoming tearing. Tensive pain in dorsum of tibia, above ankle, when sitting. Drawing to and fro in l. calf, down to malleoli. Heaviness a hand's breadth above r. malleolus, extending into foot.

Foot.—*Sticking in heels extending outward;* S. in r. heel, by sole in night; tingling, on outer side of r. sole when sitting. Tearing in l. little and fourth metatarsal bones; in dorsum, < touch; *in metatarsal bones, with pressure;* burning, in r. sole during rest. Pain in l. metatarsal bones; intermittent P. in lower part of l. heel when sitting.

Toes.—Jerks in l. Sticking in great; in ball of l. great; tickling, in ball of l. great, shocking the whole body, when sitting. Tearing in last joints of r. *Painful drawing in phalanges of r., < walking.* Burning pain in l. fourth.

Skin.—Jaundiced appearance. Exhaled the odor of the drug. Red areola on cheeks and about nasal wings, swollen and painful on pressure. Comedones that can be easily pressed out in cheeks and about nose. Elevations on elbows, without redness, with itching, < tips of the pimples, preceded by paralytic pain. Pimples on cheeks near mouth, and on temples, with sore pain, < touch; P. containing a hard substance between chin and lower lip, after squeezing out their contents they form ulcers. Spot on inner side of l. leg scratched raw and ulcerated, in morning, this ulcer was again painful and itching, next morning the scab was scratched off leaving an impure base, in evening a painful itching areola. Painful and stinging boil on upper part of natis. Vesicles about root of nose.

Creeping in nape extending over back. Sticking itching. Itching of legs towards morning, > scratching; I. on calf, transiently > scratching; now on l., now on r. calf, on the scratched places pimples causing smarting; in l. heel and sole, with sticking, after scratching burning almost as in frozen feet; < night, > scratching, the places scratched raw burn, pain and ooze water, then scabs and ulcers; in a red spot on outer part of r. leg below middle in morning, after scratching excoriation with burning pain and oozing of water, after three days a thick scab which lasts eight days, itching in border of scab and when this is scratched off bleeding, then a red cicatrized skin painful to pressure, similar spots in upper and inner part of l. ear.

Sleep.—Sleepless almost all night. *Restless sleep;* with orgasm, heat and sweat; and he says many commonplace things in sleep and snores on expiration; and dreams about several things which he had begun; with confused dreams, frequent waking, after which he must toss about long before going to sleep again. Dreams towards morning, with reflection and mental exertion; in morning that men fell dead from a height; constant D., full of invention and mental exertion; anxious, waking him frequently, < towards morning; that she is disputing with some one, this wakes her in tears.

Fever.—Chilliness all day; in evening on lying down; < towards evening, then heat, then sweat at night. Frequent shuddering, with gooseflesh; S. all over and extending across hairy scalp in evening before going to bed; with blackness before eyes, then sleepiness; in back. Cold feet; and hands, with hot face; r. leg, as if standing in cold water.

Heat; after walking in open air; internal, after dinner, with restlessness, constant necessity to move limbs, without thirst; wherever the affected part is touched; in ears in evening; internal, in border of l. ear and lobule, with slight redness; in face, with fulness in vessels; in face, with flushes; in face in flushes, with frequent chilliness in rest of body.

Sweat at night; on feet extending above malleoli in morning in bed.

Salicylicum Acidum.

Pure Salicylic acid is triturated for use.

General Action.—Very few observations concerning this acid are recorded, nearly all experiments having been made with Sodium or Potassium salts. It acts, however, as an antipyretic, similarly to *Quinine*, reducing temperature and causing profuse perspiration.

Like *Quinine* it causes headache, deafness and blindness; it also paralyzes the third nerve, more or less, causing ptosis and squint. It is eliminated by the kidneys and causes albuminuria.

Generalities.—Rheumatic pains, < walking out of doors. Discomfort, with disinclination for mental or physical exertion. Dulness on waking after a good night's rest, with nervousness, ringing in ears, < l., and fulness in head. Weakness; > open air. Nervous prostration after mental labor and nervous excitement. Feeling as if I had walked far; in evening. Symptoms return in evening.

Mind.—Delirium; it was difficult for him to collect his ideas, then he laughed without cause, talked incessantly and disconnectedly, often looked about him. Excitement; after walking. Gloomy, don't know what to begin. Unconsciousness, with loud groans.

Head.—Aching; in morning, > during the day, < evening, > next morning; with dull, bruised feeling in r. side of head; agonizing; threatening of nervous. Bruised feeling. Dulness; with general oppression. Buzzing sensation in interior of brain as if blood were forced through a contracted vessel. Rush of blood. *Vertigo; and confusion, a sensation on rising suddenly after lying a long time*, soon afterward he thought he heard music, this often woke him, later sounds as of a swarm of bees or the buzzing of flies, with sweat. Pain above r. eye; above l. side of forehead, changing to l. ear; in l. side of head; in r. side of head in afternoon; drawing, back of r. temple; in a spot in vertex, as if struck by a hammer, in night. Itching, with feeling as if hair stood on end.

Clinical.—Vertigo, tendency to fall to l. side, surrounding objects seem to fall to the right, headache.

Eyes.—Burning and dryness. Itching of r. upper lid; of canthi, with burning. Bruised pain in bones below l. eye. Boring in l. brow, with tenderness when pressed. Dim vision.

Ears and Nose.—Stoppage of ears; < l.; in l. after removal of wax, with pain; when walking, > drawing breath strongly through nostrils, but returning. *Roaring in ears; with difficult hearing. Ringing in ears. Deafness.* Dryness of nostrils, with itching. Sneezing.

Clinical.—Meniere's disease. Nasal catarrh, with persistent sneezing.

Face.—Pain in l. lower jaw, with pain in parotid on touch, affecting side of throat. Soreness at r. corner of lips.

Mouth.—Mucous membrane white. Sore feeling on sides of jaw under tongue in evening. Burning, and in epigastric region; in M. and pharynx, with dryness; in M. and throat, with scraping; on tongue, with scratching. Taste disgusting; T. bitter, bilious; bitter, tenacious saliva hawked up with difficulty.

Throat.—Hæmorrhagic pharyngitis, with difficulty in swallowing. Scraping in l. side; S. causing cough. Pharynx dry. Burning; after a plain supper. Swallowing difficult; and violent effort to swallow waking him at night, afterwards the difficulty confined to r. side of throat, with pain and with sticking along Eustachian tube to within ear, swelling of r. tonsil, perceptible externally below angle of jaw, with sensitiveness to touch and heat in vicinity, mucous membrane of throat and posterior palate red and swollen, and small ulcers, later expectoration of a cheesy lump of strong odor, with bluish-red blood.

Stomach.—Vomiting. Erosions and ulcers, and in abdomen; (ulcers, with ecchymoses). Weight after salad. Burning in epigastric region.

Clinical.—Flatulent dyspepsia, with hot, sour belching. Indigestion, with headache and putrid fermentation.

Abdomen.—Rumbling. Flatulence in evening; F., with inability to expel it. Bloated feeling towards noon. Pain in evening, < pressure, with discomfort; P. in groin when coughing; in hypogastrium and bladder without urging to urinate and only small discharge; at one time in hypochondrium, at another in hypogastrium, with feeling of incarcerated flatus, with constipation; strained, in r. groin.

Anus and Stool.—Constriction in anus after stool. Itching in anus and ineffectual attempt at stool, six hours later slimy, insufficient stool. Stool tedious and insufficient. Constipation.

Clinical.—Dysentery, stools like green frogs' spawn. Putrid diarrhœa in children.

Urinary Organs.—Micturition difficult in morning on rising; D., slow and less in quantity. Urine red, with copious sediment.

Sexual Organs.—Emission of semen (or prostatic fluid), somewhat bloody, at night, and on waking pain in genitals as if overstrained. Excitement; more physical than mental.

Respiratory Organs.—Cough returns every day from 3 till 5 P.M.; C. on lying down, as if mucus flowed from Eustachian tubes into throat, causing scratching; hacking, with scratching in throat and hawking up of small pieces of thick yellow phlegm, with occasional sneezing and discharge from nose. Dyspnœa, respiration very deep, so that the lower margin of the lungs is moved 4 to 5 C.M., auxiliary muscles are set to work, expiration is more active, number of respirations unchanged or slightly increased, sometimes complaints of air-hunger, such D. may appear without preceding surring in ears, in some cases the D. disappears during the night and increases after every dose in the daytime, sometimes the symptom is noticed only on certain days.

Chest, Heart and Pulse.—Aching in l. clavicle; at side of sternum, with feeling as if bone were sore. Oppression of chest. Palpitation; after moderate exercise, with intermittent pulse. Rapid pulse.

Back.—Stiffness at night on waking; S. in muscles of middle, with pain; in muscles along spine in afternoon when lying down, with aching.

Extremities.—*Rheumatic pains. Pain in fingers and little toes; drawing, in l. calf, extending into thigh, then transferred to l. arm. Soreness and pain in r. deltoid and r. gastrocnemius, changing next day to l. wrist and forearm, with soreness to touch and soreness on moving limb, third day same pain on palmar surface of l. index, when the pain appeared in one part it disappeared in the previous one. Strained pain in r. shoulder in morning. Pain in knuckles of r. hand; in sinews of l. forearm*, extending into third and little fingers, then tingling; burning, in inside of joint of r. thumb; *rheumatic, in lower limbs and feet at night, and burning in ball of great toe.* Stinging in a r. toe.

Clinical.—Sciatica, with burning pain, < night.

Skin.—Swelling under skin of fingers, with burning itching on inside of l. hand. Itching pimples here and there, one on r. cheek; red P. here and there, and small whitish ones, the latter in groups, itching and filled with water. Exanthema bullosum. Pustules on face and head; watery itching, between r. fingers; itching, < l. arm, skin becomes rough when scratched. Itching vesicles in a group on l. little finger. Itching after undressing, > in bed; I. on back, below jaws and under chin; of r. toes; < over breast and stomach; voluptuous, at night, > scratching, then a pimple, sometimes burning of skin after scratching.

Sleep.—Yawning in evening. Night restless, longing to sleep, but unable to do so. Amorous dream, with bloody emission, then erections in morning.

Fever.—Heat of skin. Burning in ball of great toe. Sweat.

Sambucus.

A tincture is made of the fresh leaves and flowers of Sambucus nigra, L.

Generalities and Mind.—*Dropsical swellings. Most pains occur during rest and disappear during motion, only a few are caused by motion. Starting at things to which he is accustomed.* Periodical delirium, saw frightful things on the wall. *Fretful.*

Head.—Aching at night; stupefying A., as in catarrh; stupefying, as from intoxication. Pressure outward to all sides. Vertigo in morning on rising; and < forenoon; V. on moving head, with tensive sensation as if water were in it; with obscuration of head. Pain in forehead and a sudden painful jerk through brain from one side to other. Tearing in upper part of forehead, with pain streaming down into eye; T. in bone over l. temple on stooping; intermittent, in temples, < bones. Pressure outward in temples. Burrowing in vertex. Intermittent tearing stitch through l. half of occiput, with dulness in the place during the intervals.

Eyes, Ears, Nose and Face.—Pupils contracted, then dilated. Sticking in r. ear, with cramplike pain. Itching and crawling in ears and throat, somewhat > in throat by tongue. Pressure forward in tip of nose, with heaviness, as if it would bleed. Face flushed. Tensive pain as from swelling in cheek, with numbness. Tension in l. cheek, with gnawing pressure upon upper jaw. Painless pustule, with red areola, on l. side of lower lip.

Clinical.—Suffocating nasal catarrh in children, with sudden starting up.

Mouth.—Tearing in teeth extending into incisors, with stitches, later the pain extended to eye, with sensation as if cheek were swollen, which was not the case. M. and throat sore. Dryness of palate without thirst.

Stomach.—Thirst, though drink has not a pleasant taste. Hiccough; during and after eating. Incipient nausea in and below pit of stomach. *Vomiting;* tinged with blood. Pressure in epigastric region. Sticking just below S. when sitting, < pressure.

Abdomen.—Rumbling. Spasmodic tearing in muscles in evening after lying down, < moving them. Griping; if it leans against a sharp corner; *as after taking cold, with emission of flatus.* Tormina every half hour. Pain if it presses against anything, with nausea. Bruised feeling internally. Tenderness; and distention. Griping in muscles of r. hypochondrium. Tearing in l. side. Stitches in l. obliquus muscle when sitting and standing; S. over l. hip, with rhythmical pulsation.

Stool, Urinary and Sexual Organs.—Several thin, slimy stools, with much flatus, then renewed urging, distention of abdomen, pressure in stomach and umbilical region, then no more symptoms. Itching in orifice of urethra. *Frequent desire to urinate, with copious discharge;* with scanty discharge. Obliged to urinate at night. Micturition in a thin stream. Frequent M. of dark yellow urine. Emission after midnight.

Clinical.—Urine becomes changed in character and deposits a heavy sediment; Bœnninghausen emphasizes the increased watery urine. It is found clinically that the American Sambucus (and also the European) is of great value in acute inflammation of the kidneys, with dropsy, especially for vomiting of bile, distress in stomach after eating. Profuse urine, with dry heat of the skin.

Respiratory Organs and Chest.—Hoarseness from much tenacious, glutinous mucus in larynx. Intermittent cutting in front, on third false rib, < moving trunk. Cutting griping in last ribs towards spine. Sudden internal clawing in both sides, about fourth rib. *Oppression below l. nipple, with stitches; O. beneath sternum, with pressure, and with pressure in pit of stomach and epigastric region, nausea and weakness.*

Clinical.—Suffocative respiration, with stitches in the chest. Laryngismus stridulus, starts up in great suffocation, cannot exhale the breath, face grows purple (compare Chlorine). Acute laryngitis, with spasmodic cough and attacks of suffocation. Croup, with spasm of the glottis, wheezing respiration, < after midnight. Violent dry cough, with hoarseness and tough mucus in the larynx, < night. Whooping cough, with suffocative spasm, expectoration of tough mucus during the day; cough, < after midnight or from lying with the head low.

Pulse.—Rapid; and small. Slow; but full.

Neck and Back.—Cutting stitches deep in muscles on sides of neck, < moving neck. Heaviness in nape, making motion of head difficult. Pain in middle of spine. Sticking outward in inner surface of r. scapula during rest; cutting S. in scapulæ during rest; pulsating S. beneath r. scapula when sitting. Cutting thrusts in sacrum, < bending forward, with tensive pain. Drawing pressure in sacrum extending to muscles on inside of ilium when standing.

Upper Extremities.—Pinching in axilla. Sticking in middle of inner side of upper arm. Upper arm feels as if it would break as soon as he supports himself upon it. Paralytic heaviness of elbows. Sticking in outer condyle of wrist; cutting S. in wrists, rhythmical with pulse, > motion. Drawing pain in bones of wrist during rest, and along radius. Hands tremble when writing. Tearing in finger-joints.

Lower Extremities.—Drawing sticking through anterior muscles of upper part of r. thigh during rest. Tearing around above hip-joint on walking. Cramplike drawing in thigh at insertion of large gluteal muscle when walking. Hamstrings tense and seem too short so that standing is difficult. Deeply piercing sticking in inner side of tibia, somewhat > motion. Dead sensation, as if asleep, in middle of r. tibia when standing, with coldness. Weariness of legs when standing, with sensation of a cold wind on them. Tearing in r. external malleolus in evening in bed, and in muscles on side of leg.

Skin.—Red spots here and there on cheeks, with burning. Sudden painful drawing over surface of body when sitting. Itching on forehead, > rubbing; I. on back of nose, with numbness; on patella, with rough scraping, a sensation as if eruption would break out; sticking, on inner sides of thighs, changing to burning after rubbing.

Sleep.—*Sleepiness, without sleep.* Frequent waking. Restless sleep, on sitting up in bed it seemed as if the symptoms extended downward and she felt easier. Starting out of sleep, with anxiety, suffocation and trembling. Slumber, with half-open eyes and mouth, on waking could not catch his breath, obliged to sit up, when the breathing was rapid, with whistling in chest, as if he would suffocate, he beat about with his hands, head and hands bluish and puffy, with heat without thirst, when the attacks came on he cried out, aggravation at night, from 12 till 4. Dreams; vivid, unremembered; lascivious, with emission.

Fever.—Chilliness, with warmth of face; C. creeping over whole body, < hands and feet, which are cold to touch, though the latter may be warmly wrapped up; shaking, before sleep. Shivering in attacks; S. over whole body, < from feet to knees, with sticking crawling here and there, and cold hands and feet. *Cold feet; with internal heat in face, without thirst;* hands; fingers, with crawling in them.

Heat; when walking; soon after lying down, without thirst; in flushes in afternoon, after half an hour sweat on face. *Dry heat; with dread of uncovering*, it seems as if he would take cold and have colic. External H., < palms and soles; E., without thirst. Heat in head and neck; flushing, in face. Orgasm of blood in evening after lying down, with trembling sensation.

Sweat when awake *from* 7 P.M. *till* 1 A.M., **without thirst,** *after sleep he was more hot than sweaty, without thirst; S. at night on waking;* after midnight, but not on head; first on face, several hours after the dry heat had disappeared.

Clinical.—The suppression of the ordinary perspiration during sleep is very marked; the skin becomes perfectly dry and burning when the patient falls asleep, but he breaks into profuse sweat immediately on waking.

Sanguinaria.

A tincture is made of the fresh root of the "blood-root," Sanguinaria Canadensis, L.

General Action.—An irritant of the mucous membranes of the stomach and air-passages, causing vomiting as well as nasal and bronchial catarrh. Its remarkable power to cure migraine is fully substantiated by the provings.

Allies.—Ipec., Squills, Nat. m., Rumex, Iris v., Bry.

Generalities.—Tremors. Involuntary motions of muscles. Tetanic rigidity of whole body. *Pain over upper part of l. side of head, < eye*, with pain in l. foot; in superficial bony parts (not in flesh nor in joints) at 10 P.M., > touch, but suddenly appearing in other places; *on touch in head*, breasts, loins and other parts where pain had been severe, in afternoon; *rheumatic, in nape, shoulders and arms;* neuralgic, in various parts; racking and burning. Nervous thrill through whole system. Pulsation through whole body. *Weakness;* in morning; *in morning on waking*, with disinclination to rise; in afternoon; in afternoon, with qualmish sickening feeling all over body; and sensitiveness; and stupidity. Torpor and frequent yawning. Faintness. Insensibility. Constant change of symptoms. Aggravation morning and evening; A. from a long ride in the country.

Mind.—Anxiety; before vomiting. Irritability; in morning, she could break things to pieces without cause; in afternoon, with impatience and dyspnœa. Inability to fix mind in afternoon. Inability to attend to business during the fever. Stupor.

Head.—Enlarged veins. **Aching;** *in morning;* in morning on waking; in evening, with tickling in throat; when lying; < *stooping and moving about;* **with nausea and chilliness, then flushes of heat extending from head to stomach;** *with fever; with bitter vomiting;* with earache; with stiffness of limbs and rheumatic pains; **paroxysmal;** *as if head would burst in afternoon, < r. temple, > walking in open air. Throbbing pain, < motion; < stooping* (Bry.); *with bitter vomiting.* Cerebral functions excited by small doses. Sensation as if it would be drawn forward. Confusion, > eructations. Heaviness of brain. *Fulness.* **Determination of blood, with whizzing in ears and transitory heat, then waterbrash as if vomiting would occur,** but instead there are cutting drawings in abdomen, then stool. **Vertigo;** in morning; *in morning on rising quickly from stooping or turning head quickly* (Bry.), *with faintness;* in afternoon *and inability to turn quickly without fear of falling* (Ipec.); *on rising from a seat; with heaviness in stomach;* with singing in ears; with singing before ears.

Forehead.—Sticking. Lightning-like pain in r. side of F. and temple at 5 and 7 P.M., and at 11 P.M. pain like an electric shock through forehead. Dizzy tearing above r. eye, extending to r. temple, in afternoon, after an hour sensation like driving a nail into brain alternating with boring. Burrowing in upper part of sinciput. *Pain;* and through temples; *over eyes; in morning, < exercise, sympathizing with stomach, like sick headache; over eye on waking, lasting all day; on rising from a seat, with vertigo;* pain and sore feeling in F. and temples, with strong pulsation in temporal arteries; extending into cheek-bones; *as if it would burst*, with chilliness and burning in stomach; in sinciput like a fulness in afternoon; like a pressure in r. side when standing still. Bandlike constriction above brows in afternoon. Pressive drawing.

Temples.—Periodic sticking in l. Sharp darting from one to the other through brain. Pain in morning; in afternoon, with occasional darting pain through head; in l. in morning, at times like a nail driven into brain, with violent throbbing in temporal arteries. Feeling as if pressed together, with darting pain over upper part of eyeballs. *Dulness < r., with inclination to ache.*

Pain in l. side; and in l. foot; in vertex. Vertex feels as if cleaved from base of head. Pressure on vertex in region of anterior fontanelle, > walking. *Pain in occiput and nape in afternoon*, gradually extending to region of kidneys, where it is severe, dull and heavy. Scalp loose on one side on raising eyes, with drawing in it; r. side loose; S. sore to touch; pain on moving it.

Clinical.—Extremely valuable remedy for headaches of various sorts; periodic neuralgia, pain commencing in the occiput and settling over r. eye, with nausea and vomiting, photophobia, etc.; the attacks commence in the forehead and vertex of r. side, *begin in the morning and last till evening*, < every motion, > sleep, passing off with profuse flow of urine. Headache at the climacteric, with rush of blood to the head, buzzing in the ears, nausea and chilliness, sometimes vomiting of bile, shivering, > open air and sleep.

Eyes.—Staring and protruding. Sunken, dull, burning, injected. Dim in afternoon, and feeling as if hairs were in them. Shooting into inner corner of r. and thence to forehead. Pain. Sensation as of acid fumes at 2 P.M. Feel weak in morning, and lids smart on closing them tightly, lachrymation if open, balls tender to touch. Lachrymation of r., which is painful to touch, then fluent coryza, with flow of clear water from r. nostril, > evening by diarrhœa twice; L., with burning in eyes.

Pupils dilated; and insensible. Sticking in upper lid. *Pain in r. ball in afternoon, < attempting to roll it outward or upward; in balls on motion; on touch. Balls sore, with darting through them and dim vision.* Vision dim; in afternoon, it requires effort and rubbing to see distinctly, a feeling somewhat like snow-blindness. Twitching before eyes.

Clinical.—Conjunctivitis, especially of r. eye. Blepharadenitis, with dryness under the upper lid, neuralgia about the eye.

Ears.—Sticking in l. Pain in r. at every stroke of a blacksmith's hammer; deep in l. during the pain in forehead. Throbbing under E. Cracking in r. on stroking r. cheek with finger-tips. Humming, with determination of blood. Beating whizzing in l.

Clinical.—Polypus of the ear. Humming and roaring in the ears, with painful sensitiveness to sudden sounds, in women at the climacteric.

Nose.—*Pain about root* (Nat. m.); *at root in afternoon, with tingling like coryza;* heavy, at root, with dizziness, somewhat like effects of alcoholic stimulus, with lassitude. Heat. *Sneezing; with tingling. Coryza, with heavy pain at root of nose and stinging in nose; painful C. during the fever; dry, as from a sudden cold; alternately fluent and dry; fluent, with frequent sneezing; watery, acrid.* Odor of roasted onions in nose. Aversion to the odor of syrup. *Smell and taste lost* (Nat. m.).

Clinical.—Gelatinous tumor of l. nostril, polypus. Nasal catarrh, with pain over the root of nose, sore throat, dry cough.

Face.—Redness; with heat; with puffiness and stiff feeling. Pale. Haggard. Jerking in bones extending towards eyes. *Pain in cheek-bones.* Feeling of fulness. Jaws stiff. *Lips dry.* Lips swollen towards evening.

Clinical. — Facial neuralgia spreading all over the head, bends over and holds head tightly towards floor to get relief (Ign.).

Mouth.—Teeth. Looseness; with salivation. Boring in molar, ending in gnawing. Pain in upper; in incisors and hollow molar; in a r. lower hollow molar mornings after cold drinks; when picking them; in a hollow one, < touch of food; in a r. upper hollow on waking, with pain in r. side of forehead, extending into ear, the toothache < cold water and hot drinks, but > warm water.

Tongue.—Coated yellowish-white; with bad taste; C. yellow in morning; white, with loss of appetite. Sticking in l. side. Prickling in tip; in tongue and hard palate, almost as from Mezereum (he had tobacco in his mouth). *Burnt feeling.* Crawling in tip on waking, then rough sensation extending over tongue. Dryness in r. side in morning after waking, extending over whole tongue, with raw sensation as from something acrid.

Burning in mouth and fauces. Clammy and feverish; C. in morning, with disagreeable taste, abundant accumulations about teeth and fetid breath. Taste impaired; fatty; slimy; bitter to cake, then burning in fauces; disagreeable in morning on waking.

Throat.—Feeling as if he had swallowed something sharp. *Swollen sensation on swallowing; < r. side, < swallowing, with pain; sensation as if closed by swelling, with pain on swallowing, as if he would suffocate,* and with loss of voice. Spasmodic constriction beneath jaw in afternoon. *Rawness in T. and mouth, with difficulty in swallowing,* at 12.30 P.M. mouth, fauces, etc., sensitive, as from holding hot water in mouth, making it difficult to chew food. *Tickling in evening, with hacking cough and headache.* Irritation in fauces. **Dryness,** *in afternoon,* **with dry, teasing, hacking cough; D., with tickling cough;** not > drinking. Burning in pharynx; in fauces in afternoon, < soft palate, extending to centre of sternal region; from 6 till 7 P.M.; in fauces after eating sweet things; in fauces, < soft palate, with relaxation.

Clinical.—Soreness of the roof of the mouth, extending through the pharnyx, feeling as if it had been burnt or scalded, sore throat on r. side, pains extending to the ear and to the chest, with burning of the stomach, nausea and vomiting. Rheumatic soreness of the muscles of palate after influenza. Ulcerated sore throat, with dryness, loss of smell and taste, etc.

Stomach.—Appetite craving; in morning. *Longing for spiced food; for indefinite things,* with loss of appetite. Appetite poor; in morning. A. lost; for breakfast; for breakfast, and heaviness in stomach after eating a little. Aversion to butter, which leaves a sweetish taste. Thirst. Empty eructations; spasmodic; then tickling in throat, provoking cough. Hiccough on smoking.

Nausea; at breakfast; in afternoon, with eructation, heaviness in stomach and feeling of indigestion; after eating; on stooping; *not > vomiting; with salivation; with headache* (Ipec.), *chill and heat;* with chilliness; with pallor and offensive eructations; with urging to stool; with weakness; then headache, with rheumatic pain and stiffness in limbs and nape; intermittent; periodic; sudden, as if she would faint when in church, where she was surrounded by various odors.

Vomiting; with desire to eat in order to quiet the nausea; with diarrhœa; with weakness; violent; of bitter water.

Jumping as of something alive in epigastric region. *Pain;* in epigastric region; after eating; extending downward to S. and abdomen in afternoon, causing rumbling. Soreness in epigastric region in morning; in E. region, < eating. Discomfort. Uneasiness in epigastrium. Heaviness as from indigestion. *Burning;* in evening; with weight. Burning pain in epigastric region, with soreness in chest on full inspiration. *Emptiness* in morning, *with faint feverish feeling;* E. soon after eating. Digestion weak. Agreeable sensation. Amelioration from eating, though food lies like a load. Digestion is excited by small doses.

Clinical.—Gastric derangements, with nausea, not > vomiting. Nausea during pregnancy, with salivation, constant spitting. Ulcer in the stomach, vomiting, burning pain, > vomiting, tenderness, flushes of heat rising into the head; the characteristics were the rising of heat into the head and the amelioration from vomiting.

Abdomen.—Flatulency. Discharge of flatus, then of excrement, with abatement of nausea, etc.; frequent emissions of offensive flatus, afterwards in evening hard stool. Cramp extending from place to place. Shooting through A., extending to lower limbs, in afternoon. Cutting, then watery stool. Cutting drawing. Griping, then semi-solid stool. Digging at night, with pain in small of back. Pain; and in sacrum; paroxysmal; extending to rectum and causing sharp spasmodic pain low down in rectum; as before menses; as before menses, all night. Throbbing.

Pain in upper A. in morning, then diarrhœa. Griping in umbilical region; at 5.30 P.M., with flatulency and fulness in head. Pain in region of spleen; in morning on waking; with soreness on pressure. Pain in hypochondria; *r., and r. side of chest;* l. H.; burning in r. H. and r. side of chest in morning.

Hypogastrium.—Cutting from r. to l. iliac fossa, thence to rectum, and then causing sharp spasmodic pain. Twisting pain midway between pubes and crest of l. ilium, < sitting, standing and bending towards r. and on pressure, > walking erect, afterwards it shifted to l. hip and behind short ribs, < bending to right.

Rectum.—Spasmodic cutting low down in evening. Desire for stool, with emission of flatus; frequently. Ineffectual desire, with sensation of a thick mass in anus; I. desire, then vomiting.

Stool.—*Diarrhœa, with much flatus;* frequent D. Soft, on latter days hard. At first of wind, then of scanty fæces, relieving the desire for stool. Constipation. In hard lumps. Undigested. Contained bright yellow bile. Frequent. Scanty, twice in one day.

Clinical.—Has been used for dysentery from taking cold, or for diarrhœa especially associated with cough (Ipec.).

Urinary Organs.—Pain in bladder. Constant desire to urinate, but no increase of urine. Urging and micturition every hour, but scanty each time. Frequent micturition; at night, always much watery urine; quantity normal, dark yellow; and copious. Difficult micturition. Urine copious; more C. in evening than in daytime, high-colored, sediment reddish. Scanty, red urine in morning.

Sexual Organs.—Burning pain in glans. Emissions two nights in succession, after which he felt very well. Uterine hæmorrhage. Menses too early and black; M. profuse, with less pain and weakness in small of back than usual, *but with pain in r. side of forehead and side of head and sensation as if eyes would be forced out of head, < r.*

Clinical.—Polypus of the uterus. Metrorrhagia, with cough, sick headache, flush of the face, etc. Delayed menstruation, or amenorrhea, with cough, periodical neuralgia on r. side, with flushing of face. Sore, painful nipples.

Respiratory Organs.—It sometimes promotes the excretion of mucus or muco-purulent matter in bronchi and sometimes restrains it, according to different circumstances.

Cough; from tickling in larynx, with expectoration of thick, tenacious mucus; paroxysmal, in morning. **Hacking cough; evenings after lying down, from tickling in throat** (Rumex, Puls., Hyos.); < after eating; *dry.* **Dry cough, with tickling in throat-pit and crawling extending beneath sternum,** *the C. caused pain beneath upper part of sternum; D. cough waking him, > sitting up in bed and* **discharging flatus upward and downward.**

Dyspnœa in morning, with sighing; *D. and inclination to inspire deeply.* Respiration hurried.

Clinical.—Croup, with a whistling cough. Swelling of the larynx, dryness of the throat. Aphonia. Larnygitis, with soreness, dryness, swelling, sometimes expectoration of thick mucus. Whooping cough, < night, with diarrhœa. Œdema of the glottis, great dyspnœa, respiration sawing or rasping, voice lost, cough dry and harsh, < lying down, scanty, glairy expectoration. (Compare Rumex).

Chest.—*Sticking in r. side; near r. nipple;* beneath sternum; in breasts; near l. axilla; in l. side in region of short ribs; in l. side near last ribs; in breasts in morning; in l. side on moving; l. lower part, extending to shoulder. *Sharp pain beneath r. nipple in afternoon, with difficulty in inspiring deeply and dyspnœa. Sharp myalgic pain midway between sternum and r. nipple, with tenderness of surface to pressure.*

Pain; *beneath sternum and in r. breast;* in side; under fifth rib; under l. nipple; beneath præcordial region; in l. in morning; in breasts in morning; *under l. clavicle in morning on waking, with as tired a feeling as when I retired;* in breasts in afternoon, < r.; under l. nipple, < deep inspiration; and in back; *in upper part, with heaviness and with difficult breathing;* from l. breast to shoulder; in breasts extending to r. shoulder; *in r. breast, extending to shoulder, in afternoon, so that it is difficult to put hand on vertex; in r. breast, extending to stomach and causing nausea* and lasting all night. *Burning pain between breasts in afternoon, < r. side;* tearing B. pain through breasts beneath sternum during the fever. Peculiar pains, deep but not as sharp as I supposed pleuritic pains to be, never on both sides at once. Soreness during inspiration; sore pain beneath r. nipple, < touch; nipples sore and painful. (Compare chest symptoms with Bry., Kali c., Squills).

Constriction of breasts, with inclination to inspire deeply, which aggravates the C. and causes tearing through breasts, < r. Sickening sensation from r. breast to stomach, causing nausea, in afternoon. *Burning under sternum; below r. arm and clavicle, streaming down to hepatic region at* 4 P.M.

Clinical.—Not infrequently indicated in pneumonia of a subacute type, > *lying on the back.* Typhoid pneumonia, face livid and dark red. Particularly valuable in hypostatic pneumonia (compare Verat. viride). Phthisis, with hectic fever, burning in the chest and sensation of congestion, soreness of the muscles. Ulceration of the lung, with hectic flush, circumscribed redness of the cheeks, hæmoptysis.

Heart.—Palpitation.

Pulse.—Rapid; and full, strong; and tense, but not full; and weak; in morning, and weak; and small; and small, tense; and diminished in fulness and force; and irregular; and irregular in fulness and force, from nausea; afterwards slow. *Slow and irregular; and feeble.* Irregular. Suppressed.

Neck.—Pain in l. side of nape. Strained pain in r. side. Stiffness of nape.

Back.—Pain, < lumbar region, and then down limbs to feet; P. under scapula, with chill; along inner border of r. scapula, with heat and chills alternating, and extending to kidneys, where there are heat and pain. Lumbar pain; in morning; in morning, and down limbs; > bending forward, with weakness in lower limbs; in kidneys, penetrating into r. iliac fossa, then shooting through to sigmoid flexure of colon, then extending to rectum; sore, on touch; heavy, across kidneys in morning, urine high-colored and not quite as easily voided as usual.

Extremities.—Convulsive rigidity. Pain in morning; P. in r. arm and l. foot; in r. hand and arm when warm and quiet in bed, and on top of l. foot, then in heels, then in toes. Rheumatic pains.

Upper Extremities.—*Pain in shoulders; on top of r.;*

in r. and down scapula in morning; in l. in evening; in upper part of joint on motion; *rheumatic in r.*, < forenoon after holding arm long in one position, extending to elbow; sudden rheumatic, in joint. Rheumatic pain in arm and hand; in r. forearm in evening. Hands red and burning. Pain in r. hand in morning; ulcerative, in r. palm close to index. Sticking in tip of r. little finger; from r. thumb to symphysis menti during the day. Cutting in second joint of l. middle finger. Pain in ball of r. thumb; ulcerative, in root of nail of r. thumb, then l., then extending to all fingers, one after another; rheumatic, in r. ring finger, just above second joint.

Clinical.—Rheumatism in r. arm and shoulder, < night in bed (Mag. car.).

Lower Extremities.—Rheumatic pains; wandering, in afternoon, < r.; and so severe in r. ankle and toe-joint as to cause lameness, with swelling of great toe-joint. Weakness when walking. Rheumatic pain in l. hip. Pains through hips and extending down r. limb, goutlike in metatarsal joint of r. great toe. Bruised pain in l. hip-joint on walking, < rising from a seat. Knees and legs weak in evening when walking. Stiffness in hollows and sides of knees, with tension. Cramp in l. calf, with crawling. Drawing in calves extending into heels, < r. Sticking in r. ankle; below r. outer malleolus. Sharp pain in r. ankle and great toe-joint. Sticking in heels in morning in bed. Pain in corns.

Skin.—*Ulcers about the nail.* Increased itching on an old tubercle-like eruption.

Sleep.—Yawning; with disposition to lie down; disposed to Y. and deep inspiration, which cause tearing in r. breast, in afternoon. Sleepiness; when reading. Waking late. Waking early; in night in fright, as if falling. Sleepless. Restless night; till towards morning, when sweat broke out and relieved most of the pains. Dreams frightful and disagreeable; troublesome, with tossing about all night, painful sighing and dyspnœa; that he helped dissect a corpse; of a sea voyage two nights in succession though he had never been at sea.

Fever.—*Chills;* at 2 P.M., then hot flashes, pulse 95, then burning fever, with exacerbation of all symptoms, fever and pains abating at 10 P.M.; in evening in bed, with shivering in back as if he had gooseflesh; on motion, with shaking and pain beneath scapulæ; *and shivering suddenly alternating with heat;* with nausea. Cold skin, < limbs. Cold wrists, with sweat on forehead.

Heat; in morning; every day between 2 and 3 P.M., > between 8 and 9 P.M.; with flushed face and hot hands; always with the pains, whether in head, chest or stomach; in flushes, then chills; *flying from head to stomach;* in palm; in soles and palms in forenoon; in soles, < night; through r. shoulder and clavicle to r. breast, extending to stomach and bowels. Sweat; cold.

Sanguinaria Nitrate.

This preparation should be triturated for use.

Generalities and Mind.—Discomfort as from a severe cold, affecting whole body, at 9.30 P.M., awoke frequently with dry mouth and throat from breathing with open mouth, nose being obstructed, woke at 6 A.M. in sweat, feeling better. Irritable.

Head.—Pain, with soreness. Fulness and inclination to ache. Fulness, waking him in morning, > discharge of thick, yellow mucus. Vertigo. Discomfort, < night. Pain in forehead and eyes, partially > discharge of mixed watery, clear, stringy, thick, yellow mucus from nose, tinged with blood; burning pain in forehead and root of nose. Fulness in forehead and over eyes and at root of nose. Pain in l. temple. Drawing in l. temple. Pain in l. side of head, with heat extending to parietal ridge and mastoid process, with stiffness of muscles of l. side of neck and top of l. shoulder as from exposure to a draught of cold or damp, raw air.

Eyes.—Swollen, red and painful to touch. Smarting. Aching. Burning; and sore pain. Lachrymation, tears flow down r. cheek. Pain in l. ball extending over orbit and l. side of head. Sore pain in balls; < pressure; in l., extending to supraorbital region, then across forehead and deep above root of nose. Burning in balls, > night, with pressure, leaving fulness and soreness, as in ordinary catarrh. Lids and conjunctiva red; conjunctiva red, with smarting and burning at l. inner canthus, eye sore to touch. Aching, in orbits, extending into forehead and to l. side of head.

Nose.—*Sensation as if he had taken horse-radish, causing gush of tears from eyes, which soon became blurred as from a film of mucus. Dryness of nostrils, forehead and bronchia, with soreness and rawness.* Obstruction. *Burning; extending into forehead and probably frontal sinuses;* in l. nostril, later extending to r. nostril, forehead and eyes, *with smarting of eyes, lachrymation and pain in eyes, the pain > sneezing, then watery mucus from r. nostril, then heat and fulness through nasal passages, woke at 3 A.M. with pressure, heat and fulness in forehead,* **extending to root of nose,** *restlessness and but little sleep till morning, on rising nostrils plugged with mucus, which on moving about was discharged, was thick, yellowish, that from r. nostril tinged with blood,* after discharging for ten days it left *posterior nares and soft palate feeling stiff, sore and cracked.* **Sneezing.**

Discharge of sweetish yellow mucus; *D. thick, yellow, tinged with blood; from posterior nares,* < l. side. *Watery discharge; trickling of water from r. nostril;* trickling from l. nostril, when lying on l. side; *with frequent sneezing, lachrymation, dim vision, redness and soreness of inner canthi, which feel swollen, later increase of secretions of nose, eyes, mouth and throat, with burning in these parts, without thirst* (compare Euphrasia).

Clinical.—Sang. nit. has been used quite extensively for polypus of the nose, chronic catarrh, with sneezing and burning, larnygitis, hoarseness, dry, hollow cough. Soreness behind the sternum, violent convulsive cough. Irritation at the bifurcation of the bronchi, with expectoration of blood-streaked mucus; also in general for catarrhal inflammation of mucous membranes, with great irritability of them. Rawness and soreness in posterior nares and hawking of thick yellow, sometimes bloody mucus.

Mouth.—Acrid burning on tongue. Tongue, palate, tonsils and pharynx feel sore, raw. Roughness of tongue; as if burnt; extending to fauces and tonsils and rising to posterior nares, with rawness and soreness; in M. and throat, with dryness and with constriction of throat. Burning. Taste bitter; and acrid; T. acrid, soon extending to pharynx and posterior nares; T. dry to everything, coffee did not taste natural.

Throat.—Red irritable spot. Uvula swollen and

elongated, palate and upper part of pharynx red, swollen, mucous follicles enlarged and bright red, the whole surface covered with white tenacious mucus. Pain in r. tonsil. Soreness of r. tonsil, with roughness and rawness, difficulty in swallowing, obstruction of Eustachian tube, difficulty in distinguishing sounds, roaring in r. ear. Burning in œsophagus and stomach.

Stomach and Abdomen.—Little appetite, wanted something succulent, not pungent, but soothing to mouth and throat, which felt hot, dry and raw. Eructations of putrid-smelling gases at 10 P.M., though she had eaten nothing since morning. Borborygmi, with colic as before diarrhœa; B. at night, with cutting in abdomen as if stool or flatus would be discharged.

Urinary Organs.—Micturition three times at night, urine high-colored, bright yellow sediment; M. nearly every hour at night, weighing twenty-eight ounces, and depositing a white sediment.

Respiratory Organs.—Air-passages feel as if lined with thick, stiff mucus or pus. *Burning in air-passages; in nostril, forehead, eyes, throat and bronchi, then trickling of watery mucus from nose, lachrymation, watery coryza, with burning pain in posterior nares and trachea, then tension, burning and mucus behind sternum, mucus in bronchia and throat.*

Cough short, hacking; harsh C., leaving soreness and rawness in throat and chest, with scraping rawness in pharynx; deep and rattling C., mucus came up easily. Expectoration of thin, frothy, tenacious mucus; easy E. of clear mucus, *becoming thick and yellow towards evening; of thick, yellow, sweet mucus; thick, yellow and greenish mucus.* Desire for fresh air.

Chest.—*Soreness. Pressure behind sternum, spreading to lungs and increasing the sense of suffocation. Tightness, > coughing up thick, yellow, sweet mucus, with fulness and soreness;* T. causing short, hacking cough. *Heat behind centre of sternum, with tension.*

Sleep.—*Restless; from feverishness and irritable condition. Poor, on* **account of pressure behind centre of sternum** *and soreness, with raw and rough feeling in r. side of throat.* Bad, from frequent desire to urinate and obstruction of nose and bronchi, *as soon as she moved she raised thick, yellow, sweetish mucus, this lasted all day, with apparent dryness of nose and throat.* Sleeplessness.

Fever.—Heat in forehead, > warm bathing.

Santoninum.

A solution is made with alcohol (1 to 99).

General Action.—A narcotic poison, producing unconsciousness, generally with convulsions, collapse, feeble respiration and pulse, free perspiration and sudden heart failure. The remarkable colored vision has been thought due to a coloring of the vitreous rather than to a specific action on the nerve fibres.

Generalities.—Trembled; and found it difficult to keep on my feet. Cramps. Convulsions; of limbs and face; beginning in face and extending to limbs, also affecting respiration, the irritation seemed to be in third to seventh nerves, pupils dilated; with unconsciousness, head hot, face purplish; unconsciousness, head hot, face bloated and violet, eyes rolling convulsively, pupils dilated and insensible, foam before mouth, jaws drawn together, snoring and convulsions of limbs; general, with unconsciousness, staring eyes, red, hot face, pupils dilated, < l., and insensible, pulse rapid, weak and irregular, limbs and face constantly convulsed; more like tetanus, throwing head back, eyes rolling, face distorted, body sometimes nearly curved, with legs turned back, in the intervals grasping at everything, gnawing of fingers; clonic, without warning, beginning at l. angle of mouth and spreading over l. side of face, then similar spasms in r. arm beginning in fingers, later in l. side of face and l. arm, leaving fibrillary twitching of l. angle of mouth and eyelid, two more convulsive attacks on the same evening, in one of which respiration threatened to stop though the heart was beating strongly and pulse was normal, two or three similar fits daily for the next four or five days; clonic, of side of face at 4 P.M., beginning with twitching and distortion of corner of mouth, and then going into l. orbital muscles, at first simultaneous twitching of both bulbi, the convulsion turning to the left, pupils dilated, < l., after a few minutes clonic C. of l. arm beginning in fingers and going up whole arm, voice quavering at beginning of fit, stopped after ten minutes, after fifteen minutes a second C. of l. side of face and arm, later only fibrillary twitchings at l. corner of mouth and l. eyelids, l. pupil dilated longer than r., then contraction of both and then normal state, after the fit complete euphonia, at 5.30 a similar attack, at 7 P.M. spasm began in l. side of face and l. arm, then l. leg, voice quavering and indistinct, eyes staring towards the left, with dilated pupils, voice gone, at 8 P.M. twitchings of abdominal and thoracic muscles, then r. side of face convulsed and eyeballs turned towards r., trismus, heart's action strong, stridor, artificial respiration, without it breathing was uncertain and at long intervals, spontaneous stool, then vomiting, then short clonic fits of r. leg, while spasms of l. leg was slighter, spasms repeated next day.

Malaise. Restlessness; as soon as the child lay down at night; with moaning, afterwards coma. Necessity to lie down. Weakness. Faint feeling. Collapse in morning. Partial paralysis of one side of the child, the hand appearing like induration of cellular tissue of the hand of an infant, the whole side blue, increasing till death. Amelioration in air and on motion.

Clinical.—It is said to have cured epilepsy.

Mind.—Delirium; during restless sleep. Excitement and inclination to laugh and dance. Hysterical laughter. Depression, with irresolution and lack of self-confidence, beginning with dulness and heaviness. Irritable, and restless, next day wanted everything, satisfied with nothing. Coma. Unconsciousness.

Head.—Turning and twisting, restless. Aching; in forehead. Dulness. Vertigo. Fulness in temples.

Eyes.—Surrounded by blue rings. Immovable and injected. Distorted. Rolled convulsively. Inclined to roll upward and have a sluggish motion. Pressure. Pupils dilated; and insensible; P. insensible. Pressure in supraorbital region.

Photophobia and lachrymation. Visions. Vision flickering. Objects seemed to totter and dance, and the child saw various figures, cherries, animals, etc. Vision yellow; to light-colored objects, afterwards light and dark objects became yellow-green and red seemed violet; yellowish to the gas flame, chandeliers, fire and all white objects strongly illuminated; and misty. V. green; of the blue sky in the twilight; bright; yellowish; yellowish, to the white glass-globes and writing paper. V. violet. Could not recognize violet. The fire had a curious red color and the light outside a peculiar yellow. Carmine red looked fallow, brick-red bronze, Berlin blue-greenish. Red and blue are seen in their complementary colors green and orange. Yellow egg-soup looked red and had a peculiar smell. The colors in some people's dresses were most vivid and shot up perpendicularly, and I had to quicken my pace to pass them.

Clinical.—Hyperæsthesia of the retina, then the sight becomes suddenly dim. Amblyopia. Retinal anæmia; after eating, the eyesight becomes suddenly dim, rubbing clears the eye for a few moments. After diphtheria, flashes of light, etc.

Ears and Nose.—Earache. Hallucinations of smell.

Face.—Pale; around mouth, < afternoon. L. cheek red; and r. white. Yellowish. Swollen and purple. Pinched about mouth and nose in morning, with drawing in of lips over teeth. Twitching; < lips and lids. Lips red and swollen.

Mouth.—Teeth clenched. Frothing. Tongue deep red; T. dry; T. stiff. Stomatitis ulcerosa. Apparently burning pain, as she forces everything into her mouth. Hallucinations of taste.

Throat.—Swelling of glands beginning nearly under centre of chin and spreading both ways, < towards l. parotid, increasing so as to nearly prevent swallowing.

Stomach. — Appetite deficient. Thirst; continual, for ice-water, which she swallowed greedily, in morning. Eructations. Nausea; > cold water, with deathly feeling and thirst. Vomiting; with profuse diarrhœa; with purging and abdominal pains; with pain in stomach and abdomen; with pain in epigastrium; with epigastric pressure, colic and diarrhœa, face sunken, bluish circles around eyes, body cold and covered with sweat; of yellowish, slimy mucus from 11 P.M. till forenoon. After a spoonful of nourishment he choked, vomited blood and pus and died without a struggle. Pain in pit.

Abdomen.—Tympanitic. Swollen, but soft. Rumbling. Commotion, waking him at midnight, with general sick feeling and desire for stool, stool with urging. Pain; every night before stool. Sensitive. Hot, full.

Stool.—Tenesmus. Watery, flaky, offensive, every ten to fifteen minutes, diminishing at 10 A.M., then only three till after noon, but copious, grayish and smelling putrid.

Urinary Organs.—Urging, and during micturition irritation and smarting, urine saffron-yellow, staining like bile, scanty, sp. gr. 1028, urea increased. Frequent micturition; efforts at, but *only a few drops each time.* Ischuria. *Dysuria.* Painful micturition on account of burning in urethra, with constant desire, only a few drops staining intensely yellow. M. involuntary and copious towards morning; *involuntary, by drops,* urine deep orange-colored, becoming blood-red by admixture of azotic acid.

Urine. — Pale, copious, alkaline. Yellowish and scanty. Intensely yellow. Dark. Orange-colored. Saffron-colored and increased. Dark lemon-yellow, scanty, depositing dark yellow crystals of uric acid, nitric acid caused transient brownish-red color, alkalies caused an amaranth red color. Sulphur-yellow, thick, depositing a sulphur-yellow sediment, the urine above which was slightly greenish. Pinkish-red after standing. Turbid when voided, frequent and painful desire, urine scanty, dysury. *Greenish;* yellowish-green; light green and stained linen so that it could not be washed out; greenish-yellow, liquor ammonia caused a clear, red tint; green, becoming transiently purplish from nitric acid, but when sulphuric acid is added by drops it becomes reddish-brown, if a globule of potassium be dropped on the urine a bright red track is left, if a few drops of liquor ammonia are poured down the side of the test tube a red zone will mark the junction of the two liquids, but potash is a more delicate reagent, the red alkaline fluid is not altered by boiling, but the color is destroyed by any acid, the subsequent addition of an alkali restores the color as before, bicarbonate of sodium causes no immediate change, but on boiling some time the reddish tint gradually develops and is discharged by continued boiling, carbonate of sodium gives similar results, except that it requires longer boiling before the color is discharged, phosphate of sodium gives no results, the red stratum soon subsides to lower part of test tube, carried down by the phosphates, prolonged exposure to light in contact with excess of alkali bleaches the color and chlorine at once dissipates it, when the red liquid is examined with the spectroscope the red, orange and yellow rays are transmitted, while the blue end is absorbed, in a more dilute state the red and blue rays are transmitted. Cherry-red when caustic potash is added, but no sugar is obtained with the copper test. A pint was treated with neutral acetate of lead and then filtered, to the filtrate, neutralized with potash, basic acetate of lead was added as long as any precipitate was formed and it became colorless, neutralized, filtered and washed, the yellow precipitate was transferred to a beaker and decomposed by dilute sulphuric acid, spirit of wine was added, and after twenty-four hours filtered, removed excess of sulphuric acid by barytic water, filtered, the clear fluid now gave the pink reaction with potash, but ammonia had no effect, the red alkaline filtrate gave a bulky precipitate with alum, and when this precipitate was filtered off neither the precipitate nor the filtrate afforded any color with potash, the liberated coloring substance did not combine with nitrate of silver, was not affected by corrosive sublimate, sulphocyanide of potassium, chloride of gold or bichromate of potassium, with persalts of iron it gave a rich, brown color.

Clinical.—Chronic inflammation of the bladder, with incontinence of urine, or dysuria, emission of only few drops at a time, urine has a peculiar green color.

Respiratory Organs.—Cough all night from tickling in larynx and windpipe. Respiration stertorous and broken; R. embarrassed; rattling; rapid and sighing; rapid and catching; rapid, afterwards irregular and stertorous; light and at long intervals, and there was no desire to respire. Snoring. Symptoms of paralysis of lungs.

Pulse.—Rapid; and feeble; but easily compressed. Slow and small, also soft. Lowered. Gone on l. side, thready and soft in r. radial artery.

Extremities.—Flaccid. Spasms. Jerking of upper; of fingers; of hands and feet. Trembling. Gait tottering.

Skin. — Blue. Subicteric color. Urticaria, with œdema of skin of nose, lips and lids; U. over greater part of body, with vomiting, after second dose a white wheal on nose, surrounded by an erythematous blush, and similar eruption rapidly covered the body, lips greatly swollen and viscid saliva issuing from them, eyes almost closed from swelling of lids, œdema and rash, > a warm bath.

Sleep.—Sleepy; and tired. Grating of teeth in sleep. Sleep restless. Disturbed, and I awoke unrefreshed, with sickness, frontal headache and deficient appetite. Troubled dreams.

Fever.—Coldness; with blue lips and ears and white face; cool skin, < limbs; cold feet; feet and legs; limbs in morning, the clammy coldness creeping upward during the day. Fever all the afternoon; F., with rapid pulse, skin hot, face puffy, eyes red, brilliant, fixed. Hot head; < every afternoon and evening. Hot sweat on occiput, more clammy in front. Cold sweat; and viscous.

Sarsaparilla.

A tincture is made of the dried root of the Smilax officinalis, H. and B. (from Honduras).

Generalities.—Trembling of whole body, with anxiety; T. of hands and feet in forenoon, with tearing in forehead and pinching in abdomen. Mobility of whole body, hands and feet feel very light. Racking effects. Stinging now in head, now in r. ear, now in l.; in forehead and l. side of chest, mornings on walking out-doors. Lightning-like tensive pains here and there in body and about head. Sensation in all bones as if breaking. Drawing pain in scapulæ and legs. Pain partially waking her at night without knowing where, but in morning she thought it must have been in abdomen (the day before menstruation). Feeling of strength. No exertion seemed to tire. *Weakness;* in forenoon, > a meal; < thighs, knees and feet, also during menses; with torpor, which induced him to lie on the ground, with unwillingness to move. *Faintness in evening during stool.* Aggravation from vinegar. Amelioration out of doors; A. from smelling camphor.

Clinical.—Bone-pains following gonorrhœa, or after the use of mercury, < dampness. Marasmus, with sore mouth, white sand in the urine, emaciation and shrivelled skin.

Mind.—*Cheerful.* Lively and happy. Merry; all day, and full of fun. Changeable mood. Ill humor; all day, > evening; in morning, with heaviness of head; in forenoon, with inclination to weep; in afternoon; with disposition to work; with indisposition to work and heat in face; without disinclination to work. Easily vexed and cannot forget the cause of the vexation. Silent moroseness. Aversion to everything in forenoon. Inclination to work in afternoon. Anxiety, with fear and palpitation; A., with constriction in throat; A. in head in forenoon, then in whole body, with trembling, < feet. Sadness; on account of pains, with moans; with sluggishness; and absorbed in himself. Thinks that she cannot bear the headache. Inactive and awkward. Absent-minded. Inaptitude for mental application. Stupor, with weakness of head.

Head.—Sticking so that he shudders. Pain like lightning. Tearing here and there, < motion and walking; T. deep in brain on talking and walking. Hammering pain evenings, < night, with nausea and sour vomiting. Pain; < touching or walking; with unconsciousness and inability to speak; with blackness before eyes; with flickering before eyes; with cough; or lightness; slowly increasing and decreasing, < upper part; as if screwed together at 2 P.M.; externally, like compressions and incisions. Throbbing till towards noon. Tingling as if a large bell had been struck, towards noon. *Heaviness* at 11 A.M., with stupidity, sometimes as if temples would be compressed together; H. < moving it, with tension in r. side of neck; with inclination to sink forward; with toothache. Dulness in forenoon, with stupidity; D. after sitting long, with mist before eyes, lassitude of limbs, stoppage of nose and gloomy mood; D. > towards evening; with flatulency. Weakness as after a fever, with stupor. Waving sensation at 2 P.M., with dull tremor. Vertigo frequently in forenoon; V. on gazing long at an object; when sitting and walking, with inclination of head to drop forward; when standing at a window he fell back unconscious, with swelling of throat, sour eructations before and afterwards, with pressure upon chest, and at night sweat; with unsteady gait; with general heat as from close air (on a cold, rainy day).

Forehead.—Sticking in middle; in l. side; on l. protuberance; in forenoon, > open air; in r. protuberance at 7 P.M.; in l. protuberance in evening; in r. protuberance, with pain; pulsating. Tearing; at 6.30 P.M. *Pain in l. side;* P. in forenoon and after dinner, with heaviness; and in occiput; in l. protuberance, then stinging. Throbbing in r. side on walking in open air. Heaviness.

Temples.—Sticking in r. at 1 P.M.; S. < touch; from r. to lower teeth at 2 P.M.; at root of r. mastoid process, > touch; burning, on l. bone. Stinging drawing from r. mastoid process to l. frontal protuberance. Drawing pressure on r. bone and on cartilage of ear. Heaviness in l.; in l. till noon; H., with desire to lie down.

Vertex.—Sticking on r. side, with pressing; tearing S. on l. bone.

Sides.—*Sticking;* in l. in morning, with *pressing;* from l. to nape; tearing, in r., so that he shudders. Stinging drawing on r. parietal and temporal bones. Pressure-like tearing in l. Pain in l., < temple; deep in r. half in morning, with itching; cramplike, in one, beginning with flickering and blackness before eyes, he seems unconscious, must lie down and cannot speak, because every word reverberates in his head. Sensation as if screwed together after breakfast. Throbbing deep in r. side of brain; in forenoon, with sounding.

Occiput.—Twitching on l. side. Stinging in l. side; drawing S. towards forehead, with pressure in r. temple.

Scalp.—Sensitiveness to touch, with falling out of hair. Itching of r. half; on posterior part; > scratching; not > scratching; pricking.

Clinical.—Nervous headaches in the occiput, extending to the eyes, syphilitic or mercurial. Shooting headache from left ear to root of the nose; base of the nose and eyes swollen. Neuralgic headaches of r. side, pulsative and stitching, starting from the occiput.

Eyes.—Stinging on closing them; and pain when the closed lids are pressed upon, *with a red stripe from cornea to outer canthus,* the inner corners blue and are swollen. Sensation as from sand, > open air; as from sand in l. Pain on looking at anything in the daylight; P. on reading by candle-light, paper looks red; in l., then r., with dim vision; alternating with burning. Affected by all objects in morning. Lachrymation every other day; L. when gaping. Pupils dilated. Pressing in ball in evening when reading by candlelight, with red shine on paper. Lids inflamed and dry; quivering of r. upper; agglutination in morning and lachrymation in daytime; then agglutination in morning on waking, with burning; burning, sometimes alternating with pain. Vision dim; in l. eye in afternoon.

Ears.—Swelling of a gland under r., with inflammation and suppuration. Sticking deep in r. in forenoon; beneath and in front of l. in morning. Tearing in cartilage and external meatus of r.; in r. mornings; upward behind l. in afternoon. Ulcerative pain deep in l. in morning, and around anterior part. Constriction about r. external; in r. Compression up into temple, with pressure. Drawing in lobule of l., with twitching, later in either r. or l. Itching in l. external meatus at 6 A.M., not > scratching. Ringing in l. Tolling of bells in l. in afternoon.

Nose.—Eruption in l. nostril. Pricking in tip. Burning on blowing it; with dry cough. Stoppage in forenoon; of r. nostril on waking. Sneezing in morning after rising; only in morning, with fluent coryza; fails in the attempt to sneeze. Coryza, < r. side; C., with cough; with nausea, prostration, necessity to lie down, inability to move, pulse retarded; stopped. Thick mucus. Bleeding; from r. nostril; from l. nostril on blowing nose; each time she vomits; with feeling as if small bubbles burst in nose; light-colored, from r. nostril in evening on blowing nose.

Face.—Bruised pain about inferior orbital margins in morning on pressure, when waking. Stinging on lower inner edge of r. lower jaw on touch and on bending head back. Drawing stinging, tearing in r. masseter muscles, which are spasmodically contracted. Pain as if jaws would break. Tension in masseter muscles and joints of jaws in forenoon on motion, with stiffness. Limpid vesicle on r. side of lower lip. Tetter on upper lip, with sticking. Twitching of r. side of upper lip.

Mouth.—Teeth. Stinging in forenoon in one that had been painful for a long time. Tearing from a draught of cold air or cold drink. Aching evenings; A. in molars of l. side and one of r.; in r. in evening, > picking till they bled, with crawling, tingling in roots; drawing, in r. lower from 4 A.M. till evening, with heaviness of head, < r. side. Sensitiveness of r. upper when biting on them.

Gums.—Swelling inside lower, with sore pain. Tearing in r. lower in evening; stinging, in gum and root of last r. lower molar. Pain in l. lower in afternoon on smoking tobacco.

Aphthæ on tongue and palate. Tongue coated whitish in morning; sticking in T.; roughness mornings on waking, > eating. Mouth slimy in morning. Drawing pain in soft palate. Mouth and throat dry mornings in bed; mouth, in forenoon, without thirst. Salivation; in forenoon till 1 P.M. Offensive breath.

Taste.—*Bitter in morning* after rising; on upper lip mornings; to rye bread. Sweetish, like liquorice; insipid, S.; S. when smoking tobacco. Herbaceous; nauseous. Metallic. Fishy, disagreeable, on waking. Sour, slimy in fauces mornings, like sour dough.

Throat.—Mucus tasting like blood; M. all day, which she could not detach nor swallow; tough, mornings, which cannot be removed by hawking. Constant hawking of mucus in morning. Stinging extending out at ear. Pain in r. side as from a spelt of barley, extending out at ear, > afternoon after lying down. Pain on swallowing, rawness of larynx, a pressing moving about in larynx, with cough at night and in morning, with colorless, tasteless expectoration, the pain in larynx < coughing. Constriction posteriorly; in T. and chest frequently during the day, with difficult breathing; spasmodic; with irritation. Tickling ulcerative sensation in fauces, causing cough. Roughness mornings during cough; in morning on waking, with hoarseness and dryness; exciting cough. Irritation posteriorly. Dryness in morning, with stinging on swallowing. Spasmodic urging or straining all night and frequent vomiting. Burning in œsophagus in morning.

Stomach.—Appetite increased; for dinner. Appetite lost; for breakfast; and he ate but little at noon; and food had not enough flavor, and after a meal it seemed as if he had eaten nothing, or as if stomach were without sensation; for smoking tobacco, the taste of which is changed; (for everything except juicy fruit). Thirst all day, with warmth; T. often during the day; for water at 2 P.M., after chill before dinner. Absence of thirst; during meals.

Eructations in forenoon, with shuddering and goose-flesh; imperfect E.; hiccoughing; empty, in forenoon and evening; tasting of blood after dinner. Sour eructations; after breakfast; of water in afternoon. Bitter eructations during dinner; in morning after rising, with bitter taste; of water before and after dinner; of "wasser soup" after drinking cold water; and sour, then empty; of bitter, sour matter evenings. Hiccough at 6 P.M.; after dinner.

Nausea in morning when gazing long at an object, with vertigo; N. mornings increased to vomiting, with increased herbaceous taste; all the forenoon, with ineffectual inclination to vomit; in afternoon, without inclination to vomit; after breakfast; after breakfast, with sour eructations, and when standing by an open window vertigo, unconsciousness, falling backward to the floor, afterwards tension across chest; after dinner, with exhaustion; at the thought of food eaten; in throat from rising of a nauseous vapor into mouth, with affection of head; > night, with constriction of stomach; with headache; with acrid sensation on tongue and in swallow. Retching. Vomiting; sour.

Distention after eating a little. Griping in pit extending towards sacrum; during menses. Spasmodic twisting; after dinner, with ineffectual inclination to eructate. Spasmodic sensation in pit. Pain in pit in evening when singing; P., then vomiting of breakfast; in epigastrium and under ensiform cartilage, < touch; in region, with soft stool. Heaviness and indigestion. Weak feeling. Burning; after a mouthful of bread, as after spirituous drinks.

Abdomen.—Distention; after eating or drinking. *Rumbling;* after eating, with pinching, later passing up l. side towards stomach, > doubling up; *with emptiness;* with emptiness and clucking; with growling. Loud quacking, as in spasms, > eructations. Rolling; from 5 P.M. till midnight, with pinching, preventing sleep; during diarrhœa, with fermentation and offensive flatus. Motion, with coldness; M., with burning; all day, as before diarrhœa. Emission of flatus; all day; offensive; offensive, evenings.

Stinging an hour after dinner, and under r. ribs.

Cutting at 5 P.M., then semi-fluid stool; C. waking him after midnight, > morning; with scanty stool; with consistent stool. Griping during menses. Pinching; during menses; then painful contraction of sphincter ani. Pain in morning; at 10 A.M. on pressure; with frequent diarrhœa. Constriction; in forenoon, then rumbling and grumbling, now around umbilicus, now towards chest, now downward, as before diarrhœa. Pressing drawing as after cold. Spasmodic sensations. Emptiness after breakfast, with feeling as if disembowelled. Feeling of inactivity. Internal chilliness. Burning.

Stinging in l. hypochondrium in forenoon, < bending towards r. Pain in hepatic region in morning on waking, > walking. Bruised pain in l. hypochondrium at 1 P.M., with throbbing. Stinging in l. side; now r., now l.; in l. in morning when sitting, > walking. Cutting in l. side on a line transversely towards back, then rolling in abdomen. Pain in l. Pressure inward in a spot in l., < deep inspiration, with pinching.

Cutting in a spot above umbilicus in morning; around U. in forenoon, then movements in abdomen, > emission of flatus; around U. on gaping. Moving in hypogastrium all day, as after a purgative. Pinching in l. groin. Straining constriction in hypogastrium in evening and forenoon, > passage of flatus. Tension in r. groin. Soreness in r. groin before menses, so that she can hardly walk; S. in bend of r. groin on appearance of menses, with urging to urinate.

Rectum.—Cutting and tearing. Acridity during diarrhœa. Urging during stool, with straining; U., then stool, scanty, soft, difficult from contraction of rectum; with contraction of intestines and pressure as if contents of abdomen would be pressed out, at last something passes with a jerk, with tearing and cutting in rectum, then immediate U. as if rectum would be pressed out; frequent, with scanty discharges and then tenesmus; ineffectual.

Anus.—Ulcer bearing a black pustule, opening with pain. Soreness waking him at night, then changing to burning itching, lasting all day. Burning after fluid stools. Itching on r. side, > scratching. Tenesmus after stool; after soft stool.

Stool.—Fluid evenings, then burning in anus; semi-fluid towards the end. Diarrhœa twice. Soft; and copious. *Hard;* and frequent micturition; at first, then soft; first part, last soft, then burning in anus. *Constipation.* Consistent, twice in one day. Pitchy, sticky. Hurried before breakfast. S. and micturition delayed; and infrequent, scanty.

Clinical.—Obstinate constipation, with violent urging to urinate, pressure as if the bowels would be pressed out.

Urinary Organs.—Constriction of bladder without urging. Urging nearly all day, but scanty urine; U. waking him every morning; on appearance of menses; > perfect discharge of menses; *frequent, with scanty discharge and burning.* Strangury, with pressure in bladder, yet urine will not come, and when it comes cutting; S., as in case of stone, with discharge of mucus and of white, acrid, turbid matter. Micturition without sensation in the passage; M. frequently stops, scanty, with straining and burning; in a thin, weak stream, also urine pale, with flakes in it; but once during the day, with burning during the discharge, but in sufficient quantity; omitted in forenoon, then three times in afternoon and pale, then again omitted. Wakes at night to urinate. Frequent micturition; and copious; *and copious, urine pale; copious, two or three times at night,* at first with burning; copious, pale, growing turbid on standing, like clay-water; and urine deposits a cloud.

Urethra.—Discharge of yellow pus, with redness and inflammation of glans and fever in evening, with rigors. Cutting. Scraping during micturition. *Burning during micturition;* with copious watery urine; with discharge of elongated flakes.

Urine.—Copious; in morning; during menstruation. *Scanty and turbid like clay-water as soon as it is passed;* S. and red mornings; and red, clear, with urging; with straining. *Urine passed towards the end is mingled with blood, then with blood* and pus, *then the pain when urinating abates.* Fiery, but without burning. Deep yellow, depositing a thin cloud. Turbid when passed, with burning; T. on standing, with much clay-colored sediment. Iridescent pellicle. (Compare with Chimaphila.)

Clinical.—Inflammation of the bladder, bloody urine, characterized by pain in neck of the bladder at close of micturition and chill running up the back from the bladder. Excess of gravel in the urine, especially in children. Fermentation in the bladder, as shown by the discharge of gas with urine.

Sexual Organs.—Intolerable odor. Glans red and inflamed. Tearing from glans to root of penis; after micturition, with burning and itching. Erections diminished. *Herpes on prepuce.* Itching on scrotum and perineum, and after scratching pimples oozing moisture. *Emissions at night;* with restless sleep; frequent E. several days, with inclination for coition; painful, nearly every night, with lascivious dreams. Inclination to coitus, with restless sleep. Slimy leucorrhœa when walking. Menses too early; too late; scanty, intermittent, acrid, with burning in inner part of thighs, so that she cannot approximate them on account of pain.

Clinical.—Swelling of the spermatic cord, with soreness, especially following sexual excitement. Nocturnal emissions followed by backache, dim vision, etc. Has been found useful in some conditions of secondary syphilis. Dysmenorrhœa characterized by retracted nipples.

Respiratory Organs.—Sticking in thyroid cartilage. Hoarse; every other day. Cough in forenoon, without expectoration; C., with nausea, vomiting of bile and diarrhœa; hard, in daytime, from tickling ulcerative sensation in fauces; dry, in forenoon, from roughness in throat; dry, with burning in nose on blowing it. Asthma, he is often forced to breathe short. Short breath; from slightest exertion; after dinner, and heavy; with pressure on chest. Difficult breathing; when working. Frequent deep inspiration after dinner. Stoppage of breath in evening and morning, with oppression of chest; S. as by an impediment in lungs or a spasm, with constriction in throat and anxiety.

Chest.—Nipples soft, insensible and not irritable. Stinging under last true ribs; in middle of sternum in morning; in r. breast at 1 P.M.; in r. side in afternoon on motion while standing; in r. side at 8.30 P.M., with tearing on upper surface of l. upper arm extending to wrist; in l. costal region, doubling him up in evening when sitting; in l. side when walking; in r. side, not affecting respiration; in middle, beside sternum, not affecting respiration; drawing, from r. clavicle into hyoid bone.

Pain; at night and in morning, with tightness; in centre, with inclination to keep still in order to relieve it; tensive, externally, as if too short, on straightening up and walking erect. Tension about clavicle next to sternum. Constriction alternating with sudden expansion. Intermittent sensation as if screwed together when breathing and walking, so that he must loosen his clothes. Tightness, with dyspnœa and exhaustion so that he must loosen his necktie. Oppression mornings, impeding respiration. Pressure at 11 A.M., with tearing from l. shoulder to tips of fingers; P. in afternoon; on sternum, worse during palpitation. Heat.

Heart and Pulse.—Palpitation; during the day. Pulse febrile. Pulse slow.

Neck.—Swelling of r. side of N. and throat, with pain on touch. Sticking in muscles, < touch and motion. Tearing in nape passing thence across vertex towards r. side of forehead in afternoon. Pain in nape in morning on moving head; wrenching, in a tendon in l. side on moving head. Tension in nape on moving head, with stitches. Chuckling in l. side, or else pulling.

Back.—Pain as if something were sticking fast to it on deep inspiration. Sticking between scapulæ; from r. scapula down beside spine to last rib, < inspiration, with tearing, and on deep inspiration arrest of breath. Drawing in scapulæ. Stinging under l. ribs, in lumbar region. Pain in lower part of back and sides; in lower part in forenoon on stooping and afterwards; *in lower part, passing around sides of pelvis towards genitals, < night and motion;* in lumbar region, < protracted stooping, so that walking is impeded, > rest when sitting or lying, reappearing as stitches on slighest turning of body, > afternoon. Bruised pain in sacral region evenings. Tensive pain from sacrum across l. hip on least motion, interfering with walking.

Extremities. — Mobility. Tearing at night, then headache; T. now here, now there, in all joints of body. Weakness.

Upper Extremities.—Shoulder. Cracking in r. joint on moving it. Stitches on raising arm. Tearing from r. joint to wrist in afternoon; from joints into elbows; intermittent, from l. into fingers in afternoon. Pain as from a thrust or blow on moving arm, > rest; in r. joint as from a thrust or blow on moving arm. Pain in r. joint, somewhat laming, in afternoon on moving arms, till lying down.

Stiffness of arms on motion after rest. Stinging above and in front of humerus; pulsating S. in arms near shoulder-joints. Pain in elbow as if tendon had snapped from place, on rapid pronation of forearm. Paralytic weakness of elbows. Twitching of forearms. Sticking in muscles of ulnæ; tearing S. upward above l. wrist; stinging-drawing, on inside of r. forearm. Tearing on ulna, sometimes extending to metacarpal bones; T. across above wrist, with drawing-tearing stitches towards fingers; paralytic, in forearms near elbows, < rest. Tearing in l. wrist at 2 P.M. Sprained pain in r. wrist, drawing towards ring finger. Hands tremble. Intermittent sticking in metacarpal bone of r. index. Pain in hands. Stiffness of hands, > motion, with itching, burning, and swollen veins.

Fingers.—Inflammation of thumb, < night, with throbbing and burning. Sticking in first joint of r. little; in muscles of l. thumb; in first joint of thumb, later pain on touch. Tearing on backs of l. towards tips at 1.30 P.M.; drawing, through bones of r. ring, < motion. Cutting under one thumb-nail at 7 A.M., then under the other. *Pain in tips on pressure, as from ulceration or as from salt in a wound.* Numbness (going to sleep); N., < third and fourth.

Lower Extremities.—Lassitude.

Thigh.—Stinging on r. ischium; near l. patella; in l. popliteal space, then tearing. Tearing upward and outward near knee. Pressure on inside near l. knee; on r. above popliteal space when sitting. Hip-joints lame, bruised and tired. *Weariness* during menses. Heaviness in l. when sitting and walking. Stiffness in r., as if contracted, in popliteal space and calf, with swollen feeling under toe-nails.

Knee.—Swelling, with stiffness and stinging, so that he could hardly move it sideways. Sticking on inner side; S. about r. Tearing in l. at 2 P.M.; in r. when gaping while standing; intermittent, about l. from evening till midnight. Weariness all day.

Cramp in calf; at night; from tibia down into toes, has to try to find an easier position. Tearing in muscles of r. leg; T. down r. tibia at 1 P.M.; deep in l. tibia at 3 P.M. Pain in calves as after cramp. Drawing upward above r. tibia. Legs weak; in forenoon; during menses. Cracking in l. ankle on every motion.

Foot.—Swelling; of r. tarsus, < afternoon, with redness and pain. Tearing in l. sole from heel towards toes after midnight, then itching, and after scratching sticking through heel into dorsum of foot. Sole sensitive. Drawing in sole, with itching; painful D. on dorsum of r. foot changed into twitching. Painful throbbing on inside of r. sole when sitting, with pressing and pricking, then on whole sole. Tensive feeling in tendons and toes of l., as if toes were drawn inward, in morning; T. feeling in r., as if swollen. Swollen feeling, > exercise, with itching and heat in soles. Tired when standing.

Toes.—Tearing in l. great, more towards tips, evenings; T. in r. great, with drawing. Aching about nails as if swollen.

Skin.—Warts. Red, rough elevations on forehead. Itching eruptions under nose. Tetters on all parts; on hands. Red herpetic spots on calves, with itching. Nettle-rash on neck, chest, eyelids, hands and whole body, with burning after rubbing. Eruption itching, burning and moist after rubbing, three days before menses. Inflammation like a run-around, around nail of r. index, then on l.

Pimples on face; fingers; rashlike, on going into cold air from a warm room; red, on r. knee, with itching at first; red, on back and thighs, with corroding itching in warmth, > scratching; itching, on chin; itching P. and pustules on sides of chin; itching, on cheek, inflamed far around, with burning, ending in a thick scab and causing tearing burning pain in open air.

Cracks on r. thumb, with burning pain. Herpes phlyctenodes on l. side of neck in one case, in two others irregular patches on face and l. arm, with pustules on hand wherever skin was abraded. Pustule in middle of forehead; on face; r. side of nose; dorsum of r. foot; r. side of nose, r. dorsal side of foot, l. gluteal region, sometimes with stinging on touch; itching; P. which have been scratched open leave ulcers suppurating for a long time. Ulcerations running around ends of fingers. Boil on l. buttock, stinging on touch; B. or pimples on face, < cheeks. Itching blister under chin. Clear vesicle on inside of r. wrist, behind little finger, itching, then burning, after opening the V. discharge of watery fluid, increased burning, inflammation and a scab, itching < night.

Scab on lobule of ear, with burning pain, then itching. Thick, dirty, yellowish-brown crusts, with inflamed areola and suppurating border, beneath labial commissure, extending towards mesial line of chin, afterwards the patches united and covered chin, with occasional pustules around the borders, with patches and pustules on l. hip, extending from anterior superior spine upward and backward towards lumbar region, the crusts were removed by the clothing and the eruption appeared like herpes zoster, a new crop began by small pustules on an inflamed base, later the eruption covered cheeks, with pustules on nose, forehead and neck, and the patch on hip extended to spine, with itching, disturbing sleep.

Pricking in calves; over r. external malleolus; outward, < about neck, with heat on chest, back and face. Formication in sacral region in forenoon; on l. foot at 5 P.M. on raising it and putting it down.

Itching, now here, now there; I. on l. side of nose and around eyes; about nipples; on hand and back of fingers; on outer edge of r. foot in evening, he has to scratch the ankle till it bleeds; at night, preventing sleep; towards hand and on inside above hollow of knee, < evenings in bed; every night, > in bed. I. < scratching, before and after lying down; here and there, < evening before and after lying down. I. > scratching, in r. flank; on hips in forenoon; on abdomen in evening; I. on top of r. foot in afternoon, after scratching it appears on l. tibia, > scratching. I. not > scratching, here and there; on face; in l. ear; on r. wing of nose; around umbilicus; on r. hip; under knees, and in front above them; in front of wrist in forenoon; on back in afternoon. I. returning after scratching; on forehead; above l. knee afternoons; on r. buttock evenings. I., with vesicles, or with pimples after scratching. I. on chin, then small pimples; I. on r. calf in evening, then pimples; on tendon below calves in evening and morning, and burning after scratching; on thighs, and after scratching pimples; on inside of r. forearm, and after scratching vesicles; in hollows of knees afternoons and mornings, after scratching little vesicles; on outside and front of l. thigh in afternoon, after scratching little vesicles. Burning I. on abdomen, over thighs; over whole body, with rigors. Pricking I. from 5 till 7 P.M. over whole body, and in morning on rising; in face and scalp, about neck and shoulders, with warmth in these parts, on scratching it begins in another place.

Clinical.—Eruptions like roseola, with itching. Moist eruptions, with excoriating discharge. Eruptions during hot weather becoming ulcers. Syphilitic eruptions.

Sleep.—Gaping; in forenoon, with crawling. Sleepiness; in forenoon, with sluggishness; with internal chill. Falls asleep in evening, with starting; and with dreams of falling, slipping, etc. Finds himself lying on his back on waking at night and in morning. Sleepless almost all night; before midnight from restlessness in body and soul, and mobility in limbs; for a long time after 2 A.M. Little sleep, with starting up. Starting up in fright five times in one night, with difficulty in falling asleep again; started up hurriedly, scratched above her knee unconsciously and then slept again immediately. Sleep restless; with dreams of disaster; with inclination to coitus, emissions and twitching in forearms; and unrefreshing. Sleep interrupted. Waking as if frightened by a sound.

Dream of relatives long dead. D. towards morning that white spectres come into his room and near his bed, he was frightened at first, but he struck them down with both fists, after which his nose bled and he woke, and he thought he had struck himself on his nose. Horrible, in a deep sleep; horrible, for instance, of a big soldier. Heavy, frightful, unremembered. Of vexation. That she was sleigh-riding, the sleigh upset, she started and woke. Of the business of the day before. Of what was talked about the day before. Lascivious without erections; but waking him.

Fever.—Chilliness; frequently during the day, with blue nails; in morning in bed; in forenoon; *in forenoon*, then till evening warmth and sweat; in evening; in evening on lying down, > in bed; in evening, with fever; at night, on waking; at night, waking her frequently; at night, in bed, with cold feet and heat in face and chest; from below upward over whole body; running over her in forenoon; running over her on going into open air; internal, with sleepiness. Shaking chill at night; before dinner, > "wasser soup," with chattering of teeth; without external coldness; with gaping, internal coldness and external heat, or both mixed, thirst, cough and vomiting. Cold hands, < towards tips of fingers; on arms, thighs, back and inside abdomen.

Heat; all day, with thirst; at 10 A.M.; after breakfast; *in evening, with* mirth and *feeling of strength; in evening in bed*, an hour before sleep, blood boils, heart beats and sweat stands on forehead. Heat in face; and scalp, neck, shoulders, with prickling; and chest and back, with frontal sweat and with pricking outward, < about neck. Heat in head during dinner, with sweat on forehead. Sweat; at night; *on forehead;* on hands; on forehead in evening in bed; on joints at night on waking.

Secale Cornutum.

A tincture is made of the fresh fungus, ergot of rye.

General Effects.—The chief interest in the action of ergot centres about its power to produce tonic contractions of involuntary muscle fibre; the arterioles are violently and persistently contracted, causing dry coldness of the surface and even gangrene of the lower extremities; the peristaltic muscles of the bowels are affected and the gravid uterus contracts violently. Convulsions are liable to occur. Anæsthesia and paralysis result, particularly tremblings and paraplegia.

Allies.—Tabac., Ars., Phos., *Ustil.*, Carbo v., Sabin., Verat. a., Plumb.

Generalities.—Emaciation. Consumption. Secretions diminished. Gangrene of stomach, lungs and liver, preceded by inflammation. *Unsteadiness of whole body. Trembling;* from every effort, even stretching out of tongue. Painful stretching. Irregular movements, < limbs. Voluntary muscles responded irregularly, with occasional spasms of limbs and back. *Cramps in legs, arms and chest.* Tetanic cramps; with stiffness of limbs, so that she often fell when walking. Tetanic contractions of face and limbs, > hot baths.

Twitchings; of limbs and face; under skin; here and there, similar to epileptic ones, then contractions of flexors, fingers strongly bent into palms, pulse small, not frequent, irregular. Twitching tremulous sensation in single muscular fibres and in whole muscles, in face and hands.

Convulsions; from excitement, then weakness and sopor; at every excitement, < forenoon, then weakness, sometimes stiffness of joints, the patient > rubbing and stretching limbs; < night, gradually > towards noon, with sweat from anxiety; of all *extensors,* and puerperal convulsions; with cold sweat; without previous unpleasant symptoms; sudden vertigo and blindness, entire or partial unconsciousness, falling to the ground, contractions of joints, twitching of limbs, trembling, ineffectual retching, elbows pressed against chest, wrists flexed, fingers doubled into hands, heels drawn upward, toes bent under soles; ending in sweat; then tetanus; then distortion of limbs, dilated pupils, unconsciousness, delirium, weakness of mind or insensibility, in which they kept to themselves, stared at any one who spoke to them, answered nothing, others felt paralyzed, were unable to stand or walk; then insensibility and paralysis of parts affected; then insensibility, fingers and hands numb and lips pale; then anæsthesia, loss of sight and hearing and coma; periodic; *tonic;* clonic, with pain, preceded by crawling, becoming tonic, then tetanic; often changed from clonic to tonic, even to tetanus and trismus; clonic, that in some parts changed to tonic or alternated with them. *Epileptiform spasms;* in children; with unconsciousness; at intervals of about a month, during which she lost her memory, became foolish and spoke with difficulty. *Epilepsy;* especially in children; then gradual idiocy. Opisthotonos; with tonic contractions of muscles, anxiety and loud cries. Emprosthotonos.

Wandering sticking tearing. Gnawing boring in flesh, < night, preventing sleep. **Pain, < heat applied to any part** (Sabin., Carb. v.), *and if on a cold day any additional covering was laid upon him while asleep he woke almost instantly and threw it off, in the coldest weather he lay in bed with only an old cloak over him;* P. over whole body, < back and small of back; in every nerve, with emptiness in head, then swelling of palpebræ, lips and fauces, lachrymation, coryza, difficult breathing through nose and injection of conjunctiva, lips and palpebræ livid, power of deglutition nearly lost, voice feeble, jaws fixed and difficulty in answering; sudden P., so that he cried aloud and ran about as if mad; periodical; every ten or twenty minutes, with contractions of limbs.

Drawing and crawling changing sometimes rapidly, sometimes slowly into pains and spasms, limbs flexed and skin covered with sweat. Soreness all over body, could not lie with ease and could not be moved without taking hold of her hands. Tingling all over body in morning on waking, sometimes painful. Discomfort. **Restlessness;** with wailing or screams. Typhoid symptoms. Indolence; then stupefaction, coldness and insensibility of limbs, then gangrene.

Debility; all day; after sleep; from moving or speaking; on walking across the room, with vertigo; with depressed temperature; with slow, feeble pulse; with numbness and occasional insensibility of limbs; with inability to move lower limbs and but little control over upper; *then limbs painful, cold, rigid, almost insensible, with internal pain,* < **heat, somewhat > cool air,** *the pain gradually extended from toes to legs and thighs and from fingers to arms and shoulders, till sphacelus supervened, the affected parts dead, black and dropped off.* Faintness.

Loss of voluntary motion and even power of utterance. Inability to move though not very weak. Rigidity and soreness of muscles, < lower limbs; R. and loss of sensation and pains, < warmth, > cold, but in its place coldness of whole body. Heaviness. *Senses benumbed. Paralysis;* so that he could not stand, with weakness in small of back and trembling of feet. Paralytic symptoms; < during daytime. Aggravation on appearance of menses. Amelioration from vomiting; from vomiting of mucus or worms; from sweat; from extension of the flexed limbs; of the paroxysms at night.

Clinical.—General tendency to spasm of extensor muscles, hysterical. Paralysis of flexor muscles (Plumb.). Paralysis, with internal heat and external coldness. In general, indicated in diseases of putrescence, with threatening collapse; the pulse, however, is flighty and rapid. Collapse, with blue rings round the eyes, sometimes with unnatural appetite and thirst. The characteristic aversion to being covered and to heat seems to be associated with a sense of burning up internally.

Mind.—*Delirium;* in children, with red face and thirst; with violence; then heavy sleep and snoring, she could be aroused to low muttering wanderings; he understands nothing and makes no answer; she abandons her relatives and does absurd things; muttering; muttering, with restlessness and fear of death; raving, and patient difficult to restrain, then vomiting, then deep sleep, then vertigo and exhaustion. *Raving;* with attempts to jump into the water. Sensorium disturbed at night, could not get rid of the impression that there were two sick persons in the bed, one of whom recovered and the other did not. The room appeared like the "foaming of a troubled sea." Illusions of sense. Excitement and confusion; E., with wild look and impaired vision.

Jolly. **Anxiety; with fear of death** (Acon.); *with difficult respiration.* Fear. *Moaning;* and swaying of arms to and from head; sighing; plaintive, changing to loud screams. Sadness. Rage. Irritability. Obstinacy. Ill at ease, stupid, sleepy. Strong desire to recover. Loathing of life, despair. Disinclination to work. Disinclination to answer. Desire to be left undisturbed. Apathy. *Stupor.* Thought and speech difficult. Thought disturbed. Imbecility. Foolish. Memory weak. **Consciousness till the last breath,** *and just before death it seemed as if he would improve.* Insensibility. Coma; incomplete.

Clinical.—Occasionally useful in puerperal mania. Delirium, with restlessness, throwing off the clothes, etc.

Head.—Pendulum-like movements. Sharp pain, > diarrhœa, with dizziness after the chill, the pain returned next morning after the diarrhœa had ceased. *Aching;* with delirium; burning. *Dulness. Stupefaction.* Throbbing. Agreeable sensation, then heaviness and confusion, < occiput, and general exhilaration. *Heaviness;* and uneasiness; sometimes H. and throbbing, sometimes lightness and vertigo. Oppression, with incapacity for mental exertion. Lightness, < occiput. Vacant, with feeling as if something whirled around in it. Emptiness, and the lowest word reverberated through head and passed through every nerve of body. Discomfort. Congestion. Apoplexy. *Vertigo;* on moving; < eating bread.

Forehead.—Throbbing pain. Burning pain day and night; B. pain, so that he would willingly die, with a sad expression, mouth drawn and filled with saliva from submaxillary glands, which were swollen. Heaviness of sinciput.

Pain in l. side of head; in occiput; lightning-like in occiput, extending down nape. Hair fell out; and dry and gray. Sensation as if hair were pulled. Biting on head.

Eyes.—Sunken; and surrounded by a blue margin. *Cataracts (two cases of hard, twelve of soft, nine mixed), with headache, vertigo and roaring in ears.* Glistening. Yellow. Retina and discs pale, < r. **Staring**; and blind; and wild, with dilatation of pupils; and wild, with redness of face, inarticulate moans and movements of head to and fro, arms rigid and immovable, hands drawn over to chest. Squinting. Rolling. Spasmodic distortion. Pain. Conjunctiva yellow; C. and sclerotic yellow and injected. *Pupils dilated;* and sluggish. Pupils contracted; spasmodically. Pressure in balls. Photophobia. *Vision dim;* < rising or moving in bed; and blurred; and confused, then double, then blindness. Vision troubled. V. double; and triple. V. flickering. V. of sparks. Blindness. Everything looks black on rising in bed; on moving head.

Ears.—Stopped sensation. *Roaring; with difficult hearing.* Surring. *Deafness.*

Nose.—Dryness. **Bleeding** (Carbo v.). Smell acute.

Face. — Drawn. Sunken; and often discolored. **Pale; in morning, and collapsed; and sunken, hippocratic**; and haggard. **Anxious.** *Risus sardonicus.* Ashy. Livid. Yellow. Red; and warm; dark. F. and head suddenly became purplish after stimulants and warmth were applied. Swollen. Distorted. Suffering expression. Stupid expression. Trismus. *Lips bluish.* Lips distorted; retracted, so as to expose teeth.

Mouth. — Teeth. Loose and fell out. Sordes; bloody. Gnashing.

Tongue. — *Clean. White;* and tremulous, heavy, difficult to protrude between the immovable teeth, so that speech was almost unintelligible; coated white at noon, dry and brown at tip, next day coated brown and pointed at tip, third day coated brown, dry at tip, edges stiff and swollen, fourth day brown and dry, fifth day dry, brown at tip and lead-colored at root, sixth day brownish lead-colored coat in centre, red at tip and edges, seventh day clean, dry and red at tip, eighth day dry, glazed and stiff, ninth day clear, red, pointed, tenth day red and dry, eleventh day red, dry, cracked and bleeding. Coated whitish-yellow in morning, and dry. Covered with mucus. Creamy. Brown, at last black. Scarlet at edges, crimson and black in middle, and dry. Swelling; and twitching, with suffocated voice and salivation. Bitten; during the convulsions. Prickling. *Crawling, with pain;* painful C., with spasmodic movements of tip. *Speech difficult; S. slow and weak, with feeling on every motion as if there were resistance to be overcome.* Inability to speak distinctly. Stammering; and hesitation in answering questions.

Mouth spasmodically closed or drawn. Flow of frothy, bloody mucus. Froth bloody, yellow or green. Sore and bleeding; sore as if salivated. Scalding, and in throat and stomach. Dryness; not > drinking. Constant inclination to spit. Expectoration of bloody saliva. *Salivation;* sour-tasting. Frequent running of water from mouth. *Breath fetid.* Taste bitter in morning; bitter, spoiled; nauseous, bitter; nauseous; fetid; flat, disagreeable; as if he had smoked tobacco long or taken ethereal oil; blunted; inability to taste or bear food.

Throat.—Hawking up of tenacious mucus all the forenoon, with pain in r. tonsil. Soreness and tightness; S. at 10 A.M., with difficulty in swallowing, œsophagitis, and at 8 P.M. inability to swallow when lying. *Dryness;* with irritation and injection, and on l. side of soft palate a dark patch looking like an effusion of blood beneath mucous membrane. Crawling. Burning; in fauces, extending down œsophagus to stomach. Tearing in œsophagus and bronchi.

Stomach.—Appetite unnatural, even when dying from exhausting stools. *Appetite ravenous;* especially for bread; especially for acids. A. lost. Aversion to food; and drink; with occasional coldness in stomach, that thence pervaded the whole frame; to everything except sour drinks. **Thirst**; *with dryness of mouth and throat, with burning and tingling of tongue;* for sour drinks; for undiluted wine at dinner; but inability to drink much because it distressed the stomach; **unquenchable.**

Eructations; offensive; sour. **Singultus.** *Nausea;* all day; after eating; *with debility and scanty vomiting of coffee-grounds fluid;* with sinking at stomach; alternating with heavy confusion in head. Sensation similar to seasickness. Retching, with pressure in pit of stomach; ineffectual R.

Vomiting; at 8 P.M.; soon after bread, < a hearty meal, without diminished appetite; with spasmodic constriction of stomach; easy; *violent;* in sudden attacks at night, with pain over whole body; *of food; of all food, drink and medicine; of blood;* brownish water streaked with blood; *of coffee or chocolate-colored matter;* hardened black bile; dark, bilious matter; raw, offensive, bilious substances; shreds of mucous membrane; sour, dark green matter; sour, dark green mucus, containing shreds of disorganized membrane; sour matter or tenacious mucus; dark brown mucus and everything taken into stomach; tenacious mucus in morning fasting; slimy substance and frequently round or thread-worms.

Cramp. *Pain;* in pit; in epigastric region; in morning, with pyrosis; with soreness; with waterbrash; obstructing respiration, with great appetite. *Epigastrium tender. Oppression;* in epigastrium; in pit; *and distress.* Cardialgia; in pit, without loss of appetite. Constriction in epigastrium. Uneasiness. Prickling, almost agreeable, > open air, recurring in a warm room. Heartburn. *Burning, with pain in abdomen;* B. in epigastric region, also with excitement.

Clinical.—Hiccough. Vomiting of blood, sudden, violent, with cold sweat. Extreme pressure and contraction in the stomach, followed by vomiting. Terrible distress in the stomach and abdomen, with burning, accompanied by vomiting.

Abdomen.—*Distention. Tympanitic.* Tense; and hard, painful to touch. Very soft. Rumbling. Sticking when coughing, suddenly extending into r. testicle. Pain as if a hundred knives were drawn through parts down to womb, ovaries, urethra and vulva. Griping, with stools. *Pain;* in morning, with urging to stool,

> normal stool; with inability to stand erect; every fifteen minutes; extending into testicles, > stroking, with drawing; flatulent; convulsive. Spasmodic tension. Soreness. *Coldness, and in back.* Heat, < epigastric region. Paralysis of intestines.

Liver torpid. Pain in liver. Tenderness in r. hypochondrium. Painful contractions in upper abdomen. *Pain in hypogastrium;* occasionally; burning; sudden circumscribed, after delivery; extending into scrotum evenings, with dragging as from flatus; from l. groin to calf, then legs and feet swollen, covered with phlyctenæ and gangrene on lower third of legs, descending towards feet and ascending to upper part of legs.

Rectum and Anus.—*Anus wide open* (Phos.). *Hæmorrhage from bowels* (Phos.); the blood does not clot, is thin and almost black. Cutting in rectum; stinging, with irritability of sphincter, with spasms. Excruciating pains in hæmorrhoidal veins. Pain in r., with spasm. Ineffectual desire; frequent. *Paralysis of r.*

Stool.—**Diarrhœa;** > hot baths; *exhausting; pernicious; offensive; frequent, brown, slimy, next day fetid and dark;* dark gray, looking as if meal had been stirred through it, and of sickly odor. **Thin, olive-green,** for the second time in forenoon, then burning extending high up in rectum and itching in anus; *thin, involuntary.* Watery. *Constipation.* At first mucous, then mucous or sanguinolent. Contained disorganized mucous membrane, as in dysentery. Evacuation of worms; in children.

Clinical.—Watery diarrhœa, sudden, with unquenchable thirst, drinking and vomiting, suppression of urine, shrivelled skin, icy coldness and an aversion to heat, would not be covered. Dysentery, particularly valuable in the collapsed stage, stools involuntary, grumous; with these conditions it has saved many apparently holpeless cases. Asiatic cholera, particularly with the icy coldnesss and *intolerance of being covered* (of first importance).

Urinary Organs.—Bladder and ovarian region sensitive. *Paralysis of bladder.* Frequent urging, not without effort; ineffectual U. Inability to urinate. Micturition frequent and copious; involuntary M.; rare, dribbling and without relief; difficult, with constant desire. Urine retained. Did not urinate at night, contrary to habit, and no desire in morning, but much clear urine passed vigorously during stool. Spasm of meatus urinarius. Cutting in urethra on attempting to urinate, with smarting. Burning in urethra during micturition.

Urine.—Copious. Scanty, watery, clear; S. and dark, next day "prune-juice" colored, third day *suppressed, on introducing catheter a gill of prune-colored urine, full of gritty sediment and of disagreeable odor, afterwards urine contained mucus and albumen, later involuntary micturition with blood and albumen.* Pale. Clear like water; but at times turbid. White sediment like cheese. Thick red sediment.

Clinical.—Suppression of the urine. Hæmorrhage from kidneys or bladder. Albuminous urine, after scarlet fever, with dropsy.

Sexual Organs.—Numerous erections, even after coition. Dragging in spermatic cord, so that testicles seemed drawn up to groins.

Female.—*Gangrene of vaginal mucous membrane, with a dark slate color. Discharges almost black, fluid and fetid;* D. of the color of prune-juice. Vagina hot. Pain in vulva; with soreness and throbbing. Vulva tender. Sensation of boiling water running from vulva up to mouth.

Uterus.—**Hæmorrhage** (Ustil., Carbo v.); *and apparent death of a new-born child. Irregular stormy contractions. U. and r. ovary congested and sensitive to touch,* sphincter vaginæ and vagina relaxed. Os wide open (before delivery), thick and soft. Os tinca open, sensitive to touch, hot and engorged, with profuse flowing. *Descended so that it almost protruded from labia, was hot and painful, os was open, with urging to urinate and labor-pains, > wet bandages or by pressure upon abdomen, the woman went to the eighth month, when she miscarried.* **Expulsive pains.** *Labor-pains. Pain, and in ovaries.* **Cessation of lochia, with fever, inflammation of uterus,** *later an abscess that opened through vagina.* Retention of placenta due to hour-glass contraction of uterus and subsequent sterility. *Puerperal state. Abortion;* at two months, mass perfectly black; at six months, after discharge of placenta, vomiting, jactitation, præcordial pain, pallor, cold skin, uterine contraction at irregular intervals, then unconsciousness, strabismus and death; between seventh and eighth months; then tearing in limbs. Death of fœtus.

Metrorrhagia. Menses suppressed; too profuse, congestion of blood to uterus, metrorrhagia, contractions of uterus so that it seemed ready to burst, all symptoms worse previous to menses.

Clinical.—It has cured various tumors of the uterus and appendages, with profuse menstruation or hæmorrhage thin and black, often fetid, with expulsive pains. Uterine displacements. Subinvolution of the uterus. During labor or uterine hæmorrhages it should be used with great discretion; it is extremely dangerous when there is albuminuria, for it is liable to bring on convulsions; if used too freely during labor it is extremely apt to cause puerperal metritis. Menstrual colic, with coldness, intolerance of heat, forcing pains. Lochia offensive, greenish and purulent. In puerperal fever it has made some brilliant cures when there was danger of putrefaction, with putrid discharges, tympanitis, chills, coldness, intolerance of covering, suppressed urine, tendency to collapse.

Respiratory Organs.—*Voice weak, unintelligible, stammering.* Cough, with easy expectoration of much tenacious mucus. **Expectoration of blood during violent efforts to breathe.** Asthma after suppression of itch, > reappearance of the eruption. *Respiration difficult; as from a weight on chest, so that he must take deep and forced inspirations* (Phos.); from contractions of diaphragm. **Sighs. Anxious respiration** (Phos.). Respiration slow; and small. Costal respiration.

Clinical.—Cough, apparently from spinal anæmia, pain all through the chest caused by pressure on the spine.

Chest.—*Milk suppressed.* Pleurospasmus, with suffocative, catarrhal loss of speech and twitching of muscles. Pain; in sternum and l. upper part; sharp, in sternum. Oppression.

Clinical.—Hæmorrhage of the lungs, dark venous. Gangrene of the lungs (Phos., Caps.).

Heart.—Pain in præcordial region. Præcordial anxiety. P. anguish and dyspnœa. P. tenderness. P. discomfort. Spasmodic throbbing. Beating rapidly at times during the day, in the earlier part of which she lay motionless. Palpitation; with contracted, frequently intermittent pulse. Action slow.

Pulse.—**Rapid; and small; and small, contracted, often intermittent;** and small, hard; and small, feeble; *and fluttering, depressed;* on least exertion, and feeble; and weak; and weak, intermittent, variable. *Slow;*

and full, tense; and at times full, at times small and tense; *and small, suppressed;* and small, weak; and small, thin; and small, soft; during the spasms, and small, at times intermittent and scarcely perceptible; and weak. *Weak, depressed. Small;* and contracted.

Neck and Back.—Stiffness of nape; of muscles of r. side of neck in morning, with pain on turning head. *Pain in back;* > stooping, with dragging and pressure in hypogastrium; *in lumbar region.*

Extremities.—Pale, cold and wrinkled, as if they had been long in hot water. Swelling, sometimes with rash, vesicles, furuncles, ulcers and exanthema. Nails purple. Falling off of nails from thumbs and fingers and from one of l. toes, the denuded parts covered with flabby granulations secreting a fetid discharge. *Trembling;* < exertion; and pain.

Cramps, with excruciating pains and formication; C. of hands and feet, which are painfully contracted. Arms and legs semi-flexed and semi-pronated and rigid, pain on attempting to straighten limbs. Alternately flexed and extended, with irresistible desire to stop the spasm by the will, which he was imperfectly able to do. *Convulsive movements; several times during the day, in the intervals fingers numb and often contracted.* Spasms and twitchings; tonic S. *Contractions of hands, feet, fingers and toes; sudden periodic C., with tensive pain;* C. till they became cold and immovable, with pains in various muscles, in some cases becoming tetanic, with trismus and opisthotonos or epilepsy, then weakness of memory, the attacks often occurred suddenly in the night; of flexor tendons, as if we would hop about. Distortion, even fingers bent backward; D. of hands and feet; of hands and feet, < in children, with slow pandiculations. Jerking so that he could not move or bend fingers.

Tearing. *Pain;* and bruised sensation; with cramps in flexors; *spasmodic;* spasmodic, and in gum; spasmodic, in hands and feet, changing from place to place, with constant crying; periodic drawing, extending downward in knees and elbows, with insensibility, coldness of skin and difficult movement. *Drawing,* < arms; in hands and feet; *with crawling;* and tearing; in hands and feet, with tearing; D. or tearing in limbs or joints, sometimes with crawling, < limbs. *Tingling;* of fingers and feet.

Weakness; < upper. *Heaviness;* with pain in calves. **Insensibility; of fingers and toes;** *of tips of fingers and toes;* **and coldness. Fuzzy feeling** (Phos.). *Sensation as if asleep, with formication.* Stiffness; after the spasms. Paralysis.

Clinical.—Cramps in the legs, with coldness, cold sweat. Paralysis of the extremities, with cramps, numbness and formication.

Upper Extremities.—Tonic spasms. Tearing in r. shoulder and upper arm as from a string around it, then pain in muscles. Pain in l. shoulder. *Falling asleep of arms.* Paralysis of arm. Paralytic symptoms of arm (with drawing and tearing), with rigid flexion of fingers and acute pains. Spasms of forearms, hands drawn inward and approximated to chest, pain > attempting to extend the flexed part. Hands contracted. Hands weak. Soft, painful, watery swelling of wrists.

Fingers.—*Contractions.* Flexed tightly into hands. Bent backward, difficulty in carrying hands to mouth and distortion of eyes. Cramps, especially in children. Pain in tips; then lymphatic swelling extending up arms, then loss of ends of fingers. *Prickling in tips, with sensitiveness to cold,* then suppuration; then falling of nails leaving an unhealthy granulating surface. Drawing. Rigid, cold, shrivelled, painful to pressure, dry, hands covered with red erysipelatous spots, scales and cracks. *Numbness; of tips* (Phos., Tab.); crawling.

Lower Extremities.—Reeling. Flexed, they could not stand upright and reeled. Twitching. Spasmodic contractions so that they could walk only on tips of toes. Convulsions and pain. Pain and weakness. Weakness, with painful rigidity; W. so that gait was stumbling. Walking difficult; impossible. Paralysis. Creeping insensibility anteriorly in thigh and calf during the day. *Cramp in legs and feet; in calves.* Pain in calves and feet. Weakness in legs, then pain, < night. Weight in calves and ankles; in legs and feet, with want of tone. Swelling of feet; dropsical. Inversion of feet. Cramp in feet, with weakness. *Feet asleep and stiff.* Anæsthesia of soles. Cramp in toes.

Skin.—*Swelling and pain without inflammation, then coldness, blue color, cold gangrene and death of the limb; S. of hands and feet, with gangrene, black and suppurating eruption;* emphysematous S. *Discolored; on fingers and toes, then gangrene, then dropping off of limbs.* Purple color of hands, feet, ears and nose, and much of skin mottled; ends of toes purple, suppurated and fell off. *Ecchymoses.* Red. Yellow; muddy, and dry. Jaundice of a child when born. Yellowish-brown, hot and dry. Lead-colored, wrinkled, disappearance of vessels and insensibility, so that she could be cut and pricked without pain and without bleeding. Soft, flabby. Dry; and rough; and withered. Capillary action slow. Capillaries seemed empty. Spots like flea-bites on feet. Livid spots over body. Exhalations of a vinous odor; fetid E.

Gangrene of fingers and toes; of feet and legs; *of limbs, they suddenly become cold, lead-colored and insensible; of limbs without pain when pricked or cut, though often motion is not entirely lost; with separation of the part from the body; the dead part separated at the joint;* in toes and legs, and dropping of joints, ending in death or fatuity; of fingers and toes; with separation of soft parts, general weakness, paralysis, desquamation of affected parts, stools thin, involuntary, then apoplexy and death; of limbs, with coldness, legs came off without loss of blood, all dead parts were dry, hard and black. *Cold gangrene of limbs;* of nose, fingers, hands, arms, feet, tibiæ and thighs; *C. and dry; C. and painless, so that fingers and toes drop off.* Hot gangrene that eats the flesh and bones. *Lost both feet and most of his fingers.*

Eruptions; changing to gangrene, on fingers and toes, spreading rapidly over limbs. *Anthrax changing into gangrene of limbs. Petechiæ.* Desquamation. Boils; on neck; on neck, discharging yellow matter, with burning pain; on lower limbs, with petechial exanthema, outer parts of limbs, < fingers, dark blue, gangrenous and dead and fell off; on back, nates and abdomen, with cutting, surrounded by erysipelatous redness and becoming gangrenous, the gangrene extended over trunk and thighs, with separation of epidermis and cadaverous odor, then bloating of abdomen, hiccough, coma and death. Blood ulcers. Blisters covering the swollen hands and feet; *gangrenous B.;* painless, on l. index, discharging ichor, the base of the sore blackish, all fingers insensible.

Sticking here and there, > scratching, but returning, with heat in the scratched places. Burning, torpid, prickling sensation over whole surface, with difficulty in moving limbs, with sensation as in a limb on pressure upon trunk of a nerve, when we say that the limb is asleep. Pain. Disagreeable sensation. **Formication; under skin;** *on face, gum and other parts; face, arms and legs; limbs; hands and arms; tips of fingers, hands, neck and other parts; hands and feet; limbs, with tearing stinging; tips of fingers, with partial loss of sensibility; < upper lip and at times all about mouth, with prickling; extending into forearms, with insensibility; jerking, under skin.* Itching all over body; on lower limbs like formication.

Clinical.—Senile gangrene.

Sleep.—*Sleepiness.* Stupefied slumber for days. Sleep profound; and long-continued. Sleeplessness; nearly all night, with exhilaration; with restlessness, fever and agitation. Restless sleep; with heavy dreams; interrupted by anxious dreams. Sudden waking with a wild, staring look; S. waking, with wild, frightened look, then palpitation. Anxious dreams.

Fever.—*Coldness;* with gooseflesh; sensitive to cold; then diarrhœa; then nausea, > diarrhœa; then nausea, sharp pain in head, vertigo and partial blindness; then heat and unquenchable thirst; then heat, < internal parts, with anxiety so that many lose their reason, with thirst; shaking. Shivering; sudden; in limbs. Coldness in different parts as from cold water or snow. **Cold skin** (Ars.); *< face; < limbs; and dryness.* Coldness of face, with pallor; C. over back and abdomen; in back, abdomen and limbs, with horripilation; creeping over limbs, later chill over whole body; C. and anæsthesia beginning in tips of fingers and toes and extending over whole body.

Heat; with dulness of head; with thirst; *in internal organs* (Ars.); internal, during pains in stomach, abdomen and limbs, with anxiety and thirst; as if sparks fell on different parts; *in hands and feet;* hands and feet, < fingers and toes, which were bent and stiff. Hot skin; and dry.

Sweat; over whole body except face; on forehead; from head to pit of stomach; *cold; cold, clammy* (Acon., Ars., Verat. a.); cold on limbs; clammy, then epileptiform spasms and death.

Selenium.

The pure metal is triturated for use.

Ally.—Phos.

Generalities.—Emaciation, < face, hands, loins and calves. Tearing in l. side of trunk and head, with stiffness in nape and cervical muscles, impeding turning of head. Intolerance of slightest draught of air, he takes cold therefrom and then has tearing in limbs. *Weakness; after coition, with irritability* (Phos.); after eating, with desire to lie down, but sleep prevented by pulsation in all vessels, < *abdomen.* Irresistible desire to lie down and sleep, then aggravation of all symptoms. Obliged to lie down during the heat of the day and remain half asleep, even his imagination was relaxed; suddenly obliged to lie down when sitting and working, with no other effects than that it was impossible to do anything. Aggravation after sleep, to which he is much inclined; < hot days.

Clinical.—Occasionally indicated in the prostration following typhoid fever. A remedy particularly adapted to old age; easy exhaustion, mental and physical. Useful for debility following exhausting diseases.

Mind.—Talkative when excited, < evening; T., light-hearted, excited. Fretful, sleepy, lazy, with frequent vomiting and stretching. Dread of people and of his occupation. Exhaustion after mental work late at night. Unfit for work, though he constantly begins he is obliged soon again to leave off. Forgetful, especially about business, but when lying half asleep everything recurs to him.

Head.—Sticking internally; deep. Aching every afternoon; A. after tamarind water; after lemonade and wine, and sometimes after tea. Dulness, < evening. Vertigo in morning; in evening; in evening when riding in a carriage; on standing up; with staggering, attacks of faintness, pale and distorted face and anxious sweat, and when riding in a carriage after lunch he was obliged to turn back to the house, where he vomited and was so weak that he had to go to bed; so that he must close his eyes, < motion, then nausea and anxious sweat over whole body, then vomiting of all food, then vomiting of water and mucus, at last of sour water, the paroxysms < an hour after breakfast and dinner, then weakness, with thirst for cold water, which was always vomited, taste flat, stool large, soft, colored with bile, stitches in forepart of chest as from incarcerated flatus, feeling of a board before forehead, then feeling as if head were pressed against the pillow by a warm hand on forehead, hiccough, eructations, stupefaction of head, inability to collect his thoughts and frequent lying in a doze, urine scanty, red, symptoms > emission of flatus, these attacks returned every half to one hour except at night, most relief from spirits of camphor taken alternately with black coffee, when he was obliged to hawk up much mucus.

Sticking in forehead, temples and eyes in forenoon and evening after going from cold air into warm room. Pain in temples; in occiput on standing up, with vertigo. Heaviness in occiput, at times waving in brain, fluttering in ears, twitching and pressure in eyeballs. (Drawing in occiput, with ringing and stoppage in ears.) *Hair falls out on combing.*

Clinical.—Headache from tea drinking. Neuralgic headache over left eye, < the sun, strong odors, and especially tea and strong acids. Headaches of drunkards, sometimes > liquor, for which there is a craving.

Eyes.—Inflammation. Lachrymation, with pressure in l. Blisters on inner margin of lid, with itching and pressure as from a grain of sand. Twitching of lids, with indistinct vision. Burning on margin of r. lids, with itching. Twitching in l. ball. Pain deep in orbits. Falling of hair from brows. Vision obscured. Myopia increased.

Ears.—Wax increased in the l. deaf ear, it is harder and in r. softer than usual. Throbbing in r. Stopped as from a membrane in front of them, moderately > shaking head and boring finger into ear. Distant rumbling in l. in evening in bed, with sensation as if ears were stopped.

Nose.—Pain in septum as if a pimple would form. *Itching in nostrils;* on septum. Frequent involuntary boring into it. Coryza; with distressing dry cough; then fever, next evening headache, and in upper part of middle of forehead, extending towards vertex, a pain that lasted all the next day, the hat annoyed him, heat in the painful part, the hand felt pleasant, with bruised feeling and heaviness in all limbs so that he could scarcely walk, and during the headache he woke at night with cough; fluent every evening; sudden fluent, disappearing suddenly. Yellow, thick, lumpy mucus. Gelatinous mucus, at times containing small yellow masses. Loss of smell.

Face.—Twitching. Red cheeks on waking. Cracking in lower jaw. Crack in lip; in middle of upper.

Mouth.—Teeth. Free from mucus, smoother and harder, so that on rubbing they cracked, with thickly-coated white tongue. Boring in hollow. Pain as if decayed internally, obliged to pick it till it bled. Pain in a hollow one as if it were being drawn up, > taking cold water and cold air into mouth, by eating, drinking and smoking, with coldness extending into cheek, the pains < evening in bed, with throbbing extending into l. eye, l. temple and jaws, > olfaction of Bryonia.

Tongue coated white; in morning. Pain in region of root of T. Burning on tip of tongue woke him at night. Stammering so that he misplaced syllables and could not articulate many words. Mouth full of tenacious mucus after midday nap. Dryness of M., fauces and pharynx on waking in afternoon and night, was obliged to drink much water, then sweat. Salivation. Disagreeable sweet taste on lips when smoking.

Throat.—*Hawking of lumps of transparent mucus every morning* (Argent.); of bloody mucus in evening; of mucus, with a spot of blood on it. Tickling, with scraping and necessity to raise mucus. Dryness; < towards evening.

Stomach.—Hunger immediately in morning; in middle of the night, when he happens to rise; H. increased; little in morning. Desire for brandy; late in evening; D. for salt things, then aversion to them. Thirst in evening. Hiccough from smoking before eating, with eructations. Nausea; then drawing sticking in a l. lower molar. Very sick after sleep. Cramp. Pressure as if cramp would occur.

Abdomen.—Rumbling before eating. Cutting in evening, > emission of flatus, repeated in the night. Splenetic sticking between tip of l. ilium and umbilicus when walking, so that he could scarcely move. *Pain in r. side around under last ribs, < inspiration*, extending to region of kidneys, which were sensitive to pressure.

Clinical.—Enlargement of the liver, and stitches < motion and pressure, soreness over the liver, white tongue, loss of appetite, < morning.

Stool.—Tenesmus; with frequent semi-fluid stools. Pasty, then sensation in anus as after a hard stool. *Constipation. Hard, with blood at the end* (Alumina); *H. and accumulated in rectum so that it could scarcely be evacuated.* Difficult, at the end slimy. Containing threads like hairs.

Clinical.—Constipation from paralysis of the rectum.

Urinary Organs.—*Dribbling after urinating*, especially after stool; *D. when walking* (Phos.). Frequent micturition at night. Always obliged to urinate some time after stool. Obliged to wait a long time when urinating. Discharge from urethra of fluid before micturition; *D. of watery, sticky substance just before stool and soon afterwards; of a drop of prostatic fluid when sitting, with disagreeable sensation. Dribbling of prostatic fluid. Sensation in tip of urethra as if a biting drop were forcing its way out.* Twinging forward along urethra, with *sensation as if drops were passing out. Red urine; in evening.* U. dark and scanty. Urine had the odor of violets. Brick-dust sediment. Red sandy sediment.

Genital Organs.—Erections, with itching in urethra; violent E. in morning on waking, without voluptuous sensation; incomplete E.; weak E. during sexual excitement. *Impotency, with lascivious thoughts.* Something thicker than natural and stony behind l. testicle. Jerking pain in r. testicle in evening. Itching of scrotum. *Semen thin and odorless; dribbling of S. in sleep;* discharge of S., with rheumatic pains. *Desire mentally, not physically, erection slow and incomplete, too speedy emission, but long-continued pleasurable sensation.* Menses delayed.

Clinical.—Nocturnal emissions, with sexual dreams followed by weakness in small of the back; seminal discharge thin, without odor; seminal discharges when walking; ejaculation too easy; neurasthenia from sexual excess.

Respiratory Organs.—*Hoarseness when singing, especially at the beginning; H. alternating with necessity to clear his throat* (Phos.). *Cough in morning*, slight, but affecting whole chest, *and expectoration of lumps of mucus with blood;* C. from deep in chest, with expectoration of opaque mucus and blood. Oppressed breathing in evening when lying, from raw pain in l. side of chest and here and there in small of back; O. in open air, with stitches in side. Frequent deep breathing as when sighing. (Compare Phos.)

Clinical. — Paralysis of the vocal cords; hoarseness from singing or talking. Cough, with scraping of chest and bloody expectoration. Very valuable for the hoarseness of singers, especially when it is frequently necessary to clear the throat of clear, starchy mucus (compare Stann.).

Chest.—Blood in breasts. Sticking in l. side at night, > next day, but in evening stitches in sides and stiffness in neck, then quiet sleep, next day stitches in sides in morning and evening, and when walking in open air oppression of breathing. Pain in middle on raising arm and on pressure. Oppression, and about heart; O., with stoppage of nose, dryness of throat, alternations of heat and cold, thirst, cough and sleeplessness.

Neck.—Cramp. (Drawing sticking in l. side of nape extending into l. eye every half hour, with lachrymation.) Tearing through l. side and down posterior surface of l. leg. Pain in glands above l. carotid, < pressure, with at times tearing along neck.

Back.—Paralytic pain in small of B., > lying on abdomen, < bending backward. Soreness in tuberosities of ischia, in a lean person. Lame feeling in lumbar region in morning, without pain.

Extremities.—Pain in joints. Pain as after taking cold. Stiffness and cramps; S. as if beaten in morning, < wrists. Increased cracking of wrists when stretched. Internal twitching in l. hand, on side of little finger. *Tearing in hands at night.* Tearing down posterior surface of l. thigh through half of leg. Cracking of knee on moving it while lying. Cramp in calves, heels, ankles, malleoli and flexor tendons of great toe in evening when lying. Pain in calves and toes. Swelling of ankles. Cramp in soles at night and towards morning on motion, when lying. Stitches in corns. Pain in feet, with seminal emissions.

Skin.—Fatty on face. A piece separates from sides of nails till it becomes sore and painful. Lump in skin to inner side of r. tendo-achillis. Swelling of glabella as if pimples would form; hard S. on back. Rash on forearms; red itching, in hepatic region. Pimples behind ears. Itching pimples on hands; on back; on nates; on l. calf, he must scratch it till sore, the spot is moist a long time. A plug of mucus escapes from a comedone near nose, then pus, then inflammation of the spot. Flat, painless pustules on l. inner malleolus becoming ulcers. Ulcers; herpetic, on feet. A vesicle that has been rubbed off in morning, on middle joint of second l. toe; V. about ankles scratched sore were moist several days, then very sensitive. Itching vesicles on eyebrows; on ulnar margin of l. hand; between thigh and scrotum, with smarting.

Biting in all parts, < palms. Crawling in spots about mouth, cheeks and chin, > scratching. *Itching about ankles;* on inside of wrist; in a spot between third and fourth fingers; between tendo-achillis and malleolus; of soles; of soles in evening; on balls of fingers, after scratching a white spot with red areola.

Sleep.—Sleepiness early in evening, necessity to lie down and immediate falling asleep; S. early in evening, then only partial sleep with much waking, in the middle of the night quite awake, after reading sleepy again, sound sleep only towards morning; (S., with yawning). Could hardly arouse himself in morning. Sleep as if dead all the forenoon.

Sleepless after 3 A.M., and feeling well. Late falling asleep; and early waking. Jerking in whole body in evening on falling asleep. Waking at every noise; W. early in morning, and lively; early, always at the same hour, however late he may fall asleep; from a sound sleep full of dreams in afternoon, at the minute he had determined upon. On waking he was at first unconscious, then indolent, but all the more wide awake after washing. Sleep full of dreams, with calculations. Dreams, many unremembered; D. of the occurrences of the day; of quarrels and of unnatural cruelty; historical, of distant people; of journeys and of coition, with violent erections on waking.

Fever.—Chill at 7 P.M., then fever, with headache and nausea, and at night waking in sweat. External heat of skin, as if it came from a stove, after midday nap, < after eating, with heat in different spots, now in side, now in chest or abdomen, or loins. (Burning in ulcers on feet.) Sweat in forenoon on going out; S. when walking and during a nap; on hypogastrium and pubic region when sitting; on chest and in axillæ, causing stiff white spots on linen.

Senecio.

A tincture is made of the entire fresh plant of Senecio aureus, L.

Generalities.—Trembling; nervous. Sticking in different parts; in feet, nape, arms and forehead; about noon, before dinner, moving from one part to another, in groins, lower jaw, shoulders, forearms and temples. Lancinations occasionally through the day in arms, legs, feet, chest and face, occasionally during the day in r. shoulder, l. heel and r. side of face. Migratory cutting in different parts. Weakness; in evening; with malaise and desire to lie down. Syncope from slight exertion. Aggravation in afternoon.

Mind.—Good spirits. Nervous and irritable. Homesick. Sad; in evening; sometimes, and elated sometimes; and anxious, afraid that she was going to die, but complaining constantly that she was tired and if we would only let her die she would be satisfied. Anxiety preventing sleep, with restlessness, and if she dozed for a few minutes she woke with a start, no sleep for four days. Meditative in evening, serious, disposed to think of the past and future. Confusion. Inability to fix mind.

Head.—*Stupefying pain;* oppressive pain. Fulness at night. Lightness. Vertigo; in open air; as if brain were pressed forward. Vertigo like a wave from occiput to forehead; suddenly; suddenly when walking in the street, so that I almost fell on my face. Shooting outward in forehead; and eyes. Darting pain in forehead and eyes. Cutting over eyes. Pressure outward in anterior part of head; in forehead in afternoon; in temples. Lancinations in l. temple, upper part of l. eye and inside of l. half of lower jaw.

Eyes.—Shooting outward in l. Lachrymation on going into open air.

Nose.—Tightness in morning on rising, with yawning. Full sensation; but no mucus; with burning, but little mucus; > copious flow of mucus, with sneezing. Dryness. Inclination to sneeze. Lubrication of nostrils in evening. *Coryza.* Much mucus; and in bronchi; transparent, and in trachea; white, transparent, and in trachea. Smell acute.

Face.—Pale, appeared depressed. Agonized expression. Lancinations in l. side Tenderness in front of l. ear. Cutting inside l. angle of lower jaw. Lips and gums pale.

Mouth.—Pain in a carious molar. Teeth tender. Tongue coated in evening, and dry. *Dryness at night, and in throat;* in evening, *and in fauces;* and in throat, requiring constant drinking of small quantities of water, but this caused nausea as soon as it became warm in stomach. Feverish breath in evening.

Throat.—Hawking; of white, transparent mucus; of tough, white, transparent mucus. Seemed stopped by a ball. Tightness, with desire to attempt to relieve it by swallowing.

Stomach.—Appetite lost in evening; lost, whatever was taken had a bitter metallic taste and caused nausea. Thirst; in afternoon and evening. Drinking much cold water. Eructations of air; of sour air; sour E. Nausea; in morning on rising; in morning on rising, with yawning; in evening; with cold sweat. Sharp pain in epigastrium; in diaphragm. Sensation of a ball rising into throat in afternoon. Uneasiness in evening.

Abdomen.—Rumbling in evening. Flatulence. Discharge of flatus. Griping in afternoon; in evening and night, > watery stool; in evening, < umbilical region; > bending forward. Colic; in evening, with diarrhœa; in evening, with watery diarrhœa; on rising, with urging to stool, which soon passes away; < umbilical region; > watery stool; flatulent. Sticking in hypochondria; in umbilical region. Cutting in umbilical region. Pain in umbilicus before breakfast, spreading in all directions, > stool. Griping in hypogastrium. Smarting pain in l. groin.

Stool.—Tenesmus. Watery; in evening and night; with tenesmus; containing hard lumps; frequent, containing small hard lumps, some mucus and blood, with tenesmus, afterwards exhaustion. Thin, dark; thin in morning, after supper a thin dark one, with straining. Copious diarrhœa in morning, with debility. In hard lumps mixed with yellow mucus. Containing blood.

Urinary and Sexual Organs.—*Urging to urinate, with heat in neck of bladder, pain in region of kidneys and frequent micturition. Urging after chilliness, urine bloody.* Frequent micturition at night, urine inodorous. Smarting about fossa navicularis before micturition. *Urine copious;* in morning, *and bloody, with tenesmus of bladder; and dark, with tenesmus of bladder. Urine scanty; and high-colored. Prostate gland enlarged and hard. Heavy pain moving along l. spermatic cord to testicle.*

Clinical.—Chronic inflammation of the neck of the bladder, tenesmus, bloody urine, etc. Inflammation of the kidneys, with intense pain and fever, great pain on urinating, urine red and hot. Nephritis, urine scanty, great pain over the kidney, < motion. Urine alternately profuse and scanty, with constant desire to urinate day and night, œdematous face and extremities. Abdominal dropsy, with scanty high-colored urine. Menses early, profuse, with backache. Suppressed menstruation, with bronchial catarrh.

Respiratory Organs. — Hoarse, but trachea and bronchi seemed clear. *Bronchi and lungs seemed full, but she could not raise anything, although she had fits of coughing which seemed as if it would raise almost anything.* Could only breathe by leaning forward. Respiration as if fatigued.

Clinical.—Night-cough. Bronchial catarrh.

Heart and Pulse.—Palpitation; from motion or drinking water, with pain in abdomen. Pulse scarcely perceptible.

Back and Extremities.—*Pain in back and loins at night; in l. lumbar region; in lumbar region in morning. Lancinations in lumbar region.* Lumbar region tired. Rheumatic pains in joints. Sticking in l. shoulder. Sharp pain in region of sciatic nerve about 4 P.M., shooting down thigh. Œdema of r. leg extending to abdomen and thorax (had had rheumatism of l. leg for months). Lower limbs weary.

Sleep.—Yawning; in morning on rising; in forenoon, with shivering; with inclination to stretch. Sleepiness all day. Restless before midnight; R. and sleepless. Restless sleep; with lascivious dreams. Frequent waking; and so imperceptible that sometimes I could not tell whether I had been asleep or not. Dreams vivid. Dreams lascivious; with an emission. Many dreams (fifth night), mostly intellectual and about events in my life, showing uncommon activity of memory and mind (sixth night), indistinct (seventh night), about ships and cargoes, wagons and teams, writing, fighting and breakneck adventures, always coming off lucky (ninth night), mostly about the events of the day (tenth night), afterwards pleasant.

Clinical.—Sleeplessness, especially caused by uterine irritation or prolapsus.

Fever.—Chilliness; before noon, then fever at night, with sweat and moderate thirst; < towards evening, with heat. Sensitive to cold air. Feverish; in afternoon. Heat of forehead; lips in evening. Disposition to sweat. Sweat towards morning; on forehead in evening. Skin dry and scaly except in morning, when she sweat freely. Skin dry and nails brittle.

Senega.

A tincture is made of the dried root of Polygala Senega, L.

General Action.—It presents imperfectly two important phases: (1) Laryngo-bronchial catarrh, with numerous characteristic indications, and (2) paralytic symptoms everywhere, but most pronounced in the eye and larynx. Closely allied to *Causticum*, partly to Phos. and Spongia.

Generalities.—*Weakness, with trembling of upper limbs* (Caust.); W., stretching of limbs, confusion, heaviness and beating in head; with yawning; with mental indolence and bruised pain in muscles of thighs; even to nausea; physical and mental. *Faintness in afternoon on walking in open air.* Amelioration from sweat.

Mind.—Cheerful; and childishly playful, but a slight cause made him mad and vehement; (and disposed to work). Hypochondriac and irritable; H. in evening. (Fretful in forenoon.) Anxiety; with accelerated breathing. Phlegmatic, inclined to quarrel and to give offense. Suddenly remembers unimportant regions which he saw long ago and which never made a deep impression upon him.

Head.—Boring stitches. Aching; in morning; > cold; beating, with pressure in eyes, diminished appetite, bruised feeling and malaise. **Dulness; with pressure and weakness of eyes.** *Heaviness.* Emptiness. Rush of blood on stooping, < eyeballs, where there is painful pressure. *Vertigo;* in morning, with flat taste; with roaring in ears; as if blood ceased to flow and as if ideas were arrested.

Forehead.—Tearing in l. half. *Pain; over orbits;* over l. eye; in r. half; *after dinner, and in orbits, < l. side of head, > open air; in sinciput and occiput every day, < sitting in a warm room, with pressure in eyes, which did not bear touch,* on the fifth day nausea after dinner, the pain > leaning head on arm, but exercise in open air gave the greatest relief, with sensation as if diarrhœa would come on, which was not the case, after the nausea a peculiar but not unpleasant sensation in parotid and external pain in præcordial region. Beating pain in evening. Painful drawing.

Tearing in temples extending into face, with drawing pain. Pain in temples; r.; towards forehead, in forenoon. Pain in occiput; afterwards extending to temples and finally to whole head; stupefying, towards evening. Itching on scalp in morning.

Eyes.—Staring, with sensation as if it were difficult to move eyes. Pressing; towards evening, with burning; in evening by candle-light; as if it would be pressed out of the socket in morning, then dull feeling; as if a fluid pressed into balls and distended them, on stooping. *Dryness, with smarting as from soap; D., with sensation as if balls were too large for orbits. Burning when reading or writing.* Drawing changing into coolness, then lachrymation. *Lachrymation* in open air; and sensation as if threads were hanging before eyes, < r.; *l. on looking intently, with trembling of eyes.* Pupils contracted and sluggish.

Lids.—Swelling; with burning and pain; of r., < towards inner canthus, with inflammation and pain. Pimple on margin of r. lower. Vesicle on margin of l. upper, causing pressure in eye, on being opened it discharged clear fluid. Lashes full of hard mucus in morning. Jerking; of r. upper; of lower, causing lachrymation. Lower spasmodically drawn towards nose. Pressure in r. upper, towards inner canthus; burning P. in margins in morning. Burning when writing. Pulsation in r. lower. Crawling, with sensation of sand in them.

Much mucus in Meibomian glands; hard, tenacious

mucus in canthi at night. Twitching in r. outer canthus. Pain in orbits; in balls; r. ball; now r., now l. ball; *in balls, with drawing and diminished vision;* sharp, deep in l. ball.

Sensitiveness to light; with tension in eyes. *Weakness; when reading, with lachrymation on exerting eyes too much; on continuing to read or write, with flickering; when reading, with flickering, obliging one to wipe eyes often,* but which were aggravated thereby; *with burning and lachrymation. Objects looked shaded. Vision dazzled; when reading. Flickering when reading, with running together of letters.* Illusions. *When walking towards the setting sun and looking down he saw an oval smaller sun hovering below the other,* > **bending backward and closing eyes.** A shining spot on wall at side of eye at noon, > looking directly at it.

Clinical.—Opacities of the vitreous. Valuable to promote absorption of fragments of lens after operation. Paralysis of the l. oculo-motor nerve, with double vision, > *only by bending the head backward.* Partial paralysis of the upper lid. Catarrh of conjunctiva. Muscular asthenopia (Caust.).

Ears.—Pain in r.; in r. when chewing. Warmth in r. Coolness often extends through l. Hearing painfully sensitive. Humming, with stopped sensation.

Nose.—*Dryness;* with discharge of a few drops of blood. Itching in nostrils. Sneezing; and tickling in nostrils; *causing heaviness of head and vertigo, then flow of much watery mucus from nose.* Coryza. Smell before nose as of a malignant ulcer.

Face.—*Paralytic feeling in l. half.*

Mouth.—Burrowing in l. upper molars. Pain in teeth and jaws. Lower incisors sensitive on inhaling through mouth cold or damp air. Tongue coated white; coated yellowish-white; slimy in morning, with unpleasant slimy taste; creeping under T.; dry in middle; burning in tip. Mouth and fauces burnt. Smarting burning in palate as if skin were detached. Tension in palate extending to articular fossæ of lower jaw. Astringent acridity, and < uvula. Dryness; in morning and forenoon, and in larynx; and in throat, with tenacious mucus in throat; then salivation. Salivation; with prickling and stinging in mouth; with contractive sensation in mouth; watery, when smoking. Viscid saliva. Putrid smell. Taste metallic; T. of urine; bad, with rumbling in stomach; acrid, < fauces; nauseating sweetish in throat; flat in morning; diminished.

Throat.—Inflammatory swelling of fauces, < uvula. Hawking, easy of white mucus; *H. up lumps of gray mucus in morning, with irritation in larynx inducing hacking cough; of mucus from trachea; of small lumps of tenacious mucus from larynx.* Tenacious mucus; in fauces in morning; whitish. Constant inclination to clear T. and to swallow. Scraping; in fauces; with roughness and tenacious mucus; and in back part of tongue, with salivation; with dryness, making it difficult to talk and obliging him to cough; obliging hawking; in fauces, obliging one to clear the throat often and to swallow saliva; burning, obliging frequent swallowing; tickling, in evening.

Pressure on swallowing food. Soreness. *Roughness* in forenoon; *in evening, with dry cough and oppression of chest;* in morning on waking, with dryness; with dryness and dry cough. *Rawness when clearing it.* Constriction; in fauces. Constrictive irritation in fauces. *Burning; in fauces.* Dryness, which makes speech difficult; D. of fauces, < uvula, with stitches.

Œsophagus.—*Irritation; and roughness. Sensation as if membrane had been abraded. Burning, with discharge of mucus from trachea.* Disagreeable sensation.

Clinical.—Catarrhal inflammations of the throat and fauces, with scraping, hoarseness, etc.

Stomach.—Gnawing hunger below pit in morning. Appetite diminished; lost; lost at breakfast. Thirst; with dryness of palate; with roughness and dryness in fauces. Eructations; of air. Nausea; after dinner; during the siesta; with salivation. Retching; fatiguing, with vomiting and discharge of much watery mucus. Vomiting, with diarrhœa; V., with anxiety; copious; violent, all night, with violent purging and profuse sweat.

Digging below pit after supper, with discomfort in whole body. Pain; in pit; all day; almost cramplike, disturbing sleep every night at 3 A.M. Oppression. Burning; changing into fatiguing retching and vomiting of much watery mucus. Emptiness. Digestion disturbed.

Abdomen.—Rumbling; and motions. Emission of flatus. Cutting extending to pit of stomach. Griping, with inclination to stool. Pinching, > liquid stools. Colic; during dinner; > diarrhœa. Burning.

Rumbling in l. hypochondrium. Boring in l. hypochondrium in evening. Upper A., cutting; digging towards evening, with disposition to flatulence and sudden outbreaks of ill humor; pain towards noon; gnawing before a meal, without appetite; oppression during inspiration, with warmth. Rumbling in l. side, with pinching. Sudden pressure in r. side of A. and chest in evening when sitting. When walking, drawing as of a foreign body between integuments on r. side. Shifting boring in umbilical region. Pain in umbilical region; in afternoon, < evening and rest. Pressing in hypogastrium, then emission of flatus.

Anus.—(Beating) pressure after stool.

Stool.—Watery. Diarrhœa; copious, light-colored, spurting away almost without sensation; indications of D., which did not take place. Papescent; with rumbling and emission of flatus. Constipation. Hard, large and difficult; H., scanty, rare; H., scanty, then pressing in rectum. Delayed. Frequent. Increased.

Urinary Organs.—Micturition frequent and increased; frequent, but less urine at a time and lighter colored; frequent, urine grayish, depositing a cloudy sediment. Involuntary micturition at night in sleep; when dreaming (he did not urinate before retiring). Sticking along urethra in morning after emission of dark yellow urine. Burning when urinating; in morning, with sensation as if urine had to open a passage; in evening, with pressure; B. pain along urethra after micturition.

Urine.—Copious; every time that he drinks; and *acrid;* with pressure in urethra. *Diminished. Frothy and dark;* F. in a patient whose chest was affected. Orange-colored, clear, becoming turbid when standing and depositing on all sides of vessel a white sediment. *Mixed with threads of mucus, after cooling it was thick and cloudy.* Turbid in morning as soon as it cools; T. after standing, and depositing a reddish sediment mixed with mucous flocks. As soon as it cooled in morning it deposited a thick sediment, the lower layer yellowish-red, the upper yellow, flocculent.

Clinical.—Urine greatly diminished; loaded with shreds and mucus; with scalding before and after urinating.

Sexual Organs.—Cramplike pain in glans. Tickling in prepuce and glans. Burning in glans when urinating. Erections at night; painful E., and desire increased, then diminished.

Respiratory Organs.—*Sudden hoarseness when reading. Tearing and stinging in larynx and trachea. Cough; from sudden tickling in throat;* at breakfast. Dry cough; from tickling in throat; with concussion of whole chest. **Hacking cough from irritation in larynx**; *H. cough in forenoon from mucus in larynx, < open air and walking fast; in open air; from mucus in throat. Cough, with expectoration of tenacious mucus. Expectoration; desire for.* Frequent and deep inspirations. *Short breath on ascending stairs, with oppression of chest.*

Clinical.—Loss of voice in singers, with severe burning and hawking. Catarrh of the larynx, the voice is very unsteady, and the vocal cords are partially paralyzed, sometimes expectoration of tough mucus (Caust.). Laryngeal catarrh, with cough, < before breakfast. Bronchial catarrh, with soreness of the walls of the chest, much mucus, great oppression of breathing and sensation of weight in chest (Phos.). Bronchial catarrh, cough < evening and night, in warm room and lying on r. side (Spong.). Bronchial affections in cold weather, in the aged, much difficulty in raising tough, profuse mucus, with hard, loud, accelerated breathing and anxiety (Ammon.). Whooping cough, tough expectoration, like the white of egg.

Chest.—Shifting twitching in various parts. Sticking through l. half; under l. short ribs; in a spot in l. side in evening, with sore pain; in l. half in evening when lying on r. side, with burning pain; on inspiration during rest; in a spot in l. when walking; when walking in open air, then oppression, with debility in lower limbs, sweat and almost faintness; in a spot in l. during rest, with burning pain; in r. lower intercostals, more internally; in l. half, < sitting or lying; l. upper part, < rest, with burning pain; deep in a spot in l. half, < cough and various motions; in middle, > deep inspiration; r. upper part, with clawing; intermittent, in middle; shifting, with tightness, difficult breathing, shuddering over back and occasional pain here and there about head.

Pinching. Boring in l. side, < region of heart; in lower half, < above heart; B. becoming seated in region of heart, whence it shoots to l. axilla. Clawing in different parts; in l. half in afternoon, alternating with pulsations; in l. half, < lying on r. side; < l. half, with restlessness and anxiety during rest. Racking as if everything in it were sore when stepping hard or running.

Pain; below sternum; in morning on waking; in front in morning on touch and during inspiration; in afternoon after smoking tobacco; *at night on waking;* below sternum when sitting erect; in sides of lower part when sitting; beneath sternum when sitting, next day it increased and descended towards pit of stomach; through middle on concussion, < along dorsal vertebræ; *in walls, < touch, > deep inspirations;* < pressure; < rest; in middle, < rest; superficially in pleura, < rest; < l. half, whence it proceeds; under upper part of sternum on bending head forward, gradually changing into colic; sudden, in a spot in r. side when walking; shifting; beating, at a spot below short ribs, < inspiration and < r. side.

Sore pain in l. side; S. pain on bending forward, with pulsations, but vertigo on bending backward; between third and fourth l. ribs, < pressure or increased to sticking; as if it would burst, on sneezing, though sneezing relieves chest; pulling backward (as if in mediasteum) on stepping hard, walking fast or running, making every movement difficult; *burning, under sternum, < motion and deep inspiration* (Caust., Sang.). Burning pain; in a spot in l. in afternoon, with disagreeable mood; in l. half in evening when sitting; in l. in evening when lying on l. side; in l. in evening, with anxiety in chest.

Oppression; < rest; < open air and during a walk, with pain through chest towards scapulæ; in l. side, increased almost to pain. *Tightness;* in upper part, with crawling; on certain movements, < stooping, with disposition to expand chest by stretching, this leaves soreness. Compression; in upper part, < rest; from sides towards front towards evening. Pressure outward. Tension in lower part during deep inspiration. Drawing extending to axillæ; deep burning.

Crawling; in spots in pleura; in upper part, < rest, with twitching; in lower part, with prickling. *Orgasm of blood* in afternoon, *with oppression of chest,* flushes of heat in face and frequent pulse; orgasm of blood towards evening when at rest, with creeping; with stitches; when sitting, almost causing faintness. Burning; under sternum, extending to back. Pulsations. Sensation of stagnation in upper part of lungs, < rapid walking.

Clinical.—Congestion of lungs, with great dyspnœa. Œdema of lungs, with rattling in chest. Pneumonia of r. lung, violent stitches, rattling of mucus in chest, etc. Hydrothorax. Great soreness of walls of chest from coughing, pressure, sneezing or moving arms. Very valuable for exudations in pleura after Bry. has ceased to act.

Heart.—*Boring in region;* more on outside. Pain in region during deep inspiration; in region when walking, with oppression and difficult breathing. Violent beating, shaking the whole chest.

Pulse.—Rapid; and hard; and full; and full, irregular; and soft, unequal; afterwards slow. Slow.

Neck and Back.—Drawing in cervical glands. Pain in back; in region of sacrum; under l. scapula when sitting, < evening; between scapulæ, < stepping hard or by any movements that concuss chest; drawing, along base of l. scapula.

Extremities.—Tensive pain in joints, < knees and ankles. Paralytic drawing downward in l. arm. Paralytic pain from l. elbow to little finger, with drawing. Sprained pain in r. wrist. Sticking in l. palm; in palms, with crawling and prickling. Painful drawing in metacarpal bone of l. thumb; in finger-joints. Lower limbs weary. Bruised pain in thighs and gluteals. Sprained pain in hip-joint on turning thigh when standing. Pain in hip, knee and ankle as after a long walk. Pain in l. ankle. Weariness of feet, < forenoon.

Skin.—Pimple painful on touch; pimples burning and itching when touched, on upper lip, near nose and l. corner of mouth. Itching between nates, > scratching; of legs, < evening in bed, scratching causes burning.

Sleep.—Sleepiness in evening. Stupefying sleep. Sleep sound, full of dreams, with confusion of head on waking. Anxious jerking of upper arm during siesta. Sleep restless; and full of dreams; with unremembered dreams; and interrupted, owing to oppression of chest; and frequent waking on account of sticking and tightness in chest.

Fever.—Shivering, with weakness in feet; S. over scalp. Febrile excitement, with shuddering over back, heat in face, weak, burning eyes, beating headache, difficult breathing, sticking in chest, general bruised feeling and frequent pulse. Heat in l. half of face. Heat of skin; under skin of back, < between scapulæ, with itching. Sweat.

Sepia.

Triturations should be made of the pure Sepia (the inky juice of the cuttle-fish).

General Action. — It produces general relaxation, fatigue and exhaustion, with loss of power of upper lids, extremities, abdominal muscles, etc., etc. Many symptoms point to an inactive, even congested liver. Weakness of the female sexual organs seems to be its most prominent feature. The indications of herpetic eruptions are marked and have proved very useful in practice.

Allies.—Nat. m., Puls., Sulph., Lyc.; Pod., Lil. tig., Murex, Carbo v.; Rhus t., Graph., Berb.

Generalities.—Swelling of whole body, face, abdomen, legs and arms to wrists, with shortness of breath, fever every two or three days, chills alternating with heat, sweat with the heat. Unpleasant exhalation from body after getting warm in bed. *Trembling;* anxious, with cold sweat on forehead. Jerking here and there, with sticking; J. sensation here and there in body, also in head, r. and l. sides. Spasms as from nervous weakness, pulse sometimes weak, sometimes spasmodic.

Paralytic sticking here and there, then immobility of the part. Pains in various parts; P. on l. side; in all parts on which she sits or lies; in muscles of abdomen and limbs on waking; sudden; wandering; burning, in different parts, < lower part of l. hypochondrium. Burning constriction in shoulders, chest and throat evenings. General drawing, even in bones of arm; cramping, in r. shoulder and whole r. side. Lame sore feeling all day. Sensation of a heavy cold. Symptoms of catarrhal fever, with weakness in lower limbs and drawing in arms. Feeling as if she could easily strain herself. Fulness about 1 or 2 P.M. in l. axilla, then r., then in groin. *Pulsation through body, < in whole l. chest;* in head and limbs, < night; sensation as if heart filled all cavities of body, with labored, muffled beating. Wavelike sensation through body and down arms and legs, then sudden interruption of wave and expansion, with sharp rheumatic pain. Excitement of whole body. *Restlessness;* he must rise at night and walk about; during menses, with drawing pain in lower limbs and abdomen, with rumbling, so that she must remain in bed two days, in second forenoon palpitation and dyspnœa.

Goneness, especially in **stomach. Weakness; in morning during menses**; *in morning; in morning on waking; in morning on rising;* in morning, with uneasiness in abdomen; at 9 A.M.; about breakfast time; in forenoon; in afternoon after sleep; at 7 P.M.; at 9.45 P.M.; from continued speaking; after an emission, with sensitiveness to damp air, vertigo, turbid urine and constipation; with short breath; with stupid feeling in head and tightness on chest; *as from nausea, in morning on waking;* from walking half an hour, so that he was nauseated and could not breathe, air-passages seemed drawn together as far as pit of stomach.

Indolence; in afternoon after a meal, with sleepiness; *after a meal;* of mind and body, with difficult breathing. Heaviness. Heavy stupid feeling towards evening. **Faintness** in forenoon; in morning on rising in bed, with loss of thought, then chilliness, with gooseflesh and yawning, tongue pale, pulse weak and slow; F. about midnight, with sweat, consciousness, but inability to talk or move a finger, in the midst of the paroxysm a sort of dream that he was fighting with a ghost, soon a second faint, with dream of being lost in a forest; during a slow ride; **with heat and then coldness.** Numbness in all nerves in evening, and in tongue, with dulness of head and absence of thought. Paralyzed feeling from vexation.

Aggravation from about 12 *till* 1 P.M. *and from* 4 *till* 6 P.M.; in afternoon after sleep, vascular excitement, general soreness and lameness and desire not to move; evenings and nights; on l. side; of pains during and after meals; when lying, amelioration after supper. Symptoms returned on taking a dose of Nux vomica. Amelioration of pain at 4.30 P.M., after eating; A. in open air; at rest and lying; of pain by local application of warmth; on eating supper; of all symptoms except dryness of throat by supper; *during violent exercise, and aggravation in forenoon and evening when sitting quietly;* from Rhus.

Clinical. — Jaundice. General tendency to emaciation. Anæmia and chlorosis. Indurations, especially of the breasts and ovaries. Epithelial cancer, with burning pain (lip, stomach, vagina). Especially suitable for persons with dark hair. General aggravation twice a day, forenoon and evening, from washing in water, at rest. Pains begin in morning immediately on waking, become very intense, and gradually decrease until in the afternoon they vanish. Pains are burning, worse after eating, also worse before menses.

Mind.—Fanciful pictures at night if he closes eyes, > opening eyes. Cheerful and inclined to sing. Laughing and crying alternately without corresponding change of mood. **Apathy** (Phos., Puls.). *Sadness; in morning on waking;* during menses, < morning; < morning; < *evening;* < *walking in open air; with attacks of weeping;* with loss of ambition; *about her health;* at the news of the slight illness of a friend (which at another time would have made no impression), increasing till I felt that *I should scream unless I held on to something;* alternating with liveliness. Oppressed in sultry weather, but more cheerful when it thunders and lightens.

Forebodings about his disease. Fear; when riding in a carriage; to be alone. *Anxiety;* all day after coition, with restlessness; in morning, > rising; *towards evening;* in evening, with intermittent redness of face; intermittent; about her health, with irritation and weakness; about her health, thinks that she shall have consumption and soon die. Anguish as if in blood; A. in attacks; A. when eating, and heat so that face was red and bloated, also eyes, ears and nose were affected and sweat stood in drops on finger-tips. Desire to be alone and to lie with closed eyes.

Irritability; at 7 A.M.; at 7 A.M., do not want to talk or be talked to; at the recollection of past unpleasant events; before menses, an attack of furious gestures, with sobbing, she throws herself on the bed, where she remains all day without eating; < morning; *and out of humor for all business. Vexed and disposed to scold. Discontented. Fault-finding; with weeping* and heat of face. Irritable tearfulness. Quarrelsome (feeling ashamed of it at the same time). Loathing of life. Aversion to company.

Anger; in morning; so that she fears apoplexy,

with blackness before eyes; over past times, so that he did not know what to do, with anxiety, palpitation and sweat. Ebullition of passion, with trembling, < hands. *Impatience when sitting, like uneasiness in bones.* Hastiness, with restlessness. *Nervous;* at 10 A.M., and so confused that I could not keep my mind on study. Nervous irritability, forcing me to be quiet. *Nerves sensitive to least noise.* Much affected by piano playing. Inclination to wonder over the future.

Intellect unusually clear; and memory quick. Mistakes in writing. *Language comes slowly, forget the chief points, etc. Indisposition for mental labor, which aggravates the headache.* Thinks of things he does not wish to think of, uses expressions which he knows are incorrect, undertakes things opposed to his intentions and finds such contradictions with himself that he is uncomfortable and uneasy. Inattentive. *Absent-minded and not desirous to work;* A., spoke incorrectly and misplaced words.

Heavy flow of ideas (Lyc., Ph. ac.). *Dulness in afternoon. Dulness of comprehension, inability to collect or express thoughts, building air-castles. Stupid feeling. Stupidity* in paroxysms, with shuddering and arrest of breath, she must then take a deep breath. *Forgetful;* and thoughtless, but desirous to work. *Inability to think in forenoon and afternoon; when spoken to, could follow the ideas when the same question was addressed to another person. Unable to collect thoughts at* 9.30 A.M., *or to answer the simplest questions, which caused unhappiness, felt better after crying.*

Clinical.—Hypochondriasis and hysteria; valuable for the various forms of mental depression of women, complete indifference, without interest in their own affairs or those of others (Puls. and Nat. mur.).

Head.—Jerking forward in morning; backward in morning on rising. Pinching jerks in morning on rising. Painful cracking as if something in it broke on turning head, with pain in neck. Stitches; after a meal; through head; coming up back at every step; outward through eyes all day; lastly in occiput, making him feel inactive. Tearing in a spot in brain during cough, as if something tore loose.

Aching; all day; all day, < from 5 till 6 P.M.; *all day, with mental depression; in morning;* every morning on rising; every morning after rising; *from morning till noon, with nausea;* at night, with vomiting; almost all night and till next noon; on waking, > moving about; on waking, > rising, through temples at 9.45 P.M.; after a papescent stool; < *towards evening and* < *shaking head;* < walking in open air, with weakness; *with pain and heat in eyes; with drooping of lids and feeling as if I had not sense enough to lift them;* with mental depression and inability to collect my thoughts; *as if brain were crushed, in forenoon;* as after jolting, after noonday nap; digging itching, with sensitiveness of head to touch and stiffness of neck. Throbbing pain in evening; at night; on every movement. *Aching as if it would burst;* when coughing. *Pressure outward;* as if eyes would fall out; as if everything would issue from forehead and eyes, with jerking, beating and heat.

Compression after eating, any covering is oppressive. Superficial drawing and boring, < night, driving her out of bed, about midnight it extended into temples, ear and teeth. Fulness. Swollen feeling. Strange feeling, as if on the point of falling asleep. *Dulness;* in morning on rising; < walking in open air, with pressure in eyes; with unsteadiness in it and tension of muscles of throat and nape; with heaviness and with excoriated feeling in nose, posterior nares and pharynx, < r. side, with thick, yellow discharge from r. side, and on putting finger into nose it is bloody; as from coryza, with reeling. Heaviness; every morning on rising; in evening, and after lying down one-sided headache. *Weakness so that she can scarcely think,* < *afternoon;* so that it could hardly be lifted from the pillow.

Rush of blood (Sulph.). Pulsation in evening in bed, with sensation as if head were in motion. Shaking of brain from striking foot against anything. Movement in brain on shaking head. Sensation as if brain moved in waves, with hunger. *Vertigo;* every morning on rising; in afternoon; every day from 3 till 5 P.M.; every day from 4 till 6 P.M., when sitting and walking; at night on rising in bed; *when walking; when walking in open air; when walking in open air, with palpitation;* on rising to walk; on moving arms; after a meal; on stooping after supper; on blowing nose; when she sees a large plain; when sitting after a harmless drink, then flush of heat; on moving head, and on moving head from side to side feeling as if brain moved; *with nausea and anxiety;* with cold hands and feet; with dislike for work; so that on looking up when walking he stumbles; sudden, as if the street were rising, at 5 P.M. when walking; in attacks, as if something were rolling about in head, when walking in open air, then in evening headache and humming in ears; as if fainting, with short breath. Symptoms < sleep; afternoon after sleep.

Forehead.—Stitches here and there; S. when walking fast, with nausea; *over eyes,* < *motion in the house,* > *walking in open air;* > *lying down, with nausea (she cannot eat); outward over left orbit,* after rising in morning till noon, > open air, with drawing together of eye; in F. and occiput, towards vertex, with tearing and drawing. *Tearing in r. upper part; in l. eminence;* over eyes; in F. and eyes from 2 P.M. till going to sleep in evening; after a meal; extending down beside r. wing of nose. Boring digging all day from slightest motion. *Painful jerking. Jerking pain in forepart. Pain;* over eye; during the day, with queer feeling in head; at 10 A.M., and in temples, with drooping of lids; *over l. eye in afternoon,* < *evening, and delaying sleep;* at 3 P.M., > eating; at root of nose, between 4 and 5 P.M., and going to temples; from 7 till 8 P.M., with heat in it; after a stool which was not hard; over eyes if he goes into bright sunlight; *during menses,* with hard offensive matter from nose; < morning, noon and evening, and in temples; *with heaviness of eyelids;* in F. and eyes, with tension and burning; *and in vertex, then anxiety in pit of stomach, with trembling, then nosebleed;* over r. eye and going into eye; over eyes, alternating from one to other; passing around on r. side to occiput, in evening; intermittent, during the day; as from catarrh. Drawing pain; *externally, extending back to occiput.* Heaviness, and in temples. *Heavy pain over l. eye extending towards side of head at* 3.30 P.M., *at* 4 P.M. *fulness deep in l. orbit,* the headache > *evening and open air,* < *shaking head,* next day the *same headache and fulness,* **with occasional dartings from l. eye over side of head towards occiput, headache > after meals,** *with occasional darts through eyeball, afterwards headache,* < *mental labor.* Pressure on upper part of sinciput; intermittent P. on brain in sinciput, < towards forehead; P. outward at

5 P.M., < lying, with sinking feeling in vertex, sensation as if brain moved in waves, and hunger. *Fulness, and in temples, with throbbing in carotids. Dulness;* in F. and over eyes, with heaviness. Sensation of paralysis.

Temples.—Sticking; in l.; in evening; in l. at 6 P.M.; in l. from 12 till 7 P.M., with pain about anterior inferior angle of parietal bone; in r. on waking; six stitches in l. at 11 P.M. on lying down, three of them severe and at equal intervals. **Tearing from l. to upper part of l. side of head.** *Pain;* in r. and over r. eye; extending into forehead at noon; running from r. into l. and into eyes and nose at 2 P.M.; throbbing. Pressure outward from 6 P.M. till morning. Weight as from too much blood, as during coryza. Fulness. Pressing together, running from one to other. Tickling in l., then sensation as if skin were drawn upward.

Vertex.—Pinching in V. and upper part of occiput, with soreness, which became a burning. *Pain; after mental labor; beating, in morning after rising; contractive.* Vibratory contraction in morning. Compression all day, with dyspnœa. Beating, < turning eyes or any motion of head or body to a forcing outward.

Sides.—Sticking over ears; S. in l. in afternoon, in occiput in evening. *Paroxysmal pinching.* Occasional twinges of pain. Pain deep in one, with pain in molars. Rheumatic drawing in l. Beating in one on which she lies. Heaviness of r.

Occiput.—Stitches extending towards vertex. Tearing; intermittent, in l. side near neck. Pain in a spot; P. in r. side; in evening till midnight; running down; sore, in l. side; as if hollow and ulcerated, < night and lying upon it, > pressure of hand; drawing, and on touch P. as from subcutaneous ulceration. Painful drawing inferiorly, now in r., now in l. side. Drawing. Painful beating. Dulness of l. side. Heaviness, < morning; H. extending down spine, > about an hour after rising.

Scalp.—**Falling out of hair** (Sulph., Graph.). *Swelling above temples. Scurf. Moisture.* Itching pustule towards nape, which became an ulcer, with rough scabs beneath. Movements backward and forward, he must press molars together. *Pain on touch, as if roots of hair were sore. Itching;* < afternoon; when headache passed off; on occiput in evening; on vertex, with falling of hair.

Clinical.—The headache of Sepia is usually neuralgic, frequently extending from the occiput to the eye; or congestive, on the vertex, with great despondency and desire to be alone; neuralgic, over one eye, pulsating or sticking, with great sensitiveness, especially associated with uterine complaints; occasionally used for chronic congestive headaches or for headaches associated with disordered liver and the peculiar yellow appearance around the mouth and across the nose. Eruptions on scalp and behind the ear, with soreness from scratching. Sensitiveness of the roots of the hair. Falling of the hair. Numerous pimples on the forehead near the hair. Sour perspiration on the head.

Eyes.—Congestion and dryness. *Redness* in morning on waking, with smarting in canthi; R. of r., with sore feeling in it; *of white; of white in morning on waking, with burning, smarting and pressure. Inflammation, with redness of white and sticking and pressure;* I. with a stye; with intolerance of cold water; on r., with burning of eyes and lachrymation. *Swelling, with burning and lachrymation, which relieves;* S., with headache on same side. Glassy. Surrounded by dark rings. Jerking under eyes.

Sticking in l. Darting in r. at 7 A.M. on waking, then in l. **Pain in r. as from sand** (Nat. m., Zinc.), **< pressing lids together and by rubbing.** *Pain at night;* P. in l. in afternoon, then in evening feeling as if head were stuffed; P. on turning them to the right; with heat and glittering. **Soreness in evening after a walk in cold wind, < gaslight and attempting to read, with roughness and burning** (Sulph.). *Bruised feeling. Smarting;* **in r. in evening, with inclination of lids to close against one's wish.** *Fatigued by reading and writing,* with sore pain in inner canthus. *Constrictive sensation when reading or writing by candle-light. Heaviness, with tendency to keep them closed.* Dragging. Feel pulled downward. Feeling as if they would draw within themselves during a lecture, the lecturer seemed to recede slowly from my vision, ending in nausea. *Burning; in morning,* with weakness of them; with dryness; *with soreness to touch and desire to close them;* in l. in morning, with swelling of inner canthus; *like balls of fire, < l., which is injected.* Itching.

Lachrymation; morning and evening (Puls.); of r. in morning on going into cold, open air; *in open air.* Ball, occasionally shooting during the day; digging; aching in l.; pressure on upper part, < r.; pressure on lower part of r.; sensation as if weights were attached to posterior parts; itching.

Lids.—Swelling beneath eyes; beneath eyes in morning after waking; of r. upper in morning, with redness; *red, of lower, with pressing and burning pain.* **Red herpetic spot on upper, scaly and peeling off.** Agglutination in evening; in morning, with ulceration. Drawn together in morning on waking. Jerking; > open air; in l. lower, with sensation as if tears would flow. *Heavy pain on waking. Heat of margins, with dryness* (Sulph.); H. of margin of l. lower, towards outer canthus. *Itching; of margins;* inside l. upper, with soreness of outer corner, next day lids swollen and sore to touch and on closing eye, later the I. caused lachrymation.

Burning in outer canthus often during the day for an hour. Itching in l. outer canthus, with sore pain after rubbing it; I. in inner in morning after waking, and after rubbing smarting and lachrymation, then sore feeling in outer canthi, which were agglutinated. Itching smarting in l. inner canthus, with lachrymation and reddened conjunctiva. *Pustules on l. conjunctiva,* and before eyes a mist in which floated black objects like tadpoles with their heads pointing to the centre, at 7 A.M., > 11 A.M., < 2 P.M., the mist causing nausea. Scurf in brows. Sticking as if in bone, extending from under r. lid down to upper canine tooth. Tearing in orbits, < l. Pain in bone above eyes at 9.30 P.M. Creeping on inner margin of l. orbit.

Vision—*Intolerance of reflected light from bright objects.* Dazzled by daylight, which caused headache. Dim; when writing; of one-half of an object. *Of fiery zigzags. Of a zigzag circle of colors when looking into the light. Of sparks, with weakness. Of black spots; passing in all directions, all day.* White, flickering. Of a green halo around candle-light. Vanished; *during menses, > lying down, with weakness.*

Clinical.—Supraorbital neuralgia, usually r., associated with heaviness of the upper lids; the attack is brought on by fatigue or anxiety. Conjunctivitis, scrofulous. Paralysis of the upper lid, with uterine disease or irregular menstruation. Retinal anæmia, with sudden vanishing of sight. Asthenopia. Asthenopia, with uterine complaints, worse in the evening. A general aggravation of eye troubles twice a day, morning and evening, will be found

quite important; this is true not only of the asthenopia, but also of the inflammatory symptoms. Blepharitis ciliaris. Tarsal tumors. Granular lids. Phlyctenular conjunctivitis. Pustular keratitis. It has been found useful in arresting the progress of cataract in women.

Ears.—Swelling at orifice of external meatus, pressure near antitragus causes sticking; S. of r. parotid in evening; of parotid, with stitches and on moving head tensive pain. Sticking; in l. and in l. cheek; in the weak one; through l. parotid; drawing outward, in middle. Tearing in prominence back of r.; in l., as if it were being torn out. Pain; in l. in morning, on waking; in evening; at night; in r. after midnight, after walking in wind, and next night after midnight, > warmth and sleep, with coldness over head; extending outward at 4.30 P.M., when walking in a cold wind, next day at 5 P.M. dragging in ears extending into parotid and mastoid process from walking in wind, > warmth of room, next day earache at 5 P.M. from open air, > entering warm room; sore; as from subcutaneous ulceration in external meatus on putting finger into it; drawing in r., with heat.

Pressure inward below and in front of ears; P. outward when straining at stool. Feeling as if plugged up, with deafness. Creeping in r. Tingling. *Itching in the weak one;* I. in r. at night, with moisture in it; with discharge of pus; with roaring and accumulation of purulent whitish cerumen.

Sensitiveness to noise. Loud sounds and humming. Crackling before E. as from the rattling of papers. Singing before E. Whizzing and beating; W. before E. in evening when writing, interpolated with whistling. Roaring in r. at night, with pulsative blowing; R., then she cannot hear with it; R., with whizzing and sensation as if stopped; deep-toned, synchronous with pulse, at night. Clucking noise on rising from stooping. Noise in r.

Nose.—*Swollen, inflamed, and nostrils ulcerated;* S., inflamed and painful. Ulcer in nostril. *Nostrils scabby.* Sticking in tip on touch. Pain at root. Bruised feeling in r. side of median line of tip of nose and of chin, next day the spot on the nose was red. *Soreness and rawness;* S. of l. wing; sore pain, < inspiration; at tip, then eruption there; S. feeling around r. wing with raw feeling, but thick yellow discharge from that nostril, with rawness in posterior nares. *Stuffed,* in evening discharge of watery, colorless mucus. Obstructed at night, < r. nostril; O., and difficult breathing; and discharge of hard mucus; suddenly in morning. *Dryness* (Nat. m.); *and in fauces; of l. nostril, with swollen feeling, yet without coryza.* Tingling in l. nostril, with ineffectual inclination to sneeze. Itching in nostrils, with soreness on scratching.

Clinical.—Nasal polypi. Nasal catarrh, with discharge of solid pieces of mucus from the posterior nares. Dry catarrh in l. nostril.

Sneezing; every day at 6 A.M. in bed; *almost without coryza.* Coryza, with continual snuffling; C., with diarrhœa; with headache all day, vertigo and tearfulness; with sore throat and rawness in chest, headache and toothache, < eating. *Dry coryza;* in l. nostril; with roaring in head and ears; with prickling in forehead and eyes, constant irritation to cough and dry cough in sleep. Fluent coryza; with sneezing preceded by crawling in nose; with pain in occiput and painful drawing in hips and thighs. Viscid mucus. Discharge yellow; thick yellow; of yellow water after blowing, with cutting in forehead; blowing out a piece of yellowish-green skin with blood at the edges; bloody mucus on blowing. Plugs. *Blowing out of blood; strings of blood. Bleeding; in morning after rising; evenings during menses; in evening on blowing it* (Carbo v.); appearing and disappearing suddenly. Smell acute.

Face.—Yellow, and whites of eyes (Lyc., Nat. m.). **Y. spots and Y. saddle across upper part of cheeks and nose**; *Y. around mouth.* **Pale**; in morning, with sickly look and dim red eyes. *Red; and flushes of heat. Swelling.* Many black pores. Tearing on r. malar-bone below temple; in l. cheek, extending over ear towards occiput. Crampy pain in bones. Drawing pain, with swelling of cheek. Pain in malar and nasal bones. Sticking in l. lower jaw and in glands underneath, < touch. Tearing in upper jaw; in lower, below incisors; in l. joint, in front of ear. Jaws seemed as if they could not be opened when chewing, and as if joint would crack.

Lips.—**Herpetic eruption.** Eruption in corner, with pain on touch; scurfy E. on red border after a journey in the cold. Swelling of lower in morning. Pimples in centre of red border of upper; *moist P. on margin of upper.* Painful pustule in middle of lower. Painful ulcer on inside of lower, the pain > cold water. Vesicles sore to touch, on r. side of upper. Cutting in upper. Lower feels sore inside and is full of painful blisters. Sore pain on lower near r. corner; S. and smarting and disposed to crack. *Dryness;* and cracks. Tension in lower.

Clinical.—Facial neuralgia during pregnancy; intermittent, severe only at night.

Mouth.—Teeth.—*Quick decay.* Bleeding in morning, Loose and painful, and gums bleed easily when spitting; lower incisors loose. *Sticking;* in incisors; in upper incisors; in second r. upper molar; in l. upper bicuspid about 8 A.M.; in l. molars, < from 11 till 12 o'clock; *and in jaw, extending to ear, preventing sleep at night, and during the day she had to tie a cloth over it.* Tearing from 6 P.M. or 2 A.M. every day, with jerking; *extending out through l. ear during and after eating.* Drawing cutting. Jerking in lower molars; in teeth in afternoon at every fourth inspiration, < lying, with tearing and with ptyalism; from a draught of air in mouth or ear, then grumbling causing restlessness; in molars, < stooping; rheumatic, through T. and forehead. Wrenching pain in all. Digging in upper. Gnawing in posterior molars. *Aching;* in morning after rising, from a draught of air; at night, preventing sleep, in morning she was so agitated that though weak she could not sleep; *during menses, with throbbing in gums;* when biting and on pressure of tongue; on touch and when talking; *in all, < a hollow molar, which pains as if elongated and swollen, then swelling of gums and cheeks;* in old roots, with sensitiveness to cold; in molars, with pain in submaxillary glands; in a r. upper molar after eating, extending into forehead, head, cheeks and both rows of r. teeth, > evening after going to bed; shifting. Elongated feeling in incisor. *Beating pain,* becoming sticking, with rapid decay; B. in molars extending over cheeks towards occiput, at night waking him frequently; sticking, in roots of several, renewed on entering room after walking in cold air, after eating and biting, < touch of anything warm, with burning in gums, afterwards the tooth turned black and decayed. Drawing in upper molars; in lower back molars; *if anything hot or cold is taken into mouth;* when air got into it, not when in cold air; from molars to forehead at night, waking him frequently; in hollow, extending into ear, < cold water; *extending into cheek, which swells, during menses;* as from a cupping-glass. Grumbling in incisors; in molars at night. Sensitiveness to cold air. Painful heaviness in upper incisors. Tingling in upper incisors. Teeth on edge. Coldness in lower incisors; drawing, in single upper incisors.

Gums.—*Swelling* of inner part; *S., with pain; with sore pain;* with sore pain, they recede and bleed on touch; about decayed teeth, with pain and with swelling of cheek; *with dark redness and painful throbbing as if beginning to suppurate;* and of inner mouth, with burning in mouth extending into throat. *Sore, ulcerated.* Blister, with burning pain on touch. *Bleeding,* almost without cause; on touch. Stitches. Drawing about upper incisors.

Tongue.—Coated; with pain on r. side, hindering chewing and distinct speaking; *white;* with mucus one or two hours after eating; with putrid-tasting mucus; brown, with red edges, next day tip and edges red, middle and posterior part yellow; yellow, and l. side of T. and mouth covered with stinging vesicles; dirty yellow and sticky, with putrid taste causing nausea. Pimple on tip, with sweet saliva. Pustules covering T. and throat. *Blisters* in middle; covering l. side; covering l. side of T., throat and corner of mouth; covering l. side of T., throat and l. nostril; painful, above and below tip; *with pain as if burnt.* Tearing posteriorly on r. side, with smarting. *Sore pain.* Acrid smarting on forepart. *Pain as if burnt;* on smoking the accustomed tobacco; *in tip;* with feeling as if too large; with redness and elevated papillæ. *Dryness, and in mouth and throat, and in morning roughness;* D. of tongue and palate, with roughness; D. in morning on waking, as if burnt.

Swelling of inner mouth; on mucous membrane and inner part of gums. White blisters inside cheeks. Mucus on soft palate. Pain anteriorly in palate as if burned; just back of teeth, on touch of finger or tongue. Burning in roof of palate. Dryness without thirst; D. in morning on waking, and in throat, so that she could not utter a sound. Salivation; in evening; > eating; salt. *Offensive smell;* as from mucus in chest. Taste foul, as from old catarrh; *different kinds of foul; unpleasant in morning, mouth dry and slimy;* sour; *sour in morning on waking;* sour after eating; sour, with constipation; *bitterish sour; bitter in morning;* bitter on clearing throat; bitter to food; sweet; as of manure; putrid after beer; mawkish; insipid.

Clinical.—Neuralgic toothache, > cold air, resulting from the use of tobacco. (Like Puls. there is relief from cold. Both drugs are frequently called for in the toothaches of pregnancy.)

Throat.—Throbbing in carotids. Bruised pain in submaxillary glands, with pain on touch. Swelling of submaxillary glands, with pain on swallowing; S. of l. submaxillary gland and tonsil; of l. tonsil, which was covered with pustules; of l. tonsil, with inflammation and suppuration, inability to swallow from pain, general heat, thirst and burning in eyes. Redness and dryness. Inflammation; of upper part, with swelling. Mucus, almost suffocating her. Expectoration of mucus from fauces. Hawking up of mucus; in morning; bloody.

Sticking on swallowing; S. in uvula, with redness of sides of throat, sensitive on swallowing, with shaking chill and mucus that cannot be loosened. Cutting, with rawness and much mucus; C. on swallowing, < hawking up mucus, with pressure, then bleeding, dulness of head, fever, pulse 108, then stupidity, in which he did not know whether he was awake or asleep, at night frequent waking, with much mucus in throat and distressing dreams, on rising next morning weakness, sweat on forehead and nausea, so that he lay down again. Pinching from larynx upward. Pain; in r. upper side; towards back on swallowing food and drink; and contraction; *in region of tonsil, as if neckcloth were too tight;* as if choked with something that would not go down.

Painful jerking to pit of stomach in morning when sitting up in bed. *Soreness;* at 7 A.M.; on swallowing; *with swelling of cervical glands;* with swelling, trapezius muscles very sore, can scarcely turn my head, and neck sensitive to touch; scratching, during empty swallowing; like a cramp at inside of cervical vertebræ, after a meal. Constriction, above and on larynx; in fauces on smoking. Sensation of a plug; in evening on swallowing; which he must swallow, mucus is raised by hawking or coughing.

Feeling as if skinned; and in nose. Smarting in l. side of pharynx, then cutting and at times pressing; S. posteriorly in fauces and above on palate, with burning, as before coryza. Scraping in evening; S. on swallowing. *Roughness in fauces, < hawking, with burning.* Creeping, with hoarse sensation, which causes hawking. Heat; in afternoon. Difficult swallowing as from paralysis, evenings. Numbness in r. tonsil.

Dryness; in fauces; all day; in afternoon, < 8 P.M., with heat and paroxysms of pain and lachrymation, rawness in posterior nares, redness of fauces, when swallowing it seemed as if the opposing parts would not blend, next day throat < after sleep, temporarily > detaching mucus, which had to be swallowed; in evening before sleep, not > drinking; < evenings; *in posterior nares, with much mucus in mouth, with urging to swallow;* with sense of thickness.

Stomach.—Hunger on waking, preventing sleep again; on seeing food, with salivation. *Craving hunger;* at noon; in evening; and if he only thinks of eating salivation; and if it is not appeased salivation; and after eating weariness and eructations tasting of food. *Desire for vinegar;* for acids; for sweets and meat., Little appetite, yet he relishes everything; L., but much thirst; and everything tastes too salt. *Appetite lost;* and taste; but thirst. *Aversion to meat;* to all food, *especially meat,* could eat only bread, butter and soup; to smoking tobacco.

Thirst; all day, with sickness and fever; in morning after waking; in evening; for wine; sudden and uncontrollable at 9 P.M., but water tastes insipid unless very cold. *Thirstless.*

Eructations; after eating a little (Lyc.); *after eating and drinking;* with retching; alternating with hiccough; *sour;* sour after supper; tasting like rotten eggs; empty after supper; gurgling, empty; of blood in a warm room; painful, of blood, after rapid riding; bitter, after breakfast; bitter, with nausea; bitter, in morning on rising, with bitter taste in mouth and throat, the bitter taste > eating.

Hiccough after a meal; after supper; during habitual smoking, with contraction of throat and sensation of a plug in it, causing nausea and salivation.

Nausea. **Morning nausea, > eating;** *on waking, towards evening and at night; on washing mouth; before breakfast;* on riding in a carriage; with no desire for stool; *on walking, with blackness before eyes,* fever from 1 till 6 P.M., with tearing in limbs and nausea, *in evening weakness even to faintness, with melancholy, easily startled,* at night much fetid flatus; with salivation and griping in abdomen; *then vomiting of food, then retching.* N. every day at 10 A.M.; at 11 A.M., with chilliness; in forenoon after a walk, with blackness before eyes and loss of appetite, before dinner heat with pain in limbs, nausea, headache, and in company weakness even to faintness, every trifle affected him and he was easily startled; at night waking him; after lunch; *on exerting eyes, with anxiety;* at the thought of eating; before each liquid stool; on coughing, at times retching, causing heat and sweat; on movement, with weakness forcing him to lie on the ground, and in open air the limbs felt relaxed; *with weakness;* with chilliness; with bitterness in throat; with cutting in abdomen; with digging in abdomen; then drawing in limbs; *as if everything in abdomen were turning around, in morning; intermittent, all day and after a meal, with watery salivation, bitterish sour taste, loss of appetite, yet food tasted natural;* in two attacks per day, with contractive griping in hypochondrium extending like a stitch into back, with stitches in chest and yawning till he vomits bile and food.

Vomiting during pregnancy, straining her so that blood comes up; V. of milky water during pregnancy, though she had not drunk milk; bilious, mornings.

Rumbling. *Sticking in pit;* S. in afternoon, and in the distended abdomen; beneath pit during inspiration; in pit, l. side and between scapulæ during eructations; sudden, in pit on swallowing food quickly. Tearing around pit. Cutting extending to breast, with motion of flatus, which cannot find exit. Cramplike pain, and in abdomen; burning-contracting cramps from a cold. Griping as if something would tear loose in morning during eructations. **Gnawing, > supper, with weakness;** G. in pit at night when awake, with intolerance of weight of clothes.

Distress, < afternoon, > supper, with sensitiveness to clothes, aching and throbbing, > eructations, with pain from the jar of walking, in evening flatulence. Pain in pit; P. in morning in bed; from morning till 1 P.M.; in evening, then headache; every night; in pit at night, with drawing; *in region on pressure; after a meal and on touch;* at cardiac orifice when food is descending; in epigastrium an hour after dinner and after walking in open air, with tension; in pit, > fermenting movement downward; *sore, internally;* sticking tensive, in pit and hypochondria during movement when stooping; drawing, an hour after dinner and earlier, with gnawing extending to back, where it is most painful, then prostration.

Pressure as from a stone; in pit, < bread. Contraction in region. Fulness at noon. **Emptiness** (Pod., Puls., Ign.); **with nausea as soon as she thinks of food she would like** (Puls.). *Uneasiness at 7 A.M. Pulsation in pit in morning, then ebullition in chest like palpitation, then internal heat of face and body without redness or thirst, but with sweat;* P. in pit when eating, worse the more he eats (Nat. m.). Heaviness, with pain in abdomen. Coldness. *Burning, and in pit;* B. after eructations; and in pit, with feeling as if eating would relieve it; extending upward. Heartburn in pit extending to throat in forenoon and afternoon, and in throat sourish taste and scraping.

Clinical.—Acid dyspepsia, with bloated abdomen, sour or putrid eructations, sometimes nausea and vomiting. Vomiting of pregnancy, with the characteristic sensation of emptiness in the stomach. Gastric catarrh, with excessive acidity, heartburn. Dyspepsia, with hypochondriac mood, especially at the climacteric of women, or as the result of overwrought brain, or sexual excess. Atonic dyspepsia, with amenorrhœa, the nausea and vomiting generally > eating and lying down. A longing for acids, with flatulent dyspepsia, soreness over the abdomen and liver, blisters in the mouth, and especially with a feeling of something twisting about in the stomach and rising into the throat.

Abdomen.—*Distention;* in evening, then eructations; *after dinner;* after dinner, at 6 P.M.; after soup; after eating, < supper; after least food, not > discharge of flatus; after least food, at first > then < loosening clothes; when walking, with emission of flatus; around waist during menses, with discomfort; < evening; < evening, with hardness and with congestion of superficial abdominal veins and sticking in a hernia; with noise and whistling in it; with pain and soreness; with slimy diarrhœa; with diarrhœa and griping; without stool; hard, with cutting; flatulent, after dinner, lasting till evening; painful, when riding in a carriage; tympanitic, at 4 P.M.

Rumbling. Noises. Grumbling; in evening, with motion of flatus; when lying; and motion of flatus, as in diarrhœa. Flatulence; in evening; when walking in open air; after walking in open air. Emissions of flatus; and from vagina; offensive.

Tearing in afternoon, as if intestines were torn out. Cramp. Cutting in morning; after midnight; at night, with urging to urinate; in attacks, so that she must bend up; flatulent, transversely across, > motion, with cutting in l. testicle; griping, with groaning anxiety, as if involuntary stool would pass. Griping; > eructations; with sensation as if bowels would turn inside out; alternating with sticking, in attacks of ten minutes. Griping diarrhœic feeling, then exhausting diarrhœa. Digging, with contraction and emission of flatus.

Pain; at 6 A.M. on moving, with sudden urging to stool, which was thin, yellow and scanty, with tenesmus; in muscles at night on motion; every night, waking him at 2 A.M., with at times pain above and around umbilicus, with trembling of heart, which can be felt outwardly (without palpitation), full pulse, nausea, weakness and dryness of mouth; during supper, then three stools, with urging; before stool; *before menses, with faintness;* a few days before menses, then soreness in perineum and swelling of pudendum before menses; < eating, with dulness of head and tension of skin of forehead; > stool; with many gelatinous stools; so that she must bend double; flatulent, before stool, with groans and sobs; as if intestines had been beaten to pieces.

Soreness as if menses would appear (Sulph.). Smarting after a thin stool. Tension in morning; *drawing T.* **Heaviness; during motion. Emptiness;** *after stool* (Sul. ac., Pod.). Beating here and there. Uneasiness; as before diarrhœa. *Weakness after two hard stools, with loss of appetite.* Burning when walking in open air; when sitting, > walking.

Hypochondria.—Gurgling in r. *Sticking; in hepatic*

region; in hepatic region in evening, with pain on touch and with constipation; when coughing; in r., with short, dry, evening cough; passing under H. transversely through epigastrium; tensive, impeding motion, < walking; cutting, in gall-bladder. Pinching in hepatic region, > eructations and emission of flatus; paroxysmal P. in liver. Jerks in liver. *Pain in hepatic region* (Pod.); in gall-bladder; deep in a spot over spleen from 2 till 3 P.M.; *in l., > lying;* in liver when walking; drawing, in hepatic region in evening. *Sore pain in hepatic region* (Pod.); at noon in location of a former congestion, felt next day on turning or reaching, and afterwards on sudden movement; when riding over rough roads, obstructing breathing. *Full sensation in hepatic region* (Pod.). Beating in hepatic region.

Sticking in transverse colon, beginning in splenic flexure and passing to hepatic flexure, after stool, < walking, > sitting; intermittent S. just under pit of stomach, radiating obliquely up into l. side. Pain in transverse colon; in upper A. in afternoon; in upper A., at times > internal fermentation, with tension and with pressure and sticking in umbilical region.

Sides.—Grumbling in l., with emptiness. *Sticking in l.;* in r. muscles, with twitches; then difficult breathing; transversely through from r. to l. *Pain in r.; attacks of contractive, in r., < morning, then constriction in stomach extending to chest, > eructations;* as from a stiff body or plug, making stooping painful or impossible; drawing. Burning in r. when walking far.

Umbilicus.—Sticking extending to pudendum when coughing and gagging. Smarting boring to right of U. Pain in region, < coughing and stooping; P. extending to pudendum, < touch; in centre of abdomen as from a lump from afternoon till bedtime, extending upward towards evening, with sleepiness, but inability to sleep at night; drawing, in region, then discharge of mucus from rectum, with urging and sticking, then congestion of blood to chest, with anxiety and restlessness, which after dinner changed to alternations of internal heat and chilliness, with sweat on head from 1 till 4 P.M., then headache, then pain in nape, next day the same condition; burning, to left of and below U. Sore spot in wall to right of and below U., next day tender to pressure and from movements of muscles in walking, afterwards on sudden turning.

Hypogastrium.—Swelling of l. inguinal glands, painful on walking. Fulness in r. groin when walking; F., with aching in ovaries, heaviness in head and sleepiness. Gurgling over l. hip. Sticking; in sides; in l. in morning; transversely through just over hips; upward in l. groin during stool. Sticking tearing in groin, extending into thigh on stepping. Cutting during breakfast, with urging to stool; C. in afternoon, with jerks; then free, loose stool. Griping, > 10 A.M.; G. all day in quarter-hour attacks, with hard daily stool. Pain in l. side; in r. side of front; in r. groin near Poupart's ligament; in place of a hernia during violent laughter; with bruised feeling waking her at night; across; *across at night on lying down, > micturition;* across, extending down inside of thighs, with soreness of abdomen and thighs on touch, at times inability to stand, with piles and constipation; *in pelvis, beginning in sacrum and passing forward and down to r. knee at 7.30 A.M., > pressing against something hard,* **the pelvic pain > crossing limbs,** but the pain in knee aggravated; flatulent, deep in r. side after a meal, later only on moving and bending forward. **Pressing downward; during menses** (Bell.); *> knee-elbow position, which caused eructations and sleep; in pelvis at 9 A.M., < forenoon, with sick feeling, and < 4 P.M. on waking, with gloomy feeling, > supper at 6 P.M., the P. returned at 9 P.M., next day at 9 A.M.* **Pressure as if contents would issue through genitals.** *P. as if bladder would fall out over os pubis, partially > hard pressure, the pelvic distress always felt at night on waking, > transiently by lying on side with legs flexed on thighs and thighs on abdomen,* returning third morning on stirring, *during the day sensation as of an overdistended bladder, < sitting and lying, > walking and supper, fourth day P. as if uterus would issue through vulva, > from supper till 9 P.M., on eighth day pelvic symptoms < 4 P.M. after sleep, a week later P. all day, with dulness in head and desire to sit or lie still with eyes closed, amelioration after supper.* Pressure outward low down in pelvis, with twisting and contraction; undulating P. outward in r. groin. Pulling pain in r. iliac region near crest at 10 P.M. Drawing above r. hip, extending to ribs and towards kidneys, > emission of flatus. Spasmodic contraction in r. side. Sudden distress in pelvis at 9 A.M., < forenoon, with sickness. *Singular feeling in pelvic region at 4 P.M., a weakness about small of back, pubic bones, and around anus a dragging.* Burning in r. flank.

Clinical.—Enlargement of the liver, with heaviness in the hepatic region. Torpid liver, with aching, weight and soreness, involving even the right shoulder, with occipital headache, sallow complexion, and especially a yellow stripe across the bridge of the nose.

Rectum.—*Prolapsus* (Pod.). Sticking; at night; in perineum, pressing towards rectum, in evening when sitting. Cutting during stool, with discharge of blood; C. in afternoon, drawing towards hypogastrium, then ineffectual urging. Pain during stool and when sitting afterwards; tensive P., and in anus. Contractive pain before and during hard stool; C. pain extending into vagina and perineum. Smarting after stool. *Weak feeling in evening in bed,* causing restlessness, so that he cannot sleep. *Itching. Burning all day;* during latter part of a soft stool; with hard stools. Urging, with pain in lumbar region; constant U., but scanty stool; at 6 A.M., stool in hard lumps and with bleeding, then free stools at 7 and 10 P.M. Ineffectual urging; towards evening, next morning stool hard and lumpy; *passes only wind and mucus, with sensation of a plug in rectum.*

Clinical.—Inactivity of the rectum, which feels constantly full, even after a stool; even a soft stool is expelled with difficulty. Hæmorrhoids, with bleeding at stool. A distressing feeling as of a lump in the rectum (Anac.).

Anus.—*Hæmorrhoids; bleeding when walking;* seem indurated. **Protruding H.; during stool; when walking;** after stool, of a humid, painless one; and itching. **Painful H.; when walking;** *after stool;* on touch, with intermittent sore pain pressing outward, < between stools, even when lying.

Swelling of margin, with heat. *Congestion after dinner. Expulsion of ascarides.* Discharge of bloody mucus after stool. Painful contractions. *Sticking;* from after morning stool till afternoon; < retracting it and by pressure; and tearing. Cutting at night, and in rectum. Sudden **aching** during constipation, > walking fast, ceased when fæces began to pass. *Soreness;* with intermittent tenesmus. Raw sensation during stool. Scraping during stool. Contractive sensation,

> after fermentation in abdomen; C. pain during stool, then extending forward and upward into abdomen. Tension after stool. *Burning;* during stool. *Itching;* with creeping in rectum.

Clinical.—Hæmorrhoids, with bleeding at stool; distress when walking about.

Stools.—Watery, yellow, with pain and flatulence. *Diarrhœa;* after milk; *after boiled milk;* then constipation; exhausting; almost like grits; slimy, with discharge of round and thread-worms; acrid, three times a day, then protrusion of hæmorrhoids, which ooze moisture and which pain on sitting. Pappy, sour-smelling, evacuated very quickly. Soft, thin-shaped, difficult.

Constipation; causing bleeding, weight and pain in rectum. *Hard,* with cutting in rectum; H., then soft; at night, and difficult; and large, difficult; *and difficult, mixed with mucus; and knotty,* insufficient; in small lumps, unsatisfactory, with feeling as if I had lost the power of expulsion. *Whitish. Brownish, scanty, difficult, but not hard. Bloody;* but not hard. Scanty, with loss of power to expel it; S. and difficult in evening, next morning a small soft one. Frequent; with pain and tenesmus during stool; natural, about every two hours till afternoon, towards night diarrhœa with tenesmus before and during stool, burning in anus after stool and bearing down in region of anus. Difficult. Putrid, sourish.

Clinical.—Diarrhœa; green, mucous, especially from boiled milk, in children during teething, with turbid, offensive urine and reddish sediment adherent to the vessel, rapid exhaustion and emaciation.

Urinary Organs.—Bladder. Spasm. Sticking through B. before micturition. Pinching. Aching at neck after urinating. Sensation as if drops came out, < during rest. Burning, without desire to urinate. *Distended feeling.* **Pressure on B.** (Lil. tig.) **and frequent micturition and tension in hypogastrium;** *P. in evening, with burning after micturition.* **Urging;** in morning, **with bearing down in pelvis;** *in morning, but micturition only after waiting several minutes; in neck of bladder; continual; frequent;* frequent, with scanty discharge alternating with retention of urine; ineffectual, at 11 A.M.

Frequent micturition; during the day; in afternoon; *at night;* as often as he woke at night, with thirst; with uneasiness, as from fulness in bladder; with pressure on bladder, but he must wait long before the urine comes, if he endeavors to retain the urine he is attacked with anxiety and pressure on bladder.

Urethra.—Discharge of moisture after micturition; milky D. after micturition; of prostatic fluid after micturition; of prostatic fluid, with difficult stool. *Sticking;* and cutting. Tearing; in forepart. *Smarting;* near meatus; in orifice; *during micturition;* astringent, in forepart in morning on waking. Tingling; in meatus; in meatus between 1 and 2 P.M.; for about an inch back from head of penis at 9.30 A.M. Itching. *Burning; in forepart;* in forepart after emission.

Urine.—Copious; and water-colored; next day scanty. *Scanty; with red deposit;* and deep red, no desire to urinate; with constant desire; with much thirst. **Thick, slimy, offensive, depositing a yellowish, pasty sediment next morning. Turbid; and clay-colored, with reddish sediment** (Berb.); *when passed, as if mixed with mucus, and dark; after standing, and offensive, with white sediment; with red sandy sediment* (Lyc., Berb.); and offensive; and acid, with bile pigment. *High-colored, soon becoming turbid and* **staining bottom of vessel.** *Looks like powdered brick.* Blood-red. Pale yellow. *Fetid; with much white sediment.* Acid, *deposit of white adherent film, sediment at bottom of tube pinkish,* the sediment readily dissolved on slight heat (not by nitric acid), showed amorphous particles, and on standing forty-eight hours crystals of uric acid appeared. *White, filmy, adherent sediment. Brick-dust sediment* (Lyc., Berb.), *and vessel covered with a white substance* and looking like ground glass. Deposits blood. *Yellowish-red, adherent deposit.*

Clinical.—Chronic cystitis, with slow micturition, but with constant desire and a bearing-down sensation above the pubis. Very slow micturition from atony of the bladder. It has been found valuable to relieve the distressing bearing-down feeling of cystocele. Nocturnal enuresis, especially in the forepart of the night. Chronic urethritis. The characteristic urine of Sepia deposits a red sediment which adheres tightly to the vessel.

Sexual Organs.—Sweat on male; on scrotum. Glans, *red spots;* red, almost sore indurations coming and going on inner side of G. and prepuce, tickling on touch; on lower part a purulent fluid having a sourish salt smell, with itching; itching inflammation, increasing the excitement during coition; sticking; burning during coition; heat and itching, with soreness of prepuce; heat, with pale red and at times itching eruption. Ulceration of prepuce, with itching. Sticking in prepuce and frænum, with smarting raw feeling and congestion of the integument.

Erections after coition and after nocturnal emissions; after coition, then weakness of thought, vertigo, discouragement, relaxation of body, and in evening low-spirited and inclined to start; persistent, at night; painful, when sitting after the siesta; strong, but short, with quick emission during coition; insufficient, with coition; wanting.

Pinching tearing in testicles. Cutting in testicles. Rheumatic drawing in testicles and along side of thigh. Heat in testicles. Emissions nightly, with sexual dreams; imperfect E., with lascivious dreams; weak and watery; suppressed by his waking. Sexual thoughts without erections. But little pleasurable sensation during coition. Desire increased; D., with rapid emission, but slight voluptuous feeling, then tension in hypogastrium extending to spermatic cord.

Female.—Dilated feeling before menses. *Soreness of labia, perineum and between thighs, with redness;* S. of labia, with inflamed feeling. Sticking in pudendum; extending almost to umbilicus. Burning in pudendum before menses. Vulva feels enlarged.

Vagina.—Sticking in orifice; intermittent S.; extending into body of uterus, > bending double. Jerking upward in morning after a dream. **Dryness after menses, and of vulva, causing discomfort when walking** (Nat. m.). **Leucorrhœa;** *after micturition; with itching in vagina; with eructations, retching and pallor;* **yellow; acrid, before menses, with soreness of pudenda** (Lil. tig.); **like milk** (Puls., Calc. c.), **only by day, with burning pain and excoriation between thighs** (Puls.); *looking like pus* (Calc. c.); *lumpy, fetid, with drawing pain in hypogastrium;* as clear as water; excoriating, causing pain when walking. *Discharge bloody, slimy* (Murex); *of a few drops of blood fifteen days before time for the menses;* of blood after coition;

of blood when walking; greenish-red, during pregnancy.

Uterus.—**Beginning to prolapse, congested, and yellowish leucorrhœa pouring from it** (Lil. tig.). *Prolapsus, with inclination of fundus to l.* (*Puls.*, *Murex* r. side), *causing numbness in l. lower half of body, with pain, and the same pain in pelvic region,* > *lying, especially on r. side, tenderness of os uteri.* Sticking; upward; spasmodic through U.; from cervix to fundus and then to r. ovary, causing nausea. Cramps all night during menses and next day on moving about; before and at beginning of menses. *Pain, and in l. ovary; P. passing into vagina. Feeling as if clutched and suddenly released,* at 7 P.M., *causing nausea.* **Pressure as if everything would issue through vulva** (Lil. tig. [Cap.]), **in afternoon; P. downward as if everything would fall out, with oppression of breath and pain in abdomen, she must cross her limbs to prevent protrusion of vagina, yet nothing protrudes, but there is increase of gelatinous leucorrhœa.** Painful stiffness in region.

Ovaries.—Sticking through l. (Graph.) at 4 P.M., next day at 4.30 P.M., and through acetabulum. Darting pain in r. (Pod.), next day pain as of a tight thread running to uterus. Sharp pains, with urging to urinate, the pain > micturition, later in the day heavy pain in l. ovary. Pain in r. (Pod.), < afternoon; in r., < inspiration; in r., with pain in back, next afternoon in r., with soreness on pressure after sleeping, felt too badly to move (Pod.). *Heaviness; with urging to urinate; in lower part, with urging to urinate.*

Menses—*Too early; and scanty, appearing only in the morning; and scanty, lasting only one day;* and scanty, dark, fetid. *Too late; at the full moon;* (after-effect). Reappeared in an elderly woman after they had been absent several months; with drawing from teeth into the swollen cheek. Increased and brighter colored. Scanty, pale, acrid; S., dark, clotted, painful.

Clinical.—Chronic dry catarrh of the vagina, which is painful, especially on coition. The symptoms of pressure as if everything would protrude, and the feeling of emptiness in the stomach and abdomen have led to the very successful use of this drug in displacements of the uterus, especially in simple prolapsus; there is a feeling as if everything would protrude from the pudenda and the woman even crosses her legs to prevent protrusion. Induration of the neck of the uterus. Chronic endometritis, with tenderness over the uterine region, constant desire to urinate, etc. (Aur. mur. nat.). Disorders of menstruation, amenorrhœa, dysmenorrhœa, with scanty flow, nervous palpitation, sinking at the epigastrium, morning nausea, etc., threatening abortion, with the extreme pressure of the drug. Flushes at the climacteric period. Tumors of the breast, with sharp pains.

Respiratory Organs.—Mucus in larynx, difficult to cough up but easy to swallow, even with deep inspiration. Frequent pressure in larynx in morning, without pain. Dryness of trachea; of larynx in morning. Hoarseness; in evening; with weakness and chilliness; sudden; inability to speak aloud. Voice as in coryza, in evening.

Cough every morning till 9 A.M., with coryza and with sneezing in bed; *in evening;* **at night preventing sleep** (Puls.); *at night waking him;* < **evening after lying down;** < **evening in bed,** with vomiting (Puls.); on going to sleep; with sticking in back; with sticking in hypochondria; **spasmodic;** *irritation to C. so sudden that he cannot breathe quickly enough, and it causes spasmodic contraction of chest; causing pain in pit of stomach, day and night; affecting chest and stomach;* harsh, distressing, < going from cold air to warm room, and *vice versa,* lungs are sore; scraping, it seems to have settled on chest; tickling scraping, and again loose, phlegmy. *Dry cough* towards morning, from tickling in trachea; D. in evening in bed, with vomiting of bitter fluid; *after a meal; from tickling in larynx;* from tickling in throat; > lying, but when lying at night dry coryza; with stitches in r. chest; *as if from stomach and abdomen, or from constipation, or as if something lodged in stomach; and hard, concussive; and short, in evening, with intermittent sticking in r. hypochondrium; often dry, whooping and choking, with pain in pit of stomach and scraping, raw, sore pain in larynx,* > *swallowing food, the C. does not wake her, but is worse after waking, at times rattling in trachea, ending in mucous expectoration;* and tickling, > morning, with spasm of chest. **Hacking cough in evening after lying down** (Sang.), with expectoration of pure coagulated blood. *Loose cough,* < *night. Cough, with expectoration;* day and night, *C. wakes her at night,* with sensation as if chest were hollow and sore; *C. from 8 till 9* P.M., > *expectoration; only before midnight, as soon as he gets into bed; C., with almost loss of breath if she cannot expectorate;* of blood every morning; *scanty E. evenings in bed, but mostly with bitter vomiting; purulent E., with oppression of chest, rattling in throat, the slightest motion takes away her breath and she is exhausted;* gray and yellowish E.; C. in sudden attacks, E. full and easy *only* after breakfast; violent C., with much E. of white mucus.

Expectoration.—From chest without much cough. *Salt* (Lyc.) *from chest.* Of white mucus. Yellow, tasting like rotten eggs. Blood-streaked, after a meal. Putrid-tasting, with putrid breath. Scanty, with wheezing rattling in chest.

Respiration.—Asthmatic attack at night, lay with head bent forward, then cough with expectoration of tenacious saliva; A. during mental exertion, worse during palpitation. *Breath lost on slightest motion;* when standing still. Dyspnœa; *in morning on waking, lasting four hours, with sweat;* with mucus in chest difficult to loosen. *Short;* when walking; *as if chest were full, when walking.* Oppressed in evening by pain under short ribs, which prevents motion; O. towards evening from pressure over pit of stomach. Snoring inspiration. Inclination to sigh. Inclined to take a long breath.

Clinical.—Whooping cough < before midnight, followed by expectoration which is generally thick, greenish-yellow and salty, with relief; the cough seems to come from the abdomen. Whooping cough, with violent retching, frequent desire to eat, < especially the forepart of the night. Chronic bronchitis, < morning on waking, particularly with hepatic symptoms, pale yellow face. Sepia has proved itself valuable, certainly as an intercurrent, in chronic pulmonary diseases (phthisis), particularly when there are soreness in the chest, faintness in the stomach and other symptoms; more frequently called for in women.

Chest.—Gurgling. Rattling till the expectoration is coughed up; R. of mucus, then cough and expectoration causing raw and sore pain in throat. A cold from riding in a railway car, voice hoarse, deep and unnatural. *Sticking in one mamma;* in r. side; deep in; in r. side in morning after a half sleep; in r. towards evening during inspiration; *in l. on coughing;* in r. when walking in open air; in r. during expiration; in r. side and scapula during inspiration and cough; on inspiration, he dared to take only a short breath, from this the head became affected; in r. mamma, < cold when riding or walking; in region of

r. lowest ribs towards pit of stomach, > eructations; *in l., with palpitation;* in l. without relation to breathing; occasional, in l. lung on expiration.

Tearing in r. lower ribs; near l. shoulder-joint, > eructations, but returning. Paroxysmal piercing pain in lower lobe of r. lung. Sharp pain near heart in middle of afternoon and about 10 P.M.; in a spot in ensiform cartilage, as if a nerve were tense, < inspiration and ascending stairs. Pain; in upper lobe of l. lung; in r. fourth and fifth ribs, near sternum, returning from 12 till 1 P.M.; in l. at 5 P.M.; *in evening in bed;* in r. upper on retiring at 10.45 P.M., then boring in point of l. testicle, these symptoms came and went till sleep; in upper part of sternum when coughing; in tendons of pectoral muscles, near head of humerus, on bending arm backward and from touch; < certain movements; in r. side, < stooping and lying on r. side; near l. axilla, < strong expiration, and on touch bruised pain; in sides, passing around between scapulæ.

Burning pain in sternum when drinking beer. Soreness of lungs; of mammæ on touch; of mammæ on touch, < moving, turning or stepping; burning, in upper part of l., even from touch. Rawness; from cough and expectoration.

Oppression morning and evening (see Ferr., Phos.); in evening, < lying, with difficult breathing and flickering before eyes; < walking; anxious, in upper part. Pressure on l. lower ribs on walking; P. on stooping and deep breathing; on l. lower ribs, even from touch; paroxysmal, on r., > empty eructations; tensive, < l. side. Contraction in morning; in morning on waking; at night on waking, with oppression, he had to breathe heavily and deeply, and on waking in morning some C.; with oppression, and on deep breathing sticking; with tightness; with fulness, interfering with breathing; around lower part, so that he cannot breathe deeply. Tension in attacks; T. as from a cold, posteriorly at l. side. Pressing drawing on r. false ribs, towards back, > motion and rubbing. Dragging in r. side. Weight; on upper part of sternum; necessitating deep breathing. Bubbling in l. Beating in l.; in C. and abdomen as if heart occupied the whole body. Burning in sternum. Orgasm and congestion as if hæmoptysis would follow. Tickling in lower part. Crawling causing irritation to cough.

Heart.—Sticking in afternoon; through H. about noon. Impulse increased and rapid, < inspiration. Convulsive beating, with anxiety and trembling of fingers and lower limbs. Intermittent beating after dinner; < a meal; with anxiety. Palpitation; in evening; *in evening in bed, with beating in all arteries;* > walking far and fast; with anxious feeling, which necessitates deep breathing, without influence on the spirits.

Clinical.—Sympathetic affections of the heart, palpitation and a tremulous feeling, with flushes, in women. Occasionally used for cardiac dropsy.

Pulse.—Rapid; if he thinks of past troubles, with failure of breath; with rash. Slow. Irregular.

Neck.—Stretching out, with distortion of face. Jerking in nape, with shaking of head. Sticking in nape, with drawing, arresting breathing. Pain, then cramplike pain in lower jaw; P. in r. side in evening, > dinner; sore, in lower cervical vertebræ in evening when walking in open air; drawing and expanding, in side; drawing, in r. side, < bending head to l.; contractive, in nape, < r. side. Tension; in one side as if swollen. Swollen sensation in nape. Stiffness of nape; from easy straining during work, with tense feeling.

Back.—*Tearing during menses, preventing sleep, with chills, heat, thirst and contraction of chest.* Aching; in afternoon; when sitting; when sitting bent over at writing; on walking, arresting breath; *dragging, and in sacrum, < between lumbar region and crista ilii, more on r. side, at 6 P.M., with strained feeling when walking,* afterwards the pain caused nausea and when standing faintness; burning, in spine; sudden hammering, > pressure against a hard substance, with sticking tearing, so that he felt as if he would sink together and lose his breath. Tired feeling, with pain in small of back, and on sitting down he had to sit very straight. *Heaviness in morning on waking, almost as if asleep.* Stiffness > walking; S. after a second stool, with hardness, and with tightness in pit of stomach and oppressed breathing.

Scapulæ.—Sticking; in l.; between S.; extending into side of chest when sitting and walking fast, < evening and afternoon; from r. through ribs during inspiration, > walking in open air. Tearing in l. after slight exposure; in l., as from a cold. *Pain between S. and down back;* under r. shoulder; in a spot between upper parts; between r. and vertebræ; in upper part of back in morning if she laces herself at all tightly; *between S. and under l., extending into l. lung, < expiration.* Sprained pain under l. shoulder-joint. Drawing pain above r.; near l., near spine, at times drawing to neck; under r., at one time more in back, then in side, < sitting with arm held out free from body. Drawing between S. and in upper chest; D., with jerks. Tension between S.; in l. towards evening; under r., < lying on l. side.

Lumbar Region.—Gurgling in r. Sticking in kidneys and liver; across coccyx before stool; extending to l. lung; *posteriorly over r. hip, so that she could not lie on r. side, and on touch pain as from subcutaneous ulceration;* sudden, when lifting, he had to walk bent forward and had stitches if his foot struck against anything. *Sprained pain over hips in evening in bed and in afternoon.* Rending over r. hip, extending backward. Sharp pressure on and below sacrum. **Pain**; in kidney region; *in sacrum;* in l. side; **in afternoon when walking;** *in sacrum in evening, > pressure; on waking from a nap at 7.30 P.M., < l. side, pain in lumbar region all night; across loins, < moving;* intermittent, over r. hip. **Tired pain**; in lower part of spine from walking, so that it feels broken; causing nausea, and a faint feeling when standing. Pressure on spine above lumbar region, with rheumatic drawing in neck. Pressive drawing in l. Deep-seated tension. Heavy pulling in r. at 3 P.M. Heat in kidney region on taking a long breath. Stiffness of lower part of back.

Extremities.—Swelling at wrist, bend of elbow and around malleoli in evening, > next morning, but parts were painful to touch. Jerking at night; J. on moving them; intermittent, of r. leg during the day, then trembling of r. hand. Tearing in elbows and knees; drawing, extending upward all day during rest, with weakness. Pain, < hips; of all kinds in long bones, < their ends, when walking in open air. Bruised pain in thighs and upper arms at night during sleep, with exhaustion of them. Sticking smarting in l.

knee and on inside of thighs and arms; intermittent, along inside of l. arm and leg when sitting or at rest, < from 5 P.M. till late in evening. Drawing pains in r. forearm and thigh. Drawing; arthritic, in knee and finger-joints. Anxiety. Uneasiness; at night. Purring in arms, hands and lower limbs. Weakness in morning on waking; W. in joints, < knees; with chilliness. *Heaviness.* Go to sleep easily.

Upper Extremities.—Axillary glands. Swelling; of l., with suppuration. Soreness. Full sensation in l., then r.

Shoulder.—Tearing in l. joint; in joint, as if it would tear off, > belching; drawing, in joint, as if sprained. Sprained pain in joint when resting arm while writing. Pain; in the one which was higher than the other from disease, also on touch; in joints on lifting the slightest weight or when resting elbow in an elevated position, with trembling of hands; as if excoriated; intermittent bruised, in sockets, extending to elbows, generally in only one arm at a time. Weary pain in l. joint; in r. and in muscles of nape. *Drawing pain* in joint in morning. Drawing at top during rest. Tension in l. joint, > moving it, with drawing. Pressure at night, with sprained feeling and sensation as if asleep. Stiffness of l.; of r., with lameness.

Arm.—Jerking in l. biceps in evening; J. upward in r., then trembling of hands. Shooting along inside of r. Drawing extending to fingers. Weakness on waking; W., they go to sleep during rest. Stiffness, with internal coldness. Paralytic sensation in l.; P. sensation, then throbbing. Falling asleep when resting head on it; F. asleep of arms and hands, < when under covers, in which case there is painful stiffness in them.

Upper Arm.—Jerking. Tearing in a spot above l. elbow. Bruised pain; in l.; during motion. Creeping tingling pain extending to shoulder-joint, and causing uneasiness in arm, < motion and stooping, > rest and lying in bed. Drawing pain in one, then other.

Elbow.—Sticking; in tip at night during frequent waking. Tearing at bend of l. Bruised feeling in l., in region of ulnar nerve. Tension as if too short.

Forearm.—Cramp when walking. Tearing near wrist, now r., now l.; drawing, in lower part. Pain in r. Tingling.

Wrist.—Sticking tearing in l. Tearing extending to shoulder, so that he could scarcely move arm, > during the day and when at rest, on letting arm hang down it was blue and rigid. Darting pain, and on dorsum of r. hand to between first and second fingers, then on corresponding part of palm. Drawing pain in r. Weakness of r.

Hand.—Jerking in palm, with sticking. Tearing. Tearing drawing from outer side of l. to elbow. Smarting on outer side of r. Weakness. Numbness if he holds anything tightly or carries anything, with falling asleep of it. Falling asleep at night.

Fingers.—Flexion of index, he could not straighten it. Thumb immovably bent towards little finger. Sticking in middle joints; in tip of little; in tip of l. thumb; in inner sides of tips; in l., with drawing. Tearing in first phalanx of r. thumb; in first phalanx of r. index; under nail of r. index. Sharp tingling pains in tips. Sore feeling in last joints on clenching fist, if pressed they are painful. *Tension in metacarpal joints,* < during flexion. Arthritic drawing in joints. Painful tickling under nail of r. thumb; almost painful, under nail of l. index. Numbness of r. in evening.

Lower Extremities.—Jerking in l.; upward of l. in forenoon when sitting. *Bruised feeling, she desires to sit down and when sitting feels as if she must stand up;* B. feeling, > dancing, with pain in every nerve, pain on touch. Uneasiness in one in evening, as from internal imperfect itching. Sensation in l. as if a mouse were running up and down. *Weakness.* Stiffness extending up to hip-joints; S. after sitting a short time, with falling asleep and crawling. Numbness of one when standing, with sudden paralytic sensation. Falling asleep when sitting.

Thigh.—Trembling, and of knee, with jerking in thigh. Jerking, and in buttock; J. when walking. *Cramp* when walking; in inner side when walking. Cramping pain in hip-joint, > walking; sudden tearing, in hips extending to feet, when walking. Sticking in l. when walking; tearing, in l. during rest, then ulcerative pain; tearing, when walking, almost paralyzing lower limbs, with chilliness. Tearing in r. on walking, with pain on touch; T. after dinner and supper, < knees; from hip-joint to foot at night, preventing sleep; burning, at inner part of l. buttock. Pain in posterior muscles when sitting; in hip, < walking; in femora when sitting, she must change her seat often; in r. hip-joint, close to body, beginning and ending gradually; in r. every evening after lying down, so that she could not move; in nates, so that he could scarcely sit; undulating, in upper part of femur. Bruised pain on touch, with tension when walking; in r. hip-joint when lying on r. side; in hip-joint, < rising from a seat, > continued walking, with weakness. Pulling pain in hip after moving. Pain drawing upward in femora; intermittent D. pain over r. buttock. *Drawing;* from r. hip to sole all day. *Soreness between T., with burning pain.* Tension in l. as if asleep, extending to sole; paralytic, in r. when walking, and in hip-joint. Weight.

Knee.—Painful swelling, with tension; numb S. of patella, and when kneeling the knee is unyielding and tense. Cracking. Sticking; under patella on walking fast; in hollow, with cutting; tearing, between K. and patella. Tearing in r. as soon as she grows cold; around K. and malleoli when sitting and lying. Twisting in r., with drawing pain on inside above r. knee. Boring in l. during rest. Pain in r.; from K. to toes, > walking, with drawing. Bruised pain in K. and tibia, more when sitting than when walking. Lame feeling. Drawing pain; in evening; on walking and rising from a seat. Arthritic drawing. Tension; when walking in open air; in tendons over K. on ascending stairs. Weakness; after coition.

Leg.—Swelling; between tibia and calf; < sitting and standing, > walking. Cramp in calves at night after a cold; in calves at night in bed on stretching legs, afterwards tension in calves as if too short. Tickling sticking on lower part of r. tibia. Tearing anteriorly under r. knee; between l. knee and calf; now above, now below r. calf; in tibia during menses. Aching, and in ankles; A. in afternoon, and in feet; in tibia, next day between 12 and 1 P.M. in lower part; in tibia and fibula, < malleoli, as if bones would be forced apart; cramplike, in calves, with shooting in ankles; in lower part of r. calf, as if cramp would set in; sore, in tibiæ during motion. Bruised pain in tibiæ; in calves and hamstrings; in legs, with lassitude, she unavoidably sank into a slumber full of anxious dreams. Tensive pain in calf; in tendo-achillis. Drawing pain deep in r. extending over malleolus; in leg to heel, where there was stinging. Uneasiness in evening, with cramp in them. Heaviness as if they would fall asleep. Sudden paralyzed feeling in one.

Ankle.—Pain in tendons about r.; in l. as if boot were too tight; sprained, when walking in open air; as if tendons were too short, when walking. Compression after walking in open air. Tension in bend as if too short, when walking; drawing T. from malleoli to knees like cramp in calves.

Foot.—Fetid odor of (the generally sweaty) feet. *Swelling;* from much walking; with burning and dryness. Inflammation of corns. Sticking on inner side of l. after going to bed, and beneath toes; in dorsum, < walking on pavement; in corns, < knocking against them; in corns, with burning. Tearing in lower part of r. Tenderness all day, > walking. Tensive pain in dorsum, preventing walking on pavement. Burning pain in corns. Drawing pain in corns in evening. Drawing in corns all night. Burning swollen feeling. Tingling. *Heaviness* when walking; H. extending to knees from early in morning. Falling asleep of r.; F. asleep when sitting, < morning.

Heel.—*Sticking;* during the day, *and in corns;* only at night; < treading, with tearing, they were pale, cold and numb; spasmodic, as if tendons were too short, evenings on undressing, and extending to feet; burning, nights, waking her; burning, when sitting, with smarting, sore pain.

Sole.—Cramp in internal borders; C. in evening in bed. Sticking; on touch; in l. when sitting. Tearing in r. close to toes. Pain along l. to between fourth and fifth. Prickling, with pain in corns. Crawling or prickling sticking in S. and under toes, < rest.

Toes.—A nail that had been crippled for years suppurated and a healthy one formed. Inflammation and sensitiveness to touch, with soreness of corns on them. Cramp; in second. Sticking in l. great, < rest; burning, in tip of great. Tearing in great; in r. little. Cutting at night, < lying on back, with redness of tips. Pain in corns; corroding, on upper part; bone, in ball of great. Tickling in last joint of l. great, then smarting.

Skin.—Wart on outer side of hand. *Swelling on forehead;* on nape; of a sore spot, with heat and burning pain; red, on forearm, with pain as from pressure on a boil. *Red roughness on face. Roundish red spot on ball of r. hand in evening, with itching, not > scratching.* Wine-red spots on neck and under chin. Redness over whole body after being stung by a bee, with itching red rash, inflamed eyes and drops of sweat on face. *Reddish herpetic spots above hips; on sides of neck, with itching.* Red rash on face, then on trunk, then on limbs, with fever, pulse 120. *Brown spots on elbows, surrounded by a herpetic-looking skin; yellowish B. spots about neck, scaling off on rubbing.* Eruption on head, back and shoulder, itching in evening and night; *painful E. on tip of nose;* E. on pubes increased. Scurf on chin. Desquamation on palm; D. in roundish spots, < hands and fingers.

Pimples on r. cheek; on chin, with ulcerative pain on touch; *red, on forehead, with roughness of forehead;* resembling a blood-blister, near nose; near r. nostril, afterwards forming a scab; painful, on forehead. *Itching pimples on chin;* on face; legs; dorsum of foot; pointed, on calves, up to knees, with sticking where clothes touch. Induration at root of nose; painful, on forehead; red, insensible, on hands, oozing on pricking.

A sore from any break or burn. Bleeding of a cicatrix on tip of index. Purulent eruption on outer ear. Panaritium on l. index, with beating and sticking in it. Pustules on cheeks before and during menses, with burning and soreness, preceded by prickling, when opened discharging pus and blood and leaving a pit; sore P. on cheeks and wrists, later resembling chicken-pox; hard, in r. groin and between coccyx and anus, next day those in groin were painful and there were a number along posterior border and inferior angle of l. scapula, next day on crista ilii from spine to middle of each bone. Boils on thighs; on r. nates; blood, on neck below l. jaw, with stinging.

Blisters on heel from walking; on scalp, chest, back of shoulders, on calves and knees, a few became pustules and when squeezed yielded a tough sticky matter, but pressure was painful and made them look angry, those on scalp itched, brushing the hair was agreeable, but combing or scratching made pustules sore, the brush brought off more scales than usual, and skin of nose peeled. Itching blisters on upper arm; r. thumb; I. blisters and blotches on face, hands and feet.

Sticking in evening after he gets warm in bed; in an ulcer, < night, with burning. Pain as if sore. Sensitive to slightest knock. Drawing in part which had once been injured, with tearing. Tension, < forehead, with contraction. Formication in abdomen; in feet when standing; in attacks from thighs to toes. Tickling on tip of r. great toe. *Itching acridity posteriorly on elbows.*

Itching; on bends of elbows (Rhus., Sulph.); *tip of nose; face, arms, hands, back, hips, feet, abdomen and pubes; in an ulcer;* on upper part of sternum; chest; nape; axillæ; on tibia; outer side of l. sole; toes; on joints, < *bends of elbows, popliteal space,* and ankles, < evening and morning, with itching pimples; on r. side of pubes, < night on going to bed, *becoming moist after scratching* and forming a thin scale, easily pulled off; *in various parts, > scratching, then a pinkish color; of nipples, that at times bleed and seem about to suppurate;* changing to burning; on upper part of cheeks, and after rubbing burning smarting; voluptuous, in l. groin in evening in bed, < rubbing, > tickling with tips of fingers.

Clinical.—Erysipelas of the face. Herpes and other eruptions on the face. Herpetic and eczematous eruptions. Acne. Ulcers around the joints, especially of the fingers (Borax, Mez.). Brown "liver spots" on the abdomen.

Sleep.—Yawning and stretching; in morning in bed; Y. at noon and in afternoon after a walk. Sleepiness; *during the day, with aversion to everything;* during the day, with weakness; at 6 A.M. on waking, with aversion to motion, desire to stretch, and all day dulness and aversion to motion; at 9 A.M.; at noon; in evening, with dulness in head; at 8 P.M., with chilliness in back and languid, dull feeling; when sitting, and falling asleep on reading; < *forenoon. Sleep during the day as soon as she sits down;* S. afternoons; from 4.30 till 7.30 P.M., after eating; almost all day every third day (in a child), it fell asleep when it sat down and complained of pain in forehead; sound, with many vivid dreams. *Difficult, late waking, with weariness in limbs. No desire to rise in morning.*

Sleeplessness all night, with excitement, but vigor all day; S. except from 10 till 4; before midnight; after 1 A.M.; *after* 3 A.M.; for an hour or two after 3 A.M., then sleep lying on face; from 3 till 4 A.M., from rush of ideas, then sweat, < bend of r. elbow and knee, then quiet sleep; after 4.30 A.M.; on account of rush of thoughts; with restlessness; with fancies during slumber. Little sleep on account of pain in hip-joint on moving it. Late falling asleep; if she does not lie down early, and then early waking in morning.

Waking in a fright, with screams; W. frequently; at night after a short sleep, with restlessness; at night, with anxiety and spasms in abdomen, then in mouth, chest and hip-joints, with palpitation; about midnight, with chilliness, anxiety, jerking and spasmodic drawing in thighs, chest and jaws; every morning at 4; at 5 A.M., then sleep again, and on waking dull and languid feeling; early, with weariness, but inability to sleep again.

Sleep unrefreshing. Sleep light, with vivid dreams of the events of the day. *Disturbed S. from cough* and pain in feet; D., with pain in small of back. Restlessness in evening in bed, and early waking in morning; at night, < closing eyes. *Restless sleep;* after midnight, with frequent waking; *from ebullition of blood; with weight on thighs; from anxious dreams and heat; with confused dreams;* with vexatious dreams, he calls loudly, stamps, raises his arms, which he then slowly lays down again.

Talking in sleep; screaming in sleep; groaning and grunting; biting teeth together, causing pain; starting, at noon. On falling asleep, frequent starting; startled by oppressive ebullition of blood; jerking of leg; internal trembling, with itching of thighs, > scratching. Raised himself about midnight as if in delirium and laughed, on being questioned he closed his eyes tightly, sat quite stiff, with outstretched arms and hands and tightly set teeth, after drinking a swallow of water he asked what he was to do with so much water in his stomach, yet drank more, held up his hand as if holding a glass and said, "It is nice, I have relished the water after all," afterwards talked of three couriers who were coming and referred to persons as if they were standing about.

Dreams.—Many, with loud talking. Frightful, with loud screams; F., of murder; that she was falling from a mountain. Anxious, driving him out of bed; A., of being threatened with rape; as if the body were disfigured; as if he were chased and had to run backward, on waking he imagined something was coming from above, which oppressed his chest, then crawling and sticking in chest. Distressing, could see mice, rats and snakes, heard noises in the street and people talking, running, etc., next night could not sleep for the sights I saw and noises I heard. Vexatious, dreadful. Full of dispute. Tiresome. Unpleasant; and vivid. Foolish (of a man of seventy years running away from his wife and being suspected of marrying another). That he was urinating in the chamber, instead of which he was wetting the bed. Lascivious; with erections.

Fever.—*Chilliness; all day;* in morning on waking, with restlessness; in morning, then thirst; in morning, then all day heat of face and hands, with pallor, without thirst or sweat, and in forenoon pain in stomach and headache on stooping; from 4 till 5 P.M., with heat in forehead; at 5 P.M., then flushes of heat at 6 P.M., with slight sweat; at 6 P.M., he must lie down; *towards evening, with thirst, then night-sweat;* in evening, then thirst; *every night; during headache, yet intolerance of external warmth;* in church; on motion; *sensitive to cold;* sensitive to cold north wind; after getting wet, then attacks of faintness, then coryza; after a glass of water, lasting till sleep, with watery, slimy diarrhœa; with pinching in abdomen; or else heat and sweat; alternating with heat till in the night.

Shaking chill, then heat, with inability to collect one's senses, then sweat in evening, urine brown and of acrid smell. Shivering all day two days before menses; in morning after waking, also at intervals, with short breath; during noonday rest; till going to bed, and in bed heat of face; with the pains; without chilliness; even of head, with cold hands, yawning and weakness.

Coldness of head, < night; nose cold and pinched; in back and r. shoulder at 10 P.M., running downward, C. in back if lying on side, > lying on back; as from a cold hand between scapulæ, then C. over whole body, then spasm of chest as if suffocating, then clonic convulsions of r. lower limb, and jerking of r. arm when leg is held quiet, then trembling of lower limb; of lower limbs from forenoon till bedtime; knees at night. *Hands cold, but moist; cold sending chilliness through body;* but feet warm, or *vice versa*, or often both cold at once; H. and feet cold and clammy.

Cold feet; *all day, with dampness as if I had stood in cold water; about* 11 A.M. *when writing, then general shaking chill, he had to lie down, then warmth, and at* 4 A.M. *heat, with disposition to sweat, having had slight general sweat during the night;* at noon, with hot and red face; *in afternoon and evening when sitting;* < **towards evening and in morning, with headache;** < *evening, even long after going to bed;* < *evening in bed, then cold hands.*

Heat; all day, with sicknesss and thirst; all day, with chilly shivering, dull and heavy pain in forehead (after flickering, heat and pressure in eyes), nausea, constriction of chest, yet without shortness of breath; in morning on waking; at noon; *every day from* 1 *till* 6 P.M.; at 5 P.M., first chill and after drinking cold water chilliness and inclination to lie down, then sleep and inclination to sweat; evenings, with oppression; every night till midnight; *at night causing restlessness;* at night, with anxious fancies, fanciful dreams and sweat on head; *from indigestion, with palpitation;* after dinner; after dinner, with sweat; from a short walk; from the accustomed tobacco-smoking, with oppression and anxiety; with weakness and hot urine; with redness of face and sweat of head and body, headache like a heaviness, palpitation and trembling, after the heat chilliness with deadness of hands; with intermittent pressing first in temples, all night short breath as from internal heat, in morning weakness of lower limbs, thirst, want of appetite, sleepiness, during the day shivering, pain in throat and swelling of submaxillary glands; then coldness, with faintness.

Heat in flushes; *about* 8.30 P.M.; *in evening, then itching; after slight exercise;* then chills; **as if hot water**

were poured over me, with redness of face, general sweat and anxiety, without thirst, yet with dryness of throat. Orgasm of blood; *with congestion to head and chest. Anxious heat from 4 till 5 A.M. and from 5 till 6 P.M.*; A. waking him at night. Dry heat, with redness of face, thirst, painful swallowing, sticking in l. scapula arresting the breathing and tearing in limbs. Intermittent fever, returning frequently during the day, first heat with sweat in face, thirst and bitterness of mouth, then chill, nausea, pressure in forehead extending into temples, during the heat vertigo as if he would fall.

Heat of head; in evening; *in evening, and of face;* in morning, with sensation as if nose would bleed; of forehead in afternoon, with drawing in thighs; *at 5 P.M., with fulness;* after a walk, and of face; *rising to it every five minutes;* like a burning coming out of ears, causing difficult hearing and dim vision; alternating with chilliness in lower limbs. Heat of l. ear, with redness of it. *Heat of face* every morning on waking; in morning, pallor in evening; *from talking;* after a meal. Hot lips; under nose. Tickling burning in r. axilla. Burning on skin on outside below shoulder-joint, as from a blister. Heat of hands in daytime, during excitement; in lower half of legs at night in bed; in feet at night; dry, in soles; in tips of l. toes, shooting through l. side to head and leaving there weakness.

Sweat; in morning; in morning after waking; mornings, with anxiety; every morning after waking, < lower limbs; at 5.30 A.M. on waking; in evening before sleep; *all night;* every other night; *on walking; on walking in open air, even against cold winds; on walking, < bends of joints;* on walking, with exhaustion; *during sleep, < on head;* from slightest exercise, even writing; after coughing; all day, weakening him so by evening that he could not stand; sour-smelling; *sourish, every morning;* smelling almost like elder-blossoms, also during exercise; as from a cold; sometimes hot, sometimes cold, < hands and feet; on face during sleep; on face after warm food; above anus before and during stool; *on feet;* on feet, < toes; lower limbs during the day; from above downward to middle of calves at night; of intolerable smell, on feet, toes became sore; *cold, at night, on breast, back and thighs.*

Clinical.—It has been prescribed for intermittent fever, with the general symptoms and debilitating sweats. Partial sweats.

Silica.

Pure silica (Silicic acid) is triturated for use.

General Action.—It produces a well-defined irritability of the nervous system, with extreme sensitiveness (Nux v.); the spine is sore and pressure on it causes remote pains, the sphincters are irritable and close spasmodically; painful parts are extremely sensitive, and must be wrapped up warmly. Its tendency to suppurative processes, especially to fistulous burrowings, is very clear and useful. It is adapted to some forms of deeply-seated scrofulous cachexia, and occasionally antidotes septic infection.

Allies.—Fluoric ac., Phos. ac., Pic. ac., Mur. ac.; *Hep. s.*, Merc., Nit. ac.; Calc. c., Sulph., Kali c.; *Nux v.*, Op., Arn., Hyper., Ruta.

Generalities.—**Emaciation**; *with pale, suffering expression. Trembling when writing.* Actions unsteady and confused. *Coldness of l. side of body,* then slumbering and starting up as if she would go away without knowing whither, then *she spoke unintelligibly, recognized no one, was so weak that she could not turn over alone, then convulsions, with staring, distortion of eyes, twitching of lips, lolling of tongue, stretching and distortion of head and limbs,* then roaring, dropping of tears from eyes, frothing at mouth, then general warm sweat and slumber.

Epileptic attack at night, about the time of new moon, the body was stretched out, then tossed about, without cries and without biting of tongue. In evening after slumbering he unconsciously began to thrash about with hands and feet, and to jerk, with closed eyes and snoring, froth from mouth, then he lay as if dead, and if one attempted to arouse him he became stiff, opened his eyes that were fixed and began to mumble (epileptic attack?).

Loss of appetite, pale, suffering expression, **every morning sweat** (Phos. ac., Mur. ac., Calc. c.), *heaviness and weariness of lower limbs, forcing her to lie down, nausea, chilliness every evening before sleep, sticking here and there, in sides of chest, in abdomen, limbs, so that sometimes she started in fright, pain beneath sternum on inspiration, itching on arms and lower limbs, with pimples.* Paroxysm, became pale, quiet, lost her appetite, complained in a weeping manner of sticking in ear, vomiting, weakness of hands.

Sticking in different parts, < r. side of head and r. hand; *in l. side, so that she cannot lie on it; in various parts of l. side of body, < chest, < deep inspiration;* in different parts, with tingling. *Feeling as if knives were running into her. Pain in all parts; in whole body in morning before waking,* < r. upper arm and l. shoulder, > rising; *in all muscles on motion;* **as if ulcerating, in whole side on which he was lying, with shivering on slightest uncovering** (Hep. s., Nux v., Rhus t.), **thirst and flushes of heat in head;** acute, here and there in bones, < morning on rising.

Bruised pain in whole body (Arn., Hep., Ruta); **after coition; at night, as if he had lain in an uncomfortable position** (Rhus t.); < morning, on stooping or turning suddenly, < small of back and r. side. Drawing in ears, jaws, hands and tibiæ. Sensation as if divided in half and as if l. side did not belong to her. Easily strained by lifting, which causes sticking in pit of stomach and vomiting at night, often cutting in hypogastrium, with accumulation of flatus. Painless shocks through whole body. **Took cold easily; and had a cough therefrom** (Kali c., Nux v., Dulc., Hep. s.). **Restlessness;** after sitting a long time; **with excitement.** *She feels in head and limbs every change of weather* (Merc.).

Indolence in afternoon, walking was irksome. **Weakness;** *in morning after waking; in morning on rising;* at noon, before dinner; *in evening after walking, with trembling; at night, even to faintness;* when walking, on the approach of a storm, with sleepiness, heaviness and heat; **with desire to lie all the time;** *with stupid feeling; with tension in eyes and forehead; so that she could not keep out of bed, with sensation as if whole body had been broken;* sudden, when walking in open air, with sleepiness; like that of ravenous hunger, > eating again (without relish). Stiffness at night, as if asleep, with anxiety, so that she could not fall asleep. **Symptoms mostly occur at time of the new moon. Aggravation of pain from motion** (Nux v., Hep. s.).

Clinical.—Epilepsy, the aura begins in the solar plexus. Bad effects from foreign bodies penetrating the flesh, splinters or needles. General bad effects of changes of the weather to damp-

ness (Hep. s., Merc.). In diseases of the bones it may be compared with Fluoric acid. Caries of bones, especially of long bones, with stabbing pains. Enchondroma. Loss of power like paralysis, in rickets. Diseases of joints, especially the hip-joint, with acute pain extending to knee. General aggravation at night, from open air, cold and wet, lying on painful side, wine, pressure, change of weather; general amelioration from warm wrapping.

Mind.—Sensitive (Nux v., Ign.), *even lachrymose;* **S. to noise and anxious therefrom.** *Annoyed by loud talking. Easily startled. Gloomy; and irritable;* felt as if she would die, and lost her memory. *Excessive conscientious scruples. Excitement; with easy orgasms of blood.* Longing for home. *Anxiety* at night after an anxious dream, with audible beating of heart; woke in A. about midnight, was unable to move, imagined that thieves were breaking in, became quiet on rising, A. returned after lying down; on waking, with stupefying vertigo; on waking, > moving about the house, with incarceration of flatus, without emission of flatus; *from a start;* with tightness of head and chest; about himself; in attacks, so that he could not remain sitting.

Peevishness; in forenoon. Anger. Whimsical and faultfinding. Irritable, though lively; I., and skin sensitive to touch. Obstinacy in a child. Waywardness when free from fever (in a child), with crying when touched or spoken to. Quarrelsome in evening. Discontentment. Loathing of life.

Activity. Facility of thought and fluency of expression. *Thought difficult. Attention difficult to fix.* Distraction; in forenoon, with uneasiness in head and pit of stomach. Mistakes in talking; M. and confusion, half knowing what she is about but unable to control herself. Indolence. Inability to read, write or think, < from noon till 6 P.M., > evening after eating. Memory weak; lost. Senses lost.

Clinical.—Occasionally suitable for chronic effects of fright and nervous shock. Great irritability (the general mental and physical characteristic of the drug), constant restlessness.

Head.—Stitches at 11 A.M., sometimes like tearing, < r. frontal eminence; through H.; extending upward in brain; confused, with depression of spirits and peevishness; jerking, extending over temple to l. ear, with sticking extending from l. ear to root of nose. Tearing; in afternoon, with stitches; < stooping and motion, < parietal bones; sudden, frequent, in evening in bed; jerking; intermittent, < forehead, with pain in forehead and temples; like a pulling up of scalp, < r. temple, extending to vertex. Pinching when walking.

Aching; from 3 till 5 P.M., then weariness and sleepiness; at night; *at night, with inability to remember where she was,* everything turned around, with throbbing at heart; *from hunger; with unconsciousness, groans and cries for help;* < sitting and walking, < middle of forehead, with vertigo; < l. side, with stitches; in brain, with weakness of body; with ill humor and heaviness in limbs; with nausea; which seems to come from stomach, heaviness in forehead, with tearing that drew head sideways; *waking him at night; bursting; extending into eyes in morning, with chill in afternoon, nausea and weakness as if she would faint, pain in eyes on turning them sideways or closing them, and when closed the pain was < touch;* alternately in different parts, for an hour in sinciput, then in whole head, tearing in r. temple, occiput, then in l. temple, about 1 P.M.; tearing throbbing, with eructations.

Pressing asunder, with tension; P. as if brain and eyes were forced outward. *Shattering in brain when stepping hard or knocking foot against anything, with roaring.* Sensitiveness as after violent aching. Sensation as if everything in it were alive and twisting about. Jerking through H. in evening in bed; ending in sticking in occiput; painless J. Feeling as if falling off, causing straining pain in nape as if head were hanging by a piece of skin at nape. *It seems as if she could not hold it up.* Heaviness; of brain; in forenoon, stitches in temple towards forehead in afternoon; in afternoon till night, with fulness; of brain, < from forenoon till night.

Compression of brain. Dulness; from a little conversation, with general exhaustion; with suffering in sinciput; as from too much blood. Weariness. Stupefaction. Feeling as if water-pipes were bursting in it. Rush of blood at night; *at 4 P.M., with burning in the red face;* waking him at 2 A.M., with heat and sticking; on rising from a seat, with fulness in brain; with sticking in occiput; with jerking and starting in sleep; with throbbing in vertex and forehead and heaviness of head.

Vertigo; all day while stooping at work; in morning, with forgetfulness; in morning on rising; in morning on rising in bed, so that she must fall back again, with nausea; in morning fasting; in morning when walking and sitting, < stooping, with headache; at noon when eating; in evening when sitting and standing; in forepart of night; at night when lying on l. side; at night in a dream, with nausea; about midnight in sleep, with heat in head; *on rising up;* on rising, > riding in open air, with dizzy stupefaction of head, nausea and vomiting, returning on entering house; when walking; when sitting, < riding in a carriage, when he suddenly lost consciousness; on raising eyes; while eyes are closed, after the usual smoke and snuff; with pain in sinciput; with dim vision; with ringing in ears; with nausea; with nausea, water is regurgitated; then heat in head, then sweat and weakness; even to falling, on rising from bed; waking him at night, < rest, especially rising after stooping, lasting a part of next day; *in attacks, rising from back through nape, so that she did not know where she was, and was inclined to fall forward;* in attacks towards evening in open air, < reflection; stupefying, in morning on rising; as if head would fall to left during breakfast, with heat in face and sweat on forehead; as if something moved to and fro in head, > lying; as if he were being raised up; as if he were walking backward, when walking forward; drawing her to the right in morning when walking, < afternoon, with nausea.

Forehead.—*Sticking;* in r. side; in morning, with throbbing; in r. side at 9 A.M. on stooping; from 8 till 11 P.M.; extending from one side to other, alternating with pain; tensive, in l., extending to r.; drawing over brows and in vertex. *Tearing;* in sinciput every day from 4 till 7 P.M.; at times extending to vertex; extending towards parietal bone all day, < towards evening and by motion; lancinating, in sinciput; sticking, in sinciput, then in r. temple, then in l.; arthritic, in sinciput and r. temple; tingling, extending to vertex and temples. Boring. **Bruised pain above eyes, so that he could scarcely open eyes, at first in l. side, it was a sticking extending towards other side by eye, <opening eyes.** Pain; in sinciput in

side; in middle; *in a spot over l. eye;* in morning after rising; from morning till evening; at noon; from slight mental work; in sinciput, < forehead and eyes, < motion; with tearing extending towards sinciput; *above eyes so that he could scarcely open them;* wandering; tensive, above eyes; as in coryza, and in eyes; in anterior part of brain as from pressure, increasing from 12 till 2 o'clock. *Jerking pain in middle, renewed by suddenly turning around, stooping or talking;* J. pain < night. Throbbing pain in afternoon; T. pain in l. side. *Weight over eyes;* W. in morning after rising and in afternoon; above eyes before menses. Dulness; and in nose, extending into upper teeth. Numbness. Rush of blood. Vertigo at night.

Temples.—*Stitches;* in r. in evening; with pain as if head were open. Tearing in r.; in r., with various kinds of headache; through T. Pain; *in l.;* in r. in afternoon; after a slight cold, and over r. eye; in r. after a soft stool, with pressure, then eructations of gas; extending across forehead and towards vertex, < forehead; in l., sometimes throbbing. Fluttering, with pain in occiput. Rush of blood to r.

Vertex.—Sticking. Tearing; **as if it would burst, extending through head, with throbbing and chilliness, necessity to lie down and tossing about the bed, > binding head tightly.** *Bruised pain. Jerking pain extending deep into brain;* J. like electric sparks. Pressure on it in evening, extending into eyes; P. as if a weight fell on it, on coming into the dark.

Sides.—Sticking in l., with frequent contraction of forehead. Pain in r.; sickening, in l., < pressure or movement. Paralyzed sensation in r. after coition.

Occiput.—Stitches. **Tearing in protuberances extending upward and forward over sides of head;** T. extending upward and forward through r. side of head; rheumatic. **Pain** *in sides; in bone; in morning, and in nape; in protuberance, from the hat;* **> warm wrapping of head; then stitches in forehead, with chilliness in nape and back; rising from nape to vertex,** *as if coming from back;* cold; itching, in r. side.

Scalp.—Hair falls out (Sep.). Feeling as if hair would fall out. **Soreness to touch** (Bell.). **The itching spots are painful, as if sore after scratching.** *Tenderness,* a feeling as if she had been lifted by her hair (Sep.). Creeping as if hair bristled; during dinner. *Itching; on occiput;* on l. side; and pricking.

Clinical.—Headache usually in the occiput, > warm wraps, with great sensitiveness to cold or any external impression, such as noise or light, flickering before vision, etc. Headache from nervous exhaustion. Neuralgic headache from occiput to over the eye, > warm wraps. Offensive eruptions on the occiput, which become ulcerated and scabby (Hep. s.).

Eyes.—Swelling in region of r. lachrymal gland and lachrymal sac. *Redness around E., then also of whites, with inflammation and lachrymation; R. of whites,* with pain. Ulcer on l. *Piercing stinging in l. Sudden piercing in l. Tearing on pressing them together, with burning;* T. above eyes, with sticking so that he must press lids together; extending from one to other through head. Painful cramp so that it is difficult to open them. Griping beneath r. in evening in bed. Pain every day at 4 P.M.; *as if dry and full of sand, in morning. Smarting;* in l., with pricking. Feeling as if dragged back into head by strings. Pain as if being drawn out. Tension. Twittering sensation in r. Feeling as if l. were full of water. *Weakness. Heat.* Itching of r. in evening; I. of the sore one. Lachrymation in outer canthus; L., with water from nose; L., with dimness of eyes.

Lids.—*Agglutination in morning; at night, with smarting. Twitching.* (Swelling [after the erysipelatous swelling of feet had disappeared], < morning, with burning and stinging pain, < morning and evening, with redness, > middle of the day, in evening photophobia, a mist about the light and a red and green halo, thick, slimy discharge, with agglutination.) Tearing in margins. Pain; in upper, with sticking and vanishing of vision. Soreness, smarting and inability to close them. Burning biting in r. lower in morning. Heaviness; with sleepiness. Itching of upper; burning I.

Hardened mucus in inner canthi. Biting in canthi in morning. Pain in l. canthus; in orbits, with smarting. *Vision dim;* all day; after eating, eyes seem blinded, inability to raise them; *and flickering.* Photophobia; in morning; alternating with inflammation of white of eye and lachrymation. Blinded by daylight in paroxysms. *Blackness before eyes after headache. Letters run together when reading and writing.* Fluttering. Muscæ volitantes. Speck before r. eye. Everything seemed pale during menses.

Clinical.—Caries of the orbit. Inflammation of the lachrymal sac. Acute lachrymal fistula. Blepharitis. Tarsal tumors. Ulceration of the cornea. Hypopyon, sclero-choroiditis. Irido-choroiditis. Senile cataract, ciliary neuralgia.

Ears.—*Swelling of outer and thin discharge from inner, with hissing affecting hearing.* S. of parotid, with sticking; hard, of parotid, with tensive pain on moving head and on touch. Margins inflamed and moist. Thin discharge from l. Much thin wax.

Sticking; in l.; near l.; < l., with aching and itching; in r., with tearing; in l., with feeling as if humor were flowing from it; from l. to l. temple. Tearing in and on ear; behind r.; behind and beneath r. at 1 P.M. Jerking cutting in bone behind E. Pain in r.; in meatus; in l. on blowing nose; jerking, in l. *Drawing pain in meatus.* In r. ear and down neck. Cramp-like drawing in r. Throbbing in r.; in the one on which he lies at night; shaking eyes, so that objects move up and down. *Itching; < swallowing. Seemed stopped.*

Sensitiveness to loud sounds. Ringing in evening. Chirping as of crickets. *Roaring;* in l. before and after eating; with thundering and grumbling; like the sound of a bell, forcing him to rise at night and walk about. Humming, < morning on rising, with difficult hearing and sensation as if something were in ear. Cracking on swallowing. Bubbling in r.; in r. as if something were beating on drum, which tingles in head and makes him anxious. Fluttering noise; rhythmical F. in l. *Difficulty in hearing the human voice; D. from roaring in ears;* < eating; D. coming and going suddenly. Deafness in afternoon.

Clinical.—Acute and chronic inflammation of the middle ear, especially chronic suppuration. Inflammation following bathing. Deafness in consequence of inflammation. Caries of the mastoid (Caps.). Inflammation in middle ear, with hissing sound. The discharges from the ear are generally curdy and ichorous.

Nose.—*Smarting, painful scab deep in r. nostril.* Burning stitch on side; in tip, flying up to forehead. Tearing in l. wing; drawing T. Pain in septum; biting, about nostrils as if ulcerating, streaming up into brain, causing tense, throbbing pain in forehead, tip of nose painful to touch as if suppurating. *Soreness* *on back as if beaten. Drawing in root and in r. malar-bone.* Pressure over nose in morning. *Stoppage;* in morning, then coryza in afternoon; in afternoon, preventing sleep; with running from it. Crawling in tip, with burrowing. *Itching in nostrils. Sneezing;* in afternoon and next forenoon; unsatisfactory; *ineffectual efforts at S.*

Coryza; > towards evening; with cough, swelling of submaxillary glands, pain in throat on swallowing, chilliness, necessity to lie down, then heat in bed; *fluent; alternately dry and fluent; dry;* dry, in morning on waking; dry, with rough voice. *Running out of acrid water without coryza, making nose sore and bloody internally,* with odor of blood or freshly slaughtered animals before nose. *Discharge of much mucus without coryza;* thick D.; bloody mucus. *Bleeding; after inserting finger, with dryness of nose;* in drops on stooping; dark blood from r. nostril during dinner, relieving headache.

Clinical.—Nasal catarrh, generally offensive or with an offensive purulent discharge. Catarrh, with ulceration and bloody discharge; especially when it involves the Eustachian tube. Hay fever occasionally.

Face.—Pallor. Swelling, and of lips and cervical glands, with chilliness. Tearing in cheeks, then sensation as if l. molars were on edge; T. in r. cheek extending upward in forenoon during menses. Drawing pain in bones of cheeks, < touch, and behind ears. Jaw, cramp in l. joint, then in temple; aching; pain in angle of lower when yawning, extending into ear; bruised pain in l. joint when touched and on chewing; tension in joint.

Lips.—Swelling of lower; of upper and gum, painful to touch. Pimples on upper; *painful on margin of lower;* only felt externally in r. corner, with ulcerative pain. Blisters on upper; *on margin of upper, with sticking or smarting on touch; on margin of upper,* at first with itching, then, when scabby, smarting; in red of upper, with smarting pain; painful inside and on gums. *Ulcer in corner, with itching and scabs; painful U. in corner;* fungoid, on inside of lower. Itching scab on margin of upper. Dryness; with soreness of palate; and hardness. Heat.

Clinical.—Necrosis of the jaw. Tumors on the lip.

Mouth.—*Inflammation of molar, with swelling and soreness of gum. Looseness, with pain in gum on pressure;* L., with sensitiveness on chewing; with feeling as if elongated. Sticking in an incisor when eating; S. from a strong wind, with ulcerative pain on touch, then swelling of lower jaw; preventing sleep at night, with heat in cheek and inability to take anything warm into mouth; so that he could take nothing warm nor cold into mouth; tearing, in hollow when eating; burning, with pain after eating, the pain < night and inhaling cold air, with heat of head and cheeks. Tearing when eating and afterwards; drawing, with soreness of gums. Jerkings in r. upper molars; J., and in lower jaw, preventing sleep all night. Pain; in hollow; in morning on waking; after eating; after dinner and from drink, < molars; < warm food and taking cold air into mouth; > eating, < night, preventing sleep; as if a molar were ulcerating when biting; tensive. Drawing pain in lower incisors; in a hollow T.; paroxysmal, in a hollow T. Feel too large and long for her mouth; pain in a lower molar as if too long. On edge; upper. Teething fever, although he had all his teeth he drooled, bored into his mouth and had heat in head in evening.

Gum.—*Swelling, with gumboil on it;* S., with burning from warm drinks and pain on chewing; *painful, inflamed.* Inflammation. *Gumboils.* **Sensitive to cold water** (Merc., Hep. s.). *Sore.* Constriction. Cool feeling in upper.

Tongue.—Swelling of r. half. Coated; white in morning. **Sensation of a hair on forepart;** *on tip, extending into trachea, where it caused crawling, so that he must cough;* lengthwise, coming from windpipe. Sore, with painful spots on tips; *S. feeling.* Dryness, with sensation as from pungent spices. Numbness.

Palate pale yellow and sore. Ulcer on palate reaching to gum. Stitches in curtain of palate. Palate sore. *Dryness;* when walking in open air; *without thirst.* Itching on hard and soft palate. Salivation. Heat from M. *Bad odor in morning,* almost like salivation of mercury. *Taste sour after eating;* as of rotten eggs in morning; clammy and putrid; offensive, slimy; oily; as of soapsuds; bad in morning on waking; of food long after eating; metallic in throat when sneezing; bloody in morning; T. and appetite defective; T. and appetite lost. Bitter taste; in morning; in morning after rising; to everything; and sour; with dryness of mouth and thirst; in throat, as if coming from stomach.

Clinical.—Abscesses at roots of teeth.

Throat.—*Submaxillary glands, swelling, painful on touch, with drawing pain in them and sore throat on swallowing as from an internal swelling;* S. of submaxillary glands, with sticking in them; (discharge recommenced from an old abscess that had discharged years before, but was now covered with a scab); *pain on touch;* pain in l. on deep pressure; contractive pain. *Swelling of uvula;* S., with pain; of thyroid cartilage, with itching and sticking on touch; of l. side, with tensive pain, fauces red and irritated. Hawking of mucus; *of balls of greenish-yellow offensive mucus;* of thick mucus; of salt mucus; of balls of offensive greenish-yellow mucus. Rising of mucus, without cough. Food gets into choanæ on swallowing.

Sticking on swallowing, with pain even on touch; S. on coughing; < yawning and swallowing, with burning; causing cough. Scraping in morning, sticking in evening; S. low down in evening; at night when lying on r. side, with roughness, causing cough and expectoration of mucus; < morning on waking and in evening after lying down, provoking hacking cough, with rawness in bronchi. Rawness; during cough; after dinner, provoking cough. *Soreness on l. side on swallowing; in spot on swallowing, with at times stitches in it;* in pharynx from singing; with much mucus in it. *Sensation of a lump on l. side on swallowing.*

Nauseous sensation in afternoon. Dryness; of choanæ; deep below throat; with elongation of uvula; with hoarseness and itching in meatus auditorius. Burning; and in chest. Tickling provoking cough. Tickling itching in region of pit, threatening suffocation till a deep shattering cough breaks out, which causes pain in hypogastrium and throat. Swallowing difficult, food descended slowly, first gurgling in pharynx, gradually descending to stomach, then food descends.

Clinical.—Tonsillitis, threatening suppuration; after suppuration when it does not heal.

Stomach.—Appetite. *Ravenous;* in morning; in

evening; towards evening and after eating nausea in pit of stomach; *before supper, with loss of appetite and trembling in limbs, then coldness over whole body, with heat in chest;* > lying still; and he eats as usual and then everything seems to be up in his throat; with salivation; but no desire for warm food; *so that it was difficult to fall asleep.* Appetite for he knows not what; for only cold, raw food; A., but she will swallow no food. *Diminished.* Lost. Aversion to meat.

Thirst; at night; without desire to drink, even during the chill. *Eructations;* after supper; then pressure, then pinching in stomach; loud; violent, with inclination to yawn; warm; of water; of gas; of cool air, with an odor; of food after eating. *Sour eructations* in evening; in morning, and bitter; *after a meal, with burning in throat;* after eating, and horrible tasting, lasting till eating again. Hiccough; in evening in bed; before and after eating.

Nausea; in morning; in morning on rising; in morning after waking, with slimy mouth; in pit of stomach, even in morning fasting, *with good appetite and natural taste to food;* in morning, then weakness and chilliness till noon; in forenoon, with pain in epigastric region and ineffectual inclination to eructate; at 5 P.M., during supper, > lying, with general discomfort; in evening, with pressure in stomach and aversion to food; at night; on waking after midnight, with burning in stomach, then empty eructations of food eaten the previous evening; during dinner; after eating, > lying; when walking in open air; during coition (in a woman); with loud eructations; with ineffectual retching and waterbrash; with emptiness in stomach; sudden, when smoking his usual tobacco, with faintness and trembling; as if in lower abdomen, which at one time rises, at another descends.

Vomiting of food at 9 A.M.; V. after eating, she scarcely dared to eat thin soup.

Sticking; in r. side of epigastric region. Cutting in pit, alternating with weight and tightness. Griping and clawing; G. > lying with legs drawn up, with gnawing, nausea, cold creeping over back and neck and rumbling in abdomen; paroxysmal, above S. and in hypochondria, with pinching and pressure; drawing, in pit and hypochondria, extending to hip-joints, with sticking. Twisting in pit in morning, < rising, then nausea rising to throat, > eating, with palpitation, pressure in sternum and eructations of bitter water. Screwing together in epigastric region in forenoon, then soft stool.

Pain; in pit; *after eating;* in pit after violent cough; < walking in open air, with empty eructations; in pit, with weight and crampy sensation; every half hour, with cutting in intestines; spasmodic, after eating; waking him often at night, afterwards pinching; as from a stone; as from a cold stone in epigastrium; like indigestion, in epigastrium; in epigastrium, as from having eaten too much; like a lump, from flatulent food, vomiting. Anxiety in pit during menses, so that she wished to drown herself. Discomfort after eating. Fulness after eating, > eructations; F. after eating, with sensation of a stone in it. Disordered feeling. Seemed inactive though he had a good appetite. Weakness after eating. *Heaviness;* after dinner. Heartburn, with weight at epigastrium; *H. rising* from S. after eating, with salivation. *Burning in pit;* above pit, almost like heartburn.

Abdomen.—Tense, hard; *T. and hot, with rumbling, grumbling and constant diarrhœa. Distention; and after eating tension;* with rumbling and constriction, the pain and rumbling > emission of flatus; *with weight; with pain in place of a hernia; with tension* and pressure; with eructations; with pain, the pain > emissions of flatus; with constriction about umbilical region and at times sticking, the pain > thin stool accompanied by flatus; < umbilical region, with feeling as if intestines were tossed about, and offensive flatus; *hard; flatulent.*

Retraction after eating, with feeling as if clothes pressed him. Emissions of flatus; **offensive.** Flatulence causing stitches in small of back; incarceration of flatus at night, causing contraction of chest. *Rumbling;* in morning, with pain and emission of flatus; in afternoon after the pain had ceased; < vicinity of inguinal hernia, *with gurgling.* Gurgling; with pain as if intestines were shaken up and watery stools. Movements; after eating, with colic, then four watery stools with emission of flatus and transient relief of pain; then soft stool.

Sticking and contraction. Tearing. Cutting; > olfaction of Hepar sulph., then disappearance of symptoms in stomach and tearing in limbs; paroxysmal; intermittent, at night, causing restless sleep; wandering griping. Griping; nearly every afternoon; before every emission of flatus; when walking in open air; intermittent, after eating. Twisting; after eating. Acute pain at noon after eating a little and in evening, > eructations. Pain; after eating; on rising, > stool; after warm beer, > after rumbling and eructations of gas; before emission of flatus; > emission of flatus; > applications of warm cloths; > stool, then exhaustion and a doze, colic on waking; with constipation; with inclination to stretch; with feeling as if she were stiff, hands yellow and nails blue, as if dead; then watery leucorrhœa after urinating; as from incarcerated flatus, with pressure towards rectum. Burning.

Upper A.—Cutting after dinner. Pain. Sticking burning in morning after rising, imperfectly > stool, with pressure in rectum.

Hypochondria.—Sticking; below H.; in r. at 2.30 P.M. when sitting, extending through abdomen and out at opposite side, > bending up, with pain in pit of stomach; burning in r. in afternoon. *Pain in r.;* cramplike, across H., extending into back, < motion; drawing, extending to spine, > night. Burning in r. in afternoon.

Umbilical Region.—Sticking on deep inspiration. Intermittent cutting; after midnight and in forenoon, with pain and desire for stool; extending through to back. Pinching; then in whole abdomen, with watery leucorrhœa. Griping at 9.30 A.M., with cutting; constrictive G. Digging in afternoon. Pain; then emission of flatus; beneath U. region before and during stool. Constriction; after dinner, then pasty stool.

Side.—Sticking in r.; below l. hypochondrium; in l. in evening; in l. when walking, more externally; in r., with flatulence.

Hypogastrium.—*Inguinal glands as large as peas, painful to touch.* Sticking in l. flank; in iliac regions. Tearing in groins in evening; through r. inguinal canal, with drawing; in pelvis extending to hollow of knee; in place of a hernia, as if something would be torn out. *Cutting; with incarceration of flatus, pain at every step* (after lifting a light weight). Griping. Pain in r. groin; in inguinal hernia; with straining, the pain < during stool; contracting, at night, then general sweat. Oppression at noon and in evening, like a falling, partly towards rectum, partly towards genitals. Swollen sensation in l. groin as if a hernia were pressing out.

Clinical.—Hepatic abscess, with induration and ulcerating pain.

Rectum.—Stinging (Nit. ac., Sulph., Nux v.); extending towards genitals, when walking. **Cutting** (Sulph., Nux v.). *Jerking, almost sticking pain. Burning during stool* (Sulph.). Itching in evening; *stinging I. during stool.* **Constant, ineffectual desire** *in evening* (Sulph.). **Frequent desire; but discharge of only mucus, with chilliness of body** *and nausea in throat.* Urging to a copious rather soft stool. **Stool remains long in R.,** *as if there were no power to expel it* (Hep. s.).

Anus.—Hæmorrhoids sensitive *though protruding but little; H. protrude during stool, return with difficulty and with bloody mucus from rectum;* protruded during stool, became strangulated in anus; protrusion of a vein, with itching and pressure; sticking; itching, and of anus. **Moisture** (Carbo, Nit. ac., Sulph.). Discharge of blood and mucus; of a round worm, with stool. *Sticking. Boring cramplike pain extending into rectum and testicles.* **Constriction during stool** (compare Nit. ac., Op.); C. extending into perineum. **Tension.** Pressure after soft stool. **Burning; after dry stool** (compare Mag. c. and m., Sul.). Burning pain in perineum, < after coition.

Clinical.—Hæmorrhoids intensely painful, with spasm of the sphincter. Fissure of the anus, with very great irritability.

Stool.—Watery; twice in one day, with tenesmus; and frequent, with emissions of flatus; *and frequent, scanty, as offensive as carrion. Diarrhœa;* day and night; *exhausting* at night; and profuse, with urging; and slimy, frothy, then burning and biting in anus; partly, partly hard, with urging. *Pasty;* twice in one day; with slimy membranous portions, then biting burning in anus. Soft, frequent.

Constipation; in spite of frequent straining, on following days hard, difficult, unsatisfactory stool; before and during menses. **Stool that has protruded slips back again, after urging and straining till abdominal walls are sore. Hard; with burning in anus, and lumpy, difficult** *and light-colored.* **Offensive. Scanty, difficult.** *Natural, with pressure and straining. With mucus,* then itching in anus; with reddish mucus; with bloody mucus, then biting in anus. Light-colored. Copious two hours after eating; C., and urine. At night on waking.

Clinical.—Diarrhœa of cadaverous odor, < cold air, with sour, offensive perspiration on the head, cold, but becoming warm when lightly covered, also with offensive perspiration of the feet, which makes them sore, etc. Constipation, with irritable *sphincter ani.*

Urinary Organs.—Pressure upon bladder when urinating, then burning. *Urging at night;* at night, with erections; at night, with sweat; U., with smarting in urethra; frequent; constant; constant, urine passed guttatim, with burning pain in urethra, the pain > Cantharis; frequent, ineffectual. Micturition every quarter hour about 7 A.M., every day; frequent scanty M. Involuntary, when sitting after urinating. *Prostatic fluid discharged when straining at stool;* with every stool. Dragging in prostate gland, extending forward. Urethra, sticking in forepart; cutting when urinating; smarting when urinating; burning pain when urinating. Urine copious; scanty; scanty, with burning; red; pale, burning; turbid; very sedimentous; deposits yellow sand; deposits red sand; that passed in morning has a reddish-brown sandy sediment.

Clinical. — Occasionally prescribed in albuminuria and diabetes. Nocturnal enuresis, especially in children who suffer from worms. Chronic gonorrhœa, with thick, fetid, purulent discharge.

Sexual Organs.—*Hydrocele.* Sticking through them. Disagreeable sensation, afterwards extending over sides of trunk like a cutting, to shoulders and thence into arms, with tension in them, they seemed asleep, this occurred every quarter hour during rest, < sitting and standing, not at night. Itching when urinating; I. beneath prepuce; on glans, with red spots. Redness of corona glandis, as if denuded, with itching. Swelling of prepuce, with moist itching pimples. Pricking pain in penis. Burning pain in prepuce after stool. Erections in evening and in morning in bed, with lascivious thoughts. *Violent erections* during the day; *at night,* without desire; with relaxed scrotum; with drawing pain in testicles. Erections follow slowly; no E.

Scrotum, *itching and moist spot; I. and sweat; sweat in evening;* crawling. Testicle, pain when lying down, < night; distending or compressing pain in l., as from swelling; jerking pain in l.; pain in r. as if indurated. Pressure in spermatic cords, with hanging down of testicles. *Lascivious thoughts.* Desire increased; and erections every half hour, testicles retracted; *weak;* weak, and fewer erections. *Emissions at night;* with sweat on back and waking about 2 A.M.; E. in a married man, with heavy dreams.

Female.—Painful pimples on mons veneris. *Burning in pudenda during menses, with soreness and with eruption on inner sides of thighs. Itching of pudenda;* with discharge of white water from uterus. *Bearing-down pain in vagina.* Discharge of bloody mucus after menses; of blood for several days at time of new moon, eleven days before the right time for menses; of white watery fluid, unlike ordinary leucorrhœa. *Leucorrhœa;* in evening; causing biting pain, < acid food. The child of a pregnant woman moves much. Menses too early; too late; *increased; increased, with attacks of coldness on their appearance;* suppressed. Silica taken during menses suppresses them for four days, afterwards they flow for four or five days and then remain away for six weeks; scanty; lasted only five days, were scanty and painless (they usually last ten to fourteen days); strong odor.

Clinical.—Elephantisis of the scrotum. Balanitis. Seminal emissions. Leucorrhœa chronic, purulent. Leucorrhœa acrid, excoriating, or sometimes milky, with paroxysmal discharge. Excessive menstruation. Abscess of the labium, with tendency to fistulous openings.

Respiratory Organs.—Pain in region of larynx on lifting a weight. Rawness of larynx when breathing. *Hoarseness;* < morning; < morning and evening, with pain in chest; *with tickling in larynx and cough;* with pain as if throat were swollen internally.

Cough; in morning and after going to bed; at night; *at night after lying down and in morning after waking;* in evening and all night, > warming abdomen, with fever; *from tickling and irritation in throat; at first from tickling in throat, gradually coming from lower down till it came from chest and shook abdomen, during the day sudden, explosive, without expectoration,* < *evening;* with shattering in abdomen; with scraping in throat, leaving rawness; *fatiguing, in evening in bed, with rattling of mucus;* hoarse; spasmodic; distressing, at night till 4 A.M.; causing vomiting of mucus. *Hacking cough from irritability in throat; from nightly tickling in pharynx; dry; dry, causing soreness in chest. Dry cough; during the day and waking her at night;* during the day, but greenish lumpy expectoration in morning; in morning after waking, with pain in upper part of sternum; towards evening; at night, < after going to bed; from cold drinks; violent in morning; *even to vomiting, with anxious sweat at night, necessity to rise from bed;* paroxysmal; spasmodic, every quarter hour, with rawness in chest and throat. Cough with expectoration and scraping in throat; C. with E., scraping in chest, disinclination to work, fretfulness and weariness; C., with vomiting when expectorating; **C., with purulent expectoration;** *with vomiting of masses of purulent mucus;* < *morning and forenoon, lumps of yellow mucus expectorated, with sore pain in trachea and chest;* C., < between 8 and 9 A.M., with E. of mucus and scraping in throat; C. < eating, with expectoration of white mucus; with E. of mucus from morning till evening, and mucous expectoration without cough; yellowish-green E. in morning, with rawness in throat; C. from 7 till 10 A.M., with yellowish-green expectoration; fatiguing C., with E.; hacking C. in morning, with easy E.; deep hollow C. towards noon, with expectoration of bright blood, then attacks of faintness. *Violent cough on lying down in bed,* **with thick, yellow, lumpy expectoration**; V. in morning, with bloody E.; with transparent mucous E.; V., with lachrymation, afterwards < laughter, during the C. sticking below angle of scapula and in middle of sternum, C. < morning, with stitches in chest, more in middle of sternum than at sides, with stitches in middle of sternum on inspiration, *with the morning C.* (on rising) *thick yellow expectoration* (Calc. c.), C. during the day slight and without expectoration, C. for half an hour or more at 9 P.M. on going to bed, without expectoration or pain, stoppage of nose, *difficulty of hearing, at times ringing in ears,* white slimy discharge from nose.

Expectoration in morning and during the day, at times salt, at times salt and brownish; *E. which makes water turbid, and offensive odor to that which sinks to the bottom; of thick purulent mucus from trachea;* of mucus in morning without cough; of mucus from trachea after eating; of bloody mucus.

Dyspnœa in morning on waking. Sighing.

Clinical.—It has proved serviceable in the suppurative stage of phthisis, with muco-purulent expectoration. Cough of sickly children, with night-sweats. Bronchorrhœa of old people, with offensive expectoration.

Chest.—**R. breast hard, painful, and swollen at nipple, it feels as if it were "gathering;"** l. breast hard. **Darting in l. nipple, with burning pain.** *Sticking; in r. side;* in l. breast; in l. side; in short ribs; through r. side; beneath l. breast at 2 P.M., on expiration; behind l. breast all night and next day, with chilliness; *in side on inspiration;* in l., then r. side on deep inspiration; beneath r. ribs on respiration; behind and beneath l. breast during dinner; in sternum after dinner, < inspiration; < deep breathing; beneath l. ribs, < deep breathing, ribs painful to touch; in l., with pressure; in sternum, extending around to back; in l., extending to elbow, then to wrist; in l. extending to last ribs, at night on every inspiration; sudden, in r.

Tearing in l. side; beneath l. ribs as if something would be torn away. Pinching jerking in l. intercostal muscles often during the day. *Pain in sternum,* towards pit of stomach; in l. false ribs; in various parts; in l. in morning on rising; at night; with paralyzed feeling in lower limbs after sitting long; in r. side, extending towards axilla, with drawing; beneath r. arm, as from pressure of clothes; as if it would burst when sneezing. *Bruised pain on coughing;* even on breathing. Scraping on breathing.

Tension; < l. side. Tightness; as if tied with a tape; alternating with pains in back (after taking cold?). Constriction; < eating; in forepart coming from back, on walking, > standing quietly and leaning against something, with oppression of chest and short breath. *Oppression;* after stool; at lower part of sternum; when walking so that he must stop every four or five steps and must often take a deep breath, which is difficult; *with inability to breathe deeply, without pain;* as if throat were constricted, < eating. Pressure on sides; on lower part of sternum; in morning in bed; towards evening; when she wishes to cough, she cannot cough on account of the pain; sharp, on l. Rush of blood. Burning pain. Heat, with coldness over whole body. Weakness, when talking he must use the whole chest.

Heart.—Orgasm. Heaviness in region. *Palpitation* in afternoon and evening; after noonday meal, with anxiety; in evening; from 7 P.M. till going to bed, causing anxiety and orgasm of blood in whole body; *on movement; when sitting, with throbbing over whole body;* when sitting quietly, with trembling of hand in which he was holding something; < standing, also with anxiety.

Clinical.—It has occasionally been prescribed for irregular action of the heart when the person is suffering from spinal irritation, nervous exhaustion, etc. Indurated tumors of the mammæ, with sharp pains.

Neck.—*Swelling of glands;* of r. glands. Stitches in glands. Tearing in middle of nape at 10 A.M. Pinching in r. side at 9 A.M., > laying hand on it, but returning. Pressure on l. side as if vessels were swollen. Tension in nape. **Stiffness of nape;** *of one side;* **of nape, with headache;** on nape, with chilliness.

Back.—Tearing or beating pressure, with chilliness, changing to headache and heat in head; arthritic T. Cutting all day. Griping in r. side. Pain; *in the curved spine;* in centre; in morning on beginning to move. *Throbbing. Weakness, with paralyzed feeling in lower limbs, difficulty in walking.* Stiffness; after sitting; stiff, sore feeling down r. side of spine, then across loins and over r. hip-joint.

Scapulæ.—*Sticking in r.;* between S. *Tearing between S.; beneath S. when walking;* T. asunder pain between S. Burning pain in l. Rheumatic pressure between S., < moving arm on waking from a dream of a battle about 4 A.M. Paroxysmal drawing pain, then in nape and head, when she became dizzy. Drawing between S. at night during menses, > bending backward; tensive, in r. Weight, < morning during rest, they seemed swollen, and the pain took away the breath when leaning against back.

Lumbar Region.—*Stitches between hips;* in lower part

of back; in sacral region; **in os coccygis on rising, with pain on pressure** (compare Ph. ac.); in lower part of spine, extending sideways and upward; down legs. **Pain in coccyx as after a long carriage ride** (Pic. ac.). **Bruised pain at night**; *in lumbar region and hips,* < *stooping. Pain;* in r.; beneath r. ribs (in region of kidneys) in evening; *at night,* and in shoulder on which he was lying; *on stooping; on rising from seat, with stiffness;* with tension; as if lame in region of sacrum; as if lame in morning on rising. Lameness. Desire to stretch. Drawing extending from ilium to feet, with tension, as from chilliness.

Clinical.—Spinal irritation. Diseases of the bones of the spine; in Potts' disease, with curvature, abscesses, emaciation, night-sweats, etc., it has proved exceedingly valuable. In nervous affections following injuries of the spine, epilepsy, chronic neuritis, etc., particularly when pressure upon the spine causes pain in remote parts, especially in the head. Posterior spinal sclerosis.

Extremities.—*Nails gray, dirty, as if decayed, when cut scattering like powder and splitting into layers.* Hands and feet seem dead in morning. *Trembling,* < hands; < arms, they seemed paralyzed in morning. Sticking in middle of r. thigh, then in one or other foot and in arms; in joints; tearing, in l. foot and heel at 10 A.M., then in r. shoulder, so that he must let it hang down. Tearing in l. leg and posteriorly in upper arm; in l. calf towards bend of knee, in evening in bed, with chilliness, then T. in l. shoulder; in shoulders and arms in evening in bed, then jerking pain from hips to ankles till 4 A.M., with restless sleep; in joints and soles, with jerking of feet as in chorea, causing sleeplessness; in hips, extending along outside of r. thigh to knee, where there was a stitch, > sitting, returning on moving, with inability to walk from stiffness of knee, afterwards sticking and tension in second phalanges of l. fingers.

Spasmodic pains alternately in thighs and arms from 10 till 11 P.M. Biting; in arms and legs; in arms and legs in evening, < in bed. Drawing pains, < l. side, now in leg, now in upper limbs, < l. knee and l. forearm. Drawing, partly cramplike, partly sharp. Bruised feeling, she cannot lie long in any position on account of pain. Lame feeling on rising from a seat, > continuing to walk. Uneasiness in joints when walking and sitting, with lameness. **Weakness**; of joints; < upper. Heaviness. Paralyzed feeling; after subsidence of fever. Paralytic pain on outer condyle of humerus on motion, and on inner side of thigh. Stiffness; with numbness, inability to use his hands and inability to walk without falling.

Upper Extremities. — Axilla. *Swelling of glands.* Biting pain. Drawing pain in glands.

Shoulder.—Sticking; on top of r.; in joint in morning; in r. joint, with tearing; extending to hand; back and forth from r. to elbow. Tearing in r.; T. on moving it; extending to wrists; and in wrists, with inability to lift anything; arthritic, in r.; throbbing, in l. Sharp pain in r. joint. Pain in r.; in r. extending to elbow on uncovering and becoming cold, < night; like a pressure, extending to hand, with sensation as if she could lift nothing heavy, though she could use the hand as usual. Jerking in r. joint; painful, in r. joint in evening, throwing arm high up. Drawing pain in l.; in S. and upper arm. Drawing. Weakness, and of upper arms.

Arm.—Twitching. Trembling of l.; of r., with uneasiness. Sticking. Tearing; jerking, extending into thumb. Pain in l. as if in marrow. Bruised pain in bones on deep pressure. Biting. Drawing extending into little finger. Throbbing in r. after eating; in r., so that the jerking could be felt with the other hand, thereupon arm seemed paralyzed, and it returned if he held the arm high up. Rush of blood when at work and stooping, with swelling and trembling. Weariness in morning in bed. *Heaviness.* Rheumatic stiffness of l., < motion. Numbness in r. like pins and needles. Falling asleep when lying upon it.

Upper Arm.—Sticking in upper part; posteriorly in r.; in upper and anterior part of l.; in l., with drawing pain. Tearing on inside and lower part of l.; on lower and posterior part of l.; arthritic, in r.; in middle of l. as if in marrow, at 9 A.M. Pain on inner side and lower part of l.; in lower part of l.; P. on pressure; drawing, in lower part of l.; jerking, in upper.

Elbow.—Sticking; through r. A pain between drawing and sticking. Drawing pain as if in marrow. Sensation of bursting bubbles in flexor surface of l.

Forearm.—Twitching of l. Sticking in r.; S. in lower part. Tearing in l. ulna near elbow; T. in upper part of l. during the day, at times the pain was sticking; arthritic; arthritic, in l.; paralytic, in l.; drawing, in l., the pain was at times constrictive when near wrist, while in forenoon it was near elbow. Bruised pain in l. Jerking pain in l. Drawing pain in r.; D. pain in middle of ulna. Painful drawing; in lower part of l. ulna in forenoon, then drawing pain in l. ulna near elbow and sudden stitches in radius near elbow, also sticking and tearing in upper part of forearm, at times a drawing tearing. Drawing in l. Paralytic pain in extensor tendons. Conscious of pulsations in ulnar artery.

Wrist.—Trembling. Sticking in r.; in r. when writing. *Tearing; and in ball of hand;* and in palm; in r., and in thumb; in region in forenoon; in l.; with drawing; and on motion and touch pain as if it would break; in l., with pain in l. middle finger and swelling of fingers; in l. extending to shoulder; in r. extending to elbow and then into shoulder. Pain in r.; sprained P. Constriction in r. Lameness in morning. Weakness.

Hand.—Cramps when writing. *Cramplike pain after slight exertion, with lameness.* Stinging in ball of r. Drawing; D. pain in r. *Lameness of r. so that she must often lay down the pen when writing.* Sensitiveness, with coldness. Weakness. *Numbness, with pricking in arms;* N. and pricking. **Falling asleep at night**; of r.

Fingers.—**Nails rough and yellow.** *L. middle flexed and stiff and on bending it pain along extensor tendon in back of hand. Sticking in flexor surface of one;* S. in r.; in little; in r. little; in tip of l. index; in l. middle; in thumbs; *ball of thumb;* last phalanx of thumb; deep in inner surface of middle joint of r. ring, at 9 A.M., with burning pain on outer part; *as if asleep, now in one, now in another, then in arms;* jerking, in l. middle; prickling, in r. *Tearing; in middle; in r. middle;* in thumbs; *in joints of F. and thumbs;* in second joint of r. middle, with trembling. **Sensation in tips as if suppurating. Pain as if a panaritium would form on l. index.** Cramplike pain in joint of thumb. Jerking pain in index. Drawing in l. little; *paralytic D.;* in joints of r. as if they would be pulled out of their sockets. *Dryness of tips in afternoon.* Burnt sensation on back of one. Weakness of r. thumb. Stiffness of little at night. *Numbness of one as if it were thick and the bone enlarged.*

Clinical.—Finger-nails are yellow, brittle and crumpled.

Lower Extremities.—Gait shuffling, heavy. Twitching of l.; T. together, then sensation as if head were shaking, with bristling of hair. Trembling, with nervousness. Tearing here and there in l. at 11 A.M.; in l., becoming seated in posterior part. **Weakness**; *in morning; from a short walk. Heaviness;* when walking in open air. Falling asleep of r.; F. in evening when sitting, then stiffness till she moves them again.

Thigh.—Jerking in middle and upper part of r.; periodical, above r. knee. *Sticking;* in posterior part; in upper part of r.; in l. when walking; *with drawing pain. Tearing;* in r., afterwards extending to malleoli; back and forth above l. knee, as if in the marrow, then in knee, > standing; throbbing in l.; arthritic, in l. **Pain in hips**; in l. hip on stooping; *bruised in femur when sitting, walking and lying, even in morning on waking;* twittering; jerking, in muscles of r.; drawing jerking, in r. hip-joint preventing motion; drawing, in lower part of l.; *P. between drawing and sticking, below groin. Drawing extending to feet;* D. in r. Dragging from r. hip to toes. Biting; on inner and posterior surface. *Pulsation in r.* Sensation of bursting bubbles in r.; sensation in l. as if a bladder arose under skin and suddenly burst. Weakness. Falling asleep when sitting.

Knee.—Sticking; through r.; intermittent, at night; deep in when walking. *Tearing when sitting, > motion;* about r., extending to foot, < forenoon; sticking, in l., with drawing pain. Pinching in l. K. and tibia. **Pain as if tightly bound.** Tensive pain when walking. Drawing pain in bones, extending along outer side of thighs to hips like a tight cord; sticking, in l. Drawing in l. Soreness of l. patella. Sensation of bursting bubbles in hollow of r. *Weakness;* extending to middle third of thigh. Stiffness when walking and standing.

Leg.—Swelling; of calves, with numbness. Cramp in r. calf in morning in bed. *Calves tense and contracted; calves tense as from cramp when walking.* Painful contraction in r. calf. Sticking above calf when walking in open air; in tendo-achillis when walking in open air; in legs and feet, < standing, with drawing; in calves on stepping. Tearing, < malleoli; in middle of tibia; in r. from 2 till 5 P.M.; < warmth and sitting; in legs and feet, < walking, then in l. foot, < calf, with spasmodic contraction of it, that continued even when sitting; in l., with drawing pain; drawing, in tibia; arthritic, in r., afterwards extending to shoulder. Boring in a sore spot. Pain; in l. tibia; in l. calf; in one, with numbness of other; as if in bone, from middle down to ankles and along backs of feet, < standing and walking and causing uneasiness in feet, which made it necessary to rest them. Drawing pain down legs in evening, ending with jerking. Painful drawing in lower part of tibia. *Calves feel too short when walking.* Feeling of something alive in them, like a trembling, from 6 till 7 P.M. Lameness of r., with sensitiveness of ball of diseased toe when walking. Pulsations; in l. Weakness; and below calves and in feet.

Ankle.—Sticking about r. malleoli; in r. external M., even at night. Tearing, > lying. Pain; *sprained.* Drawing in l. Tension, even when sitting. Feet give way when walking. Stiffness and weariness, with swelling about malleoli.

Foot.—**Carrion-like odor every evening without sweat** (Graph.); *sour odor without sweat.* **Cramp in soles;** *in r. sole,* during a long walk, < great toe. *Swelling; of l.;* < morning on rising, very tense on walking; *with redness, in which pressure caused a white spot, with pain extending from toes to malleoli. Sticking in corns;* in soles; in l. heel; in heel and great toe when standing and sitting; *in corns,* jerking up the feet. Tearing; *in heels;* in l. sole; in middle of r. sole, towards inner margin, in forenoon, with tension externally; in soles till 6 P.M., then extending upward and becoming seated above knee, where it lasted all night; arthritic, in top of l. Cutting in soles. Pain in back of r.; in ball; in ball of r.; in corn on touch; bruised, on back. Easily sprained. *Soles sore, < towards toes.* Drawing in sole. *Weakness.*

Toes.—Corn on great, with burning. Sticking in great; in joint of great; in the indurated; in great, so that it jerked lower limb; cramplike; cutting, in r. great. Tearing in r. great; in ball of r. great at 11 A.M.; *in r. great* in evening. *Itching cutting beneath nail. Boring in great. Pain beneath nail of great, and stitches in it; P. in great, so that he can scarcely step;* sprained, in joint of great; as if ulcerating, in great toe that had been healed, when stepping upon it; as from pressure of boot, when walking. Drawing in joints as if being pulled out of their sockets. Stiffness.

Clinical.—Ingrowing nails. Exostosis of thigh.

Skin.—Small wounds heal with difficulty and easily suppurate. Twitching on scapulæ. White spots on cheeks. Red and white spots on face; *R., sensitive smarting spot on r. tibia;* R. spots on cheeks, < eating, with red nose and burning pain from slight exertion; R. elevations on chest, with biting pain. **Sore painful spots below septum of nose, with sticking on touch.** Eruption on face. White scales on face and neck, then desquamation, with itching. *Nettle-rash on nape.* Itching rash on sternum; on calves; heat rash on fingers, with crawling itching. Red itching tetter on chin. Blotches with red areola on thighs, with biting and with itching, < evening and in bed. (Red, shiny erysipelas on foot and about ankle, with stinging.)

Bursa between second and third metacarpal bones; *on back of hand,* between third and fourth metacarpal bones, with sprained feeling on bending hand and bruised pain on moving it. Pimples on forehead; on eyebrow; on nose; on chin; on nape; *itching, on head and nape;* itching, on left side of nose; painful, as if a ganglion were forming on inside of first joint of middle finger. *Pustules on back of hand;* **painful, variola-like on forehead, occiput, sternum and spine, becoming suppurating ulcers.** Eruption like varioloid over whole body, preceded, accompanied and followed by itching. **Boils on different parts; on nape; posteriorly on thighs;** *cheek near nose; arms; calves; chin,* **with stinging on touch.**

Ulcers about nails; corrosive, on heel, with itching. Vesicles with red areola beneath nostrils; *corroding V. on first joint of l. index, with itching;* itching, about wings of nose; red, on nose, with scabs; hard, on a red base on forearm, lasting one night, with itching. *Scabs behind ears;* **itching suppurating S. on toes** *that* *had been frozen; scabby elevation on coccyx above fissure of nates. Cracks on arms and hands; a C. on index begins to burn and pain, a lymphatic gland is inflamed, extending over wrist, and in the sore spot a corroding vesicle, with burning pressing stinging.*

Sticking in ulcer on leg; and about it, with burning; S. like flea-bites here and there. Sticking prickling in many places on lower limbs, > scratching. Tearing posteriorly on r. upper arm and on l. calf. Smarting in usually painless ulcers. *Pain in ulcer on leg;* at night; *as if suppurating, in ulcer on leg.* Crawling in l. scapula; C. in different parts, < evening on undressing, becoming fixed at different points, where there was itching.

Itching; *of outer ears; back; nates; legs;* eyebrows; *nose;* in beard; l. lower limb; inner side of thighs; scapulæ and thighs; beneath skin of l. palm; on forehead extending down nose; *in various parts, < night, with sticking;* after lying down, not > scratching, with biting; face, arms and neck, with pricking; in furrow behind wing of nose, with sore pain; *burning, about mouth; voluptuous, about nose in evening;* crawling over whole body and head.

Clinical.—Indurated tumors of the mammary glands, with sharp stinging pains (it follows Conium well). Abscesses of joints, hip, knee, etc., especially with fistulous openings and offensive perspiration. Generally valuable in abscesses and in carbuncles, which spread to a large size, with hectic fever, offensive discharges and offensive sweat; in all these diseases there is extreme sensitiveness of the whole nervous system, general aggravation from cold. Felons are very frequently aborted (Fluoric acid), there is general relief from warmth (unlike Fluoric acid); there is said to be general aggravation at full moon. Glandular swellings, which threaten to suppurate. Papular eruptions on the forehead; eczema which has an offensive oozing; herpes zoster, frequently relieving the distressing pain following the eruption. Results of impure vaccination.

Sleep.—*Yawning. Sleepiness;* all day; during the day, obliged to sleep before dinner; from 1 till 9 P.M.; from 2 till 5 P.M.; *in afternoon, with frequent starting up in fright;* **in evening;** in evening, with weakness; at 7 P.M.; *after eating,* with weakness; after eating, with shivering; overpowering, in forenoon. Deep and long sleep in afternoon, then weakness.

Sleeplessness; before midnight; till towards morning; after 2 A.M.; *after 2 A.M., from rush of thoughts;* for many nights, absorbed in wonderful fancies and reveries. **Restless sleep;** *with frequent waking and chilliness; with frequent waking and dreams crowding upon each other;* with anxious dreams; with starting up and talking. The boy is restless at night and cries out. *Starting up in sleep; with trembling;* in midday nap; in evening, with waking. Jerking in sleep; with frequent rushes of blood to head; of arms and r. lower limb on falling asleep, with grasping of hands; in head in evening on falling asleep, then throbbing in r. ear. On falling asleep in evening, throbbing in head and heart and shuddering through whole body.

Talking in sleep. Constant loud laughter in S. after midnight. Attempts to rise from bed in S.; she gets up, climbs over a chair, table and piano and lies down again without knowing anything about it. Sleep interrupted. Difficult falling asleep; on account of rush of ideas.

Waking with rapid pulse, palpitation, heat, eructations, pressure in pit of stomach, then vomiting of bitter mucus, with retching; W. after midnight, with uneasiness, difficult breathing and dryness of skin; in night, with weeping, cannot collect his senses, cries anxiously and mumbles; every night about 11 P.M. after a sleep of an hour and a half, and then falling asleep again; anxious, about 3 A.M.; early. Frequent waking; then after midnight sleeplessness; after midnight, and on falling asleep about 2 or 3 he fell into a reverie; with restlessness and chilliness; and he had scarcely fallen asleep again when he dreamed of his business.

Dreams as soon as she falls asleep; much, with crying out. **D. of his youth,** *waking him and so vivid that on waking it was difficult to free himself from them;* of the events of his childhood. *Vivid of past events.* **Frightful;** in first part of night; *on falling asleep, with cries. Of being seized by a finger,* so that he awoke in fright. **Anxious, of one choking her,** she could not cry out, could only kick; A., of drowning; of a flood; of snakes; of being pursued; that he had committed murder and was apprehended; of robbers, with whom he fought, he woke in heat, anxious oppression and sweat; when half awake, as if a heavy rough beast were lying upon him so that he could not stir nor utter a loud sound. Half waking, as if many ghosts grasped him, he awoke, but could not move, with anxiety and palpitation, then fear. *Bad, with weeping.* That a ghost pursued him, after midnight. Of murders; murderers and robbers, during which he woke and said he would catch them; of being murdered, from which he woke with anxiety as if he would suffocate, without ability to speak. Of earthquakes, frightful storms, fire, etc. Full of cruelty without anger. That he must die. That he had an epileptic attack and that his head was drawn to one side. That his head was excessively large. *Restless, with loud talking. Confused, with frequent uneasy waking;* C., of everything that had happened or that he had heard during the day. Disgusting. Vexatious. Full of quarrels and humiliation. Disconnected. Of the occurrences of the day and that large dogs followed him. Of distant journeys. Somnambulistic, that he saw distant regions that he had never seen and objects which he desired to have. Full of reveries, he gets up like a somnambulist. With raving, he gets up and walks about the room without knowing where he is for a long time. Amorous, of marriage; A. and historical. *Lascivious;* in evening and morning, with erections; *with emissions;* with great sexual desire; very offensive to her; of being disturbed during coition, waking with erection and sexual fancy.

Fever.—Chilliness; all day; *all day* **on movement,** *in morning weariness even to falling asleep;* in forenoon, without thirst; at 11 A.M., with fever; **in afternoon, in a warm room,** *< arms;* **in evening;** in evening, < shoulders; in evening in bed, with heat and therefrom pain in stomach; till 8.30 P.M.; *at night when half awake;* at night, with ravenous hunger; **sensitive to cold air;** *if she put her hand out of bed;* after eating; with sticking pain; *with occasional fever;* sudden; **cramplike, in evening in bed, so that he shivered. Shivering creeping over whole body;** S., with cold, starved feeling; frequent S. during the day, then heat mostly in head and face. *Shaking C.* at 5 P.M. after bread and beer; *at 6 P.M., with necessity to lie down. Trembling C. in open air. Internal C.;* with loss of appetite; from taking cold at night, with loss of appetite and sticking burning headache. Alternating with heat; during the day.

Coldness of nose; across vertex, about the breadth of two fingers, in a line with forepart of ears; in back; extending down back, with cold hands, then heat, with tension in abdomen; **of legs in a warm room**; of knees and arms after walking in open air, finger-nails white. **Cold feet**; *all day; during the day, but at night heat of hands and feet, with drawing pains in feet and legs;* **in evening in bed; in evening in bed, preventing sleep;** *every evening, and cold legs;* **during menses**; and cold hands, with hot and red face; on beginning to walk; > *night.*

Heat; in afternoon, with heat in head, dark redness of face and thirst, headache began half an hour before the heat; in afternoon, with thirst and short breath; *in evening,* with thirst; till 7.30 P.M., then limbs seemed paralyzed; **all night, with thirst and catching respiration;** without thirst; in a child, with red, puffy face, hard glands about throat and down shoulders, distention of abdomen and constant diarrhœa; in flashes during the day; *in flashes, then sweat, then on slightest movement she is covered with sweat;* dry, every evening, with thirst, then pain in abdomen and head. *Orgasm of blood at night, throbbing in all vessels.* The intermittent fever of Silica has little sweat, usually occurring from 10 A.M. till 8 P.M., or from midnight till 8 A.M.

Heat of head; and lobules of ears; with anxiety; as if flames were coming out of mouth in evening. Heat of face; in evening, and in lobules of ears; after eating; after washing with cold water; of cheeks and palms in morning. *Burning in back when walking in open air and becoming warm. Burning of feet; soles;* on back of r.; at night; r. sole at night.

Sweat; at night; at night, with loss of appetite and prostration, as if he were going into a decline; at night, < *trunk;* **towards morning**; *in morning;* when eating and talking; **of strong odor**; *trickling, at night,* < *loins;* **on head; on head only, running down the face; offensive, on feet; offensive, on soles and between toes, they become sore when walking**; *on hands;* on chest at night; on sides of spine, then warmth in upper part of body, then sweat on face, < forehead.

Clinical.—Hectic fever, with night-sweats. Results of sudden suppression of habitual sweating of the feet.

Sinapis Nigra.

A tincture is made of the ripe seeds of the black mustard.

Generalities.—Sore feeling, with late rising and stiffness. Weakness. Aggravation in evening; from 7 till 9 P.M., amelioration by lying down at night, except dreams.

Mind.—Irritable and dissatisfied; I., don't wish to be spoken to, unfit for mental exertion. Mind worked rapidly at night, study easier and perception clearer.

Head.—Aching at night, < r. side and over r. eye, < *stooping* and motion, even opening and closing eye, > lying still; heavy A. during the day, > being busy or studying, returning on stooping, > open air, next day head the same till 11 A.M., then burning prickling in face, with full pulse and dulness of vertex as if empty, this lasted all day, with marked clearness of perception. Heaviness, < forehead, over eyes and in temples, never in occiput and only occasionally in vertex, > lying and open air, was forgotten when mind was occupied, < thinking about it, < a warm, especially a narrow room, it seldom amounted to a pain. Fulness. Dulness in forenoon. Vertigo.

Forehead.—Sharp pain over l. eye and passing over eye from l. to r. Pain above eyes; P. commencing about noon, beginning at outer canthi, < around edges of orbits and over bridge of nose, < a warm room, > cold, open air, partly > eating, but returning after eating, forehead hot and dry; towards evening, < over l. eye, > retiring, returned next morning on rising, afterwards nausea, > retiring; in F. and temples and around edges of orbits, > cold air, < warm room; as if I had taken cold, < towards night, with general tired feeling and pain in small of back; heavy, in F. and temples all the morning, > shutting eyes, disappeared on eating a hearty meal at 2 o'clock. Heaviness; in anterior part of head, forgotten during mental exertion, < thinking about it.

Dragging downward in temples, next day with pain, which was < thinking of it and forgotten during mental application. Heavy drawing pain in r. temple towards night and in evening. Heavy aching in vertex and sides of head. Pain in l. side. Scalp feels as if adherent to bones in afternoon.

Eyes.—*Sticking in l. in afternoon. Pain in l., with smarting. Sore, weak, pressure on ball causes sticking. Tired feeling in afternoon. Lachrymation; with smarting of eyes.* Balls feel as if pressed from above, > closing eyes, > a hearty meal at 2 o'clock, with tired feeling in them, pain and difficulty in keeping them open.

Nose.—Stoppage of l. nostril in afternoon and evening (Lyc., r.); **of l. all day.** *Scanty acrid discharges from anterior nares. Sneezing.*

Clinical.—Hay fever, the nose is dry and hot, no discharge, nostrils apt to be alternately affected. Acute coryza, thin, watery, excoriating discharge, with sharp hacking cough, > lying down, with smarting and itching of the eyes. Hay fever, eyes red, smarting, burning, itching. Lachrymation, sneezing, thick acrid discharge. Hay fever, with great swelling of the nose, thin, acrid discharge, dyspnœa, oppression of the chest, < night lying down. Hay fever, with rattling wheezing in chest and difficult breathing. Acrid nasal discharge. Acute catarrh of the pharynx, hot, inflamed, feels scalded, sometimes with violent burning of the stomach, < eating. Dryness of anterior nares and pharynx, of posterior nares, with slightly lumpy secretion.

Face.—Shrunken. Redness around mouth, with smarting of lips. Burning prickling. Sensation as if cheek were bulged out by a bubble of air just below malar-bone, in afternoon. Lips dry and feel as if integuments were stiff.

Mouth.—Teeth sensitive to warm drinks and cold air, < those that have been filled. Tongue coated dirty white in middle, < towards back part; a fissure along median line at the point where I was in the habit of taking the drug from the bottle, did not disappear on taking the drug in a different manner; sore and raw, could hardly bear weight of teeth on it, with soreness of gums; burning scalded feeling; forepart sore, feeling as of a blister on tip; feels dry and sticky. Burning extending to stomach. Dryness. Salivation. Breath offensive, as after onions. Taste of garlic all day; in morning, with tingling of tongue; T. of horse-radish.

Throat.—Soreness on r. side, soon extending to l.; on l. side, next day felt on swallowing and on forcing mucus from posterior nares, whole throat injected behind uvula, light red.

Stomach.—Eructations at first tasting of horse-radish, then tasteless; E. of gas; of gas all the evening, with heartburn. *Singultus.* Nausea till breakfast; in evening; with headache. Copious vomiting at 4 P.M.

Pain in epigastric region; in cardiac region all day; in region, > bending forward and sitting, with faintness; across epigastric region, tears ran from eyes and it seemed to double me up, could hardly stand; running across epigastric region when sitting leaning forward, > sitting straight; burning, then sharp, intermittent. Burning. Load, with heartburn.

Abdomen.—Rumbling; before stool. Emissions of flatus, generally noiseless and odorless. Accumulation of flatus, with occasional twinges of pain about umbilicus extending to l. iliac region, pain > retiring. Heavy pain. Pain in l. hypochondrium. Twisting pain in small intestines; in umbilical region; in umbilical region, extending in l. iliac region. Pain in umbilical and lumbar regions; in U. region in forenoon; to l. of umbilicus, extending to l. iliac region, on the fifth day it ascended to r. side, to ascending colon. Burning in umbilical region. Weight in umbilical region in forenoon; below umbilicus in afternoon. Swelling of a gland in l. groin, with pain (may have come from a sore heel caused by a tight shoe). Pain in r. groin in afternoon, > pressure; sharp, in r. inguinal gland in afternoon; remittent heavy, in l. iliac region, at times sticking.

Rectum and Stool.—Smarting cutting low down in rectum and in anus after stool, with sensation as if more should be discharged. Sharp smarting in lower part of rectum and in anus after stool, with sensation as if more should be discharged. Ineffectual desire. Two stools in one day, the second loose, difficult, rather scanty, did not seem to be through after stool, next day desire to go to stool all day, stools difficult, in lumps, which at first were large and then tapered off, same sense of not being through, some efforts fruitless, third day difficult, in small hard lumps, with desire to remain long at stool. Stool hard, like balls; hard, large, only about once every three days.

Urinary Organs.—Pain in bladder in morning before urinating. Frequent desire. Frequent micturition, urine pale; F. and copious; F. and copious at night, always preceded by erections which woke him; sometimes followed by continued desire, urine copious, pale; and urine pale, after passage it seemed as if more would come, in about half a minute dribbling, was able to retain urine without *much* discomfort. Urine copious.

Sexual Organs.—Erections sometimes with lascivious dreams; at night, with lascivious dreams and emissions; violent, day and night. Desire.

Respiratory Organs.—Hoarseness in evening; with frequent attempts to clear the throat. Cough in evening; hacking, in evening, with expectoration of small lumps of mucus; hacking, beginning generally about 7 or 8 P.M., sometimes with feeling of something low down in trachea which must be dislodged, sometimes dislodged small chunks of tenacious white mucus, but mostly dry, < cold air, > lying and temporarily > eating, excited by laughing, and during the day, < forenoon, continual attempts to clear throat, difficult raising of small lumps of white mucus, at night same sensation, with greater difficulty in raising mucus, and from posterior nares difficult discharge of cold, tasteless, tenacious, white masses of mucus. Respiration at base of l. lung roughened, with pain there.

Clinical.—Loud coughing spells, with barking expiration heard at a great distance.

Chest.—Suppuration reaching down to sternum, with gangrenous inflammation, muscles, vessels and nerves laid bare. Sticking, and in r. side. Pain in a spot an inch above and an inch to r. of apex beat of heart; wandering P.; wandering, and in abdomen.

Heart.—Sharp pain. Pain towards apex in evening; P. > afternoon; every day about 10 A.M. and from 4 till 6 P.M. and sometimes at night when studying, with dread and oppression, sometimes with a peculiar pain in r. side as if heart were there and as if I were conscious of its beating. Oppression in region, with pricking. Uneasiness, with occasional pain in cardiac region.

Pulse.—Rapid. Slow. Full; and usually soft.

Back.—Pulsating pain under lower angle of l. scapula in afternoon; in intercostal muscles under lower angle of l. S. in forenoon. Pain in lumbar region, < towards bedtime, then all night restlessness and sleeplessness from pain in back and hips, next day pain through back and hips, > motion.

Extremities.—Weariness, with cramp in calves. Occasional pains in l. shoulder-joint. Drawing at inferior insertion of r. biceps brachialis on flexion and extension of arm. Pain in calves and ankles; heavy, in leg. Weakness of calves.

Skin.—Redness.

Sleep.—Sleepiness; during the day, with weakness; during the day, then sleeplessness at night before midnight, then sleepiness in morning and late rising. Sleep but three or four hours out of the twenty-four, but no suffering therefrom, afterwards could sit up all night and not suffer from loss of sleep. Vivid dreams. Lascivious dreams.

Fever.—Chilliness, with chattering of teeth, shivering and shrunken features. Heat, with stitches in skin; H., < down spine; as from hot water in bloodvessels, > when nausea came on, also with sweat. Sweat, < forehead and upper lip; S. from least exertion, mental or physical, and from external heat.

Spigelia.

A tincture is made of the freshly dried herbs of the "Pink root," Spigelia Anthelmia, L.

General Action.—The action of this drug on the nervous system has been utilized principally for the cure of neuralgic pains which affect every part of the body, but chiefly the head, chest and heart. Its febrile symptoms are not marked and it seems not to be useful for inflammatory affections, more than as palliative of the pains accompanying such conditions. It has none of the mental anguish of Aconite, Arsenic, etc., etc.

Allies.—Bry., Puls.; Bell., China, Nux v., Sulph.; Rhus t., Kalm., Arn., Cact.

Generalities.—Convulsions, then death. Stitches in many parts on ascending stairs after a moderate walk. *Sensitiveness to touch, the slightest knock causes pain and shuddering about the place, even on stepping shattering in body; if he knocks against any part there is sudden painful crawling through whole body to head* (Arn., Bell., China, Nux v., Puls.). Everything hurt him as if he were bruised (Arn.), and on rising from a seat he was dizzy and unsteady in his legs as if reeling. Sick in evening in open air, with anxiety and internal heat. Discomfort in whole body, with heaviness and lassitude in limbs and disinclination to work.

Weakness; in morning; *in morning on waking; in morning, from confused busy dreams;* in morning on rising; in morning, and overpowering sleepiness when sitting soon after rising; *after walking;* after slight exertion; when hungry; soon after beginning to walk in open air, < thighs, with anxious pressure upon chest so that he would be glad to eructate but cannot, then desire for stool and emission of flatus, with relief in abdomen; < ascending stairs; with trembling of hands on taking hold of anything; of mind and body, < standing.

Aggravation from 10 A.M. till 12 M.; from 10 till 12 morning and night, amelioration at 3 or 4 P.M.; in afternoon; at 8 P.M., with red burning cheeks, cutting low down across abdomen, settling in lower limbs and back. Amelioration about 3 or 4 P.M., then stupor.

Clinical.—The Spigelia patient is worse from any motion of the arms and from lying on the back (Bry.).

Mind.—Joyful. Lively, contented and trustful mood alternating with palpitation and anxious oppression of chest. Earnest, vexed if any one jokes with him. Talks unwillingly. Anger. Peevish; in evening, he could kill himself, with chilliness of body. Unable to enjoy himself with others though he was not sad. Sad and peevish; and red in face; S. and fearful; S., then cheerful, then S. again in afternoon. Anxiety about the future; with inclination to peevish, indolent mood. Uneasiness and apprehension, inability to remain anywhere. Deep thought about his future. Sits lost in thought and stares at a single point. Inattention. *Mental exertion difficult. Loss of memory;* and mental indolence. Memory more active than before.

Head.—Burrowing tearing in brain *towards evening,* **< l. parietal bone, on motion, on walking, < a false step.** Cutting, waking her after a short sleep, with general restlessness and nausea, slept towards morning, on rising listlessness and languor, urine scanty and high-colored. Thrust inward in one point towards middle of brain at every step in open air. *Neuralgia flying from one part to another,* < r. side, and settling in cervical vertebræ, with feeling of imperfect support. *Pain in brain on shaking head, with vertigo* (Bry.); *P., < stooping* (Bry.); < open air; < lying, > walking; on shaking it, with heaviness; *with pressure above r. orbit; flying; like a heaviness, on drawing facial muscles it seems as if skull would burst at the top;* like confusion. Soreness as if bruised, and in eyes. Pressure outward on speaking loud or coughing; in brain on stooping. *Sensation in brain as if head were tightly bound.* Fulness, and in eyes, causing redness of eyes, lachrymation and vertigo.

Dulness; in evening; with **pressure outward in forehead;** *so that reflection was difficult.* Stupefied as after smoking strong tobacco. *Swashing sensation in brain when walking; and he feels every step. Vertigo; if he looks down he thinks that he will fall over;* if he turns his head when walking in open air; when standing; when sitting, with emptiness of head; when walking; (*> lying*), *head sinks backward, with nausea at palate, discomfort in abdomen and thorax, in abdomen pinching, with urging to stool, whereupon he loses consciousness;* with staggering to the left; as if the sidewalk were rising before me when walking; as if he would fall forward on looking in front of him.

Forehead.—**Shooting through F.; behind and above r. eminence;** in front of head and in eyes, with sore compressed feeling through balls, nausea, dread of motion or noise, face red, hands and feet cold; pulsating, from evening till morning, with hammering before ears. **Tearing externally on bone;** *in F., occiput and temples;* from l. eminence to occiput; **tensive, < beneath l. eminence, extending towards orbit; thrust-like,** *when sitting and standing,* **< r. eminence,** *causing staring. Boring. Burrowing in F., occiput and l. side of vertex, < motion, loud noise, speaking loudly or opening mouth, > lying, with burrowing tearing. Burning pain in l. bone;* in F. and l. temple; **in r. side, extending to eyes, so that he could not turn them without pain** (compare Bry.). *Pain;* in sinciput; above orbits; in cerebrum and cerebellum, causing vertigo; heavy, beneath l. eminence; confused, and in temples, with compression forward in sides. *Pressure outward; in l. side; in r. eminence; on stooping; > pressure of hand.* Pressure inward internally and externally in l. eminence. Shaking and swashing. Confusion in upper part, with emptiness, scalp is sensitive to touch and hair seems to bristle.

Temples.—*Sticking as from electric sparks in l.* Tearing thrusts in r. Pain; in r., gradually extending more and more; frequent drawing, in l. *Pressure inward, < r.*

Vertex.—Pain; in a spot. *Pressive drawing in r. side of V. and occiput.*

Side.—Jerks in l., with thrusts. Tearing sticking in l.; intermittent contractive, in a spot externally in parietal bone, < posteriorly. Pain in l. half of brain; **deep-seated, in r. side, involving r. eye, in morning in bed, < motion, even < straining at stool, and on suddenly turning head the brain seemed loose;** *pressing asunder, in r.* Dulness in r.

Occiput.—Sticking in a point in l. side. Boring in O. and vertex, as if it would draw head backward. *Jerks when walking in open air, and then in temples on every step.* Pain, < lying upon it; P. in O. and nape about 3 or 4 A.M, > rising and dressing, with stiffness; P. as after a blow; as if arteries were beating against obstacles; bubbling, > leaning backward while sitting, < lying horizontally and at first by walking, afterwards by slightest motion. Pressure inward in l. side, < stooping unless he pressed hard against the spot. Drawing dulness in evening when walking in open air. Heaviness.

Scalp.—(Covered with miliary pimples.) *Sore to touch; < moving scalp.* Pain as if ulcerating in region of vertex, with intermittent sticking jerking penetrating into brain. Seems contracted and tense. Itching crawling in l. side of vertex.

Clinical.—Neuralgic headache, *generally beginning at one point and radiating in different directions,* pains burning, jerking and tearing, < stormy weather, sometimes ending with vomiting, sometimes beginning in the morning and ending in the evening, at times a feeling as if the head were opening.

Eyes.—Surrounded by yellow rings. Sparkling, as before eruption of smallpox or measles. Look dim and weak. Hardened mucus. Redness of whites, with injected vessels; R. of white in morning, with inflammation and with heaviness of lids. Seem distended. *Burrowing stitch in middle of eye and in inner canthus, pressing upper lid downward. Pain;* **on turning them** (see Kalm.); with sensation and vision as in lachrymation, without lachrymation; **on motion, as if too large for their orbits** (Comocl.); as from sand

Burning in l. towards temple; B. pain forcing him to close them, with anxiety as if he could never open them again, on opening them after the pain had disappeared vision was prevented by a sea of blood-red masses rising up, with lachrymation and dilatation of pupils. Pressure inward at side of r. Dry heat in afternoon. Crawling. Weakness, apparently with an internal impediment, wherever he turns them they remain and he does not know what he is looking at, like one whose vision has vanished. Lachrymation; acrid, trickling.

Balls.—*Sticking in r.; on moving it; itching, in r., returning after rubbing. Pain;* < **turning eyes, and on attempting to look with eyes turned vertigo, forcing him to turn the whole head;** *tensive, in l.; contractive burning, in r.* Itching in l., > rubbing.

Pupils dilated; with relaxed and paralyzed lids. Burning pain in r. external canthus. Ulcerating and biting soreness of margins of lids. Sticking beneath lids; in l. lids; in margin of r. upper; in r. inner canthus. Cutting on margin of l. lower lid. Burning pain beneath r. lid. Pain as if upper lids were hard and immovable, with difficulty in raising them (Rhus t.). Sensation as if a hard substance were under r. upper lid, > rubbing. Swelling on temporal side of orbit, with pain and soreness on touch. *Pain in l. orbit* near malar-bone, then swelling of bone, sore to touch. *Pressure downward in l. orbit.* Burning pain in l. brow. Farsighted. *Vision dim*, or sensation as if feathers or hairs were in the lashes, < rubbing eyes; dim, and when writing he must make a great effort, as if water were in eyes. Vision vanishes when he fixes gaze.

Clinical.—Ciliary neuralgia, the pains radiate in every direction and are extremely severe. Ptosis, with sharp pains and hot lachrymation. Rheumatic iritis, indicated by the ciliary pains. Asthenopia.

Ears.—Twitching in r. auricle. Itching-sticking in l.; boring-stitching in r. Boring sticking jerking, at times shooting through Eustachian tube to throat. Jerking pain extending to eye and lower jaw. Pinching on posterior part of r. auricle. Thrusting tearing in r. Boring back of ears, < confining eyes, as in reading or writing. Pain in l.; *in margin of l.; in r.*, extending to malar-bone and r. molars; *as from a plug in l. Drawing pain in l. antitragus;* in l. ear, extending to malar-bone. Burning pain in auricle. Pressing asunder in r.; P. inward in auditory canal. Jumping sensation as from swashing of water, on stepping suddenly. Beating in l. Itching prickling in r. Itching crawling in r. Stopped sensation; on blowing nose, > boring in with finger, with loss of hearing; in l., without difficulty in hearing; as with a finger, when wind blows into them; in evening, as if something were in front of drum, which seems contracted.

Hearing difficult, as if ear were closed by a finger, with fluttering noise in it. Sensitive to loud noises. *Distant ringing, with sensation as if loosely stopped or as if a mist were before it;* R. when talking, with re-echoing through head. Sudden crackling and buzzing before them extending into forehead, > holding hands over eyes, with wavelike pulsation in them. Sound in l. as if a wind blew rapidly across it. Humming, < evening, with bubbling. Roaring before ears. Fluttering as of a bird, then moist discharge and very clear hearing.

Nose.—Tetter-like eruption in and on r. nostril. Itching boring in r. nostril forcing him to sneeze. Burning in wings provoking rubbing, but not relieved thereby. Sticking crawling in nostrils, transiently > scratching. Itching in nares. Stoppage; *of anterior part, with discharge through posterior nares;* at root. No irritation from tobacco when snuffing. Sneezing; in morning, with discharge of bloody mucus. *Discharge of mucus, at one time white, at another yellow, with discharge of mucus from mouth; D. only through posterior nares*, on blowing nose violently only a little tenacious yellowish mucus is discharged, forepart of nose is always dry. Fluent coryza; with hoarseness, external heat, prominent eyes, headache and weeping mood. Dry catarrh after eating; sudden C., dry, then fluent.

Clinical.—Frequently useful in nasal catarrh, especially of the posterior nares.

Face.—Redness, then pallor; R., sometimes of one cheek, then of both, sometimes upper lip hot and swollen, as if my breath scorched it. Sallow after flushes. Yellowish after pain in heart. Swelling on waking from midday sleep, with pallor and sickly look, S. again next morning after waking, more about eyes; muscles seem swollen and distorted in morning on rising. Sticking in l. cheek. *Tearing in l. zygomatic process*, and as the pain became a little better dulness as from swelling; *jerking T. in r. zygoma. Burning pain in r. malar-bone;* in l. cheek. Pressure on zygomata.

Jaw.—Drawing sticking from r. upper to vertex. **Tearing in lower, extending to ear and about it** *as far as nape,* < *moving head; pain in r. lower as if it would be torn out of joint* when chewing, at other times dull pain in articulation. Pressure on r. angle of lower. (Tensive pain in articulation.)

Lip.—Blackish painless pimple in red of lower. *Burning in r. side of upper, even when moved. Burning tension in upper during rest.* Burning in upper.

Clinical.—Facial neuralgia, pains radiating in every direction, shooting, burning, tearing.

Mouth.—Teeth. Sharp and brittle. *Throbbing tearing,* < *cold water,* > *lying.* Gnawing in hollow T. **Aching in evening from the customary smoke;** A. in l. molars; at night preventing sleep and driving him out of bed, not during the next day except just after eating; cramplike, in upper, so that when mouth was closed the lower jaw seemed spasmodically pressed against them; *like a pressure outward,* < lying on r. side, > eating and drinking, but it began immediately afterwards, it often woke him at night; throbbing, in a l. molar; drawing, in a hollow T. *Intermittent jerking through both rows,* < *a hollow tooth; intermittent J. in nerve of a hollow T.*, < afternoon, < water or drawing air into mouth, > *tobacco-smoke.* Coldness of upper, with sticking jerking in them.

Tongue.—*Full of cracks*, as if it would scale off. Blisters, with burning on touch, now on T., now on palate. Coated white; dark brown. *Sticking in r. side;* boring, extending forward in r. side, with acid taste in mouth. Sensation as if swollen posteriorly; when chewing.

Mucus at one time white, at another yellow, in mouth and fauces in morning. Burning pain in palate. Dryness in morning on waking, it seemed as if mouth were full of pins and needles and as if it stuck together, without thirst, even with much saliva. *Salivation white, frothy;* S. posteriorly in mouth, with excessive hunger in chest. Offensive breath. Taste bad; insipid. Does not relish his tobacco.

Clinical.—Neuralgic toothache of the most violent shooting character, < cold water.

Throat.—*Discharge of mucus from fauces all day, most from posterior nares;* D. of mucus from posterior nares so that he must hawk it up to avoid suffocation, waking him at night. Accumulation of saliva in fauces. Swelling on l. side of fauces and sticking when swallowing. Sticking in region of larynx, > swallowing, but returning; in r. side, and on swallowing S. in parotid and within ear, something between an earache and a throatache. Soreness, with cold on lungs and in head. Tingling in back part. Tickling itching in œsophagus, with sensation as if a semi-fluid substance would rise into fauces, hollow cough, waterbrash, anxiety and fear that he would faint. Inability to swallow saliva because he always brought it up again as by nausea, necessity to spit it out.

Stomach.—Appetite and thirst great; ravenous A., with nausea. Loathing of food, especially sweets. Aversion to smoking and snuffing tobacco; to smoking tobacco and to coffee. Thirst; late in evening; great, with loss of appetite; unquenchable, while face is red and hot. Eructations; sour; of gas; of gas after eating. Nausea; in morning and lasting into afternoon; rising into throat.

Sticking in pit, < inspiration, with oppression of chest; in pit during expiration, > lying; in pit and above it and between pit and where beat of heart is felt, with oppression of chest; intermittent, to left of pit; intermittent burning, near l. side of pit. Pain. Weight in pit; as of a lump, > pressure with hand and changing to pressure and tension in chest. Pressure in pit as if he would eructate and be relieved thereby, but no eructations till he has swallowed air. Chilliness in pit, spreading to abdomen and lower limbs, and at times to back.

Abdomen. — Distressing fulness after a moderate meal. Rumbling; before stool, that occurred twice in morning and once in evening, thin; like croaking of frogs. Flatus of the odor of bad eggs. Pinching sticking, with emission of flatus, then desire for stool. Pinching. Griping when lying; G., then difficult, soft stool, that constantly became thinner; *as if intestines would be constricted, causing anxiety and making respiration difficult;* extending like a stitch to chest, with emission of flatus; wandering, every day about 3 P.M., > emission of flatus. Burning, with tasteless eructations, as if mingled with water.

Sticking in hepatic region on walking rapidly and jumping, > walking quietly; rhythmical, deep below r. ribs, > breathing deeply, returning on expiration. Rumbling in l. side, then in r. Cutting in sides, extending towards middle, in morning in bed, with emission of flatus. Sticking to left of umbilicus on inspiration; to left of U. when walking. Umbilical region, cutting every day from 5 till 6 P.M., with chilliness, diarrhœa and much micturition; griping in l. side; pain as from a hard swelling in evening.

Hypogastrium.—Rumbling here and there, now and then painful. Sticking in groin; *in region of os innominatum when walking, > thirty or forty steps;* above groins, with stitchlike oppression of chest; in region of ring, with cutting, the intestines protruded like a hernia (which formerly was seldom the case), the spot sore to touch; from pelvic region down limbs; intermittent, in l. side just above ilium; boring, in ilium; tensive, in r. groin when walking; burning, posteriorly on margin of l. ilium on every inspiration; itching biting, in muscles of l. os innominatum. Cutting on sitting down, > rising from a seat, with burrowing, as from incarcerated flatus. Boring digging in r. groin. Tearing drawings through H. *Griping;* alternating with rumbling and gurgling, and during every paroxysm of pain desire to urinate, which was unchanged though much urine was passed. *Pain as if it would burst, < evening before a soft stool, then slight relief.* Pain in groin and thigh towards perineum as after a long ride on horseback. Tensive pain in r. groin on touch. Sensation as if a weight fell down, < inspiration.

Clinical.—Neuralgia of the bowels. Frequently useful in pains associated with worms in children.

Rectum and Anus.—Discharge of pieces of thick mucus, it seemed as if flatus passed, stool like sheep-dung and enveloped in mucus. *Boring stitch in perineum.* Itching in anus, > scratching; *in A. and coccyx,* with difficulty > scratching. Crawling as of thread-worms. Sensation as if a thin stool passed during emission of flatus, which did not occur. Pressure in rectum when not at stool. Cramplike urging. Ineffectual urging; after complete stool.

Stool.—Watery. Diarrhœa; frequent, mixed with tenacious, yellow mucus. Constipation. Nodular, with pressure. First part hard, then thin, then thrusts outward in forehead. White. Omitted, next day hard, difficult.

Urinary Organs.—*Prostatic fluid passes out.* Urging; with burning stitch in urethra; constant, urine bright straw-colored and smelling strong. Frequent micturition; and profuse; at night, with copious urine and pressive pain upon bladder during micturition. Difficult micturition at night, then burning. Sudden involuntary dribbling in afternoon on rising from a seat, with burning in forepart of urethra. (Spurting of urine on external pressure upon bladder.) Urine watery. Urine high-colored and scanty; almost blood-colored, on standing the lower part became gray, by shaking it all assumed that color. Large deposit of uric acid. Whitish sediment.

Sexual Organs.—Swelling of half of glans. *Itching stitch extending forward in penis and r. testicle;* I. stitch in l. testicle; burning S. in penis and r. testicle. Crawling about glans every day. *Frequent erections without internal physical sexual excitement, though with voluptuous thoughts.* Quivering of scrotum. Emission in morning, with lascivious dream, without subsequent exhaustion.

Female.—Heat in vagina, with fulness and pressure, < standing; H. in uterine region, with pain and pressure, with dislike to move. Tendency to leucorrhœa. Menses too soon, profuse, dark clots of disgusting odor; too soon, copious, bright red, of foul odor, with pressure, fulness and tearing in uterine region and stinging extending into limbs, after menses brownish leucorrhœa; too soon, with giving out of osseous, muscular and nervous systems, ending in a relaxed condition of system; fetid, bright red, with pain, making face and feet cold, beginning with depressing headache.

Respiratory Organs.—Cough in morning after coryza had mostly disappeared; at night, with catarrh;

sudden violent, on getting water into trachea; suffocative, as from water running down into glottis; short dry, in open air, causing soreness of chest; dry, violent, hollow, taking away the breath, from irritation low down in trachea, < stooping. Slow and deep sighing.

Chest.—Enlargement of mammæ and pain originating from centre of lobes deep in and proceeding to surface, causing irregular flashes of heat in head, eyes, neck and shoulders.

Sticking at the point where the beat of the heart is felt; S. in r. side; *in r. side during inspiration; in l. during inspiration and expiration; with drawing together so that he could not get his breath; beneath l. ribs in evening, bending him over; extending outward, unconnected with breathing; extending outward transversely through C., < sternum; towards l. clavicle in evening, preventing respiration; rhythmical with pulse at the point where impulse of heart is felt, or rather more externally; intermittent, extending inward above l. nipple when bending over at writing, suddenly > becoming erect;* jerking, below axilla; sudden drawing, near sternum, extending downward; *pinching, in l. side of diaphragm, taking away his breath and forcing him to remain standing; beneath heart,* changing to crawling, then to sticking again; itching, beneath clavicle; itching, in l. pectoral muscles; boring, in r. side, in region of diaphragm, during inspiration and expiration; tensive boring, in l. side during expiration; tensive drawing, in r. true ribs during inspiration and expiration, < pressure. Tensive sticking in r. false ribs during expiration; in l. side, < expiration; in r. side, < inspiration and expiration; in r. side of C. and abdomen during inspiration and expiration, < walking.

Cutting tearing beneath l. nipple, extending to region of scapula and upper arm, < inspiration and deep breathing. *Tearing boring extending outward beneath r. nipple, extending to sternum and becoming a tearing. Sticking pinching extending outward beneath r. nipple, < inspiration.* Sudden jerking as from electric sparks in forepart. Sprained pain in upper and l. side on turning body to r. side, making a false step or on turning l. arm. (Pain after hawking and clearing throat); intermittent P.; bruised, in first four l. ribs when straining at stool; ending in gastritis, aggravated by stricture in œsophagus an inch and a half above cardiac orifice and about middle of the tube, at latter place the pain passes through to back below inferior angle of r. scapula, the P. at these points < swallowing and by frequent sour, acrid, clear, bitter and frothy vomiting, especially in morning fasting, œsophagus spasmodically contracted so that I could not rest nor sleep without the almost constant use of ice, with pain in chest, trembling of stomach and beating of heart.

Pressure beneath l. clavicle; upon middle; towards evening; when standing, with drawing; above ensiform cartilage when standing. Suffocated feeling; constricted. *Cutting constriction, with anxiety. Tearing constriction in pectoral muscles when standing; T. constriction above pit of stomach, with oppression, then the same pain below pit of throat, with palpitation.*

Clinical.—Intercostal neuralgia. It has been prescribed for hydrothorax.

Heart.—*Stabbing through H. on deep inspiration.* Spasmodic pain through H., frequent stoppage, apparently of heart, the blood merely gurgling through it, which produced no fear, a listless, disgusted indifference towards everything. *Heavy aching in region of apex, with feeling as if a dull pointed knife were slowly driven through it.*

Palpitation (Ars., Puls., China, *Nat. m.*, Sulph., Cact.); *in morning when sitting,* **with anxious oppression trembling of heart; < sitting down and bending forward;** *on deep inspiration and on holding breath, with increase of anxiety,* **the palpitation was felt by the hand at pit of stomach. Violent beating in morning as soon as he sat down after rising, with weight upon chest above the point where the beating was felt, with cutting and digging in hypogastrium as from incarcerated flatus, which lasted longer than the palpitation.** *Irregularity of action, with suffocation.* **Beats audible and visible through the clothes;** *audible, < lying, with pain, causing desire for fresh air* (Cact.).

Clinical.—Inflammations of the heart, both pericardial and endocardial, with violent irregular action, severe pain. Pericarditis, with profuse sweat, sticking pain, palpitation, dyspnœa from lying on the back, dry cough. Inflammation of the heart and aorta, pain under the sternum, with numbness of the arm, irregular pulse. Neuralgia about heart, extending to arm; angina pectoris. Frequently useful for irregular and tumultuous action of the heart, nervous.

Pulse.—Rapid. Slow during the morning fever; S. and feeble. *Weak and irregular, now rapid, now slow.*

Neck.—Swelling of glands. Intermittent drawing in muscles of nape and up to occiput. Pain in nape as if he could not raise head after stooping; P. in nape as if asleep in morning after rising, > motion. Paralyzed sensation in l. side.

Back.—Twitching of dorsal and costal muscles. *Bruised pain in spine even during rest.* Sticking opposite heart; in upper dorsal vertebræ; extending to l. side when walking; periodical, in r. scapula; boring in l.; itching, in r. dorsal muscles; S. in sacrum when sitting, < inspiration and expiration. Bubbling sensation in l. scapula, as if blood were dropping through a valve. Tired aching over crest of ilium and down into pelvis, < r. side, with general languor and desire to lie down, later the tired aching < morning and forenoon.

Extremities.—Trembling; of lower, then of upper. Nails brittle and many white spots on them. Shooting through all at a false step. Tearing in bones near joints, as if scraped. Uneasiness at night preventing sleep. *Fatigue, < walking, with bruised feeling in spine.* Heaviness, and after ascending stairs difficult breathing; H. so that writing and walking were difficult.

Upper Limbs.—*Trembling.* Axilla, itching biting stitches towards forepart of l.; burning pain in l.; tensive pain in l. during rest. Jerking in r. shoulder; in top of r. L. shoulder and arm hang down as if heavy when walking, with tension in forepart of upper arm. Sprained pain in shoulder-joint and proximal joints of thumb and index. Cutting drawing across above deltoid. Drawing pain in l. deltoid, < hard pressure. Heaviness of r. arm when at rest. Arm falls asleep when writing, so that he cannot hold a pen. Twitching in l. upper arm. Tearing on middle and inner side of upper arm, < touch. Stitches in bend of elbow and in fingers; itching S. in bend of r. elbow; itching S. in tip of l. elbow.

Forearm.—*Twitching above l. wrist during rest;* sticking, above wrist. Boring stitches in r. Sticking cutting above l. wrist, on moving index while holding arm firmly against body. Pinching in bones of r. during rest. Pain in r.; *above r. wrist during rest.*

Hand.—Pale yellow. Involuntary drawing in tendons of l. so that all fingers were bent, with spasmodic pain in hollow of hand. Rhythmical tearing in joints of l., at times extending into metacarpus, then cramplike tearing in palm. Cramplike pain in l. metacarpus extending from side of thumb to that of little finger, as if hand were squeezed. Drawing pains transversely through bones. Crawling as if asleep on compressing hand. Falling asleep when at rest, > wetting them and taking firm hold of anything, with crawling in tips of fingers.

Fingers.—Sticking jerks near proximal joints. Itching sticking in tips; throbbing S. in tips, as if they had been frozen. *Tearing in phalanges of r. thumb;* in tip of l. little; in metacarpo-phalangeal joints; rhythmical, in phalanges of r. Burning pain on back of proximal phalanx of little finger; on joint of l. thumb. Paralytic pain in r. index. *Painful drawing in metacarpal joint of thumb.*

Lower Extremities.—Weakness, < thighs. Heaviness; with tingling and with difficulty in walking.

Thigh.—*Itching stitch on l.; tensive sticking in l. when walking, > standing, returning when sitting;* intermittent burning S. in muscles below neck of l. femur, in a spot externally and posteriorly, when sitting, slightly > rising, on sitting down again worse than before. *Drawing tearing in r. when sitting;* tearing outward in l. extending from knee to os innominatum, as if in periosteum, < pressure on bone. Boring above r. knee during rest. Pain above r. knee when sitting; in r., < pressure; bruised, in anterior muscles when walking; drawing, in muscles and in hip. Tension in r. when sitting; in muscles in anterior surfaces when walking; in l. gluteals when walking. Sensation of gooseflesh on r., without chilliness. Movement downward, almost like chilliness, caused by sneezing.

Knee.—Sticking through middle on bending it, momentarily > walking; deep in r. patella when sitting. *Tearing in l. as if sprained when walking, so that he limped at times, since he could not bend knee as usual.* Digging in l., with uneasiness preventing sleep. Jerking in patella. Bruised pain on touch; on inner surface on bending it. Tearing tension on outer side of l. at every step on ascending stairs. Compressive pain, < walking, with drawing and sticking.

Leg.—Cramp in l. calf. Sticking jerks above ankle. *Sticking in calf and pulsation in patellæ if knees are held stiffly outstretched;* tensive S. in l. tibia during rest. Digging on inner side of r. calf, < walking; itching, in l. tibia below patella during rest. Burning pain above r. inner malleolus. Drawing extending downward, with sensation as if warmth had penetrated them, and warmth of feet; tensive D. in l. calf when walking. Bubbling sensation in r. calf, as if blood were dropping through a valve. Heaviness in r. when sitting.

Ankle.—Boring sticking in r. malleolus during rest. Acute pain in l. in morning when stepping on it. Cramplike pain as if tendons were too short on bending foot up and down. Pressure as from a stone when standing, with drawing in it. Smarting drawing, with soreness.

Foot.—Sticking in l. sole when sitting; in l. sole as if too short and tense when stepping on it; itching, in r. sole during motion; itching boring, on back of r. during rest. Jerking tearing on back; intermittent tearing in l. above toes; intermittent, in l. metatarsal bones. Suppurative pain in sole in morning on first stepping on them. Burning pain in back of l. Digging in r. above toes during rest.

Toes.—Itching stitch in second r.; boring-itching S. in balls of second and third. Tearing in muscles of l.

Skin.—Swelling on l. side of chin, which itches during midday nap. Wartlike growth on second l. toe, with biting pain, pressure of boot caused burning pain as in a corn, it left a thick white scar. Elevations like hives on lower limbs after scratching. Pimples red and sore to touch, on neck. Pustules on chin; on r. middle finger exuding yellow pus on pressure.

Biting pain on l. side of forehead. *Tickling on back of nose as if the hairs there were lightly touched or as from a wind across it.* Crawling in calves; in tips of r. toes during rest; boring, in a spot in r. palm; itching, on r. sole.

Itching in r. auricle; externally in ears; over whole side of nose; in l. groin; in axillæ, < l.; r. forearm; *more on thighs than on legs, returning after scratching;* on l. scapula, not > scratching; on back of l. foot during rest, not > scratching; biting, in thighs, not > scratching, > night in bed; as if palms and tips of fingers had been frozen; crawling, on forehead; crawling, on r. thigh, > scratching. Burning itching in middle of palms; in r. eyebrow, > scratching; in a spot in l. palm, next day a hard red pimple, with burning itching.

Sleep.—Yawning; in forenoon, with irresistible sleepiness; without sleepiness. Sleepiness. Irresistible sleepiness; in morning; in evening so long as he was up, but late falling asleep after lying down. Sleep heavy and stupid. Sleep long at midday and on waking he could not persuade himself to rise and kept falling asleep again.

Sleepless before midnight. *Late falling asleep;* on account of mental activity, then uneasy sleep disturbed by vivid unremembered dreams, and after midnight frequent waking, tossing about and a half waking condition. Sleep unrefreshing. *Restless sleep; with frequent waking,* full of frightful dreams, for example, that lightning had struck off his shoulder; with vivid dreams of fire and quarrels and about 1 A.M. he thought it time to rise. Dreams anxious; vivid, anxious, of fire and ghosts; vivid, of well-known past occurrences, long dreams of one subject; indistinctly remembered; voluptuous, with emission without erection; lascivious, with emission.

Fever.—*Chilliness in morning, without thirst; every morning after rising; every day at 7 A.M., on rising, then at noon heat, < trunk and face, with redness, without special thirst;* in afternoon, then heat and thirst for beer; in evening on going to bed, then offensive sweat; in evening on lying down, then heat, then sweat nearly all night; in evening, with cold hands and distended abdomen, without thirst, afterwards in night when lying on back bruised pain in all joints, vivid, fatiguing dreams, talking in sleep, dry heat of body, with dryness of mouth, nose and eyes, without thirst; waking me between 2 and 3 A.M., then paroxysms of labor-like pain, < lying on back, menses bright scarlet; *on slight motion;* after dinner, obliging him to lie in bed; sensitive to cold air.

Shaking chill in morning without thirst, with lightness of movements of fingers and mental activity. Shivering towards evening in open air, with tensive pain below l. ear, next morning glandular swelling in that spot, hard and painful to touch, with sticking in l. side of throat on swallowing, swelling of gum and difficulty in opening jaw, the sticking on swallowing > pressing the swollen glands inward, with sweat two mornings. Creeping shivering; with heat, without thirst; intermittent, starting from chest; over whole body except arms, with sensation as if hair bristled.

Intermittent chilliness every morning after rising. Internal chilliness with external warmth, < chest. Alternations of chill and heat all day, with redness of face; alternations of C. and heat, C. < back, heat in hands and face.

Coldness of finger-tips; hands and feet; arms and shoulders; *in back extending to umbilical region;* extending through limbs all day, without thirst; in arms, with gooseflesh, did not dare to bring arms against body on account of shivering; *hands seemed cold when held against face, while to touch they seemed warmer than usual, only clammy in palms;* of hands, with heat of face, without thirst; hands, with cold, clammy sweat, < inner surface; chills nights after retiring, beginning about region of heart, causing restlessness and hyperæsthesia of nervous system, which sensibility lasted longer than chill; internal C. and heat alternately in l. side of forehead; *intermittent, every morning, extending upward from feet;* intermittent creeping, in morning, starting from pit of stomach and extending over trunk, head and upper limbs, with external heat, without thirst; *sudden creeping, every morning,* at one time in feet, at another in head and hands, at another in back or chest and abdomen, at another over whole body, without thirst.

Heat; in evening, < face, yet longing for warmth of bed; (while eating cold food); after slight exertion, with sweat, < head, without thirst; on moderate exertion, <in face, on more violent exertion general sweat; with thirst for beer; in paroxysms, with red lips and cheeks; internal, in forenoon; internal at night, with dryness of mouth, without thirst.

Heat in head; in skin of r. temple near eye; in skin in front of r. ear; externally in l. temple; over spine; in cheeks and lips, with redness; of lower limbs at night, without sweat or thirst; internal, in face and hands, while hands seemed cold when held to face and face seemed cold to hands; flushing, in face, without redness; flushing, over back after supper.

Sweat on slightest uncovering.

Spongia.

A tincture is made of Turkey-sponge, toasted brown.

Allies.—It is interesting to observe that both the pathogenesis and our clinical experience emphasize the similarity of this substance to Carbo v., Iod. and Brom.; compare also Phos., Stannum, etc.

Generalities.—Bruised feeling on waking; B. feeling in upper part of body. Intolerance of tight clothing about body, < region of stomach.

Weakness after slight motion, with orgasm of blood in chest, heat of face, body began to glow, vessels hard and distended, and breath left her; *W. of mind and body;* with sleepiness; with sleepiness, dull look of eyes and swelling of eyelids; with headache, loss of appetite, sleepiness and fretfulness; with dulness of head, unfitting him for mental effort; < arms; *sudden, after exertion,* **chest especially affected, she could scarcely talk** (Carbo v., Stann., Sulph.), *heat in face and nausea, after a few hours heaviness of head; sudden, after moderate motion in open air, with swaying about upon the chair, anxiety, nausea, pallor,* **short, panting respiration, surging from heart into chest, as if it would force out upward,** with involuntary closing of eyes, almost spasmodic, with forcing out of tears between the closed lashes, she was conscious but unable to make the will act upon the limbs.

Heaviness when walking in open air, so that he must sit down on the ground. Numbness of lower half of body. *Feels best when lying.*

Mind.—*Joy and irresistible desire to sing, then distraction of mind and disinclination to work.* Alternately lively and lachrymose, and peevish, quarrelsome mood. Pert, witty. Fretful, scornful, obstinate; F., he talked unwillingly; F. and lazy, little inclined to talk. Taciturn and discontented. Dissatisfied with what she accomplishes, she cannot help herself at work, does not succeed. Anxious, as if he foresaw a misfortune to himself. Fearful and tormented by a frightful image of a past sad event. Easily frightened, it seemed to shoot into her feet, and then heaviness of them.

Head.—Aching from staring at one point, with lachrymation. Feeling as if everything would press out at forehead. Dull and stupid; D. and staggering when walking. Heaviness; all day; on raising it from the table; < stooping, with fulness. Rush of blood; with external heat of forehead and perceptible pulsation in arteries of neck. Vertigo; with tendency to fall backward; when sitting, as if head would fall to one side, with heat in head.

Forehead.—Sticking transversely in l. side; S. alternately in F. and occiput on motion, with heat extending from behind ear over occiput to nape; jerking, < walking; boring outward, in l. side when walking in open air. Pain; in l. side; externally above r. eye; from above eyes to occiput and nape, till sleep; as if F. and occiput were pressed towards each other at noon; extending outward in r. eminence. Pressure outward in l. upper part when sitting. *Sensation of accumulation of blood.*

Temples.—*Stitches externally in l. extending to forehead.* Tearing in l. close to orbit, causing aching in l. half of l. eye. Pressure outward in r.; sharp, externally. Throbbing in l.

Pain in vertex; drawing. Jerking through sides of head, < temples, extending to vertex on moving arms or stooping. *Pain in r. half of brain on entering a warm room from the open air;* drawing down in r. side of head and neck. Pressure outward in r. parietal bone when lying. Whizzing in region of whichever ear she lay upon, like pulsation, with a double beating.

Occiput.—Pain in l. side as if it would burst. Paroxysmal heaviness on walking; H. in afternoon on turning head, with stitching in it, *heat of face,* hands and feet, chilliness of rest of body, inclination to coryza, weakness of body, bitter taste, then in evening after undressing shaking chill, then in bed heat except on thighs, which were numb and chilly, at night sweat.

Scalp.—Gnawing pain on vertex. Sensitiveness, <

moving it. Sensation as if hair on vertex were bristling, or as if some one moved it, < motion of body.

Eyes.—Sunken. Redness of white. Suppuration. Sticking; in evening, then pain; in r., with pressure. Tension of l. by temple. Lachrymation. Tensive sticking in l. external canthus, < moving eyes, > touch. Drawing together of l. lids in morning in bed. Pain around about beneath lids; burning, on outer surface of l. lower lid. Heaviness of lids. Itching of lids. Burning about l. ball. Sudden sticking drawing in outer angle of l. orbit, extending around eye towards inner angle. Difficulty in recognizing distant objects.

Ears.—Sticking outward in r., as if through drum. Cramplike pain in l. when walking in open air; sore P. in cartilages; drawing P. in r. middle; tensive, in a swelling at entrance of meatus, with crawling as if it would break into an ulcer, and intermittent sticking. Pressure and forcing. Constriction. Burning in orifice of r. Ringing; in r. Hearing difficult.

Nose.—Crawling stitches in l. bone. Tearing. Contracted sensation over root. (Stoppage.) *Coryza and sneezing; C. and cough; stopped.* Bleeding at dinner, from slight blowing of nose (Carbo v.).

Face. — Pallor. Redness of cheeks, with usual warmth. Swelling of cheeks. Sticking in cheek; beneath lower lip. Tearing in r. malar-bone. Suppurative pain on l. side of chin as far as corner of mouth, on touch. Jaw, *swollen gland beneath l. lower, painful to touch;* swollen glands beneath r. lower, preventing motion of neck, with tensive pain on touch; *sticking transversely through l. upper;* jerking sticking from behind r. upper into inner ear in evening in bed; *cramplike pang from l. joint to cheek in evening when eating;* cramplike pain in l. upper; pain in lower on touch.

Mouth.—Stitches in upper incisors. Pain in teeth as if he had bitten something between them; (burning) pain in l. upper molars; P. in r. lower molars as if gums and teeth were swollen and the latter elongated. On chewing, sensation as if molars were on edge and loose. Itching of teeth. Gum swollen and painful on chewing. Blisters on margin of tongue, with sore pain; B. on margin of tongue and inside of cheeks, with burning stinging so that she could eat no solids. Salivation. Taste sweetish; T. rancid in mouth and fauces when smoking the usual tobacco; bitter; bitter low down in throat.

Throat.—Hawking of mucus. Sticking internally morning and evening, < eating, and on neck sensation as if something pressed outward. Scraping. Pain as if glands near larynx and trachea were swelling. Tension in l. side near larynx on turning head to r. side. Relaxed sensation in pharynx and stomach as if he had drunk too much warm water. Burning in T. and larynx, then in ears.

Goitre (Iod.).—*Sticking; in lower part;* on swallowing, at other times aching. *Pressure.* Sensation of working, distention and pressure, as if everything would force out. Sensation as if it were loose, < swallowing, and as if everything were moving about in it. Jerking aching over whole side on which there was a G., a throbbing in head extending into cheeks and neck as a tearing.

Stomach.—*Appetite increased;* diminished. Thirst after smoking; T. for cold water in evening. Eructations; empty; bitter; sour. *Hiccough.* Nausea; when smoking as usual; with accumulation of water in mouth. Pain in epigastric region in forenoon; in pit in evening. Constriction in l. side below S. when sitting, < lying on r. side. Internal coldness in pit, with fulness.

Abdomen.—Tense. Rumbling; before stool, with stitches in anus. Emission of flatus and soft stool. Cutting in morning after eating, forcing him to bend up, with urging to a scanty stool. Cramps. Griping; > emission of flatus. Difficulty after eating, with fulness, as if digestion stopped. Heat extending into chest on smoking, with chilliness of rest of body.

Cutting in upper part in morning after eating. Tensive pain in upper when sitting; in upper when walking, < stooping. Sticking in hepatic region; externally in umbilicus. Strangulated sensation in l. side, < pressure of hand.

Hypogastrium.—Swelling of a gland in r. groin, with tensive pain when walking. Burrowing stitches in l. side on expiration, < stooping. Tearing in rings when sitting. Cutting extending into l. chest in evening after eating. Griping, with rumbling; G. when sitting, > standing bent over, with urging to stool. Burrowing as of something alive under skin above l. hip in morning when lying upon it. Cramplike pain in l. groin when sitting. Tensive pain from middle down to anus. Pain in groin as in a hernia. Strangulated sensation, > emission of flatus, soon becoming worse.

Anus.—Passage of thread-worms daily and crawling in rectum every evening. Sore pain during stool. Bruised, almost sore pain. Tenesmus with every stool; T. during stool, as if diarrhœa would occur.

Stool.—Frequent diarrhœa, with qualmishness in abdomen; white D. (First part hard, the second soft.) Hard, delayed.

Urinary Organs.—(Pain in neck of bladder like a warning to urinate.) *Frequnt micturition.* Micturition in a thin stream. (Inability to retain urine.) (Urine frothy like yeast.) Clear, bright yellow urine, depositing on standing a yellow sediment. Thick grayish-white sediment.

Sexual Organs.—Drawing stitches in body of penis, out through glans. Itching on scrotum and body of penis, with burning; voluptuous I. on tip of penis. **Spermatic cord swollen, painful** (Puls.). **Testicles, painful swelling** (Ars., Clem., Rhod.); **pinching** (Clem.), **bruised** (Rhod.), **squeezing pain in T.**; *sticking extending into spermatic cords; pain; pain on touch.* Menses too early and profuse.

Respiratory Organs.—Region of thyroid gland seems indurated (Con., Iod.). Jerking sticking externally in region of larynx. *Pain in region of larynx, when singing;* P. above thyroid cartilage, < touch. *Scraping in larynx, with burning and constriction. Dryness in region of larynx, < hawking* (Bell.). *Sensation in region of thyroid and cervical glands on breathing as if air forced in and out.* **Hoarseness** (Iod., Brom.). (Cough at night, with fretful look); **C. from low down in chest, where it pains as if sore and bloody, from coughing** (see Sang.); **dry C.**; **dry, day and night,** > **eating and drinking, with burning in chest** (*Carbo v.*); hollow, day and night, with expectoration.

Respiration difficult as if a plug were sticking in larynx and the breath could not get through on account of constriction of larynx (compare Lach.). (Dyspnœa.) Rapid panting after dancing. Respiration slow, deep, as after exhaustion.

Clinical.—Goitre; hard, with suffocative spells at night, sometimes with hoarse cough or staring eyes. Laryngitis, harsh, croupy cough, with suffocative spells rousing from sleep, larynx sensitive to touch, < turning the head; (in croup Spongia is always indicated by the suffocative attacks, resembling Brom.); it is not useful in the acute febrile stage, but it follows Aconite; it is possible, however, now to prescribe Iodine or Bromine, as occasion demands, with great accuracy, and thus avoid the necessity of giving Spongia (which combines in a feeble way some properties of both these drugs). It has been used for phthisis of the larynx and for diphtheritic croup. Chronic hoarseness, especially if the voice gives out in talking or singing (Phos.). Oppression of breathing, > eating a little. Bronchial catarrh, with wheezing asthmatic cough, > eating or drinking, < cold air; sometimes in bronchitis, with profuse expectoration and suffocative attacks, < lying with the head low and in a hot room, > eating. It has been prescribed with success in the dry suffocative cough associated with aneurism or with enlarged bronchial glands. Occasionally useful in whooping cough, < midnight and cold air.

Chest.—Sticking in l. side, with pressure; S. in r. side, and on rubbing the place sensation as if a weight were drawing downward under skin; in muscles of l. side of C. and back, with sudden pain as if a broad pointed substance were forced up; intermittent, in l.; outward, in r.; boring, in r. costal muscles during inspiration and expiration; drawing, beneath l. second ribs when walking; drawing, in l. side when sitting with back bent, < deep, slow inspiration.

Cutting in l. side on deep inspiration. **Pain when coughing, and in trachea, with rawness in throat** (compare Caust., Stan.). Painful pressure beneath short ribs on coughing. Pinching jerking outward in l. side. Sticking-pinching crawling in region of l. sixth and seventh ribs, < external pressure.

Clinical.—Occasionally prescribed in pneumonia (see Iodine); in pneumonia, when the patient cannot lie down. It has also been prescribed in pulmonary consumption, particularly the form following pneumonia, characterized by the suffocative spells of coughing, < dry, cold air.

Heart.—(Pain about heart, palpitation, with dyspnœa, cyanosis and fear of death.)

Clinical.—Rheumatic endocarditis, inability to lie down, wakes with suffocation, etc.

Pulse.—*Rapid and full.*

Neck.—Jerking in r. muscles when lying. Cracking in nape on stooping. Sticking in l. side; in r. muscles on waking, > swallowing, but returning; drawing, through l. side. Cramp in muscles, which drew jaw downward, after opening mouth wide and biting teeth together hard, with heaviness in joint of jaw as if dislocated. Frequent cracking pain in nape close to l. scapula. Intermittent pressure in r. side as if skin were pressed between fingers, and pain on touch in region of jugular vein. Sensation as if glands were swollen. Tension in muscles, < r., on bending head backward. Stiffness; *in l. side on turning head to right.*

Back.—Pain, then palpitation all day, before menses; pain extending up and down through spine when sitting erect. Sticking on r. scapula; in scapulæ, with soreness; in r. lumbar muscles; in sacrum. Tearing from r. side of sacrum to l. and upward when sitting. Pain in sacrum when walking, < stepping with l. foot; at union of sacrum and r. ilium when standing; flatulent, in lumbar region during stool. Numbness of sacrum and nates.

Extremities.—Stretching. Jerking like drawing pressure in hollow of l. knee on bending knee, alternating with similar sensation in axilla. Weakness, < muscles of lower, with bruised sensation.

Upper Extremities.—*Twitching about l. shoulder-joint.* Sticking in axilla when sitting. Stretching of arms. Sticking drawing through upper arm. Stitches in elbow on motion; in tip on flexing arm, then tearing in joint while arm was bent. Pain in tip of l. elbow. Forearms and hands tremble; boring outward stitches in internal muscles of r. F.; cramplike pain below elbow, < leaning on arm, with slow bubbling; drawing pains; pain in l. as if bones were compressed; heaviness. Wrist, stitches in r. during rest; tensive pain in l.; drawing pain upon r.; drawing in l.; tired sensation in and above them.

Swelling of hand, with inability to bend fingers. Pinching drawing inward in middle of palm. Middle joint of l. middle finger was thick, red and stiff. Sticking in distal joint of thumb, with sore pain. *Cramplike pain in ball of r. thumb all day, and on moving hand extending into thumb;* in ball of l. thumb all day on moving hand. Pain in proximal joints of r. fingers. Painful drawing in proximal phalanx of l. thumb extending into forearm. Tips of index fingers insensible.

Lower Extremities.—Weariness. Stiffness. Sudden jerking in muscular fibres of r. nates. Sticking in inner side of r. thigh; above r. knee when sitting, with pain; pulsating, above r. knee in morning in bed; drawing, below l. groin, < walking; boring outward, near r. hip. Tension in upper end of thigh, as if a muscle were too short, on every step, with sticking. Pressure extending backward on inner side above r. knee. Drawing in thighs and legs during menses.

Knee, sticking in l. in evening; pain in external tendon of flexor of r. popliteus, < walking; drawing in l. at night, then sweat; weakness when walking; heaviness when walking. Sticking in r. calf when walking. Tearing in tibia all the afternoon. Uneasiness in legs. Tearing heaviness in l. tibia close to ankle. Sensation in lower part of l. tibia as if a weight were hanging upon it when walking rapidly. Falling asleep of r. leg after a nap at noon, then of l., with spasmodic drawing of l. towards thigh when walking and sitting.

Tearing in malleoli, with heaviness of feet extending into tibiæ; drawing T. extending from r. ankle to knee. Heel, (sticking when sitting after a long walk); S. extending out of r. when standing; extending upward in r. when sitting; intermittent, extending outward in l. when standing, > motion. Pain in r. heel, < walking. Drawing pain extending from r. foot into thigh.

Skin.—Eruption on tip of nose and on lips. Itching eruption and itching red spots. Red swelling of r. antitragus, with a pimple discharging like an ulcer, ear painful to external pressure. Pimples painful to pressure beneath chin. Inflamed node in l. concha at entrance to meatus, at last covered with a scab and painful to touch. Boils painful to touch on l. ear. Blisters on r. forearm. *Yellow crusty eruption, painful to touch, on l. eyebrow.*

Sticking externally on chest and arm; in various parts, provoking scratching; itching, here and there, not > rubbing. Crawling on neck; in l. foot; in different spots, then redness and heat, then biting itching, then urticaria-like blisters, < scratching.

Itching on l. cheek; on ball of l. thumb, not > rubbing; if he scratches the itching spot the I. occurs in many other places; *as at the outbreak of sweat, in morn-*

ing on waking, recurring after rubbing; voluptuous, of backs of r. toes in morning on waking; tickling, on l. thigh close to groin; burning, at night, < back, he only slumbers and tosses about constantly, with thirstless heat over whole body, < towards morning. Sticking itching in l. cheek; on chest towards l. shoulder; beneath l. eye, somewhat > rubbing. Prickling itching in l. axilla when sitting; in hollows of knees when walking. Biting itching on chest, < cold, on pit of stomach, on back, lower part of upper arms, at other times only on feet, the biting < rubbing, then redness of the spots, then blisters.

Sleep.—*Sleepiness in afternoon, with yawning, without inactivity.* Talking in sleep. Frequent waking as from fright. Sleepless till midnight; almost all night, and frightful dreams of death and murder; and as soon as he fell asleep he was full of fancies, his forehead seemed thick and sore to touch, pain over eyes, < stooping, as if everything would press out at forehead, with chilliness. *Dreams interrupting sleep;* fatiguing D.; sad; vexatious and lachrymose, anxious; many, before midnight, then sleeplessness on account of uneasiness, on closing his eyes while awake vivid images passed before him, > opening eyes, at one time it seemed as if a battery were discharged, at another everything was enveloped in flames, at another scientific subjects crowded upon him.

Fever.—In morning pain in head and abdomen, then shaking chill, with cold blue hands and thirst, then when lying dry heat, with thirst and restless slumbering, for thirty-six hours, throughout the night on waking and moving nausea and vertigo, at intervals of twelve hours sweat, when from time to time the heat moderated, afterwards tearing and sticking in l. eye and l. cheek and eruption on lips. Coldness of hands; lower limbs; in back in region of last ribs; *in back, not > warmth of stove.* Shivering, < back, without thirst; on back in afternoon, alternating with heat on forehead, without thirst.

Heat with thirst; H. of whole body, with coldness, paleness and sweat of face; *sudden apprehensive, over whole body, with heat and redness of face and sweat; in several attacks daily, with pain in præcordial region, anxiety, weeping and inconsolable, she longed to die on the spot;* internal, in whole body in evening when sitting, with cold sweat on face. Burning in r. side of scalp; on l. shoulder; in arms and hands; feverish in limbs, with inclination to stretch; in one side of face, renewed by thinking of it; flushing, in face and blood, with nervous excitement; beneath r. corner of mouth, as if an eruption would appear, < making skin tense; internal, in forehead, with hard, rapid pulse.

Sweat in morning on waking.

Squilla.

A tincture is made of the fresh bulbs of Scilla Maritima, L.

General Action.—This acrid drug irritates the mucous membranes of the air-passages and digestive tract; for diseases of the former it is frequently prescribed, rarely for those of the latter. It stimulates the secretion of urine; it may cause bloody urine or even suppress it altogether.

Allies.—*All. cepa*, Sulph., and the Kalis (Caust., Kali c., and Tartar emetic).

Generalities.—Twitching; from nervous weakness. Convulsions. Sticking now in one part, now in another. Pains over whole body; rheumatic, > rest, < motion. Discomfort. **Weakness**; in morning after waking and rising, < thighs and region of hips; *on walking far;* more from a sleepless night than from diarrhœa, head confused yet he is cheerful and good-humored; after dinner, with sleepiness. Heaviness as from weakness.

Mind.—Lively, joyous (probably curative). Courage, sedateness. Ill-humored; at every work, he was cool to people and did not answer; and averse to mental work. Whining on account of pain in stomach. Vexed; about trifles. Anxious; and fearful of death. Indolent in morning and averse to mental work. Disinclined to think and write; to think, and depressed.

Head.—(Tearing, which does not prevent mental work.) Tingling aching in morning after rising. Heaviness; in morning, with confusion of it and quiet sleep; as if he could not hold it still when sitting. Weak and dreamy. Stupefaction every morning, with sensitiveness of vertex. Swashing on shaking it. Vertigo, with nausea; *cloudy V.;* as if he would fall sideways in morning on rising.

Forehead.—*Sticking extending into r. side of F.;* in r. eminence, extending to nose; drawing, extending into r. ear; from l. to r. side, with drawing. Piercing thrust in l. eminence. Burrowing. Pain in a spot in l. eminence; drawing P. Dulness in sinciput and occiput as after intoxication, with pressure.

Temples.—Drawing stitches in r., constricting half of brain; twitching S. in r., extending to forehead. Drawing in r., ending in sticking. *Contractive pain.*

Heaviness of whole upper part of head in morning after waking. Vertex sensitive. Pinching in sides. Occiput, drawing sticking when sitting; tearing; pain; *drawing from l. side to r.*

Eyes.—Staring. Contractive sensation in r. Itching of l. They seem swimming in cold water. Lachrymation and sneezing. *Pupils contracted;* dilated. L. upper lid swollen and hanging down. Canthus, sticking in l. external; tickling in l. external; burning in external. Tearing behind ball and in eyes.

Ears.—(Tearing); *behind l.*

Nose.—*Sore sensation on margins of nostrils.* (Sneezing at night.) *Coryza, with ulcerated nostrils; C. and eyes have a dim, weak look and are full of water in forenoon; fluent, in morning; fluent, and constant violent sneezing; biting, with frequent sneezing;* dry. *Acrid mucus* (compare Allium cepa.)

Face.—Red and burning. Drawn, tense, with large eyes and dilated pupils, staring and redness of cheeks. Varying expression, now dejected, now lively.

Mouth.—Sticking upward in upper canine teeth, as if cold sharp air penetrated them, when eating and drinking cold or warm things. Vesicles on tongue. Roughness far back on palate, with scraping. Burning in palate and throat; scraping, similar to heartburn, in palate. Mouth sticky and slimy. Salivation. Taste bitter; (bitter to everything, and sour); unpleasant, with whitish-yellow tongue; disgusting, sweetish to all food, especially meat and broth; burnt in palate except while swallowing food; blunted; lost when smoking tobacco.

Throat.—Pain in submaxillary glands.

Stomach.—Hunger ravenous; insatiable when eating what tastes good, yet stomach seems full; diminished; lost; lost, partly on account of fulness, partly because food tastes burnt, partly because food has no taste, for example, broth and meat, also on account of disgusting sweetish taste, as bread and butter. Thirst; in evening, with chilliness.

Eructations; empty; short; sour; of disgusting taste. *Nausea; in back of throat, with salivation;* in epigastric region; in pit of stomach, alternating with symptoms of diarrhœa in lower abdomen, but more indications of diarrhœa; after dinner, with eructations tasting of the food; with eructations, retching and colic. Retching. Vomiting.

Gastric and intestinal catarrh. Sticking in l. side of pit. Pinching in pit. Cardialgia. Pain; intermittent; as from a stone. Discomfort. Indigestion. Warmth.

Abdomen.—Distention. Rumbling and gurgling. Flatulence. Emission of flatus; on touching abdomen; short, abrupt; offensive; offensive, noisy, only temporarily relieving abdomen. Enteritis. Griping. Pain; intermittent; drawing, < walking. Tension; though it was soft. Tenderness so that no covering could be borne. Emptiness as if hungry. Warmth. Tearing through A. below umbilicus. Griping in umbilical region. Stinging in muscles of l. side. Pain in sides as if intestines were forcing through when coughing and walking. Gurgling bubbling in muscles of r. side.

Hypogastrium.—Paroxysmal rumbling above pubic region, < walking and standing, > eating, with rattling. Incarceration of flatus and cutting. Griping renewed next day at the same hour, > emission of flatus. Cutting griping. (Acute pain as from flatus, or as from a purge, or as before diarrhœa.)

Clinical.—Abdominal dropsy, with scanty urine.

Anus.—Sticking when walking. Itching.

Stool.—Almost liquid, smelling of sulphuretted hydrogen, with pain in small of back and tenesmus, then relief of griping in abdomen. Diarrhœa; from 2 till 7 A.M., at last watery, almost without flatulence; copious brown, slimy, offensive fæces, without pain or tenesmus, with spluttering of flatus, with thread-worms and white unformed fibres. Soft; and frequent, with burning in anus. Pasty. Constipation. Hard; and scanty. Colored with blood. Diminished at first. Sluggish.

Urinary Organs. — Strangury after micturition though there is no urine to pass. *Urging* (the prover was in the habit of urinating moderately only twice a day); *and copious urine looking like water; with scanty urine;* and on urinating a thin stool without colic; at first with profuse urine, especially of urine as clear as water, or at least watery urine, not profuse, then the opposite condition; constant ineffectual; infrequent desire and scanty urine.

Unable to retain urine because the amount was too large, it would have passed involuntarily if he had not hastened. Waking at night to urinate. Frequent micturition without increase of urine; F., urine as clear as water, *the desire sudden.* Micturition seldom and scanty, but urine not dark. Sticking in urethra while pressing at stool; S. in orifice and farther back.

Urine copious. Scanty; and watery. Bloody. Reddish, with reddish sediment, with little desire to urinate. (Hot urine and offensive stool, with undigested portions.)

Clinical.—Cystitis; tenesmus, frequent urging, urine scanty, dark. Atony of the bladder, urine is discharged involuntarily with cough (Caust.).

Sexual Organs.—Sticking in glans causing anxiety. Compressive pain in testicles. Hæmorrhage from uterus.

Respiratory Organs.—*Tickling beneath thyroid cartilage, irritating to short dry cough in four or five shocks; T. in region of thyroid cartilage, provoking cough, which increases the tickling. Irritation to cough in upper part of trachea,* with hawking. *Cough, with pressure outward in chest and painful contraction of abdominal muscles; C. even to retching* (preceded by rattling); *violent, dry, causing shattering in abdomen and dryness in throat;* **at first with expectoration; C. in morning, with profuse slimy expectoration; sudden violent C., with expectoration in morning, with sticking in side at every C.** (Kali c.). **Constant expectoration of mucus. Dyspnœa, with stitches in chest, < inspiration** (Kali c.); D., with rapid respiration and anxiety. *Difficult respiration. Frequent necessity to take a deep breath, which provokes cough.* Heavy, slow respiration.

Clinical.—Bronchitis, acute and chronic; cough brought on by drinking, generally with much mucus in the chest, which rattles and causes violent spasms of cough, with involuntary micturition; the patient generally coughs a long time before a little mucus is raised, which affords relief. Violent paroxysms of cough, with sneezing and lachrymation. Whooping cough. (Compare rattling mucus in the bronchi with Tartar emetic; Squills has less prostration and has almost always severe sticking pains in the sides, especially l.; Tartar emetic has profound prostration and sweat, but no pain.) Occasionally called for in the latest stages of pneumonia. Violent spasmodic cough, ending in a choking, almost explosive; cough from a sort of spasm in the pit of the stomach, quite dry, but always followed by the need to clear the nose (worse 5 till 7 A.M.)

Chest.—**Sticking in true ribs; in l. side** (Sulph.); in middle of ensiform cartilage; *in scapular end of clavicle during inspiration and expiration; extending downward near sternum, so that breathing was difficult;* **recurrent in side; jerking, in sides not far from sternum, on inspiration; broad in last l. rib,** *waking him in morning; broad, beneath last ribs on both sides during expiration; drawing, from last true rib to shoulder; contracting, beneath last rib* from rapid walking. Pleuro-pneumonia. *Compressive pain in r. side ending in a stitch. Drawing pain. Oppression as if too tight.* Pressure (tension?) extending to lower part of abdomen on expanding chest during inspiration. (Pain below r. arm, and on stooping throbbing pain, when touched pain as if flesh were loosened.)

Clinical.—Occasionally useful in pneumonia and pleuro-pneumonia.

Heart and Pulse.—Palpitation. Pulse rapid in one, slow in another, normal in a third; slow while vomiting; small, contracted; small, hard, tense.

Neck and Back.—*Painful jerking above l. scapula.* Pinching in cervical muscles, with drawing. Rheumatic pain in muscles on sides of neck. Stiffness of nape; of l. cervical muscles. *Painless drawing on l. scapula.* Bubbling sensation beneath scapulæ, in back and l. upper arm.

Extremities.—Pain. Uneasiness. Weakness and trembling. Falling asleep of hands when resting head upon them during the day and in lower limbs when crossing legs. Twitching of l. arm when standing; of upper arm, with pulsation. Jerking pain transversely through wrists. Stitchlike drawing from l. wrist to fingers. Sticking in joints of hands; in middle of l. metacarpus. Soreness between lower limbs. Jerking in thighs and legs when sitting. Thighs, sticking; bruised sensation; drawing pain in muscles; intermittent drawing pain when sitting and walking; bubbling extending in a streak from upper part to toes; weariness. Drawing pain in leg. Constrictive pain in hollow of l. knee when standing, forcing him to bend knee. Burning pain in ball of r. foot as after freezing.

Skin.—Eruption not unlike purpura hæmorrhagica, with collapse. Scirrhus. Pimples on neck, painful when rubbed; P. in a group between scapulæ, with tickling (crawling) itching, which changed after scratching to burning-sticking itching, then crawling itching. Red spots over whole body becoming itch-like pustules, on hands, between fingers, on feet and abdomen, with burning itching after some days. Red pustules on back, with sticking itching and after scratching burning-sticking itching, next day a crust on each one. Cold gangrene. Ulcerations, with fever, and inflammation may be expected. Moist eruption, biting like an ulcer, above middle of upper lip, with sticking itching. (Blisters on hands from handling fresh Squills.)

Sticking extending from shoulder to middle of upper arm. Neck sensitive to rubbing of neckband, with red, almost denuded spots; S. across back from one hip to the other Itching from handling Squills, with burning; sticking, on neck and jaws, momentarily > scratching; crawling, below r. arm, momentarily > scratching; biting, on forehead and chin, as if eruption would appear, momentarily > scratching.

Sleep.—*Yawning without sleepiness; but with stretching of upper limbs.* Sleepiness in evening. *Restless sleep.* Sleepless. Waking frequently and tossing about; W. at 1 A.M., with nausea, anxiety and deep respiration. Merry dreams. Vivid dream that his body was excessively swollen.

Fever.—Chilliness; then heat; internal, in evening after lying down, with external heat; internal, in night, with external heat, without thirst. Shivering, with coldness of skin. *Cold hands and feet;* feet every afternoon, with heat of body, without thirst; feet, with heat in head; feet, with heat over whole body as from hot drinks, without thirst or sweat; back and arms, even when walking in a warm room, > sitting.

Heat without redness or thirst; H. on slightest exertion and on talking, with redness, < face; internal, when coughing, talking, or on slightest exertion; dry, without thirst; (dry, then internal dry heat, both without thirst); in face, more internally, < motion of body, without thirst, with chilliness of rest of body on slightest uncovering.

Sweat in axillæ; on toes.

Stannum.

Precipitated metallic tin is triturated for use.

General Action.—Its sphere of action is not well known; it, however, seems to produce derangements of the nervous system (convulsions and paralysis) in a way somewhat similar to its ally, Zinc. Its curative power in bronchial and pulmonary diseases is well established. It was formerly supposed to be a vermifuge.

Allies.—Caust., Phos., Cina.

Generalities.—*Emaciation* and consumption. Trembling of whole body, hand trembles more when resting it lightly upon anything than when grasping anything tightly. (Epilepsy in a boy who often had convulsive attacks, < morning fasting. Tin was given to destroy the worms which were supposed to be present, thereupon the fits increased to epilepsy.) Sticking griping alternately in different parts. Many pains, especially the drawing, begin slight, increase slowly, become severe and slowly disappear. Uneasiness; at 1 A.M. after waking from deep sleep, with burrowing on tibiæ.

Weakness; *during the day, with necessity to lie down,* but inability to sleep, and when he slumbered vertigo, vanishing of senses and dulness of mind; when walking, especially in the sun, with giving way of knees and sweat of weakness on face; *< ascending steps;* < walking slowly, so that he must walk fast; > walking fast, but felt all the more afterwards; *and when about to sit down he falls upon the chair because he has not the power to sit down slowly;* and sleepiness; *as if limbs were beaten; of mind and body,* with irresistible sleepiness, but frequent waking with indifferent dreams; *sudden, so that she could scarcely breathe, when dressing after rising;* so that she could scarcely breathe, after descending steps.

Heaviness now in one, now in another bone. Sensation of agreeable lightness on deep breathing. All symptoms except weakness > walking, but returning during rest, the weakness < walking.

Clinical.—General nervous weakness. Anæmia.

Mind.—Joyful. Talkative. Quiet, good humor. Quiet, absorbed in himself, with discomfort in body; quiet, absorbed in himself, solicitous for the future. Disinclined to talk. *Fretful;* all day, > open air; *and he answers unwillingly and abruptly;* and indolent, with heat in face, he would do everything but really does nothing. Anger; transient. **Sad.** *Anxious for a week before menses,* > appearance of the flow, with apprehension. *Discontented. Discouraged. Aversion and dread of people. Restless and distracted, not persistent in work. Fruitlessly busy* as if a rush of ideas prevented him from completing his work at a certain time. Inclination to do no work and inability to think. Dulness of mind, with indifference to external objects, pallor and darkness about eyes. Want of memory in morning on waking.

Clinical.—The mental symptoms may be compared with Puls. and Nat. mur., especially the hypochondriac and tearful mood.

Head.—Pain in morning on waking, with heat in it; P. every morning, with loss of appetite, nausea and fretfulness; suppurative, externally; cramplike, *as if constricted by a band;* as if screwed inward frequently, with jerks or drawing pressure here and there at times; *as if brain were forced asunder and tense;* as if brain were loose and beating against skull, on shaking head; dizzy. *Heaviness;* all day; *in evening;* now here, now there; sometimes only on top; sometimes only in forehead or temples; < evening, with dulness; with tearing. Sensitive stupefaction, with sudden jerks on upper margin of r. orbit and in other parts. Dulness as before coryza, with sneezing. Discomfort. Tingling, with resounding of noise. Weakness, with sleepiness. *Vertigo;* when sitting; with vanishing of thought; in sudden attacks when sitting; as if objects were at too great a distance; as if he had not slept enough, in morning on waking from a long sleep; stupefying, when walking in open air.

Forehead.—Jerking, alternating with pressure; sudden jerking in l. F. and temple. Sticking in middle; in l. eminence; in l. side; deep in brain above arch of l. orbit; from anterior part of brain to r. side; and on stooping pressure outward. *Tearing;* and in l. parietal bone; and in vertex and occiput, afterwards wandering about, sometimes affecting whole head, < forehead; *intermittent, in r. half, < stooping;* jerklike drawing, externally above l. brow. Intermittent cutting in l. anterior part of brain. *Pain;* all day, < noon, cold and motion, as when riding, > warmth, rest and pressure; < bending backward, > pressure; > pressure, and in temples and vertex; in F. and vertex, with drawing through them; in middle, extending deep into brain; *as from a crashing; sharp jerking, in r. anterior lobe of brain, above orbit;* stupefying, in brain above brows; burning, in one-half all day, and in nose and eyes, with external heat in the parts, necessity to lie down, nausea and retching. *Pressure outward;* > pressure, with sleepiness. Drawing in half of F. and in one temple, causing confusion. Burning tension in scalp above r. side of forehead.

Temples.—Pulsating stitches, with heat in head, chilliness of body, weakness of head, so that he almost loses his reason, with slumbering and insensibility. Boring in l. all day; in r., > pressure. Sharp pains, < l.; intermittent, in r. Pain in r. when lying upon it; outward in r., almost as if external; *throbbing.* **Pressure inward in l., beginning slight, then increasing and again diminishing**; *P. inward all day.* Compression, and in occiput.

Vertex.—Burning stitches; sudden S. in r. side. Tearing in l. side. Pain in V. and occiput in evening; after lying down. *Constriction in whole upper part of head,* **slowly increasing and decreasing,** *with sudden pressure.* Sudden sharp pressure, with sensation as if hair moved. Heaviness near forehead; intermittent H., with now and then shootings in r. parietal region.

Sides.—Dartings at times in l. or in occiput. Tearing in r. half; through r.; in sides of brain extending to top of skull. Boring stupefying pain on l. surface of brain. Pressure outward in r. Drawing pressure from parietal bone to orbit. Heaviness in l. half of brain, with emptiness.

Occiput.—Shooting in l. side. Tearing in l. bone; in l. side. Pressure outward in l. side. Constrictive pain in r. side. Compression below vertex. Heaviness; in bones, with boring.

Clinical.—Headache, as from a hoop; the pains gradually become worse, < motion, then gradually diminish until they disappear; the gradual increase and decrease of the headache and other pains are said to be characteristic of the drug. Neuralgia about the eyes; in one case pains extended to the vertex, feeling as though the head would burst from internal blows, great sensitiveness to noise; this recurred several days, beginning at 10 and lasting till 4, being worse at noon.

Eyes.—Dim; and weak, sunken. Prominent and painful as after weeping. Jerking; in l. Burning sticking in r. towards outer canthus. Pain; in l. as from a stye on lid; as from rubbing with a woolen cloth, also > moving lids. Burning. Pupils contracted, then dilated. Ball, shooting in l. in evening; tensive stitching in l., < moving it; dartings in r.; itching in l., somewhat > rubbing. Nightly agglutination, with weakness during the day. Lids, burning stitches in r., < towards outer canthus; sensation of a hard substance behind r.; pain in upper; burning pain in l. lower; constriction, with redness of whites and burning; itching of upper, with swelling. Canthus, *pustular swelling on l. inner,* like a lachrymal fistula; stye in r. inner; twitching in r. inner; pain in r. inner; *pain in l. inner as from a stye, with lachrymation;* sticking burning in l.; itching in inner. Itching in r. lachrymal caruncula. Orbit, shooting in upper part of r., extending backward into brain; sudden thrusts in outer side of upper margin of l.; drawing pressure in upper margin of l. A rainbow around candle-light.

Ears.—Shooting in cartilage of r.; drawing, in upper part of l. concha. Tearing in r. meatus; griping, through lobule of l., with at times sensation of a cold wind in it. Boring in r., with cold feet. Cramplike pain in r. Drawing pain in l.; in outer. Drawing internally and externally in r., < moving lower jaw. Pressure externally on bone behind ear. Stopped sensation in l. in morning after rising, > blowing nose, with deafness. Itching in l. Ringing in l. Screaming when blowing nose. Creaking in l. and in front of it as of a door, in evening. Noise as of the rustling of a grasshopper in l. Rushing as from a stream of blood. Painful resounding of the jar of his steps.

Nose.—Stoppage in morning; S. from congestion of palato-nasal mucous membrane; in upper part, with heaviness; of l. nostril, with external swelling, redness and pain on touch. Sneezing; in evening. Coryza; of l. nostril; all day; alternating with stoppage of nose; fluent, with sticking headache, < l. side of forehead; stopped, can get air only through r. nostril. Bleeding in morning on rising; in morning on waking; blowing out of blood in morning.

Face.—*Pale, sunken, sickly, features elongated.* Cutting sticking in forepart of chin; burning itching S. on malar-bones. Tearing in malar-bone, extending into lower jaw near corner of mouth. Gnawing in l. side, < malar-bone. Pain in malar-bone on touch before menses, during menses bruised pain even on moving muscles of face; stupefying P., < forehead; *paroxysmal drawing, in bones of r. side, < malar-bone and orbit;* cramplike, in muscles on l. malar-bone; burning cramplike, in l. cheek in evening, then swelling of cheek, with cutting on drawing up face, as if splinters of glass were between cheek and teeth; burning, beneath r. eye. Constriction internally beneath r. cheek, with pressure; in bones of face and teeth of r. side, as if they would be drawn up shorter. Pain in upper jaw, with swelling, with redness of cheeks and sticking in them. Sticking tearing in a spot in lower lip.

Mouth.—Teeth, looseness; jerking pain after eating, > open air, with heat in face; tingling in roots of lower incisors; seem too long. Ulcer on l. gum, with painful swelling of l. cheek, the pain preventing sleep. *Tongue yellow; coated yellow;* burning in morning; itching in tip; itching of anterior third. Talking irksome; difficult on account of weakness. Tenacious mucus. Mouth and fauces corrugated, he could scarcely swallow. Acidity in velum pendulum. Sensation in velum pendulum and in posterior nares as of a foreign body or of mucus which cannot be swallowed nor hawked up. Sensation in velum pendulum palati as from snuff, which by strong inspiration is drawn down to throat, in evening. Salivation. Acid saliva runs from mouth in morning on waking. *Bad odor.* Taste bitter, sour; bitter to food; stale and acid-bitter to beer; herby to beer; sharp and dry to tobacco when smoked; insipid.

Throat.—Painful swelling of submaxillary glands. Bad odor. *Mucus; difficult hawking of thick, viscid blood-streaked; hawking of thick gray-green, mixed with blood; adherent, and efforts to raise it excite vomiturition; thick adherent, with nausea on attempting to raise it; a mass of thick viscid, bloody, efforts to expel which caused nausea; expulsive efforts to detach thick, grayish and bloody, causing nausea; inclination to hawk up M. in evening, then sore pain.* (Compare Argent. met.)

Sticking in upper part of fauces causing dryness, > swallowing; boring, in fauces extending to cervical muscles. *Cutting in pharynx on swallowing. Rawness; in morning; < deglutition, with dryness, without thirst, and efforts to raise adherent thick grayish or greenish mucus causing nausea;* with dryness, without thirst, also in morning; in r. side, with dryness and ulcerated sensation, without thirst. *Scraping in morning;* in evening. *Scraping roughness below pit. Pain as if swollen, with sore pain, and after hawking of mucus the voice is much higher than usual. Dryness;* in r. tonsil, > hawking and swallowing, *with sticking provoking cough; in r. side, with ulcerated sensation; with soreness like swelling and drawing tensive pain; (in larynx?) with tickling crawling compelling cough.*

Clinical.—Chronic catarrh of the pharnyx, with hawking up of hard lumps of mucus.

Stomach.—Hunger, with distention of stomach; *insatiable H.;* lost; lost at noon, with emptiness in stomach; the child leaves the breast of the mother who has taken Tin and will not drink. Thirst increased.

Eructations bitter after eating; empty; sweet; of flat taste; like bad eggs in morning, then of gas; acid, when walking in open air, then rawness in pharynx; acid, five hours after a meal, with uneasiness in epigastric region as from slow digestion. Hiccough; when smoking as usual after eating. Nausea; in pharynx; in fauces and pharynx; after eating; after soup, with bitter bilious vomiting; with bitter taste; with spasmodic griping in stomach and about umbilicus, and anxious uprisings to pit of stomach; shuddering, with nauseating fulness in pit of stomach. Retching; in evening, then sour, then bitter taste; then vomiting of undigested food. *Vomiting of blood;* sour V.; of mucus; of thick dark green mucus.

Swelling under skin in epigastric region when walking, with griping in abdomen. Digestion slow, acid water comes up to throat long after dinner. Cutting. Pain; in epigastric region; in forenoon; after soup, with discomfort; beneath cartilages of l. lowest rib, > pressure; *in pit, with obstruction,* and on touch pain as if suppurating; tensive, in pit; anxious, in pit, as if gush of blood would occur, when lying, > pressure. Sensation in pit as if disordered.

Clinical.—Chronic gastralgia, characterized by gradual increase and decrease of pain.

Abdomen.—Distention; after eating; painful, with sensitiveness to touch; in evening, with frequent desire as for diarrhœa, griping and painful movements as from taking cold, thrusts in l. side as from a child in the uterus, then thin stool, then urging and colic till she went to bed. Rumbling; on stretching body; when lying after a meal; when a morsel is not far from orifice of stomach; after stool, with distress; with intermittent griping as before diarrhœa. Bubbling. Flatulence. Incarcerated flatus. Griping movements as from incarcerated flatus.

Sudden sticking as with a knife through from l. to r. side on breathing. Griping, < umbilical region, with pressure and with urging to stool. *Digging* before stool. Pain, and in rectum; P. at 4.30 P.M., > passage of wind, later P. increased till 7 P.M., then profuse whitish, frothy and offensive stool, with burning in anus, then empty feeling; with fetid flatus; extending to stomach and to sides beneath ribs when pressing upon umbilical region; paroxysmal; wind colic during the day; wind colic in morning; as if suppurating, on touch, with shortness of breath; smarting; burning; drawing here and there; tensive, < towards small of back, < stooping. *Soreness,* < touch. *Emptiness* after eating much; E. (without hunger), > eating much, with weakness of body.

Upper A.—Griping between pit of stomach and umbilicus, as if muscles were pinched. Digging above umbilical region and on pressure pain as upon a sore spot. Burning beneath diaphragm. (Hysterical and hypochondriac cramps in region of abdomen and diaphragm.)

Hypochondria.—Boring stitches in l. when walking. Cutting in r., < sitting bent over. Pain in hepatic region; in upper part of liver; then thrusts from l. to r. side, < pressure upon r. side; cramplike, in l., now better, now worse; burning, in hepatic region after stool; bruised, in l.

Sides.—Sticking in r., < coughing and breathing; in r., then drawing in r. shoulder, necessity to lie down, with sweat on face and arms, then creeping chilliness. Burning pain in r. Crawling in r. as from a purge.

Umbilical Region.—Griping cutting. Griping as from taking cold. Pain in r. side; spasmodic, above and below umbilicus, > lying over a table.

Hypogastrium.—Rumbling. Sticking; in l. symphysis pubis; in r. groin on stooping, as if he had sprained himself, > rising. Cutting transversely across; drawing C. close to r. ilium. Griping in l. groin. Pinching above l. ilium on stooping, as if intestines were overstretched. Sensation as if stretched in muscles above r. anterior spine of ilium. Pain here and there, with urging to stool; P. in inguinal glands, with swelling; as before menses, < pressure. Sensation in l. groin as if a hernia would protrude. Jerking pulsations in r. inguinal cord. Burning.

Clinical.—Neuralgia of the bowels, with nausea and retching, even vomiting of blood. Colic of children, > hard pressure or by being carried over the shoulder.

Rectum.—Sticking; at end; at base, extending to anus; itching. Pain. Pressure after stool. Frequent urging; but scanty stool, at times only of mucus; sudden U., the first part of stool natural, then pasty, at last thin, with shivering downward through whole body and drawing through small of back down through thighs, when he attempts to rise it seems as if he had not finished; *ineffectual;* frequent, ineffectual.

Anus.—Pimple like a hæmorrhoid in l. side, with soreness on touch. Soreness after stool, with smarting and sticking. Corroding pain when walking and sitting. Itching. Burning.

Stool.—Soft, in forenoon, and in afternoon a thin

one; S. in evening preceded by colic for a moment before the urging, also with fetid flatus. Dysentery; stools at first loose, with urging and tormina, then discharges bloody and mucous with tenesmus. Evacuation of mucus after stool; E. of mucus in the form of worms. Constipation. Hard; in lumps; in one piece, with pressure; and seems slippery, but is not; and large, with cutting. Difficult, not hard, as from insufficient power of intestines to expel it. Scanty; and greenish. Delayed.

Clinical.—Helminthiasis.

Urinary Organs.—Pain in neck of bladder after urinating, and along urethra, it seems as if more urine would pass and some drops follow, when the pressure is worse. Desire to urinate only like a fulness in bladder, urine scanty, offensive and infrequent; frequent D. even at night, then infrequent micturition and scanty urine. Blister on margin of meatus. Soreness in tip of urethra. Burning in forepart of urethra, < urinating, he had urging every minute and passed much. Urine retained.

Sexual Organs.—Jerking in penis almost as when evacuating semen. Sticking in glans; burning. Burning pain in glans, then desire to urinate. Erections at night without lascivious dreams; E., on following days want of E. *Emissions* without lascivious dreams; E. when sleeping on back. Burning as in excessive irritation to discharge semen. Voluptuous excitement in whole body, even to emission of semen.

Female.—*Prolapsus of vagina,* < hard stool. White transparent mucus from vagina. Itching of vulva. Profuse menses.

Clinical.—Leucorrhœa, transparent and yellow, with great debility; at times thin and watery, with bearing down. Prolapsus uteri. With the uterine symptoms we find particularly a weak drawn feeling in chest (Sepia in the pit of the stomach).

Respiratory Organs.—Hoarseness on beginning to sing, with weakness and emptiness in chest, so that she must stop constantly and take a deep breath, at times the H. > expulsive cough (compare Ph. ac., Caust.). *Voice husky and hollow. Rawness in larynx.* **Mucus in trachea in forenoon easily expelled by forcible cough, with weakness of chest as if eviscerated, with weakness of whole body and of limbs,** *in which the weakness extended upward and downward, every morning.* **Irritation to cough on breathing as from mucus in trachea,** *with neither loose nor dry cough, felt more when sitting bent over than when walking.* Constriction in trachea causing inclination to cough. Tingling in trachea in evening, provoking fits of dry cough.

Cough.—**Shattering, deep. Short, weak, hoarse, as from weakness in chest. Fatiguing, paroxysmal, so that epigastric region was painful as if beaten** (Dros.). *Tickling, as from soreness deep in trachea, with scraping extending upward into throat.* Hacking, in paroxysms; *constant inclination to H. as from mucus in chest, with scraping and rattling.* **Inclination to cough before midnight, with scanty expectoration. Scraping, from irritation low down in trachea, with greenish expectoration of offensive sweet taste** (Calc. c.), **< evening before lying down, with hoarseness, and after every cough soreness in chest and trachea** (Caust.). *Frightful, with expectoration and spitting of blood.*

Expectoration.—**Of a globular, grayish lump of thick mucus,** *containing a clot of black blood and appearing to come from throat. Yellow, of foul taste from trachea. Salt, from chest. Of viscid, thick mucus, which seems to come from velum pendulum.*

Respiration.—**Short, difficult, from weakness of respiratory organs, with emptiness in stomach**; short in evening, with anxiety, necessity to breathe rapidly for a long time, > deep breathing. *Dyspnœa, > opening clothes; on motion, with want of breath;* in paroxysms in evening, with short breath and anxiety.

Clinical.—Acute bronchial catarrh, with aggravation from noon till midnight every day. Acute and chronic bronchial catarrhs; the cough is generally dry the forepart of the night, during the day there is greenish salty expectoration or expectoration of balls of mucus having a sweet taste; cough < talking, laughing, lying on r. side (Cina), or from warm drinks; expectoration of small, hard balls of sweetish mucus that will roll on the floor is quite characteristic; with the cough there is sense of great weakness in the chest, can only speak a few words at a time.

Chest.—Twitching near l. axilla; in muscles of false ribs. Sticking in clavicle; in wall in a line with apex of heart; in last r. true and in l. false ribs; in ensiform cartilage after eating; on breathing, and in shoulder-joints; *in C. and sides preventing respiration* forenoons, in afternoon distention of abdomen; *sudden, in l.; sudden, a hand's breadth beneath l. axilla;* cutting, extending upward and outward in forepart of upper ribs, not affected by respiration; burning, in l. when walking in open air, < expiration. *Tensive sticking in l. during respiration, < stooping;* in sternum during respiration; in r., almost taking away his breath.

Tearings at inner surface of sternum, in a line with fifth and sixth ribs, extending into l. chest. Cutting in r.; pinching, in r. on inspiration when walking; tearing, in l. when walking and standing. Pinching when sitting, < inspiration. Gnawing internally in a spot in l. forepart; boring, sometimes before, sometimes behind l. scapula. Burrowing extending into abdomen, with desire for stool. **Sore pain** starting from throat. *Bruised pain.* Aching, < inspiration, < above pit of stomach. Wandering pains and drawing; W. pain near l. scapula in night, with sweat on chest.

Sudden drawing beneath l. breast on rising in bed, then sticking extending into clavicle towards shoulder, where it persisted, and in l. side extending into hypogastrium, < bending inward, pressure and especially by inspiration and hacking, which caused a painful shock; D. from l. clavicle into axilla. Drawing pressure on the conjoined cartilages of last left ribs.

Oppression when coughing (Phos.); *O. in upper part, with frequent necessity to breathe deeply and emptiness in pit of stomach* (Ign.); as if something rose into throat and took away his breath. *Constriction* in evening, with anxiety; C. beneath r. arm, and on moving about a sticking; C., with sensation as if the inspired air were very dry. Sudden compression beneath true ribs. Weight in lower part. Tension across upper part in morning on rising, with pressure. Pressure outward beneath r. nipple. At times feeling as if dilated, with anxiety, as in palpitation. *Sensation of mucus, with rattling when breathing.* Intermittent sensation in a spot in r. side as if a liquid dropped rapidly into a vessel, all day.

Clinical.—Intercostal neuralgia. Phthisis, with great weakness of the chest, expectoration characteristic. Pleurisy, with knife-like stitches, < bending forward, mostly in l. side.

Pulse.—100. Slow. Indistinct and fluttering.

Neck.—Cracking in vertebræ on shaking head suddenly. Nape drawn upward, with stiffness. Sudden sticking in lower part of nape; itching stitches in nape in morning in bed. Pain in nape on bending head forward; on touch, in muscles near their insertion into occiput; raising or bowing head caused pain in muscles involved in these movements; rheumatic, in fibres of r. trapezius, < night. Weakness as if she could not hold up the head, with pain on moving head.

Back.—Sticking extending outward; jerking S. in l. side and in l. thigh. Stitchlike tearing upward in l. side when standing. Pain in B. and lower limbs as if beaten in morning on rising, with general weariness.

Scapulæ. — Sticking extending outward in spine between S.; intermittent S. in middle towards spine; burrowing, in r. dorsal muscles during respiration; burning, in upper part, transiently > rubbing; burning, in a spot in middle of back. Drawing tearing in l., partly towards back, partly towards shoulder. Sudden sprained pain between S. on lifting a weight, < l. side, with sticking on slightest movement, breathing or yawning, and on bending backward intolerable pain. Pressive drawing in spine below and between S., < motion, especially turning body.

Lumbar Region.—Sticking inward in kidney region. Dull thrusts, with sensation of external coldness against him. Sticking griping by false ribs. Tearing from both sides of vertebræ into region of kidneys, < motion of trunk. Acute pain in r. loin in morning. Pressure downward above l. hip. Wavelike shock above l. ilium.

Extremities.—Bruised pain; and above small of back; with coldness. *Weakness of arms and lower E.* Heaviness, with weakness of chest and alternating anxiety. Paralysis of l. arm and foot from fright, > night.

Upper Extremities.—Itching stitches in and beneath axilla. Shoulder, burning stitch in top of r.; burrowing stitch in r. deltoid; tearing on l.; paralytic tearing in and beneath r. joint, < motion; sharp pain in fibres of r. trapezius in night, < lifting arm and by touch; sudden acute beating on r.; compression; drawing in l. deltoid as from weakness.

Arm.—Jerking now in arm, now in hand, now in a finger, as after a blow. Tearing deep in l., < upper arm; paralytic, in l., < wrist, < motion. Sprained pain in joints, < bending arm. *Weakness from moderate exercise, so that he lets everything fall; paralytic, if he holds a light weight only a short time* (Caust.); *paralytic,* < r., chiefly in upper arm and joints, < *motion, with heaviness* and at times dyspnœa. Arms and fingers almost immovable.

Upper Arm.—Twitching above elbow during rest; internal, in l. when resting arm on anything. Tearing in anterior and upper part of r.; posteriorly and internally in middle of l.; in middle of r. suddenly appearing and disappearing; intermittent. Bruised pain in lower part of l. Intermittent pain as if l. humerus were crushed. Paralytic sprained pain beneath shoulder-joint, transiently > motion. Pressure in outer part and drawing as from a weight on l. shoulder and extending from elbow to deep-lying muscles of forearm, > in the house.

Elbow.—Drawing extending to upper arm. Tension in tip, < bending arm, with soreness.

Forearm.—Paralytic tearing in r. Pinching on radial side above wrist. Sprained pain in l. styloid process. Pressure on r. towards anterior and outer part. Cramplike stiffness of r.

Wrist. — Tearing in r., < motion. Pain in r.; sprained, in l.; intermittent sharp, in r. in evening, at night and towards morning, sometimes extending into forearm. Sudden intermittent drawing from radial side to hand.

Hand.—*Swelling* in evening. Trembling of l., with heat in it; T., < lying on table and when writing, with weakness of them. Jerking in l. above joint; wavelike drawing, as if in nerves, at night after waking. Intermittent tearing in bones of H. and wrist and in first finger-joints. Acute thrusts in second l. metacarpus, as if a tense nerve were struck by a hammer, and in other parts of hand. Sharp pain in first l. metacarpus and in r. wrist; in first r. metacarpus every few minutes. Cramplike pain on back between l. index and middle fingers. Jerking pain between thumb and index when holding a pen. Intermittent pain in posterior surface of l. metacarpus in evening. Cramplike contraction in l. palm. Sticking burning on outer margin of l. fifth metacarpus.

Fingers.—Cramp. Sticking in tips; in tip of l. middle; in second joint of l. middle; from metacarpal joint of l. index to tip; drawing, in first joint of l. index, towards tip. Tearing in first phalanges of r., < motion; in first joint of index, > moving hand; jerklike, extending into hand. Cutting in ball of l. little, < bending it up. Pain in middle joint of l. middle; near metacarpal joints of index; at inner surface of posterior end of first phalanx of l. index; sharp, in second joint of l. ring; sprained, in l. index. Cramplike drawing pain in l. middle, with jerking; sharp drawing pain in second joint of l. ring. Drawing in first phalanx of l. thumb and below wrist; sharp, in second joint of l. middle.

Lower Extremities.—Uneasiness in evening. Weakness; when standing, with tottering; after walking, with heaviness; on descending steps, and on ascending them bruised pain; of r., < femur, so that it was painful when standing and he was forced to rest upon l. limb. *Heaviness; paralytic, < thighs and knees, with weariness.*

Thigh.—Twitching in l. natis. Sticking on inner side of l.; in muscles of r. when standing; itching, in l. natis near anus; itching, high up in inner side. Tearing in forepart of r. joint, extending inward and beneath patella; drawing, in l.; drawing, in femur from knee to middle of thigh when sitting. Cutting in l.; on inner side of l. Pain in ischii when sitting; in muscles of hip on raising thigh; sharp, in upper part of r. above crural nerve at night; intermittent sharp jerking, anteriorly in r., then l.; sprained, beneath hip-joint when walking; sprained, in r. hip when walking; paralytic, in hip-joint when walking. Pulsating pressure on inner side of middle. Drawing in l. hip; in outer side of r. thigh when resting over l. while sitting; in inner side of l., in groin, from ascending ramus of ischium to back part of thigh, then from hip over small of back to r. side, with at times grumbling in ischium. Weakness.

Knee.—Itching twitching beneath patella. Sticking in r. when sitting, and in hollow; on outer side of r. when standing, > moving limb, and when sitting. Tearing in ligaments in inner side of l. Burning scraping on outer side of l. Pressure in r. Drawing from hollow of r. to calf; jerklike D., < standing, with weariness in feet extending up leg, < l. leg, and with sore pain in soles. Tensive pain in hollow of l. Weakness, with inclination to slumber. Stiffness in hollow of r.; sudden S.

Leg.—Cramp in calves almost all night. Lancinations in outer surface of l. tibia near femoral joint. Cramplike tearing in r. when walking; drawing T. when sitting. Pinching in upper part of inner muscles of calves. Bruised pain in calves and hollows of knees in evening, as after a long walk. Pressure in r. calf; below l. calf; pulsative, in r. tibia. Painful drawing on outer side of calf. Tension in l.; on inner side of l. calf when standing. Sensation as if tightly bound. Uneasiness in evening preventing slumber. Pain as if a weight were hanging upon l. when sitting if it rests over the other leg and hangs down. Heaviness in outer muscles of l. calf when walking.

Malleoli.—Sudden swelling in evening. Itching stitch beneath l. Tearing in r. extending to toes when sitting, > standing, with jerking, but when standing tearing extends upward from toes.

Foot.—Red swelling, < about malleoli, with sensation as if feet were tightly bound. Sticking in tarsal bone below r. ankle; in outer side of r. heel extending to calf, when stepping, > raising foot. Tearing in r. heel; in heels in evening in bed; drawing, between two last bones. Pain from above malleoli to soles when sitting, > standing and walking; cramplike, in r. sole when sitting; sharp, transversely across r. sole when sitting. Crawling as after a long walk or as if they would fall asleep, gradually extending into legs.

Toes.—Shooting in tip of r. great; in metatarsal joint of r. great; in metatarsal joint of r. second; in second joint of r. middle.

Skin.—Round yellow spots on l. leg. Red spots on backs of hands. Chilblains on hands in mild weather. Itching eruption over whole body. Itching hives below wrist through the day, the itching < rubbing. Swelling, with a red point on tibia, with pain on touch as if flesh were loose from bone. Red elevation on forepart of neck, with a white painless pimple in the middle of it. Burning pimple on l. eyebrow, with pain on touch; itching P. on l. thigh; itching, on face, with soreness on touch or on washing. Red, sharply circumscribed pustule on middle of sternum, with itching evenings. Red boil in r. angle of lower jaw, with drawing pain, < touch. Ulceration in the hole for the ear-ring. Painful hang-nails on fingers.

Sticking over whole l. side of body, next day on r. side; itching burning, over whole body, < rump, < morning in bed. Crawling in small of back. Itching of nipple; on back of l. foot; biting, over whole body on undressing; sticking, on outer side of thigh, transiently > rubbing; stinging burning, on back of hand, not > rubbing.

Sleep.—Yawning; when walking in open air, with oppression as from a cord about chest; with stretching of arms; inability to yawn sufficiently however wide he opens his mouth. Sleepiness; after walking in open air, < music, and a vivid dream on closing eyes. Early falling asleep and late waking. Deep sleep.

Sleep restless and interrupted by pain; R. and full of dreams about business. Frequent waking, as if he had slept enough. Starting up as from fright. The child moans, cries, begs and is frightened. (Talking about the uselessness of an external remedy for an internal trouble.) Woke lying upon back with r. leg stretched out and l. drawn up and half uncovered.

Dreams.—Of a loud noise. Of fire. Confused, unremembered. Of earthly splendor and greatness, which kept her in good humor after waking. Anxious, of quarrels, strife and battles; A., about neglected business. Vivid, anxious; V., full of terror; and confused, half-remembered; confused, in which many things go wrong with her, sometimes she talks aloud, tosses about, wakes often and always finds herself sitting up in bed. Lascivious, with emission, without erections; with erections, without emissions; with physical enjoyment, without emission.

Fever.—*Chilliness;* in whole body, with bruised pain in limbs; < along back; in knees and feet. Goose-flesh over arms, with chattering of teeth, with slight coldness and moderate shivering. Shivering several days about 10 A.M., with coldness in hands, deadness of fingers and insensibility of their tips; S. in l. arm, with jerking up of it; in l. foot extending half way to thigh in evening.

Heat; every day from 4 till 5 P.M., with sweat, then chilliness, thirst during and after the heat; < evening, < head and forehead, with redness of face and thirst; anxious, on slightest movement, with sweat; intermittent anxious, as if sweat would break out. Internal heat; after walking in open air, < chest and abdomen, without thirst; < chest and back, with sensation as if hot sweat were running down, without external heat. Hot and dry skin. Heat in forehead; in hands and feet; thighs and back; in small of back, somewhat to r. side; in feet, < internally; flushing, in face; flushing, in feet.

Sweat every morning after 4 A.M.; *in morning,* < neck, nape and forehead (Calc. c.); *at night;* cold, clammy; *hot, even on slight movement, with exhaustion.*

Staphisagria.

A tincture is made of the seeds of Delphinium Staphisagria, L. (a European Lark-spur).

Allies.—Its closest allies are the Ranunculaceæ, *Puls.*, Clem., Cimicif., Acon.; also Lyc., Sulph.

Generalities.—Sticking in face and other parts of body; *itching, in various parts. Drawing tearing here and there in all muscles when sitting* (Puls.). *Bruised sensation when walking, < calves. Pain in all bones;* drawing (?), in joints of shoulder, elbow, wrist, fingers, back, knees, on moving them, > rest, especially in evening. Paralytic drawing in various parts, < joints, if limbs are kept long in an unusual or uncomfortable position.

Weakness in morning; in morning in bed, **limbs pain as if bruised and as if there were no strength in them;** in morning on waking; in afternoon when sitting, with sleepiness; *after eating, with sleepiness and need to lie down,* wakes confused and heavy in limbs and dreads to walk, on continuing to walk, which is irksome, < ascending a hill, he feels more active and lively; *when walking, < knees;* < motion, *with bruised pain.*

Clinical.—Chronic gout, with nodosities. Neuralgia after operations. Frequently an antidote to the chronic effects of Mercury.

Mind.—Peevish in morning, he wishes to throw away everything which he takes in his hands; *P. and disin-*

clined to mental work; and restless; and quiet, vexed at things which do not concern him; at every word, she cries if any one only speaks to her. Quarrelsome and yet lively. Lachrymose; and she wraps up her face and will not hear about anybody or anything. Sad; and fears the worst results from slight causes and cannot quiet himself; and her mind seems dead; and apathetic; everything seems indifferent to him, he would rather die. The most attractive things make no impression upon him. Indifference to his surroundings, with mental exhaustion. Earnest, quiet, busy with himself, speaks but little.

Anxiety; and fear; so that he cannot remain in any place, but without complaints; and past events came before him, causing anxious sweat, then blackness before eyes, he did not know whether the images were real or illusory, then everything seemed indifferent and he lost all desire to live; (when walking rapidly, as if some one were coming behind him, and he is constantly obliged to look behind him).

Alternations of mood, at first joyous, then anxious, at last quiet and contented (the first is a transient reaction from one of fear and depression, then the primary action is noticed in anxiety, then the reaction is seen again).

Memory weak; disturbed by fantasies. Ideas vanish on attempting to grasp them; if any one interrupts him or suggests a different subject from the one of which he is thinking. He does not know whether the things presented to him are from out his memory, are real or whether he is dreaming of them, from 5 till 7 P.M. Dulness keeping him from work. *Disinclination for earnest work.*

Clinical.—Violent temper, throws things into the fire, ravenous hunger, very irritable mood, these attacks may alternate with rush of blood to the head. Has been found useful for bad effects of anger. Patients generally are extremely sensitive and feel acutely the slightest wrong. Sickness from wounded pride or chagrin.

Head.—Falls forward almost involuntarily on bending forward while sitting. Sticking all day; in evening, < stooping and walking, with tingling. Tearing in brain in morning on waking, > spasmodic yawning; *T. extending through cheeks into teeth, with pulling. Pain, stupefying, < forehead,* < moving head and standing; alternately stupefying and boring; like a tingling; on stooping, as if everything would come out at forehead; as from too much blood in brain in evening, < occiput towards bones; as if brain would fall out, on motion, and even during rest sensation as if brain were pressed together and lying loose within skull. *Compression of brain, < forehead, with paroxysmal roaring in ears, which ceases sooner than the headache.*

Dulness; in morning, with constriction in vertex; when standing and talking, as if vertigo would occur; with vertigo in forehead; intermittent; as in coryza. Heaviness; > *resting it upon the hand;* with weakness of cervical muscles, he must lean head back or to one side. *Vertigo;* in forenoon on rising from a seat, with pallor and falling to one side as in a faint, a similar attack about the same time the next day; in evening in bed; < sitting, > walking; and he runs against a door; as if stupefied, > open air; as if everything turned in a half circle on stooping and suddenly turning head.

Forehead.—*Sticking in l. side, with drawing pain;* sudden, in upper part of frontal bone; *boring, extending outward in l. half, waking him twice in morning; burning, externally on bone.* Tearing in evening when sitting, and on stooping a sticking, > walking; drawing cutting, in side. Pinching, > walking, returning on sitting and standing, and stitches in temples. Pressure above r. eye and a drawing upward; *hard P. in r. side;* as from something hard behind r. brow; intermittent drawing. Pressure outward in l. half, with pressing asunder; P. outward, at times sticking, afterwards in l. eminence, > rest, < motion. *Dulness in a spot anteriorly in middle,* like a stupefaction, on the street he does not know whether he is going to the r. or l. Heaviness above r. orbit in open air; *H. as from a ball of lead which would not loosen, in a spot in the middle, on shaking head;* upon cribiform plate of ethmoid bone, like a compression on both sides.

Temples.—Sticking in l.; *burning, in l.; internally, and externally as if bones would be pressed out, < touch;* pulsative drawing-tearing, in l. bone, on following days now in l., now in r. temple, then in l. frontal eminence. Burning tearing close to r. eye. *Pain internally and externally in l. as from pressure of a finger.*

Vertex.—Stitches extending from skull into brain, with external soreness, < touch; *burning S. externally;* boring, extending outward. *Hard pressure, and in r. temple;* sharp P. at times. Constriction and pain.

Sides.—Burning sticking in l. parietal bone. Tearing through l. half of brain, < forehead, gradually increasing and gradually diminishing. Burning pain extending inward in bone above l. ear. Soreness of r. parietal bone on touch, preventing lying on it at night.

Occiput.—Burning stitches, on first days extending from r. to l., afterwards from below upward. *Compression internally and externally.* Pressing asunder when walking in open air. Painful drawing on and beneath O. on motion of head; rheumatic D. beginning at articulation on bending head forward.

Scalp.—*Itching scurfy eruption above and behind ear. Hair falls out* (Nit. ac., Sep., Graph., Sulph.). Tearing externally in head and in teeth. *Painful drawing externally in places on head, < touch. Itching biting, < rubbing. Itching; with scurf and moisture; biting, on occiput, < scratching* (Nat. m.); *biting, on upper part of occiput, and sore pain, recurring in evening;* sticking, with fine papules towards forehead.

Clinical.—Neuralgic headache, with sensation of a ball in forehead or of a lump which cannot be shaken off. Moist fetid eruptions on the back of the head and behind the ears; painful sensitiveness of the scalp.

Eyes.—*Sunken, with blue raised rings around them. Inflammation of white, with pain.* Dim and so hot that the eye-glasses were dim. Stitches on exerting them. Pressure, with frequent necessity to wink. Burning pain about l. *Dryness all day* (Nat. m., Lyc.); *in evening, with pressure; in morning on waking,* with pressure in them so that she cannot open them unless they are moistened. Biting when writing, < afternoon and < light, with burning and with biting discharge. Feeling as if full of sleep. Biting lachrymation in morning. *Pupils dilated;* contracted. Sticking thrusts in ball, as if it would burst. Pain in upper part of r. ball. Pain in upper wall of r. orbit, pressing the eye outward.

Lids close, without sleepiness; r. wider open than usual; cutting beneath l. upper; *pain in upper all day, < closing eye; pain as if a hard substance were beneath l.*

upper; constriction in upper, forcing out tears; **itching of margins** (Sep.); *itching of margin of upper in open air,* recurring after two hours in other eye, > rubbing. Canthi, agglutination in morning; dry matter during the day; dry matter at night and in open air, and upon lashes; tensive stitch in r. outer; tearing in outer and in region of lachrymal gland; *biting smarting in inner;* hard pressure in r. inner; pain in l. inner, more biting than itching; paroxysmal burning in r. outer extending behind eye towards ear; itching in inner, < open air.

Vision.—Dim; as if eyes were full of water, with itching and sticking in inner canthus. Of a pillar of fire when in bed in a dark night; of black lightnings like a flickering, on looking in open air; small black lightnings before the letters when reading and then whole lines vanished. Of a white veil over objects, making them invisible. Halo around candle-light in evening. Illusion, on rising from a seat he seems to himself larger than natural and everything beneath him seems too low down.

Clinical.—Extremely valuable for the cure of tumors of the lids; chalazion; steatoma (Bar. c.). Scrofulous ophthalmia, styes in lids, edges inflamed and hard.

Ears.—Sticking in l.; deep in r. in evening; deep in l., then r.; *tensive, in l.* Cramplike burning pain posteriorly on l. concha. Pinching in l., with twinging. (Drawing pain.) Coldness streaming into r. meatus. Ringing on moving head; R. in l. Reports as if wind blew into them.

Clinical.—Deafness, especially after the use of Mercury.

Nose.—Soreness internally, with a scab deep internally. When touched, pain on septum in l. nostril as if it would suppurate. Smarting in one nostril as if ulcerated. Itching in l. nostril, > touch. (Stoppage in evening.) *Sneezing; without coryza.* Coryza; and cough; with tickling in nose and sneezing, discharge now profuse, mild, watery, now thick, mucous, afterwards thick, slimy substances (Puls.); sudden, at 2 P.M., lasting a quarter of an hour, with catarrhal voice; *first discharge of thick mucus, then of thin water* (Puls.); fluent, with stoppage of one nostril, sneezing, lachrymation and cracked lips.

Face. — Haggard and hollow-eyed. Swelling of cheek over lower jaw; S. as from coryza. *Induration anteriorly beneath chin by symphysis, with pain on swallowing, on touch and when rubbed by the neck-band.* Sticking in l. malar-bone; burning, in r. cheek-bone; *itching burning, in l. cheek;* itching (biting), in cheeks. Tearing in l. malar-bone, affecting teeth. When yawning, pain in l. cheek as if suppurating. Drawing in malar-bones; cutting, in l. malar-bone. Tension as if a pimple would form anteriorly on chin below margin of jaw. R. jaw is apt to get out of joint when yawning, with sticking. Pain in joint of jaw when yawning.

Lips.—Pimple covered with a scab in red of upper, with burning. Vesicles on margin of lower, with sticking burning on touch. Ulcer, with gnawing-drawing pain; U. discharging pus, then greenish water; on margin of lower, with red shiny look, sticking-drawing pain, with at times a not disagreeable itching, then sticking; scurfy, in middle of upper. Sticking extending outward in upper. Cutting as if cracked. Burning on outer margin of upper, almost in the middle.

Mouth.—Teeth. *Black* (Merc.), *she must clean them twice a day and still there are black streaks across them. One that had long been a little decayed rapidly became more hollow. A piece scales off from posterior surface of an incisor. Tickling sticking in r. lower molars. Tearing first in roots of hollow ones after chewing, then extending into crowns, < open air, with pressure on the crowns extending towards the roots, and on touch of finger the other teeth begin to pain; T. after chewing or cold drinks,* < motion, especially in open air; *in roots,* with drawing in muscles of face, first to one, then to other side; *in roots of all,* with feeling as if on edge when biting on them. *Cold drink penetrates T. as if they were hollow. Hollow T. sensitive to touch and if food remains in cavities pain extending into roots, and the gum becomes sore. Aching from drawing air into mouth;* on eating, they wabble about when touched, he cannot chew properly because when they touch each other it seems as if they were pressed deeper into gum, and gum is white. Drawing pain in a hollow one in morning; in r. from cold water; with swelling of cheek, headache in same side and heat in face; *biting, in a hollow one (in incisors a pressure) after eating, < open air; piercing, in one that becomes hollow and in corresponding one on other side, in morning;* as after Mercury, in anterior ones, < towards morning. Intermittent tugging, then throbbing in gum. Throbbing even when chewing; T. and pressive pain extending through face into eye. Biting pain in lower incisors, < night.

Gum.—*Bleeding on cleaning teeth and on pressure* (Merc.). Pale and white. Eaten away. Swelling, with heat in cheek; S. of inner surface, with pain. Pimple, painful when pressed by anything hard. Vesicle on inner side, changing to an ulcer, with sticking drawing pain. Spasmodic contraction of r. so that she cannot separate teeth on account of pain. *Tearing in gums of lower incisors and their roots when eating.* Pain on touch. Painful drawing in gums of molars and in their roots; in gum of r. incisor and canine teeth and in their roots, extending into muscles of lower jaw.

Tongue.—Coated white. Stitches in tip; on margin when pressed against palate, > eating. Sore pain anteriorly. Dryness, with stoppage of posterior nares by tough mucus; D., with collection of sour water in mouth and hard mucus stopping choanæ.

Mouth in General.—*Constant accumulation of mucus.* Blister. Sticking in palate in evening when it is dry; in palate extending into brain. Palate raw and scraped, but moist. Burning scratching in palate. Smarting posteriorly on palate when not swallowing. Salivation. Bloody saliva. Taste disgusting, bitter; to food; biting T. on smoking tobacco; sour to bread; qualmish, insipid; watery; none to food, but he has an appetite.

Clinical.—Spongy excrescences on the gums, which bleed readily and are painful. Dental fistula. Carious teeth which crumble. Teeth grow black and become brittle. Valuable for decaying teeth in pregnancy. Toothache shooting into the ear and temple, < open air or cold. Menstrual toothache. Hard pressure frequently relieves the toothache, which may be aggravated by light pressure. Aphthous sore mouth.

Throat.—Submaxillary glands swollen, preventing swallowing; swollen, and tonsils; painful; *painful as if swollen and bruised. Roughness when talking and swallowing.* Scraping in fauces behind nares as if one had drawn snuff through. (Scraping, disagreeable taste from drinking beer.) Painful drawing extending from hyoid bone deep into throat, < touching side of neck. Dryness, < evening before sleep, and on swallowing sticking.

Stomach.—Ravenous hunger; with salivation. Great desire for milk. Apparent hunger, as if stomach hung down relaxed, yet without appetite. *Thirstless.* Eructations; empty; tasting of food; mucus from upper part of throat; scraping, affecting larynx and causing cough (scraping heartburn); of tasteless liquid after eating. Waterbrash after eating. *Hiccough*, when smoking as usual; H. after eating; half an hour after supper; with nausea and stupefaction of head. Nausea; in morning; in mouth and pharynx from eating; with pressure like soreness above pit of stomach; with collection of water in mouth and short isolated eructations as from an emetic which would not act; with salivation and tension in abdomen as if he had eaten too much and then pressed upon abdomen. Vomiting every morning. Pinching in pit, > sitting and bending forward. Burrowing. Tensive pain in epigastric region. Fulness in pit, with pressure and sticking. Weight in morning after waking. Heartburn during the usual smoke.

Abdomen.—Rumbling; and gurgling; and cutting; after dinner, like forming and bursting of bubbles. Emissions of flatus; with griping; *hot;* offensive.

Cutting in morning before stool; C. < eating and drinking, with nausea so that water collects in mouth, with weakness, after the pain heat in face and rush of blood to head, even veins on hands swell up; with urging to stool, then thin scanty stool with internal chilliness in head, tenesmus after the stool; spasmodic, during the day on motion, < after urinating, with trembling of knees, in evening C. even when not moving, > bending up. Griping transversely across, with drawing in sides, in muscles, as if diarrhœa would occur; *twisting G. here and there.* Pain, heaviness and tension. Bruised pain. Drawing pain transversely through; D. pain as from flatulence. Heaving sensation and intimations of diarrhœa. Compression causing tightness of breath.

Upper A.—Griping in morning as if diarrhœa would occur, though he could not go to stool. Cutting and digging in upper and lower, with desire for stool, then thin scanty stool, then renewed desire and cutting, but without stool in spite of every effort, a kind of tenesmus, which with the colic was > rising from stool.

Hypochondria.—Rumbling in l. Sticking in r. on beginning to walk in open air. Pain as from incarcerated flatus. Constriction, oppressing chest and impeding respiration. Tension transversely across in morning in bed while fasting, causing anxiety and dyspnœa.

Umbilical Region.—Sticking, < expiration and pressure; rhythmical pinching, to left above umbilicus. Paroxysmal cutting externally in evening in bed. *Hard pressure in r. side beneath umbilicus.*

Sides.—*Pinching stitch in l. viscera;* tensive S. in l. muscles. Drawing extending downward, as if menses would appear.

Hypogastrium.—*Incarceration of flatus.* Rumbling and drawing. Swelling of inguinal glands, most noticed when walking and standing. Sticking in l. groin, < pressure, > inspiration and expiration; *drawing-burning, extending from r. ring, as if in spermatic cord, into r. testicle,* when sitting, standing and walking, < stooping (compare Puls.).

Clinical.—Atony of the stomach and abdomen, feeling as if they hung down relaxed. Colic from cold water, < heat.

Rectum.—Pain when sitting; *sore P. after stool;* bruised, deep in after a hard stool. Ineffectual urging after stool.

Anus.—*Itching when sitting;* I., with pimples.

Stool.—*A thin one passes unconsciously, with sensation as if flatus would pass* (Aloes); several thin ones. Diarrhœa mixed with flatus; with colic, the last part slimy; in morning, preceded by cutting and nausea, the last stool only of mucus. Soft; but difficult, as from constriction in anus, as from hæmorrhoids. *Constipation.* Hard, next day omitted, H. again on third day; H., mixed with flatus; in morning, then immediately a thin, copious, yellow one; and scanty, with burning cutting in anus; and scanty, thin-shaped, with pain in anus; and scanty, frequent, with pain in anus as if it would split. Difficult, first hard, then softer, with distress and straining as if rectum were constricted, with continued but ineffectual effort, then tenesmus. Delayed by want of peristaltic action in large intestine; D. and in small pieces.

Clinical.—Diarrhœa, evacuation hot, odor of rotten eggs, < after drinking cold water; particularly valuable in children whose teeth become black and crumble, and who have fetid eruptions on the scalp.

Urinary Organs.—*Pressure upon bladder,* on waking, copious urine and after an hour renewed urging. *Urging, scarcely a spoonful was passed, mostly dark yellow-red, in a thin stream, at times dribbling of urine, then sensation as if bladder were not empty;* frequent U., with copious discharge. Urine spurted from her on coughing. Micturition at night, with erection, at last only dribbling, with burning in neck of bladder and ineffectual desire for stool, relief from lying bent up. *Micturition frequent and copious;* frequent, watery at first, afterwards dark yellow; *frequent, scanty, dark;* frequent scanty; scanty every quarter of an hour, afterwards the usual amount of dark color every hour.

Discharge of prostatic fluid during hard stool. Cutting in urethra during micturition, worse afterwards. Sprained pain in upper part of urethra after micturition. *Burning in urethra during micturition;* in middle when not urinating; far back when sitting. Biting-burning crawling in orifice of urethra when not urinating. Urine scanty; copious, red.

Clinical.—Occasionally useful in enlarged prostate, especially with piles, pains over the kidneys, etc.

Sexual Organs.—Moisture on corona glandis beneath prepuce. A soft moist growth on corona glandis and one in fossa behind it, in both itching from rubbing of shirt. Sticking in r. side of glans when standing and walking. Erections all night without emission; and without lascivious thoughts. *Pain in l. testicle when walking and after rubbing, < touch. Drawing* (tearing) *in r. testicle as if compressed.* Painless bubbling in scrotum. Itching of scrotum somewhat > pressure and rubbing; voluptuous, < rubbing, so that it becomes a superficial sore pain, while the deeper I. continues and at last causes an emission. Emission every night; without dreams; with lascivious dreams; in afternoon sleep, in an old man. Great desire, then reaction.

Female.—Biting vesicle posteriorly within r. labia majora, with sore pain on touch. *Sensitiveness, it hurts to sit down.* Spasmodic pain, and in vagina. Biting. Sticking itching. Menses that had ceased for a year reappeared at the new moon, with cutting colic and rumbling (did not return on following months).

Clinical. — Occasionally indicated in secondary syphilis. Soft excrescences, which are moist and offensive on the penis. Orchitis, with burning, stinging pain, metastasis of mumps (Puls.). Often called for in the effects of masturbation, peculiar melancholia. Ovaritis. Prolapsus uteri, with feeling as though the abdomen would sink down. Irregular menses, with aching around the hips, loss of power in the legs, etc., especially following love affairs.

Respiratory Organs.—Vocal organs weak. Mucus in larynx, which he cannot loosen by coughing. Cough during the day from tickling; from irritation in larynx after eating; which threatens to tear open larynx, as from constriction of trachea, without special previous irritation; sharp, after eating, with accumulation of water in mouth, it seems as if this water would force through pharynx and causes cutting in it; with expectoration of mucus; with tenacious expectoration, after lying down in evening and at noon; with yellow expectoration like pus, < 9 A.M. till noon. Easy expectoration of much mucus by hacking. *Dyspnœa towards the end of coition.*

Chest.—*Adherent mucus* mornings, during the day easy expectoration. Sticking in r. side when sitting, on bending obliquely forward and to r. side; in cartilages of last ribs on stooping, and soreness on touch; on attempts to eructate S. and pressure extending into chest; < expiration; in intercostal muscles when sitting, < leaning backward and persistent during inspiration and expiration; in l. costal cartilages, with sticking cutting; intermittent, in l.; *intermittent, extending outward in region of fourth costal cartilages, without relation to breathing; itching, in sternum beneath pit of throat;* boring, in l.; beginning in posterior part of r. ribs and extending in a serpentine course to the cartilages; tensive, in l. side when lying and on moving, worse during expiration than inspiration, < ascending steps, at last sticking that almost took away the breath.

Pinching beneath r. short ribs; below sternum, to left of ensiform cartilage. Pain in l. side, not affected by respiration; P. externally on touch; when sitting, > walking, with heaviness; as if suppurating, behind sternum when coughing; as if beaten, in pectoral muscles in morning on moving in bed and during the day on crossing arms. Soreness behind sternum; in middle of sternum, < rising and stretching body, with pain on touch like a tension and pressure, at times taking away the breath. Scraping, then cough, with expectoration of blood. Constriction causing slow and difficult inspiration, > expiration and walking, < sitting, with anxiety and uneasiness. Uneasiness; driving him about in afternoon, with oppression. Weakness, with something adherent in trachea that compels hacking cough. *Sticking itching between costal cartilages.*

Heart.—Palpitation on waking from afternoon nap; on motion; when walking and when listening to music.

Neck.—Tensive stitches in l. muscles; jerklike S. almost behind ear in evening. Tearing in muscles. Rheumatic pain like drawing and stiffness at its union with shoulder on bending neck forward; R. pain like a drawing in nape and between scapulæ mornings preventing motion of arms on rising, could not turn neck in forenoon, with general weakness till noon; R. drawing pain in side on bending it forward. Pressive drawing on r. side. Tension in side; in muscles of nape and l. shoulder, with pressure; in l. side of neck and occiput at night, waking him often, preventing his lying on either side. Pressure downward. Stiffness of nape.

Back.—Stitches extending upward. (Pain like a beating and jerking from evening till 5 A.M., taking away his breath, with slumbering.) Sticking between last cervical and first dorsal vertebræ. Tearing on head of l. scapula, < motion. Burning pain beneath r. scapula close to spine, with heaviness in r. side of chest. Hard pressure in l. dorsal muscles near spine. Drawing pressure in two first dorsal vertebræ, with soreness. Paralytic drawing in spinous process of first dorsal vertebra.

Sacrum.—*Sticking during rest, > walking, with sprained pain; itching S. in region of kidneys;* drawing, when sitting, at times jerking. *Pain less when walking than on rising from a seat, turning in bed and on every motion sideways; as if broken in morning in bed, and on rising she could raise nothing from the ground till* 8 *or* 9 *o'clock, then hunger, then cutting in abdomen and diarrhœa, which at last was slimy;* extending downward, worse when stooping than when standing erect, > sitting; as if beaten all night, waking her about 4 A.M., > rising; bruised, in loins, extending to umbilicus, on stooping and on touch.

Extremities.—Internal trembling in morning if held long in one position. Intermittent deeply-piercing sticking in various parts. *Feel beaten and painful as after a long walk, below shoulders and below hip-joints.* Fatigue more in forenoon than in afternoon and pain everywhere, in muscles on touch and in joints on motion. Stiffness of joints in morning on rising in bed, < shoulders, *sacrum and hip-joints.*

Upper Extremities.—Pressive drawing here and there, < touch. Stitches in l. axilla; *itching, in A.;* itching, in r. Pain in r. axilla.

Shoulder.—*Sticking in joint, < touch and motion;* S. extending upward in r.; drawing, in l. joint, < moving arm towards chest. *Pain in l. joint; sprained, in r. on motion.* Pressive drawing in joints in morning, < motion. Paralytic drawing in joint, and at times in whole arm when lying under head in bed. Weight when sitting; loose, when walking, with pain on touch as if flesh were loose.

Arm.—Pain in bones during motion; *paralytic, < motion and touch.* Weakness after a nocturnal emission, with heaviness.

Upper Arm.—Tearing in muscles close to l. elbow; in l. deltoid when sitting, > motion; stitchlike, in muscles near r. elbow. *Paralytic pain in l., < motion and touch, the arm is weak.* Pain in periosteum of r. humerus, < touch. Pressive drawing in r. in evening in bed; in deltoid. Pressure inward on r., < touch.

Elbow.—Sensation near bend, more towards forearm, as from an eruption or as if it were irritated by a needle, a kind of feeling of gooseskin, somewhat burning, painful on touch. Paralytic weakness in region.

Forearm.—Jerking in l. during rest. Stitches in middle. Sticking tearing in l.; drawing T., < moving arm and hand. Drawing like a pinching on outer side of radius, beneath l. elbow. Pressive drawing in muscles, and on back of hand.

Wrist.—Sticking tearing in l. Cramplike pain about r., > stretching out fingers, returns on bending them up and then associated with a tearing stitch extending to shoulder. Pressure extending transversely across, < motion.

Hand.—Tingling stitches in palm. Intermittent pain in first l. metacarpus, < touch. Drawing pain through bones on back, < motion. Pressure on second l. metacarpus, < touch and motion.

Fingers.—Convulsive movement up and down when outstretched. Cramp, and in various parts of limbs. Sticking in middle joint of r. index and in joint next it, persistent during motion; *burning itching in l. thumb;* tensive, in tip of l. thumb. Tearing in muscles of ball of l. thumb, > motion; *jerking, in muscles, < tips; jerking, in muscles of thumb, < tip.* Cramplike pain in ball of r. little finger on moving hand. Pain in middle joint of r. middle, extending forward; *paralytic drawing, in metacarpal joints, < motion.* Painful drawing in r. phalanges; in middle joint of r. index. *Sensation in tips of l. as if a hard skin were over them, touch suspended.* Crawling as if they would go to sleep.

Lower Extremities.—Thigh. Sticking on inner side above l. knee; in middle of l., towards outer part; *itching, on inner side;* burning, in posterior surface of l.; almost scraping, internally above r. knee. Boring in l. gluteals when sitting. *Pain when walking,* < l.; *in nates after sitting;* about hip-joints when walking and sitting; sprained, in middle of l., < walking; sore, on upper and inner part; bruised, in muscles when walking rapidly; paralytic, like a drawing in middle anteriorly. Tension in large outer muscles when walking. Weakness, and in leg, < knee, necessity to drag his leg, with sticking tearing in calf and pain in sacrum; W. transversely across when lying, with bruised feeling, with stiffness in joints and trembling and uneasiness in them. Numbness in l. hip when standing, extending to abdomen.

Knee.—Jerking above r. patella. Sticking on inner margin; *in r. in morning after rising, < motion;* on outer side when stepping and on touch; *near patella, changing on touch to pain. Drawing stitches in r., < motion;* in l. when sitting, at times jerking in it. Drawing tearing beneath l. patella. Pain (sprained?) in r. when walking and on moving foot. Drawing up in hollows on lying down, a kind of voluptuous uneasiness in them, forcing him to rise; paralytic D., like weakness in r., when walking and afterwards, and in heads of muscles of calves. Weakness in morning after rising; sensation in hollows as if they would give way, on rising from a seat, a trembling, irritable drawing up.

Leg.—Cramp on waking, < upper and lower part of calf, < thinking of it, not > stretching nor bending up leg; of the calf and sole of the side on which he was lying, waking him from afternoon nap. *Burning stitches on outer side beneath l. knee, sometimes in paroxysms; boring S. in r. tibia during rest;* itching S. in r. calf when walking and standing, > scratching. *Tearing in muscles of one or other when sitting and standing; sticking in and beneath r. calf and above l. heel.* Pain in calves in evening in bed, preventing sleep and forcing her to move them constantly, the same when she rose in the night, and on lying down again. Pressive drawing on tibia when sitting. Tension in calf, with heaviness. Paralytic pressure outward in muscles of r. calf, < touch.

Ankle.—Drawing pressure transversely across, < motion.

Foot.—Swelling of back; of metatarsal bone of r. little toe, with pain on touch. Tearing in l. metatarsal bones close to ankle. Pain on inner side of l. sole during rest. Crawling and prickling as if asleep in the sole of the leg which rests over the other. Constrictive heaviness in l. metatarsal bones close to ankle.

Skin.—Tetter on thighs and legs; *on hands, itching in evening and* **burning after scratching**; itching only at night. A kind of gooseskin on thighs and legs, without chilliness, especially red and white pimples on them, with whitish pus at tips. On forearm a red elevation in the middle of which is a pustule, with burning pain during rest, and on touch pain like a boil. Skin of ulcerated leg becomes covered with a thin crust, from which yellow water exudes, with jerking and pricking pain.

Rash on chest, when warm it was red and itching. Pimples about the inflamed eye; on neck; on elbow and towards hand; *itching, on nape; itching, on body and thighs, when scratched off they are moist and then have a burning pain;* small (itching?) on face; on legs, with burning itching pain; on face, forehead, cheeks and about mouth and wrist, causing drawing itching, transiently > scratching and returning as a sticking; small, thick, red, on lower ribs, with burning-itching sticking and after rubbing pain, with creeping chill over the part and over upper abdomen; fine, on face, forehead, cheeks, and near corners of mouth, with sticking itching and on touch pain as if suppurating; on face, causing tensive sore pain, and when touched pain as if suppurating; large, with white papules on top of it, in fossa behind lobule of ear.

Tearing jerking in an ulcer. Sticking here and there. Tearing about ulcers in morning and evening, > walking, with jerking. Burning pain in ulcers in evening after lying down, preventing sleep. Biting in an ulcer, as from salt; burning-itching, on nates as if woolen were drawn over skin in evening in bed, on scratching changing to another place. Crawling on inner surfaces of toes, as if they had been asleep; C. on thighs and legs (that had been swollen, hard, elastic, for many years), with sensation as if parts were internally hot, would burst and were heavy.

Itching on cheeks; on nape; on tendo-achillis; on r. tibia above outer malleolus, not > rubbing; on leg in evening in bed, and after rubbing a painful flat ulcer; salty biting, in an ulcer; creeping, going from place to place, < morning, with crawling; tickling, in l. palm. *Sticking itching in gluteals and in several places on body; above r. outer malleolus;* on r. great toe. Burning itching on r. inner malleolus; on inner side of two toes, as if they had been frozen; in little toes in evening, as if they had been frozen, with redness and pain on touch; in r. little toe as if it had been frozen, in evening, with pain on slight pressure.

Clinical.—Eruptions, moist, offensive, itching, after scratching the itching reappears at another place. Scorbutic ulcers, with burning; spongy, bleeding gums, fetid breath. Lichen, violent itching. Herpes zoster, with shooting pains, extending down the thighs.

Sleep.—*Yawning; and stretching,* she cannot stretch enough; *forcing tears from eyes. Sleepiness in afternoon;* from 2 till 4 P.M.; during the day, and falling asleep whenever he sat down. He cannot reach the bed in the evening before he falls asleep and he falls asleep as soon as he gets into bed. Sleepless all night; till 11 P.M., then waking about 4 A.M., several nights; till midnight, then as soon as he fell asleep vivid dreams of strife and quarrels. Jerking of whole body as if some one suddenly tickled arms and legs, with heat, but without thirst or sweat. Sleep restless; and unsound, with half waking every hour; and he could lie on neither side, before midnight he was full of various thoughts; in a child, and it calls its mother constantly. Waking every hour after 2 A.M.; W. in morning as if he had slept enough, but sleeps again immediately.

Dream of the business of the day as soon as he fell asleep; of murder; full of bitterness; restless, anxious; restless, busy now with one, now with another subject, at one time he started up and woke, but could not collect himself; as soon as he fell asleep, at one time he was fighting, at another he had anxious visions, when he woke and dreamed again; that he was struggling with an animal, as soon as he fell asleep, so that he started up frightened. Vivid, connected dreams; V., unremembered; V., disagreeable, towards morning. *Amorous, with emission;* without emission.

Fever.—Chilliness in morning in bed; in morning in bed, then heat and disinclination to rise; in evening; *waking him frequently at night, with inability to collect his senses;* an hour later heat in face, without thirst; shaking, in evening before sleep; shaking, in whole body, with warm forehead, hot cheeks, cold hands, without thirst. Shivering every day about 3 P.M., > open air, with gooseflesh; S. all night; *when eating, without thirst,* two hours before the heat; *over whole body, without thirst or immediate subsequent heat;* then slight heat; with sleepiness and dryness of mouth; internal. about 3 P.M., with thirst; over back and arms in morning after rising, towards nape, and over head and face; down back after eating. Chilliness in back; cold feet in evening in bed.

Heat in afternoon when sitting quietly, with sweat, without thirst; H. towards evening in open air, with headache; at night, < about forehead, preventing sleep after 3 A.M., then shaking chill about 9 A.M.; with orgasm of blood and thirst. Heat here and there in limbs; externally on lower part of sacrum; about head in morning in bed, with sweat on forehead; of hands and feet at night; over back three hours after eating; in tip of r. great toe during rest; internally in r. hand, with redness and with tearing in middle joints of its fingers; paroxysmal, creeping over lower part of back; sticking, here and there in skin; on forehead, as from a warm breath against it, at times also a cold breath, with redness of cheeks and external warmth of body.

Sweat; at night; after midnight, every night; *of the odor of bad eggs* towards midnight; of bad odor at night; on abdomen, feet and genitals at night on waking, though moderately covered, on uncovering so cold that the sweat disappears and he thinks he has taken cold.

Sticta Pulmonaria.

A tincture is made of the fresh lichen (that growing on the maple seems the best).

Burning biting-sticking all over body, increasing in intensity all day. *Weariness.* Feeling of dulness. "Feel the medicine all over me." Inactivity of mind, inability to collect thoughts. *Dulness of head,* with **heavy pressure in forehead and root of nose, increasing in intensity during the day**; *D. of head, with sharp darting pain through vertex, side of face and lower jaw.* Heavy intermittent pain in forehead at noon, < 2 P.M., < r. supraorbital region, < 4 P.M., when it extended through brain, < r. side of head. Darting pain in temples increasing all day. Intermittent shooting in r. temple at 7 A.M., < 8 A.M., when it extended through frontal and r. parietal regions deep into brain, the pain < 11 A.M., when it was heavy and intermittent, < r. supraorbital region, almost intolerable at 5 P.M. and extending through brain. Scalp feels too small or as if drawn too tight.

Eyes feel heavy. *Burning in eyelids, increasing in intensity all day, with soreness of balls on closing lids or turning eye.* **Fulness at root of nose.** Dull oppressive pain in cardiac region. Fulness in l. hypochondrium. Pain in r. hypochondrium. *Oppression of lungs.* Lancinations in second joint of middle finger, increasing in intensity all day. Darting pains in muscles of arms, then in finger-joints and shoulders, next in thighs, knees and toes.

Clinical.—Headache, with violent pains in the eyes, which are sore on turning them. Earache, with noise and beating in the back of the head. Nasal catarrh, with profuse discharge of bloody pus, distressing cough and oppression of the chest, cough < evening and night, becoming almost incessant, < lying down. Nasal catarrh, dryness of the nose and palate, they feel as stiff as leather, with occasional discharges of scabby mucus, < evening and night. Catarrh, with constant blowing of the nose, but no discharge. Hay fever, incessant sneezing, with fulness in forehead and root of the nose and tingling. Nasal catarrh for many years, sneezing, with green discharge, frontal headache and occasional bleeding. Diarrhœa, with much mucus, associated with cough. Cough, incessant, dry, spasmodic, < evening and night, sometimes with feeling of hard masses in chest, pressure at root of nose. Hacking cough in nervous and hysterical patients, particularly such as are subject to sick headache. Cough dry, racking, with splitting headache in forehead; cough caused by inspiration, < lying down at night. Cough, with hoarseness, nightly expectoration. Very noisy coughs, often spasmodic, like whooping cough; frequently suitable for the incessant cough of measles, which prevents sleep at night, with stuffy and dry nose. Hysterical chorea, < evening and night, constant jumping about, feet and legs feel as if floating in the air.

Inflammatory rheumatism of small joints, intense pain in the neck and head. Rheumatism of the wrists. Rheumatism of the knee. Housemaid's knee.

Stillingia Sylvatica.

A tincture is made of the fresh root.

Generalities.—Distress, miserable feeling all the forenoon, headache, eyes inflamed and watery, soreness of all muscles, feeling as if he had taken a severe cold. Malaise; about bedtime, > after sleeping all night. Weakness; with feeling as if emaciated; with sleepiness, heaviness < legs, soreness of whole body, disinclination to move, desire to go where I will not be annoyed, the duties of my profession are irksome, head heavy, relaxation of muscle of neck, brain feels too large for skull, difficulty in keeping eyes open. Aggravation from exposure of the parts to cold or even to the air, amelioration from covering with flannel or by getting into bed. Amelioration after a good night's rest.

Mind.—**Gloomy forebodings.** *Spirits depressed.* Stupid.

Head.—Aching; < forehead and vertex; running from anterior part of temples. Dizziness; and *throbbing.* Shooting in r. frontal bone running down to eye. Darting pain in sinciput extending to occiput; over l. eye, with lachrymation, < r. eye, more profuse when reading. Pain in forehead; like a current running from median line to occipital process and l. cerebellum, also in evening; as from a weight on brain, the pain became darting and almost unbearable; heavy. Pain in temples; through T. and forehead; intermittent; darting, in l. Pain in r. side of head. Darting pain in r. occipital protuberances.

Clinical.—Moist, brown excoriating eruption on the scalp.

Nose and Face.—Abscesses in side of r. nostril. Discharge from nose at first watery, then muco-purulent, nostrils sore inside. Sharp burning in r. nostril at 6 A.M. on waking. Stinging-darting pain in face. Pain under malar-bone, extending transversely through face.

Mouth.—Spells of neuralgia in teeth. Tongue coated; white; yellowish-white. Tongue feels rough and sore. Heat in mouth, fauces, œsophagus and stomach. Rough, dry feeling. Salivation. Taste salt; T. bitter in morning.

Throat.—Inflammation of fauces; of l. tonsil. Choking resembling globus hystericus, > Nux. vom. and Chelid. Sensation of a ball preventing sleep till after 1 A.M. *Smarting. and stinging.* Rawness in fauces. Soreness of pharynx. Irritation of fauces. Tickling, with hacking cough; T. in fauces, with dryness and hacking cough. Dryness of fauces. Burning in fauces; increasing till throat became very sore; in throat extending to stomach, as if deprived of epithelium, < swallowing.

Stomach.—Appetite increased; lost. Regurgitations of food and vomiting of ingesta. Pyrosis every day from 2 P.M. till bedtime; every day from 3 P.M. till bedtime. Nausea. Vomiting. Cramps. Griping in epigastrium, then diarrhœa; G. in epigastrium at 6 P.M., then diarrhœa, with much flatus, next day feeling of impending diarrhœa. Distress in epigastrium. Burning. Faint, empty feeling.

Abdomen.—Rumbling; > escape of flatus and smoking. Darting pain; in l. hypochondrium, beginning in ascending colon and passing through descending colon, then escape of flatus. Cramps in hypochondria. Pain in umbilical region; heavy, in hypogastrium.

Anus.—Piles. Pain in sphincter during stool, and in rectum. Bruised pain in sphincter. Burning during stool, with tenesmus; B. during stool, with tenderness, afterwards uneasiness in rectum.

Stool.—Loose, with tenesmus and burning in anus; L. and bilious; L., two near together, with tenesmus and burning in anus, which lasted half an hour; L. and irregular, afterwards constipation with nausea, and when lying down slow and irregular pulse, afterwards sensation of impending diarrhœa. Acrid, frothy, bilious, copious, twice in one day, with tenderness and burning in anus. Six within two hours, three copious, the last three scanty white, resembling dysentery, then another, *white and resembling curds.* Urgent immediately after breakfast. Delayed; and during the evacuation pain in rectum and sphincter.

Clinical.—White, pasty, fetid stools.

Urinary Organs.—Pain in urethra; during micturition; *smarting burning,* < micturition, with difficulty in voiding urine and pain in region of kidneys. Scalding in urethra during micturition, with uneasiness at neck of bladder as if inflamed. Urine increased; and scalding and high-colored, inclined to foam; and containing brick-dust sediment, also high-colored; and thick, milky, containing much chloride of sodium. White sediment. Dark brownish sediment (before the proving the sediment was flocculent mucous.)

Sexual Organs.—Sharp pain in glans extending up urethra during micturition, causing sweat, next day sharp pain on walking. Drawing up of r. testicle. Heavy pain in l. testicle. Pain in ovaries.

Clinical.—Syphilitic eruptions. Secondary syphilis, especially bone-pains, sciatica, particularly of l. side. Bone-pains, with nodosities on the skull and long bones (Asaf., Sil., Merc.).

Respiratory Organs.—Constriction of larynx. Bruised feeling in trachea on pressure; B. feeling, with irritation in bronchi. Lame feeling in cartilages of trachea. Uneasiness in trachea and bronchi on going to bed, < next morning on rising, with tickling. *Cough, hacking; C. dry in evening, from tickling in trachea,* C. afterwards loose and deep; *dry spasmodic, towards evening, from tickling,* next day deep and loose.

Clinical.—Laryngitis, with sensation of lameness of the cartilages, feeling of constriction and soreness.

Chest.—Pain in l. clavicular space; sore, along l. clavicle in evening, and in shoulder. Darting pain through chest; and through shoulders. Raw feeling in sternum. Oppression.

Heart and Pulse.—Boring in region of heart. Pulse rapid. *Pulse irregular;* in morning; and full; and rapid, weak, but regular during the heat and sweat.

Back.—Pain in evening, extending down thighs and legs; in r. scapula, running up to neck; in r. kidney; across region of kidneys; shooting forward in l. loin when sitting. Darting pain in l. kidney on waking at 6 A.M., then in r., with heavy pain in l. testicle.

Extremities.—*Pulsating pain in r. elbow and r. leg in evening, with soreness.* (Aching in bones and muscles, with increase of the soreness caused by severe exercise and felt before the proving).

Upper Extremities.—*Shooting from middle third of humeri down to fingers.* Aching in humerus, on and above olecranon, with soreness. Pain in r. elbow, forearm and wrist, < motion; sharp, in bend of l. elbow, < hanging down; in l. elbow, extending towards shoulder and hand, as if bones were sore and would separate, < l., temporarily > change of position, with aching in l. carpal and metacarpal bones. *Shooting in upper third and inner side of forearm* at 9.30 A.M., < letting limb hang down and > pressure. Pain in finger-joints.

Lower Extremities.—Aching in evening; in r. hip and l. foot; in hip-joint when riding, < bending backward or forward, and walking, with stiffness; on outside of r. thigh and leg, running down to foot; heavy, in r. thigh and leg; drawing, in l. knee, affecting gastrocnemius and biceps. Stabbing in r. knee. Sensations in popliteal spaces. *Pain in r. leg;* in calves; in tendo-achillis; in leg and sole in morning; *in lower anterior third of l. leg* in afternoon when driving; posteriorly in r. leg after retiring. Dull feeling in calves. Pain in external malleoli; darting, in outer part of r. ankle. Aching in foot over r. instep; < standing and attempting to walk. Uneasiness of l. foot. Pain in third r. toe when in the house; in metatarsal joints of toes when walking, extending to heels.

Skin.—Smarting from rubbing on it the juice of the root, with irritation. Itching below knees; burning, below knees, < exposure to air.

Clinical.—Enlarged cervical glands. Tubercular eruptions, which tend to ulcerate.

Sleep.—Sleepiness early in evening; by spells during the day.

Fever.—Coldness on going to bed, but soon sweat and heat. Feeling as if the room were too warm by spells during the day, with sweat. Heat in face like catarrhal fever. Burning in l. ear at night before sleep, next morning vesicles upon it. Sweat.

Stramonium.

A tincture is made of the seeds of Datura Stramonium, L.

General Action.—Stramonium acts like other plants of the Solanum family in producing cerebral excitation, particularly delirium, which here assumes a peculiar form. Its scarlatina-like eruption is similar to that of Belladonna. Suppression of urine is one of the peculiarities to be noted.

Allies.—*Hyosc.*, Bell., Merc., Secale c., Verat. alb.

Generalities.—Suppression of all excretions (Secale c.). *Wildness of manners.* Inarticulate cries. Lying on their backs; upon stomach, boring head into pillow; prostrate and helpless; on the floor, cold, senseless, weak, and breathing feebly. Muscles hard. Contraction of muscles; except sphincter of bladder. Relaxation of voluntary muscles. Sat upright on a lounge supported by an assistant on each side and refused to be placed recumbent. Falling over when sitting, especially towards r. side, making a circular sweep. Threatens to fall on rising. Sways to and fro like a drunken man. Tottering so as to almost fall from its chair. Imperfect control over voluntary motions. Inability to perform co-ordinate movements. Loss of voluntary motion. Inability to take food, to see, hear, speak or feel.

Trembling of whole body (Arg. n., Gels., Cimicif., Merc.); with rigidity of trunk and limbs, constant moans, occasional shrieks, appeared as if terribly frightened, could not stand and would not lie down, pupils dilated and insensible, the least noise startled him, holding a candle before eyes caused convulsions of limbs, especially a drawing backward and increased rigidity, a nervous effort to swallow, inability to articulate, loss of voluntary motion; < abdomen, on becoming warm in bed, with prickling over whole body, mind timid and restless, preventing sleep, aggravation of every symptom after paregoric, with clammy sweat, on closing eyes hideous, menacing spectres, and the bed seemed suspended and tantalized like a feather between the two floors.

Constant restless movements (Hyosc., Merc., Rhus t., Bell.). *Subsultus tendinum* (Hyosc.). *Chorea-like movements; and features continually changing, at times laughing, at times expressing astonishment, lips moved as if trying to speak, sometimes puckered as in whistling, mouth often opened and snapped together, tongue often run out rapidly and licked about cheeks, head thrown backward and forward, spasmodic twisting of spine and whole body, limbs in constant motion, not jerking, anxiety and restlessness, rubbing nose and mouth, pulling at lips, groping about, fingering the bed-covers, scratching face or throat, at times the arm suddenly sank down relaxed for a moment, whole body exhausted, then the spasms would begin anew* (see Merc.).

Twitching; and inability to swallow or talk (Hyosc., Op.); of limbs and neck; of jaw, lips and limbs, r. side; of jaw, lips, l. arm and r. lower limb; of head from side to side, then general T., trismus, spasms of neck, difficult swallowing, stupefaction, then he lay unconscious on his back, when he was raised the neck and spine bent backward, limbs in constant convulsive motion and frequent shaking of body as from electric shocks; changing to movements as if the boy were acting in pantomime, but at times convulsions, after a bath he moved his mouth as if he wanted to speak, he seemed in an ideal childish world, **all his ideas seemed reproductions.**

Convulsions; at sight of a lighted candle, a mirror or of water; < *being touched or loudly spoken to,* **and when a cup of drink touched their lips**; < arms, face and neck; beginning in face and extending to other parts; with blowing or hissing expirations; with screams; with flushed face and full, slow pulse; with hot head, dark red face, red limbs, dilated pupils, salivation, grating of teeth and trembling; of every muscle, he beat his breast, jaws set as in tetanus, moans, stertorous breathing, occasional rattling in throat, limbs cold, pulse nearly obliterated, cold, clammy sweats, face hippocratic; then paralysis of lower limbs; *with shrieks and hoarseness, alternating with torpor; alternating with rage, during the latter he beat and bit those who attempted to hold him;* alternating with excitement of mind; alternating with opisthotonus.

Opisthotonus. Bent backward as in opisthotonus, muscles of limbs very active, *he grasped at his mouth and face, tried to get out of bed and made efforts to grasp small objects, but had no spasms.* Tetanus. Hysterical symptoms. Cramps.

Pain and anxiety. Aura running swiftly from r. heel to occiput, all along posterior r. side, when walking in the street, and I was occasionally suddenly arrested as if tripped up by a backward thrust in popliteal space, causing knees to give way and causing dead stops. Hyperæsthesia; to touch, and every motion aggravated. **Restlessness; and calling for water, swallowing difficult** (Hyosc.); with itching; with yawning and sleepiness; with moans, tossing about the bed, throwing about limbs, < arms, frequent opening and shutting of hands and many motions of fingers; and stretched himself at full length, threw his limbs about and sometimes seized his neck with both hands. *Great strength.*

Weakness; in morning on waking, also went back to bed several times; in afternoon; at 5.30 P.M.; when walking; from least exertion; and loss of sensation (touch, taste, etc.), diminution of sensorial power; sudden, with violent beating of heart. Desire to lie down. Dislike to moving about and inability to sit straight any length of time. Faintness; in paroxysms; with trembling. Collapse. Stiffness of whole body. Motionless. A boy did not feel a whipping. Paralysis of various parts; of l. side; muscular, with retention of urine. Aggravation in forenoon. Relieved for a few seconds by drinking. Sedative, anodyne and cooling.

Clinical.—Chorea, with the peculiar fright of the drug, with constantly changing spasms; chorea, particularly of the muscles of the face, which assume all kinds of expressions (rarely useful for chorea, which persistently attacks certain muscles). Hysterical convulsions, with frothing at mouth, distorted features. Convulsions resulting from fright, especially from being frightened by animals.

Mind. — Delirium; noisy; frightened by strange

objects that obtrude upon his fancy; under the impression of danger, clinging to the person who held him in her lap; he sees more horrifying images at his side than in front of him; he seems at times to be chasing or fleeing from imaginary objects; her gaze was fixed and she tried to reach towards something which she saw; staring about, then fixed gaze, with startings of limbs, low mutterings, then sudden and furious screaming, biting, scratching and tearing with hands and kicking; picked the bed-clothes, saw bugs, etc.; large dogs, cats and other horrible beasts seem to grow out of the ground at his side and he springs away from them in terror; he saw a long train of bedbugs and after them a procession of beetles, then a host of cockroaches crawled over him, he shrank back in alarm, then said "I believe I know they are not really bugs, but except once in a while they seem real;" he saw black objects, *spoke of black people and black clouds and grasped at the air;* **symptoms resembling hydrophobia; rage on attempting to administer liquids, like hydrophobia, spasm of pharynx so that anything taken choked him and was regurgitated;** *at first looked stupid and gave incoherent answers, afterwards looked like an idiot, afterwards bit a man's hand,* **sometimes cried out that she saw cats, dogs and rabbits at the top, sides and middle of the room,** *at other times caught eagerly at imaginary objects and declared she saw persons who were not present; he saw an executioner standing before him, yet he was lively, talkative, laughed and made jokes about his hallucination,* **but it seemed to him a reality;** *walks about the room absorbed in himself, with fixed, sparkling eyes, surrounded by blue rings,* **solely occupied with the objects of his fancy.**

Delirium, with sexual excitement (Hyosc.); *D., with incoherent talking; with restlessness, constant incoherent talking, dancing and singing; violent; intermittent; pleasant, incoherent; muttering; raving; sudden, with ridiculous gestures; he converses with absent persons as if they were present, and addresses inanimate objects by the names of such persons, but observes none of those standing about him; talkative, complained that a dog was tearing and biting the flesh of his chest; unintelligible muttering, looked around wildly, could not be made to do what he was told, although he apparently understood all that was going on, tried to clutch at imaginary persons, but could not use his arms; caught at the bed-clothes and everything around her; picking at bed-clothes and frequent, violent laughter; picking at imaginary objects; confused talking, grasping at the air and scratching on the bed-covers; grasps at things quickly and thinks he has seized a thing before touching it, and if he does not hold the object he does not feel that he has got it; constant tremulous reaching forward and upward of arms,* while lower limbs were motionless and paralyzed; *she began to cry when her mother took her up, and she became furious and began to scratch and bite; desire to escape; jumped, danced about the bed and knocked against the wall, with incessant and disconnected talking, laughing and staring; wild, ran about the room, jumped, talked nonsense, saw chickens and cats, spoke to them and to their toys; joyful; joyous, made known his wants by gestures without speaking, and ran about; lively, alternating with dread of an approaching monster and piteous appeals for help; laughing, making faces, behaving like an intoxicated person or a fool, pulling his clothes, staring; laughing, grasping with his hands, rolling and creeping around in bed; sings, talks, fancies there are dogs in the room, which he describes and attempts to chase, suddenly springing to his feet and as suddenly toppling over,* talks of the events of the day as if they were taking place; *constant motion of limbs, co-ordinate only as far as they related to the corresponding limb, constant motion as if picking something from the clothes or bed-clothes, and paroxysms of laughter,* ceasing suddenly, at times smiles; laughing, crying, singing, dancing, *no correct estimation of distances or size of objects,* they tried to pick up the nail-heads in the floor, which they thought to be money, a boy caught a hat, thrust his foot into it, pulled the brim and fretted because he could not "get on his trousers"; *thought she was falling; imagines that he is abandoned in a wilderness, animals jump out of the ground at his side, so that he moves quickly to the other side, where others start up and pursue him, so that he runs forward; difficult to hold in the lap, it threw out its legs wide apart and stiffened them, arms constantly thrown out as if trying to reach something, and sometimes it seemed as if something had been secured and was fumbled in the fingers, pupils dilated, eyes wild, screams, froth from mouth, skin hot; sudden starting as if in terror, with outstretched arms and staring eyes, difficulty in holding her,* incoherent cries, then a calm with laughter, grasping at imaginary objects, conveying her hands to her mouth as if eating berries, pointing at something on the floor, etc.; eyes following an imaginary object, *then striking at it, screaming, sobbing, starting back and frightened look, afterwards she struck at, pushed or attempted to bite every person or object near her,* afterwards coma, then return of excitement without ocular spectra or spasms; *sometimes she appeared for a moment free from anxiety, sat silent, with eyes fixed on the ground but picking at whatever was before her, then starting as if in fright with a shriek, distortions and apparently pain and anxiety,* at other times in the interval of ease singing and laughing, but would not utter a word or notice anything said to her, with **aversion to fluids.**

Delirium alternating with insensibility, **voice squeaking,** staggering and falling to the ground; fury and running about; periodic raving, he attacked people and tried to bite them; *symptoms resembling delirium tremens, and struggling to get out of bed, rolling from side to side, unless supported she fell forward to the ground;* he tried to get out of bed at night, but uttered no sound, preceded and followed by insensibility; jumped from bed at midnight, ran about the room, caught at every one as he passed them, said a man was chasing him, said repeatedly "You shan't have me"; on waking the child held out its hands as if it wanted a glass of water, then brought them to its mouth and sipped as if drinking, bit its own fingers and its mother's if she put them into its mouth, and screamed incessantly; one would blow up a feather in the air, another would dart straws at it in fury, another was sitting naked in a corner like a monkey, grinning and making mouths at them, a fourth would fondly kiss and paw his companions and sneer in their faces; busy D., < women, then sopor, then weariness, pain in limbs and disinclination to think; often lay down upon his knees, stretched out his arms and groped about as if seeking something; grasping outward, at times at nose or head; caught at the blaze of the fire in a singular way and fell to the floor as if paralyzed on one side; motions so fast that finally he cannot move any more and all turns black before his eyes; recognized no one, paid no attention to calls, constantly turned head from side to side; their attention could not be aroused and they resisted interference, with piteous cries and violent struggles; imagines that he is tall and large and that surrounding objects are too small; after waking all things appear to him new, even his friends, as if he had never seen them; the boy said repeatedly that there were "big sores" on him; thought that one side of him was alive and the other buried; thought that he was dying, was glad that he was and prepared for his funeral, with otherwise perfect reason and without feeling remarkably sick; with the facetious leer often seen in drunkenness; he dances at night in a churchyard; happy, incoherent talking, tottering and falling down; chatters nonsense, and when his friends set him right he excuses himself, saying they have suggested them to him, and begins to speak on the same subject; the apartment seemed all on fire; saw objects that did not exist and saw lightnings; thought that she was engaged in her usual vocation; at one time he was off to hitch up his team, at another he gathered sticks and placed them together to build a fire, then motioned as if he would scrape lice and bugs together, shake them out of hats, pull paper off the wall to get them out, pick them off himself and tramp on them, tried to catch rats, talkative, did not know his wife nor where he was, wanted to go home, etc. They tried to walk around each other on their hands and knees, heads forcibly inclined to the right, with disposition to manége if left alone, the mother muttering incoherently, the boy at intervals of a few minutes uttering a low whispering scream.

Mind clouded, I upset everything I touched, a person talking to me seemed a figure in a vision or as if talking out of a cloud, I subsided into bewilderment when he ceased talking, my writing was an almost unintelligible scrawl, vertigo, aching on vertex, could not realize anything, my wife sitting by my bed seemed like a phantom, before this I was forgetful, used wrong words, speech was thick.

All motions hasty *and forcible, he is anxious if he cannot finish them at once.* **Apprehension. Starting up in fright; shuddering and fright.** *Imagines that he is alone and is frightened.* Fear of sudden death. *Sadness in evening in bed, with thoughts of death and violent weeping;* S., with tears; and indisposition to converse, next day buoyancy. Anxiety. Despair. Crying and almost convulsive agitation. Inconsolable after the fall equinox, affected by trifles, disposed to weep, sometimes easily vexed, sometimes neglects her duties, sometimes thinks she is not fitted for her position, *aggravation from the darkness, being alone and in the morning, she wants sunshine and company.*

Talking much, but speech difficult; continued incoherent T.; talks little and utters single, broken words with a higher voice. Quarrelsome. Passionate and feeble. Furious anger; A. when pinched or tickled, with incoherent muttering, turning upon his face and kicking backward, with alternate movements of feet. Peevishness; and pacing up and down the room; when spoken to, and he answered by a sharp cry or said sharply "let me alone," all his words being curtailed; then disposition to laugh. Would not answer. Variable humor. Laughing and whining; L. for an hour, then crying; alternations of L., weeping and singing. Inclined to smile and jest. *Disinclination for real work.* Dread of cold water, but warm water relieved the symptoms. Watchfulness.

Memory lost; from inward uneasiness; M. diminished. Absence of mind. *Confusion of intellect. Always miscalled the same things,* > sound sleep. Misplaced words, called his head his foot, his arm his leg. Difficulty in speaking the right word when answering. Answered in a disconnected and lolling manner. Stammered disconnected words and shed tears. Mistakes in spelling when writing and when speaking puts words in the wrong place.

Stupefaction; from which he at times started up wildly, opened his eyes, which were partly closed, but could not keep them open, spoke disconnectedly, quarrelled with his mother, whom he did not know, face red, cheeks hot, dry heat over whole body, at times moved his lips and tongue, called for liquid, throbbing in carotids, full, rapid pulse, rapid respiration, pupils dilated, insensible, swallowing difficult; < drinking coffee, > vinegar, with anxiety, convulsions of limbs and involuntary weeping; then insomnia, and in one case delirium tremens; drunken, with restlessness, twisting his fingers and catching at imaginary objects or grasping the bed-clothes, tongue rolling, pulse quick, he often shrank as if suffering from creeping over body.

Unconsciousness; and limbs fell flaccid and lifeless when lifted; with stupid and wild appearance, when aroused she looked around vacantly; half U., sitting with upper part of body bent backward, gagging and pushing out of his mouth white froth, lips bluish, swollen, lids closed, eyes dim, pupils dilated, thirst and weariness, amelioration the next day after vinegar. Coma. Sopor; alternating with delirium.

Clinical.—Raving, with attempts to escape; talking, laughing or singing; *especially with symptoms of terror,* thinks he will be killed or that wild beasts are chasing him. Mania, wild delirium, with terrifying hallucinations. The child screams in fright or an adult is horrified or loquacious, is particularly afraid of the dark. Hallucinations; he particularly imagines that he is surrounded by black insects or by small animals of a dark color. The loquacity of this drug may be compared with that of Hyos. and Lach.; Stram. is persistent in being confined to one subject; he imagines he is talking with spirits or absent people. Very frequently useful in delirium tremens, with visions of animals from which he attempts to escape. In delirium of fever, characterized by an abnormal sense of the proportions of his body, it is similar to Bapt.; the Stram. patient is apt to imagine that certain parts are of unnatural size, or that they are double. Hydrophobia; of all drugs known to us this seems most nearly a specific for this dreadful disease, and some cases supposed to be genuine have been cured.

Head.—Swelling and internal fulness as if it would burst. Raised frequently from the pillow. Moved to and fro. Spasm to either side after a swoon, with redness of face. Dartings in different directions through it, extending to eyeballs and down r. side of nose. *Aching;* in evening; deep in brain; < over eyes, with heaviness; with vertigo and heaviness of head; alternating with lightness and disposition to faint; squeezing; throbbing. Deep-seated throbbing. Fulness. Heaviness; heavy pain in morning on waking. Lightness, with weak feeling. Confusion; with hollow feeling and sensitiveness to every sound and inability to think much. Stupid feeling. **Rush of blood.** Apoplexy. *Drunkenness;* in morning; and heavy feeling in body.

Vertigo; every morning after rising, with want of thought, weakness of memory and vision as through a gauze; at 8 P.M. when writing by gaslight; when standing; when sitting and standing in a room; on raising head from pillow; when walking, with unsteady gait and faint feeling; with nausea; with staggering; with flickering before eyes; with numbness of head; with feeling as if head were drawn backward, also with sleepiness; with loss of senses, sleepiness, sleep with more or less open eyes, when disturbed she jumped up in rage and said a few unintelligible words, when others sang she danced, pulse slow and full, mouth dry, this state lasted twenty-four hours, without eating or drinking; sudden, at noon when reading in open air and walking, with staggering as if he *would fall forward and to the left.*

Forehead.—Wrinkled. Stitches. Pain; in r. side; in morning; in r. side in morning; in afternoon, < walking in open air, > resting indoors; in the room at 4.45 P.M.; at 11 P.M.; on waking and during the morning; sudden, over l. eye at 10 A.M. when walking in open air, and in opposite part of occiput. Tingling as if pins and needles were in it. *Throbbing, and in vertex* and eyeballs; over r. eye; painful, in evening after mental work; sudden attacks of painful, in l. side in evening indoors. Confusion in sinciput, with vertigo.

Temples.—Sticking in r. from 8 P.M. till falling asleep at 11 P.M.; S. to occiput, with thirst. Pain in r. Throbbing, < r.

Vertex.—Pain, making me unwilling to get up till 4 or 5 P.M. Pressure every day, late in afternoon and evening and waking me about 4 A.M., always woke nearly on back, with inclination to r. side, and arms, < r., stretched up and bent across vertex, so that muscles of upper arm felt strained and bruised. Sudden attack of throbbing in r. anterior part, repeated in evening when indoors.

Occiput.—Pain in r. side, occasionally throbbing; P. in l., occasionally throbbing, at noon and 8 P.M.

Clinical.—Vertigo when walking in the dark. It has been prescribed for congestive headache, with fear of going mad from the violent pain. Boring frontal headache, preceded by obscure vision; it has been noticed that when the sight of one eye is blurred the pain is on the opposite side of the head; hydrocephalus. Cerebro-spinal meningitis.

Eye.—Staring; and wild; alternating with unsteadiness. **Prominent; and wide open, pupils dilated, insensible, with injected conjunctiva, as if vessels were filled with dirty fluid** (Bell., Hyosc.); and half closed. Swelling, with dilated pupils and contortions of balls. *Glistening; and restless, wide open, staring, with a peculiar intoxicated look;* and restless, suspicious and roving. Dull and heavy; D. and dark. Sunken. *Redness;* about r., with swelling; < near inner canthus. Inflammation, < r., with lachrymation. Rolling. Surrounded by a blue margin. Pricking. Pressure and tension; P. in l. Feeling in r. as if water twitched about in it.

Lachrymation; with sensitiveness to daylight. **Pupils dilated;** *and insensible;* contracted; contracted after drinking vinegar; insensible. Balls feel sore on turning them; feel enlarged and as if protruding; throbbing at 11 A.M., < l., with lachrymation. Cornea very bright. *Conjunctiva injected;* and bluish. Redness of whites and of margins of lids, with lachrymation. Sclerotic coat pink at 9 P.M., < l.

Lids.—Squinting; of r. Closed; and swollen; half C. and eyes listless. Agglutination at night. Drooping; as from cramp of orbicularis. Swollen and inflamed. Pressure as if swollen, which is the case, or as if oppressed with sleep, hence sleepiness. Quivering like live blood in r. upper at midnight. Paralysis.

Vision.—**Complained that it was dark and called for a light.** *Lost;* almost, afterwards pressure outward from middle of ball at every change of light. *Dim;* in afternoon when reading print; and things seem dissolved and too distant. Amblyopia. Weak, with pressure in eyes. Better at the beginning of twilight. Presbyopia. Impaired. If the hand was held before the eye he felt for it at varying distances. On descending stairs he takes two steps for one and falls. Dazzled by rays of sun. Things appear smaller and at a greater distance, as if dazzled. Smoky appearance to the atmosphere. Things look blue and smoky, and at times he can see only half an object. As if through coarse linen, only by pieces, for instance, of a face he saw only a nose. Confused; when reading. All things appear oblique. Dark and flickering on beginning to read. Photophobia to gaslight. Illusions. Black things seem gray. A reddish-gray border around white things. Double; and confused; at other times only parts of objects can be seen; and things awry, he sees small objects at their places, but a little higher up and sideways a second image; black letters seem gray and as if a second light gray one were placed sideways or above it. Objects appear multiplied, diversified and variously colored. Of black spots; moving with the eye by daylight and by gaslight; and fiery sparks. Of a bright spot when reading by gaslight; when looking at the gas flame. Before l. eye in bed in the dark. Of a bright bar directed upward and to the right on looking at the cloudy sky by daylight. Bright green tremulous spots low down in field, before closed eyes. Bright blue spot before l. eye. Dark blue spot in a dark room. Fiery. Of sparks; occasionally entering at a high point and disappearing in lower point of field. Of balls of fire rolling over the counterpane. Luminous vibrations before l. eye at 8.30 A.M. Sheet-lightnings in the dark.

Clinical.—Strabismus.

Ear.—Shooting. Tearing in r., with shooting through forehead and vertex. Pain; in l., pressing down to cheek. Dryness in r. Eustachian tube. *Deafness.* Hearing obtuse at times; very acute. Hallucinations. Ringing; < l. Roaring, and hearing almost lost.

Nose.—Stopped; feels S., but he can get air enough through it. Dryness; and redness, with loss of smell; of r. nostril, r. posterior nares and r. Eustachian tube. Itching. Sneezing; from dryness of nostrils. Coryza from 10 A.M. till noon, nostrils stuffed, but not much flow. Mucus diminished in morning, increased in evening. Blowing out offensive yellow mucus, becoming fluent. Black hæmorrhage, then warm sweat and general relief.

Face.—Redness; of cheeks; at 1 P.M., and of forehead; and of eyes; *with heat;* without heat of head; *and swelling;* and lips swollen; and of lips, with swelling about lips and eyes, swelling of neck beginning under l. angle of jaw and extending around to right; of cheeks, with bloating, but upper part of face looked contracted and gloomy; purplish, with swelling. *Pallor;* at 5.30 P.M. Brown; dark. *Swollen;* below eyes; on l. side; *and hot.* **Expression of terror** (Atropine). *Anxious* (Secale c.). *Wild* (Bell.). *Vacant, bewildered.* Idiotic. Besotted appearance. Risus sardonicus. Sunken. Drawn. Distorted as by anxiety, with furrowed and wrinkled forehead. Furrows from inner canthi to cheeks and from nasal wings to corners of mouth, knitting of brows, eyes sparkling, afterwards eyes dim. L. side feels swollen, afterwards redness of l. cheek.

Jaw hanging down; clenched; tetanic spasms. Lips and teeth separated; swelling of lower lip; deep redness; bright red (afterwards almost black), feeling stiff and hard and trembling; stick together and have a yellow streak along their red part; dry; *dry and sticky;* sore, parched, chapped, then peeling.

Clinical.—Neuralgia of the face, with twitches, delirium, etc.

Mouth.—Teeth. Grinding. Throbbing in l. lower T. and jaw; in l. lower molars and in submaxillary glands of same side; as if some teeth would fall out.

Tongue.—*Swollen and stiff.* Protruded; *and swollen;* and flabby. Red; on edges and thin, but white in centre. Whitish, with red dots, and tip redder than usual. Papillæ enlarged and projecting through white fur. Furred; white; white, with dryness, burning and scraping in mouth and fauces; yellowish, with disgusting bitter taste. Felt blistered. Boys scratch them with their finger-nails. *Dryness, and on palate;* D. and swelling of T. and fauces; *and white color; and redness;* at apex, and redness; and black color; and its tip curled up; except on edges, and tremulous; and stiff and felt as if its edges rolled up as hard and stiff as sole leather; and felt spongy; and of palate, without thirst at first; so that it glistened, with redness, and with dryness and redness of fauces. Heaviness. Immovable. Paralyzed and trembled if she put it out. **Stammering** (Merc.); and talking between his teeth. **Speech difficult and unintelligible** (Merc.); D. and whispering; *indistinct;* incoherent and rapid; faltering; thick as in quinsy; impeded, as if tongue were too thick or slightly paralyzed; impossible; impossible, apparently from paralysis of tongue. Dumb.

Velum palati drawn down, food and drink pass with difficulty and with scratching in velum. Mouth feels raw and sore. *Dryness;* of palate; at night, and in throat; of M., throat and nostrils from 1 till dinner at 5 P.M.; so that he cannot spit, though tongue looks moist; so that swallowing of dry food is difficult, at dinner obliged to sip frequently to help down the food which seems arrested in œsophagus. Foaming; thick; bloody; bloody every morning. Black frothy mucus issued. **Dribbling of glairy saliva** (Merc.). *Drooling* (Merc.). Salivation. Bitter taste; in forenoon; to food. Taste pasty; like sand to food, and it balls up in œsophagus and threatens to suffocate her; like leather to water, like sulphur to eggs; flat after sunset and next morning; like straw to food; lost; lost to rice-water, which feels like apple-cores in stomach.

Throat.—Externally swollen as in mumps. Difficult hawking of tenacious mucus. Blush one-third the extent of pharynx and œsophagus, a band of vascularity half an inch broad at junction of air tube with pharynx, larynx less injected, rima glottidis thickened and turgid. *Grasping at throat.* **Spasm on attempting to swallow, as in hydrophobia. Constriction; of muscles on attempting to swallow;** of fauces after a meal; of fauces, making respiration difficult; **spasmodic, with paralysis.** *Choking;* in fauces; so that the child could scarcely vomit; on attempting to swallow the first bite of food, C. like a dry stripe extending to stomach, which he was trying to swallow but could not get down.

Stitches in pharnyx. Soreness; and in fauces. Scraping; on swallowing. Pain; drawing, in fauces; constrictive burning, with sensation as if a ball were sticking in it. Burning; as if a hot stone were in it, and thirst not diminished by drinking. Feeling as if boiling water rose in it. **Dryness;** *of fauces;* **of fauces, with redness and difficult swallowing;** of fauces, which are almost white; **not > water, with difficulty in swallowing;** < swallowing saliva; *of fauces, but he would not swallow when water was forced into his mouth;* with saliva like stiff froth mixed with cotton-wool. Uneasiness, with shivering. Feeling of mucus at back; after sunset; > hawking; causing swallowing; causing hoarseness and hawking. *Paralysis of pharynx.*

Œsophagus.—*Seems drawn together. Constriction and spasm* (Merc.). **Swallowing difficult;** *of water;* with stinging in throat; with pain in submaxillary glands. *Swallowed drink hastily* (Merc.). Swallowing impossible; of bread and milk; during coma, from paralysis of the parts that had been affected by spasm, with stertor from a similar change in larynx.

Stomach.—Hunger, with tearing in abdomen, but inability to take food. Appetite increased; diminished; poor at breakfast; lost; lost for breakfast; lost, with oppression at pit of stomach. *Great desire for acids* (Verat.). **Thirst;** *not > water;* with drooling; with the headache; *for sour drinks.* Eructations in evening; sour E.; odorless; offensive bilious, in evening. *Hiccough.*

Nausea; at 5.30 P.M., with retching, causing pain in stomach, and vomiting of whitish fluid; with discomfort in middle line of chest (in œsophagus ?); with inability to vomit and then dizziness, faintness and difficulty in swallowing and breathing. Retching; ineffectual. Vomiting; of mucus at night; of sour-smelling mucus; bilious, after least motion; of a dark greenish substance mixed with food; difficult, of food mixed with nearly black clotted blood, soon after eating and causing shooting at stomach pit, retching before and after the vomiting.

Sticking in region. Shooting inward in l., then in r. side; in pit; in pit and r. side of abdomen. Pain; in pit; in epigastrium; in region of S. and bowels; on pressure; (towards the heart, < external pressure); corroding; intermittent burning. Epigastric tenderness. Smarted and felt ragged, as if full of sores. Distress at 7 P.M. Anxiety; in pit; in pit, with difficult breathing. Sourness. Irritation. Sensation as of sparks of fire rushing to eyes. Weak feeling as if everything were gone.

Abdomen.—Spasmodic retraction. *Distention;* < region of pit of stomach; with burning; with anxiety in pit of stomach, cold sweat, chilliness of limbs, confusion of mind, stupefied half slumber and anxious evacuations upward and downward. *Meteorism.* Tympanitic. Hard. Tense; and hard; and retracted. Rumbling and growling; R. and pain. Rolling during micturition, with rigors. Gurgling. Emission of flatus.

Tearing, > brothlike stools. Griping; with shooting and looseness. Twisting before stool, during stool colic, distention, rolling in abdomen, vomiting and pallor. Writhing before every stool, blackish diarrhœa every hour. Pain; sudden, in evening, with fainting and shivering; as if abdomen were puffed up, pain even when touching side. Feeling as if a living animal were moving in it. *Sensitiveness.* Sensation as if expanded to the extremest degree.

Tearing as if umbilicus would be torn out, the pain then goes into chest. Drawing in direction of transverse colon changing into tearing, with hunger, but inability to eat. Pain in hepatic region; in lower colon. Shooting backward in hypogastrium after dinner. Griping in pubic region; during stool; in centre of hypogastrium.

Rectum and Anus.—Hæmorrhoidal flux. *Discharge of coagulated blood.* Ineffectual desire. She seemed to have a motion to stool and passed a living lumbricus teres, fourteen inches long, with a little water, but without fæces or relief of symptoms.

Stool.—Watery, preceded by cramps in abdomen; W. and large; and frequent; and brown, several times from 3 till 7 P.M., preceded by pain in abdomen, sometimes brownish-yellow and frothy, full feeling in rectum, during the stools scalding in anus. Diarrhœa; with flatulence, borborygmus and occasional sharp pains; with and followed by shooting downward in rectum; chocolate-brown; fæculent dark brown at night and all next day, with griping across hypogastrium before stool, straining during stool, and straining with the urine at the same time. Two in one day, next day relaxed stool when straining on bladder, third day relaxed, dark brown. Constipation. Hard. Difficult, painful, the last part could not be evacuated by straining, but came easily after the straining ceased. (Bloody.) **S. and urine suppressed.** Decreased.

Clinical.—Diarrhœa during typhoid, black, putrid, with loquacious delirium, desire for light, fright, etc.

Urinary Organs. — *Bladder empty.* Paralysis of bladder. Retention of urine, with muscular paralysis. *Micturition only after twelve hours. Micturition dribbling;* M. by drops, urine warm and sensation as if a cylinder were pushed through urethra, after vinegar a thin stream and less frequent desire. M. stops except when straining; but frequent and copious. Frequent M. at night; F. by drops, the emission delayed for a minute before it came, yet much was discharged in the forenoon. Involuntary M.; and copious; and involuntary bloody stool. M. without effort, he was able to retain the urine, but felt as if he had not the power to retain it and to close the neck of the bladder; at the same time sensation as if urethra were too narrow and unable to expand. M. painful and urine alkaline. M. difficut and urine high-colored. Urine increased; and almost watery; and clear, like spring water. Urine dark and of strong odor. U. thick and turbid.

Clinical.—Suppression of urine, especially in typhoid.

Sexual Organs.—Constant uncovering (Hyosc.). Priapismus. Testicles retracted, penis erect as in chordée. Scrotum œdematous. Energy lost. Excitement; insatiable in women. Discharge of black blood from uterus. *Menses increased* and in large clots. Menorrhagia, with drawing pains in abdomen, thighs and other limbs.

Clinical.—Dysmenorrhœa. Puerperal convulsions. Puerperal mania. Nymphomania, either puerperal or menstrual, with great violence.

Respiratory Organs.—Suffocative *spasms of glottis* from vomiting. Pain in region of larynx. **Voice hoarse; and croaking; V. high, squeaking and out of tone, speech unintelligible; lost, she could only utter a hoarse croaking sound that alternated with a sonorous, croupy, barking cough, and inability to swallow from spasm of muscles of deglutition;** *weak;* loud and harsh.

Cough, with palpitation, anxiety, constriction of chest and convulsions; *spasmodic C.,* < evening and next morning; dry; dry, rasping, loud, from dryness in throat; loose rattling, in morning, with expectoration. Expectoration of white, frothy liquid; of thick mucus, without regard to where it fell; of blood..

Respiration. — *Suffocation.* Stertorous; and slow, deep; and blowing at each expiration. *Difficult; and rapid;* and slow; and slow, deep. *Oppressed, with tightness across chest; O., with desire for the open air. Unable to inspire a sufficient amount.* Expirations blowing or hissing, forcing reddish saliva through the closed lips, during the convulsive movements. Gasps and sobs. Sighs. Moans. Rapid; during coma; and at times gasping and choking. Slow; and irregular.

Clinical.—Spasmodic suffocative cough, with jerking of the extremities. Asthma, desire for open air. Spasmodic asthma (very important), < talking, hardly able to inspire. Most violent paroxysms of whooping cough, with suffocation almost convulsive, the child starts up in fright. Occasionally useful in pneumonia, with (the peculiar) delirium.

Chest.—Sticking in a spot in vicinity of fifth and sixth ribs. Cutting in sternum in evening after lying down, > emission of flatus, but returning. Pain from talking, and in sternum; sharp P. about junction of middle and lower third, l., then r. side, < walking, > warmth. Hard pressure on cartilages of third and fourth ribs, with difficult breathing. Tightness at night, obliging me to take frequent deep, forcible inspirations. Feeling as if something in it turned around; then heat in face. Dryness; with girding across it.

Heart.—Pressure in region. Uneasiness in region, with faintness. *Palpitation;* in afternoon on slight exertion. Violent beating; waking her from deep sleep. Action feeble; and intermittent. Pulsation slow.

Pulse. — *Rapid;* and full, strong; and hard; in evening, and hard; *and soft, feeble;* and feeble; and feeble, faltering, intermittent; and intermittent; and contracted; and small; and small, compressible; and small, and heart's action irregular; and small, soft, also could not be felt at r. wrist, nor the beating of the heart; afterwards slow, with prostration. Febrile. Strong, tumultuous. Hard. Tense and intermittent; T. in morning and unequal. Heavy beating in arteries at 7 A.M., < head and chest. Full; and hard; and irritable. Slow; and heavy; and full; and small, feeble. Intermittent. Irregular, a few rapid beats following some slow ones; I., sometimes hurried, fluttering, sometimes tense and strong, often indiscernible. Weak; and small; and tremulous, unequal, sometimes intermittent. Almost imperceptible, but during the coma it returned, was quick, small, sharp and thready. Imperceptible; afterwards rapid and strong, then rapid, unequal and intermittent.

Neck.—Swelling. *Spine sensitive, the slightest pressure caused outcries and ravings.* Stiffness.

Back.—Drawing tearing, and in upper abdomen. Pain in a spot. Pain as if beaten, and in shoulder; in B. and abdomen on motion. *Drawing pain in middle of spine; and opposite in posterior part of stomach;* D. pain in a spot on touch. Stiffness. Pain between scapulæ when coughing. Sticking in loins midway between hypochondria and iliac crests in evening when playing the piano. *Drawing pain in sacrum.* Rheumatic pains in lumbar region.

Clinical.—Sometimes useful in early stages of locomotor ataxia.

Extremities.—Swelling of hands and feet. Motions; < hands; peculiar, almost convulsive, in upper, while the lower were nearly paralyzed. Thrown to and fro; with screams and cries. **Trembling**; *of hands and feet;* of one; with shuddering; as in chill, yet heat of skin; < hands, with movements as if she were afraid of falling, body bent backward. **Twitching; of tendons**; every five minutes; **of hands and feet**; of hands, feet and legs, < l. fingers; of legs and < arms; alternating with opisthotonus, and during the coma T. of limbs still alternated with spasmodic motions of hands and arms. Convulsions; alternating with stiffness, the C. sometimes caused by external impressions, such as touching skin.

Aching. Sensation as if joints were separated; in hands and legs; as if arms and legs were separated from the body. Tingling. Weakness. Little control over. Immobility; a kind of catalepsy. *Falling asleep.* Numbness of hands and feet. Paralysis.

Upper Extremities.—Arm. Trembling when eating; choreic T. Jerking; of muscles, then darting pain through forehead. Pain in l.; twinging, near external condyle of humerus; drawing, above r. elbow. Jerking twinging pain in muscles and tendons of back side of l. forearm, extending to index. Sticking in forearm, with rheumatic constrictive pain in deltoid.

Hand.—Trembling when eating; when he seizes anything. Motions of H. and arms as if spinning and weaving; M. as in chorea, with twitching of fingers; violent M. and subsultus tendinum. Grasped a glass convulsively after drinking though she wished to set it down. Tingling in back of l. Could not be closed to make a fist. Finger-nails purple, limbs cold.

Lower Extremities.—Redness and heat, R. < anterior part of thighs. Walking difficult; impossible. Bending when walking. Stumbles against a door whenever he goes through it. Swaying to either side or forward in evening when walking. Staggering; and falling to the right; *after sunset, next day at* 1 P.M. *walked somewhat in a circle to the left;* tendency to S. backward at 9.45 P.M.; and convulsive gait; with convulsive starting of lower limbs and backward flexure of spine; yet the limbs obey the will so readily that he feels as if he had none, they feel longer than they are, so that he thinks he has touched the floor when the foot is a span away, hence he always put the foot down too quickly. Convulsion of l., beginning with shocks, drawing the limb inward and upward. Weakness. Rigidity, so that on attempting to stand he fell over; spasmodic R. Paralysis; with coldness and with agitation of the rest of the body.

Thigh.—Paroxysmal jerking and drawing upward and inward of anterior muscles. Sudden shooting in outer part of r. in afternoon when walking, it felt numb on rubbing it. Drawing pain. Pain in muscles on outer side of r. hip-joint on walking.

Knees gave way and feet staggered. When placed on his legs he would kick them outward but could not stand, and they did not remain quiet a moment. Sticking on r. tibia. Pain in r. leg, < patella. Heaviness of legs when walking. Numbness of l. leg, with stiffness and with tickling creeping under cutis, > rubbing and stretching. Paralysis of legs. Rheumatic drawing in l. ankle in evening. Sudden sharp pain in r. heel. Feet and legs swollen, hard, skin tight. Feet weak. He cannot stand on his feet.

Skin.—*Redness; first on upper part of body;* of an old cicatrix on forehead; in patches of irregular shape on face; < face and trunk, with roughness; with heat and moisture; **scarlatinous** (Bell.); *scarlet spots;* erysipelatous, of face and upper part of body, > venesection; crimson; crimson, > pressure, but returning rapidly. Copper color on l. knee; down to knees; on face and chest, and mottled; suddenly. When the copper-colored eruptions began to decline the alæ nasi and space around mouth and a spot on each temple were white. Of leaden hue, cold and clammy. Pale and cold.

Red rash; as in scarlet fever, but more shining; *as in scarlatina simplex, > pressure, but returning immediately, on hands, arms, face, neck and back;* as in scarlet fever, on face, neck and back. **Scarlet efflorescence,** *brighter than in scarlatina;* S. efflorescence, elevated and rough, with heat of skin. Itching eruption; with swelling and inflammation; E. resembling rubeola but more prominent, covering body. (Spots like flea-bites on arms.) Small, brilliant petechiæ, many stellated, covering face, neck and breast. Pimples covering body, with fever; P. like blotches on several parts of body and in palms, with stinging itching, < rubbing; on r. side of nose, painful to touch and occasional stinging in it, next day full of pus. Inflamed, painful pustules exuding acrid water, on l. thigh. Boil in groin. Vesications after the violent symptoms had subsided; painful V., oozing hot, acrid fluid, near l. calf and spreading over whole leg.

Formication in abdomen; in limbs; from l. side into thigh. Itching, < face.

Clinical.—Erysipelas of the head and face. Occasionally called for during the cure of abscesses, especially of l. hip; in this disease there may be most violent pain, which we do not often find in the Stram. patient. Scarlet fever, quite frequently indicated before the eruption appears, sometimes afterwards, particularly in the malignant type. Suppressed eruptions, with delirium, etc.

Sleep.—*Sleepiness;* in evening; at 9.30 P.M.; on waking; after the excitement, with depression of pulse and prostration; *then coma;* but she woke as soon as she fell asleep and began to prattle and laugh in a senseless manner. Narcotism, then wakefulness for twenty-four hours. Slumber, with rattling breathing, bloody foam at mouth, dark-brown face and death. Sleeps in the daytime and wakes with a pompous look. Falls asleep frequently, and on waking assumes a comically majestic appearance. Sleeps twenty-four hours. Wakes late. *Deep sleep, with snoring;* D. sleep, with difficult, deep breathing and snorting; with various dreams and apparitions; full of dreams, with an emission, then dizziness and vision as through a gauze.

Stupefied half slumber. Sleeplessness all night, with tossing about and screams; S., with walking about the room and hallucinations. Frequent waking; with sickness and vomiting. Restless sleep. Starting up in sleep; with rising up in bed, looking around vacantly and talking incoherently; waking with a start, as if dreaming. When slumbering he hears two persons talk, but does not know who they are. Dreams of different kinds; agreeable; wonderful; frightful; vivid, about things that have happened; wandering, indistinct; amorous.

Fever.—*Coldness;* from 6 till 7 P.M.; with cold sweat; with heat in head, during the hot stage cold feet, during the sweat cannot bear to be uncovered; then heat in face; sudden; shuddering, whenever he takes a dose; shaking, through whole body, with single jerks, partly of whole body, partly of single limbs, of elbows and knees; shivering, with uneasiness about throat; *S., on chin. Coldness and pallor, except of head and face, which were red and hot.* Cold face. **Cold limbs**; at night, with shuddering; and trunk; C. and heat alternately in limbs, which trembled; *hands and feet, often bluish,* also face; lower limbs; feet in morning, they are sensitive to least cold draught. Cold skin; with moisture; with clammy sweat, hands and feet livid.

Fever; in afternoon; in evening when walking, with thirst and burning above knee; on least motion, with sweat; with sweat, without thirst; with quick, small pulse and red face; with redness of skin, itching eruption over face and trunk, but feet and legs were cool and pale; he covers himself carefully during the heat, if he merely puts a finger out from under the covers the pains are very violent; then coldness and shivering, hands constantly cold, general chill, trembling and feeling as if cold water were poured down her back; *dry;* remittent typhoid, with pains beginning in l. ear and ending in l. side of chest, the pains < dry cough. **Heat of face. Heat of head**; as if fire mounted to it, also affecting stomach; then general coldness, then general heat with anguish, sleep during the heat, thirst after waking, stinging in palate until he drinks. Heat rising from abdomen, with anxiety, causing redness of face. Burning on dorsum of foot. **Hot skin; and dry, scarlet**; on face and upper limbs; on trunk, with sweat; < face and upper limbs, with congestion.

Sweat; at night; cold, clammy; *cold, on whole body* (Verat. a.); on head; on head all day; on forehead while rest of body was red, dry and hot; on face; on back; on limbs; on lower part of paralyzed lower limb; cold, on paralyzed limbs. Dryness of whole body.

Strophanthus Hispidus.

A tincture is made of the seeds of this plant, which belongs to that great order of cardiac poisons, namely, the *Apocynaceæ.* It acts directly upon the cardiac muscle. Compare Apocynum can., and allies.

From a toxic dose, the heart, together with other muscles of the body, passes at the first onset from contraction to cadaveric rigidity, and its muscular fibre assumes an acid reaction. The action upon the heart is accompanied by an increase of blood-pressure, and in certain conditions by increase of urine and by lowering of the temperature. Face flushed, lips scarlet, eyes brilliant, temperature high, skin dry, pupils dilating and contracting alternately every few seconds, pulse 140, arteries distended, l. ventricle contracting with unusual vigor, aortic valves closing with a loud and distinct "tup," a slight mitral regurgitant murmur, loquacity, no micturition for ten hours. Purging and vomiting.

Clinical.—It has been found valuable for weak heart, the pulse becomes slower, stronger and more regular; it acts well in chronic nephritis, it increases the flow of urine and diminishes the dropsy, it, however, does not seem to act well when there is much œdema of the lungs. It acts best in functional disturbance of the heart, from alcohol, tobacco, tea.

Sulfur.

Pure sublimed Sulphur is triturated for use (a tincture, saturated solution with alcohol, represents the first centesimal dilution).

General Action.—A tissue remedy of widest range. Since Sulphur is an integral part of every form of protoplasm, it follows that all tissues become affected by its abnormal exhibition, and no particular limit or character can be assigned to it. Its action on the dermoid tissues is, however, very pronounced.

Allies.—**Lyc.**, *Puls.*, Phos., Rhus t., Calc. c., Nat. m., Sep., Aloe, Hep. s.

Generalities.—**Emaciation** (Iod., Nat. m.). Blood darker in color and richer in white corpuscles; the venous blood seemed partly melanotic, changed less in the air and in part did not become red, the arterial blood was redder and turbid, dependent on the dissolved coloring matter of the blood, the blood took up less oxygen and gave out less carbonic acid than before the use of the Sulphur, coagulum formed slowly, clot three per cent. larger than before; from large doses death of so many corpuscles that they cannot be eliminated, but if continued smaller doses are taken the blood is freed from blood-corpuscles *which are dissolved;* solid constituents of both serum and albumen diminished; solid constituents and blood-corpuscles diminished, it gave out more carbonic acid and took up more oxygen; diminution of solid constituents, of serum, albumen, fat, fibrin, blood-corpuscles and clot, in only two observations was there increase of fibrin, in a third increase of fat and clot, in a fourth of serum and albumen, in a fifth of serum and clot, *in general every secretion and excretion is increased* (Phos.; Calc. c.).

Stretching at night. *Trembling; when walking* after smoking a cigar, *with weakness;* in evening, with anxious sweat, then vomiting, with anxious urging to stool, then heaviness of head and weakness of arms; of l. scapula, arm and hand in forenoon. *Starting in forenoon when awake, with shivering through whole body.* Jerking here and there; J. in whole body after supper, with pain in back and r. side of abdomen; of muscles of face and limbs in morning, becoming a general convulsion, then consciousness returned slowly, as soon as reaction was established after a chill the spasm returned in a tonic form, first in r. side, then in front of body, then in back, finally jaws were set, muscles relaxed and the child died instantly.

Hysterical paroxysm, with choreic jerkings. Conclusions; tossing the body up high. Epileptic paroxysm after starting up or after running violently; E. paroxysm starting from back or arm, as a running like a mouse, drawing the mouth to right or left and moving about painfully in abdomen, then twisting l. arm, with retracted thumb, then trembling of r. arm, then the whole body was shaken up and down, with shortness of breath, which after the paroxysm was shorter, screaming during the paroxysm, but inability to speak.

Sticking, < morning and late in evening, > motion and sometimes pressure. Sudden tearing here and there, with jerking; frequent sudden T. in evening, in l. cheek, r. cervical muscles and r. tibia; intermittent sticking T., at one time through various parts of head, at another pain through bones of cheeks, in region of ear, lower jaw and other parts of face. Pinching here and there in muscles. Tearing scraping in middle of r. thigh and on vertex and in r. ulna and radius. *Pains throughout body;* in root of nose, between shoulders and all over back; occasional flying, in phalanges of fingers and in other parts of body. Pinching here and there in muscles. Bruised feeling in morning after rising; in morning after waking, < arms.

Drawing pain in lower incisors, thighs, l. fingers and below r. scapula; in abdomen and all limbs, lasting for hours in arms, for days in thighs; in upper jaw and limbs, alternately r. and l.; alternately in r. wrist and in forehead; in one part, then in another, < r. wrist and thumb, with weakness, the pain < motion; in forenoon, now in r. hip, now in l. forehead, now in l. occiput; at 8 A.M. in l. side of jaws, then in r. thigh, r. metacarpus and r. fingers, next evening alternately in r. and l. thigh, third afternoon in middle of l. thigh, then in r. forearm and r. thumb, then in l. zygoma towards l. parietal bone, then in r. molars and r. middle finger, fourth forenoon in l. great toe, then in r. upper molars and metacarpal bone of r. thumb, then in middle of internal aspect of l. thigh, then in first phalanx of r. index; in afternoon during rest, now in head of fibula, now in l. side of forehead, now in l. elbow, now in r. great toe. Sudden drawing in r. thumb and index, r. forearm and in top of l. ear towards occiput.

Contractive pains, < muscles of thighs, impeding walking, afterwards the pains were in the bones, < femora and r. tibia, head of r. tibia painful and intolerant of touch. *Inclined to take cold. Sensitive to open air* (Hep. s.). Feeling of illness; in morning. *Discomfort;* at noon; in evening; as if whole body were dislocated. Full feeling in body. Tightness in whole body in afternoon and evening, < about chest, as if externally, with anxiety, after lying down sweat and then relief. Tremulous sensation in morning; sensation as if everything on him trembled and throbbed at night when half awake. Throbbing in temples, on neck and about heart. Nervous feeling. **Uneasiness** (Rhus t., Puls.); **the day before menses, with apprehension**; in morning; *at noon, with excitation of nervous system;* in evening; in bed; **with orgasm of blood**; with pain in forehead and heat; *in blood,* with swollen veins on hands.

Weakness; all day; *in morning; in morning, with swollen eyes and inclination to stretch* (Rhus t.); in morning, with bruised feeling in limbs; on waking at 4 A.M., with tensive pain in l. loin; at noon; towards noon when walking; **in afternoon;** *in afternoon, < sitting, with tensive headache and cramplike pressure in hollows of knees extending to malleoli;* at 2 P.M., sleep disturbed by confused dreams; every day from 2 till 3 P.M., with sleepiness; *in evening;* in evening, with yawning; *after waking;* on waking from a dreamful sleep; *after dinner;* after dinner, > walking in open air, with fulness; after eating; *after stool; from a short walk;* when walking after dinner, with aching in stomach; when walking in open air, with eructations and nausea; when walking in open air, with paroxysms of dim vision, pressure and beating in head and nausea; after walking, with nausea and trembling of limbs; from riding in a carriage, afterwards he slept all day; from exercise during menses, with irritability; from slight movement, with loss of breath, constant distention of abdomen and frequent swelling of feet; > **walking** (Rhus t.); > *walking in open air* (Puls.); *with aversion to everything, even to talking; with trembling of hands and feet;* at night, as if he had ridden or swum far; on lying down, making him faint; faint-like, on appearance of menses, with vomiting of blood and black tasteless liquid.

Walking was irksome, heaviness of feet, with tension across chest. Faintness; in afternoon, with vertigo, vomiting and sweat; like a weakness of limbs. Weight in bones of arm and chest in forenoon. Want of life, like an internal coldness, heat alternating with chilliness, pale look, with blue rings around eyes, dread of heat in the cold and dread of cold in the heat. Falling asleep of arms, cervical muscles, scalp, nates and feet, < lying. **Symptoms occur mostly during rest, > moving the affected part or walking** (Rhus t., Puls.); S. occur when walking in open air, especially in head and stomach. Aggravation in l. half of body; A. from beer; when standing; of pains by cold, amelioration from external warmth. Amelioration after hard stool; after emission of flatus smelling of rotten eggs.

Clinical.—It is very frequently valuable in acute diseases when the carefully selected remedy fails to act on account, probably, of constitutional disease; a few doses of Sulphur will temporarily modify the condition so that the indicated remedy can antidote the acute trouble. Chorea. Neuralgia of various sorts, sometimes periodic. Chlorosis. Marasmus. General effects of the suppression of eruptions. Various forms of scrofulous diseases. It is peculiarly indicated for people who have very red lips and redness of the other orifices of the body, often with soreness and burning. It is particularly suited to people with light complexions. Frequently indicated for diseases which alternate with some phase of skin trouble, especially when there is a general disagreeable odor of the exhalations of the body, general aggravation from bathing and aversion to it. Suitable for people who have harsh, rough skins, whose hair is course, but who are weak and liable to eruptions. Lithæmia, some of its various aspects, indicated by its numerous characteristic symptoms.

Mind.—Delirium, she destroys her things, throws them away, thinking that she has a superfluity of everything, and she wastes to a skeleton. Fancies that she has beautiful clothes, old rags look like fine things. Imagines that she has given injurious things to people from which they are going to die. Fancies that she is becoming emaciated. She talks nonsense. Excitement at night on going to bed; *on violent motion, with passion;* after tea; indolent, almost as after coffee. Earnest exaltation in forenoon. Agitation, with sore throat. Cheerful; in morning on rising, and clear, decided, but the confusion returns at 9 o'clock and is aggravated by earnest thought.

Ill humor (Calc. c., *Lyc.*, Ph. ac.); *in morning after rising;* in morning, **with restlessness;** < *morning and evening,* **with lachrymose mood** (Lyc., Nat. m.); **at herself; and no desire to talk; and absorbed in himself; and faultfinding; with confusion of head as in outbreak of coryza; with dulness in head and bitter taste;** *and impetuosity; he answers no one and will tolerate no one about him, he cannot obtain quickly enough what he desires; and melancholy, discontentment with himself and all about him, which unfitted him for serious occupation, cheerfulness returned for a short time on satisfying his appetite, but in* *the evening he was absorbed in himself, could not command his thoughts to read and stared at the same page upward of two hours.*

Out of sorts with everything in evening (Lyc., Puls.), *for work, pleasure, talking or movement, uncomfortable and does not know what is the matter.* **Quarrelsome** (Nux v.). **Impatience**; before urinating. Embittered mood, as if he had been insulted *Violence in a child. Vexatious and morbid ideas of the past associate themselves with indifferent things,* with courage. *Morbid ideas causing rancor* (but also joyous thoughts and melodies) mostly from the past, < *evening in bed, when they prevent sleep, with neglect of business. Obstinacy.*

Anxiety; *in evening; in evening in bed,* at the full moon; **in evening, preventing sleep** (Lyc., Puls.); **at night on waking, with heat** and cramplike sensation; > drinking a few glasses of cold water; **with heat of head and coldness of feet,** *he forgets what he wishes to do;* with involuntary thin stool; (with feverish delirium, dyspnœa, burning in stomach, vomiting, twitching of whole body and death); *as if he would die;* about my health.

Pleasure in nothing. Low spirits; *during the day, becomes lachrymose if one attempts to console her; in afternoon in open air; about her illness; and sighing,* so that he could not speak a loud word; *in attacks during the day, with desire to die; sudden, in evening, with disinclination to everything; sudden when walking in open air, which made her anxious, suspicious, peevish and lachrymose;* alternating with cheerfulness. *Despondency; and indifference. Complaining, moaning, wringing of hands, thirst and little appetite, though she swallows her food hastily. Discouraged; and weary of life.*

Weeping mood; during the nightly cough, with restlessness; during the morning stool, with obstinacy; alternating with laughing. *Disinclination to talk. Starting up even when his name is called.* Fright on waking, with distress and horror of instant death. Fear that he would take cold in the open air. Timid. *Haste when taking anything and when walking; H. during the day, with uneasiness and inability to steady himself.* Inclined to philosophical and religious reveries. *Aversion to business. Indolent;* mornings, with pain in back and lower limbs, forcing her to sit down often; and irresolute; and immovable, without definite thought.

Distraction of mind; and awkwardness at his work. Forgetful; of proper names; in respect to well-known localities. *Stupid;* and soon fell asleep. Weak-minded and could not connect two thoughts. Mistakes as to time, thinks that it is earlier than it is. Thoughts of the business that had been accomplished thronged upon him in the evening. Words and sentences that he hears revolve involuntarily in his mind. Feels great need of rest of mind and is in constant motion.

Clinical.—The well-known disposition of the Sulphur patient is irritability, sometimes alternating with mental indolence. Melancholia, with sadness, absentmindedness, sometimes a sense of disgrace. Melancholia after labor. Religious melancholia, particularly associated with abdominal plethora.

Head.—Hung sideways after waking (in a child) and after raising it it fell to the other side, lips and face pale, eyes staring, then it sneezed and eyes were closed tightly for a moment and mucus ran from mouth, then quiet sleep. Moved constantly in bed, because every place seemed too hard. **Sticking; and out at eyes**; sometimes at night, with tearing in lower jaw or followed by bruised pain in side of head, sometimes > compression of head, at times forcing him to lie down. Thrust when coughing. Tearing more in afternoon than in forenoon, > laying it on the table, with weakness and thirstless heat; T. < sides and forehead, > moving head, pressure or free air, with drawing and sticking and ulcerating pain; extending into ear; **as with a saw**; as if skull would be torn open, at night.

Aching; in morning after rising; in morning on waking, < externally on vertex; morning, noon and evening on going to bed, with shivering and pain in limbs; in forenoon; every other day from 8 or 9 A.M. till going to sleep; at 10 A.M.; from 11 A.M. till noon, returning in evening over r. eye; about noon, with heat in it; in afternoon when walking, with weariness, changing in evening to toothache and sleepiness; towards evening; towards evening, with shooting in throat; **in evening and till late at night**; in evening, with coryza; in evening, with attacks of oppression; *at night, disturbing sleep; at every step; on ascending steps; on moving head, with beating of brain against skull;* on coughing and in abdomen; in middle, caused by coughing and sneezing; on pressure, for example, by a tight hat; after eating, with pressure in eyes; in the house, > uncovering head, with tightness of scalp; < *stooping;* < open air, > in the house; > *shutting eyes* and sitting still, with vertigo, afterwards > open air, in the afternoon the vertigo was worse, with nausea, twisting and turning in stomach, yawning, prostration, trembling in limbs and occasionally noises in head and ears, the vertigo > sitting still, < stooping or moving about; *with nausea;* with sensation as if head and ears were stuffed.

Jerking pain. Tensive pain. Hammering pain; on vivacious talking; *after midnight, with pressure in stomach; as if brain beat against skull on nodding.* **Pain in morning, < vertex, as if eyes would be pressed down. Pain as from a cord around head,** *and as from a weight on top of brain;* P. as if head were drawn forward and downward, < forenoon; as if screwed together in evening, with flying heat in face; as if beaten and torn on coughing; as if raw, with intolerance of touch; stupefying; so that eyes seem to close; as from incarceration of flatus. Compression in morning; as from a band at base of brain at 10 A.M., < towards 5 P.M.

Disturbance so that she thought she had lost her reason. *Throbbing in morning;* in all arteries at 2 A.M. **Fulness, as if filled with blood** (see Acon.); *F. in afternoon, with heat. Seems distended,* with loud noises in ears. **Heaviness**; *when sitting, lying, moving and stooping;* < motion; as if he would fall forward, with dulness, both > walking, but then sticking in head. Occasional creeping, < parietal and occipital regions. Sudden paroxysm when walking across the street, blackness before eyes, she walked backward and sat down suddenly and was carried to the house unconscious, then stiffness of joints. Empty feeling in morning. Stupefaction. Stupefied weakness when walking in open air, with gloomy ideas.

Confusion; *in morning;* **in morning,** *and pressure in forehead till noon; in morning as soon as he rose,* also lasting till noon; *in morning on waking unusually early; in morning, > rising;* in morning on waking, > discharge of flatus and going into open air; **in forenoon**; *till noon,* **with pain in forehead** *as from alcoholic drink;*

at noon; in afternoon; in afternoon *after sleep,* > walking in open air; in afternoon, with roaring extending outward at l. ear and drawing pain on l. side of forehead, which soon alternated with cramplike pain in l. knee or l. wrist, or with shooting in root of r. great toe-nail when walking and frequent cramplike pain in l. calf; *at* 5 P.M.; at 5 P.M., < walking in open air, > sweat; at 5 P.M., with digging in l. side of forehead; at 7 P.M. in open air; **in evening; in evening, with pressing in forehead**; in evening, with waving; **at night in bed, with heat and rush of blood**; at night on waking; **after walking in open air**; *on waking, with weight; after dinner,* > *walking in open air;* during dinner, lasting till evening, with weakness; with aching in vertex; with pain in l. side; **as from rush of blood,** < *ascending steps; as from insufficient sleep; intermittent;* vacant, in morning on waking; like commencing vertigo, towards evening; amounting to stupefaction about 4 or 5 P.M., when walking in open air. **Giddy confusion** (Gels.); *in morning on waking; about* 11 A.M., *with dim vision;* at 2 P.M., with heat and redness of face and throbbing in arteries of head and neck, then sweat on face.

Rush of blood; during menses; *during soft stool; when in bed, and he felt the beating in all arteries of head;* after riding in a wagon; from gentle exercise, with burning and creeping in skin of face; *and a pressure in it and out at eyes,* and numbness before ears. Intoxicated in afternoon after a glass of wine.

Vertigo (Acon., Gels., Lyc., Puls.); *in morning; in morning, with nosebleed;* in morning soon after rising, till 5 P.M.; in morning on rising, with weakness (Bry., Lyc., Puls.); in morning, he falls back on the bed as soon as he attempts to stand; *in forenoon;* at 9 A.M.; at 11 A.M., with stupefaction and weakness, necessity to lie down till 3 A.M., in an uneasy slumber in which she heard everything; at noon when sitting; in afternoon; in evening when standing, with rush of blood to heart; at night on waking; at night when lying on back; at night during sweat, with nausea; **on stooping**; *when walking;* **on walking in open air** (Calc., Lyc.) after supper, **she dared not stoop nor look down**; *when walking on an elevation in the open air, with inability to step firmly and obscuration of senses;* on rising from stooping, with weight in head; when sitting, and reeling when standing; with sticking in head; with nausea; with sensation of a fog in head, making him sad, indefinite ideas, with irresolution; then shooting in anus; *to falling forward on suddenly rising from a seat; even to falling down, when walking over running water,* and all parts seem paralyzed; to falling sideways; to falling sideways when walking in open air, with nausea; sudden, during the day, < walking near a declivity; < the accustomed beer at night; in attacks when walking, with apprehension on looking in front of her and crawling ("kriebelig"); preventing clear thought; as if he would faint in evening in bed; like obscuration before eyes, when walking, with reeling to the left; like a tingling and buzzing out at forehead, if she walks rapidly or moves her head suddenly.

Forehead.—Contraction. Stitches; and above it; in bone; above l. eye; in evening; when walking; in r. half, extending into orbit; in l. side at night before falling asleep, stretching to occiput, > pressure; extending outward every day from 11 A.M. till evening; extending outward all day on every step, and on loud talking and coughing necessity to wrinkle the forehead; extending outward so that she must hold it when coughing, and also on loud talking, < evening; flying, in l. supraorbital ridge in afternoon; digging, in a spot deep in r. side at night in bed. *Tearing;* in afternoon, extending into temple, with pain. *Boring above root of nose;* over l. eye. Digging at night. **Pain; in bone;** *above brows;* in r. side; during the day; **in morning**; *in morning on waking and in occiput;* in l. side in morning; in l. side in morning after waking, till noon; in l. side in morning, > rising; in bone in morning after waking, with boring in r. supraorbital ridge; *at* 6 A.M., > *rising and washing;* on both sides of sagittal suture at 8 A.M.; deep in l. side after 11 A.M., sometimes increasing to drawing throbbing pain; in sinciput in forenoon, with confusion; *till noon,* < *above r. eye;* on l. side till noon; about noon, < stooping, and in occiput; above l. eye in afternoon; in l. side of cerebrum in afternoon when driving; in bones towards evening; in evening; in l. side in evening; in bones in evening, and in pit of stomach; at 5 P.M. on waking, > evening after sneezing, the pain recurred next day at 3 P.M., the following day at 8 P.M., with flying shoots in l. orbit; in l. protuberance on waking before midnight; in l. side at night on waking; in bone at night after waking, with boring; *during fever,* > *sweat,* **with restlessness**; *during menses,* < *afternoon;* in l. side on ascending stairs; at every step, with sweat on forehead; after dinner, and in stomach; < **motion**; < *forenoon;* above eyes, with nausea after eating, then heaviness of head; extending across nasal and malar-bones; on l., then r. side, extending to mastoid process, in morning; sudden, in l. side; sudden, about r. supraorbital arch in forenoon; alternating with pains in joints, in afternoon; now deep in F., then in occiput, alternating with gouty pains through joints of limbs; now in F., now in occiput, in forenoon during rest, alternating with gouty pains in joints; **in sinciput as from a band around forehead, with confusion**; *as from a board; as if screwed together, and over it; over eyes, as from stopped coryza every morning,* with sneezing; jerking, above r. eye; stupefying, in afternoon; as after night-watching, changing after a few days to a glowing tearing in r. side of head and teeth, < cold water; contractive, in evening, and in temples. Drawing pain towards noon, which after a few minutes alternated with a similar pain in r. wrist; in l. side during rest, with a similar pain now in l. knee, now in l. outer malleolus, now in l. wrist; in r. side alternating with cramplike drawing pain in r. inner malleolus; sudden, frequent, alternately in r. and l. side and in r. parietal region; throbbing, deep in r. side. Sudden drawing above r. brow; frequent, deep in l. side; D. in F. and temples as if a worm were crawling through them. *Tension. Pressure outward;* in frontal and cheek-bones in morning on waking, with boring, and after midnight much pain. Weight on getting up, < open air and walking, afterwards pulsative pain. Vacancy in sinciput in evening. Confusion, and in temples. Sinciput confused; morning, noon and evening, and heavy; in morning after waking, with vacancy; *in forenoon;* in evening; in evening when lying; at night, with weight in it and frequent waking; on frequent waking from restless, dreamful sleep, with weight in it; and heavy; as if intoxicated, next day more on l. side.

Temples.—Jerking in r. near ear. *Sticking;* in r.; *close to eyes on moving them or looking at anything;* flying, in l. in afternoon. Tearing in l. in evening, with drawing;

in l. T. and eye, with pressure; intermittent itching, in l. bone in afternoon when walking. *Frequent pinching in brain from one T. to the other.* Boring, and in ears. **Pressure from one to the other in morning after rising.** Aching in forenoon; at noon; in evening after reading; *on reflection and mental work, with tension in brain;* after dinner; periodical, then acute drawing pain; throbbing, in l. at 10 A.M., < walking, suddenly > 6 P.M.; throbbing, after walking, < ascending stairs; cramplike, in r. mastoid process; in morning. Cramplike tensive pain below r. mastoid process; close to r. mastoid process in afternoon during rest, extending into deepest part of bone, then shooting in r. temple; frequently in muscles of mastoid processes during the day. Constriction mornings. Painful turning and crawling. Drawing, and in occiput; D. in l. at 10 A.M.; cramplike, below r. mastoid process. Tenderness.

Vertex.—Sticking. Tearing, > noon, returned in afternoon in open air, with burning as if raw; *T. in evening as if hair would be torn out, it bristles on the most painful spots.* **Sensitiveness to touch;** *with boring beneath V.; in spots. Pain; in morning; in morning on waking; at noon, with burning;* about noon; towards noon, < open air, increasing after dinner to heaviness, > evening; in spots in afternoon; *in evening;* at night, and in lower part of occiput, with pressure on eyes, which he must close, and with chilliness, not > covering, offensive sweat and necessity to walk up and down the room; superiorly on chewing, coughing and blowing nose; after dinner, > open air, with drawing in occiput, the pain in V. returned on entering the room, > sitting awhile; on r. side, with rigor; **as from pressure on top of brain;** *throbbing, in morning;* drawing burning, in bone from 1 till 2 A.M., < touch; feverish, several mornings and lasting twelve hours; like tingling, with pain beneath r. ribs from short cough. *Intermittent pressure inward deep into brain, < late in evening and night in bed, obliging him to wrinkle the forehead and draw eyes together.* Tingling superiorly. *Heaviness.* Confusion.

Sides.—Sticking in parietal and occipital bones when coughing; sudden, in r. half of head at night before sleep, with hot cheeks and ears. Thrusts in r. in evening when sitting. Pain in r. half of brain; in one side as if brain were torn or sore, on opening eyes after midday nap; sharp, beneath l. parietal bone after supper; screwing together, in l. Paroxysmal tension in l. parietal bone at 2 A.M., as if skin were too tight and covered with ulcers, with drawing pains in lower third of thigh.

Occiput.—Sticking in r. side, with burning; drawing S. in l. side after lying down. Aching in forenoon, with drawing pain; A. from noon on, a stupefying tingling in it on stepping; in evening; *at night;* at 2 A.M. on waking; < pressure; extending into nape in morning after rising, with heaviness; *in l. side, as from congestion of blood, after waking;* as from an ulcer on coughing; throbbing, in r. half, also at 5 A.M., with pain in l. loin, the former lasted half an hour, the latter > rising in bed; burning, beneath bone, > afternoon; intermittent burning, in a spot by nape, < scratching; tensive, in l. side; drawing, in forenoon, extending to nape; drawing, when chewing. Drawing; and in nape. Weight in morning, with heat. *Pulsation in l. side, changing to jerking.*

Scalp.—**Hair falls out** (Lyc., Phos.); **in morning on combing. Painful elevations on sinciput and vertex,** one between occiput and r. mastoid process particularly sensitive; *E. on r. parietal region, sensitive to touch; painless E. on vertex.* **Pimples;** on vertex; **itching;** *inflamed;* **inflamed, on occiput.** *Painful pimples;* **on vertex;** *on middle of vertex; over r. parietal bone;* on occiput; *on vertex, then tender elevations in the same place.* **Pustules near nape; grainlike, on vertex, drying into honey-like scabs. Tender scabby elevations on vertex.** Scabs; near nape; painful, on l. parietal bone. *Scales;* white, difficult to get away. Movements from nape over vertex to forehead. Tearing and drawing. Feeling in vertex during the day as if pulled by the hair though he had been bald there a long time. Aching above forehead in morning on waking, > forenoon; *extending from vertex to forehead;* on a spot on r. temple covered with a scab; on l. side as if suppurating, on touch. **Sensitiveness;** *on scratching; on vertex.* Throbbing. Creeping and tension; C. in temples. **Itching; on occiput; near nape;** *in morning; on occiput in morning; on occiput and nape in morning after rising;* **with impatience.**

Clinical.—Neuralgic headaches, with sense of congestion or tightness, < warmth. Congestive headaches, with heaviness; there are apt to be heavy pressure and heat on the vertex, associated with abdominal symptoms. Pulsating headache, < stooping and moving (Bry.). Tendency to hydrocephalus in children, with stupor, suppressed urine and diarrhœa. In hydrocephalus it is to be compared with Apis, especially in the retrocession of eruptions. Tubercular hydrocephalus. Meningitis, secondary stage. The fontanelles close very late in sickly, scrofulous children. Eruptions on the head, usually dry, bleeding easily, burning and sore, sometimes cracking; general relief from scratching. Falling of the hair, with great dryness and soreness of the scalp, excessive itching in the evening when warm in bed.

Eyes.—**Redness; during the day, itching in evening;** of white; with swelling and with pimples on lids. *Surrounded by blue rings; and sunken. Purulent mucus. Matter in morning. White vesicle on the white, close to cornea.* Trembling. **Sticking in r.; burning, as from sand beneath l. lids** (Nat. m.). **Cutting in r.;** jerking, in r. spreading to temple, renewed by touching r. side of tip of nose. **Pain in l. as if rubbed against spiculæ of glass and drawn in towards pupil, necessity to close eye, then burning in eye and lachrymation.** *Sensation of a foreign body in l. in forenoon; in r. in afternoon; in r. in evening. Feeling of sand in morning on waking, with raw pain on rubbing them;* in r. at 3 P.M.

Aching; in l.; in r. in forenoon, and sometimes feeling as if balls were swollen; in l. about 4 P.M. after a glass of beer; in l. in evening; on looking at the flame of a candle; on touch when closed; < working in the sun; as if sleepy, in evening, without sleepiness; bruised, on pressing it together and on touch; tensive, in morning on raising them when waking. *Sensitiveness. Sensation as before inflammation.* Biting; *evenings, with lachrymation.* Smarting, with feeling as if they watered; S. in evening, the candle-light seemed to be a red ring, wherewith he could not see. *Heaviness.* Sensation of fulness of blood. *Dryness* (Lyc., Nat. m.); at 2 A.M. *Itching;* of l. in morning, < rubbing, and extending over face; of l. at noon, with lachrymation.

Burning; and easy fatigue when reading (Nat. m.); *towards outer canthus; in morning* (Zinc.); *in morning after rising; in morning, with adhesion;* in morning, > latter part of the day, with photophobia, but in evening he could not read long by lamplight without fatigue and lachrymation; *after breakfast; in forenoon; in forenoon, with itching, then lachrymation;* in l. in forenoon, with lachrymation; *towards noon, < edges of lids; at noon; in evening; in l. in evening, then lachrymation; after getting up, < external canthus; intermittent, in r.*

Lachrymation in morning (Puls.), **with burning;** *in morning, then dryness;* in open air; from the least light; acrid; feeling fatty. Pupils contracted; dilated from 3 till 4 P.M.; l. distorted. *Shooting through middle of l. pupil deep into eye when reading.*

Ball.—Jerking tearing in l. after dinner. **Aching in evening, with weight and loss of vision;** A. in l. in afternoon; *on moving them; on walking in open air; and in brows.* **Dryness and sensation as if they rubbed against lids.**

Lids.—*Redness, and of conjunctiva;* of palpebral conjunctiva, with a red, itching and burning spot on skin near l. outer canthus. Inflammation of lower. *Swelling; with pain and lachrymation;* of upper, with redness and burning pain; of upper, with dry matter in lashes. Pimple on upper. Stye on upper by inner canthus. Much mucus from Meibomian glands. Gum in lashes; in morning. **Agglutination mornings** (Puls., Rhus t.). **Jerking;** *of lower;* of l. lower; in evening; < afternoon; burning, in r. Frequent closure in morning after rising. Sticking in upper in evening; burning, as from sparks in l. upper. *Prickling.* Sudden tearing in l. upper in evening. *Cutting-burning pain in borders after dinner, < external canthi.* **Smarting sore pain on inner side after midnight, then rubbing dryness on inner surfaces. Smarting as from dryness of margins;** *S. in evening and inclination to rub them, eyes can hardly bear the light.* Aching; in upper; *in evening. Edges sensitive in morning.* **Dryness of inner surface; rubbing,** *in borders of r.* **in morning after waking; rubbing like sand, in mucous surface** *in bed.* **Itching; on edges;** edges of r.; *during the day, with prickling and smarting; in morning, with smarting;* after *dinner,* < r.; *in afternoon, forcing him to rest them every moment, eyes can scarcely endure the light in the evening;* **of r., as if they would become inflamed. Burning externally;** *B. of edges;* in upper; **in morning, with redness, swelling and itching; in edges in morning;** in morning after rising, < r.; *in forenoon; in edges in forenoon; in edges in afternoon, with itching and redness,* and the same on outside of nose; *in afternoon, with lachrymation; with inflammation, redness and tension on motion;* as from sparks in r. upper in evening; as from sparks, and they are drawn together. Heaviness in evening.

Canthi.—Redness of outer. Adhesion of external; A. in morning; with redness, inflammation and exudation. Pain in outer. Tickling in l. outer in afternoon after a glass of wine, increased to itching and preventing work in evening and felt in night on waking, next day T. at 4 P.M., then itching, extending in evening by candle-light to inner canthus and changing into shooting, preventing sleep till midnight, > cold compresses, the second morning afterwards the affected lid covered with a dry cake of mucus, upper lid felt stiff on first opening, on going out lachrymation. Itching in l. outer after walking in open air; I. in r., with shooting; in inner, with biting; in l. external in evening by candle-light and I. of upper lid, the I. increased in evening to burning, lids winked and light hurt the eyes, next morning lids stiff, lids and caruncula bright red, during the day I. on borders, in evening at sight of the candles photophobia and burning of edges of l. lids, lachrymation on reading or writing, with increase of pain, next day vision obscured by mucus, afterwards slighter blepharoblennorrhœa of r. eye. Itching biting in outer. *Burning; in outer; towards noon; in outer in evening, with sensation of a foreign body between edges of lids towards outer canthi;* in outer in evening, with sticking and dim vision; *in outer after rising;* in r. external, with sensation of a grain of sand in it; *with itching and smarting.*

Orbit.—Shooting in upper border of l. before going to sleep. Pain; drawing; cramplike, deep in r., extending into frontal sinus, then alternating with a similar pain in l.

Brow.—Tearing in l. in afternoon. Drawing pain in region of l. at night, with aching in l. ball as if it were swollen and pushed out. Drawing in l. in evening. Burning pain above and beneath it in afternoon.

Vision.—**Dim;** in forenoon; in forenoon, sometimes double, sight lost when sewing; in evening by candle-light, objects seemed enveloped in smoke; *when reading;* **with weakness of eyes and confused dark spots floating before eyes.** *Objects seem more distant than they are.* **Intolerance of sunlight.** *Photophobia.* **Flickering;** after breakfast, with a luminous appearance. **Of dark specks** (Phos.). *Of black flies floating not far from eyes. Dazzled by looking long at an object.* Of a white spot. Of lightnings at night on going to sleep. Illusions as if her skin were yellow. Blinded in morning.

Clinical.—Blepharitis, with itching and burning. Eczema of the lids. Styes and tarsal tumors. Ulcerations of the lids, which are very red and burning. Conjunctivitis, from foreign bodies, after Aconite. Catarrhal conjunctivitis. Trachoma, acute and chronic, with sharp pains like splinters. Pustular inflammation of conjunctiva and cornea, always with great photophobia, sharp pain, etc., < bathing; ulcers, abscesses. Keratitis, parenchymatosa. Kerato-iritis. Iritis, sometimes syphilitic, often in rheumatics. Retinitis. Opacities of the vitreous. Asthenopia. In all the eye troubles of Sulphur there are photophobia, nightly aggravation, sharp, stinging pains, like splinters of glass, and great dread of having any water touch the eye and face. Cataract.

Ear.—Copious wax; < l.; and viscid, fluid. **Sticking in l.;** behind l. in evening; in r. concha after dinner; through r. external meatus towards evening in open air; *as far as pharynx. Tearing in l.,* extending into head. Boring, < r., and in temples; in meatus. Gnawing in bones in front of l., also on swallowing; G. in l. external meatus, with crawling. **Aching** in l.; in l. about noon; in r. external meatus towards tympanum in afternoon and evening; *on swallowing and sneezing;* on cleaning; *as if ulcerated, on swallowing;* sore, in a spot in l. auricle; squeezing, close to meatus, in l., then in r. auricle. Sensitiveness in cavity of r. tympanum. Drawing in bones in front of l.; on swallowing; D. behind ear; in r. after lying down; in l., with eructations.

Sensation as if air were forced into them on blowing nose. *Something seems to come before l.,* so that though he hears everything he cannot understand the human voice. Stopped sensation; on blowing nose. *Tingling* and pulsation; T. and deafness; at times in one, at times in the other, with difficult hearing. Tickling. *Itching in l.;* in l. external meatus, with sweat in it; then burning. Asleep sensation in outer.

Roaring; in evening in bed, with rush of blood to head; ringing, in head coming out at ears. *Ringing;* in morning in bed; *during dinner, with deafness;* when sitting; *< lying down, with roaring as from wind; with humming or roaring in head.* Cracking on chewing, and in joint of jaw; C. as if a string broke in them; like the bursting of bubbles. Noises; in r.; loud, with distention of head; like boiling water, with frequent painful drawing in r. ear. Fluttering; before l. at 5 P.M. Intolerance of noise. Hearing hypersensitive; to the crack of a whip, with *swashing in ears;* in one who hears with difficulty, so that playing the piano causes nausea. Difficult hearing in l. ear after dinner. *Deafness.*

Clinical.—Deafness, with a variety of inflammations in external and middle ear, and perhaps also in the internal ear.

Nose.—Inflammation; *of wings, with swelling. Swelling; with pain and internal ulceration; of tip, with shining redness, whereby anterior angle of l. nostril felt thick, hard and painful to touch,* afterwards on inside the swollen part a hard, transparent, bright yellow mass, detached with difficulty and pain. Redness of tip in evening, with itching and tickling; R. of r. nostril, with sensitiveness to touch, next day r. wing inflamed and painful to touch, < septum, afterwards branlike scales.

A kind of cramp. Tearing after dinner, transiently > pressure. Cutting in evening, with thin discharge. Smarting in forenoon, and in l. lid. Aching; at root; in bones; in a spot on l. nostril; in root during the day; in bones during the day; during the day, with fulness as if one of the bones were thickened and loose; during breakfast, extending into frontal sinus; in bones in forenoon; in nostrils towards noon; at noon; in root at noon; in bones towards noon and after dinner; *in r. bones in evening;* in root in evening; in tip on touch; on touch, < its l. outer edge, next morning tensive sore pain in nose, < tip, feeling as if nose were swollen, inside covered with scabs; intermittent; intermittent, in bones; raw, on edge of r. nostril. Soreness; of mucous membrane; in a spot in l. nostril; in morning after rising, pain severe at noon and acrid flow from r. nostril; in evening, < septum, < touch; of mucous membrane on smoking.

Feeling during dinner and all the afternoon as if mucous membrane detached itself from the bone and rose as a blister, with frequent sneezing. Cracking in upper part, or feeling as of the bursting of a bubble. Rush of blood, < open air. *Crawling as in coryza.* Tickling; in l. nostril at 8 P.M., then discharge of bright, thickish blood containing many sulphates. **Itching; of nostrils, with burning as if sore**; *on outside, < margins, with swollen feeling. Burning in septum* in morning; intermittent, in l. wing in morning.

Dryness (Lyc., Nat. m.); towards tip; of borders of wings, with irritation of Schneiderian membrane as if coryza were coming on; in morning; *in forenoon in open air, with feeling as if mucous membrane were swollen;* in forenoon, with tension; in forenoon, with aching about root; in forenoon, < root, with aching; at noon; at noon, with stiffness; at noon, with escape of one or two drops of fluid and aching in nasal bones; in afternoon; in evening; in evening, with burning on outer borders of wings, which are sensitive to touch; dry feeling in evening though it is moist; in l. nostril after a glass of beer, with sensitiveness of mucous membrane on inspiring air of room; in upper part, with aching; with stiffness; with tension; alternating with watery discharge.

Constant desire to blow it though there was no mucus in forepart, and difficult discharge of viscid, long, narrow pieces. *Stoppage;* of r. nostril; and on blowing it discharge of clots of blood. Stopped sensation at root in morning, with catarrhal voice; in upper part in afternoon and evening, with fluent coryza, burning soreness, discharge of biting water and rough bass voice.

Sneezing; in evening and morning; *in morning, with sensation as if a cold were coming on and frequent blowing out of mucus mixed with blood;* at noon; in forenoon; in afternoon; preceded by nausea; *always relieving head.*

Coryza; *with chilliness and cough;* with rawness in chest, cough and much expectoration; with headache; sudden, at noon, during dinner; paroxysmal; *dry, causing obscuration of head, < eating;* stopped, during the day, with dry cough and stitches in r. side of abdomen. *Fluent coryza;* in morning; *and on blowing nose bloody mucus;* mucus must be drawn through nares. Discharge; from l. nostril at noon. Copious discharge in morning; in evening; with dryness of nose. Frequent blowing in morning; after dinner, with burning in septum. *Blood-streaked mucus;* in morning. Blowing out of thick mucus; in morning, with expectoration; in forenoon; in forenoon in open air, later in the room nose dry and its borders stiff, in afternoon profuse secretion; *yellow, purulent. Watery discharge;* from r. nostril; from l. nostril; at noon; after dinner; in evening; *with dry cough, hoarseness and dryness of throat; trickling; dropping of yellow, glutinous strong-smelling liquid mornings and evenings, without coryza;* burning; burning, at noon. Acrid, watery discharge; in evening; *at one time, then dryness and stiffness, the next moment blowing out thick phlegm, then dryness.*

Bleeding; in morning on blowing; two days in succession at 3 P.M., then pain in nose on touch; third evening of menses; just before and after menses; *on blowing;* blowing out blood at night; clotted, always on blowing.

Intolerance of odors. **Offensive odor of mucus on blowing nose** (Puls.). *Odor of old, offensive mucus* (Puls.); of burnt horn; of sulphur; of soaked peas; of soapsuds; of flowers; sharp biting, as from smoke; bad, to the dinner, which tastes well; like lime to food, but it has a good taste; blunted; lost.

Clinical.—Catarrhs of various sorts, according to the symptoms above.

Face.—Pale; and suffering as after long illness, with discomfort; *and collapsed, expression anxious.* Redness at 3 P.M.; after dinner, with sweat; in spots on r. cheek; on cheek-bones, with burning; dark, on walking in open air, with heat. Yellow. Dirty, earthy. *Distorted, as from long suffering. Swelling in morning;* S. of cheeks, with sticking and pain on touch; red, of cheeks. Roughness of cheeks, with heat and sensation as if they had been exposed to severe cold, then branlike desquamation. *Looks ill;* and has double rings around eyes. Twitching, at times on malar-bone, at times on chin.

Shooting in r. cheek-bone at 11.30 A.M.; in l. zygoma, with drawing. *Tearing in r. half; in malar-bone and at other times in lower jaw, as if they would be torn out;* in r. cheek in evening; flying, in cheeks. Pressure and burning in cheeks and cheek-bones. *Painful pressure on malar-bone and beneath eye.* Bruised pain in r. malar-bone, even at night. Drawing pain in skin of l.

side, above eye, on temples and on malar-bone as far as lobule of ear, < morning. Tension in skin around mouth in morning on waking; around mouth, with dryness and branlike desquamation; as if beginning to swell.

Jaws.—**Glandular swelling of lower;** painful S. of upper above gum; painful, on lower beneath gum; painless on lower, tender on chewing. Cracking in joint on chewing. **Drawing jerking in l. lower.** Sticking in lower, extending out of ear. Tearing in r. upper in evening; occasionally in l. lower during the day. Pain in l.; in l. lower in morning after waking, with swelling around a tooth, as if a gumboil would form; ulcerative, in l. upper. Cramplike pain in l. lower; in l. angle of lower. Drawing-tensive pain in r. Drawing in r. upper; in l. lower in morning after rising; in l. lower towards joint about noon; in l. lower in afternoon; in l. upper about 5 P.M., and in zygoma; spasmodic; sudden, in r. lower in evening.

Lips.—**Swelling of lower** (Hep.), **with eruption on it;** *S. of upper;* of upper in evening, with pain. Upper red and sensitive on its inner surface; red spot on upper; red itching point in middle of upper. Red itching elevation on upper. Elevated tetter in corners towards cheeks. *Painful inflamed spot in red of upper, next day swollen and burning, third day changed into aphthæ.* Cracks painful in middle of upper. *Pimple;* on lower; *on margin of lower, with sticking on touch; painful to touch on upper.* Painless elevation inside upper near r. corner, changing into a pedunculated wart, with three free apices. Aphthæ on r. side of lower; upper; burning, on upper; *group of painful, grayish-white, on inside of l. lower,* afterwards A. on r. upper. *Scabby ulcer on margin of lower, with burning pain.* Vesicles near l. corner; on upper; r. side of upper; middle of lower; that burst and let out acrid, yellowish fluid, on upper, with tension in skin around mouth, which was covered with branlike scales; filled with dark blood, on inside of lower, disappeared after dinner; white, transparent, in middle of lower, appearing next day like herpes labialis; painful, on l. side of upper; painful humid, on lower; *painful group near r. corner,* they burst and left round spots, which next day appeared lardaceous, then dried up and were covered with a scab. Trembling. Twitching. Soreness of l. corner. *Sore pain in corners* in afternoon. Pain in l. corner; in a spot in red of upper, next day a pustule there; on touch. Raw pain in l. corner. Tenderness of upper; after rising. Sensation of a fissure in red of lower, but there was none. Smarting in corners as if raw, < l.; burning, of lower. Sensation as if covered with salt. *Swollen feeling in upper.* **Dryness;** *in morning, with tension; in morning mucous membrane in folds, whitish scales in corners;* in morning on waking, and wrinkles; *when speaking;* and shrivelling; of upper, with sensitiveness; of red of lower, with scabs and tensive pain; **upper lip and margins of nose dry, scaly, rough and burning. Burning; in upper; in upper in morning after rising; with sticking; as if raw.**

Clinical.—Facial neuralgia, involving especially r. side of face and head, < night. (Upper lip more affected.)

Mouth.—Teeth. Decayed, < molars. Looseness, with bleeding of gums; L. of molar, it seems too long and pains on touch and eating. Elongated. Brown mucus on them. Bleeding. Red, salt-sour water exuded from a l. lower molar. Sticking; in hollow, from 7 till 8 A.M. three mornings before menses; in second r. molar at 7.15 P.M.; < biting; through them from a cold drink; *extending into ear, waking him at night;* periodically, with jerking, also after midnight and in morning. Sticking burning extending into orbits and ear, with throbbing. Tearing in a lower incisor in forenoon on inspiring cold air; T. < cold water, at times > warmth, with drawing and often with jerking in tips; intermittent drawing, now r., now l. side, also at night on waking; boring, in a carious T. day and night, preventing sleep. Cutting in r. from a draught of cold air. **Boring and throbbing;** B. in a hollow T. in evening and till late at night, during wet weather; after eating, and externally on head; *as with a hot iron.* Digging in a r. molar, > strong pressure. Jerks through single; in hollow, after dinner. Aching in l. lower from 9 till 10 P.M.; in incisors at night; *from slightest draught of air; in open air;* in almost all during dinner; in molar on touch; renewed by cold rinsing of mouth; *with pain in submaxillary glands;* with swelling of cheek; with inflammatory swelling of gum near stump; in paroxysms, then burrowing, cold is tolerated better than warmth; as if they would be broken off, > in bed, with chilliness. Sensitiveness of tips of upper, < cold water, with shooting. Pain as if too long and tingling; incisors seem too long, with sensitiveness on pressure and in open air, when jerking and tearing extending into l. temple, which is painful to pressure. **Drawing;** in r. molars; lower incisors; upper, l., then r.; in forenoon; in crowns in evening; in incisors till 11 P.M., then sleeplessness till towards morning; in r. upper at night in bed; *in open air;* in molars, < inhaling cold air; with grumbling; in l. upper, with ulcerative pain in their gums; occasional, in morning; throbbing; in a l. lower after midnight, extending over whole lower jaw to temple and ear, lasting till rising next morning, afterwards < open air and extending over whole side of face, pain in spot on lower border of jaw, < touch. On edge; and painful when bitten upon. Loose feeling in evening; L. feeling on biting, and on eating paralyzed feeling.

Gum.—*Swelling about old stumps; S., with throbbing pain;* of r. lower, with sensitiveness. Inflammation, with burning and tearing spreading over head and waking him at 2 A.M., with sensation as if l. cheek were swollen, which was not the case. Painful abscess. *Bleeding; on spitting.* Aching in r. lower in morning on waking and after dinner, with sore pain; A. as if loose, and on inhaling air shooting into it; around a r. lower stump in evening, as if a parulis would form. Sensation of swelling and ulceration in l. upper at noon.

Tongue.—**Coated;** in morning; white; white in morning; dirty yellow; dirty whitish-yellow in morning, with dryness and burning. White. Red, with white papillæ like fungi; redness of root towards evening, with swelling and pain as from pressure, speech obstructed and a hard painful pimple beneath l. side of root. *Hard elevation on r. anterior border, and on moving tongue shooting in it.* Vesicle on l. border; *smarting, on r. side.* Salt mucus sticks to it every morning. Twitching. Shooting in tip in morning; convulsive S. in tip. Biting as from blisters. *Dryness; in morning; in morning on waking, and in palate;* then after an hour slimy taste. *Burning pain.* Burning in evening, and in pharynx; B. in tip. Faltering when speaking. Talking difficult and painful.

Desquamation of inside of cheek. Blisters, with burning pain; B. painful when eating; painful sore, slightly salted food causes biting; on hard palate, preventing talking and eating. Mucus in morning; after midnight, with tickling obliging hawking; bitter, < morning. Roughness, and in throat. Constriction; spasmodic, at the first morsels. Tickling posteriorly on palate. Burning in morning; *at night, with thirst;* with eruption about it; without thirst; causing thirst, not > drinking.

Dryness; in palate; **in morning, with insipidity and stickiness;** *in morning on waking;* in palate in morning after waking; *after eating;* **of palate, with thirst;** with taste of blood; with agglutination and thirst; with scraping in throat as if food would not go down; in l. side of palate, gradually extending to r. side, with tensive pain. *Bloody saliva. Salt saliva;* in morning. **Salivation;** at 9.30 A.M.; waking him at 3 A.M., with aching in œsophagus and clammy taste; after breakfast, with nausea; **after eating;** on beginning to eat; after dinner, with sudden digging in r. parotid; when at stool; sweetish, about 8 P.M.; sour and bitter; water runs from mouth with hawking up of mucus. Bloody salivation in forenoon; in afternoon; in evening.

Taste.—**Pasty in morning.** Doughy. *Insipid;* in forenoon; with loss of appetite. Clammy; in morning. Like bad wood to food. *Metallic. Coppery; in morning on waking.* Resinous. Of sulphur. Of blood in morning after waking. Too salt to all food. As if food were not salted, though it is very salt. **Bitter bilious when fasting, though food has a good taste. Bitter in morning on waking;** in morning, > eating; in palate and throat in morning on waking, > coughing up mucus; *after eating;* to food; acrid, after breakfast. **Vinegary all day; V. after drinking milk. Sour** (Lyc.); **in morning; till after breakfast;** *in evening before going to bed; after drinking milk,* **with sour eructations;** the next day after eating too much; bitter, at noon after eating; salt, when eating. Sweetish; in morning on waking, with mucus; in forenoon; in evening; with hawking of blood; as from fasting, with hawking of mucus. *Offensive sweetish;* all day; *in forenoon, causing nausea.* Disagreeable; in morning; after breakfast; in evening after eating an ice, with nausea. Long after-taste to beer. Loss of T. to food.

Breath.—*Sour. Bad;* in morning; in morning on rising; in evening; after dinner; when coughing.

Throat.—*Swelling of submaxillary glands;* of l.; with sensitiveness to touch; of r., with tension. *Sticking in submaxillary glands, with pain on touch. Swelling of parotids, with stitches; S. of tonsils, with redness and with sore throat, cough, dyspnœa, agitation and sleeplessness;* S., also felt externally about angles of jaws, with stitches in throat when eating. *Redness of tonsils, with painful swallowing.* Elongation of uvula. Mucus; in morning on waking, and in larynx; in morning waking him and requiring to be hawked up; and in chest; salt, at back of fauces, causing frequent expectoration. **Hawking; with clearing of it and scraping** (Nit. ac.); at night from tickling in larynx, with dry tussiculation; on deep breathing; of mucus in morning after waking; of mucus at noon; blackish-gray masses of mucus during the day; jellylike mucus in morning; thick mucus at night; thick disgusting mucus in evening; pieces of hard mucus like starch. Dry food sticks in it, it takes away his breath and he must cough it up.

Stitches towards evening; **on swallowing** (Hep. s., Nit. ac.); in l. tonsil from 6 till 8 P.M., which on swallowing extended into l. ear; < swallowing, with constriction; more on empty swallowing than on swallowing food, when not swallowing pain as from a plug. T. and chest feel cut to pieces on coughing. *Choking, with soreness as if tonsils were swollen, with stitches extending into ears on swallowing. Pain on swallowing;* on swallowing, extending into r. ear; in upper part on swallowing, with pain in upper part of chest; intermittent, at back of pharynx at night till towards morning; *as from swelling of palate on swallowing;* as from a plug. Swollen sensation, with hawking up of a large piece of white mucus. *Soreness, with swelling of cervical glands; S. on empty swallowing, as if she swallowed meat* or as from elongation of uvula; after dinner, with contraction of pharnyx. Sensitiveness in morning.

Spasmodic contraction at middle of pharynx, food will not go down. Constriction of pharynx. *A hard ball seems to rise and close the pharnyx and take away the breath.* When eating, sensation as if something stuck in pharynx. Upper part of pharynx feels closed after eating. Sensation as if stretched. *Irritation in morning, with hoarseness. Rawness. Roughness; of fauces and uvula;* of pharynx; all day, with inclination to cough; of fauces in morning after waking; when swallowing, with pain; of fauces and uvula, < swallowing; with hoarseness and irritation, causing cough, which results in expectoration of round pieces of blue mucus. *Scraping;* all day; in morning after rising, then in afternoon bloody expectoration and hoarseness, at last with headache, which was < going to bed; in evening, with rawness and thirst; in evening in bed, with irritation to cough; *and irritation to cough;* in fauces, causing hawking. Sensation of a hair in it on waking from afternoon nap. Tickling causing hawking; in posterior wall of pharynx all day, causing hacking.

Fermentation in upper part. Disgust and retching. Feeling as of a fatty exhalation from stomach. Rancidity like heartburn on swallowing, < pressure upon trachea. Coldness on inspiration. *Burning in fauces;* B. in morning on waking, with hot breath; *in pharynx, with sour eructation;* like heartburn, just before menses. *Dryness;* in pharynx; in morning, with warmth; in morning, then salt taste in mouth, > eating; at 5 P.M.; *at night,* and on waking much mucus on tongue; *with burning on swallowing and hoarseness;* and tongue sticks to palate, but is moist with frothy mucus; *exciting cough.* Swallowing difficult.

Clinical.—Tonsillitis. Chronic catarrh of the pharynx (see symptoms above).

Stomach.—Appetite. **Increased;** *at noon.* **Ravenous** (Calc. c., China, Cina, Iod., Lyc., Verat.), **if he does not eat headache, lassitude and necessity to lie down.** Great, but a little food causes distention; hunger in abdomen, but fulness from a few morsels. Irresistible desire for sugar. Hunger without much appetite at noon after walking much, the last of the meal was not relished. Little; for breakfast; at noon; at noon, and no thirst; at noon, and after eating fulness in stomach and aching in scrobiculus cordis; and stomach feels overloaded after a little food. For only soft food, not for bread or meat. **Lost**; in forenoon; at noon; for supper; **as soon as he sees food, and he feels full in abdomen and aversion to it when he begins to eat** (Lyc.); and food has no taste and sticks in her gullet; he desires only acids; as from contraction in pit of stomach. *Smoking tobacco is not relished. Aversion to food*, especially to supper; to dinner; *to sour* and sweet things; *to meat*, it makes her qualmish; to meat at noon; to the usual beer in the evening; sudden, to sweets, and to milk.

Thirst; during the day; in morning; *at noon;* in afternoon, *with full feeling in stomach;* after drink; not > drink, which distresses stomach; for sugar-water; for coffee. Thirst for beer; in evening; < an hour after eating.

Eructations. — After breakfast. From milk, till vomiting of mucus. **Empty** (Puls., Phos., Sep.); in forenoon; in evening; **after eating** (Phos.); after breakfast; after breakfast, with sensation as if about to have heartburn; after breakfast, then of food, nausea, and in half an hour vomiting of the breakfast and sulphur; *after dinner;* with taste of the dinner; smelling of sulphur; with relief of symptoms. **Sour** (Lyc.); **during the day**; *after eating; after dinner;* when walking in open air; with distress in stomach from acids; tasting of lead; like heartburn. *Tasting of bad eggs.* Smelling of sulphuretted hydrogen; in evening. Smelling of sulphur; in forenoon. As after onions. Rancid after Weiss beer. Bitter, rancid, of food. Bitter, scraping, of milk. Sweetish in morning. Of the breakfast; in evening, of food eaten at noon; of food an hour after eating; of undigested food; tasting of the food (Lyc., Puls.). Hiccough-like, with pain in posterior part of palate. Tasteless, with insipid feeling in stomach. Ineffectual on going to bed.

Waterbrash in morning on rinsing mouth and hawking up mucus, with retching and discharge of water from stomach; W. in evening, water runs from mouth and he cannot speak, then vomiting of food eaten seven hours previously; two hours after eating, with eructations, running of water from mouth, vomiting of food, nausea and shivering; twice daily, a working in pit of stomach, retching and rising of much water from stomach; > eating; before dinner, making him dizzy and qualmish, then discharge of much water from stomach.

Hiccough in morning fasting; about noon, with fulness in stomach; in evening in bed; on going into open air after eating.

Nausea; during the day; *every morning;* in morning, with retching and vomiting of mucus; in morning on waking, with heat in face; in forenoon; at 9.30 A.M.; about noon, with heat of face; towards 2 P.M.; towards evening, with eructations, rolling in abdomen, emission of flatus and weakness; in evening; *in evening during stool;* at night, with working at pit of stomach as in waterbrash; *before meal-time;* an hour after eating, with waterbrash and pressure in stomach; on waking, caused by mucus that collects in chest at night; before, during and after stool, with burning in anus; with eructations, at first like mucus, then bitter rancidity; with twisting and turning in stomach; with cutting in abdomen and sweat; with trembling of whole body; even to faintness.

Vomiting; when coughing; as soon as she eats or drinks; with sweat; *of food* in morning, with trembling of hands and feet; *in evening of food eaten at noon;* bitter, in afternoon; of a salt liquid as clear as water; sour; frequent, of sour, colorless, watery liquid from 4 till 6 P.M., with faintness.

Swelling of pit. *Stitches;* in pit; *in pit in morning on standing;* at 3 P.M.; in cardiac region in evening; *in pit on deep breathing;* in pit, with several watery stools; from r. side of epigastric region to lumbar region in evening on inspiration. Cramps; at night; before dinner, then sweat till late in evening. Cutting in afternoon. Griping in epigastric region, extending downward. Clawing in morning on waking. Gnawing, then in abdomen, then two stools. Biting.

Pain in region; in pit; beneath pit; in pit during the day; in morning after rising; in pit in morning, with weight; in region in morning on waking, with full feeling; in forenoon; in pit in forenoon; in pit in forenoon, with heaviness; in forenoon after two thin stools; in pit at noon and in evening after eating, then waterbrash; in afternoon after coffee; in evening, with burning; in evening from meat or fat food, with drawing up of abdomen and delay of stool; in pit in evening on touch, with tension in stomach and chest extending to back, as if he had eaten too much; *at night, > eructations;* at night, with burning; **in pit during menses**; *beneath S. when lying; in epigastric region, on touch*, even of bed-clothes; *after eating;* in region after breakfast; after dinner; in region and chest after dinner; in pit, with weight; in pit, with scratching in stomach; extending into back, *after eating;* paroxysmal, in pit and upper abdomen, < morning, > pressure; as if disordered; burning, towards morning, > emission of fetid flatus and diarrhœa.

Screwing-together bruised pain, and in r. lower rib and hip. Squeezing pain all day in pit and chest; in pit, with anxiety, gradually changing into constriction, and at last a burning pain. *Anxious pain;* in pit; *in pit at night, with palpitation.* Tensive pain in l. side of region waking him at night, gradually going to r. side on turning upon r. side, then pain in small of back. Compressive pain at night after waking, > bending up body. Constriction; in pit; in region; all day before menses, < eating, with boring in nape and sensitiveness of scalp; in epigastric region, taking away her breath; cramplike, in pit at noon before eating, taking away the breath; anxious, in region towards noon; burning, waking him in morning and recurring twice in forenoon.

Full feeling; after breakfast; *after eating a little* (Lyc.), declining on rumbling in abdomen; without enlargement; yet good appetite for dinner. **Heaviness**; in pit; in region; in pit in morning on waking; in evening; in region after eating. *Distress from milk, it is vomited curdled.* Anxiety from acids; A., as in nausea. Oppression of pit. Throbbing in pit when sitting, with orgasm in chest, as if it would take away her breath, and faintness. *Loss of digestive power.* Emptiness; in region; in forenoon. Feeling of flabbiness in morning. Crawling, extending to throat.

Coldness; in epigastric region. *Burning;* in and about pit; *in morning;* in region in morning after waking, went from one side to the other when he turned over, > rising; after breakfast, and in œsophagus; in epigastric region when sitting quietly, with hacking in it; < walking and standing, and in abdomen; with cutting and twisting; then rumbling in abdomen and diarrhœa. *Heartburn; all day;* in morning a crawling and burning in forepart of chest; in evening; in afternoon; after dinner; for half an hour after two soft-boiled eggs. Symptoms in pit > dinner.

Clinical.—Seasickness, vomiting of pregnancy, chronic catarrh of the stomach. Weakness and faintness at 11 A.M., with need to eat. Dyspepsia from carbonaceous food, *especially from milk.*

Abdomen.—Distention (Lyc.); *in morning; in morning in bed, > emission of flatus;* in forenoon, > discharge of inodorous flatus, with qualmishness in abdomen; towards noon; in afternoon; *in afternoon, with sore pain upon l. os ilii;* about 6 P.M., with fulness about anus; in evening, with qualmishness; *between 10 and 11 P.M., with emissions of flatus smelling like sulphuretted hydrogen, also at night;* with cutting about navel and frequent waking; *after eating a little; after eating, with heaviness; after a little food, with dyspnœa;* after dinner; after a good stool; *< evening, with hardness; with tympanitis; with tension and bearing down towards anus and tickling there; with bearing down towards colon, the latter < dinner;* with rigor; with insufficient difficult stool; then semi-fluid stool; *then soft stool in evening, with tenesmus and burning in anus, then hot offensive flatus, with griping in small of back;* flatulent, in morning, during scanty menses, with pain in abdomen and small of back, in afternoon flow more profuse, with diminution of pains, which are generally > violent motion.

Rumbling; *all day;* at 5.15 A.M., after stool; in morning, with rattling; *in afternoon, > emission of fetid flatus, with griping and feeling as if a loose stool would pass;* **at night;** *at night, with gurgling; at night, then copious, pappy, yellowish-green, fetid stool; after eating; after breakfast;* after breakfast, with pinching; after breakfast, with burning in anus; *after dinner;* > breakfast, then warmth in stomach; **with diarrhœa**; with rattling; with movement, then thin scanty stool; *then watery stool every half hour;* as from foaming beer, morning and evening, then sudden urging to stool, with cutting, first part of stool hard, the rest liquid.

Gurgling. Bubbling. Grumbling after dinner, not > afternoon stool (an unusual thing for me). Wanderings. *Movements of flatus, causing sticking, < l. hypochondrium;* M. as of the fist of a child. **Flatulence** (Lyc.). **Emission of flatus;** in morning on rising and in evening; after dinner; < **evening and night; offensive; smelling of sulphuretted hydrogen,** *also at* 2 P.M., *then liquid stool of the same odor; smelling of sulphur; smelling of sulphur, then thin and pasty stool; inodorous.* (Ulcers in intestines.)

Stitches; in morning, with griping; *at night,* then frequent emissions of flatus; with cutting, waking her about midnight; here and there in parietes, < groins, now r., now l., > warmth of bed; extending into anus; sudden, shooting through whole body. Cutting; in morning in bed; about 4 and 6 P.M., > warm cloths, with tenesmus and diarrhœa; in A. and small of back, waking her after midnight, then diarrhœa and tenesmus, then also three times next morning; after dinner; before urinating; after a stool that was first hard, then soft; *with frequent pasty stools;* with diarrhœa and stitches in anus; with sore feeling deep in A.; *then soft stool, with bloody mucus;* as if menses would come on, in evening, with weakness on ascending steps.

Griping (Puls., etc.); *in morning before stool;* at 9 A.M. when walking in open air, < umbilical region, > 9 P.M.; at noon, then liquid stool; in afternoon; in afternoon, with tension; at 4 P.M., then call to stool, which was pappy, yellowish-green; in evening, and frequent fluid stools; *at night; at night, then two thin fetid stools;* at night, with diarrhœa three times; **before and during stool,** *which occurred four times a day;* before a soft stool; before stool, with working and emission of flatus, at times with pain as if anus would be torn apart, with straining at stool or tenesmus after stool; *then soft fetid stool, pain in umbilical region and tympanitic distention of abdomen, not < emission of flatus, smelling of sulphuretted hydrogen;* **after stool** (Aloe); after stool, < r. side; *> liquid stool; with diarrhœa;* with ineffectual urging to stool.

Pinching; about noon, then discharge of flatus; in evening, > discharge of flatus; then at dawn copious stool; after breakfast, with grumbling; after dinner; after dinner, with coldness. Burrowing.

Pain; in evening; after 5 P.M., < hypochondria and umbilical region, with contractive pain, and in hypogastrium feeling of paralysis; at 9 P.M.; at night when lying on her back, with cutting in sides of A. and drawing together about umbilicus, next night threatened with a similar attack when lying on back, > turning quickly on to side, then pinching about umbilicus, > emission of flatus; **before every stool;** *after eating; on touch and on walking;* from every draught of air; before going to sleep; then leucorrhœa; < night in bed, > emission of flatus; > diarrhœa; with evacuation of round worms and hard stool; with red slimy stool, fever, loss of appetite and lying down; *waking him at 5 A.M., with desire for stool,* desire > emission of flatus smelling like sulphuretted hydrogen, repeated at 7 and 8, when there were scanty but consistent stools; forcing one to bend up; occasional, in forenoon, < hypochondria, with pinching.

Bruised pain in muscles on touch; in parietes in forenoon at every step; after stool; pain at night as if internally bruised and congested with blood. *Clothes press upon A. Parietes sensitive; after dinner. Soreness after stool; as if raw, < a full breath, cough or violent exercise; as if everything in it were raw, as after childbirth,* and something in it seemed to move, or a sudden sticking in it shooting into head. *Flatulent nightly pain, with retching, anxiety and dulness of head. Pain as if a hernia would form. Drawing pain during menses.*

Pressure downward at night, waking her. Constriction during stool; C. < uterine region; sudden, at night; spasmodic, extending to chest, groins and genitals. **Tension** (Hep. s., Lyc.); *in morning;* in evening, > two liquid stools; > diarrhœa; **of muscles, so that he could not easily straighten up; as from incarcerated flatus;** tense, pressed sensation after dinner, < hypochondrium, with anxious mood. *Anxiety, then weakness in feet extending above malleoli, like an internal trembling.* Uneasiness after a short sleep. Feeling as if something were forced up through the intestines. Qualmishness. Troubles from farinaceous food. Chilliness after eating. Burning, with anxiety.

Upper A.—*Rumbling; as of great bubbles on waking before midnight.* Sticking in small intestines. Cutting, as if in chest. Pain as if everything were loosened and congested with blood, on motion and breathing. *Sensitiveness so that the clothes pressed disagreeably.*

Hypochondria.—Pain extending over sacrum into coccyx and feeling as if everything would come out at anus; P. transversely across beneath ribs (diaphragm?) on coughing and blowing nose. *Soreness on touch in morning; in evening.* Painful drawing in forenoon. Discomfort in H. and præcordial region in afternoon, extending to throat, caused by tension, pinching and tearing, now in stomach and now in region of spleen and back, slightly > empty eructations.

Hepatic Region.—**Bile increased** (Aloe, Pod., etc.). Liver seemed swollen, which hindered breathing. Action of liver impaired, with bilious vomiting and diarrhœa. *Sticking;* < walking in open air; *outward;* backward through liver at noon; *burning, when sitting bent over.* Griping when walking. Boring after dinner. *Pain;* after dinner; *on touch; with dry cough;* with constriction; in liver, waking him at night, with yellowness of white of eye; sudden, and under r. clavicle; drawing, taking away her breath, with necessity to walk bent over all day; tensive and burning. Intermittent throbbing and twitching.

Splenic Region.—Incarceration of flatus, with anxiety. *Shooting;* towards evening, > lying; after a hard stool. Cramp before menses. Pain; in forenoon when walking; at 8 P.M. when sitting; then eructations; wandering.

Sides.—Rumbling in l. *Sticking; on deep breathing* and on walking in open air; *in r. flank, taking away the breath; burning, in l. flank in evening.* Pinching in l. *Pain after midnight.* Flatulent pain in morning, not > emission of flatus; in l. when she had had no stool for a long time, < movement. Heat in l. Falling asleep of l., with chilliness.

Umbilical Region.—Paroxysmal protrusion in one pregnant, at night in bed, as from uterus. Fulness. Sticking; burning, in a spot. Cutting beneath umbilicus; C. in morning, < stooping; after midnight, with tensive pain; after getting up. **Griping**; beneath umbilicus; after luncheon (10 o'clock); *at noon, > discharge of inodorous flatus; beneath umbilicus, with frequent diarrhœa and with burning and tenesmus in anus;* **extending towards stomach in afternoon and evening, > emission of flatus.** Pinching; in evening, compelling him to draw up his legs; paroxysmal, sometimes impeding respiration and bending him double, with frequent fluid stools. **Pain**; > 3 A.M., then in l. side of abdomen, > rising; *across umbilicus, preventing sleep;* at night, waking him frequently; flatulent, below umbilicus in morning on waking. Contractive pain; in forenoon; *pinching, in umbilicus when sitting,* > rising; *below umbilicus, as before diarrhœa, about noon, recurring every half hour, with pressure on bladder, as if it were forced upon groins, and straining at sphincter muscles as in retention of urine.* **Tension**; in a circle about umbilicus on waking, with drawing.

Hypogastrium.—*An incipient hernia forced downward with a bruised pain and cannot be reduced with the hand;* the place of an old hernia protrudes. Inguinal glands swollen and painful. *Fulness;* from 10 A.M., till evening; after dinner; with weight and feeling as if something pressed on bladder. *Rumbling.* Sticking in r. groin; in l. groin, with pain; low down, with burning there and spasmodic pain in r. lower limb; in r. groin, with jerking pain there and sticking in anus; in H. and urethra, with cutting; boring, between 4 and 5 P.M., now in r. groin, now in spermatic cord, extending to testicles, now within inguinal ring, then cutting in r. great toe. Tearing in inguinal glands. **Cutting in morning, with thin stool**; deep in at 4 P.M., after a good stool, > discharge of flatus; on pressure, bending backward, or on effort at stool; *alternating with constriction, during menses.* **Griping** in morning; **G. during menses, with pain in small of back and general chilliness**; then yellowish leucorrhœa; *intermittent, so that she could scarcely walk, after entering the house, preceded by rumbling in abdomen and emission of flatus;* paroxysmal, from umbilical region to symphysis pubis about 4 A.M. Cramplike pain at night; C. pain as if intestines were knotted by threads, during menses, she could not walk nor lie, but was forced to sit upright. *Pain;* in l. groin, with heat; in r. side when standing or walking against the wind, or when turning on to l. side after lying on back; during menses, with heat, chilliness and a kind of epilepsy, she was stiff, she distorted her mouth and moved to and fro without speaking, with cold forehead and cold hands; in l. side as from something hard, obliging him to walk bent to one side; in groin over whole pubic region, as if tightly bound; sore, after dinner; drawing, in r. groin and l. side of abdomen.

Clinical.—Engorgement of the liver, with piles, constipation, bad taste, feeling of fulness, with soreness over the stomach and abdomen. Incarcerated flatulence in l. side, and constipation. Colic, with hæmorrhoids. Abdominal dropsy. In abdominal complaints Sul. follows well after Nux. Peritonitis. Colitis, with soreness along the transverse colon, < bending forward. Heavy weight and dragging in the hypogastric region, has to stoop over when walking.

Rectum.—Prolapsus during stool. *Gurgling.* **Sticking** (Nit. ac.); **< evening; taking away the breath;** jerking, in evening. Tearing. **Cutting during normal stool** (Sil., Nit. ac.); extending far up at night before a good stool. *Throbbing pain all day after stool. Burning pain during hard stool and in anus.* Worrying sore pain when lying. **Crawling in evening when sitting, with biting as from worms. Itching; during the day;** in evening; from thread-worms; < walking; > stool. Tickling. Coldness on waking, with irritation in it. **Burning; during stool** (Aloe, Nit. ac.).

Straining at stool; before and after stool. Fulness. Sensation after stool as if something remained. Pressure; during soft stool; *and on bladder; in R. and anus after a soft stool, as after a hard stool;* as if it would protrude during stool, with pressure on bladder, forced to rise three times at night on account of it. **Tenesmus; in morning after waking, then a copious fluid stool,** *later a second and in afternoon a third similar stool;* at 11 A.M. when sitting; *at night, with swelling of piles; when sitting; after stool, she cannot sit down on account of pain in anus;* after stool, a contraction, with flatus pressing high up into bowels, this flatus felt like a great sausage lying from l. to r. above umbilicus. *Urging, even in bed, then diarrhœa;* in morning and after great effort insufficient, dark, hard stool; in morning, then difficult, hard, insufficient stool, after eating renewed U. and after straining soft-formed stool; morning, noon and evening, with drawing and tension down muscles of loins; in evening and stool difficult, hard, dark; < dinner; but difficult, soft stool; then difficult scanty stool; **constant U. at night, cannot lie nor sit on account of sticking and sore pain in anus, it seems as if everything had been pressed out, < retracting anus, with pain**; *constant U. to stool and to urinate, with discharge of a few drops of blood after urinating, sticking in urethra, apprehension and discomfort;* sudden, which continued after he had passed a hard lump; frequent, but discharge of only a few drops of dark blood, with burning in anus.

Ineffectual urging; in morning; waking him in morning; in morning, with emission of flatus, towards noon after straining a soft-formed stool; in morning, but towards noon after a painful effort a scanty, firm, blackish-brown stool; in afternoon, then at night an unsatisfactory stool after much effort, with increase of urine; waking him after midnight; after dinner; with dryness in rectum; with burning and itching in anus, extrusion of hæmorrhoids, hard stool; then shooting in rectum; only at noon an unsatisfactory stool; **frequent.**

Anus.—Hæmorrhoids (Æsc. h., Aloe, Puls.); **moist,** *even after natural stool;* **increased congestion of hæmorrhoidal vessels** (Aloe); *with sticking; with burning pain on walking and touch, < stool, sometimes shooting out of it through anus, and in the first days blood passed during stool.* Moist pimples, with smarting and sticking when walking and sitting. *Red, inflamed, and covered with red veins, with burning during stool. Swelling, with burning itching;* S. of borders, tickling as if a worm were creeping about and escape of slimy fluid. *Discharge of liquid, then fæces at night in sleep; D. of moisture, with sore feeling and itching around it; involuntary, of moisture, then itching; of viscid slimy fluid causing soreness; of blood,* with easy stool; of blood after stool; a clot of blood slipped out in afternoon when walking; of thread-worms; *of thread-worms during stool.*

Sticking; during the day; in afternoon, and in neck of bladder; extending into rectum, after a difficult, not hard stool; flying, after dinner; throbbing, from border through rectum and into r. hip at 7 P.M. when standing. Jerking stitches in forenoon when standing; out at anus at noon, then sensitiveness so that he cannot sit; through r. half, with itching in anus, feeling as if it were sore, swollen and moist; jerking, out of r., then l. half towards evening, with tenderness around it.

Aching; towards noon when sitting, with straining; at noon; at noon when sitting; at noon when sitting, and feeling as if there were a pile there, but there was not; in evening after waking; *after hard stool;* after loose stool; paroxysmal, in afternoon when sitting after stool, with forcing; raw; straining, ulcerative, on touch after a loose fetid stool, and sensation long afterwards as if he would have diarrhœa. Soreness after fluid stool; after a copious loose stool. Constriction after stool. Sensation as if a worm crept out in morning on waking; a not disagreeable creeping at noon when sitting. **Itching; around it** (Æsc. h.); **at border, with sore feeling** (Æsc. h.); *in morning;* in morning, with tenesmus; *in evening; at night,* next morning escape of acrid itching fluid; with soft stool.

Burning; in morning when sitting; *in forenoon when sitting, with aching; at noon, < sitting;* at noon when sitting, with sore feeling; *in afternoon; in evening, and in urethra;* in evening when sitting; *when sitting;* when sitting after walking; when sitting, with sensation of a foreign body; *after sitting;* after moderate exercise; *before, during and after stool; after stool;* **after a thin stool; after a soft-formed stool;** *after a good stool;* after a semi-fluid stool; after a loose stool; *after an insufficient stool;* after a hard stool; so that she cannot sit; sudden.

Bearing down; in forenoon; in forenoon when sitting; *in forenoon when sitting, with tenesmus;* in forenoon when sitting, with shooting; in forenoon when walking, with cutting; towards noon, with itching shoots; at noon; at noon, with burning; at noon when sitting; at noon when sitting, with sore feeling; at noon when sitting, with shooting; at noon when sitting, suddenly disappearing, but recurring; at noon, < sitting, > walking, with shooting; > afternoon by walking, with aching, returning by fits in evening when sitting; afternoon; afternoon and evening; evening when sitting; when sitting; when sitting, > after dinner, with sore feeling; *after sitting;* after dinner; after dinner, with burning; an hour after a loose stool; when sitting after a loose stool; after a good stool, with aching; sudden, in forenoon when sitting; sudden, at noon. Paroxysmal bearing down in evening; at noon, with aching; in evening when sitting, with aching; when sitting, > 9 P.M.

Perineum.—Constriction. Sore pain at raphe. *Itching, with soft stool;* I., with shooting.

Stool.—*Fluid;* in morning; and copious; *and frequent; frequent in evening, involuntary when sneezing or laughing* (Aloe); frequent, afterwards hard and insufficient; twice a day; smelling of rotten eggs; light-colored and lienteric, with nausea, griping and rumbling, till the third day when *the diarrhœa became painless and almost involuntary,* lasting till the seventh day, then symptoms in lungs and head; stool normal in morning on rising, then straining, fluid fæces and raw pain in anus; last part; *half fluid, half lumpy, mixed with gas and noisy flatus, in morning, afternoon and evening, always soon after eating,* next day no stool. **Semi-fluid; and frequent**; at an unusual hour, and copious.

Diarrhœa; in morning on rising; after breakfast, then qualmishness in abdomen; in evening; after dinner, though he had a normal stool in forenoon; with relief to abdomen; with tenesmus; *copious;* copious, at 3 P.M., though I had had the usual stool in morning, next day none; copious, dark gray, fetid, with the spasms; scanty, with tenesmus and burning in anus; yellowish-green, slimy; mixed with mucus and full of holes, morning, noon and evening; nearly black, viscid, greasy, urgent, smelling of sulphuretted hydrogen. *Involuntary diarrhœa during emission of flatus* (Aloe), and during the day two watery stools, with pinching in abdomen; *I. and bilious, with sensation as if wind would pass;* I., with anxiety, then sweat. Frequent diarrhœa; *twice in morning; during the day, with burning in anus and gripes; and frothy, even at night, with tenesmus;* offensive, two or three times daily; even to faintness, at first with heat and sweat, then with cold sweat on forehead and feet and white tongue. Alternating with constipation.

Soft and frequent in morning; S. and fetid; with flatus smelling like rotten eggs; and insufficient; soft-formed, difficult and frequent; soft-formed, scanty, after straining; solid-soft, copious. **Pappy yellowish-green, copious fetid in morning,** *then feeling of perfect health;* P., yellow, copious, after dinner, flatus smelling of sulphuretted hydrogen, next afternoon two fluid stools mixed with mucous flakes and one at night, with burning in anus, third day three fluid stools, then constipation for three days, then sudden urging and diarrhœa; P. and scanty after straining and cutting in anus, after the stool sensation as if mucous membrane were pressed out.

Hard; after rising, causing cutting in rectum; after rising, causing smarting sticking in rectum; after dinner, then soreness in anus; after straining, with rigor and cold feeling in limbs; with congestion to head; with evacuation of a tape-worm; *soon followed by one of* *ordinary consistence;* **and difficult, only every two, three or four days**; and difficult; and difficult, covered with blood, with soreness in anus; *and black, crumbly*; and lumpy, with burning in anus; and delayed, with pressure and burning in anus; and unsatisfactory. *Scanty, hard; then burning and sore feeling in anus;* causing burning shooting in anus; and delayed; and clawing, with sensation as if rectum would prolapse. First part hard, then loose, difficult; last part loose, causing cutting in rectum; and lumpy, with raw shooting pain in rectum, the last part soft and of the color and consistence of bird-lime, scanty.

Constipation; at times; for two days, then involuntary stool. *Knotty;* in morning; *but not hard; mixed with mucus;* and difficult; and insufficient; and insufficient, causing burning pain in rectum. **Scanty; and unsatisfactory**; in morning and afternoon; and half fluid. Difficult; *on rising;* and unsatisfactory; *had to strain long, with aching in small of back.*

Tough, gluey, fetid, so urgent that some escaped prematurely, yet not diarrhœa, after getting up, *a similar stool two hours later.* **Slimy**; without fæces, frequent, mixed with red veins. Covered with mucus; and slipped out quickly. *Bloody in evening.* Light-colored. Sour-smelling. Containing undigested food. Copious; and frequent; and tough, smeary. *Rapid; and almost involuntary.* Unusually easy. Frequent; with mucus; twice in a day. Stool after dinner.

Clinical.—Dysentery, subacute, with burning, tenesmus, not violent, but persistent. Diarrhœa in great variety; stools are generally thin, watery, sometimes mucous, white or green, sometimes with bloody streaks, sometimes undigested, generally very fetid; nearly always < early in morning in bed; the necessity urgent and frequently without pain. In the chronic diarrhœa of scrofulous children we may find aversion to meat, tendency to stupor, with cold sweat, generally disagreeable odor of the body, with aversion to washing. Valuable for habitual constipation, especially when the rectum is irritable and dry, frequent ineffectual desire for stool in the rectum, with piles, soreness and burning at the anus, often with congestive headache, engorged liver, etc.

Urinary Organs.—Bladder. Sticking, or in hypogastrium; in region of neck in morning on urinating, with sticking through anus; flying, in region about 6 P.M., with soreness on pressure. Aching in region of neck at 11 A.M.; in region at 3 P.M. *Dragging in morning after urinating. Pressure; soon after micturition, with sensation as if urine were retained by contraction of sphincter,* and the same sensation in anus; *as if too full, without call to urinate.*

Urging; at night; in morning after rising, with cutting over symphysis pubis as in strangury; on waking after an emission, not > copious micturition, on account of irritation in orifice of urethra. **Constant desire; with scanty urine**; *and a few drops passed involuntarily.* **Frequent urging**; *in afternoon and evening;* with feeling of obstruction in sphincter of bladder; **sudden.**

Micturition when emitting flatus; on coughing; *in a thin stream;* in a weak stream; *intermittent;* by jerks; forcible. Dysuria. **Frequent micturition**; in forenoon; in afternoon; in evening; *at night; at night, and copious;* twice at night, and slow; always preceded by cutting in hypogastrium; with voluptuous pressure reaching as far as anus; *of watery urine; and much at a time;* and copious, pale and towards the end smelling mouldy; and scanty; and scanty, difficult, painful; of small quantities as clear as water.

Urethra.—Inflammation of orifice. Discharge of prostatic fluid; in long threads after micturition and stool. **Sticking; in forepart**; in morning; *in morning on urinating;* about noon; in afternoon; *in front of it* in evening when sitting; *with tearing; with rigor;* extending along it at 5.30 P.M.; sometimes in a spot, sometimes extending to pubes; to above pubes in evening on urinating; sudden, in orifice towards evening. Cutting before and during stool; C. as if the urine were acrid at close of micturition and afterwards. *Pain as in the beginning of gonorrhœa.* Smarting in female. *Constant urging to urinate.* **Itching in middle**; in mouth; *at mouth, as at beginning of gonorrhœa;* sudden shooting, in navicular fossa in evening. Tickling in evening. *Burning;* at 10 P.M., > Canthar.; *in forepart when not urinating.* **Burning when urinating**; *in morning;* in front part at night; *in mouth.*

Urine.—*Copious; all day;* in evening; in evening after beer; **at night**; at night, then symptoms diminished; *after midnight; and reddish;* and dark yellow; and bright yellow; of the color of sherry in morning, of the color of white wine in evening; with increase of water, urea, uric acids, mucus, inorganic salts and phosphates, but diminution of solid constituents, organic salts and extractives; with increase of water, solid matters, urea, uric acid, mucus, organic salts and extractives, but diminution of incinerated salts and phosphates. *Scanty;* after eating and of the color of dark sherry. **Turbid**; at night, and offensive; at night, and copious sediment. *Fatty pellicle. Offensive* (Sep., Benz. ac.); like sweaty feet. Smelt like chamomile tea. Bloody, slimy. Of the color of sherry. Dark. Dark brown. Red in evening, and copious sediment. Whitish. Pale, white-wine color, appearing almost like spastic urine, clear, sp. gr. diminished, reaction acid, increase of uric acid, earthy phosphates, sulphates, phosphates of soda, diminution of nitrate of urea and uroxanthin, afterwards little ammonia, later dark sherry-colored, sp. gr. and urea diminished, the earthy phosphates, sulphates and uric acid increased, afterwards chlorides decreased, later the uroxanthin abundant, urea diminished, later the morning urine was usually of a pale sherry color, that passed after dinner and in evening dark sherry-colored, for three days it contained free ammonia, on two days there were traces of iron. Increase of nitrogenous constituents, urea, uric acid and mucus, sometimes the stable salts, earthy phosphates, unstable salts and extractives were increased, sometimes diminished. Sediment reddish; white, mealy.

Clinical.—Catarrh of the bladder, burning micturition, urine contains mucus. Painful ineffectual efforts to urinate, with retention. Nocturnal enuresis. Hæmaturia. Chronic gonorrhœa, with burning and smarting during micturition. *Chronic nephritis.*

Sexual Organs.—Tingling, and in testicles. Resistance to complete emission of semen. Coldness in morning.

Glans.—Pustules. Redness of G. and inner surface of prepuce, with sore feeling, burning and smarting, with a pimple on glans, afterwards desquamation of skin and prepuce, the inflammation extended to pubes. Fetid smegma causing burning and itching (when a child there was often viscid fluid between foreskin and glans, causing itching and burning, and micturition was painful). Penis stiff and hard like leather, its inner surface shining and secreting a thin offensive ichor. *Stitches in penis;* in morning on urinating, < glans, as if urethra were pierced, at first the urine dribbles, then it is retained. Cramplike pain. **Itching.** Erections at night, with vivid, not lascivious, dreams. Phimosis, with oozing of offensive mucus under prepuce.

Prepuce.—*Redness and burning;* R. and swelling. Epididymis swollen. Hangs over glans and is divided into four or five lobes by furrows. Retracted, and penis cold, bluish. *Cold, and glans.* Itching at night, then voluptuous sensation.

Scrotum.—*Itching; in morning on waking, and on inside of thighs; about noon,* with tickling, itching and sore feeling at outer border of anus; *towards evening;* with sweat.

Testicles.—*Hang down flabby. Relaxed in evening in bed, and scrotum.* Sticking; in l. *Pressure and tension in T. and spermatic cords.* Drawing in r. T. and spermatic cord at 7 P.M.

Power increased; *weakened.* Impotency, with amorous fancies. *Desire;* in morning after waking, with erections at first strong, then weak, changing to a burning pain, gradually > emission; *at night;* for an emission, without erection; **almost lost.** *Emissions* at night; with voluptuous dreams; in midday sleep when sitting; in an old man; with burning pain in urethra; profuse, watery.

Female.—*Bearing down. Feeling of weakness. Itching, with papules about them; I. on mons veneris, with moisture.* Inflammation of one labia, with burning pain, < urinating. Pudenda, painless blisters externally; sore spot, and one on perineum; burning. *Vagina, burning so that she could scarcely sit; itching;* soreness during coition; *biting discharge.* Leucorrhœa two days before menses; *profuse L.; causing soreness and burning pain;* like nasal mucus, fourteen days after menses; thin, in morning after rising, preceded by griping in abdomen. *Itching of clitoris.* Almost daily bloody discharge from uterus for several weeks after return of long-suppressed menses. Contractive pain in region of uterus towards pudenda, as before menses, from morning till night.

Menses.—*Too early;* preceded by cutting downward in hypogastrium; and scanty; and profuse, with pain in abdomen and back, preceded by general chilliness. **Too late** (Nat. m., Puls., Sep., etc.); **with constipation and distended abdomen**; *with sickness and oppression;* lasting eight days, with pains the first days. **Profuse, stopped immediately after flowing two days and a half;** P. and long-lasting; with sour odor; and black, thick, acrid; and black, clotted, sticky. Changed to a sulphur-colored discharge, and so it continued for at least three months, ever since for a week before each monthly illness she has this discharge, which smells and looks like sulphur, < purgatives (which do not act on the bowels), and the urine at the same time will smell of sulphur, the discharge leaves a yellow stain, with sulphur-like odor upon her linen.

Clinical.—Hydrocele. Pruritus of the vulva, with burning and stinging; with miliary eruption, < heat of bed. Prolapsus uteri, with aching across the sacrum, constipation. Various forms of uterine inflammations, called for by general indications. Suppressed menstruation, with congestive headache and cold feet. Scanty menstruation, with burning heat in hands and soles at night, weight on top of the head, etc. Dysmenorrhœa, pains running from the groins to the back. Anteversion, uterus presses on the bladder, < walking. Leucorrhœa, corrosive, yellow, menstrual flow corrosive (see Kreos.).

Respiratory Organs.—Larynx. Swollen gland on thyroid cartilage, with pain on touch. Painful thrust when coughing. *Drawing at times, with dryness.* Swollen feeling. Tickling; and in bronchi. Crawling, and talking causes cough. Sensation as if mucus stuck in glottis. *Hoarseness;* **in morning**; in forenoon; in forenoon, and speaking requires an effort; in afternoon; *in evening;* in attacks. Voice rough at noon; during the day, < evening, and toneless, with occasional cough. Voice deep. Voice lost. Rattling in bronchi, *with shooting beneath l. lowest rib, towards back, < breathing deeply.*

Cough; in morning; in forenoon; afternoon; afternoon, *with shooting in chest;* afternoon, > open air, < returning to the warm room; in evening; in evening, from irritation deep in air-passages; in evening in bed before menses, > rising; *only at night;* at night, then sleeplessness for a long time; woke him about midnight, > expectoration, recurred in morning on dressing; at 1 A.M., from irritation in larynx and trachea; **from rawness in larynx** (Phos., Puls.); *from roughness in throat; on going to sleep, with heat in head and eyes and cold hands.* Provocation to cough in two or three attacks with every breath, < afternoon; P. after eating, so violent that he cannot cough soon enough, it draws his chest together spasmodically and he retches; ineffectual desire, with blackness before eyes. Tickling C. at 6 P.M., > expectoration of tenacious mucus. Fatiguing C. during the day; in morning; at night. Sudden shaking C. after dinner. Paroxysmal, generally dry, waking him at midnight; sudden, at night, with contraction of air-passages, usually dry; barking, waking him at 2 A.M., from irritation in trachea, generally dry.

Dry cough; in morning; in morning in bed, from irritation in trachea; in morning after rising, from tickling in larynx; at noon; afternoon and evening. **In evening before sleep, worse than during the day;** in evening from tickling in throat; in evening and night, and towards morning, with expectoration and sensation as if bubbles burst internally; from 5 P.M. onward, next morning cough, with whitish mucous expectoration; at night; **at night waking him;** at night after going to bed, with expectoration of two lumps of albuminous-looking blue mucus; after dinner; from irritation in larynx; from constant irritation; with pain in r. hypochondrium; sudden, as if lungs would be torn out, with aggravated headache; convulsive, waking him in morning, leaving soreness in chest; spasmodic, at noon from fulness in the chest.

Short cough in evening when sitting asleep. Dry, short cough; sometimes during the day, sometimes cough with copious mucous expectoration; in morning; morning on waking; forenoon; noon; afternoon; evening; evening after lying down, causing heat, the cough woke her about 3 A.M.; after dinner; when walking in open air; < open air, > lying down, with sore burning in pharynx; *with pain in sternum and sticking in chest;* as from irritation in trachea; paroxysmal; fatiguing, in morning, with pain in chest.

Coughing up mucus; in morning; in morning on waking; from larynx in morning; morning and evening; afternoon; night; copious mucus in evening on going to bed and in night on waking; scanty mucus in afternoon, cough < entering a warm room and on smoking tobacco, > open air and drinking wine in evening, cough wakes her at night; sweetish plugs; yellowish globular mucus in morning, cough dry during the day. Coughing up thick mucus; in morning; in morning, with sore pain in chest; in forenoon; at noon; at night; at night, with soreness in trachea; with soreness or pressure upon chest, rattling in trachea and hoarseness; jelly-like.

Expectoration in morning; E. from chest tasting like old catarrh; of bloody saliva, with sweet taste in throat; of blood at night, with fatty, sweetish taste in mouth; jelly-like. Expectoration of mucus; in morning; without cough; thick, viscid, in morning; thick in evening.

Respiration.—Threatenings of asthma. Suffocation during the day; S., with constriction of chest; in paroxysms at night in sleep; threatened at night as soon as she fell asleep, and she started up with a scream, towards morning palpitation, then exhausting sweat. *Arrested even when talking;* during sleep, she must be awakened to avoid suffocation; paroxysmally, at night; paroxysmally, > forcible deep breathing; suddenly at night on turning to l. side, > sitting up. **Dyspnœa;** *in evening in bed;* on walking rapidly; several hours after eating, then yawning. Difficult; in forenoon; afternoon; *at night when lying on back, with pressure and anxiety in chest,* and general sweat; on bending forward; on pressure upon chest; more when sitting than when walking, with necessity to breathe deeply. Short, towards evening; S. *from talking much; on walking* in open air. Deep breathing impossible. Gasping on account of constriction of larynx, face hot and turgid, eyes projecting, veins of forehead and temples distended, speech difficult, shrill whistling on inspiration, < ascending stairs. Rapid during and after getting into bed. Excretion of carbonic acid increased. Expired air is hot.

Clinical.—Aphonia. Cough is usually dry day and night, < lying down, especially at night. Larnygeal and bronchial catarrh, with attacks of suffocation. Whooping cough (it is said to "kill" the disease if burned in the room or house). Chronic asthma, with suffocative fits in the forepart of the night, and with burning in the chest.

Chest.—A swollen gland on ensiform cartilage is painful to touch. Swelling of r. nipple in morning, with pain on touch and on deep breath, afterwards sensitiveness. Twitching in one breast, with swelling as if milk rushed into it. Cracking in sternum on motion. Mucus; obliging hacking. Rattling at night; R., > expectoration, with snoring.

Sticking; in l. side; *in sternum;* beneath sternum; under l. breast; in l. pleura; externally in r.; in walls, r., then l., then on r. side of abdomen; and in dorsal muscles; between l. fourth and fifth ribs in morning after waking; in r. side in forenoon; *l. side in forenoon, < walking quickly and ascending stairs;* l. pleura at 10 A.M.; under sternum at noon on full breathing; *side in afternoon;* under heart about 3 P.M.; in evening; r. ribs in evening; r. pleura in evening; under r. breast at 10 P.M.; in side at 10 P.M. and at night; *in r. or in region of heart at night on motion when lying on back;* **in l. on breathing;** *beneath r. breast on coughing;* in region of ensiform cartilage on coughing; *pectoral muscles on moving arms;* on moving chest forward and to the left, and on deep breathing; in bend of l. false ribs on movement of body and on deep breathing, > washing with cold water, with pain; l. intercostal muscles when walking and once on speaking, forcing him to hold his breath; in r. till dinner-time; in r. after dinner; in l. before sleep; in l. ribs before sleep; in sternum, < touch; in l., transiently > deep breathing; S. or twinging in middle of sternum, more externally; in muscles, with drawing; **extending to back; extending from r. side into scapula;** *in l., extending towards heart, taking away the breath, with thirst; in r., through stomach and pit of stomach;* r. ribs, extending to shoulder, at night in bed; outward like blows, where mediasternum is attached to r. side of sternum, in direction of diaphragm, ending inside chest, on exertion of chest, > noon; *shattering, in r.; in l. side towards heart, taking away her breath, at night, with thirst; in l. side,* not affecting respiration; paroxysmal, in l. side during the day.

Cramp at times; C. in evening in a warm room, < motion, > lying down in bed, with difficult breathing and palpitation. Tearing in l. pectoralis major after dinner, < pressure. Cutting in middle, extending to pit of stomach; in l. lower ribs, with burning; deep in after walking in open air, with burning. Sticking griping on last rib and above hips. Sudden pinching in r. half in afternoon, went off with a shoot towards front of chest. Shattering when coughing, and in abdomen.

Pain in sternum; in r. side; deep in r. side; in morning; in ribs, dorsal vertebræ and muscles in morning after rising, so that he could scarcely bend forward, > holding himself upright; beneath sternum towards noon; l. side at 6 P.M.; sides at 8 P.M.; *on moving arm;* after breakfast, with sore feeling; in sternum on walking; upper part of sternum on walking in open air, > continuing to walk; r. side on coughing, with soreness on touch; after a bruise, < evening; under wall, < sneezing; r. ribs, < touch; in a spot beneath r. wall near sternum, < deep breathing and bending forward; on and beneath sternum late in evening, < deep breathing, moving body and rough handling, with sore feeling; *in sternum, with oppression of breath;* sudden, in middle of sternum frequently during the day; periodical, posteriorly in r. lower part, proceeding from the inside.

Raging pain in middle of sternum frequently in afternoon. Pain deep in in evening as if some one would grasp it, twist it, lift it up, rub it to pieces or burst it. Squeezing pain in upper part after rising, < r. side. *Bruised pain in upper part;* in upper part on touch; under sternum on leaning forward, felt next morning on deep breathing, < forenoon, > afternoon; in l. pectoral muscles, < motion, breathing and touch, with drawing or tearing in l. shoulder and muscles of upper arm. Sore feeling; in a spot deep in centre all day, < movement and inspiration, > night. Rawness; in morning on waking. Lungs feel as if resting against back when coughing.

Pressure (Phos.); in morning, > rising; *at 8 A.M., so that she could hardly breathe;* in afternoon; declining on rumbling in abdomen; transversely across middle, as from swallowing too large a morsel. **Oppression;** all day, often obliged to rise hurriedly from a seat; in forenoon; from 9 A.M. till 3 P.M.; in afternoon; at 2 P.M., deep inspirations cause pain towards r. ninth rib; in evening; < moving at night, forced to sit up; *with strained pain;* of upper part, with sensitiveness. *Constriction;* in forenoon; *on deep breathing; after rising;* on motion; on walking; in a spot in sternum, rather externally, with burning; *sticking, in pectoral muscles, with soreness on touch;* spasmodic, beneath sternum when sitting.

Tension; in muscles after dinner; in muscles on breathing deeply, and contracted feeling in anterior wall of chest; on r. lower rib, > pressure, with throbbing; r. side and r. shoulder; externally, now below sternum, now under arms, now in back; chilly. *Tightness;* l. half; in morning fasting, > eating, the hindrance to breathing seemed to be in pit of stomach; in evening; after breakfast; after walking, often obliged to breathe deeply till evening; *as if something had grown fast. Fulness before menses, forcing a deep breath;* F., and at first insipid and clammy, but suddenly a sweetish taste, sensitiveness of uvula, tickling in throat, spitting of slimy fluid mixed with bright red blood, repeated several times (he had had something similar six or seven years previously). *Heaviness;* in l. side; towards evening, with fulness.

Anxiety (Phos.); in afternoon; so that he can hardly expand it during inspiration. Trembling in C. and pit of stomach towards noon, with throbbing. Throbbing deep in at night; T. in sternum as in an ulcer; crackling, in l. side when sitting and lying, > holding his breath. *Sensation of mucus, after the raising of which respiration was freer. Rush of blood; in morning on waking;* with qualmishness amounting to faintness, and trembling of r. arm. Heat; in morning on waking; deep in middle of r. clavicle, extending to sternum; in r. side, coming and going suddenly. Coldness, and in abdomen. Emptiness during dry cough. *Weakness at night, < getting into bed so that he cannot lie long on one side and longs for morning;* **W. when talking** (Phos., Stann.); *on reading aloud; with difficulty in breathing.*

Clinical.—Valuable in the later stage of pneumonia, when the inflammatory process fails to resolve, the lung continues dull and the cough dry, the patient begins to have fever at night, hot hands and feet and hot head; a few doses of Sulphur will then generally cause the cough to loosen and the hepatization to resolve. In hydrothorax it follows Bry. well. In the earliest stage of tuberculosis, need of fresh air, feet and head hot, hands and feet burn at night, palpitation, atonic dyspepsia, with need to eat at 11 A.M., etc.

Heart.—Sticking in præcordial region; after dinner. Strange motion in præcordial region. Pain in præcordial region towards evening. Sensation as if it had not room enough. Hollow sensation in præcordial region. **Palpitation**; every forenoon; at noon after a short walk, with trembling of hands; on lying down for midday nap; *in evening;* **at night in bed**; *at night on turning in bed; at night on falling asleep; with the first movement of a child, with heat of face, then burning in abdomen; during stool;* after walking in open air; at the moment of rising; after dinner; *with anxiety as if he would faint;* **anxious.** *Rush of blood. Sudden beating in evening after turning in bed.* Irregular action. Increased pulsations of aorta from heart to clavicle, with a purring noise, when he lay on l. side the pulsation was troublesome along back. Pulsations diminished in number.

Clinical.—It seems as though the blood rushed to the heart, causing a gasping and need of fresh air, heart feels too large. Sometimes useful in cardiac dropsies.

Pulse.—Rapid; *in evening; and hard, full;* and small, soft. Pulsation in l. carotid. Feeble and intermittent.

Neck.—*Inflammation of a gland on nape close to hair, with itching.* Painful swelling anteriorly and externally. *Cracking in vertebræ;* on bending head backward and pressing it upon the pillow; *on bending head backward, with stiffness of nape.* Drawing jerking in muscles. *Sticking; in nape on stooping;* in nape on sitting bent over, with tension. *Tearing in l. side after waking before midnight, < moving head, > rest, with tension and feeling as if too short.* Pain if she talks much; in r. side on bending head to right; rheumatic, in nape in morning. *Bruised pain and tension in nape and between scapulæ, which on moving head go to shoulder;* tensive, in nape, extending to over eye, where it is a sticking. *Drawing pain in r. side; in nape and scapulæ.* Drawing on l. side to shoulder; *up nape. Stiffness; and paralytic sprained pain in nape.*

Back.—Rumbling along inside of spine. Sticking at every breath; on walking; itching. Tearing; in evening in bed, and in knees and legs. Aching; in evening when driving; **at night, with bruised sensation in small of back, preventing sleep** (Rhus t.), **with orgasm of blood**; *on stooping;* < motion, lasting till night; *sprained, on a false step; as after long stooping;* tensive, in l. side on moving arm. *Bruised feeling; in one spot; in muscles of spine.* Drawing in spine extending upward, on stooping. Weariness in l. side on moving arm; W. in morning, as if he had not slept enough, with heaviness as if he had lain uncomfortably. Heaviness in morning on rising, and in lower limbs. Stiffness after sitting; on sitting a long time, > walking; as after taking cold, and in sides; *now in back, now in hips, < turning over in bed, forced to hold his breath.*

Scapulæ.—Sticking in lower angle of l. in morning; between S. in evening, with tearing; in l. when leaning on l. arm; *beneath S., taking away the breath and preventing stooping;* in lower third of l. at night, preventing sleep, in morning it extended towards upper part of scapula and spread to muscles of nape and l. ear, < moving or turning neck, the pain was more drawing and tearing, > daytime, returned at night in warmth of bed; intermittent, along l. in morning; pulsative, undulating, in a spot below end of l. in afternoon, causing a jerk through whole body and forcing him to hold his breath (as when straining at stool), with sensitiveness to touch, movement and deep inspiration, the pain lasted all night and was felt in sleep next day, > lying on l. side, < turning in bed, next day he was often forced to stop speaking because the pain took away his breath. Tearing in l. when sitting; drawing, in r., < movement. Pain on coughing; *beneath S. in evening.* Sprained pain in r. on moving arm; between S. and in region of l. pelvis during rest, with painful jerking on motion. Drawing pain in r. in evening on going to sleep. *Tension between S.; when lying and moving; and on side of neck;* T. close to r., as if muscles were too short, at 7 P.M.

Lumbar Region.—Cracking extending to anus. Jerking in evening in bed. **Stitches**; *in bones on expiration; transversely across; pulsating;* taking away the breath till evening, with pain in head and nape, frequent alternations of chill and heat, with apprehension in pit of stomach; inward in l. sacro-iliac symphysis at 3 P.M. Tearing in l. on motion; sudden, in lumbar and sacral vertebræ in afternoon. Shooting cutting above anterior superior spinous process of r. ilium in afternoon during rest. Gnawing in a spot, after pressure upon it only bruised pain. Cramp pain in lumbar and sacral vertebræ towards evening, impeding every motion of body, > night, repeated the following evening, leaving stiffness, which made it difficult to lean forward and forced him to stretch. Sharp pain towards sacrum. Pain; in a spot in sacral region; in l.; *above lumbar region;* all day, < urinating; in region of r. sacro-iliac symphysis at 4 A.M., and in r. shoulder; in morning after waking; in morning when sitting; in forenoon when sitting; in forenoon, < walking; in afternoon; at 4 P.M., forcing him to bed; in evening; in evening after a short drive, < sitting down and rising again; at night; on waking, > rising; *after long stooping;* on rising from a seat; during stool; after dinner; above lumbar region when walking; in l. sacro-lumbar region, < turning in bed; < sitting down and rising up; < walking and standing; > walking, also returning when sitting; with hypochondriacal discomfort; *so that she could not stand erect; across loins;* occasionally extending up back and into chest, with shooting forward; extending towards middle of back and between scapulæ; sudden; sudden, after getting up. **Bruised pain** (Rhus t.); *in coccyx; all day; during the day on stooping and rising; in afternoon; in evening;* < touch. Sprained pain in l. sacral region and hip when walking; extending across pelvis to l. trochanter when stepping and causing limping; sudden, and in lower part of back; sudden, on sneezing, then drawing pain close to spine extending into l. groin and testicles, < rising from a seat and walking; shooting, in sacro-lumbar region extending across pelvis to l. trochanter on stepping, causing limping. Tension; in l.; in l. sacral region and hip; at 2 A.M.; in evening; in l. loin and hip, then sudden cutting through r. knee from bend to patella, which soon alternated with a similar pain from bend of l. elbow to its apex, the pain in back > rising; *on stooping, extending over abdomen to pit of stomach and to knee;* in l. extending to region of l. great trochanter in morning on waking, > rising; in l. sacral region and hip and in pelvis, in bed, sometimes as if pelvic bones were separating; in l. sacro-lumbar region as if muscles were too short, it spread over l. side of pelvis to trochanter and involved abdominal muscles above crest of l. ilium, when lying on l. side, on turning it attacked the same parts on r. side. Burning pain near anus. *Drawing pain. Drawing* all day, < sitting; towards evening; at night; *with weakness.* Weight; in forenoon, < stooping. Bearing down extending into groins, during menses; B. down as if menses would come on. Lightness. Stiffness.

Clinical.—Spinal irritation, with suppression of the menses or hæmorrhoids, with dry heat; also with weakness of the chest and stomach, and sleeplessness. Has been used for so-called congestions of the spinal cord.

Extremities.—Affection of all. Cracking of knees and elbows. *Unsteadiness of joints. Trembling;* < hands; of hands in afternoon, with unsteadiness of gait. Jerking of one hand and foot during the day; J., with clenched teeth and moaning, then slumber, then again J. and spasmodic drawing in limbs, then weakness.

Sticking in l. hip-joint and ball of l. hand during the day; in r. calf and r. upper arm in evening; thighs, r. hip and l. shoulder at night before sleep; in r. knee from standing, then in l. wrist; now in l. great toe, now in l. thumb. Tearing in wrists and ankles during rest, with stiffness; frequent T. during the day, with shooting in soles; sudden, in fingers and dorsa of feet; when walking T. and shooting in r. knee and tibia, then the pain jumped into l. and then into r. humerus, and so on, changing all day. Cramplike pain in muscles of l. upper arm close to bend of elbow at noon, and after two hours alternating with similar pain in sinews of l. popliteal space. Griping, now in l. shoulder, now in feet.

Pain in joints; in r. leg, r. shoulder and r. upper arm in morning; r. metatarsal bone in afternoon, then in r. elbow, then in r. wrist, then in r. metacarpal bone; after midnight; in bones on touch, as if flesh were loose; gouty, in joints in forenoon, alternating with cramplike pain in their voluntary muscles, the same in afternoon, the former pain < rest, the latter < moving. *Dragging, almost like a drawing. Bruised feeling;* all day, < upper, with heaviness; in morning; *in morning on waking, with heaviness;* in morning after waking; in morning after rising; at noon. Dislocation pain in forenoon, even on slight movement.

Drawing pain in evening; in afternoon during rest, now over l. inner ankle, now in r. shoulder-joint, now in r., now in l. wrist, often alternating with shooting in rectum; intermittent, in thigh during the day when walking, < one forenoon, when it was now in r., now in l., usually posteriorly, and at the same time paralytic pain in upper arms almost all day, and in upper part of trunk feeling as if I had taken cold; (tearing), < the feather bed; penetrating into marrow of bones (as from holding ice a long time) at night in bed, now in metacarpal bone of r. index, now in r. knee.

Drawing; here and there; in knees, arms and shoulders; l. hand and r. thigh; r. thigh, r. shoulder and up nape; r. calf, r. thigh and r. thumb; along r. radius and in outside of r. leg; r. metacarpal in afternoon, and in l. metatarsal bones; bones after dinner; in bones in evening, < forearm; occasionally in morning, < r. thigh; sometimes D., sometimes tearing, sometimes shooting, leaping from one side to the other; sudden, here and there; sudden, in l. thigh and l. third and fourth fingers; sudden, in r. fingers, l. great toes and r. tendo-achillis in afternoon, < inner surface of r. thigh; in r. forearm near elbow, like a breath over the part, causing paralytic feeling, next day similar drawing in tibia, with sensation in small of back as if a cool breath passed over it, a similar drawing near r. wrist and little finger and back of hand, the D. generally began at dorsal side of limbs, near joint and penetrated deeply.

Tension after a short walk, and in tendons of feet; in r. shoulder-joint in morning, with tearing on inside of l. thigh; as if too short, with necessity to stretch them; *cramplike, on moving, now in posterior muscles of l. thigh, now in l. calf, now in other muscles of limbs.* Desire to extend and flex hands and toes. Desire to stretch in night after waking. Waving sensation.

Weakness; all day, with heaviness; > walking, returned in the house; with trembling on motion; so that she could find no comfortable position in bed. Feeling as from long illness. Heaviness in bones of arms and legs; H. after dinner, < lower. Pressure as if they would fall asleep. *Falling asleep on lying down;* F. asleep, < pressure. Paralytic feeling on outside of l. leg and l. forearm. No sensation when sitting.

Clinical.—Synovitis, especially when there is considerable exudation, particularly in the knee. Rheumatic gout, especially beginning in the feet and extending upward, with burning heat in feet at night.

Upper Extremities.—Axilla. Swelling of glands,

purulent; oozing in r. *Sticking beneath r.* Tearing in l. in afternoon when knitting or sewing.

Shoulder.—Tearing jerks in S. or elbows, extending through limbs, < joints, making him wrinkle his forehead and draw up his eyes. Sticking in evening; *S. on motion, extending into chest;* from joint into arm when lying upon it and on inspiration and expiration. Tearing in r.; in l. joint in morning after waking; in l. S. and in r. upper arm in morning in bed, > walking in open air, with shooting in l. shoulder; in r. till noon; in S. or S. joints, < night, at first <, then > moving arm, with gnawing or bruised pain and sticking; in joints, > motion; in r., > morning, leaving a weak paralytic feeling; in l., with drawing; in joint, extending into humerus; sudden, in l. S. and first joint of l. index about 5 P.M. Frequent cutting in r. in forenoon when walking. Pain in r. on breathing; *rheumatic;* **rheumatic, in l.**; as if dislocated in joint, < night when lying; attacks of shooting throbbing, in l. in morning in bed. Throbbing in bone of l. *Drawing pain; in joint and arm;* in r., > rubbing, alternating with scraping in fauces. Drawing in r. joint and thumb; in l. in evening, extending to elbow. Tension from r. towards back in morning, impeding movement of arm. *Weight on walking in open air.*

Arm.—Cramp after midnight. Shootings through it in evening. **Tearing; in r., with paralysis;** *in arms and hands, with drawing;* in bones of r. during the day, with gnawing. Sudden pinching. Pain < motion, especially stretching or raising it, with drawing; *bruised P.;* sprained, < raising it. Drawing in r. in forenoon; jerking, from one joint to another at night in bed, < joints. Weight in r. towards noon. Paralytic feeling in r. in morning on waking. Falling asleep; < work.

Upper Arm.—Shooting from r. deltoid to middle of upper arm; twinging S. in r. Tearing in l. in evening; on anterior surface of l. humerus; jerking, in r. in evening and in l. fingers; drawing, in r., < rest, > motion, alternating with paralytic feeling. Cutting at 3 A.M., darting from deltoid to middle of r. upper arm. Pain in humeri; *jerking, in deltoid;* cramplike, in flexors of l.; bruised, in l., with sensitiveness to pressure; *drawing, in humeri after midnight;* drawing, above r. elbow. Drawing in r. *Weakness. Heaviness; in humerus; humerus, with tension.* Paralytic feeling in evening and next morning on rising.

Elbow.—Tearing in and above r., > moving arm; T. extending into upper arm and forearm. Pain on motion; bruised, about r. on lifting arm and on clenching hand; burning, in skin of flexor surface of l. *Painful drawing in nerves, extending to wrists;* acute D. in r. Tension in tendons; T. in bend of r. on flexing and extending forearm. Paralyzed feeling in r. in afternoon.

Forearm.—Tearing in bones, sometimes > pressure and motion. Aching boring in bones, with rigor. Boring-squeezing pain in r. at 3 P.M. Sensitiveness of l. to touch and exertion. Burning pain below bend of elbow, and on touch it felt dead. Drawing in r. Tension in a spot on r. as if skin were raised by a needle, changing to itching after rubbing. Heaviness of r., with sensation of falling asleep. Paralytic pain in l. all day. L. felt paralyzed and insensible at night when lying on l. side, > rubbing.

Wrist.—Stitches outward through it. Tearing; in r. in forenoon. *Sprained pain;* in r., > violent motion. Pain in l.; in l. at 7.30 A.M.; in ulnar side of l. on touch. Sensitiveness in morning, < moving them, and in finger-joints. Drawing in r. Weakness of r., with feeling of dislocation. *Stiffness, < morning, > during the day.*

Hand.—Swelling; of veins. Smelling of sulphur; palms. Trembling of r. in morning; T. on writing; and < r. thumb. Involuntary grasping, < afternoon. Cramp in l. Sticking in l. palm about 10 P.M.; S., alternating with drawing; burning, suddenly on back. Tearing in knuckles; in joints and fingers of l. in evening on moving them; on radial side of l., extending to little finger; on back of r., at times in bones, at times in extensor tendons. Cramplike pain in l. metacarpus in evening in bed. Burning gnawing in l. beginning in articular end of radius and extending in bone to phalanx of index, late in evening, < touch, lasting till sleep, returning in morning, < after dinner, < touch, > evening by exercise. Drawing pain through metacarpal bone of l. index in forenoon. Tearing contraction in r. Tendons in palms above two first fingers seem short and hard, so that hands cannot be stretched out flat. Tenderness as on entering a warm room after hands have been chilled. *Tremulous sensation.* Anxiety, forced to grasp something. Weakness in morning after rising; W. of r., with tearing in thumb. Falling asleep after immersing in water, with crawling.

Fingers.—Swelling in morning; of three middle of both hands; of joints, with stiffness and redness as if swollen and with crawling. The lunula of thumb-nails almost gone. Semi-lunar furrow across thumb-nails near their roots, afterwards on l. little finger. Jerking; burning, in l. middle. *Cramp in three middle;* in l. ring in evening, extending along common extensor to elbow, with stiffness and coldness. **Sticking in tips** (Petrol.); *on flexor surface of r. middle; in tips at night;* through tip of l. little at night and in morning; *tearing, above nail of l. ring, < evening;* intermittent, in ungual phalanx of r. index, at the end of which an almost cartilaginous wart had existed for years, pain > next day; sudden, in middle joint of r. litttle at night; burning tearing, on back of middle. **Tearing**; in first joint of l. thumb; in second phalanx of l. little in morning; in l. joints in forenoon; on inside of phalanx of l. little in forenoon, < pressure; in r. ring and little in forenoon, then creeping in them; under nail of l. thumb at night in bed; in joints before going to sleep; in first joint of thumb, extending to middle joint and over half of back of hand. Pinching in ball of l. little, every five minutes when resting upon elbow, streaming into arm, with pressure and chilliness, during the day the pain changed to sticking, with chilliness and with feeling in all limbs as after hard work. Pain in joints; in tips in morning, as if nails had been cut too short; *sprained, in first joint of thumb.* Bruised feeling in metacarpal joint of r. thumb in morning; in middle joints of third and fourth during menses, with cramplike and swollen sensation. Swollen sensation. Painful contraction of last r. **Drawing pain in single short jerks in afternoon**; D. pain through first phalanx of l. index in evening. Drawing in thumb; sudden D. almost all the evening; semi-lunar painful D. in root of nail of r. little at night in bed. Sensation, < l. thumb, as if tendons were too short on extending them and grasping anything, causing a paralyzed sensation. Falling asleep of two last in evening in bed; when playing the piano, < l.; of little, with numbness. Deadness in forenoon; *in morning*, with wrinkled skin on tips. Numbness.

Lower Extremities.—Uncertain gait in afternoon, < ascending stairs. *Tearing, forcing him to put them out of bed;* T. in l., with drawing. Tearing thrusts in r. and in hip-joint in evening when walking, forced to stretch the limb and cannot sit upon a low seat without pain. Pain in r., > forenoon by walking. *Bruised sensation* after walking in open air; in evening, with drawing. *Drawing pain; in morning and evening in bed;* in muscles of r., so that he could scarcely move it. Tendons seem too short on standing. *Uneasiness in evening till going to bed, so that she could not remain in the house.* Tingling as from weariness. *Weakness* in morning, > rising, with heaviness; in evening; after dinner; *after a short walk, with heaviness;* in r. when walking, with anxiety in it; *with pain as if there were no marrow in the bones;* sudden, after a short walk, < legs. *Heaviness; in morning in bed, with falling asleep;* when walking; < night, with tension in knees and thighs. Falling asleep of l. evenings. Numbness of r. even when lying.

Hip.—Jerking deep in l., > motion; *sudden cramplike, painful, about joint. Sticking in l. joint at night before sleep;* in l. joint at night, with weakness of l. foot; above l. extending into small of back, when coughing; *in r. joint, extending through r. half of pelvis down r. femur, avoiding knee and appearing in foot, in morning, keeping him in bed, as it was difficult to move,* then tenderness in these joints; *in l. extending to upper third of thigh in evening, < rest, > motion and pressure. Pain in joint, inability to step, pain at night even on touch.* Sprained pain in l. in morning on walking; in l. joint in forenoon on walking; in l. in forenoon when walking and standing; *in r. joint on motion in bed, so that he cannot tread in the morning, pain even on touch;* in l. when walking, and at head of l. fibula, causing limping. *Bruised pain on motion and on touch;* even on sitting, and in pubic region; in r. on sitting down and on moving body to one side. *Tensive pain in joint on walking;* drawing, in r. in afternoon, extending down thigh. *Drawing pain in l.;* in l. in afternoon, and in thigh. A kind of paralysis above nates.

Thigh.—Jerking, and in legs; J. as if in bones. **Cramp in r.** Sticking in l. T. and leg towards noon, < next day; above r. patella at 5 P.M. on walking; in l. in direction of crural nerve at night before sleep, < morning on waking, > rising, with weakness, at night traces of the pain; on inner side of l., > rubbing, with burning; sudden, in course of l. crural nerve in evening, > walking. Tearing in T. and legs at night in bed, coldness in bed; in T. and femora, often extending to knees, mostly > walking. Pain in middle of external aspect of r.; in r. nates; all night; *in posterior muscles when sitting;* in ischia after long sitting; *crampy, in lower third of l. before going to sleep, with lassitude;* in ischia as if weight of body were too great, in afternoon when sitting; as from a wound on inner side in evening; as if ischium were suppurating, preventing sitting and lying, even on touch, on rising from a seat thighs feel asleep, with pinching in ischii; *sore, between nates. Soreness between T., < walking in open air;* of nates and ischium after sitting long. Bruised pain; in anterior surface; *in r. in morning on waking, with drawing;* at night; outer side on touch; *anterior surface of r. towards evening, < pressure, with drawing and tension, causing limping,* > next forenoon when walking, returned at noon when sitting, then feeling in lower limbs as from a cold wind, pain < afternoon when sitting, > walking, returned in evening and disturbed sleep at night. Constriction in r. at 8 A.M., < walking; C. as from a band. **Drawing pain**; in tubera ischii, hip-joint and upper half of r. femur; in l. in evening; *in evening when walking,* next morning drawing pains when walking, < r. thigh, the pains lasted all the evening, even when sitting, and only once gave place to paralytic pain in l. forearm, next forenoon pain deep in r. thigh, < beginning to walk; in muscles of upper third of r. and in r. gluteal when walking, < stooping, afterwards in l. thigh; in r. in morning, < walking, alternating with similar pain in r. heel. Drawing in r.; on inside of l. during the day; in l. in morning after rising; in inside of r. in afternoon; in l. in afternoon; in l. when walking; in l. when sitting; r. during dinner, with tension, then in l.; < sitting; *intermittent cramplike, in muscles of anterior internal surface of r. at noon, then sudden aching tension in l. side of occiput;* downward on inside of l. in forenoon; backward in l. in evening, < middle, returned in morning on waking, < beginning to walk, > sitting. Tension in r. down to knee; in r. in forenoon when walking; *cramplike, in forenoon, now in muscles of anterior internal aspect of l. thigh, now in l. calf.* Weakness, and of legs.

Knee.—*Cracking.* **Sticking; in r.;** *on outermost tip;* in r. in morning on walking in open air, when sitting warmth and numbness (the pain was like that of a periostisis he had had three years before, from a fall), the pain > afternoon when walking, next morning on waking pain in lower part of knees, on walking two cracks in patella and boring, difficulty in ascending stairs; in r. in forenoon when standing; r., then l. at 11.30 P.M. when sitting, with horripilation on one side of chest; r., < standing; *on slight motion* (a cracking in it) and on ascending steps, > walking on a level; *causing shivering and fright;* burning, in bend of l. **Tearing** *in l. about noon;* in r. K. and ankle at 3 P.M.; *in l. on walking; l. on stepping, > lying, with sprained feeling, both returning in morning; externally in l. patella, > continued walking; through K. and tibia, < evening, with drawing, she does not know where to lay the legs;* **extending to feet when walking and sitting;** to toes, with heaviness of feet; from r. to crest of ilium, then general prostration. **Pain** *on moving it;* through r. at night in bed, with shooting under nail of r. great toe; **as from stiffness on rising from a seat.** Dislocation pain in l. when walking; in l. at every step, and in ankle. Sprained soreness on descending steps. Bruised pain on rising from a seat and on bending it. Cramplike drawing pain from hollow through joint, alternately in r. and l., between 10 and 11 P.M. in bed, < r. **Tension in hollows as if too short on stepping;** *T. on rising from a seat, < ascending steps; in r., so that he could not stretch leg; in hollow extending to feet, in bed, K. often spasmodically flexed and extended. Pressure on l. patella when sitting and walking.* Sensation as if grasped by both hands in evening. Weakness; in morning in bed; < forenoon, and after ascending steps burning in joints; give way when walking. Stiffness; *in hollows;* < rising from a seat, with weight.

Leg.—Swelling of veins. *Trembling, with weariness, sticking and tearing, when sitting more a tearing, when walk-*

ing sticking and tension, during which the toes are cold. Inclination to cramp on stretching out foot. Shooting in l. tendo-achillis in afternoon; in l. T. A. near os calcis at 2 P.M. during rest; periodical, in T. A. Tearing in lower end of r. in forenoon, with burning; in r. towards ankle at noon; lower part of l. in afternoon; *extending into middle of thighs;* jerking, on inner side of r. Pain in r.; in r. after dinner; in r. at night, preventing lying on r. side; along bone of r. at night, preventing lying on r. side; in r. up to hip-joint in morning, < noon, especially in hip-joint; burning, in r.; paralytic, in l. Tension in r. in morning; in r. in afternoon when sitting, with burning; in r. when standing after dinner, with weight; in r. so that he could not lie on r. side; in l. tendo-achillis in evening, < morning, < rest, > walking. Weakness of l.; W. in morning, with heaviness; when sitting and standing, > walking; and heaviness. Heaviness at night in bed. Tearing feeling of weight and weariness in morning in bed. Feeling when lying as if he could not raise it, which was not the case. Feel asleep on rising, with burning crawling in them.

Tibia.—**Sticking**; in l. in evening. Painful twitching in direction of long muscles of l., making walking difficult. Tearing in l. at noon; in l. in afternoon; paroxysmal, in l. in evening when walking, with digging. Bruised pain in evening on touch, as if flesh were loose from bone; intermittent B. pain outside of l. in afternoon. Sore pain in a spot in middle of r. at noon, it gave place towards evening to pain in small of back. Drawing pain; in r., with prickling in legs; along periosteum of l. at 7 P.M. during rest, then stitches in back near l. scapula. Drawing.

Calf.—Swelling. Gurgling as from drops of water extending down l. **Cramp** *in morning in bed;* in forenoon on walking; in l. in evening in bed on stretching out legs; *at night on stretching out legs;* **even when walking, when they are painful as if too short**; when dancing; in r. on stretching out leg in bed. Cramplike pain in lower part of l. between 7 and 8 P.M., on walking, with dislocation pain in l. ankle; C. pain in l. at every step, with pain in corns on l. foot. *Sticking in r.; back and forth to toes in evening when standing and sitting, with tearing,* the foot jerks inward, with tremulous sensation in whole body, heaviness and tearing in back, chilliness, with red cheeks, afterwards it affected pit of stomach, a tension and constriction under ribs, with oppressed respiration, and stitches in chest and upper abdomen. Boring in r. in evening, with burning. Pain on ascending steps. Drawing in l.; in muscles of r. at 6 P.M. when walking; alternately in C., tibiæ and soles; griping, when sitting, > walking. Tension; in r.; in r. in forenoon; on ascending stairs; in r. as if it were too short and made of wood in morning on walking, afterwards alternating with tension in l. occiput. Constriction. Tremulous sensation when standing. *Weary pain at night in bed.*

Ankle.—Cracking on motion. Swelling of malleoli, with sprained pain on motion. Turns when walking; < descending steps. Sticking beneath l. malleolus, < motion. Boring in r. inner malleolus at noon. *Sprained pain in l. on standing and walking;* over l. inner malleolus when walking. Drawing gnawing about l. in morning on waking. Burning griping, the burning < rubbing. Pain on movement, > next morning by continued walking; squeezing, in l. at night before going to bed, giving place to shooting in l. sole; burning, in a spot over r. internal malleolus at noon. Drawing in r. at 6 P.M.; cramplike, painful, from r. inner to outer. Tension in malleolus when walking. Weakness in l. at night, with numbness. **Stiffness of malleoli.**

Foot.—Swelling in warmth of bed; of r. when walking in open air. *Sticking in r.; in ball of r.; in the sore foot at night, with tearing; sudden burning, on back of l.;* pinching, in back of r., < motion. *Tearing in r.; T. at night, with rigidity, preventing sleep;* drawing, in r. metatarsus and toes at night. Shooting dislocation pain in metatarsal bone of r. great toe at 8 A.M. on every step up-stairs, and in afternoon when walking beneath l. outer malleolus. Cramplike pain in l. metatarsal bones, with ulcerative pain in l. sole; *C. pain in l. metatarsal bones extending to sole and ankle after midnight, then in r. Drawing pain in r. in morning on waking,* slightly > rising. *Drawing extending into hips, with cracking in joints on motion.* Tension in r.; in hollow; *in r. in morning; in r. after dinner; in r. on moving toes;* in l. metatarsus and great toe, < touch or motion. Throbbing in hollow of l. in evening; as from the jumping of a mouse in outer border of r. Weariness. **Heaviness**; in morning in bed; *< ankles; on walking in open air, > continued walking.*

Heel.—Sticking in r.; sudden, on outside of l. bone. Tearing in r.; T. extending into thighs and hip-joints when standing, < knee, > walking. Cutting extending to hollow of foot. Pain in l. Drawing in outer part of l. in evening after lying down.

Sole. — Jerking, > motion. *Cramp at every step.* Soft, sensitive, painful on walking. Stitches; in l. Tearing in r. in evening, > rubbing. Pain; as if suppurating, when stepping on them; cramplike, extending to toes on walking. Tension in narrow part of r. at noon on walking; T. as if too short on stepping. Drawing pain in morning. Falling asleep of l. in evening. Numbness, > rubbing, with crawling.

Corns. — Inflammation, with pain. **Sticking**; *in evening in bed; at night in bed.* **Pain; as from a tight shoe**; *as if boot pressed them in afternoon and alternations of drawing pain combined with stiffness, now in joints of l. great toe, now in r. ankle, now in ligamentous connection of r. ankle with metatarsus.* Sticking burning.

Toes.—Swelling. Inflammation of great, with pain. Nails, < middle, thick, horny and misshapen. Hæmorrhage below nail of little. *Cramp on stretching out feet;* C. during menses, > violent pressure, with flexion and bruised pain. *Sticking in l. great;* forepart of l. great; middle and great; *in great, now r., now l., in forenoon; in root of nail of r. great in evening, in bed;* in tips when sitting and lying. Tearing in first joint of r. great. *Cutting extending forward in l. great in morning in bed;* extending forward along inner border of l. great in evening during rest. *Pain in nail of great;* in balls of l.; in a corn on r. little; *on inside of nail of great, with soreness.* Painful drawing in first joint of l. great during rest, then on motion cramplike pain, at one time in inner malleolus, then in lower part of calf, again in knee and great toe. Tension in l. great, and in its metatarsal bone, < walking.

Skin.—Groups of black points like comedones on forehead, but they cannot be squeezed out. Black comedones on nose, *upper lip and chin.* **Hands hard and dry. Hang-nails.** Increased excretion of carbonic acid. Smelt of sulphur; in morning. *Cracked, < open air;* C., < hands; *hands, < about joints, with* *soreness; above roots of fingers;* about knuckles of hands, with rawness and roughness. Rough and atra-bilious. Liver-spots on back and chest, with itching in evening. Blue spots about malleoli, with varices.

Redness of hands and fingers in evening, with swelling as if frozen, with tension on motion; red inflamed spot on dorsum of nose; R. on back of r. arm, with burning; R. spots on arms after washing with soap and water, with burning; R. spot on l. cheek near ala nasi, then itching and elevations, with redness and heat of cheeks, traces of a similar elevation on r. cheek, < dinner and evening after wine, afterwards desquamation in round scales, which were transparent in centre, the skin beneath the detached scale elevated, red and sensitive, afterwards new scales on the spots that had desquamated, the eruption always < alcoholic liquors; bluish-red spot suddenly on inside of l. index; red, dry, dirty, with an attempt at formation of vesicles, perhaps artificial eczema, then pityriasis, with much itching.

Eruption; **burning itching**; itching, on hand; *painful, about chin. Tetter on nape.* Erythema on back of l. hand; on outside of leg, with itching, < night in bed, after scratching soreness, after the erythema smarting, < heat of bed. Desquamation; on face; on fingers in round spots. *A scaly eruption which had been driven away by external applications returned* **after scratching, with burning itching.** *Erysipelas of breast, inflammation, hardness and heat, with red rays extending from nipple and sticking in it.* (Herpes circinatus on r. middle finger became more swollen and shining), the ducts of the affected sebaceous glands filled with the products of inflammation appear more plainly, while the whitish scaly vesicles are more easily washed off.

Rash over whole body, with itching sticking; R. on r. leg, preceded by fever, leg swollen, hot, red, painful, with blisters containing yellowish serum, after the blisters burst some places were covered with thin yellowish-brown scabs, others became superficial ulcers. **Heat rash on neck**; *biting R. on face, arms and lower limbs;* itching R. over whole body, then desquamation. *Nettle-rash; with fever; on back of hand; over whole body, hands and feet;* under hips. *Chilblains on fingers, the itching < warmth.* Elevations covering back; reddish, on trunk and limbs; red burning, in r. palm; hard, hot, on l. upper arm, with sticking in it; wrinkled, colored like liver-marks, with scales.

Pimples on forehead; face; r. cheek; nose and upper lip; chin, neck, shoulders and behind ears; nape; l. side of neck; upper arm and lower limbs; about malleoli; here and there, with scabby eruptions; beneath skin on dorsum of hands; in a group under skin on back of r. hand, at joint of middle finger; of the color of the skin on thighs and arms, afterwards some had a red areola and at their apices a vesicle filled with limpid fluid, afterwards desquamation in fine scales, < region of elbows, thighs, < inside and near knees, rough; *irregularly shaped, on back of hands, < r. thumb, with itching, < forenoon. Furunculous pimples, < face, with red areola and itching;* F. pimple on l. temple and r. mastoid process. Hard pimple on l. cheek; l. angle of jaw; red, painful, near l. angle of jaw. *Inflamed pimple on forehead; above l. brow; side of forehead;* face; r. whisker; cheek; r. cheek; nape; lumbar region; back of r. hand; r. index and middle fingers; l. index, middle and ring fingers; back of third joint of r. index, at the apex a vesicle filled with opaque fluid, changing to pus, and the pimple became painful; at division between nates, making walking difficult. Painful inflamed pimples behind ear; on nates. Red pimples on thighs and r. hand, then on l. upper arm; on back of r. hand, with itching; *on nose, upper lip, chin and forearms, with itching,* **and at times burning after scratching**; nose, cheek, forehead and chin, with pain. **Pimples painful to touch on forehead.** *Painful pimples above brows;* on r. ear; r. brow; l. side of nape superiorly; white, between toes. Itching pimples; below l. corner of mouth; on arm; outside of l. elbow; backs of hands; *inside of thighs;* thighs, with red spots; **on forehead, on rubbing a sticking in them;** back of r. hand, when scratched they excrete a clear fluid, with twitching and smarting between fingers; between l. thumb and index, with areola, a vesicle filled with clear fluid formed in the apex, which burned when scratched; on face, moist after scratching; P. on outside of l. elbow, itching in morning; P. behind r. ear, with itching in evening; P. on inside of l. knee and on elbow, itching after going to bed.

Pustules above l. brow; in r. brow; on forehead; dorsum of nose; cheek; which let out fluid when scratched, on back near loins; pulsating, on l. ala nasi; reddish, with rough areola near union of ring and little fingers, itching in the heat; red, on l. forearm, itching on touch; reddish itching, on r. thumb near metacarpus; itching, in bends of elbows; on back of hand, itching in warmth of bed. Pustules similar to itch in bends of elbows and on wrists; on dorsum of r. hand; anteriorly on l. thigh. Onychia at l. thumbnail after a slight injury, pain extending to metacarpus, inflammation of first joint of thumb. Redness at tip of r. thumb, on side next index, back of thumb, bearing the nail, painful as if gathering, next day a whitish spot in centre of the redness, then a purulent deposit with a pale red areola imbedded in skin, afterwards the deposit became a brownish swelling, a transparent fluid had exuded beneath the pus and raised it up, but the pus gradually mingled with it, in the whole hand throbbing pain, < touch, ending with burning smarting, the bed of the nail was not involved.

Eruption like that after vaccination. Suppuration of abraded skin. *Boils;* on tragus; on r. whisker; l. shoulder; *inflamed, on l. side of forehead;* painful blue, on each side of lower jaw; on back, when squeezed discharging blood and pus. Scabs on nose causing tension in its tip. *Ulcer about a nail* (panaritium); U., with tensive pain; offensive, on nail; scabby, with sour-smelling matter; bleeding of an old U.

Vesicles on each frontal protuberance; below l. nostril; on r. ring finger; here and there on hands, index fingers and l. thumb, afterwards roughness of the parts; on sole after walking; ulcerating, on soles; *a slight injury on finger becomes sore, with pulsation, then a corrosive V. and hands swell, with pain on touch.* **Itching vesicles on back of hand;** between l. ring and middle fingers, filled with clear fluid; scabious, on first phalanx of r. ring finger, afterwards between l. thumb and index.

A small cut is sore and smarts, then burning, then inflammation, with throbbing pain. Stitchlike prickling over whole body in evening in warmth of bed. Sticking on cheeks, shoulders and thighs; here and there in forenoon; in an old wart (under eye), with tickling; creeping and flying S. in a wart and parts of the wart fell off. *Burning pain in parts on which he was lying at night, disturbing rest. After rubbing, pain as if denuded. Creeping shivering without chilliness.* **Formication over whole body**; on face; in hands; over l. zygoma in afternoon, with burning; *in finger-tips*, < hanging arm down, *with prickling*, hot, down back; *sticking, in r. heel;* tickling, in l. arm and lower limb in evening in bed, obliging frequent drawing up. Tickling on calf at 5 A.M. *Itching biting on nates;* in B. as from fleas in evening after lying down, preventing sleep, appearing in another spot after scratching.

Itching all over body; now here, now there; in brows *and tip of nose;* **chest; axillæ and hollows of knees; palms; fingers; between fingers;** *forehead; above l. brow; externally in ears; about chin;* r. concha; *neck;* back and l. hand; *backs of hands; about knees; toes;* lower third of l. forearm and on l. thigh; external aspect of fingers; legs; outer side of thigh; small of back; except on inside of limbs. Itching in morning; *of r. hand,* < **between fingers**; on back of hand near wrist; < above crest of l. os ilii; *after waking*, < eyelids, foreskin, glans and feet, *with smarting.* I. in afternoon on outside of thigh; *of l. hand from wrist to little finger*, < **scratching** (Puls.), **which causes burning. I. in evening between finger-joints**; on legs; legs, < l.; **general, < on and between fingers, with smarting and formication, parts not sensitive itched on touch**; *on forehead, with burning;* over r. ankle, with burning; *various parts, face, chest and hands, and after scratching redness;* on back, then pimples; l. whisker, after scratching soreness; **in bed, < arms and legs; on dorsum of r. hand in bed, with burning, it became covered with elevated, red and itching pustules,** *which went off during the night.* **I. at night over whole body;** *on upper and lower abdomen; thighs and legs; here and there*, < scrotum; wrists and inside of l. fingers, < scratching; legs, and after scratching sore feeling; **in spots, with frequent waking; general, before falling asleep; general, in bed; in heat of bed, now in one place, now in another,** < *nape;* in warmth in bed, on back and sides of trunk; *when he got warm in bed*, from hips to toes, < hollows of knees, after rubbing pimples discharging a fluid, when the itching ceased, but it returned the next night. I. of r. leg on waking; on several parts of l. hand after rising, after scratching red spots on which were papules close together and itching periodically; *on forehead after dinner; about abdomen after dinner, and on rubbing griping in intestines and tenesmus, < groins, as if towards the middle, < stooping and deep breathing, > walking; externally on nose after menses; of toes that had once been frozen;* I. < **night and morning on waking**; *on elbows and wrists, < hands, < evening, then vesicles full of yellow water;* **in spots, mostly > scratching, sometimes followed by sticking or burning**; *obliged to scratch old tetters till they bleed;* I. on scrotum and thighs, with sweat on those parts; in places, with redness; in spots below r. knee, with redness; *of fingers, with redness, which was > pressure*, but returned immediately, *next day white vesicles on inside of r. ring and little fingers, third day vesicles on inside of second phalanx of r. middle finger;* on dorsum of r. hand, < heat of bed, with redness and roughness, and red, itching pimples on r. thumb towards metacarpus, and roughness between r. thumb and index, the pimples gradually became pustules; on l. wrist, with burning, then pimples, with red areola and a white spot at their apex; in bend of elbow, with smarting, then pimples on a red spot; between r. fingers, with smarting, with a scabious-looking pimple on back of hand; **in spots that bleed and bite after scratching; in spots that are painful after scratching**; in bend of r. elbow, exudation of moisture after scratching; on legs, and after scratching burning pain; in a spot on l. lower jaw towards cheek, rubbing caused redness and elevations; in a white spot on cheek; **crawling I., with pain after scratching**; crawling, on inner side of thigh; *sticking, < walking in open air;* sudden, on r. hand in evening, < palm and between fingers.

Clinical.—Intertrigo, acne, eczema, herpes, in short, all forms of skin eruptions, generally < bathing, associated with burning itching, temporarily relieved by scratching, with the peculiar characteristics of the drug.

Sleep.—Yawning; *during the day, with sleepiness;* and stretching without sleepiness; spasmodic, in evening before going to bed. *Sleepiness; in daytime during menses;* at 8 A.M., with disinclination to work; in morning; at noon; *in afternoon; towards evening;* at night, but inability to sleep; after dinner; after two glasses of beer; after a glass of beer, with ebullition of blood. **Irresistible sleepiness during the day,** *she fell asleep when sitting at work; he fell asleep as soon as he sat down during the day; I. in evening.* Sleeps with arms over head. *Sleeps with half open eyes. Disinclination to rise in morning.* Waking difficult.

Sleeplessness all night; till midnight; **before midnight, then frequent waking and tossing about; till midnight, then disagreeable dreams, only tranquil towards morning;** for a long time after midnight; *from 12 till 3 o'clock; from 1 till 2* A.M.; **every night after 3 A.M.**; *every morning after 4; every morning after 5; on account of irritability and uneasiness; with weariness;* **with mounting of blood to head. Late falling asleep**; often not till 1 or 2 A.M.; *on account of flow of thoughts; and waking every hour; with inclination to sweat; then dreams of fire and death.* **Frequent waking; with beating of blood in head, then also in chest**; with nausea; *every half hour, could only sleep a few hours towards morning;* partly, and coldness. **Waking early.** *Waking in anxiety, heat and sweat.*

Sleep disturbed; *partly by indistinct stitches and partly by anxious dreams.* **Sleep restless**; first half of night, with sighs; *after midnight;* after midnight, dream that she was going to have a fever and woke in sweat, with heat, < face, thirst, shivering < motion, even to chattering of teeth; after 3 A.M., moaning, groaning and occasionally whistling respiration. **Frequent turning over without waking. Starting up on falling asleep**; *S. in midday nap; S. up anxiously. Jerking in lower jaw on falling asleep;* of feet in sleep. *Stretching in sleep. Sighing in sleep. Moans and lamentations. Loud talking;* of the conversation of the day; *talking before midnight, as in anxious dreams.* Unintelligible murmuring. Crying out that she was black, etc. *Sleep unrefreshing;* and too long; like a half slumber, disturbed by vivid dreams of the ordinary occupations. Sleep light.

Dreams.—Immediately on closing eyes. **Vexatious. Vivid; out of which he often woke and could not fall asleep again for a long time**; *waking him frequently; but unremembered; so V. that she was sitting on the chamber that she urinated in the bed;* of business transacted long ago. **Frightful**; *of fire; that* *he had been bitten by a dog; of the dead and dying, she wakes herself by weeping and shouting and then is confused; with palpitation,* and on waking sometimes rigor, sometimes heat and fear of robbers; after midnight, waking him; waking him, and then anxious thoughts as of ghosts; *of dangers of death and of dead people.* **Anxious; as if something oppressed him** (nightmare); *that fire came down from heaven; of danger from fire and water; as if pursued by wild beasts; and half remembered; partly A., partly indifferent;* in which she rose from bed unconscious, then headache; before midnight, she walked about like a somnambulist, thought there was a fire, dressed herself, talked out of the window, was frightened when she heard that it was nothing, for three days afterwards she was weak and felt bruised. *Disagreeable. That he was falling from a height.* Of horrible grimaces immediately on closing eyes. Of murders, from which he woke at 4 A.M., with fatigue. Of unfortunate and dishonorable events. Disturbing, with frequent waking and pain around navel. Of things she saw the next day. Confused. *Disconnected. Comic, with loud laughter, which continued after waking.* Laughable fancies in a half dream before falling asleep, many evenings, she laughed aloud. Lively. Amorous; with an emission. On waking a number (figure) appeared to her stretched out and the lines were a quarter of a yard long, > lying on other side. Rose from bed in a somnambulistic way, cried "My head, my head, I am crazy!" and grasped his forehead, after walking about a little he came to himself. She ran about the room for five minutes without knowing where she was, with open eyes.

Fever.—*Chilliness; in morning;* in morning, head soon became hot and limbs cold, a few hours later chill, then fever and sweat, which lasted eight or ten hours, then chill more severe than before; after performing his ablutions till noon; in forenoon, sensation of heat in afternoon though she was cold to touch; from 9 A.M. till 5 P.M.; from 10 till 11 A.M., then rest till 3 P.M., then heat in head and hands for two hours, with thirst for beer; from 10 A.M. till 6 P.M., > in bed, then heat in palms, then general warmth except on head; till 11 A.M., then heat from 12 till 2 P.M., with glowing cheeks, then cold from 3 till 5 P.M. and then heat before bedtime; at noon; from noon till midnight, with internal heat, redness of face, weariness of limbs as if bruised, then sweat for three hours. H. in afternoon; with thirst; with heat and palpitation; < hands and feet, with horripilation; with sensitiveness to open air, hands rigid and reddish-brown; every afternoon, then heat with thirst, cold feet, sweat on face and hands, and dry cough at night as soon as he got into bed. **C. in evening,** > *lying down,* **with headache;** in E., then sweat at night; every E., not > warmth of stove, in bed heat, and sour sweat every morning; with burning in skin above forehead extending over forehead; then in bed heat; when writing; in bed, then swarming fancies, then heat and sweat. C. from 4 till 6 P.M., then shivering starting from toes; from 5 till 6 P.M.; at 5.30 P.M., then heat, then C., with thirst till 8 o'clock; from 7 P.M. through the night and next day; at 7 P.M., then heat, with full and rapid pulse; every day at 8 P.M., then at night on waking heat without thirst; at 11 P.M. on going to bed, till sleep, with aching on r. side of vertex, it returned next morning on waking and next evening in bed, on third day C. not > the fire, with blue nails, face pale, head giddy and heavy, C. recurred on moving and after swallowing saliva, with sensation as if humeri were broken, coldness as from a draught of air diagonally across above navel. *C. at night;* in bed, < abdomen; in bed, preceded by colic, together with heat without thirst, with sweat the next night; in bed, preceded by colic, with heat without sweat, sweat next night. *C. after dinner; from dinner till 4 P.M., with thirst;* before going to sleep; after disagreeable news; in open air. C., with diarrhœa. C., then heat, with thirst, sweat, headache, hoarseness, weakness and loss of appetite; then burning in parts rubbed (thighs).

C. in two attacks in morning; tiresome C. in forenoon; alternating with heat at night. Shaking C. in evening; and pallor; from 7 till 8 P.M., with cold hands and heaviness in stomach, then thirst. Shivering at 8 A.M.; at noon, with blueness of nails and gooseskin, first on outside of arms, then on back down small of back, lastly on abdomen, where he felt as if stroked across with something cold, it was > fire and < movement, was accompanied by weariness, pallor, suffering expression, pains in middle of upper arms and of thighs and legs as if broken, and pains shooting through outside of feet, but appetite good; *in evening, then heat of face and hands, with thirst;* from 5 till 6 P.M., then after lying down heat of hands and soles, without thirst; from 8 till 9 P.M., till lying down; *at night on waking, yet warmth to touch, then heat; on least movement in bed;* in bed, then heat, then sweat smelling of sulphur; after dinner; **on body, with flushing heat in face;** with heat; *from feet over back into arms at 6 P.M.; through skin in evening in bed.*

Internal C., *without thirst;* I. about 10 A.M.; till noon, worse daily, with vertigo as if head would sink down, then weakness, with sweat day and night on head, which was puffy. Horripilation in forenoon, with weight in chest and arms; H. all the afternoon and evening after dinner; from spine over abdomen, back and upper limbs in forenoon and at 7 P.M.; in arms.

C. after drinking coffee, except in r. cheek and concha, which burned; C. on head; in a spot on vertex; paroxysmally in face, as if dashed with cold water, with perceptible coldness; externally in epigastric region; over abdomen. **C. in back;** and limbs; and on chest and arms; **in evening;** towards evening, and over scalp, *with heat in face; with dry heat in thighs and small of back;* **creeping from small of B. up B.** from 6 till 8 P.M.; *creeping up B. in evening, > stove;* as if a cold breath passed over small of B., with drawing in tibia; spreading from lower third of spine over body and lower limbs; proceeding from lumbar vertebræ in evening during firm stool after straining, with cold feeling in limbs, < lower ones; from lumbar region to abdomen and limbs; from lumbar vertebræ over abdomen when urinating and afterwards; from r. side of lumbar vertebræ over r. side of body in bed; from lumbar vertebræ over limbs, with bursting feeling in abdomen, the C. recurred at 4 P.M., with shooting in urethra and boring in bones of arms.

C. in limbs in forenoon; at 3 P.M.; l. upper arm. *Cold hands; and feet; and feet and nose;* and feet in afternoon, then shaking chill for half an hour, with blue face, then heat and sweat till 9.30. Cold fingers; l. lower limb; legs in evening. *Cold feet;* soles; *all day and evening till going to sleep;* in afternoon; in evening in bed; *in evening, with heat of head;* at night; at night in bed; at night, before sleep, with heat of head and hands; at night, with sweat on abdomen as far as groins and cutting in soles; during dinner, with itching of nostrils, from which water drops, with impatience, which makes everything difficult; *after dinner, with palpitation;* < *evening.*

Heat; all day, > night, with thirst; in morning on waking; from noon till evening, with thirst; in afternoon; evening; *night;* night, with sweat; *in the room;* when at stool, with salivation; **orgasm of blood;** *orgasm from a little beer; flushing;* anxious, in morning, with sweat and dryness of throat; dry; *dry, in morning in bed;* as if sweat would break out towards morning; internal, with thirst; internal, in whole body, a burning extending upward in chest, but she must force herself to drink; prickling, about 2 A.M., with disposition to sweat. Intermittent fever, first rigor with thirst, then heat without thirst, but with rush of blood to head (whether this fever, which lasted six weeks and left me very weak, and whether the decay of five teeth was due to the Sulphur, I cannot decide).

Burning in skin of whole body; of the spots scratched; *of skin in evening, with dryness;* of skin at 2 A.M., with tendency to sweat; **itching, in various parts, after scratching it hurts as if sore.**

Heat in head; in morning; in morning, > washing, with confusion; at 4 P.M. after a glass of beer; from 7 P.M., with confusion; from 7 to 9 P.M., with fulness in head; with fulness; *in flashes, with orgasm of blood; in flashes towards* 2 P.M.; *delaying sleep; dry, in morning on waking, with glowing face.* H. in forehead. *Burning in skin of forehead;* all day till late in evening; in morning; in morning after rising; in evening when sitting. Burning in scalp on temples at noon; *B. on vertex in morning on washing, then coolness.* Heat in occiput; in morning, > rising; in morning, with pain; on entering a heated room; > walking in open air, returning on entering the room, with pain; in sudden attacks, with pain.

H. of face; < cheeks and around eyes; *all day,* with burning on malar-bones and redness of nose; *during the day,* then between 5 and 6 P.M. every day chilliness for half an hour, then general heat for an hour; *every day from 5 till* 9 P.M.; in evening, with redness and with squeezing in cardiac region; **and in throat, without redness;** *with redness, H.* < *about mouth;* with red spots between eye and ear; and in throat, with red spots in face; first on face, with sensation as after severe illness, then chilliness, with thirst; as from drops of hot fluid on r. cheek at noon; flying, in evening; in flushes in l. cheek for an hour in forenoon and afternoon; *in flashes, then general coldness,* then weakness in bones of lower limbs as if there were no marrow in them, < sitting.

Burning in back; *in skin;* beneath axillæ; between scapulæ; about lower angle of l. scapula; in skin about noon, < between scapulæ, changing after scratching into sore pain; in skin in afternoon, with perceptible throbbing in arteries beneath skin of the affected part; with biting; corrosive, between shoulders, beneath r. shoulder-joint, in small of back and nates, in evening after lying down.

Burning at 2 A.M. extending from shoulder over l. upper arm and between scapulæ; in skin spreading from r. shoulder over upper arm and r. side of chest; in skin of extensor side of r. upper arm, and after scratching a raw pain; in skin of flexor side of l. elbow; in skin of l. elbow at 9 A.M., gradually extending over extensor side. **Heat in hands;** in forenoon; after eating. **H. in palms;** *at night;* **itching-sticking.** *Burning in tips of fingers; balls* in forenoon. Dry heat in lower limbs. Burning on r. leg; skin of r. leg and foot; r. leg in morning; r. leg in morning and evening after exercise; legs at 8 P.M. **B. in feet;** *across dorsum; in evening;* **in evening in bed, with necessity to uncover them, then uneasiness, itching and crawling;** *in hollow of l. sole in evening;* **in soles** *on stepping after long sitting; in soles,* < *walking, with itching.*

Sweat; during the day; at 3 A.M.; towards morning, with anxiety, causing him to throw off the bed-clothes; in morning on waking; in morning after waking; in morning when walking; *in morning,* > *waking; always after waking about* 6 *or* 7 A.M.; in forenoon; in forenoon when walking; in forenoon, with weakness; in afternoon; *in evening in bed;* in evening before lying down, < hands, and after lying down heat and difficult falling asleep; in evening from slight work, then a waking dream, as if she had on a garment that she must take great care to avoid soiling; **at night; at night, with restless sleep;** at night after waking; at night, then disappearance of skin symptoms; *on motion;* on movement, < forenoon and < occiput; when walking; *when walking in open air;* after walking rapidly, < occiput; when sitting; when sitting, reading, writing and talking; after thin stool, < forehead, relieving the confusion of head, then only transient pressure in forehead.

Sweat smelling of sulphur; in morning on waking; in forenoon; < hands, and metal articles about his person turn black. Sour sweat at night; with little sleep; and a burnt odor.

Sweat in axillæ; offensive, in axillæ; *S. on itching parts in morning;* head; occiput; occiput when walking; face; face and nape in morning in bed, with bruised sensation in limbs on rising; on face when eating, with redness of white of eye; face from least effort; face and neck from least exertion; nape nearly all day, at times with coldness and shivering; nape at night; hands and feet in morning; clammy, on hands and feet during the day; *hands; on palms; between fingers; about knees at night;* legs in morning; legs in evening as soon as he lay down in bed; legs at night; r. leg; r. leg at 5 A.M.; r. leg at night; feet; r. foot at night; soles; *cold on feet;* cold, on l. sole.

Clinical.—It is indicated in various types of fever, idiopathic or symptomatic; in the malarial types there is tendency to torpor, with nocturnal aggravation; heat of the head, with cold feet, or heat of the palms and soles at night. In eruptive fevers the eruption is partial and scanty; the tongue is usually dry and red at the tip and edges (compare Rhus t.).

Sulfuricum Acidum.

It is diluted with distilled water (1 to 9) for use.

General Action.—Compare Sulphur.

Generalities.—Lying on back, body and lower limbs immovable; on r. side, with knees drawn up and body bent forward; doubled up almost in the shape of a ball. Emaciation. Appearance as in collapsed stage of cholera, extremities livid, cold clammy feel, pulse gone. Tremor. Twisting about on all sides. Convulsions; with falling to the ground; with unconsciousness; with cramps in pharynx preventing swallowing;

every half hour, with dyspnœa, distorted eyes, gnashing of teeth, frothing from mouth and cold sweat on face; epileptiform, with rush of blood to head, unconsciousness; clonic, of upper limbs and dorsal muscles, convulsions of facial muscles, eyes sunken.

Agony, with occasional hysterical fits, with spastic rigidity of muscles of lower jaw, loss of speech, sudden weakness, weak and fluttering pulse, pallor and dejection of countenance. Rheumatic tearing and drawing in whole body. Pain; in every part; in spots, at first increasing, then suddenly disappearing; intermittent, with drawing up of legs and moanings. Consumption. Symptoms of last stage of croup. Rush of blood upward, with anxiety and tossing about. Tremulous sensation over whole body, without trembling, > morning. Hyperæsthesia over trunk. Sensation as if he would fall to one or other side when walking. Restlessness; and loud screams. The odor of coffee is disagreeable and causes weakness and trembling. **Weakness**; in morning after taking milk; after eating; > open air, with pain in forehead; and marasmus. Collapse; with restlessness; with irregular, finally suppressed pulse, cold sweat, etc. Faintness. Paralysis, with epileptiform spasms. Inability to move or talk. Symptoms appear immediately after dinner. Aggravation in open air; A. from cold, wet and windy weather, amelioration when warm and dry. Amelioration from pressure over epigastrium.

Clinical.—General tendency to hæmorrhage in various parts.

Mind.—Delirium; at night. Excitement. Jocose. Exaltation of mind and disposition. *Fretful*; all day, she avoids speaking to every one; in morning on waking; *if his work is not done to suit, and impatient;* and quarrelsome, averse to answering; and sick, so that she started at everything; and sad. Mistrustful. Sedate, earnest. Lachrymose. Fright. Melancholy and weary of life; M. in morning. *Despondent*. Apprehensive; from morning till evening. Anxiety; with tossing about; with burning pain and heat in stomach; with nausea, then vomiting of mucus. Averse to talking. Hasty mood, she can finish nothing quickly enough though it fatigues her. Distraction, often gave inappropriate answers. (Stupor); in paroxysms. Roused with difficulty, and when aroused resisted, saying "Let me alone, let me die." Inclined to coma. Unconsciousness.

Head.—Stitches here and there when walking in open air. Tearing. Aching; as if shattered in morning after waking, with sleepiness; as if it would burst; as if full; drawing, in evening; drawing, < r. side towards forehead. Drawing and tension. Dulness; in morning, with heaviness; with burning in stomach. Heaviness and pain as if brain fell forward and came through; H., fulness and necessity to hold it forward. Weakness. Vertigo on rising; in afternoon when sewing; when sitting; > open air.

Forehead.—Sudden jerking beneath l. eminence, suddenly disappearing; sudden painful J. above l. eminence. Sticking in r. side of sinciput in evening, > pressure, with tearing; S. above l. orbit, increasing, then disappearing; deep in brain below l. eminence, suddenly increasing, then diminishing, at last suddenly disappearing; now r., now l. side of sinciput, extending deep into brain; sudden, below l. eminence, extending into brain; alternately in F. and occiput. Tearing in middle towards l. side. Pressive and burning pain, and in eyes. Pain as from a blow, increasing, then suddenly disappearing, in r. side; near l. eminence. Painful soreness above l. eminence, more acute in isolated jerks. Pain in r. eminence on shaking head, as if brain were loose and knocked against skull. Feeling as if brain were loose and fell backward and forward. Constriction, increasing, then suddenly disappearing. Dulness in forenoon, with fulness.

Temples. — Shooting jerks in r. Sticking in r. Tearing in r. towards evening; in l. during breakfast. Wavelike burning pain as from a bruise. Intermittent grumbling in bones. Drawing rather externally in a spot in l. Pressure inward.

Pain in vertex when standing. Stupefying throbbing pain in r. side on rising after stooping. Screwed in sensation above l. ear. Heaviness in l. side. Sudden confusion as from smoke in r. side when sitting. Sticking in l. side of occiput, with pressure. Compressive pain in sides of occiput, > holding hands towards head without touching it. *Pain in scalp as from suppuration, with pain on touch.* Hair becomes gray and falls out. Itching. Tension in l. side of scalp and in l. ear, more in front of ear.

Eyes.—Sparkling. Lustreless and watery; L., and pupils dilated. Ghastly, and face. Redness, lachrymation and photophobia. Protruding. Sunken and expressive of suffering. Fixed, and pupils contracted. Look unsteady. Burning; on reading in the commencing twilight, with lachrymation; with inflammation, lids swollen, r. eye looked dull and opaque, on fourth day r. conjunctiva acquired a jelly-like consistence, on eighth day the cornea, which all along had been opaque, sloughed away, giving exit to the lens and part of the vitreous humor, for more than a week this eye continued inflamed and discharged much purulent matter, it is still suppurating and wasting away; biting, in l. when reading during the day, with lachrymation. Biting in r.

Lachrymation. Burning pain anteriorly in ball in open air, but in the house pain only on looking intently. Lids agglutinated in morning; mostly closed, but pupils small and piercing; sink down and he cannot open them; sticking outward above margin of r. at every paroxysm of cough; sticking itching on lower. Canthus, twitching in r. inner; *sensation of a foreign body in r. outer in morning when walking,* > in the house; pressure in outer. Subcutaneous tearing on margin of r. orbit, extending towards temple. Photophobia. Twitching sensation before vision, with weakness. Vision dim in morning.

Ears.—Tearing in front of l. and up into temple; in front of l., extending into cheek, where it became a crawling; deep in l., then crawling; rather externally in r., with sticking. Pain, and in fauces. Drawing outward in r. meatus. Exit of agreeable warmth from r., then jerking in it. Tickling in concha. Ringing in r. Roaring; in evening; rhythmical; as of a waterfall in l. on opening mouth during dinner. Diminished hearing as from a leaf before ear.

Nose.—Stinging prickling in r. side. Ineffectual inclination to sneeze. Vapor mounted through nose, then incessant sneezing, then stoppage of nose. Discharge of dark brown froth. Coryza, with sore eyes; C., with loss of smell; fluent; running out of much water, with stoppage of one nostril; dry; dry, at times he could get no air through one or the other nostril. Bleeding in evening when sitting and standing.

Clinical.—When the discharge trickling down from nose is thin and lemon-colored (Puls.).

Face.—*Pale;* and puffy; and sunken; and restless, drawn; and hippocratic, drawn; dingy, deathlike; with movement in stomach. Red; and puffy; r. cheek, and hot; covered with red spots, which in a few hours scabbed over and became brown. Dark blue. Cheeks livid. Gangrenous look. Distorted; and livid. Swelling of cheeks; l. cheek; S., with frequent changes of color, lips swollen and sore. Sunken; and anxious, the patient frequently sprang from bed, and died in collapse, with offensive odor from mouth and involuntary discharges. Expression of anxiety; E. of collapse. Jerking about l. ear always on moving head, afterwards also during rest. Convulsions, and of lips. Sticking frequently extending upward in r. cheek. Tearing in l. bones, then in r. side of head; here and there in lower jaw. Pinching in skin beneath r. eye, increasing then disappearing. Bruised pain in l. malar bone, increasing then suddenly disappearing. Sensation as if cheeks were puffy and as if albumen had dried upon skin. Trismus.

Lips.—White, and tongue; and mouth and fauces; and sodden, and tongue and mouth as far as could be seen; and mucous membrane thickened; in corners, and sore as if ulcerated; and excoriated, and tongue, mouth and fauces; and shrivelled and had blisters inside, with similar appearances on mouth and tongue; pearly, and mouth and throat; inner surface and gum grayish-white, thick and wrinkled. Violet. Reddish-brown. Smooth, dry, brownish. Cracked and scaly. Peeling of inner side. Swelling, redness and pain on touch; S. of inside, tongue and fauces, with appearance as if smeared with thin arrowroot; and tongue and mouth, and covered with white aphthous spots exuding offensive bloody ichor; of lower lip and tongue, the margins of which were black, mucous membrane of mouth swollen, with burning in mouth, pharynx and stomach. Dark grayish sloughs across upper, descending down angles of mouth, similar but slighter marks on forepart of neck, chest and on r. arm. Excoriation, and of chin. Sore pain in corners. Pressure as with a finger above l. corner.

Mouth.—Teeth. Chalky white and had lost their polish. Yellow and black fur, like the sordes of fever. Broke off and fell out in pieces. Tearing in l.; in l. lower in bed in evening till midnight; in l. eye-tooth all night during menses, and in lower jaw. Gnawing in r. lower in evening, < lying down till 2 A.M.; in molar and incisor when biting on something hard. Digging in a hollow molar during and after chewing something hard. Pain in l. lower in evening after lying down; P. < cold, > warmth, preventing sleep all night; pressing inward in r. upper incisor. *On edge;* in afternoon.

Gum.—Ulceration. Swelling of r. lower, when pressed pus exudes. Feels fuzzy and bleeds on slightest touch.

Tongue.—White; and thick and denuded; and swollen, corrugated, and mouth; and eroded, dry; and denuded, and mouth and throat; T. and mouth, with much tenacious glairy mucus, white patches on throat; T. and mouth, and corrugated, dry, as far as lower lip, where there was a distinct line of demarcation; and mouth, afterwards the pellicles dropped, the mucous membrane beneath was bright red and very sensitive; and mouth and fauces, and covered with a white viscid secretion; covered with grayish-white crusts, tip and edges red. Dark. Very red, often bluish-red and shining. Swollen. Shrivelled, small. Phlyctenæ on back and on palatine arch. Denuded at tip and very red, parts of it coated white. Cast off its cuticle and was red, with prominent papillæ. (Dry). Insensible, dry in centre. Speech difficult; indistinct; short, abrupt, hoarse, with at times hoarse hacking cough; only whispering, could scarcely open the mouth, from which exuded a ropy mucus. Speechless.

Mouth in General.—Swollen; *palate and pharynx, and injected, ulcerated;* M. and fauces S. and inflamed, corners of lips burnt, with burning in pharynx and œsophagus. Inflamed, and fauces and pharynx. Brown. Ashy-gray. Bleached. White and ragged. Coated white, and pharynx, swallowing difficult, voice without sound; coated white, and fauces, peeling off in parts, leaving a raw reddish-brown surface, < dorsum of tongue and end of uvula. Covered with a fuzzy membrane, and fauces. Shrivelled and dry, and fauces. *Aphthæ.* Covered with fungoid blackish red masses, and fauces. Vesicles on inside of l. cheek. Superficial ulceration, with discharge of bloody liquid. All parts touched by the acid from mouth as far as could be seen covered with crusts and exuding an offensive ichor, then aphthæ and gangrene. Brown, bloody liquid in it. Frothing, with constant retching. Black froth issued. Brownish mucus. Mucus often comes into it, which causes choking, hacking, obliged to swallow it constantly; stringy copper-colored mucus and froth from the dependent corner of mouth. Discharge of frothy, viscid, tenacious fluid, with retching caused by the fluid irritating the fauces, the fluid ejected was reddish-brown, contained shreds of mucous membrane and seemed to be a mixture of mucus and saliva, reaction on test paper was neutral.

Pain; and heat. Burning pain; and in throat, speaking difficult and painful; extending along œsophagus to stomach. Dryness. Salivation; with nausea and constriction in stomach and abdomen; with swelling of parotids and constipation; saltish, even in morning. *Breath offensive.* Taste bad; in morning after waking; insipid and pasty in morning, > rising; bitter like bile, to bread, bread causes pressure in stomach; lost.

Clinical.—Sore mouth, aphthæ occurring during protracted diseases, especially in children with marasmus, with salivation, sour vomiting, stools like chopped eggs.

Throat.—*Swelling of submaxillary glands, with inflammation* and at times sticking. *Pain as if swollen in submaxillary gland, as far as into tongue, with burnt feeling in tongue.* Painful swelling of l. parotid, with suppuration. *Swelling; of uvula and root of palate;* of fauces; of fauces, which is whitish-gray; near cricoid, with pain; *as if there were a lump in it.* Redness and sensitiveness; dark R. of pharynx. Tough mucus. Rattling of mucus, and in chest, with difficult respiration, restlessness, with pains in larynx and chest, then death. Hawking; of mucus; of tenacious masses of mucous membrane; with retching and vomiting of bloody, reddish-brown mucus, which was so acid that it burnt holes in the linen.

Sticking in l. side of pharynx on swallowing, also in evening, with pain externally on touch; paroxysmal, in T. and chest, stopping the breath, when standing and walking, > open air. Cutting in side on swallowing. Scraping. *Rawness. Sensitiveness. Soreness in evening on swallowing,* < *l. side.* Tenderness from pharynx down to epigastrium. Pain; in fauces; and as far as stomach, < swallowing, talking or turning body. *Constriction;* in pharynx; < r. side. Burning pain; in pharynx. Burning; in pharynx; fauces and gullet; and œsophagus to stomach, with coldness of rest of body. Dryness. Feeling of mucus. Acidity.

Œsophagus. — Stricture; with frequent painful vomiting. Exfoliation of mucous membrane in the form of a tube, the cast was very offensive. Pain; on pressure; extending to umbilical and epigastric regions; burning, in upper part. Heat. *Swallowing difficult;* from swelling opposite cricoid cartilage extending down trachea and moving on deglutition; as from an obstruction in pit of throat; of fluid, causing pain and convulsive cough, sometimes the fluid returned through the mouth and nares; impossible. Spasmodic dysphagia.

Clinical.—Tonsillitis, with tenacious, gray yellowish exudation, difficult swallowing, salivation, extreme fetor of the mouth. Diphtheria; valuable in the worst forms, regurgitation of liquids through the nose; drowsiness; characterized by a great quantity of exudation; diphtheritic croup, with drowsiness.

Stomach.—Hunger; and yet she eats without appetite, discomfort in stomach after eating; great, but nausea after eating, so that he must stop eating before he is satisfied; distressing, but inability to retain any nourishment; ravenous, > eating, with rumbling and gurgling in abdomen; desire for fresh plums. Appetite lost; with discomfort. Aversion to eating, > towards evening.

Thirst; after vomiting; during menses, with dry tongue; with inability to drink; burning.

Eructations. — *Sour;* when walking in open air. Bitter; after dinner; sour. Like onions. Empty; in morning after coughing, then bitter, slimy. Of food; after coughing. Of water; > dinner; sweetish; salt, before vomiting.

Hiccough; at night; when smoking; < after drinking, with vomiting.

Nausea; in morning, with oppression of chest; in mouth towards noon, though food and drink are relished; from slightest liquid, with retching; > eructations; everything turns around in stomach and rises up, is obliged to swallow it; with constriction in stomach; feeling as if stomach were disordered; with chilliness; sudden, then vomiting of clear water; faintlike, with griping cutting and twisting in abdomen and labor-like pain as if everything would press out. Retching.

Vomiting; after eating; with purging; then shivering, then ineffectual retching; of all food; of all fluid as soon as taken; of clear water, then of food taken the previous evening, then continued nausea; the matter effervescing as soon as it came in contact with the dust; of scanty coffee-like liquid; of slimy substances like coffee-grounds; brown substances; serous liquid, with white flakes at night; glairy mucus mixed with shreds of coagulated membrane; of the color of porter and of acid reaction; a fluid of the consistence of treacle and color of carbonate of lime. Of blood; convulsive; and mucus; mucus and black fibres; mixed with sour-smelling liquid, pieces of membrane and curdled milk; and dark grumous and viscid matter, afterwards brighter-colored and mixed with patches of tough mucus; streaks of B., with pieces of membrane; in clots, with watery brownish-red liquid and pieces of membrane; mixed with black clots of B., with neuralgia, then thin black stools. Black; and glairy; and flocculent mass; violent, of fluid mixed with flakes. Causing distress. Of casts of œsophagus. An elongated false membrane, evidently made up of mucous membrane of œsophagus. A backish mass formed from mucous membrane of stomach (after a fit of suffocation). Mixed with blood at 3 P.M., with pain and anxiety, then V. of a wide membranous tube, a part seemed charred, in other parts it was tinged with bile, the branching of vessels could be seen, it was tenacious and probably a part of stomach, V. and anxiety continued, and at 8 P.M. a tube was cast up, consisting of mucous and nervous coats of œsophagus, a part charred, and transverse muscular fibres could be traced round one of its ends, then she was comparatively easy and swallowed with more facility, but œsophagus was painful.

Distention; of epigastric region, also with pain on touch. Contraction of epigastric region. Sticking. Cutting in epigastric region; near l. side of S., extending to back; extending to hypochondria; paroxysmal, in region when sitting and walking, with painful moving about in it. Clawing every evening, as after taking cold. Griping beneath pit, and on pressure upon stomach bruised pain in it. Cardialgia. Distress, < eating hastily or taking indigestible food.

Pain; in pit; in region; in epigastric region; epigastrium on touch; *epigastric region after eating,* < *hard food, with sensitiveness of S.;* epigastric region, > vomiting; epigastric region, with tension; epigastric region, with a round hard swelling as large as a child's head; with ineffectual inclination to eructate; with feeling as if a hard, bitter substance rose into chest, with frequent risings of mucus, which is afterwards felt only in throat; in pit, extending to shoulders; so that he must keep his body bent, supported by two persons; as if a stone rose up, then salivation. Sensitiveness; of epigastrium. Tightness as if it would burst, after eating. Constriction, and in abdomen; in pit; sudden anxious, in pit, preventing respiration. Heaviness in pit. Coldness; *from every drink unless some spirit is mixed with it;* and relaxed feeling, with loss of appetite. Burning; sudden.

Clinical.—Dyspepsia, with vomiting of food and drink and craving for stimulants. Vomiting of drunkards. Vomiting of pregnancy, with constant salivation, feeling of lump in throat, soreness in pit of stomach, great thirst, vomiting > drinking hot water. Vomiting of pregnancy, intolerance of the smell of coffee, vomiting when lying on r. side. A valuable remedy for the desire of alcoholic drinks. Valuable for dyspepsia from alcohol, with persistent sour breath; the patient is shrivelled and cold, and cannot eat, liver is enlarged, chronic diarrhœa, etc.

Abdomen.—Distended; and tense; with emission of flatus. Muscles hard and rigid, with pain on pressure. Retraction; with sensitiveness to touch; with emptiness on percussion; painful spasmodic. Spasms. Resonant, with tenderness, < between umbilicus and ensiform cartilage. Flatulence caused by milk. Short, abrupt, difficult emission of flatus. Rumbling after emission of flatus. Gurgling on moving body by breathing when lying.

Stitches during menses, and in vagina. Neuralgia. Griping; in evening; at night; at night, with cutting and urging to stool. Pain; on pressure; < epigastric region and back; after eating, then digging and uneasiness in it; > pressure; with dragging down of parietes; with "bilious" symptoms; as if in uterus, with burning; labor-like, extending into hips, then bruised sensation in small of back; bubbling, in r. side, extending almost to back. Anxiety in morning in bed. **Weak feeling** *as if menses would come on.* Relaxed feeling in intestines after stool.

Flank.—Jerking in l., with pressure outward as with a finger. Sticking in l.; in l. in evening on inspiration after lying down, then sticking in l. upper part of chest. Griping in l. Burning in r., with hacking cough.

Hypochondria.—Distention of l. Sticking in hepatic region near stomach; in l. on leaning to r. side; in l., > pressure; in l., often with sticking in chest. Griping during stool. Burning all day when sitting.

Umbilicus.—Protruded and abdomen for about an inch and a half above U. red, with pain on pressure upon umbilicus or reddened part. Rumbling in region in evening before lying down and next morning after rising; R. in region, with feeling as if stool would occur. Sticking in l. side, extending into abdomen. Cutting in region, worse when walking in open air than in the house; C. and moving about. Pressure. Sickly warmth or heartburn in region.

Hypogastrium.—Sticking in l. side on movement; S. in region of inguinal hernia. Tearing in l. groin when sitting. Cutting in region of cæcum. Pinching in r. groin. Sharp jerking, almost like intermittent jerking colic, rather superficial. Griping before, during and after micturition; G. extending into lumbar region, causing cold sweat. Pain in r. groin as if a hernia protruded when walking and standing, so that he dared not cough or inspire, afterwards a hernia protruded at times, < talking, with pain, it returned on holding quietly, especially on sitting, and then he could breathe and cough without trouble. Forcing out in a hernia at abdominal ring, with pain in the ring even after reducing the hernia; F. in r. groin as if a hernia would occur, in morning on waking, > rising, frequently recurring; suddenly in r. groin as if a hernia would occur on rising from stool, not affected by cough or respiration. Throbbing in place of inguinal hernia.

Clinical.—Enlarged spleen, which is painful on coughing, with hæmorrhages in various parts. Sometimes indicated in inguinal hernia.

Rectum.—*Hæmorrhoids, itching; H., with burning and sticking; with moisture* and pain on touch. Pain as if it would be torn asunder during stool. Rush of blood. Sticking in anus before soft stool. *Pressing in anus during and after pasty stool.* Ineffectual desire for stool.

Stool.—Liquid, black, fetid, relieving the pain for a moment; *partly L., partly solid, offensive, with much thin mucus and streaks of blood;* (L., green). *Diarrhœa;* dysenteric; till evening, of only fermented mucus, with burning in rectum, flatulence and rumbling. **Soft, then empty feeling in abdomen.** Constipation; with pain in abdomen. Like sheep-dung. Hard and infrequent; H., delayed, painful; and bloody; in small connected black lumps mixed with blood, during menses, with sticking in anus so that she must stand up; first part, then soft; at first, and bloody, then soft, with burning in anus. **As if chopped, saffron yellow, stringy and slimy.** *Yellowish-white.* Colored with blood. Black, mixed with blood. *Frequent, green,* painful. Large, formed. The child's napkins when washed went into holes. Indolent. Omitted; in the primary action, and urine retained.

Clinical.—Diarrhœa, like chopped eggs, of yellow mucus, sometimes frothy, said to be < eating oysters; often indicated in children; the evacuations are extremely fetid, and there is a general sour odor over the whole body.

Urinary Organs.—*Pain in bladder if the desire to urinate is not immediately satisfied.* Pressure upon neck of bladder as if everything would force out, when standing, walking and sitting, obliging him to press thighs together, > coition. Frequent micturition of only a few drops. Obliged to rise at night to urinate. Constant desire, always before the last drops cutting in urethra, for seven days, afterwards there is every time a dragging in loins and groins. Frequent desire, with pain behind symphysis and on urinating cutting, the catheter met with an obstruction in region of neck of bladder, which was found to be a swollen and very sensitive prostate. Burning in urethra after coition. Burning in urethra during micturition, with diminished urine; with increased then diminished urine; with micturition only morning and evening.

Urine.—Increased. Diminished, thick. Suppressed. None passed in morning. Red and fiery; brownish-red. Like water; and soon desposits a thin mucous sediment. Becomes turbid when standing and deposits an earthy sediment. Has a fine pellicle on its surface and a bloody sediment. White sediment. An ounce of pale U., which had a powerful effect on litmus paper. Four ounces of clear amber-colored U., acid reaction, sp. gr. 1030, 1000 grains of it yielded 54 grains of solid residue, half of this residue was soluble in alcohol, the alcoholic solution showed free Sulphuric acid, the insoluble residue furnished 16.9 grains of sulphate of baryta. Albuminous and containing much Sulphuric acid; A., light brown, very acid, highest sp. gr. 1038, containing free Sulphuric acid, afterwards pale cylinders, with fatty degeneration, copious sediment of urate of ammonia, afterwards urine scanty, sp. gr. 1028, no chlorides; A., containing sulphates, pale cylinders, free blood-corpuscles and varying amounts of urates; and containing casts; and red, acid, sp. gr. 1020, containing Sulphur, on standing many pale or yellowish granular cylinders; with brownish-red sediment containing hæmatin, but no blood-corpuscles; and containing blood, with acute nephritis, in one case fibrinous casts and epithelia, and in the other cellular elements only, the albumen diminished from day to day, microscopical examination of kidneys after death showed a recent inflammatory process (granular opacity and fatty degeneration of epithelial elements, recent cleaving of the nuclei of interstitial tissue, especially along course of vessels).

Sexual Organs.—Warmth, and in scrotum. Itching pain in upper margin of glans. Erections during the day without amorous thoughts. Relaxation of scrotum. Emission without voluptuous sensation.

Female.—Miscarriage. Discharge of corroding mucus; of bloody mucus, as if menses would come on. Burning leucorrhœa. Transparent or milk-like leucorrhœa without sensation. Menses too late; with pain in abdomen and small of back; too early.

Desire after menses; D. rather in external genitals, yet she was not much excited by coition. Aversion to coition after menses.

Respiratory Organs. — Rattling in trachea and bronchi. Sticking in air-passages. Bronchitis with prostration. Glossitis. Larynx, rattling of mucus; movements as in croup; sticking; constriction; sprained pain on talking and on external pressure; pain on touch; sensitiveness; pain, talking was irksome, as from immobility of parts. Hoarseness; with dryness and roughness in throat and larynx; and hollow voice, almost unintelligible; without sound. Voice croaking, almost unintelligible; low muttering; feeble; weak, croupy, then lost; lost.

Cough; caused by open air; on walking in open air; fatiguing; distressing, with whistling respiration and croupy voice; rattling, hoarse; rattling, shaking, interrupted; hacking. Dry C., afterwards loose with improvement; short D., with paroxysms of gasping; in paroxysms; also in morning after rising. Cough in morning with slimy expectoration; C. from irritation in fauces, with white frothy expectoration; paroxysmal, with copious expectoration, at times with vomiting, then diarrhœa, fever and night-sweats, pain in chest, offensive breath, percussion at apex of r. lung was dull, expiration prolonged, vesicular and hollow, and a peculiar purring over whole chest, gradual collapse and the patient died in slight delirium, the post mortem showed upper lobes of lungs adherent to œsophagus and an opening from œsophagus to a cavity which occupied nearly all of the upper and part of the middle lobes of r. lung, the cavity was filled with blackish-brown offensive fluid with lung tissue, pleura was almost gangrenous, etc.

Expectoration perpetual; copious; offensive. Hæmoptysis when walking slowly.

Respiration.—Suffocation; in spasms. Dyspnœa; at night, with cough; at night, with choking in larynx; and larynx moved up and down violently, child lay with head bent backward as in croup, lost consciousness and soon died; with distress and pain about region of stomach and r. lower ribs; with rattling in trachea; rattling; noisy; intermittent; and breathing irregular; causing anxiety. Stertor. Short; and difficult; and rapid. Rapid; with shooting in cervical muscles and movements in wings of nose; and heaving, with spasmodic motion of muscles of neck, and at each inspiration depression of lower jaw, so as to form a sort of gasping motion. Slow and weak. Moaning; and slow. Superficial and rattling.

Chest.—Moist râles. Rattling in evening in bed, with rapid pulse and short breath; R. in l. lung, then dulness with bronchial respiration and pneumonia; at base of lungs without dulness on percussion, with rapid pulse, cough, tenacious sputa, afterwards pallor with circumscribed redness of cheeks, next day oppression of chest, bronchial respiration, in r. side some râles, on l. side moist and rattling râles, respiration 40, headache, next day pallor, clammy sweat and death. Dulness at base of r. lung, then pneumonia, collapse and death. Painful spasms.

Stitches; in r. breast; in l. side of sternum by costal cartilage; in front of and beneath r. axilla; in front of l. axilla on putting down a heavy weight, then bruised pain over a large part of sternum; in r. costal region during menses, < inspiration; in l. side when walking, < inspiration and cough, > rest; deep in l. side with arrest of breathing, then sensitiveness in a spot to left and above ensiform cartilage; in r. breast, extending deeper upon pressure; in sternum extending to other side of chest in evening on entering house; sudden, in l. upper part, extending into back; paroxysmal, in lower ribs, extending next day to tract of lumbar nerves, with hyperæsthesia of skin extending over whole body, with rest in no position; paroxysmal, in r. lower part, < deep inspiration, with pain near spine between fourth and tenth vertebræ and along axillary line from fifth to tenth intercostal space and at union of ribs with their cartilages, hyperæsthesia of skin between linea-axilla mammillaris.

Neuralgia in intercostal nerves, between r. tenth and sixth ribs, paroxysmal, from deep inspiration, < night. Cutting in front of l. axilla. Scraping deep in middle with burning and tearing. Pain along sternum; P. on inspiration; in middle of sternum, as from a thrust; acute drawing, in middle, preventing deep inspiration; pulsating bubbling, beneath l. ribs. *Pressure on l. side and in pit of stomach;* inward in r. ribs, worse at intervals. Drawing tension in l. side. Oppression; from catarrh in morning on waking, with irritation to cough without anything to be loosened, after several hours easy expectoration of mucus. Constriction. Fulness. Burning pain, extending down behind sternum, causing anxiety. Burning in l. side in attacks; B. in l. outer part, as from boiling water; worse at intervals. Weakness so that talking is difficult.

Heart.—Stitches through it, then sore pain. Pain in præcordial region. Anxiety in præcordial region extending over whole chest. Palpitation; when upper part of body is pressed forward resting upon arms, with inclination to take a deep breath. Beat of H. and arteries scarcely perceptible.

Pulse.—Rapid; and tense, full; and small; and feeble; and contracted; and intermittent. Slow; and large; and small; and feeble. Hard and full; H. and tense. Small; and thready, irregular, tremulous; and tremulous, with coldness; and weak; and weak, trembling; and scarcely perceptible, at times intermittent; and irregular; and irregular, scarcely perceptible; and contracted, irregular, almost convulsive and tremulous, sometimes rapid, sometimes intermittent. Thready; and almost imperceptible. Weak; in humeral arteries, could not be felt at wrists and temples.

Neck.—Swollen. Pain in l. side on pressure; as from a weight between side and l. shoulder. Drawing beneath r. ear.

Back.—Sticking in spine and l. side of nape. Pain; as if sore and beaten; drawing, on motion and on stooping. Stiffness in morning, > during the day on motion. *Lumbar pain;* bruised, when sitting and standing; on movement, like a soreness or like a spasmodic drawing; burning. Weakness in lumbar region and lower limbs so that he could scarcely stand alone.

Extremities.—Livid. Swelling of wrists and other large joints, with pain. Convulsive movements of arms and legs. (Twitching of tendons.) Inclination to cramps in hands and feet. Tearing during menses, < evening. Pain in joints during sleep. Sensitiveness.

Upper Extremities.—Pain as from an ulcer in l. axilla, extending into chest, < ascending stairs and walking, forcing her to sit down. L. axillary glands sensitive. Shoulder, jerking in r. on writing; stitches on raising arm; sticking tearing in l.; cutting, with burning, as if it would cut through; intermittent, tremulous sensation in l. Arm, stitches in joint; intermittent drawing and spasmodic constrictive, paralytic pain in r. when writing; heaviness. Tearing posteriorly beneath r. shoulder-joint and extending up about it. Cutting extending down l. arm. Tensive pain in elbows. Smarting as if bruised on outer side of l. elbow. Sudden bruised pain in l. ulna close to wrist every three seconds, extending up into arm. Drawing in wrists, with weariness.

Hand.—Jerking in metacarpal bone of r. index extending into arm; painful, in joint of metacarpal bone of thumb, extending into wrist and at times into arm. Tensive pain in r. metacarpus when walking in open air with arm hanging down, with heaviness as if blood accumulated in it. Painful beatings in metacarpal bone of r. index.

Fingers.—Stitches in middle of joints; burning or smarting S. on r. side of middle. Tearing in first joint of r. thumb; beneath nail of index, as in a whitlow, < cold water; jerking, extending from r. thumb to chest when sitting. Jerking pain in tips; through r. thumb, starting from tip. Burning stinging crawling as if asleep in tip of little and in a spot on middle.

Lower Extremities.—Staggering and falling in the street, then collapse. Stretching. Heaviness. R. inclined to numbness. Cramp in r. hip.

Thigh.—Sticking externally in middle of l. Tearing in varicose veins of T. and leg in morning in bed; T. up and down in l., > rubbing. Cutting. Intermittent pinching in a spot on inner side of l. Acute pain as from a blow obliquely above l. knee in wave-like intervals. Pain in l. near knee, feeling as if it would soon become cutting. Intermittent pressure on upper and inner part of r. Constriction low down, extending at intervals into leg. Spasmodic constrictive paralytic pain in r. T. and leg.

Knee.—Stitches like thrusts in middle of r. when sitting, then pain; prickling S. in hollow of l.; burning, in l. Painful jerks like thrusts in inner side of l. Burning pain in hollow of r. Painful weakness when standing, with jerking in them.

Prickling stitches in l. tendo-achillis. Pain in calves more when sitting than when walking. Crawling in l. tibia; in calves when walking, with cramp. Falling asleep of l. leg when sitting still, < walking. Intermittent pain like thrusts or jerks beneath l. outer malleolus. Stiffness of malleoli when walking. Stitches in a corn; burning S. in heels. Tearing in l. heel in morning on waking; T. in a corn, forcing him to draw up the foot. Bruised pain on l. sole, at first increasing, then jerking, then suddenly disappearing. Acute pressure in r. instep, increasing and decreasing. Falling asleep of l. foot in evening when sitting. Prickling stitches beneath great toe. Intermittent jerking griping in toes.

Skin.—Jaundice. Pale, cold and covered with sweat. Livid, dry and desquamating in small scales. Bluish spots on forearms as from settling of blood. Lower lip, cheeks, back of hand and forearm swollen, red and painful, as after a scald, next day, cuticle of hands, etc., black, dry and rough, on third day the pellicles of tongue, lips and cheeks had fallen off, all mucous membranes of mouth bright red. Red patches on forearms, > pressure, but returning immediately on its removal. Eruption on head, face and nape; on hands and between fingers, itching < after midnight. Chilblains on fingers, with acute pain.

Pimples on forehead and side of nose. Burning-itching red spots on tibia with a pimple in the middle, after scratching the part swells, after the swelling ceases the itching begins again. Skin of l. side of face partially removed and the whole presented a white disorganized appearance, eyelids inflamed and swollen, l. eyeball involved, inside of lips white and swollen, white excoriated streaks on back of l. hand and between fingers, the white marks turned brown, pain in l. eye extending into head, bursting of cornea and discharge of aqueous humor and crystalline lens, towards the close of the fifth day a shivering fit, next morning acute pain in bend of r. arm where he had been bled, inflammation around the orifice, swelling of arm, afterwards febrile symptoms, difficult breathing and other signs of pulmonary inflammation, death on the thirteenth morning. Sloughs on r. buttock close to anus, a probe passed some distance into pelvic cavity and towards gluteal region. Dark red elevations on back of hand, with a scab, under which there seems to be matter. Boils on back. Ulcers on hands and feet.

Stitches in the scar of a burn; S. as from woolen clothing. Intermittent burning cutting crawling like a corrosive soreness. Corroding sensation in an ulcer. Itching, appearing in another spot on scratching.

Clinical.—Purpura hæmorrhagica. Itching over whole body was cured by Sul. ac.

Sleep.—Yawning after dinner. *Sleepiness;* in morning after waking. Wakeful all night. *Falls asleep late;* and wakes easily; and sleeps uneasily, wakes often. Wide awake after two hours, as if he had slept enough. Wakes after midnight; with heat, dryness of throat, thirst, intolerance of being uncovered. Sleep light and seldom. Restless. Frequent starting from sound sleep. Jerking, causing starting up, and salivation; J. together of fingers and doubling up of them, so that he started up. Dreams unremembered; anxious, even to crying out; anxious, of fire, dead persons and danger; by a woman that she had coition twice, and orgasm twice; by a woman of desire for coition and on waking a tumultuous desire therefor, which was especially seated in the clitoris. Nightmare as if a weight were lying upon her or as if some one were holding her by the throat, she could not speak, she woke in perspiration, two days before menses.

Fever.—Chilliness; all day; in morning, > open air; external, with internal heat and prostration; alternating with heat. Shivering, with gooseflesh; internal, through trunk; down trunk, without chilliness. Cold skin; < limbs. Cold face and limbs; face and hands; limbs; limbs, and livid nails; limbs, and cyanotic; hands, with transient warmth of body; hands and feet; feet and forehead.

Heat; in evening after lying down; during or after dinner; with delirium and excitement; with small, rapid pulse; with small, rapid, hard pulse; with full, hard pulse, then fever with raving, then pulse soft and small, then rapid, skin covered with cold sweat; in attacks; dry, in evening after a journey of eight hours, till 8 P.M., with thirst, burning in eyes and once creeping chilliness; in skin; extending from throat along back; cool burning in l. cheek.

Sweat; during the day; in morning; on every motion; when sitting, < upper part of body; with scarcely perceptible pulse; sour, in morning, then hoarseness. Cold sweat; after taking anything warm, < face and forehead; and clammy; on forehead. Skin dry, forehead covered with drops of sweat. Skin hot and dry.

Clinical.—Typhoid fever, with phosphoric-acid symptoms of great drowsiness and slow answering, desire for stimulants, which give relief, vomiting of food, sour discharges. Typhoids, with hæmorrhages, rapid sinking, deathly paleness of the face, thick, soft pulse, sense of general trembling.

Sumbul.

A tincture is made of the dried root of Ferula Sumbul, Hooker fil.

General Action.—A feeble narcotic; used in Russia for a nervous stimulant, especially in low fevers, dysentery, delirium tremens, hysteria, *et cetera*.

Closely allied to Asafœtida and Moschus.

Generalities.—Emaciation. Strong odor of the medicine from the breath and skin, < palms, which felt sticky. Darting pains in l. lumbar region, in chest, sides and abdomen during the day. Bruised sensation in muscles, < l. triceps. Tingling. Throbbing in nape, abdomen and lumbar region. Clogged sensation, < head and stomach. Sensation as of cobwebs being moved over different parts, first of cerebellum and then over face. Sickliness. It feels especially good to sit down. Weakness; in morning; in morning, with sleepiness; in evening, with stretching and yawning; from walking; from least exertion, < arms and hands, and chiefly l.; with trembling; with oppression; with listlessness; as from insufficient, unrefreshing sleep. Faintness; on hearing music, the loud notes jar in the head; with vertigo on stooping; tendency to, from stooping or excitement.

Mind.—Fit of hysterical laughter and tears. Nervous excitement in evening after listening to a disputation, with heat, < head. Excitability, easily depressed, easily aroused to passion, sensation as if least provocation would enrage, with mirth, with the excitability fulness in temples and forehead and cerebellum, < l. side, and pulsations below l. ear. Mirthful, smiling, disturbed by nothing; M., witty. Cheerful; and excited; and disposed for intellectual occupation, happy enthusiastic state as after performing a noble deed; and mirth, alternating with despondency as if ill-treated by every one. Vivacity, hastiness. Cannot feel compassion. Amorous. Fond of the society of women. Anxious. Easily frightened. Despairing. Melancholy, no desire for labor, even intellectual. Irritable; in afternoon and evening; in evening, from harsh music, and agitated. Restless when reading. Tranquil and indolent. Activity; anxious, with physical weakness. *Intellect dull in morning, clear in evening.* Thought disturbed in morning. *Mistakes in writing and summing.*

Head.—Aching; < 6 P.M., with tensive fulness. Constriction, < from forehead to occiput; benumbing, in brain as if contracted, in morning. Confusion; during the day, but in afternoon he was more overwhelmed, with tendency to snore and he did so when awake; with contracted feeling in forehead; with contractive pain in l. half of forehead. Fulness. Affected by sunbeams, it feels full of blood, and in cerebellum heat, uneasiness and fulness extending to spinal cord. Uneasiness, < forehead and cerebellum, with heat, light and ebullition of blood. Ebullition of blood, with lightness and exalted feeling. Blood seems to circulate quickly, < l. side. Heaviness; with compression from one temple to the other and heat in forehead. Vertigo; in evening on stooping; on stooping; from using warm water; on rising from a seat and when lying.

Forehead.—Constriction of skin. Pain; over eyes; in l. eminence; after dinner; with heat; pushing, in a spot in l. eminence; tensive, in F. and over eyes at 6 P.M. and in evening, < l. temple. Constriction on rising. Confusion. Oppression. Fulness; and over eyes; and in cerebellum; in F. and occiput, with dulness. Heaviness.

Pain in temples; in l. Painful pulsation in l. temple at 7 P.M. Oppression in temples, < l., and over l. eye. Pressure in a spot on vertex. Weight extending from vertex to brows. Pain in occiput; from cerebellum to frontal region during menses. Painful uneasiness in l. cerbellum, with stiffness in adjoining muscles on moving head. Round sore elevations over l. parietal bone, painful on touch, dry, coming off in dry scabs, < in a line over ear.

Eyes.—Dull. Brilliant and face fresher. Sensitive to light; l. to artificial light. Seem too tight, with biting in lids and blinking. Sudden sensation of a foreign body in l., spreading over ball and obscuring vision, intolerance of light at 5 P.M., < 6 P.M., lachrymation, can be closed only half way, as if lids were swollen, and very painful when closed, so as to disturb sleep, woke next morning with pain in l. eye, pressure of closed lid was very painful, red streaks across cornea towards external canthus, inflammation of conjunctiva towards external canthus, sensation of a sharp body grating against ball when turned outward, pain in l. eye, < moving it. Biting in l. lids. Twitching in l. brow. Vision dim; dim transiently, with stupefying pressure in eyes; quivering; flickering, > eructations.

Ears.—Singing and hissing; S. (as of a kettle) in r. in evening.

Nose.—Swelling of l. ala. Alæ sore, < morning and towards night. Picking. Teasing tickling. Itching inside tip; in evening; intermittent. Sneezing. *Coryza; < morning;* yellow; thick, bright yellow, gummy; tenacious yellow, < l. nostril, nose dry towards alæ; thick whitish, in morning, with diminished smell; watery; watery, at 8 P.M.; watery, cold, with soreness about edges of nose. Stuffing; at root; in evening; > olfaction of Camphor; with diminished smell; extending down its chamber; in chambers extending towards throat, in morning; of yellow mucus, extending into throat; of thick yellow tenacious mucus; of yellow tenacious mucus on waking, < 9 A.M. Obstructing mucus in root extending into throat, so that he speaks through the nose. Bleeding. Smell lost.

Face.—Pale and thin. Cramplike pain in masseter muscles at noon and in afternoon, with stiffness on moving jaw and pain in meatus auditorius. Sensation of cobwebs moving over it at 10 P.M. in bed. Sensation as if skin were tight. Swelling of upper lip and of gum. Heat and dryness in lips and mouth.

Mouth.—Shooting in first l. lower molar in morning; in first l. upper molar, extending into cheek.

Tongue—Elongated, red. Flabby, showing imprint of teeth, papillæ at apex enlarged. Papillæ red, enlarged in morning. Glazed. White, with brown crust at back; W. in morning, and elongated; in morning, brown in centre and at back; in morning, with brown crust in centre and at back. Coated white, rough; coated white, with brown crust at back, papillæ conicæ and filliformæ enlarged; dirty white. Dirty brown at back in morning. Brown coat in morning on waking; B. coat, with rough feeling as if scraped; moist; moist in morning, but towards evening it became red and elongated and papillæ like deep red spots, with wedge-shaped brown crust at back. Heat, and in throat and stomach.

Salivation; in morning, with tenacious mucus in throat and constant want to swallow; thin; watery, and swallowing frequent. Watery saliva, with pressure in pit of stomach. (Saliva frothy and speech difficult on account of difficult motion of tongue.) Dryness, and in throat, without thirst. Hot breath; in evening; at times, and offensive; and balmy. Flat odor. Taste clammy; at noon, with eructations and taste of food (herring) many hours after eating; deficient T.; of horse-chestnuts at night; of bread at 7.30 P.M.; flat and heavy to food and beer. Want of relish; for animal food and stout.

Throat.—Mucus; obstructing; obstructing, sweetish. Tenacious mucus; in morning; hence it is convenient to keep the mouth constantly open; with erosion, heat and rawness; greenish; sweet; sweet, causing hawking, but without detaching it upward; thick, in T. and mouth on waking at 4 A.M., with *constriction at top of gullet, constant swallowing,* attempts to clear throat by sounds like croup, breathing impeded but better when lying on back, sensation of film around top of gullet, *choking constriction,* l. side of chest oppressed.

Stitches in fauces > swallowing saliva, with rawness and soreness. Snatching sensation. Scraping. Rawness in evening; towards night, with hoarseness; and soreness. Excoriated feeling in l. side of upper part of T. and back of mouth at noon; near l. tonsil at noon, < speaking. Tickling; at 6 P.M., inciting to cough; with harshness and roughness. Heat in evening. *Constant swallowing.* Dryness of œsophagus.

Clinical.—Spasm of pharyngeal muscles.

Stomach.—Appetite great; at 6 P.M.; for bread; and assimilation increased; A. variable, large at one meal, absent at the next; deficient, especially for animal food; lost; no desire for animal food or beer, little appetite at dinner. Thirst for stimulants; in evening, especially for wine; for wine; for wine, it tastes very agreeable, while stout tastes heavy and leaves a clammy insipid taste.

Eructations; at 4 and 10 P.M., after beer, with burning pyrosis and taste of beer, with rumbling and twisting in abdomen; with odor of musk; with taste of musk; tasting of bread at 7 P.M. Empty eructations; at 11 P.M.; before stool; with taste of last food (bread), also pyrosis. Pyrosis after stout at dinner. Hiccough, with cough. Nausea; in throat; all day; in throat from 3 till 5 P.M.; at 11 P.M., with oppression of forehead, < l. temple; with salivation. Bilious vomiting.

Shooting in cardiac end in evening; in cardiac end (l. hypochondrium). Cutting at 4 P.M. Pain in pit; in S. or intestines; in epigastric region; with rumbling; deep in pit, with anxiety and loud breathing, then rumbling, tensive, in cardiac end and through l. breast. Emptiness, then bulimia. Heat rising into throat; pleasant warmth in S. and abdomen.

Abdomen.—Flabby, doughy. Hard, heavy. Distention; and heaviness; and sensitiveness deep in umbilical region, < retracting abdomen; extending to sternum, heaviness, with discomfort, < stooping or lifting leg. Rumbling; and gurgling. Bubbling. Emission of flatus; fetid; fetid, hot. Cutting. Pinching. Forcing-down pain, < l. side, with commotion and sickliness. Sensation of diarrhœa. Dry heat, which flushes to skin. Bubbling in l. side. Intermittent pressure between stomach and navel, < pressure, fulness in epigastric region. Pain in umbilical region on gentle pressure, with drawing in of abdomen. Heat under umbilicus, rising into throat and head and flushing to the skin, which becomes moist. Shooting in r. hypochondrium; in evening when walking; tensive, in r. lower. Gnawing in r. hypochondrium; in evening. Gnawing in r. hypogastrium; in morning; in evening; < deep inspiration, with tensive pain. Throbbing pain in r. hypogastrium in evening. Twitching pain in l. iliac region. Sickly pain in l. iliac and inguinal regions before stool. Sensation in hypogastrium of approaching diarrhœa.

Rectum.—Sticking in lower part. Pain in morning, with uneasiness as if protruding. Sensation as if it protruded after stool and as if anus were not closed. Sensation of something moving in it at 8 P.M.; near anus at night, with biting. Inclination to stool; frequent; frequent ineffectual, to diarrhœa. Hæmorrhoids excited. Raw sensation in anus during stool. Uneasy dryness, with sensation as if not closed, painful when walking.

Stool.—*Diarrhœa;* with urging, burning and biting in anus and rectum, with painful tension extending to tip of penis, then drops of mucus from anus; fetid; scanty; scanty, then burning and cutting at anus and frequent chilliness through back, with weakness; consisting at last of bits of mucus, scanty, with urging and cutting in orifice of anus, constant sensation as if another stool would follow, with erection, dribbling of urine and almost involuntary contraction of levator and sphincter ani; then constipation. Soft; preceded by flatus; with straining; and scanty; and abundant, fetid; and small, delayed; and brown, with bitings in rectum; and sudden; and sudden, with rawness in anus; and long and thin, with great expulsive efforts, preceded by sickliness, commotion of intestines and sickly pains in l. iliac and inguinal regions, with the stool sensation as if rectum protruded and as if anus were not closed.

Constipation; without desire, as from constriction of anus. Hard; in lumps; in pieces, slight; in pieces, preceded and followed by sweat and external heat, which soon changes to external coldness, with tremblings and cold sweat; (first part, then soft, copious, then blood). Scanty; and hard. Consisting almost only of empty urging, with much urine, then ineffectual urging to stool with emission of flatus. Large, fetid. Difficult, in pieces and gritty. Preceded by tremor, cold clammy sweat and forcing. Increased secretion of mucus in intestinal canal.

Clinical.—Has proved useful in chronic dysentery and diarrhœa.

Urinary Organs.—Frequent desire; in evening, with sensation as if bladder were nearly empty, and small emission; in small quantities; constant, and for stool. Ineffectual desire, then constant pressure and urine had to be forcibly restrained; frequent ineffectual efforts to urinate, with urging to stool, cutting in anus and coldness in back.

Urine.—Reddish-brown, with white cloud; R., with oily pellicle adhering to side of vessel, also with rosy sediment. Brownish-red, with light cloud at bottom. Yellowish-red, a floating cloud forms at the bottom, oily pellicle on surface; Y., with white floating shreds, which fall into a cloud at bottom, like white spots. Bright reddish-yellow, passes quickly, feels hot, after some time a white floating cloud could be seen at the bottom. Clear, with white floating particles; C., with white shreds, after standing pink tenacious sediment, oily pellicle; with white floating shreds, after some hours there forms at the bottom a white floating cloud, easily disturbed, in which the shreds appear like white spots; and scanty, deposits a rosy, tenacious sediment; and deposits a whitish tenacious sediment. Muddy, clear on surface, with oily pellicle. Increased. Diminished; and of strong ammoniacal odor; and turbid, micturition frequent. Sediment whitish, and covered with an oily pellicle; reddish-brown, with oily pellicle; rosy, with rosy coating.

Genital Organs.—Itching, with increased desire. Heat at 6 P.M., at 8 P.M. chiefly in perineum, between thighs and penis. Penis and lining of prepuce painful and irritable, tingling in glans, l. scrotum hot and inflamed, skin excoriated in places, leaving a bright red surface, in l. testis shooting, heat and burning pain, erythema of l. side of scrotum exactly to raphe and of glans and lining of prepuce, smegma behind glans near frænum, next day burning tingling in glans, prepuce and glans moist, with watery, saltish-smelling fluid, excoriation of l. scrotum, end of prepuce thickened, phimosis, whitish, curdy matter between glans and prepuce, which are bluish red and swollen, l. testis dark red, excoriated, third day shooting in end of penis, greenish yellow pus from the excoriated scrotum, voluptuous itching, tickling in prepuce, fourth day want of desire, aqueous discharge from glans, in evening intermittent itching in end of prepuce (biting, stinging, pleasurable sensation), fifth day phimosis, constriction of prepuce a little above end (which is swollen), retaining drops of urine, afterwards tickling in end of prepuce, afterwards itching tingling in prepuce, itching in prepuce at night and in morning, afterwards tickling in lining membrane of prepuce, tingling in end of prepuce. Soreness of end of penis from friction of clothes in walking. Intermittent tingling in glans. Frequent erections. Itching of prepuce. L. testis suspended. Aching in l. testis. Sensation of flabbiness and rawness in l. scrotum in morning. Shooting in l. spermatic cord when walking. Tensive pulsation in l. spermatic cord when walking. Desire; absent (since l. scrotum healed), as from physical weakness, erections few and without pleasure.

Female.—*White leucorrhœa, < after sitting.* Menses retarded; too early, scanty and of short duration.

Respiratory Organs.—Increased mucus. Tickling in windpipe. Hoarseness; at 8 A.M.; after 9 A.M.; on rising, and bass voice. Voice obstructed by mucus in throat. Cough in morning; in evening; from tickling in throat; and hiccough; in series, from 10 to 11 A.M.; two or three single C. in succession; dry; ejects sweet mucus into mouth. Hacking cough; in morning; in morning, excited by speaking and tickling in throat; in the daytime from irritation in throat as from air ascending spirally, also morning, noon and evening; from tickling in throat; from tickling in larynx, < morning; shaking; which detaches sweet mucus into mouth.

Chest.—Shrill, whiffing, jerking tubular sound anteriorly under l. clavicle on inspiration, the jerks perceptible throughout inspiration but the shrill, tubular whiffing only at beginning of inspiration. Lancinations in l. breast, < deep inspiration, with biting pain. Prickings in r.; under ribs; externally in a line with nipples; under l. ribs in evening; in a spot below l. breast in evening; in l. pectoral muscle on moving arm. Darting under lower sternum. Pain like a knife under l. ribs; in sides; in r. at noon; darting through after meals, > towards night; below l. breast, darting through side of chest, also slightly in r. chest, < inspiration. Pain under l. axilla in a line with nipple in evening; through l. side, < moving l. arm or leaning forward; paroxysmal, under sternum; bruised, in l. clavicle in evening, < moving arm.

Tensive pain below l. axilla; and near nipple, in a line with it externally; under l. ribs, in a line with nipple, at 9 A.M., < inspiration; in l. breast in evening; like a string pulling in r. breast. Tightness under l. breast; in l. breast and between it and sternum in morning, < inspiration; under l. breast, < inspiration; in l. side on blowing nose; with diminished mucus. Oppression of l., as if it were difficult to force the blood through the lung, < stooping. Uneasiness in l. lung.

Clinical.—Asthma.

Heart.—Sinking, and it beats softly, as if in water. Palpitation; at 9 P.M.; after running up-stairs; P. after beer, < paying attention to it; from least exertion; with flushes of heat. Jerkings in evening; intermittent J., worse during the flush of heat and after drinking stout, with palpitation.

Pulse.—Rapid; in afternoon; in evening, and strong; and full. Compressible during a chill. *Irregular;* in morning, and rapid; in evening, and full, compressible; and strong; and strong, compressible; and rapid; now rapid, now slow, and narrow, compressible and weak, slow, with occasional quick, full beats, *compressible;* and slow, compressible, afterwards rapid, then sweat in morning, then pulse narrow; and weak, low.

Neck.—Shooting from l. muscles up to temple. Tensive pain in muscles along l. shoulder over upper edge of scapula. Pulsation in nape and between scapulæ, with heat. Uneasiness in nape and spinal cord, < l. side, < heat, especially of sun, with sensation of swelling, prickings and throbbings as if about to inflame; U. in nape, < l. side, extending in a less degree down spine to sacrum, with trembling heat. Stiffness extending towards ears and temples; S. in muscles of neck and back on rotating head, with pain.

Back.—Posteriorly over l. scapula an indistinct mixed murmur and purring sound similar to that which is supposed to depend on muscular contraction and often associated with rheumatism, and laterally on a line with l. nipple, when the inspiratory inflation is about half completed two respiratory jerks, and the same below l. nipple over the seat of pain. Pain in l. loin; in lumbar region in evening; tensive, near l.

side of top of sacrum when walking. Throbbing in l. side of sacrum; in sacrum at 6 P.M., with shooting.

Extremities.—Uneasiness, > motion in open air, with vibrations along nerves. Fulness of hands and feet. Dry, tremulous tingling in palms and feet. Weakness, < l. arm and leg.

Upper Extremities.—Strap falls over l. shoulder as if it were emaciated. Uneasiness in l. shoulder above superior edge of scapula, with tensive pain.

Arm.—Pain down l. and in knuckle of l. index; in belly of l. biceps when extended or touched. Bruised feeling; in muscles, < l. triceps; down l. Weakness of l.; of l. with numbness and heaviness; inside of l. and in triceps, with beaten sensation. Loss of elasticity of vessels of l. Numbness down r. to thumb; tingling pricking, from slightest cold or from resting it on anything.

Weakness of forearms. Hands red and their veins distended, < l.; on depressing hands. Fingers swollen. Shooting from back of l. ring F. to wrist (along ulnar nerve), at 10 P.M.; wiry, laterally up l. and in joints of second and fourth. Lateral surfaces of F. sore.

Lower Extremities.—Pain in knee, with stiffness of leg; (P. as if internal ligaments and coverings of r. knee were loosened in morning on stepping). Rheumatic pain externally from r. knee to ankle when walking. Legs felt as if they were not his own and he could not trust himself to walk. Weakness of legs in morning on waking, with heaviness; W. of feet, with unsteadiness on walking. Trembling of feet.

Skin.—Pale, cold, dry, with empty vessels, then clammy sweat; intermittent pallor in afternoon. Red spots on scapula, with itching and bleeding when scratched; smooth R. spots on face, < forehead. Skin peels off nose in dry patches. Soreness between l. fingers when rubbed. Itching; on upper inner part of thighs; on nose in morning; in miliary spot on back at 10 P.M., < r. scapula and hip; between r. thumb and index, where there is a red spot, that reappears after pressure and obliges scratching, afterwards another red itching spot.

Sleep.—Sleepiness in afternoon and at 6 P.M., with protracted sleep at night (till 1 A.M.); in evening after a walk; in the cold; without thought. Sleep at night long and sound, next day sleepiness and especially weakness in feet. Sleep prolonged in morning; with vivid dreams, also with difficult rousing from suddenly falling asleep again; in a half-waking sleep, with vivid dream of having risen and dressed, dream influenced by occurrences in the next room. Wakeful at night, but soon fell asleep again.

Dreams.—Many. Of falling from a height. Of personal diseases and injuries. Agreeable. Vivid; and agreeable, of recent events. Amorous in morning. Of coition, with profuse *sudden* emission and waking on r. side; of C.; with profuse *sudden* ejaculation and waking, then in morning dulness over eyes and in forehead and difficulty in retaining or collecting ideas.

Fever.—Coldness; during the day; in morning; in morning, flushing heat after dinner; in morning, < hands and feet, those of l. side feel icy and numb; sensitiveness to cold air, < a draught; with dry white shrunken skin; external, in morning, hands and lumbar region cold; creeping, < region of lumbar vertebræ, thence extending upward and downward, fingers cool and backs of hands shrivelled. Shivering; in back in morning, with cold hands.

Coldness occasionally above l. zygoma, as from the trickling of a drop of water. Coldness in back; internally; deep in spine; in lumbar region; frequently in spine, with sensation as if soft stool would follow; over lumbar region, as from cold air, also in morning; creeping, with nausea, salivation, inclination to urinate, pressure in stomach and rumbling in abdomen. Chilliness extending to upper arms, with cold skin. *Cold hands;* in morning; in morning, and clammy; and fingers; with flushes of heat and red hands, veins painfully distended; internally, and feet, fingers seem cold when put against the warm cheeks.

Heat; in afternoon, with easy sweat; at 8 P.M. when walking slowly, with sweat; in evening, with sweat; in evening, then sweat; at night in bed, with sweat; after least exertion; when walking after warm drinks, < tea, with sweat; during and after walking, with sweat, the heat rises to head and l. side of nape, causing faintness and vertigo, < rising from a seat, moving quickly, or after a little wine, running up-stairs, looking steadily at any object not directly before eyes, hands feel cool, with heat in head, face, < l. cheek, and neck, throbbings on l. side of neck, heat increases the symptoms; then sweat, < palms and face.

Nervous heat. Dry heat, or clammy sweat; D. tremulous, when walking, then sweat, hands cold; tingling, in skin; tingling, in skin, in hands and feet, with sweat. Heat in flushes; in evening; in evening, then sweat; during and after walking, with sweat; with sweat; with trembling; then sweat; ascending to throat, mouth and head; coming from back; welling from lumbar region over whole body in evening, in the sunbeams, when walking *and during and after mesmerizing*, with beatings of the heart. Dry H. in flushes in evening; with trembling, then sweat; D., in flushes, from within to surface, < exertion, heat in skin, which is ruddy and becomes moist.

Heat near surface; of skin; of skin, < hands (which are ruddy and veins distended), and in feet; rising to head; head and face in evening, then sweat; in face; l. side and cheek; face, hands and feet; nape; l. side of nape, with throbbing; along cervical spinal cord, with uneasiness; flushing, in back; trembling, along nerves of back and neck during the day, with feeling of insecurity and want of confidence in self-control over movements; tingling, in feet and palms, heat in flushes to the skin; as if hot water flowed through different parts, at one time in spine, < lumbar region, at another in abdomen, thence it extended into stomach and dorsal vertebræ, at times pressure deep in navel, at times higher up, with almost constant urging to stool.

Sweat; in flushes; greasy; with the odor of musk; cold, clammy; clammy, at 6 P.M., and flies continually settle on the skin; on l. cheek in evening. Skin dry.

Tabacum.

A tincture is made of the dried leaves of Havana tobacco.

General Action.—A powerful depressant, causing nausea and vomiting, feeble heart and pulse, low temperature, vertigo, delirium and collapse. It produces also violent gastro-enteritis. In some cases convulsions, of spinal origin, as well as a tetanic rigidity.

It may cause long-continued spasms of arterioles (Ergot), with persistent coldness of the surface. Its long-continued use favors degeneration of nerve tissue, as witnessed in atrophy of the optic nerve and general muscular paralysis (Phos.). Palpitation is a frequent and persistent symptom.

Allies. — *Arsen.*, Lobelia, Verat. alb., Phosphorus, Coccul.

Generalities. — Emaciation; < back and cheeks. Marasmus. Consumption. Gout. Appearance parched. Muscles rigid. Flaccid, pallid. Collapse, with cold sweat (Verat. alb.). Hands doubled into a fist and drawn tightly across chest, fingers could not be stretched nor arm moved, muscles of chest and arms felt hard, with vibrating contractions of different fibres. Walks bent double, pressing hand over spine and groaning at every step. Cloro-anæmia in children. Congestion to head and chest. Blood deteriorated; red corpuscles diminished; thin, with passive congestions; thin, red corpuscles scattered, non-confluent and crenated.

Trembling; of tongue and limbs; of head and hands; head and hands after dinner, with mirth as in intoxication; and when he walked his legs seemed bowed, he had lost the full use of lower limbs and climbed into bed with difficulty, while in bed continual movement of muscles of arms and legs and sometimes facial muscles, moved involuntarily; convulsive; hysterical, from conversation, rapid walking or violent motion of attendants, with twitching of all flexors, apprehension of some rapidly approaching physical catastrophe, the result of which would be death, he would clutch the arm of any bystander and beseech him to save his life, to relieve him from the præcordial distress and threatening suffocation.

Cramp. Twitching; of single muscles; in whole body, with pulsation in head and palpitation; of tendo-achillis and other muscles, < night, with restlessness and sleeplessness; of all muscles, with appearance of frightful pain, constantly placed his hand on his abdomen and tore at his penis; at night preventing sleep, and something seemed to draw l. shoulder down irresistibly.

Convulsions; of eyelids and masseter muscles, inability to open mouth; of arms, then of legs, afterwards of whole body, then prostration; and limbs forcibly contracted against body; and head drawn back, nape rigid; with copious dark greenish-brown diarrhœa; with rattling; with bending forward of body and stretching of limbs and subdued cries on account of pain in stomach; with rigidity of limbs, contractions of abdominal muscles, bending backward of body, distended bloodvessels on head; and sank to the floor, I noticed two short inspirations and all was ended, he was lying on l. side, mouth wide open, tongue protruding, lips, tongue and inside of mouth dark blue, eyes open, pupils contracted, general appearance of a man who had been struck dead suddenly, petechiæ all over body, with ecchymoses in places, rigor mortis very great; tetanic, < back; clonic, < limbs, teeth grit together, hands clenched, legs rapidly flexed and extended. Epilepsy. Spasmodic attack in morning, constant necessity to stretch and yawn, with rolling sensation through chest, abdomen and calves, then leaden heaviness of feet.

Neuralgia, universal, < night; different N., as of N. pudendas ext., waking him at 4 A.M., with painful erections and strangury, > about noon after watery micturiction six or eight times, neuralgia of plexus cœliacus, with sour eructations, of fifth l. intercostal nerve, of r. plexus brachialis, as soon as one neuralgia ceases another starts up. Pain during low barometer and during a wind, > hot applications to stomach, lying on back and strict diet; drawing P. over whole body. Drawing in l. lower limb, between shoulders and beneath sternum.

Feeling as if blood circulated rapidly and violently. Shuddering through whole body, then nausea and violent vomiting, with from 1 till 4 A.M. convulsions of arms, lower limbs and in muscles of back. *Restlessness; requiring continual change of place* (Ars.); with pain and anxious perspiration. Hyperæsthesia of different nervous branches. Feeling of increased vigor in muscles, with disinclination for movement.

Weakness (Ars., Phos.); in morning after interrupted, restless sleep; greater in forenoon than in afternoon; towards evening, and on moving a part shivering and coldness between shoulders, with dizziness and stitches in temples, forehead and vertex; all night; of muscles, with flabbiness; of voluntary muscles, with vertigo on motion; with smarting and warm palms; and motionless, apparently insensible. Inclination to lie down, but when he goes to bed he cannot close his eyes to sleep. Loss of co-ordination of antagonistic muscles, so that when standing knees gave way and on sitting down I fell with my full weight upon the chair, unable to draw my clothes on my limbs without supporting myself, at times *gait slow and shuffling, difficulty in ascending stairs*, especially if the steps were high, such an ascent caused anxiety and dread of falling backward, so that I went bent forward, with attacks of vertigo on walking in open air, < looking upward suddenly, with weakness and at times nosebleed. Disturbance of motility.

Faintness; sudden. Paralysis. Hemiplegia. Numbness; < l. limb and tip of tongue; beginning in tips of fingers, toes and tongue; of feet, gradually working up and causing paralysis of whole system; in one hand, gradually losing the use of it, then in the other, and in feet, slowly working towards the vitals, became helpless and for weeks before he died he could not swallow even liquids. Loss of sensation, voluntary motion and respiration. Aggravation on l. side; A. from great heat, great cold and especially in stormy weather; from walking, riding in a carriage, and jar of a railway train. Amelioration in open air; A. from vomiting.

Clinical.—Effects of sunstroke.

Mind.—Delirium, with vomiting and diarrhœa; quiet D., murmuring to himself; mania-a-potu, sleepless, excitable, talkative and fantastic imagination, pulse soft, full, 85, look wild, skin cold and moist, tongue coated, moist, constipation, hearing excellent (had been hard of hearing), spoke rapidly and distinctly (had talked with difficulty for years, probably from partial paralysis of tongue); delirium tremens, tossing about the bed, with hallucinations of snakes, lions, bears, etc., thought he saw his father's head cut off and the blood running from the body, during these wild paroxysms he tried to get out of bed, it taking several men to hold him, he lolled like a dog and then tried to set an imaginary dog trot or some like imaginary animal, snapped at the attendants, drank eagerly, then he had beautiful visions, saw a beautiful lake, said he would drown himself in that lake and attempted to get out of bed, on being prevented from rising he tried to choke himself and made himself black in the face before his hands could be loosened, begged some one take him out-doors and shoot him, but while under the influence of Belladonna catalepsy, eyes staring, eyeballs could be touched without his winking, afterwards no recollection of what happened on the first day, though he was rational till 4 P.M., urine high-colored, strong-smelling, passed by a catheter, stool omitted, would not eat, but drank eagerly, weak, dizzy on becoming erect.

Nervous excitability; with irregular action of muscles, < lids, mouth and upper limbs, then ease and contentment. Joyful and talkative; J. and lively; and danced about on one leg for joy. Singing all day. Laughter without cause. Agitation. Silly. Misanthropic. Taciturn. Morose. Despondent; > vomiting after dinner, with nausea; and irresolute, weak and incapacitated for business; and nervous; and fearful of death, yet attempting suicide; and apprehensive of sudden death. Apprehensive towards evening; A. of immediate death; and insensible. Nervous and timid; N. on smoking, and shaking. Timid, startled or trembling at any ordinary noise, afraid to be alone at night, aspect haggard, wild. Anxiety; in afternoon, with uneasiness; afternoons, > weeping; at night on being alone; when walking; with restless manner and frightened look; as if she dreaded death, two days at 4 P.M. Indifferent, would not answer, immovable. Indolent. Aversion to moving about. Psychical uneasiness. Cowardly, inactive.

Copious flow of ideas, often lasting all night, during which I would conceive and elaborate about twenty undertakings, of which probably not one would ever come to light, leaving me in the morning worn out and sick. *Difficulty of concentration* (Phos.). Confusion of ideas; and lack of words to express them. Inability to grasp an idea, which is crowded out by other thoughts, > vomiting after dinner, with heaviness and dulness of head. Unintelligible answers. Inferior intelligence in children. Dulness. Sluggishness. Loss of power. Memory failed. Inability to move or speak after waking suddenly about midnight, with cold sweat, then insensibility, then loss of memory, > pouring a bucket of water on his head, then vivid recollection of a variety of ideas and events which appeared to have passed through his mind and occupied him during his supposed insensibility.

Stupor; then wild intoxication, started up in bed, with ridiculous, foolish talking, with convulsive movements and spasm of facial muscles. Sopor, with half-closed eyes, staring, pupils dilated, trembling of limbs, rapid respiration, violent beating of heart and carotids, thirst, sweat and cold limbs. Insensible and dumb. Coma; then he was aroused by pain, made automatic movements, arose, walked a few steps as if intoxicated, threw himself upon the bed and tossed about; but when aroused by loud calls and vigorous shaking he clutched his forehead, crying "Oh, my head! oh, my head!" stared wildly about, conduct and appearance as in delirium tremens. Unconsciousness; with the appearance of sleep; without apparent respiration; and falling to the ground; screamed out that the smokers must go out of the room, though no one was smoking, that the fumes took away his breath, etc., then he became quiet and talked incessantly and irrationally, with staring eyes, spoke of his past life.

Head.—Trembling when reading. Thrown back, almost opisthotonos. Stitches deep in, extending towards vertex. *Aching;* and in eyes; in afternoon < above r. eye; after dinner, < forehead, < motion; suddenly when urinating, then vomiting; > *open air;* as if something in it were shaking in morning, on moving, > rest. Compression, < occiput. *Heaviness;* after dinner; on stooping; and it sinks forward. Oppression as if the world rested upon him, with weakness. Confusion; with pressure at root of nose and stopped sensation in ears. Congestion; and flushing heat. Sensation of rush of blood. Rising sensation like an aura. Shocks, then sensation of rush of blood. Apoplexy.

Vertigo; on motion; on attempting to rise; when standing and sitting; on entering the house after walking, with nausea and inclination to eructate, the nausea < a warm room, so that she must go into open air, where she vomits the food eaten at noon; with reeling; with no steadiness of body; with weakness; with nausea; with pain in forehead and temples; with bruised sensation in head; with fulness of head; with pain deep in orbits and weakness of eyes; with colic; everything seemed to move from r. to l. or from above downward or the reverse; amounting to unconsciousness; paroxysmal; in attacks, preceded by pinching headache, compressed feeling as if the world rested upon him, disordered vision, everything around him seemed to move in all directions, after the attacks great weakness.

Forehead.—Contraction in muscles. Stitches extending to occiput, > open air, returned if he stood still, > lying down. Pain; deep in; above eyes; above eyes, with flickering vision, < walking; above eyes, with heat of head; and at root of nose; drawing, in l. half of forehead and through l. eye; as if brain were compressed, < bending head towards painful side. Sensation as if brain were pressed backward.

Temples.—Stitches in l.; sore S.; alternating with pressure; drawing, extending from l. over forehead to vertex. Tearing in muscles. Pain. Compression towards evening. Contraction. Throbbing.

Vertex.—Stitches. Pain; on waking, lasting nearly all day, and in temples; after eating; at times with stitches; as from a board.

Sides.—Stitches in l.; in parietal bone, extending towards occiput, on walking rapidly. Pain in r. during dinner; in bones in morning on waking, > rising; when pressing on r. bone; as if broken.

Pain in occiput; extending to temple. Giddiness in occiput. Hair falls out on combing. Formication above l. temple. Itching.

Clinical.—Neuralgic headaches, sensation of sudden blows, as if struck by a hammer. Persistent headache, from one temple to the other, involving the orbits, or with shooting in left eye, > cold.

Eyes.—Surrounded by dark redness. Sparkling. Lost their brilliancy. Listless and heavy. Sunken; and seeming small. Turned upward. Staring. Haggard. Red; and pain in base of orbits; and cornea vascular and semiopaque; cornea, with photophobia. Cornea dim, covered with mucus. Exophthalmus from weakness of recti muscles. Sticking in l. Pain; on looking intently, with flickering; < moving them;

in r. extending into occiput; as after long weeping. Tension from l. into upper jaw, with drawing. Feeling as if a hair were in r. towards evening. Burning; in evening when reading; in l., with sensation of coldness.

Lachrymation; with heat of eyes; on looking intently; with contraction of lids. Irregular irritation of retina, sometimes central scotoma, with improved vision in the dark, diminished extent of accommodation, at times increased intraocular pressure.

Optic Nerve.—Brilliant white, areas enlarged and their outlines clearly defined. Atrophy, the inner (apparent) half white and non-vascular, the outer red and vascular; white or gray atrophy (in a few cases bluish-white), beginning at outer part of disc, usually with sharply defined margin and with diminishing size of retinal vessels, in a few cases signs of congestion, in two cases neuritis with indistinct outline of disc, in some cases centre of disc depressed and atrophied, l. eye affected first and more than r. in nearly every case, vision failed suddenly in a few, rapidly in many, in others the progress of the disease was fitful, some had flashes of light, others fog, but most simply indistinct vision, as the atrophy advanced the pupils were dilated and insensible, in a few cases divergence of eyes (compare Phosph.). Disc too large and irregularly circular, the tissue of tendinous whiteness; congested, swollen and hazy. Vision failed, first in r. eye, it began as if a drop of water were before the eye, this increased in size, also floating muscæ before each, discs pale, the r. only on yellow-spot side.

Ball.—Pressure. Digging-drawing pains, < motion, and in temples, with distended vessels and throbbing in them. Heat.

Pupil.—Dilated; and sluggish; and insensible; irregularly; l., and not circular, r. contracted, both insensible. Contracted; and sluggish; and insensible.

Lids.—Closed; and photophobia. Granular. Squinting when trying to read. Twitching of l. upper. Contraction, with biting in balls. In persistent motion, half voluntary. Numbness of orbicular oris. Itching in r. inner canthus, with burning after rubbing.

Injection of conjunctiva. Sensation of a foreign body in conjunctiva. Sticking in upper part of orbit; extending from r. outer to inner margin of brow, into orbit. Heat in orbits.

Vision.—Dim; as from mucus; and glimmering, with pains through temples, can see better on a cloudy day and nearly as well as ever when it begins to grow dark, if he sees a distant team coming towards him it looks like two; suddenly when walking, as if a lot of gnats came before the sight. Presbyopia increased. Imperfect, so that he could not see small objects. Failing, < a bright light, especially for distant vision, optic discs pale at their temporal portion. Failed, could not find suitable glasses, l. pupil larger than r., optic discs pale, < yellow-spot side, retina dim around discs. Blind; on looking at a white object; almost; almost, towards evening, < rubbing eyes. Flickering. Amblyopia, with intolerance of light, especially blue, vision < pressure on balls. Double, < stimulants, with black dots filling field of vision, insufficiency of internal recti, double V. for distant objects, cannot diverge both eyes, discs pale, partly atrophied. Of black points; black spots; things looked black, slight hypermetropia, but sight not improved by glasses, discs pale at their temporal portion, the physiological cup very large in each, and in one eye spontaneous pulsation of the vein.

Ears.—Redness and burning. Stitches; in l.; during music; < open air; in lobule of r., with tearing; behind r., with hard, red swelling. Tearing in r.; in front of and beneath r.; jerklike, in r., and in front of it externally. Gnawing in r. Pain; within on touching outer ear. Tickling. Stopped sensation; < r. Sensitive to slightest noise; to music and loud talking. Hearing dull. Ringing. Humming < loud noises or going into open air. Roaring; < morning; and rushing. Noises.

Nose.—Ulceration. Inflammation of wings, with erosion and pustules. Pressure in Schneiderian membrane, with formication. Burning under it as from fluent coryza; sudden B. in l. nostril. Dryness; and in throat, < evening and at bedtime. Stoppage. Crawling in nostrils. Constant desire to sneeze. Sneezing several times, then head felt easier. Catarrh dry; C. spreading to throat, where there was a raw feeling; fluent; fluent, with acute smell. Constant discharge of watery mucus. Bleeding; and from lungs; black, from l. nostril; thick, dark, tenacious. Smell acute; in morning; for tobacco and cologne water; diminished; weak, but very sensitive to the odor of wine, so that from an empty wineglass standing in the room she became almost befogged.

Face.—Pale; and collapsed, covered with cold sweat (Verat. alb.); *and contracted;* and drawn; *eyes sunken, surrounded by blue rings;* and emaciated, stupid looking; suddenly, and lips livid, all indications of syncope; and red alternately. Pale gray; dullish gray, a chlorotic tinge with the color belonging to certain cachexias. Dirty hue. Bluish and drawn. Violet. Livid. Yellowish, resembling the carcinomatous physiognomy. Cheek sallow and sunken. Red and swollen; red spots; circumscribed redness of cheeks, < l.; dark red; brownish red. Reddish brown. *Sunken.* Pinched and contorted. Drawn. Muscles of l. side contracted as in apoplexy. Anæmic or cachectic look. Expression altered; indicating exhaustion; stupid; austere, gloomy, as if indifferent to everything on account of being discouraged. Dead feeling through the middle.

Jaws.—Dropped. Contraction. Sticking in joints on laughing; drawing pain in angles of lower. Painful drawing in r. side of lower.

Lips.—Cancer. Eruption in corners. Pale. Livid. Drawn back showing the teeth, which were covered with dark sordes. Cracked, painful. Upper rough, dry and burning. Upper feels elongated.

Mouth.—Teeth. Dirty and stained. Caries. Chattering in evening from cold. Sticking in hollow when biting on it; tearing, about r. lower. *Tearing in evening, and in bones of face;* drawing, in upper, extending towards forehead. Drawing in upper, > pressure on cheeks. Throbbing in hollow. Aching; sudden, with heat of face and vertigo; and enamel altered in structure and color, fangs denuded of their periosteum, rough at the extremities, the fangs of the color of horn, porous, differing from the usual dense substance which envelops them. Uneasiness about the crowns, gradually extending to the fangs, teeth tender to touch and if bitten on a sudden pain, afterwards jumping pain at bottom of the alveolar process, aggravations of symptoms from sudden changes of temperature, alcoholic stimulants or anything that accelerated the circulation, sometimes if there were a space (from previous extraction) between the affected teeth a sensation as if electric shocks passed continuously from tooth to tooth.

Gums.—Pale and parched. Drawing.

Tongue.—Cracked. Coated; brown-yellow, smooth, papillæ prominent. Yellowish, not coated. Dry; and lips; and white; and dark red; and coated with a blackish-brown crust. Trembling; and whitish, not coated. Swollen glands under it, painful to external touch. Stitches. Feels swollen, so that his words run into each other. When reading he cannot articulate, he reads very slowly. Speech difficult; and unintelligible; faltering and mind uncertain; low, broken, complaints of exhaustion, confusion of head and a mouldy taste of tobacco; want of power.

Mouth full of white tenacious mucus which must be expectorated frequently; yellowish mucus. *Frothing.* Ulceration. Hyperæmia of M. and pharynx, pharynx covered with granulations, with dryness and varnished appearance. *Burning, and in throat.* **Salivation.** *Watery saliva running constantly from mouth.* Dryness.

Taste.—Bad. As of burnt milk. Sour; to everything. Bitter; in morning. Insipid in morning. Flat slimy in morning. To water as if it were mixed with wine. As if back of tongue were filled with settlings of his pipe, mixed itself up with his food and drink. Of rancid oil; > during a meal, after a few weeks a yellowish spot like dried lichen on edge of the tongue, on sucking it it seemed as if the bad taste came from this spot, soon a similar spot on arches of palate.

Throat.—Tensive pain in submaxillary gland, with feeling as if swollen and as if lower jaw had lost its mobility. Fauces red; F. and roof of mouth red and dry. Uvula œdematous. Tonsils enlarged. Catarrhal inflammation of tonsils. Hawking of mucus; (gray). Tenacious mucus. Choking.

Angina. Scraping; in afternoon; with rawness; in T. and larynx, with pressure; in pharynx, with biting; in pharynx, with rawness; in pharynx, with burning. Scratching and irritation to cough. Pressure as if something were sticking in it. Pain in pharynx on swallowing. Soreness in r. side of pharynx when not swallowing. Nocturnal attacks of tightness, with palpitation and neuralgic pains in neck. Crawling, with pain on swallowing. Tickling and rawness; T. rising up and provoking cough. Dryness; and irritation. Heat in pharynx; in pharynx after swallowing; stinging, in pharynx; burning-scraping, in T. and œsophagus, extending to stomach. Periodic sensation of a plug in œsophagus, with constant pressure. Pain in lower part of œsophagus on swallowing food. Swallowing difficult; painful, owing to spasms of throat; impossible; impossible, except when the article was placed low in throat.

Stomach.—Appetite immediately after vomiting; A., but cannot eat; ravenous; paroxysms of canine; incessant, if she eats nothing she is nauseated; for alcoholic drinks; craving for stimulants and narcotics; little; bad in morning; lost; lost, and food at noon disgusts her. *Thirst;* in evening; *< night;* frequent, for small quantities of water; almost none; none, water will not go down. Aversion to drinking water.

Eructations; loud, all day, < eating; empty; empty, after eating; sour; sour, hot in morning; of food; tasting of food. Hiccough; spasmodic; **Nausea;** in morning on rising; in morning on hawking up mucus, with insipid taste in mouth; *on motion;* with irrational talking; with stitches in l. temple; with salivation; *with relaxed sensation in stomach;* with sensation of a hard substance in stomach; with coldness in stomach; with twisting movement in pit of stomach, lachrymation and salivation; with griping in abdomen; with pain in hypogastrium; then apprehension of misfortune, with oppression of chest, > weeping; **paroxysmal, as in seasickness, with vertigo and cold sweat;** *amounting almost to faintness, > open air;* sudden; rising up from pit of stomach. *Retching.*

Vomiting; nearly all night; on motion; and diarrhœa. *Violent;* from irritation in larynx; with diarrhœa, anxiety and weakness; of blood, then of mucus three times. Spasmodic. *Easy, of sour liquid;* of sour liquid, with mucus, then great relief; sour and slimy in morning, with considerable effort. *Watery, sometimes insipid, sometimes bitter, in morning, even before breakfast;* of water, with which it becomes green and yellow before the eyes; of a mass of liquid in one long stream. Of whitish mucus. Of blood. Of food.

Placed his hands on pit of stomach and often drew up his legs as from pain in abdomen. Distention of epigastrium. Stitches in pit; above pit, > rest; in pit, extending to back. Cramp. Pain; in pit; in epigastric region; in pit during and after dinner; in region of cardiac orifice when eating; after eating, then vomiting; in pit on pressure; in epigastric region on pressure; in pit, < night, at times with pulsation and anxiety; spasmodic, in region of cardiac orifice; in morning, as if he had swallowed something too large, he can hardly eat breakfast on account of pain as if the bolus were forced through too small an opening, and when the food is in the stomach it causes bursting pain, fluids cause pain, warm drinks cause less suffering than cold while swallowing, but they alleviate the burning pain in stomach, and on full inspiration sticking extending from epigastrium to spine, with feeling as if it would be relieved by eructation, but it is not.

Gastrodynia. Gastralgia. Cardialgia. Clawing after eating. Pinching after eating, then diarrhœa, which occurred habitually three or four times a day. Constriction after eating. Shocks in epigastrium; at night and before breakfast; on going to sleep, but after awhile in the daytime, with sweat. Feeling as if it would turn over. Dyspepsia; with nervous palpitation and acidity, hypochondriasis and epigastric sinking. Oppression of pit. Discomfort. Inclination to eructate. Heartburn; rising into throat. Burning; in epigastric region. Coldness, and along spine. **Sinking at pit;** at epigastrium; sudden, at pit, with faintness. *Weakness;* after vomiting. Faintness from fasting a short time.

Clinical.—Persistent nausea and vomiting of pregnancy, with deathly nausea, pale face, coldness in the stomach, gall-stone colic. Gastralgia, starting from the cardiac end of the stomach, pains extending into l. arm. Seasickness.

Abdomen.—Distended; and hard, tense, painful to touch; and heaviness. Retracted. Violent contractions of muscles. Flatulence. Rumbling; in afternoon when walking; on deep breathing, with gurgling; with gurgling and griping; with general coldness. Movements as before diarrhœa. Sudden stitches.

Tearing at night. Griping; and pinching; then clawing in stomach. Pain; in morning; in evening, with movements of flatus, then diarrhœa, with tenesmus; with constipation; with diarrhœa; then cramp in stomach, nausea and salivation; as from a purge, towards evening; burning, < epigastrium. Heat. Sensitiveness on waking after midnight, > soft stool, the same symptoms at 4 A.M.; S. to touch of clothes, and < pit of stomach and hepatic region. Shocks at night on getting into a drowse, afterwards in the daytime, with epigastric sinking, costiveness and dyspepsia.

Hypochondria.—Liver enlarged. Liver inflamed. Stitches; in hepatic region; in hepatic region towards evening; in liver, < breathing; in hepatic region, > stooping, preventing stretching; in liver extending towards pit of stomach, when walking; burning, externally in l. Lancinations, abdomen felt large, painful, insensible to touch, difficulty in articulating from numbness of tongue and muscles of cheeks and lower jaw, which were agitated when I tried to speak, then on eating soup sudden piercing pain in stomach, threw myself back in my chair, pale, covered with cold sweat, breathless, > hot cloths, pain returned on attempting to eat, vomiting (after taking warm water and tickling uvula) of food and bitter fluid, which relieved by causing sweat, the paroxysms always > sweat, tongue furred. Pain; on pressure in hepatic region, extending to pit of stomach; paroxysmal, in l. below heart, < motion, > slight pressure; as if a round weight were lying in r., with pain on touch.

Umbilicus.—Painful retraction, < stooping; cramplike R., with pain in region. Tearing in region as from a bruise every afternoon, spreading over abdomen and concentrating in spine, > night. Cutting in region. Pain in region, with digging; cramplike P. in region.

Sticking in r. flank. Pressure in upper A. Rumbling, with inclination to stool; R. in transverse colon. Pain in hypogastrium, > emission of flatus; P. in hypogastrium, with looseness; with general chilliness. Weakness in r. groin.

Clinical.—Strangulated hernia.

Rectum and Anus.—Hæmorrhoids. Sore pain in A. during diarrhœa. Straining in A. during stool, with burning. Burning pain in A. after stool. Itching in A. Desire for stool with frequent pinching in rectum. Frequent urging in morning. Frequent U. but always scanty stool preceded and followed by sore pain in abdomen; ineffectual U., afterwards hard delayed stool. Paralysis of rectum and bladder.

Stool.—*Resembling those of cholera.* Watery, offensive, then tenesmus; *W., urgent, painless, five or six times every morning;* frequent involuntary and unconscious evacuation of bloody and W. fæces and watery urine. Diarrhœa; about 2 A.M.; after eating, with emission of flatus; with griping, then constipation, then vomiting of much brownish fluid mixed with tobacco; afterwards stools like sheep-dung; copious; serous; green, slimy, with tenesmus; involuntary; frequent; frequent in morning, the first generally about 4 A.M.; five times at night, with burning and tenesmus in anus; in sudden attacks, with cutting in lower part of hypogastrium, as from incarcerated flatus, > expelling it per rectum, but soon returning, at the same time faint feeling with nausea, then sudden urging, stool profuse, gushing, fluid, offensive, with faintness and giddiness, perhaps three or four attacks in one day, then constipation for a week or more, then stools natural for a long time, once or twice dysenteric diarrhœa, with tenesmus for two or three days. Soft; with tenesmus and pain in small of back; with straining and pressure as if fæces were retained; twice at night; and frequent, then internal sensitiveness in abdomen; and small, frequent, then straining. Pasty, frequent; P., copious, often slimy, with emission of flatus; and yellow-green, almost involuntary, then tenesmus.

Constipation; changing at times to diarrhœa. Hard and delayed; and dark. Irregular. Indolent, with at times diarrhœa, with weakness of sphincter ani. Black, fetid. Diminished. Frequent. Involuntary, and micturition.

Clinical.—Cholera infantum, with icy coldness of the extremities, feeble, irregular pulse, deathly nausea and vomiting, > uncovering (Secale).

Urinary Organs.—Frequent desire; constant; D. waking him at night, and on rising he fell in a fainting fit, then coldness, weakness and cold sweat, pulse slow and small. Frequent micturition, at times involuntary dribbling; F. at night, almost involuntary; urine pale, copious; F. and copious, once involuntary at night.

Urethra.—Inflammation of orifice, with agglutination. Discharge of prostatic fluid. Prickling during micturition. Itching before urinating. Burning-itching pain after urinating. Burning when urinating; B. and tickling, then emission at night.

Urine.—Dark red, smelling of tobacco. *Copious;* and pale; and yellowish-red; and deep yellowish-brown; and red, offensive, ammoniacal. Scanty, dark, sp. gr. 1025, acid reaction; deposits urates and mucus; diminished, with increase of free acid, uric acid, phosphoric acid and sulphuric acid and diminution of urea and chlorine. Suppressed. Albuminuria.

Clinical.—Renal colic.

Sexual Organs.—Flabby. Varicocele. Crawling in glans. Erections towards morning; many E. without voluptuous sensations; no E. or desire. Impotency. Emissions; at night; at night without waking. Discharge from vagina of a few drops like meat-water fourteen days after menses. Menses deranged; profuse.

Clinical.—Hyperæsthesia and neuralgia of glans penis.

Respiratory Organs.—Irritation in upper part of trachea, then expectoration. Larynx, constriction; burning, with almost constant cough; tickling, with alteration of voice. Voice hoarse; weak; weak and low.

Cough, with emaciation and weakness; C. and hiccough at the same time, as if she would suffocate; tickling; whooping, day and night, intermitting only during a meal; with dry sputa. Dry cough; all the morning, with stitching in pit of stomach; towards evening; and short; in violent fits from irritation in throat and larynx, < night. Hæmoptysis, cough with expectoration of blood and mucus.

Respiration.—Asphyxia and syncope. Suffocative feeling; in attacks; in paroxysms, from which he frequently woke in anxiety; in nightly attacks, causing him to spring out of bed in anguish, > smoking and slow walking. Stertorous; and the cheeks flopping with each expiration. *Difficult;* on ascending; on ascending stairs or an eminence, with palpitation and distress in cardiac region; and rapid; and sighing; with long sighs; and moaning, deep; suddenly; with sibilant râles. Sighing and irregular. Moaning. Short. Prolonged. Rapid; and short, at times slow and deep, apparently omitting at times. Slow; and thorax scarcely expanded; interrupted by continual yawning; and spasmodic, deep; and stertorous. Feeble. (Easier when bending towards l. side and pressing.) Increase of carbonic acid expired. Decrease of aqueous vapor expired.

Chest.—Various diseases. Pulmonary phthisis. Lungs flaccid and tendency to marasmus. Angina pectoris. Stitches; in sternum; beneath l. ribs; in r. side; in r. side on talking; on deep breathing; beneath sternum on deep breathing; on breathing, and in side, with weakness of head as if intoxicated and flickering vision; near r. axilla, > inspiration; beneath sternum, with impossibility to breathe deeply; in middle, extending to sternum; backward through it, < deep breathing; burning, beneath l. breast; sore, in r. side, < rest. Cutting in intercostal muscles from front towards back on deep breathing, < touch.

Pain; beneath sternum; with anxiety; in l. side, < præcordial region; behind sternum and rather to l. side, usually in afternoon, sometimes interfering with sleep, > before morning, with oppression; flitting; in sides alternating with sore throat; sudden, with gasping for breath and *sensation as if a crowbar were pressed tightly from r. breast to l. and twisted in a knot round the heart, which stopped for a minute and then leaped like a dozen frogs, afterwards the heart missed every fourth beat*, frequent recurrence of the attacks; sudden, as if squeezed in a vise, in evening when smoking, with insensible pulse. Soreness during rest; sore pain in r. female breast, with feeling as if the nipple were bitten off.

Constriction; across upper front part, with dyspnœa and disposition to inspire fully, with darting pain from heart to vertex; and inability to breathe deeply, with anxiety, inability to rid herself of the thought that some misfortune would happen to her. *Tightness on breathing deeply;* T. during dinner, with stitches beneath r. short ribs. Oppression, > deep breathing; O. in female breast. Anxiety beginning in C. and præcordial region. Heaviness of sternum. Shocks in C. and region of heart at night but afterwards in the daytime, with rush of blood to head, causing unconsciousness.

Clinical.—Asthma.

Heart.—Systolic murmur in aortic arch and in large vessels. Sounds muffled and almost running into each other; sounds inaudible and its movement scarcely felt. Disease. Pain in region, < night, with intermission of pulse and heart's action; P. in region, with soreness and inability to lie long on l. side; sudden, in region in morning, with transverse constriction in upper part of chest, inability to walk or speak, pulse insensible, hands cold. *Præcordial oppression; in paroxysms, < night, with palpitation and pain between shoulders.* Præcordial anxiety suddenly in evening, then sleeplessness and springing from bed. Disturbance.

Palpitation (Thea, Spig.); all night; when lying on l. side; < lying on l. side, with trembling of heart; with bruit in carotids; with pain in cardiac region; with tightness of throat; in attacks in evening or night, with pain and constriction of chest; in attacks at night, with oppression and pain about shoulders. Beating violently, so that he must give up active exercise. *Action weak;* and intermittent; and slow, intermittent. Beating irregularly, with slight anæmic murmur. Movements like the purring tremor which is likely to accompany aortic regurgitation. Paralysis.

Clinical.—Angina pectoris, pains radiate from centre of sternum, with cold extremities, pinched features, suffocation. Dilatation of the heart, with feeble irregular pulse, chest pains, extending down the left arm, clammy sweat, etc.

Pulse.—*Rapid;* and full; and full, hard; *and small;* and small, hard; and small, irregular; and soft; and feeble. *Slow;* and full; and full, large, movement increases the beats more than in a healthy state; and small; and intermittent; and intermittent, scarcely perceptible, also small. Violent. Strong in temporal arteries. Intermittent; and small; and irregular, rapid, then slow. *Weak and small;* with cold clammy sweat; *W., soft and full;* W. and irritable. Imperceptible; at wrist, action of heart scarcely perceptible.

Neck.—*Neuralgia, with tightness of throat.* Pain in nape, with heaviness, so that he must remove the neckerchief. Tension in skin of r. side, with burning. Stiffness so that she could not turn head to r. side.

Back.—Morbid feeling in different parts of spine, if affected in region of seventh cervical vertebra he felt depression and paralyzed sensation of forearms and hands, with compression of manubrium sterni, difficulty in swallowing and shrill paroxysmal cough, if the upper part of spine was painful there was only palpitation, if the part corresponding to the twelfth dorsal vertebra became painful there were compression of stomach, loss of appetite and vomiting, when the central sensations moved to the lower part of spine the gastric symptoms changed to eccentric disturbances of sacral region, as cramps or spasms of sphincter ani and emissions, then debility, unhappy looks and dejection, at times the whole spine was affected, then all the symptoms appeared simultaneously, causing unsteady action of lower limbs and difficulty in stepping over objects, sudden vertigo when walking, at times the central pain moved to l. hemisphere of brain, causing double vision. Tenderness of spine, < cervical and lumbar regions. Stiffness of spine and lower limbs. Pain in middle of spine in morning, with general bruised feeling, < upper limbs. Stitches in r. scapula. Burning beneath scapula.

Lumbar Region.—Pain in region of kidneys; before urinating; P. on rising from a seat and on beginning to walk, > walking; < sitting and lying; beating, in region of sacrum in evening. Constriction, < after stool. Feeling as if some one were blowing on the spine.

Extremities.—Relaxed; and paralyzed; and outstretched, powerless, trembling and twitching. Trembling; of hands and feet, with weakness of them. Cataleptic condition of arms and legs. Pain in all. Feeling as if fingers were longer when smoking tobacco in a pipe, if he continues smoking he feels as if he had lost the use of his legs from the knees downward, and if he smokes half a cigar in-doors his calves feel as if they did not belong to him and were dropping away. Weakness; trembling. Stiffness.

Upper Extremities.—Stitches in l. shoulder, with drawing. Pulsation beneath r. shoulder.

Arm.—Bound over chest. Spasmodic contractions, and in hands. Trembling, and in hands. Pain on raising it; P. in l., with weakness; drawing, in a spot as if an ulcer would form on l. Tension in l., < elbow. Constant inclination to stretch. Easy fatigue from holding a book, at times with stitches in fingers, < thumbs. R. seemed paralyzed, as with cramp.

Tearing in tendons of l. forearm towards hand and then in elbow. Sprained pain in r. forearm, < elbow, with stitches on exertion. Sticking in elbow, so that he could not stretch the arm quickly. Drawing pain on turning elbow.

Hands.—Joined and rigidly contracted. Trembling. Sticking in r., with tearing. Drawing, paralytic, spasmodic pain in r., extending to elbow. Drawing in l., then general paralysis. Seem paralyzed and cold, then burning and fuzziness in tip of fingers and difficult mobility, with general coldness.

Fingers.—Swollen. Cramp; in morning on washing; in three first l., with formication. Twitching of one. Tearing in little.

Lower Extremities.—Walking about as if intoxicated. Tottering; in morning after rising. Gait of an old man. Shuffling gait. Drawing. Uneasiness. Loss of control. Weakness; or paralysis, with loss of sensation and weakness of all special senses. Sticking in and above l. gluteal muscles; in r. hip towards evening. Pain in hips and knees; in r. gluteal muscles on pressure; in gluteal and femoral muscles, and tension as after a long walk.

Knee.—Cracking when walking. Tottered, and he seemed scarcely able to support his emaciated body. Cramp. Stitches in hollows; S. on bending, pressure in them during rest.

Tearing down l. calf; externally on l. tibia. Tension in legs when walking. Paralyzed feeling below knee, as if asleep. Pain in l. ankle. Foot, shaking; jerking tearing on back of l. Paralyzed feeling in r., weak as if paralyzed, could scarcely ascend stairs. Cramp from toes into knee. Acute pain in balls of l. toes, so that he could not step as usual.

Skin.—Grayish, a medium between the pallor of chlorosis and of other cachexiæ. Pallid and appeared anæmic. Livid, covered with cold sweat. Jaundice. Red spots on r. shoulder, with burning on touch. Inflammation from slightest wound. Red itching eruption on back. Gritty elevations on cheeks beneath eyes, perceptible only on touch. Pimples; on forehead, with itching, transiently > rubbing; itching, on chest; itching, on back, small of back and fingers. Pustules on nape and upper limbs. Itching blisters filled with yellow liquid, with red areola, with sore pain on touch.

Trembling sensation as if it were being torn. Formication from l. knee to toes. *Itching of whole skin;* here and there; with turgescence and sweat; on face in evening; on arm and neck; r. hypochondrium; thighs.

Sleep.—Yawning; after dinner; after dinner, with sleepiness. Sleepiness; in forenoon; towards evening; > open air; with heat and restlessness. Sleeping after dinner, could not arouse herself till after palpitation. Deep sleep, then sweat. Heavy sleep, with irregular rattling respiration, from which he could not be awakened, face and back covered with cold sweat, eyes staring, features drawn. Stupefying, unrefreshing sleep. Cannot be awakened in the morning.

Sleeplessness; first part of night; > smoking. Could not fall asleep in the evening, could not wake in the morning. Sleep light, often interrupted, sometimes by cough and colic. Frequent waking. Wakes before midnight, but soon falls asleep again. Starting on falling asleep; with shock through epigastrium and sometimes through chest. Restless sleep; with coldness; with frequent waking on account of pain in l. wrist and ankle; with anxious dreams; with constant nightmare.

Dreams.—Uneasy. Frightful. Anxious, of fire. Of snakes, apprehension of death, etc. Painful, that a tooth had fallen out. Nightmare, dream that she wished to talk and could not on account of her large tongue, which extended out of her mouth and up to her nose, she tried to cry out and could not, wept and was inconsolable, at last woke in anxiety.

Fever.—*Chilliness;* from 5 till 7 P.M., with thirst about 6; *with cold sweat;* with rush of heat, without thirst. Internal, with hot face, now cold, now warm, sweaty hands, without thirst. Shaking C. in evening; in evening in bed; in evening, with inclination to stretch. Shivering; nearly all day; all day, with pain between shoulders; all day, with shaking, and towards evening sweat in palms; in morning in open air; in afternoon after eating, alternating with heat, during the coldness sweat under arms; in evening; in open air; with yawning and stretching of arms; with flushes of heat; internal, with bruised sensation, heat and disinclination to work. Gooseflesh all day.

Coldness of skin; of skin, < limbs; of nose, with moisture; of limbs, with blue color; limbs; hands, with warmth of body; l. hand, with heat of r.; from knees to toes, with burning in thighs and much heat; legs, with heat of body; feet; feet all night; suddenly creeping along back in evening when drinking beer and smoking, with general weakness, then pain on lower part of frontal bone, when undressing shaking chill, then dry heat, then sweat, then vivid dreams, from which I woke with sweat, exhaustion and confusion of head, and in morning on rising pain in frontal region as from pressure downward in skull, headache > horizontal position, with thirst, coated tongue and loss of appetite, on attempting to walk pain in loins and nape, gait slow and anxious, with vertigo and pressing headache, l. foot often failed to make a step, headache > afternoon by bleeding from l. nostril, < evening on making visits, concentrated in l. side, > going to bed, vivid dreams, headache returned in morning.

Heat; with restlessness; with intoxication; dry; flushing, after vomiting. Orgasm of blood. Symptoms similar to intermittent fever on ceasing to smoke. Dry heat of skin. Heat of head; and face; mounting suddenly; then formication, loss of appetite, sticking in ears, then coldness and shivering. H. of face, with redness; rising into it; r. cheek, while l. was pale; l. cheek towards evening, with redness, without thirst. In palms. In knee, and on touch feeling as if pins were in it. On side of sole, < towards evening.

Sweat; at night; in sleep. **Cold sweat;** all night; **and clammy;** and trickling, everywhere except on forehead; *on hands;* forehead; face. Viscous. Smelling of tobacco before midnight. Sweat on head; and chest; on forehead; running down his face during light occupation. Dryness of skin.

Tanacetum.

A tincture is made of the fresh leaves and flowers of the tansy.

Compare other compositæ, Cina and Absinth.

Generalities. — Trembling. Remarkable gestures, stretched, drew up the feet, stood on his head, said, "Let me do as I wish, I cannot do anything else," so he drew up his legs and when the muscles would draw them no farther he pulled them up with his hands and then suddenly stretched them.

Convulsions; during pregnancy; with frothing at mouth, labored respiration and irregular pulse; with features horribly distorted, unconsciousness and inability to swallow; then vomiting, then catalepsy; every five or ten minutes, head thrown back, respiration suspended, arms raised and rigidly extended, fingers contracted, in about half a minute a tremulous motion, sometimes shaking the room, with faint and imperfect attempts at inspiration, the time from the beginning of the convulsion to the first full inspiration varied from a minute to a minute and a half, occasionally the tongue was wounded by the teeth, after a convulsion face pallid and livid, pulse slow and weak, often after a convulsion the head was drawn slowly backward and eyelids opened wide, between the convulsions the limbs were mostly relaxed but jaws were clenched; supposed to be epileptic, in which the shoulder was dislocated; tonic contraction of flexors, forearms drawn forcibly against chest, face congested and livid, foamy saliva ejected from mouth, eyes wide open; clonic; sudden, clonic, with trembling of arms, which were thrown forward of and at right angles with the body, wrists bent at right angles, forearms supinated, tips of fingers nearly in contact, fingers straight and slightly bent at metacarpal joints, muscles of respiration strongly affected, air forced from chest slowly but steadily and hissed as it escaped from the lips, between the spasms muscles were flexible except jaws, which were rigidly closed the first hour, but afterwards rigid during the spasms and relaxed between them, the spasms more frequent as the patient grew weaker.

Rheumatic symptoms. Sensation approaching a thrill through the whole body. Weariness. Numbness, with sensation as if arms and legs were suddenly swelling. Paralysis of all voluntary motion, including muscles of deglutition.

Clinical.—Chorea, with strange gesticulations. Affections from worms, with twitchings in sleep and wakening from fright.

Mind.—Exhilaration. Shrieked and fell senseless to the ground, > vomiting. Nervous. Indifference to my questions and incoherence in her replies. Dulness of all senses. Impossible to fix my attention and it seemed as if my reason would leave me. Confusion. Mind fatigued after least mental exertion. Intellect feeble, with tendency to stupor. Coma. Unconsciousness; partial.

Head.—Agonizing pain. Fulness; and pain; with frontal pain; and in face. Heavy aching. Condition similar to apoplexy. Vertigo. Frontal pain, with cutting in temples. Occipito-frontal pain.

Eyes.—Inward strabismus of r. Sclerotics injected, eyes open and brilliant, pupils dilated and immovable. Sclerotic coat so congested that it was dark purple, glassy, and so swollen that the cornea seemed depressed. Slow lateral motion of balls. Aching in balls. Pupils dilated; contracted; contracted, then dilated. Lids agglutinated in morning.

Ears.—Stitches in middle. Sensation as if something closed them suddenly. Ringing. Roaring.

Nose and Face.—Coryza. Nostrils dry. Face red; and eyes; cheeks bright red. Face dusky. Features fixed, giving an expression of deep solemnity. Lips and nose drawn to r. side.

Mouth and Throat. — Tongue feels rough and is coated white. Frothing at mouth. Mouth blood-stained. Taste flat, insipid. Mucus in fauces and larynx, disturbing respiration. Feeling in throat as if I would cough, without ability to cough. Tickling in fauces and larynx causing constant inclination to cough, but no cough. Throat rough. Inability to swallow.

Stomach.—Thirst. Eructations tasting of the oil; flatulent, tasting of tansy; of sour air at night. Nausea; with faintness. Vomiting. Drawing cutting in epigastrium. Weight. Burning; and in abdomen.

Abdomen.—Rumbling. Pain; mostly in region of small intestines, from small doses it is cutting stitching, from large doses heavy pains, with frequent cutting, < night, and especially after midnight. In morning, feeling as if full of limpid secretions from taking a cathartic. Warmth over it. Dull pain in r. hypochondrium, sharp in l. Umbilical region, sticking; frequent pains through the day, < 4 A.M. Cutting at umbilicus, then papescent stools. Drawing pain in l. groin.

Stool and Urine.—Diarrhœa, then constipation; D. twice; twice and sensation as if he would have more. Stool omitted. Constant desire to urinate; with heavy pain in small of back (secondary). Frequent micturition. Obliged to rise to urinate, urine smelled of tansy. Urine scalding; U. fetid; high-colored, afterwards light-colored; copious, high-colored, smelling of the drug; suppressed, then copious.

Clinical.—Many cases of dysentery.

Sexual Organs.—Inflammation of vaginal walls of labia, ending in abscess of one labia. Menses profuse (after a suppression of several days), with labor-like pains. Abortion in the early months of pregnancy; A. prevented. At full term a child was born, not larger than a rat, and lived three weeks.

Clinical.—Dysmenorrhœa, with bearing-down pains, tenderness, drawing in the groins.

Respiratory Organs and Chest. — Voice sounded strange to his own ears. Breathing oppressed; and hurried, stertorous, obstructed by frothy mucus in air-passages and blown from between lips in expiration, breath smelled of tansy; but not stertorous, blowing mucus and saliva from fauces and mouth, this respiration most marked after each spasm, but sometimes not unlike that of sound sleep. Moaning and distressed appearance. Desire to draw a full breath, which did not relieve the oppression of chest. Pain in l. side.

Heart and Pulse.—Feeble action of heart and all the signs of impending dissolution. Pulse rapid; and forcible; and full, forcible; and feeble; and small, feeble. Pulse slow; 60, with a peculiar measured beat. Pulse full and incompressible. P. irregular. Pulseless.

Back and Extremities.—Backache; in lumbar region. Lumbago in evening. Extremities, prickling, with flashes of heat; intermittent pricking, and along spine; pain; cold numbness creeping over them, increasing almost to paralysis. Lameness of l. wrist in morning, with soreness. Weakness of legs, with general prostration. Unsteadiness of step, with indescribable feeling worse than pain.

Skin, Sleep and Fever.—Eruption like variola. Drowsy. Chill, then heat. Skin cold and moist; cold, < towards extremities. Heat; of skin. Cold, clammy sweat.

Taraxacum.

A tincture is made of the entire fresh plant of the Dandelion.

Allies.—Chel., Puls. (Hydrast.).

Generalities.—Inner feeling as if very sick, all limbs painful on touch or when in an uncomfortable position. Restlessness and discomfort. Weakness, so that he wished to lie or sit, when he was semi-conscious, as on falling asleep. Most symptoms appear when sitting and disappear when walking.

Mind.—Talkative. Inclined to laugh. Religious, happy, contented. Ill humor in morning and disinclined to any occupation or to talking. Gloomy when unoccupied, does not know what to do, cannot make up his mind to do anything. Irresolute and dreading work, though it progresses well as soon as he undertakes it.

Head.—Pain extending outward; burning P., extending upward. Sensation composed of pressure and itching. Constriction of brain from all sides. Heaviness, with redness of face. Vertigo on walking in open air, with dulness of head; V. on walking in open air, head fell now to r., now to l.; on walking in open air, with insecure step, as if he would fall forward.

Forehead.—Sticking; *externally in l. side;* tearing, in l. Pain; in forepart of head, extending outward towards forehead; crawling, as from something alive, extending from the middle of it on walking in open air; drawing, on bone when standing. Stupefying pain, as after intoxication; S. pain when sitting, so that he lost his senses when reading and did not know where he was, > open air, with nausea. Contraction above nose, with whirling, at another time painless sensation as if brain were distended here and there.

Temples.—*Stitches in l. when sitting, > standing;* in l. when walking in open air, > standing. *Pain in r.* Drawing pain; *in l. when sitting, > walking and standing.*

Sticking in l. side. *Tearing in occiput* when walking, > standing still; externally when walking; sticking, behind r. ear. Heaviness in occiput, > stooping, < rising and holding head erect; *H. deep down, with pressure.* Pimple above r. temple, painful on touch. Anterior part of scalp tense, as if tight over vertex.

Eyes.—Hard mucus, more in morning than during the day. Sticking in r. A kind of ophthalmia, eyes cannot endure light and constantly water, with pressure on r. upper lid. Ball, *burning sticking in l. towards external canthus; burning in l.;* burning in r. towards inner canthus; sticking burning pain in l. Pupils dilated; contracted. Lids agglutinated in morning. Sticking burning in lids. Pressure as from sand in r. inner canthus, with feeling as if lid were swollen there.

Ears.—Sticking extending outward in r. and always again inward; S. behind ear, with tearing down side of neck; itching burning, in r. Tearing in outer meatus and sharp pressure behind ramus of lower jaw. *Drawing pain in outer.* Pressure inward in l. Chirping in l. like grasshoppers. (Hearing difficult as from stoppage of ear, in evening.)

Nose and Face.—Sneezing when walking in open air. Bleeding from l. nostril at noon, before dinner. Stitching in cheek. Sharp pressure in r. cheek. Crack in middle of upper lip. *Pustule in r. corner of lips.*

Mouth.—Sour-tasting blood flowed from r. hollow teeth. Pain like blows in incisors, < crowns. Drawing pain in r. hollow teeth, extending into cheek and to brow. Teeth on edge when chewing food. **Tongue covered with a white film, with raw sensation in it, afterwards the film comes off in pieces, leaving dark red and sensitive spots;** *coated white, gradually peeling off in spots;* coated white; coated yellowish-brown at back; brown in morning on waking; and dry; burning stitches in l. side. *Salivation, with feeling as if larynx were compressed;* sour-tasting S. *Taste bitter before eating; bitter, rising from œsophagus into mouth* (Chel., Puls.); sour to meat, especially to gravy from roast meat, when it touches tip of tongue; salty-sour to butter when it touches tip of tongue; none to tobacco-smoke, it causes burning in throat, almost like heartburn, and takes away the breath, > drinking.

Throat.—Hawking up of sour mucus that sets the teeth on edge. Acute pain in lower part of parotid and in cervical muscles and extending from sternum to mastoid process, on moving jaws and neck. Tickling irritation to hacking cough in region of pit of throat, he always had a few minutes' warning of the paroxysm, but was never able to suppress it. Dryness, with a ring of inflammation around isthmus faucium; D. in fauces, with bitter mucus, making the voice husky; D., with stitches. Swallowing difficult, as from a swelling. Sharp pressure on anterior wall of œsophagus and larynx, provoking cough, > swallowing.

Stomach.—*Bitter eructations and hiccough;* empty E., < drinking. Nausea; in œsophagus; when sitting, > standing, with anxiety; *as from fat,* > open air, with stupefying pain in forehead. Tension in pit when stooping, with pressure in ensiform cartilage. Stitches in r. side of diaphragm when lying on that side. Tensive pain in region of diaphragm during violent inspiration.

Abdomen.—Rumbling and movements. Griping; then emission of flatus. *Stitches partly in l. hypochondrium, sometimes in l. or r. side of abdomen, sometimes in hypogastrium;* in side; *l. side;* tense, in r. side; itching, in r. muscles. Pain in l. side. Rumbling in umbilical region towards l. side. Boring outward in umbilical region, extending towards r. side. *Sudden persistent motion as if bubbles formed and burst in hypogastrium.* Burning stitches in l. hypogastrium, extending towards genitals. Sprained sensation in l. groin on walking, > standing and touch. Painless bubbling in muscles of l. hypogastrium.

Clinical.—This is a remedy for bilious diarrhœa, chilliness after eating or drinking, pain and soreness over the liver, *bitter taste, mapped tongue.*

Stool and Urine.—*Stool difficult,* not hard. Stool

pasty and early, then ineffectual urging. Constipation. *Pressure to urinate, without pain; frequent desire to urinate and copious urine*, afterwards frequent desire and scanty discharge. Urine high-colored and diminished.

Sexual Organs.—Boring in glans. Long-continued erections. Tickling on prepuce. Stitch in l. testicle; burning, in r. Emission every other night.

Chest.—*Twitching in r. costal muscles;* l. costal muscles. Stitches in sternum; side; on last l. rib; beneath r. axilla; in region of sixth rib; in r. side when walking; beneath last l. rib, towards back, on every breath; in r. side, > violent inspiration and expiration, on pressure it returned more violently and extended over a larger space; in l., extending towards back; extending inward during inspiration when standing. Boring in r. breast, < walking, with digging. Boring-sticking drawing in scapular end of r. clavicle. Pressure beneath l. axilla; beneath l. ribs; outward against r. ribs, from hepatic region into chest, during expiration while standing; burning, in sternum, worse during expiration than inspiration.

Heart and Pulse.—Uneasy sinking in præcordia. Pulse rapid, full, soft.

Neck.—*Twitching in l. lower part;* behind l. ear. Sticking in nape; *in l. side when standing, > sitting down;* boring, outward in l.

Back.—Sticking in spine towards r. side when lying, especially in small of back, with difficult breathing; *tensive, towards r. side; outward in r. scapula. Vibration in r. scapula, with quivering* (see Chel.). Pressure in sacrum; when standing; outward in l. loin. Painless creeping in sacrum.

Extremities.—Easy motion, but it seems to him as if motor power were restrained. Twitching on top of l. shoulder. Throbbing on l. shoulder; with general chilliness. Stitch on outer side of l. arm. Pain on inner side of l arm.

Upper Arm.—Twitching; in outer part of l. Sticking on inner side of l.; S. posteriorly, > rubbing; intermittent, on outer side of middle of r. during rest. Pain like electric shocks on outer side of l. Pain in muscles of l. Intermittent throbbing.

Stitches in r. elbow; in l. forearm; r. forearm, > touch. *Twitching in muscles of l. forearm.* Pain on inner side of r. forearm. Frequent drawing pains in forearms. Tearing drawing in l. wrist, extending to three last fingers. Sticking in l. fourth finger. *Pain in three last r. fingers;* burning, in l. third and fourth.

Lower Extremities.—Twitching in upper part; in l. gluteals extending downward. *Sticking in l.;* boring, on inner side when sitting; pinching, high up on forepart, as if beaten, more on touch than when walking. Pressure on inner side of r. when sitting and standing.

Knee.—Sticking; drawing, on outer side of r. Tearing on outer tendon in hollow when sitting. Sharp pressure on outer side on bending leg. Burning pain in forepart of r.; in l. patella.

Leg.—Stitches in r. calf; upward on outer side of l. leg when standing; drawing, upward in r. when standing, > sitting; throbbing, in r. calf just beneath hollow of knee; burning, in calf when standing. Tearing on outer margin of l. when standing. Gnawing in r. when standing. *Pain in l. calf; jerking, in r. calf, suddenly > touch;* drawing, when sitting and walking; burning, in lower part of r.; burning, on outer side of. r. Burning on forepart of tibia. Weakness, < ascending steps; W. of r. when walking, yet the muscles seem tenser than in l.

Ankle.—Stitch in r. inner malleolus when sitting; itching, in inner M. Tearing drawing in l.

Foot.—Stitches extending from dorsum into sole; on dorsum of l. extending towards great toe; *in r. sole,* extending outward, when sitting; itching, in r. sole. Boring in r. sole; burning, in l. sole, extending towards little toe. *Pressure on back of r. when sitting. Drawing pain on back of r. when standing;* on back of l. when standing. Burning pain on r. sole towards outer side; in r. sole towards toes when sitting. Burning drawing on back of l.

Toes.—Stitches in r. great, towards second toe; tearing S.; burning, in r. great when walking. Pulling from little toe up tibia, when sitting.

Skin.—Rash on upper part of body, with tingling and itching, scratching temporarily relieved the itching, but caused more eruption and redness, face red in patches and swollen, on forearms and hands lichen and urticaria, the lichen was purple, thicker about wrists and bindings of elbows, where it was in patches on an inflamed base, the papillæ were covered with a brownish crust as if blood had hardened, the urticaria was principally on the front of the arms, < scratching, coming and going two or three times a day, worse in morning, chest and waist were thickly covered and very red. Pimple in middle of l. brow, painful on touch; itching, on hands, < sides of fingers and backs of hands. Pustules on r. wing of nose; on upper part of l. cheek, with red areola and gnawing on touch. Itching vesicles on back of foot.

Itching on l. gluteals; on fourth toes; suddenly below chin; on l. calf in evening on lying down, not > scratching, then redness and moisture; on back of r. foot, > scratching; corrosive, on l. thigh; voluptuous, in perineum, then biting pain; tickling, in perineum, between anus and pudendum.

Sleep.—Yawning when sitting. Sleepiness during the day when reading, > moving about; overpowering, after eating, on waking necessity to urinate, with burning before and after micturition. He fell asleep when listening to scientific conversation and immediately had vivid dreams. Restless nights. Frequent waking as if he had slept enough; F. waking and tossing about. *Dreams vivid, unremembered;* and anxious; D. of quarrels; voluptuous.

Fever.—Chilliness; *after eating, < drinking;* with headache; shaking, on walking in open air. *Finger-tips cold.* Heat; without thirst; suddenly when walking in open air, without thirst; *in face, with redness; in attacks in toes,* < back of r. great toe; in r. forearm. Sweat; in evening on falling asleep, lasting all night; as soon as he fell asleep, waking him, with heat, < cheeks; on waking, causing itching biting; between toes, < r.

Clinical.—During a fever great restlessness, with tearing pains in the legs, intolerable while at rest, constant muttering delirium, violent tearing in the occiput, chilliness after eating or drinking, mapped tongue.

Tarentula.

The live Spanish spider is triturated with sugar of milk.

General Action.—(The remarkable nervous symptoms require confirmation.)

Generalities.—Yelled and fell down, was carried to

the house in agony, smarting pain, hot and cold, starting from the bite to small of back and then returning to the bite, this alternating pain lasted all night. Falling suddenly as if struck by apoplexy, then shortness of breath, blackness of face, hands, etc., he revived as he heard music, sighed, moved first his feet, then hands and rest of body, and on being raised to his feet danced vigorously, sighed deeply, rolled upon the ground, kicked vigorously, the dance was repeated for three days and he was restored by the perspiration thus induced, but each year, about the time of the bite, pain reappeared in the affected part, with the above symptoms in less intensity, again > music and dancing.

Stretched upon the ground and seemed about to expire, when he heard the music he got up as quick as lightning, seemed awakened by a frightful vision, stared wildly about, still moving every joint, when I stopped playing he fell down in an instant and cried, every part was distorted, he scraped the earth with his hands, on hearing the music again he arose as before and danced wildly, keeping perfect time but jumping and running to and fro, making comical postures, somewhat like Chinese dances, and everything he did was very wild. Twitching, < arms, alternating with opisthotonos. Convulsions; and subsultus in all limbs, penis erect, abdominal muscles contracted and rigid.

Pain and swelling; P. immediately in bitten part, he fell to the ground, with coldness of body, bristling of hair, tension of trunk, weakness of legs, sighing, complaints, said that he was suffocating, wished to cry out but could not, on hearing music the next morning he began to dance, was bathed in sweat, was sleepless for a week, drank pure wine, had no stool for four days, desired nothing, wished to be bathed with water, liked a red color, pursued anything blue, tore it to pieces and trampled it under foot, at night he held his heels in his hands to scratch them, in which manner he could sleep a little, ate little or nothing, but dancing for almost a week, he was cured by sweat and music.

A few hours after the bite, anguish of heart, dejection, difficulty in breathing, they complain in a mournful voice, roll their eyes, when asked where they suffer they do not reply or place the hand upon the heart, the symptoms vary according to the variety of Tarentula, the temperament of the patient and the degree of summer heat, the T. in northern Apulia are fiercer and the symptoms severer, the patients are charmed by various colors, green, blue, etc., rarely by dark colors, at the sight of an annoying color anguish of heart and renewal of symptoms, the T. subalbida causes slight pain followed by itching, sharp pain in abdomen and diarrhœa, the T. stellata causes severer pain and itching, stupor, heaviness and pain in head, general trembling, etc., the T. uvea causes, besides the above symptoms, swelling, great pain in the bitten part, spasm, chill, cold sweat of whole body, aphonia, nausea, tension of trunk and chest, distention of abdomen, etc., in general, after the severer symptoms have declined, there is a peculiar melancholy, a bending forward of neck, sometimes > music or dancing, desperation, they court dissolution, otherwise virtuous women sigh deeply, howl, make indecent gestures, expose their sexual organs, etc., others like to whip buttocks, feet, back, etc., others have great desire to run.

Restlessness, must keep in motion though walking aggravates the symptoms. Weakness; so that he could hardly be moved from side to side, with constriction of chest and anguish of heart. When urged to dance she replied with tears that she could not on account of pain in joints of feet and weakness. Return of all symptoms every year at the time of the bite, all symptoms > dancing. Aggravation of all symptoms from drinking two fluid ounces of whisky.

Clinical.—The Spanish Tarentula has been used very largely for hysteria, characterized by most violent alternations of moods, especially with sudden, stealthy and destructive impulses; its curative powers in these and other forms of mental disturbance rest upon a very slender basis, for it is probable that most of the mental symptoms attributed to the bite of this spider are purely imaginary. Hystero-epilepsy, with wild shrieks. Hysteria, with constant movement of the extremities, especially of the hands. Paralysis agitans. Chorea, especially of the extremities. Nocturnal chorea in children. General hyperæsthesia.

Mind.—Agitation. Melancholy, anguish, restlessness, peevishness, haste in whatever I undertook from fear that something would prevent my finishing it, I would start up and hastily change my position through fear that something would fall on me, when walking I would stop short or suddenly throw my head to one side through fear of striking it against an imaginary object which appeared to be suspended a few inches above my head, fear of impending calamity, desire to be alone, with fear of being alone, even during daylight, frightful images as soon as the eyes closed, with inability to sleep.

Head, etc.—Headache. Weakness of head. Eyes glaring, red. Eyes inflamed, conjunctiva injected, *r. pupil dilated*, l. contracted, vision lost in r. eye, objects seen in l. eye appeared bright red. Roaring and rumbling in ears, with dulness of hearing. Profuse hæmorrhage of black blood from nose, each drop coagulated and sank at once like a bullet to the bottom of a vessel partly filled with water, and formed a large black clot. Face pale, earthy, in strong contrast with the nearly purple neck. Countenance expressive of terror.

Mouth, Throat and Stomach.—Tongue moist. Tongue coated dark-brown, edges and tip fiery red. Said that her tongue was drawn backward, so that she could not speak. Swelling of external throat. Throbbing pain in submaxillary and cervical glands, with occasional stinging. Fauces swollen, purplish, swallowing difficult, as from partial paralysis. Swallowing painful. Appetite lost. *Thirst;* burning, with internal heat; burning, with constant desire for large quantities of cold water. Vomiting, with incessant paroxysms of cough and scanty expectoration of mucus; V. of everything taken into stomach soon after eating, preceded by burning pain in stomach and œsophagus, which the V. relieved.

Abdomen, Stool and Urine.—Colic, then fever, then fatal symptoms. Stools three or four times daily, dark, fetid, partly-formed, difficult, containing much mucus followed by smarting and burning at anus, stools always immediately on having head washed. Urine scanty, high-colored, passed with difficulty, a dense precipitate after standing.

Sexual Organs. — Clinical. — Dysmenorrhœa, with extremely sensitive ovaries. It has been used in various forms of disease of the sexual organs of women; chronic vaginitis, granular; induration of the cervix and body of uterus; cancerous ulceration of the os, with induration; subinvolution, with leucorrhœa, burning, smarting pain in the coccyx, > standing, uterine neuralgias, extending to the sacrum and spine, with convulsive movement. Intense pruritus of the vulva. Nymphomania. "Fidgets" in the legs, associated with menstrual irregularities.

Respiratory Organs and Chest.—Aphonia. Breathing difficult; with peculiar incessant sighing; B. short and hurried, < attempting to lie down. Pain at base of lungs when coughing or inhaling. Constriction of chest. Chest expands with difficulty.

Heart and Pulse.—Anguish of heart; preventing lying down, did not go to bed nor sleep for four nights. Painful throbbing in carotids, > nosebleed, with fulness of head, < region of medulla oblongata. Pulse irregular.

Neck and Extremities.—Neck felt sore. Trembling of knees when standing, the joints felt stiff and sore. Knuckles and toes pain so that he cannot bear the lightest weight of linen. Legs and lower joints gradually became numb and insensible to pinching, in the bitten part there was a reddish and almost livid tumor of the size of a lentil.

Clinical.—Spinal irritability, the slightest touch causes spasmodic pains in chest. Multiple sclerosis, with trembling, intense pain at night.

Skin. — Inflammation of the bitten toe; I. of the scratch, with burning and itching in it, axillary, submaxillary and cervical glands swollen and sensitive to touch, nearly purple swelling of throat in a line from chin to sternum and in a line from occipital protuberance to scapulæ, the swelling > profuse nosebleed. Each year pain in the toes from the reopened wound, they were inflamed and a thin ichor exuded from the nails, deeply corroding the neighboring parts.

Inflamed pimple, with scarlet areola, with a red erysipelatous line from it marking the course of the spider after biting, the pimple and erysipelatous inflamed areola spread, chills followed by fever generally supervene on second or third day, with thirst, anxiety, restlessness, headache, delirium, sweat and retention of urine, the pimple becomes a hard painful abscess, ending in mortification of the integuments over it and having several small openings, discharging a thick sanious matter, containing pieces of mortified cellular tissue, fasciæ and tendons, the openings run into each other and form large cavities, now the fever becomes intermittent with evening paroxysms, accompanied by diarrhœa and prostration.

Felt a prick as from an ant or fly, with pain in joint of l. ring finger (from bite on l. forearm), next day the affected part was red and had a golden areola, on the third day the areola was swollen, with continuance of the pain, a black scab formed again and again, till on the fifteenth day the yellow circle reappeared. Burning on scalp, then vesicles resembling *crusta lactea*, five ulcers on different parts of scalp, which discharged thin greenish, offensive, ichorous pus, vesicles on different parts of body, soon becoming pustular and turning to ulcers.

Sleep and Fever.—Irresistible sleepiness. *Sleeplessness.* Chills spreading from lumbar region over whole body, < slightest cold draught and artificial heat. Cold sweat.

Clinical.—Intermittent fever, with chorea-like convulsions.

Tarentula Cubensis.

The live Cuban spider is irritated in a bottle and the virus diluted with alcohol.

Clinical.—This spider has been used for various forms of unhealthy or malignant suppuration, especially carbuncles, with burning stinging pain; with great weakness and diarrhœa; with most terrible pains; bubo; diphtheria. In all these diseases there is usually a purplish hue with burning stinging pains (compare with Lach.).

Tartaric Acid.

Pure Tartaric acid is triturated for use.

Compare other organic acids, Acetic, Citric, etc.

Convulsions. Bruised sensation, < lower limbs. Weakness; *in evening, can scarcely drag himself along.* Amelioration in open air. Vertigo. Face suddenly became red, he exclaimed that he was poisoned and then was speechless. Lips dry; lips brown and blackish at their inner edge; burning; (burning on upper, at a spot where a pimple had been cured). Teeth set on edge. *Tongue brown and dry.* Taste pasty in morning, > eating. Burning in throat and stomach. *Thirst.* Eructations. Nausea. *Vomiting; dark green.* Pinching in abdomen; below navel, with emission of flatus and cold feeling in abdomen. *Pain in umbilical region. Many stools at night. Fæces of the color of coffee-grounds.* Hoarseness, with scraping in larynx. Respiration difficult and slow; accelerated, then laborious and slow. Heart's action weak. *Pulse feeble. Sharp pain in loins.* Tearing in soles near heels, preventing setting feet on ground, after luncheon. Paralysis of thighs and legs. Yawning; and stretching. Coldness in evening in bed.

Tellurium.

Pure metallic Tellurium is triturated.

General Action.—See symptoms of spine and skin. *Allies.*—Ars., Rhus t., Cepa.

Generalities.—Pains over whole body, < limbs and scapulæ, < r. side, < waking; fugitive and indistinct P., "first r., then l." **Restless** (Ars., Rhus t.). **Weakness,** then sharp, quick pains in elbows, ankles and various parts. Heaviness in morning after deep sleep and bad dreams, with dulness.

Mind.—*Forgets and neglects much, it is too much trouble to observe and write down the symptoms, when thinking of any business he forgets everything else.* Quiet.

Head.—Aching; in afternoon, < l. side, and at 6 P.M., < forepart; towards evening; < vertex. Brain felt bruised on every movement. Dulness. Heavy, full and sleepy. Sudden rush of blood when sitting quietly working, with head bent forward, almost twice daily, now in morning, now in afternoon, with reddening of face. Every evening on getting to sleep, vertigo as if he were wafted and drawn forth quickly in the direction of his legs, always waking him.

Forehead.—Stitches anteriorly, pressure above eyes as after lack of sleep. Linear pain behind l. brow. Congestive pain in F. and temples in morning on waking, < stooping, when there was weight, > lying. Pressure outward deep in a long line above eyes, < r. side. Pain in a spot in l. sinciput, pressing like a hazelnut, at night and through next morning.

Tensive pain externally in l. half in morning when lying on l. side. Pressure upon a spot behind vertex. Occiput, pain in r. side; confusion at sides and < towards back part; numbness, and in nape.

Eyes.—Red, dropsical, biting, itching swelling of l. upper lid towards inner angle, secreting some fluid, then a scab, globe reddened. Itching of l. upper lid towards inner canthus towards evening, with pressure as if a hair had grown in the wrong direction.

Clinical.—Eczema impetiginoides of the lids and conjunctiva. Scrofulous ophthalmia.

Ears.—Sudden obstruction in forenoon and at 10 P.M., < l. Air catches itself in l. Eustachian tube; on taking a pinch of snuff and on eructation of wind. Itching within, with thin wax. **Itching of l., with burning and swelling and with aching and throbbing in external meatus, then discharge from ear, copious, watery, smelling like fish-pickle, acrid, causing vesicles wherever it touched ear or neck, the inflammation of ear generally was not vesicular, ear was bluish-red and appeared infiltrated with water.**

Clinical.—Eczema of the external ear, with itching and swelling and painful throbbing, discharge smelling like old fish-brine, vesicular eruption externally. Numerous cases of otorrhœa have been cured. Deafness.

Nose.—Obstruction of r. nostril; of l. in forenoon, slime running off posteriorly. Sudden dryness (as from sudden stoppage of fluent coryza or as from an abortive attempt to sneeze) in r. side of N. and fauces between 4 and 5 P.M., then painful heat in r. eye, with lachrymation. **Fluent coryza** *when walking in clear air (from 11 A.M. till noon)*, > *stay in open air*, **with hoarseness and lachrymation** (Allium cep.), *short cough and pressure under sternum;* C., with thick mucus. Thick slime on waking, he had breathed through the mouth at night, nose sometimes stopped. Dry coryza, worse at irregular intervals.

Face and Mouth.—Distortion of l. facial muscles when speaking, l. angle of mouth drawn to the left and upward. Burning in lips in afternoon after being in cold air in the forenoon; in middle of upper in afternoon. Pain in l. teeth, which had been filled with lead. *Garlicky breath.* Mouth and pharynx cool as after peppermint, < drawing in air. Taste metallic, earthy.

Throat.—In morning much slime from posterior nares tasting salt, like smoked herring. The slime in posterior nares has been deposited as a yellow-reddish resin, which is hawked out in morning. Suffocative feeling in upper part. Scratching; < towards evening. Soreness in evening on empty swallowing; < l. side; prickly, in fauces on swallowing, < r. side. Pressure in tonsils. Dryness at 5 P.M.; in fauces towards evening; in fauces, < r. side; in fauces, > eating or drinking, with pain; in fauces in morning, < l. side, > walking in open air from 11 A.M. till noon, then pain in r. side extending into ear, < empty swallowing, stoppage of r. ear, the D. always felt morning and evening; prickly, in fauces in morning, < l. side, > after breakfast; painful, in back part, as from sudden stoppage of fluent coryza or as from an abortive attempt to sneeze, in morning. Itching in fauces above larynx, with burning, as if he had scalded himself. Feels fauces and pharynx, and at times has a sensation as if round waves pushed against pharynx below. Swallowing painful.

Stomach.—Sudden desire for apples at 11.30 P.M. on going to sleep, making him wide awake. Good appetite, with desire for beer, later both ceased. No desire to smoke in evening. Eructations tasting of the food. Nausea before evening meal, > eating, with headache; N., caused by vertigo, and after eating rice vomiting; N. with frequent pulse. Contracting sensation in epigastrium as if it folded together, then pain in l. side, with soreness. *Empty and weak feeling*, yet no appetite. Discomfort, something comes up to pharynx, as if a wet eructation would occur, but nothing comes up, then difficult retching, then accumulation of water in mouth, then retching, then yawning. Heartburn in epigastrium and on both sides of it, as after spirituous drinks.

Abdomen.—Pinching at 8 A.M., and stool, first thick, then diarrhœic; P. at 10 P.M., > emission of flatus. Spasmodic pain as from incarcerated flatus, < afternoon, one day at 6 P.M. while eating, with urging to stool, then copious stool, then only feeling of flatulence, the pain returned four days afterwards between 3 and 4 P.M., > copious stools. Full after supper, but not bloated. Warmth as after spirituous drinks.

Fulness in region of upper A. and liver. Pressure of incarcerated flatus in l. hypochondrium after breakfast, then in r. *Burning in hepatic region* as if blistered inside, in forenoon when sitting, then heavy pressure. Gnawing *rubbing* pain in r. side, < low in back. Pain anteriorly on sides and above pubic region; in l. flank, within crest of ilium. Numbness of walls began below umbilicus on each side, extended around and upward to ribs while lying on sofa after supper.

Rectum and Stool.—Blind hæmorrhoids. Itching in anus; in rectum after stool. Diarrhœa, then urging, with burning in rectum, then stronger retraction of abdomen. Constipation; with much wind. Stool only every other day and difficult. Stool omitted for two days, then one not hard, composed of crumbs enveloped in brown-reddish slime, next day the first part was similar, but the last part softer.

Urinary and Sexual Organs.—Urine dark; deep red, scanty, acid, sp. gr. 1030, abundant coloring matter, hydrochloric acid caused striking change of color. Erections all night. Sexual desire and power increased; desire powerful, then extinct.

Respiratory Organs.—Hoarseness in morning after rising. In larynx a sensation between roughness and pressure, generally provoking cough, gradually passing into tickling. Cough, with pressure under sternum. Easy expectoration of white mucus.

Chest.—Stitches, < l. side; above l. rib. Drawing cutting in l. nipple and around it, extending towards scapula. Pain in clavicle; in middle of sternum; above first l. rib. Oppression. Feeling in middle lobe of r. lung as if a fluid wanted to discharge itself (pressing downward) in afternoon. Bubbling in middle lobe of r. lung, < afternoon. Undulatory throbbing as from wind-balls under r. ribs, somewhat towards epigastrium, when lying on l. side, flatus does not pass off as freely in the morning as usual, and the hitherto rather diarrhœic stool intermits, flatus becomes stinking.

Heart.—Palpitation, with throbbing through whole body and fulness of pulse, then sweat.

Neck.—Sharp pain extending into ear when lying on l. ear.

Back.—**Spine sensitive from last cervical to about fifth dorsal vertebra, with dread of having the part touched or approached** (compare Chin. s.), *the dread was greater than the actual sensibility, from these vertebræ a peculiar irritation radiated into neck and shoulders and to sternum, this sensation < fatigue, but only partially > repose.*

Drawing and pressure in r., then l. scapula. Pain between scapulæ; in region of kidneys, extending downward and towards abdomen, < night, with soreness and weight, the pains < next morning, especially the soreness; P. in sacrum, < stooping or rising from sitting or lying, it passes down r. thigh in direction of sciatic nerve, it is almost impossible for him to press at stool, sometimes on moving the pain in sacrum and sacral ligaments is like a stab; P. in os sacrum as if beaten in morning, < stooping, not > rising again, extending after a time into renal region, > walking in open air, returning when sitting, returning next day when standing in a stooping posture, > walking, < lying on back, but when lying on l. side it is worse towards the right, on third day the pain in sacrum and leg > motion in open air, < pressing at stool, and when coughing and laughing the pain extends from sacral plexus through large foramen ischiaticum along great sciatic nerve into thigh, < r. side.

Extremities.—Sprained and bruised sensation in knees, hips, elbows and shoulder-joint on returning from a walk after supper. Sensation of an internal tumor at anterior margin of l. axilla, with pain on pressure and motion. Sometimes tearing towards elbow and in palm towards thumb-joint. Drawing cramplike pain in l. supinator longus, just below bend of elbow. Heaviness of l. forearm and hand about 10 P.M., with numbness. Pain through metacarpal bone of r. fourth finger. Drawing in r. hand, afterwards involving forearm. Sensation as if skin of hands and fingers, < r., were contracted, with sensation as if ends of fingers were dead. Rheumatic pain in r. little finger (except last joint), < strong pressure or movement. Pain in first phalanx of l. little finger as if he had fallen upon it, with pain on motion.

Lower Extremities.—Burning aching anteriorly at outside of r. knee. Knees and legs, < r., feel tired, all the evening drawing in r. leg posteriorly from posterior spinous process to calf, < kneeholder and after lying down (11.30), so as to prevent sleep and obliging him to turn frequently, the sleep is very good, with amelioration of all pain. Pain in r. metatarsal bone as if pressed.

Clinical.—Sciatica, < lying down at night, straining at stool, coughing or laughing, < r. side.

Skin.—*Red points shining through the skin of l. hand, sometimes with itching, with itching of feet*, < *l.*, after several days similar points on calves and then extending up thighs, the itching < where the skin perspires most, after a few days similar pimples on epigastrium, the points more visible on rubbing, from epigastrium the eruption extends towards l. nipple, then turns towards l. axilla, at the same time itching in various parts of back, a spot on r. side of forehead is sore on pressure, as if bruised, now itching on posterior and superior parts of head.

Pimples on face; small, *red, sharply defined, with vesicles upon them, on lower limbs, then also on upper*, < **l. side**, *they began on outside of calves and then on inside of forearms, above wrists, and spread from that point, with itching*, < **night after going to bed**; red itching P. on abdomen, inside of thighs and perineum, the itching < cold weather.

Vesicles in a cluster on an inflamed base, on forehead, above r. external canthus, they dried into thin scales and spread, with itching and pricking, afterwards the herpetic spot was circular, about half an inch in diameter, consisting of an elevated ring of vesicles, some larger than others, on an inflamed base, enclosing a depressed area of red skin, which desquamated but contained no vesicles, it itched and had successive crops of thin white scales, one evening the stinging was very annoying when sitting still, wandering all over body, a similar herpetic spot midway between l. ribs and crest of ilium, with itching, which changed into smarting on rubbing, with indications of another spot just above it, afterwards itching vesicles on a slightly inflamed base, falling off in white scales, on scalp, < occiput, in border of hair on nape, and posteriorly on ears, the spot on forehead is breaking up now, but just above it is a similar smaller one, afterwards the spot on forehead is red.

Sticking pricking in various parts, < rest. Pricking itching at scrotum in afternoon, < r. side, then high up on inside of l. thigh, then low on r. side of abdomen, then on l. side, then between buttocks.

Clinical.—Herpes circinatus. Eczema.

Sleep.—Sleepy in evening, went to sleep while sitting. The sleepy, heavy condition which he had before the proving vanished, and instead thereof a restlessness on going to bed. Waking about 4 A.M., with sweat. Nightmare. Dream of smoking cigars, which he never does.

Fever.—Internal chilliness, with shudderings. Skin hot and dry, with bruised sensation, as if he had taken cold. Sweat; when sitting writing; offensive; of offensive Tellurium odor at night (from taking cold); offensive, on feet, < toes.

Terebinthina.

One part of oil of turpentine is dissolved in 99 parts of alcohol.

General Action.—It inflames the kidneys and urinary tract, causing profuse hæmorrhage from the kidneys as well as strangury; it irritates the bronchial and intestinal mucous membrane, causing cough and loose, bloody evacuations, *with marked tympanitis.* It has caused hæmorrhages from the lungs and uterus (as well as from the kidneys and bowels).

Allies.—*Secale c.*, Carbo v., *Canth.*, Erigeron, Phos.

Generalities.—Swayed backward and forward when dressing and undressing, though his feet were far apart. Relaxation of muscles. *Occasional subsultus.* Opisthotonos at intervals of ten or fifteen minutes. Convulsions (Secale c.); when she heard water poured out or when water was offered to her, or if a looking-glass was presented to her she suddenly jumped to her feet, muscles of body were rigid, spine stiff, but arms, hands and face were convulsed, groaned, and on being approached she attempted to scratch and bite the person coming near her, eyes wide open, look savage, the attacks lasted from two to five minutes, then she gradually relaxed all muscles and lay down, the spasms were preceded by strangury, no urine all day.

Symptoms resembling those of malignant cholera (Secale c.). Neuralgia in various parts, < one or other lower limb. Mucous membranes dry. **Weakness;** through the day; with inability to walk, staggering and falling; so that when limbs were raised they fell heavily back by their own weight. Faint. Stiffness of whole body; of muscles, he walks slowly and bent over. Inability to ride horseback.

Mind.—Excitement. Anxiety; with weakness on

going to bed. Facility of thought. *Dulness, inability to fix attention.* Stupefaction. *Coma.* Insensibility.

Head.—Tearing; extending towards r. side; intermittent, till evening. *Aching;* with colic; intermittent, with nausea. Dulness. Fulness in evening; F. and pressure, so that he constantly cried out "My head! my head!" and apoplexy was apprehended. Intoxication; and sometimes a kind of trance; drenched in sweat all night and stupid, woke next morning weak and with head bewildered, staggering about when undertaking to stand still, > profuse discharge of urine, which smelled of violets. *Vertigo;* with dulness of head and sick feeling in whole body; with nausea and diminished appetite; sudden, even to falling, with blackness before eyes.

Forehead.—Sticking. Tearing extending out towards r. ear, which is hot, while l. ear is cold to touch. Heavy pain over l. eye when sitting and during mental work. Drawing in bones of F. and r. half of face in evening.

Sticking in r. mastoid process. Intermittent smarting tickling pain in l. temple in evening in bed, > rubbing.

Eyes.—Sunken; and surrounded by dark rings. Pupils contracted. Vision of black, floating points and spots when walking in open air, > looking at a distance, with vertigo.

Clinical.—Ciliary neuralgia over r. eye (Cedron). Episcleritis, with intense pain in eye and side of the head. Rheumatic iritis, with intense pain, especially with burning in the kidneys, dark urine. Adhesions of the iris. Amblyopia from alcohol.

Ears and Nose.—Ringing and singing before ears, like the striking of a clock. Coryza, peculiar, watery, at times from one nostril, at times from both, without the usual accompanying symptoms. *Nosebleed.*

Clinical.—Deafness, with discharges from l. ear.

Face.—*Pale;* and anxious, shrunken. Red. Anxious. Sensation of spasm beginning under chin and extending to cheek-bones, with nervous drawings in cheeks, without visible contraction of face, then supraorbital pain as if bruised. Herpes of lips. Lips could scarcely be moved.

Mouth and Throat.—Drawing in teeth. Burning in tip of tongue, with prominent papillæ. Agreeable coolness in M. Breath cold (Secale c., Carbo v.). Scraping in throat; in evening, provoking hacking cough; in pharynx and in stomach, with warmth. No power over deglutition.

Stomach.—Hunger and thirst; sudden H. for rue on bread and butter (of which he had already eaten freely) in evening during enjoyable mental work; H. diminished; *lost.* Thirst. Rancid eructations. Nausea; in morning; from meat; with eructations and griping beneath stomach-pit; with inability to vomit owing to weakness. *Vomiting; of mucus; of yellowish mucus.*

Rumbling in S. and abdomen after dinner, with pain extending into side. Symptoms of gastro-enteritis. Inflammation of S. and intestines, so that slight touch of abdomen, especially epigastric region, could not be endured. Pain; in a spot in pit, > stooping, lying and deep breathing; in evening when lying on l. side, preventing sleep, > emission of flatus while lying on r. side; becoming nausea, > eructations; in pit after eating, as if food had been swallowed too hastily. In pit sensation as if he had swallowed a ball. In pit pressure as from without. In pit sensation between pain and burning. *Heat;* in epigastric region.

Abdomen.—**Distention** (Carbo v.); after food which was relished; with constipation; *obliging him to rest.* **Meteorismus.** Rumbling; in morning, with gurgling; and gurgling, then colic in evening; and griping and thin stool. Griping. *Colic;* with violent movements in abdomen; with heaviness and emission of flatus; bending the patient up; extending into legs. Feeling as before violent purging. Irritation. Sensation as if intestines were drawn back to spine. Heaviness after midday nap. Coldness as if naked, after dinner.

Cutting in upper. Pressure beneath diaphragm, extending from l. to r. side, after eating. Sticking in r. side after stool, with griping. Tearing cutting in l. side in evening when lying on r. side, then also on r. side. Umbilical region retracted, cold, as if a cold round plate were pressed against it, when lying after dinner.

Hypochondria.—Jerking sticking in l. in evening when urinating. Cutting in l. when sitting, > motion, with pain. Griping. Pressure in l., with drawing; burning P. Burning in r.

Hypogastrium.—Swelling of inguinal glands when sitting in evening, with pain. Movement as if a hernia would protrude in groin, < sitting with legs outstretched. Cramp, now in r., now in l. groin, > walking, with dragging and pressure outward. Tearing in symphysis pubis. Cutting; with distention of some parts as if a hernia would protrude. Feeling as if pubes were suddenly forced asunder. Drawing in groins and thighs. Cutting drawing in r. groin; from ring into r. testicle, > stooping. Dragging in r. groin, with cutting.

Clinical.—Abdominal dropsy. It has proved valuable in pelvic peritonitis, especially when complicated with bladder troubles and with excessive tympanitis.

Anus.—Burning; when standing; after stool; and tickling; and crawling and sensation as if worms crept out; itching, after stool, as from blind hæmorrhoids. Urging; ineffectual.

Stool.—Diarrhœa; yellow, with discharge of tapeworm, also round worms; greenish-yellow, frequent, with discharge of tape-worm. Pasty, with colic and burning in anus. Constipation. Hard, scanty; H. and dark chestnut-brown. Diminished (two instead of one). Two in evening.

Clinical.—Diarrhœa, with red, sore, shining tongue.

Urinary Organs.—Bladder. Movement in region during stool, as if B. were suddenly distended and bent forward. *Inflammation.* Twinging and cutting alternating with a similar pain above navel, > walking in open air, < rest. Spasmodic pain when sitting. *Burning, and when urinating, also in urethra. Frequent desire, with scanty urine each time.*

Strangury, bloody urine, then soreness of bladder (Canth.); **S., bloody urine** *and total suppression of urine. Dysuria. Incontinence of urine. Difficult micturition.* **Urethritis, with painful erections** (Canth.). *Burning in urethra; when urinating.*

Urine.—**Bloody** (Canth., Phos., *Erigeron*); **and scanty.** Scanty; and red, sometimes bloody, or else copious and light-colored. Copious. *Suppressed* (effects from use for stone). *Smelling of violets;* has a wine color and deposits a thick, slimy, whitish-yellow sediment. Contains sugar. Clear, but on standing becomes turbid, with reddish-white sediment. Slimy sediment.

Clinical.—Inflamed kidneys, with dull pain and burning, pain extends to the bladder, strangury, bloody urine; particularly useful when this condition follows any acute disease. Congestion of the kidneys, with great quantity of blood in the urine. Acute cystitis, with burning pain in region of kidney. Dysuria and constant tenesmus.

Sexual Organs.—Drawing in l. testicle when sitting; spasmodic, in l. extending along l. spermatic cord. Burning posteriorly in r. testicle. Emission at night. Tearing in mons veneris. Menstruation delayed and scanty.

Respiratory Organs.—Dryness. Prickling in trachea as in commencing bronchitis. Voice gone. Cough as from a foreign substance in trachea, with cramp in larynx as in whooping cough, inspiration in six or seven catches, the cramp became so violent that he could scarcely inspire, then scraping in throat. (Aggravation of short, dry cough, especially when lying after eating.) *Expectoration streaked with blood. Breathing difficult;* and *lungs seem overdistended.* Breathing stertorous. *B. short; and hurried, anxious.* Increase of respiratory movements.

Clinical.—Hæmoptysis relieving the congestion of the lungs. Capillary bronchitis, especially with scanty, bloody urine.

Chest.—Spastic contraction of muscles of C. and neck in evening. Mucous râles in lungs, with minute crepitation. Pain behind sternum; itching, in l. pectoralis major. Soreness in lower part. Burning along sternum, gradually extending over C. and disappearing, with stitches at nipples (after warm drinks).

Heart.—Oppression of præcordial region. Warmth in evening when sitting, forcing her to yawn much, with collection of water in mouth. Palpitation; in evening.

Pulse.—*Rapid;* and respiration; and full; and hard; and hard, small; *small, compressible, and almost imperceptible;* and small, irregular; and small, weak; and weak. *Scarcely perceptible; and thready* (Carbo v., Secale c.). Weak, irregular and intermittent in evening.

Neck.—Gradual painful drawing up nape into occiput and then to forehead.

Back.—Pain; extending up to between shoulders and there becoming a throbbing; drawing, when sitting, < evening. Drawing in dorsal and lumbar muscles, with heaviness and indolence on moving in open air. Pain in lumbar and hypogastric regions, with warmth, then sensitiveness to pressure. *Kidney region painful in morning when sitting; P. and heavy;* and diabetes, and died dropsical; l. **Burning drawing pain in kidney region.** *Drawing in r. kidney extending into r. hip.* Drawing pain in small of back.

Extremities.—Acute pain in all joints. Heaviness. Partial loss of use of r. arm and l. leg. But little use of r. arm, she could advance it from the body but a short distance, she could raise shoulder-blade and bend elbow, but the hand fell with a jerk into the position in which she wished to place it. Sprained pain in muscles of l. upper arm. Drawing in humeri in morning. Trembling of hands. Fingers insensible and asleep in evening.

Lower Extremities.—Tottering. She limped with l. foot and dragged the leg in walking, ankle was stiff. Drawing along thighs; in outer side of r., as if in fascia lata; along course of large vessels; with colic as if menses would appear, though she had them eight days previously; in r. hip-joint, with tearing. Drawing paralytic pain in l. thigh. Feet were placed far apart when standing or walking. Pain in feet.

Skin.—Rubefaction and sometimes vesicles. Livid spots on back and abdomen. Scarlet eruption. Nettle-rash. Eruption, sudden, erythematous, papular, often vesicular, analogous to that caused by certain forms of sea-food. Exanthema like scarlet rash on affected knee, extending to ankle, then on chest and r. foot, gradually extending over largest part of body.

Warmth in bend of elbow (from local applications), with itching, redness and distention of vessels of corium, sticking, sensitiveness to touch, which especially caused sticking, the breath from the mouth was felt more acutely there than elsewhere and caused burning, the reddened cutis was swollen and numb when brushed with a feather or finger, burning stinging extending over inner half of joint to olecranon process, pulsative burning, with pressure and tension over the red surface and sometimes deep pulsation, at times stitches over the whole surface, at other times only in spots in the reddened place, smarting soreness, red spots on the margin of diffused redness, swelling of hair-follicles, burning, < inner side of joint, pressure caused pain, then aggravation of the burning, pain in inner half of joint on putting arm down, afterwards appearance similar to extravasation of blood, spots incompletely raised by exudation, sore pain on touch, desquamation.

Sensitiveness of limbs, < lower, with at times acute pains following the large nerves. Burning itching on r. groin.

Clinical.—Bed-sores in paralytics. Purpura hæmorrhagica. Urticaria.

Sleep.—Sleepiness; in evening; but the day nap did not interfere with his night's rest. Sleeplessness and excitement; S. for two hours at night, with tossing about. Restless sleep and frequent waking. Awoke alarmed, but unable to cry out. Nightmare waking him as soon as he fell asleep. Anxious dreams.

Fever.—Coldness; causing tossing about the bed; of skin; of limbs. Heat; with sweat of lower limbs, < the affected one and along the nerve affected; of trunk; of skin; of skin, with sweat. Sweat; *cold and clammy over whole body;* on lower limbs in evening in bed.

Clinical.—Typhoid fever, with hæmorrhage from the bowels, bloody albuminous urine, excessive tympanitis.

Thallium.

The pure metal is triturated.

Emaciation. Hyperæmia, < application to conjunctiva, with swelling and excessive secretion. *Trembling;* and chorea-like movements. Pains < lower limbs, with lassitude. Conjunctivitis, with much mucus (and perhaps disturbance of vision). Ptyalism. Appetite lost. Nausea. Vomiting. *Lancinations following each other with the rapidity of electric shocks, in stomach and bowels.* Abdomen retracted. Pain in intestinal canal. Diarrhœa and even bloody stools. Constipation. Respiration slow and difficult. Pulse slow. *Paralysis of lower limbs.* (Compare Plumbum, to which it is closely allied physically.)

Clinical.—It has relieved the violent pains of locomotor ataxia.

Thea.

A tincture is made of Pekœ-tea (Camellia Thea, Link).

Generalities.—Loss of weight diminished. Lean; and pale. Trembling. Convulsions, < limbs. Epilepsy. Twitching like the sensation caused by electric sparks, in different parts, < forearms, hands and finger-joints. Agitation; first in limbs, extending from muscles to nervous centres. Inclination to lie down. Weakness; for two hours after breakfast; < every meal; with pain in small of back; as if knees would not support body. Sinking, craving, fluttering feeling. Faintness; which vexed him; becoming a cramplike pain after every meal, reaching into throat and often waking her at night. Incapable of muscular action. Symptoms of paralysis, numbness of limbs and partial loss of use of limbs. If wine or beer were drunk after the tea the sleeplessness and malaise were not felt, but if strong beer were drunk before the tea it diminished the frequency of the pulse and caused comfort and buoyancy of mind and body. Aggravation in afternoon; A. if I drank it fasting. Feeling of great ease.

Mind.—Delirium; and unconsciousness, ecstasy, he laughs and talks in rhyme; delirium tremens, wandering about the house, imagining that evil spirits and people were seeking to harm her, sleeplessness, twitching of face and limbs, later wandering about the wharves and attempting to drown herself. Agreeable exhilaration of mind and body, contentment, placidity, increase of intellectual and physical vigor, without noticeable reaction. Temporary exaltation, greater confidence in himself. Excitement from animated conversation and intense thinking, then refreshing sleep; E., with clearness of intellect; then debilitating influence upon nervous system and lumbar portion of spinal marrow. Cordiality, brilliancy of intellect, conversation fluent, interesting, witty, then the opposite state, with irritability, sensitiveness and quarrelsome mood.

Sensation as if impelled to commit suicide, to jump out of the window, to put her baby into the boiler with the clothes, to cut its throat when cutting the bread, to throw it down stairs. Nervousness at the sound of the night-bell; N., > beer, with want of confidence. Anguish. Terror. Fright at night, sinister thoughts, invincible propensity to analyze his life, to look at it on the dark side and to resolve it into its most hopeless realities. Anxiety. Apprehension of something dreadful about to happen, fear of sudden death, would never go out alone, at times impulse to commit some horrible crime, to murder her children, so that she trembled for their safety. Weeps easily. Peevish; and taciturn; and disinclined to write or think; and averse to everything and to fatigue. Averse to movement; to conversation. Sadness in some, cheerfulness in others. Gloomy, heavy and dizzy in forehead.

Aptitude for study increased, more capable of sustained attention. Greater power of receiving impressions, it disposes to pensive meditation, causes activity of ideas, attention is easily fixed, sensation of health and gayety, but after an hour nervous troubles, such as yawning, irritability, pains in epigastrium, palpitation, trembling of limbs and sadness, with these symptoms insupportable insomnia, with excitation, then lassitude and headache. Ideas dull and confused. Memory weak; lost. Incapable of any occupation. Insensibility in evening.

Head.—Aching; in morning and evening, often with nausea; with throbbing of carotids; or backache, Sick headache; every week, with soreness of head, then weakness; < during menses, pain begins in l. ovary and stomach and passes to head, throbbing shooting through temples, extending down nose, with acuteness of smell, vomiting of bile when the pain is at its height, exertion causes vomiting during the headache. Congestion; with fulness, < over eyes. Vertigo; with darkness before eyes; sudden, as if about to lose consciousness in evening when walking in open air.

Frontal pain. Frontal heaviness, < walking, with vertigo; < walking, with compression. Vertigo in vertex, with heat and pulsation. On both sides of base of cerebellum and in nape, neuralgic pain like a cold flat-iron between skin and skull, extending over cranium and over forehead to eyes. Sharp twitching pain in r. occipital protuberance, with feeling of damp coldness, afterwards the pain extends to nape, r. shoulder and r. arm, > application of hand or warm cloth. Sudden tensive pain in occiput, almost in nape. Scalp painful to touch; on vertex.

NOTE—Tea is one of the most fruitful causes of "sick-headache."

Eyes.—Glittering. Dryness from mental exercise during a sleepless night, then neuralgia of them. Pupils dilated. Vision dim. Vision of sparks; flashing, fiery lines darting from eyes and radiating outward from axis of vision.

Ears.—Neuralgic pain in cartilages, with coldness, the pains extending to molars and cheek-bones. Ringing. Roaring. Hallucinations of hearing, for five nights he thought he heard the door-bell, it often woke him with a start.

Nose.—Soreness of internal edge. Constant desire to pick it. Dryness. Sensation at root as if epistaxis would occur.

Face.—Pale; with circumscribed redness; and lips; and cheeks easily flushed. Red; cheeks. Wild and distressed expression.

Mouth.—Teeth diseased. Tongue pale; T. red, with white slime; stinging as from blisters, with pain as if scalded, and on top red spots and white blisters. Scraping of soft palate. Dryness and sensitiveness. Salivation, with hunger, afterwards dryness of mouth, scanty viscid saliva, with satiety and a little thirst. Offensive breath in morning on waking. Filled with viscid saliva after drinking. Taste bitter. Taste of tea extending from throat to stomach.

Throat.—Diphtheritic soreness. Painless swelling of mucous membrane of pharynx. Dryness. Uneasiness as from a foreign body in pharynx.

Stomach.—Appetite great, with faintness at the dinner-hour; great, but easily satisfied, then satiety. Craving for acids; especially lemons. Longing for tea, which removed the goneness and gave vigor for a short time, often loathed the tea, but could not resist it, thirsty, but could not bear cold water, every mouthful affected her head like a shock. Lost; with craving at pit of stomach. Loathing of food till noon, then she eats sparingly. Dislikes cold water. Lack of thirst.

Exhausting eructations. Nausea; in pit of stomach; > diarrhœa, with general discomfort and sweat; > a glass of sherry or beer, with weakness and irregular pulse; with discomfort in stomach; with salivation, weak feeling in stomach, which seems to hang in his body like an empty bag. Vomiting; of bile; of the meal which she had lately taken. Spasms from slight exertions. Pyrosis. Pain in epigastrium; < eating, > before breakfast, and in umbilical region; cramplike and pressing, after every meal, reaching into throat and often waking her at night. Sensitiveness of epigastrium; with feeling as if caved in. Tickling in pit, causing dry cough, which shakes the whole digestive organization, bringing on neuralgic head symptoms. Heartburn. Burning in region of pylorus.

Emptiness; in epigastrium; in pit after eating, with pain; with craving; with craving and with fluttering in l. side; with excitability and constriction, preventing deep breathing; with oppression, benumbed feeling and with tossing about, groans at every breath, occasionally rubbing her stomach violently.

Abdomen.—Borborygmi, and < epigastric region. Relaxation of fibres of intestines. Paroxysmal stitches below ribs, extending from r. towards l. side, after luncheon. Liability to hernia. Cutting above umbilicus, extending to pit of stomach, there becoming intense and radiating thence over chest, causing sick faint feeling, sometimes three or four pains in quick succession, but oftener one long slow pain every four or five minutes, then spasmodic belching, pain < towards morning, then frequent watery stools, with flatus and pain, then nervous depression, the least thought of any exertion seemed overpowering, heavy sleep the second night and exhaustion, < next morning, eyes sunken, face pallid, tremor of hands, even on lifting a small vial, all movements slow, halting, feeling in brain that everything must stop.

Rectum and Stool.—Tumefaction of lower end of R., with itching. Diarrhœa frequent; chronic D., < beer, > port wine. Constipation. Stool hard in part, the rest scarcely formed; S. irregular and costive; S. scanty; frequent.

Urinary Organs.—Pain in vesical region, with tenderness and frequent desire to urinate, scanty discharge, biting and smarting after urinating. Urine diminished. Urea increased. Urine decreased, contains less water, solids, urea, uric acid, oxalic acid, sulph. acid, sulph. of potash, chlorine, chloride of sodium, phosphate of magnesia and salts by incineration, but more ammonia, muriate of ammonia, potash, chloride of potassium, phos. acid, phosphate of soda, phosphate of lime, volative salts and extractives.

Genital Organs.—Erections. Excitement. Soreness of r. ovary. Menses only once in seven weeks, scanty, with cramplike, bearing-down pain, generally has nosebleed before menses (it is not quite evident that tea caused these symptoms, but it undoubtedly aggravated them).

Respiratory Organs.—Symptoms of swelling of mucous lining of R. and digestive tracts. Scraping in larynx. Constriction of larynx, with dry hacking cough. Hoarseness, almost aphonia. Cough, with bloody expectoration; dry C. during one day. Suffocation. Apparent asphyxia every five or six minutes. Gasping. Respiration irregular and oppressed. Respiration increased; in frequency and amplitude. Breathless at least attempt to walk; on ascending stairs, with palpitation.

Chest.—Oppression; and anxiety. Constriction. Tightness across upper part, obliging her to sit up in bed. Fulness in clavicles, with feeling of suffocation; F. about clavicles, with fluttering in l. side.

Heart.—Sibilant râle. Spasmodic pain in region; with feeling as if continually falling into deliquium. Anguish in region. Anxious oppression. Præcordial anxiety after tea at supper, with a sleepless night, but if excited by lively conversation or by continued thinking the anxiety disappeared and he had a refreshing sleep. Uneasiness. Præcordial distress as if about to faint. Palpitation; at night, with inability to lie on l. side; with dilatation and thinning of heart; with pain in region of heart; at times, at other times heart seemed motionless. Fluttering, then momentary suspension of its action and long-continued swoonings.

Pulse.—Rapid; and full; and irregular, often intermittent; then slower, irregular and intermittent; and small, feeble. Slow and weak in some cases, in others fluttering or intermittent; S., irregular, small, at times hardly perceptible. Irregular and scarcely perceptible. Irregular, intermittent, almost imperceptible, with anxiety in præcordium or sensation in pit of stomach as in incipient faintness, then frequent paroxysms of asphyxia like nightmare, with spasmodic pain in præcordial region, with intermittent, irregular, at times suppressed respiration.

Extremities.—Trembling. Pain on inside of arms above elbows, waking her at night. Joints of hands and feet tender and sensitive to touch. Nervous excitability of wrists, feet and hands. Trembling of hand; and arm. Pain in sciatic nerve. Sensation on under side of thighs as if circulation had ceased, with sensation of paralysis, causing nervousness and desire to kick in order to restore sensibility. Neuralgic pain in outer hamstrings. Inability to lift the affected leg, sometimes r., sometimes l. Restlessness of feet in evening. Sensation as if the weight of a sheet would crush toes.

Skin. — Peeling of ends of fingers from dryness. Pimples, red, indolent or slightly painful, sometimes in clusters, over neck, shoulders and < thighs, they are easily broken, bleed a little and dry up soon. Tumor, circumscribed, almost indolent, movable, in thickness of derma, in lumbar region, the skin covering it is a lively pink, tension of integuments is felt even to the hips, with itching, afterwards a similar tumor on outer and upper part of r. thigh, and on one palmar aspect of r. wrist, the hand engorged, preventing writing, then the same symptoms simultaneously on scrotum, penis and prepuce, appearing like an enormous hydrocele and a phimosis, the parts are indolent, all these tumefactions require two days for their resolution. Crawling under various parts of skin, with pricking and itching, causing irritability. Itching of different parts, < anteriorly on thighs, next day it extends to legs and < ankles and insteps.

Sleep.—Sleepy; in the daytime. Sleeplessness; till morning; all night; from 10 P.M. till 2 A.M., with irritation and persistent thinking; > beer; with vascular excitement; with restlessness; with dryness and heat of skin and tossing about. Tardy slumbers, with anxiety in limbs, more rapid action of heart, sweat on præcordial region, dry heat of other parts. Troubled sleep, waking at intervals. Frequent starting from sleep. Woke suddenly as from a struggle of incubus. Waking in night in agitation (from green tea after a hearty dinner), with oppression of head, sensation of approaching death, or sometimes he seemed dragged from the lowest abyss of darkness back to the world, from which during his paroxysm he felt himself gradually sink. Nightmare. Dream that I murdered in cold blood boys and girls, these crimes caused no emotion, and long after waking I found pleasure in the remembrance of the dream.

Fever. — Coldness; of skin; passing over head; deathly, of cartilages of ears from least draught of air; of hands and feet, with clammy sweat on them. Heat; internal, with flushes upon the surface. Sweat; chilly. Dry skin.

Theridion.

A tincture is made of the live Curacoa spider (with three orange spots posterially and one square orange spot on its belly).

It may be compared with Aranea.

Generalities. — Tetanus, with trismus (?). *Every penetrating sound and reverberation penetrates her whole body, < teeth, and increases the vertigo, which then causes nausea.* Pain in all bones, as if every part would fall asunder, feeling as if broken from head to foot, then coldness. Weakness; in morning, with sleepiness; with tremulousness and perspiration. Sudden, violent symptoms, > Acon.; later symptoms > Graph.

Clinical.—Hysteria, with loquacity and feeling as though head did not belong to her, or as if she could lift it off, great sensitiveness to light, etc. Scrofulous diseases of bones, rickets, caries and necrosis.

Mind.—Joyous, he sings though the head is internally hot, oppressed and heavy. Imaginative excitement in head at night, with rushing in ears. Talkative after spirituous beverages. Inclined to talk and to occupy his mind, remains awake late in evening. *Inclined to be startled. Time appears to pass rapidly*, although he does little. Despair, want of self-confidence, he gives himself up. Tries to occupy himself constantly, but finds pleasure in nothing. Sluggishness, with disinclination to rising in morning. *Aversion to work;* to professional labor. Thinking is hard when it is of a comparative nature, but not when it is creative.

Head.—*Aching at the beginning of every motion;* evening when walking, with depression; deep in brain, so that she must sit or walk, it is impossible to lie. *Thick feeling, with nausea and vomiting on least motion, < closing eyes; T. feeling, as if it were another head, or if she had something else upon it.* Oppression and heaviness; O., hindering his studies. Painless, indescribable sensation. *Vertigo* on turning around; V. < stooping; *with nausea increased to vomiting;* in sleep, waking her at 11 P.M., she could not remain lying, fell as if in a swoon, straining to vomit until cold sweat broke out, repeated every quarter of an hour, with attacks of painless diarrhœa, at first vomiting of acrid, slimy water, almost arresting her breath, ineffectual retching, vertigo and vomiting on least motion, even *vertigo* and nausea *on closing her eyes* from weakness, sleep after Mentha pip., in morning on rising nausea and vomiting of bile, throat felt scalded, back was tired, pulse accelerated, head ached. Headache like a band in root of nose and around ears. *Aching behind eyes.* Stinging in l. temple. Pressing together in temples. Oppression behind ears, with fulness. Itching on head and nape in evening.

Clinical.—Violent headache, with nausea, cannot bear the least noise; a feeling as if the vertex was separated from the rest of the head, or as if she would like to lift it off. Effects of sunstroke, with most intolerant headache, nausea and vomiting.

Eyes, Ears and Nose.—Twitching in r. eye. Burning pain internally above inner canthus on waking. Vision lost, everything seemed very far, as if a veil were before her, with blazing and flickering, necessity to lie down, even flickering when closing eyes, then affection of head and weakness. Loud noises make too strong an impression, > Acon. Roaring in ears. Rushing in ears, with impaired hearing. Nose dry, as if too much air passed in. Itching in nose. Sneezing in evening, with running coryza; S. all day, with discharge of water from nose, but without coryza; violent, with frequent necessity to blow the nose, then heaviness deep above nose.

Clinical.—Nasal catarrh, with offensive, greenish, yellow discharge.

Mouth and Œsophagus.—Jaw immovable in morning on waking and at other times of the day, then opening involuntarily. *Teeth feel as if cool water were too cold.* Burning and tensive pain in teeth, gums and palate. Raging pain in all teeth in afternoon and evening, causing weeping, but drawing particularly in roots of sound eye-teeth. Gums, mouth and nose dry, and feeling as if too much air passed into mouth. Gums sore. (Burnt and numb feeling in tongue.) Sliminess of mouth. There is no proper taste, her mouth feels furred (benumbed). Pressure in lower part of œsophagus towards epigastrium; as if something were slipping towards the epigastrium, taking away the breath.

Stomach and Abdomen.—*Constant desire to eat and drink, he knows not what.* Appetite for acidulous fruit. Increased desire to smoke tobacco. *Thirst;* after midday sleep; for wine and brandy. Nausea in morning; on rising; from vertigo on least motion; on opening eyes, > Mosch. Emission of flatus. Pain in groins after coition; in region of groin on motion, when she draws up her leg it seems as if some one tapped her hard on the groin.

Clinical.—Seasickness in women, nausea < closing the eyes.

Anus and Stool.—Anus protrudes and is painful, < sitting. (Spasmodic contraction of rectum and anus returns again.) Heaviness in perineal region, which he has had for a long time, is now felt at every step, with feeling of a lump there. Stool papescent, scanty, urgent, next day thin and scanty, omitted on third day; scanty, with tenesmus; difficult towards the end, though not hard; delayed and less urgent than usual; once instead of twice as usual.

Urinary and Sexual Organs.—Urine increased. (Red spots on glans.) Erections strong in morning, without desire; weak E. during coition; no E., desire vanished. Scrotum shrivelled. Violent and profuse emission during nap after dinner (had taken anise during the day).

Clinical.—Dysmenorrhœa, intense, in l. ovary, with intense headache, extreme sensitiveness of the cervix, chilliness, etc. (compare Lil.). Syphilitic cases.

Respiratory Organs and Chest.—Cough at night. Increased inclination to take a deep respiration, to sigh. *Stitches in chest* beneath l. shoulder, felt even in throat; pinching, in l. pectoral muscle.

Clinical.—It has been used in some form of phthisis, violent stitches in upper part of l. chest, extending to the back. Convulsive cough, with the peculiar vertigo. Violent cough, with spasmodic jerking of the head forward and the knees upward.

Back and Extremities.—Pain between shoulders. Loins affected after vomiting. Heaviness in all limbs after breakfast, necessity to lie down, sleepiness, internal chill so that he trembles. Stinging from elbow to shoulder. Peculiar drawing in r. hip, passing down thigh in evening when sitting and afterwards, with internal coldness below knee. Knees trouble her in afternoon. Feet swollen. Pain in little toe as if pressed in walking.

Skin, Etc.—Hard pimple beside ball of thumb. Itching on back; calf; nape; at edge of shoulder in morning; *on nates, with knots;* burning, on inner and upper part of l. ring finger, with redness. Sleepy in morning. Sleeps all day. Deep sleep at night. He often bites the tip of his tongue in sleep, so that it is sore the next day (similar to Phos. ac., which, however, has it only laterally). Sleep long and dreamful at midday, dreams of journeys in distant regions and of riding on horses (in one who scarcely ever sat upon a horse). Dream that he broke off a tooth. Shaking chill, with foam at mouth; shaking chill, with headache and vomiting. Sweat after walking and driving.

Thlaspi.

A tincture is made of the entire plant, T. Bursa-pastoris, ("Shepherd's purse").

Compare with the mustards, Sinapis.

Vesicles at the place of application (chest) and its vicinity, with pustules, the skin between them being bright red, with swelling of the face so that the eyes were closed, and vesicles and bullæ on the reddened face. Coarse miliary rash, particularly vesicular, with stinging and itching, soothed by contact, but followed by burning, also swelling of eyelids and prepuce (from local applications).

Clinical.—*Leucorrhœa*, preceding and following menses, which are profuse and dark; dark, fetid. Profuse hæmorrhages from all parts of the body. It has been found very valuable for hæmorrhages from the kidneys, especially when associated with symptoms of calculus in the kidney. Useful for the pains of kidney gravel. To some extent valuable for uric acid diathesis (compare Ocimum).

Thuja.

A tincture is made of the fresh leaves of the arbor vitæ, Thuja occidentalis, L.

General Action.—It appears to act vigorously on the genito-urinary tract, producing urethritis (closely simulating gonorrhœa) as well as vesical catarrh. It is believed to have caused excrescences similar to figwarts and other symptoms allied to the sequelæ of gonorrhœa, and in some degree to syphilis.

Allies.—Aur., Nit. ac., Sulph., Puls., Ign.

Generalities.—Swelling of veins, < arm. Odor of the prover intolerably increased. Intermittent trembling. Jerking in upper part of body during the day; in flexors of l. thumb, in r. cheek and under scapulæ; sudden cramplike, of under lip in evening and here and there in *circumscribed spots on skin.* Walking seems very easy, as if she had wings. Delightful feeling of corporeal well-being in afternoon, with inclination to intellectual labor.

Stitches in all parts; in and on almost every part; in l. palm, r. shoulder and near pit of chin; in different parts, elbow, tibia, nipple, chin, scorbiculus, scapula, shoulder-joints; in forehead and different parts, < shoulders, arms and thighs; (in ear, lower jaw, splenic region, hip-joint, iliac region, middle of thigh and leg, tarsus, shoulder-joint, upper arm, forearm and metacarpus), < r. side; flying, in different parts; now in l. knee, now in head and now in elbow and finger-joints in evening; now here, now there, with tearing; and tearing, sometimes in the same part, sometimes in others (ear, ear-cartilage, ala of nose, near sternum, in epigastrium, between scapulæ) and sometimes in all limbs, in evening in bed.

Tearing in concha, eyeball, pit of stomach, scapulæ, shoulder and hip-joints, thigh from ischium to knee, leg, arm and forearm; (in small of back, nape, over temple, in knee, tarsi and some phalanges of fingers), < r. side; *T., drawing or sticking*, with attacks of vertigo and *stiffness in feet* and back *to nape;* alternating with drawing pain, < limbs, < rest, but also in r. tibia when walking, making me limp. Drawing tearing now here, now there, on l. side of body; in r. arm, < along ulnar nerve, in r. thigh, r. zygoma and r. side of chest, after rising, then less in l. side of body.

Pinching and pressing pain under shoulder, in dorsum of foot and different parts of external chest. Twitching pain as if tendons of patellæ were drawn out and then suffered to return, when sitting and walking, and a similar pain in temples. Pain as from a thrust in spots on chest and limbs, < touch. Shocks in insolated muscular parts, < middle of upper part of r. thigh and l. arm. Crawling pain. Sensitiveness to touch. Muscular pains were generally in the middle instead of in tendinous portions. Pressure in various parts, with scraping prickling, seeming to be in bones. Bruised sensation in small of back and in feet.

Drawing pain in different parts; in arms and feet and especially in small of back, at night; now here, now there; flying, in various parts, < hands; in r. thumb when writing, then in index, later in middle and finally in little finger, and in afternoon in l. arm, shifted to upper part of l. thigh, then in mastoid processes, then in frontal eminence, where it was more of a digging twitching, finally in limbs, next day the pains wandered about, next forenoon it was for several hours near l. wrist and all the afternoon in upper part of l. thigh; tearing, during rest, sometimes in frontal eminences and occipital protuberances, sometimes in middle of l. arm and thigh.

Drawing in hands, feet, small of back and between shoulders; in scapulæ, in direction of nape and from knees to malleoli and from elbows to wrists; here and there under skin, in tendinous expansions; in r. thumb and forearm in evening, then in l. thumb and r. upper teeth; at night in hands and feet, with tearing, then in epigastrium, hypochondria, on chest, < small of back, ending in sweat; in various parts, with stitches like electric shocks; now here, now there, also < evening; now here, now there, < l. side of body;

now here, now there, < upper part of thigh; sudden, here and there, < r. fingers.

Illusory sensation, as if the body were thin and delicate and he must avoid every touch, as if the connection of different parts were in danger of being severed. Discomfort; in forenoon, with sensitiveness to cold air; > dinner. Malaise in afternoon, with sensation as if a chill were coming on; M. at 8.30 P.M. in the street, with debility and weakness in stomach, amelioration from a glass of cordial, but at 10 P.M. indisposition not easy to describe; two hours after dinner; with ill humor; with internal shivering; with internal chills. Uneasiness; after dinner; before falling asleep; (on walking rapidly, with ill humor).

Weakness; all day; in morning; in morning, with confusion of head; in morning on waking, with bruised feeling; in morning on rising; on rising, < upper arms and thighs; in afternoon, with sleepiness; in afternoon, with bruised sensation and aversion to motion; in afternoon, with prostrated feeling in limbs; in evening; in evening, with discomfort and with confusion of head; in evening, and unwell; at night; before dinner; after dinner, with ill humor; after dinner, with pain in forehead; after eating, with necessity to lie down; (after stool); with gloomy mood, obliged to take a little wine, then amelioration of all symptoms; with faintness, without being able to say what ails her; of body, with perfect mental activity; with chill, forcing him to bed at 6 P.M.; during the day, as if he had not slept enough at night; sudden, with pain in calves, then internal chill, with hot, dry skin, forcing him to lie down, such debility that it was difficult to move his limbs, at 10 P.M. the chill merged into dry heat, and towards morning sweat, no appetite, much thirst, no urine all day and during the access of heat full, quick pulse and headache, next morning scanty, dark red urine, sweat till noon, could not leave his bed for weakness, that evening a chill, then a sleepless night, next day debility, no appetite, tongue furred, urine copious.

Symptoms appear in morning on waking; appear during rest, are transient, < spirituous drinks, except the customary beer. Aggravation of pains after 3 A.M. and 3 P.M., they prevent sleep in evening; A. during rest; during rest, but by remaining quiet symptoms are developed which disappear on motion in open air; A. and amelioration on alternate days. Amelioration in open air; A. from movement.

Clinical.—In general, good for bad effects of vaccination.

Mind.—Cheerful. Lively and loquacious (effects of the alcohol?). Inclination for exertion in evening. **Loathing of life** (Aur., Nit. ac.). **Ill humor** (Sulph.); in afternoon; *with indisposition to do anything; with heaviness of head and disinclination to talk;* with restlessness; with fulness in head and drowsiness. *Discontentment.* **Sadness** (Aur., Puls., Sulph., etc.); every forenoon; in afternoon; afternoon and next morning; before going to sleep; *with disposition to weep;* with discouragement. Excited and inclined to anger. Uneasy, everything seems burdensome and distressing. Anxiety. Averse to everything, anxious about the future. Apprehensive of becoming sick. Earnest in evening. Excessively thoughtful about a trifle. Indifferent to the opposite sex.

Power of thought increased, but rather for analytical than synthetical reasoning. Clearer during the febrile paroxysm and he is inclined to all kinds of work. *Indisposed to intellectual labor.* Intellectual exercise soon fatigues in evening. *Speaks slowly and in monosyllables. Collects his thoughts and speaks slowly, he seeks for words while talking. Could scarcely collect his senses for half an hour in morning on waking.* Inattentive to what was going on around him. Distracted, unsteady, inclined to do now this, now that. He could not get rid of a thought that he had just had. Stupefied, with sleepiness and weakness; as if intoxicated, < morning. Coma.

Clinical.—Melancholia, with a fixed idea that he is made of a brittle substance, will not allow persons to touch him, for fear that he will be broken. Great emotional sensitiveness, music causes weeping and trembling (Ign.). Fixed idea of a living animal in the abdomen; of the soul separated from the body; of strange people by his side, etc.

Head.—*Sticking; and in r. eye;* in morning on rising, < moving; in afternoon when walking; in evening, > evacuation; *in centre of brain, extending through centre of l. eye;* upward through brain, also < coughing; through brain, generally in direction of eyebrows and from eyeball to occiput; jerklike, through head, leaving a pressing. Sticking crawling pain in morning. Tearing in brain extending into r. eyeball. *Boring.*

Aching; all day; in morning; in morning on waking after a restless night; towards noon; towards noon, and in eyes, with gastric uneasiness and red urine, afterwards < wine at dinner, smoking increased it to vertigo; in afternoon; in afternoon, with burning in r. eye; in evening; in evening till 10 P.M.; in evening till midnight; in spots in skull in evening; at night, and in eyes; with chilliness; with heat; with heat in cheeks; *in morning, > walking in open air, at one time forcing asunder at malar-bone and upper jaw, at another time in vertex,* **as if pierced by a nail** (Ign., Hep. s.), **as by a jerk,** *at another, as if forehead would fall out, with internal chilliness;* momentary, here and there; in morning, as after too deep sleep or after stooping, a pulsation or pressing short jerking in forehead, with redness of face; as if compressed externally with pulselike beating and sticking in temples, the pains > pressure and bending backward, returning on bending forward; as if brain were distended in morning on waking after deep sleep, with nausea and vomiting three times of bitter water, with chill for five hours, loss of appetite, without thirst; like a stupefaction; drawing.

Drawing from H. over nape to small of back. Several times sensation as if brain were raised. Internal weakness, brain seems numb and dead. Empty feeling when sitting and walking. Fulness; in afternoon, with drawing pain in neck. Feeling as if lead lay in brain on turning head to one side. Heaviness, < occiput, < motion; H. as if a weight were pressing brain inward. Stupefaction; in morning. Rush of blood, even when undressed, with sweat on face and desire for cold drinks. Drunkenness as from alcohol, heat in head and face, uncertain gait, etc.

Confusion; in morning; in morning, < forehead and temples, after an hour extending over vertex; in forenoon; in forenoon, with vanishing of objects on attempting to fix them; in forenoon, with paroxysms of drawing pain in middle of forehead, < *l. frontal eminence,* extending thence to posterior part of l. eyeball and at times to occiput, changing at 3 P.M. into digging pain and lasting till 10 P.M.; at noon; in afternoon; in evening, < forehead; after dinner; after supper; when standing, so that he does not know where he is; with dim vision; and incapable of thought.

Vertigo; at 1.30 P.M. *on closing eyes;* in evening on going out; after a siesta; on being waked from his siesta, with trouble in collecting his thoughts; in bed; on moving head sideways; after talking long and when walking; when sitting or lying; when sitting, with staggering on walking; < sitting and closing eyes, > lying; with heat; with vanishing of letters when reading; like a moving to and fro when sitting, < lying; as if his seat were balancing to and fro when closing eyes, > opening eyes; sudden, on looking up after dinner; sudden, at 11 A.M. when writing, from a feeling as if a current of air ascended from occiput and penetrated towards forepart of head, with loss of thought; in attacks; returning as in pushes every minute when seated; as if stupefied in morning.

Forehead.—Maddening twitching in r. eminence in evening. Sticking; in eminences; l. eminence; side; l. eminence in afternoon; l. eminence at 6 P.M.; l. eminence on waking; > walking in open air; above l. eye, extending towards r. Tearing; *in r. side of sinciput and face, transversely across nose to zygoma and over eyes, < morning and evening;* beating, in eminence, with heat. **Transitory pain as if a nail had been driven into l. eminence** *in evening, also when walking in street; in l. eminence, > touch, but returning immediately in superior posterior angle of l. parietal bone, as if a convex button were pressed against it,* next day at 5 P.M. digging in l. eminence alternating with pressure as of a convex button near vertex, this sensation > touch, but returned immediately, was felt in r. mastoid process, l. parietal bone and r. side of pit of throat. Pain; in middle; in r. side; externally above r. eye; over r. superciliary eminence; all day; in morning, with obstruction of nose; in l. side at 9 A.M. when writing, lasting all the forenoon; in evening; in evening, with failure of sight; at 6 P.M.; at 8 P.M., and in temples; on waking; on waking, > rising, returned at 9.30, became heavy; with warmth; with heat in cheeks; with burning in eyes; transversely across; in evening after much conversation, gradually extending towards vertex; over l. brow, extending to r. side of forehead in forenoon when walking in open air; *merging into a sensation as if a wedge were driven into temple,* < motion of head or swallowing; as before catarrh, and in brows; stunning, and in vertex; consisting of pressure, bruised and tearing sensation extending to occiput, on waking, > sleeping again. Twitching pain, and in l. side of face; in l. eminence; r. eminence extending to eye. Clawing pain in l. eminence, becoming fixed in a small spot, with rumbling in bowels. *Drawing pain* in r. side; in l. eminence in evening after lying down and next morning on waking; *intermittent, in l. side,* with colic and emission of flatus; paroxysmal, in r. eminence at 5.30 A.M. on waking, extending to r. orbit and r. nasal bone, ending at 8 o'clock; transversely across, as if a weight were sinking into it; sudden, over l. eyelid, extending through middle of l. brow and dividing l. eminence into threads and rays, which penetrated deep into brain, after waking. Drawing over l. brow; painful, in l. eminence at 10 A.M. when walking in open air; intermittent painful, in r. side at 10 A.M. Pain as if compressed in anterior part of head covered with hair, in evening. Constriction externally on l. eminence, pressing upper lip downward. Confusion; in r. side; at noon; in evening.

Temples.—Swelling of veins. *Sticking; externally in l.;* in r.; in mastoid process, with drawing behind r. ear; *suddenly through l., as if an awl had been forced through brain,* then sensitiveness; *drawing, in l. muscle, < chewing, > touch;* boring, from one to the other. Drawing tearing in l. mastoid process in evening and then in eyeballs. Periodical pinching in r. mastoid process as from pressure of a convex button. Pain deep in r.; P. in evening; in r. in evening; in l. after dinner, lasting all the evening; in morning, now in r., now in l., and again in vertex; raging, extending inward, as if brain would be pressed outward; intermittent contractive, in r. Pressure inward in r. in forenoon. Drawing pain in muscles, < chewing. Drawing below r. mastoid process in evening, with tension and with roaring in l. ear and occasional drawing in l. frontal eminence towards temple; pressive D. in l.; downward from r. mastoid process. Sensitiveness of l. Throbbing in r. towards noon on rising from a seat.

Vertex.—*Sticking; as if a needle pierced bone near sagittal suture* in evening. *Feeling as if a nail were driven outward.* Drawing tearing extending towards middle of brain. *Pain;* in morning, returned in evening, with burning in stomach; in morning, > rising; in morning on waking, afterwards extending to frontal eminences and eyes and returning to vertex, pain > evening, but it threatens to return when he thinks about it; towards noon, > evening; in evening; in evening till midnight; after dinner; in V. and occiput, < moving head and a false step, with sensation as if lead were in it and feeling as if brain moved about loosely; heavy, in upper surface in evening and next forenoon, > cool air and rubbing forehead, eyes and face, with intermittent sticking, head and eyes sensitive to touch, next evening crawling in these places. Weight. Sensation as if brain were pressed out on nodding forward. Drawing in pericranium, at times in vertex, at times in occiput, with tearing. Sensitiveness in morning; S. to touch in a spot in r. side, with redness. Sensation as if upper part of skull were beaten in.

Sides.—Sticking in r.; in l. parietal bone; in l. on bowing; in l. on waking, then dulness of head all day. **Sensation as if a nail were driven into r. parietal bone** (Coffea), **> touch; in r. bone,** *after dinner;* **in angles of bones,** *then itching gnawing.* Tearing in l. and l. teeth; in r. on going to bed. Pain in r., < vertex and above eye; in l. parietal bone, with pressure in r., extending over whole head; in posterior and inferior angle of l. parietal bone, extending to r. frontal eminence during rest, waking him one day at 5 A.M., > rising, then stupidity and dulness of head. Cramplike sensation in l., then warmth. Spot in middle of l. parietal bone sensitive to touch. Pressure as from a convex button in l.; in superior and posterior angle of l. parietal bone, > touch. Painless drawing in r. parietal bone, with pressure and with almost agreeable warmth of whole body. Numbness and tingling in l. half of brain and in l. ear.

Occiput.—Sticking downward through O.; from foramen magnum through brain to vertex; in brain from neck to vertex; upward in brain from occipital foramen. Tearing stab through r. half to forehead.

Tearing in protuberance and in petrous portion of temporal bone; jerking, < r. side. Pain; in evening; on moving head to one side, with stupefaction; in a spot on l. side on touch, so that he was disinclined to lie on l. side at night. Drawing; and tension; painful, in l. side. Tension from one ear to the other. Fulness in evening when walking in open air, with pressure. Dulness, with floating black points before vision, even on closing eyes; D. ending in headache. Crawling on l. side of bone. Heaviness.

Scalp.—Twitching on r. side of occiput. Hair comes off of vertex. Red painful pimples on temples. Painless tubercles. Feels shrunken and hard on temples and forehead. Tearing in tendinous aponeurosis on vertex. Jerking constriction at beginning of dinner. Compression on occiput, with crawling. Pain as if tense. *Sensitive to touch on vertex*, and shining; sensitive where cool air was felt on forehead by an open window after dinner. Biting and corroding smarting on r. side in evening; corroding biting on occiput, with sensation as if something were crawling in the hair. Itching on occiput.

Clinical.—Neuralgic headache in the occiput, extreme soreness and screaming, cannot sleep nor chew. Violent neuralgic headache, as though a nail were driven in. Neuralgia of the head and face, with stabbing, unendurable pains; neuralgia of the head and face from tea-drinking. Neuralgia at night, extending from vertex over the whole head.

Eyes.—Congestion of r. *White of E., is blood-red;* white of l. near cornea red in morning; *white of E. red and inflamed*, with biting and pressure as from sand. Much gum. Sticking in morning in sharp air; S. in a bright light. Boring above r. inner canthus. *Pressure. Dryness;* of r., and in margin of lower lid a burning spot as if a stye would form. *Burning;* in r.; in morning; in morning on rising; at 10 A.M.; at 2 P.M., *and in lids;* in evening; in evening, *with stinging and with injection of cornea;* in evening, < inner canthi; after dinner; during headache, with pain from the light; in r. during headache, > washing with cold water; with heaviness of lids and heat in r. ear; in l. near internal canthus, compelling him to rub it; as if room were smoky. Sensitiveness; of r. in morning. *Weakness;* when reading; < writing; *with pressure as from sand.*

Lachrymation of l. eye; L. in the air; of l. eye when walking in open air; when walking against the wind. *Pupils dilated;* in evening. Pupils contracted.

Balls.—Sticking in l. Tearing in l.; drawing T. in evening. Pain in r.; leaving sensitiveness to touch, the pain returned next morning on waking. Burning pain on upper surface of l. in evening, < touch.

Lids.—Swelling of upper. Red pimple on margin of lower. Agglutination; on waking. Quivering of upper; l. lower; r. Closed. Inability to open on waking, they were painful and closed involuntarily. Cutting in upper. *Feeling as if swollen and as if a foreign body were in eyes. Burning;* in evening, with dim vision; *in edges in evening, with stinging* (even the smoke of tobacco burns in the nose).

Canthi.—Hardened mucus in inner. Sticking in r. outer, with dryness, as from sand; S. in l. inner, with moisture which obscures vision; intermittent, in r. inner, piercing deeply. Feeling as of sand in r. inner till bedtime, and pain on moving lid. Biting in r. at 5 P.M., with swimming of objects. Burning; in outer; in l. outer in forenoon; in outer after rising; in l. outer, with dryness. Burning pressure in l. outer.

Orbits.—Pressing in lower border of r., then sensitiveness to touch and to closing of eye. Drawing pain in bottom of r. in morning. Tension in bottom of l.; at 7.30 P.M.; in l. in morning after waking, with pressure, then in r. *Tearing in l. brow, > touch.* Roots of hair of l. brow sensitive to touch.

Vision.—*Shortsighted. Dim;* when writing; *in open air, with confusion of head; with pressure in eyes as if they would be pressed out of head or as if they were swollen;* with muscæ volitantes. Failed when reading. Dark with the eye that is not inflamed; D. when reading, with sensation about eyes as if he had not slept enough. Trembling of objects after eating. *Luminous disc like a firefly hovering before eyes* on entering a dark room; < twilight, in the room, afterwards this circle, which followed the movements of eyeball and hovered at various distances, now before one, now before both eyes, became more ellipitical, had a dark violet or blackish nucleus in the centre. On going to dinner, sudden sparkling, and black shining, swimming points, disappearing first in r. eye.

Clinical.—Ciliary neuralgia, pain extends over the face and head, with great soreness, cannot lie on the face nor chew. Kerato-iritis, with excessive photophobia, opacity, etc. Episcleritis, with great soreness and violent pain. Iritis, especially syphilitic, with gummata on the iris, severe nocturnal pain.

Ears.—Quivering extending to l. corner of mouth. (Wax increased.) Sticking in r.; in r. meatus; in r. meatus, with twitching; in r., with ringing; outward from r. and under lobule; from depth of r. through external meatus; squeezing, in l. when sitting after dinner; from external meatus to internal, compelling him to hold his breath, at night as he entered the house from the cold air, leaving ear sensitive, less severe attack next morning, with sensation as if free access of air were prevented, after dinner feeling as if external meatus were filled with water, as when one dips his head under the surface, afterwards the earache threatened to return when he thought of it, afterwards slight sticking in l. ear.

Tearing in evening in bed till midnight, with hammering and with micturition every half hour and with cold feet as far as knees; T. in l. concha, then in l. eye, ending with a darting stitch through middle of ball. Pinching in r. Cramplike pain in r.; in r. outer; in r. external meatus, < drawing scalp down from highest point of skull; cramp in middle like an aching and compression, then a stitch like lightning, frequently in evening. Pain behind l.; in meatus at noon; burning, behind r.

Sensation as if something were squeezed out. Compression in outer meatus. Tension in lower part of outer, as if a band were pulling downward. Drawing behind r., with constriction in ear; D. behind r. after dinner, with stitches in mastoid processes. Heat in r. Stoppage; with tension; of l. morning and noon, with diminished hearing; of r. in morning, with fulness and sneezing, which returned in evening, then itching in nostrils towards point of nose, then thin mucus.

Ringing; during the day; sudden, in r. after dinner, suddenly changing after a few hours to buzzing and groaning, then gradually changing to a noise as of a spurting liquid, which lasted most of the night. Creaking like the turning of a wooden screw, <

empty swallowing, with sticking; C. like the turning of a wooden screw on swallowing, with dryness in r. outer canthus as from sand. Buzzing. Roaring; in l.; early in bed; at noon, with buzzing; in afternoon on entering house, with painful thumping; in l., *with creaking when swallowing saliva;* in r., with boiling; like a draught through a stove.

Clinical.—Polypi of the ear, with otorrhœa, easy bleeding, shooting pains. Otorrhœa smelling of putrid meat.

Nose.—Ulceration half an inch within, where there is a scab (Aur., Nit. ac.). *Swelling of l. wing, with induration and tensive pain. Red itching spot, sore to touch, in fissure of r. wing. Feeling of soreness or ulceration in r. nostril,* < *pressure on ala.* Stitches in l. wing. *Painful pressure at root.* Pain at root at noon, with warmth, as if cold would set in. Tension above r. wing, > rubbing. Crawling as in coryza. *Sensation of dry catarrh in upper part,* < *evening. Stoppage;* with nasal voice; in morning and blowing out of blood all day, with frontal pain. Burning, with swollen feeling and with sensitiveness of septum, on which are vesicles; B. in lower border of r. nostril at noon, with sensitiveness to touch.

Dryness; in evening, and in frontal sinuses; at noon, > open air, returning in the house, moist after smoking a cigar; on smoking a cigar; with tickling; in r. nostril extending into frontal sinuses, with burning; *and sensitiveness,* this sensation gradually extended to frontal sinuses and eyes became sensitive, amelioration in afternoon, two days afterwards on rising the same feeling in l. nostril and r. frontal sinus; D. and pressure in nose and frontal sinuses in forenoon, catarrhal flow for an hour at noon, then pressure on root of nose and copious mucus, afterwards the pressure drew off towards ears, causing tension and stoppage of ears, next day D. and tension in nose, with swollen feeling in whole mucous membrane.

Sneezing; in morning, ending with dulness in head; in morning on waking, with tickling in nose and burning in eyes, as if catarrh were coming on; in morning, and stoppage of r. nostril alternating with running, this catarrh lasted two hours, then ceased suddenly, returned in evening and again ceased suddenly; at noon; in evening and morning; in evening, with tickling in nose; after dinner, without catarrh; caused by vapor rising from stomach into nose; with stoppage of r. nostril and internal chilliness of feet; with obstruction in nose and roughness in throat, symptoms < evening, with aching in forehead and weight and pressure in eyes, then a restless night, on waking next morning throat was obstructed with phlegm, and after hawking larynx and trachea were painful, then malaise and ill humor, aching in forehead, burning in eyes, obstruction of nose, hoarseness, he felt better at noon when walking in open air, but aggravation when at rest, much flowing from nose, feet cold, general ill feeling sent him to bed early, it was long before he could get warm, dulness of head, cough, stoppage of nose, next morning uneasiness and weakness, at noon dulness and buzzing in head, dry cough, amelioration in evening, febrile symptoms at night, > after midnight, sweat towards morning.

Coryza all day; at night, with cough; with headache; *sudden;* intermittent; dry, in open air, becoming fluent by sneezing. Fluent coryza; in morning; towards evening, with hoarseness; disturbing nights' rest; in the house. Blowing out thick mucus at noon. Mucus mixed with clotted blood. Bleeding; in morning on blowing, on rising; in afternoon, relieving the head; in evening; *on blowing;* < becoming heated. Smell and taste dull.

Clinical.—Nasal catarrh, with quantities of thick, green mucus, pus and blood that seem to come from the frontal sinuses. Painful scabs in the nostrils. Warts on the nose.

Face.—Wan. Pale and earthy. Red in afternoon, and limbs cool. Bloated and sickly-looking. Sunken. Swelling of a gland on l. cheek. Twitching extending towards zygomata, with crawling. Jerking sticking in muscles of cheek when walking in open air. Burning tearing in periosteum of l. side during dinner. Cramp-like pain in r. cheek when the part is at rest. *Boring in l. malar-bone,* > *touch.* Drawing pain between mouth and nose, as if periosteum were tense, with pain like a saddle over nasal bones. In r. half from temple to teeth drawing, sometimes darting pain, then sensitiveness of whole face. Crawling drawing in zygomata; in l. zygoma, then dulness, appeared again next day, then on r. side. Crawling in zygomata and l. upper jaw, with drawing. Sensation as if a spot under r. nostril would become indurated. Burrowing itching in l. malar-bone.

Jaws.—Cracking on yawning. Stitches in l. lower; in lower coming out of ear; *between l. ear and zygomatic arch* as if jaw had been suddenly dislocated in evening and morning when chewing; boring, in r. lower; drawing, in angle of l. lower, > touch. Tearings in l. upper extending towards eye; in lower in region of joints, uniting at chin and disappearing together; drawing, in r. lower in evening; paroxysmal drawing, in l. upper; in single jerks from angle to os hyoides, deep in integuments. Gnawing boring in l. upper. Drawing in r. upper in morning; in l. upper at 1 P.M.; l. upper at 5 P.M. Stiffness of l. masseter muscles, painful on opening jaws.

Lips.—*Red itching elevation on upper* in forenoon. Itching tubercle on upper near r. corner. Itching pimples on margin of upper towards middle. On edge of upper, dark red burning spots, on which elevations developed, dried up and fell off, then new spots ran the same course. Redness of upper in morning, with burning. Upper swollen and burning. Twitching of upper; of upper near corner. (Stitches.) Cutting in l. side of upper; upward through l. half of lower. *Sensitiveness of upper.* Burning, and in palate. Dryness without thirst. Itching in inner side of upper.

Mouth.—Teeth. Loose in morning. Sticking in incisor; jumping, in l. lower hollow. Tearing in l. in afternoon; sudden, in first l. lower molar, suddenly extending over whole lower jaw. Digging in two r. upper hollow molars, with burning pain, pain > Merc. sol., returning in a warm room, > cold water and > inhaling air at an open window, later D. in these teeth > cold water, < warm soup and tobacco-smoke. Pain in hollow on blowing nose; as from touch upon a nerve from evening till midnight, with intermittent jerking; jerking, in hollow in morning; like a hacking or sharp throbbing in the gum; in first l. lower molar as if split asunder, after every cup of tea, afterwards extending over upper and lower jaw; sore, beneath last r.; corroding, in hollow, affecting whole side of head, < cold (drinks or air) and chewing. Drawing in lower incisors; wandering D. in hollow; sharp, extending upward, < eating.

Gums.—Swollen and painfully sore; swelling of G. and tongue, with pain when she takes anything hard into her mouth or eats. Jerking sticking in r. upper at 4.30 P.M. during siesta. Sticking jerking through G. of last lower molars. G. of molars sensitive at noon; l. lower sensitive to touch.

Tongue.—*White blister on side close to root, painfully sore; white V. returned, with burning, < after warm food.* Coated; and half dry; white; white, with rough, scraping sensation, with a painful white blister in front of the middle. Sticking beneath r. side, < swallowing. Cutting in tip and on its under surface. **Tip painful to touch.** *Sore.* Roughness, and of hard palate and throat. Dryness; at tip. Burning.

Mouth filled with blisters, as if burnt, with thirst at night. Sticking from r. velum palati into internal ear at night. Soreness of palate; about hard palate, as if burnt and covered with vesicles. On swallowing saliva, sore pain in palate as if air penetrated a wound, extending towards l. ear internally. Pressure in curtain of palate, with heaviness. Dryness; of palate; of palate, without thirst; of palate, with inclination to cough; with thirst and loss of appetite; of back part, with thirst. Bloody saliva. Frequent spitting of saliva and mucus, with hollowness at stomach and insipid taste. Salivation; in morning; after breakfast, with weakness of stomach; in evening; with drawing in r. masseter; with swelling of salivary glands; sweet; acid-tasting; acid, at 6 P.M.; insipid, at night; metallic-tasting, with swelling of salivary glands.

Taste.—Bitter; in morning; at night; to bread. Bitter sharp after food, < root of tongue and in fauces, at noon, even an unpleasant after-taste to black coffee. Bitter mucous. Bitter sharp salt, < about root of tongue. Sweetish salt, < back part of mouth and root of tongue. As if food were salted too little. Sharp. Sweetish; slimy, after eating; insipid, in evening. Resinous, constrictive. Nauseous; after eating. Bad in morning. Unpleasant after eating ices. Insipid; with sensation as if stomach were disordered. (Mouldy when smoking tobacco.) Dull; in afternoon.

Clinical.—Violent toothache from decayed teeth, particularly useful when the teeth decay next the gums, with retraction of the gums, leaving a healthy crown; teeth extremely sensitive to cold water. Aphthous sore mouth.

Throat.—Swelling; of tonsils; of tonsils, and pain inducing frequent swallowing. Uvula seemed lengthened in afternoon. Tonsils red; in afternoon. Rising of a nauseating rancid vapor, perceptible to smell. Mucus in fauces which cannot be hawked up; M. when eating, which she must hawk up or else she cannot swallow the food. Hawking, with cough; H., with soreness of throat; and hacking. Hawking up mucus; of a sharp resinous taste; blood-red, from fauces; tough; thick, in morning; thick tenacious, from larynx in morning; tough white, at night.

Sticking; in pit; beneath larynx; in r. side of fauces, suddenly extending into ear, with sensation in ear on opening and closing mouth as of an opening through which air could penetrate. Scraping; after eating ices; with inclination to cough. *Roughness;* in morning; in morning, > breakfast, with deep voice and inclination to hawk; till afternoon; in evening; then feeling of a painless tumor; as from snuff. Pain on swallowing; in back part on swallowing; in r. side of pharynx, extending to ear, impeding swallowing. Soreness like a swelling from taking cold. Sensation in r. side as if about to inflame, and during the day stinging on swallowing.

Sensation as if he could not swallow on account of mucus and as if œsophagus were contracted, and after hawking the throat feels rough. Burning forcing him to hawk. *Dryness;* of pharynx; in evening; of fauces at night; and constriction; with salivation, hawking and spitting of white tough mucus. Inclination to swallow. Swallowing painful; difficult, without apparent cause in throat.

Stomach.—Appetite. Great; towards evening; at dinner; without thirst. A., but does not relish food, and after eating anxiety and palpitation. Little. *Lost;* in evening. Aversion to dinner; to meat. Tobacco-smoke is not as agreeable as at other times, in evening.

Thirst; in morning on waking; in afternoon; after dinner; with coldness and drowsiness; with alternations of heat and cold, the latter < back, with hot head and face during the day, coldness before midnight, warmth towards morning, sweat finally; for cold drinks all day, without thirst; for cold drinks before and after dinner; little.

Eructations; when smoking; foul, late in evening; rancid; as of rancid grease; tasting of food when eating; of food, tasting of the drug all the afternoon; (bitter after eating). Empty eructations; all day; in afternoon; during a walk, with emission of flatus. Hiccough after eating, then pressure in pit of stomach, then flatulence and eructations.

Nausea; at 10 A.M., with rapid pulse; at night, with pain in stomach and vomiturition; all night, with retching of only mucus; after the customary smoke, with sweat, both > stool; when walking in open air, with vertigo, heat in face, anxious sweat, could scarcely get his breath, heaviness of legs so that he staggered; (from all food); in pit of stomach; in epigastric region; mounting from abdomen; with apprehension mounting from pit of stomach and back again; with dulness of head; with salivation; with chill. Vomiting, then shaking chill, with heaviness of limbs and tearing in occiput; V. of sourish-tasting liquid and food.

Swelling of region, > emissions of flatus. Stitches in pit; on l. side near pit; outward on l. side near pit; gnawing, in bed, > rising. Tearing in pit on bending body to r. side. Cutting on l. side near pit. Cramp, < towards evening. Pinching in forenoon; frequently in epigastric region during dinner. Boring above pit.

Pain; in epigastrium towards r. hypochondrium in morning, < rest; in forenoon; in pit at night; after roast meat eaten in evening; after eating; in pit after eating; in pit after eating, so that he cannot bear his hand upon it; in pit after eating, on moving body and feeling of epigastric region; extending into fauces; in pit and chest, impeding respiration; spasmodic, in pit; on r. side near pit, as from a foreign body, < morning, with stitches. Soreness of pit; in region on pressure, < evening. Constriction in forenoon, then eructation. Feeling as if deranged, with pressure over pit, which impeded respiration. Throbbing as in an artery, in middle of pit. Uneasiness; in region, with eructations of the drug.

Heartburn; in afternoon; at 7 P.M.; on stooping; intermittent, after dinner. Burning in region; B. in morning; in forenoon; in forenoon, with pressing; in afternoon; in afternoon, with pressing; from 4 till 6 P.M.; in evening; in evening on eating fish, with pressing; after dinner; after dinner, with pressing; after dinner till evening and again in the night; after supper, with pressing and occasional constriction; < movement and speaking.

Abdomen.—*Distention;* in afternoon; in afternoon, with rumbling and colic; *after eating;* after eating, with stitches, pressure, dragging and emission of flatus; after dinner, with griping; after dinner, embarrassing respiration; > eructations; with colic and constipation; *flatulent. Rumbling;* after breakfast, with cutting; in afternoon, *with emission of flatus;* in afternoon and evening, with gurgling, sticking and shifting of flatus; at night, with grumbling; with rolling; with shifting of flatus and with sticking in all parts of body. Gurgling. Flatulence at night. *Emission of flatus;* towards morning; at night; with moisture; *noiseless;* odorless; loud, inodorous.

Occasional sticking. Paroxysmal tearing upward, beginning in r. groin. Griping; in evening, with emission of flatus; with pinching now here, now there. Colic; in forenoon when walking in open air; at noon; at noon, so that he could scarcely stand straight, < driving, headache and chilliness, the C. > copious liquid stool and emission of flatus, C. < again towards evening; in evening; at 7 P.M., with movements, as before diarrhœa, violent diarrhœa at 8.30, then sensitiveness of abdomen; at night; < from morning till noon, > dinner, returned in evening till midnight, *with pressure in hypogastrium;* with diarrhœa; disturbing sleep; sudden, during dinner; sudden, in evening, as if all bowels were pulled towards a point behind umbilicus, > liquid stools and emission of flatus, with distention of abdomen, headache and rapid pulse. Sprained pain in muscles on bending backward. **Sensation of something alive.** Sensation as if a child's knee were pushed out against anterior walls in morning. *Tension.* Burning compression transversely across, externally. Incommoded by supper, which was eaten with a hearty appetite. (Burning, still more in chest, hypochondria and pit of stomach, all of which parts are externally hot.)

Hypochondria.—Jerking in l. towards epigastrium. Stitches deep in; in r. in evening, < respiration; in hepatic region when sitting; in liver when walking; drawing, in liver. Sticking in splenic region; during a meal; when sitting after dinner; < dinner and supper; with pale look; then soreness; deep, in forenoon. Cutting in side above liver on inspiration when walking, > pressure and standing still. Pressure as from a stone on lower part of liver when walking. Sensation of something alive moving in r.; in l. in bed. (Burning, < hepatic region.)

Upper A.—Cutting from the spine outward. Constrictive cramp. Colic in small intestines.

Sides.—Stitches in l. making walking difficult; in r. when lying on r. side, > pressure, returning on walking in open air. Cutting deep in l.; in l., with griping. Pinching in l. Pain in l. muscles as if a hook were drawn upward. Pain in r., > pressure, returning on deep inspiration or forcible expiration. Fulness in r., in lumbar region, making breathing difficult, at 2 or 3 A.M. in bed.

Umbilical Region.—Cutting above umbilicus extending into small of back. Pinching. Griping; above umbilicus; at 2 P.M., with wandering; drawing towards r. groin, causing there intermittent pressing, > open air. Constriction.

Hypogastrium.—*Swelling of inguinal glands;* of groin; S., with frequent urging to urinate; with sensitiveness to pressure and to jar of foot on the ground; with constrictive pains like cramps. Rumbling in r. after stool. *Sticking in inguinal glands;* on r. side of pelvis near linea alba; in r. groin and between sacrum and anus; in l. iliac region all day; in groin frequently during the day, with feeling as if inguinal glands were swollen; deep in r. groin in forenoon when walking in the street; in r. groin when coughing; from groin down through thigh when sitting; throbbing, in r. groin. *Cutting;* in r. iliac region. Boring inward in region of r. iliac bone; attacks of B., with painful drawing up of testes and occasional urging to stool. Pain, < above symphysis pubis; in r. iliac region when walking in the room; flatulent, before stool, < towards sides; as from a foreign body in r. side of pelvis, near linea alba. **Movement as of something living** (Croc.), **like a pushing of muscles by the arm of a child, without pain.** *Sudden bounding as of something alive in r. iliac region.* Pressure outward; inward in r. groin. Bruised feeling over crest of r. ilium on touch. Drawing pain in groin on standing and walking; D. pain from inguinal glands to knees, < when going to sleep, then heaviness of limbs. Drawing in r. groin; l. groin at noon; in l. side, with pain on touch; from crest of r. iliac bone to upper part of thigh. Tension; in forenoon (with empty stomach), < deep inspiration, with occasional sticking. Constriction. Fatigue in groins; in groins, changing to drawing pain extending to glans.

Rectum.—Stitches after stool; S. < evening; occasional; upward; extending into urethra beneath frænum; burning, when not at stool. Cutting. Jerklike constriction and tearing upward, and in anus. Boring outward as from a worm, after stool. Pain during stool, so that she must desist. Itching after stool. Urging, with erections; frequent ineffectual U.; ineffectual, with itching in anus extending into urethra; ineffectual, afterwards loose stool, next day loose stool, third day no stool.

Anus.—*Swelling of hæmorrhoidal veins;* with urging to stool and itching and burning in anus. Protrusion of hæmorrhoidal vessels in afternoon when walking, with sticking in them. (Red painless pimples like figwarts.) *Moisture. Discharge of bloody slime by day and night. Sticking; at 1 P.M. when sitting;* in evening; > walking in open air; *extending into region of l. iliac bone* in morning; alternating with burning in prepuce, also in morning after walking. *Hæmorrhoidal pressure;* at 11 A.M.; in evening when sitting; in evening, *with burning; when seated; on touch. Soreness* in morning; *after a slimy discharge, as if skin were cracked. Constriction with almost every stool.* Squeezing in hæmorrhoids; S. in hæmorrhoidal vessels in forenoon; in forenoon, with pressing. Sensation of alternate congestion and emptiness in hæmorrhoidal vessels.

Burning; in hæmorrhoidal vessels; in morning; in forenoon; at noon, with soreness; after a loose stool; after stool, with drawing inward; after a hard, scanty stool, with pressing; after stool, then discharge of mucus, *with stitches in rectum in direction of a line from anus to small of back,* as the stitches ceased the itching and burning returned. Biting. *Itching;* in hæmorrhoids, with squeezing; *in hæmorrhoidal vessels in fore-*

noon, with dragging; in hæmorrhoidal vessels in forenoon when walking, with burning; at 10 A.M.; in evening, with pressing; in evening, with burning; after dinner; < morning; < evening, with burning and tenesmus; < evening after stool, with burning; with sweat; passing into burning after a hard stool.

Clinical.—Warts about anus. Fistula. Piles.

Perineum.—R. side of raphe prominent and felt thickened. Clammy moisture in sulcus between nates. Stitches extending outward, > retracting anus. Cutting extending into urethra. Soreness; a sore painful spot in sulcus between nates, not far from anus. *Burning pain, raphe prominent, and an inch from anus a tubercle, which became moist and smarted on walking.* Burning in fossa between nates when walking. Itching in forenoon when seated.

Clinical.—Excessive perspiration on perineum.

Stool.—Liquid; and copious; and scanty; half liquid, scanty, with sensation as if rectum were inactive. **Diarrhœa**; in evening; *nearly watery, painless;* with pain; scanty, with urging, then feeling of inactivity of rectum. Soft; and copious; and frequent, also copious. Papescent, three times in one day, next day no stool; every day after dinner, with emission of flatus; and scanty; and scanty, after dinner; and fetid, twice in one day; and copious, frequent, affording great relief.

Constipation; with shifting of flatulence; next day copious fluid stools in morning and after dinner; for eight days, then copious hard stool; for several days, after a profuse nocturnal emission. Hard; after much straining, then pain in anus, with borborygmus, after three hours a more liquid stool, then burning in anus; and delayed; in large brown balls covered with streaks of blood; and difficult, then the opposite, secondary action. Hard and unsatisfactory, with tenesmus; H. and U., with copious, inodorous flatus; afterwards another papescent one; then itching and burning in anus. Unsatisfactory; after much straining. Copious. Large, hard at first, then papescent, clayish and fetid. Scanty; with griping. *Frequent; and normal.* Ending with discharge of mucus, also itching and burning. Violent, with bellyache and burning in anus, that night another stool with borborygmi.

Clinical.—Chronic diarrhœa. Stools forcible, pale, copious, greasy, expelled with gurgling, like water from a bung-hole, < after breakfast; particularly diarrhœa after vaccination.

Urinary Organs.—Bladder. Seemed larger. Sticking from neck towards urethra. Cutting in afternoon; C. in region, < walking. Attacks of boring *in region, with painful drawing up of testes.* Sensitiveness in region, with inflated feeling and frequent urging. *Urging;* all day; all night, and much light-colored urine; hasty, with copious urine. *Frequent urging,* even when there was but little in bladder; with copious urine; then copious watery urine, even at night.

Dribbling from urethra (not bladder) *after urinating. Micturition stops five or six times before bladder is emptied. Frequent micturition; at night;* at night, with itching in urethra; at night, with hasty, incessant urging; at night, urine copious, straw-yellow; at night, urine copious, and after micturition renewed urging and discharge of a few drops; *and copious;* of limpid urine; every minute, obliged to press, urine passes only by paroxysms, when there is burning pain in urethra. Micturition infrequent.

Urethra.—*Orifice closed by a slimy fluid consisting of serous liquid and a lump of mucus,* which could be drawn out into threads, in morning, after removing this liquid burning on urinating. Discharge of prostatic fluid, which can be drawn out into threads, in morning after waking. Mucous discharge from female. Sticking; in evening; in fossa navicularis at 4 P.M.; at night, with frequent erections, so that he could not sleep; with urging to urinate; in anterior end when not urinating; in forepart, penis being relaxed; extending forward, > while urinating; sudden, from bulbus almost to middle of it, forcing him to bend over, towards noon when walking in open air; jerking cutting, when not urinating; burning, near meatus when not urinating; tearing, in forepart. Tearing like lightning, hither and thither in afternoon when sitting, with stitches in anus. Cutting in perineal portion; C. when urinating; drawing, when walking. Attacks of sticking beating in fossa navicularis. *Sensation as if a few drops ran down it after urinating; sensation of moisture running forward in it,* < evening; sensation as if a drop of viscid fluid pressed forward at 4.45 P.M. when sitting. *Jerking voluptuous formication in fossa navicularis; in forepart* at 9 A.M. when walking in the street, penis being relaxed. Itching; when urinating; voluptuous, in forepart after dinner, with relaxed penis; voluptuous, in forepart, penis being relaxed, with sensation as if a few drops would flow out. Burning; in forepart; towards bulbus; in orifice in evening; after rising; after a pollution, when not urinating; after micturition, and in fundus of bladder; after micturition in morning, with stitches from urethra to anus, pressing in region of neck of bladder and urging; in forepart, with sticking; then voluptuous feeling, < after micturition. Burning during micturition; after dinner; in navicular fossa (Petrosel.); and afterwards; with dark urine; with red urine; *with gleety discharge, the stream small and split, next day the discharge was yellow, the symptoms were those of gonorrhœa.*

Urine.—*Watery, after standing it becomes cloudy.* Red; and deposits a thick brick-dust sediment. Of penetrating odor. Copious; in afternoon, and limpid; at night; in evening and night, *yellowish wine-colored;* with stitches in l. testicle. *Scanty, dark, burning;* S., soon becomes turbid and deposits a clayey sediment. None all day, next day scanty, dark red, afterwards copious. Turbid, deposits a sediment; flocky, mucous sediment.

Clinical.—Dysuria. High-colored, strong smelling urine. Gonorrhœa, with thin, greenish discharge and scalding during micturition. Repressed gonorrhœa, especially with rheumatism or inflamed prostate.

Sexual Organs.—Sticking in condylomata. *Sweat* on waking; S. on male. Flat dirty ulcer on corona glandis, with burning pain, surrounded by redness, with sticking. (Degeneration of epididymus like variocele.)

Glans.—*Moisture. Secreted thin mucus.* Covered with greenish-yellow, ill-smelling secretion, and on dorsum, near hinder border, four tubercles with a vesicle on the summit, and in sulcus near attachment of foreskin an eroded spot surrounded by a red circle, vesicles broke and left painless erosions surrounded by a red margin and yielding the secretion, then red, sensitive granular elevations, afterwards sebaceous glands of prepuce inflamed. Depressed vesicle, with stinging when urinating. Smooth red excrescences behind G. under prepuce, with crawling. Red at aperture of urethra, next day bruised pain in l. testicle, afterwards eroded spot in middle of furrow of glans discharging puslike fluid, aggravation from wine, inner surface of prepuce sore in spots, inflamed at frænulum, glans sensitive and painful when walking. Red spots, with inflammation of inner surface of foreskin, next day burning on glans, red eroded spots exuding a thin yellowish, ill-smelling secretion on furrow behind corona, afterwards the spots ran together and were covered with granular elevations, feeling as if glans were ulcerating, afterwards the furrow as far as frænulum was sore and covered with papillæ, then reddish excrescences on hinder parts of glans and inner surface of prepuce full of granular tubercles, sebaceous glans of prepuce swollen. Stitches; in tip when not urinating, < pressure; near urethra, with desire to urinate, urine passed guttatim, stitches intermittent during micturition; burning; burning, in penis extending to testicles and umbilical region, < sitting, > walking. *Painful jerking in penis*, with sensation as if a viscid liquid exuded from urethra, which was not the case. Jerking pain in penis. Bruised sensation when sitting. *Sensitiveness;* on waking; with swelling of sebaceous glands; with darting stitches through it. Excoriated feeling near frænulum; on touch. Painful throbbing at base. *Intermittent burning between glans and prepuce.* Itching; when walking; *in G. and prepuce, alternating with stitches in anus;* sticking, in side; burning, in tip when urinating; tickling, between G. and prepuce.

Erections in morning when half awake; in morning on waking, with strong desire, but no emission, which was not usually the case; in afternoon; long-continued at night.

Prepuce.—**Red growth like condylomata on inner surface.** *Swelling.* Red itching spot on inner surface. Red gritty spot on outer surface, becomes an ulcer covered with a scab, with itching and sometimes with burning pain. On inner surface moist tetter, depressed in middle, painful to touch. Stitches on inner surface. Burning on inner surface; B. alternating with stitches in anus. Biting in morning after walking; B., and on upper surface of glans. Itching; *on inner surface;* in afternoon, with biting.

Scrotum.—*Sweat;* in morning on waking, *and on perineum and inner surface of thighs;* on one half. Moist pimple. Sticking; burning, extending through S. and spermatic cord. Bruised sensation in r. side. Corroding aching of r. half. Itching on l. in evening; I. and crawling, with burning pain after rubbing.

Testicles.—L. drawn up against abdomen, with swelling of inguinal glands. Stitches. Bruised tearing sideways in r. Pain as if they would be crushed when sitting, < walking. Compression. Drawing; in l.; in l., with weight in it, also > walking in open air. *Feeling as if they moved,* > walking in open air.

Excitement at noon, especially tickling in prepuce and glans. Desire great; lost. *Emission* towards morning; at night; *at night,* whereupon he woke; at night, with pain in orifice of urethra as if too tight.

Female.—Cramplike pain on rising from a seat, and in perineum; C. pain extending into hypogastrium. Pain like a pressure and contraction when sitting. *Biting during and after micturition, < urethra, with itching.* Labiæ, swelling, with burning pain when walking and on touch; (whitish ulcer on inner surface of majora, at first sore on touch, then itching). Pudenda, sticking on walking far; *pain as if sore and biting,* also < during micturition; *itching when walking. Burning in vagina when walking and sitting, with biting. Leucorrhœa;* yellow-green.

Menses.—Scanty and early; D. and delayed. Lasted only one day; and scanty; and consisted of a clot of black blood, next time lasted only one day and consisted of three clots of black blood, third time lasted a day and a night. Weak.

Clinical.—Secondary syphilis; roseola, iritis, with condylomata, etc. Chancroidal ulcers on the genitals. Epithelioma of the vagina and uterus. Uterine polypi, with terrible pain. Ovaritis, l. Chronic ovaritis following gonorrhœa. Prolapsus, < driving, with great pain in the back. *Condylomata.* Vagina extremely sensitive in coition (Kreos., Sulph.).

Respiratory Organs.—Larynx. Mucus at night, and in trachea. Constriction and burning; C. in region of os hyoides after eating ices. Pressure. Voice rough. Voice deep and hoarse in morning on waking. Hoarseness during the lecture, with inclination to hawk; H., with violent cough and stitches in l. breast and l. scapula; as from constriction in pharynx.

Trachea.—Sticking in region of pit of throat on breathing; in l. side below larynx, < swallowing. Scraping causing cough.

Cough.—In morning on rising, > noon, with roughness in throat; C., with oppression of chest; inclination to, with burning in l. side of throat near larynx, which afterwards extended towards l. ear, with more soreness; as from pungent food, in morning on rising. Dry; in evening; > wine and beer, with constriction in spots on thorax and corresponding parts of lungs, compelling deep inspirations; interrupted, when sitting smoking a cigar. *Hacking dry;* in morning; in morning on waking; in afternoon and evening; in evening, from tobacco-smoke; after dinner; two hours after dinner; from tension, now in l. chest, now in l. hypochondrium. Dry, short, barking in morning. *Short interrupted, convulsive* at night and on waking, from irritation in larynx and leaving dryness in it. Coughing up mucus; in morning and evening; when eating and after eating; tough M.; thick M. in morning; tickling, in forenoon; thick, at night; tenacious, towards noon, irritation to vomit and retching, then illness and weakness and return of headache.

Expectoration of thick mucus; of mucus in morning after rising, leaving sensitiveness in larynx; of tough mucus in morning; of blood when walking.

Respiration.—Breathlessness when walking in afternoon, with heat and weight on chest, dry cough and sticking in head. Difficult; in evening, with pressing in chest towards back; before bedtime, with pressure on chest, delaying sleep; on going to bed, with pressing on chest and sticking in side; on ascending stairs; < ascending stairs, with weak feeling in chest and pressure under sternum; with anxiety; also with great desire for water; almost panting. *Short at night,* necessity to breathe deeply; S. on walking; with weight on chest. Hurried at night. Necessity for frequent deep breathing.

Clinical.—Polypi of the vocal cords. Cough in the morning after rising and during the day, sometimes in evening after lying down; immediately after eating.

Chest.—Stitches in side; l.; l. lung; under sternum; region of r. fifth rib; in r. fourth rib near sternum; on side near middle of sternum; in lower half of side; on r. side near lower part of middle of sternum; under mammæ, not affected by respiration; in l. often during the day; in r. lower part at 6 A.M.; in l. in forenoon; on r. side near sternum at noon, > deep inspiration, returned on expiration; lower part of r. lung at 3 P.M. after sneezing; lower part of r. lung from 3 till 11 P.M., < sneezing, deep breathing and coughing; at 4 P.M. after sneezing; in l. side often in evening; in l. side in evening, < inspiration; low down in l. side in evening when going home; in l. during inspiration and expiration; now in r., now in l.; double, in breast; like lightning transversely through it; in sides extending to axillæ; backward through upper part of l. breast, then twitching feeling; forward through lower part of lungs, with bruised sensation in chest, dulness of head, sadness and discouragement; sudden, backward, in r. half in forenoon, next day in l. half; periodical, deep in l. pectoralis major; intermittent, inward, from l. axilla; throbbing, in l.; crawling, in r.

Cutting in different directions; upward on r. side near sternum; upward through middle to pit of throat, often during the day; from sternum to r. elbow; under sternum, embarrassing respiration. Pinching in region of fifth and sixth ribs. Knocking under sternum extending to sacrum, when lying on back. Clawing in sternum at 2 P.M. Cramplike pain under sternum (< deep inspiration), and in inguinal region. Tearing drawing in region of l. fifth and sixth ribs when standing and sitting, > moving and deep inspiration.

Pain in l. side; at r. lower part; under sternum; under l. short ribs; in l. side, < region of fifth rib; in r. side in afternoon, accompanied in evening by sticking, which extended into small of back; in middle of sternum at 6 P.M.; in l. side in evening, > stool; in upper part, < pressure; in r. side, < deep breathing and bending; in lower lobe of l. lung, < deep breathing; in middle, with sticking on deep inspiration; in a spot under sternum, gradually extending to scorbiculus, in afternoon and evening; in middle up to throat, causing difficult respiration; crawling, in a spot in l. side of sternum, leaving soreness.

Sensitiveness of spots. Sore pain in region of ribs on touch. Internal smarting as if sore, < dry cough. Scraping causing cough. Sprained sensation in l. side close to pit of stomach. Bruised sensation in afternoon; under r. arm; under sternum, with fulness; with oppression under sternum. Sticking beating in middle of r. side.

Feeling in spots as if chest from without and corresponding parts of lungs from within were constricted, < rest, causing deep sighs. Constriction of lower part as from a bandage, at noon; C. in lower half, with compression. Compression when laughing, with shortness of breath; C. backward when sitting, < stretching body. Oppression; of lower part; with pain on inspiration; with inclination to cough; at noon before dinner, with difficult respiration and pain in anterior surface of stomach on deep inspiration as from external pressure; as from internal adhesion. Sensation as if distended from within.

Tightness obliging deep breathing. Tension on deep inspiration; T. from first false rib to l. axilla, < raising arm; in lungs, becoming sticking on deep inspiration. Pressure; after eating; on sternum, not affecting respiration; in middle when sitting, not impeding respiration; with cramplike constriction; in attacks about axilla; from within towards nipple. All diameters seem shorter. Want of pliability and sufficiency of inspired air. Heat; under sternum. Weakness.

Heart.—*Sticking in region.* Tearing in region extending into l. scapula, in open air. Twitching pain under it. Pain; in forenoon, with tension; in a spot in evening; in a spot in region on touch. Palpitation; *visible, without anxiety.* Pulsation imperceptible at night, then trembling of it and anxiety.

Pulse.—Rapid; during the access of heat, and full; and full, hard, also in evening. Feverish in evening, with headache. Slow, weak.

Neck.—Swelling; of glands; of glands, with pain so that he could not lie down at night. Vessels distended and blue. Creaking in vertebræ on certain movements of head. Sticking over joint of atlas in evening; in muscles on motion; pinching, in r. side, > moving it. Tearing in nape; in tendinous expansion on r. side; in nape, extending into shoulder; intermittent sticking, in r. muscles in evening, extending to scapula; digging, in r. muscles, extending to scapula, in evening, > touch, with roaring in l. ear and creaking on swallowing saliva. Sticking cutting in l. side as far as ear in morning.

Pain in nape; in l. side as from a hard bed; in nape close to occiput, as from a hard bed, during the day this spread over r. side of back as if muscles were sprained, < bending head forward and raising r. arm, in the evening the pain moved more into region of r. shoulder and neck, next day on bending head forward pain as if muscles were too short, with roaring and boiling in r. ear, afterwards the pain was a sort of *tumultuous digging*, as if muscles had been crushed and as if a gathering were taking place in subcutaneous and intermuscular areolar tissue, > sweat. Sensation in nape as if beaten to pieces.

Pressing and drawing pain upward in r. side. *Drawing in nape* in evening, with sticking from nape to r. ear and shoulder; D. in l. side in evening before sleep and next day till afternoon; in l. side on waking; painful, in l. side close to occiput alternating with a similar pain in r. frontal eminence, at 11.30. *Tension in l. side; in r. side and in small of back;* in l. side, darting to occiput and scapula, preventing turning of head, afterwards < morning; drawing, in nape, < l. sde. *Stiffness* of l. side; *of nape* in afternoon; *of nape and l. side extending into ear, even during rest, not impeding movement.* Uneasiness or intermittent pinching in muscles, nape and in chest, with nausea.

Back.—Stitches; (extending upward through chest); from spine through upper abdomen to pit of stomach. Cutting from spine to pit of stomach. Dislocated feeling in middle of spine, < sudden bending to right. Boring in a spot. Pain in spots when sitting; P. as from long stooping, in evening after lying down. Bruised feeling. *Drawing pain when sitting.* Drawing along spine and calves, with weakness in feet. Soreness; in middle. Pulsation in spine when sitting. Heaviness and tension. Stiffness in spine as after standing bent a long time.

Scapulæ.—Twitching under l. Sticking between; on r.; under r.; burning, between S. when sitting. Tearing in l. Cutting under l.; from point of l.

through chest to edge of middle of sternum. Pressing between; on waking. Bruised pain. Constriction between S., hindering respiration and motion of arms. Drawing between.

Lumbar Region.—Twitching in l. at 2 P.M. Sticking between coccyx and anus at 7 P.M. when walking; close to spine when standing and leaning sideways; in l. side of vertebræ when walking, not affected by sitting; from l. side of sacrum into l. testicle; from sacral bones into side of pelvis; jerklike burning, in r. side close to sacrum, > violent rubbing. Cutting when walking. Sudden cramplike pain in sacrum if he moves his feet after standing long in one spot, he threatens to fall. Pain; in renal region; in sacrum on stooping; in vertebræ on leaning forward in sitting; in sacrum and lower half of spine, < bending body; in a spot in sacrum when lying, > motion. Bruised sensation, and in feet; in region and sacrum in morning after rising, < standing or turning trunk, > walking. Tensive pain in sacrum. Pressure outward in l. when sitting. Drawing pain in l. *Drawing in sacrum;* towards nates in morning on rising; in forenoon, with pressing; at noon; in muscles at noon when walking; < sitting; *painful, in sacrum, coccyx and thighs, which after sitting long prevented his standing erect.* Burning, then frequent burning micturition, next day the B. in renal region increased and was accompanied by drawing along ureter to vesica. Weakness when sitting, with pain in coccyx.

Extremities.—*Trembling of hand and foot.* Stretching; and uneasiness. Cracking in elbows, knees and ankles on stretching limbs. Sticking in shoulders and r. knee; in sole and metacarpus; in external malleolus, hip-joint, middle metacarpal bone, on inner edge of foot, in heel; in joints, with tearing; drawing, in r. upper to elbow and in r. thigh to knee. Tearing in l. upper arm, then in l. leg; in a spot in middle of r. thigh and in l. upper arm, < muscles; in outside of r. ankle, then in l. elbow, then drawing in inner side of l. upper thigh, then T. in second joint of r. thumb. Bruised sensation; in shoulders and thighs, with weariness; at times in shoulders, at times in thighs.

Drawing pains in hands and feet. Drawing; in joints of hands and feet; in inner surface of r. thigh, in r. knee, r. calf, bend of elbow, in popliteal spaces, < l.; hands and feet, then in forearm; l. calf, then from r. elbow to wrist; l. ankle, then in r. ulna, then on radial side of r. upper arm; r. leg, < outside towards ankle, and in r. hand, < thumb, at noon; in evening, < upper arm and forearm near wrist, with bruised sensation and dulness; during rest, < inner surface of upper part of l. thigh and forearm; < r. forearm, < movement; from r. wrist to tips of fingers and from r. calf to malleoli, with sensation as if that foot were lame, then drawing from r. elbow to wrist, then paralytic feeling in thighs; now here, now there; sudden; occasional; in slow accesses, in r. arm and thigh at 10 A.M.; painful, in second joint of l. thumb in morning during rest, the same in course of forenoon in almost all finger-joints during rest, for an instant in inner side of l. foot as far as sole, suddenly on inner side of l. metatarsus.

Tension now here, now there in extensor muscles of E. and nates, then heat in evening. Sticking beating in r. hand extending to tips of fingers and in anterior part of r. foot, in morning in bed. Weariness; in afternoon when sitting. Stiffness and heaviness. Falling asleep of arms and legs at night on waking.

Upper Extremities.—Axilla. Stitches in r. Drawing from l. to elbow; paroxysmal laming, in r.

Shoulder.—Swelling of r., with elevation and with inability to tie his cravat behind or hang his watch-chain around his neck. Cracking in joint on bending arm backward and inability to move arm on account of pain as if dislocated. *Stitches;* in joint; in r. deltoid when walking in open air; > walking in open air; in r. near clavicle, with tearing; drawing, in r. joint and in bend of elbow. Tearing in l.; in l. at night; in l., at times going to r. and nape. Cutting in r. joint. Pressings on r. Bruised pain in joints and upper arms. Drawing in r.; in l. in morning after rising, > afternoon; at night, and in upper arm, preventing his lying on that side, > next morning by warm wrappings, leaving a lame feeling in arm, at 9.30 A.M. attacks of tearing, returning in evening, and in r. arm, < forearm, a condition bordering on paralysis, with coldness; laming, in r. S. and thumb at 5 P.M., then tearing in palm near wrist; laming, in l. in evening, with tearing, next day in r. Throbbing in joint.

Arm.—Jerking during the day. Trembling after writing, with drawing pain. Raging pain from 3 A.M. till rising at 6 A.M. Burrowing drawing pain in periosteum of bone, extending to fingers, with pressure outward, and on deep pressure upon periosteum pain as if flesh were loosened from bone. Drawing in l.; in r. in afternoon; in bones. Tension in extensors of r. when writing. Weakness, with frequent tearing in them. Difficult to move, as if joints were dry. Paralytic feeling as if he had carried a weight.

Upper Arm.—Twitching in muscles of r.; pulselike, in r. in afternoon and evening, < r. deltoid. Stitches in r., > touch. Tearing in anterior tuberosity of l. humerus, < motion, increased to burning pain by touch; *drawing,* in r., also in morning, also in forenoon. Pain and weakness; P. now in r., now in l.; on pressure, as if flesh were loosened from humerus. Bruised pain; after dinner. Paralytic pain in muscles of middle of l. Drawing in l. in evening; intermittent, painful, in outer surface near olecranon. Heaviness from middle of l. to fingers.

Elbow.—Stitches; in r.; in l. several times during the day; < outer side of l., > touch; drawing from r. to wrist in evening in a crowded theatre. Drawing tearing from l. to two middle fingers. Boring. Pain in bone of l.; bruised, as if crushed and limp, and in wrists. Soreness in bend of r. in forenoon on extending it. Pain as after a knock, in prominences of r. Drawing in r. in forenoon. Tension in bend of r. when writing. Throbbing in l. during the day, in evening drawing in arm extending into fingers.

Forearm.—Sticking near elbow; in r. to finger-joints; in posterior surface of l. ulna near elbow an hour after dinner; intermittent tearing, on outer side of r.; tearing, from l. elbow to fingers, so that they were suddenly flexed; burning, above r. wrist. Tearing in bones of l. F. and wrist. Sticking tearing where l. ulna joins carpus; on inner side of l. from hand to elbow. Quick drawing boring through F. and metacarpal bone of index. Sore pain on r. Drawing pain in l.; in inner side of l. in forenoon, < rest. Drawing in r.; in inner side of l. in morning, and in r. fingers; along r. radius and into little finger at noon; sticking, on inner surface of l. towards wrist. Burning pain in muscles on moving hand quickly and strongly. Paralytic burning in muscles, extending to tips of fingers, > rest. Coursing and gurgling as if single drops of blood rolled over each other. Debility of r. in forenoon, > writing, with lameness and with trembling of r. hand, in which the veins swelled. Heaviness. Stiffness of l. as far as fingers.

Wrist.—Stitches in r.; in l. extending to tip of index; inward crosswise where radius and carpus unite, during rest. Tearing in l.; in r. carpus. Pain in r. as if dislocated. Crushing pain in inner side of l., in head of radius, in evening, with swelling and pain on touch. Paralytic feeling.

Hand.—Trembling when writing. Sticking in metacarpus; in middle bone of l.; in metacarpal bone of little finger; in l. palm in evening. Tearing; in r. metacarpus; in metacarpal bone of index; in metacarpal bone of little finger; in l. in evening; in dorsum of l. at noon when writing; paroxysms of T. and sticking, so violent in middle of r. elbow when writing that he had to give it up, in afternoon when driving in a carriage T. in l. forearm, < anterior tuberosity of humerus, that region becoming sensitive to touch, with pricking in l. hand, amelioration from sweat in evening in a crowded theatre. Cramplike pressure in l. between little and ring fingers on their inner sides, with heat of l. fingers, but coldness of l. metacarpus and r. hand. Tension in r., < thumb; in extensors of r. Dry feeling. Stiff and tired on motion.

Fingers.—Redness of balls of index, with swelling; of distal phalanges of three l. middle, with swelling and with stinging extending into tips at 5 P.M. Twitching in r. middle. Sticking; in tip of r. third; in r. thumb; nail of l. thumb; first joints; metacarpal joints of thumb and index; l. ring at 10 A.M.; tips of three l. middle in afternoon; above middle joint of middle, < bending finger; outward in third phalanx of index; drawing, in r. index and middle. Tearing in r. little; sticking, in little. Drawing pain in l. middle in afternoon. Drawing; in thumbs; in little; l. thumb; dorsum of r. ring; first joint of r. index; third joint of r. ring; r. thumb in morning on rising; l. index at 11 A.M.; l. thumb at 11 A.M.; r. index at 10.30 A.M., > movement; in first joint of r. thumb at noon, so that it was not easily moved; in r. at 4 P.M., then in r. elbow; in first joint of r. thumb at 7 P.M., > motion; > walking in open air, with pressure in l. upper arm; occasional, in r. thumb; intermittent painful, in l. thumb at 10 A.M.; sudden, in l. thumb and r. little in forenoon, > during touch; in thumbs extending into wrists. (Numbness.) *Crawling in tips of three l. middle as if asleep.*

Lower Extremities.—Staggering when walking in the air; S. after stooping. Burning stitches extending thence in every direction. Pain in l. in bed; drawing tensive, in r. at night, with heaviness and difficult motion. Weariness, < legs. Stiffness when walking, with heaviness.

Thigh.—Quivering above l. knee. Sticking high up on it; in l. as far as knee; in external tuberosity of l. when walking; paroxysmal, in l. acetabulum down to calf, deep in bone, when walking in the street; drawing, in head of l. femur. Tearing in r.; in r. hip-joint; posteriorly from r. ischium to popliteal space. Cramplike pain above l. knee when sitting. Pain as if dislocated in r. T. and leg on being carried forward when walking; in hip-joints and knees, < walking in open air. Pain in hip; anteriorly in lower third of r.; in l., as if it would break in evening on walking; circumscribed, in inner side, as after a long walk; as if beaten, above middle on walking in open air. Scraping soreness in inner side of r. Drawing; in inner side of l. upper, in r. hip and r. knee; through outer surface in afternoon; in evening; in hips, inward and downward towards genitals; in upper part of l., making walking difficult; through T. to head and thence to pit of stomach, with blackness before eyes and nausea; painful, extending from bend to internal surface of r. during rest. Tension in outside of r. extending into knee, < walking and bending; in hip-joint extending to groin and posteriorly to hollow of knee, < walking, > standing. *Painful laxity in hip-joints as if the capsules were weak*, as if they could not support the body when standing, > walking, with general weakness. Paroxysms of weakness in inner muscles. T. and leg fell asleep when sitting.

Knee.—Involuntary motion (with pain). Cracking. Sticking in l.; on outside of l.; in l. in morning in bed; on inner side of l. when standing; when walking; in l. patella on ascending stairs; on beginning to walk, < rising from a seat; in r. coming from popliteal space; in hollow, impeding stretching of leg; burning-biting, anteriorly in l.; burning-biting, near inner hamstring. Tearing in l.; in r. popliteal space on bending body to the right; in l. extending to middle of calf when sitting; drawing, in r. at 5 P.M. Pinching near and beneath r. patella on bending and stretching leg. Gnawing in patellæ and heels, latter < walking. Pain; in r. in forenoon when sitting, then coldness in K., then pressing and tension in heart, then coldness again in K.; throbbing, on outer side when sitting, < walking; bruised, on walking in evening, the weight of body seemed too great. Pressing on inner side of r.; P. inward on inner side when sitting. Drawing in r. Tension in r. popliteal space in afternoon; in K. and heels in evening, < rising after sitting long, afterwards only on walking. Strong extension impossible on account of a painful obstacle in popliteal spaces. Weakness; lasting longest in l.

Leg.—(Shaft of tibia swollen.) Sticking beneath knee; under r. knee; in r. tendo-achillis; in tendo-achillis above heel; in bones from tarsus to knee. Tearing; in r. tendo-achillis; downward in r. tibia all day; downward in l.; in r. shin-bone from knee down and from tarsus to knee. Intermittent pinching in calves; periodical, in middle of l. calf, as from pressure of a convex button. Pain in r.; in r. at night, so that he must lie on l. side; in r. twice during the day, felt next morning after rising, and a spot next to tibia, near a varicose dilatation, smarted as if sore, was red and sensitive to touch, pain again as if sore on its upper surface in evening. Burning pain on inner side of r. in afternoon; sticking, in external tuberosity of l. tibia, beginning when sitting, < pressure. Bruised pain; in r. shin-bone. Drawing pain in l. shin-bone at 9 P.M.; paroxysmal, downward in r. Drawing in r.; in r. calf all day. Tension in flexor surface of r.; in r. in forenoon, > dinner, with pain in skin as if ulcerated; in r. at noon when walking; in r., with weight; like weariness. Pressure outward in tibia. Weakness; *of l. when sitting, changing into cutting in muscles of calf when walking*, which returned paroxysmally when sitting. Heaviness; of r. in evening, with burning; of r., with burning on inner surface.

Ankle.—Stitches in l.; in r. malleolus; like bites of insects in bend; burning, near r. outer malleolus during rest. Tearing inside r. in afternoon; sticking, in r. in forenoon when walking. Pain as from a false step, in r. outer malleolus on walking. Benumbing pain in r. inner malleolus. Drawing pains below r. inner malleolus at 5 P.M.; sharp, in l. inner malleolus, gradually extending into calf. Tension in r. when walking. Compression in region of l. malleoli.

Foot.—Back of F. and toes swollen, red, painful as if numb, with tension on motion. Red spot on dorsum, impeding walking. Jerking up (with pain); clawing J. in soles as after a long walk. Stitches in l. sole near great toe; in middle metatarsal bones; in heels; l. heel and great toe; heel and ball of r. foot in evening; outward in middle of sole; tearing, in a corn. Tearing in r.; outer border of r. sole; r. metatarsal bones; r. middle metatarsal bone. Cutting in the joint on back of l. when walking, then warmth. Pinching in dorsum of l.; intermittent P. near metatarsal bone of little toe. Ulcerative pain in soles on stepping. Drawing in r. heel at 10 A.M. Weakness; of l. when sitting; of l. sole when sitting; when walking; of l. on going out; of l. when walking in the room, with falling asleep of it; with lameness; of r. sole as after a long journey and as if bruised, when sitting and walking. Heaviness of r.; H. in evening, with tension, so that walking was painful; and coldness. *Falling asleep of l.*, > walking in open air; of l. sole when sitting. Pain in heel as if asleep in morning on rising. Feeling of paralysis in l. in afternoon when sitting.

Toes.—Shining, red, swollen, itching, and after rubbing burning. Stitches in l. great; and fourth and little; l. fourth, l. sole and r. thigh; noon and evening on bending body to l. side; superficial, in tips of fourth and little; tearing, in sides of nails. Tearing in r. great, and in tarsus; in l. little. Pain in r. middle; drawing, in great on waking. Drawing in great; l. great; in all, extending into leg; cramplike, in distal phalanx of r. great, less when walking than when sitting, with warmth; painful, in r. great towards evening. Feeling in little as if skin were pulled in spots.

Clinical.—Sciatica of l. side from fright. Toe-nails crumble, are very brittle.

Skin.—Wartlike excrescences *on back of r. hand, on chin and other places; on hands*, in shape of a truncated cone, smooth, in epidermis, later the largest were rough and split, the larger ones became depressed in centre. Warts on hands; on backs of hands and fingers, the old horny ones were painful on touch and washing, with red areola, afterwards there were four sets, the oldest still with red areola, the next rough and irregular, the smaller ones of the second crop smooth and shaped like truncated cones and the third crop very small, old ones less painful and the areola paler on appearance of menses.

Blue about clavicles. Red streak on forehead over root of nose. Red mottled spot on l. forearm; on back of r. foot. *Red itching spots* on inside of r. arm near wrist in evening; *round, on inside of l. forearm, with white vesicles* raised upon it, which burst, poured out a clear lymph and left a yellowish crust. Eruption on an inflamed surface on l. side of chin; scabby E. on cheek, not far from corner of mouth. Blotch with red areola on dorsum of r. foot, making walking in boots difficult, changing to a dark red elevation with a lighter areola, later another blotch in the still existing red spot, impeding walking.

Pimples over face; red, in a streak extending forward on sides of neck, with soreness on touch; red, full of serum, itching, behind l. wing of nose; painful, in raphe of perineum; painless, near raphe of perineum; itching, on chin; itching, with burning on touch and after scratching, on r. nates, also on knees. Tubercle on inner side of r. thigh, *feeling like a wart*, dark red, *areola bright red, tip dingy white*, pain on touching or moving it, next day filled with pus, later changed to brown scab; *red T. between scrotum and r. thigh;* inflamed, on face; painless, in sulcus between nates; painful, in middle of l. eyebrow; painful inflamed, on r. side of forehead, also on various parts. Node on l. side of nape near border of hair, next day a rough place; white, on calf, with itching in and around them, and after rubbing sticking-burning pain. (Nettle-rash.)

Condylomata about anus, sore even to touch; C. bleeding profusely; *by anus, with stitches when walking;* burning and stinging; itching stinging; burning pain on touch; tickling; tickling itching. Pustules between eyebrows, with itching; red, bleeding on scratching, above lip; like chicken-pox on knee; like chicken-pox, with red areola, on thighs, elbows and forearms. Boil, with red areola and itching, near sacrum; B. behind r. ear, formed a scab which exuded a glutinous moisture, this fell off and another formed, it was sensitive to touch. Ulcer on back.

Stitches on l. elbow; *in various parts changing to burning;* biting, on r. patella, with jerking; in spots, leaving itching. Sensitive to cool air. Tension in nape on moving head. Biting on whole body. Crawling on toes; l. toes, with pain on treading; corrosive, on nose.

Itching on face; forepart of neck; lower part of sacrum; in hollow below os coccygis; on r. knee, l. shoulder, scrotum and other parts; in distinct points on inside of thigh and on hairy parts of genitals, also with scraping; general, on going to bed, < abdomen; in spots, with burning pain after rubbing; *as from flea-bites on abdomen, back, arms and legs,* < evening and night. *Sticking itching on different parts,* < breasts; on chest and sides of neck towards noon; over whole body at night till after 1 A.M., > rubbing. Crawling itching over whole body; in upper arm, then stitching in a spot. Voluptuous itching between r. toes; on inner side of back of r. foot.

Clinical.—Fungoid excrescences from various parts of the body, which bleed easily on the slightest touch. Molluscum, tubercular, umbilicated. Numerous crops of warts, and condylomata, which bleed readily. Lupus. Varicose ulcers. Pemphigus, eczema. It was used by Bœnninghausen in variola as soon as the vesicles filled; he believed it caused rapid desiccation and prevented scars.

Sleep.—Yawning; in evening. **Sleepiness;** all day; in morning, afternoon and evening; in morning, with disinclination to rise, fretfulness and weariness; in afternoon, the eyes close when sitting; towards evening, without ability to sleep; in evening, with the fever; before dinner; after dinner; when sitting; early, but sleep uneasy with dreams, and waking early in morning with fretfulness and disinclination to rise. Sleeps much during the day.

Sleeplessness; before midnight and waking about 4 A.M.; before midnight, from emissions of flatus, itching and burning in anus, flying stitches in rectum and repeated micturition; after midnight, was not sleepy in the morning; till towards morning; with restlessness; with restlessness and coldness, if he slumbers for a moment *he dreams of dead people.* Late falling asleep and early waking next morning; sleep came late and was unrefreshing. Unrefreshing sleep, interrupted by terrible dreams of the dead; U., disturbed by starting and horrible images. Frequent waking. Uneasiness at night, with apprehension, could scarcely sleep, with coldness of legs, which are covered with cold sweat. *Restless sleep;* before midnight; on account of heat; *with dreams;* with odorless sweat; interrupted by straining cough; and awake from 2 till 3 A.M., then frequent waking; with moaning; with frequent waking and passing from one dream into another, with an emission. Quiet talking in sleep. Cries. Full of dreams and starting up. Sudden bounding up in abdomen during siesta at 5 P.M., with starting in whole upper part of body as from fright. Sudden anxiety after half an hour's sleep, then sweat, then sleep, but continual starting up again.

Dreams; immediately on falling asleep; long, caused by conversation in evening, with deep reflection, he relies upon his good conscience when accused of a crime; lively and pleasant; vivid; restless; heavy, harassing; frightful, from which he woke in heat; of danger of death when lying on l. side. Anxious D.; with loud cries; on falling asleep, he felt thrusts in l. side, woke and gasped for air. Confused; about absurd things. *Voluptuous;* with pollution; of coition, but without emission, on waking a painful erection.

Fever.—Coldness; all day; all day, < back, with weakness, in evening headache, heat of skin, full, rapid pulse, sticking in r. hypochondrium (< respiration), extending into sacral region, so that she went to bed, then heat, then quiet sleep; every morning, without thirst; in forenoon, also without thirst; all the forenoon, with internal shivering and with confusion of head; in forenoon, alternating in heat in afternoon; at noon, < limbs; at 3 P.M.; every day from 6 till 7.30 P.M., with external heat of body, dryness of mouth and thirst; in evening, without thirst, pulse 100, full and hard; in evening, passing into heat on lying down; in night on appearance of menses, next day alternating with heat, with weakness even to falling (for several days past heat and sweat during dinner), sleepless after 3 A.M. on account of heat, coldness before dinner, next afternoon heat when walking, in evening coldness in back, heat in head, drowsiness and thirst; after dinner; with headache; with thirst; with vomiturition; with numbness of l. foot. Alternating with heat in forenoon. Creeping chill; during dinner. *Shaking chill, with yawning, the warm air seems cold and the sun has no power to warm him;* S. chill without external coldness; at 3 A.M., then thirst, then sweat, except on head, which was only warm; on l. side of body, which feels cold, in evening in bed.

Shivering; in the daytime; in evening in bed; when dressed; *from slightest uncovering in warm air,* with or without gooseflesh, while hands and face were warm; with dryness of throat, painful deglutition, nausea and illness driving him to bed early; with want of appetite, peevishness and weak, small pulse, she now took Nux vom., after an hour shaking chill for half an hour, then heat; gradually extending over whole body at night, then sweat; creeping, < back, with hot face; creeping over body in evening, with agreeable warmth of body, cold fingers, < l., without thirst, with sensation of gooseflesh; beginning in head; in back.

Coldness of face, with heat of forehead, hands warm and their veins distended; C. running from nape to small of back on lying down, < movement, > rising. Coldness of back not > warmth of stove; of back in afternoon and evening, with debility and stiffness in limbs; in evening, alternating with heat in it. Cool limbs in evening, with redness of face, but in evening after Cocc. 30th sweat and amelioration. *Cold hands; and internal heat in face;* hands and feet in forenoon, hands purple; H., feet and anterior surface of thigh when sitting in a warm room. Coldness of tips of fingers, with external heat of rest of body, without thirst; C. of tips of fingers, the rest of hands lukewarm, rest of body hot to touch, and internal heat in face. Cold feet internally in night, with external warmth of them; after going to bed; after going to bed, with anxiety, trembling of heart, then sweat.

Heat; in morning, and chill in evening, then heat and sleepiness; towards morning, with sweat; in evening, then creeping chilliness, with cold hands; in evening; *with activity of mind and thirst;* with vertigo; with feverish pulse; dry, at night, with uneasy sleep. Feeling as if sweat would break out. Orgasm of blood, heart beats violently, on ascending stairs she must rest often; O. every evening, throbbing in vessels on every motion, > sitting.

Heat in forehead in forenoon; externally in a spot in occiput, corresponding with which H. and pressure in brain. Heat in face; all day; in evening, with redness of cheeks; when sitting, with redness, without thirst; of l. cheek, with redness of it and with chilliness on back on motion, fingers dead; *flushing, without thirst;* sudden, with redness. H. externally over r. lower ribs. In lumbar region. Burning in r. leg in morning; in r. leg at noon; in skin of r. leg; inner side of r. leg; in hollow of l. knee as if an eruption would break out. On dorsum of r. foot. In corns. In spots under skin, < r. side of chest.

Sweat in evening after warm soup, then diminution of pain in nape; at night; on all covered parts at night as soon as he fell asleep; in axillæ; on hands and feet; *feet,* < toes; inner side of thighs and legs on waking; thighs near genitals when sitting; cold; sour-smelling, almost every night. Dry sensation in skin, < hands.

Clinical.—Extremely fetid sweat on feet.

Trillium.

A tincture is made of the fresh root of Trillium pendulum, Ait.

Weakness. Aggravation at night and in morning; of pain on motion and after eating; and on l. side. Amelioration of pain by exercise in open air. Melancholy. Repugnance to conversation. Irritability, disposition to get angry at trifles. Fear that he is going to be sick, anguish, agitation, tossing about, impossibility of keeping still. Headache, < noise, walking or coughing; H.

in l. temporal fossa, < noise; in forehead, > bending forward, returning on becoming erect. Weariness of head when walking. Confusion of head. Vertigo; < morning on rising; in attacks, with tottering. Pain as if eyeballs were too large and would fall out of their sockets. Burning in inner canthus, with lachrymation. Vision blurred, everything looks bluish.

Grumbling toothache, with dull pain in face. Tongue and gums feel greasy. Salivation. Taste foul; < morning on rising; T. insipid and appetite lost. Pungent sensation in throat. Continual inclination to drink ice-water. Disgust for everything except cold water. Nausea, with empty eructations; N., with aching in stomach. Pain in epigastrium; crampy, in stomach, with pinchings, gnawing and fulness; the pains in stomach < eating and morning. Sensation of contractions in stomach. Swelling of abdomen, as in ascites, with sensation as if the contents were drawn against spine. Abdominal parietes flabby, with goneness, a want of support in front and intermittent lancinations extending backward, causing one to bend forward. Flatulence, with grumbling in abdomen. Diarrhœa painless, tinged with blood. Constipation, then watery, offensive diarrhœa. Cutting in urethra when urinating. Urine copious, offensive. Itching of genitals, < scratching.

Sensation of a foreign substance in larynx, causing continual cough. Difficult breathing, feeling as if chest were bound up. Palpitation, with anxiety. Pain in l. shoulder, extending into hand; crampy, in muscles of arms and calves; crampy, in fingers when writing. Sleeplessness, with tossing about. Sleep disturbed by dreams, dreams of festivities, sleigh-rides, etc. Fever during pain in abdomen, then sweat. Head and face feel hot. Skin hot and dry, with itching and burning, < scratching.

Clinical.—Hæmorrhagic diathesis. Hæmorrhages from the kidneys, nose, uterus; blood is generally dark and clotted. Threatening abortion; it has arrested numerous cases, with gushing of bright blood on the least movement, especially in women who are subject to too profuse or too frequent menstruation. Hæmorrhages from fibroid tumors. Prolapsus uteri, with great bearing down. copious yellow, stringy leucorrhœa, characteristics of the menses, Uterine hæmorrhage with a marked *sensation as though the hips and back were falling to pieces,* > *tight bandages.*

Trombidium Muscæ Domesticæ.

A tincture is made of the red acarus, found under the wings of the common house-fly.

Generalities and Mind.—Rheumatic pains in l. shoulder, arm, knee and region of heart. Inability to keep quiet. Weakness. Felt better in evening; better in open air. Talkative during the day; and disposed to be contrary. Inability to collect ideas, absence of ideas. Loss of memory.

Head.—Oppressive aching. Dulness in forenoon. Congestion in evening, with red face and ears. Lightness. Dizziness; on every attempt to rise from bed, with faintness. Heavy, sometimes sharp pains in temples, extending over forehead, at 9.30 P.M., < l. side. Pain in l. mastoid process on waking at 7 A.M.; in l. side of head at 10 P.M., < shaking head and walking. Shooting above r. temple at 3 P.M.; near r. parietal eminence at 11 A.M. Itching at 7 A.M., < vertex and occiput.

Eyes, Ears and Nose.—Redness of internal part of conjunctiva, similar to a pterygium. Lachrymation in open air. Itching at r. inner canthus at 9 P.M. Shooting in ears in afternoon, < r.; frequently in r. during the day and evening; in r. in forenoon, < swallowing or blowing nose. Itching in ears after rising. Nose obstructed on rising. Fluent coryza in open air and on eating. Mucous discharge from nose, worse during dinner. Dryness of nose in evening, with scabs. Nosebleed in morning; afternoon.

Mouth, Throat and Stomach.—Aching in l. decayed tooth on waking at 7 A.M., renewed by breakfast, lasting till noon; in evening; in evening from reading aloud, preventing sleep almost all night, lasting next day, < lying down, eating, talking and cold air, > warm drinks, > Staph. Tongue coated white. Throat sore on r. side. Appetite lost. Eructations after meals; tasting of the ingesta. (Vomiting after breakfast, thought it was from drinking coffee.) Griping in pit of stomach, < dinner.

Abdomen.—Flatulent distention; at 10 P.M.; at 11 P.M., causing pain. Shooting, beginning in l. hypochondrium. *Griping on rising, obliging stool, which was brown and diarrhœic and which relieved the pain until after breakfast, when it returned with greater violence and induced a second stool, with tenesmus causing prolapsus, then burning about anus; sudden G. at* 1.30 P.M., < *l. side, which induced a stool,* the stool passed quickly, then tenesmus and prolapsus, then pain as if excoriated, the stool relieved the pain only temporarily, as it returned with such violence as to force sweat from all parts, abated gradually, < dinner, causing another stool of soft brown fæces mixed with mucus, then tenesmus, prolapsus, weakness, < knees. Pain in morning, with urging to stool; P. at 3 P.M., > diarrhœa; on eating, with desire for stool; < pressure; darting, at 10 A.M., < above r. hip; as from incarcerated flatus at 3 P.M.; sore, waking about 5 A.M., with urging to stool; heavy, in forenoon, < drinking cold water and eating dinner, the same pain next day, < pressure. Pain in hepatic region, just under ends of floating ribs; in forenoon, sore to pressure; sore, in evening, with sensitiveness to touch. Darting pain in liver at 10 P.M.

Clinical.—Congestion of the liver, with internal sore pain in the abdomen and urgent loose stools on rising from bed, during the stool sharp pain in l. side, shooting downward; the pain is not > stool; with the stool tenesmus, chilliness in the back; followed by great prostration, coldness; the stools return after dinner and after supper, but not after breakfast.

Anus and Stool.—Stitches upward along l. side of anus. Diarrhœa, with straining and expulsion of flatus; D. at 5 A.M., during the day several small, loose stools, always preceded by sore pain in intestines, with the stool tenesmus and shivering along the back, on following days several stools daily, mostly small, consisting of mucus with tenesmus, > Merc.; *light brown D. at* 10 A.M. *and* 2 P.M., *preceded and followed by pain in abdomen, straining with the second stool.* Constipation, afterwards pappy stool.

Clinical.—Dysenteric stools, worse from 4 P.M. till 4 A.M., with a dry skin, etc. Dysentery, with brown, thin discharges, sometimes bloody, sometimes with violent colic and severe tenesmus.

Respiratory Organs and Chest.—Hoarseness. Hacking cough from irritation in throat. Cutting to right of lower part of sternum at 7 A.M. Sharp pain in lower part of chest at 7 A.M. Throbbing all over chest from 9 till 11 A.M.

Heart and Pulse.—Shooting in region of heart at

7.30 A.M. Pain in region of heart at 4 P.M., < a long breath; darting rheumatic, in region. Pulse 100 and full at 9 A.M. Intermittent pulse.

Extremities.—Shooting in different joints during the day; in joints in afternoon and evening; in l. heel and wrist; in phalangeal joints of third finger and in l. knee, in forenoon. Heaviness. Shoulder, shooting in r. joint at 2 P.M.; shocks in l. joint in afternoon and next forenoon; pain in l.; rheumatic pain in l. Forearm, aching down l.; pain in bones of l. at noon; frequent pains in l. in forenoon; intermittent pain in l. at 11 P.M., then shooting. Shooting in a spot on inner side of dorsum of wrist at 4 P.M.; in r. wrist at noon, intermittent at first; in phalangeal joints of second l. finger at 8.30 A.M.; in palmar surface of ungual phalanx of r. thumb; intermittent, in finger-joints, elbows and wrists in forenoon, also in r. finger-joints, elbow and wrist in forenoon. Pain in l. hip-joint on rising from a seat and beginning to walk, causing limping, usually > a few steps. Thigh, tearing in lower part of l. at 2.30 P.M.; flying, sharp pains in l. at 9 A.M. Knee, rheumatic pain in l.; intermittent pain in r. at 9 A.M. Boring in r. tibia in forenoon. Pain in inner part of l. ankle at 12 P.M., < bearing weight on it. Tearing in l. tarsus at 1 P.M. Shooting in r. ankle at 3 P.M.; in l. tarsus at 6 P.M.; in outer side of r. metatarsus at 3 P.M.; in inner side of l. heel.

Skin, etc.—Pimples on nape in evening. Itching in spots on chin and among whiskers; in evening, and about neck. Constant inclination to gape through the day; in afternoon. Sleepiness. Restless sleep. Wakefulness after 4 A.M., with restlessness. Lewd dreams. Chilliness at night, < morning on waking. Fever in afternoon, with pulsation in arteries of head and aching in occiput and small of back. Burning in pinnæ of ears in evening, < r.

Uranium Nitricum.

Pure nitrate of Uranium is triturated for use.

Generalities and Mind.—Feeling as if he had taken cold. Languor; on rising from bed. Ill humor; and not feeling well all day.

Head.—(Aching caused by a violent cold from exposure to wet, with sore throat for four days, leaving me well except cough in morning on rising, > expectoration.) Heaviness on waking. Vertigo twice in evening. Pain in forehead; over l. eye; in evening, and in occiput; in temple; in occipital protuberances; in occiput on waking. Neuralgia on posterior edge of l. temporal bone (formerly on r.) from 2 till 4 P.M., leaving dull aching, N. woke me at 1 A.M. that night, lasted an hour and prevented sleep, ill from the pain during the next day, two days later pain in the old place (r. side) came on gradually, > dinner.

Eyes, Nose, Etc.—*Stye in l. upper lid.* (Œdema of lower lids worse than usual.) Shooting from r. orbit to occipital protuberance in evening. Itching in nose. L. nostril stuffed. Dry coryza. Painless ulcer, with one elevated side, in mouth opposite l. anterior upper molar, more tender next day, < evening. Acid saliva. Hawking of tenacious mucus. Contracted feeling in throat.

Stomach.—Appetite lost. Eructations; tasteless; putrid at 11 and 3 o'clock. Indigestion in afternoon a quarter of an hour before dinner, with gnawing sinking at cardiac end of stomach, not hungry nor faint. Dyspepsia, flatus after food, acidity, pain from cardiac end of stomach to suprarenal region, > movement, lasted all day, bowels slightly moved, pale clay-colored fæces (query, if from the drug, as I had had similar but slighter attacks), afterwards epigastric pain as above returned, > food, with occasional twisting-screwing feeling lower down.

Clinical.—Vomiting of food, with agonizing, burning pain in the stomach, and soreness, apparently from an ulcer, associated with crops of styes on the eyelids. Enormous appetite and thirst, but the patient emaciates, with this there is excessive flow of urine. Repeated cases of ulceration of the stomach have been cured.

Abdomen and Stool.—Flatus. Borborygmi. Sharp colic, with tenesmus and with raw feeling in rectum, afterwards in sleep unconscious seminal emission. Urging in rectum and bladder, waking me at 2 A.M., borborygmi, soft stool. Stool twice in one day. Constipation.

Urinary Organs.—Sore pain in vesical region in evening. Burning in urethra. Urine contained bile. Urine high-colored, a few lithates on standing, afterwards it contained mucus, here and there a cast, uric acid crystals (uncertain pus or blood-cells in two specimens out of five), later a thick mucous sediment, acid in passing, soon becoming alkaline and offensive, many uric acid crystals and lithate of ammonia, with pavement epithelium, no sugar or albumen, later muco-purulent sediment after standing all night, deposits of urates and mucus, phosphates abundant, muco-purulent appearance on standing, this material was dissolved by boiling; average sp. gr. increased, maximum diminished, average quantity unchanged, maximum quantity decreased, minimum quantity increased; sp. gr. sometimes diminished, sometimes increased, sometimes acid, sometimes albuminous, sometimes much mucus, phosphates sometimes scanty, sometimes copious, some days frequent micturition, one day desire to urinate immediately after micturition, one day fishy odor, one day urine high-colored and turbid, more chlorides than usual, average of sp. gr. increased, maximum of sp. gr. increased, average of quantity increased, minimum of quantity unchanged; slight sediment, a few crystals of urate of soda, here and there a dumb-bell, very indistinct and only in two specimens out of five. "It produces acute parenchymatous nephritis; sugar is found in the urine, this generally does not come on until after albumen has appeared; glycosuria is very characteristic and persistent; it also produces at times a large amount of oxalate of lime."

Clinical.—Numerous cases of diabetes are reported cured with this drug; it seems particularly indicated by the excessive thirst, emaciation, and, perhaps, also tympanitis.

Chest, Etc.—Intermittent pain radiating from l. side of ensiform cartilage, < fasting. Loins stiff. Night restless, with shivering and heat.

Urtica Urens.

A tincture is made of the stinging nettle.

Generalities.—Symptoms returned at the same time every year.

Head.—Aching, < over eyes; A., with stitches in region of spleen. Fulness, sensation of rush of blood and dulness; F. all day, with giddiness, like a rush of blood. Pain in r. side of sinciput; and in r. side of face, extending to malar-bone; over r. eye and in eyeball; over eyes during the day and evening; neuralgic, in r. side of forehead and face at 9 P.M. Stinging pain in r. parietal bone forcing me to rub and press it. Pain in occiput and over eyes.

Eyes.—Pain in r.; in l. at 3 P.M.; in balls as from a blow, with feeling as if sand were in eyes. Feel weak and sore.

Throat.—Burning; with frequent hawking of frothy mucus; causing cough, expectoration scanty, frothy.

Stomach and Abdomen.—Nausea. Soreness of abdomen at 10 A.M. when lying, and on pressure sound as if full of water. Pain in l. hypochondrium at 10 P.M.

Anus and Stool.—Hæmorrhoid, with raw burning in anus during and after stool, and in afternoon and evening itching and burning. Stool omitted in morning, but at 2 P.M. scanty dysenteric stool, a greenish-brown slime, with urging and tenesmus, afterwards constipation, then small stool with straining, later dysentery, frequent urging, small painful stool, mucus mixed with white matter like boiled white of eggs, at times a little blood, pain in abdomen for a week; S. omitted for three days, then six hours after Nux vom. a natural stool, four hours later several dysenteric stools of whitish slime, with pain around umbilicus, then for the next five days daily two to four white and yellow stools mixed with mucus, with colic and tenesmus.

Chest and Pulse.—Sore feeling as from a blow in l. side of chest; intermittent soreness in r. side during the day. Pulse accelerated by six beats.

Extremities.—Rheumatic pain in arms and ankles, < r. arm. Pain in r. deltoid, < 9 P.M., could not put on his coat alone; cramplike, in r. deltoid in evening, < rotating arm inward, with soreness to touch, with rheumatic feeling in l. arm, next day aggravation of the pain in r. arm by lying on it, and on moving it a stitch darted through the arm, the pain extended over front of humerus, and at times a similar but lighter pain in l. arm, muscles of r. arm feel sore as if bruised, cannot raise or stretch r. arm on account of pain, afterwards rheumatic stiffness and pain in r. wrist, later rheumatic pain in l. arm, wrist and fingers. Stiff soreness on inside of l. knee.

Skin.—*Itching swellings all over fingers and hands*, resembling "bold hives;" lumps and red spots on hands and fever blisters on lips, itching. *Heat in skin of face, arms, shoulders and chest, with formication, numbness and itching*, lips, nose and ears swollen, lids so œdematous that they could scarcely be opened, after awhile upper part of body as far as navel œdematous and pale, transparent blisters filled with serum and looking like sudamina, becoming confluent and making the skin look wrinkled, lids closed, forming transparent, here and there bluish shining swellings as large as hen's eggs, the woman, who had had no children for three years and a half and had nursed none of her children, had *at first great swelling of breasts, which discharged serum, then copious milk*, urine suppressed for eight days, everything disappeared with desquamation.

Sleep and Fever.—Drowsiness when reading. General heat on getting into bed, with soreness over abdomen.

Clinical.—It has been found valuable for absence of milk after confinement (Ricinus). Pruritus of the vulva; of the scrotum; of the perineum. General urticaria, with intolerable itching and burning, especially from eating shell-fish. Whooping cough has been cured.

Usnea Barbata.

A tincture is made of the fresh lichen.

Headache, I had to go to the house, I could feel the blood press to the brain, my wife worked over me and I got to sleep, next morning felt well. At 8 P.M., pain (l. head) went down to sacrum, increased all the evening, and bursting headache in front. 9-12 P.M., sharp, shooting, steady pain in back. Sleep from after midnight till 8 A.M. Sore next day all over. Headache comes and goes slowly.

Clinical.—"Cured several cases of headache; the pain is over the entire head, or front head, with feeling as if the temples would burst, or the eyes would burst out of the sockets; I have always used the tincture."

Ustilago.

A tincture is made of the fresh ripe fungus, "cornsmut," Ustilago maidis.

Allies.—*Secale corn.*, Sabina.

Generalities.—Neuralgic pains in forehead, hands and feet. Rheumatic pains all up and down l. side, with cutting in l. knee and calf if I pressed any weight upon toes or flexed knee with any weight upon it; R. pains in muscles of arms, hands, fingers and small of back, those in back < walking. Symptoms of a cold. Malaise as if I had taken cold; felt *sick* with a cold, continual watery flow from nose and eyes, with occasional chills. Sick all over, could scarcely tell where. Languor; during the day, with headache, < noon, and with burning frontal headache at 9 P.M.; in morning on rising; on waking early, yet could not rest; in morning on rising; at 2 P.M. Faint feeling at 11 A.M. in a warm lecture-room; F. spells beginning in epigastrium, with small pains in hypochondrium and bowels.

Mind.—Depression of spirits in afternoon. Could not bear to see or talk with any one. Irritability, < being asked a question or to repeat anything. The day seemed like a dream.

Head.—Aching; all the morning; at 7 A.M.; in evening, < forehead; < walking. Vertigo in attacks, sometimes with double vision, sometimes white specks blot out everything else, later attacks of V. with internal heat. Frontal pain in morning; in forenoon, with smarting in eyes; all day, with aching distress in eyeballs and with fulness in head in morning; with distress in epigastrium; sharp. Prickling in l. temple. Loss of hair.

Eyes.—Attacks of twitching, and eyes appear to look (revolve) in circles and dart from one object to another. Spasms, with vanishing of vision and head seems to whirl. Aching and lachrymation. Hot feeling on closing lids. Weakness. Lachrymation in open air. Lids agglutinated in morning. Vision of spots dancing to and fro.

Nose and Face.—Boil in r. nostril. Dryness of nostrils in forenoon, with dry feeling in skin. Bright epistaxis, > pressure. Sudden pallor when sitting and in evening.

Mouth.—Sometimes looseness of teeth. Aching all day in decayed upper first and second molars. Tongue coated in morning. Prickling in tongue, with feeling as if something were pressing the roots upward, with dryness of nostrils. Salivation; bitter; thin, bitter. Taste coppery; in morning; slimy coppery; slimy coppery in morning; slimy; slimy, with burning distress in stomach.

Throat.—L. tonsil enlarged, congested, dark reddish, r. painful on swallowing at 2 P.M., l. painful at 9 P.M., next morning congestion of l. extending along Eustachian tube and causing pain in ear. Lancinations in r. tonsil (fauces were somewhat inflamed when the medicine was taken), next day fauces hotter and more sensitive to motion. Roughness of fauces. Dryness of fauces, with burning dryness in stomach; D. of fauces, with difficulty in swallowing, feeling of a lump behind larynx, later frequent efforts to swallow, with feeling as if something had lodged in fauces, afterwards irritation of fauces, and on swallowing feeling of a lump in larynx. Burning in œsophagus.

Stomach.—Appetite craving; poor. Thirst; at night. Eructations of sour fluid; of sour food. Cutting. Pain; frequently in afternoon; on full inspiration; in epigastrium, with drawing pain in joints of fingers; in spells, and in small intestines, with distress in r. hypochondrium; burning, in cardiac region. Distress; in forenoon; in afternoon, > supper.

Abdomen. — Periodical cutting in umbilical and hypogastric regions, at 6 P.M., > 8 P.M. by a constipated stool, afterwards grumbling pains in whole abdomen. Pain occasionally; P. in r. lobe of liver; in umbilicus; umbilicus before natural stool; l. groin when walking; drawing, in r. hypochondrium all day. Distress in umbilicus and r. hypochondrium.

Stool.—Natural at 4 A.M. Loose at 4 A.M., with pain and rumbling in abdomen. Light-colored diarrhœa. Soft, next day dry, lumpy, two days later black, dry, lumpy. Constipated.

Urinary Organs.—Tenesmus of bladder and incontinence of urine. Urging, urine light-colored. No desire, but uneasiness. Urine increased; scanty, red; acid, high-colored.

Sexual Organs.—Relaxed. Erections when reading at 4 o'clock; frequently during the day and night. Scrotum relaxed and cold sweat on it. Pain in testicles, < r.; P. in testicles, sometimes neuralgic; in paroxysms, sometimes causing faintish feeling. Desire depressed. *Yellow and offensive leucorrhœa. Tenderness of l. ovary, with pain and swelling.* (*Aching distress at mouth of womb.*) Menses that had just ceased returned, bright-colored, soreness and bearing down in l. side preceding the flow and partially ceasing with it; *M. copious, bright red, not coagulating easily* (in a woman who thought she had passed the climacteric, as there had been no discharge for over a year), it stopped as suddenly as it began, no pain, only faintness and confused feeling in head.

Clinical.—Uterine hæmorrhage, bright red, partly thin, partly clotted; the uterus is soft and spongy, and suffers from passive congestion. Uterine hæmorrhage, with pain extending down to the knees. In the uterine region soreness, especially on l. side, with ovarian irritability, bearing-down pain, the pains often shoot down the legs. It has proved curative in amenorrhœa. At the period sharp pains from hip to hip, followed by expulsive pains. Numerous cases of menorrhagia. Left ovarian neuralgia, with habitual profuse menstruation, which is followed by brownish and yellowish leucorrhœa. Membranous dysmenorrhœa, lancinating pains shooting down the leg. Chronic uterine hæmorrhage, with persistent oozing of dark blood, with black clots. It is especially suited to the climacteric period and to tall, slim women, with clear, white skin. Pain in l. mammary region in intermenstrual period; ovarian congestion, with burning pains.

Chest.—Spasmodic tearing at top of l. side and passing to sixth or seventh rib, at 3 P.M. when standing and reading, < breathing. Pain in l. infraclavicular region in morning; drawing, in l. imframammary region, waking me at 3 A.M., > turning on back from r. side. Aching, burning distress in sternum and under it in stomach, with neuralgic pains. Oppression along median line. Constriction, with pain. Heat and pressure.

Heart.—Sudden flying pain from it to stomach, arresting breathing.

Back.—Pain; extending to extreme end of spine; in lumbar region; in region of r. kidney, < sitting still, next day in region of l. kidney, > moving about, with heat, fulness, soreness on deep pressure (but it relieved the pain), with uneasiness in l. thigh, frequent desire to urinate, stream very small, the following day it requires considerable effort of will to empty the bladder, which is done slowly, pain and soreness in l. loin continue; heavy, in lumbar region, in bed with uneasiness about bladder (had had no desire to urinate on going to bed), woke early in morning with distended feeling in bladder, micturition slow and difficult, urine scarcely colored, pain in B. < next night, < lying on face, > lying on r. side; bearing down, in sacral region as in dysmenorrhœa, changing to l. ovarian region and gradually extending through hip.

Extremities.—Cutting in bones of r. hand and foot. Frequent rheumatic symptoms in arms, fingers and legs. Pain in shoulder-joints; rheumatic, in muscles of r. shoulder. Intermittent numb tingling sensation in r. arm and hand every day. Pain in r. elbow, < motion. Stitching along metacarpal bone of r. index. Rheumatic drawing pain in finger-joints, < second joint of r. index, all the afternoon. Pain in l. knee when walking, increasing to cramp, obliging me to lean upon the arm of a friend, the pain, with occasional cramps, lasted all the evening, < raising foot so as to press upon toes. Cramplike stiffness in l. leg, < raising foot so as to press upon toes. Feet swollen; in morning.

Skin.—The scalp one filthy mass of inflammation, two-thirds of the hair came out, the rest matted together, with oozing of watery serum from scalp, eruption like rubeola on neck and chest, gradually extending to feet, thickest on chest and joints, itching < night, rubbing any part brought out the eruption, on face and neck it was in patches like ringworm, but not vesicular. Boils on nape. Congested feeling.

Sleep.—Difficult falling asleep and then unpleasant dreams. Restless night; with fever; with troubled dreams. Gloomy and disappointing dreams. Sexual dreams; without emission; and disgusting, in which I was a principal actor, waking me, arose and urinated with difficulty and tenesmus.

Fever.—Chills running up and down back. Heat at night. Internal heat; with vertigo; < eyes, which are inflamed and sensitive to light, eyeball sore to touch; intermittent, < eyes. Burning in face and scalp. Skin dry; at night; and hot.

Uva-Ursi.

A tincture is made of the fresh leaves of Arctostaphylos Uva-ursi, Spr.

Headache. Vertigo. Flushing of face. Urinary troubles. Burning after discharge of slimy urine. Involuntary micturition. Green urine. *Bloody urine.* Pulse varied slightly in number of beats; slightly accelerated and soft; slightly accelerated, afterwards harder; slightly accelerated and fuller, afterwards slower, weak and flowing; rose one beat, then smaller, slightly slower; slower, with at first small increase in fulness, then it was smaller; irregular and small.

Clinical.—Cystitis. Frequent urging, with severe spasm of the bladder, burning and tearing pain; urine contains blood and tough mucus, which can be rolled out of the vessel in large masses. Uterine inertia during labor. Uterine hæmorrhage (said to be quite equal to Ergot.).

Valeriana.

A tincture is made of the dried root of Valeriana officinalis, L.

General Action.—A "nervine" to be compared with Ignatia, Moschus, and especially *Pulsatilla.*

Generalities. — Twitching superficially in various parts of muscles. Tremulousness, with rest nowhere, as when expecting a joyful event. **Drawing like transient jerks now here, now there** (Puls.). Smarting pressure as if excoriated or sticking as with a hard blunt tool, in small spots; in region of shoulder and in other places. Malaise. Discomfort. Weakness in morning; in evening, with drowsiness; < lower limbs. Aggravation at noon and first part of afternoon and evening and the hours before midnight; of abdominal symptoms in evening (Puls.).

Clinical.—Hysteria, with dread of being left alone; overexcitability, especial dread of the dark or being left alone, very restless and excitable. Globus hystericus, with sensation of something warm rising from stomach into throat. Neuralgia.

Mind.—Joyfulness; all day; in evening, and greater activity; as after drinking coffee, he comprehended everything more easily than before; almost amounting to mischievousness. Delirium, attempted to get out of the window, threatened and vociferated violently, complained that he could not see, recognized no one, imagined himself away from home and beset with all sorts of dangers, from which he attempted to escape, but he was unable to walk without staggering. Agitation. Fear in evening when sitting in the dark (imagined some one might hurt him). Anxious; and hypochondriac, as if objects around him were estranged from him, the room appears desolate, he does not feel at home and is impelled to leave the room. Peevish. Irritation of nerves in forenoon, though he appears more cheerful and vigorous than before, his eyes, arms and knees feel weak. (Seriousness.) Great flow of ideas, confused, faint recollections of former thoughts and actions, chasing each other so rapidly that he became stupefied, he felt like one dreaming. Disinclination for mental work.

Head.—Stitches. *Aching;* in one or another part; *at* 11 P.M., < *over orbits;* at night. Excited feeling as after intoxication. Symptoms of congestion of brain, pain extending from r. frontal region over whole head, sometimes to eyes, making them sensitive to slight effort, sometimes to r. angle of lower jaw and causing an asleep sensation. Heaviness. Rush of blood; with fulness, < under vertex. Confusion; changing to drawing pain, < forehead. Stupid feeling when stooping; sudden stupefaction when standing, causing him to stagger and almost fall to one side. Vertigo on stooping, sensation as if everything were turning around with her, with intoxicated feeling.

Forehead.—Intermittent sticking deep in middle. *Pain;* in r. side; above r. brow; **alternating with darting sticking,** < *over orbits,* **as if it would pierce the eyes from within outward;** in l. half, with drawing together; above r. orbit, ending in heaviness; in r. side, periodically extending to l. side; extending from r. side over whole head, > sound sleep at night, returned next morning; extending to vertex, < towards eyes, so that moderate exertion of eyes caused pain in balls; over eyes, as if balls would be pressed out, at 1 P.M., an hour after dinner, < moving them. Constrictive drawing transversely across F. Numb tension behind eminence. Confusion in sinciput.

Temple, jerking in r.; intermittent pressure inward in r.; heaviness. Vertex, sticking at 10 P.M.; pain; P. below bone; contractive stupefying P. as from a blow, extending over head, lasting longest at V. Drawing pain in r. side at 5 P.M. from a current of air; D. pain in r. side, with flushes of heat over cheeks, later the pain extends as an aching into r. orbit. Pressure and drawing penetrating into side of occiput. Internal hammering in occiput in evening when half asleep, so that he forcibly turned his head to and fro.

Clinical.—Violent headache, appearing in jerks, with faintness.

Eyes.—Shining. *Smarting as from smoke* at 3 P.M.; burning S. at 10 A.M. *Pressure* in morning after rising, *margins of lids seem swollen and sore,* < region of l. inner canthus, they look red; P. as from a stye in r. at noon. Pupils dilated at 9 A.M.; D. even when approached by a lighted candle. Tearing in r. ball. Pain in lids from 1 till 2 P.M., with swelling. Stitches in inner canthus at 11 A.M. Painful drawing around orbits, < towards side, < stooping. Vision very distinct for distant objects. V. dim in morning, with pain in eyes as if he had not slept enough. Scintillations before eyes. Lights before eyes at 10 P.M., the closed and dark room seemed filled with the light of twilight, so that he imagined he distinguished objects, with a sensation as if he felt that things were near him even when not looking at them, and on looking he saw that the things were really there.

Ears and Nose.—Jerking in r. meatus auditorius. Crampy drawing in l. ear. Ringing in ears in evening in bed, he imagines that he hears the clock strike, at 10 P.M. sneezing.

Face.—Injected. Twitching sensation beneath skin of l. cheek, transiently > moving hand over it; crampy T. in region of l. malar-bone. Crampy drawing in r. malar bone. Dartings as of electricity in r. ramus of jaw. Pressure almost like a darting in r. side of lower lip and in gum of r. canine tooth.

Clinical.—Trismus from decayed tooth, with the characteristic symptom of a thread hanging down the œsophagus, which cannot be got rid of.

Mouth.—*Toothache;* shooting; drawing backward in lower and forward in upper. Constriction of tongue. Dryness of tip of tongue in morning, without thirst. Gradually increasing sticking in region of velum pendulum palati, with, towards the end, bitter taste and salivation inducing cough. Dryness, and in pharynx, then salivation. Offensive *salivation.* **Taste flat, slimy in morning after waking** (Puls.); *T. and smell of fetid tallow at noon, before dinner;* bitter on tip of tongue when licking lips a quarter of an hour after eating meat and vegetables.

Throat.—Scraping; with ineffectual desire to hawk.

Spasmodic constriction of pharynx. Dryness; of pharynx.

Stomach.—Appetite great; violent at dinner, causing nausea; little for dinner; although he is indifferent when thinking of eating, yet he eats much with relish at noon; lost; lost for supper. Disgust for food, from large doses. Aversion to tobacco, in a great smoker. Thirst; till noon.

Eructations; *of rancid fluid*, not rising into mouth (heartburn), at 4 P.M.; *empty;* empty before a meal; tasting of Hepar sul. in morning after waking; offensive; insipid; warm, from epigastric region, arresting breathing. **Nausea;** in morning on rising, > eating and open air; with salivation; with faintness, lips white, body icy cold, then vomiting of bile and mucus, with shaking chill; **as if a thread were hanging in the throat**, *gradually rising from umbilical region to fauces and causing salivation. Vomiting;* nightly.

Rumbling and grumbling. Intermittent sticking on l. side and over pit of stomach, in region of costal cartilage. Shooting cutting from pit to umbilical region. *Pressure in pit;* in epigastric region; with heaviness; sudden transient, in pit, with gurgling in abdomen. Fulness; in epigastric region; in epigastric region, < region of cardia, with pressure; changing to ravenous hunger; F. and peculiar scraping irritation in S. and abdomen, causing nausea, rising through œsophagus and arresting breathing. Heaviness in epigastric region. Weakness. Heat; in pit; epigastric region; epigastric region, with cramps.

Clinical.—Gastralgia, with great tympanitis, and putrid eructation.

Abdomen.—*Distention;* causing restlessness at night. Hardness. Rumbling and gurgling; R. < umbilical region, with motions and cutting. Offensive flatus. (When emitting flatus the baby cries and presses, occasionally he passes a little blood by the rectum.) Cutting, then diarrhœa twice; C. on retracting it, with pinching. Pain; in various parts in evening, at one time in umbilical region for an hour; in muscles as if bruised or as from a cold, < inspiration. Burrowing. Feeling as if it would be distended, even to bursting. Inclination to retract, he does it even involuntarily (alternate action).

Rumbling in small intestines, with gurgling and cutting, then after half an hour normal stool; R. in upper abdomen. Upper A. and hepatic region painful to touch at 11 P.M. Hypochondrium, stitches in l.; painful jerks in r.; (pressing in l. in morning in bed, on coughing or deep breathing it became a cutting, possibly from a cold). Sudden pain as from subcutaneous ulceration in l. side, two days in succession at 10 P.M. Cutting in umbilical region.

Hypogastrium.—Pinching in evening in bed. Crampy pain in l. side at 11 P.M when sitting. Sprained pain in l. side at 7 P.M. when sitting. Twisting, with nausea, as if menses would come on. Bruised pain, < parts covering os pubis, increasing in paroxysms, as a painful pressure or drawing. Drawing pain from 10 till 11 P.M.; in r. inguinal glands on crossing thighs, the place is painful to touch; in l. iliac region, as if bruised at 2 P.M., spreading to middle of abdomen, then rumbling in bowels.

Rectum and Anus.—Stitches in R. when standing. Boring in R. at 10 P.M.; in l. side of sphincter at 1 P.M. when standing. Tearing in anus at 2 P.M. on moving a little when sitting. Tenesmus in A. as if diarrhœa would set in on rising from stool, disappears gradually, returns in a few hours forcing him to stool, when he has a natural evacuation.

Stool.—*Diarrhœa;* twice in evening, with tickling in anus; violent, in morning; (the baby has had frequent loose S., has now many more, looser and watery discharges, in which solid particles like curdled milk float). Pasty; and greenish, with blood. Frequent; with effort.

Urinary Organs.—Clawing in region of bladder in evening. Constant desire to urinate, which he insisted upon doing through the window. *Frequent micturition.* When urinating the baby presses very hard, causing the dark red rectum to protrude, when a few drops of blood fall out. Urine dark brown; dark red in morning, but became clear on standing; contained brownish flakes; smells of the drug; seems to contain bile. Copious urine; and high-colored, also of strong odor; and on standing a sediment of brown flakes. Turbid urine; in morning, depositing a whitish sediment; depositing a slimy white sediment; and dark red, depositing a vermilion red sediment; and brownish, with brick-dust sediment. Sediment in urine; turbid; mealy; white in morning; copious, the upper part of which is pale, the lower turbid and reddish.

Sexual Organs.—Frequent erections in morning, next day creeping and drawing in penis as if asleep. Tensive gurgling pain in r. testicle at 5 P.M. when sitting.

Respiratory Organs and Chest.—Dry cough. Hacking cough. Difficult breathing after breakfast, with anxiety in chest. Stitches in chest at 5 P.M. during a horseback ride; *sudden S.* **outward** *in C. and region of liver at* 2 P.M.; *in region of last true ribs* at 8 P.M., *when standing*, **with pressure outward;** *outward below l. axilla during inspiration*, < *deep inspiration*, and on pressure a sore pain. Jerks like electric shocks below axilla. Twitching pain in C. *Pressure across lower half of C. at* 10 P.M. *when walking, with oppression of breath.* Oppression in region of r. lower true rib.

Heart and Pulse.—Sudden stitches in region of H. during inspiration, when sitting erect or standing, > stooping. Palpitation. Pulse rapid; with rush of blood to head, feeling of fulness and warmth in face; and irregular, tense; and irregular, tremulous; and in the first quarter of an hour full and vigorous, in the second the diastole is shorter, the whole body agreeably warm, and a tremulous anxiety seems to come out of abdomen; 78, the beats of heart scarcely felt (86); 60 in one minute, 90 the next, and weak and small, in forenoon; slow, then rapid. Pulse small.

Neck and Back.—Piercing drawing from nape to occiput at 11 A.M. on bending head backward, with pressure. Drawing pain in back. Rheumatic pain in scapulæ. Stitches in kidney region when sitting down. *Strained pain above l. hip*, **worse when standing, and especially when sitting, than when walking.** Bubbling pressure above anus, in region of os coccygis, at 9 A.M. Drawing transversely across lumbar region in evening in bed.

Extremities.—Bruised pain. *Drawing, slow, painful, in bones* **when sitting quietly,** *with jerking; painful D. in muscles from l. shoulder to fingers, with single stitches, a sort of tearing*, the tearing returned after a second dose, > **walking** (Puls., Rhus t.), *after a stitch in knee (so that she could scarcely walk), then pain which moved* *from knee to toes and back again* (**less when walking than when sitting**), finally felt in r. foot; sudden crampy D. in muscles just above bend of elbow at noon, and in outer muscles of thigh. Paralytic pain in knees, elbows and shoulder-joints on ceasing to walk. Paralytic numbness. Stiffness in elbows and knees at 5 P.M. after walking a little, with weariness.

Clinical.—Neuralgia of the limbs; sciatica, < sitting, > walking.

Upper Extremities.—*Crampy jerking shooting through humerus.* Stinging in region of posterior border of deltoid at 11 P.M. *Crampy drawing downward in region of r. biceps when writing.* Drawing pain downward in l. deltoid and bend of elbows when laying arm on the table and bending it, if the arm hangs down the drawing changes into heaviness in fingers as if they were turgid with blood. Pressure as with tip of finger in region of head of humerus. (Tearing in elbow.) Bruised pain in bends of elbows from 7 till 9 A.M. when writing, afterwards extending as a drawing pain along biceps. Stitches below tip of elbow at 6 P.M. Tearing upward in inner side of forearm at 4 P.M. Tremor of hands when writing at 10 A.M., with heat and redness of cheeks and warmth of rest of body. Sudden jerks in hands, then pain on touch. Crampy jerks through thumb, as from electricity. Stitches in bones of middle phalanges of fingers at 11 P.M.

Lower Extremities.—Thigh. Jerking in muscles of r. hip. Darts as of electric sparks in middle of l. when standing, then bruised pain. *Crampy tearing (jerking) in outer side of hip-bone, extending into hip,* in afternoon. Crampy pain in front part extending to groin at 10 P.M. Clawing pain above bend of r. knee at 4 P.M. on beginning to walk, < a false step. Bruised pain from middle of r. along outer side to knee, in afternoon when riding in a carriage, < jolting. Burning pain in l. hip at 11 P.M. in bed. Intermittent pressure transversely across above l. knee, afterwards descending to knee. Paralytic pain from r. ischiatic region and great trochanter down to patella, so that walking was difficult. Drawing downward in outer side in morning on extending the limb sideways.

Knee.—Tearing in bends from 11 till 12 P.M. when sitting or standing. Pain in patellæ. Tensive pain from bend through calf at 1 P.M. when sitting. Weakness in bends of K. and ankles in morning after rising, with bruised pain transversely across thighs and in small of back.

Leg.—Stitches in front region of tuberosity of fibula at 11 A.M. *Twinging pain in outer side of calf at* 5 P.M. **when sitting.** *Tearing in l. calf* at 4 P.M., when laying r. limb across l.; *pulsative, in r. calf* **in afternoon when sitting.** *Drawing along tendo-achillis towards heel* **when sitting,** > **rising,** *with weak feeling.* Bruised pain anteriorly in middle of tibia as if fibrillæ had been broken, when walking. Pressure as with tip of finger on l. side below l. knee. Lassitude when standing, with heaviness; L. in calves in afternoon when standing, with tension. Heaviness in calves, when walking she feels as if she could not get along.

Ankle.—Sticking over l. malleolus in region of tendo-achillis at 1 o'clock. *Sprained pain in r. after running upstairs,* < **standing,** > **walking**; *sudden, in r. outer malleolus,* **more when standing than when walking.** Bruised pain in l. *in afternoon* when the carriage jolted. *Drawing in tarsal joints* **when sitting** at 4 P.M.

Foot.—Jerking as from electricity in inner border of r. Tearing in balls of soles *in afternoon,* then warmth. *Pain in heels; when sitting,* < r.; **when sitting,** *with stinging.*

Toes.—Tearing in dorsum from 11 till 12 P.M., < great. Pain in tips *in evening.* Heaviness in tips of three middle at 4 P.M., with drawing pain, feeling of subcutaneous ulceration and cooling sensation as from a current of air through soles to calves.

Skin.—Eruption first red and confluent, then white, hard, elevated pimples, on arm and chest. Pimples and white vesicles on an elevated red border, painful to touch, in white of upper lip and on cheek. Smarting as if excoriated in outer side of l. knee; S. as if excoriated in spots that could be covered with the tip of finger. Itching in axilla at 3 P.M.

Sleep.—Yawning, with stretching of limbs; Y., with chilliness. Sleepiness; irresistible; then profound sleep for two hours, on waking the headache had disappeared. *Sleeplessness. Unusually wide awake in evening and restless at night, sleep only towards morning, when he had vivid dreams.* Restless sleep; disturbed by cramp-like pain in stomach. Sleep disturbed by vivid dreams, by confused dreams, tired in morning; by dreams partly voluptuous, partly anxious, for instance, that he was driving through deep water. Many dreams.

Fever.—Chilliness; tremulous, at 11 A.M.; intermittent, in evening; in thrills creeping downward over whole body; in upper half of head at 5 P.M., when pressing the hat firmly on the head; in region of hip, as if cold water were poured over her, with warmth of rest of body. Shuddering in paroxysms from nape downward.

Heat; all day, < motion, with sweat on face, forehead, etc., pulse strong and rapid; in forenoon, with sweat on slightest motion; during dinner, with sweat in hair on forehead; as soon as he begins to walk, < face, with sweat; *with uneasiness. Dry heat;* **in evening when sitting.** Heat of skin. Heat in head on stooping; of cheeks at noon in open air, with redness of them, after fifteen minutes general sweat, < face; *in flushes over cheeks* **in evening,** with dry feeling in tongue, without thirst. Synochus. *Sweat;* at night; with the odor of the drug; on forehead about noon, after dinner the eyes feel weak as after revelry; in hair of forehead about noon, with stiffness of loins, pulse being 90.

Veratrum Album.

A tincture is made of the dried root.

General Action.—It produces profound prostration, weak heart, cold skin, with cold sweat and collapse. Most violent vomiting and purging, with terrible colic and at times cramps. Muscular spasms, rigid contraction of muscles, even tetanic.

Allies.—Colchicum, Iris v., Secale c., Acon., Ars., Cupr., Zinc., Rhus t.

Generalities.—Activity on diminution of pains and emotional disturbances, with mobility. Movements slow. Muscles relaxed. *Trembling.* Convulsive movements of face and limbs. *Spasms;* epileptic. **Cholera.** New attack of gout. Stitches here and there; S. in r. cheek and r. chest, with salivation; in part S. here and there, in part sticking colic, with peppery biting in throat. Pain in sides, breasts and thighs. Bruised pain in bones; *in muscular parts, with pressure.* Drawing pain in head and sacrum. Itching sensation in bones. Distress from open air, as after acute illness. Restlessness; undertakes several things, but is soon weary and accomplishes nothing. Desire to lie down.

Weakness; in morning; *in morning, with shivering;* in morning, with sleepiness, preventing rising; after breakfast, with sleepiness; in forenoon, > a glass of wine, with dizziness and inability to work; in afternoon and evening, then fatiguing, dreamy sleep; in evening, on account of mental excitement; in evening, all work, especially mental, is irksome, with uneasiness, heaviness of head, which is painful, then stupid sleep; *on going to stool;* after a short walk, with indisposition; < breakfast, with heaviness of limbs; **with sinking down**; with disinclination to work; *then twisting in abdomen and back, > stool;* **as from too great heat in the air; paralytic; rapid,** inviting sleep in forenoon; *in attacks when walking;* as if he had walked too far; as if he had not slept enough, head stupid, *on attempting to rise he sank back in bed in a dreamy half sleep, with sweat and apprehension* (Acon.).

Faintness; at noon for three days, *with pallor, twitching in cheeks* and sparks before l. eye, *then vomiting of white froth. All symptoms except weakness > lying,* they return on rising; all except headache > sitting.

Clinical.—Rheumatic pains, like electric jerks, < heat of the bed, > walking about. Attacks of sudden faintness. Violent tonic spasms, palms and soles drawn inward. General tetanic rigidity of muscles, face drawn and pinched, tendency to cramp, especially in the calves, etc. Tendency to collapse, with cold sweat.

Mind.—Raging, *with heat of body. Delirium; with general coldness, open eyes, with cheerful, at times laughing expression, he prattles about religious subjects, about vows to be performed, prays, believes that he is not in his own house. Beside himself, groans* and does not know how to calm himself. *Cursing and howling all night,* and complaining of being stupid, with headache and salivation.

Inconsolable over a fancied misfortune, runs about the room howling and screaming, looking upon the ground, or sits brooding in the corner, wailing and weeping in an inconsolable manner, *< evening, sleeps only till* 2 *o'clock. Despair. Despondency and discouragement,* with weeping and inclination to hang the head. Melancholia, with chilliness as if dashed with cold water, with frequent nausea. *Fear;* (ending with eructations). **Anxiety**; in morning; all night; in evening and after dinner; (in evening in bed till almost midnight, with waking sopor, and drawing movement in abdomen, which causes roaring in head); *if he stands,* **with cold sweat on forehead and vomiting**; during stool, with fear of apoplexy; caused by crawling in fingers; *taking away the breath; as if he had committed a crime. Anguish.*

Ill humor; in forenoon, with no inclination to work; at every work that does not go to suit him, with impatience and weakness; at every interruption at work; with anxiety, palpitation and rapid audible respiration. *Taciturn;* he speaks in a low weak voice; (and rages and tears his clothes); says nothing except when excited to do so, and then he scolds. (Cannot endure to have any one speak to him.) Seeks out faults in others and taunts them with them. (Talkative.) Inclination to work. Indifference all day, so that he often rubs his forehead in order to collect his thoughts. Sensation as if gradually nearing his end, though with tranquillity.

Oversensitiveness, increased mental power. When he has nothing to do he seems dazed, cannot think easily, is quiet and absorbed in himself. *Conscious only as in a dream.* Waking sopor, one eye is open, the other closed or half open, frequent starting up as if frightened. Unconsciousness. (Does not recognize his relatives.) Loss of ideas; of memory.

Clinical.—Raging delirium, sometimes with rapid talking, at other times refusal to talk; sometimes with rage and swearing, tearing clothes. Hallucinations of physical diseases; of having committed crime, obscene delirium. In delirium he tries to get out of bed. Melancholia, hangs his head and wants to be alone. Delirium after severe illness; people crowd about her. Despairing melancholia after great disappointments or religious excitement.

Head.—Sticking, and in r. shoulder. *Aching;* < walking, even to reeling, > sitting; > appearance of menses; *with vomiting of green mucus;* with nausea, colic and pain in back; with buzzing in front of forehead; with heat in eyes; with painful inflammation of eyes, preventing sleep at night; with stiffness; with toothache; with flow of urine; *(tearing?) during menstruation (which had not occurred for six weeks), < morning, > evening, with nausea; paroxysmal bruised, here and there in brain, with pressure;* as if brain were broken; tensive; constrictive, with constrictive pain in œsophagus; throbbing; intermittent throbbing; stupefying.

(Shattering, with jerking in l. arm and paleness of fingers.) Confusion; in forenoon, with heaviness, emptiness, peevishness and disinclination to do anything; < sitting erect and standing, > stooping and lying on back, with tensive pressure now in temples, now in vertex, and contracted pupils; with nausea; with heaviness and with difficulty in talking as if he could not think of the words; dizzy. Heaviness. *Rush of blood on stooping. Vertigo;* in morning; in morning on rising; towards noon before menses, and sweat at night; when walking; < rising from a seat, with pressure in vertex, pain in arms, vanishing of vision and creeping coldness through arms; and intoxication; with aversion to food; as if nothing were firm in his head.

Forehead.—Stitches in l. side; single, even when sitting. Pinching. Pain in sinciput; and heat and heaviness; throbbing, over l. eye. Tension, and in occiput; in sinciput; in head between temples.

Temples.—Sticking. Pain extending to forehead, < bending forward, > bending backward and pressure, recurring on rising up. (Sensation of a drop of water, not cool, running down.)

Cutting in vertex. *Pressing on vertex in morning after waking; pain like a flattening pressure on V., which on movement becomes a throbbing.* Pain in one side, with pain in stomach. Sticking in occiput, neck and r. shoulder in morning on waking, < motion, with tearing; S. deep in occiput, with tension. Sudden pain in O. Tearing and tension in O. and nape. *Crawling and bristling sensation in r. side as if a bunch of hair were electrified, with shivering under scalp.* Itching biting stitch in scalp. (Itching.)

Clinical.—Persistent vertigo, with cold sweat on the forehead, with great weakness. Neuralgic headaches, especially characterized by feeling of ice on vertex. Neuralgia in the head in convulsive shocks immediately on raising the head, with vomiting, > pressure on vertex.

Eyes.—*Surrounded by black rings; by blue rings, and looked dull. Distorted, protruding.* Turned upward so that only whites could be seen. Staring. Without lustre. Redness of white of r. Inflammation; of r.; of r., with febrile heat; with tearing. Blueness of l., with frequent eructations. Pain; and he moved the hands over head; with loss of appetite and inflamed appearance of blood (buffy coat). Heat; < open air, with sticking; with lachrymation, cutting and dry sensation. Weak sensation. Seem watery, as if covered with albumen. *Lachrymation; with redness of eyes, as in coryza.*

Pupils contracted; with compressing pain in eyes; then dilated, with weakness and sleepiness, even when walking; *dilated;* dilated at 7 P.M., with weak vision. Balls rotated. Paroxysmal pain as if beaten in r. ball at outer canthus, > pressure. Sticking in canthi.

Lids.—Agglutination on rising. Sticking in upper by outer canthus. **Dryness** (Arsen., Zinc.); after midday nap, then lachrymation; < *after sleep, painful as if rubbed sore, are stiff and agglutinated; of upper, as if salt were between it and ball* at noon after dinner. Burning. Sticking itching internally. Paralysis.

Vision.—*Double.* Of sparks; and black spots on rising from a seat, forcing him to sit or lie. Shining spots flit before eyes. Blindness.

Clinical.—Hemeralopia preceding menstruation, with other Veratrum symptoms.

Ears.—Stitches deep in l.; behind l. E. and jaw. (Tearing in lobule.) Pain in external meatus; P. in r. in morning. Sensation as if a membrane were stretched over it. Alternations in r. of heat and sensation of a cold breath. Hearing diminished; one or other ear seems stopped. Ringing. Whistling in r. preceded by dulness of hearing, once after the W. the hearing was clear, after two minutes it was dull again. Roaring on rising from a seat, with rushing in them and bright fire before eyes; R. during menses, with pain in limbs and thirst; like a storm.

Nose.—Sensation as if ulcerated internally. Compression in bones, with pressure inward. Sharp burning in l. nostril. *Dryness as from dust;* D. and heat. Sneezing. Catarrh; then gelatinous mucus in fauces and throat, with membranes of yellow-brown mucus. *Bleeding;* from r. nostril; (at night in sleep); before menses. Smell of dung in nose.

Face.—**Sunken, and expression anxious** (Ars.). **Pale** (Ars.); and lips; **with frequent stools** (Ars.); alternating suddenly with redness and heat. Red and hot; red, with great thirst and flow of urine. *Bluish* (Cupr.); towards end of menses, with grinding of teeth. Dark, with anxious expression. Swelling. Drawing and tensive pains in r. side and r. ear. (Jerking pinching in muscular parts.)

Jaws.—*Closed.* Stitches in r. frequently during the day; in joints on opening them, so that he cannot draw down jaw as usual. Sore pain in forepart of lower. Bruised feeling in muscles of lower when eating, so that he must stop chewing. Pressure in muscles of l. as from a dull point of wood. *Stiffness of muscles.*

Lips.—Cracked. Painful pimple on margin of red near corner, < touch. Vesicles in l. corner. Lips and mouth dry in evening.

Clinical.—Facial neuralgia, drawing tearing pains, with pinched features, cold extremities, cold sweat, nausea and vomiting.

Mouth.—Teeth. Loose. Grating. Boring in upper incisors. Aching, with inflammation of tonsils and weakness; A., then swollen red face; then when chewing ending in drawing streaming into roots, even when something soft was taken between teeth; in l. upper molars as if filled with lead. Acutely affected by cold wind. Swelling of gum and lower jaw.

Tongue.—Swelling. **Coldness** (Cupr., Camph.). Burning; and in œsophagus; with stinging; in tip and in mouth, with sticking and coolness; and in throat and stomach, with coldness in mouth as from peppermint; sharp, on tip. *Dryness* (Nux mos., Rhus t.). *Inability to talk.* Stammering.

Inflammation of mouth. Frothing. Mucus running out towards noon; tenacious M. in mouth and palate, < drinking water; much M., and in fauces and throat, expectoration of large lumps of M. without cough, next day M. in mouth and throat after eating, and in evening constant spitting of M. after a glass of wine, with cold hands. Pain, then inflammation, then red swollen tongue, preceded by nausea. **Dryness, and of palate, with thirst for water** (Acon., Ars., Nux mos.); D. in morning after rising, only slightly > rinsing, *with stickiness; with stickiness,* without special thirst. Burning; posteriorly and in fauces. Numbness of palate as if covered with the skin of a plum. Seemed sore.

Salivation; **running from mouth like waterbrash;** tenacious; alternating with dryness and stickiness of mouth; with acrid, salt taste and heat in palm and pit of stomach. *Tasteless saliva, with tastelessness in mouth.* Salt saliva. *Taste and coolness in M. and throat as from peppermint; biting T. in throat as from peppermint, with heat rising from œsophagus into mouth,* with nausea; *pasty;* as of dung; putrid, herby, almost like pestwursel; (sour, with watery salivation); *diminished.*

Throat.—Swelling of l. submaxillary glands, with internal soreness, < l. side, and with choking and constriction during and after swallowing. Pinching in submaxillary glands. Swelling; of tonsils, with redness of pharynx. Tenacious mucus. **Scraping;** burning. Pain; and in œsophagus, with burning stinging in pharynx. Drawing pain, with thirst and colic. *Roughness.* Paroxysmal constriction and choking as from unripe pears. *Dryness;* in pharynx; in fauces, with heat and secretion of mucus; not > drinking. *Burning;* in pharynx; in fauces.

Œsophagus.—Swelling. Distention, with feeling as if he would suffocate. Contraction as from pressure of a swelling. Coldness comes up into it (also a spot far back on palate is cold), then warm, sweetish, salt, slimy liquid rises like waterbrash, then coldness returns. Burning. Swallowing impossible.

Clinical.—Neuralgic toothache, pulsating, driving to madness, teeth feel heavy, as if filled with lead.

Stomach.—**Hunger violent; H. in stomach,** *with undisturbed appetite; with thirst and profuse urine;* ravenous, without thirst. **Appetite for fruit;** with aversion to warm food. *Longing for only cold food, herring, sardines; for acids;* for gherkins; for citric acid. Little appetite, and nausea when eating. Appetite lost. **Thirst** (Bry.); in afternoon and evening; **during sweat; for cold drinks.**

Eructations; after breakfast, with shivering and weakness; after eating, with pressure in stomach and tension in upper abdomen; bitter; sour; qualmish, with terrific cough; (tasting of food); *violent, mostly of air. Empty eructations;* after eating; in evening after lying down, then scraping, scratching in larynx, almost as after heartburn. Waterbrash choking him. Efforts to eructate. *Hiccough;* in morning during the customary smoke.

Nausea; in pit of stomach; from breakfast, > meat at noon; after dinner; while eating, with hunger and pressure in epigastric region; after eating a little, with pressure and heaviness in stomach; *with bilious taste; with salivation and closure of jaws; with great thirst* and flow of urine; *with frothing from mouth; with weakness;* with red sweaty face; with crawling in stomach.

Vomiting (Acon., Cupr.); **and diarrhœa ten times, with pale, sunken face, covered with cold sweat**; with purging, then unconsciousness; *with exhaustion as if thighs would separate from hip-joints;* with sinking of strength and pulse; with heat of body; **forcible; violent, of slimy acid liquid with food,** *with painful distortion of face;* **of food;** *of food, with green mucus;* of food, with mucus and green substances; **green** (Merc. c.); *bloody;* black bloody, frequent V. and stools; paroxysmal, sour-smelling, > drinking cold milk, then chill in bed; of bile, then of tenacious mucus; of froth, then of yellowish-green, sour-smelling mucus; (black). **Vomiting of mucus** (Cupr., Sec. c.); **with cold sweat**; with weakness; **green**; green, then of froth; green, then chilliness; dark green (Sec. c.), with diarrhœa, and yet appetite and thirst; *bloody, with cold sweat;* white, at night; white, with good appetite; tenacious, at night; bitter, sour, brown M. and food in evening two hours after coffee; and of bile, then of black bile, at last of blood.

Painful distention of pit. Fulness after eating a little. Cramp, with burning pressure in pit and in middle of chest, and with eructations after breakfast. Pinching in pit, < walking. Cardialgia. *Pain;* in epigastric region and side; after dinner; *acute, in epigastrium; extending into sternum, hypochondria and to ilia; as from ravenous hunger;* pressing and drawing, in pit. Burning; in region of pit; in epigastrium and along œsophagus; like heartburn, in evening, and in chest, with cold shivering over back. Heaviness after breakfast, and in chest. (Sensation of weakness, with internal coldness in epigastric region and pressure.)

Clinical.—Craving juicy things. Most violent retching and vomiting, of food, or of whatever is taken into the stomach; the ejecta are always very profuse, and the vomiting is attended with cold sweat, great prostration, burning in the stomach and great sensitiveness to touch. The violent retching and vomiting is the most characteristic feature of the Veratrum patient, unlike Arsenic and Cuprum; the ejecta are profuse, though many of the other symptoms correspond. Vomiting of great quantities of blood, at times even bright red, usually dark and thick. A few cases of dyspepsia from chewing tobacco, without vomiting or diarrhœa.

Abdomen.—*Distention;* with colic and emission of flatus; flatulent, with colic as from constipation and uneasiness. Rumbling; with nausea in it, a sensation as if diarrhœa would come on, without desire for stool; with diuresis; and unusual troubles with a hernia. Flatulence in evening; after dinner. Emission of flatus; noisy, at night; unnoticed after dinner, with thin stool, then acrid diarrhœa, with tenesmus. Twitching, with not disagreeable warmth of chest.

Stitches extending through abdominal ring along spermatic cord when coughing. **Cutting**; here and there; *early in morning, with diarrhœa.* Griping; drawing, then emission of flatus and tenacious stool. **Pain** (Colch., Coloc.); nightly, with sleeplessness; **with feeling as if intestines were twisted into a knot**; with thirst and increased urine; from back towards navel; **flatulent, here and there, the longer delayed the emission of flatus the more difficult it is to pass** (Coloc.); sudden (griping?) in morning in bed, then desire for stool, stool yellowish-green, pasty, the last part consisted of mucus, the desire lasted after the stool, then almost clear mucus, then feeling above pubes as if beaten and an unsettled feeling in pit of stomach. Drawing pain in evening when walking; D. as from a purge. Bruised feeling because flatus refuses to pass.

Sticking in region of spleen when walking after a moderate meal. Pain in hypochondria and chest from non-emission of flatus; tensive P. as from flatulence in hypochondria. Warmth in upper abdomen; extending over chest to throat. Urging to stool in upper A., but stool follows with difficulty or not at all from inactivity of rectum.

Umbilical Region.—Cutting, with thirst and increased urine. *Griping at times above, at times below navel, in afternoon soon after eating,* which while standing changes to another place than when walking, and the reverse. Pain; before pains in back; *as from flatus.*

Hypogastrium.—Indications of protrusion of inguinal hernia. Symptoms as if a hernia would protrude. *Cutting sticking soon after eating.* Deep drawing tearing, mostly above pubis. Pain in groin; in cæcal region as from spasmodic incarcerated flatus; bruised, in pubic region in morning, with sensation in l. groin as if a hernia would form, < sitting. Sensation of impending faintness before stool.

Clinical.—The whole abdomen is usually swollen and very sensitive. It is adapted to the most terrible attacks of colic, the pain begins in the stomach, radiates upward to the shoulders and then involves the whole abdomen, associated with retching, vomiting, purging, coldness, cold sweat, etc.

Rectum and Anus.—Blind hæmorrhoids; with pressure towards anus. Tenesmus. Burning in anus during stool. (Sore pain in anus.)

Stool.—**Diarrhœa**; in evening; **with profuse sweat**; *with desire for eating and drinking;* with pain during and after stool; **frequent and painful** (Ars.); passed unnoticed with emission of flatus (Aloe); *watery, involuntary.* Soft, sudden; S., scanty, brownish-yellow. **Constipation; on account of hardness and large size of stool** (compare Iris v.); with heat and pain in head. Dry. **Copious. Frequent, with shivering.** Acrid. Bloody. First part large, the latter consisting of thin strings of fæces of normal consistence. Indolent. Evacuations suppressed.

Clinical. — Diarrhœa, < night, by drinking, after fruit (China), associated with terrible colic, cold sweat on the forehead, feeble pulse; stools very profuse, watery, with flakes, sometimes blackish, followed by great emptiness and weakness in the abdomen; the evacuations are often accompanied by violent vomiting. Frequently called for in worst cases of cholera morbus and true cholera. Chronic constipation, evacuations black, hard, large, with faintness, cold sweat, etc.

Urinary Organs.—Pain in bladder and on urinating burning. Tenesmus. Frequent desire, urine retained at first, then watery urine with smarting in forepart of meatus. *Dysuria.* Involuntary micturition. Difficult micturition of pale watery urine in a weak stream. Stitching in orifice of urethra after urinating. Pinching in urethra when not urinating. Pain as if contracted behind glans, with ineffectual desire since bladder was empty. Burning in forepart of urethra when urinating. *Diuresis;* with constipation; with coryza. Urine colorless like water; scanty, yellow, turbid, even when passed; burning; acrid.

Clinical.—Dysuria, with burning. Suppression of urine (Stram.). Green urine.

Sexual Organs.—Sensitiveness. Stiffness of penis. Excoriation of prepuce. Drawing pain in testicles. Pimples on r. labia before menses. Abortion. Irrestrainable flooding. *Menses too early; M. profuse;* M. that had been suppressed for many years reappeared; that had been suppressed a long time returned at the full moon.

Clinical.—Dysmenorrhœa, with vomiting, abdominal weakness; sexual mania precedes the menses. Puerperal mania. Suppressed menses, with cold sweat, vomiting and diarrhœa. Uterus enlarged and inflamed, very sensitive, could not tolerate the least touch, with diarrhœa and coldness. Endometritis, with great agony.

Respiratory Organs. — *Constriction of larynx; spasmodic, with contracted pupils; spasmodic, with attacks of suffocation* and protruding eyes; suffocative. *Tickling low down in air-tubes, provoking cough, with slight expectoration;* without expectoration. Loss of voice.

Cough.—**Hollow, in long shocks,** *with cutting in abdomen;* **deep H., always in three or four shocks,** which seem to come from abdomen, in evening. *Violent,* in evening, with salivation. *Dry;* with tickling in pharynx; then expectoration; violent, at night and in morning; biting, < evening, with shivering; hacking, from tickling in lowest part of sternum; hoarse, at night; almost D., with pain in side and head. *With much expectoration, blueness of face and involuntary micturition.*

Respiration.—**Suffocative.** *Difficult. Short on slightest motion, a kind of oppression of chest* (Ferr., Phos.). *Weak, interrupted. Stopped;* for several minutes at times, was spasmodic and rattling.

Clinical.—Bronchitis, especially of old people, rattling of mucus, with inability to expectorate, great prostration, cold sweat (Ant. tart.). Violent fits of coughing, followed by eructations of gas, the cough seems to start from the abdomen, which has to be held when coughing, < in a warm room. Suffocative spasm, with cough from constriction of the larynx or chest. Whooping cough. Cough < in a warm room, eating or drinking and cold water, from crying. Every attack of whooping cough is followed by great exhaustion and cold sweat; attacks sometimes accompanied by vomiting and diarrhœa.

Chest.—Catarrh without involuntary cough, tenacious mucus must be raised by hawking. Spasmodic contraction of l. intercostal muscles, impeding respiration. Stitches in r. side; near nipples, which at last itch; paroxysmal, in r. side, taking away the breath, during the day. Cutting. Pinching in region of sternum, more after drinking than after eating. Griping in r. side. Pain; in ribs; in region of sternum; *in region of sternum after eating and drinking;* beneath ribs, < expiration; with dry cough; in l. side, with cough, weakness and difficult respiration; in l. side, then in back; beneath last r. ribs, ending with a stitch, < inspiration; stinging-throbbing, in a spot in l.

Tightness *even when sitting* (Phos., Ferr., Ars.), **with difficult respiration** and headache; T. when standing; *when walking, with fulness, so that breath fails;* he cannot inspire sufficient air on account of contraction of air-passages by tenacious, firm mucus. *Constriction;* periodical cramplike, in l. side. *Oppression when coughing;* O. after burning in throat and gnawing in stomach; frequent, < morning on rising, with pain in side on breathing. Pressure; painful rhythmical, on upper part of sternum; pulselike, as with a dull point in region of l. rib, and on touch pain as if suppurating. Fulness forcing him to eructate. Cold drawing at times, with sensitiveness to cold air. Tickling in middle of sternum as if it would provoke cough.

Heart.—Cutting burning in præcordial region at night. Paroxysmal anxiety, then violent beating and warmth. *Violent beating.* **Palpitation, with anxiety and rapid, audible respiration** (Acon.).

Clinical.—Cardiac debility, with very weak pulse; any exertion brings on irregular action of the heart and thready pulse; the face is flushed when lying, and on rising suddenly it becomes very pale, with cold sweat, faintness, etc. (Compare other plants of same family, Convallaria, Strophanthus, etc.)

Pulse.—*Rapid. Slow; and almost lost;* and small, tense. *Small, irregular, at times intermittent. Imperceptible.*

Neck.—Bent, with pain on motion, less on pressure, with tension and tearing in r. side. Sticking in vertebræ; in neck and r. shoulder, with stiffness of nape. Pain in nape and shoulders in morning on waking; in nape in morning, with stiffness of shoulder; in l. side, with drawing; *rheumatic, in nape, extending to sacrum,* < going to stool; as if skin were excoriated. Tension in nape; and shoulders and between scapulæ, < motion, with sticking. Stiffness in nape; painful, in nape during the headache; rheumatic, in nape, causing vertigo, < moving. Heaviness in nape, cervical muscles no longer support the head. *Muscles of nape seem paralyzed.*

Back.—Sticking and burning; burning S., with tension in small of back. Pain in B. and shoulder, with sticking and tension; P. in spine when walking, then drawing pressure as if bruised, > pressure; as if broken, in morning on stooping and on rising up. Painful stiffness. Scapulæ, pain extending over back, with diuresis, thirst and constipation; pain between S. even when sitting, on turning it becomes a tugging; bruised pain. Stitches in sacrum on stooping; intermittent, in coccyx when standing, rather itching than sticking. Pain in loins; in sacrum when standing; in sacrum when walking upon a level; in loins, with arthritic tearing in lower limbs; tensive and pinching, in loins and above hips at noon when walking and standing; tensive, in small of back; bruised, in l. side of sacrum on stooping and on rising; bruised and paralytic, in joints of sacrum and knee on moving after rising from a seat.

Extremities. — **Nails blue on account of coldness** (Nux v.). Stretching. Painful lameness. Trembling, with anxiety at heart and inclination to faint. (Twitching, with sweat, then vertigo and much drinking.) Tearing in extensor muscles when sitting. Electric shocks in knee and elbow, then bruised pain. *Pain as from fatigue;* (as if the bed were hard, in those upon which he lies); arthritic, in deltoid, upper arm and knee. Drawing pain; when walking, > night by continuing to walk. Spasmodic drawing above joints on moving. **Weakness.** Stiffness, < forenoon and after standing; S. and insensibility. *Falling asleep;* of arms and feet even when lying. *Paralysis.*

Upper Extremities.—Sticking in r. axilla extending to elbow. Pain in r. axilla.

Shoulder.—Sticking in l. joint; in r., with tensive

pain, the S. extends to back, impeding movement, the pain > pressure, < hawking and coughing, even respiration is painful, after removal of pressure there is burning in skin. A single cutting on it. Pain; in r. joint; during rainy weather, and in arms, all symptoms > warm weather and a dose of Rhus; extending to head like lightning, then loss of vision.

Arm. — Trembling on taking hold of anything. (Twitching.) Pain as if beaten in r. after a little effort; paralytic, with difficulty in raising them. Sensation as if too full and swollen. Weakness, and of hands. Stiffness in muscles of l., with drawing; S. of muscles of l., with numbness and pain. Numbness of r.; with heaviness. Paralytic feeling in r.

Upper Arm.—Smarting on inner side as from sore flesh. Pain in muscles of r.; in muscles of l., then r.; paralytic bruised, in l. on stretching it; drawing downward, in middle of l. humerus, as if sore from lying on it.

Drawing pain in bend of elbow on flexing it, it seems swollen so that it cannot be completely flexed, with paralytic feeling in arm. *Pain in middle of l. forearm as if bones were pressed together.* Jerking in r. wrist and towards elbow. Hands fall asleep. *Crawling in hands as if falling asleep.*

Fingers.—Pain in bones of second phalanges on grasping anything; P. in thumb-joint as if dislocated; tensive, in middle on motion; burning-itching, in first phalanx of little, as if it had been frozen. Rigid, insensible. Falling asleep.

Lower Extremities. — Tottering gait. Heaviness. *Lameness in r. hip, then also in l., so that walking was difficult.*

Thigh.—Rhythmical twitching in large external muscle when sitting and standing, recurred after walking. Cramplike pain in T. or calf if he supports himself less upon that foot when standing. Pain as if broken when sitting; rheumatic drawing P. in muscles when standing. Cramplike drawing in upper gluteals when standing. Weakness, and in knees; and in hips, with aching as if lame.

Knee.—Cracking. Painful jerking in r. Raised high up every quarter or half hour in afternoon, > evening on lying down. (Sticking, and in ankle.) Single cutting. Bruised pain on descending stairs. Spasmodic drawing pain from hollow of r. into thigh when standing. Drawing at times when standing, walking or sitting. Tension in hollow when standing and walking. Cold sore sensation externally. Heaviness of K. and feet when walking, with clumsiness.

Leg.—*Cramp in calves* (Cupr., Rhus t.); in outer part of calves in evening after walking and jumping. Tearing in muscles of l.; extending downward in tibia. Pain, and in ankles; *in bone below knee as if broken when stepping upon it;* in calves and tibia as if they would break down. Crawling, a painful surging. Heaviness; in morning, as if paralysis impended. Stiffness in calf, with drawing; S. in r. calf, with pain.

Ankle.—Sprained pain in evening when walking, when previously while sitting the soles had been stretched backward, so that they rested upon backs of toes. Pressure in r.; P. as if bones were pressed.

Foot.—Sudden swelling. Jerking in the weak foot when standing. Cramp. Stitching in a corn on l. when sitting. Cramplike pain on stretching it. Pain in corns; sore, in corn on raising foot, so that he stood only on the toes, in evening; in r. as if a plug were pushed upward on tarsal and metatarsal bone of little toe; as from fatigue, as if stones were tied upon them, < knees, > motion. Painful drawing transversely through joints when sitting. Burning itching deep internally under l. heel.

Toes.—*Stinging in r. when standing;* in great; in r. great, with burning. Tensive pain in external tendons on walking.

Skin.—Whole body pale. Desquamation. Red eruption about mouth and on chin; copper red, about mouth and chin. Red spots on nose, next day vesicles close together on nose. Rash on cheeks, with pain in face; rash (only about joints?) itching when warm, after scratching burning and hives as from stinging nettles. Painful tetter in various places; (dry T. between thumb and index). Red pimples on back of fingers, between second and third joints; painful P. on lower jaw, and on touch constricting pain, changing to a pustule, with inflamed areola. Eruption like the itch. Burning blisters like anthrax on l. thigh, elevated pustules with depressed tips, with dark red swollen areola, with tensive pain when walking, next day burning sticking when walking.

Stinging on throat and chest, > stroking (with redness and elevations like urticaria, which is noticed only on touch). Tension on forehead, with feeling as if it were difficult to move and a pressure. Sensitiveness, pain in every part on which he lies. Crawling on hands and fingers.

Itching on forehead; hollows of knees; great toe; (face); (here and there); shoulders, back, face, arms and fingers, with burning and shivering; palmar surface of l. middle finger and ball of thumb, with biting and stinging; legs, on rubbing painful pimples in skin; arms and legs, as if eruption would appear; as if pimples would appear here and there on face and behind ears, with sore sensation behind ears. Corroding itching; on inner side of wrist. Biting itching, with crawling, beneath lobule of r. ear; in calves when standing. Crawling itching on various parts of face, rather biting than stinging, then red pimples with hard, red, elevated margins, then brown tips, filled with yellow pus, when fully developed sore to touch.

Sleep.—*Yawning;* in morning; in morning, with stretching, with weakness and bruised feeling in joints as if he had not slept enough; after midday nap, with stretching; in evening; in evening, with stretching, weariness and sleepiness; with lachrymation; causing roaring in ears. *Sleepiness* at noon, so that the head nods, and when making an effort to talk the lids close and thoughts vanish; S. < afternoon; with starting up preventing sleep, then febrile attack. Falls asleep in afternoon when reading; when sitting, with partial consciousness. Sleeps with arms over head. Sleep heavy, dreamy; S. long, interrupted; stupefied; stupefying, a waking sopor; (too sound).

Sleeplessness; till midnight from mental activity, with heat and tossing about; with constant moving, after a while knees began to be cold, at 10 o'clock drawing in legs, then cold creeping as from snow-water, from knees to feet, with restlessness till 3 o'clock, only two hours of restless sleep in morning. Late falling asleep; on account of cold feet. Restless sleep; from 12 till 3 o'clock, then pain in shoulder. Whining in sleep. Sleep interrupted by anxiety and emotional disturbances, with complaints that the blood burns in the veins, < head, and of a spasm rising from chest to throat, with special heat of head and hands, the heat and anxiety > open air, then yawning. Frequent waking, with pain in forehead and temples and heaviness of head; (waking at night, with chilly trembling of r. arm).

Dreams; confused; indistinct, and waking early; of hunting; quarrelsome; frightful, then vomiting of tenacious green mucus; vivid, of robbers, he woke in fright and then believed that the dream was a reality; that he was violently pursued; anxious, for instance, that a dog was biting him and he could not get away; fatiguing, of climbing, jumping, fear of being pursued by armed men, then weakness in morning on waking, with heaviness of head and limbs; heavy (of difficult pushing through a narrow, low, dark cleft in a rock), with anxiety and sweat.

Fever.—Chilliness; in morning when dressing; in morning, **with thirst,** and weakness of limbs, < thighs; *with rigidity;* **creeping; running from head to toes, with thirst**; *alternating with heat and sweat;* alternations of C. and heat, with vertigo, anxiety and nausea. Shivering; all day, with smarting in skin; all day, with drawing pain in neck and back; in morning; afternoon; evening; *before vomiting; after drinking, with gooseflesh;* from every draught of air, with painful drawing through back, shoulders and arms; *with redness and heat of face;* with horripilation, for example, in face; waking from sleep, with cold feet and drawing up of legs; *in back and arms;* in back and arms, with warmth of lower limbs; over back, shoulders and arms all day; in limbs, < shoulders and arms, as if cold air streamed through the bones.

Cold skin (Camph., Sec. c.). **Coldness of head; then heat**; < sinciput; in vertex and feet; *creeping,* < **vertex**; with heat of it and with sensitiveness of hair; as from a cold wind through it. **Face cold, distorted, deathlike** (Camph.). **Coldness over back** (Sec. c.); then heat in it; *alternating with heat in it; extending into arms several times;* creeping. **Cold limbs**; upper; with drawing pain in them; arms on raising them. **Cold hands** (China, Ipec., etc.); before vomiting, after vomiting hot hands with orgasm of blood. Cold hands and feet after breakfast; in evening; preventing sleep till 3 A.M. *Cold feet, with hot red cheeks and contracted pupils;* (cold feet in afternoon when walking in melting snow, with moist feeling in them, in evening cramplike pain in them when walking); *as if cold water ran about in them, with trembling;* soles in evening in bed, forcing him to rise and walk about; to knees, as from a cold wind, waking him after midnight, > rubbing long.

Heat; every day; daily before midnight; in evening in bed, with sweat; then sweat, the room seemed obscure, could not tolerate the daylight nor hold up his head, but was forced to press it against the chest; with pale face and sweat; internal, yet he refuses drink. (Burning in skin beneath sweat.) *Heat of head;* sinciput, changing to warm then cold sweat on forehead. *Heat of face;* on and above red of upper lip; in morning in bed; (with redness and constant laughing); and of hands, *with redness of face,* indifferent mood, caring only for the things just about him, and tendency to start; and in eyes, as from hot steam, with redness of cheeks. Heat in region of scapulæ; H. streaming up back into occiput; in back as if sweat would break out in evening when walking slowly in open air. Hands hot, afterwards cold. Heat extending into tips of fingers and toes, with crawling. Burning in malleoli; in tibiæ in evening as if he had come from too great cold.

Sweat in evening when he wishes to sleep; at night; towards morning; in morning, < face, face inclined to sweat even during the day; in sleep; on motion. **Cold sweat** (Ant. t., Ars., China, Ip., Sec. c.); **on forehead; on forehead with the evacuation;** *on forehead on rising from a seat; on head and chest.* Sour sweat. Of bitter odor towards morning. Sweat on hands; (face and axillæ when walking).

Clinical.—It has been prescribed for congestive chills, which commence with coldness in the abdomen, cold breath, terrible vomiting and diarrhœa, with cold sweat, threatening collapse.

Veratrum Viride.

A tincture is made of the fresh root.

General Action.—It is a powerful respiratory poison, producing asphyxia; it paralyzes the heart and vasomotor centres and causes a low temperature (cold sweat and collapse). In large doses it produces convulsions. It excites vomiting, but not purging unless given in toxic doses.

Allies.—Bell., Hyos., Coccul., Ferr., Phos.

Generalities.—Tremor. Inability to control voluntary muscles. *Spasm, with shrieks,* body bent backward, arm rigid and thrown over head, face dark blue, breathing suspended, spasm repeated. Pains flying about in temple and l. trochanter major; in second joint of r. index, then in r. angle of lower jaw, then in l. heel, then in middle of l. neck, then in r. heel and l. knee; in l. humerus just above elbow, soon changing to region of l. nipple, then to middle of l. humerus, then to l. shoulder-joint, > 9 P.M. by eating; in different parts between 5 and 6 P.M., in l. chest, r. shoulder over clavicle, in head of l. tibia and three or four inches above the same, in tendons of r. popliteal space, in outside of r. arm and l. ulna, r. wrist, head of l. radius, back of first joint of l. middle finger and second phalanx of l. great toe. Distress.

Clothes would not fit me, seemed as if they scratched me somewhere and I could not relieve myself, constant twitching of different parts from trying to relieve the rubbing sensation; < sitting. Obliged to grasp the rails for support when walking. Muscular action interrupted after walking or jumping. *Weakness;* at 1 P.M., with trembling; with heavy pain in head; *sudden.* Faintness; on rising suddenly from reclining, with pallor. Stiffness of voluntary muscles, < temporal and extensors of head. Aggravation in morning on waking; in afternoon and evening. Amelioration from hot, strong coffee.

Clinical.—Inflammatory rheumatism. Effects of sunstroke. Most violent convulsions; epilepsy; hysteria; hystero-epilepsy; chorea, with violent congestion. Threatening tetanus. Has been used for poisoning by opium.

Mind.—Delirious; and quarrelsome, *striking and kicking with r. hand and foot* (Hyosc.), at times these movements appeared involuntary, the delirium became happy and comical. Fear of death. Thought it probable that I should die, but was not alarmed. Depression and prostration. Stupor when not vomiting. Lethargy between the vomiting spells, with slow and difficult respiration. Unconsciousness.

Clinical.—Furious delirium, with screaming, howling and striking. Delirium, with incessant muttering, dilated pupils, red streak down the tongue, etc.

Head.—Aching; at 4 P.M.; with full, heavy feeling in eyes; (with vomiting every ten or fifteen minutes); which stopped at temples and took a diagonal course across head; (central congestive), < noise and motion; heavy, with occasional painful throbbing in temples; heavy, at 7 P.M., with weakness, < lower limbs. Confusion; in afternoon and evening. *Fulness in morning, with heaviness;* (F. and congested feeling, with pain in forehead and nausea). Queer feeling. *Vertigo; in morning on rising* (Phos.); in morning, > *closing eyes and resting head, with photophobia* (Bell.); *on rising from bed, with vomiting* (Coccul.); *on rising from a seat or bed; with nausea* (Coccul.); *with nausea, then heat of surface;* in attacks, with nausea and pain in bowels.

Forehead.—Aching; over eyes; over r. eye; in morning on waking, > stool; at 6 P.M., with cold hands and feet, skin of head hot and moist; with contractive pain in skin of forehead; with vomiting and hiccough; with cold hands and feet; extending on l. side to occiput, all day after 1 P.M., < lying, especially lying on occiput; numb, constricted, pressing back to ears, sensation as if membrana tympani would break; drawing, at 2 P.M. Sharp drawing over l. eye, with contracted feeling in skin of forehead. Indescribable sensation rising towards crown and grasping, as it were, vertex and occiput, at night after a short sleep. Heaviness; over l. eye at 2 P.M. on stooping.

Neuralgic pains in temples; *in r. temple close to eye at* 10 A.M. Pain in r. temple and over r. eye and in r. malar-bone just under eye; in r. mastoid process; in l. side of head; at junction of l. parietal and temporal bones in forenoon; in l. side extending backward; in l. side back to temple; in l. side to temple in forenoon; in occiput.

Clinical. — Intense congestive headache, with throbbing stupefaction, double vision, numbness of the limbs, nausea, vomiting, etc. Cerebral apoplexy. Indicated in cerebral hyperæmia. Cerebro-spinal meningitis.

Eyes.—Glassy. Shooting in l., stopping suddenly. Pain in r.; in l. when riding in an omnibus; with cold feet. Lachrymation; with full feeling in lids as if he had cried much. **Pupils dilated** (Bell., etc.). Heaviness of lids, with soreness and sleepiness. Aching in upper part of r. orbit; over r. eye gradually extending to forehead. *Dim vision; on becoming erect, with partial syncope;* < while vomiting; (with green circles around gaslight). Vision impaired; dazzling; *unsteady;* of a green circle around candle (Phos.), which, as vertigo came on and I closed eyes, turned to red. *Blindness if he attempted to walk, with faintness.*

Ears.—Fulness in l., with audible beating in carotid. Ringing in r. at 2 P.M., moving quickly makes me deaf. *Humming, with sensitiveness to noise,* ears feel cold, with spells of deafness. (Noise.)

Clinical.—Acute inflammation in the middle ear (Ferr. phos.).

Nose.—Pinched and blue at 2 P.M. Catarrh and sneezing. Profuse mucus at 2 P.M., next day at 1 P.M.

Face. — **Flushed** (Bell.). Pale; with cadaverous look; and gray. Blue; and hippocratic. Sunken. Stinging in r. jugum malar at night. **Lips and mouth dry all day;** *lips dry, with thick mucus in mouth.* Jaws rigid. Pain in r. angle of lower jaw.

Mouth.—*Tongue feels scalded; feels scalded,* **red in centre,** *coated yellow at base; feels scalded,* **with red streak in centre,** coated yellow; coated yellow along centre in morning; (coated yellow, < along base and centre); red on edges, grayish from tip half way back, back part gray, with red spots of the size of a pin's head, strawberry tongue; bleached; bleached at centre and tip in morning, with red edges; white in centre, bright red at tip and edges. Speech lost; almost lost. Burning, and in throat; acrid B. Salivation; at 2 P.M., next day at 1 P.M. Taste flat in morning; flat, bitter in morning; bitterish, reminding one of the odor of spermatic fluid; (bitter to food); like lime-water to water.

Clinical.—The dry, red stripe through the centre of the tongue, especially when associated with a bloated, livid face, seems quite characteristic.

Throat.—Submaxillary glands swollen, sore to touch. Burning; and in œsophagus and stomach. Dryness causing short, dry cough; D. and heat in T. and fauces, which finally reached stomach. Numbness of fauces. Symptoms of globus hystericus. Inability to swallow. Sensation of a ball in œsophagus; rising as far as top of sternum, as from a gradual tonic contraction of stomach. Burning pain along œsophagus, with inclination to swallow.

Clinical.—Acute inflammation of the œsophagus, with fiery burning pains.

Stomach.—Ravenous appetite in morning on waking; at noon. Aversion to food, and after eating a little supper dyspepsia, partially > a glass of whisky. *Thirst in morning after rising, with nausea;* T. temporarily > drinking a little. Eructations of wind; acrid, sour E. *Hiccough; with spasms of upper part of œsophagus at* 2 P.M., next day at 1 P.M.; with salivation and discharge of mucus from stomach and nose. *Nausea;* > eating; > empty eructations; with desire for stool; with desire for stool, some wind passed but not much fæces; with drawing pain in lower part of chest. Retching; with pain; ineffectual.

Vomiting; *in morning on rising; with cold sweat* (Verat. alb.); with running from nose and eyes; with salivation and sweat; with collapse; with pain and weakness; without effort or nausea; without nausea, but with a sense of rising in œsophagus, which might be compared to the rumination of animals, feeling as if muscular fibres of stomach contracted gradually and steadily upon its contents until they were expelled, the diaphragm and abdominal muscles remaining inactive; of bile; of bile and then of mucus and dark blood, then retching, moaning and fear of death, > Ars.; white, ropy mucus; thick, glairy mucus and water; dinner, then thick, glairy mucus; food, mucus, etc.; food and contents of stomach, then glairy mucus; (food if ever so little is taken).

Spasm, and in respiratory organs. Cramp as if muscles were contracting, > bending forward, then pain in abdomen as if retracted. *Twisting tearing,* < motion. Neuralgic pains in cardiac portion at 7 P.M. Excruciating pain in lower part, with feeling as if the warm tea, etc., that I took to provoke vomiting went under the pain increasing the constriction; sharp P. in epigastric and umbilical regions at 11 A.M., passing down to pubes; sharp flying, in epigastric and umbilical regions in evening. Pain in epigastrium; at 9 P.M. Feeling in epigastrium as if a full dose of calomel were operating. Distress; in epigastrium, with sickness. Tightness. Feeling as if slowly contracting and forcing contents into œsophagus, causing sensation of a ball rising to top of sternum. Sensation of waves rising into chest at night on waking. Uneasiness; in epigastrium. Dyspepsia. Glow.

Abdomen.—Flatulence. Griping, with pain over epigastrium. *Pain;* in morning; at 2 and 6 P.M.; *with flatulence;* running down into scrotum; in region of gall-bladder at 8 P.M., next day at 8 A.M. Soreness across A.

Umbilical Region.—Cutting at 10 A.M., with rumbling in bowels and soft stool, at 4 P.M. pain and rumbling, at 5 P.M., with neuralgic pain in l. groin, at 8 P.M. pain in umbilicus, next day by spells shooting at 8 A.M. and noon, at 1 P.M. distress in U. region with desire for stool, at 10 P.M. mushy stool, then aching in rectum. Neuralgia in r. side passing to groin in evening. Pain; below navel; at 10 A.M., with heavy pain in region of gall-bladder; at 2 P.M.; drawing, at 11 A.M. and noon.

Hypogastrium.—(Cutting.) *Pain;* **just above pelvis** all day, *with soreness.*

Clinical.—Acute pelvic cellulitis and peritonitis.

Rectum and Anus.—Aching in R. after stool. Tenesmus at 6.30 A.M., waking him, soft stool, stringy and doughy, and at 7.30 stool of same consistence but with less tenesmus; sudden T. at 1 P.M. when riding, doubling me up, then an offensive, forcible, watery stool in one gush, then ineffectual desire and all the afternoon pain in abdomen. (Frequent desire preceded and followed by cutting in rectum); ineffectual D., with weakness and faintness. Crawling as of a worm in anus.

Stool.—Diarrhœa copious, offensive, with pale face, preceded by tenesmus and burning in anus; frequent D., with tenesmus, felt better after each stool; frequent, with tenesmus and burning, tenesmus > stool, next day constipation. Soft, frequent; S., large, bright-colored, prompt and sooner after rising than usual; S. and stringy, but seemed to stick in sphincter; alternately S. and hard every two hours, the soft one was doughy, stringy and large, the hard one was of medium size and followed by pain. Copious, free, light-colored. Doughy and hard to expel, twice in one day, tenesmus with the second one.

Urinary and Genital Organs.—Smarting in urethra on urinating. *Urine very clear;* U. increased; scanty; turbid, dark, with reddish sediment, covered with a scum. Painful testicles; l.; in morning, < l.; in evening; < l., sometimes shooting up cord into abdomen.

Clinical.—Rigid os during labor, with full bounding pulse, congested head, etc. Pelvic congestions, with tenderness, fever, etc. Puerperal fever, puerperal convulsions. Suppressed menses of plethoric women, with intense congestion of the head, sometimes with opisthotonos. Dysmenorrhœa, with most violent suffering, congested head or convulsions.

Respiratory Organs.—Tickling spasmodic cough in evening, coming from just above sternum. *Breathing difficult* (Ferr., etc.); *convulsive, almost to suffocation* (Verat. alb., Ferr., Phos.); B. heavy, almost stertorous; slow; short. Asphyxiated feeling when retching.

Clinical.—Bronchitis, with great dyspnœa, livid face, sometimes with cold extremities, irregular heart, cold sweat. Pneumonia; pulse full, hard, great difficulty of breathing, with throbbing headache, livid face, dry tongue, etc. Intense pulmonary congestion, with great arterial excitement, dyspnœa; it is generally indicated before hepatization has taken place. Occasionally useful in pleurisy.

Chest.—Feeling of dislocation in l. side in afternoon when walking (r., l.). Pain; below l. nipple; (in region of heart); about l. nipple in afternoon; most severe over front, with occasional twitchings in small intestines; burning, under sternum, in region of heart, at 2, 3 and 6 P.M. Constriction after vomiting, with anguish. Stricture. (Oppression.) Congestion of blood in lungs. Throbbing in r. side.

Heart.—Neuralgic pain in region and cardiac portion at 5 P.M. Pricking in region at noon and at 3 P.M. Hot pain in region at 3 P.M. Burning distress in region at 1 P.M. Action slow; (and weak).

Clinical. — Pericarditis and endocarditis. Hypertrophy. Valvular insufficiency.

Pulse.—Rapid on least exertion; R., full and strong; and irregular; and feeble; then slow. *Slow;* with sinking sensation about heart; and full, intermitting every sixth or seventh beat; and small, creeping; and weak; and weak, soft; and weak, small, soft. (Throbbing in carotids.) Soft; and irregular. Scarcely perceptible. Imperceptible.

Neck.—Pain in middle of l. side; in N. and arms; nape and arms, almost impossible to hold head up at 1. P.M.; at 2 P.M., < motion; at 4 P.M., and in arms; in r. sterno-mastoid near process in evening; in r. side about middle of sterno-mastoid, then itching in corresponding place on l. side. Feeling as if cords of nape were loose.

Back.—Pain. Weakness. Thrilling quivering about an inch to left of dorsal vertebræ, four inches below scapula in evening, on rising from reclining it changed into aching, later crawling with the thrilling. Pain in r. side of seventh vertebra; on r. side of dorsal spine; in l. scapula; in r. scapula in afternoon and evening; in bone of r. scapula, with darting from r. clavicle to scapula; in r. side of sacrum where it unites with pelvis.

Extremities.—Hands and feet shrivelled, as if they had been long in water. Cramplike sensation in gastrocnemii, with inability to exert them, repeated next day in G. and muscles of forearm, later sometimes calf, sometimes forearm and sometimes extensors of knees were affected.

Pain in condyles of legs and arms; middle of r. tibia and r. shoulder; l. instep and top of l. shoulder above clavicle and in l. heel; knees and elbow, generally about condyles; back part of second joint of r. middle finger and in second phalanx of r. great toe; l. elbow, lower third of l. tibia, < inner malleolus; knees, l. tibia above inner malleolus, above l. elbow and l. trochanter major; r. trochanter major, external condyle of l. humerus, l. radius and ulna, middle of r. tibia, l. ankle internally and externally; outside of middle of l. leg, in l. radius below elbow, in middle of l. femur, in outside muscles, and in l. trochanter; joints, < l. outer ankle; in forenoon in l. inner malleolus, l. great trochanter, l. shoulder and inner condyle of l. tibia; middle of r. tibia, then in muscles of l. thigh and in muscles above ridge of l. scapula; above l. elbow, rose to middle of humerus, then to shoulder-joint, then went to l. instep and outside of l. ankle, then to r. ankle; r. knee, about inner condyle of femur, soon extended to inner middle of thigh, wandered to front of thigh and above knee, then aching in inner condyle of l. femur, also inner condyle of l. humerus and l. instep, then settles in outside of r.

ankle; radial condyle of l. humerus and outer side of l. ankle, with shudderings; joints in morning on waking, till he fell asleep again, with shuddering, without chilliness, next morning woke with the shuddering and with throbbing aching in r. knee on which he was lying.

Thrilling aching in l. radius below elbow, then in inner condyle of r. femur, then in outer condyle of l. femur. Drawing pains in calves and r. elbow in evening. Feeling of clumsiness. Weakness; and stiffness; of gastrocnemii, then of all muscles of forearm.

Upper Extremities.—L. shoulder painful; in forenoon; towards back before going to bed; in upper part at night after going to bed; on top, in muscles above scapular ridge at night. Thrilling or shuddering in region of l. shoulder. Pain in arms at 11 A.M.; arms on holding something in hand; inner condyle of l. humerus; outer condyle of l. humerus in forenoon; outer condyle of l. humerus at night; humerus above elbow at night; at end of r. elbow; r. elbow, going to scapula, when riding in an omnibus; carpal end of r. ulna; middle of l. ulna in morning; r. ulna, two inches above wrist, and in third phalanx of r. index, in forenoon; r. pisiform bone in morning; second phalanx of r. thumb in afternoon and evening; sudden, in first joint of r. ring finger at night before going to bed; pulsating, in first joint of r. middle finger.

Lower Extremities.—Loss of locomotion. Sudden lancing pain in r. hip where gluteals are lost in thigh, on going to bed. Pain in l. great trochanter; inner condyle of l. femur; inner side of l. thigh just above condyle; above l. knee; great trochanter in forenoon; above l. knee in evening, and in r. knee; great trochanter when lying on it at night, r., then l.; l. hip on waking, then < r.; l. hip when sitting on it; suddenly in r. trochanter.

Knee.—Sprained pain at inner condyle of l. femur when walking, with pain in second phalanx of l. great toe. Pain in tendons about popliteal space, then in l. instep and in middle of r. tibia; in r. knee, l. inner malleolus, etc., in morning; in r. K. and ankle in morning on waking; sometimes simultaneous, sometimes alternate, at night. Throbbing aching on going to bed; in r., on which he was lying, in morning on waking, > turning on l. side and rubbing, it then appeared in l. knee, then in r., > dressing, then returned, pains are apt to come when the limb is in a constrained position.

Leg.—Cramps; in calves in morning, waking him; tendency to C. on touch or motion. Spasmodic contraction of muscles. Pain in head of l. fibula; and inner condyle of l. tibia; P. about middle of l. tibia; lower third of l. tibia; top of lower third of l. tibia, then in lower part of l. calf; r. tibia and ankle in afternoon; about middle of l. tibia when sitting; back of r. leg, two or three inches above ankle, < moving great toe. Drawing in r. calf when walking. Paralyzed sensation in extensors of feet.

Dislocated feeling in r. ankle on walking. Sharp pain about middle of l. instep towards inside. Aching inside in bend of l. foot at 9 P.M. when eating; r. side of l. sole at night when lying on r. side; in l. instep on stretching foot; second phalanx of l. great toe.

Skin.—Mortification of arm (after compound fracture of humerus). Peculiar sensation. Itching below r. corner of mouth; in malar prominence; line between r. ala nasi and face; first joint of l. thumb, l. ala nasi, l. cartilage of nose, lip under l. ala nasi, in l. ear; r. mastoid process and middle of inside of l. thigh; l. malar prominence in morning; middle of l. brow on going to bed; l. malar prominence, with crawling. Itching at night in r. malar region; about middle of l. sterno-mastoid; on back of first joint of l. index and in corresponding joint of next finger. Itching at night in bed, r. brow, r. ala nasi and l. malar prominence; about line of ala nasi and cheek; l. malar prominence, orifice of l. ear and l. groin; r., then l. ala nasi; r. ala nasi, then stinging in r. jugum of malar, > rubbing, then I. in l. ala nasi; r. ala nasi when lying on r. side, changing to l. ala when he turned to l. side.

Clinical.—Erysipelas; sometimes in the first stage of phlegmonous E. Erysipelas of the head and face, with the peculiar tongue, delirium, etc.

Sleep.—Sleepiness. Little sleep; with restlessness. Restless, with frightful dreams of people drowning. Dreaming much; *D. of water;* of water, fishing, etc.; frightful, of being on the water; odd, in which the Atlantic figured largely; in which he was continually provoked and baffled.

Fever.—Chilliness; in morning after rising; with sweat; with cold sweat on limbs. Agues. Shuddering; towards morning; and hands and feet cold and benumbed, a cold numb feeling crept up arms and legs, finally the whole body felt as if enveloped in cold damp clothing and I became prostrate; on waking S. in r., then l. shoulder, then in chest extending into abdomen. Cold skin; with clammy sweat. Cold limbs; as far as knees and elbows; hands and feet; covered with clammy sweat.

Heat of body, with cold sweat on forehead; H. of skin, then dizziness, nausea and coldness; (burning in head, with flushed face). *Sweat; with weakness; cold;* cold, on hands and face; cold, clammy, on brow.

Verbascum.

A tincture is made of the fresh plant, Verbascum Thapsus, L. (the mullein).

Generalities.—Narcotic effects. Sinking sensation.

Mind.—Excited fantasies, especially of a sensual nature. Joyfulness, with laughter. Fretfulness, with inclination to work and satisfaction in having people about him and in talking with them. Anxiety all day, > towards evening. Depression all day, all his efforts and hopes seem unavailing. Disinclination for work. Indifference. Distraction. Memory diminished. When writing, tendency to omit words or insert wrong ones in their places, or to leave out letters in well-known words.

Head.—*Benumbing pain, rather external, < forehead;* stupefying P., < sides of forehead. Tingling when walking. Confusion; with confined sensation; as if everything would press out at forehead. Heaviness; with vertigo, somewhat pleasurable. *Vertigo in attacks when head is supported by pressure on l. cheek;* sudden V. as from pressure upon middle of head.

Forehead.—Sticking outward in l. eminence; intermittent S. in l. side; intermittent, deep between l. eminence and parietal eminence. Prickling in l. sinus. Slow hammering in l. eminence. Pain; < over r. eye; sharp, in r. eminence; extending outward, > stooping; intermittent P. and beating near l. eminence; stupefying, deep in r. eminence on going from the cold into warmth; more pressing than tearing above l. orbit. Pressure outward, < between brows; benumbing P. inward in l. side of bone. Benumbing drawing in l. eminence in a draught of air.

Temples.—Sticking jerking externally in l., then r. Benumbing stitches above r.; *deep in r. when eating, < pressure, after a few hours it extended like a tearing into r. upper teeth.* **Sensation as if pinched together with pincers;** *in articular eminences of bone.* Prickling in l., with burning. Pain in r.; *in articular eminence of bone in front of l. ear;* in articular eminence of bone, < biting teeth together. Pressure forward in l.

Vertex.—Pressing pain on it. Tension in l. side, gradually becoming a sharp pressure, at the same time l. ramus of lower jaw seems pressed against upper.

Sides.—*Sticking extending forward through l. hemisphere of brain;* intermittent S. behind l. eminence. Tearing in r. half of brain. Pain extending outward in r. half of brain; jerking P. in l. half of brain; benumbing, in l. and in l. cheek.

Occiput.—Sticking in l. side. Pain; in r. protuberance.

Eyes.—Heat, with contracted sensation in orbits. Pupils dilated. Dimness of vision, watery, increase of shortsightedness, objects seem indistinct and enlarged.

Ears.—Tearing stitch in l. when eating; in front of l., extending downward. Tearing in r.; *in l., extending inward, with drawing. Sensation as if l. would be drawn inward.* Sudden pressure behind r., with stitches. *Feeling of deafness in l. Stopped sensation in l., then r.;* in ears, nose and larynx when reading aloud, not affecting hearing.

Clinical.—Deafness; feeling as though the ears were stopped (this very ancient use of the mullein has been lately revived in the local use of "mullein oil." See current literature).

Nose.—Coryza, with watery, bland discharge. Thick tenacious mucus in posterior nares, causing constant inclination to hawk, could raise but little.

Face.—Pallid. *Sticking in l. zygomatic arch;* intermittent, in l. zygomatic process. Pressure on r. malar-bone; **on l. zygomatic arch as far as ear,** *during the day, in evening before going to bed and in morning on waking, <pressure; benumbing, intermittent, on upper margin of l. zygomatic process* (compare *Plat.*). *Tension in integuments of chin, masseter muscles and throat,* but jaws can be moved easily; *in l. zygomatic process, articular elevation of temporal bone and frontal eminence on going into open air and in a draught of air.* **Pinching** *on r. side of lower jaw. Pressure in l. joint of jaw, involving whole cheek, becoming on pressure a* **benumbing tension.**

Clinical.—Facial neuralgia; the pains tend to recur periodically, they feel like the crushing of tongs, benumbing, sometimes lightning-like, particularly beginning in the malar-bone and articulation of jaw, < change of temperature, pressure, or any motion of the muscles of the face. Infraorbital and supraorbital neuralgia.

Mouth.—Tearing in r. large lower molars; intermittent, in l. small lower molars. *Tongue brown at root in morning on rising and in forenoon;* brown at root in forenoon, with flat, nauseous taste; coated brownish-yellow in morning, with flat taste and offensive breath; brownish-yellow after dinner, coated with tenacious mucus. (Collection of salt water.) Flat taste some time after a meal.

Stomach.—Hunger without appetite through the day, nothing is relished, yet he wishes to eat. Unquenchable thirst. Eructations of tasteless liquid; empty E.; bitter, qualmish. *Hiccough.* Pressure. Emptiness in pit, which disappeared with rumbling below l. ribs.

Abdomen.—Tympanitic, then rumbling beneath l. ribs, which caused loud eructations. Tearing sticking extending downward; intermittent S. in back part between r. loin and spine. Griping as from incarcerated flatus; cutting G., with eructations; cutting G. here and there, rising towards ribs, where it becomes seated. Pain extending low down, causing spasmodic contraction of sphincter ani and desire for stool. Rumbling in l. hypochondrium, with gurgling. Sticking deep in l. side where ribs cease. Sticking pinching beneath r. hypochondrium. Umbilical region, stitches round to back and in dorsal vertebræ, on deep inspiration and on stooping; intermittent stitches in r. side; intermittent stitches in l. side above navel; intermittent stitches in l. side beneath navel, < bending forward after eating; sensation as if intestines were adherent to wall and were being torn away, < pressure; *pressure as from a stone, < stooping;* constriction. Gurgling in hypogastrium. Sticking deep in r. side above pubis.

Stool.—Soft; with straining. Scanty and like sheep-dung, with pressure. Thick, pasty, nearly black. Omitted.

Urinary Organs.—*Frequent micturition, copious, afterwards scanty.* Frequent desire, with scanty discharge; with copious discharge.

Clinical.—Constant dribbling of urine. Nocturnal enuresis.

Sexual Organs. — Desire, with lascivious fancies. Emissions at night; without lascivious dream; in morning after waking and falling asleep again, with erratic dreams.

Respiratory Organs.—Hoarseness on reading aloud.

Chest.—Sticking in l. in middle axillary line; in next to last rib where it passes into the cartilage, > pressure, but returning; beneath l. nipple on inspiration, whereby another deep inspiration was caused; intermittent, near l. side of ensiform cartilage; benumbing, taking away the breath, in region of first and second costal cartilages. Intermittent, benumbing cutting near l. side of ensiform cartilage, below last ribs. Sharp pressure beneath l. nipple. Pain and oppression, with disinclination to frequent breathing. Tension in evening as soon as he lay down, with stitches in region of heart.

Clinical.—A popular remedy for asthma and chronic coughs.

Pulse.—Reduced in number, and especially in force.

Back.—Sticking in last dorsal vertebra on sitting bent over; intermittent, in l. scapula.

Extremities.—Stretching. Pain on top of shoulder, pressing rather than tearing, > motion. Cramplike pressure at l. elbow, extending into forearm. Tearing downward in shaft of l. ulna. Tensive pain in l. wrist. *Stitches like a sprain (or paralysis) where carpal bone of thumb articulates with radius.* Sticking in external condyle of palm; between metacarpal bones of r. thumb and index; tearing, in palm. Cramplike pressure now in r., now in l. metacarpus on moving arm. Pain on back of r. hand, pressing rather than tearing. Bruised pain on outer side of metacarpal bones of little fingers on touch. Sticking in proximal phalanx of l. thumb; tearing, through l. little finger; intermittent, in middle joint of index; intermittent, in distal phalanx of index, on motion the pain extended into proximal joint. Cramplike pressure in proximal phalanx of r. thumb, > motion. Paralytic drawing in l. index. Paralytic pain in l. fingers, < metacarpal joints. Insensibility of thumb (from application of juice).

Lower Extremities.—Tottering in open air. Weariness. Heaviness on ascending and descending stairs. Stitches above l. patella on stepping. *Cramplike pain in muscles of r. thigh when walking in open air;* in muscles above r. knee when sitting and standing. Drawing pressing from middle of r. thigh to knee when sitting. Paralytic pain on inner side of r. thigh when leg is drawn up in sitting, on treading sticking extending towards knee. Knees tremble. *Sudden pain through r. knee when standing, sitting and walking.* Leg, tearing downward; cramplike pressure on l. near ankle. Weakness in bone of r. when riding r. thigh over l. Intermittent sticking in metatarsal bones of l. great and adjacent toes during rest. *Cramplike pressure in r. sole when standing, > walking.*

Skin.—Pimple in front of r. ear, with stinging on touch; red, near thyroid cartilage, painful on pressure. Tingling and pricking almost like nettles (from the leaves). Itching, crawling tickling on side of l. middle finger. Itching on forearm.

Sleep.—Yawning and stretching. Sleepiness; in morning after rising, with indolence; irresistible, after dinner. Restless sleep. Sleep only till 4 A.M., filled with dreams of war and corpses, several nights.

Fever.—Coldness over whole body, perceptible externally on hands and feet; cold limbs. Shivering, < from one shoulder to thigh, as if cold water were poured over it.

Vespa.

A tincture is made of live wasps (Vespa crabo).

Generalities.—Trembling, quaking, with chattering of teeth. Nervo-muscular excitement. Stinging piercing deeply, as if a hook were pulled out; sudden S. and burning in cheek waking me at 4 A.M. (after a sting on cheek), with soreness and smarting along lymphatics into neck, cheek swollen and red, maxillary joint stiff and painful, sore feeling ran along gums to tonsil, relief from bathing, two hours later suddenly aroused by suffocation, difficulty in swallowing and renewal of former distress, the symptoms returned in paroxysms, submaxillary and cervical glands of the side became swollen and tender, pains about wound became more constant, were throbbing, smarting and burning, but there was a periodicity about the stinging for more than a month, though the wound suppurated and discharged freely, slight rigors and febrile conditions, < evening.

Sudden tearing. Cutting like electric shocks through all joints, arm, head and face swollen, eyes red and twitching, red lines along absorbents, itching over whole body, insensibility, vomiting, pulse slow, heart's action scarcely preceptible. Pain after sting in region of brows, with inflammation and mortification. Feeling as if dying, at night. Distress. Weakness; with enuresis somni, heat especially overpowers him. Faintness; all day, with trembling and nausea.

Mind.—Anxiety. Low-spirited. Insensibility. Unconsciousness, with inability to move.

Eyes.—Injection of r. conjunctiva. Itching of r. lid in evening, with swelling, afterwards pain in lid and ball, erysipelatous inflammation of lid, whole side of face painful and swollen, *almost complete chemosis of conjunctiva, it being raised up on the sclerotic membrane, more than half over eye to border of cornea, as if fatty matter were under it, caused by effusion of lymph*, an abscess opened upon inside of upper lid about its centre, later the chemosis became reddish.

Clinical.—Inflammation of r. eye, with baggy swelling of conjunctiva.

Ears and Face.—Sticking deep in r. ear. Face livid. Purulent catarrh of middle ears. Face smooth, dark red, bloated. Anxious expression. Face and eyes œdematous, F., mouth and throat appeared as in severe cynanche (after a sting on tongue).

Mouth. — Tongue swollen and tense, swelling below chin, between that and hyoid bone, pain in a point in middle line, three-quarters of an inch from apex; swollen, red, rounded, filled the mouth, immovable, could not speak, only mumbled, swallowing was painful and difficult. Swelling of palate, with inflammation, so preventing respiration that he died; S. of mouth and throat, with burning pain, nausea, vertigo, after two hours fever, delirium, face, neck, arms and chest swollen and shining red, respiration impeded, swallowing difficult, pulse 126, heart's action irregular and tumultuous, cured by Camph. Peculiar taste, a combination of palatal and nasal sensation, as when a nest of wasps is disturbed, < heat.

Throat.—Swelling. Soreness. Heat. Difficulty in swallowing.

Stomach and Abdomen.—Hunger. Thirst. Eructations. Nausea; in evening after coming indoors, with weight in stomach; with faint feeling and trembling. Vomiting, with swelling of head. Cold feeling in stomach. Heat in S. Uneasiness in abdomen.

Urinary and Sexual Organs.—Clinical.—Burning micturition, in women. Valuable in affections of l. ovary, with tenderness, frequent micturition, pain in sacrum, extending up back.

Respiratory Organs.—Hoarseness. Voice lost. Spasm of glottis (after application of diluted ammonia to tongue), face pale, drops of sweat on forehead, arms thrown out to gasp for air, he got out of bed, sank back on bed, face livid, breath and pulse stopped. Dyspnœa. Respiration hurried.

Pulse.—Rapid and small; R. and feeble; R., with violent beating of carotids.

Neck, Back and Extremities.—Pain in l. side of neck, waking her at night, preventing her from turning it to l. side, felt least when lying on back, best on r. side. Pain in scapula (place of sting), with soreness. Pain in shoulder, in region of stings, axillary glans swollen. Sprained pain in l. shoulder-joint on moving it, < lifting arm or twisting it. Aching in hand and arm.

Skin.—Redness of hands, feet and chest. Swelling of face, body and limbs; of cheek, skin soon became bright red, the redness spread over head and down neck, shoulders, back and front of chest, with pain and tenderness; of the part (r. side of neck), with aching, redness and burning, the B. > then < cold water; of thumb and face, < lids, face, < ears, soon became red as if covered with scarlet rash, restlessness at night, heat, irritation, and wherever he scratched himself there arose spots like nettle-rash, S. and redness of l. arm and hand, after forty hours œdema of lids, < lower, face pallid and puffy. Prurigo-like, pinkish, lentil-shaped spots on hand and forearm, on neck, and all over down to feet. Ulcer. Desquamation of whole surface. Abscesses over whole body, causing emaciation.

Itching of whole body; of the part every day about 3 or 4 A.M., slightly > applications of vinegar, always burning after scratching, also the same every day about 8 or 9 A.M. and at 3 P.M., the I. > applications of salt and vinegar.

Sleep and Fever.—Night restless. Sleepless all night. Heat, with sick feeling, vertigo, almost faintness. Burning (after the sting) as if something were sticking and drawing out, the part stung was bright red, elevated, with hard swelling, the redness surrounded by a circle of chilliness, soon changing to a general chill, intermittent, extending in waves over whole body; B. of the part, then swelling, red, with burning pain.

Viburnum Opulus.

A tincture is made of the fresh bark of the root of the "high cranberry." (It contains Valerianic acid !).

Generalities.—Pains flying from one part to another; wandering, tired pains extending to hips and knees, with disinclination to move about. Soreness of muscles of l. side of body. Nervous, cannot keep still. Languid and dull feeling. Tired in morning on rising. *Inability to lie on affected side;* on l. side. Aggravation in evening or night; A. in a warm room. Amelioration in open air; from pressure; from motion, walking.

Clinical.—It is used for hysteria.

Mind.—Exaltation of spirits, in some cases followed by depression. Depressed. Irritable, wishes to be alone. Confusion; and inability to concentrate it. Stupid feeling as if I could not tell where I was or what to do, in morning on waking. Inability to perform mental labor.

Head.—*Hurt by every cough.* Pain beginning about 3 P.M., < night; P., with red face; throbbing, all the evening, so severe on retiring that I felt sick all over; heavy, < over eyes, < l. side, at times extending to vertex and occiput (< when delayed menses should appear), < a sudden jar, bending over, false step or movement. Dull and sluggish. *Vertigo;* in afternoon on closing eyes; < descending stairs or walking in a dimly-lighted room; with inclination to turn to left; as if he would fall forward, on rising from a seat.

Forehead.—*Pain;* over l. eye; in r. supraorbital region; in forenoon; over eyes on opening them, the soreness extending back into head; with occasional vertigo, almost incapacitating him for study, with profuse and frequent micturition; and in supraorbital region, with profuse, clear, watery urine; beginning over r. eye and extending to vertex, with fulness in head and pressure on vertex; throbbing, extending to eyeballs, < mental exertion, > moving about; confusing, extending to temples, as after night-watching, compelling cessation of mental exertion.

Pain in l. temple, with pinching; *P. in l. side of head;* sharp, in parietal region, penetrating into brain, < coughing, moving head and stool. Aggravation on r. side. Hair feels as if pulled. Scalp sensitive to touch.

Eyes.—Swelling about r., with induration. Sclerotica streaked with blood. Sensation of sand. Pain, < r., with congestion. Sore feeling on closing lids. Burning and lachrymation. Heaviness, feel almost sick enough to go to bed; H. over eyes and in balls, at times had to look twice to be sure of seeing an object. Balls feel sore. Lids swollen.

Ears.—Stabbing. Pains in bone, waking at night. External ear sore as if bruised, cannot lie on affected side of head, had to rub ear and it seemed as if I must straighten it out, sensation as if pinned to head, lay on other side and was awakened by the same feeling in that ear, in consequence compelled to change position often.

Nose and Face.—Sneezing. Watery coryza. Face flushed and hot. Lips dry.

Mouth and Throat.—Tooth sore on pressure. Tongue broad and white, with brown centre and imprints of teeth. Dryness of tongue; of mouth. Taste disagreeable; coppery. Tickling in r. side of pharynx, causing cough.

Stomach.—Nausea; every night; during menses; for ten days after menses, with faintness at stomach; > eating, with faintness, both returning; in pit of stomach, > lying perfectly quiet, faintness always on trying to get up; *with faintness;* (without inclination to vomit), > *eating;* then vomiting. Pain; in afternoon, > stretching body and throwing stomach forward; cramplike, and in abdomen, doubling him up. Sensitiveness of region. Indigestion, food lies heavy. Goneness.

Abdomen.—Rumbling and darting pains. Darting pains, which settle about navel. Flying pains. Bearing-down pains as during menstruation, with heavy pain over pubes; B. down pain, with drawing pains in anterior muscles of thighs and occasional shooting in ovarian regions. Sensitiveness to pressure, < about umbilicus. Pressure of flatus in l. side. Throbbing pain under l. floating ribs from 11 P.M. till 3 A.M., > hard pressure and walking about the room. Throbbing in l. hypochondrium when lying on l. side. Sticking in spleen in evening, > walking about the room, with sensation as if hot fluid ran through its vessels. Pain in region of spleen causing faintness, > sweat. *Cramping pain in hypogastrium* during menstruation; *sudden C. pain; as before menstruation,* < night.

Rectum.—Hæmorrhage of dark red blood during and after stool. *Inactivity, no inclination for stool.*

Stool.—Watery, profuse, frequent, at menstrual period, with chills and cold sweat rolling off forehead. *Constipation;* with *tenesmus,* when bowels moved pain in l. orbital region; desire, with much straining; alternating with diarrhœa. *Hard, large, with cutting in rectum and anus; H., large, painful and so difficult that mechanical assistance was necessary;* scanty, in balls, difficult; and scanty, with hæmorrhage, with constriction of rectum and anus; and long, large, difficult, having a desire to evacuate, but on attempting feels as if nothing were there, stool slow and only after long straining. *Large, difficult,* with urging. Irregular. Omitted two days, then hard, with blood and *soreness of anus.*

Urinary Organs.—Sensation after micturition as if urine continued to flow. *Copious urine;* in morning, *clear, watery,* sp. gr. 1019, frequent micturition; every hour in afternoon and evening; at night, *and pale,* sp. gr. 1021; every hour or two during menses, and *clear,* *light-colored;* and watery; in afternoon, watery, clear, micturition frequent. Light-colored urine.

Clinical.—Spasmodic dysuria.

Sexual Organs.—Pain in r. side of epididymis, with swelling; of l. side of E. and l. testicle, with swelling. Emission without dream.

Female.—Leucorrhœa; thick, white and copious; thin, yellowish-white after menses; thin, colorless, except with every stool, when it was thick, white, inodorous, blood-streaked; causing redness, smarting and itching of genitals. *Sudden pain in womb and hypogastrium before menstruation. Pain in ovarian region. Congested feeling in pelvic organs, as before menses. Bearing-down pains in pelvic region, with uneasiness; B. down as before menses; as during menses, with heavy aching in sacral region and over pubes; as during menses, with drawing pains in anterior muscles of thighs,* every day after 3 P.M., *with occasional shooting over ovaries, later the same pains, with nervousness, could not sit or lie still on account of the pains. Menstrual pain, with feeling as if the breath would leave her body and heart would cease to beat.* Menses too early, profuse and offensive; *too late, scanty, thin, light-colored, lasting but a few hours, with lightness of head, faintness on attempting to sit up;* looks like jelly; stains permanently; ceased for several hours, then four large clots of the color of raw beef, and as solid as liver; for two days flow like normal M., but with cramping pain and nervousness.

Clinical.—Dysmenorrhœa, excruciating colic through the uterus and lower part of the abdomen, just preceding menstruation. It is very valuable for after-pains. The uterine pains are like those of Sepia, extending around the pelvis to the uterine region, with sensation of emptiness and goneness, but they are much more violent and become cramplike, sometimes extending down thighs. Membranous dysmenorrhœa. Cramps in the calves always between the menses, < just before the period, with scanty, delayed menstruation, dysmenorrhœa, etc.

Respiratory Organs, Chest and Heart.—Hoarse. Suffocating spells at night. Shooting over l. sixth rib near sternum. In lungs sensation as if muscles of chest failed to act, causing dyspnœa. Heart's action increased.

Neck.—Stiffness, with pain in occiput; S. in nape, with sore feeling.

Back.—*Pain as if it would break during menses.* Lame and bruised feeling in muscles. Wandering, tired pains in muscles, < l. side. Tired, bruised pain in muscles from point of scapula to wing of ilium, on both sides of spine, > firm pressure. Pain in lumbar region; between l. floating ribs and wing of ilium, > pressure, but must keep moving; in kidney region, < working in laboratory, > pressing across back with arms crossed; in l. loin and l. hypochondrium, causing faintness, > warm sweat though the night was cool; throbbing, in l. loin, < lying down, > walking with cane pressed across back; *in back, loins and hypogastrium as if menses were coming on, < early part of evening and in a close room, > open air and moving about.*

Extremities.—Pain in r. shoulder. Soreness of l. shoulder in region of subclavian muscle, < rest and wet weather, > motion, with lameness. Pain in l. biceps. Numbness of l. arm and hand. Buzzing feeling in hands as if they would burst. Swelling of fingers, < washing in cold water, with numbness. Weakness of lower, with heaviness. Feeling in feet as from the starting of circulation after constriction is removed.

Sleep and Fever.—Sleepy after dinner. Sleep restless and unrefreshing; R. and disturbed; disturbed by slight noise. Disagreeable dreams. Chill from 8 till 10 A.M. or 12 M., then headache.

Viburnum Prunifolium.

"A tincture is made of the fresh, ripe fruit." (The bark is officinal in the allopathic pharmacopœias).

Before she had swallowed the third dose she fell and had to be carried to the bed, her throat became dry, complained of loss of vision, partial loss of speech and general relaxation of system.

Clinical.—Valuable in many cases of threatening miscarriage; it checks the flow. Supposed to be a uterine tonic.

Vinca.

A tincture is made of the fresh plant. Vinca minor, L., the lesser Periwinkle.

Arthritic tearing in bones. Tremulous feeling in all vessels; T. feeling, < upper limbs, with tendency to start, < exerting the mind. Empty feeling in various parts. Weakness. Most symptoms > moving in open air. Sadness, with fear of death. Lachrymose. Peevish and quarrelsome, soon followed by repentance. Headache. Pressure externally upon head. Vertigo, with flickering before eyes. Dulness of sinciput, < stooping when writing, with slow pressure towards eyes and dimness of eyes. Sticking in l. temple, extending towards malar-bone. Pressure in temples. Tearing in vertex, with hammering outward. Matting of the hair. Moist eruption on scalp, with vermin, especially itching at night, with burning after scratching. Corrosive itching of scalp. Itching biting on scalp, < vertex.

Itching of eyelids, with burning and redness. On getting snuff into the eye there was so little secretion that he was obliged to wash it out. Vision obscured when reading, also at times when walking. Ringing and whistling in ears, with feeling of a cold wind, < l. ear. Tip of nose red from slightest cause. Eruption on septum, discharging a moisture which formed a light brown scab, the skin was dirty white, elevated, with a red areola. Dryness in nose, extending into frontal sinus, with heat. Itching in nose. Stoppage of nose, < one nostril, with discharge of much mucus through posterior nares. Nosebleed. Swelling of face, with papules. Pallor. Tearing in malar-bones. Swelling of upper lip and of corner of mouth. Itching of upper lip. Lips dry.

Toothache; tearing, > warmth of bed. Aphthæ in mouth. Salivation. Insipid taste; to all food. Hawking through the day. Ulcers in the throat (?). Sore throat, with difficulty in swallowing. Sensation of something sticking low down in œsophagus, which provokes swallowing. Hunger alternating with loss of appetite before the hunger has been satisfied. Little thirst. Empty eructations after beer, generally < taking liquids; violent empty E. Nausea; after coffee. Violent, copious vomiting of bitter, yellowish-green liquid. Gastric disturbances. Emptiness in stomach. Flatulence. Abdomen full, tense, but painless; A. distended after stool. Rumbling, with gurgling and emission of offensive flatus. Griping. Urging to stool.

Stool first hard, then soft. Stool exhausting, with burning in anus. Urine diminished. Urine pale. Excessive menstruation, with weakness.

Hoarseness. Tenacious mucus in trachea. Spasmodic cough, with little tickling in larynx. Rapid respiration. Stitches on sternum; in chest, with pains and dyspnœa. Pressure on sternum, with empty feeling in chest. Painful tension in cervical muscles, with stiffness and weight. Tearing in limbs. Inclination to stretch limbs. Swelling of first joints of fingers, with stiffness of them and with burning pain in nails. Cramplike drawing in upper arm and tips of fingers; in feet and toes. Itching moist spots on upper part of r. ankle. Burning in the ulcers like bed-sores on l. nates. Sensitiveness of skin, with redness and soreness, even from slight rubbing. Corrosive itching. Yawning. Sleepless and restless at night. Lascivious dreams. Sudden paroxysms of shivering. Heat, with full, hard pulse; H. in scalp, with prickling; in cheeks, without redness.

Clinical.—Eczema of scalp and face, with offensive odor. Eczema matting the hair together. Bald spots sometimes become covered with very fuzzy hair. Crusta lactea. Menorrhagia, continuous flow, particularly at the climacteric. It is especially useful for hæmorrhages after the climacteric. Hæmorrhages from fibroid tumors.

Viola Tricolor.

A tincture is made of the whole plant in flower (Pansy).

Generalities.—Feeling as if he had not slept enough in forenoon when sitting. Exhaustion.

Clinical.—General aggravation in winter and cold air.

Mind.—Hasty in his actions as if impelled by anxiety, yet feeling of prostration. Sad about his domestic relations. Disobedient. Morose all day, with sensitiveness and little desire to talk; M. all day, inclined to quarrel and dispute; M. all day, in evening jolly and inclined to talk; and quiet, indifferent; and weeping mood. Introspective, discouraged, discontented with his work; I., discontented with himself, distrustful of himself, especially of his future. Disinclination for mental work; D. for earnest wrok. Dulness in afternoon and evening, with disinclination to talk, which was almost impossible.

Head.—Tearing, with heat in face and thirst. Pain in brain; P., with pressure in forehead; *in brain extending outward through forehead.* Confusion; with pressure in frontal bones; with pressure in forehead, and when walking the brain shakes, with heaviness, as if a stone were in it, which extended forward into head. Heaviness, with pressure towards forehead; H. as if a weight pressed it forward, > stooping, < rising. Vertigo when walking, with reeling.

Forehead.—Burning stitch in bone. Pain above r. eye, > pressure; extending from root of nose into brain, > open air; wavelike. Tensive drawing externally in l. side, extending into cervical muscles. Tingling when sitting still.

Tearing stitch externally in l. temple. Pressure outward in temples. Pain in l. temple near eye; burning, on r. side of vertex when sitting; bruised, in parietal bone on touch. Pressure outward in r. side of head. Sticking in l. side of occiput; tensive in r. muscles of occiput.

Clinical.—Eczema of scalp, with swollen cervical glands. In crusta lactea it is similar to Vinca (but Viola has urine like cat's urine). By some considered nearly specific in eczema of the scalp, especially with matted hair.

Eyes.—Itching-cutting stitches outward in r. Biting in l. as if sweat were in it. Pupils contracted. Tensive stitch in l. ball, persistent on motion. Sensation of a hard body between balls and upper lids. Lids pressed together and difficult to open. Hardened matter in canthi. Vision obscured, especially distant objects.

Clinical.—Scrofulous ophthalmia, with crusta lactea.

Ears, Nose and Face.—Itching stitches behind l. ear. Pressure inward upon drum of ear. Itching pressure towards l. side of nose. Drawing tension in l. cheek, in front of ear. Drawing pain from l. side of lower jaw into r. side of head.

Mouth and Throat.—Tongue white. Tongue covered with bitter mucus. Salivation, with dry sensation in mouth. Sore throat in evening.

Stomach.—Loss of appetite and taste. Empty eructations. Nausea and retching. Sticking in diaphragm during inspiration and expiration. Constriction in pit on inspiration.

Abdomen. — Rumbling and emission of flatus. Stitches like lightning in r. side of A. and chest when walking; griping S. when walking, so that he must stand still. Griping. Cutting; with urging to stool; with howling and screaming, then sleep at noon, the pain returned on waking, then emission of flatus and stool with mucus in large pieces. Sticking in upper A. during inspiration and expiration; S. externally in umbilical region. Sticking cutting in hypochondrium on inspiration while sitting bent over. Stitches in l. groin when sitting and on rising up; jerklike, in forepart of hypogastrium when sitting, > standing up, leaving burning. Pinching crawling in r. side of pelvis when sitting.

Rectum and Stool.—Excessive urging to stool, which is normal. Stool soft; soft, preceded by flatulence; hard; as if chopped.

Urinary Organs.—Tenesmus. Urging; *frequent, with copious urine;* frequent, with scanty urine. Frequent copious micturition, can scarcely hold the urine. Stitch in urethra when not urinating. Urine copious, burning; scanty; turbid; offensive; *smelling like cat's urine.*

Clinical.—Incontinence of urine at night, in children, the urine smelling like cat's urine.

Sexual Organs.—Erection in morning. Penis, jerking, tending to make it stiff, in morning on waking; stitch in back; itching biting in skin; pain extending to glans. Burning in glans. Swelling of prepuce. Voluptuous itching of prepuce when standing, with erection. Itching sticking of scrotum. *Emission, with lascivious dream.* Stitch on r. side of mons veneris. Leucorrhœa.

Chest.—Twitching of r. pectoral muscles. *Sticking on l. true ribs; in l. side during inspiration and expiration* while walking; in r. side when walking; when standing; in r. side, < inspiration and expiration; in upper part of sternum, < expiration; itching, in r. pectoral muscles. Cutting on r. side, < moving trunk and arm, bruised pain on pressure.

Heart and Pulse.—Anxiety in H. in wavelike throbbing when lying. Oppression in region of H. on bending forward while sitting, with stitches. Pulse rapid.

Neck and Back.—Swelling of cervical glands. Cramplike drawing in cervical muscles, which suddenly drew the head backward. Sticking in l. scapula. Pinching contraction between scapulæ, with coldness.

Upper Extremities.—Sticking in r. axilla; cutting, in axilla, with itching; in l. shoulder joint, > motion; in l. elbow; contractive, in l. forearm near bend of elbow, when walking; in l. ring finger during rest.

Lower Extremities.—Stitches in l. gluteals when lying. Thighs feel bruised in morning on waking. Tearing bubbling in internal and upper part of thigh when sitting. Drawing in r. thigh when standing. Itching stitch in l. knee; in r. patella when lying, >motion, returning on sitting. Twitching in r. calf towards inner side; feeling of T. in l. calf. Sticking in r. tibia when walking. Pressing-out pain in r. tibia when walking and sitting, < standing. Drawing along calf and thigh when walking, with giving way of knees. Tensive sticking in middle of r. foot when walking. Tearing in heel beneath inner malleolus, > motion, leaving burning. Pain in r. sole; in r. sole when sitting; in r. sole when walking, < joints. Pressing burning in l. great toe.

Skin.—Thick and hard on face. *Eruption over face (except eyelids) and behind ears, with burning itching, < night, a thick, hard scab formed, cracked here and there, from which a tenacious yellow pus exuded and hardened into a substance like gum.* Pimple beneath l. zygoma, with pain on touch; itching P. on last joint of index. Nettle-rash over whole body, with stinging biting. Hives on l. cheek, with itching, not < scatching.

Burning stitches on l. thigh; on upper abdomen when walking. Itching stitches below r. external malleolus; on r. side of abdomen, > touch. *Cutting and crawling, with cramplike pain in skin between scapulæ.* Itching on r. wing of nose; on r. scapula; inner upper part of r. thigh; anteriorly above l. knee; on l. inner malleolus; on ball of r. great toe when standing, < sitting; of dorsal muscles, > scratching; between scrotum and thigh when sitting, > scratching; sticking in l. brow, > rubbing.

Clinical.—Impetigo, groups of pustules, followed by scabs, on chin and upper lip.

Sleep.—Sleepiness in afternoon; in afternoon, with falling of eyelids; irresistible, in afternoon. *Frequent waking.* Restless. The child twitches the hands and closes in the thumb, with general dry heat and redness of face. Falls asleep late on account of numerous thoughts, in morning he wakes early, lies upon the unaccustomed side and cannot arouse himself on account of weakness. Amorous dreams. Vivid dreams.

Fever.—Chilliness in cold, open air; creeping, in forenoon, with vertigo and pulling asunder sensation in middle of brain. Heat without thirst; H. after eating, < face, with sweat, oppression of chest, with anxiety, driving him about; in scalp above forehead; in skin of temple by r. eye; in side of face on which he was not lying in evening; suddenly in face when sitting, without thirst. Sweat at night.

Vipera.

The fresh poison of the German viper (adder) is triturated with sugar of milk.

Compare other serpent venoms.

Generalities.—Œdema; with coma. Swelling, < lips and eyelids; of whole r. side of body; of lymphatics extending from the bite, with inflammation; with insensibility. Bitten part swollen; with blackness, hardness and spots; with inflammation; with œdema, redness and heat, parts hard and tender, with tensive pain; with pain, then numbness and rigidity, afterwards suppuration successively of finger, forearm and axilla; and of mouth and abdomen (he sucked the wound), with general weakness, hands black and cold, bloody vomiting and diarrhœa. Swelling of face after bite on cheek, parts about the bite livid, next day diffuse cellular inflammation extended from the wound to neck and sternum and opposite side of face.

Swelling of bitten tongue, he fell to the ground in asphyxia, respiration and pulse stopped, face purple, the circumference of neck exceeded that of head; tongue blue, immovable, protruding, with constant dribbling of saliva, S. of submaxillary and parotid glands, gasping for air, pallor, anxious expression; and vessels on under surface gorged with blood, face pale, cold sweat on forehead, pulse quick and irregular, bloody salivation, T. felt benumbed, later it appeared almost square, under surface nearly black, inability to articulate, difficulty in swallowing, the S. extended to r. nipple and had a crackling or emphysematous feel, as if air were extravasated in cellular membrane.

Swelling of the bitten limb; with darkness; with dark redness; covered with phlyctænules; with ecchymoses, and at the place of the bite ulcers exuding sanious liquid; at anniversary of the bite, with development of spots and malaise; like phlegmonous erysipelas, with ecchymoses around the bite; doughy, temperature elevated, cutaneous veins looked like red stripes, pain on motion; painful œdema every year at the first hot weather, with colic and retching, digestion disturbed, somnolence, gums fungoid, skin icteric, chilliness, physical and intellectual weariness.

Swelling of arm, shoulder, chest and back of side bitten, with inflammation; S. of hand, arm and r. side of trunk, with pain causing repeated fainting; of the bitten arm, almost purple, with anxiety, headache, vomiting and shivering, in a few hours bulla on a red base over the wound, afterwards similar bullæ all over body, even on face, the intermediate spaces red and swollen, when ruptured much turbid serum escaped, the eruption lasted from May to November, every May afterwards lassitude, anxiety, nausea, headache, etc., then after six or eight days the white cicatrix became red and painful, then tingling and swelling of arm, then bullæ lasting five or six weeks.

Swelling of arm and hand, gradually extended over chest, with nausea and vomiting, arm hot, livid, covered with black and dark red spots, skin tense, the livid red color > pressure, but the spots of ecchymoses were not affected thereby, at the bite phlyctenular blisters with reddish serum, also phlyctenulæ on back of hand, cephalalgia, vertigo, rapid pulse, pale tongue, hand began to diminish in size, but shoulder was large, covered with black mottled spots, l. scapular region and part of r. livid red, with spots of ecchymoses, the redness and spots extended over anterior part of chest, r. breast œdematous, hard and ecchymosed (the trouble in breast was apparently caused by a blow), afterwards the ecchymoses and infiltration spread over nates, sclerotica yellow.

Swelling of arm to shoulder, with vomiting and diarrhœa of bilious and sour liquid, then of substances smelling like broth, thirst, pulse scarcely perceptible, skin pale and covered with clammy sweat, tongue and affected arm œdematous as far as elbow, the latter colorless and insensible, delirium at times, next day skin hot and dry, axillary glands swollen and sensitive, swelling extending along spine to r. hip, afterwards bluish redness of the swelling, the places upon which he lay were bluish-black, skin over swollen parts insensible.

Swelling of the bitten hand; with stitches; with stitches on motion; with tingling pain and coolness, gangrene threatened, temperature of arm low, S. extended to axilla; extending finally to hypogastrium; and wrist, burning pain when bitten, soon extending to middle of elbow and thence to axilla, diminishing in the wound as it extended, when the pain reached axilla there were constriction and heat in head, throat and r. side of tongue.

Swelling of the bitten finger; and of hand, with stupefaction; with heat and contraction, the contraction soon affected arm, and arm was swollen, < about joints; extending to shoulders and chest, with uneasiness, vomiting and sleeplessness; œdematous, and of forearm; slight, white, back of hand swollen, red lines reaching to elbow, forearm tender, next day arm swollen and ecchymosed, axillary glands swollen and inflamed, that evening ecchymoses extended down side to crest of ilium, afterwards hardness of forearm and elbow, with stiffness and pain on bending elbow; head hanging down, tongue protruding, face and lids swollen, œdema of submucous tissue of mouth and pharynx, ptyalism, vomiting, pain at pit of stomach, pain in r. axilla, in a few hours arm was swollen, axillary glands inflamed and painful, next morning back and inner part of arm ecchymosed, the finger (bitten part) was the last to become painful and swell.

Œdematous swelling of arm (after bite on index), tongue furred, pulse rapid and irregular, oppression at præcordia, hurried respiration, depression of nervous energy, red lines in absorbent glands, which were tender and enlarged. Arm and hand swollen, grayish-yellow, the bitten finger bluish-black, the wound surrounded by blisters, scarification over the wound caused oozing of black blood.

Swelling of the bitten thumb, and hand and forearm, shiny, tense, elastic, not pitting on pressure, peculiar redness of arm, red line of absorbents along arm to axilla, thence it separated into three lines which spread over chest, from elbow to axilla they appeared inflamed, in patches, fingers swollen and immovable, bursting sensation in hand and arm, smarting in axilla, pain on pressure in axillary glands and along absorbents, pulse weak and sluggish. Bitten thumb black, hand swollen and spotted, next day arm covered with spots, above elbow sores filled with liquid.

Swelling of bitten limbs as far as abdomen, with feverish coldness of the limbs; as far as A., blue and yellow; as far as A., and black; S., with black spots, the S. extended to abdomen, then syncope and death; up to knee and soon to abdomen, green, red and yellow; to knee, immovable and insensible, the bitten spot dark blue; and covered with bluish-red spots (after bite on toe); and hard, insensible, with inflammation of superficial veins (after bite on toe). Swelling of the bitten leg, with yellow color; as far as abdomen, bluish-brown, with blackish spots about the bite.

Swelling of the bitten foot, with chronic suppuration; dorsum and whole toe, with blue color; with pain as if blown up with air, with two bluish-yellow stripes gradually extending along leg to thigh and abdomen; becomes indurated and bluish-red; as far as knee, hard and bluish-red, S. remained for years; pain in the wound, afterwards foot was inflamed and swollen as far as knee, later paralysis of foot so that he was unable to ride horseback; and leg and abdomen, with almost black color; as far as abdomen, grayish-yellow, covered with blisters, after fourteen years the knee was still stiff and leg drawn backward; and leg and thigh, with redness, veins and superficial lymphatics swollen, bluish-red above popliteal space, rest of body œdematous, < upper lids and tongue, which he could scarcely move, pulse small, rapid, respiration difficult, prostration, anxiety, pressure in præcordial region, nausea, the wound became bluish-red, comatose, afterwards tongue, < tip, was denuded and blisters formed, lymphatic vessels and glands, < popliteal space, were hard and painful.

Swelling of the toes to near knee, with a red circle around the wound, the wound was filled with a drop of lymph, which was no sooner wiped off than it was succeeded by another.

Black blood flows from a wound near the bite, cellular tissue green and blue. Apparent modification of the functions of the blood, fibrin is altered, globules less able to perform their functions, with tendency to hæmoptysis, especially epistaxis, imperfect coagulation. Ecchymoses in endocardium and pericardium, lungs hyperæmic, mucous membrane covered with ecchymoses, the tissue œdematous, mucous membrane of intestines ecchymosed, blood did not coagulate. Persons become prematurely old, developement of children is arrested. Falling down when standing. Cramps, < flexor muscles. Subsultus tendinum. Spasms; with raging pains in head, jaws and abdomen. Epilepsy. Collapse.

Sticking in the bitten part; on every change of weather, with tearing; extending through whole body; then leaden gray color and swelling. Appearance as of a nettle-sting, then creeping up arm, veins distended, with feeling as if they would burst; piercing tip of thumb, then spreading over arm, then sensation of a flame flickering through arm. Sticking in knee and head on every change of weather, with tearing.

Pain. Pain in the bitten part; extending through whole body; returned every year; with stitches in finger-tips; and sinking down in a faint, with heat and shivering shooting through body for half an hour, when he was first able to call for help, relief from vomiting of bile, thirst, cold, clammy sweat, features drawn, eyes protruding, staring, color dark yellow, pulse slow, hard and full, jaws spasmodically closed, talking and swallowing difficult; burning.

Smarting in the bitten thumb, with burning, then white color, with lividity of forearm (intermittent at first), stiffness, swelling of arm, next morning the part looks sloughy and inflamed, lividity begins on posterior aspect of thumb, becomes bluish on inner side of dorsum of hand, gradually assumes the appearance of ecchymoses as it approaches the forearm, ecchymoses of arm, bright red in places, in others blue and black, everywhere tinctured with livid spots, pain on pressing the thumb, soreness of the limb.

Disease of the bitten leg, painful, at times spotted yellow, at times spotted blue, after various remedies these disappeared and attacked the eyes, after long suffering she became blind for two years, then eyes improved, but there were pains in various parts of abdomen and limbs, at last she became almost numb. Feeling as if the poison extended from the bite on thumb to shoulder and then to abdomen. Sensitive to every change of weather. Malaise every year, with pain in the bitten arm and lassitude. Chronic cachexia. Restlessness. Periodic symptoms, with tendency of cachectic symptoms to return.

Weakness; every year at the anniversary of the bite, with indigestion; with swelling of bloodvessels; with stammering of a few unintelligible words and sleepiness; so that he fainted every time he raised his head; so that he fainted every time he rose. Faintness; with warmth in head; with flow of white saliva from mouth; with vomiting of black blood, then bloody stools; with falling to the ground, vomiting, lying as if paralyzed and unconscious, involuntary stools and urine, then death in half an hour, without swelling or spasms; alternating with anxiety and restlessness.

Loss of acuteness of special senses. Numbness of foot after bite in heel, then heat extending from the point to abdomen, chest and at last to throat and tongue, causing burning thirst, then restlessness, febrile shivering, trembling and weakness. Torpor. Immobility. Inability to move muscles and tendons. Stiffness, movement impossible. Paralysis of limbs and even of the whole body; of the bitten limb; of the bitten limb, involving half of the body; yearly, with pain and insensibility. Amelioration from sweat; from vomiting; bilious vomiting.

Mind.—Delirium; and raving; with vomiting; alternating with sopor. Wandering, as if drunk, answers mumbling, incoherent. Irrational talking, with sleeplessness and pains. Screaming, then convulsions. Premonition of death. Anguish. Anxiety; and agitation. Depression. Uneasiness. Confusion. Stupor; with cutting in abdomen. Torpor. Coma, with thirst for water. Loss of functions, with drawn features. Unconsciousness; with sinking down.

Head.—Ecchymoses in membrane of brain, infusion of bloody serum in ventricles. Tearing at every change of weather, with sticking. Aching; with coated tongue and bad appetite; with inclination to sigh, which pain prevented, restlessness even to despair, eyes glistening, face yellow, cheeks red, thirst, with moist tongue, which is white in middle, red on edges, pulse weak and small, faint feeling, pain in loins, warm, dry skin, constipation, copious clear urine. Confusion. Heaviness. Stupefaction. Apoplexy. Intoxication, with sleep, exhaustion, loss of vision, difficulty in breathing, retching, vomiting, spasms, pain in umbilical region, tension of abdomen, pulse small, rapid, voice lost, sleepiness. Vertigo; with falling forward; with nosebleed and anxiety; with nausea and vomiting, so that he fainted; with loss of vision.

Eyes.—Dark yellow. Red, inflamed and watery. Staring. Sunken. Pupils dilated; l., r. contracted. Balls immovable. Paralysis of lids. Lids dropped over eyes. Vision dim; dim in l. eye, lost in r.; lost.

Nose.—Bleeding.

Face.—Swelling; and neck; with pressing out of eyes; tense and blackish, not very painful, with closure of throat. Convulsed. Red. Pale; and hippocratic, with cold sweat on forehead; and anxious, covered with drops of sweat. Livid, with subicteric color. Yellowish and anxious. Expression of anxiety; of terror, wild and woe-begone. Raging pain in jaws. No power in jaw. Lips blue; lips and tongue swollen, covered with saliva and pale; lips and tongue swollen, livid and protruding. Acid burning in lips, mouth and throat.

Mouth.—Scorbutic line on gums. Swelling of salivary glands; of mouth; of mouth and throat, with dryness, so that swallowing was impossible.

Tongue.—Swollen; and brownish-black, protruding from mouth; so that he could not speak; with closed jaws and difficult speech; can be protruded but slightly and slowly, is directed to the side affected, voice hesitating, thick and as in intoxication. Protruding. Discolored. Black. Fuliginous and breath fetid. Yellow, tip red. Pale, jerking, protruded between teeth, not swollen. White, tremulous; W. in middle, moist on edges, with thirst; coated white. Dry. Replies difficult, in a deep voice. Speech inarticulate; and thick; lost on account of weakness.

Throat.—Swelling like a goitre. Closure so that she could swallow only water and milk, afterwards biting in fauces, the swelling of which became blackish. Pain; with difficulty in swallowing, viscid mucus adheres to pharynx.

Stomach.—Appetite lost. Thirst; just before death, with hunger; with the heat; with moist tongue; for cold drinks. Nausea; with shuddering; with attack of faintness. Retching; with suffocative sensation.

Vomiting; after milk; of all food and drink; with weakness; with faintness; with erysipelas; with shivering and thirst; with coldness of body; with distention; with colic; with colic and thirst; with purging and urinating; with diarrhœa; with diarrhœa and weak irregular pulse; spasmodic; of blood; bilious; of mucous and bilious matter; bitter yellow fluid; green substances; green liquid; viscid greenish fluid, in color and taste like inspissated bile, then bilious diarrhœa.

Cardialgia. Pain; in epigastrium; in epigastrium, < pressure; in epigastric or umbilical region, with anxiety and vomiting, thirst though he cannot tolerate much liquid, bloody and mucous vomiting, bloody diarrhœa; excruciating, in pit and in abdomen; sudden, in pit, with thirst. Uneasiness in epigastrium. Digestion slow.

Abdomen.—Tense, pressure causes distention of facial muscles. Swelling, with raging pains and spasms even to faintness, and after drinking milk vomiting of a mass of round worms, then freedom from worm troubles which he had before. Sudden flatulent distention, with colic, pain in back and vomiting. Rumbling. Cutting. Griping. Pain; and in back; with diarrhœa; with stupefying headache, vomiting, and with swelling and blueness of the foot; in umbilical region, < pressure. Hypochondria tense; H. sore.

Rectum.—Discharge of black coagulated blood; of blood just before death. Pain and tenesmus. Urging to pass stool and urine; desire for stool, with coldness to touch.

Stool.—Diarrhœa; frequent; bilious. Fetid; and

black. Bloody; in masses of dark offensive blood, apparently from scarification of tongue. Copious. Numerous, with urging, shivering and thirst. Involuntary; and frequent, mixed with blood and mucus; and involuntary micturition.

Clinical.—After diarrhœa, greenish and bloody, most violent pain in the enlarged liver, with jaundice and fever, pain extending from the liver to the shoulder and down to the hip; Vipera immediately removed the pain in the shoulder and reduced the liver to its normal size.

Urinary Organs.—Ineffectual desire. Strangury. Involuntary micturition. Frequent watery micturition. Urine increased; suppressed; *dark yellow, as in jaundice.*

Respiration.—Suffocation. Dyspnœa; with sticking in heart. Anxious; as in croup, threatening asphyxia. Oppressed and short. Ceased suddenly, heart stopped, face became livid, etc., tracheotomy was performed, blood drawn from arm flowed scantily, was dark, mixed with bright streaks.

Chest.—Veins of C. and abdomen thick and hard. Swelling, with difficult breathing; S. as far as umbilicus after bite on face. Œdema of lungs before death. Double pneumonia. Pain; in l. side; over four or five r. ribs on pressure; flying. Oppression, with anxiety; O., with præcordial anxiety; with violent efforts to breathe and swallow.

Heart.—Sticking; with cold sweat and faintness; with weakness, difficulty in breathing and cold sweat. Pain, with faintness. Dragging pain so that he tears his clothes, becomes faint and sinks down with weakness, with distress in abdomen, violent vomiting ten times, pallor, coldness of body, blueness and blackness of the bitten finger. Anxiety; at the same time for four years, with soreness of the bitten foot and paralysis of r. arm. Action slow. Action feeble; and no pulsation in radial or carotid arteries, but that in crural was very strong.

Clinical.—Vipera is a very valuable remedy for varicose veins and for acute phlebitis, the vein is swollen, bordered by an area of inflammation, which is very sensitive to touch, but particularly with the sensation, on letting the leg hang down, as if it would burst from the fulness of the veins. A gold-beater, who had used his r. hand for years in his business, found that the veins of the whole arm had become excessively swollen and painful; he could no longer use his arm or permit it to hang down, but he carried it in a short sling, and when sitting had to rest it on a table or something high, on account of the bursting feeling on letting it hang down; immediately cured by Vipera.

Pulse.—Rapid; with unquenchable thirst; R. and feverish; and full and strong in the healthy arm, but small and low in the wounded arm; and soft; and thready; and small; and small, scarcely perceptible; and small, with chilliness and cold sweat; and small, contracted, irregular; and small, intermittent, irregular, contracted, with fever; and small, hard, heart's action tremulous, with oppression of præcordium; and low, interrupted. Slow, febrile; S. and weak; S., full and hard, with stiffness, coldness and sweat. Febrile. Small; and contracted; and intermittent. Intermittent and thready. Irregular. Weak, with sopor; W., with violent pains; and intermittent; and irregular. Scarcely perceptible.

Back.—Sticking in kidneys. Pain in loins.

Extremities.—Swelling; and red, covered with yellow spots; and blue and black. Livid spots on the bitten limb every year at the time of the bite. Yellowish, livid, mottled. Yellowish-green, with livid spots. Erysipelatous inflammation. Painful trembling. Pain; < touch; alternating with pains in abdomen. Benumbed. Relaxed.

Clinical.—Bursting feeling in limbs, in three cases neurasthenia, an old sprain and varicose veins.

Upper Extremities.—Paralysis after a bite on foot. Pain in shoulders; in arm extending to chest. Arm swollen; and of a sickly color; and reddish-blue; and livid red; and red, covered with spots, soft; and painful. Arm deep red. Paralysis of r. arm recurring for years after a bite on foot. Forearm yellow. Swelling of the hand not bitten; S. of hand, not pitting on pressure, *with pain as if it would burst*, with pain on touch; and stiffness. Hands violet-colored, covered with phlyctenules. Skin of hand dead and detached in large plates, subjacent tissues livid. The bitten finger bluish-black. Stitches in finger-tips after bite on arm. Tearing from bitten fingers to chest, with uneasiness, vomiting and sleeplessness.

Lower Extremities.—Shuffling gait caused by paralysis. Convulsive movements. Cramps. Weakness. Feeling as if something moved up along thigh (after bite on ankle). Tension in knees and ankles. Knees stiff. Leg swollen, cold and insensible; swollen as if puffed up with air, and painful. Paralysis of leg, with feeling as if dead. Foot swollen and blue. Dragging of foot. Foot seemed shortened, so that he limped. Paralysis of foot, with shuffling gait; P., then ulcers.

Skin.—Pale. Yellowish. Jaundiced on face and trunk, with red patches on limbs. Livid; in spots. Black spots on limb and abdomen; reddish-black spots on abdomen and face; bluish-black spots discharging disorganized blood about bite; black petechial spots over whole body, which was cold to touch. Bright blue or almost black spots about the wound. Herpetic eruption, with itching about the wound. Roseola-like eruption on inside of arm and down side of body. Pus sometimes at the point of the bite. Ulcers. Blisters; about the bite, bursting and leaving ulceration, muscles were laid bare, were dark red, dry, looked like smoked meat, insensible to touch, the sore was offensive. Gangrenous spots; on limbs; G. slough at the bite. Gangrene of foot, with swelling extending to knee. Crawling in soles, then also in palms.

Sleep.—Disposed to yawn. Sleepiness; and heaviness; with inability to sleep and also constant necessity to change the position. Sleeplessness; from pain. Night restless.

Fever.—Chilliness; with sweat; with cold sweat; with rigidity and clammy sweat; then fever. Temperature diminished, resists cold badly. Shivering; with flushes of heat; with thirst. Coldness of head and upper limbs; of finger.

Heat; in morning, with thirst, restlessness and moderate pains; towards evening; at night, with delirium; then shivering. Fever of irregular type; intermittent F. Hot skin; and dry. Heat shooting through body when bitten. Burning in the bitten foot; spreading from the bitten part through the whole limb; extending from the bitten spot on arm to chest; B. running up arm; rising from heel to tongue; on chest and abdomen, with longing for cold applications though skin was cold to touch; of fingers (from rubbing a stick with which a snake had been bruised), with swelling.

Sweat; after vomiting; after chamomile tea, except over the bitten limb from abdomen to toes; cold; cold, clammy. Skin dry.

Viscum Album.

A tincture is made of the fresh berries and leaves of the mistletoe.

A kind of aura epileptica, feeling as if he must fall, a glow rising from the feet to the head, feeling as if he were on fire, with pallor of face. Paralysis of every muscle, except of those of the eye. Inability to speak or swallow, and death from starvation. Frequent recurrence of the symptoms during two years. Inclined to be violent. Spectral illusions. Insensibility. Stupor, then insensibility, lying motionless with closed eyes, but easily aroused by a loud noise and then answered any question, but when she relapsed into her former condition there was a slight disposition to stertor. Giddiness. Conjunctiva injected. Pupils dilated and fixed; contracted and at first insensible. Face red. Lips livid. Alimentary canal paralyzed. Constipation. Breathing slow and stertorous. Pulse quick, small and irregular; slow, full and bounding. Sensation as if a spider were crawling over dorsum of l., then of r. hand. Sudden pain from within outward in r. foot, compelling him to take off his boot, as it felt too tight. Drowsiness. Skin warm and moist.

Clinical.—Deafness in l. ear. Numerous cases of retained placenta. Metrorrhagia, partly bright, partly clotted and dark, with dull headache, stitches in the temples, numbness of the extremities, blue rings around the eyes, sunken eyes. It causes uterine contractions and stops hæmorrhages. Chronic endometritis (granular endometritis), characterized by enlargement, either subinvolution, alveolar hyperplasia or hypertrophy. A case of whooping cough was cured in two days. Several cases of sciatica. Chorea from fright.

Wyethia.

A tincture is made of the fresh root of Wyethia helenioides, Nutt.

Weak as after a severe illness; W., nervous, uneasy, apprehensive of some calamity. Unable to make much exertion, the least exercise causes sweat. Aggravation in afternoon. Headache; over r. eye, sharp at first, then fulness. Rush of blood to head. Dizziness. Itching in r. ear. Mouth feels as if it had been scalded. Increased flow of tough, ropy saliva. *Dryness of fauces, constant desire to clear throat by hemming* (Argent. nit.); *pricking D. in posterior nares, sensation as if something were in nasal passages, no relief from an effort to clear them through throat. Throat feels swollen, epiglottis dry and burning, constant desire to swallow saliva to relieve the dryness, yet no relief, swallowing difficult.* Uvula feels elongated. Heat in œsophagus and stomach, < eating.

Belching of wind alternating with hiccough. Nausea and vomiting. Weight in stomach as from indigestible food. Pain and bearing down in r. side. Sharp, deep-seated pain below r. ribs, then soreness. Itching in anus. Dark brown diarrhœa. Stool dark brown, small, looked burned; dark, regular, soft (previously light-colored, irregular and constipated). Constipation, with hæmorrhoids. Leucorrhœa. Pain in l. ovary, shooting down to knee. Menses appear for the first time in over a year, since birth of last child, purple, scanty, painful. Burning in bronchial tubes. Dry, hacking cough from tickling in epiglottis. Pulse slow. Pain in back extending to extreme point of spine. Pain in r. arm, with stiffness of wrist and hand. Cold sweat over whole body, coming and going by flashes.

Clinical.—Pricking, dry sensation in posterior nares; granular appearance of pharynx. Chronic pharyngitis, dryness, with constant desire to clear the throat, tendency to atrophy of the mucous membrane. Pharynx dark red, sensitive; also soreness of the muscles of the palate, following severe influenza. Granular sore throat, with burning and enlarged follicles, frequent inclination to clear the throat. Tendency to get hoarse from talking or singing (Phos.), the throat is hot and dry (Bell.). Dry asthma.

Xanthoxylum.

A tincture is made of the fresh bark of the prickly ash, Xanthoxylum fraxineum, Willd.

Generalities.—Sharp shooting pain. Neuralgic pain in r. side. Aching all over; in side; in l. side under l. scapula and l. hip. Indescribable sensation at 4 P.M., thought I was dying, whole body seemed falling to pieces, could not walk straight, the atmosphere seemed blue, light flashed before my eyes, body seemed elastic and as if on the stretch, tongue seemed to alternately expand and contract, distant ringing in l. ear, could not eat but craved ice-water, which relieved the nausea, l. leg heavy, on lying down pain in sacral region, amelioration at 10 P.M.

Malaise; in morning on rising. Thrill over whole body. Sensation in bed as if I were sunken deep, on sitting up sensation as if floating. Restless, felt rather easier lying. Weakness; in morning on waking. Inability to walk straight or talk straight. Falling asleep of l. side if I sat still any time. Numbness of whole body in morning on waking; in morning on rising; of l. side in morning on rising; of l. side from head to foot, affecting half of nose. Aggravation at night and in morning. Amelioration from vomiting; A after lunch; after eating, but was tired and ached all over.

Mind.—Nervous, frightened feeling. Feeling as if something would happen. Depression; in morning on waking, with languor. Felt as if I would rather die than live. Felt as though I would like to take enough to kill myself, during the headache. Indifference and malaise. No life nor ambition to do anything. Stupid feeling after supper.

Head.—Aching; in morning, with sleepiness; and dulness; and weight in it, intolerance of motion or shock, every step sends a shock to head; throbbing; delaying sleep, with bright star-shaped spots dancing up and down on shutting eyes. *Fulness.* Felt large; with intolerance of light. Tightness, with pain increasing over eyes. Dull, heavy feeling. Soreness to touch. Throbbing, and in neck. Feeling as if dropping to pieces, fear that something would happen. Feeling of looseness or quivering in brain on shaking head. Vertigo; in morning on rising; when walking; on lifting head; with black spots dancing before eyes; as if falling forward, in morning on attempting to rise, everything became black, with nausea preventing me from eating breakfast, vomiting of the coffee and toast that I had succeeded in eating.

Forehead.—Aching; in a spot over nose; over r. eye; > open air and cool water; in upper part, < r. side, pain extends to base of brain, with soreness; extending into orbits; waking her at 4 A.M.; throbbing, over r. eye, with nausea; burning, < sudden motion of head, extending to vertex and into orbits, with heaviness in eyelids and bright spots before eyes.

Temples.—Pain; with feeling as if top of head were lifted off; intermittent darting, in l.; sudden screwing P. through T., spreading over head, at 6 P.M., with heavy pressure on vertex, after the pain has lasted an hour blur before eyes, as if looking through a blue lace veil, dizziness and nausea, at 9 P.M. loud noise in l. ear (like a windmill?), the pain prevented sleep till 12.30, awakened at 4 A.M. by nausea, attempted to rise, but was so giddy that I pitched forward, the dizziness > lying down, but not the nausea.

Weight on vertex. Pain in vertex; in upper part of cranium, with flashes of throblike pain as if the top of head would be taken off; in l. side of head and in l. elbow; in occiput, with bewildered sensation. Tightening of scalp, with heavy pain in temples, afterwards increase of head difficulties, with heat and quiet menstrual flow (two days too early).

Eyes.—Bloodshot, with red margins, feeling as if full of sand; B. and heavy, with red burning lids; B. and sensitive to light, bright images before eyes, dilated pupils. Heavy grinding pain in l. Motion is painful if much out of field of vision, and eyes are sore on pressure. Pain in r. lid. Vision of blue sparks. Things looked far away.

Ears.—Pain in r. or in jaw-socket, he does not know whether it is ear or tooth that aches; darting, under and back of r. Sensitive. Ringing; in r. Roaring. Noise in r. like a valve opening and shutting.

Nose.—Dryness. R. nostril seems filled up. Catarrhal symptoms, watering of eyes and nose. Discharge of mucus, with congested feeling as if about to bleed; D. of dry and bloody scales of mucus. Bleeding.

Face.—Flushed; but body cold. Pain in lower jaw and l. side.

Clinical.—Neuralgia of the face, of l. lower jaw.

Mouth.—Tongue coated; white; whitish-yellow. Burning and dry feeling in M. and tongue. Peppery taste; extending to stomach.

Throat.—Aching; in r. side; on touch; and it tired me to talk. Feeling as if in a vise in morning on rising. Soreness of r. side; S., with expectoration of tough mucus. Feeling of enlargement. Feeling of a bunch in l. side when swallowing after dinner, on going to bed it shifted to r. side. Dryness and hoarseness; D., and it was a great exertion to talk. Burning in œsophagus, with stinging.

Stomach.—Loss of appetite; with great thirst, craved coffee and lemonade. Thirst for large quantities at a time. Empty eructations, with slight taste of ingesta. Nausea; at the smell of breakfast; > a glass of ice-water; with frequent chills; with headache; with oppression of stomach. Fulness or pressure at epigastrium. Faintness as if fasting, but I did not care to eat more than a few mouthfuls, which nauseated me.

Abdomen.—Rumbling, with soreness on pressure. Flatulence. Griping at 7 A.M., soon after waking, with brown diarrhœa mixed with mucus, next morning G. on waking, continued at intervals through the day, with indifference and malaise; G. and pain, then watery diarrhœa, fever and chill (the diarrhœa could not be reproduced by large doses). Boring deep in r. hypochondrium, > hot compresses, steady pressure and constant motion, < lying or sitting. Pain in r. side below ribs. Dragging in lower part of pelvis and back.

Rectum and Stool.—Stinging in r. after stool, with burning and hæmorrhage as from hæmorrhoids. Urging, stool large, dark brown, rather loose, causing excoriation and pain. Stools watery, small, dark, offensive, frequent, followed by burning pain in rectum and anus; loose S., then burning and smarting. Constipation in morning, stool after supper, next day three S., on third day S. before and after breakfast. Slight S., twice in one day.

Urine.—Profuse; slightly increased, sp. gr. varied from 1015 to 1019. Scanty and high-colored at night and next morning; S., high-colored, sp. gr. 1025, micturition frequent. Thirty oz. in twenty-four hours, sp. gr. 1030, reaction acid. High-colored.

Sexual Organs.—Leucorrhœa milky, white; whitish after menses. Shooting from region of r. ovary to hip, thigh and back, causing me to walk the floor and hold my breath, with gushing milk-white leucorrhœa, ceasing suddenly. Cutting in r. ovarian region, extending down thigh and over hip, in morning on waking, could find no position comfortable. Sudden sharp pain in region of r. ovary, which later radiated down thigh and across to l. hip, > lying down and drawing up legs. Pain in ovaries > drawing up knees and by heat; in l., extending down thigh; in l. during menses, sudden, gradually increasing and dying away as it came.

Menses profuse; and too early; and early, preceded by leucorrhœa; and too early, bright red, slight dysmenorrhœa, > walking and hot applications, very nervous, easily startled and hysterical. *Menses too early and painful;* too early, with intermittent cramp-like pain in head and abdomen, inability to lie still, hungry, but food nauseated, drank much, urine profuse, l. side numb, nape lame, eye twitched, pupils dilated, face flushed, blue light before eyes, chill, nausea, when vomiting it seemed as if stomach rose and fell, pulse rapid, restless night, sleep at intervals, next day awoke with pain in r. ovarian region, frontal headache, head light, l. side numb, l. foot went to sleep, menses profuse.

Clinical.—Amenorrhœa from getting her feet wet, scanty, high-colored urine, nausea at the sight of food, complete discouragement. After-pains. Ovarian neuralgia, with violent pains in the loins and lower part of the abdomen, < l. side, extending down the thigh. Neuralgic dysmenorrhœa, pains going down the anterior portions of the thighs, mostly left-sided. Neuralgic dysmenorrhœa, with neuralgic headaches, especially over l. eye, congestion of head and eyes, photophobia, great bearing down in the abdomen, pains in the back and down the legs, menses very scanty, thick, almost black.

Respiratory Organs.—Vocal cords affected. Hoarseness; in open air; with frequent necessity to clear the throat. Aphonia. Cough in open air; C. < cold draught, > warm room; hacking; hacking, without expectoration, sometimes from tickling in throat, again deep in bronchi; spasmodic, voiceless, stifled, about every twenty minutes, with scraping, even sore feeling under sternum, during each attack in evening sharp pain in lower part of r. lung. Suffocated sensation waking him at night. Dyspnœa, with increased action of heart; D., with cutting in lower part of r. lung. Every inspiration an exertion and unsatisfactory, as deep breathing caused pain in lower part of r. lung and in heart. Could not get air enough into lungs. Desire to take long breaths; and deep.

Chest.—Shooting in r. side like pleuritic pains, occasionally extending to scapula, constant desire to take a long breath. Pain in lower part of r. lung on deep inspiration or coughing. Strained pain on deep inspiration, < waking in night and turning in bed. Constriction as from running or as from weight on lungs. Tightening, with inclination to gape.

Heart. — Intermittent cutting in region passing through body antero-posteriorly, making me hold my breath and turn pale even to lips, < inspiration, after each attack was thirsty, flushed and exhausted. Pain in region starting me out of a sound sleep, apex beat to be seen and felt over large area, with suffocating feeling, had to sit up in bed and turn one way and then another, with cough without expectoration, three attacks at night, once almost unconscious from the tremulous beating of heart, pulse rapid, temperature high, slept hardly at all.

Pulse.—Rapid; and feeble, irregular. Slow; and soft. Throbbing in carotids.

Neck. — Pain in nape; in nape, > pressing head backward, with stiffness; in neck and r. shoulder, extending down back, inability to turn head to l.; rheumatic, in nape, > pressing head backward; drawing, in nape, extending down r. scapula. Tired feeling in nape. Stiffness.

Back.—Twitching of muscles. Pain, < cervical region and upper part of sacral region; in spine. Muscles tired. Coccyx seemed elongated, sensitive to pressure and aching, could not sit except on a cushion.

Extremities.—Heavy to lift. Joints seemed loosened. Pain in r. arm; inside r. just above elbow; in r. beginning just above elbow. Arms better from being twisted. Arms felt as if I had carried a weight. Numbness of l. shoulder and arm. Pain in elbows; in l. elbow, passing to palm, then to shoulder; in l. knee and l. elbow extending to hand, then in l. side and top of l. foot; in wrist extending to thumb; sudden cramplike, in wrists and knees, ending in a steady ache; flashing, in r. thumb, extending to hand.

Lower Extremities. — Inability to walk straight. Weakness. Pain; in l. thigh; in knee. Twitching in l. knee and trembling in r. Pain in r. leg in morning; flash of pain in r. calf. Legs weak; and feet. Pain in r. ankle; in l. heel; shooting from feet to knees. It seemed as if the floor were cotton-wool.

Clinical.—Sciatica, < hot weather. Sciatica of the anterior crural nerve, after *Gnaph.*

Skin.—Blotches on face, with boils.

Sleep.—Gaping. Drowsiness; all the morning; in evening. Sleep from 4 till 7 P.M. and then from 10 P.M. till 7 A.M. Slept hard all night; hard and heavy, dreamed of flying about over tops of houses; heavy, with constant dreams. Frequent waking. Sleep restless, frightful dreams of being killed or burned. Night restless, although very sleepy, constantly twisted and turned, and when I did sleep dreamed of being chased and when overtaken and about to be killed I could not make a sound to call for help. Dream of suffocation, waking me. Dream that my throat grew up, I woke in fright about 2 A.M., with shaking, and l. arm felt like lead and was numb, the position may have caused the numbness.

Fever.—Temperature low. Chilliness; frequently, with pain in limbs; in feet in morning on rising. Temperature high. Heat; in all veins, with desire to be bled, flash of heat from head to foot; in flashes; in flushes over face and head.

Zincum.

Pure metallic zinc is triturated for use.

General Action.—Zinc produces a marked derangement of the whole cerebro-spinal system; delirium, spasms, violent neuralgias, tremblings, extreme hyperæsthesia and paralysis. There seems no doubt that it affects not only the meninges of the brain and cord, but also the nerve-structure itself. Its action on mucous membranes is particularly seen in the eye, gastro-intestinal canal and bronchi. Its action on the blood is well established; marked anæmia (deficiency of red corpuscles) with profound prostration results. Its action on the skin is shown in the eczematous eruptions which it produces.

Allies.—Plumb., Puls., Argent., Stram., Bell.

Generalities.—Emaciation; with feeble appearance, face wrinkled and bluish. Paleness of mucous surfaces, with disappearance of subcutaneous cellular tissue and atrophy of muscular system, < r. side. **Twitching of various muscles** (Hyosc., Bell.); *of body and face.* Trembling after every excitement (Arg. nit., Stram.). Stretching of body and limbs, with pale, sunken face.

Sticking here and there in evening; tearing S. above l. eye and at the same time in umbilical region. Sticking cutting in r. side. *Pain between skin and flesh;* P. in l. groin, near l. side of navel, in l. chest and l. side of head; in abdomen, head and eyes in evening on lying down; in whole body, > rest; cramplike, here and there in muscles; cramplike, off and on all day.

Next after lung and digestive disturbances, and the so-called night-blindness, there appears after ten to twelve years' work, in the smelters, a peculiar affection, pain in back, sensitiveness of soles, formication of lower limbs, numbness and coldness in the same, sensation of a band around abdomen and occasionally pain in muscles of lower half of body from crampy twitchings in them, sense of touch diminished, reflex excitability increased, but muscular sensibility weakened, so that there is staggering on closing eyes, and in the dark control of muscular power ceases, muscles remain well nourished and strong for a long time, but at each intentional movement diffused muscular tremor (Arg. nit.), later the gait becomes stiff, spasmodic, trembling and uncertain, the step is made on the full sole, finally weakness of lower and sometimes of upper extremities.

Pressing asunder upon walls of trunk, without trace of flatulence, caused by the nerves, < r. side. Swollen sensation. Sensation of trembling without trembling. Discomfort. *Throbbing through whole body.* Muscular soreness; towards evening, with malaise. Dulness like slight nausea two hours after dinner, with tremulous feeling in chest, pain in forehead and inability to understand what he was reading. Unfitted for work (after vomiting), feels best when lying with eyes closed. Increase of vigor at first when walking, with lightness, afterwards weakness.

Weakness; all day, with sleepiness, aversion to noise, yet difficult hearing, a dreamy condition as after a sleepless night, with shivering and cold creeping; in morning on waking; in morning, < lower limbs, with indolence; in evening; < r. side; < after dinner, at times with tremulousness and heaviness of head; with aching in lumbar region; with pains in limbs;

with sensation as if beaten; sudden, faintlike, when standing; dizzy, nauseating, as after smoking too strong tobacco, on remaining up long in evening.

Faintness; then prostration and numbness. Necessity to lie down during the day. Heaviness in morning; *in morning in bed, with weariness in lower limbs.* Numbness on lying down, with fear of apoplexy. Decrease of sensibility to touch, but tickling was more quickly responded to than in the normal state. Inability to move head or limbs every morning on waking, with sensibility to contact over whole surface, after an hour staggering with tendency to fall to the left. **Aggravation from wine though symptoms seem to have been > camphor;** *A. from wine and Nux vom., especially uneasiness at night and constipation.* **Most symptoms appear after dinner and towards evening** (Puls.); *appear when sitting and during rest, less during motion and in open air* (Puls.). Amelioration in morning; A. on waking; from sweat.

Clinical.—Occasionally useful in locomotor ataxia with trembling, unsteadiness of the extremities and lightning-like pains. Epilepsy, especially in young children. Physical exhaustion, with acute sensitiveness of all cutaneous nerves and muscular unsteadiness. Very marked relief from discharges and appearance of eruptions (compare Sul.). The Zinc. patients are always relieved of their chest symptoms by expectoration, of pains by menstruation, of head symptoms by the re-appearance of alvine evacuations or of eruptions, etc., etc. Varicose veins, particularly of the lower extremities; extremely valuable, especially in the subacute or chronic condition which underlies and determines the development of this disease; it works well when associated with Puls.; the two drugs should never be given together, but consecutively; Zinc. follows Puls., acting better after Puls. has relieved some of the acute symptoms; neither of these drugs, however, is often indicated in acute phlebitis (see Vipera). Convulsions from suppression of menses, suppression of eruptions, from fright, etc. Chorea, with incessant movements, mostly twitching, especially during sleep, the feet particularly affected. Anæmia of teething children.

Mind.—Illusion when holding head down as if she had a goitre which she could not see over. Very happy at times. Lively and excited. Joyful, < towards evening, and excited. Laughs excessively over a trifle, and is just as easily vexed. Loquacity. *Easily offended.* Anger causing weakness; easily excited to A., but quiet. Wishes that he could get hold of some one on whom he could vent his anger. Impatient. Ill humor; in morning; at noon, > evening, and terrified; in afternoon, and disgusted with everything; during menses, and lachrymose; when obliged to speak; at much talking of other people, and impatient; < *evening, and sullen mood;* and frightened easily; and indolence, later liveliness and joyfulness; so that he whined, with pain in vertex.

Anxiety; during menses; on account of thieves or horrible apparitions when awake; as if he had done evil; restless, in morning. Apprehension and ennui, she seeks society; A. > evening, with lachrymose mood; as if he had committed a crime. Despondent. Sadness. Hypochondriac mood three hours after dinner, with pressure under short ribs, < r., with aversion to work and general discomfort, without trace of flatulence or of overloading stomach. Sensitive to noise. Talking and listening were distressing. Dread of work. Indolence after dinner, with sleepiness. Variable mood, sad at noon, in evening contented and happy. Alternately irritable, easily frightened, wrathful and despondent. Quiet thoughts of death in afternoon, with weakness. Indifferent.

Imaginative powers excited. **Dulness and thoughtlessness.** *Forgetful. Mental operations difficult. Difficulty in grasping ideas and in co-ordinating thoughts.* Ideas disconnected. Answers slow and as if in bad temper. Uses wrong words when talking. Omits letters in writing. Inability to fix the attention when reading and writing.

Clinical.—Delirium, with subsultus tendinum, coldness of extremities and trembling of hands. Melancholia. The mental condition is generally lethargic, stupid, and is associated with tendency to convulsions, sometimes with feeling of paralysis, so that the extremities have to be rubbed. It is said that a suicidal tendency or fear that one is to be arrested on account of crime is a marked indication for the drug in mental alienation. It is sometimes indicated in general paresis.

Head.—Tearing in brain; T. from morning till after lying down in evening, < r. frontal region, with throbbing; during and after dinner, with sticking in it, cutting in abdomen and yawning; sticking, and in eyes. Raging here and there. *Aching;* at night; **after a glass of accustomed wine,** *and in eyes;* > open air; > washing with cold water; with shivering; in brain, almost driving one mad, then vomiting of bile and trembling; congestive, mostly frontal and temporal, with beating in forehead and temples, < stooping and exposure to the heat of the sun; gnawing, especially in forehead, < over r. eye, on stooping this gnawing and heaviness became a beating headache; stupefying, obliged to lie down; stupefying, as from coal-gas, all the morning. Tingling when speaking loud, with resounding. Throbbing felt with pulse-beat. Oppression. Heaviness as if it would fall down. Fulness and heat. Inability to support it in evening. Weak feeling, < eyes. Dulness; in morning on waking; in forenoon, with pain in forehead and eyes and sleepiness; on waking; after dinner. Paroxysms of dizzy stupefaction, < afternoon and evening, with blackness before eyes and general weakness. Intoxication.

Vertigo; in morning, with headache; in morning, with heaviness and confusion of head as from loss of sleep; from morning till noon; at noon, with stunned feeling; after dinner; on sitting up in bed; when sitting and standing, > walking; after rising from stooping, with buzzing in head; with flushing heat; with weakness of head and abdomen so that she must lie down; *so that he could not stand; in attacks, preceded by sharp pressure at root of nose and sensation of drawing together of eyes as by a cord, followed by nausea, faintness and trembling of hands;* as if he would fall over, when standing, < occiput, not affecting eyes; as if he saw through a mist, after eating; as if he would have apoplexy, with anxiety and fear of falling headlong; as if head moved up and down in morning on waking, with similar floating of the images of his fancy, with semi-consciousness.

Forehead.—Pulsation perceptible to hand. Sticking, with drawing in it, and pain as if vertex were split in two; S., with tearing as if head would burst; tearing, in skin above l. brow; boring, above r. eminence. Tearing; in forepart; in l. eminence; *in l. eminence after dinner;* in sinciput after dinner, with throbbing; in forepart during supper, with crawling; in r. eminence, extending to orbit and upper lid; sticking, towards noon, with ineffectual inclination to sneeze. *Sharp pain in a spot in evening;* S. pain in morning on waking, becoming a pressure in temples. *Pain;* in sinciput; in r. eminence; l. side; every morning; *in sinciput*, at noon and in evening, *with dulness;* in l. eminence after dinner; *in sinciput* after dinner, *with dulness extending into eyes;* < stooping or mental work; with dulness, rendering thought difficult; with impatience; across sinuses, with sensibility of cartilages of ear and nose; sudden, after ascending stairs, settling in r. frontal region; sudden, above r. eye, with pressure downward in lids; throbbing, in l. region, then in r. *Pressure upon a spot in middle* at times. Sensitiveness. Sensation as if air forced itself too sensitively into sinuses. Drawing and throbbing. Tension; in sinciput. Dulness, with pinching in root of nose; D., with constriction in bone beneath and in front of r. ear; in sinciput, with heaviness. Heaviness; in evening during menses, with feeling as if head would be drawn backward.

Temples.—Sticking in l.; above r. at night, with tearing; inward suddenly in r.; intermittent, in r. Tearing; in r.; *in r. or also just above it; after dinner, with stitches in r. ear; intermittent pinching;* sticking; jerking, above l. Pinching in l. Pain; in l.; and in r. eye; in l., < moving or jarring head, not noticed when the mind is occupied with something else, with feeling as if the pulse beat against a tender place; alternately in T. and occiput. Cramplike pressure inward. Tightness.

Vertex.—Burning stitches in middle. Tearing in V. and above forehead; in V. and l. parietal bone; behind V.; *drawing, in attacks*, and more in forehead. *Ulcerative pain on touch in evening.*

Sides.—Tearing on r. near vertex; in r. half; in l. anterior half, above forehead; in r. and in teeth in afternoon; in r. after dinner, with sticking; drawing, in l. half. Boring in l. parietal bone; in r. side and occiput in evening; in r. parietal bone in evening when standing, with sensation of bursting; in r., with pain; drawing, in l. after dinner. Pain in l. half; temporary sharp, in l. Screwing-together pain in evening. Throbbing pain in r. in evening; in r., with twinging.

Occiput.—Sticking in a spot on O. Tearing in sides; in r. side when laughing; in r. side, with stitches on vertex. Gnawing in upper part; in r. protuberance, as by a mouse. Pain; in r. side; after walking in open air; extending to eyes; raging like the beating of waves in a spot in r. side in evening, with heat extending over vertex. Bruised pain. Pressing-asunder pain in r. side; in l. close to vertebræ. Drawing in l. side; D., with gnawing in forehead as from worms; dizzy, deep in r. side when sitting. **Heaviness and dulness.** *Vertigo as if he would fall to the left when walking;* V. in evening when sitting and smoking as usual, with desire for stool.

Scalp.—Falling of hair. Itching pimples. Itching moist eruption on and above temples. Suppurating pain on one side. Pain on touching hair on vertex. Sore feeling in a spot on r. side; S. feeling, not affected by touch. Drawing on vertex; S. feels drawn together to one spot. Sensation as if hair bristled, < above l. ear. Sore itching in a spot in middle.

Clinical.—Neuralgic headaches, the result of brain fag, sometimes with blurring of one half of the vision, photophobia, vertigo, etc. Headaches extending from the forehead to the vertex and occiput, > hard pressure on sides of head, sometimes a feeling of a heavy weight on the top of the head, always < stimulants. Occipital headache, with feeling of a heavy weight dragging the occiput downward, sometimes associated with a heavy weight on the vertex, scalp sore, photophobia, restlessness, aggravation from alcoholic stimulants. Violent headaches in school children who are overtaxed, with soft pulse; some cases have been cured when there seemed to be decided symptoms of beginning meningitis. Hydrocephalus; a very valuable remedy in different forms, following infantile cholera or even idiopathic and apparently tubercular; the general indications are roaring in the head, starting in fright, base of the head hot, photophobia, tremulousness of the muscles, constant motion of the feet, sometimes curative even after convulsions have set in; (the late Dr. Dunham usually advised low triturations in these conditions); many brilliant cures are reported. Meningitis consequent upon suppressed exanthemata or during teething, always characterized by the peculiar hyperæsthesia of all the special senses, trembling, twitchings, squinting, and even convulsions.

Eyes.—Inflammation during menses. Turned outward. Moisture during the day, agglutination in morning. Stitch in l.; cutting, in r. Tearing in l. **Pain as from sand, < evening and night, with lachrymation, even upper lid towards inner canthus was red and swollen,** *with inflammation and redness of r. conjunctiva, suppuration in inner canthus.* Pain; *in l. in evening;* in l. when walking in open air; in l., with uneasiness in it, often with weakness of head; tensive, in r., like rheumatism; as if pressed inward. Pressure; towards evening.

Burning in afternoon; in E. and lids in morning and evening, with dryness and pressure; *with biting, photophobia and lachrymation* (< *evening*), *with agglutination in morning;* pressing when reading, < l. lid. Biting in l., > rubbing; *sore, towards evening, < r.;* prickling, in lower part of l. and below it, upon cheek. Feeling as if she had wept much. *Constantly affected.* Weak, sick feeling. *Tickling as from dust in r.* Itching; *of l.*, > rubbing.

Lachrymation in morning on waking, also in open air. Twitching in l. ball. *Dry feeling in ball.* Sticking in r. ball. Aching in balls. Pupils alternately dilated and contracted, but usually dilated. Lid, twitching of l. lower; falling of upper and œdema of lower; sticking in r. lower and l. upper; *pressure on margin of l. lower, near inner canthus; burning of l. as if too dry;* sore feeling on r. upper; itching on margin of l. upper; paralysis of upper. *Canthi,* **agglutination of inner, in morning, with pressing sore feeling** (Puls.); **sore feeling in inner,** (Puls.); soreness in outer, with biting pain; **itching in inner with sticking and with cloudy vision;** *painful pressure in r. inner, with redness of conjunctiva; biting in r. inner, > rubbing.* Jerking in l. brow. Sticking tearing in and above l. brow. Bruised sensation in orbit and bones of face.

Vision.—*Dim;* in morning after waking. *Photophobia;* with dim, watery eyes. Flickering. Objects appear elongated and at times double. Diplopia, < l. eye, then strabismus. Vanishing, with absence of mind; V. after dinner and when writing, with lachrymation and burning. Of fiery flakes floating in circles on looking at the sky. Of yellow, blue and green rings, with suffering look and sleepiness.

Clinical.—Pterygium, smarting, lachrymation, itching and burning, all the symptoms worse in inner canthus, etc. Catarrhal conjunctivitis, worse in inner canthus. Note the marked affinity of Zinc. for the inner, and of Graph. for the outer canthi. It has been found useful in blurred vision, associated with the severe headaches of brain fag, neuralgic pain extending from over the eye to the occiput.

Ears.—Wax in l. increased, thin and impeding hearing, the beating of the pulse is distinct and causes roaring in ear. Discharge from l.; offensive from l.; purulent from l., orifices swollen and hot, with left-sided headache. Stitches; in r.; with itching; in l., close to lobule, with tearing; *cutting-tearing, near r. drum. Tearing;* in bone in front of l.; at times with itching, or in morning with crawling, or in evening with burning. Cramp in lobule of l.; in lobule of l. extending into neck, on boring finger into ear. Jerking pain from mouth along Eustachian tube; pinching J. Pain; bruised, in bone beneath and in front of r. on touch. Pinching drawing behind l. extending into lower jaw. Tickling in l., not > rubbing. Itching in r., > boring into it; in l., with feeling on putting finger into it as if fleas were jumping about.

Ringing; in r. at night. Crash as of the breaking of a pane of glass on falling asleep. Cracking after breakfast, with beating. Whizzing, and in evening pulsation; W. in front of r. Noises. Roaring. Hearing lost.

Nose.—Swelling on r. side; of l. wing, with pain. Sticking in septum on touch. Tearing externally on r. side; jerking, in r. side. Cutting on inner margin of l. wing. *Cutting crawling in evening, then sneezing.* Pinching in root, extending into eye; in root, with stitches in jaws. Throbbing pain in root, with full sensation. *Sore feeling high up, and in r. nostril tearing. Pressure upon root as if it would be pressed into head,* < noon. Drawing in r. nostril after dinner, with tearing. Tickling in mucous membrane, with irritation as if it would provoke sneezing. Itching in r. nostril; in l., then sneezing, then bleeding, > cold water. Stuffed feeling. *Stoppage;* with apprehension and oppression; with mucus in larynx and posterior nares and nasal speech.

Sneezing; in morning and afternoon; after a meal. Increased discharge of mucus, without coryza. Feeling of coryza, with sore sensitiveness of nostrils. Coryza, with irritation of nasal mucous membrane, impeding respiration; C., with stoppage of nose, but running from nose; sudden, in evening after lying down; dry all day, with pain in back, < sitting. Fluent coryza, afterwards dry; F. towards evening, with pressure in r. tonsil on swallowing and yawning; with raw throat; with crawling in nose and frequent sneezing; alternating with dry, < evening. Blowing out of blood. Bleeding after dinner on blowing, then stupefaction in forehead as from apoplexy, with swimming of objects before eyes.

Face.—*Pale.* Earthy. Cachectic look, bluish-white. Swelling of l. cheek, with itching. Expression vacant and apathetic or irritable; morose and gloomy, even in morning. Flushed. Cadaverous, pinched. Twitching, with nausea and vomiting; T. of musculi risores, with constant inclination to laugh. Jerklike stitches; *sudden S. from r. zygoma to upper margin of orbit, deep in bone, in evening, then sensitiveness of the spot;* tearing, in chin and on throat, passing into one another. Tearing in l. cheek; *in malar-bone extending into upper jaw;* in r. malar-bone, with bruised pain on pressure. Sticking in joint of jaw, beneath and in front of l. ear, on moving jaw backward and biting strongly and on pressing finger on joint. Cramplike tearing here and there in lower jaw, < chin. Pain in jaw, near l. wing of nose.

Lips.—Swelling; of upper. Thick glutinous moisture. Pimples on upper; yellowish-white itching, on lower; flat red, painful to touch in middle of upper. Water-blisters or suppurating pimples in upper. Ulcers in corners; yellow, inside lower. Upper sore, ulcerating in middle. Twitching in l. side of upper. *Dry; and cracked.* Sticking in upper. Pain, a jerking tearing in r. side of upper. Tensive smarting on lower; burning S. on inner surface of lower. Burning in r. corner.

Mouth.—Teeth. Bleeding, and of gums. Water seemed to come from last r. lower molar, and on touch of tongue sticking in it. Sticking in roots of l. upper canine and in adjacent incisors; in l. lower molars in evening; in l. T. and jaw, extending into neck; jerking, in l. lower molars, also in evening, waking him suddenly. Picking, with prickling and with drawing pains in jaws. Tearing in l. upper molars; in roots of r. upper; in last l. lower molars in evening; *in hollow molar,* < pressure, on sucking it blood comes; l. lower, < incisors, with drawing; last l. molars, then in cheek extending to temple and forehead; extending from root of a r. upper towards temple in evening after lying down; jerking, in last r. lower molar. Pain in hollow before menses. *Jerking;* in r. lower molars in evening after lying down till sleep; intermittent, in l. *Drawing in roots of incisors;* in r. lower molars; l. upper incisors; *upper incisors* towards noon, with sore feeling on gums; in roots of upper incisors and at the same time in pharynx, extending into cervical muscles; now in r., now in l. last lower molars; *sharp jerking, in two last molars;* sharp jerklike, suddenly in all incisors; throbbing, in last molars, alternately r. and l. Throbbing pain in hollow after eating or after becoming heated or getting cold. Sensitiveness of upper molars, with drawing sore pain in a l. lower molar, which protrudes from its socket and is loose, with swelling on l. submaxillary gland. Painful burning in incisors, with biting on lower surface of tongue. Feeling as if on edge. Seemed blunted, but on separating molars sensation of softness and agglutination.

Gum.—*Bleeding; on slightest touch.* Swelling; sore painful. White. White pellicles. The ulcer on the root of a bad tooth is sensitive to touch, with elongated feeling in tooth, when pressing upon it blood comes. Pain when chewing, and in palate; P. on inner side as if sore, as if separated from teeth. Biting on inner surface, with itching.

Tongue.—*Blisters;* painful on eating. Swelling of l. side preventing talking. Whitish; covered with white mucus; coated white as from cheese, in morning, with icy coldness; coated yellowish-white, < towards root. Dirty moist. Painful as if sore. Dry.

Inflammation of palate. Swelling of palate behind incisors, with pain. Yellow ulcer on inside of l. cheek, painful, < morning. Pain posteriorly on palate and on velum palati, < yawning. *Sticking biting on palate close to and in roots of incisors.* Crawling as from large bubbles on inside of cheeks. *Salivation; with crawling on inside of cheeks;* with nausea; with metallic taste; with metallic taste and stitches in tip of tongue; sour-bitter. Fetid breath.

Taste.—Metallic. Coppery. Clammy. Salt, with dryness in throat. As after eating raw peas. Of bad cheese in forepart of mouth, > swallowing, to which he was impelled by mucus in throat. Bitter. Bitter slimy in morning on waking. Sweet beneath forepart of tongue; as of a sweetish powder in throat; and flat. Of blood, and a disagreeable sweetness rising from stomach; of B., with dryness in throat and soreness rising from chest.

Clinical.—Difficult dentition; the child is weak, cold, pulse soft, bores the head into the pillow, tends to squint, cries out in sleep, and particularly has restless feet.

Throat.—Twitching of l. sterno-cleido-mastoid muscle. Swelling of submaxillary glands; of tonsils, with ulceration; of tonsils, with pain, < swallowing. Inflammation, and on pharynx and tonsils round, sharply-defined ulcers, with red, everted edges, they gradually coalesced and were filled with yellowish-white matter. Lumps of white mucus pass through posterior nares into mouth without hawking. Greenish mucus seated low down is expectorated, with sore pain in upper part of chest. Rising of hot vapor. Something like blood with sweetish taste comes into it in evening after lying down.

Jerking tearing in pharynx extending into l. cervical muscles. Pain, and at angle of jaw and in laryngeal region; in tonsils on swallowing in evening and night; on swallowing, with swelling externally and in tonsils; *as from internal swelling*, also on empty swallowing. *Tearing drawing posteriorly on sides of pharynx, more when not swallowing than on empty swallowing.* Sore pain, with fulness in œsophagus; anxious sore feeling, < night; cramplike retching soreness, rather externally in muscles, on swallowing even drink. Soreness on swallowing. Biting scraping posteriorly in fauces. Rawness; in evening, with hacking cough; so that she could scarcely breathe, with hoarseness; scraping in pharynx towards evening.

Constriction on swallowing, with desire to swallow frequently; C. and spasm. Choking sensation in r. side when not swallowing. Pressure from pharynx down into abdomen, as if a hard body were opposing from below; spasmodic P. upward in pit or upper part of œsophagus. *Sensation of mucus posteriorly in pharynx, with inclination to hawk.* Food seems to stick in pharynx after dinner. *Dryness;* posteriorly in fauces in morning on waking and afterwards, with thirst; in morning when walking, with rawness, hawking of mucus and sore pain low down in throat, then raising of black clotted blood, then all day sweet taste, dryness in throat and bloody saliva; *in evening;* after dinner; < morning or after dinner, *and in larynx*, at times > food, *with rawness*, often forcing him to hawk or cough; *with mucus in larynx and constant inclination to hawk up tenacious mucus, which soon collects again.* Burning; like heartburn, even on swallowing. Dysphagia. Constriction in œsophagus during deglutition, with spasm.

Clinical.—Globus hystericus, rising from the pit of the stomach.

Stomach.—Appetite. *Ravenous;* at noon and in evening, but after eating distended feeling; in evening. Insatiability, but no relish for food. Desire to eat in pharynx, even after a meal, after satisfying it overloaded feeling in stomach and pressure in head. Haste in eating. Dinner better relished than usual. Desire for salt and salty things. Diminished; at noon; at dinner; and capricious, at times lost. Dinner is not relished, with pain in stomach as from fasting. *Lost;* in morning and evening; and almost no taste; with disgust at the sight of food. *Aversion to the sweetness of sugar;* to food, with colic; to fish; to meat and warm cooked food; to veal in evening, the morsels swelled up in her mouth; *to wine and brandy, which they took to excite their appetites.*

Thirst; from morning till evening; *in afternoon;* in afternoon during menses; *in afternoon, with heat in palm;* in evening till lying down, with heat; during dinner or afterwards; with hasty drinking, which was very refreshing; for beer in evening; burning.

Eructations; after beef-tea; during breakfast, tasting of it; tasting of milk in afternoon; tasting of the meat eaten; at night of the food eaten at noon; loud, with at times rapid, with at times weak, slow pulse; sweetish; acrid, after sweets, causing scraping in larynx like heartburn; qualmish, an hour and a half after a moderate dinner, with burning in stomach. Pyrosis. Sour E.; after food; after breakfast of bread and milk. *Empty E.;* in evening or forenoon; with pressure upon chest; then tasting of the fat eaten; bitter; *sour* after drinking or *after dinner;* the gas of which burned in the daylight with a pale flame, indicating the presence of hydrogen. Bitter E.; after supper; of yellow water and bile after eating, then vomiting. Ineffectual efforts to eructate, with pressure in middle of spine; I., then empty eructations with relief.

Hiccough; in evening or after breakfast; > eructations of bile.

Nausea; through the day; in morning; in morning, > rising; during breakfast; after breakfast and dinner; after midday nap, obliged to spit much; after supper; after dinner and supper, > emission of flatus, with distention of stomach and inclination to eructate; after stooping, with shuddering on washing and while sitting down; < **a sip of wine, with headache**; with chilliness; with shivering; with sweat; with trembling and weariness; with general sick feeling; with sick feeling in head and chest; with stomachache as from emptiness; with colic; with eructations and salivation; with risings as in vomiting on attempting to hawk; in stomach-pit, with tense sensation above navel; so that he must sit down, but inability to vomit, with eructations and desire for stool.

Retching; with sour taste and sour water in mouth; *of bloody mucus.*

Vomiting; of thin liquid; of food immediately after swallowing it; of mucus; of water and mucus; of mucus, then bile; acrid, of contents of stomach, causing burning where it touched the face, while drinking, without nausea, afterwards rawness of throat; regularly three or four times a day, with acid reaction, smelling of rancid oil, besides the remains of food butyric acid and lactic acid and a large number of sarcinæ and cryptogams; bilious; easy, of watery bile, then relief; of bitter, yellow, bilious water; of bitter, slimy liquid and at last food, with shocks of coughing, warmth < abdomen, sweat, chilliness over arms, shuddering, empty eructations, hiccough, rumbling and griping in abdomen, the nausea > sitting bent over, the nausea and vomiting returned on sitting erect, on moving and on pressure upon abdomen.

Gurgling at noon and in evening when yawning, with rumbling. Movements at noon, with coldness. Dilated as far as navel, its peristaltic movements at times appreciable through abdominal wall, pylorus hypertrophied, sunken and movable, forming a tumor sensible to touch, sometimes to r., sometimes to l. of umbilicus, at last under r. false ribs another hard, slightly indented tumor, painful when pressed, the size was variable, it disappeared under prolonged pressure of fingers, it was most evident during the violent gastric crisis, it was caused by contractions of the hypertrophied muscle resting upon a solid surface formed by the increased mass of the liver. Fulness, with heaving.

Sticking in diaphragm; in diaphragm and between shoulders; *in and beneath pit, with tearing; from both sides towards each other*, with S. in middle of sternum. Pinching in pit. Griping deep in region of pit, < deep breathing. Cramplike pain; in pit; in pit and chest; pit and epigastric region. Sharp pain, and in pit.

Pain; *in pit;* in epigastrium; epigastrium and r. side of umbilicus; in region and in abdomen in morning; in morning after rising, then sticking in præcordial region; at noon, with coldness in it; in evening after eating; in pit in evening, with burning soreness on pressure; on pressure; in pit during inspiration, the breath was held back, after dinner; in epigastric region, with fulness; in pit extending to chest, > eructations; in diaphragm and between shoulders, extending to sacrum; in epigastric region, causing excitement and spasmodic pressure; heavy.

Cramplike dragging in pit and epigastric region. Drawing in and beneath pit. Constriction from both sides, with anxiety and heat over whole body. Compression in morning fasting. Oppression; in pit; sudden, in epigastric region during menses, with tightness so that everything must be loosened. Screwing-together sensation in pit. Discomfort after a meal; D. in cardiac orifice extending to œsophagus. Sinking for hours after eating acids. Emptiness in S. and abdomen, with hunger two hours after dinner; E., with nausea. *Burning; in epigastric region;* in upper part when fasting. Acidity. Digestion difficult.

Clinical.—Gastric derangement, < alcoholic stimulants, especially flatulence, with much rumbling in abdomen (see Arg. nit.). Atonic dyspepsia, feeling as if the stomach were collapsed; (note a goneness in the stomach in the later part of the forenoon, similar to Sul.).

Abdomen.—*Distention; in evening* on going to bed without supper; towards evening, with pressure and odorless flatus; after eating; with stitches. *Gurgling. Rumbling* in morning; in morning, *with rolling; in morning in bed, with grumbling and flatulent pain;* after milk, with cutting and emissions of flatus; < *evening, with movements* and emissions of flatus, or with cutting in hypogastrium after dinner; with dragging pains; with gurgling, then painful retracting and urging to stool. Flatulence; which presses out the hæmorrhoids, which are then painful, < lying. Emission of flatus; *hot* in evening; offensive; hot, offensive, passes often after dinner till midnight; offensive, noisy in evening, without flatulent troubles in abdomen, the first emissions were odorless.

Sticking after normal stool; after supper, > rest, and in middle of spine; intermittent; every seven days or once in three weeks; into scrotum; burning. *Cutting* all night; *C., then leucorrhœa* and yawning. *Griping;* here and there; *at various times* (also in sides of A. and about navel), *sometimes when yawning*, **or after breakfast, or with cutting after dinner;** in evening, with diarrhœa; anteriorly in evening, with emission of flatus; after soup, < upper; with tendency to diarrhœa; or cutting, sometimes in morning, often followed by soft or diarrhœa-like stools; as far as stomach, where it is a constriction, obliging her to bend up, in evening; tensive, on a jar or on retracting abdomen, then sticking towards pit of stomach. Twisting in morning in bed before emission of flatus. Rachialgia, with exhaustion caused by want of sleep and anorexia.

Pain; at night, and in lumbar region, with stitches in l. side and drawing pain in lower limbs; *after a light meal, with tympanitis;* after dinner and supper, changing to sticking while walking, > emission of flatus; after copious stool; with every stool and emission of flatus; at times with nausea and running of water from mouth, often with offensive mucus, which took away her appetite; then cramplike feeling in bladder; waking her at night, then thick leucorrhœa; so that he rolled on the floor; as if diarrhœa would come on. Flatulent pain; in evening, < hypogastrium; after dinner, < movement. Flatulent, throbbing pain, extending towards chest. Acute drawing extending into urethra, with crawling. Constriction even when lying after midnight, < rising; C. taking away the breath. Uneasiness. Heaviness. Internal coldness. Empty feeling, with discharge of flatus.

Upper.—Distention from pit of stomach to below navel, with pain in it and with sensitiveness of r. upper lid. *Gurgling*, and in lower; *in upper after eating, with pain. Griping tearing in U. and in side of chest after dinner, < walking and standing, > rest of body and mind.* Griping during dinner; in evening, with emission of flatus and itching over hips. Cutting; when eating. Sharp pain between pit of stomach and navel, < retracting abdomen, but > the eructations caused thereby. Biting. Throbbing in skin beneath pit of stomach.

Hypochondria.—*Cramplike pain alternating with oppression of chest and difficult breathing.* Pain as from flatulence, and in sides of abdomen and in back, even in morning in bed, < walking, somewhat > stool, renewed by walking. Heaviness; and in loins, with pain, then prostration.

Hepatic Region.—*Liver voluminous. Sticking* in r. side and middle; in H. region and r. hip; during sour eructations and on inspiration; *sometimes also in hip, or with burning or biting externally, at times also in evening or after dinner;* jerking, after supper. Intermittent tearing. Pinching; as from incarcerated flatus, < motion, and in r. side of abdomen. Pinching griping in a spot. Pain in a spot; P., with jerklike tearing drawing.

Region of Spleen.—*Sticking;* in evening when walking and standing; with pain; deep, < pressure. *Intermittent pinching.* Slow pulsating sore feeling. Pressure.

Sides.—Rumbling in l. in evening; in r., then croaking. Stitches in r.; in l. flank in morning after waking; sudden, in l. at night, < breathing and pressure. Tension. Tensive colic in l., > eructations.

Umbilical Region.—Stitches as from an internal ulcer in a spot in r. side above navel, < touch and motion; cutting S. transversely across; tearing. Tearing from one side to the other below navel till evening. Cutting transversely below navel. *Sticking griping;* griping as from flatus, when walking. *Pain;* and below navel; in middle of abdomen after a moderate supper; in middle of abdomen, with cramplike drawing; *as from an internal induration in a spot beneath navel,* < pressure and retracting abdomen.

Hypogastrium. — Protrusion of inguinal hernia. Jerking from groin towards penis. Stitches; in l.; above groin; near genitals, then tearing drawing in root of penis; cutting, in l. after emission of flatus;

downward through r. ilium on bending over, with a hard abdomen. Tearing low down in r. side, extending into groin; deep in l. side, beginning in region of hip. Pinching in r. groin and flank as in retention of urine, renewed by rising from a seat. *Pain in pubic region;* P. close to r. hip; after a dry stool; > normal stool; in groin and pubic region, with drawing; intermittent, on rising; jerking, in r. groin. Prickling in l. groin at night, alternating with drawing, disturbing sleep. Bruised sensation in r. side. Drawing pain in l. groin when sitting. Drawing in l. groin. Screwing-together sensation in l. groin, extending into chest. Constriction in l. side on walking and on pressure, > sitting after dinner. Pressing feeling low down, extending to beginning of urethra, with crawling. A hernia presses down forcibly. Painful retching in l. groin as if a hernia would occur. Feeling as if an inguinal gland were swollen.

Clinical.—It has been used for flatulent colic, for lead colic, neuralgia of the bowels, with retraction of the abdomen (Plumb.), etc. Enlargement of the liver, with flatulent dyspepsia, etc. Enlarged, indurated liver, which is sore. Reflex symptoms from floating kidney.

Rectum.—Jerking stitches extending into root of penis. Cutting and smarting. Boring extending into abdomen, with pressing, so that she could not sit down. Drawing pain extending into abdomen. Soreness. Itching. Heaviness when standing, > emission of flatus. Feeling as if pressed by flatus, though none passes; feeling as if flatus pressed against coccyx, by which it was retained, in evening. Tenesmus. Desire for stool in morning and after eating; D. for stool, with movement in abdomen; long, then difficult, soft stool; ineffectual.

Anus.—Discharge of blood. Protrusion of hæmorrhoids, with smarting pain. Stitches; crawling, in morning; burning, in evening when walking; twinging, like lightning into rectum. Tearing. Jerklike cutting. Burning soreness in evening. Crawling pressure. *Crawling;* sore. *Itching;* in evening; after soft stool; with oozing of corrosive moisture; ending in pain. *Burning; during stool;* after stool.

Stool.—*Diarrhœa;* at night, with griping and tenesmus; with emission of flatus; then no stool for three days; frequent, then leucorrhœa; involuntary, in morning on waking; brown; brown, gushing, flatulent, preceded and followed by griping; yellowish, gushing; pasty, with straining after stool; offensive, alternating with constipation; bilious, then no stool for twenty-four hours; bilious, then great relief. Soft, twice at night; S. after dinner, with cessation of pain in abdomen; S. several times a day, enveloped in bright red frothy blood, preceded by colic; and difficult, with emission of prostatic fluid.

Constipation; but some desire for stool. **Hard, small** (Plumb.), *with pressure and rumbling in abdomen; H. often crumbling, with pressure and clawing in anus; and unsatisfactory,* only every two o rthree days; in morning, another after dinner soft, accompanied and followed by vertigo and roaring in head; and scanty in evening, then several small soft ones; and difficult; with blood; then renewed urging; at first, then liquid; first part, last part easy, soft. *Large in size, with great effort of abdominal muscles.* Tenacious, light yellow, with sticking in anus. Scanty, tenacious, then straining and heat in anus. Light-colored, the first part large and hard, the last soft. Profuse. Normal, four times a day, with griping in abdomen. Intermittent.

Clinical.—Cholera infantum with green mucous discharges, sometimes with tenesmus (Merc. dulc.), with boring of the head into the pillow, restless extremities. Sudden cessation of diarrhœa followed by the cerebral symptoms above noted. Involuntary stools and urine. It has been used for chronic dysentery with the particularly marked symptoms of Zinc.

Urinary Organs.—Pressure upon bladder, but not to urinate. Urging to urinate, urine copious; U. after micturition every evening on lying down, but only three or four drops pass; frequent at night, with scanty discharge. Micturition slow and in a thin stream; dribbling, every evening; involuntary, on blowing nose (after a difficult stool); frequent after midnight, urine light yellow, not very copious; frequent, urine rather increased, watery or lemon-colored.

Urethra.—Emission of prostatic fluid. Flow of blood; after painful micturition. Stitches through U.; in orifice; twinging backward like lightning. Cutting in orifice in evening when sitting; tearing, in middle extending forward. Sore pain in forepart when not urinating. Drawing and tearing in forepart; *acute D. in forepart and in penis.* Biting in orifice after micturition; in forepart when not urinating, with tearing. Itching. Burning before and during micturition; after micturition; when urinating during menses; tearing B.

Urine.—Increased in evening; at night. Scanty; in evening and morning, and pale; after dinner; and high-colored; and nearly blood-red; and becomes turbid like clay-water. Reddish. Very yellow, deposits white flakes. *That passed at night is very turbid in morning.* Dark and turbid; with copious sediment of urate of ammonia, with a few crystals of oxalate of lime and a few cells of renal epithelium, at times a pellicle after standing, urine clearer on boiling, odor after standing from previous evening (in a corked bottle) sickening, wheylike, reaction acid, sugar present; turbid when it left the urethra except towards the end of micturition. Sediment flocculent; mealy in that passed at night.

Clinical.—Hysterical retention of urine. Paralysis of the bladder. Can urinate only when sitting. Occasionally useful for symptoms occuring during albuminuria, with œdema, irregular heart, spasmodic breathing and hæmorrhages.

Sexual Organs.—Falling of hair. Tearing in tip of glans. Painful jerking in root of penis. Penis sensitive when walking, as if the shirt rubbed it. Itching of end of penis in morning on waking. Erections, with pain; *strong E.;* strong, with pain in abdomen. Scrotum shrivelled; and neighboring parts; with shivering in it; sore red pimple at the root of a hair; stitches extending into glans; pain in r. side, < touch; sore sensation, and in contiguous parts of thigh; itching every evening not > scratching.

Stitches in l. testicle during rest. Drawing pain in testicles; prickling, < sitting and stooping. *Drawing up of r. or l. testicle, with pain and swelling; D. in testicles extending along spermatic cords;* in l., then r. T.; in l., at times extending along spermatic cord, with prickling pressure. Testicles feel sore and bruised. Desire in the company of women and discharge of semen too soon; D., but difficult seminal discharge. *Emissions at night without lascivious dreams.*

Female.—Pudenda, varices; pressure, and on rectum; pressure towards P., with cutting about navel; sticking biting during menses, with itching and swollen feeling. *Discharge of bloody mucus causing itching on pudenda, after menses. Leucorrhœa;* < every stool; *thick,* < morning and evening, also before and during menses; acrid, with burning in pudenda; slimy, with griping in upper abdomen. Lochia suppressed and milk diminished. *Menses too early;* and profuse, lasting three days; delayed; delayed and profuse, < night and walking, with cutting and drawing in abdomen and small of back; *discharged in large clots,* < *walking;* only three days; termination prolonged; returned (after a suppression of three months) with alternations of paleness and redness of face. *Excitement* at night without lascivious dreams.

Clinical.—Seminal emissions, with hypochondriasis, general irritability and depression. Neuralgia of the testicles, < walking. Irregular menstruation. Sometimes vicarious menstruation, hæmorrhage from the urethra, or bowels, or lungs, with the general Zinc. symptoms. Neuralgia of left ovary, preceding menses, > the flow. Pruritus of the vulva. Unnatural sexual excitement in women. All the symptoms of derangement of the female organs are associated with the general restlessness, depression, tendency to coldness, spinal tenderness and especially the restless feet of Zinc.

Respiratory Organs.—Tickling in region of larynx; from mucus; on it, with sticking in it. Voice weak when talking loud. *Hoarseness,* with burning in trachea; H. as if chest were filled with mucus.

Cough; with oppression; with stitches in head; preventing sleep all night, with sticking in chest and thirst; *violent;* tickling, fatiguing, < night; suffocative, a tickling irritation takes away the breath; short, from tickling beneath sternum. *Dry cough; morning and evening,* **before and during menses,** *with bloody expectoration and with burning and sore pain in chest;* in evening, > lying down, with heaviness on chest; from tickling in larynx; waking her at night during menses; with stitches in chest, feeling as if it would burst, difficulty in breathing and talking; *and spasmodic;* and hacking. Cough and expectoration; incessant tendency to; day and night, E. thick, purulent; E. of tenacious mucus like old catarrh, then sensation as if chest were hollow and cold; bloody E. Expectoration of much mucus of milky color; constant, of metallic-tasting mucus.

Asthma and other chest troubles. Croupy condition, with symptoms of paralysis of cervical muscles. *Respiration oppressed;* < l. lung; heavy and deep. R. and chest unusually free and easy.

Clinical.—Spasmodic cough, sometimes whooping cough, particularly in children; said to be characteristic when during the spasms of cough the child grasps the genitals. Bronchitis, with easy, profuse, frothy expectoration, < night, lying down, must sit up. Asthmatic bronchitis, with constriction of the chest. Asthma.

Chest. — Mucus loosened by hawking. Angina. *Stitches in r.;* in l.; deep in r.; in sternum; in upper part of l.; in l. clavicle; beneath r. nipple; beneath l. mamma; on r. short ribs; in l. mamma in morning; above heart in evening; in l. in evening when standing, with bruised pain; in region of l. ribs opposite pit of stomach in evening, with ulcerative pain; in side at night; beneath sternum when eating; when walking in open air, extending to l. side of neck, with difficult breathing; in l. side on moving arm; in a spot on deep breathing; in middle during and after inspiration, with tightness; in r. side, at times on turning body to r., or after dinner, followed by pressure, or alternating with stitches in r. flank and side of abdomen; in middle of sternum at times on stooping, at times followed by pressure deep internally extending into throat; in r. side, < violent expiration; in l., < breathing, > stretching; *in a spot in l., with feeling as if corroded and bruised;* beneath r. axilla, with tension; in r. side, with tension and bruised pain; in l., with pain; in l., with pain in l. nipple; in side, then cough, with expectoration of bloody mucus; in upper part of sternum extending into l. loin in morning, with fear of stooping; pleuritic, beneath heart in evening; tearing, beneath axilla, then sore feeling.

Tearing above pit of stomach; beneath l. axilla; in r.; in lower part of l.; in r. upper ribs, almost in the back; sticking, in l. Cramp extending to stomach and abdomen from 7 till 8 P.M. Pinching in forepart of r., then stitches in r. hypochondrium, extending to præcordial region, with long-remaining bruised pain in the part; intermittent, in morning, with nausea; intermittent, with twinging. Sharp pain near r. axilla.

Pain; in l., then in r.; in r. mamma; beneath l. nipple; here and there, or in l. side; in l. nipple, with sensitiveness; in l. ribs, with sensitiveness to touch; as if blood forced its way into the finest vessels in lungs, < r. Sore pain in l. pectoral muscles; about r. nipple. Bruised pain when riding in a carriage; internally in a spot in upper part. *Roughness* at night, *with rawness,* heat and sweat. Rheumatic drawing beneath clavicle near shoulder-joint; sharp D. about l. nipple, with sore pain on touch, which soon became a pulsation. Painful throbbing by l. axilla at noon. *Anxiety;* > evening, with headache.

Oppression; in morning. Tightness beneath sternum in evening; *T. in evening, with sticking and pressure in middle of sternum, with small, rapid pulse.* Constriction; with pain as if cut to pieces; as by a band, on walking in open air. Pressure; on l. clavicle; here and there upon C. and back; upon r. end of l. clavicle in morning; upon upper part of sternum or upon lower part of chest after eating; outward, intermittent, here and there in l., with drawing tension; as if a foreign substance were rising into throat; as from rheumatism and incarcerated flatus. Tensive pain; in l. clavicle, with drawing. Distended feeling in l. mamma. *Burning in side;* in l. side and l. scapula; in a spot in r. side, near pit of stomach, and above l. nipple; in sternum, with weakness; on r., as if in skin, extending to back. Affection of l. lung. Symptoms < motion, when she lifts or takes hold of anything.

Clinical.—The chest feels as if oppressed with quantities of mucus. Intercostal neuralgia.

Heart.—First sound hoarse and prolonged. *Stitches at apex; in præcordial region, with tension;* S., < violent expiration. Cramplike feeling, and in lungs. Pain at apex; in region, with external swelling and tenderness; sharp at apex. Pressure, heaviness and spasmodic tension. Præcordial anxiety towards evening. *Palpitation;* and a stitch with every beat of the heart.

Pulse.—*Rapid in evening,* at times with heat; R., wiry and irregular; and full, and tense, irregular, hard. Slow and intermittent; S. and feeble; and compressible. Hard; and small. Irregular.

Neck.—Stitches in muscles. *Tearing in r. side* posteriorly; and below jaw and behind and beneath ear;

T. in l. side in morning, > pressure; in l. side, extending behind ear; sticking, posteriorly and inferiorly in a spot in r. side. Pinching on sides near trunk. *Pain in N. and small of back as if beaten and wearied; P. in muscles at night, even during sleep, as if head had been in an uncomfortable position;* in nape as if it could not support the head when sitting and writing. Cramplike drawing in r. side on holding head erect; down cervical muscles when chewing. Pressure as with a finger on r. side when talking. Tension in l. side; T. in anterior muscles; in r. side, with drawing. **Weariness in nape in evening when writing**. *Stiffness in cervical and upper dorsal muscles* every morning, *with pain;* S. in side in morning in bed, with pain extending to shoulder; cramplike, in l. side.

Back.—*Sticking when sitting and walking.* Pinching in spots, with burning pain. *Bruised pain when walking in open air, with weakness.* Pain < sitting. Burning drawing pain in morning during sleep, with sensation of falling asleep in shoulder-joint, disturbing sleep, > waking. Tensive, rheumatic pain in spine. Drawing and burning. Sticking in middle when standing. Pain in r. side near middle of spine. *Burning pressure upon spine above small of back.*

Scapulæ.—Stitches beneath r.; close to upper part of r., < during eructations; on inner margin of r., with pressure; extending into l.; from r. to l.; beneath l.; extending into l. chest; in margin of l. extending towards axilla, with rising of heat to head; jerking, beneath and near l. Tearing between S.; in r.; burning, between r. and spine. Sharp pain close to r. Pain beneath l.; between S.; in upper dorsal muscles every night, < movement, with stiffness; between S., extending to sacrum. Throbbing under lower third of l. Tensive pain between S. *Tension beneath r.*, extending down back and towards axilla; as from an adhesive plaster near inner margin of r. Tensive pressure upon a spot by border of r.

Lumbar Region.—Cracking when walking. *In kidney region,* stitches; r.; l. when standing and walking, with bruised pain; after dinner or in evening, at times extending towards chest; intermittent, in l. Tearing in region of r. kidney, at times sticking; *cutting, at times in r. kidney region, at times drawing pressure;* intermittent, in region of l. kidney; sticking, in sacrum. Cutting extending into calves and feet on motion. Pinching in kidney region. *Pain; in spine;* above r. hip; in kidney region; *in region of l. kidney,* at times pinching; at night on turning over in bed; on stooping; on walking and sitting down; *when walking, often forcing him to stand still, > continuing to walk;* in region of l. kidney on touch; < lying on back, > lying on side; with languor; sore, in region of l. kidney; tensive, rheumatic, and in shoulder; paralytic, when lying in an uncomfortable position, < rising from a seat and beginning to walk. Screwed-in sensation in evening on rising from a seat. Drawing just above r. nates; in spine and lumbar region like painful weakness, when sitting and stooping. Dragging in coccyx, at times pinching. Pressure upon lower part of spine. *Weakness when walking;* all day when walking, and in hollows of knees; on beginning to walk, and in lower limbs; when sitting, with tension in it and abdomen. Paralyzed feeling extending to hips and afterwards to l. side.

Clinical.—Spinal irritation; the whole spine is sensitive, especially the last dorsal vertebræ, the symptoms < sitting still and stimulants. Muscular rheumatism of the lumbar region, extending to the hips and thighs, < rising from a chair, stooping, etc.

Extremities.—Trembling; with twitching of muscles of thighs. Cramp. Sticking in joints; S. in all, extending into tips of fingers when sitting, < after heat, with tearing. *Tearing;* in bones of l. forearm, then in knee; after physical effort; *drawing in middle of almost all bones, so that they had no steadiness.* Aching. Darting pain through all joints, < ankles, knees and elbows, with numbness of adjacent parts and an exhausted paralyzed sensation in muscles of upper arms and thighs, < r. *Bruised feeling,* < lower; *B. in morning on waking, with weariness.* Drawing; here and there, ending in slow stitches. *Weakness;* of hands and feet during menses; sudden, at noon, more when standing than when sitting, with trembling and ravenous hunger. Heaviness on walking in open air. *Stiffness;* with soreness; *of joints, with lancinations* **transversely across** *above joints,* pressure upon joints caused soreness and pricking.

Upper Extremities.—Axilla. Stitches in l. and down forepart of chest arresting the breathing, in evening. Tearing extending into l.; sticking, in r. Sore feeling in a spot.

Shoulder.—Jerking in r., then bruised pain in l. scapula. Stitches in l.; beneath r. after dinner. Tearing; deep in r.; upon l., about beginning of neck; deep in the bone of the joint upon which she was lying in evening; on r., > scratching, with pressure in middle of upper arm; in joints, with tension; sticking, on top of r. Tearing arthritic pain extending to fingers. Heaviness on waking, with pressure. Falling asleep of joint.

Arm.—Twitching, and of hands. Tearing, and in hands. Bruised pain, < morning and evening; B. pain in l., he is unable to raise it on account of pain in deltoid. Inclination to stretch; I. to move himself with his arms. Weakness and tension; W., with pain in wrist as if wrenched. R. fails at times to respond to her demand.

Upper Arm.—Sticking in r. in morning when dressing; in anterior surface of l. after dinner, with burning. *Tearing near l. shoulder;* close to elbows; in anterior surface of l. near elbow and in r. near shoulder; in deltoids extending down upper arms; intermittent, in middle of inner side of l. Pain in r.; rheumatic, in deltoids, < raising arm. Bruised pain in r. humerus; in l. deltoid. Drawing in l. close to elbow; acute rheumatic, in deltoids from top of shoulders down arms, < raising arms. Rheumatic tension in head of l. humerus. Bubbling in l.

Elbow.—Sticking in r. in evening when yawning, with tension. Tearing in bends; *in r. in morning, > rubbing;* up and down in l., in a spot of a hand's breadth. Rheumatic pressure. Rheumatic drawing. Relaxed sensation in r. Heaviness as if paralyzed in bend of l.

Forearm.—Tearing in l., < upper part; bubbling, in muscles on inner side of r., not far from elbow. Cramplike drawing, or in fingers. Drawing pain as if in bone. Bruised pain on touch and on turning arm, at times with tearing in thick part of it. Rheumatic tension above l. wrist.

Wrist.—Tearing; in r.; in region of pisiform bone; in middle of r., then towards back of fingers; in r., with painful drawing; in bend of l., with tearing stitches on back of l. hand; extending to first phalanx of thumb when riding in a carriage. Burning pain in r., and in ball of hand. Drawing pain in r. as if sprained. Rheumatic drawing in r. Tension in r. as if muscles were too short.

Hand. — *Trembling; when writing, with weakness* (China, Phos.); *during menses;* more when resting it quietly upon the table than when leaning upon elbow. Tearing in r. just beneath wrist; in r. palm near fingers; in metacarpal bones of index fingers; on back of r. fourth and fifth metacarpal bones and in wrist; *in back of l.*, at times alternating with tearing on r. hand; sticking, in r., in bend of wrist and in palm near little finger; tensive, in r. palm. Pinching or sticking in ball of l. above little finger. Pressure on ball of l. Tearing drawing in palm between l. thumb and index. Tension in metacarpal bone of little finger extending towards wrist. Rigidity, < r.; of back when playing the piano, with feeling of cramp in extensor muscles of thumb. Asleep in morning on waking. Paralysis of r., it was blue, cadaverous, heavy, insensible, with small, thready, scarcely perceptible pulse.

Fingers.—Jerking in first joints of r. Stitches; through first phalanx of l. thumb; tearing; tearing, in middle joints of three last fingers of both hands; cutting, in tips of thumbs. *Tearing in first joints and phalanges;* in tips of index, middle and little fingers; in r. thumb and above it and in two adjacent fingers; beneath nail of r. thumb; in l. thumb towards tip, with painful throbbing, falling asleep and numb sensation and externally perceptible heat; sticking, in last joint of r. thumb; jerking, from first joints of l. towards tips in evening; drawing, in r. thumb. Pain in middle joint of r. index and at intervals in its first phalanx. Tearing drawing in last phalanges of l. middle and ring fingers. Drawing pain in tips, extending up arms (though the passes were downward). Throbbing in thumb, with crawling and internal heat.

Lower Extremities.—*Rheumatic drawing in r.* Tensive pain in l. Discomfort in morning in bed when bent. Feeling of congestion of blood in l., < leg. **Uneasiness at night.** Difficult to use and control. Weakness of l. in evening; in evening, with pain in them and sensitiveness to every draught through the room; on rising from a seat, < calves; attacks of tremulous, > walking, with paleness of face; paralytic W. and heaviness in afternoon on beginning to walk, > continuing to walk. *Heaviness;* and tearing; during menses, with drawing about knees as if they would be twisted around.

Nates.—Tearing on l. beneath hip; sticking, on r. below hip. Drawing pain after drinking wine. Bubbling in r. Pulsation in l.

Hip.—Tearing in l.; anteriorly on crest of ilium when sitting; drawing, posteriorly on l., with burning. Pain posteriorly in l. Bruised pain in joint, with tension and pain on motion; B. pain in l. extending to middle of thigh when walking and standing, > sitting, with pinching, heat and sensitiveness in it and with weakness of lower limb; in joint, as if flesh were loosened from bone.

Thigh.—*Varices extending to labiæ.* Stitches in middle; about great trochanter; on posterior surface in evening when yawning; tearing, when walking and lying. *Tearing* beneath hips and posteriorly on r. hip; < thick portion; on inner side of l., > motion; on outer side of femur, extending from hip to middle of thigh while sitting; drawing, in articular extremity to l. and beneath hip. Jerking pain on inner side. Bruised pain in gluteals and posterior femoral muscles; on anterior surface of l., with soreness on pressure. Paralytic pain in r., first in upper part, then extending towards knee, in evening when standing, > sitting. Drawing sore pain on outer muscles. Drawing pain on inner side of r.; intermittent D. pain in evening. Drawing posteriorly, with pressing, so that he could not sit down, > walking; *rheumatic D.* Feeling in bend when walking as if muscles were too short. Heaviness of r. when walking, with lameness; H. in l. femur above knee in evening, with paralytic pain.

Knee.—Stitches; on inner side of r. during rest; like a flea-bite on inner side of r. Tearing on outer side of l. patella; in bends in morning, < walking, > sitting, with bruised pain; in r., > rubbing; in bone of l., with contraction; and outer margin of bend, extending into calf; in l. extending to middle of thigh; extending upward and downward in l., with gnawing; in l. or also extending upward, with bruised pain. Pain, and in ankles; in r. patella in evening and then in l. and in heel; in a dream, and almost immovable, and on waking unusually early they were painful as after fatigue, < rest; gradually increasing and decreasing. Boring in evening, < r.; in l., with gnawing in it and tension in upper part of calf, renewed after sitting down. Burrowing. Bruised feeling. Drawing pain at night. Rheumatic drawing in r. and downward in tibia. Tensive pain in r. when walking; in hollows when walking in open air. Beating when sitting after a long walk. Crawling in l. Stiffness.

Leg.—*Œdema.* Cramp in morning in bed, drawing it up. Stitch above r. foot when running. Tearing in l. between tibia and ankle; in forepart of r. beneath knee, then bruised pain; *drawing, in tendines-achilles and about inner malleoli;* pulsating, in tendines-achilles. Drawing pain in evening. *Drawing in r. tendo-achillis.* Pressure on inner side of l. below calf, then tearing; alternating P. and drawing in bones of r. *Weakness, < walking. Stiffness so that she could not walk.* Falling asleep of r. at night.

Tibia.—*Sticking;* when walking. Tearing on r.; in lower end of r.; *to back of foot.* **Burning pain.** Drawing pain in r. Rheumatic drawing in r., with tension. Tension and pressure; T. beneath r. knee, then burning.

Calf.—Jerking in l. Cramp; threatens on turning over. *Tearing;* extending to malleoli. Cramplike pain in l. C. and foot; in l. at night. Drawing down; D. and tension. Stiffness when walking, with tightness.

Ankle.—Swelling about malleoli of a formerly diseased foot. Tearing in r. outer malleolus; > rubbing; T. in bend and on margin and back of l. foot; beneath r. inner malleolus extending to heel in evening when sitting. Sprained pain; on moving foot. Pain beneath outer malleolus. Rheumatic tension in l. during rest.

Foot.—Trembling; on raising them while sitting; with difficulty in raising them and frequent stumbling. *Nervous movement for hours after retiring and in sleep.* Stitches in ball; burning, here and there in bone on back. Tearing on outer margin of r. towards toes, > rubbing; on back of l., > walking, with crawling on it and numbness of soles; *on margin of r., with tension;* drawing, in r., extending into malleoli, with heaviness during rest. Pain in outer margin of r. as if bones would break when walking, on raising foot, also on holding it sideways and resting it upon tip. Tension in r., downward on heel, as if foot had been sprained or as if muscles were too short. Drawing in bones of l. *Weakness in morning in bed, > rising and walking;* in evening during menses, with soft stool. Paralyzed feeling in r. Falling asleep towards evening.

Heel.—Stitches. Tearing and pain, the feet seem beaten from the body. *Boring* **after drinking wine.** *Ulcerative pain, worse when walking than when sitting.*

Sole.—Tearing; sticking, and in bend of joints of r. little toe. Ulcerative pain in morning, with burning. Pain on stepping upon them, they seem swollen, with feeling as if scratched by a toothed instrument. Tension in r. as if tendons were too short in evening when stepping.

Toes.—Sticking in ball of great during rest, with burning, as after freezing; prickling, in l. great; pulsating, in tip of r. great; crawling, as after falling asleep in bend of first joint of l. great, on inner side. Tearing in lower part of two first r.; in r. little in evening; in r. great, with jerking tearing in outer side of l. calf; *sticking, in first joints of r. great;* sticking, in bends of first joints of first two r.; drawing, and in forepart of foot. *Sprained pain in bends of first joints.* Ulcerative pain in r. great in evening; in nail of great on touch. Pain as if sore from walking; tearing sore pain in tip of great beneath nail. Feeling as if blistered.

Clinical.—Sciatica, with restlessness of the feet, the pain extending the whole length of the leg, < night and walking.

Skin.—*Erysipelatous inflammation of tendo-achillis, with painful swelling.* Inflamed swelling on foot. Red swelling, hard, painful, on l. wing of nose, painful to pressure. Red round spots on hands and fingers. Bunion on little toe and ball of foot, with stinging when walking. Chilblains on hands. Rash in bend of elbow; itching, in hollows of knees and bends of elbows. Eruption between scapulæ, with itching in evening; E. of crust on face; on r. hand, with painful fissures. Cracks on hands from slight cold, with pain; painful burning C. between two fingers of l. hand. Roughness of back of r. hand, < catching cold and cold weather, with irritation when rubbed that goes through the whole body and with discharging vesicles.

Pimples on face; beneath skin of bend of last joint of ring finger; on forehead, back and third l. toe, with sore pain on touch; on r. side of neck, with ulcerative pain on pressure; red, on chest and face; on forearm, itching by day. Itching pimples in middle of chin; on back of hand; on thighs, calves and about knees, > scratching.

Red spot on leg becoming covered with a scab, with itching. Itching pustules beneath chin. White pimples with moisture, on upper lip, chin and forehead after drinking wine. Profuse bleeding of a slight injury. Ulcerative blisters as after a burn on back of r. foot. Boils on shoulders; on l. upper arm; on back, between scapulæ and in other parts; red, finally dark blue, with hard areola, containing dark pus, on l. side of pubic region.

Tearing sticking above l. eyebrow. *Formication;* through all limbs; on calves extending to toes; > rubbing; with here and there oscillatory movements. Biting and burning pain in an ulcer; B. on back of r. hand, extending above wrist, as if an eruption would appear.

Itching; over whole body; in points, < hands; on upper lip, chin and about mouth; about nipples; on lower limbs; on sole; r. sole; *r. knee;* flexor surface of joints; on limbs, except joints; *all joints in succession,* at last on hip-joint; on face in evening; *thighs and* **hollows of knees** *in evening* (Sulph.), with nettle-rash after scratching; anteriorly above knee every evening, with pimples that are easily scratched off; on r. toes in evening, < scratching, with heat, redness and swelling as if they had been frozen; at night, < back and abdomen; at night, after scratching it appears in another place; on soles, calves and thighs, < night; of nose and scalp, > scratching; under eyes, > scratching, also behind r. ear; over protruding part of chin, with redness; in spots on back, with tetter painful to touch; on almost every part, at times with burning, or with redness, or with pimples and eruption after scratching, at times sore to touch; of great toes as if they had been frozen; sudden here and there, < evening in bed, > touch. Sticking itching in evening in bed; on anterior ball of great toe in evening; over whole body, with sour sweat; with nettle-rash after rubbing; in a spot on l. fourth finger, then a red pustule with throbbing burning pain.

Clinical.—Formication of feet and legs, as from bugs crawling over the skin, preventing sleep. *Eczema.*

Sleep.—Yawning; all day; in forenoon after a good night's sleep. Sleepiness; in morning; in forenoon; when reading before dinner; with tensive spasmodic dulness of head and inability to sleep; irresistible, at 2 P.M. when working, > open air. Deep exhausting sleep with many dreams.

Sleeplessness; almost all night, then heaviness in morning. Falls asleep late; on account of mental activity; and wide awake early in morning. **Jerking through whole body in sleep at night,** *and at noon;* of l. arm in morning; between olecranon and inner condyle of humerus when lying down to sleep at noon; *unconscious starting during menses. Starting from sleep with jerking in l. lower extremity. Loud screaming without knowing it.* Talking. Immediately after lying down in evening she rises up in bed, talks unintelligibly, with short tremulous respiration. Restless sleep; after midnight, early waking, with weariness and feeling as if eyes lay deep in head; and unrefreshing; and full of dreams; full of fantasies and thoughts upon which he was obliged to reflect; he woke screaming as if delirious, as if geese were biting him; could sleep but little at night, but slept long in morning. Sleep disturbed by headache and cramps in calves. *Frequent waking; from frightful dreams; in spite of great sleepiness, with palpitation and* **screaming,** *from anxious dreams of thieves;* and the night seemed very long; with anxious dreams of water and of drowning; with difficult falling asleep again, anxious dreams towards morning; then sleepless after 5 A.M. Waking about midnight from vivid dreams, with internal but not external heat, with necessity to uncover limbs.

Dreams.—With mental excitement and talking about midnight about his dream. Mostly of work or study, rose at 11 P.M. with feeling as if I must urinate and was lost in my own room, when thoroughly awake found that the desire to urinate was a false alarm. Disgusting, of being smeared with human excrement. Vexatious or quarrelsome or sad. Vivid; after midnight. Roving, in morning, that he went all over the continent, that he was in Chicago helping to settle the Republican ticket. Anxious; the anxiety of which continued after waking. Frightful. Of fire, falling, coining counterfeit money, then sweat. Of falling from the roof of a house, about midnight, two hours later, of a wedding feast, the parties being masked and in fancy costumes. Of corpses and horses, which changed into dogs under him. That she was being strangled, and in moving after waking fear lest the man who strangled her would return. Nightmare.

Clinical.—Somnambulism.

Fever.—Chill; all day during menses; in morning on waking; in forenoon, but in afternoon frequent rising of heat, with redness of face; in evening; till evening, then nausea, eructations and accumulation of sour water; from afternoon till evening; after dinner till evening; while writing, with sensation of a stony substance in throat, with yawning; with internal heat; then febrile symptoms over whole body, with chill creeping and drawing through back. Sensitiveness to open air in afternoon and evening; S. to cold, < feet and tips of fingers. Paroxysmal chilliness several times a day, with shivering, flushes of heat over whole body, *trembling of limbs*, sickness even to faintness, qualmish taste, with loathing of the food in the mouth, emptiness in stomach, *throbbing in whole body, short, hot breath*, dry mouth, hot, dry hands. Creeping C. on going into open air, > in house; C. over upper and lower part of body; over upper and lower abdomen.

Shaking chill from 4 till 8 P.M.; *in evening*, also on taking hold of anything cold, > lying down; with pale, sunken face, weak, rapid and irregular pulse, often with nausea and vomiting, at last pulse large and full, with heat, red face, skin swollen, then restless sleep with distressing dreams and exhaustion, at last sweat, the attacks usually begin at the end of a day's work, last eight to ten hours and cease in morning. Shivering; in evening in bed; in evening in open air; in evening, then sometimes indistinct cold stage, but always sweat; from a penetrating wind, not from cold; with headache; with shuddering nausea; with trembling of limbs; with general indisposition; for two or three hours, then cold sweats, or more frequently the sweat is preceded by flushes of heat and violent febrile reaction; *down back*. Shivering discomfort like the premonition of a storm.

Cold body in forenoon, with heat of face; cold nose; face; *limbs*; hands; hands and feet; feet in evening in bed; feet, waking him at night; forehead in evening, with feeling of heat; skin over most of body in evening, with thirst and heat. External parts (lobules of ears, tip of nose, etc.) are easily frozen.

Heat; in evening after lying down, with anxiety all night; *all night, with sweat*; in company; < back, not in feet; with sweat in axillæ; then cold sweat; agreeable, in afternoon, with slight sweat; in flushes; in flushes, then cold sweat; internal, after 6 P.M.; internal, < head, with redness of cheeks; flushing, with sudden crying out to be fanned, and thirst; of whole body except feet, as if sweat would break out, in afternoon; of whole body in evening, except coldness in abdomen.

Burning on skin of r. scapula; in l. axilla; in hands, with sweat in palms; in a spot in l. hand; in skin on margin of r. hand; on flexor surface of fingers; l. side and l. scapula; in skin on lower part of r. calf; beneath r. inner malleolus; of head, with redness of face; fingers, then about throat and in face, with redness of face, then coldness in nape. Evening, heat in head and eyes; in soles; head and cheeks, with redness of cheeks; in head, after two hours chilliness; beneath r. heel, worse when walking than when sitting. *Burning on l. forearm* at night; above r. wrist on moving arm; in spots when sitting; biting, posteriorly in upper part of skin on l. upper arm; itching, on outer side above r. knee.

Sweat; towards morning; towards morning, then gradual disappearance of symptoms; at night; at night, < lower limbs; when walking in open air; on hands; easy, on head and hands; *offensive, on feet*, he walked the feet sore; sour-smelling; sour, with sticking itching over whole body; cold, often preceded by heat; on neck and head, < behind ears, around nose and in folds of skin.

Zingiber.

A tincture is made of the dried root of the ginger, Amomum Zingiber, L.

Generalities and Mind.—Twitching over r. eye and in neck. Cold rheumatism. Feels very unwell all day. Inclination to lie down. Weakness; in afternoon; all day and evening, with sleepiness, felt better in afternoon and in the air; with feverishness; with fluttering of heart and empty sensation. Irritability in evening, with chilliness. Increased activity of brain. Memory strengthened.

Head.—Aching in morning, with heat in head; A. from 7 till 9 P.M., < moving; < moving and stooping; < noise, > dinner; with soreness to touch; with heat in head; with stiffness of l. side of neck; externally, > touch; drawing, settling in r. temple; drawing, as if r. eye were pressing out, all day; encircling it, heavy pain as from a board pressing through the whole head, at noon; heavy, at noon, < forehead, with stiff neck. Feeling as if pressed. On stooping, sensation as if contents pressed into forehead and root of nose. Heavy pressure inward when walking in cold damp air, afterwards affecting the whole body. Confusion and empty feeling. Rush of blood in afternoon, < temples, with weak, full pulse. Dizziness.

Forehead.—Stitches; over l. eye at 5 P.M., then frontal pain, and eyes sensitive to light. Pain in morning; P. over eye; over l. side at 11 A.M., then changing about in head; over l. eye from 9 till 10 P.M.; < over eyes, < laughing, talking or stooping; over l. eye in afternoon and evening, < cold open air, with stitches now and then, next day heavy P. with stitches now and then. Drawing pain, < over root of nose; D. pain at noon, < l. side; over l. eye at 7 P.M.; over l. eye, extending towards r., when in church, settling in r. occiput, where she felt a heavy drawing pain, with frontal headache, nausea, faint sensation and chilliness, all symptoms > in a warm room; sharp, over brows, with aching of brows, then nausea in a warm room, later (at noon) more aching and heavier sensation extending around the head, heavier on l. vertex, afterwards heavier over r. eye and l. occiput, later pain over r. eye and heavy pain in l. occiput. Drawing pressure on bone when he exerts himself. Drawing, with heat.

Temples.—Pain; in afternoon; in evening; in l. till sleep, 8 P.M.; at 11 P.M., with dull and sore feeling over l. eye; after bread; with numbness in them, pressure over eyes, heat in face and fainting weakness; beating, in l.; drawing, in l. and over l. brow at 5 P.M.

Pulsating pain in r. side of vertex, < rising. Heavy pain in l. side of vertex at 11 A.M. Sore feeling in l. side of vertex, < touch. Pain in l. side in evening, with heat in head and thirst; drawing, internally above temples when walking in open air, > standing still, disappearing on uncovering head in a warm room; in a circle through cerebellum, then heavy P. encircling the head above the eyes, extending to occiput. Beating pressure in l. side of occiput; in evening. Itching of scalp; during the morning, and of cheeks.

Eyes.—Sensation of sand in l., > rubbing. Pressure; in l.; in and over l. Smarting burning pain. Sensitiveness to light; in evening; in afternoon and evening, with stinging in balls. Watery. Stitches inside lids. Cutting downward in margins of lids. Sharp drawing pain through and around balls and through superciliary ridges. Sudden glimmerings.

Ears.—Tearing in r. at 7 P.M.; drawing T. in r. Sensitive to noise during the day. Humming.

Nose.—Itching in nostrils, not > scratching. Dryness. Frequent sneezing at 6 P.M., with many ineffectual attempts to sneeze. Obstructed feeling, with thick discharge; O. feeling, with watery discharge. Discharge, watery, from r. then l. nostril, < open air; watery, streaked with blood, while her cough is worse; serous, then thicker, posterior nares obstructed.

Face.—Looks exhausted in morning before menstruation, with blue rings below eyes. Drawing stinging in l. lower jaw to first incisor at 10 P.M. and in night. Drawing pain in l. upper jaw; l. lower at 9 P.M.; in l. lower from second molar to first incisor; from upper to temple. Drawing from l. upper jaw to temples. Soreness in r. lower jaw in morning, with swelling.

Mouth.—Drawing pain in first two l. lower molars; in all l. lower teeth at 5 P.M.; in l. lower to first incisor (she has a decayed tooth on this side) at 7 P.M., later it returns after being in the air. Sensitiveness of all lower teeth, with pressing drawing in their roots. Dryness of roof, and of posterior nares, which are stopped. Burning. Salivation; with vesicles on tongue and gums, which feel sore. *Breath smells foul* to herself. *Slimy taste in morning.*

Throat.—Looseness of mucus, with soreness in T. and pit of stomach. Tickling from 3 P.M. till evening, < l. side; in evening, irritating to cough. Dryness on waking, with difficult swallowing as over an obstacle, afterwards the same at night, with raising of hard mucus; D. at 10 P.M., on going home, with feeling of swelling externally, constant desire to swallow, pressure and stinging; of posterior nares, with obstruction and also with thick discharge.

Stomach.—Loss of desire to smoke. Thirst; at night, in morning dry lips and mouth; with headache; with heat in head. Eructations; in evening; empty; sickening; incomplete. *Nausea;* on rising at 7 A.M., with wind and rumbling in bowels, preceded by drawing pain in hypogastrium; from 7 till 8 P.M. and next day from 7 till 8 A.M.; at 7.30 P.M., with empty feeling in stomach; at night after a short unrefreshing sleep, then sleeplessness; rising into chest. Pain in S. and back, > going to bed; P. from bread; drawing, going from pit under sternum, where it feels like flatulence. Heaviness in evening with inability to sleep, nervous, fidgety feeling, cramps in soles and palms, and a hoarseness such as she had during cholera. Digestion weak, retarding the stool.

Clinical.—Vomiting of old drunkards, with heavy feeling like a stone in the stomach, slimy, bad taste in the morning, and bad breath.

Abdomen.—Distention. Rolling. Flatulence; in evening; before supper; on rising from bed. Stinging at 6.15 P.M., < l. iliac region. Contracting colic passing through it when standing, then desire for stool. Drawing pain all night, with weight and flatulency. Drawing downward; at 8 P.M.; towards evening, < sides, then nausea. Nausea in morning, two hours after the usual stool.

Rumbling in l. side at 10 P.M., sometimes pain through bowels. Stitches in l. hypochondrium; at night. Heavy pain in r. hypochondrium, towards back, at noon, < deep breathing. Cutting in l. umbilical region. Sore pain in a spot in the middle of a line from umbilicus to r. hip. Sudden drawing stinging pain in l. iliac region, going upward, at 3 P.M. *Sharp pain in l. iliac region* after supper and after breakfast next morning. Pain in iliac region from 5 P.M. till sleep, next day in l. in evening, on third day at 5 P.M., with soreness; in l. groin at 2 P.M., with superficial soreness in a spot, the same over Poupart's ligament at 8 P.M. Drawing pain in hypogastrium; passing from r. to l. side, then it went higher up; at 10 P.M., and in back, then a stool, some days later drawing at 7 P.M., < l. side.

Anus and Stool.—*Hæmorrhoids hot and painful* (after chewing ginger for asthma, which it did not relieve), > Nux v. Redness in and around anus, with inflammation, and with burning itching extending up back. Diarrhœa before breakfast; twice after breakfast; with acidity of stomach and slimy taste; mucous, frequently through the day; brown, mucous, with wind. Soft stool.

Clinical.—Anus sore and hot during pregnancy. Diarrhœa from drinking bad water, with much flatulence, cutting pain, relaxation of sphincter. Chronic intestinal catarrh.

Urinary and Sexual Organs.—Yellow discharge from urethra at night. Stinging burning pain in orifice of urethra, not while urinating, urine pale. Acute pain in orifice of urethra when urinating, > Nux v. Dribbling after micturition. Urine profuse; and bright-colored; and of strong smell. Urine dark brown. Urine thick, turbid, > Nux v. Prepuce cold and moist. Itching of prepuce. Painful erections, > Nux v. Sperma increased. Emission at night. Sexual desire. Menstruation too early, copious, dark, clotted, with sick and irritable feeling.

Clinical.—Complete suppression of urine after typhoid.

Respiratory Organs.—Hoarseness. Soreness like a ridge in upper larynx. Scratching in larynx, which irritates to a dry cough; with rancid feeling, which makes her drink water. *Smarting below larynx, then cough and expectoration of mucus.* Cough at night; before midnight; from tickling and dryness in larynx; from contraction of skin in region of larynx; excited by burning and smarting; < morning, with expectoration, which she has to swallow; scraping; dry, from scratching in larynx, waking him often between 1 and 2 A.M. Short breath. Breathing difficult, from pain in r. lung; *with necessity to sit up.*

Clinical.—Asthma, necessity to sit up in order to breathe, without anxiety, < towards morning.

Chest.—Stitches in r. side; in l. lower lung; through chest; intermittent, in lungs, after motion; in lower part of r. lung, waking her at 2 A.M., *with difficult breathing, necessity to sit up,* < dry, hacking cough, in the morning expectoration, all day pain in r. lung, with external soreness. Pain under sternum all day; under sternum at 4 P.M.; in r. lung from second to sixth rib in front, at 7 P.M., worse at intervals, then difficult breathing; in lungs at 9 P.M.; through middle lobe of l. lung at 9 P.M.; drawing, from r. axilla to sternum, from third to sixth rib, in intercostal muscles, at 9 A.M. after working. Broken feeling around it in evening. Pressure when walking, the time when he does not cough; outward under upper part of sternum, afterwards < r. side.

Heart and Pulse.—Stinging in region of heart at 5 P.M. Fluttering of H. Pulse rapid; slow, full and hard in evening.

Neck.—Cracking sound in region of first cervical vertebra in evening on looking upward; on rising from a seat, with stiffness in l. side of neck. Stiffness; < l. side; < motion.

Back.—Lameness after much walking. Aching in afternoon; in sacral region; r. loin; loins, < l., during menstruation; loins, < r., > leaning against something; first low down, but passing off she feels it higher up, at 8 P.M., several times, with nausea; as from weakness, > sitting and leaning against something; as from weakness, in sacral region, in evening after lying down, > Nux v.; as if beaten in small of B. when walking and standing. Drawing pain between scapulæ at 6 P.M.; in l. sacral region in evening, the first day of menstruation; lower part in evening; drawing, sometimes stitching pain in small of B. and lower down in abdomen at 7 P.M., < deep breathing, with inability to sit erect, this pain went with stitches through the chest and settled as a stinging under l. scapula. Stitches in small of B. In loin, a shock-like moving downward, as from a dropping fluid. Stiffness of lower part, > going to bed, with heaviness in it and pain in abdomen.

Extremities.—Twitching in muscles of back part of r. humerus and in r. thigh at 5.30 P.M. Cramp in soles and palms. Heavy pain in arms and legs at 11 A.M. Heaviness. Weakness; in joints after walking.

Upper Extremities.—Drawing pain in l. shoulder-joint at 11 P.M.; in l. joint, with weakness. Shoulder-joint felt paralyzed after a fall which strained it, with pain on raising it. Arm, twitching extending downward in l. at 4 and 6 P.M.; pain in r., going to wrist; drawing pain in l.; drawing pain in l. in afternoon and evening, < entering a warm room, < upper arm; drawing in l., next day in r., then l.; heaviness of l. at 10 A.M., with numbness, < forearm. Upper arm, twitching in muscles of r.; drawing pain in r. in evening; heavy feeling, a kind of lameness. Pain along l. deltoid, as from overwork, a lame sensation at 8 P.M., < motion. Pulling tearing along r. triceps at 7 P.M. Drawing pain from lower part of inner side of humerus to middle of forearm at 4 P.M. Felt a loud crack in l. elbow on motion. Forearm, twitching in muscles of l. at 4 P.M.; internal trembling of muscles when holding something tight; drawing pain in r. towards wrist at 9 P.M. Rheumatic drawing over back of hand. Drawing, cramplike pain in l. palm at 5 P.M.

Lower Extremities.—Thigh, drawing; drawing pain in outer side of l. at 5 P.M. Hip, broken feeling, also tired when standing, feels best when sitting; soreness in l. returned long after a fall; two drawing pains, then a rest, then the pain again, at 10 A.M., < l., then lameness; stiffness at 5 P.M., a lame feeling. Pain as from a strain in bend of knee. Drawing pain in l. knee, then in both knees, extending to feet; along inner side of r. patella; below l. patella in afternoon; acute (digging), on top of foot when outstretched. Aching in heels after long standing. Prickling, crawling pains in sole when walking or standing; almost like a sore pain when sitting; as if asleep in soles and balls of feet in evening when sitting. Burning pricking crawling in soles, heels and toes when sitting, especially burning in corns and soles.

Skin.—Redness; with heat and stinging. Red pimples on l. cheek; face, neck and forepart of head; wings of nose. Feels relaxed, soft and pliable. Itching in beard; on pubic parts; pricking, in calves when sitting.

Sleep.—Sleepiness; in morning after good sleep at night, with yawning; in afternoon; towards evening; and laziness; sleep from 6 till 9 P.M., with lively dreams. Sleepless the latter part of the night; till towards morning, falls from one dream into another, dreams of fire, fright, etc.; from 3 A.M. till late in morning, > Nux v.; and nervous, fidgety feeling; half awake, dreamed all night. Waking early. Sleep unrefreshing; irritable, lazy; restless, after 2 A.M., with many dreams (of the church). Dreams many; many (dancing, throwing of somersets by an old man), incomplete emissions; pleasant; unpleasant; anxious; wandering, varied, cheerful, vivid and aspiring.

Fever.—Chilliness, with faintness and sick headache; creeping C. in evening, < about trunk; extending upward; four or five times in evening, beginning in lower limbs and creeping to back. Cold shivering. Cold hands and feet alternately; feet towards noon, then hands. Temperature increased. Heat at 11 A.M., with hard, full pulse, redness of the face and humming in ears; H. in head all day; in head, < ears, with headache; ears; face; face, with redness; face and r. cheek at 5 P.M., with pain in temples; palms. Sweat.

Zizia.

A tincture is made of the entire fresh plant, Thaspium aureum, Nutt. (Zizia aurea, Koch.).

Generalities.—Spasmodic movements of muscles of face and limbs. Convulsions; and swooning. Increase of strength, with inclination for muscular exertion. Pains, < movement, noise, light or contact.

Clinical.—Hysteria. Chorea, especially during sleep, fidgety legs (Tarent.). Epilepsy.

Mind.—Exhilaration; then depression; of all faculties, then sleepiness. Laughing and weeping alternately. Depression, with irritability and indifference; D., with disgust of life; D., then exhilaration and desire for conversation. Desire to move about, with apparent increase of strength, but slight exercise causes fatigue. Dreamy, imaginative mood.

Clinical.—Hypochondriasis, desire to commit suicide.

Head.—Pain and lightness. Affection of brain and nervous system. Tightness. Rush of blood to H. and face, with feeling of fulness. Giddiness. Tightness in forehead and occiput. Pressure upon top of brain. Pain in r. temple, with nausea; P. in l. side, < light or noise; in occiput, extending to muscles of neck.

Clinical.—Neuralgia of the head and face.

Eyes.—Red. Sensitive to light. Lachrymation. Lids agglutinated in morning by a yellowish mucopurulent secretion. Stye on r. lid. Smarting of lids. Shooting through orbits. Sharp pain in r. orbit, < moving balls, stooping or stepping.

Nose and Face.—Obstruction of r. nostril, with pain on touch and soreness. Catarrhal, asthmatic and pleuritic maladies. Face pale and puffy. One cheek red, the other pale. Boring in cheek-bones. Pain in jaws.

Mouth and Throat.—Tongue coated white; coated yellow, and respiration oppressed; T. red and sensitive to cold and warm drinks. Mouth dry. Taste bitter. Inflammation of pharynx. Tonsils and palate red and throat sore. Increased mucus in throat.

Stomach.—Craving for acids and stimulants. Appetite diminished; lost. Thirst. Nausea. Vomiting; acid and bilious. Pressure causing nausea and faintness. Sensitive to touch.

Sexual Organs.—Excitement of male. Emission at night. Power enhanced. Uterine affections characterized by vascular and nervous excitement. Leucorrhœa acrid; bland and profuse. Menses profuse for one day, then acrid leucorrhœa; M. suppressed suddenly.

Clinical.—Intermittent neuralgia of l. ovary.

Respiratory Organs.—Roughness in upper part of larynx on inspiring or coughing. Rawness of larynx from coughing, with smarting. Trachea sensitive to touch. Tight cough from inspiring deeply; from dryness of larynx. *Dry cough, with shooting in chest;* D., short, with stitches in r. side and sense of suffocation; D., hard, short, with stitches in r. side from beneath sixth rib to two inches below xiphoid cartilage. Respiration asthmatic, with inability to recline; R. oppressed and accelerated.

Clinical.—Dry cough, with stitches in the chest, dyspnœa, aggravation in evening and night.

Chest.—Stitches, with feverish symptoms; S. from front part to scapula; pleuritic, in r. side, < coughing or attempting to take a long breath. Pain in intercostal muscles on pressure; sharp, from sides to scapulæ. Bruised feeling in muscles.

Back and Extremities.—Pain under r. scapula; in loins, < movement; smarting burning, in small of back. Pricking in r. arm, with diminished sensibility. Lameness of muscles of upper arms. Dragging in hips. Legs tired after slightest exertion.

Skin.—Whole body pale; and puffy. Face and ankles œdematous. Itching pimples on forehead, wrists and legs. Sensitive to touch.

Sleep.—Drowsiness; with lassitude. Sleep prevented by pain. Twitching in sleep. Talking in sleep. Disturbed by unpleasant dreams.

Fever.—Chilliness, with twitchings of muscles of face and upper limbs, then fever; C. and heat alternating with faintness, nausea, pain in r. temple, redness of eyeballs, dry and red tongue and thirst for cold water; C. of hands and feet, with flushed cheeks, hot head, visible pulsations of carotid and temporal arteries, drowsiness and irritability. Fever, with headache, pain in back and thirst. Heat in cheeks, with redness; in cheeks, with sense of fulness. Hot flushes in face and head, then sweat.

CORRECTIONS.

P. 39, 2d column, 30th line from top, before "<" insert "*in r.*,".
P. 149, 2d column, 12th line from bottom, for "<" read ">".
P. 156, 2d column, 21st line from bottom, for "<" read ">".
P. 178, 1st column, 14th line from top, before "olecranon" insert "l."
P. 178, 1st column, 16th line from bottom, before "**knee**" insert "**r.**"
P. 184, 2d column, 21st line from top, omit "*l.*"
P. 191, 1st column, 25th line from top, for "lower" read "inner".
P. 200, 1st column, 8th line from top, for "<" read ">".
P. 208, 1st column, 29th line from top, read "*afternoon than in forenoon.*"
P. 210, 1st column, 23d line from bottom, for "<" read ">".
P. 211, 1st column, 22d line from top, after "*rise*" insert "*from stooping*".
P. 217, 2d column, 13th line from bottom, after "*forward*" for ";" read ",".
P. 218, 2d column, 2d line from bottom, for "," read ";".
P. 324, 2d column, 11th line from top, after "<" add "**forehead,**".
P. 338, 1st column, 27th line from top, before "*humerus*" insert "*r.*"
P. 358, 2d column, 1st line, after "reflecting" add "> stooping,".
P. 358, 22d line from top, for ">" read "<".
P. 403, 2d column, 17th line from top, for "<" read ">".
P. 442, 1st column, 20th line from top, after "I," read "*with tearing in head and return of anxiety and pressure in chest, especially while sitting, then violent pulsation of heart;*".
P. 477, 1st column, 9th line from bottom, for "<" read ">".
P. 499, 2d column, 28th line from top, for "flatus" read "mucus".
P. 501, 1st column, 32d line from top, after "head" insert "(which seemed enlarged)".
P. 520, 1st column, 27th line from bottom, read "*swallowing, and especially on empty swallowing constrictive retching*".
P. 554, 2d column, 8th line from bottom, for "<" read ">".
P. 561, 2d column, 2d line from bottom, before "from" insert "as".
P. 718, 1st column, 4th line from bottom, after "*rest*" insert "*;*".
P. 786, 1st column, 19th line from top, before "Stitches" insert "Knee.—".
P. 793, 2d column, 8th line from bottom, for "back" read "spine".
P. 802, 1st column, 28th line from top, for "or" read "on".
P. 809, 2d column, 6th line from bottom, for "D." read "B."
P. 821, 2d column, 17th line from top, omit "**but no power to expel its contents** (Carbo v.), > **catheter**;".
P. 927, 1st column, 19th line from top, for ">" read "<".